D1606664

2013
STANDARD POSTAGE
STAMP CATALOGUE

ONE HUNDRED AND SIXTY-NINTH EDITION IN SIX VOLUMES

VOLUME 6

COUNTRIES OF THE WORLD
San-Z

EDITOR	Charles Snee
EDITOR EMERITUS	James E. Kloetzel
ASSISTANT EDITOR /NEW ISSUES & VALUING	Martin J. Frankevicz
ASSOCIATE EDITORS	David Akin, Donna Houseman
VALUING ANALYST	Steven R. Myers
ADMINISTRATIVE ASSISTANT/CATALOGUE LAYOUT	Eric Wiessinger
PRINTING AND IMAGE COORDINATOR	Stacey Mahan
CREATIVE DIRECTOR	Mark Potter
ADVERTISING	Angela Nolte
CIRCULATION /PRODUCT PROMOTION MANAGER	Tim Wagner
VICE PRESIDENT/EDITORIAL AND PRODUCTION	Steve Collins
PRESIDENT	William Fay

Released September 2012

Includes New Stamp Listings through the July 2012 *Linn's Stamp News Special Edition* Catalogue Update

Copyright© 2012 by

Scott Publishing Co.

911 Vandemark Road, Sidney, OH 45365-0828

A division of AMOS PRESS, INC., publishers of *Linn's Stamp News, Linn's Stamp News Special Edition, Coin World* and *Coin World Special Edition*.

Table of Contents

See Volume 1 for United States, United Nations and Countries of the World A-B
See Volume 2, 3, 4, 5 for Countries of the World, C-Sam

Volume 2: C-F
Volume 3: G-I
Volume 4: J-M
Volume 5: N-Sam

Scott Publishing Mission Statement
The Scott Publishing Team exists to serve the recreational,
educational and commercial hobby needs of stamp collectors and dealers.
We strive to set the industry standard for philatelic information and products by developing and
providing goods that help collectors identify, value, organize and present their collections.
Quality customer service is, and will continue to be, our highest priority.
We aspire toward achieving total customer satisfaction.

Scott Publishing Co.

SCOTT   911 VANDEMARK ROAD, SIDNEY, OHIO 45365   937-498-0802

Fellow Scott Catalogue User:

New minimum catalogue value is 25¢.

Welcome to the sixth and final volume of the *2013 Scott Standard Postage Stamp Catalogue*, which provides listings and values for countries of the world San-Z, specifically San Marino through Zululand. More than 14,500 value changes are spread among the 96 countries in this volume. This total is on par with the average number of value changes recorded during the past several years.

Not included in this total are the thousands of 20¢ minimum values that were raised to 25¢. That's right: the Scott minimum catalogue value is now 25¢. This significant change was effective with the 2013 Volume 1. The minimum catalogue value represents a part of the cost incurred by a dealer to prepare and stock an individual stamp for resale. Beginning with the 2001 catalogues, Scott raised its minimum value from 15¢ to 20¢. After more than a decade, economic realities dictated that the editors raise the minimum value an additional 5¢.

A somewhat stronger dollar affects values in the 2013 Vol. 6.

Overall, the stamp market is rather flat and quiet. Scarce and rare items continue to perform well, both in auctions and in retail transactions. However, the values of many stamps are holding steady, or have declined somewhat, mainly due to a modest strengthening of the dollar against major foreign currencies. These downward adjustments were needed to keep Scott values in line with retail activity.

This year, a thorough review of Yugoslavia resulted in almost 4,000 value changes, tops among all Vol. 6 countries. These value changes cover all periods, and increases far outnumber decreases. As we have seen with other countries this year, modern postage issues show sizable gains. The 2002 16-dinar stamp celebrating the 750th anniversary of the Moraca Monastery (Scott 2574) leaps to $20 mint, never hinged and $12 used, from just $2 both ways in 2012. Substantial increases of 50 percent or more are seen among the Ljubljana issues of 1941-45.

Other Vol. 6 countries with large numbers of value changes include: South West Africa (1,093), Tanzania (1,066), Sri Lanka (1,063), Ukraine (1,046) and Turks & Caicos Islands (848). In general, the market has slowed for stamps issued during the 1960s, 1970s and the early 1980s. Stocks of these stamps are deep, and demand is lethargic. This, coupled with a modest strengthening of the dollar against major foreign currencies, has pushed down some values.

However, value increases often are seen for issues of the past 10 years or so. For example, values for Serbia are up sharply for issues 2003-present. The 2006 World Cup set, Scott 336-338, soars to $45 mint and used, from $13 both ways in 2012. Values for South Georgia issues of 1999-2011 are up 10 percent to 20 percent or more. The Preservation of Polar Regions sheet of two, Scott 375, rises from $6.50 mint and used last year to $11.50 both ways in 2013. Values also are up noticeably for all modern Ukraine issues.

In some cases, smaller print runs are fueling these increases. Demand from collectors simply exceeds the available supply, particularly after new-issue dealers have satisfied the needs of their customers. Stamps depicting popular topical themes, such as various flowers and animals, are appreciating in value. Modern topicals related to China, including various Lunar New Year stamps, also are advancing in value.

In general, solid value increases are seen for selected classic stamps of many other Vol. 6 countries. Pay particular attention to used values, which are strengthening as collectors more aggressively pursue true very fine examples with desirable postmarks.

Values of error stamps from the classic period also continue to exhibit healthy gains. A standout example is the Virgin Islands 1867 1-shilling rose and black with central figure omitted, Scott 8c, which rockets from $92,500 unused in 2012 to $225,000 this year.

Significant editorial enhancements for Yemen, Yugoslavia.

Collectors of Yemen will be pleased to see numerous new listings among the postage, air post and postage due issues of the 1960s. Many of these 26 new sets of stamps were previously described in editorial notes. In addition, almost 80 new sets issued during 1967-72 and not mentioned previously in the Scott catalogue are now listed and valued for the first time. Specialists have confirmed that these stamps were legitimately issued and were used to carry mail. New editorial notes identify stamps that the editors need to examine before they can be listed. Two notes, following Nos. 94 and C19, provide explanations for sets of stamps that do not meet Scott listing criteria.

There are 17 new listings in Yugoslavia. Among these are new minor numbers, Scott C7a-C14, for the perf. 12½ varieties of the 1937 air post set depicting various scenes. Never-hinged totals have been added for dozens of sets scattered throughout the postage and back-of-the-book sections. New footnotes call attention to and provide values for many imperforate varieties.

For a summary of these and other listing-related changes, you are encouraged to review the Number Additions, Deletions & Changes listing, which may be found on page 1571 in this volume.

Each year, we strive to make the catalogues more visually useful. Dozens of overprinted and surcharged stamps are now illustrated in color, in place of the verbal descriptions that once headlined the respective listings. Also, various black-and-white drawings of different type designs, some of which have been in the catalogue for decades, are now illustrated with actual stamps.

Detailed listing criteria for personalized stamps are now included in the catalogue Introduction, under the section titled "Catalogue Listing Policy."

The relentless pursuit of perfection.

That, my fellow collectors, is what we at Scott are all about. Each year, we strive to capture the most accurate snapshot of the stamp-hobby marketplace, while improving and expanding the editorial content of each catalogue.

Pursuing these objectives would be much more challenging were it not for the many catalogue users out there who carefully review the catalogues and notify us of any mistakes they encounter. If you come across any mistakes, or have suggestions for the Scott catalogues, please notify me at csnee@scottonline.com.

Final thoughts.

If you are a newcomer to the Scott catalogues, you might not be aware that the covers of each year's volumes are united under a common theme. This year, stamps depicting lighthouses take center stage on the 2013 covers. The Vol. 6 cover spotlights stamps from Seychelles, the Solomon Islands, Sri Lanka and Turkey. The stamps on the U.S. Specialized and Classic Specialized covers yet to be revealed are just as eye-catching and attractive.

Now go and have fun with your collection. Cheers!

Charles Snee/Catalogue Editor

Acknowledgments

Our appreciation and gratitude go to the following individuals who have assisted us in preparing information included in this year's Scott Catalogues. Some helpers prefer anonymity. These individuals have generously shared their stamp knowledge with others through the medium of the Scott Catalogue.

Those who follow provided information that is in addition to the hundreds of dealer price lists and advertisements and scores of auction catalogues and realizations that were used in producing the catalogue values. It is from those noted here that we have been able to obtain information on items not normally seen in published lists and advertisements. Support from these people goes beyond data leading to catalogue values, for they also are key to editorial changes.

A special acknowledgment to Liane and Sergio Sismondo of The Classic Collector for their extraordinary assistance and knowledge sharing that has aided in the preparation of this year's Standard and Classic Specialized Catalogues.

Donald R. Alexander
Roland Austin
Robert Ausubel (Great Britain Collectors Club)
Jack Hagop Barsoumian (International Stamp Co.)
John Birkinbine II
Brian M. Bleckwenn (The Philatelic Foundation)
John D. Bowman (Carriers and Locals Society)
Roger S. Brody
Mahdi Bseiso
Mike Bush (Joseph V. Bush, Inc.)
Tina & John Carlson (JET Stamps)
Richard A. Champagne (Richard A. Champagne, Inc.)
Henry Chlanda
Ron Cipolla
Bob Coale
Leroy P. Collins III (United Postal Stationery Society)
Frank D. Correl
Tom Cossaboom
Tony L. Crumbley (Carolina Coin & Stamp, Inc.)
Ernesto Cuesta
Christopher Dahle
Stephen R. Datz
Tony Davis
Charles Deaton
Chris de Haer
Ubaldo Del Toro
Bob Dumaine
Sister Theresa Durand
Mark Eastzer (Markeet Stamp Co.)
Paul G. Eckman
George Epstein
Mehdi Esmaili
Leon Finik
Henry Fisher
Robert A. Fisher
Jeffrey M. Forster
Robert S. Freeman
Ernest E. Fricks (France & Colonies Philatelic Society)
Bob Genisol (Sultan Stamp Center)
Stan Goldfarb
Daniel E. Grau
Jan E. Gronwall
John Heaton
Bruce Hecht (Bruce L. Hecht Co.)
Clifford O. Herrick (Fidelity Trading Co.)

Peter Hoffman
Philip J. Hughes
Doug Iams
Robert Jack
Peter Jeannopoulos
Stephen Joe (International Stamp Service)
William A. Jones
Allan Katz (Ventura Stamp Co.)
Stanford M. Katz
Lewis Kaufman
George Krieger
John R. Lewis (The William Henry Stamp Co.)
Ulf Lindahl
Ignacio Llach (Filatelia Llach S.L.)
Robert L. Markovits (Quality Investors, Ltd.)
Marilyn R. Mattke
William K. McDaniel
Allen Mintz (United Postal Stationery Society)
William E Mooz
Gary Morris (Pacific Midwest Co.)
Peter Mosiondz, Jr.
Bruce M. Moyer (Moyer Stamps & Collectibles)
Richard H. Muller
Behruz Nassre
Gregg Nelson
Albert Olejnik
Nik & Lisa Oquist
Dr. Everett Parker
John E. Pearson (Pittwater Philatelic Service)
Donald J. Peterson (International Philippine Philatelic Society)
Stanley M. Piller (Stanley M. Piller & Associates)
Todor Drumev Popov
Peter W. W. Powell
Ghassan D. Riachi
Eric Roberts
Robert G. Rufe
Michael Ruggiero
Frans H. A. Rummens
Mehrdad Sadri (Persiphila)
Richard H. Salz (Canal Zone Study Group)
Alex Schauss (Schauss Philatelics)
Jacques C. Schiff, Jr. (Jacques C. Schiff, Jr., Inc.)

Bernard Seckler (Fine Arts Philatelists)
Guy Shaw
Jeff Siddiqui
Sergio & Liane Sismondo (The Classic Collector)
Jay Smith
Merle Spencer (The Stamp Gallery)
Frank J. Stanley, III
Kenneth Thompson
Peter Thy
Scott R. Trepel (Siegel Auction Galleries)
Philip T. Wall
Kristian Wang
Giana Wayman
William R. Weiss, Jr. (Weiss Expertizing)
Ed Wener (Indigo)
Don White (Dunedin Stamp Centre)
Kirk Wolford (Kirk's Stamp Company)
Robert F. Yacano (K-Line Philippines)
Ralph Yorio
Val Zabijaka
Michal Zika
Alfonso G. Zulueta, Jr.

Addresses, Telephone Numbers, Web Sites, E-Mail Addresses of General & Specialized Philatelic Societies

Collectors can contact the following groups for information about the philately of the areas within the scope of these societies, or inquire about membership in these groups. Aside from the general societies, we limit this list to groups that specialize in particular fields of philately, particular areas covered by the Scott Standard Postage Stamp Catalogue, and topical groups. Many more specialized philatelic society exist than those listed below. These addresses are updated yearly, and they are, to the best of our knowledge, correct and current. Groups should inform the editors of address changes whenever they occur. The editors also want to hear from other such specialized groups not listed. Unless otherwise noted all website addresses begin with http://

American Philatelic Society
100 Match Factory Place
Bellefonte PA 16823-1367
Ph: (814) 933-3803
www.stamps.org
E-mail: apsinfo@stamps.org

American Stamp Dealers Association, Inc.
P.O. Box 692
Leesport PA 19553
Ph: (800) 369-8207
www.americanstampdealer.com
E-mail: asda@americanstampdealer.com

National Stamp Dealers Association
Dick Keiser, President
2916 NW Bucklin Hill Road #136
Silverdale WA 98383-8514
Ph: (800) 875-6633
www.nsdainc.org
E-mail: gail@nsdainc.org

International Society of Worldwide Stamp Collectors
Joanne Berkowitz, MD
P.O. Box 19006
Sacramento CA 95819
www.iswsc.org
E-mail: executivedirector@iswsc.org

Royal Philatelic Society
41 Devonshire Place
London, W1G 6JY
UNITED KINGDOM
www.rpsl.org.uk
E-mail: secretary@rpsl.org.uk

Royal Philatelic Society of Canada
P.O. Box 929, Station Q
Toronto, ON, M4T 2P1
CANADA
Ph: (888) 285-4143
www.rpsc.org
E-mail: info@rpsc.org

Young Stamp Collectors of America
Janet Houser
100 Match Factory Place
Bellefonte PA 16823-1367
Ph: (814) 933-3820
www.stamps.org/ysca/intro.htm
E-mail: ysca@stamps.org

Philatelic Research Resources

(The Scott editors encourage any additional research organizations to submit data for inclusion in this listing category)

American Philatelic Research Library
100 Match Factory Place
Bellefonte PA 16823
Ph: (814) 933-3803
www.stamplibrary.org

Institute for Analytical Philately, Inc.
P.O. Box 751833
Las Vegas NV 89136-1833
Ph: (877) 213-2387
www.analyticalphilately.org
E-mail: info@analyticalphilately.org

The Western Philatelic Library
P.O. Box 2219
1500 Partridge Ave.
Sunnyvale CA 94087
Ph: (408) 733-0336
www.fwpf.org

Groups focusing on fields or aspects found in worldwide philately (some might cover U.S. area only)

American Air Mail Society
Stephen Reinhard
P.O. Box 110
Mineola NY 11501
www.americanairmailsociety.org
E-mail: sreinhard1@optonline.net

American First Day Cover Society
Douglas Kelsey
P.O. Box 16277
Tucson AZ 85732-6277
Ph: (520) 321-0880
www.afdcs.org
E-mail: afdcs@afdcs.org

American Revenue Association
Eric Jackson
P.O. Box 728
Leesport PA 19533-0728
Ph: (610) 926-6200
www.revenuer.org
E-mail: eric@revenuer.com

American Topical Association
Vera Felts
P.O. Box 8
Carterville IL 62918-0008
Ph: (618) 985-5100
www.americantopicalassn.org
E-mail: americantopical@msn.com

Christmas Seal & Charity Stamp Society
John Denune
234 E. Broadway
Granville OH 43023
Ph: (740) 587-0276
www.charityseals.org
E-mail: jdenune@roadrunner.com

Errors, Freaks and Oddities Collectors Club
Don David Price
5320 Eastchester Drive
Sarasota FL 34134-2711
Ph: (717) 445-9420
www.efocc.org
E-mail: ddprice98@hotmail.com

First Issues Collectors Club
Kurt Streepy, Secretary
3128 E. Mattatha Drive
Bloomington IN 47401
www.firstissues.org
E-mail: secretary@firstissues.org

International Society of Reply Coupon Collectors
Peter Robin
P.O. Box 353
Bala Cynwyd PA 19004
E-mail: peterrobin@verizon.net

The Joint Stamp Issues Society
Richard Zimmermann
124, Avenue Guy de Coubertin
Saint Remy Les Chevreuse, F-78470
FRANCE
www.jointstampissues.net
E-mail: contact@jointstampissues.net

National Duck Stamp Collectors Society
Anthony J. Monico
P.O. Box 43
Harleysville PA 19438-0043
www.ndscs.org
E-mail: ndscs@ndscs.org

No Value Identified Club
Albert Sauvanet
Le Clos Royal B, Boulevard des Pas Enchantes
St. Sebastien-sur Loire, 44230
FRANCE
E-mail: alain.vailly@irin.univ nantes.fr

The Perfins Club
Jerry Hejduk
P.O. Box 490450
Leesburg FL 34749-0450
Ph: (352) 326-2117
E-mail: flprepers@comcast.net

Postage Due Mail Study Group
John Rawlins
13, Longacre
Chelmsford, CM1 3BJ
UNITED KINGDOM
E-mail: john.rawlins2@ukonline.co.uk.

Post Mark Collectors Club
Beverly Proulx
7629 Homestead Drive
Baldwinsville NY 13027
Ph: (315) 638-0532
www.postmarks.org
E-mail: stampdance@yahoo.com

Postal History Society
Kalman V. Illyefalvi
869 Bridgewater Drive
New Oxford PA 17350-8206
Ph: (717) 624-5941
www.stampclubs.com
E-mail: kalphyl@juno.com

Precancel Stamp Society
Jerry Hejduk
P.O. Box 490450
Leesburg FL 34749-0450
Ph: (352) 326-2117
www.precancels.com
E-mail: psspromosec@comcast.net

United Postal Stationery Society
Stuart Leven
P.O. Box 24764
San Jose CA 95154-4764
www.upss.org
E-mail: poststat@gmail.com

United States Possessions Philatelic Society
David S. Durbin
2270 Rule Ave., Unit C
Maryland Heights MO 63043
Ph: (573) 230-6921
www.uspps.net
E-mail: patlabb@aol.com

Groups focusing on U.S. area philately as covered in the Standard Catalogue

Canal Zone Study Group
Tom Brougham
737 Neilson St.
Berkeley CA 94707
www.CanalZoneStudyGroup.com
czsgsecretary@gmail.com

Carriers and Locals Society
Martin Richardson
P.O. Box 74
Grosse Ile MI 48138
www.pennypost.org
E-mail: martinr362@aol.com

Confederate Stamp Alliance
Patricia A. Kaufmann
10194 N. Old State Road
Lincoln DE 19960
Ph: (302) 422-2656
www.csalliance.org
E-mail: trishkauf@comcast.net

Hawaiian Philatelic Society
Kay H. Hoke
P.O. Box 10115
Honolulu HI 96816-0115
Ph: (808) 521-5721

Plate Number Coil Collectors Club
Gene Trinks
16415 W. Desert Wren Court
Surprise AZ 85374
Ph: (623) 322-4619
www.pnc3.org
E-mail: gctrinks@cox.net

Ryukyu Philatelic Specialist Society
Laura Edmonds, Secy.
P.O. Box 240177
Charlotte NC 28224-0177
Ph: (704) 519-5157
www.ryukyustamps.org
E-mail: secretary@ryukyustamps.org

United Nations Philatelists
Blanton Clement, Jr.
P.O. Box 146
Morrisville PA 19067-0146
www.unpi.com
E-mail: bclemjr@yahoo.com

United States Stamp Society
Executive Secretary
P.O. Box 6634
Katy TX 77491-6631
www.usstamps.org
E-mail: webmaster@usstamps.org

U.S. Cancellation Club
Roger Rhoads
6160 Brownstone Court
Mentor OH 44060
bob.trachimowicz.org/indfk.html
E-mail: rrrhoads@aol.com

U.S. Philatelic Classics Society
Rob Lund
2913 Fulton St.
Everett WA 98201-3733
www.uspcs.org
E-mail: membershipchairman@uspcs.org

Groups focusing on philately of foreign countries or regions

Aden & Somaliland Study Group
Gary Brown
P.O. Box 106
Briar Hill, Victoria, 3088
AUSTRALIA
E-mail: garyjohn951@optushome.com.au

American Society of Polar Philatelists (Antarctic areas)
Alan Warren
P.O. Box 39
Exton PA 19341-0039
www.polarphilatelists.org
E-mail: alanwar@att.net

Andorran Philatelic Study Circle
D. Hope
17 Hawthorn Drive
Stalybridge, Cheshire, SK15 1UE
UNITED KINGDOM
apsc.free.fr
E-mail: apsc@free.fr

Australian States Study Circle of The Royal Sydney Philatelic Club
Ben Palmer
GPO 1751
Sydney, N.S.W., 2001
AUSTRALIA

Austria Philatelic Society
Ralph Schneider
P.O. Box 23049
Belleville IL 62223
Ph: (618) 277-6152
www.austriaphilatelicsociety.com
E-mail: rschneider39@charter.net

Baltic States Philatelic Society
Anatoly Chlenov
5719 Drysdale Court
San Jose CA 95124
Ph: (650) 863-1552
www.baltic-philately.com
E-mail: achlenov@localstamps.com

American Belgian Philatelic Society
Edward de Bary
11 Wakefield Drive Apt. 2105
Asheville NC 28803
E-mail: belgam@charter.net

Bechuanalands and Botswana Society
Neville Midwood
69 Porlock Lane
Furzton, Milton Keynes, MK4 1JY
UNITED KINGDOM
www.nevsoft.com
E-mail: bbsoc@nevsoft.com

Bermuda Collectors Society
John Pare
405 Perimeter Road
Mount Horeb WI 53572
www.bermudacollectorssociety.org
E-mail: science29@comcast.net

Brazil Philatelic Association
William V. Kriebel
1923 Manning St.
Philadelphia PA 19103-5728
Ph: (215) 735-3697
www.brazilphilatelic.org
E-mail: info@brazilphilatelic.org

British Caribbean Philatelic Study Group
Dr. Reuben A. Ramkissoon
11075 Benton St. #236
Loma Linda CA 92354-3182
www.bcpsg.com
E-mail: rramkissoon@juno.com

The King George VI Collectors Society (British Commonwealth)
Brian Livingstone
21 York Mansions, Prince of Wales Drive
London, SW11 4DL
UNITED KINGDOM
www.kg6.info
E-mail: livingstone484@btinternet.com

British North America Philatelic Society (Canada & Provinces)
David G. Jones
184 Larkin Drive
Nepean, ON, K2J 1H9
CANADA
www.bnaps.org
E-mail: shibumi.management@gmail.com

British West Indies Study Circle
John Seidl
4324 Granby Way
Marietta GA 30062
Ph: (770) 642-6424
www.bwisc.org
john.seidl@gmail.com

Burma Philatelic Study Circle
Michael Whittaker
1, Ecton Leys, Hillside
Rugby, Warwickshire, CV22 5SL
UNITED KINGDOM
www.burmastamps.homecall.co.uk
E-mail: manningham8@mypostoffice.co.uk

Cape and Natal Study Circle
Dr. Guy Dillaway
P.O. Box 181
Weston MA 02493
www.nzsc.demon.co.uk

Ceylon Study Circle
R. W. P. Frost
42 Lonsdale Road, Cannington
Bridgewater, Somerset, TA5 2JS
UNITED KINGDOM
www.ceylonsc.org
E-mail: rodney.frost@tiscali.co.uk

Channel Islands Specialists Society
Moira Edwards
86, Hall Lane, Sandon
Chelmsford, Essex, CM2 7RQ
UNITED KINGDOM
www.ciss1950.org.uk
E-mail: membership@ciss1950.org.uk

China Stamp Society
Paul H. Gault
P.O. Box 20711
Columbus OH 43220
www.chinastampsociety.org
E-mail: secretary@chinastampsociety.org

Colombia/Panama Philatelic Study Group (COPAPHIL)
Thomas P. Myers
P.O. Box 522
Gordonsville VA 22942
www.copaphil.org
E-mail: tpmphil@hotmail.com

Association Filatelic de Costa Rica
Giana Wayman
c/o Interlink 102, P.O. Box 52-6770
Miami FL 33152
E-mail: scotland@racsa.co.cr

Society for Costa Rica Collectors
Dr. Hector R. Mena
P.O. Box 14831
Baton Rouge LA 70808
www.socorico.org
E-mail: hrmena@aol.com

International Cuban Philatelic Society
Ernesto Cuesta
P.O. Box 34434
Bethesda MD 20827
www.cubafil.org
E-mail: ecuesta@philat.com

Cuban Philatelic Society of America ®
P.O. Box 141656
Coral Gables FL 33114-1656
www.cubapsa.com
E-mail: cpsa.usa@gmail.com

Cyprus Study Circle
Colin Dear
10 Marne Close, Wem
Shropshire, SY4 5YE
UNITED KINGDOM
www.cyprusstudycircle.org/index.htm
E-mail: colindear@talktalk.net

Society for Czechoslovak Philately
Tom Cassaboom
P.O. Box 4124
Prescott AZ 86302
www.csphilately.org
E-mail: klfck1@aol.com

Danish West Indies Study Unit of the Scandinavian Collectors Club
Arnold Sorensen
7666 Edgedale Drive
Newburgh IN 47630
Ph: (812) 480-6532
www.scc-online.org
E-mail: valbydwi@hotmail.com

East Africa Study Circle
Michael Vesey-Fitzgerald
Vernalls Orchard, Gosport Lane
Lyndhurst, SO43 7BP
UNITED KINGDOM
www.easc.org.uk
E-mail: secretary@easc.org.uk

Egypt Study Circle
Mike Murphy
109 Chadwick Road
London, SE15 4PY
UNITED KINGDOM
Dick Wilson: North American Agent
egyptstudycircle.org.uk
E-mail: egyptstudycircle@hotmail.com

Estonian Philatelic Society
Juri Kirsimagi
29 Clifford Ave.
Pelham NY 10803
Ph: (914) 738-3713

Ethiopian Philatelic Society
Ulf Lindahl
21 Westview Place
Riverside CT 06878
Ph: (203) 866-3540
home.comcast.net/~fbheiser/ethiopia5.htm
E-mail: ulindahl@optonline.net

Falkland Islands Philatelic Study Group
Carl J. Faulkner
Williams Inn, On-the-Green
Williamstown MA 01267-2620
Ph: (413) 458-9371
www.fipsg.org.uk

Faroe Islands Study Circle
Norman Hudson
40 Queenís Road, Vicarís Cross
Chester, CH3 5HB
UNITED KINGDOM
www.faroeislandssc.org
E-mail: jntropics@hotmail.com

Former French Colonies Specialist Society
COLFRA
BP 628
75367 Paris, Cedex 08
FRANCE
www.colfra.com
E-mail: clubcolfra@aol.com

France & Colonies Philatelic Society
Edward Grabowski
111 Prospect St., 4C
Westfield NJ 07090
www.franceandcolonies.org
E-mail: edjjg@alum.mit.edu

Germany Philatelic Society
P.O. Box 6547
Chesterfield MO 63006
www.germanyphilatelicusa.org

Gibraltar Study Circle
David R. Stirrups
34 Glamis Drive
Dundee, DD2 1QP
UNITED KINGDOM
E-mail: drstirrups@dundee.ac.uk

Great Britain Collectors Club
Steve McGill
10309 Brookhollow Circle
Highlands Ranch CO 80129
www.gbstamps.com/gbcc
E-mail: steve.mcgill@comcast.net

International Society of Guatemala Collectors
Jaime Marckwordt
449 St. Francis Blvd.
Daly City CA 94015-2136
www.guatemalastamps.com

Haiti Philatelic Society
Ubaldo Del Toro
5709 Marble Archway
Alexandria VA 22315
www.haitiphilately.org
E-mail: u007ubi@aol.com

Hong Kong Stamp Society
Ming W. Tsang
P.O. Box 206
Glenside PA 19038
www.hkss.org
hkstamps@yahoo.com

Society for Hungarian Philately
Robert Morgan
2201 Roscomare Road
Los Angeles CA 90077-2222
www.hungarianphilately.org
E-mail: bwilson1951@aol.com

India Study Circle
John Warren
P.O. Box 7326
Washington DC 20044
Ph: (202) 564-6876
www.indiastudycircle.org
E-mail: warren.john@epa.gov

Indian Ocean Study Circle
Mrs. S. Hopson
Field Acre, Hoe Benham
Newbury, Berkshire, RG20 8PD
UNITED KINGDOM

Society of Indo-China Philatelists
Ron Bentley
2600 N. 24th St.
Arlington VA 22207
www.sicp-online.org
E-mail: ron.bentley@verizon.net

Iran Philatelic Study Circle
Mehdi Esmaili
P.O. Box 750096
Forest Hills NY 11375
www.iranphilatelic.org
E-mail: m.esmaili@earthlink.net

Eire Philatelic Association (Ireland)
David J. Brennan
P.O. Box 704
Bernardsville NJ 07924
www.eirephilatelicassoc.org
E-mail: brennan704@aol.com

Society of Israel Philatelists
Michael Bass
P.O. Box 507
Northfield OH 44067
www.israelstamps.com
israelstamps@gmail.com

Italy and Colonies Study Circle
Andrew DiAnneo
1085 Dunweal Lane
Calistoga CA 94515
www.icsc.pwp.blueyonder.co.uk
E-mail: audanneo@napanet.net

International Society for Japanese Philately
William Eisenhauer
P.O. Box 230462
Tigard OR 97281
www.isjp.org
E-mail: secretary@isjp.org

Korea Stamp Society
John E. Talmage
P.O. Box 6889
Oak Ridge TN 37831
www.pennfamily.org/KSS-USA
E-mail: jtalmage@usit.net

Latin American Philatelic Society
Jules K. Beck
30½ St. #209
St. Louis Park MN 55426-3551

Liberian Philatelic Society
William Thomas Lockard
P.O. Box 106
Wellston OH 45692
Ph: (740) 384-2020
E-mail: tlockard@zoomnet.net

Liechtenstudy USA (Liechtenstein)
Paul Tremaine
410 SW Ninth St.
Dundee OR 97115
Ph: (503) 538-4500
www.liechtenstudy.org
E-mail: editor@liechtenstudy.org

Lithuania Philatelic Society
John Variakojis
3715 W. 68th St.
Chicago IL 60629
Ph: (773) 585-8649
lithuanianphilately.com/lps
E-mail: variakojis@sbcglobal.net

Luxembourg Collectors Club
Gary B. Little
7319 Beau Road
Sechelt, BC, V0N 3A8
CANADA
lcc.luxcentral.com
E-mail: gary@luxcentral.com

Malaya Study Group
David Tett
P.O. Box 34
Wheathampstead, Herts, AL4 8JY
UNITED KINGDOM
www.m-s-g.org.uk
E-mail: davidtett@aol.com

Malta Study Circle
Alec Webster
50 Worcester Road
Sutton, Surrey, SM2 6QB
UNITED KINGDOM
E-mail: alecwebster50@hotmail.com

Mexico-Elmhurst Philatelic Society International
Thurston Bland
1022 Ramona Ave.
Corona CA 92879-2123
www.mepsi.org

Asociacion Mexicana de Filatelia
AMEXFIL
Jose Maria Rico, 129, Col. Del Valle
Mexico City DF, 03100
MEXICO
E-mail: alejandro.grossmann@gmail.com

Society for Moroccan and Tunisian Philately
206, bld. Pereire
75017 Paris
FRANCE
members.aol.com/Jhaik5814
E-mail: splm206@aol.com

Nepal & Tibet Philatelic Study Group
Roger D. Skinner
1020 Covington Road
Los Altos CA 94024-5003
Ph: (650) 968-4163
www.fuchs-online.com/ntpsc/
E-mail: colinhepper@hotmail.co.uk

American Society for Netherlands Philately
Hans Kremer
50 Rockport Court
Danville CA 94526
Ph: (925) 820-5841
www.asnp1975.com
E-mail: hkremer@usa.net

New Zealand Society of Great Britain
Keith C. Collins
13 Briton Crescent
Sanderstead, Surrey, CR2 0JN
UNITED KINGDOM
www.cs.stir.ac.uk/~rgc/nzsgb
E-mail: rgc@cs.stir.ac.uk

Nicaragua Study Group
Erick Rodriguez
11817 SW 11th St.
Miami FL 33184-2501
clubs.yahoo.com/clubs/
nicaraguastudygroup
E-mail: nsgsec@yahoo.com

Society of Australasian Specialists/ Oceania
Stuart Leven
P.O. Box 24764
San Jose CA 95154-4764
Ph: (408) 978-0193
www.sasoceania.org
E-mail: sas_oceania@yahoo.com

Orange Free State Study Circle
J. R. Stroud
28 Oxford St.
Burnham-on-sea, Somerset, TA8 1LQ
UNITED KINGDOM
orangefreestatephilately.org.uk
E-mail: richardstroudph@gofast.co.uk

Pacific Islands Study Circle
John Ray
24 Woodvale Ave.
London, SE25 4AE
UNITED KINGDOM
www.pisc.org.uk
E-mail: info@pisc.org.uk

Pakistan Philatelic Study Circle
Jeff Siddiqui
P.O. Box 7002
Lynnwood WA 98046
E-mail: jeffsiddiqui@msn.com

Centro de Filatelistas Independientes de Panama
Vladimir Berrio-Lemm
Apartado 0823-02748
Plaza Concordia Panama
PANAMA
E-mail: panahistoria@gmail.com

Papuan Philatelic Society
Steven Zirinsky
P.O. Box 49, Ansonia Station
New York NY 10023
Ph: (718) 706-0616
www.communigate.co.uk/york/pps
E-mail: szirinsky@cs.com

International Philippine Philatelic Society
Donald J. Peterson
7408 Alaska Ave., NW
Washington DC 20012
Ph: (202) 291-6229
www.theipps.info
E-mail: dpeterson@comcast.net

Pitcairn Islands Study Group
Dr. Everett L. Parker
249 NW Live Oak Place
Lake City FL 32055-8906
Ph: (386) 754-8524
www.pisg.net
E-mail: eparker@hughes.net

Polonus Philatelic Society (Poland)
Robert Ogrodnik
P.O. Box 240428
Ballwin MO 63024-0428
Ph: (314) 821-6130
www.polonus.org
E-mail: rvo1937@gmail.com

International Society for Portuguese Philately
Clyde Homen
1491 Bonnie View Road
Hollister CA 95023-5117
www.portugalstamps.com
E-mail: cjh1491@sbcglobal.net

Rhodesian Study Circle
William R. Wallace
P.O. Box 16381
San Francisco CA 94116
www.rhodesianstudycircle.org.uk
E-mail: bwall8rscr@earthlink.net

Rossica Society of Russian Philately
Edward J. Laveroni
P.O. Box 320997
Los Gatos CA 95032-0116
www.rossica.org
E-mail: ed.laveroni@rossica.org

St. Helena, Ascension & Tristan Da Cunha Philatelic Society
Dr. Everett L. Parker
249 NW Live Oak Place
Lake City FL 32055-8906
Ph: (386) 754-8524
www.atlanticislands.org
E-mail: eparker@hughes.net

St. Pierre & Miquelon Philatelic Society
James R. (Jim) Taylor
2335 Paliswood Road SW
Calgary, AB, T2V 3P6
CANADA

Associated Collectors of El Salvador
Joseph D. Hahn
1015 Old Boalsburg Road Apt G-5
State College PA 16801-6149
www.elsalvadorphilately.org
E-mail: jdhahn2@gmail.com

Fellowship of Samoa Specialists
Donald Mee
23 Leo St.
Christchurch, 8051
NEW ZEALAND
www.samoaexpress.org
E-mail: donanm@xtra.co.nz

Sarawak Specialists' Society
Stu Leven
P.O. Box 24764
San Jose CA 95154-4764
Ph: (408) 978-0193
www.britborneostamps.org.uk
E-mail: stulev@ix.netcom.com

Scandinavian Collectors Club
Donald B. Brent
P.O. Box 13196
El Cajon CA 92020
www.scc-online.org
E-mail: dbrent47@sprynet.com

Slovakia Stamp Society
Jack Benchik
P.O. Box 555
Notre Dame IN 46556

Philatelic Society for Greater Southern Africa
Alan Hanks
34 Seaton Drive
Aurora, ON, L4G 2K1
CANADA
Ph: (905) 727-6993
www.psgsa.thestampweb.com
Email: alan.hanks@sympatico.ca

Spanish Philatelic Society
Robert H. Penn
1108 Walnut Drive
Danielsville PA 18038
Ph: (610) 760-8711
E-mail: roberthpenn@aol.com

Sudan Study Group
c/o North American Agent
Richard S. Wilson
53 Middle Patent Road
Bedford NY 10506
www.sudanstamps.org
E-mail: dadu1@verizon.net

American Helvetia Philatelic Society (Switzerland, Liechtenstein)
Richard T. Hall
P.O. Box 15053
Asheville NC 28813-0053
www.swiss-stamps.org
E-mail: secretary2@swiss-stamps.org

Tannu Tuva Collectors Society
Ken R. Simon
513 Sixth Ave. S.
Lake Worth FL 33460-4507
Ph: (561) 588-5954
www.tuva.tk
E-mail: yurttuva@yahoo.com

Society for Thai Philately
H. R. Blakeney
P.O. Box 25644
Oklahoma City OK 73125
E-mail: HRBlakeney@aol.com

Transvaal Study Circle
Jeff Woolgar
c/o 9 Meadow Road
Gravesend, DA11 7LR
UNITED KINGDOM
www.transvaal.org.uk

Ottoman and Near East Philatelic Society (Turkey and related areas)
Bob Stuchell
193 Valley Stream Lane
Wayne PA 19087
www.oneps.org
E-mail: rstuchell@msn.com

Ukrainian Philatelic & Numismatic Society
Michael G. Matus
157 Lucinda Lane
Wyomissing PA 19610-1026
Ph: (610) 927 3838
www.upns.org
E-mail: michael.matus@verizon.net

Vatican Philatelic Society
Sal Quinonez
1 Aldersgate, Apt. 1002
Riverhead NY 11901-1830
Ph: (516) 727-6426
www.vaticanphilately.org

British Virgin Islands Philatelic Society
Giorgio Migliavacca
P.O. Box 7007
St. Thomas VI 00801-0007
www.islandsun.com/FEATURES/
bviphil9198.html
E-mail: issun@candwbvi.net

West Africa Study Circle
Dr. Peter Newroth
Suite 603
5332 Sayward Hill Crescent
Victoria, BC, V8Y 3H8
CANADA
www.wasc.org.uk/

Western Australia Study Group
Brian Pope
P.O. Box 423
Claremont, Western Australia, 6910
AUSTRALIA
www.wastudygroup.com
E-mail: black5swan@yahoo.com.au

Yugoslavia Study Group of the Croatian Philatelic Society
Michael Lenard
1514 N. Third Ave.
Wausau WI 54401
Ph: (715) 675-2833
E-mail: mjlenard@aol.com

Topical Groups

Americana Unit
Dennis Dengel
17 Peckham Road
Poughkeepsie NY 12603-2018
www.americanaunit.org
E-mail: info@americanaunit.org

Astronomy Study Unit
John W. G. Budd
29203 Coharie Loop
San Antonio FL 33576-4643
Ph: (352) 588-4706
www.astronomystudyunit.com
E-mail: jwgbudd@earthlink.net

Bicycle Stamp Club
Tony Teideman
P.O. Box 90
Baulkham Hills, NSW, 1755
AUSTRALIA
members.tripod.com/~bicyclestamps
E-mail: tonimaur@bigpond.com

Biology Unit
Alan Hanks
34 Seaton Drive
Aurora, ON, L4G 2K1
CANADA
Ph: (905) 727-6993

Bird Stamp Society
Graham Horsman
23A E. Main St.
Blackburn West Lothian
Scotland, EH47 7QR
UNITED KINGDOM
www.bird-stamps.org/bss
E-mail: graham_horsman7@msn.com

Canadiana Study Unit
John Peebles
P.O. Box 3262, Station A
London, ON, N6A 4K3
CANADA
E-mail: c.s.u@sympatico.ca

Captain Cook Study Unit
Brian P. Sandford
173 Minuteman Drive
Concord MA 01742-1923
www.captaincooksociety.com
E-mail: US@captaincooksociety.com

Casey Jones Railroad Unit
Roy W. Menninger MD
85 SW Pepper Tree Lane
Topeka KS 66611-2072
www.uqp.de/cjr/index.htm
E-mail: roymenn@sbcglobal.net

Cats on Stamps Study Unit
Mary Ann Brown
3006 Wade Road
Durham NC 27705
www.catsonstamps.org
E-mail: mabrown@nc.rr.com

Chemistry & Physics on Stamps Study Unit
Dr. Roland Hirsch
20458 Water Point Lane
Germantown MD 20874
www.cpossu.org
E-mail: rfhirsch@cpossu.org

Chess on Stamps Study Unit
Ray C. Alexis
608 Emery St.
Longmont CO 80501
E-mail: chessstuff911459@aol.com

Christmas Philatelic Club
Linda Lawrence
312 Northwood Drive
Lexington KY 40505
www.web.295.ca/cpc/
E-mail: stamplinda@aol.com

Christopher Columbus Philatelic Society
Donald R. Ager
P.O. Box 71
Hillsboro NH 03244-0071
Ph: (603) 464-5379
ccps.maphist.nl/
E-mail: meganddon@tds.net

Collectors of Religion on Stamps
Verna Shackleton
425 N. Linwood Ave. #110
Appleton WI 54914
www.coros-society.org
E-mail: corosec@sbcglobal.net

Dogs on Stamps Study Unit
Morris Raskin
202A Newport Road
Monroe Township NJ 08831
Ph: (609) 655-7411
www.dossu.org
E-mail: mraskin@cellurian.com

Earth's Physical Features Study Group
Fred Klein
515 Magdalena Ave.
Los Altos CA 94024
epfsu.jeffhayward.com

Ebony Society of Philatelic Events and Reflections, Inc. (African-American topicals)
Manuel Gilyard
800 Riverside Drive, Suite 4H
New York NY 10032-7412
www.esperstamps.org
E-mail: gilyardmani@aol.com

Europa Study Unit
Tonny E. Van Loij
3002 S. Xanthia St.
Denver CO 80231-4237
www.europastudyunit.org/
E-mail: tvanloij@gmail.com

Fine & Performing Arts
Deborah L. Washington
6922 S. Jeffery Blvd., #7 - North
Chicago IL 60649
E-mail: brasslady@comcast.net

Fire Service in Philately
John Zaranek
81 Hillpine Road
Cheektowaga NY 14227-2259
Ph: (716) 668-3352
www.firestamps.com

Gay & Lesbian History on Stamps Club
Joe Petronie
P.O. Box 190842
Dallas TX 75219-0842
www.glhsc.org
E-mail: glhsc@aol.com

Gems, Minerals & Jewelry Study Unit
George Young
P.O. Box 632
Tewksbury MA 01876-0632
Ph: (978) 851-8283
www.rockhounds.com/rockshop/gmjsuapp.txt
E-mail: george-young@msn.com

Graphics Philately Association
Mark H. Winnegrad
P.O. Box 380
Bronx NY 10462-0380
www.graphics-stamps.org
E-mail: indybruce1@yahoo.com

Journalists, Authors & Poets on Stamps
Ms. Lee Straayer
P.O. Box 6808
Champaign IL 61826
E-mail: lstraayer@dcbnet.com

Lighthouse Stamp Society
Dalene Thomas
8612 W. Warren Lane
Lakewood CO 80227-2352
Ph: (303) 986-6620
www.lighthousestampsociety.org
E-mail: dalene@lighthousestampsociety.org

Lions International Stamp Club
John Bargus
108-2777 Barry Road RR 2
Mill Bay, BC, V0R 2P2
CANADA
Ph: (250) 743-5782

Mahatma Gandhi On Stamps Study Circle
Pramod Shivagunde
Pratik Clinic, Akluj
Solapur, Maharashtra, 413101
INDIA
E-mail: drnanda@bom6.vsnl.net.in

Mask Study Unit
Carolyn Weber
1220 Johnson Drive, Villa 104
Ventura CA 93003-0540
E-mail: cweber@venturalink.net

Masonic Study Unit
Stanley R. Longenecker
930 Wood St.
Mount Joy PA 17552-1926
Ph: (717) 669-9094
E-mail: natsco@usa.net

Mathematical Study Unit
Estelle Buccino
5615 Glenwood Road
Bethesda MD 20817-6727
Ph: (301) 718-8898
www.math.ttu.edu/msu/
E-mail: montystrauss@gmail.com

Medical Subjects Unit
Dr. Frederick C. Skvara
P.O. Box 6228
Bridgewater NJ 08807
E-mail: fcskvara@optonline.net

Military Postal History Society
Ed Dubin
1 S. Wacker Drive, Suite 3500
Chicago IL 60606
www.militaryPHS.org
E-mail: dubine@comcast.net

Mourning Stamps and Covers Club
James Bailey, Jr.
P.O. Box 937
Brownwood TX 76804
E-mail: jfbailey238@directv.net

Napoleonic Age Philatelists
Ken Berry
7513 Clayton Drive
Oklahoma City OK 73132-5636
Ph: (405) 721-0044
www.nap-stamps.org
E-mail: krb2@earthlink.net

Old World Archeological Study Unit
Caroline Scannel
11 Dawn Drive
Smithtown NY 11787-1761
www.owasu.org
E-mail: editor@owasu.org

Petroleum Philatelic Society International
Dr. Chris Coggins
174 Old Bedford Road
Luton, England, LU2 7HW
UNITED KINGDOM
E-mail: WAMTECH@Luton174.fsnet.co.uk

Philatelic Computing Study Group
Robert de Violini
P.O. Box 5025
Oxnard CA 93031-5025
www.pcsg.org
E-mail: dviolini@adelphia.net

Rotary on Stamps Unit
Gerald L. Fitzsimmons
105 Calla Ricardo
Victoria TX 77904
rotaryonstamps.org
E-mail: glfitz@suddenlink.net

Scouts on Stamps Society International
Lawrence Clay
P.O. Box 6228
Kennewick WA 99336
Ph: (509) 735-3731
www.sossi.org
E-mail: lclay3731@charter.net

Ships on Stamps Unit
Les Smith
302 Conklin Ave.
Penticton, BC, V2A 2T4
CANADA
Ph: (250) 493-7486
www.shipsonstamps.org
E-mail: lessmith440@shaw.ca

Space Unit
Carmine Torrisi
P.O. Box 780241
Maspeth NY 11378
Ph: (917) 620-5687
stargate.1usa.com/stamps/
E-mail: ctorrisi1@nyc.rr.com

Sports Philatelists International
Mark Maestrone
2824 Curie Place
San Diego CA 92122-4110
www.sportstamps.org
Email: president@sportstamps.org

Stamps on Stamps Collectors Club
Alf Jordan
156 W. Elm St.
Yarmouth ME 04096
www.stampsonstamps.org
E-mail: ajordan1@maine.rr.com

Windmill Study Unit
Walter J. Hollien
P.O. Box 346
Long Valley NJ 07853-0346
Ph: (862) 812-0030
E-mail: whollien@earthlink.net

Wine On Stamps Study Unit
Bruce L. Johnson
115 Raintree Drive
Zionsville IN 46077
www.wine-on-stamps.org
E-mail: indybruce@yahoo.com

Women on Stamps Study Unit
Hugh Gottfried
2232 26th St.
Santa Monica CA 90405-1902
E-mail: hgottfried@adelphia.net

Zeppelin Collectors Club
Cheryl Ganz
P.O. Box 77196
Washington DC 20013
www.americanairmailsociety.org

Expertizing Services

The following organizations will, for a fee, provide expert opinions about stamps submitted to them. Collectors should contact these organizations to find out about their fees and requirements before submiting philatelic material to them. The listing of these groups here is not intended as an endorsement by Scott Publishing Co.

General Expertizing Services

American Philatelic Expertizing Service (a service of the American Philatelic Society)
100 Match Factory Place
Bellefonte PA 16823-1367
Ph: (814) 237-3803
Fax: (814) 237-6128
www.stamps.org
E-mail: ambristo@stamps.org
Areas of Expertise: Worldwide

B. P. A. Expertising, Ltd.
P.O. Box 1141
Guildford, Surrey, GU5 0WR
UNITED KINGDOM
E-mail: sec@bpaexpertising.org
Areas of Expertise: British Commonwealth, Great Britain, Classics of Europe, South America and the Far East

Philatelic Foundation
70 W. 40th St., 15th Floor
New York NY 10018
Ph: (212) 221-6555
Fax: (212) 221-6208
www.philatelicfoundation.org
E-mail: philatelicfoundation@verizon.net
Areas of Expertise: U.S. & Worldwide

Philatelic Stamp Authentication and Grading, Inc.
P.O. Box 56-2111
Miami FL 33256-2111
Customer Service: (305) 345-9864
www.stampauthentication.com
E-mail: info@stampauthentication.com
Areas of Expertise: U.S., Canal Zone, Hawaii, Philippines, Canada & Provinces

Professional Stamp Experts
P.O. Box 6170
Newport Beach CA 92658
Ph: (877) STAMP-88
Fax: (949) 833-7955
www.collectors.com/pse
E-mail: pseinfo@collectors.com
Areas of Expertise: Stamps and covers of U.S., U.S. Possessions, British Commonwealth

Royal Philatelic Society Expert Committee
41 Devonshire Place
London, W1N 1PE
UNITED KINGDOM
www.rpsl.org.uk/experts.html
E-mail: experts@rpsl.org.uk
Areas of Expertise: Worldwide

Expertizing Services Covering Specific Fields Or Countries

China Stamp Society Expertizing Service
1050 W. Blue Ridge Blvd.
Kansas City MO 64145
Ph: (816) 942-6300
E-mail: hjmesq@aol.com
Areas of Expertise: China

Confederate Stamp Alliance Authentication Service
Gen. Frank Crown, Jr.
P.O. Box 278
Capshaw AL 35742-0396
Ph: (302) 422-2656
Fax: (302) 424-1990
www.csalliance.org
E-mail: csaas@knology.net
Areas of Expertise: Confederate stamps and postal history

Errors, Freaks and Oddities Collectors Club Expertizing Service
138 East Lakemont Drive
Kingsland GA 31548
Ph: (912) 729-1573
Areas of Expertise: U.S. errors, freaks and oddities

Estonian Philatelic Society Expertizing Service
39 Clafford Lane
Melville NY 11747
Ph: (516) 421-2078
E-mail: esto4@aol.com
Areas of Expertise: Estonia

Hawaiian Philatelic Society Expertizing Service
P.O. Box 10115
Honolulu HI 96816-0115
Areas of Expertise: Hawaii

Hong Kong Stamp Society Expertizing Service
P.O. Box 206
Glenside PA 19038
Fax: (215) 576-6850
Areas of Expertise: Hong Kong

International Association of Philatelic Experts
United States Associate members:

Paul Buchsbayew
119 W. 57th St.
New York NY 10019
Ph: (212) 977-7734
Fax: (212) 977-8653
Areas of Expertise: Russia, Soviet Union

William T. Crowe
P.O. Box 2090
Danbury CT 06813-2090
E-mail: wtcrowe@aol.com
Areas of Expertise: United States

John Lievsay
(see American Philatelic Expertizing Service and Philatelic Foundation)
Areas of Expertise: France

Robert W. Lyman
P.O. Box 348
Irvington on Hudson NY 10533
Ph and Fax: (914) 591-6937
Areas of Expertise: British North America, New Zealand

Robert Odenweller
P.O. Box 401
Bernardsville NJ 07924-0401
Ph and Fax: (908) 766-5460
Areas of Expertise: New Zealand, Samoa to 1900

Sergio Sismondo
10035 Carousel Center Drive
Syracuse NY 13290-0001
Ph: (315) 422-2331
Fax: (315) 422-2956
Areas of Expertise: British East Africa, Camerouns, Cape of Good Hope, Canada, British North America

International Society for Japanese Philately Expertizing Committee
132 North Pine Terrace
Staten Island NY 10312-4052
Ph: (718) 227-5229
Areas of Expertise: Japan and related areas, except WWII Japanese Occupation issues

International Society for Portuguese Philately Expertizing Service
P.O. Box 43146
Philadelphia PA 19129-3146
Ph and Fax: (215) 843-2106
E-mail: s.s.washburne@worldnet.att.net
Areas of Expertise: Portugal and Colonies

Mexico-Elmhurst Philatelic Society International Expert Committee
P.O. Box 1133
West Covina CA 91793
Areas of Expertise: Mexico

Ukrainian Philatelic & Numismatic Society Expertizing Service
30552 Dell Lane
Warren MI 48092-1862
Areas of Expertise: Ukraine, Western Ukraine

V. G. Greene Philatelic Research Foundation
P.O. Box 204, Station Q
Toronto, ON, M4T 2M1
CANADA
Ph: (416) 921-2073
Fax: (416) 921-1282
www.greenefoundation.ca
E-mail: vggfoundation@on.aibn.com
Areas of Expertise: British North America

Information on Catalogue Values, Grade and Condition

Catalogue Value

The Scott Catalogue value is a retail value; that is, an amount you could expect to pay for a stamp in the grade of Very Fine with no faults. Any exceptions to the grade valued will be noted in the text. The general introduction on the following pages and the individual section introductions further explain the type of material that is valued. The value listed for any given stamp is a reference that reflects recent actual dealer selling prices for that item.

Dealer retail price lists, public auction results, published prices in advertising and individual solicitation of retail prices from dealers, collectors and specialty organizations have been used in establishing the values found in this catalogue. Scott Publishing Co. values stamps, but Scott is not a company engaged in the business of buying and selling stamps as a dealer.

Use this catalogue as a guide for buying and selling. The actual price you pay for a stamp may be higher or lower than the catalogue value because of many different factors, including the amount of personal service a dealer offers, or increased or decreased interest in the country or topic represented by a stamp or set. An item may occasionally be offered at a lower price as a "loss leader," or as part of a special sale. You also may obtain an item inexpensively at public auction because of little interest at that time or as part of a large lot.

Stamps that are of a lesser grade than Very Fine, or those with condition problems, generally trade at lower prices than those given in this catalogue. Stamps of exceptional quality in both grade and condition often command higher prices than those listed.

Values for pre-1900 unused issues are for stamps with approximately half or more of their original gum. Stamps with most or all of their original gum may be expected to sell for more, and stamps with less than half of their original gum may be expected to sell for somewhat less than the values listed. On rarer stamps, it may be expected that the original gum will be somewhat more disturbed than it will be on more common issues. Post-1900 unused issues are assumed to have full original gum. From breakpoints in most countries' listings, stamps are valued as never hinged, due to the wide availability of stamps in that condition. These notations are prominently placed in the listings and in the country information preceding the listings. Some countries also feature listings with dual values for hinged and never-hinged stamps.

Grade

A stamp's grade and condition are crucial to its value. The accompanying illustrations show examples of Very Fine stamps from different time periods, along with examples of stamps in Fine to Very Fine and Extremely Fine grades as points of reference. When a stamp seller offers a stamp in any grade from fine to superb without further qualifying statements, that stamp should not only have the centering grade as defined, but it also should be free of faults or other condition problems.

FINE stamps (illustrations not shown) have designs that are quite off center, with the perforations on one or two sides very close to the design but not quite touching it. There is white space between the perforations and the design that is minimal but evident to the unaided eye. Imperforate stamps may have small margins, and earlier issues may show the design just touching one edge of the stamp design. Very early perforated issues normally will have the perforations slightly cutting into the design. Used stamps may have heavier than usual cancellations.

FINE-VERY FINE stamps will be somewhat off center on one side, or slightly off center on two sides. Imperforate stamps will have two margins of at least normal size, and the design will not touch any edge. For perforated stamps, the perfs are well clear of the design, but are still noticeably off center. *However, early issues of a country may be printed in such a way that the design naturally is very close to the edges. In these cases, the perforations may cut into the design very slightly.* Used stamps will not have a cancellation that detracts from the design.

VERY FINE stamps will be just slightly off center on one or two sides, but the design will be well clear of the edge. The stamp will present a nice, balanced appearance. Imperforate stamps will be well centered within normal-sized margins. *However, early issues of many countries may be printed in such a way that the perforations may touch the design on one or more sides. Where this is the case, a boxed note will be found defining the centering and margins of the stamps being valued.* Used stamps will have light or otherwise neat cancellations. This is the grade used to establish Scott Catalogue values.

EXTREMELY FINE stamps are close to being perfectly centered. Imperforate stamps will have even margins that are slightly larger than normal. Even the earliest perforated issues will have perforations clear of the design on all sides.

Scott Publishing Co. recognizes that there is no formally enforced grading scheme for postage stamps, and that the final price you pay or obtain for a stamp will be determined by individual agreement at the time of transaction.

Condition

Grade addresses only centering and (for used stamps) cancellation. *Condition* refers to factors other than grade that affect a stamp's desirability.

Factors that can increase the value of a stamp include exceptionally wide margins, particularly fresh color, the presence of selvage, and plate or die varieties. Unusual cancels on used stamps (particularly those of the 19th century) can greatly enhance their value as well.

Factors other than faults that decrease the value of a stamp include loss of original gum, regumming, a hinge remnant or foreign object adhering to the gum, natural inclusions, straight edges, and markings or notations applied by collectors or dealers.

Faults include missing pieces, tears, pin or other holes, surface scuffs, thin spots, creases, toning, short or pulled perforations, clipped perforations, oxidation or other forms of color changelings, soiling, stains, and such man-made changes as reperforations or the chemical removal or lightening of a cancellation.

Grading Illustrations

On the following two pages are illustrations of various stamps from countries appearing in this volume. These stamps are arranged by country, and they represent early or important issues that are often found in widely different grades in the marketplace. The editors believe the illustrations will prove useful in showing the margin size and centering that will be seen on the various issues.

In addition to the matters of margin size and centering, collectors are reminded that the very fine stamps valued in the Scott catalogues also will possess fresh color and intact perforations, and they will be free from defects.

Examples shown are computer-manipulated images made from single digitized master illustrations.

Stamp Illustrations Used in the Catalogue

It is important to note that the stamp images used for identification purposes in this catlaogue may not be indicative of the grade of stamp being valued. Refer to the written discussion of grades on this page and to the grading illustrations on the following two pages for grading information.

Fine-Very Fine

SCOTT
CATALOGUES
VALUE
STAMPS IN
THIS GRADE

Very Fine

Extremely Fine

Fine-Very Fine

SCOTT
CATALOGUES
VALUE
STAMPS IN
THIS GRADE

Very Fine

Extremely Fine

Fine-Very Fine →

**SCOTT
CATALOGUES
VALUE
STAMPS IN
THIS GRADE**

Very Fine →

Extremely Fine →

Fine-Very Fine →

**SCOTT
CATALOGUES
VALUE
STAMPS IN
THIS GRADE**

Very Fine →

Extremely Fine →

For purposes of helping to determine the gum condition and value of an unused stamp, Scott Publishing Co. presents the following chart which details different gum conditions and indicates how the conditions correlate with the Scott values for unused stamps. Used together, the Illustrated Grading Chart on the previous pages and this Illustrated Gum Chart should allow catalogue users to better understand the grade and gum condition of stamps valued in the Scott catalogues.

Gum Categories:	MINT N.H.	ORIGINAL GUM (O.G.)				NO GUM
	Mint Never Hinged *Free from any disturbance*	**Lightly Hinged** *Faint impression of a removed hinge over a small area*	**Hinge Mark or Remnant** *Prominent hinged spot with part or all of the hinge remaining*	**Large part o.g.** *Approximately half or more of the gum intact*	**Small part o.g.** *Approximately less than half of the gum intact*	**No gum** *Only if issued with gum*
Commonly Used Symbol:	★ ★	★	★	★	★	(★)
Pre-1900 Issues (Pre-1881 for U.S.)	*Very fine pre-1900 stamps in these categories trade at a premium over Scott value*			Scott Value for "Unused"		Scott "No Gum" listings for selected unused classic stamps
From 1900 to breakpoints for listings of never-hinged stamps	Scott "Never Hinged" listings for selected unused stamps	Scott Value for "Unused" (Actual value will be affected by the degree of hinging of the full o.g.)				
From breakpoints noted for many countries	Scott Value for "Unused"					

Never Hinged (NH; ★★): A never-hinged stamp will have full original gum that will have no hinge mark or disturbance. The presence of an expertizer's mark does not disqualify a stamp from this designation.

Original Gum (OG; ★): Pre-1900 stamps should have approximately half or more of their original gum. On rarer stamps, it may be expected that the original gum will be somewhat more disturbed than it will be on more common issues. Post-1900 stamps should have full original gum. Original gum will show some disturbance caused by a previous hinge(s) which may be present or entirely removed. The actual value of a post-1900 stamp will be affected by the degree of hinging of the full original gum.

Disturbed Original Gum: Gum showing noticeable effects of humidity, climate or hinging over more than half of the gum. The significance of gum disturbance in valuing a stamp in any of the Original Gum categories depends on the degree of disturbance, the rarity and normal gum condition of the issue and other variables affecting quality.

Regummed (RG; (★)): A regummed stamp is a stamp without gum that has had some type of gum privately applied at a time after it was issued. This normally is done to deceive collectors and/or dealers into thinking that the stamp has original gum and therefore has a higher value. A regummed stamp is considered the same as a stamp with none of its original gum for purposes of grading.

Understanding the Listings

On the opposite page is an enlarged "typical" listing from this catalogue. Below are detailed explanations of each of the highlighted parts of the listing.

① **Scott number** — Scott catalogue numbers are used to identify specific items when buying, selling or trading stamps. Each listed postage stamp from every country has a unique Scott catalogue number. Therefore, Germany Scott 99, for example, can only refer to a single stamp. Although the Scott catalogue usually lists stamps in chronological order by date of issue, there are exceptions. When a country has issued a set of stamps over a period of time, those stamps within the set are kept together without regard to date of issue. This follows the normal collecting approach of keeping stamps in their natural sets.

When a country issues a set of stamps over a period of time, a group of consecutive catalogue numbers is reserved for the stamps in that set, as issued. If that group of numbers proves to be too few, capital-letter suffixes, such as "A" or "B," may be added to existing numbers to create enough catalogue numbers to cover all items in the set. A capital-letter suffix indicates a major Scott catalogue number listing. Scott generally uses a suffix letter only once. Therefore, a catalogue number listing with a capital-letter suffix will seldom be found with the same letter (lower case) used as a minor-letter listing. If there is a Scott 16A in a set, for example, there will seldom be a Scott 16a. However, a minor-letter "a" listing may be added to a major number containing an "A" suffix (Scott 16Aa, for example).

Suffix letters are cumulative. A minor "b" variety of Scott 16A would be Scott 16Ab, not Scott 16b.

There are times when a reserved block of Scott catalogue numbers is too large for a set, leaving some numbers unused. Such gaps in the numbering sequence also occur when the catalogue editors move an item's listing elsewhere or have removed it entirely from the catalogue. Scott does not attempt to account for every possible number, but rather attempts to assure that each stamp is assigned its own number.

Scott numbers designating regular postage normally are only numerals. Scott numbers for other types of stamps, such as air post, semi-postal, postal tax, postage due, occupation and others have a prefix consisting of one or more capital letters or a combination of numerals and capital letters.

② **Illustration number** — Illustration or design-type numbers are used to identify each catalogue illustration. For most sets, the lowest face-value stamp is shown. It then serves as an example of the basic design approach for other stamps not illustrated. Where more than one stamp use the same illustration number, but have differences in design, the design paragraph or the description line clearly indicates the design on each stamp not illustrated. Where there are both vertical and horizontal designs in a set, a single illustration may be used, with the exceptions noted in the design paragraph or description line.

When an illustration is followed by a lower-case letter in parentheses, such as "A2(b)," the trailing letter indicates which overprint or surcharge illustration applies.

Illustrations normally are 70 percent of the original size of the stamp. Oversized stamps, blocks and souvenir sheets are reduced even more. Overprints and surcharges are shown at 100 percent of their original size if shown alone, but are 70 percent of original size if shown on stamps. In some cases, the illustration will be placed above the set, between listings or omitted completely. Overprint and surcharge illustrations are not placed in this catalogue for purposes of expertizing stamps.

③ **Paper color** — The color of a stamp's paper is noted in italic type when the paper used is not white.

④ **Listing styles** — There are two principal types of catalogue listings: major and minor.

Major listings are in a larger type style than minor listings. The catalogue number is a numeral that can be found with or without a capital-letter suffix, and with or without a prefix.

Minor listings are in a smaller type style and have a small-letter suffix or (if the listing immediately follows that of the major number)

may show only the letter. These listings identify a variety of the major item. Examples include perforation and shade differences, multiples (some souvenir sheets, booklet panes and se-tenant combinations), and singles of multiples.

Examples of major number listings include 16, 28A, B97, C13A, 10N5, and 10N6A. Examples of minor numbers are 16a and C13Ab.

⑤ **Basic information about a stamp or set** — Introducing each stamp issue is a small section (usually a line listing) of basic information about a stamp or set. This section normally includes the date of issue, method of printing, perforation, watermark and, sometimes, some additional information of note. *Printing method, perforation and watermark apply to the following sets until a change is noted.* Stamps created by overprinting or surcharging previous issues are assumed to have the same perforation, watermark, printing method and other production characteristics as the original. Dates of issue are as precise as Scott is able to confirm and often reflect the dates on first-day covers, rather than the actual date of release.

⑥ **Denomination** — This normally refers to the face value of the stamp; that is, the cost of the unused stamp at the post office at the time of issue. When a denomination is shown in parentheses, it does not appear on the stamp. This includes the non-denominated stamps of the United States, Brazil and Great Britain, for example.

⑦ **Color or other description** — This area provides information to solidify identification of a stamp. In many recent cases, a description of the stamp design appears in this space, rather than a listing of colors.

⑧ **Year of issue** — In stamp sets that have been released in a period that spans more than a year, the number shown in parentheses is the year that stamp first appeared. Stamps without a date appeared during the first year of the issue. Dates are not always given for minor varieties.

⑨ **Value unused and Value used** — The Scott catalogue values are based on stamps that are in a grade of Very Fine unless stated otherwise. Unused values refer to items that have not seen postal, revenue or any other duty for which they were intended. Pre-1900 unused stamps that were issued with gum must have at least most of their original gum. Later issues are assumed to have full original gum. From breakpoints specified in most countries' listings, stamps are valued as never hinged. Stamps issued without gum are noted. Modern issues with PVA or other synthetic adhesives may appear ungummed. Unused self-adhesive stamps are valued as appearing undisturbed on their original backing paper. Values for used self-adhesive stamps are for examples either on piece or off piece. For a more detailed explanation of these values, please see the "Catalogue Value," "Condition" and "Understanding Valuing Notations" sections elsewhere in this introduction.

In some cases, where used stamps are more valuable than unused stamps, the value is for an example with a contemporaneous cancel, rather than a modern cancel or a smudge or other unclear marking. For those stamps that were released for postal and fiscal purposes, the used value represents a postally used stamp. Stamps with revenue cancels generally sell for less.

Stamps separated from a complete se-tenant multiple usually will be worth less than a pro-rated portion of the se-tenant multiple, and stamps lacking the attached labels that are noted in the listings will be worth less than the values shown.

⑩ **Changes in basic set information** — Bold type is used to show any changes in the basic data given for a set of stamps. These basic data categories include perforation gauge measurement, paper type, printing method and watermark.

⑪ **Total value of a set** — The total value of sets of three or more stamps issued after 1900 are shown. The set line also notes the range of Scott numbers and total number of stamps included in the grouping. The actual value of a set consisting predominantly of stamps having the minimum value of 25 cents may be less than the total value shown. Similarly, the actual value or catalogue value of se-tenant pairs or of blocks consisting of stamps having the minimum value of 25 cents may be less than the catalogue values of the component parts.

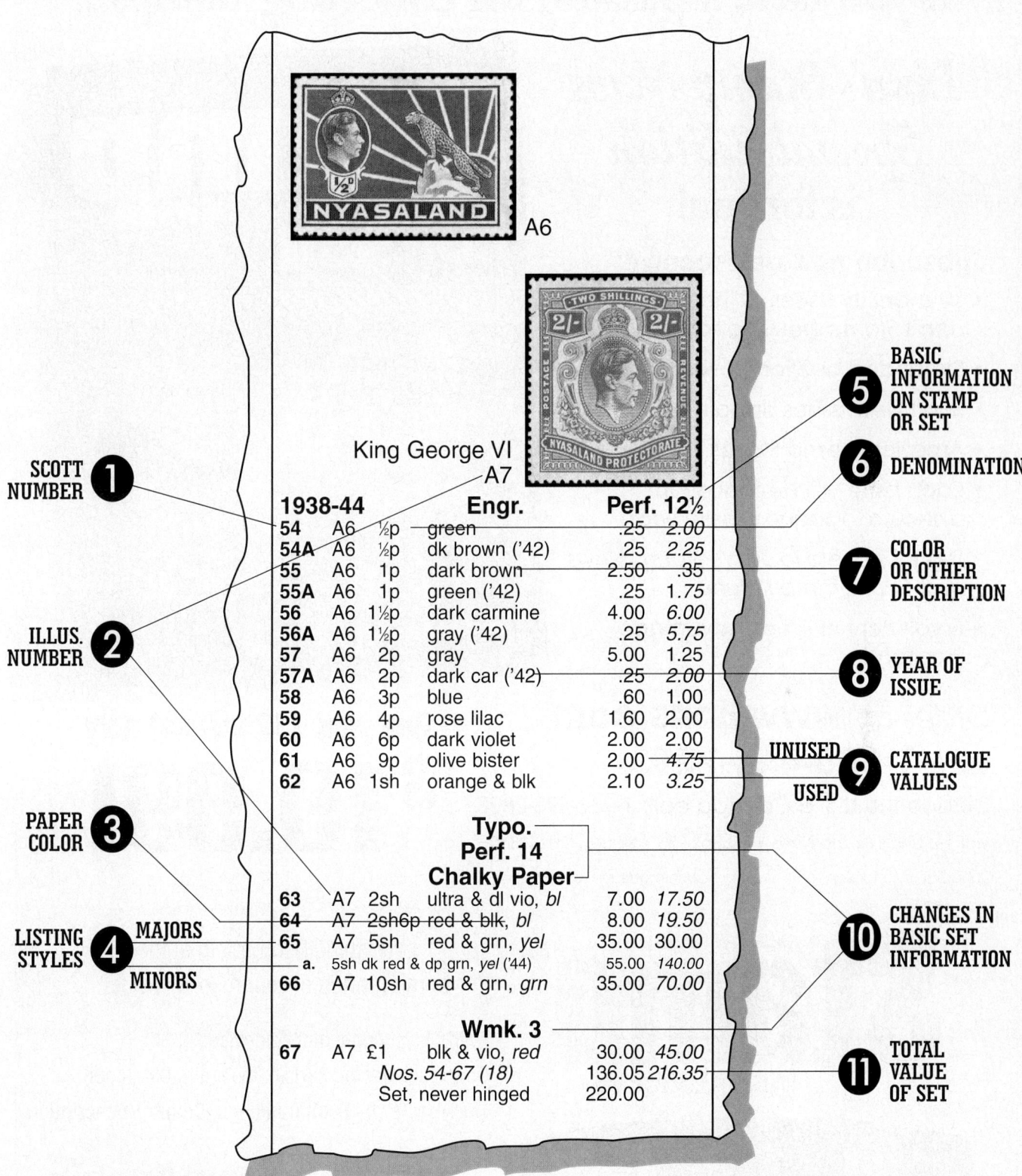

A6

King George VI
A7

SCOTT NUMBER **1**

ILLUS. NUMBER **2**

PAPER COLOR **3**

LISTING STYLES **4**
MAJORS
MINORS

5 BASIC INFORMATION ON STAMP OR SET

6 DENOMINATION

7 COLOR OR OTHER DESCRIPTION

8 YEAR OF ISSUE

9 CATALOGUE VALUES
UNUSED
USED

10 CHANGES IN BASIC SET INFORMATION

11 TOTAL VALUE OF SET

1938-44			**Engr.**	**Perf. 12½**	
54	A6	½p	green	.25	*2.00*
54A	A6	½p	dk brown ('42)	.25	*2.25*
55	A6	1p	dark brown	2.50	.35
55A	A6	1p	green ('42)	.25	1.75
56	A6	1½p	dark carmine	4.00	*6.00*
56A	A6	1½p	gray ('42)	.25	5.75
57	A6	2p	gray	5.00	1.25
57A	A6	2p	dark car ('42)	.25	*2.00*
58	A6	3p	blue	.60	1.00
59	A6	4p	rose lilac	1.60	2.00
60	A6	6p	dark violet	2.00	2.00
61	A6	9p	olive bister	2.00	*4.75*
62	A6	1sh	orange & blk	2.10	*3.25*

Typo.
Perf. 14
Chalky Paper

63	A7	2sh	ultra & dl vio, *bl*	7.00	*17.50*
64	A7	2sh6p	red & blk, *bl*	8.00	*19.50*
65	A7	5sh	red & grn, *yel*	35.00	30.00
a.			5sh dk red & dp grn, *yel* ('44)	55.00	*140.00*
66	A7	10sh	red & grn, *grn*	35.00	*70.00*

Wmk. 3

67	A7	£1	blk & vio, *red*	30.00	*45.00*
			Nos. 54-67 (18)	136.05	*216.35*
			Set, never hinged	220.00	

Catalogue Listing Policy

It is the intent of Scott Publishing Co. to list all postage stamps of the world in the *Scott Standard Postage Stamp Catalogue*. The only strict criteria for listing is that stamps be decreed legal for postage by the issuing country and that the issuing country actually have an operating postal system. Whether the primary intent of issuing a given stamp or set was for sale to postal patrons or to stamp collectors is not part of our listing criteria. Scott's role is to provide basic comprehensive postage stamp information. It is up to each stamp collector to choose which items to include in a collection.

It is Scott's objective to seek reasons why a stamp should be listed, rather than why it should not. Nevertheless, there are certain types of items that will not be listed. These include the following:

1. Unissued items that are not officially distributed or released by the issuing postal authority. If such items are officially issued at a later date by the country, they will be listed. Unissued items consist of those that have been printed and then held from sale for reasons such as change in government, errors found on stamps or something deemed objectionable about a stamp subject or design.

2. Stamps "issued" by non-existent postal entities or fantasy countries, such as Nagaland, Occusi-Ambeno, Staffa, Sedang, Torres Straits and others. Also, stamps "issued" in the names of legitimate, stamp-issuing countries that are not authorized by those countries.

3. Semi-official or unofficial items not required for postage. Examples include items issued by private agencies for their own express services. When such items are required for delivery, or are valid as prepayment of postage, they are listed.

4. Local stamps issued for local use only. Postage stamps issued by governments specifically for "domestic" use, such as Haiti Scott 219-228, or the United States non-denominated stamps, are not considered to be locals, since they are valid for postage throughout the country of origin.

5. Items not valid for postal use. For example, a few countries have issued souvenir sheets that are not valid for postage. This area also includes a number of worldwide charity labels (some denominated) that do not pay postage.

6. Intentional varieties, such as imperforate stamps that look like their perforated counterparts and are usually issued in very small quantities. Also, other egregiously exploitative issues such as stamps sold for far more than face value, stamps purposefully issued in artificially small quantities or only against advance orders, stamps awarded only to a selected audience such as a philatelic bureau's standing order customers, or stamps sold only in conjunction with other products. All of these kinds of items are usually controlled issues and/or are intended for speculation. These items normally will be included in a footnote.

7. Items distributed by the issuing government only to a limited group, club, philatelic exhibition or a single stamp dealer or other private company. These items normally will be included in a footnote.

8. Stamps not available to collectors. These generally are rare items, all of which are held by public institutions such as museums. The existence of such items often will be cited in footnotes.

The fact that a stamp has been used successfully as postage, even on international mail, is not in itself sufficient proof that it was legitimately issued. Numerous examples of so-called stamps from non-existent countries are known to have been used to post letters that have successfully passed through the international mail system.

There are certain items that are subject to interpretation. When a stamp falls outside our specifications, it may be listed along with a cautionary footnote.

A number of factors are considered in our approach to analyzing how a stamp is listed. The following list of factors is presented to share with you, the catalogue user, the complexity of the listing process.

Additional printings — "Additional printings" of a previously issued stamp may range from an item that is totally different to cases where it is impossible to differentiate from the original. At least a minor number (a small-letter suffix) is assigned if there is a distinct change in stamp shade, noticeably redrawn design, or a significantly different perforation measurement. A major number (numeral or numeral and capital-letter combination) is assigned if the editors feel the "additional printing" is sufficiently different from the original that it constitutes a different issue.

Commemoratives — Where practical, commemoratives with the same theme are placed in a set. For example, the U.S. Civil War Centennial set of 1961-65 and the Constitution Bicentennial series of 1989-90 appear as sets. Countries such as Japan and Korea issue such material on a regular basis, with an announced, or at least predictable, number of stamps known in advance. Occasionally, however, stamp sets that were released over a period of years have been separated. Appropriately placed footnotes will guide you to each set's continuation.

Definitive sets — Blocks of numbers generally have been reserved for definitive sets, based on previous experience with any given country. If a few more stamps were issued in a set than originally expected,

they often have been inserted into the original set with a capital-letter suffix, such as U.S. Scott 1059A. If it appears that many more stamps than the originally allotted block will be released before the set is completed, a new block of numbers will be reserved, with the original one being closed off. In some cases, such as the U.S. Transportation and Great Americans series, several blocks of numbers exist. Appropriately placed footnotes will guide you to each set's continuation.

New country — Membership in the Universal Postal Union is not a consideration for listing status or order of placement within the catalogue. The index will tell you in what volume or page number the listings begin.

"No release date" items — The amount of information available for any given stamp issue varies greatly from country to country and even from time to time. Extremely comprehensive information about new stamps is available from some countries well before the stamps are released. By contrast some countries do not provide information about stamps or release dates. Most countries, however, fall between these extremes. A country may provide denominations or subjects of stamps from upcoming issues that are not issued as planned. Sometimes, philatelic agencies, those private firms hired to represent countries, add these later-issued items to sets well after the formal release date. This time period can range from weeks to years. If these items were officially released by the country, they will be added to the appropriate spot in the set. In many cases, the specific release date of a stamp or set of stamps may never be known.

Overprints — The color of an overprint is always noted if it is other than black. Where more than one color of ink has been used on overprints of a single set, the color used is noted. Early overprint and surcharge illustrations were altered to prevent their use by forgers.

Personalized Stamps — Since 1999, the special service of personalizing stamp vignettes, or labels attached to stamps, has been offered to customers by postal administrations of many countries. Sheets of these stamps are sold, singly or in quantity, only through special orders made by mail, in person, or through a sale on a computer website with the postal administrations or their agents for which an extra fee is charged, though some countries offer to collectors at face value personalized stamps having generic images in the vignettes or on the attached labels. It is impossible for any catalogue to know what images have been chosen by customers. Images can be 1) owned or created by the customer, 2) a generic image, or 3) an image pulled from a library of stock images on the stamp creation website. It is also impossible to know the quantity printed for any stamp having a particular image. So from a valuing standpoint, any image is equivalent to any other image for any personalized stamp having the same catalogue number. Illustrations of personalized stamps in the catalogue are not always those of stamps having generic images.

Personalized items are listed with some exceptions. These include:
1. Stamps or sheets that have attached labels that the customer cannot personalize, but which are nonetheless marketed as "personalized," and are sold for far more than the franking value.
2. Stamps or sheets that can be personalized by the customer, but where a portion of the print run must be ceded to the issuing country for sale to other customers.
3. Stamps or sheets that are created exclusively for a particular commercial client, or clients, including stamps that differ from any similar stamp that has been made available to the public.
4. Stamps or sheets that are deliberately conceived by the issuing authority that have been, or are likely to be, created with an excessive number of different face values, sizes, or other features that are changeable.
5. Stamps or sheets that are created by postal administrations using the same system of stamp personalization that has been put in place for use by the public that are printed in limited quantities and sold above face value.
6. Stamps or sheets that are created by licensees not directly affiliated or controlled by a postal administration.

Excluded items may or may not be footnoted.

Se-tenants — Connected stamps of differing features (se-tenants) will be listed in the format most commonly collected. This includes pairs, blocks or larger multiples. Se-tenant units are not always symmetrical. An example is Australia Scott 508, which is a block of seven stamps. If the stamps are primarily collected as a unit, the major number may be assigned to the multiple, with minors going to each component stamp. In cases where continuous-design or other unit se-tenants will receive significant postal use, each stamp is given a major Scott number listing. This includes issues from the United States, Canada, Germany and Great Britain, for example.

Special Notices

Classification of stamps

The *Scott Standard Postage Stamp Catalogue* lists stamps by country of issue. The next level of organization is a listing by section on the basis of the function of the stamps. The principal sections cover regular postage, semi-postal, air post, special delivery, registration, postage due and other categories. Except for regular postage, catalogue numbers for all sections include a prefix letter (or number-letter combination) denoting the class to which a given stamp belongs. When some countries issue sets containing stamps from more than one category, the catalogue will at times list all of the stamps in one category (such as air post stamps listed as part of a postage set).

The following is a listing of the most commonly used catalogue prefixes.

Prefix .... Category
C.........Air Post
M........Military
P.........Newspaper
N.........Occupation - Regular Issues
O........Official
Q........Parcel Post
J..........Postage Due
RA......Postal Tax
B........Semi-Postal
E.........Special Delivery
MR......War Tax

Other prefixes used by more than one country include the following:
H.........Acknowledgment of Receipt
I..........Late Fee
CO......Air Post Official
CQ......Air Post Parcel Post
RAC....Air Post Postal Tax
CF......Air Post Registration
CB......Air Post Semi-Postal
CBO...Air Post Semi-Postal Official
CE......Air Post Special Delivery
EY.......Authorized Delivery
S.........Franchise
G........Insured Letter
GY......Marine Insurance
MC.....Military Air Post
MQ.....Military Parcel Post
NC......Occupation - Air Post
NO......Occupation - Official
NJ........Occupation - Postage Due
NRA....Occupation - Postal Tax
NB......Occupation - Semi-Postal
NE......Occupation Special Delivery
QY......Parcel Post Authorized Delivery
AR......Postal-fiscal
RAJ.....Postal Tax Due
RAB....Postal Tax Semi-Postal
F.........Registration
EB.......Semi-Postal Special Delivery
EO......Special Delivery Official
QE......Special Handling

New issue listings

Updates to this catalogue appear each month in the *Linn's Stamp News Special Edition* magazine. Included in this update are additions to the listings of countries found in the *Scott Standard Postage Stamp Catalogue* and the *Specialized Catalogue of United States Stamps and Covers*, as well as corrections and updates to current editions of this catalogue.

From time to time there will be changes in the final listings of stamps from the *Linn's Stamp News Special Edition* to the next edition of the catalogue. This occurs as more information about certain stamps or sets becomes available.

The catalogue update section of the *Linn's Stamp News Special Edition* is the most timely presentation of this material available. Annual subscriptions to *Linn's Stamp News* are available from Linn's Stamp News, Box 926, Sidney, OH 45365-0926.

Number additions, deletions & changes

A listing of catalogue number additions, deletions and changes from the previous edition of the catalogue appears in each volume. See Catalogue Number Additions, Deletions & Changes in the table of contents for the location of this list.

Understanding valuing notations

The *minimum catalogue value* of an individual stamp or set is 25 cents. This represents a portion of the cost incurred by a dealer when he prepares an individual stamp for resale. As a point of philatelic-economic fact, the lower the value shown for an item in this catalogue, the greater the percentage of that value is attributed to dealer mark up and profit margin. In many cases, such as the 25-cent minimum value, that price does not cover the labor or other costs involved with stocking it as an individual stamp. The sum of minimum values in a set does not properly represent the value of a complete set primarily composed of a number of minimum-value stamps, nor does the sum represent the actual value of a packet made up of minimum-value stamps. Thus a packet of 1,000 different common stamps — each of which has a catalogue value of 25 cents — normally sells for considerably less than 250 dollars!

The *absence of a retail value* for a stamp does not necessarily suggest that a stamp is scarce or rare. A dash in the value column means that the stamp is known in a stated form or variety, but information is either lacking or insufficient for purposes of establishing a usable catalogue value.

Stamp values in *italics* generally refer to items that are difficult to value accurately. For expensive items, such as those priced at $1,000 or higher, a value in italics indicates that the affected item trades very seldom. For inexpensive items, a value in italics represents a warning. One example is a "blocked" issue where the issuing postal administration may have controlled one stamp in a set in an attempt to make the whole set more valuable. Another example is an item that sold at an extreme multiple of face value in the marketplace at the time of its issue.

One type of warning to collectors that appears in the catalogue is illustrated by a stamp that is valued considerably higher in used condition than it is as unused. In this case, collectors are cautioned to be certain the used version has a genuine and contemporaneous cancellation. The type of cancellation on a stamp can be an important factor in determining its sale price. Catalogue values do not apply to fiscal, telegraph or non-contemporaneous postal cancels, unless otherwise noted.

Some countries have released back issues of stamps in canceled-to-order form, sometimes covering as much as a 10-year period. The Scott Catalogue values for used stamps reflect canceled-to-order material when such stamps are found to predominate in the marketplace for the issue involved. Notes frequently appear in the stamp listings to specify which items are valued as canceled-to-order, or if there is a premium for postally used examples.

Many countries sell canceled-to-order stamps at a marked reduction of face value. Countries that sell or have sold canceled-to-order stamps at *full* face value include United Nations, Australia, Netherlands, France and Switzerland. It may be almost impossible to identify such stamps if the gum has been removed, because official government canceling devices are used. Postally used examples of these items on cover, however, are usually worth more than the canceled-to-order stamps with original gum.

Abbreviations

Scott Publishing Co. uses a consistent set of abbreviations throughout this catalogue to conserve space, while still providing necessary information.

COLOR ABBREVIATIONS

amb. amber	crim. crimson	ol ..... olive
anil.. aniline	cr ..... cream	olvn . olivine
ap.... apple	dk .... dark	org... orange
aqua aquamarine	dl ..... dull	pck .. peacock
az .... azure	dp.... deep	pnksh pinkish
bis ... bister	db.... drab	Prus. Prussian
bl..... blue	emer emerald	pur... purple
bld... blood	gldn. golden	redsh reddish
blk... black	gryshgrayish	res ... reseda
bril... brilliant	grn... green	ros ... rosine
brn... brown	grnsh greenish	ryl.... royal
brnsh brownish	hel ... heliotrope	sal ... salmon
brnz. bronze	hn.... henna	saph sapphire
brt.... bright	ind... indigo	scar . scarlet
brnt . burnt	int .... intense	sep .. sepia
car... carmine	lav ... lavender	sien . sienna
cer ... cerise	lem .. lemon	sil..... silver
chlky chalky	lil ..... lilac	sl...... slate
chamchamois	lt ...... light	stl ..... steel
chnt. chestnut	mag. magenta	turq.. turquoise
choc chocolate	man. manila	ultra ultramarine
chr... chrome	mar.. maroon	Ven.. Venetian
cit .... citron	mv ... mauve	ver ... vermilion
cl...... claret	multi multicolored	vio ... violet
cob .. cobalt	mlky milky	yel ... yellow
cop .. copper	myr.. myrtle	yelsh yellowish

When no color is given for an overprint or surcharge, black is the color used. Abbreviations for colors used for overprints and surcharges include: "(B)" or "(Blk)," black; "(Bl)," blue; "(R)," red; and "(G)," green.

Additional abbreviations in this catalogue are shown below:

Adm.	Administration
AFL...............	American Federation of Labor
Anniv.............	Anniversary
APS	American Philatelic Society
Assoc.	Association
ASSR.	Autonomous Soviet Socialist Republic
b.	Born
BEP...............	Bureau of Engraving and Printing
Bicent............	Bicentennial
Bklt.	Booklet
Brit.	British
btwn.	Between
Bur...............	Bureau
c. or ca..........	Circa
Cat.	Catalogue
Cent.	Centennial, century, centenary
CIO	Congress of Industrial Organizations
Conf.	Conference
Cong.	Congress
Cpl.	Corporal
CTO	Canceled to order
d.	Died
Dbl.	Double
EDU...............	Earliest documented use
Engr.	Engraved
Exhib.............	Exhibition
Expo.............	Exposition
Fed.	Federation
GB	Great Britain
Gen...............	General
GPO	General post office
Horiz.	Horizontal
Imperf.	Imperforate
Impt...............	Imprint

Intl.	International
Invtd.	Inverted
L	Left
Lieut., lt........	Lieutenant
Litho.............	Lithographed
LL	Lower left
LR	Lower right
mm	Millimeter
Ms.	Manuscript
Natl.	National
No.................	Number
NY	New York
NYC	New York City
Ovpt.	Overprint
Ovptd............	Overprinted
P	Plate number
Perf..............	Perforated, perforation
Phil..............	Philatelic
Photo............	Photogravure
PO	Post office
Pr.	Pair
P.R.................	Puerto Rico
Prec..............	Precancel, precanceled
Pres..............	President
PTT...............	Post, Telephone and Telegraph
R...................	Right
Rio.................	Rio de Janeiro
Sgt.................	Sergeant
Soc...............	Society
Souv.	Souvenir
SSR..............	Soviet Socialist Republic, see ASSR
St..................	Saint, street
Surch.	Surcharge
Typo.	Typographed
UL.................	Upper left
Unwmkd.	Unwatermarked
UPU..............	Universal Postal Union
UR	Upper Right
US	United States
USPOD	United States Post Office Department
USSR	Union of Soviet Socialist Republics
Vert...............	Vertical
VP	Vice president
Wmk.............	Watermark
Wmkd.	Watermarked
WWI	World War I
WWII	World War II

Examination

Scott Publishing Co. will not comment upon the genuineness, grade or condition of stamps, because of the time and responsibility involved. Rather, there are several expertizing groups that undertake this work for both collectors and dealers. Neither will Scott Publishing Co. appraise or identify philatelic material. The company cannot take responsibility for unsolicited stamps or covers sent by individuals.

All letters, E-mails, etc. are read attentively, but they are not always answered due to time considerations.

How to order from your dealer

When ordering stamps from a dealer, it is not necessary to write the full description of a stamp as listed in this catalogue. All you need is the name of the country, the Scott catalogue number and whether the desired item is unused or used. For example, "Japan Scott 422 unused" is sufficient to identify the unused stamp of Japan listed as "422 A206 5y brown."

Basic Stamp Information

A stamp collector's knowledge of the combined elements that make a given stamp issue unique determines his or her ability to identify stamps. These elements include paper, watermark, method of separation, printing, design and gum. On the following pages each of these important areas is briefly described.

Paper

Paper is an organic material composed of a compacted weave of cellulose fibers and generally formed into sheets. Paper used to print stamps may be manufactured in sheets, or it may have been part of a large roll (called a web) before being cut to size. The fibers most often used to create paper on which stamps are printed include bark, wood, straw and certain grasses. In many cases, linen or cotton rags have been added for greater strength and durability. Grinding, bleaching, cooking and rinsing these raw fibers reduces them to a slushy pulp, referred to by paper makers as "stuff." Sizing and, sometimes, coloring matter is added to the pulp to make different types of finished paper.

After the stuff is prepared, it is poured onto sieve-like frames that allow the water to run off, while retaining the matted pulp. As fibers fall onto the screen and are held by gravity, they form a natural weave that will later hold the paper together. If the screen has metal bits that are formed into letters or images attached, it leaves slightly thinned areas on the paper. These are called watermarks.

When the stuff is almost dry, it is passed under pressure through smooth or engraved rollers - dandy rolls - or placed between cloth in a press to be flattened and dried.

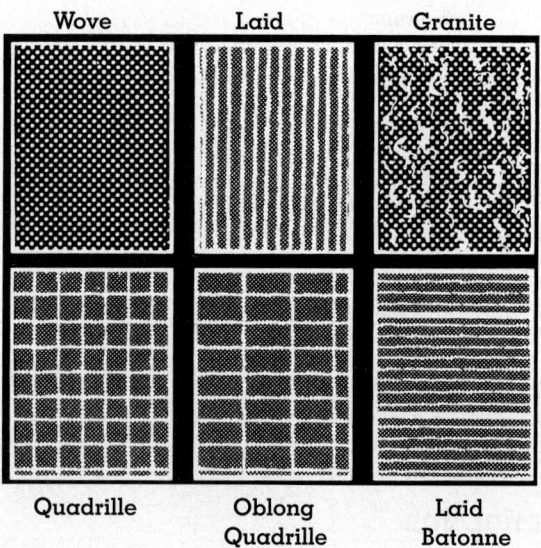

Wove   Laid   Granite

Quadrille   Oblong   Laid
Quadrille   Batonne

Stamp paper falls broadly into two types: wove and laid. The nature of the surface of the frame onto which the pulp is first deposited causes the differences in appearance between the two. If the surface is smooth and even, the paper will be of fairly uniform texture throughout. This is known as *wove paper*. Early papermaking machines poured the pulp onto a continuously circulating web of felt, but modern machines feed the pulp onto a cloth-like screen made of closely interwoven fine wires. This paper, when held to a light, will show little dots or points very close together. The proper name for this is "wire wove," but the type is still considered wove. Any U.S. or British stamp printed after 1880 will serve as an example of wire wove paper.

Closely spaced parallel wires, with cross wires at wider intervals, make up the frames used for what is known as *laid paper*. A greater thickness of the pulp will settle between the wires. The paper, when held to a light, will show alternate light and dark lines. The spacing and the thickness of the lines may vary, but on any one sheet of paper they are all alike. See Russia Scott 31-38 for examples of laid paper.

Batonne, from the French word meaning "a staff," is a term used if the lines in the paper are spaced quite far apart, like the printed ruling on a writing tablet. Batonne paper may be either wove or laid. If laid, fine laid lines can be seen between the batons.

Quadrille is the term used when the lines in the paper form little squares. *Oblong quadrille* is the term used when rectangles, rather than squares, are formed. Grid patterns vary from distinct to extremely faint. See Mexico-Guadalajara Scott 35-37 for examples of oblong quadrille paper.

Paper also is classified as thick or thin, hard or soft, and by color. Such colors may include yellowish, greenish, bluish and reddish.

Brief explanations of other types of paper used for printing stamps, as well as examples, follow.

Colored — Colored paper is created by the addition of dye in the paper-making process. Such colors may include shades of yellow, green, blue and red. *Surface-colored papers*, most commonly used for British colonial issues in 1913-14, are created when coloring is added only to the surface during the finishing process. Stamps printed on surface-colored paper have white or uncolored backs, while true colored papers are colored through. See Jamaica Scott 71-73.

Pelure — Pelure paper is a very thin, hard and often brittle paper that is sometimes bluish or grayish in appearance. See Serbia Scott 169-170.

Native — This is a term applied to handmade papers used to produce some of the early stamps of the Indian states. Stamps printed on native paper may be expected to display various natural inclusions that are normal and do not negatively affect value. Japanese paper, originally made of mulberry fibers and rice flour, is part of this group. See Japan Scott 1-18.

Manila — This type of paper is often used to make stamped envelopes and wrappers. It is a coarse-textured stock, usually smooth on one side and rough on the other. A variety of colors of manila paper exist, but the most common range is yellowish-brown.

Silk — Introduced by the British in 1847 as a safeguard against counterfeiting, silk paper contains bits of colored silk thread scattered throughout. The density of these fibers varies greatly and can include as few as one fiber per stamp or hundreds. U.S. revenue Scott R152 is a good example of an easy-to-identify silk paper stamp.

Silk-thread paper has uninterrupted threads of colored silk arranged so that one or more threads run through the stamp or postal stationery. See Great Britain Scott 5-6 and Switzerland Scott 14-19.

Granite — Filled with minute cloth or colored paper fibers of various colors and lengths, granite paper should not be confused with either type of silk paper. Austria Scott 172-175 and a number of Swiss stamps are examples of granite paper.

Chalky — A chalk-like substance coats the surface of chalky paper to discourage the cleaning and reuse of canceled stamps, as well as to provide a smoother, more acceptable printing surface. Because the designs of stamps printed on chalky paper are imprinted on what is often a water-soluble coating, any attempt to remove a cancellation will destroy the stamp. *Do not soak these stamps in any fluid.* To remove a stamp printed on chalky paper from an envelope, wet the paper from underneath the stamp until the gum dissolves enough to release the stamp from the paper. See St. Kitts-Nevis Scott 89-90 for examples of stamps printed on this type of chalky paper.

India — Another name for this paper, originally introduced from China about 1750, is "China Paper." It is a thin, opaque paper often used for plate and die proofs by many countries.

Double — In philately, the term double paper has two distinct meanings. The first is a two-ply paper, usually a combination of a thick and a thin sheet, joined during manufacture. This type was used experimentally as a means to discourage the reuse of stamps.

The design is printed on the thin paper. Any attempt to remove a cancellation would destroy the design. U.S. Scott 158 and other Banknote-era stamps exist on this form of double paper.

The second type of double paper occurs on a rotary press, when the end of one paper roll, or web, is affixed to the next roll to save time feeding the paper through the press. Stamp designs are printed over the joined paper and, if overlooked by inspectors, may get into post office stocks.

Goldbeater's Skin — This type of paper was used for the 1866 issue of Prussia, and was a tough, translucent paper. The design was printed in reverse on the back of the stamp, and the gum applied over the printing. It is impossible to remove stamps printed on this type of paper from the paper to which they are affixed without destroying the design.

Ribbed — Ribbed paper has an uneven, corrugated surface made by passing the paper through ridged rollers. This type exists on some copies of U.S. Scott 156-165.

Various other substances, or substrates, have been used for stamp manufacture, including wood, aluminum, copper, silver and gold foil, plastic, and silk and cotton fabrics.

Watermarks

Watermarks are an integral part of some papers. They are formed in the process of paper manufacture. Watermarks consist of small designs, formed of wire or cut from metal and soldered to the surface of the mold or, sometimes, on the dandy roll. The designs may be in the form of crowns, stars, anchors, letters or other characters or symbols. These pieces of metal - known in the paper-making industry as "bits" - impress a design into the paper. The design sometimes may be seen by holding the stamp to the light. Some are more easily seen with a watermark detector. This important tool is a small black tray into which a stamp is placed face down and dampened with a fast-evaporating watermark detection fluid that brings up the watermark image in the form of dark lines against a lighter background. These dark lines are the thinner areas of the paper known as the watermark. Some watermarks are extremely difficult to locate, due to either a faint impression, watermark location or the color of the stamp. There also are electric watermark detectors that come with plastic filter disks of various colors. The disks neutralize the color of the stamp, permitting the watermark to be seen more easily.

Multiple watermarks of Crown Agents and Burma

Watermarks of Uruguay, Vatican City and Jamaica

WARNING: Some inks used in the photogravure process dissolve in watermark fluids (Please see the section on Soluble Printing Inks). Also, see "chalky paper."

Watermarks may be found normal, reversed, inverted, reversed and inverted, sideways or diagonal, as seen from the back of the stamp. The relationship of watermark to stamp design depends on the position of the printing plates or how paper is fed through the press. On machine-made paper, watermarks normally are read from right to left. The design is repeated closely throughout the sheet in a "multiple-watermark design." In a "sheet watermark," the design appears only once on the sheet, but extends over many stamps. Individual stamps

may carry only a small fraction or none of the watermark.

"Marginal watermarks" occur in the margins of sheets or panes of stamps. They occur on the outside border of paper (ostensibly outside the area where stamps are to be printed). A large row of letters may spell the name of the country or the manufacturer of the paper, or a border of lines may appear. Careless press feeding may cause parts of these letters and/or lines to show on stamps of the outer row of a pane.

Soluble Printing Inks

WARNING: Most stamp colors are permanent; that is, they are not seriously affected by short-term exposure to light or water. Many colors, especially of modern inks, fade from excessive exposure to light. There are stamps printed with inks that dissolve easily in water or in fluids used to detect watermarks. Use of these inks was intentional to prevent the removal of cancellations. Water affects all aniline inks, those on so-called safety paper and some photogravure printings - all such inks are known as fugitive colors. *Removal from paper of such stamps requires care and alternatives to traditional soaking.*

Separation

"Separation" is the general term used to describe methods used to separate stamps. The three standard forms currently in use are perforating, rouletting and die-cutting. These methods are done during the stamp production process, after printing. Sometimes these methods are done on-press or sometimes as a separate step. The earliest issues, such as the 1840 Penny Black of Great Britain (Scott 1), did not have any means provided for separation. It was expected the stamps would be cut apart with scissors or folded and torn. These are examples of imperforate stamps. Many stamps were first issued in imperforate formats and were later issued with perforations. Therefore, care must be observed in buying single imperforate stamps to be certain they were issued imperforate and are not perforated copies that have been altered by having the perforations trimmed away. Stamps issued imperforate usually are valued as singles. However, imperforate varieties of normally perforated stamps should be collected in pairs or larger pieces as indisputable evidence of their imperforate character.

PERFORATION

The chief style of separation of stamps, and the one that is in almost universal use today, is perforating. By this process, paper between the stamps is cut away in a line of holes, usually round, leaving little bridges of paper between the stamps to hold them together. Some types of perforation, such as hyphen-hole perfs, can be confused with roulettes, but a close visual inspection reveals that paper has been removed. The little perforation bridges, which project from the stamp when it is torn from the pane, are called the teeth of the perforation.

As the size of the perforation is sometimes the only way to differentiate between two otherwise identical stamps, it is necessary to be able to accurately measure and describe them. This is done with a perforation gauge, usually a ruler-like device that has dots or graduated lines to show how many perforations may be counted in the space of two centimeters. Two centimeters is the space universally adopted in which to measure perforations.

Perforation gauge

perce en arc   perce en lignes

perce en points   oblique roulette

perce en scie   perce serpentin

To measure a stamp, run it along the gauge until the dots on it fit exactly into the perforations of the stamp. If you are using a graduated-line perforation gauge, simply slide the stamp along the surface until the lines on the gauge perfectly project from the center of the bridges or holes. The number to the side of the line of dots or lines that fit the stamp's perforation is the measurement. For example, an "11" means that 11 perforations fit between two centimeters. The description of the stamp therefore is "perf. 11." If the gauge of the perforations on the top and bottom of a stamp differs from that on the sides, the result is what is known as *compound perforations*. In measuring compound perforations, the gauge at top and bottom is always given first, then the sides. Thus, a stamp that measures 11 at top and bottom and 10½ at the sides is "perf. 11 x 10½." See U.S. Scott 632-642 for examples of compound perforations.

Stamps also are known with perforations different on three or all four sides. Descriptions of such items are clockwise, beginning with the top of the stamp.

A perforation with small holes and teeth close together is a "fine perforation." One with large holes and teeth far apart is a "coarse perforation." Holes that are jagged, rather than clean-cut, are "rough perforations." *Blind perforations* are the slight impressions left by the perforating pins if they fail to puncture the paper. Multiples of stamps showing blind perforations may command a slight premium over normally perforated stamps.

The term *syncopated perfs* describes intentional irregularities in the perforations. The earliest form was used by the Netherlands from 1925-33, where holes were omitted to create distinctive patterns. Beginning in 1992, Great Britain has used an oval perforation to help prevent counterfeiting. Several other countries have started using the oval perfs or other syncopated perf patterns.

A new type of perforation, still primarily used for postal stationery, is known as microperfs. Microperfs are tiny perforations (in some cases hundreds of holes per two centimeters) that allows items to be intentionally separated very easily, while not accidentally breaking apart as easily as standard perforations. These are not currently measured or differentiated by size, as are standard perforations.

ROULETTING

In rouletting, the stamp paper is cut partly or wholly through, with no paper removed. In perforating, some paper is removed. Rouletting derives its name from the French roulette, a spur-like wheel. As the wheel is rolled over the paper, each point makes a small cut. The number of cuts made in a two-centimeter space determines the gauge of the roulette, just as the number of perforations in two centimeters determines the gauge of the perforation.

The shape and arrangement of the teeth on the wheels varies. Various roulette types generally carry French names:

Perce en lignes - rouletted in lines. The paper receives short, straight cuts in lines. This is the most common type of rouletting. See Mexico Scott 500.

Perce en points - pin-rouletted or pin-perfed. This differs from a small perforation because no paper is removed, although round, equidistant holes are pricked through the paper. See Mexico Scott 242-256.

Perce en arc and *perce en scie* - pierced in an arc or saw-toothed designs, forming half circles or small triangles. See Hanover (German States) Scott 25-29.

Perce en serpentin - serpentine roulettes. The cuts form a serpentine or wavy line. See Brunswick (German States) Scott 13-18.

Once again, no paper is removed by these processes, leaving the stamps easily separated, but closely attached.

DIE-CUTTING

The third major form of stamp separation is die-cutting. This is a method where a die in the pattern of separation is created that later cuts the stamp paper in a stroke motion. Although some standard stamps bear die-cut perforations, this process is primarily used for self-adhesive postage stamps. Die-cutting can appear in straight lines, such as U.S. Scott 2522, shapes, such as U.S. Scott 1551, or imitating the appearance of perforations, such as New Zealand Scott 935A and 935B.

Printing Processes

ENGRAVING (Intaglio, Line-engraving, Etching)

Master die — The initial operation in the process of line engraving is making the master die. The die is a small, flat block of softened steel upon which the stamp design is recess engraved in reverse.

Master die

Transferring the design to the plate

Photographic reduction of the original art is made to the appropriate size. It then serves as a tracing guide for the initial outline of the design. The engraver lightly traces the design on the steel with his graver, then slowly works the design until it is completed. At various points during the engraving process, the engraver hand-inks the die and makes an impression to check his progress. These are known as progressive die proofs. After completion of the engraving, the die is hardened to withstand the stress and pressures of later transfer operations.

Transfer roll

Transfer roll — Next is production of the transfer roll that, as the name implies, is the medium used to transfer the subject from the master die to the printing plate. A blank roll of soft steel, mounted on a mandrel, is placed under the bearers of the transfer press to allow it to roll freely on its axis. The hardened die is placed on the bed of the press and the face of the transfer roll is applied to the die, under pressure. The bed or the roll is then rocked back and forth under increasing pressure, until the soft steel of the roll is forced into every engraved line of the die. The resulting impression on the roll is known as a "relief" or a "relief transfer." The engraved image is now positive in appearance and stands out from the steel. After the required number of reliefs are "rocked in," the soft steel transfer roll is hardened.

Different flaws may occur during the relief process. A defective relief may occur during the rocking in process because of a minute piece of foreign material lodging on the die, or some other cause. Imperfections in the steel of the transfer roll may result in a breaking away of parts of the design. This is known as a relief break, which will show up on finished stamps as small, unprinted areas. If a damaged relief remains in use, it will transfer a repeating defect to the plate. Deliberate alterations of reliefs sometimes occur. "Altered reliefs" designate these changed conditions.

Plate — The final step in pre-printing production is the making of the printing plate. A flat piece of soft steel replaces the die on the bed of the transfer press. One of the reliefs on the transfer roll is positioned over this soft steel. Position, or layout, dots determine the correct position on the plate. The dots have been lightly marked on the plate in advance. After the correct position of the relief is determined,

the design is rocked in by following the same method used in making the transfer roll. The difference is that this time the image is being transferred from the transfer roll, rather than to it. Once the design is entered on the plate, it appears in reverse and is recessed. There are as many transfers entered on the plate as there are subjects printed on the sheet of stamps. It is during this process that double and shifted transfers occur, as well as re-entries. These are the result of improperly entered images that have not been properly burnished out prior to rocking in a new image.

Modern siderography processes, such as those used by the U.S. Bureau of Engraving and Printing, involve an automated form of rocking designs in on preformed cylindrical printing sleeves. The same process also allows for easier removal and re-entry of worn images right on the sleeve.

Following the entering of the required transfers on the plate, the position dots, layout dots and lines, scratches and other markings generally are burnished out. Added at this time by the siderographer are any required *guide lines, plate numbers* or other *marginal markings*. The plate is then hand-inked and a proof impression is taken. This is known as a plate proof. If the impression is approved, the plate is machined for fitting onto the press, is hardened and sent to the plate vault ready for use.

On press, the plate is inked and the surface is automatically wiped clean, leaving ink only in the recessed lines. Paper is then forced under pressure into the engraved recessed lines, thereby receiving the ink. Thus, the ink lines on engraved stamps are slightly raised, and slight depressions (debossing) occur on the back of the stamp. Prior to the advent of modern high-speed presses and more advanced ink formulations, paper had to be dampened before receiving the ink. This sometimes led to uneven shrinkage by the time the stamps were perforated, resulting in improperly perforated stamps, or misperfs. Newer presses use drier paper, thus both *wet* and *dry printings* exist on some stamps.

Rotary Press — Until 1914, only flat plates were used to print engraved stamps. Rotary press printing was introduced in 1914, and slowly spread. Some countries still use flat-plate printing.

After approval of the plate proof, older *rotary press plates* require additional machining. They are curved to fit the press cylinder. "Gripper slots" are cut into the back of each plate to receive the "grippers," which hold the plate securely on the press. The plate is then hardened. Stamps printed from these bent rotary press plates are longer or wider than the same stamps printed from flat-plate presses. The stretching of the plate during the curving process is what causes this distortion.

Re-entry — To execute a re-entry on a flat plate, the transfer roll is re-applied to the plate, often at some time after its first use on the press. Worn-out designs can be resharpened by carefully burnishing out the original image and re-entering it from the transfer roll. If the original impression has not been sufficiently removed and the transfer roll is not precisely in line with the remaining impression, the resulting double transfer will make the re-entry obvious. If the registration is true, a re-entry may be difficult or impossible to distinguish. Sometimes a stamp printed from a successful re-entry is identified by having a much sharper and clearer impression than its neighbors. With the advent of rotary presses, post-press re-entries were not possible. After a plate was curved for the rotary press, it was impossible to make a re-entry. This is because the plate had already been bent once (with the design distorted).

However, with the introduction of the previously mentioned modern-style siderography machines, entries are made to the preformed cylindrical printing sleeve. Such sleeves are dechromed and softened. This allows individual images to be burnished out and re-entered on the curved sleeve. The sleeve is then rechromed, resulting in longer press life.

Double Transfer — This is a description of the condition of a transfer on a plate that shows evidence of a duplication of all, or a portion of the design. It usually is the result of the changing of the registration between the transfer roll and the plate during the rocking in of the original entry. Double transfers also occur when only a portion of the design has been rocked in and improper positioning is noted. If the worker elected not to burnish out the partial or completed design, a strong double transfer will occur for part or all of the design.

It sometimes is necessary to remove the original transfer from a plate and repeat the process a second time. If the finished re-worked image shows traces of the original impression, attributable to incomplete burnishing, the result is a partial double transfer.

With the modern automatic machines mentioned previously, double transfers are all but impossible to create. Those partially doubled images on stamps printed from such sleeves are more than likely re-entries, rather than true double transfers.

Re-engraved — Alterations to a stamp design are sometimes necessary after some stamps have been printed. In some cases, either the original die or the actual printing plate may have its "temper" drawn (softened), and the design will be re-cut. The resulting impressions from such a re-engraved die or plate may differ slightly from the original issue, and are known as "re-engraved." If the alteration was made to the master die, all future printings will be consistently different from the original. If alterations were made to the printing plate, each altered stamp on the plate will be slightly different from each other, allowing specialists to reconstruct a complete printing plate.

Dropped Transfers — If an impression from the transfer roll has not been properly placed, a dropped transfer may occur. The final stamp image will appear obviously out of line with its neighbors.

Short Transfer — Sometimes a transfer roll is not rocked its entire length when entering a transfer onto a plate. As a result, the finished transfer on the plate fails to show the complete design, and the finished stamp will have an incomplete design printed. This is known as a "short transfer." U.S. Scott No. 8 is a good example of a short transfer.

TYPOGRAPHY (Letterpress, Surface Printing, Flexography, Dry Offset, High Etch)

Although the word "Typography" is obsolete as a term describing a printing method, it was the accepted term throughout the first century of postage stamps. Therefore, appropriate Scott listings in this catalogue refer to typographed stamps. The current term for this form of printing, however, is "letterpress."

As it relates to the production of postage stamps, letterpress printing is the reverse of engraving. Rather than having recessed areas trap the ink and deposit it on paper, only the raised areas of the design are inked. This is comparable to the type of printing seen by inking and using an ordinary rubber stamp. Letterpress includes all printing where the design is above the surface area, whether it is wood, metal or, in some instances, hardened rubber or polymer plastic.

For most letterpress-printed stamps, the engraved master is made in much the same manner as for engraved stamps. In this instance, however, an additional step is needed. The design is transferred to another surface before being transferred to the transfer roll. In this way, the transfer roll has a recessed stamp design, rather than one done in relief. This makes the printing areas on the final plate raised, or relief areas.

For less-detailed stamps of the 19th century, the area on the die not used as a printing surface was cut away, leaving the surface area raised. The original die was then reproduced by stereotyping or electrotyping. The resulting electrotypes were assembled in the required number and format of the desired sheet of stamps. The plate used in printing the stamps was an electroplate of these assembled electrotypes.

Once the final letterpress plates are created, ink is applied to the raised surface and the pressure of the press transfers the ink impression to the paper. In contrast to engraving, the fine lines of letterpress are impressed on the surface of the stamp, leaving a debossed surface. When viewed from the back (as on a typewritten page), the corresponding line work on the stamp will be raised slightly (embossed) above the surface.

PHOTOGRAVURE (Gravure, Rotogravure, Heliogravure)

In this process, the basic principles of photography are applied to a chemically sensitized metal plate, rather than photographic paper. The design is transferred photographically to the plate through a halftone, or dot-matrix screen, breaking the reproduction into tiny dots. The plate is treated chemically and the dots form depressions, called cells, of varying depths and diameters, depending on the degrees of shade in the design. Then, like engraving, ink is applied to the plate and the surface is wiped clean. This leaves ink in the tiny cells that is lifted out and deposited on the paper when it is pressed against the plate.

Gravure is most often used for multicolored stamps, generally using the three primary colors (red, yellow and blue) and black. By varying the dot matrix pattern and density of these colors, virtually any color can be reproduced. A typical full-color gravure stamp will be created from four printing cylinders (one for each color). The original multicolored image will have been photographically separated into its component colors.

Modern gravure printing may use computer-generated dot-matrix screens, and modern plates may be of various types including metal-coated plastic. The catalogue designation of Photogravure (or "Photo") covers any of these older and more modern gravure methods of printing.

For examples of the first photogravure stamps printed (1914), see Bavaria Scott 94-114.

LITHOGRAPHY (Offset Lithography, Stone Lithography, Dilitho, Planography, Collotype)

The principle that oil and water do not mix is the basis for lithography. The stamp design is drawn by hand or transferred from engraving to the surface of a lithographic stone or metal plate in a greasy (oily) substance. This oily substance holds the ink, which will later be transferred to the paper. The stone (or plate) is wet with an acid fluid, causing it to repel the printing ink in all areas not covered by the greasy substance.

Transfer paper is used to transfer the design from the original stone or plate. A series of duplicate transfers are grouped and, in turn, transferred to the final printing plate.

Photolithography — The application of photographic processes to lithography. This process allows greater flexibility of design, related to use of halftone screens combined with line work. Unlike photogravure or engraving, this process can allow large, solid areas to be printed.

Offset — A refinement of the lithographic process. A rubber-covered blanket cylinder takes the impression from the inked lithographic plate. From the "blanket" the impression is *offset* or transferred to the paper. Greater flexibility and speed are the principal reasons offset printing has largely displaced lithography. The term "lithography" covers both processes, and results are almost identical.

EMBOSSED (Relief) Printing

Embossing, not considered one of the four main printing types, is a method in which the design first is sunk into the metal of the die. Printing is done against a yielding platen, such as leather or linoleum. The platen is forced into the depression of the die, thus forming the design on the paper in relief. This process is often used for metallic inks.

Embossing may be done without color (see Sardinia Scott 4-6); with color printed around the embossed area (see Great Britain Scott 5 and most U.S. envelopes); and with color in exact registration with the embossed subject (see Canada Scott 656-657).

HOLOGRAMS

For objects to appear as holograms on stamps, a model exactly the same size as it is to appear on the hologram must be created. Rather than using photographic film to capture the image, holography records an image on a photoresist material. In processing, chemicals eat away at certain exposed areas, leaving a pattern of constructive and destructive interference. When the phororesist is developed, the result is a pattern of uneven ridges that acts as a mold. This mold is then coated with metal, and the resulting form is used to press copies in much the same way phonograph records are produced.

A typical reflective hologram used for stamps consists of a reproduction of the uneven patterns on a plastic film that is applied to a reflective background, usually a silver or gold foil. Light is reflected off the background through the film, making the pattern present on the film visible. Because of the uneven pattern of the film, the viewer will perceive the objects in their proper three-dimensional relationships with appropriate brightness.

The first hologram on a stamp was produced by Austria in 1988 (Scott 1441).

FOIL APPLICATION

A modern tecnique of applying color to stamps involves the application of metallic foil to the stamp paper. A pattern of foil is applied to the stamp paper by use of a stamping die. The foil usually is flat, but it may be textured. Canada Scott 1735 has three different foil applications in pearl, bronze and gold. The gold foil was textured using a chemical-etch copper embossing die. The printing of this stamp also involved two-color offset lithography plus embossing.

COMBINATION PRINTINGS

Sometimes two or even three printing methods are combined in producing stamps. In these cases, such as Austria Scott 933 or Canada 1735 (described in the preceding paragraph), the multiple-printing technique can be determined by studying the individual characteristics of each printing type. A few stamps, such as Singapore Scott 684-684A, combine as many as three of the four major printing types (lithography, engraving and typography). When this is done it often indicates the incorporation of security devices against counterfeiting.

INK COLORS

Inks or colored papers used in stamp printing often are of mineral origin, although there are numerous examples of organic-based pigments. As a general rule, organic-based pigments are far more

subject to varieties and change than those of mineral-based origin.

The appearance of any given color on a stamp may be affected by many aspects, including printing variations, light, color of paper, aging and chemical alterations.

Numerous printing variations may be observed. Heavier pressure or inking will cause a more intense color, while slight interruptions in the ink feed or lighter impressions will cause a lighter appearance. Stamps printed in the same color by water-based and solvent-based inks can differ significantly in appearance. This affects several stamps in the U.S. Prominent Americans series. Hand-mixed ink formulas (primarily from the 19th century) produced under different conditions (humidity and temperature) account for notable color variations in early printings of the same stamp (see U.S. Scott 248-250, 279B, for example). Different sources of pigment can also result in significant differences in color.

Light exposure and aging are closely related in the way they affect stamp color. Both eventually break down the ink and fade colors, so that a carefully kept stamp may differ significantly in color from an identical copy that has been exposed to light. If stamps are exposed to light either intentionally or accidentally, their colors can be faded or completely changed in some cases.

Papers of different quality and consistency used for the same stamp printing may affect color appearance. Most pelure papers, for example, show a richer color when compared with wove or laid papers. See Russia Scott 181a, for an example of this effect.

The very nature of the printing processes can cause a variety of differences in shades or hues of the same stamp. Some of these shades are scarcer than others, and are of particular interest to the advanced collector.

Luminescence

All forms of tagged stamps fall under the general category of luminescence. Within this broad category is fluorescence, dealing with forms of tagging visible under longwave ultraviolet light, and phosphorescence, which deals with tagging visible only under shortwave light. Phosphorescence leaves an afterglow and fluorescence does not. These treated stamps show up in a range of different colors when exposed to UV light. The differing wavelengths of the light activates the tagging material, making it glow in various colors that usually serve different mail processing purposes.

Intentional tagging is a post-World War II phenomenon, brought about by the increased literacy rate and rapidly growing mail volume. It was one of several answers to the problem of the need for more automated mail processes. Early tagged stamps served the purpose of triggering machines to separate different types of mail. A natural outgrowth was to also use the signal to trigger machines that faced all envelopes the same way and canceled them.

Tagged stamps come in many different forms. Some tagged stamps have luminescent shapes or images imprinted on them as a form of security device. Others have blocks (United States), stripes, frames (South Africa and Canada), overall coatings (United States), bars (Great Britain and Canada) and many other types. Some types of tagging are even mixed in with the pigmented printing ink (Australia Scott 366, Netherlands Scott 478 and U.S. Scott 1359 and 2443).

The means of applying taggant to stamps differs as much as the intended purposes for the stamps. The most common form of tagging is a coating applied to the surface of the printed stamp. Since the taggant ink is frequently invisible except under UV light, it does not interfere with the appearance of the stamp. Another common application is the use of phosphored papers. In this case the paper itself either has a coating of taggant applied before the stamp is printed, has taggant applied during the papermaking process (incorporating it into the fibers), or has the taggant mixed into the coating of the paper. The latter method, among others, is currently in use in the United States.

Many countries now use tagging in various forms to either expedite mail handling or to serve as a printing security device against counterfeiting. Following the introduction of tagged stamps for public use in 1959 by Great Britain, other countries have steadily joined the parade. Among those are Germany (1961); Canada and Denmark (1962); United States, Australia, France and Switzerland (1963); Belgium and Japan (1966); Sweden and Norway (1967); Italy (1968); and Russia (1969). Since then, many other countries have begun using forms of tagging, including Brazil, China, Czechoslovakia, Hong Kong, Guatemala, Indonesia, Israel, Lithuania, Luxembourg, Netherlands, Penrhyn Islands, Portugal, St. Vincent, Singapore, South Africa, Spain and Sweden to name a few.

In some cases, including United States, Canada, Great Britain and Switzerland, stamps were released both with and without tagging. Many of these were released during each country's experimental period. Tagged and untagged versions are listed for the aforementioned countries and are noted in some other countries' listings. For at least a few stamps, the experimentally tagged version is worth far more than its untagged counterpart, such as the 1963 experimental tagged version of France Scott 1024.

In some cases, luminescent varieties of stamps were inadvertently created. Several Russian stamps, for example, sport highly fluorescent ink that was not intended as a form of tagging. Older stamps, such as early U.S. postage dues, can be positively identified by the use of UV light, since the organic ink used has become slightly fluorescent over time. Other stamps, such as Austria Scott 70a-82a (varnish bars) and Obock Scott 46-64 (printed quadrille lines), have become fluorescent over time.

Various fluorescent substances have been added to paper to make it appear brighter. These optical brighteners, as they are known, greatly affect the appearance of the stamp under UV light. The brightest of these is known as Hi-Brite paper. These paper varieties are beyond the scope of the Scott Catalogue.

Shortwave UV light also is used extensively in expertizing, since each form of paper has its own fluorescent characteristics that are impossible to perfectly match. It is therefore a simple matter to detect filled thins, added perforation teeth and other alterations that involve the addition of paper. UV light also is used to examine stamps that have had cancels chemically removed and for other purposes as well.

Gum

The Illustrated Gum Chart in the first part of this introduction shows and defines various types of gum condition. Because gum condition has an important impact on the value of unused stamps, we recommend studying this chart and the accompanying text carefully.

The gum on the back of a stamp may be shiny, dull, smooth, rough, dark, white, colored or tinted. Most stamp gumming adhesives use gum arabic or dextrine as a base. Certain polymers such as polyvinyl alcohol (PVA) have been used extensively since World War II.

The *Scott Standard Postage Stamp Catalogue* does not list items by types of gum. The *Scott Specialized Catalogue of United States Stamps and Covers* does differentiate among some types of gum for certain issues.

Reprints of stamps may have gum differing from the original issues. In addition, some countries have used different gum formulas for different seasons. These adhesives have different properties that may become more apparent over time.

Many stamps have been issued without gum, and the catalogue will note this fact. See, for example, United States Scott 40-47. Sometimes, gum may have been removed to preserve the stamp. Germany Scott B68, for example, has a highly acidic gum that eventually destroys the stamps. This item is valued in the catalogue with gum removed.

Reprints and Reissues

These are impressions of stamps (usually obsolete) made from the original plates or stones. If they are valid for postage and reproduce

obsolete issues (such as U.S. Scott 102-111), the stamps are *reissues*. If they are from current issues, they are designated as *second, third*, etc., *printing*. If designated for a particular purpose, they are called *special printings*.

When special printings are not valid for postage, but are made from original dies and plates by authorized persons, they are *official reprints*. *Private reprints* are made from the original plates and dies by private hands. An example of a private reprint is that of the 1871-1932 reprints made from the original die of the 1845 New Haven, Conn., postmaster's provisional. *Official reproductions* or imitations are made from new dies and plates by government authorization. Scott will list those reissues that are valid for postage if they differ significantly from the original printing.

The U.S. government made special printings of its first postage stamps in 1875. Produced were official imitations of the first two stamps (listed as Scott 3-4), reprints of the demonetized pre-1861 issues (Scott 40-47) and reissues of the 1861 stamps, the 1869 stamps and the then-current 1875 denominations. Even though the official imitations and the reprints were not valid for postage, Scott lists all of these U.S. special printings.

Most reprints or reissues differ slightly from the original stamp in some characteristic, such as gum, paper, perforation, color or watermark. Sometimes the details are followed so meticulously that only a student of that specific stamp is able to distinguish the reprint or reissue from the original.

Remainders and Canceled to Order

Some countries sell their stock of old stamps when a new issue replaces them. To avoid postal use, the *remainders* usually are canceled with a punch hole, a heavy line or bar, or a more-or-less regular-looking cancellation. The most famous merchant of remainders was Nicholas F. Seebeck. In the 1880s and 1890s, he arranged printing contracts between the Hamilton Bank Note Co., of which he was a director, and several Central and South American countries. The contracts provided that the plates and all remainders of the yearly issues became the property of Hamilton. Seebeck saw to it that ample stock remained. The "Seebecks," both remainders and reprints, were standard packet fillers for decades.

Some countries also issue stamps *canceled-to-order (CTO)*, either in sheets with original gum or stuck onto pieces of paper or envelopes and canceled. Such CTO items generally are worth less than postally used stamps. In cases where the CTO material is far more prevalent in the marketplace than postally used examples, the catalogue value relates to the CTO examples, with postally used examples noted as premium items. Most CTOs can be detected by the presence of gum. However, as the CTO practice goes back at least to 1885, the gum inevitably has been soaked off some stamps so they could pass as postally used. The normally applied postmarks usually differ slightly from standard postmarks, and specialists are able to tell the difference. When applied individually to envelopes by philatelically minded persons, CTO material is known as *favor canceled* and generally sells at large discounts.

Cinderellas and Facsimiles

Cinderella is a catch-all term used by stamp collectors to describe phantoms, fantasies, bogus items, municipal issues, exhibition seals, local revenues, transportation stamps, labels, poster stamps and many other types of items. Some cinderella collectors include in their collections local postage issues, telegraph stamps, essays and proofs, forgeries and counterfeits.

A *fantasy* is an adhesive created for a nonexistent stamp-issuing authority. Fantasy items range from imaginary countries (Occusi-Ambeno, Kingdom of Sedang, Principality of Trinidad or Torres Straits), to non-existent locals (Winans City Post), or nonexistent transportation lines (McRobish & Co.'s Acapulco-San Francisco Line).

On the other hand, if the entity exists and could have issued stamps (but did not) or was known to have issued other stamps, the items are considered *bogus* stamps. These would include the Mormon postage stamps of Utah, S. Allan Taylor's Guatemala and Paraguay inventions, the propaganda issues for the South Moluccas and the adhesives of the Page & Keyes local post of Boston.

Phantoms is another term for both fantasy and bogus issues.

Facsimiles are copies or imitations made to represent original stamps, but which do not pretend to be originals. A catalogue illustration is such a facsimile. Illustrations from the Moens catalogue of the last century were occasionally colored and passed off as stamps. Since the beginning of stamp collecting, facsimiles have been made for collectors as space fillers or for reference. They often carry the word "facsimile," "falsch" (German), "sanko" or "mozo" (Japanese), or "faux" (French) overprinted on the face or stamped on the back. Unfortunately, over the years a number of these items have had fake cancels applied over the facsimile notation and have been passed off as genuine.

Forgeries and Counterfeits

Forgeries and counterfeits have been with philately virtually from the beginning of stamp production. Over time, the terminology for the two has been used interchangeably. Although both forgeries and counterfeits are reproductions of stamps, the purposes behind their creation differ considerably.

Among specialists there is an increasing movement to more specifically define such items. Although there is no universally accepted terminology, we feel the following definitions most closely mirror the items and their purposes as they are currently defined.

Forgeries (also often referred to as *Counterfeits*) are reproductions of genuine stamps that have been created to defraud collectors. Such spurious items first appeared on the market around 1860, and most old-time collections contain one or more. Many are crude and easily spotted, but some can deceive experts.

An important supplier of these early philatelic forgeries was the Hamburg printer Gebruder Spiro. Many others with reputations in this craft included S. Allan Taylor, George Hussey, James Chute, George Forune, Benjamin & Sarpy, Julius Goldner, E. Oneglia and L.H. Mercier. Among the noted 20th-century forgers were Francois Fournier, Jean Sperati and the prolific Raoul DeThuin.

Forgeries may be complete replications, or they may be genuine stamps altered to resemble a scarcer (and more valuable) type. Most forgeries, particularly those of rare stamps, are worth only a small fraction of the value of a genuine example, but a few types, created by some of the most notable forgers, such as Sperati, can be worth as much or more than the genuine. Fraudulently produced copies are known of most classic rarities and many medium-priced stamps.

In addition to rare stamps, large numbers of common 19th- and early 20th-century stamps were forged to supply stamps to the early packet trade. Many can still be easily found. Few new philatelic forgeries have appeared in recent decades. Successful imitation of well-engraved work is virtually impossible. It has proven far easier to produce a fake by altering a genuine stamp than to duplicate a stamp completely.

Counterfeit (also often referred to as *Postal Counterfeit* or *Postal Forgery*) is the term generally applied to reproductions of stamps that have been created to defraud the government of revenue. Such items usually are created at the time a stamp is current and, in some cases, are hard to detect. Because most counterfeits are seized when the perpetrator is captured, postal counterfeits, particularly used on cover, are usually worth much more than a genuine example to specialists. The first postal counterfeit was of Spain's 4-cuarto carmine of 1854 (the real one is Scott 25). Apparently, the counterfeiters were not satisfied with their first version, which is now very scarce, and they soon created an engraved counterfeit, which is common. Postal counterfeits quickly followed in Austria, Naples, Sardinia and the Roman States. They have since been created in many other countries as well, including the United States.

An infamous counterfeit to defraud the government is the 1-shilling Great Britain "Stock Exchange" forgery of 1872, used on telegraph forms at the exchange that year. The stamp escaped detection until a stamp dealer noticed it in 1898.

Fakes

Fakes are genuine stamps altered in some way to make them more desirable. One student of this part of stamp collecting has estimated that by the 1950s more than 30,000 varieties of fakes were known. That number has grown greatly since then. The widespread existence of fakes makes it important for stamp collectors to study their philatelic holdings and use relevant literature. Likewise, collectors should buy from reputable dealers who guarantee their stamps and make full and prompt refunds should a purchased item be declared faked or altered by some mutually agreed-upon authority. Because fakes always have some genuine characteristics, it is not always possible to obtain unanimous agreement among experts regarding specific items. These students may change their opinions as philatelic knowledge increases. More than 80 percent of all fakes on the philatelic market today are regummed, reperforated (or perforated for the first time), or bear forged overprints, surcharges or cancellations.

Stamps can be chemically treated to alter or eliminate colors. For example, a pale rose stamp can be re-colored to resemble a blue shade of high market value. In other cases, treated stamps can be made to resemble missing color varieties. Designs may be changed by painting, or a stroke or a dot added or bleached out to turn an ordinary variety into a seemingly scarcer stamp. Part of a stamp can be bleached and reprinted in a different version, achieving an inverted center or frame. Margins can be added or repairs done so deceptively that the stamps move from the "repaired" into the "fake" category.

Fakers have not left the backs of the stamps untouched either. They may create false watermarks, add fake grills or press out genuine grills. A thin India paper proof may be glued onto a thicker backing to create the appearance an issued stamp, or a proof printed on cardboard may be shaved down and perforated to resemble a stamp. Silk threads are impressed into paper and stamps have been split so that a rare paper variety is added to an otherwise inexpensive stamp. The most common treatment to the back of a stamp, however, is regumming.

Some in the business of faking stamps have openly advertised fool-proof application of "original gum" to stamps that lack it, although most publications now ban such ads from their pages. It is believed that very few early stamps have survived without being hinged. The large number of never-hinged examples of such earlier material offered for sale thus suggests the widespread extent of regumming activity. Regumming also may be used to hide repairs or thin spots. Dipping the stamp into watermark fluid, or examining it under longwave ultraviolet light often will reveal these flaws.

Fakers also tamper with separations. Ingenious ways to add margins are known. Perforated wide-margin stamps may be falsely represented as imperforate when trimmed. Reperforating is commonly done to create scarce coil or perforation varieties, and to eliminate the naturally occurring straight-edge stamps found in sheet margin positions of many earlier issues. Custom has made straight-edged stamps less desirable. Fakers have obliged by perforating straight-edged stamps so that many are now uncommon, if not rare.

Another fertile field for the faker is that of overprints, surcharges and cancellations. The forging of rare surcharges or overprints began in the 1880s or 1890s. These forgeries are sometimes difficult to detect, but experts have identified almost all. Occasionally, overprints or cancellations are removed to create non-overprinted stamps or seemingly unused items. This is most commonly done by removing a manuscript cancel to make a stamp resemble an unused example. "SPECIMEN" overprints may be removed by scraping and repainting to create non-overprinted varieties. Fakers use inexpensive revenues or pen-canceled stamps to generate unused stamps for further faking by adding other markings. The quartz lamp or UV lamp and a high-powered magnifying glass help to easily detect removed cancellations.

The bigger problem, however, is the addition of overprints, surcharges or cancellations - many with such precision that they are very difficult to ascertain. Plating of the stamps or the overprint can be an important method of detection.

Fake postmarks may range from many spurious fancy cancellations to a host of markings applied to transatlantic covers, to adding normally appearing postmarks to definitives of some countries with stamps that are valued far higher used than unused. With the increased popularity of cover collecting, and the widespread interest in postal history, a fertile new field for fakers has come about. Some have tried to create entire covers. Others specialize in adding stamps, tied by fake cancellations, to genuine stampless covers, or replacing less expensive or damaged stamps with more valuable ones. Detailed study of postal rates in effect at the time a cover in question was mailed, including the analysis of each handstamp used during the period, ink analysis and similar techniques, usually will unmask the fraud.

Restoration and Repairs

Scott Publishing Co. bases its catalogue values on stamps that are free of defects and otherwise meet the standards set forth earlier in this introduction. Most stamp collectors desire to have the finest copy of an item possible. Even within given grading categories there are variances. This leads to a controversial practice that is not defined in any universal manner: stamp *restoration*.

There are broad differences of opinion about what is permissible when it comes to restoration. Carefully applying a soft eraser to a stamp or cover to remove light soiling is one form of restoration, as is washing a stamp in mild soap and water to clean it. These are fairly accepted forms of restoration. More severe forms of restoration include pressing out creases or removing stains caused by tape. To what degree each of these is acceptable is dependent upon the individual situation. Further along the spectrum is the freshening of a stamp's color by removing oxide build-up or the effects of wax paper left next to stamps shipped to the tropics.

At some point in this spectrum the concept of *repair* replaces that of restoration. Repairs include filling thin spots, mending tears by reweaving or adding a missing perforation tooth. Regumming stamps may have been acceptable as a restoration or repair technique many decades ago, but today it is considered a form of fakery.

Restored stamps may or may not sell at a discount, and it is possible that the value of individual restored items may be enhanced over that of their pre-restoration state. Specific situations dictate the resultant value of such an item. Repaired stamps sell at substantial discounts from the value of sound stamps.

Terminology

Booklets — Many countries have issued stamps in small booklets for the convenience of users. This idea continues to become increasingly popular in many countries. Booklets have been issued in many sizes and forms, often with advertising on the covers, the panes of stamps or on the interleaving.

The panes used in booklets may be printed from special plates or made from regular sheets. All panes from booklets issued by the United States and many from those of other countries contain stamps that are straight edged on the sides, but perforated between. Others are distinguished by orientation of watermark or other identifying features. Any stamp-like unit in the pane, either printed or blank, that is not a postage stamp, is considered to be a *label* in the catalogue listings.

Scott lists and values booklet panes. Modern complete booklets also are listed and valued. Individual booklet panes are listed only when they are not fashioned from existing sheet stamps and, therefore, are identifiable from their sheet stamp counterparts.

Panes usually do not have a used value assigned to them because there is little market activity for used booklet panes, even though many exist used and there is some demand for them.

Cancellations — The marks or obliterations put on stamps by postal authorities to show that they have performed service and to prevent their reuse are known as cancellations. If the marking is made with a pen, it is considered a "pen cancel." When the location of the post office appears in the marking, it is a "town cancellation." A "postmark" is technically any postal marking, but in practice the term generally is applied to a town cancellation with a date. When calling attention to a cause or celebration, the marking is known as a "slogan cancellation." Many other types and styles of cancellations exist, such as duplex, numerals, targets, fancy and others. See also "precancels," below.

Coil Stamps — These are stamps that are issued in rolls for use in dispensers, affixing and vending machines. Those coils of the United States, Canada, Sweden and some other countries are perforated horizontally or vertically only, with the outer edges imperforate. Coil stamps of some countries, such as Great Britain and Germany, are perforated on all four sides and may in some cases be distinguished from their sheet stamp counterparts by watermarks, counting numbers on the reverse or other means.

Covers — Entire envelopes, with or without adhesive postage stamps, that have passed through the mail and bear postal or other markings of philatelic interest are known as covers. Before the introduction of envelopes in about 1840, people folded letters and wrote the address on the outside. Some people covered their letters with an extra sheet of paper on the outside for the address, producing the term "cover." Used airletter sheets, stamped envelopes and other items of postal stationery also are considered covers.

Errors — Stamps that have some major, consistent, unintentional deviation from the normal are considered errors. Errors include, but are not limited to, missing or wrong colors, wrong paper, wrong watermarks, inverted centers or frames on multicolor printing, inverted or missing surcharges or overprints, double impressions, missing perforations, unintentionally omitted tagging and others. Factually wrong or misspelled information, if it appears on all examples of a stamp, are not considered errors in the true sense of the word. They are errors of design. Inconsistent or randomly appearing items, such as misperfs or color shifts, are classified as freaks.

Color-Omitted Errors — This term refers to stamps where a missing color is caused by the complete failure of the printing plate to deliver ink to the stamp paper or any other paper. Generally, this is caused by the printing plate not being engaged on the press or the ink station running dry of ink during printing.

Color-Missing Errors — This term refers to stamps where a color or colors were printed somewhere but do not appear on the finished stamp. There are four different classes of color-missing errors, and the catalog indicates with a two-letter code appended to each such listing what caused the color to be missing. These codes are used only for the United States' color-missing error listings.

FO = A *foldover* of the stamp sheet during printing may block ink from appearing on a stamp. Instead, the color will appear on the back of the foldover (where it might fall on the back of the selvage or perhaps on the back of the stamp or another stamp). FO also will be used in the case of foldunders, where the paper may fold underneath the other stamp paper and the color will print on the platen.

EP = A piece of *extraneous paper* falling across the plate or stamp paper will receive the printed ink. When the extraneous paper is removed, an unprinted portion of stamp paper remains and shows partially or totally missing colors.

CM = A misregistration of the printing plates during printing will result in a *color misregistration*, and such a misregistraion may result in a color not appearing on the finished stamp.

PS = A *perforation shift* after printing may remove a color from the finished stamp. Normally, this will occur on a row of stamps at the edge of the stamp pane.

Measurements – When measurements are given in the Scott catalogues for stamp size, grill size or any other reason, the first measurement given is always for the top and bottom dimension, while the second measurement will be for the sides (just as perforation gauges are measured). Thus, a stamp size of 15mm x 21mm will indicate a vertically oriented stamp 15mm wide at top and bottom, and 21mm tall at the sides. The same principle holds for measuring or counting items such as U.S. grills. A grill count of 22x18 points (B grill) indicates that there are 22 grill points across by 18 grill points down.

Overprints and Surcharges — Overprinting involves applying wording or design elements over an already existing stamp. Overprints can be used to alter the place of use (such as "Canal Zone" on U.S. stamps), to adapt them for a special purpose ("Porto" on Denmark's 1913-20 regular issues for use as postage due stamps, Scott J1-J7) or to commemorate a special occasion (United States Scott 647-648).

A *surcharge* is a form of overprint that changes or restates the face value of a stamp or piece of postal stationery.

Surcharges and overprints may be handstamped, typeset or, occasionally, lithographed or engraved. A few hand-written overprints and surcharges are known.

Personalized Stamps — In 1999, Australia issued stamps with se-tenant labels that could be personalized with pictures of the customer's choice. Other countries quickly followed suit, with some offering to print the selected picture on the stamp itself within a frame that was used exclusively for personalized issues. As the picture used on these stamps or labels vary, listings for such stamps are for any picture within the common frame (or any picture on a se-tenant label), be it a "generic" image or one produced especially for a customer, almost invariably at a premium price.

Precancels — Stamps that are canceled before they are placed in the mail are known as precancels. Precanceling usually is done to expedite the handling of large mailings and generally allow the affected mail pieces to skip certain phases of mail handling.

In the United States, precancellations generally identified the point of origin; that is, the city and state. This information appeared across the face of the stamp, usually centered between parallel lines. More recently, bureau precancels retained the parallel lines, but the city and state designations were dropped. Recent coils have a service inscription that is present on the original printing plate. These show the mail service paid for by the stamp. Since these stamps are not intended to receive further cancellations when used as intended, they are considered precancels. Such items often do not have parallel lines as part of the precancellation.

In France, the abbreviation *Affranchts* in a semicircle together with the word *Postes* is the general form of precancel in use. Belgian precancellations usually appear in a box in which the name of the city appears. Netherlands precancels have the name of the city enclosed between concentric circles, sometimes called a "lifesaver." Precancellations of other countries usually follow these patterns, but may be any arrangement of bars, boxes and city names.

Precancels are listed in the Scott catalogues only if the precancel changes the denomination (Belgium Scott 477-478); if the precanceled stamp is different from the non-precanceled version (such as untagged U.S. precancels); or if the stamp exists only precanceled (France Scott 1096-1099, U.S. Scott 2265).

Proofs and Essays — Proofs are impressions taken from an approved die, plate or stone in which the design and color are the same as the stamp issued to the public. Trial color proofs are impressions taken from approved dies, plates or stones in colors that vary from the final version. An essay is the impression of a design that differs in some way from the issued stamp. "Progressive die proofs" generally are considered to be essays.

Provisionals — These are stamps that are issued on short notice and intended for temporary use pending the arrival of regular issues. They usually are issued to meet such contingencies as changes in government or currency, shortage of necessary postage values or military occupation.

During the 1840s, postmasters in certain American cities issued stamps that were valid only at specific post offices. In 1861, postmasters of the Confederate States also issued stamps with limited validity. Both of these examples are known as "postmaster's provisionals."

Se-tenant — This term refers to an unsevered pair, strip or block of stamps that differ in design, denomination or overprint.

Unless the se-tenant item has a continuous design (see U.S. Scott 1451a, 1694a) the stamps do not have to be in the same order as shown in the catalogue (see U.S. Scott 2158a).

Specimens — The Universal Postal Union required member nations to send samples of all stamps they released into service to the International Bureau in Switzerland. Member nations of the UPU received these specimens as samples of what stamps were valid for postage. Many are overprinted, handstamped or initial-perforated "Specimen," "Canceled" or "Muestra." Some are marked with bars across the denominations (China-Taiwan), punched holes (Czechoslovakia) or back inscriptions (Mongolia).

Stamps distributed to government officials or for publicity purposes, and stamps submitted by private security printers for official approval, also may receive such defacements.

The previously described defacement markings prevent postal use, and all such items generally are known as "specimens."

Tete Beche — This term describes a pair of stamps in which one is upside down in relation to the other. Some of these are the result of intentional sheet arrangements, such as Morocco Scott B10-B11. Others occurred when one or more electrotypes accidentally were placed upside down on the plate, such as Colombia Scott 57a. Separation of the tete-beche stamps, of course, destroys the tete beche variety.

Currency Conversion

Country	Dollar	Pound	S Franc	Yen	HK $	Euro	Cdn $	Aus $
Australia	0.9755	1.5780	1.0673	0.0121	0.1257	1.2822	0.9867	–
Canada	0.9886	1.5992	1.0816	0.0123	0.1274	1.2994	–	1.0134
European Union	0.7608	1.2307	0.8324	0.0095	0.0981	–	0.7696	0.7799
Hong Kong	7.7590	12.551	8.4891	0.0966	–	10.199	7.8485	7.9539
Japan	80.298	129.89	87.854	–	10.349	105.55	81.224	82.315
Switzerland	0.9140	1.4785	–	0.0114	0.1178	1.2014	0.9245	0.9370
United Kingdom	0.6182	–	0.6764	0.0077	0.0797	0.8126	0.6253	0.6337
United States	–	1.6176	1.0941	0.0125	0.1289	1.3144	1.0115	1.0251

Country	Currency	U.S. $ Equiv.
San Marino	euro	1.3144
Saudi Arabia	riyal	.2666
Senegal	Community of French Africa (CFA) franc	.0020
Serbia	dinar	.0118
Seychelles	rupee	.0720
Sierra Leone	leone	.0002
Singapore	dollar	.8044
Slovakia	euro	1.3144
Slovenia	euro	1.3144
Solomon Islands	dollar	.1385
Somalia	shilling	.0006
South Africa	rand	.1294
S. Georgia & S. Sandwich Isls	British pound	1.6176
Spain	euro	1.3144
Sri Lanka	rupee	.0079
Sudan	pound	.3739
Surinam	dollar	.3054
Swaziland	emalangeni	.1294
Sweden	krona	.1480
Switzerland	franc	1.0941
Syria	pound	.0174
Tajikistan	somoni	.2102
Tanzania	shilling	.0006
Thailand	baht	.0323
Timor	U.S. dollar	1.0000
Togo	Community of French Africa (CFA) franc	.0020
Tokelau	New Zealand dollar	.7997
Tonga	pa'anga	.5827
Niuafo'ou	pa'anga	.5827
Trinidad & Tobago	dollar	.1563
Tristan da Cunha	British pound	1.6176
Tunisia	dinar	.6496
Turkey	lira	.5670
Turk. Rep. of Northern Cyprus	lira	.5670
Turkmenistan	manat	.3509
Turks & Caicos Islands	U.S. dollar	1.0000
Tuvalu	Australian dollar	1.0251
Uganda	shilling	.0004
Ukraine	hryvnia	.1243
United Arab Emirates	dirham	.2722
Uruguay	peso	.0503
Uzbekistan	sum	.0005
Vanuatu	vatu	.0110
Vatican City	euro	1.3144
Venezuela	bolivar	.2326
Viet Nam	dong	.00005
Virgin Islands	U.S. dollar	1.0000
Wallis & Futuna Islands	Community of French Pacific (CFP) franc	.0110
Yemen	rial	.0047
Zambia	kwacha	.0002
Zaire (Congo Dem. Rep.)	franc	.0011
Zimbabwe	U.S. dollar	1.0000

Source: xe.com May 3, 2012. Figures reflect values as of May 3, 2012.

COMMON DESIGN TYPES

Pictured in this section are issues where one illustration has been used for a number of countries in the Catalogue. Not included in this section are over-printed stamps or those issues which are illustrated in each country.

EUROPA
Europa, 1956

The design symbolizing the cooperation among the six countries comprising the Coal and Steel Community is illustrated in each country.

Belgium	496-497
France	805-806
Germany	748-749
Italy	715-716
Luxembourg	318-320
Netherlands	368-369

Europa, 1958

"E" and Dove — CD1

European Postal Union at the service of European integration.

1958, Sept. 13

Belgium	527-528
France	889-890
Germany	790-791
Italy	750-751
Luxembourg	341-343
Netherlands	375-376
Saar	317-318

Europa, 1959

6-Link Enless Chain — CD2

1959, Sept. 19

Belgium	536-537
France	929-930
Germany	805-806
Italy	791-792
Luxembourg	354-355
Netherlands	379-380

Europa, 1960

19-Spoke Wheel CD3

First anniverary of the establishment of C.E.P.T. (Conference Europeenne des Admin-istrations des Postes et des Telecommunica-tions.) The spokes symbolize the 19 founding members of the Conference.

1960, Sept.

Belgium	553-554
Denmark	379
Finland	376-377
France	970-971
Germany	818-820
Great Britain	377-378
Greece	688
Iceland	327-328

Ireland	175-176
Italy	809-810
Luxembourg	374-375
Netherlands	385-386
Norway	387
Portugal	866-867
Spain	941-942
Sweden	562-563
Switzerland	400-401
Turkey	1493-1494

Europa, 1961

19 Doves Flying as One — CD4

The 19 doves represent the 19 members of the Conference of European Postal and Tele-communications Administrations C.E.P.T.

1961-62

Belgium	572-573
Cyprus	201-203
France	1005-1006
Germany	844-845
Great Britain	383-384
Greece	718-719
Iceland	340-341
Italy	845-846
Luxembourg	382-383
Netherlands	387-388
Spain	1010-1011
Switzerland	410-411
Turkey	1518-1520

Europa, 1962

Young Tree with 19 Leaves CD5

The 19 leaves represent the 19 original members of C.E.P.T.

1962-63

Belgium	582-583
Cyprus	219-221
France	1045-1046
Germany	852-853
Greece	739-740
Iceland	348-349
Ireland	184-185
Italy	860-861
Luxembourg	386-387
Netherlands	394-395
Norway	414-415
Switzerland	416-417
Turkey	1553-1555

Europa, 1963

Stylized Links, Symbolizing Unity — CD6

1963, Sept.

Belgium	598-599
Cyprus	229-231
Finland	419
France	1074-1075
Germany	867-868
Greece	768-769
Iceland	357-358
Ireland	188-189
Italy	880-881
Luxembourg	403-404
Netherlands	416-417
Norway	441-442
Switzerland	429
Turkey	1602-1603

Europa, 1964

Symbolic Daisy — CD7

5th anniversary of the establishment of C.E.P.T. The 22 petals of the flower symbolize the 22 members of the Conference.

1964, Sept.

Austria	738
Belgium	614-615
Cyprus	244-246
France	1109-1110
Germany	897-898
Greece	801-802
Iceland	367-368
Ireland	196-197
Italy	894-895
Luxembourg	411-412
Monaco	590-591
Netherlands	428-429
Norway	458
Portugal	931-933
Spain	1262-1263
Switzerland	438-439
Turkey	1628-1629

Europa, 1965

Leaves and "Fruit" CD8

1965

Belgium	636-637
Cyprus	262-264
Finland	437
France	1131-1132
Germany	934-935
Greece	833-834
Iceland	375-376
Ireland	204-205
Italy	915-916
Luxembourg	432-433
Monaco	616-617
Netherlands	438-439
Norway	475-476
Portugal	958-960
Switzerland	469
Turkey	1665-1666

Europa, 1966

Symbolic Sailboat — CD9

1966, Sept.

Andorra, French	172
Belgium	675-676
Cyprus	275-277
France	1163-1164
Germany	963-964
Greece	862-863
Iceland	384-385
Ireland	216-217
Italy	942-943
Liechtenstein	415
Luxembourg	440-441
Monaco	639-640
Netherlands	441-442
Norway	496-497
Portugal	980-982
Switzerland	477-478
Turkey	1718-1719

Europa, 1967

Cogwheels CD10

1967

Andorra, French	174-175
Belgium	688-689
Cyprus	297-299
France	1178-1179
Germany	969-970
Greece	891-892
Iceland	389-390
Ireland	232-233
Italy	951-952
Liechtenstein	420
Luxembourg	449-450
Monaco	669-670
Netherlands	444-447
Norway	504-505
Portugal	994-996
Spain	1465-1466
Switzerland	482
Turkey	B120-B121

Europa, 1968

Golden Key with C.E.P.T. Emblem CD11

1968

Andorra, French	182-183
Belgium	705-706
Cyprus	314-316
France	1209-1210
Germany	983-984
Greece	916-917
Iceland	395-396
Ireland	242-243
Italy	979-980
Liechtenstein	442
Luxembourg	466-467
Monaco	689-691
Netherlands	452-453
Portugal	1019-1021
San Marino	687
Spain	1526
Switzerland	488
Turkey	1775-1776

Europa, 1969

"EUROPA" and "CEPT" CD12

Tenth anniversary of C.E.P.T.

1969

Andorra, French	188-189
Austria	837
Belgium	718-719
Cyprus	326-328
Denmark	458
Finland	483
France	1245-1246
Germany	996-997
Great Britain	585
Greece	947-948
Iceland	406-407
Ireland	270-271
Italy	1000-1001
Liechtenstein	453
Luxembourg	475-476
Monaco	722-724
Netherlands	475-476
Norway	533-534
Portugal	1038-1040
San Marino	701-702
Spain	1567
Sweden	814-816

Switzerland..............................500-501
Turkey.....................................1799-1800
Vatican....................................470-472
Yugoslavia..............................1003-1004

Europa, 1970

Interwoven
Threads
CD13

1970

Andorra, French 196-197
Belgium...................................741-742
Cyprus....................................340-342
France.....................................1271-1272
Germany..................................1018-1019
Greece 985, 987
Iceland....................................420-421
Ireland....................................279-281
Italy...1013-1014
Liechtenstein 470
Luxembourg............................489-490
Monaco...................................768-770
Netherlands............................483-484
Portugal 1060-1062
San Marino..............................729-730
Spain 1607
Switzerland.............................515-516
Turkey.....................................1848-1849
Yugoslavia..............................1024-1025

Europa, 1971

"Fraternity,
Cooperation,
Common
Effort"
CD14

1971

Andorra, French 205-206
Belgium...................................803-804
Cyprus....................................365-367
Finland....................................504
France.....................................1304
Germany..................................1064-1065
Greece....................................1029-1030
Iceland....................................429-430
Ireland....................................305-306
Italy...1038-1039
Liechtenstein 485
Luxembourg............................500-501
Malta.......................................425-427
Monaco...................................797-799
Netherlands............................488-489
Portugal 1094-1096
San Marino..............................749-750
Spain 1675-1676
Switzerland.............................531-532
Turkey.....................................1876-1877
Yugoslavia..............................1052-1053

Europa, 1972

Sparkles, Symbolic
of Communications
CD15

1972

Andorra, French 210-211
Andorra, Spanish 62
Belgium...................................825-826
Cyprus....................................380-382
Finland....................................512-513
France.....................................1341
Germany..................................1089-1090
Greece....................................1049-1050
Iceland....................................439-440
Ireland....................................316-317
Italy...1065-1066
Liechtenstein 504
Luxembourg............................512-513
Malta.......................................450-453
Monaco...................................831-832

Netherlands............................494-495
Portugal 1141-1143
San Marino..............................771-772
Spain 1718
Switzerland.............................544-545
Turkey.....................................1907-1908
Yugoslavia 1100-1101

Europa, 1973

Post Horn
and Arrows
CD16

1973

Andorra, French 219-220
Andorra, Spanish 76
Belgium...................................839-840
Cyprus....................................396-398
Finland....................................526
France.....................................1367
Germany..................................1114-1115
Greece....................................1090-1092
Iceland....................................447-448
Ireland....................................329-330
Italy...1108-1109
Liechtenstein 528-529
Luxembourg............................523-524
Malta.......................................469-471
Monaco...................................866-867
Netherlands............................504-505
Norway....................................604-605
Portugal 1170-1172
San Marino..............................802-803
Spain 1753
Switzerland.............................580-581
Turkey.....................................1935-1936
Yugoslavia 1138-1139

Europa, 2000

CD17

2000

Albania....................................2621-2622
Andorra, French 522
Andorra, Spanish 262
Armenia...................................610-611
Austria 1814
Azerbaijan...............................698-699
Belarus....................................350
Belgium...................................1818
Bosnia & Herzegovina (Moslem) 358
Bosnia & Herzegovina (Serb) 111-112
Croatia....................................428-429
Cyprus....................................959
Czech Republic 3120
Denmark..................................1189
Estonia....................................394
Faroe Islands..........................376
Finland....................................1129
Aland Islands..........................166
France.....................................2771
Georgia 228 229
Germany..................................2086-2087
Gibraltar..................................837-840
Great Britain (Guernsey).........805-809
Great Britain (Jersey)..............935-936
Great Britain (Isle of Man) 883
Greece.....................................1959
Greenland................................363
Hungary...................................3699-3700
Iceland.....................................910
Ireland.....................................1230-1231
Italy..2349
Latvia.......................................504
Liechtenstein 1178
Lithuania..................................668
Luxembourg.............................1035
Macedonia...............................187
Malta..1011-1012
Moldova...................................355
Monaco....................................2161-2162
Poland......................................3519
Portugal 2358
Portugal (Azores).....................455
Portugal (Madeira)...................208

Romania...................................4370
Russia......................................6589
San Marino..............................1480
Slovakia 355
Slovenia 424
Spain 3036
Sweden....................................2394
Switzerland..............................1074
Turkey......................................2762
Turkish Rep. of Northern Cyprus....500
Ukraine 379
Vatican City.............................1152

The Gibraltar stamps are similar to the stamp illustrated, but none have the design shown above. All other sets listed above include at least one stamp with the design shown, but some include stamps with entirely different designs. Bulgaria Nos. 4131-4132 and Yugoslavia Nos. 2485-2486 are Europa stamps with completely different designs.

PORTUGAL & COLONIES
Vasco da Gama

Fleet Departing
CD20

Fleet Arriving at
Calicut — CD21

Embarking at
Rastello
CD22

Muse of
History
CD23

San Gabriel,
da Gama and
Camoens
CD24

Archangel
Gabriel, the
Patron Saint
CD25

Flagship San
Gabriel — CD26

Vasco da
Gama — CD27

Fourth centenary of Vasco da Gama's discovery of the route to India.

1898

Azores......................................93-100
Macao.......................................67-74
Madeira.....................................37-44
Portugal 147-154
Port. Africa 1-8
Port. Congo..............................75-98
Port. India................................189-196
St. Thomas & Prince Islands ...170-193
Timor..45-52

Pombal
POSTAL TAX
POSTAL TAX DUES

Marquis de
Pombal — CD28

Planning
Reconstruction
of Lisbon,
1755 — CD29

Pombal Monument,
Lisbon — CD30

Sebastiao Jose de Carvalho e Mello, Marquis de Pombal (1699-1782), statesman, rebuilt Lisbon after earthquake of 1755. Tax was for the erection of Pombal monument. Obligatory on all mail on certain days throughout the year. Postal Tax Dues are inscribed "Multa."

1925

Angola RA1-RA3, RAJ1-RAJ3
Azores RA9-RA11, RAJ2-RAJ4
Cape Verde RA1-RA3, RAJ1-RAJ3
Macao............... RA1-RA3, RAJ1-RAJ3
Madeira............. RA1-RA3, RAJ1-RAJ3
Mozambique..... RA1-RA3, RAJ1-RAJ3
Nyassa.............. RA1-RA3, RAJ1-RAJ3
Portugal RA11-RA13, RAJ2-RAJ4
Port. Guinea RA11-RA13, RAJ2-RAJ4
Port. India......... RA1-RA3, RAJ1-RAJ3
St. Thomas & Prince
Islands RA1-RA3, RAJ1-RAJ3
Timor RA1-RA3, RAJ1-RAJ3

Vasco da Gama
CD34

Mousinho de
Albuquerque
CD35

Dam
CD36

Prince Henry
the Navigator
CD37

Affonso de
Albuquerque
CD38

Plane over
Globe
CD39

1938-39

Angola 274-291, C1-C9
Cape Verde 234-251, C1-C9
Macao......................289-305, C7-C15
Mozambique 270-287, C1-C9
Port. Guinea 233-250. C1-C9
Port. India 439-453, C1-C8
St. Thomas & Prince
Islands ... 302-319, 323-340, C1-C18
Timor 223-239, C1-C9

Lady of Fatima

Our Lady of the Rosary, Fatima, Portugal — CD40

1948-49

Angola	315-318
Cape Verde	266
Macao	336
Mozambique	325-328
Port. Guinea	271
Port. India	480
St. Thomas & Prince Islands	351
Timor	254

A souvenir sheet of 9 stamps was issued in 1951 to mark the extension of the 1950 Holy Year. The sheet contains: Angola No. 316, Cape Verde No. 266, Macao No. 336, Mozambique No. 325, Portuguese Guinea No. 271, Portuguese India Nos. 480, 485, St. Thomas & Prince Islands No. 351, Timor No. 254. The sheet also contains a portrait of Pope Pius XII and is inscribed "Encerramento do Ano Santo, Fatima 1951." It was sold for 11 escudos.

Holy Year

Church Bells and Dove CD41

Angel Holding Candelabra CD42

Holy Year, 1950.

1950-51

Angola	331-332
Cape Verde	268-269
Macao	339-340
Mozambique	330-331
Port. Guinea	273-274
Port. India	490-491, 496-503
St. Thomas & Prince Islands	353-354
Timor	258-259

A souvenir sheet of 8 stamps was issued in 1951 to mark the extension of the Holy Year. The sheet contains: Angola No. 331, Cape Verde No. 269, Macao No. 340, Mozambique No. 331, Portuguese Guinea No. 275, Portuguese India No. 490, St. Thomas & Prince Islands No. 354, Timor No. 258, some with colors changed. The sheet contains doves and is inscribed 'Encerramento do Ano Santo, Fatima 1951.' It was sold for 17 escudos.

Holy Year Conclusion

Our Lady of Fatima — CD43

Conclusion of Holy Year. Sheets contain alternate vertical rows of stamps and labels bearing quotation from Pope Pius XII, different for each colony.

1951

Angola	357
Cape Verde	270
Macao	352
Mozambique	356
Port. Guinea	275
Port. India	506
St. Thomas & Prince Islands	355
Timor	270

Medical Congress

CD44

First National Congress of Tropical Medicine, Lisbon, 1952. Each stamp has a different design.

1952

Angola	358
Cape Verde	287
Macao	364
Mozambique	359
Port. Guinea	276
Port. India	516
St. Thomas & Prince Islands	356
Timor	271

Postage Due Stamps

CD45

1952

Angola	J37-J42
Cape Verde	J31-J36
Macao	J53-J58
Mozambique	J51-J56
Port. Guinea	J40-J45
Port. India	J47-J52
St. Thomas & Prince Islands	J52-J57
Timor	J31-J36

Sao Paulo

Father Manuel da Nobrega and View of Sao Paulo — CD46

Founding of Sao Paulo, Brazil, 400th anniv.

1954

Angola	385
Cape Verde	297
Macao	382
Mozambique	395
Port. Guinea	291
Port. India	530
St. Thomas & Prince Islands	369
Timor	279

Tropical Medicine Congress

CD47

Sixth International Congress for Tropical Medicine and Malaria, Lisbon, Sept. 1958. Each stamp shows a different plant.

1958

Angola	409
Cape Verde	303
Macao	392
Mozambique	404
Port. Guinea	295
Port. India	569
St. Thomas & Prince Islands	371
Timor	289

Sports

CD48

Each stamp shows a different sport.

1962

Angola	433-438
Cape Verde	320-325
Macao	394-399
Mozambique	424-429
Port. Guinea	299-304
St. Thomas & Prince Islands	374-379
Timor	313-318

Anti-Malaria

Anopheles Funestus and Malaria Eradication Symbol — CD49

World Health Organization drive to eradicate malaria.

1962

Angola	439
Cape Verde	326
Macao	400
Mozambique	430
Port. Guinea	305
St. Thomas & Prince Islands	380
Timor	319

Airline Anniversary

Map of Africa, Super Constellation and Jet Liner — CD50

Tenth anniversary of Transportes Aereos Portugueses (TAP).

1963

Angola	490
Cape Verde	327
Mozambique	434
Port. Guinea	318
St. Thomas & Prince Islands	381

National Overseas Bank

Antonio Teixeira de Sousa — CD51

Centenary of the National Overseas Bank of Portugal.

1964, May 16

Angola	509
Cape Verde	328
Port. Guinea	319
St. Thomas & Prince Islands	382
Timor	320

ITU

ITU Emblem and the Archangel Gabriel — CD52

International Communications Union, Cent.

1965, May 17

Angola	511
Cape Verde	329
Macao	402
Mozambique	464
Port. Guinea	320
St. Thomas & Prince Islands	383
Timor	321

National Revolution

CD53

40th anniv. of the National Revolution. Different buildings on each stamp.

1966, May 28

Angola	525
Cape Verde	338
Macao	403
Mozambique	465
Port. Guinea	329
St. Thomas & Prince Islands	392
Timor	322

Navy Club

CD54

Centenary of Portugal's Navy Club. Each stamp has a different design.

1967, Jan. 31

Angola	527-528
Cape Verde	339-340
Macao	412-413
Mozambique	478-479
Port. Guinea	330-331
St. Thomas & Prince Islands	393-394
Timor	323-324

Admiral Coutinho

CD55

Centenary of the birth of Admiral Carlos Viegas Gago Coutinho (1869-1959), explorer and aviation pioneer. Each stamp has a different design.

1969, Feb. 17

Angola	547
Cape Verde	355
Macao	417
Mozambique	484
Port. Guinea	335
St. Thomas & Prince Islands	397
Timor	335

Administration Reform

Luiz Augusto Rebello da Silva — CD56

Centenary of the administration reforms of the overseas territories.

1969, Sept. 25

Angola	549
Cape Verde	357
Macao	419
Mozambique	491
Port. Guinea	337
St. Thomas & Prince Islands	399
Timor	338

Marshal Carmona

CD57

Birth centenary of Marshal Antonio Oscar Carmona de Fragoso (1869-1951), President of Portugal. Each stamp has a different design.

1970, Nov. 15

Angola	563
Cape Verde	359
Macao	422
Mozambique	493
Port. Guinea	340
St. Thomas & Prince Islands	403
Timor	341

Olympic Games

CD59

20th Olympic Games, Munich, Aug. 26-Sept. 11. Each stamp shows a different sport.

1972, June 20

Angola	569
Cape Verde	361
Macao	426
Mozambique	504
Port. Guinea	342
St. Thomas & Prince Islands	408
Timor	343

Lisbon-Rio de Janeiro Flight

CD60

50th anniversary of the Lisbon to Rio de Janeiro flight by Arturo de Sacadura and Coutinho, March 30-June 5, 1922. Each stamp shows a different stage of the flight.

1972, Sept. 20

Angola	570
Cape Verde	362
Macao	427
Mozambique	505
Port. Guinea	343
St. Thomas & Prince Islands	409
Timor	344

WMO Centenary

WMO Emblem — CD61

Centenary of international meterological cooperation.

1973, Dec. 15

Angola	571
Cape Verde	363
Macao	429
Mozambique	509
Port. Guinea	344
St. Thomas & Prince Islands	410
Timor	345

FRENCH COMMUNITY
Upper Volta can be found under Burkina Faso in Vol. 1
Madagascar can be found under Malagasy in Vol. 3
Colonial Exposition

People of French Empire CD70

Women's Heads CD71

France Showing Way to Civilization CD72

"Colonial Commerce" CD73

International Colonial Exposition, Paris.

1931

Cameroun	213-216
Chad	60-63
Dahomey	97-100
Fr. Guiana	152-155
Fr. Guinea	116-119
Fr. India	100-103
Fr. Polynesia	76-79
Fr. Sudan	102-105
Gabon	120-123
Guadeloupe	138-141
Indo-China	140-142
Ivory Coast	92-95
Madagascar	169-172
Martinique	129-132
Mauritania	65-68
Middle Congo	61-64
New Caledonia	176-179
Niger	73-76
Reunion	122-125
St. Pierre & Miquelon	132-135
Senegal	138-141
Somali Coast	135-138
Togo	254-257
Ubangi-Shari	82-85
Upper Volta	66-69
Wallis & Futuna Isls.	85-88

Paris International Exposition
Colonial Arts Exposition

"Colonial Resources"
CD74   CD77

Overseas Commerce CD75

Exposition Building and Women CD76

"France and the Empire" CD78

Cultural Treasures of the Colonies CD79

Souvenir sheets contain one imperf. stamp.

1937

Cameroun	217-222A
Dahomey	101-107
Fr. Equatorial Africa	27-32, 73
Fr. Guiana	162-168
Fr. Guinea	120-126
Fr. India	104-110
Fr. Polynesia	117-123
Fr. Sudan	106-112
Guadeloupe	148-154
Indo-China	193-199
Inini	41
Ivory Coast	152-158
Kwangchowan	132
Madagascar	191-197
Martinique	179-185
Mauritania	69-75
New Caledonia	208-214
Niger	72-83
Reunion	167-173
St. Pierre & Miquelon	165-171
Senegal	172-178
Somali Coast	139-145
Togo	258-264
Wallis & Futuna Isls.	89

Curie

Pierre and Marie Curie CD80

40th anniversary of the discovery of radium. The surtax was for the benefit of the Intl. Union for the Control of Cancer.

1938

Cameroun	B1
Cuba	B1-B2
Dahomey	B2
France	B76
Fr. Equatorial Africa	B1
Fr. Guiana	B3
Fr. Guinea	B2
Fr. India	B6
Fr. Polynesia	B5
Fr. Sudan	B1
Guadeloupe	B3

Indo-China	B14
Ivory Coast	B2
Madagascar	B2
Martinique	B2
Mauritania	B3
New Caledonia	B4
Niger	B1
Reunion	B4
St. Pierre & Miquelon	B3
Senegal	B3
Somali Coast	B2
Togo	B1

Caillie

Rene Caillie and Map of Northwestern Africa — CD81

Death centenary of Rene Caillie (1799-1838), French explorer. All three denominations exist with colony name omitted.

1939

Dahomey	108-110
Fr. Guinea	161-163
Fr. Sudan	113-115
Ivory Coast	160-162
Mauritania	109-111
Niger	84-86
Senegal	188-190
Togo	265-267

New York World's Fair

Natives and New York Skyline CD82

1939

Cameroun	223-224
Dahomey	111-112
Fr. Equatorial Africa	78-79
Fr. Guiana	169-170
Fr. Guinea	164-165
Fr. India	111-112
Fr. Polynesia	124-125
Fr. Sudan	116-117
Guadeloupe	155-156
Indo-China	203-204
Inini	42-43
Ivory Coast	163-164
Kwangchowan	121-122
Madagascar	209-210
Martinique	186-187
Mauritania	112-113
New Caledonia	215-216
Niger	87-88
Reunion	174-175
St. Pierre & Miquelon	205-206
Senegal	191-192
Somali Coast	179-180
Togo	268-269
Wallis & Futuna Isls.	90-91

French Revolution

Storming of the Bastille CD83

French Revolution, 150th anniv. The surtax was for the defense of the colonies.

1939

Cameroun	B2-B6
Dahomey	B3-B7
Fr. Equatorial Africa	B4-B8, CB1
Fr. Guiana	B4-B8, CB1
Fr. Guinea	B3-B7
Fr. India	B7-B11
Fr. Polynesia	B6-B10, CB1
Guadeloupe	B4-B8
Indo-China	B15-B19, CB1
Inini	B1-B5
Ivory Coast	B3-B7

Kwangchowan	B1-B5
Madagascar	B3-B7, CB1
Martinique	B3-B7
Mauritania	B4-B8
New Caledonia	B5-B9, CB1
Niger	B2-B6
Reunion	B5-B9, CB1
St. Pierre & Miquelon	B4-B8
Senegal	B4-B8, CB1
Somali Coast	B3-B7
Togo	B2-B6
Wallis & Futuna Isls.	B1-B5

Plane over Coastal Area
CD85

All five denominations exist with colony name omitted.

1940

Dahomey	C1-C5
Fr. Guinea	C1-C5
Fr. Sudan	C1-C5
Ivory Coast	C1-C5
Mauritania	C1-C5
Niger	C1-C5
Senegal	C12-C16
Togo	C1-C5

Defense of the Empire

Colonial Infantryman — CD86

1941

Cameroun	B13B
Dahomey	B13
Fr. Equatorial Africa	B8B
Fr. Guiana	B10
Fr. Guinea	B13
Fr. India	B13
Fr. Polynesia	B12
Fr. Sudan	B12
Guadeloupe	B9
Indo-China	B19B
Inini	B7
Ivory Coast	B13
Kwangchowan	B7
Madagascar	B9
Martinique	B9
Mauritania	B14
New Caledonia	B11
Niger	B12
Reunion	B11
St. Pierre & Miquelon	B8B
Senegal	B14
Somali Coast	B9
Togo	B10B
Wallis & Futuna Isls.	B7

Colonial Education Fund

CD86a

1942

Cameroun	CB3
Dahomey	CB4
Fr. Equatorial Africa	CB5
Fr. Guiana	CB4
Fr. Guinea	CB4

Fr. India	CB3
Fr. Polynesia	CB4
Fr. Sudan	CB4
Guadeloupe	CB3
Indo-China	CB5
Inini	CB3
Ivory Coast	CB4
Kwangchowan	CB1
Malagasy	CB5
Martinique	CB4
Mauritania	CB4
New Caledonia	CB4
Niger	CB4
Reunion	CB4
St. Pierre & Miquelon	CB3
Senegal	CB5
Somali Coast	CB3
Togo	CB3
Wallis & Futuna	CB3

Cross of Lorraine & Four-motor Plane
CD87

1941-5

Cameroun	C1-C7
Fr. Equatorial Africa	C17-C23
Fr. Guiana	C9-C10
Fr. India	C1-C6
Fr. Polynesia	C3-C9
Fr. West Africa	C1-C3
Guadeloupe	C1-C2
Madagascar	C37-C43
Martinique	C1-C2
New Caledonia	C7-C13
Reunion	C18-C24
St. Pierre & Miquelon	C1-C7
Somali Coast	C1-C7

Transport Plane
CD88

Caravan and Plane
CD89

1942

Dahomey	C6-C13
Fr. Guinea	C6-C13
Fr. Sudan	C6-C13
Ivory Coast	C6-C13
Mauritania	C6-C13
Niger	C6-C13
Senegal	C17-C25
Togo	C6-C13

Red Cross

Marianne
CD90

The surtax was for the French Red Cross and national relief.

1944

Cameroun	B28
Fr. Equatorial Africa	B38
Fr. Guiana	B12
Fr. India	B14
Fr. Polynesia	B13
Fr. West Africa	B1
Guadeloupe	B12
Madagascar	B15
Martinique	B11
New Caledonia	B13
Reunion	B15
St. Pierre & Miquelon	B13
Somali Coast	B13

Wallis & Futuna Isls.	B9

Eboue

CD91

Felix Eboue, first French colonial administrator to proclaim resistance to Germany after French surrender in World War II.

1945

Cameroun	296-297
Fr. Equatorial Africa	156-157
Fr. Guiana	171-172
Fr. India	210-211
Fr. Polynesia	150-151
Fr. West Africa	15-16
Guadeloupe	187-188
Madagascar	259-260
Martinique	196-197
New Caledonia	274-275
Reunion	238-239
St. Pierre & Miquelon	322-323
Somali Coast	238-239

Victory

Victory — CD92

European victory of the Allied Nations in World War II.

1946, May 8

Cameroun	C8
Fr. Equatorial Africa	C24
Fr. Guiana	C11
Fr. India	C7
Fr. Polynesia	C10
Fr. West Africa	C4
Guadeloupe	C3
Indo-China	C19
Madagascar	C44
Martinique	C3
New Caledonia	C14
Reunion	C25
St. Pierre & Miquelon	C8
Somali Coast	C8
Wallis & Futuna Isls.	C1

Chad to Rhine

Leclerc's Departure from Chad — CD93

Battle at Cufra Oasis — CD94

Tanks in Action, Mareth — CD95

Normandy Invasion — CD96

Entering Paris — CD97

Liberation of Strasbourg — CD98

"Chad to the Rhine" march, 1942-44, by Gen. Jacques Leclerc's column, later French 2nd Armored Division.

1946, June 6

Cameroun	C9-C14
Fr. Equatorial Africa	C25-C30
Fr. Guiana	C12-C17
Fr. India	C8-C13
Fr. Polynesia	C11-C16
Fr. West Africa	C5-C10
Guadeloupe	C4-C9
Indo-China	C20-C25
Madagascar	C45-C50
Martinique	C4-C9
New Caledonia	C15-C20
Reunion	C26-C31
St. Pierre & Miquelon	C9-C14
Somali Coast	C9-C14
Wallis & Futuna Isls.	C2-C7

UPU

French Colonials, Globe and Plane — CD99

Universal Postal Union, 75th anniv.

1949, July 4

Cameroun	C29
Fr. Equatorial Africa	C34
Fr. India	C17
Fr. Polynesia	C20
Fr. West Africa	C15
Indo-China	C26
Madagascar	C55
New Caledonia	C24
St. Pierre & Miquelon	C18
Somali Coast	C18
Togo	C18
Wallis & Futuna Isls.	C10

Tropical Medicine

Doctor
Treating
Infant
CD100

The surtax was for charitable work.

1950

Cameroun	B29
Fr. Equatorial Africa	B39
Fr. India	B15
Fr. Polynesia	B14
Fr. West Africa	B3
Madagascar	B17
New Caledonia	B14
St. Pierre & Miquelon	B14
Somali Coast	B14
Togo	B11

Military Medal

Medal, Early Marine
and Colonial
Soldier — CD101

Centenary of the creation of the French Military Medal.

1952

Cameroun	322
Comoro Isls.	39
Fr. Equatorial Africa	186
Fr. India	233
Fr. Polynesia	179
Fr. West Africa	57
Madagascar	286
New Caledonia	295
St. Pierre & Miquelon	345
Somali Coast	267
Togo	327
Wallis & Futuna Isls.	149

Liberation

Allied Landing, Victory Sign and Cross
of Lorraine — CD102

Liberation of France, 10th anniv.

1954, June 6

Cameroun	C32
Comoro Isls.	C4
Fr. Equatorial Africa	C38
Fr. India	C18
Fr. Polynesia	C22
Fr. West Africa	C17
Madagascar	C57
New Caledonia	C25
St. Pierre & Miquelon	C19
Somali Coast	C19
Togo	C19
Wallis & Futuna Isls.	C11

FIDES

Plowmen
CD103

Efforts of FIDES, the Economic and Social
Development Fund for Overseas Possessions

(Fonds d' Investissement pour le Developpement Economique et Social). Each stamp has a different design.

1956

Cameroun	326-329
Comoro Isls.	43
Fr. Equatorial Africa	189-192
Fr. Polynesia	181
Fr. West Africa	65-72
Madagascar	292-295
New Caledonia	303
St. Pierre & Miquelon	350
Somali Coast	268
Togo	331

Flower

CD104

Each stamp shows a different flower.

1958-9

Cameroun	333
Comoro Isls.	45
Fr. Equatorial Africa	200-201
Fr. Polynesia	192
Fr. So. & Antarctic Terr.	11
Fr. West Africa	79-83
Madagascar	301-302
New Caledonia	304-305
St. Pierre & Miquelon	357
Somali Coast	270
Togo	348-349
Wallis & Futuna Isls.	152

Human Rights

Sun, Dove
and U.N.
Emblem
CD105

10th anniversary of the signing of the Universal Declaration of Human Rights.

1958

Comoro Isls.	44
Fr. Equatorial Africa	202
Fr. Polynesia	191
Fr. West Africa	85
Madagascar	300
New Caledonia	306
St. Pierre & Miquelon	356
Somali Coast	274
Wallis & Futuna Isls.	153

C.C.T.A.

CD106

Commission for Technical Cooperation in
Africa south of the Sahara, 10th anniv.

1960

Cameroun	339
Cent. Africa	3
Chad	66
Congo, P.R.	90
Dahomey	138
Gabon	150
Ivory Coast	180
Madagascar	317
Mali	9
Mauritania	104
Niger	104
Upper Volta	89

Air Afrique, 1961

Modern and Ancient Africa, Map and
Planes — CD107

Founding of Air Afrique (African Airlines).

1961-62

Cameroun	C37
Cent. Africa	C5
Chad	C7
Congo, P.R.	C5
Dahomey	C17
Gabon	C5
Ivory Coast	C18
Mauritania	C17
Niger	C22
Senegal	C31
Upper Volta	C4

Anti-Malaria

CD108

World Health Organization drive to eradicate malaria.

1962, Apr. 7

Cameroun	B36
Cent. Africa	B1
Chad	B1
Comoro Isls.	B1
Congo, P.R.	B3
Dahomey	B15
Gabon	B4
Ivory Coast	B15
Madagascar	B19
Mali	B1
Mauritania	B16
Niger	B14
Senegal	B16
Somali Coast	B15
Upper Volta	B1

Abidjan Games

CD109

Abidjan Games, Ivory Coast, Dec. 24-31,
1961. Each stamp shows a different sport.

1962

Chad	83 84
Cent. Africa	19-20
Congo, P.R.	103-104
Gabon	163-164, C6
Niger	109-111
Upper Volta	103-105

African and Malagasy Union

Flag of
Union
CD110

First anniversary of the Union.

1962, Sept. 8

Cameroun	373
Cent. Africa	21

Chad	85
Congo, P.R.	105
Dahomey	155
Gabon	165
Ivory Coast	198
Madagascar	332
Mauritania	170
Niger	112
Senegal	211
Upper Volta	106

Telstar

Telstar and Globe Showing Andover
and Pleumeur-Bodou — CD111

First television connection of the United
States and Europe through the Telstar satellite, July 11-12, 1962.

1962-63

Andorra, French	154
Comoro Isls.	C7
Fr. Polynesia	C29
Fr. So. & Antarctic Terr.	C5
New Caledonia	C33
Somali Coast	C31
St. Pierre & Miquelon	C26
Wallis & Futuna Isls.	C17

Freedom From Hunger

World Map
and Wheat
Emblem
CD112

U.N. Food and Agriculture Organization's
"Freedom from Hunger" campaign.

1963, Mar. 21

Cameroun	B37-B38
Cent. Africa	B2
Chad	B2
Congo, P.R.	B4
Dahomey	B16
Gabon	B5
Ivory Coast	B16
Madagascar	B21
Mauritania	B17
Niger	B15
Senegal	B17
Upper Volta	B2

Red Cross Centenary

CD113

Centenary of the International Red Cross.

1963, Sept. 2

Comoro Isls.	55
Fr. Polynesia	205
New Caledonia	328
St. Pierre & Miquelon	367
Somali Coast	297
Wallis & Futuna Isls.	165

African Postal Union, 1963

UAMPT
Emblem,
Radio Masts,
Plane and
Mail
CD114

Establishment of the African and Malagasy Posts and Telecommunications Union.

1963, Sept. 8

Cameroun	C47
Cent. Africa	C10
Chad	C9
Congo, P.R.	C13
Dahomey	C19
Gabon	C13
Ivory Coast	C25
Madagascar	C75
Mauritania	C22
Niger	C27
Rwanda	36
Senegal	C32
Upper Volta	C9

Air Afrique, 1963

Symbols of Flight — CD115

First anniversary of Air Afrique and inauguration of DC-8 service.

1963, Nov. 19

Cameroun	C48
Chad	C10
Congo, P.R.	C14
Gabon	C18
Ivory Coast	C26
Mauritania	C26
Niger	C35
Senegal	C33

Europafrica

Europe and Africa
Linked — CD116

Signing of an economic agreement between the European Economic Community and the African and Malagasy Union, Yaounde, Cameroun, July 20, 1963.

1963-64

Cameroun	402
Chad	C11
Cent. Africa	C12
Congo, P.R.	C16
Gabon	C19
Ivory Coast	217
Niger	C43
Upper Volta	C11

Human Rights

Scales of
Justice and
Globe
CD117

15th anniversary of the Universal Declaration of Human Rights.

1963, Dec. 10

Comoro Isls.	58
Fr. Polynesia	206
New Caledonia	329
St. Pierre & Miquelon	368
Somali Coast	300
Wallis & Futuna Isls.	166

PHILATEC

Stamp Album, Champs Elysees
Palace and Horses of Marly
CD118

Intl. Philatelic and Postal Techniques Exhibition, Paris, June 5-21, 1964.

1963-64

Comoro Isls.	60
France	1078
Fr. Polynesia	207
New Caledonia	341
St. Pierre & Miquelon	369
Somali Coast	301
Wallis & Futuna Isls.	167

Cooperation

CD119

Cooperation between France and the French-speaking countries of Africa and Madagascar.

1964

Cameroun	409-410
Cent. Africa	39
Chad	103
Congo, P.R.	121
Dahomey	193
France	1111
Gabon	175
Ivory Coast	221
Madagascar	360
Mauritania	181
Niger	143
Senegal	236
Togo	495

ITU

Telegraph,
Syncom Satellite
and ITU Emblem
CD120

Intl. Telecommunication Union, Cent.

1965, May 17

Comoro Isls.	C14
Fr. Polynesia	C33
Fr. So. & Antarctic Terr.	C8
New Caledonia	C40
New Hebrides	124-125
St. Pierre & Miquelon	C29
Somali Coast	C36
Wallis & Futuna Isls.	C20

French Satellite A-1

Diamant Rocket and Launching
Installation — CD121

Launching of France's first satellite, Nov. 26, 1965.

1965-66

Comoro Isls.	C15-C16
France	1137-1138
Reunion	358-359
Fr. Polynesia	C40-C41
Fr. So. & Antarctic Terr.	C9-C10
New Caledonia	C44-C45
St. Pierre & Miquelon	C30-C31
Somali Coast	C39-C40
Wallis & Futuna Isls.	C22-C23

French Satellite D-1

D-1 Satellite in Orbit — CD122

Launching of the D-1 satellite at Hammaguir, Algeria, Feb. 17, 1966.

1966

Comoro Isls.	C17
France	1148
Fr. Polynesia	C42
Fr. So. & Antarctic Terr.	C11
New Caledonia	C46
St. Pierre & Miquelon	C32
Somali Coast	C49
Wallis & Futuna Isls.	C24

Air Afrique, 1966

Planes and Air Afrique
Emblem — CD123

Introduction of DC-8F planes by Air Afrique.

1966

Cameroun	C79
Cent. Africa	C35
Chad	C26
Congo, P.R.	C42
Dahomey	C42
Gabon	C47
Ivory Coast	C32
Mauritania	C57
Niger	C63
Senegal	C47
Togo	C54
Upper Volta	C31

African Postal Union, 1967

Telecommunications Symbols and Map
of Africa — CD124

Fifth anniversary of the establishment of the African and Malagasy Union of Posts and Telecommunications, UAMPT.

1967

Cameroun	C90
Cent. Africa	C46
Chad	C37
Congo, P.R.	C57
Dahomey	C61
Gabon	C58
Ivory Coast	C34
Madagascar	C85
Mauritania	C65
Niger	C75
Rwanda	C1-C3
Senegal	C60
Togo	C81
Upper Volta	C50

Monetary Union

Gold Token of the
Ashantis, 17-18th
Centuries — CD125

West African Monetary Union, 5th anniv.

1967, Nov. 4

Dahomey	244
Ivory Coast	259
Mauritania	238
Niger	204
Senegal	294
Togo	623
Upper Volta	181

WHO Anniversary

Sun,
Flowers
and WHO
Emblem
CD126

World Health Organization, 20th anniv.

1968, May 4

Afars & Issas	317
Comoro Isls.	73
Fr. Polynesia	241-242
Fr. So. & Antarctic Terr.	31
New Caledonia	367
St. Pierre & Miquelon	377
Wallis & Futuna Isls.	169

Human Rights Year

Human Rights
Flame — CD127

1968, Aug. 10

Afars & Issas	322-323

Comoro Isls. 76
Fr. Polynesia.........................243-244
Fr. So. & Antarctic Terr. 32
New Caledonia 369
St. Pierre & Miquelon...................382
Wallis & Futuna Isls. 170

2nd PHILEXAFRIQUE

CD128

Opening of PHILEXAFRIQUE, Abidjan, Feb. 14. Each stamp shows a local scene and stamp.

1969, Feb. 14

Cameroon.................................C118
Cent. Africa C65
Chad C48
Congo, P.R. C77
Dahomey C94
Gabon C82
Ivory Coast C38-C40
Madagascar C92
Mali C65
Mauritania C80
Niger C104
Senegal C68
Togo C104
Upper Volta C62

Concorde

Concorde in Flight
CD129

First flight of the prototype Concorde supersonic plane at Toulouse, Mar. 1, 1969.

1969

Afars & Issas C56
Comoro Isls. C29
France......................................C42
Fr. Polynesia C50
Fr. So. & Antarctic Terr. C18
New Caledonia C63
St. Pierre & Miquelon C40
Wallis & Futuna Isls. C30

Development Bank

Bank Emblem — CD130

African Development Bank, fifth anniv.

1969

Cameroun..................................499
Chad...217
Congo, P.R..........................181-182
Ivory Coast 281
Mali.....................................127-128
Mauritania 267
Niger 220
Senegal 317-318
Upper Volta 201

ILO

ILO Headquarters, Geneva, and Emblem — CD131

Intl. Labor Organization, 50th anniv.

1969-70

Afars & Issas 337
Comoro Isls. 83
Fr. Polynesia 251-252
Fr. So. & Antarctic Terr. 35
New Caledonia 379
St. Pierre & Miquelon 396
Wallis & Futuna Isls. 172

ASECNA

Map of Africa, Plane and Airport
CD132

10th anniversary of the Agency for the Security of Aerial Navigation in Africa and Madagascar (ASECNA, Agence pour la Securite de la Navigation Aerienne en Afrique et a Madagascar).

1969-70

Cameroun...................................500
Cent. Africa 119
Chad 222
Congo, P.R. 197
Dahomey 269
Gabon 260
Ivory Coast 287
Mali 130
Niger 221
Senegal 321
Upper Volta 204

U.P.U. Headquarters

CD133

New Universal Postal Union headquarters, Bern, Switzerland.

1970

Afars & Issas 342
Algeria......................................443
Cameroun.............................503-504
Cent. Africa 125
Chad 225
Comoro Isls. 84
Congo, P.R. 216
Fr. Polynesia 261-262
Fr. So. & Antarctic Terr. 36
Gabon 258
Ivory Coast 295
Madagascar 444
Mali 134-135
Mauritania 283
New Caledonia 382
Niger 231-232
St. Pierre & Miquelon 397-398
Senegal 328-329
Tunisia 535
Wallis & Futuna Isls. 173

De Gaulle

CD134

First anniversay of the death of Charles de Gaulle, (1890-1970), President of France.

1971-72

Afars & Issas 356-357
Comoro Isls. 104-105
France................................1322-1325
Fr. Polynesia 270-271
Fr. So. & Antarctic Terr. 52-53
New Caledonia 393-394
Reunion 377, 380
St. Pierre & Miquelon..........417-418
Wallis & Futuna Isls. 177-178

African Postal Union, 1971

UAMPT Building, Brazzaville, Congo — CD135

10th anniversary of the establishment of the African and Malagasy Posts and Telecommunications Union, UAMPT. Each stamp has a different native design.

1971, Nov. 13

Cameroun.................................C177
Cent. Africa C89
Chad C94
Congo, P.R. C136
Dahomey C146
Gabon C120
Ivory Coast C47
Mauritania C113
Niger C164
Rwanda C8
Senegal C105
Togo C166
Upper Volta C97

West African Monetary Union

African Couple, City, Village and Commemorative Coin — CD136

West African Monetary Union, 10th anniv.

1972, Nov. 2

Dahomey 300
Ivory Coast 331
Mauritania 299
Niger 258
Senegal 374
Togo 825
Upper Volta 280

African Postal Union, 1973

Telecommunications Symbols and Map of Africa — CD137

11th anniversary of the African and Malagasy Posts and Telecommunications Union (UAMPT).

1973, Sept. 12

Cameroun...................................574
Cent. Africa 194
Chad 294
Congo, P.R. 289
Dahomey 311
Gabon 320
Ivory Coast 361
Madagascar 500
Mauritania 304
Niger 287

Rwanda 540
Senegal 393
Togo..849
Upper Volta 297

Philexafrique II — Essen

CD138

CD139

Designs: Indigenous fauna, local and German stamps. Types CD138-CD139 printed horizontally and vertically se-tenant in sheets of 10 (2x5). Label between horizontal pairs alternately commemoratives Philexafrique II, Libreville, Gabon, June 1978, and 2nd International Stamp Fair, Essen, Germany, Nov. 1-5.

1978-1979

Benin C285-C206
Central Africa C200-C201
Chad C238-C239
Congo Republic C245-C246
Djibouti C121-C122
Gabon C215-C216
Ivory Coast C64-C65
Mali C356-C357
Mauritania C185-C186
Niger C291-C292
Rwanda C12-C13
Senegal C146-C147
Togo.................................C363-C364

BRITISH COMMONWEALTH OF NATIONS

The listings follow established trade practices when these issues are offered as units by dealers. The Peace issue, for example, includes only one stamp from the Indian state of Hyderabad. The U.P.U. issue includes the Egypt set. Pairs are included for those varieties issued with bilingual designs se-tenant.

Silver Jubilee

Windsor Castle and King George V
CD301

Reign of King George V, 25th anniv.

1935

Antigua 77-80
Ascension 33-36
Bahamas 92-95
Barbados 186-189
Basutoland 11-14
Bechuanaland Protectorate......117-120
Bermuda 100-103
British Guiana 223-226
British Honduras 108-111
Cayman Islands 81-84
Ceylon 260-263
Cyprus 136-139
Dominica 90-93
Falkland Islands 77-80
Fiji 110-113
Gambia 125-128

Gibraltar....................................100-103
Gilbert & Ellice Islands.............33-36
Gold Coast...............................108-111
Grenada.....................................124-127
Hong Kong.................................147-150
Jamaica......................................109-112
Kenya, Uganda, Tanganyika 42-45
Leeward Islands..........................96-99
Malta...184-187
Mauritius.....................................204-207
Montserrat....................................85-88
Newfoundland..............................226-229
Nigeria..34-37
Northern Rhodesia........................18-21
Nyasaland Protectorate................47-50
St. Helena...................................111-114
St. Kitts-Nevis..............................72-75
St. Lucia.......................................91-94
St. Vincent..................................134-137
Seychelles..................................118-121
Sierra Leone...............................166-169
Solomon Islands...........................60-63
Somaliland Protectorate...............77-80
Straits Settlements.....................213-216
Swaziland......................................20-23
Trinidad & Tobago.........................43-46
Turks & Caicos Islands.................71-74
Virgin Islands................................69-72

The following have different designs but are included in the omnibus set:

Great Britain...............................226-229
Offices in Morocco......67-70, 226-229,
    422-425, 508-510
Australia......................................152-154
Canada...211-216
Cook Islands.................................98-100
India...142-148
Nauru...31-34
New Guinea....................................46-47
New Zealand................................199-201
Niue..67-69
Papua..114-117
Samoa...163-165
South Africa...................................68-71
Southern Rhodesia........................33-36
South-West Africa........................121-124

249 stamps

Coronation

Queen Elizabeth and King George VI
CD302

1937

Aden..13-15
Antigua...81-83
Ascension.......................................37-39
Bahamas...97-99
Barbados.......................................190-192
Basutoland......................................15-17
Bechuanaland Protectorate........121-123
Bermuda.......................................115-117
British Guiana..............................227-229
British Honduras...........................112-114
Cayman Islands..............................97-99
Ceylon..275-277
Cyprus..140-142
Dominica..94-96
Falkland Islands.............................81-83
Fiji..114-116
Gambia...129-131
Gibraltar.......................................104-106
Gilbert & Ellice Islands.................37-39
Gold Coast...................................112-114
Grenada..128-130
Hong Kong....................................151-153
Jamaica.......................................113-115
Kenya, Uganda, Tanganyika.........60-62
Leeward Islands...........................100-102
Malta..188-190
Mauritius......................................208-210
Montserrat......................................89-91
Newfoundland..............................230-232
Nigeria...50-52
Northern Rhodesia.........................22-24
Nyasaland Protectorate.................51-53
St. Helena....................................115-117
St. Kitts-Nevis................................76-78
St. Lucia.......................................107-109
St. Vincent...................................138-140
Seychelles....................................122-124
Sierra Leone................................170-172
Solomon Islands.............................64-66

Somaliland Protectorate...............81-83
Straits Settlements......................235-237
Swaziland.......................................24-26
Trinidad & Tobago..........................47-49
Turks & Caicos Islands.................75-77
Virgin Islands.................................73-75

The following have different designs but are included in the omnibus set:

Great Britain...................................234
Offices in Morocco...........82, 439, 514
Canada...237
Cook Islands...............................109-111
Nauru...35-38
Newfoundland..............................233-243
New Guinea.....................................48-51
New Zealand................................223-225
Niue..70-72
Papua..118-121
South Africa...................................74-78
Southern Rhodesia........................38-41
South-West Africa........................125-132

202 stamps

Peace

King George VI and Parliament Buildings, London
CD303

Return to peace at the close of World War II.

1945-46

Aden..28-29
Antigua...96-97
Ascension.......................................50-51
Bahamas......................................130-131
Barbados.......................................207-208
Bermuda.......................................131-132
British Guiana..............................242-243
British Honduras...........................127-128
Cayman Islands...........................112-113
Ceylon..293-294
Cyprus..156-157
Dominica......................................112-113
Falkland Islands.............................97-98
Falkland Islands Dep..........1L9-1L10
Fiji..137-138
Gambia...144-145
Gibraltar.......................................119-120
Gilbert & Ellice Islands.................52-53
Gold Coast...................................128-129
Grenada..143-144
Jamaica.......................................136-137
Kenya, Uganda, Tanganyika.........90-91
Leeward Islands...........................116-117
Malta..206-207
Mauritius......................................223-224
Montserrat...................................104-105
Nigeria...71-72
Northern Rhodesia.........................46-47
Nyasaland Protectorate.................82-83
Pitcairn Island.................................9-10
St. Helena....................................128-129
St. Kitts-Nevis................................91-92
St. Lucia.......................................127-128
St. Vincent...................................152-153
Seychelles....................................149-150
Sierra Leone................................186-187
Solomon Islands.............................80-81
Somaliland Protectorate..............108-109
Trinidad & Tobago..........................62-63
Turks & Caicos Islands.................90-91
Virgin Islands.................................88-89

The following have different designs but are included in the omnibus set:

Great Britain...............................264-265
    Offices in Morocco...............523-524
Aden
    Kathiri State of Seiyun.............12-13
    Qu'aiti State of Shihr and Mukalla .....
   12-13
Australia......................................200-202
Basutoland......................................29-31
Bechuanaland Protectorate........137-139
Burma..66-69
Cook Islands................................127-130
Hong Kong...................................174-175
India...195-198
    Hyderabad...................................51
New Zealand................................247-257
Niue..90-93
Pakistan-Bahawalpur.....................O16
Samoa...191-194

South Africa.................................100-102
Southern Rhodesia........................67-70
South-West Africa........................153-155
Swaziland.......................................38-40
Zanzibar......................................222-223

164 stamps

Silver Wedding

King George VI and Queen Elizabeth
CD304   CD305

1948-49

Aden..30-31
    Kathiri State of Seiyun.............14-15
    Qu'aiti State of Shihr and Mukalla .....
   14-15
Antigua...98-99
Ascension.......................................52-53
Bahamas......................................148-149
Barbados.......................................210-211
Basutoland......................................39-40
Bechuanaland Protectorate........147-148
Bermuda.......................................133-134
British Guiana..............................244-245
British Honduras...........................129-130
Cayman Islands...........................116-117
Cyprus..158-159
Dominica......................................114-115
Falkland Islands.............................99-100
Falkland Islands Dep..........1L11-1L12
Fiji..139-140
Gambia...146-147
Gibraltar.......................................121-122
Gilbert & Ellice Islands.................54-55
Gold Coast...................................142-143
Grenada..145-146
Hong Kong...................................178-179
Jamaica.......................................138-139
Kenya, Uganda, Tanganyika.........92-93
Leeward Islands...........................118-119
Malaya
    Johore......................................128-129
    Kedah...55-56
    Kelantan.....................................44-45
    Malacca..1-2
    Negri Sembilan...........................36-37
    Pahang..44-45
    Penang...1-2
    Perak...99-100
    Perlis...1-2
    Selangor.....................................74-75
    Trengganu...................................47-48
Malta..223-224
Mauritius......................................229-230
Montserrat...................................106-107
Nigeria...73-74
North Borneo...............................238-239
Northern Rhodesia.........................48-49
Nyasaland Protectorate.................85-86
Pitcairn Island.................................11-12
St. Helena....................................130-131
St. Kitts-Nevis................................93-94
St. Lucia.......................................129-130
St. Vincent...................................154-155
Sarawak.......................................174-175
Seychelles....................................151-152
Sierra Leone................................188-189
Singapore......................................21-22
Solomon Islands.............................82-83
Somaliland Protectorate..............110-111
Swaziland.......................................48-49
Trinidad & Tobago..........................64-65
Turks & Caicos Islands.................92-93
Virgin Islands.................................90-91
Zanzibar......................................224-225

The following have different designs but are included in the omnibus set:

Great Britain...............................267-268
    Offices in Morocco.....93-94, 525-526
Bahrain...62-63
Kuwait...82-83
Oman..25-26
South Africa.....................................106
South-West Africa..............................159

138 stamps

U.P.U.

Mercury and Symbols of Communications — CD306

Plane, Ship and Hemispheres — CD307

Mercury Scattering Letters over Globe CD308

U.P.U. Monument, Bern CD309

Universal Postal Union, 75th anniversary.

1949

Aden..32-35
    Kathiri State of Seiyun.............16-19
    Qu'aiti State of Shihr and Mukalla .....
   16-19
Antigua...100-103
Ascension.......................................57-60
Bahamas......................................150-153
Barbados.......................................212-215
Basutoland......................................41-44
Bechuanaland Protectorate........149-152
Bermuda.......................................138-141
British Guiana..............................246-249
British Honduras...........................137-140
Brunei...79-82
Cayman Islands...........................118-121
Cyprus..160-163
Dominica......................................116-119
Falkland Islands.............................103-106
Falkland Islands Dep..........1L14-1L17
Fiji..141-144
Gambia...148-151
Gibraltar.......................................123-126
Gilbert & Ellice Islands.................56-59
Gold Coast...................................144-147
Grenada..147-150
Hong Kong...................................180-183
Jamaica.......................................142-145
Kenya, Uganda, Tanganyika.........94-97
Leeward Islands...........................126-129
Malaya
    Johore......................................151-154
    Kedah...57-60
    Kelantan.....................................46-49
    Malacca.......................................18-21
    Negri Sembilan...........................59-62
    Pahang..46-49
    Penang..23-26
    Perak...101-104
    Perlis...3-6
    Selangor.....................................76-79
    Trengganu...................................49-52
Malta..225-228
Mauritius......................................231-234
Montserrat...................................108-111
New Hebrides, British.................62-65
New Hebrides, French.................79-82
Nigeria...75-78
North Borneo...............................240-243
Northern Rhodesia.........................50-53
Nyasaland Protectorate.................87-90
Pitcairn Islands..............................13-16
St. Helena....................................132-135
St. Kitts-Nevis................................95-98
St. Lucia.......................................131-134
St. Vincent...................................170-173

Sarawak...................................176-179
Seychelles..............................153-156
Sierra Leone...........................190-193
Singapore.................................23-26
Solomon Islands........................84-87
Somaliland Protectorate.........112-115
Southern Rhodesia...................71-72
Swaziland.................................50-53
Tonga.......................................87-90
Trinidad & Tobago....................66-69
Turks & Caicos Islands 101-104
Virgin Islands...........................92-95
Zanzibar.................................226-229

The following have different designs but are included in the omnibus set:

Great Britain...........................276-279
Offices in Morocco..................546-549
Australia.......................................223
Bahrain.....................................68-71
Burma.....................................116-121
Ceylon....................................304-306
Egypt......................................281-283
India.......................................223-226
Kuwait......................................89-92
Oman..31-34
Pakistan-Bahawalpur 26-29, O25-O28
South Africa............................109-111
South-West Africa 160-162

319 stamps

University

Arms of
University
College
CD310

Alice, Princess
of Athlone
CD311

1948 opening of University College of the West Indies at Jamaica.

1951

Antigua 104-105
Barbados................................228-229
British Guiana.........................250-251
British Honduras.....................141-142
Dominica................................120-121
Grenada.................................164-165
Jamaica.................................146-147
Leeward Islands.....................130-131
Montserrat.............................112-113
St. Kitts-Nevis.......................105-106
St. Lucia................................149-150
St. Vincent............................174-175
Trinidad & Tobago 70-71
Virgin Islands...........................96-97

28 stamps

Coronation

Queen Elizabeth
II — CD312

1953

Aden..47
Kathiri State of Seiyun.................28
Qu'aiti State of Shihr and Mukalla ....
....28
Antigua.......................................106
Ascension....................................61
Bahamas....................................157
Barbados....................................234
Basutoland...................................45
Bechuanaland Protectorate.........153
Bermuda.....................................142
British Guiana.............................252
British Honduras.........................143
Cayman Islands..........................150

Cyprus 167
Dominica...................................141
Falkland Islands 121
Falkland Islands Dependencies ...1L18
Fiji...145
Gambia.....................................152
Gibraltar...................................131
Gilbert & Ellice Islands................60
Gold Coast................................160
Grenada....................................170
Hong Kong................................184
Jamaica....................................153
Kenya, Uganda, Tanganyika 101
Leeward Islands........................132
Malaya
Johore....................................155
Kedah......................................82
Kelantan...................................71
Malacca....................................27
Negri Sembilan..........................63
Pahang.....................................71
Penang.....................................27
Perak......................................126
Perlis.......................................28
Selangor..................................101
Trengganu.................................74
Malta..241
Mauritius...................................250
Montserrat.................................127
New Hebrides, British 77
Nigeria......................................79
North Borneo.............................260
Northern Rhodesia.......................60
Nyasaland Protectorate................96
Pitcairn......................................19
St. Helena................................139
St. Kitts-Nevis..........................119
St. Lucia..................................156
St. Vincent...............................185
Sarawak....................................196
Seychelles.................................172
Sierra Leone.............................194
Singapore...................................27
Solomon Islands..........................88
Somaliland Protectorate 127
Swaziland...................................54
Trinidad & Tobago 84
Tristan da Cunha..........................13
Turks & Caicos Islands 118
Virgin Islands............................114

The following have different designs but are included in the omnibus set:

Great Britain...........................313-316
Offices in Morocco..................579-582
Australia.................................259-261
Bahrain.....................................92-95
Canada..330
Ceylon...317
Cook Islands...........................145-146
Kuwait....................................113-116
New Zealand...........................280-284
Niue.......................................104-105
Oman..52-55
Samoa....................................214-215
South Africa................................192
Southern Rhodesia........................80
South-West Africa 244-248
Tokelau Islands...............................4

106 stamps

Royal Visit 1953

Separate designs for each country for the visit of Queen Elizabeth II and the Duke of Edinburgh.

1953

Aden..62
Australia.................................267-269
Bermuda......................................163
Ceylon...318
Fiji..146
Gibraltar......................................146
Jamaica.......................................154
Kenya, Uganda, Tanganyika 102
Malta...242
New Zealand...........................286-287

13 stamps

West Indies Federation

Map of the
Caribbean
CD313

Federation of the West Indies, April 22, 1958.

1958

Antigua...................................122-124
Barbados................................248-250
Dominica................................161-163
Grenada.................................184-186
Jamaica.................................175-177
Montserrat.............................143-145
St. Kitts-Nevis.......................136-138
St. Lucia................................170-172
St. Vincent............................198-200
Trinidad & Tobago....................86-88

30 stamps

Freedom from Hunger

Protein Food
CD314

U.N. Food and Agricultural Organization's "Freedom from Hunger" campaign.

1963

Aden..65
Antigua.......................................133
Ascension.....................................89
Bahamas.....................................180
Basutoland....................................83
Bechuanaland Protectorate..........194
Bermuda.....................................192
British Guiana.............................271
British Honduras.........................179
Brunei..100
Cayman Islands..........................168
Dominica....................................181
Falkland Islands 146
Fiji...198
Gambia......................................172
Gibraltar....................................161
Gilbert & Ellice Islands................76
Grenada.....................................190
Hong Kong................................218
Malta...291
Mauritius...................................270
Montserrat.................................150
New Hebrides, British 93
North Borneo.............................296
Pitcairn.......................................35
St. Helena................................173
St. Lucia..................................179
St. Vincent...............................201
Sarawak....................................212
Seychelles.................................213
Solomon Islands.........................109
Swaziland..................................108
Tonga..127
Tristan da Cunha..........................68
Turks & Caicos Islands 138
Virgin Islands............................140
Zanzibar.....................................280

37 stamps

Red Cross Centenary

Red Cross
and
Elizabeth
II
CD315

1963

Antigua...................................134-135
Ascension.................................90-91
Bahamas................................183-184
Basutoland...............................84-85
Bechuanaland Protectorate......195-196
Bermuda................................193-194
British Guiana.........................272-273
British Honduras.....................180-181
Cayman Islands......................169-170
Dominica................................182-183
Falkland Islands 147-148
Fiji...203-204
Gambia...................................173-174
Gibraltar.................................162-163
Gilbert & Ellice Islands.............77-78
Grenada.................................191-192
Hong Kong............................219-220
Jamaica.................................203-204

Malta......................................292-293
Mauritius.................................271-272
Montserrat.............................151-152
New Hebrides, British 94-95
Pitcairn Islands..........................36-37
St. Helena..............................174-175
St. Kitts-Nevis.......................143-144
St. Lucia................................180-181
St. Vincent............................202-203
Seychelles.............................214-215
Solomon Islands.....................110-111
South Arabia..................................1-2
Swaziland...............................109-110
Tonga.....................................134-135
Tristan da Cunha......................69-70
Turks & Caicos Islands 139-140
Virgin Islands.........................141-142

70 stamps

Shakespeare

Shakespeare Memorial Theatre,
Stratford-on-Avon — CD316

400th anniversary of the birth of William Shakespeare.

1964

Antigua 151
Bahamas.....................................201
Bechuanaland Protectorate............197
Cayman Islands...........................171
Dominica....................................184
Falkland Islands 149
Gambia......................................192
Gibraltar....................................164
Montserrat.................................153
St. Lucia...................................196
Turks & Caicos Islands 141
Virgin Islands............................143

12 stamps

ITU

ITU
Emblem
CD317

Intl. Telecommunication Union, cent.

1965

Antigua 153-154
Ascension................................92-93
Bahamas................................219-220
Barbados................................265-266
Basutoland..............................101-102
Bechuanaland Protectorate......202-203
Bermuda................................196-197
British Guiana.........................293-294
British Honduras.....................187-188
Brunei....................................116-117
Cayman Islands.......................172-173
Dominica................................185-186
Falkland Islands 154-155
Fiji...211-212
Gibraltar.................................167-168
Gilbert & Ellice Islands.............87-88
Grenada.................................205-206
Hong Kong............................221-222
Mauritius...............................291-292
Montserrat.............................157-158
New Hebrides, British 108-109
Pitcairn Islands..........................52-53
St. Helena..............................180-181
St. Kitts-Nevis.......................163-164
St. Lucia................................197-198
St. Vincent............................224-225
Seychelles.............................218-219
Solomon Islands.....................126-127
Swaziland...............................115-116
Tristan da Cunha......................85-86
Turks & Caicos Islands 142-143
Virgin Islands.........................159-160

64 stamps

Intl. Cooperation Year

ICY Emblem CD318

1965

Antigua	155-156
Ascension	94-95
Bahamas	222-223
Basutoland	103-104
Bechuanaland Protectorate	204-205
Bermuda	199-200
British Guiana	295-296
British Honduras	189-190
Brunei	118-119
Cayman Islands	174-175
Dominica	187-188
Falkland Islands	156-157
Fiji	213-214
Gibraltar	169-170
Gilbert & Ellice Islands	104-105
Grenada	207-208
Hong Kong	223-224
Mauritius	293-294
Montserrat	176-177
New Hebrides, British	110-111
New Hebrides, French	126-127
Pitcairn Islands	54-55
St. Helena	182-183
St. Kitts-Nevis	165-166
St. Lucia	199-200
Seychelles	220-221
Solomon Islands	143-144
South Arabia	17-18
Swaziland	117-118
Tristan da Cunha	87-88
Turks & Caicos Islands	144-145
Virgin Islands	161-162

64 stamps

Churchill Memorial

Winston Churchill and St. Paul's, London, During Air Attack CD319

1966

Antigua	157-160
Ascension	96-99
Bahamas	224-227
Barbados	281-284
Basutoland	105-108
Bechuanaland Protectorate	206-209
Bermuda	201-204
British Antarctic Territory	16-19
British Honduras	191-194
Brunei	120-123
Cayman Islands	176-179
Dominica	189-192
Falkland Islands	158-161
Fiji	215-218
Gibraltar	171-174
Gilbert & Ellice Islands	106-109
Grenada	209-212
Hong Kong	225-228
Mauritius	295-298
Montserrat	178-181
New Hebrides, British	112-115
New Hebrides, French	128-131
Pitcairn Islands	56-59
St. Helena	184-187
St. Kitts-Nevis	167-170
St. Lucia	201-204
St. Vincent	241-244
Seychelles	222-225
Solomon Islands	145-148
South Arabia	19-22
Swaziland	119-122
Tristan da Cunha	89-92
Turks & Caicos Islands	146-149
Virgin Islands	163-166

136 stamps

Royal Visit, 1966

Queen Elizabeth II and Prince Philip CD320

Caribbean visit, Feb. 4 - Mar. 6, 1966.

1966

Antigua	161-162
Bahamas	228-229
Barbados	285-286
British Guiana	299-300
Cayman Islands	180-181
Dominica	193-194
Grenada	213-214
Montserrat	182-183
St. Kitts-Nevis	171-172
St. Lucia	205-206
St. Vincent	245-246
Turks & Caicos Islands	150-151
Virgin Islands	167-168

26 stamps

World Cup Soccer

Soccer Player and Jules Rimet Cup CD321

World Cup Soccer Championship, Wembley, England, July 11-30.

1966

Antigua	163-164
Ascension	100-101
Bahamas	245-246
Bermuda	205-206
Brunei	124-125
Cayman Islands	182-183
Dominica	195-196
Fiji	219-220
Gibraltar	175-176
Gilbert & Ellice Islands	125-126
Grenada	230-231
New Hebrides, British	116-117
New Hebrides, French	132-133
Pitcairn Islands	60-61
St. Helena	188-189
St. Kitts-Nevis	173-174
St. Lucia	207-208
Seychelles	226-227
Solomon Islands	167-168
South Arabia	23-24
Tristan da Cunha	93-94

42 stamps

WHO Headquarters

World Health Organization Headquarters, Geneva — CD322

1966

Antigua	165-166
Ascension	102-103
Bahamas	247-248
Brunei	126-127
Cayman Islands	184-185
Dominica	197-198
Fiji	224-225
Gibraltar	180-181
Gilbert & Ellice Islands	127-128
Grenada	232-233
Hong Kong	229-230
Montserrat	184-185
New Hebrides, British	118-119
New Hebrides, French	134-135
Pitcairn Islands	62-63
St. Helena	190-191
St. Kitts-Nevis	177-178
St. Lucia	209-210

St. Vincent	247-248
Seychelles	228-229
Solomon Islands	169-170
South Arabia	25-26
Tristan da Cunha	99-100

46 stamps

UNESCO Anniversary

"Education" — CD323

"Science" (Wheat ears & flask enclosing globe). "Culture" (lyre & columns). 20th anniversary of the UNESCO.

1966-67

Antigua	183-185
Ascension	108-110
Bahamas	249-251
Barbados	287-289
Bermuda	207-209
Brunei	128-130
Cayman Islands	186-188
Dominica	199-201
Gibraltar	183-185
Gilbert & Ellice Islands	129-131
Grenada	234-236
Hong Kong	231-233
Mauritius	299-301
Montserrat	186-188
New Hebrides, British	120-122
New Hebrides, French	136-138
Pitcairn Islands	64-66
St. Helena	192-194
St. Kitts-Nevis	179-181
St. Lucia	211-213
St. Vincent	249-251
Seychelles	230-232
Solomon Islands	171-173
South Arabia	27-29
Swaziland	123-125
Tristan da Cunha	101-103
Turks & Caicos Islands	155-157
Virgin Islands	176-178

84 stamps

Silver Wedding, 1972

Queen Elizabeth II and Prince Philip — CD324

Designs: borders differ for each country.

1972

Anguilla	161-162
Antigua	295-296
Ascension	164-165
Bahamas	344-345
Bermuda	296-297
British Antarctic Territory	43-44
British Honduras	306-307
British Indian Ocean Territory	48-49
Brunei	186-187
Cayman Islands	304-305
Dominica	352-353
Falkland Islands	223-224
Fiji	328-329
Gibraltar	292-293
Gilbert & Ellice Islands	206-207
Grenada	466-467
Hong Kong	271-272
Montserrat	286-287
New Hebrides, British	169-170
Pitcairn Islands	127-128
St. Helena	271-272
St. Kitts-Nevis	257-258
St. Lucia	328-329
St.Vincent	344-345
Seychelles	309-310
Solomon Islands	248-249
South Georgia	35-36

Tristan da Cunha	178-179
Turks & Caicos Islands	257-258
Virgin Islands	241-242

60 stamps

Princess Anne's Wedding

Princess Anne and Mark Phillips — CD325

Wedding of Princess Anne and Mark Phillips, Nov. 14, 1973.

1973

Anguilla	179-180
Ascension	177-178
Belize	325-326
Bermuda	302-303
British Antarctic Territory	60-61
Cayman Islands	320-321
Falkland Islands	225-226
Gibraltar	305-306
Gilbert & Ellice Islands	216-217
Hong Kong	289-290
Montserrat	300-301
Pitcairn Island	135-136
St. Helena	277-278
St. Kitts-Nevis	274-275
St. Lucia	349-350
St. Vincent	358-359
St. Vincent Grenadines	1-2
Seychelles	311-312
Solomon Islands	259-260
South Georgia	37-38
Tristan da Cunha	189-190
Turks & Caicos Islands	286-287
Virgin Islands	260-261

44 stamps

Elizabeth II Coronation Anniv.

CD326

CD327

CD328

Designs: Royal and local beasts in heraldic form and simulated stonework. Portrait of Elizabeth II by Peter Grugeon. 25th anniversary of coronation of Queen Elizabeth II.

1978

Ascension	229
Barbados	474
Belize	397
British Antarctic Territory	71
Cayman Islands	404
Christmas Island	87
Falkland Islands	275
Fiji	384
Gambia	380
Gilbert Islands	312
Mauritius	464
New Hebrides, British	258
St. Helena	317
St. Kitts-Nevis	354
Samoa	472

Solomon Islands 368
South Georgia 51
Swaziland 302
Tristan da Cunha 238
Virgin Islands 337

20 sheets

Queen Mother Elizabeth's 80th Birthday

CD330

Designs: Photographs of Queen Mother Elizabeth. Falkland Islands issued in sheets of 50; others in sheets of 9.

1980

Ascension 261
Bermuda 401
Cayman Islands 443
Falkland Islands 305
Gambia 412
Gibraltar 393
Hong Kong 364
Pitcairn Islands 193
St. Helena 341
Samoa 532
Solomon Islands 426
Tristan da Cunha 277

12 stamps

Royal Wedding, 1981

Prince Charles and Lady Diana — CD331   CD331a

Wedding of Charles, Prince of Wales, and Lady Diana Spencer, St. Paul's Cathedral, London, July 29, 1981.

1981

Antigua 623-625
Ascension 294-296
Barbados 547-549
Barbuda 497-499
Bermuda 412-414
Brunei 268-270
Cayman Islands 471-473
Dominica 701-703
Falkland Islands 324-326
Falkland Islands Dep 1L59-1L61
Fiji 442-444
Gambia 426-428
Ghana 759-761
Grenada 1051-1053
Grenada Grenadines 440-443
Hong Kong 373-375
Jamaica 500-503
Lesotho 335-337
Maldive Islands 906-908
Mauritius 520-522
Norfolk Island 280-282
Pitcairn Islands 206-208
St. Helena 353-355
St. Lucia 543-545
Samoa 558-560
Sierra Leone 509-517
Solomon Islands 450-452
Swaziland 382-384
Tristan da Cunha 294-296
Turks & Caicos Islands 486-488
Caicos Island 8-10
Uganda 314-316
Vanuatu 308-310
Virgin Islands 406-408

Princess Diana

CD332

CD333

Designs: Photographs and portrait of Princess Diana, wedding or honeymoon photographs, royal residences, arms of issuing country. Portrait photograph by Clive Friend. Souvenir sheet margins show family tree, various people related to the princess. 21st birthday of Princess Diana of Wales, July 1.

1982

Antigua 663-666
Ascension 313-316
Bahamas 510-513
Barbados 585-588
Barbuda 544-546
British Antarctic Territory 92-95
Cayman Islands 486-489
Dominica 773-776
Falkland Islands 348-351
Falkland Islands Dep 1L72-1L75
Fiji 470-473
Gambia 447-450
Grenada 1101A-1105
Grenada Grenadines 485-491
Lesotho 372-375
Maldive Islands 952-955
Mauritius 548-551
Pitcairn Islands 213-216
St. Helena 372-375
St. Lucia 591-594
Sierra Leone 531-534
Solomon Islands 471-474
Swaziland 406-409
Tristan da Cunha 310-313
Turks and Caicos Islands 530A-534
Virgin Islands 430-433

250th anniv. of first edition of Lloyd's List (shipping news publication) & of Lloyd's marine insurance.

CD335

Designs: First page of early edition of the list; historical ships, modern transportation or harbor scenes.

1984

Ascension 351-354
Bahamas 555-558
Barbados 627-630
Cayes of Belize 10-13
Cayman Islands 522-525
Falkland Islands 404-407
Fiji 509-512
Gambia 519-522
Mauritius 587-590
Nauru 280-283
St. Helena 412-415
Samoa 624-627
Seychelles 538-541
Solomon Islands 521-524
Vanuatu 368-371
Virgin Islands 466-469

Queen Mother 85th Birthday

CD336

Designs: Photographs tracing the life of the Queen Mother, Elizabeth. The high value in each set pictures the same photograph taken of the Queen Mother holding the infant Prince Henry.

1985

Ascension 372-376
Bahamas 580-584
Barbados 660-664
Bermuda 469-473
Falkland Islands 420-424
Falkland Islands Dep 1L92-1L96
Fiji 531-535
Hong Kong 447-450
Jamaica 599-603
Mauritius 604-608
Norfolk Island 364-368
Pitcairn Islands 253-257
St. Helena 428-432
Samoa 649-653
Seychelles 567-571
Solomon Islands 543-547
Swaziland 476-480
Tristan da Cunha 372-376
Vanuatu 392-396
Zil Elwannyen Sesel 101-105

Queen Elizabeth II, 60th Birthday

CD337

1986, April 21

Ascension 389-393
Bahamas 592-596
Barbados 675-679
Bermuda 499-503
Cayman Islands 555-559
Falkland Islands 441-445
Fiji 544-548
Hong Kong 465-469
Jamaica 620-624
Kiribati 470-474
Mauritius 629-633
Papua New Guinea 640-644
Pitcairn Islands 270-274
St. Helena 451-455
Samoa 670-674
Seychelles 592-596
Solomon Islands 562-566
South Georgia 101-105
Swaziland 490-494
Tristan da Cunha 388-392
Vanuatu 414-418
Zambia 343-347
Zil Elwannyen Sesel 114-118

Royal Wedding

Marriage of Prince Andrew and Sarah Ferguson CD338

1986, July 23

Ascension 399-400
Bahamas 602-603
Barbados 687-688
Cayman Islands 560-561
Jamaica 629-630
Pitcairn Islands 275-276
St. Helena 460-461
St. Kitts 181-182

Seychelles 602-603
Solomon Islands 567-568
Tristan da Cunha 397-398
Zambia 348-349
Zil Elwannyen Sesel 119-120

Queen Elizabeth II, 60th Birthday

Queen Elizabeth II & Prince Philip, 1947 Wedding Portrait — CD339

Designs: Photographs tracing the life of Queen Elizabeth II.

1986

Anguilla 674-677
Antigua 925-928
Barbuda 783-786
Dominica 950-953
Gambia 611-614
Grenada 1371-1374
Grenada Grenadines 749-752
Lesotho 531-534
Maldive Islands 1172-1175
Sierra Leone 760-763
Uganda 495-498

Royal Wedding, 1986

CD340

Designs: Photographs of Prince Andrew and Sarah Ferguson during courtship, engagement and marriage.

1986

Antigua 939-942
Barbuda 809-812
Dominica 970-973
Gambia 635-638
Grenada 1385-1388
Grenada Grenadines 758-761
Lesotho 545-548
Maldive Islands 1181-1184
Sierra Leone 769-772
Uganda 510-513

Lloyds of London, 300th Anniv.

CD341

Designs: 17th century aspects of Lloyds, representations of each country's individual connections with Lloyds and publicized disasters insured by the organization.

1986

Ascension 454-457
Bahamas 655-658
Barbados 731-734
Bermuda 541-544
Falkland Islands 481-484
Liberia 1101-1104
Malawi 534-537
Nevis 571-574
St. Helena 501-504
St. Lucia 923-926
Seychelles 649-652
Solomon Islands 627-630

South Georgia 131-134
Trinidad & Tobago 484-487
Tristan da Cunha.....................439-442
Vanuatu 485-488
Zil Elwannyen Sesel.................146-149

Moon Landing, 20th Anniv.

CD342

Designs: Equipment, crew photographs, spacecraft, official emblems and report profiles created for the Apollo Missions. Two stamps in each set are square in format rather than like the stamp shown; see individual country listings for more information.

1989

Ascension Is.............................468-472
Bahamas 674-678
Belize 916-920
Kiribati 517-521
Liberia 1125-1129
Nevis 586-590
St. Kitts 248-252
Samoa 760-764
Seychelles 676-680
Solomon Islands......................643-647
Vanuatu 507-511
Zil Elwannyen Sesel.................154-158

Queen Mother, 90th Birthday

CD343   CD344

Designs: Portraits of Queen Elizabeth, the Queen Mother. See individual country listings for more information.

1990

Ascension Is.............................491-492
Bahamas 698-699
Barbados 782-783
British Antarctic Territory..........170-171
British Indian Ocean Territory 106-107
Cayman Islands.......................622-623
Falkland Islands 524-525
Kenya 527-528
Kiribati 555-556
Liberia 1145-1146
Pitcairn Islands........................336-337
St. Helena 532-533
St. Lucia 969-970
Seychelles 710-711
Solomon Islands......................671-672
South Georgia 143-144
Swaziland 565-566
Tristan da Cunha.....................480-481
Zil Elwannyen Sesel.................171-172

Queen Elizabeth II, 65th Birthday, and Prince Philip, 70th Birthday

CD345

CD346

Designs: Portraits of Queen Elizabeth II and Prince Philip differ for each country. Printed in sheets of 10 + 5 labels (3 different) between. Stamps alternate, producing 5 different triptychs.

1991

Ascension Is. 505-506
Bahamas 730-731
Belize 969-970
Bermuda 617-618
Kiribati 571-572
Mauritius 733-734
Pitcairn Islands........................348-349
St. Helena 554-555
St. Kitts 318-319
Samoa 790-791
Seychelles 723-724
Solomon Islands......................688-689
South Georgia 149-150
Swaziland 586-587
Vanuatu 540-541
Zil Elwannyen Sesel.................177-178

Royal Family Birthday, Anniversary

CD347

Queen Elizabeth II, 65th birthday, Charles and Diana, 10th wedding anniversary: Various photographs of Queen Elizabeth II, Prince Philip, Prince Charles, Princess Diana and their sons William and Henry.

1991

Antigua 1446-1455
Barbuda 1229-1238
Dominica.................................1328-1337
Gambia 1080-1089
Grenada 2006-2015
Grenada Grenadines 1331-1340
Guyana 2440-2451
Lesotho 871-875
Maldive Islands........................1533-1542
Nevis 666-675
St. Vincent 1485-1494
St. Vincent Grenadines 769-778
Sierra Leone...........................1387-1396
Turks & Caicos Islands 913-922
Uganda 918-927

Queen Elizabeth II's Accession to the Throne, 40th Anniv.

CD348

CD349

Various photographs of Queen Elizabeth II with local Scenes.

1992 - CD348

Antigua 1513-1518
Barbuda 1306-1309
Dominica.................................1414-1419
Gambia 1172-1177
Grenada 2047-2052
Grenada Grenadines 1368-1373

Lesotho 881-885
Maldive Islands....................1637-1642
Nevis 702-707
St. Vincent 1582-1587
St. Vincent Grenadines 829-834
Sierra Leone........................1482-1487
Turks and Caicos Islands.........978-987
Uganda 990-995
Virgin Islands 742-746

1992 - CD349

Ascension Islands 531-535
Bahamas 744-748
Bermuda 623-627
British Indian Ocean Territory 119-123
Cayman Islands........................648-652
Falkland Islands 549-553
Gibraltar 605-609
Hong Kong 619-623
Kenya 563-567
Kiribati 582-586
Pitcairn Islands........................362-366
St. Helena 570-574
St. Kitts 332-336
Samoa 805-809
Seychelles 734-738
Solomon Islands......................708-712
South Georgia 157-161
Tristan da Cunha.....................508-512
Vanuatu 555-559
Zambia 561-565
Zil Elwannyen Sesel.................183-187

Royal Air Force, 75th Anniversary

CD350

1993

Ascension 557-561
Bahamas 771-775
Barbados 842-846
Belize 1003-1008
Bermuda 648-651
British Indian Ocean Territory 136-140
Falkland Is. 573-577
Fiji 687-691
Montserrat 830-834
St. Kitts 351-355

Royal Air Force, 80th Anniv.

CD350

Design CD350 Re-inscribed

1998

Ascension 697-701
Bahamas 907-911
British Indian Ocean Terr 198-202
Cayman Islands........................754-758
Fiji 814-818
Gibraltar 755-759
Samoa 957-961
Turks & Caicos Islands 1258-1265
Tuvalu 763-767
Virgin Islands 879-883

End of World War II, 50th Anniv.

CD351

CD352

1995

Ascension 613-617
Bahamas 824-828
Barbados 891-895
Belize 1047-1050
British Indian Ocean Territory 163-167
Cayman Islands........................704-708
Falkland Islands 634-638
Fiji 720-724
Kiribati 662-668
Liberia 1175-1179
Mauritius 803-805
St. Helena 646-654
St. Kitts 389-393
St. Lucia 1018-1022
Samoa 890-894
Solomon Islands......................799-803
South Georgia & S. Sandwich Is. 198-200
Tristan da Cunha.....................562-566

UN, 50th Anniv.

CD353

1995

Bahamas 839-842
Barbados 901-904
Belize 1055-1058
Jamaica 847-851
Liberia 1187-1190
Mauritius 813-816
Pitcairn Islands........................436-439
St. Kitts 398-401
St. Lucia 1023-1026
Samoa 900-903
Tristan da Cunha.....................568-571
Virgin Islands 807-810

Queen Elizabeth, 70th Birthday

CD354

1996

Ascension 632-635
British Antarctic Territory..........240-243
British Indian Ocean Territory 176-180
Falkland Islands 653-657
Pitcairn Islands........................446-449
St. Helena 672-676
Samoa 912-916
Tokelau 223-227
Tristan da Cunha.....................576-579
Virgin Islands 824-828

Diana, Princess of Wales (1961-97)

CD355

1998

Ascension	696
Bahamas	901A-902
Barbados	950
Belize	1091
Bermuda	753
Botswana	659-663
British Antarctic Territory	258
British Indian Ocean Terr.	197
Cayman Islands	752A-753
Falkland Islands	694
Fiji	819-820
Gibraltar	754
Kiribati	719A-720
Namibia	909
Niue	706
Norfolk Island	644-645
Papua New Guinea	937
Pitcairn Islands	487
St. Helena	711
St. Kitts	437A-438
Samoa	955A-956
Seycelles	802
Solomon Islands	866-867
South Georgia & S. Sandwich Islands	220
Tokelau	252B-253
Tonga	980
Niuafo'ou	201
Tristan da Cunha	618
Tuvalu	762
Vanuatu	719
Virgin Islands	878

Wedding of Prince Edward and Sophie Rhys-Jones

CD356

1999

Ascension	729-730
Cayman Islands	775-776
Falkland Islands	729-730
Pitcairn Islands	505-506
St. Helena	733-734
Samoa	971-972
Tristan da Cunha	636-637
Virgin Islands	908-909

1st Manned Moon Landing, 30th Anniv.

CD357

1999

Ascension	731-735
Bahamas	942-946
Barbados	967-971
Bermuda	778
Cayman Islands	777-781

Fiji	853-857
Jamaica	889-893
Kirbati	746-750
Nauru	465-469
St. Kitts	460-464
Samoa	973-977
Solomon Islands	875-879
Tuvalu	800-804
Virgin Islands	910-914

Queen Mother's Century

CD358

1999

Ascension	736-740
Bahamas	951-955
Cayman Islands	782-786
Falkland Islands	734-738
Fiji	858-862
Norfolk Island	688-692
St. Helena	740-744
Samoa	978-982
Solomon Islands	880-884
South Georgia & South Sandwich Islands	231-235
Tristan da Cunha	638-642
Tuvalu	805-809

Prince William, 18th Birthday

CD359

2000

Ascension	755-759
Cayman Islands	797-801
Falkland Islands	762-766
Fiji	889-893
South Georgia and South Sandwich Islands	257-261
Tristan da Cunha	664-668
Virgin Islands	925-929

Reign of Queen Elizabeth II, 50th Anniv.

CD360

2002

Ascension	790-794
Bahamas	1033-1037
Barbados	1019-1023
Belize	1152-1156
Bermuda	822-826
British Antarctic Territory	307-311
British Indian Ocean Territory	239-243
Cayman Islands	844-848
Falkland Islands	804-808
Gibraltar	896-900
Jamaica	952-956
Nauru	491-495
Norfolk Island	758-762
Papua New Guinea	1019-1023
Pitcairn Islands	552
St. Helena	788-792
St. Lucia	1146-1150
Solomon Islands	931-935
South Georgia & So. Sandwich Is.	274-278
Swaziland	706-710
Tokelau	302-306
Tonga	1059

Niuafo'ou	239
Tristan da Cunha	706-710
Virgin Islands	967-971

Queen Mother Elizabeth (1900-2002)

CD361

2002

Ascension	799-801
Bahamas	1044-1046
Bermuda	834-836
British Antarctic Territory	312-314
British Indian Ocean Territory	245-247
Cayman Islands	857-861
Falkland Islands	812-816
Nauru	499-501
Pitcairn Islands	561-565
St. Helena	808-812
St. Lucia	1155-1159
Seychelles	830
Solomon Islands	945-947
South Georgia & So. Sandwich Isls.	281-285
Tokelau	312-314
Tristan da Cunha	715-717
Virgin Islands	979-983

Head of Queen Elizabeth II

CD362

2003

Ascension	822
Bermuda	865
British Antarctic Territory	322
British Indian Ocean Territory	261
Cayman Islands	878
Falkland Islands	828
St. Helena	820
South Georgia & South Sandwich Islands	294
Tristan da Cunha	731
Virgin Islands	1003

Coronation of Queen Elizabeth II, 50th Anniv.

CD363

2003

Ascension	823-825
Bahamas	1073-1075
Bermuda	866-868
British Antarctic Territory	323-325
British Indian Ocean Territory	262-264
Cayman Islands	879-881
Jamaica	970-972
Kiribati	825-827
Pitcairn Islands	577-581
St. Helena	821-823
St. Lucia	1171-1173
Tokelau	320-322
Tristan da Cunha	732-734
Virgin Islands	1004-1006

Prince William, 21st Birthday

CD364

2003

Ascension	826
British Indian Ocean Territory	265
Cayman Islands	882-884
Falkland Islands	829
South Georgia & South Sandwich Islands	295
Tokelau	323
Tristan da Cunha	735
Virgin Islands	1007-1009

British Commonwealth of Nations

Dominions, Colonies, Territories, Offices and Independent Members

Comprising stamps of the British Commonwealth and associated nations.

A strict observance of technicalities would bar some or all of the stamps listed under Burma, Ireland, Kuwait, Nepal, New Republic, Orange Free State, Samoa, South Africa, South-West Africa, Stellaland, Sudan, Swaziland, the two Transvaal Republics and others but these are included for the convenience of collectors.

1. Great Britain

Great Britain: Including England, Scotland, Wales and Northern Ireland.

2. The Dominions, Present and Past

AUSTRALIA

The Commonwealth of Australia was proclaimed on January 1, 1901. It consists of six former colonies as follows:

New South Wales	Victoria
Queensland	Tasmania
South Australia	Western Australia

The following islands and territories are, or have been, administered by Australia: Australian Antarctic Territory, Christmas Island, Cocos (Keeling) Islands, Nauru, New Guinea, Norfolk Island, Papua.

CANADA

The Dominion of Canada was created by the British North America Act in 1867. The following provinces were former sepa- rate colonies and issued postage stamps:

British Columbia and	Newfoundland
Vancouver Island	Nova Scotia
New Brunswick	Prince Edward Island

FIJI

The colony of Fiji became an independent nation with dominion status on Oct. 10, 1970.

GHANA

This state came into existence Mar. 6, 1957, with dominion status. It consists of the former colony of the Gold Coast and the Trusteeship Territory of Togoland. Ghana became a republic July 1, 1960.

INDIA

The Republic of India was inaugurated on January 26, 1950. It succeeded the Dominion of India which was proclaimed August 15, 1947, when the former Empire of India was divided into Pakistan and the Union of India. The Republic is composed of about 40 predominantly Hindu states of three classes: governor's provinces, chief commissioner's provinces and princely states. India also has various territories, such as the Andaman and Nicobar Islands.

The old Empire of India was a federation of British India and the native states. The more important princely states were autonomous. Of the more than 700 Indian states, these 43 are familiar names to philatelists because of their postage stamps.

CONVENTION STATES

Chamba	Jhind
Faridkot	Nabha
Gwalior	Patiala

FEUDATORY STATES

Alwar	Jammu and Kashmir
Bahawalpur	Jasdan
Bamra	Jhalawar
Barwani	Jhind (1875-76)
Bhopal	Kashmir
Bhor	Kishangarh
Bijawar	Kotah
Bundi	Las Bela
Bussahir	Morvi
Charkhari	Nandgaon
Cochin	Nowanuggur
Dhar	Orchha
Dungarpur	Poonch
Duttia	Rajasthan
Faridkot (1879-85)	Rajpeepla
Hyderabad	Sirmur
Idar	Soruth
Indore	Tonk
Jaipur	Travancore
Jammu	Wadhwan

NEW ZEALAND

Became a dominion on September 26, 1907. The following islands and territories are, or have been, administered by New Zealand:

Aitutaki	Ross Dependency
Cook Islands (Rarotonga)	Samoa (Western Samoa)
Niue	Tokelau Islands
Penrhyn	

PAKISTAN

The Republic of Pakistan was proclaimed March 23, 1956. It succeeded the Dominion which was proclaimed August 15, 1947. It is made up of all or part of several Moslem provinces and various districts of the former Empire of India, including Bahawalpur and Las Bela. Pakistan withdrew from the Commonwealth in 1972.

SOUTH AFRICA

Under the terms of the South African Act (1909) the self-governing colonies of Cape of Good Hope, Natal, Orange River Colony and Transvaal united on May 31, 1910, to form the Union of South Africa. It became an independent republic May 3, 1961.

Under the terms of the Treaty of Versailles, South-West Africa, formerly German South-West Africa, was mandated to the Union of South Africa.

SRI LANKA (CEYLON)

The Dominion of Ceylon was proclaimed February 4, 1948. The island had been a Crown Colony from 1802 until then. On May 22, 1972, Ceylon became the Republic of Sri Lanka.

3. Colonies, Past and Present; Controlled Territory and Independent Members of the Commonwealth

Aden	Bechuanaland
Aitutaki	Bechuanaland Prot.
Antigua	Belize
Ascension	Bermuda
Bahamas	Botswana
Bahrain	British Antarctic Territory
Bangladesh	British Central Africa
Barbados	British Columbia and
Barbuda	Vancouver Island
Basutoland	British East Africa
Batum	British Guiana

British Honduras
British Indian Ocean Territory
British New Guinea
British Solomon Islands
British Somaliland
Brunei
Burma
Bushire
Cameroons
Cape of Good Hope
Cayman Islands
Christmas Island
Cocos (Keeling) Islands
Cook Islands
Crete,
  British Administration
Cyprus
Dominica
East Africa & Uganda
  Protectorates
Egypt
Falkland Islands
Fiji
Gambia
German East Africa
Gibraltar
Gilbert Islands
Gilbert & Ellice Islands
Gold Coast
Grenada
Griqualand West
Guernsey
Guyana
Heligoland
Hong Kong
Indian Native States
  (see India)
Ionian Islands
Jamaica
Jersey

Kenya
Kenya, Uganda & Tanzania
Kuwait
Labuan
Lagos
Leeward Islands
Lesotho
Madagascar
Malawi
Malaya
  Federated Malay States
  Johore
  Kedah
  Kelantan
  Malacca
  Negri Sembilan
  Pahang
  Penang
  Perak
  Perlis
  Selangor
  Singapore
  Sungei Ujong
  Trengganu
Malaysia
Maldive Islands
Malta
Man, Isle of
Mauritius
Mesopotamia
Montserrat
Muscat
Namibia
Natal
Nauru
Nevis
New Britain
New Brunswick
Newfoundland
New Guinea

New Hebrides
New Republic
New South Wales
Niger Coast Protectorate
Nigeria
Niue
Norfolk Island
North Borneo
Northern Nigeria
Northern Rhodesia
North West Pacific Islands
Nova Scotia
Nyasaland Protectorate
Oman
Orange River Colony
Palestine
Papua New Guinea
Penrhyn Island
Pitcairn Islands
Prince Edward Island
Queensland
Rhodesia
Rhodesia & Nyasaland
Ross Dependency
Sabah
St. Christopher
St. Helena
St. Kitts
St. Kitts-Nevis-Anguilla
St. Lucia
St. Vincent
Samoa
Sarawak
Seychelles
Sierra Leone
Solomon Islands
Somaliland Protectorate
South Arabia
South Australia
South Georgia

Southern Nigeria
Southern Rhodesia
South-West Africa
Stellaland
Straits Settlements
Sudan
Swaziland
Tanganyika
Tanzania
Tasmania
Tobago
Togo
Tokelau Islands
Tonga
Transvaal
Trinidad
Trinidad and Tobago
Tristan da Cunha
Trucial States
Turks and Caicos
Turks Islands
Tuvalu
Uganda
United Arab Emirates
Victoria
Virgin Islands
Western Australia
Zambia
Zanzibar
Zululand

**POST OFFICES IN
FOREIGN COUNTRIES**
Africa
  East Africa Forces
  Middle East Forces
Bangkok
China
Morocco
Turkish Empire

Colonies, Former Colonies, Offices, Territories Controlled by Parent States

Belgium
Belgian Congo
Ruanda-Urundi

Denmark
Danish West Indies
Faroe Islands
Greenland
Iceland

Finland
Aland Islands

France
COLONIES PAST AND PRESENT, CONTROLLED TERRITORIES
Afars & Issas, Territory of
Alaouites
Alexandretta
Algeria
Alsace & Lorraine
Anjouan
Annam & Tonkin
Benin
Cambodia (Khmer)
Cameroun
Castellorizo
Chad
Cilicia
Cochin China
Comoro Islands
Dahomey
Diego Suarez
Djibouti (Somali Coast)
Fezzan
French Congo
French Equatorial Africa
French Guiana
French Guinea
French India
French Morocco
French Polynesia (Oceania)
French Southern & Antarctic Territories
French Sudan
French West Africa
Gabon
Germany
Ghadames
Grand Comoro
Guadeloupe
Indo-China
Inini
Ivory Coast
Laos
Latakia
Lebanon
Madagascar
Martinique
Mauritania
Mayotte
Memel
Middle Congo
Moheli
New Caledonia
New Hebrides
Niger Territory
Nossi-Be
Obock
Reunion
Rouad, Ile
Ste.-Marie de Madagascar
St. Pierre & Miquelon
Senegal
Senegambia & Niger
Somali Coast
Syria
Tahiti
Togo
Tunisia
Ubangi-Shari
Upper Senegal & Niger
Upper Volta
Viet Nam
Wallis & Futuna Islands

POST OFFICES IN FOREIGN COUNTRIES
China
Crete
Egypt
Turkish Empire
Zanzibar

Germany
EARLY STATES
Baden
Bavaria
Bergedorf
Bremen
Brunswick
Hamburg
Hanover
Lubeck
Mecklenburg-Schwerin
Mecklenburg-Strelitz
Oldenburg
Prussia
Saxony
Schleswig-Holstein
Wurttemberg

FORMER COLONIES
Cameroun (Kamerun)
Caroline Islands
German East Africa
German New Guinea
German South-West Africa
Kiauchau
Mariana Islands
Marshall Islands
Samoa
Togo

Italy
EARLY STATES
Modena
Parma
Romagna
Roman States
Sardinia
Tuscany
Two Sicilies
  Naples
  Neapolitan Provinces
  Sicily

FORMER COLONIES, CONTROLLED TERRITORIES, OCCUPATION AREAS
Aegean Islands
  Calimno (Calino)
  Caso
  Cos (Coo)
  Karki (Carchi)
  Leros (Lero)
  Lipso
  Nisiros (Nisiro)
  Patmos (Patmo)
  Piscopi
  Rodi (Rhodes)
  Scarpanto
  Simi
  Stampalia
Castellorizo
Corfu
Cyrenaica
Eritrea
Ethiopia (Abyssinia)
Fiume
Ionian Islands
  Cephalonia
  Ithaca
  Paxos
Italian East Africa
Libya
Oltre Giuba
Saseno
Somalia (Italian Somaliland)
Tripolitania

POST OFFICES IN FOREIGN COUNTRIES
"ESTERO"*
Austria
China
  Peking
  Tientsin
Crete
Tripoli
Turkish Empire
  Constantinople
  Durazzo
  Janina
Jerusalem
Salonika
Scutari
Smyrna
Valona
*Stamps overprinted "ESTERO" were used in various parts of the world.

Netherlands
Aruba
Netherlands Antilles (Curacao)
Netherlands Indies
Netherlands New Guinea
Surinam (Dutch Guiana)

Portugal
COLONIES PAST AND PRESENT, CONTROLLED TERRITORIES
Angola
Angra
Azores
Cape Verde
Funchal
Horta
Inhambane
Kionga
Lourenco Marques
Macao
Madeira
Mozambique
Mozambique Co.
Nyassa
Ponta Delgada
Portuguese Africa
Portuguese Congo
Portuguese Guinea
Portuguese India
Quelimane
St. Thomas & Prince Islands
Tete
Timor
Zambezia

Russia
ALLIED TERRITORIES AND REPUBLICS, OCCUPATION AREAS
Armenia
Aunus (Olonets)
Azerbaijan
Batum
Estonia
Far Eastern Republic
Georgia
Karelia
Latvia
Lithuania
North Ingermanland
Ostland
Russian Turkestan
Siberia
South Russia
Tannu Tuva
Transcaucasian Fed. Republics
Ukraine
Wenden (Livonia)
Western Ukraine

Spain
COLONIES PAST AND PRESENT, CONTROLLED TERRITORIES
Aguera, La
Cape Juby
Cuba
Elobey, Annobon & Corisco
Fernando Po
Ifni
Mariana Islands
Philippines
Puerto Rico
Rio de Oro
Rio Muni
Spanish Guinea
Spanish Morocco
Spanish Sahara
Spanish West Africa

POST OFFICES IN FOREIGN COUNTRIES
Morocco
Tangier
Tetuan

Dies of British Colonial Stamps

DIE A

DIE B

DIE I

DIE II

DIE A:

1. The lines in the groundwork vary in thickness and are not uniformly straight.
2. The seventh and eighth lines from the top, in the groundwork, converge where they meet the head.
3. There is a small dash in the upper part of the second jewel in the band of the crown.
4. The vertical color line in front of the throat stops at the sixth line of shading on the neck.

DIE B:

1. The lines in the groundwork are all thin and straight.
2. All the lines of the background are parallel.
3. There is no dash in the upper part of the second jewel in the band of the crown.
4. The vertical color line in front of the throat stops at the eighth line of shading on the neck.

DIE I:

1. The base of the crown is well below the level of the inner white line around the vignette.
2. The labels inscribed "POSTAGE" and "REVENUE" are cut square at the top.
3. There is a white "bud" on the outer side of the main stem of the curved ornaments in each lower corner.
4. The second (thick) line below the country name has the ends next to the crown cut diagonally.

DIE Ia.
1 as die II.
2 and 3 as die I.

DIE Ib.
1 and 3 as die II.
2 as die I.

DIE II:

1. The base of the crown is aligned with the underside of the white line around the vignette.
2. The labels curve inward at the top inner corners.
3. The "bud" has been removed from the outer curve of the ornaments in each corner.
4. The second line below the country name has the ends next to the crown cut vertically.

Wmk. 1
Crown and C C

Wmk. 2
Crown and C A

Wmk. 3
Multiple Crown
and C A

Wmk. 4
Multiple Crown
and Script C A

Wmk. 4a

Wmk. 314
St. Edward's Crown
and C A Multiple

Wmk. 373

Wmk. 384

Wmk. 406

British Colonial and Crown Agents Watermarks

Watermarks 1 to 4, 314, 373, 384 and 406, common to many British territories, are illustrated here to avoid duplication.

The letters "CC" of Wmk. 1 identify the paper as having been made for the use of the Crown Colonies, while the letters "CA" of the others stand for "Crown Agents." Both Wmks. 1 and 2 were used on stamps printed by De La Rue & Co.

Wmk. 3 was adopted in 1904; Wmk. 4 in 1921; Wmk. 314 in 1957; Wmk. 373 in 1974; Wmk. 384 in 1985; Wmk 406 in 2008.

In Wmk. 4a, a non-matching crown of the general St. Edwards type (bulging on both sides at top) was substituted for one of the Wmk. 4 crowns which fell off the dandy roll. The non-matching crown occurs in 1950-52 printings in a horizontal row of crowns on certain regular stamps of Johore and Seychelles, and on various postage due stamps of Barbados, Basutoland, British Guiana, Gold Coast, Grenada, Northern Rhodesia, St. Lucia, Swaziland and Trinidad and Tobago. A variation of Wmk. 4a, with the non-matching crown in a horizontal row of crown-CA-crown, occurs on regular stamps of Bahamas, St. Kitts-Nevis and Singapore.

Wmk. 314 was intentionally used sideways, starting in 1966. When a stamp was issued with Wmk. 314 both upright and sideways, the sideways varieties usually are listed also – with minor numbers. In many of the later issues, Wmk. 314 is slightly visible.

Wmk. 373 is usually only faintly visible.

SAN MARINO

‚san mə-'rē-ˌnō

LOCATION — Eastern Italy, about 20 miles inland from the Adriatic Sea
GOVT. — Republic
AREA — 24.1 sq. mi.
POP. — 25,061 (1999 est.)
CAPITAL — San Marino

100 Centesimi = 1 Lira
100 Cents = 1 Euro (2002)

Catalogue values for unused stamps in this country are for Never Hinged items, beginning with Scott 412 in the regular postage section, Scott B39 in the semipostal section, Scott C97 in the airpost section, Scott E26 in the special delivery section, and Scott Q40 in the parcel post section.

Watermarks

Wmk. 140 — Crown

Wmk. 174 — Coat of Arms

Wmk. 217 — Three Plumes

Wmk. 277 — Winged Wheel

Wmk. 303 — Multiple Stars

Wmk. 339 — Triskelion

Nos. 1-28 were spaced very narrowly on the plates, so that perforations often cut into the design on one or two sides. Values are for stamps with perforations clear of the design. Examples with perfs cutting in the design sell for less, while examples with four clear, full margins sell for substantially more than the values shown.

A1	A2
Numeral	Coat of Arms

1877-99 Typo. Wmk. 140 Perf. 14

1	A1	2c green	37.50	17.50
2	A1	2c blue ('94)	18.00	17.50
3	A1	2c claret ('95)	16.00	17.50
4	A2	5c orange ('90)	190.00	45.00
5	A2	5c olive grn ('92)	11.00	8.50
6	A2	5c green ('99)	11.00	12.50
7	A2	10c ultra	350.00	105.00
a.		10c blue ('90)	950.00	275.00
8	A2	10c dk green ('92)	11.00	10.00
9	A2	10c claret ('99)	11.00	12.50
10	A2	15c claret ('94)	190.00	120.00
11	A2	20c vermilion	50.00	17.50
12	A2	20c lilac ('95)	11.00	15.50
13	A2	25c maroon ('90)	175.00	85.00
14	A2	25c blue ('99)	11.00	15.50
15	A2	30c brown	1,000.	125.00
16	A2	30c org yel ('92)	11.00	17.50
17	A2	40c violet	1,000.	125.00
18	A2	40c dk brown ('92)	11.00	17.50
19	A2	45c gray grn ('92)	11.00	17.50
20	A2	65c red brown ('92)		17.50
21	A2	1 l car & yel ('92)	2,000.	825.00
22	A2	1 l lt blue ('95)	1,875.	650.00
23	A2	2 l brn & yel ('94)	110.00	110.00
24	A2	5 l vio & grn ('94)	275.00	350.00

See Nos. 911-915.

Nos. 7a, 15, 11 Surcharged in Black

1892

25	A2	5c on 10c blue	100.00	27.50
a.		Inverted surcharge	110.00	35.00
b.		5c on 10c ultramarine	50,000.	9,250.
c.		As "b," inverted surch.	—	
d.		Double surcharge, one inverted	—	
e.		Pair, one without surcharge	2,100.	
f.		Pair, one without surcharge, surcharge inverted	2,100.	
26	A2	5c on 30c brown	325.00	125.00
a.		Inverted surcharge	400.00	150.00
b.		Double surch., one inverted	400.00	190.00
c.		Double invtd. surcharge	400.00	190.00
27	A2	10c on 20c ver	75.00	17.50
a.		Inverted surcharge	82.50	25.00
b.		Double surch., one inverted	90.00	32.50
c.		Double surcharge	90.00	32.50

Ten to twelve varieties of each surcharge.

No. 11 Surcharged

28	A2	10c on 20c ver	325.00	20.00

Government Palace and Portraits of Regents, Tonnini and Marcucci
A6   A7

Portraits of Regents and View of Interior of Palace — A8

Wmk. 174

1894, Sept. 30 Litho. Perf. 15½

29	A6	25c blue & dk brn	8.75	3.50
30	A7	50c dull red & dk brn	52.50	9.25
31	A8	1 l green & dk brown	37.50	11.50
		Nos. 29-31 (3)	98.75	24.25

Opening of the new Government Palace and the installation of the new Regents.

Statue of Liberty — A9

Wmk. 140

1899-1922 Typo. Perf. 14

32	A9	2c brown	3.75	1.90
33	A9	2c claret ('22)	.75	.75
34	A9	5c brown org	7.50	4.50
35	A9	5c olive grn ('22)	.75	.75
36	A9	10c brown org ('22)	.75	.75
37	A9	20c dp brown ('22)	.75	.75
38	A9	25c ultra ('22)	1.50	1.50
39	A9	45c red brown ('22)	3.00	3.00
		Nos. 32-39 (8)	18.75	13.90

Numeral of Value — A10	Mt. Titano — A11

1903-25 Perf. 14, 14½x14

40	A10	2c violet	22.50	12.00
41	A10	2c orange brn ('21)	1.50	1.10
42	A11	5c blue grn	11.50	7.50
43	A11	5c olive grn ('21)	1.50	1.10
44	A11	5c red brn ('25)	.75	.75
45	A11	10c claret	11.00	7.50
46	A11	10c brown org ('21)	1.50	1.10
47	A11	10c olive grn ('25)	.75	.75
48	A11	15c blue grn ('22)	1.50	1.10
49	A11	15c brown vio ('25)	.75	.75
50	A11	20c brown orange	150.00	60.00
51	A11	20c brown ('21)	1.50	1.10
52	A11	20c blue grn ('25)	.75	.75
53	A11	25c blue	26.00	12.00
54	A11	25c gray ('21)	1.50	1.10
55	A11	25c violet ('25)	.75	.75
56	A11	30c brown red	12.00	17.50
57	A11	30c claret ('21)	1.50	1.10
58	A11	30c orange ('25)	22.50	3.75
59	A11	40c orange red	22.50	17.50
60	A11	40c dp rose ('21)	1.50	1.10
61	A11	40c brown ('25)	.75	.75
62	A11	45c yellow	16.50	18.00
63	A11	50c brown vio ('23)	3.00	3.00
64	A11	50c gray blk ('25)	.75	.75
65	A11	60c brown red ('25)	1.50	.75
66	A11	65c chocolate	16.50	18.00
67	A11	80c blue ('21)	6.00	6.00
68	A11	90c brown ('23)	6.00	6.00
69	A11	1 l olive green	60.00	30.00
70	A11	1 l ultra ('21)	6.00	6.00
71	A11	1 l lt blue ('25)	1.50	.75
72	A11	2 l violet	1,000.	375.00
73	A11	2 l orange ('21)	22.50	26.00
74	A11	2 l lt green ('25)	7.50	7.50
75	A11	5 l slate	275.00	260.00
76	A11	5 l ultra ('25)	16.50	18.50
		Nos. 40-76 (37)	1,733.	927.30

For overprints and surcharges see Nos. 77, 93-96, 103, 107, 188-189, B1-B2, E2, E4.

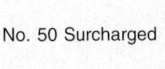
No. 50 Surcharged

1905, Sept. 1

77	A11	15c on 20c brown org	15.00	10.50
a.		Large 5 in 1905 on level with 9	90.00	45.00

Coat of Arms	
A12	A13

Two types:
I — Width 18½mm.
II — Width 19mm.

1907-10 Unwmk. Engr. Perf. 12

78	A12	1c brown, II ('10)	8.50	2.10
a.		Type I	17.00	3.25
79	A13	15c gray, I	37.50	6.75
a.		Type II ('10)	325.00	35.00

No. 79a Surcharged in Brown

1918, Mar. 15

80	A13	20c on 15c gray	6.50	4.00

St. Marinus — A14

Perf. 14½x14, 14x14½
1923, Aug. 11   Typo.   Wmk. 140
81   A14 30c dark brown   .80   .80
San Marino Intl. Exhib. of 1923. Proceeds from the sale of this stamp went to a mutual aid society.

Italian Flag and Views of Arbe and Mt. Titano A15

1923, Aug. 6
82   A15 50c olive green   .80   .80
Presentation to San Marino of the Italian flag which had flown over the island of Arbe, the birthplace of the founder of San Marino. Inscribed on back: "V. Moraldi dis. Blasi inc. Petiti impr.-Roma."

Mt. Titano and Sword — A16

1923, Sept. 29   Perf. 14x14½
83   A16 1 l dark brown   22.50 22.50
In honor of the San Marino Volunteers who were killed or wounded in WWI.

Giuseppe Garibaldi A17

Allegory-San Marino Sheltering Garibaldi A18

1924, Sept. 25   Perf. 14
84   A17 30c dark violet   4.00   4.00
85   A17 50c olive brown   4.00   4.00
86   A17 60c dull red   5.00   5.00
87   A18 1 l deep blue   10.00 10.00
88   A18 2 l gray green   12.00 12.00
     Nos. 84-88 (5)   35.00 35.00
75th anniv. of Garibaldi's taking refuge in San Marino.

No. B8 Surcharged in Black

1924, Oct. 9
89   SP1 30c on 45c yel brn & blk   2.25   2.25

Nos. B9-B11 Surcharged

90   SP2 60c on 1 l bl grn & blk   9.00   9.00
91   SP2 1 l on 2 l vio & blk   25.00 25.00
92   SP2 2 l on 3 l claret & blk   20.00 20.00
     Nos. 89-92 (4)   56.25 56.25

Nos. 67 and 68 Surcharged in Black or Red

1926, July 1
93   A11 75c on 80c blue   2.50   2.50
94   A11 1.20 l on 90c brown   2.50   2.50
95   A11 1.25 l on 90c brn (R)   4.00   4.00
96   A11 2.50 l on 80c blue (R)   8.50   8.50
     Nos. 93-96 (4)   17.50 17.50

Antonio Onofri — A19   A20

Unwmk.
1926, July 29   Engr.   Perf. 11
97   A19 10c dk blue & blk   .75   .75
98   A19 20c olive grn & blk   1.50   1.50
99   A19 45c dk vio & blk   .75   .75
100 A19 65c green & blk   .75   .75
101 A19 1 l orange & blk   6.00   6.00
102 A19 2 l red vio & blk   6.00   6.00
     Nos. 97-102 (6)   15.75 15.75
For surcharges see Nos. 104-106, 181-182.

Special Delivery Stamp No. E2 Surcharged
Perf. 14½x14
1926, Nov. 25   Wmk. 140
103 A20 1.85 l on 60c violet   .85   .85

Nos. 101 and 102 Surcharged

1927, Mar. 10   Unwmk.   Perf. 11
104 A19 1.25 l on 2 l   10.00 10.00
105 A19 2.50 l on 2 l   20.00 20.00
106 A19 5 l on 2 l   60.00 60.00
     Nos. 104-106 (3)   90.00 90.00

Type of Special Delivery Stamp of 1923 Surcharged

1927, Sept. 15   Wmk. 140   Perf. 14
107 A11 1.75 l on 50c on 25c vio   1.25   1.25
The 50c on 25c violet was not issued without 1.75-lire surcharge.

War Memorial A21

Unwmk.
1927, Sept. 28   Engr.   Perf. 12
108 A21 50c brown violet   2.25   2.25
109 A21 1.25 l blue   3.25   3.25
110 A21 10 l gray   30.00 30.00
     Nos. 108-110 (3)   35.50 35.50
Erection of a cenotaph in memory of the San Marino volunteers in WWI.

Capuchin Church and Convent A22

Design: 2.50 l, 5 l, Death of St. Francis.

1928, Jan. 2
111 A22 50c red   25.00   9.00
112 A22 1.25 l dp blue   10.50 10.50
113 A22 2.50 l dk brown   10.50 10.50
114 A22 5 l dull violet   32.50 30.00
     Nos. 111-114 (4)   78.50 60.00
7th centenary of the death of St. Francis of Assisi.
For surcharges see Nos. 183-184.

The Rocca (State Prison) A24

Government Palace A25

Statue of Liberty — A26

1929-35   Wmk. 217
115 A24 5c vio brn & ultra   1.50   .75
116 A24 10c grnsh blue & red vio   2.00   1.25
117 A24 15c dp org & emer   1.50   .75
118 A24 20c dk bl & org red   1.50   .75
119 A24 25c grn & gray blk   1.50   .75
120 A24 30c gray brn & red   1.50   .75
121 A24 50c red vio & ol gray   1.50   .75
122 A24 75c dp red & gray blk   1.50   .75
123 A25 1 l dk brn & emer   1.50   .75
124 A25 1.25 l dk blue & blk   1.50   .75
125 A25 1.75 l green & org   4.00   2.00
126 A25 2 l bl gray & red   2.00   1.25
127 A25 2.50 l car rose & ultra   2.00   1.25
128 A25 3 l dp org & bl   2.00   1.25
129 A25 3.70 l ol blk & red brn ('35)   2.00   1.25
130 A26 5 l dk vio & dk grn   4.00   3.75
131 A26 10 l bis brn & dk bl   16.00 15.00
132 A26 15 l green & red vio   75.00 90.00
133 A26 20 l dk bl & red   350.00 340.00
     Nos. 115-133 (19)   472.50 463.75

General Post Office — A27

1932, Feb. 4
134 A27 20c blue green   35.00 21.00
135 A27 50c dark red   42.50 25.00
136 A27 1.25 l dark blue   275.00 190.00
137 A27 1.75 l dark brown   170.00 100.00
138 A27 2.75 l dark violet   85.00 60.00
     Nos. 134-138 (5)   607.50 396.00
Opening of new General Post Office.
For surcharges see Nos. 151-160.

San Marino-Rimini Electric Railway — A28

1932, June 11
139 A28 20c deep green   4.00   4.00
140 A28 50c dark red   6.50   6.50
141 A28 1.25 l dark blue   16.00 16.00
142 A28 5 l deep brown   95.00 95.00
     Nos. 139-142 (4)   121.50 121.50
Opening of the new electric railway between San Marino and Rimini.

Giuseppe Garibaldi — A29

Garibaldi's Arrival at San Marino — A30

1932, July 30
143 A29 10c violet brown   12.50   5.00
144 A29 20c violet   12.50   5.00
145 A29 25c green   12.50   5.00
146 A29 50c yellow brn   17.00 10.00
147 A30 75c dark red   42.50 21.00
148 A30 1.25 l dark blue   50.00 30.00
149 A30 2.75 l brown org   100.00 60.00
150 A30 5 l olive green   340.00 425.00
     Nos. 143-150 (8)   587.00 561.00
Garibaldi (1807-1882), Italian patriot.

Nos. 138 and 137 Surcharged

1933, May 27
151 A27 25c on 2.75 l   16.00 16.00
152 A27 50c on 1.75 l   32.50 32.50
153 A27 75c on 2.75 l   65.00 65.00
154 A27 1.25 l on 1.75 l   400.00 400.00
     Nos. 151-154 (4)   513.50 513.50
Convention of philatelists, San Marino, May 28.

Nos. 134-137 Surcharged in Black

1934, Apr. 12
155 A27 25c on 1.25 l   3.25   3.25
156 A27 50c on 1.75 l   4.75   4.75
157 A27 75c on 50c   11.00 11.00
158 A27 1.25 l on 20c   40.00 40.00
     Nos. 155-158 (4)   59.00 59.00
San Marino's participation (with a philatelic pavilion) in the 15th annual Trade Fair at Milan, Apr. 12-27.

Nos. 136 and 138 Surcharged Wheel and New Value

1934, Apr. 12
159 A27 3.70 l on 1.25 l   65.00 65.00
160 A27 3.70 l on 2.75 l   80.00 80.00

Ascent to Mt. Titano
A31

Unwmk.

1935, Feb. 7   **Engr.**   *Perf. 14*

161	A31	5c choc & blk	.75	.75
162	A31	10c dk vio & blk	.75	.75
163	A31	20c orange & blk	.75	.75
164	A31	25c green & blk	.75	.75
165	A31	50c olive bis & blk	.75	.75
166	A31	75c brown red & blk	3.50	3.50
167	A31	1.25 l blue & blk	7.00	7.00
		Nos. 161-167 (7)	14.25	14.25

12th anniv. of the founding of the Fascist Movement.

Melchiorre Delfico — A32   Statue of Delfico — A33

1935, Apr. 15   **Wmk. 217**   *Perf. 12*

Center in Black

169	A32	5c brown lake	2.50	2.50
170	A32	7½c lt brown	2.50	2.50
171	A32	10c dk blue grn	2.50	2.50
172	A32	15c rose carmine	50.00	25.00
173	A32	20c orange	3.25	3.00
174	A32	25c green	3.25	3.00
175	A32	30c dull violet	3.25	3.00
176	A33	50c olive green	5.00	5.00
177	A33	75c red	15.00	15.00
178	A33	1.25 l dark blue	4.25	4.25
179	A33	1.50 l dk brown	70.00	70.00
180	A33	1.75 l brown org	100.00	100.00
		Nos. 169-180 (12)	261.50	235.75

Melchiorre Delfico (1744-1835), historian. For surcharges see Nos. 202, 277.

Nos. 99-100 Surcharged in Black

Nos. 112-113 Surcharged in Black

1936   **Unwmk.**   *Perf. 11*

181	A19	80c on 45c dk vio & blk	4.00	4.00
182	A19	80c on 65c grn & blk	4.00	4.00
		Perf. 12		
183	A22	2.05 l on 1.25 l	9.50	9.50
184	A22	2.75 l on 2.50 l	25.00	25.00
		Nos. 181-184 (4)	42.50	42.50

Issued: #181-182, 4/14; #183-184, 8/23.

Souvenir Sheet

Design from Base of Roman Column — A34

1937, Aug. 23   **Engr.**   **Wmk. 217**

185 A34   5 l steel blue   10.00   10.00

Unveiling of the Roman Column at San Marino. The date "1636 d. F. R." means the 1,636th year since the founding of the republic.

No. 185 was privately surcharged "+ 10 L 1941."

Souvenir Sheets

Abraham Lincoln — A35

1938, Apr. 7   **Wmk. 217**   *Perf. 13*

186	A35	3 l dark blue	1.50	1.50
187	A35	5 l rose red	15.00	15.00

Dedication of a Lincoln bust, Sept. 3, 1937.

No. 49 and Type of 1925 Surcharged with New Value in Black

1941   **Wmk. 140**   *Perf. 14*

188	A11	10c on 15c brown vio	.50	.50
189	A11	10c on 30c brown org	1.00	1.00

Flags of Italy and San Marino — A36

Harbor of Arbe A37

1942   **Photo.**

190	A36	10c yel brn & brn org	.30	.30
191	A36	15c brn & red brn	.30	.30
192	A36	20c gray grn & gray blk	.30	.30
193	A36	25c green & blue	.30	.30
194	A36	50c brn red & brn	.30	.30
195	A36	75c red & gray blk	.30	.30
196	A37	1.25 l bl & gray bl	.30	.30
197	A37	1.75 l brn & grnsh blk	.30	.30
198	A37	2.75 l bis brn & gray bl	.80	.80
199	A37	5 l green & brown	4.50	4.50
		Nos. 190-199 (10)	7.70	7.70

Return of the Italian flag to Arbe.

No. 190 Surcharged in Black

1942, July 30

200 A36   30c on 10c   .30   .30

Rimini-San Marino Stamp Day, Aug. 3.

No. 192 Surcharged with New Value and Bars in Black

1942, Sept. 14

201 A36   30c on 20c   .30   .30

No. 177 Surcharged with New Value in Black

1942, Sept. 28   **Wmk. 217**   *Perf. 12*

202 A33   20 l on 75c red & blk   17.50   17.50

Printing Press and Newspaper A38

Newspapers A39

Wmk. 140

1943, Apr. 12   **Photo.**   *Perf. 14*

203	A38	10c deep green	.30	.30
204	A38	15c bister	.30	.30
205	A38	20c dk orange brn	.30	.30
206	A38	30c dk rose vio	.30	.30
207	A38	50c blue black	.30	.30
208	A38	75c red orange	.30	.30
209	A39	1.25 l blue	.30	.30
210	A39	1.75 l deep violet	.30	.30
211	A39	5 l slate	1.25	1.25
212	A39	10 l dark brown	4.50	4.50
		Nos. 203-212 (10)	8.15	8.15

Nos. 206 and 207 Overprinted in Red

1943, July 1

213	A38	30c dk rose vio	.25	.25
214	A38	50c blue black	.25	.25

Rimini-San Marino Stamp Day, July 5.

A40

A41

Overprinted in Black: "28 LVGLIO 1943 1642 F. R."

1943, Aug. 27

215	A40	5c brown	.30	.30
216	A40	10c orange red	.30	.30
217	A40	20c ultra	.30	.30
218	A40	25c deep green	.30	.30
219	A40	30c brown carmine	.30	.30
220	A40	50c deep violet	.30	.30
221	A40	75c car rose	.30	.30
222	A41	1.25 l sapphire	.30	.30
223	A41	1.75 l red org	.30	.30
224	A41	2.75 l dk red brn	1.25	1.25
225	A41	5 l green	1.50	1.50
226	A41	10 l violet	2.40	2.40
227	A41	20 l slate blue	6.50	6.50
		Nos. 215-227,C26-C33 (21)	27.10	27.10

This series was prepared for the 20th anniv. of fascism, but as Mussolini was overthrown July 25, 1943, it was overprinted for the downfall of fascism.

Overprint on Nos. 222-227 adds "d." before "F.R."

Exist without overprint. Value of set $55.

A42

A43

Overprinted "Governo Provvisorio" in Black

1943, Aug. 27

228	A42	5c brown	.30	.30
229	A42	10c orange red	.30	.30
230	A42	20c ultra	.30	.30
231	A42	25c deep green	.30	.30
232	A42	30c brown carmine	.30	.30
233	A42	50c deep violet	.30	.30
234	A42	75c carmine rose	.30	.30
235	A43	1.25 l sapphire	.30	.30
236	A43	1.75 l red orange	.30	.30
237	A43	5 l green	.80	.80
238	A43	20 l slate blue	2.00	2.00
		Nos. 228-238,C34-C39 (17)	11.20	11.20

Souvenir Sheets

A44

Perf. 14, Imperf.

1945, Mar. 15   **Photo.**   **Unwmk.**

239	A44	Sheet of 3	90.00	70.00
		Never hinged	125.00	
a.		10 l dull blue	20.00	20.00
b.		15 l dull green	20.00	20.00
c.		25 l dull red brown	20.00	20.00

Sheets contain a papermaker's watermark, "Hammermill Bond, Made in U.S.A."

Nos. 239, 241 and C40 were issued to commemorate the 50th anniv. of the reconstruction of the Government Palace.

Government Palace — A45

1945, Mar. 15   Wmk. 140   Perf. 14
241 A45 25 l brown violet   6.50 6.50
         Never hinged   13.00

Coat of Arms of Faetano — A46

Coats of Arms: 20c, 60c, 25 l, Montegiardino. 40c, 5 l, 50 l, San Marino. 80c, 2 l-4 l, Fiorentino. 10 l, Borgomaggiore. 20 l, Serravalle.

1945-46   Wmk. 277
242 A46 10c dark blue   .30   .30
243 A46 20c vermilion   .30   .30
244 A46 40c deep orange   .30   .30
245 A46 60c slate black   .30   .30
246 A46 80c dark green   .30   .30
247 A46 1 l dk car rose   .30   .30
248 A46 1.20 l deep violet   .30   .30
249 A46 2 l chestnut   .30   .30
250 A46 3 l dp blue ('46)   .30   .30
250A A46 4 l red org ('46)   .30   .30
251 A46 5 l dark brown   .30   .30
251A A46 15 l dp bluc ('40)   2.25 1./5

Lithographed and Engraved
252 A46 10 l brt red &
             brown   2.25 1.75
253 A46 20 l brt red & ul-
             tra   6.00 4.75
254 A46 20 l org brn & ul-
             tra ('46)   12.00 9.50
   a. Vert. pair, imperf. btwn.   425.00
       Never hinged   600.00
255 A46 25 l hn brn & ul-
             tra ('46)   11.00 8.75

Size: 22x27mm
256 A46 50 l ol brn & ultra
             ('46)   16.00 13.00
       Nos. 242-256 (17)   52.80 42.80
       Set, never hinged   100.00

Nos. 252-256 are in sheets of 10 (2x5). Values: Nos. 252, 254-255, $90 each. No. 253, $125, No. 256, $300.
For surcharges see Nos. 258-259, B26.

"Dawn of New Hope" — A52

Engr. & Litho.
1946   Unwmk.   Perf. 14
257 A52 100 l dull yel & brn
             vio   8.75 8.75
       Never hinged   20.00
   j. Vert. pair, imperf. btwn.   700.00
       Never hinged   1,200.

UN Relief and Rehabilitation Administration. Sheets of 10 with blue coat of arms in top margin.

Franklin D. Roosevelt and Flags of San Marino and US — A52a

Designs: 1 l, 50 l, Quotation on Liberty, from Franklin D. Roosevelt. 2 l, 100 l, Roosevelt

portrait, vert. 5 l, 15 l, Roosevelt and flags (as shown).

Wmk. 277
1947, May 3   Photo.   Perf. 14
257A A52a 1 l bister & brn   .25   .25
257B A52a 2 l blue & sepia   .25   .25
257C A52a 5 l violet & multi   .25   .25
257D A52a 15 l green & multi   .25   .25
257E A52a 50 l vermilion &
             brn   .50   .50
257F A52a 100 l violet & sepia   .90   .90
       Nos. 257A-257F,C51A-C51H
             (14)   26.30 21.55
       Set, never hinged   60.00

For surcharges see #257G-257I, C51I-C51K.

Nos. 257A-257C Surcharged with New Value

1947, June 16
257G A52a 3 l on 1 l   .40   .40
257H A52a 4 l on 2 l   .40   .40
257I A52a 6 l on 5 l   .40   .40
       Nos. 257G-257I,C51I-C51K (6)   2.40 2.40
       Set, never hinged   4.75

No. 250A Surcharged with New Value in Black

1947, June 16   Wmk. 277
258 A46 6(l) on 4 l red org   .25 .25
       Never hinged   .30

No. 250A Surcharged in Black

259 A46 21 l on 4 l red org   .85 1.00
       Never hinged   2.00

"St. Marinus Raising the Republic" by Girolamo Batoni — A53

Wmk. 217
1947, July 18   Engr.   Perf. 12
260 A53 1 l brt grn & vio   .30   .30
261 A53 2 l purple & vio   .30   .30
262 A53 4 l vio brn & dk bl
             grn   .30   .30
263 A53 10 l org & bl blk   .30   .30
264 A53 25 l carmine & purple   .80   .75
265 A53 50 l dk bl grn & brn   18.00 16.00
       Nos. 260-265,C52-C53 (8)   24.00 21.70
       Set, never hinged   55.00

For overprints and surcharges see Nos. 294-295, B27-B38, C56.

United States 1847 Stamp A54

United States Stamps of 1847 and 1869 A55

A56

Wmk. 277
1947, Dec. 24   Photo.   Perf. 14
266 A54 2 l red vio & dk brn   .30   .30
267 A55 3 l sl gray, dp ultra &
             car   .30   .30

268 A54 6 l dp bl & dk gray
             grn   .30   .30
269 A56 15 l vio, dp ultra &
             car   .35   .35
270 A55 35 l dk brn, dp ultra &
             car   1.40 1.40
271 A56 50 l sl grn, dp ultra &
             car   1.40 1.40
       Nos. 266-271,C55 (7)   14.05 14.05
       Set, never hinged   35.00

1st United States postage stamps, cent.

Laborer and San Marino Flag A57

1948, June 3
272 A57 5 l brown   .40   .40
273 A57 8 l green   .40   .40
274 A57 30 l crimson   .40   .40
275 A57 50 l red brn & rose
             lil   1.60 1.50

Engr.
276 A57 100 l dk bl & dp vio   60.00 60.00
       Nos. 272-276 (5)   62.80 62.70
       Set, never hinged   125.00

See Nos. 373-374.

No. 172 Surcharged with New Value and Ornaments in Black

1948   Wmk. 217   Perf. 12
277 A32 100 l on 15c   55.00 55.00
       Never hinged   110.00

Government Palace — A58

Mt. Titano, Distant View — A59

Various Views of San Marino.

1949-50 Wmk. 277 Photo. Perf. 14
278 A58 1 l black & blue   .30   .30
279 A58 2 l violet & car   .30   .30
280 A58 3 l violet & ultra   .30   .30
281 A58 4 l black & vio   .30   .30
282 A58 5 l violet & brn   .30   .30
283 A58 6 l dp blue & sep   .80   .45
284 A59 8 l blk brn & yel
             brn   .45   .30
285 A59 10 l brn blk & bl   .60   .30
286 A58 12 l brt rose & vio   1.60   .90
287 A58 15 l vio & brt rose   4.75 1.60
288 A58 20 l dp bl & brn
             ('50)   14.00 2.10
289 A58 35 l green & violet   9.50 5.50
290 A58 50 l brt rose & yel
             brn   4.75 1.60
291 A58 55 l dp bl & dl grn
             ('50)   55.00 37.50

Perf. 14x13½
Engr.
292 A59 100 l blk brn & dk
             grn   77.50 60.00
293 A59 200 l dp blue & brn   77.50 65.00
       Nos. 278-293 (16)   247.95 176.75
       Set, never hinged   525.00

Nos. 260 and 261 Overprinted in Black

1949, June 28   Wmk. 217
294 A53 1 l brt green & vio   .40 .40
295 A53 2 l purple & olive   .40 .40
       Set, never hinged   1.60

San Marino-Riccione Stamp Day, June 28.

Francesco Nullo — A60

1 l, 20 l, Francesco Nullo. 2 l, 5 l, Anita Garibaldi. 3 l, 50 l, Giuseppe Garibaldi. 4 l, 15 l, Ugo Bassi.

Wmk. 277
1949, July 31   Photo.   Perf. 14
Size: 22x28mm
296 A60 1 l blk & car lake   .25   .25
297 A60 2 l red brn & blue   .25   .25
298 A60 3 l car lake & dk grn   .25   .25
299 A60 4 l violet & dk brn   .25   .25
Size: 26½x36½mm
300 A60 5 l purple & dk brn   .25   .25
301 A60 15 l car lake & gray bl   .80   .80
302 A60 20 l violet & car lake   1.40 1.40
303 A60 50 l red brn & violet   12.00 12.00
       Nos. 296-303,C57-C61 (13)   45.35 30.85
       Set, never hinged   60.00

Centenary of Garibaldi's escape to San Marino.
See Nos. C57-C61, 404-410.

Stagecoach on Road from San Marino — A61

1949, Dec. 29   Engr.
304 A61 100 l blue & gray
             vio   11.00 11.00
       Never hinged   22.50
       Sheet of 6   275.00 275.00
       Never hinged   350.00

UPU, 75th anniversary.

A62

A63

A63a

Perf. 13½x14, 14x13½
1951, Mar. 15   Engr.   Wmk. 277
Sky and Cross in Carmine
305 A62 25 l dk brn & red
             vio   7.50 7.50
306 A63 75 l org brn & dk
             brn   10.00 10.00
307 A63a 100 l dk brn & gray
             blk   12.50 12.50
       Nos. 305-307 (3)   30.00 30.00
       Set, never hinged   60.00

Issued to honor the San Marino Red Cross.

Christopher
Columbus
A64

Designs: 2 l, 25 l, Columbus on his ship. 3 l, 10 l, 20 l, Landing of Columbus. 4 l, 15 l, 80 l, Pioneers trading with Indians. 5 l, 200 l, Columbus and map of Americas.

1952, Jan. 28		**Photo.**	**Perf. 14**
308	A64	1 l brn org & dk grn	.30	.30
309	A64	2 l dk brown & vio	.30	.30
310	A64	3 l violet & dk brn	.30	.30
311	A64	4 l blue & org brn	.30	.30
312	A64	5 l grn & dk bl grn	.45	.45
313	A64	10 l dk brown & blk	.65	.65
314	A64	15 l carmine & blk	.95	.95

Engr.

315	A64	20 l dp bl & dk bl grn	1.40	1.40
316	A64	25 l vio brn & blk brn	6.00	6.00
317	A64	60 l choc & vio bl	8.25	8.25
318	A64	80 l gray & blk	26.00	26.00
319	A64	200 l Prus grn & dp ultra	47.50	47.50
Nos. 308-319,C80 (13)			119.90	119.90
Set, never hinged			250.00	

Issued to honor Christopher Columbus.

Type of
1952 in
New Colors
Overprinted
in Black or
Red

1952, June 29			**Photo.**	
320	A64	1 l vio & dk brn	.25	.25
321	A64	2 l carmine & blk	.25	.25
322	A64	3 l grn & dk bl grn (R)	.25	.25
323	A64	4 l dk brn & blk	.25	.25
324	A64	5 l purple & vio	.30	.30
325	A64	10 l bl & org brn (R)	.70	.70
326	A64	15 l org brn & blue	2.25	2.00
Nos. 320-326,C81 (8)			39.25	39.00
Set, never hinged			80.00	

4th Intl. Sample Fair of Trieste.

Discobolus — A65

Tennis
A66

Model
Airplane — A67

Designs: 3 l, Runner. 4 l, Cyclist. 5 l, Soccer. 25 l, Shooting. 100 l, Roller skating.

1953, Apr. 20		**Wmk. 277**	**Perf. 14**
327	A65	1 l dk brn & blk	.25	.25
328	A66	2 l black & brown	.25	.25
329	A65	3 l blk & grnsh bl	.25	.25
330	A66	4 l blk & brt bl	.25	.25
331	A66	5 l dk brn & sl grn	.25	.25
332	A67	10 l dp blue & crim	.35	.35
333	A67	25 l blk & dk brn	1.75	1.75
334	A66	100 l dk brn & slate	6.50	6.50
Nos. 327-334,C90 (9)			54.85	54.85
Set, never hinged			125.00	

See No. 438.

Type of
1953
Overprinted
in Black

1953, Aug. 24

335	A66	100 l grn & dk bl grn	16.00	16.00
Never hinged			35.00	

San Marino-Riccione Stamp Day, Aug. 24.

Narcissus
A68

Flowers: 2 l, Tulips. 3 l, Oleanders. 4 l, Cornflowers. 5 l, Carnations. 10 l, Irises. 25 l, Cyclamen. 80 l, Geraniums. 100 l, Roses.

1953, Dec. 28			**Photo.**	
336	A68	1 l multicolored	.30	.30
337	A68	2 l multicolored	.30	.30
338	A68	3 l multicolored	.30	.30
339	A68	4 l multicolored	.30	.30
340	A68	5 l multicolored	.30	.30
341	A68	10 l multicolored	.30	.30
342	A68	25 l multicolored	2.25	2.25
343	A68	80 l multicolored	13.50	13.50
344	A68	100 l multicolored	22.50	22.50
Nos. 336-344 (9)			40.05	40.05
Set, never hinged			80.00	

Walking
Racer — A69

Fencing
A70

Sports: 3 l, Boxing. 4 l, 200 l, 250 l, Gymnastics. 5 l, Motorcycling. 8 l, Javelin-throwing. 12 l, Automobiling. 25 l, Wrestling. 80 l, Walk racer.

1954-55		**Photo.**	**Wmk. 277**
345	A69	1 l violet & cer	.25	.25
346	A70	2 l dk grn & vio	.25	.25
347	A70	3 l brn & brn org	.25	.25
348	A69	4 l dk bl & brt bl	.25	.25
349	A70	5 l dk grn & dk brn	.25	.25
350	A70	8 l lil rose & pur	.25	.25
351	A70	12 l black & crim	.25	.25
352	A69	25 l bl & dk bl grn	.35	.35
353	A69	80 l dk bl & bl grn	1.00	1.00
354	A69	200 l violet & brn	4.00	4.00

Perf. 12½x13

Engr.

355	A69	250 l multi ('55)	32.50	32.50
Sheet of 4 (#355)			250.00	250.00
Nos. 345-355 (11)			39.60	39.60
Set, never hinged			80.00	

A71

A72

Liberty statue and Government palace.

1954, Dec. 16			**Perf. 13x13½**
356	A71	20 l choc & blue	.40	.40
357	A71	60 l car & dk grn	.80	.80
Nos. 356-357,C92 (3)			2.45	2.45
Set, never hinged			5.00	

1955, Aug. 27		**Wmk. 303**	**Perf. 14**
358	A72	100 l gray blk & bl	2.50	2.50
Never hinged			5.00	

7th San Marino-Riccione Stamp Fair. See No. 385.

Murata Nuova
Bridge — A73

View of La
Rocca — A74

Design: 15 l, Government Palace.

1955, Nov. 15			**Perf. 14**
Size: 22x27½mm; 27½x22mm			
359	A73	5 l blue & brown	.25	.25
360	A74	10 l org & bl grn	.25	.25
361	A74	15 l Prus grn & car	.25	.25
362	A73	25 l dk brn & vio	.25	.25
363	A74	35 l vio & red car	.25	.25
Nos. 359-363 (5)			1.25	1.25
Set, never hinged			1.25	

See Nos. 386-388, 636-638.

Ice Skater — A75

Skier
A76

3 l, 50 l, Tobogganing. 4 l, Skier going downhill. 5 l, 100 l, Ice Hockey player. 10 l, Girl ice skater.

1955, Dec. 15		**Wmk. 303**	**Perf. 14**
364	A75	3 l brown & yellow	.25	.25
365	A76	2 l brt blue & red	.25	.25
366	A76	3 l blk brn & lt brn	.25	.25
367	A75	4 l brown & green	.25	.25
368	A75	5 l ultra & sal pink	.25	.25
369	A76	10 l ultra & pink	.25	.25
370	A76	25 l gray blk & red	.50	.50
371	A76	50 l brown & indigo	1.40	1.40
372	A76	100 l blk & Prus grn	4.25	4.25
Nos. 364-372,C95 (10)			27.65	27.65
Set, never hinged			50.00	

7th Winter Olympic Games at Cortina d'Ampezzo, Jan. 26-Feb. 5, 1956.
For surcharge see No. C96.

Type of 1948 Inscribed: "50th Anniversario Arengo 25 Marzo 1906"

1956, Mar. 24		**Wmk. 303**	**Perf. 14**
373	A57	50 l sapphire	5.75	7.25
Never hinged			11.00	

50th anniv. of the meeting of the heads of families (Arengo), the beginning of the democratic era in San Marino.

Type of 1948 inscribed: "Assistenza Invernale"

1956, Mar. 24			**Photo.**
374	A57	50 l dark green	5.75	7.25
Never hinged			11.00	

Issued to publicize the Winterhelp charity.

Pointer and
Arms
A77

Dogs: 2 l, Russian greyhound. 3 l, Sheep dog. 4 l, English greyhound. 5 l, Boxer. 10 l, Great Dane. 25 l, Irish setter. 60 l, German shepherd. 80 l, Scotch collie. 100 l, Hunting hound.

1956, June 8		**Wmk. 303**	**Perf. 14**
375	A77	1 l ultra & brown	.25	.25
376	A77	2 l car lake & bl gray	.25	.25
377	A77	3 l ultra & brown	.25	.25
378	A77	4 l grnsh bl & gray vio	.25	.25
379	A77	5 l car lake & dk brn	.25	.25
380	A77	10 l ultra & brown	.25	.25
381	A77	25 l dk blue & multi	.60	1.00
382	A77	60 l car lake & multi	4.25	5.25
383	A77	80 l dk blue & multi	5.00	6.25
384	A77	100 l car lake & multi	10.50	12.00
Nos. 375-384 (10)			21.85	26.00
Set, never hinged			55.00	

Sailboat Type of 1955

1956		**Wmk. 303**	**Perf. 14**
385	A72	100 l brown & bl grn	1.25	1.75
Never hinged			2.50	

8th San Marino-Riccione Stamp Fair.

Types of 1955 with added inscription: "Congresso Internaz. Periti Filatelici San Marino-Salsomaggiore 6-8 Ottobre 1956."

Designs: 20 l, La Rocca. 80 l, Murata Nuova Bridge. 100 l, Government palace.

1956, Oct. 6			**Perf. 14**
Size: 26x36mm; 36x26mm			
386	A74	20 l blue & brown	.45	.45
387	A73	80 l vio & red car	1.75	1.75
388	A74	100 l org & bl grn	2.75	2.75
Nos. 386-388 (3)			4.95	4.95
Set, never hinged			10.00	

Intl. Philatelic Cong., San Marino, 10/6-8.

Street and
Borgo Maggiore
Church — A78

Hospital
Street — A79

Views: 3 l, Gate tower. 20 l, Covered Market of Borgo Maggiore. 125 l, View from South Bastion.

1957, May 9		**Photo.**	**Wmk. 303**
389	A78	2 l dk grn & rose red	.25	.25
390	A78	3 l blue & brown	.25	.25
391	A78	20 l dk blue green	.25	.25
392	A79	60 l brn & blue vio	.75	1.50

Engr.

393	A78	125 l dk blue & blk	.25	.25
Nos. 389-393 (5)			1.75	2.50
Set, never hinged			3.00	

See Nos. 473-476, 633-635.

Daisies and View of
San Marino — A80

Flowers: 2 l, Primrose. 3 l, Lily. 4 l, Orchid. 5 l, Lily of the Valley. 10 l, Poppy. 25 l, Pansy. 60 l, Gladiolus. 80 l, Wild Rose. 100 l, Anemone.

Wmk. 303

1957, Aug. 31		Photo.	Perf. 14

Flowers in Natural Colors

394	A80	1 l dk vio blue	.25	.25
395	A80	2 l dk vio blue	.25	.25
396	A80	3 l dk vio blue	.25	.25
397	A80	4 l dk vio blue	.25	.25
398	A80	5 l dk vio blue	.25	.25
399	A80	10 l blue, buff & lilac	.25	.25
400	A80	25 l blue, yel & lilac	.25	.25
401	A80	60 l blue, yel & dl red brn	.30	.35
402	A80	80 l blue & dl red brn	.55	.90
403	A80	100 l bl, yel & dl red brn	1.00	1.75
		Nos. 394-403 (10)	3.60	4.75
		Set, never hinged	7.00	

Type of 1949 Inscribed:
"Commemorazione 150 Nascita G. Garibaldi."

Portraits: 2 l, 50 l, Anita Garibaldi. 3 l, 25 l, Francesco Nullo. 5 l, 100 l, Giuseppe Garibaldi. 15 l, Ugo Bassi.

1957, Dec. 12	Wmk. 303	Perf. 14

Size: 22x28mm

404	A60	2 l vio & dull bl	.25	.25
405	A60	3 l lake & dk grn	.25	.25
406	A60	5 l brn & ol gray	.25	.25

Size: 26½x37mm

407	A60	15 l blue & vio	.25	.25
408	A60	25 l green & dk gray	.25	.25
409	A60	50 l violet & brn	.80	1.25
410	A60	100 l brown & vio	.80	1.25
		Nos. 404-410 (7)	2.85	3.75
		Set, never hinged	6.00	

Nos. 409-410 are printed se-tenant. Birth of Giuseppe Garibaldi, 150th anniv.

Panoramic
View
A81

1958, Feb. 27	Engr.	Perf. 14
411	A81	500 l green & blk	75.00	75.00
		Never hinged	125.00	
		Sheet of 6	525.00	525.00
		Never hinged	800.00	

Catalogue values for unused stamps in this section, from this point to the end of the section, are for Never Hinged items.

Fair Emblem and
San Marino
Peaks — A82

1958, Apr. 12	Photo.	Perf. 14
412	A82	40 l yel green & brn	.25	.25
413	A82	60 l brt blue & mar	.55	.55

World's Fair, Brussels, Apr. 17-Oct. 19.

Madonna
and Fair
Entrance
A83

Design: 60 l, View of Fair Grounds.

1958, Apr. 12		
414	A83	15 l yellow, grn & bl	.25	.25
415	A83	60 l green & rose red	.60	.50
		Nos. 414-415,C97 (3)	4.10	4.00

San Marino's 10th participation in the Milan Fair.

Wheat — A84

Designs: 2 l, 125 l, Corn. 3 l, 80 l, Grapes. 4 l, 25 l, Peaches. 5 l, 40 l, Plums.

1958, Aug. 30	Wmk. 303	Perf. 14
416	A84	1 l dk blue & yel org	.25	.25
417	A84	2 l dk grn & red org	.25	.25
418	A84	3 l blue & ocher	.25	.25
419	A84	4 l green & rose car	.25	.25
420	A84	5 l blue, yel & grn	.25	.25
421	A84	15 l ultra & brn org	.25	.25
422	A84	25 l multicolored	.25	.25
423	A84	40 l multicolored	1.00	.50
424	A84	80 l multicolored	1.25	.60
425	A84	125 l bl, grn & org ver	6.00	4.00
		Nos. 416-425 (10)	10.00	6.85

Bay and
Stamp of
Naples
A85

1958, Oct. 8		Photo.
426	A85	25 l lilac & red brn	.25	.25

Cent. of the stamps of Naples. See No. C100.

Pierre de
Coubertin — A86

Portraits: 3 l, Count Alberto Bonacossa. 5 l, Avery Brundage. 30 l, Gen. Carlo Montu. 60 l, J. Sigfrid Edstrom. 80 l, Henri de Baillet Latour.

1959, May 19	Wmk. 303	Perf. 14
427	A86	2 l brn org & blk	.25	.25
428	A86	3 l lilac & gray brn	.25	.25
429	A86	5 l blue & dk grn	.25	.25
430	A86	30 l violet & blk	.25	.25
431	A86	60 l dk grn & gray brn	.25	.25
432	A86	80 l car rose & dp grn	.25	.25
		Nos. 427-432,C106 (7)	6.25	4.75

Leaders of the Olympic movement; 1960 Olympic Games, Rome. See Nos. 1060-1062.

Lincoln and
his Praise
of San
Marino,
May 7,
1861
A87

Lincoln Portraits and: 10 l, Map of San Marino. 15 l, Government palace. 70 l, San Marino peaks, vert.

1959, July 1		Perf. 14
433	A87	5 l brown & blk	.25	.25
434	A87	10 l blue grn & ultra	.25	.25
435	A87	15 l gray & green	.25	.25

Perf. 13x13½

Engr.

436	A87	70 l violet	.45	.45
		Nos. 433-436,C108 (5)	7.20	6.45

Birth sesquicentennial of Abraham Lincoln.

Arch of
Augustus,
Rimini, and
Romagna
½b Stamp
A88

1959, Aug. 29	Photo.	Perf. 14
437	A88	30 l black & brown	.25	.25

Centenary of the first stamps of Romagna. See No. C109.

Type of 1953 Inscribed: "Universiade Torino"

1959, Aug. 29	Wmk. 303	Perf. 14
438	A65	30 l red orange	.75	.55

Turin University Sports Meet, 8/27-9/6.

Messina
Cathedral Portal
and Stamp of
Sicily 1859 — A89

Stamp of Sicily and: 2 l, Greek temple, Selinus. 3 l, Erice Church. 4 l, Temple of Concordia, Agrigento. 5 l, Ruins of Castor and Pollux Temple, Agrigento. 25 l, San Giovanni degli Eremiti Church. 60 l, Greek theater, Taormina, horiz.

1959, Oct. 16		
439	A89	1 l ocher & dk brn	.25	.25
440	A89	2 l olive & dk red	.25	.25
441	A89	3 l blue & slate	.25	.25
442	A89	4 l red & brown	.25	.25
443	A89	5 l dull bl & rose lil	.25	.25
444	A89	25 l multicolored	.25	.25
445	A89	60 l multicolored	.25	.25
		Nos. 439-445,C110 (8)	4.75	4.75

Centenary of stamps of Sicily.

Golden
Oriole
A90

Nightingale — A91

Birds: 3 l, Woodcock. 4 l, Hoopoe. 5 l, Red-legged partridge. 10 l, Goldfinch. 25 l, European Kingfisher. 60 l, Ringnecked pheasant. 80 l, Green woodpecker. 110 l, Red-breasted flycatcher.

1960, Jan. 28	Photo.	Perf. 14

Centers in Natural Colors

446	A90	1 l blue	.25	.25
447	A91	2 l green & red	.25	.25
448	A90	3 l green & red	.25	.25
449	A91	4 l dk green & red	.25	.25
450	A90	5 l dark green	.25	.25
451	A91	10 l blue & red	.25	.25
452	A91	25 l grnsh blue	.80	.40
453	A90	60 l blue & red	2.40	1.50
454	A91	80 l Prus blue & red	4.50	3.00
455	A91	110 l blue & red	10.00	4.50
		Nos. 446-455 (10)	19.20	10.90

Shot Put — A92

Sports: 2 l, Gymnastics. 3 l, Walking. 4 l, Boxing. 5 l, Fencing, horiz. 10 l, Bicycling. 15 l, Hockey, horiz. 25 l, Rowing, horiz. 60 l, Soccer. 110 l, Equestrian, horiz.

1960, May 23	Wmk. 303	Perf. 14
456	A92	1 l car rose & vio	.25	.25
457	A92	2 l gray & org	.25	.25
458	A92	3 l brn ol & pur	.25	.25
459	A92	4 l rose red & brn	.25	.25
460	A92	5 l brown & blue	.25	.25
461	A92	10 l red brn & bl	.25	.25
462	A92	15 l emer & lilac	.25	.25
463	A92	25 l bl ol & gray	.25	.25
464	A92	60 l dp grn & org	.25	.25
465	A92	110 l emer, red & blk	.30	.25
		Set of 3 souvenir sheets	11.00	11.00
		Nos. 456-465,C111-C114 (14)	3.65	3.50

17th Olympic Games, Rome, 8/25-9/11. Souvenir sheets are: (1.) Sheet of 4, one each of 1 l, 2 l, 3 l and 60 l, all printed in deep green and brown. (2.) Sheet of 4, one each of 4 l and 10 l plus a 20 l and 40 l in designs of Nos. C111-C112 but without "Posta Aerea" inscribed-all 4 printed in rose red and brown. (3.) Sheet of 6, one each of 5 l, 15 l, 25 l and 110 l plus an 80 l and 125 l in designs of Nos. C113-C114 but without "Posta Aerea"- all 6 printed in emerald and brown.

Mt. Titano — A93

Founder Melvin Jones and Lions
Headquarters — A94

60 l, Government Palace and statue of Liberty. 115 l, Clarence L. Sturm, president. 150 l, Finis E. Davis, vice president.

1960, July 1	Photo.	Wmk. 303
466	A93	30 l red brn & dk bl	.25	.25
467	A94	45 l bl vio & bis brn	.50	.50
468	A93	60 l dull rose & bl	.25	.25
469	A94	115 l green & blk	.50	.50
470	A94	150 l brn & dk bl	3.50	2.75
		Nos. 466-470,C115 (6)	13.50	12.75

Lions Intl.; founding of the Lions Club of San Marino.

Beach of
Riccione
and San
Marino
Peaks
A95

1960, Aug. 27		Perf. 14
471	A95	30 l multicolored	.35	.25

12th San Marino-Riccione Stamp Day, Aug. 27. See No. C116.

Boy with Basket of Fruit, by Caravaggio — A96

1960, Dec. 29   Wmk. 303   Perf. 14

472	A96	200 l multicolored	11.00	8.50

350th anniversary of the death of Michelangelo da Caravaggio (Merisi), painter.

Types of 1957

Views: 1 l, Hospital street. 4 l, Government building. 30 l, Gate tower. 115 l, Covered market of Borgo Maggiore.

1961, Feb. 16   Perf. 14

473	A79	1 l dk blue grn	.25	.25
474	A78	4 l dk blue & blk	.25	.25
475	A78	30 l brt vio & brn	.75	.75
476	A78	115 l brown & blue	.40	.40
		Nos. 473-476 (4)	1.65	1.65

Hunting Roebuck A97

Hunting Scenes (16th-18th century): 2 l, Falconer, vert. 3 l, Wild boar hunt. 4 l, Duck shooting with crossbow. 5 l, Stag hunt. 10 l, Mounted falconer, vert. 30 l, Hunter with horn and dogs. 60 l, Hunter with rifle and dog, vert. 70 l, Hunter and beater. 115 l, Duck hunt.

Wmk. 303

1961, May 4   Photo.   Perf. 14

477	A97	1 l lil rose & vio bl	.25	.25
478	A97	2 l gray, dk red & blk	.25	.25
479	A97	3 l red org, brn & blk	.25	.25
480	A97	4 l lt bl, red & blk	.25	.25
481	A97	5 l yellow grn & brn	.25	.25
482	A97	10 l org, blk, brn & vio	.25	.25
483	A97	30 l yel, bl & dk grn	.25	.25
484	A97	60 l ocher, brn, blk & red	.25	.25
485	A97	70 l green, blk & car	.25	.25
486	A97	115 l brt pink, blk & dk bl	.75	.75
		Nos. 477-486 (10)	3.00	3.00

Mt. Titano and Cancelled Stamp of Sardinia, 1862 — A98

Photogravure and Embossed

1961, Sept. 5   Wmk. 303   Perf. 13

487	A98	30 l multicolored	.50	.50
488	A98	70 l multicolored	1.00	1.00
489	A98	200 l multicolored	.50	.50
		Nos. 487-489 (3)	2.00	2.00

Cent. of Independence Phil. Exhib., Turin, 1961.

Europa Issue, 1961

View of San Marino A99

Wmk. 339

1961, Oct. 20   Photo.   Perf. 13

490	A99	500 l brn & blue grn	35.00	15.00
		Sheet of 6	300.00	150.00

King Enzo's Palace and Neptune Fountain, Bologna — A100

Views of Bologna: 70 l, Loggia dei Mercanti. 100 l, Two Towers.

1961, Nov. 25   Wmk. 339   Perf. 14

491	A100	30 l grnsh bl & blk	.25	.25
492	A100	70 l dk ol grn & blk	.25	.25
493	A100	100 l red brown & blk	.25	.25
		Nos. 491-493 (3)	.75	.75

Bophilex, philatelic exhibition, Bologna.

Duryea, 1892 A101

Automobiles (pre-1910): 2 l, Panhard-Levassor. 3 l, Peugeot. 4 l, Daimler. 5 l, Fiat, vert. 10 l, Decauville. 15 l, Wolseley. 20 l, Benz. 25 l, Napier. 30 l, White, vert. 50 l, Oldsmobile. 70 l, Renault, vert. 100 l, Isotta Fraschini. 115 l, Bianchi. 150 l, Alfa.

1962, Jan. 23   Wmk. 303   Perf. 14

494	A101	1 l red brn & bl	.25	.25
495	A101	2 l ultra & org brn	.25	.25
496	A101	3 l black, brn & org	.25	.25
497	A101	4 l gray & dk red	.25	.25
498	A101	5 l violet & org	.25	.25
499	A101	10 l black & org	.25	.25
500	A101	15 l black & ver	.25	.25
501	A101	20 l black & ultra	.25	.25
502	A101	25 l gray & org	.25	.25
503	A101	30 l black & ocher	.25	.25
504	A101	50 l black & brt pink	.25	.25
505	A101	70 l black, gray & grn	.25	.25
506	A101	100 l black, yel & car	.30	.30
507	A101	115 l blk, org & bl grn	.40	.40
508	A101	150 l multicolored	.50	.50
		Nos. 494-508 (15)	4.20	4.20

Wright Plane, 1904 A102

Historic Planes (1907-1910): 2 l, Ernest Archdeacon. 3 l, Albert and Emile Bonnet-Labranche. 4 l, Glenn Curtiss. 5 l, Farman. 10 l, Louis Bleriot. 30 l, Hubert Latham. 60 l, Alberto Santos Dumont. 70 l, Alliott Verdon Roe. 115 l, Faccioli.

Wmk. 339

1962, Apr. 4   Photo.   Perf. 14

509	A102	1 l blk & dull yel	.25	.25
510	A102	2 l red brn & grn	.25	.25
511	A102	3 l red brn & gray grn	.25	.25
512	A102	4 l brown & blk	.25	.25
513	A102	5 l magenta & blue	.25	.25
514	A102	10 l ocher & bl grn	.25	.25
515	A102	30 l ocher & ultra	.25	.25
516	A102	60 l black & ocher	.30	.30
517	A102	70 l dp orange & blk	.60	.60
518	A102	115 l grn & ocher	.70	.70
		Nos. 509-518 (10)	3.35	3.35

Mountaineer Descending A103

Designs: 2 l, View of Sassolungo. 3 l, Mt. Titano. 4 l, Three Peaks of Lavaredo. 5 l, Matterhorn. 15 l, Skier on downhill run. 30 l, Climbing an overhang. 40 l, Cutting steps in ice. 85 l, Giant's Tooth. 115 l, Mt. Titano.

1962, June 14   Wmk. 339   Perf. 14

519	A103	1 l bis brn & blk	.25	.25
520	A103	2 l Prus grn & blk	.25	.25
521	A103	3 l lilac & blk	.25	.25
522	A103	4 l brt bl & blk	.25	.25
523	A103	5 l dp org & blk	.25	.25
524	A103	15 l org yel & blk	.25	.25
525	A103	30 l carmine & blk	.25	.25
526	A103	40 l grnsh bl & blk	.25	.25
527	A103	85 l lt green & blk	.25	.25
528	A103	115 l vio bl & blk	.40	.40
		Nos. 519-528 (10)	2.65	2.65

Hunter with Dog A104

Modern Hunting Scenes: 2 l, Hound master on horseback, vert. 3 l, Duck hunt. 4 l, Stag hunt. 5 l, Partridge hunt. 15 l, Lapwing (hunt). 50 l, Wild duck hunt. 70 l, Duck hunt from boat. 100 l, Boar hunt. 150 l, Pheasant hunt, vert.

1962, Aug. 25   Photo.   Perf. 14

529	A104	1 l brown & yel grn	.25	.25
530	A104	2 l dk bl & org	.25	.25
531	A104	3 l blk & Prus bl	.25	.25
532	A104	4 l black & brown	.25	.25
533	A104	5 l brn & yel grn	.25	.25
534	A104	15 l blk & org brn	.25	.25
535	A104	50 l brn, dp grn & blk	.25	.25
536	A104	70 l grn, sal pink & blk	.25	.25
537	A104	100 l blk, brick red & sep	.25	.25
538	A104	150 l grn, lil & blk	.40	.40
		Nos. 529-538 (10)	2.65	2.65

Europa Issue, 1962

Mt. Titano and "Europa" A105

1962, Oct. 25   Wmk. 339

539	A105	200 l gray & car	1.50	1.25
		Sheet of 6	10.00	10.00

Egyptian Cargo Ship A106

Ancient Ships: 2 l, Greece, 2nd Cent. B.C. 3 l, Roman galley. 4 l, Vikings, 10th Cent. 5 l, "Santa Maria," 1492. 10 l, Cypriote galleon, vert. 30 l, Galley, 1600. 60 l, "Sovereign of the Seas," 1637, vert. 70 l, Danish ship, 1750, vert. 115 l, Frigate, 1850.

1963, Jan. 10

540	A106	1 l blue & org yel	.25	.25
541	A106	2 l mag, tan & brn	.25	.25
542	A106	3 l brown & lil rose	.25	.25
543	A106	4 l vio brn & gray	.25	.25
544	A106	5 l brown & yellow	.25	.25
545	A106	10 l brn & brt yel grn	.25	.25
546	A106	30 l blk, bl & sep	.60	.60
547	A106	60 l lt vio bl & yel grn	.60	.60
548	A106	70 l blk, gray & dl red	1.10	1.10
549	A106	115 l blk, brn & gray bl	2.50	1.40
		Nos. 540-549 (10)	6.30	5.20

Lady with Veil, by Raphael — A107

Paintings by Raphael: 70 l, Self-portrait. 100 l, St. Barbara from Sistine Madonna. 200 l, Portrait of a Young Woman (Maddalena Strozzi).

Size: 26½x37mm

Wmk. 339

1963, Mar. 28   Photo.   Perf. 14

550	A107	30 l multicolored	.40	.40
551	A107	70 l multicolored	.25	.25
552	A107	100 l multicolored	.35	.25

Size: 26½x44mm

553	A107	200 l multicolored	.40	.40
		Nos. 550-553 (4)	1.40	1.30

Jousting with "Saracen," Arezzo — A108

Medieval "Knightly Games": 2 l, French knights, horiz. 3 l, Crossbow contest. 4 l, English knight receiving lance, horiz. 5 l, Tournament, Florence. 10 l, Jousting with "Quintana," Ascoli Piceno. 30 l, "Quintana," Foligno, horiz. 60 l, Race through Siena. 70 l, Tournament, Malpaga, horiz. 115 l, Knights challenging.

1963, June 22   Wmk. 339   Perf. 14

554	A108	1 l lilac rose	.25	.25
555	A108	2 l slate	.25	.25
556	A108	3 l black	.25	.25
557	A108	4 l violet	.25	.25
558	A108	5 l rose violet	.25	.25
559	A108	10 l dull green	.25	.25
560	A108	30 l red brown	.25	.25
561	A108	60 l Prus green	.25	.25
562	A108	70 l brown	.25	.25
563	A108	115 l black	.25	.25
		Nos. 554-563 (10)	2.50	2.50

Butterfly — A109

Various butterflies. 70 l, 115 l, horiz.

Wmk. 339

1963, Aug. 31   Photo.   Perf. 14

564	A109	25 l multicolored	.25	.25
565	A109	30 l multicolored	.25	.25
566	A109	60 l multicolored	.25	.25
567	A109	70 l multicolored	.25	.25
568	A109	115 l multicolored	.55	.35
		Nos. 564-568 (5)	1.55	1.35

St. Marinus Statue, Government Palace — A110

1963, Aug. 31

569	A110	100 l shown	.25	.25
570	A110	100 l Modern fountain	.25	.25

San Marino-Riccione Stamp Fair.

Europa Issue, 1963

Flag and "E" — A111

1963, Sept. 21   Wmk. 339   *Perf. 14*
571 A111 200 l blue & brn org   .60 .50

Women's Hurdles A112

Sports: 2 l, Pole vaulting, vert. 3 l, Women's relay race. 4 l, Men's high jump. 5 l, Soccer. 10 l, Women's high jump. 30 l, Women's discus throw, vert. 60 l, Women's javelin throw. 70 l, Water polo. 115 l, Hammer throw.

1963, Sept. 21
572	A112	1 l	org & red brn	.25 .25
573	A112	2 l	lt grn & dk brn	.25 .25
574	A112	3 l	bl & dk brn	.25 .25
575	A112	4 l	dp bl & dk brn	.25 .25
576	A112	5 l	red & dk brn	.25 .25
577	A112	10 l	lil rose & claret	.25 .25
578	A112	30 l	gray & red brn	.25 .25
579	A112	60 l	brt yel & dk brn	.25 .25
580	A112	70 l	brt bl & dk brn	.25 .25
581	A112	115 l	grn & dk brn	.25 .25
		Nos. 572-581 (10)		2.50 2.50

Publicity for 1964 Olympic Games.

Modern Pentathlon A113

Designs: 1 l, Runner, vert. 2 l, Woman gymnast, vert. 3 l, Basketball, vert. 5 l, Dual rowing. 15 l, Broad jumper. 30 l, Swimmer in racing dive. 70 l, Woman sprinter. 120 l, Bicycle racers, vert. 150 l, Fencers, vert.

Inscribed "Tokio, 1964"

1964, June 25   Wmk. 339   *Perf. 14*
582	A113	1 l	brn & yel grn	.25 .25
583	A113	2 l	blk & red brn	.25 .25
584	A113	3 l	blk & brown	.25 .25
585	A113	4 l	blk & org red	.25 .25
586	A113	5 l	blk & brt bl	.25 .25
587	A113	15 l	dk brn & org	.25 .25
588	A113	30 l	dk vio & bl	.25 .25
589	A113	70 l	red brn & grn	.25 .25
590	A113	120 l	brn & brt bl	.25 .25
591	A113	150 l	blk & crimson	.25 .25
		Nos. 582-591 (10)		2.50 2.50

18th Olympic Games, Tokyo, Oct. 10-25.

Same Inscribed "Verso Tokio"

1964, June 25   Photo.
592 A113 30 l indigo & lilac   .25 .25
593 A113 70 l brn & Prus grn   .25 .25

"Verso Tokyo" Stamp Exhibition at Rimini, Italy, June 25-July 6.

Murray-Blenkinsop Locomotive, 1812 — A114

History of Locomotive: 2 l, Puffing Billy, 1813. 3 l, Locomotion I, 1825. 4 l, Rocket, 1829. 5 l, Lion, 1838. 15 l, Bayard, 1839. 20 l, Crampton, 1849. 50 l, Little England, 1851. 90 l, Spitfire, c. 1860. 110 l, Rogers, c. 1865.

1964, Aug. 29   Wmk. 339   *Perf. 14*
594	A114	1 l	blk & buff	.25 .25
595	A114	2 l	blk & green	.25 .25
596	A114	3 l	blk & rose lilac	.25 .25
597	A114	4 l	blk & yellow	.25 .25
598	A114	5 l	blk & salmon	.25 .25
599	A114	15 l	blk & yel grn	.25 .25
600	A114	20 l	blk & dp pink	.25 .25
601	A114	50 l	blk & pale bl	.25 .25
602	A114	90 l	blk & yel org	.25 .25
603	A114	110 l	blk & brt bl	.35 .35
		Nos. 594-603 (10)		2.60 2.60

Baseball Players A115

1964, Aug. 29   Photo.
604 A115 30 l shown   .30 .30
605 A115 70 l Pitcher   .30 .30

8th European Baseball Championship, Milan.

Europa Issue, 1964

"E" and Globe A116

1964, Oct. 15   Wmk. 339   *Perf. 14*
606 A116 200 l dk blue & red   2.25 1.00

President John F. Kennedy (1917-1963) — A117

130 l, Kennedy and American flag, vert.

1964, Nov. 22   Photo.   *Perf. 14*
607 A117 70 l multicolored   .25 .25
608 A117 130 l multicolored   .25 .25

Start of Bicycle Race from Government Palace — A118

Designs: 70 l, Cyclists (going right) and view of San Marino. 200 l, Cyclists (going left) and view of San Marino.

1965, May 15   Photo.   Wmk. 339
609 A118 30 l sepia   .25 .25
610 A118 70 l deep claret   .25 .25
611 A118 200 l rose red   .25 .25
    Nos. 609-611 (3)   .75 .75

48th Bicycle Tour of Italy.

Brontosaurus — A119

Dinosaurs: 2 l, Brachiosaurus, vert. 3 l, Pteranodon. 4 l, Elasmosaurus. 5 l, Tyrannosaurus. 10 l, Stegosaurus. 75 l, Thaumatosaurus victor. 100 l, Iguanodon. 200 l, Triceratops.

1965, June 30   Wmk. 339   *Perf. 14*
612	A119	1 l	dk brn & emer	.25 .25
613	A119	2 l	blk & sl bl	.25 .25
614	A119	3 l	sl grn, ol grn & yel	.25 .25
615	A119	4 l	brn & slate bl	.25 .25
616	A119	5 l	claret & grn	.25 .25
617	A119	10 l	claret & grn	.30 .30
618	A119	75 l	dk bl & blk grn	.30 .30
619	A119	100 l	green & claret	.60 .60
620	A119	200 l	brown & grn	.85 .85
		Nos. 612-620 (9)		3.30 3.30

Europa Issue, 1965

Rooks on Chessboard A120

1965, Aug. 28   Photo.   *Perf. 14*
621 A120 200 l brown & multi   1.25 .65

Dante by Gustave Doré A121

Doré's Illustrations for Divina Commedia: 90 l, Charon ferrying boat across Acheron. 130 l, Eagle carrying Dante from Purgatory to Paradise. 140 l, Dante with Beatrice examined by Sts. Peter, James and John on faith.

Perf. 14x14½
1965, Nov. 20   Engr.   Wmk. 339
Center in Brown Black
622 A121 40 l indigo   .25 .25
623 A121 90 l car rose   .25 .25
624 A121 130 l red brown   .25 .25
625 A121 140 l ultra   .25 .25
    Nos. 622-625 (4)   1.00 1.00

Dante Alighieri (1265-1321), poet.

Stylized Peaks, Flags of Italy and San Marino A122

1965, Nov. 25   Photo.   *Perf. 14*
626 A122 115 l grn, red, ocher & bl   .30 .30

Visit of Giuseppe Saragat, president of Italy.

Trotter A123

Horses: 20 l, Cross Country, vert. 40 l, Hurdling. 70 l, Gallop. 90 l, Steeplechase. 170 l, Polo, vert.

Perf. 14x13, 13x14
1966, Feb. 28   Photo.   Wmk. 339
627	A123	10 l	multicolored	.25 .25
628	A123	20 l	multicolored	.25 .25
629	A123	40 l	multicolored	.25 .25
630	A123	70 l	multicolored	.25 .25
631	A123	90 l	multicolored	.25 .25
632	A123	170 l	multicolored	.25 .25
		Nos. 627-632 (6)		1.50 1.50

Scenic Types of 1955-57

5 l, Hospital Street. 10 l, Gate tower. 15 l, View from South Bastion. 40 l, Murata Nuova Bridge. 90 l, View of La Rocca. 140 l, Government Palace.

1966, Mar. 29   Wmk. 339   *Perf. 14*
633	A79	5 l	blue & brn	.25 .25
634	A78	10 l	dk sl grn & bl grn	.25 .25
635	A78	15 l	dk brn & vio	.25 .25
636	A73	40 l	dk pur & brick red	.25 .25
637	A74	90 l	blk & dull bl	.25 .25
638	A74	140 l	violet & org	.25 .25
		Nos. 633-638 (6)		1.50 1.50

"Bella" by Titian A124

Titian Paintings: 90 l, 100 l, Details from "The Education of Love." 170 l, Detail from "Sacred and Profane Love."

1966, June 16   Wmk. 339   *Perf. 14*
639	A124	40 l	multicolored	.25 .25
640	A124	90 l	multicolored	.25 .25
641	A124	100 l	multicolored	.25 .25
642	A124	170 l	multicolored	.25 .25
		Nos. 639-642 (4)		1.00 1.00

Stone Bass A125

Fish: 2 l, Cuckoo wrasse. 3 l, Dolphin. 4 l, John Dory. 5 l, Octopus, vert. 10 l, Orange scorpionfish. 40 l, Electric ray, vert. 90 l, Jellyfish, vert. 115 l, Sea Horse, vert. 130 l, Dentex.

Perf. 14x13½, 13½x14
1966, Aug. 27   Wmk. 339
643	A125	1 l	multicolored	.25 .25
644	A125	2 l	multicolored	.25 .25
645	A125	3 l	multicolored	.25 .25
646	A125	4 l	multicolored	.25 .25
647	A125	5 l	multicolored	.25 .25
648	A125	10 l	multicolored	.25 .25
649	A125	40 l	multicolored	.25 .25
650	A125	90 l	multicolored	.25 .25
651	A125	115 l	multicolored	.25 .25
652	A125	130 l	multicolored	.25 .25
		Nos. 643-652 (10)		2.50 2.50

Europa Issue, 1966

Our Lady of Europe A126

1966, Sept. 24   Wmk. 339   *Perf. 14*
653 A126 200 l multicolored   .45 .35

Peony and Mt. Titano — A127

Flowers and Various Views of Mt. Titano: 10 l, Bell flowers. 15 l, Pyrenean poppy. 20 l, Purple nettle. 40 l, Day lily. 140 l, Gentian. 170 l, Thistle.

Wmk. 339

1967, Jan. 12		Photo.	Perf. 14	
654	A127	5 l multicolored	.25	.25
655	A127	10 l multicolored	.25	.25
656	A127	15 l multicolored	.25	.25
657	A127	20 l multicolored	.25	.25
658	A127	40 l multicolored	.25	.25
659	A127	140 l multicolored	.25	.25
660	A127	170 l multicolored	.25	.25
		Nos. 654-660 (7)	1.75	1.75

St. Marinus — A128

The Return of the Prodigal Son — A129

Design: 170 l, St. Francis. The paintings are by Giovanni Francesco Barbieri (1591-1666).

Wmk. 339

1967, Mar. 16			Perf. 14	
661	A128	40 l multicolored	.25	.25
662	A128	170 l multicolored	.25	.25
663	A129	190 l multicolored	.25	.25
a.		Strip of 3, #661-663	.75	.75

Europa Issue, 1967

Map Showing Members of CEPT — A130

1967, May 5		Wmk. 339	Perf. 14	
664	A130	200 l sl grn & brn org	.85	.45

Amanita Caesarea — A131

Various Mushrooms.

1967, June 15		Photo.	Perf. 14	
665	A131	5 l multicolored	.25	.25
666	A131	15 l multicolored	.25	.25
667	A131	20 l multicolored	.25	.25
668	A131	40 l multicolored	.25	.25
669	A131	50 l multicolored	.25	.25
670	A131	170 l multicolored	.25	.25
		Nos. 665-670 (6)	1.50	1.50

Amiens Cathedral A132

Designs: 40 l, Siena Cathedral. 80 l, Toledo Cathedral. 90 l, Salisbury Cathedral. 170 l, Cologne Cathedral.

Wmk. 339

1967, Sept. 21		Engr.	Perf. 14	
671	A132	20 l dk vio, bister	.25	.25
672	A132	40 l slate grn, bis	.25	.25
673	A132	80 l slate bl, bis	.25	.25
674	A132	90 l sepia, bis	.25	.25
675	A132	170 l deep plum, bis	.25	.25
		Nos. 671-675 (5)	1.25	1.25

Crucifix of Santa Croce, by Cimabue A133

1967, Dec. 5		Wmk. 339	Perf. 15	
676	A133	300 l brn & vio blue	.60	.60

The Crucifix of Santa Croce, by Giovanni Cimabue (1240-1302), was severely damaged in the Florentine flood of Nov. 1966.

Coat of Arms — A134

Coats of Arms: 3 l, Penna Rossa. 5 l, Fiorentino. 10 l, Montecerreto. 25 l, Serravalle. 35 l, Montegiardino. 50 l, Faetano. 90 l, Borgo Maggiore. 180 l, Montelupo. 500 l, State arms of San Marino.

Perf. 13x13½

1968, Mar. 14		Litho.	Wmk. 339	
677	A134	2 l multi	.25	.25
678	A134	3 l multi	.25	.25
679	A134	5 l multi	.25	.25
680	A134	10 l multi	.25	.25
681	A134	25 l multi	.25	.25
682	A134	35 l multi	.25	.25
683	A134	50 l multi	.25	.25
684	A134	90 l multi	.25	.25
685	A134	180 l multi	.25	.25
686	A134	500 l multi	.65	.25
		Nos. 677-686 (10)	2.90	2.50

Common Design Types pictured following the introduction.

Europa Issue, 1968
Common Design Type

1968, Apr. 29		Engr.	Perf. 14x13½	
Size: 37x27½mm				
687	CD11	250 l claret brown	.75	.35

"Battle of San Romano" (Detail), by Paolo Uccello — A135

Designs: Details from "The Battle of San Romano," by Paolo Uccello (1397-1475).

Photogravure and Engraved

1968, June 14		Wmk. 339	Perf. 14	
688	A135	50 l pale lil & blk	.25	.25
689	A135	90 l pale lil & blk, vert.	.25	.25
690	A135	130 l pale lil & blk	.25	.25
691	A135	230 l pale pink & blk	.30	.30
		Nos. 688-691 (4)	1.05	1.05

The Mystic Nativity, by Botticelli, Detail A136

1968, Dec. 5		Wmk. 339	Engr.	Perf. 14	
692	A136	50 l dark blue	.25	.25
693	A136	90 l deep claret	.25	.25
694	A136	180 l sepia	.25	.25
		Nos. 692-694 (3)	.75	.75

Christmas.

"Peace" by Lorenzetti A137

Designs: 80 l, "Justice." 90 l, "Moderation." 180 l, View of Siena, 14th century, horiz. All designs are from the "Good Government" frescoes by Ambrogio Lorenzetti in the Town Hall of Siena.

Wmk. 339

1969, Feb. 13		Engr.	Perf. 14	
695	A137	50 l dark blue	.25	.25
696	A137	80 l brown	.25	.25
697	A137	90 l dk blue vio	.25	.25
698	A137	180 l magenta	.25	.25
		Nos. 695-698 (4)	1.00	1.00

Young Soldier, by Bramante — A138

Designs: 90 l, Old Soldier, by Bramante. Designs are from murals in the Pinakotheke of Brear, Milan.

1969, Apr. 28		Photo.	Perf. 14	
699	A138	50 l multicolored	.30	.30
700	A138	90 l multicolored	.30	.30

Bramante (1444-1514), Italian architect and painter.

Europa Issue, 1969
Common Design Type

1969, Apr. 28		Engr.	Perf. 14x13	
Size: 37x27mm				
701	CD12	50 l dull green	.60	.60
702	CD12	180 l rose claret	.60	.60

Charabanc A139

Coaches, 19th Century: 10 l, Barouche. 25 l, Private drag. 40 l, Hansom cab. 50 l, Curricle. 90 l, Wagonette. 180 l, Spider phaeton.

Perf. 14½x14

1969, June 25		Photo.	Unwmk.	
703	A139	5 l blk, ocher & dk bl	.25	.25
704	A139	10 l blk, grn & pur	.25	.25
705	A139	25 l dk grn, pink & brn	.25	.25
706	A139	40 l ind, lil & lt brn	.25	.25
707	A139	50 l blk, dl yel & dk bl	.25	.25
708	A139	90 l blk, yel grn & brn	.25	.25
709	A139	180 l multi	.25	.25
		Nos. 703-709 (7)	1.75	1.75

Pier at Rimini A140

Paintings by R. Viola: 20 l, Mt. Titano. 200 l, Pier at Riccione, horiz.

1969, Sept. 17		Unwmk.	Perf. 14	
710	A140	20 l multicolored	.25	.25
711	A140	180 l multicolored	.25	.25
712	A140	200 l multicolored	.30	.30
		Nos. 710-712 (3)	.80	.80

"Faith" by Raphael — A141

Designs: 180 l, "Hope" by Raphael. 200 l, "Charity" by Raphael.

Perf. 13½x14

1969, Dec. 10		Engr.	Wmk. 339	
713	A141	20 l dl pur & sal	.25	.25
714	A141	180 l dl pur & lt grn	.25	.25
715	A141	200 l dp pur & bis	.25	.25
		Nos. 713-715 (3)	.75	.75

Signs of the Zodiac A142

Perf. 14x13½

1970, Feb. 18		Photo.	Unwmk.	
716	A142	1 l Aries	.25	.25
717	A142	2 l Taurus	.25	.25
718	A142	3 l Gemini	.25	.25
719	A142	4 l Cancer	.25	.25
720	A142	5 l Leo	.25	.25
721	A142	10 l Virgo	.25	.25
722	A142	15 l Libra	.25	.25
723	A142	20 l Scorpio	.25	.25
724	A142	70 l Sagittarius	.25	.25
725	A142	90 l Capricorn	.25	.25

726	A142	100 l	Aquarius	.25	.25
727	A142	180 l	Pisces	.40	.40
			Nos. 716-727 (12)	3.15	3.15

Fleet in Bay of Naples, by Peter Brueghel, the Elder — A143

Unwmk.

1970, Apr. 30   Photo.   *Perf. 14*
728	A143	230 l	multi	.40	.40

10th Europa Phil. Exhib., Naples, May 2-10.

Europa Issue, 1970
Common Design Type

1970, Apr. 30   *Perf. 14x13½*
Size: 36x27mm
729	CD13	90 l	brt yel grn & red	.50	.25
730	CD13	180 l	ocher & red	.60	.30

St. Francis' Gate and Rotary Emblem — A144

220 l, Rocca (State Prison) and Rotary emblem.

1970, June 25 Photo. *Perf. 13½x14*
731	A144	180 l	multi	.30	.30
732	A144	220 l	multi	.50	.50

65th anniv. of Rotary Intl.; 10th anniv. of the San Marino Rotary Club.

Woman with Mandolin, by Tiepolo — A145

Paintings by Tiepolo: 180 l, Woman with Parrot. 220 l, Rinaldo and Armida Surprised, horiz.

Size: 26½x37½mm

1970, Sept. 10   Unwmk.   *Perf. 14*
733	50 l	multi		.25	.25
734	180 l	multi		.30	.30

Size: 56x37½mm
735	220 l	multi		.50	.50
	a.	A145 Strip of 3, #733-735		1.10	1.10

Giambattista Tiepolo (1696-1770), Venetian painter.

Black Pete — A146

Walt Disney and Jungle Book Scene A147

Disney Characters: 2 l, Gyro Gearloose. 3 l, Pluto. 4 l, Minnie Mouse. 5 l, Donald Duck. 10 l, Goofy. 15 l, Scrooge McDuck. 50 l, Huey, Louey and Dewey. 90 l, Mickey Mouse.

Perf. 13x14, 14x13

1970, Dec. 22   Photo.
736	A146	1 l	multi	.25	.25
737	A146	2 l	multi	.25	.25
738	A146	3 l	multi	.25	.25
739	A146	4 l	multi	.25	.25
740	A146	5 l	multi	.25	.25
741	A146	10 l	multi	.25	.25
742	A146	15 l	multi	.25	.25
743	A146	50 l	multi	.50	.50
744	A146	90 l	multi	1.00	1.00
745	A147	220 l	multi	7.50	7.50
			Nos. 736-745 (10)	10.75	10.75

Walt Disney (1901-66), cartoonist & film maker.

Customhouse Dock, by Canaletto — A148

Paintings by Canaletto: 180 l, Grand Canal between Balbi Palace and Rialto Bridge. 200 l, St. Mark's and Doges' Palace.

1971, Mar. 23   Unwmk.   *Perf. 14*
746	A148	20 l	multi	.25	.25
747	A148	180 l	multi	.25	.25
748	A148	200 l	multi	.85	.85
			Nos. 746-748 (3)	1.35	1.35

Save Venice campaign.

Europa Issue, 1971
Common Design Type

1971, May 29   *Perf. 13½x14*
Size: 27½x23mm
749	CD14	50 l	org & blue	.35	.25
750	CD14	90 l	blue & org	.45	.30

Congress Emblem and Hall, San Marino Flag — A149

Design: 90 l, Detail from Government Palace door, Congress and San Marino emblems, vert.

1971, May 29   Photo.   *Perf. 12*
751	A149	20 l	violet & multi	.25	.25
752	A149	90 l	olive & multi	.25	.25
753	A149	180 l	multi	.25	.25
			Nos. 751-753 (3)	.75	.75

Italian Philatelic Press Union Congress, San Marino, May 29-30.

Duck-shaped Jug with Flying Lasa — A150

Etruscan Art, 6th-3rd Centuries B.C.: 80 l, Head of Mercury, vert. 90 l, Sarcophagus of a married couple, vert. 180 l, Chimera.

Photo. & Engr.

1971, Sept. 16   *Perf. 14*
754	A150	50 l	blk & org	.25	.25
755	A150	80 l	blk & lt grn	.25	.25
756	A150	90 l	blk & lt bl	.25	.25
757	A150	180 l	blk & org	.40	.40
			Nos. 754-757 (4)	1.15	1.15

Tiger Lily A151

Venus, by Botticelli A152

1971, Dec. 2   Photo.   *Perf. 11½*
758	A151	1 l	shown	.25	.25
759	A151	2 l	Phlox	.25	.25
760	A151	3 l	Carnations	.25	.25
761	A151	4 l	Globe flowers	.25	.25
762	A151	5 l	Thistles	.25	.25
763	A151	10 l	Peonies	.25	.25
764	A151	15 l	Hellebore	.25	.25
765	A151	50 l	Anemones	.25	.25
766	A151	90 l	Gaillardia	.25	.25
767	A151	220 l	Asters	.30	.30
			Nos. 758-767 (10)	2.55	2.55

1972, Feb. 23 *Perf. 14, 13x14 (180 l)*

Details from La Primavera, by Sandro Botticelli: 180 l, Three Graces. 220 l, Spring.

Sizes: 50 l, 220 l, 21x37mm;
180 l, 27x37mm
768	A152	50 l	gold & multi	.25	.25
769	A152	180 l	gold & multi	.50	.50
770	A152	220 l	gold & multi	.50	.50
			Nos. 768-770 (3)	1.25	1.25

Europa Issue 1972
Common Design Type

1972, Apr. 27   *Perf. 11½*
Granite Paper
Size: 22½x33mm
771	CD15	50 l	org & multi	.50	.25
772	CD15	90 l	lt bl & multi	.50	.25

St. Marinus Taming Bear A153

Designs: 55 l, Donna Felicissima asking St. Marinus for mercy for her sons. 100 l, St. Marinus turning archers to stone. 130 l, Felicissima giving mountains to St. Marinus to establish Republic.

Photo. & Engr.

1972, Apr. 27   *Perf. 14*
773	A153	25 l	dl yel & blk	.25	.25
774	A153	55 l	sal pink & blk	.25	.25
775	A153	100 l	dl bl & blk	.25	.25
776	A153	130 l	citron & blk	.25	.25
			Nos. 773-776 (4)	1.00	1.00

Allegories of San Marino after 16th century paintings.

Italian House Sparrow — A154

1972, June 30   Photo.   *Perf. 11½*
Granite Paper
777	A154	1 l	shown	.25	.25
778	A154	2 l	Firecrest	.25	.25
779	A154	3 l	Blue tit	.25	.25
780	A154	4 l	Ortolan bunting	.25	.25
781	A154	5 l	White-spotted bluethroat	.25	.25
782	A154	10 l	Bullfinch	.25	.25
783	A154	25 l	Linnet	.25	.25

784	A154	50 l	Black-eared wheater	.25	.25
785	A154	90 l	Sardinian warbler	.25	.25
786	A154	220 l	Greenfinch	.25	.25
			Nos. 777-786 (10)	2.50	2.50

Young Man, Heart, Emblem — A155

Design: 90 l, Heart disease victim, horiz.

1972, Aug. 26   *Perf. 13½x14, 14x13½*
787	A155	50 l	lt bl & multi	.25	.25
788	A155	90 l	ocher & multi	.25	.25

World Heart Month.

Italian Philatelic Federation Emblem — A156

1972, Aug. 26   *Perf. 13½x14*
789	A156	25 l	gold & ultra	.25	.25

Honoring veterans of Philately.

5c Coin, 1864 A157

Coins: 10 l, 10c coin, 1935. 15 l, 1 lira, 1906. 20 l, 5 lire, 1898. 25 l, 5 lire, 1937. 50 l, 10 lire, 1932. 55 l, 20 lire, 1938. 220 l, 20 lire, 1925.

1972, Dec. 15   Litho.   *Perf. 12½x13*
790	A157	5 l	gray, blk & brn	.25	.25
791	A157	10 l	org, blk & sil	.25	.25
792	A157	15 l	brt rose, blk & sil	.25	.25
793	A157	20 l	lil, blk & sil	.25	.25
794	A157	25 l	vio, blk & sil	.25	.25
795	A157	50 l	brt bl, blk & sil	.25	.25
796	A157	55 l	ocher, blk & sil	.25	.25
797	A157	220 l	emer, blk & gold	.30	.30
			Nos. 790-797 (8)	2.05	2.05

New York, 1673 — A158

300 l, View of New York from East River, 1973.

1973, Mar. 9   Photo.   *Perf. 11½*
Granite Paper
798	200 l	bis, och & ol grn		.50	.50
799	300 l	bl, lil & blk		1.00	1.00
	a.	A158 Pair, #798-799		2.00	2.00

New York, 300th anniv. Printed checkerwise.

Rotary Press, San Marino Towers — A159

1973, May 10 **Photo.** *Perf. 13x14*
800 A159 50 l multi .25 .25

Tourist Press Congress, San Marino.

Gymnasts and Olympic Rings — A160

1973, May 10 **Unwmk.**
801 A160 100 l grn & multi .25 .25

5th Youth Games.

Europa Issue 1973
Common Design Type

1973, May 10 *Perf. 11½*
Size: 32½x23mm
802 CD16 20 l salmon & multi .40 .25
803 CD16 180 l lt bl & multi .60 .35

Grapes — A161

1973, July 11 **Photo.** *Perf. 11½*
804 A161 1 l shown .25 .25
805 A161 2 l Tangerines .25 .25
806 A161 3 l Apples .25 .25
807 A161 4 l Plums .25 .25
808 A161 5 l Strawberries .25 .25
809 A161 10 l Pears .25 .25
810 A161 25 l Cherries .25 .25
811 A161 50 l Pomegranate .25 .25
812 A161 90 l Apricots .25 .25
813 A161 220 l Peaches .30 .30
    Nos. 804-813 (10) 2.55 2.55

Arc-en-Ciel, France — A162

Famous Aircraft: 55 l, Macchi Castoldi, Italy. 60 l, Antonov, USSR. 90 l, Spirit of St. Louis, US. 220 l, Handley Page, Great Britain.

1973, Aug. 31 **Photo.** *Perf. 14x13½*
814 A162 25 l ocher, vio bl & gold .25 .25
815 A162 55 l gray, vio bl & gold .25 .25
816 A162 60 l rose, vio bl & gold .25 .25
817 A162 90 l lem, vio bl & gold .25 .25
818 A162 220 l org, vio bl & gold .40 .40
    Nos. 814-818 (5) 1.40 1.40

Crossbowman, Serravalle Castle — A163

Designs: 10 l, Crossbowman, Pennarossa Castle. 15 l, Drummer, Montegiardino Castle. 20 l, Trumpeter, Fiorentino Castle. 30 l, Crossbowman, Borga Maggiore Castle. 50 l, Trumpeter, Guaita Castle. 80 l, Crossbowman, Faetano Castle. 200 l, Crossbowman, Montelupo Castle.

1973, Nov. 7 **Photo.** *Perf. 13½*
819 A163 5 l black & multi .25 .25
820 A163 10 l black & multi .25 .25
821 A163 15 l black & multi .25 .25
822 A163 20 l black & multi .25 .25
823 A163 30 l black & multi .25 .25
824 A163 40 l black & multi .25 .25
825 A163 50 l black & multi .25 .25
826 A163 80 l black & multi .25 .25
827 A163 200 l black & multi .25 .25
    Nos. 819-827 (9) 2.25 2.25

San Marino victories in the Crossbow Tournament, Massa Marittima, July 15, 1973.

Attendants, by Gentile Fabriano — A164

Christmas: Details from Adoration of the Kings, by Gentile Fabriano (1370-1427).

1973, Dec. 19 **Photo.** *Perf. 11½*
828 A164 5 l shown .25 .25
829 A164 30 l King .25 .25
830 A164 115 l King .25 .25
831 A164 250 l Horses .35 .35
    Nos. 828-831 (4) 1.10 1.10

Shield, 16th Century A165

16th Century Armor: 5 l, Round shield. 10 l, German full armor. 15 l, Helmet with intricate etching. 20 l, Horse's head armor "Massimiliano." 30 l, Decorated helmet with Sphinx statuette on top. 50 l, Pommeled sword and gauntlets. 80 l, Sparrow-beaked helmet. 250 l, Sforza round shield.

Engr. & Litho.
1974, Mar. 12 *Perf. 13*
832 A165 5 l blk, lt grn & buff .25 .25
833 A165 10 l blk, buff & bl .25 .25
834 A165 15 l blk, bl & ultra .25 .25
835 A165 20 l blk, tan & ultra .25 .25
836 A165 30 l blk & lt bl .25 .25
837 A165 50 l blk, rose & ultra .25 .25
838 A165 80 l blk, gray & grn .25 .25
839 A165 250 l blk & yel .35 .35
    Nos. 832-839 (8) 2.10 2.10

Head of Woman, by Emilio Greco — A166

Europa: 200 l, Nude, by Emilio Greco (head shown on 100 l).

Engr. & Litho.
1974, May 9 *Perf. 13x14*
840 A166 100 l buff & blk .60 .50
841 A166 200 l pale grn & blk 1.00 .60

Yachts at Riccione and San Marino Peaks A167

1974, July 18 **Photo.** *Perf. 11½*
Granite Paper
842 A167 50 l ultra & multi .25 .25

26th San Marino-Riccione Stamp Day.

Arms of Lucia — A168

Coats of arms of participating cities.

1974, July 18 *Perf. 12*
843 A168 15 l shown .50 .50
844 A168 20 l Massa Marittima .50 .50
845 A168 50 l San Marino .50 .50
846 A168 115 l Gubbio 1.00 1.00
847 A168 300 l Lucca 1.00 1.00
    a. Strip of 5, #843-847 4.00 4.00

9th Crossbow Tournament, San Marino.

UPU Emblem — A169

1974, Oct. 9 **Photo.** *Perf. 11½*
Granite Paper
848 A169 50 l multi .30 .30
849 A169 90 l grn & multi .30 .30

Centenary of Universal Postal Union.

Mt. Titano and Hymn by Tommaseo A170

Niccolo Tommaseo A171

1974, Dec. 12 **Photo.** *Perf. 13½x14*
850 A170 50 l lt grn, blk & red .30 .30
851 A171 150 l yel, grn & blk .30 .30

Tommaseo (1802-1874), Italian writer.

Virgin and Child, 14th Century Wood Panel — A172

1974, Dec. 12 *Perf. 11½*
852 A172 250 l gold & multi .60 .60

Christmas.

"Refuge in San Marino" — A173

1975, Feb. 20 **Photo.** *Perf. 13½x14*
853 A173 50 l multi .25 .25

Flight of 100,000 refugees from Romagna to San Marino, 30th anniversary.

Musicians, from Leopard Tomb, Tarquinia — A174

Etruscan Art: 30 l, Chariot race, from Tomb on the Hill, Chiusi. 180 l, Achilles and Troilus, from Bulls' Tomb, Tarquinia. 220 l, Dancers, from Triclinium Tomb, Tarquinia.

Litho. & Engr.
1975, Feb. 20 *Perf. 14*
854 A174 20 l multi .25 .25
855 A174 30 l multi .25 .25
856 A174 180 l multi .25 .25
857 A174 220 l multi .30 .30
    Nos. 854-857 (4) 1.05 1.05

Europa Issue 1975

St. Marinus, by Guercino (Francesco Barbieri)
A175   A176

1975, May 14 **Photo.** *Perf. 11½*
Granite Paper
858 A175 100 l multi .55 .25
859 A176 200 l multi .75 .35

The Lamentation, by Giotto — A177

Frescoes by Giotto (details): 40 l, Mary and Jesus (Flight into Egypt). 50 l, Heads of four angels (Flight into Egypt). 100 l, Mary Magdalene (Noli Me Tangere), horiz. 500 l, Angel and the elect (Last Judgment), horiz.

1975, July 10   Photo.   Perf. 11½
Granite Paper

860	A177	10 l gold & multi	.25	.25
861	A177	40 l gold & multi	.25	.25
862	A177	50 l gold & multi	.25	.25
863	A177	100 l gold & multi	.25	.25
864	A177	500 l gold & multi	.65	.65
		Nos. 860-864 (5)	1.65	1.65

Holy Year.

Tokyo, 1835, Woodcut by Hiroshige — A178

300 l, Tokyo, Business District, 1975.

1975, Sept. 5   Photo.   Perf. 11½
Granite Paper

865	A178	200 l multi	.40	.40
866	A178	300 l multi	1.00	1.00
a.		Pair, #865-866	1.40	1.40

Printed checkerwise.

Aphrodite A179

1975, Sept. 19   Photo.   Perf. 11½

867	A179	50 l vio, blk & gray	.30	.30

Europa '75 Philatelic Exhibition, Naples.

Multiple Crosses A180

1975, Sept. 19

868	A180	100 l blk, dp org & vio	.30	.30

EUROCOPHAR Intl. Pharmaceutical Cong.

Christmas — A181

Christmas: Paintings by Michelangelo: 50 l, Angel. 100 l, Head of Virgin. 250 l, Doni Madonna.

1975, Dec. 3   Photo.   Perf. 11½
Granite Paper

869	50 l multi	.25	.25
870	100 l multi	.50	.50
871	250 l multi	.50	.50
a.	A181 Strip of 3, #869-871	1.25	1.25

Woman on Balcony, by Gentilini — A183

Two Women, by Gentilini A184

230 l, Woman (same as right head on 150 l) & IWY emblem, by Franco Gentilini.

1975, Dec. 3   Granite Paper

872	A183	70 l bl & multi	.25	.25
873	A184	150 l multi	.50	.50
874	A183	230 l multi	.50	.50
		Nos. 872-874 (3)	1.25	1.25

International Women's Year.

Modesty, by Emilio Greco — A185

Capitol, Washington, D.C. — A186

"Civic Virtues": 20 l, Temperance. 50 l, Fortitude. 100 l, Altruism. 150 l, Hope. 220 l, Prudence. 250 l, Justice. 300 l, Faith. 500 l, Honesty. 1000 l, Industry. Designs show drawings of women's heads by Emilio Greco.

1976, Mar. 4   Photo.   Perf. 11½
Granite Paper

875	A185	10 l buff & blk	.25	.25
876	A185	20 l pink & blk	.25	.25
877	A185	50 l grnsh & blk	.25	.25
878	A185	100 l salmon & blk	.25	.25
879	A185	150 l lilac & blk	.25	.25
880	A185	220 l gray & blk	.30	.30
881	A185	250 l yel & multi	.35	.35
882	A185	300 l gray & blk	.40	.40
883	A185	500 l yel & blk	.65	.65
884	A185	1000 l gray & blk	1.50	1.50
		Nos. 875-884 (10)	4.45	4.45

See Nos. 900-905, 931-933.

1976, May 29   Photo.   Perf. 11½

Arms of San Marino and: 150 l, Statue of Liberty. 180 l, Independence Hall, Philadelphia.

885	A186	70 l multi	.25	.25
886	A186	150 l multi	.25	.25
887	A186	180 l multi	.40	.40
		Nos. 885-887 (3)	.90	.90

American Bicentennial.

Montreal Olympic Games Emblem A187

1976, May 29

888	A187	150 l crimson & blk	.30	.30

21st Olympic Games, Montreal, Canada, 7/17-8/1.

Decorated Plate — A188

Europa: 180 l, Seal of San Marino.

1976, July 8   Photo.   Perf. 11½
Granite Paper

889	A188	150 l multi	.75	.70
890	A188	180 l bl, sil & blk	.75	.70

"Unity" — A189

1976, July 8   Perf. 13½x14

891	A189	150 l vio blk, yel & red	.25	.25

United Mutual Aid Society, centenary.

"Peaks of San Marino" — A190

1976, Oct. 14   Photo.   Perf. 13x14

892	A190	150 l blk & multi	.30	.30

ITALIA 76 Intl. Phil. Exhib., Milan, 10/14-24.

Children and UNESCO Emblem A191

1976, Oct. 14   Perf. 11½
Granite Paper

893	A191	180 l multi	.25	.25
894	A191	220 l multi	.30	.30

UNESCO, 30th anniv

Christmas — A192

Design: 150 l, Annunciation (detail), by Titian. 300 l, Virgin and Child, by Titian.

Litho. & Engr.
1976, Dec. 15   Perf. 13x14

895	150 l multi	.35	.35
896	300 l multi	.75	.75
a.	A192 Pair, #895-896	1.10	1.10

Exhibition Emblem A193

1977, Jan. 28   Photo.   Perf. 11½
Granite Paper

897	A193	80 l multi	.25	.25
898	A193	170 l multi	.25	.25
899	A193	200 l multi	.30	.30
		Nos. 897-899,C133 (4)	1.05	1.05

San Marino 77 Phil. Exhib.

Civic Virtues Type of 1976

70 l, Fortitude. 90 l, Prudence. 120 l, Altruism. 160 l, Temperance. 170 l, Hope. 320 l, Faith.

1977, Apr. 14   Photo.   Perf. 11½
Granite Paper

900	A185	70 l pink & blk	.25	.25
901	A185	90 l buff & blk	.25	.25
902	A185	120 l lt bl & blk	.25	.25
903	A185	160 l lt grn & blk	.25	.25
904	A185	170 l cream & blk	.25	.25
905	A185	320 l lil & blk	.75	.75
		Nos. 900-905 (6)	2.00	2.00

San Marino, after Ghirlandaio A194

Europa: 200 l, San Marino, detail from painting by Guercino.

1977, Apr. 14
Granite Paper

906	A194	170 l multi	.75	.35
907	A194	200 l multi	.75	.35

Vertical Flying Machine, by da Vinci — A195

Litho. & Engr.
1977, June 6   Perf. 13x14

908	A195	120 l multi	.25	.25

Centenary of Enrico Forlanini's experiments with vertical flight

University Square, Bucharest, 1877 — A196

Design: 400 l, National Theater and Intercontinental Hotel, 1977.

1977, June 6   Photo.   Perf. 11½
Granite Paper

909	200 l bis & multi	.50	.50
910	400 l lt bl & multi	1.00	1.00
a.	A196 Pair, #909-910	1.50	1.50

Centenary of Romanian independence. Printed checkerwise.

Type A2 of
1877 — A197

1977, June 15   Engr.   *Perf. 15x14½*
911 A197   40 l slate grn   .25   .25
912 A197   70 l deep blue   .25   .25
913 A197 170 l red   .25   .25
914 A197 500 l brown   .75   .75
915 A197 1000 l purple   1.50 1.50
       Nos. 911-915 (5)   3.00 3.00
Centenary of San Marino stamps.

St. Marinus, by
Retrosi — A198

Souvenir Sheet
1977, Aug. 28   Photo.   *Perf. 11½*
Granite Paper
916 A198   Sheet of 5   15.00 15.00
  a.   1000 l single stamp   2.50 2.50
Centenary of San Marino stamps; San
Marino '77 Phil. Exhib., Aug. 28-Sept. 4.

Medicinal
Plants — A199

1977, Oct. 19   Photo.   *Perf. 11½*
917 A199 170 l multi   .30   .30
Congress of Italian Pharmacists' Union.
Design shows high mallow, tilia, camomile,
borage, centaury and juniper.

Woman
Attacked
by
Octopus,
Emblem
A200

1977, Oct. 19
918 A200 200 l multi   .30   .30
World Rheumatism Year.

Virgin   San Francisco
Mary — A201   Gate — A202

Christmas: 230 l, Palm, olive and star. 300 l,
Angel.

1977, Dec. 5   Photo.   *Perf. 11½*
919 A201 170 l sil, gray & blk   .25   .25
920 A201 230 l sil, gray & blk   .40   .40
921 A201 300 l sil, gray & blk   .75   .75
  a.   Strip of 3, #919-921   1.40 1.40

1978, May 30   Photo.   *Perf. 11½*
Europa: 200 l, Ripa Gate.
922 A202 170 l lt bl & dk bl   1.00   .40
923 A202 200 l buff & brn   1.25   .50

Baseball Player   Feather, WHO
and   Emblem — A204
Diamond — A203

1978, May 30
924 A203   90 l multi   .25   .25
925 A203 120 l multi   .25   .25
World Baseball Championships.

1978, May 30
926 A204 320 l multi   .50   .50
Fight against hypertension.

ITU Emblem,
Waves Coming
from 3
Peaks — A205

1978, July 26   Photo.   *Perf. 11½*
927 A205   10 l car & yel   .25   .25
928 A205 200 l vio bl & lt bl   .25   .25
Membership in ITU.

Seagull and
Falcon, 3
Peaks
A206

1978, July 26
929 A206 120 l multi   .25   .25
930 A206 170 l multi   .30   .30
30th San Marino-Riccione Stamp Day.

Civic Virtues Type of 1976
Drawings by Emilio Greco: 5 l, Wisdom. 35 l,
Love. 2000 l, Faithfulness.

1978, Sept. 28   Photo.   *Perf. 11½*
Granite Paper
931 A185   5 l lt vio & blk   .25   .25
932 A185   35 l gray & blk   .25   .25
933 A185 2000 l yel & blk   2.50 2.50
       Nos. 931-933 (3)   3.00 3.00

Christmas
A207

1978, Dec. 6   Photo.   *Perf. 14x13½*
941 A207   10 l Holly leaves   .25   .25
942 A207 120 l Stars   .25   .25
943 A207 170 l Snowflakes   .25   .25
       Nos. 941-943 (3)   .75   .75

Globe and Woman
Holding
Torch — A208

1978, Dec. 6   *Perf. 11½x12*
944 A208 200 l multi   .30   .30
Universal Declaration of Human Rights,
30th anniversary.

First San
Marino
Autobus,
1915
A209

Europa: 220 l, Mail coach, 1895.

1979, Mar. 29   Photo.   *Perf. 11½x12*
945 A209 170 l multi   2.00   .80
946 A209 220 l multi   2.75 1.40

Albert Einstein (1879-1955),
Theoretical Physicist — A210

1979, Mar. 29   *Perf. 11½*
947 A210 120 l gray, lt & dk brn .40   .40

San Marino   Maigret — A212
Crossbow
Federation
Emblem — A211

1979, July 12   Litho.   *Perf. 14x13*
948 A211 120 l multi   .25   .25
14th Crossbow Tournament.

Litho. & Engr.
1979, July 12   *Perf. 13x14*
Fictional Detectives: 80 l, Perry Mason. 150
l, Nero Wolfe. 170 l, Ellery Queen. 220 l, Sherlock Holmes.
949 A212   10 l multi   .25   .25
950 A212   80 l multi   .25   .25
951 A212 150 l multi   .25   .25
952 A212 170 l multi   .25   .25
953 A212 220 l multi   .35   .35
       Nos. 949-953 (5)   1.35 1.35

Girl Holding
Book — A213

IYC Emblem, Paintings by Marina
Busignani: 120 l, 170 l, 220 l, Children and
birds, diff. 350 l, Mother nursing child.

1979, Sept. 6   Litho.   *Perf. 11½*
954 A213   20 l multi   .25   .25
955 A213 120 l multi   .25   .25
956 A213 170 l multi   .25   .25
957 A213 220 l multi   .35   .35
958 A213 350 l multi   .50   .50
       Nos. 954-958 (5)   1.60 1.60

St. Apollonia, 15th   Chestnut Tree,
Century   Deer — A216
Woodcut — A214

Waterskier
A215

1979, Sept. 6   Photo.
959 A214 170 l multi   .25   .25
13th Biennial Intl. Congress of Stomatology.

1979, Sept. 6
960 A215 150 l multi   .25   .25
European Waterskiing Championship.

1979, Oct. 25   Photo.   *Perf. 11½*
Protected Trees and Animals or Birds: 10 l,
Cedar of Lebanon, falcon. 35 l, Dogwood,
racoon. 50 l, Banyan, tiger. 70 l, Umbrella
pine, hoopoe. 90 l, Siberian spruce, marten.
100 l, Eucalyptus, koala bear. 120 l, Date
palm, camel. 150 l, Sugar maple, beaver.
170 l, Adansonia, elephant.

961 A216   5 l multi   .25   .25
962 A216   10 l multi   .25   .25
963 A216   35 l multi   .25   .25
964 A216   50 l multi   .25   .25
965 A216   70 l multi   .25   .25
966 A216   90 l multi   .25   .25
967 A216 100 l multi   .25   .25
968 A216 120 l multi   .25   .25
969 A216 150 l multi   .25   .25
970 A216 170 l multi   .25   .25
       Nos. 961-970 (10)   2.50 2.50

Holy Family,
by Antonio
Alberto de
Ferrara, 15th
Century
Fresco
A217

Christmas (de Ferrara Fresco): 80 l, St.
Joseph. 170 l, Infant Jesus. 220 l, One of the
Three Kings.

1979, Dec. 6   Photo.   *Perf. 12*
971 A217   80 l multi   .25   .25
972 A217 170 l multi   .25   .25
973 A217 220 l multi   .50   .50
974 A217 320 l multi   .75   .75
       Nos. 971-974 (4)   1.75 1.75

Disturbing Muses, by Giorgio de Chirico — A218

1979, Dec.
975	A218	40 l shown	.25	.25
976	A218	150 l Ancient horses	.25	.25
977	A218	170 l Self-portrait	.25	.25
		Nos. 975-977 (3)	.75	.75

Giorgio de Chirico, Italian surrealist painter.

St. Benedict, 15th Century Fresco — A219

Granite Paper
1980, Mar. 27   Photo.   Perf. 12x11½
978	A219	170 l multi	.25	.25

St. Benedict of Nursia, 1500th birth anniversary.

Fight Against Cigarette Smoking — A220

Designs: Sketches of smokers and cigarettes by Giuliana Consilivio.

1980, Mar. 27
979	A220	120 l multi	.25	.25
980	A220	220 l multi	.25	.25
981	A220	520 l multi	.75	.75
		Nos. 979-981 (3)	1.25	1.25

Naples, 17th Century Engraving A221

1980, Mar. 27   Perf. 14x13½
982	A221	170 l multi	.30	.30

20th Intl. Phil. Exhib., Europa '80, Naples, Apr. 26-May 4.

View of London, 1850 — A222

1980, May 8   Perf. 11½x12
983		200 l shown	.50	.50
984		400 l London, 1980	1.00	1.00
a.	A222	Pair, #983-984	1.60	1.60

London 1980 Intl. Stamp Exhib., May 6-14. Printed checkerwise.
See Nos. 1001-1002, 1032-1033, 1054-1055, 1069-1070, 1098-1099, 1110-1111, 1141-1142, 1339-1340.

A223

Europa: 170 l, Giovanbattista Belluzzi (1506-54), military architect. 220 l, Antonio Orafo (1460-1552), goldsmith and jeweler.

1980, May 8   Perf. 11½
985	A223	170 l multi	1.25	.60
986	A223	220 l multi	2.00	1.00

A224

Granite Paper
1980, July 7   Photo.   Perf. 11½
987	A224	70 l Bicycling	.25	.25
988	A224	90 l Basketball	.25	.25
989	A224	170 l Running	.25	.25
990	A224	350 l Gymnast	.50	.50
991	A224	450 l High jump	.75	.75
		Nos. 987-991 (5)	2.00	2.00

22nd Summer Olympic Games, Moscow, July 19-Aug. 3.

Ancient Fortifications A225   Weight Lifting A226

Photogravure and Engraved
1980, Sept. 18   Perf. 13½x14
992	A225	220 l multi	.35	.35

World Tourism Conf., Manila, Sept. 27.

1980, Sept. 18   Photo.   Perf. 14x13½
993	A226	170 l multi	.30	.30

European Junior Weight Lifting Championship, Sept.

Robert Stolz, "Philatelic Waltz" Score A227

Photo. & Engr.
1980, Sept. 18   Perf. 14
994	A227	120 l lt bl & blk	.30	.30

Robert Stolz (1880-1975) composer.

Madonna of the Harpies, by Andrea Del Sarto — A228

Annunciation by Del Sarto (Details): 250 l, Virgin Mary. 500 l Angel.

1980, Dec. 11   Perf. 13½
995	A228	180 l multi	.30	.30
996	A228	250 l multi	.45	.45
997	A228	500 l multi	1.00	1.00
		Nos. 995-997 (3)	1.75	1.75

Christmas; 450th death anniv. of Del Sarto.

St. Joseph's Eve Bonfire — A229

Europa Issue 1981
1981, Mar. 24   Photo.   Perf. 12
Granite Paper
998	A229	200 l shown	.85	.55
999	A229	300 l San Marino Day fireworks	1.90	.85

Intl. Year of the Disabled — A230

1981, May 15   Photo.   Perf. 11½
Granite Paper
1000	A230	300 l multi	.40	.40

Exhibition Type of 1980

St. Charles' Square, Vienna, by Jakob Alt, 1817.

1981, May 15
Granite Paper
1001	A222	200 l shown	.40	.40
1002	A222	300 l Vienna, 1981	.60	.60
a.		Pair, #1001-1002	1.00	1.00

WIPA '81 Intl. Phil. Exhib., Vienna, 5/22-31.

Woman Playing Flute — A232   Grand Prix Motorcycle Race — A233

Drawings based on Roman sculptures.

1981, July 10   Photo.   Perf. 11½
Granite Paper
1003	A232	300 l shown	.60	.60
1004	A232	550 l Soldier	.75	.75
1005	A232	1500 l Shepherd	2.00	2.00
a.		Souv. sheet of 3, #1003-1005	6.50	6.50

Virgil's death bimillennium. No. 1005a has continuous design.

1981, July 10   Litho.   Perf. 14x15
1006	A233	200 l multi	.30	.30

Natl. Urban Development Plan (Housing) — A234

1981, Sept. 22   Photo.
Granite Paper
1007	A234	20 l shown	.25	.25
1008	A234	80 l Parks	.25	.25
1009	A234	400 l Energy plants	.50	.50
		Nos. 1007-1009 (3)	1.00	1.00

European Junior Judo Championship, Oct. 30-Nov. 1 — A235

1981, Sept. 22   Photo.   Perf. 11½
Granite Paper
1010	A235	300 l multi	.40	.40

World Food Day — A236

1981, Oct. 23
Granite Paper
1011	A236	300 l multi	.50	.50

A237

Designs: 150 l, Child Holding a Dove, by Pablo Picasso (1881-1973). 200 l, Homage to Picasso, by Renato Guttuso.

1981, Oct. 23   Granite Paper
1012	A237	150 l multi	.25	.25
1013	A237	200 l multi	.50	.50

A238

Christmas; 500th Birth Anniv. of Benvenuto Tisi da Garofalo Adoration of the Kings and St. Bartholomew): 200 l, One of the Three Kings with Goblet, by Garafalo. 300 l, King with a Jar. 600 l, Virgin and Child.

Photo. & Engr.
1981, Dec. 15   Perf. 13½
1014	A238	200 l multi	.30	.30
1015	A238	300 l multi	.50	.50
1016	A238	600 l multi	1.00	1.00
		Nos. 1014-1016 (3)	1.80	1.80

Postal Stationery Centenary A239

1982, Feb. 19 **Photo.** *Perf. 12*
1017 A239 200 l multi   .30 .30

Savings Bank Centenary A240

1982, Feb. 19
1018 A240 300 l multi   .40 .40

Europa 1982 — A241

Designs: 300 l, Convocation of the Assembly of Heads of Families, 1906. 450 l, Napoleons's Treaty of Friendship offer, 1797.

1982, Apr. 21 **Photo.** *Perf. 11½*
Granite Paper
1019 A241 300 l multi   3.25 1.60
1020 A241 450 l multi   4.75 2.25

Archimedes A242   800th Birth Anniv. of St. Francis of Assisi A243

1982, Apr. 21 **Photo.** *Perf. 14x13½*
1021 A242 20 l shown   .25 .25
1022 A242 30 l Copernicus   .25 .25
1023 A242 40 l Newton   .25 .25
1024 A242 50 l Lavoisier   .25 .25
1025 A242 60 l Marie Curie   .25 .25
1026 A242 100 l Robert Koch   .25 .25
Litho. & Engr.
1027 A242 200 l Thomas Edison   .25 .25
1028 A242 300 l Guglielmo Marconi   .40 .40
1029 A242 450 l Hippocrates   .60 .60
Engr.
1030 A242 5000 l Galileo   6.50 6.50
   Nos. 1021-1030 (10)   9.25 9.25
   See Nos. 1041-1046.

1982, June 10 **Photo.**
1031 A243 200 l multi   .30 .30

Exhibition Type of 1980
1982, June 10
1032 A222 300 l Notre Dame, 1806   .50 .50
1033 A222 450 l 1982   .75 .75
   a.   Pair, #1032-1033   1.25 1.25
PHILEXFRANCE '82 Stamp Exhibition, Paris, June 11-21.

Visit of Pope John Paul II — A245

1982, Aug. 29 **Litho.** *Perf. 13½x14*
1034 A245 900 l multi   1.40 1.40

Natl. Flags of ASCAT Members — A246

Granite Paper
1982, Sept. 1 **Photo.** *Perf. 11½*
1035 A246 300 l multi   .40 .40
Inaugural Meeting of ASCAT (Assoc. of Editors of Philatelic Catalogues), 1977.

A247   A248

1982, Sept. 1 **Unwmk.**
1036 A247 700 l blk & red   .90 .90
15th Amnesty Intl. Congress, Rimini, Italy, Sept. 9-15.

Photo. & Engr.
1982, Dec. 15 *Perf. 13½*
Christmas: Paintings by Gregorio Sciltian (1900-85).
1037 A248 200 l Angel   .40 .40
1038 A248 300 l Virgin and Child   .55 .55
1039 A248 450 l Angel, diff.   .80 .80
   Nos. 1037-1039 (3)   1.75 1.75

Secondary School Centenary A249

1983, Feb. 24 **Photo.** *Perf. 13½x14*
1040 A249 300 l Begni Building   .45 .45

Scientist Type of 1982
1983, Apr. 21 *Perf. 14x13½*
1041 A242 150 l Alexander Fleming   .25 .25
1042 A242 250 l Alessandro Volta   .40 .40
1043 A242 350 l Evangelista Torricelli   .50 .50
1044 A242 400 l Carolus Linnaeus   .75 .75
1045 A242 1000 l Pythagoras   1.50 1.50
1046 A242 1400 l Leonardo da Vinci   2.00 2.00
   Nos. 1041-1046 (6)   5.40 5.40

3rd Formula One Grand Prix A250

1983, Apr. 20 **Photo.** *Perf. 14x13½*
1047 A250 50 l multi   .25 .25
1048 A250 350 l multi   .75 .75

Auguste Piccard — A251

1983, Apr. 20 *Perf. 12x11½*
Granite Paper
1049 A251 400 l Aerostat   2.50 1.50
1050 A251 500 l Bathyscaph   3.75 2.25
Europa. Piccard (1884-1962), Swiss scientist.

World Communications Year — A252

1983, Apr. 28 **Engr.** *Perf. 14x13*
1051 A252 400 l Ham radio operator   .70 .70
1052 A252 500 l Mailman   .85 .85

Manned Flight Bicentenary A253

Lithographed and Engraved
1983, May 22 *Perf. 13½x14*
1053 A253 500 l Montgolfiere, 1783 .65 .65

Exhibition Type of 1980
Designs: Botafogo Bay and Monte Corcovado, Rio de Janeiro.

1983, July 29 **Photo.** *Perf. 11½x12*
Granite Paper
1054 A222 400 l 1845   .50 .50
1055 A222 1400 l 1983   2.00 2.00
   a.   Pair, #1054-1055   2.75 2.75
BRASILIANA '83 Intl. Stamp Show, Rio de Janeiro, July 29-Aug. 7.

20th Anniv. of World Food Program A255

1983, Sept. 29 **Photo.** *Perf. 14x13½*
1056 A255 500 l multi   .70 .70

Christmas A256

Paintings, Raphael (1483-1520): 300 l, Our Lady of the Grand Duke. 400 l, Our Lady of the Goldfinch. 500 l, Our Lady of the Chair.

Photo. & Engr.
1983, Dec. 1 *Perf. 13½*
1057 A256 300 l multi   .45 .45
1058 A256 400 l multi   .65 .65
1059 A256 500 l multi   1.00 1.00
   a.   Strip of 3, #1057-1059   2.25 2.25

Olympic Type of 1959
IOC Presidents: 300 l, Demetrius Vikelas, 1894-96. 400 l, Lord Killanin. 550 l, Antonio Samaranch, 1984.

1984, Feb. 8 **Photo.** *Perf. 14x13½*
1060 A86 300 l multi   .60 .60
1061 A86 400 l multi   1.00 1.00
1062 A86 550 l multi   1.50 1.50
   Nos. 1060-1062 (3)   3.10 3.10

Flag-wavers Group, 2nd Anniv. — A257

Litho. & Engr.
1984, Apr. 27 *Perf. 13x14*
1063 A257 300 l Flag   .50 .50
1064 A257 400 l Flags   .75 .75

Europa (1959-1984) A258

1984, Apr. 27 **Photo.** *Perf. 11½*
Granite Paper
1065 A258 400 l multi   2.75 1.00
1066 A258 550 l multi   3.75 1.50

A259

1984, June 14 **Photo.** *Perf. 13½x14*
1067 A259 450 l multi   .70 .70
Motorcross Grand Prix, Baldasserona.

A260

Souvenir Sheet
1984, June 14   Litho.   Perf. 13x14
1068   Sheet of 2   3.25 3.25
  a. A260 550 l Man   1.00 1.00
  b. A260 1000 l Woman   2.00 2.00
    1984 Summer Olympics.

Exhibition Type of 1980
Ausipex '84: Views of Melbourne. Se-tenant.

1984, Sept. 21   Photo.   Perf. 11½
Granite Paper
1069 A222 1500 l 1839   2.25 2.25
1070 A222 2000 l 1984   2.75 2.75
  a. Pair, #1069-1070   5.00 5.00

Visit of
Italian Pres.
Pertini
A262

1984, Oct. 20   Photo.   Perf. 14x13½
1071 A262 1950 l multi   3.00 3.00

School and
Philately — A263

Sketches by Jacovitti.

1984, Oct. 30   Perf. 13½x14
1072 A263 50 l Universe   .25 .25
1073 A263 100 l Evolution   .25 .25
1074 A263 150 l Environment .25 .25
1075 A263 200 l Mankind   .25 .25
1076 A263 450 l Science   .60 .60
1077 A263 550 l Philosophy .70 .70
    Nos. 1072-1077 (6) 2.30 2.30

Christmas — A264

Details of Madonna of San Girolamo by Correggio, 1527.

1984, Dec. 5   Litho.   Perf. 13½x14
1078 400 l multi   .75 .75
1079 450 l multi   1.00 1.00
1080 550 l multi   1.25 1.25
  a. A264 Strip of 3, #1078-1080 3.00 3.00

Composers and
Music — A265

Europa: 450 l, Johann Sebastian Bach (1685-1750), Toccata and Fugue. 600 l, Vincenzo Bellini (1801-1835), Norma.

1985, Mar. 18   Photo.   Perf. 12
1081 A265 450 l ocher & gray blk 2.50 1.10
1082 A265 600 l yel grn & gray
               blk   3.50 1.40

Olympiad of the
Small States, May
23-26 — A266

Sportphilex '85: Natl. Olympic Committee and Sportphilex '85 emblems, flags of Andorra, Cyprus, Iceland, Liechtenstein, Luxembourg, Malta, Monaco, San Marino.

1985, May 16   Litho.   Perf. 13½x14
1083 A266 50 l Diving   .25 .25
1084 A266 350 l Running   .50 .50
1085 A266 400 l Rifle shooting .60 .60
1086 A266 450 l Cycling   .70 .70
1087 A266 600 l Basketball   .95 .95
    Nos. 1083-1087 (5) 3.00 3.00

Emigration
A267

1985, May 16
1088 A267 600 l Birds migrating 1.00 1.00

Intl. Youth
Year — A268

1985, June 24   Photo.   Perf. 12
Granite Paper
1089 A268 400 l Boy, dove   .50 .50
1090 A268 600 l Girl, dove, horse 1.00 1.00

Helsinki
Conference, 10th
Anniv. — A269

1985, June 24   Perf. 13½x14
1091 A269 600 l Sapling, sun-
           burst, clouds 1.00 1.00

City Hall, by
Renzo Bonelli,
Camera
Lens. — A270

1985, June 24   Perf. 13½x14½
1092 A270 450 l multi   .75 .75

Intl. Fed. of Photographic Art, 18th Congress.

World Angling
Championships,
Arno River,
Florence, Sept.
14-15 — A271

1985, Sept. 11   Photo.   Perf. 14½x15
1093 A271 600 l Hooked fish 1.00 1.00

Alessandro Manzoni (1785-1873),
Novelist & Poet — A272

19th century engravings from Manzoni's I Promessi Sposi (1825-27): 400 l, Don Abbondio encounters Don Rodrigo's henchmen. 450 l, The attempt to force the curate to perform a dubious marriage ceremony. 600 l, The Plague at Milan.

1985, Sept. 11   Engr.   Perf. 14x13½
1094 A272 400 l multi   .60 .60
1095 A272 450 l multi   .70 .70
1096 A272 600 l multi   1.00 1.00
    Nos. 1094-1096 (3) 2.30 2.30

Intl. Feline
Fed.
Congress
A273

Mosaic detail: Cat, Natl. Museum, Naples.

1985, Oct. 25   Photo.   Perf. 12
Granite Paper
1097 A273 600 l multi   1.00 1.00

Exhibition Type of 1980
ITALIA '85: Views of the Colosseum, Rome.

1985, Oct. 25   Perf. 11½x12
Granite Paper
1098 A222 1000 l multi   1.50 1.50
1099 A222 1500 l multi   2.50 2.50
  a. Pair, #1098-1099   4.50 4.50

Christmas
A275

Photo. & Engr.
1985, Dec. 3   Perf. 14
1100 A275 400 l Angel   1.00 1.00
1101 A275 450 l Mother and
               Child   1.50 1.50
1102 A275 600 l Angel, diff. 2.50 2.50
  a. Strip of 3, #1100-1102 6.00 6.00

Hospital,
Cailungo
A276

1986, Mar. 6   Photo.   Perf. 12x11½
1103 A276 450 l multi   .60 .60
1104 A276 650 l multi   .85 .85

Natl. social security org., ISS, 30th anniv., and World Health Day.

Halley's
Comet — A277

Designs: 550 l, Giotto space probe. 1000 l, Adoration of the Magi, by Giotto (1276-1337).

1986, Mar. 6   Perf. 11½x12
1105 A277 550 l multi   1.00 1.00
1106 A277 1000 l multi 1.50 1.50

Europa Issue 1986

Deer — A278

1986, May 22   Photo.   Perf. 13½x14
1107 A278 550 l shown 10.00 7.50
1108 A278 650 l Falcon 15.00 10.00

3rd Veterans
World Table
Tennis
Championships
A279

1986, May 22   Engr.
1109 A279 450 l multicolored .80 .80

AMERIPEX '86, Chicago, May 22-
June 1 — A280

Views of Old Water Tower, Chicago: 2000 l, Lithograph, 1870, by Charles Shober. 3000 l, Photograph, 1986.

Perf. 11½x12
1986, May 22   Photo.   Unwmk.
1110 2000 l multi   3.00 3.00
1111 3000 l multi   4.25 4.25
  a. A280 Pair, #1110-1111 7.50 7.50

Intl. Peace
Year — A281

1986, July 10   Photo.   Perf. 11½x12
1112 A281 550 l multi   .80 .80

Souvenir Sheet

Terra Cotta Statuary, Tomb of Emperor
Qin Shi Huang Di (259-210
B.C.) — A282

Litho. & Engr.

1986, July 10			Perf. 13½	
1113	Sheet of 3		6.50	6.50
a.	A282 550 l Bearded man		1.00	1.00
b.	A282 650 l Horse, horiz.		1.50	1.50
c.	A282 2000 l Bearded man, diff.		3.50	3.50

Normalization of diplomatic relations with
the People's Republic of China, 15th anniv.

UNICEF, 40th
Anniv. — A283

1986, Sept 16	Photo.		Perf. 12	
1114	A283 650 l multi		1.00	1.00

European Boccie
Championships
A284

1986, Sept 16			Perf. 14x15	
1115	A284 550 l multi		.80	.80

Choral Society,
25th
Anniv. — A285

Painting (detail): Apollo Dancing with the
Muses, by Giulio Romano (1492-1546).

1986, Sept 16				
1116	A285 450 l multi		.70	.70

Christmas
A286

Design: Oil on wood triptych, 15th cent., by
Hans Memling (1435-1494), Kunsthistorisches
Museum, Vienna.

Photo. & Engr.

1986, Nov. 26			Perf. 14	
1117	A286 450 l St. John the			
	Baptist		1.25	1.25
1118	A286 550 l Virgin and Child		1.75	1.75
1119	A286 650 l St. John the			
	Evangelist		2.00	2.00
a.	Strip of 3, #1117-1119		5.25	5.25

Europa Issue 1987

Our Lady of
Consolation
Church,
Borgomaggiore
A287

Church designed by Giovanni Michelucci,
architect: 600 l, Architect's sketch of interior.
700 l, Actual interior.

1987, Mar. 12	Photo.		Perf. 12	
1120	A287 600 l multi		8.50	5.00
1121	A287 700 l multi		13.00	6.50

Motoring
Events
A288

Designs: 500 l, 80th anniv., Peking-Paris
Race. 600 l, 15th San Marino Rally. 700 l,
Mille Miglia Race, 60th anniv.

1987, Mar. 12			Perf. 11½	
1122	A288 500 l multi		.70	.70
1123	A288 600 l multi		.85	.85
1124	A288 700 l multi		1.00	1.00
	Nos. 1122-1124 (3)		2.55	2.55

Sculptures,
Open-air
Museum
A289

Seventh Natl. Art
Biennale
A290

Perf. 14½x13½

1987, June 13			Photo.	
1125	A289	50 l Reffi		
		Busignani	.25	.25
1126	A289	100 l Bini	.25	.25
1127	A289	200 l Guguianu	.40	.40
1128	A289	300 l Berti	.50	.50
1129	A289	400 l Crocetti	.65	.65
1130	A289	500 l Berti, diff.	.80	.80
1131	A289	600 l Messina	1.00	1.00
1132	A289	1000 l Minguzzi	1.50	1.50
1133	A289	2200 l Greco	3.50	3.50
1134	A289	1000 l Sassu	17.00	17.00
	Nos. 1125-1134 (10)		25.85	25.85

1987, June 13			Perf. 11½	

Abstract works: 500 l, Dal Diario del Brasile-
foresta Vergine, by Emilio Vedova. 600 l,
Invenzione Cromatica con Brio, by Corrado
Cagli.

Granite Paper

1135	A290 500 l multi		.75	.75
1136	A290 600 l multi		.85	.85

Air Club of San Marino Ultra-
lightweight Aircraft — A291

1987, June 13		Granite Paper		
1137	A291 600 l multi		1.00	1.00

Mahatma
Gandhi
A292

1987, Aug. 2	Photo.		Perf. 14x13½	
1138	A292 500 l Gandhi Square,			
	bust		.85	.85

A293

1987, Aug. 29			Perf. 12	

Granite Paper

1139	A293 600 l Olympic em-			
	blem, athlete		1.10	1.10

OLYMPHILEX '87, Rome.

A294

1987, Aug. 29		Granite Paper		
1140	A294 700 l ultra, blk & red		1.10	1.10

First Representation of San Marino at the
Mediterranean Games, Syria, Sept. 11-15.

Exhibition Type of 1980

HAFNIA '87: Views of Copenhagen (1836-
1986), as seen from the Round Tower.

1987, Oct. 16	Photo.		Perf. 11½x12	

Granite Paper

1141	A222 1200 l multi		2.50	2.50
1142	A222 2200 l multi, diff.		4.00	4.00
a.	Pair, #1141-1142		6.75	6.75

Christmas
A296

Details from Triptych of Cortona and The
Annunciation, by Fra Angelico (c. 1400-1455),
Diocesan Museum of Cortona: No. 1143,
Angel. No. 1144, Madonna and child. No.
1145, Saint. Printed se-tenant.

Photo. & Engr.

1987, Nov. 12			Perf. 13½	
1143	A296 600 l multi		1.75	1.75
1144	A296 600 l multi		1.75	1.75
1145	A296 600 l multi		1.75	1.75
a.	Strip of 3, #1143-1145		5.50	5.50

High Speed
Train — A297

Europa Issue 1988
Granite Paper

1988, Mar. 17	Photo.		Perf. 12	
1146	A297 600 l shown		5.50	4.50
1147	A297 700 l Fiber optics		9.25	5.00

Promote
Stamp
Collecting
A298

Stamps, cancellations, covers: 50 l, Nos. 81,
B25 and 859. 150 l, No. C11. 300 l, Nos. 349
and 1006. 350 l, Nos. 944 and 1031. 1000 l,
Nos. 303, 1081 and 308.

1988, Mar. 17			Perf. 11½	

Granite Paper

1148	A298	50 l multi	.25	.25
1149	A298	150 l multi	.25	.25
1150	A298	300 l multi	.50	.50
1151	A298	350 l multi	.65	.65
1152	A298	1000 l multi	1.75	1.75
	Nos. 1148-1152 (5)		3.40	3.40

See Nos. 1179-1183, 1225-1229.

A299

Historic sites and distinguished professors:
550 l, Carlo Malagola. 650 l, Pietro Ellero.
1300 l, Giosue Carducci (1835-1907), professor of literary history, 1861-1904, and Nobel
Prize winner for literature, 1906. 1700 l, Giovanni Pascoli (1855-1912), lyric poet, Pascoli's
successor as professor at Bologna.

1988, May 7	Photo.		Perf. 13½x14	
1153	A299 550 l multi		.80	.80
1154	A299 650 l multi		1.00	1.00
1155	A299 1300 l multi		1.75	1.75
1156	A299 1700 l multi		2.50	2.50
	Nos. 1153-1156 (4)		6.05	6.05

Bologna University, 900th anniv.

A300

Posters from Fellini Films: 300 l, La Strada.
900 l, La Dolce Vita. 1200 l, Amarcord.

1988, July 8	Photo.		Perf. 13½x14	
1157	A300 300 l multi		.40	.40
1158	A300 900 l multi		1.25	1.25
1159	A300 1200 l multi		1.75	1.75
	Nos. 1157-1159 (3)		3.40	3.40

Federico Fellini, Italian film director and winner of the 1988 San Marino Prize.
See Nos. 1187-1189, 1202-1204.

Mt. Titano
and Sand
Dunes of
the Adriatic
Coast
A301

1988, July 8			Perf. 14x13½	
1160	A301 750 l multi		1.10	1.10

40th Stamp Fair, Riccione.

Souvenir Sheet

1988 Summer Olympics,
Seoul — A302

1988, Sept. 19 Photo.   Perf. 13½x14

1161	A302	Sheet of 3		4.25	4.25
a.		650 l	Running	1.00	1.00
b.		750 l	Hurdles	1.10	1.10
c.		1300 l	Gymnastics	1.90	1.90

Intl. AIDS
Congress,
San
Marino,
Oct. 10-14
A303

1988, Sept. 19   Perf. 14x13½

1162	A303	250 l	shown	.55	.55
1163	A303	350 l	"AIDS"	.70	.70
1164	A303	650 l	Virus, knot	1.25	1.25
1165	A303	1000 l	Newspaper	2.00	2.00
		Nos. 1162-1165 (4)		4.50	4.50

Kurhaus Scheveningen, The
Hague — A304

1988, Oct. 18   Photo.   Perf. 11½x12
Granite Paper

1166	1600 l	Lithograph, c. 1885		2.00	2.00
1167	3000 l	1988		4.00	4.00
a.	A304	Pair, #1166-1167		6.25	6.25

FILACEPT '88, Holland.
See Nos. 1190-1191.

Christmas — A305

Paintings by Melozzo da Forli (1438-1494):
No. 1168, Angel with Violin, Vatican Art Gallery. No. 1169, Angel of the Annunciation, Uffizi Gallery, Florence. No. 1170, Angel with Lute, Vatican Art Gallery.

1988, Dec. 9   Photo.   Perf. 13½
Size of No. 1169: 21x40mm

1168	650 l	multi	1.75	1.75
1169	650 l	multi	1.75	1.75
1170	650 l	multi	1.75	1.75
a.	A305	Strip of 3, #1168-1168	5.50	5.50

Europa Issue 1989
Souvenir Sheet

Children's Games — A306

1989, Mar. 31   Photo.   Perf. 13½x14

1171		Sheet of 2		32.50	30.00
a.	A306	650 l	Sledding	12.50	11.00
b.	A306	750 l	Hopscotch	12.50	11.00

Nature Conservation — A307

Illustrations by contest-winning youth: 200 l, Federica Sparagna. 500 l, Giovanni Monteduro. 650 l, Rosa Mannarino.

1989, Mar. 31   Perf. 14x13½

1172	A307	200 l	multi	.35	.35
1173	A307	500 l	multi	.75	.75
1174	A307	650 l	multi	1.00	1.00
		Nos. 1172-1174 (3)	2.10	2.10

Sporting Anniversaries and
Events — A308

1989, May 13   Photo.   Perf. 12
Granite Paper

1175	A308	650 l	Olympics	.85	.85
1176	A308	750 l	Soccer	.95	.95
1177	A308	850 l	Tennis	1.10	1.10
1178	A308	1300 l	Car racing	1.60	1.60
		Nos. 1175-1178 (4)		4.50	4.50

Natl. Olympic Committee, 30th anniv. (650 l); admission of San Marino Soccer Federation to the UEFA and FIFA (750 l); San Marino '89, the tennis grand prix (850 l); Grand Prix of San Marino, Imola (1300 l).

Stamp Collecting Type of 1988

Covers and canceled stamps (postal history): 100 l, No. 916a with Iserravalle cancel, Sept. 1, 1977. 200 l, No. 1151 with Montegiardino cancel, May 3, 1986. 400 l, Italy No. 47 canceled on San Marino parcel card #422, 1895. 500 l, Type SP3 essay proposed by Martin Riester di Parigi, March 1865. 1000 l, Stampless cover, 1862.

1989, May 13   Perf. 12
Granite Paper

1179	A298	100 l	multi	.35	.35
1180	A298	200 l	multi	.45	.45
1181	A298	400 l	multi	.90	.90
1182	A298	650 l	multi	1.10	1.10
1183	A298	1000 l	multi	2.25	2.25
		Nos. 1179-1183 (5)	5.05	5.05

French
Revolution,
Bicent. — A309

1989, July 7   Litho.   Perf. 12½x13

1184	A309	700 l	The Tennis Court Oath	1.25	1.25
1185	A309	1000 l	Arrest of Louis XVI	1.75	1.75
1186	A309	1800 l	Napoleon	2.75	2.75
		Nos. 1184-1186 (3)		5.75	5.75

Show Business Type of 1988

Scenes from: 1200 l, Marguerite et Armand. 1500 l, Apollon Musagete. 1700 l, Valentino.

1989, Sept. 18 Photo.   Perf. 13½x14

1187	A300	1200 l	multi	2.00	2.00
1188	A300	1500 l	multi	2.50	2.50
1189	A300	1700 l	multi	3.00	3.00
		Nos. 1187-1189 (3)		7.50	7.50

Rudolf Nureyev, Russian ballet dancer and winner of the 1989 San Marino Prize.

Exhibition Type of 1988

Views of The Capitol, Washington, DC.: 2000 l, In 1850. 2500 l, In 1989.

1989, Nov. 17   Photo.   Perf. 11½
Granite Paper

1190	A304	2000 l	multi	3.00	3.00
1191	A304	2500 l	multi	4.00	4.00
a.		Pair, #1190-1191	7.25	7.25

World Stamp Expo '89.

A310

Christmas: Panels from a Polyptych, c. 1540, by Coda Studio of Rimini, in the Church of the Servants of Mary, Valdragone.

Size of No. 1193: 50x40mm

1989, Nov. 17   Granite Paper

1192		650 l	Angel	1.25	1.25
1193		650 l	Holy family	1.25	1.25
1194		650 l	Praying Madonna	1.25	1.25
a.	A310	Strip of 3, #1192-1194	4.00	4.00

A311

Europa: Post offices.

1990, Feb. 22   Photo.   Perf. 13½x14

1195	A311	700 l	Palazzeto delle Poste, 1842	1.50	1.10
1196	A311	800 l	Dogana	2.00	1.40

A312   A313

Design: The Martyrdom of Saint Agatha, by Giambattista Tiepolo, and occupation force departing by the Porta del Loco.

1990, Feb. 22   Perf. 12
Granite Paper

1197	A312	3500 l	multicolored	5.00	5.00

Liberation from Cardinal Alberoni's occupation force, 250th anniv.

1990, Mar. 23   Photo.   Perf. 11½x12
Granite Paper

European Tourism Year: No. 1198, The republic pinpointed on a map of Italy. No. 1199, San Marino atop Mt. Titano in proximity

to other cities in the region. No. 1200, Rocca Guaita, San Marino.

1198	A313	600 l	shown	1.00	1.00
1199	A313	600 l	multicolored	1.00	1.00
1200	A313	600 l	multicolored	1.00	1.00
		Nos. 1198-1200 (3)	3.00	3.00

See Nos. 1209a, 1260-1262.

Souvenir Sheet

1990 World Cup Soccer
Championships, Italy — A314

Various athletes: a, Germany. b, Italy. c, Great Britain. d, Uruguay. e, Brazil. f, Argentina.

1990, Mar. 23   Perf. 13½x14

1201	A314	Sheet of 6	6.25	6.25
a.-f.		700 l any single	1.00	1.00

Show Business Type of 1988

Scenes from: 600 l, Hamlet. 700 l, Richard III. 1500 l, Marathon Man.

1990, May 3   Photo.   Perf. 13½x14

1202	A300	600 l	multi	1.00	1.00
1203	A300	700 l	multi	1.25	1.25
1204	A300	1500 l	multi	2.75	2.75
		Nos. 1202-1204 (3)		5.00	5.00

Sir Laurence Olivier (1907-1989), British actor, winner of the 1990 San Marino Prize. Name misspelled "Lawrence" on the stamps.

President
of Italy,
State Visit
A315

1990, June 11 Litho.   Perf. 13x12½

1205	A315	600 l	multicolored	.90	.90

Statue of Saint
Marinus — A316

#1207, Liberty statue. #1208, Government Palace. #1209, Flag of San Marino.

1990, June 11   Photo.   Perf. 11½
Granite Paper
Booklet Stamps

1206	A316	50 l	multicolored	.40	.40
1207	A316	50 l	multicolored	.40	.40
1208	A316	50 l	multicolored	.40	.40
1209	A316	50 l	multicolored	.40	.40
a.		Bklt. pane of 7, #1198-1200, perf. 11½ vert., #1206-1209		5.25	
		Nos. 1206-1209 (4)		1.60	1.60

See Nos. 1256-1259.

Discovery
of America,
500th
Anniv. (in
1992)
A317

1990, Sept. 6   Litho.   Perf. 13x12½

1210	A317	1500 l	Artifacts, map	2.25	2.25
1211	A317	2000 l	Native plants, map	3.00	3.00

See Nos. 1230-1231.

Pinocchio, by
Carlo Collodi
(1826-1890)
A318

Flora and Fauna
A319

Cartoon style drawings from Pinocchio.

1990, Sept. 6   Photo.   Perf. 11½x12
Granite Paper
1212	A318	250 l	shown	.40	.40
1213	A318	400 l	Geppetto	.60	.60
1214	A318	450 l	Blue fairy	.70	.70
1215	A318	600 l	Cat & wolf	1.50	1.50
		Nos. 1212-1215 (4)		3.20	3.20

1990, Oct. 31   Photo.   Perf. 14x13½
Designs: 200 l, Papilio machaon, Ephedra major. 300 l, Apoderus coryli, Corylus avellana. 500 l, Eliomys quercinus, Quercus ilex. 1000 l, Lacerta viridis, Ophrys bertolonii. 2000 l, Regulus ignicapillus, Pinus nigra.

1216	A319	200 l	multicolored	.25	.25
1217	A319	300 l	multicolored	.40	.40
1218	A319	500 l	multicolored	.75	.75
1219	A319	1000 l	multicolored	1.50	1.50
1220	A319	2000 l	multicolored	2.75	2.75
		Nos. 1216-1220 (5)		5.65	5.65

A320

Christmas: Cuciniello Crib, San Martino Museum of Naples.

1990, Oct. 31   Perf. 11½
Granite Paper
1221	A320	750 l	shown	1.50	1.50
1222	A320	750 l	Nativity, diff.	1.50	1.50
a.		Pair, #1221-1222		3.25	3.25

A321

1991, Feb. 12   Photo.   Perf. 13½x14
1223	A321	750 l	Ariane 4 rocket	5.00	5.00
1224	A321	800 l	ERS-1 satellite	5.00	5.00
		Europa.			

Stamp Collecting Type of 1988
Areas of philately: 100 l, Stamp store. 150 l, Clubs. 200 l, Exhibitions. 450 l, Albums, catalogues. 1500 l, Magazines, books.

1991, Feb. 12   Perf. 12
Granite Paper
1225	A298	100 l	multicolored	.25	.25
1226	A298	150 l	multicolored	.25	.25
1227	A298	200 l	multicolored	.35	.35
1228	A298	450 l	multicolored	1.00	1.00
1229	A298	1500 l	multicolored	2.50	2.50
		Nos. 1225-1229 (5)		4.35	4.35

Italian Philatelic Press Union, 25th anniv. (No. 1229).

Discovery of America Type

1991, Mar. 22   Litho.   Perf. 13x12½
1230	A317	750 l	Map, instruments	1.10	1.10
1231	A317	3000 l	Columbus' fleet	4.00	4.00

1992
Summer
Olympics,
Barcelona
A323

Olympic torch relay.

1991, Mar. 22   Perf. 15x14
1232	A323	400 l	Athens	.75	.75
1233	A323	600 l	San Marino	1.00	1.00
1234	A323	2000 l	Barcelona	3.00	3.00
		Nos. 1232-1234 (3)		4.75	4.75

Basketball,
Cent. — A324

Fauna — A325

Designs: 750 l, James Naismith (1861-1939), creator of basketball, players.

1991, June 4   Photo.   Perf. 13½x14
1235	A324	650 l	multicolored	1.00	1.00
1236	A324	750 l	multicolored	1.25	1.25

1991, June 4   Perf. 14x13½
1237	A325	500 l	House cat	.75	.75
1238	A325	550 l	Hamster on wheel	.80	.80
1239	A325	750 l	Great Dane, poodle	1.10	1.10
1240	A325	1000 l	Tropical fish	1.50	1.50
1241	A325	1200 l	Birds in cage	1.75	1.75
		Nos. 1237-1241 (5)		5.90	5.90
		Children's Day.			

See Nos. 1251-1255.

James Clerk Maxwell (1831-1879),
Physicist — A326

1991, Sept. 24   Photo.   Perf. 14x13½
1242	A326	750 l	multicolored	1.10	1.10
		Radio, cent. (in 1995).			

See Nos. 1263, 1279, 1300.

Souvenir Sheet

Birth of New Europe — A327

Designs: No. 1243a, Dove, broken chains, Brandenburg Gate. b, Pres. Gorbachev, rainbow, Pres. Bush. c, Flower, broken barbed wire, map.

1991, Sept. 24   Litho.
1243	A327	1500 l	Sheet of 3, #a.-c.	7.00	7.00

La Rocca
fortress — A328

Christmas: Diff. winter views of 10th cent.

1991, Nov. 13   Litho.   Perf. 14½
1244	A328	600 l	multicolored	.90	.90
1245	A328	750 l	multicolored	1.10	1.10
1246	A328	1200 l	multicolored	1.75	1.75
		Nos. 1244-1246 (3)		3.75	3.75

No. 1246 is airmail.

Gioacchino Rossini (1792-1868),
Composer — A329

Designs: 750 l, Bianca e Falliero, Rossini opera festival 1989. 1200 l, The Barber of Seville, La Scala 1982-83.

1992, Feb. 3   Photo.   Perf. 14x13½
1247	A329	750 l	multicolored	1.25	1.25
1248	A329	1200 l	multicolored	1.75	1.75

Discovery
of America,
500th
Anniv.
A330

Designs: 1500 l, Columbus, ships at anchor, natives. 2000 l, Map of voyages.

1992, Feb. 3   Litho.   Perf. 12
1249	A330	1500 l	multicolored	2.10	2.10
1250	A330	2000 l	multicolored	2.75	2.75

Fauna Type of 1991

Flora.

1992, Mar. 26   Litho.   Perf. 13½
1251	A325	50 l	Roses	.25	.25
1252	A325	200 l	House plant	.30	.30
1253	A325	300 l	Orchids	.50	.50
1254	A325	450 l	Cacti	.75	.75
1255	A325	5000 l	Geraniums	6.50	6.50
		Nos. 1251-1255 (5)		8.30	8.30

Tourism Types of 1990
Designs: No. 1256, Crossbowman. No. 1257, Tennis player. No. 1258, Motorcyclist. No. 1259, Race car. No. 1260, Couple in moonlight. No. 1261, Man in restaurant. No. 1262, Woman reading beneath umbrella.

1992, Mar. 26   Perf. 14½x13½
Booklet Stamps
1256	A316	50 l	multicolored	.25	.25
1257	A316	50 l	multicolored	.25	.25
1258	A316	50 l	multicolored	.25	.25
1259	A316	50 l	multicolored	.25	.25

Perf. 13½ Vert.
1260	A313	600 l	multicolored	1.10	1.10
1261	A313	600 l	multicolored	1.10	1.10
1262	A313	600 l	multicolored	1.10	1.10
a.		Bklt. pane of 7, #1256-1262+label		4.50	

Physicist Type of 1991
Design: Heinrich Rudolf Hertz (1857-94).

1992, Mar. 26   Photo.   Perf. 14x13½
1263	A326	750 l	multicolored	1.10	1.10
		Radio, cent. (in 1995).			

Discovery of
America, 500th
Anniv. — A331

1992, May 22   Photo.   Perf. 12x11½
Granite Paper
1264	A331	750 l	Globe, ship at sea	2.10	2.10
1265	A331	850 l	Ship in egg	2.40	2.40
		Europa.			

Souvenir Sheet

1992 Summer Olympics,
Barcelona — A332

a, Soccer. b, Shooting. c, Swimming. d, Running.

1992, May 22   Litho.   Perf. 14
1266	A332	1250 l	Sheet of 4, #a.-d.	8.00	8.00

Mushrooms — A333

Designs: Nos. 1267, Poisonous mushrooms. No. 1268a, Edible mushrooms in bowl. No. 1268b, Edible mushrooms on table.

1992, Sept. 18   Photo.   Perf. 11½x12
Granite Paper
1267	A333	Pair		1.25	1.25
a.-b.		250 l any single		.55	.55
1268	A333	Pair		1.50	1.50
a.-b.		350 l any single		.70	.70

Admission to the UN — A334

Designs: a, Arms of San Marino, buildings. b, UN emblem, buildings.

1992, Sept. 18   Litho.   Perf. 12x12½
1269	A334	Pair		2.75	2.75
a.-b.		1000 l any single		1.25	1.25

The Sacred Conversation, by Piero della Francesca (1420-1492)
A335

Christmas: a, Entire painting. b, Detail of faces. c, Detail of dome.

1992, Nov. 16   Litho.   Perf. 14½
1270   Triptych   4.75   4.75
  a.-c.   A335 750 l any single   1.50   1.50

Contemporary Art — A336

Paintings: 750 l, Stars, by Nicola de Maria. 850 l, Abstract face, by Mimmo Paladino.

1993, Jan. 29   Litho.   Perf. 11½
1271   A336   750 l multicolored   .95   .95
1272   A336   850 l multicolored   1.10   1.10

Europa.

1993 Sporting Events — A337

1993, Jan. 29   Perf. 13½x14
1273   A337   300 l Tennis   .40   .40
1274   A337   400 l Cross-country skiing   .50   .50
1275   A337   550 l Women running   .70   .70
1276   A337   600 l Fisherman   .90   .90
1277   A337   700 l Men running   .90   .90
1278   A337   1300 l Sailboat, runners   1.75   1.75
  Nos. 1273-1278 (6)   5.15   5.15

No. 1273, Youth Games. No. 1274-1275, European Youth Olympic Days. No. 1276, World Championships for Freshwater Angling Clubs, Ostellato, Italy. No. 1277, Games of Small European Countries, Malta. No. 1278, Mediterranean Games, Roussillon, France.

Physicists Type of 1991

Design: 750 l, Edouard Branly (1844-1940).

1993, Mar. 26   Photo.   Perf. 14x13½
1279   A326   750 l multicolored   1.10   1.10

Radio, cent. (in 1995).

Souvenir Sheet

Inauguration of State Television — A338

Designs: a, 100-meter finals, World Track Championships, Tokyo, 1991. b, San Marino. c, Neil Armstrong on moon, 1969.

1993, Mar. 26   Litho.   Perf. 13½
1280   Sheet of 3   7.75   7.75
  a.-c.   A338 2000 l any single   2.50   2.50

Soaking may affect the hologram on #1280b.

Butterflies
A339

1993, May 26   Litho.   Perf. 14x15
1281   A339   250 l Iphiclides podalirius   .85   .85
1282   A339   250 l Colias crocea   .85   .85
1283   A339   250 l Nymphalis antiopa   .85   .85
1284   A339   250 l Melitaea cinxia   .85   .85
  a.   Block or strip of 4, #1281-1284   4.25   4.25

World Wildlife Fund.

Miniature Sheet

United Europe — A340

Village of Europe: No. 1285a, Denmark. b, England. c, Ireland. d, Luxembourg. e, Germany. f, Netherlands. g, Belgium. h, Portugal. i, Italy. j, Spain. k, France. l, Greece.

1993, May 26   Perf. 13½x14
1285   A340   750 l Sheet of 12   12.50   12.50
  a.   Any single, #a.-l.   1.00   1.00

Famous Men
A341

Designs: 550 l, Carlo Goldoni (1707-93), playwright, vert. 650 l, Horace (65-8 BC), poet and satrist, vert. 850 l, Claudio Monteverdi (1567-1643), composer. 1850 l, Guy de Maupassant (1850-93), writer.

1993, Sept. 17   Litho.   Perf. 13½x14
1286   A341   550 l multicolored   .70   .70
1287   A341   650 l multicolored   .85   .85
1288   A341   850 l multicolored   1.10   1.10
1289   A341   1850 l multicolored   2.40   2.40
  Nos. 1286-1289 (4)   5.05   5.05

Christmas
A342

Designs: 600 l, San Marino in winter, vert. Paintings by Gerard van Honthorst: 750 l, Adoration of the Child. 850 l, Adoration of the Shepherds, vert.

1993, Nov. 12   Litho.   Perf. 14½
1290   A342   600 l multicolored   .90   .90
1291   A342   750 l multicolored   1.10   1.10
1292   A342   850 l multicolored   1.25   1.25
  Nos. 1290-1292 (3)   3.25   3.25

10th Intl. Dog Show
A343

Designs: 350 l, Dachshund. 400 l, Afghan hound. 450 l, Belgian tervueren shepherd dog.

500 l, Boston terrier. 550 l, Mastiff. 600 l, Alaskan malamute.

1994, Jan. 31   Litho.   Perf. 15x14
1293   A343   350 l multicolored   .45   .45
1294   A343   400 l multicolored   .50   .50
1295   A343   450 l multicolored   .60   .60
1296   A343   500 l multicolored   .65   .65
1297   A343   550 l multicolored   .70   .70
1298   A343   600 l multicolored   .75   .75
  Nos. 1293-1298 (6)   3.65   3.65

Souvenir Sheet

1994 Winter Olympics, Lillehammer — A344

a, 90-meter ski jump. b, Downhill skiing. c, Giant slalom skiing. d, Pairs figure skating.

1994, Jan. 31   Perf. 13½
1299   A344   750 l 2 each #a.-d.   7.50   7.50

Physicists Type of 1991

Aleksandr Stepanovich Popov (1859-1905).

1994, Mar. 11   Photo.   Perf. 14x13½
1300   A326   750 l multicolored   1.10   1.10

Radio cent. (in 1995).

Gardens — A345

1994, Mar. 11   Litho.   Perf. 13
1301   A345   100 l Gate   .25   .25
1302   A345   200 l Grape arbor   .25   .25
1303   A345   300 l Well   .40   .40
1304   A345   450 l Gazebo   .60   .60
1305   A345   1850 l Pond   2.40   2.40
  Nos. 1301-1305 (5)   3.90   3.90

Intl. Olympic Committee, Cent. A346

1994, Mar. 11   Photo.   Perf. 14x13½
1306   A346   600 l multicolored   1.25   1.25

A347

Various soccer plays: a, Two players, one with #8 on shirt. b, Player in blue shirt kicking ball upward. c, Player heading ball. d, Players, one with #6 on shirt. e, Goal keeper.

1994, May 23   Litho.   Perf. 14
1307   A347   600 l Strip of 5, #a.-e.   3.75   3.75

1994 World Cup Soccer Championships, US. No. 1307 has a continuous design.

Europa (Ulysses spacecraft and: 750 l, Flight path around Sun and Jupiter. 850 l, Sun.

1994, May 23
1308   A348   750 l multicolored   .95   .95
1309   A348   850 l multicolored   1.10   1.10

Inauguration of Government Building, Cent. — A349

Designs: 150 l, Exterior in shade, vert. 600 l, Exterior in sunshine, vert. 650 l, Clock tower. 1000 l, Interior.

Perf. 13½x13, 13x13½
1994, Sept. 30   Litho.
1310   A349   150 l multicolored   .25   .25
1311   A349   600 l multicolored   .75   .75
1312   A349   650 l multicolored   .85   .85
1313   A349   1000 l multicolored   1.25   1.25
  Nos. 1310-1313 (4)   3.10   3.10

Dedication of St. Mark's Basilica, 900th Anniv. A350

1994, Oct. 8   Photo.   Perf. 13½x13
1314   A350   750 l multicolored   3.50   3.50
  a.   Souvenir sheet of 2, tete beche   4.50   4.50

No. 1314 printed with se-tenant label. No. 1314a contains No. 1314 and Italy No. 2003. Only No. 1314 was valid for postage in San Marino.

Touring Club of Italy, Cent. — A351

Vehicles traveling on road in middle of flower field: a, Traffic cop, bus. b, Tandem tanker truck. c, Sailboat, volcano. d, Truck loaded with animals, camper, fish in lake.

1994, Nov. 18   Litho.   Perf. 14x13½
1315   Block of 4   5.25   5.25
  a.-d.   A351 1000 l any single   1.25   1.25

No. 1315 is a continuous design.

A352

The Enthroned Madonna and Child with Saints, by Giovanni Santi (1440-1494) (Christmas): 600 l, Drummer, piper. 750 l, Madonna and Child. 850 l, Piper, harpist.

1994, Nov. 18   **Perf. 14x15**
1316 A352 600 l multicolored   .75 .75
1317 A352 750 l multicolored   .95 .95
1318 A352 850 l multicolored   1.10 1.10
    Nos. 1316-1318 (3)   2.80 2.80

A353

Sporting Events of 1995: 1319, Junior World Cycling Championships, Forli, San Marino. 1320, Volleyball, cent. 1321, Men's Speed Skating World Championships, Baselga di Pine, Italy. 1322, World Track & Field Championships, Goteborg, Sweden.

1995, Feb. 10   **Photo.**   **Perf. 13x14**
1319 A353 100 l Cycling   .25 .25
1320 A353 500 l Volleyball   .65 .65
1321 A353 650 l Speed skater   .85 .85
1322 A353 850 l Runner   1.10 1.10
    Nos. 1319-1322 (4)   2.85 2.85

European Nature Conservation Year — A354

Nature scenes with flowers, water: a, Snails, dragonfly, fish. b, Frog, snake. c, Ladybugs, butterfly. d, Ducklings, frog. e, Ducks, snail.

1995, Feb. 10
1323 A354 600 l Strip of 5, #a.-e. 4.50 4.50

    No. 1323 is a continuous design.

UN, 50th Anniv. — A355

Designs: 550 l, UN emblem surrounded by people. 600 l, Emblem in center of rose. 650 l, Hourglass shaped from halves of globe. 1200 l, "50," Emblem, rainbow.

1995, Mar. 24   **Litho.**   **Perf. 14x15**
1324 A355 550 l multicolored   .70 .70
1325 A355 600 l multicolored   .75 .75
1326 A355 650 l multicolored   .85 .85
1327 A355 1200 l multicolored   1.50 1.50
    Nos. 1324-1327 (4)   3.80 3.80

Peace & Freedom A356

1995, Mar. 24   **Perf. 15x14**
1328 A356 750 l shown   .95 .95
1329 A356 850 l Sheep, meadow 1.10 1.10
    Europa.

World Tourism Organization, 20th Anniv. — A357

Designs: 750 l, Mt. Titano encircled by five colored lines symbolizing continents. 850 l, Airplane over globe. 1200 l, Five lines encircling earth.

1995, May 5   **Litho.**   **Perf. 15x14**
1330 A357 600 l multicolored   .75 .75
1331 A357 750 l multicolored   .95 .95
1332 A357 850 l multicolored   1.10 1.10
1333 A357 1200 l multicolored   1.50 1.50
    Nos. 1330-1333 (4)   4.30 4.30

Santa Croce Basilica, Florence, 700th Anniv. A358

1200 l, Detail from fresco, The Legend of the True Cross, by Agnolo Gaddi, facade of the basilica. 1250 l, Painting, The Madonna and Child with Saints, by Andrea della Robbia, Santa Croce Cloister, Pazzi Chapel.

1995, May 5
1334 A358 1200 l multicolored   1.50 1.50
1335 A358 1250 l multicolored   1.60 1.60

Radio, Cent. — A359

Designs: No. 1336, Stations on radio dial. No. 1337, Guglielmo Marconi (1874-1937), transmitting equipment.

1995, June 8   **Litho.**   **Perf. 14**
1336   850 l multicolored   1.25 1.25
1337   850 l multicolored   1.25 1.25
    a. A359 Pair, #1336-1337   2.75 2.75

    Printed in sheets of 10 stamps.
    See Germany #1900, Ireland #973-974, Italy #2038-2039, Vatican City #978-979.

Miniature Sheet

Motion Picture, Cent. — A360

Different frames from films:
The General: a, 1. b, 2. c, 3. d, 4.
Il Gattopardo: e, 1. f, 2. g, 3. h, 4.
Allegro Non Troppo: i, 1. j, 2. k, 3. l, 4.
Braveheart: m, 1. n, 2. o, 3. p, 4.

1995, Sept. 14   **Litho.**   **Perf. 15x14**
1338   Sheet of 16   6.00 6.00
    a.-p. A360 250 l any single   .35 .35

Exhibition Type of 1980

Qianmen complex of Zhengyangmen Rostrum, Embrasured Watchtower, Beijing: No. 1339, In 1914. No. 1340, In 1995.

1995, Sept. 14   **Perf. 14**
1339 A222 1500 l multicolored   1.90 1.90
1340 A222 1500 l multicolored   1.90 1.90
    a. Pair, #1339-1340   4.00 4.00

    Beijing '95.

Neri of Rimini, 14th Cent. Artist — A361

Designs: 650 l, The Annunciation.

1995, Nov. 6   **Litho.**   **Perf. 14x15**
1341 A361 650 l multicolored   1.10 1.10

Christmas — A362

Designs: a, Santa, sleigh, reindeer. b, Children, Christmas tree. c, Nativity, star.

1995, Nov. 6   **Litho.**   **Perf. 14x15**
1342 A362   Strip of 3   4.00 4.00
    a.-c.   750 l any single   1.25 1.25

    No. 1342 is a continuous design.

Express Mail Service A363

1995, Nov. 6   **Perf. 15x14**
1343 A363 6000 l multicolored   7.50 7.50

A364

1996, Feb. 12   **Litho.**   **Perf. 14x15**
1344 A364 100 l Discus   .25 .25
1345 A364 500 l Wrestling   .65 .65
1346 A364 650 l Athletics   .85 .85
1347 A364 1500 l Javelin   2.25 2.25
1348 A364 2500 l Running   3.50 3.50
    Nos. 1344-1348 (5)   7.50 7.50

    1996 Summer Olympics, Atlanta.

A365

Portrait of Mother Teresa of Calcutta, by Gina Lollobrigida.

Granite Paper

1996, Mar. 22   **Photo.**   **Perf. 12**
1349 A365 750 l multicolored   1.75 1.75

    Europa.

China '96 Philatelic Exhibition, Beijing A366

1996, Mar. 22   **Perf. 14x13½**
1350 A366 1250 l multicolored   2.25 2.25

    Marco Polo's return from China, 700th anniv. (in 1995).
    See Italy No. 2070.

Nature World Exhibition A367

Photographs of wildlife: 50 l, Dolphin. 100 l, Frog. 150 l, Penguins. 1000 l, Butterfly. 3000 l, Ducks.

1996, Mar. 22   **Perf. 12**
        Granite Paper
1351 A367 50 l multicolored   .25 .25
1352 A367 100 l multicolored   .25 .25
1353 A367 150 l multicolored   .25 .25
1354 A367 1000 l multicolored   1.50 1.50
1355 A367 3000 l multicolored   4.00 4.00
    Nos. 1351-1355 (5)   6.25 6.25

China-San Marino Relations, 25th Anniv. A368

#1356, Great Wall of China. #1357, Wall surrounding Mount Titano, San Marino.

1996, May 6   **Litho.**   **Perf. 12**
1356 A368 750 l multicolored   1.10 1.10
1357 A368 750 l multicolored   1.10 1.10
    a.   Pair, Nos. 1356-1357   2.25 2.25
    b.   Souvenir sheet, No. 1357a   2.50 2.50

    No. 1357a is a continuous design.
    See People's Republic of China Nos. 2675-2676.

Medieval Days Celebration A369

Festival activities: No. 1358, Woman weaving yarn, vert. No. 1359, Potter, vert. No. 1360, Woman making brushes, vert. No. 1361, Man playing checkers, vert. No. 1362, Group blowing trumpets. No. 1363, Group holding banners. No. 1364, Men seated with crossbows. No. 1365, Street performers.

Perf. 14 on 2 Sides

1996, May 6   **Litho. & Photo.**
       Booklet Stamps
1358 A369 750 l multicolored   1.10 1.10
1359 A369 750 l multicolored   1.10 1.10
1360 A369 750 l multicolored   1.10 1.10
1361 A369 750 l multicolored   1.10 1.10
1362 A369 750 l multicolored   1.10 1.10
1363 A369 750 l multicolored   1.10 1.10
1364 A369 750 l multicolored   1.10 1.10
1365 A369 750 l multicolored   1.10 1.10
    a.   Booklet pane, #1358-1365   9.00
       Complete booklet, #1365a   9.00

Festival Bar A370

History of
Italian
Songs
A371

Singer, allegory of song: a, Enrico Caruso, "O Sole Mio." b, Armando Gill, "Come Pioveva." c, Ettore Petrolini, "Gastone." d, Vittorio de Sica, "Parlami D'Amore Mariu." e, Odoardo Spadaro, "La Porti un Bacione a Firenze." f, Alberto Rabagliati, "O Mia Bela Madonina." g, Beniamino Gigli, "Mamma." h, Claudio Villa, "Luna Rossa." i, Secondo Casadei, "Romagna Mia." j, Renato Rascel, "Arrivederci Roma." k, Fred Buscaglione, "Guarda Che Luna." l, Domenico Modugno, "Nel Blu Dipinto di Blu."

1996, May 25   Litho.   Perf. 14x13½
1366 A370 2000 l shown   3.00   3.00
Granite Paper
Photo.
Perf. 12x11½
1367 A371   750 l Sheet of 12,
      #a.-l.   12.00 12.00

Gazzetta Dello
Sport,
Cent. — A372

1996, May 25   Perf. 12
Granite Paper
1368 A372 1850 l multicolored   3.00 3.00

UNICEF,
50th Anniv.
A373

1996, Sept. 20   Photo.   Perf. 12
Granite Paper
1369 A373 550 l Hen, chicks   .80   .80
1370 A373 1000 l Baby birds   1.50 1.50

UNESCO,
50th Anniv.
A374

World Heritage Sites: 450 l, Yellowstone Natl. Park, US. 500 l, Prehistoric caves, Vézère Valley, France. 650 l, Old town center, San Gimignano, Italy. 1450 l, Church of the Wies Pilgrimage, Germany.

1996, Sept. 20   Granite Paper
1371 A374 450 l multicolored   .60   .60
1372 A374 500 l multicolored   .65   .65
1373 A374 650 l multicolored   .85   .85
1374 A374 1450 l multicolored   1.90 1.90
    Nos. 1371-1374 (4)   4.00 4.00

Christmas — A375

Scenes looking through windows of a home: a, Playing game underneath Christmas tree. b, Tags draped from holly branch. c, Girl reading book, Santa in sleigh. d, Christmas tree. e, Fruits, candles, nuts. f, Streaking star, snowflakes. g, Toys. h, Presents. i, Santa Claus puppet. j, Nativity. k, Mistletoe. l, Stocking hung by fireplace. m, Family eating, drinking. n, Christmas tree, silhouettes of mother,

father, wreath. o, Wreath, silhouettes of children & grandmother, snowman. p, Calendar, champaigne bottle popping cork.

1996, Nov. 8   Photo.   Perf. 14½
1375 A375 750 l Sheet of 16,
      #a.-p.   16.00 16.00

Souvenir Sheet

Hong Kong — A376

View from harbor: a, 1897. b, 1997.

1997, Feb. 12   Litho.   Perf. 12½
1376 A376 750 l Sheet of 2, #a.-
      b.   2.00 2.00

World Alpine
Skiing
Championships,
Sestrière,
Italy — A377

Scene of people skiing on mountain: a, Skier jumping left, birds. b, Ski lift, bird in sky. c, Coming down mountain, sleigh. d, Coming down mountain, Sestrière sign.

1997, Feb. 12   Perf. 12
Granite Paper
1377 A377 1000 l Block of 4, #a.-
      d.   5.00 5.00

No. 1377 is a continuous design.

San Marino
Townships
(Castelli)
A378

1997, Mar. 21   Photo.   Perf. 12
Granite Paper
1378 A378 100 l Acquaviva   .25   .25
1379 A378 200 l Borgomaggi-
      ore   .25   .25
1380 A378 250 l Chiesanuova   .35   .35
1381 A378 400 l Domagnano   .50   .50
1382 A378 500 l Faetano   .65   .65
1383 A378 550 l Fiorentino   .75   .75
1384 A378 650 l Montegiardi-
      no   1.00 1.00
1385 A378 750 l Serravalle   1.10 1.10
1386 A378 5000 l San Marino   6.50 6.50
    Nos. 1378-1386 (9)   11.35 11.35

Stories and
Legends — A379

St. Marinus, Mt. Titano: 650 l, St. Marinus talking to bear that killed the mule. 750 l, Mother begging St. Marinus to forgive her son for trying to kill him.

1997, Mar. 21
Granite Paper
1387 A379 650 l multicolored   .85   .85
1388 A379 750 l multicolored   .95   .95
    Europa.

Sporting
Events
A380

500 l, Giro d'Italia cycling event. 550 l, 10th Tennis Intl. 750 l, Formula 1 San Marino Grand Prix. 1000 l, Republic of San Marino (Soccer) Trophy. 1000 l, Bowls (pétanque) World Championship. 1250 l, Motorcross 250cc World Championship. 1500 l, Mille Miglia classic car spectacle.

1997, May 19   Photo.   Perf. 12
Granite Paper
1389 A380 500 l multicolored   .65   .65
1390 A380 550 l multicolored   .70   .70
1391 A380 750 l multicolored   .95   .95
1392 A380 850 l multicolored   1.10 1.10
1393 A380 1000 l multicolored   1.25 1.25
1394 A380 1250 l multicolored   1.60 1.60
1395 A380 1500 l multicolored   1.90 1.90
    Nos. 1389-1395 (7)   8.15 8.15

5th Intl.
Symposium on
UFO's and
Associated
Phenomena
A381

1997, May 19   Granite Paper
1396 A381 750 l multicolored   1.10 1.10

Trees — A382

50 l, Pinus pinea. 800 l, Quercus pubescens. 1800 l, Juglans regia. 2000 l, Pirus communis.

1997, June 27   Photo.   Perf. 12
Granite Paper
1397 A382   50 l multicolored   .25   .25
1398 A382 800 l multicolored   1.25 1.25
1399 A382 1800 l multicolored   2.50 2.50
1400 A382 2000 l multicolored   2.75 2.75
    Nos. 1397-1400 (4)   6.75 6.75

First Stamps of
San Marino,
120th
Anniv. — A383

Designs: No. 1401, G. Battista Barbavara di Gravellona, director general of Sardinian Post Office. No. 1402, Enrico Repettati, chief engraver for Officina Carte Valori, Turin. No. 1403, Otto Bickel, German stamp dealor, promoter of San Marino-Philatelist. No. 1404, Alfredo Reffi, San Marino stamp dealer, publisher of post cards, stamp catalogue.

1997, June 27   Perf. 11½
Granite Paper
1401 A383 800 l multicolored   1.10 1.10
1402 A383 800 l multicolored   1.10 1.10
1403 A383 800 l multicolored   1.10 1.10
1404 A383 800 l multicolored   1.10 1.10
    a.   Strip of 4, #1401-1404   4.50 4.50

Beatification
of
Bartolomeo
Maria Dal
Monte
(1726-78)
A384

1997, Sept. 18   Photo.   Perf. 12
Granite Paper
1405 A384 800 l multicolored   1.10 1.10

Italian
Comic Book
Characters
A385

Designs: a, "Quadratino," by Antonio Rubino. b, "Signor Bonaventura," by Sergio Tofano. c, "Kit Carson," by Rino Albertarelli. d, "Cocco Bill," by Benito Jacovitti. e, "Tex Willer," by Gian Luigi Bonelli and Arelio Galleppini. f, "Diabolik," by Angela and Luciana Giussani and Franco Paludetti. g, "Valentina," by Guido Crepax. h, "Corto Maltese," by Hugo Pratt. i, "Sturmtruppen," by Franco Bonvicini. j, "Alan Ford," by Max Bunker. k, "Lupo Alberto," by Guido Silvestri. l, "Pimpa," by Francesco Tullio Altan. m, "Bobo," by Sergio Staino. n, "Zanardi," by Andrea Pazienza. o, "Martin Mystère," by Alfredo Castelli and Giancarlo Alessandrini. p, "Dylan Dog," by Tiziano Sclavi and Angelo Stano.

1997, Sept. 18   Granite Paper
Sheet of 16
1406 A385 800 l #a.-p.   18.00 18.00

Adoration of the
Magi, by Georgio
Vasari (1511-
74) — A386

1997, Nov. 14   Photo.   Perf. 12
Granite Paper
1407 A386 800 l multicolored   1.25 1.25

Volunteer
Service,
Solidarity
A387

Designs: 550 l, St. Francis of Assisi, doves. 650 l, Mariele Ventre, children. 800 l, Children circling hands around world, Zecchino d'Oro song festival.

1997, Nov. 14   Granite Paper
1408 A387 550 l multicolored   .70   .70
1409 A387 650 l multicolored   .85   .85
1410 A387 800 l multicolored   1.00 1.00
    Nos. 1408-1410 (3)   2.55 2.55

Volkswagen
Beetle
A388

Designs: a, Maggiolino (old Beetle). b, Golf I. c, New Beetle. d, Golf IV.

1997, Nov. 14   Granite Paper
1411 A388 800 l Sheet of 4, #a.-
      d.   4.75 4.75

No. 1411 was issued with attached entry form for drawing to win a new Beetle car. Entry form is rouletted at top to separate from bottom of sheet. Values are for sheets with entry form attached.

Ferrari's Formula 1 Race Cars, 50th Anniv. A389

Model number, year: a, 125S, 1947. b, 500F2, 1952. c, 801, 1956. d, 246 Dino, 1958. e, 156, 1961. f, 158, 1964. g, 312T, 1975. h, 312T4, 1979. i, 126C, 1981. j, 156/85, 1985. k, 639, 1989. l, F310, 1996.

1998, Feb. 11   Litho.   Perf. 13
1412 A389 800 l Sheet of 12,
       #a.-l.   14.00 14.00

A390

6th World Day of the Sick: 1500 l, Rainbow pulled over earth by dove.

1998, Feb. 11   Perf. 14x14½
1413 A390 650 l shown   1.00 1.00
1414 A390 1500 l multicolored   2.25 2.25

A391

Europa (Natl. Feasts and Festivals): 650 l, Installation of the Captains Regent. 1200 l, Feast Day of the Republic's Patron Saint.

1998, Mar. 31   Litho.   Perf. 14x15
1415 A391 650 l multicolored   1.00 1.00
1416 A391 1200 l multicolored   1.75 1.75

Giacomo Leopardi (1798-1837), Poet — A392

Words from poem, illustration: 550 l, "The Infinite," 1819, hedges, hill. 650 l, "A Village Saturday," 1829, woman walking. 900 l, "Nocturne of a Wandering Asian Shepherd," 1822-30, man looking at moon. 2000 l, "To Sylvia," woman's face.

1998, Mar. 31   Perf. 15x14
1417 A392 550 l multicolored   .80 .80
1418 A392 650 l multicolored   1.00 1.00
1419 A392 900 l multicolored   1.25 1.25
1420 A392 2000 l multicolored   2.75 2.75
       Nos. 1417-1420 (4)   5.80 5.80

1998 World Cup Soccer Championships, France — A393

Soccer players: 650 l, At goal. 800 l, In black & yellow, in blue. 900 l, In red, in black & blue.

1998, May 28   Photo.   Perf. 11½x12
Granite Paper
1421 A393 650 l multicolored   1.50 1.50
  a.   Booklet pane of 4   6.00
1422 A393 800 l multicolored   1.75 1.75
  a.   Booklet pane of 4   7.00
1423 A393 900 l multicolored   2.00 2.00
  a.   Booklet pane of 4   8.00
       Complete booklet, #1421a,
       1422a, 1423a   25.00
     Nos. 1421-1423 (3)   5.25 5.25

Emigration A394

Designs: 800 l, People on ship's deck, group photograph in front of Mt. Titano, 3rd class ticket to New York, passport. 1500 l, People at work, work permit, residency permit, pay slip, US dollar.

1998, May 28   Granite Paper
1424 A394 800 l multicolored   1.25 1.25
1425 A394 1500 l multicolored   2.25 2.25

Souvenir Sheet

San Marino Natl. Flag in Space — A395

Designs: a, Launch of US space shuttle. b, Shuttle in orbit, flag of San Marino. c, Earth, space shuttle.

1998, May 28   Granite Paper
1426 A395 2000 l Sheet of 3,
       #a.-c.   8.00 8.00

A396   A397

Riccione 1998, Intl. Stamp Fair: 800 l, Sun, sail on boat as canceled stamp. 1500 l, Dolphin diving through canceled stamp.

1998, Aug. 28   Photo.   Perf. 12x11½
Granite Paper
1427 A396 800 l multicolored   1.00 1.00
1428 A396 1500 l multicolored   1.90 1.90

1998, Aug. 28   Perf. 14½
Science Fiction: a, Twenty Thousand Leagues Under the Sea, by Jules Verne (1828-1905). b, War of the Worlds, by H.G. Wells (1866-1946). c, Brave New World, by Aldous Huxley (1894-1963). d, 1984, by George Orwell (1903-50). e, Chronicles of the Galaxy, by Isaac Asimov (1920-92). f, City without End, by Clifford D. Simak (1904-88). g, Fahrenheit 451, by Ray Bradbury (b. 1920). h, The Seventh Victim, by Robert Sheckley (b. 1928). i, The Space Merchants, by Frederik Pohl (b. 1919) and C.M. Kornbluth (1923-58). j, Neighbors from the Middle Ages and the Future, by Roberto Vacca (b. 1927). k, Stranger in a Strange Land, by Robert Heinlein (1907-88). l, A Clockwork Orange, by Anthony Burgess (1917-93). m, Drowned World, by James G. Ballard (b. 1930). n, Dune, by Frank Herbert (1920-86). o, 2001, A Space Odessy, by Arthur Clarke (b. 1917). p, Blade Runner (Do Androids Dream of Electric Sheep), by Phillip K. Dick (1928-82).

Granite Paper
1429 A397 800 l Sheet of
       16, #a.-p.   17.50 17.50

Italia '98 A398

1998, Oct. 23   Photo.   Perf. 14
1430 A398 800 l Pope John Paul
       II   1.75 1.75
See Italy No. 2265, Vatican City No. 1085.

A399   A400

Christmas (Children of different races, Christmas tree made up of Santa Clauses, gifts): a, Boy running left, star on tree. b, Child from tropical region, star on tree. c, Child, rabbit, bottom of tree. d, Dog, girl, bottom of tree.

1998, Oct. 23   Perf. 12x11½
Granite Paper
1431 A399 800 l Block of 4, #a.-
              d.   4.50 4.50
   No. 1431 is a continuous design.

1998, Oct. 23   Granite Paper
1432 A400 900 l Woman   1.25 1.25
1433 A400 900 l Man   1.25 1.25
  a.   Pair, #1432-1433   2.50 2.50
Universal Declaration of Human Rights, 50th Anniv. No. 1433a is a continuous design.

A401

Italia '98: Statue, "Girl," by Emilio Greco.

1998, Oct. 23   Granite Paper
1434 A401 1800 l multicolored   2.50 2.50

For Nos. 1435-1521, denominations are shown in euros and lira. For listing purposes, face values in lira are shown.

A402

1999 World Hang Gliding Championships, Italy: 800 l, Hand using feather to write in sky. 1800 l, Man on glider, holding balloon.

1999, Feb. 12   Litho.   Perf. 13½x13
1435 A402 800 l multicolored   1.25 1.25
1436 A402 1800 l multicolored   2.75 2.75

Operas in San Marino, 400th Anniv. — A403

Opera, composer: a, "L'incoronazione di Poppea," by Monteverdi. b, "Dido and Aeneas," by Purcell. c, "Orpheus and Euridice," by Gluck. d, "Don Giovanni," by Mozart. e, "The Barber of Seville," by Rossini. f, "Norma," by Bellini. g, "Lucia di Lammermour," by Donizetti. h, "Aida," by Verdi. i, "Faust," by Gounod. j, "Carmen," by Bizet. k, "The Ring of the Nibelungen," by Wagner. l, "Boris Godonov," by Mussorgski. m, "Tosca," by Puccini. n, "Love for Three Oranges," by Prokofiev. o, "Porgy and Bess," by Gershwin. p, "West Side Story," by Bernstein.

1999, Feb. 12   Perf. 13x13½
Sheet of 16
1437 A403 800 l #a.-p.   17.00 17.00

Bonsai '99, San Marino Bonsai Exhibition A404

50 l, Pinus mugo. 300 l, Olea europaea. 350 l, Pinus silvestris. 500 l, Quercus robar.

1999, Mar. 27   Litho.   Perf. 13x13½
1438 A404 50 l multicolored   .25 .25
1439 A404 300 l multicolored   .40 .40
1440 A404 350 l multicolored   .45 .45
1441 A404 500 l multicolored   .65 .65
       Nos. 1438-1441 (4)   1.75 1.75

Mount Titano Natl. Park A405

Europa: 650 l, Eastern slopes, fortress tower. 1250 l, Walled enclosure, Cesta tower.

1999, Mar. 27
1442 A405 650 l multicolored   1.00 1.00
1443 A405 1250 l multicolored   1.75 1.75

1999 World Cycling Championships, Veneto, Italy — A406

1999, Mar. 27
1444 A406 900 l Building, em-
              blem   1.25 1.25
1445 A406 3000 l Colosseum,
              emblem   4.00 4.00

2nd Roman Republic, Garibaldi's Escape to San Marino, 150th Anniv. A407

1999, May 12   Litho.   Perf. 13x13¼
1446 A407 1250 l multicolored   1.75 1.75

Council of Europe,
50th
Anniv. — A408

1999, May 12   *Perf. 13¼x13*
1447 A408 1300 l multicolored   1.75 1.75

UPU,
125th
Anniv.
A409

800 l, Text from original UPU Treaty, Swiss Parliament Building, Bern. 3000 l, World map highlighting UPU's 22 founding countries.

1999, May 12   *Perf. 13x13¼*
1448 A409   800 l multicolored   1.00 1.00
1449 A409 3000 l multicolored   4.50 4.50

Holy Year
2000
A410

650 l, Map of route of 15th cent. European pilgrims, Canterbury Cathedral. 800 l, Fresco of priest blessing pilgrim, 11th cent., Reims Cathedral. 900 l, Fresco of hospice welcoming pilgrims, 15th cent., Duomo de Pavia. 1250 l, Bas-relief of pilgrims on the road, Cathedral of Fidenza, 12th cent. 1500 l, View of Rome from Monte Mario, by Sir Charles Eastlake, St. Peter's Basilica, Rome.

1999, June 5
1450 A410   650 l multicolored   .95   .95
1451 A410   800 l multicolored   1.10 1.10
1452 A410   900 l multicolored   1.25 1.25
1453 A410 1250 l multicolored   1.75 1.75
1454 A410 1500 l multicolored   2.10 2.10
    Nos. 1450-1454 (5)   7.15 7.15

Fauna of
San Marino
A411

1999, June 5
1455 A411   500 l Lepus
       europaeus   .75   .75
1456 A411   650 l Sciurus vul-
       garis   .95   .95
1457 A411 1100 l Meles meles   1.50 1.50
1458 A411 1250 l Vulpes vulpes   1.75 1.75
1459 A411 1850 l Hystrix cristata   2.75 2.75
    Nos. 1455-1459 (5)   7.70 7.70

Architecture — A412

Designs: 50 l, Sant'Agata Feltria, Rocca Fregosa. 250 l, San Leo, Rocca Feltresca. 650 l, Urbino, Ducal Palace. 1300 l, Sassocorvaro, Rocca Ubaldinesca. 6000 l, Montale and Rocca towers, San Marino.

1999, Sept. 20   Litho.   *Perf. 13x13¼*
1460 A412   50 l multicolored   .25   .25
1461 A412   250 l multicolored   .35   .35
1462 A412   650 l multicolored   .85   .85
1463 A412 1300 l multicolored   1.60 1.60
1464 A412 6000 l multicolored   7.50 7.50
    Nos. 1460-1464 (5)   10.55 10.55

San Marino
Red Cross,
50th Anniv.
A413

1999, Sept. 20
1465 A413 800 l St. Martin of
       Tours   1.25 1.25

Souvenir Sheet

Milan Soccer Club, 100th
Anniv. — A414

Designs: a, 1901 team, trophy on table. b, Players Gren, Nordahl and Liedholm. c, 1963 team, black and white photograph. d, 1990 team, white shirts. e, 1994 team, hanging banners. f, 1999 team, player holding trophy.

1999, Sept. 20
1466 A414 800 l Sheet of 6, #a.-
       f.   7.50 7.50

Souvenir Sheet

Audi Automobiles — A415

Designs: a, Horch. b, Audi TT. c, Audi A8. d, Auto Union.

1999, Nov. 5   Litho.   *Perf. 13x13¼*
1467 A415 1500 l Sheet of 4,
       #a.-d.   8.25 8.25

No. 1467 was issued with attached entry form for drawing to win a new Audi A3 car. Entry form is rouletted at top to separate from bottom of sheet. Values are for sheets with entry form attached.

Christmas
A416

1999, Nov. 5
1468 A416 800 l multicolored   1.25 1.25

Millennium — A417

Designs: a, Tank, soldiers and refugees of World Wars. b, Syringe and vial, MRI machine, DNA molecule. c, Washing machine, subway, Tiffany lamp. d, Radio, telephone operators, person at computer. e, Airplanes, airship, astronaut on moon. f, Pollution. g, Automobiles and truck. h, Atomic diagram, nuclear submarine, mushroom cloud. i, Charlie Chaplin in "Modern Times," comic strip, chair. j, Crossword puzzle, art gallery visitors, car and trailer, people exercising. k, Advertisements and slogans. l, Cyclist, soccer players, stadium.

2000, Feb. 2   Litho.   *Perf. 13x13¼*
1469 A417 650 l Sheet of 12,
       #a.-l.   12.00 12.00

Souvenir Sheet

Holy Year 2000 — A418

Designs: a, St. John Lateran Basilica, St. Marinus and Mt. Titano. b, Basilica of St. Paul, statue of St. Marinus, the Rocca. c, Basilica of St. Mary Major, Basilica of San Marino. d, St. Peter's Basilica, St. Marinus.

2000, Feb. 2
1470 A418 1000 l Sheet of 4,
       #a.-d.   6.00 6.00

A419   A420

Designs: 650 l, Rotary emblem and towers. 800 l, Palace, coat of arms, Statue of Liberty, Rotary emblem.

2000, Apr. 27   Litho.   *Perf. 13x13¼*
1471 A419 650 l multi   1.00 1.00
1472 A419 800 l multi   1.25 1.25
    Rotary Club of San Marino, 40th anniv.

2000, Apr. 27

Bologna, European City of Culture: 650 l, Government Palace and Statue of Liberty, San Marino, and Fiera Towers, Bologna. 800 l, Marconi's workbench, radio antenna, Bologna buildings. 1200 l, Microchip, drums, keyboards, Bologna buildings. 1500 l, Still Life, by Giorgio Morandi, antique books, Bologna buildings.

1473 A420   650 l multi   .95   .95
1474 A420   800 l multi   1.10 1.10
1475 A420 1200 l multi   1.75 1.75
1476 A420 1500 l multi   2.25 2.25
    Nos. 1473-1476 (4)   6.05 6.05

Community of San Patrignano's Fight
Against Drug Abuse — A421

Designs: 650 l, Vincenzo Muccioli, community's founder. 1200 l, Rainbow emblem. 2400 l, Muccioli and community residents.

2000, Apr. 27   *Perf. 13x13¼*
1477 A421   650 l multi   .95   .95
1478 A421 1200 l multi   1.75 1.75
1479 A421 2400 l multi   3.25 3.25
    Nos. 1477-1479 (3)   5.95 5.95

Europa, 2000
Common Design Type

2000, Apr. 27   *Perf. 13¼x13*
1480 CD17 800 l multi   1.00 1.00

Stampin'
the Future
Children's
Stamp
Design
Contest
Winner
A422

2000, May 31   *Perf. 13x13¼*
1481 A422 800 l multi   1.10 1.10

Intl. Cycling
Union,
Cent.
A423

2000, May 31
1482 A423 1200 l multi   1.75 1.75

2000 Summer Olympics,
Sydney — A424

Designs: a, Dog, butterfly. b, Hippopotamus, penguin. c, Elephant, ladybug. d, Rabbit, snail.

2000, May 31   *Perf. 13¼x13*
1483 A424 1000 l Block of 4,
       #a-d   6.00 6.00

European
Convention
on Human
Rights,
50th Anniv.
A425

2000, Sept. 15   Litho.   *Perf. 13x13¼*
1484 A425 800 l multi   1.10 1.10

Intl. Rights
of the Child
Convention,
10th Anniv.
A426

Child: 650 l, And army helmet. 800 l, In corner of room. 1200 l, As flower. 1500 l, With book.

2000, Sept. 15
1485-1488 A426   Set of 4   6.50 6.50

Art of the
Montefeltro
A427

650 l, Basilica of San Marino, Statue of St. Marinus, by Adamo Tadolini. 800 l, Santa Maria d'Antico Church, Madonna and Child statue, by Luca Della Robbia. 1000 l, San

Lorenzo Church, church door. 1500 l, Interior and exterior of San Leo Church. 1800 l, Frescoes, Santuario Madonna della Grazie.

2000, Sept. 15
1489-1493 A427 Set of 5   7.50 7.50

Republic of San Marino, 1700th Anniv. — A428

No. 1494: a, Melchiorre Delfico (1744-1835), historian. b, Giuseppe Garibaldi. c, Abraham Lincoln. d, World War II refugees. e, Jewels from Treasure of Domagnano. f, Map after 1643 war. g, Napoleon Bonaparte's offer to extend territory. h, Arengo of 1906. i, Child's head. j, Young man's head. k, Woman's head. l, Old man's head. m, St. Marinus, by Francesco Manzocchi of Forli, left half of arms. n, Right half of arms, St. Marinus, work attributed to Ghirlandaio. o, St. Marinus, by School of Guercino (blue denomination at top). p, St. Marinus in Glory, by anonymous artist. q, Double throne of Regents. r, Republican statutes, 17th cent. s, Palace Guards on parade. t, Flags of San Marino and other countries.

2000, Nov. 14   Photo.   Perf. 11¾
1494		Souvenir booklet	25.00	
a.-l.	A428 800 l Any single		1.00	1.00
m.-t.	A428 1200 l Any single		1.50	1.50
u.	Booklet pane, #1494a-1494d		4.00	
v.	Booklet pane, #1494e-1494h		4.00	
w.	Booklet pane, #1494i-1494l		4.00	
x.	Booklet pane, #1494m-1494p		6.00	
y.	Booklet pane, #1494q-1494t		6.00	

No. 1494 includes an 800 l postal card.

Virgin With the Infant Jesus, by Ludovico Carracci A429

2000, Nov. 14   Litho.   Perf. 13x13½
1495 A429 800 l multi   3.50 3.50
Christmas.

Souvenir Sheet

Ferrari, 2000 Formula 1 Racing Champion — A430

a, Car on track. b, Car, track wall.

2001, Jan. 10
1496 A430 1500 l #a-b   5.00 5.00

Heritage of the Malatesta Family A431

Sigismondo Malatesta and: 800 l, Malatestian Temple, by Leon Battista Alberti. 1200 l, Pieta by Giovanni Bellini.

2001, Feb. 19   Litho.   Perf. 13x13¼
1497-1498 A431 Set of 2   3.00 3.00

24 Hours of San Marino Regatta — A432

Hull colors: a, Green. b, Orange. c, Black. d, Brown.

2001, Feb. 19   Perf. 13¼x13
1499 A432 1200 l Block or strip of 4, #a-d   7.00 7.00

Giuseppe Verdi (1813-1901), Composer — A433

Verdi and scenes from operas: a, Nabucco. b, Ernani. c, Rigoletto. d, Il Trovatore. e, La Traviata. f, I Vespri Siciliani. g, Un Ballo in Maschera. h, La Forza del Destino. i, Don Carlos. j, Aida. k, Otello. l, Falstaff.

2001, Feb. 19   Perf. 13x13¼
1500	Sheet of 12	15.00	15.00
a.-l.	A433 800 l Any single	1.25	1.25

Europa — A434

Designs: 800 l, Safe in forest. 1200 l, Faucet on mountain.

2001, Apr. 17   Litho.   Perf. 13¼x13
1501-1502 A434 Set of 2   3.00 3.00

Emigration to the US — A435

Immigrants viewing Statue of Liberty and: 1200 l, Ellis Island Immigration Museum, New York. 2400 l, San Marino Social Club, Detroit.

2001, Apr. 17   Perf. 13x13¼
1503-1504 A435 Set of 2   5.00 5.00

Euroflora 2001, Genoa — A436

Designs: 800 l, Dahlia variabilis, ship. 1200 l, Zantedeschia aethiopica, ship. 1500 l, Helen Troubel rose, ship. 2400 l, Amaryllis hippeastrum, Lanterna.

2001, Apr. 17   Perf. 13¼x13
1505-1508 A436 Set of 4   8.50 8.50

9th Games of the Small European States — A437

No. 1509: a, Bocce, running. b, Swimming. c, Cycling. d, Shooting. e, Judo. f, Tennis, table tennis. g, Basketball and volleyball. h, Mascot carrying torch.

2001, Apr. 17
1509 A437 800 l Sheet of 8, #a-h 9.50 9.50

Opening of New State Museum A438

Various holdings: 550 l, 800 l, 1500 l, 2000 l.

2001, June 23   Perf. 13x13¼
1510-1513 A438 Set of 4   7.25 7.25

UN High Commisioner for Refugees, 50th Anniv. — A439

No. 1514: a, Emblem at bottom. b, Emblem at top.

2001, June 23   Perf. 13¼x13
1514 A439 1200 l Horiz. pair, #a-b   4.25 4.25

Foundation of the Republic, 1700th Anniv. — A440

No. 1515: a, Uninhabited land. b, People on horses. c, Small community. d, Town with highway.

2001, June 23   Perf. 13x13¼
1515 A440 1200 l Block of 4, #a-d   7.25 7.25

Homage to Artist Joseph Beuys A441

2001, Sept. 10
1516 A441 2400 l multi   3.50 3.50

Year of Dialogue Among Civilizations A442

2001, Sept. 10   Perf. 13¼x13
1517 A442 2400 l multi   3.75 3.75

United Mutual Aid Society, 125th Anniv. — A443

Allegory of assistance and: a, Old building. b, Modern building.

2001, Sept. 10   Perf. 13x13¼
1518 A443 1200 l Horiz. pair, #a-b   3.75 3.75

Christmas — A444

No. 1519: a, Angel with lute. b, Woman with basket, Magus on camel. c, Magus on camel, shepherd with sheep, woman with gift. d, Man with gift, castles, star, Holy Family. e, Man with lantern, goose, chicken, sheep. f, Angel with long, thin-mouthed, horn. g, Angel with harp. h, Magus on camel. i, Two women with baskets, dog. j, Shepherd with two sheep. k, Angel with short, wide-mouthed horn. l, Woman with gift, angel with horn. m, Angel with violin. n, Man, sleigh, gifts. o, Woman with gift, pulling sleigh. p, Angel with drum.

2001, Oct. 18   Litho.   Perf. 13
1519 A444 800 l Sheet of 16, #a-p   20.00 20.00

Introduction of the Euro (in 2002) A445

Map of Europe and: 1200 l, Coins of various countries, 1-euro coin. 2400 l, Banknotes of various countries, 100-euro banknote.

2001, Oct. 18   Perf. 13x13¼
1520-1521 A445 Set of 2   5.50 5.50

100 Cents = 1 Euro (€)

A446

Designs: 1c, Rabbits. 2c, Sunset over San Marino. 5c, Cactus. 10c, Field of grain. 25c, Aerial view of alpine landscape. 50c, Wet olive branches. €1, Sparrows. €5, Baby.

2002, Jan. 16   Litho.   Perf. 13¼x13
1522	A446	1c multi	.25	.25
1523	A446	2c multi	.25	.25
1524	A446	5c multi	.25	.25
1525	A446	10c multi	.30	.30
1526	A446	25c multi	.75	.75
1527	A446	50c multi	1.50	1.50
1528	A446	€1 multi	3.00	3.00
1529	A446	€5 multi	15.00	15.00
	Nos. 1522-1529 (8)		21.30	21.30

Manuel Poggiali, 2001 World 125cc Class Motorcycling Champion — A447

No. 1530: a, "2001" at UR. b, "2001" at UL.

2002, Jan. 16   Perf. 13x13¼
1530 A447 62c Horiz. pair, #a-b   4.00 4.00

2002 Winter Olympics, Salt Lake City — A448

No. 1531: a, Dog skiing. b, Hippopotamus skating. c, Rabbit skiing. d, Elephant playing ice hockey.

2002, Jan. 16   Perf. 13¼x13
1531 A448 41c Block of 4, #a-d   5.00 5.00

Europa — A449

Designs: 36c, Lion tamer, clown, trapeze artist, tightrope walker. 62c, Trapeze artist, horse act, clown, acrobat.

2002, Mar. 22   Litho.   Perf. 13¼x13
1532-1533 A449 Set of 2   13.00 13.00

Priority Mail A450

Designs: 62c, Cyclist. €1.24, Hurlder.

2002, Mar. 22   Perf. 13x13¼
Stamp + Etiquette
1534-1535 A450 Set of 2   5.75 5.75

2002 World Cup Soccer Championships, Japan and Korea — A451

Scenes from Italian team's victorious matches in: a, 1934. b, 1938. c, 1970. d, 1982. e, 1990. f, 1994.

2002, Mar. 22
1536 A451 41c Sheet of 6, #a-f   7.50 7.50

Maastricht Treaty, 10th Anniv. A452

2002, June 3   Litho.   Perf. 13x13¼
1537 A452 €1.24 multi   4.00 4.00

Intl. Year of Mountains — A453

No. 1538: a, Clouds at and above level of Mt. Titano. b, Clouds below Mt. Titano. c, Mt. Titano with no clouds.

2002, June 3   Perf. 13¼x13
1538 A453 41c Horiz. strip of 3, #a-c   4.00 4.00

Souvenir Sheet

San Marino Postage Stamps, 125th Anniv. — A454

No. 1539: a, Parts of #1, 7. b, Parts of #7, 11. c, Parts of #11, 15. d, Parts of #15, 17.

2002, June 3   Perf. 13¼
1539 A454 €1.24 Sheet of 4, #a-d   15.00 15.00

Intl. Amateur Radio Conference A455

Emblems of San Marino and International Amateur Radio Associations, Morse code and map in: 36c, Green. 62c, Orange.

2002, Sept. 19   Perf. 13¼x13
1540-1541 A455 Set of 2   3.25 3.25

Craftsmen — A456

Designs: 26c, Blacksmith. 36c, Broom maker. 41c, Chair mender. 77c, Scribe. €1.24, Knife grinder. €1.55, Charcoal maker.

2002, Sept. 19
1542-1547 A456 Set of 6   14.00 14.00

Souvenir Sheet

Tourist Attractions — A457

No. 1548: a, Public Palace (30x52mm). b, Guaita (First Tower), buildings at bottom (45x30mm). c, Cesta and Montale (Second and Third Towers) (45x30mm). d, Basilica del Santo (building with steps at left (45x30mm). e, Cappucini Church (building with steps at center) (45x30mm). f, Gate of San Francesco (40x40mm).

2002, Sept. 19   Perf. 12½
1548 A457 62c Sheet of 6, #a-f   11.00 11.00

Greetings — A458

Designs: No. 1549, 41c, "Da mi basia mille. . . " No. 1550, 41c, "Hello." No. 1551, 41c, "Best Wishes." No. 1552, 41c, "Ehi! Ci sono anch'io." No. 1553, 41c, "?????!!!!!" No. 1554, 41c, "Sorry."

2002, Oct. 31   Perf. 13¼x13
1549-1554 A458 Set of 6   8.00 8.00

Christmas — A459

No. 1555: a, Baby's hands grasping adult's hands. b, Baby looking up towards mother. c, Baby breastfeeding. d, Mother and baby asleep. e, Hands cradling baby. f, Baby and mother in blanket. g, Mother kissing baby. h, Mother showing open mouth to baby. i, Baby on mother's shoulder. j, Mother smiling at baby. k, Mother nuzzling baby's hand. l, Two babies.

2002, Oct. 31   Perf. 12½
1555 A459 41c Sheet of 12, #a-l   15.00 15.00

Paintings — A460

Designs: 52c, Woman with Mango, by Paul Gauguin (1848-1903). 62c, Wheatfield with Flight of Crows, by Vincent Van Gogh (1853-90). €1.55, Portrait of a Young Woman, by Il Parmigianino (1503-40).

2003, Jan. 24   Litho.   Perf. 13¼x13
1556-1558 A460 Set of 3   8.00 8.00

2003 World Nordic Skiing Championships, Val di Fiemme, Italy — A461

No. 1559: a, Skiers #4, 13. b, Skier #37. c, Skiers #6, 7.

2003, Jan. 24
1559 A461 77c Sheet of 3, #a-c   7.00 7.00

Cuisine — A462

No. 1560: a, Artichoke and mushroom salad. b, Prosciutto, sausage and cheese. c, Spaghetti with chopped tomatoes. d, Tortellini with ham. e, Shrimp. f, Octopus. g, Ravioli. h, Fettucini with tomato sauce. i, Breast of fowl. j, Fish, shrimp and salad greens. k, Dessert with red sauce in starburst design. l, Dessert with yellow sauce. m, Salad with cherry tomato garnish. n, Meat on bed of vegetables. o, Dessert with raspberry, grape and whipped cream garnishes. p, Custard in shell with lines of chocolate sauce.

2003, Jan. 24   Perf. 12½
1560 A462 41c Sheet of 16, #a-p   20.00 20.00

Girolamo Fracastoro (1478-1553), Physician and Verona, Italy — A463

2003, Mar. 18 Litho. Perf. 13x13¼
1561 A463 77c multi 2.50 2.50
100th Veronafil Philatelic Exhibition, Verona, Italy.

Europa — A464

Poster art by: 28c, Armando Testa. 77c, Henri de Toulouse-Lautrec.

2003, Mar. 18 Perf. 13¼x13
1562-1563 A464 Set of 2 10.00 10.00

Race Horses — A465

Designs: 11c, Molvedo. 15c, Tornese. 26c, Ribot. €1.55, Varenne.

2003, Mar. 18
1564-1567 A465 Set of 4 6.25 6.25

Start of Stagecoach Mail Service, 120th Anniv. A466

Designs: 41c, Stagecoach going to Rimini. 77c, Stagecoach drawn by four horses.

2003, June 7 Perf. 13x13¼
1568-1569 A466 Set of 2 3.50 3.50

Powered Flight, Cent. A467

Designs: 36c, Wright Flyer. 41c, Bleriot XI. 62c, Aermacchi MB339. 77c, Italian 313th Acrobatic Training Group (Frecce Tricolori).

2003, June 7
1570-1573 A467 Set of 4 7.00 7.00

St. Petersburg, Russia, 300th Anniv. A468

Designs: 15c, Bridge across Winter Canal, Fortress, Cathedral of Sts. Peter and Paul. 26c, Architect Bartolomeo Francesco Rastrelli, Opera House. 36c, View of city from Trinity Bridge. 41c, Aleksandr Pushkin. 77c, Empress

Catherine II (the Great). €1.55, Czar Peter I (the Great).

2003, June 7
1574-1579 A468 Set of 6 10.50 10.50

Souvenir Sheet

Bicycle Races — A469

No. 1580: a, Tour de France, cent. b, 2003 Road Cycling World Championships, Hamilton, Ont., Canada.

2003, June 7 Perf.
1580 A469 77c Sheet of 2, #a-b 5.00 5.00
No. 1580 contains two 38mm diameter stamps.

2003 Rugby World Cup, Australia — A470

Various rugby players: 41c, 62c, 77c, €1.55.

2003, Sept. 15 Litho. Perf. 13¼x13
1581-1584 A470 Set of 4 10.00 10.00

Children's Games A471

Designs: 36c, Cart racing. 41c, Blind man's buff. 62c, Hoop rolling. 77c, Marbles. €1.24, Handkerchief game. €1.55, Tug-of-war.

2003, Sept. 15 Perf. 13x13¼
1585-1590 A471 Set of 6 15.00 15.00

Puppetry — A472

No. 1591: a, Puppets with drum and cymbals. b, Puppet with horn. c, Audience, puppet with flower. d, Audience, puppets with sticks.

2003, Sept. 15
1591 A472 41c Block of 4, #a-d 5.00 5.00

Reconstruction of La Fenice Theater, Venice — A473

Litho. & Embossed
2003, Oct. 24 Perf. 13¼x13
1592 A473 €3.72 multi 20.00 20.00

Christmas — A474

No. 1593: a, Christmas cards. b, Holy Family c, Shepherds and Magi. d, Angel. e, Christmas tree, vert. f, Girl and games. g, Children, fruit and cake. h, Carolers. i, Stocking on Christmas tree, vert. j, Cornucopia. k, Arms of San Marino. l, Girl, toys and gift, vert. m, Wreath. n, Boy, sled and snowman. o, Santa Claus. p, Children, toys and Christmas tree.

2003, Oct. 24 Litho. Perf. 13½
1593 A474 41c Sheet of 16, #a-p 20.00 20.00

Manuel Poggiali, 2003 250cc Motorcycle World Champion A475

2004, Feb. 6 Litho. Perf. 13¼x13¼
1594 A475 €1.55 multi 4.75 4.75

Venice Carnival A476

Designs: 77c, Doges' Palace. €1.55, Costumed carnival participant, canal and bridge.

2004, Feb. 6
1595-1596 A476 Set of 2 7.00 7.00

Latin Union, 50th Anniv. A477

Designs: 41c, Ballerina, by Edgar Degas, tango dancers. 77c, Illustration from Don Quixote, scene from Dona Flor and Her Two Husbands. €1.55, Susanna and the Elders, by Tintoretto, and Sunday Afternoon, by Fernando Botero.

2004, Feb. 6
1597-1599 A477 Set of 3 8.25 8.25

FIFA (Fédération Internationale de Football Association), Cent. — A478

2004, Apr. 16 Litho. Perf. 13¼x13
1600 A478 €2.80 multi 8.50 8.50

European Bonsai Association, 20th Convention A479

Trees and: 45c, Black Japanese pine bonsai, by Kunjo Kobayashi. 60c, Dwarf pine bonsai, by Pius Notter.

2004, Apr. 16
1601-1602 A479 Set of 2 3.50 3.50

Souvenir Sheet

People's Republic of China, 55th Anniv. — A480

No. 1603: a, Tien-an-men Palace, Beijing, and Government Palace, San Marino. b, Mount San Marino, Great Wall of China. c, Tower of San Marino, Pagoda of the Temple of Heaven, Peace Statue, vert.

Perf. 13x13¼, 13¼x13 (#1603c)
2004, Apr. 16
1603 A480 80c Sheet of 3, #a-c 7.25 7.25

Europa — A481

Fantasy vacation vehicles made up of: 45c, Automobile, airplane and boat. 80c, Boat, camper, train and bus.

Perf. 13¼x13, 13x13¼
2004, May 21 Litho.
1604-1605 A481 Set of 2 3.75 3.75

2004 Summer Olympics, Athens A482

No. 1606: a, Chariot, boxers, javelin thrower. b, Discus thrower, wrestlers, torch bearer. c, Relay race runner, cyclist, golfer. d, Tennis player, weight lifter, gymnasts.

2004, May 21 Perf. 13x13¼
1606 Horiz. strip of 4 11.00 11.00
a.-d. A482 90c Any single 2.75 2.75

Volkswagen Automobiles in Italy, 50th Anniv. — A483

No. 1607: a, Blue Volkswagen Golf. b, Old and new Volkswagen Beetles, blue denomination. c, Old and new Volkswagen Beetles, green denomination. d, Silver Volkswagen Golf.

2004, May 21   **Perf. 13x13¼**
1607 A483 Booklet pane of 4 19.00 —
a.-d.   €1.50 Any single   4.50 4.50
           Complete booklet, #1607 19.00

Sao Paolo, Brazil, 450th Anniv. A484

Designs: 60c, Founding of city by Jesuits Manuel de Nobrega and José Anchieta. 80c, Mario de Andrade, artist, Antonio Alcantara Machado, writer, and Municipal Theater. €1.40, City skyline, monastery building.

2004, Aug. 20
1608-1610 A484 Set of 3   8.50 8.50

Writers — A485

Designs: 45c, Petrarch (1304-74). €1.50, Oscar Wilde (1854-1900). €2.20, Anton Chekhov (1860-1904).

2004, Aug. 20   **Perf. 13¼x13**
1611-1613 A485 Set of 3   13.00 13.00

Fairy Tales — A486

Designs: 45c, Hansel and Gretel. 60c, Little Red Riding Hood. 80c, Pinocchio. €1, Puss in Boots.

2004, Aug. 20
1614-1617 A486 Set of 4   8.50 8.50

Souvenir Sheet

Meeting of Rimini, 25th Anniv. — A487

No. 1618: a, Man with tie, two men with construction helmets. b, Woman wearing glasses, child, woman. c, Child, woman and man. d, Priest, rabbi and man.

2004, Aug. 20   **Perf. 13½**
1618 A487 €1 Sheet of 4,
            #a-d   12.00 12.00

Christmas — A488

No. 1619 — Angels and: a, Musical instruments. b, Bag of toys. c, Christmas tree. d, Cornucopia and "2005."

2004, Nov. 12   **Perf. 13¼x13**
1619 A488 60c Block of 4, #a-d 7.25 7.25

Paintings A489

Designs: 45c, Rebecca at the Well, by Giovanni Battista Piazzetta (1682-1754). €1.40, Piazza Navona, by Scipione Gino Bonichi (1904-33). €1.70, The Persistence of Memory, by Salvador Dali (1904-89).

2004, Nov. 12   **Perf. 14¾x14¼**
1620-1622 A489 Set of 3   11.00 11.00

Souvenir Sheet

Reopening of La Scala Theater, Milan — A490

No. 1623: a, Composer Antonio Salieri, theater's stage. b, Theater's facade. c, Conductor Riccardo Muti, audience.

2004, Nov. 12   **Perf. 13¼**
1623 A490 €1.50 Sheet of 3,
            #a-c   13.50 13.50

Dec. 26, 2004 Tsunami Relief A491

2005, Feb. 28 Litho. Perf. 13x13¼
1624 A491 €1.50 multi   5.00 5.00

Profits from the sale of this stamp went to charities involved with tsunami relief.

Intl. Weight Lifting Federation, Cent. — A492

2005, Feb. 28   **Perf. 13¼x13**
1625 A492 €2.20 multi   6.75 6.75

2004 Beatification of Alberto Marvelli — A493

Designs: 90c, Marvelli assisting injured man. €1.80, Marvelli, Pope John Paul II, Loreto Basilica.

2005, Feb. 28
1626-1627 A493 Set of 2   8.25 8.25

Ferrari Race Cars — A494

Race cars and: 1c, Juan Manuel Fangio. 4c, Niki Lauda. 5c, John Surtees. 45c, Michael Schumacher. 62c, Ferrari emblem. €1.50, Alberto Ascari.

2005, Feb. 28
1628-1633 A494 Set of 6   8.00 8.00

Europa — A495

Designs: 62c, Bread. €1.20, Wine.

2005, Apr. 25 Litho. Perf. 13¼x13
1634-1635 A495 Set of 2   5.50 5.50

78th Annual Reunion of Italian Alpine Troops — A496

Soldier: 36c, Climbing mountain. 45c, Picking flower. 62c, Assisting mother and child. €1, With other soldiers at reunion.

2005, Apr. 25
1636-1639 A496 Set of 4   7.50 7.50

Uniformed Militia — A497

Designs: 36c, Officer with saber, Third Tower. 45c, Soldier with musket, Second Tower. 62c, Standard bearer, Palazzo Pubblico. €1.50, Officer with saber, member of Military Band, First Tower.

2005, Apr. 25   **Perf. 13¼x14**
1640-1643 A497 Set of 4   9.00 9.00

History of Mail Service A498

Designs: 36c, Courier, ship, train. 45c, Man reading letter. 60c, Men reading letter. 62c, Man and woman.

2005, June 4   **Perf. 13x13¼**
1644-1647 A498 Set of 4   6.25 6.25

Coins A499

Designs: 36c, 1864 copper 5-centisimi coin. 45c, 1898 silver 5-lire coin. €1, Gold 10 and 20-lire coins, euro coins. €2.20, Euro coins.

2005, June 4
1648-1651 A499 Set of 4   12.00 12.00

Miniature Sheet

Musical Theater — A500

No. 1652: a, Erminio Macario in *Made in Italy*. b, Wanda Osiris in *Gran Baraonda*. c, Toto in *A Prescindere*. d, Anna Magnani in *Volumeide*. e, Aldo Fabrizzi in *Rugantino*. f, Renato Rascel in *Rascelinaria*. g, Nino Taranto in *Napoli che Ride*. h, Delia Scala in *Il Delia Scala Show*. i, Tino Scotti in *Ghe Pensi Mi*. j, Carlo Dapporto in *Giove in Doppiopetto*.

2005, June 4   **Perf. 13¼x13**
1652 A500 45c Sheet of 10,
            #a-j   13.50 13.50

Giovanni Pascoli (1855-1912), Poet — A501

Poetry and: 36c, Kite and child. 45c, Mt. Titano. €1, Tower and horse. €2, Pascoli and church bell tower.

2005, Aug. 26   *Perf. 13x13¼*
1653-1656 A501   Set of 4   11.50 11.50

Venice Gondola Regatta A502

Designs: €1.40, Statues of angel and devil as racing gondoliers. €2, Gondolier, vert.

Perf. 13x13¼, 13¼x13
2005, Aug. 26   *Litho.*
1657-1658 A502   Set of 2   10.50 10.50

Miniature Sheet

Italian Wine Bottle Labels — A503

No. 1659: a, Ferrari Brut. b, Amarone della Valpolicella. c, Canevel. d, Biondi-Santi. e, Vecchioflorio. f, Fazi Battaglia. g, Sassicaia, vert. h, Piano di Monte Vergine dei Feudi di San Gregorio, vert. i, Schiopetto, vert. j, Barolo, vert.

Perf. 13x13¼, 13¼x13 (vert. stamps)
2005, Aug. 26
1659 A503 45c Sheet of 10,
    #a-j   13.50 13.50

Dahlia — A504

Serpentine Die Cut 6¾ Vert.
2005, Nov. 17   **Photo.**
Self-Adhesive
Coil Stamp
1660 A504 (45c) multi   1.40 1.40

Pope Clement XIV (1705-74) A505

Designs: 80c, Wearing monk's habit and cardinal's biretta. €1, Giving blessing.

2005, Nov. 17   **Litho.**   *Perf. 13x13¼*
1661-1662 A505   Set of 2   5.50 5.50

Artists and Writers — A506

Designs: 36c, Baptistry door panel by Lorenzo Ghiberti (1378-1455), sculptor. 62c, The Annunciation, by Fra Angelico (c. 1400-

1455). €1, Jules Verne (1828-1905), writer. €1.30, Hans Christian Andersen (1805-75), writer.

2005, Nov. 17   *Perf. 13¼x13*
1663-1666 A506   Set of 4   10.00 10.00

Christmas A507

Designs: 62c, Annunciation. €1.55, Holy Family. €2.20, Adoration of the Magi.

2005, Nov. 17   *Perf. 13x13¼*
1667-1669 A507   Set of 3   13.50 13.50

2004 Winter Olympics, Turin — A508

No. 1670 — Ski slope with: a, American flag at left. b, Eagle and airplane at right. c, Finish line. d, Skaters at right.

2006, Feb. 1   *Perf. 12½x12¾*
1670 A508 45c Block of 4, #a-d   5.50 5.50

Christopher Columbus (1451-1506), Explorer — A509

Columbus and: 90c, Native American. €1.80, Ship and globe.

2006, Feb. 1   *Perf. 13x13¼*
1671-1672 A509   Set of 2   8.25 8.25

Assembly of the Patriarchs, Cent. — A510

Assembled patriarchs and: 45c, Government Palace. 62c, Statue of Liberty. €1.50, Basilica.

2006, Feb. 1   *Perf. 13¼x13*
1673-1675 A510   Set of 3   7.75 7.75

Souvenir Sheet

"Two Republics" Philatelic Exhibition — A511

2006, Apr. 5   **Photo.**   *Perf. 13x13¼*
1676 A511   Sheet, #1676a, Italy
     #2740   4.00 4.00
  a.   62c multi   2.00 2.00
See Italy No. 2740. On No. 1676, the San Marino stamp is on the left. On Italy No. 2740a, the San Marino stamp is on the right. Both stamps in No. 1676 have text printed on reverse.

2006 World Cup Soccer Championships, Germany A512

2006, Apr. 5   **Litho.**   *Perf. 13¼x13*
1677 A512 €2.20 multi   6.50 6.50

Art — A513

Designs: 36c, Bathers, by Paul Cézanne (1839-1906). 45c, Bathsheba With King David's Letter, by Rembrandt (1606-69). 60c, Coronation of the Virgin, by Gentile da Fabriano (c. 1370-1427). €1.80, The Bridal Chamber, fresco by Andrea Mantegna (1431-c. 1506).

2006, Apr. 5   *Perf. 13x13¼*
1678-1681 A513   Set of 4   9.50 9.50

Children's Health — A514

2006, June 19   *Perf. 13¼*
1682 A514 €2.20 multi + label   6.50 6.50

Europa A515

Designs: 45c, Butterfly with children's faces. 62c, Leonardo da Vinci's Vitruvian Man as jigsaw puzzle.

2006, June 19   *Perf. 13x13¼*
1683-1684 A515   Set of 2   3.25 3.25

Crossbow Federation, 50th Anniv. — A516

Designs: 36c, Flag bearers, drummer. 45c, Flag bearers carrying flags of the nine San Marino castles. 62c, Crossbowman preparing to shoot, flag of Federation. €1, Two crossbowmen positioning weapons. €1.50, Flag-throwers and drummers. €2.80, Flags of Federation and San Marino, man holding target with shot arrows.

2006, June 19   *Perf. 13¼x13*
1685-1690 A516   Set of 6   20.00 20.00

Italy's Victory in 2006 World Cup Soccer Championships A517

2006, Aug. 21
1691 A517 €1 multi   3.00 3.00

Intl. Gymnastics Federation, 125th Anniv. — A518

Emblem and: 15c, Rings. €2.80, Female gymnast.

2006, Aug. 21
1692-1693 A518   Set of 2   8.75 8.75

Italian Philatelic Press Union, 40th Anniv. — A519

Emblem and: 90c, Castle turrets. €2.20, Arch and statues.

2006, Aug. 21
1694-1695 A519   Set of 2   9.25 9.25

Duke Guidubaldo, Carlo Bo and University of Urbino — A520

2006, Nov. 13   **Litho.**   *Perf. 13*
1696 A520 €2.20 multi   6.50 6.50
University of Urbino, 500th anniv.

Famous Men — A521

Artist's interpretations of famous works by: 5c, Roberto Rossellini (1906-77), film director. 65c, Luchino Visconti (1906-76), film director. 85c, Jacopone da Todi (c. 1236-1306), poet. €1.40, Wolfgang Amadeus Mozart (1756-91), composer.

2006, Nov. 13   *Perf. 13¼x13*
1697-1700 A521   Set of 4   8.75 8.75

A522

Christmas
A523

The Nativity, by Tiepolo: No. 1701, Joseph (detail). No. 1702, Angel (detail). No. 1703, Infant Jesus (detail). No. 1704, Virgin Mary (detail). €2.80, Entire painting.

2006, Nov. 13	Litho.		Perf. 13¼	
1701 A522	60c multi + label		1.75	1.75
1702 A522	60c multi + label		1.75	1.75
1703 A522	65c multi + label		1.90	1.90
1704 A522	65c multi + label		1.90	1.90
1705 A523	€2.80 multi		8.50	8.50
a.	Booklet pane, #1701-1705,			
	+ label, perf. 13¼ on 3			
	sides		16.00	—
	Complete booklet, #1705a		16.00	
	Nos. 1701-1705 (5)		15.80	15.80

No. 1705a lacks the small labels attached to Nos. 1701-1704.

San Marino's Presidency of the Council of Europe Committee of Ministers — A524

2007, Jan. 23	Litho.	Perf. 13¼	
1706 A524	65c multi	1.75	1.75

Printed in sheets of 4.

Alessandro
Glaray,
San
Marino
Philatelic
Expert
A525

2007, Jan. 23		Perf. 13x13¼	
1707 A525	€1.80 multi	4.75	4.75

Gina Lollobrigida,
Actress and
Artist — A526

Designs: 65c, Self-portrait. 85c, "Potato Seller," photograph by Lollobrigida. €1, "Esmerelda," sculpture by Lollobrigida. €3.20, Lollobrigida and Mother Teresa.

2007, Jan. 23		Perf. 13¼x13	
1708-1711 A526	Set of 4	15.00	15.00

25th San Gabriel
Intl. Philatelic Art
Award — A527

2007, Apr. 20			
1712 A527	€1.50 multi	4.25	4.25

Items
Designed
by Bruno
Munari
(1907-98)
A528

Designs: 36c, Window-dresser's tool. 65c, Milk carton. €1.40, Shutter lock. €2, Hangable shop light.

2007, Apr. 20		Perf. 12½x12¾	
1713-1716 A528	Set of 4	12.00	12.00

Giuseppe Garibaldi (1807-82), Italian
Nationalist Leader — A529

Designs: 65c, Garibaldi, San Marino flag, men on horseback. €1.40, Garibaldi landing at Marsala, battle scene. €2, Garibaldi on horseback, Garibaldi shaking hands with King Victor Emmanuel II of Italy.

2007, Apr. 20	Litho.	Perf. 13¼x13	
1717-1719 A529	Set of 3	11.00	11.00

Europa — A530

Designs: 60c, Scouts, stylized globe, compass. 65c, Scouts, stylized globe, map of San Marino.

2007, June 2			
1720-1721 A530	Set of 2	3.50	3.50

Scouting, cent.

2007 European
Baseball Cup,
San
Marino — A531

Designs: 65c, Batter, catcher and umpire. €1, Pitcher.

2007, June 2			
1722-1723 A531	Set of 2	4.50	4.50

2007 World Track
and Field
Championships,
Osaka,
Japan — A532

Designs: 60c, High jump. 85c, Long jump, horiz. €1.50, Runners, horiz.

2007, June 2		Perf. 13	
1724-1726 A532	Set of 3	8.00	8.00

Souvenir Sheet

Postilions, 400th Anniv. — A533

Litho. & Engr.

2007, June 2		Perf. 13¼	
1727 A533	€4.50 multi	12.00	12.00

Intl. Assoc. of
Editors of Stamp
Catalogues,
Albums and
Philatelic
Publications
(ASCAT), 30th
Anniv. — A534

2007, Aug. 24	Litho.	Perf. 13¼x13	
1728 A534	65c multi	1.75	1.75

Castles — A535

No. 1729: a, Rocca, San Marino. b, Orava Castle, Slovakia.

Litho. & Engr.

2007, Aug. 24		Perf. 13	
1729 A535	65c Horiz. pair, #a-b	3.50	3.50

No. 1729 was printed in sheets containing four pairs. See Slovakia No. 525.

Miniature Sheet

European Wine Labels — A536

No. 1730: a, 1996 Porto Quinta do Estanho. b, Tarlant Cuvée Louis Brut Champagne, horiz. c, Bauget-Jouette Champagne, horiz. d, 2006 Zlahtina. e, 2006 Petri Riesling. f, 1999 Tokaji, horiz. g, Carmelo Rodero Ribera de Duero, horiz. h, Teodor Belo Simcic.

Perf. 13¼x13, 13x13¼ (horiz. stamps)

2007, Aug. 24			Litho.	
1730 A536	65c Sheet of 8, #a-h, + 2 labels		14.00	14.00

Equal
Opportunity To
All — A537

2007, Dec. 3	Litho.	Perf. 13¼x13	
1731 A537	€1 multi	3.00	3.00

Famous
People — A538

Designs: 60c, Arturo Toscanini (1867-1957), conductor. 65c, Sculpture of Paolina Borghese, by Antonio Canova (1757-1822). €1, Carlo Goldoni (1707-93), playwright. €1.80, Via Toscanella, painting by Ottone Rosai (1895-1957).

2007, Dec. 3			
1732-1735 A538	Set of 4	12.00	12.00

Christmas
A539

Designs: 60c, Government Palace, Christmas tree, and Star of Bethlehem. 65c, Santa Claus. 85c, Holy Family.

2007, Dec. 3			
1736-1738 A539	Set of 3	6.25	6.25

Milan
International
Soccer Team,
Cent. — A540

2008, Feb. 26	Litho.	Perf. 13¼x13	
1739 A540	€1 multi	3.00	3.00

San
Marino
Post
Office,
175th
Anniv.
A541

2008, Feb. 26		Perf. 13x13¼	
1740 A541	€1.80 multi	5.50	5.50

Paintings — A542

Designs: 36c, The Crucifixion, by Giovanni Bellini. 60c, Madonna and Child with St. John, by Jacopo Bassano. 65c, Venus and Love, by Gian Antonio Pellegrini. 85c, Old Man's Face, by Giandomenico Tiepolo.

2008, Feb. 26   Perf. 13¼x13
1741-1744 A542   Set of 4   7.50 7.50

Intl. Year of Planet Earth A543

Designs: 60c, Stylized skeleton and car emitting exhaust. 85c, Stylized sun and person. €1.40, Drop of water and tipped glass. €2, Earth on fire.

2008, Feb. 26   Perf. 13x13¼
1745-1748 A543   Set of 4   15.00 15.00

European Year of Intercultural Dialogue — A544

2008, Apr. 8   Litho.   Perf. 14¼x14½
1749 A544 65c multi   2.10 2.10

Printed in sheets of 3.

Concetto Marchesi (1878-1957), Historian of Italian and Latin Literature — A545

2008, Apr. 8   Perf. 13x13¼
1750 A545 €1 multi   3.25 3.25

Apparition at Lourdes, 150th Anniv. — A546

Designs: 36c, Bernadette Soubirous, first miracle healing. 60c, Procession of faithful at Lourdes. €2, Apparition of Virgin Mary before Soubirous.

2008, Apr. 8   Perf. 13¼x13
1751-1753 A546   Set of 3   9.50 9.50

Our Lady of Mercy, Bas-relief by Leonardo Blanco — A547

Litho. & Embossed
2008, June 13   Perf. 13¼x13
1754 A547 €1 multi   3.25 3.25

San Marino-America Friendship Association, 30th Anniv. — A548

2008, June 13   Litho.
1755 A548 €1.50 multi   4.75 4.75

Europa A549

Boy and girl: 60c, On ships. 65c, On globe releasing doves.

2008, June 13   Perf. 13x13¼
1756-1757 A549   Set of 2   4.00 4.00

Souvenir Sheet

2008 Summer Olympics, Beijing — A550

No. 1758: a, 36c, Table tennis. b, 65c, Fencing. c, 85c, Swimming.

2008, June 13
1758 A550   Sheet of 3, #a-c   5.75 5.75

Andrea Palladio (1508-80), Architect A551

2008, Aug. 22   Litho.   Perf. 13x13¼
1759 A551 €1 multi   3.00 3.00

A552

Road Cycling World Championships, Varese, Italy — A553

2008, Aug. 22   Perf. 13¼x13
1760 A552   85c multi   2.50 2.50
1761 A553   €3.25 multi   9.50 9.50

Famous People — A554

Designs: 60c (No. 1762), Posters for operas by Giacomo Puccini (1858-1924). 60c (No. 1763), Scenes from Cuore, by Edmondo De Amicis (1846-1908). €1, Rotonda di Palmieri and Vita Militare, paintings by Giovanni Fattori (1825-1908). €1.40, Book cover designs and actors in movie based on works by Giovannino Guareschi (1908-68), writer. €1.70, Piece of pottery and painting, The Print Collectors, by Honoré Daumier (1808-79), artist. €2.20, Scene from La Luna e i Falò, by Cesare Pavese (1908-50).

2008
1762-1767 A554   Set of 6   21.25 21.25
Issued: No. 1762, €1, €1.40, €1.70, 8/22; No. 1763, €2.20, 11/18.

International Polar Year — A555

Designs: 60c, Mountain. €1, Penguins. €1.20, Helicopter over ice sheet.

2008, Nov. 18   Perf. 13x13¼
1768-1770 A555   Set of 3   7.25 7.25

Miniature Sheet

Addition of San Marino Historic Center and Mt. Titano to UNESCO World Heritage List — A556

No. 1771: a, Cesta Tower. b, Basilica. c, Statue of Liberty, Government Palace. d, Omerelli neighborhood. e, Buildings near wall. f, Guaita Tower.

2008, Nov. 18   Perf. 13¼x13
1771 A556   €1 Sheet of 6, #a-f
                                15.50 15.50

Christmas A557

Designs: 36c, Angel playing trumpet. 60c, Holy Family. €1, Angel with gift.

2008, Nov. 18
1772-1774 A557   Set of 3   5.00 5.00

San Marino Olympic Committee, 50th Anniv. — A558

2009, Feb. 20   Litho.   Perf. 13¼x14
1775 A558 €1.80 multi   4.75 4.75

Ceramics A559

Designs: 36c, Amphora, by Libero Cellarosi. 60c, Amphora, by Umberto Masi. 85c, Vase, by Giorgio Monti.

2009, Feb. 20   Perf. 13x13¼
1776-1778 A559   Set of 3   4.75 4.75

Miniature Sheet

Futurist Manifesto, by Filippo Tomasso Marinetti, Cent. — A560

No. 1779: a, Dog on a Leash, painting by Giacomo Balla (40x30mm). b, Armored Train, painting by Giono Severini (30x40mm). c, Electric Power Plant, painting by Antonio Sant'Elia (30x45mm). d, Zang Tumb Tumb, by Marinetti (45x30mm). e, Red Horseman, painting by Carlo Carra (40x30mm). f, Noise machine, by Luigi Russolo (53x30mm). g, Cyclist, painting by Umberto Boccioni (40x30mm). h, Still Life with Red Egg, by Ardeng Soffici (30x38mm). i, Unique Forms of Continuity in Space, sculpture by Boccioni (30x38mm). j, Futurist Evening, drawing by Boccioni (45x30mm).

2009, Feb. 20   Perf. 12½ to 13¼
1779 A560 60c Sheet of 10,
           #a-j, + label   15.50 15.50

38th Intl. Criminal Police Organization and Interpol European Regional Conference, San Marino — A561

2009, May 8   Litho.   Perf. 14x13¼
1780 A561 €2 multi   5.75 5.75

San Marino Expo 2010 Pavilion and Shanghai Skyline — A562

2009, May 8   Litho.   Perf. 13
1781 A562 €2.20 multi   6.25 6.25

Europa — A563

Designs: 60c, Earth, Saturn, Neptune, astronomical instruments. 65c, Solar System, star ring of European Union flag, Mount Titano.

2009, May 8   Litho.   Perf. 13½x14
1782-1783 A563   Set of 2   3.50 3.50
    Intl. Year of Astronomy.

World Air Games, Turin — A564

Doves and: 60c, Hot-air balloon. 85c, Glider. €1.50, Helicopter. €1.80, Airplane.

2009, May 8   Litho.   Perf. 13¼
1784-1787 A564   Set of 4   13.50 13.50

Louis Braille (1809-52), Educator of the Blind — A565

Litho. & Embossed
2009, June 16   Perf. 13¼x13
1788 A565 €1.50 multi   4.25 4.25

Writers of Detective Stories A566

Designs relating to and names of characters from stories by: 36c, Edgar Allan Poe (1809-49). 85c, Arthur Conan Doyle (1859-1930). €1.40, Raymond Chandler (1888-1959).

2009, June 16   Litho.   Perf. 14x13¼
1789-1791 A566   Set of 3   7.50 7.50

16th Mediterranean Games, Pescara, Italy — A567

Designs: 60c, Running. €1.40, Cycling. €1.70, Wrestling.

2009, June 16
1792-1794 A567   Set of 3   10.50 10.50

Miniature Sheet

Wines of San Marino — A568

No. 1795: a, Tessano. b, Brugneto. c, Riserva Titano. d, Caldese. e, Roncale. f, Moscato Spumante.

2009, June 16   Perf. 13x13¼
1795 A568 60c Sheet of 6, #a-
    f   10.00 10.00

Bologna Soccer Club, Cent. A569

2009, Aug. 25
1796 A569 €1 multi   3.00 3.00

30th Rimini Meeting — A570

2009, Aug. 25   Litho.   Perf. 13½x14
1797 A570 €1.80 multi   5.25 5.25

Souvenir Sheets

Attractions of San Marino — A571

No. 1798, €1 — Interior of Palazzo Pubblico with: a, Entire denomination on vignette. b, Part of final "0" of denomination on black frame.
No. 1799, €1 — Statue of St. Marinus with: a, Entire denomination on vignette. b, Part of final "0" of denomination on black frame.

No. 1800, €1 — Statue of Liberty and Piazza della Libertà with: a, "1" of denomination below "a" of "San." b, "1" of denomination below "S."

2009, Aug. 25   Litho.   Perf. 13¾x14
1798-1800 A571   Set of 3   17.50 17.50

European Year of Creativity and Innovation. Nos. 1798-1800 were sold as a set with a €1.40 postal card that opened up to serve as a stereoscope for the stamp sheets. The set included a pair of plastic lenses for the stereoscope, an instruction card for assembling the stereoscope, a self-adhesive seal for the postal card, and an imperforate sample stereoscope card depicting the vignette shown on the postal card that was not valid for postage. Values are for the set of 3 sheets only.

Italian Language Day — A572

2009, Oct. 21   Photo.   Perf. 13¼x13
1801 A572 60c multi + label   1.90 1.90

Issued in sheets of 5 + 5 labels. See Italy No. 2966; Vatican City No. 1426.

Pets A573

Winning photographs in pet photography contest: 36c, Cat, by Natascia Stefanelli. 60c, Poodle, by Tina Woodcock. 65c, Duck, by Ettore Zonzini. 75c, Kid, foal and dog, by Anna Rosa Francioni. 85c, Turtle, by Maria Eleonora Vaglio. €1.20, Dog and butterfly, by Lorenzo Zamagni.

2009, Oct. 21   Litho.   Perf. 14x13¼
1802-1807 A573   Set of 6   13.00 13.00

Souvenir Sheet

Christmas — A574

No. 1808 — Rest on the Flight Into Egypt, by Caravaggio: a, €1.50, Joseph and angel. b, €2, Madonna and Child, horiz.

2009, Oct. 21   Perf. 13¾
1808 A574   Sheet of 2, #a-b   10.50 10.50

San Marino Association of Blood and Organ Donors, 50th Anniv. — A575

2010, Feb. 9   Litho.   Perf. 13¾
1809 A575 €1.80 multi   5.00 5.00

Flowers — A576

No. 1810: a, 10c, Daffodils. b, 85c, Hyacinths. c, €1, Grape hyacinths. d, €1.50, Tulips.

2010, Feb. 9   Perf. 13¼x13
1810 A576   Block or strip of 4,
    #a-d   9.50 9.50

Souvenir Sheet

2010 Winter Olympics, Vancouver — A577

No. 1811: a, 65c, Ski jumping, snowboarding, ice hockey, speed skating. b, 85c, Downhill skiing, cross-country skiing, curling, bobsledding. c, €1, Speed skating, figure skating, downhill skiing.

2010, Feb. 9   Perf. 13x13¼
1811 A577   Sheet of 3, #a-c   7.00 7.00

Miniature Sheet

Expo 2010, Shanghai — A578

No. 1812: a, 65c, San Marino flag, Third Tower on Mt. Titano (30x40mm). b, €1, Second Tower, Great Wall of China (30x40mm). c, €1.50, First Tower, spear of Statue of Liberty (30x40mm). d, €1.80, San Marino Government Building, Statue of Liberty (36x51mm).

Perf. 13¼x13, 13¼ (#1812d)
2010, Feb. 9
1812 A578 Sheet of 4, #a-d 13.50 13.50

Men's Volleyball World Championships, Italy — A579

2010, Mar. 17 *Perf. 13¼x14*
1813 A579 €1 multi 2.75 2.75

2010 World Cup Soccer Championships, South Africa — A580

2010, Mar. 17 *Perf. 14x13¼*
1814 A580 €1.50 multi 4.00 4.00

Italian Cyclists — A581

No. 1815: a, €1.40, Gino Bartali (1914-2000). b, €1.50, Fausto Coppi (1919-60).

2010, Mar. 17
1815 A581 Horiz. pair, #a-b 8.00 8.00

Europa A582

Designs: 60c, Girl with wings of book pages. 65c, Girl asleep on a book in space.

2010, Mar. 17 *Perf. 14¾x14*
1816-1817 A582 Set of 2 3.50 3.50

Miniature Sheet

Friendship Between San Marino and Japan — A583

No. 1818: a, Statue of La Repubblica, by Vittorio Pochini, La Rocca tower, San Marino. b, Himeji Castle, Japan. c, Apparition of Saint Marinus to His People, mural by Emilio Retrosi. d, Nihonbashi Bridge in the Morning, painting by Hiroshige.

2010, Mar. 17 *Perf. 13x13¼*
1818 A583 €1.50 Sheet of 4, #a-d 16.50 16.50
See Japan No. 3217.

San Marino Lions Club, 50th Anniv. — A584

Various photos of San Marino with country name in: 36c, Red violet. 60c, Orange brown.

2010, July 26 *Litho. Perf. 14x13¼*
1819-1820 A584 Set of 2 2.50 2.50

F.C. Internazionale, 2009-10 Italian Soccer Champions — A585

No. 1821: a, Italian flag, soccer ball, F.C. Internazionale emblem. b, Shield inscribed "18," part of soccer ball. c, Part of soccer ball, European Union flag.

2010, July 26
1821 Horiz. strip of 3 8.00 8.00
a.-c. A585 €1 Any single 2.60 2.60

Miniature Sheet

Sites in San Marino and Gibraltar — A586

No. 1822: a, Second Tower, San Marino. b, Moorish Castle, Gibraltar. c, Mt. Titano, San Marino. d, Rock of Gibraltar.

2010, July 26
1822 A586 €1.50 Sheet of 4, #a-d 16.00 16.00
See Gibraltar No. 1237.

Famous People A587

Designs: 60c, Moon, hands of Frédéric Chopin (1810-49), composer. 65c, Scenes from movies, *The Seven Samurai, Ran,* and *Dersu Uzala,* directed by Akira Kurosawa (1910-98). 85c, Symphony orchestra and conductor Gustav Mahler (1860-1911), composer. €1, *The Birth of Venus,* by Sandro Botticelli (1445-1510), vert. €1.40, *The Tempest,* by Giorgione da Castelfranco (c. 1477-1510), vert. €1.45, *The Supper at Emmaus,* by Caravaggio (1571-1610), vert. €1.50, *The Football Players,* by Henri Rousseau (1844-1910), vert. €4.95, Characters from "The Adventures of Huckleberry Finn," and Mark Twain (1835-1910), author.

2010 *Perf. 14x13¼, 13¼x14*
1823-1830 A587 Set of 8 34.00 34.00
Issued: 60c, 65c, 85c, €4.95, 10/5; others, 7/26.

Luciano Pavarotti (1935-2007), Opera Singer — A588

2010, Oct. 5 *Perf. 14x13¼*
1831 A588 €2.20 multi 6.25 6.25

Christmas A589

Christmas tree with background color of: 60c, Blue. 65c, Green. 85c, Red.

Litho. With Foil Application
2010, Oct. 5 *Perf. 13x13¼*
1832-1834 A589 Set of 3 6.00 6.00

Sport in the Philately of San Marino Exhibition A590

2011, Feb. 8 Litho. *Perf. 14¼x14¾*
1835 A590 €1.50 multi 4.25 4.25

San Marino Choir, 50th Anniv. — A591

2011, Feb. 8
1836 A591 €2.20 multi 6.00 6.00

Luigi Einaudi (1874-1961), President of Italy — A592

2011, Feb. 8 *Perf. 14¾x14¼*
1837 A592 €3.30 multi 9.00 9.00

Paintings A593

Designs: 10c, Self-portrait with a Beret, by Paul Cézanne. 50c, Horse Racing at Longchamp, by Edgar Degas. 85c, View from the Artist's Window, by Camille Pissarro. €1, Flower Beds at Vétheuil, by Claude Monet.

€2.50, Jacques Bergeret as a Child, by Pierre-Auguste Renoir.

2011, Feb. 8 *Perf. 13¾*
1838-1842 A593 Set of 5 13.50 13.50

Europa A594

Designs: 60c, Forest. 65c, Stacked logs.

2011, Apr. 5 Litho. *Perf. 14¾x14¼*
1843-1844 A594 Set of 2 3.75 3.75
Intl. Year of Forests.

First Men in Space, 50th Anniv. A595

Designs: 50c, Yuri Gagarin (1934-68), Soviet cosmonaut. €2.40, Alan B. Shepard, Jr. (1923-98), American astronaut.

2011, Apr. 5
1845-1846 A595 Set of 2 8.50 8.50

Souvenir Sheet

Flowers — A596

No. 1847: a, Delphinium "Verissimo del Titano." b, Dianthus "Sant'Agata." c, Rosa "Repubblica di San Marino."

2011, Apr. 5
1847 A596 €1.50 Sheet of 3, #a-c 13.00 13.00

Miniature Sheet

Tourism — A597

No. 1848 — Sites in San Marino: a, Prima Torre (First Tower). b, Basilica del Santo, horiz. c, Chiesa dei Cappuccini (Church of the Capuchin), horiz. d, Palazzo del Governo (Government Building). e, Chiesa di San Francesco (San Francesco Church). f, Porta San Francesco (San Francesco Gate).

2011, Apr. 5 *Perf. 14¾*
1848 A597 65c Sheet of 6, #a-f 11.50 11.50

Brescia Soccer
Team,
Cent. — A598

2011, June 4   *Perf. 14x14¾*
1849 A598 €1 multi   3.00 3.00

Visit of
Pope
Benedict
XVI to
San
Marino
A599

2011, June 4   *Perf. 14¾x14*
1850 A599 €1 multi   3.00 3.00

Souvenir Sheet

Anita and Giuseppe Garibaldi, First
Tower of San Marino — A600

2011, June 4   *Perf. 14x13¼*
1851 A600 €1.50 multi   4.50 4.50
Granting of San Marino citizenship to Gari-
baldis. See Italy No. 3070.

Miniature Sheet

World Theater Day — A601

No. 1852: a, Statue of Liberty, San Marino,
buildings. b, Mask with tassels, buildings. c,
Character with arms extended. d, Face, three
towers of San Marino. e, Face, dancers in ring.
f, Dancers in ring.

2011, June 4   *Perf. 13¾x13¼*
1852 A601 85c Sheet of 6, #a-
     f   15.00 15.00

A.C. Milan,
2010-11
Italian
Soccer
Champions
A602

2011, Oct. 11   *Perf. 14*
1853 A602 €1 multi
     2.75 2.75

Alcide De Gasperi (1881-1954), Italian
Prime Minister — A603

No. 1854 — De Gasperi and: a, 50c, Family,
scales, war damage. b, €2.64, Torch, map of
Europe.

2011, Oct. 11   *Perf. 14x13½*
1854 A603   Horiz. pair, #a-b   8.75 8.75

Souvenir Sheet

European Year of
Volunteering — A604

2011, Oct. 11   *Perf. 14¾x14¼*
1855 A604 €4.95 multi   14.00 14.00

Souvenir Sheet

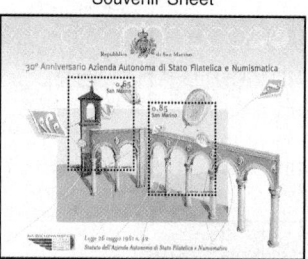

Philatelic and Numismatic Bureau of
San Marino, 30th Anniv. — A605

No. 1856: a, 65c, Tower, arches, stamp and
coins. b, 85c, Arches, stamp and coins.

2011, Oct. 11   *Perf. 13½x14*
1856 A605   Sheet of 2, #a-b   4.25 4.25

Miniature Sheet

Christmas — A606

No. 1857: a, 85c, Angels. b, €1, Magi. c,
€1.50, Shepherd and Mary. d, €2.50, Mary
and infant Jesus.

2011, Oct. 11
1857 A606   Sheet of 4, #a-d   16.00 16.00

Milano Marittima,
Italy,
Cent. — A607

2012, Feb. 29
1858 A607 €1 multi   2.75 2.75

Miniature Sheet

Paintings by Gustav Klimt (1862-
1918) — A608

No. 1859: a, 85c, The Embrace
(L'abbraccio). b, €1, The Kiss (Il bacio). c,
€1.40, The Three Ages of Woman (Le tre età
della donna). d, €1.50, Hope II (La speranza
II).

2012, Feb. 29   *Perf. 13¼x13*
1859 A608   Sheet of 4, #a-d   12.50 12.50

Souvenir Sheet

New San Marino Coat of
Arms — A609

No. 1860: a, 60c, Crown, arms in blue. b,
85c, Berry on branch, arms in silver. c, €4.95,
Old arms in circle, new arms in gold.

Litho. With Foil Application
2012, Feb. 29   *Perf. 13x13¼*
1860 A609   Sheet of 3, #a-c   17.00 17.00

SEMI-POSTAL STAMPS

Regular Issue of 1903 Surcharged

     a   b

1917, Dec. 15   **Wmk. 140**   *Perf. 14*
B1 A10(a)   25c on 2c violet   15.00 15.00
B2 A11(b)   50c on 2 l violet   60.00 60.00

Statue of
Liberty — SP1

View of
San Marino
SP2

1918, June 1   **Typo.**
B3   SP1   2c dl vio & blk   3.25 3.25
B4   SP1   5c bl grn & blk   3.25 3.25
B5   SP1   10c lake & blk   3.25 3.25
B6   SP1   20c brn org & blk   3.25 3.25
B7   SP1   25c ultra & blk   3.25 3.25
B8   SP1   45c yel brn & blk   3.25 3.25
B9   SP2   1 l bl grn & blk   20.00 24.00
B10 SP2   2 l vio & blk   17.00 17.00
B11 SP2   3 l claret & blk   17.00 17.00
   Nos. B3-B11 (9)   73.50 77.50

These stamps were sold at an advance of
5c each over face value, the receipts from that
source being devoted to the support of a hospital for Italian soldiers.
For surcharges see Nos. 89-92.

Nos. B6-B8
Overprinted

1918, Dec. 12
B12 SP1   20c brn org & blk   5.00 5.00
B13 SP1   25c ultra & blk   5.00 5.00
B14 SP1   45c yel brn & blk   5.00 5.00

Nos. B9-B11 Overprinted

B15 SP2   1 l blue grn & blk   10.00 10.00
B16 SP2   2 l violet & blk   19.00 20.00
B17 SP2   3 l claret & blk   19.00 20.00
   Nos. B12-B17 (6)   63.00 65.00

Celebration of Italian Victory over Austria.
Inverted overprints were privately produced.

Coat of   Liberty
Arms   SP4
SP3

1923, Sept. 20   **Engr.**
B18 SP3   5c + 5c olive grn   .80 .80
B19 SP3   10c + 5c orange   .80 .80
B20 SP3   15c + 5c dk green   .80 .80
B21 SP3   25c + 5c brn lake   .80 .80
B22 SP3   40c + 5c vio brn   4.00 4.00
B23 SP3   50c + 5c gray   2.40 .80
B24 SP4   1 l + 5c blk & bl   8.00 8.00
   Nos. B18-B24 (7)   17.60 16.00

St. Marinus
SP5

Wmk. 140

1944, Apr. 25   Photo.   Perf. 14
B25 SP5 20 l + 10 l gldn brn   2.40   2.40
    Never hinged   5.00   5.00
    Sheet of 8   110.00 110.00
    Never hinged   225.00

The surtax was used for workers' houses.
See No. CB1.

No. 256 Surcharged in Red "L. 10"

1946, Aug. 24   Unwmk.
B26 A46 50 l + 10 l   20.00   20.00
    Never hinged   40.00
    Sheet of 10   800.00 800.00
    Never hinged   1,500.

Third Philatelic Day, Rimini. The surtax was
for the exhibition.

Air Post Types of 1946 Surcharged
"CONVEGNO FILATELICO / 30
NOVEMBRE 1946 / + LIRE 25" (or
"LIRE 50") in Red or Violet

1946, Nov. 30   Wmk. 277
B26A AP7 3 l + 25 l dk brn (R)   .95   .70
B26B AP8 5 l + 25 l red org
    (V)   .95   .70
B26C AP6 10 l + 50 l ultra (R)   7.25   .65
    Nos. B26A-B26C (3)   9.15   2.05
    Set, never hinged   20.00

Inscription "Posta Aerea" does not appear
on these stamps.

No. 260 Surcharged
in Black

1947, Nov. 13   Wmk. 217   Perf. 12
B27 A53 1 l + 1 l brt grn & vio   .30   .30
B28 A53 1 l + 2 l brt grn & vio   .30   .30
B29 A53 1 l + 3 l brt grn & vio   .30   .30
B30 A53 1 l + 4 l brt grn & vio   .30   .30
B31 A53 1 l + 5 l brt grn & vio   .30   .30
    a.   Strip of 5, #B27-B31   2.00   2.00

Surcharged on No. 261
B32 A53 2 l + 1 l pur & olive   .30   .30
B33 A53 2 l + 2 l pur & olive   .30   .30
B34 A53 2 l + 3 l pur & olive   .30   .30
B35 A53 2 l + 4 l pur & olive   .30   .30
B36 A53 2 l + 5 l pur & olive   .30   .30
    a.   Strip of 5, #B32-B36   2.00   2.00

Surcharged on No. 262
B37 A53 4 l + 1 l   2.10   2.10
B38 A53 4 l + 2 l   2.10   2.10
    a.   Pair, #B37-B38   14.50   14.50
    Nos. B27-B38 (12)   7.20   7.20
    Set, never hinged   18.00

Surcharges on Nos. B27-B38 are arranged
consecutively, changing from ascending to
descending order of denomination on alternate rows in the sheet.

> **Catalogue values for unused
> stamps in this section, from this
> point to the end of the section, are
> for Never Hinged items.**

Refugee
Boy — SP6

1982, Dec. 15   Photo.   Perf. 11½
B39 SP6 300 l + 100 l multi   .40   .40

Surcharge was for refugee support.

AIR POST STAMPS

View of
San
Marino
AP1

Wmk. 217

1931, June 11   Engr.   Perf. 12
C1 AP1 50c blue grn   32.50   22.50
C2 AP1 80c red   32.50   22.50
C3 AP1 1 l bister brn   9.50   11.00
C4 AP1 2 l brt violet   9.50   11.00
C5 AP1 2.60 l Prus bl 65.00   80.00
C6 AP1 3 l dk gray   55.00   62.50
C7 AP1 5 l olive grn   9.50   11.00
C8 AP1 7.70 l dk brown 19.00   22.50
C9 AP1 9 l dp orange   19.00   22.50
C10 AP1 10 l dk blue   400.00   500.00
    Nos. C1-C10 (10)   651.50   765.50
    Set, never hinged   1,625.

Exist imperf.

Graf Zeppelin Issue
Stamps of Type AP1 Surcharged in
Blue or Black

1933, Apr. 28
C11 AP1 3 l on 50c org   9.50   150.00
C12 AP1 5 l on 80c ol grn 47.50 150.00
C13 AP1 10 l on 1 l dk bl
    (Bk)   47.50   200.00
C14 AP1 12 l on 2 l yel brn 47.50 250.00
C15 AP1 15 l on 2.60 l dl
    red (Bk)   47.50   260.00
C16 AP1 20 l on 3 l bl grn
    (Bk)   47.50   425.00
    Nos. C11-C16 (6) 247.00 1,435.
    Set, never hinged 600.00

Exist imperf.

Nos. C1 and C2 Surcharged

1936, Apr. 14
C17 AP1 75c on 50c blue grn   2.40   2.40
C18 AP1 75c on 80c red   14.00   14.00
    Set, never hinged   40.00

Nos. C5 and C6 Surcharged with New
Value and Bars

1941, Jan. 12
C19 AP1 10 l on 2.60 l   95.00   95.00
C20 AP1 10 l on 3 l   30.00   30.00
    Set, never hinged   250.00

View of
Arbe — AP2

Wmk. 140

1942, Mar. 16   Photo.   Perf. 14
C21 AP2 25c brn & gray blk   .30   .30
C22 AP2 50c grn & brn   .30   .30
C23 AP2 75c gray bl & red brn .30   .30
C24 AP2 1 l ocher & brn   .75   .75
C25 AP2 5 l bis brn & bl   7.00   7.00
    Nos. C21-C25 (5)   8.65   8.65
    Set, never hinged   16.00

Return of the Italian flag to Arbe.

AP3

Overprinted in Black

1943, Aug. 27
C26 AP3 25c yellow org   .30   .30
C27 AP3 50c car rose   .30   .30
C28 AP3 75c dark brown   .30   .30
C29 AP3 1 l dk rose vio   .30   .30
C30 AP3 2 l sapphire   .30   .30
C31 AP3 5 l orange red   1.50   1.50
C32 AP3 10 l deep green   2.25   2.25
C33 AP3 20 l black   7.50   7.50
    Nos. C26-C33 (8)   12.75 12.75
    Set, never hinged   25.00

See footnote after No. 227. Nos. C26-C33
exist without overprint (not regularly issued).
Value $1,500.

San Marino Map,
Fasces and
Wing — AP4

Overprinted in Black

1943, Aug. 27
C34 AP4 25c yellow org   .30   .30
C35 AP4 50c car rose   .30   .30
C36 AP4 75c dark brown   .30   .30
C37 AP4 1 l dk rose vio   .30   .30
C38 AP4 5 l orange red   1.25   1.25
C39 AP4 20 l black   3.25   3.25
    Nos. C34-C39 (6)   5.70   5.70
    Set, never hinged   9.50

Government
Palace — AP5

1945, Mar. 15   Photo.
C40 AP5 25 l bister brn   6.50   6.50

See note after No. 239.

Gulls and
San Marino
Skyline
AP6

Plane and
View of
San Marino
AP7

Planes over Mt.
Titano — AP8

Plane over
Globe
AP9

Photo., Engr. (20 l, 50 l)

1946-47   Unwmk.   Perf. 14
C41 AP6 25c blue blk   .25   .25
C42 AP7 75c red org   .25   .25
C43 AP6 1 l brown   .25   .25
C44 AP7 2 l dull green   .25   .25
C45 AP7 3 l violet   .25   .25
C46 AP8 5 l violet blue   .25   .25
C47 AP6 10 l crimson   .25   .25
C48 AP8 20 l brown lake   1.60   1.60
C49 AP8 35 l orange red   4.75   4.75
C50 AP8 50 l dk yellow grn   8.00   7.00
C51 AP9 100 l sepia ('47)   1.25   1.25
    Nos. C41-C51 (11) 17.35 16.35
    Set, never hinged   30.00

Some values exist imperforate.
Issue dates: 35 l, Nov. 3, 1946; 100 l, Mar.
27, 1947; others, Aug. 8, 1946.
For surcharges and overprint see Nos.
B26A-B26C, C54.

Roosevelt Type of Regular Issue, 1947

F. D. Roosevelt and: 1 l, 31 l, 50 l, Eagle. 2 l,
20 l, 100 l, San Marino arms. 5 l, 200 l, Flags
of San Marino and US, vert.

Wmk. 277

1947, May 3   Photo.   Perf. 14
C51A A52a 1 l dp ultra &
    sep   .25   .25
C51B A52a 2 l org red &
    sep   .25   .25
C51C A52a 5 l multicolored   .25   .25
C51D A52a 20 l choc & sep   .25   .25
C51E A52a 31 l org & sep   .50   .50
C51F A52a 50 l dk car &
    sep   .90   .90
C51G A52a 100 l bl & sepia   4.00   1.75
C51H A52a 200 l multicolored 17.50 15.00
    Nos. C51A-C51H (8) 23.90 19.15
    Set, never hinged   50.00

Nos. C51A-C51E, C51H exist imperf. Value,
set $150.

Nos. C51A-C51C Surcharged

1947, June 16
C51I A52a 3 l on 1 l dp ultra &
    sep   .40   .40
C51J A52a 4 l on 2 l org red &
    sep   .40   .40
C51K A52a 6 l on 5 l multicolored   .40   .40
    Nos. C51I-C51K (3) 1.20   1.20
    Set, never hinged   2.50

St. Marinus Type of Regular Issue, 1947

Wmk. 217

1947, July 18   Engr.   Perf. 12
Center in Bright Blue

C52 A53 25 l deep orange   1.25   1.25
C53 A53 50 l red brown   2.75   2.50
    Set, never hinged   8.00

No. C51
Overprinted
in Red

1947, July 18   Unwmk.   Perf. 14
C54 AP9 100 l sepia   1.25   1.25
    Never hinged   2.00
    a.   Double overprint   150.00

b.   Never hinged   250.00
        Inverted overprint   150.00
        Never hinged   250.00

Rimini Phil. Exhib., July 18-20.

US No. 1
and Mt.
Titano
AP11

Wmk. 277

1947, Dec. 24   Engr.   Perf. 14
C55 AP11 100 l dk pur & dk
           brn   10.00 10.00
     Never hinged   20.00
     Sheet of 10   2,500.
a.   Imperf.   160.00
     Never hinged   300.00
     As "a," sheet of 10   8,000.

1st US postage stamps, cent.

No. 264 Surcharged "POSTA AEREA"
and New Value in Black

1948, Oct. 9   Wmk. 217   Perf. 12
C56 A53 200 l on 25 l   30.00 30.00
     Never hinged   60.00

Giuseppe and
Anita Garibaldi
Entering San
Marino — AP12

Wmk. 277

1949, June 28   Photo.   Perf. 14
Size: 27½x22mm
C57 AP12 2 l brn red & ultra   .30   .30
C58 AP12 3 l dk green & se-
           pia   .30   .30
C59 AP12 5 l dk bl grn & ul-
           tra   .30   .30
Size: 37x22mm
C60 AP12 25 l dk green & vio 5.00 2.50
C61 AP12 65 l grnsh blk &
           gray blk   24.00 12.00
     Nos. C57-C61 (5)   29.90 15.40
     Set, never hinged   30.00

Garibaldi's escape to San Marino, cent.

Stagecoach
on Road
from San
Marino
AP13

1950, Feb. 9   Engr.   Perf. 14
C62 AP13 200 l deep blue   1.50 1.50
     Never hinged   2.50
a.   Perf. 13½x14 ('51)   3.50 3.50
     Never hinged   5.00
     As "a," sheet of 6   45.00 45.00
     Never hinged   80.00
b.   Imperf ('51)   25.00 25.00
     As "b," sheet of 6   325.00 325.00
     Never hinged   500.00

UPU, 75th anniv. #C62 was issued in
sheets of 25; #C62a & C62b in sheets of 6.
See #C75.

AP14   AP15

AP16

Various Views of San Marino.

1950, Apr. 12   Photo.   Perf. 14
Size: 27½x21½mm, 21½x27½mm
C63 AP14 2 l vio & dp
           grn   .35   .25
C64 AP14 3 l blue &
           brown   .35   .25
C65 AP15 5 l brn blk &
           rose red   .35   .25
C66 AP14 10 l grnsh blk &
           bl   1.40   .60
C67 AP14 15 l grnsh blk &
           vio   1.60   .75
Size: 36x26½mm, 26½x36mm
C68 AP15 55 l dp bl & dp
           grn   24.00 20.00
C69 AP14 100 l car & gray   18.00 16.00
C70 AP15 250 l violet & brn 75.00 45.00
Engr.
C71 AP16 500 l bl, dk grn &
           vio brn   75.00 100.00
     Nos. C63-C71 (9)   196.05 183.10
     Set, never hinged   425.00

See No. C78. For overprints and surcharges
see Nos. C72-C74, C76, C79.

Types of 1950
Overprinted in Black,
Blue or Brown

1950, Apr. 12   Photo.
New Colors; Sizes as Before
C72 AP15 5 l dp bl & dp grn   .25   .25
C73 AP14 15 l car & gray (Bl) .55   .55
C74 AP15 55 l vio & brn (Br) 4.00 4.00
     Nos. C72-C74 (3)   4.80 4.80
     Set, never hinged   7.50

The overprint is arranged differently on each
denomination.
San Marino's participation in the 28th Intl.
Fair of Milan, Apr., 1950.

Stagecoach Type of 1950
1951, Jan. 31   Engr.   Perf. 13½x14
C75 AP13 300 l rose brn &
           brn   20.00 20.00
     Never hinged   30.00
     Sheet of 6   200.00 225.00
     Never hinged   425.00
a.   Imperf.   800.00
     Never hinged   1,400.
     Sheet of 6   4,500.
     Never hinged   8,000.

No. C71 Surcharged in Black
"Giornata Filatelica San Marino-
Riccione 20-8-1951," New Value and
Bars

1951, Aug. 20   Perf. 14
C76 AP16 300 l on 500 l   35.00 35.00
     Never hinged   80.00

Flag and
Plane
AP17

Perf. 13½x14
1951, Nov. 22   Engr.   Wmk. 277
C77 AP17 1000 l multi   500.00 500.00
     Never hinged   700.00
     Sheet of 6   7,000. 7,000.
     Never hinged   9,000.

Type of 1950
1951, Apr. 28   Photo.   Perf. 14
Size: 36x26½mm
C78 AP16 500 l dk grn &
           brn   125.00 125.00
     Never hinged   250.00
     Sheet of 6   2,250. 2,250.
     Never hinged   3,000.

No. C70 Surcharged
in Black

1951, Dec. 6
C79 AP15 100 l on 250 l   4.00 4.00
     Never hinged   6.50

Issued to raise funds for flood victims in
northern Italy.

Columbus,
Globe,
Statue of
Liberty and
Buildings
AP18

1952, Jan. 28   Engr.
C80 AP18 200 l dk bl & blk   27.50 27.50
     Never hinged   55.00

Issued to honor Christopher Columbus.

Type of
1952
Overprinted
in Red

1952, June 29
C81 AP18 200 l blk brn & choc 35.00 35.00
     Never hinged   70.00

4th Intl. Sample Fair of Trieste.

Cyclamen — AP19

Flowers and Seacoast — AP20

2 l, As #C85-C87 with flowers omitted. 3 l,
Rose.

1952, Aug. 25   Photo.   Perf. 10x14
C82 AP19 1 l pur & lil rose   .25   .25
C83 AP19 2 l blue & bl grn   .25   .25
C84 AP19 3 l dk brn & red   .25   .25
Perf. 14
C85 AP20 5 l rose lil & brn   .25   .25
C86 AP20 25 l vio & bl grn   .25   .25
Perf. 13
Engr.
C87 AP20 200 l multi   40.00 40.00
     Sheet of 6, #C87   800.00 800.00
     Never hinged   1,000.
     Nos. C82-C87 (6)   41.25 41.25
     Set, never hinged   80.00

Riccione Phil. Exhib., Aug. 25, 1952.

Plane Making Photographic
Survey — AP21

75 l, Aerial survey, seen through window.

1952, Nov. 17   Photo.   Perf. 14
C88 AP21 25 l olive green   1.25 1.25
C89 AP21 75 l red brn & pur 4.25 4.25
     Set, never hinged   8.00

Aerial photographic survey of San Marino,
1952.

Skier
AP22

1953, Apr. 20   Engr.
C90 AP22 200 l bl grn &
           dk grn   45.00 45.00
     Never hinged   90.00
     Sheet of 6   1,000. 1,000.
     Never hinged   1,250.

Plane and
Arms of
San Marino
AP23

1954, Apr. 5
C91 AP23 1000 l dk blue
           & brn   100.00 100.00
     Never hinged   150.00
     Sheet of 6   1,000. 1,000.
     Never hinged   1,250.

Type of Regular Issue, 1954
1954, Dec. 16   Photo.   Perf. 13
C92 A71 120 l dp bl & red
          brn   1.25 1.25
     Never hinged   2.50

Hurdler
AP25

1955, June 26   Wmk. 303   Perf. 14
C93 AP25 80 l shown   1.25 1.10
C94 AP25 120 l Relay   2.00 1.75
     Set, never hinged   4.75

San Marino's first Intl. Exhib. of Olympic
Stamps, June.

Ski Jumper
AP26

1955, Dec. 15
C95 AP26 200 l blk & red org 20.00 20.00
     Never hinged   40.00

7th Winter Olympic Games at Cortina
d'Ampezzo, Jan. 26-Feb. 5, 1956.

No. 372 Overprinted in Upper Right
Corner with Plane and "Posta Aerea"
1956, Dec. 10
C96 A76 100 l blk & Prus grn 1.40 2.75
     Never hinged   2.75

Catalogue values for unused
stamps in this section, from this
point to the end of the section, are
for Never Hinged items.

Helicopter, Plane
and Modernistic
Building — AP27

Wmk. 303

1958, Apr. 12		**Photo.**		**Perf. 14**
C97	AP27	125 l lt blue & brn	3.25	3.25

10th participation in Milan Fair.
See Nos. 414-415.

View of San Marino — AP28

Design: 300 l, Road from Mt. Titano.

Wmk. 303

1958, June 23	**Engr.**		**Perf. 13**
C98	200 l brn & dk blue	4.75	4.75
C99	300 l magenta & vio	4.75	4.75
a.	AP28 Strip, Nos. C98, C99 + label	10.00	10.00

Printed in sheets containing 20 each of Nos. C98 and C99 flanking a center label with San Marino coat of arms. Nos. C98 and C99 also come se-tenant in sheet.

Naples Stamps Type of Regular Issue

Design: Bay of Naples and 50g stamp of Naples.

1958, Oct. 8		**Photo.**		**Perf. 14**
C100	A85	125 l brn & red brn	2.75	2.75

Sea Gull
AP29

Birds: 10 l, Falcon. 15 l, Mallard. 120 l, Stock dove. 250 l, Barn swallow.

1959, Feb. 12				**Perf. 14**
C101	AP29	5 l green & gray	.25	.25
C102	AP29	10 l blue & org brn	.25	.25
C103	AP29	15 l red & multi	.25	.25
C104	AP29	120 l rose red, yel & gray blk	1.25	.60
C105	AP29	250 l dp grn, yel & blk	4.00	2.25
	Nos. C101-C105 (5)		6.00	3.60

Pierre de
Coubertin
AP30

1959, May 19	**Engr.**		**Perf. 13**
C106	AP30	120 l sepia	4.75	3.25

Pierre de Coubertin; 1960 Olympic Games in Rome.

Alitalia
Viscount
Over San
Marino
AP31

1959, June 3		**Photo.**		**Perf. 14**
C107	AP31	120 l bright violet	2.00	2.00

First flight San Marino-Rimini-London.

Lincoln Type of Regular Issue, 1959

Design: Abraham Lincoln and San Marino peaks.

1959, July 1		**Engr.**		**Perf. 14x13**
C108	A87	200 l dark blue	6.00	5.25

Romagna Stamps Type

Design: Bologna view, 3b Romagna stamp.

Wmk. 303

1959, Aug. 29		**Photo.**		**Perf. 14**
C109	A88	120 l blk & blue grn	2.50	2.00

Sicily Stamps Type

Design: Fishing boats, Monte Pellegrino and 50g stamp of Sicily, horiz.

1959, Oct. 16			
C110	A89	200 l multicolored	3.00 3.00

Olympic Games Type

Sports: 20 l, Basketball. 40 l, Sprint race. 80 l, Swimming, horiz. 125 l, Target shooting, horiz.

1960, May 23		**Wmk. 303**		**Perf. 14**
C111	A92	20 l lilac	.25	.25
C112	A92	40 l bis brn & dk red	.25	.25
C113	A92	80 l ultra & buff	.25	.25
C114	A92	125 l ver & dk brn	.35	.25
	Nos. C111-C114 (4)		1.10	1.00

Souvenir sheets are valued and described below No. 465.

Lions Intl. Type

Design: 200 l, Globe and Lions emblem.

1960, July 1			**Photo.**
C115	A94	200 l ol grn, brn & ultra	8.50 8.50

12th Stamp Fair Type

1960, Aug. 27		**Wmk. 303**		**Perf. 14**
C116	A95	125 l multicolored	1.60	1.40

Helicopter
and Mt.
Titano
AP32

1961, July 6		**Engr.**		**Perf. 14**
C117	AP32	1000 l rose car	60.00	40.00
	Sheet of 6		400.00	275.00

Tupolev TU-
104A
AP33

Planes: 10 l, Boeing 707, vert. 15 l, Douglas DC-8. 25 l, Boeing 707. 50 l, Vickers Viscount 837. 75 l, Caravelle, vert. 120 l, Vickers VC10. 200 l, D. H. Comet 4C. 300 l, Boeing 727. 500 l, Rolls Royce Dart turbo-prop. 1000 l, Boeing 707.

1963-65	**Wmk. 339**	**Photo.**		**Perf. 14**
C118	AP33	5 l bl & vio brn	.30	.30
C119	AP33	10 l org & dk bl	.30	.30
C120	AP33	15 l violet & red	.30	.30
C121	AP33	25 l violet & car	.30	.30
C122	AP33	50 l grnsh bl & red	.30	.30
C123	AP33	75 l emer & dp org	.30	.30
C124	AP33	120 l vio bl & red	.30	.30
C125	AP33	200 l brt yel & blk	.50	.50
C126	AP33	300 l org & blk	.50	.50

		Perf. 13		
C127	AP33	500 l multicolored	6.00	6.00
	Sheet of 4		27.50	27.50
C128	AP33	1000 l lil rose, ultra & yel	3.00	3.00
	Sheet of 4		25.00	25.00
	Nos. C118-C128 (11)		12.10	12.10

Issued: Nos. C118-C126, Dec. 5, 1963. No. C127, Mar. 4, 1965. No. C128, Mar. 12, 1964.

Mt. Titano and
Flight
Symbolized
AP34

1972, Oct. 25	**Unwmk.**		**Perf. 11½**	
Granite Paper				
C129	AP34	1000 l multi	1.60	1.60

Glider
AP35

Designs: Each stamp shows a different type of air current in background.

1974, Oct. 9		**Photo.**		**Perf. 11½**
Granite Paper				
C130	AP35	40 l multicolored	.25	.25
C131	AP35	120 l multicolored	.25	.25
C132	AP35	500 l multicolored	.65	.65
	Nos. C130-C132 (3)		1.15	1.15

50th anniversary of gliding in Italy.

San Marino 77 Type of 1977

1977, Jan. 28		**Photo.**		**Perf. 11½**
C133	A193	200 l multicolored	.25	.25

Wright Brothers'
Flyer A — AP36

1978, Sept. 28		**Photo.**		**Perf. 11½**
C134	AP36	10 l multicolored	.25	.25
C135	AP36	50 l multicolored	.25	.25
C136	AP36	200 l multicolored	.25	.25
	Nos. C134-C136 (3)		.75	.75

75th anniversary of first powered flight.

AIR POST SEMI-POSTAL STAMP

View of San
Marino
APSP1

Wmk. 140

1944, Apr. 25		**Photo.**		**Perf. 14**
CB1	APSP1	20 l + 10 l ol grn	2.40	2.40
	Never hinged		4.75	
	Sheet of 8		110.00	110.00
	Never hinged		225.00	

The surtax was used for workers' houses.

SPECIAL DELIVERY STAMPS

SD1

Unwmk.

1907, Apr. 25		**Engr.**		**Perf. 12**
E1	SD1	25c carmine	40.00	20.00

For surcharges see Nos. E3, E5.

Type of Regular Issue of 1903 Overprinted

ESPRESSO

Perf. 14½x14

1923, May 30			**Wmk. 140**	
E2	A11	60c violet	1.25	1.25

For surcharge see No. 103.

Type of 1907 Issue Surcharged

Cent. 60

1923, July 26			**Perf. 14**	
E3	SD1	60c on 25c carmine	1.25	1.25
a.	Vert. pair, imperf. between		275.00	

No. E2 Surcharged

1926, Nov. 25			**Perf. 14½x14**	
E4	A11	1.25 l on 60c violet	1.90	1.90

No. E3 Surcharged

L. 1,25

1927, Sept. 15				
E5	SD1	1.25 l on 60c on 25c	1.25	1.25
a.	Inverted surcharge		175.00	
b.	Vert. pair, imperf. between		800.00	
c.	Double surcharge		190.00	

Statue of Liberty and View of San
Marino — SD2

Wmk. 217

1929, Aug. 29		**Engr.**		**Perf. 12**
E6	SD2	1.25 l green	.75	.75

Overprinted in Red

E7	SD2	2.50 l deep blue	1.25	1.25

Arms of
San Marino
SD3

1943, Sept. **Wmk. 140** **Photo.** **Perf. 14**
E8 SD3 1.25 l green .25 .25
E9 SD3 2.50 l reddish orange .25 .25

View of San Marino SD4

Pegasus SD5

1945-46 **Photo.** **Wmk. 140**
E12 SD4 2.50 l deep green .25 .25
E13 SD4 5 l deep orange .25 .25
Unwmk.
E14 SD4 5 l carmine rose 1.00 .50
Wmk. 277
E15 SD4 10 l sapphire ('46) 3.00 2.00
Engr.
Unwmk.
E16 SD5 30 l deep ultra ('46) 8.00 4.50
Nos. E12-E16 (5) 12.50 7.50
See Nos. E22-E23. For surcharges see Nos. E17-E21, E24-E25.

Nos. E14 and E15 Srchd. in Black

1947 **Unwmk.** **Perf. 14**
E17 SD4 15 l on 5 l car rose .25 .25
Wmk. 277
E18 SD4 15 l on 10 l saph .25 .25

No. E16 Surcharged with New Value and Bars in Carmine
1947-48 **Unwmk.**
E19 SD5 35 l on 30 l ('48) 77.50 37.50
E20 SD5 60 l on 30 l 4.25 4.25
E21 SD5 80 l on 30 l ('48) 40.00 21.00
Nos. E19-E21 (3) 121.75 62.75

Types of 1945-46
1950, Dec. 11 **Photo.** **Wmk. 277**
E22 SD4 60 l rose brown 7.50 7.50
E23 SD4 80 l deep blue 7.50 7.50
Set, never hinged 30.00

Nos. E22-E23 Surcharged with New Value and Three Bars
1957, Dec. 12 **Perf. 14**
E24 SD4 75 l on 60 l rose brn 3.00 3.00
E25 SD5 100 l on 80 l dp blue 3.00 3.00
Set, never hinged 8.00

> Catalogue values for unused stamps in this section, from this point to the end of the section, are for Never Hinged items.

Crossbow SD6

Design: No. E27, "Espresso" at left; crossbow casts two shadows.
1965, Aug. 28 **Photo.** **Wmk. 339**
E26 SD6 120 l on 75 l blk, gray & yel .25 .25
E27 SD6 135 l on 100 l blk & org .25 .25

Without Surcharge
Design: 80 l, 100 l, "Espresso" at left; crossbow casts two shadows.
1966, Mar. 29
E28 SD6 75 l blk, gray & yel .25 .25

E29 SD6 80 l blk & lilac .25 .25
E30 SD6 100 l blk & orange .25 .25
Nos. E28-E30 (3) .75 .75

SEMI-POSTAL SPECIAL DELIVERY STAMP

SPSD1

1923, Sept. 20 **Engr.** **Perf. 14**
EB1 SPSD1 60c + 5c brown red 1.75 1.75

POSTAGE DUE STAMPS

D1

Wmk. 140
1897-1920 **Typo.** **Perf. 14**
J1 D1 5c bl grn & dk brn 1.60 1.60
J2 D1 10c bl grn & dk brn 1.60 1.60
a. Numerals inverted 375.00
J3 D1 30c bl grn & dk brn 3.25 3.25
J4 D1 60c bl grn & dk brn 4.00 4.00
a. Numerals inverted 375.00 —
J5 D1 60c bl grn & dk brn 47.50 21.00
J6 D1 1 l claret & dk brn 9.50 10.50
J7 D1 3 l claret & brn ('20) 32.50 32.50
J8 D1 5 l claret & dk brn 95.00 72.50
J9 D1 10 l claret & dk brn 40.00 45.00
Nos. J1-J9 (9) 234.95 191.95
See Nos. J10-J36. For surcharges see Nos. J37-J60, J64.

1924
J10 D1 5c rose & brown 2.40 2.25
J11 D1 10c rose & brown 2.40 2.25
J12 D1 30c rose & brown 4.00 4.00
J13 D1 50c rose & brown 4.75 4.75
J14 D1 60c rose & brown 16.00 16.00
J15 D1 1 l green & brown 24.00 24.00
J16 D1 3 l green & brown 65.00 65.00
J17 D1 5 l green & brown 80.00 80.00
J18 D1 10 l green & brown 375.00 425.00
Nos. J10-J18 (9) 573.55 623.25

1925-39 **Perf. 14**
J19 D1 5c blue & brn 1.60 .80
a. Numerals inverted 300.00
J20 D1 10c blue & brn 1.60 .80
a. Numerals inverted 300.00
J21 D1 15c blue & brn ('39) 1.60 .80
J22 D1 20c blue & brn ('39) .75 .80
J23 D1 25c blue & brn ('39) 1.25 1.25
J24 D1 30c blue & brn 1.50 .80
J25 D1 40c blue & brn ('39) 9.50 9.50
J26 D1 50c blue & brn 2.50 1.25
a. Numerals inverted 300.00
J27 D1 60c blue & brn 6.50 1.60
J28 D1 1 l buff & brn 9.50 1.60
J29 D1 2 l buff & brn ('39) 4.75 4.75
J30 D1 3 l buff & brn 125.00 67.50
J31 D1 5 l buff & brn 35.00 9.50
J32 D1 10 l buff & brn 47.50 27.50
J33 D1 15 l buff & brn ('28) 4.00 2.25
J34 D1 25 l buff & brn ('28) 67.50 47.50
J35 D1 30 l buff & brn ('28) 14.50 20.00
J36 D1 50 l buff & brn ('28) 16.00 20.00
Nos. J19-J36 (18) 350.55 218.20

Postage Due Stamps of 1925 Surcharged in Black and Silver

1931, May 18
J37 D1 15c on 5c bl & brn 1.60 1.60
J38 D1 15c on 10c bl & brn 1.60 1.60
J39 D1 15c on 30c bl & brn 1.60 1.60
J40 D1 20c on 5c bl & brn 1.60 1.60
J41 D1 20c on 10c bl & brn 1.60 1.60
J42 D1 20c on 30c bl & brn 1.60 1.60
J43 D1 25c on 5c bl & brn 4.00 4.00
J44 D1 25c on 10c bl & brn 4.00 4.00
J45 D1 25c on 30c bl & brn 32.50 32.50
J46 D1 40c on 5c bl & brn 4.00 1.60
J47 D1 40c on 10c bl & brn 4.75 2.00

J48 D1 40c on 30c bl & brn 4.75 2.00
J49 D1 2 l on 5c bl & brn 65.00 60.00
J50 D1 2 l on 10c bl & brn 150.00 110.00
J51 D1 2 l on 30c bl & brn 95.00 87.50
Nos. J37-J51 (15) 373.60 313.20

Nos. J19, J24-J25, J30, J34, J33, J22 Surcharged in Black

Perf. 14, 14½x14
1936-40 **Wmk. 140**
J52 D1 10c on 5c ('38) 4.75 4.75
J53 D1 25c on 30c ('38) 17.50 17.50
J54 D1 50c on 5c ('37) 17.50 17.50
J55 D1 1 l on 30c 80.00 12.00
J56 D1 1 l on 40c ('40) 14.00 14.00
J57 D1 1 l on 3 l ('37) 80.00 4.75
J58 D1 1 l on 15 l ('38) 125.00 35.00
J59 D1 2 l on 15 l ('38) 55.00 35.00
J60 D1 3 l on 20c ('40) 45.00 35.00
Nos. J52-J60 (9) 438.75 180.50

Coat of Arms — D6

1939 **Typo.** **Perf. 14**
J61 D6 5c blue & brown .80 .80

Nos. J61 and J36 Surcharged with New Values and Bars
1940-43
J62 D6 10c on 5c .80 .40
J63 D6 50c on 5c 3.25 1.60
J64 D1 25 l on 50 l ('43) 4.75 4.75
Nos. J62-J64 (3) 8.80 6.75

Coat of Arms — D7

Unwmk.
1945, June 7 **Photo.** **Perf. 14**
J65 D7 5c dk green .25 .25
J66 D7 10c orange brn .25 .25
J67 D7 15c rose red .25 .25
J68 D7 20c dp ultra .25 .25
J69 D7 25c dk purple .25 .25
J70 D7 30c rose lake .25 .25
J71 D7 40c bister .25 .25
J72 D7 50c slate blk .25 .25
J73 D7 60c chestnut .25 .25
J74 D7 1 l dp orange .25 .25
J75 D7 2 l carmine .25 .25
J76 D7 5 l dull violet .25 .25
J77 D7 10 l dark blue .25 .25
J78 D7 20 l dark green 6.75 6.00
J79 D7 25 l red orange 6.75 6.00
J80 D7 50 l dark brown 6.75 6.00
Nos. J65-J80 (16) 23.50 21.25

PARCEL POST STAMPS

These stamps were used by affixing them to the way bill so that one half remained on it following the parcel, the other half staying on the receipt given the sender. Most used halves are right halves. Complete stamps were and are obtainable canceled, probably to order. Both unused and used values are for complete stamps.

PP1

Engraved, Typographed
1928, Nov. 22 **Unwmk.** **Perf. 12**
Pairs are imperforate between
Q1 PP1 5c blk brn & bl .80 .80
a. Imperf. 75.00
Q2 PP1 10c dk bl & bl .80 .80
Q3 PP1 20c gray blk & bl .80 .80
a. Imperf. 75.00
Q4 PP1 25c car & blue .80 .80
Q5 PP1 30c ultra & blue .80 .80
Q6 PP1 50c orange & bl .80 .80
Q7 PP1 60c rose & blue .80 .80

Q8 PP1 1 l violet & brn .80 .80
a. Imperf. 75.00
Q9 PP1 2 l green & brn 1.60 1.50
Q10 PP1 3 l bister & brn 2.00 2.00
Q11 PP1 5 l gray & brn 2.40 2.40
Q12 PP1 10 l rose lilac & brn 4.75 4.75
Q13 PP1 12 l red brn & brn 18.00 18.00
Q14 PP1 15 l olive grn & brn 27.50 27.50
a. Imperf. 75.00
Q15 PP1 20 l brn vio & brn 45.00 45.00
Nos. Q1-Q15 (15) 107.65 107.55

Halves Used
Q1-Q8 .20
Q9-Q10 .20
Q11 .20
Q12 .35
Q13 .65
Q14 2.75
Q15 3.00

1945-46 **Wmk. 140** **Perf. 14**
Pairs are perforated between
Q16 PP1 5c rose vio & red org .25 .25
Q17 PP1 10c red org & blk .25 .25
Q18 PP1 20c dark red & grn .25 .25
Q19 PP1 25c yel & blk .25 .25
Q20 PP1 30c red vio & org red .25 .25
Q21 PP1 50c dull pur & blk .25 .25
Q22 PP1 60c rose lake & blk .25 .25
Q23 PP1 1 l brown & dp bl .25 .25
Q24 PP1 2 l dk brn & dk bl .25 .25
Q25 PP1 3 l olive brn & brn .25 .25
Q26 PP1 4 l blue grn & brn .25 .25
Q27 PP1 10 l bl blk & brt pur .25 .25
Q28 PP1 12 l myr grn & dl bl 3.50 1.60
Q29 PP1 15 l green & purple 2.25 1.60
Q30 PP1 20 l rose lil & brn 1.90 1.60
Q31 PP1 25 l dp car & ultra ('46) 37.50 25.00
Q32 PP1 50 l yel & dp org ('46) 57.50 35.00
Nos. Q16-Q32 (17) 105.65 67.80

Halves Used
Q16-Q27 .20
Q28 .20
Q29 .20
Q30 .20
Q31 .30
Q32 .60

Nos. Q32 and Q31 Surcharged with New Value and Wavy Lines in Black
1948-50
Q33 PP1 100 l on 50 l 42.50 32.50
Half, used 1.00
Q34 PP1 200 l on 25 l ('50) 140.00 90.00
Half, used 1.00

1953, Mar. 5 **Wmk. 277** **Perf. 13½**
Pairs Perforated Between
Q35 PP1 10 l dk grn & rose lil 32.50 12.00
Half, used 1.40
Q36 PP1 300 l pur & lake 150.00 110.00
Half, used 1.40

1956 **Wmk. 303** **Perf. 13½**
Q37 PP1 10 l gray & brt pur .25 .25
Half, used .20
Q38 PP1 50 l yel & dp org 1.00 .80
Half, used .25

No. Q38 Surcharged with New Value and Wavy Lines In Black
Q39 PP1 100 l on 50 l .65 .60
Half, used .30

> Catalogue values for unused stamps in this section, from this point to the end of the section, are for Never Hinged items.

1960-61
Q40 PP1 300 l violet & brn 55.00 40.00
Half, used .75
Q41 PP1 500 l dk brn & car ('61) 2.40 2.40
Half, used .30

1965-72 **Wmk. 339** **Perf. 13½**
Pairs Perforated Between
Q42 PP1 10 l gray & brt pur .25 .25
Q43 PP1 50 l yel & red org .25 .25
Q44 PP1 100 l on 50 l yel & red org .80 .80
Q45 PP1 300 l violet & brown .30 .30
Q46 PP1 500 l brn & red ('72) 6.00 6.00
Q47 PP1 1000 l bl grn & lt red brn ('67) 8.40 8.40
Nos. Q42-Q47 (6) 8.40 8.40

Halves Used
Q42-Q43 .20
Q44-Q45 .25
Q46 .30
Q47 .50

SARAWAK

sə-'rä-ˌwäḵ

LOCATION — Northwestern part of the island of Borneo, bordering on the South China Sea
GOVT. — Former British Crown Colony
AREA — 48,250 sq. mi. (approx.)
POP. — 1,954,300 (1997 est.)
CAPITAL — Kuching

The last ruling Raja, who retired in 1946 when he ceded Sarawak to the British Crown, was Sir Charles Vyner Brooke, an Englishman. He inherited the title from his father, Sir Charles Johnson Brooke, who in turn received it from his uncle, Sir James Brooke. The title of Raja was conferred on Sir James by Raja Muda Hassim after Sir James had aided him in subduing a rebellion. The title and right of succession were duly recognized by the Sultan of Brunei and by Great Britain.
Sarawak joined the Federation of Malaysia in 1963.

100 Cents = 1 Dollar

> **Catalogue values for unused stamps in this country are for Never Hinged items, beginning with Scott 155.**

Watermarks

Wmk. 47 — Multiple Rosettes   Wmk. 71 — Rosette

Wmk. 231 — Oriental Crown

Unused examples of Nos. 1-7, 25 and 32-35 are valued without gum. Stamps with original gum are worth more.

Sir James Brooke — A1   Sir Charles Johnson Brooke — A2

1869, Mar. 1   Unwmk.   Litho.   Perf. 11
1	A1	3c brown, *yellow*	70.00	275.00

1871, Jan.
2	A2	3c brown, *yellow*	3.00	5.00
a.		Vertical pair, imperf between	575.00	
b.		Horizontal pair, imperf between	900.00	
c.		Period after "THREE"	55.00	70.00

No. 2 surcharged "TWO CENTS" is believed to be bogus.
There are a number of lithographic flaws, including narrow A, "period" after THREE, etc. Imperfs. of Nos. 1, 2 are proofs.
A papermaker's watermark, "LNL," usually appears once or twice in each pane.
For surcharges see Nos. 25, 32.

1875, Jan. 1   Perf. 12
3	A2	2c gray lilac, *lilac*	19.00	22.00
4	A2	4c brown, *yellow*	5.00	4.00
b.		Vertical pair, imperf between	925.00	900.00
5	A2	6c green, *green*	5.00	5.75
6	A2	8c blue, *blue*	5.00	6.25
7	A2	12c red, *rose*	9.00	9.00
		Nos. 3-7 (5)	43.00	47.00

Nos. 3-7 have each five varieties of the words of value.
Imperfs are proofs.
A papermaker's watermark usually appears once or twice in each pane of Nos. 3-7, "LNT" on No. 5, "LNL" on others.
Some examples of No. 7 have the appearance of being on laid paper, but the lines are accidental and not constant within the sheets.
For surcharges see Nos. 33-35.

Sir Charles Johnson Brooke — A4

1888-97   Typo.   Perf. 14
8	A4	1c lilac & blk ('92)	4.50	1.25
9	A4	2c lilac & carmine	5.50	3.00
10	A4	3c lilac & blue	7.50	6.25
11	A4	4c lilac & yellow	32.50	62.50
12	A4	5c lilac & grn ('91)	27.50	4.25
13	A4	6c lilac & brown	24.00	65.00
14	A4	8c green & car	17.00	4.75
a.		8c green & rose ('97)	30.00	17.50
15	A4	10c grn & vio ('91)	50.00	16.50
16	A4	12c green & blue	16.00	12.00
17	A4	16c gray grn & org ('97)	62.50	90.00
18	A4	25c green & brown	60.00	50.00
19	A4	32c gray grn & blk ('97)	47.50	70.00
20	A4	50c gray green ('97)	65.00	120.00
21	A4	$1 gray grn & blk ('97)	100.00	100.00
		Nos. 8-21 (14)	519.50	605.50

No. 21 shows the numeral on white tablet.
Three higher values — $2, $5, $10 — were prepared but not issued. Value $950 each.
For surcharges see Nos. 22-24, 26-27.

Nos. 14 and 16 Surcharged in Black

2c. — No. 22   5c. — No. 23

5c. — No. 24

1889-91
22	A4	2c on 8c	3.50	8.00
a.		Double surcharge	525.00	
b.		Pair, one without surcharge	8,000.	
c.		Inverted surcharge	4,250.	
23	A4	5c on 12c ('91)	29.00	55.00
a.		Double surcharge	1,400.	
b.		Pair, one without surcharge	12,000.	
c.		No period after "C"	37.50	60.00
d.		Without "C"	675.00	725.00
e.		Double surch., one vert.	4,000.	
24	A4	5c on 12c ('91)	300.00	325.00
a.		No period after "C"	140.00	150.00
b.		Double surcharge	1,500.	
c.		"C" omitted	950.00	1,000.

No. 2 Surcharged in Black

ONE CENT

1892, May 23   Perf. 11
25	A2	1c on 3c brown, *yel*	3.00	3.50
b.		Without bar	425.00	250.00
c.		Period after "THREE"	50.00	55.00
d.		Double surcharge	525.00	575.00
e.		Vertical pair, imperf between	800.00	
f.		Vertical pair, imperf horiz.	750.00	

Examples of No. 25b must be from the first printing, wherein the bar was applied after the surcharge. Examples of No. 25 with parts of the surcharge and/or bar omitted are stamps

that had gum on the face prior to the surcharging operation. The ink was removed when the gum was washed off.

No. 10 Surcharged in Black

one cent. — e   One Cent. — f

1892   Perf. 14
26	A4(e)	1c on 3c lil & bl	4.00	4.00
a.		No period after "cent"	250.00	250.00
27	A4(f)	1c on 3c lil & bl	65.00	40.00
b.		Double surcharge	750.00	850.00

Issued: #26, Feb.; #27, Jan. 12.

Sir Charles Johnson Brooke
A11   A12

A13   A14

1895, Jan. 1   Engr.   Perf. 11½, 12
28	A11	2c red brn	14.00	11.00
a.		Perf. 12½	22.00	6.00
b.		Vertical pair, imperf between	600.00	
c.		Horizontal pair, imperf between	450.00	
d.		As "a," horiz. pair, imperf between	700.00	
29	A12	4c black	14.00	4.00
a.		Horizontal pair, imperf between	800.00	
30	A13	6c violet	17.50	11.50
31	A14	8c deep green	37.50	7.00
		Nos. 28-31 (4)	83.00	33.50

The 2c and 8c imperf are proofs. Perforated stamps of these designs in other colors are color trials, which exist surcharged with new values in pence. These surcharged varieties were used in trial printings of a British South African issue.

Stamps of 1871-75 Surcharged in Black or Red

2 CENTS.

1899   Perf. 11
32	A2	2c on 3c brown, *yel*	2.75	2.00
a.		Period after "THREE"	75.00	75.00
b.		Vertical pair, imperf between	1,000.	

Perf. 12
33	A2	2c on 12c red, *rose*	3.50	3.75
a.		Inverted surcharge	975.00	1,400.
34	A2	4c on 6c green, *grn* (R)	45.00	90.00
35	A2	4c on 8c blue, *bl* (R)	7.00	11.00
		Nos. 32-35 (4)	58.25	106.75

Sir Charles J. Brooke — A16

1899-1908   Typo.   Perf. 14
36	A16	1c blue & car ('01)	1.40	1.40
37	A16	2c gray green	2.25	1.00
38	A16	3c dull violet ('08)	17.50	.75
39	A16	4c analine carmine	2.75	.30
40	A16	8c yellow & black	2.50	.90
41	A16	10c ultra	3.75	1.10
42	A16	12c light violet ('99)	5.50	5.00
43	A16	16c org brn & grn	6.50	

44	A16	20c brn ol & vio ('00)	6.25	4.75
45	A16	25c brown & ultra	8.50	5.75
46	A16	50c ol grn & rose	27.50	32.50
47	A16	$1 rose & green	90.00	125.00
		Nos. 36-47 (12)	174.40	180.45

A 5c was prepared but not issued. Value $13.50.
See the *Scott Classic Catalogue* for listings of shades.

1901   Wmk. 71
48	A16	2c gray green	45.00	19.00

Sir Charles Vyner Brooke — A17

1918-23   Unwmk.
50	A17	1c slate bl & rose	2.60	3.00
51	A17	2c deep green	3.00	1.75
52	A17	2c violet ('23)	2.25	3.00
53	A17	3c violet brown	3.75	3.00
54	A17	3c dp grn ('22)	3.25	1.40
55	A17	4c carmine rose	7.50	3.75
56	A17	4c purple brn ('23)	2.25	2.50
57	A17	5c orange ('23)	2.25	2.50
58	A17	6c lake brown ('22)	1.75	1.60
59	A17	8c yellow & blk	14.00	70.00
60	A17	8c car rose ('22)	5.25	35.00
61	A17	10c ultra	5.00	5.00
a.		10c blue	5.00	5.00
62	A17	10c black ('23)	3.25	4.75
63	A17	12c violet	18.00	42.50
64	A17	12c ultra ('22)	12.50	21.00
65	A17	16c brn & blue grn	6.50	8.50
66	A17	20c olive bis & vio	8.00	7.50
a.		20c olive green & violet	8.00	7.50
67	A17	25c brown & blue	4.75	20.00
68	A17	30c bis & gray ('22)	4.25	4.75
69	A17	50c olive grn & rose	11.50	17.00
70	A17	$1 car rose & grn	28.00	32.50
		Nos. 50-70 (21)	149.60	291.00

In 1918 a supply of the 1c (No. 50) had the value tablet printed, by error, in slate blue instead of rose. It is officially stated that this stamp was never issued and had no franking power. Value $22.
The $1 denomination shows numeral of value in color on white tablet.

Nos. 61 and 63 Surcharged

ONE cent

1st Printing — Bars 1¼mm apart.
2nd Printing — Bars ¾mm apart.

1923, Jan.
77	A17	1c on 10c ultra	16.50	62.50
a.		"cnet"	450.00	975.00
b.		Bars ¾mm apart	160.00	450.00
78	A17	2c on 12c violet	11.00	47.50
a.		Bars ¾mm apart	92.50	300.00

Type of 1918 Issue
1928-29   Typo.   Wmk. 47
79	A17	1c slate blue & rose	1.75	.40
80	A17	2c dull violet	2.75	1.40
81	A17	3c deep green	3.75	5.75
82	A17	4c purple brown	2.10	.25
83	A17	5c orange ('29)	14.00	5.75
84	A17	6c brown lake	1.50	.35
85	A17	8c carmine	4.00	26.00
86	A17	10c black	2.00	1.40
87	A17	12c ultra	4.00	35.00
88	A17	16c dp brn & bl grn	4.00	4.50
89	A17	20c olive & vio	4.00	7.50
90	A17	25c dk brown & ultra	6.50	9.75
91	A17	30c olive bis & gray	5.50	11.50
92	A17	50c olive grn & rose	12.00	24.00
93	A17	$1 car rose & grn	20.00	27.50
		Nos. 79-93 (15)	87.85	161.05
		Set, never hinged	170.00	

Sir Charles Vyner Brooke
A18   A19

Wmk. 231

1932, Jan. 1   **Engr.**   *Perf. 12½*

94	A18	1c indigo	1.00	1.10
95	A18	2c dark green	1.25	2.25
96	A18	3c deep violet	5.00	1.10
97	A18	4c deep orange	9.00	.85
98	A18	5c brown lake	8.50	1.40
99	A18	6c deep red	9.75	11.00
100	A18	8c orange yel	11.00	9.75
101	A18	10c black	2.75	3.75
102	A18	12c violet blue	5.00	11.00
103	A18	15c orange brown	8.25	9.75
104	A18	20c violet & org	8.00	9.00
105	A18	25c org brn & yel	15.00	25.00
106	A18	30c org red & ol brn	12.50	35.00
107	A18	50c olive grn & red	17.50	15.00
108	A18	$1 car & green	25.00	40.00
		Nos. 94-108 (15)	139.50	175.95

1934-41   **Unwmk.**   *Perf. 12*

109	A19	1c brown violet	1.50	.25
110	A19	2c blue green	1.75	.25
111	A19	2c black ('41)	4.75	1.75
112	A19	3c black	1.40	.25
113	A19	3c blue grn ('41)	8.00	5.00
114	A19	4c magenta	2.25	.25
115	A19	5c violet	2.25	.25
116	A19	6c deep rose	3.00	.70
117	A19	6c red brn ('41)	8.75	9.00
118	A19	8c red brown	2.50	.25
119	A19	8c dp rose ('41)	9.25	.25
120	A19	10c red	4.25	.45
121	A19	12c deep ultra	3.50	.30
122	A19	12c orange ('41)	7.50	6.25
123	A19	12c orange	7.50	12.00
124	A19	15c deep blue ('41)	9.75	20.00
125	A19	20c dp rose & olive	7.50	1.50
126	A19	25c orange & vio	7.50	2.00
127	A19	30c violet & red brn	7.75	3.25
128	A19	50c red & violet	9.00	1.00
129	A19	$1 dk brn & red	4.00	1.00
130	A19	$2 violet & mag	24.00	24.00
131	A19	$3 bl grn & rose	45.00	50.00
132	A19	$4 red & ultra	45.00	80.00
133	A19	$5 red brn & red	65.00	85.00
134	A19	$10 orange & blk	30.00	85.00
		Nos. 109-134 (26)	322.65	389.95

Issue dates: May 1, 1934. Mar. 1, 1941.
For overprints see #135-154, 159-173, N1-N22.

Stamps of 1934-41
Overprinted in Black
or Red

1945, Dec. 17

135	A19	1c brown violet	.85	.70
136	A19	2c black (R)	2.00	1.40
137	A19	3c blue green	.85	1.75
138	A19	4c magenta	1.90	.35
139	A19	5c violet (R)	2.75	1.10
140	A19	6c red brown	2.40	.90
141	A19	8c deep rose	9.50	20.00
142	A19	10c red	1.10	.80
143	A19	12c orange	2.75	4.25
144	A19	15c deep blue	4.75	.45
145	A19	20c dp rose & ol	2.75	4.00
146	A19	25c org & vio (R)	3.00	3.00
147	A19	30c vio & red brn	5.50	3.00
148	A19	50c red & violet	1.00	.40
149	A19	$1 dk brn & red	1.90	3.75
150	A19	$2 violet & mag	6.75	17.50
151	A19	$3 bl grn & rose	20.00	90.00
152	A19	$4 red & ultra	26.00	60.00
153	A19	$5 red brn & red	140.00	250.00
154	A19	$10 org & blk (R)	125.00	250.00
		Nos. 135-154 (20)	360.75	713.35
		Set, never hinged	525.00	

> Catalogue values for unused stamps in this section, from this point to the end of the section, are for Never Hinged items.

Sir James Brooke, Sir Charles V.
Brooke and Sir Charles J. Brooke
A20

1946, May 18

155	A20	8c dark carmine	3.25	1.25
156	A20	15c dark blue	3.50	2.50
157	A20	50c red & black	3.75	3.50
158	A20	$1 sepia & black	4.00	32.50
		Nos. 155-158 (4)	14.50	39.75

Type of 1934-41
Overprinted in Blue or
Red

1947, Apr. 16   **Wmk. 4**   *Perf. 12*

159	A19	1c brown violet	.25	.30
160	A19	2c black (R)	.25	.25
161	A19	3c blue green (R)	.25	.25
162	A19	4c magenta	.25	.25
163	A19	6c red brown	.30	1.00
164	A19	8c deep rose	1.00	.25
165	A19	10c red	.35	.25
166	A19	12c orange	.70	1.00
167	A19	15c deep blue (R)	.50	.55
168	A19	20c dp rose & ol (R)	2.25	.65
169	A19	25c orange & vio (R)	.65	.55
170	A19	50c red & violet (R)	1.25	.90
171	A19	$1 dk brown & red	1.50	1.50
172	A19	$2 violet & magenta	3.75	4.25
173	A19	$5 red brown & red	4.50	4.00
		Nos. 159-173 (15)	17.75	16.05

Common Design Types
pictured following the introduction.

Silver Wedding Issue
Common Design Types
1948, Oct. 25   **Photo.**   *Perf. 14x14½*

174	CD304	8c scarlet	.40	.40

Engraved; Name Typographed
Perf. 11½x11

175	CD305	$5 light brown	52.50	55.00

UPU Issue
Common Design Types
Engr.; Name Typo. on 15c, 25c
Perf. 13½, 11x11½

1949, Oct. 10   **Wmk. 4**

176	CD306	8c rose carmine	1.50	.60
177	CD307	15c indigo	3.50	2.50
178	CD308	25c green	2.00	1.50
179	CD309	50c violet	2.00	6.50
		Nos. 176-179 (4)	9.00	11.10

Troides
Brookiana
A21

Western
Tarsier — A22

Designs: 3c, Kayan tomb. 4c, Kayan girl and boy. 6c, Bead work. 8c, Dyak dancer. 10c, Scaly anteater. 12c, Kenyah boys. 15c, Fire making. 20c, Kelemantan rice barn. 25c, Pepper vines. 50c, Iban woman. $1, Kelabit smithy. $2, Map of Sarawak. $5, Arms of Sarawak.

Perf. 11½x11, 11x11½

1950, Jan. 3   **Engr.**

180	A21	1c black	.75	.30
181	A22	2c orange red	.40	.50
182	A22	3c green	.40	.80
183	A22	4c brown	.65	.25
184	A22	6c aquamarine	.45	.25
185	A21	8c red	1.00	.30
186	A21	10c orange	2.50	6.00
187	A21	12c purple	4.50	1.75
188	A21	15c deep blue	3.50	.25
189	A21	20c red org & brn	2.75	.50
190	A21	25c carmine & grn	4.25	.60
191	A21	50c purple & brn	7.00	.45
192	A21	$1 dk brn & bl grn	26.00	5.00
193	A21	$2 rose car & blue	37.50	18.50

Engr. and Typo.

194	A21	$5 dp vio, blk, red & yel	30.00	18.50
		Nos. 180-194 (15)	121.65	53.95

1952, Feb. 1

195	A21	10c orange *(Map)*	2.75	.80

Coronation Issue
Common Design Type
1953, June 3   **Engr.**   *Perf. 13½x13*

196	CD312	10c ultra & black	2.00	2.25

Logging — A23

Hornbill
A24

Elizabeth II — A25

Designs: 2c, Young Orangutan. 4c, Kayan Dancing. 8c, Shield with spears. 10c, Kenyah ceremonial carving. 12c, Barong Panau (sailboat). 15c, Turtles. 20c, Melanau basket making. 25c, Astana, Kuching (Governor's Residence). $1, $2, Queen Elizabeth II (Portrait like Fiji A39). $5, Arms.

Perf. 11x11½, 11½x11, 12x12½ (A25)

1955-57   **Wmk. 4**   **Engr.**

197	A23	1c green	.25	.30
198	A23	2c red orange	.35	.55
199	A23	4c brown carmine	1.00	.60
200	A23	6c greenish blue	3.75	3.50
201	A24	8c rose red	.40	.30
202	A24	10c dark green	.30	.25
203	A24	12c purple	4.25	.55
204	A24	15c ultra	2.25	.30
205	A24	20c brown & olive	1.25	.25
206	A24	25c brt green & brn	7.50	.25
207	A25	30c violet & red brn	8.00	.30
208	A25	50c car rose & blk	3.00	.40
209	A25	$1 orange brn & grn	14.00	2.50
210	A25	$2 green & violet	22.50	3.75

Engr. and Typo.

211	A24	$5 dp vio, blk, red & yel	32.50	19.00
		Nos. 197-211 (15)	101.30	32.80

Issued: 30c, 6/1/55; others, 10/1/57.
See Nos. 215-222.

Freedom from Hunger Issue
Common Design Type
Perf. 14x14½
1963, June 4   **Photo.**   **Wmk. 314**

212	CD314	12c sepia	1.60	1.75

STATE OF MALAYSIA
Types of 1955-57
Perf. 11x11½, 11½x11

1964-65   **Engr.**   **Wmk. 314**

215	A23	1c green	.25	1.00
216	A23	2c red orange	1.00	13.50
217	A24	6c green blue	7.00	5.25
218	A24	10c dark green	2.25	1.40
219	A24	12c purple	3.75	12.00
220	A24	15c ultra	1.50	17.50
221	A24	20c brown & olive	1.00	2.00
222	A24	25c brt grn & brn	4.25	6.00
		Nos. 215-222 (8)	21.00	58.65

Issued: 20c, 6/9/64; 2c, 15c, 8/17/65; others, 9/9/64.

Orchid Type of Johore (Malaysia), 1965, with State Crest
Wmk. 338
1965, Nov. 15   **Photo.**   *Perf. 14½*
Flowers in Natural Colors

228	A14	1c black & lt grnsh bl	.25	1.25
229	A14	2c black, red & gray	.30	2.50
230	A14	5c black & Prus blue	1.50	.25
231	A14	6c black & lt lilac	.90	2.25
232	A14	10c black & lt ultra	1.25	.25
233	A14	15c black, lil rose & grn	1.75	.25
234	A14	20c black & brown	2.50	.55
		Nos. 228-234 (7)	8.45	7.30

Clipper and
State
Crest — A26

Perf. 13½x13

1971, Feb. 1   **Litho.**   **Unwmk.**

235	A26	1c Delias ninus	.85	2.25
236	A26	2c Danaus melanip-pus	.95	2.25
237	A26	5c Parthenos sylvia	2.00	.25
a.		Booklet pane of 4 ('73)	9.00	
238	A26	6c Papilio demoleus	2.00	3.00
239	A26	10c Hebomnia glaucippe	2.00	.25
a.		Booklet pane of 4 ('73)	9.00	
240	A26	15c Precis orithya	3.00	.25
a.		Booklet pane of 4 ('73)	13.00	
241	A26	20c Valeria valeria	3.00	1.50
		Nos. 235-241 (7)	13.80	9.75

Clipper and
New State
Crest — A27

Changed Colors, Designs as Before

1977-78   **Photo.**   **Unwmk.**

242	A27	1c multi ('78)	8.50	15.00
243	A27	2c multi ('78)	20.00	16.00
244	A27	5c multicolored	2.50	2.00
245	A27	10c multicolored	1.50	.80
246	A27	15c multicolored	3.00	.30
247	A27	20c multi ('78)	7.00	5.75
		Nos. 242-247 (6)	42.50	39.85

Flower Type of Johore, 1979, with State Crest

1979, Apr. 30   **Wmk. 47**   *Perf. 14½*

248	A16	1c multicolored	.25	.40
249	A16	2c multicolored	.25	.40
250	A16	5c multicolored	.25	.50
251	A16	10c multicolored	.30	.25
252	A16	15c multicolored	.30	.25
253	A16	20c multicolored	.60	.25
254	A16	30c multicolored	.90	.70
		Nos. 248-254 (7)	2.85	2.75

1983-86   **Unwmk.**

250a	A16	5c ('86)	1.00	1.25
251a	A16	10c ('85)	1.00	1.10
253a	A16	20c	1.00	1.10
		Nos. 250a-253a (3)	3.00	3.45

Agriculture and State Arms Type of Johore Shield Divided into 3 Parts of Different Colors
Wmk. 388
1986, Oct. 25   **Litho.**   *Perf. 12*

255	A19	1c multicolored	.25	.25
256	A19	2c multicolored	.25	.25
257	A19	5c multicolored	.30	.25
258	A19	10c multicolored	.40	.25
259	A19	15c multicolored	.55	.25
260	A19	20c multicolored	.55	.25
261	A19	30c multicolored	1.00	.25
		Nos. 255-261 (7)	3.30	1.75

Agriculture and Arms Type of Johore

Yellow Shield
Divided by Diagonal
Bands of Black and
Red

1986-96   **Litho.**   **Wmk. 388**   *Perf. 12*

262	A19	1c multicolored	.25	.25
263	A19	2c multicolored	.25	.25
a.		Perf. 15x14½	3.00	
264	A19	5c multicolored	.25	.25
a.		Perf 14 ('96)	.90	.25
265	A19	10c multicolored	.25	.25
a.		Perf. 14 ('95)	2.00	
b.		Perf. 15x14½ ('95)	2.00	
c.		Perf. 14x14½ ('96)	4.50	.35
266	A19	15c multicolored	.25	.25
267	A19	20c multicolored	.30	.25
268	A19	30c multicolored	.40	.25
a.		Perf. 14 ('94)	1.75	.35
b.		Perf. 15x14½ ('94)	4.25	.45
c.		Perf. 14x14½ ('94)	4.25	.45
		Nos. 262-268 (7)	1.95	1.75

Flowers and Arms Type of Johore of 2007

Perf. 14x13¾

2007, Dec. 31		**Litho.**	**Wmk. 388**	
269	A20	5c multi	.25	.25
270	A20	10c multi	.30	.25
271	A20	20c multi	.35	.25
272	A20	30c multi	.50	.25
273	A20	40c multi	.60	.30
274	A20	50c multi	.75	.35
a.		Souvenir sheet of 6, #269-274	3.00	2.50
		Nos. 269-274 (6)	2.75	1.65

OCCUPATION STAMPS

Issued under Japanese Occupation

Stamps of 1934-41
Handstamped in Violet

1942		**Unwmk.**	**Perf. 12**	
N1	A19	1c brown violet	45.00	85.00
N2	A19	2c blue green	125.00	200.00
N3	A19	2c black	150.00	160.00
N3A	A19	3c black	500.00	500.00
N4	A19	3c blue green	80.00	110.00
N5	A19	4c magenta	110.00	120.00
N6	A19	5c violet	130.00	140.00
N7	A19	6c deep rose	180.00	180.00
N8	A19	6c red brown	120.00	130.00
N8A	A19	8c red brown	450.00	450.00
N9	A19	8c deep rose	100.00	120.00
N10	A19	10c red	110.00	130.00
N11	A19	12c deep ultra	190.00	200.00
N12	A19	12c orange	190.00	200.00
N12A	A19	15c orange	550.00	550.00
N13	A19	15c deep blue	150.00	160.00
N14	A19	20c dp rose & ol	90.00	120.00
N15	A19	25c orange & vio	130.00	150.00
N16	A19	30c violet & red brn	90.00	120.00
N17	A19	50c red & violet	100.00	120.00
N18	A19	$1 dk brown & red	150.00	170.00
N19	A19	$2 violet & mag	325.00	400.00
N19A	A19	$3 blue grn & rose	2,750.	2,750.
N20	A19	$4 red & ultra	325.00	475.00
N21	A19	$5 red brown & red	325.00	475.00
N22	A19	$10 orange & blk	325.00	475.00
		Nos. N1-N22 (26)	7,790.	8,690.

Stamps overprinted with Japanese characters in oval frame or between 2 vertical black lines were not for paying postage.

SASENO

ˈsə-ˈzā-ˌnō

LOCATION — An island in the Adriatic Sea, lying at the entrance of Valona Bay, Albania.
GOVT. — Italian possession
AREA — 2 sq. mi.

Italy occupied this Albanian islet in 1914, and returned it to Albania in 1947.

100 Centesimi = 1 Lira

Used values in italics are for postally used stamps. CTO's or stamps with fake cancels sell for about the same as unused, hinged stamps.

Italian Stamps of 1901-22 Overprinted

1923		**Wmk. 140**	**Perf. 14**	
1	A48	10c claret	26.00	72.50
2	A48	15c slate	26.00	72.50
3	A50	20c brown orange	26.00	72.50
4	A49	25c blue	26.00	72.50
5	A49	30c yellow brown	26.00	72.50
6	A49	50c violet	26.00	72.50
7	A49	60c carmine	26.00	72.50
8	A46	1 l brown & green	26.00	72.50
a.		Double overprint	400.00	
		Nos. 1-8 (8)	208.00	580.00
		Set, never hinged	500.00	

Superseded by postage stamps of Italy.

SAUDI ARABIA

ˈsau̇-dē ə-ˈrā-bē-ə

LOCATION — Southwestern Asia, on the Arabian Peninsula between the Red Sea and the Persian Gulf
GOVT. — Kingdom
AREA — 849,400 sq. mi.
POP. — 17,880,000 (1995 est.)
CAPITAL — Riyadh

In 1916 the Grand Sherif of Mecca declared the Sanjak of Hejaz independent of Turkish rule. In 1925, Ibn Saud, then Sultan of the Nejd, captured the Hejaz after a prolonged siege of Jedda, the last Hejaz stronghold.

The resulting Kingdom of the Hejaz and Nejd was renamed Saudi Arabia in 1932.

40 Paras = 1 Piaster = 1 Guerche (Garch, Qirsh)

11 Guerche = 1 Riyal (1928)

110 Guerche = 1 Sovereign (1931)

440 Guerche = 1 Sovereign (1952)

20 Piasters (Guerche) = 1 Riyal (1960)

100 Halalas = 1 Riyal (1976)

Catalogue values for unused stamps in this country are for Never Hinged items, beginning with Scott 178 in the regular postage section, Scott C1 in the airpost section, Scott J28 in the postage due section, Scott O7 in official section, and Scott RA6 in the postal tax section.

Watermarks

Wmk. 337 — Crossed Swords and Palm Tree

Watermark lines are thicker than the paper.

Wmk. 361 — Crossed Swords, Palm Tree and Arabic Inscription

HEJAZ

Sherifate of Mecca

Adapted from Carved Door Panels of Mosque El Salih Talay, Cairo — A1

Taken from Page of Koran in Mosque of El Sultan Barquq, Cairo — A2

Taken from Details of an Ancient Prayer Niche in the Mosque of El Amri at Qus in Upper Egypt — A3

Perf. 10, 12

			Unwmk.	Typo.
1916, Oct.				
L1	A1	¼pi green	50.00	32.50
L2	A2	½pi red	50.00	30.00
a.		Perf. 10	225.00	90.00
L3	A3	1pi blue	20.00	11.00
a.		Perf. 12	160.00	140.00
b.		Perf. 10x12		1,100.
		Nos. L1-L3 (3)	120.00	73.50

Exist imperf. Forged perf. exist.
See Nos. L5-L7, L10-L12. For overprints see Nos. L16-L18, L26-L28, L52-L54, L57-L59, L61-L66, L67, L70-L72, L77-L81, 37.

Central Design Adapted from a Koran Design for a Tomb. Background is from Stone Carving on Entrance Arch to the Ministry of Wakfs — A4

1916-17			**Roulette 20**	
L4	A4	⅛pi orange ('17)	5.00	1.40
L5	A1	¼pi green	6.00	1.40
L6	A2	½pi red	9.00	1.40
L7	A3	1pi blue	9.50	1.40
		Nos. L4-L7 (4)	29.50	5.60

See #L9. For overprints & surcharge see #L15a, L16c, L17b, L18d, L25, L51, L56, L69, 33.

Adapted from Stucco Work above Entrance to Cairo R. R. Station A5

Adapted from First Page of the Koran of Sultan Farag — A6

1917			**Serrate Roulette 13**	
L8	A5	1pa lilac brown	4.10	1.40
L9	A4	⅛pi orange	4.75	1.40
L10	A1	¼pi green	5.25	1.40
L11	A2	½pi red	5.75	1.40
L12	A3	1pi blue	6.00	1.40
L13	A6	2pi magenta	10.00	9.00
		Nos. L8-L13 (6)	35.85	16.00

Designs A1-A6 are inscribed "Hejaz Postage."
For overprints and surcharge see #L14-L31, L55-60, L62, L65-L75, L79a-81.

Kingdom of the Hejaz

Stamps of 1917-18 Overprinted in Black, Red or Brown

1921, Dec. 21   *Serrate Roulette 13*

L14	A5	1pa lilac brown	65.00	14.00
a.	Date omitted at right		150.00	
b.	Date omitted at left		275.00	
L15	A4	⅛pi orange	35.00	16.00
a.	Inverted overprint		110.00	
b.	Double overprint		225.00	
c.	Roulette 20		800.00	
d.	As "c," invtd. overprint		1,750.	*1,400.*
e.	Double overprint, one inverted		500.00	
f.	Double overprint, both inverted		500.00	
g.	Date omitted at right		100.00	
L16	A1	¼pi green	35.00	5.50
a.	Inverted overprint		110.00	
b.	Double overprint		225.00	
c.	Roulette 20		800.00	
d.	As "c," invtd. overprint		1,750.	
e.	Double overprint, one inverted		600.00	
f.	Double overprint, both inverted		200.00	
g.	Date omitted at right		100.00	
L17	A2	½pi red	35.00	6.75
a.	Inverted overprint		200.00	77.50
b.	Roulette 20		800.00	
c.	Double overprint		500.00	
d.	Double overprint, both inverted		500.00	
e.	Date omitted at right		100.00	
L18	A3	1pi blue (R)	35.00	6.25
a.	Brown overprint		30.00	18.00
b.	Black overprint		40.00	27.50
c.	As "b," invtd. overprint		400.00	
d.	Roulette 20		800.00	
e.	Date omitted at right		100.00	
L19	A6	2pi magenta	35.00	9.00
a.	Double overprint		3,250.	
b.	Date omitted at right		100.00	
c.	As "a," date omitted at left		7,000.	
	Nos. L14-L19 (6)		240.00	57.50

Nos. L15-L17, L18b and L19 exist with date (1340) omitted at left or right side.

All values except No. L15 exist with gold overprint.

No. L14 With Additional Surcharge

a

b

L22	A5(a)	½pi on 1pa	350.00	125.00
L23	A5(b)	1pi on 1pa	350.00	125.00

Forgeries of Nos. L14-L23 abound.

Stamps of 1917-18 Overprinted in Black

1922, Jan. 7

L24	A5	1pa lilac brown	12.50	2.75
a.	Inverted overprint		150.00	
b.	Double overprint		110.00	
c.	Double ovpt., one inverted		225.00	
L25	A4	⅛pi orange	20.00	6.25
a.	Inverted overprint		110.00	
b.	Double ovpt., one inverted		225.00	
L26	A1	¼pi green	8.00	2.75
a.	Inverted overprint		110.00	
b.	Double ovpt., one inverted		225.00	
L27	A2	½pi red	10.00	1.75
a.	Inverted overprint		110.00	
b.	Double ovpt., one inverted		225.00	
L28	A3	1pi blue	5.00	.80
a.	Inverted overprint		95.00	
b.	Double overprint		175.00	
L29	A6	2pi magenta	9.00	5.50
a.	Double overprint		175.00	

With Additional Surcharge of New Value

L30	A5(a)	½pi on 1pa lil brn	40.00	14.00
L31	A5(b)	1pi on 1pa lil brn	4.00	.90
a.	Inverted surcharge		105.00	
b.	Double surcharge		100.00	
c.	Dbl. surch., one invtd., ovpt. invtd.		300.00	
d.	Inverted overprint		115.00	
e.	Inverted overprint and surcharge		225.00	
f.	Inverted overprint, double surcharge		225.00	
g.	Words of surcharge transposed		225.00	
h.	Overprint and surcharge inverted, words of surcharge transposed		500.00	

i.	Right hand character of surcharge inverted		100.00
	Nos. L24-L31 (8)	108.50	34.70

The 1921 and 1922 overprints read: "The Arab Hashemite Government, 1340."

The overprint on No. L28 in red is bogus. Forgeries abound.

Types A7 and A8
Very fine examples will be somewhat off center but perforations will be clear of the framelines.

Arms of Sherif of Mecca — A7

1922, Feb.   **Typo.**   *Perf. 11½*

L32	A7	⅛pi red brown	3.00	.45
L34	A7	½pi red	3.25	.45
L35	A7	1pi dark blue	3.50	.45
L36	A7	1½pi violet	4.00	.45
L37	A7	2pi orange	5.00	.45
L38	A7	3pi olive brown	4.00	.45
a.	3pi brown		3.00	.25
L39	A7	5pi olive green	4.25	.55
	Nos. L32-L39 (7)		27.00	3.25

Numerous shades exist. Some values were printed in other colors in 1925 for handstamping by the Nejdi authorities in Mecca. These exist without handstamps.
Exist imperf.
Forgeries exist, usually perf. 11.
Reprints of Nos. L32, L35 exist; paper and shades differ.
See Nos. L48A-L49. For surcharges and overprints see Nos. L40-L48, L76, L82-L159, 7-20, 38A-48, 55A-58A, LJ11-LJ16, LJ26-LJ39, J1-J8, J10-J11, P1-P3, Jordan 64-72, 91, 103-120, J1-J17, O1.

Stamps of 1922 Surcharged with New Values in Arabic

c   d

1923

L40	A7(c)	¼pi on ⅛pi org brn	40.00	32.50
a.	Double surcharge		150.00	
b.	Double inverted surcharge		375.00	
c.	Double surch., one invtd.		400.00	
L41	A7(d)	10pi on 5pi ol grn	45.00	27.50
a.	Double surch., one invtd.		200.00	
b.	Inverted surcharge		175.00	

Forgeries exist.

Caliphate Issue

Stamps of 1922
Overprinted in Gold

1924

L42	A7	⅛pi orange brown	5.50
L43	A7	½pi red	4.00
L44	A7	1pi dark blue	6.00
a.	Inverted overprint		225.00
L45	A7	1½pi violet	5.75
L46	A7	2pi orange	5.25
a.	Inverted overprint		225.00
L47	A7	3pi olive brown	6.00
L48	A7	5pi olive green	7.00
a.	Inverted overprint		225.00
	Nos. L42-L48 (7)		39.50

Assumption of the Caliphate by King Hussein in Mar., 1924. The overprint reads "In commemoration of the Caliphate, Shaaban, 1342."

The overprint was typographed in black and dusted with "gold" powder while wet. Inverted overprints on other values are forgeries. So-called black overprints are either forgeries or gold overprints with the gold rubbed off. No genuine black overprints are known.

The overprint is 18-20mm wide. The 1st setting of the ½p is 16mm.
Forgeries exist.
Nos. L43-L44, L46 exist with postage due overprint as on Nos. LJ11-LJ13.

Type of 1922 and

Arms of Sherif of Mecca — A8

1924   *Perf. 11½*

L48A	A7	¼pi yellow green	7.50	5.75
	Tête bêche pair		50.00	
L49	A7	3pi brown red	11.00	9.00
a.	3pi dull red		3.50	4.50
L50	A8	10pi vio & dk brn	7.00	4.50
a.	Center inverted		60.00	55.00
c.	10pi purple & sepia		4.00	4.50
	Nos. L48A-L50 (3)		25.50	19.25

Nos. L48A, L50, L50a exist imperf.
Several printings of Nos. L48A-L50 exist; paper and shades differ.
A plate flaw in position 13 of No. L48A, which appears as a large white gash in the upper left portion of the stamp, exists. Values: unused single, $50; unused tête-bêche pair, $250.
Forgeries exist, usually perf. 11.
For overprint see No. L76A, Jordan 121.

Jedda Issues
Stamps of 1916-17 Overprinted

The Jedda overprints on Nos. L51-L159 read: "Al-hukuma al Hejaziyeh, 5 Rabi al'awwal 1343"
(The Hejaz Government, October 4, 1924). This is the date of the accession of King Ali. Counterfeits exist of all Jedda overprints.

Jedda issues were also used in Medina and Yambo.
Used values for #L51-L186 and LJ17-LJ39 are for genuine cancels. Privately applied cancels exist for "Mekke" (Mecca, bilingual or all Arabic), Khartoum, Cairo, as well as for Jeddah. Many private cancels have wrong dates, some as early as 1916. These are worth half the used values.

Red Overprint

1925, Jan.   *Roulette 20*

L51	A4	⅛pi orange	40.00	14.00
a.	Inverted overprint		110.00	
b.	Ovptd. on face and back		225.00	
c.	Normal ovpt. on face, double ovpt. on back		325.00	
L52	A1	¼pi green	40.00	14.00
a.	Inverted overprint		75.00	
b.	Double overprint		75.00	
c.	Double overprint, one invtd.		175.00	
L53	A2	½pi red	90.00	67.50
a.	Inverted overprint		175.00	
b.	Double ovpt., one invtd.		175.00	
	Nos. L51-L53 (3)		170.00	95.50

Serrate Roulette 13

L55	A5	1pa lilac brown	30.00	12.50
a.	Inverted overprint		75.00	
b.	Double overprint		70.00	
c.	Ovptd. on face and back		200.00	
d.	Normal ovpt. on face, double ovpt. on back		150.00	
L56	A4	⅛pi orange	60.00	35.00
L57	A1	¼pi green	37.50	20.00
a.	Pair, one without overprint		1,750.	
b.	Inverted overprint		75.00	
c.	Double ovpt., one inverted		300.00	
L58	A2	½pi red	55.00	27.50
a.	Inverted overprint		175.00	
L59	A3	1pi blue	60.00	32.50
a.	Inverted overprint		125.00	
L60	A6	2pi magenta	45.00	35.00
a.	Inverted overprint		150.00	
	Nos. L55-L60 (6)		287.50	162.50

Gold Overprint
Roulette 20

L61	A1	¼pi green, gold on red ovpt.	2,250.	
	Never hinged		3,000.	
a.	Gold on blue ovpt.		4,000.	*7,000.*

Serrate Roulette 13

L62	A1	¼pi green, gold on red ovpt.	45.00	22.50
a.	Inverted overprint		250.00	

The overprint on No. L61 was typographed in red or blue (No. L62 only in red) and dusted with "gold" powder while wet.

Blue Overprint
Roulette 20

L63	A1	¼pi green	150.00	22.50
a.	Inverted overprint		175.00	
a.	Ovptd. on face and back		225.00	
L64	A2	½pi red, invtd. ovpt.	150.00	80.00
a.	Upright overprint		200.00	

Serrate Roulette 13

L65	A1	¼pi green	35.00	16.00
a.	Inverted overprint		75.00	
b.	Vertical overprint		1,000.	
L66	A2	½pi red	55.00	27.50
a.	Inverted overprint		110.00	
L66B	A6	2pi mag, invtd. ovpt.		1,800.

Blue overprint on Nos. L4, L8, L9 are bogus.

Same Overprint in Blue on Provisional Stamps of 1922
Overprinted on No. L17

L67	A2	½pi red		2,750.

Overprinted on Nos. L24-L29

L68	A5	1pa lilac brn	200.00	160.00
L69	A4	⅛pi orange	2,500.	1,800.
a.	Inverted overprint		4,500.	
L70	A1	¼pi green	80.00	65.00
a.	Inverted overprint		800.00	
L71	A2	½pi red	100.00	85.00
a.	Inverted overprint		900.00	
L72	A3	1pi blue	125.00	110.00
a.	Inverted overprint		800.00	
L73	A6	2pi magenta	175.00	160.00
a.	Inverted overprint		1,500.	

Same Overprint on Nos. L30 and L31

L74	A5(a)	½pi on 1pa	105.00	90.00
L75	A5(b)	1pi on 1pa	90.00	75.00
a.	Inverted overprint		800.00	

Same Overprint in Blue Vertically, Reading Up or Down, on Stamps of 1922-24
Perf. 11½

L76	A7	½pi red	900.00	900.00
L76A	A8	10pi vio & dk brn		1,800. 1,800.

Nos. L5, L10 Overprinted Reading Up in Blue or Red

(Overprint reads up in illustration)

Roulette 20

L77a	A1	¼pi green (Bl)	550.00	500.00
L78	A1	¼pi green (R)	500.00	450.00

Serrate Roulette 13

L79a	A1	¼pi green (Bl)	350.00	300.00
L80	A1	¼pi green (R)	75.00	60.00

Overprint Reading Down
Roulette 20

L77	A1	¼pi green (Bl)	200.00	175.00

Serrate Roulette 13

L79	A1	¼pi green (Bl)	105.00	90.00
L80a	A1	¼pi green (R)	225.00	200.00
L80b	A1	¼pi green (R), double ovpt.	450.00	
L80c	A1	¼pi green (R), double ovpt., 1 reading up and 1 reading down	500.00	
L80d	A1	¼pi green (R), triple ovpt., all reading up	600.00	

Nos. L10, L32-L39, L48A, L49a, L50 Overprinted

Serrate Roulette 13
Red Overprint (vertical, reading down)

L81	A1	¼pi green	1,350.	
a.		Overprint reading up	1,500.	
b.		Overprint horizontal	1,750.	
c.		As "b," overprint inverted	1,750.	

Perf. 11½

Blue Overprint

L82	A7	⅛pi red brown	13.00	5.50
a.		Inverted overprint	55.00	
L83	A7	½pi red	15.00	7.25
a.		Double overprint	75.00	
b.		Inverted overprint		45.00
c.		Double ovpt., one invtd.	100.00	
d.		Overprint reading up	175.00	
L84	A7	1pi dark blue	500.00	
a.		Inverted overprint	500.00	
L85	A7	1½pi violet	22.50	11.00
a.		Inverted overprint	50.00	45.00
L86	A7	2pi orange	22.50	11.00
		On cover, single franking		200.00
a.		Double ovpt., one invtd.	75.00	
b.		Inverted overprint	50.00	
c.		Double overprint	75.00	
L87	A7	3pi olive brown	20.00	9.00
a.		Inverted overprint	50.00	
b.		Double ovpt., one invtd.	75.00	
c.		Overprint reading up	180.00	
d.		Dbl. ovpt., both invtd.	105.00	
L88	A7	3pi dull red	24.00	11.00
a.		Inverted overprint	50.00	
b.		Double ovpt., one invtd.	75.00	
L89	A7	5pi olive green	21.00	11.00
a.		Inverted overprint	55.00	

Some values exist in pairs, one without overprint.

Black Overprint

L90	A7	⅛pi red brown	90.00	
a.		Inverted overprint	175.00	
L91	A7	½pi red	11.00	4.50
a.		Inverted overprint	75.00	
L92	A7	1pi dark blue	500.00	
a.		Inverted overprint	500.00	
L93	A7	1½pi violet	26.00	12.00
a.		Inverted overprint	75.00	
L94	A7	2pi orange	15.00	7.25
a.		Inverted overprint	50.00	
L95	A7	3pi olive brown	12.00	5.50
a.		Inverted overprint	75.00	67.50
L96	A7	3pi dull red	15.00	7.25
a.		Inverted overprint	50.00	
L97	A7	5pi olive green	20.00	9.00
a.		Inverted overprint	50.00	

Red Overprint

L98	A7	⅛pi red brn, invtd.	900.00	
L99	A7	¼pi yellow grn	35.00	16.00
a.		Tête bêche pair	100.00	
b.		Inverted overprint	50.00	
c.		Tête bêche pair, one with inverted overprint	125.00	
L100	A7	½pi red	1,000.	500.00
a.		Inverted overprint	1,100.	500.00
L101	A7	1pi dark blue	20.00	8.00
a.		Inverted overprint	50.00	
b.		Double ovpt., one invtd.	40.00	
L102	A7	1½pi violet	11.00	4.50
a.		Inverted overprint	50.00	
L103	A7	2pi orange	27.50	12.00
a.		Inverted overprint	50.00	
b.		Overprint reading up	200.00	
L104	A7	3pi olive brown	27.50	12.00
a.		Inverted overprint	50.00	
L105	A7	3pi dull red, invtd.	1,700.	
L106	A7	5pi olive green	20.00	7.25
a.		Inverted overprint	50.00	
b.		Inverted overprint	175.00	
c.		Overprint reading down	175.00	
L107	A8	10pi vio & dk brn	35.00	16.00
a.		Inverted overprint	50.00	
b.		Center inverted	125.00	
c.		As "b," invtd. ovpt.	175.00	

Nos. L98, L105 with normal overprint are fakes.

Gold Overprint

L108	A7	⅛pi red brown	35.00	27.50
L109	A7	½pi red	35.00	27.50
L110	A7	1pi dark blue	40.00	27.50
L111	A7	1½pi violet	125.00	110.00
L112	A7	2pi orange	110.00	90.00
L113	A7	3pi olive brown	45.00	35.00
L114	A7	3pi dull red	130.00	100.00
L115	A7	5pi olive green	105.00	85.00
		Nos. L108-L115 (8)	625.00	502.50

Inverted overprints are forgeries.

Same Overprint on Nos. L42-L48
Blue Overprint

L116	A7	⅛pi red brown	50.00	42.50
a.		Double ovpt., one invtd.	300.00	
L117	A7	½pi red	95.00	80.00
L118	A7	1pi dark blue	80.00	55.00
L119	A7	1½pi violet	90.00	65.00
L120	A7	2pi orange	300.00	275.00
a.		Inverted overprint	500.00	
L121	A7	3pi olive brown	125.00	110.00
a.		Inverted overprint	225.00	
L122	A7	5pi olive green	50.00	37.50
a.		Inverted overprint	250.00	
		Nos. L116-L122 (7)	790.00	665.00

Black Overprint

L123	A7	⅛pi red brown	50.00	42.50
a.		Inverted overprint	275.00	
L125	A7	1½pi violet	150.00	140.00
a.		Inverted overprint	300.00	
L127	A7	3pi olive brown	125.00	110.00
a.		Inverted overprint	300.00	
L128	A7	5pi olive green	155.00	140.00
a.		Inverted overprint	300.00	
		Nos. L123-L128 (4)	480.00	432.50

Red Overprint

L129	A7	1pi dark blue	125.00	90.00
L130	A7	1½pi violet	135.00	110.00
L131	A7	2pi orange	150.00	90.00
		Nos. L129-L131 (3)	410.00	290.00

Overprints on stamps or in colors other than those listed are forgeries.

Stamps of 1922-24 Surcharged

a

and Handstamp Surcharged

b — 1/4pi

b — 1pi   b — 10pi

1925   Litho.   Perf. 11½

L135	A7	¼pi on ¼pi on ⅛pi red brn	75.00	47.50
b.		1pi on ¼pi on ⅛pi red brown	150.00	
L136	A7	¼pi on ¼pi on ½pi red	50.00	30.00
c.		1pi on ¼pi on ½pi	75.00	55.00
L138	A7	1pi on 1pi on 2pi orange	50.00	30.00
a.		¼pi on 1pi on 2pi org	125.00	
b.		10pi on 1pi on 2pi org	105.00	
c.		¼pi on 1pi on 2pi org	55.00	
d.		10pi on ¼pi on 2pi org	105.00	
L139	A7	1pi on 1pi on 3pi ol brn	30.00	22.50
L140	A7	1pi on 1pi on 3pi dl red	45.00	35.00
b.		¼pi on 1pi on 3pi dl red	125.00	
L141	A7	1pi on 10pi on 5pi ol grn	25.00	16.00
b.		1pi on 10 pi on 5 pi	110.00	
		Nos. L135-L141 (6)	275.00	181.00

The printed surcharge (a) reads "The Hejaz Government. October 4, 1924." with new denomination in third line. This surcharge alone was used for the first issue (Nos. L135a-L141a). The new denomination was so small and indistinct that its equivalent in larger characters was soon added by handstamp (b) at bottom of each stamp for the second issue (Nos. L135-L141).

The handstamped surcharge (b) is found double, inverted, etc. It is also known in dark violet.

Without Handstamp "b"

L135a	A7	¼pi on ⅛pi red brn	110.00	
L136b	A7	¼pi on ½pi red	110.00	
L138e	A7	1pi on 2pi orange	110.00	
L139a	A7	1pi on 3pi olive brn	110.00	
L140a	A7	1pi on 3pi dull red	110.00	
L141a	A7	1pi on 10pi on 5pi olive grn	110.00	
		Nos. L135a-L141a (6)	660.00	

Stamps of 1922-24 Surcharged

Black Surcharge

L142	A7	⅛pi on ½pi red	10.00	7.25
a.		Inverted surcharge	40.00	
L143	A7	½pi on ½pi red	11.00	7.25
a.		Inverted surcharge	40.00	
L144	A7	½pi on ½pi red	12.50	7.25
a.		Inverted surcharge	25.00	
L145	A7	1pi on 1½pi vio	12.50	7.25
a.		Inverted surcharge	40.00	
L146	A7	1pi on 2pi org	10.00	7.25
a.		"10pi"	150.00	
b.		Inverted surcharge	40.00	
c.		As "a," inverted surcharge	150.00	
L147	A7	1pi on 3pi olive brn	12.50	7.25
a.		"10pi"	100.00	
b.		Inverted surcharge	55.00	
c.		As "a," inverted surcharge	150.00	
L148	A7	10pi on 5pi olive grn	20.00	14.00
a.		Inverted surcharge	75.00	
		Nos. L142-L148 (7)	88.50	57.50

Blue Surcharge

L149	A7	⅛pi on ½pi red	17.50	11.00
a.		Inverted surcharge	75.00	
b.		Double surcharge	225.00	
L150	A7	¼pi on ½pi red	15.00	11.00
a.		Inverted surcharge	75.00	
L151	A7	½pi on ½pi red	15.00	11.00
a.		Inverted surcharge	75.00	
b.		Double surcharge	125.00	
L152	A7	1pi on 1½pi vio	20.00	11.00
a.		Inverted surcharge	75.00	
L153	A7	1pi on 2pi org	17.50	11.00
a.		"10pi"	100.00	
L154	A7	1pi on 3pi olive brn	30.00	22.50
a.		"10pi"	110.00	
b.		Inverted surcharge	75.00	
L155	A7	10pi on 5pi olive grn	35.00	25.00
a.		Inverted surcharge	75.00	
		Nos. L149-L155 (7)	150.00	102.50

Red Surcharge

L156	A7	1pi on 1½pi vio	30.00	22.50
a.		Inverted surcharge	90.00	
L157	A7	1pi on 2pi org	30.00	22.50
a.		"10pi"	100.00	
b.		Inverted surcharge	90.00	
L158	A7	1pi on 3pi olive brn	32.50	22.50
a.		"10pi"	125.00	
b.		Inverted surcharge	90.00	
L159	A7	10pi on 5pi olive grn	32.50	22.50
a.		Inverted surcharge	90.00	
		Nos. L156-L159 (4)	125.00	90.00
		Nos. L142-L159 (18)	363.50	250.00

The "10pi" surcharge is found inverted on Nos. L146a, L147a. The existence of genuine inverted "10pi" surcharges on Nos. L153a, L154a, L157a and L158a is in doubt. The 10pi on 1½pi is bogus.

King Ali Issue

A9

A10

A11

A12

1925, May-June   Perf. 11½
Black Overprint

L160	A9	⅛pi chocolate	2.25	1.50
L161	A9	¼pi ultra	2.25	1.50
L162	A9	½pi car rose	2.25	1.50
L163	A10	1pi yellow green	3.00	1.75
L164	A10	1½pi orange	3.00	1.75
L165	A10	2pi blue	3.50	2.25
L166	A11	3pi dark green	3.50	2.25
L167	A11	5pi orange brn	3.50	2.25
L168	A12	10pi red & green	6.00	4.50
a.		Center inverted	90.00	
		Nos. L160-L168 (9)	29.25	19.25

Red Overprint

L169	A9	⅛pi chocolate	4.00	2.75
L170	A9	¼pi ultra	2.50	1.60
L171	A10	1pi yellow green	3.00	2.00
L172	A10	1½pi orange	3.00	2.00
L173	A10	2pi deep blue	3.50	2.50
L174	A11	3pi dark green	3.25	2.75
a.		Horiz. pair, imperf. vert.	75.00	
L175	A11	5pi org brn	4.00	2.75
L176	A12	10pi red & green	6.50	5.50
		Nos. L169-L176 (8)	29.75	21.85

Blue Overprint

L177	A9	⅛pi chocolate	2.75	1.75
L179	A9	½pi car rose	2.75	1.75
L180	A10	1pi yellow green	2.75	1.75
L181	A10	1½pi orange	2.75	1.75
L182	A11	3pi dark green	2.75	1.75
L183	A11	5pi orange brn	6.75	5.50
L184	A12	10pi red & green	9.00	7.25
L185	A12	10pi red & org	275.00	
		Nos. L177-L184 (7)	29.50	21.50

Without Overprint

L186	A12	10pi red & green	8.00	6.75
a.		Dbl. impression of center	90.00	

The overprint in the tablets on Nos. L160-L185 reads: "5 Rabi al'awwal, 1343" (Oct. 4, 1924), the date of the accession of King Ali.

The tablet overprints vary slightly in size. Each is found reading upward or downward and at either side of the stamp. These control overprints were first applied in Jedda by the government press.

They were later made from new plates by the stamp printer in Cairo. In the Jedda overprint, the bar over the "0" figure extends to the left.

Some values exist with 13m or 15mm instead of 18mm between tablets. They sell for more. The lines of the Cairo overprinting are generally wider, but more lightly printed, usually appearing slightly grayish and the bar is at center right. The Cairo overprints are believed not to have been placed in use.

Imperforates exist.

Nos. L160-L168 are known with the overprints spaced as on type D3 and aligned horizontally.

Examples of these stamps (perforated or imperforate) without the overprint, except No. L186 were not regularly issued and not available for postage.

No. L185 exists only with Cairo overprint. Imperfs of No. L185 sell for much less than No. L185. Fake perfs have been added to the imperfs.

The ¼pi with blue overprint is bogus.

No. L186 in other colors are color trials.

For overprints see #58B-58D, Jordan 122-129.

NEJDI ADMINISTRATION OF HEJAZ

Handstamped in Blue, Red, Black or Violet

The overprint reads: "1343. Barid al Sultanat an Nejdia" (1925. Post of the Sultanate of Nejd).

The overprints on this and succeeding issues are handstamped and, as usual, are found double, inverted, etc. These variations are scarce.

1925, Mar.-Apr.   Unwmk.   Perf. 12
On Stamp of Turkey, 1915, With Crescent and Star in Red

1	A22	5pa ocher (Bl)	30.00	27.50
2	A22	5pa ocher (R)	30.00	20.00
3	A22	5pa ocher (Bk)	30.00	22.50
4	A22	5pa ocher (V)	30.00	18.00

On Stamp of Turkey, 1913

5	A28	10pa green (Bl)	40.00	16.00
a.		Inverted overprint	500.00	
6	A28	10pa green (R)	40.00	12.50

On Stamps of Hejaz, 1922-24
Perf. 11½

7	A7	⅛pi red brn (R)	27.50	24.00
8	A7	⅛pi red brn (Bk)	40.00	35.00
9	A7	⅛pi red brn (V)	30.00	24.00
10	A7	½pi car (R)	35.00	30.00
11	A7	½pi car (Bk)	40.00	35.00
12	A7	½pi car (V)	30.00	27.50
13	A7	½pi red (Bl)	40.00	22.00
14	A7	½pi red (V)	40.00	18.00
15	A7	1½pi vio (R)	60.00	24.00
16	A7	2pi yel buff (R)	85.00	57.50
a.		2pi orange (R)	110.00	
17	A7	2pi yel buff (V)	85.00	57.50
a.		2pi orange (V)	100.00	32.50

18	A7	3pi brn red (Bl)	70.00	30.00
19	A7	3pi brn red (R)	70.00	22.50
20	A7	3pi brn red (V)	70.00	25.00

Many Hejaz stamps of the 1922 type were especially printed for this and following issues. The re-impressions are usually more clearly printed, in lighter shades than the 1922 stamps, and some are in new colors.
Counterfeits exist.

Arabic Inscriptions
R1   R2

On Hejaz Bill Stamp

22	R1	1pi violet (R)	40.00	15.00

On Hejaz Notarial Stamps

23	R2	1pi violet (R)	50.00	20.00
24	R2	2pi blue (R)	50.00	30.00
25	R2	2pi blue (V)	50.00	27.50

For overprint see No. 49.

Locomotive — R3

Type I

Type II

On Hejaz Railway Tax Stamps

Two design types appear on the basic revenue stamps. Type 1 depicts the cab's window and the band at the center of the boiler as a series of horizontal lines, the top of the cab does not touch the frame line above it, and the coupler at rear of car appears as a fine hook that does not touch the right frame. Type 2 depicts the cab's window and band on boiler as open vertical spaces, the top of the cab touches the frame line above it, and the coupler appears as a blob connected to the right frame line. Type 2 appears in position 12 in the sheet of 18 (6x3) of the 500pi value, and in position 30 in the 36-stamp (6x6) sheets in which the other values were printed.

Type 1

26	R3	1pi blue (R)	40.00	9.00
a.		Type 2	60.00	
27	R3	2pi ocher (R)	60.00	14.00
a.		Type 2	90.00	
28	R3	2pi ocher (V)	60.00	14.00
a.		Type 2	90.00	
29	R3	3pi lilac (R)	60.00	20.00
a.		Type 2	90.00	
		Nos. 1-20,22-29 (28)	1,332.	698.50

For overprints and surcharges see Nos. 34, 50-54, 55, 59-68, J12-J15.

Pilgrimage Issue
Various Stamps Handstamp Surcharged in Blue and Red in Types "a" and "b" and with Tablets with New Values

a

b

Surcharge "a" reads: "Tezkar al Hajj al Awwal Fi 'ahd al Sultanat al Nejdia, 1343" (Commemorating the first pilgrimage under the Nejdi Sultanate, 1925).
"b" reads: "Al Arba" (Wednesday.)

1925, July 1   **Perf. 12**
On Stamps of Turkey, 1913

30	A28	1pi on 10pa grn (Bl & R)	100.00	55.00
31	A30	5pi on 1pi bl (Bl & R)	100.00	55.00

On Stamps of Hejaz, 1917-18
Serrate Roulette 13

32	A5	2pi on 1pa lil brn (R & Bl)	125.00	67.50
33	A4	4pi on ½pi org (R & Bl)	400.00	350.00

On Hejaz Railway Tax Stamp
Perf. 11½

34	R3	3pi lilac, type 1 (Bl & R)	200.00	40.00
a.		Type 2	300.00	
		Nos. 30-34 (5)	925.00	567.50

No. 30 with handstamp "a" in black was a favor item. Nos. 30 and 33 with both handstamps in red are forgeries.

Handstamped in Blue, Red, Black or Violet

This overprint has practically the same meaning as that described over No. 1. The Mohammedan year (1343) is omitted.
This handstamp is said to be in private hands at this time. Extreme caution is advised before buying rare items.

1925, July-Aug.   **Perf. 12**
On Stamp of Turkey, 1915,
with Crescent and Star in Red

35	A22	5pa ocher (Bl)	50.00	24.00

On Stamps of Turkey, 1913

36	A28	10pa green (Bl)	60.00	20.00
a.		Black overprint	120.00	
b.		As "a," ovpt inverted	650.00	

On Stamps of Hejaz, 1922 (Nos. L28-L29)
Serrate Roulette 13

37	A3	1pi blue (R)	75.00	67.50
38	A6	2pi magenta (Bl)	75.00	67.50

On Stamps of Hejaz, 1922-24
Perf. 11½

38A	A7	⅛pi red brn (Bk)	4,500.	
38B	A7	⅛pi red brn (Bl)	3,750.	
39	A7	½pi red (Bl)	12.50	10.00
a.		Imperf., pair	25.00	22.50
39B	A7	½pi red (Bk)	20.00	18.00
c.		Imperf., pair	50.00	37.50
40	A7	1pi gray vio (R)	35.00	29.00
		1pi black violet (R)	50.00	
41	A7	1½pi dk red (Bk)	35.00	30.00
a.		1½pi brick red (Bk)	50.00	
42	A7	2pi yel buff (Bl)	47.50	
a.		2pi orange (Bl)	60.00	55.00
43	A7	2pi deep vio (Bl)	55.00	52.50
44	A7	3pi brown red (Bl)	35.00	34.00
45	A7	5pi scarlet (Bl)	40.00	37.50
		Nos. 35-38,39-45 (12)	542.50	433.50

Overprint on Nos. 38A, 39B, 39C is blue-black.
See note above No. 35.

---

c

d

e

With Additional Surcharge of New Value Typo. in Black

Color in parenthesis is that of overprint on basic stamp.

46	A7(c)	1pi on ½pi (Bl)	12.50	1.75
a.		Imperf, pair	40.00	
b.		Ovpt & surch. inverted	90.00	
47	A7(d)	1½pi on ½pi (Bl)	17.50	7.25
a.		Imperf., pair	30.00	
b.		Black overprint	20.00	
48	A7(e)	2pi on 3pi (Bl)	17.50	16.00
		Nos. 46-48 (3)	47.50	25.00

Several variations in type settings of "c," "d" and "e" exist, including inverted letters and values.

On Hejaz Notarial Stamp

49	R2	2pi blue (Bk)	50.00	20.00

On Hejaz Railway Tax Stamps

50	R3	1pi blue, type 1 (R)	40.00	25.00
a.		Type 2	60.00	
51	R3	1pi blue, type 1 (Bk)	60.00	9.00
a.		Type 2	90.00	
52	R3	2pi ocher, type 1 (Bl)	60.00	9.00
a.		Type 2	90.00	
53	R3	3pi lilac, type 1 (Bl)	70.00	22.50
a.		Type 2	100.00	
54	R3	5pi green, type 1 (Bl)	60.00	20.00
a.		Type 2	90.00	
		Nos. 49-54 (6)	340.00	105.50

Hejaz Railway Tax Stamp Handstamped in Black

This overprint reads: "Al Saudia. — Al Sultanat al Nejdia." (The Saudi Sultanate of Nejd.)

1925-26

Small Handstamp

55	R3	1pi blue, type 1	—	200.00
b.		Type 2	—	400.00

On Nos. L34, L36-L37, L41

55A	A7	½ pi red	—	350.00
56	A7	1½pi violet	—	375.00
57	A7	2pi orange	—	375.00
57A	A7	10pi on 5pi ol green	—	375.00

On Nos. L95 and L97

58	A7	3pi olive brown	—	400.00
58A	A7	5pi olive green	—	400.00

On Nos. L162-L163, L173
Perf. 11½

58B	A9	½pi car rose	350.00	
58C	A10	1pi yel grn	—	225.00
58D	A10	2pi blue	—	350.00

Large Handstamp

58K	R3	1pi blue		7,000.
58L	A7	3pi brown (#L95b)		1,000.
		reading up		
a.		Overprint reading down		1,000.
58M	A10	1pi yel grn (#L163)	1,500.	1,000.

Nos. 55-58M were provisionally issued at Medina after its capitulation.
Only one example of No. 58K, a single stamp used on piece, is known.
This overprint exists on Nos. L160-L161, L164-L172, L174-L175, L180-L183. These 17 are known as bogus items, but may exist genuine.
Lithographed overprints are forgeries.

Medina Issue

Hejaz Railway Tax Stamps Handstamped

and Handstamp Surcharged in Various Colors

The large overprint reads: "The Nejdi Posts — 1344 — Commemorating Medina, the Illustrious." The tablet shows the new value.

1925

59	R3	1pi on 10pi vio, type 1 (Bk & V)	70.00	70.00
a.		Type 2	100.00	
60	R3	2pi on 50pi lt bl, type 1 (R & Bl)	70.00	70.00
a.		Type 2	100.00	
61	R3	3pi on 100pi red brn, type 1 (Bl & Bk)	70.00	70.00
a.		Type 2	100.00	
62	R3	4pi on 500pi dull red, type 1 (Bl & Bk)	70.00	70.00
a.		Type 2	100.00	
63	R3	5pi on 1000pi dp red, type 1 (Bl & Bk)	70.00	70.00
a.		Type 2	100.00	
		Nos. 59-63 (5)	350.00	350.00

JEDDA ISSUE

Hejaz Railway Tax Stamps Handstamped and Tablet with New Value in Various Colors

This handstamp reads: "Commemorating Jedda — 1344 — The Nejdi Posts."

1925

64	R3	1pi on 10pi vio, type 1 (Bk & Bl)	70.00	70.00
b.		Type 2	100.00	
65	R3	2pi on 50pi lt bl, type 1 (R & Bk)	70.00	70.00
a.		Type 2	100.00	

66 R3 3pi on 100pi red
brn, type 1 (R
& Bl)   70.00   70.00
  a. Type 2   100.00
67 R3 4pi on 500pi dl red,
type 1 (Bk & Bl)   70.00   70.00
  a. Type 2   100.00
68 R3 5pi on 1000pi dp
red, type 1 (Bk
& Bl)   70.00   70.00
  a. Type 2   100.00
Nos. 64-68 (5)   350.00   350.00

Nos. 59-63 and 64-68 were prepared in anticipation of the surrender of Medina and Jedda.

Kingdom of Hejaz-Nejd

Arabic
Inscriptions
and
Value — A1

A2

Inscriptions in upper tablets: "Barid al Hejaz wa Nejd" (Posts of the Hejaz and Nejd)

1926, Feb. Typo. Unwmk. Perf. 11
69 A1 ¼pi violet   45.00   17.00
70 A1 ½pi gray   45.00   17.00
71 A1 1pi deep blue   45.00   21.00
72 A2 2pi blue green   45.00   17.00
73 A2 3pi carmine   45.00   18.00
74 A2 5pi maroon   45.00   12.00
Nos. 69-74 (6)   270.00   102.00

Nos. 69-72, 74 exist imperf. Value, each $40.
Used values are for favor cancels.

1926, Mar.   Perf. 11
75 A1 ¼pi orange   12.00   10.00
  a. Horiz. pair, imperf between   100.00
76 A1 ½pi blue green   5.25   15.00
  a. Horiz. pair, imperf between   100.00
  b. Vertz. pair, imperf between   100.00
77 A1 1pi carmine   4.25   7.50
  a. Horiz. pair, imperf between   100.00
  b. Vert. pair, imperf between   100.00
78 A2 2pi violet   5.25   12.50
  a. Horiz. pair, imperf between   100.00
  b. Vert. pair, imperf between   100.00
79 A2 3pi dark blue   5.25   7.50
  a. Horiz. pair, imperf between   100.00
  b. Vert. pair, imperf between   100.00
80 A2 5pi lt brown   10.00   20.00
  a. 5pi olive brown
  b. Horiz. pair, imperf between   100.00
  c. Vert. pair, imperf between   100.00
Nos. 75-80 (6)   42.00   72.50

Nos. 75-80 also exist imperf. Value, twice the values shown above. Examples that are perforated 14, 14x11 and 11x14 were privately produced.
Counterfeits of types A1 and A2 are perf. 11½. They exist with and without overprints.
Types A1 and A2 in colors other than listed are proofs.

Pan-Islamic Congress Issue

Stamps of
1926
Hstmpd.

1926   Perf. 11
92 A1 ¼pi orange   12.00   4.00
93 A1 ½pi blue green   12.00   4.00
94 A1 1pi carmine   12.00   4.00
95 A2 2pi violet   12.00   4.00
96 A2 3pi dark blue   12.00   4.00
97 A2 5pi light brown   12.00   4.00
Nos. 92-97 (6)   72.00   24.00

The overprint reads: "al Mootamar al Islami 20 Zilkada, Sanat 1344." (The Islamic Congress, June 1, 1926.)
See counterfeit note after No. 80.

Tughra of King Abdul
Aziz — A3

1926-27   Typo.   Perf. 11½
98 A3 ⅛pi ocher   5.00   .60
99 A3 ¼pi gray green   6.00   1.50
100 A3 ½pi dull red   6.00   1.50
  b. Horiz. pair, imperf between   400.00
101 A3 1pi deep violet   6.50   1.50
102 A3 1½pi gray blue   18.00   2.25
103 A3 3pi olive green   14.00   4.75
104 A3 5pi brown orange   27.50   5.00
105 A3 10pi dark brown   70.00   7.00
Nos. 98-105 (8)   153.00   24.10
Set, never hinged   225.00

Inscription at top reads: "Al Hukumat al Arabia" (The Arabian Government). Inscription below tughra reads: "Barid al Hejaz wa Nejd" (Post of the Hejaz and Nejd).

Stamps of 1926-27
Handstamped in
Black or Red

1927
107 A3 ⅛pi ocher   13.00   4.75
108 A3 ¼pi gray grn   13.00   4.75
109 A3 ½pi dull red   13.00   4.75
110 A3 1pi deep violet   13.00   4.75
111 A3 1½pi gray bl (R) 13.00   4.75
112 A3 3pi olive green   13.00   4.75
113 A3 5pi brown orange 14.50   4.75
114 A3 10pi dark brown   16.00   4.75
Nos. 107-114 (8)   108.50   38.00
Set, never hinged   175.00

The overprint reads: "In commemoration of the Kingdom of Nejd and Dependencies, 25th Rajab 1345."
Inverted varieties have not been authenticated.

Turkey No.
258
Surcharged in
Violet

1925   Perf. 12
115 A28 1g on 10pa green   175.00

Similar surcharges of 6g and 20g were made in red, but were not known to have been issued. Values: 6g, $350; 20g, $500.

A4   A5

1929-30   Typo.   Perf. 11½
117 A4 1¾g gray blue   40.00   4.50
119 A4 20g violet   50.00   10.00
120 A4 30g green   80.00   22.50

1930   Perf. 11, 11½
125 A5 ½g rose   19.00   3.25
126 A5 1½g violet   19.00   2.10
127 A5 1¾g ultra   19.00   2.75
128 A5 3½g emerald   19.00   4.25
    Perf. 11
129 A5 5g black brown   30.00   6.50
Nos. 125-129 (5)   106.00   18.85

Anniversary of King Ibn Saud's accession to the throne of the Hejaz, January 8, 1926.

A6   A7

1931-32   Perf. 11½
130 A6 ⅛g ocher ('32)   22.50   3.25
131 A6 ¼g blue green   22.50   2.50
133 A6 1¾g ultra   37.50   3.25
Nos. 130-133 (3)   82.50   9.00

1932   Perf. 11½
135 A7 ¼g blue green   16.00   32.50
  a. Perf 11
136 A7 ½g scarlet   47.50   5.25
  a. Perf 11
137 A7 2⅛g ultra   90.00   8.50
  a. Perf 11
Nos. 135-137 (3)   153.50   46.25

Kingdom of Saudi Arabia

A8

1934, Jan.   Perf. 11½, Imperf.
138 A8 ¼g yellow green   11.00   10.00
  Never hinged   15.00
139 A8 ½g red   11.00   10.00
  Never hinged   15.00
140 A8 1½g light blue   21.00   19.00
  Never hinged   27.50
141 A8 3g blue green   21.00   19.00
  Never hinged   27.50
142 A8 3½g ultra   37.50   7.75
  Never hinged   47.50
143 A8 5g yellow   50.00   37.50
  Never hinged   65.00
144 A8 10g red orange   90.00
  Never hinged   120.00
145 A8 20g bright violet 110.00
  Never hinged   150.00
146 A8 ¼s claret   225.00
  Never hinged   300.00
147 A8 30g dull violet 140.00
  Never hinged   180.00
148 A8 ½s chocolate   475.00
  Never hinged   700.00
149 A8 1s violet brown 1,075.
  Never hinged   1,750.
Nos. 138-149 (12)   2,266.

Proclamation of Emir Saud as Heir Apparent of Arabia. Perf. and imperf. stamps were issued in equal quantities.
Favor cancels exist on Nos. 144-149.

Tughra of King
Abdul
Aziz — A9

1934-57   Perf. 11, 11½
159 A9 ⅛g yellow   5.25   .45
160 A9 ¼g yellow grn   5.25   .45
161 A9 ½g rose red ('43) 3.75   .25
  a. ½g dark carmine   12.00   1.40
162 A9 ⅞g lt blue ('56)   6.50   .55
163 A9 1g blue green   5.25   .45
164 A9 2g olive grn ('57) 9.00   2.25
  a. 2g olive bister ('57) 25.00   7.25
165 A9 2⅞g violet ('57)   6.50   .55
166 A9 3g ultra ('38)   6.50   .25
  a. 3g light blue   20.00   1.75
167 A9 3½g lt ultra   35.00   2.25
168 A9 5g orange   6.50   .55
169 A9 10g violet   19.00   1.75
170 A9 20g purple brn   32.50   1.10
  a. 20g purple black   25.00   2.25
171 A9 100g red vio ('42) 90.00   5.25
172 A9 200g vio brn ('42) 115.00   7.00
Nos. 159-172 (14)   346.00   23.10
Set, never hinged   450.00

The ½g has two types differing in position of the tughra.
No. 162 measures 31x22mm. No. 164 30½x21½mm. No. 165, 30½x22mm. No. 166 30x21mm. No. 171, 31x22mm. No. 172, 30½x21½mm. Rest of set, 29x20½mm. Grayish paper was used in 1946-49 printings.
No. 168 exists with pin-perf 6.
For overprint see No. J24.

Yanbu Harbor
near
Radwa — A10

1945   Typo.   Perf. 11½
173 A10 ½g brt carmine   7.75   .35
174 A10 3g lt ultra   10.00   1.10
175 A10 5g purple   27.50   1.40
176 A10 10g dk brown vio 60.00   3.25
Nos. 173-176 (4)   105.25   6.10
Set, never hinged   145.00

Meeting of King Abdul Aziz and King Farouk of Egypt at Jebal Radwa, Saudi Arabia, Jan. 24, 1945.

> **Catalogue values for unused stamps in this section, from this point to the end of the section, are for Never Hinged items.**

Arms of Saudi
Arabia and
Afghanistan
A12

1950, Mar.   Perf. 11
178 A12 ½g carmine   9.00   1.10
179 A12 3g violet blue   13.50   1.10

Visit of Zahir Shah of Afghanistan, March 1950. One 3g in each sheet inscribed POSTFS, value $45.

Old City
Walls,
Riyadh
A13

1950   Center in Red Brown
180 A13 ½g magenta   67.50   .40
181 A13 1g lt blue   13.00   .40
182 A13 3g violet   19.00   .90
183 A13 5g vermilion   42.50   1.75
184 A13 10g green   77.50   4.50
  a. Singular "guerche" in Arabic 575.00   67.50
Nos. 180-184 (5)   219.50   7.95

50th lunar anniversary of King Ibn Saud's capture of Riyadh, Jan. 16, 1902.
No. 184a: On the 3g, 5g and 10g the currency is expressed in the plural in both French (grouche) and Arabic. One stamp in each sheet of 20 (4x5), position 11, of the 10g shows the Arabic characters in the singular form of "guerche," as on the ½g and 1g.

Arms of Saudi
Arabia and
Jordan — A14

1951, Nov.   Perf. 11
185 A14 ½g carmine   12.50   1.75
  a. "BOYAUME"   250.00
186 A14 3g violet blue   17.50   2.75
  a. "BOYAUME"   250.00

Visit of King Tallal of Jordan, Nov. 1951.

Bedouins and
Train — A15

1952, June   Engr.   Perf. 12
187 A15 ½g redsh brown   9.75   1.50
188 A15 1q deep green   9.75   1.50
189 A15 3q violet   20.00   1.00
190 A15 10q rose pink   40.00   7.50
191 A15 20q blue   82.50   16.00
Nos. 187-191 (5)   162.00   27.50

Inaugural trip over the Saudi Government Railroad between Riyadh and Dammam.

Saudi Arabia Arms and Lebanon Emblem — A16

1953, Feb.   Typo.   Perf. 11
192 A16 ½g carmine   7.50 1.25
193 A16 3g violet blue   15.00 2.00

Visit of President Camille Chamoun of Lebanon.

Arms of Saudi Arabia and Emblem of Pakistan A17

1953, Mar.
194 A17 ½g dark carmine   9.00 1.25
195 A17 3g violet blue   18.00 1.90

Visit of Gov.-Gen. Ghulam Mohammed of Pakistan.

Arms of Saudi Arabia and Jordan — A18

1953, July   Unwmk.
196 A18 ½g carmine   8.00 1.25
    a.   "GOERCHE"   75.00
197 A18 3g violet blue   19.00 1.90

Visit of King Hussein of Jordan, July, 1953.

Globe — A18a

1955, July   Litho.
198 A18a ½g emerald   3.50   .60
199 A18a 3g violet   9.50 1.25
200 A18a 4g orange   14.00 3.00
    Nos. 198-200 (3)   27.00 4.85

Founding of the Arab Postal Union, July 1, 1954.

Ministry of Communications Building, Riyadh — A19

1960, Apr. 12   Photo.   Perf. 13
201 A19 2p bright blue   1.40   .25
202 A19 5p deep claret   2.75   .25
203 A19 10p dark green   7.50   .95
    Nos. 201-203 (3)   11.65 1.45

Arab Postal Union Conference, at Riyadh, Apr. 11. Imperfs. exist.

Arab League Center, Cairo A20

1960, Mar. 22   Perf. 13x13½
204 A20 2p dull grn & blk   2.50   .30

Opening of the Arab League Center and the Arab Postal Museum in Cairo. Exists imperf.

Radio Tower and Waves A21

1960, June 4
205 A21 2p red & black   2.50   .35
206 A21 5p brown blk & mar   4.25   .40
207 A21 10p bluish blk & ultra   6.75   .95
    Nos. 205-207 (3)   13.50 1.70

1st international radio station in Saudi Arabia. Imperfs. exist.

Map of Palestine, Refugee Camp and WRY Emblem — A22

1960, Oct. 30   Litho.   Perf. 13
208 A22 2p dark blue   .45   .30
209 A22 8p lilac   .45   .30
210 A22 10p green   1.40   .30
    Nos. 208-210 (3)   2.30   .90

World Refugee Year, July 1, 1959-June 30, 1960. Imperfs. exist.

Wadi Hanifa Dam, near Riyadh — A23

Type I (Saud Cartouche) (Illustrated over No. 286)
1960-62   Unwmk.   Photo.   Perf. 14
Size: 27½x22mm
211 A23 ½p bis brn & org   1.75   .30
212 A23 1p ol bis & pur   1.75   .30
213 A23 2p blue & sepia   1.75   .30
214 A23 3p sepia & blue   1.75   .30
215 A23 4p sepia & ocher   1.75   .30
216 A23 5p blk & dk violet   1.75   .30
217 A23 6p brn blk & car
         rose ('62)   1.75   .50
    a.   6p black & carmine rose 1.75   .40
218 A23 7p red & gray ol   1.75   .30
219 A23 8p dk bl & brn blk   1.75   .35
220 A23 9p org brn & scar   1.75   .40
    c.   9p yel brn & metallic red 1.75 .55
221 A23 10p emer grn &
         mar ('62)   2.10   .50
    a.   10p blue green & maroon 2.10   .85
222 A23 20p brown & green   5.00   .50
223 A23 50p black & brown   27.50 2.50
224 A23 75p brown & gray   77.50 2.75
225 A23 100p dk bl & grn bl   72.50 3.25
226 A23 200p lilac & green   110.00 8.50
    Nos. 211-226 (16)   312.10 21.35

Gas-Oil Separating Plant, Buqqa — A24

1960-61
227 A24 ½p maroon & org   1.50 1.50
228 A24 1p blue & red org   1.50 1.50
229 A24 2p ver & blue   1.50 1.50
230 A24 3p lilac & brt grn   1.50 1.50
231 A24 4p yel grn & lilac   1.50 1.50
232 A24 5p dk gray & brn
         red   1.50 1.50
233 A24 6p brn org & dk
         vio   1.50 1.50
234 A24 7p vio & dull grn   1.50 1.50
235 A24 8p blue grn &
         gray   1.50 1.50
236 A24 9p ultra & sepia   4.75 1.50
237 A24 10p blue & rose   2.50   .45
238 A24 20p org brn & blk   8.75   .65
239 A24 50p red & brn grn   25.00 1.90
240 A24 75p red & blk brn   40.00 4.00
241 A24 100p dk bl & red brn   60.00 3.50
242 A24 200p dk gray & ol
         grn   100.00 8.00
    Nos. 227-242 (16)   254.50 33.50

Nearly all of Nos. 211-242 exist imperf; probably not regularly issued.

See Nos. 258-273, 286-341, 393-450, 461-483.

Dammam Port — A25

Wmk. 337
1961, Aug. 16   Litho.   Perf. 13
243 A25 3p lilac   1.75   .30
244 A25 6p light blue   2.50   .40
245 A25 8p dark green   4.25   .40
    Nos. 243-245 (3)   8.50 1.10

Expansion of the port of Dammam. Imperf min. sheets of 4 were for presentation purposes and have wmk. sideways. Value, set $425. Imperforate pairs or margined imperfs with upright watermark come from full sheets not perforated by the print shop.

Globe, Radio and Telegraph A26

Perf. 13x13½
1961, Aug. 7   Photo.   Unwmk.
246 A26 3p dull purple   1.50   .25
247 A26 6p gray black   2.75   .40
248 A26 8p brown   4.25   .65
    Nos. 246-248 (3)   8.50 1.30

Arab Union of Telecommunications. Imperfs. exist.

Arab League Building, Cairo — A27

Malaria Eradication Emblem — A28

1962, Apr. 22   Wmk. 337   Perf. 13
249 A27 3p olive green   1.50   .30
250 A27 6p carmine rose   3.00   .40
251 A27 8p slate blue   4.75   .45
    Nos. 249-251 (3)   9.25 1.15

Arab League Week, Mar. 22-28.

Imperforate or missing-color varieties of Nos. 249-285 and 344-353 were not regularly issued.

1962, May 7   Litho.   Wmk. 337
252 A28 3p red org & blue   1.50   .30
253 A28 6p emerald & Prus bl   2.00   .35
254 A28 8p black & lil rose   3.00   .60
    a.   Souv. sheet of 3, #252-254,
         imperf.   32.50 32.50
    Nos. 252-254 (3)   6.50 1.25

WHO drive to eradicate malaria.
Nos. 252-254 are known unofficially overprinted with new dates only or with "AIR MAIL" and two plane silhouettes.
A 4p exists as an essay.

Koran A29

1963, Mar. 12   Wmk. 337   Perf. 11
255 A29 2½p lilac rose & pink   1.00   .25
256 A29 7½p blue & pale grn   2.10   .40
257 A29 9½p green & gray   3.25   .40
    Nos. 255-257 (3)   6.35 1.05

First anniversary of the Islamic Institute, Medina. A 3p exists as an essay. Copies of the 2½p exist with virtually all the pink background omitted. No copies are known with the pink completely omitted.

**Dam Type of 1960 Redrawn
Type I (Saud Cartouche)**
Perf. 13½x13
1963-65   Wmk. 337   Litho.
Size: 28½x23mm
258 A23 ½p bis brn & org   15.00 1.10

Nos. 258, 264-265 are widely spaced in the sheet, producing large margins.

Perf. 14
Photo.
Size: 27½x22mm
259 A23 ½p bis brn & org
         ('65)   22.50 1.75
260 A23 3p sepia & blue   9.00   .65
261 A23 4p sepia & ocher
         ('64)   12.50   .80
262 A23 5p black & dk vio   12.50   .80
263 A23 20p dk car & grn   22.50 1.60
    Nos. 258-263 (6)   94.00 6.70

A 1p was prepared but not issued. It is known only imperf.

**Gas-Oil Plant Type of 1960 Redrawn
Type I (Saud Cartouche)**
Perf. 13½x13
1963-65   Wmk. 337   Litho.
Size: 28½x23mm
264 A24 ½p maroon & or-
         ange   13.50 1.25
265 A24 1p blue & red org
         ('64)   7.25   .45

Photo.
Perf. 14
Size: 27½x22mm
266 A24 ½p mar & org ('64)   11.50   .60
267 A24 1p blue & red org   9.75   .45
268 A24 3p lilac & brt grn   22.50 1.10
269 A24 4p yel grn & lilac   13.50   .60
270 A24 5p dk gray & brn
         red   13.50   .60
271 A24 6p brn org & dk vio
         ('65)   19.00   .75
272 A24 8p dull grn & blk   35.00 1.40
273 A24 9p blue & sepia   35.00 1.75
    Nos. 264-273 (10)   180.50 8.95

The 3p, 4p and 6p exist imperf.

Hands Holding Wheat Emblem — A30

1963, Mar. 21   Litho.   Perf. 11
274 A30 2½p lilac rose & rose   1.10   .25
275 A30 7½p brt lilac & pink   1.10   .35
276 A30 9p red brn & lt blue   2.75   .45
    Nos. 274-276 (3)   4.95 1.05

FAO "Freedom from Hunger" campaign. The 3p imperf in various colors are essays.

Jet over Dhahran Airport — A31

1963, July 27   Litho.   Perf. 13
277 A31 1p blue gray & ocher   1.60   .35
278 A31 3½p ultra & emer   3.25   .35
279 A31 6p emerald & rose   5.75   .45
    a.   "Thahran" for "Dharan" in Arabic 8.75
280 A31 7½p lilac rose & lt bl   5.75   .55
281 A31 9½p ver & dull vio   8.25   .60
    Nos. 277-281 (5)   24.60 2.30

Opening of the US-financed terminal of the Dhahran Airport and inauguration of international jet service.
On No. 279a the misspelling consists of an omitted dot over one character near top left in one horiz. row of five.
Nos. 277-281 with a second impression of the frame are forgeries.

Flame — A32

1964, Apr.   Wmk. 337   Perf. 13x13½
282 A32 3p lil, pink & Prus bl ... 3.50 .30
283 A32 6p yel grn, lt bl & Prus bl ... 4.00 .35
284 A32 9p brn, buff & Prus bl ... 9.00 .45
Nos. 282-284 (3) ... 16.50 1.10

15th anniv. of the signing of the Universal Declaration of Human Rights.
The 3p in other colors is an essay.

King Faisal and Arms of Saudi Arabia A33

1964, Nov.   Litho.   Perf. 13
285 A33 4p dk blue & emerald ... 7.50 .60

Installation of Prince Faisal ibn Abdul Aziz as King, Nov. 2, 1964.

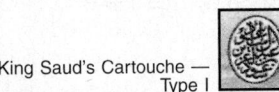

King Saud's Cartouche — Type I

King Faisal's Cartouche — Type II

Dam Type of 1960 Redrawn Type I (Saud Cartouche)
1965-70   Litho.   Unwmk.   Perf. 14
Size: 27x22mm

286 A23 1p ol bis & pur ... 32.50 1.60
287 A23 2p dk blue & sep ... 6.25 .45
288 A23 3p lilac & blue ... 4.75 .50
289 A23 4p sepia & ocher ... 9.00 .50
290 A23 5p blk & dk vio ... 8.00 .50
291 A23 6p blk & car rose ... 19.00 .90
292 A23 7p brown & gray ... 19.00 .50
293 A23 8p dk bl & gray ... 110.00 8.00
294 A23 9p org brn & scar ... 100.00 8.00
295 A23 10p bl grn & mar ... 92.50 5.00
296 A23 11p red & yel grn ... 8.75 3.25
297 A23 12p org & dk bl ... 8.75 .50
298 A23 13p dk ol & rose ... 8.75 .60
299 A23 14p org brn & yel grn ... 8.75 .60
300 A23 15p sepia & gray grn ... 8.75 3.25
301 A23 16p dk red & dl vio ... 10.50 .70
302 A23 17p rose lil & dk bl ... 10.50 3.50
303 A23 18p green & brt bl ... 10.50 .70
304 A23 19p black & bister ... 14.50 .85
305 A23 20p brn & grn ... 13.50 1.60
306 A23 23p mar & lilac ... 11.50 3.25
307 A23 24p ver & blue ... 14.50 .95
308 A23 26p olive & yel ... 18.00 1.10
309 A23 27p ultra & red brn ... 18.00 1.10
310 A23 31p gray & dull bl ... 18.00 1.25
311 A23 33p ol grn & lilac ... 18.00 1.25
312 A23 100p dk bl & grnsh bl ... 550.00 80.00
313 A23 200p dull lil & grn ... 550.00 80.00
Nos. 286-313 (28) ... 1,702. 210.40

A 50p exists but was never placed in use.
Issue years: 1966, 2p, 4p, 10p-20p, 1968, 6p-9p. 1970, 100p-200p.

Gas-Oil Plant Type of 1960 Redrawn Type I (Saud Cartouche)
1964-70   Litho.   Unwmk.
Size: 27x22mm

314 A24 1p bl & red org ... 7.25 .25
315 A24 2p vermilion & bl ... 11.00 .25
316 A24 3p lilac & brt grn ... 4.50 .25
317 A24 4p yel grn & lilac ... 6.50 .25
318 A24 5p dl gray vio & dk red brn ... 24.00 1.75
319 A24 6p brn org & dk vio ... 50.00 4.50
320 A24 7p vio & dull grn ... 27.50 1.75
321 A24 8p bl grn & gray ... 6.00 .30
322 A24 9p ultra & sepia ... 12.50 .70
323 A24 10p dk blue & rose ... 375.00 32.50
324 A24 11p olive & org ... 4.00 .30
325 A24 12p bister & grn ... 4.00 .30
326 A24 13p rose red & dk bl ... 4.00 .35
327 A24 14p vio & lt brown ... 5.50 .35
328 A24 15p rose red & sep ... 6.00 .45
329 A24 16p green & rose red ... 8.00 .45
330 A24 17p car rose & red brn ... 12.50 1.40
331 A24 18p gray & ultra ... 8.00 .55
332 A24 19p brown & yel ... 8.00 .55
333 A24 20p dull org & dk gray ... 27.50 1.75
334 A24 23p orange & car ... 7.25 .65
335 A24 24p emer & org yel ... 8.00 .70
336 A24 26p lil & red brn ... 11.00 .70
337 A24 27p ver & dk gray ... 11.00 .70
338 A24 31p dull grn & car ... 19.00 1.40
339 A24 33p red brn & gray ... 17.00 1.40
340 A24 50p red brn & dull grn ... 500.00 45.00
341 A24 200p dk gray & ol gray ... 500.00 45.00
Nos. 314-341 (28) ... 1,685. 144.50

A 100p exists but was never placed in use.
Issue years: 1965, 4p, 8p, 9p, 23p-33p. 1966, 1p, 2p, 5p, 11p-14p, 16p-20p. 1967, 15p. 1968, 6p, 7p. 1969, 50p. 1970, 200p. Others, 1964.

Holy Ka'aba, Mecca — A34

1965, Apr. 17   Wmk. 337   Perf. 13
344 A34 4p salmon & blk ... 4.50 .30
345 A34 6p brt pink & blk ... 6.50 .35
346 A34 10p yel grn & blk ... 9.00 .45
Nos. 344-346 (3) ... 20.00 1.10

Mecca Conf. of the Moslem World League.

Arms of Saudi Arabia and Tunisia A35

1965, Apr.   Litho.
347 A35 4p car rose & silver ... 3.50 .30
348 A35 8p red lilac & silver ... 4.50 .45
349 A35 10p vio & silver ... 6.50 .45
Nos. 347-349 (3) ... 14.50 1.20

Visit of Pres. Habib Bourguiba of Tunisia, Feb. 22-26.

Highway, Hejaz Mountains — A36

1965, June 2   Wmk. 337   Perf. 13
350 A36 2p red & blk ... 2.00 .35
351 A36 4p blue & blk ... 4.00 .50
352 A36 6p lilac & blk ... 5.75 .85
353 A36 8p brt green & blk ... 7.25 1.00
Nos. 350-353 (4) ... 19.00 2.70

Opening of highway from Mecca to Tayif.

ICY Emblem A37

1965, Nov. 13   Unwmk.   Perf. 13
354 A37 1p yellow & dk brn ... 1.75 .25
355 A37 2p orange & ol grn ... 1.75 .25
356 A37 3p lt blue & gray ... 1.75 .25
357 A37 4p yel grn & dk sl grn ... 2.00 .25
358 A37 10p orange & magenta ... 4.50 1.25
Nos. 354-358 (5) ... 11.75 2.25

International Cooperation Year, 1965.

ITU Emblem, Old and New Communication Equipment — A38

1965, Dec. 22   Litho.   Perf. 13
359 A38 3p blue & blk ... 2.25 .25
360 A38 4p lilac & dk grn ... 2.25 .25
361 A38 8p emerald & dk brn ... 2.25 .40
362 A38 10p dull org & dk grn ... 2.25 .40
Nos. 359-362 (4) ... 9.00 1.30

Centenary of the ITU.

Library Aflame and Lamp A39

1966, Jan.   Litho.   Perf. 12x12½
363 A39 1p orange ... 1.90 .25
364 A39 2p dark red ... 1.90 .25
365 A39 3p red violet ... 2.50 .25
366 A39 4p violet ... 3.00 .25
367 A39 5p lilac rose ... 4.50 .35
368 A39 6p vermilion ... 9.50 .45
Nos. 363-368 (6) ... 23.30 1.80

Burning of the Library of Algiers, June 7, 1962. Nos. 363-368 were withdrawn from sale Jan. 26, 1966, due to incorrect Arabic inscriptions. Later some values were inadvertently again placed in use.

Arab Postal Union Emblem — A40

1966, Mar. 15   Litho.   Perf. 14
369 A40 3p dull pur & olive ... 1.25 .30
370 A40 4p deep blue & olive ... 1.25 .30
371 A40 6p maroon & olive ... 4.50 .30
372 A40 7p deep green & olive ... 4.50 .45
Nos. 369-372 (4) ... 11.50 1.35

10th anniv. (in 1964) of the APU. Printed in sheets of two panes, so horizontal gutter pairs exist.

Dagger in Map of Palestine — A41

1966, Mar. 19   Litho.   Perf. 13
373 A41 2p yel grn & blk ... 2.25 .50
374 A41 4p lt brown & blk ... 4.00 1.00
375 A41 6p dull blue & blk ... 5.00 1.25
376 A41 8p ocher & blk ... 8.00 1.50
Nos. 373-376 (4) ... 19.25 4.25

Deir Yassin massacre, Apr. 9, 1948.

Emblems of World Boy Scout Conference and Saudi Arabian Scout Association A42

1966, Mar. 23   Unwmk.
377 A42 4p yel, blk, grn & gray ... 4.75 .55
378 A42 8p yel, blk, org & lt bl ... 4.75 .55
379 A42 10p yel, blk, sal & bl ... 10.00 .80
Nos. 377-379 (3) ... 19.50 1.90

Arab League Rover Moot (Boy Scout Jamboree).

WHO Headquarters, Geneva, and Flag — A43

1966, May   Litho.   Perf. 13
380 A43 4p aqua & multi ... 1.75 .50
381 A43 6p yel brn & multi ... 3.50 1.00
382 A43 10p pink & multi ... 6.75 1.25
Nos. 380-382 (3) ... 12.00 2.75

Opening of the WHO Headquarters, Geneva.

UNESCO Emblem — A44

1966, Sept.   Unwmk.   Perf. 12
383 A44 1p apple grn & multi ... 1.75 .25
384 A44 2p dull org & multi ... 1.75 .30
385 A44 3p lilac rose & multi ... 2.50 .40
386 A44 4p pale green & multi ... 2.50 .55
387 A44 10p gray & multi ... 3.50 1.00
Nos. 383-387 (5) ... 12.00 2.45

20th anniv. of UNESCO.

Radio Tower, Telephone and Map of Arab Countries — A45

1966, Nov. 7   Litho.   Perf. 12½
Design in Black, Carmine & Yellow
388 A45 1p vio blue ... 1.90 .25
389 A45 2p bluish lilac ... 1.90 .25
390 A45 4p rose lilac ... 3.75 .25
391 A45 6p lt olive grn ... 3.75 .35
392 A45 7p gray green ... 5.00 .50
Nos. 388-392 (5) ... 16.30 1.60

Issued to publicize the 8th Congress of the Arab Telecommunications Union, Riyadh.

Dam Type of 1960 Redrawn
Type II (Faisal Cartouche)
(Illustrated over No. 286)

1966-76　Litho.　Unwmk.　Perf. 14
Size: 27x22mm

393	A23	1p ol bis & pur	*200.00*	*22.50*
394	A23	2p dk blue & sep	19.00	1.50
395	A23	3p blk & dk bl	11.00	.80
396	A23	4p sepia & ocher	15.00	.40
397	A23	5p blk & dk vio	40.00	7.50
398	A23	6p blk & car rose	32.50	6.75
399	A23	7p sepia & gray	18.00	1.75
400	A23	8p dk bl & gray	11.00	.45
401	A23	9p org grn & scar	7.50	.80
402	A23	10p bl grn & mar	15.00	1.40
403	A23	11p red & yel grn	11.00	1.40
404	A23	12p org & dk bl	6.50	1.40
405	A23	13p blk & rose	22.50	1.40
406	A23	14p org brn & yel grn	19.00	1.40
407	A23	15p sep & gray	19.00	1.75
408	A23	16p dk red & dl vio	27.50	3.25
409	A23	17p rose lil & dk bl	32.50	1.75
410	A23	18p green & brt bl	22.50	2.50
411	A23	19p black & bister	7.25	.80
412	A23	20p brown & grn	72.50	2.25
413	A23	23p maroon & lil	350.00	4.50
414	A23	24p ver & blue	52.50	5.50
415	A23	26p olive & yel	6.75	.70
416	A23	27p ultra & red brn	7.75	.70
417	A23	33p ol grn & lilac	42.50	2.25
419	A23	50p black & brown	*250.00*	*35.00*
420	A23	100p dk bl & grnsh bl	*400.00*	*45.00*
421	A23	200p dull lilac & grn	*400.00*	*72.50*
		Nos. 393-421 (28)	2,118.	227.90

A 31p has been reported.

Issue years: 1966, 1p. 1967, 2p, 10p. 1968, 3p, 4p, 6p, 7p, 20p; 1969, 5p, 8p. 1970, 9p, 23p; 1972, 12p, 15p, 16p. 1973, 11p; 1974, 17p, 50p-200p; 1975, 19p, 24p-33p; 1976, 18p.

Gas-Oil Plant Type of 1960 Redrawn
Type II (Faisal Cartouche)
(Illustrated over No. 286)

1966-78　　　　Unwmk.
Size: 27x22mm

422	A24	1p bl & red org	37.50	3.00
423	A24	2p ver & dull bl	7.75	.35
424	A24	3p lilac & brt grn	15.00	.60
425	A24	4p grn & dull lil	9.00	.35
426	A24	5p dl gray vio & dk red brn	40.00	1.90
427	A24	6p brn org & dull pur	25.00	3.75
428	A24	7p vio & dull grn	35.00	1.90
429	A24	8p bl grn & grnsh gray	6.00	.35
430	A24	9p ultra & sep	4.25	.35
431	A24	10p dk bl & rose	5.00	.60
432	A24	11p olive & org	80.00	8.00
433	A24	12p bister & grn	5.00	.75
434	A24	13p rose red & dk bl	47.50	.35
435	A24	14p vio & lt brn	45.00	2.50
436	A24	15p car & sepia	11.50	.65
437	A24	16p grn & rose red	15.50	.75
438	A24	17p car rose & red brn	11.00	.60
439	A24	18p gray & ultra	15.50	1.60
440	A24	19p brown & yel	17.50	1.60
441	A24	20p brn org & gray	13.00	1.60
442	A24	23p orange & car	22.50	1.90
443	A24	24p emer & org yel	19.00	.75
444	A24	26p lilac & red brn	*190.00*	
445	A24	27p ver & dk gray	37.50	3.75
446	A24	31p green & rose car	12.00	.75
447	A24	33p brown & gray	22.50	1.25
448	A24	50p red brn & dl grn	450.00	150.00
449	A24	100p dk bl & red brn	450.00	50.00
450	A24	200p dk gray & ol gray	450.00	62.50
		Nos. 422-450 (29)	2,090.	302.45

Issue years: 1967, 20p; 1968, 3p, 5p-9p; 15p, 16p; 1969, 100p; 1970, 11p, 14p, 200p; 1973, 13p, 18p, 24p; 1974, 19p, 50p; 1975, 12p, 17p, 27p-33p; 1978, 26p; others, 1966.

No. 442 with a double impression of the frame is a forgery.

Emblem of Saudi Arabian Scout Association A46

1967, Mar. 28　Litho.　Perf. 13½
Emblem in Green, Red, Yellow & Black

451	A46	1p dk blue & blk	2.25	.75
452	A46	2p blue grn & blk	2.75	.75
453	A46	3p lt blue & blk	4.25	.75
454	A46	4p rose brn & blk	5.25	.75
455	A46	10p brown & blk	12.50	2.00
		Nos. 451-455 (5)	27.00	5.00

2nd Arabic League Rover Moot, Mecca, March 13-28.

Meteorological Instruments and WMO Emblem — A47

1967, July　Unwmk.　Perf. 13

456	A47	1p brt magenta	1.25	.30
457	A47	2p violet	2.50	.30
458	A47	3p olive	2.50	.30
459	A47	4p blue green	9.00	.35
460	A47	10p blue	13.00	.75
		Nos. 456-460 (5)	28.25	2.05

Issued for World Meteorological Day.

Dam Type of 1960 Redrawn
Type II (Faisal Cartouche)

1968-76　Wmk. 361　Litho.　Perf. 14

461	A23	1p ol bis & pur ('68)	*1,100.*	*275.00*
462	A23	2p dk blue & sep	110.00	6.50
463	A23	3p blk & dk bl	70.00	3.50
464	A23	4p sepia & ocher	625.00	110.00
465	A23	5p blk & dk vio	92.50	6.50
466	A23	6p blk & car rose	85.00	5.00
467	A23	7p sepia & gray	125.00	10.00
468	A23	8p dk bl & gray	65.00	3.25
469	A23	9p org brn & ver	240.00	22.50
470	A23	10p bl grn & mar	160.00	13.00
471	A23	11p red & yel grn	200.00	20.00
472	A23	12p org & sl bl	175.00	16.00
473	A23	13p black & rose	240.00	24.50
		Nos. 462-473 (12)	2,187.	240.75

Issue years: 1968, 2p, 10p; 1969, 3p; 1970, 8p; 1971, 1p, 5p; 1972, 6p, 9p, 11p, 12p; 1973, 4p; 1974, 13p; 1976, 9p.

Gas-Oil Plant Type of 1960 Redrawn
Type II (Faisal Cartouche)

1968-76　　　　　Perf. 14

474	A24	1p bl & red org	9.50	.90
475	A24	2p ver & dull bl	5.75	.45
476	A24	4p grn & dl lil	95.00	9.50
477	A24	5p dk brn & red brn ('73)	26.00	1.75
478	A24	6p brn org & dk vio ('73)	32.50	2.25
479	A24	9p dk bl & sep ('76)	52.50	4.50
480	A24	10p dk bl & rose	8.50	.60
481	A24	11p ol & org ('72)	40.00	2.25
482	A24	12p bis & grn ('72)	42.50	3.50
483	A24	23p org & car ('74)	70.00	3.50
		Nos. 474-483 (10)	382.25	29.20

Map Showing Dammam to Jedda Road, and Dates — A48

Wmk. 361
1968, Aug.　Litho.　Perf. 14

484	A48	1p yellow & multi	1.60	.25
485	A48	2p orange & multi	1.60	.25
486	A48	3p multicolored	3.25	.25
487	A48	4p multicolored	3.25	.25
488	A48	10p multicolored	10.00	.45
		Nos. 484-488 (5)	19.70	1.45

Issued to commemorate the completion of the trans-Saudi Arabia highway in 1967.

Several positions in the sheet have the dots representing Dammam and Riyadh omitted. Most had the dots added by pen before issuance.

Prophet's Mosque, Medina — A49

New Arcade, Mecca Mosque — A50

Wmk. 361, 337 (#489, 493)
1968-76　Litho.　Perf. 13½x14
Design A49

489	A49	1p org & grn ('70)	2.10	.30
490	A49	2p brn & grn, redrawn ('72)	3.50	.35
a.		2p red brn & grn, wmk. 337	6.25	.30
b.		As "a," redrawn	200.00	
491	A49	3p vio & grn ('72)	3.25	.35
a.		3p vio & grn, wmk. 337 ('70)	2.75	.30
492	A49	4p ocher & grn ('72)	3.50	.35
a.		Redrawn ('71)	5.50	.45
b.		4p ocher & green, redrawn, wmk. 337	6.25	
493	A49	5p dp lil rose & grn ('71)	7.75	.90
494	A49	6p blk & grn ('73)	9.75	.90
a.		6p gray & green ('76)	18.00	.90
495	A49	10p brown & grn	12.00	.90
a.		Redrawn	9.00	
496	A49	20p dk brn & grn ('70)		
a.		Redrawn	18.00	
497	A49	50p sepia & grn ('75)	19.00	5.75
498	A49	100p blk & grn ('75)	15.00	4.50
499	A49	200p red & grn ('75)	19.00	6.25
		Nos. 489-499 (11)	109.85	22.30

See redrawn note following design A55. No. 494 exists imperf.

Warning: Stamps of design A49 in other colors, double frames, inverted centers or centers omitted are forgeries. They are printed on sheet selvage.

1968-69　　　　　Wmk. 361

500	A50	3p dp org & gray ('69)	350.00	90.00
501	A50	4p green & gray	5.75	.45
502	A50	10p mag & gray	8.25	.90
		Nos. 500-502 (3)	364.00	91.35

Expansion of Prophet's Mosque — A51

Madayin Saleh — A52

1968-76　　　　　Wmk. 361

503	A51	1p org & grn ('72)	4.50	.25
504	A51	2p brn & grn ('72)	7.25	.25
c.		As No. 504, redrawn		
505	A51	3p blk & grn ('69)	6.25	.35
b.		3p gray & grn ('76)	18.00	1.75
c.		As No. 505, redrawn	4.50	
506	A51	4p org & grn ('70)	6.25	.45
a.		Redrawn	4.50	.45
507	A51	5p red & grn, redrawn ('74)	6.75	.90
508	A51	6p Prus bl & grn ('72)	9.00	.90
509	A51	8p rose red & grn ('76)	22.50	1.75
510	A51	10p brn red & grn ('74)	8.25	.55
b.		10p org & grn, redrawn ('76)	18.00	.90
511	A51	20p vio & grn ('74)	18.00	2.25
		Nos. 503-511 (9)	88.75	7.50

Wmk. 337

503a	A51	1p	5.00	.35
504a	A51	2p ('70)	6.75	.35
b.		As "a," redrawn	35.00	
505a	A51	3p ('71)	7.25	.70
d.		As "a," redrawn		
506b	A51	4p Redrawn ('72)	9.00	
507a	A51	5p ('70)	4.50	.45
508a	A51	6p ('72)	6.25	.45
510a	A51	10p ('70)	11.00	.60
c.		As "a," redrawn	18.00	
511a	A51	20p ('72)	8.25	.70
		Nos. 503a-511a (8)	58.00	3.70

See redrawn note following design A55.

1968-75

512	A52	2p ultra & bis brn ('70)	26.00	4.50
513	A52	4p dk & lt brown	6.50	.90
514	A52	7p org & lt brn ('75)	50.00	1.10
515	A52	10p sl grn & lt brn	16.00	2.25
516	A52	20p lil rose & brn ('71)	18.00	1.75
		Nos. 512-516 (5)	116.50	10.50

Arabian Stallion — A53

Camels and Oil Derrick — A54

517	A53	4p mag & org brn	7.25	.95
518	A53	10p blk & org brn	20.00	3.75
519	A53	14p dk org & grn ('71)	30.00	7.50
520	A53	20p ol grn & ocher ('71)	11.00	2.40
		Nos. 517-520 (4)	68.25	14.60

1969-71

521	A54	4p dk pur & redsh brn ('71)	29.00	5.00
522	A54	10p ultra & hn brn	26.50	3.75

Holy Ka'aba, Mecca — A55

Original

Redrawn

On the original stamps the knob-shaped Arabic letter, located under the two square dots in the middle of the top panel, has a small central dot. The dot often is missing.

On the redrawn stamps the dot has been enlarged into a conspicuous irregular oval. The 3p also has a period added after the value and the 4p has the "4" under the "T" instead of the "S." There are other small differences.

Numeral & "Postage" on Gray Background, 8p on White

1969-75

523	A55	4p dp grn & blk ('70)	7.75	.70
a.		Redrawn, value corner white ('74)	16.00	1.75
b.		Redrawn ('75)	14.00	
524	A55	6p dp lil rose & blk ('71)	4.50	.35
a.		Value corner white ('74)	22.50	2.75
525	A55	8p red & blk ('75)	27.50	2.75
526	A55	10p dk gr & blk ('69)	16.00	1.40
a.		Redrawn, value corner white ('74)	14.00	1.75
b.		Redrawn ('75)	18.00	
		Nos. 523-526 (4)	55.75	5.20

Rover Moot Badge — A56

Perf. 13½x14
1969, Feb. 19   Litho.   Wmk. 337
607 A56 1p orange & multi   1.75   .25
608 A56 4p dull purple & multi   5.75   .25
609 A56 10p orange brn & multi   15.00   .85
    Nos. 607-609 (3)   22.50 1.35

3rd Arab League Rover Moot, Mecca, Feb. 19-Mar. 3.

Traffic Light and Intersection — A57

1969, Feb.   Wmk. 361   Perf. 13½
610 A57 3p dl bl, red & brt bl grn   2.75   .25
  a. 3p dull blue, red & gray green   30.00 1.25
611 A57 4p org brn, red & gray grn   2.75   .25
612 A57 10p dl pur, red & gray grn   5.50   .60
    Nos. 610-612 (3)   11.00 1.10

Issued for Traffic Day.

WHO Emblem — A58

1969, Oct. 20   Wmk. 337   Perf. 14
613 A58 4p lt bl, vio bl & yel   13.00   .25

20th anniv. (in 1968) of WHO.

Islamic Conference Emblem A59

1970, Mar. 23   Litho.   Wmk. 361
614 A59 4p blue & black   3.50   .25
615 A59 10p yellow bis & blk   5.25   .55

Islamic Conference of Foreign Ministers, Jedda, March 1970.

Open Book and Satellite Earth Receiving Station — A60

Perf. 14x13½
1970, Aug. 1   Litho.   Wmk. 337
616 A60 4p violet bl & multi   5.75   .25
617 A60 10p green & multi   11.50   .60

World Telecommunications Day.

Steel Rolling Mill, Jedda A61

1970, Oct. 26   Wmk. 337   Perf. 13½
618 A61 3p yellow org & multi   5.25   .25
619 A61 4p violet & multi   8.00   .25
620 A61 10p brt green & multi   14.00   .95
    Nos. 618-620 (3)   27.25 1.45

Inauguration of 1st steel mill in Saudi Arabia.

Rover Moot Emblem — A62

1971, Feb.   Litho.   Perf. 14
621 A62 10p brt blue & multi   10.50   .80

4th Arab League Rover Moot, 1971.

Telecommunications Symbol — A63

1971, May 17   Wmk. 337   Perf. 14
622 A63 4p blue & blk   2.50   .25
623 A63 10p lilac & blk   6.00   .50

World Telecommunications Day.

University Emblem — A64   Arab League Emblem — A65

Wmk. 337; Wmk. 361 (4p)
1971, Aug.   Litho.   Perf. 14
624 A64 3p brt green & black   2.10   .25
625 A64 4p brown & black   4.25   .25
626 A64 10p blue & black   7.75   .60
    Nos. 624-626 (3)   14.10 1.10

King Abdul Aziz National University.

1971, Nov.   Wmk. 337   Perf. 13½
627 A65 10p multicolored   8.00   .45

Arab League Week.

Education Year Emblem — A66   OPEC Emblem — A67

1971, Nov.   Litho.
628 A66 4p apple grn & brn red   7.25   .25

International Education Year 1970.

1971, Dec.   Perf. 14
629 A67 4p light blue   8.00   .25

10th anniversary of OPEC (Organization of Petroleum Exporting Countries).

Globe A68

1972, Aug.   Wmk. 361   Perf. 14
630 A68 4p multicolored   8.00   .25

4th World Telecommunications Day.

Telephone — A69

1972, Oct.   Wmk. 337, 361 (5p)
631 A69 1p red, blk & grn   2.50   .25
632 A69 4p dk grn, blk & grn   2.50   .25
633 A69 5p lil, blk & grn   4.75   .25
634 A69 10p tan, blk & grn   10.50   .50
    Nos. 631-634 (4)   20.25 1.25

Inauguration of automatic telephone system (1969).

Writing Hand — A70

1972, Sept. 8   Litho.   Wmk. 361
635 A70 10p multicolored   10.50   .45

World Literacy Day, Sept. 8.

Holy Ka'aba and Grand Mosque, Mecca A71

Rover Moot Emblem and: 4p, Prophet's Mosque, Medina. 10p, Plains of Arafat.

1973
636 A71 4p lt blue & multi   4.50   .25
637 A71 6p lilac & multi   9.00   .45
638 A71 10p salmon & multi   13.50   .75
    Nos. 636-638 (3)   27.00 1.45

5th Arab League Rover Moot.

Globe and Map of Palestine A71a

1973   Litho.   Wmk. 361   Perf. 14
639 A71a 4p black, yel & red   4.50   .25
640 A71a 10p blue, yel & red   9.25   .50

Palestine Week.

Leaf and Emblem — A72

1973
641 A72 4p yellow & multi   8.00   .35

International Hydrological Decade 1965-74.

Arab Postal Union Emblem — A73

1973, Dec.   Litho.   Perf. 14
642 A73 4p sepia & multi   5.50   .40
643 A73 10p purple & multi   13.50   .65

25th anniversary (in 1971) of the Conference of Sofar, Lebanon, establishing the Arab Postal Union.

Balloons and Pacifier — A74

1973, Dec.
644 A74 4p lt blue & multi   10.00   .25

Universal Children's Day (stamp dated 1971).

Arab Postal and UPU Emblems A75

1974, July 7   Wmk. 361   Perf. 14
645 A75 3p yellow & multi   62.50 3.50
646 A75 4p rose & multi   62.50 6.75
647 A75 10p lt green & multi   62.50 10.50
    Nos. 645-647 (3)   187.50 20.75
Centenary of the Universal Postal Union.

Handshake and UNESCO Emblem — A76

1974, May 21   Perf. 13½
648 A76 4p orange & multi   3.00 .30
649 A76 10p green & multi   14.00 .80
International Book Year, 1972.

Desalination Plant — A77

1974, Sept. 3   Wmk. 361   Perf. 14
650 A77 4p dp orange & bl   2.75 .25
651 A77 6p emerald & vio   5.75 .30
652 A77 10p rose red & blk   8.75 .65
    Nos. 650-652 (3)   17.25 1.20
Opening (in 1971) of sea water desalination plant, Jedda.

A78

Design: INTERPOL emblem.
1974, Nov. 1
653 A78 4p ocher & ultra   9.50 .25
654 A78 10p emerald & ultra   17.50 .60
50th anniversary (in 1973) of International Criminal Police Organization.

APU emblem, tower and letter.
1974, Oct. 26   Litho.   Wmk. 361
655 A79 4p multicolored   9.00 .25
Arab Consultative Council for Postal Studies, 3rd session.

UPU Headquarters, Bern — A80

1974, Nov. 15   Perf. 13½
656 A80 3p orange & multi   4.50 .30
657 A80 4p lilac & multi   7.50 .60
658 A80 10p blue & multi   10.50 1.50
    Nos. 656-658 (3)   22.50 2.40
Opening of new Universal Postal Union Headquarters, Bern, May 1970.

Tank, Planes, Rockets and Flame A81

1974, Dec. 15   Perf. 14
659 A81 3p slate & multi   2.50 .25
660 A81 4p brown & multi   5.00 .30
661 A81 10p lilac & multi   13.50 .85
    Nos. 659-661 (3)   21.00 1.40
King Faisal Military Cantonment, 1971.

A82

Red Crescent flower.
1974, Dec. 17   Perf. 14x14½
662 A82 4p gray & multi   2.25 .30
663 A82 6p lt green & multi   5.75 .60
664 A82 10p lt blue & multi   11.50 1.10
    Nos. 662-664 (3)   19.50 2.00
Saudi Arabian Red Crescent Society, 10th anniversary (in 1973).

A83

Saudi Arabian scout emblem and minarets.
1974, Dec. 23   Wmk. 361   Perf. 14
665 A83 4p brown & multi   6.00 .25
666 A83 6p blue blk & multi   11.50 .40
667 A83 10p purple & multi   17.50 .70
    Nos. 665-667 (3)   35.00 1.35
6th Arab League Rover Moot, Mecca.

A84

Design: Reading braille.
1975, Mar. 31   Perf. 14x13½
668 A84 4p multicolored   14.00 .30
669 A84 10p multicolored   10.00 .50
    Day of the Blind.

Anemometer and Weather Balloon with WMO Emblem — A85

Perf. 13½x14
1975, May 8   Litho.   Wmk. 361
670 A85 4p multicolored   10.50 .30
Centenary (in 1973) of International Meteorological Cooperation.

King Faisal — A86

1975, July 6   Unwmk.   Perf. 14
671 A86 4p green & rose brn   3.50 .35
672 A86 16p violet & green   4.50 .90
673 A86 23p dk green & vio   9.25 1.50
    Nos. 671-673 (3)   17.25 2.75
Miniature Sheet
Imperf
674 A86 40p Prus bl & ocher   400.00
King Faisal ibn Abdul-Aziz Al Saud (1906-1975). Size of No. 674: 71x80mm.

Conference Emblem — A87

1975, July 11   Perf. 14
675 A87 10p rose brn & blk   6.25 .55
6th Islamic Conference of Foreign Ministers, Jedda, July 12.

Wheat and Sun — A88

1975, Sept. 17   Litho.   Wmk. 361
676 A88 4p lilac & multi   4.00 .25
677 A88 10p blue & multi   11.00 .50
Charity Society, 20th anniversary.

Holy Ka'aba, Globe, Clasped Hands — A89

1975, Sept. 17   Perf. 14
678 A89 4p olive bis & multi   9.50 .30
679 A89 10p orange & multi   19.00 .55
Conference of Moslem Organizations, Mecca, Apr. 6-10, 1974.

Saudia Tri-Star and DC-3 — A90

1975, Sept.   Litho.   Unwmk.
680 A90 4p buff & multi   9.50 .35
681 A90 10p lt blue & multi   19.00 .65
Saudia, Saudi Arabian Airline, 30th anniversary.

Conference Centers in Mecca and Riyadh A91

1975, Sept.   Perf. 14
682 A91 10p multicolored   14.50 .70

Friday Mosque, Medina, and Juwatha Mosque, al-Hasa — A92

1975, Oct. 26   Litho.   Unwmk.
683 A92 4p green & multi   8.00 .40
684 A92 10p vermilion & multi 11.00 .70
Ancient Islamic holy places.

FAO Emblem — A93

1975, Oct. 26
685 A93 4p gray & multi   5.50 .25
686 A93 10p buff & multi   16.00 .65
World Food Program, 10th anniversary (in 1973). Stamps are dated 1973.

Conference Emblem — A94

1976, Mar. 20   Unwmk.   Perf. 14
687 A94 4p multicolored   19.00 .35
Islamic Solidarity Conference of Science and Technology.

Saudi Arabia Map, Transmission Tower, TV Screen — A95

1976, May 26   Litho.   Perf. 14
688 A95 4p multicolored   26.00 .35
Saudi Arabian television, 10th anniversary.

Grain, Atom Symbol, Graph A96

1976, June 28   Litho.   Perf. 14
689 A96 20h yellow & multi   5.00 .40
690 A96 50h yellow & multi   9.50 .80
Second Five-year Plan.

Holy Ka'aba A97

Two types:
I — "White" minarets. Gray vignette.
II — Black minarets and vignette. Design redrawn, strengthened, darkened, clarified.

1976-79   Litho.   Wmk. 361   Perf. 14
Type II
691 A97 5h lilac & blk   .25 .25
692 A97 10h lt violet & blk   .35 .25
693 A97 15h salmon & blk   .50 .25
  a. Type I   4.25 .25
694 A97 20h lt bl & blk, II   5.50 .25
  a. Type I   5.00 .25
695 A97 25h yellow & blk   1.50 .25
696 A97 30h gray grn & blk   2.10 .25
697 A97 35h bister & blk   1.25 .25
698 A97 40h lt green & blk   4.75 .25
  a. Type I ('77)   6.00 .30
699 A97 45h dull rose & blk   1.60 .25
700 A97 50h pink & blk   1.50 .25
703 A97 65h gray blue & blk   1.90 .25

710 A97 1r lt yel grn & blk   2.50 .25
711 A97 2r green & black   9.75 .50
  Nos. 691-711 (13)   33.45 3.50
No. 698 imperf exists as an issued error. Value, $110. Nos. 691-711 also exist as imperfs not regularly issued.
  Issue years: 20h, 1977; 5h-15h, 25h-50h, 1r, 1978; 65h, 2r, 1979.
  See Nos. 872-882, 961-968.

Quba Mosque, Medina, built 622 — A98

1976-77
719 A98 20h orange & blk   2.25 .25
720 A98 50h emer & lilac ('77)   4.00 .25
Reissued in 1978 in different shades.
No. 720 exists imperf as an issued error.

Globe, Telephones 1876 and 1976 A100

1976, July 17   Unwmk.   Perf. 13½
721 A100 50h multicolored   9.00 .35
Centenary of first telephone call by Alexander Graham Bell, Mar. 10, 1876.

Arab Leaders A101

1976, Oct. 30   Litho.   Perf. 14
722 A101 20h ultra & emerald   5.50 .30
Arab Summit Conference, Riyadh, October. Leaders pictured: Pres. Elias Sarkis, Lebanon; Pres. Anwar Sadat, Egypt; Pres. Hafez al Assad, Syria; King Khalid, Saudi Arabia; Amir Sabah, Kuwait; Yasir Arafat, Palestine Liberation Organization chairman.

WHO Emblem and Eye A102

1976, Nov. 28   Litho.   Perf. 14
723 A102 20h multicolored   14.50 .25
World Health Day; Prevention of Blindness.

Holy Ka'aba — A103

1976, Nov. 28   Unwmk.
724 A103 20h multicolored   10.00 .30
50th anniversary of installation of new covering of Holy Ka'aba, Mecca.

Conference Emblem A104

Unwmk.
1977, Feb. 18   Litho.   Perf. 14
725 A104 20h multicolored   10.00 .25
Islamic Jurisprudence Conference, Riyadh, Oct. 24-Nov. 2, 1976.

A105

Design: Sharia College emblem.

1977, Feb. 25   Perf. 14
726 A105 4p multicolored   9.00 .25
25th anniversary (in 1974) of the founding of Sharia (Islamic Law) College, Mecca.

A106

1977
727 A106 20h dk brn & brt grn   2.50 .25
  a. Incorrect date   22.50
728 A106 80h bl blk & brt grn   4.75 .65
  a. Incorrect date   22.50
2nd anniversary of installation of King Khalid ibn Abdul-Aziz. Nos. 727a-728a, issued Mar. 3, have incorrect Arabic date in bottom panel, last characters of 2nd and 3rd rows identical "ir." Stamps withdrawn after a few days and replaced Aug. 14 with corrected date, last characters in 3rd row changed to "ro."

Diesel Train and Map of Route A107

1977, May 23   Litho.   Perf. 14
729 A107 20h multicolored   27.50 .25
Dammam-Riyadh railroad, 25th anniversary.

Arabic Ornament and Names — A108

Designs (Names from Left to Right): UL, Malik Ben Anas (715-795). UR, Mohammad Ben Idris Al-Shafi'i (767-820). LL, Abu Hanifa an-Nu'man (699-767). LR, Ahmed Ben Hanbal (780-855).

1977, Aug. 15   Litho.   Perf. 14
730 A108 Block of 4   65.00 3.75
  a.-d. 20h, single stamp   9.00 .70
Famous Imams (7th-9th centuries), founders of traditional schools of Islamic jurisprudence. Sheets of 60 stamps (15 blocks).
No. 730 exists with a double impression of the blue color. Stamps with double impressions of the black color are forgeries.

Al Khafji Oil Rig — A109

1976-80   Wmk. 361
731 A109 5h vio blue & org   .25   .25
732 A109 10h yel grn & org   .25   .25
733 A109 15h brown & org   .25   .25
734 A109 20h green & org   .25   .25
735 A109 25h dk pur & org   .25   .25
736 A109 30h blue & orange   .30   .25
737 A109 35h sepia & org   .40   .25
738 A109 40h mag & org   .40   .25
  a. 40h dull purple & org   175.00
739 A109 45h violet & orange   .50   .25
740 A109 50h rose & orange   .65   .25
  a. 50h dull org & org (error)   75.00 6.75
741 A109 55h grnsh bl & org   27.50 4.25
743 A109 65h sepia & org   1.50   .40
750 A109 1r gray & orange   1.90   .25
751 A109 2r dk vio & org
              ('80)   4.25 1.25
  Nos. 731-751 (14)   38.65 9.05
All values exist with extra dot in Arabic "Al Khafji." The 20h, 25h, 50h, 65h and 1r were retouched to remove the dot.
Color of flame varies from light orange to vermilion.
No. 737 imperf exists as an issued error. Value, $275. Nos. 731-751 also exist as imperfs not regularly issued.
See Nos. 885-892, 1300A.

Mohenjo-Daro Ruins — A110

1977, Oct. 23   Litho.   Unwmk.
761 A110 50h multicolored   10.00 .40
UNESCO campaign to save Mohenjo-Daro excavations in Pakistan.

Idrisi's World
Map,
1154 — A111

1977, Nov. 1   Litho.   Perf. 14
762 A111 20h multicolored   3.50   .40
763 A111 50h multicolored   7.00   .70
First International Symposium on Studies in
the History of Arabia at the University of
Riyadh, Apr. 23-26, 1977.

King Faisal Specialist Hospital,
Riyadh — A112

1977, Nov. 13   Litho.   Unwmk.
764 A112 20h multicolored   4.25   .30
765 A112 50h multicolored   6.75   .50

Conference
Emblem — A113

1978, Jan. 24   Litho.   Perf. 14
766 A113 20h vio blue & yel   5.50   .25
1st World Conf. on Moslem Education.

APU
Emblem,
Members'
Flags
A114

1978, Jan. 21
767 A114 20h multicolored   2.50   .25
768 A114 80h multicolored   4.75   .60
25th anniversary of Arab Postal Union.

Taif-Abha-Gizan Highway — A115

1978, Oct. 15   Litho.   Perf. 14
769 A115 20h multicolored   2.50   .25
770 A115 80h multicolored   4.75   .50
Inauguration of Taif-Abha-Gizan highway.
No. 770 exists with black (road) missing and
with black double.

Pilgrims, Mt. Arafat and Holy
Ka'aba — A116

Unwmk.
1978, Nov. 6   Litho.   Perf. 14
771 A116 20h multicolored   2.50   .25
772 A116 80h multicolored   4.75   .50
Pilgrimage to Mecca.
No. 772 exists with inscriptions (black and
blue colors) omitted.

Gulf Postal
Organization
Emblem — A117

1979, Feb. 6   Litho.   Perf. 14
773 A117 20h multicolored   1.75   .25
774 A117 50h multicolored   3.25   .40
1st Conf. of Gulf Postal Organization,
Baghdad.

Saudi
Arabia No.
129, King
Abdul Aziz
ibn Saud
A118

Unwmk.
1979, June 4   Litho.   Perf. 14
775 A118 20h multicolored   2.00   .25
776 A118 50h multicolored   4.25
777 A118 115h multicolored   6.75   .75
      Nos. 775-777 (3)   13.00 1.35

Souvenir Sheet
Imperf
778 A118 100h multicolored   110.00
1st commemorative stamp, 50th anniv. No.
778 contains one stamp with simulated perforations. Size: 101x76mm.

Crown
Prince
Fahd
A119

1979, June 25   Perf. 14
779 A119 20h multicolored   2.50   .25
780 A119 50h multicolored   4.70   .35
Crown Prince Fahd ibn Abdul Aziz.

Dome of
the Rock,
Jerusalem
A120

1979, July 2   Wmk. 361
781 A120 20h multi (shades)   2.75   .55
No. 781 exists with inscriptions (green and
mauve colors) omitted.
Imperfs. exist. See No. 866.

Gold Door, Holy
Ka'aba — A121

1979, Oct. 13   Litho.   Perf. 14
782 A121 20h multicolored   2.25   .25
783 A121 80h multicolored   4.25   .50
Installation of new gold doors. Imperfs. exist.

Pilgrims at Holy Ka'aba, Mecca
Mosque — A122

1979, Oct. 27
784 A122 20h multicolored   1.50   .25
785 A122 50h multicolored   3.25   .35
Pilgrimage to Mecca. Imperfs. exist.

Birds in Trees, IYC Emblem — A123

IYC Emblem and: 50h, Child's drawing.

1980, Feb. 17   Litho.   Perf. 14
786 A123 20h multicolored   12.50   .25
787 A123 50h multicolored   19.00   .40
Intl. Year of the Child (1979). Imperfs. exist.

King Abdul
Aziz ibn
Saud on
Horseback,
Saudi Flag
A124

1980, Apr. 5   Litho.   Perf. 14
788 A124 20h multicolored   1.75   .25
789 A124 80h multicolored   4.25   .40
Saudi Arabian Army, 80th anniv. (1979).
Imperfs. exist.

Arab League,
35th Anniversary
A125

1980, Apr. 27   Litho.   Perf. 14
790 A125 20h multicolored   2.25   .25
Imperfs. exist.

International Bureau of Education,
50th Anniversary — A126

1980, May 4
791 A126 50h multicolored   2.75   .35
Imperfs. exist.

Smoke Entering
Lungs, WHO
Emblem — A127

1980, May 20
792 A127 20h shown   1.75   .25
793 A127 50h Cigarette, horiz. 4.25   .30
Anti-smoking campaign. Imperfs. exist.

20th
Anniversary
of OPEC
A128

Design: 50h, Workers holding OPEC
emblem (Organization of Petroleum Exporting
Countries).

1980, Sept. 1   Litho.   Perf. 14
794 A128 20h multicolored   1.75   .25
795 A128 50h multi, vert.   3.25   .35

Pilgrims
Arriving at
Jedda
Airport
A129

1980, Oct. 18
796 A129 20h multicolored   1.10   .25
797 A129 50h multicolored   2.50   .40
Pilgrimage to Mecca.

Conference
Emblem
A130

Holy Ka'aba,
Mecca
Mosque — A131

1981, Jan. 25   Litho.   Perf. 14
798 A130 20h shown   1.25   .25
799 A131 20h shown   1.25   .25
800 A131 20h Prophet's Mosque,
            Medina   1.25   .25

801 A131 20h Dome of the Rock,
Jerusalem   1.25   .25
Nos. 798-801 (4)   5.00 1.00

Third Islamic Summit Conference, Mecca.

Hegira,
1500th
Anniv.
A132

1981, Jan. 26
802 A132   20h multicolored   1.10 .25
803 A132   50h multicolored   2.10 .35
804 A132   80h multicolored   4.00 .60
Nos. 802-804 (3)   7.20 1.20
Souvenir Sheet
805 A132 300h multicolored   125.00

Industry
Week
A133

1981, Feb. 21
806 A133 20h multicolored   1.00 .25
807 A133 80h multicolored   3.25 .55

Line Graph
and
Telephone
A134

Map of
Saudi
Arabia,
Microwave
Tower
A135

1981, Feb. 28
808 A134   20h shown   .75 .30
809 A135   80h shown   3.25 .55
810 A134 115h Earth satellite
station   4.00 .85
Nos. 808-810 (3)   8.00 1.70
Souvenir Sheets
811 A134 100h like #808   65.00
812 A135 100h like #809   65.00
813 A135 100h like #810   65.00

Ministry of Posts and Telecommunications
achievements.

Arab City
Day — A135a

1981, Apr. 2   **Litho.**   *Perf. 14*
814 A135a 20h multicolored   .50 .25
815 A135a 65h multicolored   1.50 .50
816 A135a 80h multicolored   2.25 .50
817 A135a 115d multicolored   3.00 .90
Nos. 814-817 (4)   7.25 2.15

Jedda
Airport
Opening
A136

1981, Apr. 12
818 A136 20h shown   .75 .25
819 A136 80h Plane over airport,
diff.   3.75 .65

1982 World
Cup
Soccer
Preliminary
Games — A137

1981, July 26   **Litho.**   *Perf. 14*
820 A137 20h multicolored   2.75 .35
821 A137 80h multicolored   5.50 .55

Intl. Year of the
Disabled — A138

1981, Aug. 5
822 A138 20h Reading braille   2.00 .25
823 A138 50h Man weaving rug   4.00 .35

3rd Five-year Plan (1981-
1985) — A139

1981, Sept. 5
824 A139 20h multicolored   1.75 .25

King Abdul
Aziz, Map
of Saudi
Arabia
A140

1981, Sept. 23   **Litho.**   *Perf. 14*
825 A140   5h multicolored   .25 .25
826 A140   10h multicolored   .25 .25
827 A140   15h multicolored   .25 .25
828 A140   20h multicolored   .45 .25
829 A140   50h multicolored   .90 .35
830 A140   65h multicolored   1.25 .50
831 A140   80h multicolored   3.25 .50
832 A140 115h multicolored   4.25 .75
Nos. 825-832 (8)   10.85 3.10
Souvenir Sheet
Imperf
833 A140 10r multicolored   110.00

50th anniv. of kingdom. No. 833 shows king,
map, document. Size: 100x75mm.

Pilgrimage
to Mecca
A141

1981, Oct. 7
834 A141 20h multicolored   2.25 .25
835 A141 65h multicolored   3.75 .60

World Food
Day
A142

1981, Oct. 16
836 A142 20h multicolored   3.00 .50

2nd Session of
the Gulf
Cooperative
Council Summit
Conference,
Riyadh, Nov.
10 — A143

1981, Nov. 10   **Litho.**   *Perf. 14*
837 A143 20h multicolored   1.25 .35
838 A143 80h multicolored   3.50 .75

King Saud
University,
25th Anniv.
A144

1982, Mar. 10   **Litho.**   *Perf. 14*
839 A144 20h multicolored   1.10 .30
840 A144 50h multicolored   2.40 .40

New
Regional
Postal
Centers
A145

1982, July 14   **Litho.**   *Perf. 14*
841 A145   20h Riyadh P.O.   .45 .25
842 A145   65h Jedda   1.50 .40
843 A145   80h Dammam   1.90 .40
844 A145 115h Automated sorting   2.25 .65
Nos. 841-844 (4)   6.10 1.70

Four 300h souvenir sheets exist in same
designs as Nos. 841-844 respectively. Value,
$26.50 each.

Riyadh Television
Center — A146

1982, Sept. 4
845 A146 20h multicolored   1.50 .25

25th Anniv.
of King's
Soccer Cup
A147

1982, Sept. 8
846 A147 20h multicolored   1.00 .25
847 A147 65h multicolored   2.25 .40

30th Anniv.
of Arab
Postal
Union
A148

1982, Sept. 8
848 A148 20h Emblem   1.00 .25
849 A148 65h Map, vert.   2.25 .50

Pilgrimage
to Mecca
A149

1982, Sept. 26
850 A149 20h multicolored   1.00 .25
851 A149 50h multicolored   2.25 .50

World
Standards
Day
A150

1982, Oct. 14
852 A150 20h multicolored   1.75 .25

World Food
Day
A151

1982, Oct. 16
853 A151 20h multicolored   1.50 .25

Coronation
of King
Fahd, June
14, 1982
A152

Installation
of Crown
Prince
Abdullah,
June 14,
1982
A153

1983, Feb. 12   **Litho.**   *Perf. 14*
854 A152 20h multicolored   .45 .25
855 A153 20h multicolored   .45 .25
856 A152 50h multicolored   .90 .40
857 A153 50h multicolored   .90 .40
858 A152 65h multicolored   1.40 .45
859 A153 65h multicolored   1.40 .45

860	A152	80h multicolored	1.60	.50
861	A153	80h multicolored	1.60	.50
862	A152	115h multicolored	2.50	.80
863	A153	115h multicolored	2.50	.80
	Nos. 854-863 (10)		13.70	4.80

Two one-stamp souvenir sheets contain
Nos. 862-863, perf. 12½. Value $300.

6th Anniv. of United Arab Shipping
Co. — A154

Various freighters.

1983, Aug. 9   Litho.   Perf. 14

864	A154	20h multicolored	.75	.25
865	A154	65h multicolored	2.50	.25

Dome of
the Rock,
Jerusalem
A155

1983, Sept.   Wmk. 361   Perf. 12

866	A155	20h multicolored	.90	.25

See No. 781.

Pilgrimage
to Mecca
A156

1983, Sept. 16   Litho.   Perf. 14

867	A156	20h brt blue & multi	.50	.25
868	A156	65h dk black & multi	1.75	.25

World
Communications
Year — A157

1983, Oct. 8   Litho.   Perf. 14

869	A157	20h Post and UPU emblems	.35	.25
870	A157	80h Telephone and ITU emblems	1.90	.35

Holy Ka'ba Type of 1976
Type II
Perf. 14x13½

1982-86   Litho.   Wmk. 361
Size: 26x21mm

872	A97	10h lt vio & blk ('83)	.25	.25
874	A97	20h lt blue & blk	.25	.25
880	A97	50h pink & blk ('83)	.45	.25
881	A97	65h gray bl & blk	.60	.25
882	A97	1r lt yel grn & blk	1.40	.25

Perf. 13½

874c	A97	20h lt blue & blk	.25	.25
880a	A97	50h pink & blk ('83)	.45	.25
881a	A97	65h gray bl & blk	.60	.25
882a	A97	1r lt yel grn & blk	1.40	.25

Perf. 12

872b	A97	10h lt vio & blk		—
873	A97	15h sal & blk ('85)	.25	.25
874a	A97	20h lt blue & blk ('84)	.25	.25
880b	A97	50h pink & blk ('86)	.30	.25
881b	A97	65h gray bl & blk ('84)	.60	.25
882b	A97	1r lt yel grn & blk ('83)	1.40	.25

Perf. 12
Unwmk.

872a	A97	10h lt vio & blk ('87)	.25	.25
874b	A97	20h lt blue & blk	.25	.25
881c	A97	65h gray bl & blk ('84)	.60	.25
882c	A97	1r lt yel grn & blk ('85)	1.40	.25
	Nos. 872-882c (7)		4.60	1.75

Counterfeits of the 1r are perf. 11.

Al Khafji Oil Rig Type of 1976
Perf. 14x13½

1982-84   Litho.   Wmk. 361
Size: 26x21mm

885	A109	5h vio bl & org	.25	.25
886	A109	10h yel grn & org	.25	.25
887	A109	15h bis brn & org	.25	.25
888	A109	20h green & org	.25	.25
890	A109	50h rose & org	.30	.25
891a	A109	65h sepia & orange	2.75	1.40
892	A109	1r gray & org	.60	.30

Perf. 13½

885a	A109	5h	.25	.25
886a	A109	10h	.25	.25
887a	A109	15h	.25	.25
888a	A109	20h	.25	.25
890a	A109	50h	.25	.25
891	A109	65h sepia & org ('84)	.35	.25
892a	A109	1r	.55	.30

1983   Perf. 12

886b	A109	10h	.25	.25
887b	A109	15h	.25	.25
888b	A109	20h	.25	.25
889	A109	25h dk pur & org	.25	.25
890b	A109	50h	.30	.25
891b	A109	65h	.35	.25
892b	A109	1r	.45	.30
	Nos. 885-892b (8)		2.50	2.05

Opening of King Khalid International
Airport — A158

1983, Nov. 16   Litho.   Perf. 13½x14

893	A158	20h shown	.60	.25
894	A158	65h blue & multi	2.10	.25

World Food
Day — A159

1983, Nov. 29   Litho.   Perf. 14

895	A159	20h Wheat, Irrigation, Silos	1.75	.25

Aqsa
Mosque,
Jerusalem
A160

1983, Dec. 13   Litho.   Perf. 14

896	A160	20h multicolored	.70	.30

Old and Modern Riyadh — A161

Shobra Palace, Taif — A162

Old and New Jedda
(Waterfront) — A163

Damman — A164

1984-95   Litho.   Wmk. 361   Perf. 12

897	A161	20h lilac rose & multi	.25	.25
898	A162	20h Prus grn & multi	.25	.25
899	A161	50h black & multi	.50	.25
900	A162	50h brown & multi	1.00	.55

Unwmk.

901	A161	50h multicolored	.70	.40
902	A162	50h multicolored	1.00	.55
903	A163	50h multicolored	1.40	.70
904	A164	50h green & multi	.65	.25
905	A161	75h green & multi	1.00	.55
906	A162	75h multicolored	1.00	.55
907	A163	75h pink & multi	1.40	.70
908	A164	75h blue & multi	.95	.55
909	A161	150h pink & multi	2.40	1.10
910	A162	150h green & multi	2.40	1.10
911	A163	150h green & multi	2.50	1.10
911A	A164	150h red lilac & multi	2.00	.95
	Nos. 897-911A (16)		19.40	9.80

Issued: #897, 6/27/84; #898, 10/13/84;
#899, 8/29/84; #900, 3/10/87; #910, 9/3/87;
#902, 11/3/87; #909, 5/4/88; #903, 911,
1/31/89; #906, 1990; #901, 907, 1991; #905,
1992; #904, 908, 911A, 1995.

Estate Development Fund, 10th
Anniv. — A165

1984, July 28   Unwmk.

912	A165	20h multicolored	.80	.30

Opening of
Solar
Village,
near Al-
Eyenah
A166

1984, Aug. 14   Litho.   Perf. 12

913	A166	20h multicolored	.50	.25
914	A166	80h Stylized sun, solar panels	1.50	.35

Imperf
Size: 81x81mm

915	A166	100h like 20h	35.00	
916	A166	100h like 80h	35.00	

Pilgrimage to Mecca — A167

Al-Kheef Mosque: 65h, Aerial view.

1984, Sept. 4   Litho.   Perf. 14

917	A167	20h brown & multi	.60	.25

Perf. 12

918	A167	65h olive gray & multi	2.10	.25

Participation of
Saudi Arabian
Soccer Team in
1984
Olympics — A168

1984, Sept. 25   Litho.   Perf. 12

919	A168	20h blue & multi	2.00	1.25
920	A168	115h green & multi	6.50	2.00

"Games" and "Olympiad" are misspelled on
both stamps.

World Food
Day
A169

1984, Oct. 16   Litho.   Perf. 12

921	A169	20h multicolored	.70	.30

Beginning with Nos. 922-923 some
issues are printed in sheets that have
labels inscribed in Arabic. Generally
there are from 2 to 6 labels per sheet.
Stamps with label attached command a
premium.

90th Anniv. International Olympic
Committee — A170

1984, Dec. 23   Litho.   Perf. 12

922	A170	20h multicolored	.75	.50
923	A170	50h multicolored	3.75	.50

Launch of ARABSAT — A171

1985, Feb. 9   Litho.   Perf. 12

924	A171	20h ARABSAT, view of Earth	2.40	.25

7th Holy Koran Competition — A172

1985, Feb. 10   Litho.   Perf. 12
925 A172 20h multicolored   .55   .25
926 A172 65h multicolored   1.25   .25

4th Five-Year Development Plan,
1985-1990 — A173

Portrait of King Fahd, industry emblems
and: 20h, Dhahran Harbor, Jubail. 50h, Television tower, earth receiver, microwave tower.
65h, Agriculture. 80h, Harbor, Yanbu.

1985, Mar. 23   Litho.   Perf. 13x12
927   20h multicolored   .50   .25
928   50h multicolored   1.25   .25
929   65h multicolored   1.50   .25
930   80h multicolored   2.10   .35
   a. A173 Block of 4, #927-930   6.25   1.25

Intl. Youth
Year
A174

1985, May 4   Perf. 12
931 A174 20h multicolored   .55   .25
932 A174 80h multicolored   1.25   .35

Self-sufficiency in
Wheat Production
A175

1985, May 4
933 A175 20h multicolored   .70   .30

East-West Pipeline — A176

1985, June 9
934 A176 20h Tanker loading
              berth, Yanbu   .75   .25
935 A176 65h Pipeline, map   1.75   .25

Shuttle
Launch — A177

Shuttle, Missions Emblem — A178

1985, July 7
936 A177 20h multicolored   1.25   .55
937 A178 115h multicolored   6.00   1.10
   Prince Sultan Ibn Salman Al-Saud, 1st
Arab-Moslem astronaut, on Discovery 51-G.

UN, 40th
Anniv.
A179

1985, July 15
938 A179 20h multicolored   .80   .30

Highway, Map, Holy Ka'aba in Mecca
to Prophet's Mosque in
Medina — A180

1985, July 22
939 A180 20h multicolored   .60   .30
940 A180 65h multicolored   1.40   .30
   Mecca-Medina Highway opening, 10/11/84.

Post Code Inauguration — A181

1985, July 24
941 A181 20h Covers   .75   .30

1984 Asian
Soccer
Cup
Victory
A182

1985, July 30
942 A182 20h multicolored   .50   .40
943 A182 65h multicolored   1.25   .40
944 A182 115h multicolored   3.25   .70
   Nos. 942-944 (3)   5.00   1.50

Pilgrimage to Mecca — A183

1985, Aug. 25   Litho.   Perf. 12
945 A183 10h multicolored   .30   .30
946 A183 15h multicolored   .30   .30
947 A183 20h multicolored   .45   .30
948 A183 65h multicolored   1.00   .30
   Nos. 945-948 (4)   2.05   1.20

1st Gulf
Olympics
Day,
Riyadh,
May 2
A184

1985, Sept. 8
949 A184 20h multicolored   .50   .25
950 A184 115h multicolored   2.40   .50

World Food
Day
A185

1985, Oct. 16
951 A185 20h multicolored   1.00   .50
952 A185 65h multicolored   3.50   .50

King Abdul Aziz, Masmak Fort and
Horsemen — A186

1985, Dec. 1
953 A186 15h multicolored   .30   .30
954 A186 20h multicolored   .30   .30
955 A186 65h multicolored   1.00   .30
956 A186 80h multicolored   1.25   .35
   Nos. 953-956 (4)   2.85   1.25
   Intl. Conference on the History of King
Abdul Aziz Al-Sa'ud, Riyadh. An imperf. souvenir sheet showing smaller versions of Nos.
953-956 and the conference emblem exists.
Sold for 10r. Value $26.50.

King Fahd Koran Publishing Center,
Medina — A187

1985, Dec. 18
957 A187 20h multicolored   .30   .30
958 A187 65h multicolored   1.50   .30

OPEC,
25th Anniv.
A188

1985, Dec. 24
959 A188 20h multicolored   .40   .30
960 A188 65h multicolored   2.10   .30

Holy Ka'aba Type of 1976
Type II
1986, Feb. 17   Litho.   Perf. 12
Booklet Stamps
Size: 29x19mm
961 A97 10h lt vio & blk   8.00
   a.   Booklet pane of 4   37.50
965 A97 20h bluish grn & blk   13.50
968 A97 50h pink & black   27.50
   a.   Bklt. pane of 4, #961, 2 #965,
         #968   60.00
   Nos. 961-968 (3)   49.00
   Due to vending machine breakdowns, distribution of this set has been very limited. The
government does have stocks of these stamps
but they are not currently being sold.

A189

1986, Jan. 8   Litho.   Perf. 12
971 A189 20h multicolored   1.40   .30
   Intl. Peace Year.

A190

1986, Mar. 24   Perf. 14, 12 (65h)
972 A190 20h multicolored   .60   .25
   a.   Perf. 12   .60   .25
973 A190 65h multicolored   1.40   .25
   Riyadh Municipality, 50th aAnniv.

A191

1986, Apr. 21   Perf. 12
974 A191 20h multicolored   .75   .25
975 A191 50h multicolored   1.25   .25
   UN child survival campaign.

General Establishment for Electric
Power, 10th Anniv. — A192

1986, Apr. 26
976 A192 20h multicolored   .40   .30
977 A192 65h multicolored   1.60   .30

Continental Maritime Cable
Inauguration — A193

1986, June 1   Litho.   Perf. 12
978   A193   20h multicolored   .75   .35
979   A193   50h multicolored   1.50   .35

Natl. Guard Housing Project, Riyadh,
Inauguration — A194

1986, July 19
980   A194   20h multicolored   .50   .25
981   A194   65h multicolored   1.50   .25

Islamic Arch, Holy
Ka'aba — A195

1986-98   Litho.   Perf. 12
984   A195   30h blk & bluish
                  grn   .25   .25
985   A195   40h black & lilac
                  rose   .45   .25
986   A195   50h black & brt
                  green   1.10   .60
987   A195   75h black & Prus
                  bl   1.40   .70
   a.   Perf. 13½x14   1.10   .60
987B A195 100h black & red
988   A195 100h blk & bl green   1.60   .80
989   A195 150h black & rose li-
                  lac   2.75   1.40
   a.   Perf. 13½x14   2.50   1.25
990   A195   2r blk & vio blue   3.00   1.60
          Nos. 984-990 (8)   10.55   5.60

   Issued: 30h, 40h, 8/5; 75h, 150h, 7/30/90;
50h, 10/9/90; #987a, 6/13/92; #989a, 6/6/92;
2r, 4/99; #987B, 988, 9/21/96.
   This is an expanding set. Numbers may
change.

Pilgrimage to Mecca — A196

   Designs of: a, A116. b, A129. c, A156. d,
A149. e, A141. f, A122. g, A183. h, A167.

1986, Aug. 13   Litho.   Perf. 12
1002 A196   Block of 8   22.50 22.50
   a.-h.   20h, any single

Discovery of Oil,
50th
Anniv. — A197

1986, Sept. 16
1003 A197   20h Well, refinery   .50   .25
1004 A197   65h Well, map   2.25   .25

   Because of difficulty in separation most
stamps have damaged perfs.

World Food
Day — A198

1986, Oct. 18
1005 A198   20h shown   .35   .35
1006 A198 115h Stylized plant   1.90   .65

Massacre of
Palestinian
Refugees, Sept.
17, 1982 — A199

1986, Nov. 1   Litho.   Perf. 12
1007 A199   80h multicolored   1.25   .60
1008 A199 115h multicolored   1.90   .95

   Definitive stamps generally do not
have an official date of issue. Any dates
shown probably reflect sales at the
Riyadh or Dammam post offices only.

Saudi Universities

Imam
Mohammed ibn
Saud — A200

Umm al-
Qura — A201

King
Saud — A202

King Fahd
Petroleum and
Minerals — A203

King
Faisal — A204

King Abdul
Aziz — A205

Medina
Islamic — A206

1986-91
1009 A200   15h sage grn &
                  blk   .25   .25
1010 A200   20h ultra & black   .25   .25
1011 A200   50h ultra & black   .65   .40
1012 A200   65h brt bl & blk   .80   .40
1013 A200   75h brt bl & blk   1.00   .55
1014 A200 100h rose & black   1.10   .55
1015 A200 150h rose cl & blk   2.00   .95
1016 A201   50h ultra & black   .80   .50
1017 A201   65h brt bl & blk   1.00   .40
1018 A201   75h brt bl & blk   1.00   .55
1019 A201 100h dull rose &
                  blk   1.60   .80
1020 A201 150h rose cl & blk   2.40   1.10
1021 A202   50h ultra & black   .85   .50
1022 A202   75h brt bl & blk   1.00   .55
1023 A202 100h dull rose &
                  blk   1.60   .80
1024 A202 150h rose cl & blk   2.25   1.00
1025 A203   50h ultra & black   .65   .40
1026 A203   75h brt bl & blk   1.00   .55
1027 A203 150h rose cl & blk   2.00   .95
1028 A204   50h ultra & black   .65   .40
1029 A204   75h brt bl & blk   1.00   .55
1030 A204 150h rose cl & blk   2.25   .70
1031 A205   50h ultra & black   .65   .40
1032 A205   75h brt bl & blk   1.00   .65
1033 A205 150h rose cl & blk   2.25   1.00
1034 A206   50h ultra & black   .70   .25
1035 A206   75h brt bl & blk   1.00   .55
1036 A206 150h rose cl & blk   2.00   .40
          Nos. 1009-1036 (28)   33.70 16.35

   Issued: #1009-1010, 1012, 1014, 11/26;
#1019, 3/29; #1023, 7/22; #1016, 1020, 8/8;
#1015, 1027, 1036, 1/31/89; #1011, 1025,
1028, 1031, 2/25/89; #1017, 3/89; #1024,
1030, 1033, 4/29/89; #1034, 7/4/89; #1021,
1989; #1013, 1018, 1026, 1990; #1022, 1029,
1032, 1035, 1991.

Saudi-Bahrain Highway
Inauguration — A207

1986, Nov. 26   Perf. 14
1039   Strip of 2   3.25   .45
   a.-b.   A207 20h any single 1.40   .25

   Printed se-tenant in a continuous design.

1st Modern
Olympic
Games,
Athens,
90th Anniv.
A208

1986, Dec. 27
1040 A208   20h multicolored   1.50   .70
1041 A208 100h multicolored   8.00   1.25

General Petroleum and Minerals
Organization (Petromin), 25th
Anniv. — A209

**   Unwmk.**
1987, Feb. 23   Litho.   Perf. 12
1042 A209   50h multicolored   .80   .45
1043 A209 100h multicolored   1.90   .80

Restoration and Expansion of Quba
Mosque, Medina — A210

   Design: View of mosque and model of
expanded mosque.

1987, Mar. 21
1044 A210   50h multicolored   1.00   .40
1045 A210   75h multicolored   1.50   .55

Vocational
Training
A211

   Designs: a, Welding. b, Drill press operation. c, Lathe operation. d, Electrician.

**   Unwmk.**
1987, Apr. 8   Litho.   Perf. 12
1046   Block of 4   8.50   8.50
   a.-d.   A211 50h any single 1.75   1.75

Cairo Exhibition
A212

   Design: Desert fortifications in silhouette,
Riyadh television tower, King Khalid Intl. Airport hangars and pyramid of Giza.

**   Unwmk.**
1987, June 17   Litho.   Perf. 12
1047 A212   50h multicolored   .90   .50
1048 A212   75h multicolored   1.60   .65

A213

Inauguration of King Fahd
Telecommunications Center,
Jedda — A214

1987, July 21
1049 A213   50h multicolored   .90   .50
1050 A214   75h multicolored   1.60   .65

Afghan Resistance Movement A215

1987, July 25
1051 A215 50h multicolored .90 .50
1052 A215 100h multicolored 1.60 .90

Pilgrimage to Mecca — A216

Design: View of Ihram and Meqat Wadi Muhrim Mosque from Wadi Muhrim Meqat.

1987, Aug. 3
1053 A216 50h multicolored 1.00 .50
1054 A216 75h multicolored 1.50 .60
1055 A216 100h multicolored 1.75 .90
Nos. 1053-1055 (3) 4.25 2.00

Home for Disabled Children, 1st Anniv. — A217

1987, Oct. 3
1056 A217 50h multicolored 1.10 .55
1057 A217 75h multicolored 1.75 .75

World Post Day — A218

1987, Oct. 10
1058 A218 50h multicolored .70 .40
1059 A218 150h multicolored 2.00 .95

World Food Day A219

1987, Oct. 17
1060 A219 50h multicolored .85 .40
1061 A219 75h multicolored 1.40 .50

Social Welfare Society, 25th Anniv. — A220

1987, Oct. 26
1062 A220 50h multicolored .95 .45
1063 A220 100h multicolored 1.75 .75

Dome of the Rock — A221

1987, Dec. 5
1064 A221 75h multicolored 2.25 .60
1065 A221 150h multicolored 4.25 1.10

Restoration and Expansion of the Prophet's Mosque, Medina — A222

1987, Dec. 15 *Perf. 14*
1066 A222 50h multicolored .90 .35
1067 A222 75h multicolored 1.25 .50
1068 A222 150h multicolored 2.50 .95
Nos. 1066-1068 (3) 4.65 1.80

An imperf. 300h souvenir sheet exists. Value $52.50.

Battle of Hattin, 800th Anniv. A223

Warriors in silhouette and Dome of the Rock.

1987, Dec. 21 *Perf. 12*
1069 A223 75h multicolored 2.25 .50
1070 A223 150h multicolored 4.25 1.10

Saladin's conquest of Jerusalem.

A224

1987, Dec. 26
1071 A224 50h multicolored 1.00 .50
1072 A224 75h multicolored 1.50 .60

8th session of the Supreme Council of the Gulf Cooperation Council.

A225

1988, Feb. 13 *Litho.* *Perf. 12*
1073 A225 50h multicolored 1.10 .60
1074 A225 75h multicolored 1.75 .85

3rd Regional Highways Conf. of the Middle East.

A226

Inauguration of King Fahd Intl. Stadium — A227

1988, Mar. 2
1075 A226 50h multicolored 1.00 .45
1076 A227 150h multicolored 2.75 1.25

Blood Donation — A228

1988, Apr. 13 *Litho.* *Perf. 12*
1077 A228 50h multicolored 1.00 .45
1078 A228 75h multicolored 1.25 .60

WHO, 40th Anniv. — A229

1988, Apr. 7
1079 A229 50h multicolored 1.10 .50
1080 A229 75h multicolored 1.40 .60

King Fahd, Custodian of the Holy Mosques — A230

King Fahd and mosques at Medina and Mecca.

1988, Apr. 23 *Litho.* *Perf. 12*
1081 A230 50h multicolored .65 .40
1082 A230 75h multicolored .95 .50
1083 A230 150h multicolored 2.10 .95
Nos. 1081-1083 (3) 3.70 1.85

A 75h souvenir sheet exists containing an enlarged version of No. 1082. Sold for 3r. Value $67.50.

Environmental Protection A231

1988, June 5
1084 A231 50h multicolored 1.00 .35
1085 A231 75h multicolored 1.50 .55

Palestinian Uprising, Gaza and the West Bank A232

1988, July 10
1086 A232 75h multicolored 1.50 .60
1087 A232 150h multicolored 3.00 1.10

Pilgrimage to Mecca — A233

1988, July 23 *Litho.* *Perf. 12*
1088 A233 50h multicolored 1.10 .40
1089 A233 75h multicolored 1.60 .55

World Food Day A234

1988, Oct. 16 *Litho.* *Perf. 12*
1090 A234 50h multicolored 1.25 .50
1091 A234 75h multicolored 1.90 .70

Qiblatain Mosque Expansion — A235

1988, Nov. 9
1092 A235 50h multicolored 1.00 .35
1093 A235 75h multicolored 1.50 .55

5th World Youth Soccer Championships, Riyadh, Dammam, Jedda and Taif — A250

1989, Feb. 16 *Litho.* *Perf. 12*
1094 A250 75h multicolored 1.75 .65
1095 A250 150h multicolored 3.25 1.25

World Health Day — A251

1989, Apr. 8 *Litho.* *Perf. 12*
1096 A251 50h multicolored 1.10 .35
1097 A251 75h multicolored 1.60 .55

Sea Water Desalination Plant — A252

1989, May 30   Litho.   Perf. 12
1098 A252 50h multicolored   .70 .40
1099 A252 75h multicolored   1.10 .60

Proclamation of the State of Palestine,
Nov. 15, 1988 — A253

1989, June 6   Litho.   Perf. 12
1100 A253 50h multicolored   1.00 .25
1101 A253 75h multicolored   1.50 .35

Pilgrimage to Mecca — A254

Design: Al-Tan'eem Mosque, Mecca.

1989, July 12   Litho.   Perf. 12
1102 A254 50h multicolored   .90 .25
1103 A254 75h multicolored   1.40 .40

World Food
Day
A255

1989, Oct. 16   Litho.   Perf. 12
1104 A255 75h multicolored   .75 .50
1105 A255 150h multicolored   1.50 1.00

Holy Mosque Expansion — A256

1989, Dec. 30   Litho.   Perf. 12
1106 A256 50h multicolored   .75 .35
1107 A256 75h multicolored   1.10 .55
1108 A256 150h multicolored   2.10 1.10
          Nos. 1106-1108 (3)   3.95 2.00

A souvenir sheet containing an enlarged
version of design A256 exists. Sold for 5r.
Value, perf or imperf, each $35.00.

Youth Soccer
Cup
Championships
A257

1989, Dec. 20
1109 A257 75h multicolored   1.10 .45
1110 A257 150h multicolored   2.10 .95

UNESCO World
Literacy
Year — A258

1990, Jan. 9
1111 A258 50h multicolored   .95 .40
1112 A258 75h multicolored   1.50 .55

World Health Day — A259

Unwmk.
1990, Apr. 7   Litho.   Perf. 12
1113 A259 75h multicolored   1.00 .50
1114 A259 150h multicolored   2.10 .95

Flowers — A262

1990
1115   Sheet of 21   12.00
 a.-u. A262 50h any single   .60 .25
1116   Sheet of 21   18.00
 a.-u. A262 75h any single   .75 .40
1117   Sheet of 21   35.00
 a.-u. A262 150h any single   1.50 .80
          Nos. 1115-1117 (3)   65.00

21 Different species pictured on the sheets.
Issued: 50h, 75h, Feb. 6; 150h, Jan. 17.
See No. 1292A.

Islamic Conference, 20th
Anniv. — A263

1990, Feb. 20   Litho.   Perf. 12
1118 A263 75h blue & multi   .70 .35
1119 A263 150h gray & multi   1.50 .70

Islamic
Heritage
A264

Designs: b, Arabic script in rectangle. c, Circular design. d, Mosque and minaret.

1990, July 29
1120   Block of 4   4.50 2.50
 a.-d. A264 75h any single   1.00 .60

Horses
A265

1990, Apr. 14   Color of Horse
1121   Block of 4   4.00 1.40
 a.   A265 50h white, red tassels
            on bridle   .95 .35
 b.   A265 50h black   .95 .35
 c.   A265 50h white, brown bridle   .95 .35
 d.   A265 50h chestnut   .95 .35
1122 A265 50h like #1121d   .65 .35
1123 A265 75h like #1121b   1.00 .50
1124 A265 100h like #1121a   1.40 .65
1125 A265 150h like #1121c   2.00 1.00
          Nos. 1121-1125 (5)   9.05 3.90

No. 1121 has white border on two sides.
Nos. 1122-1125 have white border on four
sides.

Pilgrimage to Mecca — A266

1990, June 28
1126 A266 75h multicolored   1.00 .50
1127 A266 150h multicolored   2.10 1.00

Television
Tower — A267

1990, July 21
1128 A267 75h multicolored   1.00 .50
1129 A267 150h multicolored   2.10 1.00

Saudi Arabian Airlines Route
Map — A268

1990, Sept. 3
1130   75h Global routes   .75 .40
1131   75h Domestic routes   .75 .40
 a.   A268 Pair, #1130-1131   1.75 1.00
1132   150h like #1130   1.50 .90
1133   150h like #1131   1.50 .90
 a.   A268 Pair, #1132-1133   3.25 2.10
          Nos. 1130-1133 (4)   4.50 2.60

World Food
Day
A269

1990, Oct. 16   Litho.   Perf. 12
1134 A269 75h multicolored   1.10 .65
1135 A269 150h multicolored   2.50 1.25

Organization of Petroleum Exporting
Countries (OPEC), 30th
Anniv. — A270

1990, Sept. 26
1136 A270 75h multicolored   1.75 .60
1137 A270 150h multicolored   2.75 1.10

Fifth Five Year Development
Plan — A271

Designs: a, Oil refinery, irrigation, and oil
storage tanks. b, Radio tower, highway, and
mine. c, Monument, sports stadium, and vocational training. d, Television tower, environmental protection, and modern architecture.

1990, Oct. 30
1138 A271 75h Block of 4, #a.-d. 5.50 2.10

Battle of
Badr,
624 — A272

1991, Apr. 3   Litho.   Perf. 12
1139 A272 75h org, dk grn &
                 grn   1.00 .50
1140 A272 150h lt bl, dk bl & grn   1.90   .95

A273

1991, Apr. 9
1141 A273 75h multicolored   1.00 .45
1142 A273 150h multicolored   1.90 .90

World Health Day.

A274

Animals: a, k, Impala. b, l, Ibex. c, m, Oryx. d, n, Fox. e, o, Bat. f, p, Hyena. g, q, Cat. h, r, Dugong. i, s, Leopard.

Blocks of 9

1991		**Litho.**		**Perf. 12**
1143	A274	25h Block, #a.-i.	3.50	1.75
1144	A274	50h Block, #a.-i.	8.00	4.00
1145	A274	75h Block, #a.-i.	11.50	6.25
1146	A274	100h Block, #a.-i.	16.00	7.75
1146J	A274	150h Block, #k.-s.	22.50	18.00
t.		Perf 14x13½	27.50	19.00
		Nos. 1143-1146J (5)	61.50	37.75

Issued: #1143-1146, May 1; #1146J, Dec. 1. No. 1146J exists imperf.

Pilgrimage to Mecca — A275

1991, June 20		**Litho.**		**Perf. 14**
1147	A275	75h blue & multi	.90	.45
1148	A275	150h green & multi	1.60	.80

World Telecommunications Day — A276

1991, June 3				**Perf. 12**
1149	A276	75h multicolored	.90	.45
1150	A276	150h multicolored	1.60	.80

A277

1991, May 11				
1151	A277	75h multicolored	1.10	.70
1152	A277	150h multicolored	2.25	1.40

Liberation of Kuwait.

A278

1991, Sept. 8		**Litho.**		**Perf. 12**
1153	A278	75h blue & multi	1.50	.75
1154	A278	150h buff & multi	3.00	1.50

Literacy Day.

A279

1991, Oct. 16		**Litho.**		**Perf. 12**
1155	A279	75h green & multi	.90	.50
1156	A279	150h orange & multi	1.60	1.00

World Food Day.

A280

1991, Dec. 7				
1157	A280	75h green & multi	1.75	.75
1158	A280	150h dk blue & multi	2.75	1.75

Childrens' Day.

A281

1992, Apr. 8		**Litho.**		**Perf. 12**
1159	A281	75h lt blue & multi	1.00	.60
1160	A281	150h lt org & multi	2.10	1.10

World Health Day.

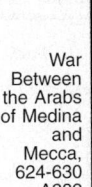

War Between the Arabs of Medina and Mecca, 624-630
A282

1992, Apr. 18				
1161	A282	75h lt org & grn	.90	.55
1162	A282	150h lt bl, dk bl & grn	2.00	.95

Pilgrimage to Mecca — A283

Unwmk.

1992, June 9		**Litho.**		**Perf. 12**
1163	A283	75h lt blue & multi	1.00	.60
1164	A283	150h lt orange & multi	2.10	1.10

Population and Housing Census — A284

1992, Sept. 26		**Litho.**		**Perf. 14**
1165	A284	75h blue & multi	.75	.50
1166	A284	150h org yel & multi	1.50	.95

World Food Day
A285

1992, Oct. 17				**Perf. 12**
1167	A285	75h Vegetables	1.25	.65
1168	A285	150h Fruits	2.40	1.25

Consultative Council — A286

Document: d, g, 12 lines. e, h, 13 lines. f, i, 11 lines. 5r, Scrolls of 12, 11, & 13 lines.

1992, Dec. 12		**Litho.**		**Perf. 12**
1168A	A286	75h Strip of 3, #d.-f.	2.25	1.40
1168B	A286	150h Strip of 3, #g.-i.	5.75	3.00

Imperf
Size: 120x79mm

1168C	A286	5r multicolored	27.50	13.50

Birds — A287

a, k, Woodpecker. b, l, Arabian bustard. c, m, Lark. d, n, Turtle dove. e, o, Heron. f, p, Partridge. g, q, Hoopoe. h, r, Falcon. i, s, Houbara bustard.

1992-97				**Perf. 14x13½**
		Blocks of 9		
1169	A287	25h #a.-i.	5.25	5.25
j.		Perf. 12, #k.-s.	27.50	
1170	A287	50h #a.-i.	10.00	
j.		Perf. 12, #k.-s.		
1171	A287	75h #a.-i.	11.50	5.50
j.		Perf. 12, #k.-s.	11.50	5.75
1172	A287	100h #a.-i.	24.50	12.00
j.		Perf. 12, #k.-s.	24.50	12.00
1173	A287	150h #a.-i.	40.00	19.00
j.		Perf. 12, #k.-s.	40.00	19.00
		Nos. 1169-1173 (5)	91.25	41.75

Issued: 150h, 3/18/92; 75h, 7/14/92; 100h, 3/1/93; 25h, 50h, 11/6/94; #1171j, 1173j, 8/94; 1169j, 1996; 1170j, 1997(?).

World Health Day
A288

1993, Apr. 7		**Litho.**		**Perf. 12**
1175	A288	75h red & multi	.90	.50
1175A	A288	150h blue & multi	2.00	.90

King Fahd Championship Soccer Cup — A289

1993, Mar. 15				
1176	A289	75h green & multi	1.75	.70
1176A	A289	150h rose red & multi	2.75	1.75

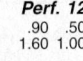

Pilgrimage to Mecca — A290

1993, May 30		**Litho.**		**Perf. 12**
1177	A290	75h green & multi	.90	.50
1178	A290	150h blue & multi	1.60	1.00

Intl. Telecommunications Day — A291

1993, May 17			**Inscription Color**	
1179	A291	75h dark blue	.90	.50
1180	A291	150h red lilac	1.60	1.00

Battle of Alkandk
A292

1993, May 15				
1181	A292	75h lt org & grn	.90	.50
1182	A292	150h lt bl, dk bl & grn	1.60	1.00

World Food Day — A293

1993, Dec. 14		**Litho.**		**Perf. 12**
1183	A293	75h black & multi	1.10	.55
1184	A293	150h red & multi	2.50	1.10

World Dental Health Day
A294

1994, Apr. 9		**Litho.**		**Perf. 12**
1185	A294	75h multicolored	1.00	.50
1186	A294	150h multicolored	1.90	1.00

Intl. Olympic Committee, Cent.
A295

1994, Apr. 23		**Litho.**		**Perf. 12**
1187	A295	75h blue & multi	1.10	.65
1188	A295	150h red & multi	2.50	1.10

Battle of Khaybar
A296

1994, June 14   Litho.   Perf. 12
1189 A296 75h bister & green   1.00   .50
1190 A296 150h sil, bl & grn   1.90   1.00

Pilgrimage to Mecca — A297

1994, May 14
1191 A297 75h green & multi   .90   .50
1192 A297 150h red & multi   1.60   1.10

Consultative Council — A298

Design: 150h, Different view of building, inscription tablet at right.

1994, July 12   Litho.   Perf. 12
1193 A298 75h multicolored   .90   .50
1194 A298 150h multicolored   2.00   .90
  a. Souv. sheet of 2, #1193-
        1194, imperf.   32.50

No. 1194a sold for 5r.

A299

1994 World Soccer Cup Championships, U.S. — A300

1994, June 18
1195 A299 75h multicolored   .90   .50
1196 A300 150h multicolored   2.00   .90

King Abdul Aziz Port, Dammam — A301

1994-95   Litho.   Perf. 12
1198 A301 25h multicolored   .75   .50
1199 A301 50h multicolored   .75   .50
1200 A301 75h multicolored   1.00   .65

1201 A301 100h multicolored   1.40   .75
1202 A301 150h multicolored   2.10   1.00
  Nos. 1198-1202 (5)   6.00   3.40
  Issued: 75h, 8/22/94; 150h, 11/5/94; 100h, 3/11/95; 50h, 11/28/95; 25h, 12/27/95.

A304

World Food Day
A305

1994, Oct. 16   Litho.   Perf. 12
1212 A304 75h Green house   1.75   .70
1213 A305 150h Foods   2.75   1.75

A306

Arab League, 50th Anniv.
A307

1995, Mar. 25   Litho.   Perf. 12
1214 A306 75h multicolored   .95   .50
1215 A307 150h multicolored   1.75   1.00

A308

UN, 50th Anniv. — A309

1995, Feb. 19
1216 A308 75h multicolored   1.00   .50
1217 A309 150h multicolored   1.90   1.00

Refugee Care
A310

1995, Apr. 9   Litho.   Perf. 12
1218 A310 75h green & multi   .95   .50
1219 A310 150h tan & multi   1.75   1.00

Pilgrimage to Mecca
A311

1995, May 3   Litho.   Perf. 12
1220 A311 75h blue & multi   .95   .50
1221 A311 150h tan & multi   1.75   1.00

Deaf Week — A312

1995, May 3   Litho.   Perf. 12
1222 A312 75h shown   1.00   .50
1223 A312 150h Hand sign, ear   1.90   1.00

Saudi Arabian Airlines, 50th Anniv.
A313

1995, Aug. 21
1224 A313 75h Anniv. emblem,
             vert.   1.00   .50
1225 A313 150h shown   1.90   1.00

FAO, 50th Anniv. — A314

1995, Oct. 16   Litho.   Perf. 12
1226 A314 75h shown   1.75   .70
1227 A314 150h Emblem over
             globe   2.75   1.75

Jeddah Port — A315

1996   Litho.   Perf. 12
1228   A315 25h multicolored   .45   .35
1229   A315 50h multicolored   .90   .45
1230   A315 75h multicolored   1.40   .70
1230A A315 100h multicolored   2.25   2.25
1230B A315 150h multicolored   3.00   1.75
  Nos. 1228-1230B (5)   8.00   5.50
  Issued: 25h and 50h, 1/27/96; 75h, 2/7/96; 100h, 11/25/96; 150h, 3/30/96.

1996 Summer Olympics, Atlanta
A316

1996, June 23
1231 A316 150h orange & multi   2.10   1.10
1232 A316 2r blue & multi   3.25   1.50

Pilgrimage to Mecca — A317

1996, Apr. 21
1233 A317 150h black & multi   2.10   1.10
1234 A317 2r rose red &
             multi   3.00   1.40
1235 A317 3r green & multi   4.25   2.10
  Nos. 1233-1235 (3)   9.35   4.60

World Health Organization
A318

1996, July 14   Litho.   Perf. 12
1236 A318 2r green & multi   2.50   1.25
1237 A318 3r red & multi   4.00   2.00

FAO, 50th Anniv.
A319

1996, Oct. 16   Litho.   Perf. 12
1238 A319 2r blue & multi   3.75   1.60
1239 A319 3r red & multi   5.25   2.50

UNICEF, 50th Anniv.
A320

1996, Nov. 12
1240 A320 150h buff & multi   2.00   1.00
1241 A320 2r blue & multi   2.75   1.25

King Abdul Aziz Research Center, 25th Anniv.
A321

1997, Jan. 8   Litho.   Perf. 12
1242 A321 150h brown & multi   2.00   1.00
1243 A321 2r green & multi   2.75   1.25

Rabigh Steam Power Plant A322

Designs: 150h, Power plant. 2r, Power plant, electrical power lines.

1996, Dec. 31
1244 A322 150h multicolored 2.00 1.00
Size: 51x26mm
1245 A322 2r multicolored 2.75 1.25

Yanbu Port — A323

1996   Litho.   Perf. 12
1245A A323 50h multicolored 1.10 .60
1246 A323 2r multicolored 3.75 1.90
Issued: 1245A, 12/21; 1246 11/25.
See No. 1273.

Opening Mecca A324

1997, Jan. 30
1247 A324 1r brt grn & multi 1.40 .65
1248 A324 2r lt yel grn & multi 2.75 1.40

King Fahd, Birthday A325

1997, Mar. 10
1249 A325 100h green & multi 1.40 .60
1250 A325 150h pink & multi 1.90 .95
1251 A325 2r tan & multi 2.50 1.40
Nos. 1249-1251 (3) 5.80 2.95

An imperf souvenir sheet containing an enlarged version of design A325 exists. Sold for 5r. Value $18.

Jubail Port — A326

1996-97
1251A A326 50h multicolored .85 .50
1251B A326 100h multicolored .85 .40
1252 A326 150h multicolored 1.25 .65
1252A A326 2r multicolored 3.00 1.50
1252B A326 4r multicolored 3.50 1.75
Nos. 1251A-1252B (5) 9.45 4.80

Issued: 50h, 10/17/96; 100h, 6/29/96; 150h, 7/8/96; 2r, 9/97(?); 4r, 7/24/96.

Campaign Against Use of Illegal Drugs A327

1997, Feb. 26
1253 A327 150h blue & multi 4.00 2.00
1254 A327 2r red & multi 5.50 2.75

Battle of Hunain A328

1997, Mar. 10   Litho.   Perf. 12
1255 A328 150h multicolored 1.90 1.00
1256 A328 2r multicolored 2.75 1.40

World Health Day A329

1997, Apr. 7   Litho.   Perf. 14
1257 A329 150h multicolored 1.90 1.00
1258 A329 2r multicolored 2.75 1.40

A330

Al-Hijjah A331

1997, Apr. 8
1259 A330 1r multicolored 1.25 .65
1260 A331 2r multicolored 2.75 1.25

King Fahd Natl. Library A332

1997, July 94   Litho.   Perf. 12
1261 A332 1r shown 1.25 .65
1262 A332 2r Open book 2.75 1.25

A333

1997, July 26
1263 A333 150h Emblem, rays 2.10 1.10
1264 A333 2r shown 3.25 1.50
King Abdul Aziz Public Library.

A334

1997, July 15   Litho.   Perf. 12
1265 A334 1r red & multi 1.25 .70
1266 A334 2r green & multi 2.75 1.25
Montreal Protocol on Substances that Deplete Ozone Layer, 10th anniv.

3rd GCC Stamp Exhibition, Riyadh A335

1997, Sept. 30   Litho.   Perf. 12
1267 A335 1r multicolored 1.50 .70

Prince Salman Center — A336

1997, Dec. 27   Litho.   Perf. 12
1268 A336 1r multicolored 1.50 .70

Battle of Tabuk A337

1998, Jan. 24   Litho.   Perf. 12
1269 A337 1r multicolored 1.40 .70

World Food Day — A338

1998, Feb. 22
1270 A338 2r multicolored 2.75 1.50

Disabled Persons Day — A339   Al Hijjah — A340

1998, Mar. 8   Litho.   Perf. 12
1271 A339 1r multicolored 1.40 .70

1998, Mar. 29
1272 A340 2r multicolored 2.75 1.40

Yanbu Port Type of 1997
1996, Sept. 3   Litho.   Perf. 12
1273 A323 100h multicolored 1.90 .90
1273A A323 150h multi 3.00 1.90
1273B A323 4r multi 4.00 1.75
Nos. 1273-1273B (3) 8.90 4.55
Issued: 150h, 8/28/96; 4r, 11/8/97.

WHO, 50th Anniv. — A341   Dam — A342

1998, May 18
1274 A341 1r multicolored 1.25 .60

1998, May 9
1275 A342 1r multicolored 1.25 .60

A343   A344

1998, May 31   Litho.   Perf. 12
1276 A343 1r multicolored 1.25 .60
Islamic Organization for Education and Science.

1998, Sept. 30
1277 A344 2r multicolored 2.50 1.25
Arab Stamp Day.

A345

KSA, Cent. A346

Designs: No. 1278, Forts. No. 1279, Military equipment. No. 1280, Entrance to fort, vert. 2r, King Fahd, KSA emblem, outline of map of Saudi Arabia, vert.

1999, Jan 22   **Litho.**   *Perf. 12*
1278	A345	1r multicolored	2.25	1.10
1279	A346	1r multicolored	2.25	1.10
1280	A345	1r multicolored	2.25	1.10
1281	A345	2r multicolored	4.50	2.25
		Nos. 1278-1281 (4)	11.25	5.55

#1278-1279 exist imperf in souvenir sheets of 1. There are some color variations. #1280-1281 exist imperf in a souvenir sheet of 2. The three sheets sold for 5r each. Value, set of three sheets $55.

King Fahd Intl. Airport — A347

1999, Feb. 6
1282	A347	1r multicolored	1.25	.65

Size: 26x38mm
1283	A347	2r Jet, control tower	2.50	1.25

Development of Palace of Justice Area — A348

1999, Jan. 22
1284	A348	1r multicolored	2.25	1.10

Exists imperf in a souvenir sheet of 1. It sold for 5r. Value $18.

World Food Day — A348a

1999, Mar. 16   **Litho.**   *Perf. 12*
1285	A348a	1r multicolored	2.50	1.25

Al-Hijjah — A349

1999, Mar. 18   **Litho.**   *Perf. 12*
1286	A349	2r multicolored	2.50	1.10

A350

1999, Mar. 6
1287	A350	1r multicolored	2.25	1.10

Kingdom of Saudi Arabia, cent. Exists in an imperf. souvenir sheet of 1. It sold for 5r. Value $18.

A351

1999, May 22   **Litho.**   *Perf. 12*
1288	A351	1r Traffic signals	1.40	.70

Academy for Security Sciences — A352

1999, May 29   **Litho.**   *Perf. 12*
1289	A352	150h multicolored	2.00	1.00

Intl. Holy Koran Competition — A353

1999, Oct. 3   **Litho.**   *Perf. 12*
1290	A353	1r multicolored	1.40	.70

UPU, 125th Anniv. — A354

1999, Oct. 26   **Litho.**   *Perf. 12*
1291	A354	1r multi	2.50	1.10

World Meteorological Organization, 50th Anniv. — A355

2000, Mar. 23   **Litho.**   *Perf. 12*
1292	A355	1r multi	1.40	.70

Flowers Type of 1990

Designs like Nos. 1115a-1115u.

2000, Feb. 1   **Litho.**   *Perf. 12*
1292A		Block of 21	40.00
b.-v.		A262 1r Any single	

Pilgrimage to Mecca A356

2000, Mar. 11   *Perf. 14x14¼*
1293	A356	1r black & multi	1.10	.60
1294	A356	2r red & multi	2.10	1.10

Scouting — A357

2000, July 18   **Litho.**   *Perf. 14*
1295	A357	1r multi	1.10	.50

Riyadh, Arabian Cultural Capital, 2000 — A358

2000, July 4   **Litho.**   *Perf. 14*
1296	A358	1r multi	1.60	1.00

Water Conservation A359

2000, June 18
1297	A359	1r multi	1.60	1.00

Consultative Council, 75th Anniv. — A360

2000, June 7
1298	A360	1r multi	1.60	1.00

UN High Commissioner for Refugees, 50th Anniv. — A361

2000, Sept. 23
1299	A361	2r multi	2.00	1.00

Jizan Port — A362

2000, Sept. 16   **Litho.**   *Perf. 14*
1299A	A362	50h multi	.50	.50
1299B	A362	1r multi	1.00	1.00
1300	A362	2r multi	1.90	1.90
		Nos. 1299A-1300 (3)	3.40	3.40

Al Khafji Oil Rig Type of 1976-80 Redrawn With Palm Trees and Swords at Upper Right
Perf. 14x13½

2000, Sept. 13   **Litho.**   **Unwmk.**

Size: 26x21mm
1300A	A109	25h dk pur & org	.35	.35

King Abdul Aziz City for Science and Technology A363

2000, Oct. 28
1301	A363	1r multi	1.10	.50

King Khalid University A364

2000, Dec. 5   *Perf. 14*
1302	A364	1r multi	1.10	.50

Buraydah — A365

2000   *Perf. 13¾x14*
1303	A365	50h blue & multi	.50	.50
1304	A365	1r grn & multi	1.00	1.00
1305	A365	2r blk & multi	1.90	1.90
		Nos. 1303-1305 (3)	3.40	3.40

Buraydah — A366

2000-01   *Perf. 13¾x14*
1306	A366	50h blue & multi	.50	.50
1307	A366	1r grn & multi	1.00	1.00
1308	A366	2r blk & multi	1.90	1.90
		Nos. 1306-1308 (3)	3.40	3.40

No. 1308 issued 2/2/01.

King Fahd Printing Press A367

Denomination color: 50h, Pink. 1r, Blue. 2r, Black.

2001, Apr. 25   **Litho.**   *Perf. 14*
1309-1311	A367	Set of 3	3.25	3.25

King Abdul Aziz
Center for Gifted
Care — A368

2001, May 13
1312 A368 1r multi   1.00 .50

Pilgrimage to Mecca — A369

No. 1313: a, Mosque, tower at center, b, Holy Ka'aba. c, Mosque, tower at left and center. d, Mosque, tower and two men at left. e, Mosque, tower at right, mountain in background. f, Mosque, tower and five pilgrims at left. g, Mosque, tower at right. h, Mosque, orange background.

2001, Feb. 28   *Perf. 13¾x14*
1313 A369 1r Block of 8, #a-h 8.00 8.00

Palestinian
Intifada
A370

Designs: 1r, Map of Israel, Palestinian boy and father. 2r, Barbed wire, boy and father, vert.

2001, May 30   *Litho.* *Perf. 14*
1314-1315 A370 Set of 2 3.25 3.25

A souvenir sheet containing an imperforate 49x36mm example of No. 1314 sold for 5r. Value $35.

King Abdul Aziz Historical
Center — A371

No. 1316: a, Building with curved, pointed wall. b, Building with one tree in front. c, Building with towers. d, Aerial view of building.

2001, June 25
1316 A371 1r Block of 4, #a-d 4.00 4.00

World Teacher's
Day — A372

2001, Oct. 6
1317 A372 1r multi   1.00 1.00

Paintings
A373

No. 1318: a, Abstract cityscape in green and yellow. b, Horse and geometric designs. c, Building windows. d, Landscape in yellow, orange and brown. e, Building with blue sky.

2001, Oct. 15
1318   Horiz. strip of 5 5.00 5.00
  a.-e. A373 1r Any single   .95 .95

7th Five-
Year Plan
A374

2002, Jan. 19 *Litho.* *Perf. 14*
1319 A374 1r multi   .95 .95

A375

Abha — A376

2002, Jan. 19
1320 A375 1r blue & multi 1.00 1.00
1321 A376 2r green & multi 1.90 1.90

Islamic Educational, Scientific and
Cultural Organization — A377

2002, Jan. 29
1322 A377 1r multi   .95 .95

Pilgrimage
to Mecca
A378

2002, Feb. 13
1323 A378 1r multi   .95 .95

20 Years of
Achievements
Under King
Fahd — A379

Litho. with Foil Application
2002, Apr. 13
1324 A379 1r multi   .95 .95

An imperforate 3r souvenir sheet overprinted in gold and depicting an example of No. 1324 and various other stamps, in whole or in part, exists. Value $3.

King Fahd
Port, Yanbu
A380

2002, May 26 *Litho.* *Perf. 14*
1325 A380 1r yel & multi 1.00 1.00
1326 A380 2r gray & multi 1.90 1.90

King Fahd
Port, Al
Jubail
A381

2002, May 26
1327 A381 1r black & multi 1.00 1.00
1328 A381 2r multi   1.90 1.90

   Issued: 1r, 7/13.

Pilgrimage
to Mecca
A382

2003, Feb. 7 *Litho.* *Perf. 14*
1329 A382 1r multi   .95 .95

Water Conservation — A383

Designs: No. 1330, 1r, Two water drops. No. 1331, 1r, One water drop, vert.

2003, Mar. 30 *Litho.* *Perf. 14*
1330-1331 A383 Set of 2 2.00 2.00

Civil
Defense
A384

2003, Apr. 29
1332 A384 1r multi   .95 .95

Saudi
Arabian Red
Cresecent
Society
A385

2003, May 20
1333 A385 1r multi   .95 .95

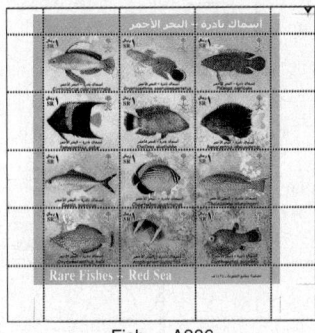

Fish — A386

Designs: Nos. 1334a, 1335a, Cirrhilabrus rubriventralis. Nos. 1334b, 1335b, Cryptocentrus caeruleopunctatus. Nos. 1334c, 1335c, Plesiops nigricans. Nos. 1334d, 1335d, Pomacanthus asfur. Nos. 1334e, 1335e, Cheilinus abudjubbe. Nos. 1334f, 1335f, Pomacentrus albicaudatus. Nos. 1334g, 1335g, Caesio suevicus. Nos. 1334h, 1335h, Chaetodon austriacus. Nos. 1334i, 1335i, Thalassoma klunzingeri. Nos. 1334j, 1335j, Oxymonacanthus halli. Nos. 1334k, 1335k, Amphirion bicinctus. Nos. 1334l, 1335l, Canthigaster pygmaea.

2003
1334 A386 1r Sheet of 12, #a-l 13.50 13.50
1335 A386 2r Sheet of 12, #a-l 22.50 18.00

   Issued: No. 1334, 5/26; No. 1335, 6/21.

Dialogue
Among
Civilizations
A387

2003, July 1
1336 A387 1r multi   .95 .95

Electricity Conservation — A388

2003, Sept. 27
1337 A388 1r multi   .95 .95

World Post Day — A389

2003, Oct. 9
1338 A389 1r multi .95 .95

Ninth Gulf Cooperation Council Stamp Exhibition — A390

2003, Oct. 18
1339 A390 1r multi .95 .95

First Saudi Commemorative Stamp, 75th Islamic Year Anniv. — A391

2003, Oct. 20
1340 A391 1r No. 129 .95 .95

Supreme Council for Handicapped Affairs — A392

2003, Nov. 11
1341 A392 1r multi .95 .95

King Abdul Aziz Equestrian Race Course, Janadriyah A393

2003, Dec. 17
1342 A393 1r multi .95 .95

Pilgrimage to Mecca A394

2003, Dec. 24
1343 A394 1r multi .95 .95
   a. Arabian "1" missing in denomination — —

Mosque, Buraydah A395

Mosque, Medina A396

Mosque, Riyadh A397

Mosque, Dammam A398

Mosque, Baha A399

Mosque, Khobar A400

Mosque, Taif — A401

Mosque, Najran A402

2003, Dec. 24
1344   Sheet of 8   6.25 6.25
   a. A395 1r bl & multi .80 .80
   b. A396 1r bl & multi .80 .80
   c. A397 1r bl & multi .80 .80
   d. A398 1r bl & multi .80 .80
   e. A399 1r bl & multi .80 .80
   f. A400 1r bl & multi .80 .80
   g. A401 1r bl & multi .80 .80
   h. A402 1r bl & multi .80 .80
1345   Sheet of 8   13.50 13.50
   a. A395 2r red & multi 1.60 1.60
   b. A396 2r red & multi 1.60 1.60
   c. A397 2r red & multi 1.60 1.60
   d. A398 2r red & multi 1.60 1.60
   e. A399 2r red & multi 1.60 1.60
   f. A400 2r red & multi 1.60 1.60
   g. A401 2r red & multi 1.60 1.60
   h. A402 2r red & multi 1.60 1.60

Mosques built in reign of King Fahd.

Tabouk — A403

2004, Jan. 19
1346 A403 1r blk & multi 1.00 1.00
1347 A403 2r red & multi 1.90 1.90

MD-11 A404

Boeing 747 — A405

Boeing 777 — A406

MD-90 A407

2004, Jan. 19
1348   Block of 4   4.00 4.00
   a. A404 1r multi .90 .90
   b. A405 1r multi .90 .90
   c. A406 1r multi .90 .90
   d. A407 1r multi .90 .90

New airplanes of Saudi Arabian Airlines.

Judicial Systems A408

2004, Apr. 5   Litho.   *Perf. 14*
1349 A408 1r multi .95 .95

Hail — A409

2004, Oct. 16   Litho.   *Perf. 13¾x14*
1350 A409 1r blk & multi 1.00 1.00
1351 A409 2r red & multi 1.90 1.90

Tourism — A411

No. 1353: a, Sand dune. b, Funicular cars. c, Sea coast. d, Rock climbers.

2004, Nov. 1
1353 A411 2r Block of 4, #a-d 8.00 8.00

"Islam is Peace" A412

2004, Dec. 27
1354 A412 2r multi 2.00 2.00

Pilgrimage to Mecca A413

2005, Jan. 4
1355 A413 1r multi .95 .95

Municipal Elections — A414

2005, Jan. 8   Litho.   *Perf. 14*
1356 A414 1r multi .95 .95

Islamic Solidarity Games — A415

2005, Apr. 2
1357 A415 1r multi .95 .95

World Summit on the Information Society A410

2004, Nov. 1   *Perf. 14*
1352 A410 1r multi .95 .95

Anti-Terrorism
Campaign
A416

2005, July 9   Litho.   **Perf. 14**
1358 A416 1r multi   .95 .95

An imperf. souvenir sheet with simulated perfs sold for 3r. Value $9.

Arar
A417

2005, July 16   Litho.   **Perf. 14**
1359 A417 1r multi   .95 .95

Ancient Artifacts — A418

Ruins — A419

No. 1360: a, Bowl. b, Head of animal. c, Head of human. d, Inscribed tablet.
No. 1361: a, Ruin with two towers, walls in foreground, year in black. b, Building with one tower, year in white. c, Fort with towers at corners, year in white. d, Ruins on hilltop, year in black.

2005, Aug. 20
1360 A418 1r Block of 4, #a-d   4.25 4.25
1361 A419 2r Block of 4, #a-d   7.75 7.75

Mecca, Capital of
Islamic
Culture — A420

2005, July 16   Litho.   **Perf. 14**
1362 A420 3r multi   2.50 2.50

A souvenir sheet of one exists. Value, $20.

King Fahd (1923-
2005)
A421

Denominations: 2r, 3r.

2005, Dec. 21
1363-1364 A421   Set of 2   4.00 4.00

An imperf 105x80mm stamp with picture reversed sold for 5r. Value $18.

Pilgrimage
to Mecca
A422

2005, Dec. 28
1365 A422 2r multi   1.50 1.50

An imperf 80x105mm stamp depicting pilgrims to Mecca sold for 5r.

King
Abdullah — A423

Crown Prince
Sultan — A424

Litho. with Foil Application
2006, Jan. 18
1366 A423 2r multi   1.60 1.60
1367 A424 2r multi   1.60 1.60
1368 A423 3r multi   2.50 2.50
1369 A424 3r multi   2.50 2.50
Nos. 1366-1369 (4)   8.20 8.20

Installation of new king and crown prince. An imperf 106x80mm stamp depicting the new king and crown prince sold for 5r. Value $22.50.

National
Society for
Human
Rights
A425

2006, Jan. 30   Litho.   **Perf. 14**
1370 A425 2r multi   1.60 1.60

An 80x105mm imperforate stamp depicting a stylized person sold for 5r. Value $22.50.

OPEC Intl. Development Fund, 30th
Anniv. — A426

2006, Mar. 13
1371 A426 2r multi   1.60 1.60

King Faisal International Prize — A427

Color of denomination: 2r, Blue. 3r, Green.

2006, Apr. 3
1372-1373 A427   Set of 2   4.00 4.00

Saudi Post
Mailboxes
A428

2006, Apr. 22
1374 A428 2r multi   1.60 1.60

King Saud
University
A429

2006, May 14
1375 A429 2r multi   1.60 1.60

2006 World Cup
Soccer
Championships,
Germany
A430

Emblem and: 2r, Players. 3r, World map.

2006, May 20
1376-1377 A430   Set of 2   4.00 4.00

Gulf Cooperation Council, 25th
Anniv. — A431

Litho. With Foil Application
2006, May 25
1378 A431 2r multi   1.60 1.60

An imperf. 165x105mm stamp depicting flags of Gulf Cooperation council members sold for 5r. Value $13.50.
See Bahrain Nos. 628-629, Kuwait Nos. 1646-1647, Oman Nos. 477-478, and Qatar Nos. 1007-1008.

Saudi Center for
Organ
Transplantation
A432

2006, June 17   Litho.
1379 A432 2r multi   1.60 1.60

Al Medina
Al
Munawara
A433

2006, Sept. 5
1380 A433 2r multi   1.50 1.50

An imperf. 105x80mm stamp depicting a smaller version of No. 1380 and the doorway shown at the lower left of No. 1380 sold for 5r.

Riyadh Intl.
Book Fair
A434

2006, Sept. 9
1381 A434 2r multi   1.50 1.50

National
Day
A435

2006, Sept. 23
1382 A435 2r multi   1.50 1.50

Arabian
Horses
A436

No. 1383: a, Brown horse facing right, no shadow. b, Brown horse facing left, no shadow. c, Brown horse facing right, with shadow. d, Brown horse facing left, with shadow. e, White horse. f, Horse and colt.

2006, Nov. 13
1383   Block of 6   9.00 9.00
a.-f. A436 2r Any single   1.50 1.50

Pilgrimage
to Mecca
A437

2006, Dec. 11
1384 A437 2r multi   1.50 1.50

Kingdom of Humanity A438

2007, Apr. 23
1385 A438 2r multi   1.50 1.50

An imperf. 105x80mm stamp depicting flag and King Abdullah sold for 5r.

2006 World Cup Soccer Championships, Germany A439

2007, May 14
1386 A439 2r multi   1.50 1.50

Elimination of Poliomyelitis From Saudi Arabia — A440

2007, June 9
1387 A440 2r multi   1.50 1.50

Butterflies A441

Nos. 1388 and 1389: a, Junonia hierta. b, Melitaea deserticola. c, Funonia orithya cheesmani. d, Eyrema hecabe. e, Papilio demoleus. f, Colotis calas. g, Colotis phisadia. h, Vanessa cardui. Backgrounds differ on Nos. 1388 and 1389.

2007, Aug. 20
1388   Sheet of 8   12.00 12.00
a.-h.   A441 2r Any single   1.50 1.50
1389   Sheet of 8   18.00 18.00
a.-h.   A441 3r Any cingle   2.25 2.25

Direct Mail Conference, Riyadh — A442

No. 1390: a, PosTech 2007 emblem. b, Flags and emblems of postal services of Gulf Cooperation Council countries. c, Emblem of 13th Gulf Cooperation Council Postage Stamp Exhibition. d, Emblem for UPU Regional Roundtable and map.

2007, Nov. 11
1390 A442 2r Block of 4, #a-d   6.00 6.00

Women in Science and Education — A443

No. 1391: a, Woman teaching children. b, Woman at microscope. c, Women in classroom. d, Woman at computer in laboratory.

2007, Nov. 11
1391 A443 2r Block of 4, #a-d   6.00 6.00

Third OPEC Summit, Riyadh A444

2007, Nov. 17
1392 A444 2r multi   1.50 1.50

National Day A445

2007, Dec. 1
1393 A445 2r multi   1.50 1.50

Pilgrimage to Mecca A446

2007, Dec. 9   Litho.   Perf. 14
1394 A446 2r multi   1.50 1.50

Harmony Through Intellectual Dialogue — A447

2007, Dec. 29
1395 A447 2r multi   1.50 1.50

Camels — A448

No. 1396: a, Al majaheem. b, Al wad'h. c, Al shog'h. d, Al shoe'l.

2008, Apr. 21
1396 A448 2r Block of 4, #a-d   6.00 6.00

An imperf. 105x75mm stamp depicting smaller versions of Nos. 1396a-1396d sold for 5r.

Aramco, 75th Anniv. — A449

No. 1397: a, Workmen on oil drilling platform. b, Scuba diver and fish. c, Child's drawing of oil drilling. d, Child's drawing of Saudi people.

2008, May 20   Perf. 13¾x14
1397 A449 2r Block of 4, #a-d   6.00 6.00

Development of Riyadh, 50th Anniv. — A450

2008, June 21   Perf. 14
1398 A450 2r multi   1.50 1.50

An imperf. 105x80mm stamp depicting Riyadh and King Abdullah sold for 5r.

Intl. Electrotechnical Commission, Cent. — A451

2008, July 19
1399 A451 2r multi   1.50 1.50

A souvenir sheet containing two perf. 13¾x13¼ stamps for Arab Postal Day sold for 10r.

Pilgrimage to Mecca A452

2008, Dec. 1   Litho.   Perf. 14
1400 A452 2r multi   1.50 1.50

Compare with types A437 and A446.

King Abdullah University of Science and Technology — A453

2009, Sept. 23   Perf. 13¾x14
1401 A453 2r multi   1.50 1.50

An imperf. 105x75mm stamp depicting King Abdullah and the university sold for 5r.

Jerusalem, Capital of Arab Culture — A454

2009, Oct. 25   Perf. 14
1402 A454 2r multi   1.50 1.50

National Day A455

2009, Nov. 18
1403 A455 2r multi   1.50 1.50

Pilgrimage to Mecca — A456

2009, Nov. 18   Perf. 13¾x14
1404 A456 2r multi   1.50 1.50

Organization of Petroleum Exporting Countries, 50th Anniv. — A457

2010, Jan. 9   Perf. 14
1405 A457 2r multi   1.50 1.50

Janandriyah
Festival, 25th
Anniv. — A458

2010, Nov. 9   *Perf. 14*
1406 A458 2r multi   1.50 1.50

National Day — A459

2010, Nov. 10   *Perf. 13¾x14*
1407 A459 2r multi   1.50 1.50

Souvenir Sheet

Pilgrimage to Mecca — A460

No. 1408: a, Pilgrims and train. b, Pilgrims, train, King Abdullah, Mecca Royal Clock Hotel Tower, Holy Ka'aba. c, Mecca Royal Clock Hotel Tower, Holy Ka'aba, clock.

2010, Nov. 10   *Perf. 14*
1408 A460 2r Sheet of 3, #a-c, + 3 labels   4.50 4.50

Miniature Sheets

Jewelry — A461

No. 1409: a, Bracelet with ruby. b, Gold bracelet. c, Three horseshoe bracelets. d, Silver armlets. e, Silver bangles. f, Two bracelets.
No. 1410 — Stamps with gray brown background: a, Headdress ornament. b, Earrings. c, Earrings with hooks visible at top. d, Head ornament. e, Rings. f, Forehead ornament.
No. 1411 — Stamps with pink background: a, Gold, cornelian and ruby necklace. b, Silver necklace with red stone. d, Waist belt. e, Necklace. f, Silver necklace with large square pendants.

2010-11   *Perf. 14*
1409 A461 2r Sheet of 6, #a-f   9.00 9.00
1410 A461 2r Sheet of 6, #a-f   9.00 9.00
1411 A461 2r Sheet of 6, #a-f   9.00 9.00
   Nos. 1409-1411 (3)   27.00 27.00

Issued: No. 1409, 12/29. No. 1410, 4/4/11; No. 1411, 9/12/11.

AIR POST STAMPS

Catalogue values for unused stamps in this section are for Never Hinged items.

Airspeed Ambassador Airliner — AP1

1949-58   **Unwmk.**   **Typo.**   *Perf. 11*
C1 AP1 1g blue green   4.50 .50
C2 AP1 3g ultra   5.75 .50
  a. 3g blue ('58)   20.00 1.75
C3 AP1 4g orange   5.75 .50
C4 AP1 10g purple   16.00 1.00
C5 AP1 20g brn ('58+)   13.50 2.25
  a. 20g chocolate ('49)   22.50 2.40
C6 AP1 100gviolet rose   150.00 22.50
   Nos. C1-C6 (6)   195.50 27.25

Imperfs. exist, not regularly issued.
The 1st printings are on grayish paper and sell for more.
No. C3 exists with pin-perf 6.
+ The date for No. C5 is not definite.

Saudi Airlines Convair 440 — AP2

Type I (Saud Cartouche)
(Illustrated over No. 286)

1960-61   **Photo.**   *Perf. 14*
C7 AP2 1p dull pur & grn   .80 .30
C8 AP2 2p grn & dull pur   .80 .30
C9 AP2 3p brn red & bl   .80 .30
C10 AP2 4p bl & dull pur   .80 .30
C11 AP2 5p grn & rose red   .80 .30
C12 AP2 6p ocher & slate   1.40 .30
C13 AP2 8p rose & gray ol   1.50 .30
C14 AP2 9p purple & red brn   2.25 .30
C15 AP2 10p blk & dl red brn   6.50 .60
C16 AP2 15p bl & bis brn   6.50 .30
C17 AP2 20p bis brn & emer   6.50 .45
C18 AP2 30p sep & Prus grn   15.00 1.40
C19 AP2 50p green & indigo   32.50 .95
C20 AP2 100p gray & dk brn   65.00 2.50
C21 AP2 200p dk vio & black   100.00 3.75
   Nos. C7-C21 (15)   241.15 12.35

Nos. C7-C18 exist imperf., probably not regularly issued.

1963-64   **Photo.**   **Wmk. 337**
   Size: 27½x22mm
C24 AP2 1p lilac & green   3.25 .30
C25 AP2 2p green & dull pur   12.00 .30
C26 AP2 4p blue & dull pur   4.50 .30
C27 AP2 6p ocher & slate   12.00 .95
C28 AP2 8p rose & gray olive   22.50 1.90
C29 AP2 9p pur & red brn ('64)   15.00 1.25
   Nos. C24-C29 (6)   69.25 5.00

Redrawn
   Perf. 13½x13
1964   **Wmk. 337**   **Litho.**
   Size: 28½x23mm
C30 AP2 3p brn red & dull bl   9.00 1.00
C31 AP2 10p blk & dk red brn   16.00 1.50
C32 AP2 20p bis brn & emer   35.00 3.50
   Nos. C30-C32 (3)   60.00 6.00

Nos. C30-C32 are widely spaced in the sheet, producing large margins.

Saudi Airline Boeing 720-B Jet — AP3

Type I (Saud Cartouche)
(Illustrated over No. 286)

1965-70   **Unwmk.**   **Litho.**   *Perf. 14*
C33 AP3 1p lilac & green   110.00 3.75
C34 AP3 2p grn & dull pur   3,850. 125.00
C35 AP3 3p rose lil & dull bl   13.00 .25
C36 AP3 4p blue & dull pur   7.75 .25
C37 AP3 5p ol & rose red   2,525. 550.00
C38 AP3 6p ocher & slate   140.00 2.40
C39 AP3 7p rose & ol gray   8.75 .45
C40 AP3 8p rose & gray ol   110.00 2.40
C41 AP3 9p purple & red brn   7.25 .40
C42 AP3 10p blk & dk red brn   110.00 7.75
C43 AP3 11p green & bister   110.00 25.00
C44 AP3 12p orange & gray   7.75 .40
C45 AP3 13p dk green & yel grn   6.00 .40
C46 AP3 14p dk blue & org   6.00 .45
C47 AP3 15p blue & bis brn   100.00 7.75
C48 AP3 16p black & ultra   8.75 .60
C49 AP3 17p bister & sepia   7.00 .45
C50 AP3 18p dk bl & yel grn   7.00 .45
C51 AP3 19p car & dp org   7.75 .60
C52 AP3 20p bis brn & emer   190.00 8.75
C53 AP3 23p olive & bister   210.00 15.00
C54 AP3 24p dk blue & sep   7.00 .60
C55 AP3 26p ver & blue grn   7.00 .60
C56 AP3 27p ol brn & ap grn   8.00 .60
C57 AP3 31p car rose & rose red   10.00 .75
C58 AP3 33p red & dull pur   13.00 .75

The 50p, 100p and 200p exist but were not placed in use.
Issue years: 1966, 1p, 3p, 7p, 10p, 12p-14p; 16p-19p; 1969, 5p, 11p; 1970, 2p, 6p, 8p, 15p, 20p; others, 1965.

Type II (Faisal Cartouche)
1966-78   **Unwmk.**   **Litho.**   *Perf. 14*
C59 AP3 1p dull pur & pur   25.00 1.10
C60 AP3 2p green & dull pur   25.00 1.75
C61 AP3 3p brn red & dull bl   25.00 .55
C62 AP3 4p blue & dull pur   12.50 .30
C63 AP3 5p ol & rose red   2,250. 550.00
C64 AP3 6p ocher & slate   150.00 11.00
C65 AP3 7p rose & ol gray   70.00 7.75
C66 AP3 8p rose & gray ol   95.00 13.50
C67 AP3 9p purple & red brn   6.25 .65
C68 AP3 10p blk & dull red brn   20.00 1.10
C69 AP3 11p green & bister   15.00 .55
C70 AP3 12p orange & gray   55.00 4.25
C71 AP3 13p dk grn & yel grn   17.50 1.10
C72 AP3 14p dk blue & org   16.00 1.75
C73 AP3 15p blue & bis brn   13.50 .85
C74 AP3 16p black & ultra   20.00 3.25
C75 AP3 17p bister & sepia   17.50 1.75
C76 AP3 18p dk bl & yel grn   16.00 2.75
C77 AP3 19p carmine & org   22.50 1.10
C78 AP3 20p brn & brt grn   210.00 15.00
C79 AP3 23p olive & bister   27.50 3.25
C80 AP3 24p dk blue & blk   32.50 3.25
C83 AP3 31p car rose & rose red   —
C84 AP3 33p red & dull pur   13.50 .55
C85 AP3 50p emer & ind   700.00 210.00
C86 AP3 100p gray & dk brn   950.00 325.00
C87 AP3 200p dk vio & blk   1,125. 210.00

The existence of 26p and 27p denominations has been reported.
The status of the 31p has been questioned. If it exists it may not have been issued.
Issue years: 1968, 4p, 33p; 1969, 7p; 1970, 8p, 9p, 20p; 1971, 13p, 16p; 1974, 50p, 200p; 1975, 12p, 14p, 15p, 17p, 19p, 24p; 1976, 18p; 1978, 31p, 100p; others, 1966.

1968-71   **Wmk. 361**   **Litho.**   *Perf. 14*
C88 AP3 1p lilac & green   8.25 .25
C89 AP3 2p green & lilac   10.50 .25
C90 AP3 3p rose lil & dull bl   50.00 2.40
C91 AP3 4p blue & dull pur   13.00 1.50
C92 AP3 7p rose & gray   13.00 2.10
C93 AP3 8p red & gray ol   52.50 8.25
C94 AP3 9p pur & red brn   72.50 10.00
C95 AP3 10p blk & dull red brn   45.00 4.75
   Nos. C88-C95 (8)   264.75 29.50

Issue years: 1969, 3p, 10p; 1970, 4p; 1971, 7p-9p; others, 1968.

Falcon — AP4

   Perf. 13½x14
1968-71   **Litho.**   **Wmk. 361**
C96 AP4 1p green & red brn   18.50 .30
C97 AP4 4p dk red & red brn   275.00 19.00
C98 AP4 10p blue & red brn   32.50 4.75
C99 AP4 20p green & red brn ('71)   60.00 9.75
   Nos. C96-C99 (4)   386.00 33.80

Nine other denominations were printed but are not known to have been issued.

HEJAZ POSTAGE DUE STAMPS

From Old Door at El Ashraf Barsbai in Shari el Ashrafiya, Cairo — D1

   Serrate Roulette 13
1917, June 27   **Typo.**   **Unwmk.**
LJ1 D1 20pa red   3.25 2.00
LJ2 D1 1pi blue   3.50 2.00
LJ3 D1 2pi magenta   3.75 2.00
   Nos. LJ1-LJ3 (3)   10.50 6.00

For overprints see Nos. LJ4-LJ10, LJ17-LJ25, J9.

Nos. LJ1-LJ3 Overprinted in Black or Red — a

Type a
1921, Dec.
LJ4 D1 20pa red   20.00 2.75
  a. Double overprint, one at left   140.00
  b. Overprint at left   30.00 20.00
LJ5 D1 1pi blue (R)   7.00 3.50
LJ6 D1 1pi bl, ovpt. at left   30.00 18.00
  a. Overprint at right   27.50 32.50
LJ7 D1 2pi magenta   12.50 7.25
  a. Double overprint, one at left   62.50
  b. Overprint at left   27.50
   Nos. LJ4-LJ7 (4)   69.50 31.50

Nos. LJ1-LJ3 Overprinted in Black — b

Type b
1922, Jan.
LJ8 D1 20pa red   25.00 27.50
  a. Overprint at left   35.00
LJ9 D1 1pi blue   5.00 3.25
  a. Overprint at left   45.00
LJ10 D1 2pi magenta   5.00 3.25
  a. Overprint at left   32.50
   Nos. LJ8-LJ10 (3)   35.00 34.00

Regular issue of
1922 Overprinted

Black Overprint

1923			**Perf. 11½**	
LJ11	A7	½pi red	4.25	1.40
a.		Inverted overprint	50.00	
LJ12	A7	1pi dark blue	7.50	1.40
a.		Inverted overprint	80.00	
b.		Double overprint	125.00	
LJ13	A7	2pi orange	5.00	1.75
a.		Inverted overprint	47.50	
		Nos. LJ11-LJ13 (3)	16.75	4.55
1924				
Blue Overprint				
LJ14	A7	½pi red	17.50	2.75
a.		Inverted overprint	80.00	
LJ15	A7	1pi dark blue	37.50	2.75
a.		Inverted overprint	100.00	
LJ16	A7	2pi orange	27.50	4.50
a.		Inverted overprint	80.00	
		Nos. LJ14-LJ16 (3)	82.50	10.00

This overprint reads "Mustahaq" (Due).

Jedda Issues

Nos. LJ1-LJ3
Overprinted in Red or
Blue (Overprint reads
up in illustration)

Jedda issues were also used in Medina and
Yambo. **Used values for #L51-L186 and
LJ17-LJ39 are for genuine cancels.** Privately applied cancels exist for "Mekke"
(Mecca, bilingual or all Arabic), Khartoum,
Cairo, as well as for Jeddah. Many private
cancels have wrong dates, some as early
as 1916. These are worth half the used
values.

1925, Jan.		**Serrate Roulette 13**		
LJ17	D1	20pa red (R)	375.00	350.00
LJ18	D1	20pa red (Bl)	75.00	
LJ19	D1	1pi blue (R)	20.00	18.00
LJ20	D1	1pi blue (Bl)	27.50	25.00
LJ21	D1	2pi mag (Bl)	15.00	14.00
Overprint Reading Down				
LJ17a	D1	20pa	550.00	550.00
LJ18a	D1	20pa	450.00	
LJ19a	D1	1pi	18.00	18.00
LJ20a	D1	1pi	67.50	80.00
LJ21a	D1	2pi	60.00	60.00

Nos. LJ1-LJ3
Overprinted in Blue or
Red

1925				
LJ22	D1	20pa red (Bl)	450.00	425.00
a.		Inverted overprint	325.00	325.00
LJ24	D1	1pi blue (R)	25.00	27.50
a.		Inverted overprint	32.50	32.50
LJ25	D1	2pi magenta (Bl)	20.00	18.00
a.		Inverted overprint	35.00	45.00
b.		Double overprint	350.00	

No. LJ2 with this overprint in blue is bogus.

Regular Issues of 1922-24 Overprinted

a

---

and Handstamped

b

1925			**Perf. 11½**	
LJ26	A7	⅛pi red brown	20.00	18.00
b.		Pair, one without hand-		
		stamp	100.00	—
c.		Overprint inverted	60.00	—
d.		Violet handstamp	75.00	—
LJ27	A7	½pi red	27.50	25.00
b.		Pair, one without hand-		
		stamp	100.00	—
c.		Overprint inverted	60.00	—
LJ28	A7	1pi dark blue	20.00	18.00
b.		Pair, one without hand-		
		stamp	100.00	—
c.		Overprint inverted	60.00	—
LJ29	A7	1½pi violet	22.50	18.00
b.		Pair, one without hand-		
		stamp	100.00	—
c.		Overprint inverted	60.00	—
d.		Violet handstamp	75.00	—
LJ30	A7	2pi orange	25.00	20.00
b.		Pair, one without hand-		
		stamp	100.00	—
c.		Overprint inverted	60.00	—
d.		Violet handstamp	75.00	—
LJ31	A7	3pi olive brown	25.00	20.00
b.		Pair, one without hand-		
		stamp	100.00	—
c.		Overprint inverted	60.00	—
LJ32	A7	3pi dull red	50.00	45.00
b.		Pair, one without hand-		
		stamp	100.00	—
c.		Overprint inverted	60.00	—
d.		Violet handstamp	75.00	—
LJ33	A7	5pi olive green	25.00	20.00
b.		Pair, one without hand-		
		stamp	100.00	—
c.		Overprint inverted	60.00	—
LJ34	A7	10pi vio & dk brn	30.00	25.00
b.		Pair, one without hand-		
		stamp	100.00	—
c.		Overprint inverted	60.00	—
d.		Violet handstamp	75.00	—
		Nos. LJ26-LJ34 (9)	245.00	209.00

The printed overprint (a), consisting of the
three top lines of Arabic, was used alone for
the first issue (Nos. LJ26a-LJ34a). The "postage due" box was so small and indistinct that
its equivalent in larger characters was added
by boxed handstamp (b) at bottom of each
stamp for the second issue (Nos. LJ26-LJ34).
The handstamped overprint (b) is found
double, inverted, etc. It is also known in dark
violet.
Counterfeits exist of both overprint and
handstamp.

Without Boxed Handstamp "b"

LJ26a	A7	⅛pi red brown	42.50
LJ27a	A7	½pi red	42.50
LJ28a	A7	1pi dark blue	42.50
LJ29a	A7	1½pi violet	42.50
LJ30a	A7	2pi orange	42.50
LJ31a	A7	3pi olive brown	42.50
LJ32a	A7	3pi dull red	42.50
LJ33a	A7	5pi olive green	55.00
LJ34a	A7	10pi vio & dk brn	55.00
		Nos. LJ26a-LJ34a (9)	407.50

Regular Issue of
1922 Overprinted

and Handstamped

LJ35	A7	½pi red	150.00	140.00
LJ36	A7	1½pi violet	150.00	140.00
a.		Overprint in red, boxed		
		handstamp violet		1,400.
LJ37	A7	2pi orange	200.00	175.00
LJ38	A7	3pi olive brown	150.00	140.00
LJ39	A7	5pi olive green	150.00	140.00
		Nos. LJ35-LJ39 (5)	800.00	735.00
		Set, never hinged	1,000.	

Counterfeits exist of Nos. LJ4-LJ39.

Arabic Numeral of Value
D2   D3

1925, May-June			**Perf. 11½**	
LJ40	D2	½pi light blue	3.00	
LJ41	D2	1pi orange	3.00	
LJ42	D2	2pi lt brown	3.00	
LJ43	D2	3pi pink	3.00	
		Nos. LJ40-LJ43 (4)	12.00	

Nos. LJ40-LJ43 were not issued without overprint.
Nos. LJ40-LJ43 exist imperforate. Impressions in colors other than issued are trial color
proofs.

Black Overprint

1925				
LJ44	D3	½pi light blue	3.00	
LJ45	D3	1pi orange	3.00	
LJ46	D3	2pi light brown	3.00	
LJ47	D3	3pi pink	3.00	
		Nos. LJ44-LJ47 (4)	12.75	

Nos. LJ44-LJ47 exist with either Jedda or
Cairo overprints and the tablets normally read
upward. Values are for Cairo overprints; Jedda
overprints sell for more.

Red Overprint

LJ48	D3	½pi light blue	3.75
LJ49	D3	1pi orange	3.75
LJ50	D3	2pi light brown	3.75
LJ51	D3	3pi pink	3.75

Blue Overprint

LJ52	D3	½pi light blue	3.75	
LJ53	D3	1pi orange	3.75	
LJ54	D3	2pi light brown	3.75	
LJ55	D3	3pi pink	3.75	
		Nos. LJ40-LJ55 (16)	54.75	

Red and blue overprints are from Cairo.
Nos. LJ44-LJ55 exist imperf.

NEJDI ADMINISTRATION OF HEJAZ POSTAGE DUE STAMPS

Nos. LJ11-LJ16
Handstamped in
Blue, Red or Black

1925, Apr.-June Unwmk. Perf. 11½				
J1	A7	½pi red (Bl)	27.50	27.50
J2	A7	1pi lt blue (R)	55.00	55.00
a.		1pi dark blue (R)	35.00	35.00
J3	A7	2pi yel buff (Bl)	55.00	55.00
a.		2pi orange (Bl)	47.50	47.50
		Nos. J1-J3 (3)	137.50	137.50

The original boxed overprint is printed on
Nos. J1, J2a and J3a. Nos. J2-J3 are overprinted on a new printing of the basic stamps
with handstamped boxed overprints.

Same, with Postage Due Overprint in Blue

J4	A7	½pi red (Bl)	140.00
J5	A7	1pi dk blue (R)	550.00
J6	A7	2pi orange (Bl)	175.00

On Hejaz Stamps of 1922-24

Handstamped in
Blue

J7	A7	½pi red (Bl & Bl)	16.00	16.00
J8	A7	3pi brn red (Bl & Bl)	19.00	19.00

Handstamped in Blue,
Black or Violet

See note before No. 35.

On Hejaz No. LJ9
Serrate Roulette 13½

J9	D1	1pi blue (V)	60.00	27.50

Same Overprint on
Hejaz Stamps of
1924 with additional
Handstamp in
Black, Blue or Red

Perf. 11½

J10	A7	3pi brn red (Bl & Bk)	11.00	11.00
J11	A7	3pi brn red (Bk & Bl)	11.00	11.00

Same Handstamps on Hejaz Railway Tax Stamps

J12	R3	1pi blue, type 1 (Bk & R)	12.00	12.00
a.		Type 2	40.00	
		never hinged	60.00	
J13	R3	2pi ocher, type 1 (Bl & Bk)	12.00	12.00
a.		Type 2	40.00	
		never hinged	60.00	
J14	R3	5pi green, type 1 (Bk & R)	20.00	20.00
a.		Type 2	60.00	
		never hinged	90.00	
J15	R3	5pi green, type 1 (V & BK)	20.00	9.00
a.		Type 2	60.00	
		never hinged	90.00	
		Nos. J10-J15 (6)	86.00	75.00

The second handstamp, which is struck on
the lower part of the Postage Due Stamps, is
the word Mustahaq (Due) in various forms.
#J13 exists with 2nd handstamp in blue.

Hejaz-Nejd

D1

1926		**Typo.**	**Perf. 11**	
J16	D1	½pi carmine	4.00	.65
J17	D1	2pi orange	4.00	.65
J18	D1	6pi light brown	4.00	.65
		Nos. J16-J18 (3)	12.00	1.95

Nos. J16-J18 exist with perf. 14, 14x11 and
11x14, and imperf. These sell for six times the
values quoted.
Nos. J16-J18 in colors other than listed
(both perf. and imperf.) are proofs.
Counterfeit note after No. 80 also applies to
Nos. J16-J21.

Pan-Islamic Congress Issue
Postage Due Stamps of 1926
Handstamped like Regular Issue

J19	D1	½pi carmine	5.50	4.50
J20	D1	2pi orange	5.50	4.50
J21	D1	6pi light brown	5.50	4.50
		Nos. J19-J21 (3)	16.50	13.50

D2

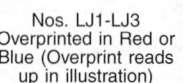

1927			Perf. 11½	
J22	D2	1pi slate	18.00	.45
a.	Inscription reads "2 piastres" in upper right circle		200.00	100.00
J23	D2	2pi dark violet	5.75	.45

Saudi Arabia

Saudi Arabia
No. 161
Handstamped
in Black

1935			
J24	A9	½g dark carmine	350.00

Two types of overprint.

D3

1937-39				Unwmk.	
J25	D3	½g org brn ('39)	20.00	20.00
J26	D3	1g light blue	20.00	20.00
J27	D3	2g rose vio ('39)	29.00	13.50
	Nos. J25-J27 (3)		69.00	53.50

Catalogue values for unused stamps in this section, from this point to the end of the section, are for Never Hinged items.

D4

1961			Litho.	Perf. 13x13½	
J28	D4	1p purple	5.00	5.00
J29	D4	2p green	8.50	4.00
J30	D4	4p rose red	10.00	10.00
	Nos. J28-J30 (3)		23.50	19.00

The use of Postage Due stamps ceased in 1963.

OFFICIAL STAMPS

Official stamps were normally used only on external correspondence.

O1

1939		Unwmk.	Typo.	Perf. 11½	
O1	O1	3g deep ultra	5.25	2.40
		Perf. 11, 11½		
O2	O1	5g red violet	6.75	3.00
		Perf. 11		
O3	O1	20g brown	14.00	6.25
O4	O1	50g blue green	27.50	13.00
O5	O1	100g olive grn	110.00	60.00
O6	O1	200g purple	90.00	40.00
	Nos. O1-O6 (6)		253.50	124.65

Catalogue values for unused stamps in this section, from this point to the end of the section, are for Never Hinged items.

O2

1961		Litho.	Perf. 13x13½	
		Size: 18x22-22½mm		
O7	O2	1p black	1.75	.30
O8	O2	2p dark green	2.75	.50
O9	O2	3p bister	3.25	.60
O10	O2	4p dark blue	4.50	.75
O11	O2	5p rose red	5.50	.90
O12	O2	10p maroon	8.75	2.75
O13	O2	20p violet blue	15.00	5.25
O14	O2	50p dull brown	35.00	14.50
O15	O2	100p dull green	70.00	25.00
	Nos. O7-O15 (9)		146.50	50.55

Nos. O8, O10-O15 exist imperf., probably not regularly issued.

1964-65		Wmk. 337	Perf. 13½x13	
		Size: 21x26mm		
O16	O2	1p black	2.50	.55
O17	O2	2p green ('65)	4.00	1.10
O18	O2	3p bister	12.50	3.75
O19	O2	4p dark blue	9.00	2.75
O20	O2	5p rose red	11.50	1.60
	Nos. O16-O20 (5)		39.50	9.75

1965-70		Wmk. 337	Typo.	Perf. 11	
O21	O2	1p dark brown	7.00	2.40
O22	O2	2p green	7.00	2.40
O23	O2	3p bister	7.00	2.40
O24	O2	4p dark blue	7.00	2.40
O25	O2	5p deep orange	12.50	3.00
O26	O2	6p red lilac	12.50	3.00
O27	O2	7p emerald	12.50	3.00
O28	O2	8p car rose	12.50	3.00
O29	O2	9p red	250.00	
O30	O2	10p red brown	55.00	3.00
O31	O2	11p pale green	105.00	
O32	O2	12p violet	450.00	
O33	O2	13p blue	17.50	4.50
O34	O2	14p purple	17.50	4.50
O35	O2	15p orange	250.00	
O36	O2	16p black	250.00	
a.	"19" instead of "16"		750.00	
O37	O2	17p gray green	250.00	
O38	O2	18p yellow	250.00	
O39	O2	19p dp red lilac	250.00	
O39A	O2	20p lt blue green		1,500.
O40	O2	23p ultra	375.00	
O41	O2	24p yellow green	250.00	
O42	O2	26p bister	275.00	
O43	O2	27p pale lilac	275.00	
O44	O2	31p pale salmon	375.00	
O45	O2	33p yellow green	300.00	
O46	O2	50p olive bister	850.00	
O47	O2	100p ol gray ('70)	1,350.	500.00
	Nos. O21-O39,O40-O47 (27)		6,273.	

Nos. O21-O28, O30 and O33-O34 were released to the philatelic trade in 1964. Nos. O21-O47 were printed from new plates; lines of the design are heavier. The numerals have been enlarged and the P's are smaller. Head of "P" 2mm wide on 1964-65 issue, 1mm wide on 1965-70 issue.
No. O39A is only known used. All known examples are faulty.

O3

Wmk. 361, 337 (7p, 8p, 9p, 11p, 12p, 23p)				
1970-72		Litho.	Perf. 13½x14	
O48	O3	1p red brown	4.50	1.50
O49	O3	2p deep green	4.50	1.50
O50	O3	3p rose red	6.00	2.40
O51	O3	4p bright blue	7.50	3.00
O52	O3	5p brick red	7.50	3.00
O53	O3	6p orange	7.50	3.00
a.	Wmk. 337		175.00	45.00
O54	O3	7p deep salmon	175.00	
O55	O3	8p violet	325.00	
O56	O3	9p dk blue grn	325.00	
O57	O3	10p blue	9.50	9.50
a.	Wmk. 337		175.00	
O58	O3	11p olive green	325.00	
O58A	O3	12p black brown	400.00	
O59	O3	20p gray violet	24.00	7.75
a.	Wmk. 337		175.00	90.00
O59B	O3	23p ocher ('72)	375.00	
O60	O3	31p deep plum	75.00	29.00
O61	O3	50p light brown	700.00	500.00
O62	O3	100p green	700.00	325.00

Use of official stamps ceased in 1974.

NEWSPAPER STAMPS

Nos. 8, 9 and 14 with Additional Overprint in Black

1925		Unwmk.	Perf. 11½	
P1	A7	⅛pi red brown (Bk)	1,800.	1,800.
P2	A7	⅛pi red brown (V)	1,400.	900.
P3	A7	⅛pi red (V)	2,750.	1,800.

Overprint reads: "Matbu'a" (Newspaper), but these stamps were normally used for regular postage. Counterfeits exist.
The status of this set in question. The government may have declared it to be unauthorized.

POSTAL TAX STAMPS

PT1

1934, May 15		Unwmk.	Perf. 11½	
RA1	PT1	½g scarlet	100.00	4.50

No. RA1 collected a "war tax" to aid wounded of the 1934 Saudi-Yemen war.

Nos. RA2-RA8 raised funds for the Medical Aid Society.

General Hospital, Mecca PT2

PT2a

1936, Oct.			Size: 37x20mm	
RA2	PT2	½g scarlet	400.00	9.00

Type of 1936, Redrawn

1937-42			Size: 30½x18mm	
RA3	PT2a	½g scarlet	35.00	.90
a.	½g rose ('39)		60.00	1.75
b.	½g rose car, perf. 11 ('42)		125.00	6.75

General Hospital, Mecca — PT3

1943		Typo.	Perf. 11½, 11	
		Grayish Paper		
RA4	PT3	½g car rose	35.00	.25
a.	½g scarlet		35.00	.25

The 1g green and 5g indigo were not for postal use.
See Nos. RA5-RA8.

Map of Saudi Arabia Type I — (Flag inscriptions intact) — PT4

Type II — (Flag inscriptions scratched out)

1946		Unwmk.	Perf. 11½	
RA4B	PT4	½g magenta (II)	16.00	.90
c.	Type I		55.00	.90
d.	Type I, perf. 11		45.00	.90
e.	Type II, perf. 11		67.50	

Return of King Ibn Saud from Egypt.
This stamp was required on all mail during Jan.-July.

Type of 1943, Redrawn

1948-53		Litho.	Perf. 10	
RA5	PT3	⅛g rose brn ('53)	20.00	.25
c.	Perf. 11x10		27.50	2.75

Catalogue values for unused stamps in this section, from this point to the end of the section, are for Never Hinged items.

1950			Rouletted	
RA6	PT3	⅛g red brown	5.50	.25
a.	⅛g rose		7.25	.25
b.	⅛g carmine		9.00	.25

All lines in lithographed design considerably finer; some shading in center eliminated.

Type of 1943

1955-56		Photo.	Perf. 11	
RA7	PT3	⅛g rose car	8.00	.25
RA8	PT3	¼g car rose ('56)	4.75	.25

The tax on postal matter was discontinued in May, 1964.

Coat of Arms, Waves and View — PT5

		Wmk. 361		
1974, Oct.		Litho.	Perf. 14	
RA9	PT5	1r blue & multi	200.00	

Obligatory on all mailed entries in a government television contest during month of Ramadan in 1974 and 1975. The tax aided a benevolent society.

SCHLESWIG

'shles-ˌwig

LOCATION — In the northern part of the former Schleswig-Holstein Province, in northern Germany.

Schleswig was divided into North and South Schleswig after the Versailles Treaty, and plebiscites were held in 1920. North Schleswig (Zone 1) voted to join Denmark, South Schleswig to stay German.

100 Pfennig = 1 Mark
100 Ore = 1 Krone

Watermark

Wmk. 114 —
Multiple Crosses

Plebiscite Issue

Arms — A11

View of
Schleswig
A12

Perf. 14x15

1920, Jan. 25   Typo.   Wmk. 114

1	A11	2½pf gray	.25	.80
2	A11	5pf green	.25	.80
3	A11	7½pf yellow brown	.25	.80
4	A11	10pf deep rose	.25	.80
5	A11	15pf red violet	.25	.80
6	A11	20pf deep blue	.25	.80
7	A11	25pf orange	.35	.80
8	A11	35pf brown	.45	1.00
9	A11	40pf violet	.35	.80
10	A11	75pf greenish blue	.45	.80
11	A12	1m dark brown	.45	.80
12	A12	2m deep blue	.70	1.20
13	A12	5m green	1.50	1.60
14	A12	10m red	2.75	3.25
	Nos. 1-14 (14)		8.50	15.05
	Set, never hinged		40.00	

The colored portions of type A11 are white, and the white portions are colored, on Nos. 7-10.

Types of 1920
Overprinted in Blue

1920, May 20

15	A11	1o dark gray	.25	2.40
16	A11	5o green	.25	1.60
17	A11	7o yellow brn	.25	1.60
18	A11	10o rose red	.25	1.60
19	A11	15o lilac rose	.25	2.40
20	A11	20o dark blue	.25	2.75
21	A11	25o orange	.25	8.00
22	A11	35o brown	.85	14.50
23	A11	40o violet	.25	4.75
24	A11	75o greenish blue	.45	8.00
25	A12	1k dark brown	.65	13.00
26	A12	2k deep blue	7.00	47.50
27	A12	5k green	3.50	47.50
28	A12	10k red	8.00	87.50
	Nos. 15-28 (14)		22.45	243.10
	Set, never hinged		165.00	

OFFICIAL STAMPS

Nos. 1-14 Overprinted

C·I·S

1920   Wmk. 114   Perf. 14x15

O1	A11	2½pf gray	65.00	92.50
O2	A11	5pf green	65.00	110.00
O3	A11	7½pf yellow brn	65.00	92.50
O4	A11	10pf deep rose	65.00	120.00
O5	A11	15pf red violet	42.50	60.00
O6	A11	20pf dp blue	65.00	67.50
a.		Double overprint	1,500.	
O7	A11	25pf orange	125.00	175.00
a.		Inverted overprint	1,050.	
O8	A11	35pf brown	125.00	175.00
O9	A11	40pf violet	110.00	100.00
O10	A11	75pf grnsh blue	125.00	250.00
O11	A12	1m dark brown	125.00	250.00
O12	A12	2m deep blue	185.00	275.00
O13	A12	5m green	275.00	425.00
O14	A12	10m red	500.00	625.00
	Nos. O1-O14 (14)		1,937.	2,817.
	Set, never hinged		3,800.	

The letters "C.I.S." are the initials of "Commission Interalliée Slesvig," under whose auspices the plebiscites took place.

Counterfeit overprints exist.

SENEGAL

ˌse-ni-'gäl

LOCATION — West coast of Africa, bordering on the Atlantic Ocean
GOVT. — Republic
AREA — 76,000 sq. mi.
POP. — 10,051,930 (1999 est.)
CAPITAL — Dakar

The former French colony of Senegal became part of French West Africa in 1943. The Republic of Senegal was established Nov. 25, 1958. From Apr. 4, 1959, to June 20, 1960, the Republic of Senegal and the Sudanese Republic together formed the Mali Federation. After its breakup, Senegal resumed issuing its own stamps in 1960.

100 Centimes = 1 Franc

Catalogue values for unused stamps in this country are for Never Hinged items, beginning with Scott 195 in the regular postage section, Scott B16 in the in the semi-postal section, Scott C26 in the airpost section, Scott CB2 in the airpost semi-postal section, Scott J32 in the postage due section, and Scott O1 in the official section.

French Colonies Nos. 48, 49, 51, 52, 55, Type A9, Surcharged

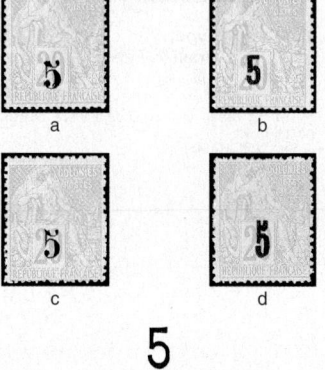

1887   Unwmk.   Perf. 14x13½
Black Surcharge

1	(a) 5c on 20c red, grn	210.00	210.00
a.	Double surcharge	500.00	
2	(b) 5c on 20c red, grn	375.00	375.00
3	(c) 5c on 20c red, grn	1,250.	1,250.
4	(d) 5c on 20c red, grn	260.00	260.00
5	(e) 5c on 20c red, grn	475.00	475.00
6	(a) 5c on 30c brn, bis	325.00	325.00
7	(b) 5c on 30c brn, bis	1,400.	1,400.
8	(d) 5c on 30c brn, bis	475.00	475.00
	Nos. 1-8 (8)	4,770.	4,770.

See Madagascar #6-7 for stamps with surcharge like "d" on 10c and 25c stamps.

f   g

h   i

j   k   l   m

9	(f) 10c on 4c cl, lav	160.00	160.00
10	(g) 10c on 4c cl, lav	240.00	240.00
11	(h) 10c on 4c cl, lav	120.00	120.00
12	(i) 10c on 4c cl, lav	120.00	120.00
a.	"1" without top stroke		
13	(f) 10c on 20c red, grn	725.00	725.00
14	(g) 10c on 20c red, grn	750.00	750.00
15	(h) 10c on 20c red, grn	650.00	650.00
16	(i) 10c on 20c red, grn	1,500.	1,500.
17	(j) 10c on 20c red, grn	750.00	750.00
18	(k) 10c on 20c red, grn	2,800.	2,800.
19	(l) 10c on 20c red, grn	750.00	750.00
20	(m) 10c on 20c red, grn	750.00	750.00

o   p

q   r

s   t

15151515

n   u   v   w

21	(n) 15c on 20c red, grn	130.00	130.00
22	(o) 15c on 20c red, grn	110.00	110.00
23	(p) 15c on 20c red, grn	87.50	87.50
24	(q) 15c on 20c red, grn	160.00	160.00
25	(r) 15c on 20c red, grn	100.00	100.00
26	(s) 15c on 20c red, grn	100.00	100.00
27	(t) 15c on 20c red, grn	260.00	260.00
28	(u) 15c on 20c red, grn	87.50	87.50
29	(v) 15c on 20c red, grn	120.00	120.00
30	(w) 15c on 20c red, grn	425.00	425.00
	Nos. 21-30 (10)	1,580.	1,580.

Counterfeits exist of Nos. 1-34.

French Colonies Stamps of 1881-86
Surcharged

1892

Black Surcharge

31	A9 75c on 15c blue	450.00	200.00
a.	"SENEGAL" double		950.00
32	A9 1fr on 5c grn, grnsh	450.00	200.00
a.	"SENEGAL" double		14,750.
b.	"SENEGAL" omitted		2,800.
c.	"1F" double		325.00

"SENEGAL" in Red

33	A9 75c on 15c blue	15,250.	5,500.
34	A9 1fr on 5c grn, grnsh	6,500.	1,600.

Navigation and
Commerce — A24

1892-1900   Typo.   Perf. 14x13½
Name of Colony in Blue or Carmine

35	A24	1c blk, lil bl	1.60	1.20
36	A24	2c brn, buff	2.75	2.40
37	A24	4c claret, lav	2.75	2.00
38	A24	5c grn, grnsh	3.25	2.40
39	A24	5c yel grn ('00)	2.75	1.60
40	A24	10c blk, lav	8.00	6.50
41	A24	10c red ('00)	6.00	2.00
42	A24	15c bl, quadrille paper	15.00	2.40
43	A24	15c gray ('00)	7.25	2.75
44	A24	20c red, grn	12.00	6.50
45	A24	20c blk, rose	18.50	7.25
46	A24	25c blue ('00)	45.00	37.50
47	A24	30c brn, bis	20.00	9.50
48	A24	40c red, straw	28.00	24.00
49	A24	50c car, rose	45.00	32.50
50	A24	50c brn, az ('00)	52.50	47.50
51	A24	75c vio, org	22.50	21.00
52	A24	1fr brnz grn, straw	26.00	23.00
	Nos. 35-52 (18)		318.85	232.00

Perf. 13½x14 stamps are counterfeits.
For surcharges see Nos. 53-56, 73-78.

Stamps of 1892 Surcharged

1903

53	A24	5c on 40c red, straw	20.00	20.00
54	A24	10c on 50c car, rose	28.00	28.00
55	A24	10c on 75c vio, org	28.00	28.00
56	A24	10c on 1fr brnz grn, straw	92.50	92.50
	Nos. 53-56 (4)		168.50	168.50

General
Louis
Faidherbe
A25

Oil Palms — A26

Dr. Noel
Eugène
Ballay
A27

1906   **Typo.**
"SÉNÉGAL" in Red or Blue

57	A25	1c slate	1.60	1.60
a.		"SENEGAL" omitted	160.00	160.00
58	A25	2c choc (R)	2.00	1.60
58A	A25	2c choc (Bl)	3.25	2.40
59	A25	4c choc, *gray bl*	2.75	2.40
60	A25	5c green	3.25	1.20
a.		"SENEGAL" omitted		130.00
61	A25	10c car (Bl)	13.50	1.20
a.		"SENEGAL" omitted	500.00	500.00
62	A25	15c violet	8.00	4.00
63	A26	20c blk, *az*	9.50	4.75
64	A26	25c bl, *pnksh*	4.00	3.25
65	A26	30c choc, *pnksh*	9.50	6.50
66	A26	35c blk, *yellow*	32.50	3.25
a.		"SENEGAL" double	240.00	260.00
67	A26	40c car, *az* (Bl)	13.00	7.25
67A	A26	45c choc, *grnsh*	25.00	17.00
68	A26	50c dp violet	13.50	7.25
69	A27	75c bl, *org*	10.50	8.75
70	A27	1fr blk, *azure*	32.50	32.50
71	A27	2fr blue, *pink*	40.00	40.00
72	A27	5fr car, *straw* (Bl)	72.50	72.50
		Nos. 57-72 (18)	296.85	217.40

Stamps of 1892-1900 Surcharged in
Carmine or Black

1912

73	A24	5c on 15c gray (C)	1.20	1.20
74	A24	5c on 20c red, *grn*	2.40	2.40
75	A24	5c on 30c brn, *bis* (C)	1.60	1.60
76	A24	10c on 40c red, *straw*	2.00	2.00
77	A24	10c on 50c car, *rose*	4.75	5.50
78	A24	10c on 75c vio, *org*	7.25	8.75
		Nos. 73-78 (6)	19.20	21.45

Two spacings between the surcharged
numerals found on Nos. 73 to 78. For detailed
listings, see the *Scott Classic Specialized Catalogue of Stamps and Covers.*

Senegalese
Preparing
Food
A28

1914-33   **Typo.**

79	A28	1c ol brn & vio	.25	.25
80	A28	2c black & blue	.30	.30
81	A28	4c gray & brn	.30	.30
82	A28	5c yel grn & bl grn	.50	.25
83	A28	5c blk & rose ('22)	.25	.25
a.		Center double	340.00	
84	A28	10c org red & rose	1.45	.25
85	A28	10c yel grn & bl grn ('22)	.30	.30
86	A28	10c red brn & bl ('25)	.40	.40
87	A28	15c red org & brn vio ('17)	.40	.40
88	A28	20c choc & blk	.40	.30
89	A28	20c grn & bl grn ('26)	.55	.55
90	A28	20c db & lt bl ('27)	.80	.80
91	A28	25c ultra & bl	1.20	1.00
92	A28	25c red & blk ('22)	.65	.30
93	A28	30c black & rose	.75	.30
94	A28	30c red org & rose ('22)	.65	.30
95	A28	30c gray & bl ('26)	.55	.30
96	A28	30c dl grn & dp grn ('28)	.80	.55
97	A28	35c orange & vio	.70	.50
98	A28	40c violet & grn	.90	.50
99	A28	45c bl & ol brn	1.90	1.25
100	A28	45c rose & bl ('22)	.95	.50
101	A28	45c rose & ver ('25)	.80	.80
102	A28	45c ol brn & org ('28)	3.50	3.00
103	A28	50c vio brn & bl	1.90	1.20
104	A28	50c ultra & bl ('22)	2.40	2.10

105	A28	50c red org & grn ('26)	.65	.40
106	A28	60c vio, *pnksh* ('26)	.65	.40
107	A28	65c rose red & dp ('28)	1.75	1.60
108	A28	75c gray & rose	1.20	.70
109	A28	75c dk bl & lt bl ('25)	1.20	1.20
110	A28	75c rose & gray bl ('26)	2.00	1.05
111	A28	90c brn red & rose ('30)	5.50	5.50
112	A28	1fr violet & blk	1.20	.70
113	A28	1fr blue ('26)	1.05	.40
114	A28	1fr blk & gray bl ('28)	1.75	1.05
115	A28	1.10fr bl grn & blk ('28)	4.25	4.50
116	A28	1.25fr dp grn & dp org ('33)	1.60	1.60
117	A28	1.50fr dk bl & bl ('30)	3.25	3.25
118	A28	1.75fr dk brn & Prus bl ('33)	7.25	1.60
119	A28	2fr carmine & bl	4.00	2.60
120	A28	2fr lt bl & brn ('22)	2.75	1.05
121	A28	3fr red vio ('30)	4.00	2.40
122	A28	5fr green & vio	5.50	2.00
		Nos. 79-122 (44)	73.10	49.10

Nos. 79, 82, 84 and 97 are on both ordinary
and chalky paper.
For surcharges see Nos. 123-137, B1-B2.

No. 108
and Type of
1914
Srchd.

1922-25

123	A28	60c on 75c vio, *pnksh*	1.10	1.10
a.		Double surcharge	140.00	
124	A28	65c on 15c red org & dl vio ('25)	1.60	1.60
125	A28	85c on 15c red org & dl vio ('25)	1.60	1.60
126	A28	85c on 75c ('25)	1.60	1.60

No. 87
Srchd. in
Various
Colors

1922

127	A28	1c on 15c (Bk)	.80	.80
128	A28	2c on 15c (Bl)	.80	.80
129	A28	4c on 15c (G)	.80	.80
130	A28	5c on 15c (R)	.80	.80
		Nos. 123-130 (8)	9.10	9.10

Stamps and Type of 1914 Surcharged
with New Value and Bars in Black or
Red

1924-27

131	A28	25c on 5fr grn & vio	.95	.95
132	A28	90c on 75c brn red & cer ('27)	1.60	1.20
a.		Double surcharge	140.00	125.00
133	A28	1.25fr on 1fr bl & lt bl (R) ('26)	1.20	1.20
134	A28	1.50fr on 1fr dk bl & ultra ('27)	1.60	1.20
135	A28	3fr on 5fr mag & ol brn ('27)	4.00	2.40
136	A28	10fr on 5fr dk bl & red org ('27)	8.75	4.00
137	A28	20fr on 5fr vio & ol bis ('27)	8.75	8.00
		Nos. 131-137 (7)	26.85	18.95

> Common Design Types
> pictured following the introduction

Colonial Exposition Issue
Common Design Types
Name of Country Typographed in
Black

1931   **Engr.**   **Perf. 12½**

138	CD70	40c deep green	4.50	4.50
139	CD71	50c violet	4.50	4.50
140	CD72	90c red orange	4.50	4.50
a.		"SENEGAL" double	175.00	
141	CD73	1.50fr dull blue	4.50	4.50
		Nos. 138-141 (4)	18.00	18.00

Faidherbe
Bridge, St.
Louis
A29

Diourbel
Mosque
A30

1935-40   **Perf. 12½x12**

142	A29	1c violet blue	.25	.25
143	A29	2c brown	.25	.25
144	A29	3c violet ('40)	.30	.30
145	A29	4c gray blue	.25	.25
146	A29	5c orange red	.25	.25
147	A29	10c violet	.25	.25
148	A29	15c black	.25	.25
149	A29	20c dk carmine	.30	.25
150	A29	25c black brn	.30	.25
151	A29	30c green	.30	.30
152	A29	40c rose lake	.30	.30
153	A29	45c dk blue grn	.30	.30
154	A30	50c red orange	.30	.25
155	A30	60c violet ('40)	.30	.30
156	A30	65c dk violet	.30	.30
157	A30	70c red brn ('40)	.80	.80
158	A30	75c brown	.80	.65
159	A30	90c rose car	2.10	1.60
160	A30	1fr violet	10.50	2.60
161	A30	1.25fr redsh brn	1.35	.95
162	A30	1.25fr rose car ('39)	.95	.95
163	A30	1.40fr dk bl grn ('40)	.95	.95
164	A30	1.50fr dk blue	.30	.30
165	A30	1.60fr pck bl ('40)	.95	.95
166	A30	1.75fr dk blue grn	.40	.30
167	A30	2fr blue	.80	.30
168	A30	3fr green	.75	.50
169	A30	5fr black brn	.80	.75
170	A30	10fr rose lake	1.75	1.10
171	A30	20fr grnsh slate	1.75	1.10
		Nos. 142-171 (30)	29.15	17.85

Nos. 143, 148 and 156 surcharged with new
values are listed under French West Africa.
For surcharges see Nos. B9, B11-B12.

Paris International Exposition Issue
Common Design Types

1937   **Perf. 13**

172	CD74	20c deep violet	2.00	2.00
a.		Sénégal omitted	100.00	110.00
173	CD75	30c dark green	2.00	2.00
174	CD76	40c car rose	2.00	2.00
175	CD77	50c dark brown	1.60	1.60
176	CD78	90c red	1.60	1.60
177	CD79	1.50fr ultra	2.00	2.00
		Nos. 172-177 (6)	11.20	11.20

Colonial Arts Exhibition Issue
Souvenir Sheet
Common Design Type

1937   **Unwmk.**   **Imperf.**

178	CD76	3fr rose violet	8.75	10.50
a.		Inscriptions inverted	1,600.	

Senegalese
Woman — A31

1938-40   **Perf. 12x12½, 12½x12**

179	A31	35c green	.65	.65
180	A31	55c chocolate	.65	.65
181	A31	80c violet	1.10	.75
182	A31	90c lt rose vio ('39)	.80	.80
183	A31	1fr car lake	2.10	1.20
184	A31	1fr cop brn ('40)	.70	.70
185	A31	1.75fr ultra	1.10	.80
186	A31	2.25fr ultra ('39)	1.05	1.05
187	A31	2.50fr black ('40)	1.50	1.50
		Nos. 179-187 (9)	9.65	8.10

For surcharge see No. B10.

Caillié Issue
Common Design Type

1939   **Engr.**   **Perf. 12½x12**

188	CD81	90c org brn & org	.80	.80
189	CD81	2fr brt vio	1.20	1.20
190	CD81	2.25fr ultra & dk bl	1.20	1.20
		Nos. 188-190 (3)	3.20	3.20

For No. 188 surcharged 20fr and 50fr, see
French West Africa.

New York World's Fair Issue
Common Design Type

1939   **Perf. 12½x12**

191	CD82	1.25fr car lake	.95	.95
192	CD82	2.25fr ultra	1.05	1.05

Diourbel
Mosque
and
Marshal
Pétain
A32

1941   **Engr.**

193	A32	1fr green	1.00	
194	A32	2.50fr blue	1.00	

Nos. 193-194 were issued by the Vichy government in France, but were not placed on
sale in Senegal.
For surcharges, see Nos. B15A-B15B.

Types of 1935-38 Without "RF"
1943-44   **Perf. 12½**

194A	A29	40c rose lake	1.00	
194B	A30	1fr dk red vio & blk	1.60	
194C	A30	1.50fr bl grn & blk	1.10	
194D	A30	2fr Prus blue & red	1.10	
194E	A30	3fr grn & red vio	1.40	
194F	A30	5fr dp ol brn & lake	1.40	
194G	A30	10fr rose lake & blue	1.40	
194H	A30	20fr gray bl & red	3.50	
		Nos. 194A-194H (8)	12.50	

Nos. 194A-194H were issued by the Vichy
government in France, but were not placed on
sale in Senegal.

See French West Africa No. 69 for
additional stamp inscribed "Senegal"
and "Afrique Occidentale Francaise."

> Catalogue values for unused
> stamps in this section, from this
> point to the end of the section, are
> for Never Hinged items.

Republic

Roan
Antelope — A33

Animals: 10fr, Savannah buffalo, horiz. 15fr,
Wart hog. 20fr, Giant eland. 25fr, Bushbuck,
horiz. 85fr, Defassa waterbuck.

1960   **Unwmk.**   **Engr.**   **Perf. 13**

195	A33	5fr brn, grn & claret	.30	.25
196	A33	10fr grn & brn	.55	.25
197	A33	15fr blk, claret & org brn	.65	.30
198	A33	20fr brn, grn, ocher & sal	.85	.40
199	A33	25fr brn, lt grn & org	1.40	.60
200	A33	85fr brn, grn, olive & bis	3.25	1.40
		Nos. 195-200 (6)	7.00	3.20

Imperforates
Most Senegal stamps from 1960
onward exist imperforate in issued
and trial colors, and also in small
presentation sheets in issued colors.

72 SENEGAL

Allegory of Independent State — A34

1961, Apr. 4
201 A34 25fr bl, choc & grn .80 .25
Independence Day, Apr. 4.

Wrestling
A35

1fr, Pirogues racing. 2fr, Horse race. 30fr, Male tribal dance. 45fr, Lion game.

1961, Sept. 30 **Perf. 13**
202 A35 50c ol, bl & choc .25 .25
203 A35 1fr grn, bl & maroon .25 .25
204 A35 2fr ultra, bis & sepia .70 .25
205 A35 30fr carmine & claret 1.10 .55
206 A35 45fr indigo & brn org 1.75 .65
Nos. 202-206 (5) 4.05 1.95

UN Headquarters, New York and Flag — A36

1962, Jan. 6 **Engr.** **Perf. 13**
207 A36 10fr grn, ocher & car .35 .25
208 A36 30fr car, ocher & grn .65 .40
209 A36 85fr grn, ocher & car 2.25 .65
Nos. 207-209 (3) 3.25 1.30

1st anniv. of Senegal's admission to the United Nations, Sept. 28, 1960.

Map of Africa, ITU Emblem and Man with Telephone
A37

1962, Jan. 22 **Photo.** **Perf. 12½x12**
210 A37 25fr blk, grn, red & ocher .80 .30
Meeting of the Commission for the Africa Plan of the ITU, Dakar.

African and Malgache Union Issue
Common Design Type

1962, Sept. 8 **Unwmk.**
211 CD110 30fr grn, bluish grn, red & gold .80 .50

Boxing — A38

15fr, Diving, horiz. 20fr, High jump, horiz. 25fr, Soccer. 30fr, Basketball. 85fr, Running.

1963, Apr. 11 **Engr.** **Perf. 13**
Athletes in Dark Brown
212 A38 10fr ver & emer .30 .25
213 A38 15fr dk bl & bis .40 .25
214 A38 20fr ver & dk bl .45 .25
215 A38 25fr grn & dk bl .65 .25

216 A38 30fr ver & grn 1.25 .50
217 A38 85fr vio bl 2.75 1.10
Nos. 212-217 (6) 5.80 2.60
Friendship Games, Dakar, Apr. 11-21.

UPU Monument, Bern A39

1963, June 14 **Unwmk.** **Perf. 13**
218 A39 10fr grn & ver .45 .25
219 A39 15fr dk bl & red brn .45 .25
220 A39 30fr red brn & blk 1.00 .40
Nos. 218-220 (3) 1.90 .90

2nd anniv. of Senegal's admission to the UPU.

Charaxes Varanes — A40

Butterflies: 45fr, Papilio nireus. 50fr, Colotis danae. 85fr, Epiphora bauhiniae. 100fr, Junonia hierta. 500fr, Danaus chrysippus.

Butterflies in Natural Colors

1963, July 20 **Photo.** **Perf. 12½x13**
221 A40 30fr bl gray & blk 1.25 .50
222 A40 45fr org & blk 1.75 .75
223 A40 50fr brt yel & blk 2.00 .95
224 A40 85fr red & blk 4.50 1.25
225 A40 100fr bl & blk 5.25 2.00
226 A40 500fr emer & blk 18.00 6.50
Nos. 221-226 (6) 32.75 11.95

Prof. Gaston Berger (1896-1960), Philosopher, and Owl — A41

1963, Nov. 13 **Perf. 12½x12**
227 A41 25fr multi .75 .30

Scales, Globe, Flag and UNESCO Emblem A42

1963, Dec. 10
228 A42 60fr multi 1.25 .50
15th anniv. of the Universal Declaration of Human Rights.

Flag, Mother and Child — A43

1963, Dec. 21 **Perf. 12x12½**
229 A43 25fr multi .80 .30
Issued for the Senegalese Red Cross.

Dredging of Titanium-bearing Sand — A44

Designs: 10fr, Titanium extraction works. 15fr, Cement works at Rufisque. 20fr, Phosphate quarry at Pallo. 25fr, Extraction of phosphate ore at Taiba. 85fr, Mineral dock, Dakar.

1964, July 4 **Engr.** **Perf. 13**
230 A44 5fr grnsh bl, car & dk brn .25 .25
231 A44 10fr ocher, grn & ind .25 .25
232 A44 15fr dk bl, brt grn & dk brn .35 .25
233 A44 20fr ultra, ol & pur .55 .25
234 A44 25fr dk bl, yel & blk .70 .25
235 A44 85fr bl, red & brn 2.00 .85
Nos. 230-235 (6) 4.10 2.10

Cooperation Issue
Common Design Type

1964, Nov. 7 **Engr.** **Perf. 13**
236 CD119 100fr dk grn, dk brn & car 1.60 .85

St. Theresa's Church, Dakar A45

10fr, Mosque, Touba. 15fr, Mosque, Dakar, vert.

1964, Nov. 28 **Unwmk.** **Perf. 13**
237 A45 5fr bl, grn & red brn .25 .25
238 A45 10fr dk bl, ocher & blk .25 .25
239 A45 15fr brn, bl & sl grn .90 .25
Nos. 237-239 (3) 1.40 .75

Leprosy Examination — A46

Leprosarium, Peycouk Village — A47

1965, Jan. 30 **Engr.** **Perf. 13**
240 A46 20fr brn red, grn & blk .50 .30
241 A47 65fr org, dk bl & grn 1.50 .55
Issued to publicize the fight against leprosy.

Upper Casamance Region — A48

Views: 30fr, Sangalkam. 45fr, Forest along Senegal River.

1965, Feb. 27 **Unwmk.** **Perf. 13**
242 A48 25fr red brn, sl bl & grn .55 .25
243 A48 30fr indigo & lt brn .65 .30
244 A48 45fr yel grn, red brn & dk brn 1.40 .50
Nos. 242-244,C41 (4) 5.10 2.05

Abdoulaye Seck — A49

General Post Office, Dakar A50

1965, Apr. 24 **Unwmk.** **Perf. 13**
245 A49 10fr dk brn & blk .35 .25
246 A50 15fr brn & dk sl grn .45 .25

Berthon-Ader Telephone — A51

Designs: 60fr, Cable laying ship "Alsace." 85fr, Picard's cable relay for submarine telegraph.

1965, May 17 **Engr.**
247 A51 50fr bl grn & org brn .65 .30
248 A51 60fr mag & dk bl 1.25 .45
249 A51 85fr ver, bl & red brn 1.40 .50
Nos. 247-249 (3) 3.30 1.25
ITU, centenary.

Plowing with Ox Team A52

Designs: 60fr, Harvesting millet, vert. 85fr, Men working in rice field.

1965, July 3 **Unwmk.** **Perf. 13**
250 A52 25fr dk ol grn, brn & pur .55 .30
251 A52 60fr ind, sl grn & dk brn 1.25 .50
252 A52 85fr dp car, sl grn & brt grn 1.75 .55
Nos. 250-252 (3) 3.55 1.35

Gorée Sailboat A53

Designs: 20fr, Large Seumbediou canoe. 30fr, Fadiouth one-man canoe. 45fr, One-man canoe on Senegal River.

1965, Aug. 7 **Photo.** **Perf. 12½x13**
253 A53 10fr multi .25 .25
254 A53 20fr multi .55 .25
255 A53 30fr multi 1.00 .30
256 A53 45fr multi 1.75 .60
Nos. 253-256 (4) 3.55 1.40

Cashew — A54

1965   **Photo.**   **Perf. 12½**
257 A54 10fr shown   .25 .25
258 A54 15fr Papaya   .45 .25
259 A54 20fr Mango   .65 .30
260 A54 30fr Peanuts   1.25 .30
Nos. 257-260 (4)   2.60 1.10
Issued: 10fr, 15fr, 20fr, Nov. 6. 30fr, Dec. 18.

"Elegant Man" — A55   Drummer and Map of Africa — A56

Dolls of Gorée: 2fr, "Elegant Woman." 3fr, Woman peddling fruit. 4fr, Woman pounding grain.

1966, Jan. 22   **Engr.**   **Perf. 13**
261 A55 1fr brn, rose car & ultra   .25 .25
262 A55 2fr brn, bl & org   .25 .25
263 A55 3fr brn, red & bl   .25 .25
264 A55 4fr brn, lil & emer   .25 .25
Nos. 261-264 (4)   1.00 1.00

1966
15fr, Sculpture; mother & child. #267, Music; stringed instrument. 75fr, Dance; carved antelope headpiece (Bambara). 90fr, Ideogram.
265 A56 15fr dk red brn, bl & ocher   .35 .25
266 A56 30fr brn, red & grn   .70 .25
267 A56 30fr dk red brn, bl & yel   1.10 .60
268 A56 75fr dk red brn, bl & blk   1.75 .60
269 A56 90fr dk red brn, org & sl grn   2.10 .65
a. Souv. sheet of 4, #265, 267-269   6.25 6.25
Nos. 265-269 (5)   6.00 2.35
Intl. Negro Arts Festival, Dakar, Apr. 1-24.
Issued: #266, 2/5; others, 4/2. See #364.

Fish — A57

1966, Feb. 26   **Photo.**   **Perf. 12½x13**
270 A57 20fr Tuna   .50 .25
271 A57 30fr Merou   .60 .30
272 A57 50fr Girella   1.25 .65
273 A57 100fr Parrot fish   2.75 .85
Nos. 270-273 (4)   5.10 2.05

Arms of Senegal — A58   Flowers — A59

1966, July 2   **Litho.**   **Perf. 13x12½**
274 A58 30fr multi   .80 .25

1966, Nov. 19   **Photo.**   **Perf. 11½**
275 A59 45fr Mexican poppy   1.25 .25
276 A59 55fr Mimosa   1.25 .35
277 A59 60fr Haemanthus   1.60 .45
278 A59 90fr Baobab   2.10 .65
Nos. 275-278 (4)   6.20 1.70

Harbor, Gorée Island A60

Designs: 25fr, S.S. France in roadstead, Dakar and seagulls. 30fr, Hotel and tourist village, N'Gor. 50fr, Hotel and bay, N'Gor.

1966, Dec. 25   **Engr.**   **Perf. 13**
279 A60 20fr mar & vio bl   .25 .25
280 A60 25fr red, grn & blk   2.00 .30
281 A60 30fr dk red & dp bl   .40 .25
282 A60 50fr brn, sl grn & emer   .65 .30
Nos. 279-282 (4)   3.30 1.10

Laying Urban Water Pipes A61

Symbolic Water Cycle — A62

20fr, Cattle at water trough. 50fr, Village well.

1967, Mar. 25   **Engr.**   **Perf. 13**
283 A61 10fr org brn, grn & dk bl   .25 .25
284 A61 20fr grn, brt bl & org brn   .65 .25
Typo.
Perf. 13x14
285 A62 30fr sky bl, blk & org   .70 .25
Engr.
Perf. 13
286 A62 50fr brn red, brt bl & bis   1.50 .35
Nos. 283-286 (4)   3.10 1.10
Intl. Hydrological Decade (UNESCO), 1965-74.

Lions Emblem A63

1967, May 27   **Photo.**   **Perf. 12½x13**
287 A63 30fr lt ultra & multi   1.00 .40
50th anniversary of Lions International.

Blaise Diagne A64

1967, June 10   **Engr.**   **Perf. 13**
288 A64 30fr ocher, sl grn & dk red brn   .80 .30
Blaise Diagne (1872-1934), member of French Chamber of Deputies and Colonial Minister.
For surcharge see No. 380.

City Hall and Arms, Dakar A65

1967, June 10
289 A65 90fr bl, dk grn & blk   1.75 .50

Eagle and Antelope Carvings — A66

150fr, Flags, maple leaf and EXPO '67 emblem.

1967, Sept. 2   **Photo.**   **Perf. 13x12½**
290 A66 90fr red & blk   2.00 .50
291 A66 150fr red & multi   2.50 .80
EXPO '67 Intl. Exhib., Montreal, 4/28-10/27.

International Tourist Year Emblem — A67

Tourist Photographing Hippopotamus and Siminti Hotel — A68

1967, Oct. 7   **Typo.**   **Perf. 14x13**
292 A67 50fr blk & bl   .90 .40
Perf. 13
Engr.
293 A68 100fr blk, sl grn & ocher   3.50 1.10
International Tourist Year.

Monetary Union Issue
Common Design Type
1967, Nov. 4   **Engr.**   **Perf. 13**
294 CD125 30fr multi   .60 .25
West African Monetary Union, 5th anniv.

Lyre-shaped Megalith, Kaffrine — A69

70fr, Ancient covered bowl, Bandiala.

1967, Dec. 2   **Engr.**   **Perf. 13**
295 A69 30fr grn, grnsh bl & red brn   1.25 .35
296 A69 70fr red brn, ocher & brt bl   2.10 .85

Nurse Feeding Child — A70   Human Rights Flame — A71

1967, Dec. 23
297 A70 50fr bl grn, red & red brn   1.00 .40
Issued for the Senegalese Red Cross.

1968, Jan. 20   **Photo.**   **Perf. 13x12½**
298 A71 30fr brt grn & gold   .80 .30
International Human Rights Year.

Parliament, Dakar A72

1968, Apr. 16   **Photo.**   **Perf. 12½x13**
299 A72 30fr car rose   .80 .25
Inter-Parliamentary Union Meeting, Dakar.

Pied Kingfisher — A73

Goose Barnacles — A74

10fr, Green lobster. 15fr, African jacana. 20fr, Sea cicada. 35fr, Shrimp. 70fr, African anhinga.

1968-69   **Photo.**   **Perf. 11½**
Dated "1968" or (70fr) "1969"
Granite Paper
300 A73 5fr brn & multi   .35 .25
301 A74 10fr red & multi   .50 .25
302 A74 15fr yel & multi   .75 .35
303 A74 20fr ultra & multi   .90 .35
304 A74 35fr car rose & ol grn   2.25 .40
305 A73 70fr Prus bl & multi   2.75 1.00
306 A74 100fr yel grn & multi   6.50 1.75
Nos. 300-306 (7)   14.00 4.35
Issued: 5fr, 7/13/68; 15fr, 12/21/68; 70fr, 4/26/69; others 5/18/68. Nos. 300-306 exist as tete-beche pairs. Value, set of pairs $30.
See Nos. C53-C57.

Steer and Hypodermic Syringe — A75

1968, Aug. 17   **Engr.**   **Perf. 13**
307 A75 30fr dk grn, dp bl & brn red   1.00 .40
Campaign against cattle plague.

Boy and WHO Emblem — A76   Bambara Antelope Symbol — A77

1968, Nov. 16   **Engr.**   **Perf. 13**
308 A76 30fr blk, grn & car   .55 .30
309 A76 45fr red brn, grn & blk   1.10 .30
WHO, 20th anniversary.

1969, Jan. 13   **Engr.**   **Perf. 13**
Design: 30fr, School of Medicine and Pharmacology, Dakar, horiz.
310 A77 30fr emer, brt bl & ind   .80 .30
311 A77 50fr red, gray ol & bl grn   .90 .30
6th Medical Meeting, Dakar, Jan. 13-18.

Panet, Camels and Mogador-St. Louis Route — A78

1969, Feb. 15   Engr.   Perf. 13
312   A78   75fr ultra, Prus bl & brn   2.50   .80
Leopold Panet (1819-1859), first explorer of the Mauritanian Sahara.

ILO Emblem A79

1969, May 3   Photo.   Perf. 12½x13
313   A79   30fr blk & grnsh bl   .55   .25
314   A79   45fr blk & dp car   .80   .25
ILO, 50th anniversary.

Arms of Casamance — A80

Design: 20fr, Arms of Gorée Island.

1969, July 26   Litho.   Perf. 13½
315   A80   15fr rose & multi   .25   .25
316   A80   20fr bl & multi   .75   .25

Development Bank Issue
Common Design Type

1969, Sept. 10   Engr.   Perf. 13
317   CD130   30fr gray, grn & ocher   .65   .25
318   CD130   45fr brn, grn & ocher   .90   .25

Mahatma Gandhi — A81

1969, Oct. 2   Engr.   Perf. 13
319   A81   50fr multi   1.50   .35
   a.   Miniature sheet of 4   6.00   3.00
Mohandas K. Gandhi (1869-1948), leader in India's fight for independence.

Rotary Emblem and Symbolic Ship — A82

1969, Nov. 29   Photo.   Perf. 12½x13
320   A82   30fr ultra, yel & blk   .80   .30
Dakar Rotary Club, 30th anniversary.

ASECNA Issue
Common Design Type

1969, Dec. 12   Engr.   Perf. 13
321   CD132   100fr dark gray   1.60   .50

Niokolo-Koba Campsite — A83

Tourism: 20fr, Cape Skiring, Casamance. 35fr, Elephants at Niokolo-Koba National Park. 45fr, Millet granaries, pigs and boats, Fadiouth Island.

1969, Dec. 27
322   A83   20fr bl, red brn & ol   .75   .25
323   A83   30fr bl, red brn & ocher   1.00   .25
324   A83   35fr grnsh bl, blk & ocher   4.00   .65
325   A83   45fr vio bl & hn brn   2.00   .55
   Nos. 322-325 (4)   7.75   1.70

Bottle-nosed Dolphins A84   Lenin (1870-1924) A85

1970, Feb. 21   Photo.   Perf. 12x12½
326   A84   50fr dl bl, blk & red   7.50   1.50

1970, Apr. 22   Photo.   Perf. 11½
327   A85   30fr brn, buff & ver   2.50   .65

Souvenir Sheet
Perf. 12x11½
327A   A85   50fr brn, buff & ver   4.00   1.75
No. 327A contains one 32x48mm stamp.

UPU Headquarters Issue
Common Design Type

1970, May 20   Engr.   Perf. 13
328   CD133   30fr dk red, ind & dp cl   .55   .25
329   CD133   45fr dl brn, dk car & bl grn   1.00   .30

Textile Plant, Thies — A86

Design: 45fr, Fertilizer plant, Dakar.

1970, Nov. 21   Engr.   Perf. 13
330   A86   30fr grn, brt bl & brn red   .65   .25
331   A86   45fr brn red & brt bl   1.00   .30
Industrialization of Senegal.

Boy Scouts — A87   Three Heads and Sun — A88

Design: 100fr, Lord Baden-Powell, map of Africa with Dakar, and fleur-de-lis.

1970, Dec. 11   Photo.   Perf. 11½
332   A87   30fr multi   .55   .25
333   A87   100fr multi   2.25   .60
1st African Boy Scout Conf., Dakar, Dec. 11-14.

1970, Dec. 19   Engr.   Perf. 13
Design: 40fr, African man and woman, globe with map of Africa.
334   A88   25fr ultra, org & vio brn   .65   .25
335   A88   40fr brn ol, dk brn & org   1.00   .40
International Education Year.

Senegal Arms — A89

1970-76   Photo.   Perf. 12
336   A89   30fr yel grn & multi   .50   .25
336A   A89   35fr brt pink & multi ('71)   .50   .25
   b.   Bklt. pane of 10 ('72)   5.00
336C   A89   50fr bl & multi ('75)   .50   .25
336D   A89   65fr lil rose & multi ('76)   .50   .25
   Nos. 336-336D (4)   2.00   1.00
The booklet pane has a control number in the margin.
See No. 654.

Refugees and UN Emblem A90

1971, Jan. 16   Perf. 12½x12
337   A90   40fr ver, blk, yel & grn   1.00   .30
High Commissioner for Refugees, 20th anniversary. See No. C94.

Mare "Mbayang" A91

Horses: 25fr, Mare Madjiguene. 100fr, Stallion Pass. 125fr, Stallion Pepe.

1971   Photo.   Perf. 11½
338   A91   25fr multi   1.00   .50
339   A91   40fr multi   1.50   .65
340   A91   100fr multi   4.00   2.25
341   A91   125fr multi   5.25   1.90
   Nos. 338-341 (4)   11.75   5.30
Improvements in horse breeding.
For surcharge see No. 392.

UN Emblem, Black and White Children A92   Globe and Telephone A94

UN Emblem, Four Races A93

Perf. 13x12½, 12½x11
1971, Mar. 21   Litho.
342   A92   30fr multi   .85   .35
343   A93   50fr multi   1.40   .60
Intl. Year against Racial Discrimination.

1971, May 17   Engr.   Perf. 13
Design: 40fr, Radar, satellite, orbits.
344   A94   30fr pur, grn & brn   .45   .25
345   A94   40fr Prus bl, dk brn & red brn   1.10   .30
3rd World Telecommunications Day.

Drummer (Hayashida) — A95

50fr, Dwarf Japanese quince and grape hyacinth. 65fr, Judo. 75fr, Mt. Fuji.

1971, Aug. 7   Photo.   Perf. 13½
346   A95   35fr lt ultra & multi   1.25   .30
347   A95   50fr yel & multi   1.50   .45
348   A95   65fr dp org & multi   2.25   .60
349   A95   75fr grn & multi   2.75   .95
   Nos. 346-349 (4)   7.75   2.30
13th Boy Scout World Jamboree, Asagiri Plain, Japan, Aug. 2-10.

Map of West Africa with Senegal, UNICEF Emblem A97

100fr, Nurse, children, UNICEF emblem.

1971, Oct. 30   Perf. 12½
352   A97   35fr dl bl, org & blk   .90   .35
353   A97   100fr multi   3.00   .65
UNICEF, 25th anniv.

Basketball and Games' Emblem — A98

40fr, Basketball. 75fr, Emblem.

1971, Dec. 24   Photo.   Perf. 13½x13
354   A98   35fr lt vio & multi   .70   .25
355   A98   40fr emer & multi   1.00   .30
356   A98   75fr ocher & multi   1.60   .65
   Nos. 354-356 (3)   3.30   1.20
6th African Basketball Championships, Dakar, Dec. 25, 1971-Jan. 2, 1972.

"The Exile of Albouri" — A99

Design: 40fr, "The Merchant of Venice."

1972, Mar. 25   Perf. 13x12½
357   A99   35fr dk red & multi   .55   .30
358   A99   40fr dk red & multi   .90   .30
Intl. Theater Day. See No. C112.

WHO Emblem and Heart A100

Design: 40fr, Physician with patient, WHO emblem and electrocardiogram.

1972, Apr. 7   Engr.   Perf. 13
359 A100 35fr brt bl & red brn   .50 .25
360 A100 40fr slate grn & brn   1.00 .25

"Your heart is your health," World Health Month.

Containment of the Desert, Environment Emblem — A101

1972, June 3   Photo.   Perf. 13x12½
361 A101 35fr multi   1.60 .60

UN Conference on Human Environment, Stockholm, June 5-16. See No. C113.

Tartarin Shooting the Lion — A102

Design: 100fr, Alphonse Daudet.

1972, June 24   Engr.   Perf. 13
362 A102 40fr brt grn, rose car & brn   2.00 1.10
363 A102 100fr Prus bl, bl & brn   3.00 1.10

Alphonse Daudet (1840-1897), French novelist, and centenary of the publication of his "Tartarin de Tarascon."

Souvenir Sheet

Stringed Instrument — A103

1972, July 1   Engr.   Perf. 11½
364 A103 150fr rose red   4.00 3.00

Belgica 72, Intl. Phil. Exhib., Brussels, June 24-July 9. No. 364 contains one stamp in design similar to No. 267.

Wrestling, Olympic Rings — A104

1972, July 22   Photo.   Perf. 14x13½
365 A104 15fr shown   .35 .25
366 A104 20fr 100-meter dash   .80 .25
367 A104 100fr Basketball   2.50 .50
368 A104 125fr Judo   3.00 .65
Nos. 365-368 (4)   6.65 1.65

Souvenir Sheet
Perf. 13½x14½
369 A104 240fr Torchbearer and Munich   6.25 3.25

20th Olympic Games, Munich, 8/26-9/11.

Book Year Emblem, Children Reading A105

1972, Sept. 16   Photo.   Perf. 13
370 A105 50fr gray & multi   .90 .35

International Book Year.

Senegalese Fashion — A106

1972-76   Engr.
371 A106 25fr black   .35 .25
  a.   Booklet pane of 5   2.00
  b.   Booklet pane of 10   5.00
372 A106 40fr brt ultra   .50 .25
  a.   Booklet pane of 5   3.00
  b.   Booklet pane of 10   7.50
372C A106 60fr brt grn ('76)   .50 .25
372D A106 75fr lil rose   .50 .25
  Nos. 371-372D (4)   1.85 1.00

See Nos. 563-573, 1153-1164, 1249-1257D, 1345A-1345C.

Aleksander Pushkin A107

Amphicra-sphedum Murrayanum A108

1972, Oct. 28   Photo.   Perf. 11½
373 A107 100fr salmon & purple   3.00 .65

Aleksander Pushkin (1799-1837), Russian writer.

West African Monetary Union Issue
Common Design Type

Design: 40fr, African couple, city, village and commemorative coin.

1972, Nov. 2   Engr.   Perf. 13
374 CD136 40fr ol brn, bl & gray   .50 .30

1972-73   Photo.   Perf. 11½
Marine Life: 10fr, Pterocanium tricolpum. 15fr, Ceratospyris polygona. 20fr, Cortiniscus typicus. 30fr, Theopera cortina.

375 A108 5fr multi   1.00 .35
376 A108 10fr multi   1.25 .40
377 A108 15fr multi   2.50 .40
378 A108 20fr multi   1.50 .40
379 A108 30fr multi   4.00 .50
  Nos. 375-379,C115-C118 (9)   34.75 7.30

Issued: #375-377, 11/25/72; #378-379, 7/28/73.

No. 288 Surcharged in Vermilion

1972, Dec. 9   Engr.   Perf. 13
380 A64 100fr on 30fr multi   2.25 .60

Blaise Diagne (1872-1934).

Melchior — A109

1972, Dec. 23   Photo.   Perf. 13x13½
381 A109 10fr shown   .25 .25
382 A109 15fr Caspar   .25 .25
383 A109 40fr Balthasar   .80 .35
384 A109 60fr Joseph   .85 .40
385 A109 100fr Virgin and Child   1.50 .65
  a.   Strip of 5, #381-385   5.25 2.00

Christmas. No. 385a has continuous design, showing traditional Gorée dolls.

Black and White Men Carrying Emblem — A110

Europafrica Issue
1973, Jan. 20   Engr.   Perf. 13
386 A110 65fr blk & grn   1.40 .40

Earth Station, Gandoul A111

1973, May 17   Engr.   Perf. 13
387 A111 40fr multi   .80 .30

Phases of Solar Eclipse A112

Designs: 65fr, Moon between earth and sun casting shadow on earth. 150fr, Diagram of areas of partial and total eclipse, satellite in space.

1973, June 30   Photo.   Perf. 13x14
388 A112 35fr dk bl & multi   .75 .30
389 A112 65fr dk bl & multi   1.25 .45
390 A112 150fr dk bl & multi   2.75 1.00
  Nos. 388-390 (3)   4.75 1.75

Total solar eclipse over Africa, June 30.

Men Holding Torch over Africa — A113

1973, July 7   Perf. 12½x13
391 A113 75fr multi   1.00 .40

Org. for African Unity, 10th anniv.

No. 338 Surcharged with New Value, 2 Bars, and Overprinted in Ultramarine: "SECHERESSE / SOLIDARITE AFRICAINE"

1973, July 21   Photo.   Perf. 11½
392 A91 100fr on 25fr multi   2.25 .85

African solidarity in drought emergency.

African Postal Union Issue
Common Design Type
1973, Sept. 12   Engr.   Perf. 13
393 CD137 100fr dk grn, vio & dk red   1.60 .50

Child, Map of Senegal, WMO Emblem A114

1973, Sept. 22
394 A114 50fr multi   .80 .35

Intl. meteorological cooperation, cent.

INTERPOL Headquarters, Paris — A115

1973, Oct. 6   Engr.   Perf. 13
395 A115 75fr ultra, bis & slate grn   1.60 .50

50th anniv. of Intl. Criminal Police Org.

Souvenir Sheet

John F. Kennedy (1917-1963) — A116

1973, Nov. 22   Engr.   Perf. 13
396 A116 150fr ultra   2.75 2.75

Amilcar Cabral — A117

1973, Dec. 15   Photo.   Perf. 12½x13
397   A117   75fr multi   1.25   .40

Cabral (1924-1973), leader of anti-Portuguese guerrilla movement in Portuguese Guinea.

Victorious Athletes and Flag — A118

1974, Apr. 6   Photo.   Perf. 12½x13
398   A118   35fr shown   .80   .25
399   A118   40fr Folk theater   .80   .25

National Youth Week.

Soccer Cup, Yugoslavia-Brazil Game, Our Lady's Church, Munich — A119

Soccer Cup and Games: 40fr, Australia-Germany (Fed. Rep.) and Belltower, Hamburg. 65fr, Netherlands-Uruguay and Tower, Hanover. 70fr, Zaire-Italy and Church, Stuttgart.

1974, June 29   Photo.   Perf. 13x14
400   A119   25fr car & multi   .35   .25
401   A119   40fr car & multi   .65   .25
402   A119   65fr car & multi   .90   .30
403   A119   70fr car & multi   1.50   .40
      Nos. 400-403 (4)   3.40 1.20

World Cup Soccer Championship, Munich, June 13-July 7.
For surcharge see No. 406.

UPU Emblem, Envelopes and Means of Transportation — A120

1974, Oct. 9   Engr.   Perf. 13
404   A120   100fr multi   3.00   .85

Centenary of Universal Postal Union.

Fair Emblem — A121

1974, Nov. 28   Engr.   Perf. 12½x13
405   A121   100fr bl, org & dk brn   1.75   .50

Dakar International Fair.

No. 401 Surcharged in Black on Gold

1975, Feb. 1   Photo.   Perf. 13x14
406   A119   200fr on 40fr multi   3.25 1.25

World Cup Soccer Championships, 1974, victory of German Federal Republic.

Pres. Senghor and King Baudouin — A122

1975, Feb. 28   Photo.   Perf. 13x13½
407   A122   65fr lil & dk bl   .80   .35
408   A122   100fr org & grn   2.00   .50

Visit of King Baudouin of Belgium.

ILO Emblem A123

1975, Apr. 30   Photo.   Perf. 13½x13
409   A123   125fr multi   1.75   .50

International Labor Festival.

Globe, Stamp, Letters, España 75 Emblem — A124

1975, June 6   Engr.   Perf. 13
410   A124   55fr indigo, grn & red   1.25   .40

Espana 75 Intl. Phil. Exhib., Madrid, 4/4-13.

Apollo of Belvedere, Arphila 75 Emblem, Stamps — A125

1975, June 6
411   A125   95fr dk brn, brn & bis   2.25   .80

Arphila 75 International Philatelic Exhibition, Paris, June 6-16.

Professional Instruction — A126

1975, June 28   Engr.   Perf. 13
412   A126   85fr multi   1.25   .40

Dr. Albert Schweitzer (1875-1965), Medical Missionary, Lambarene Hospital — A127

1975, July 5
413   A127   85fr grn & vio brn   1.75   .65

Senegalese Soldier, Batallion Flag, Map of Sinai — A128

1975, July 10   Litho.   Perf. 12½
414   A128   100fr multi   1.75   .50

Senegalese Battalion of the UN' Sinai Service, 1973-74.

Women and Child — A129

55fr, Women pounding grain, vert.

1975, Oct. 18   Photo.   Perf. 13½
415   A129   55fr silver & multi   1.75   .35
416   A129   75fr silver & multi   2.25   .50

International Women's Year.

Staff of Aesculapius and African Mask — A130

1975, Dec. 1   Photo.   Perf. 12½x13
417   A130   50fr multi   .80   .30

40th French Medical Cong., Dakar, Dec. 1-3.

Map of Africa with Senegal and Namibia, UN Emblem A131

1976, Jan. 5   Photo.   Perf. 13
418   A131   125fr vio bl & multi   1.00   .35

International Human Rights and Namibia Conference, Dakar, Jan. 5-8.

Sailfish Fishing A132

200fr, Racing yachts & Oceanexpo 75 emblem.

1976, Jan. 28   Photo.   Perf. 13½x13
419   A132   140fr multi   5.25 1.50
420   A132   200fr multi   3.50 1.60

Oceanexpo 75, 1st Intl. Oceanographic Exhib., Okinawa, July 20, 1975-Jan. 1976.

Servals — A133

Designs: 3fr, Black-tailed godwits. 4fr, River hogs. 5fr, African fish eagles. No. 425, Okapis. No. 426, Sitatungas.

1976, Feb. 26   Photo.   Perf. 13
421   A133   2fr gold & multi   .30   .25
422   A133   3fr gold & multi   .65   .25
423   A133   4fr gold & multi   .30   .25
424   A133   5fr gold & multi   1.00   .50
425   A133   250fr gold & multi   6.25 1.75
426   A133   250fr gold & multi   6.25 1.75
  a.   Strip of 2, #425-426 + label   14.50
       Nos. 421-426 (6)   14.75 4.75

Basse Casamance National Park.
See Nos. 473-478.

A. G. Bell, Telephone, ITU Emblem — A134

1976, Mar. 31   Litho.   Perf. 12½x13
427   A134   175fr multi   2.50   .80

Centenary of first telephone call by Alexander Graham Bell, Mar. 10, 1876.

Map of African French-speaking Countries — A135

1976, Apr. 12   Litho.   Perf. 13½
428   A135   60fr yel grn & multi   .80   .30

Scientific and Cultural Meeting of the African Dental Association, Dakar, Apr. 12-17.

Family and Graph A136

1976, Apr. 26
429   A136   65fr multi   1.00   .40

1st population census in Senegal, Apr. 1976.

Thomas Jefferson and 13-star
Flag — A137

1976, June 19   Engr.   Perf. 13
430   A137   50fr bl, red & blk   1.00   .30
American Bicentennial.

Planting Seedlings — A138

1976, Aug. 21   Litho.   Perf. 12
431   A138   60fr yel & multi   1.00   .25
Reclamation of Sahel region.

Campfire
A139

Jamboree
Emblem, Map of
Africa — A140

1976, Aug. 30   Litho.   Perf. 12½
432   A139   80fr multi   .90   .40
433   A140   100fr multi   1.75   .55
1st All Africa Scout Jamboree, Sherehills,
Jos, Nigeria, Apr. 2-8, 1977.

A140a

1976 Summer Olympics,
Montreal — A140b

1976, Sept. 11   Litho.   Perf. 13½
433A   A140a   5fr Swimming   .25   .25
433B   A140a   10fr Weightlifting   .25   .25
433C   A140a   15fr Hurdles,
                          horiz.   .25   .25
433D   A140a   20fr Equestrian,
                          horiz.   .25   .25

433E   A140a   25fr Steeple-
                          chase,
                          horiz.   .35   .25
433F   A140a   50fr Wrestling   .55   .25
433G   A140a   60fr Field hockey   .70   .25
433H   A140a   65fr Track   .80   .25
433I   A140a   70fr Women's
                          gymnastics   1.00   .40
433J   A140a   100fr Cycling,
                          horiz.   1.25   .50
433K   A140a   400fr Boxing   4.50   .95
433L   A140a   500fr Judo   5.75   1.10
          Nos. 433A-433L (12)   15.90   4.95
Litho. & Embossed
433M   A140a   1000fr Basketball   9.00   3.75
Souvenir Sheet
433Q   A140b   1000fr Boxers,
                          city sky-
                          line   9.00   3.75
          Nos. 433K-433Q are airmail.

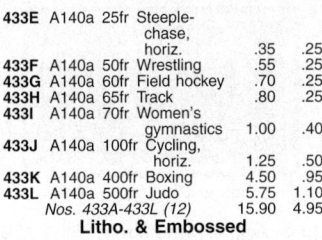

Mechanized Tomato Harvest — A141

1976, Oct. 23   Photo.   Perf. 13
434   A141   180fr multi   3.00   1.25

Map of
Dakar and
Gorée
A142

Designs: 60fr, Star over Africa. 70fr, Students in laboratory and library. 200fr, Handshake over world map, Pres. Senghor.

1976, Oct. 9   Litho.   Perf. 13½x14
435   A142   40fr multi   .35   .25
436   A142   60fr multi   .50   .25
437   A142   70fr multi   1.00   .25
438   A142   200fr multi   2.75   .85
          Nos. 435-438 (4)   4.60   1.60
70th birthday of Pres. Leopold Sedar
Senghor.

Scroll with Map of
Africa,
Senegalese
People — A143

1977, Jan. 8   Perf. 12½
439   A143   60fr multi   .80   .30
Day of the Black People.

Joe Frazier and Muhammad
Ali — A144

Design: 60fr, Ali and Frazier in ring, vert.

1977, Jan. 7   Photo.   Perf. 13x13½
440   A144   60fr blue & blk   .65   .25
441   A144   150fr emerald & blk   2.25   .60
World boxing champion Muhammad Ali.

Dancer
and
Musician
A145

Festival Emblem and: 75fr, Wood carving
and masks. 100fr, Dancers and ancestor
statuette.

1977, Feb. 10   Litho.   Perf. 12½
442   A145   50fr yellow & multi   .55   .25
443   A145   75fr green & multi   1.25   .30
444   A145   100fr rose & multi   1.40   .50
          Nos. 442-444 (3)   3.20   1.05
2nd World Black and African Festival,
Lagos, Nigeria, Jan. 15-Feb. 12.

Cogwheels and Symbols of
Industry — A146

1977, Mar. 28   Engr.   Perf. 13
445   A146   70fr yel grn & ocher   .80   .30
Dakar Industrial Zone, 1st anniversary.

Burning Match
and Burnt
Trees — A147

60fr, Burnt trees and house, fire-truck, horiz.

1977, Apr. 30   Litho.   Perf. 12½
446   A147   40fr green & multi   1.00   .35
447   A147   60fr slate & multi   1.75   .55
Prevention of forest fires.

Drummer, Telephone, Agriculture and
Industry — A148

Electronic Tree
and ITU
Emblem — A149

1977, May 17   Litho.   Perf. 13
448   A148   80fr multi   .80   .40
449   A149   100fr multi   1.25   .60
World Telecommunications Day.

Symbol of
Language
Studies — A150

Sassenage Castle, Grenoble — A151

Perf. 12x12½, 12½
1977, May 21   Litho.
450   A150   65fr multi   .65   .25
451   A151   250fr multi   2.75   1.00
10th anniv. of Intl. French Language Council.

Woman in
Boat,
Wooden
Shoe
A152

Design: 125fr, Senegalese woman, symbolic tulip and stamp, vert.

1977, June 4   Perf. 13½x14, 14x13½
452   A152   50fr blue grn & multi   .50   .25
453   A152   125fr ocher & multi   1.50   .45
Amphilex '77 International Philatelic Exhibition, Amsterdam, May 26-June 5.

Adult
Reading
Class
A153

Design: 65fr, Man learning to read.

1977, Sept. 10   Litho.   Perf. 12½
454   A153   60fr multi   .70   .25
455   A153   65fr multi   .70   .25
National Literacy Week, Sept. 8-14.

A154

Paintings: 20fr, Mercury, by Rubens. 25fr,
Daniel in the Lions' Den, by Peter Paul
Rubens (1577-1640). 40fr, The Empress, by
Titian (1477-1576). 60fr, Flora, by Titian. 65fr,
Jo, the Beautiful Irish Woman, by Gustave
Courbet (1819-1877). 100fr, The Painter's
Studio, by Courbet.

1977, Nov.   Photo.   Perf. 13x13½
456   A154   20fr multi   .55   .25
457   A154   25fr multi   .55   .25
458   A154   40fr multi   .55   .25
459   A154   60fr multi   1.00   .25

460	A154	65fr multi	1.40 .55
461	A154	100fr multi	3.00 1.00
		Nos. 456-461 (6)	7.05 2.55

A155

Christmas: 20fr, Adoration by People of Various Races. 25fr, Decorated arch and procession. 40fr, Christmas tree, mother and child. 100fr, Adoration of the Kings, horiz.

1977, Dec. 22   Litho.   Perf. 12½

462	A155	20fr multi	.25 .25
463	A155	25fr multi	.40 .25
464	A155	40fr multi	.65 .25
465	A155	100fr multi	1.25 .65
		Nos. 462-465 (4)	2.55 1.40

Regatta at
Soumbedioun
A156

Tourism: 10fr, Senegalese wrestlers. 65fr, Regatta at Soumbedioun. 100fr, Dancers.

1978, Jan. 7   Litho.   Perf. 12½

466	A156	10fr multi	.25 .25
467	A156	30fr multi	.35 .25
468	A156	65fr multi, horiz.	.80 .40
469	A156	100fr multi, horiz.	1.75 .50
		Nos. 466-469 (4)	3.15 1.40

Acropolis,
Athens,
and African
Buildings
A157

1978, Jan. 30

470	A157	75fr multi	.80 .30

UNESCO campaign to save world's cultural heritage.

Solar-powered Pump, Field and
Sheep — A158

Energy in Senegal: 95fr, Pylon bringing electricity to villages and factories.

1978, Feb. 25

471	A158	50fr multi	.55 .25
472	A158	95fr multi	1.25 .40

Park Type of 1976

5fr, Caspian terns in flight, royal terns on ground. 10fr, Pink-backed pelicans. 15fr, Wart hog & gray heron. 20fr, Greater flamingoes, nests, eggs & young. #477, Gray heron & royal terns. #478, Abyssinian ground hornbill & wart hog.

1978, Apr. 22   Photo.   Perf. 13

473	A133	5fr gold & multi	.25 .25
474	A133	10fr gold & multi	.55 .25
475	A133	15fr gold & multi	1.10 .25
476	A133	20fr gold & multi	1.25 .40
477	A133	150fr gold & multi	5.25 1.00

478	A133	150fr gold & multi	5.25 1.00
a.		Strip of 2, #477-478 + label	11.50
		Nos. 473-478 (6)	13.65 3.15

Salum Delta National Park.

Dome of the
Rock, Jerusalem
A159

1978, May 15   Litho.   Perf. 12½

479	A159	60fr multi	.80 .25

Palestinian fighters and their families.

Vaccination, Dr. Jenner, WHO
Emblem — A160

1978, June 3

480	A160	60fr multi	.80 .35

Eradication of smallpox.

Soccer, Flags:
Argentina,
Hungary, France,
Italy — A161

Soccer, Cup, Argentina '78 Emblem and Flags of: 40fr, No. 486a, Poland, German Democratic Rep., Tunisia, Mexico. 65fr, 125fr, Austria, Spain, Sweden, Brazil. 75fr, No. 484, Netherlands, Iran, Peru, Scotland. 150fr, like 25fr.

1978, June 24   Photo.   Perf. 13

481	A161	25fr multi	.25 .25
482	A161	40fr multi	.55 .25
483	A161	65fr multi	.80 .30
484	A161	100fr multi	1.50 .30
		Nos. 481-484 (4)	3.10 1.10

Souvenir Sheets

485		Sheet of 2	2.75
a.	A161	75fr multi	.60
b.	A161	125fr multi	1.10
486		Sheet of 2	2.75
a.	A161	100fr multi	.85
b.	A161	150fr multi	1.10

11th World Cup Soccer Championship, Argentina, June 1-25.

Mahatma
Gandhi — A162

Design: 150fr, No. 489a, Martin Luther King. No. 489b, like 125fr.

1978, June 27   Perf. 12

487	A162	125fr multi	1.75 .35
488	A162	150fr multi	2.25 .60

Souvenir Sheet

489		Sheet of 2	4.00
a.	A162	200fr multi	1.60
b.	A162	200fr multi	1.60

Mahatma Gandhi and Martin Luther King, advocates of non-violence.

Homes and Industry — A163

1978, Aug. 5   Litho.   Perf. 12½

490	A163	110fr multi	1.25 .40

3rd Intl. Fair, Dakar, Nov. 28-Dec. 10.

Wright Brothers and Flyer — A164

Designs: 150fr, like 75fr. 100fr, 250fr, Yuri Gagarin and spacecraft. 200fr, 300fr, US astronauts Frank Borman, William Anders, James Lovell Jr. and spacecraft.

1978, Sept. 25   Litho.   Perf. 13½x14

491	A164	75fr multi	.90 .25
492	A164	100fr multi	1.25 .40
493	A164	200fr multi	2.25 .85
		Nos. 491-493 (3)	4.40 1.50

Souvenir Sheet

494		Sheet of 3	6.25
a.	A164	150fr multi	.60
b.	A164	250fr multi	1.40
c.	A164	300fr multi	2.00

75th anniv. of 1st powered flight; 10th anniv. of the death of Yuri Gagarin, first man in space; 10th anniv. of Apollo 8 flight around moon.

Henri Dunant (1828-1910), Founder of
Red Cross, and Patients — A165

Design: 20fr, Henri Dunant, First Aid station, Red Cross flag.

1978, Oct. 28   Photo.   Perf. 11½

495	A165	5fr brt blue & red	.25 .25
496	A165	20fr multi	.45 .25

Bedside Lecture and Emblem — A166

100fr, Pollution, fish and mercury bottles.

1979, Jan. 15   Litho.   Perf. 13½x13

497	A166	50fr multi	.45 .25
498	A166	100fr multi	1.10 .30

9th Medical Days, Dakar, Jan. 15-20.

Map of
Senegal with
Shortwave
Stations
A167

60fr, Children on vacation, ambulance, soccer player. 65fr, Rural mobile post office.

1978, Dec. 27   Litho.   Perf. 13½x13

499	A167	50fr multi	.55 .25
500	A167	60fr multi	.55 .25
501	A167	65fr multi	.70 .25
		Nos. 499-501 (3)	1.80 .75

Achievements of postal service.

Farmer
A168

Design: 150fr, Factories, communication, transportation, fish, physician and worker.

1979, Feb. 17   Litho.   Perf. 12½

502	A168	30fr multi	.35 .25
503	A168	150fr multi	1.40 .50

Pride in workmanship.

Children's Village and
Children — A169

Design: 60fr, Different view of village.

1979, Mar. 30   Perf. 12x12½

504	A169	40fr multi	.45 .25
505	A169	60fr multi	.70 .25

Children's SOS villages.

Infant, Physician
Vaccinating Child,
IYC
Emblem — A170

65fr, Boys with book, globe, IYC emblem.

1979, Apr. 21   Litho.   Perf. 13½x13

506	A170	60fr multi	.65 .25
507	A170	65fr multi	.65 .25

International Year of the Child.

Drum, Carrier Pigeon,
Satellite — A171

Design: 60fr, Baobab tree and flower, Independence monument with lion, vert.

1979, June 8   Perf. 12½x13

Size: 36x48mm

508	A171	60fr multi	1.75 .85

Perf. 12½

Size: 36x36mm

509	A171	150fr multi	3.50 1.50

Philexafrique II, Libreville, Gabon, June 8-17. Nos. 508, 509 each printed with labels showing UAPT '79 emblem.

People Walking through Open Book A172

1979, Sept. 15 Photo. Perf. 11½x12
510 A172 250fr multi 2.50 .80

Intl. Bureau of Education, Geneva, 50th anniv.

Sir Rowland Hill (1795-1879), Originator of Penny Postage, Type AP3 with Exhibition Cancel — A173

1979, Oct. 9 Perf. 11½
511 A173 500fr multi 5.25 2.00

Black Trees, by Hundertwasser A174

Litho. & Engr.
1979, Dec. 10 Perf. 13½x14
512 A174 60fr shown 45.00 11.00
  a. Souvenir sheet of 4 175.00 175.00
513 A174 100fr Head of a man 45.00 13.00
  a. Souvenir sheet of 4 175.00 175.00
514 A174 200fr Rainbow windows 45.00 15.00
  a. Souvenir sheet of 4 175.00 175.00
  Nos. 512-514 (3) 135.00 39.00

Paintings by Friedensreich Hundertwasser, pseudonym of Friedrich Stowasser (b. 1928).

Running, Championship Emblem A175

1980, Jan. 14 Litho. Perf. 13
515 A175 20fr shown .25 .25
516 A175 25fr Javelin .25 .25
517 A175 50fr Relay race .55 .25
518 A175 100fr Discus 1.25 .45
  Nos. 515-518 (4) 2.30 1.20

1st African Athletic Championships.

Mudra Afrique Arts Festival A176

1980, Mar. 22 Photo. Perf. 14
519 A176 50fr Musicians .45 .25
520 A176 100fr Dancers, festival building 1.00 .45
521 A176 200fr Drummer, dancers 1.75 .85
  Nos. 519-521 (3) 3.20 1.55

Lions Emblem, Map of Dakar Harbor A177

1980, May 17 Litho. Perf. 13
522 A177 100fr multi 1.10 .40

22nd Cong., Lions Intl. District 403, Dakar.

Chimpanzees — A178

1980, June 2 Photo. Perf. 13½
523 A178 40fr shown .85 .25
524 A178 60fr Elephants 1.25 .40
525 A178 65fr Derby's elands 1.50 .45
526 A178 100fr Hyenas 2.25 .50
527 Pair 9.00 5.00
  a. A178 200fr Herd 4.25 1.00
  b. A178 200fr Guest house 4.25 1.00
  Nos. 523-527 (5) 14.85 6.60

Souvenir Sheet
528 Sheet of 4 8.00 8.00
  a. A178 125fr like #523 1.50 1.50
  b. A178 125fr like #524 1.50 1.50
  c. A178 125fr like #525 1.50 1.50
  d. A178 125fr like #526 1.50 1.50

Niokolo Koba National Park. No. 527 printed in continuous design with label showing location of park.

Tree Planting Year — A179

1980, June 27 Litho. Perf. 13
529 A179 60fr multi .90 .40
530 A179 65fr multi 1.00 .40
  Nos. 529-530

Rural Women Workers A180

Rural women workers. 50fr, 200fr, horiz.

1980, July 19
531 A180 50fr multi .35 .25
532 A180 100fr multi 1.25 .35
533 A180 200fr multi 2.00 .80
  Nos. 531-533 (3) 3.60 1.40

Wrestling, Moscow '80 Emblem — A181

1980, Aug. 21 Perf. 14½
534 A181 60fr shown .45 .25
535 A181 65fr Running .55 .30
536 A181 70fr Sports, map showing Moscow .55 .30
537 A181 100fr Judo .80 .40
538 A181 200fr Basketball 1.75 .80
  Nos. 534-538 (5) 4.10 2.05

Souvenir Sheet
539 Sheet of 2 2.00
  a. A181 75fr like #534 .65 .25
  b. A181 125fr like #535 1.00 .35
540 Sheet of 2 2.00
  a. A181 75fr like #527 .65 .25
  b. A181 125fr like #538 1.00 .35

22nd Summer Olympic Games, Moscow, July 19-Aug. 3.

Caspian Tern and Sea Gulls, Kalissaye Bird Sanctuary A182

National Park Wildlife: 70fr, Laughing gulls and Hansel's tern, Barbarie Spit. 85fr, Turtle and crab, Madeleine Islands. 150fr, Cormorant, Madeleine Islands.

1981, Jan. 31 Litho. Perf. 14½x14
541 A182 50fr multi 3.50 .50
542 A182 70fr multi 3.50 .70
543 A182 85fr multi 1.75 .70
544 A182 150fr multi 7.00 1.75
  Nos. 541-544 (4) 15.75 3.65

Souvenir Sheet
545 Sheet of 4 22.50 22.50
  a. A182 125fr like #541 3.50 2.75
  b. A182 125fr like #542 3.50 2.75
  c. A182 125fr like #543 3.50 2.75
  d. A182 125fr like #544 3.50 2.75

Anti-Tobacco Campaign — A183

1981, June 20 Litho. Perf. 13
546 A183 75fr Healthy people .70 .30
547 A183 80fr shown .90 .30

4th Intl. Dakar Fair, Nov. 25-Dec. 7 A184

1981, Sept. 19 Litho. Perf. 12½
548 A184 80fr multi .80 .30

Natl. Hero Lat Dior A185

1982, Jan. 11 Photo. Perf. 14
549 A185 80fr Portrait, vert. .55 .35
550 A185 500fr Battle 4.50 1.40

Local Flora — A186

1982, Feb. 1 Perf. 11½
551 A186 50fr Nymphaea lotus .55 .25
552 A186 75fr Strophanthus sarmentosus .90 .30
553 A186 200fr Crinum moorei 2.25 .65

554 A186 225fr Cochlospermum tinctorium 2.25 .85
  Nos. 551-554 (4) 5.95 2.05

Inscribed 1981.

Euryphrene Senegalensis — A187

1982, Feb. 27 Litho. Perf. 14
555 A187 45fr shown 2.25 .50
556 A187 55fr Hypolimnas salmacis 3.00 .60
557 A187 75fr Cymothoe caenis 3.25 .75
558 A187 80fr Precis cebrene 4.00 .90
  Nos. 555-558 (4) 12.50 2.75

Souvenir Sheet Perf. 14½
559 Sheet of 4 20.00 20.00
  a. A187 100fr like 45fr 2.00 1.50
  b. A187 150fr like 55fr 3.00 2.50
  c. A187 200fr like 75fr 4.00 3.50
  d. A187 250fr like 80fr 5.00 4.00

Destructive Insects — A188

Various insects. 80fr, 100fr horiz.

1982, Apr. 7 Litho. Perf. 14
560 A188 75fr multi 1.75 .40
561 A188 80fr multi 3.25 .70
562 A188 100fr multi 2.50 .90
  Nos. 560-562 (3) 7.50 2.00

Fashion Type of 1972
1982-93 Engr. Perf. 13
563 A106 5fr Prus blue .25 .25
564 A106 10fr dull red .25 .25
565 A106 15fr orange .25 .25
566 A106 20fr dk purple .25 .25
567 A106 30fr henna brn .25 .25
568 A106 45fr orange yellow .35 .25
569 A106 50fr bright magenta .40 .25
570 A106 90fr brt carmine .50 .30
571 A106 125fr ultramarine .95 .50
572 A106 145fr orange .85 .35
573 A106 180fr gray blue 1.40 .70
  Nos. 563-573 (11) 5.70 3.60

Issued: 5, 10, 15, 20, 30fr, Apr. 30; 90fr, Dec., 1984; 180fr, 1991; 45, 50, 125fr, 1993; 145fr, 1995.

Banner and Stamp — A189

1982, Dec. 30 Photo. Perf. 13
575 A189 100fr shown .70 .35
576 A189 500fr Stamp, arrows 4.50 1.50

PHILEXFRANCE Intl. Stamp Exhibition, Paris, June 11-21.

Senegambia Confederation, Feb. 1 — A190

1982, Nov. 15   Litho.   Perf. 12½
577 A190 225fr Map, flags   2.00 .65
578 A190 350fr Arms   2.75 1.00

Local Birds — A191   1982 World Cup — A192

1982, Dec. 1   Photo.   Perf. 11½
Granite Paper
579 A191 45fr Godwit   .65 .25
580 A191 75fr Jabiru   1.10 .35
581 A191 80fr Francolin   1.25 .55
582 A191 500fr Eagle   6.25 2.25
        Nos. 579-582 (4)   9.25 3.40

1982, Dec. 11   Litho.   Perf. 12½x13
583 A192 30fr Player   .25 .25
584 A192 50fr Player, diff.   .35 .25
585 A192 75fr Ball   .80 .25
586 A192 80fr Cup   .90 .35
        Nos. 583-586 (4)   2.30 1.10

Souvenir Sheets
Perf. 12½
587 A192 75fr like 30fr   .80 .80
588 A192 100fr like 50fr   1.10 1.10
589 A192 150fr like 75fr   1.50 1.50
590 A192 200fr like 80fr   2.25 2.25
        Nos. 587-590 (4)   5.65 5.65

A193

Designs: 60fr, Exhibition poster, viewers, horiz. 70fr, Simulated butterfly stamps. 90fr, Simulated stamps under magnifying glass. 95fr, Coat of Arms over Exhibition Building.

1983, Aug. 6   Litho.   Perf. 12½
591 A193 60fr multi   .55 .25
592 A193 70fr multi   1.40 .30
593 A193 90fr multi   1.75 .30
594 A193 95fr multi   1.75 .40
        Nos. 591-594 (4)   5.45 1.25
        Dakar '82 Stamp Exhibition.

A194

1983, Oct. 25   Litho.   Perf. 12½x13
595 A194 90fr Electricity   .85 .40
596 A194 95fr Gasoline   1.00 .45
597 A194 260fr Coal, wood   2.25 .65
        Nos. 595-597 (3)   4.10 1.50
        Energy conservation.

Namibia Day — A195

1983, Nov. 14   Litho.   Perf. 13½x13
598 A195 90fr Torch   .80 .35
599 A195 95fr Chain, fist   .90 .35
600 A195 260fr Woman bearing
                 torch   2.75 .65
        Nos. 598-600 (3)   4.45 1.35

West African Monetary Union, 20th Anniv. — A196   Dakar Alizes Rotary Club, First Anniv. — A197

Designs: 60fr, Mask emblem, Ziguinchor Agency building, Dakar, horiz. 65fr, Monetary Union headquarters, emblem.

Perf. 13½x13, 13x13½
1983, Nov. 28
601 A196 60fr multi   .65 .25
602 A196 65fr multi   .65 .25

1983, Dec. 5   Perf. 13x13½
603 A197 70fr green & multi   .90 .35
604 A197 500fr blue & multi   4.50 1.75

Customs Cooperation Council, 30th Anniv. — A198

1983, Dec. 23   Perf. 12½x13
605 A198 90fr multi   .65 .25
606 A198 300fr multi   3.00 .80

Economic Comm. for Africa, 25th Anniv. — A199

1984, Jan. 10   Perf. 12½
607 A199 90fr multi   .70 .35
608 A199 95fr multi   .90 .35

SOS Children's Village A200

1984, Mar. 29   Perf. 13½x13, 13x13½
609 A200 90fr Village   .80 .25
610 A200 95fr Mother & child,
                 vert.   1.00 .40
611 A200 115fr Brothers & sis-
                 ters   1.10 .40
612 A200 260fr House, vert.   2.50 .85
        Nos. 609-612 (4)   5.40 1.90

Scouting Year A201

1984, May 28   Litho.   Perf. 13
613 A201 60fr Sign   .55 .25
614 A201 70fr Emblem   .55 .25
615 A201 90fr Scouts   .70 .30
616 A201 95fr Baden-Powell   .90 .30
        Nos. 613-616 (4)   2.70 1.10

1984 Olympic Games — A202

1984, July 28   Litho.   Perf. 13
617 A202 90fr Javelin   .70 .25
618 A202 95fr Hurdles   .90 .35
619 A202 165fr Soccer   1.50 .50
        Nos. 617-619 (3)   3.10 1.10

Souvenir Sheet
Perf. 13x12½
620   Sheet of 3   4.50 4.50
  a.   A202 125fr like 90fr   .95 .95
  b.   A202 175fr like 95fr   1.50 1.50
  c.   A202 250fr like 165fr   1.75 1.75

World Food Day A203

Perf. 13x12½, 12½x13
1984, Dec. 16   Litho.
621 A203 65fr Food production   .55 .30
622 A203 70fr Cooking, vert.   .70 .30
623 A203 225fr Dining   2.25 .85
        Nos. 621-623 (3)   3.50 1.45

No. 612 Overprinted "AIDE AU SAHEL 84"

1984, Dec.   Perf. 13x13½
624 A200 260fr multi   2.25 1.25
        Drought relief.

UNESCO World Heritage Campaign — A204   Water Emergency Plan — A205

1984, Dec. 6   Litho.   Perf. 13½
625 A204 90fr William Ponty
                 School   1.10 .40
626 A204 95fr Island map,
                 horiz.   1.10 .40
627 A204 250fr History Muse-
                 um   3.25 1.00
628 A204 500fr Slave Prison,
                 horiz.   6.00 2.25
        Nos. 625-628 (4)   11.45 4.05

Souvenir Sheet
Perf. 13x12½, 12½x13
629   Sheet of 4   11.00 11.00
  a.   A204 125fr like No. 625   1.00 .75
  b.   A204 150fr like No. 626   1.25 1.00
  c.   A204 325fr like No. 627   2.25 2.00
  d.   A204 675fr like No. 628   5.25 5.00

Restoration of historic sites, Goree Island.

1985, Mar. 28   Perf. 13x12½, 12½x13
630 A205 40fr Well and pump   .60 .25
631 A205 50fr Spigot and crops .70 .35
632 A205 90fr Water tanks, live-
                 stock   1.40 .55
633 A205 250fr Women at well   3.00 1.10
        Nos. 630-633 (4)   5.70 2.25
        Nos. 631-633 horiz.

World Communications Year — A206

Designs: 95fr, Maps of Africa and Senegal, transmission tower. 350fr, Globe, pigeon with letter.

1985, Apr. 13   Litho.   Perf. 13
634 A206 90fr multi   .70 .35
635 A206 95fr multi   .90 .35
636 A206 350fr multi   3.25 1.25
        Nos. 634-636 (3)   4.85 1.95

Traditional Musical Instruments — A207

50fr, Gourd fiddle, bamboo flute. 85fr, Drums, stringed instrument. 125fr, Musician playing balaphone, drums. 250fr, Rabab, shawm & single-string fiddles.

1985, May 4   Perf. 12½x13, 13x12½
637 A207 50fr multi   .75 .25
638 A207 85fr multi   1.10 .45
639 A207 125fr multi   1.60 .60
640 A207 250fr multi   3.25 1.00
        Nos. 637-640 (4)   6.70 2.30

Nos. 638-640 vert. For surcharge see No. 676.

PHILEXAFRICA '85, Lome, Togo, Nov. 16-24 — A208

1985, Oct. 21   Perf. 13
641 A208 100fr Political and civic
                 education   .70 .25
642 A208 125fr Vocational train-
                 ing   1.00 .40
643 A208 150fr Culture, space
                 exploration   1.25 .50
644 A208 175fr Self-sufficiency in
                 food production 2.25 .85
        Nos. 641-644 (4)   5.20 2.00

Intl. Youth Year A209

1985, Nov. 30   Perf. 14
645 A209 40fr Vocational train-
                 ing   .35 .25
646 A209 50fr Communications   .45 .25
647 A209 90fr World peace   .80 .30
648 A209 125fr Cultural ex-
                 change   1.25 .35
        Nos. 645-648 (4)   2.85 1.15

Senegal Arms Type of 1970
1985, Dec.   Litho.   Perf. 13
Background Color
654 A89 95fr bright orange   .80 .25

Fishing at Kayar A210

1986, Jan. 28   Litho.   Perf. 14
659 A210 40fr Hauling boat .35 .25
660 A210 50fr Women on beach .55 .25
661 A210 100fr Fisherman, catch 1.00 .35
662 A210 125fr Women buying fish 1.40 .50
663 A210 150fr Unloading fish 1.60 .60
Nos. 659-663 (5) 4.90 1.95
Nos. 661-662 vert.

Folk Costumes — A211

1985, Dec. 28   Litho.   Perf. 13½
664 A211 40fr multi .25 .25
665 A211 95fr multi, vert., diff. .80 .30
666 A211 100fr multi, vert., diff. .90 .30
667 A211 150fr multi, vert., diff. 1.25 .50
Nos. 664-667 (4) 3.20 1.35

Coiffures — A212   1986 Africa Soccer Cup, Cairo — A213

1986, Mar. 3   Perf. 13
668 A212 90fr Perruque, Ceeli .70 .35
669 A212 125fr Ndungu, Kearly, Rasta 1.00 .40
670 A212 250fr Jamono Kura, Kooraa 2.25 .75
671 A212 300fr Mbaram, Jeere 2.75 .90
Nos. 668-671 (4) 6.70 2.40

1986, Mar. 7   Perf. 13½
672 A213 115fr Soccer ball, flags 1.00 .30
673 A213 125fr Athlete, map 1.00 .35
674 A213 135fr Pyramid, heraldic lion 1.10 .40
675 A213 165fr Flag, lions, map 1.40 .50
Nos. 672-675 (4) 4.50 1.55

No. 638 Surcharged with Lions Intl. Emblem, Two Bars, and "Ve CONVENTION / MULTI-DISTRICT / 403 / 8-10 / MAI / 1986" in Dark Ultramarine

1986, May 8   Litho.   Perf. 13x12½
676 A207 165fr on 85fr multi 1.40 .50

World Wildlife Fund — A214

Ndama gazelles.

1986, June 30   Perf. 13
677 A214 15fr multi 1.00 .40
678 A214 45fr multi 1.75 .60
679 A214 85fr multi 3.00 1.25
680 A214 125fr multi 5.00 2.00
Nos. 677-680 (4) 10.75 4.25

UN Child Survival Campaign — A215

1986, Sept. 5   Litho.   Perf. 14
681 A215 50fr Immunization .45 .25
682 A215 85fr Nutrition .70 .30

1986 World Cup Soccer Championships, Mexico — A216

Various plays, world cup and artifacts: 125fr, Ceremonial vase. 135fr, Mayan mask, Palenque. 165fr, Gold breastplate. 340fr, Porcelain mask, Teofihuacan, 7th cent. B.C.

1986, Nov. 17   Perf. 12½x12
683 A216 125fr multi 1.00 .40
684 A216 135fr multi 1.10 .40
685 A216 165fr multi 1.40 .55
686 A216 340fr multi 2.75 1.10
Nos. 683-686 (4) 6.25 2.45

Nos. 683-686 Overprinted "ARGENTINE 3 / R.F.A. 2" in Scarlet
1986, Nov. 17
687 A216 125fr multi 1.00 .40
688 A216 135fr multi 1.10 .45
689 A216 165fr multi 1.40 .55
690 A216 340fr multi 2.75 1.10
Nos. 687-690 (4) 6.25 2.50

Guembeul Nature Reserve A217

1986, Dec. 4   Litho.   Perf. 13½
691 A217 50fr Ostriches 1.25 .25
692 A217 65fr Kob antelopes .45 .25
693 A217 85fr Giraffes .60 .40
694 A217 100fr Ostrich, buffalo, kob, giraffe 2.00 .50
695 A217 150fr Buffaloes 1.25 .60
Nos. 691-695 (5) 5.55 2.00

Christmas A218

1986, Dec. 22   Litho.   Perf. 14
696 A218 70fr Puppet, vert. .55 .25
697 A218 85fr Folk musicians .80 .25
698 A218 150fr Outdoor celebration, vert. 1.25 .50
699 A218 250fr Boy praying, creche 2.25 .85
Nos. 696-699 (4) 4.85 1.85
Inscribed 1985.

Statue of Liberty, Cent. — A219

1986, Dec. 30   Litho.   Perf. 12½
700 A219 225fr multi 2.00 .65

Marine Life A220

1987, Jan. 2   Perf. 14
701 A220 50fr Jellyfish, coral .55 .25
702 A220 85fr Sea urchin, starfish 1.00 .25
703 A220 100fr Spiny lobster 1.60 .50
704 A220 150fr Dolphin 2.10 .65
705 A220 200fr Octopus 3.25 .90
Nos. 701-705 (5) 8.50 2.55

Senegal Stamp Cent. — A221

1987, Apr. 8   Perf. 13
706 A221 100fr Intl. express mail 1.40 .30
707 A221 130fr #37 1.60 .40
708 A221 140fr Similar to #201 1.75 .40
709 A221 145fr #151, similar to #154 1.75 .50
710 A221 320fr #27 5.00 1.10
Nos. 706-710 (5) 11.50 2.70
Designs of Nos. 37, 151 and 27 same as originally released but perfs simulated.
For overprint see No. 784.

Paris-Dakar Rally — A222

1987, Jan. 22   Perf. 14
711 A222 115fr Motorcycle, truck, vert. 1.25 .40
712 A222 125fr Official, race 1.75 .40
713 A222 135fr Sabine, truck 1.75 .55
714 A222 340fr Eiffel Tower, Dakar huts, vert. 3.25 1.25
Nos. 711-714 (4) 8.00 2.60
Homage to Thierry Sabine. Inscribed 1986.

Ferlo Nature Reserve — A223

1987, Feb. 5   Perf. 13½
715 A223 55fr Antelope .80 .30
716 A223 70fr Ostrich 1.10 .45
717 A223 85fr Warthog 1.10 .45
718 A223 90fr Elephant 1.25 .50
Nos. 715-718 (4) 4.25 1.70
Inscribed 1986.

Agena-Gemini 8 Link-up in Outer Space, 20th Anniv. — A224

1987, Feb. 27   Litho.   Perf. 13
719 A224 320fr multi 2.75 1.25
Souvenir Sheet   Perf. 12½
720 A224 500fr multi 6.25 6.25
Nos. 719-720 inscribed 1986 and have erroneous "10e Anniversaire" inscription.

Solidarity Against South African Apartheid — A225

1987, July 31   Litho.   Perf. 13
721 A225 130fr shown 1.00 .40
722 A225 140fr Mandela, hand, broken chain, vert. 1.10 .45
723 A225 145fr Mandela, dove, death 1.10 .50
Nos. 721-723 (3) 3.20 1.35
Inscribed 1986.

Intelsat, 20th Anniv. A226

1987, Aug. 31   Perf. 14
724 A226 50fr Emblem .45 .25
725 A226 125fr Satellite 1.00 .40
726 A226 150fr Emblem, globe 1.10 .50
727 A226 200fr Earth, satellite in space 2.00 .70
Nos. 724-727 (4) 4.55 1.85
Inscribed 1985. Nos. 726-727 vert.

West African Union, 10th Anniv. — A227

1987, Sept. 7
728 A227 40fr shown .35 .25
729 A227 125fr Emblem, handshake 1.00 .45
Inscribed 1985.

Dakar Rotary Club, 45th Anniv. — A228

1987, Sept. 29   Perf. 13
730 A228 500fr multi 4.50 1.75
Inscribed 1985.

United Nations, 40th Anniv. — A229

1987, Oct. 8   *Perf. 14*
731 A229 85fr Emblem, NYC office .90 .30
732 A229 95fr Emblem .90 .30
733 A229 150fr Hands, emblem 1.25 .55
    Nos. 731-733 (3) 3.05 1.15
Inscribed 1985.

Cathedral of African Memory, 50th Anniv. A230

130fr, Statue of saint, Fr. Daniel Brottier, vert.

1987, Oct. 16   *Perf. 12½x13, 13x12½*
734 A230 130fr multi 1.25 .65
735 A230 140fr multi 1.25 .65
Inscribed 1986.

Lat Dior, King of Cayor (d. 1887) A231

1987, Oct. 27   *Litho.*   *Perf. 14*
736 A231 130fr Battle of Dekhele 1.25 .50
737 A231 160fr Lat Dior 1.25 .50

World Food Day A232

1987, Oct. 30   *Litho.*   *Perf. 12½*
738 A232 130fr Earth storing grain, vert. 1.00 .60
739 A232 140fr shown 1.25 .60
740 A232 145fr Emblem, vert. 1.50 .60
    Nos. 738-740 (3) 3.75 1.80
Inscribed 1986.

A233

Fauna, Bassa Casamance Natl. Park — A234

1987, Nov. 9   *Perf. 13*
741 A233 115fr Felis servalina 1.00 .55
742 A233 135fr Galagoides demi-dovii 1.40 .60
743 A233 150fr Potamochoerus porcus 1.50 .65
744 A233 250fr Panthera pardus 2.75 1.25
745 A234 300fr Aigrette 12.50 3.75
746 A234 300fr Guepier 12.50 3.75
   a.   Pair, #745-746 + label 27.50 8.00
    Nos. 741-746 (6) 31.65 10.55

Inscribed 1986. No. 745-746 has continuous design with corner label picturing map of Senegal with park highlighted.

Traditional Wrestling — A235

Various moves.

1987, Nov. 30   *Litho.*   *Perf. 14*
747 A235 115fr multi, horiz. 1.10 .45
748 A235 125fr multi, diff., horiz. 1.10 .50
749 A235 135fr multi, diff. 1.25 .55
750 A235 165fr multi, diff. 1.60 .75
    Nos. 747-750 (4) 5.05 2.25

Birds in Djoudj Natl. Park — A236

1987, Dec. 4
751 A236 115fr Stork 1.75 .40
752 A236 125fr Pink flamingos, horiz. 2.00 .40
753 A236 135fr White pelicans, horiz. 2.50 .65
754 A236 300fr Pelicans in water 5.00 1.25
755 A236 350fr like 125fr, horiz. 5.25 1.75
756 A236 350fr like 135fr, horiz. 5.25 1.75
   a.   Pair, #755-756 + label 11.50 11.50
    Nos. 751-756 (6) 21.75 6.20

Christmas A237

Designs: 145fr, Youth dreaming of presents. 150fr, Madonna and child. 180fr, Holy Family, congregation praying. 200fr, Holy Family, candle and Christmas tree.

1987, Dec. 24   *Perf. 12½x13*
757 A237 145fr multi 1.25 .40
758 A237 150fr multi 1.25 .40
759 A237 180fr multi 1.75 .65
760 A237 200fr multi 2.00 .65
    Nos. 757-760 (4) 6.25 2.10

Dakar Intl. Fair, 10th Anniv. (in 1985) — A238

1988, Feb. 27   *Litho.*   *Perf. 13*
761 A238 125fr multi .90 .45
Inscribed 1985.

Fish — A239

1988, Feb. 29   *Litho.*   *Perf. 13*
762 A239 5fr Amelurus nebulosus .30 .30
763 A239 100fr Heniochus acuminatus 1.25 .60
764 A239 145fr Anthias anthias 2.25 .90
765 A239 180fr Cyprinus carpio 4.00 1.50
    Nos. 762-765 (4) 7.80 3.30

World Meteorology Day — A240

1988, Mar. 15   *Perf. 13½*
766 A240 145fr multi 1.25 .55

Paris-Dakar Rally, 10th Anniv. (in 1987) — A241

Various motorcycle and automobile entries in desert settings.

1988   *Perf. 13*
767 A241 145fr Motorcycle 1.60 .55
768 A241 180fr Race car 2.00 .60
769 A241 200fr Race car, truck 2.10 .90
770 A241 410fr Thierry Sabine 4.50 1.75
    Nos. 767-770 (4) 10.20 3.80

Inscribed 1987. For surcharges, see Nos. 1051, 1194A.

Mollusks A242

1988, Apr. 20   *Perf. 12½*
771 A242 10fr Squid .25 .25
772 A242 20fr Donax trunculus .25 .25
773 A242 145fr Achatina fulica, vert. 1.75 .65
774 A242 165fr Helix nemoralis 2.25 .85
    Nos. 771-774 (4) 4.50 2.00

1988 African Soccer Cup Championships, Rabat — A243

1988, May 10   *Litho.*   *Perf. 13*
775 A243 80fr Cameroun (winner) .70 .30
776 A243 100fr Kick, CAF emblem .90 .35
777 A243 145fr Map, players, final score 1.25 .40
778 A243 180fr Trophy 1.75 .60
    Nos. 775-778 (4) 4.60 1.65
    Nos. 776-778 vert.

US Peace Corps in Senegal, 25th Anniv. — A244

1988, May 11   *Litho.*   *Perf. 13*
779 A244 190fr multi 1.50 .65

Marine Flora — A245

1988, June 13   *Litho.*   *Perf. 12½*
780 A245 10fr Dictyota atomaria .25 .25
781 A245 65fr Agarum gmelini .65 .25
782 A245 145fr Saccorrhiza bulbosa 1.40 .50
783 A245 180fr Rhodymenia palmetta 1.75 .65
    Nos. 780-783 (4) 4.05 1.65
Inscribed 1987.

No. 710 Overprinted

1988, Aug. 27   *Litho.*   *Perf. 13*
784 A221 320fr multi 2.75 1.25

Stamp Fair, Riccione, Aug. 27-29, 1988. Stamp incorrectly overprinted "89," instead of "88."

ENDA — A246

1988 Litho. Perf. 13

785 A246 125fr Thierno Saidou Nourou Tall Center — 1.00 .50

For surcharge, see No. 824.

1988 Summer Olympics, Seoul — A247

1988, Sept. 17 Litho. Perf. 13

786 A247 5fr shown — .25 .25
787 A247 75fr Running, swimming, soccer — .70 .35
788 A247 300fr Character trademark, torch — 2.75 1.00
789 A247 410fr Emblems, running — 3.50 1.40
Nos. 786-789 (4) — 7.20 3.00

Industries A248

1988, Nov. 7 Litho. Perf. 13

790 A248 5fr Phosphate, Thies — .25 .25
791 A248 20fr I.C.S. — .25 .25
792 A248 145fr Seib Mill, Diourbel — 1.25 .45
793 A248 410fr Mbao refinery — 3.75 1.60
Nos. 790-793 (4) — 5.50 2.55

Postcards, c. 1900 — A249

20fr, Boys, Government Palace. 145fr, Wrestlers, St. Louis Great Mosque. 180fr, Dakar Depot, young woman in folk costume. 200fr, Governor's Residence, housewife using mortar & pestle.

1988, Nov. 26

794 A249 20fr red brn & blk — .25 .25
795 A249 145fr red brn & blk — 1.25 .55
796 A249 180fr red brn & blk — 1.60 .75
797 A249 200fr red brn & blk — 1.90 1.00
Nos. 794-797 (4) — 5.00 2.55

Indigenous Flowers — A250

1988, Dec. 4 Perf. 13x12½

798 A250 20fr Packia biglobosa — .25 .25
799 A250 60fr Eurphorbia pulcherrima — .55 .25
800 A250 65fr Cyrtosperma senegalense — .65 .25
801 A250 410fr Bombax costatum — 3.75 1.50
Nos. 798-801 (4) — 5.20 2.25

11th Paris-Dakar Rally A251

1989, Jan. 13 Litho. Perf. 13½

802 A251 10fr Mask, vehicle, Eiffel Tower — .25 .25
803 A251 145fr Helmet, desert scene — 1.50 .50
804 A251 180fr Turban, rallyist in desert — 1.75 .65
805 A251 220fr Thierry Sabine — 2.25 .85
Nos. 802-805 (4) — 5.75 2.25

For surcharge see No. 1050.

Tourism A252

1989, Feb. 15 Perf. 13

806 A252 10fr Teranga — .25 .25
807 A252 80fr Campement — .70 .30
808 A252 100fr Saly — .90 .40
809 A252 350fr Dior — 2.75 1.10
Nos. 806-809 (4) — 4.60 2.05

Inscribed 1988.

Tourism — A253

1989, Mar. 11

810 A253 130fr Natl. tourism emblem, vert. — 1.00 .40
811 A253 140fr Visiting rural community — 1.10 .45
812 A253 145fr Sport fishing — 1.40 .65
813 A253 180fr Water skiing, polo — 1.40 .80
Nos. 810-813 (4) — 4.90 2.30

Inscribed 1987.

French Revolution, Bicent. — A254

Designs: 180fr, Governor's Palace, St. Louis. 220fr, Declaration of Human Rights and Citizenship, vert. 300fr, Flag, revolutionaries.

1989, May 24 Litho. Perf. 13

814 A254 180fr shown — 1.75 1.00
815 A254 220fr multi — 2.00 1.00
816 A254 300fr multi — 3.00 1.60
Nos. 814-816 (3) — 6.75 3.60

PHILEXFRANCE '89 — A255

1989, July 7 Litho. Perf. 13x12½

817 A255 10fr shown — .25 .25
818 A255 25fr Simulated stamp, map of France — .25 .25
819 A255 75fr Exhibit — .65 .30
820 A255 145fr Affixing stamp — 1.25 .50
Nos. 817-820 (4) — 2.40 1.30

Antoine de Saint-Exupery (1900-1944), French Aviator and Writer — A256

Scenes from novels: 180fr, Southern Courier, 1929. 220fr, Night flier, 1931. 410fr, Bomber pilot, 1942.

1989, Aug. 30 Litho. Perf. 13

821 A256 180fr multi — 1.50 .50
822 A256 220fr multi — 1.75 .85
823 A256 410fr multi — 4.00 1.40
Nos. 821-823 (3) — 7.25 2.75

No. 785 Surcharged in Bright Green

1989 Litho. Perf. 13

824 A246 555fr on 125fr multi — 4.25 2.00

3rd Francophone Summit on the Arts and Culture — A257

Designs: 5fr, Palette, quill pen in ink pot, dancer, vert. 30fr, Children reading. 100fr, Architecture, women, Earth. 200fr, Artist sketching, easel, gear wheels, chemist, computer operator.

1989 Perf. 13x13½, 13½x13

825 A257 5fr multicolored — .25 .25
826 A257 30fr multicolored — .25 .25
827 A257 100fr multicolored — .80 .45
828 A257 200fr multicolored — 1.75 .95
Nos. 825-828 (4) — 3.05 1.90

Pottery A258

1989, Nov. 1 Perf. 13

829 A258 15fr shown — .25 .25
830 A258 30fr Potter, three-handled urn — .35 .25
831 A258 75fr Vases — .65 .35
832 A258 145fr Woman carrying pottery — 1.25 .45
Nos. 829-832 (4) — 2.50 1.30

"30," Dakar Cancel — A259

Natl. Archives, 75th Anniv. — A260

30fr, Telephone handset, map. 180fr, Map, simulated stamp, phone handset. 220fr, Telecommunications satellite, globe, map.

1989, Oct. 9 Perf. 13½

833 A259 25fr multicolored — .25 .25
834 A259 30fr multicolored — .25 .25
835 A259 180fr multicolored — 1.50 .50
836 A259 220fr multicolored — 1.75 .65
Nos. 833-836 (4) — 3.75 1.65

Conference of Postal and Telecommunication Administrations of West African Nations (CAPTEAO), 30th anniv.

1989, Oct. 23 Perf. 11½

Designs: 15fr, Stacks, postal card of 1922. 40fr, Document, 1825. 145fr, Document, Archives building. 180fr, Tome.

837 A260 15fr multicolored — .25 .25
838 A260 40fr multicolored — .35 .25
839 A260 145fr multicolored — 1.25 .55
840 A260 180fr multicolored — 1.40 .65
Nos. 837-840 (4) — 3.25 1.70

Jawarharlal Nehru, 1st Prime Minister of Independent India — A261

1989, Nov. 14 Perf. 13

841 A261 220fr Portrait, vert. — 1.75 .65
842 A261 410fr shown — 3.75 1.40

Marine Life A262

1989, Nov. 27

843 A262 10fr Grapsus grapsus — .25 .25
844 A262 60fr Hippocampus guttulatus — .85 .30
845 A262 145fr Lepas anatifera — 1.75 .55
846 A262 220fr Beach flea — 1.90 .95
Nos. 843-846 (4) — 4.75 2.05

Children's March to the Sanctuary A263

1989, Dec. 9 Litho. Perf. 13½

847 A263 145fr shown — 1.10 .40
848 A263 180fr Church — 1.50 .60

Pilgrimage to Notre Dame de Popenguine, cent.

Birds A263a

Designs: 10fr, Phalacrocovax carbolucidus, Anhinga rufa. 45fr, Lavius cirrocephalus. 100fr, Dwarf bee-eater, Lophogetus occipitalis. 180fr, Egretta gularis.

1989, Dec. 11 Perf. 13

849 A263a 10fr multicolored — .35 .30
850 A263a 45fr multicolored — 1.00 .40
851 A263a 100fr multicolored — 2.00 .60
852 A263a 180fr multicolored — 6.00 1.00
Nos. 849-852 (4) — 9.35 2.30

Natl. parks: Djoudj (10fr), Langue de Barbarie (45fr), Basse Casamance (100fr) and Saloum (180fr).

Christmas
A264

Joan of Arc
Institute, 50th
Anniv.
A265

1989, Dec. 22　　Litho.　　Perf. 13
853　A264　10fr shown　　　　　　.25　.25
854　A264　25fr Teddy bear　　　　.25　.25
855　A264　30fr Manger　　　　　　.25　.25
856　A264　200fr Mother and child　1.75　.80
　　　　Nos. 853-856 (4)　　　　　2.50　1.55

1989, Dec. 26　　　　　　　Perf. 13½
857　A265　20fr shown　　　　　　.25　.25
858　A265　500fr Institute　　　　4.25　1.40

Flight of the 1st Seaplane, Mar. 28,
1910 — A266

Perf. 13x12½, 12½x13
1989, Dec. 30　　　　　　　Litho.
859　A266　125fr shown　　　　　1.00　.30
860　A266　130fr Seaplane, Fabre　1.10　.40
861　A266　475fr Fabre, schematic
　　　　　　　of aircraft, vert.　4.25　1.00
　　　　Nos. 859-861 (3)　　　　6.35　1.70

Souvneir Sheet

862　A266　700fr like 475fr, vert.　6.00　5.00

Henri Fabre (1882-1984), aviator.

1992 Summer Olympics,
Barcelona — A267

Various athletes and monuments or
architecture.

1990, Jan. 8　　　　　　　Perf. 12½
863　A267　10fr Basketball　　　.25　.25
864　A267　130fr High jump　　　.90　.25
865　A267　180fr Discus　　　　1.25　.30
866　A267　210fr Running　　　1.50　.40
867　A267　315fr Tennis　　　　2.25　.50
868　A267　475fr Equestrian　　3.75　.60
　　　　Nos. 863-868 (6)　　　9.90　2.30

Souvenir Sheet

869　A267　600fr Soccer　　　　4.50　1.00

Fight AIDS
Worldwide
A268

1989, Dec. 1　　Litho.　　Perf. 13½
870　A268　5fr shown　　　　　　.25　.25
871　A268　100fr Umbrella　　　　.90　.35
872　A268　145fr Fist crushing vi-
　　　　　　rus　　　　　　　　1.10　.50
873　A268　180fr Hammering away
　　　　　　at virus　　　　　　1.50　.65
　　　　Nos. 870-873 (4)　　　　3.75　1.75

12th Paris-Dakar Rally — A269

1990, Jan. 16　　　　　　　Perf. 13
874　A269　20fr shown　　　　　　.25　.25
875　A269　25fr Motorcycle　　　　.25　.25
876　A269　180fr Trophy winner,
　　　　　　crowd　　　　　　　1.60　.65
877　A269　200fr Thierry Sabine　1.60　.80
　　　　Nos. 874-877 (4)　　　　3.70　1.95

1990 World Cup Soccer
Championships, Italy — A270

Various athletes and: 45fr, Trophy, the
Piazza Della Signoria, Florence. 140fr, Piazza
Navona, Rome. 180fr, *The Virgin with St.
Anne and the Infant Jesus,* by Leonardo da
Vinci. 220fr, Portrait of Giuseppe Garibaldi
(1807-1882), Risorgimento Museum, Turin.
300fr, *The Sistine Madonna,* by Raphael.
415fr, *The Virgin and Child,* by Daniele da
Volterra. 700fr, Columbus Monument, Milan.

1990, Jan. 31　　Litho.　　Perf. 13x12½
878　A270　45fr multicolored　　　.35　.25
879　A270　140fr multicolored　　1.00　.40
880　A270　180fr multicolored　　1.40　.45
881　A270　220fr multicolored　　1.50　.55
882　A270　300fr multicolored　　2.50　.75
883　A270　415fr multicolored　　3.50　1.25
　　　　Nos. 878-883 (6)　　　10.25　3.65

Souvenir Sheet

Nos. 878-883 exist in souvenir sheets of 1.

884　A270　700fr multicolored　　6.00　3.00

1990 African Soccer
Cup
Championships,
Algeria — A271

1990, Mar. 2　　Litho.　　Perf. 13
885　A271　20f shown　　　　　　.25　.25
886　A271　60f Goalie　　　　　　.55　.25
887　A271　100f Exchange of
　　　　　　flags　　　　　　　　.90　.40
888　A271　500f Ball, trophy　　4.50　1.75
　　　　Nos. 885-888 (4)　　　　6.20　2.65

Postal
Services
A272

1990, Apr. 30　　Litho.　　Perf. 13
889　A272　5fr Facsimile trans-
　　　　　　mission　　　　　　.25　.25
890　A272　15fr Express mail　　.25　.25
891　A272　100fr Postal money or-
　　　　　　ders　　　　　　　　.75　.30
892　A272　180fr CNE　　　　　1.25　.50
　　　　Nos. 889-892 (4)　　　　2.50　1.30

A273

1990, May 31　　　　　　　Perf. 13½
893　A273　145fr shown　　　　1.25　.45
894　A273　180fr Hand, wreath,
　　　　　　envelope　　　　　1.50　.75

Multinational Postal School, 20th anniv.

A274

1990, May 31
895　A274　5fr shown　　　　　　.25　.25
896　A274　500fr Family　　　　3.75　1.25

S.O.S. Children's Village appeal for aid.

Boy
Scouts
A275

Scouting emblems and: 30fr, Camping.
100fr, Hiking at lakeshore. 145fr, Following
trail. 200fr, Scout, vert.

1990, Nov. 5　　Litho.　　Perf. 11½
897　A275　30fr multicolored　　.25　.25
898　A275　100fr multicolored　　.70　.30
899　A275　145fr multicolored　　1.00　.50
900　A275　200fr multicolored　　1.60　.60
　　　　Nos. 897-900 (4)　　　　3.55　1.65

Medicinal
Plants — A276

1990, Nov. 30　　　　　　Perf. 13x13½
901　A276　95fr Cassia tora　　1.00　.40
902　A276　105fr Tamarindus indi-
　　　　　　ca　　　　　　　　1.10　.45
903　A276　125fr Cassia oc-
　　　　　　cidentalis　　　　1.40　.55
904　A276　175fr Leptadenia has-
　　　　　　tata　　　　　　　1.75　.65
　　　　Nos. 901-904 (4)　　　5.25　2.05

A277

1990, Dec. 24　　Litho.　　Perf. 13½
905　A277　25fr shown　　　　　.25　.25
906　A277　145fr Angel, stars, peo-
　　　　　　ple　　　　　　　　1.25　.65
907　A277　180fr Adoration of the
　　　　　　Magi　　　　　　　1.60　.65

908　A277　200fr Animals, baby in
　　　　　　manger　　　　　1.75　.65
　　　　Nos. 905-908 (4)　　　4.85　2.20
　　　　Christmas.

A278

1991, Jan. 2　　Litho.　　Perf. 13x12½
909　A278　180fr multicolored　　1.50　.65

Intl. Red Cross, 125th Anniv., Senegalese
Red Cross, 25th anniv. No. 909 inscribed
1988.

Paris-Dakar Rally — A279

1991, Jan. 17
910　A279　15fr shown　　　　　.25　.25
911　A279　125fr Car, motorcycle　.90　.40
912　A279　180fr Car racing in
　　　　　　water　　　　　　1.50　.65
913　A279　220fr Two motorcycles,
　　　　　　beach　　　　　　2.00　.85
　　　　Nos. 910-913 (4)　　　4.65　2.15

Reptiles
A280

1991, Jan. 31　　　　　　Perf. 13½x13
914　A280　15fr Python sebae　　.25　.25
915　A280　60fr Chelonia mydas　.90　.25
916　A280　100fr Crocolylus
　　　　　　niloticus　　　　　1.50　.50
917　A280　180fr Chameleo sene-
　　　　　　galensis　　　　　2.50　.85
　　　　Nos. 914-917 (4)　　　5.15　1.85

　　　　Inscribed 1990.

African Film
Festival
A281

Designs: 30fr, Sphinx, slave house, cave
paintings, tomb of Mohammed. 60fr, Dogon
mask, mosque of Dioulasso, drawing of Osiris,
man on camel. 100fr, Ruins, drum, statue of
scribe, camels. 180fr, mask, mosque of
Djenne, pyramids, Moroccan architecture.

1991, Feb. 23　　　　　　Perf. 11½
918　A281　30fr org & multi　　.25　.25
919　A281　60fr org & multi　　.50　.25
920　A281　100fr org & multi　　1.00　.45
921　A281　180fr org & multi　　1.75　.65
　　　　Nos. 918-921 (4)　　　3.50　1.60

Alfred Nobel (1833-1896),
Industrialist — A282

Designs: 145fr, Drawing of Nobel.

1991, Mar. 29   Litho.   Die Cut
Self-adhesive
922 A282 145fr multi, vert.   2.00   .65
923 A282 180fr shown   2.50   .85

Antelope — A283

1991, Apr. 24   Litho.   Perf. 13½x13
924 A283   5fr Ouerbia ourebi   .25   .25
925 A283   10fr Gazella dorcas   .25   .25
926 A283 180fr Kobos kob kob   1.40   .60
927 A283 555fr Alcelaphus buce-
                    laphus major   5.00 2.00
        Nos. 924-927 (4)   6.90 3.10

Trees
A284

1991, May 30   Perf. 13½x13, 13x13½
928 A284   90fr Ancardium oc-
                    cidentalus   .75   .40
929 A284 100fr Mangifera indica   1.00   .50
930 A284 125fr Borassus flabel-
                    lifer, vert.   1.00   .50
931 A284 145fr Elaeis guineen-
                    sis, vert.   1.25   .60
        Nos. 928-931 (4)   4.00 2.00

Christopher Columbus — A285

100fr, Meeting Haitian natives. 145fr, Columbus' personal coat of arms, vert. 180fr, Santa Maria, Columbus. 200fr, 220fr, Columbus, ships. 500fr, Details of voyages. 625fr, Columbus at chart table.

1991, July 8   Litho.   Perf. 13
932 A285 100fr multicolored   .90   .40
  a.   Sheet of 1, perf. 12½   .90   .40
933 A285 145fr multicolored   1.25   .55
  a.   Sheet of 1, perf. 12½   1.25   .60
934 A285 180fr multicolored   1.60   .65
  a.   Sheet of 1, perf. 12½   1.75   .75
935 A285 200fr multicolored   1.75   .75
  a.   Sheet of 1, perf. 12½   1.75   .75
936 A285 220fr multicolored   2.00   .80
  a.   Sheet of 1, perf. 12½   2.00   .80
937 A285 500fr multicolored   4.50 1.90
  a.   Sheet of 1, perf. 12½   4.50 2.00
938 A285 625fr multicolored   5.75 2.25
  a.   Sheet of 1, perf. 12½   5.75 2.50
        Nos. 932-938 (7)   17.75 7.30

Tourism
A286

Designs: 10fr, Canoe excursion, Basse-Casamance. 25fr, Shore at Boufflers Hotel, Goree Island. 30fr, Huts built on stilts, Fadiouth Island. 40fr, Salt collecting on lake.

1991, July 30   Litho.   Perf. 13
939 A286   10fr multicolored   .25   .25
940 A286   25fr multicolored   .25   .25
941 A286   30fr multicolored   .35   .25
942 A286   40fr multicolored   .35   .25
        Nos. 939-942 (4)   1.20 1.00
            Dated 1989.

Louis Armstrong, Jazz Musician, 20th Death Anniv. — A287

1991, Oct. 7   Perf. 13½
943 A287   10fr shown   .25   .25
944 A287 145fr Singing   1.25   .60
945 A287 180fr With trumpets   1.50   .75
946 A287 220fr Playing trumpet 1.75   .90
        Nos. 943-946 (4)   4.75 2.50

Yuri Gagarin, First Man in Space, 30th Anniv. — A288

Various portraits of Gagarin with Vostok I in Earth orbit.

1991, Nov. 25   Litho.   Perf. 13½
947 A288   15fr multicolored   .25   .25
948 A288 145fr multicolored   1.25   .60
949 A288 180fr multicolored   1.50   .75
950 A288 220fr multicolored   1.75   .90
        Nos. 947-950 (4)   4.75 2.50

Rural Water Supply Project — A289

1991, Dec. 2   Litho.   Perf. 13½
951 A289   30fr Bowl of water   .25   .25
952 A289 145fr Water faucet,
                    huts   1.25   .65
953 A289 180fr Dripping faucet,
                    flags   1.60   .80
954 A289 220fr Water tower, huts 1.90 .95
        Nos. 951-954 (4)   5.00 2.65

6th Islamic Summit — A290

1991, Dec. 9
955 A290   15fr shown   .25   .25
956 A290 145fr Upraised hands   1.25   .65
957 A290 180fr Congress Center,
                    Dakar   1.60   .80
958 A290 220fr Grand Mosque,
                    Dakar   1.90   .95
        Nos. 955-958 (4)   5.00 2.65

A291

Basketball, Cent.: 145fr, Player dribbling ball. 180fr, Couple holding trophy. 220fr, Lion, basketball, trophies.

1991, Dec. 21   Litho.   Perf. 13½
959 A291 125fr multicolored   1.00   .50
960 A291 145fr multicolored   1.25   .60
961 A291 180fr multicolored   1.50   .75
962 A291 220fr multicolored   1.75   .90
        Nos. 959-962 (4)   5.50 2.75

A292

1991, Dec. 24   Litho.   Perf. 13½
963 A292   5fr Jesus   .25   .25
964 A292 145fr Madonna and
                    Child   1.25   .60
965 A292 160fr Angels   1.40   .70
966 A292 220fr Christ Child, ani-
                    mals   1.90   .95
        Nos. 963-966 (4)   4.80 2.50

Christmas. For surcharge see No. 975.

A293

Musical score and: 5fr, Bust of Mozart. 150fr, Mozart conducting. 180fr, Mozart at piano. 220fr, Portrait.

1991, Dec. 31
967 A293   5fr multicolored   .25   .25
968 A293 150fr multicolored   1.25   .65
969 A293 180fr multicolored   1.60   .80
970 A293 220fr multicolored   1.90   .95
        Nos. 967-970 (4)   5.00 2.65

Wolfgang Amadeus Mozart, death bicent.

A293a

Mermoz and: 145fr, Outline maps of South America, Africa. 180fr, Airplane. 200fr, Aiplane in flight.

1991?   Litho.   Perf. 13½
970A A293a   15fr multicolored   .25   .25
970B A293a 145fr multicolored   1.00   .35
970C A293a 180fr multicolored   1.50   .35
970D A293a 200fr multicolored   2.00   .65
        Nos. 970A-970D (4)   4.75 1.60

Jean Mermoz (1901-36), pilot.
Nos. 970A-970D exist in imperf. souvenir sheets of 1.

A294

1992, Jan. 12   Litho.   Perf. 13½
971 A294   10fr shown   .25   .25
972 A294 145fr Map, soccer balls 1.25 .60
973 A294 200fr Lion, trophy   1.60   .85
974 A294 220fr Players   1.75   .90
        Nos. 971-974 (4)   4.85 2.60

18th African Soccer Cup Championships.

No. 965 Surcharged

1992, Feb. 19   Litho.   Perf. 13½
975 A292 180fr on 160fr   2.00 1.00

Natl. Parks
A295

1992, Mar. 20   Perf. 13½x13
976 A295   10fr Delta Du Saloum   .45   .25
977 A295 125fr Djoudj   1.60   .50
978 A295 145fr Niokolo-Koba   2.25   .60
979 A295 220fr Basse
                    Casamance   2.75   .90
        Nos. 976-979 (4)   7.05 2.25

Senegal's Participation in Gulf War — A296

Designs: 30fr, Oil wells, flag and missiles. 145fr, Oil wells, soldier. 180fr, Holy Ka'aba, soldier with gun. 220fr, Peace dove with flag, map.

1992, Apr. 4   Perf. 13½
980 A296   30fr multicolored   .25   .25
981 A296 145fr multicolored   1.25   .60
982 A296 180fr multicolored   1.50   .75
983 A296 220fr multicolored   1.75   .90
        Nos. 980-983 (4)   4.75 2.50

Fish Industry
A297

Stylized designs: 5fr, Catching fish. 60fr, Retail outlets. 100fr, Processing plant. 150fr, Packaging.

1992, Apr. 6   Litho.   Perf. 13½
984 A297   5fr multicolored   .25   .25
985 A297   60fr multicolored   .55   .30
986 A297 100fr multicolored   .90   .45
987 A297 150fr multicolored   1.25   .65
        Nos. 984-987 (4)   2.95 1.65

Tourism — A298

1992, May 5   *Perf. 13½x13*
988 A298   5fr Niokolo complex   .25   .25
989 A298 10fr Casamance River   .25   .25
990 A298 150fr Dakar region   1.25   .65
991 A298 200fr Saint-Louis ex-
                 cursion   1.75   .95
     Nos. 988-991 (4)   3.50 2.10

Planting
Trees
A299

Various designs showing children planting trees.

1992, May 29 *Perf. 13½x13, 13x13½*
992 A299 145fr multi   1.25   .65
993 A299 180fr multi   1.60   .80
994 A299 200fr multi   1.75   .90
995 A299 220fr multi, vert.   1.90   .95
     Nos. 992-995 (4)   6.50 3.30

Public
Works
Projects
A300

Various scenes of people cleaning and repairing public walkways.

Perf. 13½x13, 13x13½
1992, June 1   Litho.
996 A300 25fr multi   .25   .25
997 A300 145fr multi   1.25   .65
998 A300 180fr multi, vert.   1.60   .80
999 A300 220fr multi, vert.   2.00 1.00
     Nos. 996-999 (4)   5.10 2.70

Children's Rights — A301

1992, June 12   *Perf. 13*
1000 A301 20fr Education   .25   .25
1001 A301 45fr Guidance   .40   .25
1002 A301 165fr Instruction   1.40   .70
1003 A301 180fr Health care   1.60   .80
      Nos. 1000-1003 (4)   3.65 2.00

African
Integration
A302

1992, June 29   Litho.   *Perf. 13*
1004 A302 10fr Free trade   .25   .25
1005 A302 30fr Youth activities   .25   .25
1006 A302 145fr Communications   1.25   .60
1007 A302 220fr Women's move-
                  ments   2.00 1.00
      Nos. 1004-1007 (4)   3.75 2.10

1992 Summer
Olympics,
Barcelona
A303

1992, July 25   Litho.   *Perf. 13½*
1008 A303 145fr Map, horiz.   1.10   .55
1009 A303 180fr Runner   1.50   .70
1010 A303 200fr Sprinter, horiz.   2.00   .75
1011 A303 300fr Torch bearer   2.75 1.10
      Nos. 1008-1011 (4)   7.35 3.10

Blue
Train — A304

1992, Aug. 3
1012 A304 70fr shown   .70   .30
1013 A304 145fr Train yard   1.40   .55
1014 A304 200fr Train, passen-
                  gers   2.00   .75
1015 A304 220fr Station   2.10   .85
      Nos. 1012-1015 (4)   6.20 2.45

Intl. Maritime
Heritage
Year — A305

25fr, Map of Antarctica. 100fr, Ocean, sea life. 180fr, Man addressing UN. 220fr, Hands holding globe, flags, ship, fish.

1992, Sept. 4
1016 A305 25fr multi, horiz.   .25   .25
1017 A305 100fr multi   1.00   .40
1018 A305 180fr multi   2.00   .70
1019 A305 220fr multi   2.25   .85
      Nos. 1016-1019 (4)   5.50 2.20

Corals
A306

Various coral formations.

Perf. 13½x13, 13x13½
1992, Sept. 18   Litho.
1020 A306 50fr multicolored   .40   .25
1021 A306 100fr multicolored   1.10   .40
1022 A306 145fr multi, vert.   1.50 1.10
1023 A306 220fr multicolored   2.25   .90
      Nos. 1020-1023 (4)   5.25 2.65

Konrad Adenauer (1876-1967) — A307

Designs: 5fr, Portrait, vert. 145fr, Schaumburg Palace, Bonn. 180fr, Hands clasped. 220fr, Map of West Germany.

Perf. 13x13½, 13½x13
1992, Sept. 30   Litho.
1024 A307   5fr multicolored   .25   .25
1025 A307 145fr multicolored   1.25   .60
1026 A307 180fr multicolored   1.50   .75
1027 A307 220fr multicolored   1.75   .90
      Nos. 1024-1027 (4)   4.75 2.50

Shellfish — A308

1992, Oct. 1   Litho.   *Perf. 13½*
1028 A308 20fr Crab   .25   .25
1029 A308 30fr Spider crab   .35   .25
1030 A308 180fr Lobster   1.75   .70
1031 A308 200fr Shrimp   2.10   .75
      Nos. 1028-1031 (4)   4.45 1.95

Fruit-bearing
Plants — A309

1992, Oct. 16   Litho.   *Perf. 13x13½*
1032 A309 10fr Parkia biglobosa   .25   .25
1033 A309 50fr Balanites ae-
                  gyptiaca   .45   .25
1034 A309 200fr Parinari
                  macrophylla   1.60   .70
1035 A309 220fr Opuntiatuna   1.75   .90
      Nos. 1032-1035 (4)   4.05 2.10

John Glenn's
Orbital Flight,
30th
Anniv. — A310

15fr, Astronaut in spacesuit, flag, map, spacecraft, horiz. 145fr, American flag, Glenn, horiz. 180fr, Flag, lift-off of rocket, Glenn in spacesuit, horiz. 200fr, Astronaut in spacesuit, spacecraft.

1992, Nov. 30   Litho.   *Perf. 13½*
1036 A310 15fr multicolored   .25   .25
1037 A310 145fr multicolored   1.25   .60
1038 A310 180fr multicolored   1.60   .70
1039 A310 200fr multicolored   1.75   .80
      Nos. 1036-1039 (4)   4.85 2.35

Maps Featuring Bakari II — A311

100fr, Map from Spanish Atlas, 1375. 145fr, Stone head, Vera Cruz, Mexico, world map, 1413.

1992, Dec. 2   *Perf. 13*
1040 A311 100fr multicolored   1.50   .40
1041 A311 145fr multicolored   2.25   .60

No. 1041 issued only with black bar obliterating "Mecades."

Biennial of
Dakar — A312

20fr, Picture frame. 50fr, Puppet head, stage. 145fr, Open book. 220fr, Musical instrument.

1992, Dec. 14   *Perf. 13½*
1042 A312 20fr multicolored   .25   .25
1043 A312 50fr multicolored   .45   .25
1044 A312 145fr multicolored   1.25   .60
1045 A312 220fr multicolored   2.10   .90
      Nos. 1042-1045 (4)   4.05 2.00

Christmas
A313

Designs: 15fr, Children dancing around large ornament, horiz. 145fr, Christmas tree. 180fr, Jesus Christ. 200fr, Santa Claus.

1992, Dec. 24   *Perf. 13½*
1046 A313 15fr multicolored   .25   .25
1047 A313 145fr multicolored   2.00   .60
1048 A313 180fr multicolored   2.50   .70
1049 A313 200fr multicolored   2.75   .90
      Nos. 1046-1049 (4)   7.50 2.45

Nos. 770,
804 Srchd.
in Red

1993, Jan. 17   Litho.   *Perf. 13½*
1050 A251 145fr on 180fr #804   1.75 1.00
               Perf. 13
1051 A241 220fr on 410fr #770   2.75 1.25

Size and location of surcharge varies.

Environmental Protection — A314

Accident
Prevention
A315

Designs: 20fr, Medical clinic. 25fr, Preventing industrial accidents. 145fr, Preventing chemical spills. 200fr, Red Cross helicopter, airline crash.

Perf. 13 (#1052, 1055), 13½
1993, Mar. 22   Litho.
1052 A314 20fr multicolored   .25   .25
1053 A315 25fr multicolored   .25   .25
1054 A315 145fr multicolored   1.10   .60
1055 A314 200fr multicolored   1.60   .80
      Nos. 1052-1055 (4)   3.20 1.90

Abdoulaye Seck
Marie Parsine
(1873-1931), PTT
Director — A316

1993, Apr. 21   Litho.   *Perf. 13½*
1056 A316 220fr multicolored   2.10   .90

Wild
Animals
A317

30fr, Crocuta crocuta. 50fr, Panthera leo. 70fr, Panthera pardus. 150fr, Giraffa camelopardalis peratta, vert. 180fr, Cervus.

1993, Nov. 26   Litho.   Perf. 13½
1057 A317 30fr multicolored .25 .25
1058 A317 50fr multicolored .25 .25
1059 A317 70fr multicolored .55 .25
1060 A317 150fr multicolored 1.00 .30
1061 A317 180fr multicolored 1.60 .35
  Nos. 1057-1061 (5) 3.65 1.40

Christmas
A318

Designs: 80fr, Two children seated by Christmas tree. 145fr, Santa holding presents, three children. 150fr, Girl, Santa with present.

1993, Dec. 24   Litho.   Perf. 13x13½
1062 A318 5fr multicolored .25 .25
1063 A318 80fr multicolored .30 .25
1064 A318 145fr multicolored .55 .30
1065 A318 150fr multicolored .60 .30
  Nos. 1062-1065 (4) 1.70 1.10

Paris-Dakar Rally, 16th Anniv. — A319

Designs: 145fr, Truck, car, motorcycle racing by tree. 180fr, Racing through desert, men with camel. 220fr, Car, truck, village.

1994, Jan. 5   Perf. 13½
1066 A319 145fr multicolored .70 .30
1067 A319 180fr multicolored .90 .35
1068 A319 220fr multicolored 1.00 .45
  Nos. 1066-1068 (3) 2.60 1.10

Assassination of John F. Kennedy, 30th Anniv. — A320

1993, Dec. 31   Litho.   Perf. 13
1069 A320 80fr shown .30 .25
1070 A320 555fr Kennedy, White House 2.25 1.10

Fishing Industry A321

5fr, Drying eels. 90fr, Sifting for shellfish. 100fr, Salting fish. 200fr, Cooking fish.

1994, Feb. 28
1071 A321 5fr multicolored .25 .25
1072 A321 90fr multicolored .35 .25
1073 A321 100fr multicolored .40 .25
1074 A321 200fr multicolored .80 .40
  Nos. 1071-1074 (4) 1.80 1.15

Flowers — A321a

Design: 80fr, Gloriosa superba. 100fr, Erythrina senegalensis. 145fr, Spathodea campanulata. 220fr, Hibiscus rosa-sinensis. 250fr, Satanocrater berhautii.

Perf. 13¼x13½
1994, Feb. 28   Litho.
1074A A321a 80fr multi 4.00 —
1074B A321a 100fr multi 5.00 —
1074C A321a 145fr multi 7.25 —
1074D A321a 220fr multi —
1074E A321a 250fr multi 11.00 —
  Dated 1993.

Conservation of the Seashore — A322

Stylized designs: 5fr, Halting removal of sand. 75fr, Fight against drifting sand dunes. 100fr, Dams, dikes against beach erosion. 200fr, Healthy, aesthetic environment.

1994, Mar. 7
1075 A322 5fr multicolored .25 .25
1076 A322 75fr multicolored .30 .25
1077 A322 100fr multicolored .55 .40
1078 A322 200fr multicolored .80 .60
  Nos. 1075-1078 (4) 1.90 1.50

Save the Elephant A323

1994, Apr. 18
1079 A323 30fr shown .25 .25
1080 A323 60fr Elephant in "SOS" .65 .25
1081 A323 90fr Elephants forming "SOS" 1.25 .45
1082 A323 145fr Elephant, tusks 1.60 .50
  Nos. 1079-1082 (4) 3.75 1.45

Arrival of Portuguese in Senegal, 550th Anniv. A324

1994, Nov. 17   Litho.   Perf. 12
1083 A324 175fr multicolored .80 .40
  See Portugal No. 2036.

A325

Shells: 20fr, Murex saxatilis, horiz. 45fr, Nerita senegalensis. 75fr, Polymita picea, horiz. 175fr, Scalaria pretiosa. 215fr, Conus gloria maris.

1994, Oct. 3   Litho.   Perf. 13½
1084 A325 20fr multicolored .25 .25
1085 A325 45fr multicolored .25 .25
1086 A325 75fr multicolored .30 .25
1087 A325 175fr multicolored .75 .40
1088 A325 215fr multicolored .95 .50
  Nos. 1084-1088 (5) 2.50 1.65

A326

1994, Nov. 4
1089 A326 175fr multi, horiz. .75 .40
1090 A326 215fr multi, horiz. .95 .50
1091 A326 275fr multicolored 1.25 .60
1092 A326 290fr multi, diff. 1.25 .65
  Nos. 1089-1092 (4) 4.20 2.15

Intl. Olympic Committee, Cent.

Wild Animals A327

1994, Oct. 28   Litho.   Perf. 13½
1093 A327 60fr Canis aureus .30 .25
1094 A327 70fr Aonyx capensis .30 .25
1095 A327 100fr Herpestes ichneumon .45 .25
1096 A327 175fr Manis gigantea .75 .40
1097 A327 215fr Varanus niloticus .95 .45
  Nos. 1093-1097 (5) 2.75 1.60

Lions Club Intl., 13th Multidistrict Convention, Dakar — A328

1994, May 5   Litho.   Perf. 13½x13
1098 A328 30fr shown .25 .25
1099 A328 60fr Emblem, butterfly .30 .25
1100 A328 175fr Emblem, "L's" .85 .40
1101 A328 215fr Colors, emblem 1.00 .50
  Nos. 1098-1101 (4) 2.40 1.40

African Children's Day A329

UNICEF emblem and: 175fr, Children playing. 215fr, Family, huts.

1994, June 16   Litho.   Perf. 13½
1102 A329 175fr multicolored 2.00 .40
1103 A329 215fr multicolored 2.25 .50

1994 World Cup Soccer Championships, US — A330

Designs: 45fr, Flags of participants, soccer ball, vert. 175fr, Top of globe, bottom of soccer ball, vert. 215fr, Player. 665fr, Two players.

1994, June 17
1104 A330 45fr multicolored .25 .25
1105 A330 175fr multicolored .80 .40
1106 A330 215fr multicolored 1.00 .50
1107 A330 665fr multicolored 3.00 1.50
  Nos. 1104-1107 (4) 5.05 2.65

UPU Congress, Seoul — A331

Designs: 10fr, Rainbow. 175fr, Dove with wings like postage stamp. 300fr, 260fr, Stylized stamp. Stylized globe, air mail envelope, hands.

1994, Aug. 16   Litho.   Perf. 13½x13
1108 A331 10fr multicolored .30 .25
1109 A331 175fr multi 1.50 1.00
1110 A331 260fr multicolored 2.00 1.10
1111 A331 300fr multicolored 2.25 1.25

Intl. Year of the Family A333

UN emblem and: 5fr, People of different races, national flags, peace dove, globe, sun. 175fr, Globe, flags, people. 215fr, Globe, mother & child. 290fr, Buildings, family, dove, sun, globe.

1994, Aug. 19   Perf. 13½x13
1113 A333 5fr multicolored .25 .25
1114 A333 175fr multicolored .80 .40
1115 A333 215fr multicolored 1.00 .50
1116 A333 290fr multicolored 1.40 .70
  Nos. 1113-1116 (4) 3.45 1.85

10th Toulouse to Saint-Louis Air Rally — A334

1994, Apr. 10   Perf. 13½
1117 A334 100fr Breguet 14 .50 .25
1118 A334 145fr Guillaumet .65 .35
1119 A334 180fr Jean Mermoz .85 .40
1120 A334 220fr Saint-Exupery 1.00 .50
  Nos. 1117-1120 (4) 3.00 1.50
  Dated 1993.

Christmas — A335

175fr, Santa Claus, Christ, children, presents. 215fr, Christmas trees, religious scenes. 275fr, Magi, Christ Child. 290fr, Madonna & Child.

Perf. 13x13½, 13½x13
1994, Nov. 24
1121 A335 175fr multi, vert. .80 .40
1122 A335 215fr multi, vert. 1.00 .50
1123 A335 275fr multi 1.25 .65
1124 A335 290fr multi, vert. 1.40 .70
  Nos. 1121-1124 (4) 4.45 2.25

Historical Sites — A336

Designs: 100fr, Goree Chateau. 175fr, Soudan Mansion. 215fr, Goree Island. 275fr, Pinet Laprade fort, Sedhiou.

1994, Mar. 20   Litho.   Perf. 13½x13
1125	A336	100fr multicolored	.45	.25
1126	A336	175fr multicolored	.80	.40
1127	A336	215fr multicolored	1.00	.50
1128	A336	275fr multicolored	1.25	.65
		Nos. 1125-1128 (4)	3.50	1.80

Kallisaye Natl. Park A337

Water birds: 100fr, Ardea melanocephala, vert. 275fr, Sterna caspia, vert. 290fr, Egretta gularis, vert. 380fr, Pelecanus rufescens.

1995, Feb. 2   Perf. 13½
1129	A337	100fr multicolored	.50	.25
1130	A337	275fr multicolored	1.40	.70
1131	A337	290fr multicolored	1.60	.75
1132	A337	380fr multicolored	2.00	.95
		Nos. 1129-1132 (4)	5.50	2.65

Dinosaurs A338

1995, Jan. 27
1133	A338	100fr Diplodocus	.45	.25
1134	A338	175fr Brontosaurus	.75	.40
1135	A338	215fr Triceratops	1.00	.50
1136	A338	290fr Stegosaurus	1.75	.70
1137	A338	300fr Tyrannosaurus	2.50	1.00
		Nos. 1133-1137 (5)	6.45	2.85

House of Slaves, Goree A339

1994   Litho.   Perf. 13½
1138	A339	500fr multicolored	2.50	1.25

Flowers — A340

Designs: 30fr, Bombax costatum. 75fr, Allamanda cathartica. 100fr, Catharantus roseus. 1000fr, Clerodendron speciossimum.

1995, Apr. 9
1139	A340	30fr multicolored	.25	.25
1140	A340	75fr multicolored	.40	.25
1141	A340	100fr multicolored	.50	.25
1142	A340	1000fr multicolored	5.00	2.50
		Nos. 1139-1142 (4)	6.15	3.25

A341

1995, May 11   Litho.   Perf. 11½
1143	A341	260fr shown	1.25	.65
1144	A341	275fr Emblem, dove	1.40	.70

District 9100 Conference of Rotary, Intl.

A342

Map of Africa with countries highlighted, native item or animal: 10fr, Sudan, musical instrument. 15fr, Dahomey (Benin), huts, canoes. 30fr, Ivory Coast, elephant. 70fr, Mauritania, camel. 175fr, Guinea, string instrument, bananas. 180fr, Upper Volta (Burkina Faso), ox, vegetables, drum. 215fr, Niger, Cross of Agadès. 225fr, Senegal, lions.

1995, June 17
1145	A342	10fr multicolored	.25	.25
1146	A342	15fr multicolored	.25	.25
1147	A342	30fr multicolored	.25	.25
1148	A342	70fr multicolored	.35	.25
1149	A342	175fr multicolored	.90	.45
1150	A342	180fr multicolored	.95	.45
1151	A342	215fr multicolored	1.10	.55
1152	A342	225fr multicolored	1.25	.60
		Nos. 1145-1152 (8)	5.30	3.05

Fashion Type of 1972

1995, June 30   Perf. 13½x13
Size: 21x26mm
1153	A106	5fr yel brown	.25	.25
1154	A106	10fr bright green	.25	.25
1155	A106	20fr henna brown	.25	.25
1156	A106	25fr olive	.25	.25
1157	A106	30fr light olive	.25	.25
1158	A106	40fr yellow green	.25	.25
1159	A106	100fr slate blue	.50	.25
1160	A106	150fr deep blue	.75	.35
1161	A106	175fr dull brown	.90	.45
1162	A106	200fr black	1.00	.50
1163	A106	250fr red	1.25	.60
1164	A106	275fr rose carmine	1.40	.80
		Nos. 1153-1164 (12)	7.30	4.45

Economic Community of West African States (ECOWAS), 20th Anniv. — A343

Designs: 175fr, Satellite dish, telephone, computer, map, dam, vert. 215fr, Flags of member nations, fruits, vegetables.

1995, Sept. 11   Litho.   Perf. 13½
1165	A343	175fr multicolored	.90	.45
1166	A343	215fr multicolored	1.10	.55

Louis Pasteur (1822-95) — A345

275fr, Holding vial. 500fr, In laboratory.

1995, Sept. 28   Litho.   Perf. 11½
1168	A345	275fr multicolored	1.25	.60
1169	A345	500fr multicolored	2.25	1.25

Motion Pictures, Cent. A346

Early developments by Lumiere Brothers: 100fr, Scene from "The Water Sprinkler." 200fr, First pulbic showing of motion picture. 250fr, Auguste, Louis Lumiere watching picture of train arriving at station. 275fr, Demonstrating cinematography.

1995, Oct. 2   Perf. 13½
1170	A346	100fr multicolored	.45	.25
1171	A346	200fr multicolored	1.00	.45
1172	A346	250fr multicolored	1.25	.55
1173	A346	275fr multicolored	1.75	.70
		Nos. 1170-1173 (4)	4.45	1.95

FAO, 50th Anniv. A347

Designs: 175fr, Farmer, oxen. 215fr, Technician, bringing water to arid regions. 260fr, Gathering fish. 275fr, Nutrition of infants.

1995, Oct. 16
1174	A347	175fr multicolored	.80	.40
1175	A347	215fr multicolored	.95	.50
1176	A347	260fr multicolored	1.10	.55
1177	A347	275fr multicolored	1.25	.60
		Nos. 1174-1177 (4)	4.10	2.05

A348

1995, Oct. 24   Perf. 11½
1178	A348	275fr shown	1.25	.60
1179	A348	1000fr Building	4.25	2.00

UN, 50th anniv.

A349

1995, Nov. 2
1180	A349	150fr shown	.70	.35
1181	A349	500fr Contestants	2.25	1.10

La Francophonie, 25th anniv.

Wild Animals A350

Designs: a, 90fr, Syncerus nanus savanensis. b, 150fr, Phacochoerus aethiopicus. c, 175fr, Tragelaphus scriptus. d, 275fr, Goechelone sulcata. e, 300fr, Hystrix cristata.

1995, Nov. 13   Perf. 13½
1182	A350	Strip of 5, #a.-e.	5.75	5.75

Endangered Birds — A351

1995, Nov. 30   Perf. 13½x13
1183	A351	90fr Hydroprogne caspia	.45	.25
1184	A351	145fr Gelochelidon nilotica	.80	.30
1185	A351	150fr Sterna maxima	1.40	.35
1186	A351	180fr Sterna hirunda	1.75	.55
		Nos. 1183-1186 (4)	4.40	1.45

Butterflies A352

Designs: 45fr, Meganostoma eurydice. 100fr, Luehdorfia japonica. 200fr, Hebomoia glaucippe. 220fr, Aglais urticae.

1995, Dec. 4   Perf. 13
1187	A352	45fr multicolored	.40	.25
1188	A352	100fr multicolored	.80	.30
1189	A352	200fr multicolored	1.90	.50
1190	A352	220fr multicolored	2.25	.80
		Nos. 1187-1190 (4)	5.35	1.85

Tourism A353

1995, Dec. 28   Perf. 13½
1191	A353	100fr Bassari Festival	.45	.25
1192	A353	175fr Baawnaan, vert.	.80	.40
1193	A353	220fr Traditional huts	1.00	.50
1194	A353	500fr Turu	2.25	1.10
		Nos. 1191-1194 (4)	4.50	2.25

No. 770 Surcharged

1995 ?   Litho.   Perf. 13
1194A	A241	275fr on 410fr #770	—

A354   A355

Paris-Granada-Dakar Rally, 17th Anniv.: 215fr, Car, silhouettes of three people. 275fr, Man racing on motorcycle, vert. 290fr, Car under Eiffel Tower, car racing toward finish line. 665fr, Two cars going over hill.

1996, Jan. 16   Litho.   Perf. 11½
1195	A354	215fr multicolored	1.10	.60
1196	A354	275fr multicolored	1.50	.75
1197	A354	290fr multicolored	1.60	.80
1198	A354	665fr multicolored	3.50	1.75
		Nos. 1195-1198 (4)	7.70	3.90

1996, Feb.2

Flowers: 175fr, Gossypium barbadense. 275fr, Hibiscus sabdariffa. 290fr, Hibiscus asper. 500fr, Nymphaea lotus.

1199	A355	175fr multicolored	.95	.45
1200	A355	275fr multicolored	1.50	.75
1201	A355	290fr multicolored	1.60	.80
1202	A355	500fr multicolored	2.75	1.40
		Nos. 1199-1202 (4)	6.80	3.40

Sports
A356

1996, Mar. 29   Litho.   Perf. 11½

1203	A356	125fr Boxing	.65	.35
1204	A356	215fr Judo	1.10	.60
1205	A356	275fr Javelin	1.50	.75
1206	A356	320fr Discus	1.75	.90
		Nos. 1203-1206 (4)	5.00	2.60

Art by Serge
Correa, Hall
of Pearls
A357

1996,Apr. 18

1207	A357	260fr Corridor 1	1.25	.70
1208	A357	320fr Symphony 1	1.75	.85

National
Parks
A358

Designs: 175fr, Dolphin, flamingo, heron, Saloum Delta. 200fr, Chimpanzee, giraffe, elephant, Niokolo-Koba. 220fr, Crustaceans, bird in cave, Madeleine Island. 275fr, Abyssinia hornbill, crocodile, hippopotamus, Basse Casamance.

1996, Mar. 4

1209	A358	175fr multicolored	.95	.50
1210	A358	200fr multicolored	1.10	.55
1211	A358	220fr multicolored	1.25	.60
1212	A358	275fr multicolored	1.50	.75
		Nos. 1209-1212 (4)	4.80	2.40

Intl.
Olympic
Committee,
Cent.
A359

1996, July 1   Litho.   Perf. 12½

1213	A359	215fr multicolored	1.25	.60

1996
Summer
Olympic
Games,
Atlanta
A360

1996, July 15   Perf. 13

1214	A360	10fr Swimming	.25	.25
1215	A360	80fr Gymnastics	.40	.25
1216	A360	175fr Running	1.00	.50
1217	A360	260fr Hurdles	1.40	.70
		Nos. 1214-1217 (4)	3.05	1.70

Decade of
UN Against
Illegal Drug
Abuse and
Trafficking
A361

215fr, UN emblem, hand holding red stop sign, drug paraphernalia.

1996, June 21   Perf. 13½

1218	A361	175fr multicolored	.95	.50
1219	A361	215fr multicolored	1.10	.60

Red Cross of
Senegal — A362

1996, Oct. 21   Perf. 12½

1220	A362	275fr multicolored	1.50	.75

Primates
A363

Designs: 10fr, Cercopithecus aethiops. 30fr, Erthrocebus patas. 90fr, Cercopithecus campbelli. 215fr, Pantroglodytes verus. 260fr, Papio papio.

1996, Nov. 29   Litho.   Perf. 13x13½

1221	A363	10fr multicolored	.30	.25
1222	A363	30fr multicolored	.30	.25
1223	A363	90fr multicolored	.50	.25
1224	A363	215fr multicolored	.90	.50
1225	A363	260fr multicolored	1.00	.60
a.		Strip of 5, #1221-1225	4.00	3.00

UNICEF,
50th
Anniv.
A364

1996, Dec. 11   Perf. 13½x13

1226	A364	75fr shown	.30	.25
1227	A364	275fr Child, diff.	1.25	.60

19th Dakar-Agades-Dakar
Rally — A365

25fr, Semi-truck. 75fr, Man pushing car, figure of man. 215fr, Race car. 300fr, Man on motorcycle.

1997, Jan. 19   Litho.   Perf. 13x13½

1228	A365	25fr multicolored	.25	.25
1229	A365	75fr multicolored	.30	.25
1230	A365	215fr multicolored	.90	.45
1231	A365	300fr multicolored	1.25	.65
		Nos. 1228-1231 (4)	2.70	1.60

Trees — A366

Designs: 80fr, Faidherbia albida. 175fr, Eucalyptus. 220fr, Khaya senegalensis. 260fr, Casuarina equisetifolia.

1997, Mar. 31

1232	A366	80fr multicolored	.35	.25
1233	A366	175fr multicolored	.75	.35
1234	A366	220fr multicolored	.90	.45
1235	A366	260fr multicolored	1.00	.50
		Nos. 1232-1235 (4)	3.00	1.55

Birds — A367

25fr, Platalea leucorodia. 70fr, Leptilos crumeniferus. 175fr, Balcarica pavonina. 215fr, Ephippiarhychus senegalensis. 220fr, Numenius arquata.

1997, Feb. 28

1236	A367	25fr multicolored	.25	.25
1237	A367	70fr multicolored	.30	.25
1238	A367	175fr multicolored	.75	.35
1239	A367	215fr multicolored	.90	.45
1240	A367	220fr multicolored	.95	.50
a.		Strip of 5, #1236-1240	5.00	5.00

Insects
A368

Designs: 10fr, Mantis religiosa. 50fr, Forficula auricularia. 75fr, Schistocerca gregaria. 215fr, Cicindela lunulata. 220fr, Gryllus campestris.

1997, Jan. 31   Perf. 13½x13

1241	A368	10fr multicolored	.25	.25
1243	A368	50fr multicolored	.25	.25
1244	A368	75fr multicolored	.30	.25
1245	A368	215fr multicolored	.90	.45
1246	A368	220fr multicolored	.95	.45
a.		Strip of 5, #1241-1246	4.00	4.00

Postal officials in Senegal have declared Greenpeace sheets of nine with values of 250fr and 425fr "fake" and "illegal".

Cheikh Anta Diop (1923-86),
Historian — A369

Diop: 175fr, And Egyptian hieroglyphs, Sphinx. 215fr, Performing carbon 14 test.

1996, Feb. 26   Litho.   Perf. 13¼

1247-1248	A369	Set of 2	3.50 1.50

Fashion Type of 1972

1996-97   Engr.   Perf. 13½x13
Size: 21x26mm

1249	A106	15fr green		
1250	A106	50fr green	.25	.25
1251	A106	60fr olive grn	.40	
1251A	A108	70fr olive green	.40	
1252	A106	80fr green	.60	—
1253	A106	190fr olive green	.75	
1254	A106	215fr dark blue	.80	.40
1254A	A106	225fr dark blue	1.00	—
1255	A106	240fr brown	1.40	
1256	A106	260fr red brown	1.00	.50
1256A	A106	300fr red lilac	1.40	
1256B	A106	320fr rose lilac	1.50	
1257	A106	350fr henna brown	1.60	
1257B	A106	410fr lake	1.75	
1257C	A106	500fr brn violet	2.25	
1257D	A106	1000fr carmine	4.50	

Issued: 80fr, 225fr, 4/13/96. 50fr, 70fr, 215fr, 260fr, 4/13; 190fr, 240fr, 300fr, 350fr, 1000fr, 6/97.

Additional stamps were released in this set. The editors would like to examine them. Numbers will change if necessary.

Third World
A370

Design: 500fr, Hot air balloon in flight.

1996, Apr. 13   Litho.   Perf. 13½

1258	A370	215fr shown	.75	.40
1259	A370	500fr multicolored	1.75	.90

See Mali Nos. 812-813.

Pres.
Leopold
Senghor,
90th
Birthday
A371

Pictures of Senghor and: 175fr, Map of Senegal. 275fr, Quotation, vert.

1996, Oct. 9   Litho.   Perf. 13¼

1260-1261	A371	Set of 2	1.75 1.75

Niokolo-Badiar Natl. Park — A372

Designs: 30fr, Haliaetus vacifer. 90fr, Hippopotamus amphibius. 240fr, Loxindonta africana oxyotis. 300fr, Taurotragus derbianus.

1997, July 21   Litho.   Perf. 13½x13

1262	A372	30fr multicolored	.65	.25
1263	A372	90fr multicolored	.65	.25
1264	A372	240fr multicolored	1.00	.50
1265	A372	300fr multicolored	1.25	.65
		Nos. 1262-1265 (4)	3.55	1.65

Shells
A373

Designs: a, 15fr, Cassis tesselata. b, 40fr, Pugilina meria. c, 190fr, Cyprea mappa. d, 200fr, Natica adansoni. e, 300fr, Bullia miran.

1997, Aug. 19   Perf. 13x13½

1266	A373	Strip of 5, #a.-e.	4.00	4.00

Wild
Animals
A374

a, 25fr, African buffaloes. b, 90fr, Gazelles. c, 100fr, Gnu. d, 200fr, Wild dogs. e, 240fr, Cheetah.

1997, June 27
1267 A374 Strip of 5, #a.-e.   4.00 4.00

Goree Island A375

1997, May 30   *Perf. 13½*
1268 A375 180fr multicolored   .75 .40

No. 1268 is dated 1992 and has word "almadies" obliterated.

Dakar-Dakar Rally, 20th Anniv. — A376

Designs: 20fr, Truck traveling across Sahel. 45fr, Motorcycle arriving at Lake Rose. 190fr, Sports utility vehicle crossing Mauritanian Desert. 240fr, Car at Senegal River.

1998, Jan. 1   Litho.   *Perf. 13½x13*
1269 A376 20fr multicolored   .25 .25
1270 A376 45fr multicolored   .25 .25
1271 A376 190fr multicolored   .80 .40
1272 A376 240fr multicolored   1.00 .50
    Nos. 1269-1272 (4)   2.30 1.40

Food Day A377

190fr, Receiving grain through cereal bank. 200fr, Proper nutrition for women.

1997, Oct. 16
1273 A377 190fr multicolored   .80 .40
1274 A377 200fr multicolored   .85 .45

A378   A379

Masks: 45fr, Planche, Burkina Faso. 90fr, Kpeliyehe, Ivory Coast. 200fr, Nimba, Guinea Bissau. 240fr, Walu, Mali. 300fr, Dogon, Mali.

1997, Nov. 28
1275 A378 45fr multicolored   .25 .25
1276 A378 90fr multicolored   .45 .25
1277 A378 200fr multicolored   .85 .40
1278 A378 240fr multicolored   1.00 .50
1279 A378 300fr multicolored   1.25 .65
   a.   Strip of 5, #1275-1279   4.00 2.50

1997   *Perf. 11½*
1280 A379 310fr multicolored   1.25 .65

Heinrich von Stephan (1831-97).

Vasco de Gama (1460-1524), Expedition Around Cape of Good Hope, 500th Anniv. A380

De Gama and: 40fr, Route of spices. 75fr, Port of Zanzibar. 190fr, Caravel revolution. 200fr, Maps being printed.

1997, Nov. 22
1281 A380 40fr multicolored   .35 .25
1282 A380 75fr multicolored   .35 .25
1283 A380 190fr multicolored   1.40 .40
1284 A380 200fr multicolored   1.40 .40
    Nos. 1281-1284 (4)   3.50 1.30

Trains A381

Designs: 15fr, CC2400. 90fr, Loco-tractor. 100fr, Mountain train. 240fr, Maquinista. 310fr, Freight train, series 151-A.

1997, Dec. 16   *Perf. 13x13½*
1285 A381 15fr multicolored   .25 .25
1286 A381 90fr multicolored   .50 .25
1287 A381 100fr multicolored   .55 .30
1288 A381 240fr multicolored   1.00 .55
1289 A381 310fr multicolored   1.25 .70
   a.   Strip of 5, #1285-1289   3.50 2.75

Musical Instruments A382

1997, Nov. 22   *Perf. 13x13½*
1290 A382 125fr Riiti   .75 .25
1291 A382 190fr Kora   1.00 .40
1292 A382 200fr Fama   1.25 .45
1293 A382 240fr Dioung dioung   1.50 .50
    Nos. 1290-1293 (4)   4.50 1.60

World Wildlife Fund A383

Profelis aurata: 100fr, Climbing on tree limb. 240fr, Lying on tree limb. 300fr, Two cubs.

1997, Dec. 24   Litho.   *Perf. 11½*
1294 A383 45fr multicolored   .50 .30
1295 A383 100fr multicolored   .75 .40
1296 A383 240fr multicolored   1.25 .95
1297 A383 300fr multicolored   1.75 1.25
    Nos. 1294-1297 (4)   4.25 2.90

SOS Children's Village, Ziguinchor A384

1998, Jan. 14   Litho.   *Perf. 11½*
1298 A384 190fr shown   .80 .40
1299 A384 240fr Child, buildings   1.00 .50

Club Aldiana, 25th Anniv. — A385

Designs: 290fr, Hut, people at market, mother and baby. 320fr, People on boats, woman in traditional dress, fish in basket.

1998, Jan. 12   *Perf. 13½*
1300 A385 290fr multicolored   2.25 .60
1301 A385 320fr multicolored   2.50 .65

Diana, Princess of Wales (1967-97) A386

Various portraits.

1998
1302 A386 240fr like #1304g   1.00 .50

Sheets of 9
1303 A386 200fr #a.-i.   7.50 3.75
1304 A386 250fr #a.-i.   9.50 4.75

Nos. 1303-1304 are continuous designs.

Souvenir Sheets
1305 A386 1000fr Portrait   4.25 2.10
1306 A386 1500fr With her sons   6.25 3.25
1307 A386 2000fr Wearing tiara   8.25 4.25

1998 World Cup Soccer Cup Championships, France — A387

Designs: 25fr, Soccer players. 50fr, Player's legs kicking ball. 150fr, Mascot, ball in air. 300fr, Country flags in shape of soccer players.

1998, June 10   Litho.   *Perf. 13x13½*
1308 A387 25fr multicolored   .25 .25
1309 A387 50fr multicolored   .25 .25
1310 A387 150fr multicolored   .60 .25
1311 A387 300fr multicolored   1.00 .50
    Nos. 1308-1311 (4)   2.10 1.25

Henriette Bathily Women's Museum A388

1998, May 16   Litho.   *Perf. 13*
1312 A388 190fr shown   1.25 .60
1313 A388 270fr Emblem at right   1.90 .90

Abolition of Slavery, 150th Anniv. — A389

Designs: 20fr, Slavery Museum, Goree. 40fr, Frederick Douglass. 190fr, Mother, child. 290fr, Victor Schoelcher.

1998, Apr. 27
1314 A389 20fr multicolored   .25 .25
1315 A389 40fr multicolored   .25 .25
1316 A389 190fr multicolored   1.40 .65
1317 A389 290fr multicolored   2.00 1.00
    Nos. 1314-1317 (4)   3.90 2.15

SOS Children's Village — A390

Children's drawings: 30fr, House, car. 50fr, shown. 180fr, Sun, flowers. 300fr, Lakes, trees.

1998, June 16
1318 A390 30fr multicolored   .25 .25
1319 A390 50fr multicolored   .25 .25
1320 A390 180fr multicolored   .70 .35
1321 A390 300fr multicolored   1.10 .55
    Nos. 1318-1321 (4)   2.30 1.40

Navigational Aids — A391

Designs: 50fr, Red buoy. 100fr, Mamelles Lighthouse. 190fr, Lighted buoy. 240fr, Port entrance lighthouse.

1998, July 3   *Perf. 12*
1322 A391 50fr multicolored   .25 .25
1323 A391 100fr multicolored   .40 .25
1324 A391 190fr multicolored   .70 .35
1325 A391 240fr multicolored   .90 .45
    Nos. 1322-1325 (4)   2.25 1.30

21st Paris-Dakar Rally — A392

Designs: 150fr, Race car broken down, hood up, helicopter, rescue van. 175fr, Man with shovels, vehicle stuck in sand, helicopter. 240fr, Motorcycles racing, one down, camel. 290fr, Motorcycle racing, man walking, vehicle broken down.

1999, Jan. 17   Litho.   *Perf. 11½*
1326 A392 150fr multicolored   .55 .30
1327 A392 175fr multicolored   .65 .35
1328 A392 240fr multicolored   .90 .45
1329 A392 290fr multicolored   1.00 .50
    Nos. 1326-1329 (4)   3.10 1.60

Women's Hair Styles, Headdresses A393

Designs: 100fr, Long hair over shoulders. 240fr, Shorter hair. 300fr, Head wrapped.

1998, Nov. 30
1330 A393 40fr red brn & blk   .25 .25
1331 A393 100fr brt grn & blk   .35 .25
1332 A393 240fr violet & black   .90 .45
1333 A393 300fr blue & black   1.10 .55
    Nos. 1330-1333 (4)   2.60 1.50

Endangering Marine Fauna A394

Designs: 50fr, Intensive net fishing. 100fr, Sewage and pollutants in sea. 310fr, Use of dynamite for fishing. 365fr, Oil slicks released from tanker ships.

1998, Dec. 29

1334	A394	50fr multicolored	.25	.25
1335	A394	100fr multicolored	.40	.25
1336	A394	310fr multicolored	1.25	.65
1337	A394	365fr multicolored	1.50	.75
		Nos. 1334-1337 (4)	3.40	1.90

Intl. Year of the Ocean A395

1998, Oct. 30   *Perf. 13x13½*

| 1338 | A395 | 190fr shown | .70 | .35 |
| 1339 | A395 | 790fr Sea life, diff. | 2.75 | 1.50 |

Universal Declaration of Human Rights, 50th Anniv. A396

1998, Dec. 9

| 1340 | A396 | 200fr Prisoner | 1.25 | .70 |
| 1341 | A396 | 350fr Free people | 2.25 | 1.10 |

Hotel Palm Beach, Voyages of Fram, 50th Anniv. A397

Designs: 240fr, Huts, trees, aerial view of hotel grounds. 300fr, Woman braiding another's hair, beach at hotel.

1998, Nov. 6   **Litho.**   *Perf. 13½x13*

| 1342 | A397 | 240fr multicolored | 1.60 | .80 |
| 1343 | A397 | 300fr multicolored | 2.00 | 1.00 |

Italia '98 Intl. Philatelic Exhibition — A398

Design: Leaning Tower of Pisa.

1998, Oct. 23

| 1344 | A398 | 290fr multicolored | 1.00 | .50 |

Italia '98 Intl Philatelic Exhibition A398a

No. 1344A — Race drivers and automobiles: b, Alberto Ascari. c, Giuseppe Farina. d, Ricardo Patrese. e, Michele Alboreto. f, Elio de Angelis. g, Andrea de Cesaris.

1998, Oct. 23   **Litho.**   *Perf. 13¼*

| 1344A | A398a | 100fr Sheet of 6, #b-g | 8.00 | 8.00 |

Souvenir Sheet

Ferrari Automobiles, 50th Anniv. — A399

1998, Oct. 23   **Litho.**   *Perf. 13½*

| 1345 | A399 | 1000fr multicolored | 4.75 | 4.75 |

Italia '98.

Fashion Type of 1972

1998   **Engr.**   *Perf. 13½x13*
Size: 21x26mm

1345A	A106	125fr dark olive	.50	.40
1345B	A106	290fr violet	1.25	1.00
1345C	A106	310fr purple brown	1.40	1.10

Souvenir Sheet

De Tomaso Automobiles, 40th Anniv. — A400

Automobile colors: a, black, shown. b, silver. c, black, diff. d, red.

1999, Feb. 28   **Litho.**   *Perf. 12¼*

| 1346 | A400 | 250fr Sheet of 4, #a-d | 9.50 | 9.50 |

Italia '98. Dated 1998.

Actors & Actresses — A401

No. 1347: a, Romy Schneider. b, Yves Montand. c, Catherine Deneuve. d, Gina Lollobrigida. e, Marcello Mastroianni. f, Sophia Loren. g, Frank Sinatra. h, Dean Martin. i, Marilyn Monroe.

1500fr, Monroe, diff. 2000fr, Mastroianni, diff.

1999, Feb. 28 Litho.   *Perf. 12x12¼*

| 1347 | A401 | 200fr Sheet of 9, #a-i. | 7.00 | 7.00 |

Souvenir Sheets
Perf. 13½

| 1348 | A401 | 1500fr multicolored | 6.00 | 6.00 |
| 1349 | A401 | 2000fr multicolored | 9.50 | 9.50 |

Italia '98. Dated 1998.

Elvis Presley — A402

Various portraits.

1999, Feb. 28 Litho.   *Perf. 12x12¼*

| 1350 | A402 | 250fr Sheet of 9, #a-i | 9.50 | 9.50 |

Dated 1998.
A sheet similar to No. 1350 exists. Stamps are perf 13¼ and have Italia '98 logo. The top margins of the sheet are not inscribed.

PhilexFrance 99 — A403

1999, July 2   **Litho.**   *Perf. 13*

| 1351 | A403 | 240fr multicolored | 1.25 | 1.10 |

No. 1351 has a holographic image. Soaking in water may affect hologram.

Chess Pieces and Scenes of the Crusades A404

Designs: No. 1353, Pope Urban II, 1053. No. 1354: a, Muslim army. b, Bishopric of St. George. c, Army of Karbugha. d, Muslim troops attacking Christians. e, Baldwin I, King of Jerusalem. f, Christian Army. g, Third crusade, Richard the Lion-Hearted. h, Capture of Acre, 1191. i, Crusaders leave for Jaffa, 1191. No. 1355: a, Pope Urban II, 1095. b, Peter the Hermit. c, Byzantine Emperor Alexius. d, People's Crusade, 1096. e, Godfrey of Bouillon. f, Crusaders at Constantinople, 1097. g, Knights of St. John. h, Crusaders cross Alps. i, Capture of Jerusalem. No. 1356: a, Chateau-gaillard of Richard the Lion-Hearted. b, Capture of Arsuf, 1191. c, Truce between Richard the Lion-Hearted and

---

Saladin, 1192. d, Arrival of Louis IX at Damietta, 1248. e, Children's Crusade. f, Capture of Louis IX. g, Flood at El Mansurah. h, Treaty between Sultan al-Kamil and Frederick II. i, Monks record history of Crusades.

1999, July 16   **Litho.**   *Perf. 13½*

| 1353 | A404 | 250fr multicolored | 1.25 | 1.25 |

Sheets of 9

1354	A404	200fr #a.-i.	7.50	7.50
1355	A404	250fr #a.-i.	9.25	9.25
1356	A404	400fr #a.-i.	15.00	15.00

Athletes — A405

No. 1357, Jackie Robinson with bat behind back. No. 1358, Muhammad Ali, arm raised by referee.
No. 1359: a-h, various portraits of Jackie Robinson.
No. 1360: a-h, various portraits of Muhammad Ali.
1000fr, Muhammad Ali in robe. 1500fr, Close-up of Jackie Robinson like No. 1359g. No. 1363, Robinson at bat. No. 1364, Ali with both fists clenched.

1999, July 16   **Litho.**   *Perf. 13½*

| 1357 | A405 | 250fr multicolored | 1.00 | 1.00 |
| 1358 | A405 | 300fr multicolored | 1.25 | 1.25 |

Sheets of 9

| 1359 | A405 | 250fr #1357, 1359a.-h. | 9.25 | 9.25 |
| 1360 | A405 | 300fr #1358, 1360a.-h. | 11.50 | 11.50 |

Souvenir Sheets

1361	A405	1000fr multicolored	4.25	4.25
1362	A405	1500fr multicolored	6.25	6.25
1363	A405	2000fr multicolored	8.25	8.25
1364	A405	2000fr multicolored	8.25	8.25

Nos. 1361-1364 each contain one 36x42mm stamp.

Sports A405a

Designs: 200fr, Ayrton Senna, Formula 1 racing champion. 300fr, Ludger Beerbaum, equestrian competitor, vert. 400fr, Pete Sampras, tennis player, vert.
No. 1366 — Formula 1 racing champions: a, Juan Manuel Fangio. b, Alberto Ascari. c, Graham Hill. d, Jim Clark. e, Jack Brabham. f, Jackie Stewart. g, Niki Lauda. h, Like No. 1365, no white margin. i, Alain Prost.
No. 1367 — Equestrian competitors, vert.: a, Martin Schaudt. b, Klaus Balkenhol. c, Nadine Capellman-Biffar. d, Willi Melliger. e, Like No. 1365A, without printer's name at LL. f, Ulrich Kirchhoff. g, Sally Clark. h, Bettina Overesch-Boker. i, Karen O'Conner.
No. 1368 — Tennis and table tennis players, vert.: a, Liu Guoliang. b, Martina Hingis. c, Deng Yaping. d, Andre Agassi. e, Jean-Philippe Gatien. f, Anna Kournikova. g, Mikael Appelgren. h, Like No. 1365B, no white margin. i, Jan-Ove Waldner.
1500fr, German Equestrian jumping team. No. 1370, Ayrton Senna. No. 1370A, Table tennis players Vladimir Samsonov, Deng Yaping, Jörg Rosskopf.

1999, July 16   **Litho.**   *Perf. 13½*

| 1365-1365B | A405a | Set of 3 | 3.75 | 3.75 |

Sheets of 9, #a-i

1366	A405a	200fr multi	7.50	7.50
1367	A405a	300fr multi	11.00	11.00
1368	A405a	400fr multi	15.00	15.00

Souvenir Sheets

1369	A405a	1500fr multi	6.25	6.25
1370	A405a	2000fr multi	8.00	8.00
1370A	A405a	2000fr multi	8.00	8.00

Transportation — A406

Designs: 250fr, Sailboat of Sir Thomas Lipton. 300fr, Sinking of Titanic. 325fr, Bentley coupe. 350fr, Prussian locomotive. 375fr, Ducati Motorcycle. 500fr, Concorde.

1999, July 23   Litho.   Perf. 13½

1371	A406	250fr multicolored	1.00	1.00
1372	A406	300fr multicolored	1.25	1.25
1373	A406	325fr multicolored	1.40	1.40
1374	A406	350fr multicolored	1.40	1.40
1375	A406	375fr multicolored	1.50	1.50
1376	A406	500fr multicolored	2.00	2.00
	Nos. 1371-1376 (6)		8.55	8.55

See Nos. 1385-1399.

Intl. Year
of Older
Persons
A407

30fr, Picture in book. 150fr, Man with mallet. 290fr, Musicians. 300fr, Scientists, vert.

Perf. 13¼x13, 13x13¼
1999, Aug. 10   Litho.

1377	A407	30fr multicolored	.25	.25
1378	A407	150fr multicolored	.60	.60
1379	A407	290fr multicolored	1.10	1.10
1380	A407	300fr multicolored	1.25	1.25
	Nos. 1377-1380 (4)		3.20	3.20

Mushrooms
A408

Scouting emblem and: 60fr, "Amanite phalloide." 175fr, Coprinus atramentarius. 220fr, "Amanite vireuse." 250fr, Agaricus campester.

Perf. 13¼x13½
1999, Aug. 27   Litho.

1381	A408	60fr multicolored	.30	.30
1382	A408	175fr multicolored	.75	.75
1383	A408	220fr multicolored	1.00	1.00
1384	A408	250fr multicolored	1.10	1.10
	Nos. 1381-1384 (4)		3.15	3.15

Transportation Type of 1999

No. 1385 — Boats and ships: a, France. b, United States. c, Finnjet. d, Chusan. e, Sheers. f, Vendredi 13. g, Like No. 1371 without white margin. h, Pen Duick 11. i, Jester.
No. 1386 — Titanic: a, Construction. b, Launching. c, Departing. d, At start of voyage. e, Collision with iceberg. f, Like No. 1372 without white margin. g, Exploration of wreckage. h, Bow, passengers. i, Captain Edward John Smith.
No. 1387 — Automobiles: a, Duryea. b, Menon. c, Petite Renault. d, Zero Fiat. e, Spa. f, Packard. g, Like No. 1373 without white margin. h, Mercedes-Benz. i, Morris Minor.
No. 1388 — Trains: a, Mikado. b, 241P. c, Ten-wheeler. d, The Milwaukee. e, Class 1.S. f, Prussian locomotive G12. g, Like No. 1374 without white margin. h, KK-SEB Series 310. i, Outrance.
No. 1389 — Motorcycles and bicycles: a, Brooklands. b, Moto Brough Superior. c, 1903 race. d, Like No. 1375 without inscription at LL. e, Dave Thorpe Moto-cross Yamaha. f, Kevin Schwantz Moto Suzuki. g, Michaux bicycle. h, Racing bicycle with helmeted rider. i, Women on bicycles.
No. 1390 — Rockets, vert.: a, R.D. 107, USSR. b, Soyuz, USSR. c, Proton, USSR. d, Atlas-Centaur, US. e, Atlas-Agena, US. f, Atlas-Mercury, US. g, Titan 2, US. h, Juno 2, US. i, Saturn 1, US.
No. 1391 — Express trains: a, Acela, US. b, Class 332, Great Britain. c, ICE, Germany. d, TEE, Luembourg. e, Nevada Super Speed, US. f, Inter City 250, Great Britain. g, Korean

High Speed. h, Eurostar, France & Great Britain. i, Thalys PBA, France.
No. 1392 — Supersonic aircraft or prototypes: a, SR-71. b, Maglifter. c, S.M. d, Super Concorde. e, TU-144. f, Boeing X. g, X-33. h, Like No. 1376 without white margin. i, X-34.
1000fr, Eric Tabarly and Pen Duick IV. No. 1394, Marc Seguin, arrival of train at Mont-Saint-Michel, vert. No. 1395, Walter P. Chrysler, 1924 Chrysler. No. 1396, Etienne Chambron, TGV trains, vert. No. 1397, Bobby Julich on racing bicycle. No. 1398, Concorde, diff. 2500fr, Neil Armstrong.

1999, July 23   Litho.   Perf. 13½
Sheets of 9

1385	A406	250fr #a.-i.	9.25	9.25
1386	A406	300fr #a.-i.	11.00	11.00
1387	A406	325fr #a.-i.	12.00	12.00
1388	A406	350fr #a.-i.	13.00	13.00
1389	A406	375fr #a.-i.	14.00	14.00
1390	A406	400fr #a.-i.	15.00	15.00
1391	A406	450fr #a.-i.	17.00	17.00
1392	A406	500fr #a.-i.	18.00	18.00

Souvenir Sheets

1393	A406	1000fr multicolored	4.25	4.25
1394	A406	1500fr multicolored	5.50	5.50
1395	A406	1500fr multicolored	6.00	6.00
1396	A406	2000fr multicolored	8.25	8.25
1397	A406	2000fr multicolored	8.25	8.25
1398	A406	2000fr multicolored	8.25	8.25
1399	A406	2500fr multicolored	10.50	10.50

No. 1390 contains nine 35x50mm stamps. Nos. 1393, 1395, 1397-1399 each contain one 50x35 stamp. Nos. 1394 and 1396 each contain one 35x50mm stamp.

UPU, 125th   Mother
Anniv. — A409   Teresa — A411

First Manned Moon Landing, 30th
Anniv. — A410

UPU emblem and: 270fr, Rainbows, envelope. 350fr, "125."

1999, Oct. 9   Litho.   Perf. 11½x11¾

1400	A409	270fr multi	1.10	1.10
1401	A409	350fr multi	1.40	1.40

1999, Oct. 9   Perf. 13½x13, 13x13½

Designs: 25fr, Two astronauts on moon, flag. 145fr, Neil Armstrong, flag, astronaut on moon, vert. 180fr, Astronaut, flag, rocket, vert. 500fr, Astronaut on moon, space shuttle, vert.

1402	A410	25fr multi	.25	.25
1403	A410	145fr multi	.60	.60
1404	A410	180fr multi	.70	.70
1405	A410	500fr multi	2.00	2.00
	Nos. 1402-1405 (4)		3.55	3.55

1999, Oct. 9   Perf. 11½x11¾

Mother Teresa and: 75fr, Child, facing away. 100fr, Three children. 290fr, Priest. 300fr, Child.

1406	A411	75fr multi	.25	.25
1407	A411	100fr multi	.40	.40
1408	A411	290fr multi	1.10	1.10
1409	A411	300fr multi	1.25	1.25
	Nos. 1406-1409 (4)		3.00	3.00

Awarding of Nobel Peace Prize to Mother Teresa, 20th anniv.

Fauna
A412

Designs: 60fr, Hippotragus equinus. 90fr, Haematopus ostralegus. 300fr, Dendrocygna viduada. 320fr, Demochelys coriacea.

1999, Oct. 9   Perf. 13½x13

1410	A412	60fr multi	.25	.25
1411	A412	90fr multi	.35	.35
1412	A412	300fr multi	1.25	1.25
1413	A412	320fr multi	1.25	1.25
	Nos. 1410-1413 (4)		3.10	3.10

Paintings by Paul Cézanne — A413

Various paintings.

1999   Perf. 13¼

1414	A413	200fr Sheet of 9, #a.-i.	8.00	8.00

Betty
Boop — A414

Designs: No. 1415, 250fr, With red guitar. No. 1416, 250fr, With microphone. No. 1417, 400fr, On chair.
No. 1418, 250fr: a, With saxophone. b, With tambourine. c, Like #1415 (continuous design). d, With pink guitar. e, On piano keys. f, With drumsticks. g, With earphones. h, Like #1416 (continuous design). i, With purple jacket.
No. 1419, 400fr: a, With red dress. b, With flowers. c, With blue pants. d, With purple dress. e, Like #1417 (continuous design). f, With black pants. g, With ankh earrings. h, With black dress. i, With purple shirt and pants.
No. 1420, 1000fr, With saxophone. No. 1421, 1500fr, With red dress. No. 1422, 2000fr, With purple shirt.

1999   Litho.   Perf. 13¼

1415-1417	A414	Set of 3	3.75	3.75

Sheets of 9, #a-i

1418-1419	A414	Set of 2	24.00	24.00

Souvenir Sheets

1420-1422	A414	Set of 3	12.00	12.00

Actors and Actresses — A415

No. 1423, 250fr: a, Clark Gable. b, Rudolph Valentino. c, Errol Flynn. d, Cary Grant. e, Robert Taylor. f, Gary Cooper. g, James Dean. h, Humphrey Bogart. i, Marlon Brando.

No. 1424, 425fr: a, Grace Kelly. b, Marilyn Monroe. c, Audrey Hepburn. d, Greta Garbo. e, Jean Harlow. f, Loretta Young. g, Jane Russell. h, Dorothy Lamour. i, Veronica Lake.
No. 1425, 450fr: a, Ginger Rogers, Fred Astaire. b, Cary Grant, Katharine Hepburn, James Stewart. c, Melvyn Douglas, Greta Garbo. d, Vivien Leigh, Clark Gable. e, Burt Lancaster, Deborah Kerr. f, Humphrey Bogart, Lauren Bacall. g, Steve McQueen, Jacqueline Bisset. h, Gene Kelly, Rita Hayworth. i, Ingrid Bergman, Cary Grant.

1999   Sheets of 9, #a-i

1423-1425	A415	Set of 3	32.50	32.50

I Love Lucy — A416

Designs: No. 1426, 300fr, Fred, Ethel and Lucy with chick boxes. No. 1427, 300fr, Lucy reading murder mystery, vert.
No. 1428: a, Ethel, Lucy holding box. b, Ricky, Lucy, Fred and Ethel. c, Fred, Ethel and Lucy standing. d, Lucy with chicks. e, Fred, Ethel, Lucy and Ricky at table. f, Ethel and Lucy bending over. g, Lucy. h, Lucy, Ethel and Fred at table.
No. 1429, vert. — Lucy with: a, Telephone. b, Green dress. c, Black vest. d, Black hair bow. e, Spoon and bottle. f, Salad. g, Lilac jacket. h, Tan coat.
No. 1430, 1000fr, Lucy holding box, vert. No. 1431, 2000fr, Lucy holding bag, vert.

1999

1426-1427	A416	Set of 2	2.40	2.40
1428	A416	300fr Sheet of 9, #1426, 1428a-1428h	11.00	11.00
1429	A416	300fr Sheet of 9, #1427, 1429a-1429h	11.00	11.00

Souvenir Sheets

1430-1431	A416	Set of 2	12.00	12.00

The Three Stooges — A417

Designs: No. 1432, 400fr, Larry with scissors, Curly, Moe with drill.
No. 1433: a, Larry and Moe on bed. b, Larry, Moe, Curly in police uniforms. c, Moe, Larry on telephone. d, Larry and Moe with scissors, Curly. e, Larry, Curly, Moe behind operating room equipment. f, Moe on floor, Larry, Curly. g, Moe, Curly, Larry with ladder. h, Moe with plank, Larry, Curly.
No. 1434, 1000fr, Moe with feathers in hair, Curly, vert. No. 1435, 1500fr, Curly with hat, vert.

1999

1432	A417	400fr multi	1.60	1.60
1433	A417	400fr Sheet of 9, #1432, 1433a-1433h	14.50	14.50

Souvenir Sheets

1434-1435	A417	Set of 2	10.00	10.00

Picasso Paintings — A418

No. 1436: a, Country name in yellow, denomination at UL. b, Country name in white. c, Country name in yellow, denomination at UR. d, Country name in red.

1999
1436 A418 375fr Sheet of 4,
#a-d 5.50 5.50

22nd Paris-Cairo-Dakar Rally — A419

Designs: 75fr, Motorcycles, car, truck, helicopter, Pyramids. 100fr, Cars, truck, Sphinx, Pyramid, camel and driver. 220fr, Motorcycle, truck, helicopter. 320fr, Camel and driver, motorcycle, car, Pyramids.

2000   Litho.   Perf. 11¾x11½
1437-1440 A419 Set of 4 3.50 3.50

World Meteorological Organization, 50th Anniv. A420

Designs: 100fr, Satellite dish, map, weather station. 790fr, Weather measuring equipment, vert.

2000   Perf. 11¾x11½, 11½x11¾
1441-1442 A420 Set of 2 3.25 3.25

23rd Paris-Cairo-Dakar Rally — A421

Stylized head and: 190fr, Motorcyclist. 220fr, Facial features with text, vert. 240fr, Camel, vert. 790fr, Car.

Perf. 13½x13¼, 13¼x13½
2001, Jan. 6
1443-1446 A421 Set of 4 6.50 6.50

Advent of New Millennium A422

Millennium emblem and: 20fr, National Festival of Arts and Culture. 100fr, Pan-African Plastic Arts. 150fr, National Heritage Day. 300fr, Goree Memorial, horiz.

2001, Feb. 13   Perf. 13½x13, 13x13½
1447-1450 A422 Set of 4 2.50 2.50
Dated 2000.

2000 Summer Olympics, Sydney — A423

Designs: 40fr, Swimming, weight lifting. 80fr, Taekwondo. 240fr, 200-meter race. 290fr, Handball.

2001, Feb. 28   Perf. 13¼x13½
1451-1454 A423 Set of 4 3.25 3.25
Dated 2000.

Kermel Artisan Market — A424

Building and: 50fr, Woman, flowers. 90fr, Mask, drum. 250fr, Masks, bowls, horiz. 350fr, Woman, carvings.

Perf. 13¼x13½, 13½x13¼
2001, Mar. 15
1455-1458 A424 Set of 4 3.25 3.25

Medicinal Plants — A425

Designs: 240fr, Maytenus senegalensis. 320fr, Boscia senegalensis. 350fr, Euphorbia hirta. 500fr, Guierra senegalensis.

2001, Apr. 16   Litho.   Perf. 13¼x13
1459-1462 A425 Set of 4 6.00 6.00

19th Lions Intl. Convention, Dakar A426

Lions Intl. emblem and: 190fr, People in canoe, map of Senegal. 300fr, Lion, vert.

Perf. 13½x13¼, 13¼x13½
2001, May 21
1463-1464 A426 Set of 2 2.40 2.40

UN High Commissioner for Refugees, 50th Anniv. — A427

Emblem and: 240fr, Tank, refugees. 320fr, Refugee, globe, vert.

Perf. 13½x13¼, 13¼x13½
2001, June 20
1465-1466 A427 Set of 2 2.00 2.00

Intl. Teacher's Day — A428

UNESCO emblem and: 225fr, Book, teacher, vert. 290fr, Teacher, world map.

Perf. 13¼x13, 13x13¼
2001, Oct. 5
1467-1468 A428 Set of 2 1.75 1.75
Dated 2000.

National Parks A429

Designs: 75fr, Antelope, lion. 125fr, Heron and marabou stork. 275fr, Cranes and elephant. 300fr, Zebras, vert.

Perf. 13¾x13½
2001, Nov. 12   Litho.
1469 A429 75fr multi .50 .25
1470 A429 125fr multicolored .90 .25
1471 A429 275fr multicolored 1.75 1.00
1472 A429 300fr multi 1.90 1.00
Nos. 1469-1472 (4) 5.05 2.50
Dated 2000.

Tourism A430

Tourism emblem and: 145fr, Drummer and dancer. 290fr, Tree, windsurfer, person on air mattress, vert.

Perf. 13x13¼, 13¼x13
2001, Dec. 3   Litho.
1473-1474 A430 Set of 2 1.60 1.60
Dated 2000.

2002 African Cup Soccer Tournament, Mali A431

Tournament emblem and: 250fr, Flags, player holding cup, players and soccer ball. 380fr, Players near goal. 425fr, Players kicking ball at goal. 440fr, Player, cup, vert.

2002, Jan. 9
1475-1478 A431 Set of 4 5.25 5.25

Peulh Woman — A433a
A433

Linguère — A434a
A434

On types A433a and A434a, the numerals in the denominations have thin serifs and zeroes that are thin at top and bottom. On types A433 and A434 the lines of these numerals are the same thickness.

2002		**Litho.**	**Perf. 13½x13**	
1483	A433	5fr lilac rose	—	—
1483A	A433a	5fr lilac rose	—	—
1484	A433	10fr brt orange	—	—
1484A	A433a	10fr orange	—	—
1485	A433	20fr orange	—	—
1485A	A433a	20fr orange	—	—
1486	A433	25fr rose red	—	—
1486A	A433a	25fr rose red	—	—
1487	A433	40fr bright pink	—	—
1488	A433	50fr light blue	—	—
1488A	A433a	50fr light blue	—	—
1489	A433	60fr light green	—	—
1490	A433	70fr light yel green	—	—
1490A	A433	75fr dark green	—	—
1490B	A433	80fr dark blue	—	—
1490C	A433	90fr brown	—	—
1491	A433	100fr brt yel grn	—	—
1491A	A433	125fr silver	—	—
1491B	A433a	125fr silver	—	—
1492	A433	150fr olive green	—	—
1493	A433	175fr yellow brown	—	—
1494	A434	200fr olive green	—	—
1494A	A434	225fr lilac	—	—
1495	A434	250fr ocher	—	—
1496	A434	290fr red brown	—	—
1497	A434	300fr brt rose lil	—	—
1497A	A434a	350fr brt rose li-lac	—	—
1498	A434	360fr violet	—	—
1499	A434	370fr blue	—	—
1499A	A434	380fr brt green	—	—
1500	A434	390fr Prussian blue	—	—
1500A	A434	400fr light brown	—	—
1501	A434	425fr bright green	—	—
1502	A434	500fr olive brown	—	—
1502A	A434a	600fr gray	—	—
1502B	A434a	700fr bright lilac	—	—
1503	A434	800fr black	—	—
1504	A434	1000fr brt blue	—	—
1504A	A434a	1000fr brt blue	—	—

Issued: 10fr (#1484), 10fr (#1484A), 50fr (#1488A), 75fr, 100fr, 300fr, 500fr, 1000fr, 2002; 5fr, 20fr, 25fr, 40fr, 50fr (#1488), 60fr, 150fr, 175fr, 200fr, 250fr, 290fr, 360fr, 370fr, 390fr, 425fr, 800fr, 3/12/02; 225fr, 400fr, 2003; 125fr, 350fr, 600fr, 700fr, 4/5/04. Issue dates for Nos. 1483A, 1485A, 1486A, 1490B, 1490C, 1491B, 1499, 1499A and 1504A are uncertain, because examples seen used are from 2005 and 2006. Nos. 1490B, 1490C, 1491B, and 1499A have "2003" year dates, while others have "2002" year dates.

Proclamation of the Act of African Union — A435

Map of Africa and: 330fr, Handshake, vert. 390fr, Hands, flags.

2002   Litho.   Perf. 13¼x13, 13x13¼
1505-1506 A435 Set of 2 2.50 2.50

Door of the Third Millennium A436

Various depictions with frame colors of: 200fr, Orange. 290fr, Blue. 390fr, Olive green. 725fr, Rose pink.

2002   *Perf. 13¼x13*
1507-1510 A436   Set of 4   4.50 4.50

Dak'Art 2002
A437

Art by: 200fr, Zehirum Yetmgeta. 380fr, Moustapha Dime, vert. 400fr, Abdoulaye Konate. 425fr, Gora Mbengue.

2002, Apr. 30   *Perf. 13x13¼, 13¼x13*
1511-1514 A437   Set of 4   5.00 5.00

Star and Map of Senegal — A438

Denomination color: 200fr, Green. 380fr, Red.

2002, May 15   *Perf. 13¼x13*
1515-1516 A438   Set of 2   2.00 2.00

Horses
A440

Designs: 30fr, Mbayar du Baol. 200fr, Mpar du Cayor. 250fr, Narougor. 300fr, Foutanke.

2002, Dec. 20   Litho.   *Perf. 13x13¼*
1519-1522 A440   Set of 4   2.50 2.50

Ecotourism
A441

Designs: 90fr, Sacred baobab tree. 250fr, Birds, Djoudj National Park. 300fr, Mangroves. 380fr, Wood and vine bridge.

2002, Dec. 20   Litho.   *Perf. 13x13¼*
1523-1526 A441   Set of 4   7.75 7.75

Fauna
A442

Designs: 75fr, Gorilla gorilla. 290fr, Ceratotherium simum. 360fr, Geochelone sulcata, ostrich and snake. 380fr, Giraffa camelopardalis, vert.

2002, Dec. 26   *Perf. 13x13¼, 13¼x13*
1527-1530 A442   Set of 4   5.75 5.75

25th Paris-Dakar Rally
A443

Designs: 360fr, Automobiles, man with camel. 425fr, Motorcyclists.

2003, Jan. 19   Litho.   *Perf. 13x13¼*
1531-1532 A443   Set of 2   4.25 4.25

Dated 2002.

A444

A445

New Partnership for African Development — A446

Designs: 250fr, Map of Africa, symbols of industry. 290fr, Map of Africa, bird, model of atom.

     Perf. 13¼x13, 13x13¼
2003, June 22   Litho.
1533 A444 200fr shown   .70 .70
1534 A444 250fr multi   .85 .85
1535 A445 250fr shown   .85 .85
1536 A444 290fr multi   1.00 1.00
1537 A446 360fr shown   1.25 1.25
   Nos. 1533-1537 (5)   4.65 4.65

Traditional Costumes — A447

Designs: 250fr, Goumbé Lébou. 360fr, Badiaranké. 390fr, Grand Boubou. 500fr, Bowede.

2003, July 16   *Perf. 13¼x13*
1538-1541 A447   Set of 4   5.25 5.25

Marine Life
A448

Designs: 290fr, Cymbium cymbium. 370fr, Herring. 380fr, Catfish. 400fr, Chelonia mydas.

2003, July 16   Litho.   *Perf. 13¼x13*
1542-1545 A448   Set of 4   5.00 5.00

Sculptures
A449

Designs: 200fr, Le Cailcédrat Mort. 300fr, Tete d'un Sorcier. 380fr, Le Laard. 440fr, Le Thioury.

2003, July 16   Litho.   *Perf. 13¼x13*
1546-1549 A449   Set of 4   11.50 11.50

26th Paris-Dakar Rally — A451

Designs: 390fr, Motorcyclists. 500fr, Motorcyclist and car.

2004, Jan. 14   Litho.   *Perf. 13x13¼*
1553-1554 A451   Set of 2   3.50 3.50

Dated 2003.

Intl. Cycling Union, Cent. (in 2000)
A452

2004?   Litho.   *Perf. 13¼x13*
1555 A452   45fr multi   — —
1557 A452   275fr multi   — —

Dated 2000.

Historic Sites
A453

Designs: 240fr, Dakar Railroad Station. 370fr, Fort Podor. 390fr, Dakar City Hall. 500fr, Notre Dame des Victoires Cathedral.

2004, Apr. 29   Litho.   *Perf. 13x13¼*
1559-1562 A453   Set of 4   5.50 5.50

Dated 2003.

Land Transportation — A453a

Design: 200fr, Small bus (Car rapide).

2004   Litho.   *Perf. 13x13¼*
1562A A453a 200fr multi

   Three additional stamps exist in this set. The editors would like to examine any examples.

African Cup of Nations Soccer Tournament
A454

Designs: 200fr, Cup, emblem. 300fr, Cup, soccer ball, stadium, television, horiz. 400fr, Emblems, players shaking hands, horiz. 425fr, Players in action, horiz.

2004   *Perf. 13¼x13, 13x13¼*
1563-1566 A454   Set of 4   5.50 5.50

Houses of Worship
A455

Designs: 200fr, Omarienne de Guédé Mosque. 225fr, Popenguine Basilica, vert. 250fr, Grand Mosque, Touba. 300fr, Grand Mosque, Tivaouane.

     Perf. 13x13¼, 13¼x13
2004, Oct. 9   Litho.
1567-1570 A455   Set of 4   3.75 3.75

Locally Produced Crops — A456

Designs: 100fr, Millet. 150fr, Cowpeas, millet and corn, horiz. 200fr, Corn. 300fr, Rice.

2004, Dec. 6   *Perf. 13¼x13, 13x13¼*
1571-1574 A456   Set of 4   3.00 3.00

27th Paris-Dakar Rally — A457

Designs: 450fr, Automobile, motorcycle and truck. 550fr, Motorcycle, vert.

     Perf. 13x13¼, 13¼x13
2005, Jan. 16   Litho.
1575-1576 A457   Set of 2   4.00 4.00

Children's Art — A458

Various drawings by: 50fr, Mbaye Gnilane. 75fr, Pape Cheick Diack, horiz. 100fr, Aly Gueye, horiz. 425fr, Abdourahim Diallo, horiz.

     Perf. 13¼x13, 13x13¼
2005, Feb. 28   Litho.
1577-1580 A458   Set of 4   2.75 2.75

28th Paris-Dakar Rally
A459

Design: 500fr, Rally emblem, camels, tents, automobile. 1000fr, Rally emblem, helicopter, man repairing car, men carrying car doors.

2006, Jan. 14   Litho.   *Perf. 13x13¼*
1581 A459   500fr multi   — —
1582 A459   1000fr multi   —

Dolls — A460

Designs: 200fr, Tooiodo Peulh. 250fr, La Reine Siguare. 375fr, Zulu doll. 425fr, Woloff stuffed dolls.

Litho., Litho & Engr. (375fr)
2006, Apr. 5   *Perf. 13¼x13*
1583-1586 A460   Set of 4   7.25 7.25

Campaign Against HIV A461

Designs: 200fr, Family discussing HIV and AIDS, map of Senegal. 250fr, Woman, molecular model, drop of water, vert. 290fr, Couples with thought balloons. 425fr, Group of seated men, huts.

Perf. 13x13¼, 13¼x13
2006, Apr. 5   Litho.
1587-1590 A461   Set of 4   4.50 4.50
      Dated 2004.

World Numerical Solidarity Day — A462

Designs: 200fr, Satellite, computer screen, Earth's hemispheres. 250fr, Earth, people using telephones, clasped arms. 370fr, Satellite, map of Senegal, city skyline, horiz. 380fr, Satellite, computer screen, hand with computer disk, horiz.

Perf. 13½x13, 13x13½
2006, May 3   Litho.
1591-1594 A462   Set of 4   4.75 4.75

Flowers A463

Designs: 100fr, Malva silvestris. 150fr, Moringa olifera, vert. 300fr, Cichorum intybus, vert. 450fr, Dandelion.

Perf. 13x13¼, 13¼x13
2006, July 10   Litho.
1595-1598 A463   Set of 4   9.00 9.00
      Dated 2005.

Wrestling A464

Designs: 100fr, Two wrestlers standing. 200fr, Two wrestlers in ring. 250fr, Wrestler, vert. 500fr, Wrestler pouring water on himself, vert.

Perf. 13x13¼, 13¼x13
2007, July 10   Litho.
1599-1602 A464   Set of 4   9.50 9.50

Demba and Dupont Memorial, Dakar — A465

Various views of statue: 200fr, 450fr.

2006, Aug. 23   Litho.   *Perf. 13¼x13*
1603-1604 A465   Set of 2   3.75 3.75

Pres. Léopold Sedar Senghor (1906-2001) A466

Denomination color: 200fr, Red. 450fr, Green.

2006, Oct. 9   Litho.   *Perf. 13¼x13*
1605-1606 A466   Set of 2   5.75 5.75

Campaign Against Mutilation of Female Genitalia — A467

Designs: 50fr, Woman grabbing another woman, man holding sign. 200fr, Two women, two children, razor blade. 350fr, Woman, health workers, razor blade. 370fr, Women, girl with raised hand.

2006, Dec. 8   Litho.   *Perf. 13¼x13*
1607-1610 A467   Set of 4   4.00 4.00

Air Transport A468

Design: 250fr, Airship and airplane.

2006   Litho.   *Perf. 13x13¼*
1612 A468   250fr multi   —
1614 A468   500fr multi   —
Two additional stamps were issued in this set. The editors would like to examine any examples.

Birds A469

Designs: 30fr, Luscinia phoenicurus. 75fr, Rouge-gorge bleu (robin), vert. 200fr, Pica pica, vert. 400fr, Corneille (crow), vert.

2006   Litho.   *Perf. 13x13¼, 13¼x13*
1615-1618 A469   Set of 4   12.50 12.50

Fishing — A469a

Design: 15fr, Fishermen removing catch from boat. 50fr, Fishermen in boat pulling in net. 150fr, Fisherman in boat casting net. 300fr, Fishermen in boat and in water drawing in net.

2006   *Perf. 13x13¼*
1618A A469a   15fr multi   —   —
1618B A469a   50fr multi   —   —
1618C A469a   150fr multi   —   —
1618D A469a   300fr multi   —   —

National Solidarity Day A471

Designs: 50fr, Exchange of books and corn. 100fr, Shell, hands, star, map of Senegal. 200fr, Map of Senegal, hands, bowl. 500fr, Map of Senegal, items produced in Senegal.

2007, Sept. 11   Litho.   *Perf. 13¼x13*
1621-1624 A471   Set of 4   3.75 3.75
      Dated 2006.

Gorée Diaspora Festival — A472

Designs: 50fr, Emblem. 200fr, Emblem, pendant and prism, horiz. 450fr, Hands with quill pen, building. 525fr, Ship, emblem, Gorée Island.

Perf. 13¼x13, 13x13¼
2007, Sept. 11
1625-1628 A472   Set of 4   5.50 5.50

Tourism A473

Designs: 200fr, Lion, elephant and giraffes, Niokolo-koba Park.

2008, Feb. 27   Litho.   *Perf. 13x13¼*
1631 A473   200fr multi   —
Three additional stamps were issued in this set. The editors would like to examine any examples.

Environmental Protection — A474

Designs: 100fr, Do not cut down trees. 200fr, Fire is dangerous, vert. 300fr, Man picking up litter. 450fr, Protect the vegetation.

Perf. 13x13¼, 13¼x13
2008, June 5   Set of 4   5.00 5.00
      Dated 2007.

Flora A475

Designs: 200fr, Strichnos nux vomica. 290fr, Conium maculatum, vert. 300fr, Tree bud, vert. 450fr, Pitcher plant, vert.

Perf. 13x13¼, 13¼x13
2008, Sept. 5   Litho.
1637-1640 A475   Set of 4   5.50 5.50
      Dated 2007.

Miniature Sheet

Native Dishes — A476

No. 1641: a, 50fr, Bassi (seasoned meat and vegetables). b, 200fr, Yassa poulet (marinated chicken and vegetables). c, 250fr, Thieboudiene (marinated fish. d, 500fr, Yassa poisson (marinated fish and vegetables).

2008, Sept. 5   Litho.   *Perf. 13x13¼*
1641 A476   Sheet of 4, #a-d   4.50 4.50

30th Paris-Dakar Rally — A476a

Designs: 450fr, Motorcyclist, van, camel. 550fr, Motorcyclist, car, horiz.

Perf. 13¼x13, 13x13¼
2009, Jan. 29   Litho.
1643-1644 A476a   Set of 2   4.00 4.00
      Dated 2008.

Mother's Day A477

Mothers receiving flowers from daughters, with background color of: 200fr, Lilac. 450fr, Yellow, vert.

Perf. 13x13¼, 13¼x13
2009, June 3   Litho.
1645-1646 A477   Set of 2   2.75 2.75

Blind Boy Reading Braille Book — A478

Designs: 200fr, Shown. 450fr, "9" in Braille text.

Litho. & Embossed
2009, May 20   **Perf. 13¼x13**
1647-1648 A478   Set of 2   2.75 2.75
Louis Braille (1809-52), educator of the blind.

Independence, 50th Anniv. — A479

Denomination color: 300fr, Green. 500fr, Red.

2010, Apr. 4   Litho.   Perf. 13x13¼
1649-1650 A479   Set of 2   3.50 3.50

West African Economic and Monetary Union, 11th Anniv. (in 2005) — A480

Designs: 500fr, Coin, balls and emblem. 790fr, Map of member countries, emblems, building, birthday cake with candle, horiz.

2010, Apr. 5   Perf. 13¼x13, 13x13¼
1651-1652 A480   Set of 2   5.50 5.50
Dated 2006.

Democracy and Liberty — A481

Designs: 150fr, Peaceful protest. 250fr, Woman holding election card. 400fr, Woman casting ballot. 450fr, Newspapers, radio, television.

2010, Apr. 5   Litho.   Perf. 13¼x13
1653-1656 A481   Set of 4   5.25 5.25
Dated 2006.

Dances — A482

Designs: 100fr, Ndaw rabine. 200fr, Niary gorom, horiz. 250fr, Daganthe. 450fr, Ndaa daly.

2010, Apr. 21   Perf. 13¼x13, 13x13¼
Granite Paper
1657-1660 A482   Set of 4   4.25 4.25

Insects A483

Designs: 150fr, Praying mantis. 200fr, Wasp. 250fr, Grasshopper. 500fr, Ant.

2010, Apr. 21   Litho.   Perf. 13x13¼
1661-1664 A483   Set of 4   4.50 4.50

Grand Agricultural Offensive for Food Security — A484

Designs: 100fr, Map of Africa, farmers with team of oxen, fruits and vegetables. 500fr, People and vegetables.

2010, Aug. 5   Litho.   Perf. 13¼x13¼
1665 A484 100fr multi
1668 A484 500fr multi
Dated 2009. Two additional stamps were issued in this set. The editors would like to examine any examples.

SOS Children's Village A485

Denomination in: 300fr, Orange. 400fr, Yellow.

2010, Sept. 15 Litho.   Perf. 13x13¼
1669-1670 A485   Set of 2   3.00 3.00

Fifth Gorée Diaspora Festival A486

Festival emblem and: 190fr, Men and buildings.

2010, Nov. 4   Litho.   Perf. 13x13¼
1671 A486 190fr multi   —
Dated 2009. Three additional stamps were issued in this set. The editors would like to examine any examples.

World Festival of Negro Arts — A487

Designs: 200fr, Woman with arms raised, vert. 300fr, Map of Africa. 450fr, Sphere, stylized people with arms raised, vert. 500fr, Carving of woman smoking pipe, table, vert.

Perf. 13x13¼, 13¼x13¼
2010, Dec. 21   Litho.
1675 A487 200fr multi   —
1676 A487 300fr multi   —
1677 A487 450fr multi   —
1678 A487 500fr multi   —
Dated 2007.

Birds — A488

Designs: 10fr, Ibis religionas, horiz. 200fr, Ardea pavonia. 450fr, Spoonbill (spatule). 500fr, Himantopus himantopus.

2011, Apr. 6   Litho.   Perf. 13x13¼
1679 A488 10fr multi   — —
            Perf. 13¼x13
1680 A488 200fr multi   — —
1681 A488 450fr multi   — —
1682 A488 500fr multi   — —
Dated 2009.

Pottery — A489

Design: 150fr, Water container and lid (canari réservoir d'eau). 200fr, Drinking cup (canari de libation).

2011, Apr. 6   Litho.   Perf. 13¼x13
1683 A489 150fr multi   —
1684 A489 200fr multi   —
Dated 2007. Two additional stamps were issued in this set. The editors would like to examine any examples.

Islands A490

Design: 100fr, Ile aux Oiseaux (Bird Island).

2011   Litho.   Perf. 13x13¼
1688 A490 100fr multi   —
Dated 2009. Three additional stamps were issued in this set. the editors would like to examine any examples.

SEMI-POSTAL STAMPS

No. 84 Surcharged in Red

1915   Unwmk.   Perf. 14x13½
B1 A28 10c + 5c org red & rose   2.00 2.00
  a. Chalky paper   2.00 2.00
No. B1 is on both ordinary and chalky paper.

Same Surcharge on No. 87

1918
B2 A28 15c + 5c red org & brn vio   2.00 2.00

Curie Issue
Common Design Type
1938   Engr.   Perf. 13
B3 CD80 1.75fr + 50c brt ultra   13.00 13.00

French Revolution Issue
Common Design Type
Photo., Name & Value Typo. in Black

1939
B4 CD83 45c + 25c green   9.50 9.50
B5 CD83 70c + 30c brown   9.50 9.50
B6 CD83 90c + 35c red org   9.50 9.50
B7 CD83 1.25fr + 1fr rose pink   9.50 9.50
B8 CD83 2.25fr + 2fr blue   9.00 9.00
        Nos. B4-B8 (5)   47.00 47.00

Stamps of 1935-38 Surcharged in Red or Black

1941   Perf. 12x12½, 12
B9 A30   50c + 1fr red org   3.25
B10 A31   80c + 2fr vio (R)   7.25
B11 A30   1.50fr + 2fr dk bl   7.25
B12 A30   2fr + 3fr blue   7.25
        Nos. B9-B12 (4)   25.00

Common Design Type and

Bambara Sharpshooter SP1   Colonial Soldier SP2

1941   Photo.   Perf. 13½
B13 SP1   1fr + 1fr red   1.25
B14 CD86 1.50fr + 3fr maroon   1.25
B15 SP2   2.50fr + 1fr blue   1.25
        Nos. B13-B15 (3)   3.75

The surtax was for the defense of the colonies.
Nos. B13-B15 were issued by the Vichy government, but it is doubtful whether they were placed in use in Senegal.

Nos. 193-194 Srchd. in Black or Red

1944   Engr.   Perf. 12½x12
B15A 50c + 1.50fr on 2.50fr deep blue (R)   .80
B15B + 2.50fr on 1fr green   .80
Colonial Development Fund.
Nos. B15A-B15B were issued by the Vichy government in France, but were not placed on sale in Senegal.

Catalogue values for unused stamps in this section, from this point to the end of the section, are for Never Hinged items.

Republic
Anti-Malaria Issue
Common Design Type
Perf. 12½x12
1962, Apr. 7   Engr.   Unwmk.
B16 CD108 25fr + 5fr brt grn   1.10 .65

Freedom from Hunger Issue
Common Design Type
1963, Mar. 21   Perf. 13
B17 CD112 25fr + 5fr dp vio, grn & brn   .80 .50

SP3

2002 World Cup Soccer Championships, Japan and Korea — SP4

World Cup: 290fr+50fr, Soccer ball and stadium. 360fr+50fr, Soccer field and crowd.

2002		Litho.	Perf. 13½	
B18	SP3	75fr +100fr shown	.75	.75

			Perf. 13x13¼	
B19	SP4	200fr +100fr shown	1.25	1.25
B20	SP4	290fr +50fr multi	1.40	1.40
B21	SP4	360fr +50fr multi	1.60	1.60
		Nos. B18-B21 (4)	5.00	5.00

Value for No. B18 is for example with surrounding selvage.

AIR POST STAMPS

Landscape AP1

Caravan AP2

Perf. 12½x12, 12x12½

1935		Engr.	Unwmk.	
C1	AP1	25c dk brown	.30	.30
C2	AP1	50c red orange	.65	.50
C3	AP1	1fr rose lilac	.30	.30
C4	AP1	1.25fr yellow grn	.30	.30
C5	AP1	2fr blue	.30	.30
C6	AP1	3fr olive grn	.50	.30
C7	AP2	3.50fr violet	.50	.30
C8	AP2	4.75fr orange	.95	.50
C9	AP2	6.50fr dk blue	1.45	1.10
C10	AP2	8fr black	1.75	1.75
C11	AP2	15fr rose lake	1.75	1.40
		Nos. C1-C11 (11)	8.75	7.05

No. C8 surcharged "ENTR' AIDE FRANCAIS + 95f 25" in green, red violet or blue, was never issued in this colony.

Common Design Type

1940		Engr.	Perf. 12½x12	
C12	CD85	1.90fr ultra	.55	.55
C13	CD85	2.90fr dk red	.55	.55
C14	CD85	4.50fr dk gray grn	.65	.65
C15	CD85	4.90fr yellow bis	.95	.95
C16	CD85	6.90fr dp orange	1.30	1.30
		Nos. C12-C16 (5)	4.00	4.00

Common Design Types

1942				
C17	CD88	50c car & bl	.30	
C18	CD88	1fr brn & blk	.50	
C19	CD88	2fr dk grn & red brn	.50	
C20	CD88	3fr dk bl & scar	1.05	
C21	CD88	5fr vio & brn red	.70	

Frame Engr., Center Typo.

C22	CD89	10fr ultra, ind & hn	.70	
C23	CD89	20fr rose car, mag & choc	1.10	
C24	CD89	50fr yel grn, dl grn & yel	2.10	2.75

Engr. & Photo.
Size: 47x26mm

C25	CD88	100fr dk red & bl	2.50	3.75
		Nos. C17-C25 (9)	9.45	

There is doubt whether Nos. C17 to C23 were officially placed in use.

> **Catalogue values for unused stamps in this section, from this point to the end of the section, are for Never Hinged items.**

Republic

Abyssinian Roller — AP3

Designs: 50fr, Carmine bee-eater, vert. 200fr, Violet touraco, vert. 250fr, Red bishop, vert. 500fr, Fish eagle, vert.

Perf. 12½x13, 13x12½

1960-63		Photo.	Unwmk.	
		Birds in Natural Colors		
C26	AP3	50fr blk & gray bl		
C27	AP3	100fr blk, yel & lil ('61)	2.25	.50
			4.00	1.00
C28	AP3	200fr blk, grn & bl ('61)	9.00	2.50
C29	AP3	250fr blk & pale grn ('63)	9.00	3.00
C30	AP3	500fr blk & bl	25.00	5.25
		Nos. C26-C30 (5)	49.25	12.25

Air Afrique Issue
Common Design Type

1962, Feb. 17		Engr.	Perf. 13	
C31	CD107	25fr vio brn, sl grn & ocher	.80	.30

African Postal Union Issue
Common Design Type

1963, Sept. 8		Photo.	Perf. 12½	
C32	CD114	85fr choc, ocher & red	1.75	.50

Air Afrique Issue, 1963
Common Design Type

1963, Nov. 19		Unwmk.	Perf. 13x12	
C33	CD115	50fr multicolored	2.00	.65

Independence Monument — AP4

1964, Apr. 4		Photo.	Perf. 12x13	
C34	AP4	300fr ultra, tan, ocher & grn	5.00	1.75

Symbolic European and African Cities — AP5

1964, Apr. 18		Engr.	Perf. 13	
C35	AP5	150fr grn, brn red & blk	4.00	1.40

Congress of the Intl. Federation of Twin Cities, Dakar.

Europafrica Issue, 1964

Peanuts, Globe, Factory, Figures of "Africa," and "Europe" — AP6

1964, July 20		Photo.	Perf. 13x12	
C36	AP6	50fr multicolored	2.00	.60

See note after Madagascar No. 357.

Basketball AP7

1964, Aug. 22		Engr.	Perf. 13	
C37	AP7	85fr shown	2.50	.65
C38	AP7	100fr Pole vault	2.75	1.00

18th Olympic Games, Tokyo, Oct. 10-25.

Launching of Syncom 2 — AP8

1964, Oct. 24		Unwmk.	Perf. 13	
C39	AP8	150fr grn, red brn & ultra	3.00	1.00

Communication through space.

Pres. John F. Kennedy (1917-1963) AP9

1964, Dec. 5		Photo.	Perf. 13	
C40	AP9	100fr brt yel, dk grn & brn red	2.75	1.00
a.		Souvenir sheet of 4	12.00	12.00

Scenic Type of Regular Issue, 1965

View: 100fr, Shore of Gambia River in Eastern Senegal.

1965, Feb. 27		Engr.	Perf. 13	
		Size: 48x27mm		
C41	A48	100fr brn blk, grn & bis	2.50	1.00

Mother and Child, Globe and Emblems AP10

1965, Sept. 25		Unwmk.	Perf. 13	
C42	AP10	50fr choc, brt bl & grn	1.25	.40

International Cooperation Year.

A-1 Satellite and Earth — AP11

Designs: No. C44, Diamant rocket. 90fr, Scout rocket and FR-1 satellite.

1966, Feb. 19		Engr.	Perf. 13	
C43	AP11	50fr yel brn, dk grn & blk	1.00	.40
C44	AP11	50fr Prus bl, lt red brn & car rose	1.00	.40
C45	AP11	90fr dk red brn, dk gray & Prus bl	2.50	.85
		Nos. C43-C45 (3)	4.50	1.65

French achievements in space.

D-1 Satellite over Globe — AP12

1966, June 11		Engr.	Perf. 13	
C46	AP12	100fr dk car, sl & vio	2.50	.80

Launching of the D-1 satellite at Hammaguir, Algeria, Feb. 17, 1966.

Air Afrique Issue, 1966
Common Design Type

1966, Aug. 31		Photo.	Perf. 13	
C47	CD123	30fr red brn, blk & lem	.80	.30

Mermoz Plane "Arc-en-Ciel" — AP13

Jean Mermoz — AP14

Designs: 35fr, Latecoére 300 "Croix du Sud." 100fr, Map showing last flight from Dakar to Brazil.

1966, Dec. 7   Engr.   Perf. 13
C48 AP13 20fr bl, rose lil & indigo   .80   .25
C49 AP13 35fr slate, brn & grn   1.00   .30
C50 AP13 100fr grn, lt grn & mar 1.75   .50
C51 AP14 150fr blk, ultra & mar   3.50 1.00
     Nos. C48-C51 (4)   7.05 2.05

Jean Mermoz (1901-36), French aviator, on the 30th anniv. of his last flight.

Dakar-Yoff Airport — AP15

1967, Apr. 22   Engr.   Perf. 13
C52 AP15 200fr red brn, ind & brt bl   3.50 1.00

Knob-billed Goose — AP16

Flowers and Birds: 100fr, Mimosa. 150fr, Flowering cactus. 250fr, Village weaver. 500fr, Bateleur.

1967-69   Photo.   Perf. 11½
Granite Paper
Dated "1967"
C53 AP16 100fr gray, yel & grn   3.00 1.00
C54 AP16 150fr multicolored   5.00 1.50
Dated "1968"
C55 AP16 250fr gray & multi   8.00 1.75
Dated "1969"
C56 AP16 300fr brt bl & multi   12.50 3.00
C57 AP16 500fr orange & multi   17.50 4.25
     Nos. C53-C57 (5)   46.00 11.50

Issued: 100fr, 6/24/67; 500fr, 7/13/68; 300fr, 12/21/68; 250fr, 4/26/69.

The Girls from Avignon, by Picasso AP17

1967, July 22   Perf. 12x13
C59 AP17 100fr multicolored   3.50 1.00

African Postal Union Issue, 1967
Common Design Type

1967, Sept. 9   Engr.   Perf. 13
C60 CD124 100fr brt grn, vio & car lake   1.75   .50

Konrad Adenauer AP18

1968, Feb. 17   Photo.   Perf. 12½
C61 AP18 100fr dk red, ol & blk   2.25   .60
a.   Souvenir sheet of 4   10.00 10.00

Konrad Adenauer (1876-1967), chancellor of West Germany (1949-63).

Weather Balloon, Vegetation and WMO Emblem — AP19

1968, Mar. 23   Engr.   Perf. 13
C62 AP19 50fr blk, ultra & bl grn 1.25   .40

8th World Meteorological Day, Mar. 23.

19th Olympic Games, Mexico City, Oct. 12-27 — AP20

1968, Oct. 12   Engr.   Perf. 13
C63 AP20 20fr Hurdling   .55   .25
C64 AP20 30fr Javelin   .70   .30
C65 AP20 50fr Judo   1.40   .35
C66 AP20 75fr Basketball   2.25   .65
     Nos. C63-C66 (4)   4.90 1.55

PHILEXAFRIQUE Issue

Young Woman Reading Letter, by Jean Raoux AP21

1968, Oct. 26   Photo.   Perf. 12½
C67 AP21 100fr buff & multi   3.50 2.00

PHILEXAFRIQUE, Phil. Exhib. in Abidjan, Feb. 14-23, 1969. Printed with alternating buff label.

2nd PHILEXAFRIQUE Issue
Common Design Type
Senegal #160 and Boulevard, Dakar.

1969, Feb. 14   Engr.   Perf. 13
C68 CD128 50fr grn, gray & pur   2.00 1.40

Tourist Emblem with Map of Africa and Dove — AP22

1969   Photo.   Perf. 13
C69 AP22 100fr red, lt grn & lt bl 1.75 .50

Year of African Tourism, 1969.

Pres. Lamine Gueye (1891-1968) AP23

Design: 45fr, Pres. Gueye wearing fez.

1969, June 10   Photo.   Perf. 12½
C70 AP23 30fr brn, org & blk   .45   .25
C71 AP23 45fr brn, lt grnsh bl & blk 1.25   .30
a.   Min. sheet, 2 ea #C70-C71   3.50 3.50

"Transmission of Thought" Tapestry by Ousmane Faye — AP24

Fari, Tapestry by Allaye N'Diaye — AP25

1969, Oct. 25   Photo.   Perf. 12½
C72 AP24 25fr multicolored   .90   .35

Perf. 12x12½
C73 AP25 50fr multicolored   2.00   .65

Europafrica Issue

Baila Bridge — AP26

1969, Nov. 15   Photo.   Perf. 13x12
C74 AP26 100fr multicolored   2.00   .50

Emile Lécrivain, Plane and Toulouse-Dakar Route — AP27

1970, Jan. 31   Engr.   Perf. 13
C75 AP27 50fr grn, slate & rose brn   1.25   .40

40th anniv. of the disappearance of the aviator Emile Lécrivain (1897-1929).

René Maran, Martinique AP28

Portraits: 45fr, Marcus Garvey, Jamaica. 50fr, Dr. Price Mars, Haiti.

1970, Mar. 21   Photo.   Perf. 12½
C76 AP28 30fr red brn, lt grn & blk   .35   .25
C77 AP28 45fr blue, pink & blk   1.00   .25
C78 AP28 50fr grn, buff & blk   1.10   .40
     Nos. C76-C78 (3)   2.45   .90

Issued to honor prominent Negro leaders.

"One People, One Purpose, One Faith" AP29

1970, Apr. 3   Photo.   Perf. 11½
C79 AP29 500fr gold & multi   7.50 3.00
a.   Souvenir sheet   10.00 10.00

10th anniv. of independence. No. C79 sold for 600fr.

Bay of Naples and Dakar Post Office — AP30

1970, May 2   Photo.   Perf. 13x12½
C80 AP30 100fr multicolored   2.00   .60

10th Europa Phil. Exhib., Naples, May 2-10.

Blue Cock,
by
Mamadou
Niang
AP31

Tapestries: 45fr, Fairy. 75fr, "Lunaris," by Jean Lurçat.

1970, June 20 Photo. *Perf. 12½x12*
C81 AP31 30fr black & multi   .55   .35
C82 AP31 45fr dk red brn & multi   2.00   .50
C83 AP31 75fr yellow & multi   3.00   .65
   Nos. C81-C83 (3)   5.55 1.50

Head of the Courtesan Nagakawa, by Chobunsai Yeishi, and Mt. Fuji, by Hokusai — AP32

EXPO Emblem and: 25fr, Woman Playing Guitar, by Hokusai, and Sun Tower, vert. 150fr, "One of the Present-day Beauties of Nanboku" by Katsukawa Shuncho, vert.

1970, July 18 Engr. *Perf. 13*
C84 AP32 25fr red & green   .65   .25
C85 AP32 75fr yel grn, dk bl &
           red brn   1.75   .35
C86 AP32 150fr bl, red brn &
           ocher   2.75   .80
   Nos. C84-C86 (3)   5.15 1.40

EXPO '70 Intl. Exhib., Osaka, Japan, Mar. 15-Sept. 13.

Tuna, Processing Plant and
Ship — AP33

Urban Development in Dakar — AP34

1970, Aug. 22 Engr. *Perf. 13*
C87 AP33 30fr dl red, blk & brt bl 1.00   .25
C88 AP34 100fr chocolate & grn   1.75   .60

Progress in industrialization and urbanization in Dakar.

Beethoven;
Napoleon and
Allegory of
Eroica
Symphony
AP35

Design: 100fr, Beethoven holding quill.

1970, Sept. 26 Engr. *Perf. 13*
C89 AP35 50fr ol, brn & ocher   2.25   .50
C90 AP35 100fr Prus grn & dp
           claret   4.50 1.10
Ludwig van Beethoven (1770-1827), composer.

Globe, Scales and Women of Four
Races — AP36

1970, Oct. 24 Engr. *Perf. 13*
C91 AP36 100fr grn, ocher & red   2.25   .80
   25th anniversary of United Nations.

De Gaulle, Map
of Africa,
Symbols — AP37

100fr, Charles de Gaulle & map of Senegal.

1970, Dec. 31 Photo. *Perf. 12½*
C92 AP37 50fr multicolored   1.75   .85
C93 AP37 100fr blue & multi   3.50 1.60

Honoring Pres. Charles de Gaulle as liberator of the colonies.

"A Roof for Every Refugee" — AP38

1971, Jan. 16
C94 AP38 100fr multicolored   1.75   .65
   High Commissioner for Refugees, 20th anniv.

Phillis Wheatley,
American
Poet — AP39

Prominent Blacks: 40fr, James E. K. Aggrey, Methodist missionary, Ghana. 60fr, Alain Le Roy Locke, American educator. 100fr, Booker T. Washington, American educator.

1971, Apr. 10 Photo. *Perf. 12½*
C95 AP39 25fr multicolored   .25   .25
C96 AP39 40fr blk, bl & bis   .45   .30
C97 AP39 60fr blk, bl & emer   1.00   .40
C98 AP39 100fr blk, bl & red   1.50   .60
   Nos. C95-C98 (4)   3.20 1.55

Napoleon
as First
Consul, by
Ingres
AP40

Designs: 25fr, Napoleon in 1809, by Robert Lefevre. 35fr, Napoleon on his death bed, by Georges Rouget. 50fr, Awakening into Immortality, sculpture by Francois Rude.

1971, June 19 Photo. *Perf. 13*
C99   AP40 15fr gold & multi   .70   .40
C100 AP40 25fr gold & multi   1.00   .50
C101 AP40 35fr gold & multi   1.40   .60
C102 AP40 50fr gold & multi   2.75 1.00
   Nos. C99-C102 (4)   5.85 2.50

Napoleon Bonaparte (1769-1821).

Gamal Abdel   Alfred
Nasser — AP41   Nobel — AP41a

1971, July 17 *Perf. 12½*
C103 AP41 50fr multicolored   1.00   .30
   Nasser (1918-1970), President of Egypt.

1971, Sept. 25 Photo. *Perf. 13½x13*
C103A AP41a 100fr multicolored   2.25   .60
   Alfred Nobel (1833-1896), inventor of dynamite who established the Nobel Prizes.

Iranian Flag and Senegal Coat of
Arms — AP42

1971, Oct. 15 *Perf. 13x12½*
C104 AP42 200fr multicolored   3.00 1.00
   2500th anniversary of the founding of the Persian empire by Cyrus the Great.

African Postal Union Issue, 1971
Common Design Type
   Design: 100fr, Arms of Senegal and UAMPT Building, Brazzaville, Congo.

1971, Nov. 13 *Perf. 13x13½*
C105 CD135 100fr blue & multi   1.60   .50

Louis Armstrong (1900-1971),
American Jazz Musician — AP43

1971, Nov. 27 Photo. *Perf. 12½*
C106 AP43 150fr gold & dk brn   6.75 1.60

Sapporo Olympic Emblem and Speed
Skating — AP44

Sapporo '72 Emblem and: 10fr, Bobsledding. 125fr, Skiing.

1972, Jan. 22 *Perf. 13*
C107 AP44 5fr multicolored   .25   .25
C108 AP44 10fr multicolored   .25   .25
C109 AP44 125fr multicolored   3.00   .60
   Nos. C107-C109 (3)   3.50 1.10

11th Winter Olympic Games, Sapporo, Japan, Feb. 3-13.

Fonteghetto della Farina, by
Canaletto — AP45

Design: 100fr, San Giorgio Maggiore, by Giovanni Antonio Guardi, vert.

1972, Feb. 26
C110 AP45 50fr gold & multi   1.25   .65
C111 AP45 100fr gold & multi   2.50 1.25
   UNESCO campaign to save Venice.

Theater Type of Regular Issue
150fr, Daniel Sorano as Shylock, vert.

1972, Mar. 25 Photo. *Perf. 12½x13*
C112 A99 150fr multicolored   4.00 1.50

Environment Type of Regular Issue
100fr, Protection of the ocean (oil slick).

1972, June 3 Photo. *Perf. 13x12½*
C113 A101 100fr multicolored   2.25   .60

Emperor Haile
Selassie,
Ethiopian and
Senegalese
Flags — AP46

1972, July 23 Photo. *Perf. 13½x13*
C114 AP46 100fr gold & multi   1.75   .60

80th birthday of Emperor Haile Selassie of Ethiopia.

Swordfish — AP47

Designs: 65fr, Killer whale. 75fr, Rhincodon. 125fr, Common rorqual (whale).

1972-73 Photo. *Perf. 11½*
C115 AP47 50fr multi   3.75   .75
C116 AP47 65fr multi   5.00 1.25
C117 AP47 75fr multi   7.25 1.50
C118 AP47 125fr multi   8.50 1.75
   Nos. c115-c118 (4)   24.50 5.25

Issued: #C115, C118, 11/25/72; #C116-C117, 7/28/73.

Palace of the Republic — AP48

1973, Apr. 3   Photo.   *Perf. 13*
C119 AP48 100fr multi   1.75 .60

Hotel Teranga, Dakar — AP49

1973, May 26   Photo.   *Perf. 13*
C120 AP49 100fr multi   1.75 .60

Emblem of African Lions Club — AP50

1973, June 2
C121 AP50 150fr multi   2.50 .80

15th Congress of Lions Intl., District 403, Dakar, June 1-2.

"Couple with Mimosa," by Marc Chagall AP51

1973, Aug. 11   Photo.   *Perf. 13*
C122 AP51 200fr multi   7.00 2.75

Map of Italy with Riccione AP52

Human Rights Flame and People AP54

Raoul Follereau and World Map — AP53

1973, Aug. 25   Engr.
C123 AP52 100fr dk grn, red & pur   2.25 .60
Intl. Phil. Exhib., Riccione 1973.

1973, Dec. 22   Engr.   *Perf. 13*
100fr, Dr. Armauer G. Hansen & leprosy bacilli.
C124 AP53 40fr sl grn, pur & red brn   1.10 .25
C125 AP53 100fr sl grn, mag & plum   2.40 .75
Centenary of the discovery of the Hansen bacillus, the cause of leprosy.

1973, Dec. 15   Photo.   *Perf. 13½*
65fr, Human Rights flame and drummer.
C126 AP54 35fr grn & multi   .70 .25
C127 AP54 65fr org & multi   1.00 .40
25th anniv. of the Universal Declaration of Human Rights.

Men of Four Races, Arms of Dakar, Congress Emblem — AP55

50fr, Key joining twin cities & emblem, vert.

1973, Dec. 26   Photo.
C128 AP55 50fr org & multi   .90 .35
C129 AP55 125fr red & multi   1.75 .50
8th Congress of the World Federation of Twin Cities, Dakar, Dec. 26-29.

Finfoots — AP56

1974, Feb. 9   Photo.   *Perf. 13*
C130 AP56 1fr shown   .25 .25
C131 AP56 2fr Spoonbills   .25 .25
C132 AP56 3fr Crested cranes   .30 .25
C133 AP56 4fr Egrets   .30 .25
C134 AP56 250fr Flamingos   7.00 1.60
C135 AP56 250fr Flamingos   7.00 1.60
a.   Strip of 2 + label   12.50
Nos. C130-C135 (6)   15.10 4.20
Djoudj Park bird sanctuary. Denomination in gold on No. C134, in black on No. C135.

Tiger Attacking Wild Horse, by Delacroix — AP57

Design: 200fr, Tiger Hunt, by Eugéne Delacroix (1798-1863).

1974, Mar. 23   Photo.   *Perf. 13*
C136 AP57 150fr gold & multi   3.00 .80
C137 AP57 200fr gold & multi   3.75 1.25

Intl. Fair, Dakar — AP57a

1974, Nov. 28   Embossed   *Perf. 10½*
C137A AP57a 350fr silver   5.75 4.50
C137B AP57a 1500fr gold   27.50 18.00

Soyuz and Apollo, Space Docking Emblem — AP58

1975, May 23   Engr.   *Perf. 13*
C138 AP58 125fr multi   2.00 .60
US-USSR space cooperation.
For overprint see No. C140.

Senegal Type D6, Tuscany Type A1, Map of Italy AP59

1975, Aug. 23   Engr.   *Perf. 13*
C139 AP59 125fr org, vio & dk red 2.00 .65
Intl. Phil. Exhib., Riccione 1975.

No. C138 Overprinted: "JONCTION / 17 Juil. 1975"

1975, Oct. 21   Engr.   *Perf. 13*
C140 AP58 125fr multi   2.00 .60
Apollo-Soyuz link-up in space, July 17, 1975.

Boston Massacre — AP60

Design: 500fr, Lafayette, Washington, Rochambeau and Battle of Yorktown.

1975, Dec. 20   Engr.   *Perf. 13*
C141 AP60 250fr ultra, red & brn   3.00 1.10
C142 AP60 500fr bl & ver   6.75 2.50
American Bicentennial.

Concorde and Map — AP61

1976, Jan. 21   Litho.   *Perf. 13*
C143 AP61 300fr multi   2.00 2.00
First commercial flight of supersonic jet Concorde, Paris to Rio de Janeiro, Jan. 21. For overprint see No. C145.

2nd Intl. Fair, Dakar — AP61a

1976, Dec. 3   Embossed   *Perf. 10½*
C143A AP61a 500fr silver   6.50 6.50
C143B AP61a 1500fr gold   27.50 27.50

Spaceship and Control Room — AP62

1977, June 25   Litho.   *Perf. 12½*
C144 AP62 300fr multi   3.25 1.25
Viking space mission to Mars.

No. C143 Overprinted in Red: "22.11.77 / PARIS NEW-YORK"
1977, Nov. 22   *Perf. 13*
C145 AP61 300fr multi   4.00 2.00
Concorde, 1st commercial flight, Paris-New York.

Evolution of Fishing — AP62a

Designs: 10fr, Fishermen hauling in netted catch. 15fr, Two fishermen in canoe. 20fr, Ship, man holding fish. 25fr, Fisherman holding net.

1977   Litho.   *Perf. 12¾*
C145A AP62a 5fr shown   — —
C145B AP62a 10fr multi   — —
C145C AP62a 15fr multi   — —
C145D AP62a 20fr multi   — —
C145E AP62a 25fr multi   — —

Philexafrique II-Essen Issue
Common Design Types

Designs: No. C146, Lion & Senegal #C28. No. C147, Capercaillie & Schleswig-Holstein #1.

1978, Nov. 1   Litho.   *Perf. 12½*
C146 CD138 100fr multi   2.00 1.50
C147 CD139 100fr multi   2.00 1.50
a.   Pair, #C146-C147   10.00 4.00

J. Dabry, L. Gimie, and J. Mermoz, Airplane, Map of Route (St. Louis-Natal) — AP63

1980, Dec.   Photo.   *Perf. 13*
C148 AP63 300fr multi   3.25 1.00
1st airmail crossing of So. Atlantic, 50th anniv.

1st Transatlantic Commercial Airmail
Flight, 55th Anniv. — AP64

1985, May 12   Litho.   Perf. 13
C149 AP64 250fr multi   2.75 1.00

Clement Ader (1841-1926), Engineer
and Aviation Pioneer — AP65

Ader and: 145fr, Automobile, microphone.
180fr, 615fr, 940fr, Bat-winged steam powered
airplane.

1991, June 7   Litho.   Perf. 13
C150 AP65 145fr multicolored   2.00   .40
C151 AP65 180fr multicolored   2.25   .65
C152 AP65 615fr multi, vert.   7.50 2.25
Nos. C150-C152 (3)   11.75 3.30

Souvenir Sheet
C153 AP65 940fr multi, vert.   7.00 3.50

AIR POST SEMI-POSTAL STAMPS

French Revolution Issue
Common Design Type
1939 Unwmk. Photo. Perf. 13
Name and Value Typo. in Orange
CB1 CD83 4.75 + 4fr brn blk   16.00 16.00
Surtax used for the defense of the colonies.

Dahomey types SPAP1-SPAP3
inscribed Senegal
Perf. 13½x12½, 13 (#CB4)
Photo, Engr. (#CB4)
1942, June 22
CB2 SPAP1 1.50fr + 3.50fr
green   .80 6.50
CB3 SPAP2 2fr + 6fr brown   .80 6.50
CB4 SPAP3 3fr + 9fr car red   .80 6.50
Nos. CB2-CB4 (3)   2.40 19.50

Native children's welfare fund.

Colonial Education Fund
Common Design Type
Perf. 12½x13½
1942, June 22   Engr.
CB5 CD86a 1.20fr + 1.80fr blue
& red   .80 6.50

Catalogue values for unused
stamps in this section, from this
point to the end of the section, are
for Never Hinged items.

Republic

Nile Gods Uniting Upper and Lower
Egypt (Abu Simbel) — SPAP1

1964, Mar. 7   Engr.   Perf. 13
CB6 SPAP1 25fr + 5fr Prus bl,
red brn & sl
grn   1.60   .65
UNESCO campaign to save historic monuments in Nubia.

POSTAGE DUE STAMPS

Postage Due Stamps of
French Colonies
Surcharged

1903   Unwmk.   Imperf.
J1 D1 10c on 50c lilac   105.00 105.00
J2 D1 10c on 60c brown,
buff   105.00 105.00
J3 D1 10c on 1fr rose, buff   475.00 475.00
Nos. J1-J3 (3)   685.00 685.00

D2   D3

1906   Typo.   Perf. 14x13½
J4 D2 5c green, grnsh   6.50 4.75
J5 D2 10c red brown   8.00 5.50
J6 D2 15c dark blue   8.00 7.25
J7 D2 20c black, yellow   10.50 7.25
J8 D2 30c red, straw   11.00 11.00
J9 D2 50c violet   13.50 13.50
J10 D2 60c black, buff   17.00 17.00
J11 D2 1fr black, pinkish   26.00 26.00
Nos. J4-J11 (8)   100.50 92.25

1914
J12 D3 5c green   .55   .55
J13 D3 10c rose   .55   .55
J14 D3 15c gray   .95   .80
J15 D3 20c brown   1.20 1.10
J16 D3 30c blue   1.60 1.40
J17 D3 50c black   1.90 1.75
J18 D3 60c orange   2.25 1.60
J19 D3 1fr violet   2.25 1.90
Nos. J12-J19 (8)   11.25 9.65

Type of 1914 Issue
Surcharged

1927
J20 D3 2fr on 1fr lilac rose   8.00 8.00
J21 D3 3fr on 1fr orange
brown   8.00 8.00

D4

1935   Engr.   Perf. 12½x12
J22 D4 5c yellow green   .30   .30
J23 D4 10c red orange   .30   .30
J24 D4 15c violet   .30   .30
J25 D4 20c olive green   .30   .30
J26 D4 30c reddish brown   .30   .30
J27 D4 50c rose lilac   1.10 1.10
J28 D4 60c orange   1.50 1.50
J29 D4 1fr black   1.10 1.10
J30 D4 2fr dark blue   1.10 1.10
J31 D4 3fr dark carmine   1.50 1.50
Nos. J22-J31 (10)   7.80 7.80

Catalogue values for unused
stamps in this section, from this
point to the end of the section, are
for Never Hinged items.

Republic

D5   Lion — D6

1961, Feb. 20   Typo.   Perf. 14x13½
J32 D5 1fr orange & red   .25   .25
J33 D5 2fr ultra & red   .25   .25
J34 D5 5fr brown & red   .25   .25
J35 D5 20fr green & red   .60   .60
J36 D5 25fr red lilac & red 1.25 1.25
Nos. J32-J36 (5)   2.60 2.60

1966-83   Typo.   Perf. 14x13
Lion in Gold
J37 D6 1fr red & black   .25   .25
J38 D6 2fr yel brn & black   .25   .25
J39 D6 5fr red lilac & black .25   .25
J40 D6 10fr brt blue & black .25   .25
J41 D6 20fr emerald & black .40   .40
J42 D6 30fr gray & black   .80   .80
J43 D6 60fr blue & black   .40   .40
J44 D6 90fr rose & black   .60   .40
Nos. J37-J44 (8)   3.20 3.00
Issued: 1fr-30fr, 12/1/66; others, 10/1983.

OFFICIAL STAMPS

Catalogue values for unused
stamps in this section are for
Never Hinged items.

Arms — O1   Baobab
Tree — O2

Perf. 14x13½
1961, Sept. 18   Typo.   Unwmk.
Denominations in Black
O1 O1 1fr sepia & bl   .25   .25
O2 O1 2fr dk bl & org   .25   .25
O3 O1 5fr maroon & grn   .25   .25
O4 O1 10fr ver & blk   .25   .25
O5 O1 25fr vio bl & ver   .65   .25
O6 O1 50fr ver & gray   1.00   .45
O7 O1 85fr lilac & org   2.00   .60
O8 O1 100fr ver & yel grn   2.75 1.10
Nos. O1-O8 (8)   7.40 3.40

1966-77   Typo.   Perf. 14x13
O9 O2 1fr yel & blk   .25   .25
O10 O2 5fr org & blk   .25   .25
O11 O2 10fr red & blk   .25   .25
O12 O2 20fr dp red lil & blk .25   .25
O13 O2 25fr dp lil & blk ('75) .45 .25
O14 O2 30fr bl & blk   .45   .25
O15 O2 35fr bl & blk ('73)   .55   .25
O16 O2 40fr grnsh bl & blk ('75) .55 .25
O17 O2 55fr emer & blk   1.00   .45
O18 O2 60fr emer & blk ('77) .55   .25
O19 O2 90fr dk bl grn & blk 1.40   .25
O20 O2 100fr brn & blk   1.75   .25
Nos. O9-O20 (12)   7.70 3.20
See Nos. O22-O25.

No. O17 Surcharged with New Value
and Two Bars
1969
O21 O2 60fr on 55fr emer & blk   1.75 .25

1983, Oct.   Typo.   Perf. 14x13
O22 O2 90fr dk grn & blk   .60 .25
"90F" is shorter and wider than on Nos. O9-
O22.

1991   Litho.   Perf. 13x13¼
O22B O2 45fr blue & black
O23 O2 50fr red & blk   1.00 1.00
O24 O2 145fr brt grn & blk 2.75 2.75
O25 O2 180fr org yel & blk 3.25 3.25
Nos. O23-O25 (3)   7.00 7.00

An additional stamp was issued in this set.
The editors would like to examine any
example.

No. O22B Surcharged

2010 ?   Litho.   Perf. 13x13¼
O26 O2 100fr on 45fr #O22B

SENEGAMBIA & NIGER

,se-nə-'gam-bē-ə and 'nī-jər

A French Administrative unit for the Senegal and Niger possessions in Africa during the period when the French possessions in Africa were being definitively divided into colonies and protectorates. The name was dropped in 1904 when this territory was consolidated with part of French Sudan, under the name Upper Senegal and Niger.

100 Centimes = 1 Franc

Navigation and
Commerce — A1

1903 Unwmk. Typo. *Perf. 14x13½*
Name of Colony in Blue or Carmine

1	A1	1c black, *lil bl*	2.40	3.25
2	A1	2c brown, *buff*	2.50	3.25
3	A1	4c claret, *lav*	5.50	7.25
4	A1	5c yel grn	6.75	8.50
5	A1	10c red	7.50	9.00
6	A1	15c gray	14.00	16.00
7	A1	20c red, *green*	12.50	16.00
8	A1	25c blue	21.00	20.00
9	A1	30c brn, *bister*	17.50	21.00
10	A1	40c red, *straw*	25.00	30.00
11	A1	50c brn, *azure*	50.00	55.00
12	A1	75c deep vio, *org*	55.00	62.50
13	A1	1fr brnz grn, *straw*	67.50	80.00
		Nos. 1-13 (13)	287.15	331.75

Perf. 13½x14 stamps are counterfeits.

SERBIA

'sər-bē-ə

LOCATION — In southeastern Europe, bounded by Romania and Bulgaria on the east, the former Austro-Hungarian Empire on the north, Greece on the south, and Albania and Montenegro on the west
GOVT. — Kingdom
AREA — 18,650 sq. mi.
POP. — 2,911,701 (1910)
CAPITAL — Belgrade

A powerful kingdom during the Middle Ages, Serbia was conquered by the Ottoman Turks in 1389 and remained under Turkish rule until 1829, when it became an autonomous region. In 1878 it became fully independent and led the movement to unite the southern Slavs into a single state under Serbian rule. Occupied by Germany, Austria-Hungary and Bulgaria during World War I, the collapse of Austria-Hungary in the autumn of 1918 made it possible for Serbia to realize its national ambitions.

On December 1, 1918, Serbia absorbed Montenegro, Bosnia and Herzegovina, Croatia, Dalmatia and Slovenia, to form the Kingdom of the Serbs, Croats and Slovenes, which became the Kingdom of Yugoslavia in 1929.

During World War II, Yugoslavia was broken up by its Axis occupiers, and a German satellite regime was established in Serbia. After the war, it became one of the constituent republics of the Socialist Federal Republic of Yugoslavia.

In 1992, with the dissolution of the greater Yugoslav republic, only Montenegro remained associated with Serbia, first in the Federal Republic of Yugoslavia and, after 2002, in the looser federation of Serbia & Montenegro.

After a referendum on independence on May 21, 2006, Montenegro seceded from Serbia and Montenegro, declaring independence on June 3, 2006. Serbia formally accepted this secession on June 7. While some stamps issued after

June 7 bear the "Serbia and Montenegro" inscription, they were sold only in Serbia.

100 Paras = 1 Dinar

> **Catalogue values for unused stamps in this country are for Never Hinged items, beginning with Scott 180 in the regular postage section and Scott RA2 in the postal tax section.**

Coat of Arms — A1   Prince Michael (Obrenovich III) — A2

1866 Unwmk. Typo. *Imperf.*
Paper colored Through

1	A1	1p dk green, *dk vio rose*	55.00

Surface Colored Paper, Thin or Thick

2	A1	1p dk green, *lil rose*	55.00
a.		1p olive green, *rose*	55.00
b.		1p yel grn, *pale rose* (thick paper)	375.00
3	A1	2p red brown, *lilac*	75.00
a.		2p red brn, *lil gray* (thick paper)	250.00
b.		2p dl grn, *lil gray* (thick paper)	800.00
		Nos. 1-3 (3)	185.00

Vienna Printing
Perf. 12

4	A2	10p orange	1,100.	675.00
5	A2	20p rose	750.00	30.00
6	A2	40p blue	750.00	125.00
a.		Half used as 20p on cover		
		Nos. 4-6 (3)	2,600.	830.00

Belgrade Printing
Perf. 9½

7	A2	1p green	22.50	
8	A2	2p bister brn	32.50	
9	A2	20p rose	15.00	22.50
a.		Pair, imperf. between		
10	A2	40p ultra	240.00	275.00
a.		Half used as 20p on cover		
		Nos. 7-10 (4)	310.00	

Pelure Paper

11	A2	10p orange	90.00	110.00
12	A2	20p rose	75.00	15.00
a.		Pair, imperf. between		
13	A2	40p ultra	55.00	37.50
a.		Pair, imperf. between		
b.		Half used as 20p on cover		
		Nos. 11-13 (3)	220.00	162.50

Nos. 1-3, 7-8, 14-16, 25-26 were used only as newspaper tax stamps.

1868-69 Ordinary Paper *Imperf.*

14	A2	1p green	37.50	
a.		1p olive green ('69)	3,750.	
15	A2	2p brown	75.00	
a.		2p bister brown ('69)	260.00	

Counterfeits of type A2 are common.

Prince Milan (Obrenovich IV)
A3   A4

Perf. 9½, 12 and Compound
1869-78

16	A3	1p yellow	5.50	110.00
17	A3	10p red brown	9.00	4.75
a.		10p yellow brown	475.00	75.00
18	A3	10p orange ('78)	2.25	6.00
19	A3	15p orange	85.00	30.00
20	A3	20p gray blue	1.50	2.50
a.		20p ultramarine	4.50	2.25
b.		Half used as 10p on cover		
21	A3	25p rose	2.25	7.50
22	A3	35p lt green	4.50	4.50

23	A3	40p violet	2.25	3.00
a.		Half used as 20p on cover		
24	A3	50p blue green	11.00	7.50
		Nos. 16-24 (9)	123.25	175.75

The first setting, which included all values except No. 18, had the stamps 2-2½mm apart. A new setting, introduced in 1878, had the stamps 3-4mm apart, providing wider margins. Only Nos. 17, 18, 20 and 21 exist in this new setting, which differs also in shades from the earlier setting.

The narrow-spaced Nos. 17, 20 and 21 are rarer, especially unused, as are the early shades of Nos. 23 and 24.

All values except Nos. 19 and 24 are known in various partly perforated varieties.
Counterfeits exist.
See No. 25.

1872-79 *Imperf.*

25	A3	1p yellow	6.75	19.00
a.		Tête bêche pair		
26	A4	2p blk, thin paper ('79)	.75	.75
a.		Thick paper ('73)	2.25	19.00

Used value of No. 26 is for canceled-to-order.

King Milan
I — A5

King Alexander (Obrenovich V) — A6

1880 *Perf. 13x13½*

27	A5	5p green	1.90	.35
a.		5p olive green	550.00	3.75
28	A5	10p rose	2.25	.35
29	A5	20p orange	1.10	.75
a.		20p yellow	4.50	1.90
30	A5	25p ultra	1.50	1.10
a.		25p blue	1.90	1.10
31	A5	50p brown	1.50	5.50
a.		50p brown violet	210.00	4.50
32	A5	1d violet	6.75	6.00
		Nos. 27-32 (6)	15.00	14.05

1890

33	A6	5p green	.35	.25
34	A6	10p rose red	1.25	.25
35	A6	15p red violet	1.10	.25
36	A6	20p orange	.75	.25
37	A6	25p blue	.90	.35
38	A6	50p brown	2.25	2.25
39	A6	1d dull lilac	11.00	9.00
		Nos. 33-39 (7)	17.60	12.60

King Alexander — A7

1894-96 *Perf. 13x13½*
Granite Paper

40	A7	5p green	4.00	.25
a.		Perf. 11½	7.50	.40
41	A7	10p car rose	5.50	.25
b.		Perf. 11½	90.00	1.50
42	A7	15p violet	9.00	.25
43	A7	20p orange	67.50	.75
a.		Half used as 10p on cover		375.00
44	A7	25p blue	19.00	.35
45	A7	50p brown	22.50	.75
46	A7	1d dk green	1.50	3.00
47	A7	1d red brn, *bl* ('96)	19.00	3.75
		Nos. 40-47 (8)	148.00	9.35

1898-1900 *Perf. 13x13½, 11½*
Ordinary Paper

48	A7	1p dull red	.30	.25
49	A7	5p green	3.75	.25
50	A7	10p rose	60.00	.25
51	A7	15p violet	7.50	.25
52	A7	20p orange	6.25	.25
53	A7	25p deep blue	7.00	.35
54	A7	50p brown	15.00	3.00
		Nos. 48-54 (7)	99.80	4.60

Nos. 49-54 exist imperf.
Nos. 49-51, 53 and 56-57 exist with perf. 13x13½x11½x13½.

Type of 1900 Stamp Surcharged

1900

56	A7	10p on 20p rose	5.50	.75

Same, Surcharged

1901

57	A7	10p on 20p rose	1.75	.25
58	A7	15p on 1d red brn, *bl*	5.25	1.00
a.		Inverted surcharge	100.00	110.00

King Alexander (Obrenovich V)
A8   A9

1901-03 Typo. *Perf. 11½*

59	A8	5p green	.35	.35
60	A8	10p rose	.35	.35
61	A8	15p red violet	.35	.35
62	A8	20p orange	.35	.35
63	A8	25p ultra	.35	.35
64	A8	50p bister	.75	.75
65	A9	1d brown	1.10	1.90
66	A9	3d brt rose	11.00	15.00
67	A9	5d deep violet	11.00	15.00
		Nos. 59-67 (9)	25.60	34.40

Counterfeits of Nos. 66-67 exist. Nos. 59-67 imperf. value of set of pairs, $100.

Arms of Serbia on Head of King Alexander — A10

Two Types of the Overprint

Type I — Overprint 12mm wide. Bottom of mantle defined by a single line. Wide crown above shield.
Type II — Overprint 10mm wide. Double line at bottom of mantle. Smaller crown above shield.

Arms Overprinted in Blue, Black, Red and Red Brown

1903-04 Type I *Perf. 13½*

68	A10	1p red lil & blk (Bl)	.90	1.10
a.		Inverted overprint	10.00	
69	A10	5p yel grn & blk (Bl)	.75	.35
70	A10	10p car & blk (Bk)	.50	.35
a.		Double overprint	8.75	
71	A10	15p ol gray & blk (Bk)	.50	.35
a.		Double overprint	8.75	
72	A10	20p org & blk (Bk)	.75	.35
73	A10	25p bl & blk (Bk)	.75	.35
a.		Double overprint	10.00	
74	A10	50p gray & blk (R)	4.50	1.10

There were two printings of the type I overprint on Nos. 68-74, one typographed and one lithographed.

Type II

75	A10	1d bl grn & blk (Bk)	11.00	4.50

#68-75 with overprint omitted, value, set $75.

Perf. 11½
Type I

75A	A10	5p (Bl)	.75	1.50
75B	A10	50p (R)	2.25	7.50
75C	A10	1d (Bk)	2.25	15.00

Type II

76	A10	3d vio & blk (R Br)	3.00	3.75
a.		Perf. 13½	110.00	110.00
77	A10	5d lt brn & blk (Bl)	3.00	3.75

Type I With Additional Surcharge

78	A10	1p on 5d (R)	2.25	11.00
a.		Perf. 13½	750.00	750.00
		Nos. 68-78 (14)	33.15	50.95

Karageorge and Peter I — A11

Insurgents, 1804 A12

1904   **Typo.**

79	A11	5p yellow green	1.50	.75
80	A11	10p rose red	.75	.75
81	A11	15p red violet	.75	.75
82	A11	25p blue	1.50	1.50
83	A11	50p gray brown	1.50	1.50
84	A12	1d bister	2.25	5.25
85	A12	3d blue green	3.00	7.50
86	A12	5d violet	3.75	9.00
		Nos. 79-86 (8)	15.00	27.00

Centenary of the Karageorgevich dynasty and the coronation of King Peter. Counterfeits of Nos. 79-86 exist.

King Peter I Karageorgevich
A13   **A14**

Perf. 11½, 12x11½

1905   **Wove Paper**

87	A13	1p gray & blk	.25	.25
88	A13	5p yel grn & blk	.90	.25
89	A13	10p red & blk	2.50	.25
90	A13	15p red lil & blk	3.00	.25
91	A13	20p yellow & blk	5.25	.25
92	A13	25p ultra & blk	6.25	.25
93	A13	30p sl grn & blk	4.50	.25
94	A13	50p dk brown & blk	5.50	.50
95	A13	1d bister & blk	.90	.35
96	A13	3d blue grn & blk	.90	.90
97	A13	5d violet & blk	3.75	2.75
		Nos. 87-97 (11)	33.70	6.25

Counterfeits of Nos. 87-97 abound.
The stamps of this issue may be found on both thick and thin paper.

1908   **Laid Paper**

98	A13	1p gray & blk	.35	.25
99	A13	5p yel grn & blk	2.25	.25
100	A13	10p red & blk	6.75	.25
101	A13	15p red lilac & blk	9.00	.25
102	A13	20p yellow & blk	9.00	.35
103	A13	25p ultra & blk	6.75	.35
104	A13	30p gray grn & blk	10.00	.35
105	A13	50p dk brn & blk	13.00	.75
		Nos. 98-105 (8)	57.10	2.80

Nos. 90, 98-100, 102-104 are known imperforate but are not believed to have been issued in this condition.
Values of Nos. 98-105 are for horizontally laid paper. Four values also exist on vertically laid paper (1p, 5p, 10p, 30p).

1911-14   **Thick Wove Paper**

108	A14	1p slate green	.25	.25
109	A14	2p dark violet	.25	.25
110	A14	5p green	.25	.25
111	A14	5p pale yel grn ('14)	.25	.25
112	A14	10p carmine	.25	.25
113	A14	10p red ('14)	.25	.25
114	A14	15p red violet	.35	.25
115	A14	15p slate blk ('14)	.25	.25
a.		15p red (error)	900.00	—
116	A14	20p yellow	.30	.25
117	A14	20p brown ('14)	.50	.30
118	A14	25p deep blue	.45	.25
119	A14	25p indigo ('14)	.25	.25

120	A14	30p blue green	.30	.30
121	A14	30p olive grn ('14)	.25	.30
122	A14	50p dk brown	.50	.35
123	A14	50p brn red ('14)	.45	.35
124	A14	1d orange	22.50	45.00
125	A14	1d slate ('14)	3.75	7.50
126	A14	3d lake	30.00	90.00
127	A14	3d olive yel ('14)	150.00	1,100.
128	A14	5d violet	27.50	62.50
129	A14	5d dk violet ('14)	6.00	19.00
		Nos. 108-129 (22)	244.85	1,328.

Counterfeits exist.

King Peter and Military Staff — A15

1915   **Perf. 11½**

132	A15	5p yellow green	.35	—
133	A15	10p scarlet	.35	—
134	A15	15p slate	5.50	
135	A15	20p brown	1.50	
136	A15	25p blue	11.00	
137	A15	30p olive green	7.50	
138	A15	50p orange brown	30.00	
		Nos. 132-138 (7)	56.20	

Nos. 134-138 were prepared but not issued for postal use. Instead they were permitted to be used as wartime emergency currency. Some are known imperf. The 15p also exists in blue from an erroneous cliche in the 25p plate; value $325.

Stamps of France, 1900-1907, with this handstamped control were used in 1916-1918 by the Serbian Postal Bureau, in the Island of Corfu. On the 1c to 35c, the handstamp covers 2 or 3 stamps. It was applied after the stamps were on the cover.

King Peter and Prince Alexander — A16

1918-20   **Typo.**   **Perf. 11, 11½**

155	A16	1p black	.25	.25
156	A16	2p olive brown	.25	.25
157	A16	5p apple green	.25	.25
158	A16	10p red	.25	.25
159	A16	15p black brown	.25	.25
160	A16	20p red brown	.25	.25
161	A16	20p violet ('20)	1.60	.90
162	A16	25p deep blue	.25	.25
163	A16	30p olive green	.25	.25
164	A16	50p violet	.25	.25
165	A16	1d violet brown	1.10	.25
166	A16	3d slate green	1.50	.90
167	A16	5d red brown	1.90	1.10
		Nos. 155-167 (13)	8.35	5.40

#157-160, 164 exist imperf. Value each $9.

1920   **Pelure Paper**   **Perf. 11½**

169	A16	1p black	.25	.25
170	A16	2p olive brown	.25	.25

Catalogue values for unused stamps in this section, from this point to the end of the section, are for Never Hinged items.

SERBIA & MONTENEGRO
100 Paras = 1 Dinar

Yugoslavia became Serbia & Montenegro Feb. 4, 2003, with each section of the country maintaining and operating their own postal service, and each having their own currency. After a referendum on independence on May 21, 2006, Montenegro seceded from Serbia and Montenegro, declaring independence on June 3. On June 7, Serbia recognized the dissolution of the union.
The listings below contain stamps bearing the dinar currency, for use in Serbia, or those bearing both the dinar and euro currencies, which were issued for use in either Serbia or Montenegro. Stamps inscribed in euro currency only were used in Montenegro and may be found in listings for that country.

Council of Europe — A20

Map color: 16d, Red violet. 28.70d, Blue.

2003, Apr. 3   **Litho.**   **Perf. 13¾**
180-181 A20 Set of 2   2.75 2.75

Easter — A21

Religious paintings: 12d, From 16th cent. 16d, By D. Bacevic. 26.20d, From 1616. 28.70d, By Giovanni Bellini.

2003, Apr. 18
182-185 A21   Set of 4   4.75 4.75

Belgrade Choral Society, 150th Anniv. A22

2003, Apr. 22   **Perf. 13¼ Syncopated**
186 A22   16d multi   2.00 2.00

Europa — A23

Man pasting poster on: 28.70d, Pillar. 50d, Wall.

2003, May 9   **Perf. 13¾**
187-188 A23   Set of 2   4.50 4.50

Flowers — A24

2003, May 13

189		Horiz. strip of 4 + central label	4.75	4.75
a.	A24	16d Galanthus nivalis	.75	.75
b.	A24	24d Erythronium dens-canis	1.00	1.00
c.	A24	26.20d Hepatica nobilis	1.10	1.10
d.	A24	28.70d Anemone ramunculoides	1.25	1.25

Actors and Actresses — A25

No. 190: a, Ilija Stanojevic (1859-1930). b, Dobrivoje Dobrica Milutinovic (1880-1956). c, Zivana Zanka Stokic (1887-1947). d, Ljubinka Bobic (1897-1978). e, Radomir-Rasa Plaovic (1899-1977). f, Milivoje Zivanovic (1900-76). g, Miloslav Mija Aleksic (1923-95). h, Zoran Radmilovic (1933-85).

2003, May 20
190 A25 16d Sheet of 8, #a-h, + 8 labels   6.00 6.00

First Automobile in Belgrade, Cent. — A26

2003, June 3   **Perf. 13¼ Syncopated**
191 A26 16d multi   7.00 7.00

Nature Protection A27

Views of Zasavicz Nature Reserve: 28.70d, River. 50d, Swamp, vert.

2003, June 12
192-193 A27   Set of 2   4.50 4.50

Yugoslavia No. F1 and Type of Yugoslavia No. 2258 Surcharged

2003, July 3   **Litho.**   **Perf. 12½**
194	RL1	1d on (R) ultra	2.10	2.10
195	A751	12d on 20p lil rose & pale vio	3.75	3.75

No. 189b Under Magnifying Glass — A28   **Postal Van and Parcels — A29**

Woman With Headset A30   **Postal Van A31**

Cable Television System — A32

2003　　　**Litho.**　　　**Perf. 12½**
196 A28 1d multi　　　.60　.60
197 A29 8d multi　　　.80　.80
198 A30 12d multi　　1.20　1.20
199 A31 16d multi　　1.60　1.60
200 A32 32d multi　　3.75　3.75
　　　Nos. 196-200 (5)　7.95 7.95
　　Issued: 16d, 8/4; others 8/7.

Military Museum, Belgrade, 125th Anniv. — A33

2003, Aug. 27　　　**Perf. 13x13¾**
201 A33 16d (25c) multi　　.90　.90

Serbian Women's Circle, Cent. — A34

Perf. 13¼ Syncopated
2003, Aug. 28
202 A34 16d (25c) multi　　.90　.90

Serbian and Montenegrin States, 125th Anniv. — A35

Designs: No. 203, 16d (25c), Serbian arms, denomination at UR. No. 204, 16d (25c), Montenegrin arms, denomination at UL.

2003, Sept. 10
203-204 A35　Set of 2　　1.50 1.50

Ninth European Model Rocketry Championship, Sremska Mitrovica A36

2003, Sept. 12　　　**Perf. 13x13¾**
205 A36 16d (25c) multi　　.90　.90

Second Danube Countries Conference on Art and Culture — A37

Carved rocks with: No. 206, 16d (25c), Denomination at UL. No. 207, 16d (25c), Denomination at UR.

2003, Sept. 17
206-207 A37　Set of 2　　1.50 1.50

Nos. 206-207 were each printed in sheets of 8 + label.

Souvenir Sheet

Serbiafila XIII Philatelic Exhibition — A38

No. 208: a, Belgrade in the 17th century. b, Sculpture.

2003, Sept. 22　　　**Perf. 13½**
208 A38 32d (50c) Sheet of 2,
　　　　#a-b　　　4.25 4.25

Joy of Europe — A39

Children's drawings: 28.70d (50c), Man, woman, bird and flower. 50d (80c), Rabbit, flowers, horiz.

2003, Oct. 14　　　**Perf. 13¼**
209-210 A39　Set of 2　　4.25 4.25

Vecernje Novosti Newspaper, 50th Anniv. — A40

2003, Oct. 16
211 A40 32d (50c) multi　　1.75 1.75

Stamp Day — A41

2003, Oct. 24
212 A41 16d (25c) multi　　3.75 3.75

Association of Applied Artists and Designers, 50th Anniv. — A42

2003, Oct. 29
213 A42 16d (25c) multi　　.90　.90

National Theater of Montenegro, 50th Anniv. — A43

2003, Nov. 1　　　**Perf. 13¾x13**
214 A43 32d (50c) multi　　1.75 1.75

City of Pancevo, 850th Anniv. — A44

2003, Nov. 12　　　**Perf. 13x13¾**
215 A44 32d (50c) multi　　2.00 2.00

Christmas — A45

Designs: 10d, Santa Claus and reindeer. 13.50d, Ornaments. 26.20d, Snowflakes.

2003, Nov. 24　　　**Perf. 13¼**
216-218 A45　Set of 3　　3.00 3.00
　　Complete booklet, 10 #216　7.00
　　Complete booklet, 10 #217　8.00

Serbian Orthodox Church Museum Exhibits — A46

No. 219: a, Painting of St. John the Baptist, 1645. b, Cross, 1602. c, Miter, 15th cent. d, Tabernacle, 1550-51.

2003, Nov. 26　　　**Perf. 13¾x13**
219　Horiz. strip of 4 + central
　　　label　　　　5.25 5.25
　a. A46 16d (25c) multi　　.90　.90
　b. A46 24d (35c) multi　　1.20 1.20
　c. A46 26.20d (40c) multi　1.40 1.40
　d. A46 28.70d (50c) multi　1.50 1.50

Christmas A47

Religious paintings: 12d (20c), Nativity, 1983. 16d (25c), Nativity, 18th cent. 26.20d (40c), Madonna and Child, 2000. 28.70d (50c), Adoration of the Magi, by Albrecht Durer.

2003, Dec. 2　　　**Perf. 13x13¼**
220-223 A47　Set of 4　　4.25 4.25

Submarine Units, 75th Anniv. A48

2003, Dec. 10　　　**Perf. 13¼**
224 A48 32d (50c) multi　　3.00 3.00

Printed in sheets of 8 + label.

Powered Flight, Cent. — A49

Designs: 16d (25c), Wright Brothers and airplane. 28.70d (50c), Airplane in flight, horse-drawn carriages.

2003, Dec. 17
225-226 A49　Set of 2　　10.00 10.00

Politika Newspaper, Cent. — A50

Centenary emblem and: No. 227, 16d (25c), Typewriter. No. 228, 16d, (25c), Office building, vert.

2004, Jan. 21
227-228 A50　Set of 2　　2.00 2.00

Worldwide Fund for Nature (WWF) A51

No. 229 — Insects: a, Parnassius apollo. b, Rosalia alpina. c, Aeshna viridis. d, Saga pedo.

2004, Jan. 30　　　**Perf. 13¼**
229　Horiz. strip of 4 + central
　　　label　　　　5.00 5.00
　a. A51 12d (20c) multi　　.60　.60
　b. A51 16d (25c) multi　　.75　.75
　c. A51 26.20d (40c) multi　1.25 1.25
　d. A51 28.70d (50c) multi　1.50 1.50

First Serbian Rebellion, Bicent. — A52

Bicentennial emblem and: No. 230, 16d (25c), Flag, Karageorge (George Petrovic). No. 231, 16d (25c), Children and map of Europe.

2004, Feb. 13　　　**Perf. 13x13¾**
230-231 A52　Set of 2　　1.50 1.50

Flora and Butterflies — A53

No. 232: a, Ramonda serbica. b, Ramonda nathaliae. c, Heodes virgaureae. d, Lysandra bellargus.

2004, Feb. 16　　　**Perf. 13¾x13**
232　Horiz. strip of 4 + central
　　　label　　　　5.25 5.25
　a. A53 16d (25c) multi　　.80　.80
　b. A53 24d (35c) multi　　1.10 1.10
　c. A53 26.20d (40c) multi　1.25 1.25
　d. A53 28.70d (50c) multi　1.60 1.60

2004 Summer Olympics, Athens — A54

Serbia and Montenegro Olympic Committee emblem and: 32d (50c), Runner. 56d (80c), Wrestlers.

2004, Feb. 27　　　**Perf. 13x13¾**
233-234 A54　Set of 2　　4.25 4.25

First Serbian
Rebellion,
Bicent.
A55

Designs: 12d, Rebels. 16d, Flag, gun, vert.
28.70d, Karageorge (George Petrovic), vert.
32d, Children, globe, vert.

2004, Mar. 1   Litho.   Perf. 13¼
235-238 A55   Set of 4   4.75 4.75

Campaign Against
Terrorism — A56

2004, Mar. 12   Perf. 13¾x13
239 A56 16d (25c) multi   1.25 1.25

Easter — A57

Designs: 16d (25c), The Crucifixion, by
Vlasios Coconis. 28.70d (50c), The Resurrection, by Klemens Katounakis.

2004, Mar. 15   Perf. 13x13¾
240-241 A57   Set of 2   2.50 2.50

Milutin
Milankovic
(1879-1958),
Climatologist
A58

2004, Mar. 22
242 A58 16d (25c) multi   1.10 1.10

Albert Einstein
(1879-1955),
Physicist — A59

2004, Mar. 31   Perf. 13¾x13
243 A59 16d (25c) multi   7.75 7.75
Printed in sheets of 8 + label.

Selection of
Kotor as World
Heritage Site,
25th
Anniv. — A60

2004, Apr. 7   Perf. 13x13¾
244 A60 16d (25c) multi   .95   .95

Printing of
First History of
Montenegro,
by Vasilije
Petrovic, 250th
Anniv. — A61

2004, Apr. 29
245 A61 16d (25c) multi   1.50 1.50

Europa — A62

Designs: 16d (25c), Paragliders. No. 247,
56d (80c), Sailboat, swimmer, horiz.
No. 248: a, 32d (50c), Sailboats, paraglider,
horiz. b, 56d (80c), Rowboats, horiz.

2004, May 5   Perf. 13¾x13, 13x13¾
246-247 A62   Set of 2   4.00 4.00
Souvenir Sheet
248 A62   Sheet of 2, #a-b   8.00 8.00

Church of St. Sava,
Belgrade — A63

Designs: 16d (25c), Church, St. Sava.
28.70d (50c), Church, statue of St. Sava,
horiz.

2004, May 10   Perf. 13¾x13, 13x13¼
249-250 A63   Set of 2   2.50 2.50

Michael Pupin
(1854-1935),
Inventor — A64

2004, May 13   Engr.   Perf. 13¼
251 A64 16d (25c) violet   .95   .95

FIFA
(Fédération
Internationale
de Football
Association),
Cent. — A65

2004, May 21 Litho.   Perf. 13x13¾
252 A65 28.70d (50c) multi   1.75 1.75

Nature
Protection
A66

Designs: 32d (50c), Ravnjak River. 56d
(80c), Sara National Park.

2004, June 10
253-254 A66   Set of 2   5.00 5.00
Each stamp printed in sheet of 8 + label.

Souvenir Sheet

JUFIZ XII Philatelic Exhibition,
Belgrade — A67

No. 255: a, Lion from Terazije Fountain. b,
Entire fountain.

2004, June 21   Perf. 13¼
255 A67 32d (50c) Sheet of 2,
          #a-b   4.50 4.50

2004 Summer
Olympics,
Athens — A68

Athens Olympics emblem, ancient Greek
ruins and: 16d (25c), Runners. 28.70d (50c),
Runners, diff. 32d (50c), Long jumper. 57.40d
(80c), Hurdlers.

2004, June 24   Perf. 13x13¾
256-259 A68   Set of 4   7.75 7.75
Each stamp printed in sheets of 8 + label.

Yugoslavia Nos. 2255-
2256 Surcharged

Methods as Before
2004, June 25   Perf. 12½
260 A751 12d on 1p #2255a   2.50   2.50
 a.   on #2255, perf. 13¼   150.00 150.00
261 A751 32d on 5p #2256a   5.00   5.00
 a.   on #2256, perf. 13¼   450.00 450.00
See Yugoslavia No. 2577 for stamp similar
to No. 260, but with violet surcharge.

Volujica
Telegraph
Station,
Cent. — A69

2004, Aug. 3 Litho.   Perf. 13x13¾
262 A69 16d (25c) multi   1.75 1.75

Joy of
Europe — A70

Children's drawings: 32d (50c) Bridge and
city skyline. 56d (80c), City buildings, vert.

2004, Oct. 2   Perf. 13¾
263-264 A70   Set of 2   4.75 4.75
Each stamp printed in sheets of 8 + label.

Port of Bar, 125th
Anniv. — A71

2004, Oct. 12
265 A71 32d (50c) multi   1.75 1.75

Stamp Day — A72

2004, Oct. 22   Perf. 13¾x13
266 A72 16d (25c) multi   2.40 2.40

National Bank of
Serbia, 120th
Anniv. — A73

Designs: 16d (25c), Bank building. 32d
(50c), Bank building, George Vajfert.

Perf. 13¼ Syncopated
2004, Oct. 28   Engr.
267-268 A73   Set of 2   2.50 2.50
Each stamp printed in sheet of 8 + label.

Silver Objects
From 1899 — A74

2004, Nov. 2 Litho.   Perf. 13¾x13
269   Horiz. strip of 4 + central
        label   5.00 5.00
 a. A74 16d (25c) Plate on pedestal .75   .75
 b. A74 24d (35c) Box   1.10 1.10
 c. A74 26.20d (40c) Bowl   1.25 1.25
 d. A74 28.70d (50c) Bowl with lid 1.50 1.50

Buildings
A75

2004, Nov. 15   Perf. 13¾x13¾
270   Horiz. strip of 4 + central
        label   5.00 5.00
 a. A75 16d (25c) Lombardic Palace .75   .75
 b. A75 24d (35c) Pima Palace   1.10 1.10
 c. A75 26.20d (40c) Grgurina Palace 1.25 1.25
 d. A75 28.70d (50c) Bizanti Palace 1.50 1.50

Christmas
A76

Designs: 16d (25c), Nativity, by Vasilis Leurac. 28.70d (50c), Nativity, by Ememija Profeta.

2004, Dec. 1
271-272 A76   Set of 2   2.50 2.50

Endangered Birds — A77

2005, Jan. 31   Litho.   Perf. 13¼
273   Horiz. strip of 4 + central
         label   6.00 6.00
a. A77 16.50d (25c) Egretta alba   .70 .70
b. A77 33d (40c) Podiceps nigricollis 1.25 1.25
c. A77 41.50d (50c) Aythya nyroca   1.75 1.75
d. A77 49.50d (60c) Ciconia nigra   2.00 2.00

Yugoslavia No. F1, Serbia Nos. 199, 200 Surcharged in Blue or Black

2005, Feb. 3   Litho.   Perf. 12½
274 RL1 50p on R #F1
          (Bl)   60.00 15.00
275 A31 16.50d on 16d #199   30.00 7.50
276 A32 33d on 32d #200   45.00 7.50
     Nos. 274-276 (3)   135.00 30.00
            Surcharge styles differ.

Stamp Collecting — A78

2005, Feb. 3   Litho.   Perf. 12½
277 A78 50p multi   1.40 1.40

Flora and Fauna — A79

2005, Feb. 16   Perf. 13x13¾
278   Horiz. strip of 4 + central
         label   6.00 6.00
a. A79 16.50d (25c) Capparis spinosa .70 .70
b. A79 33d (40c) Mustela erminea   1.25 1.25
c. A79 41.50d (50c) Trollius
         europaeus   1.75 1.75
d. A79 49.50d (60c) Rupicapra rupi-
         capra   2.00 2.00

Montenegrin Table Tennis Assoc., 50th Anniv. — A80

2005, Feb. 28
279 A80 16.50d (25c) multi   15.00 15.00

Easter — A81

Designs: 16.50d (25c), Fresco, 18th cent. 28.70d (50c), Crucifixion, 1602.

2005, Mar. 1
280-281 A81   Set of 2   2.75 2.75

Mountain Scenes — A82

2005, Mar. 7   Litho.   Perf. 12½
282 A82 16.50d Zlatibor   1.10 1.10
283 A82 33d Kopaonik   3.25 3.25

Serbian Law University, Cent. — A83

2005, Mar. 12   Perf. 13x13¾
284 A83 16.50d (25c) multi   .95 .95

Miniature Sheet

Theater Celebrities — A84

No. 285: a, Jovan Djordjevic (1826-1900). b, Milan Predic (1881-1972). c, Milan Grol (1876-1952). d, Mira Trailovic (1924-89). e, Soja Jovanovich (1922-2002). f, Hugo Klajn (1894-1981). g, Mata Milosevic (1901-97). h, Bojan Stupica (1910-70).

2005, Mar. 25   Perf. 13¾x13
285 A84 16.50d (25c) Sheet of 8,
          #a-h, + central
          label   7.00 7.00

European Philatelic Cooperation, 50th Anniv. (in 2006) — A85

Elements of Europa common design types (CD) or Yugoslavian stamps: No. 286, CD12. No. 287, CD13. No. 288, CD14. No. 289, CD15. No. 290, CD16. No. 291, Yugoslavia #1206. No. 292, Yugoslavia #1678. No. 293, CD13, CD15 and Yugoslavia #1678.

2005, Mar. 31   Perf. 13x13¾
Background Color
286 A85 16.50d (25c) green   .70 .70
287 A85 16.50d (25c) claret   .70 .70
288 A85 16.50d (25c) claret   .70 .70
289 A85 16.50d (25c) blue   .70 .70
a.   Souvenir sheet, #286-289   7.50 7.50
290 A85 41.50d (50c) claret   1.75 1.75
291 A85 41.50d (50c) olive
          gray   1.75 1.75
292 A85 41.50d (50c) blue   1.75 1.75
293 A85 41.50d (50c) orange   1.75 1.75
a.   Souvenir sheet, #290-293   11.00 11.00
     Nos. 286-293 (8)   9.80 9.80

Europa stamps, 50th anniv. (in 2006).

Hans Christian Andersen (1805-75), Author — A86

Silhouette of Andersen and: 41.50d (50c), The Little Mermaid. 58d (70c), The Snow Queen.

2005, Apr. 1   Perf. 13¾x13
294-295 A86   Set of 2   4.00 4.00

Mountain Scenes Type of 2005
Design: 5d, Goc, 13d, Jastrebac.

2005, Apr. 1   Litho.   Perf. 12¾x12¼
295A A82 5d multi   1.10 .25
295B A82 13d multi   2.25 .45

Europa — A87

Designs: No. 296, 41.50d (50c), Dumplings and rolls. No. 297, 73d (90c), Fish dish, tomato, lettuce, garlic, oil cruet, pepper mill. No. 298: a, 41.50d (50c), Cake, flower, cup of coffee. b, 73d (90c), Slice of pie, apples.

2005, May 5   Perf. 13¾x13¾
296-297 A87   Set of 2   4.75 4.75

Souvenir Sheet
298 A87 Sheet of 2, #a-b   4.75 4.75

Captains and Their Ships A88

2005, May 13   Perf. 13¼
299   Horiz. strip of 4 + central
         label   6.00 6.00
a. A88 16.50d (25c) Marko Ivanovic   .70 .70
b. A88 33d (40c) Petar Zelalic   1.40 1.40
c. A88 41.50d (50c) Matija Balovic   1.75 1.75
d. A88 49.50d (60c) Ivan Bronza   2.00 2.00

Emblem of Red Star Sports Club — A89

Emblem of Partisan Sports Club — A90

No. 302 — Knight with shield with emblem of: a, Red Star. b, Partisan.

2005, May 23   Perf. 13x13¾
300 A89 16.50d (25c) multi   .90 .90
301 A90 16.50d (25c) multi   .90 .90

Souvenir Sheet
302   Sheet of 2   2.00 2.00
a. A89 16.50d (25c) multi   .90 .90
b. A90 16.50d (25c) multi   .90 .90

Souvenir Sheet

Danube Regatta, 50th Anniv. — A91

No. 303: a, 41.50d (50c), Rowers in boats. b, 49.50d (60c), Rowers in boats, map.

2005, June 6
303 A91 Sheet of 2, #a-b   4.00 4.00

Intl. Year of Physics A92

Theory of Relativity, Cent. — A93

2005, June 10
304 A92 41.50d (50c) multi   1.75 1.75
305 A93 58d (70c) multi   2.50 2.50

European Nature Protection A94

Various views of Koviljsko-Petrovaradinski Rit Special Nature Reserve: 41.50d (50c), 58d (70c).

2005, June 20
306-307 A94   Set of 2   4.25 4.25

European Volleyball Championships, Belgrade and Rome — A95

2005, Sept. 2   Litho.   Perf. 13x13¾
310 A95 16.50d (25c) multi   3.00 3.00
         Printed in sheets of 8 + label.

European Basketball Championships, Serbia & Montenegro — A96

2005, Sept. 16
311 A96 16.50d (25c) multi   3.00 3.00
         Printed in sheets of 8 + label.

A97

Joy of
Europe — A98

Perf. 13¾x13, 13x13¾
2005, Sept. 21
312 A97 41.50d (50c) multi 1.60 1.60
313 A98 58d (70c) multi 2.40 2.40
Each stamp printed in sheets of 8 + label.

World Youth
Day — A99

2005, Sept. 30 **Perf. 13x13¾**
314 A99 41.50d (50c) multi 1.75 1.75
Printed in sheets of 8 + label.

Start of European
Union Accession
Negotiations — A100

2005, Oct. 10 **Perf. 13¾x13**
315 A100 16.50d (25c) multi .90 .90

World Air
Sports
Federation,
Cent. — A101

Emblem and: 49.50d (60c), Alberto Santos-
Dumont's 14-bis airplane. 58d (70c), Parachute, glider, ultra-light aircraft.

2005, Oct. 14 **Perf. 13x13¾**
316-317 A101 Set of 2 4.50 4.50
Each stamp printed in sheets of 8 + label.

Stamp
Day — A102

2005, Oct. 24
318 A102 16.50d (25c) multi .90 .90

United
Nations, 60th
Anniv.
A103

2005, Oct. 24
319 A103 16.50d (25c) multi .90 .90

St. Petar of
Cetinje (1782-
1830),
Montenegrin
Leader
A104

2005, Oct. 28
320 A104 16.50d (25c) multi .90 .90

First
Montenegrin
Constitution,
Cent. — A105

2005, Nov. 14
321 A105 16.50d (25c) multi .90 .90

Stevan Sremac
(1855-1906),
Humorist — A106

2005, Nov. 23 **Perf. 13¼**
322 A106 16.50d (25c) multi .90 .90

Paintings of
Monasteries
A107

No. 323: a, Studenica Monastery, by Djordje
Krstic. b, Sopocani Monastery, by Paja Jovanovic. c, Zica Monastery, by Krstic. d, Gracanica Monastery, by Milan Milanovic.

2005, Nov. 28
323 Horiz. strip of 4 + central
label 6.00 6.00
a. A107 16.50d (25c) multi .70 .70
b. A107 33d (40c) multi 1.40 1.40
c. A107 41.50d (50c) multi 1.75 1.75
d. A107 49.50d (60c) multi 2.00 2.00

Paintings in
Museums
A108

No. 324: a, Girl with a Blue Ribbon, by F. X.
Winterhalter. b, Adoration of the Child, by
Andrea Alovidi. c, Madonna and Child with
Saints, by Biagio d'Antonio. d, Remorse, by
Vlaho Bukovac.

2005, Dec. 9
324 Horiz. strip of 4 + central
label 6.00 6.00
a. A108 16.50d (25c) multi .70 .70
b. A108 33d (40c) multi 1.40 1.40
c. A108 41.50d (50c) multi 1.75 1.75
d. A108 49.50d (60c) multi 2.00 2.00

Christmas
A109

Designs: 16.50d (25c), Nativity. 46d (50c),
Nativity, diff.

2005, Dec. 12 **Perf. 13x13¾**
325-326 A109 Set of 2 2.75 2.75

Stevan Stojanovic
Mokranjac (1856-
1914), Composer
A110

2006, Jan. 9 **Perf. 13¾x13**
327 A110 46d (50c) multi 2.00 2.00

Jovan Sterija
Popovic (1806-56),
Writer — A111

2006, Jan. 13
328 A111 33d (40c) multi 1.50 1.50

2006 Winter
Olympics,
Turin — A112

Designs: 53d (60c), Ski jumping. 73d (80c),
Downhill skiing.

2006, Feb. 10 **Perf. 13x13¾**
329-330 A112 Set of 2 5.00 5.00
Each stamp printed in sheets of 8 + label.

National Theater,
Belgrade — A113

2006, Feb. 1 **Litho.** **Perf. 13¼**
331 A113 46d multi 2.00 2.00

Easter — A114

Designs: 16.50d (20c), Easter egg with
Cyrillic inscription. 46d (50c), Basket of Easter
eggs.

2006, Mar. 1 **Perf. 13¾x13¼**
332-333 A114 Set of 2 2.50 2.50

Danube
Commission,
150th Anniv.
A115

No. 334: a, Novi Sad (shown). b, Smederevo. c, Belgrade. d, Tabula Traiana.

2006, Mar. 6 **Perf. 13¼x13¾**
334 Horiz. strip of 4 + central label 5.25 5.25
a.-b. A115 16.50d (20c) Either single .70 .70
c.-d. A115 46d (50c) Either single 1.90 1.90

Fauna
A116

No. 335: a, Canis lupus. b, Otis tarda. c,
Vormela peregusna. d, Ursus arctos.

2006, Apr. 3
335 Horiz. strip of 4 + central label 5.25 5.25
a.-b. A116 16.50d (20c) Either single .70 .70
c.-d. A116 46d (50c) Either single 1.90 1.90

2006 World Cup
Soccer
Championships,
Germany — A117

2006 World Cup emblem and: 33d (40c),
Soccer players. 46d (50c), Soccer player and
stadium.
No. 338, horiz.: a, Stadium, text in Cyrillic
letters. b, Stadium, text in Latin letters.

2006, Apr. 12 **Perf. 13¾x13¼**
336-337 A117 Set of 2 20.00 20.00
Souvenir Sheet
Perf. 13¼x13¾
338 A117 46d (50c) Sheet of
2, #a-b 25.00 25.00

Europa
A118

Children's drawings: No. 339, 46d (50c),
Beach umbrella, person in winter jacket on
beach towel, penguin. No. 340, 73d (80c),
Lion and lamb.
No. 341: a, 46d (50c), Girls talking. b, 73d
(80c), Children at open door, rainbow.

2006, May 4 **Perf. 13¼x13¾**
339-340 A118 Set of 2 5.00 5.00
Souvenir Sheet
341 A118 Sheet of 2, #a-b 6.00 6.00

Nikola Tesla (1856-
1943), Electrical
Engineer — A119

Designs: 16.50d (20c), Tesla, lightning. No. 343, 46d (50c), Tesla, electrical generator. No. 344, horiz.: a, 46d (50c), Tesla. b, 112d (€1.30), Turbine.

2006, May 26 — *Perf. 13¾x13¼*
342-343 A119 Set of 2   2.75 2.75
Souvenir Sheet
Perf. 13¾
344 A119 Sheet of 2, #a-b   7.50 7.50

Rose Varieties A120

No. 345: a, Aqua. b, Vendela. c, Sphinx. d, Red Berlin.

Perf. 13¼x13¾
2006, June 20 — Litho.
345   Horiz. strip of 4 + central label   5.25 5.25
a.-b. A120 16.50d Either single   .70 .70
c.-d. A120 46d Either single   1.90 1.90

As these stamps were released after the breakup of Serbia and Montenegro, they were sold only in Serbia.

Nature Protection A121

Designs: 46d, Fusoski Park, Novi Sad. 58d, Gradski Park, Vrsac.

2006, June 20
346-347 A121 Set of 2   4.00 4.00

As these stamps were released after the breakup of Serbia and Montenegro, they were sold only in Serbia. Each stamp was printed in a sheet of 8 + label.

Battle of Mishar, by Paja Jovanovic A122

2006, June 30
348 A122 46d multi   2.00 2.00

Battle of Mishar, 200th anniv.

Flag — A123

Coat of Arms — A124

2006, June 30 — *Perf. 12½*
349 A123 16.50d multi   .70 .70
350 A124 20d multi   .90 .90

European Water Polo Championships, Belgrade — A125

2006, Sept. 1 — *Perf. 13¼x13¾*
351 A125 46d multi   1.90 1.90

Serbian Victory at European Water Polo Championships — A126

2006, Sept. 13
352 A126 46d mult   2.25 2.25

Joy of Europe A127

Children's drawings: 46d, Buildings. 73d, Girl touching bird.

2006, Sept. 29
353-354 A127 Set of 2   5.25 5.25

Zhica Monastery — A128

2006, Oct. 7 — *Perf. 12½*
355 A128 8d multi   .55 .55

Stamp Day — A129

2006, Oct. 24 — *Perf. 13¾x13¼*
356 A129 46d Serbia #1   2.25 2.25

First Serbian postage stamps, 140th anniv.

Bridal Jewelry A130

No. 357: a, Bracelet, 19th cent. b, Ring, 17th-19th cent. c, Earrings, 20th cent. d, Necklace, 19th cent.

2006, Oct. 30 — *Perf. 13¼x13¾*
357   Horiz strip of 4 + central label   6.00 6.00
a.-b. A130 16.50d Either single   .80 .80
c.-d. A130 46d Either single   2.10 2.10

Atelie 212 Theater, 50th Anniv. — A131

2006, Nov. 10 — *Perf. 13¾x13¼*
358 A131 46d multi   1.90 1.90

Wolfgang Amadeus Mozart (1756-91), Composer A132

Rembrandt (1606-69), Painter — A133

2006, Nov. 16
359 A132 46d multi   2.25 2.25
360 A133 46d multi   2.25 2.25

A134

Christmas A135

2006, Nov. 20 — *Perf. 13¼x13¾*
361 A134 16.50d multi   .80 .80
362 A135 46d multi   2.10 2.10

New Year 2007 — A136

2006, Dec. 1
363 A136 46d multi   2.10 2.10

UNICEF, 60th Anniv. A137

2006, Dec. 11
364 A137 16.50d multi   .80 .80

Liberation of Belgrade, 200th Anniv. A138

2006, Dec. 13
365 A138 16.50d multi   .80 .80

Flower — A139

Flowers A140

Apple Orchard A141

River — A142

Goc A143

Zlatibor A144

Kopaonik A145

Belgrade — A146

2007, Jan. 1 — Litho. *Perf. 13¾x13¼*
366 A139 50p multi   .35 .35
Perf. 13¼x13¾
367 A140 1d multi   .35 .35
368 A141 5d multi   .35 .35
369 A142 10d multi   .50 .50
Perf. 13¼
370 A143 13d multi   .65 .65
371 A144 33d multi   1.60 1.60
372 A145 50d multi   2.60 2.60
373 A146 100d multi   5.25 5.25
     Nos. 366-373 (8)   11.65 11.65

Intl. Polar
Year — A147

2007, Jan. 30   **Perf. 13¼x13¾**
374 A147 46d multi   2.00 2.00

Miniature Sheet

Actors and Actresses — A148

No. 375: a, Petar Dobrinovic (1853-1923). b, Milka Grgurova Aleksic (1840-1924). c, Ljubisa Jovanovic (1908-71). d, Rahela Ferari (1911-94). e, Miodrag Petrovic Ckalja (1924-2003). f, Branko Plesa (1926-2001). g, Ljuba Tadic (1929-2005). h, Danila Bata Stojkovic (1934-2002).

2007, Feb. 16
375 A148 16.50d Sheet of 8, #a-
h, + central la-
bel   6.00 6.00

Easter — A149

Designs: 20d, Crucifixion. 46d, Crucifixion in silhouette.

2007, Mar. 1   **Perf. 13¾x13¼**
376-377 A149   Set of 2   3.00 3.00

2007 European Table Tennis
Championships, Belgrade — A150

2007, Mar. 23   **Perf. 13¼x13¾**
378 A150 46d multi   2.25 2.25

Souvenir Sheet
Perf. 13¾
379 A150 112d Player, net   5.00 5.00

No. 378 printed in sheets of 8 + label.

Art From St.
Sava Church
— A150a

2007, Apr. 1   **Litho.**   **Perf. 13¼**
379A A150a 10d multi   .50 .50

Rose — A151

2007, Apr. 4   **Perf. 13¼**
380 A151 40d multi   2.00 2.00

Worldwide Fund
for Nature
(WWF) — A152

No. 381 — Dryocopus martius: a, Facing right. b, Facing right, feeding chicks. c, Facing left, feeding chicks. d, Facing left.

2007, Apr. 6   **Perf. 13¾x13¼**
381   Horiz. strip of 4 + central label   5.75 5.75
a.-b. A152 20d Either single   .85 .85
c.-d. A152 40d Either single   1.75 1.75

Parks — A153

Designs: 40d, Vrnacka Banja Park. 46d, Pionirski Park, Belgrade.

2007, Apr. 20   **Perf. 13¼x13¾**
382-383 A153   Set of 2   4.00 4.00

Europa
A154

International and Serbian Scouting emblems and: No. 384, 20d, Scouts, tents and compass. 46d, Scouts in canoe, Scout hat, neckerchief and backpack.
No. 386: a, c, e, Milos Popovic and compass. b, d, f, Lord Robert Baden-Powell, Scout hat, neckerchief and backpack.

2007, May 3   **Litho.**   **Perf. 13¼x13¾**
384-385 A154   Set of 2   3.00 3.00

Miniature Sheet
386   Sheet of 6   5.25 5.25
a. A154 20d multi, perf. 13¼x13¾,
imperf. at top   .85 .85
b. A154 20d multi, perf. 13¾x13¾,
imperf. at top   .85 .85
c. A154 20d multi, perf. 13¼x13¾,
imperf. at top and right   .85 .85
d. A154 20d multi, perf. 13¼x13¾,
imperf. at bottom   .85 .85
e. A154 20d multi, perf. 13¼x13¾,
imperf. at bottom   .85 .85
f. A154 20d multi, perf. 13¼x13¾,
imperf. at bottom and right   .85 .85

Scouting, cent. Nos. 384-385 each printed in sheets of 8 + label. No. 386 was sold with but not attached to a booklet cover.

Serbian
Chairmanship
of Council of
Europe
A155

2007, May 10   **Perf. 13¼x13¾**
387 A155 20d multi   1.10 1.10

First Air
Crossing of
Atlantic by
Amelia
Earhart, 75th
Anniv.
A156

2007, May 21   **Litho.**
388 A156 50d multi   2.50 2.50

Printed in sheets of 8 + label.

Dositej
Obradovic's
Arrival in Serbia,
Bicent. — A157

2007, May 28   **Perf. 13¾x13¼**
389 A157 20d multi   .80 .80

Jovan Zmaj's
Children's
Games, 50th
Anniv.
A158

2007, June 1   **Perf. 13¼x13¾**
390 A158 20d multi   .80 .80

Souvenir Sheet

Srbijafila XIV, Belgrade — A159

No. 391: a, 20d, Stefan Lazarevic. b, 46d, Castle.

2007, June 11   **Perf. 13¾**
391 A159   Sheet of 2, #a-b   2.50 2.50

Souvenir Sheet

European Olympic Youth Festival,
Belgrade — A160

No. 392: a, Swimmer. b, Runner.

2007, June 20
392 A160 46d Sheet of 2, #a-d   3.75 3.75

Equestrian
Events
A161

No. 393: a, Endurance jumping. b, Carriage pull. c, Dressage. d, Show jumping.

2007, June 28   **Perf. 13¼x13¾**
393   Horiz. strip of 4 + central label   5.50 5.50
a.-b. A161 20d Either single   .85 .85
c.-d. A161 40d Either single   1.75 1.75

Scientists — A162

Designs: 40d, William Thomson, Lord Kelvin (1824-1907), physicist. No. 395, 46d, Giuseppe Occhialini (1907-93), physicist. No. 396, 46d, Dmitri Mendeleev (1834-1907), chemist.

2007, July 10   **Perf. 13¾x13¼**
394-396 A162   Set of 3   6.00 6.00

Petar
Lubarda
(1907-74),
Painter
A163

2007, July 27   **Perf. 13¼**
397 A163 20d multi   .90 .90

Kalenic
Monastery, 600th
Anniv. — A164

2007, Aug. 28   **Perf. 13¾x13¼**
398 A164 20d multi   .90 .90

Haliaeetus
Albicilla
A165

2007, Sept. 7   **Photo.**   **Perf. 13¾**
399 A165 46d multi   1.90 1.90

See Austria No. 2116.

Ozone Layer
Protection
A166

Perf. 13¾x13¼
2007, Sept. 17   **Litho.**
400 A166 20d multi   .90 .90

Printed in sheets of 8 + label.

Archaeological Sites — A167

Gamzigrad-Romulijana site: 46d, No. 401, Cyrillic inscriptions, denomination at UL. No. 402, Latin inscriptions, denomination at UR.

2007, Sept. 21   **Perf. 13¼x13¾**
401-402 A167   Set of 2   4.75 4.75

Nos. 401-402 each were printed in sheets of 9 + label.

Joy of Europe A168

2007, Sept. 28
403 A168 46d multi   1.90 1.90

Launch of Sputnik 1, 50th Anniv. A169

2007, Oct. 4
404 A169 46d multi   2.25 2.25

Belgrade Observatory, 120th Anniv. — A170

2007, Oct. 15
405 A170 20d multi   .90 .90
  Printed in sheets of 24 + label.

Evzhen Deroko (1860-1944) and Serbia No. 24 — A171

2007, Oct. 24
406 A171 46d multi   2.25 2.25
  Stamp Day.

Paintings — A172

  Paintings by: 20d, Dura Jaksic (1832-78). No. 408, 46d, Uros Predic (1857-1953). No. 409, 46d, Frida Kahlo (1907-54).

2007, Nov. 1   **Perf. 13¾x13¼**
407-409 A172   Set of 3   4.75 4.75

Christmas A173

  Nativity paintings: 20d, 46d.

2007, Nov. 9   **Perf. 13¼x13¾**
410-411 A173   Set of 2   3.25 3.25

Danube River Harbors and Ships — A174

  Ships and: 20d, Novi Sad, Serbia. 46d, Orsova, Romania.

No. 414 — Ships: a, 40d, Sirona. b, 50d, Orsova.

2007, Nov. 14   **Perf. 13¼x13¾**
412-413 A174   Set of 2   3.25 3.25
    Souvenir Sheet
    Perf. 13¾
414 A174   Sheet of 2, #a-d   4.25 4.25
  See Romania Nos. 5003-5005.

Diplomatic Relations Between Serbia and Japan, 125th Anniv. A175

    Perf. 13¼x13¾
2007, Dec. 23   **Litho.**
415 A175 46d multi   2.25 2.25
  Printed in sheets of 8 + label.

Vinca Archaeological Excavations, Cent. — A176

2008, Jan. 28
416 A176 20d multi   1.00 1.00

Paintings of Predrag-Peda Milosavljevic (1908-87) A177

  Designs: 20d, Cluny Museum, Paris. 46d, Notre Dame Cathedral, Paris.

2008, Feb. 4
417-418 A177   Set of 2   2.75 2.75

Intl. Swimming Federation (FINA), Cent. — A178

2008, Feb. 18
419 A178 50d multi   2.25 2.25
  Printed in sheets of 8 + label.

2008 Summer Olympics, Beijing A179

  Designs: 46d, Tennis. 50d, Hurdlers.

2008, Mar. 7
420-421 A179   Set of 2   3.75 3.75
  Nos. 420-421 each were printed in sheets of 8 + label.

Easter — A180

  Designs: 20d, Shown. 46d, Jesus, cross, diff.

2008, Mar. 21   **Perf. 13¾x13¼**
422-423 A180   Set of 2   3.00 3.00

2008 Serbian Olympic Tennis Team — A181

  Designs: 20d, Janko Tipsarevic. No. 425, 30d, Nenad Zimonjic. No. 426, 30d, Jelena Jankovic. 40d, Ana Ivanovic. 46d, Novak Djokovic.

2008, Apr. 8   **Perf. 13¼x13¾**
424-428 A181   Set of 5   10.00 10.00

Endangered Animals — A182

  No. 429: a, Cervus elaphus. b, Meles meles. c, Felis silvestris. d, Sus scrofa.

2008, Apr. 7   **Perf. 13¾x13¼**
429   Horiz. strip of 4 + central label   6.00 6.00
a.-b. A182 20d Either single   .90 .90
c.-d. A182 46d Either single   2.00 2.00

    Souvenir Sheet

2008 Eurovision Song Contest, Belgrade — A183

2008, Apr. 11   **Perf. 13¾**
430 A183 177d multi   8.00 8.00

Europa A184

  Stamped cover, letter and: 46d, Quill pen. 50d, Letter opener.

2008, May 5   **Perf. 13¼x13¾**
431-432 A184   Set of 2   4.00 4.00
  Nos. 431-432 each were printed in sheets of 8 + label.

European Nature Protection A185

  Designs: 20d, Vlasina Lake. 46d, Djavolja Varos rock formations.

2008, May 23
433-434 A185   Set of 2   3.00 3.00
  Nos. 433-434 each were printed in sheets of 8 + label.

Oriental Express, 125th Anniv. — A186

  Train and: 20d, Eiffel Tower and Arc de Triomphe. 50d, Hagia Sophia, Istanbul.

2008, June 9
435-436 A186   Set of 2   3.00 3.00
  Nos. 435-436 each were printed in sheets of 8 + label.

Television Belgrade, 50th Anniv. — A187

2008, June 16   **Litho.**
437 A187 46d multi   1.90 1.90
  Printed in sheets of 8 + label.

University of Belgrade, Bicent. A188

2008, July 10   **Perf. 13¼x13¾**
438 A188 20d multi   .90 .90

Grapes and Vineyards A189

  No. 439: a, Riesling grapes, vineyard in Fruska Gora (grapes at left). b, Sauvignon Blanc grapes, vineyard in Oplenac (grapes at right). c, Prokupac grapes, vineyard in Zupa. d, Frankovka grapes, vineyard in Vrsac.

2008, Sept. 25
439   Horiz. strip of 4 + central label   6.25 6.25
a.-b. A189 20d Either single   1.00 1.00
c.-d. A189 46d Either single   2.00 2.00

Joy of Europe A190

2008, Sept. 26
440 A190 46d multi   1.90 1.90
  Printed in sheets of 8 + label.

First Telephone Station in Belgrade, 125th Anniv. — A191

2008, Oct. 24
441 A191 46d multi 1.90 1.90
Stamp Day.

Traditional Children's Costumes A192

Girl from: 46d, Sumadija. 50d, Kumodraz.

2008, Nov. 10 *Perf. 13¾x13¼*
442-443 A192 Set of 2 3.75 3.75
Nos. 442-443 each were printed in sheets of 9 + label.

Danube Navigation Convention, 60th Anniv. — A193

2008, Nov. 20 *Perf. 13¼x13¾*
444 A193 46d multi 1.90 1.90
Printed in sheets of 8 + label.

Christmas A194

Designs: 20d, Nativity, by unknown artist. 46d, Nativity, by Dimitrije Bacevic.

2008, Nov. 28 *Perf. 13¾x13¼*
445-446 A194 Set of 2 2.75 2.75

Dadov Theater, Belgrade, 50th Anniv. — A195

2008, Dec. 5
447 A195 20d multi .90 .90

Osisani Jez Magazine, 75th Anniv. — A196

2009, Jan. 5 Litho. *Perf. 13¾x13¼*
448 A196 20d multi .90 .90
Printed in sheets of 8 + central label.

Louis Braille (1809-52), Educator of the Blind — A197

2009, Jan. 5 *Perf. 13¼x13¾*
449 A197 46d multi 1.90 1.90

Coat of Arms Type of 2006 Surcharged

2009, Jan. 28 Litho. *Perf. 13¼*
450 A124 22d on 20d multi .90 .90

Belt and Buckle — A198   Ring — A199

Embroidery A200   Kalemegdan, Belgrade A201

2009, Jan. 28 *Perf. 13¾*
451 A198 11d multi .45 .45
452 A199 22d multi .90 .90
453 A200 44d multi 1.90 1.90
454 A201 55d multi 2.25 2.25
Nos. 451-454 (4) 5.50 5.50

Protected Mammals — A202

No. 455: a, Mustela ermina. b, Micromys minutus. c, Sicista subtilis. d, Spermophilus citellus.

2009, Feb. 16 *Perf. 13¾x13¼*
455 Horiz. strip of 4 + central label 4.50 4.50
a.-b. A202 22d Either single .70 .70
c.-d. A202 46d Either single 1.50 1.50

Politikin Zabavnik Magazine, 70th Anniv. — A203

2009, Feb. 28 *Perf. 13¼x13¾*
456 A203 22d multi .90 .90
Printed in sheets of 8 + central label.

Birds A204

Designs: 22d, Scolopax rusticola. 46d, Monticola saxatilis.

2009, Mar. 2 *Perf. 13¾x13¼*
457-458 A204 Set of 2 2.25 2.25
458a Souvenir sheet, #457-458 2.25 2.25
See Bulgaria Nos. 4498-4499.

Easter A205

Icons from church in Topola: 22d, Last Supper. 46d, Entombment of Jesus.

2009, Mar. 9 *Perf. 13¼*
459-460 A205 Set of 2 2.25 2.25

Miniature Sheet

Actors and Actresses — A206

No. 461: a, Vela Nigrinova (1862-1908). b, Milan Ajvaz (1897-1980). c, Nevenka Urbanova (1909-2007). d, Stevo Zigon (1926-2005). e, Slobodan Perovic (1926-78). f, Stevan Salajic (1929-2002). g, Neda Spasojevic (1941-81). h, Milos Zutic (1939-93).

2009, Mar. 27 *Perf. 13¼x13¾*
461 A206 22d Sheet of 8, #a-h, + central label 6.50 6.50

25th Summer Universiade, Belgrade A207

Belgrade skyline, emblem, and birds in sports: 22d, Diving, fencing, basketball, soccer, swimming. 46d, Handball, gymnastics, tennis, judo, hurdling.

2009, Mar. 31 Litho.
462-463 A207 Set of 2 2.25 2.25

Paintings — A208

Designs: 22d, Self-portrait with a Veil, by Milena Pavlovic Barili (1909-45). No. 465, 46d, Young Woman in a Pink Dress, by Paja Jovanovic (1859-1957). No. 466, 46d, Still Life with Parrot, by Jovan Bijelic (1884-1964).

2009, Apr. 6 *Perf. 13¾x13¼*
464-466 A208 Set of 3 4.00 4.00

Europa A209

Designs: 46d, Goddess Urania, Galileo's telescope, Milky Way. 50d, Radio telescope, Horsehead Nebula.

2009, May 5 *Perf. 13¼x13¾*
467-468 A209 Set of 2 3.50 3.50
Intl. Year of Astronomy. Nos. 467-468 were each printed in sheets of 8 + central label.

Laying of Cornerstone of St. Sava Cathedral, 70th Anniv. A210

2009, May 9 *Perf. 13¼*
469 A210 22d multi .90 .90

European Nature Protection A211

Designs: 22d, Gyps fulvus over Uvac River. 46d, Pcinja Valley.

2009, May 20 *Perf. 13¾x13¼*
470-471 A211 Set of 2 2.50 2.50
Nos. 470-471 were each printed in sheets of 8 + central label.

Miniature Sheet

Composers — A212

No. 472: a, Kornelije Stankovic (1831-65). b, Josif Marinkovic (1851-1931). c, Petar Konjovic (1883-1970). d, Stevan Hristic (1885-1958). e, Miloje Milojevic (1884-1946). f, Mihovil Logar (1902-98). g, Lyubica Maric (1909-2003). h, Vasilije Mokranjac (1923-84).

2009, May 29
472 A212 22d Sheet of 8, #a-h, + central label 6.00 6.00

Battle of Cegar, 200th Anniv. A213

Designs: 22d, Battle of Cegar, painting by Boza Ilic. 46d, Stevan Sindelic, soldiers at Skull Tower.

2009, May 29 *Perf. 13¼x13¾*
473-474 A213 Set of 2 2.50 2.50

Painting of Frescoes in Church of the Virgin Mary, Studenica, 800th Anniv. — A214

2009, June 8   *Perf. 13¼*
475 A214 22d multi   .90 .90

Famous Men — A215

Designs: No. 476, 22d, Pavle Savic (1909-94), physicist. No. 477, 22d, Dimitrije Putnikovic (1859-1910), educator. No. 478, 46d, Pierre Curie (1859-1906), physicist. No. 479, 46d, Charles Darwin (1809-82), naturalist.

2009, June 22   *Perf. 13¾x13¼*
476-479 A215   Set of 4   5.00 5.00

Railroads in Serbia, 125th Anniv. — A216

Designs: 22d, CS No. 1 steam locomotive, Belgrade Station. 46d, JZ 441 electric locomotive, Nis Station.

2009, Sept. 8   *Litho.*   *Perf. 13¼*
480-481 A216   Set of 2   2.25 2.25

Golden Pen International Biennale of Illustrations, 50th Anniv. — A217

2009, Sept. 21   *Perf. 13¾x13¼*
482 A217 22d gold & black   .90 .90

Joy of Europe A218

2009, Sept. 30   *Perf. 13¼x13¾*
483 A218 46d multi   1.90 1.90
    Printed in sheets of 8 + label.

Gold Medalists at 2009 FINA World Swimming Championships, Rome — A219

Designs: No. 484, 46d, Nadja Higl (shown). No. 485, 46d, Milorad Cavic. 50d, Serbian Water Polo team.

2009, Oct. 9
484-486 A219   Set of 3   5.50 5.50
    Nos. 484-486 each were printed in sheets of 8 + label.

Stamp Day — A220

2009, Oct. 23   *Perf. 13¾x13¼*
487 A220 46d multi   1.90 1.90
    Michel Stamp Catalogs, Cent.

Exhibition of Dinosaurs From Argentina, Belgrade A221

Designs: 22d, Herrerrasaurus ischigualastensis. 46d, Giganotosaurus carolinii.

2009, Nov. 9   *Perf. 13¼x13¾*
488-489 A221   Set of 2   2.50 2.50
    Nos. 488-489 each were printed in sheets of 8 + label.

Christmas A222

Frescoes from Krusedol Monastery by Jov Vasilijevic: 22d, Christ's Birth. 46d, Epiphany.

2009, Nov. 23   *Litho.*   *Perf. 13¼*
490-491 A222   Set of 2   2.50 2.50

NIN Magazine, 75th Anniv. — A223

2010, Jan. 26   *Perf. 13¾x13¼*
492 A223 22d multi   .75 .75

New Year 2010 (Year of the Tiger) — A224

Tiger at: 22d, Right. 50d, Left.

2010, Jan. 27   *Perf. 13¼x13¾*
493-494 A224   Set of 2   2.40 2.40

European Nature Protection A225

Paeonia officinalis and: 22d, Deliblato Sands. 46d, Vrsac Mountains.

2010, Feb. 10   *Perf. 13¼x13¾*
495-496 A225   Set of 2   2.25 2.25
496a   Souvenir sheet, #495-496,   2.25 2.25
       perf. 13¾

2010 Winter Olympics, Vancouver A226

Designs: 22d, Cross-country skiing. 50d, Downhill skier.

2010, Feb. 12   *Perf. 13¾*
497-498 A226   Set of 2   2.50 2.50
    Nos. 497-498 each were printed in sheets of 8 + central label.

Serbian Olympic Committee, Cent. — A227

2010, Feb. 23   *Litho.*   *Perf. 13¾*
499 A227 22d multi   .80 .80

Expo 2010, Shanghai A228

Serbian Pavilion and: 22d, People, birds. 50d, Shanghai buildings.

2010, Feb. 26   *Perf. 13¾x13¼*
500-501 A228   Set of 2   2.50 2.50

Frédéric Chopin (1810-49), Composer A229

2010, Mar. 1
502 A229 50d multi   1.75 1.75
    Printed in sheets of 8 + central label.

Easter — A230

Red Easter egg and: 22d, Crucifixion painting. 46d, Egg depicting resurrected Jesus.

2010, Mar. 2   *Perf. 13¼x13¾*
503-504 A230   Set of 2   2.25 2.25

Military Academy, Belgrade, 160th Anniv. A231

       Perf. 13¼x13¾
2010, Mar. 18   *Litho.*
505 A231 22d multi   .60 .60

Zastava 750, 55th Anniv. A232

2010, Apr. 8
506 A232 22d multi   .80 .80

Birds A233

No. 507: a, Passer domesticus. b, Phoenicurus ochruros. c, Columba livia. d, Parus major.

2010, Apr. 12   *Perf. 13¾*
507   Horiz. strip of 4 + central
      label   5.00 5.00
   a.   A233 22d multi   .70 .70
   b.   A233 33d multi   1.00 1.00
   c.   A233 46d multi   1.40 1.40
   d.   A233 50d multi   1.60 1.60

Industrialization of Serbia, 140th Anniv. — A234

2010, Apr. 19   *Perf. 13¾*
508 A234 22d multi   .80 .80

Europa — A235

Designs: 66d, Girl reading on stack of books, vine, house, rabbit, giraffe, chicks. 77d, Girl standing on stack of books, boy in sling under moon, pumpkins, fairies.

2010, May 5
509-510 A235   Set of 2   4.00 4.00
    Nos. 509-510 each were printed in sheets of 8 + central label.

2010 World Cup Soccer Championships, South Africa — A236

Emblem of 2010 World Cup and: 22d, Map of Africa, two players. 50d, Map of Africa, two players, flags of South Africa and Serbia. 177d, Feet of soccer player, soccer balls, horiz.

2010, May 6   *Perf. 13¾*
511-512 A236   Set of 2   2.25 2.25

Souvenir Sheet
Perf. 13¾x¼
513 A236 177d multi   4.50 4.50

No. 513 contains one 43x35mm stamp. Nos. 511-512 each were printed in sheets of 8 + label.

50th Tour de Serbie Bicycle Race — A237

2010, June 1   *Perf. 13¾x13¼*
514 A237 50d multi   1.75 1.75

Printed in sheets of 8 + label.

Icons — A238

No. 515: a, Archangel Michael, by Andrei Rublev, 15th cent., Russia. b, Odigitria Virgin, Belgrade, 14th cent.

2010, June 28   *Perf. 13¼x13¾*
515 A238 50d Pair, #a-b   2.75 2.75

No. 515 was printed in sheets of 8, containing 4 of each stamp, + central label. See Russia No. 7221.

50th Trumpet Festival, Guca A239

2010, Aug. 13   *Perf. 13¾*
516 A239 44d multi   1.50 1.50

Printed in sheets of 8 + label. See Bosnia & Herzegovina (Serb Administration) No. 402.

2010 Youth Olympics, Singapore — A240

2010, Aug. 14
517 A240 51d multi   1.50 1.50

Printed in sheets of 8 + label.

Mother Teresa (1910-97), Humanitarian A241

2010, Aug. 26   *Perf. 13¾x13¼*
518 A241 50d multi   1.50 1.50

Miniature Sheet

Writers — A242

No. 519: a, Laza Kostic (1841-1910). b, Branislav Nusic (1864-1938). c, Borisav Stankovic (1876-1927). d, Ivo Andric (1892-1975). e, Milos Crnjanski (1893-1977). f, Mesa Selimovic (1910-82). g, Borislav Pekic (1930-92). h, Danilo Kis (1935-89).

2010, Nov. 26   *Perf. 13¼*
519 A242 22d Sheet of 8, #a-h, + central label   5.25 5.25

Plate, 16th Cent. — A243

Figurine, 19th Cent. — A244

2010, Nov. 26
520 A243 22d multi   .65 .65
521 A244 44d multi   1.30 1.30

Belgrade Art Museum, 60th anniv.

Serbian Postal Service, 170th Anniv. A245

2010, Nov. 26   *Perf. 13¼*
522 A245 46d multi   1.50 1.50

Stamp Day.

Joy of Europe A246

2010, Nov. 26
523 A246 46d multi   1.50 1.50

Printed in sheets of 8 + central label.

Christmas A247

Nativity paintings from church in Zemun by: 22d, Arsenija Teodorovic. 46d, Unknown artist.

2010, Nov. 30
524-525 A247   Set of 2   2.00 2.00

Ivan Saric (1876-1966), Aviation Pioneer, and Saric No. 1 Airplane — A248

Airplanes — A249

No. 527: a, 44d, Breguet 14. b, 55d, Spartan Cruiser. c, 66d, Rogozarski IK-3. d, 77d, McDonnell Douglas DC-9.

2010, Dec. 9   *Perf. 13¼*
526 A248 22d multi   .65 .65

Perf. 13¾
527 A249   Sheet of 4, #a-d   6.75 6.75

Souvenir Sheet

Preservation of Polar Regions and Glaciers — A250

No. 528: a, 46d, Iceberg. b, 66d, Glacier.

2011, Jan. 31   Litho.   *Perf. 13¼*
528 A250   Sheet of 2, #a-b   3.00 3.00

New Year 2011 (Year of the Rabbit) A251

Rabbit, ring of Chinese Zodiac animals and: 22d, Geometric design. 55d, Chinese character for "rabbit."

2011, Feb. 7   Set of 2
529-530 A251   2.00 2.00

Serbian Membership in Intl. Telecommunications Union, 145th Anniv. — A252

2011, Feb. 9   *Perf. 13¼x13¾*
531 A252 46d multi   1.25 1.25

Printed in sheets of 8 + label.

Rebuilding of Avala Telecommunications Tower, Belgrade — A253

2011, Feb. 14   *Perf. 13¼*
532 A253 44d multi   1.25 1.25

Art — A254

Designs: 22p, Self-portrait of Katarina Ivanovic (1811-82). 33d, Woman in Traditional Dress, by Uros Knezevic (1811-76). 44d, Self-portrait, sculpture, by Djordje Jovanovic (1861-1953). 66d, Self-portrait with Wife and Son, by Bora Baruh (1911-42).

2011, Feb. 25   *Perf. 13¾x13¼*
533-536 A254   Set of 4   4.50 4.50

Kornilije Stankovic (1831-65), Composer A255

2011, Mar. 15   *Perf. 13¼x13¾*
537 A255 22d multi   .65 .65

Stankovic Music School, cent.

Easter — A256

Religious paintings by Arsenije Teodorovic (1767-1826): 22d, Christ's Arrival in Jerusalem. 112d, Resurrection.

2011, Mar. 25   *Perf. 13¾*
538-539 A256   Set of 2   4.00 4.00

Serbian National Theater, Novi Sad, 150th Anniv. A257

2011, Mar. 28
540 A257 22d multi   .65 .65
Printed in sheets of 24 + central label.

Rotary International Polio Plus Program A258

2011, Mar. 31   *Perf. 13¾x13¼*
541 A258 50d multi   1.50 1.50

Worldwide Fund for Nature (WWF) A259

No. 542 — Phalacrocorax pygmaeus: a, Two birds, one on branch. b, Bird on rock. c, Two birds in flight. d, Two birds in water.

2011, Apr. 11   *Perf. 13¼x13¾*
542   Horiz. strip of 4 + central
         label   4.75 4.75
  a. A259 22d multi   .65   .65
  b. A259 33d multi   .95   .95
  c. A259 44d multi   1.25 1.25
  d. A259 66d multi   1.90 1.90

Intl. Year of Biodiversity — A260

2011, Apr. 15   *Perf. 13¾*
543 A260 50d multi   1.50 1.50

Europa A261

Forest and: 33d, Logs. 66d, Tree leaves.

2011, May 5   *Litho.*
544-545 A261   Set of 2   3.00 3.00
Intl. Year of Forests. Nos. 544-545 each were printed in sheets of 8 + central label.

Scouting in Serbia, Cent. — A262

2011, May 6   *Perf. 13¼x13¾*
546 A262 22d multi   .65 .65

Bora Stankovic Gymnasium, Vranje, 130th Anniv. — A263

2011, May 10   *Perf. 13¾x13¼*
547 A263 22d multi   .65 .65

Dr. Laza Lazarevic (1851-91), Writer and Psychiatrist A264

2011, May 13
548 A264 22d multi   .65 .65

Berries A265

No. 549: a, Rubus idaeus. b, Fragaria vesca. c, Ribes rubrum. d, Vaccinium macrocarpon.

2011, May 27   *Perf. 13¼x13¾*
549   Horiz. strip of 4 + central
         label   5.00 5.00
  a. A265 22d multi   .65   .65
  b. A265 33d multi   .95   .95
  c. A265 44d multi   1.40 1.40
  d. A265 66d multi   2.00 2.00

Campaign Against AIDS, 30th Anniv. — A266

2011, June 1   *Perf. 13¾x13¼*
550 A266 50d multi   1.50 1.50

Digital Serbia — A267

Designs: 22d, Keyhole on Earth, key. 44d, Stylized eye, "@" and "www."

2011, June 3   *Perf. 13¼*
551-552 A267   Set of 2   2.00 2.00

European Nature Protection A268

Waterfalls: 22d, Mokranjska Stena. 46d, Beli Izvorac.

2011, June 13   *Perf. 13¾x13¼*
553-554 A268   Set of 2   2.00 2.00

Franz Liszt (1811-86), Composer — A269

2011, June 14   *Perf. 13¾*
555 A269 50d multi   1.40 1.40

Bridges A270

Designs: 22d, Danube River Bridge, near Beska. 44d, Sava River Railway Bridge, Belgrade. 46d, Danube River Bridge, Novi Sad.

2011, June 20   *Litho.*
556-558 A270   Set of 3   3.25 3.25

Duzijanca Harvest Festival, Cent. — A271

Designs: 22d, Model of cathedral in Subotica. 55d, Centenary wheat crown.

2011, July 1
559-560 A271   Set of 2   2.25 2.25
Nos. 559-560 each were printed in sheets of 9 + label.

Belgrade Zoo, 75th Anniv. A272

Designs: 22d, Lion, white lion and cubs. No. 562, vert. — White or albino animals: a, 33d, Panthera tigris tigris. b, 44d, Neophron percnopterus. c, 46d, Macropus rufogriseus. d, 50d, Panthera leo.

2011, July 12   *Perf. 13¾*
561 A272 22d multi   .65 .65
562 A272 Sheet of 4, #a-d   5.00 5.00
No. 562 was sold with, but unattached to, a booklet cover.

Computer Mouse Flower — A273

2011, July 13
563 A273 22d multi   .65 .65

Soko Galeb Jet, 50th Anniv. A274

2011, July 20   *Perf. 13¼x13¾*
564 A274 50d multi   1.40 1.40
Printed in sheets of 8 + central label.

First Conference of Non-Aligned Countries, 50th Anniv. — A275

2011, Sept. 1   *Perf. 13¾x13¼*
565 A275 22d multi   .60 .60

European Women's Volleyball Championships, Italy and Serbia — A276

2011, Sept. 20   *Perf. 13¾*
566 A276 46d multi   1.25 1.25
Printed in sheets of 8 + central label.

Joy of Europe A277

2011, Sept. 30   *Perf. 13¼x13¾*
567 A277 46d multi   1.25 1.25
Printed in sheets of 8 + central label.

First Serbian Motion Picture, Cent. A278

2011, Oct. 3   *Perf. 13¾*
568 A278 22d multi   .60 .60

Stamp
Day — A279

2011, Oct. 25   *Perf. 13¾x13¼*
569 A279 46d multi   1.25 1.25

Beogradfila Stamp Exhibition, Belgrade.

Writers
A280

Designs: 22d, Rachel de Queiroz (1910-2003), Brazilian writer. 46d, Ivo Andric (1892-1975), Yugoslvian writer, and Nobel medal.

2011, Oct. 26   *Perf. 13¾*
570-571 A280 Set of 2   1.90 1.90

See Brazil Nos.

Christmas
A281

Designs: 22d, Birth of Christ, icon, c. 1780. 112d, Birth of Christ, by Arsenije Teodorovic.

2011, Jan. 15
572-573 A281 Set of 2   3.50 3.50

Journalist's Association of Serbia,
130th Anniv. — A282

2011, Nov. 25
574 A282 22d multi   .60 .60

Moravica
Hydroelectric
Plant,
Cent. — A283

2011, Dec. 19   *Perf. 13¼x13¾*
575 A283 22d multi   .55 .55

Serbian
Victories at
2011 Men's and
Women's
European
Volleyball
Championships
A284

Designs: No. 576, 22d, Two male players.
No. 577, 22d, Three female players.

2011, Dec. 20   *Perf. 13¾x13¼*
576-577 A284 Set of 2   1.10 1.10

African National
Congress,
Cent. — A285

2012, Jan. 6   *Litho.*
578 A285 46d multi   1.25 1.25

New Year
2012 (Year of
the Dragon)
A286

Designs: 22d, Dragon. 55d, Dragon, diff.

2012, Feb. 6   *Perf. 13¼x13¾*
579-580 A286 Set of 2   1.90 1.90

Architecture
A287

Designs: 22d, Department store, Belgrade. 33d, Telephone Exchange Building, Belgrade, horiz. 46d, Hotel Moskva, Belgrade, horiz. 55d, City Hall, Subotica, horiz.

    Perf. 13¾x13¼, 13¼x13¾
2012, Mar. 2
581-584 A287 Set of 4   3.75 3.75

National
Theater,
Nis,
125th
Anniv.
A288

2012, Mar. 9   *Perf. 13¼*
585 A288 22d multi   .55 .55

Easter — A289

Designs: 22d, Ceremonial cross. 46d, Resurrection of Christ.

2012, Mar. 15   *Perf. 13¾*
586-587 A289 Set of 2   1.60 1.60

POSTAGE DUE STAMPS

Coat of Arms
   D1   D2

1895   Unwmk.   Typo.   *Perf. 13x13½*
       Granite Paper

J1	D1	5p red lilac	6.00 1.00
J2	D1	10p blue	6.00 .40
J3	D1	20p orange brown	47.50 8.00
J4	D1	30p green	.40 .80
J5	D1	50p rose	.40 1.10
a.		Cliché of 5p in plate of 50p	80.00 100.00
		Nos. J1-J5 (5)	60.30 11.30

No. J1 exists imperf. Value $75.

1898-1904   **Ordinary Paper**
J6	D1	5p magenta ('04)	.70 .70
J7	D1	20p brown	6.00 1.00
a.		Tête bêche pair	150.00 150.00
J8	D1	20p dp brn ('04)	6.00 1.00
		Nos. J6-J8 (3)	12.70 2.70

1906   **Granite Paper**   *Perf. 11½*
J9	D1	5p magenta	5.25 1.00

1909   **Laid Paper**
J10	D1	5p magenta	.80 .60
J11	D1	10p pale blue	4.75 7.50
J12	D1	20p pale brown	.40 .80
		Nos. J10-J12 (3)	5.95 8.90

1914   **White Wove Paper**
J13	D1	5p rose	.40 2.00
J14	D1	10p deep blue	6.00 9.00

1918-20   *Perf. 11*
J15	D2	5p red	.40 .85
J16	D2	5p red brown ('20)	.40 .85
J17	D2	10p yellow green	.40 .85
J18	D2	20p olive brown	.40 .85
J19	D2	30p slate green	.40 .85
J20	D2	50p chocolate	.90 1.50
		Nos. J15-J20 (6)	2.90 5.75

NEWSPAPER STAMPS

N1

Overprinted with Crown-topped Shield
in Black

1911   Unwmk.   Typo.   *Perf. 11½*
P1	N1	1p gray	.80 .80
P2	N1	5p green	.80 .80
P3	N1	10p orange	.80 .80
a.		Cliché of 1p in plate of 10p	225.00
P4	N1	15p violet	.80 .80
P5	N1	20p yellow	.80 .80
a.		Cliché of 50p in plate of 20p	85.00 140.00
P6	N1	25p blue	.80 .80
P7	N1	30p slate	7.50 7.50
P8	N1	50p brown	6.25 6.25
P9	N1	1d bister	6.25 6.25
P10	N1	3d rose red	7.50 7.50
P11	N1	5d gray vio	6.25 6.25
		Nos. P1-P11 (11)	38.55 38.55

POSTAL TAX STAMPS

> **Catalogue values for unused
> stamps in this section are for
> Never Hinged items.**

Red Cross and
Disabled
People — PT2

2006, Sept. 14   *Litho.*   *Perf. 13¾*
RA2 PT2 8d multi   .25 .25

Obligatory on mail Sept. 14-21.

Red Cross and
Children — PT3

2006, Sept. 22
RA3 PT3 8d multi   .25 .25

Obligatory on mail Sept. 22-29.

Children's
Week — PT4

2006, Oct. 2   *Litho.*   *Perf. 12½*
RA4 PT4 8d multi   .25 .25

Obligatory on mail Oct. 2-8.

AIDS
Prevention — PT5

2006, Oct. 9   *Perf. 13¾*
RA5 PT5 8d multi   .25 .25

Obligatory on mail Oct. 9-31.

European Olympic
Youth Festival,
Belgrade — PT6

2006, Dec. 1   *Litho.*   *Perf. 13¾*
RA6 PT6 8d multi   .30 .30

Obligatory on mail Dec. 1-31.

2007 European
Judo
Championships,
Belgrade — PT7

2007, Jan. 22
RA7 PT7 8d multi   .30 .30

Obligatory on mail Jan. 22-27.

Red Cross
Week — PT9

2007, May 8   *Litho.*   *Perf. 13¾*
RA9 PT9 10d multi   .35 .35

Obligatory on mail May 8-15.

Red Cross Solidarity
Week — PT11

2007, Sept. 14   Litho.   Perf. 13¾
RA11 PT11 10d multi .40 .40
Obligatory on mail Sept. 14-21.

Campaign Against
AIDS — PT13

2007, Nov. 1   Litho.   Perf. 13¾
RA13 PT13 10d multi .40 .40
Obligatory on mail Nov. 1-30.

Campaign
Against Sex
Slavery
PT15

2008, Jan. 21   Litho.   Perf. 13¼
RA15 PT15 10d multi .35 .35
Obligatory on mail Jan. 21-26.

Red Cross Solidarity
Week — PT20

2008, Sept. 14   Litho.   Perf. 13¾
RA20 PT20 10d multi .35 .35
Obligatory on mail Sept. 14-21.

Avala
Telecommunications
Tower,
Belgrade — PT23

2008, Nov. 3   Litho.   Perf. 13¾
RA23 PT23 10d multi .30 .30
Obligatory on mail Nov. 3-29.

Red Cross
Week — PT25

2009, May 8   Litho.   Perf. 13¾
Dated "2009"
RA25 PT25 10d multi .30 .30
Obligatory on mail May 8-15. See No. RA35.

King Alexander I
(1888-1934) — PT26

2009, June 8
RA26 PT26 10d multi .30 .30
Obligatory on mail June 8-13.

St. Sava Cathedral,
Belgrade — PT27

2009, June 29
RA27 PT27 10d multi .30 .30
Obligatory on mail June 29-Aug. 29.

Red Cross Solidarity
Week — PT28

2009, Sept. 14
RA28 PT28 10d multi .35 .35
Obligatory on mail Sept. 14-21.

Homeless
Children — PT31

2009, Dec. 23   Litho.   Perf. 13¾
RA31 PT31 10d multi .30 .30
Obligatory on mail Dec. 23-31.

Refugees — PT32

2010, Feb. 1
RA32 PT32 10d multi .30 .30
Obligatory on mail Feb. 1-6.

European Water Polo Championships,
Zagreb — PT34

2010, Apr. 16   Litho.   Perf. 13¼x13¾
RA34 PT34 10d multi .30 .30
Obligatory on mail Apr. 16-24.

Red Cross Week Type of 2009
2010, May 8   Perf. 13¾
Dated "2010"
RA35 PT25 10d multi .25 .25
Obligatory on mail May 8-15.

ISSUED UNDER AUSTRIAN OCCUPATION

100 Heller = 1 Krone

Stamps of Bosnia,
1912-14,
Overprinted

1916   Unwmk.   Perf. 12½
1N1 A23 1h olive green 2.25 5.25
1N2 A23 2h brt blue 2.25 5.25
1N3 A23 3h claret 2.25 5.25
1N4 A23 5h green .40 .75
1N5 A23 6h dk gray 1.50 3.75
1N6 A23 10h rose carmine .40 .75

1N7 A23 12h dp olive grn .80 2.25
1N8 A23 20h orange brown .80 1.40
1N9 A23 25h ultra .80 2.25
1N10 A23 30h orange red .80 2.25
1N11 A24 35h myrtle grn .80 2.25
1N12 A24 40h dk violet .80 2.25
1N13 A24 45h olive brown .80 2.25
1N14 A24 50h slate blue .80 2.25
1N15 A24 60h brown violet .80 2.25
1N16 A24 72h dark blue .80 2.25
1N17 A25 1k brn vio, *straw* 1.50 2.25
1N18 A25 2k dk gray, *bl* 1.50 2.25
1N19 A26 3k carmine, *grn* 1.50 2.25
1N20 A26 5k dk vio, *gray* 1.50 2.25
1N21 A25 10k dk ultra, *gray* 15.00 30.00
Nos. 1N1-1N21 (21) 38.05 81.65

Stamps of Bosnia, 1912-14,
Overprinted "SERBIEN" Horizontally at
Bottom

1916
1N22 A23 1h olive green 8.00 19.00
1N23 A23 2h bright blue 8.00 19.00
1N24 A23 3h claret 8.00 19.00
1N25 A23 5h green .50 3.00
1N26 A23 6h dark gray 8.00 19.00
1N27 A23 10h rose carmine .50 3.00
1N28 A23 12h dp olive grn 8.00 19.00
1N29 A23 20h orange brn 8.00 19.00
1N30 A23 25h ultra 8.00 19.00
1N31 A23 30h orange red 8.00 19.00
1N32 A24 35h myrtle green 8.00 19.00
1N33 A24 40h dark violet 8.00 19.00
1N34 A24 45h olive brown 8.00 19.00
1N35 A24 50h slate blue 8.00 19.00
1N36 A24 60h brown violet 8.00 19.00
1N37 A24 72h dark blue 8.00 19.00
1N38 A25 1k brn vio, *straw* 19.00 40.00
1N39 A25 2k dk gray, *bl* 19.00 40.00
1N40 A26 3k carmine, *grn* 22.50 47.50
1N41 A26 5k dk vio, *gray* 27.50 60.00
1N42 A25 10k dk ultra, *gray* 52.50 100.00
Nos. 1N22-1N42 (21) 253.50 559.50

Nos. 1N22-1N42 were prepared in 1914, at the time of the 1st Austrian occupation of Serbia. They were not issued at that time because of the retreat. The stamps were put on sale in 1916, at the same time as Nos. 1N1-1N21.

ISSUED UNDER GERMAN OCCUPATION

In occupied Serbia, authority was ostensibly in the hands of a government created by the former Yugoslav General, Milan Nedich, supported by the Chetniks, a nationalist organization which turned fascist. Actually the German military ran the country.

Types of Yugoslavia,
1939-40, Overprinted
in Black

1941   Unwmk.   Typo.   Perf. 12½
Paper with colored network
2N1 A16 25p blk (*lt grn*) .30 7.50
2N2 A16 50p org (*pink*) .30 3.75
2N3 A16 1d yel grn (*lt grn*) .30 3.75
2N4 A16 1.50d red (*pink*) .30 3.75
2N5 A16 2d dp mag (*pink*) .30 3.75
2N6 A16 3d dl red brn (*pink*) 1.10 30.00
2N7 A16 4d ultra (*lt grn*) .75 6.00
2N8 A16 5d dk bl (*lt grn*) 1.10 15.00
2N9 A16 5.50d dk vio brn (*pink*) 1.10 15.00
2N10 A16 6d sl bl (*pink*) 1.10 15.00
2N11 A16 8d sep (*lt grn*) 1.50 22.50
2N12 A16 12d brt vio (*lt grn*) 1.50 22.50
2N13 A16 16d dl vio (*pink*) 2.10 75.00
2N14 A16 20d bl (*lt grn*) 3.50 275.00
2N15 A16 30d brt pink (*lt grn*) 13.50 1,000.
Nos. 2N1-2N15 (15) 28.75 1,498.
Set, never hinged 72.50

Double overprints exist on 50p, 1d, 5d, 5.50d and 12d. Value, $250.

Stamps of
Yugoslavia, 1939-40,
Overprinted in Black

Paper with colored network
2N16 A16 25p blk (*lt grn*) .25 22.50
2N17 A16 50p org (*pink*) .25 5.25
2N18 A16 1d yel grn (*lt grn*) .25 5.25
2N19 A16 1.50d red (*pink*) .25 5.25
2N20 A16 2d dp mag (*pink*) .25 5.25
2N21 A16 3d dl red brn (*pink*) .60 20.00
2N22 A16 4d ultra (*lt grn*) .65 5.25
2N23 A16 5d dk bl (*lt grn*) .65 9.75
2N24 A16 5.50d dk vio brn (*pink*) 1.00 20.00
2N25 A16 6d sl bl (*pink*) 1.00 20.00
2N26 A16 8d sep (*lt grn*) 1.25 30.00
2N27 A16 12d brt vio (*lt grn*) 1.75 30.00
2N28 A16 16d dl vio (*pink*) 1.75 97.50
2N29 A16 20d bl (*lt grn*) 1.75 300.00
2N30 A16 30d brt pink (*lt grn*) 9.00 975.00
Nos. 2N16-2N30 (15) 20.65 1,551.
Set, never hinged 47.50

Lazaritza
Monastery — OS1

Ruins of
Manassia
Monastery
OS4

Designs: 1d, Kalenica Monastery. 1.50d, Ravanica Monastery. 3d, Ljubostinja Monastery. 4d, Sopocane Monastery. 7d, Tsitsa Monastery. 12d, Goriak Monastery. 16d, Studenica Monastery.

1942-43   Typo.   Perf. 11½
2N31 OS1 50p brt violet .25 .40
2N32 OS1 1d red .25 .40
2N33 OS1 1.50d red brn .75 5.25
2N34 OS1 1.50d green ('43) .25 .40
2N35 OS4 2d dl rose violet .25 .40
2N36 OS4 3d brt blue .75 5.25
2N37 OS4 3d rose pink ('43) .25 .40
2N38 OS4 4d ultra .25 .40
2N39 OS4 7d dk slate grn .25 .40
2N40 OS1 12d lake .25 2.50
2N41 OS1 16d grnsh blk 1.00 3.00
Nos. 2N31-2N41 (11) 4.50 18.80
Set, never hinged 5.25

For surcharges see Nos. 2NB29-2NB37.

Post
Rider — OS10

Post
Wagon — OS11

9d, Mail train. 30d, Mail truck. 50d, Mail plane.

1943, Oct. 15   Photo.   Perf. 12½
2N42 OS10 3d copper red & gray lilac .80 4.50
2N43 OS11 8d vio rose & gray .80 4.50
2N44 OS10 9d dk bl grn & sep .80 4.50

2N45 OS10 30d chnt & sl grn .80 4.50
2N46 OS10 50d dp bl & red brn .80 4.50
    Nos. 2N42-2N46 (5) 4.00 22.50
    Set, never hinged 8.00

Centenary of postal service in Serbia. Printed in sheets of 24 containing 4 of each stamp and 4 labels.

OCCUPATION SEMI-POSTAL STAMPS

Smederevo Fortress on the Danube OSP1

Refugees OSP2

Perf. 11½x12½
1941, Sept. 22 Typo. Unwmk.
2NB1 OSP1 50p + 1d dk brn .30 1.60
2NB2 OSP2 1d + 2d dk gray grn .30 2.00
2NB3 OSP2 1.50d + 3d dp cl .55 3.50
  a. Perf. 12½ 4.25 16.00
    Never hinged 8.50
2NB4 OSP1 2d + 4d dk bl .80 4.75
    Nos. 2NB1-2NB4 (4) 1.95 11.85
    Set, never hinged 4.25

Souvenir Sheets
2NB5 Sheet of 2 55.00 450.00
    Never hinged 110.00
  a. OSP2 1d + 49d rose lake 19.00 45.00
  b. OSP1 2d + 48d gray 19.00 45.00

Imperf
2NB6 Sheet of 2 55.00 450.00
    Never hinged 110.00
  a. OSP2 1d + 49d gray 19.00 45.00
  b. OSP1 2d + 48d rose lake 19.00 45.00

The surtax aided the victims of an explosion at Smederevo and was used for the reconstruction of the town.

Christ and Virgin Mary — OSP4

a

b

1941, Dec. 5 Photo. Perf. 11½
With Rose Burelage
2NB7 OSP4 50p + 1.50d brn red .35 6.25
2NB8 OSP4 1d + 3d sl grn .35 6.25
2NB9 OSP4 2d + 6d dp red .35 6.25
2NB10 OSP4 4d + 12d dp bl .35 6.25
    Nos. 2NB7-2NB10 (4) 1.40 25.00
    Set, never hinged 3.00

With Symbol "a" Outlined in Cerise
2NB7a OSP4 50p 11.00 72.50
2NB8a OSP4 1d 11.00 72.50
2NB9a OSP4 2d 11.00 72.50
2NB10a OSP4 4d 11.00 72.50
    Nos. 2NB7a-2NB10a (4) 44.00 290.00
    Set, never hinged 87.50

With Symbol "b" Outlined in Cerise
2NB7b OSP4 50p 11.00 72.50
2NB8b OSP4 1d 11.00 72.50
2NB9b OSP4 2d 11.00 72.50
2NB10b OSP4 4d 11.00 72.50
    Nos. 2NB7b-2NB10b (4) 44.00 290.00
    Set, never hinged 87.50

Without Burelage
2NB7c OSP4 50p 1.60 20.00
2NB8c OSP4 1d 1.60 20.00
2NB9c OSP4 2d 1.60 20.00
2NB10c OSP4 4d 1.60 20.00
    Nos. 2NB7c-2NB10c (4) 6.40 80.00
    Set, never hinged 12.40

These stamps were printed in sheets of 50, in 2 panes of 25. In the panes, #8, 12, 13, 14, 18, forming a cross, are without burelage. #7, 17 are type "a," #9, 19 type "b." 16 of the 25 stamps have overall burelage.
Surtax aided prisoners of war.

1942, Mar. 26
Thicker Paper, Without Burelage
2NB11 OSP4 50p + 1.50d brn 1.00 4.00
2NB12 OSP4 1d + 3d dk grn 1.00 4.00
2NB13 OSP4 2d + 6d mag 1.00 4.00
2NB14 OSP4 4d + 12d ultra 1.00 4.00
    Nos. 2NB11-2NB14 (4) 4.00 16.00
    Set, never hinged 8.50

OSP5

OSP6

OSP7

OSP8

Designs: Anti-Masonic symbolisms.

1942, Jan. 1
2NB15 OSP5 50p + 50p yel brn .30 3.50
2NB16 OSP6 1d + 1d dk grn .30 3.50
2NB17 OSP7 2d + 2d rose car .40 6.25
2NB18 OSP8 4d + 4d indigo .40 6.25
    Nos. 2NB15-2NB18 (4) 1.40 19.50
    Set, never hinged 3.00

Anti-Masonic Exposition of Oct. 22, 1941. The surtax was used for anti-Masonic propaganda.

Mother and Children — OSP9

1942
2NB19 OSP9 2d + 6d brt pur 4.75 10.50
2NB20 OSP9 4d + 8d dp bl 4.75 10.50
2NB21 OSP9 7d + 13d dk bl 4.75 10.50
2NB22 OSP9 20d + 40d dp rose lake 4.75 10.50
    Nos. 2NB19-2NB22 (4) 19.00 42.00
    Set, never hinged 40.00

Nos. 2NB19-2NB22 were issued in sheets of 16 consisting of a block of four of each denomination. The surtax aided war orphans.

Broken Sword — OSP10

Wounded Flag-bearer OSP11

Designs: 1.50d+48.50d, Broken sword. 3d+5d, 2d+48d, Wounded soldier. 3d+47d, Wounded flag-bearer. 4d+10d, 4d+46d, Tending casualty.

1943
2NB23 OSP10 1.50d + 1.50d dk brn 1.00 3.25
2NB24 OSP11 2d + 3d dk bl grn 1.00 3.25
2NB25 OSP11 3d + 5d dp rose vio 2.00 4.75
2NB26 OSP10 4d + 10d dp bl 2.00 5.75
    Nos. 2NB23-2NB26 (4) 6.00 17.00
    Set, never hinged 13.00

Souvenir Sheets
Thick Paper
2NB27 Sheet of 2 50.00 3,000.
  a. OSP10 1.50d + 48.50d dk brn 16.00 1,350.
  b. OSP10 4d + 46d dp bl 16.00 1,350.
2NB28 Sheet of 2 55.00 3,000.
  a. OSP11 2d + 48d dk bl grn 18.00 1,350.
  b. OSP11 3d + 47d dp rose vio 18.00 1,350.

The sheets measure 150x110mm. The surtax aided war victims.

Stamps of 1942-43 Surcharged in Black

1943, Dec. 11
Pale Green Burelage
2NB29 OS1 50p + 2d brt vio .25 47.50
2NB30 OS1 1d + 3d red .25 47.50
2NB31 OS1 1.50d + 4d dp grn .25 47.50
2NB32 OS4 2d + 5d dl rose vio .25 47.50
2NB33 OS4 3d + 7d rose pink .25 47.50
2NB34 OS4 4d + 9d ultra .25 47.50
2NB35 OS4 7d + 15d dk sl grn .50 47.50
2NB36 OS1 12d + 25d lake .50 225.00

2NB37 OS1 16d + 33d grnsh blk 1.10 350.00
    Nos. 2NB29-2NB37 (9) 3.60 907.50
    Set, never hinged 7.00

The surtax aided the victims of the bombing of Nisch.

OCCUPATION AIR POST STAMPS

Types of Yugoslavia, 1937-40, Overprinted in Carmine or Maroon

Nos. 2NC1-2NC3, 2NC5-2NC7, 2NC9

Nos. 2NC4, 2NC8, 2NC10

1941 Unwmk. Perf. 12½
Paper with colored network
2NC1 AP6 50p brown 4.00 175.00
2NC2 AP7 1d yellow grn 4.00 175.00
2NC3 AP8 2d blue gray 4.00 175.00
2NC4 AP9 2.50d rose red (M) 4.00 175.00
2NC5 AP6 5d brown vio 4.00 175.00
2NC6 AP7 10d brn lake (M) 4.00 175.00
2NC7 AP8 20d dk green 4.00 175.00
2NC8 AP9 30d ultra 4.00 175.00
2NC9 AP10 40d Prus grn & pale grn (C) 9.50 625.00
2NC10 AP11 50d sl bl & gray bl (C) 13.50 1,100.
    Nos. 2NC1-2NC10 (10) 55.00 3,125.
    Set, never hinged 125.00
Nos. 2NC1-2NC2 exist without network.

Same Surcharged in Maroon or Carmine

No. 2NC13

No. 2NC14

Without colored network
2NC11 AP7 1d on 10d 3.00 200.00
2NC12 AP8 3d on 20d 3.00 200.00
2NC13 AP9 6d on 30d 3.00 200.00
2NC14 AP10 8d on 40d 6.00 400.00
2NC15 AP11 12d on 50d 10.00 850.00
    Nos. 2NC11-2NC15 (5) 25.00 1,850.
    Set, never hinged 60.00

Regular Issue of Yugoslavia, 1939-40, Surcharged in Black

1942 Green Network
2NC16 A16 2d on 2d dp mag .25 2.00
2NC17 A16 4d on 4d ultra .25 2.00
2NC18 A16 10d on 12d brt vio .25 4.00
2NC19 A16 14d on 20d blue .25 4.00
2NC20 A16 20d on 30d brt pink .50 16.00
    Nos. 2NC16-2NC20 (5) 1.50 28.00
    Set, never hinged 3.00

OCCUPATION POSTAGE DUE STAMPS

Types of Yugoslavia
Similar to OD3-OD4
Overprinted

1941   Unwmk.   Typo.   Perf. 12½

2NJ1	OD3	50p violet	.80	40.00
2NJ2	OD3	1d lake	.80	40.00
2NJ3	OD3	2d dark blue	.80	40.00
2NJ4	OD3	3d red	1.25	60.00
2NJ5	OD4	4d lt blue	1.60	140.00
2NJ6	OD4	5d orange	1.60	140.00
2NJ7	OD4	10d violet	2.75	350.00
2NJ8	OD4	20d green	6.75	950.00
		Nos. 2NJ1-2NJ8 (8)	16.35	1,760.
		Set, never hinged	32.50	

OD3   OD4

1942   Perf. 12½

2NJ9	OD3	1d maroon & grn	1.25	8.00
2NJ10	OD3	2d dk blue & red	1.25	8.00
2NJ11	OD3	3d vermilion & bl	1.25	12.00
2NJ12	OD4	4d blue & red	1.25	12.00
2NJ13	OD4	5d orange & bl	1.60	16.00
2NJ14	OD4	10d violet & red	1.60	24.00
2NJ15	OD4	20d green & red	8.00	95.00
		Nos. 2NJ9-2NJ15 (7)	16.20	175.00
		Set, never hinged	32.50	

OD5

2NJ16	OD5	50p black	.75	6.25
2NJ17	OD5	3d violet	.75	6.25
2NJ18	OD5	4d blue	.75	6.25
2NJ19	OD5	5d dk slate grn	.75	6.25
2NJ20	OD5	6d orange	1.25	16.00
2NJ21	OD5	10d red	1.60	20.00
2NJ22	OD5	20d ultra	4.00	60.00
		Nos. 2NJ16-2NJ22 (7)	9.85	121.00
		Set, never hinged	22.50	

OCCUPATION OFFICIAL STAMP

OOS1

1943   Unwmk.   Typo.   Perf. 12½

2NO1	OOS1	3d red lilac	.80	2.00
		Never hinged	1.60	

SEYCHELLES

sā-'shelz̧

LOCATION — A group of islands in the Indian Ocean, off the coast of Africa north of Madagascar.
GOVT. — Republic
AREA — 175 sq. mi.
POP. — 79,164 (1999 est.)
CAPITAL — Victoria

The islands were attached to the British colony of Mauritius from 1810 to 1903, when they became a separate colony. Seychelles achieved internal self-government in October 1975 and independence on June 29, 1976.

100 Cents = 1 Rupee

> Catalogue values for unused stamps in this country are for Never Hinged items, beginning with Scott 149 in the regular postage section and Scott J1 in the postage due section.

Watermark

Wmk. 380 — "POST OFFICE"

Queen Victoria — A1

Two dies of 2c, 4c, 8c, 10c, 13c, 16c:
Die I — Shading lines at right of diamond in tiara band.
Die II — No shading lines in this rectangle.

1890-1900   Typo.   Wmk. 2   Perf. 14

1	A1	2c grn & rose (II)	3.50	1.25
a.		Die I	5.00	14.00
2	A1	2c org brn & grn ('00)	2.50	1.75
3	A1	3c dk vio & org ('93)	2.00	.75
4	A1	4c car rose & grn (II)	3.50	1.75
a.		Die I	37.50	15.00
5	A1	6c car rose ('00)	4.50	.75
6	A1	8c brn vio & ultra (II)	12.00	2.50
a.		8c brn vio & bl (I)	15.00	4.50
7	A1	10c ultra & brn (II)	13.00	4.25
a.		10c bl & brn (I)	9.50	27.50
8	A1	12c ol gray & grn ('93)	3.50	.85
9	A1	13c slate & blk (II)	4.25	2.50
a.		Die I	8.00	15.00
10	A1	15c ol grn & vio ('93)	6.00	2.75
11	A1	15c ultra ('00)	10.00	4.50
12	A1	16c org brn & bl (I)	9.50	5.50
a.		16c org brn & ultra (II)	52.50	14.50
13	A1	18c ultra ('97)	8.50	1.50
14	A1	36c brn & rose ('97)	35.00	6.00
15	A1	45c brn & rose ('93)	30.00	45.00
16	A1	48c ocher & green	25.00	15.00
17	A1	75c yel & pur ('00)	70.00	87.50
18	A1	96c violet & car	67.50	60.00
19	A1	1r vio & red ('97)	16.00	5.75
20	A1	1.50r blk & rose ('00)	90.00	110.00
21	A1	2.25r vio & grn ('00)	125.00	110.00
		Nos. 1-21 (21)	541.25	469.85

Numerals of 75c, 1r, 1.50r and 2.25r of type A1 are in color on plain tablet.
For surcharges see Nos. 22-37.

Surcharged in Black

1893

22	A1	3c on 4c car rose & green (II)	1.50	2.00
a.		Inverted surcharge	375.00	450.00
b.		Double surcharge	600.00	
d.		Pair, one without surcharge	14,000.	
23	A1	12c on 16c org brn & ultra (II)	18.50	3.50
a.		12c on 16c org brn & bl (I)	4.00	5.00

b.		Inverted surcharge (I)	575.00	
d.		Double surcharge (I)	15,750.	11,000.
e.		Double surcharge (II)	5,500.	5,500.
24	A1	15c on 16c org brn & ultra (II)	18.50	4.00
a.		15c on 16c org brn & bl (I)	12.00	17.50
b.		Inverted surcharge (I)	400.00	375.00
c.		Inverted surcharge (II)	1,100.	1,250.
d.		Double surcharge (I)	1,500.	1,500.
e.		Double surcharge (II)	825.00	875.00
f.		Triple surcharge (II)	5,000.	
25	A1	45c on 48c ocher & grn	32.50	7.00
26	A1	90c on 96c vio & car	70.00	42.50
		Nos. 22-26 (5)	141.00	59.00

No. 15 Surcharged in Black

18 CENTS

1896

27	A1	18c on 45c brn & rose	10.00	4.25
a.		Double surcharge	1,850.	1,850.
b.		Triple surcharge	2,750.	
28	A1	36c on 45c brn & rose	12.00	70.00
a.		Double surcharge	1,850.	

Surcharged in Black

3 cents   **6 cents**

1901

29	A1	3c on 10c bl & brn (II)	2.00	.90
a.		Double surcharge	950.00	
b.		Triple surcharge	3,250.	
30	A1	3c on 16c org brn & ultra (II)	4.50	6.50
a.		"3 cents" omitted (II)	675.00	675.00
b.		Inverted surcharge (II)	800.00	800.00
c.		Double surcharge (II)	625.00	650.00
31	A1	3c on 36c brn & rose	1.00	1.10
a.		Without bars	—	—
b.		Double surcharge	950.00	1,100.
c.		"3 cents" omitted	800.00	850.00
32	A1	6c on 8c brn vio & ultra (II)	3.25	4.50
a.		Inverted surcharge	800.00	925.00
		Nos. 29-32 (4)	10.75	13.00

Stamps of 1890-1900 Surcharged

2 cents

1902, June

33	A1	2c on 4c car rose & grn (II)	3.00	3.50
34	A1	30c on 75c yel & pur	2.25	4.75
a.		Narrow "0" in "30"	12.50	57.50
35	A1	30c on 1r vio & red	11.00	40.00
a.		Narrow "0" in "30"	27.50	110.00
b.		Double surcharge	1,750.	
36	A1	45c on 1r vio & rod	8.50	60.00
37	A1	45c on 2.25r vio & grn	52.50	160.00
a.		Narrow "5" in "45"	250.00	450.00
		Nos. 33-37 (5)	77.25	268.25

King Edward VII — A6

Numerals of 75c, 1.50r and 2.25r of type A6 are in color on plain tablet.

1903, May 26   Typo.   Wmk. 2

38	A6	2c red brn & grn	2.25	2.50
39	A6	3c green	1.25	1.60
40	A6	6c carmine rose	3.50	1.60
41	A6	12c ol gray & grn	3.50	3.25
42	A6	15c ultra	5.00	3.25
43	A6	18c pale yel grn & rose	5.25	8.25
44	A6	30c purple & grn	8.75	13.50
45	A6	45c brown & rose	8.75	13.50
46	A6	75c yel & pur	12.50	35.00
47	A6	1.50r black & rose	55.00	87.50
48	A6	2.25r red vio & grn	40.00	110.00
		Nos. 38-48 (11)	145.75	279.95

Nos. 42-43, 45 Surcharged

3 cents

1903

49	A6	3c on 15c	1.40	4.25
50	A6	3c on 18c	4.00	52.50
51	A6	3c on 45c	4.25	4.25
		Nos. 49-51 (3)	9.65	61.00

Type of 1903

1906   Wmk. 3

52	A6	2c red brn & grn	1.90	5.50
53	A6	3c green	1.90	1.90
54	A6	6c car rose	2.50	1.00
55	A6	12c ol gray & grn	4.00	4.00
56	A6	15c ultra	4.00	2.50
57	A6	18c pale yel grn & rose	4.00	8.00
58	A6	30c purple & grn	7.75	10.00
59	A6	45c brown & rose	4.00	8.00
60	A6	75c yellow & pur	11.00	67.50
61	A6	1.50r black & rose	65.00	72.50
62	A6	2.25r red vio & grn	47.50	72.50
		Nos. 52-62 (11)	153.55	253.40

King George V
A7   A8

Numerals of 75c, 1.50r and 2.25r of type A7 are in color on plain tablet.

1912   Perf. 14

63	A7	2c org brn & grn	1.00	5.75
64	A7	3c green	3.50	.70
65	A7	6c car rose	4.75	1.50
66	A7	12c ol gray & grn	1.40	4.50
67	A7	15c ultra	4.00	1.75
68	A7	18c pl yel grn & rose	3.50	6.75
69	A7	30c pur & grn	8.00	1.50
70	A7	45c brn & rose	3.00	42.50
71	A7	75c yell & pur	3.25	6.00
72	A7	1.50r blk & rose	8.50	1.10
73	A7	2.25r vio & grn	65.00	2.75
		Nos. 63-73 (11)	105.90	74.80

Die I

For description of dies I and II see Dies of British Colonial Stamps in the Table of Contents.
The 5c of type A8 has a colorless numeral on solid-color tablet. Numerals of 9c, 20c, 25c, 50c, 75c, and 1r to 5r of type A8 are in color on plain tablet.

1917-20

74	A8	2c org brn & grn	.55	3.00
75	A8	3c green	2.25	1.40
76	A8	5c brown ('20)	2.50	8.50
77	A8	6c carmine rose	3.00	1.60
78	A8	12c gray	1.75	1.10
79	A8	15c ultra	1.90	1.60
80	A8	18c violet & grn	4.00	35.00
a.		Die II ('20)	1.90	21.00
81	A8	25c blk & red, yel ('20)	2.00	42.50
a.		Die II ('20)	2.50	12.00
82	A8	30c dull vio & ol grn	1.60	10.00
83	A8	45c dull vio & org	3.50	40.00
84	A8	50c dull vio & blk ('20)	8.00	40.00
85	A8	75c blk, bl grn, ol back	1.75	21.00
a.		75c blk, emer (Die II) ('20)	1.50	21.00
86	A8	1r dl vio & red ('20)	15.00	60.00
87	A8	1.50r vio & bl, bl	10.00	57.50
a.		Die II ('20)	18.00	35.00
88	A8	2.25r gray grn & dp vio	55.00	150.00
89	A8	5r gray grn & ultra	120.00	260.00
		Nos. 74-89 (16)	232.80	733.20

Die II

1921-32   Wmk. 4

Ordinary Paper

91	A8	2c org brn & grn	.30	.25
92	A8	3c green	1.90	.25
93	A8	3c black ('22)	1.10	.35
94	A8	4c green	1.10	2.75
95	A8	4c ol grn & rose red ('28)	7.25	19.00
96	A8	5c dk brown	1.25	6.00
97	A8	6c car rose	3.00	10.00
98	A8	6c violet ('22)	1.25	.25

99	A8	9c rose red ('27)	3.50	4.75
100	A8	12c gray	3.00	.25
a.		Die I ('32)	20.00	.65
101	A8	12c carmine ('22)	1.50	.35
102	A8	15c ultra	2.25	65.00
103	A8	15c yellow ('22)	1.10	3.00
104	A8	18c violet, yel	2.75	14.00
105	A8	20c ultra ('22)	1.60	.40

Chalky Paper

106	A8	25c blk & red, yel ('22)	3.00	22.50
107	A8	30c dull vio & ol grn	1.60	17.00
108	A8	45c dull vio & org	1.40	5.75
109	A8	50c dull vio & blk	2.75	2.50
110	A8	75c blk, emerald	9.00	24.00
111	A8	1r dull vio & red	20.00	20.00
a.		Die I ('32)	12.00	37.50
112	A8	1.50r vio & bl, bl	14.00	25.00
113	A8	2.25r green & vio	16.50	16.00
114	A8	5r green & ultra	110.00	175.00
		Nos. 91-114 (24)	211.10	434.35

Common Design Types pictured following the introduction.

Silver Jubilee Issue
Common Design Type

1935, May 6   Engr.   Perf. 11x12

118	CD301	6c black & ultra	1.25	3.00
119	CD301	12c indigo & green	4.75	2.25
120	CD301	20c ultra & brown	3.50	3.75
121	CD301	1r brn vio & indigo	8.00	21.00
		Nos. 118-121 (4)	17.50	30.00
		Set, never hinged	30.00	

Coronation Issue
Common Design Type

1937, May 12   Perf. 11x11½

122	CD302	6c olive green	.30	.25
123	CD302	12c deep orange	.45	.55
124	CD302	20c deep ultra	.45	1.10
		Nos. 122-124 (3)	1.20	1.90
		Set, never hinged	2.00	

Coco-de-mer Palm — A9

Seychelles Giant Tortoise — A10

Fishing Canoe — A11

Ordinary or Chalky Paper

Perf. 13½x14½, 14½x13½

1938-41		Photo.		Wmk. 4
125	A9	2c violet brown	.40	1.75
126	A10	3c green	5.50	2.50
127	A10	3c orange	.50	1.50
128	A11	6c orange	8.50	3.75
129b	A11	6c green	.45	2.40
130	A9	9c rose red	9.50	3.25
131	A9	9c peacock blue ('45)	4.25	3.25
132	A10	12c violet	30.00	1.75
133	A10	15c copper red	4.00	4.25
134	A9	18c rose lake	4.75	3.00
135	A11	20c bright blue ('41)	25.00	6.50
136	A11	20c ocher	1.90	3.25
137	A9	25c ocher	30.00	15.00
138	A10	30c rose lake	30.00	10.00
139	A9	30c bright blue	1.90	5.50
140	A11	45c brown	2.25	2.50
141	A9	50c dull lilac ('49)	2.50	3.00
142	A10	75c gray blue	50.00	45.00
143	A10	75c dull violet	2.00	5.00
144	A11	1r yel grn	72.50	70.00
145	A11	1r gray	2.00	5.00
146	A9	1.50r violet	3.75	13.00
147	A10	2.25r olive bister	16.00	29.00
148	A11	5r copper red	13.00	11.00
		Nos. 125-148 (24)	320.65	251.15
		Set, never hinged	600.00	

Issued: #126, 128, 132, 135, 137, 1/1; #125, 130, 138, 140-142, 144, 146-148, 2/10; others, 8/8/41.

See Nos. 158-169, 174-188.

For detailed listings, see the Scott Classic Specialized catalogue.

> Catalogue values for unused stamps in this section, from this point to the end of the section, are for Never Hinged items.

Peace Issue
Common Design Type

Perf. 13½x14

1946, Sept. 23   Engr.   Wmk. 4

149	CD303	9c light blue	.25	.25
150	CD303	30c dark blue	.35	.25

Silver Wedding Issue
Common Design Types

1948, Nov. 11   Photo.   Perf. 14x14½

151	CD304	9c bright ultra	.25	.75

Engraved; Name Typographed
Perf. 11½x11

152	CD305	5r rose carmine	16.00	37.50

UPU Issue
Common Design Types

Perf. 13½, 11x11½

1949, Oct. 10				Engr.
153	CD306	18c red violet	.25	.25
154	CD307	50c dp rose violet	2.25	2.00
155	CD308	1r gray	.55	.35
156	CD309	2.25r olive	.55	1.25
		Nos. 153-156 (4)	3.60	3.85

Types of 1938-41 Redrawn and

Sailfish — A12

Map — A13

Perf. 14½x13½, 13½x14½

1952, Mar. 3		Photo.		Wmk. 4
157	A12	2c violet	.75	.75
158	A10	3c orange	.75	.30
159	A9	9c peacock blue	.70	1.75
160	A11	15c yellow green	.60	1.00
161	A13	18c rose lake	1.75	.25
162	A11	20c ocher	2.00	1.50
163	A10	25c bright red	.80	2.25
164	A12	40c ultra	1.25	2.00
165	A11	45c violet brown	1.50	.35
166	A9	50c brt violet	1.40	1.75
167	A13	1r gray	4.75	4.25
168	A9	1.50r brt blue	11.00	16.00
169	A10	2.25r olive bister	17.50	18.00
170	A13	5r copper red	18.00	19.00
171	A12	10r green	25.00	45.00
		Nos. 157-171 (15)	87.75	114.15

The redrawn design shows a new portrait of King George VI surrounded by crown, as on type A12.

Nos. 157-170 exist with watermark 4a (error). See the Scott Classic Specialized Catalogue of Stamps and Covers for listings.

Coronation Issue
Common Design Type

1953, June 2   Engr.   Perf. 13½x13

172	CD312	9c dark blue & blk	.80	.80

Types of 1938-52 with Portrait of Queen Elizabeth II
Perf. 14½x13½, 13½x14½

1954-56				Photo.
173	A12	2c violet	.25	.25
174	A10	3c orange	.25	.25
175	A9	9c peacock blue	.25	.25
176	A9	10c blue ('56)	.70	2.25
177	A11	15c yellow grn	2.50	.30
178	A13	18c rose lake	.25	.25
179	A11	20c ocher	1.50	.50
180	A10	25c bright red	2.50	1.25
181	A13	35c mag ('56)	6.50	1.75
182	A12	40c ultra	1.00	.25
183	A11	45c violet brn	.25	.25
184	A10	50c brt violet	.35	.80

185	A11	70c vio brn ('56)	7.50	2.25
186	A13	1r gray	1.75	.60
187	A9	1.50r brt blue	6.00	10.00
188	A10	2.25r olive bister	6.00	8.50
189	A13	5r copper red	18.00	10.00
190	A12	10r green	28.00	20.00
		Nos. 173-190 (18)	83.55	59.70

Issued: 10c, 35c, 70c, 9/15/56; others, 2/1/54.

For surcharge see No. 193.

"Stone of Possession" — A14

Perf. 14½x14

1956, Nov. 15				Wmk. 4
191	A14	40c ultra	.25	.25
192	A14	1r gray black	.35	.35

Bicentenary of French colonization.

No. 183 Surcharged "5 cents" and Bars

1957, Sept. 16   Perf. 13½x14½

193	A11	5c on 45c violet brn	.70	.70
a.		Double surcharge		325.00
b.		Thick bars omitted		650.00

The "c," "e" or "s" of surcharge may be found in italic.

Flying Fox — A15

1957, Oct. 25   Perf. 14½x13½

194	A15	5c light violet	2.75	.30

Mauritius Stamp of 1859 with Seychelles "B64" Cancellation A16

Engr. & Typo.
Perf. 11½x11

1961, Dec. 11				Wmk. 314
		Stamp in Dull Blue & Black		
195	A16	10c lilac	.30	.30
196	A16	35c dull green	.40	.40
197	A16	2.25r orange brown	1.50	1.50
		Nos. 195-197 (3)	2.20	2.20

1st post office in Victoria, Seychelles, cent.

Black Parrot — A17

Anse Royal Bay — A18

Designs: 10c, Vanilla. 15c, Fisherman. 20c, Denis Island Lighthouse. 25c, Clock Tower, Victoria. 30c, 35c, Anse Royal Bay. 40c, Government House. 45c, Fishing boat. 50c, Cascade Church. 60c, Flying fox. 70c, 85c, Sailfish. 75c, Coco-de-mer palm. 1r, Cinnamon. 1.50r, Copra. 2.25r, Map of Indian Ocean. 3.50r, Settlers' homes. 5r, Regina Mundi Convent. 10r, Badge of Seychelles.

Perf. 14½x13½, 13½x14½

1962-69		Photo.		Wmk. 314
		Size: 24x31mm, 31x24mm		
198	A17	5c multicolored	3.25	2.00
a.		Wmkd. sideways ('67)	.35	.25
199	A17	10c multicolore	1.50	.25
a.		Wmkd. sideways ('68)	.30	.25
200	A17	15c multicolored	.35	.25
201	A17	20c multicolored	.40	.25
202	A17	25c multicolored	.50	.25
202A	A18	30c multicolored	8.50	5.50
203	A18	35c multicolored	2.00	2.25
204	A18	40c multicolored	.25	1.00
204A	A17	45c multicolored	3.75	5.75
205	A17	50c multicolored	.45	.30
b.		Wmkd. sideways ('69)	1.75	3.75
205A	A17	60c multicolored	2.00	.50
206	A17	70c multicolored	6.50	3.25
206A	A17	75c multicolored	2.75	4.25
206B	A17	85c multicolored	1.25	.45
207	A18	1r multicolored	.40	.25
208	A18	1.50r multicolored	5.50	7.00
209	A18	2.25r multicolored	5.50	8.00
210	A18	3.50r multicolored	2.50	7.00
211	A18	5r multicolored	4.25	2.75

Perf. 13x14

Size: 22½x39mm

212	A17	10r multicolored	13.00	4.00
		Nos. 198-212 (20)	64.60	55.25

Issued: 45c, 75c, 8/1/66; #198a, 2/7/67; 30c, 60c, 85c, 7/15/68; others 2/21/62.

The 60c and 85c have watermark sideways.

For surcharges and overprints see Nos. 216-217, 233-236, 241-243.

For overprints see British Indian Ocean Territory Nos. 1-15.

Freedom from Hunger Issue
Common Design Type

1963, June 4   Perf. 14x14½

213	CD314	70c lilac	.90	.40

Red Cross Centenary Issue
Common Design Type

1963, Sept. 2   Litho.   Perf. 13

214	CD315	10c black & red	.25	.25
215	CD315	75c ultra & red	.85	.65

Nos. 203 and 206 Surcharged with New Value and Bars

Perf. 14x14½, 14½x14

1965, Apr.		Photo.		Wmk. 314
216	A18	45c on 35c	.25	.25
217	A17	75c on 70c	.70	.70

ITU Issue
Common Design Type

Perf. 11x11½

1965, June 1				Wmk. 314
218	CD317	5c orange & vio bl	.25	.25
219	CD317	1.50r red lil & apple grn	.70	.35

Intl. Cooperation Year Issue
Common Design Type

1965, Oct. 25   Perf. 14½

220	CD318	5c blue grn & claret	.25	.25
221	CD318	40c lt violet & green	.70	.40

Churchill Memorial Issue
Common Design Type

1966, Jan. 24   Photo.   Perf. 14
Design in Black, Gold and Carmine Rose

222	CD319	5c bright blue	.30	.30
223	CD319	15c green	.40	.30
224	CD319	75c brown	1.25	.35
225	CD319	1.50r violet	2.00	1.10
		Nos. 222-225 (4)	3.95	2.05

World Cup Soccer Issue
Common Design Type

1966, July 1   Litho.   Perf. 14

226	CD321	15c multicolored	.25	.25
227	CD321	1r multicolored	.70	.70

WHO Headquarters Issue
Common Design Type

1966, Sept. 20   Litho.   Perf. 14

228	CD322	20c multicolored	.45	.30
229	CD322	50c multicolored	.80	.45

UNESCO Anniversary Issue
Common Design Type

1966, Dec. 1   Litho.   Perf. 14

230	CD323	15c "Education"	.25	.25
231	CD323	1r "Science"	.60	.60
232	CD323	5r "Culture"	1.75	1.75
		Nos. 230-232 (3)	2.60	2.60

Nos. 200, 204A, 206A and 210
Overprinted: "UNIVERSAL / ADULT / SUFFRAGE / 1967"

Perf. 14½x14, 14x14½

1967, Sept. 18   **Photo.**   **Wmk. 314**

233	A17	15c multicolored	.25	.25
234	A18	45c brt blue & yel	.25	.25
235	A17	75c multicolored	.25	.25
236	A18	3.50r multicolored	.40	.50
		Nos. 233-236 (4)	1.15	1.25

Cowries: Tiger, Mole, Money — A19

Sea Shells (ITY Emblem and): 40c, Textile, betulinus and virgin cones. 1r, Arthritic spider conch. 2.25r, Triton and subulate auger.

Perf. 14x13½

1967, Dec. 4   **Photo.**   **Wmk. 314**

237	A19	15c multicolored	.30	.25
238	A19	40c multicolored	.45	.25
239	A19	1r multicolored	.65	.40
240	A19	2.25r multicolored	1.10	1.10
		Nos. 237-240 (4)	2.50	2.00

Issued for International Tourist Year, 1967.

Nos. 204, 204A and 206A Surcharged

Perf. 14x14½, 14½x14

1968, Apr. 16   **Photo.**   **Wmk. 314**

241	A18	30c on 40c multicolored	.30	.25
242	A18	60c on 45c blue & yel	.30	.25
243	A17	85c on 75c multicolored	.35	.35
		Nos. 241-243 (3)	.95	.85

The surcharge on No. 241 includes 2 bars; on Nos. 242-243 it includes 3 bars and "CENTS."

Family, Rising Sun and Human Rights Flame — A20

1968, Sept. 2   **Litho.**   **Wmk. 314**

244	A20	20c chocolate & multi	.25	.25
245	A20	50c vio blue & multi	.25	.25
246	A20	85c black & multi	.25	.25
247	A20	2.25r brown & multi	.25	.75
		Nos. 244-247 (4)	1.00	1.50

International Human Rights Year.

First Landing on Praslin Island — A21

Designs: 50c, La Digue and La Curieuse at anchor, vert. 85c, Coco-de-mer and black parrot, vert. 2.25r, La Digue and La Curieuse under sail.

Litho.; Head Embossed in Gold

Perf. 14x14½

1968, Dec. 30   **Wmk. 314**

248	A21	20c multicolored	.25	.25
249	A21	50c dk blue, blk & red	.35	.35
250	A21	85c rose red & multi	.85	.65
251	A21	2.25r ultra & multi	1.25	2.25
		Nos. 248-251 (4)	2.50	3.50

Landing on Praslin Island of the Chevalier Marion Dufresne expedition, 200th anniv.

Separation of Rocket and Spacecraft — A22

5c, Launching of Apollo XI, vert. 50c, Landing module & men on the moon. 85c, Seychelles tracking station. 2.25r, Moonscape & earth.

1969, Sept. 9   **Litho.**   *Perf. 13½*

252	A22	5c multicolored	.25	.25
253	A22	20c multicolored	.25	.25
254	A22	50c multicolored	.35	.25
255	A22	85c multicolored	.50	.50
256	A22	2.25r multicolored	.80	1.40
		Nos. 252-256 (5)	2.15	2.65

See note after US No. C76.

Lazare Picault Landing in 1741 — A23

History of Seychelles: 10c, US satellite tracking station. 15c, German cruiser Königsberg at Aldabra, 1915. 20c, British fleet refueling, St. Anne, 1939-45. 25c, Ashanti King Prempeh in exile, 1896. 30c, 40c, Stone of Possession placed, 1756. 50c, 65c, Pirates. 60c, Corsairs. 85c, 95c, Jet and airport. 1r, First capitulation of the French to the British, 1794. 1.50r, Battle between the sailing vessels Sybille and Chiffone, 1801. 3.50r, Visit of Duke of Edinburgh, 1956. 5r, Chevalier Queau de Quincy. 10r, Map of Indian Ocean, 1574. 15r, Seychelles coat of arms.

Perf. 13x12½

1969-72   **Litho.**   **Wmk. 314**

257	A23	5c multicolored	.25	.25
258	A23	10c multicolored	.25	.25
259	A23	15c multicolored	3.00	2.25
260	A23	20c multicolored	2.00	.25
261	A23	25c multicolored	.25	.25
262	A23	30c multicolored	1.25	4.00
262A	A23	40c multicolored	3.00	1.25
263	A23	50c multicolored	.40	.25
264	A23	60c multicolored	1.25	1.50
264A	A23	65c multicolored	6.00	8.00
265	A23	85c multicolored	3.50	2.00
265A	A23	95c multicolored	5.50	3.25
266	A23	1r multicolored	.40	.25
267	A23	1.50r multicolored	2.00	2.25
268	A23	3.50r multicolored	1.25	2.25
269	A23	5r multicolored	1.25	3.00
270	A23	10r multicolored	2.75	8.00
271	A23	15r multicolored	4.50	14.00
		Nos. 257-271 (18)	38.80	53.25

Issued: 40, 65, 95c, 12/11/72; others, 11/3/69.

For overprints & surcharges see Nos. 294-298, 323-330, 361-369.

St. Anne Island, Ship and Gulls — A24

Designs: 50c, Flying fish, island and ship. 85c, Map of Seychelles and compass rose. 3.50r, Anchor, chain on sea bottom.

1970, Apr. 27   *Perf. 14*

272	A24	20c multicolored	1.00	.80
273	A24	50c multicolored	.65	.55
274	A24	85c multicolored	.65	.55
275	A24	3.50r multicolored	.90	.90
		Nos. 272-275 (4)	3.20	2.80

Bicentenary of first settlement on St. Anne.

Girl and Eye Chart — A25

Designs: 50c, Infant on scales and milk bottles. 85c, Mother and child, vert. 3.50r, Red Cross branch headquarters.

1970, Aug. 4   **Litho.**   **Wmk. 314**

276	A25	20c lt blue & multi	.40	.25
277	A25	50c multicolored	.60	.50
278	A25	85c multicolored	.80	.80
279	A25	3.50r multicolored	2.00	2.00
		Nos. 276-279 (4)	3.80	3.55

Centenary of British Red Cross Society.

Pitcher Plant — A26

Flowers: 50c, Wild vanilla. 85c, Tropic-bird flower. 3.50r, Vare hibiscus.

1970, Dec. 29   *Perf. 14½*

280	A26	20c multicolored	.35	.25
281	A26	50c multicolored	.45	.45
282	A26	85c multicolored	1.00	1.00
283	A26	3.50r multicolored	3.50	2.25
a.		Souvenir sheet of 4, #280-283	8.00	12.00
		Nos. 280-283 (4)	5.30	3.95

Souvenir Sheet

Map Showing Location of Seychelles — A27

Perf. 13½x14

1971, Apr. 20   **Litho.**   **Wmk. 314**

| 284 | A27 | 5r yellow grn & multi | 4.00 | 9.50 |

Issued to publicize Seychelles' location.

Consolidated Catalina Amphibian — A28

Designs: 5c, Piper Navajo, vert. 20c, Westland Wessex, vert. 60c, Grumman Albatross amphibian, vert. 85c, "G" class Short Brothers flying boat. 3.50r, Vickers supermarine "Walrus" amphibian.

Perf. 14x14½, 14½x14

1971, June 28   **Litho.**   **Wmk. 314**

285	A28	5c orange & multi	.25	.25
286	A28	20c purple & multi	.25	.25
287	A28	50c olive & multi	.65	.25
288	A28	60c sepia & multi	.80	.30
289	A28	85c brown & multi	1.10	.40
290	A28	3.50r blue & multi	8.00	2.25
		Nos. 285-290 (6)	11.05	3.70

Completion of Seychelles Airport.

Santa Claus, by Jean-Claude Waye Hive — A29

Christmas (Children's Drawings): 15c, Santa Claus riding a tortoise, by Edison Thérésine. 3.50r, Santa Claus on the seashore, by Isabelle Tirant.

1971, Oct. 12   *Perf. 13½*

291	A29	10c dark blue & multi	.25	.25
292	A29	15c dark green & multi	.25	.25
293	A29	3.50r violet & multi	.60	.85
		Nos. 291-293 (3)	1.10	1.35

Nos. 262, 264-265 Surcharged with New Value and 5 Bars

1971, Dec. 21   *Perf. 13x12½*

294	A23	40c on 30c multicolored	.55	.85
295	A23	65c on 60c multicolored	.65	1.00
296	A23	95c on 85c multicolored	.80	1.40
		Nos. 294-296 (3)	2.00	3.25

Nos. 260, 269 Overprinted in Black or Gold: "ROYAL VISIT 1972"

1972, Mar. 21   **Litho.**   **Wmk. 314**

| 297 | A23 | 20c multicolored | .25 | .25 |
| 298 | A23 | 5r multicolored (G) | 1.60 | 2.25 |

Visit of Elizabeth II and Prince Philip.

Brush Warbler — A30

1972, July 15   *Perf. 14x13½*

299	A30	5c shown	1.00	.50
300	A30	20c Scops owl	2.50	.50
301	A30	50c Blue pigeons	2.75	.60
302	A30	65c Magpie robin	3.00	.65
303	A30	95c Paradise flycatchers	3.00	2.75
304	A30	3.50r Kestrel	8.00	12.00
a.		Souvenir sheet of 6, #299-304	35.00	40.00
		Nos. 299-304 (6)	20.25	17.00

Fireworks — A31

1972, Sept. 18   **Litho.**   *Perf. 14*

305	A31	10c shown	.25	.25
306	A31	20c Canoe race, horiz.	.25	.25
307	A31	25c Women in local costumes	.25	.25
308	A31	5r Water-skiing, horiz.	.70	.70
		Nos. 305-308 (4)	1.45	1.45

Seychelles Festival 1972.

Silver Wedding Issue, 1972
Common Design Type

Design: Queen Elizabeth II, Prince Philip, giant tortoise and leaping sailfish.

1972, Nov. 20   **Photo.**   *Perf. 14x14½*

| 309 | CD324 | 95c multicolored | .25 | .25 |
| 310 | CD324 | 1.50r multicolored | .70 | .70 |

Princess Anne's Wedding Issue
Common Design Type

1973, Nov. 14   **Litho.**   *Perf. 14*

| 311 | CD325 | 95c ocher & multi | .30 | .30 |
| 312 | CD325 | 1.50r slate & multi | .50 | .50 |

Soldierfish — A32

Wmk. 314

1974, Mar. 5   **Litho.**   *Perf. 14*

313	A32	20c shown	.30	.25
314	A32	50c Filefish	.55	.25
315	A32	95c Butterflyfish	1.10	.70
316	A32	1.50r Gaterin	2.75	2.75
		Nos. 313-316 (4)	4.70	3.95

Envelope and Globe — A33

UPU, cent.: 50c, Globe with location of Seychelles and radio tower. 95c, Cancellation and globe. 1.50r, "UPU" with emblems.

Perf. 12½x12

1974, Oct. 9			**Wmk. 314**	
317	A33	20c multicolored	.25	.25
318	A33	50c multicolored	.25	.25
319	A33	95c multicolored	.40	.40
320	A33	1.50r multicolored	.65	.65
		Nos. 317-320 (4)	1.55	1.55

Winston Churchill A34

Design: 1.50r, Churchill, different portrait.

1974, Nov. 30		**Litho.**	**Perf. 14½**	
321	A34	95c lt blue & multi	.25	.25
322	A34	1.50r lt green & multi	.60	.60
a.		Souvenir sheet of 2, #321-322	.90	1.50

Sir Winston Churchill (1874-1965).

Nos. 260, 263, 265A and 267 Overprinted in Black or Silver

Perf. 13x12½

1975, Feb. 8			**Wmk. 314**	
323	A23	20c multi (B)	.30	.25
324	A23	50c multi (B)	.30	.25
325	A23	95c multi (S)	.40	.40
326	A23	1.50r multi (B)	.55	.95
		Nos. 323-326 (4)	1.55	1.85

Visit of cruise ship Queen Elizabeth II, Mahe, Seychelles.

Nos. 260, 264A, 266, 268 Overprinted in Gold

1975, Oct. 1		**Litho.**	**Wmk. 314**	
327	A23	20c multicolored	.25	.25
328	A23	65c multicolored	.35	.35
329	A23	1r multicolored	.65	.55
330	A23	3.50r multicolored	1.75	1.25
		Nos. 327-330 (4)	3.00	2.40

Queen Elizabeth I A35

Portraits: 15c, Gladys Aylward. 20c, Elizabeth Fry. 25c, Emmeline Pankhurst. 65c, Florence Nightingale. 1r, Amy Johnson. 1.50r, Joan of Arc. 3.50r, Eleanor Roosevelt.

Wmk. 314				
1975, Dec. 15		**Litho.**	**Perf. 13½**	
331	A35	10c dp brown & multi	.25	.25
332	A35	15c dk brown & multi	.25	.25
333	A35	20c dk green & multi	.25	.25
334	A35	25c purple & multi	.25	.25
335	A35	65c dk blue & multi	.50	.40

336	A35	1r Prus blue & multi	.75	.65
337	A35	1.50r dp violet & multi	1.00	1.25
338	A35	3.50r dk olive & multi	2.00	2.50
		Nos. 331-338 (8)	5.25	5.80

International Women's Year.

Praslin Map and Grand Anse Postmark, 1907 — A36

Designs: 65c, La Digue map and postmark, 1916. 1r, Partial map of Mahé and Victoria postmark, 1917. 1.50r, Southern part of Mahé and Anse Royale postmark, 1938.

1976, Mar. 30		**Wmk. 373**	**Perf. 14**	
339	A36	20c lt blue & multi	.25	.25
340	A36	65c lt blue & multi	.40	.40
341	A36	1r lt blue & multi	.55	.55
342	A36	1.50r lt blue & multi	.75	.75
a.		Souvenir sheet of 4, #339-342	3.00	3.50
		Nos. 339-342 (4)	1.95	1.95

Rural posts of Seychelles.

First Landing, 1609, and James Mancham — A37

Designs: 25c, Stone of Possession. 40c, Arrival of 1st settlers, 1770 (ship). 75c, Le Chevalier Quéau de Quincy. 1r, Sir Bickham Sweet-Escott. 1.25r, Government House. 1.50r, Coat of arms of Internal Self-government. 3.50r, Seychelles flag.

1976, June 29			**Perf. 14**	
343	A37	20c rose & multi	.25	.25
344	A37	25c yellow & multi	.25	.25
345	A37	40c lilac & multi	.25	.25
346	A37	75c green & multi	.45	.45
347	A37	1r salmon & multi	.70	.70
348	A37	1.25r multicolored	.80	.80
349	A37	1.50r ocher & multi	1.00	1.00
350	A37	3.50r blue & multi	2.25	2.25
		Nos. 343-350 (8)	5.95	5.95

Seychelles' independence, June 29, 1976.

Flags of Seychelles and US — A38

US bicent.: 10r, State House, Seychelles, and Independence Hall, Philadelphia.

1976, July 12		**Litho.**		
351	A38	1r blue & multi	.30	.30
352	A38	10r red & multi	2.00	2.75

Swimming — A39

Designs (Olympic Rings and): 65c, Hockey. 1r, Basketball. 3.50r, Soccer.

1976, July 26			**Perf. 14½**	
353	A39	20c vio blue & blk	.30	.25
354	A39	65c dk grn, yel grn & blk	.55	.25

355	A39	1r brown, grn & blk	.55	.25
356	A39	3.50r car rose & blk	.85	1.75
		Nos. 353-356 (4)	2.25	2.50

21st Olympic Games, Montreal, Canada, July 17-Aug. 1.

Seychelles Sunbird — A40

Seychelles Birds (James R. Mancham, Congress Emblem and): 20c, Paradise flycatcher, vert. 1.50r, Gray white-eye. 5r, Black parrot, vert.

		Wmk. 373		
1976, Nov. 8		**Litho.**	**Perf. 14½**	
357	A40	20c multicolored	.25	.25
358	A40	1.25r multicolored	1.25	.80
359	A40	1.50r multicolored	1.60	1.10
360	A40	5r multicolored	2.75	3.75
a.		Souvenir sheet of 4, #357-360	8.00	10.50
		Nos. 357-360 (4)	5.85	5.90

4th Pan-African Ornithological Cong., Mahe Beach Hotel, Nov. 6-13.

Nos. 260, 263, 265A-266, 268-271, 264A Overprinted or Surcharged: "Independence / 1976"

Perf. 13x12½

1976, Nov. 22		**Litho.**	**Wmk. 314**	
361	A23	20c multicolored	1.00	1.90
362	A23	50c multicolored	.90	2.25
363	A23	95c multicolored	2.50	2.25
364	A23	1r multicolored	.90	2.25
365	A23	3.50r multicolored	4.00	4.75
366	A23	5r multicolored	3.50	6.50
367	A23	10r multicolored	4.75	12.50
368	A23	15r multicolored	5.25	12.50
369	A23	25r on 65c multi	6.50	19.00
		Nos. 361-369 (9)	29.30	63.90

Washington's Inauguration — A41

American Bicentennial: 2c, Jefferson and map of Louisiana Purchase. 3c, Seward and map of Alaska Purchase. 4c, Pony Express, 1860. 5c, Lincoln's Emancipation Proclamation, 1863. 1.50r, Completion of Transcontinental Railroad, 1869. 3.50r, Wright Brothers' 1st flight, 1903. 5r, Ford assembly line, 1913. 10r, Kennedy and Apollo 11 moon landing, 1969. 25r, Declaration of Independence, 1776.

		Perf. 14x13½		
1976, Dec. 21			**Wmk. 373**	
370	A41	1c rose & plum	.25	.25
371	A41	2c lilac & vio	.25	.25
372	A41	3c blue & vio bl	.25	.25
373	A41	4c yellow & brn	.25	.25
374	A41	5c brt yel & grn	.25	.25
375	A41	1.50r yel brn & brn	.50	.50
376	A41	3.50r brt grn & bl grn	.75	.75
377	A41	5r yellow & brn	1.00	1.00
378	A41	10r dull bl & dk bl	1.75	1.75
		Nos. 370-378 (9)	5.25	5.25

Souvenir Sheet

379	A41	25r lilac rose & pur	5.50	5.50

Seychelles Islands and Arms — A42

The Orb — A43

Designs: 40c, 5r, 10r, similar to 20c. 1r, St. Edward's Crown. 1.25r, Ampulla and Spoon. 1.50r, Scepter with Cross.

1977, Sept. 5		**Litho.**	**Perf. 14**	
380	A42	20c multicolored	.25	.25
381	A42	40c multicolored	.25	.25
382	A43	50c multicolored	.25	.25
383	A43	1r multicolored	.25	.25
384	A42	1.25r multicolored	.25	.25
385	A43	1.50r multicolored	.25	.25
386	A42	5r multicolored	.45	.45
387	A42	10r multicolored	.80	.80
a.		Souv. sheet of 4, #380, 382, 383, 387	2.00	2.25
		Nos. 380-387 (8)	2.75	2.75

25th anniv. of reign of Elizabeth II.

Coral Reef — A44

Perf. 14, 14x14½ (40c, 1, 1.25, 1.50r)

1977-91		**Litho.**	**Wmk. 373**	

Sizes: 40c, 1, 1.25, 1.50r, 30x25mm, Others 28x23mm

Without Date Imprint

388	A44	5c Reef fish	.25	1.00
389	A44	10c Hawksbill turtle	.25	.25
a.		Inscribed "1979"	.30	.25
c.		Inscribed "1982"	.30	.25
d.		Inscribed "1988"	.35	.35
390	A44	15c Coco de mer	.25	1.00
a.		Inscribed "1979"	.30	.25
391	A44	20c Wild vanilla	1.20	.25
c.		Inscribed "1982"	4.00	3.25
392	A44	25c Butterfly	1.20	.50
a.		Inscribed "1979"	3.25	3.25
b.		Inscribed "1988"	1.50	1.50
393	A44	40c Coral reef	.25	.25
a.		Inscribed "1979"	.30	.25
b.		Inscribed "1981"	.30	.25
c.		Inscribed "1982"	.30	.25
394	A44	50c Giant tortoise	.25	.25
a.		Inscribed "1979"	.60	.25
d.		Inscribed "1988"	.60	.25
e.		Inscribed "1991"	.60	.25
f.		Wmk. 384, perf. 14x14½, inscr. "1991"	.30	.30
395	A44	75c Crayfish	.25	.25
a.		Inscribed "1979"	.75	.15
396	A44	1r Madagascar cardinal	.35	.30
a.		Inscribed "1979"	12.00	1.10
d.		Inscribed "1988"	1.50	1.10
e.		Inscribed "1991"	1.50	1.10
397	A44	1.25r Fairy tern	1.00	.40
398	A44	1.50r Flying fox	1.00	.45
a.		Inscribed "1979"	3.00	.75
398A	A44	3r like #399, wmk. 384	2.00	1.75
399	A44	3.50r Green gecko	1.25	2.50

Perf. 13

Size: 27x35mm

400	A44	5r Octopus, vert.	1.90	1.60
401	A44	10r Tiger cowrie, vert.	3.75	3.25
402	A44	15r Pitcher plant, vert.	5.25	3.25
403	A44	20r Arms, vert.	5.75	3.25
		Nos. 388-403 (17)	26.15	20.50

Issued: 40c, 1r, 1.25r, 1.50r, 10/31/77; #394a, 398A, 11/1991; others, 1978. For surcharge and overprint see #446, 605.

Denomination "R" Instead of "Re." or "Rs."

Perf. 14x14½, 14 (1.10r)

1981, Jan. 6			**Litho.**	

Sizes: 1.10r, 28x23mm, Others, 30x25mm

"1980" Imprint Beneath Design

403A	A44	1r like No. 396	.45	.45
b.		Inscribed "1982"	.45	.45
d.		Inscribed "1986"	.45	.45
e.		Inscribed "1988"	.45	.45
f.		Inscribed "1990"	.45	.45
403B	A44	1.10r like No. 399	.85	.85
a.		Inscribed "1981"	1.75	1.50

403C	A44	1.25r like No. 397	.65	.65
i.		Wmk. 384 ('89)	.70	.70
403D	A44	1.50r like No. 398	.70	.70
b.		Inscribed "1982"	.75	1.10
g.		Inscribed "1991"	.75	1.10

Perf. 13

403E	A44	5r like No. 400	2.50	2.50
c.		Inscribed "1985"	2.00	2.00
j.		Perf. 14x14½, Wmk 384 ('90)	3.25	3.25
403F	A44	10r like No. 401	5.25	5.25
403G	A44	15r like No. 402	7.50	7.50
403H	A44	20r like No. 403	10.50	10.50
		Nos. 403A-403H (8)	28.40	28.40

See No. 576 for No. 403C with commemorative inscription.

Cruiser Aurora, Star and Flag — A45

1977, Nov. 7   Unwmk.   Perf. 12

404	A45	1.50r red, black & gold	.80	.65
a.		Souvenir sheet	2.00	2.00

60th anniv. of Russian Oct. Revolution.

St. Roch Roman Catholic Church, Bel Ombre — A46

Christmas: 1r, Anglican Cathedral, Victoria. 1.50r, R. C. Cathedral, Victoria. 5r, St. Mark's Anglican Church, Praslin.

Perf. 13½x14

1977, Dec. 5   Wmk. 373

405	A46	20c multicolored	.25	.25
406	A46	1r multicolored	.25	.25
407	A46	1.50r multicolored	.25	.25
408	A46	5r multicolored	.40	.40
		Nos. 405-408 (4)	1.15	1.15

Calendar Page, June 5, 1977 — A47

1.25r, Hands holding rifle, torch & Seychelles flag. 1.50r, Fisherman & farmer holding hands. 5r, Soldiers & waving children.

Perf. 14x13½

1978, June 5   Litho.   Wmk. 373

409	A47	40c multicolored	.25	.25
410	A47	1.25r multicolored	.25	.25
411	A47	1.50r multicolored	.25	.25
412	A47	5r multicolored	.50	.50
		Nos. 409-412 (4)	1.25	1.25

First anniversary of Liberation Day.

Edward VII, George V, George VI — A48

Designs: 1.50r, Queens Victoria and Elizabeth II. 3r, Queen Victoria Monument, Seychelles. 5r, Queen's Building, Victoria, Seychelles.

1978, Aug. 21   Litho.   Perf. 14

413	A48	40c multicolored	.25	.25
414	A48	1.50r multicolored	.25	.25
415	A48	3r multicolored	.25	.25
416	A48	5r multicolored	.35	.35
a.		Souvenir sheet of 4, #413-416	1.40	1.40
		Nos. 413-416 (4)	1.10	1.10

25th anniv. of coronation of Elizabeth II.

Gardenia from Aride Island — A49

Designs (Coat of Arms and): 1.25r, Magpie robin of Fregate Island. 1.50r, Seychelles paradise flycatchers. 5r, Green turtle.

Perf. 13½x14

1978, Oct. 16   Litho.   Wmk. 373

417	A49	40c multicolored	.25	.25
418	A49	1.25r multicolored	2.25	.75
419	A49	1.50r multicolored	2.25	.75
420	A49	5r multicolored	2.25	1.90
		Nos. 417-420 (4)	7.00	3.65

"Stone of Possession" — A50

1978, Dec. 15   Litho.   Perf. 13½

421	A50	20c shown	.25	.25
422	A50	1.25r Map, 1782	.25	.25
423	A50	1.50r Clock tower	.25	.25
424	A50	5r Pierre Poivre	.40	.40
		Nos. 421-424 (4)	1.15	1.15

Bicentennary of the founding of Victoria.

Seychelles Fody — A51   Patrice Lumumba — A52

Birds: No. 426, Green-backed heron. No. 427, Seychelles bulbul. No. 428, Seychelles cave swiftlets. No. 429, Grayheaded lovebirds.

1979, Feb. 27   Litho.   Perf. 14

425	A51	2r multicolored	.90	.90
426	A51	2r multicolored	.90	.90
427	A51	2r multicolored	.90	.90
428	A51	2r multicolored	.90	.90
429	A51	2r multicolored	.90	.90
a.		Strip of 5, #425-429	4.75	4.75
		Nos. 425-429 (5)	4.50	4.50

1979, June 5   Litho.   Perf. 14½

African Liberation Heroes: 2r, Kwame Nkrumah. 2.25r, Dr. Eduardo Mondlane. 5r, Amilcar Cabral.

430	A52	40c violet & blk	.25	.25
431	A52	2r dark blue & blk	.25	.25
432	A52	2.25r orange brn & blk	.25	.25
433	A52	5r olive grn & blk	.45	.45
		Nos. 430-433 (4)	1.20	1.20

Coat of Arms, Rowland Hill, Seychelles No. 412 — A53

Coat of Arms, Hill, Seychelles stamps: 2.25r, No. 301. 3r, No. 205. 5r, No. 4.

1979, Aug. 27   Litho.   Perf. 14x14½

434	A53	40c multicolored	.25	.25
435	A53	2.25r multicolored	.35	.35
436	A53	3r multicolored	.45	.45
		Nos. 434-436 (3)	1.05	1.05

Souvenir Sheet

437	A53	5r multicolored	.90	.90

Sir Rowland Hill (1795-1879), originator of penny postage.

Schoolboy, IYC Emblem — A54

IYC Emblem and: 2.25r, Children. 3r, Boy with ball, vert. 5r, Girl with puppet, vert.

Perf. 14½x14, 14x14½

1979, Oct. 25   Litho.

438	A54	40c multicolored	.25	.25
439	A54	2.25r multicolored	.25	.25
440	A54	3r multicolored	.25	.25
441	A54	5r multicolored	.35	.35
		Nos. 438-441 (4)	1.10	1.10

International Year of the Child.

Three Kings Bearing Gifts A55

Christmas (Stained Glass Windows): 20c, Angel, vert. 2.25r, Virgin and Child, vert. 5r, Flight into Egypt.

1979, Dec. 3   Litho.   Perf. 14½

442	A55	20c multicolored	.25	.25
443	A55	2.25r multicolored	.35	.35
444	A55	3r multicolored	.45	.45
		Nos. 442-444 (3)	1.05	1.05

Souvenir Sheet

445	A55	5r multicolored	.85	.85

No. 399 Surcharged

Wmk. 373

1979, Dec. 7   Litho.   Perf. 14

446	A44	1.10r on 3.50r multicolored	.50	.50

Seychelles Kestrel — A56

Seychelles Kestrel: a, shown. b, Pair. c, Female, eggs. d, Mother and chick. e, Chicks nesting.

1980, Feb. 29   Litho.   Perf. 14

447		Strip of 5	6.50	6.50
a.-e.		A56 2r any single	1.25	1.25

See Nos. 468, 483.

50-Rupee Bank Note, London 1980 Emblem — A57

New Currency: 40c, 1.50r, horiz.

1980, Apr. 18   Litho.   Perf. 14

448	A57	40c multicolored	.25	.25
449	A57	1.50r multicolored	.40	.40
450	A57	2.25r multicolored	.50	.50
451	A57	5r multicolored	.85	.85
a.		Souvenir sheet of 4, #448-451	2.25	2.25
		Nos. 448-451 (4)	2.00	2.00

London 1980 Intl. Stamp Exhib., May 6-14.

Sprinting, Moscow '80 Emblem — A58

1980, June 13   Perf. 14½

452	A58	40c shown	.25	.25
453	A58	2.25r Weight lifting	.25	.25
454	A58	3r Boxing	.40	.40
455	A58	5r Yachting	.95	.95
a.		Souvenir sheet of 4, #452-455	2.75	2.75
		Nos. 452-455 (4)	1.85	1.85

22nd Summer Olympic Games, Moscow, July 19-Aug. 3.

Boeing 747 A59

1980, Aug. 22   Litho.   Perf. 14

456	A59	40c shown	.25	.25
457	A59	2.25r Tour bus	.35	.35
458	A59	3r Ocean liner, pirogue	.55	.55
459	A59	5r Tour motor boat	.95	.95
		Nos. 456-459 (4)	2.10	2.10

World Tourism Conf., Manila, Sept. 27.

Female Coco-de-Mer Palm Tree — A60

1980, Oct. 31   Litho.   Perf. 14

460	A60	40c shown	.25	.25
461	A60	2.25r Male tree	.40	.40
462	A60	3r Bowls	.55	.55
463	A60	5r Gourds, canoes	.85	.85
a.		Souvenir sheet of 4, #460-463	3.50	3.50
		Nos. 460-463 (4)	2.05	2.05

Vasco da Gama's San Gabriel, 1497
A61

Wmk. 373
1981, Feb. **Litho.** *Perf. 14½*
464 A61 40c shown .25 .25
465 A61 2.25r Mascarenhas' Caravel, 1505 .55 .55
466 A61 3.50r Darwin's Beagle, 1831 .75 .75
467 A61 5r Queen Elizabeth 2, 1968 .95 .95
 a. Souvenir sheet of 4, #464-467 3.75 3.75
 Nos. 464-467 (4) 2.50 2.50

Bird Type of 1980
1981, Apr. 10 **Litho.** *Perf. 14*
468 Strip of 5, multi 7.25 7.25
 a. A56 2r Male fairy tern 1.40 1.40
 c. A56 2r Female 1.40 1.40
 d. A56 2r Female, diff. 1.40 1.40
 e. A56 2r Adult bird, chick 1.40 1.40

Prince Charles, Lady Diana, Royal Yacht Charlotte A61a

Prince Charles and Lady Diana — A61b

Wmk. 380
1981, June 23 **Litho.** *Perf. 14*
469 A61a 1.50r Couple, Victoria & Albert I .25 .25
 a. Bklt. pane of 4, perf. 12 1.10
470 A61a 1.50r Couple .50 .50
471 A61a 5r Cleveland .60 .60
472 A61b 5r like #470 1.75 1.75
 a. Bklt. pane of 2, perf. 12 2.00
473 A61a 10r Britannia 1.50 1.50
474 A61b 10r like #470 3.50 3.50
 Nos. 469-474 (6) 8.10 8.10

Each denomination issued in sheets of 7 (6 type A61a, 1 type A61b).
For surcharges see Nos. 528-533.

Souvenir Sheet
1981 **Litho.** *Perf. 12*
474A A61b 7.50r Couple 2.50 2.50

Seychelles Intl. Airport, 10th Anniv. — A62

Wmk. 373
1981, July 27 **Litho.** *Perf. 14½*
475 A62 40c Britten-Norman Islander .25 .25
476 A62 2.25r Britten-Norman Trislander .70 .70
477 A62 3.50r Vickers VC-10 1.00 1.00
478 A62 5r Boeing 747 1.40 1.40
 Nos. 475-478 (4) 3.35 3.35

A63   A65

Designs: Various flying foxes.

1981, Oct. 9 **Litho.** *Perf. 14*
479 A63 40c multicolored .25 .25
480 A63 2.25r multicolored .40 .40
481 A63 3r multicolored .60 .60
482 A63 5r multicolored 1.10 1.10
 a. Souvenir sheet, #479-482 4.25 4.25
 Nos. 479-482 (4) 2.35 2.35

Bird Type of 1980
a, Male Chinese bittern. b, Female. c, Hen on nest. d, Nest, eggs. e, Hen, chicks.

1982, Feb. 4 **Litho.** *Perf. 14*
483 Strip of 5 17.50 17.50
 a.-e. A56 3r any single 3.25 3.25

1982, Apr. 22 **Litho.** *Perf. 14½*
487 A65 40c Map of Silhouette Island and La Digue .25 .25
488 A65 1.50r Denis & Bird Islds. .40 .40
489 A65 2.75r Curieuse Isld., Praslin .70 .70
490 A65 7r Mahe 1.75 1.75
 a. Souvenir sheet of 4, #487-490 4.50 4.50
 Nos. 487-490 (4) 3.10 3.10

5th Anniv. of Liberation A66

1982, June 5 *Perf. 14*
491 A66 40c Bookmobile .25 .25
492 A66 1.75r Mobile dental clinic .30 .30
493 A66 2.75r Farming .50 .50
494 A66 7r Construction site 1.50 1.50
 a. Souvenir sheet of 4, #491-494 5.00 5.00
 Nos. 491-494 (4) 2.55 2.55

Tourism A67

Hotels.
1982, Sept. 1
495 A67 1.75r Northolme .40 .40
496 A67 1.75r Reef .40 .40
497 A67 1.75r Barbarons Beach .40 .40
498 A67 1.75r Coral Strand .40 .40
499 A67 1.75r Beau Vallon Bay .40 .40
500 A67 1.75r Fisherman's Cove .40 .40
501 A67 1.75r Mahe Beach .40 .40
502 A67 1.75r Island scene .40 .40
 Nos. 495-502 (8) 3.20 3.20

Tata Bus A68

Wmk. 373
1982, Nov. 18 **Litho.** *Perf. 14*
503 A68 20c shown .25 .25
504 A68 1.75r Mini moke .40 .40
505 A68 2.75r Ox cart .65 .65
506 A68 7r Truck 1.60 1.60
 Nos. 503-506 (4) 2.90 2.90

World Communications Year — A69

1983, Feb. 25
507 A69 40c Radio control room .25 .25
508 A69 2.75r Satellite earth station .55 .55

509 A69 3.50r TV control room .70 .70
510 A69 5r Postal services 1.00 1.00
 Nos. 507-510 (4) 2.50 2.50

Commonwealth Day — A70

1983, Mar. 14
511 A70 40c Agricultural research .25 .25
512 A70 2.75r Food processing plant .30 .30
513 A70 3.50r Fishing industry .40 .40
514 A70 7r Flag 1.10 1.10
 Nos. 511-514 (4) 2.05 2.05

Denis Isld. Lighthouse, 1910 — A71

1983, July 14 *Perf. 14x13½*
515 A71 40c shown .25 .25
516 A71 2.75r Seychelles Hospital, 1924 .30 .30
517 A71 3.50r Supreme Court, 1894 .50 .50
518 A71 7r State House, 1911 1.00 1.00
 a. Souvenir sheet of 4, #515-518 5.50 5.50
 Nos. 515-518 (4) 2.05 2.05

Manned Flight Bicentenary — A72

1983, Sept. 15 *Perf. 14*
519 A72 40c Royal Vauxhall balloon, 1836 .25 .25
520 A72 1.75r DeHavilland D.H.-50j .60 .60
521 A72 2.75r Grumman Albatross .90 .90
522 A72 7r Swearingen Merlin 1.50 1.50
 Nos. 519-522 (4) 3.25 3.25

First Intl. Air Seychelles Flight — A73

1983, Oct. 26 **Litho.**
523 A73 2r DC10 aircraft 2.50 2.50

Paintings, Marianne North — A74

1983, Nov. 17 **Litho.** *Perf. 14*
524 A74 40c Swamp Plant and Moorhen .25 .25
525 A74 1.75r Wormia flagellaria .50 .50
526 A74 2.75r Asiatic Pancratium .75 .75
527 A74 7r Pitcher Plant 1.75 1.75
 a. Souvenir sheet of 4, #524-527 6.75 6.75
 Nos. 524-527 (4) 3.25 3.25

Nos. 469-474 Surcharged
Wmk. 380
1983, Dec. 28 **Litho.** *Perf. 14*
528 A61a 50c on 1.50r multi .25 .25
529 A61b 50c on 1.50r multi .25 .25
530 A61a 2.25r on 5r multi 1.40 1.40
531 A61b 2.25r on 5r multi 1.40 1.40
532 A61a 3.75r on 10r multi 2.25 2.25
533 A61b 3.75r on 10r multi 2.25 2.25
 Nos. 528-533 (6) 7.80 7.80

Handicrafts — A75

Wmk. 373
1984, Feb. 29 **Litho.** *Perf. 14*
534 A75 50c Coconut kettle .25 .25
535 A75 2r Scarf, doll .45 .70
536 A75 3r Coconut-fiber roses .70 1.00
537 A75 10r Carved fishing boat, doll 2.10 3.00
 Nos. 534-537 (4) 3.50 4.95

Lloyd's List Issue
Common Design Type
1984, May 21 **Litho.** *Perf. 14½x14*
538 CD335 50c Port Victoria .25 .25
539 CD335 2r Steamship, 1930s .80 .80
540 CD335 3r Cruise liner 1.10 1.10
541 CD335 10r Ennerdale 3.50 3.50
 Nos. 538-541 (4) 5.65 5.65

People's United Party, 20th Anniv. A76

1984, June 2 **Litho.** *Perf. 14*
542 A76 50c Original headquarters .25 .25
543 A76 2r Liberation statue, vert. .50 .50
544 A76 3r New headquarters .70 .70
545 A76 10r Pres. Rene, vert. 1.75 1.75
 Nos. 542-545 (4) 3.20 3.20

Souvenir Sheet

UPU Congress — A77

1984, June 18 *Perf. 14½*
546 A77 5r No. 156 3.00 3.00

1984 Summer Olympics A78

1984, July 28 *Perf. 14*
547 A78 50c Long jump .25 .25
548 A78 2r Boxing .50 .50
549 A78 3r Diving .70 .70
550 A78 10r Weight lifting 2.50 2.50
 a. Souvenir sheet of 4, #547-550 4.25 4.25
 Nos. 547-550 (4) 3.95 3.95

Scuba Diving A79

1984, Sept. 24
551	A79	50c shown	.25	.25
552	A79	2r Paragliding	1.00	1.00
553	A79	3r Sailing	1.50	1.50
554	A79	10r Water skiing	5.00	5.00
		Nos. 551-554 (4)	7.75	7.75

Whale Conservation — A80

1984, Nov. **Litho.**
555	A80	50c Humpback whale	3.00	3.00
556	A80	2r Sperm whale	5.00	5.00
557	A80	3r Right whale	6.00	6.00
558	A80	10r Blue whale	10.00	10.00
		Nos. 555-558 (4)	24.00	24.00

Audubon Birth Bicent. — A81

Bare-legged scops owls.

1985, Mar. 11 **Litho.** **Perf. 14**
559	A81	50c multicolored	2.75	2.75
560	A81	2r multicolored	4.50	4.50
561	A81	3r multicolored	4.75	4.75
562	A81	10r multicolored	8.00	8.00
		Nos. 559-562 (4)	20.00	20.00

EXPO '85, Tsukuba — A82

Wmk. 373
1985, Mar. 15 **Litho.** **Perf. 14**
563	A82	50c Giant tortoise	.35	.35
564	A82	2r Fairy tern	1.75	1.75
565	A82	3r Wind surfing	2.40	2.40
566	A82	5r Coco de mer	4.00	4.00
a.		Souvenir sheet of 4, #563-566	10.00	10.00
		Nos. 563-566 (4)	8.50	8.50

See No. 604.

Queen Mother 85th Birthday
Common Design Type
Perf. 14½x14
1985, June 7 **Litho.** **Wmk. 384**
567	CD336	50c Queen Elizabeth, 1930	.25	.25
568	CD336	2r With grandchildren, 1970	.80	.80
569	CD336	3r 75th birthday celebration	1.25	1.25
570	CD336	5r Holding Prince Henry	1.75	1.75
		Nos. 567-570 (4)	4.05	4.05

Souvenir Sheet
571	CD336	10r Exiting from helicopter	5.50	5.50

2nd Indian Ocean Islands Games A83

1985, Aug. 24
572	A83	50c Boxing	.25	.25
573	A83	2r Soccer	.85	.85
574	A83	3r Swimming	1.40	1.40
575	A83	10r Wind surfing	4.50	4.50
		Nos. 572-575 (4)	7.00	7.00

A83a

1985, Nov. 1 **Wmk. 384**
576	A83a 1.25r Fairy tern	4.00	4.00

Air Seychelles 1st Airbus.

A84

1985, Nov. 28
577	A84	50c Agriculture	.25	.25
578	A84	2r Construction	.80	.80
579	A84	3r Carpentry	1.25	1.25
580	A84	10r Science education	3.75	3.75
		Nos. 577-580 (4)	6.05	6.05

Intl. Youth Year.

Vintage Cars A85

1985, Dec. 18
581	A85	50c 1919 Ford Model T	.30	.30
582	A85	2r 1922 Austin Seven	1.50	1.50
583	A85	3r 1924 Morris Bullnose Oxford	1.75	1.75
584	A85	10r 1929 Humber Coupe	6.00	6.00
		Nos. 581-584 (4)	9.55	9.55

Halley's Comet — A86

1986, Feb. **Wmk. 384** **Perf. 14x14½**
585	A86	50c Transit instrument	.25	.25
586	A86	2r Quadrant	1.00	1.00
587	A86	3r Trajectory diagram	1.50	1.50
588	A86	10r Edmond Halley	4.25	4.25
		Nos. 585-588 (4)	7.00	7.00

Giselle, Performed by the Ballet Louvre, Apr. 4-8 — A87

Wmk. 384
1986, Apr. 4 **Litho.** **Perf. 14**
589	A87	2r Heroine	.80	.80
590	A87	3r Hero	1.10	1.10

Souvenir Sheet
591	A87	10r United	4.00	4.00

First ballet performed in the Seychelles.

Queen Elizabeth II 60th Birthday
Common Design Type

Designs: 50c, Marrying the Duke of Edinburgh, 1947. 1.25r, State opening of Parliament, 1982. 2r, Greeting child aboard the Britannia, Qatar Harbor. 3r, Silver Jubilee celebration. 5r, Visiting Crown Agents' offices, 1983.

1986, Apr. 21 **Perf. 14½**
592	CD337	50c scarlet, blk & sil	.25	.25
593	CD337	1.25r ultra & multi	.30	.30
594	CD337	2r green & multi	.50	.50
595	CD337	3r violet & multi	.75	.75
596	CD337	5r rose vio & multi	1.25	1.25
		Nos. 592-596 (5)	3.05	3.05

For overprints see Nos. 625-629.

AMERIPEX '86, Inter-island Communications — A88

Wmk. 384
1986, May 22 **Litho.** **Perf. 14**
597	A88	50c La Digue Ferry	.35	.35
598	A88	2r Phone booth, vert.	1.40	1.40
599	A88	3r Victoria P.O., vert.	2.40	2.40
600	A88	7r Air Seychelles trislander	5.50	5.50
		Nos. 597-600 (4)	9.65	9.65

Coptic Catholic Knights of Malta Celebration Day — A89

Perf. 14½x14
1986, June 7 **Litho.** **Wmk. 384**
601	A89	5r Natl. arms, assoc. emblem	2.00	2.00
a.		Souvenir sheet of 1	4.25	4.25

Royal Wedding Issue, 1986
Common Design Type

2r, Informal portrait. 10r, Andrew, helicopter.

1986, July 23 **Litho.** **Perf. 14**
602	CD338	2r multicolored	.50	.50
603	CD338	10r multicolored	2.00	2.00

Tsukuba Expo Type of 1985
Souvenir Sheet
Wmk. 384
1986, July 12 **Litho.** **Perf. 14**
604		Sheet of 4	6.50	6.50
a.	A82	50c multicolored	.25	.25
b.	A82	2r multicolored	1.25	1.25
c.	A82	3r multicolored	1.75	1.75
d.	A82	5r multicolored	3.00	3.00

No. 604 inscribed "Seychelles Philatelic Exhibition-Tokyo-1986" and printed without EXPO '85 emblem on margin or on individual stamps. Nos. 604a-604d inscribed "1986."

No. 396 Overprinted

Perf. 14½x14
1986, Oct. 28 **Wmk. 373**
605	A44 1r multicolored	4.00	4.00

Intl. Creole Day.

State Visit of Pope John Paul II — A90

Pope and: 50c, Seychelles Airport. 2r, Cathedral. 3r, Baie Lazare parish church. 10r, People's Stadium.

1986, Dec. 1 **Wmk. 384** **Perf. 14½**
606	A90	50c multicolored	.25	.25
607	A90	2r multicolored	2.00	2.00
608	A90	3r multicolored	2.75	2.75
609	A90	10r multicolored	9.00	9.00
a.		Souvenir sheet of 4, #606-609	20.00	20.00
		Nos. 606-609 (4)	14.00	14.00

Butterflies — A91

Wmk. 384
1987, Feb. 18 **Litho.** **Perf. 14½**
610	A91	1r Melanitis leda	1.00	1.00
611	A91	2r Phalanta philiberti	2.00	2.00
612	A91	3r Danaus chrysippus	2.75	2.75
613	A91	10r Euploea mitra	9.25	9.25
		Nos. 610-613 (4)	15.00	15.00

Seashells — A92

1987, May 7 **Wmk. 373**
614	A92	1r Gloripallium pallium	1.25	1.25
615	A92	2r Spondylus aurantius	2.40	2.40
616	A92	3r Harpa ventricosa, Lioconcha ornata	3.50	3.50
617	A92	10r Strombus lentiginosus	11.00	11.00
		Nos. 614-617 (4)	18.15	18.15

Liberation, 10th Anniv. — A93

Perf. 14x14½, 14½x14
1987, June 5 **Wmk. 384**
618	A93	1r Liberation monument	.30	.30
619	A93	2r Hospital, horiz.	.50	.50
620	A93	3r Orphanage, horiz.	.85	.85
621	A93	10r Fish monument	2.10	2.10
		Nos. 618-621 (4)	3.75	3.75

Natl. Banking Cent. — A94

1987, June 25 **Perf. 14½x14**
622	A94	1r Savings Bank, Praslin	.30	.30
623	A94	2r Development Bank	.45	.45
624	A94	10r Central Bank	1.75	1.75
		Nos. 622-624 (3)	2.50	2.50

Nos. 592-596
Ovptd. in Silver

Wmk. 384
1987, Dec. 9   Litho.   Perf. 14½
625	CD337	50c scar, blk & sil	.25	.25
626	CD337	1.25r ultra & multi	.30	.30
627	CD337	2r green & multi	.60	.60
628	CD337	3r violet & multi	.85	.85
629	CD337	5r rose vio & multi	1.40	1.40
	Nos. 625-629 (5)		3.40	3.40

Fishing
Industry
A95

Wmk. 384
1987, Dec. 11   Litho.   Perf. 14
630	A95	50c Tuna cannery	.25	.25
631	A95	2r Fishing trawler	.85	.85
632	A95	3r Weighing fish	1.25	1.25
633	A95	10r Hauling catch from net	4.50	4.50
	Nos. 630-633 (4)		6.85	6.85

Beach
Scenes
A96

Wmk. 384
1988, Feb. 9   Litho.   Perf. 14½
634	A96	1r Para-sailing, wind-surfing, kayaks	.50	.50
635	A96	2r Boating	1.25	1.25
636	A96	3r Yacht at anchor	1.75	1.75
637	A96	10r Hotel, cabanas	5.50	5.50
	Nos. 634-637 (4)		9.00	9.00

Green
Turtles — A97

No. 638, Newly hatched turtles headed toward ocean. No. 639, Offspring hatching. No. 640, Female emerging from ocean. No. 641, Female laying eggs in sand. Stamps of same denomination printed se-tenant in a continuous design.

1988, Apr. 22   Wmk. 373
638	A97	2r multicolored	2.75	2.75
639	A97	2r multicolored	2.75	2.75
640	A97	3r multicolored	3.50	3.50
641	A97	3r multicolored	3.50	3.50
	Nos. 638-641 (4)		12.50	12.50

A98

Designs: 1r, No. 647a, Shot put. Nos. 643, 647b, High jump. 3r, No. 647c, Medal winner, grandstand and flags. 4r, No. 647d, Running. 5r, No. 647e, Javelin. 10r, Tennis.

1988, July 29   Wmk. 384   Perf. 14½
642	A98	1r multicolored	.35	.35
643	A98	2r multicolored	.75	.75
644	A98	3r multicolored	1.10	1.10
645	A98	4r multicolored	1.50	1.50
646	A98	5r multicolored	1.75	1.75
647		Strip of 5	3.50	3.50
a.-e.		A98 2r any single	.70	.70
	Nos. 642-647 (6)		8.95	8.95

Souvenir Sheet
Wmk. 373
648	A98	10r multicolored	8.00	8.00

No. 647 has a continuous design. 1988 Summer Olympics, Seoul, (1r-5r). Intl. Tennis Fed., 75th anniv. (10r). No. 648 contains one stamp, size: 28x39mm.

Lloyds of London, 300th Anniv.
Common Design Type
Designs: 1r, Leadenhall Street, London, 1928. 2r, Cinq Juin, horiz. 3r, Queen Elizabeth II, horiz. 10r, Explosion of the Hindenburg, Lakehurst, New Jersey, 1937.

Wmk. 384
1988, Sept. 30   Litho.   Perf. 14
649	CD341	1r multicolored	1.10	1.10
650	CD341	2r multicolored	1.25	1.25
651	CD341	3r multicolored	2.50	2.50
652	CD341	10r multicolored	9.25	9.25
	Nos. 649-652 (4)		14.10	14.10

Defense
Forces
Day, 1st
Anniv.
A99

1988, Nov. 25   Litho.   Wmk. 373
653	A99	1r Motorcycle police	1.40	1.40
654	A99	2r Air force helicopter	2.75	2.75
655	A99	3r Navy patrol boat	4.25	4.25
656	A99	10r Tank	14.50	14.50
	Nos. 653-656 (4)		22.90	22.90

Christmas
A100

Illustrations by local artists.

1988, Dec. 1   Litho.   Wmk. 373
657	A100	50c Selwyn Hoareau	.25	.25
658	A100	85c Robin Leste	.85	.85
659	A100	3r France Anacoura	1.40	1.40
660	A100	10r Andre McGaw	4.50	4.50
	Nos. 657-660 (4)		7.00	7.00

Orchids
A101

Wmk. 384
1988, Dec. 21   Litho.   Perf. 14
661	A101	1r Dendrobium, vert.	.70	.70
662	A101	2r Arachnis hybrid	1.40	1.40
663	A101	3r Vanda caerulea, vert.	2.00	2.00
664	A101	10r Dendrobium phalaenopsis	6.75	6.75
	Nos. 661-664 (4)		10.85	10.85

Jawaharlal
Nehru
(1889-1964),
1st Prime
Minister of
Independent
India
A102

1989, Mar. 30   Perf. 13½
665	A102	2r India Type A409	1.40	1.40
666	A102	10r Portrait	7.25	7.25

People's United
Party (SPUP),
25th
Anniv. — A103

1989, June 5   Perf. 14
667	A103	1r Rally, old office	.40	.40
668	A103	2r Maison Du Peuple	.70	.70
669	A103	3r Pres. Rene, banner, torch	1.10	1.10
670	A103	10r Torch, flag, Rene	3.50	3.50
	Nos. 667-670 (4)		5.70	5.70

Moon Landing, 20th Anniv.
Common Design Type
Apollo 15: 1r, Saturn 5 lift-off. 2r, David R. Scott, Alfred M. Worden and James B. Irwin. 3r, Mission emblem. 5r, Irwin salutes flag in front of the Hadley Delta. 10r, Buzz Aldrin about to step onto the Moon, Apollo 11 mission.

1989, July 20
Size of Nos. 677-678: 29x29mm
676	CD342	1r multicolored	.50	.50
677	CD342	2r multicolored	1.25	1.25
678	CD342	3r multicolored	1.90	1.90
679	CD342	5r multicolored	3.00	3.00
	Nos. 676-679 (4)		6.65	6.65

Souvenir Sheet
680	CD342	10r multicolored	10.00	10.00

Intl. Red Cross and Red Crescent
Organizations, 125th Annivs. — A104

1989, Sept. 12   Perf. 14½
681	A104	1r Ambulance, 1870	1.40	1.40
682	A104	2r H.M. Hospital Ship Liberty, 1914-18	3.00	3.00
683	A104	3r Sunbeam Standard Army Ambulance, 1914-18	5.00	5.00
684	A104	10r The White Train, 1899-1902	16.00	16.00
	Nos. 681-684 (4)		25.40	25.40

Island
Birds — A105

1989, Oct. 16   Perf. 14½x14
685	A105	50c Black parrot	.35	.35
686	A105	2r Sooty tern	3.75	3.75
687	A105	3r Magpie robin	5.50	5.50
688	A105	5r Roseate tern	9.00	9.00
a.		Souvenir sheet of 4, #685-688	20.00	20.00
	Nos. 685-688 (4)		18.60	18.60

French Revolution Bicent., World
Stamp Expo '89 — A106

1989, Nov. 17   Perf. 14
689	A106	2r Flags	2.00	2.00
690	A106	5r Storming of the Bastille	5.00	5.00

Souvenir Sheet
691	A106	10r Raising French flag, Seychelles, 1791	11.00	11.00

African
Development
Bank, 25th
Anniv. — A107

Orchids — A108

1r, Beau Vallon School, horiz. 2r, Fishing Authority headquarters, horiz. 3r, Variola. 10r, Deneb.

1989, Dec. 29   Wmk. 384
692	A107	1r multicolored	1.10	1.10
693	A107	2r multicolored	2.10	2.10
694	A107	3r multicolored	3.25	3.25
695	A107	10r multicolored	11.50	11.50
	Nos. 692-695 (4)		17.95	17.95

1990, Jan. 26
696	A108	1r Disperis tripetaloides	1.40	1.40
697	A108	2r Vanilla phalaenopsis	3.00	3.00
698	A108	3r Angraecum eburneum superbum	4.25	4.25
699	A108	10r Polystachya concreta	15.00	15.00
	Nos. 696-699 (4)		23.65	23.65

Expo '90
(International
Garden &
Greenery
Exposition),
Japan — A109

Designs: 2r, Fumiyo Sako. 3r, Coco-de-mer, male and female plants. 5r, Pitcher plant, Aldabra lily. 7r, Gardenia, Arms of Seychelles.

1990, June 8   Litho.   Wmk. 373
700	A109	2r multicolored	1.60	1.60
701	A109	3r multicolored	2.25	2.25
702	A109	5r multicolored	4.00	4.00
703	A109	7r multicolored	5.50	5.50
a.		Souvenir sheet of 4, #700-703	14.50	14.50
	Nos. 700-703 (4)		13.35	13.35

Penny Black 150th Anniv., Stamp
World London '90
A110

Exhibition emblem and stamps on stamps: 1r, Seychelles #38, Great Britain #80 canceled. 2r, Seychelles #81, Great Britain #64 canceled. 3r, Seychelles #74, Great Britain #62 canceled. 5r, Seychelles #2, Great Britain

#3 canceled. 10r, Seychelles #197, Great Britain #1 canceled.

1990, May 3   *Perf. 12½*

704	A110	1r multicolored	1.10	1.10
705	A110	2r multicolored	2.25	2.25
706	A110	3r multicolored	3.00	3.00
707	A110	5r multicolored	5.50	5.50
		Nos. 704-707 (4)	11.85	11.85

Souvenir Sheet

708	A110	10r multicolored	17.00	17.00

Boeing 767-200ER
A111

Perf. 14½x14½

1990, July 27   **Litho.**   **Wmk. 384**

709	A111	3r multicolored	6.25	6.25

Printed in panes of 10 (2 strips of 5 separated by pictorial gutter).

Queen Mother, 90th Birthday
Common Design Types

1990, Aug. 4   **Wmk. 384**   *Perf. 14x15*

710	CD343	2r Queen Elizabeth in coronation robes, 1937	1.25	1.25

Perf. 14½

711	CD344	10r Visiting workshops, 1947	5.75	5.75

A112   A113

1990, Sept. 8   **Wmk. 373**   *Perf. 14*

712	A112	1r Blackboard	1.00	1.00
713	A112	2r Reading mail	2.10	2.10
714	A112	3r Reading directions	3.00	3.00
715	A112	10r Crossword puzzle	10.00	10.00
		Nos. 712-715 (4)	16.10	16.10

Intl. Literacy Year.

1990, Oct. 27   *Perf. 13½x14*

Various Sega Dancers: a, Pink and white skirt, white blouse. b, Yellow dress. c, Blue, sky blue and pink dress. d, Yellow, green and pink dress. e, White and pink skirt, green blouse.

716		Strip of 5	17.00	17.00
a.-e.	A113	2r any single	3.25	3.25

Festival Kreol 1990.

First Regional Seminar, Indian Ocean Petroleum Exploration
A114

1990, Dec. 10   **Wmk. 384**   *Perf. 14½*

717	A114	3r Beach	3.25	3.25
718	A114	10r Geological map	11.00	11.00

Orchids — A115

1991, Feb. 1   *Perf. 14*

719	A115	1r Bulbophyllum intertextum	1.10	1.10
720	A115	2r Agrostophyllum occidentale	2.25	2.25
721	A115	3r Vanilla planifolia	3.50	3.50
722	A115	10r Malaxis seychellarum	11.00	11.00
		Nos. 719-722 (4)	17.85	17.85

Elizabeth & Philip, Birthdays
Common Design Types

1991, June 17   *Perf. 14½*

723	CD345	4r multicolored	2.00	2.00
724	CD346	4r multicolored	2.00	2.00
a.		Pair, #723-724 + label	5.00	5.00

Butterflies
A116

Perf. 14½x14

1991, Nov. 15   **Litho.**   **Wmk. 373**

725	A116	1.50r Precis rhadama	1.75	1.75
726	A116	3r Lampides boeticus	3.75	3.75
727	A116	3.50r Zizeeria knysna	4.75	4.75
728	A116	10r Phalanta phalanta aethiopica	13.50	13.50
		Nos. 725-728 (4)	23.75	23.75

Souvenir Sheet

729	A116	10r Eagris sabadius	14.50	14.50

Phila Nippon '91.

Christmas
A117

Woodcuts: 50c, The Holy Virgin, Joseph, the Holy Child and St. John by Raphael, engraved by S. Vouillemont. 1r, The Holy Virgin, the Child and an Angel by Van Dyck, engraved by A. Blooting. 2r, The Holy Family, St. John and St. Anna by Rubens, engraved by Lucas Vorsterman. 7r, The Holy Family, an Angel and St. Catherine, painting and engraving by Cornelius Bloemaert.

1991, Dec. 2   **Wmk. 384**   *Perf. 14*

730	A117	50c multicolored	.25	.25
731	A117	1r multicolored	1.40	1.40
732	A117	2r multicolored	3.00	3.00
733	A117	7r multicolored	9.50	9.50
		Nos. 730-733 (4)	14.15	14.15

Queen Elizabeth II's Accession to the Throne, 40th Anniv.
Common Design Type

1992, Feb. 6   **Wmk. 373**

734	CD349	1r multicolored	.80	.80
735	CD349	1.50r multicolored	1.10	1.10
736	CD349	3r multicolored	2.40	2.40
737	CD349	3.50r multicolored	2.50	2.50
738	CD349	5r multicolored	4.00	4.00
		Nos. 734-738 (5)	10.80	10.80

Flora and Fauna
A118

Designs: 10c, Brush warbler. 25c, Bronze gecko, vert. 50c, Seychelles tree frog. 1r, Seychelles splendid palm, vert. 1.50r, Seychelles skink, vert. 2r, Giant tenebrionid beetle. 3r, Seychelles sunbird. 3.50r, Seychelles killifish. 4r, Magpie robin. 5r, Seychelles vanilla, vert. 10r, Tiger chameleon. 15r, Coco-de-mer, vert. 25r, Paradise flycatcher, vert. 50r, Giant tortoise.

Wmk. 373

1993, Mar. 1   **Litho.**   *Perf. 13½*
"1993" Date Imprint Beneath Design

739	A118	10c multicolored	.25	.25
b.		Inscribed "1996"	.40	.25
d.		Inscribed "2000"	—	.25
740	A118	25c multicolored	.25	.25
b.		Inscribed "1996"	.40	.25
d.		Inscribed "2000"	—	.25
741	A118	50c multicolored	.25	.25
b.		Inscribed "1996"	.40	.25
d.		Inscribed "2000"	—	.25
742	A118	1r multicolored	.35	.35
a.		Inscribed "1994"	1.00	1.00
d.		Inscribed "2000"	—	—
743	A118	1.50r multicolored	.55	.55
b.		Inscribed "1996"	.75	.75
744	A118	2r multicolored	.75	.75
b.		Inscribed "1996"	1.50	1.50
745	A118	3r multicolored	1.10	1.10
c.		Inscribed "1998"	3.00	3.00
d.		Inscribed "2000"	—	—
746	A118	3.50r multicolored	1.40	1.40
d.		Inscribed "2000"	—	—
e.		Perf. 14x13¾	—	15.00
747	A118	4r multicolored	1.50	1.50
748	A118	5r multicolored	1.90	1.90
a.		Inscribed "1994"	6.00	6.00
749	A118	10r multicolored	3.75	3.75
a.		Inscribed "1994"	11.00	11.00
750	A118	15r multicolored	5.50	5.50
b.		Inscribed "1996"	11.00	11.00
d.		Inscribed "2000"	—	—
751	A118	25r multicolored	9.25	9.25
a.		Inscribed "1994"	27.50	27.50
752	A118	50r multicolored	19.00	19.00
		Nos. 739-752 (14)	45.80	45.80

No. 746e is dated 2000.
For surcharges see Nos. 844-850.

First Visit to Seychelles by Archbishop of Canterbury — A119

Archbishop and: 3r, Anglican Cathedral, Victoria. 10r, Air France, Air Seychelles airplanes.

1993, June 8   *Perf. 13½*

753	A119	3r multicolored	2.75	1.25
754	A119	10r multicolored	9.25	4.50

4th Indian Ocean Island Games — A120

1993, Aug. 21   *Perf. 14½*

755	A120	1.50r Running	1.10	1.10
756	A120	2r Soccer	2.00	2.00
757	A120	3.50r Cycling	2.40	2.40
758	A120	10r Sailing	6.50	6.50
		Nos. 755-758 (4)	12.00	12.00

Telecommunications, Cent. — A121

Designs: 1r, Cable ship Scotia, Victoria, 1893. 3r, Eastern Telegraph Company's Office, Victoria, 1904. 4r, HF Transmitting Station, operational 1971. 10r, New Telecoms House, Victoria, 1993.

1993, Nov. 12   *Perf. 13*

759	A121	1r multicolored	.95	.95
760	A121	3r multicolored	2.75	2.75
761	A121	4r multicolored	4.00	4.00
762	A121	10r multicolored	10.00	10.00
		Nos. 759-762 (4)	17.70	17.70

Zil Elwannyen Sesel Nos. 59, 61, 63, 64 Srchd.

1994, Feb. 18   *Perf. 14x14½*

763	A9	1r on 2.10r #59	.70	.70
764	A9	1.50r on 2.75r #61	1.10	1.10
765	A9	3.50r on 7r #63	2.10	2.10
766	A9	10r on 15r #64	6.75	6.75
		Nos. 763-766 (4)	10.65	10.65

Hong Kong '94. Size and location of surcharge varies.

Butterflies
A122

1994, Aug. 16   **Wmk. 384**   *Perf. 14*

767	A122	1.50r Eurema floricola	1.50	1.50
768	A122	3r Coeliades forestan	3.25	3.25
769	A122	3.50r Borbo borbonica	3.50	3.50
770	A122	10r Zizula hylax	11.00	11.00
		Nos. 767-770 (4)	19.25	19.25

A123   A124

1995, Sept. 26   **Wmk. 373**

771	A123	1.50r Age 9	.95	.95
772	A123	3r Wedding day	1.75	1.75
773	A123	3.50r 1936 Portrait	2.00	2.00
774	A123	10r 1975 Photograph	5.75	5.75
		Nos. 771-774 (4)	10.45	10.45

Queen Mother, 95th birthday.

Wmk. 384

1996, July 12   **Litho.**   *Perf. 14*

Black Paradise Flycatcher.

775	A124	1r Female on branch	1.00	1.00
776	A124	1r Male in flight	1.00	1.00
777	A124	1r Male on branch	1.00	1.00
778	A124	1r Female, young	1.00	1.00
a.		Strip of 4, #775-778	4.75	4.75

Souvenir Sheet

779	A124	10r Female, male birds	9.00	9.00

World Wildlife Fund.
Stamps in No. 778a may be out of Scott number sequence.

A125

1996, July 15

780	A125	50c Swimming	.25	.25
781	A125	1.50r Running	1.10	1.10
782	A125	3r Sailing	2.50	2.50
783	A125	5r Boxing	4.00	4.00
		Nos. 780-783 (4)	7.85	7.85

Modern Olympic Games, cent.

A126

Wmk. 373
1996, Aug. 19   Litho.   Perf. 14
784 A126 3r shown   2.25 2.25
785 A126 10r Portrait up close   6.75 6.75

Archbishop Makarios of Cyprus, Exiled in Seychelles, 40th anniv.

Birds — A127

#786, Aldabra souimanga sunbird. #787, Seychelles sunbird. #788, Aldabra blue pigeon. #789, Seychelles blue pigeon. #790, Aldabra red headed fody. #791, Seychelles fody. #792, Aldabra white-eye. #793, Seychelles white-eye.

Wmk. 373
1996, Nov. 11   Litho.   Perf. 14½
786 3r multicolored   2.50 2.50
787 3r multicolored   2.50 2.50
  a. A127 Pair, #786-787   5.00 5.00
788 3r multicolored   2.50 2.50
789 3r multicolored   2.50 2.50
  a. A127 Pair, #788-789   5.00 5.00
790 3r multicolored   2.50 2.50
791 3r multicolored   2.50 2.50
  a. A127 Pair, #790-791   5.00 5.00
792 3r multicolored   2.50 2.50
793 3r multicolored   2.50 2.50
  a. A127 Pair, #792-793   5.00 5.00
     Nos. 786-793 (8)   20.00 20.00

Zil Elwannyen Sesel No. 58 Srchd.

1997, Feb. 12   Perf. 14x14½
794 A9 1.50r on 2r   4.00 4.00

Hong Kong '97.

Queen Elizabeth II and Prince Philip, 50th Wedding Anniv. — A128

Designs: No. 795, Queen in red & white dress. No. 796, Prince driving four-in-hand team. No. 797, Prince in business suit. No. 798, Queen, horse. No. 799, Prince Charles, Princess Anne. No. 800, Prince, Queen.
10r, Queen and Prince in open carriage, horiz.

Wmk. 373
1997, Nov. 20   Litho.   Perf. 13
795 1r multicolored   .95   .95
796 1r multicolored   .95   .95
  a. A128 Pair, #795-796   1.90 1.90
797 1.50r multicolored   1.25 1.25
798 1.50r multicolored   1.25 1.25
  a. A128 Pair, #797-798   2.50 2.50

799 3r multicolored   2.50 2.50
800 3r multicolored   2.50 2.50
  a. A128 Pair, #799-800   5.00 5.00
     Nos. 795-800 (6)   9.40 9.40
Souvenir Sheet
801 A128 10r multicolored   8.00 8.00

Diana, Princess of Wales (1961-97)
Common Design Type

Designs: a, In red dress. b, Wearing white blouse, printed vest. c, In blue dress, flowers. d, Wearing white dress.

Perf. 14½x14
1998, Mar. 31   Litho.   Wmk. 373
802 CD355 3r Sheet of 4, #a.-d.   6.50 6.50

No. 802 sold for 12r + 3r, with surtax from international sales being donated to the Princess Diana Memorial Fund and surtax from national sales being donated to designated local charity.

Intl. Year of the Ocean — A129

Designs: a, Blue and yellow fish. b, School of gold-colored fish. c, Lionfish. d, Various small fish. e, Anemones. f, Turtle.

1998   Litho.   Perf. 14
803 A129 3r Strip of 6, #a.-f.   9.50 9.50
     Complete booklet, 2 #803   20.00

Australia '99, World Stamp Expo A130

18th Cent. ships: 1.50r, Vierge du Cap, 1721. 3r, Elizabeth, 1741. 3.50r, Curieuse, 1768. 10r, Le Flèche, 1801.
20r, The Cheval Marin, 1774, vert.

1999   Litho.   Wmk. 384   Perf. 14
804 A130 1.50r multicolored   .85   .85
805 A130 3r multicolored   1.75 1.75
806 A130 3.50r multicolored   2.00 2.00
807 A130 10r multicolored   5.50 5.50
     Nos. 804-807 (4)   10.10 10.10
Souvenir Sheet
808 A130 20r multicolored   12.00 12.00

Nos. 804-807 each issued with se-tenant label.

Wedding of Prince Edward and Sophie Rhys-Jones A131

Wmk. 373
1999, Sept. 1   Litho.   Perf. 13¼
809 A131 3r shown   2.25 2.25
810 A131 15r In carriage   7.75 7.75

Christmas and Millennium A132

1r, Cathedral of the Immaculate Conception. 1.50r, Fairy tern. 2.50r, Dolphin. 10r, Comet.

Perf. 14x14½
1999, Dec. 14   Litho.   Wmk. 373
811 A132 1r multi   .75   .75
812 A132 1.50r multi   1.10 1.10
813 A132 2.50r multi   1.90 1.90
814 A132 10r multi   7.25 7.25
     Nos. 811-814 (4)   11.00 11.00

Queen Mother, 100th Birthday — A133

Designs: 3r, As child. 5r, As young woman. 7r, With King George VI. 10r, As old woman.

Wmk. 373
2000, Aug. 4   Litho.   Perf. 14¼
815 A133 3r multi   1.50 1.50
816 A133 5r multi   2.50 2.50
817 A133 7r multi   3.50 3.50
818 A133 10r multi   5.00 5.00
     Nos. 815-818 (4)   12.50 12.50

Anniversaries — A134

Designs: 1r, Arrival of the Jacobin deportees, 200th anniv. 1.50r, Victoria as capital of Seychelles, 160th anniv. 3r, Arrival of Father Leon Des Avanchers, 150th anniv. 3.50r, Victoria Fountain, cent., vert. 5r, Botanical Gardens, cent. 10r, Independence, 25th anniv., vert.

Wmk. 373
2001, July 25   Litho.   Perf. 14
819-824 A134 Set of 6   8.00 8.00

Nos. 819 and 824 lack Age of Victoria emblem.

Ducks A135

Designs: No. 825, 3r, Garganey. No. 826, 3r, Northern shoveler. No. 827, 3r, Ruddy shelduck. No. 828, 3r, White-faced whistling duck.

Wmk. 384
2001, Oct. 4   Litho.   Perf. 14
825-828 A135 Set of 4   9.00 9.00

Birdlife International World Bird Festival — A136

Seychelles Scops owl: a, In flight. b, In tree. c, Standing on branch, vert. d, Standing on tip of broken branch, vert. e, Standing on branch.

Perf. 14¼x14½, 14½x14¼
2001, Oct. 4
829 A136 3r Sheet of 5, #a-e   13.00 13.00

Queen Mother Elizabeth (1900-2002)
Common Design Type
Souvenir Sheet

No. 830: a, 5r, As young woman, without hat. b, 10r, As old woman, wearing hat.

Perf. 14½x14¼
2002, Aug. 5   Litho.   Wmk. 373
Without Purple Frames
830 CD361 Sheet of 2, #a-b   7.00 7.00

Worldwide Fund for Nature (WWF) A137

Frogs: No. 831, 1r, Seychelles frog. No. 832, 1r, Palm frog. No. 833, 1r, Thomasset's frog. No. 834, 1r, Gardiner's frog.
20r, Seychelles tree frog.

Wmk. 373
2003, Feb. 3   Litho.   Perf. 14
831-834 A137 Set of 4   5.00 5.00
Souvenir Sheet
835 A137 20r multi   11.50 11.50

Fish A138

Designs: 10c, Seychelles blenny. 50c, Seychelles anemonefish. 1r, Indian butterflyfish. 1.50r, Goldbar wrasse. 3r, Seychelles squirrelfish. 5r, Greenthroat parrotfish. 50r, Whale shark.

Wmk. 373
2003, Nov. 3   Litho.   Perf. 14
836 A138 10c multi   .25   .25
837 A138 50c multi   .25   .25
838 A138 1r multi   .45   .45
839 A138 1.50r multi   .65   .65
840 A138 3r multi   1.10 1.10
841 A138 5r multi   1.75 1.75
  a. Wmk. 406, dated "2010"   .80   .80
842 A138 50r multi   17.50 17.50
  a. Wmk. 406, dated "2010"   8.00 8.00
     Nos. 836-842 (7)   21.95 21.95

See Nos. 852-858, 893-896.
Issued: Nos. 841a, 842a, 7/5/10.

Indian Ocean Commission, 20th Anniv. — A139

Wmk. 373
2004, Feb. 16   Litho.   Perf. 13¼
843 A139 15r multi   6.75 6.75

Nos. 743, 745, 748-752 Surcharged

Methods and Perfs As Before
2004, July 1   Wmk. 373
844 A118 1r on 1.50r #743   .50   .50
845 A118 2r on 3r #745   .90   .90
846 A118 3.50r on 5r #748   1.75 1.75
847 A118 3.50r on 10r #749   1.75 1.75
848 A118 3.50r on 15r #750   1.75 1.75
849 A118 4r on 25r #751   1.90 1.90
850 A118 4r on 50r #752   1.90 1.90
     Nos. 844-850 (7)   10.45 10.45

Pope John Paul II
(1920-2005)
A140

Wmk. 373

2005, Aug. 18		Litho.	**Perf. 14**
851	A140	5r multi	3.00 3.00

Fish Type of 2003

Designs: 25c, African pygmy angelfish. 2r, Picasso triggerfish. 3.50r, Palette surgeonfish. 4r, Longfin batfish. 10r, Masked moray eel. 15r, Lyretail grouper. 25r, Emperor snapper.

2005, Oct. 3		Wmk. 373		**Perf. 14**
852	A138	25c multi	.25	.25
853	A138	2r multi	.85	.85
854	A138	3.50r multi	1.60	1.60
a.		Wmk. 406, dated "2010"	.55	.55
855	A138	4r multi	1.75	1.75
a.		Wmk. 406, dated "2010"	.65	.65
856	A138	10r multi	3.50	3.50
a.		Wmk. 406, dated "2010"	1.60	1.60
857	A138	15r multi	4.75	4.75
a.		Wmk. 406, dated "2010"	2.40	2.40
858	A138	25r multi	8.00	8.00
a.		Wmk. 406, dated "2010"	4.00	4.00
		Nos. 852-858 (7)	20.70	20.70

Issued: Nos. 854a, 855a, 856a, 857a, 858a, 7/5/10.

Exile of
Archbishop
Makarios in
Seychelles, 50th
Anniv. — A141

Designs: 3.50r, Archbishop Makarios and Seychelles natives. 15r, Archbishop Makarios.

Wmk. 373

2006, June 28		Litho.	**Perf. 14**
859-860	A141	Set of 2	10.00 10.00

Independence,
30th
Anniv. — A142

Designs: 50c, Possession Stone. 1r, Seychelles flag. 1.50r, Valee de Mai World Heritage Site. 2r, School children. 3.50r, Jacob Marie holding bonm. 4r, Ship "Seychelles Progress." 15r, Independence anniversary emblem.

Wmk. 373

2006, June 28		Litho.	**Perf. 14**
861-867	A142	Set of 7	16.00 16.00

Selection of
Aldabra as
UNESCO World
Heritage Site,
25th
Anniv. — A143

Designs: 2r, Zangiv flowers. 3.50r, Dugongs. 10r, Giant tortoises.

Perf. 12½x13

2007, Nov. 19		Litho.	Wmk. 373
868-870	A143	Set of 3	4.00 4.00

2008
Summer
Olympics,
Beijing
A144

Designs: 1r, Bamboo, kayaking. 1.50r, Dragon, swimming. 2r, Lantern, sailing. 3.50r, Fish, javelin.

Wmk. 373

2008, Apr. 30		Litho.	**Perf. 13¼**
871-874	A144	Set of 4	2.00 2.00

Aldabra
Drongos
A145

Aldabra Red-headed Fodies — A146

Wmk. 373

2008, Oct. 1		Litho.	**Perf. 14**
875	A145	1r shown	.25	.25
876	A145	1r Drongos, diff.	.25	.25
877	A146	1r shown	.25	.25
878	A146	1r Fodies, diff.	.25	.25
		Nos. 875-878 (4)	1.00	1.00

Souvenir Sheet

879	A146	20r Fody and drongo	4.75 4.75

Worldwide Fund for Nature (WWF).

Explorers and
Ships — A147

Designs: 1.50r, Ferdinand Magellan. 3.50r, Sir Martin Frobisher. 6.50r, Sir Francis Drake. 8r, Henry Hudson. 15r, Abel Tasman. 27r, Sir John Franklin.
7r, The Ascension.

Wmk. 406

2009, May 25		Litho.	**Perf. 14**
880-885	A147	Set of 6	7.75 7.75

Souvenir Sheet

886	A147	7r multi	1.00 1.00

Space
Exploration
A148

Designs: 3.50r, X-1 jet being loaded under Superfortress, 1951. 7r, Lunar landing research vehicle, 1964. 8r, Apollo 11 launch site, 1969. 13r, Space Shuttle flight STS-86 on launch pad, 1997. 20r, Soyuz TMA-13 rolls out to launch pad, 2008.
24r, Astronaut on Moon, painting by Capt. Alan Bean, vert.

Wmk. 406

2009, July 20		Litho.	**Perf. 13¼**
887-891	A148	Set of 5	7.75 7.75

Souvenir Sheet
Perf. 13x13¼

892	A148	24r multi	3.75 3.75

No. 892 contains one 40x60mm stamp. Nos. 887-891 each were printed in sheets of 6.

Fish Type of 2003

Designs: 6.50r, Queen coris. 7r, White-lined goatfish. 8r, Three-spot angelfish. 100r, Coral grouper.

Wmk. 406

2010, July 5		Litho.	**Perf. 14**
893	A138	6.50r multi	1.00	1.00
894	A138	7r multi	1.10	1.10
895	A138	8r multi	1.25	1.25
896	A138	100r multi	16.00	16.00
		Nos. 893-896 (4)	19.35	19.35

Wedding of Prince William and
Catherine Middleton — A149

Couple: 3.50r, Waving in coach. 4r, Kissing, vert. 7r, Standing and waving, vert. 25r, Holding hands, vert.

2011, Aug. 1			
897-900	A149	Set of 4	6.50 6.50

State
House,
Cent.
A150

2011, Nov. 11			
901	A150	3.50r multi	.55 .55

Seychelles Post Office, 150th
Anniv. — A151

Designs: 3.50r, Post Office, Victoria, 2011. 7r, Old Post Office, Victoria, 1900s.

2011, Dec. 12			
902-903	A151	Set of 2	1.60 1.60

POSTAGE DUE STAMPS

> Catalogue values for unused stamps in this section are for Never Hinged items.

D1

Engr.; Denomination Typo. in Carmine

1951, Mar. 1		Wmk. 4	**Perf. 11½**
J1	D1	2c carmine	1.50	3.00
J2	D1	3c blue green	2.25	3.00
J3	D1	6c ocher	2.25	2.25
J4	D1	9c brown orange	2.25	4.00
J5	D1	15c purple	2.10	12.50
J6	D1	18c deep blue	2.75	12.50

J7	D1	20c black brown	2.75	12.50
J8	D1	30c red brown	2.75	9.00
		Nos. J1-J8 (8)	18.60	58.75

Engr.; Denomination Typo.

1964-65			**Wmk. 314**
J9	D1	2c carmine	2.00	12.00
J10	D1	3c green & red	2.00	14.00

Issue dates: July 7, 1964, Sept. 14, 1965.

Dated "1980"

1980		Litho.	**Perf. 14**
J11	D1	5c lilac rose & red	.30	1.60
J12	D1	10c dk green & red	.30	1.60
J13	D1	15c bister & red	.30	1.60
J14	D1	20c brown org & red	.30	1.60
J15	D1	25c violet & red	.30	1.60
J16	D1	75c dk red brown & red	.35	1.60
J17	D1	80c dk blue & red	.40	1.75
J18	D1	1r claret & red	.40	1.75
		Nos. J11-J18 (8)	2.65	13.10

ZIL ELWANNYEN SESEL

LOCATION — South of Seychelles

The islands of Aldabra, Farquhar and Des Roches. Formerly part of the British Indian Ocean Territory.

> Catalogue values for unused stamps in this country are for Never Hinged items.

Type of Seychelles, 1977-78

Perf. 14, 14½x14 (40c, 1r, 1.25r, 1.50r)

1980-81   Litho.   Wmk. 373
Imprinted "1980" Beneath Design
Size: 30x26mm (40c, 1r, 1.25r, 1.50r)

1	A44	5c Reef fish	.25	.25
2	A44	10c Hawksbill turtle	.25	.25
3	A44	15c Coco-de-mer	.25	.25
4	A44	20c Wild vanilla	.30	.25
5	A44	25c Butterfly	1.25	.25
6	A44	40c Coral reef	.45	.25
7	A44	50c Giant tortoise	.45	.25
8	A44	75c Crayfish	.55	.25
9	A44	1r Madagascar fody	1.50	.75
10	A44	1.10r Green gecko	.60	.75
11	A44	1.25r Fairy tern	2.00	.80
12	A44	1.50r Flying fox	.75	.60

Size: 27x35mm

13	A44	5r Octopus, vert.	1.10	1.40
a.		Perf. 13 ('81)	1.50	1.50
14	A44	10r Giant tiger cow-rie, vert.	1.25	2.25
a.		Perf. 13 ('81)	2.50	2.50
15	A44	15r Pitcher plant, vert.	1.50	3.50
a.		Perf. 13 ('81)	3.50	3.50
16	A44	20r Natl. arms, vert.	1.50	4.75
a.		Perf. 13 ('81)	4.75	4.75
		Nos. 1-16 (16)	13.95	16.80

Nos. 13a-16a have "1981" date imprint beneath design.

Inscribed "1981"

1981

1a	A44	5c multicolored	.25	.25
2a	A44	10c multicolored	.25	.25
3a	A44	15c multicolored	.25	.25
4a	A44	20c multicolored	.30	.25
5a	A44	40c multicolored	1.50	.25
6a	A44	40c multicolored	.60	.25
7a	A44	50c multicolored	.60	.25
8a	A44	75c multicolored	.60	.25
9a	A44	1r multicolored	1.50	.75
10a	A44	1.10r multicolored	.90	.75
11a	A44	1.25r multicolored	2.00	.80
12a	A44	1.50r multicolored	.90	.60
		Nos. 1a-12a (12)	9.65	4.90

Traveling
Post
Office
A1

1980, Oct. 24			**Perf. 14**
17	A1	1.50r Cinq Juin	.25	.25
18	A1	2.10r Canceling letters	.25	.25
19	A1	5r Map	.50	.50
		Nos. 17-19 (3)	1.00	1.00

The 5r showing Agalega as part of the Seychelles was not issued.

Marine Life — A2

1980, Nov. 28
20	A2	1.50r Yellowfin Tuna	.40	.40
21	A2	2.10r Blue marlin	.45	.45
22	A2	5r Sperm whale	.85	.85
		Nos. 20-22 (3)	1.70	1.70

Royal Wedding Types of Seychelles
1981, June 23   Wmk. 380   Perf. 14
23	A61a	40c Royal Escape	.25	.25
a.		Bkt. pane of 4, perf. 12½x12, unwmkd.	1.10	1.10
24	A61b	40c Couple	.40	.40
25	A61a	5r Victoria & Albert II	.80	.80
26	A61b	5r like #24	1.25	1.25
a.		Bkt pane of 2, perf. 12½x12, unwmkd.	3.00	3.00
27	A61a	10r Britannia	1.50	1.50
28	A61b	10r like #24	2.50	2.50
		Nos. 23-28 (6)	6.70	6.70

Souvenir Sheet
Perf. 12½x12
29	A61b	7.50r like #24	2.50	2.50

Each denomination issued in sheets of 7 (6 type A61a, 1 type A61b).
For surcharges see Nos. 70-75.

Wildlife A3

1981, Dec. 11   Wmk. 373   Perf. 14
30	A3	1.40r Wright's skink	.25	.25
31	A3	2.25r Tree frog	.30	.30
32	A3	5r Robber crab	.50	.50
		Nos. 30-32 (3)	1.05	1.05

Workboats — A4

1982, Mar. 11   Perf. 14x14½
33	A4	1.75r Cinq Juin	.55	.45
34	A4	2.10r Junon	.65	.55
35	A4	5r Diamond M. Dragon	.80	.70
		Nos. 33-35 (3)	2.00	1.70

Mailboats A5

1982, July 22   Wmk. 373   Perf. 14
36	A5	40c Paulette	.45	.35
37	A5	1.75r Janette	.60	.60
38	A5	2.75r Lady Esme	.75	.80
39	A5	3.50r Cinq Juin	.80	.95
		Nos. 36-39 (4)	2.60	2.70

Aldabra, World Heritage Site — A6

1982, Nov. 19
40	A6	40c Birds flying over island	.25	.25
41	A6	2.75r Map	.55	.55
42	A6	7r Giant tortoises	1.25	1.25
		Nos. 40-42 (3)	2.05	2.05

Wildlife A7

1983, Feb. 25   Perf. 14x14½
43	A7	1.75r Red land crab	.40	.40
44	A7	2.75r Black terrapin	.75	.75
45	A7	7r Madagascar green gecko	1.60	1.60
		Nos. 43-45 (3)	2.75	2.75

Maps — A8

1983, Apr. 27   Perf. 14½
46	A8	40c Poivre Island, Ile du Sud	.25	.25
47	A8	1.50r Ile des Roches	.25	.25
48	A8	2.75r Astove Island	.45	.45
49	A8	7r Coetivy Island	1.25	1.25
a.		Souvenir sheet of 4, #46-49	4.50	4.50
		Nos. 46-49 (4)	2.20	2.20

Birds — A9

Perf. 14x14½
1983, July 13   Wmk. 373
50	A9	5c Aldabra brush warbler	.25	.25
51	A9	10c Barred ground dove	.25	.25
52	A9	15c Aldabra nightjar	.25	.25
53	A9	20c Malagasy grass warbler	.25	.25
54	A9	25c Aldabra white-eye	.25	.25
55	A9	40c Aldabra fody	.25	.25
56	A9	50c Aldabra rail	.25	.25
57	A9	75c Aldabra bulbul	.30	.30
58	A9	2r Dimorphic little egret	1.10	1.10
59	A9	2.10r Aldabra sunbird	1.25	1.40
60	A9	2.50r Aldabra turtle dove	1.50	1.50
61	A9	2.75r Aldabra sacred ibis	1.60	1.75

Perf. 14½x14
62	A9	3.50r Aldabra coucal	2.00	2.10
63	A9	7r Aldabra kestrel	4.25	4.50
64	A9	15r Aldabra blue pigeon	9.00	9.50
65	A9	20r Greater flamingo	11.50	12.00
		Nos. 50-65 (16)	34.25	35.90

Nos. 62-65 vert. See Nos. 96-100. For surcharges see Seychelles Nos. 763-766.

World Tourism Day A10

1983, Sept. 27   Perf. 14
66	A10	50c Windsurfing	.25	.25
67	A10	2r Hotel	.25	.25
68	A10	3r Beach	.40	.40
69	A10	10r Sunset	1.25	1.25
		Nos. 66-69 (4)	2.15	2.15

Nos. 23-28 Surcharged
1983   Wmk. 380   Perf. 14
70	A61a	30c on 40c multi	.35	.35
71	A61b	30c on 40c multi	.35	.35
72	A61a	2r on 5r multi	1.40	1.40
73	A61b	2r on 5r multi	1.40	1.40

74	A61a	3r on 10r multi	2.00	2.00
75	A61b	3r on 10r multi	2.00	2.00
		Nos. 70-75 (6)	7.50	7.50

Each denomination issued in sheets of 7 (6 type A61a, 1 type A61b).

Aldabra Post Office, Reopening — A11

1984, Mar. 30   Wmk. 373   Perf. 14
76	A11	50c Map, postmark	.25	.25
77	A11	2.75r Aldabra rail	.90	.90
78	A11	3r Giant tortoise	1.00	1.00
79	A11	10r Red-footed booby	3.50	3.50
		Nos. 76-79 (4)	5.65	5.65

Game Fishing A12

1984, May 31
80	A12	50c Fishing boat	.25	.25
81	A12	2r Hooked fish, vert.	.60	.60
82	A12	3r Weighing catch, vert.	.80	.80
83	A12	10r Fishing boat, stern view	3.00	3.00
		Nos. 80-83 (4)	4.65	4.65

Crabs A13

1984, Aug. 24   Perf. 14½
84	A13	50c Giant hermit crab	.25	.25
85	A13	2r Fiddler crabs	.75	.75
86	A13	3r Ghost crab	1.00	1.00
87	A13	10r Spotted pebble crab	3.75	3.75
		Nos. 84-87 (4)	5.75	5.75

Constellations A14   Mushrooms A15

1984, Oct. 16   Perf. 14
88	A14	50c Orion	.25	.25
89	A14	2r Cygnus	.65	.65
90	A14	3r Virgo	.90	.90
91	A14	10r Scorpio	2.75	2.75
		Nos. 88-91 (4)	4.55	4.55

Wmk. 373
1985, Jan. 31   Litho.   Perf. 14
92	A15	50c Lenzites elegans	.25	.25
93	A15	2r Xylaria telfairei	1.60	1.60
94	A15	3r Lentinus sajor-caju	2.25	2.25
95	A15	10r Hexagonia tenuis	7.75	7.75
		Nos. 92-95 (4)	11.85	11.85

Bird Type of 1983
Inscribed "Zil Elwannyen Sesel"
Wmk. 373, 384 (5c)
1985-88   Perf. 14x14½
Year Imprint ( ) Beneath Design
96	A9	5c Like #50 (1988) ('88)	5.50	5.50
97	A9	10c Like #51 (1985)	5.50	5.50
a.		Inscribed "1987"	5.50	5.50
b.		Wmk. 384 (1988) ('88)	5.50	5.50

98	A9	25c Like #54 (1985)	5.50	5.50
99	A9	50c Like #56 (1987) ('87)	5.50	5.50
a.		Wmk. 384 ('88)	5.50	5.50
100	A9	2r Like #58	7.50	7.50
a.		Wmk. 384 ('88)	7.50	7.50
b.		As "a," inscribed "1990"	7.50	7.50
		Nos. 96-100 (5)	29.50	29.50

Common Design Types pictured following the introduction.

Queen Mother 85th Birthday
Common Design Type
Perf. 14½x14
1985, June 1   Wmk. 384
101	CD336	1r Coronation portrait	.30	.30
102	CD336	2r With Princess Anne	.70	.70
103	CD336	3r Wearing tiara	1.10	1.10
104	CD336	5r Holding Prince Henry	1.90	1.90
		Nos. 101-104 (4)	4.00	4.00

Souvenir Sheet
105	CD336	10r In river taxi, Venice	4.00	4.00

World Wildlife Fund A16

1985, Sept. 27   Perf. 14
106	A16	50c Giant tortoise	8.25	3.00
107	A16	75c Tortoises crossing stream	9.00	1.00
108	A16	1r Three tortoises	9.75	4.00
109	A16	2r Tortoise facing right	13.00	5.50
		Nos. 106-109 (4)	40.00	13.50

Souvenir Sheet
Perf. 13x13½
110	A16	10r Two tortoises	29.00	29.00

See Nos. 131-134.

Famous Visitors A17

Visitors and their ships: 50c, Phoenician trader, 600 B.C. 2r, Sir Hugh Scott, HMS Sealark, 1908. 10r, Vasco de Gama, Sao Gabriel, 1502.

1985, Oct. 25   Wmk. 373   Perf. 14
111	A17	50c multicolored	.30	.30
112	A17	2r multicolored	1.40	1.40
113	A17	10r multicolored	6.50	6.50
		Nos. 111-113 (3)	8.20	8.20

Queen Elizabeth II, 60th Birthday
Common Design Type

Designs: 75c, As princess. 1r, With Prince Philip. 1.50r, Wearing blue cape. 3.75r, Portrait. 5r, Wearing red hat.

Perf. 14½x14
1986, Apr. 21   Wmk. 384
114	CD337	75c scar, blk & sil	.25	.25
115	CD337	1r blue & multi	.25	.25
116	CD337	1.50r grn & multi	.25	.25
117	CD337	3.75r vio & multi	.65	.65
118	CD337	5r rose vio & multi	1.00	1.00
		Nos. 114-118 (5)	2.40	2.40

For overprints see Nos. 135-139.

Royal Wedding
Common Design Type

3r, Sarah Ferguson, Prince Andrew. 7r, Andrew.

1986, July 23   Perf. 14
119	CD338	3r multicolored	.75	.75
120	CD338	7r multicolored	1.75	1.75

Coral — A18   Flowers — A19

Continuous design: a, Acropora palifera, Tubastraea coccinea. b, Echinopora lamellosa, Favia pallida. c, Sarcophyton sp, Porites lutea. d, Goniopora sp, Goniastrea retiformis. e, Tubipora musica, Fungia fungites.

1986, Sept. 17
121 A18   2r Strip of 5, #a.-e.   13.00   13.00

1986, Nov. 12
122 A19   50c Hibiscus tiliaceus   .30   .30
123 A19   2r Crinum angustum   1.60   1.60
124 A19   3r Phaius tetragonus   2.50   2.50
125 A19   10r Rothmannia annae   8.25   8.25
   Nos. 122-125 (4)   12.65   12.65

Fish — A20   Trees — A21

Continuous design: a, Chaetodon unimaculatus. b, Ostorhincus fleurieu. c, Platax orbicularis. d, abudefduf annulatus. e, Chaetodon lineolatus.

1987, Mar. 26
126 A20   2r Strip of #126a-126e   10.00   10.00

1987, Aug. 26   *Perf. 14½*
127 A21   1r Coconut   .85   .85
128 A21   2r Mangrove   2.00   2.00
129 A21   3r Pandanus palm   3.25   3.25
130 A21   5r Indian almond   5.25   5.25
   Nos. 127-130 (4)   11.35   11.35

Nos. 106-110 Redrawn
World Wildlife Fund Emblem
without Circle

1987, Sept. 9   Wmk. 384   *Perf. 14*
131 A16   50c multicolored   9.75   5.50
132 A16   75c multicolored   12.50   7.00
133 A16   1r multicolored   15.00   8.50
134 A16   2r multicolored   20.00   11.50
   Nos. 131-134 (4)   57.25   32.50

Nos. 114-118 Ovptd. in Silver
"40TH WEDDING ANNIVERSARY"

1987, Dec. 9   *Perf. 14½x14*
135 CD337   75c scar, blk & sil   .25   .25
136 CD337   1r blue & multi   .35   .35
137 CD337   1.50r grn & multi   .55   .55
138 CD337   3.75r vio & multi   1.40   1.40
139 CD337   5r rose vio & multi   2.00   2.00
   Nos. 135-139 (5)   4.55   4.55

Mai Valley Tropical Forest — A22

Continuous design: b, Trunk of palm tree at right. c, Bamboo.

1987, Dec. 16   *Perf. 14*
140 A22   3r Strip of 3, #a.-c.   11.50   11.50

Insects A23

1988, July 28   **Wmk. 373**
141 A23   1r Yanga seychellensis   2.10   2.10
142 A23   2r Belenois aldabraensis   3.50   3.50
143 A23   3r Polyspilota seychelliana   4.25   4.25
144 A23   5r Polposipus herculeanus   5.25   5.25
   Nos. 141-144 (4)   15.10   15.10

Souvenir Sheet

1988 Summer Olympics, Seoul — A24

1988, Aug. 31   **Wmk. 384**
145 A24   10r multicolored   8.00   8.00

Lloyds' of London, 300th Anniv.
Common Design Type

Designs: 1r, Lloyd's building, 1988. 2r, Cable ship Retriever, horiz. 3r, Chantel, horiz. 5r, Torrey Canyon aground off Cornwall, 1967.

1988, Oct. 28   **Wmk. 373**
146 CD341   1r multicolored   1.25   1.25
147 CD341   2r multicolored   2.10   2.10
148 CD341   3r multicolored   3.25   3.25
149 CD341   5r multicolored   5.50   5.50
   Nos. 146-149 (4)   12.10   12.10

Christmas — A25

Perf. 13½x14, 14x13½
1988, Nov. 18   **Wmk. 384**
150 A25   1r Santa, toys in canoe   .45   .45
151 A25   2r Church, vert.   .80   .80
152 A25   3r Santa riding bird, vert.   1.25   1.25
153 A25   5r Sleigh over island   2.00   2.00
   Nos. 150-153 (4)   4.50   4.50

Moon Landing, 20th Anniv.
Common Design Type

Apollo 18: 1r, Firing room, Launch Control Center. 2r, Astronauts Slayton, Stafford, Brand and cosmonauts Leonov and Kubasov. 3r, Mission emblem. 5r, Apollo and Soyuz docking in space. 10r, Apollo 11 lifted aboard USS Hornet.

Perf. 14x13½, 14 (#155-156)
1989, July 20
Size of Nos. 155-156: 29x29mm
154 CD342   1r multicolored   1.25   1.25
155 CD342   2r multicolored   2.10   2.10
156 CD342   3r multicolored   3.25   3.25
157 CD342   5r multicolored   5.25   5.25
   Nos. 154-157 (4)   11.85   11.85

Souvenir Sheet
158 CD342   10r multicolored   17.00   17.00

Poisonous Plants — A26

1989, Oct. 9   *Perf. 14*
159 A26   1r Dumb cane   1.50   1.50
160 A26   2r Star of Bethlehem   3.25   3.25
161 A26   3r Indian licorice   4.75   4.75
162 A26   5r Black nightshade   7.50   7.50
   Nos. 159-162 (4)   17.00   17.00
   See Nos. 173-176.

Creole Cooking — A27

1989, Dec. 18
163 A27   1r Tec-tec broth   1.50   1.50
164 A27   2r Pilaf a la Seychelloise   3.00   3.00
165 A27   3r Mullet grilled in banana leaves   4.25   4.25
166 A27   5r Daube   7.00   7.00
   a.   Souvenir sheet of 4, #163-166   17.00   17.00
   Nos. 163-166 (4)   15.75   15.75

No. 166a has continuous design.

Stamp World London '90 A28

Designs: 1r, #22. 2r, #13. 3r, #61. 5r, #32.

Wmk. 373
1990, May 3   Litho.   *Perf. 12½*
167 A28   1r multicolored   1.50   1.50
168 A28   2r multicolored   3.25   3.25
169 A28   3r multicolored   4.50   4.50
170 A28   5r multicolored   8.25   8.25
   a.   Souvenir sheet of 4, #167-170   17.50   17.50
   Nos. 167-170 (4)   17.50   17.50

Queen Mother 90th Birthday
Common Design Types

Designs: 2r, As Duchess of York with infant Elizabeth. 10r, With King George VI viewing bomb-damaged London, 1940.

1990, Aug. 4   Wmk. 384   *Perf. 14x15*
171 CD343   2r multi   1.50   1.50
    Perf. 14½
172 CD344   10r yel brn & blk   7.50   7.50

Poisonous Plants Type of 1989
Wmk. 373

1990, Nov. 5   Litho.   *Perf. 12½*
173 A26   1r Ordeal plant   1.40   1.40
174 A26   2r Thorn apple   2.75   2.75
175 A26   3r Strychnine tree   4.00   4.00
176 A26   5r Bwa zasmen   7.25   7.25
   Nos. 173-176 (4)   15.40   15.40

Elizabeth & Philip, Birthdays
Common Design Types
Wmk. 384

1991, June 17   Litho.   *Perf. 14½*
177 CD345   4r multicolored   3.25   3.25
178 CD346   4r multicolored   3.25   3.25
   a.   Pair, #177-178 + label   7.00   7.00

Shipwrecks — A29

Wmk. 373
1991, Oct. 28   Litho.   *Perf. 14*
179 A29   1.50r St. Abbs, 1860   2.40   2.40
180 A29   3r Norden, 1862   4.25   4.25
181 A29   3.50r Clan Mackay, 1894   4.75   4.75
182 A29   10r Glenlyon, 1905   12.00   12.00
   Nos. 179-182 (4)   23.40   23.40

Queen Elizabeth II's Accession to
the Throne, 40th Anniv.
Common Design Type

1992, Feb. 6
183 CD349   1r multicolored   .80   .80
184 CD349   1.50r multicolored   1.10   1.10
185 CD349   3r multicolored   2.00   2.00
186 CD349   3.50r multicolored   2.40   2.40
187 CD349   5r multicolored   3.75   3.75
   Nos. 183-187 (5)   10.05   10.05

Aldabra World Heritage Site, 10th Anniv. — A30

Designs: 1.50r, Lomatopyllum aldabrense. 3r, Dryolimnas cuvieri aldabranus. 3.50r, Birgus latro. 10r, Dicrurus aldabranus.

1992, Nov. 19   *Perf. 14½*
188 A30   1.50r multicolored   2.25   2.25
189 A30   3r multicolored   4.25   4.25
190 A30   3.50r multicolored   5.00   5.00
191 A30   10r multicolored   13.50   13.50
   Nos. 188-191 (4)   25.00   25.00

SHANGHAI

shäŋ-'hī

LOCATION — A city on the Whangpoo River, Kiangsu Province, China
POP. — 3,489,998

A British settlement was founded there in 1843 and by agreement with China settlements were established by France and the United States. Special areas were set aside for the foreign settlements and a postal system independent of China was organized which was continued until 1898.

   16 Cash = 1 Candareen
   100 Candareens = 1 Tael
   100 Cents = 1 Dollar (1890)

Watermark

Wmk. 175 — Kung Pu (Municipal Council)

Dragon — A1

Antique Numerals
Roman "I" in "I6"
"Candareens" Plural

1865-66   Unwmk.   Typo.   *Imperf.*
Wove Paper
1   A1   2ca black   775.00   *6,750.*
   a.   Pelure paper   825.00
2   A1   4ca yellow   1,000.   *5,250.*
   a.   Pelure paper   1,000.
   b.   Double impression   —
3   A1   8ca green   650.00   *6,000.*
   a.   8ca yellow green   775.00
4   A1   16ca scarlet   2,250.   *6,000.*
   a.   16ca vermilion   2,250.
   b.   16ca yellow green   2,250.
   Nos. 1-4 (4)   4,675.   *24,000.*

No. 1: top character of three in left panel as illustrated. No. 5: top character is two horiz. lines.

Nos. 2, 3: center character of three in left panel as illustrated. Nos. 6, 7: center character much more complex.

Antique Numerals
"Candareens" Plural
Pelure Paper

5	A1	2ca black	650.00	
a.		Wove paper	650.00	6,250.
6	A1	4ca yellow	825.00	3,750.
7	A1	8ca deep green	875.00	—
		Nos. 5-7 (3)	2,350.	

Antique Numerals
"Candareen" Singular
Laid Paper

8	A1	1ca blue	700.00	5,500.
9	A1	2ca black	10,000.	
10	A1	4ca yellow	2,750.	
		Nos. 8-10 (3)	13,450.	

Wove Paper

11	A1	1ca blue	500.00	7,750.
12	A1	2ca black	650.00	7,750.
13	A1	4ca yellow	775.00	8,000.
14	A1	8ca olive green	650.00	—
15	A1	16ca vermilion	700.00	
a.		"1" of "16" omitted	26,000.	
		Nos. 11-15 (5)	3,275.	

Roman "I," Antique "2"
"Candareens" Plural Except on 1ca
Wove Paper

16	A1	1ca blue	950.00	3,800.
17	A1	12ca fawn	375.00	
18	A1	12ca chocolate	550.00	
		Nos. 16-18 (3)	1,875.	

Antique Numerals
"Candareens" Plural Except on 1ca
Wove Paper

19	A1	1ca indigo, pelure paper	450.00	5,500.
a.		1ca blue, wove paper	425.00	5,750.
20	A1	3ca orange brown	500.00	4,250.
a.		Pelure paper	525.00	3,750.
21	A1	6ca red brown	350.00	
22	A1	6ca fawn	875.00	—
23	A1	6ca vermilion	500.00	
24	A1	12ca orange brown	325.00	
25	A1	16ca vermilion	325.00	1,500.
a.		"1" of "16" omitted	500.00	
		Nos. 19-25 (7)	3,325.	

Examples of No. 22 usually have the straight lines cutting through the paper.

Antique Numerals
Roman "I"
"Candareens" Plural Except on 1ca
Laid Paper

26	A1	1ca blue	32,000.	
27	A1	2ca black	7,000.	
28	A1	3ca red brown	28,000.	—

Examples of No. 28 usually have the straight lines cutting through the paper.

Modern Numerals
"Candareen" Singular

29	A1	1ca slate blue	250.00	4,500.
a.		1ca dark blue	250.00	4,250.
30	A1	3ca red brown	250.00	5,000.

"Candareens" Plural Except the 1c

31	A1	2ca gray	225.00	
32	A1	3ca red brown	225.00	3,400.

Coarse Porous Wove Paper

33a	A1	1ca blue	160.00	
34a	A1	2ca black	210.00	
b.		Grayish paper	275.00	
35a	A1	3ca red brown	150.00	
36a	A1	4ca yellow	350.00	
37a	A1	6ca olive green	190.00	
38a	A1	8ca emerald	225.00	
39a	A1	12ca orange vermilion	160.00	
40a	A1	16ca red	250.00	875.00
41a	A1	16ca red brown	225.00	875.00
		Nos. 33a-41a (9)	1,920.	

Chinese characters change on same denomination stamps.

Nos. 1, 2, 11 and 32 exist on thicker paper, usually toned. Most authorities consider these four stamps and Nos. 33a-41a to be official reprints made to present sample sets to other post offices. The tone in this paper is an acquired characteristic, due to various causes. Many shades and minor varieties exist of Nos. 1-41a.

A2

A3

A4

A5

1866 Litho. Perf. 12

42	A2	2c rose	27.50	35.00
43	A3	4c lilac	47.50	60.00
44	A4	8c gray blue	52.50	55.00
45	A5	16c green	82.50	110.00
		Nos. 42-45 (4)	210.00	260.00

Nos. 42-45 imperf. are proofs. See No. 50. For surcharges see Nos. 51-61, 67.

A6

A7

A8

A9

1866 Perf. 15

46	A6	1ca brown	11.00	15.50
a.		"CANDS"	200.00	200.00
47	A7	3ca orange	45.00	60.00
48	A8	6ca slate	47.50	55.00
49	A9	12ca olive gray	72.50	110.00
		Nos. 46-49 (4)	176.00	240.50

See Nos. 69-77. For surcharges see Nos. 62-66, 68, 78-83.

1872

50	A2	2c rose	170.00	200.00

Handstamp
Surcharged in Blue, Red or Black — a

1873 Perf. 12

51	A2	1ca on 2c rose	60.00	65.00
52	A3	1ca on 4c lilac	25.00	37.50
a.		Inverted surcharge	625.00	
b.		Double surcharge	725.00	
53	A3	1ca on 4c lilac (R)	9,000.	3,750.
54	A3	1ca on 4c lilac (Bk)	25.00	37.50
a.		Inverted surcharge	300.00	
55	A4	1ca on 8c gray bl	52.50	55.00
a.		Double surcharge	625.00	
56	A4	1ca on 8c gray bl (R)	22,000.	16,000.
57	A5	1ca on 16c green	4,250.	3,250.
a.		Double surcharge	10,000.	
58	A5	1ca on 16c green (R)	32,000.	13,500.

Perf. 15

59	A2	1ca on 2c rose	72.50	75.00

1875 Perf. 12

60	A2	3ca on 2c rose	300.00	250.00
61	A5	3ca on 16c green	4,250.	3,250.

Perf. 15

62	A7	1ca on 3ca orange	38,000.	18,000.
63	A8	1ca on 6ca slate	875.00	650.00
64	A8	1ca on 6ca slate (R)	12,000.	4,500.
65	A9	1ca on 12ca ol gray	1,100.	900.00
66	A9	1ca on 12ca ol gray (R)	8,000.	4,000.

67	A2	3ca on 2c rose	875.00	750.00
68	A9	3ca on 12ca olive gray	6,000.	6,000.

Counterfeits exist of Nos. 51-68.

Types of 1866

1875 Perf. 15

69	A6	1ca yel, yel	42.50	37.50
70	A7	3ca rose, rose	42.50	37.50

Perf. 11½

71	A6	1ca yel, yel	900.00	650.00

1876 Perf. 15

72	A6	1ca yellow	25.00	30.00
73	A7	3ca rose	95.00	95.00
74	A8	6ca green	140.00	160.00
75	A9	9ca blue	250.00	300.00
76	A9	12ca light brown	275.00	325.00
		Nos. 72-76 (5)	785.00	910.00

1877 Engr. Perf. 12½

77	A6	1ca rose	2,250.	3,000.

Stamps of 1875-76 Surcharged type "a" in Blue or Red

1877 Litho. Perf. 15

78	A7	1ca on 3ca rose, rose	550.00	475.00
79	A7	1ca on 3ca rose	170.00	150.00
a.		Double surcharge	2,250.	
80	A8	1ca on 6ca green	300.00	250.00
81	A9	1ca on 9ca blue	550.00	550.00
82	A9	1ca on 12ca lt brn	3,250.	2,000.
83	A9	1ca on 12ca lt brn (R)	8,500.	5,500.

Counterfeits exist of Nos. 78-83.

A11

A12

A13

A14

1877 Perf. 15

84	A11	20 cash blue violet	16.50	15.00
a.		20 cash violet	13.00	10.00
85	A12	40 cash rose	22.50	20.00
86	A13	60 cash green	25.00	23.00
87	A14	80 cash blue	32.50	35.00
88	A14	100 cash brown	30.00	32.50
		Nos. 84-88 (5)	126.50	125.50

Handstamp
Surcharged in Blue — b

1879 Perf. 15

89	A12	20 cash on 40c rose	45.00	37.50
a.		Inverted surcharge	550.00	
90	A14	60 cash on 80c blue	55.00	70.00
91	A14	60 cash on 100c brn	65.00	65.00
		Nos. 89-91 (3)	165.00	172.50

Types of 1877

1880 Perf. 11½

92	A11	20 cash violet	11.00	11.00
a.		Horiz. pair, imperf. btwn.	800.00	
b.		Vert. pair, imperf. horiz.	850.00	
93	A12	40 cash rose	17.50	15.00
a.		Horiz. pair, imperf. btwn.	900.00	
94	A13	60 cash green	20.00	20.00
95	A14	80 cash blue	21.00	20.00
96	A14	100 cash brown	24.00	22.50

Perf. 15x11½

97	A11	20 cash lilac	170.00	150.00
		Nos. 92-97 (6)	263.50	238.50

Surcharged type "b" in Blue

1884 Perf. 11½

98	A12	20 cash on 40c rose	24.00	22.00
a.		Double surcharge	700.00	
99	A14	60 cash on 80c blue	35.00	36.00
100	A14	60 cash on 100c brn	42.50	42.50
		Nos. 98-100 (3)	101.50	100.50

Types of 1877

1884

101	A11	20 cash green	10.50	10.00

1885 Perf. 15

102	A11	20 cash green	8.25	5.00
103	A12	40 cash brown	10.00	9.00
104	A13	60 cash violet	17.50	17.00
a.		60 cash red violet	22.50	25.00
b.		Vert. pair, imperf. btwn.	1,000.	
105	A14	80 cash buff	16.50	15.00
a.		Horiz. pair, imperf. btwn.	800.00	
106	A14	100 cash yellow	20.00	20.00

Perf. 11½x15

107	A11	20 cash green	16.50	15.00
108	A13	60 cash red vio	20.00	20.00
		Nos. 102-108 (7)	106.25	96.00

Surcharged type "b" in Blue or Red

1886 Perf. 15

109	A14	40 cash on 80c buff	13.50	12.00
a.		Inverted surcharge	20.00	18.00
b.		Red surcharge	550.00	
110	A14	60 cash on 100c yellow	20.00	18.00
a.		Inverted surcharge	100.00	100.00
b.		Double surcharge	225.00	
c.		Red surcharge	600.00	

Types of 1877

1888 Perf. 15

111	A11	20 cash gray	9.50	5.50
112	A12	40 cash black	9.50	9.50
113	A13	60 cash rose	13.00	12.00
a.		Third character at left lacks dot at top	27.50	20.00
114	A14	80 cash green	14.00	10.00
115	A14	100 cash lt blue	17.50	17.50
		Nos. 111-115 (5)	63.50	54.50

Nos. 106, 103, 105 Handstamp
Surcharged in Blue or Red Type "b" or

c

d

1888 Perf. 15

116	A14(b)	40 cash on 100c yel	16.50	16.00
a.		Inverted surcharge	125.00	
b.		Double surcharge	140.00	
c.		Red surcharge	32.50	30.00
118	A12(c)	20 cash on 40c brn	27.50	25.00
a.		Inverted surcharge	200.00	175.00
b.		Double surcharge	350.00	
c.		Red surcharge	400.00	
119	A14(c)	20 cash on 80c buff	14.50	12.00
a.		Inverted surcharge	250.00	140.00
b.		Double surcharge	650.00	550.00
c.		Red surcharge	425.00	
120	A12(d)	20 cash on 40c brn	27.50	26.00
a.		Inverted surcharge	300.00	175.00
		Nos. 116-120 (4)	86.00	79.00

Omitted surcharges paired with normal stamp exist on Nos. 116, 119.

Handstamp
Surcharged in Black and Red (100 cash) or Red (20 cash) — e

1889 Unwmk.

121	A14(e)	100 cash on 20c on 100c yel	200.00	225.00
a.		Without the surcharge "100 cash"	500.00	
b.		Blue & red surcharge	1,800.	—
122	A14(c)	20 cash on 80c grn	16.50	15.00
a.		Inverted surcharge	140.00	

123 A14(c) 20 cash on
      100c bl   16.50 15.00
  a. Double surcharge   350.00
    Nos. 121-123 (3) 233.00 255.00

Counterfeits exist of Nos. 116-123.

1889	**Wmk. 175**	*Perf. 15*	
124 A11	20 cash gray	5.75	4.25
125 A12	40 cash black	8.50	7.00
126 A13	60 cash rose	27.50	27.50
a.	Third character at left lacks dot at top	30.00	30.00

          Perf. 12

127 A14	80 cash green	11.00	22.00
a.	Horiz. pair, imperf. btwn.	2,000.	
128 A14	100 cash dk bl	17.50	22.00
	Nos. 124-128 (5)	70.25	82.75

Nos. 124-126 are sometimes found without watermark. This is caused by the sheet being misplaced in the printing press, so that the stamps are printed on the unwatermarked margin of the sheet.

Shield with Dragon
Supporters — A20

1890	**Unwmk.**	**Litho.**	*Perf. 15*	
129 A20	2c brown		4.25	4.75
130 A20	5c rose		12.00	8.00
131 A20	15c blue		27.50	15.00

Nos. 129-131 imperforate are proofs.

        Wmk. 175

132 A20	10c black	17.50	12.00
a.	Perf. 12	1,000.	550.00
133 A20	15c blue	25.00	18.00
134 A20	20c violet	17.50	14.00
	Nos. 129-134 (6)	103.75	71.75

See Nos. 135-141. For surcharges and overprints see Nos. 142-152, J1-J13.

1891		*Perf. 12*	
135 A20	2c brown	3.00	2.00
136 A20	5c rose	13.00	7.00

1892			
137 A20	2c green	3.50	2.50
138 A20	5c red	8.25	7.25
139 A20	10c orange	22.00	22.00
140 A20	15c violet	13.50	10.00
141 A20	20c brown	14.50	13.00
	Nos. 137-141 (5)	61.75	54.75

No. 130 Handstamp
Surcharged in Blue — f

1892	**Unwmk.**	*Perf. 15*	
142 A20	2c on 5c rose	130.00	80.00
a.	Inverted surcharge	850.00	750.00

Counterfeits exist of Nos. 142-152.

Stamps of 1892 Handstamp
Surcharged in Blue

    g   h

1893	**Wmk. 175**	*Perf. 12*	
143 A20	½c on 15c violet	20.00	13.00
a.	Double surcharge	375.00	
b.	Vert. pair, imperf. btwn.	350.00	325.00
144 A20	1c on 20c brown	20.00	13.00
a.	½c on 20c brown (error)	26,000.	

Nos. 144 and 144a exist in se-tenant pairs. Example pairs with black surcharge come from a trial printing.

Surcharged in Blue or Red (#152) on Halves of #136 (#145-147), #138 (#148-150), #135 (#151), #137 (#152):

    i   j   k   m

145 A20(i)	½c on half of 5c	13.50	10.00
146 A20(j)	½c on half of 5c	13.50	10.00
147 A20(k)	½c on half of 5c	275.00	200.00
148 A20(i)	½c on half of 5c	13.50	10.00
149 A20(j)	½c on half of 5c	13.50	10.00
150 A20(k)	½c on half of 5c	225.00	160.00
151 A20(m)	1c on half of 2c	3.50	3.00
c.	Dbl. surch., one in green	1,600.	350.00
d.	Dbl. surch., one in black	1,700.	350.00
152 A20(m)	1c on half of 2c	16.50	12.00
	Nos. 145-152 (8)	574.00	415.00

The ½c surcharge setting of 20 (2x10) covers a vertical strip of 10 unsevered stamps, with horizontal gutter midway. This setting has 11 of type "i," 8 of type "j" and 1 of type "k." Nos. 145-152 are perforated vertically down the middle.

Inverted surcharges exist on Nos. 145-151. Double surcharges, one inverted, are also found in this issue.

Handstamped provisionals somewhat similar to Nos. 145-152 were issued in Foochow by the Shanghai Agency.

Coat of Arms — A24

Typo. (Dot)

Litho. (No Dot)

1893		*Perf. 13½x14*	
Frame Inscriptions in Black			
Lithographed			
153 A24	½c orange	7.25	3.00
b.	Horiz. pair, imperf vert.	225.00	
154 A24	1c brown	7.25	1.75
155 A24	2c vermilion	8.00	2.50
a.	Imperf, pair	225.00	
156 A24	5c blue	1.10	.65
a.	Black inscriptions inverted	1,800.	
b.	Black inscriptions double	900.00	
157 A24	10c green	10.00	11.00
158 A24	15c yellow	1.10	.90
159 A24	20c lilac	11.00	9.00
	Nos. 153-159 (7)	45.70	28.80

          Typographed

153a A24	½c orange	.55	.50
154a A24	1c brown	.55	.50

        Typo & Litho

157a A24	10c green	2.75	3.00
159a A24	20c lilac	3.00	5.00

On Nos. 157 and 159, frame inscriptions are lithographed, rest of design typographed.

See Nos. 170-172. For overprints and surcharges see Nos. 160-166, 168-169.

Stamps of 1893
Overprinted in Black

1893, Dec. 14			
160 A24	½c (On #153a)	.50	.50
a.	Inverted overprint	165.00	150.00
161 A24	1c (On #154a)	.65	.65
a.	Double overprint	67.50	50.00
162 A24	2c (On #155)	.90	.90
a.	Inverted overprint	165.00	120.00
163 A24	5c (On #156)	3.50	5.00
a.	Inverted overprint	325.00	
164 A24	10c (On #157a)	11.00	12.00
165 A24	15c (On #158)	7.25	6.50
166 A24	20c (On #159)	9.50	10.00
	Nos. 160-166 (7)	33.30	35.55

50th anniv. of the first foreign settlement in Shanghai.

Mercury — A26

1893, Nov. 11	**Litho.**	*Perf. 13½*	
167 A26	2c vermilion & black	1.10	1.00

Nos. 158 and 159
Handstamp
Surcharged in Black

1896		*Perf. 13½x14*	
168 A24	4c on 15c yellow & blk	11.00	8.00
169 A24	6c on 20c lilac & blk (#159)	11.00	8.00
a.	On #159a	55.00	25.00

Surcharge occurs inverted or double on Nos. 168-169.

      Arms Type of 1893

1896			
170 A24	2c scarlet & blk	.30	1.60
a.	Black inscriptions inverted	2,000.	1,800.
b.	Black inscriptions double	1,400.	1,200.
171 A24	4c orange & blk, yel	7.25	5.50
172 A24	6c car & blk, *rose*	8.25	8.50
	Nos. 170-172 (3)	15.80	15.60

    POSTAGE DUE STAMPS

Postage Stamps of
1890-92 Handstamped
in Black, Red or Blue

1892	**Unwmk.**	*Perf. 15*	
J1 A20	2c brown (Bk)	900.00	900.00
a.	Inverted overprint	2,500.	
J2 A20	5c rose (Bk)	25.00	14.00
a.	Inverted overprint	425.00	
J3 A20	15c blue (Bk)	52.50	47.50
a.	Inverted overprint	400.00	
b.	Blue overprint	425.00	

        Wmk. 175

J4 A20	10c black (R)	35.00	32.50
J5 A20	15c blue (R)	30.00	27.50
a.	Inverted overprint	600.00	
b.	Double overprint	300.00	
c.	Pair, one without ovpt.	1,300.	
J6 A20	20c violet (Bk)	22.50	20.00
	Nos. J1-J6 (6)	1,065.	1,041.

1892-93		*Perf. 12*	
J7 A20	2c brown (Bk)	3.75	3.75
a.	Inverted overprint	175.00	160.00
b.	Double overprint	400.00	
c.	Pair, one without ovpt.	1,000.	
J8 A20	2c brown (Bl)	3.50	3.00
J9 A20	5c rose (Bl)	15.50	9.00
a.	Inverted overprint	225.00	
J10 A20	10c orange (Bk)	250.00	225.00
J11 A20	10c orange (Bl)	20.00	15.00
a.	Inverted overprint	325.00	
J12 A20	15c violet (R)	32.50	30.00
J13 A20	20c brown (R)	32.50	30.00
	Nos. J7-J13 (7)	357.75	315.75

          D2

1893	**Litho.**	*Perf. 13½*	
J14 D2	½c orange & blk		.55	.55

      Perf. 14x13½

J15 D2	1c brown & black	.65	.55
a.	Horiz. pair, imperf. vert.	350.00	
J16 D2	2c vermilion & black	.65	.55
a.	Horiz. pair, imperf. vert.	350.00	
J17 D2	5c blue & black	1.00	.90
J18 D2	10c green & black	6.00	2.00
J19 D2	15c yellow & black	4.75	4.00
J20 D2	20c violet & black	1.75	1.50
	Nos. J14-J20 (7)	15.35	10.05

Stamps of Shanghai were discontinued in 1898.

SHARJAH & DEPENDENCIES

ʼshär-jə

LOCATION — Oman Peninsula, Arabia, on Persian Gulf
GOVT. — Sheikdom under British protection
POP. — 5,000 (estimated)
CAPITAL — Sharjah

The dependencies on the Gulf of Oman are Dhiba, Khor Fakkan, and Kalba.

Sharjah is one of six Persian Gulf sheikdoms to join the United Arab Emirates which proclaimed independence Dec. 2, 1971. See United Arab Emirates.

100 Naye Paise = 1 Rupee

Catalogue values for all unused stamps in this country are for Never Hinged items.

Sheik Saqr bin
Sultan al Qasimi,
Flag and
Map — A1

      Perf. 14½x14

1963, July 10 **Photo.** **Unwmk.**
Black Portrait and Inscriptions;
        Lilac
        Rose Flag

1 A1	1np lt bl grn & pink	.25	.25
2 A1	2np grnsh bl & sal	.25	.25
3 A1	3np violet & yel	.25	.25
4 A1	4np emerald & gray	.25	.25
5 A1	5np aqua & lt grn	.25	.25
6 A1	6np dl grn & brt yel	.30	.25
7 A1	8np Prus bl & bis	.30	.25
8 A1	10np aqua & tan	.40	.25
9 A1	16np ultra & bis	.40	.25
10 A1	20np lt vio & lem	.50	.30
11 A1	30np rose lil & brt yel grn	.95	.35
12 A1	40np dk bl & yel grn	1.40	.50
13 A1	50np green & fawn	1.75	.75
14 A1	75np ultra & fawn	3.00	1.00
15 A1	100np ol bis & rose	4.00	1.50
	Nos. 1-15 (15)	14.15	6.65

Exist imperf. Value, set $14.

Malaria Eradication Emblem — A2

1963, Aug. 8

16	A2	1np grnsh blue	.25	.25
17	A2	2np dull blue	.25	.25
18	A2	3np violet blue	.30	.25
19	A2	4np emerald	.40	.25
20	A2	90np yellow brown	3.50	1.50
		Nos. 16-20 (5)	4.70	2.50

Miniature Sheet

Imperf

21	A2	100np bright blue	8.50	3.75

WHO drive to eradicate malaria. No. 21 contains one 39x67mm stamp.

See Nos. C1-C6. For surcharge and overprints see Nos. 35, C7-C12, O1-O9.

Red Crescent and Sheik — A3

1963, Aug. 25   **Perf. 14x14½**

22	A3	1np purple & red	.25	.25
23	A3	2np brt green & red	.25	.25
24	A3	3np dark blue & red	.25	.25
25	A3	4np dark green & red	.25	.25
26	A3	5np dark brown & red	.25	.25
27	A3	85np green & red	2.75	.90
		Nos. 22-27 (6)	4.00	2.15

Miniature Sheet

Imperf

28	A3	100np plum & red	6.50	3.75

Cent. of the Intl. Red Cross. Imperfs. exist. Value, set $12. No. 28 contains one 67x39m stamp.

Nos. 36-40 and No. 20 Surcharged

Nos. 29-34

No. 35

1963, Oct. 6   **Photo.**   **Perf. 14½x14**

29	A4	10np on 1np brt grn	.40	.30
30	A4	20np on 2np red brn	.80	.60
31	A4	30np on 3np ol grn	1.25	1.00
32	A4	40np on 4np dp ultra	1.60	1.25
33	A4	75np on 90np carmine	3.00	2.00
34	A4	80np on 90np carmine	4.25	2.50
35	A2	1r on 90np yel brn	4.75	3.75
		Nos. 29-35 (7)	15.55	11.40

Due to a stamp shortage the surcharged set appeared before the commemorative issue.

Wheat Emblem and Hands with Broken Chains — A4

1963, Oct. 15   **Perf. 14½x14**

36	A4	1np brt green	.25	.25
37	A4	2np red brown	.25	.25
38	A4	3np olive green	.25	.25
39	A4	4np deep ultra	.25	.25
40	A4	90np yellow brown	3.00	1.00
		Nos. 36-40 (5)	4.00	2.00

Miniature Sheet

Imperf

41	A4	100np purple	5.00	3.00

"Freedom from Hunger" campaign of the FAO. Imperfs. exist. Value, set $12. No. 41 contains one 39x67mm stamp.

For surcharges see Nos. 29-34.

Orbiting Astronomical Observatory — A5

Satellites: 2np, Nimbus weather satellite. 3np, Pioneer V space probe. 4np, Explorer XIII. 5np, Explorer XII. 35np, Relay satellite. 50np, Orbiting Solar Observatory.

1964, Feb. 5   **Photo.**   **Perf. 14**

42	A5	1np blue	.25	.25
43	A5	2np red brn & yel grn	.25	.25
44	A5	3np blk & grnsh bl	.25	.25
45	A5	4np lemon & blk	.25	.25
46	A5	5np brt pur & lem	.25	.25
47	A5	35np grnsh bl & pur	1.25	.80
48	A5	50np ol grn & redsh brn	2.75	1.25
		Nos. 42-48 (7)	5.25	3.30

Space research. Exist imperf. Value, set $8.

A 100np imperf. souvenir sheet shows various satellites, the Earth and stars. Colors: dark blue, gold, green & pink. Size: 112x80mm. Value $9.

Runner — A6

1964, Mar. 3   **Unwmk.**

49	A6	1np shown	.25	.25
50	A6	2np Discus	.25	.25
51	A6	3np Hurdler	.25	.25
52	A6	4np Shot put	.25	.25
53	A6	20np High jump	.40	.25
54	A6	30np Weight lifting	.90	.25
55	A6	40np Javelin	1.25	.30
56	A6	1r Diving	2.75	1.00
		Nos. 49-56 (8)	6.30	2.80

18th Olympic Games, Tokyo, Oct. 10-25, 1964.

Exist imperf. Value, set $10.

An imperf. souvenir sheet contains one 1r stamp similar to No. 56. Size of stamp: 67x67mm, size of sheet: 102x102mm. Value $10.

Girl Scouts A7

1964, June 30   **Perf. 14x14½**

57	A7	1np grnsh gray	.25	.25
58	A7	2np emerald	.25	.25
59	A7	3np brt blue	.25	.25
60	A7	4np brt violet	.25	.25
61	A7	5np carmine rose	.40	.25
62	A7	2r dark red brown	4.00	2.00
		Nos. 57-62 (6)	5.40	3.25

Exist emerald. Value, set $9.

An imperf. souvenir sheet contains one 2r bright red stamp. Size of stamp: 67x40mm. Size of sheet: 102½x76mm. Value $7.

Sharjah Boy Scout — A8

Marching Scouts With Drummers — A9

Designs: 3np, 2r, Boy Scout portrait.

Perf. 14½x14, 14x14½

1964, June 30   **Photo.**   **Unwmk.**

63	A8	1np gray green	.25	.25
64	A9	2np emerald	.25	.25
65	A8	3np brt blue	.25	.25
66	A9	4np brt violet	.40	.30
67	A9	5np brt carmine rose	.60	.40
68	A8	2r dk red brown	3.00	1.25
		Nos. 63-68 (6)	4.75	2.70

Issued to honor the Sharjah Boy Scouts. Exist imperf. Value, set $4.10.

An imperf. souvenir sheet exists with one 2r bright red stamp in design of No. 68. Size of stamp: 39½x67mm. Size of sheet: 77x103mm. Value $7.

Olympic Torch and Rings — A10

1964, Oct. 15   **Litho.**   **Perf. 14**

69	A10	1np olive green	.25	.25
70	A10	2np ultra	.25	.25
71	A10	3np orange brown	.25	.25
72	A10	4np blue green	.25	.25
73	A10	5np dark violet	.30	.25
74	A10	40np brt blue	.50	.30
75	A10	50np dark red brown	.80	.40
76	A10	2r bister	4.25	1.25
		Nos. 69-76 (8)	6.85	3.20

18th Olympic Games, Tokyo, Oct. 10-25. Exist imperf. Value, set $12.

An imperf. souvenir sheet exists with one 2r yellow green stamp. Size of stamp: 82mm at base. Size of sheet: 107x76mm. Value $12.

Early Telephone — A11

Designs: No. 78, Modern telewriter. No. 79, 1895 car. No. 80, American automobile, 1964. No. 81, Early X-ray. No. 82, Modern X-ray. No. 83, Mail coach. No. 84, Telstar and Delta rocket. No. 85, Sailing vessel. No. 86, Nuclear ship "Savannah." No. 87, Early astronomers. No. 88, Jodrell Bank telescope. No. 89, Greek messengers. No. 90, Relay satellite, Delta rocket and globe. No. 91, Early flying machine. No. 92, Caravelle plane. No. 93, Persian water wheel. No. 94, Hydroelectric dam. No. 95, Old steam locomotive. No. 96, Diesel locomotive.

         Unwmk.

1965, Apr. 23   **Litho.**   **Perf. 14**

77	A11	1np rose red & blk	.25	.25
78	A11	1np rose red & blk	.25	.25
79	A11	2np orange & indigo	.25	.25
80	A11	2np orange & indigo	.25	.25
81	A11	3np dk brn & emer	.25	.25
82	A11	3np emer & dk brn	.25	.25
83	A11	4np yel grn & dk vio	.25	.25
84	A11	4np dk vio & yel grn	.25	.25
85	A11	5np bl grn & brn	.25	.25
86	A11	5np bl grn & brn	.25	.25
87	A11	30np gray & bl	.25	.25
88	A11	30np blue & gray	.25	.25
89	A11	40np vio bl & yel	.45	.25
90	A11	40np vio bl & yel	.45	.25
91	A11	50np blue & sepia	.55	.30
92	A11	50np blue & sepia	.55	.30
93	A11	75np brt grn & dk brn	.65	.40
94	A11	75np brt grn & dk brn	.65	.40
95	A11	1r yellow & vio bl	3.25	1.25
96	A11	1r yellow & vio bl	3.25	1.25
		Nos. 77-96 (20)	12.80	7.40

Issued to show progress in science, transport and communications. Each two stamps of same denomination are printed se tenant. Exist imperf.

Two imperf. souvenir sheets exist. One contains one each of Nos. 89-90 and the other, of Nos. 95-96. Size: 102x75mm.

Stamps of Sharjah & Dependencies were replaced in 1972 by those of United Arab Emirates.

AIR POST STAMPS

Type of Regular Issue, 1963

Black Portrait and Inscriptions; Lilac Rose Flag

Perf. 14½x14

1963, July 10   **Photo.**   **Unwmk.**

C1	A1	1r ultra & fawn	1.75	.40
C2	A1	2r lt violet & lemon	3.25	.70
C3	A1	3r dl grn & brt yel	4.00	1.00
C4	A1	4r grnsh bl & sal	6.50	1.40
C5	A1	5r emerald & gray	8.00	1.60
C6	A1	10r olive bis & rose	14.00	3.50
		Nos. C1-C6 (6)	37.50	8.60

Exist imperf.

Nos. C1-C6
Overprinted

**Black Portrait and Inscriptions;
Lilac
Rose Flag**

1964, Apr. 7

C7	A1	1r ultra & fawn	3.50	3.50
C8	A1	2r lt violet & lem	7.00	7.00
C9	A1	3r dull grn & brt yel	12.00	12.00
C10	A1	4r grnsh blue & sal	15.00	15.00
C11	A1	5r emerald & gray	22.50	22.50
C12	A1	10r olive bis & rose	32.50	32.50
		Nos. C7-C12 (6)	92.50	92.50

Pres. John F. Kennedy (1917-63).
Exist imperf. Value, set $100.

World
Map
and
Flame
AP1

1964, Apr. 15   *Perf. 14x14½*

C13	AP1	50np red brown	.70	.35
C14	AP1	1r purple	1.50	.85
C15	AP1	150np Prus green	2.50	1.40
		Nos. C13-C15 (3)	4.70	2.60

Issued for Human Rights Day.
Exist imperf. Value, set $7.
An imperf. souvenir sheet contains one 3r carmine rose stamp. Size of stamp: 67x40mm. Size of sheet: 89x64mm. Value $6.

View of Khor Fakkan — AP2

Designs: 20np, Beni Qatab Bedouin camp near Dhaid. 30np, Oasis of Dhaid. 40np, Kalba Castle. 75np, Sharjah street with wind tower. 100np, Sharjah Fortress.

1964, Aug. 13   Photo.   Unwmk.

C16	AP2	10np multi	.25	.25
C17	AP2	20np multi	.35	.25
C18	AP2	30np multi	.45	.25
C19	AP2	40np multi	.65	.35
C20	AP2	75np multi	1.40	.45
C21	AP2	100np multi	2.25	.65
		Nos. C16-C21 (6)	5.35	2.20

Unisphere and
Sheik
Saqr — AP3

20np, Offshore oil rig. 1r, New York skyline.

     Perf. 14½x14

1964, Sept. 1   Photo.   Unwmk.

     Size: 26x45mm

C22	AP3	20np multi	.40	.25
C23	AP3	40np multi	.75	.25

     Size: 86x45mm

C24	AP3	1r multi, horiz.	2.50	.60
a.		Strip of 3, Nos. C22-C24	5.00	5.00

New York World's Fair, 1964-65.

Exist imperf. Value, strip $6.
An imperf. souvenir sheet exists with one 40np stamp in AP3 design. Size of stamp: 40x68mm. Size of sheet: 76x108mm. Value $6.

J. F. Kennedy,
Statue of
Liberty — AP4

1964, Nov. 22   *Perf. 14x13½*

C25	AP4	40np multicolored	1.50	.85
C26	AP4	60np multicolored	1.75	.85
C27	AP4	100np multicolored	1.75	.85
		Nos. C25-C27 (3)	5.00	2.55

Pres. John F. Kennedy.
Exist imperf. Value, set $17.50.
A souvenir sheet contains one each of Nos. C25-C27, imperf. Size: 107x76mm. Value $11.50.

Rock
Dove
AP5

Birds: 40np, 2r, Red jungle fowl. 75np, 3r, Hoopoe.

     Perf. 14x14½

1965, Feb. 20   Photo.   Unwmk.

C28	AP5	30np gray & multi	.85	.25
C29	AP5	40np multicolored	1.00	.35
C30	AP5	75np brt blue & multi	1.50	.50
C31	AP5	150np blue & multi	2.75	.90
C32	AP5	2r multicolored	3.50	1.25
C33	AP5	3r red & multi	5.25	1.75
		Nos. C28-C33 (6)	14.85	5.00

Exist imperf. Value, set $17.50.

OFFICIAL STAMPS

Nos. 7-15
Overprinted

     Perf. 14½x14

1965, Jan. 13   Photo.   Unwmk.

O1	A1	8np multi	.25	.25
O2	A1	10np multi	.25	.25
O3	A1	16np multi	.25	.25
O4	A1	20np multi	.35	.35
O5	A1	30np multi	.40	.40
O6	A1	60np multi	.60	.60
O7	A1	50np multi	1.50	1.50
O8	A1	75np multi	4.00	4.00
O9	A1	100np multi	7.00	7.00
		Nos. O1-O9 (9)	14.60	14.60

SIBERIA

sī-'bir-ē-ə

LOCATION — A vast territory of Russia lying between the Ural Mountains and the Pacific Ocean.

The anti-Bolshevist provisional government set up at Omsk by Adm. Aleksandr V. Kolchak issued Nos. 1-10 in 1919. The monarchist, anti-Soviet government in Priamur province issued Nos. 51-118 in 1921-22.

(Stamps of the Czechoslovak Legion are listed under Czechoslovakia.)

100 Kopecks = 1 Ruble

**Russian Stamps of 1909-18
Surcharged**

     a   b

On Stamps of 1909-12

1919   Unwmk.   *Perf. 14x14½*
     Wove Paper
     Lozenges of Varnish on Face

1	A14(a)	35k on 2k dull grn	.60	2.00
a.		Inverted surcharge	100.00	
b.		"5" omitted	150.00	
c.		Double surcharge	—	
2	A14(a)	50k on 3k car	.60	2.00
a.		Inverted surcharge	100.00	
3	A14(a)	70k on 1k dl org yel	1.00	4.50
a.		Inverted surcharge	100.00	
4	A15	1r on 4k car	1.25	2.00
a.		Dbl. surch., one inverted	200.00	110.00
b.		Inverted surcharge	100.00	
c.		Double surcharge	200.00	
5	A14(b)	3r on 7k blue	7.00	9.50
a.		Double surcharge	100.00	30.00
b.		Inverted surcharge	100.00	25.00
c.		Pair, one without surcharge	400.00	
d.		"3" omitted	—	
6	A11(b)	5r on 14k dk bl & car	9.50	20.00
a.		Double surcharge	100.00	40.00
b.		Inverted surcharge	100.00	40.00

On Stamps of 1917
     Imperf

7	A14(a)	35k on 2k gray grn	1.25	4.50
a.		Inverted surcharge	100.00	
8	A14(a)	50k on 3k red	1.00	4.50
a.		Inverted surcharge	200.00	
b.		Double surcharge	—	
9	A14(a)	70k on 1k orange	.75	4.50
a.		Inverted surcharge	100.00	
b.		Dbl. surch., one inverted	—	
10	A15(b)	1r on 4k car	9.50	16.00
		Nos. 1-10 (10)	32.45	69.50

Nos. 1-10 were first issued in Omsk during the regime of Admiral Kolchak. Later they were used along the line of the Trans-Siberian railway to Vladivostok.
Some experts question the postal use of most off-cover canceled examples of Nos. 1-10.

25 P 1-

Similar surcharges, handstamped as above are bogus.

**Priamur Government Issues
Nikolaevsk Issue**

   A5   A6

     A7

**1909-17 Russian Stamps
Handstamp Surcharged or
Overprinted**

1921   Unwmk.   *Perf. 14x14½, 13½*

51	A5	10k on 4k carmine	250.00
52	A5	10k on 10k dark blue	2,000.
53	A6	15k on 14k dark blue & carmine	200.00
54	A6	15k on 15k red brown & deep blue	90.00

55	A6	15k on 35k red brown & green	100.00
56	A6	15k on 50k brown violet & green	100.00
57	A6	15k on 70k brown & red orange	250.00
58	A7	15k on 1r brn & org	200.00
59	A5	20k on 20k dull blue & dark carmine	350.00
60	A5	20k on 14k dk blue & car (#118)	200.00
a.		15k on 20k on 14k dark blue & carmine (error)	1,100.
61	A7	20k on 3½r maroon & light green	250.00
62	A7	20k on 5r indigo, grn & lt blue	950.00
63	A7	20k on 7r dark green & pink	950.00

Nos. 59-60 are overprinted with initials but original denominations remain.
A 10k on 5k claret (Russia No. 77) and a 15k on 20k blue & carmine (Russia No. 82a) were not officially issued. Some authorities consider them bogus.
Reprints exist.

On Semi-Postal Stamp of 1914

64	SP6	20k on 3k mar & gray grn, *pink*	950.00

On Stamps of 1917
     Imperf

65	A5	10k on 1k orange	100.00
66	A5	10k on 2k gray green	100.00
67	A5	10k on 3k red	100.00
68	A5	10k on 5k claret	700.00
69	A6	15k on 1r pale brn, brn & red org	150.00
70	A7	20k on 1r pale brn, brn & red org	200.00
71	A7	20k on 3½r maroon & light green	350.00
72	A7	20k on 7r dark green & pink	950.00

The letters of the overprint are the initials of the Russian words for "Nikolaevsk on Amur Priamur Provisional Government."
As the surcharges on Nos. 51-72 are handstamped, a number exist inverted or double.
A 20k blue & carmine (Russia No. 126) with Priamur overprint and a 15k on 20k (Russia No. 126) were not officially issued. Some authorities consider them bogus.
No evidence found of genuine usage of Nos. 51-72.

Stamps of Far Eastern
Republic Overprinted

1922

78	A2	2k gray green	25.00	25.00
a.		Inverted overprint	200.00	
79	A2a	4k rose	25.00	25.00
a.		Inverted overprint	250.00	
80	A2	5k claret	25.00	25.00
81	A2a	10k blue	25.00	25.00
		Nos. 78-81 (4)	100.00	100.00

Anniv. of the overthrow of the Bolshevik power in the Priamur district.
The letters of the overprint are the initials of "Vremeno Priamurski Pravitel'stvo" i.e. Provisional Priamur Government, 26th May.

Russian Stamps of 1909-21 Overprinted in Dark Blue or Vermilion

On Stamps of 1909-18

1922   *Perf. 14x14½*

85	A14	1k dull org yel	75.00	100.00
86	A14	2k dull green	125.00	110.00
87	A14	3k carmine	35.00	50.00
88	A14	4k carmine	25.00	35.00
89	A14	5k dk claret	35.00	40.00
90	A14	7k blue (V)	100.00	45.00
91	A15	10k dark blue (V)	65.00	70.00
92	A14	14k dk bl & car	75.00	85.00
93	A11	15k red brn & dp bl	15.00	25.00
94	A8	20k dl bl & dk car	50.00	25.00
95	A11	25k dull green & blue & carmine	120.00	150.00
96	A11	25k on 14k dark blue & dark violet (V)	40.00	50.00
97	A11	35k red brn & grn	10.00	15.00
a.		Inverted overprint	200.00	
98	A8	50k brn vio & grn	20.00	30.00
99	A11	70k brn & red org	50.00	55.00
		Nos. 85-99 (15)	840.00	885.00

On Stamps of 1917
Imperf

100	A14	1k orange		10.00	25.00
a.	Inverted overprint			250.00	100.00
101	A14	2k gray green		15.00	25.00
102	A14	3k red		20.00	25.00
103	A15	4k carmine		100.00	100.00
104	A14	5k claret		35.00	25.00
105	A11	15k red brn & dp bl		140.00	125.00
106	A8	20k blue & car		125.00	75.00
107	A9	1r pale brn, brn &			
		red org		30.00	40.00
	Nos. 100-107 (8)			475.00	440.00

On Stamps of Siberia, 1919
Perf. 14½x15

108	A14	35k on 2k green		100.00	100.00

Imperf

109	A14	70k on 1k orange		110.00	120.00

On Stamps of Far Eastern Republic, 1921

110	A2	2k gray green		20.00	20.00
111	A2a	4k rose		20.00	7.00
112	A2	5k claret		20.00	25.00
a.	Inverted overprint			100.00	
113	A2a	10k blue (R)		20.00	30.00
	Nos. 109-113 (5)			190.00	202.00

Same, Surcharged with New Values

114	A2	1k on 2k gray grn		20.00	25.00
115	A2a	3k on 4k rose		20.00	25.00

The overprint is in a rectangular frame on stamps of 1k to 10k and 1r; on the other values the frame is omitted. It is larger on the 1 ruble than on the smaller stamps.

The overprint reads "Priamurski Zemski Krai," Priamur Rural Province.

Far Eastern Republic
Nos. 30-32 Overprinted
in Blue

Perf. 14½x15

116	A14	35k on 2k green		20.00	25.00

Imperf

117	A14	35k on 2k green		60.00	120.00
118	A14	70k on 1k orange		30.00	15.00
	Nos. 116-118 (3)			110.00	160.00

Counterfeits of Nos. 51-118 abound.

SIERRA LEONE

sē-,er-ə lē-'ōn

LOCATION — West coast of Africa, between Guinea and Liberia
GOVT. — Republic in British Commonwealth
AREA — 27,925 sq. mi.
POP. — 5,296,651 (1999 est.)
CAPITAL — Freetown

Sierra Leone was a British colony and protectorate. In 1961 it became fully independent, remaining within the Commonwealth. It became a republic April 19, 1971.

12 Pence = 1 Shilling
20 Shillings = 1 Pound
100 Cents = 1 Leone (1964)

Catalogue values for unused stamps in this country are for Never Hinged items, beginning with Scott 186 in the regular postage section and Scott C1 in the air post section.

Watermark

Wmk. 336 — St. Edwards Crown & SL, Multiple

Queen Victoria
A1   A2

1859-74   Unwmk.   Typo.   Perf. 14

1	A1	6p bright violet ('74)		55.00	30.00
a.	6p dull violet ('59)			220.00	45.00
b.	6p gray lilac ('65)			300.00	45.00

1872   Perf. 12½

5	A1	6p violet	425.00	70.00

1872   Wmk. 1 Sideways   Perf. 12½

6	A2	1p rose		85.00	40.00
8	A2	3p yellow buff		160.00	42.50
9	A2	4p blue		200.00	45.00
10	A2	1sh yellow green		525.00	62.50

1873   Wmk. 1 Upright

6a	A2	1p		140.00	35.00
7	A2	2p magenta		150.00	55.00
8a	A2	3p		550.00	95.00
9a	A2	4p		375.00	57.50
10a	A2	1sh		525.00	110.00

1876-96   Wmk. 1 Upright   Perf. 14

11	A2	½p bister		3.50	9.50
12	A2	1p rose		55.00	16.00
13	A2	1½p violet ('77)		55.00	10.00
14	A2	2p magenta		72.50	4.50
15	A2	3p yellow buff		55.00	5.00
16	A2	4p blue		190.00	7.25
17	A1	6p brt violet ('85)		67.50	27.50
a.	Half used as 3p on cover				2,750.
18	A1	6p violet brn ('90)		21.00	16.00
19	A1	6p brown vio ('96)		3.00	7.75
20	A2	1sh green		67.50	7.25
	Nos. 11-20 (10)			590.00	110.75

For surcharge see No. 32.

1883-93   Wmk. Crown and C A (2)

21	A2	½p bister		27.50	57.50
22	A2	½p dull green ('84)		3.50	2.00
23	A2	1p carmine ('84)		5.50	1.10
a.	1p rose carmine			32.50	9.50
b.	1p rose			225.00	40.00
24	A2	1½p violet ('93)		3.25	7.25
25	A2	2p magenta		57.50	9.50
26	A2	2p slate ('84)		42.50	3.00
27	A2	2½p ultra ('91)		13.50	1.75
28	A2	3p org yel ('92)		4.00	11.00
29	A2	4p blue		1,000.	32.50
30	A2	4p bister ('84)		2.75	2.25
31	A2	1sh org brn ('88)		25.00	13.50
	Nos. 21-28,30-31 (10)			185.00	108.85

For surcharge see No. 33.

Nos. 13 and 24
Surcharged in Black

1893   Wmk. 1

32	A2	½p on 1½p violet		525.00	800.00
a.	"PFNNY"			3,300.	4,500.

Wmk. 2

33	A2	½p on 1½p violet		5.00	3.50
a.	"PFNNY"			82.50	82.50
b.	Inverted surcharge			125.00	125.00
c.	Same as "a," inverted			8,000.	5,500.
d.	Double surcharge			1,200.	

A4

1896-97

34	A4	½p lilac & grn ('97)		2.75	3.50
35	A4	1p lilac & car		4.75	2.00
36	A4	1½p lilac & blk ('97)		4.50	24.00
37	A4	2p lilac & org		2.75	5.50
38	A4	2½p lilac & ultra		2.75	1.40
39	A4	3p lilac & sl ('97)		9.50	7.75
40	A4	4p lilac & car ('97)		14.50	14.50
41	A4	5p lilac & blk		14.50	16.00
42	A4	6p lilac ('97)		9.00	27.50
43	A4	1sh green & blk		6.75	22.50
44	A4	2sh green & ultra		27.50	67.50
45	A4	5sh green & car		80.00	200.00
46	A4	£1 violet, red		190.00	500.00
	Nos. 34-46 (13)			365.25	892.15

Numerals of Nos. 39-46 of type A4 are in color on plain tablet.

A5   A6

a   b

c   d

e   f

1897   Wmk. C A over Crown (46)

47	A5	1p lilac & grn		5.25	4.25
a.	Double overprint			1,800.	1,800.
48	A6(a)	2½p on 3p lil &			
		grn		13.50	17.50
a.	Double surcharge			35,000.	
b.	Double surcharge, types "a" and "b"			30,000.	
c.	Double surcharge, types "a" and "c"			45,000.	
49	A6(b)	2½p on 3p		67.50	80.00
50	A6(c)	2½p on 3p		200.00	215.00
51	A6(d)	2½p on 3p		400.00	525.00
52	A6(a)	2½p on 6p lil &			
		grn		10.50	17.50
53	A6(b)	2½p on 6p		50.00	67.50
54	A6(c)	2½p on 6p		150.00	175.00
55	A6(d)	2½p on 6p		325.00	400.00
56	A6(a)	2½p on 1sh lilac		110.00	80.00
57	A6(b)	2½p on 1sh lilac		1,100.	1,100.
58	A6(c)	2½p on 1sh lilac		525.00	500.00
59	A6(e)	2½p on 1sh lilac		1,750.	2,000.
59A	A6(f)	2½p on 1sh lilac		1,750.	1,500.
60	A6(a)	2½p on 2sh lilac		4,000.	2,500.
61	A6(b)	2½p on 2sh lilac		20,000.	
62	A6(c)	2½p on 2sh lilac		11,500.	13,500.
a.	Italic "N" in "REVENUE"			50,000.	50,000.
63	A6(e)	2½p on 2sh lilac		47,500.	
63A	A6(f)	2½p on 2sh lilac		47,500.	50,000.

The words "POSTAGE AND REVENUE" on Nos. 56-63A are set in two lines and overprinted below instead of above "2½d."

The "d" in type "f" is 3½mm wide; that in type "a" is 3mm.

Very fine examples of Nos. 47-63A will have perforations touching the frameline on one or more sides.

Nos. 56-59A are often found discolored. Such stamps sell for about half the values quoted.

King Edward VII — A7

Numerals of 3p to £1 of type A7 are in color on plain tablet.

1903   Wmk. Crown and C A (2)

64	A7	½p violet & grn		3.25	5.00
65	A7	1p violet & car		2.25	1.10
66	A7	1½p violet & blk		1.50	11.00
67	A7	2p violet & brn org		4.50	17.50
68	A7	2½p violet & ultra		5.00	9.00
69	A7	3p violet & gray		11.00	15.00
70	A7	4p violet & car		8.00	9.00
71	A7	5p violet & blk		9.00	35.00
72	A7	6p violet & dull vio		12.50	17.50
73	A7	1sh green & blk		18.00	67.50
74	A7	2sh green & ultra		50.00	70.00
75	A7	5sh green & car		75.00	110.00
76	A7	£1 violet, red		260.00	275.00
	Nos. 64-76 (13)			460.00	649.60

1904-05   Wmk. 3   Chalky Paper

77	A7	½p violet & grn		5.75	5.25
78	A7	1p violet & car		4.50	1.75
79	A7	1½p violet & blk		3.50	15.00
80	A7	2p violet & brn org		4.75	4.50
81	A7	2½p violet & ultra		5.25	2.25
82	A7	3p violet & gray		40.00	4.00
83	A7	4p violet & car		8.00	8.00
84	A7	5p violet & blk		12.00	30.00
85	A7	6p violet & dl vio		4.50	3.50
86	A7	1sh green & blk		8.50	10.00
87	A7	2sh green & ultra		25.00	30.00
88	A7	5sh green & car		35.00	57.50
89	A7	£1 violet, red		240.00	260.00
	Nos. 77-89 (13)			396.75	431.75

The 1p also exists on ordinary paper.

1907-10   Ordinary Paper

90	A7	½p green		1.00	.60
91	A7	1p carmine		6.25	.80
92	A7	1½p orange ('10)		1.40	2.25
93	A7	2p gray		1.40	1.75
94	A7	2½p ultra		4.00	3.25

Chalky Paper

95	A7	3p violet, *yel*		8.50	3.25
96	A7	4p blk & red, *yel*		2.60	1.75
97	A7	5p vio & ol grn		9.00	5.75
98	A7	6p vio & red vio		10.00	9.00
99	A7	1sh black, *green*		9.00	12.50
100	A7	2sh vio & bl, *bl*		17.50	22.50
101	A7	5sh grn & red, *yel*		42.50	62.50
102	A7	£1 vio & blk, *red*		300.00	210.00
	Nos. 90-102 (13)			410.40	329.15

The 3p also exists on ordinary paper. Value, unused $12.50, used $15.

King George V and Seal of the Colony
A8   A9

Die I

For description of dies I and II see "Dies of British Colonial Stamps" in Table of Contents.

Numerals of 3p, 4p, 5p, 6p and 10p of type A8 are in color on plain tablet. Numerals of 7p and 9p are on solid-color tablet.

1912-24   Ordinary Paper   Wmk. 3

103	A8	½p green		2.50	2.50
104	A8	1p scarlet		4.00	.80
a.	1p carmine			2.00	.45
105	A8	1½p orange		2.25	2.75
106	A8	2p gray		1.50	.25
107	A8	2½p ultra		1.25	1.00

Chalky Paper

108	A9	3p violet, *yel*		3.50	3.75
109	A9	4p blk & red, *yel*		3.25	9.50
a.	Die II ('24)			5.00	6.00
110	A9	5p violet & ol grn		1.50	7.00
111	A9	6p vio & red vio		3.75	6.75
112	A8	7p violet & org		3.50	9.50
113	A8	9p violet & blk		5.75	14.00
114	A8	10p violet & red		3.50	20.00
115	A9	1sh black, *green*		5.00	5.25
a.	1sh black, *emerald*				190.00
116	A9	2sh vio & ultra, *bl*		15.00	6.25
117	A9	5sh grn & red, *yel*		15.00	30.00
118	A9	10sh grn & red, *grn*		75.00	140.00
119	A9	£1 vio & blk, *red*		175.00	260.00
120	A9	£2 violet & ultra		650.00	900.00
121	A9	£5 gray grn & org		1,900.	2,500.
	Nos. 103-119 (17)			321.25	519.30

The status of #115a has been questioned.

Die II

1921-27   Ordinary Paper   Wmk. 4

122	A8	½p green		1.40	1.10
123	A8	1p violet ('26)		3.50	.25
a.	Die I ('24)			1.75	.90
124	A8	1½p scarlet		2.00	1.50
125	A8	2p gray ('22)		1.10	.25
126	A8	2½p ultra		1.40	9.00
127	A8	3p ultra ('22)		1.40	1.40

128	A8	4p blk & red, *yel*	2.00	*3.75*
129	A8	5p vio & ol grn	1.40	1.40

Chalky Paper

130	A8	6p dp vio & red vio	1.40	*2.75*
131	A8	7p vio & org ('27)	3.25	22.50
132	A8	9p dl vio & blk ('22)	3.25	19.00
133	A9	10p violet & red	4.00	30.00
134	A9	1sh blk, *emerald*	8.50	8.00
135	A9	2sh vio & ultra, *bl*	9.00	11.50
136	A9	5sh grn & red, *yel*	9.00	57.50
137	A9	10sh grn & red, *grn*	110.00	225.00
138	A9	£2 violet & ultra	600.00	850.00
139	A9	£5 gray grn & org	1,700.	2,500.
		Nos. 122-137 (16)	162.60	394.90

Rice Field — A10

Palms and Kola Tree — A11

1932, Mar. 1   Engr.   Perf. 12½

140	A10	½p green	.25	.25
141	A10	1p dk violet	.30	.25
142	A10	1½p rose car	.35	1.40
143	A10	2p yellow brn	.35	.25
144	A10	3p ultra	.75	2.00
145	A10	4p orange	.75	8.00
146	A10	5p olive green	1.00	3.50
147	A10	6p light blue	.75	3.50
148	A10	1sh red brown	2.75	6.50

Perf. 12

149	A11	2sh dk brown	6.00	8.25
150	A11	5sh indigo	14.00	22.50
151	A11	10sh deep green	80.00	160.00
152	A11	£1 deep violet	150.00	275.00
		Nos. 140-152 (13)	257.25	491.40

Wilberforce Issue

Arms of Sierra Leone — A12

Slave Throwing Off Shackles — A13

Map of Sierra Leone — A14

Old Slave Market, Freetown A15

Fruit Seller — A16

Government Sanatorium — A17

1933, Oct. 2

153	A12	½p deep green	1.00	*1.25*
154	A13	1p brown & blk	.85	.25
155	A14	1½p orange brn	6.00	4.75
156	A15	2p violet	3.50	.25
157	A16	3p ultra	4.00	1.75
158	A17	4p dk brown	7.00	10.00
159	A18	5p red brn & sl grn	7.50	11.00
160	A19	6p dp org & blk	8.50	7.00
161	A20	1sh dk violet	5.00	17.50
162	A21	2sh bl & dk brown	30.00	45.00
163	A22	5sh red vio & blk	160.00	200.00
164	A23	10sh green & blk	240.00	350.00
165	A24	£1 yel & dk vio	475.00	550.00
		Nos. 153-165 (13)	948.35	1,198.

Abolition of slavery in the British colonies and cent. of the death of William Wilberforce, English philanthropist and agitator against the slave trade.

Common Design Types pictured following the introduction.

Silver Jubilee Issue
Common Design Type

1935, May 6   Perf. 11x12

166	CD301	1p black & ultra	1.25	*2.50*
167	CD301	3p ultra & brown	2.25	*8.00*
168	CD301	5p indigo & green	3.00	*17.50*

Bullom Canoe — A18

Punting near Banana Islands — A19

Government Buildings, Freetown A20

Old Slavers' Resort, Bunce Island — A21

African Elephant — A22

George V A23

Freetown Harbor — A24

169	CD301	1sh brown vio & ind	12.00	8.50
		Nos. 166-169 (4)	18.50	36.50
		Set, never hinged	29.00	

Coronation Issue
Common Design Type

1937, May 12   Perf. 11x11½

170	CD302	1p deep orange	.40	.75
171	CD302	2p dark violet	.65	.75
172	CD302	3p deep ultra	.90	3.00
		Nos. 170-172 (3)	1.95	4.50
		Set, never hinged	3.75	

Freetown Harbor A25

Rice Harvesting A26

1938-44   Perf. 12½

173	A25	½p green & blk	.25	.50
174	A25	1p dp cl & blk	.30	.70
175	A26	1½p rose red	12.50	1.25
175A	A26	1½p red vio ('41)	.25	*.70*
176	A26	2p red violet	30.00	3.00
176A	A26	2p dark red ('41)	.25	*2.10*
177	A26	3p ultra & blk	.30	*.60*
178	A25	4p red brn & blk	.55	4.50
179	A26	5p olive green	3.75	4.00
180	A26	6p gray	.55	.60
181	A25	1sh ol grn & blk	1.40	.90
181A	A26	1sh3p org yel ('44)	.30	*.60*
182	A25	2sh sepia & blk	2.75	2.50
183	A26	5sh red brown	6.00	9.50
184	A26	10sh emerald	15.00	11.50
185	A25	£1 dk blue	11.00	26.50
		Nos. 173-185 (16)	85.15	69.45
		Set, never hinged	130.00	

> Catalogue values for unused stamps in this section, from this point to the end of the section, are for Never Hinged items.

Peace Issue
Common Design Type

Perf. 13½x14

1946, Oct. 1   Engr.   Wmk. 4

186	CD303	1½p lilac	.25	.25
187	CD303	3p bright ultra	.25	.25

Silver Wedding Issue
Common Design Types

1948, Dec. 1   Photo.   Perf. 14x14½

188	CD304	1½p brt red violet	.25	.25

Engraved; Name Typographed
Perf. 11½x11

189	CD305	£1 dark blue	24.50	24.50

UPU Issue
Common Design Types

Engr.; Name Typo. on 3p, 6p

1949, Oct. 10   Perf. 13½, 11x11½

190	CD306	1½p rose violet	.25	.35
191	CD307	3p indigo	.50	1.75
192	CD308	6p gray	.85	2.00
193	CD309	1sh olive	1.40	1.00
		Nos. 190-193 (4)	3.00	5.10

Coronation Issue
Common Design Type

1953, June 2   Engr.   Perf. 13½x13

194	CD312	1½p purple & black	.40	.40

Cape Lighthouse A27

Cotton Tree, Freetown — A28

1p, Queen Elizabeth II Quay. 1½d, Piassava workers. 3p, Rice harvesting. 4p, Iron ore production, Marampa. 6p, Whale Bay, York Village. 1sh, Bullom boat. 1sh3p, Map of Sierra Leone & plane. 2sh6p, Orugu Bridge. 5sh, Kuranko chief. 10sh, Law Courts, Freetown. £1, Government House.

Perf. 13 (A27), 13½ (A28)
1956, Jan. 2   Engr.   Wmk. 4
Center in Black

195	A27	½p lt violet	1.00	*2.00*
196	A27	1p reseda	.70	.25
197	A27	1½p ultra	1.75	*5.00*
198	A28	2p lt brown	.55	.25
199	A28	3p ultra	.95	.25
a.		Perf 13x13½	1.75	10.00
200	A27	4p gray blue	2.50	2.00
201	A27	6p violet	1.00	.30
202	A28	1sh carmine	1.25	.50
203	A27	1sh3p gray brown	12.00	.50
204	A28	2sh6p brown org	15.00	10.00
205	A28	5sh green	3.75	*4.00*
206	A27	10shred violet	4.00	3.00
207	A27	£1 orange	17.00	*22.50*
		Nos. 195-207 (13)	61.45	50.55

For surcharges and overprints see Nos. 242-247, 251-253, 255-256, 319, 322, C1-C7, C13.

Independent State

Carrying Oil Palm Fruit — A29

Diamond Miner and Badge A30

Badge and: 1½p, 5sh, Bundu mask. 2p, 10sh, Bishop Crowther and Old Fourah Bay College. 3p, 6p, Sir Milton Margai. 4p, 1sh3p, Lumley Beach, Freetown. £1, Bugler.

Perf. 13x13½, 13½x13
1961, Apr. 27   Engr.   Wmk. 336

208	A29	½p blue grn & dk brn	.25	.25
209	A30	1p gray grn & brn org	1.50	.25
210	A29	1½p green & blk	.25	.25
211	A29	2p vio blue & blk	.25	.25
212	A30	3p brn org & ultra	.25	.25
213	A30	4p rose red & grnsh bl	.25	.25
214	A30	6p lilac & gray	.25	.25
215	A29	1sh org & dk brn	.35	.25
216	A30	1sh3p vio & grnsh bl	.35	.25
217	A30	2sh6p black & grn	2.75	.40
218	A29	5sh rose red & blk	1.00	*1.50*
219	A29	10shemerald & blk	1.25	*1.50*
220	A29	£1 carmine & yel	8.50	*10.00*
		Nos. 208-220 (13)	17.20	15.65

Sierra Leone's Independence.
For surcharges see Nos. 254, 274, 279-280, 285-286, 290-291, 294, 296, 299, C10, C29-C31, C132-C133.

Royal Charter, 1799 — A31

House of Representatives, Freetown, 1924 — A32

Designs: 4p, King's Yard Gate, Freetown, 1817. 1sh3p, Yacht "Britannia."

1961, Nov. 25   Engr.   Wmk. 336
221 A31   3p vermilion & blk   .25   .25
222 A31   4p violet & blk   .80   .80
223 A32   6p orange & blk   .95   .95
224 A32   1sh3p blue & blk   1.90   1.90
Nos. 221-224 (4)   3.90   3.90

Visit of Elizabeth II to Sierra Leone, Nov., 1961.
For overprints and surcharges see Nos. 272, 278, C8-C9, C11-C12.

Malaria Eradication Emblem — A33

1962, Apr. 7   Perf. 11x11½
225 A33   3p crimson   .25   .25
226 A33   1sh3p green   .40   .40

WHO drive to eradicate malaria.

Fireball Lily — A34

Jina Gbo — A35

Plants: 1½p, Stereospermum. 2p, Black-eyed Susan. 3p, Beniseed. 4p, Blushing hibiscus. 6p, Climbing lily. 1sh, Beautiful crinum. 1sh3p, Bluebells. 2sh6p, Broken hearts. 5sh, Ra-ponthi. 12sh, Blue plumbago. £1, African tulip tree.

1963, Jan. 1   Photo.   Perf. 14
Flowers in Natural Colors
227 A34   ½p olive brown   .25   .25
228 A35   1p org ver & dk red   .25   .25
229 A34   1½p green   .25   .25
230 A34   2p lemon   .25   .25
231 A34   3p dark green   .25   .25
232 A34   4p lt violet blue   .25   .25
233 A35   6p indigo   .25   .25
234 A34   1sh brt yel grn & red   .40   .25
235 A35   1sh3p dk yellow grn   1.00   1.00
236 A34   2sh6p dk gray   1.25   .70
237 A34   5sh deep violet   1.50   .90
238 A34   10sh red lilac   3.50   1.50
239 A35   £1 bright blue   6.00   6.00
Nos. 227-239 (13)   15.40   11.35

For surcharges see Nos. 271, 273, 276-277, 283-284, 289, 295, 300-305, 317-318, 320-321, 329-332, C37-C41, C57-C60, C134.

Wheat Emblem, Grain Bin and Threshing Machine A36

1sh3p, Bullom woman examining onion crop.

Perf. 11½x11
1963, Mar. 21   Engr.   Wmk. 336
240 A36   3p orange yel & blk   .25   .25
241 A36   1sh3p green & brown   .40   .40

FAO "Freedom from Hunger" campaign.
For surcharges see Nos. 275, C28.

Nos. 195, 197 and 199 Surcharged in Red, Brown, Orange, Violet or Blue

On A27

On A28

Perf. 13, 13½
1963, Apr. 27   Wmk. 4
Center in Black
242 A27   3p on ½p lt vio (R)   .40   .25
243 A27   4p on 1½p ultra (Br)   .25   .25
244 A27   6p on ½p lt vio (O)   .30   .25
245 A28   10p on 3p ultra (R)   .50   .50
246 A28   1sh6p on 3p ultra (V)   .40   .40
247 A28   3sh6p on 3p ultra (Bl)   .50   .50
Nos. 242-247 (6)   2.35   2.15

Type "a" exists in two settings, varying in the width of the line "19 Progress 63." In each sheet of 60, this line measures 19½p-21mm on 55 stamps, and 17½-18mm on 5 stamps. See Nos. C1-C7.

Centenary Emblem — A37

Design: 6p, Red Cross. 1sh3p, Centenary Emblem with curved-lines background.

Perf. 11x11½
1963, Nov. 1   Engr.   Wmk. 336
248 A37   3p purple & red   .25   .25
249 A37   6p black & red   .25   .25
250 A37   1sh3p dark green & red   1.10   1.10
Nos. 248-250 (3)   1.60   1.60

Centenary of International Red Cross.
For surcharge see No. C56.

Nos. 199, 197, 216 and 195 Ovptd. or Srchd. in Pink, Red, Violet or Brown

Perf. 13, 13½, 13½x13
1963, Nov. 4   Engr.   Wmk. 4
Center in Black except No. 254
251 A28   3p (P)   .25   .25
252 A27   4p on 1½p ultra (P)   .25   .25
253 A27   9p on 1½p (V)   .25   .25
254 A28   1sh on 1sh3p (R)   .25   .25
255 A27   1sh6p on ½p (R)   .40   .30
256 A28   2sh on 3p (Br)   .40   .30
Nos. 251-256, C8-C13 (12)   33.55   32.85

Oldest postal service (1st stamps in 1859) and the newest GPO in West Africa. Overprint in 5 lines on Nos. 251 and 256. A number of surcharge varieties and errors exist.

Map and Lion of Sierra Leone — A38

Engraved and Lithographed
1964, Feb. 10   Unwmk.   Die Cut
Self-adhesive
257 A38   1p multicolored   .25   .25
258 A38   3p multicolored   .25   .25
259 A38   4p multicolored   .25   .25
260 A38   6p multicolored   .25   .25
261 A38   1sh multicolored   .25   .25
262 A38   2sh multicolored   .30   .30
263 A38   5sh multicolored   .60   .60
Nos. 257-263,C14-C20 (14)   5.40   5.40

New York World's Fair, 1964-65.
For surcharges see Nos. 288, 297, 335 and note under No. 299.

"John F. Kennedy, American Patriot, World Humanitarian" A39

1964, May 11   Self-adhesive
264 A39   1p multicolored   .25   .25
265 A39   3p multicolored   .25   .25
266 A39   4p multicolored   .25   .25
267 A39   6p multicolored   .25   .25
268 A39   1sh multicolored   .25   .25
269 A39   2sh multicolored   .35   .35
270 A39   5sh multicolored   .60   1.25
Nos. 264-270,C21-C27 (14)   4.95   6.75

For surcharges see Nos. 281-282, 287, 292-293, 298, 333, 336, and note under No. 299.

Issues of 1961-63 Surcharged in Red, Black, Dark Blue, Violet or Orange
1964, Aug. 4
271 A35   1c on 6p (#233) (R)   .25   .25
272 A31   2c on 3p (#221)   .25   .25
273 A34   3c on 3p (#231)   .25   .25
274 A29   5c on ½p (#208) (DB)   .25   .25
275 A36   8c on 3p (#240) (R)   .25   .25
276 A35   10c on 1sh3p (#235) (R)   .30   .25
277 A34   15c on 1sh (#234)   .40   .40
278 A32   25c on 6p (#223) (V)   .60   .60
279 A30   50c on 2sh6p (#217) (O)   1.20   1.20
Nos. 271-279,C28-C31 (13)   5.95   5.90

Issues of 1961-64 Surcharged in Black or Gold
1965, Jan. 20
280 A30   1c on 3p (#212)   .25   .25
281 A39   2c on 1p (#264)   .25   .25
282 A39   4c on 3p (#265)   .25   .25
283 A35   5c on 2p (#230)   .25   .25
284 A34   1 le on 5sh (#237) (G)   2.50   2.50
285 A29   2 le on £1 (#220)   5.25   5.25
Nos. 280-285 (6)   8.75   8.75

The surcharges on Nos. 284-285 are given in numerals and spelled out in two lines; numeral on Nos. 280-283.

Issues of 1961-64 Surcharged in Red, Black, Orange, Blue or Pink
1965, Apr.
286 A29   1c on 1½p (#210) (R)   .25   .25
287 A39   2c on 4p (#265)   .25   .25
288 A38   2c on 4p (#259)   .25   .25
289 A35   3c on 1p (#228)   .25   .25
290 A29   3c on 2p (#211) (O)   .25   .25
291 A30   5c on 1sh3p (#216) (O)   .25   .25
292 A39   15c on 6p (#267)   2.75   2.75
293 A39   15c on 1sh (#268) (O)   5.00   5.00
294 A30   20c on 6p (#214) (O)   1.25   1.25
295 A35   25c on 6p (#233) (R)   1.60   1.60
296 A30   50c on 3p (#212) (R)   3.25   3.25
297 A38   60c on 5sh (#263) (Bl)   7.50   7.50
298 A39   1 le on 4p (#266) (P)   9.75   9.75
299 A29   2 le on £1 (#220) (Bl)   18.00   18.00
Nos. 286-299 (14)   50.60   50.60

Additional surcharges exist: "1c" on Nos. 260, 262, 269-270. See note after No. C41 for airmails. Value $4 each.
For surcharges see Nos. 333, 335-336.

Nos. 228, 231, 234, 235, 232, 237 Srchd.

Designs of Surcharge: Nos. 301, 304, Sir Milton Margai. Nos. 302, 305, Sir Winston Churchill.

Wmk. 336
1965, May 19   Photo.   Perf. 14
300 A35   2c on 1p multi   .40   .25
301 A34   3c on 3p multi   .25   .25
302 A34   10c on 1sh multi   .60   .30
303 A35   20c on 1sh3p multi   1.10   .30
304 A34   50c on 4p multi   1.00   .50
305 A34   75c on 5sh multi   4.00   2.00
Nos. 300-305,C37-C41 (11)   25.90   12.35

For surcharges see Nos. 329-332.

Cola Nut and Plant — A40

Coat of Arms A41

Typographed; Embossed on Silver Foil
1965   Unwmk.   Die Cut
Self-adhesive
310 A40   1c multicolored   .25   .25
311 A40   2c multicolored   .25   .25
312 A40   3c multicolored   .25   .25
313 A40   4c multicolored   .50   .40
314 A40   5c multicolored   .50   .40

Engr.; Embossed on Paper
315 A41   20c multi, cream   2.00   .75
316 A41   50c multi, cream   4.00   4.00
Nos. 310-316,C53-C55 (10)   14.80   12.70

Various advertisements printed on peelable paper backing. Nos. 310-316 have side tabs for handling and come packed in boxes of 100. Nos. 310-312 and 314 were released during November due to a stamp shortage; official release date for set, Dec. 17, 1965. See #338-356, C67, C97. For surcharges see #334, 337, 364-368.

Nos. 197-198, and 232-234, 236 Surcharged with New Value in Black or Ultramarine and Overprinted: "FIVE YEARS / INDEPENDENCE / 1961-1966"
1966, Apr. 27   Wmk. 4, 336
317 A35   1c on 6p multi   .25   .25
318 A34   2c on 4p multi   .25   .25
319 A27   3c on 1½p ultra & blk (U)   .25   .25
320 A34   8c on 1sh multi (U)   .25   .25
321 A34   10c on 2sh6p multi (U)   .25   .25
322 A28   20c on 2p lt brown (U)   .55   .55
Nos. 317-322,C56-C60 (11)   8.30   8.30

5th anniv. of independence. The surcharge on No. 317 includes an "X" over old denomination.

Lion's Head Coin — A42

Designs: 2c, 3c, ¼ Golde coin. 5c, 8c, ½ Golde coin. 25c, 1 le, 1 Golde coin. (3c, 8c, 1 le, Map of Sierra Leone.)

Litho.; Embossed on Gilt Foil
1966, Nov. 12   Unwmk.   *Die Cut*
Self-adhesive

Diameter: 2c, 3c, 38mm; 5c, 8c, 54mm; 25c, 1 le, 82mm

323	A42	2c orange & dp plum	.25	.25
324	A42	3c red lilac & emerald	.25	.25
325	A42	5c vio blue & red org	.25	.25
326	A42	8c black & Prus blue	.25	.25
327	A42	25c emerald & violet	.50	.50
328	A42	1 le red & orange	2.75	2.75
		Nos. 323-328,C61-C66 (12)	12.20	12.20

1st gold coinage of Sierra Leone. Advertising printed on paper backing.

Nos. 297-298, 303-305 and 316 Surcharged in Red, Silver, Violet, Green, Blue or Black

on A34, A35

on A38, A39

on A41

1967, Dec. 2

329	A34	6½c on 75c on 5sh (R)	.30	.30
330	A34	7½c on 75c on 5sh (S)	.30	.30
331	A34	9½c on 50c on 4p (G)	.40	.40
332	A35	12½c on 20c on 1sh3p (V)	.50	.50
333	A39	17½c on 1 le on 4p (Bl)	3.50	3.50
334	A41	17½c on 50c	3.50	3.50
335	A38	18½c on 60c on 5sh	10.00	10.00
336	A39	18½c on 1 le on 4p	3.50	3.50
337	A41	25c on 50c	1.00	1.00
		Nos. 329-337,C67-C69 (12)	24.90	24.90

Self-adhesive & Die Cut
Nos. 338-421 are self-adhesive and die cut.

Cola Nut Type of 1965
Typographed; Embossed on White Paper

1967-68   Unwmk.
White Numeral Tablet

338	A40	½c brt car, grn & yel	.25	.25
339	A40	1c brt car, grn & yel	.25	.25
340	A40	1½c orange, grn & yel	.25	.25
341	A40	2c brt car, grn & yel	.25	.25
342	A40	2½c emer, bl grn & yel	.40	.40
343	A40	3c brt car, grn & yel	.25	.25
344	A40	3½c olive, rose & ultra	.25	.25
345	A40	4½c gray ol, grn & yel	.40	.40
346	A40	5c brt car, grn & yel	.40	.40
347	A40	5½c red brn, grn & yel	.45	.45
		Nos. 338-347 (10)	3.15	3.15

Advertisements printed on peelable backing except on the 2c, 3c, 3½c and 5c.

Colored Numeral Tablet

348	A40	½c brt car, grn & yel	.25	.25
349	A40	1c brt car, grn & yel	.25	.25
350	A40	2c pink, brn & car	.25	.25
351	A40	2c brt car, grn & yel	.75	.60
352	A40	2½cbl grn, vio & org	1.00	.75
353	A40	2½cemer, bl grn & yel	.30	.25
354	A40	3c brt car, grn & yel	.25	.25
355	A40	3½clilac rose, grn & yel	.30	.30
356	A40	4c brt car, grn & yel	.25	.25
		Nos. 348-356 (9)	3.60	3.15

Nos. 344, 348-354 issued in 1968. Advertisements printed on peelable backing on the 3½c and 4c.

Map of Africa Showing Rhodesia A43

Each denomination shows map of Africa with map of one of the following countries—Portuguese Guinea, South Africa, Mozambique, Rhodesia, South West Africa or Angola.

1968, Sept. 25   Unwmk.   Litho.

357	A43	½c multicolored	.25	.25
358	A43	2c multicolored	.25	.25
359	A43	3c multicolored	.25	.25
360	A43	3½c multicolored	.25	.25
361	A43	10c multicolored	.30	.30
362	A43	11½c multicolored	.35	.35
363	A43	15c multicolored	.40	.40
		Nos. 357-363 (7)	2.05	2.05
		7 Strips of 6 (1 of each design) (42)		17.50

Intl. Human Rights Year. Sheets of 30 have 5 horizontal rows containing one stamp of each design. Advertisements printed on peelable backing.
See #C72-C78. For surcharges see #C106-C111.

No. 316 Surcharged

Engraved; Embossed on Paper
1968, Nov. 30

364	A41	6½c on 50c multi	.25	.25
365	A41	17½c on 50c multi	.30	.30
366	A41	22½c on 50c multi	.60	.60
367	A41	45c on 50c multi	.75	.75
368	A41	50c on 50c multi	1.25	1.25
		Nos. 364-368,C79-C83 (10)	6.70	6.70

19th Olympic Games, Mexico City, 10/12-27.

Sierra Leone Type A1, 1859 A44

2c, Design A40, 2c, 1965. 3½c, #220. 5c, #315. 12½c, #189. 1 le, Design A9, #2, 1912.

1969, Mar. 1   Litho.

369	A44	1c multicolored	.25	.25
370	A44	2c multicolored	.25	.25
371	A44	3½c multicolored	.25	.25
372	A44	5c multicolored	.25	.25
373	A44	12½c multicolored	.40	.40
374	A44	1 le multicolored	2.75	2.75
		Nos. 369-374,C84-C89 (12)	17.65	17.65

5th anniv. of free-form self-adhesive postage stamps. Various advertisements printed on peelable paper backing. No. 369 has side tab for handling and comes packed in boxes of 50. Nos. 370-374 are without side tabs and come 20 stamps attached to one sheet.

Globe, Freighter, Flags of Sierra Leone and Japan — A45

Map of Europe and Africa, Freighter, Flags of Sierra Leone and Netherlands — A46

Anvil Shape with Flags of Sierra Leone and: 3½c, Union Jack. 10c, 50c, West Germany. 18½c, Netherlands.

1969, July 10

375	A45	1c multicolored	.25	.25
376	A46	2c multicolored	.25	.25
377	A46	3½c multicolored	.25	.25
378	A46	10c multicolored	.25	.25
379	A46	18½c multicolored	.45	.45
380	A46	50c multicolored	1.00	1.00
		Nos. 375-380,C90-C95 (12)	8.20	8.20

Completion of the Pepel Port iron ore carrier terminal. Various advertisements printed on peelable paper backing. No. 375 has side tab for handling and comes packed in boxes of 50. Nos. 376-380 are without side tabs and come 20 stamps attached to one sheet.

African Development Bank Emblem — A47

Lithographed; Gold Impressed
1969, Sept. 10

381	A47	3½c lt blue, grn & gold	.30	.30

5th anniv. of the African Development Bank. Advertising printed on peelable paper backing, 20 imperf. stamps to a sheet of backing, roulette 10. See No. C96.

Diamond and Boy Scout Emblem A48

1969, Dec. 6   Litho.

382	A48	1c multicolored	.25	.25
383	A48	2c multicolored	.25	.25
384	A48	3½c multicolored	.25	.25
385	A48	4½c multicolored	.25	.25
386	A48	5c multicolored	.30	.30
387	A48	75c multicolored	8.00	8.00
		Nos. 382-387,C100-C105 (12)	82.55	67.35

60th anniv. of the Sierra Leone Boy Scouts. Various advertising printed on peelable paper backing. No. 382 has side tab for handling and comes packed in boxes of 100. Nos. 383-387 are without side tabs and come 20 stamps attached to one sheet.

EXPO '70 Emblems, Torii, Maps of Sierra Leone and Japan — A49

1970, June 22

388	A49	2c multicolored	.25	.25
389	A49	3½c multicolored	.25	.25
390	A49	10c multicolored	.25	.25
391	A49	12½c multicolored	.30	.30
392	A49	20c multicolored	.35	.35
393	A49	45c multicolored	.60	.60
		Nos. 388-393,C112-C117 (12)	6.15	6.15

EXPO '70 Intl. Exhib., Osaka, Japan, Mar. 15-Sept. 13. Various advertising printed on peelable paper backing.

Diamond A50

Palm Kernel — A51

Lithographed and Embossed
1970, Oct. 3   Unwmk.
Light Blue Background

394	A50	1c carmine & blk	.25	.25
395	A50	1½c brt green & car	.25	.25
396	A50	2c lilac & yel grn	.25	.25
397	A50	2½c ocher & dk bl	.25	.25
398	A50	3c vio bl & org red	.45	.45
399	A50	3½c dk blue & grn	.50	.50
400	A50	4c olive & ultra	.50	.25
401	A50	5c black & lilac	.50	.25

Orange Brown Background

402	A51	6c bright green	.60	.25
403	A51	7c rose lilac	.65	.30
404	A51	8½c orange	.70	.30
405	A51	9c lilac	.70	.30
406	A51	10c dark blue	.75	.30

407 A51 11½c blue 1.00 .50
408 A51 18½c yellow green 2.00 .75
Nos. 394-408,C118-C124 (22) 48.55 40.40

Advertisements printed on peelable paper backing. Packed in boxes of 500.

Sewa Diadem in Jewelry Box — A52

1970, Dec. 30
409 A52 2c multicolored .50 .25
410 A52 3½c multicolored .50 .25
411 A52 10c multicolored .90 .35
412 A52 12½c multicolored 1.00 .45
413 A52 40c multicolored 2.75 1.50
414 A52 1 le multicolored 13.00 11.00
Nos. 409-414,C125-C130 (12) 58.30 51.60

Diamond industry. Advertisement printed on peelable paper backing. Sheets of 20.

Traffic Pattern — A53

1971, Mar. 1 Litho.
415 A53 3½c orange & vio blue 1.50 1.50

Right hand traffic change-over. See No. C131. Advertisements printed on peelable paper backing.

Flag and Lion's Head — A54

Litho.; Embossed in Silver
1971, Apr. 27
416 A54 2c multicolored .25 .25
417 A54 3½c multicolored .25 .25
418 A54 10c multicolored .25 .25
419 A54 12½c multicolored .25 .25
420 A54 40c multicolored .80 .80
421 A54 1 le multicolored 1.75 1.75
Nos. 416-421,C137-C142 (12) 9.75 9.75

10th anniversary of independence. Advertisements printed on peelable paper backing. Stamps are in shape of Sierra Leone map.

Pres. Siaka Stevens — A55

1972 Litho. *Perf. 13*
422 A55 1c pink & multi .25 .25
423 A55 2c violet & multi .25 .25
424 A55 4c lt ultra & multi .25 .25
425 A55 5c buff & multi .25 .25
426 A55 7c rose & multi .25 .25

427 A55 10c olive & multi .25 .25
428 A55 15c emerald & multi .25 .25
429 A55 18c yellow & multi .30 .30
430 A55 20c lt blue & multi .35 .35
431 A55 25c orange & multi .40 .40
432 A55 50c brt green & multi 1.00 .60
433 A55 1 le multicolored 1.60 1.25
434 A55 2 le red org & multi 2.50 2.50
435 A55 5 le multicolored 4.00 8.50
Nos. 422-435 (14) 11.90 15.65

Shades from later printings are found on several denominations including 1c, 2c, 7c, 10c, 1 le, 2 le.

Guma Valley Dam and Bank Emblem — A56

1975, Jan. 14 Litho. *Perf. 13½*
436 A56 4c multicolored 125.00 50.00

African Development Bank, 10th anniversary. See No. C143.

Pres. Siaka Stevens and Opening of Congo Bridge — A57

1975, Aug. 24 Litho. *Perf. 13x13½*
437 A57 5c multicolored 15.00 15.00

Congo Bridge opening and Pres. Siaka Stevens' 70th birthday. See No. C144.

Pres. Tolbert and Stevens, Hands across Mano River — A58

1975, Oct. 3 Litho. *Perf. 13x13½*
438 A58 4c multicolored 1.40 1.40

Mano River Union Agreement between Liberia and Sierra Leone, signed Oct. 3, 1973. See No. C145.

Mohammed Ali Jinnah, Flags of Sierra Leone and Pakistan — A59

1977, Jan. 28 Litho. *Perf. 13 rough*
439 A59 30c multicolored 1.00 1.00

Mohammed Ali Jinnah (1876-1948), First Governor General of Pakistan.

Elizabeth II — A60

1977, Nov. 28 Litho. *Perf. 12½x12*
440 A60 5c multicolored .25 .25
441 A60 1 le multicolored 1.25 1.25

25th anniv. of the reign of Elizabeth II.

Fourah Bay College — A61

Design: 20c, Old College, vert.

Perf. 12x12½, 12½x12
1977, Dec. 19 Litho.
442 A61 5c multicolored .25 .25
443 A61 20c multicolored .35 .35

Fourah Bay College, Mt. Aureol, Freetown, founded 1827.

St. Edward's Crown and Scepters — A62

Designs: 50c, Elizabeth II in coronation coach. 1 le, Elizabeth II and Prince Philip on coronation day.

1978, Sept. 14 Litho. *Perf. 14½x14*
444 A62 5c multicolored .25 .25
445 A62 50c multicolored .50 .50
446 A62 1 le multicolored .70 .70
Nos. 444-446 (3) 1.45 1.45

25th anniv. of coronation of Elizabeth II.

Fig Tree Blue A63

Butterflies: 15c, Narrow blue-banded swallowtail. 25c, Pirate. 1 le, African giant swallowtail.

1979, Apr. 9 Litho. *Perf. 14½*
447 A63 5c multicolored .25 .25
448 A63 15c multicolored .55 .55
449 A63 25c multicolored .90 .90
450 A63 1 le multicolored 3.75 3.75
Nos. 447-450 (4) 5.45 5.45

Child, IYC and SOS Emblems — A64

Designs (Emblems and): 27c, Girl and infant. 1 le, Mother and infant.

Perf. 14x13½
1979, Aug. 13 Litho. *Wmk. 373*
451 A64 5c multicolored .25 .25
452 A64 27c multicolored .55 .55
453 A64 1 le multicolored 1.00 1.00
a. Souvenir sheet of 1 2.00 2.00
Nos. 451-453 (3) 1.80 1.80

Intl. Year of the Child and 30th anniv. of SOS villages (villages for homeless children).

Presidents Stevens and Tolbert, Pigeon Post, Mano River — A65

1979, Oct. 3 *Perf. 13½*
454 A65 5c multicolored .25 .25
455 A65 22c multicolored .30 .30
456 A65 27c multicolored .40 .40
457 A65 35c multicolored .45 .45
458 A65 1 le multicolored 1.40 1.40
a. Souvenir sheet of 1 1.40 1.40
Nos. 454-458 (5) 2.80 2.80

Mano River Union, 5th anniv.; Postal Union, 1st anniv.

Sierra Leone No. 9, Hill — A66

1979, Dec. 19 Litho. *Perf. 14½x14*
459 A66 10c Grt. Britain #6 .25 .25
460 A66 15c shown .25 .25
461 A66 50c Sierra Leone #220 .90 .90
Nos. 459-461 (3) 1.40 1.40

Souvenir Sheet
462 A66 1 le Sierra Leone #119 1.25 1.25

Sir Rowland Hill (1795-1879), originator.

Touraco A67

1980, Jan. 29 *Perf. 14*
No Date Inscription Below Design
463 A67 1c shown .25 .25
464 A67 2c Olive-bellied sunbird .25 .25
465 A67 3c Black-headed oriole .25 .25
466 A67 5c Spur-winged goose .25 .25
467 A67 7c White-bellied didric cuckoo .25 .25
468 A67 10c Gray parrot, vert. .25 .25
469 A67 15c African blue quail, vert. .45 .45
470 A67 20c West African wood owl, vert. .60 .60
471 A67 30c Blue plantain eater, vert. .90 .90
472 A67 40c Nigerian blue-breasted kingfisher, vert. 1.10 1.10
473 A67 50c Black crake, vert. 1.60 1.60
474 A67 1 le Hartlaub's duck 3.00 3.00
475 A67 2 le Black bee-eater 6.00 6.00
476 A67 5 le Denham's bustard 15.00 15.00
Nos. 463-476 (14) 30.15 30.15

For surcharges see Nos. 632-636. For overprints see Nos. 637-638.

1981 **Inscribed "1981"**
463a A67 1c multicolored 1.00 1.00
464a A67 2c multicolored 1.00 1.00
465a A67 3c multicolored 1.00 1.00
466a A67 5c multicolored 1.00 1.00

468a	A67	10c multicolored	.75	.75
469a	A67	15c multicolored	1.75	1.75
470a	A67	20c multicolored	2.50	2.50
471a	A67	30c multicolored	2.00	2.00
472a	A67	40c multicolored	2.00	2.00
473a	A67	50c multicolored	2.00	2.00
474a	A67	1 le multicolored	3.00	3.00
475a	A67	2 le multicolored	6.00	6.00
476a	A67	5 le multicolored	12.00	12.00
		Nos. 463a-476a (13)	36.00	36.00

For surcharges see Nos. 632a-636a. For overprints see Nos. 637a, 638a.

1982　　　　Inscribed "1982"

463b	A67	1c multicolored	1.00	1.00
464b	A67	2c multicolored	1.00	1.00
465b	A67	3c multicolored	1.00	1.00
466b	A67	5c multicolored	1.00	1.00
467b	A67	7c multicolored	10.00	10.00
468b	A67	10c multicolored	.75	.75
469b	A67	15c multicolored	1.75	1.75
470b	A67	20c multicolored	2.50	2.50
471b	A67	30c multicolored	2.00	2.00
472b	A67	40c multicolored	2.00	2.00
473b	A67	50c multicolored	2.00	2.00
474b	A67	1 le multicolored	3.00	3.00
475b	A67	2 le multicolored	6.00	6.00
476b	A67	5 le multicolored	12.00	12.00
		Nos. 463b-476b (14)	46.00	46.00

For surcharges see Nos. 632b-636b. For overprints see Nos. 637b, 638b.
For this design dated 1983, without watermark, see Nos. 600A-600K.

Rotary Intl., 75th Anniv. A68

1980, Feb. 23　　　　Perf. 14

477	A68	5c orange & multi	.25	.25
478	A68	27c red & multi	.30	.30
479	A68	50c green & multi	.50	.50
480	A68	1 le blue & multi	1.00	1.00
		Nos. 477-480 (4)	2.05	2.05

Mail Ship "Maria," 1884, London '80 Emblem A69

1980, May 6　　Litho.　　Perf. 14

481	A69	6c shown	.30	.30
482	A69	31c "Tarquah," 1902	.50	.50
483	A69	50c "Aureol," 1951	1.10	1.10
484	A69	1 le "Africa Palm," 1974	1.75	1.75
		Nos. 481-484 (4)	3.65	3.65

London 80 Intl. Stamp Exhib., May 6-14.

Conf. Emblem — A70

1980, July 1　　Litho.　　Perf. 14½

485	A70	20c multicolored	.25	.25
486	A70	1 le multicolored	1.00	1.00

17th African Summit Conf., Freetown, July 1-4.

Small Striped Swordtail — A71

1980, Oct. 6　　Litho.　　Perf. 14

487	A71	5c shown	.25	.25
488	A71	27c Pearl charaxes	1.00	1.00
489	A71	35c White barred charaxes	1.25	1.25
490	A71	1 le Zaddach's forester	3.50	3.50
		Nos. 487-490 (4)	6.00	6.00

Freetown Airport — A72

1980, Dec. 5　　Litho.　　Perf. 13½

491	A72	6c shown	.25	.25
492	A72	26c Mammy Yoko Hotel	.30	.30
493	A72	31c Freetown Cotton Tree	.35	.35
494	A72	40c Beindomgo Falls	.50	.50
495	A72	50c Water skiing	.60	.60
496	A72	1 le Elephant	1.25	1.25
		Nos. 491-496 (6)	3.25	3.25

Servals — A73

Cats and Kittens: No. 498, Serval kittens. No. 500a, African golden cats. No. 502a, Leopards. No. 504a, Lions. Pairs have continuous design.

1981, Feb. 23　　Litho.　　Perf. 14

497	A73	6c multicolored	.25	.25
498	A73	6c multicolored	.25	.25
a.		Pair, #497-498	.25	.25
499	A73	31c multicolored	.65	.65
500	A73	31c multicolored	.65	.65
a.		Pair, #499-500	1.60	1.60
501	A73	50c multicolored	1.25	1.25
502	A73	50c multicolored	1.25	1.25
a.		Pair, #501-502	3.00	3.00
503	A73	1 le multicolored	3.00	3.00
504	A73	1 le multicolored	3.00	3.00
a.		Pair, #503-504	6.00	6.00
		Nos. 497-504 (8)	10.30	10.30

Ambulance Clinic — A74

Wmk. 373
1981, Apr. 18　　Litho.　　Perf. 14½

505	A74	6c Soldiers, vert.	.40	.40
506	A74	31c shown	1.75	1.75
507	A74	40c Traffic policeman, vert.	2.40	2.40
508	A74	1 le Coast Guard ship	5.50	5.50
		Nos. 505-508 (4)	10.05	10.05

Anniv.: independence, 20th; republic, 10th.

Royal Wedding Issue
Common Design Type

1981　　Litho.　　Perf. 12, 14

509	CD331	31c Bouquet	.40	.40
510	CD331a	35c Sandringham	.60	.60
511	CD331	45c Charles	.75	.75
512	CD331a	60c Charles	.75	.75
513	CD331a	70c like 35c	2.00	2.00
514	CD331	1 le Couple	1.00	1.00
515	CD331a	1.30 le Charles	2.00	2.00
516	CD331a	1.50 le Couple	1.00	1.00
517	CD331a	2 le Couple	4.00	4.00
		Nos. 509-517 (9)	12.50	12.50

Souvenir Sheet

518	CD331	3 le Royal landau	3.00	3.00

31c, 45c, 1 le, 3 le issued July 22, perf. 14. 35c, 60c, 1.50 le issued in sheets of 5 plus label; perf. 12, Sept. 9. 70c, 1.30 le, 2 le issued in booklets only, perf. 14.
For surcharges see #540-546, 714, 716, 721.

Soccer Player — A75

Wmk. 373
1981, Sept. 30　　Litho.　　Perf. 14

519	A75	6c shown	.25	.25
520	A75	31c Boys planting trees	.45	.45
521	A75	1 le Duke of Edinburgh	1.00	1.00
522	A75	1 le Pres. Stevens	1.00	1.00
		Nos. 519-522 (4)	2.70	2.70

Duke of Edinburgh's Awards and Pres. Steven's Awards, 25th anniv.

Pineapples — A76

Woman Tending Rice Plants — A77

Perf. 14, 14½ (A77)

1981　　Litho.　　Wmk. 373

523	A76	6c shown	.25	.25
524	A77	6c Peanuts for export	.25	.25
525	A76	31c Peanuts	.50	.50
526	A77	31c Crushing, eating cassava	.50	.50
527	A76	50c Cassava fruits	.85	.85
528	A77	50c shown	.85	.85
529	A76	1 le Rice plants	1.25	1.25
530	A77	1 le Men tending pineapple plants	1.25	1.25
		Nos. 523-830 (8)	5.70	5.70

World Food Day. Issue dates: Nos. 523, 525, 527, 529, Oct. 16; others, Nov. 2.

Princess Diana Issue
Common Design Type

1982, July　　　　Perf. 14½

531	CD332	31c Caernarvon Castle	.50	.50
532	CD332	50c Honeymoon	.85	.85
533	CD332	2 le Wedding	2.50	2.50
		Nos. 531-533 (3)	3.85	3.85

Souvenir Sheet

534	CD332	3 le Diana	3.75	3.75

Also issued in sheetlets of 5 + label.
For overprints and surcharges see Nos. 552-555, 713, 715, 717-720, 722-723.

Scouting Year A78

1982, Aug. 23　　　　Perf. 14

535	A78	20c Studying animal husbandry	.30	.30
536	A78	50c Botanical study	.85	.85
537	A78	1 le Baden-Powell	1.60	1.60
538	A78	2 le Fishing at campsite	2.50	2.50
		Nos. 535-538 (4)	5.25	5.25

Souvenir Sheet

539	A78	3 le Raising flag	4.25	4.25

For surcharges see Nos. 694-698.

Nos. 509-512, 514, 516, 518 Surcharged

1982, Aug. 30　　　　Wmk. 373

540	CD331	50c on 31c	1.60	1.60
541	CD331	50c on 35c	1.60	1.60
542	CD331	50c on 45c	1.60	1.60
543	CD331	50c on 60c	1.60	1.60
544	CD331	90c on 1 le	2.75	2.75
545	CD331	2 le on 1.50 le	6.00	6.00
		Nos. 540-545 (6)	15.15	15.15

Souvenir Sheet

546	CD331	3.50 le on 3 le	2.50	2.50

1982 World Cup — A79

Designs: Various soccer players.

1982, Sept. 7

547	A79	20c multicolored	.50	.50
548	A79	30c multicolored	.70	.70
549	A79	1 le multicolored	2.50	2.50
550	A79	2 le multicolored	4.50	4.50
		Nos. 547-550 (4)	8.20	8.20

Souvenir Sheet

551	A79	3 le multicolored	6.00	6.00

For overprints see Nos. 561-565.

Nos. 531-534 Overprinted: "ROYAL BABY/ 21.6.82"

1982, Oct. 15　　Litho.　　Perf. 14½

552	CD332	31c multicolored	.30	.30
553	CD332	50c multicolored	.50	.50
554	CD332	2 le multicolored	1.25	1.00
		Nos. 552-554 (3)	2.05	1.80

Souvenir Sheet

555	CD332	3 le multicolored	2.50	2.50

Birth of Prince William of Wales, June 21. Also issued in sheetlets of 5 + label.
For surcharges see #715, 719-720, 723.

George Washington — A80

Various paintings of Washington. 31c, 1 le, vert.

1982, Oct. 30　　Litho.　　Perf. 14

556	A80	6c multicolored	.25	.25
557	A80	31c multicolored	.45	.45
558	A80	50c multicolored	.60	.60
559	A80	1 le multicolored	1.00	1.00
		Nos. 556-559 (4)	2.30	2.30

Souvenir Sheet

560	A80	2 le multicolored	2.25	2.25

Nos. 547-551 Overprinted with Finalists and Score

1982, Nov. 9　　　　Perf. 14

561	A79	20c multicolored	.30	.30
562	A79	30c multicolored	.45	.45
563	A79	1 le multicolored	1.25	1.25
564	A79	2 le multicolored	1.75	1.75
		Nos. 561-564 (4)	3.75	3.75

Souvenir Sheet

565	A79	3 le multicolored	2.50	2.50

Italy's victory in 1982 World Cup.

Christmas — A81

Stained-glass Windows, St. George's Cathedral, Freetown.

1982, Nov. 18   **Perf. 14**
566	A81	6c Temptation of Christ	.25	.25
567	A81	31c Baptism of Christ	.45	.45
568	A81	50c Annunciation	.60	.60
569	A81	1 le Nativity	1.00	1.00
		Nos. 566-569 (4)	2.30	2.30

Souvenir Sheet
570	A81	2 le Mary and Joseph	2.25	2.25

Charles Darwin (1809-82) A82

1982, Dec. 10
571	A82	6c Long-snouted crocodile	1.75	1.75
572	A82	31c Rainbow lizard	2.25	2.25
573	A82	50c River turtle	3.00	3.00
574	A82	1 le Chameleon	4.50	4.50
		Nos. 571-574 (4)	11.50	11.50

Souvenir Sheet
575	A82	2 le Royal python, vert.	3.75	3.75

500th Birth Anniv. of Raphael — A83

School of Athens, Fresco, Vatican. Nos. 576-579 show details.

1983, Jan. 28   **Litho.**   **Perf. 14**
576	A83	6c Diogenes	.25	.25
577	A83	31c Euclid, Ptolemy	.45	.45
578	A83	50c Euclid and his Students	.75	.75
579	A83	2 le Pythagoras, Heraclitus	2.00	2.00
		Nos. 576-579 (4)	3.45	3.45

Souvenir Sheet
580	A83	3 le Entire painting	2.75	2.75

A83a

1983, Mar. 14   **Litho.**   **Perf. 14**
581	A83a	6c Agricultural training	.25	.25
582	A83a	10c Tourism development	.25	.25
583	A83a	50c Broadcast training	.75	.75
584	A83a	1 le Airport services	1.50	1.50
		Nos. 581-584 (4)	2.75	2.75

Commonwealth Day.

25th Anniv. of Economic Commission for Africa — A84

1983, Apr. 29   **Litho.**   **Perf. 13½x13**
585	A84	1 le multicolored	1.25	1.25

Endangered Chimpanzees, World Wildlife Fund Emblem — A85

Various chimpanzees from Outamba-Kilimi Natl. Park. 10c, 31c, vert.

1983, May   **Litho.**   **Perf. 14**
586	A85	6c multicolored	2.10	2.10
587	A85	10c multicolored	2.75	2.75
588	A85	31c multicolored	5.00	5.00
589	A85	60c multicolored	7.75	7.75
		Nos. 586-589 (4)	17.60	17.60

Souvenir Sheet
590	A85	3 le Elephants	7.00	7.00

For surcharges see No. 2906-2909.

World Communications Year — A86

1983, July 14   **Perf. 14**
591	A86	6c Traditional communications	.25	.25
592	A86	10c Mano River mail	.25	.25
593	A86	20c Satellite ground station	.30	.30
594	A86	1 le English packet, 1805	1.25	1.25
		Nos. 591-594 (4)	2.05	2.05

Souvenir Sheet
595	A86	2 le Map, phone, envelope	2.00	2.00

Manned Flight Bicentenary — A87

1983, Aug. 31   **Litho.**   **Perf. 14**
596	A87	6c Montgolfiere, 1783, vert.	.30	.30
597	A87	20c Deutschland blimp, 1897	.80	.80
598	A87	50c Norge I blimp, North Pole, 1926	1.90	1.90
599	A87	1 le Cape Sierra sport balloon, Freetown, 1983, vert.	3.75	3.75
		Nos. 596-599 (4)	6.75	6.75

Souvenir Sheet
600	A87	2 le Futuristic airship	3.00	3.00

Birds Type of 1980

1983, Oct. 1   **Unwmk.**   **Perf. 14**
Inscribed "1983"
600A	A67	1c Touraco	1.50	1.50
600B	A67	2c Olive-bellied sunbird	1.50	1.50
600C	A67	5c Spur-winged goose	1.00	1.00
600D	A67	10c Gray parrot, vert.	1.25	1.25
600E	A67	15c African blue quail, vert.	1.75	1.75

600F	A67	20c West African wood owl, vert.	2.75	2.75
600G	A67	30c Blue plantain eater, vert.	2.50	2.50
600H	A67	40c Nigerian blue-breasted kingfisher, vert.	3.50	3.50
600I	A67	50c Black crake, vert.	3.50	3.50
600J	A67	2 le Black bee-eater	10.00	10.00
600K	A67	5 le Denham's bustard	15.00	15.00
		Nos. 600A-600K (11)	44.25	44.25

For surcharges see Nos. 632A-636E. For overprints see Nos. 638C-638D.

Walt Disney, Space Ark Fantasy — A88

1983, Nov.
601	A88	1c Hippopotamus, Huey, Dewey and Louie	.25	.25
602	A88	1c Mickey Mouse and Snake	.25	.25
603	A88	3c Elephant and Donald Duck	.25	.25
604	A88	3c Zebra and Goofy	.25	.25
605	A88	10c Lion and Ludwig von Drake	.25	.25
606	A88	10c Rhinoceros and Goofy	.25	.25
607	A88	2 le Giraffe and Mickey Mouse	1.75	1.75
608	A88	3 le Monkey and Donald Duck	2.50	2.50
		Nos. 601-608 (8)	5.75	5.75

Souvenir Sheet
609	A88	5 le Mickey Mouse and animals	5.50	5.50

10th Anniv. of Mano River Union A89

1984, Feb. 8   **Litho.**   **Perf. 15**
610	A89	6c Teaching Program graduates	.25	.25
611	A89	25c Emblem	.25	.25
612	A89	31c Map, presidents	.25	.25
613	A89	41c Guinea Accession signing	.35	.35
a.		Souvenir sheet of 1	.50	.50
		Nos. 610-613 (4)	1.10	1.10

23rd Olympic Games, Los Angeles, July 28-Aug. 12 — A90

1984, Mar. 15   **Perf. 14**
614	A90	90c Gymnastics	.55	.55
615	A90	1 le Hurdles	.70	.70
616	A90	3 le Javelin	1.25	1.25
		Nos. 614-616 (3)	2.50	2.50

Souvenir Sheet
617	A90	7 le Boxing	3.75	3.75

For surcharges see Nos. 699-702.

Apollo 11, 15th Anniv. — A91

1984, May 14   **Litho.**   **Perf. 14**
618	A91	50c Lift off	.40	.40
619	A91	75c Lunar landing	.60	.60
620	A91	1.25 le 1st step on moon	1.00	1.00
621	A91	2.50 le Walking on moon	2.00	2.00
		Nos. 618-621 (4)	4.00	4.00

Souvenir Sheet
622	A91	5 le TV transmission, horiz.	4.00	4.00

UPU Congress A92

1984, June 19
623	A92	4 le Concorde	5.00	5.00

Souvenir Sheet
624	A92	4 le UPU emblem, von Stephan	3.25	3.25

UN Decade for African Transportation — A93

Various cars.

1984, July 16   **Perf. 14½x15**
625	A93	12c Citroen	.25	.25
626	A93	60c Locomobile	.70	.70
627	A93	90c AC Ace	.95	.95
628	A93	1 le Vauxhall Prince Henry	1.25	1.25
629	A93	1.50 le Delahaye-185	1.75	1.75
630	A93	2 le Mazda	2.25	2.25
		Nos. 625-630 (6)	7.15	7.15

Souvenir Sheet
Perf. 15
631	A93	6 le Volkswagon Beetle	6.50	6.50

Nos. 466, 468, 475 Surcharged
Wmk. 373

1984, Aug. 3   **Perf. 14**
632	A67	25c on 10c multi	7.50	7.50
633	A67	40c on 10c multi	7.50	7.50
634	A67	50c on 2 le multi	7.50	7.50
635	A67	70c on 5c multi	7.50	7.50
636	A67	10 le on 5c multi	7.50	7.50
		Nos. 632-636 (5)	37.50	37.50

Nos. 466a, 468a, 475a Surcharged
632a	A67	25c on 10c multi	7.50	7.50
633a	A67	40c on 10c multi	7.50	7.50
634a	A67	50c on 2 le	7.50	7.50
635a	A67	70c on 5c	7.50	7.50
636a	A67	10 le on 5c	7.50	7.50
		Nos. 632a-636a (5)	37.50	37.50

Nos. 466b, 468b, 475b Surcharged
632b	A67	25c on 10c multi	7.50	7.50
633b	A67	40c on 10c multi	7.50	7.50
634b	A67	50c on 2 le	7.50	7.50
635b	A67	70c on 5c	7.50	7.50
636b	A67	10 le on 5c	7.50	7.50
		Nos. 632b-636b (5)	37.50	37.50

Nos. 600C, 600D, 600J Surcharged

1984, Aug. 3   **Unwmk.**   **Perf.**
636A	A67	25c on 10c multi	1.40	1.40
636B	A67	40c on 10c multi	1.00	1.00
636C	A67	50c on 2 le multi	1.00	1.00
636D	A67	50c on 5c multi	1.00	1.00
636E	A67	10 le on 5c multi	4.50	4.50
		Nos. 636A-636E (5)	8.90	8.90

#473, 476 Ovptd.: "AUSIPEX 84"
Wmk. 373

1984, Aug. 22   **Litho.**   **Perf. 14**
637	A67	50c multi (#473)	6.00	6.00
a.		On #473a	6.00	6.00
b.		On #473b	6.00	6.00
638	A67	5 le multi (#476)	16.00	16.00
a.		On #476a	16.00	16.00
b.		On #476b	16.00	16.00

On Nos. 600I, 600K
638C	A67	50c multicolored	2.00	2.00
638D	A67	5 le multicolored	4.00	4.00

Portuguese Caravel Da Sintra — A94

1984

639	A94	2c shown	.80	1.50
640	A94	5c Merlin of Bristol	.80	.80
641	A94	10c Golden Hind	1.25	.60
642	A94	15c Interloper Morduant	2.00	.60
643	A94	20c Navy Board Transport Atlantic	1.50	.60
644	A94	25c Navy Vessel Lapwing	1.50	.60
645	A94	30c Brig Traveller	1.50	.60
646	A94	40c Schooner Amistad	1.60	.90
647	A94	50c Teazer	1.75	1.10
648	A94	70c Cable Ship Scotia	2.00	1.60
649	A94	1 le Alecto	2.50	2.25
650	A94	2 le Blonde	5.00	4.50
651	A94	5 le Fox	14.00	12.00
652	A94	10 le Mail ship Accra	24.00	24.00
		Nos. 639-652 (14)	60.20	51.65

Issued: #639-649, 9/5; #650-651, 10/9; 10 le, 11/7.

See #739-740. For surcharges see #809-812.

1985   Perf. 12½x12

639a	A94	2c	.25	.25
640a	A94	5c	.25	.25
641a	A94	10c	.25	.25
643a	A94	20c	.25	.25
644a	A94	25c	.25	.25
645a	A94	30c	.25	.25
646a	A94	40c	.25	.25
647a	A94	50c	.25	.25
648a	A94	70c	.25	.25
649a	A94	1 le	1.50	1.50
650a	A94	2 le	3.00	3.00
651a	A94	5 le	7.25	7.25
652a	A94	10 le	14.50	14.50
		Nos. 639a-652a (13)	28.50	28.50

125th Anniv. of Sierra Leone Postage Stamps A95

1984, Oct. 9

653	A95	50c Mail messenger, No. 2	.45	.45
654	A95	2 le Post Master receiving letters, No. 2	2.00	2.00
655	A95	3 le Cover	3.00	3.00
		Nos. 653-655 (3)	5.45	5.45

Souvenir Sheet

656	A95	5 le Penny Black, No. 2	3.25	3.25

50th Anniv. of Donald Duck — A95a

1984, Nov.   Litho.   Perf. 14x13½

657	A95a	1c Wise Little Hen	.25	.25
658	A95a	2c Boat Builders	.25	.25
659	A95a	3c Three Caballeros	.25	.25
660	A95a	4c Mathematic Land	.25	.25
661	A95a	5c Mickey Mouse Club	.25	.25
662	A95a	10c On Parade	.25	.25
663	A95a	1 le Don Donald	1.40	1.40
663A	A95a	2 le Donald gets drafted, p. 12½x12	3.00	3.00
664	A95a	4 le Tokyo Disneyland	6.00	6.00
		Nos. 657-664 (9)	11.90	11.90

Souvenir Sheet

665	A95a	5 le Sketches	9.00	9.00

Christmas — A96

Mother and Child paintings.

1984, Nov. 28   Perf. 14

666	A96	20c Pisanello	.25	.25
667	A96	1 le Memling	.50	.50
668	A96	2 le Raphael	1.00	1.00
669	A96	3 le van der Werff	1.25	1.25
		Nos. 666-669 (4)	3.00	3.00

Souvenir Sheet

670	A96	6 le Picasso	4.25	4.25

Songbirds A97

1985, Jan. 31   Litho.

671	A97	40c Straw-tailed whydah	1.25	1.25
672	A97	90c Spotted flycatcher	2.75	2.75
673	A97	1.30 le Garden warbler	4.25	4.25
674	A97	3 le Speke's weaver	7.50	7.50
		Nos. 671-674 (4)	15.75	15.75

Souvenir Sheet

675	A97	5 le Great gray shrike	5.75	5.75

International Youth Year — A98

1985, Feb. 14   Litho.

676	A98	1.15 le Fishing	.75	.75
677	A98	1.50 le Timber	.90	.90
678	A98	2.15 le Rice farming	1.40	1.40
		Nos. 676-678 (3)	3.05	3.05

Souvenir Sheet

679	A98	5 le Diamond polishing	5.00	5.00

Intl. Civil Aviation Org., 40th Anniv. A100

Early aviators and their aircraft: 70c, Eddie Rickenbacker, Spad XIII (1918). 1.25 le, Samuel P. Langley, Aerodrome No. 5. 1.30 le, Orville and Wilbur Wright, Flyer 1. 2 le, Charles Lindbergh, Spirit of St. Louis.

1985, Feb. 28   Litho.   Perf. 14

680	A100	70c multicolored	1.40	1.40
681	A100	1.25 le multicolored	2.40	2.40
682	A100	1.30 le multicolored	2.40	2.40
683	A100	2 le multicolored	4.50	4.50
		Nos. 680-683 (4)	10.70	10.70

Souvenir Sheet

684	A100	5 le Jet over Freetown	4.00	4.00

Easter A101

Religious paintings: Nos. 685, 687, 689 by Botticelli (1445-1510). Nos. 686, 688 by Velazquez (1599-1660).

1985, Apr. 29

685	A101	45c The Temptation of Christ	.25	.25
686	A101	70c Christ at the Column	.35	.35
687	A101	1.55 le Pieta	.95	.95
688	A101	10 le Christ on the Cross	7.00	7.00
		Nos. 685-688 (4)	8.55	8.55

Souvenir Sheet

689	A101	12 le Man of Sorrows	6.00	6.00

Queen Mother, 85th Birthday — A102

Designs: 1 le, Queen Mother at St. Peter's Cathedral, London, vert. 1.70 le, With Double Star at Sandown Racetrack. 10 le, Attending the gala ballet at Covent Garden, 1971, vert. 12 le, With Princess Anne at Ascot, vert.

1985, July 8   Litho.   Perf. 14

690	A102	1 le multicolored	.30	.30
691	A102	1.70 le multicolored	.60	.60
692	A102	10 le multicolored	3.25	3.25
		Nos. 690-692 (3)	4.15	4.15

Souvenir Sheet

693	A102	12 le multicolored	4.00	4.00

Nos. 535-539 Surcharged "75th Anniversary / of Girl Guides," Black Bar and New Value

1985, July 25

694	A78	70c on 20c multi	1.00	1.00
695	A78	1.30 le on 50c multi	2.25	2.25
696	A78	5 le on 1 le multi	1.50	1.50
697	A78	7 le on 2 le multi	2.75	2.75
		Nos. 694-697 (4)	7.50	7.50

Souvenir Sheet

698	A78	15 le on 3 le multi	6.00	6.00

Nos. 614-617 Surcharged with Winners Names, Country, "Gold Medal," Black Bar and New Value

1985, July 25

699	A90	2 le on 90c Ma Yanhonjg, China	.90	.90
700	A90	4 le on 1 le E. Moses, USA	1.60	1.60
701	A90	8 le on 3 le A. Haerkoenen, Finland	3.25	3.25
		Nos. 699-701 (3)	5.75	5.75

Souvenir Sheet

702	A90	15 le on 7 le M. Taylor, USA	6.00	6.00

1905 Chater-Lea, Hill Station House — A103

Designs: 2 le, Honda XR 350 R, QE II Quay. 4 le, Kawasaki Vulcan, Bo Clock Tower. 5 le, Harley-Davidson Electra-Glide, Makeni. 12 le, 1893 Millet.

1985, Aug. 15

703	A103	1.40 le multicolored	1.10	1.10
704	A103	2 le multicolored	1.50	1.50
705	A103	4 le multicolored	3.00	3.00
706	A103	5 le multicolored	3.75	3.75
		Nos. 703-706 (4)	9.35	9.35

Souvenir Sheet

707	A103	12 le multicolored	8.00	8.00

Motorcycle cent., Decade for African Transport.

A104

1985, Sept. 3

708	A104	70c Viola pomposa	.50	.50
709	A104	3 le Spinet	2.50	2.50
710	A104	4 le Lute	3.25	3.25
711	A104	5 le Oboe	3.50	3.50
		Nos. 708-711 (4)	9.75	9.75

Souvenir Sheet

712	A104	12 le Portrait	8.00	8.00

Johann Sebastian Bach (1685-1750), composer. Nos. 708-712 show music from "Clavier Ubang."

Nos. 510, 512, 516, 531-534, 552-555 Surcharged

1985, Sept. 30   Perfs. as Before
Designs CD331-CD332

713		70c on 31c #531	.65	.65
714		1.30 le on 60c #512	3.00	3.00
715		1.30 le on 31c #552	1.40	1.40
716		2 le on 35c #510	4.00	4.00
717		4 le on 50c #532	4.00	4.00
718		5 le on 2 le #533	4.75	4.75
719		5 le on 50c #553	4.75	4.75
720		7 le on 2 le #554	6.75	6.75
721		8 le on 1.50 le #516	12.50	12.50
		Nos. 713-721 (9)	41.80	41.80

Souvenir Sheets

722		15 le on 3 le #534	12.00	12.00
723		15 le on 3 le #555	12.00	12.00

Christmas — A105

Madonna and child paintings by: 70c, Carlo Crivelli (c. 1430-1494). 3 le, Dirk Bouts (c. 1400-1475). 4 le, Antonello de Messina (c. 1430-1479). 5 le, Stefan Lochner (c. 1400-1451). 12 le, Miniature from the Book of Kells, 9th cent., Ireland.

1985, Oct. 18   Litho.   Perf. 14

724	A105	70c multicolored	.25	.25
725	A105	3 le multicolored	1.10	1.10
726	A105	4 le multicolored	1.25	1.25
727	A105	5 le multicolored	1.75	1.75
		Nos. 724-727 (4)	4.35	4.35

Miniature Sheet

728	A105	12 le multicolored	3.50	3.50

Jacob and Wilhelm Grimm, Fabulists — A106

Mark Twain, American Humorist A107

Walt Disney characters acting out Twain quotes (A107) or in Rumpelstiltskin (A106).

1985, Oct. 30	Litho.	Perf. 14	
729 A106	70c multicolored	.35	.35
730 A106	1.30 le multicolored	.50	.50
731 A107	1.50 le multicolored	1.25	1.25
732 A106	2 le multicolored	.75	.75
733 A107	3 le multicolored	1.50	1.50
734 A107	4 le multicolored	1.60	1.60
735 A107	5 le multicolored	1.75	1.75
736 A106	10 le multicolored	3.25	3.25
Nos. 729-736 (8)		10.95	10.95

Souvenir Sheets

737 A106	15 le multicolored	4.75	4.75
738 A107	15 le multicolored	6.00	6.00

Nos. 731, 733-735 bear the Intl. Youth Year emblem.

Ship Type of 1984

1985, Nov. 15			
739 A94	15 le Favourite	4.50	4.50
740 A94	25 le Euryalus	7.50	7.50

UN, 40th Anniv. A108

Stamps of UN and famous men: 2 le, No. 30, Kennedy. 4 le, No. 59, Einstein. 7 le, No. 44, Maimonides (1135-1204), medieval Judaic scholar. 12 le, Martin Luther King, Jr. (1929-1968), civil rights leader, vert.

1985, Nov. 28	Litho.	Perf. 14½	
741 A108	2 le multicolored	1.40	1.40
742 A108	4 le multicolored	2.50	2.50
743 A108	7 le multicolored	4.75	4.75
Nos. 741-743 (3)		8.65	8.65

Souvenir Sheet

744 A108	12 le multicolored	3.50	3.50

1986 World Cup Soccer Championships A109

Various soccer plays.

1986, Mar. 3		Perf. 14	
745 A109	70c multicolored	.40	.40
746 A109	3 le multicolored	1.50	1.50
747 A109	4 le multicolored	2.10	2.10
748 A109	5 le multicolored	2.75	2.75
Nos. 745-748 (4)		6.75	6.75

Souvenir Sheet

749 A109	12 le multicolored	3.50	3.50

For overprints and surcharges see Nos. 788-792.

Statue of Liberty, Cent. — A110

New York City: 40c, Times Square, 1905. 70c, Times Square, 1986. 1 le, Tally Ho Coach, c. 1880, horiz. 10 le, Liberty Lines express bus, 1986. 12 le, Statue of Liberty.

1986, Mar. 11			
750 A110	40c multicolored	.25	.25
751 A110	70c multicolored	.25	.25
752 A110	1 le multicolored	.55	.55
753 A110	10 le multicolored	3.50	3.50
Nos. 750-753 (4)		4.55	4.55

Souvenir Sheet

754 A110	12 le multicolored	4.50	4.50

Halley's Comet — A112

15c, Johannes Kepler (1571-1630), German astronomer, & Paris Observatory. 50c, US space shuttle landing, 1985. 70c, Bayeux Tapestry (detail), 1066 sighting. 10 le, Arthurian magician, Merlin, sights comet, 530. 12 le, Comet over Sierra Leone.

1986, Apr. 1			
755 A111	15c multicolored	.25	.25
756 A111	50c multicolored	.25	.25
757 A111	70c multicolored	.35	.35
758 A111	10 le multicolored	5.25	5.25
Nos. 755-758 (4)		6.10	6.10

Souvenir Sheet

759 A112	12 le multicolored	3.25	3.25

For overprints and surcharges see Nos. 813-817.

Queen Elizabeth II, 60th Birthday
Common Design Type

1986, Apr. 21			
760 CD339	10c Cranwell, 1951	.25	.25
761 CD339	1.70 le Garter Ceremony	.55	.55
762 CD339	10 le Braemar Games, 1970	2.75	2.75
Nos. 760-762 (3)		3.55	3.55

Souvenir Sheet

763 CD339	12 le Windsor Castle, 1943	2.75	2.75

For surcharges see Nos. 793-795.

AMERIPEX '86 — A113

Locomotives.

1986, May 22			
764 A113	50c Hiawatha, Milwaukee	1.40	1.40
765 A113	2 le The Rocket, Rock Is.	2.50	2.50
766 A113	4 le Prospector, Rio Grande	4.00	4.00
767 A113	7 le Daylight, So. Pacific	4.75	4.75
Nos. 764-767 (4)		12.65	12.65

Souvenir Sheet

768 A113	12 le Broadway, Pennsylvania	7.00	7.00

Royal Wedding Issue, 1986
Common Design Type

Designs: 10c, Prince Andrew and Sarah Ferguson. 1.70 le, Andrew with shotgun. 10 le, Andrew saluting. 12 le, Couple, diff.

1986, July 23			
769 CD340	10c multi	.25	.25
770 CD340	1.70 le multi	.40	.40
771 CD340	10 le multi	1.90	1.90
Nos. 769-771 (3)		2.55	2.55

Souvenir Sheet

772 CD340	12 le multi	3.00	3.00

For surcharges see Nos. 796-798.

Indigenous Flowers — A114

1986, Aug. 25	Litho.	Perf. 15	
773 A114	70c Monodora myristica	.25	.25
774 A114	1.50 le Gloriosa simplex	1.00	1.00
775 A114	4 le Mussaenda erythrophylla	.45	.45
776 A114	6 le Crinum ornatum	.70	.70
777 A114	8 le Bauhinia purpurea	.80	.80
778 A114	10 le Bombax costatum	1.00	1.00
779 A114	20 le Hibiscus rosa-sinensis	1.75	1.75
780 A114	30 le Cassia fistula	2.25	2.25
Nos. 773-780 (8)		8.20	8.20

Souvenir Sheets

781 A114	40 le Clitoria ternatea	4.50	4.50
782 A114	40 le Plumbago auriculata	4.50	4.50

US Peace Corps in Sierra Leone, 25th Anniv. A115

1986, Aug. 26	Litho.	Perf. 14	
783 A115	10 le multi	1.40	1.40

Intl. Peace Year A116

1986, Sept. 1			
784 A116	1 le Transportation	.40	.40
785 A116	2 le Education	.60	.60
786 A116	5 le Communications	1.25	1.25
787 A116	10 le Fishing	2.25	2.25
Nos. 784-787 (4)		4.50	4.50

Nos. 745-749 Ovptd. or Surcharged "WINNERS / Argentina 3 / West Germany 2" in Gold

1986, Sept. 1		Perf. 14	
788 A109	70c multi	.40	.40
789 A109	3 le multi	.90	.90
790 A109	4 le multi	1.25	1.25
791 A109	40 le on 5 le multi	10.50	10.50
Nos. 788-791 (4)		13.05	13.05

Souvenir Sheet

792 A109	40 le on 12 le multi	5.00	5.00

Nos. 760, 762-763 Surcharged in Silver or Black

1986, Sept. 15			
793 CD339	70c on 10c multi	.50	.25
794 CD339	45 le on 10 le multi	4.00	4.00

Souvenir Sheet

795 CD339	50 le on 12 le (B)	5.00	5.00

Nos. 769, 771-772 Surcharged in Silver

1986, Sept. 15			
796 CD340	70c on 10c multi	.25	.25
797 CD340	45 le on 10 le multi	2.50	2.50

Souvenir Sheet

798 CD340	50 le on 12 le multi	5.00	5.00

STOCKHOLMIA '86 — A117

Disney characters in Mother Goose fairy tales.

1986, Sept. 22		Perf. 11	
799 A117	70c Jack and Jill	.25	.25
800 A117	1 le Wee Willie Winkie	.25	.25
801 A117	2 le Little Miss Muffet	.25	.25
802 A117	4 le Old King Cole	.55	.55
803 A117	5 le Mary Quite Contrary	.85	.85
804 A117	10 le Little Bo Peep	1.25	1.25
805 A117	25 le Polly Put the Kettle On	3.25	3.25
806 A117	35 le Rub-a-Dub-Dub	4.50	4.50
Nos. 799-806 (8)		11.15	11.15

Souvenir Sheets

807 A117	40 le Old Woman in the Shoe	5.25	5.25
808 A117	40 le Simple Simon	5.25	5.25

Nos. 639, 645-646 and 648 Surcharged

1986, Oct. 15			
809 A94	30 le on 2c multi	2.75	2.75
810 A94	40 le on 30c multi	3.00	3.00
811 A94	45 le on 40c multi	3.50	3.50
812 A94	50 le on 70c multi	3.50	3.50
Nos. 809-812 (4)		12.75	12.75

Nos. 755-759 Ovptd. or Srchd. with Halley's Comet Emblem in Black or Silver

1986, Oct. 15			
813 A111	50c multi	.25	.25
814 A111	70c multi	.25	.25
815 A111	1.50 le on 15c multi	.25	.25
816 A111	45 le on 10 le multi	7.25	7.25
Nos. 813-816 (4)		8.00	8.00

Souvenir Sheet

817 A112	50 le on 12 le multi (S)	6.00	6.00

Christmas A118

Paintings by Titian: 70c, Virgin and Child with St. Dorothy. $1.50 le, The Gypsy Madonna, vert. 20 le, The Holy Family. 30 le, Virgin and Child in an Evening Landscape, vert. 40 le, Madonna with the Pesaro Family.

1986, Nov. 17	Litho.	Perf. 14	
818 A118	70c multi	.25	.25
819 A118	1.50 le multi	.25	.25
820 A118	20 le multi	3.25	3.25
821 A118	30 le multi	4.25	4.25
Nos. 818-821 (4)		8.00	8.00

Souvenir Sheet

822 A118	40 le multi	12.00	12.00

Statue of Liberty, Cent. A119

Pictures of the statue by Peter B. Kaplan before and after renovation. Nos. 823, 825-826, 828-829, 831, vert.

1987, Jan. 2   **Perf. 14**

823	A119	70c Torch assembly	.25	.25
824	A119	1.50 le Liberty holding torch	.25	.25
825	A119	2 le Torch assembly, diff.	.25	.25
826	A119	3 le Man, torch	.25	.25
827	A119	4 le Crown	.25	.25
828	A119	5 le Lighting of the statue	.30	.30
829	A119	10 le Lighting, diff.	.60	.60
830	A119	25 le Liberty Is.	1.50	1.50
831	A119	30 le Face	1.75	1.75
	Nos. 823-831 (9)		5.40	5.40

UNICEF, 40th Anniv. A120

1987, Mar. 18   **Litho.**   **Perf. 14**

832	A120	10 le multi	.80	.80

Nomoli Soapstone Sculpture — A121

An early view of Freetown

Tall Ship in Harbor, Freetown — A122

1987, Jan. 2   **Perf. 15**

833	A121	2 le shown	.25	.25
834	A121	5 le King's Yard Gate, 1817	.30	.30

Souvenir Sheet

835	A122	60 le shown	4.00	4.00

First settlement of liberated slaves returned to the African continent by the British, Freetown, bicent.

America's Cup — A123

Constellation, 1964 — A124

1987, June 15   **Litho.**   **Perf. 14**

836	A123	1 le USA, 1987	.25	.25
837	A123	1.50 le New Zealand, 1987	.25	.25
838	A123	2.50 le French Kiss, 1987	.25	.25

839	A123	10 le Stars & Stripes, 1987	1.10	1.10
840	A123	15 le Australia II, 1983	1.50	1.50
841	A123	25 le Freedom, 1980	2.40	2.40
842	A123	30 le Kookaburra III, 1987	2.40	2.40
	Nos. 836-842 (7)		8.15	8.15

Souvenir Sheet

843	A124	50 le shown	4.00	4.00

Nos. 837, 839 and 842 horiz.
For overprint see No. 964.

CAPEX '87 — A125

Disney characters, Canadian sights.

1987, June 15   **Perf. 11**

849	A125	2 le Parliament	.25	.25
850	A125	5 le Totem poles	.45	.45
851	A125	10 le Perce Rock	.75	.75
852	A125	20 le Canadian Rockies	1.40	1.40
853	A125	25 le Old Quebec City	1.90	1.90
854	A125	45 le Aurora Borealis	3.00	3.00
855	A125	50 le Yukon P.O.	3.25	3.25
856	A125	75 le Niagara Falls	5.50	5.50
	Nos. 849-856 (8)		16.50	16.50

Souvenir Sheets

857	A125	100 le Exploring Newfoundland	6.00	6.00
858	A125	100 le Calgary Exhibition and Stampede	6.00	6.00

Butterflies — A126   1988 Summer Olympics, Seoul — A127

1987, Aug. 4   **Perf. 14**

859	A126	10c Blue salamis	2.10	.70
b.		Inscribed "1989"	1.75	1.00
860	A126	20c Pale-tailed blue	2.10	.70
b.		Inscribed "1989"	1.75	1.00
861	A126	40c Acraea swallowtail	2.10	.70
b.		Inscribed "1989"	1.75	.75
862	A126	1 le Broad blue-banded swallowtail	2.10	.70
b.		Inscribed "1989"	2.50	1.10
863	A126	2 le Giant blue swallowtail	2.10	.70
b.		Inscribed "1989"	3.00	1.50
864	A126	3 le Blood-red cymothoe	2.50	1.10
b.		Inscribed "1989"	4.25	2.25
865	A126	5 le Green-spotted swallowtail	2.50	1.10
866	A126	10 le Small-striped swordtail	4.25	1.50
867	A126	20 le Congo long-tailed blue	7.75	3.50
868	A126	25 le Blue monarch	8.00	4.50
869	A126	30 le Black and yellow swallowtail	8.00	4.75
870	A126	45 le Western blue charaxes	13.50	6.50
871	A126	60 le Violet-washed charaxes	3.25	5.25
872	A126	75 le Orange admiral	3.75	4.75
873	A126	100 le Blue-patched judy	5.75	9.00
	Nos. 859-873 (15)		69.75	45.45

See Nos. 1257-1260, 1332A-1332L.

1988-89   **Perf. 12x12½**

859a	A126	10c	.60	.25
860a	A126	20c	.90	.25
861a	A126	40c	.90	.25
862a	A126	1 le	.90	.25
863a	A126	2 le	1.10	.25
864a	A126	3 le	1.10	.25
865a	A126	5 le	1.10	.25
866a	A126	10 le	1.10	.40
867a	A126	20 le	1.40	.80
868a	A126	25 le	1.40	1.00
869a	A126	30 le	1.50	1.25
870a	A126	45 le	1.75	1.75
873a	A126	100 le	6.25	5.00
	Nos. 859a-873a (13)		20.00	11.95

1987, Aug. 10

874	A127	5 le Cycling	.25	.25
875	A127	10 le Equestrian	.60	.60
876	A127	45 le Running	2.75	2.75
877	A127	50 le Tennis	3.00	3.00
	Nos. 874-877 (4)		6.60	6.60

Souvenir Sheet

878	A127	100 le Gold medal, map	6.50	6.50

Works of Art by Marc Chagall, (1887-1985) A128

1987, Aug. 17   **Perf. 14**

879	A128	3 le The Quarrel, 1911-1912	.25	.25
880	A128	5 le Rebecca Giving Abraham's Servant a Drink	.25	.25
881	A128	10 le The Village	.50	.50
882	A128	20 le Ida at the Window, 1924	.85	.85
883	A128	25 le Promenade, 1913	1.50	1.50
884	A128	45 le Peasants	3.25	3.25
885	A128	50 le Turquoise Plate	4.00	4.00
886	A128	75 le Cemetery Gate, 1917	5.50	5.50
	Nos. 879-886 (8)		16.10	16.10

Size: 111x95mm

Imperf

887	A128	100 le Wedding Feast, Stravinsky's Ballet, 1945	8.00	8.00
888	A128	100 le The Falling Angel	8.00	8.00

Nos. 879-886 printed in sheets of 10 (5x2). Stamp selvage inscribed with name of painting.

Transportation Innovations — A129

1987, Aug. 28   **Perf. 15**

889	A129	3 le Apollo 8, 1968, vert.	.25	.25
890	A129	5 le Blanchard's Balloon, 1793	.25	.25
891	A129	10 le Lockheed Vega, 1932	.50	.50
892	A129	15 le Vicker's Vimy, 1919	.80	.80
893	A129	20 le Tank Mk1, c. 1918	1.40	1.40
894	A129	25 le Sikorsky VS-300, 1939	1.60	1.60
895	A129	30 le Flyer 1, 1903	2.10	2.10
896	A129	35 le Bleriot XI, 1909	2.25	2.25
897	A129	40 le Paraplane, 1983, vert.	2.75	2.75
898	A129	50 le Daimler's motorcycle, 1885	3.25	3.25
	Nos. 889-898 (10)		15.15	15.15

Rhinegold Express, Ireland (1st Electric Railroad, 1884) — A129a

1987, Aug. 28   **Litho.**   **Perf. 15**

898A	A129a	100 le multi	7.00	7.00

Wimbledon Tennis Champions — A130

2 le, Evonne Goolagong, Australia. 5 le, Martina Navratilova, US-Czechoslovakia. 10 le, Jimmy Connors, US. 15 le, Bjorn Borg, Sweden. 30 le, Boris Becker, West Germany. 40 le, John McEnroe, US. 50 le, Chris Evert Lloyd, US. 75 le, Virgina Wade, Great Britain. #907, Steffi Graf, German Open 1986. #908, Boris Becker.

1987, Sept. 4   **Perf. 14**

899	A130	2 le multicolored	.30	.30
900	A130	5 le multicolored	.75	.75
901	A130	10 le multicolored	1.10	1.10
902	A130	15 le multicolored	1.50	1.50
903	A130	30 le multicolored	3.00	3.00
904	A130	40 le multicolored	3.25	3.25
905	A130	50 le multicolored	3.50	3.50
906	A130	75 le multicolored	4.75	4.75
	Nos. 899-906 (8)		18.15	18.15

Souvenir Sheets

907	A130	100 le multicolored	9.00	9.00
908	A130	100 le multicolored	9.00	9.00

For overprints see Nos. 965, 1023-1024.

Discovery of America, 500th Anniv. (in 1992) A131

5 le, Ducats, Santa Maria, Issac Abravanel (1437-1508), fund raiser. 10 le, Astrolabe, Pinta, Abraham Zacuto (1452-1515), astronomer. 45 le, Maravedis (coins), Nina, Luis de Santangel (1448-1498), fund raiser. 50 le, Tobacco leaves, plant, Luis de Torres (1453-1522), translator.

1987, Sept. 11

909	A131	5 le multicolored	1.00	1.00
910	A131	10 le multicolored	1.25	1.25
911	A131	45 le multicolored	3.75	3.75
912	A131	50 le multicolored	4.50	4.50
	Nos. 909-912 (4)		10.50	10.50

Souvenir Sheet

913	A131	100 le Columbus, map	6.00	6.00

For overprint see No. 966.

Fauna and Flora A132

1987, Sept. 15

914	A132	3 le Cotton tree	.25	.25
915	A132	5 le Dwarf crocodile	.25	.25
916	A132	10 le Kudu	.65	.65
917	A132	20 le Yellowbells	1.60	1.60
918	A132	25 le Hippopotamus	2.10	2.10
919	A132	45 le Comet orchid	3.50	3.50
920	A132	50 le Baobab tree	4.00	4.00
921	A132	75 le Elephant	6.25	6.25
	Nos. 914-921 (8)		18.60	18.60

Souvenir Sheets

922	A132	100 le Banana, papaya, coconut, pineapple	5.00	5.00
923	A132	100 le Leopard	5.00	5.00

16th World Scout Jamboree, Australia, 1987-88 A133

Scouts, jamboree emblem, map of Australia and: 5 le, Ayers Rock. 15 le, Sailing. 40 le, Sydney skyline. 50 le, Sydney Harbour Bridge, Opera House. 100 le, Flags of Sierra Leone, Australia and Scouts.

1987, Oct. 5   Litho.   Perf. 15

924	A133	5 le multicolored	.50	.50
925	A133	15 le multicolored	1.10	1.10
926	A133	40 le multicolored	2.40	2.40
927	A133	50 le multicolored	4.00	4.00
		Nos. 924-927 (4)	8.00	8.00

Souvenir Sheet

928	A133	100 le multicolored	5.50	5.50

1.50 le stamps like the 50 le were printed but not issued.

US Constitution Bicentennial — A134

Designs: 5 le, White House. 10 le, George Washington. 30 le, Patrick Henry. 65 le, New Hampshire state flag. 100 le, John Jay.

1987, Nov. 9   Perf. 14

929	A134	5 le multi	.25	.25
930	A134	10 le multi, vert.	.85	.85
931	A134	30 le multi, vert.	1.25	1.25
932	A134	65 le multi	2.75	2.75
		Nos. 929-932 (4)	5.10	5.10

Souvenir Sheet

933	A134	100 le multi, vert.	5.00	5.00

Tokyo Disneyland, 5th Anniv. — A135

Disney animated characters and attractions at Tokyo Disneyland.

1987, Dec. 9   Litho.   Perf. 14

934	A135	20c Space Mountain	.25	.25
935	A135	40c Country Bear Jamboree	.25	.25
936	A135	80c Mickey Mouse Review	.25	.25
937	A135	1 le Mark Twain's River Boat	.25	.25
938	A135	2 le Western River Railroad	.25	.25
939	A135	3 le Pirates of the Caribbean	.25	.25
940	A135	10 le Big Thunder Mountain train	.80	.80
941	A135	20 le It's a Small World	1.75	1.75
942	A135	30 le Park entrance	2.50	2.50
		Nos. 934-942 (9)	6.55	6.55

Souvenir Sheet

943	A135	65 le Cinderella's Castle	10.00	10.00

Mickey Mouse, 60th anniv.

Christmas — A136

Paintings by Titian: 2 le, The Annunciation. 10 le, Madonna and Child with Saints. 20 le, Madonna and Child with Saints Ulfus and Brigid. 35 le, Madonna of the Cherries. 65 le, Pesaro Altarpiece, vert.

1987, Dec. 21

944	A136	2 le multicolored	.30	.30
945	A136	10 le multicolored	1.00	1.00
946	A136	20 le multicolored	1.75	1.75
947	A136	35 le multicolored	3.00	3.00
		Nos. 944-947 (4)	6.05	6.05

Souvenir Sheet

948	A136	65 le multicolored	6.50	6.50

40th Wedding Anniv. of Queen Elizabeth II and Prince Philip A137

Mushrooms A138

1988, Feb. 15   Litho.   Perf. 14

949	A137	2 le Ceremony, 1947	.30	.30
950	A137	3 le Elizabeth, Charles, 1948	.30	.30
951	A137	10 le Elizabeth, Anne, Charles, c. 1950	.90	.90
952	A137	50 le Elizabeth, c. 1970	4.50	4.50
		Nos. 949-952 (4)	6.00	6.00

Souvenir Sheet

953	A137	65 le Wedding portrait	6.00	6.00

1988, Feb. 29

954	A138	3 le Russula cyanoxantha	.25	.25
955	A138	10 le Lycoperdon perlatum	1.75	1.75
956	A138	20 le Lactarius deliciosus	3.50	3.50
957	A138	30 le Boletus edulis	5.50	5.50
		Nos. 954-957 (4)	11.00	11.00

Miniature Sheet

958	A138	65 le Amanita muscaria	10.00	10.00

Fish A139

1988, Apr. 13   Perf. 15

959	A139	3 le Golden pheasant	.30	.30
960	A139	10 le Banded toothcarp	.60	.60
961	A139	20 le Jewel fish	1.00	1.00
962	A139	35 le Butterfly fish	1.60	1.60
		Nos. 959-962 (4)	3.50	3.50

Miniature Sheet

963	A139	65 le African longfin	4.00	4.00

Nos. 841, 903 and 911 Ovptd. for Philatelic Exhibitions in Black

a

b

c

1988, Apr. 19   Litho.   Perf. 14

964	A123(a)	25 le multicolored	2.75	2.75
965	A130(b)	30 le multicolored	3.25	3.25
966	A131(c)	45 le multicolored	4.50	4.50
		Nos. 964-966 (3)	10.50	10.50

Intl. Fund for Agricultural Development (IFAD), 10th Anniv. — A140

1988, May 3   Litho.   Perf. 14

967	A140	3 le Cocoa, coffee	.25	.25
968	A140	15 le Tropical fruit	1.10	1.10
969	A140	25 le Rice harvest	1.90	1.90
		Nos. 967-969 (3)	3.25	3.25

1988 Summer Olympics, Seoul — A141

Birds — A142

1988, June 15

970	A141	3 le Basketball	.25	.25
971	A141	10 le Judo	.55	.55
972	A141	15 le Gymnastics	.70	.70
973	A141	40 le Synchronized swimming	2.10	2.10
		Nos. 970-973 (4)	3.60	3.60

Souvenir Sheet

974	A141	65 le Torch-bearer	3.00	3.00

1988, June 25

975	A142	3 le Swallow-tailed bee-eater	1.25	1.25
976	A142	5 le Tooth-billed barbet	1.50	1.50
977	A142	8 le African golden oriole	1.90	1.90
978	A142	10 le Red bishop	1.90	1.90
979	A142	12 le Red-billed shrike	1.90	1.90
980	A142	20 le European bee-eater	2.25	2.25
981	A142	35 le Barbary shrike	3.00	3.00
982	A142	40 le Black-headed oriole	3.50	3.50
		Nos. 975-982 (8)	17.20	17.20

Souvenir Sheets

983	A142	65 le Saddlebill stork	4.00	4.00
984	A142	65 le Purple heron	4.00	4.00

For surcharges see Nos. 2892-2896.

Merchant Marine A143

1988, July 1

985	A143	3 le Aureol	.95	.95
986	A143	10 le Dunkwa	2.50	2.50
987	A143	15 le Melampus	3.25	3.25
988	A143	30 le Dumbaia	4.25	4.25
		Nos. 985-988 (4)	10.95	10.95

Souvenir Sheet

989	A143	65 le Loading containers	4.75	4.75

Paintings by Titian A144

1 le, The Concert, 1512. 2 le, Philip II of Spain, c. 1550-51. 3 le, St. Sebastian, c. 1520-22. 5 le, Martyrdom of St. Peter Martyr, c. 1528-30. 15 le, St. Jerome, 1560. 20 le, St. Mark Enthroned with Saints Cosmas and Damian, Roch & Sebastian, c. 1508-09. 25 le, Portrait of a Young Man, 1506. 30 le, St. Jerome in Penitence, 1555. #998, Self-portrait, 1567. #999, Orpheus and Eurydice, 1508.

1988, Aug. 22   Litho.   Perf. 13½x14

990	A144	1 le multicolored	.25	.25
991	A144	2 le multicolored	.25	.25
992	A144	3 le multicolored	.25	.25
993	A144	5 le multicolored	.60	.60
994	A144	15 le multicolored	1.50	1.50
995	A144	20 le multicolored	1.75	1.75
996	A144	25 le multicolored	2.10	2.10
997	A144	30 le multicolored	2.40	2.40
		Nos. 990-997 (8)	9.10	9.10

Souvenir Sheets

998	A144	50 le multicolored	3.25	3.25
999	A144	50 le multicolored	3.25	3.25

John F. Kennedy A145

Kennedy half-dollar and space achievements: 3 le, Recovery of a Mercury capsule by the US Navy. 5 le, Splashdown and recovery of Liberty Bell 7, July 21, 1961, piloted by Virgil "Gus" Grissom, vert. 15 le, Launch of Freedom 7, piloted by Alan B. Shepard, May 5, 1961, vert. 40 le, Friendship 7 in orbit, piloted by John Glenn, Feb. 20, 1962. 65 le, Kennedy, speech excerpt.

1988, Sept. 26   Litho.   Perf. 14

1000	A145	3 le multicolored	.35	.35
1001	A145	5 le multicolored	.90	.90
1002	A145	15 le multicolored	3.00	3.00
1003	A145	40 le multicolored	3.75	3.75
		Nos. 1000-1003 (4)	8.00	8.00

Souvenir Sheet

1004	A145	65 le multicolored	4.75	4.75

Intl. Red Cross and Red Crescent Organizations, 125th Annivs. — A146

1988, Nov. 1

1005	A146	3 le Africa food relief	.90	.90
1006	A146	10 le Battle of Solferino	3.00	3.00
1007	A146	20 le WWII Pacific	4.00	4.00
1008	A146	40 le WWI Europe	5.00	5.00
		Nos. 1005-1008 (4)	12.90	12.90

Souvenir Sheet
Size: 41x28mm
1009 A146 65 le Alfred Nobel,
       Dunant,
       horiz.   6.00   6.00

Miniature Sheet

Christmas, Mickey Mouse 60th
Anniv. — A147

Walt Disney characters dancing: No. 1010a,
Huey, Dewey and Louie. No. 1010b,
Clarabelle Cow. No. 1010c, Goofy. No. 1010d,
Scrooge McDuck and Grandma Duck. No.
1010e, Donald Duck. No. 1010f, Daisy Duck.
No. 1010g, Minnie Mouse. No. 1010h, Mickey
Mouse. No. 1011, Dance, c. 1920. No. 1012,
Dance, c. 1950.

1988, Dec. 1			**Perf. 13½x14**	
1010	A147	Sheet of 8	9.00	9.00
a.-h.		10 le any single	.85	.85

Souvenir Sheets
1011	A147	70 le multicolored	5.75	5.75
1012	A147	70 le multicolored	5.75	5.75

Christmas
A148

Paintings by Rubens (details): 3 le, Adora-
tion of the Magi (Virgin and Child). 3.60 le,
Adoration of the Shepherds (shepherds and
child). 5 le, Adoration of the Magi (Magi). 10 le,
Adoration of the Shepherds (Virgin and Child).
20 le, Virgin and Child Surrounded by Flowers.
40 le, St. Gregory the Great and Other Saints
(Virgin and Child). 60 le, Adoration of the
Magi, (Virgin, Child and Magi), diff. 80 le,
Madonna and Child with Saints. No. 1021, St.
Gregory the Great and Other Saints. No.
1022, Virgin and Child Enthroned with Saints.

1988, Dec. 15		**Litho.**	**Perf. 13½x14**	
1013	A148	3 le multicolored	.25	.25
1014	A148	3.60 le multicolored	.25	.25
1015	A148	5 le multicolored	.45	.45
1016	A148	10 le multicolored	.65	.65
1017	A148	20 le multicolored	1.25	1.25
1018	A148	40 le multicolored	2.50	2.50
1019	A148	60 le multicolored	3.50	3.50
1020	A148	80 le multicolored	4.75	4.75
Nos. 1013-1020 (8)			13.60	13.60

Souvenir Sheets
1021	A148	100 le multicolored	6.00	6.00
1022	A148	100 le multicolored	6.00	6.00

No. 907 Ovptd. "GRAND SLAM WINNER" in Gold
Set of 4

1989, Jan. 16			**Perf. 14**
Souvenir Sheets			
1023A-	A130 100 le		
1023D			26.00 26.00

Gold marginal overprints: No. 1023A, "AUS-
TRALIAN OPEN / JANUARY 11-24, 1988 /
GRAF v EVERET / 6-1 / 7-6." 1023B,
"FRENCH OPEN / MAY 23-JUNE 5, 1988 /
GRAF v ZVEREVA / 6-0 / 6-0." 1023C, "WIM-
BLEDON / JUNE 20-JULY 4, 1988 / GRAF v
NAVRATILOVA / 5-7 / 6-2 / 6-1." 1023D, "U.S.
OPEN / AUGUST 29-SEPTEMBER 11, 1988 /
GRAF v SABATINI / 6-3 / 3-6 / 6-1."

No. 907 Ovptd. "GOLD MEDALIST" in Gold

1989, Jan. 16		**Litho.**	**Perf. 14**	
1024	A130	100 le multi	6.50	6.50

Marginal overprint: "SEOUL OLYMPICS
1988 / GRAF v SABATINI / 6-3 / 6-3."

Medalists
of the
1988
Summer
Olympics,
Seoul
A149

Designs: 3 le, Christian Schenk, German
Democratic Republic, decathlon. 6 le, Hitoshi
Saito, Japan, heavyweight judo. 10 le, Jutta
Niehaus, Federal Republic of Germany,
women's road race. 15 le, Tomas Lange, German Democratic Republic, single sculls. 20 le,
Matthew Biondi, US, 50m and 100m freestyle.
30 le, Carl Lewis, US, 100m sprint. 40 le,
Nicole Uphoff, Federal Republic of Germany,
individual dressage. 50 le, Andras Sike, Hungary, 126-pound Greco-Roman wrestling. No.
1033, Gold medal, five-ring emblem. No.
1034, Torch, five-ring emblem.

1989, Apr. 28		**Litho.**	**Perf. 14**	
1025	A149	3 le multicolored	.85	.85
1026	A149	6 le multicolored	1.10	1.10
1027	A149	10 le multicolored	1.75	1.75
1028	A149	15 le multicolored	1.75	1.75
1029	A149	20 le multicolored	1.75	1.75
1030	A149	30 le multicolored	2.25	2.25
1031	A149	40 le multicolored	2.75	2.75
1032	A149	50 le multicolored	2.75	2.75
Nos. 1025-1032 (8)			14.95	14.95

Souvenir Sheets
1033	A149	100 le multicolored	6.50	6.50
1034	A149	100 le multicolored	6.50	6.50

Name of athlete not inscribed on No. 1031.

1990 World Cup
Soccer
Championships,
Italy — A150

1989, May 8

1035	A150	3 le Brazil vs. Sweden	.25	.25
1036	A150	6 le Germany vs. Hungary	.55	.55
1037	A150	8 le England vs. Germany	.70	.70
1038	A150	10 le Argentina vs. The Netherlands	.90	.90
1039	A150	12 le Brazil vs. Czechoslo-vakia	1.10	1.10
1040	A150	20 le Germany vs. The Netherlands	1.75	1.75
1041	A150	30 le Italy vs. Germany	2.75	2.75
1042	A150	40 le Brazil vs. It-aly	3.50	3.50
Nos. 1035-1042 (8)			11.50	11.50

Souvenir Sheets
1043	A150	100 le Uruguay vs. Brazil	5.50	5.50
1044	A150	100 le Argentina vs. Germa-ny	5.50	5.50

Mano
River
Union,
15th
Anniv.
A151

Designs: 1 le, Sierra Leone-Guinea postal
service. 3 le, Presidents Momoh, Conte of
Guinea and Doe of Liberia. 10 le, Freetown-
Monrovia Highway under construction. 15 le,
Presidents signing the Communique at a 1988
summit.

1989, May 19			**Perf. 14**	
1045	A151	1 le multicolored	.75	.75
1046	A151	3 le multicolored	1.25	1.25
1047	A151	10 le multicolored	2.00	2.00
Nos. 1045-1047 (3)			4.00	4.00

Souvenir Sheet
1048	A151	15 le multicolored	3.50	3.50

Ahmadiyya Muslim
Centenary
Thanksgiving
Celebrations
A152

1989, June 8

1049	A152	3 le black & brt blue	.60	.60

Miniature Sheets

Shakespeare's 425th Birth
Anniv. — A153

Scenes from the playwright's works.
No. 1050: a, Richard III. b, Othello (Desde-
mona and two men). c, The Two Gentlemen of
Verona. d, Macbeth (chamber). e, Hamlet. f,
Taming of the Shrew (scene with dog). g, The
Merry Wives of Windsor. h, Henry IV (assem-
bly room).
No. 1051: a, Macbeth (horsemen). b,
Romeo and Juliet. c, Merchant of Venice. d,
As You Like It. e, Taming of the Shrew (ruined
meal). f, King Lear. g, Othello (death scene).
h, Henry IV (street scene).

1989, May 30			**Perf. 13**	
1050		Sheet of 8 + label	9.00	9.00
a.-h.		A153 15 le any single	1.00	1.00
1051		Sheet of 8 + label	9.00	9.00
a.-h.		A153 15 le any single	1.00	1.00

Souvenir Sheets
1052	A153	100 le Portrait	7.00	7.00
1053	A153	100 le Portrait, coat of arms	7.00	7.00

Nos. 1050-1051 contain center label picturing Shakespeare's portrait (No. 1050) or his
birthplace in Stratford (No. 1051).

Paintings by Takeuchi Seiho (1864-
1942) — A154

Designs: 3 le, Lapping Waves. 6 le, Hazy
Moon, vert. 8 le, Passing Spring, vert. 10 le,
Mackerels. 12 le, Calico Cat. 30 le, The First
Time To Be a Model, vert. 40 le, Kingly Lion.
75 le, After a Shower, vert. No. 1062, Domesticated Monkeys and Rabbits. No. 1063, Dozing
in the Midst of All the Chirping, vert.

Perf. 14x13½, 13½x14
1989, July 3			**Litho.**	
1054	A154	3 le multicolored	.25	.25
1055	A154	6 le multicolored	.35	.35
1056	A154	8 le multicolored	.55	.55
1057	A154	10 le multicolored	.70	.70
1058	A154	12 le multicolored	.75	.75
1059	A154	30 le multicolored	2.00	2.00
1060	A154	40 le multicolored	2.75	2.75
1061	A154	75 le multicolored	5.25	5.25
Nos. 1054-1061 (8)			12.60	12.60

Souvenir Sheets
1062	A154	150 le multicolored	7.50	7.50
1063	A154	150 le multicolored	7.50	7.50

Hirohito (1901-89) and enthronement of
Akihito as emperor of Japan.
See Nos. 1098-1129.

PHILEXFRANCE '89, French
Revolution Bicent. — A155

Famous people, sites, exhibition and anniv.
emblems: 6 le, Robespierre (1758-94), the
Bastille. 20 le, Georges Jacques Danton
(1759-94), the Louvre. 45 le, Marie Antoinette
(1755-93), Notre Dame Cathedral interior. 80
le, Louis XVI (1754-93), Palace of Versailles.
150 le, Revolutionaries in Paris, vert.

1989, July 14		**Litho.**	**Perf. 14**	
1064	A155	6 le multicolored	.65	.65
1065	A155	20 le multicolored	1.25	1.25
1066	A155	45 le multicolored	2.25	2.25
1067	A155	80 le multicolored	3.75	3.75
Nos. 1064-1067 (4)			7.90	7.90

Souvenir Sheet
1068	A155	150 le multicolored	6.25	6.25

Miniature Sheets

Space Exploration — A156

Satellites, probes and spacecraft.
No. 1069: a, Sputnik, 1957. b, Telstar, 1962.
c, Rendezvous of Gemini 6 and 7, 1965. d,
Yuri Gagarin, 1st man in space, 1961. e, Mari-
ner, 1964. f, Surveyor on Mars, 1966. g, US-
Canadian Alouette satellite, 1962. h, Edward
White, 1st American to walk in space, 1965. i,
OGO-4 satellite, 1967.
No. 1070: a, Buzz Aldrin on the Moon,
Apollo 11 mission, 1969. b, Apollo 15 mission
lunar rover. c, Apollo 15 crew member. d, Conducting experiments on the lunar surface. e,
Splitrock, Valley of Taurus-Littrow. f, Saluting
the flag, Apollo 15 lunar module. g, Solar wind
experiment. h, Lunar rover, diff. i, Apollo command module.
No. 1071: a, Module separation. b, Docking
maneuvers. c, Lunar module in space. d, Second stage separation. e, Module transposition.
f, Lunar module controlled descent, Moon's
surface. g, Apollo 11 liftoff, 1969. h, Lunar
module separates from command module. i,
Neil Armstrong's first step on the Moon.
No. 1072: a, Mariner-Mars, 1971. b, Mariner
10, 1973. c, Viking, 1975. d, Skylab, 1974. e,
Soyuz-Salyut, 1974. f, Viking robot craft, 1974.
g, Pioneer 2, 1973. h, Apollo-Soyuz, 1975. i,
Pioneer-Venus, 1978.
No. 1073: a, Apollo 17 lunar module, 1972.
b, Command module jettison of service module before reentry. c, Soyuz 11, 1971. d, Lunar
module liftoff. e, U.S. Navy recovery operation.
f, Mars 2, 1971. g, Command module in docking position. h, Luna 17, 1970. i, Mars 3, 1971.
No. 1074: a, Voyager 1 and 2, 1977. b,
Columbia space shuttle, 1981. c, Mir space
station, 1986. d, IUE-Ultraviolet Explorer, US,
U.K. and the European Space Agency, 1978.
e, Astronaut operating out of shuttle cargo
bay, 1983. f, Magellan, 1989. g, Soyuz-Salyut,
1978. h, STS-10, 1984. i, Shuttle, space telescope, 1989.
No. 1075, Spacelab. No. 1076, Future
space station. No. 1077, Voyager.

1989, July 20		**Litho.**	**Perf. 14**	
1069		Sheet of 9	5.50	5.50
a.-i.		A156 10 le any single	.60	.60
1070		Sheet of 9	5.50	5.50
a.-i.		A156 10 le any single	.60	.60
1071		Sheet of 9	5.50	5.50
a.-i.		A156 10 le any single	.60	.60
1072		Sheet of 9	8.50	8.50
a.-i.		A156 15 le any single	.90	.90
1073		Sheet of 9	8.50	8.50
a.-i.		A156 15 le any single	.90	.90

1074		Sheet of 9	8.50	8.50
a.-i.	A156	15 le any single	.90	.90

Souvenir Sheets

1075	A156	100 le multicolored	7.50	7.50
1076	A156	100 le multicolored	7.50	7.50
1077	A156	100 le multicolored	7.50	7.50

Nos. 1069f is incorrectly inscribed "Mars" instead of "Moon."

Orchids — A157   Butterflies — A158

1989, Sept. 8   Litho.   Perf. 14

1078	A157	3 le Bulbophyl-		
		lum barbigerum	.85	.85
1079	A157	6 le Bulbophyl-		
		lum fal- catum	1.25	1.25
1080	A157	12 le Habenaria macrara	1.75	1.75
1081	A157	20 le Eurychone rothchildi- ana	2.25	2.25
1082	A157	50 le Calyp- trochilum christy- anum	3.25	3.25
1083	A157	60 le Bulbophyl- lum distans	3.75	3.75
1084	A157	70 le Eulophia guineensis	3.75	3.75
1085	A157	80 le Diapha- nanthe pel- lu-cida	4.50	4.50
		Nos. 1078-1085 (8)	21.35	21.35

Souvenir Sheets

1086	A157	100 le Cyrtorchis arcuata	12.00	12.00
1087	A157	100 le Butterflies, Eulophia cucullata	12.00	12.00

1989, Sept. 11

1088	A158	6 le Salamis temora	1.25	1.25
1089	A158	12 le Pseudacraea lucretia	1.60	1.60
1090	A158	18 le Charaxes boueti	2.10	2.10
1091	A158	30 le Graphium antheus	3.50	3.50
1092	A158	40 le Colotis protomedia	4.50	4.50
1093	A158	60 le Asterope pechueli	5.00	5.00
1094	A158	72 le Coenura aurantiaca	5.75	5.75
1095	A158	80 le Precis octa- via	5.75	5.75
		Nos. 1088-1095 (8)	29.45	29.45

Souvenir Sheets

1096	A158	100 le Charaxes cithaeron	12.00	12.00
1097	A158	100 le Euphaedra themis	12.00	12.00

Nos. 1088-1090, 1095 and 1097 horiz.

Art Type of 1989

Paintings by Hiroshige in the series Fifty-three Stations on the Tokaido: No. 1098, Coolies Warming Themselves at Hamamatsu. No. 1099, Imakiri Ford at Maisaka. No. 1100, Pacific Ocean Seen from Shirasuka. No. 1101, Futakawa Street Singers. No. 1102, Repairing Yoshida Castle. No. 1103, The Inn at Akasaka. No. 1104, The Bridge to Okazaki. No. 1105, Samurai's Wife Entering Narumi. No. 1106, Harbour at Kuwana. No. 1107, Autumn in Ishiyakushi. No. 1108, Snowfall at Kameyama. No. 1109, The Frontier Station of Seki. No. 1110, Teahouse at Sakanoshita. No. 1111, Kansai Houses at Minakushi. No. 1112, Kusatsu Station. No. 1113, Ferry to Kawasaki. No. 1114, The Hilly Town of Hodogaya. No. 1115, Lute Players at Fujisawa. No. 1116, Mild Rainstorm at Oiso. No. 1117, Lake Ashi and Mountains of Hakone. No. 1118, Twilight at Numazu. No. 1119, Mount Fuji From Hara. No. 1120, Samurai's Children Riding Through Yoshiwara. No. 1121, Mountain Pass at Yui. No. 1122, Harbour at Ejiri. No. 1123, Stopping at Fujieda. No. 1124, Misty Kanaya on the Oi River. No. 1125, The Bridge to Kakegawa. No. 1126, Teahouse at Fukuroi. No. 1127, The Ford at Mitsuke. No. 1128, Sanjo Bridge in Kyoto. No. 1129, Nibonbashi Bridge in Edo.

1989, Nov. 13   Litho.   Perf. 14x13½

1098-1127	A154	25 le Set of 30	37.50	37.50

Souvenir sheets

1128-1129	A154	120 le each	8.00	8.00

Hirohito (1901-1989) and enthronement of Akihito as emperor of Japan.

Souvenir Sheet

Jefferson Memorial, Washington, DC — A159

1989, Nov. 17   Litho.   Perf. 14

1136	A159	100 le multicolored	2.00	2.00

World Stamp Expo '89.

Endangered Species — A160

1989, Nov. 29   Perf. 14

1137	A160	6 le Humpback whale	.25	.25
1138	A160	9 le Formosan sika deer	.30	.30
1139	A160	16 le Spanish lynx	.65	.65
1140	A160	20 le Goitered ga- zelle	.95	.95
1141	A160	30 le Japanese sea lion	1.40	1.40
1142	A160	50 le Long-eared owl	2.25	2.25
1143	A160	70 le Chinese copper pheasant	3.25	3.25
1144	A160	100 le Siberian ti- ger	4.50	4.50
		Nos. 1137-1144 (8)	13.55	13.55

Souvenir Sheets

1145	A160	150 le Mauritius kestrel fal- con	9.00	9.00
1146	A160	150 le Crested ibis	9.00	9.00

World Stamp Expo '89.

Christmas — A161

Disney characters and classic automobiles: 3 le, 1934 Phantom II Rolls-Royce Roadstar. 6 le, 1935 Mercedes-Benz 500K. 10 le, 1938 Jaguar SS-100. 12 le, 1941 Jeep. 20 le, 1937 Buick Roadmaster Sedan Model 91. 30 le, 1948 Tucker. 40 le, 1933 Alfa Romeo. 50 le, 1937 Cord. No. 1155, 1938 Fiat Topolino. No. 1156, 1931 Pontiac Model 401, 1929 Pontiac Landau.

1989, Dec. 18   Perf. 14x13½

1147	A161	3 le multicolored	.90	.90
1148	A161	6 le multicolored	1.10	1.10
1149	A161	10 le multicolored	1.40	1.40
1150	A161	12 le multicolored	1.60	1.60
1151	A161	20 le multicolored	2.25	2.25
1152	A161	30 le multicolored	2.50	2.50
1153	A161	40 le multicolored	2.75	2.75
1154	A161	50 le multicolored	3.00	3.00
		Nos. 1147-1154 (8)	15.50	15.50

Souvenir Sheets

1155	A161	100 le multicolored	12.00	12.00
1156	A161	100 le multicolored	12.00	12.00

Christmas — A162

Religious paintings by Rembrandt: 3 le, Adoration of the Magi. 6 le, The Holy Family with a Cat. 10 le, The Holy Family with Angels. 15 le, Simeon in the Temple. 30 le, The Circumcision. 90 le, The Holy Family. 100 le, The Visitation. 120 le, The Flight into Egypt. No. 1165, The Adoration of the Shepherds. No. 1166, The Presentation of Jesus in the Temple.

1989, Dec. 22   Perf. 14

1157	A162	3 le multicolored	.60	.60
1158	A162	6 le multicolored	.75	.75
1159	A162	10 le multicolored	1.10	1.10
1160	A162	15 le multicolored	1.25	1.25
1161	A162	30 le multicolored	1.90	1.90
1162	A162	90 le multicolored	3.50	3.50
1163	A162	100 le multicolored	3.50	3.50
1164	A162	120 le multicolored	3.50	3.50
		Nos. 1157-1164 (8)	16.10	16.10

Souvenir Sheets

1165	A162	150 le multicolored	5.50	5.50
1166	A162	150 le multicolored	5.50	5.50

Miniature Sheets

Exploration of Mars — A163

No. 1167: a, Kepler. b, Galileo. c, Drawings by Huygens in 1672 and Schiaparelli in 1886. d, Sir W. Herschel. e, Percival Lowell in Arizona, 1896-1907. f, Mars. g, Mariner 4, 1965. h, Mars 2, 1971. i, Mars 3, 1971.
No. 1168: a, Mariner 9, 1971. b, Mariner 9, Phobos. c, Cydonia Region. d, South polar cap. e, Profile of Mars. f, Polar cap, diff. g, Nix Olympica. h, Grand Canyon of Mars. i, North Pole.
No. 1169: a, Olympus Mons. b, Viking 1, July 1976. c, Viking 2 releases Lander, Sept. 1976. d, Lander entering Mars's atmosphere. e, Parachute deployed. f, Terminal descent. g, Viking Lander on Mars. h, Soil sampler (robotic arm). i, Soil Sampler (US flag, machine).
No. 1170: a, Martian dusk. b, Project Deimos. c, Exploration of Mars (astronauts surveying land). d, Return to Rombus. e, US rocket bound for Mars. f, Spacecraft bound for Mars. g, Spacecraft in Martian orbit. h, Mission to Mars (astronauts weightless in spacecraft cabin). i, Space station.
No. 1171, "The Face," Mars.

1990   Litho.   Perf. 14

1167		Sheet of 9	25.00	25.00
a.-i.	A163	175 le any single	2.75	2.75
1168		Sheet of 9	25.00	25.00
a.-i.	A163	175 le any single	2.75	2.75
1169		Sheet of 9	25.00	25.00
a.-i.	A163	175 le any single	2.75	2.75
1170		Sheet of 9	25.00	25.00
a.-i.	A163	175 le any single	2.75	2.75

Souvenir Sheet

1171	A163	150 le multicolored	6.00	6.00
1171A	A163	150 le Space station	6.00	6.00

Issued: No. 1171A, Dec. 24; others, Jan. 15.
Extreme speculation has occured with this issue, centered around No. 1171, the face on Mars stamp.

World War II — A164

USAF aircraft.

1990, Feb. 5   Litho.   Perf. 14

1172	A164	1 le Doolittle Raid B-25	.25	.25
1173	A164	2 le B-24 Libera- tor	.25	.25
1174	A164	3 le A-20 Boston	.25	.25
1175	A164	9 le P-38 Light- ning	.50	.50
1176	A164	12 le B-26	.55	.55
1177	A164	16 le B-17 F	.80	.80
1178	A164	50 le B-25 D Mitchell	2.40	2.40
1179	A164	80 le Boeing B-29	3.50	3.50
1180	A164	90 le B-17 G	4.25	4.25
1181	A164	100 le The Enola Gay	4.75	4.75
		Nos. 1172-1181 (10)	17.50	17.50

Souvenir Sheets

1182	A164	150 le B-25, USS Hornet	7.00	7.00
1183	A164	150 le B-17 G	7.00	7.00

Stage and Screen Roles Played by Sir Laurence Olivier (1907-1989) — A165

1990, Apr. 27

1184	A165	3 le Antony & Cleopatra, 1951	.25	.25
1185	A165	9 le Henry V, 1943	.25	.25
1186	A165	16 le Oedipus, 1945	.45	.45
1187	A165	20 le Wuthering Heights, 1939	.65	.65
1188	A165	30 le Marathon Man, 1976	.90	.90
1189	A165	70 le Othello, 1964	2.10	2.10
1190	A165	175 le Beau Geste, 1929	5.50	5.50
1191	A165	200 le Richard III, 1956	6.25	6.25
		Nos. 1184-1191 (8)	16.35	16.35

Souvenir Sheets

1192	A165	250 le The Battle of Britain, 1969	7.00	7.00
1193	A165	250 le Hamlet, 1947	7.00	7.00

Walt Disney Characters, Settings in Sierra Leone — A166

1990, Apr. 23

1194	A166	3 le Bauxite mine	.25	.25
1195	A166	6 le Panning for gold	.25	.25
1196	A166	10 le Lungi Intl. Airport	.25	.25
1197	A166	12 le Old Fourah Bay Col- lege	.30	.30
1198	A166	16 le Mining baux- ite	.40	.40
1199	A166	20 le Rice harvest	.50	.50
1200	A166	30 le The Cotton Tree	.90	.90
1201	A166	100 le Rutile Mine	3.25	3.25
1202	A166	200 le Fishing at Goderich	6.50	6.50
1203	A166	225 le Bintumani Hotel	7.00	7.00
		Nos. 1194-1203 (10)	19.60	19.60

Souvenir Sheets

1204	A166	250 le Market Place, King Jimmy	6.50	6.50
1205	A166	250 le Diamond mining	6.50	6.50

Penny Black, 150th
Anniv. — A167

1990, May 3   **Perf. 14**
1206	A167	50 le deep ultra	2.00	2.00
1207	A167	100 le violet brown	5.00	5.00

Souvenir Sheet
1208	A167	250 le black	7.50	7.50

World Cup Soccer Championships,
Italy — A168

Team photographs.

1990, May 11   **Litho.**   **Perf. 14**
1209	A168	15 le Colombia	.60	.60
1210	A168	15 le United Arab Emirates	.60	.60
1211	A168	15 le South Korea	.60	.60
1212	A168	15 le Cameroun	.60	.60
1213	A168	15 le Costa Rica	.60	.60
1214	A168	15 le Romania	.60	.60
1215	A168	15 le Yugoslavia	.60	.60
1216	A168	15 le Egypt	.60	.60
1217	A168	30 le Netherlands	1.25	1.25
1218	A168	30 le Uruguay	1.25	1.25
1219	A168	30 le USSR	1.25	1.25
1220	A168	30 le Czechoslovakia	1.25	1.25
1221	A168	30 le Scotland	1.25	1.25
1222	A168	30 le Belgium	1.25	1.25
1223	A168	30 le Austria	1.25	1.25
1224	A168	30 le Sweden	1.25	1.25
1225	A168	45 le W. Germany	1.75	1.75
1226	A168	45 le England	1.75	1.75
1227	A168	45 le United States	1.75	1.75
1228	A168	45 le Ireland	1.75	1.75
1229	A168	45 le Spain	1.75	1.75
1230	A168	45 le Brazil	1.75	1.75
1231	A168	45 le Italy	1.75	1.75
1232	A168	45 le Argentina	1.75	1.75
		Nos. 1209-1232 (24)	28.80	28.80

No. 1209 spelled "Columbia," No. 1218
"Uraguay," No. 1220 "Czecheslovakia" on
stamps.

Great
Crested
Grebe
A169

1990, June 4
1233	A169	3 le shown	.25	.25
1234	A169	6 le Green woodhoo-poe	.25	.25
1235	A169	10 le African jacana	.25	.25
1236	A169	12 le Avocet	.25	.25
1237	A169	20 le African finfoot	.45	.45
1238	A169	80 le Glossy ibis	2.00	2.00
1239	A169	150 le Hamerkop	3.50	3.50
1240	A169	200 le Greater honey guide	4.50	4.50
		Nos. 1233-1240 (8)	11.45	11.45

Souvenir Sheets
1241	A169	250 le Painted snipe	6.25	6.25
1242	A169	250 le Palm swift	6.25	6.25

Mickey as
Yeoman
Warder
A170

Disney characters: 6 le, Scrooge as lamp-
lighter. 12 le, Knight Goofy. 15 le, Clarabell as
Anne Boleyn. 75 le, Minnie Mouse as Queen
Elizabeth I. 100 le, Donald Duck as chimmey
sweep. 125 le, Pete as King Henry VIII. 150 le,
May dancers in Salisbury. No. 1251, Boadi-
cea, Queen of the Iceni. No. 1252, Lawyers at
Parliament House.

1990, June 6   **Perf. 13½x14**
1243	A170	3 le multicolored	.25	.25
1244	A170	6 le multicolored	.25	.25
1245	A170	12 le multicolored	.25	.25
1246	A170	15 le multicolored	.30	.30
1247	A170	75 le multicolored	2.10	2.10
1248	A170	100 le multicolored	2.75	2.75
1249	A170	125 le multicolored	3.50	3.50
1250	A170	150 le multicolored	4.25	4.25
		Nos. 1243-1250 (8)	13.65	13.65

Souvenir Sheets
1251	A170	250 le multicolored	5.50	5.50
1252	A170	250 le multicolored	5.50	5.50

Queen Mother,
90th
Birthday — A171

1990, July 5   **Perf. 14**
1253		75 le shown	1.50	1.50
1254		75 le Wearing black hat	1.50	1.50
1255		75 le Wearing yellow hat	1.50	1.50
a.	A171	Strip of 3, #1253-1255	5.00	5.00
		Nos. 1253-1255 (3)	4.50	4.50

Souvenir Sheet
1256	A171	250 le Like No. 1253	5.00	5.00

Butterfly Type of 1987

1990   **Perf. 12½x11½**
1257		3 le like No. 861	.25	.25
1258		9 le like No. 864	.25	.25
1259	A126	12 le like No. 859	.25	.25
1260	A126	16 le like No. 860	.30	.30
		Nos. 1257-1260 (4)	1.05	1.05

Inscribed 1989.

Miniature Sheet

Wildlife — A172

Designs: No. 1261a, Golden cat. b, White-
backed night heron. c, Bateleur eagle. d, Marabou stork. e, White-faced whistling duck. f,
Aardvark. g, Royal antelope. h, Pygmy hippopotamus. i, Leopard. j, Sacred ibis. k, Mona
monkey. l, Darter. m, Chimpanzee. n, African

elephant. o, Potto. p, African manatee. q, African fish eagle. r, African spoonbill.

1990, Sept. 24   **Litho.**   **Perf. 14**
1261		Sheet of 18	22.50	22.50
a.-r.	A172	25 le any single	1.00	1.00

Souvenir Sheet
1262	A172	150 le Crowned eagle, vert.	12.50	12.50

No. 1261 printed in continuous design
showing map of Sierra Leone in background.

A173   A174

Carousel animals.

1990, Oct. 22   **Litho.**   **Perf. 14**
1263	A173	5 le Rabbit	.25	.25
1264	A173	10 le Horse with panther saddle	.25	.25
1265	A173	20 le Ostrich	.35	.35
1266	A173	30 le Zebra	.55	.55
1267	A173	50 le White horse	.90	.90
1268	A173	80 le Sea monster	1.40	1.40
1269	A173	100 le Giraffe	1.75	1.75
1270	A173	150 le Armored horse	2.75	2.75
1271	A173	200 le Camel	3.50	3.50
		Nos. 1263-1271 (9)	11.70	11.70

Souvenir Sheets
1272	A173	300 le Centaur, Lord Baden-Powell	7.25	7.25
1273	A173	300 le Horse head	7.25	7.25

1990, Nov. 12   **Litho.**   **Perf. 14**
1274	A174	5 le Men's 100-meter race	.25	.25
1275	A174	10 le Men's 4x400-meter relay	.25	.25
1276	A174	20 le Men's 100-meter race, diff.	.40	.40
1277	A174	30 le Weight lifting	.70	.70
1278	A174	40 le Freestyle wrestling	1.00	1.00
1279	A174	80 le Water polo	2.00	2.00
1280	A174	150 le Women's gymnastics	3.50	3.50
1281	A174	200 le Cycling	5.00	5.00
		Nos. 1274-1281 (8)	13.10	13.10

Souvenir Sheets
1282	A174	400 le Boxing	7.25	7.25
1283	A174	400 le Olympic flag	7.25	7.25

1992 Summer Olympics, Barcelona.

Christmas
A175

Paintings: 10 le, The Holy Family Resting by
Rembrandt. 20 le, The Holy Family with St.
Elizabeth by Andrea Mantegna. 30 le, Virgin
and Child with an Angel by Correggio. 50 le,
The Annunciation by Bernardo Strozzi. 100 le,
Madonna and Child Appearing to St. Anthony
by Filippino Lippi. 175 le, Virgin and Child by
Giovanni Boltraffio. 200 le, The Esterhazy
Madonna by Raphael. 300 le, Coronation of
Mary by Orcagna. No. 1292, Adoration of the
Shepherds by Bronzino. No. 1293, Adoration
of the Shepherds by Gerard David.

1990, Dec. 17   **Perf. 13**
1284	A175	10 le multicolored	.25	.25
1285	A175	20 le multicolored	.30	.30
1286	A175	30 le multicolored	.50	.50
1287	A175	50 le multicolored	.80	.80
1288	A175	100 le multicolored	2.00	2.00
1289	A175	175 le multicolored	4.00	4.00

1290	A175	200 le multicolored	4.25	4.25
1291	A175	300 le multicolored	6.00	6.00
		Nos. 1284-1291 (8)	18.10	18.10

Souvenir Sheets
1292	A175	400 le multicolored	8.50	8.50
1293	A175	400 le multicolored	8.50	8.50

Christmas
A176

Walt Disney characters in "The Night Before
Christmas."

No. 1294a, 'Twas the night. . . b, Not a creature. . . c, The stockings were hung. . . d, And
Mama in her kerchief. . . e, When out on the
lawn. . . f, I sprang from my bed. . . g, Away to
the window. . . h, Tore open the shutter. . .

No. 1295a, The moon on the breast. . . b,
When what to my wondering. . . c, With a little
old driver. . . d, More rapid than eagles. . . e,
To the top of the porch. . . f, And then in a
twinkling. . . g, As I drew in my head. . . h, He
was dressed. . .

No. 1296a, A bundle of toys. . . b, The
stump of a pipe. . . c, He had a broad face. . .
d, He was chubby and plump. . . e, A wink of
his eye. . . f, Then turned with a jerk. . . g, And
giving a nod. . . h, He sprang to his sleigh. . .

No. 1297, The children were nestled. . . No.
1298, His eyes, how they twinkled. . . No.
1299, He spoke not a word. . . No. 1300, And
he whistled. . . No. 1301, As dry leaves. . . No.
1302, But I heard him exclaim. . .

1990, Dec. 17   **Litho.**   **Perf. 13**
Miniature Sheets of 8
1294	A176	50 le #a.-h.	7.50	7.50
1295	A176	75 le #a.-h.	22.50	22.50
1296	A176	100 le #a.-h.	11.50	11.50

Souvenir Sheets
1297	A176	400 le multi	5.00	5.00
1298	A176	400 le multi, horiz.	5.00	5.00
1299	A176	400 le multi	5.00	5.00
1300	A176	400 le multi, horiz.	5.00	5.00
1301	A176	400 le multi, horiz.	5.00	5.00
1302	A176	400 le multi	5.00	5.00

Peter Paul
Rubens
(1577-1640),
Painter
A177

Entire paintings or different details from:
5 le, Helena Fourment as Hagar in the Wilderness. 10 le, Isabella Brant. 20 le, 60 le, Countess of Arundel and Her Party. 80 le, Nicolaas
Rockox. 100 le, Adriana Perez. 150 le, George
Villiers, Duke of Buckingham. 300 le, Countess of Buckingham. No. 1311, Veronica Spi-
nola Doria. No. 1312, Giovanni Carlo Dorio.

1990, Dec. 24   **Perf. 14**
1303	A177	5 le multicolored	.25	.25
1304	A177	10 le multicolored	.25	.25
1305	A177	20 le multicolored	.30	.30
1306	A177	60 le multicolored	.95	.95
1307	A177	80 le multicolored	1.25	1.25
1308	A177	100 le multicolored	1.60	1.60
1309	A177	150 le multicolored	2.75	2.75
1310	A177	300 le multicolored	5.25	5.25
		Nos. 1303-1310 (8)	12.60	12.60

Souvenir Sheets
1311	A177	350 le multicolored	7.50	7.50
1312	A177	350 le multicolored	7.50	7.50

Mushrooms — A178

Designs: 3 le, Chlorophyllum molybdites. 5 le, Lepista nuda. 10 le, Clitocybe nebularis. 15 le, Cyathus striatus. 20 le, Bolbitius vitellinus. 25 le, Leucoagaricus naucinus. 30 le, Suillus luteus. 40 le, Podaxis pistillaris. 50 le, Oudemansiella radicata. 60 le, Phallus indusiatus. 80 le, Macrolepiota rhacodes. 100 le, Mycena pura. 150 le, Volvariella volvacea. 175 le, Omphalotus olearius. 200 le, Sphaerobolus stellatus. 250 le, Schizophyllum commune.

Each 350 le: No. 1329, Agaricus campestris. No. 1330, Hypholoma fasciculare. No. 1331, Suillus granulatus. No. 1332, Psilocybe coprophila.

1990, Dec. 31   **Perf. 14**

1313	A178	3 le multicolored	.25	.25
1314	A178	5 le multicolored	.25	.25
1315	A178	10 le multicolored	.25	.25
1316	A178	15 le multicolored	.25	.25
1317	A178	20 le multicolored	.35	.35
1318	A178	25 le multicolored	.50	.50
1319	A178	30 le multicolored	.60	.60
1320	A178	40 le multicolored	.80	.80
1321	A178	50 le multicolored	.95	.95
1322	A178	60 le multicolored	1.10	1.10
1323	A178	80 le multicolored	1.60	1.60
1324	A178	100 le multicolored	2.50	2.50
1325	A178	150 le multicolored	3.25	3.25
1326	A178	175 le multicolored	4.00	4.00
1327	A178	200 le multicolored	4.75	4.75
1328	A178	250 le multicolored	5.75	5.75
		Nos. 1313-1328 (16)	27.15	27.15

Souvenir Sheets

1329-1332	A178	Set of 4	26.50	26.50

Butterfly Type of 1987 With "Sierra Leone" in Blue

1991   **Litho.**   **Perf. 14**

1332A	A126	50c Like #861	—	
m.		Perf. 12½x11½	—	
1332B	A126	1 le Like #862	—	
1332C	A126	2 le Like #863	—	
1332D	A126	5 le Like #865	—	
1332E	A126	10 le Like #866	—	
1332F	A126	20 le Like #867	—	
1332G	A126	30 le Like #864	—	
1332H	A126	50 le Like #859	—	
n.		Perf. 12½x11½	—	
1332I	A126	60 le Like #871	—	
1332J	A126	80 le Like #860	—	
o.		Perf. 12½x11½	—	
1332K	A126	100 le Like #873	—	
1332L	A126	300 le Like #869	—	
p.		Perf. 12½x11½	—	

Every sixth perforation hole on Nos. 1332Am, 1332Hn, 1132Jo, and 1332Lp is larger. These stamps are not known used. All stamps are dated "1990."

Easter A179

Entire works or details from paintings by Rubens: 10 le, Flight of St. Barbara. 20 le, No. 1341, The Last Judgement. 30 le, St. Gregory of Nazianzus. 50 le, Doubting Thomas. 80 le, No. 1342, The Way to Calvary. 100 le, St. Gregory with Sts. Domitilla, Maurus and Papianus. 175 le, Sts. Gregory, Maurus and Papianus. 300 le, Christ and the Penitent Sinners.

1991, Apr. 8   **Litho.**   **Perf. 13½x14**

1333	A179	10 le multicolored	.25	.25
1334	A179	20 le multicolored	.40	.40
1335	A179	30 le multicolored	.65	.65
1336	A179	50 le multicolored	1.10	1.10
1337	A179	80 le multicolored	1.60	1.60
1338	A179	100 le multicolored	2.10	2.10
1339	A179	175 le multicolored	3.50	3.50
1340	A179	300 le multicolored	6.00	6.00
		Nos. 1333-1340 (8)	15.60	15.60

Souvenir Sheets

1341-1342	A179	400 le Set of 2	16.00	16.00

Phila Nippon '91 — A180

Japanese locomotives: 10 le, Class 1400 steam. 20 le, Streamlined C55 steam. 30 le, ED17 electric. 60 le, EF13 electric. 100 le, Baldwin Mikado steam. 150 le, C62 steam. 200 le, KiHa 81 class diesel. 300 le, Class 8550 steam.

Each 400 le: No. 1351, Hikari bullet train. No. 1352, Class 7000 electric. No. 1353, D51 steam. No. 1354, Class 9600 steam.

1991, May 13   **Litho.**   **Perf. 14**

1343	A180	10 le multicolored	.25	.25
1344	A180	20 le multicolored	.35	.35
1345	A180	30 le multicolored	.55	.55
1346	A180	60 le multicolored	1.00	1.00
1347	A180	100 le multicolored	1.75	1.75
1348	A180	150 le multicolored	2.50	2.50
1349	A180	200 le multicolored	3.50	3.50
1350	A180	300 le multicolored	5.25	5.25
		Nos. 1343-1350 (8)	15.15	15.15

Souvenir Sheets

1351-1354	A180	Set of 4	26.00	26.00

Fish — A181

1991, June 3   **Litho.**   **Perf. 14**

1355	A181	10 le Aphyosemion ghana	.25	.25
1356	A181	20 le Black-lipped panchax	.35	.35
1357	A181	30 le Peter's killie	.65	.65
1358	A181	60 le Micro-walkeri killie	1.25	1.25
1359	A181	100 le Butterfly fish	2.25	2.25
1360	A181	150 le Green panchax	3.00	3.00
1361	A181	200 le Six-barred panchax	4.25	4.25
1362	A181	300 le Banded puffer	6.00	6.00
		Nos. 1355-1362 (8)	18.00	18.00

Souvenir Sheets

1363	A181	400 le Spotfin synodontis	8.00	8.00
1364	A181	400 le Two-striped panchax	8.00	8.00

Paintings by Vincent Van Gogh — A182

Designs: 10c, The Langlois Bridge at Arles. 50c, Trees in the Garden of Saint-Paul Hospital, vert. 1 le, Wild Flowers and Thistles in a Vase, vert. 2 le, Still Life: Vase with Oleanders and Books. 5 le, Farmhouses in a Wheat Field Near Arles. 10 le, Self-Portrait, Sept. 1889, vert. 20 le, Portrait of Patience Escalier, vert. 30 le, Portrait of Doctor Felix Rey, vert. 50 le, The Iris, vert. 60 le, The Shepherdess, vert. 80 le, Vincent's House in Arles (The Yellow House). 100 le, The Road Menders. 150 le, The Garden of Saint-Paul Hospital, vert. 200 le, View of the Church of Saint-Paul-De-Mausole. 250 le, Seascape at Saintes-Maries. 300 le, Pieta, vert.

Each 400 le: No. 1381, Church at Auvers Sur Dise, vert. No. 1382, Vineyards with a View of Auvers. No. 1383, The Trinquetaille Bridge. No. 1384, Two Poplars on a Road Through the Hills, vert. No. 1385, Haystacks in Provence. No. 1386, The Garden of Saint-Paul Hospital, diff.

1991, June 28   **Litho.**   **Perf. 13½**

1365	A182	10c multicolored	.25	.25
1366	A182	50c multicolored	.25	.25
1367	A182	1 le multicolored	.25	.25
1368	A182	2 le multicolored	.25	.25
1369	A182	5 le multicolored	.25	.25
1370	A182	10 le multicolored	.25	.25
1371	A182	20 le multicolored	.25	.25
1372	A182	30 le multicolored	.40	.40
1373	A182	50 le multicolored	.75	.75
1374	A182	60 le multicolored	.90	.90
1375	A182	80 le multicolored	1.25	1.25
1376	A182	100 le multicolored	1.60	1.60
1377	A182	150 le multicolored	2.40	2.40
1378	A182	200 le multicolored	3.25	3.25
1379	A182	250 le multicolored	4.25	4.25
1380	A182	300 le multicolored	4.75	4.75
		Nos. 1365-1380 (16)	21.30	21.30

Size: 102x76mm

Imperf

1381-1386	A182	Set of 6	27.00	27.00

Royal Family Birthday, Anniversary
Common Design Type

1991, July 5   **Litho.**   **Perf. 14**

1387	CD347	10 le multi	.25	.25
1388	CD347	20 le multi	.30	.30
1389	CD347	30 le multi	.50	.50
1390	CD347	80 le multi	1.25	1.25
1391	CD347	100 le multi	1.60	1.60
1392	CD347	200 le multi	3.25	3.25
1393	CD347	250 le multi	4.00	4.00
1394	CD347	300 le multi	4.75	4.75
		Nos. 1387-1394 (8)	15.90	15.90

Souvenir Sheets

1395	CD347	400 le Elizabeth, Philip	6.50	6.50
1396	CD347	400 le Charles, Diana, sons	6.50	6.50

10 le, 30 le, 200 le, 250 le, No. 1395, Queen Elizabeth II, 65th birthday. Others, Charles and Diana, 10th wedding anniversary.

Butterflies A183

1991, Aug. 5   **Litho.**   **Perf. 14x13½**

1397	A183	10 le Coppery swallowtail	.25	.25
1398	A183	30 le Orange forester	.90	.90
1399	A183	50 le Large striped swordtail	1.50	1.50
1400	A183	60 le Lilac beauty	1.75	1.75
1401	A183	80 le African leaf	2.25	2.25
1402	A183	100 le Blue diadem	3.00	3.00
1403	A183	200 le Beautiful monarch	6.00	6.00
1404	A183	300 le Veined swallowtail	8.50	8.50
		Nos. 1397-1404 (8)	24.15	24.15

Souvenir Sheets
Perf. 13x12

1405	A183	400 le Blue banded nymph	8.50	8.50
1406	A183	400 le Western red charaxes	4.50	4.50
1407	A183	400 le Broad-bordered grass yellow	4.50	4.50
1408	A183	400 le African clouded yellow	5.50	5.50

While numbers 1406-1407 have the same issue date as Nos. 1397-1405, the dollar value of Nos. 1406-1407 was lower when they were released. While No. 1408 has the same issue date as Nos. 1397-1407, the value of No. 1408 was different when released.

World War II Motion Pictures A184

Designs: 2 le, To Hell and Back, Audie Murphy. 5 le, Attack, Jack Palance. 10 le, Mrs. Miniver, Greer Garson and Walter Pidgeon. 20 le, The Guns of Navarone. 30 le, The Great Dictator, Paulette Goddard and Charlie Chaplin. 50 le, The Train. 60 le, The Diary of Anne Frank. 80 le, The Bridge on the River Kwai, William Holden. 100 le, Lifeboat, Alfred Hitchcock, Tallulah Bankhead. 200 le, Sands of Iwo Jima, John Wayne. 300 le, Thirty Seconds

Over Tokyo, Van Johnson and Spencer Tracy. 350 le, Casablanca, Humphrey Bogart and Ingrid Bergman. No. 1421, Twelve O'Clock High, Gregory Peck. No. 1422, Tora! Tora! Tora!. No. 1423, Patton, George C. Scott.

1991, Oct. 14   **Litho.**   **Perf. 14**

1409	A184	2 le multicolored	.25	.25
1410	A184	5 le multicolored	.25	.25
1411	A184	10 le multicolored	.25	.25
1412	A184	20 le multicolored	.25	.25
1413	A184	30 le multicolored	.40	.40
1414	A184	50 le multicolored	.90	.90
1415	A184	60 le multicolored	1.00	1.00
1416	A184	80 le multicolored	1.40	1.40
1417	A184	100 le multicolored	1.90	1.90
1418	A184	200 le multicolored	3.50	3.50
1419	A184	300 le multicolored	5.25	5.25
1420	A184	350 le multicolored	6.00	6.00
		Nos. 1409-1420 (12)	21.35	21.35

Souvenir Sheets

1421	A184	450 le multicolored	6.25	6.25
1422	A184	450 le multicolored	6.25	6.25
1423	A184	450 le multicolored	6.25	6.25

Miniature Sheets

Botanic Gardens — A185

Munich Botanic Garden: No. 1424a, Meissen China ornament. b, Masdevallia. c, White Egyptian lotus. d, French marigold. e, Pitcher plant. f, The Palm House. g, Dog's tooth violet. h, Passion flower. i, Hedge rose. j, Sensitive plant. k, Pitcher plant, diff. l, Trillium. m, Wild plantain. n, German primrose. o, Tulip. p, Spring walk.

Kyoto Botanic Garden: No. 1425a, Flowering cherry. b, Gardenia. c, The Domed Conservatory. d, Chrysanthemums. e, Bleeding heart. f, Hibiscus. g, Hiryu azalea. h, Sweet honeysuckle. i, Goldband lily. j, Non-traditional garden art. k, Viburnum. l, Japanese iris. m, Orchid. n, Hydrangea. o, View of Kyoto Botanic Garden. p, Camelia.

Brooklyn Botanic Garden: No. 1426a, The Palm House. b, Kurume azalea. c, Southern magnolia. d, Oleander. e, Chinese wisteria. f, Sourwood tree. g, Cattleya orchid. h, Gingko tree. i, Japanese Hill and Pond Garden. j, Rose. k, German iris. l, East Indian lotus. m, Speciosum lily. n, Lilac. o, Rose bay. p, Cranford Rose Garden.

Each 600 le: No. 1427, Rhododendron, Munich, horiz. No. 1428, Chrysanthemum, Kyoto, horiz. No. 1429, Magnolia soulangeana, Brooklyn, horiz.

1991, Oct. 28

Sheets of 16

1424	A185	60 le #a.-p.	14.00	14.00
1425	A185	60 le #a.-p.	14.00	14.00
1426	A185	60 le #a.-p.	14.00	14.00

Souvenir Sheets

1427-1429	A185	Set of 3	22.00	22.00

Christmas A186

Details from paintings or engravings by Albrecht Durer: 6 le, Mary being Crowned by Two Angels. 60 le, St. Christopher. 80 le, Virgin and Child. 100 le, Madonna and Child (Virgin with the Pear). 200 le, Madonna and Child. 300 le, The Virgin in Half-Length. 700 le, The Madonna with the Siskin.

Each 600 le: No. 1437, The Feast of the Rose Garlands. No. 1438, Virgin and Child with St. Anne.

1991, Dec. 9   Litho.   Perf. 12

1430	A186	6 le pink & black	.25	.25
1431	A186	60 le blue & black	.70	.70
1432	A186	80 le multicolored	.90	.90
1433	A186	100 le multicolored	1.10	1.10
1434	A186	200 le multicolored	2.25	2.25
1435	A186	300 le multicolored	3.25	3.25
1436	A186	700 le multicolored	7.75	7.75
		Nos. 1430-1436 (7)	16.20	16.20

Souvenir Sheets
Perf. 14½

1437-1438	A186	Set of 2	14.00	14.00

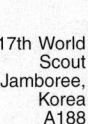

Wolfgang Amadeus Mozart, Death Bicent. A187

Mozart and: 50 le, National Theatre, Prague. 100 le, St. Peter's Abbey, Salzburg. 500 le, Scene from opera, "Idomeneo."

1991, Dec. 20   Perf. 14

1439	A187	50 le multicolored	.50	.50
1440	A187	100 le multicolored	1.00	1.00
1441	A187	500 le multicolored	5.00	5.00
		Nos. 1439-1441 (3)	6.50	6.50

Souvenir Sheet

1442	A187	600 le Bust, vert.	8.00	8.00

17th World Scout Jamboree, Korea A188

Designs: 250 le, Scouts learning to sail. 300 le, Lord Robert Baden-Powell, founder. 400 le, Scouts playing baseball. 750 le, Jamboree emblem, vert.

1991, Dec. 20

1443	A188	250 le multicolored	2.00	2.00
1444	A188	300 le multicolored	2.50	2.50
1445	A188	400 le multicolored	3.50	3.50
		Nos. 1443-1445 (3)	8.00	8.00

Souvenir Sheet

1446	A188	750 le multicolored	8.00	8.00

Miniature Sheet

Attack on Pearl Harbor, 50th Anniv. — A189

Designs: a, Japanese D3A1 Val dive bomber. b, Plane amid rising smoke over Ford Island. c, Battleships ablaze. d, Naval station, three planes. e, Drydock ablaze, tank farm. f, Two Vals over water, ships. g, USS Utah and Ford Island installations ablaze, ship underway. h, Installations on Ford Island ablaze. i, US P-40 Warhawk fighter plane. j, Two Japanese torpedo bombers, plane on fire falling from sky. k, Three Japanese bombers over Pearl City. l, Two Japanese bombers diving on four ships, one burning ship. m, Japanese plane on fire. n, Two Japanese planes. o, One Japanese plane over Waipio Peninsula.

1991, Dec. 20   Perf. 14½x15

1447	A189	75 le Sheet of 15,		
		#a.-o.	21.00	21.00

Walt Disney Christmas Cards — A190

Designs and year of issue: 12 le, Mickey and Donald decorating tree, 1952. 30 le, Characters surrounding book with "Alice in Wonderland", 1950. 60 le, Dwarf asleep with hare and tortoise, 1938. 75 le, Minnie, Donald, Mickey and Pluto mailing Christmas card, 1936. 100 le, Costumed characters in front of Magic Kingdom, 1984. 125 le, Mickey singing, Donald's nephews and Pluto reading 20,000 Leagues Under the Sea, 1954. 150 le, 101 Dalmations with season's greetings, 1960. 200 le, Donald and Mickey among gifts, 1948. 300 le, Mickey, Minnie at home for Christmas, 1983. 400 le, Donald and ducks preparing for Christmas watching Mickey Mouse Club, 1956. Characters on parade with Christmas cheer. 500 le, Disney characters, 50th birthday of Walt Disney Productions, 1972.

Each 900 le: No. 1460, Map of Magic Kingdom, 1955, vert. No. 1461, Seven dwarfs in bobsled, 1959, vert. No. 1462, Alice in Wonderland at tea party, 1950, vert.

1991, Dec. 24   Litho.   Perf. 14x13½

1448	A190	12 le multicolored	.25	.25
1449	A190	30 le multicolored	.25	.25
1450	A190	60 le multicolored	.45	.45
1451	A190	75 le multicolored	.50	.50
1452	A190	100 le multicolored	.70	.70
1453	A190	125 le multicolored	1.00	1.00
1454	A190	150 le multicolored	1.10	1.10
1455	A190	200 le multicolored	1.60	1.60
1456	A190	300 le multicolored	2.10	2.10
1457	A190	400 le multicolored	2.75	2.75
1458	A190	500 le multicolored	3.50	3.50
1459	A190	600 le multicolored	4.25	4.25
		Nos. 1448-1459 (12)	18.45	18.45

Souvenir Sheets
Perf. 13½x14

1460-1462	A190	Set of 3	18.00	18.00

Disney Characters on World Tour A192

Designs: 6 le, Chiquita Minnie in Central America. 10 le, Gold Medal Goofy in Ancient Greece. 20 le, Donald, Daisy having Flamenco Fun in Spain. 30 le, Goofy guarding Donald at London's Buckingham Palace. 50 le, Mickey and Minnie dressed in Paris originals. 100 le, Goofy with mountain goat in Switzerland. 200 le, Daisy, Minnie as luau ladies in Hawaii. 350 le, Mickey, Donald and Goofy as ancient Egyptian comic strips, horiz. 500 le, Daisy and Minnie as can-can dancers in Paris, horiz.

Each 700 le: No. 1479, Mickey playing bagpipes in Scotland. No. 1480, Goofy fishes from Donald's gondola in Venice, Italy. No. 1481, Mickey and Goofy taking crash course in Greek.

Perf. 13x13½, 13½x13

1992, Feb.   Litho.

1470	A192	6 le multicolored	.25	.25
1471	A192	10 le multicolored	.25	.25
1472	A192	20 le multicolored	.25	.25
1473	A192	30 le multicolored	.30	.30
1474	A192	50 le multicolored	.50	.50
1475	A192	100 le multicolored	.95	.95
1476	A192	200 le multicolored	1.90	1.90
1477	A192	350 le multicolored	3.25	3.25
1478	A192	500 le multicolored	4.75	4.75
		Nos. 1470-1478 (9)	12.40	12.40

Souvenir Sheets

1479-1481	A192	Set of 3	20.00	20.00

Queen Elizabeth II's Accession to the Throne, 40th Anniv.
Common Design Type

1992, Feb. 6   Litho.   Perf. 14

1482	CD348	60 le multi	.65	.65
1483	CD348	100 le multi	1.10	1.10
1484	CD348	300 le multi	3.00	3.00
1485	CD348	400 le multi	4.25	4.25
		Nos. 1482-1485 (4)	9.00	9.00

Souvenir Sheets

1486	CD348	700 le Queen, hillside	7.25	7.25
1487	CD348	700 le Queen, houses	7.25	7.25

Spanish Art — A193

Paintings by Francisco de Zurbaran: 1 le, The Visit of St. Thomas Aquinas to St. Bonaventure. 10 le, St. Gregory. 30 le, St. Andrew. 50 le, St. Gabriel the Archangel. 60 le, The Blessed Henry Suso. 100 le, St. Lucy. 300 le, St. Casilda. 400 le, St. Margaret of Antioch. 500 le, St. Apollonia. 600 le, St. Bonaventure at the Council of Lyons. 700 le, St. Bonaventure on His Bier. 800 le, The Martyrdom of St. James (detail). No. 1496, St. Hugh in the Refectory, horiz. No. 1497, The Martyrdom of St. James. No. 1497A, The Young Virgin.

1992, May 25   Litho.   Perf. 13

1487A	A193	1 le multi	.25	.25
1488	A193	10 le multi	.25	.25
1489	A193	30 le multi	.25	.25
1490	A193	50 le multi	.40	.40
1491	A193	60 le multi	.45	.45
1491A	A193	100 le multi	.50	.50
1491B	A193	300 le multi	1.50	1.50
1492	A193	400 le multi	3.00	3.00
1493	A193	500 le multi	4.00	4.00
1494	A193	600 le multi	4.75	4.75
1495	A193	700 le multi	3.50	3.50
1495A	A193	800 le multi	4.00	4.00

Size: 120x95mm
Imperf

1496	A193	900 le multi	7.25	7.25
1497	A193	900 le multi	6.75	6.75
1497A	A193	900 le multi	4.75	4.75
		Nos. 1487A-1497A (15)	41.60	41.60

Granada '92.
While Nos. 1487A-1497A all have the same issue date, the dollar value of Nos. 1487A, 1489-1490, 1491A-1491B, 1492, 1495, 1497-1497A was lower when they were released.

Prehistoric Animals — A194

Designs: No. 1498a, Rhamphorhynchus. b, Pteranodon. c, Dimorphodon. d, Pterodactyl. e, Archaeopteryx. f, Iguanodon. g, Hypsilophodon. h, Nothosaurus. i, Brachiosaurus. j, Kentrosaurus. k, Plesiosaurus. l, Trachodon. m, Hesperornis. n, Henodus. o, Steneosaurus. p, Stenopterygius. q, Eurhinosaurus. r, Placodus. s, Mosasaurus. t, Mixosaurus. No. 1499, Herperornis, diff.

1992, June 8   Perf. 14

1498	A194	50 le Sheet of 20, #a.-t.	22.50	22.50

Souvenir Sheet

1499	A194	50 le multicolored	3.00	3.00

"Sierra Leone" is 22mm wide on No. 1499.

A195

Tropical Birds: 30 le, Greater flamingo. 50 le, White-crested hornbill. 100 le, Verreaux's touraco. 170 le, Yellow-spotted barbet. 200 le, African spoonbill. 250 le, Saddlebill stork. 300 le, Red-headed lovebird. 600 le, Yellow-billed barbet. No. 1508, Fire-bellied woodpecker. No. 1509, Swallow-tailed beeeater.

1992, July 20   Litho.   Perf. 14

1500	A195	30 le multi	.40	.40
1501	A195	50 le multi	.65	.65
1502	A195	100 le multi	.80	.80
1503	A195	170 le multi	1.50	1.50
1504	A195	200 le multi	2.40	2.40
1505	A195	250 le multi	2.00	2.00
1506	A195	300 le multi	2.50	2.50
1507	A195	600 le multi	7.50	7.50
		Nos. 1500-1507 (8)	17.75	17.75

Souvenir Sheets

1508	A195	1000 le multi	11.00	11.00
1509	A195	1000 le multi	7.00	7.00

While Nos. 1500-1509 all have the same release date, the value of Nos. 1502-1503, 1505-1506, 1509 was lower when they were released.

A196

1992 Summer Olympics, Barcelona: 10 le, Marathon. 20 le, Gymnastics, parallel bars. 30 le, Discus. 50 le, 110-meter hurdles, horiz. 60 le, Women's long jump. 100 le, Gymnastics, floor exercise, horiz. 200 le, Windsurfing. 300 le, Road race cycling. 400 le, Weight lifting. 900 le, Soccer, horiz.

1992   Litho.   Perf. 14

1510	A196	10 le multicolored	.25	.25
1511	A196	20 le multicolored	.25	.25
1512	A196	30 le multicolored	.40	.40
1513	A196	50 le multicolored	.55	.55
1514	A196	60 le multicolored	.75	.75
1515	A196	100 le multicolored	1.25	1.25
1516	A196	200 le multicolored	2.40	2.40
1517	A196	300 le multicolored	3.50	3.50
1518	A196	400 le multicolored	4.75	4.75
		Nos. 1510-1518 (9)	14.10	14.10

Souvenir Sheet

1519	A196	900 le multicolored	8.50	8.50

1992 Winter Olympics, Albertville A197

Designs: 250 le, Women's biathlon, vert. 500 le, Speed skating, vert. 600 le, Men's downhill skiing.

Each 900 le: No. 1523, Men's single luge. No. 1524, Ice dancing, vert.

1992, Sept. 8   Litho.   Perf. 14

1520	A197	250 le multicolored	2.00	2.00
1521	A197	500 le multicolored	4.00	4.00
1522	A197	600 le multicolored	4.75	4.75
		Nos. 1520-1522 (3)	10.75	10.75

Souvenir Sheets

1523-1524	A197	Set of 2	11.50	11.50

Discovery of America, 500th Anniv. A198

Designs: 300 le, Ferdinand, Isabella, Columbus. 500 le, Landing in New World. 900 le, Columbus, vert.

1992, Oct.   Litho.   Perf. 14

1525	A198	300 le multicolored	2.25	2.25
1526	A198	500 le multicolored	3.25	3.25

Souvenir Sheet

1527	A198	900 le multicolored	6.00	6.00

Birds — A199

Designs: 50c, Pygmy goose. 1 le, Spotted eagle owl. 2 le, Verreaux's touraco. 5 le, Saddlebill stork. 10 le, African golden oriole. 20 le, Malachite kingfisher. 30 le, Fire-crowned bishop. 40 le, Fire-bellied woodpecker. 50 le, Red-billed fire-finch. 80 le, Blue fairy flycatcher. 100 le, Crested malimbe. 150 le, Vitelline masked weaver. 170 le, Blue plantaineater. 200 le, Superb sunbird. 250 le, Swallow-tailed bee-eater. 300 le, Cabani's yellow bunting. 500 le, Crocodile bird. 750 le, White-faced owl. 1000 le, Blue cuckoo-shrike. 2000 le, Bare-headed rock-fowl. 3000 le, Red-tailed buzzard.

1992-93   Litho.   Perf. 14x15
No Date Imprint

1528	A199	50c multi	.25	.25
1529	A199	1 le multi	.25	.25
1530	A199	2 le multi	.25	.25
1531	A199	5 le multi	.25	.25
1532	A199	10 le multi	.25	.25
1533	A199	20 le multi	.25	.25
1534	A199	30 le multi	.25	.25
1535	A199	40 le multi	.25	.25
1536	A199	50 le multi	.25	.25
a.		Inscribed "1994"	—	—
c.		Inscribed "1997"	—	—
1537	A199	80 le multi	.40	.40
1538	A199	100 le multi	.50	.50
a.		Inscribed "1994"	—	—
b.		Inscribed "1996"	—	—
c.		Inscribed "1997"	—	—
d.		Inscribed "1999"	—	—
e.		Inscribed "2000"	—	—
1539	A199	150 le multi	.80	.80
a.		Inscribed "1994"	—	—
1540	A199	170 le multi	.90	.90
1541	A199	200 le multi	1.00	1.00
a.		Inscribed "1994"	—	—
b.		Inscribed "1996"	—	—
c.		Inscribed "1997"	—	—
d.		Inscribed "1999"	—	—
e.		Inscribed "2000"	—	—
g.		Inscribed "2006"	—	—
1542	A199	250 le multi	1.25	1.25
c.		Inscribed "1997"	—	—
e.		Inscribed "2000"	—	—
f.		Inscribed "2002"	—	—
g.		Inscribed "2006"	—	—
1543	A199	300 le multi	1.90	1.90
a.		Inscribed "1994"	—	—
b.		Inscribed "1996"	—	—
c.		Inscribed "1997"	—	—
d.		Inscribed "1999"	—	—
e.		Inscribed "2000"	—	—
g.		Inscribed "2006"	—	—
1544	A199	500 le multi	3.25	3.25
b.		Inscribed "1996"	—	—
c.		Inscribed "1997"	—	—
e.		Inscribed "2000"	—	—
f.		Inscribed "2002"	—	—
g.		Inscribed "2006"	—	—
1545	A199	750 le multi	4.75	4.75
e.		Inscribed "2000"	—	—
g.		Inscribed "2006"	—	—
1546	A199	1000 le multi	6.25	6.25
b.		Inscribed "1996"	—	—
d.		Inscribed "1999"	—	—
e.		Inscribed "2000"	—	—
f.		Inscribed "2002"	—	—
g.		Inscribed "2006"	—	—
1546A	A199	2000 le multi	19.00	19.00
e.		Inscribed "2000"	—	—
f.		Inscribed "2002"	—	—
g.		Inscribed "2006"	—	—
1546B	A199	3000 le multi	19.00	19.00
b.		Inscribed "1996"	—	—
e.		Inscribed "2000"	—	—
f.		Inscribed "2002"	—	—
g.		Inscribed "2006"	—	—
		Nos. 1528-1546B (21)	61.25	61.25

Issued: #1528-1546, 9/92; #1546A-1546B, 1993.

See Nos. 2152-2155.

Model Trains A200

Lionel models: No. 1547a, Pennsylvannia RR GG-1 electric #6-18306, O gauge, 1992. b, Wabash RR Hudson #8610, O gauge, 1985. c, Locomotive #1911, standard gauge, 1911. d, Chesapeake & Ohio 4-4-2 #6-18627, O gauge, 1992. e, Gang car #50, O gauge, 1954. f, #8004, 1980 model of Rock Island &

Peoria RR engine built for Columbian Exposition of 1893, O gauge. g, Western Maryland RR Shay #6-18023, O gauge, 1992. h, (Kenner-Parker) Boston & Albany Hudson #784, O gauge, 1986. i, Locomotive #6, standard gauge, 1906.

No. 1548a, Pennsylvania RR Torpedo #238EW, O gauge, 1936. b, Denver & Rio Grande Western Alco Pa No. 6-18107, O gauge, 1992. c, #408E Locomotive, standard gauge, 1930. d, Mickey Mouse 60th birthday boxcar No. 19241, O gauge, 1991. e, Polished brass locomotive, No. 54, standard gauge, 1913. f, Broadway limited #392E, standard gauge, 1936. g, Great Northern RR EP-5 #18302, O gauge, 1988. h, 4-4-0 Locomotive #6, standard gauge, 1918. i, 4-4-4 Locomotive No. 400E, standard gauge, 1933.

No. 1549a, Special F-3 diesel engine, O gauge, 1947. b, Pennsylvannia RR GE 44-ton switcher #6-18905, O gauge, 1992. c, #1 trolley, standard gauge, 1913. d, Seaboard RR freight diesel, O gauge, 1958. e, Pennsylvannia S-2 turbine, O gauge, 1991. f, Western Pacific RR GP-9 diesel #6-18822, O gauge, 1992. g, #10 with Ives plates transition model, standrad gauge, 1929. h, 4-4-4 locomotive #400E, standard gauge, 1931. i, #384E, standard gauge, 1928.

Each 1000 le: No. 1550, Hudson No. 8210 Special, O gauge. No. 1551, #381E, standard gauge, 1928. No. 1552, 2-Rail electric model #300 trolley with converse body, 2⅞-inch gauge.

1992, Nov. 23   Litho.   Perf. 14
Sheets of 9

1547	A200	150 le #a.-i.	14.00	14.00
1548	A200	170 le #a.-i.	16.00	16.00
1549	A200	170 le #a.-i.	16.00	16.00

Souvenir Sheets
Perf. 13

1550-1552	A200	Set of 3	26.00	26.00

Genoa '92 (#1547-1549). Nos. 1550-1552 contains one 51x39mm stamp.

Walt Disney Characters in Christmas Scenes A201

1992, Nov. 16   Perf. 13½x14

1553	A201	10 le Minnie & Chip	.25	.25
1554	A201	20 le Goofy as Santa	.25	.25
1555	A201	30 le Daisy, Minnie	.25	.25
1556	A201	50 le Mickey, Goofy	.35	.35
1557	A201	80 le Pete	.55	.55
1558	A201	100 le Donald Duck	.70	.70
1559	A201	150 le Morty & Ferdie	1.10	1.10
1560	A201	200 le Mickey	1.40	1.40
1561	A201	300 le Goofy with ornament	2.25	2.25
1562	A201	500 le Chip & Dale	3.50	3.50
1563	A201	600 le Donald & Dale	5.00	5.00
1564	A201	800 le Huey, Dewey & Louie	6.00	6.00
		Nos. 1553-1564 (12)	21.60	21.60

Souvenir Sheets

1565	A201	900 le Mickey Mouse	8.00	8.00

Perf. 14x13½

1566	A201	900 le Angel with Chip, horiz.	8.00	8.00
1567	A201	900 le Mickey & Minnie, horiz.	8.00	8.00

Mickey Mouse Magazines and Books A202

10 le, Magazine cover, Mar. 1936, v. 1, #6. 20 le, Magazine cover, June 1936, v. 1, #9. 30 le, Magazine cover, Nov. 1936, v. 2, #2. 40 le, Magazine cover, Aug. 1937, v. 2, #11. 50 le, Magazine cover, Oct. 1937, v. 2, #13. 60 le, Magazine cover, Dec. 1937, v. 3, #3. 70 le, Magazine cover, Jan. 1938, v. 3, #4. 150 le, Cover, Big Book #4062, 1935. 170 le, Story book cover, 1936. 200 le, Comic book cover, unnumbered. 300 le, Comic book cover, No. 181. 400 le, Comic book cover #194. 500 le, Story book cover, Book 1, 1931. No. 1581, Boys' and Girls' March of Comics cover, 1948. No. 1582, First Mickey Mouse Magazine cover for June-Aug. 1935, v. 1, #1, horiz. No. 1583, Cover of early Mickey Mouse story book published in England, 1933, horiz.

1992   Perf. 13½x14

1568	A202	10 le multicolored	.25	.25
1569	A202	20 le multicolored	.25	.25
1570	A202	30 le multicolored	.25	.25
1571	A202	40 le multicolored	.25	.25
1572	A202	50 le multicolored	.30	.30
1573	A202	60 le multicolored	.35	.35
1574	A202	70 le multicolored	.40	.40
1575	A202	150 le multicolored	.80	.80
1576	A202	170 le multicolored	1.10	1.10
1577	A202	200 le multicolored	1.25	1.25
1578	A202	300 le multicolored	1.90	1.90
1579	A202	400 le multicolored	2.40	2.40
1580	A202	500 le multicolored	3.25	3.25
		Nos. 1568-1580 (13)	12.75	12.75

Souvenir Sheets

1581	A202	900 le multicolored	5.50	5.50

Perf. 14x13½

1582	A202	900 le multicolored	5.50	5.50
1583	A202	900 le multicolored	5.50	5.50

Christmas A203

Details or entire paintings: 1 le, Virgin and Child, by Fiorenzo di Lorenzo. 10 le, Madonna and Child on a Wall, by Circle of Dirk Bouts. 20 le, Virgin and Child with the Flight into Egypt, by Master of Hoogstraeten. 30 le, Madonna and Child before Firescreen, by Master of Flemalle. 50 le, Mary in a Rose Garden, by Hans Memling. 100 le, Virgin Mary and Child, by Lucas Cranach the Elder. 170 le, Virgin and Child, by Rogier van der Weyden. 200 le, Madonna and Saints, by Perugino. 250 le, Madonna Enthroned with Saints Catherine and Barbara, by Master of Hoogstraeten. 300 le, The Virgin in a Rose Arbor, by Stefan Lochner. 500 le, Madonna and Child with Angels, by Sandro Botticelli. 1000 le, Madonna and Child with Young St. John the Baptist, by Fra Bartolemmeo.

Each 900 le: No. 1596, The Virgin with the Green Cushion, by Andrea Solario. No. 1597, The Virgin and Child, by Jan Gossaert. No. 1598, The Virgin and Child, by Lucas Cranach the Younger.

1992, Dec. 7   Litho.   Perf. 13½x14

1584	A203	1 le multi	.25	.25
1585	A203	10 le multi	.25	.25
1586	A203	20 le multi	.25	.25
1587	A203	30 le multi	.25	.25
1588	A203	50 le multi	.40	.40
1589	A203	100 le multi	.70	.70
1590	A203	170 le multi	1.25	1.25
1591	A203	200 le multi	1.40	1.40
1592	A203	250 le multi	1.75	1.75
1593	A203	300 le multi	2.25	2.25
1594	A203	500 le multi	3.75	3.75
1595	A203	1000 le multi	7.25	7.25
		Nos. 1584-1595 (12)	19.75	19.75

Souvenir Sheets

1596-1598	A203	Set of 3	20.00	20.00

Anniversaries and Events A204

150 le, Emblems of FAO, ICN, WHO. #1600, Graf Zeppelin. #1601, Cow, emblems, grain stalk. 200 le, Starving child. #1603, Lions Intl. emblem, map. #1604, Cottonwood tree. 300 le, African elephant. 600 le, Space Shuttle. 700 le, Graf Zeppelin LZ 127, specifications.

Each 900 le: #1608, Astronaut. #1609, Count Zeppelin.

1992, Dec.   Litho.   Perf. 14

1599	A204	150 le multicolored	1.10	1.10
1600	A204	170 le multicolored	1.25	1.25
1601	A204	170 le multicolored	1.25	1.25
1602	A204	200 le multicolored	1.75	1.75
1603	A204	250 le multicolored	1.75	1.75
1604	A204	250 le multicolored	2.00	2.00
1605	A204	300 le multicolored	2.50	2.50
1606	A204	600 le multicolored	3.75	3.75
1607	A204	700 le multicolored	4.25	4.25
		Nos. 1599-1607 (9)	19.60	19.60

Souvenir Sheets

1608-1609	A204	Set of 2	12.00	12.00

Intl. Conference on Nutrition, Rome (#1599, 1601). Count Zeppelin, 75th anniv. of death (#1600, 1607, 1609). World Health Organization (#1602). Lions Intl., 75th anniv. (#1603). Earth Summit, Rio de Janeiro (#1604-1605). Intl. Space Year (#1606, 1608).

Miniature Sheet

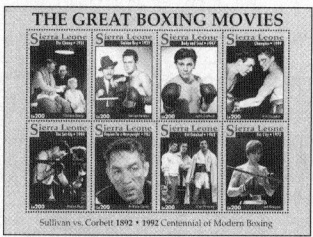

Boxing — A205

Boxing movies, stars, each 200 le: No. 1610a, The Champ, Wallace Beery. b, Golden Boy, William Holden. c, Body and Soul, John Garfield. d, Champion, Kirk Douglas. e, The Set-Up, Robert Ryan. f, Requiem for a Heavyweight, Anthony Quinn. g, Kid Galahad, Elvis Presley. h, Fat City, Jeff Bridges.

Boxing champions, each 200 le: No. 1611a, Joe Louis. b, Archie Moore. c, Muhammad Ali. d, George Foreman. e, Joe Frazier. f, Marvin Hagler. g, Sugar Ray Leonard. h, Evander Holyfield.

Each 1000 le: No. 1612, Gentlemen Jim, Errol Flynn. No. 1613, Muhammad Ali, diff. No. 1614, Rocky III, Sylvester Stallone.

1993, Feb. 8   Litho.   Perf. 13½x14

1610	A205	Sheet of 8, #a.-h.	11.50	11.50
1611	A205	Sheet of 8, #a.-h.	11.50	11.50

Souvenir Sheets

1612-1614	A205	Set of 3	19.00	19.00

Miniature Sheets

PAINTINGS FROM THE LOUVRE

BICENTENNIAL 1793 – 1993

Louvre Museum, Bicent. — A206

Details or entire paintings by Eugene Delacroix (1798-1863): Nos. 1615a-1615b, Entry of the Crusaders into Constantinople (left, right). c-d, Jews Purchasing Brides in Morocco (left, right). e-f, The Death of Sardanapalus (left, right). g-h, Liberty Guiding the People (left, right).

No. 1616a, An Orphan at the Cemetery. b-c, Women of Algiers in their Apartment (left, right). d, Dante and Virgil in the Infernal Regions. e, Self-Portrait. f-g, Massacre at Chios (left, right). h, Frederic Chopin.

No. 1617, Rape of the Sabine Women, by Jacques-Louis David (1748-1825).

1993, Mar. 8   Litho.   Perf. 12x12½

1615	A206	70 le Sheet of 8,		
		#a.-h. + label	6.75	6.75
1616	A206	70 le Sheet of 8,		
		#a.-h. + label	6.75	6.75

Souvenir Sheet
Perf. 14½

| 1617 | A206 | 900 le multicolored | 8.50 | 8.50 |

Mushrooms
A207

Butterflies
A208

Designs: 30 le, Amanita flammeola. 50 le, Cantharellus pseudocbarius. 100 le, Volvariella volvacea. 200 le, Termitomyces microcarpus. 300 le, Auricularia auricula. 400 le, Pleurotus tuberregium. 500 le, Schizophyllum commune. 600 le, Termitomyces robustus.

Each 1000 le: No. 1626, Phallus rubicundus. No. 1627, Daldina concentrica.

1993, May 5   Perf. 14

1618	A207	30 le multi	.25	.25
1619	A207	50 le multi	.30	.30
1620	A207	100 le multi	.80	.80
1621	A207	200 le multi	1.60	1.60
1622	A207	300 le multi	2.40	2.40
1623	A207	400 le multi	3.25	3.25
1624	A207	500 le multi	4.25	4.25
1625	A207	600 le multi	5.25	5.25
		Nos. 1618-1625 (8)	18.10	18.10

Souvenir Sheets

| 1626-1627 | A207 | Set of 2 | 17.00 | 17.00 |

1993, May 5

20 le, False acraea. 30 le, Blue temora. 50 le, Foxy charaxes. 100 le, Leaf blue. 150 le, Blue-banded swallowtail. 170 le, African monarch. 200 le, Mountain beauty. 250 le, Gaudy commodore. 300 le, Palla butterfly. 500 le, Pirate butterfly. 600 le, Painted lady. 700 le, Gold-banded forester.

Each 1000 le: #1640, Blue diadem. #1641, Blue swallowtail. #1642, African leaf butterfly.

| 1628-1639 | A208 | Set of 12 | 18.00 | 18.00 |

Souvenir Sheets

| 1640-1642 | A208 | Set of 3 | 19.00 | 19.00 |

Miniature Sheets

Sierra Leone • Cats of the World

Cats — A209

Designs, each 150 le: No. 1643a, Somali. b, Egyptian Mau smoke. c, Chocolate-point Siamese. d, Mi-Ke Japanese bobtail. e, Chinchilla. f, Red Burmese. g, British shorthair brown tabby. h, Blue Persian. i, British silver classic tabby. j, Oriental ebony. k, Red Persian. l, British calico shorthair.

Each 150 le: No. 1644a, Black Persian. b, Blue-point Siamese. c, American wirehair. d, Birman. e, Scottish fold (silver tabby). f, American shorthair red tabby. g, Blue & white Persian bicolor. h, Havana brown. i, Norwegian forest cat. j, Brown tortie Burmese. k, Angora. l, Exotic shorthair.

Each 1000 le: No. 1645, American shorthair blue tabby, horiz. No. 1646, Seal-point colorpoint, horiz.

1993, May 17   Litho.   Perf. 14

| 1643 | A209 | Sheet of 12, #a.-l. | 15.00 | 15.00 |
| 1644 | A209 | Sheet of 12, #a.-l. | 15.00 | 15.00 |

Souvenir Sheets

| 1645-1646 | A209 | Set of 2 | 16.00 | 16.00 |

Nos. 1643-1646 Ovptd. with Hong Kong '94 Emblem

1994   Litho.   Perf. 14

1643m	On #1643b & in sheet margin	9.50	9.50
1644m	On #1644b & in sheet margin	9.50	9.50
1645a	Ovptd. in sheet margin	5.25	5.25
1646a	Ovptd. in sheet margin	5.25	5.25

Wild Animals
A210

1993, June 17

1647	A210	30 le Gorilla	.25	.25
1648	A210	100 le Bongo	.80	.80
1649	A210	150 le Potto	1.25	1.25
1650	A210	170 le Chimpanzee	1.40	1.40
1651	A210	200 le Dwarf galago	1.60	1.60
1652	A210	300 le African linsang	2.50	2.50
1653	A210	500 le Banded duiker	4.50	4.50
1654	A210	750 le Diana monkey	6.50	6.50
		Nos. 1647-1654 (8)	18.80	18.80

Souvenir Sheets

| 1655 | A210 | 1200 le Leopard | 11.50 | 11.50 |
| 1656 | A210 | 1200 le Elephant | 11.50 | 11.50 |

Flowers
A211

30 le, Bleeding-heart vine. 40 le, Passion vine. 50 le, Hydrangea. 60 le, Wax begonia. 100 le, Hibiscus. 150 le, Crape-myrtle. 170 le, Bougainvillea. 200 le, Leadwort. 250 le, Gerbera daisy. 300 le, Black-eyed susan. 500 le, Gloriosa lily. 900 le, Sweet violet.

Each 1200 le: #1669, Gloriosa lily, diff. #1670, Passion vine, diff. #1671, Hibiscus, diff.

1993, July 15   Litho.   Perf. 14

1657	A211	30 le multi	.25	.25
1658	A211	40 le multi	.25	.25
1659	A211	50 le multi	.25	.25
1660	A211	60 le multi	.30	.30
1661	A211	100 le multi	.80	.80
1662	A211	150 le multi	1.25	1.25
1663	A211	170 le multi	1.40	1.40
1664	A211	200 le multi	1.60	1.60
1665	A211	250 le multi	2.00	2.00
1666	A211	300 le multi	2.40	2.40
1667	A211	500 le multi	4.00	4.00
1668	A211	900 le multi	5.00	5.00
		Nos. 1657-1668 (12)	19.50	19.50

Souvenir Sheets

| 1669-1671 | A211 | Set of 3 | 22.50 | 22.50 |

Coronation of Queen Elizabeth II, 40th Anniv. — A212

100 le, Queen, Princess Anne. 200 le, Coronation procession. 600 le, Official coronation photograph. 1500 le, Portrait, by Pietro Annigoni, 1954-55.

1993, Oct.   Litho.   Perf. 14

1672	A212	100 le multi	.65	.65
1673	A212	200 le black	1.60	1.60
1674	A212	600 le multi	5.25	5.25
		Nos. 1672-1674 (3)	7.50	7.50

Souvenir Sheet

| 1675 | A212 | 1500 le multi | 12.50 | 12.50 |

Copernicus
(1473-1543)
A213

Picasso (1881-1973)
A214

250 le, Early telescope. 800 le, Moon's surface.

1993, Oct.

| 1676 | A213 | 250 le multicolored | 1.75 | 1.75 |
| 1677 | A213 | 800 le multicolored | 5.50 | 5.50 |

1993, Oct.

Sculpture: 170 le, Woman with Hat, 1961. Paintings: 200 le, Buste de Femme, 1958. 800 le, Maya with a Doll, 1938. 1000 le, Women of Algiers (after Delacroix), 1955.

1678	A214	170 le multicolored	1.10	1.10
1679	A214	200 le multicolored	1.25	1.25
1680	A214	800 le multicolored	5.50	5.50
		Nos. 1678-1680 (3)	7.85	7.85

Souvenir Sheet

| 1681 | A214 | 1000 le multicolored | 7.00 | 7.00 |

Christmas
A215

Details or entire paintings, by Raphael: 50 le, 100 le, 1200 le (No. 1690), Madonna of the Fish. 150 le, Madonna & Child Enthroned with Five Saints. 800 le, The Holy Family with the Lamb.

Details or entire woodcuts, by Durer: 200 le, 250 le, 300 le, The Circumcision. 500 le, 1200 le (No. 1691), Holy Clan with Saints and Two Angels Playing Music.

1993, Dec.   Perf. 13½x14

1682	A215	50 le multi	.25	.25
1683	A215	100 le multi	.50	.50
1684	A215	150 le multi	.80	.80
1685	A215	200 le multi	1.25	1.25
1686	A215	250 le multi	1.50	1.50
1687	A215	300 le multi	1.75	1.75
1688	A215	500 le multi	3.00	3.00
1689	A215	800 le multi	5.00	5.00
		Nos. 1682-1689 (8)	14.05	14.05

Souvenir Sheets

| 1690-1691 | A215 | Set of 2 | 14.00 | 14.00 |

Christmas
A216

Disney characters celebrate Christmas: different.

Each 1200 le: #1700, Santa. #1701, Elves, horiz. #1702, Santa, horiz. #1703, Mickey, Minnie, horiz.

1993, Dec. 17   Perf. 13½x14

1692	A216	50 le multi	.25	.25
1693	A216	100 le multi	.50	.50
1694	A216	170 le multi	.90	.90
1695	A216	200 le multi	1.00	1.00
1696	A216	250 le multi	1.40	1.40
1697	A216	500 le multi	2.75	2.75
1698	A216	600 le multi	3.25	3.25
1699	A216	800 le multi	4.50	4.50
		Nos. 1692-1699 (8)	14.55	14.55

Souvenir Sheets
Perf. 13½x14, 14x13½

| 1700-1703 | A216 | Set of 4 | 27.50 | 27.50 |

1994 World Cup Soccer Championships, US — A217

Players, country: 30 le, Jose Luis Brown (R), Argentina. 50 le, Gary Lineker, England. 100 le, Carlos Valderrama, Colombia. 250 le, Skuhravy, Czechoslovakia; Marchena, Costa Rica. 300 le, Butragueno, Spain. 400 le, Roger Milla, Cameroun. 500 le, Roberto Donadoni, Italy. 700 le, Enzo Scifo, Belgium.

Each 1200 le: No. 1712, 1200 le, Socrates, Brazil. No. 1713, 1200 le, Wright, England; Demol, Belgium.

1993   Perf. 13½x14

| 1704-1711 | A217 | Set of 8 | 18.00 | 18.00 |

Souvenir Sheets

| 1712-1713 | A217 | Set of 2 | 18.00 | 18.00 |

A218

Hong Kong '94 — A219

Stamps and: No. 1714, Hong Kong #455, pagoda, Tiger Baum Garden. No. 1715, Ai Par Garden, #1084.

Carved lacquer, Qing Dynasty: No. 1716a, Bowl with "Wan-Sui-Ch'ang-Chun." b, Four-wheeled box. c, Flower container. d, Box with human figure design. e, Shishi dog (not lacquer). f, Persimmon.

1994, Feb. 18   Litho.   Perf. 14
1714 A218 200 le multicolored   1.00 1.00
1715 A218 200 le multicolored   1.00 1.00
a.   Pair, #1714-1715   2.00 2.00

Miniature Sheet
1716 A219 100 le Sheet of 6,
           #a.-f.   6.50 6.50

Nos. 1714-1715 issued in sheets of 5 pairs. No. 1715a is a continuous design.
New Year 1994 (Year of the Dog) (#1716e).

Miniature Sheet

New Year 1994 (Year of the Dog) — A220

a, 100 le, Pekingese. b, 150 le, Doberman pinscher. c, 200 le, Tibetan terrier. d, 250 le, Weimaraner. e, 400 le, Rottweiler. f, 500 le, Akita. g, 600 le, Schnauzer. h, 1000 le, Tibetan spaniel.
Each 1200 le: No. 1718, Wire-haired pointing Griffon. No. 1719, Shih Tzu.

1994, June 20   Litho.   Perf. 14
1717 A220 Sheet of 8, #a.-h.   14.50 14.50

Souvenir Sheets
1718-1719 A220 Set of 2   11.50 11.50

D-Day, 50th Anniv. A221

Designs: 500 le, British paratroops drop behind enemy lines. 750 le, US paratrooper jumps from C47 transport.
1000 le, C47 Douglas Dakota, paratroops.

1994, July 11   Litho.   Perf. 14
1720 A221 500 le multicolored   2.25 2.25
1721 A221 750 le multicolored   3.25 3.25

Souvenir Sheet
1722 A221 1000 le multicolored   5.50 5.50

A222

PHILAKOREA '94 — A223

100 le, Traditional wedding, Korea House, Seoul. 400 le, Royal tombs, Koryo Dynasty, Kaesong. 600 le, Terraced farm land, near Chungmu.
Tiger paintings, Choson Dynasty: No. 1726: a, Tiger, cubs, 19th cent. b, Munsa-pasal seated on lion. c, Extinct Korean tiger. d, Tiger, bamboo. e, Tiger guarding 3 cubs, 4 magpies. f, Tiger, 19th cent. g, Mountain Spirit. h, Tiger, bird in tree.
No. 1727, Wall painting of mounted hunters from Tomb of the Dancers of Kungnaesong, Koguryo period.

Perf. 14, 13½ (#1726)
1994, July 11   Litho.
1723-1725 A222 Set of 3   5.50 5.50

Miniature Sheet of 8
1726 A223 200 le #a.-h.   8.50 8.50
Souvenir Sheet
1727 A222 1200 le multicolored 10.00 10.00

Miniature Sheets of 6

First Manned Moon Landing, 25th Anniv. — A224

No. 1728, each 200 le: a, Edwin E. Aldrin, Jr. b, Michael Collins. c, Neil A. Armstrong. d, Apollo 11 liftoff. e, Aldrin descending to lunar surface. f, Aldrin, lunar module Eagle reflected in Aldrin's face shield.
No. 1729, each 200 le: a, Aldrin gathering soil samples. b, Eagle with Aldrin deploying solar wind experiment. c, Aldrin, ALSEP & Eagle at Tranquility Base. d, US flag, Aldrin, Tranquility Base. e, Plaque on moon. f, Apollo 11 crew, stamp ceremony.
1000 le, First footprint on moon.

1994, July 11   Perf. 14
Sheets of 6, #a-f
1728-1729 A224 Set of 2   9.50 9.50
Souvenir Sheet
1730 A224 1000 le multicolored 7.50 7.50

Miniature Sheet of 6

A225

1994 World Cup Soccer Championships, U.S. — A226

Players: No. 1731a, Kim Ho, South Korea. b, Cobi Jones, U.S. c, Claudio Suarez, Mexico. d, Tomas Brolin, Sweden. e, Ruud Gullit, Netherlands. f, Andreas Herzog, Austria.
Each 1500 le: No. 1732, Sierra Leone team. No. 1733, Giants Stadium, New Jersey.

1994, July 15
1731 A225 250 le #a.-f.   9.00 9.00
Souvenir Sheets
1732-1733 A226 Set of 2   14.00 14.00

Birds — A227

250 le, Black kite. 300 le, Superb sunbird. 500 le, Martial eagle. 800 le, Red bishop.
No. 1738 - White-necked picathartes: a, 50 le, Feeding young. b, 100 le, On brown tree limb. c, 150 le, Two at nest. d, 200 le, On gray limb, green leaves.
No. 1739, 1200 le, Greater flamingo, vert. No. 1740, 1200 le, White-necked picathartes up close, vert.

1994, Aug. 10
1734-1737 A227 Set of 4   21.00 21.00

1738 A227 Vert. Strip of 4,
           #a.-d.   5.50 5.50
Souvenir Sheets
1739-1740 A227 Set of 2   18.50 18.50

World Wildlife Fund (#1738). For surcharge see No. 2903.

Orchids — A228

Designs: 50 le, Aerangis kotschyana. 100 le, Brachycorythis kalbreyeri. 150 le, Diaphananthe pellucida. 200 le, Eulophia guineensis. 300 le, Eurychone rothschildana. 500 le, Tridactyle tridactylites. 750 le, Cyrtorchis arcuata. 900 le, Ancistrochilus rothschildianus.
Each 1500 le: No. 1749, Plectrelminthus caudatus. No. 1750, Polystachaya affinis.

1994, Sept. 1
1741-1748 A228 Set of 8   17.00 17.00
Souvenir Sheets
1749-1750 A228 Set of 2   15.00 15.00

Christmas A229

Details or entire paintings: 50 le, The Birth of the Virgin, by Murillo. 100 le, Education of the Virgin, by Murillo. 150 le, Annunciation, by Filippino Lippi. 200 le, Marriage of the Virgin, by Bernard van Orley. 250 le, The Visitation, by Nicolas Vleughels. 300 le, Holy Infant from Castelfranco altarpiece, by Giorgione. 400 le, Adoration of the Magi, Workshop of Bartholome Zeitblom. 600 le, Presentation of Infant Jesus in the Temple, by Memling.
Each 1500 le: No. 1759, Nativity Altarpiece, by Lorenzo Monado. No. 1760, Allendale Nativity, by Giorgione.

1994, Dec. 1   Litho.   Perf. 13½x14
1751-1758 A229 Set of 8   13.50 13.50
Souvenir Sheets
1759-1760 A229 Set of 2   13.00 13.00

Intl. Year of the Family A230

1994, Dec. 20   Litho.   Perf. 14
1761 A230 300 le Working in
           field   1.25 1.25
1762 A230 350 le At beach   1.40 1.40

Disney Christmas — A231

Designs: 50 le, Mickey's Christmas cat. 100 le, Goofy's Christmas tree, vert. 150 le, Daisy's Christmas gift. 200 le, Donald's Christmas surprise, vert. 250 le, Minnie's Christmas flight. 300 le, Goofy's Christmas snowball, vert. 400 le, Goofy's Christmas letters. 500 le, Christmas sled ride, vert. 600 le, Mickey's

Christmas snowman. 800 le, Pluto's Christmas treat, vert.
Each 1500 le: No. 1773, Goofy hanging outdoor lights. No. 1774, Mickey asleep in chair, vert.

Perf. 14x13½, 13½x14
1995, Jan. 23   Litho.
1763-1772 A231 Set of 10   17.50 17.50
Souvenir Sheets
1773-1774 A231 Set of 2   17.00 17.00

Donald Duck's Gallery of Old Masters A232

Name of painting, inspiration: 50 le, Madonna Duck, Leonardo da Vinci. 100 le, Portrait of a Venetian Duck, Tintoretto. 150 le, Duck with a Glove, Frans Hals. 200 le, Donald with a Pink, Quentin Massys. 250 le, Pinkie Daisy, Sir Thomas Lawrence. 300 le, Donald's Whistling Mother, Whistler. 400 le, El Quacko, El Greco. 500 le, The Noble Snob, Rembrandt. 600 le, The Blue Duck, by Gainsborough. 800 le, Modern Quack, Picasso.
Each 1500 le: No. 1785, Soup's On, Brueghel. No. 1786, Duck Dancers, Degas, horiz.

1995, Jan. 23   Perf. 13½x14, 14x13½
1775-1784 A232 Set of 10   14.50 14.50
Souvenir Sheets
1785-1786 A232 Set of 2   15.00 15.00

Miniature Sheets of 12

Olympic Medal Winners — A233

Summer Olympics: No. 1787a, Ragnar Lundberg, 1952 men's pole vault. b, Karin Janz, 1972 all-round gymnastics. c, Matthias Volz, 1936 gymnastics. d, Carl Lewis, 1988 long jump. e, Sara Simeoni, 1976 high jump. f, Daley Thompson, 1980 decathlon. g, Japan vs. Britain, 1964 soccer. h, Gabriella Dorio, 1984 1500-meters run. i, Daniela Hunger, 1988 200-meters individual medley swimming. j, Kyoko Iwasaki, 1992 200-meters breast stroke. k, Italian team member, 1960 water polo. l, David Wilkie, 1976 200-meters breast stroke.
1994 Winter Olympics, Lillehammer: No. 1788a, Katja Seizinger, downhill skiing. b, Hot air balloon (no medalist). c, Elvis Stojko, figure skating. d, Jens Weissflog, individual large hill ski jump. e, Bjorn Daehlie, 10k cross-country skiing. f, Germany, four-man bobsled. g, Markus Wasmeier, men's super giant slalom. h, Georg Hackl, luge. i, Trovill & Dean, ice dancing. j, Bonnie Blair, speed skating. k, Nancy Kerrigan, figure skating. l, Team Sweden, hockey.
Each 1000 le: No. 1789, torchbearer, horiz. No. 1790, Oksana Baiul, Nancy Kerrigan, Chen Lu, 1994 figure skating, horiz.

1995, Feb. 6   Litho.   Perf. 14
1787 A233 75 le #a.-l.   4.00 4.00
1788 A233 200 le #a.-l.   11.00 11.00
Souvenir Sheets
1789-1790 A233 Set of 2   10.00 10.00

Miniature Sheets

Dinosaurs A234

No. 1791, each 200 le: a, Ceratosaurus (d). b, Brachiosaurus. c, Pteranodon (b). d, Stegoceras. e, Saurolophus (h). f,

Ornithomumus. g, Compsognathus (j). h, Deinonychus (i). i, Ornitholestes. j, Archaeopteryx. k, Heterodontosaurus (l). l, Lesothosaurus.

No. 1792: a, 100 le, Triceratops. b, 250 le, Protoceratops (c). c, 400 le, Monoclonius (b). d, 800 le, Styracosaurus (c).

Each 2500 le: No. 1793, Deinonychus. No. 1794, Rhamphorynchus.

1995, May 4   Litho.   Perf. 14
1791 A234 Sheet of 12, #a.-l.   10.00 10.00
1792 A234 Sheet of 4, #a.-d.   8.50   8.50
Souvenir Sheets
1793-1794 A234 Set of 2   16.50 16.50

Sierra Club, Cent. A235

No. 1795, vert, each 150 le: a, L'Hoest's guenon. b, Black-footed cat. c, Colobus monkey up close. d, Colobus monkey in tree. e, Mandrill facing forward. f, Bonobo with young. g, Bonobo lying down. h, Mandrill facing right. i, Colobus monkey standing.

No. 1796, each 150 le: a, Black-faced impala facing forward. b, Herd of black-faced impala. c, Black-faced impala drinking. d, Bonobo. e, Black-footed cat. f, Black-footed cat up close. g, L'Hoest's guenon. h, L'Hoest's guenon, seated. i, Mandrills.

1995, May 10
Sheets of 9, #a-i
1795-1796 A235 Set of 2   12.50 12.50

New Year 1995 (Year of the Boar) A236

Stylized boars, each 100 le: No. 1797a, red & multi, facing left. b, green & multi, facing right. c, green & multi, facing left. d, red & multi, facing right.

500 le, Two boars, vert.

1995, May 8   Litho.   Perf. 14
1797 A236 Block of 4, #a.-d.   6.00   6.00
Souvenir Sheet
1798 A236 500 le multicolored   8.00   8.00

Singapore '95 — A237

Marine life, each 300 le: No. 1799a, Pufferfish. b, Coral grouper. c, Hawksbill turtle. d, Hogfish. e, Emperor angelfish. f, Butterflyfish. g, Lemon butterflyfish. h, Parrotfish. i, Moray eel.

Water birds, marine life, each 300 le: No. 1800a, Cape pigeons. b, Pelican. c, Puffin. d, Humpback whale. e, Greater shearwater. f, Bottlenose dolphin. g, Gurnard. h, Salmon. i, John dory.

Each 1500 le: #1801, Surgeonfish. #1802, Angelfish, vert.

1995
Sheets of 9, #a-i
1799-1800 A237 Set of 2   20.00 20.00
Souvenir Sheets
1801-1802 A237 Set of 2   12.00 12.00

Miniature Sheets of 6 or 8

A238

End of World War II, 50th Anniv. — A239

No. 1803: a, USS Idaho. b, HMS Ark Royal. c, Admiral Graf Spee. d, Destroyer. e, HMS Nelson. f, PT 109. g, USS Iowa. h, Bismark.

No. 1804: a, B-17. b, B-25. c, B-24 Liberator. d, USS Missouri. e, A-20 Boston. f, Pennsylvania, Colorado, Louisville, Portland, Columbia enter Lingayen Gulf.

No. 1805, HMS Indomitable launching aircraft. No. 1806, B-29 bomber.

1995, July 10
1803 A238 250 le #a.-h. + label   10.00 10.00
1804 A239 300 le #a.-f. + label   10.00 10.00
Souvenir Sheet
1805 A238 1500 le multi   6.00   6.00
1806 A239 1500 le multi   8.00   8.00

No. 1805 contains one 57x42mm stamp.

UN, 50th Anniv. — A240

No. 1807: a, 300 le, Dais, UN General Assembly. 400 le, Sec. Gen. U. Thant. 500 le, UN building, dove.
1500 le, Sec. Gen. Dag Hammarskjold.

1995, July 10   Litho.   Perf. 14
1807 A240 Strip of 3, #a.-c.   4.50   4.50
Souvenir Sheet
1808 A240 1500 le multicolored   5.00   5.00

No. 1807 is a continuous design.

1995 Boy Scout Jamboree, Holland A241

No. 1809: a, 400 le, Natl. flag. b, 500 le, Lord Baden-Powell. c, 600 le, Scout sign.
1500 le, Scout salute.

1995, July 10
1809 A241 Strip of 3, #a.-c.   5.00   5.00
Souvenir Sheet
1810 A241 1500 le multicolored   5.00   5.00

Queen Mother, 95th Birthday A242

No. 1811: a, Drawing. b, Holding bouquet of flowers. c, Formal portrait. d, Without hat. 1500 le, Blue hat, dress.

1995, July 10   Perf. 13½x14
1811 A242 400 le Block or strip of 4, #a.-d.   5.25   5.25
Souvenir Sheet
1812 A242 1500 le multicolored   5.00   5.00

No. 1811 was issued in sheets of 8 stamps. For surcharges see Nos. 2544-2545.

FAO, 50th Anniv. A243

No. 1813: a, 300 le, Man working with sack of food. b, 400 le, Boy carrying bundle of sticks on head. c, 500 le, Woman holding bowl of fruit.
1500 le, Woman holding baby, vert.

1995, July 10   Perf. 14
1813 A243 Strip of 3, #a.-c.   4.50   4.50
Souvenir Sheet
1814 A243 1500 le multicolored   5.00   5.00

Rotary Intl., 90th Anniv. A244

Designs: 500 le, Natl. flag, Rotary emblem. 1000 le, Paul Harris, Rotary emblem.

1995, July 10
1815 A244 500 le multicolored   3.00   3.00
Souvenir Sheet
1816 A244 1000 le multicolored   4.50   4.50

Singapore '95 — A245

Flora & fauna, each 300 le: No. 1817a, African tulip tree. b, Senegal bush locust. c, Killifish. d, Bird of paradise. e, Mandrill. f, Painted reed frog. g, Large spotted acraea. h, Carmine bee-eater.

No. 1818, each 300 le: a, Flame lily. b, Grants gazelle. c, Dogbane. d, Gold-banded forester. e, Horned chameleon. f, Malachite kingfisher. g, Leaf beetle. h, Acanthus.

Each 1500 le: No. 1819, Lion. No. 1820, African elephant.

1995, Sept. 5   Litho.   Perf. 14
Sheets of 8, #a-h
1817-1818 A245 Set of 2   26.00 26.00
Souvenir Sheets
1819-1820 A245 Set of 2   10.00 10.00

Third UN Decade for Advancement of Women — A246

Designs: 300 le, Development. 500 le, Peace. 700 le, Equality.

1995   Litho.   Perf. 14
1821-1823 A246 Set of 3   5.00   5.00

Sierra Leone Grammar School, 150th Anniv. A247

1995, Sept. 27   Litho.   Perf. 14
1824 A247 300 le multicolored   1.25   1.25

Christmas A248

Details or entire paintings: 50 le, Holy Family, by Beccafumi. 100 le, Rest on Flight into Egypt, by Barocci. 150 le, La Vierge, by Bellini. 200 le, The Flight, by d'Arpino. 600 le, Adoration of the Magi, by Francken. 800 le, The Annunciation, by da Conegliano.

Each 1500 le: No. 1831, Virgin and child, by Cranach. No. 1832, Madonna and Child, by Berlinghiero.

1995, Dec. 1   Litho.   Perf. 13½x14
1825-1830 A248 Set of 6   6.50   6.50
Souvenir Sheets
1831-1832 A248 Set of 2   12.00 12.00

Disney Christmas A249

Antique Disney toys: 5 le, Mickey Mouse doll. 10 le, Donald rag drum major. 15 le, Donald wind-up. 20 le, Toothbrush holder. 25 le, Mickey telephone. 30 le, Walking wind-up. 800 le, Movie projector. 1000 le, Goofy tricycle.

Each 1500 le: No. 1841, Black Mickey Mouse. No. 1842, First Mickey book.

1995, Dec. 4   Perf. 13½x14
1833-1840 A249 Set of 8   9.50   9.50
Souvenir Sheets
1841-1842 A249 Set of 2   10.00 10.00

Nobel Prize Fund Established, Cent. — A250

Recipients, each 250 le: No. 1843a, Andrew Huxley, medicine, 1963. b, Nelson Mandela, peace, 1993. c, Gabriela Mistral, literature, 1945. d, Otto Diels, chemistry, 1950. e, Hannes Alfven, physics, 1970. f, Wole Soyinka, literature, 1986. g, Hans G. Dehmelt, physics, 1989. h, Desmond Tutu, peace, 1984. i, Leo Esaki, physics, 1973.

No. 1844, each 250 le: a, Maria Goeppert Mayer, physics, 1963. b, Irène Joliot-Curie, chemistry, 1935. c, Mother Teresa, peace, 1979. d, Selma Lagerlöf, literature, 1909. e, Rosalyn Yalow, medicine, 1977. f, Dorothy Hodgkin, chemistry, 1964. g, Rita Levi-Montalcini, medicine, 1986. h, Mairead Corrigan, peace, 1976. i, Betty Williams, peace, 1976.

No. 1845, each 250 le: a, Tobias Asser, peace, 1911. b, Andrei Sakharov, peace, 1975. c, Frederic Passy, peace, 1901. d, Dag Hammarskjöld, peace, 1961. e, Aung San Suu Kyi, peace, 1991. f, Ludwig Quidde, peace, 1927. g, Elie Wiesel, peace, 1986. h, Bertha von Suttner, peace, 1905. i, Dalai Lama, peace, 1989.

No. 1846, each 250 le: a, Richard Zsigmondy, chemistry, 1925. b, Robert Huber, chemistry, 1988. c, Wilhelm Ostwald, chemistry, 1909. d, Johann Deisenhofer, chemistry, 1988. e, Heinrich Wieland, chemistry, 1927. f, Gerhard Herzberg, chemistry, 1971. g, Hans von Euler-Chelpin, chemistry, 1929. h, Richard Willstätter, chemistry, 1915. i, Fritz Haber, chemistry, 1918.

Each 1500 le: No. 1847, Albert Einstein, physics, 1921. No. 1848, Wilhelm Röentgen, physics, 1901. No. 1849, Sin-Itiro Tomonaga, physics, 1965.

1995, Dec. 29   Litho.   Perf. 14
Sheets of 9, #a-i
1843-1846 A250 Set of 4   50.00 50.00
Souvenir Sheets
1847-1849 A250 Set of 3   18.00 18.00

Railways of the World
A251

No. 1850, each 200 le: a, Denver and Rio Grande Western. b, Central of Georgia. c, Seaboard Air Line. d, Missouri Pacific Lines. e, Atchison, Topeka and Santa Fe. f, Chicago, Milwaukee, St. Paul and Pacific. g, Texas and Pacific. h, Minneapolis, St. Paul & Sault Saint Marie. (Soo Line). i, Western Pacific. j, Great Northern. k, Baltimore & Ohio. l, Chicago, Rock Island and Pacific.

No. 1851, each 200 le: a, Southern Pacific 4-8-4 "Daylight" express, US. b, Belgian National 4-4-2 express. c, Indian Railways 4-6-2 "WP" express. d, South Australian 4-8-4 express. e, Union Pacific 4-8-8-4 "Big Boy," US. f, UK 4-6-2 "Royal Scot" streamlined. g, German Federal, class 052 2-10-0. h, Japanese National, 4-6-4 express. i, Pennsylvania, 4-4-4-4 streamlined, US. j, East African 4-8-2+2-8-4 Beyer-Garratt. k, Milwaukee Road 4-6-4 "Hiawatha" express, US. l, Paris-Orleans, 4-6-2 Pacific, France.

No. 1852, each 250 le: a, "Eurostar" express. b, ETR 401 Pendolino four-car tilting train, Italy. c, HST 125 inter-city high speed train, UK. d, "Virgin" B-B class high speed diesel-hydraulic express, Spain. e, French Natl. Railways TGV. f, Amtrak "Southwest Chief," US. g, TGV "Atlantique," France. h, "Peloponnese Express," Greece. i, "Shin-Kansen" high-speed electric train, Japan. j, Canadian Natl. turbo train. k, XPT high-speed diesel-electric train, Australia. l, SS1 Co-Co electric locomotive, China.

No. 1853, each 300 le: a, Canadian Natl. U1-F. b, Central Pacific No. 119 at Promontory, US. c, LNER "A4" class streamlined 4-6-2, UK. d, New York Central J32 "Empire State Express," US. e, Canadian Natl. 4-8-4. f, Class 38 Pacific 4-6-2 express, Australia. g, Canadian Pacific 4-6-2 express. h, Southern "West Country" class 4-6-2, UK.i, Norfolk & Western Class J 4-8-4, US. j, RM Class 4-6-0 Pacific, China. k, P-36 class 4-8-4 express, USSR. l, Great Western "King" class 4-6-0, UK.

Each 1500 le: No. 1853M, British Railways Jubilee class 4-6-0, No. 45627 named "Sierra Leone." No. 1853N, Denver & Rio Grande Western "California Zephyr," US. No. 1853O, 1st train to cross newly opened bridge over Yangtze River, 1968, China. No. 1853P, Beijing-Shanghai Express, China. No. 1853Q, China Railways, "QJ" class 2-10-2.

1995, May 23   Litho.   Perf. 14
Sheets of 12, #a-l
1850-1851 A251 Set of 2   16.00 16.00
1852   A251 250 le multi   10.00 10.00

1853 A251 300 le multi   12.00 12.00
Souvenir Sheets
1853M-1853Q A251 Set of 5   25.00 25.00

Nos. 1853M-1853Q each contain one 56x43mm stamp. No. 1850 exists with two different top margin inscriptions, "THE COLOURFUL RAILROADS OF NORTH AMERICA" and "THE COLOURFUL RAILROADS OF THE WORLD."

New Year 1996 (Year of the Rat)
A252

Different stylized rats: No. 1854a, Facing left, purple & multi. b, Facing right, blue green & multi. c, Facing left, blue green & multi. d, Facing right, blue & multi.
No. 1856, Rat, vert.

1996, Jan. 6
1854 A252 200 le Block of 4, #a.-
              d.   3.75 3.75
Miniature Sheet of 4
1855 A252 200 le #1854a-1854d 3.75 3.75
Souvenir Sheet
1856 A252 500 le multicolored 3.75 3.75
No. 1854 was issued in sheets of 16 stamps.

Disney Characters as Circus Performers
A253

Designs: 100 le, Mickey, the magician. 200 le, Clarabelle Cow, the tightrope walker. 250 le, The clowns, Donald and Huey, Dewey and Louie. 300 le, Donald, the lion tamer. 800 le, Minnie, the bareback rider. 1000 le, Goofy and Minnie, the trapeze artists.
Each 1500 le: #1863, Mickey, horiz. #1864, Pluto, horiz.

1996, Jan. 29   Litho.   Perf. 14x13½
1857-1862 A253 Set of 6   13.00 13.00
Souvenir Sheets
Perf. 13½x14½
1863-1864 A253 Set of 2   13.00 13.00

Motion Pictures, Cent.
A254

No. 1865, each 250 le: a, Film projector. b, Pete. c, Silver. d, Rin-Tin-Tin. e, King Kong. f, Flipper. g, Jaws. h, Elsa. i, Moby Dick.
No. 1866, Directors or stars, scene from movie, each 250 le: a, Lumière Brothers. b, George Méliès. c, Toshiro Mifune d, Clark Gable, Vivien Leigh, David O. Selznick. e, Fritz Lang, Metropolis. f, Akira Kurosawa, Ran. g, Charlie Chaplin. h, Marlène Dietrich. i, Steven Spielberg, ET.
Each 1500 le: #1867, Lassie. #1868, Cecil B. de Mille.

1996, Feb. 26   Litho.   Perf. 14
Sheets of 9, #a-i
1865-1866 A254 Set of 2   17.50 17.50
Souvenir Sheets
1867-1868 A254 Set of 2   10.00 10.00

Paintings from Metropolitan Museum of Art — A255

Entire paintings or details: No. 1869, each 200 le: a, Honfleur, by Jongkind. b, A Boat on the Shore, by Courbet. c, Barges at Pontoise, by Pissarro. d, The Dead Christ with Angels, by Manet. e, Salisbury Cathedral, by Constable. f, A Lady with a Setter Dog, by Eakins. g, Tahitian Women Bathing, by Gaugin. h, Majas on a Balcony, by Goya.

By Renoir: No. 1870, each 200 le: a, In the Meadow. b, By the Seashore. c, Still Life with Peaches and Grapes. d, Marguerite (Margot) Bérard. e, Young Girl in Pink and Black Hat. f, A Waitrress at Duval's Restaurant. g, A Road in Louveciennes. h, Two Young Girls at the Piano.

No. 1871, each 200 le: a, Morning, an Overcast Day, Rouen, by Pissarro. b, The Horse Fair, by Bonheur. c, High Tide: the Bathers, by Homer. d, The Dance Class, by Degas. e, The Brioche, by Manet. f, The Grand Canal, Venice, by Turner. g, St. Thecla Interceding for Plague-stricken Este, by G. B. Tiepolo. h, Bridge at Villeneuve, by Sisley.

No. 1872, each 200 le: a, Madame Charpentier, by Renoir. b, Head of Christ, by Rembrandt. c, The Standard-Bearer, by Rembrandt. d, Girl Asleep, by Vermeer. e, Lady with a Lute, by Vermeer. f, Portrait of a Woman, by Rembrandt. g, La Grenouillère, by Monet. h, Woman with Chrysanthemums, by Degas.

Each 1500 le: No. 1873, The Death of Socrates, by J.L. David. No. 1874, Battle of Constantine and Maxentius, by Rubens. No. 1875, Samson and Delilah, by Rubens. No. 1876, The Emblem of Christ Appearing to Constantine, by Rubens.

Sheets of 8, #a-h, + label
1996   Litho.   Perf. 13½x14
1869-1872 A255 Set of 4   24.00 24.00
Souvenir Sheets
Perf. 14
1873-1876 A255 Set of 4   15.00 15.00
Nos. 1873-1876 each contain one 85x57mm.
Nos. 1874-1876 are not in the Metropolitan.

1996 Summer Olympic Games, Atlanta
A256

100 le, 1932 Olympic Stadium, Los Angeles. 150 le, Archery. 500 le, Rings (gymnastics). 600 le, Pole vault.
No. 1881: a, Field hockey. b, Swimming. c, Equestrian. d, Boxing. e, Pommel horse. f, 100-meter dash.

1996, June 11   Litho.   Perf. 14
1877-1880 A256 Set of 4   5.25 5.25
1881   A256 300 le Sheet of 6,
                 #a.-f.   6.75 6.75
Souvenir Sheet
1882   A256 1500 le Runner 6.00 6.00

Queen Elizabeth II, 70th Birthday
A257

Designs: a, Portrait. b, Receiving flowers. c, Holding flowers, wearing black hat, coat. 1500 le, Waving from balcony.

1996, July 15   Litho.   Perf. 13½x14
1886 A257 600 le Strip of 3,
            #a.-c.   6.00 6.00
Souvenir Sheet
1887 A257 1500 le multicolored 6.00 6.00
No. 1886 was issued in sheets of 9 stamps.

UNICEF, 50th Anniv.
A258

Designs: 300 le, Children reading. 400 le, Young man, woman reading. 500 le, Children in class.
1500 le, Children's faces.

1996, July 15   Perf. 14
1888-1890 A258 Set of 3   3.75 3.75
Souvenir Sheet
1891 A258 1500 le multicolored 5.50 5.50

Cats — A259

No. 1892, each 200 le a, Abyssinian. b, British tabby. c, Norwegian forest. d, Maine coon. e, Bengal. f, Asian. g, American curl. h, Devon rex. i, Tonkinese. j, Egyptian mau. k, Burmese. l, Siamese.
No. 1893, each 200 le: a, British shorthair. b, Tiffany. c, Birman. d, Somali. e, Malayan. f, Japanese bobtail. g, Himalayan. h, Tortoiseshell. i, Oriental. j, Ocicat. k, Chartreux. l, Ragdoll.
Each 2000 le: No. 1894, Persian. No. 1895, Burmilla.

1996, June 17
Sheets of 12, #a-l
1892-1893 A259 Set of 2   17.50 17.50
Souvenir Sheets
1894-1895 A259 Set of 2   10.00 10.00

Mushrooms — A260

50 le, Cinnabar-red chanterelle. 300 le, Larch suillus. 400 le, Yellow more. 500 le, Variable cort.
No. 1900, each 250 le: a, African driver ant, Indigo milky, Marshall's false monarch (e). b, Scally inky cap. c, Pyxie cup (b). d, Barometer earthstar (c), rainbow grasshopper (h). e, Feltringed agaricus, long-horned longhorn. f, Spotted mycena. g, Orange latex milky. h, Tawny grissett amanita fulva, lamellicorn larva.
No. 1901, each 250 le: a, Millar tiger, little nest polymore. b, Coral slime. c, Red-gilled cort. d, Parasitic volvamella, veined tiger. e, Onion-stalked lepiota. f, Blusher. g, Orange mock oyster. h, Lizard claw, red and yellow barbet.
Each 1500 le: No. 1902, Netted rhodotus. No. 1903, Parasitic psathyrella.

1996, June 17
1896-1899 A260 Set of 4   5.00 5.00
Sheets of 8, #a.-h.
1900-1901 A260 Set of 2   12.50 12.50
Souvenir Sheets
1902-1903 A260 Set of 2   10.00 10.00

Space Exploration — A261

Designs: a, Pioneer-Venus orbiter, 1986-92. b, Hubble space telescope. c, Voyager probe. d, Space Shuttle Challenger in orbit. e, Pioneer II. f, Mars-Viking 1 lander.
1500 le, Shuttle Challenger landing.

1996
1904 A261 300 le Sheet of 6,
　　　　#a.-f.　　　　　　4.50 4.50
Souvenir Sheet
1905 A261 1500 le multicolored 5.75 5.75

Butterflies
A262

Designs: 150 le, Charaxes pleione. 200 le, Eurema brigitta. 300 le, Charaxes ameliae. 500 le, Kallimoides rumia.
No. 1910, each 250 le: a, Precis orithya. b, Palla ussheri. c, Junonia orithya. d, Cymothoe sangaris. e, Cyrestis camillus. f, Precis rhadama. g, Precis cebrene. h, Hypolimnas misippus. i, Colotis danae.
Each 1500 le: No. 1911, Charaxes bohemani. No. 1912, Papilio antimachus.

1996, Aug. 15 Litho. Perf. 14
1906-1909 A262 Set of 4 4.25 4.25
1910 A262 Sheet of 9, #a.-i. 7.75 7.75
Souvenir Sheets
1911-1912 A262 Set of 2 9.50 9.50

Flowers — A263

Designs: 150 le, Tulipa. 200 le, Helichrysum bracteatum. 400 le, Viola. 500 le, Phalaenopsis.
No. 1917, each 200 le: a, Fountain. b, Begonia multiflora. c, Narcissus. d, Crocus speciosus. e, Chrysanthemum frutescens. Petunia. f, Cosmos pipinnatus. g, Anemone coronaria. h, Convolvulus minor.
No. 1918, each 300 le: a, Paphiopedilum. b, Cymbidium "Peach bloom." c, Sailboat. d, Miltonia. e, Parides gundalachianus. f, Laeliocatt leya. g, Lycaste aromatica. h, Brassolaeliocatt leya. i, Cymbidium "Southern Lace," Catastica teutila.
Each 1500 le: No. 1919, Helianthus annuus. No. 1920, Cymbidium "Lucifer."

1996, Aug. 19
1913-1916 A263 Set of 4 4.00 4.00
1917 A263 Sheet of 9, #a.-i. 5.50 5.50
1918 A263 Sheet of 9, #a.-i. 8.00 8.00
Souvenir Sheets
1919-1920 A263 Set of 2 9.50 9.50

Chinese
Lunar
Calendar
A264

Year of the: a, Rat. b, Ox. c, Tiger. d, Hare. e, Dragon. f, Snake. g, Horse. h, Sheep. i, Monkey. j, Rooster. k, Dog. l, Pig.

1996, July 15 Litho. Perf. 13½x14
1921 A264 150 le Sheet of 12,
　　　　#a.-l.　　　　　　4.50 4.50

Ships
A265

No. 1922, each 300 le: a, Clipper ship, "Cutty Sark," 19th cent. b, SS Great Britain, 1846. c, "Dreadnaught," 1906. d, RMS Queen Elizabeth, 1940-72. e, Ocean-going racing yacht, 1962. f, SS United States, 1952. g, Nuclear powered submarine, 1950's. h, Super tanker, 1960's. i, USS Enterprise, 1980s.
No. 1923, each 300 le: a, Greek war galley, 4th cent. BC. b, Roman war galley, 50AD. c, Viking ship, 9th cent. d, Flemish carrack, 15th cent. e, Merchant man, 16th cent. f, Tudor warship, 16th cent. g, Elizabethan galleon, 17th cent. h, Dutch Man of War, 17th cent. i, "Maestrale," Maltese galley, 18th cent.
Each 1500 le: No. 1924, Cruise ship "Legend of the Seas," 1996 Panama Canal. No. 1925, Egyptian ocean-going ship, 1480BC.

1996, Oct. 29 Litho. Perf. 14
Sheets of 9, #a-i
1922-1923 A265 Set of 2 13.50 13.50
Souvenir Sheets
1924-1925 A265 Set of 2 7.50 7.50
Nos. 1924-1925 each contain one 56x43mm stamp.

Christmas
A266

Details or entire paintings, by Filippo Lippi: 200 le, Madonna of Humility. 250 le, Coronation of the Virgin. 400 le, 500 le, Annunciation. 600 le, Barbadori Altarpiece. 800 le, Coronation of the Virgin, diff.
Each 2000 le: Paintings by Rubens: No. 1932, Adoration of the Magi. No. 1933, Holy Family with St. Anne.

1996, Dec. 12 Litho. Perf. 13½x14
1926-1931 A266 Set of 6 12.00 12.00
Souvenir Sheets
1932-1933 A266 Set of 2 10.00 10.00

Souvenir Sheets

Fantasies of the Sea — A267

Each 1500 le: #1934, Sea Dragon's Daughter. #1935, Homo Aquaticus. #1936, Chinese Sea Fairy. #1937, Sea Totem. #1938, The Turtle, horiz. #1939, Mermaid, horiz. #1940, How the Whale Got its Throat, horiz. #1941, Killer Whale Crest. #1942, Aphrodite. #1943, Ship Figurehead. #1944, Lilith. #1945, Queen of the Orkney Islands. #1946, Haida Eagle. #1947, Captain Ahab. #1948, Waskos. #1949, Jonah. #1950, Odysseus. #1951, The Little Mermaid. #1952, Squamish Indians. #1953, Boy on a Dolphin. $1954, Airship to Atlantis. #1955, Sea Bishop. #1956, 20,000 Leagues Under the Sea. #1957, Whale Song. #1958, Arion. #1959, Dragonrider of Pern. #1960, Kelpie. #1961, Natsihlane. #1962, Merman.

#1963, Albatross. #1964, City under polar ice melt. #1965, Tom Swift. #1966, The Flying Dutchman, horiz. #1967, Sea Centaur. #1968, Lang (dragon), horiz. #1969, Triton. #1970, Sea Serpent. #1971, Arthropod sea monster. #1972, The Ancient Mariner. #1973, Poseidon.

1996, Dec. 19 Litho. Perf. 14
1934-1973 A267 Set of 40 150.00 150.00

New Year 1997 (Year of the Ox)
A268

Various stylized oxen, background color: Nos. 1975-1976: a, purple. b, green. c, blue. d, claret.
800 le, like #1975d, vert.

1997, Jan. 8 Litho. Perf. 14
1975 A268 150 le Block of 4, #a.-
　　　　d.　　　　　　1.50 1.50
1976 A268 250 le Sheet of 4,
　　　　#a.-d.　　　　　6.50 6.50
Souvenir Sheet
1977 A268 800 le multicolored 2.75 2.75
No. 1975 was issued in sheets of 16 stamps.

Disney's
Aladdin in
Christmas
Scenes
A269

Designs: 10 le, Aladdin, Jasmine. 15 le, Santa, Genie. 20 le, Aladdin, Jasmine on magic carpet. 25 le, Genie as Christmas tree. 30 le, Aladdin, Genie "Santa." 100 le, Jasmine, Aladdin, Genie. 800 le, Genie's letter to Santa. 1000 le, Genie's Christmas carol.
Each 2000 le: No. 1986, Aladdin, Abu. No. 1987, Jasmine, Aladdin, horiz.

1997, Jan. 27 Perf. 14x13½
1978-1985 A269 Set of 8 12.00 12.00
Souvenir Sheets
Perf. 14x13½, 13½x14
1986-1987 A269 Set of 2 10.00 10.00

Hong
Kong — A270

Panoramic view of Hong Kong, each 500 le: No. 1988, in daytime. No. 1989, at night.

1997, Feb. 12 Litho. Perf. 14
Sheets of 4, #a-d
1988-1989 A270 Set of 2 10.50 10.50

UNESCO,
50th Anniv.
A271

World Heritage Sites: 60 le, Town of Kizhi Pogost, Russia. 200 le, Durmitor Natl. Park, Yugoslavia. 250 le, City of Nessebar, Bulgaria. 400 le, City of Bukhara, Uzbekistan. 500 le, Monastery of Kiev-Pechersk, Ukraine. 700 le, Mountain Walks, Vlkolinec, Slovakia.
No. 1996, each 300 le: a, Town of Roros, Norway. b, City of Warsaw, Poland. c, Cathedral of Notre Dame, Luxembourg. d, City of Vilnius, Lithuania. e, Jelling, Denmark. f, Old Church of Petäjävesi, Finland. g, Sweden. h, Cathedral City of Bern, Switzerland.
No. 1997, each 300 le: a, Area surrounding Mt. Kilimanjaro, Tanzania. b, Monument, Fasil Ghebbi, Ethiopia. c, Natl. Park, Mt. Ruwenzori, Uganda. d, Abu Simbel, Egypt. e, Tsingy Bemaraha Strict Nature Reserve, Madagascar. f, House, Djenne, Mali. g, Traditional house construction, Ghana. h, Large house, Aromey.
Various views of Himeji-Jo, Japan, vert: No. 1998: a, b, c, d, e.
Each 2000 le: No. 1999, Natl. Bird Sanctuary, Djudj, Senegal, horiz. No. 2000, Acropolis, Athens, Greece, horiz.

1997, Mar. 24 Litho. Perf. 13½x14
1990-1995 A271 Set of 6 6.00 6.00
Sheets of 8, #a-h, + Label
1996-1997 A271 Set of 2 13.50 13.50
Sheet of 5 + Label
1998 A271 500 le #a.-e. 6.75 6.75
Souvenir Sheets
1999-2000 A271 Set of 2 10.00 10.00

Paintings by
Hiroshige
(1797-1858)
A272

No. 2001, each 400 le: a, Hatsune Riding Grounds, Bakuro-cho. b, Mannen Bridge, Fukagawa. c, Ryogoku Bridge and the Great Riverbank. d, Asakusa River, Great Riverbank, Miyato River. e, Silk-goods Lane, Odenmacho. f, Mokuboji Temple, Uchigawa Inlet, Gozensaihata.
Each 1500 le: No. 2002, Tsukudajima from Eitai Bridge. No. 2003, Nihonbashi Bridge and Edobashi Bridge.

1997 Litho. Perf. 13½x14
2001 A272 Sheet of 6, #a.-f. 6.50 6.50
Souvenir Sheets
2002-2003 A272 Set of 2 7.50 7.50

Chernobyl
Disaster,
10th Anniv.
A273

Designs: 1000 le, UNESCO. 1500 le, Chabad's Children of Chernobyl.

1997, June 23
2004 A273 1000 le multicolored 3.25 3.25
2005 A273 1500 le multicolored 4.75 4.75

Queen Elizabeth II and Prince Philip,
50th Wedding Anniv.
A274

No. 2006: a, Queen. b, Royal arms. c, Black & white photograph, Prince in dress uniform. d, Black & white photograph, Prince in tuxedo,

bow tie. e, Palace of Holyroodhouse. f, Prince in hat guiding horses.
1500 le, Queen, Prince in colored photograph.

1997, June 23   **Perf. 14**
2006 A274 400 le Sheet of 6,
#a.-f.   13.50 13.50

Souvenir Sheet
2007 A274 1500 le mul-
ticolored   4.00 4.00

Return of Hong Kong to
China — A275

Designs: 400 le, Flag of China, map of China, Hong Kong, Victoria at night. 500 le, 650 le, Flag of China, July 1, 1997, city scene inside letters spelling "Hong Kong." 550 le, 600 le, Flag of China, Victoria harbor inside letters spelling "Hong Kong '97." 800 le, Victoria harbor, Deng Xiaoping (1904-97).

1997, June 23
2008-2013 A275 Set of 6   9.50 9.50
Nos. 2008-2013 were each issued in sheets of 3.

Souvenir Sheets

Mother Goose — A276

Designs, each 1500 le: No. 2014, Three Blind Mice. No. 2015, Woman holding out full skirt as "Myself."

1997, June 23   **Litho.**   **Perf. 14**
2014-2015 A276 Set of 2   8.00 8.00

1998 Winter
Olympic
Games,
Nagano
A277

Designs: 250 le, Stadium, Calgary, 1988, American Indian. 300 le, Freestyle aerial skiing, vert. 500 le, Ice hockey, vert. 800 le, Dan Jansen, 1000-meter speed skater, vert.
No. 2022, vert, each 300 le: a, Peggy Fleming, figure skating. b, Japanese ski jumper, Nordic combined. c, 2-man luge, Germany. d, Frank-Peter Roetsch, biathlon, E. Germany.
Each 1500 le: No. 2023, Jamaican bobsled team, vert. No. 2024, Johann Olav Koss, Norway, vert.

1997, July 16   **Litho.**   **Perf. 14**
2018-2021 A277 Set of 4   5.00 5.00
2022 A276 Strip of 4, #a.-d.   3.25 3.25

Souvenir Sheets
2023-2024 A277 Set of 2   8.00 8.00
No. 2022 was issued in sheets of 8 stamps.

1998 World Cup Soccer
Championships, France — A278

Players: 100 le, Stabile, Uruguay. 150 le, Schiavio, Italy. 200 le, Kocsis, Hungary. 250 le, Nejedly, Czechoslovakia. 500 le, Leonidas, Brazil. 600 le, Ademir, Brazil.
No. 2031, each 300 le: a, Dwight Yorke, Trinidad & Tobago. b, Dennis Bergkamp, Holland. c, Steve McManaman, England. d, Ryan Giggs, Wales. e, Romario, Brazil, f, Faustino Asprilla, Colombia. g, Roy Keane, Ireland. h, Peter Schmeichel, Denmark.
Each 1500 le: No. 2032, Pele, Brazil, horiz. No. 2033, Lato, Poland, horiz.

1997, July 23   **Perf. 13½x14, 14x13½**
2025-2030 A278 Set of 6   4.75 4.75
Sheet of 8
2031 A278 #a.-h. + 2 labels   6.50 6.50
Souvenir Sheets
2032-2033 A278 Set of 2   8.00 8.00

Classic Horror Movies — A279

Lead character, movie: No. 2034, each 300 le: a, Lon Chaney, "Phantom of the Opera," 1934. b, Boris Karloff, "The Mummy," 1932. c, Fredric March, "Dr. Jekyll & Mr. Hyde, " 1932. d, Lon Chaney, Jr., "The Wolf Man," 1941. e, Charles Laughton, "Island of Lost Souls," 1933. f, Lionel Atwill, "Mystery of the Wax Museum, " 1933. g, Bela Lugosi, "Dracula," 1931. h, Vincent Price, "The Haunted Palace," 1963. i, Elsa Lanchester, "Bride of Frankenstein," 1935.
3000 le, Bela Lugosi, Boris Karloff, "Son of Frankenstein," 1939.

1997, Aug. 15   **Perf. 14**
2034 A279 Sheet of 9, #a.-i.   8.50 8.50
Souvenir Sheet
2035 A279 3000 le multicolored   8.00 8.00

Domestic
Cats — A280

Designs: 150 le, American short hair tabby. 200 le, British short hair. 500 le, Turkish angora.
No. 2039, each 400 le: a, Chartreux. b, Abyssinian. c, Burmese. d, White angora. e, Japanese bobtail. f, Cymric.
1500 le, Egyptian mau.

1997, Aug. 29
2036-2038 A280 Set of 3   2.25 2.25

2039 A280 Sheet of 6, #a.-f.   6.50 6.50
Souvenir Sheet
2040 A280 1500 le multicolored   4.00 4.00
No. 2040 contains one 64x32mm stamp.

Butterflies   Orchids
A281   A282

Designs: 150 le, Vindula erota. 200 le, Pereutel leucodrosime. 250 le, Dynstor napolean. 300 le, Thauria aliris. 600 le, Papilio aegeus. 800 le, Amblypodia anita. 1500 le, Kallimoides rumia. 2000 le, Papilio dardanas.
No. 2049: a, Lycaena dispar. b, Graphium sarpedon. c, Euploe core. d, Papilio cresphontes. e, Colotis danae. f, Battus philenor.
No. 2050: a, Mylothris chloris. b, Argynnis lathonia. c, Elymnias agondas. d, Palla ussheri. e, Papilio glaucus. f, Cercyonis pegala.
Each 3000 le: No. 2051, Hebomoia glaucippe, horiz. No. 2052, Colias eurytheme, horiz.

1997, Aug. 1   **Litho.**   **Perf. 14**
2041-2048 A281 Set of 8   15.00 15.00
Sheets of 6
2049 A281 500 le #a.-f.   8.00 8.00
2050 A281 600 le #a.-f.   9.75 9.75
Souvenir Sheets
2051-2052 A281 Set of 2   16.00 16.00
For surcharges see Nos. 2897-2898.

1997, Sept. 1

Designs: 150 le, Ansellia africana. 200 le, Maxillaria praestans. 250 le, Cymbidium mimi. 300 le, Dendrobium bigibbum. 500 le, Encyclia vitellina. 800 le, Epidendrum prismatocarpum.
No. 2059, each 400 le: a, Laelia anceps. b, Paphiopedilum fairrieanum. c, Restrepia lansbergii. d, Yamadara cattleya. e, Cleistes divaricata. f, Calypso bulbosa.
Each 1500 le: No. 2060, Odontoglossum schlieperianum. No. 2061, Paphiopedilum tonsum.

2053-2058 A282 Set of 6   6.00 6.00
2059 A282 Sheet of 6, #a.-f.   6.50 6.50
Souvenir Sheets
2060-2061 A282 Set of 2   8.00 8.00

Motion
Pictures
Directed by
Alfred
Hitchcock
A283

No. 2062, each 350 le: a, Ray Milland in "Dial M for Murder." b, James Stewart, Kim Novak in "Vertigo." c, Cary Grant, Ingrid Bergman in "Notorious." d, John Dall, James Stewart in "Rope." e, Cary Grant in "North by Northwest." f, Grace Kelly, James Stewart in "Rear Window." g, Joan Fontaine, Laurence Olivier in "Rebecca." h, Tippi Hedren in "The Birds." i, Janet Leigh in "Psycho."
1500 le, Alfred Hitchcock.

1997, Aug. 15   **Litho.**   **Perf. 14**
2062 A283 Sheet of 9, #a.-i.   8.50 8.50
Souvenir Sheet
2063 A283 1500 le multicolored   4.00 4.00

Dogs — A284

Designs: 100 le, Shetland sheep dog. 250 le, Alaskan husky. 600 le, Jack Russell terrier.
No. 2067, each 400 le: a, Basset hound. b, Irish setter. c, St. Bernard. d, German shepherd. e, Dalmatian. f, Cocker spaniel.
1500 le, Boxer.

1997, Aug. 29
2064-2066 A284 Set of 3   2.50 2.50
2067 A284 Sheet of 6, #a.-f.   6.50 6.50
Souvenir Sheet
2068 A284 1500 le multicolored   4.00 4.00
No. 2068 contains one 31x63mm stamp.

Disney
Christmas
Stamps
A285

Designs: 150 le, Huey, Dewey, & Louie. 200 le, Mickey's kids. 250 le, Daisy Duck. 300 le, Minnie. 400 le, Mickey. 500 le, Donald Duck. 600 le, Pluto. 800 le, Goofy.
No. 2077, each 50 le: a, like #2071. b, like #2069. c, like #2074. d, like #2072. e, like #2070. f, like #2073.
Each 2000 le: No. 2078, Mickey in sleigh. No. 2079, Mickey, Donald, Daisy in Santa suits, horiz.

1997, Oct. 1   **Perf. 13½x14, 14x13½**
2069-2076 A285 Set of 8   8.50 8.50
2077 A285 Sheet of 6, #a.-f.   1.60 1.60
Souvenir Sheets
2078-2079 A285 Set of 2   12.00 12.00
For overprints see Nos. 2117-2119.

Civilian
Airliners
A286

No. 2080, each 600 le: a, SUD Caravelle 6. b, DeHavilland comet. c, Boeing 707. d, Airbus industrie A-300.
No. 2080E, each 600 le: f, Benoist Type XIV. g, Junkers JU52/3m. h, Douglas DC-3. i, Sikorsky S-42.
Each 2000 le: #2081, Concorde. #2081A, Lockheed L-1649A Starliner.

1997, Oct. 6   **Perf. 14**
2080 A286 Sheet of 4, #a.-d.
+ label   6.50 6.50
2080E A286 Sheet of 4, #f.-i.
+ label   6.50 6.50
Souvenir Sheets
2081-2081A A286 Set of 2   12.00 12.00
Nos. 2081-2081A contain one 91x34mm stamp.

Christmas
A287

Entire paintings or details: 100 le, 150 le, The Annunciation, by Titian (diff. details). 200 le, Madonna of Foligno, by Raphael. 250 le, The Annunciation, by Michelino. 500 le, The Prophet Isaiah, by Michelangelo. 600 le, Three Angels, by Master of the Rhenish Housebook.
Each 2000 le: No. 2088, The Fall of the Rebel Angels, by Peter Bruegel the Elder, horiz. No. 2089, Unidentified painting of Angel pointing hand in air, man with book, horiz.

1997, Dec. 24
2082-2087 A287 Set of 6   4.75   4.75
Souvenir Sheets
2088-2089 A287 Set of 2   10.50 10.50

Diana, Princess of Wales (1961-97) — A288

Various portraits, each 400 le, color of sheet margin: No. 2090, Pale pink. No. 2091, Pale blue. No. 2092, Pale yellow.
Each 1500 le: No. 2093, Wearing wide-brimmed hat. No. 2094, With Prince Harry (in margin). No. 2095, Helping to feed needy.

1998, Jan. 12   Litho.   Perf. 14
Sheets of 6, #a.-f.
2090-2092 A288 Set of 3   19.50 19.50
Souvenir Sheets
2093-2095 A288 Set of 3   12.00 12.00

New Year 1998 (Year of the Tiger) A289

Various stylized tigers in: No. 2096: a, purple. b, maroon. c, bright lilac rose. d, orange. 800 le, maroon, vert.

1998, Jan. 26   Litho.   Perf. 14
2096 A289 250 le Sheet of 4,
        #a.-d.   2.75   2.75
Souvenir Sheet
2097 A289 800 le red org & multi 2.25   2.25

Flora and Fauna A290

Designs: 200 le, Metagyrphus nitens, vert. 250 le, Lord Derby's parakeet, vert. 300 le, Narcissus, vert. 400 le, Barbus tetrazona. 500 le, Agalychnis callidryas. 600 le, Wolverine.
No. 2104, each 450 le: a, Japanese white-eyes. b, Rhododendron. c, Slow loris. d, Violet flowers. e, Orthetrum albistylum. f, Coluber jugularis.
No. 2105, each 450 le: a, Cheetah. b, Ornithogalum thyrsoides. c, Ostrich. d, Common chameleon. e, Fennec fox. f, Junonia hierta cebrene.
Each 2000 le: No. 2106, Tricolored heron, vert. No. 2107, Atheris squamiger

1998, Aug. 4   Litho.   Perf. 14
2098-2103 A290 Set of 6   5.00   5.00
Sheets of 6, #a.-f.
2104-2105 A290 Set of 2   14.50 14.50
Souvenir Sheets
2106-2107 A290 Set of 2   10.00 10.00

Dinosaurs A291

Designs: 200 le, Hypsilophodon, vert. 400 le, Lambeosaurus, vert. 500 le, Corythosaurus. 600 le, Stegosaurus, vert. 800 le, Antrodemus.
No. 2113, each 500 le, vert: a, Plateosaurus. b, Tyrannosaurus. c, Brachiosaurus. d, Iguanodon. e, Styracosaurus. f, Hadrosaurus.
No. 2114, each 500 le: a, Tyrannosaurus. b, Tenontosaurus. c, Deinonychus. d, Triceratops. e, Maiasaura. f, Struthiomimus.

Each 2000 le: No. 2115, Tyrannosaurus. No. 2116, Triceratops.

1998, Aug. 18   Litho.   Perf. 14
2108-2112 A291 Set of 5   5.50   5.50
Sheets of 6, #a.-f.
2113-2114 A291 Set of 2   13.50 13.50
Souvenir Sheets
2115-2116 A291 Set of 2   10.00 10.00

Nos. 2077-2079 Ovptd.

Perf. 13½x14, 14x13½
1998, Aug. 31
2117 A285 50 le Sheet of 6,
        #a.-f.   9.00   9.00
Souvenir Sheets
2118-2119 A285 Set of 2   19.00 19.00
Emblem and "MICKEY & MINNIE — 70TH ANNIVERSARY" appear in sheet margin on Nos. 2118-2119.

Ships of the World A292

No. 2120, each 300 le: a, Phoenician, 8th cent. BC. b, Drakkar, 6th cent. c, Carrack, 14th cent. d, Venetian Galley, 16th cent. e, Galeasse, 17th cent. f, Chebeck, 17th cent.
No. 2121, each 300 le: a, Junk, 19th cent. b, HMS Victory, 19th cent. c, Savanna, 19th cent. d, Gaissa, 19th cent. e, Warrior, 19th cent. f, Preussen, 20th cent.
Each 2000 le: No. 2122, Santa Maria, 1492. No. 2123, Titanic, 1912.

1998, Sept. 1   Perf. 14
Sheets of 6, #a.-f.
2120-2121 A292 Set of 2   18.00 18.00
Souvenir Sheets
2122-2123 A292 Set of 2   10.00 10.00
Nos. 2122-2123 each contain one 57x43mm stamp.
For surcharges see Nos. 2899-2900.

Disney's The Lion King, Simba's Pride A293

No. 2124, each 500 le: a, Kiara (with bird). b, Pumbaa. c, Kiara & Kovu. d, Kovu. e, Kiara & Kovu (red background). f, Timon (orange background).
No. 2125, each 500 le: a, Kiara (with butterfly). b, Timon & Pumbaa. c, Kiara. d, Kiara & Kovu (green background). e, Kovu (with bird). f, Kiara & Kovu (pink background).
Each 2500 le: No. 2126, Pumbaa & Timon. No. 2127, Kiara & Kovu, horiz.

Perf. 13½x14, 14x13½
1998, Sept. 15
Sheets of 6, #a.-f.
2124-2125 A293 Set of 2   25.00 25.00
Souvenir Sheets
2126-2127 A293 Set of 2   22.50 22.50

Paintings by Picasso — A294

Paintings: 400 le, Man with Straw Hat and Ice Cream Cone, 1938. 600 le, Woman in Red Armchair, 1932. 800 le, Nude in a Garden, 1934.
2000 le, Child Holding a Dove, 1901.

1998, Dec. 15   Litho.   Perf. 14½
2128-2130 A294 Set of 3   7.00   7.00
Souvenir Sheet
2131 A294 2000 le multicolored 4.00   4.00

Gandhi — A295

1998, Dec. 15   Perf. 14
2132 A295 600 le Portrait   5.00   5.00
Souvenir Sheet
2133 A295 2000 le Close-up   5.00   5.00
No. 2132 printed in sheets of 4.
For surcharge see No. 2904.

Royal Air Force, 80th Anniv. A296

No. 2134, each 800 le: a, McDonnell Douglas Phantom FRG2. b, Two Panavia Tornado GR1. c, Jaguar GR1A. d, Hercules C-130.
Each 2000 le: No. 2135, Eagle, biplane. No. 2136, Lysander, Eurofighter.

1998, Dec. 15
2134 A296 Sheet of 4, #a.-d. 13.00 13.00
Souvenir Sheets
2135-2136 A296 Set of 2   15.00 15.00

19th World Scouting Jamboree, Chile A297

No. 2137, each 1500 le: a, Dan Beard, Robert Daden-Powell, 1937. b, Kuwaiti Scouts. c, Scout leader bottle feeding bear cub.
No. 2138, each 1500 le, vert: a, William D. Boyce, Lone Scouts founder. b, Guion S. Bluford. c, Ellison S. Onizuka.
Each 3000 le: No. 2139, Lord, Lady Robert Baden-Powell. No. 2140, Bear cub drinking from bottle.

1998, Dec. 15
Sheets of 3, #a.-c.
2137-2138 A297 Set of 2   18.00 18.00
Souvenir Sheets
2139-2140 A297 Set of 2   13.50 13.50
For surcharge see No. 2901.

Christmas A298

Entire paintings or details: 200 le, Penitent of Mary Magdalen, by Titian. 500 le, Lamentation of Christ, by Veronese. 1500 le, The Building of Noah's Ark, by Guido Reni. 2000 le, Abraham and Isaac, by Rembrandt.
Each 3000 le: No. 2145, Adoration of the Shepherds, by Bartolomé Estéban Murillo. No. 2146, The Assumption of the Virgin, by Murillo.

1998, Dec. 14   Litho.   Perf. 14
2141-2144 A298 Set of 4   9.00   9.00
Souvenir Sheets
2145-2146 A298 Set of 2   12.00 12.00

Ferrari Automobiles — A298a

No. 2146A, each 800 le: c, 400 Superamerica. d, 250 GT Lusso. e, 342 America. 2000 le, 330 GTC.

1998, Dec. 15   Litho.   Perf. 14
2146A A298a Sheet of 3, #c-e   3.00   3.00
Souvenir Sheet
2146B A298a multi   2.60   2.60
No. 2146A contains three 39x25mm stamps.

Diana, Princess of Wales (1961-97) — A299

1998, Dec. 15   Perf. 14½x14
2147 A299 600 le multicolored 2.00   2.00
No. 2147 was issued in sheets of 6.

New Year 1999 (Year of the Rabbit) A300

Color of stylized rabbits — #2148: a, red. b, red violet. c, blue. d, light violet. 1500 le, Rabbit, vert.

1998, Dec. 24   Perf. 14
2148 A300 700 le Sheet of 4,
        #a.-d.   7.00   7.00
Souvenir Sheet
2149 A300 1500 le multicolored 6.00   6.00

Paintings by Eugène Delacroix (1798-1863) — A301

Designs: a, Rocks and a Small Valley. b, Jewish Musicians from Magador. c, Moroccans Traveling. d, Women of Algiers in their Apartment. e, Moroccan Military Exercises. f, Arabs Skirmishing in the Mountains. g, Arab Chieftan Reclining on a Carpet. h, Procession in Tangier.

No. 2151, Chopin, vert.

1998

2150	A301	400 le Sheet of 8, #a.-h.	11.00	11.00

Souvenir Sheet

2151	A301	400 le multicolored	6.00	6.00

Bird Type of 1992

Designs: 4000 le, Gray-headed bush-shrike. 5000 le, Black-backed puffback. 6000 le, Crimson-breasted shrike. 10,000 le, Northern shrike.

1999   **Litho.**   **Perf. 14x15**

No Date Imprint

2152	A199	4000 le multi	12.00	12.00
2153	A199	5000 le multi	14.00	14.00
a.		Inscribed "2002"	14.00	
b.		Inscribed "2006"	14.00	
2154	A199	6000 le multi	18.00	18.00
2155	A199	10,000 le multi	22.50	22.50
b.		Inscribed "2006"	22.50	
		Nos. 2152-2155 (4)	66.50	66.50

Issued: 4000 le, 5000 le, 2/18/99.

Birds, Marine Life — A302

150 le, Powder blue surgeon. 250 le, Frilled anemone. 600 le, Red beard sponge. 800 le, Red-finned batfish.

No. 2160, each 400 le: a, Eastern reef egret. b, Dolphins. c, Sailing ship, Humpback whale. d, Red and green macaw. e, Blue tangs. f, Guitarfish. g, Manatees. h, Hammerhead shark. i, Blue shark. j, Lemon goby, moorish idol. k, Ribbon eels. l, Loggerhead turtle.

Sharks — #2161, each 500 le: a, Blue shark. b, Tiger shark. c, Bull shark. d, Great white. e, Scalloped hammerhead. f, Oceanic whitetip. g, Zebra shark. h, Leopard shark. i, Horn shark.

Dolphins, whales — #2162, each 500 le: a, Hector's dolphin. b, Tucuxi. c, Hourglass dolphin. d, Bottlenose dolphin. e, Gray's beaked whale. f, Bowhead whale. g, Fin whale. h, Gray whale. i, Blue whale.

Each 3000 le: No. 2163, Purple firefish. No. 2164, Spotted eagle ray. No. 2165, Leatherback turtle.

1999, Feb. 22   **Perf. 14**

2156-2159	A302	Set of 4	3.00	3.00
2160	A302	Sheet of 12, #a.-l.	8.00	8.00

Sheets of 9, #a.-i.

2161-2162	A302	Set of 2	15.00	15.00

Souvenir Sheets

2163-2165	A302	Set of 3	22.50	22.50

Intl. Year of the Ocean (#2160-2162, #2164-2165).

Airplanes A303

200 le, Grumman X-29. 300 le, Rocket-powered Bell X-1. 400 le, MiG-21 Fishbed, 1956, USSR. 600 le, Blériot X1 Monoplane, 1909. 800 le, Southern Cross, Fokker F.VII, 1928. 1500 le, Supermarine S.6B.

No. 2172, each 600 le: a, Grumman F3F-1, 1940. b, North American F-86A Sabre Jet, 1949. c, Cessna 377 Super Skymaster. d, F-16 Fighting Falcon, 1973. e, Voyager, Experimental Aircraft, Dick Rutan, Jeana Yeager. f, Fairchild A10A Thunderbolt II, 1975. g, Lockheed Vega, 1933. h, Lockheed Vega, 1930.

No. 2173, each 800 le: a, Sopwith Tabloid, 1914. b, Vickers F.B.5 Gun Bus, 1915. c, Savoia Marchetti S.M. 79-II Sparviero, 1940. d, Mitsubishi A6M3 Zero Sen, 1942. e, Morane-Saulnier L, 1915. f, Shorts 360. g, Tupolev TU-160, 1988. h, Mikoyan-Gurevich MiG-15, 1948.

No. 2174, each 1500 le: a, Nieuport 11C. 1, 1915. b, D.H. Vampire N.F. 10, 1951. c, Aerospatiale-Aeritalia ATR 72. d, Fiat CR.32, 1933. e, Curtiss P-6E Hawk, 1932. f, Saab JA 37

Viggen, 1977. g, Piper Pa-46 Malibu. h, F-14 Tomcat.

Each 3000 le: No. 2175, Spirit of St. Louis. No. 2176, Canadair CL-215.

1999, Mar. 22   **Litho.**   **Perf. 14**

2166-2171	A303	Set of 6	6.00	6.00

Sheets of 8, #a.-h.

2172-2174	A303	Set of 3	26.00	26.00

Souvenir Sheets

2175-2176	A303	Set of 2	13.00	13.00

Australia '99 World Stamp Expo A304

Flowers: 150 le, Geranium wallchianum. 200 le, Osmanthus x burkwoodu. 250 le, Iris pallida, vert. 500 le, Rhododendron, vert. 600 le, Rose, vert. 800 le, Papoose, vert. 1500 le, Viola labradorica, vert. 2000 le, Rosa banksiae, vert.

No. 2185, each 600 le: a, Jack snipe. b, Alstroemeria ligtu. c, Lilium (yellow). d, Marjorie fair. e, Aemone coranaria. f, Clematis ranncu.

No. 2186, each 600 le: a, Aquilegiaa olympica. b, Lilium (orange). c, Magnolia grandiflora. d, Polygonatum x hybridum. e, Clematis montana. f, Vinca minor.

No. 2187, each 600 le: a, Colchicum speciosum. b, Scandere. c, Helianthus annuus. d, Lady Kerkrade. e, Clematix x durandil. f, Lilium regale.

No. 2188, each 600 le, vert.: a, Clematis hybrida. b, Cardiospermum halicacabum. c, Fritillaria imperialis. d, Iris ibetidiisima. e, Pyracantina. f, Hepatica transsilvanica.

Each 4000 le: No. 2189, Clerodendrum trichotomum. No. 2190, Holboellia. No. 2191, Crocus angustifolius, vert. No. 2192, Rubus fruitcosus, vert.

1999, Apr. 14

2177-2184	A304	Set of 8	8.50	8.50

Sheets of 6, #a-f

2185-2188	A304	Set of 4	20.00	20.00

Souvenir Sheets

2189-2192	A304	Set of 4	29.00	29.00

Birds — A305   Fauna — A306

No. 2193, each 600 le: a, Cattle egret. b, White-fronted bee-eater. c, African gray parrot. d, Cinnamon-chested bee-eater. e, Malachite kingfisher. f, White-throated bee-eater. g, Yellow-billed stork. h, Hildebrandt's starling.

No. 2194, each 600 le: a, Great white pelican. b, Superb starling. c, Red-throated bee-eater. d, Woodland kingfisher. e, Purple swamphen. f, Pied kingfisher. g, African spoonbill. h, Crocodile bird.

Each 3000 le: No. 2195, African fish-eagle. No. 2196, Richenow's weaver.

1999, May 18   **Litho.**   **Perf. 14**

Sheets of 8, #a.-h.

2193-2194	A305	Set of 2	19.00	19.00

Souvenir Sheets

2195-2196	A305	Set of 2	12.00	12.00

For surcharge see No. 2902.

1999, May 31   **Litho.**

Designs: 300 le, Diana monkey. 400 le, Red-vented malimbe. 500 le, Eurasian kestrel. 600 le, Little owl. 800 le, Bush pig. 1500 le, Lion.

No. 2203, each 900 le: a, Flap-necked chameleon. b, Golden oriole (c). c, Europeon bee-eater. d, Leopard. e, Lion (d). f, Chimpanzee (e).

No. 2204, each 900 le: a, Senagal galago. b, Hoopoe. c, Long-tailed pangolin (f). d, Hippopotamus. e, African elephant (d). f, Red-billed hornbill.

Each 3000 le: No. 2205, West African linsang. No. 2206, Gray parrot.

2197-2202	A306	Set of 6	9.00	9.00

Sheets of 6, #a-f

2203-2204	A306	Set of 2	19.00	19.00

Souvenir Sheets

2205-2206	A306	Set of 2	13.50	13.50

Queen Mother (b. 1900) — A307   Trains — A308

No. 2207, each 1300 le: a, With Duke of York and Princess Elizabeth, 1926. b, In 1979. c, In Nairobi, 1959. d, In 1991. 4000 le, With crown, 1937.

1999, Aug. 4   **Litho.**   **Perf. 14**

Gold Frames

2207	A307	Sheet of 4, #a.-d. + label	11.00	11.00

Souvenir Sheet

Perf. 13½

2208	A307	4000 le multi	10.00	10.00

No. 2208 contains one 38x51mm stamp. See Nos. 2512-2513.

1999, Aug. 4   **Perf. 14**

Designs: 100 le, Rocket. 150 le, Benguela Railway, horiz. 200 le, Sudan Railways 310 2-8-2, horiz. 250 le, Chicago, Burlington & Quincy Railroad, horiz. 300 le, Terrier, horiz. 400 le, Dublin-Cork Express, horiz. 500 le, George Stephenson, horiz. 600 le, Shay, horiz. 1500 le, South Wind, horiz.

No. 2218, each 800 le, horiz.: a, American. b, Flying Scotsman. c, Lord Nelson. d, Mallard. e, Evening Star. f, Britannia.

No. 2219, each 800 le, horiz.: a, Class 19D 4-8-2. b, Double-headed train. c, Egyptian Railways Bo-Bo. d, GMAM Garratt 4-8-2+2-8-4. e, Passenger train, Rabat. f, Rhodesian Railway 14A Class 2-2 Garratt.

Each 3000 le: No. 2220, Mountain Class Garratt. No. 2221, Royal train.

2209-2217	A308	Set of 9	7.00	7.00

Sheets of 6, #a-f

2218-2219	A308	Set of 2	18.00	18.00

Souvenir Sheets

2220-2221	A308	Set of 2	13.00	13.00

Inscription on No. 2218f is misspelled.

Paintings of Fu Baoshi (1904-65) A309

No. 2222: a, Interpretation of a Poem of Shi-Tao. b, Autumn of Ho-Pao. c, Landscape in Rain (bridge). d, Landscape in Rain, diff. e, Landscape in Rain (house on mountain). f, Portrait of To-Fu. g, Classic Lady (trees with leaves). h, Portrait of Li-Pai. i, Sprite of the Mountain. j, Classic Lady (bare trees).

No. 2223: a, 800 le, Four Seasons — Winter, horiz. b, 1500 le, Four Seasons — Summer, horiz.

1999, Aug. 4   **Perf. 12¾**

2222	A309	400 le Sheet of 10, #a.-j.	10.00	10.00

Perf. 13

2223	A309	Sheet of 2, #a.-b.	8.00	8.00

China 1999 World Philatelic Exhibition. No. 2223 contains 51x38mm stamps.

1999 Return of Macao to People's Republic of China — A310

1999, Aug. 4   **Perf. 14**

2224	A310	1200 le multi	8.00	8.00

China 1999 World Philatelic Exhibition. Issued in sheets of 3 stamps.

Hokusai Paintings — A311

#2225, each 1000 le: a, Hanging Cloud Bridge. b, Timber Yard by the Tate River. c, Bird Drawings (owl). d, As "c," (ducks). e, Travelers Crossing the Oi River. f, Travelers on the Tokaido Road at Hodogaya.

No. 2226, each 1000 le: a, People Admiring Mount Fuji from a Tea House. b, People on a Temple Balcony. c, Sea Life (crustacean). d, Sea Life (clam). e, Pontoon Bridge at Sano in Winter. f, A Shower Below the Summit.

Each 1000 le: No. 2227, A View of Mount Fuji and Travelers by a Bridge, vert. No. 2228, A Sudden Gust of Wind at Eijiri, vert.

1999, Aug. 4   **Perf. 13¾**

Sheets of 6, #a-f.

2225-2226	A311	Set of 2	19.00	19.00
2227-2228	A311	Set of 2	12.00	12.00

Johann Wolfgang von Goethe (1749-1832), German Poet — A312

No. 2229: a, Witch besieges faust. b, Goethe and Friedrich von Schiller. c, Margaret places flowers before the niche of Mater Dolorosa.

No. 2230: a, Helena with her chorus. b, Faust takes a seat beside Helena.

Each 3000 le: #2231, Angelic spirit. #2232, Ariel, vert.

1999, Aug. 4   **Perf. 14**

Sheets of 3

2229	A312	1600 le #a.-c.	8.50	8.50
2230	A312	1600 le #a.-b.		
		2229b	8.50	8.50

Souvenir Sheets

2231-2232	A312	Set of 2	13.00	13.00

Souvenir Sheets

PhilexFrance '99 — A313

Designs, each 3000 le: No. 2233, Crampton locomotive. No. 2234, De Glehn compound with Lemaitre front end 4-4-2.

1999, Aug. 4   **Perf. 13¾**

2233-2234	A313	Set of 2	12.00	12.00

IBRA '99 — A314

1999   *Perf. 14x14½*
2235 A314 1500 le Class 4-4-0   3.50 3.50
2236 A314 2000 le Class 05   4.50 4.50

Rights of the
Child — A315

No. 2237: a, Girl holding candle. b, Two children. c, Girl, diff.
   2000 le, Child, horiz.

1999, Aug. 4   **Litho.**   *Perf. 14*
2237 A315 1600 le Sheet of 3,
         #a.-c.   10.00 10.00
Souvenir Sheet
2238 A315 3000 le multi   8.00   8.00

Wedding of Prince
Edward and
Sophie Rhys-Jones
A316

No. 2239: a, Sophie, close-up. b, Edward (shirt and tie). c, Sophie, diff. d, edward, diff.
   4000 le, Couple.

1999, Aug. 4   *Perf. 13¾x13¼*
2239 A316 2000 le Sheet of 4,
        #a.-d.   11.00 11.00
Souvenir Sheet
Perf. 13¼x13¾
2240 A316 4000 le multi   11.00 11.00

Birds of
Africa
A317

No. 2241, each 600 le: a, African paradise monarch. b, Lilac-breasted roller. c, Common Scops owl. d, African emerald cuckoo. e, Blue monarch. f, African golden oriole. g, White-throated bee eater. h, Black-bellied seed-cracker. i, Hoopoe.
   No. 2242, each 600 le: a, White-faced whistling duck. b, Black-headed heron. c, Black-headed gonolek. d, Malachite kingfisher. e, Fish eagle. f, African spoonbill. g, African skimmer. h, Black heron. i, Allen's gallinule.
   No. 2243, each 600 le: a, Scimitarbill. b, Bateleur. c, Black-headed weaver. d, Variable sunbird. e, Blue swallow. f, Black-winged red bishop. g, Namaqua dove. h, Golden-breasted bunting. i, Hartlaub's bustard.
   No. 2244, each 600 le: a, Montagu's harrier. b, Booted eagle. c, Yellow crested helmet-shrike. d, Scarlet-tufted malachite sunbird. e, Pin-tailed whydah. f, Red-headed malimbe. g, Western violet-backed sunbird. h, Yellow white eye. i, Brubru.
   Each 4000 le: 2245, Rwenzori turaco, vert. No. 2246, African pygmy kingfisher, vert. No. 2247, Gray crowned crane, vert. No. 2248, Shoebill, vert.

1999   **Litho.**   *Perf. 14*
Sheets of 9, #a.-i.
2241-2244 A317 Set of 4   32.50 32.50
Souvenir Sheets
2245-2248 A317 Set of 4   24.00 24.00
   For surcharge see No. 2905.

New Year
2000
(Year of
the
Dragon)
A318

No. 2249 (dragon color): a, Brown red. b, Blue green. c, Bright red. d, Lilac.
   4000 le, Red dragon, vert.

2000, Feb. 5   **Litho.**   *Perf. 14*
2249 A318 1500 le Sheet of 4,
        #a.-d.   8.00 8.00
Souvenir Sheet
2250 A318 4000 le multi   7.50 7.50

Sammy
Davis,
Jr. — A319

No. 2251: a, As child. b, With motorcycle. c, With red checked shirt. d, With microphone. e, With leg on chair. f, Holding cigarette.
   5000 le, With other people.

2000, Mar. 8   *Perf. 13¾*
2251 A319 1000 le Sheet of 6,
        #a.-f.   6.25 6.25
Souvenir Sheet
2252 A319 5000 le multi   5.25 5.25

Flowers — A320

Various flowers making up a photomosaic of Princess Diana.

2000, Mar. 28
2253 A320 800 le Sheet of 8,
        #a.-h.   6.50 6.50
   See Nos. 2359-2360.

Millennium — A321

Highlights of 1600-1650: a, Election of Michael Romanov as Russian tsar. b, William Shakespeare publishes "Hamlet." c, Kung Hsien paints "Thousand Peaks and Myriad Ravines." d, Francis Bacon publishes his works. e, Founding of Jamestown, Virginia. f, Reign of Louis XIV of France. g, Founding of Quebec. h, Birth of Isaac Newton. i, Nicholas Poussin paints "Rape of the Sabine Women." j, Johannes Kepler publishes "The New Astronomy." k, The Mayflower arrives in America. l, King James Bible is published. m, Dutch East India Company introduces tea to Europe. n, René Descartes develops his philosophy. o, Galileo defends Copernican system. p, Queen Elizabeth I dies (60x40mm). q, Miguel de Cervantes publishes "Don Quixote."

2000, Mar. 28   *Perf. 12¾x12½*
2254 A321 400 le Sheet of 17,
       #a.-q., + label 6.75 6.75

Paintings of Anthony Van
Dyck — A322

No. 2255, each 1000 le: a, Portrait of a Man. b, Anna Wake, Wife of Peter Stevens. c, Peter Stevens. d, Adriaen Stevens. e, Maria Bosschaerts, Wife of Adriaen Stevens. f, Portrait of a Woman.
   No. 2256, each 1000 le: a, Self-portrait, 1617-18. b, Self-portrait, 1620-21. c, Self-portrait, 1622-23. d, Andromeda Chained to the Rock. e, Self-portrait, late 1620s-early 1630s. f, Mary Ruthven.
   No. 2257, each 1000 le: a, The Betrayal of Judas (detail of The Taking of Christ.) b, Ecce Homo, 1625-26. c, Christ Carrying the Cross (showing woman with blue garment). d, The Raising of Christ on the Cross. e, The Crucifixion, c. 1627 f, The Lamentation, c. 1616 (actually the "Mocking of Christ").
   No. 2258, each 1000 le: a, The Taking of Christ. b, The Mocking of Christ. c, Ecce Homo, 1628-32. d, Christ Carrying the Cross (showing poleax). e, The Crucifixion, c. 1629-30. f, The Lamentation 1618-20.
   No. 2258G, each 1000 le: h, The Duchess of Crow With Her Son. i, Susanna Fourment and Her Daughter. j, Geronima Brignole-Sale With Her Daughter Maria Aurelia. k, A Woman With Her Daughter. l, A Genoese Noblewoman (Paola Adorno) and Her Son. m, A Genoese Noblewoman (Paola Adorno) and Her Son.
   Each 5000 le: No. 2259, Self-portrait With a Sunflower. No. 2260, Self-portrait with Endymion Porter. No. 2261, Young Woman With a Child. No. 2262, Porzia Imperiale With Her Daughter Maria Francesca. No. 2263, Portrait of a Mother and Her Daughter. No. 2264, A Woman and a Child, horiz.

2000, Apr. 10   *Perf. 13¾*
Sheets of 6, #a.-f.
2255-2258G A322 Set of 5   32.50 32.50
Souvenir Sheets
2259-2264 A322 Set of 6   32.50 32.50
   Easter (Nos. 2257-2258).

Mario Andretti — A323

No. 2265: a, Behind wheel. b, With helmet, facing left. c, In pits. d, In crash. e, Inspecting tire. f, With white shirt. g, Without shirt. h, In car #50.
   5000 le, With others in front of old car.

2000, Mar. 28   **Litho.**   *Perf. 13¾*
2265 A323 600 le Sheet of 8,
        #a-h   5.50 5.50
Souvenir Sheet
2266 A323 5000 le multi   5.50 5.50

Scenes from "The Little Colonel" with
Shirley Temple — A324

Temple — No. 2267: a, With Colonel Lloyd (Lionel Barrymore), standing. b, With Walker (Bill Robinson). c, With two children. d, With soldiers. e, With mother (Evelyn Venable), Becky (Hattie McDaniel). f, Hugging Colonel Lloyd.
   No. 2268: a, With Becky and Walker. b, With Walker, diff. c, Alone. d, Tugging Colonel Lloyd's coat.
   No. 2269, Holding chair.

2000, Mar. 28
Sheets of 6 and 4
2267 A324 1200 le #a-f   8.00 8.00
2268 A324 1500 le #a-d   6.75 6.75
Souvenir Sheet
2269 A324 5000 le multi   5.50 5.50
   See also Nos. 2550-2552.

Parrots — A325

Designs: 200 le, African gray parrot. 1500 le, Sulfur-crested cockatoo, horiz.
   No. 2272, each 800 le: a, Monk parakeet. b, Citron-crested cockatoo. c, Queen-of-Bavaria conure. d, Budgerigar. e, Yellow-chevroned parakeet. f, Cockatiel. g, Amazon parrot. h, Sun conure. i, Malabar parakeet.
   No. 2273, each 800 le: a, Grand eclectus parrot. b, Sun parakeet. c, Red fan parakeet. d, Fischer's lovebird. e, Blue masked lovebird. f, White belly rosella. g, Plum-headed parakeet. h, Striated lorikeet. i, Gold-mantled rosella.
   4000 le, Blue and gold macaw.

2000, May 16   *Perf. 13¾x14, 14x13¾*
2270-2271 A325 Set of 2   1.90   1.90

Sheets of 9, #a-i
2272-2273 A325 Set of 2   16.00 16.00
Souvenir Sheet
2274 A325 multi   4.50 4.50

The Stamp Show 2000, London (Nos. 2272-2274). Size of stamps: Nos. 2272-2273, 28x42mm; No. 2274, 38x50mm.

Orchids
A326

Designs: 300 le, Aeranthes henrici. 500 le, Ophrys apifera. 600 le, Disa crassicornis. 2000 le, Aeranthes grandiflora.

No. 2279, each 1100 le: : a, Oeleoclades maculata. b, Polystachya megaglossa. c, Polystachya pubescens. d, Tridactyle bicaudata. e, Angraecum veitcii. f, Sobennikoffia robusta.

No. 2280, each 1100 le: a, Aerangis curnowiana. b, Aerangis fastudsa. c, Angraecum magdalenae. d, Angraecum sororium. e, Eulophia speciosa. f, Ansellia africana.

Each 4000 le: No. 2281, Angraecum compactum. No. 2282, Angraecum eburneum.

2000, May 16   Perf. 14
2275-2278 A326 Set of 4   3.75 3.75
Sheets of 6, #a-f
2279-2280 A326 Set of 2   15.00 15.00
Souvenir Sheets
2281-2282 A326 Set of 2   9.00 9.00

Prince William, 18th Birthday — A327

Various photos.

2000, May 29   Perf. 14
2283 A327 1100 le Sheet of 4,
    #a-d   5.00 5.00
Souvenir Sheet
    Perf. 13¾
2284 A327 5000 le multi   5.50 5.50

No. 2284 contains one 38x50mm stamp.

Souvenir Sheet

2000 Summer Olympics,
Sydney — A328

Designs: a, Hurdler. b, Soccer player. c, Finnish flag, Helsinki Stadium. d, Ancient Greek wrestlers.

2000, May 29   Perf. 14
2285 A328 1500 le Sheet of 4.
    #a-d   6.75 6.75

First Zeppelin Flight, Cent. — A329

No. 2286: a, LZ-129. b, LZ-4. c, LZ-6.
4000 le, LZ-127.

2000, May 29   Perf. 14
2286 A329 2000 le Sheet of 3,
    #a-c   6.75 6.75
Souvenir Sheet
    Perf. 14¼
2287 A329 4000 le multi   4.50 4.50

Size of stamps: No. 2286, 38x24mm.

Betty Boop — A330

No. 2288: a, Wearing flowered dress. b, Carrying shopping bags. c, Wearing baseball cap. d, Holding shoes. e, Sitting in chair. f, Wearing jacket. g, Playing guitar. h, Holding lasso. i, Holding flower.

Each 5000 le: No. 2289, Pointing at dog. No. 2290, Riding bicycle.

2000, Mar. 8   Litho.   Perf. 13¾
2288 A330 800 le Sheet of 9,
    #a-i   8.25 8.25
Souvenir Sheets
2289-2290 A330 Set of 2   11.50 11.50

I Love Lucy — A331

No. 2291, each 800 le — Lucy: a, Wearing blue cap. b, With arms in front, with Vitameatavegamin bottle. c, Wearing pink nightgown. d, Wearing pink nightgown, sticking out tongue. e, Wearing blue cap on television screen. f, Holding bottle near table. g, With arms at side, with bottle. h, Holding bottle near cheek. i, Pouring out liquid in bottle.

Each 5000 le: No. 2292, Wearing blue cap on television, Desi touching television. No. 2293, Lucy and Fred Mertz.

Illustration reduced.

2000, Mar. 8
2291 A331 Sheet of 9, #a-i   8.25 8.25
Souvenir Sheets
2292-2293 A331 Set of 2   11.50 11.50

Berlin Film Festival, 50th
Anniv. — A332

No. 2294, each 1100 le: a, Las Palabras de Max. b, Ascendancy. c, Deprisa, Deprisa. d, Die Sehnsucht der Veronika Voss. e, Heartland. f, La Colmena.
5000 le, Las Truchas.

2000, May 29   Perf. 14
2294 A332 Sheet of 6, #a-f   7.50 7.50
Souvenir Sheet
2295 A332 5000 le multi   5.75 5.75

Souvenir Sheet

Public Railways, 175th Anniv. — A333

No. 2296, each 3000 le: a, Locomotion No. 1, George Stephenson. b, James Watt's original design for a separate condenser engine.

2000, May 29
2296 A333 Sheet of 2, #a-b   7.00 7.00

Souvenir Sheet

Johann Sebastian Bach (1685-1750) — A334

2000, May 29
2297 A334 5000 le multi   5.75 5.75

Sea Birds
A335

Designs: 400 le, Herring gull. 600 le, Caspian tern. 800 le, Red phalarope. 2000 le, Magnificent frigatebird.

No. 2302, each 1000 le: a, Caspian tern, diff. b, Glaucous gull. c, Northern gannet. d, Long-tailed jaeger. e, Brown pelican. f, Great skua.

No. 2303, each 1000 le: a, Wandering albatross. b, Fork-tailed storm petrel. c, Great shearwater. d, Blue-footed booby. e, Great cormorant. f, Atlantic puffin.

Each 5000 le: No. 2304, Brown booby, vert. No. 2305, Red-tailed tropicbird, vert.

2000, May 16   Litho.   Perf. 14
2298-2301 A335 Set of 4   3.75 3.75
Sheets of 6, #a-f
2302-2303 A335 Set of 2   12.00 12.00
Souvenir Sheets
2304-2305 A335 Set of 2   10.00 10.00

Richard Petty, Stock Car
Racer — A336

No. 2306, each 800 le: a, Car in pits. b, With family. c, Wearing red jacket. d, Wearing Pontiac cap. e, Wearing white hat, uniform with two STP logos. f, Wearing STP cap. g, Standing in car. h, Profile, wearing STP logos on shoulder. i, Wearing headphones.

No. 2307, each 800 le: a, Holding trophy. b, Wearing Winston cap. c, Wearing black hat. d, Hatless, blue background. e, Wearing shirt with red collar. f, Holding helmet. g, Leaning on blue and red car. h, With arm in car. i, Leaning head out of car.

No. 2308, each 800 le: a, Wearing red shirt, white hat. b, Hatless, orange background. c, Wearing Pontiac cap. d, Strapped in car, without helmet. e, Holding timer. f, Wearing red and blue helmet. g, Wearing white hat, blue uniform. h, With trophy, wearing STP cap. i, With white hat, reclining.

Each 5000 le: No. 2309, Standing in car, diff. No, 2310, In race, horiz.

Illustration reduced.

2000, Aug. 15   Perf. 13¾
    Sheets of 9, #a-i
2306-2308 A336 Set of 3   21.00 21.00
Souvenir Sheets
2309-2310 A336 Set of 2   10.00 10.00

Popes — A337

No. 2311, each 1100 le: a, Gregory VI (1045-46). b, Celestine V (1294). c, Honorius IV (1285-87). d, Innocent IV (1243-54). e, Innocent VII (1404-06). f, John XXII (1316-34).

No. 2312, each 1100 le: a, Martin IV (1281-85). b, Nicholas II (1059-61). c, Nicholas IV (1288-92). d, Urban IV (1261-64). e, Urban V (1362-70). f, Urban VI (1378-89).

Each 5000 le: No. 2313, Nicholas IV (1288-92), diff. No. 2314, Clement XI (1700-21).

2000, Aug. 21
Sheets of 6, #a-f
2311-2312 A337 Set of 2   13.00 13.00
Souvenir Sheets
2313-2314 A337 Set of 2   10.00 10.00

Monarchs — A338

No. 2315, each 1100 le: a, Emperor Hung Wu of China. b, Emperor Hsuan Te of China. c, King Sejong of Korea. d, Emperor T'ung Chih of China. e, Emperor T'ai Tsu (Chao K'uang-yin) of Chin. f, Empress Yung Ching of China.
No. 2316, Kublai Khan of China.

2000, Aug. 21
2315 A338 Sheet of 6, #a-f   6.50 6.50
Souvenir Sheet
2316 A338 5000 le multi   5.00 5.00

European Soccer
Championships — A339

No. 2317, each 1300 le — Germany: a, Worns. b, Team photo. c, Babbel. d, Franz Beckenbauer. e, Selessin Stadium, Liege, Belgium. f, Stefan Kuntz.
No. 2318, each 1300 le — Italy: a, Walter Zenga. b, Team photo. c, Roberto Bettega. d, Totti. e, Philips Stadium, Eindhoven, Netherlands. f, Vieri.
No. 2319, each 1300 le — Portugal: a, Dimas. b, Team photo. c, Pinto. d, Santos. e, Gelredome Stadium, Arnhem, Netherlands. f, Sousa.
No. 2320, each 1300 le — Romania: a, Munteanu. b, Team photo. c, Petre. d, Petrescu, e, Popescu.
Each 5000 le: No. 2321, German coach Erich Ribbeck, vert. No. 2322, Italian coach Dino Zoff, vert. No. 2323, Portuguese coach Humberto Coelho, vert. No. 2324, Romanian coach Emerich Jenei, vert.
Illustration reduced.

2000, Aug. 21
Sheets of 6, #a-f (#2317-2319);
Sheet of 6 #a-e, #2319e (#2320)
2317-2320 A339 Set of 4   30.00 30.00
Souvenir Sheets
2321-2324 A339 Set of 4   20.00 20.00

Albert Einstein (1879-1955) — A340

2000, May 29   Litho.   Perf. 14
2325 A340 5000 le multi   5.00 5.00

Apollo-Soyuz Mission, 25th
Anniv. — A341

No. 2326, each 1200 le, vert.: a, Apollo 18. b, Soyuz 19. c, Apollo and Soyuz docked. 5000 le, Apollo and Soyuz docking.

2000, May 29
2326 A341 Sheet of 3, #a-c   3.50 3.50
Souvenir Sheet
2327 A341 5000 le multi   5.00 5.00

Queen Mother, 100th Birthday — A342

Litho. & Embossed
2000, Aug. 4   Die Cut Perf. 8¾
Without Gum
2328 A342 18,000 le gold & multi

Dogs and
Cats
A343

500 le, Bulldog. 800 le, Brown tabby. 1500 le, Burmese. 2000 le, Dachshund.
No. 2333, 1000 le: a, Beagle. b, Scottish terrier. c, Bloodhound. d, Greyhound. e, German shepherd. f, Cocker spaniel.
No. 2334, 1000 le: a, Red tabby stumpy Manx. b, Red self. c, Maine Coon cat. d, Black smoke. e, Chinchilla. f, Russian Blue.

Souvenir Sheet

No. 2335, 1100 le: a, Pointer. b, Doberman pinscher. c, Collie. d, Chihuahua. e, Afghan hound. f, Boxer.
No. 2336, 1100 le: a, Singapura. b, Himalayan. c, Abyssinian. d, Black cat. e, Siamese. f, North African wild cat.
No. 2337, 5000 le, Fox terrier, vert. No. 2338, 5000 le, Calico, vert.

2000, Oct. 2   Litho.   Perf. 14
2329-2332 A343 Set of 4   5.00 5.00
Sheets of 6, #a-f
2333-2336 A343 Set of 4   26.00 26.00
Souvenir Sheets
2337-2338 A343 Set of 2   10.50 10.50

Paintings from the Prado — A344

No. 2339, 1000 le: a, The Transport of Mary Magdalen, by José Antolinez. b, The Holy Family, by Francisco de Goya. c, Our Lady of the Immaculate Conception, by Antolinez. d, Charles IV as Prince, by Anton Raphael Mengs. e, Louis XIII of France, by Philippe de Champaigne. f, Prince Ferdinand VI by Jean Ranc.
No. 2340, 1000 le: a, Adam, by Albrecht Dürer. b, Moor, by Manuel Benedito Vives. c, Eve, by Dürer. d, A Gypsy, by Raimundo Madrazo y Garreta. e, Maria Guerrero, by Joaquin Sorolla y Bastida. f, The Model Aline Masson with a White Mantilla, by Madrazo y Garreta.
No. 2341, 1000 le: a, Figure in yellow robe from Madonna and Child Between Saints Catherine and Ursula, by Giovanni Bellini. b, Madonna and Child from Madonna and Child Between Saints Catherine and Ursula. c, Figure in red robe from Madonna and Child Between Saints Catherine and Ursula. d, Giovanni Mateo Ghiberti, by Bornardino India. e, The Marchioness of Santa Cruz, by Agustin Esteve. f, Self-portrait, by Orazio Borgianni.
No. 2342, 1000 le: a, Mary from The Holy Family with a Bird, by Bartolomé Esteban Murillo. b, Jesus from The Holy Family with a Bird. c, Joseph, from The Holy Family with a Bird. d, Cardinal Carlos de Borja, by Andrea Procaccini. e, St. Dominic de Guzmán, by Claudio Coello. f, Christ Supported by an Angel, by Alonso Cano.
No. 2343, 1000 le: a, Woman from The Seller of Fans, by José del Castillo. b, Allegory of Summer, by Mariano Salvador Maella. c, Man with basket from The Seller of Fans. d, Portrait of a Girl, by Carlos Luis de Ribera y Fieve. e, The Poultry Keeper, by Pensionante del Saraceni. f, The Death of Cleopatra, by Guido Reni.
No. 2344, 1000 le: a, Feliciana Bayeu, by Francisco Bayeu y Subias. b, Tomás de Iriarte by Joaquin Inza. c, St. Elizabeth of Portugal, by Francisco de Zurbarán. d, Christ from The Vision of St. Francis at Porziuncola, by Murillo. e, Monk from The Vision of St. Francis at Porziuncola. f, Woman from The Vision of St. Francis at Porziuncola.
No. 2345, 5000 le, Lot and His Daughters, by Francesco Furini. No. 2346, 5000 le, The Execution of Torrijos and His Companions, by Antonio Gisbert Pérez. No. 2347, 5000 le, the Concert, by Vicente Palmaroli y González. No. 2348, 5000 le, The Finding of Joseph's Cup in Benjamin's Bag, by Jacopo Amigoni. No. 2349, 5000 le, Vulcan's Forge, by Diego Velázquez. No. 2350, 5000 le, The Two Friends, by Joaquin Agrasot y Juan, horiz.
Illustration reduced.

2000, Oct. 6   Perf. 12x12¼, 12¼x12
Sheets of 6, #a-f
2339-2344 A344 Set of 6   37.50 37.50
Souvenir Sheets
2345-2350 A344 Set of 6   32.50 32.50
Espana 2000 Intl. Philatelic Exhibition.

Mushrooms — A345

Designs: 600 le, Tuberous polyphore. 900 le, Cultivated agaricus. 1200 le, Scarlet wax cap. 2500 le, Blue-green psilocybe.
No. 2355, 1000 le, vert.: a, Armed stinkhorn. b, Red-staining inocybe. c, Amanitopsis vaginata. d, Inocybe jurana. e, Xerula longipes. f, Tricholoma matsutake.
No. 2356, 1000 le, vert.: a, Orange-staining mycena. b, Russula amoema. c, Cinnabar chanterelle. d, Calodon aurantiacum. e, Lentinus lepidus. f, Gomphidius roseus.
No. 2357, 5000 le, Orange latex lactarius. No. 2358, 5000 le, Common morel, vert.

2000, Oct. 30   Litho.   Perf. 14
2351-2354 A345 Set of 4   5.50 5.50
Sheets of 6, #a-f
2355-2356 A345 Set of 2   12.50 12.50
Souvenir Sheets
2357-2358 A345 Set of 2   10.50 10.50

Flower Photomosaic Type of 2000

No. 2359, 800 le: Various flowers making up a photomosaic of the Queen Mother.
No. 2360, 900 le: Various photographs of religious scenes making up a photomosaic of Pope John Paul II.

2000, Oct. 30   Perf. 13¾
Sheets of 8, #a-h
2359-2360 A320 Set of 2   14.50 14.50

Massacre of Israeli Olympic Athletes,
1972 — A346

No. 2361, horiz.: a, Kahat Shor. b, Andrei Schpitzer. c, Joseph Romano. d, Yaakov Springer. e, Eliazer Halffin. f, Amitsur Shapira. g, Moshe Weinberg. h, Mark Slavin. i, Torchbearer, Israeli flag. j, Joseph Gottfreund. k, Ze'ev Friedman. l, David Berger.

2000, Nov. 9   Perf. 14
2361 A346 500 le Sheet of 12,
                #a-l   6.25 6.25
Souvenir Sheet
2362 A346 5000 le Torchbearer 5.25 5.25

Circus
A347

Designs: 800 le, Tightrope rider. 1000 le, Bear and ball. 1500 le, Tiger on ball. 2000 le, Camels.
No. 2367, 1100 le: a, Polar bear on roller. b, Ape. c, Clown, green background. d, Tightrope walker. e, Seals. f, Camel.
No. 2368, 1100 le: a, Clown, brown background. b, Tiger on wires. c, Monkey. d, Dogs. e, Bear on skates. f, Trapeze artists.
No. 2369, 1100 le, vert.: a, Acrobat. b, Giraffe. c, Bear on poles. d, Elephant. e, Horse. f, Fire eater.
No. 2370, 5000 le, Trainer on elephant's trunk, vert. No. 2371, 5000 le, Tiger jumping through flaming hoop, vert. No. 2372, 5000 le, Cannon flyer, vert.

2000, Dec. 1   Litho.
2363-2366 A347 Set of 4   5.75 5.75
Sheets of 6, #a-f
2367-2369 A347 Set of 3   21.00 21.00
Souvenir Sheets
2370-2372 A347 Set of 3   16.00 16.00

Queen Mother,
100th
Birthday — A348

2000, Dec. 18
2373 A348 1100 le multi   1.10 1.10
Issued in sheets of 6.

New Year 2001 (Year of the
Snake) — A349

No. 2374, horiz.: a, Blue snake. b, Red
snake. c, Purple snake. d, Green snake.

2001, Jan. 2
2374 A349   800 le Sheet of 4,
             #a-d   3.50 3.50
Souvenir Sheet
2375 A349 2500 le Green snake 2.60 2.60

History of the Orient Express — A350

No. 2376, 1000 le: a, First sleeping car,
1872. b, Dining car #193, 1886. c, Dining car
#2422, 1913. d, Sleeping car Type S1. e,
Metal sleeping car #2645. f, Metal sleeping car
#2644, 1922.
No. 2377, 1000 le: a, Dining car, Series
#8341. b, Dining car, Series #3342. c, Sleep-
ing car, Series #3312 Type Z. d, Sleeping car,
Series #3879, 1950. e, Sleeping car, Series
#3311 Type Z. f, Dining car, Series #3785,
1932.
No. 2378, 1100 le: a, Ostend-Vienna. b,
Engine East 230, #3175. c, Dual cylinder locomotive. d, Simplon Orient Express, 1919. e,
Engine East 220, #2405. f, Caboose of Simplon Express, c. 1906.
No. 2379, 1100 le: a, Sleeping car #507,
1897. b, Sleeping car #438, 1894. c, Sleeping
car #313, 1880. d, Sleeping car #190, 1886. e,
Sleeping car #102, 1882. f, Sleeping car #77,
1881.
No. 2380, 5000 le, Locomotive. No. 2381,
5000 le, Georges Nagelmackers, vert. No.
2382, 5000 le, Mata Hari, vert. No. 2383,
5000 le, Agatha Christie, vert.

2001, Jan. 15   *Perf. 14*
Sheets of 6, #a-f
2376-2379 A350 Set of 4   26.00 26.00
Souvenir Sheets
2380-2383 A350 Set of 4   21.00 21.00

Reptiles
A351

Designs: 250 le, Natal Mixands dwarf chameleon. 400 le, Cape cobra. 500 le, Western
sand lizard. 600 le, Pan-hinged terrapin.
800 le, Many-horned adder. 1500 le, Hawequa
flat gecko.
No. 2390, 1200 le: a, Reticulated desert lizard. b, Ball python. c, Gaboon viper. d,
Dumeril's boa. e, Common egg-eater. f, Helmet turtle.
No. 2391, 1200 le: a, Asian saw-scaled
viper. b, Namibian sand snake. c, Angolan
garter snake. d, Striped skaapsteker. e, Brown
house snake. f, Shield-nosed cobra.
No. 2392, 5000 le, Green water snake. No.
2393, 5000 le, Flap-necked chameleon.

2001, Jan. 15
2384-2389 A351 Set of 6   4.25 4.25
Sheets of 6, #a-f
2390-2391 A351 Set of 2   15.00 15.00
Souvenir Sheets
2392-2393 A351 Set of 2   10.50 10.50

Rijksmuseum, Amsterdam, Bicent. (in
2000) — A352

No. 2394, 1100 le, vert.: a, Gentleman Writ-
ing a Letter, by Gabriel Metsu. b, Self-portrait,
by Carel Fabritius. c, The Windmill at Wijk bij
Duurstede, by Jacob van Ruisdael. d,
Bentheim Castle, by van Ruisdael. e, Ships on
a Stormy Sea, by Willem van de Velde, the
Younger. f, David from David Playing the Harp,
by Jan de Bray.
No. 2395, 1100 le, vert.: a, St. Paul from St.
Paul Healing the Cripple at Lystra, by Karel
Dujardin. b, Two hatless men from The Mea-
gre Company, by Frans Hals and Pieter
Codde. c, Man from Elegant Couple in an Inte-
rior, by Eglon van der Neer. d, Laid Table With
Cheese and Fruit, by Floris van Dijck. e, Bac-
chanal, by Moses van Uyttenbroeck. f, Kneel-
ing woman from St. Paul Healing the Cripple
at Lystra.
No. 2396, 1100 le, vert.: a, Lady Reading a
Letter, by Metsu. b, Portrait of Titus, by Rembrandt. c, Portrait of Gerard de Lairesse, by
Rembrandt. d, Portrait of a Family in an Interior, by Emanuel de Witte. e, The Letter, by
Gerard Terborch. f, Three Women and a Man
in a Courtyard Behind a House, by Pieter de
Hooch.
No. 2397, 1100 le, vert.: a, Candlebearers
from David Playing the Harp. b, Hand of St.
Paul from St. Paul Healing the Cripple at Lys-
tra. c, Two men, one with hat, from The Mea-
gre Company. d, The Gray, by Ohilips
Wouwerman. e, Couple from Elegant Couple
in an Interior. f, The Hut, by Adriaen van de
Velde.
No. 2398, 5000 le, Road in the Dunes With
a Passenger Coach, by Salomon van Ruys-
dael. No. 2399, 5000 le, Cows in the Meadow,
by Albert Gerard Bilders. No. 2400, 5000 le,
Lot and His Daughters, by Hendrick Goltzius.
No. 2401, 5000 le, Arrival of Queen Wilhelmina at the Frederiksplein in Amsterdam, by
Otto Eerelman.

2001, Jan. 15   *Perf. 13¾*
Sheets of 6, #a-f
2394-2397 A352 Set of 4   27.50 27.50
Souvenir Sheets
2398-2401 A352 Set of 4   21.00 21.00

Battle of Britain, 60th Anniv. — A353

No. 2402, 1000 le: a, Bombed village near
London. b, The Underground as a bomb shel-
ter. c, Firemen. d, Home Guard. e, Setting
lights out time. f, Pilots resting between flights.
g, Brendan "Paddy" Finucane, ace pilot. h,
Hawk 75.
No. 2403, 1000 le: a, St. Paul's Cathedral.
b, Eastenders leaving London. c, Winston
Churchill being cheered by British crew. d,
Rescue pilot. e, Boy Scouts helping children. f,
Big gunners, 1940. g, Plane spotter lights. h,
Survey watchers.
No. 2404, 1000 le: a, Post Office Engineer,
WAFF. b, Women munitions workers. c,
Churchill as prime minister and defense minis-
ter. d, German Dornier DO17. e, Church fires
from Nazi bombs, London, 1940. f, All-night
raid on London, 1940. g, Lunchtime in the
Underground. h, People in the Underground,
1940.
No. 2405, 1000 le: a, London Bridge. b, Sur-
rey Home Guard. c, British Cruiser tank MK III.
d, Newfoundland men at the guns, 1940. e,
Lady Astor's Constituency hit, 1940. f, Chur-
chill worried with war, 1940. g, Bomb blast at
Parliament. h, Development of radar, 1940.
No. 2406, 6000 le, Churchill and wife
inspecting harbor damage. No. 2407, 6000 le,
London, 1940. No. 2408, 6000 le, British
Supermarine Spitfire. No. 2409, 6000 le,
Bombing crew preparing for flight, 1940, vert.

2001, Jan. 30   *Perf. 14*
Sheets of 8, #a-h
2402-2405 A353 Set of 4   35.00 35.00
Souvenir Sheets
2406-2409 A353 Set of 4   25.00 25.00

Biblical Scenes by Rembrandt — A354

No. 2410, 1000 le: a, The Song of Simeon.
b, Study for Adoration of the Magi. c, Mary
With the Child by a Window. d, The Rest on
the Flight Into Egypt. e, The Circumcision. f,
The Shepherds Worship the Child.
No. 2411, 1000 le: a, The Angel Rises Up in
the Flame of Manoah's Sacrifice. b, Tobias
Frightened by the Fish. c, The Angel of the
Lord Stands in Balaam's Path. d, The Angel
Appears to Hagar in the Desert. e, Jacob's
Dream. f, The Healing of Tobit.
No. 2412, 5000 le, Simeon's Prophecy to
Mary. No. 2413, 5000 le, The Angel Prevents
the Sacrifice of Isaac. No. 2414, 5000 le, The
Angel Leaves Tobit and His Family, vert. No.
2415, 5000 le, The Adoration of the Magi, vert.

2001, Feb. 13   *Perf. 13¾*
Sheets of 6, #a-f
2410-2411 A354 Set of 2   12.50 12.50
Souvenir Sheets
2412-2415 A354 Set of 4   21.00 21.00

Racehorses
A355

Designs: 200 le, Native Dancer. 500 le,
Citation. 1500 le, Spectre. 2000 le, Carbine.
No. 2420, 1200 le: a, Arkle. b, Golden Miller.
c, Phar Lap. d, Battleship. e, Kelso. f, Nijinsky.
No. 2421, 1200 le: a, Red Rum. b, Sir Ken.
c, War Admiral. d, Troytown. e, Shergar. f,
Allez France.
No. 2422, 5000 le, Cigar. No. 2423, 5000 le,
Desert Orchid. No. 2424, 5000 le, Trophy. No.
2425, 5000 le, Horses on turf track, horiz.

2001, Feb. 27   *Perf. 14*
2416-2419 A355 Set of 4   4.50 4.50
Sheets of 6, #a-f
2420-2421 A355 Set of 2   15.00 15.00
Souvenir Sheets
2422-2425 A355 Set of 4   21.00 21.00

Automobiles — A356

No. 2426, 1000 le: a, 1898 Benz Velo. b,
1909 Rolls-Royce Silver Ghost. c, 1912 Ford
Model T. d, 1937 Duesenberg SJ. e, 1938-40
Grosser Mercedes. f, 1938 Citroen Light 15.
No. 2427, 1000 le: a, 1939 Lincoln Zephyr.
b, 1947 Volkswagen Beetle. c, 1959 Jaguar
Mark II. d, 1968 Ford Shelby Mustang GT500.
e, 1987-94 Opel/Vauxhall Senator. f, 2002
Mercedes Maybach.
No. 2428, 5000 le, 1928 Bentley 3-liter short
chassis Tourer. No. 2429, 5000 le, 1999 Fer-
rari 360 Modena.

2001, Apr. 30   *Perf. 13¾*
Sheets of 6, #a-f, + 6 labels
2426-2427 A356 Set of 2   12.50 12.50
Souvenir Sheets
2428-2429 A356 Set of 2   10.50 10.50

Butterflies
A357

Designs: 250 le, Eurema floricola. 400 le,
Papilio dardanus. 800 le, Amauris nossima.
1500 le, Gideona lucasi.
No. 2434, 1100 le: a, Papilio dardanus. b,
Cymothoe sangaris. c, Epiphora albida. d,
African giant swallowtail. e, Papilio nobilis
nobilis. f, Charaxes hadnanus.
No. 2435, 1100 le: a, Charaxes lucretia. b,
Euxanthe closslex. c, Charaxes phenix. d,
Charaxes acraeades. e, Charaxes protoclea
azota. f, Charaxes lydiae.
No. 2436, 5000 le, Clotis zoe. No. 2437,
5000 le, Acraea ranaualona, vert.

Perf. 13¼x13½, 13½x13¼
2001, Apr. 30   *Litho.*
2430-2433 A357 Set of 4   3.25 3.25
Sheets of 6, #a-f
2434-2435 A357 Set of 2   14.50 14.50
Souvenir Sheets
2436-2437 A357 Set of 2   11.00 11.00

Queen Elizabeth II, 75th Birthday — A358

No. 2438: a, Wearing hat. b, With infant. c, Wearing crown. d, Wearing black blouse.

2001, June 18　　Litho.　　**Perf. 14**
2438　A358　2000 le Sheet of 4,
　　　　#a-d　　　　　　8.25　8.25
　Souvenir Sheet
　　Perf. 13¾
2439　A358　5000 le　As older wo-
　　　　man　　　　　　　5.25　5.25
No. 2438 contains four 28x42mm stamps.

Japanese
Art — A359

Designs: 50 le, Iziu Chinuki No Hi, by Hokkei, horiz. 100 le, A Visit to Enoshima, by Kiyonaga Torii, horiz. 150 le, Inn on a Harbor, by Sadahide, horiz. 200 le, Entrance to Foreigner's Establishment, by Sadahide, horiz. 250 le, Courtesans at Cherry Blossom Time, by Kiyonaga, horiz. 300 le, Cherry Blossom Viewing at Ueno, by Toyohara Chikanobu, horiz. 400 le, A Summer Evening at a Restaurant by the Sumida River, by Torii, horiz. 500 le, Ichikana Yaozo I As Samurai, by Buncho. 600 le, The Actor Nakamura Noshoi II as a Street Walker, by Shunzan Katsukawa. 800 le, Arashi Sangoro II, by Shokosai. 1500 le, bando Mitsugoro I by Shunko. No. 2451, 2000 le, Matsumoto Koshiro II, by Masanobu.

No. 2452, 2000 le: a, Nakamura Shikan II and Nakamura Baiko, by Shigeharu. b, Women Making Rice Cakes, by Shunsho. c, Youth Sending Letter by Arrow, by Harushige. d, Woman with green sash from Six Girls, by Eisho.

No. 2453, 2000 le: a, Woman with checked kimono, from Six Girls. b, Courtesan on a Bench, by Eiri. c, Courtesan and Her Two Kamuro, by Suzuki Harunobu. d, Clearing Weather at Awazu, by Shigemasa.

No. 2454, 2000 le — Paintings by Harunobu: a, Promenade. b, Wine Tasters. c, Rain in May. d, Lovers by the Wall.

No. 2455, 2000 le — Paintings by Harunobu: a, Young Woman Attended by Maid. b, Lovers by Lespedeza Bush. c, Girl Contemplating a Landscape. d, Young Man Unrolling a Hanging Scroll.

No. 2456, 5000 le, Searching for the Hermit, by Harunobu. No. 2457, 5000 le, Courtesan and Two Kamuro, by Harunobu. No. 2458, 5000 le, Drying Clothes, by Harunobu. No. 2459, 5000 le, Komachi Praying For Rain, by Harunobu. No. 2460, 5000 le, Girl Contemplating Landscape, by Harunobu.

2001, July 2　　　　　　**Perf. 13½**
2440-2451　A359　Set of 12　7.25　7.25
　Sheets of 4, #a-d
2452-2455　A359　Set of 4　32.50 32.50
　Souvenir Sheets
2456-2460　A359　Set of 5　26.00 26.00
　Phila Nippon '01, Japan (#2452-2460).

Marlene Dietrich — A360

No. 2461: a, Looking over shoulder. b, Wearing necklace. c, Wearing coat with flower. d, Holding cigarette.

2001, June 18　　Litho.　　**Perf. 13¾**
2461　A360　2000 le Sheet of 4,
　　　　#a-d　　　　　　8.25　8.25

Toulouse-Lautrec Paintings — A361

No. 2462, horiz.: a, A La Mie. b, A Corner of the Moulin de la Gallete. c, The Start of the Quadrille.
5000 le, La Goulue.

2001, June 18
2462　A361　2200 le Sheet of 3,
　　　　#a-c　　　　　　7.00　7.00
　Souvenir Sheet
2463　A361　5000 le multi　5.25　5.25

Monet Paintings — A362

No. 2464, horiz.: a, The Road to Vétheuil, Winter. b, The Church at Vétheuil, Snow. c, Breakup of the Ice Near Vétheuil. d, The Boulevard de Pontoise at Argenteuil, Snow.
5000 le, Irises by the Pond.

2001, June 18
2464　A362　1500 le Sheet of 4,
　　　　#a-d　　　　　　6.25　6.25
　Souvenir Sheet
2465　A362　5000 le multi　5.25　5.25

Giuseppe Verdi (1813-1901), Opera Composer — A363

No. 2466: a, Vladimir Popov. b, Enrico Caruso. c, Rudolf Bockelmann. d, Stage.
5000 le, Aprile Millo and Barseg Tumanyan.

2001, June 18　　　　　　**Perf. 14**
2466　A363　1700 le Sheet of 4,
　　　　#a-d　　　　　　7.00　7.00
　Souvenir Sheet
2467　A363　5000 le multi　5.25　5.25

Royal Navy Submarines, Cent. — A364

No. 2468: a, C Class submarine. b, HMS Spartan. c, HMS Exeter. d, HMS Chatham. e, HMS Verdun. f, HMS Marlborough.
5000 le, HMS Vanguard.

2001, June 18
2468　A364　1100 le Sheet of 6,
　　　　#a-f　　　　　　7.00　7.00
　Souvenir Sheet
2469　A364　5000 le multi　5.25　5.25

U.S. Civil War — A365

No. 2470, 2000 le — Generals: a, Ulysses S. Grant. b, John Bell Hood. c, Jeb Stuart. d, Robert E. Lee.
No. 2471, 2000 le: a, Gen. Joshua Chamberlain. b, Gen. Stonewall Jackson. c, Gen. George McClellan. d, Adm. David Farragut.
No. 2472, 2000 le — Battle scenes: a, Shiloh. b, Bull Run. c, Fair Oaks. d, Chattanooga.
No. 2473, 2000 le — Battle scenes: a, Fredericksburg. b, Gettysburg. c, Mobile Bay. d, Fort Sumter.

No. 2474, 5000 le, Gen. William Tecumseh Sherman. No. 2475, 5000 le, Gen. George A. Custer. No. 2476, 5000 le, Battle of Vicksburg. No. 2477, 5000 le, Battle of Antietam.

2001, Aug. 27
　Sheets of 4, #a-d
2470-2473　A365　Set of 4　32.50 32.50
　Souvenir Sheets
2474-2477　A365　Set of 4　21.00 21.00

Horses in Literature and Mythology — A366

No. 2478, 1100 le: a, Piebald, from National Velvet, by Enid Bagnold. b, Strider, by Leo Tolstoy. c, Black Beauty, by Anna Sewell. d, Red Pony, by John Steinbeck. e, Black Stallion, by Walter Farley. f, Misty of Chincoteague, by Marguerite Henry.
No. 2479, 1100 le: a, Arvak Alsvid. b, Pegasus. c, Sleipnir. d, Veillanfif. e, Grani. f, Galathe, from Troilus and Cressida, by William Shakespeare.
No. 2480, 5000 le, Rosinante, from Don Quixote, by Miguel de Cervantes. No. 2481, 5000 le, Xanthus and Balius.

2001, Feb. 27　　Litho.　　**Perf. 14**
　Sheets of 6, #a-f
2478-2479　A366　Set of 2　14.00 14.00
　Souvenir Sheets
2480-2481　A366　Set of 2　10.50 10.50

Dinosaurs — A367

No. 2482, 1000 le: a, Acrocanthosaurus. b, Edmontosaurus. c, Archaeopteryx. d, Hadrosaurus. e, Mongolian avimimus. f, Pachyrhinosaurus. g, Iguanodons (with tree trunk). h, Iguanodons, diff.
No. 2483, 1000 le, horiz.: a, Albertosaurus. b, Pteranodon ingens. c, Asiatic iguanodon. d, Sordes. e, Coelophysis. f, Saichania. g, Bactrosaurus. h, Triceratops.
No. 2484, 5000 le, Corythosaurus. No. 2485, 5000 le, Stenonychosaurus.

2001, Mar. 1　　　　　　**Perf. 13½**
　Sheets of 8, #a-h
2482-2483　A367　Set of 2　17.00 17.00
　Souvenir Sheets
2484-2485　A367　Set of 2　10.50 10.50
　Hong Kong 2001 Stamp Exhibition.

Souvenir Sheets

Dinosaurs — A367a

Designs: No. 2485A, 5000 le, Dryosaurus. No. 2485B, 5000 le, Diplodocids. No. 2485C, 5000 le, Allosaurus.

2001, Mar. 1   Litho.   Perf. 13½
2485A-2485C A367a Set of 3   15.00 15.00
Nos. 2485A-2485C were not available in the marketplace until 2002.

Butterflies — A368

No. 2486, 1100 le: a, Teinopalpus imperialis. b, Swallowtail. c, Doris. d, Northern Jezebel. e, Beautiful monarch. f, Gaudy commodore.
No. 2487, 1100 le: a, Plain tiger. b, Tiger. c, Morpho cypris. d, Castnia litus. e, Dismorphia nemesis. f, Blue and yellow butterfly (inscribed African violets).
No. 2488, 5000 le, Scarce swallowtail. No. 2489, 5000 le, Clouded yellow, vert.

2001, Apr. 30
Sheets of 6, #a-f
2486-2487 A368 Set of 2   14.50 14.50
Souvenir Sheets
2488-2489 A368 Set of 2   11.00 11.00

Photomosaic of Queen Elizabeth II — A369

2001, June 18   Perf. 14
2490 A369 1000 le multi   1.10 1.10
Printed in sheets of 8.

Mao Zedong (1893-1976) — A370

No. 2492, 1100 le — Map of China and Mao: a, Without hat. b, With green cap. c, With blue cap.
No. 2493, 1100 le — Red frame and Mao with: a, Uniform. b, Shirt with open collar. d, Cap.
No. 2493, 5000 le, Mao wearing black suit. No. 2494, 5000 le, Mao in white.

2001, June 18
Sheets of 3, #a-c
2491-2492 A370 Set of 2   7.00 7.00
Souvenir Sheets
2493-2494 A370 Set of 2   10.50 10.50

Ferrari Automobiles — A371

Designs: 100 le, 2001 360 Challenge. 500 le, 1971 712 Can Am. 600 le, 1970 512M. 1000 le, 1988 F40. 1500 le, 1982 365 GT4/BB. 2000 le, 1972 365 GTB/4.

2001, Oct. 8   Perf. 13¾
2495-2500 A371 Set of 6   6.00 6.00

Souvenir Sheets

Horses — A372

Chinese Character for Horse — A373

No. 2501: a, Green background. b, Blue background.
No. 2502 — "2002" in: a, Green. b, Red. c, Orange. d, Purple.

2001, Nov. 29   Perf. 13
2501 A372 1200 le Sheet of 2, #a-b   2.50 2.50

Perf. 13x13¼
2502 A373 1200 le Sheet of 4, #a-d   5.00 5.00
New Year 2002 (Year of the Horse).

2002 World Cup Soccer Championships, Japan and Korea — A374

No. 2503, 1400 le: a, Newspaper article, 1950. b, Jules Rimet, 1954. c, Pele and teammates, 1958. d, Vava and Schroiff, 1962. e, Bobby Charlton, 1966. f, Pele, 1970.
No. 2504, 1400 le: a, Daniel Passarella, 1978. b, Karl-Heinz Rummenigge, 1982. c, Diego Maradona, 1986. d, Roger Milla, 1990. e, Romario, 1994. f, Zinedine Zidane, 1998.
No. 2505, 5000 le, Head from Jules Rimet trophy, 1930. No. 2506, 5000 le, Head and globe from World Cup trophy, 2002.

2001, Dec. 7   Perf. 13¾x14¼
Sheets of 6, #a-f
2503-2504 A374 Set of 2   17.00 17.00
Souvenir Sheets
Perf. 14½x14¼
2505-2506 A374 Set of 2   10.00 10.00

Christmas — A375

Paintings by Filippo Lippi: 300 le, Madonna of Humility. 600 le, Annunciation. 1500 le, Annunciation, vert. 2000 le, Adoration of the Child and Saints, vert.
5000 le, Barbadori Altarpeice, vert.

2001, Dec. 26   Perf. 14
2507-2510 A375 Set of 4   4.50 4.50
Souvenir Sheet
2511 A375 5000 le multi   5.00 5.00

Queen Mother Type of 1999 Redrawn

No. 2512: a, With Duke of York and Princess Elizabeth, 1926. b, In 1979. c, In Nairobi, 1959. d, In 1991.
4000 le, With crown, 1937.

2001, Dec.   Perf. 14
Yellow Orange Frames
2512 A307 1300 le Sheet of 4, #a-d, + label   5.25 5.25
Souvenir Sheet
Perf. 13¾
2513 A307 4000 le multi   4.00 4.00

Queen Mother's 101st birthday. No. 2513 contains one 38x51mm stamp with a slightly darker backdrop than that found on No. 2208. Sheet margins of Nos. 2512-2513 lack embossing and gold arms and frames found on Nos. 2207-2208.

SOS Children's Village — A376

2002, Jan. 24   Perf. 14
2514 A376 2000 le multi   2.00 2.00

Steam and Electric Inventions and Their Inventors — A377

No. 2515, 1100 le: a, The Rocket steam locomotive, 1829. b, High-speed electric passenger train. c, 1863 Steam pumper. d, Early electric trolley. e, 1893 Steam automobile. f, Electric monorail.
No. 2516, 1100 le: a, Early steam pumper. b, Telephone. c, Steam liner. d, Battery and light bulb. e, 1770 Steam carriage. f, Electric passenger train.
No. 2517, 1100 le: a, Robert Fulton and steamboat. b, Thomas Edison and light bulb. c, 1899 T9 steam locomotive. d, Radio and antennae. e, James Watt, and steam engine diagram. f, Alexander Graham Bell and telephone.
No. 2518, 5000 le, 1899 Steam locomotive. No. 2519, 5000 le, Telephone, radio and light bulb. No. 2520, 5000 le, Benjamin Franklin, vert.

Perf. 13¼x13½, 13½x13¼
2002, Jan. 24
Sheets of 6, #a-f
2515-2517 A377 Set of 3   20.00 20.00
Souvenir Sheets
2518-2520 A377 Set of 3   15.00 15.00

United We Stand — A378

2002, Feb. 6   Perf. 13½x13¼
2521 A378 2000 le multi   2.25 2.25

Reign of Queen Elizabeth II, 50th Anniv. — A379

No. 2522: a, With young Prince Charles and Princess Anne. b, Wearing tiara and stole, looking forward. c, Wearing tiara and stole, looking right. d, Wearing hat.
5000 le, Wearing hat and gloves.

2002, Feb. 6   **Perf. 14¼**
2522 A379 2000 le Sheet of 4,
     #a-d   9.00 9.00
     Souvenir Sheet
2523 A379 5000 le multi   5.50 5.50

2002
Winter
Olympics,
Salt Lake
City
A380

Designs: Nos. 2524, 2525, 2000 le, Curling.
Nos. 2524A, 2525A, 2000 le, Ice hockey.

2002, Apr. 22   **Litho.**   **Perf. 14**
     Olympic Rings in Color
2524-
2524A   A380   Set of 2
                      4.00 4.00
2524Ab   Souvenir sheet, #2524-
     2524A   4.00 4.00

Olympic Rings in White on Black
Background
     Perf. 13¼x13½
2525-
2525A   A380   Set of 2
                      4.00 4.00
2525Ab   Souvenir sheet, #2525-
     2525A   4.00 4.00

Flowers — A381

Designs: 400 le, Jerusalem artichoke.
500 le, Painted trillium. 600 le, Bluebells.
1000 le, Rough-fruited cinquefoil. 1500 le,
Wake robin. 2000 le, Seashore mallow.
   No. 2532, 1300 le, horiz.: a, Hepatica. b,
Star of Bethlehem. c, Wood lily. d, Wild gera-
nium. e, Hedge bindweed. f, Gloxinias.
   No. 2533, 1300 le, horiz.: a, Laevigata iris.
b, Dietes. c, Day lily. d, Cardinal flower. e,
Mountain pink. f, Seaside gentian.
   No. 2534, 5000 le, Dame's rocket. No. 2535,
5000 le, Pinxter flower.

2002, Apr. 29   **Litho.**   **Perf. 14x14½**
2526-2531 A381   Set of 6   6.00 6.00
     Perf. 14
     Sheets of 6, #a-f
2532-2533 A381   Set of 2   15.00 15.00
     Souvenir Sheets
2534-2535 A381   Set of 2   10.00 10.00

Nos. 2532-2533 contain six 42x38mm
stamps; Nos. 2534-2535 contain one
38x42mm stamp.

Wildlife — A382

Designs: 200 le, Giraffe. 400 le, L'Host's
guenon. 1500 le, Jentik's duiker.
   No. 2539, 1100 le, horiz.: a, Kudu. b, Caracal. c, Oribi. d, Aardwolf. e, Bushpig. f,
Suricates.
   No. 2540, 1100 le, horiz.: a, African buffalo.
b, Wild dog. c, Black-backed jackal. d, Aardvark. e, Impala. f, Waterbuck.
   No. 2541, 8000 le, Vervet monkey. No.
2542, 8000 le, Springbok.

2002, Apr. 29   **Perf. 14**
2536-2538 A382   Set of 3   2.10 2.10
     Sheets of 6, #a-f
2539-2540 A382   Set of 2   13.00 13.00
     Souvenir Sheets
2541-2542 A382   Set of 2   16.00 16.00

Chiune Sugihara,
Japanese Diplomat
Who Saved Jews
in World War
II — A383

2002, July 1   **Litho.**   **Perf. 14**
2543 A383 2000 le multi   2.00 2.00
   Printed in sheets of 4.

Nos. 1811-
1812
Surcharged

Methods & Perfs. As Before
2002, July 1
2544 A242   800 le on 400 le
     Block or
     strip of 4,
     #a-d   3.25 3.25
     Souvenir Sheet
2545 A242 5000 le on 1500 le
     multi   5.00 5.00
   Queen Mother Elizabeth (1900-2002). No.
2544 was issued in sheets of eight stamps.
Sheet margins of 2544-2544 were overprinted
with black border and "In Memoriam / 1900-
2002."

Intl Year of Ecotourism — A384

   No. 2546: a, Bullom boats. b, Dinkongor
Falls. c, Rokel River. d, Pygmy hippopotamus.
e, Hills of Soa Chiefdom. f, Long Beach.
5000 le, Photo safari.

2002, July 1   **Litho.**   **Perf. 14**
2546 A384 1300 le Sheet of 6,
     #a-f   7.75 7.75
     Souvenir Sheet
2547 A384 5000 le multi   5.00 5.00

First Non-stop Solo Transatlantic
Flight, 75th Anniv. — A385

   No. 2548, horiz. — The Spirit of St. Louis: a,
Being towed from Ryan Airlines factory. b,

Being towed May 20, 1927. c, Taking off, May
20, 1927.
   No. 2549, Charles Lindbergh.

2002, July 1
2548 A385 2500 le Sheet of 3,
     #a-c   7.50 7.50
     Souvenir Sheet
2549 A385 2500 le multi   2.50 2.50

Shirley Temple Movie Type of 2000

   Temple in scenes from "Wee Willie Winkie"
— No. 2550: a, With woman, man in army
uniform, two men wearing turbans. b, Resting
head near mirror. c, With boy wearing army
uniform and kilt. d, With man wearing turban.
e, With man in army uniform. f, Giving note to
man in prison.
   No. 2551, vert: a, With woman. b, With man
wearing turban. c, With woman and man. d,
With man in army uniform.
   5000 le, With man in army uniform, vert.

2002, July 1   **Perf. 12¼**
2550 A324 1100 le Sheet of 6,
     #a-f   6.50 6.50
2551 A324 1300 le Sheet of 4,
     #a-d   5.25 5.25
     Souvenir Sheet
2552 A324 5000 le multi   5.00 5.00

20th World Scout Jamboree,
Thailand — A386

   No. 2553: a, Boys on rocks fishing. b,
Scouts without caps. c, Scouts in water holding fish. d, Scouts with caps.
   5000 le, Scouts in sailboat.

2002, July 1   **Perf. 14**
2553 A386 2000 le Sheet of 4,
     #a-d   8.00 8.00
     Souvenir Sheet
2554 A386 5000 le multi   5.00 5.00

Intl. Year of Mountains — A387

   No. 2555: a, Mt. Etna, Italy. b, Cotopaxi,
Ecuador. c, Mt. Everest, Nepal. d, Mt. Popo-
catepetl, Mexico.
   5000 le, Mt. Machhapuchare, Nepal.

2002, July 1
2555 A387 2000 le Sheet of 4,
     #a-d   8.00 8.00
     Souvenir Sheet
2556 A387 5000 le multi   5.00 5.00

Pokémon — A388

   No. 2557, vert.: a, Sudowoodo. b, Aipom. c,
Shuckle. d, Miltank. e, Hitmontop. f, Ledian.
5000 le, Lugia.

2002, Aug. 26   **Perf. 13¾**
2557 A388 1500 le Sheet of 6,
     #a-f   9.25 9.25
     Souvenir Sheet
2558 A388 5000 le multi   5.25 5.25

Popeye in New York — A389

   No. 2559, vert. — Popeye and : a, And Olive
Oyl on river tour. b, And Olive Oyl in Central
Park. c, And Olive Oyl near Brooklyn Bridge.
d, Statue of Liberty. e, Flatiron Building. f,
Empire State Building.
   5000 le, Popeye and Olive Oyl skating at
Rockefeller Center.

2002, Aug. 26   **Perf. 12¼**
2559 A389 1300 le Sheet of 6,
     #a-f   8.00 8.00
     Souvenir Sheet
2560 A389 5000 le multi   5.25 5.25
   No. 2559 contains six 38x50mm stamps.

A390

Teddy Bears, Cent. — A391

No. 2561: a, Bear with green bow. b, Bears with harlequin costumes. c, Bear with red headdress. d, Bear with black and gold neckband.
No. 2562: a, Baby girl bear. b, School girl bear. c, Bear in overalls. d, Bear in pajamas.

2002, Sept. 23   *Perf. 14*
2561 A390 1700 le Sheet of 4,
    #a-d   6.50 6.50
2562 A391 2000 le Sheet of 4,
    #a-d   7.75 7.75

Elvis Presley (1935-77) — A392

No. 2563: a, Wearing flowered shirt. b, Wearing jacket, holding light-colored guitar. c, Seated in chair. d, Wearing sweater. e, With arms raised. f, With black guitar.

2002, Oct. 7   Litho.
2563 A392 1000 le Sheet of 6,
    #a-f   5.75 5.75

2002 World Cup Soccer Championships, Japan and Korea — A393

No. 2564, 1400 le — Germany vs. Paraguay: a, Michael Ballack. b, Oliver Kahn. c, Miroslav Klose. d, Diego Gacilan. e, Jose Luis Chilavert. f, Guido Alvarenga.
No. 2565, 1400 le — Denmark vs. England: a, Jesper Gronkjaer. b, Thomas Helveg. c, Dennis Rommedahl. d, Michael Owen. e, David Seaman. f, Rio Ferdinand.
No. 2566, 1400 le — Mexico vs. U.S.: a, Rafael Marquez. b, Oscar Perez. c, Jared Borgetti. d, Landon Donovan. e, Brad Friedel. f, DaMarcus Beasley.
No. 2567, 1400 le — Japan vs. Turkey: a, Ryuzo Morioka. b, Kazuyuki Toda. c, Atsushi Yanagisawa. d, Fatih Akyel. e, Yildiray Basturk. f, Umit Davala.
No. 2568, 2500 le — Germany: a, Coach Rudi Voeller. b, Dietmar Hamann.
No. 2569, 2500 le — Paraguay: a, Julio Cesar Caceres. b, Coach Cesare Maldini.
No. 2570, 2500 le — Denmark: a, Coach Morten Olsen. b, Jon Dahl Tomasson.

No. 2571, 2500 le — England: a, David Beckham. b, Coach Sven Goran Eriksson.
No. 2572, 2500 le — Mexico: a, Coach Javier Aguirre. b, Jesus Arellano.
No. 2573, 2500 le — United States: a, Brian McBride. b, Coach Bruce Arena.
No. 2574, 2500 le — Japan: a, Coach Philippe Troussier. b, Junichi Inamoto.
No. 2575, 2500 le — Turkey: a, Vildiray Basturk. b, Coach Senol Gunes.

2002, Nov. 18   *Perf. 13¼*
Sheets of 6, #a-f
2564-2567 A393 Set of 4   40.00 40.00
Souvenir Sheets of 2, #a-b
2568-2575 A393 Set of 8   47.50 47.50

Christmas — A394

Designs: 50 le, Madonna and Child Between Saints John the Baptist and Catherine of Alexandria, by Perugino. 100 le, Madonna and Child Enthroned Between Angels and Saints, by Domenico Ghirlandaio. 150 le, The Virgin, by Giovanni Bellini. 500 le, Stories of the Virgin Birth of Mary, by Ghirlandaio. 5000 le, Adoration of the Magi, by Ghirlandaio.
6000 le, Madonna Enthroned with Saints, by Ghirlandaio.

2002, Nov. 18   *Perf. 14*
2576-2580 A394 Set of 5   6.75 6.75
Souvenir Sheet
2581 A394 6000 le multi   7.00 7.00

Pres. Ronald Reagan — A395

No. 2582, 1700 le — Country name in black: a, Wearing brown tie. b, Wearing red tie.
No. 2583, 1700 le — Country name in white: a, Wearing spotted tie. b, Wearing striped tie.

2002, Dec. 30   Litho.
Pairs, #a-b
2582-2583 A395 Set of 2   6.75 6.75
Nos. 2582-2583 each were printed in sheets containing two pairs.

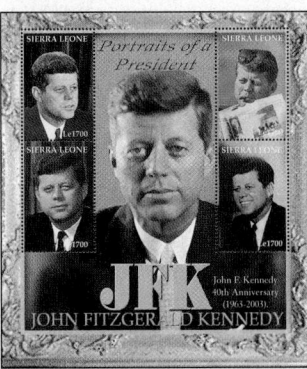

Pres. John F. Kennedy (1917-63) — A396

No. 2584, 1700 le: a, Wearing red tie. b, With newspaper. c, In front on brown curtain. d, In front of brown and tan background.
No. 2585, 1700 le — John and Jacqueline: a, In formal wear greeting man. b, With purple background. c, Playing with child. d, At Love Field, Nov. 22, 1963.

Princess Diana (1961-97) — A397

Designs: No. 2586, 1700 le, Wearing black dress. No. 2587, 1700 le, Wearing blue dress and tiara.

2002, Dec. 30
2586-2587 A397 Set of 2   3.50 3.50
Nos. 2586-2587 each were printed in sheets of 4.

2002, Dec. 30   *Perf. 14*
Sheets of 4, #a-d
2584-2585 A396 Set of 2   13.50 13.50

Birds, Flowers and Insects of Africa — A398

No. 2588, 1300 le — Birds: a, Great blue turaco. b, Helmet vanga. c, Scarlet-tufted malachite sunbird. d, African pitta. e, African jacana. f, Southern carmine bee-eater.
No. 2589, 1300 le — Flowers: a, Ancistrochilus rothschildianus. b, Oeceoclades maculata. c, Eulophia guineensis. d, Angraecum distichum. e, Disa uniflora. f, Vanilla imperialis.
No. 2590, 1300 le — Insects: a, Panther-spotted grasshopper. b, Basker moth. c, Charaxes samagdalis. d, Carpenter ant. e, Worker bee. f, Ten-spot dragonfly.
No. 2591, 5000 le, European robin. No. 2592, 5000 le, Bulbophyllum lepidum. No. 2593, 5000 le, Common dotted border butterfly, horiz.

2003, Jan. 13
Sheets of 6, #a-f
2588-2590 A398 Set of 3   25.00 25.00
Souvenir Sheets
2591-2593 A398 Set of 3   16.00 16.00

New Year 2003 (Year of the Ram) — A399

No. 2594 — Color of ram: a, Green. b, Orange. c, Red violet. d, Orange brown.

2003, Feb. 10
2594 A399 900 le Sheet of 6, #a-
    c, 3 #d   5.75 5.75

Astronauts Killed in Space Shuttle Columbia Accident — A400

No. 2595: a, Mission Specialist 1 David M. Brown. b, Commander Rick D. Husband. c, Mission Specialist 4 Laurel Blair Salton Clark. d, Mission Specialist 4 Kalpana Chawla. e, Payload Commander Michael P. Anderson. f, Pilot William C. McCool. g, Payload Specialist 4 Ilan Ramon.

2003, Apr. 7   *Perf. 13½x13¼*
2595 A400 1000 le Sheet of 7,
    #a-g   6.25 6.25

A401

Teddy Bears, Cent. — A402

No. 2596, vert.: a, Bear with umbrella. b, Bear with belt. c, Bear with pink dress. d, Bear with horn.
5000 le, Bear in automobile.
12,000 le, Bear with flower.

2003   Litho.   *Perf. 14¼*
2596 A401 1500 le Sheet of
    4, #a-d   5.25 5.25
Souvenir Sheet
2597 A401 5000 le multi   4.25 4.25
Embroidered
Imperf
2598 A402 12,000 le multi   10.50 10.50
Issued: Nos. 2596, 2597, 7/1, No. 2598, Apr. No. 2598 issued in sheets of 4.

Sierra Leone

A403

Coronation of Queen Elizabeth II, 50th Anniv. — A404

Designs: No. 2599, 1500 le, Crowning of the Queen. No. 2600, 1500 le, Queen signs the oath. No. 2601, 1500 le, Sovereign's sword. No. 2602, 1500 le, Anointing of the Queen. No. 2603, 1500 le, Queen presented with Holy Bible. No. 2604, 1500 le, Royal onlookers. No. 2605, 1500 le, Ampulla and spoon. No. 2606, 1500 le, Orb and scepter.
5000 le, Queen with crown. 15,000 le, Queen with hat.

2003   **Litho.**   **Perf. 13¼**
2599-2606 A403   Set of 8   10.50 10.50
Souvenir Sheet
Perf. 14¼
2607   A403   5000 le multi   4.25 4.25
Miniature Sheet
Litho. & Embossed
Perf. 13¼x13
2608   A404   15,000 le multi   13.00 13.00
Issued: Nos. 2599-2607, 7/1; No. 2608, 4/7. No. 2607 contains one 37x50mm stamp.

Rembrandt Paintings A405

Designs: 800 le, Young Man with Pointed Beard. 1000 le, Old Man with Book. 1200 le, The Shipbuilder Jan Rijcksen and His Wife, Griet Jans, horiz. 2000 le, Portrait of a Young Jew.
No. 2613: a, Juno. b, Bellona, Goddess of War. c, Artemesia. d, Esther Preparing to Intercede with Ahasuerus.
5000 le, Two Scholars Disputing.

Perf. 14¼, 13¼ (#2613)
2003, May 13   **Litho.**
2609-2612 A405   Set of 4   4.50 4.50
2613   A405   1700 le Sheet of 4,
#a-d   6.00 6.00
Souvenir Sheet
2614   A405   5000 le multi   4.50 4.50

Japanese Art — A406

Designs: 800 le, Priest Raigo Transformed Into a Rat, by Yoshitoshi Tsukioka. 1000 le, The Spirit of Tamichi as a Great Snake, by Yoshitoshi Tsukioka. 1500 le, The Gathering and Gossiping of Various Tools, by Kuniyoshi Utagawa. 2500 le, Caricatures of Actors as Three Animals Playing Ken, by Kuniyoshi Utagawa.
No. 2619 — Paintings by Yoshitoshi Tsukioka: a, The Fox Woman Leaving Her Child. b, Fox Cry. c, The Lucky Teakettle of Morin Temple. d, The Ghost of Okiku.
5000 le, Fox in a Thunderstorm, by Kunisada Utagawa.

2003, May 13   **Perf. 14¼**
2615-2618 A406   Set of 4   5.25 5.25
2619   A406   2000 le Sheet of 4,
#a-d   7.25 7.25
Souvenir Sheet
2620   A406   5000 le multi   4.50 4.50

Paintings by Pablo Picasso A407

Designs: 400 le, Glass, Pipe and Playing Card. 500 le, Still-Life on a Pedestal in front of a Window. 600 le, Woman in a Feathered Hat. 700 le, Pedestal and Guitar. 1000 le, The Bread Carrier. 3000 le, Female Acrobat.
No. 2627: a, Portrait of a Woman. b, Woman in a Red Armchair. c, Seated Woman with Small Round Hat (Dora Maar). d, Woman with Crossed Hands.
No. 2628, Boy in Black Shorts. No. 2629, Bathers, horiz.

2003, May 13   **Perf. 14¼**
2621-2626 A407   Set of 6   5.50 5.50
2627   A407   2000 le Sheet of 4,
#a-d   7.25 7.25
Imperf
Size: 82x105mm
2628   A407   5000 le multi   4.50 4.50
Size: 103x82mm
2629   A407   5000 le multi   4.50 4.50

Painting of Mona Lisa, 500th Anniv. — A408

No. 2629A, 500th Anniversary of Mona Lisa (complete painting).
No. 2630 — Inscribed: a, Chartier: Mona Lisa — Mistress of Francis I. b, Copy of Mona Lisa, Cheramy Collection.
5000 le, 500th Anniversary of Mona Lisa (face).

2003, July 1   **Perf. 14**
2629A A408   2000 le multi   1.75 1.75
2630   A408   2000 le Sheet of 3,
#a-b, No.
2629A   5.25 5.25
Souvenir Sheet
2631   A408   5000 le multi   4.25 4.25
No. 2629A was issued in two sheets of six with different selvage in 2004.

Intl. Year of Fresh Water — A409

No. 2632 a, Waterfalls of Mount Tonkoui. b, Tagbaladougou Falls. c, Cascades d'Ouzoud. 5000 le, Little Scarcies.

2003, July 1
2632   A409   2000 le Sheet of 3,
#a-c   5.25 5.25
Souvenir Sheet
2633   A409   5000 le multi   4.25 4.25

Rotary Club of Sierra Leone, 40th Anniv. — A410

No. 2634 — Rotarians and: a, People in canoe. b, Cacheted first day cover envelope, Sierra Leone natives. c, Girl with flowers. 6000 le, Bhichal Rattakul, Rotary President.

2003, July 1
2634   A410   2500 le Sheet of 3,
#a-c   6.50 6.50
Souvenir Sheet
2635   A410   6000 le multi   5.25 5.25

Prince William, 21st Birthday — A411

No. 2636: a, Wearing solid shirt. b, Wearing striped shirt. c, Wearing sweater.
5000 le, Wearing plaid shirt.

2003, July 1
2636   A411   2500 le Sheet of 3,
#a-c   6.50 6.50
Souvenir Sheet
2637   A411   5000 le multi   4.25 4.25

Circus Performers — A412

No. 2638, 2000 le: a, Peggy Williams. b, Nico. c, Steve T. J. Tatter Smith. d, Uncle Dippy.
No. 2639, 2000 le: a, Caracal. b, Chairs. c, Elena Panova. d, Chinese Circus.

2003, July 1   **Litho.**
Sheets of 4, #a-d
2638-2639 A412   Set of 2   13.50 13.50

Powered Flight, Cent. — A413

No. 2640, 1500 le: a, Wright Brothers first plane (gray background). b, Voisin-Farmin (blue background). c, Levavasseur Antoinette (pink background). d, Nieuport (numbered 345).
No. 2641, 1500 le: a, Wright Brothers first plane (blue background). b, Voisin-Farmin (gray background). c, Levavasseur Antoinette (blue background). d, Nieuport (no number on plane).
No. 2642, 5000 le, Henri Farmin Crossing Finish Line in Voisin-Farmin plane. No. 2643, 5000 le, Roland Garros and others around airplane.

2003, July 14
Sheets of 4, #a-d
2640-2641 A413   Set of 2   10.50 10.50
Souvenir Sheets
2642-2643 A413   Set of 2   8.50 8.50
Inscriptions on No. 2640 are incorrect. See also No. 2751.

Tour de France Bicycle Race, Cent. — A414

No. 2644, 1500 le: a, Ferdinand Kubler, 1950. b, Hugo Koblet, 1951. c, Fausto Coppi, 1952. d, Louison Bobet, 1953.

No. 2645, 1500 le: a, Bobet, 1954. b, Bobet, 1955. c, Roger Walkowiak, 1956. d, Jacques Anquetil, 1957.

No. 2646, 1500 le: a, Eddy Merckx, 1970. b, Merckx, 1971. c, Merckx, 1972. d, Luis Ocana, 1973.

No. 2647, 5000 le, Bobet, 1953-55. No. 2648, 5000 le, Anquetil, 1957, diff. No. 2649, 5000 le, Bernard Hinault, 1978.

2003, July 14   **Perf. 13¼**

Sheets of 4, #a-d

2644-2646 A414   Set of 3   15.50 15.50

Souvenir Sheets

2647-2649 A414   Set of 3   13.00 13.00

Olympic Medalists A415

Designs: 300 le, Forrest Smithson, 1908. 400 le, Hannes Kolehmainen, 1912. 500 le, Larissa Latynina, 1964. 800 le, Klaus Dibiasi, 1976. 1000 le, Archie Hahn, 1904. 1500 le, M. Hurley. 2000 le, Ray Ewry, 1900. 3000 le, Henry Taylor, 1908.

2003, Nov. 17   **Perf. 13¼**

2650-2657 A415   Set of 8   7.75 7.75

Inscription on No. 2655 is incorrect as there were no cycling events in 1904 and no cycling medalists in any year named Hurley.

Christmas A416

Paintings by Pontormo Rosso Fiorentino: 100 le, Madonna and Child with St. Anne and Four Saints. 150 le, Madonna and Child with Two Saints. 500 le, Madonna and Child Enthroned with Four Saints (Ognissanti Altarpiece). 4000 le, Madonna Enthroned Between Two Saints.

5000 le, Madonna with Saints.

2003, Nov. 17   **Perf. 14¼**

2658-2661 A416   Set of 4   4.00 4.00

Souvenir Sheet

2662 A416 5000 le multi   4.25 4.25

New Year 2004 (Year of the Monkey) — A417

No. 2663 — Background color: a, Yellow orange. b, Blue. c, Rose pink. d, Dark orange 2500 le, Pink.

2004, Jan. 15   **Perf. 13¾**

2663 A417 1200 le Sheet of 4, #a-d   4.00 4.00

Souvenir Sheet
Perf. 14

2664 A417 2500 le multi   2.10 2.10

No. 2664 contains one 42x28mm stamp.

Paintings of Chiao Ping-chen (1689-1726) — A418

No. 2665: a, Untitled painting depicting courtyard. b, Untitled landscape. c, Court Ladies (woman with purple robe at LR). d, Court Ladies (woman with purple robe at center)

5000 le, The Beauty of Traditional Chinese Architecture in Painting.

2004, Jan. 21   **Perf. 13¼**

2665 A418 2000 le Sheet of 4, #a-d   6.50 6.50

Imperf

2666 A418 5000 le shown   4.25 4.25

No. 2665 contains four 38x50mm stamps.

British Council, 60th Anniv. A419

Frame colors: 500 le, Gray green. 1000 le, Dull green. 2000 le, Purple. 3000 le, Red.

2004, Jan. 29   **Perf. 14**

2667-2670 A419   Set of 4   5.50 5.50

Map & Lion Type of 1964 Redrawn
2004, Feb. 4   **Die Cut**
Self-Adhesive

2671 A38 1000 le multi   .85 .85

Printed in sheets of 10.

Paintings by Norman Rockwell — A420

No. 2672: a, Ice Cream Carrier. b, The Voyeur. c, Teacher's Birthday. d, Fisk Tires Advertisement.

5000 le, Cousin Reginald Plays Pirate.

2004, Feb. 24   **Litho.**   **Perf. 13½**

2672 A420 2000 le Sheet of 4, #a-d   6.50 6.50

Souvenir Sheet

2673 A420 5000 le multi   4.25 4.25

Cessation of Concorde Flights in 2003 — A421

No. 2674, 3000 le — Concorde 206-G BOAA and: a, Blue background. b, Top half of Brazilian flag. b, Bottom half of Brazilian flag.

No. 2675, 3000 le — Concorde G-AXDN and: a, Pink background. b, Top half of Egyptian flag (red stripe). c, Bottom half of Egyptian flag.

No. 2676, 3000 le — Concorde G-ADXN Aircraft 101 and: a, City skyline. b, Top half of Kenyan flag (black stripe). c, Bottom half of Kenyan flag.

2004, Feb. 24   **Perf. 13¼x13½**

Sheets of 3, #a-c

2674-2676 A421   Set of 3   22.50 22.50

Paintings from the Hermitage, St. Petersburg, Russia — A422

No. 2677: a, The Birth of St. John the Baptist, by Jacopo Tintoretto. b, Penitent Mary Magdalene, by Titian. c, The Death of St. Petronilla, by Simone Pignoni. d, The Assumption of the Virgin, by Bartolomé Esteban Murillo. e, St. Jerome Hears the Trumpet, by Jusepe de Ribera. f, St. George and the Dragon, by Tintoretto.

No. 2678 — Paintings by Elisabeth Vigée-Lebrun: a, Countess A. S. Stroganova and Her Son. b, Count G. I. Chernyshev Holding a Mask. c, Self-portrait. d, Baron G. A. Stroganov.

No. 2679, The Apostles Peter and Paul, by El Greco. No. 2680, A Visit to the Priest, by Jean-Baptiste Greuze, horiz.

2004, Feb. 24   **Litho.**   **Perf. 13¼**

2677 A422 1400 le Sheet of 6, #a-f   7.00 7.00

2678 A422 2000 le Sheet of 4, #a-d   6.50 6.50

Imperf

2679 A422 5000 le shown   4.25 4.25

Size: 100x69mm

2680 A422 5000 le multi   4.25 4.25

Marilyn Monroe (Larger Final Zero) — A423

Marilyn Monroe (Zeroes Same Size) — A424

Marilyn Monroe — A425

2004, May 3   **Perf. 14**

2681 A423 1000 le Pair, #a-b   1.60 1.60

Perf. 13½x13¼

2682 A424 1000 le Pair, #a-b   1.60 1.60

2683 A425 2000 le Sheet of 4, #a-d   6.50 6.50

First Orbiting Astronauts of China, US and Russia — A426

No. 2684, horiz. — Yang Lewei: a, Wearing flight jumpsuit. b, Wearing uniform. c, Wearing space suit. d, Wearing space suit, giving hand gesture.

No. 2685: a, Vostok 1. b, John Glenn. c, Friendship 7. d, Yuri Gagarin. e, Shenzhou 5. f, Yang Lewei, diff.

No. 2686, 5000 le, Yang Lewei, diff. No. 2687, 5000 le, Glenn, diff.

2004, May 10   **Perf. 13¼x13½**

2684 A426 900 le Horiz. strip of 4, #a-d   2.75 2.75

Perf. 13½x13¼

2685 A426 1200 le Sheet of 6, #a-f   5.50 5.50

Souvenir Sheets

2686-2687 A426   Set of 2   7.75 7.75

No. 2684 printed in sheets containing two strips.

Cats
A427

Designs: 100 le, Ruddy Somali. 800 le, Bombay. 1200 le, Burmese. 3000 le, British Shorthair.

No. 2692, vert.: a, Persian. b, Colorpoint Shorthair. c, Cornish Rex. d, Blue Point Balinese.

5000 le, Devon Rex.

Perf. 13¼x13½, 13½x13¼
2004, May 17
2688-2691	A427	Set of 4	4.25	4.25
2692	A427	1700 le Sheet of 4, #a-d	5.50	5.50

Souvenir Sheet
2693	A427	5000 le multi	4.00	4.00

Moths and Butterflies
A428

Designs: 200 le, Io moth. 300 le, Hackberry butterfly. 400 le, Red admiral butterfly. 4000 le, Spangled fritillary butterfly.

No. 2698: a, Pearl crescent butterfly. b, Pipevine swallowtail butterfly. c, Alfalfa looper moth. d, Tiger swallowtail butterfly.

5000 le, Cecropia moth.

2004, May 17   **Perf. 13¼x13½**
2694-2697	A428	Set of 4	4.00	4.00
2698	A428	1700 le Sheet of 4, #a-d	5.50	5.50

Souvenir Sheet
2699	A428	5000 le multi	4.00	4.00

Birds — A429

Designs: 500 le, Belted kingfisher. 1000 le, Burrowing owl. 1500 le, Crested caracara. 2000 le, Red-headed finch.

No. 2704, horiz.: a, Snail kite. b, Avocet. c, Greater flamingo. d, Bald eagle.

5000 le, Ring-necked pheasant, horiz.

Perf. 13½x13¼, 13¼x13½
2004, May 17
2700-2703	A429	Set of 4	4.00	4.00
2704	A429	1700 le Sheet of 4, #a-d	5.50	5.50

Souvenir Sheet
2705	A429	5000 le multi	4.00	4.00

Election of Pope John Paul II, 25th Anniv. (in 2003) — A431

No. 2712 — Pope John Paul II: a, Visiting Australia, 1986. b, With John Bonica, 1987. c, Visiting Croatia, 2003. d, Celebrating 25th anniversary mass, 2003.

2004, May 24   **Perf. 13¼x13½**
2712	A431	2000 le Sheet of 4, #a-d	6.50	6.50

Souvenir Sheet

Deng Xiaoping (1904-97), Chinese Leader — A432

2004, June 1   **Perf. 14**
2713	A432	5000 le multi	4.00	4.00

2004 Summer Olympics, Athens
A433

Designs: 250 le, Marathon, 1908. 300 le, Dimitrios Vikelas, first president of Intl. Olympic Committee. 1500 le, 1896 Olympic medal. 2000 le, Discus thrower.

2004, June 6   **Perf. 14¼**
2714-2717	A433	Set of 4	3.25	3.25

A434

D-Day, 60th Anniv. — A435

No. 2718: a, Gen. Dwight D. Eisenhower. b, Rear Adm. Don P. Moon. c, Lt. Gen. Omar N. Bradley. d, Rear Adm. Alan G. Kirk. e, Maj. Gen. Clarence R. Huebner. f, Maj. Gen. Maxwell D. Taylor.

No. 2719, 950 le: a, LST landing craft. b, M4 Sherman tank. c, M4 Sherman tank and soldier. d, Tank cannon. e, 70th Tank Battalion patch. f, Soldier with rifle, g, 743rd Tank Battalion patch. h, 741st Tank Battalion patch.

No. 2720, 1000 le: a, P-51 Mustang over battle. b, Paratroopers, map. c, Map. d, P-38 Lightning. e, M4 Sherman tank, diff. f, Soldiers. g, LCM landing craft, map. h, US light cruiser, map with numbers.

No. 2721, 1000 le: a, P-47 Thunderbolt. b, Paratroopers, airplanes, map. c, Tank, map. d, Soldier with rifle, map. e, US heavy cruiser. f, US light cruiser, map. g, Ships. h, US destroyer escorts.

No. 2722, 1000 le: a, Spitfire. b, Typhoon. c, Tail of Typhoon, wing of P-38 Lightning, other airplane. d, P-51 Mustang. e, C-47 Skytrain. f, Wing of Typhoon, fuselage of C-47 Skytrain, other airplane. g, P-38 Lightning. h, US Air Force patch.

No. 2723, 1000 le: a, US light cruiser, blimps. b, LST landing craft, blimps. c, Landing craft with door open. d, LST landing craft. e, US armored car. f, Soldiers, tank. g, US medical transport vehicle. h, US armored car leaving landing craft.

No. 2724, 1100 le: a, Soldier with rifle, map, diff. b, Paratrooper, 101st Airborne Division patch. c, Paratrooper, tail of plane. d, Nose of airplane. e, Gen. Eisenhower. f, Gen. Bernard Montgomery. g, Paratrooper, 82nd Airborne Division patch. h, Two paratroopers, C-47 Skytrain.

2004, June 1   **Perf. 14**
2718	A434	1400 le Sheet of 6, #a-f	7.00	7.00

Sheets of 8, #a-h
2719-2724	A435	Set of 6	40.00	40.00

British Lighthouses
A436

Designs: 1800 le, Smalls Lighthouse. 2000 le, Needles Rocks Lighthouse. 2500 le, St. John's Point Lighthouse. 3500 le, Bell Rock Lighthouse. 4000 le, Eddystone Lighthouse.

2004, June 17   **Perf. 14¾x14**
2725-2729	A436	Set of 5	11.50	11.50

American Indian Artifacts — A437

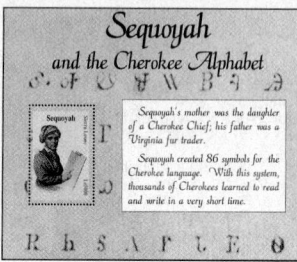

American Indians — A438

No. 2730: a, Arapaho pipe bag. b, Apache basket. c, Blackfoot parfleche. d, Crow elkhide robe. e, Iroquois moccasins. f, Hopi canteen. g, Sioux parfleche. h, Navajo rug. i, Nez Perce cradle.

No. 2731 — Ioway chiefs and warriors: a, Ne-O-Mon-Ne. b, Ma-Has-Kah. c, Moa-Na-Hon-Ga. d, Tah-Ro-Hon. e, Not-Chi-Mi-Ne. f, Shau-Hau-Napo-Tinia.

No. 2732, horiz. — Paintings by Charles Russell: a, Medicine Man. b, War Party. c, Signal Smoke.

5000 le, Sequoyah.

2004, July 5   **Perf. 14**
2730	A437	1000 le Sheet of 9, #a-i	7.50	7.50
2731	A438	1500 le Sheet of 6, #a-f	7.50	7.50
2732	A438	3000 le Sheet of 3, #a-c	7.50	7.50
Nos. 2730-2732 (3)			22.50	22.50

Souvenir Sheet
2733	A438	5000 le multi	4.00	4.00

Prehistoric Animals — A439

No. 2734, 2000 le: a, Apatosaurus. b, Styracosaurus. c, Plateosaurus. d, Pachyrhinosaurus.

No. 2735, 2000 le, horiz.: a, Camarasaurus. b, Iystrosaurus. c, Ankylosaurus. d, Herrerasaurus.

No. 2736, 5000 le, Dunklosteus. No. 2737, 5000 le, Archaeopteryx, horiz.

2004   **Perf. 14**
Sheets of 4, #a-d
2734-2735	A439	Set of 2	13.00	13.00

Souvenir Sheets
2736-2737	A439	Set of 2	8.25	8.25

No. 2734 has two labels.

Orchids — A440

Designs: 150 le, Catasetum pileatum. No. 2739, 400 le, Cattleya araguainsis. No. 2740, 400 le, Barkeria spectabilis. 3500 le, Catasetum fimbriatum.

No. 2742: a, Odontonia vesta. b, Ancistrorhothschildianus. c, Ansellia africana. d, Aspasia epidendroides.

5000 le, Bulbophyllum lobbii.

2004, May 17   Litho.   Perf. 12½
2738-2741 A440   Set of 4   3.75 3.75
2742 A440 1700 le Sheet of 4,
    #a-d   5.50 5.50
Souvenir Sheet
2743 A440 5000 le multi   4.25 4.25

Dogs — A441

Designs: 250 le, Great Pyrenees. 600 le, Kerry Blue terrier. 1300 le, Mastiff. 1800 le, English sheepdog.
No. 2748: a, Sealyham terrier. b, Norwich terrier. c, Wheaton terrier. d, Bull terrier. 5000 le, Greyhound.

2004, May 17
2744-2747 A441   Set of 4   3.25 3.25
2748 A441 1700 le Sheet of 4,
    #a-d   5.50 5.50
Souvenir Sheet
2749 A441 5000 le multi   4.25 4.25

Souvenir Sheet

Intl. Year of Peace — A442

No. 2750 — Position of olive branch carried by dove: a, Below last two zeros of denomination. b, Below three and first two zeros of denomination. c, Covered by last two zeros of denomination.

2004, June 1   Perf. 14
2750 A442 3000 le Sheet of 3,
    #a-c   7.50 7.50

Powered Flight Type of 2003
No. 2751: a, Curtiss Triad. b, Avro Biplane. c, Curtiss America. d, Farnborought Be-2.

2004, July 17
2751 A413 1500 le Sheet of 4,
    #a-d   5.00 5.00

Worldwide Fund for Nature (WWF) — A443

No. 2752 — Patas monkey: a, Monkey grooming another. b, Monkeys and flower. c, Adult and juvenile. d, Head of monkey.

2004, Oct. 11   Perf. 13¼x13½
2752 A443 1000 le Block of 4,
    #a-d   3.75 3.75
e.   Miniature sheet, 2 each
    #2752a-2752d   8.00 8.00
    for surcharge see No. 2910.

National Basketball Association Players — A444

Designs: No. 2753, 700 le, Kobe Bryant, Los Angeles Lakers. No. 2754, 700 le, Carmelo Anthony, Denver Nuggets. No. 2755, 700 le, Yao Ming, Houston Rockets. No. 2756, 700 le, Jermaine O'Neal, Indiana Pacers. No. 2757, 700 le, Leandro Barbosa, Phoenix Suns. 2000 le, Vlade Divac, Sacramento Kings.

2004   Perf. 14
2753-2758 A444   Set of 6   4.50 4.50
Issued: Nos. 2753, 2758, 11/2; No. 2754, 11/4; Nos. 2755-2756, 11/6; No. 2757, 12/13. Each stamp printed in a sheet of 12.

George Herman "Babe" Ruth (1895-1948), Baseball Player — A445

2004, Dec. 13
2759 A445 500 le multi   .40 .40
    Printed in sheet of 16.

National Soccer Team — A446

2004, Dec. 13   Perf. 12
2760 A446 2000 le multi   1.75 1.75

Pres. Ronald Reagan and Queen Elizabeth II — A447

No. 2761, Reagan and Queen: a, With spouses. b, Making a toast.

2004, Dec. 13   Perf. 13½
2761 A447 2000 le Horiz. pair,
    #a-b   3.25 3.25
Printed in sheets containing three each of Nos. 2761a and 2761b.

Ocean Liners A448

Designs: 600 le, Paris. 800 le, Statendam. 1000 le, Stavengerfjord. 1500 le, Campania. 2000 le, Drottningholm. 3000 le, Lusitania. 5000 le, United States, horiz.

2004, Dec. 13   Perf. 14¼
2762-2767 A448   Set of 6   7.25 7.25
Souvenir Sheet
2768 A448 5000 le multi   4.25 4.25

Christmas A449

Designs: 1000 le, Nativity with the Annunciation to the Shepherds, by Follower of Jan Joest. 1500 le, Christmas Snow, by Norman Rockwell. 2000 le, The Christmas Tree, by E. Osborn. 5000 le, The Spirit of Christmas, by Rockwell.
8000 le, Madonna and Child Enthroned with Two Angels, by Fra Filippo Lippi.

2004, Dec. 13   Perf. 12¼x12
2769-2772 A449   Set of 4   7.75 7.75
Souvenir Sheet
2773 A449 8000 le multi   6.50 6.50

Miniature Sheet

Yasujiro Ozu (1903-63), Film Director — A450

No. 2774 — Posters or scenes from: a, Tokyo Story. b, Late Spring. c, Early Summer. d, Equinox Flower. e, Good Morning. f, An Autumn Afternoon.

2004, Dec. 13   Perf. 13¼
2774 A450 1400 le Sheet of 6,
    #a-f   7.00 7.00

Miniature Sheets

A451

Elvis Presley (1935-77) — A452

Various depictions of Presley.

2004, Dec. 13   Perf. 13½
2775 A451 2000 le Sheet of 4,
    #a-d   6.50 6.50
2776 A452 2000 le Sheet of 4,
    #a-d   6.50 6.50

FIFA (Fédération Internationale de Football Association), Cent. — A453

No. 2777: a, Diego Simeone. b, Careca. c, Oliver Bierhoff. d, Kevin Keegan. 5000 le, David Ginola.

2004, Dec. 13   Perf. 12¾x12½
2777 A453 2000 le Sheet of 4,
    #a-d   6.50 6.50
Souvenir Sheet
2778 A453 5000 le multi   4.25 4.25

Locomotives, 200th Anniv. — A454

No. 2779, 1000 le: a, Stephenson's Rocket. b, Indonesian State Railway B50 class 2-4-0. c, Eurostar Paris-London train. d, China Railways SY Class 2-8-2. e, Baldwin 0-6-0. f, Hunsle 0-4-2T. g, Bagnall 0-6-0 ST Progress. h, North British-built 4-8-2T. i, Baldwin 0-6-2l.
No. 2780, 1000 le, vert.: a, GWR Mogul, Severn Valley Railway. b, Kitson Meyer 0-6-6-0. c, China Railways SL7 Class Pacific. d, Fireman fueling Yugoslav Class 20 2-6-0. e, Lookout man with flag. f, Workers filling sandboxes. g, Indian Railways locomotive taking water. h, Man on Indian Railways ZP Pacific Pulgeon. i, Worker cleaning smokebox.
No. 2781, 1000 le, vert.: a, LMS 8F 2-8-0, Great Central Railway. b, Rhodesia Railways 12 Class 4-8-2. c, DR German Railways 01 Class Pacific. d, Indian Railways McArthur 2-8-2. e, USATC 0-6-0T. f, China Railways KD6 2-8-0. g, Polish Feldbahn 0-8-0T. h, Indian Railways Mawd 2-8-2. i, North British 2-10-0.
No. 2782, 1000 le, vert.: a, B12 Class 4-6-0. b, Uruguay Railways Beyer Peacock Mogul 2-6-0. c, Ghana Railways Diesel-electric locomotive. d, Bagnall 0-4-0. e, Ledo Brickworks, Upper Assam. f, Train at Indian sugar mill. g, Carbon converter, Tangshan Locomotive Works, China. h, Crane loading timber on train car, Lanxiang, China. i, Worker carrying clay to train at Ledo Brickworks.
No. 2783, 5000 le, Ghan. No. 2784, 5000 le, Hudson Line. No. 2785, 5000 le, Blue Train. No. 2786, 5000 le, Bullet Train.

Perf. 13¼x13½, 13½x13¼
2004, Dec. 13
    Sheets of 9, #a-i
2779-2782 A454   Set of 4   30.00 30.00
Souvenir Sheets
2783-2786 A454   Set of 4   16.50 16.50

New Year 2005 (Year of the Rooster) — A455

No. 2787: a, Country name in blue. b, Country name in red.

2005, Feb. 23   Perf. 12
2787 A455 600 le Pair, #a-b   1.00 1.00
    Printed in sheets containing two pairs.

Pope John Paul II (1920-2005) and French President Jacques Chirac — A456

2005, May 24   Litho.   Perf. 13½x13¼
2788   A456   1800 le multi   1.60   1.60
Printed in sheet of 6.

Maimonides (1135-1204), Philosopher — A457

2005, May 24   Perf. 12
2789   A457   2000 le multi   1.75   1.75
Printed in sheets of 4.

Rotary International, Cent. — A458

No. 2790: a, Map, handshake. b, Map, people, "Service Above Self." c, Emblem. d, Founder Paul P. Harris.

2005, May 24   Perf. 12¾
2790   A458   1800 le Sheet of 4,
         #a-d   6.25   6.25

Expo 2005, Aichi, Japan — A459

No. 2791: a, Glacial polish, Toiyabe National Forest, Nevada. b, African gorilla. c, Rock climber, Yosemite Valley, California. d, Nassau grouper spawning, Caribbean Sea. e, Ladybug swarm. f, Evolution Valley, California.

2005, May 24   Perf. 12
2791   A459   1500 le Sheet of 6,
         #a-f   7.75   7.75

Hans Christian Andersen (1805-75), Author — A460

No. 2792: a, Little Claus and Big Claus. b, Little Ida's Flowers. c, The Tinderbox. 5000 le, The Princess and the Pea.

2005, May 24   Perf. 12¾
2792   A460   3000 le Sheet of 3,
         #a-c   7.75   7.75
Souvenir Sheet
Perf. 12
2793   A460   5000 le multi   4.25   4.25
No. 2792 contains three 42x28mm stamps.

Friedrich von Schiller (1759-1805), Writer — A461

No. 2794: a, Statue of Schiller, Berlin. b, Statue of Schiller, Munich. c, Statue of Schiller and Johann Wolfgang von Goethe. 5000 le, Schiller.

2005, May 24   Perf. 12¾
2794   A461   3000 le Sheet of 3,
         #a-c   7.75   7.75
Souvenir Sheet
2795   A461   5000 le multi   4.25   4.25

Jules Verne (1828-1905), Writer — A462

No. 2796: a, Verne's tomb, Amiens, France. b, Michael Arden, From the Earth to the Moon. c, Verne, Moon. 5000 le, Verne, hot air balloon.

2005, May 24
2796   A462   3000 le Sheet of 3,
         #a-c   7.75   7.75
Souvenir Sheet
2797   A462   5000 le multi   4.25   4.25

Battle of Trafalgar, Bicent. — A463

Paintings of various battle scenes: 500 le, 1000 le, 2000 le, 5000 le. 8000 le, Battle scene, diff.

2005, May 24   Perf. 12¾
2798-2801   A463   Set of 4   7.25   7.25
Souvenir Sheet
Perf. 12
2802   A463   8000 le multi   7.00   7.00

World War II Battles — A464

No. 2803, 2000 le, horiz. — Battle of Britain: a, Luftwaffe launches air strikes on Britain. b, Civilians take cover on underground station platform. c, Pilots race to planes. d, War in the sky.
No. 2804, 2000 le, horiz. — Battle of Stalingrad: a, Russians counterattack. b, Destroyed German tank. c, End of the German 6th Army. d, German prisoners of war.
No. 2805, 5000 le, Winston Churchill. No. 2806, 5000 le, Russian victory at Stalingrad, horiz.

2005, May 24   Perf. 13¼
Sheets of 4, #a-d
2803-2804   A464   Set of 2   14.00   14.00
Souvenir Sheets
2805-2806   A464   Set of 2   8.50   8.50

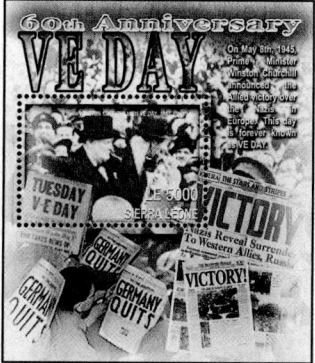

End of World War II, 60th Anniv. — A465

No. 2807, 2000 le: a, Franklin D. Roosevelt, Winston Churchill. b, Secretary of Defense Louis Johnson, Generals Douglas MacArthur and Omar Bradley. c, Meeting of Allied Expeditionary Force commanders. d, Winston Churchill.
No. 2808, 2000 le: a, Roosevelt's address to Congress after Pearl Harbor attack. b, "Little Boy" atomic bomb. c, "Fat Man" atomic bomb. d, Japanese surrender ceremony.
No. 2809, 5000 le, Winston Churchill on V-E Day. No. 2810, 5000 le, Women reading newspapers.

2005, May 24   Perf. 12¾
Sheets of 4, #a-d
2807-2808   A465   Set of 2   14.00   14.00
Souvenir Sheets
2809-2810   A465   Set of 2   8.50   8.50
The picture used for No. 2807b is not from the World War II era as Johnson was not Secretary of Defense until 1949.

Fire Fighting Apparatus — A466

Designs: 900 le, Boss Hoss Limited Edition fire motorcycle, German flag. 1200 le, Pumper

8 by 10, Austrian flag. 1500 le, Hydraulic platform truck, Germany. Ireland flag. 1800 le, Scania fire appliance, Australian flag.
No. 2815, 2000 le — Trucks from: a, Japan. b, Germany. c, Canada. d, Ireland.
No. 2816, 2000 le: a, Mercedes-Benz 2635 Thoma, Germany. b, 1997 Dennis Sabre water tender, Ireland. c, Microscopic fire truck, Japan. d, Scania fire appliance, Australia, diff.
No. 2817, 2000 le: a, 1935 Chevrolet fire truck. b, 1914 International fire truck. c, 1885 Chemical fire engine. d, 1963 Mason FD1.
No. 2818, 5000 le, Fire engine, US flag. No. 2819, 5000 le, 1890 horse-driven fire wagon, British flag.

2005, May 24   Perf. 12¾
2811-2814   A466   Set of 4   4.75   4.75
Sheets of 4, #a-d
2815-2817   A466   Set of 3   21.00   21.00
Souvenir Sheets
2818-2819   A466   Set of 2   8.50   8.50

Quesnard Lighthouse, Alderney — A467

2005, June 17
2820   A467   4500 le multi   4.00   4.00

Wedding of Prince Charles and Camilla Parker Bowles A468

Designs: No. 2821, 2000 le, Families of bride and groom. No. 2822, 2000 le, Charles and Camilla, vert. No. 2823, 2000 le, Charles, Camilla and bookstand, vert.

Perf. 13¼x13½, 13½x13¼
2005, Sept. 22   Litho.
2821-2823   A468   Set of 3   5.25   5.25

A469

Elvis Presley (1935-70) — A470

No. 2824, 2000 le — Elvis with microphone with background colors of: a, Blue. b, Dark green. c, Yellow green. d, Red and violet.
No. 2825, 2000 le — Elvis: a, Playing guitar, blue denomination. b, Holding guitar, pale olive denomination. c, Holding guitar, pink denomination. d, Playing guitar, lilac denomination.

2005, Dec. 1   Litho.   Perf. 13¼
Sheets of 4, #a-d
2824-2825   A469   Set of 2   13.50   13.50
Litho. & Embossed
Serpentine Die Cut 8¾
2826   A470   18,000 le gold &
         multi   15.50   15.50

Christmas — A471

Paintings: 500 le, The Virgin with Grapes, by Pierre Mignard. 1500 le, Adoration of the Shepherds, by Bartolomé Esteban Murillo. 2000 le, Madonna with the Child, by Murillo. 3000 le, Fountain of Life, by Hans Holbein, the Elder.

6000 le, Adoration of the Shepherds, by Murillo, diff.

2005, Dec. 13	**Litho.**	**Perf. 12½**	
2827-2830 A471	Set of 4	6.00	6.00

Souvenir Sheet

2831 A471	6000 le multi	5.25	5.25

Souvenir Sheet

Intl. Year of Microcredit — A472

No. 2832 — Woman at left and: a, Man and woman. b, Man holding stick. c, Man with scales. d, Woman and cow.

2005

2832 A472	2500 le Sheet of 4, #a-d	8.50 8.50

New Year 2006 (Year of the Dog) — A473

In its Position, by Xu Beihong: 600 le, Detail. 2000 le, Entire painting.

2006   **Perf. 13¼**

2833 A473	600 le multi	.50	.50

Souvenir Sheet
Perf. 11¼x11½

2834 A473	2000 le multi	1.75	1.75

No. 2833 printed in sheets of 4. No. 2834 contains one 26x60mm stamp.

Pope Benedict XVI — A474

2006, Jan. 24   **Perf. 13¼**

2835 A474	10,000 le multi	8.50 8.50

Printed in sheets of 4.

Miniature Sheet

Indian Chiefs — A475

No. 2836 — Chief and tribe: a, Medicine Crow, Crow. b, Quanah Parker, Comanche. c, Garfield, Jicarilla. d, Pretty Eagle, Crow. e, Plenty Coups, Crow. f, He Dog, Oglala. g, Crow King, Hunkpapa. h, Pontiac, Ottawa. i, Naiche, Chiricahua. j, Gall, Hunkpapa.

2006, Jan. 31

2836 A475	1250 le Sheet of 10, #a-j	11.00 11.00

Travels of Pope John Paul II in 2003-04 — A476

No. 2837, 2500 le: a, Madrid, Spain. b, Croatia. c, Banja Luka, Bosnia & Herzegovina. d, Slovakia.

No. 2838, 2500 le: a, Pompeii, Italy. b, Bern Switzerland. c, Lourdes, France. d, Loreto, Italy.

2006, Feb. 27   **Perf. 13½**
Sheets of 4, #a-d, + 4 Labels

2837-2838 A476	Set of 2	17.00 17.00

Children's Art — A477

No. 2839, 2000 le — Circus animals: a, Monkey. b, Red-toed elephant. c, Colored giraffe. d, Colored bird.

No. 2840, 2000 le — Reptiles: a, Green gecko. b, Frog. c, Spotted lizard. d, Orange lizard.

No. 2841, 2000 le — Flowers: a, Yellow flowers. b, Poppies. c, Orange flowers. d, Lilies.

2006   **Perf. 13¼**
Sheets of 4, #a-d

2839-2841 A477	Set of 3	21.00 21.00

2006 Winter Olympics, Turin A478

Designs: 1000 le, US #1146. 1300 le, Canada #1152. 2000 le, Poster for 1988 Calgary Winter Olympics. 3000 le, Poster for 1960 Squaw Valley Winter Olympics.

2006, Apr. 7	**Litho.**	**Perf. 13¼**	
2842-2845 A478	Set of 4	6.25	6.25

Messengers of Peace — A479

No. 2846: a, Michael Douglas, actor. b, United Nations Building, New York.

2006, May 29

2846 A479	2000 le Pair, #a-b	3.50 3.50

Printed in sheets containing 3 each #2846a-2846b.

Souvenir Sheet

US #300, Benjamin Franklin — A480

2006, May 29

2847 A480	6000 le multi	5.25 5.25

Washington 2006 World Stamp Exhibition.

Queen Elizabeth II, 80th Birthday — A481

No. 2848 — Queen wearing: a, Green hat. b, Blue hat. c, No hat. d, Yellow hat. 6000 le, Wearing tiara.

2006, June 13   **Perf. 14¼**

2848 A481	3000 le Sheet of 4, #a-d	10.50 10.50

Souvenir Sheet

2849 A481	6000 le multi	5.25 5.25

Souvenir Sheet

Ludwig Durr (1878-1956), Engineer, and Zeppelins — A482

No. 2850 — Durr and: a, Zeppelin L30. b, The Hindenburg. c, Graf Zeppelin.

2006, July 26   **Perf. 12¾**

2850 A482	4000 le Sheet of 3, #a-c	10.50 10.50

Rembrandt (1606-69), Painter A483

Designs: 800 le, Abraham Frans. 1000 le, The Rat Catcher. 2000 le, Young Man with Velvet Cap. 8000 le, The Flute Player.

No. 2855, 3000 le: a, Abraham and Isaac. b, Abraham Entertaining the Angels. c, Return of the Prodigal Son. d, Adam and Eve.

No. 2856, 3000 le — Details from The Night Watch: a, Man with black hat, neck ruffle and sash. b, Man holding gun below chin. c, Man with white hat. d, Man with red hat holding gun.

No. 2857, 6000 le, Portrait of an Amsterdam Citizen as a Militiaman. No. 2858, 6000 le, Maria Trip, Daughter of Alotte Adriaenson. No. 2859, 6000 le, Homer Dictating to a Scribe.

2006, July 26   **Perf. 12, 13¼ (#2855)**

2851-2854 A483	Set of 4	10.00 10.00

Sheets of 4, #a-d

2855-2856 A483	Set of 2	21.00 21.00

Imperf
Size: 70x100mm

2857-2859 A483	Set of 3	15.50 15.50

Souvenir Sheet

Elvis Presley (1935-77) — A484

No. 2860 — Presley in: a, White costume. b, Black and white cape. c, Army uniform. d, Blue jacket.

2006, Dec. 21   **Perf. 13¼**

2860 A484	2000 le Sheet of 4, #a-d	6.75 6.75

Christmas — A485

Details from Main Altar of the Jesuit Church, Antwerp, by Peter Paul Rubens: 1000 le, Angel. 1500 le, Madonna and Child. No. 2863, 2000 le, Angel, diff., with denomination in white at UL. 3000 le, Angel, diff.

No. 2865, 2000 le: a, Like 1000 le. b, Like 1500 le. c, Like No. 2863, with denomination in black at LR. d, Like 3000 le.

2006, Dec. 21   *Perf. 14*
2861-2864 A485   Set of 4   6.50 6.50
Souvenir Sheet
2865 A485 2000 le Sheet of 4,
         #a-d   6.75 6.75

Souvenir Sheet

Wolfgang Amadeus Mozart (1756-91),
Composer — A486

2006, Dec. 21   **Litho.**   *Perf. 13¼*
2866 A486 7000 le multi   6.00 6.00

Miniature Sheets

Pres. John F. Kennedy (1917-
63) — A487

No. 2867, 2000 le — Kennedy: a, At microphones on inauguration day. b, Portrait and cover of inaugural program. c, Taking oath, medal depicting Kennedy. d, And Robert Frost and poem.

No. 2868, 2000 le: a, Kennedy and map of Cuba. b, Map of US, Soviet Premier Nikita Khrushchev, and Soviet R-12 missile. c, Map of Cuba, Kennedy meeting with Soviet Foreign Minister Andrei Gromyko. d, Cuban President Fidel Castro, John and Robert Kennedy.

2006, Dec. 21   *Perf. 13¼*
Sheets of 4, #a-d
2867-2868 A487   Set of 2   14.00 14.00

Miniature Sheet

Marilyn Monroe (1926-62),
Actress — A488

No. 2869: a, With hand on shoulder. b, With straps of brown dress showing. c, With hand behind head. d, Leaning to left.

2006, Dec. 21
2869 A488 2000 le Sheet of 4,
         #a-d   7.00 7.00

Space Achievements — A489

No. 2870: a, Mir Space Station. b, Space Shuttle Challenger. c, Giotto Comet Probe. d, Luna 9. e, Viking 1. f, International Space Station.

No. 2871, 3000 le: a, Launch of Boeing Delta II rocket. b, Calipso. c, CloudSat. d, Aura, Parasol, Calipso, CloudSat, Aqua and OCO satellites in orbit.

No. 2872, 3000 le, vert. — Artist's conceptions of: a, NASA's crew launch. b, New spacecraft to rendezvous with International Space Station. c, New lunar lander. d, Parachutes deploying after reentry.

No. 2873, 3000 le, vert. — Photos of International Space Station from: a, June 3, 1999. b, Dec. 2, 2000. c, June 15, 2002. d, Aug. 6, 2005.

No. 2874, 6000 le, Apollo 11 Lunar Module. No. 2875, 6000 le, Impactor with Deep Impact Probe. No. 2876, 6000 le, Mars Reconnaissance Orbiter. No. 2877, 6000 le, Space Shuttle Columbia, vert.

2006, Dec. 21
2870 A489 2000 le Sheet of 6,
         #a-f   10.50 10.50
Sheets of 4, #a-d
2871-2873 A489   Set of 3   32.50 32.50
Souvenir Sheets
2874-2877 A489   Set of 4   21.00 21.00

New Year
2007
(Year of
the Pig)
A490

2007, Jan. 3   *Perf. 13¼*
2878 A490 2000 le multi   1.75 1.75
Printed in sheets of 4.

Scouting, Cent. — A491

Designs: 3000 le, Dove, inscriptions in various languages. 6000 le, Dove, inscriptions in various languages, symbols.

2007, Feb. 15
2879 A491 3000 le multi   2.60 2.60
Souvenir Sheet
2880 A491 6000 le multi   5.25 5.25

No. 2867 was printed in sheets of 4 with stamps having slightly different gradations of background color.

Princess Diana (1961-97) — A492

No. 2881, vert. — Diana wearing: a, Yellow dress, country name in red. b, Blue dress, country name in red. c, White dress, country name in green at bottom. d, Yellow dress, country name in green. e, No dress shown, country name in red. f, White dress, country name in green at top.
7000 le, Diana with blue hat.

2007, Mar. 15   **Litho.**   *Perf. 13¼*
2881 A492 1500 le Sheet of 6,
         #a-f   7.75 7.75
Souvenir Sheet
2882 A492 7000 le multi   6.00 6.00

Concorde — A493

No. 2883, 2000 le: a, Air speed indicator showng speed record. b, Concorde in flight.

No. 2884, 2000 le, horiz.: a, Concorde, Royal Air Force Red Arrows and British flag. b, Concorde over Buckingham Palace.

2007, Mar. 15   **Litho.**
Pairs, #a-b
2883-2884 A493   Set of 2   7.00 7.00

Nos. 2883-2884 each printed in sheets containing three of each stamp.

Pope Benedict
XVI — A494

2007, July 12
2885 A494 1500 le multi   1.00 1.00
Printed in sheets of 8.

Miniature Sheet

Ferrari Automobiles, 60th
Anniv. — A495

No. 2886: a, 1948 166 Inter. b, 2004 612 Scaguetti. c, 1995 F50. d, 2000 550 Barchetta Pininfarina. e, 1957 250 GT Cabriolet. f, 1963 250 P. g, 1961 246 SP. h, 1981 126 CK.

2007, July 12
2886 A495 1400 le Sheet of 8,
         #a-h   7.75 7.75

Christmas
A496

Painting details: 1000 le, The Annunciation, by Raphael. 1500 le, The Adoration of the Magi, by Raphael. 2000 le, The Presentation of the Christ Child in the Temple, by Raphael. 3000 le, The Nativity and the Arrival of the Magi, by Giovanni di Pietro.

2007, Nov. 28   *Perf. 14¾x14*
2887-2890 A496   Set of 4   5.00 5.00

Miniature Sheet

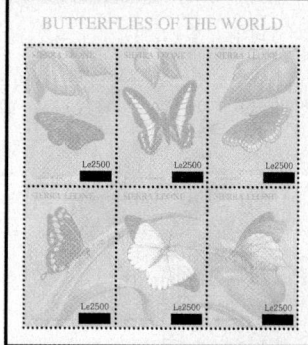

2008 Summer Olympics,
Beijing — A497

No. 2891 — 1956 Melbourne Summer Olympics: a, Murray Rose, swimming gold medalist. b, Poster for 1956 Summer Olympics. c, Vladimir Kuts, track gold medalist. d, Laszlo Papp, boxing gold medalist.

2008, Jan. 8   **Litho.**   *Perf. 14*
2891 A497 1500 le Sheet of 4,
         #a-d   4.00 4.00

Nos. 975-977,
980-981
Surcharged

Methods and Perfs. As Before
2008, Mar. 10
2892 A142 800 le on 3 le #975   .55   .55
2893 A142 800 le on 5 le #976   .55   .55
2894 A142 800 le on 8 le #977   .55   .55
2895 A142 800 le on 20 le #980   .55   .55
2896 A142 800 le on 35 le #981   .55   .55
     Nos. 2892-2896 (5)   2.75 2.75

Nos. 2049-2050 Surcharged

Methods and Perfs. As Before
2008, Mar. 10
2897 A281 2500 le on 500 le
         Sheet of
         6, #a-f,
         #2049   10.00 10.00
2898 A281 2500 le on 600 le
         Sheet of
         6, #a-f,
         #2050   10.00 10.00

Nos. 2120-2121 Surcharged

Methods and Perfs. As Before
2008, Mar. 10

2899	A292	2800 le on 300 le Sheet of 6, #a-f, #2120	11.50 11.50
2900	A292	4000 le on 300 le Sheet of 6, #a-f, #2121	16.00 16.00

No. 2138 Surcharged

Methods and Perfs As Before
2008, Mar. 10

2901	A297	2800 le on 1500 le Sheet of 3, #a-c	5.75 5.75

No. 2193 Surcharged

Methods and Perfs As Before
2008, Mar. 10

2902	A305	2800 le on 600 le Sheet of 8, #a-h, #2193	15.00 15.00

Nos. 1738a-1738d Surcharged

Methods and Perfs. As Before
2008, Mar. 10

2903		Vert. strip of 4	9.75 9.75
a.	A227	3500 le on 50 le #1738a	2.40 2.40
b.	A227	3500 le on 100 le #1738b	2.40 2.40
c.	A227	3500 le on 150 le #1738c	2.40 2.40
d.	A227	3500 le on 200 le #1738d	2.40 2.40

No. 2132
Surcharged

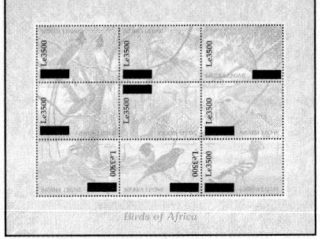

Methods and Perfs. As Before
2008, Mar. 10

2904	A295	3500 le on 600 le #2132	2.40 2.40

No. 2241 Surcharged

Methods and Perfs. As Before
2008, Mar. 10

2905	A317	3500 le on 600 le Sheet of 9, #a-i, #2241	21.00 21.00

Nos. 586-589 Surcharged

Methods and Perfs. As Before
2008, Mar. 10

2906	A85	4000 le on 6c #586	2.75 2.75
2907	A85	4000 le on 10c #587	2.75 2.75
2908	A85	4000 le on 31c #588	2.75 2.75
2909	A85	4000 le on 60c #589	2.75 2.75
		Nos. 2906-2909 (4)	11.00 11.00

No. 2752 Surcharged in Black and Red

Methods and Perfs. As Before
2008, Mar. 10

2910	A443	4000 le on 1000 le Block of 4, #a-d, #2752	11.00 11.00

2008 World Stamp Championship, Israel — A498

2008, May 14		**Litho.**	**Imperf.**
2911	A498	7500 le multi	5.25 5.25

Miniature Sheet

Discovery and Exploration of Oregon — A499

No. 2912: a, Joel Palmer locates pass through the Cascades (30x50mm). b, Sir Francis Drake, first European to view Oregon coast, horiz. (40x25mm). c, Capt. Robert Gray, discoverer of the Columbia River, horiz. (40x25mm), d, Meriwether Lewis, William Clark and Multnomah Falls (30x50mm).

2008, June 13			**Perf. 13¼**
2912	A499	1500 le Sheet of 4, #a-d	4.25 4.25

2008 National Topical Stamp Show, Portland, Oregon.

Wedding of Queen Elizabeth II and Prince Philip, 60th Anniv. — A500

No. 2913: a, Couple. b, Queen.

2008, June 19			
2913	A500	1500 le Pair, #a-b	2.10 2.10

Printed in sheets containing three of each stamp.

32nd America's Cup Yacht Races — A501

Various yachts with large panel in: a, Blue. b, Orange. c, Red. d, Olive brown.

2008, June 19			
2914		Strip of 4	8.00 8.00
a.	A501	200 le multi	.25 .25
b.	A501	500 le multi	.35 .35
c.	A501	1000 le multi	.70 .70
d.	A501	10,000 le multi	6.75 6.75

Seven Wonders of the Modern World — A502

No. 2915, vert.: a, Statue of Christ the Redeemer, Brazil. b, Roman Colosseum, Italy. c, Great Wall of China. d, Machu Picchu, Peru. e, Petra, Jordan. f, Chichén Itzá, Mexico. 7000 le, Taj Mahal, India.

2008, June 19			
2915	A502	1500 le Sheet of 6, #a-f	6.25 6.25

Souvenir Sheet

2916	A502	7000 le multi	4.75 4.75

Khilafat Ahmadiyya, Cent. — A503

Denominations: 800 le, 1000 le, 2000 le, 3000 le.

2008, June 20			**Perf. 12¾**
2917-2920	A503	Set of 4	4.75 4.75

A504

Elvis Presley (1935-77) — A505

No. 2921 — Presley: a, Both shoulders showing. b, Right shoulder showing. c, Left shoulder showing.

No. 2922: a, Denomination in yellow green, country name in blue. b, Denomination in red, country name in yellow green. c, Denomination in blue, country name in red. d, Denomination in blue, country name in yellow green. e, Denomination in yellow green, country name in red. f, Denomination in red, country name in blue.

2008, Oct. 28   **Perf. 11½**
2921   Horiz. strip of 3   3.00   3.00
a.-c.   A504 1500 le Any single   1.00   1.00
                                    Perf. 13¼
2922 A505 1500 le Sheet of 6,
                          #a-f   6.00   6.00
No. 2921 was printed in sheets containing
two of each stamp.

Intl. Polar Year — A506

No. 2923 — Penguins with background
color of: a, Red. b, Purple. c, Blue green. d,
Orange.
7000 le, Penguins on ice.

2008, Oct. 28   **Perf. 13¼**
2923 A506 3000 le Sheet of 4,
                          #a-d   8.00   8.00
                         Souvenir Sheet
2924 A506 7000 le multi   4.75   4.75

Christmas
A507

Designs: 1000 le, Nativity. 1500 le, Virgin
Mary and Jesus. 2000 le, Joseph and Jesus.
3000 le, Angels and Jesus.

2008, Dec. 11   **Perf. 14¼x14¾**
2925-2928 A507 Set of 4   5.00   5.00

Inauguration of
Barack Obama as
US
President — A508

2009, Jan. 20   **Perf. 12¼x11¾**
2929 A508 3000 le multi   2.00   2.00
      Printed in sheets of 4.

Miniature Sheets

Space Exploration, 50th Anniv. (in
2007) — A509

No. 2930, 2200 le: a, Martian North Pole
dust storms. b, Saturn. c, Jupiter's atmos-
phere. d, Craters on Mercury. e, Venus. f,
Mercury.
No. 2931, 2200 le, horiz.: a, Spitzer Space
Telescope. b, Galaxy M81. c, Hubble Space
Telescope. d, Evil Eye Galaxy (M64). e, Cat's
Eye Nebula. f, Hoag's Object.
No. 2932, 3000 le: a, Apollo 11 Lunar Mod-
ule. b, Mercury Redstone rocket. c, Space
Shuttle Atlantis on launch pad. d, Space Shut-
tle Endeavour.
No. 2933, 3000 le, horiz.: a, Sun shining,
astronaut. b, South Pole of the Sun. c, Solar
eruption. d, Solar eclipse.

2009, Jan. 27   **Perf. 12**
      Sheets of 6, #a-f
2930-2931 A509   Set of 2   17.00 17.00
      Sheets of 4, #a-d
2932-2933 A509   Set of 2   15.50 15.50
      Miniature Sheet

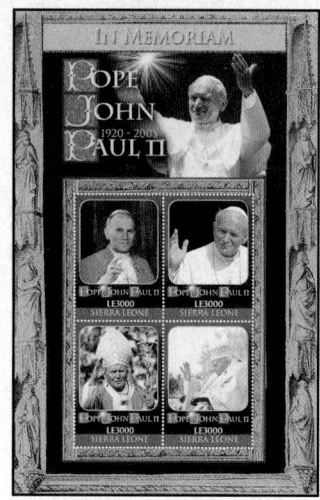

Pope John Paul II (1920-
2005) — A510

No. 2934 — Color of vestments: a, Red. b,
White. c, Green. d, Yellow.

2009, Feb. 4   **Litho.**   **Perf. 13¼**
2934 A510 3000 le Sheet of 4,
                          #a-d   7.75   7.75

Yi Jianlian,
National
Basketball
Association
Player — A511

No. 2935: a, Wearing white uniform, holding
basketball. b, Wearing dark uniform, holding
basketball. c, Wearing white uniform, without
basketball.

2009, Feb. 20
2935   Vert. strip of 3   3.00   3.00
a.-c.   A511 1500 le Any single   1.00   1.00
Printed in sheets of 6, containing two each
Nos. 2935a-2935c.

      Miniature Sheets

A512

A513

China 2009 World Stamp Exhibition,
Luoyang — A514

No. 2936 — Art of Chang Dai-chien (1899-
1983): a, Landscape of Yangshuo. b, Scholar
Admiring Plum Blossoms. c, The Golden Sum-
mit of Mount Emei. d, Lotuses After the Rain.
No. 2937 — Chinese landmarks: a, Temple
of Heaven, Beijing. b, Dalian Exhibition
Center, Dalian. c, Xian South Gate, Shaanxi
Province. d, National Grand Theater, Beijing.
No. 2938 — Sports: a, Javelin. b, Fencing.
c, Soccer. d, Weight lifting.

2009   **Litho.**   **Perf. 12¾**
2936 A512 1500 le Sheet of 4,
                          #a-d   4.00   4.00
                                    Perf. 12½
2937 A513 1500 le Sheet of 4,
                          #a-d   4.00   4.00
                                    Perf. 11½
2938 A514 2000 le Sheet of 4,
                          #a-d   5.25   5.25
Issued: No. 2938, 2/16; Nos. 2936-2937,
4/10.

Peonies
A515

2009, Apr. 10   **Perf. 13¼**
2939 A515 1500 le multi   .95   .95
      Printed in sheets of 6.

      Miniature Sheet

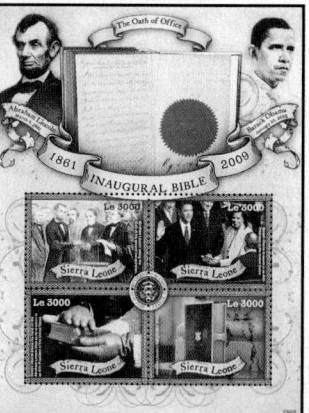

U.S. Inaugural Bibles of 1861 and
2009 — A516

No. 2940: a, Abraham Lincoln taking oath of
office, 1861. b, Barack Obama taking oath of
office, 2009. c, Obama's hand on Bible. d, Lincoln's inaugural Bible.

2009, May 14   **Perf. 11½**
2940 A516 3000 le Sheet of 4,
                          #a-d   7.50   7.50
      Miniature Sheet

Elvis Presley (1935-77) — A517

No. 2941 — Presley and: a, Light blue
denomination, purple background. b, Yellow
denomination, brown background. c, Light
blue denomination, green and black background. d, Yellow denomination, dull purple
background.

2009, May 14   **Perf. 13¼**
2941 A517 3000 le Sheet of 4,
                          #a-d   7.50   7.50
      Miniature Sheet

George Frideric Handel (1685-1759),
Composer — A518

No. 2942: a, Handel's birthplace, Halle, Germany. b, Foundling Hospital where Handel
directed concerts. c, Portrait of Handel, by
Thomas Hudson. d, Ranelagh Gardens. e,
Statue of Handel, by Louis-François Roubiliac.
f, Farinelli and Senesino from opera, "Flavio."

2009, May 14   **Perf. 11½**
2942 A518 2500 le Sheet of 6,
                          #a-f   9.50   9.50
      Miniature Sheets

2009 National Basketball Association
All-Star Teams — A519

No. 2943, 1250 le — Eastern Division All-
Stars: a, Ray Allen. b, Kevin Garnett. c, Danny
Granger. d, Devin Harris. e, Dwight Howard. f,
Allen Iverson. g, LeBron James. h, Joe John-
son. i, Rashard Lewis. j, Paul Pierce. k,
Dwayne Wade. l, Mo Williams.
No. 2944, 1250 le — Western Division All-
Stars: a, Chauncey Billups. b, Kobe Bryant. c,
Tim Duncan. d, Pau Gasol. e, Yao Ming. f, Dirk
Nowitzki. g, Shaquille O'Neal. h, Tony Parker.
i, Chris Paul. j, Brandon Ray. k, Amare
Stoudemire. l, David West.

2009, May 14   **Perf. 14¼x14¾**
Sheets of 12, #a-l
2943-2944   A519   Set of 2   19.00 19.00

Miniature Sheet

Ferrari Race Cars — A520

No. 2945: a, 1977 312 T2. b, 1982 126 C2. c, 1983 126 C3. d, 2007 F2007.

2009, July 6   **Perf. 14¼**
2945   A520   3000 le Sheet of 4,   7.50 7.50
        #a-d

Miniature Sheet

First Man on the Moon, 40th Anniv. — A521

No. 2946: a, Apollo 11 Command and Lunar Modules. b, Astronaut Neil Armstrong. c, Apollo 11 plaque. d, Apollo 11 Command Module. e, Apollo 11 Lunar Module. f, Apollo 11 crew in quarantine.

2009, July 20   **Litho.**   **Perf. 13¼**
2946   A521   2500 le Sheet of 6,   8.75 8.75
        #a-f

Souvenir Sheet

35th G8 Summit, L'Aquila, Italy — A522

2009, Sept. 30
2947   A522   8000 le multi   4.25 4.25

Miniature Sheet

Pope Benedict XVI — A523

No. 2948 — Pope Benedict XVI: a, 2600 le, Facing forward. b, 2600 le, Facing left. c, 2800 le, As "a." d, 2800 le, As "b."

2009, Sept. 30   **Perf. 11½**
2948   A523   Sheet of 4, #a-d   5.75 5.75

Miniature Sheets

Dogs — A524

No. 2949, 3000 le — Cavalier King Charles spaniel: a, In front of fence. b, In bucket. c, With head on ground. d, With flowers at left.
No. 2950, 3000 le — English Springer spaniel: a, On wooden planks. b, Head. c, Standing. d, In front of overturned bucket.

2009, Sept. 30   **Perf. 11½x12**
Sheets of 4, #a-d
2949-2950   A524   Set of 2   13.00 13.00

Cats A525

Designs: 1000 le, Birman lilac point. 1500 le, Singapura sepia agouti. No. 2953, 2000 le, Scottish Fold blue tortie tabby and white. 3000 le, Asian Shaded lilac shaded silver.
No. 2955, 2000 le: a, Somali lilac. b, British Angora red shaded silver. c, Maine coon Maine wave. d, Turkish Van tortie and white.

2009, Sept. 30   **Perf. 14¾x14¼**
2951-2954   A525   Set of 4   4.00 4.00
2955   A525   2000 le Sheet of 4,   4.25 4.25
        #a-d

A526

Wildlife — A527

Designs: 1000 le, Giraffe. 1500 le, Bonobo. No. 2958, 2000 le, African bush elephant. 3000 le, Zebra.
No. 2960, 2000 le: a, Cheetah. b, Red colobus monkey. c, Hippopotamus. d, Lion.

2009, Sept. 30   **Perf. 14**
2956-2959   A526   Set of 4   4.00 4.00
2960   A527   2000 le Sheet of 4,   4.25 4.25
        #a-d

A528

Birds — A529

Designs: 1000 le, Pied kingfisher. 1500 le, House sparrow. No. 2963, 2000 le, Skylark. 3000 le, Black-chested snake-eagle.
No. 2965, 2000 le: a, Greenfinch. b, Pangani longclaw. c, Barn swallow. d, Namaqua sandgrouse.

2009, Sept. 30   **Perf. 14¾x14¼**
2961-2964   A528   Set of 4   4.00 4.00
2965   A529   2000 le Sheet of 4,   4.25 4.25
        #a-d

A530

Orchids — A531

Designs: 1000 le, Penthea filicornis. No. 2967, 1500 le, Herschelia graminifolia. 2000 le, Satyrium princeps. 3000 le, Herschelia charpentieriana.
No. 2970, 1500 le: a, Eulophia quartiniana. b, Ansellia gigantea. c, Angraecum infundibulare. d, Disperis capensis. e, Bartholina burmanniana. f, Disa uniflora.

2009, Sept. 30   **Perf. 14¼x14¾**
2966-2969   A530   Set of 4   4.00 4.00
       Perf. 14¾x14¼
2970   A531   1500 le Sheet of 6,   5.00 5.00
        #a-f

A532

Mushrooms — A533

Designs: 1000 le, Fringed panaeolus. 1500 le, Orange latex lactarius. 2000 le, Purple laccaria. 3000 le, Liver lactarius.
No. 2975: a, Death cap. b, Cinnabar polypore. c, King bolete. d, Panther amanita. e, Fly amanita. f, Mica inky cap.

2009, Sept. 30   **Perf. 14**
2971-2974   A532   Set of 4   4.00 4.00
       Perf. 14¾x14¼
2975   A533   1700 le Sheet of 6,   5.50 5.50

Chinese Aviation, Cent. — A534

No. 2976 — Feng Ru (1884-1912), pilot: a, And newspaper story. b, With airplane in Auckland. c, With airplane in 1912. d, And Feng Ru II airplane.
7500 le, Feng Ru and airplane.

2009, Nov. 12   **Perf. 14¼**
2976   A534   2700 le Sheet of 4,   5.75 5.75
        #a-d

Souvenir Sheet

2977   A534   7500 le multi   4.00 4.00

Aeropex 2009, Beijing. No. 2976 contains four 42x28mm stamps.

Miniature Sheet

The Three Stooges — A535

No. 2978 — Moe, Larry and Curly: a, Looking over the back of a sofa. b, Holding bottles. c, With wringer washer. d, Holding glasses.

2009, Dec. 9   **Perf. 11½x11¼**
2978   A535   2700 le Sheet of 4,   5.50 5.50
        #a-d

Bridges — A536

No. 2979: a, Tower Bridge, London. b, Hangzhou Bay Bridge, Zhejiang, China. c, Juscelino Kubitschek Bridge, Brasilia, Brazil. d, Sydney Harbour Bridge, Sydney. e, Ponte Vecchio, Florence, Italy. f, Bosporus Bridge, Istanbul.
7000 le, Golden Gate Bridge, San Francisco.

2009, Dec. 9
2979   A536   2000 le Sheet of 6,   6.25 6.25
        #a-f
      Souvenir Sheet
2980   A536   7000 le multi   3.75 3.75

Miniature Sheet

Chinese Zodiac Animals — A537

No. 2981: a, Rat. b, Ox. c, Tiger. d, Rabbit. e, Dragon. f, Snake. g, Horse. h, Ram. i, Monkey. j, Rooster. k, Dog. l, Pig.

2010, Jan. 4		Litho.	Perf. 12
2981	A537	800 le Sheet of 12,	
	#a-l		5.00 5.00

Souvenir Sheet

New Year 2010 (Year of the Tiger) — A538

No. 2982 — Tiger with denomination at: a, Right. b, Left.

2010, Jan. 4		Perf. 11½x12
2982	A538	8000 le Sheet of 2,
	#a-b	8.25 8.25

Flag, Coat of Arms and Title of National Anthem of Sierra Leone A539

2010, Mar. 1		Perf. 13½
2983	A539	2000 le multi	1.10 1.10

Pres. Abraham Lincoln (1809-65) A540

2010, Mar. 1		Perf. 12x11½
2984	A540	2700 le multi	1.40 1.40

Printed in sheets of 4.

Miniature Sheet

Election of Pres. John F. Kennedy, 50th Anniv. — A541

No. 2985 — Kennedy: a, Standing in limousine. b, Pointing. c, Sitting in chair. d, On campaign button.

2010, Mar. 1		Perf. 12x11½
2985	A541	4000 le Sheet of 4,
	#a-d	8.50 8.50

Miniature Sheet

Charles Darwin (1809-82), Naturalist — A542

No. 2986: a, Darwin's frog. b, Darwin's fox. c, Galapagos tortoise. d, Galapagos marine iguana.

2010, Mar. 1		Perf. 13¼
2986	A542	2500 le Sheet of 4,
	#a-d	5.25 5.25

A543

A544

A545

A546

Elvis Presley (1935-77) — A547

No. 2987 — Presley: a, Holding microphone on stand. b, With arm raised and other on neck of guitar. c, With hand resting on guitar. d, Singing, not holding microphone.

2010, Mar. 1		Perf. 11½x12
2987	A543	2700 le Sheet of 4,
	#a-d	5.75 5.75

Souvenir Sheets
Perf. 13¼

2988	A544	8000 le multi	4.25 4.25
2989	A545	8000 le multi	4.25 4.25
2990	A546	8000 le multi	4.25 4.25
2991	A547	8000 le multi	4.25 4.25
	Nos. 2988-2991 (4)		17.00 17.00

Teams Participating in 2010 World Cup Soccer Championships, South Africa — A548

Team and flag of: No. 2992, 1900 le, Algeria. No. 2993, 1900 le, Argentina. No. 2994, 1900 le, Australia. No. 2995, 1900 le, Brazil. No. 2996, 1900 le, Cameroun. No. 2997, 1900 le, Chile. No. 2998, 1900 le, Denmark. No. 2999, 1900 le, England. No. 3000, 1900 le, France. No. 3001, 1900 le, Germany. No. 3002, 1900 le, Ghana. No. 3003, 1900 le, Greece. No. 3004, 1900 le, Honduras. No. 3005, 1900 le, Italy. No. 3006, 1900 le, Ivory Coast. No. 3007, 1900 le, Japan. No. 3008, 1900 le, North Korea. No. 3009, 1900 le, South Korea. No. 3010, 1900 le, Mexico. No. 3011, 1900 le, Netherlands. No. 3012, 1900 le, New Zealand. No. 3013, 1900 le, Nigeria. No. 3014, 1900 le, Paraguay. No. 3015, 1900 le, Portugal. No. 3016, 1900 le, Serbia. No. 3017, 1900 le, Slovakia. No. 3018, 1900 le, Slovenia. No. 3019, 1900 le, South Africa. No. 3020, 1900 le, Spain. No. 3021, 1900 le, Switzerland. No. 3022, 1900 le, United States. No. 3023, 1900 le, Uruguay.

2010, Mar. 1		Perf. 14¼
2992-3023	A548	Set of 32	32.00 32.00

Nos. 2992-3023 each were printed in sheets of 6.

Miniature Sheets

A549

Pope John Paul II (1920-2005) — A550

No. 3024 — Country name in yellow with Pope John Paul II: a, Waving. b, Wearing miter with large cross. c, Wearing miter with central panel of hexagons and triangles. d, With candlestick at right.

No. 3025 — Country name in black with Pope John Paul II: a, Praying. b, Wearing red vestments. c, With both arms raised. d, Wearing miter.

2010, Apr. 26		Perf. 11½x12
3024	A549	4000 le Sheet of 4,
	#a-d	8.25 8.25
3025	A550	4000 le Sheet of 4,
	#a-d	8.25 8.25

Miniature Sheets

A551

Michael Jackson (1958-2009),
Singer — A552

No. 3026 — Blue background with Jackson:
a, Looking right. b, Holding microphone with
silver head. c, Holding microphone with black
head. d, Wearing red shirt.
No. 3027 — Purple background with Jackson: a, Facing left, wearing shiny costume. b,
Wearing white jacket. c, With head raised. d,
Holding microphone.

2010, Apr. 26   *Perf. 12*
3026 A551 4000 le Sheet of 4,
     #a-d   8.25   8.25
3027 A552 4000 le Sheet of 4,
     #a-d   8.25   8.25

Miniature Sheets

A553

Boy Scouts of America, Cent. — A554

No. 3028 — Eagle-shaped cloud and: a,
Eagle Scout badge, Dog Care, Small Boat
Sailing, Law and Botany merit badges. b,
Eagle Scout badge, Astronomy, Energy, The-
ater and Home Repairs merit badges. c, Boy
Scouts of America emblem, Scout holding
branch.
No. 3029: a, Badges for Tenderfoot, Second
Class and First Class Scout ranks. b, Badges
for Star, Life and Eagle Scout ranks. c, Boy
Scouts of America emblem, Scout holding
branch, eagle-shaped cloud.

2010, Apr. 26   *Perf. 13¼*
3028 A553 4000 le Sheet of 4,
     #3028a-
     3028b, 2
     #3028c   8.25   8.25
3029 A554 4000 le Sheet of 4,
     #3029a-
     3029b, 2
     #3029c   8.25   8.25

Butterflies — A555

No. 3030: a, Protogoniomorpha parhassus.
b, Kallimoides rumia rumia. c, Precis pelarga.
d, Salamis cacta cacta.
No. 3031, 6000 le: a, Hypolimnas misippus.
b, Hypolimnas salmacis salmacis.
No. 3032, 6000 le: a, Junonia sophia
sophia. b, Junonia oenone.

2010, Apr. 26   *Perf. 12*
3030 A555 4000 le Sheet of 4,
     #a-d   8.25   8.25
   Souvenir Sheets of 2, #a-b
3031-3032 A555   Set of 2   12.50 12.50

Girl Guides, Cent. — A556

No. 3033 — Pictures of Girl Guides of the
past in frames and: a, Three Girl Guides. b,
Two Girl Guides blowing bubbles, Girl Guide
wearing balloon sculpture. c, Four Girl Guides.
d, Eight Girl Guides.
8000 le, Brownie saluting, vert.

2010, June 17   *Perf. 11½x12*
3033 A556 2700 le Sheet of 4,
     #a-d   5.50   5.50
     Souvenir Sheet
     Perf. 11½
3034 A556 8000 le multi   4.25   4.25

Henri Dunant (1828-1910), Founder of
the Red Cross — A557

No. 3035 — Dunant, Red Cross and: a, Harriet Beecher Stowe (1811-96), writer. b,
Charles Dickens (1812-70), writer. c, Bertha
von Suttner (1843-1914), writer. d, Victor
Hugo (1802-85), writer.
10,000 le, Dunant and Frédéric Passy
(1822-1912), co-winner of 1901 Nobel Peace
Prize.

2010, Oct. 14   *Perf. 11½x12*
3035 A557 4000 le Sheet of 4,
     #a-d   7.75   7.75
     Souvenir Sheet
     Perf. 11½
3036 A557 10,000 le multi   5.00   5.00

Miniature Sheets

A558

Mother Teresa (1910-97),
Humanitarian — A559

No. 3037 — Mother Teresa at left with: a,
Five children, child at left in red. b, Three children. c, Five children, all with head coverings.
d, With four children.
No. 3025 — Mother Teresa: a, Holding child
and wrapping hand around another child. b,
Speaking to woman. c, Holding child. d, Holding baby, children near hut.

2010, Oct. 14   *Perf. 13x13¼*
3037 A558 4000 le Sheet of 4,
     #a-d   7.75   7.75
3038 A559 4000 le Sheet of 4,
     #a-d   7.75   7.75

Princess Diana (1961-97) — A560

No. 3039 — Background color: a, Red vio-
let. b, Green. c, Blue violet. d, Orange.
No. 3040, 10,000 le, Red violet background.
No. 3041, 10,000 le, Blue violet background.

2010, Oct. 14   *Perf. 12*
3039 A560 4000 le Sheet of 4,
     #a-d   7.75   7.75
     Souvenir Sheets
3040-3041 A560   Set of 2   9.75   9.75

     Souvenir Sheet

New Year 2011 (Year of the
Rabbit) — A561

No. 3042 — Rabbit with: a, Head lowered.
b, Head raised.

2010, Nov. 7
3042 A561 6000 le Sheet of 2,
     #a-b   5.75   5.75

Miniature Sheets

Chinese Emperors — A562

No. 3043: a, Text "Emperor / Gaozu / Han
Dynasty" and Chinese characters. b, Portrait
of Emperor Gaozu (c. 256-195 B.C).
No. 3044: a, Text "Emperor / Hongwu / Ming
Dynasty" and Chinese characters. b, Color
portrait of Emperor Hongwu (1328-98). c, Ink
drawing of Emperor Hongwu. d, Empress Ma
(1333-82).
No. 3045: a, Text "Emperor / Kangxi / Qing
Dynasty" and Chinese characters. b, Emperor
Kangxi (1654-1722), wearing purple robe. c,
Emperor Kangxi on throne. d, Emperor Kangxi
holding calligrapher's brush.

2010, Nov. 7   *Perf. 12*
3043 A562 3000 le Sheet of 4,
     #3043a, 3
     #3043b   5.75   5.75
3044 A562 3000 le Sheet of 4,
     #a-d   5.75   5.75
3045 A562 3000 le Sheet of 4,
     #a-d   5.75   5.75
    Nos. 3043-3045 (3)   17.25 17.25
   China 2010 World Philatelic Exhibition,
Beijing.

Miniature Sheets

A563

Pope John Paul II (1920-
2005) — A564

No. 3046 — Denominations at left with Pope
John Paul II: a, Wearing miter with large cross.
b, Wearing zucchetto and red vestments,
denomination in black. c, Wearing zucchetto
and red vestments, denomination in orange. d,
Wearing miter with central panel of hexagons
and triangles.
No. 3047 — Denominations at right with
Pope John Paul II: a, Holding cross. b, Waving. c, Wearing red vestments. d, Praying.

2010, Dec. 30   *Perf. 12*
3046 A563 2700 le Sheet of 4,
     #a-d   5.25   5.25
3047 A564 2700 le Sheet of 4,
     #a-d   5.25   5.25

Miniature Sheets

A565

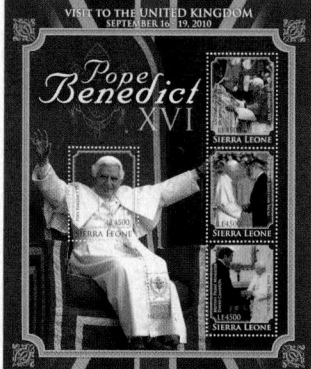

Visit of Pope Benedict XVI to United
Kingdom — A566

No. 3048 — Pope Benedict XVI: a, At Cotton Park, Birmingham. b, At Hyde Park, London. c, Celebrating mass at Westminster Cathedral, London. d, Waving at Westminster Abbey, London.
No. 3049 — Pope Benedict XVI: a, Meeting Archbishop of Canterbury Rowan Williams. b, Seated. c, Meeting Chief Rabbi Jonathan Sacks. d, Meeting British Prime Minister David Cameron.

2010, Dec. 30   Perf. 12x12½
3048 A565 4500 le Sheet of 4,
             #a-d   8.75 8.75
        Perf. 12x11½
3049 A566 4500 le Sheet of 4,
             #a-d   8.75 8.75

Souvenir Sheets

Popes and Their Coats of
Arms — A567

No. 3050, 14,000 le: a, Pope Paul VI. b, Arms of Pope Paul VI.
No. 3051, 14,000 le: a, Pope John Paul I. b, Arms of Pope John Paul I.

2010, Dec. 30   Litho.   Imperf.
       Without Gum
       Sheets of 2, #a-b
3050-3051 A567 Set of 2   27.00 27.00

A568

Whales — A569

No. 3052: a, Southern minke whale. b, Common minke whale. c, Blue whale. d, Sei whale.
No. 3053, Bryde's whale. No. 3054, Fin whale.

2011, Jan. 12   Perf. 12
3052 A568 4000 le Sheet of 4,
             #a-d   7.75 7.75
        Souvenir Sheets
        Perf. 13 Syncopated
3053 A568 8000 le multi   4.00 4.00
3054 A569 8000 le multi   4.00 4.00

Lotus Flowers — A570

No. 3055: a, Country name at LL, denomination at top right, Latin name at right reading down. b, Country name at LL, denomination at top right, Latin name at top. c, Country name at UL, denomination at LR, Latin name at right reading down. d, Country name at LR, denomination at UL, Latin name at top right.
10,000 le, Lotous flower, vert.

2011, Feb. 1   Perf. 14¾x114¼
3055 A570 4000 le Sheet of 4,
             #a-d   7.50 7.50
        Souvenir Sheet
        Perf. 14¼x14¾
3056 A570 10,000 le multi   4.75 4.75
Indipex Intl. Philatelic Exhibition, New Delhi.

Reptiles and Amphibians — A572

No. 3058, 4000 le — Reptiles: a, Nile crocodile. b, African clwed gecko. c, African spurred tortoise. d, Rainbow agama.
No. 3059, 4000 le — Frogs and toads: a, Big-eyed tree frog. b, Marbled reed frog. c, African red toad. d, African clawed frog.
No. 3060, 8000 le, Eastern green mamba.
No. 3061, 8000 le, African bullfrog.

2011, Mar. 25   Perf. 13 Syncopated
       Sheets of 4, #a-d
3058-3059 A572 Set of 2   15.00 15.00
       Souvenir Sheets
3060-3061 A572 Set of 2   7.50   7.50

Paintings by Sandro Botticelli (c. 1445-
1510) — A573

No. 3062: a, Portrait of a Young Man. b, Flight into Egypt. c, Crucified Christ. d, Three Miracles of Saint Zenobius.
8000 le, The Annunciation, horiz.

2011, Mar. 25   Perf. 12
3062 A573 4000 le Sheet of 4,
             #a-d   7.50 7.50
        Souvenir Sheet
        Perf. 12¾
3063 A573 8000 le multi   3.75 3.75
No. 3063 contains one 51x38mm stamp.

Miniature Sheets

A574

Elvis Presley (1935-77) — A575

No. 3064 — Presley wearing: a, White suit, with knees bent, facing forward. b, Leather jacket, no microphone visible. c, White suit with knees bent, facing left. d, Leather jacket, with microphone at left. e, White suit, legs straight. f, Leather jacket, microphone at right.
No. 3065 — Presley with frame in: a, Bright blue. b, Dark brown. c, Green. d, Yellow brown. e, Blue.

2011, Mar. 25   Perf. 12
3064 A574 3300 le Sheet of 6,
             #a-f   9.25 9.25
        Perf. 12½
3065 A575 4100 le Sheet of 5,
             #a-e   9.50 9.50

Miniature Sheets

President Barack Obama — A576

No. 3066, 4000 le: a, Afghanistan Pres. Hamid Karzai. b, Presidents Karzai and Obama seated. c, Presidents Karzai and Obama shaking hands. d, Pres. Obama.
No. 3067, 4000 le: a, Pres. Obama at left, flag at right. b, Pres Obama and Representative Nancy Pelosi. c, Pres. Obama and Senator Harry Reid. d, Pres. Obama in center, unidentified people in background, flag at right.

2011, Mar. 25   Perf. 13 Syncopated
       Sheets of 4, #a-d
3066-3067 A576 Set of 2   15.00 15.00

Miniature Sheets

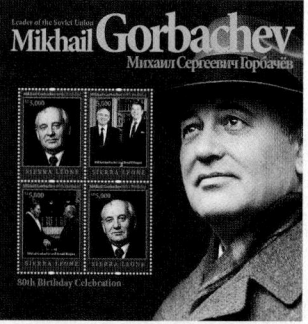

Soviet Union General Secretary
Mikhail Gorbachev — A577

No. 3068: a, Gorbachev standing next to Pres. Ronald Reagan. b, Gorbachev and Reagan shaking hands. c, Gorbachev looking forward.
No. 3069: a, Gorbachev wearing hat. b, Gorbachev looking left. c, Gorbachev and Reagan seated. d, Gorbachev and Pres. George H. W. Bush.

2011, Mar. 25   Litho.
3068 A577 5000 le Sheet of 4,
             #3068a-
             3068b, 2
             #3068c   9.25 9.25
3069 A577 5000 le Sheet of 4,
             #a-d   9.25 9.25

Engagement of Prince William and
Catherine Middleton — A578

Designs: No. 3070, 4000 le, Couple.
No. 3071, vert.: a, Prince William. b, Middleton. c, Couple, hands visible. d, Couple, hands not visible.
No. 3072, 5000 le: a, Middleton. b, Prince William.
No. 3073, 5000 le, vert: a, Middleton. b, Prince William.

2011, Mar. 25   Perf. 12
3070 A578 4000 le multi   1.90 1.90
3071 A578 4000 le Sheet of 4,
             #a-d   7.50 7.50
     Souvenir Sheets of 2, #a-b
        Perf. 13 Syncopated
3072-3073 A578 Set of 2   9.25 9.25
No. 3070 was printed in sheets of 4.

Wedding of Prince William and Catherine Middleton — A579

No. 3074: a, Prince William. b, Catherine Middleton. c, Prince Charles. d, Princess Diana. e, Prince Philip. f, Queen Elizabeth II.
No. 3075, 5500 le: a, Prince William. b, Couple in coach.
No. 3076, 5500 le: a, Middleton. b, Couple kissing.

2011 **Perf. 13 Syncopated**
3074 A579 3500 le Sheet of 6,
#a-f, + 5
labels 9.75 9.75
Souvenir Sheets of 2, #a-b, + Central Label
3075-3076 A579 Set of 2 10.50 10.50

The stated day of issue of Apr. 29 for this issue is incorrect as the stamps show photographs from the wedding held that day.

Dr. Sun Yat-sen (1866-1925), President of China — A580

2011, Oct. 3 **Perf. 12**
3077 A580 4000 le multi 1.90 1.90
Printed in sheets of 4.

Miniature Sheet

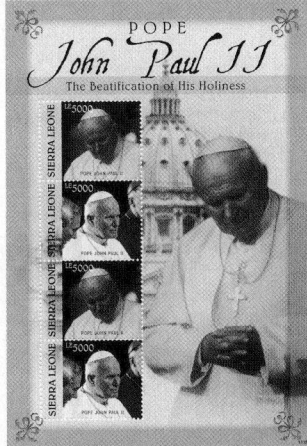

Beatification of Pope John Paul II — A581

No. 3078: a, Pope John Paul II looking down, beige under country name. b, Pope John Paul II, cardinal at right, beige area under "Leone" only. c, As "a," dark areas under country name. d, As "b," beige area under "Sierra" only.

2011, Oct. 3 **Litho.**
3078 A581 5000 le Sheet of 4,
#a-d 9.00 9.00

Worldwide Fund for Nature (WWF) — A582

No. 3079 — Forest puff adder with country name and denomination in: a, Red. b, Purple. c, Yellow. d, Blue.

2011, Oct. 3 **Perf. 13¼**
3079 Strip of 4 5.75 5.75
a.-d. A582 3100 le Any single 1.40 1.40
e. Souvenir sheet of 8, 2 each
#a-d 11.50 11.50

Miniature Sheets

Chinese Civil Engineering Projects — A583

No. 3080 — Qingdao Cross-sea Bridge: a, Bridge, both shores visible. b, Bridge span.
No. 3081 — Qingdao-Jiaozhouwan Undersea Tunnel: a, Tunnel entrance. b, Tunnel cross-section.

2011, Oct. 3 **Perf. 13 Syncopated**
3080 A583 1500 le Sheet of 6, 3
each #a-b 4.25 4.25
3081 A583 2500 le Sheet of 4, 2
each #a-b 4.50 4.50

Intl. Year of Forests — A584

No. 3082: a, Forest. b, Boy in forest. c, Red-eyed tree frog. d, Red-crested turaco. e, Logger with chain saw. f, U.N. Secretary-General Ban Ki-moon.
No. 3083: a, Intl. Year of Forests emblem. b, Forest, diff.

2011, Oct. 3 **Perf. 12x11½**
3082 A584 2500 le Sheet of 6,
#a-f, + 3 labels 6.75 6.75
Souvenir Sheet
Perf. 11½
3083 A584 5000 le Sheet of 2,
#a-b 4.50 4.50

Miniature Sheets

Jane Goodall Institute, 50th Anniv. — A585

No. 3084, 5000 le: a, Black-and-white photograph of Goodall. b, Color photograph of Goodall extending arm towards chimpanzee. c, Black-and-white photograph of Goodall and chimpanzee. d, Color photograph of Goodall.
No. 3085, 5000 le: a, Goodall writing in journal. b, Goodall, holding camera, observing chimpanzee. c, Goodall extending arm toward three chimpanzees. d, Goodall holding cup with sun on horizon.

2011, Oct. 3 **Perf. 13 Syncopated**
Sheets of 4, #a-d
3084-3085 A585 Set of 2 18.00 18.00

Princess Diana (1961-97) — A586

No. 3086 — Various photographs of Princess Diana with upper and lower panels in: a, Black. b, Pale pink. c, Red. d, Orange red. 11,000 le, Princess Diana, diff.

2011, Oct. 3 **Perf. 12**
3086 A586 5000 le Sheet of 4,
#a-d 9.00 9.00
Souvenir Sheet
3087 A586 11,000 le multi 5.00 5.00

Sept. 11, 2001 Terrorist Attacks, 10th Anniv. — A587

No. 3088: a, Memorial wall dedicated to firefighters. b, Tribute in light, Brooklyn Bridge in foreground. c, Pentagon memorial. d, Commemorative flag. e, Field with American flags. f, Cross of steel beams at Ground Zero. 11,000 le, Tribute in light, vert.

2011, Oct. 3 **Perf. 12**
3088 A587 3400 le Sheet of 6,
#a-f 9.25 9.25
Souvenir Sheet
Perf. 12½
3089 A587 11,000 le multi 5.00 5.00
No. 3089 contains one 38x51mm stamp.

Pres. Abraham Lincoln (1809-65) — A588

No. 3090: a, US flag, bust of Lincoln. b, Painting of Lincoln.
No. 3091 — Photograph of Lincoln and: a, Union soldier's cap. b, Lincoln's stovepipe hat. c, Confederate soldier's cap.

2011, Oct. 3 **Perf. 11½**
3090 A588 4000 le Sheet of 4, 2
each #a-b 7.25 7.25

Perf. 11½x12
3091 A588 6000 le Sheet of 3,
#a-c 8.25 8.25
American Civil War, 150th anniv.

First Man in Space, 50th Anniv. — A589

No. 3092, 4000 le, horiz.: a, Vostok rocket on pedestal. b, MiG 15. c, Yuri Gagarin, first man in space. d, Alan Shepard, Jr., first American in Space.
No. 3093, 4000 le, horiz.: a, Vostok rocket in space. b, Vostok capsule. c, Vostok mission patch for Gagarin's space flight. d, L. Gordon Cooper, American astronaut.
No. 3094, 8000 le, Gagarin. No. 3095, 8000 le, Vostok capsule.

2011, Oct. 3 **Perf. 12½x12**
Sheets of 4, #a-d
3092-3093 A589 Set of 2 14.50 14.50
Souvenir Sheets
Perf. 12x12½
3094-3095 A589 Set of 2 7.25 7.25

Orchids — A590

No. 3096: a, Bolusiella imbricata. b, Bulbophyllum scaberulum. c, Oeceoclades maculata. d, Ancistrochilus rothschildianus. e, Sarracenia flava. f, Phaius.
No. 3097: a, Ancistrochilus rothschildianus, diff. b, Angraecum subulatum. c, Eulophia guineensis. d, Eurychone rothschildiana.
No. 3098, 11,000 le, Monodora myristica. No. 3099, 11,000 le, Polystachya galeata.

Perf. 11½, 12x12½ (#3097)
2011, Oct. 3
3096 A590 3400 le Sheet of 6,
#a-f 9.25 9.25
3097 A590 4800 le Sheet of 4,
#a-d 8.75 8.75
Souvenir Sheets
3098-3099 A590 Set of 2 10.00 10.00
Intl. Year of Forests.

Miniature Sheet

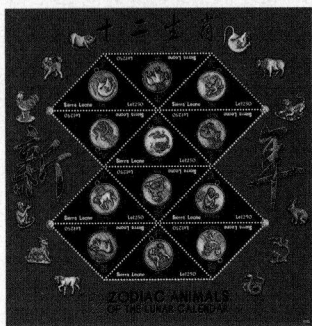

Chinese Zodiac Animals — A592

No. 3104: a, Rat. b, Ox. c, Tiger. d, Snake. e, Dragon. f, Rabbit. g, Horse. h, Ram. i, Monkey. j, Boar. k, Dog. l, Rooster.

2011, Oct. 3 **Litho.** **Perf. 12**
3104 A592 1250 le Sheet of 12,
#a-l 6.75 6.75

Miniature Sheet

Chinese Art by Lu Lv Jun — A593

No. 3105: a, Calligraphy with two red chops below left column of characters (30x40mm). b, Two birds on tree branch (30x40mm). c, Forest (60x40mm). d, Flowers, calligraphy at top red chop at left (30x40mm). e, Two birds on ground below tree (30x40mm). f, Calligraphy with two red chops to left of left column of characters (30x40mm). g, 18mm wide abstract work (30x40mm). h, Trees with red chop at lower right (30x40mm). i, Calligraphy and cat (60x40mm). j, Calligraphy and Chinese person (30x40mm). k, Flowers, calligraphy at top, two red chops at left (30x40mm). l, Flowers, calligraphy at right (30x40mm).

2011, Oct. 22   **Perf. 14**
3105 A593 1300 le Sheet of 12,
#a-l   7.25   7.25

Miniature Sheet

Freddy Will, Musician — A594

No. 3106 — Will wearing: a, T-shirt, black background. b, Suit, with hands clasped. c, Suit, brick wall in background. d, T-shirt, chain link fence in background.

2011, Oct. 22   **Perf. 13 Syncopated**
3106 A594 4000 le Sheet of 4,
#a-d   7.50   7.50

AIR POST STAMPS

> **Catalogue values for unused stamps in this section are for Never Hinged items.**

Independence — Progress Issue

Nos. 197, 199, 204 and 206 Surcharged Like Nos. 242-247 plus "AIRMAIL" in Carmine, Red, Violet, Blue or Orange

Perf. 13, 13½

1963, Apr. 27   **Wmk. 4**   **Engr.**
Center in Black

C1	A27	7p on 1½p (C)	.25	.25
C2	A27	1sh3p on 1½p (R)	.25	.25
C3	A28	2sh6p brn org (V)	2.50	.65
C4	A27	3sh on 3p (Bl)	.65	.65
C5	A28	6sh on 3p (O)	1.00	.80
C6	A27	11sh on 10sh (C)	1.75	1.00
C7	A27	11sh on £1 (C)	625.00	240.00
		Nos. C1-C6 (6)	6.40	3.60

Nos. 221, 224, 213, 223 and 207 Srchd. or Ovptd. in Brown, Red, Black, Violet, Ultra or Orange

Perf. 13x13½, 13½x13, 13

1963, Nov. 4   **Wmk. 4, 336**

C8	A31	7p on 3p (Br)	.25	.25
C9	A32	1sh3p blue & blk (R)	1.75	1.75
C10	A30	2sh6p on 4p (Bk)	1.25	1.25
C11	A31	3sh on 3p (V)	2.00	1.50

C12	A32	6sh on 6p (U)	1.50	1.50
C13	A27	£1 org & blk (O)	25.00	25.00
		Nos. C8-C13 (6)	31.70	31.20

Overprint is in 6 lines on Nos. C8, C11 and C12. A number of surcharge varieties and errors exist.

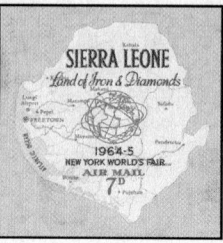

Unisphere and Map of Sierra Leone — AP1

Engraved and Lithographed
1964, Feb. 10   **Unwmk.**   **Die Cut**
Self-adhesive

C14	AP1	7p multicolored	.25	.25
C15	AP1	9p multicolored	.25	.25
C16	AP1	1sh3p multicolored	.25	.25
C17	AP1	2sh6p multicolored	.35	.35
C18	AP1	3sh6p multicolored	.50	.50
C19	AP1	6sh multicolored	.65	.65
C20	AP1	11sh multicolored	1.00	1.00
		Nos. C14-C20 (7)	3.10	3.10

New York World's Fair, 1964-65.
For surcharge see No. C33.

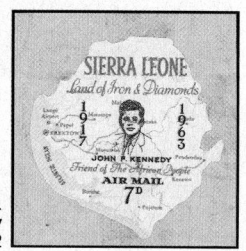

John F. Kennedy AP2

1964, May 11   **Self-adhesive**

C21	AP2	7p multicolored	.25	.25
C22	AP2	9p multicolored	.25	.25
C23	AP2	1sh3p multicolored	.25	.25
C24	AP2	2sh6p multicolored	.30	.30
C25	AP2	3sh6p multicolored	.35	.60
C26	AP2	6sh multicolored	.55	1.00
C27	AP2	11sh multicolored	.80	1.25
		Nos. C21-C27 (7)	2.65	3.80

For surcharges see Nos. C32, C34-C36.

Nos. 241, 213, 219 and 218 Surcharged in Dark Blue, Black, Red or Violet Blue

Perf. 11½x11, 13½x13, 13x13½

1964, Aug. 4   **Engr.**   **Wmk. 336**

C28	A36	7c on 1sh3p (#241) (DB)	.25	.25
C29	A30	20c on 4p (#213)	.40	.40
C30	A29	30c on 10sh (#219) (B)	.70	.70
C31	A29	40c on 5sh (#218) (VB)	.85	.85
		Nos. C28-C31 (4)	2.20	2.20

Map-shaped Issues of 1964
Surcharged in Red or Black

Engraved and Lithographed
1964-65   **Unwmk.**   **Die Cut**

C32	AP2	7c on 7p (#C21) (R)	.25	.25
C33	AP1	7c on 9p (#C15)	.85	.85
C34	AP2	60c on 9p (#C22)	1.25	1.25
C35	AP2	1 le on 1sh3p (#C23) (R)	2.00	2.00
C36	AP2	2 le on 11sh (#C27)	4.25	4.25
		Nos. C32-C36 (5)	8.60	8.60

Issue dates: Aug. 4, 1964, Nos. C35-C36. Jan. 20, 1965, Nos. C32, C34. April, 1965, No. C33.

Regular Issue of 1963 Surcharged like Nos. 300-305 with "AIRMAIL" added

Wmk. 336

1965, May 19   **Photo.**   **Perf. 14**

Designs of Surcharge: No. C37, C39-C40, Sir Milton Margai and Sir Winston Churchill. No. C38, Margai. No. C41, Churchill.

C37	A35	7c on 2p (#230)	.65	.25
C38	A34	15c on ½p (#227)	.40	.75
C39	A35	30c on 6p (#233)	1.75	.50

C40	A35	1 le on £1 (#239)	5.25	1.75
C41	A34	2 le on 10sh (#238)	10.50	5.50
		Nos. C37-C41 (5)	18.55	8.70

The portraits and inscription on No. C39 are white, the denomination and "AIRMAIL" are orange.

Ten more surcharges were issued Nov. 9, 1965: "2c" on Nos. C16, C23 and C25. "3c" on Nos. C14 and C22. "5c" on Nos. C17-C19, C24, and C26. Value $4 each.

One further surcharge was issued Jan. 28, 1966: "TWO/Leones" on No. C39. Value $10.

Type of Regular Issue and

Diamond Necklace AP3

Litho.; Reversed Embossing
1965, Dec. 17   **Unwmk.**   **Die Cut**
Self-adhesive

C53	AP3	7c blk, grn, gold & bl	.90	.25
C54	AP3	15c blk, brnz, car & bl	1.90	1.90

Engr. and Embossed on Paper

C55	A41	40c multi, cream	4.25	4.25
		Nos. C53-C55 (3)	7.05	6.40

Various advertisements printed on peelable paper backing. Nos. C54-C55 have side tabs for handling and come packed in boxes of 100. No. C53 is without side tab and comes 25 stamps attached to one sheet.
For overprints and surcharges see Nos. C68-C69, C79-C83.

Nos. 248, 229, 232, 234 and 236 Surcharged and Overprinted: "AIRMAIL/FIVE YEARS/INDEPENDENCE/1961-1966"

1966, Apr. 27   **Wmk. 336**

C56	A37	7c on 3p pur & red	.25	.25
C57	A34	15c on 1sh multi	.50	.50
C58	A34	25c on 2sh6p multi	.75	.75
C59	A34	50c on 1 ½p multi	1.50	1.50
C60	A34	1 le on 4p multi	3.50	3.50
		Nos. C56-C60 (5)	6.45	6.45

The denomination on No. C60 is spelled out "One Leone."

Self-adhesive & Die Cut
Nos. C61-C131, C135-C142 are self-adhesive and die cut.

Gold Coin Type of Regular Issue

Designs: 7c, 10c, ¼ Golde coin. 15c, 30c, ½ Golde coin. 50c, 2 le, 1 Golde coin. (7c, 15c, 50c, Map of Sierra Leone. 10c, 30c, 2 le, Lion's head.)
Diameter: 7c, 10c, 38mm; 15c, 30c, 54mm; 50c, 2 le, 82mm.

Lithographed; Embossed on Gilt Foil
1966, Nov. 12   **Unwmk.**

C61	A42	7c red & orange	.25	.25
C62	A42	10c dull blue & red	.25	.25
C63	A42	15c red & orange	.25	.25
C64	A42	30c black & rose lilac	.60	.60
C65	A42	50c rose lilac & emer	1.10	1.10
C66	A42	2 le green & black	5.50	5.50
		Nos. C61-C66 (6)	7.80	7.80

Advertising printed on paper backing.

Type of Regular Issue, 1965 and No. C55 Surcharged

1967, Dec. 2   **Engr. & Embossed**

C67	A41	10c multi (red frame), cream	.50	.50
a.		Black frame	.50	.50
C68	A41	11½c on 40c multi, cr	.40	.40
C69	A41	25c on 40c multi, cr	1.00	1.00
		Nos. C67-C69 (3)	1.90	1.90

Eagle — AP4

Embossed Foil on Black Paper
1967, Dec. 2   **Unwmk.**

C70	AP4	9½c black, gold & red	.75	.75
C71	AP4	15c black, gold & grn	1.00	1.00

Various advertisements printed on peelable paper backing. See Nos. C98-C99, C118-C124.

Map Type of Regular Issue

Designs: Each denomination shows map of Africa with map of one of the following countries — Portuguese Guinea, South Africa, Mozambique, Rhodesia, South West Africa or Angola. Sheets of 30 (6x5) have 5 horizontal rows containing one stamp of each design.

1968, Sept. 25   **Litho.**

C72	A43	7½c multicolored	.25	.25
C73	A43	9½c multicolored	.30	.30
C74	A43	14½c multicolored	.35	.35
C75	A43	18½c multicolored	.40	.40
C76	A43	25c multicolored	.50	.50
C77	A43	1 le multicolored	3.50	3.50
C78	A43	2 le multicolored	9.50	9.50
		Nos. C72-C78 (7)	14.80	14.80
		7 Strips of 6, 1 of each design (42)	122.50	

No. C55 Overprinted and Surcharged in Red Similar to Nos. 364-368

Engraved and Embossed on Paper
1968, Nov. 30

C79	A41	6½c on 40c multi	.25	.25
C80	A41	10c on 40c multi	.60	.60
C81	A41	22½c on 40c multi	.60	.60
C82	A41	28½c on 40c multi	.85	.85
C83	A41	40c multicolored	1.25	1.25
		Nos. C79-C83 (5)	3.50	3.50

Scroll Type of Regular Issue

7½c, #C54. 9½c, #C70. 20c, #C16. 30c, #C26. 50c, #165. 2 le, #207 with "2nd Year of Independence" overprint. All are horiz.

1969, Mar. 1   **Litho.**

C84	A44	7½c multicolored	.25	.25
C85	A44	9½c multicolored	.30	.30
C86	A44	20c multicolored	.50	.50
C87	A44	30c multicolored	.70	.70
C88	A44	50c multicolored	1.75	1.75
C89	A44	2 le multicolored	10.00	10.00
		Nos. C84-C89 (6)	13.50	13.50

Various advertisements printed on peelable paper backing. No. C84 has side tab for handling and comes packed in boxes of 50. No. C85-C89 are without side tabs and come 20 stamps attached to one sheet.
For surcharges see Nos. C135-C136.

Pepel Port Types of Regular Issue

Designs: 7½c, 15c, Globe, tanker, flags of Sierra Leone and Japan. Anvil Shape with Flags of Sierra Leone and: 9½c, 2 le, Union Jack. 25c, Netherlands. 1 le, West Germany.

1969, July 10

C90	A45	7½c multicolored	.25	.25
C91	A46	9½c multicolored	.25	.25
C92	A45	15c multicolored	.40	.40
C93	A46	25c multicolored	.60	.60
C94	A46	1 le multicolored	1.75	1.75
C95	A46	2 le multicolored	2.50	2.50
		Nos. C90-C95 (6)	5.65	5.65

Various advertisements printed on peelable paper backing. No. C90 has side tab for handling and comes packed in boxes of 50. Nos. C91-C95 are without side tabs and come 20 stamps attached to one sheet.

Bank Type of Regular Issue
Lithographed; Gold Impressed
1969, Sept. 10

C96	A47	9½c yel grn, vio & gold	.90	.90

Advertising printed on peelable paper backing; 20 imperf. stamps to a sheet of backing, roulette 10.

Cola Nut Type of Regular Issue and Type of 1967

Typo.; Embossed on White Paper

1969, Sept. 10

C97	A40	7c yel, mar & car	.40	.40

Embossed Foil on Black Paper

C98	AP4	9½c blk, gold & bl	7.00	7.00
C99	AP4	15c blk, gold & red	9.00	9.00
		Nos. C97-C99 (3)	16.40	16.40

No. C97 has side tab for handling and comes packed in boxes of 100. Nos. C98-C99 have advertisements printed on peelable paper backing, side tabs and come packed in boxes of 50.

Boy Scout, Lord Baden-Powell and Scout Emblem — AP5

1969, Dec. 6   **Litho.**

C100	AP5	7½c multicolored	.50	.40
C101	AP5	9½c multicolored	.60	.50
C102	AP5	15c multicolored	.90	.90
C103	AP5	22c multicolored	1.25	1.25
C104	AP5	55c multicolored	5.00	5.00
C105	AP5	3 le multicolored	65.00	50.00
		Nos. C100-C105 (6)	73.25	58.05

60th anniv. of the Sierra Leone Boy Scouts. Various advertising printed on peelable paper backing. No. C100 has side tab for handling and comes packed in boxes of 100. Nos. C101-C105 are without side tabs and come 20 stamps attached to one sheet.

No. 357 Surcharged "AIRMAIL" and New Denomination in Metallic Emerald, Lilac, Blue, Green, Bronze or Silver

1970, Mar 28

C106	A43	7½c on ½c (E)	.30	.30
C107	A43	9½c on ½c (L)	.40	.40
C108	A43	15c on ½c (Bl)	.55	.55
C109	A43	28c on ½c (G)	1.00	1.00
C110	A43	40c on ½c (Br)	1.75	1.75
C111	A43	2 le on ½c (S)	9.00	9.00
		Nos. C106-C111 (6)	13.00	13.00

See design paragraph over No. 357.

EXPO Type of Regular Issue

Maps of Sierra Leone and Japan.

1970, June 22   **Litho.**

C112	A49	7½c multicolored	.25	.25
C113	A49	9½c multicolored	.25	.25
C114	A49	15c multicolored	.35	.35
C115	A49	25c multicolored	.60	.60
C116	A49	50c multicolored	.70	.70
C117	A49	3 le multicolored	2.00	2.00
		Nos. C112-C117 (6)	4.05	4.05

Various advertising printed on peelable paper backing.

Eagle Type of 1967

1970, Oct. 3   **Embossed Foil**

C118	AP4	7½c crim & gold	.55	.55
C119	AP4	9½c emer & cop	.65	.65
C120	AP4	15c grnsh bl & sil	1.25	1.25
C121	AP4	25c brt red lil & gold	2.75	2.25
C122	AP4	50c gold & emer	5.50	4.50
C123	AP4	1 le silver & dk bl	11.00	9.00
C124	AP4	2 le gold & brt bl	17.50	17.50
		Nos. C118-C124 (7)	39.20	35.70

Advertisements printed on peelable paper backing. Issued in sheets of 10.

"Treasure of Sierra Leone" Diamond — AP6

Lithographed and Embossed

1970, Dec. 30

C125	AP6	7½c multicolored	.75	.25
C126	AP6	9½c multicolored	.90	.30
C127	AP6	15c multicolored	1.25	.50
C128	AP6	25c multicolored	1.75	1.75
C129	AP6	75c multicolored	7.50	7.50
C130	AP6	2 le multicolored	27.50	27.50
		Nos. C125-C130 (6)	39.65	37.75

Diamond industry. Advertisement printed on peelable paper backing. Sheets of 20.

Traffic Type of Regular Issue

1971, Mar. 1   **Litho.**

C131	A53	9½c vio blue & org	3.50	3.50

Advertisements printed on peelable paper backing.

Nos. 211, 215, 228 and C87 Surcharged in Dark Red, Dark Blue or Black

a

b

1971, Mar. 1   Engr.   Wmk. 336

C132	A29(a)	10c on 2p (DR)	.35	.30
C133	A29(a)	20c on 1sh (DB)	.70	.65

Photo.   Perf. 14

C134	A35(a)	50c on 1p (Bk)	1.75	1.50

Unwmk.

Litho.   Imperf.

C135	A44(b)	70c on 30c (DB)	2.75	2.50
C136	A44(b)	1 le on 30c (Bk)	4.00	3.25
		Nos. C132-C136 (5)	9.55	8.20

Lion's Head and Bugles AP7

Lithographed and Embossed (Gold)

1971, Apr. 27

C137	AP7	7½c multicolored	.25	.25
C138	AP7	9½c multicolored	.25	.25
C139	AP7	15c multicolored	.25	.25
C140	AP7	25c multicolored	.45	.45
C141	AP7	75c multicolored	1.50	1.50
C142	AP7	2 le multicolored	3.50	3.50
		Nos. C137-C142 (6)	6.10	6.10

10th anniversary of independence. Advertisements printed on peelable paper backing. Stamps are in shape of Sierra Leone map and in flag colors.

Guma Valley Dam and Bank Emblem — AP8

1975, Jan. 14   Litho.   Perf. 13½

C143	AP8	15c multicolored	1.00	1.00

African Development Bank, 10th anniv.

Congo River Type of 1975

1975, Aug. 24   Litho.   Perf. 13x13½

C144	A57	20c multicolored	.60	.60

Mano River Type of 1975

1975, Oct. 3   Perf. 13x13½

C145	A58	15c multicolored	.40	.40

SINGAPORE

ˈsiŋ-ə-ˌpor

LOCATION — An island just off the southern tip of the Malay Peninsula, south of Johore

GOVT. — Republic in British Commonwealth

AREA — 250 sq. mi.

POP. — 3,531,600 (1999 est.)

CAPITAL — Singapore

Singapore, Malacca and Penang were the British settlements which, together with the Federated Malay States, composed the former colony of Straits Settlements. On April 1, 1946, Singapore became a separate colony when the Straits Settlements colony was dissolved. Malacca and Penang joined the Malayan Union, which was renamed the Federation of Malaya in 1948. In 1959 Singapore became a state with internal self-government. Singapore joined the Federation of Malaysia in 1963 and withdrew in 1965.

100 Cents = 1 Dollar

> Catalogue values for all unused stamps in this country are for Never Hinged items.

Watermark

Wmk. 366 — S multiple

King George VI — A1

1948   Wmk. 4   Typo.   Perf. 14

1	A1	1c black	.25	1.00
2	A1	2c orange	.25	.50
3	A1	3c green	.50	.80
4	A1	4c chocolate	.30	1.25
6	A1	6c gray	.40	.85
7	A1	8c rose red	.50	.85
9	A1	10c plum	.30	.25
11	A1	15c ultra	12.00	.25
12	A1	20c dk green & blk	5.50	.45
14	A1	25c org & rose lilac	3.00	.40
16	A1	40c dk vio & rose red	9.50	5.00
17	A1	50c ultra & black	4.00	.25
18	A1	$1 vio brn & ultra	13.50	4.50
19	A1	$2 rose red & emer	67.50	5.50
20	A1	$5 chocolate & emer	150.00	6.50
		Nos. 1-20 (15)	267.50	28.35
		Set, hinged	140.00	

1949-52   Perf. 18

1a	A1	1c black ('52)	.75	3.25
2a	A1	2c orange	1.00	1.40
4a	A1	4c chocolate	1.10	.25
5	A1	5c rose violet ('52)	4.00	1.50
6a	A1	6c gray ('52)	1.75	1.40
8	A1	8c green ('52)	9.00	3.00
9a	A1	10c plum ('50)	.60	.25
10	A1	12c rose red ('52)	11.00	8.50
11a	A1	15c ultra ('50)	19.00	.35
12a	A1	20c dark green & black	4.50	3.25
13	A1	20c ultra ('52)	6.50	.75
14a	A1	25c org & rose lil ('50)	1.25	.25
15	A1	35c dk vio & rose red ('52)	6.00	3.00
16a	A1	40c dk vio & rose red ('51)	45.00	16.00
17a	A1	50c ultra & black ('50)	10.50	.25
18a	A1	$1 violet brown & ultra	21.00	.80
b.		Wmk. 4a (error)	7,000.	
19a	A1	$2 rose red & emer ('51)	140.00	3.25
b.		Wmk. 4a (error)	7,000.	
20a	A1	$5 choc & emerald ('51)	260.00	4.00
		Nos. 1a-20a (18)	542.95	51.45
		Set, hinged	300.00	

Common Design Types pictured following the introduction.

Silver Wedding Issue
Common Design Types
Inscribed: "Singapore"

1948, Oct. 25   Photo.   Perf. 14x14½
21   CD304   10c purple   1.25   .25

Engraved; Name Typographed
Perf. 11½x11
22   CD305 $5 light brown   140.00   50.00

UPU Issue
Common Design Types
Inscribed: "Malaya-Singapore"
Engr.; Name Typo. on 15c, 25c
Perf. 13½, 11x11½

1949, Oct. 10   Wmk. 4
23   CD306   10c rose violet   .60   .30
24   CD307   15c indigo   7.50   2.00
25   CD308   25c orange   7.50   3.00
26   CD309   50c slate   7.50   5.00
    Nos. 23-26 (4)   23.10   10.30

Coronation Issue
Common Design Type
1953, June 2   Engr.   Perf. 13½x13
27   CD312   10c magenta & black   2.75   .30

Chinese Sampans — A2

Sir Stamford Raffles Statue — A3

Singapore River — A4

Designs: 2c, Malay kolek. 4c, Twa-kow. 5c, Lombok sloop. 6c, Trengganu pinas. 8c, Palari. 10c, Timber tongkong. 12c, Hylam trader. 20c, Cocos-Keeling schooner. 25c, Argonaut plane. 30c, Oil tanker. 50c, Liner (M.S. Chusan). $5, Arms of Singapore.

Perf. 13½x14½
1955, Sept. 4   Photo.   Wmk. 4
28   A2   1c sepia   .25   .80
29   A2   2c orange yellow   1.75   1.10
30   A2   4c orange brown   .80   .25
31   A2   5c magenta   .40   .30
32   A2   6c gray blue   .40   .50
33   A2   8c aqua   .95   .75
34   A2   10c dark purple   2.25   .25
35   A2   12c rose red   2.75   2.25
36   A2   20c violet blue   2.50   .25
37   A2   25c orange & purple   5.00   .75
38   A2   30c purple & plum   3.25   .25
39   A2   50c brt blue & black   2.25   .25
Perf. 13½x14, 14x13½
Engr.
40   A3 $1 blue & purple   32.50   .35
41   A4 $2 blue green & red   45.00   1.90
Engr.; Arms Typo.
42   A3 $5 multicolored   50.00   4.50
    Nos. 28-42 (15)   150.05   14.45

For a later printing of the 10c and 50c, plates with finer screen (250) than normal (200) were used.

Singapore Lion and Administrative Center — A5

Perf. 11½x12
1959, June 1   Photo.   Wmk. 314
Lion in Gold
43   A5   4c deep rose red   .85   .75
44   A5   10c magenta   1.25   .40
45   A5   20c ultra   3.00   3.25
46   A5   25c yellow green   3.25   2.75
47   A5   30c bright violet   3.25   3.50
48   A5   50c bluish gray   4.50   3.50
    Nos. 43-48 (6)   16.10   14.15

New Constitution of Singapore.

State Flag of Singapore — A6

1960, June 3   Litho.   Perf. 13½
49   A6   4c blue, red & yellow   2.25   .75
50   A6   10c gray, red & yellow   3.75   1.10

Issued for National Day, June 3, 1960.

Hands and Map of Singapore — A7

1961, June 3   Photo.
51   A7   4c brown, yellow & gray   1.25   1.10
52   A7   10c green, yellow & gray   2.00   .25

Issued for National Day, June 3, 1961.

Sea Horse — A8

Malayan Fish: 4c, Tiger barb, horiz. 5c, Anemone fish, horiz. 6c, Archerfish. 10c, Harlequin fish, horiz. 20c, Butterflyfish. 25c, Two-spot gournami, horiz.

Perf. 14½x13½, 13½x14½
1962, Mar. 31   Wmk. 314
53   A8   2c lt grn & red brn   .40   1.00
54   A8   4c red orange & blk   .40   .60
  a.   Black omitted   750.00
55   A8   5c gray & red org   .25   .25
  a.   Red orange omitted   650.00
  b.   Wmkd. sideways ('67)   3.25   2.00
56   A8   6c yellow & blk   .65   .60
57   A8   10c dk gray & red org   .50   .25
  a.   Red orange omitted   400.00   300.00
  b.   Wmkd. sideways ('67)   1.60   .50
  c.   Black omitted   4,000.
58   A8   20c blue & orange   1.50   .25
  a.   Orange omitted   800.00
59   A8   25c orange & black   1.25   .25
  a.   Black omitted   900.00
  b.   Wmkd. sideways ('67)   1.60   .25
    Nos. 53-59 (7)   4.95   3.20

For surcharge see No. 370.

Symbolic of Labor's Role in Building the Nation — A9

1962, June 3   Unwmk.   Perf. 11½
60   A9   4c brt rose, blk & yel   1.40   1.40
61   A9   10c brt blue, blk & yel   1.75   .75

Issued for National Day, June 3, 1962.

Vanda Tan Chay Yan — A10

Yellow-Breasted Sunbird — A11

Designs: 1c, Arachnis Maggie Oei, horiz. 12c, Grammatophyllum speciosum. 30c, Vanda Miss Joaquim. 50c, Shama, horiz. $1, White-breasted kingfisher, horiz. $5, White-tailed sea eagle.

Perf. 12½, 13½x13 (50c, $1), 13x13½ ($2, $5)
1963, Mar. 10   Photo.   Wmk. 314
Flowers and Birds in Natural Colors
Size: 37x26mm, 26x37mm
62   A10   1c brt pink & ultra   .30   .25
  a.   Wmkd. sideways ('67)   1.50   .50
63   A10   8c lt blue & mag   1.50   .55
64   A10   12c salmon & brown   1.50   .30
65   A10   30c tan & ol green   1.50   .25
  a.   Tan omitted   125.00
Size: 35½x25½mm, 25½x35½mm
66   A11   50c yel green & blk   1.50   .25
  a.   Wmkd. sideways ('66)   9.00   4.50
67   A11 $1 yellow & blk   26.00   .25
  a.   Wmkd. sideways ('67)   25.00   7.00
68   A11 $2 dull blue & blk   16.00   1.10
69   A11 $5 pale blue & blk   32.50   2.75
    Nos. 62-69 (8)   80.80   5.70

See No. 76.

Government Housing Project — A12

1963, June 3   Perf. 12½
70   A12   4c multicolored   .80   .55
71   A12   10c multicolored   2.00   .25

Issued for National Day, June 3, 1963.

Folk Dancers — A13

1963, Aug. 8   Photo.   Perf. 14x14½
72   A13   5c multicolored   1.00   .50

Southeast Asia Cultural Festival.

Workers, Factory and Apartment House — A14

Wmk. 314 (30c), Unwmd. (15, 20c)
1966, Aug. 9   Perf. 12½x13
73   A14   15c ultra & multi   .80   .25
74   A14   20c red & multi   1.25   .25
75   A14   30c yellow & multi   2.00   1.00
    Nos. 73-75 (3)   4.05   1.50

First anniversary of the Republic.

Bird Type of 1963
Design: 15c, Black-naped tern (sterna).

1966, Nov. 9   Wmk. 314   Perf. 12½
Bird in Natural Colors
Size: 26x37mm
76   A11   15c blue & black   4.00   .25
  a.   Orange (eye) omitted   75.00

Marching Women, Chinese Inscription — A15

15c, Malay inscription. 50c, Tamil inscription.

Perf. 14x14½
1967, Aug. 9   Photo.   Unwmk.
77   A15   6c lt brown, gray & red   .70   .75
78   A15   15c multicolored   1.00   .25
79   A15   50c multicolored   2.25   1.75
    Nos. 77-79 (3)   3.95   2.75

"Build a Vigorous Singapore" campaign.

Buildings and Map of Africa and Southeast Asia — A16

1967, Oct. 7   Perf. 14x13½
Black Overprint
80   A16   10c multicolored   .60   .30
81   A16   25c multicolored   1.25   1.10
82   A16   50c multicolored   1.90   1.50
    Nos. 80-82 (3)   3.75   2.90

2nd Afro-Asian Housing Cong., Oct. 7-15. No. 80 exists without overprint.

Map of Singapore and Symbolic Worker — A17

Sword Dance — A18

Stamps are inscribed "Work for Prosperity" in English and: 6c, Chinese. 15c, Malay. 50c, Tamil.

Perf. 13½x14½
1968, Aug. 9   Photo.   Unwmk.
83   A17   6c red, black & gold   .25   .25
84   A17   15c brt yel grn, blk & gold   .50   .40
85   A17   50c brt blue, blk & gold   1.60   1.50
    Nos. 83-85 (3)   2.35   2.15

Issued for National Day, 1968.

Wmk. Rectangles (334)
1968   Photo.   Perf. 14

Designs: 6c, Lion dance. 10c, Bharatha Natyam, Indian dance. 15c, Tari Payong, Sumatran dance. 20c, Kathak Kali, Indian dance mask. 25c, Lu Chih Shen and Lin Chung, Chinese opera masks. 30c, Dragon dance, horiz. 50c, Tari Lilin, Malayan candle dance. 75c, Tarian Kuda Kepang, Javanese dance. $1, Yao Chi, Chinese opera mask.

86	A18	5c yellow & multi	.65 .25
87	A18	6c orange & multi	1.40 .25
88	A18	10c blue green & multi	.25 .25
89	A18	15c lt brown & multi	.65 .25
a.		Booklet pane of 4 ('69)	50.00
90	A18	20c brown & multi	.75 .30
91	A18	25c dp car & multi	1.25 .50
92	A18	30c pink & multi	.45 .50
93	A18	50c brown org & multi	.70 1.00
94	A18	75c brt rose & multi	3.00 1.25
95	A18	$1 olive grn & multi	4.50 2.00
		Nos. 86-95 (10)	13.60 6.55

Issue dates: 6c, 20c, 30c, 50c, 75c, Dec. 1; 5c, 10c, 15c, 25c, $1, Dec. 29.

1973			Perf. 13
86a	A18	5c yellow & multi	7.50 10.00
88a	A18	10c blue green & multi	16.00 8.50
90a	A18	20c brown & multi	12.00 15.00
91a	A18	25c deep car & multi	7.50 12.50
92a	A18	50c pink & multi	12.00 17.00
93a	A18	50c brown org & multi	12.00 26.50
95a	A18	$1 olive green & multi	22.50 21.00
		Nos. 86a-95a (7)	89.50 110.50

Cogwheel and Emblem A19

1969, Apr. 15		Unwmk.	Perf. 13
96	A19	15c blue, black & silver	.60 .25
97	A19	30c red, black & silver	1.50 1.10
98	A19	50c violet, black & silver	2.00 2.00
		Nos. 96-98 (3)	4.10 3.35

25th Plenary Session of the Economic Commission for Asia and the Far East (ECAFE), Singapore, Apr. 15-28.

"Homes for the People" A20

Plane over Docks of Singapore A21

Perf. 13x13½

1969, July 20		Litho.	Unwmk.
99	A20	25c emerald & black	1.75 .85
100	A20	50c dark blue & black	2.50 1.75

1960-69 building program of the Housing and Development Board.

1969, Aug. 9   Perf. 14x14½

30c, UN emblem and map of Singapore. 75c, Flags and map of Malaya and Borneo. $1, Uplifted hands and Singapore flag. $5, Tail of Japanese plane and searchlights. $10, Statue of Sir Thomas Stamford Raffles.

101	A21	15c yel, blk & org	3.00 .55
102	A21	30c brt blue & blk	3.00 1.60
103	A21	75c orange & multi	6.50 1.90
104	A21	$1 red & black	12.00 9.50
105	A21	$5 gray, blk & red	45.00 52.50
106	A21	$10 emerald & blk	57.50 55.00
a.		Souv. sheet of 6, #101-106	675.00 675.00
		Nos. 101-106 (6)	127.00 121.05

Sesquicent. of the founding of Singapore.

Mirudhangam, South Indian Drum — A22

Musical Instruments: 4c, Pi Pa, Chinese, 4 strings, vert. $2, Rebab, Malay violin, 3

strings, vert. $5, Vina, Indian, 7 strings. $10, Ta Ku, Chinese drum.

1969		Photo. Wmk. 366	Perf. 13
107	A22	1c multicolored	.25 2.25
108	A22	4c multicolored	.80 2.75
109	A22	$2 multicolored	6.00 1.00
110	A22	$5 multicolored	16.00 1.50
111	A22	$10 multicolored	50.00 15.00
		Nos. 107-111 (5)	73.05 22.50

Issued: 1c, 4c, $2, $5, Nov. 10; $10, Dec. 6.

Sea Shells — A23

Designs: 30c, Tropical fish. 75c, Greater flamingo and helmeted hornbill. $1, Orchids.

Perf. 13½

1970, Mar. 15		Unwmk.	Litho.
112	A23	15c pale vio & multi	1.60 .25
113	A23	30c lt blue & multi	2.90 1.00
114	A23	75c yellow & multi	8.00 4.00
115	A23	$1 lt green & multi	9.00 6.50
a.		Souvenir sheet of 4, #112-115	35.00 35.00
		Nos. 112-115 (4)	21.50 11.75

EXPO '70 International Exposition, Osaka, Japan, Mar. 15-Sept. 13.

Child Playing (Kindergarten) — A24

50c, Sports activities. 75c, Cultural activities.

1970, July		Unwmk.	Perf. 13½
116	A24	15c deep orange & blk	1.00 .25
117	A24	50c orange, blk & vio bl	3.00 2.50
118	A24	75c blk & dp lilac rose	4.50 3.75
		Nos. 116-118 (3)	8.50 6.50

People's Association, 10th anniversary.

Soldier and Map of Singapore — A25

Map and soldiers in various positions.

1970, Aug. 9		Litho.	Unwmk.
119	A25	15c emerald, blk & org	1.00 .25
120	A25	50c org, blk & brt mag	4.75 3.25
121	A25	$1 brt mag, blk & emer	6.50 7.50
		Nos. 119-121 (3)	12.25 11.00

National military service.

Runners A26

1970, Aug. 23		Photo.	Perf. 13
122	A26	10c shown	2.00 2.00
123	A26	15c Swimmers	2.50 2.50
124	A26	25c Badminton	2.75 2.75
125	A26	50c Automobile race	3.25 3.25
a.		Strip of 4, #122-125	15.00 15.00

1970 Festival of Sports.

Ship and Emblem of National Line (Neptune Oriental Lines) — A27

Designs: 30c, Ship in first container berth. 75c, Ship repairing and ship building.

1970, Nov. 1		Litho.	Perf. 12
126	A27	15c vio bl, lem & red	3.25 .75
127	A27	30c dp ultra & lemon	7.25 6.25
128	A27	75c red & lemon	11.00 11.00
		Nos. 126-128 (3)	21.50 18.00

Singapore shipping industry.

Flags of Commonwealth Nations — A28

Designs: 15c, Circular arrangement of names of Commonwealth members. 30c, Flags arranged in circle. $1, Flags (different arrangement).

1971, Jan. 14			Perf. 15x14½
		Size: 46½x31mm	
129	A28	15c gold & multi	.75 .75
130	A28	30c gold & multi	2.00 2.00
131	A28	75c gold & multi	3.75 3.75
		Size: 67x31mm	
		Perf. 14	
132	A28	$1 gold & multi	5.00 5.00
		Nos. 129-132 (4)	11.50 11.50

Commonwealth Heads of Government Meeting, Singapore, Jan. 12-14.

Cycle Rickshaws A29

Houses of Worship in Singapore — A30

		Perf. 11½	
1971, Apr. 4		Unwmk.	Litho.
133	A29	15c shown	.90 .25
134	A29	20c Sampans	1.40 .60
135	A29	30c Market place	3.75 1.40
		Perf. 13x13½	
136	A30	50c Waterfront	4.50 5.50
137	A30	75c shown	8.50 7.00
		Nos. 133-137 (5)	19.05 14.75

Tourist publicity.

Chinese New Year — A31

Singapore Festivals: 30c, Hari Raya Puasa (Moslem). 50c, Deepavali (Hindu). 75c, Christmas.

1971, Aug. 9		Litho.	Perf. 14
138	A31	15c multicolored	1.50 1.50
139	A31	30c multicolored	4.00 4.00
140	A31	50c multicolored	5.25 5.25
141	A31	75c multicolored	7.00 7.00
a.		Souvenir sheet of 4, #138-141	125.00 125.00
		Nos. 138-141 (4)	17.75 17.75

Satellite Earth Station, Sentosa Island — A32

No. 143 as 15c, enlarged to cover 4 stamps.

1971, Oct. 23		Unwmk.	Perf. 13½
142	A32	15c red & multi	3.00 1.60
143	A32	Block of 4	62.50 42.50
a.		30c (yellow numeral)	15.75 11.00
b.		30c (green numeral)	15.75 11.00
c.		30c (rose numeral)	15.75 11.00
d.		30c (orange numeral)	15.75 11.00

Establishment of Singapore's satellite earth station, Sentosa Island.

Singapore River and Fort Canning, 1843-1847 — A33

Views of Singapore, from 19th century art works: 15c, The Padang, 1851. 20c, Waterfront, 1848-1849. 35c, View from Fort Canning, 1846. 50c, View from Mount Wallich, 1857. $1, Waterfront with ships, from the sea, 1861.

1971, Dec. 5		Unwmk.	Perf. 13x12½
		Size: 52x45mm	
144	A33	10c gold & multi	3.00 3.00
145	A33	15c gold & multi	4.25 4.25
146	A33	20c gold & multi	5.50 5.50
147	A33	35c gold & multi	12.50 12.50
		Perf. 12½x13	
		Size: 68x47mm	
148	A33	50c gold & multi	17.50 17.50
149	A33	$1 gold & multi	22.00 22.00
		Nos. 144-149 (6)	64.75 64.75

George V 1c Copper Coin, 1920 A34

Singapore Coins: 35c, Silver dollar, 1969. $1, Gold $150, 1969 commemorative coin for sesquicentennial of founding of Singapore.

1972, June 4   Litho.   Perf. 13½
150	A34	15c dk grn, dp org & blk	2.25	2.25
151	A34	35c red & black	4.75	4.75
152	A34	$1 ultra, yellow & blk	4.50	4.50
		Nos. 150-152 (3)	11.50	11.50

"Moon Festival," by Seah Kim Joo — A35

Paintings by Singapore Artists: 35c, "Complimentary Force," by Thomas Yeo. 50c, "Rhythm in Blue," by Yusman Aman. $1, "Gibbons," by Chen Wen Hsi.

1972, July 9   Litho.   Perf. 12½
Size: 40x43½mm
| 153 | A35 | 15c brown org & multi | .75 | .75 |

Size: 35½x53½mm
| 154 | A35 | 35c blue green & multi | 2.25 | 2.25 |
| 155 | A35 | 50c dull violet & multi | 3.00 | 3.00 |

Size: 40x43½mm
| 156 | A35 | $1 bister & multi | 8.00 | 8.00 |
| | | *Nos. 153-156 (4)* | 14.00 | 14.00 |

Chinese New Year — A36

Festivals: 35c, Hari Raya Puasa (candles and ornament). 50c, Deepavali (incense and teapot). 75c, Christmas (candle and stained glass window).

1972, Aug. 9   Litho.   Perf. 13x12½
157	A36	15c deep rose & multi	.75	.75
158	A36	35c violet & multi	2.50	2.50
159	A36	50c green & multi	2.50	2.50
160	A36	75c blue & multi	3.75	3.75
		Nos. 157-160 (4)	9.50	9.50

Technical and Scientific Training — A37

Designs: 35c, Sport. $1, Art and culture.

1972, Oct. 1   Photo.   Perf. 12
161	A37	15c orange & multi	1.75	1.75
162	A37	35c blue & multi	3.25	3.25
163	A37	$1 orange & multi	5.00	5.00
		Nos. 161-163 (3)	10.00	10.00

Youth of Singapore.

Neptune Ruby A38

1972, Dec. 17   Litho.   Perf. 14x14½
Size: 42x28½mm
| 164 | A38 | 15c shown | .75 | .75 |

Size: 29½x28½mm
165	A38	75c Maria Rickmers	4.50	4.50
166	A38	$1 Chinese junk	15.75	15.75
a.		Souvenir sheet of 3, #164-166	50.00	50.00
		Nos. 164-166 (3)	21.00	21.00

Singapore shipping industry.

Quality and Reliability Emblem — A39

Birds, Jurong Bird Park — A40

15c, Emblem & initials of participating organizations: Singapore Institute of Standards & Industrial Research, Singapore Manufacturers' Association, Natl. Trades Union Congress. 75c, Emblem & "Prosperity through Quality & Reliability" in multiple rows. $1, Quality & Reliability emblem.

1973, Feb. 25   Litho.   Perf. 14½x14
167	A39	15c gold & multi	.90	.90
168	A39	35c gold & multi	2.40	2.40
169	A39	75c gold & multi	2.75	2.75
170	A39	$1 gold & multi	2.75	2.75
		Nos. 167-170 (4)	8.80	8.80

Prosperity through Quality and Reliability campaign.

1973, Apr. 29   Perf. 12½

Landmarks: 35c, Dancers, National Theater. 50c, City Hall and ballplayers. $1, Singapore River with boats and buildings.
171	A40	15c vermilion & blk	1.40	1.40
172	A40	35c dull green & blk	3.00	3.00
173	A40	50c brown & blk	3.75	3.75
174	A40	$1 dark violet & blk	6.25	6.25
		Nos. 171-174 (4)	14.40	14.40

Airline Emblems A41

35c, Emblem of Singapore Airlines and intl. destinations. 75c, SIA emblem on stylized tail of Boeing jet. $1, SIA emblems circling globe.

1973, June 24   Litho.   Perf. 13½
175	A41	10c multicolored	.80	.80
176	A41	35c multicolored	2.25	2.25
177	A41	75c multicolored	2.50	2.50
178	A41	$1 multicolored	3.50	3.50
		Nos. 175-178 (4)	9.05	9.05

Singapore Intl. Airport at Paya Lebar.

Entertainers A42

Composite of various forms of entertainment.

1973, Aug. 9   Litho.   Perf. 13½x14
179	A42	10c black & orange red	2.00	2.00
180	A42	35c black & orange red	2.75	2.75
181	A42	50c black & orange red	2.75	2.75
182	A42	75c black & orange red	3.00	3.00
a.		Block of 4, #179-182	12.75	12.75

National Day 1973.

Running, Judo, Boxing — A43

Designs: 15c, Bicycling, weight lifting, pistol shoot, yachting. 25c, Various balls. 35c, Tennis racket, ball, hockey stick. 50c, Swimming. $1, Singapore National Stadium.

Size: 25x25mm

1973, Sept. 1   Photo.   Perf. 14
183	A43	10c gold, silver & ind	.70	.70
184	A43	15c gold & dk brown	2.25	2.25
185	A43	25c silver, gold & blk	2.10	2.10
186	A43	35c gold, silver & dk pur	3.75	3.75

Perf. 13x14
Size: 40½x25mm
187	A43	50c gold & multi	3.00	3.00
188	A43	$1 sil, vio bl & emer	5.00	5.00
a.		Souvenir sheet of 6, #183-188	55.00	55.00
		Nos. 183-188 (6)	16.80	16.80

7th South East Asia (SEAP) Games, Singapore.

Agave A44

Mangosteen A45

Designs: Stylized flowers and fruit.

1973   Photo.   Perf. 13
189	A44	1c shown	.25	.25
190	A44	5c Coleus blumei	.25	.25
a.		Booklet pane of 10 (4 #190, 4 #191 + 2 #193)	15.00	
191	A44	10c Madagascar periwinkle	.25	.25
192	A44	15c Sunflower	.25	.25
193	A44	20c Dwarf palm	.60	.25
194	A44	25c Yellow daisy	.65	.25
195	A44	35c Chrysanthemum	1.00	.40
196	A44	50c Costus	1.40	.25
197	A44	75c Transvaal daisy	2.00	.70
198	A45	$1 shown	2.75	.25
199	A45	$2 Jackfruit	5.50	.75
200	A45	$5 Coconuts	14.00	5.50
201	A45	$10 Pineapple	27.50	11.50
		Nos. 189-201 (13)	56.40	20.85

Nos. 189-201 have fluorescent underprint "Singapore" in multiple rows.

Tiger and Orangutans — A46

Tropical Fish — A47

1973, Dec. 16   Litho.   Perf. 13
202	A46	5c shown	.80	.80
203	A46	10c Leopard and deer	.45	.45
204	A46	35c Panther and stag	6.00	6.00
205	A46	75c White horse & lion	9.25	9.25
		Nos. 202-205 (4)	16.50	16.50

Opening of Singapore Zoo.

1974, Apr. 21   Perf. 13½x14

Designs: Various poecilia reticulata fish.
206	A47	5c apple green & multi	1.00	1.00
207	A47	10c pink & multi	1.25	1.25
208	A47	35c brt blue & multi	4.50	4.50
209	A47	$1 brt green & multi	6.75	6.75
		Nos. 206-209 (4)	13.50	13.50

Scout Conference Emblem A48

1974, June 9   Perf. 13½x14½
| 210 | A48 | 10c multicolored | .50 | .50 |
| 211 | A48 | 75c multicolored | 2.50 | 2.50 |

9th Asia-Pacific Boy Scout Conf., Singapore.

UPU Emblem, Circle and "Centenary" Multiple — A49

UPU, cent.: 35c, Circle and UN emblems, multiple. 75c, Circle and pigeons, multiple.

1974, July 7   Litho.   Perf. 14½x13½
212	A49	10c orange brn & multi	.40	.40
213	A49	35c blue & multi	1.50	1.50
214	A49	75c emerald & multi	2.10	2.10
		Nos. 212-214 (3)	4.00	4.00

Family — A50

1974, Aug. 9   Litho.   Perf. 13x13½
215	A50	10c shown	.40	.40
216	A50	35c Symbols for male & female	1.40	1.40
217	A50	75c World map and WPY emblem	2.50	2.50
		Nos. 215-217 (3)	4.30	4.30

Natl. Day and World Population Year 1974.

"Sun and Tree" — A51

Children's Drawings: 10c, "My Daddy and Mommy." 35c, "A Dump Truck." 50c, "My Aunt."

1974, Oct. 1   Photo.   Perf. 14x13½
218	A51	5c multicolored	.60	.60
219	A51	10c multicolored	.75	.75
220	A51	35c multicolored	2.75	2.75
221	A51	50c multicolored	3.25	3.25
a.		Souv. sheet, #218-221, perf 13	30.00	30.00
		Nos. 218-221 (4)	7.35	7.35

Children's drawings for Children's Day (UNICEF).

Alfresco Dining A52

Tourist publicity: 20c, Singapore River. $1, "Kelong" fish traps.

1975, Jan. 26   Litho.   Perf. 14
222	A52	15c multicolored	1.00	1.00
223	A52	20c multicolored	1.90	1.90
224	A52	$1 multicolored	6.25	6.25
		Nos. 222-224 (3)	9.15	9.15

Prows of Barges and Wave Design A53

25c, Cargo ships & ship's wheel. 50c, Tanker & signal flags. $1, Container ship & propellers.

1975, Mar. 10   Litho.   Perf. 13½
225	A53	5c multicolored	.25	.25
226	A53	25c multicolored	2.25	2.25
227	A53	50c multicolored	3.00	3.00
228	A53	$1 multicolored	4.50	4.50
		Nos. 225-228 (4)	10.00	10.00

9th Biennial Conf. of the Intl. Assoc. of Ports and Harbors, Singapore, Mar. 8-15.

Satellite Earth Stations, Sentosa Island — A54

Oil Refinery — A55

Science and Industry: 75c, Brain surgery, Medical Center, Jurong.

1975, June 29   Photo.   Perf. 13½
229	A54	10c multicolored	.40	.25
230	A55	35c multicolored	2.50	2.50
231	A54	75c multicolored	2.50	2.50
		Nos. 229-231 (3)	5.40	5.25

"10" and "Homes and Gardens for the People" — A56

Crowned Cranes — A57

Tenth Natl. Day ("10" and): 35c, "Shipping and ship building." 75c, "Communications and technology." $1, "Trade, commerce and industry."

1975, Aug. 9   Litho.   Perf. 13½
232	A56	10c multicolored	.45	.45
233	A56	35c multicolored	1.25	1.25
234	A56	75c multicolored	3.00	3.00
235	A56	$1 multicolored	3.25	3.25
		Nos. 232-235 (4)	7.95	7.95

1975, Oct. 5   Litho.   Perf. 14½x13½
Birds: 10c, Great hornbill. 35c, White-breasted and white-collared kingfishers. $1, Sulphur-crested cockatoo and blue and yellow macaw.

236	A57	5c emerald & multi	2.25	2.25
237	A57	10c emerald & multi	2.25	2.25
238	A57	35c emerald & multi	11.50	11.50
239	A57	$1 emerald & multi	17.50	17.50
		Nos. 236-239 (4)	33.50	33.50

IWY Emblem, Peace Dove as "Equality" — A58

IWY Emblem: 35c, Peace dove with eggs in basket, symbolizing "Development." 75c, Peace dove & young, symbolizing "Peace."

1975, Dec. 7   Litho.   Perf. 13½
240	A58	10c blk, blue & pink	.30	.30
241	A58	35c orange & multi	2.50	2.50
242	A58	75c dp violet & multi	3.50	3.50
a.		Souvenir sheet of 3, #240-242	20.00	20.00
		Nos. 240-242 (3)	6.30	6.30

International Women's Year 1975.

Yellow Flame — A59   Aranda Hybrid — A60

Wayside Trees: 35c, Cabbage tree. 50c, Rose of India. 75c, Variegated coral tree.

1976, Apr. 18   Litho.   Perf. 14
243	A59	10c multicolored	.55	.25
244	A59	35c multicolored	2.50	2.50
245	A59	50c multicolored	2.90	2.90
246	A59	75c multicolored	4.50	4.50
		Nos. 243-246 (4)	10.45	10.15

1976, June 20   Litho.   Perf. 14
Designs: Varieties of aranda orchids.

247	A60	10c black & multi	.80	.25
248	A60	35c black & multi	4.00	2.00
249	A60	50c black & multi	5.25	2.50
250	A60	75c black & multi	7.00	3.25
		Nos. 247-250 (4)	17.05	8.00

"10" and Children's Band A61

35c, Running boys. 75c, Dancing children.

1976, Aug. 9   Litho.   Perf. 12½
251	A61	10c multicolored	.30	.30
252	A61	35c multicolored	1.75	1.75
253	A61	75c multicolored	2.10	2.10
		Nos. 251-253 (3)	4.15	4.15

Singapore Youth Festival, 10th anniversary.

Queen Elizabeth Walk — A62

Paintings of Old Singapore, c. 1905-10: 50c, The Padang. $1, Raffles Place.

1976, Nov. 14   Litho.   Perf. 14
254	A62	10c multicolored	.75	.75
255	A62	50c multicolored	3.00	3.00
256	A62	$1 multicolored	6.00	6.00
a.		Souvenir sheet of 3, #254-256, perf. 13½	25.00	25.00
		Nos. 254-256 (3)	9.75	9.75

Chinese Bridal Costume — A63   Radar, Surface to Air Missile, Soldiers — A64

Designs: 35c, Indian bridal costume. 75c, Malay bridal costume.

1976, Dec. 19   Litho.   Perf. 14½
257	A63	10c lt green & multi	.55	.55
258	A63	35c lilac & multi	2.00	2.00
259	A63	75c yellow & multi	4.50	4.50
		Nos. 257-259 (3)	7.05	7.05

1977, Mar. 12   Litho.   Perf. 14½
50c, Infantry soldiers and tank. 75c, Jet fighter, pilot, telecommunications center.

260	A64	10c multicolored	.75	.25
261	A64	50c multicolored	2.75	2.50
262	A64	75c multicolored	4.00	4.00
		Nos. 260-262 (3)	7.50	6.75

National Service, 10th anniversary.

Lyrate Cockle A65   Spotted Hermit Crab A66

Sea Shells: 5c, Folded scallop. 10c, Marble cone. 15c, Scorpion conch. 20c, Amplustre bubble. 25c, Spiral Babylon. 35c, Regal thorny oyster. 50c, Winged frog shell. 75c, Troschel's murex.

Marine Life: $2, Stingray. $5, Cuttlefish. $10, Lionfish.

1977   Perf. 13½
263	A65	1c orange & multi	1.10	1.60
264	A65	5c orange & multi	.25	.25
a.		Bklt. pane, 4 #264, 8 #265	5.00	
265	A65	10c orange & multi	.25	.25
266	A65	15c orange & multi	1.00	.40
267	A65	20c orange & multi	1.00	.25
268	A65	25c orange & multi	1.25	2.25
269	A65	35c orange & multi	1.50	1.40
270	A65	50c orange & multi	2.00	.25
271	A65	75c orange & multi	3.00	.25

Perf. 14
272	A66	$1 multicolored	2.50	.25
273	A66	$2 multicolored	2.50	.75
274	A66	$5 multicolored	3.50	3.00
275	A66	$10 multicolored	6.00	4.25
		Nos. 263-275 (13)	25.85	15.15

No. 264a has a large inscribed selvage, the size of 6 stamps.
Issued: #263-271, Apr. 9; others, June 4.

Singapore Harbor Improvements A67

Labor Day: 50c, Construction workers. 75c, Road workers.

1977, May 1   Litho.   Perf. 13x12½
276	A67	10c multicolored	.50	.50
277	A67	50c multicolored	1.75	1.75
278	A67	75c multicolored	2.50	2.50
		Nos. 276-278 (3)	4.75	4.75

"Key to Savings" — A68   Grain and Cattle — A69

Designs: 35c, "On-line Banking Service." 75c, "GIRO Service."

1977, July 16   Litho.   Perf. 13, 14
279	A68	10c multicolored	.25	.25
a.		Perf 14	25.00	25.00
280	A68	35c multicolored	1.00	1.00
a.		Perf 14	100.00	100.00
281	A68	75c multicolored	2.75	2.75
a.		Perf 14	130.00	130.00
		Nos. 279-281 (3)	4.00	4.00

Centenary of Post Office Savings Bank.

1977, Aug. 8   Litho.   Perf. 14
10c, Flags of founding members: Thailand, Indonesia, Singapore, Malaysia, Philippines. 75c, Steel, oil & chemical industries.

282	A69	10c multicolored	.35	.25
283	A69	35c multicolored	1.00	1.00
284	A69	75c multicolored	2.50	2.50
		Nos. 282-284 (3)	3.85	3.75

Association of South East Asian Nations (ASEAN), 10th anniversary.

Bus Stop — A70

Children's Drawings: 10c, Chingay procession, vert. 75c, Playground.

1977, Oct. 1   Perf. 12½
285	A70	10c multicolored	.35	.25
286	A70	35c multicolored	1.00	.65
287	A70	75c multicolored	3.25	1.50
a.		Souvenir sheet of 3, #285-287	16.00	16.00
		Nos. 285-287 (3)	4.60	2.40

Symbols of Life Sciences — A71   Botanical Gardens — A72

Singapore Science Center: 35c, "Physical sciences." 75c, "Science and technology." $1, Science Center.

1977, Dec. 10   Litho.   Perf. 14½x14
288	A71	10c multicolored	.25	.25
289	A71	35c multicolored	.60	.60
290	A71	75c multicolored	1.40	1.40
291	A71	$1 multicolored	2.40	2.40
		Nos. 288-291 (4)	4.65	4.65

1978, Apr. 22   Litho.   Perf. 14½
Singapore Parks and Gardens: 10c, Jurong Bird Park, horiz. 35c, East Coast Lagoon and Park.

292	A72	10c multicolored	.25	.25
293	A72	35c multicolored	1.10	1.10
294	A72	75c multicolored	2.25	2.25
		Nos. 292-294 (3)	3.60	3.60

Red-whiskered Bulbul — A73

Songbirds: 35c, White eyes. 50c, White-rumped shama. 75c, White-crested laughing thrush.

1978, July 1   Litho.   Perf. 13½
295	A73	10c multicolored	.75	.75
296	A73	35c multicolored	2.25	2.25
297	A73	50c multicolored	2.50	2.50
298	A73	75c multicolored	3.00	3.00
		Nos. 295-298 (4)	8.50	8.50

Thian Hock Keng Temple — A74

National Monuments: No. 303a, like No. 299. Nos. 300, 303b, Hajjah Fatimah Mosque. Nos. 301, 303c, Armenian Church. Nos. 302, 303d, Sri Mariamman Temple.

1978, Aug. 9
299	A74	10c tan & multi	.70	.70
300	A74	10c green & multi	.70	.70
301	A74	10c blue & multi	.70	.70
302	A74	10c lilac & multi	.70	.70
		Nos. 299-302 (4)	2.80	2.80

Souvenir Sheet
303		Sheet of 4	9.00	9.00
a.		A74 35c tan & multi	1.40	
b.		A74 35c green & multi	1.40	
c.		A74 35c blue & multi	1.40	
d.		A74 35c lilac & multi	1.40	

Map of Proposed Cable Network A75

1978, Oct. 30   Litho.   Perf. 14
304	A75	10c multicolored	.25	.25
305	A75	35c multicolored	.95	.95
306	A75	50c multicolored	1.25	1.25
307	A75	75c multicolored	2.10	2.10
		Nos. 304-307 (4)	4.55	4.55

ASEAN Submarine Cable Network. Nos. 304-307 printed in sheets of 100. Stamps have perforations around design and around edges. See No. 429a.

Neptune Spinel — A76

Ships: 35c, Neptune Aries. 50c, Arno Temasek. 75c, Neptune Pearl.

1978, Nov. 18   Litho.   Perf. 13½x14
308	A76	10c multicolored	1.00	.25
309	A76	35c multicolored	2.25	2.00
310	A76	50c multicolored	2.25	2.25
311	A76	75c multicolored	3.00	3.00
		Nos. 308-311 (4)	8.50	7.50

Neptune Oriental Shipping Lines, 10th anniv.

Concorde A77

Aviation Development: 35c, Boeing 747B. 50c, Vickers-Vimy, 1st aircraft to land in Singapore. 75c, Wright Brothers' Flyer I.

1978, Dec. 16   Perf. 13½
312	A77	10c yellow green & blk	.60	.40
313	A77	35c blue & black	1.40	1.25
314	A77	50c carmine & black	1.60	1.60
315	A77	75c brown & black	2.50	2.50
		Nos. 312-315 (4)	6.10	5.75

75th anniversary of 1st powered flight.

Distance Marker in Kilometers — A78

Designs: 35c, Tape measure in centimeters. 75c, Scales in grams and kilograms.

1979, Jan. 24   Litho.   Perf. 13x13½
316	A78	10c multicolored	.25	.25
317	A78	35c multicolored	.50	.50
318	A78	75c multicolored	1.25	1.25
		Nos. 316-318 (3)	2.00	2.00

Introduction of metric system.

Vanda Orchids — A79

Varieties of vanda hybrids. 10c, 35c, horiz.

Perf. 14½x14, 14x14½
1979, Apr. 14   Litho.
319	A79	10c multicolored	.30	.30
320	A79	35c multicolored	1.00	1.00
321	A79	50c multicolored	1.50	1.50
322	A79	75c multicolored	1.75	1.75
		Nos. 319-322 (4)	4.55	4.55

Envelope Addressed to Postmaster A80

50c, Envelope addressed to Philatelic Bureau.

1979, July 1   Litho.   Perf. 12½x13
323	A80	10c orange & multi	.25	.25
324	A80	50c dark blue & multi	1.00	1.00

Singapore's postal code system.

Old Phone, Telephone Lines — A81

Designs: 35c, Dial, world map. 50c, Push-button phone, skyline. 75c, Line network.

1979, Oct. 5   Litho.   Perf. 13½
325	A81	10c multicolored	.40	.40
326	A81	35c multicolored	.60	.60
327	A81	50c multicolored	1.00	1.00
328	A81	75c multicolored	1.40	1.40
		Nos. 325-328 (4)	3.40	3.40

Telephone service centenary.

IYC Emblem, Lanterns Festival A82

IYC Emblem, Children's Drawings: 35c, Singapore Harbor. 50c, "Use Your Hands." 75c, Soccer.

1979, Nov. 10   Litho.   Perf. 13
329	A82	10c multicolored	.40	.40
330	A82	35c multicolored	.60	.60
331	A82	50c multicolored	.80	.80
332	A82	75c multicolored	1.25	1.25
a.		Souvenir sheet of 4, #329-332	6.25	6.25
		Nos. 329-332 (4)	3.05	3.05

International Year of the Child.

Botanic Gardens, 120th Anniversary — A83

1979, Dec. 15   Perf. 13½
333	A83	10c shown	.25	.25
334	A83	50c Gazebo	1.10	1.10
335	A83	$1 Greenhouse	2.25	2.25
		Nos. 333-335 (3)	3.60	3.60

Hainan Junk — A84

1980   Litho.   Perf. 14
336	A84	1c shown	.25	.25
337	A84	5c Clipper	.25	.25
338	A84	10c Fujian junk	.25	.25
a.		Booklet pane of 10	4.00	
339	A84	15c Golekkan	.25	.25
340	A84	20c Palari	.25	.25
341	A84	25c East Indiaman	.25	.25
342	A84	35c Galleon	.50	.25
343	A84	50c Caravel	.70	.25
344	A84	75c Jiangsu trader	1.00	.25

Size: 41½x24½mm
Perf. 13½
345	A84	$1 Coaster	1.50	.35
346	A84	$2 Oil tanker	2.75	.55
347	A84	$5 Screw steamer	7.00	1.60
348	A84	$10 Paddle wheel steamer	15.00	15.00
		Nos. 336-348 (13)	29.95	10.25

Issued: #336-344, Apr. 26; others, Apr. 5.

Straits Settlements No. 1, Old Singapore Map, London 1980 Emblem — A85

London 1980 Emblem and: 35c, Straits Settlements No. 146, letter. $1, Singapore No. 19, map of Straits. $2, Singapore No. 106, letter, 1819.

1980, May 6   Litho.   Perf. 13
349	A85	10c multicolored	.30	.30
350	A85	35c multicolored	.60	.60
351	A85	$1 multicolored	1.25	1.25
352	A85	$2 multicolored	2.10	2.10
a.		Souvenir sheet of 4, #349-352	5.00	5.00
		Nos. 349-352 (4)	4.25	4.25

London 1980 Intl. Stamp Exhib., May 6-14.

Fund Board Emblem, Keys to Retirement — A86

1980, July 1   Litho.   Perf. 13
353	A86	10c shown	.30	.30
354	A86	50c Home ownership savings	.70	.70
355	A86	$1 Old age savings	1.40	1.40
		Nos. 353-355 (3)	2.40	2.40

Central Provident Fund Board, 25th anniv.

Map Showing Singapore-Indonesia Cable Route — A87

1980, Aug. 8   Litho.   Perf. 14
356	A87	10c multicolored	.25	.25
357	A87	35c multicolored	.80	.80
358	A87	50c multicolored	1.25	1.25
359	A87	75c multicolored	1.75	1.75
		Nos. 356-359 (4)	4.05	4.05

ASEAN Submarine Cable Network extension. Stamps perforated around design and around edges. See No. 429a.

Fair Emblem A88

1980, Oct. 3   Litho.   Perf. 13
360	A88	10c multicolored	.25	.25
361	A88	35c multicolored	.50	.50
362	A88	75c multicolored	1.10	1.10
		Nos. 360-362 (3)	1.85	1.85

Asean Trade Fair, Oct. 3-12.

A89

1980, Nov. 2   Litho.   Perf. 13½
363	A89	10c Flame of the wood	.25	.25
364	A89	35c Golden trumpet	.60	.60
365	A89	50c Sky vine	.60	.60
366	A89	75c Bougainvillea	1.50	1.50
		Nos. 363-366 (4)	2.95	2.95

A90

1981, Jan. 24   Litho.   Perf. 14x14½
367	A90	10c multicolored	.30	.30
368	A90	35c multicolored	.50	.50
369	A90	75c multicolored	.95	.95
		Nos. 367-369 (3)	1.75	1.75

Monetary Authority of Singapore, 10th anniv.

No. 54 Surcharged

Perf. 13½x14½
1981, Mar. 5   Photo.   Wmk. 314
370	A8	10c on 4c red org & blk	.45	.45

A91   A92

Unwmk.
1981, Apr. 11   Litho.   Perf. 13
371	A91	10c Technical Training (Woodworking)	.30	.30
372	A91	35c Building construction	.50	.50
373	A91	50c Electronics	.75	.75
374	A91	75c Precision machinery	.90	.90
		Nos. 371-374 (4)	2.45	2.45

1981, Aug. 25 Litho. Perf. 14

Sports For All: Various sports.

375	A92	10c multicolored	.55	.25
376	A92	75c multicolored	2.50	2.50
377	A92	$1 multicolored	3.25	3.25
		Nos. 375-377 (3)	6.30	6.00

A93

A94

1981, Nov. 24 Litho. Perf. 14½

378	A93	10c Man in wheelchair	.25	.25
379	A93	35c Group	.60	.60
380	A93	50c Teacher, student	.90	.90
381	A93	75c Blind communications worker	1.25	1.25
		Nos. 378-381 (4)	3.00	3.00

Intl. Year of the Disabled.

1981, Dec. 29 Litho. Perf. 14x13½

382	A94	10c multicolored	.30	.30
383	A94	35c multicolored	.45	.45
384	A94	50c multicolored	.80	.80
385	A94	75c multicolored	1.00	1.00
386	A94	$1 multicolored	1.25	1.25
a.		Souvenir sheet of 5, #382-386	4.00	4.00
		Nos. 382-386 (5)	3.80	3.80

Changi airport opening.

A95

1982, Mar. 3 Litho. Perf. 14x14½

387	A95	10c Clipper	.50	.50
388	A95	50c Blue grassy tiger	1.75	1.75
389	A95	$1 Raja Brooke's birdwing	2.25	2.25
		Nos. 387-389 (3)	4.50	4.50

A96

1982, June 14 Litho. Perf. 14

390	A96	10c multicolored	.25	.25
391	A96	35c multicolored	.60	.60
392	A96	50c multicolored	.75	.75
393	A96	75c multicolored	1.00	1.00
		Nos. 390-393 (4)	2.60	2.60

15th ASEAN Ministerial meeting.

A97

1982, July 9 Litho. Perf. 12

394	A97	10c multicolored	.25	.25
395	A97	75c multicolored	1.10	1.10
396	A97	$1 multicolored	1.90	1.90
		Nos. 394-396 (3)	3.25	3.25

1982 World Cup.

Sultan Shoal Lighthouse, 1896 — A98

1982, Aug. 7

397	A98	10c shown	.65	.65
398	A98	75c Horsburgh, 1851	1.75	1.75
399	A98	$1 Raffles, 1855	2.10	2.10
a.		Souvenir sheet of 3, #397-399	6.00	6.00
		Nos. 397-399 (3)	4.50	4.50

10th Anniv. of PSA Container Terminal A99

1982, Sept. 15 Litho. Perf. 13½

400	A99	10c Yard gantry cranes	.25	.25
401	A99	35c Computer	.50	.50
402	A99	50c Freightlifter	.65	.65
403	A99	75c Straddle carrier	1.10	1.10
		Nos. 400-403 (4)	2.50	2.50

Scouting Year — A100

1982, Oct. 15 Litho. Perf. 14x13½

404	A100	10c Color guard	.25	.25
405	A100	35c Hiking	.65	.65
406	A100	50c Building tower	.90	.90
407	A100	75c Kayaking	1.40	1.40
		Nos. 404-407 (4)	3.20	3.20

Productivity Movement A101

1982, Nov. 17 Perf. 13½

408	A101	10c Text	.25	.25
409	A101	35c Housing	.50	.50
410	A101	50c Quality control meeting	.70	.70
411	A101	75c Participation	1.10	1.10
		Nos. 408-411 (4)	2.55	2.55

Commonwealth Day — A102

12th Southeast Asia Games — A103

1983, May 14 Litho. Perf. 13½x13

412	A102	10c multicolored	.25	.25
413	A102	35c multicolored	.40	.40
414	A102	75c multicolored	.75	.75
415	A102	$1 multicolored	1.00	1.00
		Nos. 412-415 (4)	2.40	2.40

1983, May 28 Litho. Perf. 14x13½

416	A103	10c Soccer	.25	.25
417	A103	35c Racket games	.45	.45
418	A103	75c Athletics	.95	.95
419	A103	$1 Swimming	1.40	1.40
		Nos. 416-419 (4)	3.05	3.05

Neighborhood Watch Safety Campaign A104

1983, June 24 Litho. Perf. 14

420	A104	10c Family	.40	.25
421	A104	35c Children	.75	.75
422	A104	75c Community	1.20	.80
		Nos. 420-422 (3)	2.35	1.80

BANGKOK '83 Intl. Stamp Show, Aug. 4-13 — A105

10c, #282-284, statue of King Chulalongkorn (1868-1910). 35c, #304-307, map of southeast Asia. $1, #390-393, Declaration of ASEAN (Assoc. of South East Asian Nations) signatures, 1976.

1983, Aug. 4 Litho. Perf. 14x14½

423	A105	10c multicolored	.35	.25
424	A105	35c multicolored	.70	.55
425	A105	$1 multicolored	1.50	1.25
a.		Souvenir sheet of 3, #423-425	4.50	4.50
		Nos. 423-425 (3)	2.55	2.05

ASEAN Submarine Cable Network A106

1983, Sept. 27 Litho. Perf. 14

426	A106	10c multicolored	.30	.25
427	A106	35c multicolored	.90	.70
428	A106	50c multicolored	1.10	.90
429	A106	75c multicolored	1.75	1.40
a.		Souv. sheet of 6, #304, 359, 426-429	7.00	7.00
		Nos. 426-429 (4)	4.05	3.25

World Communications Year — A107

1983, Nov. 10 Litho. Perf. 13

430	A107	10c Telex service	.40	.25
431	A107	35c Telephone numbering plan	.75	.60
432	A107	75c Satellite transmission	1.50	1.25
433	A107	$1 Sea communications	1.90	1.60
		Nos. 430-433 (4)	4.55	3.70

Coastal Birds — A108

Perf. 14½x13½

1984, Mar. 15 Litho.

434	A108	10c Slaty-breasted rail	.55	.25
435	A108	35c Black bittern	1.40	1.40
436	A108	50c Brahminy kite	2.00	2.00
437	A108	75c Common moorhens	3.00	3.00
		Nos. 434-437 (4)	6.95	6.65

Natl. Monuments A109

10c, House of Tan Yeok Nee (merchant), 1885. 35c, Thong Chai Building (former hospital), 1892. 50c, Telok Ayer Market, 1894. $1, Nagore Durgha Muslim Shrine, 1828.

1984, June 7 Litho. Perf. 12

438	A109	10c multicolored	.25	.25
439	A109	35c multicolored	.60	.60
440	A109	50c multicolored	.90	.90
441	A109	$1 multicolored	1.90	1.90
		Nos. 438-441 (4)	3.65	3.65

A110

A111

1984, Aug. 9 Litho. Perf. 14

442	A110	10c No. 121	.25	.25
443	A110	35c No. 377	.55	.55
444	A110	50c No. 99	.75	.75
445	A110	75c No. 243	1.10	1.10
446	A110	$1 No. 386	1.50	1.50
447	A110	$2 No. 367	2.75	2.75
a.		Souvenir sheet of 6, #442-447	9.25	9.25
		Nos. 442-447 (6)	6.90	6.90

25th anniv. of self-government.

1984, Oct. 26 Litho. Perf. 12

Total Defense: a, This is our country. b, We are one. c, We work together. d, We are prepared. e, We are ready.

448		Strip of 5	1.00	1.00
a.-e.	A111	10c any single	.25	.25

Bridges A112

1985, Mar. 15 Engr. Perf. 14½x14

449	A112	10c Coleman	.25	.25
450	A112	35c Cavenagh	.50	.50
451	A112	75c Elgin	1.25	1.25
452	A112	$1 Benjamin Sheares	1.75	1.75
		Nos. 449-452 (4)	3.75	3.75

Insects — A113

1985 Litho. Perf. 13x13½

453	A113	5c Ceriagrion cerinorubellum	.25	.25
454	A113	10c Apis javana	.25	.25
455	A113	15c Delta arcuata	.25	.25
456	A113	20c Xylocopa caerulea	.25	.25
457	A113	25c Donacia javana	.30	.30
458	A113	35c Heteroneda reticulata	.60	.60
459	A113	50c Catacanthus nigripes	.85	.85
460	A113	75c Chremistica pontianaka	1.40	1.40

Litho. & Engr.
Size: 35x30mm

461	A113	$1 Homoeoxipha lycoides	1.75	1.75
462	A113	$2 Traulia azureipennis	3.50	3.50
463	A113	$5 Trithemis aurora	8.50	8.50

464 A113 $10 Scambophyllum
sangiunolen-
tum 17.00 17.00
Nos. 453-464 (12) 34.90 34.90
Issued: #453-460, 4/24; #461-464, 6/5.

Redrawn

1986			**Perf. 13x13½**		
453a	A113	5c		5.50	5.50
454a	A113	10c		10.50	10.50
455a	A113	15c		16.00	16.00
456a	A113	20c		22.50	22.50
457a	A113	25c		27.50	27.50
458a	A113	25c		37.50	37.50
459a	A113	50c		57.50	57.50
460a	A113	75c		82.50	82.50

Nos. 453a-460a (8) 259.50 259.50

Singapore is 20½mm long on Nos. 453a-454a; 21mm long on Nos. 453-454. Rock is 1½mm from bottom right on No. 455; 2½mm on No. 455a. Pink flower touches frame on No. 456; is clear of the frame on No. 456a. Feelers indistinct and left one touches frame on No. 457; feelers sharp and left one ends just below frame on No. 457a.

Vein of leaf at lower left stops short of frame on No. 458; vein touches frame on No. 458a. Leaf at top touches frame on No. 459; leaf is below frame on No. 459a. Wing ends 1½mm above frame on No. 460; wing touches frame at bottom on No. 460a.

Other differences exist in the position and sharpness of the design and colors.

People's Assoc., 25th Anniv. — A114

Montage of public services.

1985, July 1			**Perf. 13½x14**	
465	A114	10c multicolored	.25	.25
466	A114	35c multicolored	.50	.50
467	A114	50c multicolored	.85	.85
468	A114	75c multicolored	1.10	1.10

Nos. 465-468 (4) 2.70 2.70

Public Housing, 25th Anniv. — A115

Modern housing developments.

1985, Aug. 9				
469	A115	10c multicolored	.25	.25
470	A115	35c multicolored	.55	.55
471	A115	50c multicolored	.70	.70
472	A115	75c multicolored	1.10	1.10
a.	Souv. sheet of 4, #469-472		5.25	5.25

Nos. 469-472 (4) 2.60 2.60

Girl Guides, 75th Anniv. — A116

Activities.

1985, Nov 6			**Perf. 14½x14**	
473	A116	10c Brownies	.25	.25
474	A116	35c Guides	.60	.60
475	A116	50c Seniors	.80	.80
476	A116	75c Guide leaders	1.40	1.40

Nos. 473-476 (4) 3.05 3.05

Intl. Youth Year — A117

1985, Dec. 18			**Perf. 13**	
477	A117	10c Youth assoc. emblems	.25	.25
478	A117	75c Hand, sapling	1.10	.80
479	A117	$1 Dove, stick figures	1.40	1.00

Nos. 477-479 (3) 2.75 2.05

Indigenous Fruit — A118

Natl. Trade Unions Cong., 25th Anniv. — A119

1986, Feb. 26 Litho.			**Perf. 14½x14**	
480	A118	10c Psidium guajava	.45	.25
481	A118	35c Eugenia aquea	1.20	1.00
482	A118	50c Nephelium lappaceum	1.50	1.25
483	A118	75c Manilkara zapota	2.00	1.75

Nos. 480-483 (4) 5.15 4.25

1986, May 1			**Perf. 13½**	

Progress: a, Science and technology. b, Communications. c, Industry. d, Education.

484		Strip of 4	2.00	2.00
a.-d.	A119 10c any single		.25	.25

Souvenir Sheet

485		Sheet of 4	5.00	5.00
a.-d.	A119 35c any single		.50	.50

EXPO '86, Vancouver A120

1986, May 2			**Perf. 14½x14**	
486		Strip of 3	4.25	4.25
a.	A120 50c Calligraphy		.85	.85
b.	A120 75c Garland making		1.25	1.25
c.	A120 $1 Batik printing		1.75	1.75

Economic Development Board, 25th Anniv. — A121

1986, Aug. 1			**Perf. 15**	
487	A121	10c Automation	.25	.25
488	A121	35c Precision engineering	.45	.45
489	A121	75c Electronics	.75	.75
490	A121	75c Biotechnology	1.10	1.10

Nos. 487-490 (4) 2.55 2.55

Submarine Cable — A122

1986, Sept. 8			**Perf. 13½**	
491	A122	10c multicolored	.50	.25
492	A122	35c multicolored	1.00	1.00
493	A122	50c multicolored	1.40	1.40
494	A122	75c multicolored	1.75	1.75

Nos. 491-494 (4) 4.65 4.40

Citizens' Consultative Committees, 21st Anniv. — A123

1986, Oct 15			**Perf. 12**	
495	A123	Block of 4	3.00	3.00
a.		10c multicolored	.25	.25
b.		35c multicolored	.55	.55
c.		50c multicolored	.80	.80
d.		75c multicolored	1.25	1.25

Intl. Peace Year — A124

1986, Dec. 17 Litho.			**Perf. 14x13½**	
496	A124	10c People	.30	.25
497	A124	35c Southeast Asia map	.75	.50
498	A124	$1 Globe	1.75	1.50

Nos. 496-498 (3) 2.80 2.25

Views of Singapore A125

1987, Feb. 25			**Perf. 12x12½**	
499	A125	10c Orchard Road	.25	.25
500	A125	50c Central business district	.95	.95
501	A125	75c Marina Center, Raffles City	1.25	1.25

Nos. 499-501 (3) 2.45 2.45

Assoc. of Southeast Asian Nations (ASEAN), 20th Anniv. A126

National Service, 20th Anniv. A127

1987, June 15			**Perf. 12**	
502	A126	10c multicolored	.25	.25
503	A126	35c multicolored	.55	.55
504	A126	50c multicolored	.80	.80
505	A126	75c multicolored	1.25	1.25

Nos. 502-505 (4) 2.85 2.85

1987, July 1			**Perf. 15x14**	

Designs: a, Army. b, Navy. c, Air Force. d, Pledge of Allegiance. e, Singapore Lion.

506		Strip of 4	2.50	2.50
a.-d.	A127 10c any single		.25	.25
507		Sheet of 5	5.00	5.00
a.-e.	A127 35c any single		.45	.45

River Life — A128

1987, Sept. 2			**Perf. 14**	
508	A128	10c Singapore River	.40	.25
509	A128	50c Kallang Basin	1.20	.90
510	A128	$1 Kranji Reservoir	2.75	2.50

Nos. 508-510 (3) 4.35 3.65

Natl. Museum Cent. A129

Views of the museum and artifacts: 10c, Majapahis gold bracelet, 14th-15th cent. 75c, Ming fluted kendi (water jar). $1, Seventeen-wave kris (sword with silver hilt, sheath), property of Sultan Abdul Jalil Sabat, 1699.

1987, Oct. 12 Litho.			**Perf. 13½x14**	
511	A129	10c multicolored	.50	.25
512	A129	75c multicolored	1.60	1.40
513	A129	$1 multicolored	1.90	1.50

Nos. 511-513 (3) 4.00 3.15

Singapore Science Center, 10th Anniv. A130

Attractions.

1987, Dec. 10			**Perf. 14½**	
514	A130	10c Omni Theater	.40	.40
515	A130	35c Omni Planetarium	1.10	1.10
516	A130	75c Cellular model	2.25	2.25
517	A130	$1 Science exhibits	3.00	3.00

Nos. 514-517 (4) 6.75 6.75

Artillery, Cent. A131

Designs: 10c, 155-Gun Howitzer and Khatib Camp, headquarters of the Singapore Gunners. 35c, 25-Pound gun salute and Singapore City Hall. 50c, 4.5-inch Howitzer and Singapore Cricket Club, c. 1928. $1, Ft. Fullerton Drill Hall, c. 1893, and .405 Maxim gun.

1988, Feb. 22 Litho.			**Perf. 13½x14**	
518	A131	10c multicolored	.85	.25
519	A131	35c multicolored	1.75	1.40
520	A131	50c multicolored	2.00	2.00
521	A131	$1 multicolored	2.75	2.40

Nos. 518-521 (4) 7.35 6.05

Mass Transit A132

1988, Mar. 12			**Perf. 14**	
522	A132	10c Rail car, map	1.20	.25
523	A132	50c Elevated train	2.75	2.50
524	A132	$1 Urban subway	4.50	4.00

Nos. 522-524 (3) 8.45 6.75

See No. 1064.

Natl. Television Broadcast System, 25th Anniv. A133

1988, Apr. 4   Litho.   Perf. 13½x14

525	A133	10c shown	.40	.25
526	A133	35c Studio	.85	.85
527	A133	75c Television, transmission tower	1.25	1.25
528	A133	$1 Screen, satellite dish	1.90	1.60
		Nos. 525-528 (4)	4.40	3.95

Public Utilities Board, 25th Anniv. — A134

1988, May 4   Litho.   Perf. 13½

529	A134	10c Water works	.35	.25
530	A134	50c Electric company	1.20	1.20
531	A134	$1 Fossil fuels	2.10	2.00
a.		Souvenir sheet of 3, #529-531	6.00	6.00
		Nos. 529-531 (3)	3.65	3.45

Courtesy Campaign, 10th Anniv. — A135

Singa the lion (character trademark) and: 10c, Neighbors. 30c, Store service counter. $1, Helping the elderly.

1988, July 6   Litho.   Perf. 14½

532	A135	10c multicolored	.35	.25
533	A135	30c multicolored	.75	.60
534	A135	$1 multicolored	2.00	1.60
		Nos. 532-534 (3)	3.10	2.45

Fire Service, Cent. A136

1988, Nov. 1   Litho.   Perf. 13½

| 535 | A136 | 10c Turntable ladder truck | .80 | .25 |
| 536 | A136 | $1 1890s Steam pump | 4.75 | 4.75 |

Port Authority, 25th Anniv. — A137

Various facilities.

1989, Apr. 3   Litho.   Perf. 14x13½

537	A137	10c multicolored	.80	.25
538	A137	30c multi, diff.	1.20	.60
539	A137	75c multi, diff.	1.75	1.60
540	A137	$1 multi, diff.	1.90	1.75
		Nos. 537-540 (4)	5.65	4.20

Old Chinatown A138

1989, May 17   Litho.   Perf. 14½

541	A138	10c Sago St.	.55	.45
542	A138	35c Pagoda St.	1.40	1.40
543	A138	75c Trengganu St.	2.40	2.25
544	A138	$1 Temple St.	2.75	2.50
		Nos. 541-544 (4)	7.10	6.60

Maps of Singapore — A139

Early 19th cent. map Singapore Showing Principal Residences and Places of Interest: No. 545a, Upper left. No. 545b, Upper right. No. 545c, Lower left. No. 545d, Lower right.

1989, July 26   Litho.   Perf. 14½

| 545 | A139 | Block of 4 | 7.00 | 6.50 |
| a.-d. | | 15c any single | 1.75 | 1.60 |

Size: 33x31mm
Perf. 12½x13

546	A139	50c Singapore and Dependencies	3.00	2.50
547	A139	$1 Plan of the British Settlement	3.50	3.50
		Nos. 545-547 (3)	13.50	12.50

Fish — A140

1989, Sept. 6   Perf. 14

548	A140	15c Clown triggerfish	1.90	1.50
549	A140	30c Majestic angelfish	2.10	2.50
550	A140	75c Emperor angelfish	3.75	3.75
551	A140	$1 Royal empress angelfish	4.50	4.25
		Nos. 548-551 (4)	12.25	12.00

Festivals — A141

Children's drawings: 15c, Hari Raya Puasa, by Loke Yoke Yen. 35c, Chinese New Year, by Simon Koh. 75c, Thaipusam, by Henry Setiono. $1, Christmas, by Wendy Ang Lin.

1989, Oct. 25   Perf. 14½

552	A141	15c multicolored	.70	.40
553	A141	35c multicolored	.90	.70
554	A141	75c multicolored	1.60	1.25
555	A141	$1 multicolored	2.00	1.75
a.		Souv. sheet of 4, #552-555, perf. 14	6.00	6.00
		Nos. 552-555 (4)	5.20	4.10

Singapore Indoor Stadium — A142

1989, Dec. 27   Litho.   Perf. 14½

556	A142	30c North entrance	1.10	.90
557	A142	75c Interior	2.25	1.75
558	A142	$1 East entrance	2.60	2.10
a.		Souvenir sheet of 3, #556-558	6.50	6.50
		Nos. 556-558 (3)	5.95	4.75

Sports issue.

Lithographs of 19th Cent. Singapore A143

1990, Feb. 21   Litho.   Perf. 13

559	A143	15c Singapore River, 1839	1.10	.25
		Complete booklet, 10 #559	13.00	
560	A143	30c Chinatown, 1837	1.50	.75
561	A143	75c Waterfront, 1837	2.60	2.40
562	A143	$1 View from Ft. Canning, 1824	3.00	2.60
		Nos. 559-562 (4)	8.20	6.00

First Postage Stamps, 150th Anniv. — A144

Maps and: 50c, Nos. 101-106. 75c, Cover to Scotland. $1, Cover to Ireland $2, Great Britain Nos. 1, 2.

1990, May 3   Litho.   Perf. 13½

563	A144	50c multicolored	1.25	1.10
564	A144	75c multicolored	1.50	1.40
565	A144	$1 multicolored	2.40	2.10
566	A144	$2 multicolored	3.50	3.25
a.		Souvenir sheet of 4, #563-566	12.00	12.00
		Nos. 563-566 (4)	8.65	7.85

Tourism A145

1990, July 4   Perf. 14½

567	A145	5c Zoo	.25	.25
568	A145	15c Resort	.25	.25
a.		Booklet pane of 10	12.00	
569	A145	20c City	.30	.30
570	A145	25c Dragon boat race	.35	.35
571	A145	30c Hotel	.40	.40
572	A145	35c Caged birds	.50	.50
573	A145	40c Park	.55	.55
574	A145	50c Festival	.65	.65
575	A145	75c Building, diff.	1.00	1.00
		Nos. 567-575 (9)	4.25	4.25

Independence, 25th Anniv. — A146

1990, Aug. 16   Litho.   Perf. 14x14½

576	A146	15c shown	1.00	1.00
a.		Booklet pane of 10	16.00	
577	A146	35c One Singapore	1.20	1.20
578	A146	75c One hope	2.25	2.25
579	A146	$1 One people	2.50	2.50
		Nos. 576-579 (4)	6.95	6.95

Tourism A147

$1, Chinese opera singer, Siong Lim Temple. $2, Malay dancer, Sultan Mosque. $5, Indian dancer, Sri Mariamman Temple. $10, Ballet dancer, Victoria Memorial Hall.

Photo. & Engr.
1990, Oct. 10   Perf. 15x14

580	A147	$1 multicolored	1.75	1.75
581	A147	$2 multicolored	3.25	3.25
582	A147	$5 multicolored	8.25	8.25
583	A147	$10 multicolored	14.50	14.50
		Nos. 580-583 (4)	27.75	27.75

Ferns A148

1990, Nov. 14   Litho.   Perf. 14

584	A148	15c Stag's horn	.40	.25
585	A148	35c Maiden hair	.85	.60
586	A148	75c Bird's nest	1.60	1.40
587	A148	$1 Rabbit's foot	2.10	1.60
		Nos. 584-587 (4)	4.95	3.85

Houses of Worship A149

Designs: 20c, Hong San See Temple, 1912. 50c, Abdul Gattoor Mosque, 1910. 75c, Sri Perumal Temple, 1961. $1, St. Andrew's Cathedral, 1863.

1991, Jan. 23   Litho.   Perf. 14½

588		20c multicolored	.40	.40
589		20c multicolored	.40	.40
a.	A149	Pair, #588-589	1.00	1.00
590		50c multicolored	1.00	1.00
591		50c multicolored	1.00	1.00
a.	A149	Pair, #590-591	2.75	2.75
592		75c multicolored	1.50	1.50
593		75c multicolored	1.50	1.50
a.	A149	Pair, #592-593	4.00	4.00
594		$1 multicolored	2.00	2.00
595		$1 multicolored	2.00	2.00
a.	A149	Pair, #594-595	5.25	5.25
		Nos. 588-595 (8)	9.80	9.80

Vanda Miss Joaquim — A151

Design: No. 597, Dendrobium Anocha.

1991, Apr. 24   Litho.   Perf. 14

596	A151	$2 multicolored	3.00	3.00
597	A151	$2 multicolored	3.00	3.00
a.		Pair, #596-597 + label	7.50	7.50
b.		Souvenir sheet, #596-597	14.00	14.00

Singapore '95 Intl. Philatelic Exhibition.
See Nos. 615-616, 664-665, 685-686, 716-717.

Civilian Airports A152

Designs: 20c, Boeing 747, Changi Terminal II, 1991. 75c, Boeing 747, Changi Terminal I, 1981. $1, Concorde, Paya Lebar, 1955-1981. $2, DC-3, Kallang, 1937-1955.

Perf. 13½x14½

1991, July 1   Litho. & Engr.
598	A152	20c multicolored	.40	.40
599	A152	75c multicolored	1.50	1.50
600	A152	$1 multicolored	2.25	2.25
601	A152	$2 multicolored	6.00	6.00
		Nos. 598-601 (4)	10.15	10.15

Arachnopsis Eric Holttum — A153

Orchids: 30c, Cattleya Meadii. $1, Calanthe vestita.

1991, Aug. 8   Litho.   Perf. 14½x13½
602	A153	20c multicolored	1.10	1.00
603	A153	30c multicolored	1.50	1.25
604	A153	$1 multicolored	3.50	3.50
		Nos. 602-604 (3)	6.10	5.75

Birds — A154

Designs: 20c, Common tailorbird. 35c, Scarlet-backed flowerpecker. 75c, Black-naped oriole. $1, Common tora.

1991, Sept. 19   Perf. 14
605	A154	20c multicolored	.45	.25
a.		Booklet pane of 10	22.50	22.50
606	A154	35c multicolored	1.50	1.50
607	A154	75c multicolored	3.50	3.50
608	A154	$1 multicolored	3.75	3.75
		Nos. 605-608 (4)	9.20	9.00

10 Years of Productivity — A155   Phila Nippon '91 — A156

1991, Nov. 1   Litho.   Perf. 14x14½
609	A155	20c shown	.25	.25
610	A155	$1 Construction engineers	2.00	2.00

1991, Nov. 16   Perf. 14½x14

Flowers: 30c, Railway creeper. 75c, Asystasia. $1, Singapore rhododendron. $2, Coat buttons.
611	A156	30c multicolored	1.20	.75
612	A156	75c multicolored	1.60	1.40
613	A156	$1 multicolored	2.00	1.60
614	A156	$2 multicolored	3.25	2.75
a.		Souvenir sheet of 4, #611-614	11.00	11.00
		Nos. 611-614 (4)	8.05	6.50

Flower Type of 1991

Designs: No. 615, Dendrobium Sharifah Fatimah. No. 616, Phalaenopsis Shim Beauty.

1992, Jan. 22   Perf. 14
615	A151	$2 multicolored	3.50	3.50
616	A151	$2 multicolored	3.50	3.50
a.		Pair, #615-616 + label	7.50	7.50
b.		Souvenir sheet of 2, #615-616	14.00	14.00

Singapore '95 Intl. Philatelic Exhibition.

Paintings A157

1992, Mar. 11   Litho.   Perf. 14
617	A157	20c Singapore Waterfront, 1958	.40	.40
618	A157	75c Kampung Hut, 1973	1.50	1.50
619	A157	$1 Bridge, 1983	2.10	2.10
620	A157	$2 Singapore River, 1984	4.25	4.25
		Nos. 617-620 (4)	8.25	8.25

1992 Summer Olympics, Barcelona A158

1992, Apr. 24   Perf. 14
621	A158	20c Soccer	.40	.40
622	A158	35c Relay races	.65	.65
623	A158	50c Swimming	.80	.80
624	A158	75c Basketball	1.25	1.25
625	A158	$1 Tennis	1.90	1.90
626	A158	$2 Sailing	4.00	4.00
a.		Souvenir sheet of 6, #621-626	12.00	12.00
		Nos. 621-626 (6)	9.00	9.00

No. 626a exists with two different inscriptions in the bottom selvage: "XXVth Olympic Games 1992 Barcelona" and "Games of the XXVth Olympiad."

Costumes, 1910 — A159

1992, Apr. 24   Litho.   Perf. 14½
627	A159	20c Chinese family	.30	.30
628	A159	35c Malay family	.60	.60
629	A159	75c Indian family	1.60	1.60
630	A159	$2 Straits Chinese family	4.00	4.00
		Nos. 627-630 (4)	6.50	6.50

Natl. Military Forces, 25th Anniv. — A160

Designs: 35c, Frogman with gun, fighter plane, artillery. $1, Fighter, tank, ship.

1992, July 1
631	A160	20c multicolored	.40	.40
632	A160	35c multicolored	1.25	1.25
633	A160	$1 multicolored	3.25	3.25
		Nos. 631-633 (3)	4.90	4.90

Visit ASEAN Year, 25th Anniv. A161

Designs: 20c, Mask, bird, sea life. 35c, Costumed women. $1, Outdoor scenery.

1992, Aug. 8
634	A161	20c multicolored	.45	.45
635	A161	35c multicolored	1.25	1.25
636	A161	$1 multicolored	3.25	3.25
		Nos. 634-636 (3)	4.95	4.95

Crabs A162

Designs: 20c, Mosaic crab. 50c, Johnson's freshwater crab. 75c, Singapore freshwater crab. $1, Swamp forest crab.

1992, Aug. 21   Perf. 14½x15
637	A162	20c multicolored	.35	.35
a.		Booklet pane of 10	12.50	
638	A162	50c multicolored	1.00	1.00
639	A162	75c multicolored	1.90	1.90
640	A162	$1 multicolored	2.50	2.50
		Nos. 637-640 (4)	5.75	5.75

Currency, Notes and Coins — A163

1992, Oct. 2   Litho.   Perf. 14½
641		20c Coins	.40	.40
642		75c Coin, flowers on note	1.60	1.60
643		$1 Boat on note, coins	2.00	2.00
644		$2 Bird on note	4.00	4.00
a.	A163	Block of 4, #641-644	9.50	9.50
		Nos. 641-644 (4)	8.00	8.00

Wild Animals A164

1993, Jan. 13   Litho.   Perf. 14½x15
645	A164	20c Sun bear	.30	.30
646	A164	30c Orangutan	.60	.60
647	A164	75c Slow loris	1.40	1.40
648	A164	$2 Large mouse deer	4.25	4.25
		Nos. 645-648 (4)	6.55	6.55

Greetings Stamps — A165

a, Thank you. b, Congratulations. c, Best wishes. d, Happy birthday. e, Get well soon.

Perf. 14½x14 on 3 Sides
1993, Feb. 10
Booklet Stamps
649	A165	20c Strip of 5, #a.-e.	4.25	4.25
f.		Booklet pane of 2 #649	8.50	8.50

Preservation of Tanjong Pagar — A166

1993, Mar. 10   Litho.   Perf. 14
650	A166	20c shown	.35	.35
651	A166	30c Building facade, tower	.90	.90
652	A166	$2 Aerial view	6.25	6.25
		Nos. 650-652 (3)	7.50	7.50

A167

1993, May 29   Perf. 12x11½
653	A167	$2 Cranes, by Chen Wen Hsi	3.50	3.50

Indopex '93.

A168

1993, June 12   Litho.   Perf. 14
654	A168	20c Soccer	.40	.30
655	A168	35c Basketball	.95	.70
656	A168	50c Badminton	1.10	1.00
657	A168	75c Running	1.40	1.40
658	A168	$1 Water polo	1.75	1.50
659	A168	$2 Yachting	2.75	2.50
		Nos. 654-659 (6)	8.35	7.40

17th Sea Games, Singapore.

Butterflies A169

1993, Aug. 21   Litho.   Perf. 14½
660	A169	20c Plain tiger	.30	.30
a.		Booklet pane of 10	8.00	
661	A169	50c Malay lacewing	1.00	1.00
662	A169	75c Palm king	1.60	1.60
663	A169	$1 Banded swallowtail	2.10	2.10
		Nos. 660-663 (4)	5.00	5.00

Flower Type of 1991
1993, Aug. 13
Size: 26x34mm
664	A151	$2 Phalaenopsis amabilis	4.00	4.00
665	A151	$2 Vanda sumatrana	4.00	4.00
a.		Pair, #664-665 + label	8.50	8.50
b.		Souvenir sheet of 2, #664-665, perf. 15x14½	8.50	8.50

Singapore '95 World Stamp Exhibition and Taipei '93, Asian Intl. Invitation Stamp Exhibition (#665b).

Fruits — A170

1993, Oct. 1   Litho.   Perf. 14½x14
666	A170	20c Papaya	.30	.30
667	A170	35c Pomegranate	.65	.65
668	A170	75c Starfruit	1.50	1.50
669	A170	$2 Durian	3.50	3.50
a.		Souvenir sheet of 4, #666-669	7.00	7.00
		Nos. 666-669 (4)	5.95	5.95

Bangkok '93 (#669a).

Chinese
Egrets — A171

Designs: 20c, Two, one with bill in water. 25c, Two, one with fish in mouth. 30c, Two facing opposite directions. 35c, In flight.

1993, Nov. 10   Litho.   Perf. 13½x14
670	A171	20c multicolored	.85	.85
671	A171	25c multicolored	.90	.90
672	A171	30c multicolored	1.40	1.40
673	A171	35c multicolored	1.75	1.75
a.		Strip of 4, #670-673	5.50	5.50

World Wildlife Fund.

Palm Tree — A171a

1993, Nov. 24   Photo.   Die Cut
Self-Adhesive
Booklet Stamp
673B	A171a	(20c) multicolored	.90	.90
c.		Booklet pane of 15	13.50	13.50

By its nature, No. 673c is a complete booklet. The peelable backing serves as a booklet cover.

Marine
Life — A172

Perf. 13x13½, 13½x14 (#675B)
1994   Litho.
674	A172	5c Tiger cowrie	.25	.25
675	A172	20c Sea fan	.35	.35
a.		Booklet pane of 10	3.50	
675B	A172	(20c) Blue-spotted stingray	.40	.40
676	A172	25c Tunicate	.50	.50
677	A172	30c Clownfish	.55	.55
678	A172	35c Nudibranch	.65	.65
679	A172	40c Sea urchin	.70	.70
680	A172	50c Soft coral	.90	.90
681	A172	75c Pin cushion star	1.40	1.40

Litho. & Engraved
Perf. 14 Syncopated
682	A172	$1 Knob coral	2.00	2.00
683	A172	$2 Mushroom coral	3.75	3.75
684	A172	$5 Bubble coral	9.75	9.75
684A	A172	$10 Octopus coral	19.00	19.00
		Nos. 674-684A (13)	40.20	40.20

Self-Adhesive
Die Cut Perf. 8½
684B	A172	(20c) Blue-spotted stingray	1.00	1.00
c.		Booklet pane of 10	13.00	

Nos. 675B, 684B inscribed "FOR LOCAL ADDRESSES ONLY." By its nature, No. 684c is a complete booklet. The peelable paper backing serves as a booklet cover.
Issued: 5c-75c, 1/12/94; $1-$10, 3/23/94; #675B, 684B, 11/16/94.
See Nos. 816-824.

Flower Type of 1991
Designs: No. 685, Paphiopedilum vicotriaregina. No. 686, Dendrobium smillieae.

1994, Feb. 18   Litho.   Perf. 14½
Size: 26x35mm
685	A151	$2 multicolored	4.50	4.50
686	A151	$2 multicolored	4.50	4.50
a.		Pair, #685-686 + label	10.00	10.00
b.		Souvenir sheet of 2, #685-686	10.00	10.00

Singapore '95 and Hong Kong '94 (#686b).

Spring Festival — A173

1994, May 18   Litho.   Perf. 13½
687	A173	20c Ballet	.40	.25
688	A173	30c Mime, puppets	.80	.55
689	A173	50c Musicians	1.00	.65
690	A173	$1 Crafts	2.00	1.20
		Nos. 687-690 (4)	4.20	2.65

Operationally Ready Natl. Servicemen, 25th Anniv. — A174

Civilian-soldiers: 20c, Saluting flag, aiming anti-tank missile. 30c, With family, on jungle patrol with automatic rifle. 35c, Reading newspaper, aiming machine gun. 75c, Working with computer, and as commander, looking through binoculars.

1994, July 1   Litho.   Perf. 13½
691	A174	20c multicolored	.85	.65
692	A174	30c multicolored	1.00	.85
693	A174	35c multicolored	1.25	1.00
694	A174	75c multicolored	2.40	2.00
		Nos. 691-694 (4)	5.50	4.50

Herons — A175

1994, Aug. 16   Litho.   Perf. 14
695		20c Black-crowned night heron	.60	.60
a.		Booklet pane of 10	9.50	
696		50c Little heron	.90	.90
697		75c Purple heron	1.10	1.10
698		$1 Gray heron	1.60	1.60
a.		A175 Block of 4, #695-698	5.00	5.00
		Nos. 695-698 (4)	4.20	4.20

Greetings
Stamps — A175a

#698B, Birthday cake. #698C, Bouquet of flowers. #698D, Gift-wrapped present. #698E, Fireworks. #698F, Balloons.

Die Cut Perf. 11½
1994, Sept. 14   Litho.
Self-Adhesive
Booklet Stamps
698B	A175a	(20c) multicolored	.85	.85
698C	A175a	(20c) multicolored	.85	.85
698D	A175a	(20c) multicolored	.85	.85
698E	A175a	(20c) multicolored	.85	.85
698F	A175a	(20c) multicolored	.85	.85
g.		Bklt. pane, 2 ea #698B-698F	9.00	
		Nos. 698B-698F (5)	4.25	4.25

Nos. 698B-693F inscribed "For Local Addresses Only." By its nature, No. 698Fg is a complete booklet. The peelable paper backing serves as a booklet cover. The outside of the cover contains 10 peelable labels.

Modern Singapore, 175th
Anniv. — A176

Early, modern scenes: 20c, Schoolchildren reading, graduating seniors. 50c, Horse-drawn carriages, high-speed train. 75c, Small boats, container ship dock. $1, Skyline.

1994, Sept. 30   Perf. 13½x14
699	A176	20c multicolored	.45	.30
700	A176	50c multicolored	.90	.55
701	A176	75c multicolored	1.50	.90
702	A176	$1 multicolored	1.75	1.40
a.		Souvenir sheet of 4, #699-702	5.00	5.00
		Nos. 699-702 (4)	4.60	3.15

ICAO, 50th
Anniv.
A177

Designs: 35c, Control tower, passenger jet. 75c, Terminal, Concord jet. $2, Control tower, communication satellite, passenger jet.

1994, Oct. 5   Litho.   Perf. 14
703	A177	20c multicolored	.30	.30
704	A177	35c multicolored	.50	.50
705	A177	75c multicolored	1.25	1.25
706	A177	$2 multicolored	3.25	3.25
		Nos. 703-706 (4)	5.30	5.30

Love Stamps — A178

#707, "Love" in three different inscriptions. #708, Spiral of "Love." #709, "Love" on two lines. #710, "Love" in different languages. #711, Geometrical "Love."

Die Cut Perf. 11½
1995, Feb. 8   Litho.
Self-Adhesive
Booklet Stamps
707	A178	(20c) multicolored	1.25	1.25
708	A178	(20c) multicolored	1.25	1.25
709	A178	(20c) multicolored	1.25	1.25
710	A178	(20c) multicolored	1.25	1.25
711	A178	(20c) multicolored	1.25	1.25
a.		Booklet pane, 2 each #707-711	12.50	
		Nos. 707-711 (5)	6.25	6.25

Nos. 707-711 inscribed "FOR LOCAL ADDRESSES ONLY." By its nature, No. 711a is a complete booklet. The peelable paper backing serves as a booklet cover. The outside of the cover contains 10 peelable labels.

Meet in Singapore — A179

Scenes in Suntec City: (20c), Intl. Convention & Exhibition Center. 75c, High rise buildings. $1, Temasek Boulevard. $2, Fountain Terrace.

1995, Jan. 11   Perf. 13½x14
712	A179	(20c) multicolored	.30	.30
713	A179	75c multicolored	1.25	1.25
714	A179	$1 multicolored	1.75	1.75
715	A179	$2 multicolored	3.25	3.25
		Nos. 712-715 (4)	6.55	6.55

Singapore '95. No. 712 inscribed "FOR LOCAL ADDRESSES ONLY."

Souvenir Sheets of 2, #712, 715
Inscribed:
715a	FIP DAY	8.50	8.50
715b	OLYMPIC DAY-YOUTH	8.50	8.50
715c	FIAP DAY	8.50	8.50
715d	LETTER WRITING DAY	8.50	8.50
715e	STAMP COLLECTING DAY	8.50	8.50
715f	SINGAPORE '95 DAY	8.50	8.50
715g	PHILATELIC MUSEUM DAY	8.50	8.50
715h	SINGAPORE POST DAY	8.50	8.50
715i	AWARDS DAY	8.50	8.50
715j	THEMATIC PHILATELY DAY	8.50	8.50

Flower Type of 1991
Designs: No. 716, Vanda Marlie Dolera, No. 717, Vanda limbata.

1995, Mar. 15   Litho.   Perf. 14
716	A151	$2 multicolored	3.00	3.00
717	A151	$2 multicolored	3.00	3.00
a.		Pair, #716-717 + label	7.00	7.00
b.		Souvenir sheet, #716-717	12.00	12.00
c.		Souvenir sheet, #716-717	9.00	9.00

Singapore '95 (#717a-717c).
The margin of No. 717b pictures a chimpanzee in the jungle and No. 717c pictures a fish. Three limited edition sheets were issued 9/1/95 at the show. They sold for 50, 12.5 and 2.9 times face. Values, $550, $220, $350.

Independence, 30th Anniv. — A180

"My Singapore, My Country, Happy Birthday" in various languages and: 20c, "30" formed in ribbon, #471, flower. 75c, #598, Music sheet. $1, Natl. flag, #489, music sheets, vert.

Perf. 14x13½, 13½x14
1995, Apr. 19   Litho.
718	A180	(20c) multicolored	.40	.40
719	A180	50c multicolored	1.00	1.00
720	A180	75c multicolored	1.60	1.60
721	A180	$1 multicolored	1.60	1.60
a.		Souvenir sheet of 4, #718-721	6.25	6.25
		Nos. 718-721 (4)	4.60	4.60

No. 718 inscribed "For Local Addresses Only." No. 721a is a continuous design.

End of
World
War II,
50th
Anniv.
A181

Designs: (20c), Crowd celebrating, Straits Settlements #271, vert. 50c, Lord Mountbatten receiving Japanese surrender of Singapore, Straits Settlements #265, vert. 70c, Food kitchen. $2, Police road block.

Perf. 14x13½, 13½x14
1995, June 21   Litho.
723	A181	(20c) multicolored	.30	.30
724	A181	60c multicolored	.90	.90
725	A181	70c multicolored	1.00	1.00
726	A181	$2 multicolored	3.00	3.00
		Nos. 723-726 (4)	5.20	5.20

No. 723 inscribed "For Local Addresses Only" and sold for 20c on day of issue.

New Six
Digit
Postal
Code
A182

Meet in Singapore — A179

1995, Sept. 1   Litho.   Perf. 14x14½
727	A182	(20c) shown	.40	.30
728	A182	$2 Six boxes, numbers	2.90	2.75

No. 728 inscribed "For Local Addresses Only."

Philatelic
Museum,
Singapore
A183

Museum building, various stamps, featuring: 20c, #12. 50c, #157. 60c, #661. $2, Displays of stamps.

1995, Aug. 19 — **Perf. 13x13½**
729	A183	(20c) multicolored	.40	.40
730	A183	50c multicolored	1.10	1.10
731	A183	60c multicolored	1.25	1.25
732	A183	$2 multicolored	4.00	4.00
		Nos. 729-732 (4)	6.75	6.75

No. 729 inscribed "For Local Addresses Only."

Fish
A184

1995, July 19 — **Litho.** — **Perf. 13½x14**
733	A184	(20c) Yellow-faced angelfish	.40	.40
		Complete booklet, 10 #733	5.00	
734	A184	60c Harlequin sweetlips	1.25	1.25
735	A184	70c Lionfish	1.40	1.40
736	A184	$1 Longfin bannerfish	2.10	2.10
		Nos. 733-736 (4)	5.15	5.15

No. 733 inscribed "For Local Addresses Only."

Paintings in Singapore Art Museum
A185

Designs: (20c), Tropical Fruits, by Georgette Chen. 30c, Bali Beach, by Cheong Soo Pieng. 70c, Gibbons, by Chen Wen Hsi. $2, Shi (Lion), by Pan Shou (calligraphy).

1995, Oct. 20 — **Litho.** — **Perf. 12½**
737	A185	(20c) multicolored	.40	.40
738	A185	30c multicolored	.60	.60
739	A185	70c multicolored	1.25	1.25

Perf. 13½x13
740	A185	$2 multicolored	4.00	4.00
		Nos. 737-740 (4)	6.25	6.25

No. 737 inscribed "For Local Addresses Only." No. 740 is 22½x39mm.

New Year 1996 (Year of the Rat) — A186

1996, Feb. 9 — **Litho.** — **Perf. 12**
741	A186	(20c) shown	.40	.30
742	A186	$2 Rat with orange	4.00	4.00

Souvenir Sheet
742A	A186	Sheet of 2, #742, 742Ab	47.50	47.50
b.		22c like #741	.25	.25
c.		As #742A, diff. sheet margin	25.00	25.00
d.		As #742A, diff. sheet margin	27.50	27.50

No. 741 inscribed "For Local Addresses Only."
Sheet margins contain exhibition emblems for: #742A: Indonesia '96; #742Ac, China '96; #742Ad, CAPEX '96.
Issued: #742A, 3/21; #742Ac, 5/18; #742Ad, 6/8.

Architectural Styles — A187

Designs: (20c), Bukit Pasoh, Chinatown. 35c, Jalan Sultan, Kampong Glam. 70c, Dalhousie Lane, Little India. $1, Supreme Court, Civic District.

1996, Jan. 17 — **Perf. 13½x14**
743	A187	(20c) multicolored	.50	.40
744	A187	35c multicolored	.75	.75
745	A187	70c multicolored	1.60	1.20
746	A187	$1 multicolored	2.00	1.60
		Nos. 743-746 (4)	4.85	3.95

No. 743 inscribed "For Local Addresses Only."

Old Maps of Singapore
A188

Designs: (20c), Old Straits. 60c, Detail of town. $1, Part of Malay Peninsula, Singapore. $2, Town and entrance.

1996, Mar. 13 — **Litho.** — **Perf. 12**
747	A188	(20c) multicolored	.40	.40
748	A188	60c multicolored	1.10	1.10
749	A188	$1 multicolored	1.75	1.75
750	A188	$2 multicolored	3.25	3.25
		Nos. 747-750 (4)	6.50	6.50

No. 747 inscribed "For Local Addresses Only."

Greetings Stamps — A189

Children's drawings about courtesy: (22c), #755Bc, Child telling another to be quiet in library. 35c, Children helping elderly during outdoor activities. 50c, Giving seat at bus stop to expectant mother. 60c, Sharing umbrella. $1, Giving up seat on bus to senior citizen.

Die Cut Perf. 11
1996, July 10 — **Litho.**
Self-Adhesive
Booklet Stamps
751	A189	(22c) multicolored	.60	.60
a.		Booklet pane of 10	5.00	
752	A189	35c multicolored	1.10	1.10
753	A189	50c multicolored	1.50	1.50
754	A189	60c multicolored	1.75	1.75
755	A189	$1 multicolored	3.00	3.00
a.		Booklet pane of 10, 5 #751, 2 #752, 1 each #753-755	12.00	
		Nos. 751-755 (5)	7.95	7.95

Souvenir Sheet
755B	A189	Sheet of 5, #752-755, 755Bc	7.50	7.50
c.		22c multicolored	.30	.30

No. 751 inscribed "For Local Addresses Only." By their nature Nos. 751a and 755a are complete booklets. The peelable paper backing serves as a booklet cover. The outside of the cover contains 10 peelable labels.

1996 Summer Olympic Games, Atlanta — A190

Designs: (22c), #759Ab, Board, dinghy sailing. 60c, Soccer, tennis. 70c, Pole vault, hurdles. $2, Diving, swimming.

1996, July 19 — **Litho.** — **Perf. 14½**
756	A190	(22c) multicolored	.45	.30
757	A190	60c multicolored	1.20	1.00
758	A190	70c multicolored	1.40	1.00
759	A190	$2 multicolored	3.50	3.00
		Nos. 756-759 (4)	6.55	5.30

Souvenir Sheet
759A	A190	Sheet of 4, #757-759, 759Ab	6.50	6.50
b.		22c multicolored	.30	.30

No. 756 inscribed "For Local Addresses Only."

Asian Civilizations Museum — A191

(22c), Calligraphy in Caoshu, Ming Dynasty, 17th cent. 60c, Javanese Divination manuscript, Surkarta (Solo), Indonesia, 1842. 70c, Temple hanging, Tamilnadu. South India, 19th cent. $2, Calligraphic implements, Persia and Turkey, 17th-19th cent.

1996, June 5 — **Litho.** — **Perf. 13½x14**
760	A191	(22c) multicolored	.40	.25
761	A191	60c multicolored	1.10	.75
762	A191	70c multicolored	1.40	.85
763	A191	$2 multicolored	3.25	3.25
		Nos. 760-763 (4)	6.15	5.10

No. 760 inscribed "For Local Addresses Only."

Care for Nature — A192

Native trees: (22c), Cinnamomum iners. 60c, Hibiscus tiliaceus. 70c, Parkia speciosa. $1, Terminalia catappa.

1996, Sept. 11 — **Litho.** — **Perf. 13½**
764	A192	(22c) multicolored	.35	.30
a.		Booklet pane of 10	7.00	
		Complete booklet, #764a	7.50	
765	A192	60c multicolored	1.00	1.00
766	A192	70c multicolored	1.10	1.10
767	A192	$1 multicolored	1.60	1.60
		Nos. 764-767 (4)	4.05	4.00

No. 764 inscribed "For Local Addresses Only."

Panmen, Suzhou, China — A193

Design: 60c, Singapore waterfront.

1996, Oct. 9 — **Litho.** — **Perf. 13x13½**
768	A193	(22c) multicolored	.50	.50
769	A193	60c multicolored	1.75	1.75

Souvenir Sheet
769A	A193	Sheet of 2, #769, 769Ab	5.00	5.00
b.		22c like #768	.30	.30
c.		As #769A, ovptd. in sheet margin	30.00	30.00

No. 768 inscribed "For Local Addresses Only."
No. 769Ac is ovptd. in sheet margin with violet on gold Singapore-China Stamp Exhibition emblem.
See People's Republic of China Nos. 2733-2734.

First World Trade Organization Ministerial Conference — A194

1996, Nov. 20 — **Litho.** — **Perf. 14**
770	A194	(22c) pink, vio & multi	.40	.40
771	A194	60c ver, grn & multi	1.00	1.00
772	A194	$1 bl, yel org & multi	1.60	1.60
773	A194	$2 grn, car & multi	3.50	3.50
		Nos. 770-773 (4)	6.50	6.50

No. 770 inscribed "For Local Addresses Only."

New Year 1997 (Year of the Ox)
A195

Nos. 774, 775, Different stylized oxen.

1997, Jan. 10 — **Perf. 13½x14**
774	A195	(22c) multicolored	.50	.50
775	A195	$2 multicolored	4.00	4.00
a.		Sheet, 9 each #774-775	45.00	
b.		Souvenir sheet, #775, #775d	15.00	15.00
c.		As "b," diff. sheet margin	15.00	15.00
d.		22c like #774	15.00	15.00
e.		As "b," diff. sheet margin	15.00	15.00

No. 774 inscribed "For Local Addresses Only."
Sheet margin contains exhibition emblem: #775b Hong Kong '97; #775c Pacific '97; #775e Shanghai 1997.
Issued: #775b, 2/12/97; #775c, 5/29/97; #775e, 11/19/97.

Traditional Games A196 — Ground Transportation A197

1997, Feb. 21 — **Litho.** — **Perf. 14½**
776	A196	(22c) Shuttlecock	.35	.35
777	A196	35c Marbles	.55	.55
778	A196	60c Tops	.90	.90
779	A196	$1 Fivestones	1.50	1.50
a.		Souvenir sheet of 4, #776-779	4.00	4.00
		Nos. 776-779 (4)	3.30	3.30

No. 776 inscribed "For Local Addresses Only." Singpex '97 (#779a).

1997, Mar. 19 — **Perf. 13½**
780	A197	5c Bullock cart	.25	.25
781	A197	20c Bicycle	.30	.30
782	A197	(22c) Rickshaw	.35	.35
783	A197	30c Electric tram	.45	.45
784	A197	35c Trolley bus	.55	.55
785	A197	40c Trishaw	.60	.60
786	A197	50c Vintage car	.75	.75
787	A197	60c Horse-drawn carriage	.90	.90
788	A197	70c Fire engine	1.00	1.00
		Nos. 780-788 (9)	5.15	5.15

Souvenir Sheet
788A	A197	Sheet, #780-781, 783-788, 788Ab	7.00	7.00
b.		22c like #782	.35	.35

Self-Adhesive
Serpentine Die Cut Perf. 11½
Booklet Stamp
789	A197	(22c) like #782	.50	.50
a.		Booklet pane of 10	7.00	

Nos. 782, 789 are inscribed "For Local Addresses Only." Nos. 780, 783-784, 787-788 are horiz.

By its nature No. 789a is a complete book-let. The peelable paper backing serves as a booklet cover.

Greetings Stamps — A198

Litho. & Engr.
1997, Apr. 23   *Perf. 13*

$1, Taxi. $2, Bus, horiz. $5, Mass rapid transit system. $10, Light rapid transit system, horiz.

Size: 28x35mm (#790, 792), 43x24mm (#791, 793)

790	A197	$1 multicolored	1.50	1.50
791	A197	$2 multicolored	3.00	3.00
792	A197	$5 multicolored	7.50	7.50
793	A197	$10 multicolored	15.00	15.00
a.		Souvenir sheet, #790-793	27.50	27.50
		Nos. 790-793 (4)	27.00	27.00

Word "Friends" used in making designs: #794, Man's head. #795, Sharing umbrella. #796, Penguins. #797, Butterflies, hand. #798, Coffee cup. #799, Flower. #800, Candle. #801, Tree. #802, Jar holding stars. #803, Two cans connected by string.

Serpentine Die Cut 14½
1997, May 14   Litho.
Self-Adhesive
Booklet Stamps

794	A198	(22c) multicolored	.70	.70
795	A198	(22c) multicolored	.70	.70
796	A198	(22c) multicolored	.70	.70
797	A198	(22c) multicolored	.70	.70
798	A198	(22c) multicolored	.70	.70
a.		Booklet pane, 2 each #794-798	7.00	
		Nos. 794-798 (5)	3.50	3.50
799	A198	(22c) multicolored	.70	.70
800	A198	(22c) multicolored	.70	.70
801	A198	(22c) multicolored	.70	.70
802	A198	(22c) multicolored	.70	.70
803	A198	(22c) multicolored	.70	.70
a.		Booklet pane, 2 each #799-803	7.00	
		Nos. 799-803 (5)	3.50	3.50

Nos. 794-803 are inscribed "For Local Addresses Only." By their nature Nos. 798a and 803a are complete booklets. The peelable paper backing serves as a booklet cover. The outside cover contains 10 peelable labels.

Upgrading of Public Housing — A199

Designs: (22c) New look for the precinct. 30c, Outdoor facilities. 70c, Landscaped gardens. $1, Additional space, balcony.

1997, July 16   Litho.   *Perf. 14*

804	A199	(22c) multicolored	.30	.30
805	A199	30c multicolored	.40	.40
806	A199	70c multicolored	1.10	1.10
807	A199	$1 multicolored	1.75	1.75
		Nos. 804-807 (4)	3.55	3.55

No. 804 is inscribed "For Local Addresses Only."

ASEAN, 30th Anniv. — A200

Designs: (22c), 30 years of "dates," globe, hands clasped, sky. 35c, Southeast Asian cultures. 60c, Satellite dish, circuit board, map of Southeast Asia, sky. $1, Tourist attractions in ASEAN countries.

1997, Aug. 8   Litho.   *Perf. 14*

808	A200	(22c) multicolored	.40	.40
809	A200	35c multicolored	.60	.60
810	A200	60c multicolored	1.10	1.10
811	A200	$1 multicolored	2.00	2.00
		Nos. 808-811 (4)	4.10	4.10

No. 808 is inscribed "For Local Addresses Only."

Value is for stamp with surrounding selvage.

Protection of the Environment — A201

(22c), Clean Environment. 60c, Clean waters. 70c, Clean air. $1, Clean homes.

1997, Sept. 13   Litho.   *Perf. 14x13½*

812	A201	(22c) multicolored	.30	.30
a.		Booklet pane of 10	5.00	
		Complete booklet, #812a	5.00	
813	A201	60c multicolored	.80	.80
814	A201	70c multicolored	.90	.90
815	A201	$1 multicolored	1.30	1.30
		Nos. 812-815 (4)	3.30	3.30

No. 812 is inscribed "For Local Addresses Only."

Marine Life Type of 1994

1997   Photo.   *Perf. 13x13½*

816	A172	5c like #674	.40	.40
816A	A172	(20c) like #675B	1.10	1.10
817	A172	25c like #676	1.00	1.00
818	A172	30c like #677	1.40	1.40
819	A172	35c like #678	1.50	1.50
820	A172	40c like #679	1.60	1.60
821	A172	50c like #680	2.10	2.10

Photo. & Embossed
Perf. 14 Syncopated Type A (2 Sides)

822	A172	$1 like #682	4.00	4.00
822A	A172	$2 like #683	11.00	11.00
823	A172	$5 like #684	20.00	20.00
824	A172	$10 like #684A	42.50	42.50
		Nos. 816-824 (11)	86.60	86.60

No. 816A is inscribed "For Local Addresses Only."

Nos. 822-824 have embossed logo in center of stamp and denomination and country are white. Nos. 682, 684, 684A have embossed lettering for country name and denomination.

Shells of Singapore and Thailand A202

Designs: (22c), Drupa morum. 35c, Nerita chamaeleon. 60c, Littoraria melanostoma. $1, Cryptospira elegans.

1997, Oct. 9   Litho.   *Perf. 13x14*

825	A202	(22c) multicolored	.50	.50
826	A202	35c multicolored	.70	.70
827	A202	60c multicolored	1.10	1.10
828	A202	$1 multicolored	2.00	2.00
		Nos. 825-828 (4)	4.30	4.30

Souvenir Sheet

828A	A202	Sheet of 4, #826-828, #828Ab	4.50	4.50
b.		22c like #825	.50	.50

No. 825 inscribed "For Local Addresses Only."

See Thailand Nos. 1771-1774.

New Year 1998 (Year of the Tiger) A203

Different stylized tigers.

1998, Jan. 9   Litho.   *Perf. 13x14*

829	A203	(22c) multicolored	.35	.35
830	A203	$2 multicolored	3.25	3.25
a.		Horiz. or vert. pair, #829-830	3.50	3.50
b.		Sheet of 9 each, #829-830	35.00	35.00

Souvenir Sheet

830C	A203	Sheet of 2, #830, #830Cd	6.00	6.00
d.		22c like #829	.40	.40
e.		As #830C, diff. inscription	6.00	6.00

Israel '98 (#830C). Italia '98 (#830Ce).
No. 829 inscribed "For Local Addresses Only."
Stamps in No. 830b are arranged in a checkerboard fashion.
Issued: #830Ce, 10/23/98.

Dinosaurs — A204

Self-Adhesive
1998, Apr. 22   Photo.   *Die Cut*

831	A204	(22c) Pentaceratops	.45	.45
832	A204	(22c) Apatosaurus	.45	.45
833	A204	(22c) Albertosaurus	.45	.45
a.		Pane, 5 each #831-833	7.00	
		Nos. 831-833 (3)	1.35	1.35

Nos. 831-833 are inscribed "For Local Addresses Only."

A205

Songbirds: (22c), Lesser green leafbird. 60c, Magpie robin. 70c, Straw-headed bulbul. $2, Yellow-bellied prinia.

1998, May 6   Photo.   *Perf. 11½*
Granite Paper

834	A205	(22c) multicolored	.35	.35
835	A205	60c multicolored	1.00	1.00
836	A205	70c multicolored	1.10	1.10
837	A205	$2 multicolored	3.00	3.00
		Nos. 834-837 (4)	5.45	5.45

No. 834 is inscribed "For Local Addresses Only."

A206

"Hello" stamps.

Self-Adhesive
Booklet Stamps
Serpentine Die Cut 11
1998, May 20   Litho.

838	A206	(22c) yellow & multi	.80	.80
839	A206	(22c) orange & multi	.80	.80
840	A206	(22c) green & multi	.80	.80
841	A206	(22c) blue & multi	.80	.80
842	A206	(22c) black & multi	.80	.80
a.		Booklet pane, 2 each #838-842	8.00	

Nos. 838-842 are inscribed "For Local Addresses Only."

By its nature No. 842a is a complete booklet. The peelable paper backing serves as a booklet cover. The outside cover contains 10 peelable labels.

Fauna from "Fragile Forest," Singapore Zoological Gardens — A207

Serpentine Die Cut 11½
1998, June 5   Litho.
Self-Adhesive
Booklet Stamps

843	A207	(22c) Rhino beetle	.70	.70
844	A207	(22c) Surinam horned frog	.70	.70
845	A207	(22c) Atlas moth	.70	.70
846	A207	(22c) Green iguana	.70	.70
847	A207	(22c) Giant scorpion	.70	.70
a.		Booklet, 2 each #843-847	8.00	
848	A207	(22c) Hissing cockroach	.70	.70
849	A207	(22c) Two-toed sloth	.70	.70
850	A207	(22c) Archer fish	.70	.70
851	A207	(22c) Cobalt blue tarantula	.70	.70
852	A207	(22c) Greater mousedeer	.70	.70
a.		Booklet, 2 each #848-852	8.00	

Nos. 843-852 are inscribed "For Local Addresses Only."
The peelable paper backing of Nos. 847a & 852a serves as a booklet cover. In the margins of Nos. 847a & 852a there is a leaf-shaped scratch-off that reveals an animal.

The Singapore Story (Moments in History) — A208

(22c), 22c, "Turbulent years," 1955-59. 60c, "Self-government," 1959-63. $1, "Towards merger and independence," 1961-65. $2, "A nation is born," 1965.

1998   *Perf. 13x13½*

853	A208	(22c) multicolored	.30	.30
854	A208	60c multicolored	.80	.80
855	A208	$1 multicolored	1.40	1.40
856	A208	$2 multicolored	2.75	2.75
		Nos. 853-856 (4)	5.25	5.25

Souvenir Sheet

857		Souvenir sheet of 4	14.00	14.00
a.		22c multicolored	.70	.70
b.		60c multicolored	1.90	1.90
c.		$1 multicolored	3.00	3.00
d.		$2 multicolored	6.25	6.25

Issued: #853-856, 7/7/98; #857, 7/23/98.
No. 853 is inscribed "For Local Addresses Only." No. 857 has a UV varnish producing a shiny effect on portions of the design. No. 857 sold for $7.
Singpex '98 (#857).

Orchids of Singapore and Australia — A209

1998, Aug. 6   Photo.   *Perf. 11½*

858	A209	(22c) Moth orchid	.40	.40
859	A209	70c Bamboo orchid	1.25	1.25
860	A209	$1 Tiger orchid	1.75	1.75
861	A209	$2 Cooktown orchid	3.50	3.50
		Nos. 858-861 (4)	6.90	6.90

Souvenir Sheet

861A	A209	Sheet of 4, #859-861, #861Ab	10.00	10.00
b.		22c like #858	2.00	1.00

No. 858 is inscribed "For Local Addresses Only."
See Australia Nos. 1681-1684.

Flowers A210

Designs: No. 862, Wedilia trilobata. No. 863, Dillenia suffruticosa. No. 864, Canna hybrid. No. 865, Caesalpinia pulcherrima.

No. 866, Zephyranthes rosea. No. 867, Cassia alata. No. 868, Heliconia rostrata. No. 869, Allamanda cathartica.

1998, Sept. 9   Litho.   Perf. 14

862	A210	(22c) multicolored	.50	.50
863	A210	(22c) multicolored	.50	.50
864	A210	(22c) multicolored	.50	.50
865	A210	(22c) multicolored	.50	.50
a.		Strip of 4, #862-865	2.10	2.10
b.		Booklet pane, 3 each #864-865, 2 each #862-863	5.50	
		Complete booklet, #865b	5.50	
866	A210	35c multicolored	.70	.70
867	A210	35c multicolored	.70	.70
868	A210	60c multicolored	1.25	1.25
869	A210	60c multicolored	1.25	1.25
a.		Strip of 4, #866-869	3.75	3.75
b.		Souvenir sheet of 8, #862-869	5.00	5.00

Stamps in #869b are in pairs, #864-863, 862/865 horiz., #866-867, 868, 869 vert.

A211

Festivals — A212

#870, 874 Eid al-Fitr. #871, 875, Christmas. #872, 876, Chinese New Year. #873, 877, Deepavali.

1998, Oct. 7   Litho.   Perf. 13x14

870	A211	(22c) multicolored	.35	.35
871	A211	(22c) multicolored	.35	.35
872	A211	(22c) multicolored	.35	.35
873	A211	(22c) multicolored	.35	.35
a.		Block of 4, #870-873	1.90	1.90
874	A212	30c multicolored	.50	.50
875	A212	30c multicolored	.50	.50
876	A212	30c multicolored	.50	.50
877	A212	30c multicolored	.50	.50
		Nos. 870-877 (8)	3.40	3.40

Nos. 870-873 are inscribed "For Local Addresses Only."

Serpentine Die Cut

878	A211	(22c) like #870	1.10	1.10
879	A211	(22c) like #871	1.10	1.10
880	A211	(22c) like #872	1.10	1.10
881	A211	(22c) like #873	1.10	1.10
		Nos. 878-881 (4)	4.40	4.40

Historical Buildings — A213

(22c), Parliament House. 70c, Former Convent of the Holy Infant Jesus Chapel. $1, Hill Street Building. $2, Sun Yat Sen Nanyang Memorial Hall.

1998, Nov. 4   Perf. 13½

882	A213	(22c) multicolored	.35	.35
883	A213	70c multicolored	1.10	1.00
884	A213	$1 multicolored	1.60	1.40
885	A213	$2 multicolored	3.25	2.75
		Nos. 882-885 (4)	6.30	5.50

No. 882 inscribed "For Local Addresses Only."

Inter-Religious Organization, 50th Anniv. — A214

1999, Jan. 15   Litho.   Perf. 13x13½

886	A214	(22c) white & multi	.35	.25
887	A214	60c pink & multi	1.00	1.00
888	A214	$1 blue & multi	1.75	1.75
		Nos. 886-888 (3)	3.10	3.00

No. 886 is inscribed "For Local Addresses Only."

New Year 1999 (Year of the Rabbit) A215

Various stylized rabbits.

1999, Jan. 15   Perf. 14

889	A215	(22c) multicolored	.50	.50
890	A215	$2 multicolored	3.25	2.75
a.		Horiz. or vert. pair, #889-890	3.50	3.50
b.		Sheet, 9 each #829-830	32.50	

Souvenir Sheet

890C		Sheet of 2, #890 & 890Cd	5.00	5.00
d.		A215 22c like #889	1.25	.60
e.		As #890C, with PhilexFrance 99 margin	5.00	5.00
f.		As #890C, with China 1999 World Phil. Exhib. margin	5.00	5.00

No. 889 is inscribed "For Local Addresses Only."
No. 890C was issued 4/27 for IBRA '99, World Philatelic Exhibition, Nuremberg. Issued: #890Ce, 7/2/99; #890Cf, 8/21/99.

19th Century Sailing Ships — A216

1999, Mar. 19   Litho.   Perf. 14½

891	A216	(22c) Clipper	.35	.35
892	A216	70c Twakow, vert.	1.10	1.10
893	A216	$1 Fujian junk, vert.	1.75	1.75
894	A216	$2 Golekkan	3.25	3.25
		Nos. 891-894 (4)	6.45	6.45

Souvenir Sheet

894A	A216	Sheet of 4, #892-894, #894Ab	6.50	6.50
b.		22c like #891	2.75	1.25

Australia '99 World Stamp Expo (#894A). No. 891 is inscribed "For Local Address Only."

Greetings Stamps — A217

Expressions of kindness: a, "Think of others." b, "Do not litter." c, "Be kind to animals." d, "Be considerate." e, "Be generous."

Serpentine Die Cut 9½
1999, May 12   Litho.
Self-Adhesive
Booklet Stamps

895	A217	(22c) Booklet pane, 2 each #a.-e.	5.50	5.50

Nos. 895a-895e are inscribed "For Local Addresses Only."
No. 895 is a complete booklet. The peelable paper backing serves as a booklet cover. Stamps are printed 2 each #895a-895c on one side, 2 each #895d-895e on the other with 3 labels on each side.

Hong Kong and Singapore Tourism — A218

(22c), Hong Kong Harbor. 35c, Skyline of Singapore. 50c, Giant Buddha, Hong Kong. 60c, Merlion Sentosa Island, Singapore. 70c, Hong Kong Street scene. $1, Bugis Junction, Singapore.

1999, July 1   Litho.   Perf. 13½x13¼

896	A218	(22c) multicolored	.40	.40
897	A218	35c multicolored	.60	.60
898	A218	50c multicolored	.90	.90
899	A218	60c multicolored	1.10	1.10
900	A218	70c multicolored	1.25	1.25
901	A218	$1 multicolored	1.90	1.90
		Nos. 896-901 (6)	6.15	6.15

Souvenir Sheet

902		Sheet of 6, #897-901, #902a	6.25	6.25
a.		A218 22c like #896	.40	.40

No. 896 is inscribed for "For Local Addresses Only."
See Hong Kong Nos. 849-854.

Butterflies A219

Perf. 12½x12¾

903	A219	(22c) Peacock	.40	.40
904	A219	70c Blue pansy	1.25	1.25
905	A219	$1 Great egg-fly	2.00	2.00
906	A219	$2 Red admiral	3.75	3.75
		Nos. 903-906 (4)	7.40	7.40

1999, Aug. 12   Litho. & Engr.

Souvenir Sheet

907	A219	Sheet of 4, #904-906, #907a	7.50	7.50
a.		A219 22c like #903	2.50	1.25

No. 903 is inscribed "For Local Addresses Only."
See Sweden No. 2356.

Yusof bin Ishak (1910-70), First President of Singapore A220

Perf. 13¼x13¾
1999, Sept. 9   Litho. & Engr.

908	A220	$2 multicolored	3.25	3.25

Issued in sheets of 4.

Amphibians & Reptiles — A221

1999, Oct. 13   Litho.   Perf. 14

909	A221	(22c) Green turtle	.35	.35
		Complete booklet, 10 #909	3.50	
910	A221	60c Green crested lizard	1.00	1.00
911	A221	70c Copper-cheeked frog	1.10	1.10
912	A221	$1 Water monitor	1.75	1.75
		Nos. 909-912 (4)	4.20	4.20

No. 909 inscribed "For Local Addresses Only."

New Parliament House — A222

Perf. 13¼x13¾
1999, Nov. 17   Litho.

913	A222	(22c) North view	.35	.35
914	A222	60c Northeast view	1.00	.85
915	A222	$1 Southeast view	1.60	1.50
916	A222	$2 West view	3.25	2.75
		Nos. 913-916 (4)	6.20	5.45

#913 inscribed "For Local Address Only."

Singapore in the 20th Century A223

No. 917: a, Colonialism. b, Education. c, Immigration. d, Government. e, Japanese occupation. f, National service. g, Transportation. h, Tourism. i, Housing. j, Economic progress.

Perf. 13¼x12½
1999, Dec. 31   Litho.

917		Sheet of 10 + 5 labels	9.50	9.50
a.-b.		A223 (22c) Any single	.40	.40
c.-d.		A223 35c Any single	.50	.50
e.-f.		A223 60c Any single	.90	.90
g.-h.		A223 70c Any single	1.10	1.10
i.-j.		A223 $1 Any single	1.60	1.60

Nos. 917a-917b inscribed "For Local Addresses Only."

Millennium — A224

No. 918: a, (22c), Information technology. b, 60c, Arts and culture. c, $1, Heritage. d, $2, Globalization.

2000, Jan. 1   Photo.   Perf. 14¼x14¾
Granite Paper

918	A224	Horiz. strip of 4, #a-d	6.00	6.00
e.		Souvenir sheet, #918	6.00	6.00

No. 918a inscribed "For Local Addresses Only."

New Year 2000 (Year of the Dragon) A225

Dragon: (22c), 22c, Facing left. $2, $10, Facing right.

2000   Litho.   Perf. 13x13¼

919	A225	(22c) multi	.50	.50
920	A225	$2 multi	3.25	2.75
a.		Horiz. pair, #919-920	3.50	3.50
b.		Souvenir sheet, #920a	3.50	3.50

Souvenir Sheets

921		Sheet of 2, #920, 922a, with Bangkok 2000 margin	5.00	5.00
a.		A225 22c multi	.50	.50
b.		As No. 921, with The Stamp Show 2000 margin	5.00	5.00
c.		As No. 921, with Naba 2000 margin	6.00	6.00

Litho. & Embossed

922	A225	$10 gold & multi	15.00	15.00

Issued: No. 920b, 10/30; No. 921, 3/25; No. 921b, 5/22; No. 921c, 6/21; others, 1/1. No. 919 inscribed "For Local Addresses Only."

Millennium Personalized
Stamp — A225a

2000, Mar. 8   Litho.   Perf. 14x14¼
923 A225a (22c) multi + label   1.25 1.25

No. 923 printed in sheets of 20 stamps + labels that could be personalized. Sheets sold for $20 for the first sheet with additional sheets available for $10. The design on No. 923 is similar to that on No. 918a, but is 19x46mm and lacks frame.

Post Offices and Cancels
A226

Designs: (22c), Original post office, B172 cancel. 60c, General Post Office, c. 1873, 1875 cancel. $1, General Post Office, 1928, 1935 cancel. $2, Singapore Post Center, 1998 cancel.

2000, Mar. 8   Litho.   Perf. 13½
935 A226 (22c) multi   .40   .40
936 A226 60c multi   1.00 1.00
  a. Booklet pane, 4 #935, 2 #936   3.50
937 A226 $1 multi   1.60 1.60
938 A226 $2 multi   3.50 3.50
  a. Booklet pane, 4 #937, 2 #938   13.50
    Complete bklt., #936a, 938a   18.00
  Nos. 935-938 (4)   6.50 6.50
Souvenir Sheet
939 A226 Sheet of 4, #936-938, 939a   5.00 5.00
  a. A226 22c like No. 935   .25   .25

No. 935 is inscribed "For Local Addresses Only."

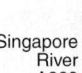

Celebrations
A227

Designs: No. 940, (22c), Yipee. No. 940A, (22c), Yeah. No. 940B, (22c), Hurray. No. 940C, (22c), Yes. No. 941, (22c), Happy.

Serpentine Die Cut 9½
2000, May 10   Litho.
Self-Adhesive
940-941 A227 Set of 5   3.00 3.00
  941a Booklet, 2 each #940-941   5.75

Nos. 940-941 are inscribed "For Local Addresses Only." Eight self-adhesive die cut labels are affixed to the opposite side of the peelable backing paper.

Singapore River
A228

No. 942: a, River community, 1920s. b, South Boat Quay, 1930s. c, Social gathering, 1950s. d, Changing skyline, 1980s. e, River Regatta, 1990s. f, At the river mouth, 1900s. g, Stevedores, 1910s. h, Lighters, 1940s. i, Men at work, 1960s. j, Working with cranes, 1970s.

2000, June 21   Perf. 14
942   Sheet of 10   7.00 7.00
  a.-e. A228 (22c) Any single   .35   .35
  f.-j. A228 60c Any single   .95   .95

Nos. 942a-942e are inscribed "For Local Addresses Only."

Stampin' the Future
A229

Children's Stamp Design Contest Winners: (22c), Future lifestyle, art by Liu Jiang Wen. 60c, Future homes, art by Shaun Yew Chuan Bin. $1, Home automation, art by Gwendolyn Soh Shihui. $2, Floating city, art by Dawn Koh.

2000, July 7   Litho.   Perf. 14x12¾
943-946 A229 Set of 4   6.00 6.00
  946a Souvenir sheet, #943-946   6.25 6.25

World Stamp Expo 2000, Anaheim (No. 946a). No. 943 is inscribed "For Local Addresses Only."

Care for Nature
A230

No. 947: a, Archer fish. b, Smooth otter. c, Collared kingfisher. d, Orange fiddler crab.

2000, Aug. 11   Photo.   Perf. 14½
Granite Paper
947   Block of 4   5.00 5.00
  a.-b. A230 (22c) Any single   .40   .40
  c.-d. A230 $1 Any single   2.00 2.00
  e. Booklet pane, 5 each #947a, 947b   12.00
    Booklet, #947e   12.00
  f. Souv. sheet, #947, 947 imperf   9.50 9.50

Nos. 947a-947b are inscribed "For Local Addresses Only."
No. 947f sold for $5.

2000 Summer Olympics, Sydney — A231

Designs: (22c), Swimming and high jump. 60c, Badminton and discus. $1, Soccer and hurdles. $2, Table tennis and gymnastics.

2000, Sept. 15   Litho.   Perf. 13½
948-951 A231 Set of 4   6.50 6.50

No. 948 is inscribed "For Local Addresses Only."

A232

Festivals and Holidays
A233

Designs: Nos. 952, 960, (22c), 956, 30c, Christmas. Nos. 953, 961, (22c), 957, 30c, Eid ul-Fitr. Nos. 954, 962, (22c), 958, 30c, Chinese New Year. Nos. 955, 963, (22c), 959, 30c, Deepavali.

2000, Oct. 11   Litho.   Perf. 13
952-955 A232 Set of 4   3.00 3.00
956-959 A233 Set of 4   3.00 3.00
Serpentine Die Cut 12¾x13¼
Self-Adhesive
960-963 A232 Set of 4   4.50 4.50

Nos. 952-955, 960-963 are inscribed "For Local Addresses Only."

New Year 2001 (Year of the Snake)
A234

Designs: (22c), Snake and branch. $2, Two snakes.

2001, Jan. 12   Perf. 14½x14
964 A234 (22c) multi   .50   .50
965 A234 $2 multi   3.25 3.00
  a. Horiz. pair, #964-965   3.75 3.75
  b. Souvenir sheet, #964-965, with Hong Kong 2001 margin   5.50 5.50
  c. Souvenir sheet, #964-965, with Belgica 2001 margin   5.50 5.50
  d. Souvenir sheet, #964-965, with Phila Nippon '01 margin 5.50 5.50

Issued: No. 965c, 6/9; No. 965d, 7/1.

Early Singaporeans
A235

Designs: No. 966, $1, Tan Tock Seng (1798-1850), philanthropist. No. 967, $1, P. Govindasamy Pillai (1887-1980), businessman. No. 968, $1, Edwin John Tessensohn (1857-1926), politician. No. 969, $1, Eunos bin Abdullah (1876-1941), politician.

2001, Feb. 28   Photo.   Perf. 11¾
Granite Paper
966-969 A235 Set of 4   6.50 6.50

Commonwealth Day, 25th Anniv. — A236

Designs: (22c), Co-operation. 60c, Education. $1, Sports. $2, Arts and culture.

2001, Mar. 12   Litho.   Perf. 14x14¼
970-973 A236 Set of 4   6.75 6.75

No. 970 inscribed "For Local Addresses Only."

Greetings — A237

Serpentine Die Cut 10
2001, Apr. 25   Litho.
Self-Adhesive
974 A237 (22c) Balloons   .50   .50
975 A237 (22c) Fireworks   .50   .50
976 A237 (22c) Roses   .50   .50
977 A237 (22c) Gifts   .50   .50
978 A237 (22c) Musical instruments   .50   .50
  a. Booklet, 2 each #974-978 + 10 labels   5.00
  Nos. 974-978 (5)   2.50 2.50

Nos. 974-978 inscribed "For Local Addresses Only."

Perf. 14
Water-Activated Gum
978B A237 (22c) Fireworks   1.00 1.00
978C A237 (22c) Musical instruments 1.00 1.00
978D A237 (22c) Roses   1.00 1.00
978E A237 (22c) Balloons   1.00 1.00

978F A237 (22c) Gifts   1.00 1.00
  g. Vert. strip, #978B-978F + 5 labels   5.00 5.00

Nos. 978B-978F were printed in sheets containing four of each stamp and 20 labels that could be personalized. Sheets sold for $11 for the first sheet with additional sheets available for $10. At least three different sheets of 6 of No. 978B and 6 non-personalizable labels exist. These sheets sold as part of a set of 8 sheets with various face values that sold for $8.50 per sheet, and later as part of another set of 8 sheets, for $9 per sheet..

Singapore Arts Festival — A238

No. 979: a, (22c), "a." b, 60c, "r." c, $1, "t." d, $2, "s."

2001, May 16   Perf. 14
979 A238 Block of 4, #a-d   5.50 5.50

No. 979a inscribed "For Local Addresses Only."

Pets — A239

No. 980: a, Fish. b, Cockatoos. c, Chicks. d, Turtle. e, Dog and fish. f, Cat and mice. g, Bird and dog. h, Dog and cat. i, Parrots. j, Cat and rabbit.

2001, July 26   Perf. 13½
980   Sheet of 10   8.00 8.00
  a.-d. (22c) Any single, 25x25mm   .45   .45
  e.-f. (22c) Any single, 25x35mm   .45   .45
  g.-h. 50c Any single, 25x42mm   1.00 1.00
  i.-j. $1 Any single, 25x42mm   1.75 1.75

Nos. 980a-980f are inscribed "For Local Addresses Only." Singpex '01.

Frame — A240

Serpentine Die Cut 15x14½
2001, July 26
Self-Adhesive
981 A240 (22c) multi   1.00 1.00
Size: 24x34mm
982 A240 (22c) multi   1.00 1.00
  a. Pane, 6 #981, 4 #982 +16 labels   10.00

Nos. 981-982 inscribed "For Local Addresses Only." No. 982a contains three examples of No. 982 with differing white paw prints, and one example without paw print. Singpex '01.

Care for
Nature — A241

Orangutans: (22c), Adult hanging on tree.
60c, Two adults. No. 983c, Adult and child. No.
983d, Two adults and child.

2001, Sept. 5   **Perf. 13½x13**
983   Horiz. strip of 4   4.25   4.25
   a.   A241 (22c) multi   .30   .30
   b.   A241 60c multi   .90   .90
   c.-d.   A241 $1 Any single   1.40   1.40
   e.   Souvenir sheet, #983   7.00   7.00
   f.   Sheet, 2 each #983c-983d, + 8
       labels, perf. 12¾(/05)   9.75   9.75

Self-Adhesive
Booklet Stamp
Serpentine Die Cut 12½

984   A241 (22c) multi   .50   .50
   a.   Booklet of 10   5.00

Nos. 983a, 984 inscribed "For Local
Addresses Only."
No. 983e sold for $3.90, with 50c of that
donated to the Care for Nature Trust Fund.
No. 983f issued 5/1/05. No. 983f sold for $6.

Flowers
A242

Designs: (22c), Melastoma malabathricum.
60c, Leontopodium alpinum. $1, Saraca cau-
liflora. $2, Gentiana clusii.

2001, Sept. 20   **Perf. 13¼x12¾**
985-988   A242   Set of 4   6.50   6.50
988a   Souvenir sheet, #985-988   6.50   6.50

No. 985 inscribed "For Local Addresses
Only." See Switzerland No. 1107.

Tropical
Fish — A243

Designs: 5c, Moorish idol. 20c, Threadfin
butterflyfish. (22c), Copperband butterflyfish.
(23c), Copperband butterflyfish. 30c, Pearl-
scale butterflyfish. 31c, Eight-banded butterflyfish. 40c, Rainbow butterflyfish. 50c, Yellow-
faced angelfish. 60c, Emperor angelfish. 70c,
Striped sailfin tang. 80c, Palette tang.

2001-05   **Perf. 13x13¼**
989   A243   5c multi   .35   .35
990   A243   20c multi   .35   .35
991   A243   (22c) multi   .45   .45
992   A243   30c multi   .65   .65
992A   A243   31c multi   .75   .75
992B   A243   (31c) multi   .75   .75
993   A243   40c multi   .80   .80
994   A243   50c multi   1.00   1.00
995   A243   60c multi   1.10   1.10
996   A243   70c multi   1.40   1.40
997   A243   80c multi   1.60   1.60
   a.   Sheet of 9, #989-997   8.75   8.75
   Nos. 989-997 (11)   9.20   9.20

Self-Adhesive
Serpentine Die Cut 12½

998   A243 (22c) multi   .50   .50
   a.   Booklet of 10   5.00
998B   A243 (23c) multi   .60   .60
   c.   Booklet pane of 10   6.00

Issued: Nos. 989-992, 993-998 issued
10/24/01. 31c, 2/3/04; (23c), 7/7/04; No. 992B,
3/18/05.
Nos. 991, 998 inscribed "For Local
Addresses Only." No. 998B is inscribed "1st
Local." No. 992B is inscribed "2nd Local."

New Year
2002 (Year
of the
Horse)
A244

Designs: Nos. 999, 1001a, (22c), One
horse. Nos. 1000, 1001b, $2, Two horses.

Litho., Litho & Embossed with Foil
Application (#1001a, 1001b)
2002, Jan. 10   **Perf. 13½x13¼**
999-1000   A244   Set of 2   4.75   4.75
1000a   Souvenir sheet, #999-1000,
      perf. 13x13¼   4.75   4.75
1001   Sheet, #1001a-1001b, 8
      each #999-1000   27.50   27.50
   a.   A244 (22c) silver & multi   .30   .30
   b.   A244 $2 gold & multi   2.75   2.75

A souvenir sheet containing one each of
Nos. 1001a and 1001b exists. It was sold only
in year sets.
No. 1000a issued 8/2/02, for Philakorea.

William Farquhar Collection of Natural
History Drawings — A245

No. 1002, (22c) — Animals and Reptiles: a,
Landak raya. b, Cipan, Badak murai. c,
Landak kelubu. d, Kongkang. e, Biawak tanah.
f, Tupai terbang merah. g, Memerang kecil. h,
Biawak pasir. i, Tupai kerawak, vert. j, Napuh,
vert.
No. 1003, (22c) — Fruits and Plants: a,
Buah rumenia. b, Manggis hutan. c,
Cempedak. d, Bunga dedap. e, Jeringau, vert.
f, Rotang, vert. g, Tuba, vert. h, Tebu gagak,
vert. i, Temu kunci, vert. j, Rambutan, vert.
No. 1004, (22c) — Birds: a, Burung gaji-gaji.
b, Kuau cermin. c, Ayam kolam. d, Kelengking.
e, Burung kuang. f, Puhung. g, Burung kunyit,
vert. h, Burung pacat sayap biru, vert. i,
Burung mural, vert. j, Burung berek-berek,
vert.
No. 1005, (22c) — Fish: a, Ikan tenggiri
papan. b, Ikan kertang. c, Ikan kakatua. d,
Ikan bambangan. e, Ikan parang. f, Ikan buntai
pisang. g, Ikan ketang. h, Pari hitam. i, Telinga
gajah. j, Ikan babi.
Designs: No. 1006, Like No. 1002. No.
1007, Like No. 1003. No. 1008, Like No. 1004.
No. 1009, Like No. 1005.

Perf. 13¼x13¾, 13¾x13¼
2002   **Litho.**
Sheets of 10, #a-j
1002-1005   A245   Set of 4   15.00   15.00

Serpentine Die Cut 12½
Sheets of 10, #a-j
Self-Adhesive

1006-1009   A245   Set of 4   17.50   17.50

Issued: Nos. 1002-1003, 2/20; Nos. 1004-
1005, 3/20. Nos. 1006-1007, 2/20; Nos. 1008-
1009, 3/20. Nos. 1002-1009 inscribed "For
Local Addresses Only."

Toys
A246

Designs: (22c), Lego blocks. 60c, Cowboys
and Indians, robot. 70c, Dolls. $1, Racing
cars.

2002, May 22   **Perf. 14½x14**
1010-1013   A246   Set of 4   4.00   4.00
No. 1010 inscribed "For local addresses
only."

Tropical
Birds — A247

Designs: (22c), Red-throated sunbird. 40c,
Asian fairy bluebird. $1, Black-naped oriole.
$2, White-bellied woodpecker.

2002, June 27   **Perf. 13¼x14**
1014-1017   A247   Set of 4   5.75   5.75
1017a   Souvenir sheet, #1014-1017   7.00   7.00
No. 1014 inscribed "For local addresses
only." See Malaysia Nos. 886-888.

Fish Type of 2001
Discus fish: $1, Blue turquoise. $2, Brown
discus. $5, Red alenquer. $10, Red turquoise.

2002, July 24   **Perf. 13½x13¼**
Size: 29x25mm
1018   A243 $1 multi   1.50   1.50
1019   A243 $2 multi   3.00   3.00
1020   A243 $5 multi   8.00   8.00
1021   A243 $10 multi   16.00   16.00
   a.   Souvenir sheet, #1018-1021   29.00   29.00
   Nos. 1018-1021 (4)   28.50   28.50

A248

Festivals
and
Holidays
A249

Designs: Nos. 1022, 50c; 1026, 1030, (22c),
Christmas. No. 1023, 50c; 1027, 1031, (22c),
Chinese New Year. Nos. 1024, 50c; 1028,
1032, (22c), Deepavali. No. 1025, 50c; 1029,
1033, (22c), Eid ul-Fitr.

Litho. with Hologram Affixed
2002, Aug. 21   **Perf. 13¼x13¾**
1022-1025   A248   Set of 4   3.25   3.25
1026-1029   A249   Set of 4   2.00   2.00

Self-Adhesive
Serpentine Die Cut 13¼x13¾
1030-1033   A249   Set of 4   4.25   4.25

Nos. 1026-1033 are inscribed "For Local
Addresses Only."

Trees — A250

Designs: Nos. 1034, 1038, (22c), Flame of
the forest. 60c, Rain tree. No. 1036, $1,
Tembusu. No. 1037, $1, Kapok tree.

2002, Sept. 25   **Litho.**   **Perf. 13½x13**
1034-1037   A250   Set of 4   4.50   4.50

Self-Adhesive
Booklet Stamp
Serpentine Die Cut 12½
1038   A250   (22c) multi   .60   .60
   a.   Booklet of 10   6.00

Nos. 1034, 1038 are inscribed "For Local
Addresses Only."
A sheet containing 2 each Nos. 1035-1036
and 2 stamps similar to No. 1034 but inscribed

"1st Local" + 6 non-personalizable labels sold
for $9.90.

Opening of
Esplanade
Performing
Arts Center
A251

Various views of complex with background
colors of: (22c), Orange. 60c, Brown. $1, Blue
green. $2, Dark blue.

2002, Oct. 12 Litho.   **Perf. 13¼x13¾**
1039-1042   A251   Set of 4   6.00   6.00
1042a   Souvenir sheet, #1039-1042   6.00   6.00
No. 1039 is inscribed "For local addresses
only."

Singapore, A Global City — A252

No. 1043: a, Sailboats. b, Conductor's
hands.

2002-04   **Perf. 14¼x14**
1043   A252 $2 Horiz. pair, #a-b +
      central label   6.50   6.50
1043c   Souvenir sheet, #1043a-
      1043b, + American Express
      label   7.00   7.00
   d.   As "c," with Coca-Cola label   7.00   7.00
   e.   As "c," with McDonald's label   7.00   7.00
   f.   As "c," with Reader's Digest la-
      bel   7.00   7.00
   g.   As "c," with Swatch label   7.00   7.00
   h.   As "c," ovptd. in margin with
      World Stamp Championship
      emblem in silver   7.00   7.00
   i.   As "d," ovptd. in margin with
      World Stamp Championship
      emblem in silver   7.00   7.00
   j.   As "e," ovptd. in margin with
      World Stamp Championship
      emblem in silver   7.00   7.00
   k.   As "f," ovptd. in margin with
      World Stamp Championship
      emblem in silver   7.00   7.00
   l.   As "g," ovptd. in margin with
      World Stamp Championship
      emblem in silver   7.00   7.00

Issued: Nos. 1043-1043g, 11/20/02. Nos.
1043h-1043l, 6/23/04. Nos. 1043h-1043l sold
for $4.53 each.

New Year
2003 (Year
of the Ram)
A253

Designs: (22c) Red violet ram. $2, Tree and
yellow green ram.

2003, Jan. 10 Litho.   **Perf. 13x13½**
1044-1045   A253   Set of 2   3.50   3.50
1045a   Sheet, 9 each #1044-1045   25.00   25.00
1045b   Souvenir sheet, #1044-
      1045, with Bangkok 2003
      margin   5.00   5.00
1045c   Souvenir sheet, #1044-
      1045, with China 2003
      margin   5.00   5.00

No. 1044 inscribed "For Local Addresses
Only."
Issued: No. 1045b, 10/4; No. 1045c, 11/20.

History of
Empress
Place
Building
A254

Designs: (22c), Government offices. 60c,
Government offices, diff. $1, Empress Place
Museum. $2, Asian Civilizations Museum.

2003, Feb. 26   **Perf. 14½**
1046-1049   A254   Set of 4   6.00   6.00
No. 1046 inscribed "For local addresses
only."

Nocturnal Animals A255

Designs: (22c), Tarsier. 40c, Barn owl. $1, Babirusa. $2, Clouded leopard.

2003, Mar. 20   Litho.   Perf. 13¼
1050-1053	A255	Set of 4	5.75 5.75
1053a		Souvenir sheet	7.00 7.00

No. 1050 inscribed "For Local Addresses Only." Glow-in-the-dark ink was applied to portions of No. 1053a by silk-screening.

Singapore Police Force — A256

Designs: (22c), Community policing. 40c, Traffic policing. $1, Maritime policing. $2, International peacekeeping.

2003, Apr. 23   Litho.   Perf. 13¼x13
1054-1057	A256	Set of 4	5.75 5.75

No. 1054 inscribed "For Local Addresses Only."

Singapore, A Global City — A257

No. 1058: a, Spacecraft. b, Robot.

2003, May 21   Litho.   Perf. 14¼x14
1058	A257	$2 Horiz. pair, #a-b + central label	6.50 6.50
c.		Souvenir sheet, #1058a-1058b + CNN label	6.50 6.50
d.		As "c," with Creative Technology label	6.50 6.50
e.		As "c," with Microsoft label	6.50 6.50
f.		As "c," with Siemens label	6.50 6.50
g.		As "c," with Singapore Airlines label	6.50 6.50
h.		As "c," ovptd. in margin with World Stamp Championship emblem in silver	6.50 6.50
i.		As "d," ovptd. in margin with World Stamp Championship emblem in silver	6.50 6.50
j.		As "e," ovptd. in margin with World Stamp Championship emblem in silver	6.50 6.50
k.		As "f," ovptd. in margin with World Stamp Championship emblem in silver	6.50 6.50
l.		As "g," ovptd. in margin with World Stamp Championship emblem in silver	6.50 6.50

Issued: Nos. 1058-1058g, 5/21/03. Nos. 1058h-1058l, 6/23/04. Nos. 1058h-1058l sold for $4.53 each.

Joy and Caring — A258

Designs and inscriptions: Nos. 1059a, 1060a, Cat (Joy). Nos. 1059b, 1060b, Running heart (Joy). Nos. 1059c, 1060c, Teddy bear (Joy). Nos. 1059d, 1060d, Laughing man (Joy). Nos. 1059e, 1060e, Ostrich head (Joy). Nos. 1059f, 1060f, Apple (Caring). Nos. 1059g, 1060g, Hand and heart (A helping hand). Nos. 1059h, 1060h, Hearts (Togetherness). Nos. 1059i, 1060i, Flower (Beauty of a caring heart). Nos. 1059j, 1060j, Stars (Keeping in touch keeps us going).

2003, June 25   Perf. 14½
1059		Sheet of 10 + 2 labels	6.00 6.00
a.-j.		A258 (22c) Any single	.60 .60
k.		Sheet, 10 each #1059c, 1059h + 20 labels	14.00 14.00
l.		Sheet of 20 #1059i + 20 labels	14.50 14.50
m.		Sheet, 10 each #1059c, 1059h + 20 labels	16.00 16.00

Self-Adhesive
Serpentine Die Cut 10x9¾
1060		Booklet of 10 + 6 labels	6.00 6.00
a.-j.		A258 (22c) Any single	.60 .60

Inscribed "For Local Addresses Only." Labels on No. 1059k could be personalized for an additional fee.
Issued: No. 1059l, 8/8; No. 1059m, 11/25/04. Nos. 1059l and 1059m each sold for $8. A sheet of 5 #1059j and 5 non-personalizable labels sold for $9.90.
See Nos. 1119-1121.

Opening of North East Line of Rapid Transit System A259

Designs: (22c), Map of Rapid Transit System, train. 60c, Entrance gates, station cross-section, train. $2, System control room, train.
No. 1064: a, (22c), Like No. 522. b, 60c, Like No. 523. c, $2, Like No. 524.

2003, July 18   Perf. 13¾
1061-1063	A259	Set of 3	4.50 4.50

Souvenir Sheet
1064	A259	Sheet of 6, #1061-1063, 1064a-1064c	8.50 8.50

Nos. 1061, 1064a are inscribed "For Local Addresses Only."

National Day — A260

Designs: (22c), Flag. 60c, National flower, Vanda Miss Joaquim orchid. $1, Merlion and buildings. $2, People of Singapore.

2003, Aug. 9   Perf. 13¼x13½
1065-1068	A260	Set of 4	6.00 6.00
1065a		Sheet of 20 + 20 labels	12.50 12.50
1068a		Souvenir sheet, #1065-1068	6.00 6.00
1068B		Sheet, 3 #1068Bc, 2#1068Bd + 10 labels	10.00 10.00
c.		A260 60c Like #1066, 35x28mm	1.50 1.50
d.		A260 $1 Like #1067, 35x28mm	2.50 2.50

No. 1065 is inscribed "For local addresses only."
No. 1065a sold for $8. Labels could be personalized.
Numerous different sheets containing 5 stamps similar to No. 1065 but inscribed "1st Local" + 10 non-personalizable labels (sheets having various labels and margins) exist. Sheets sold for $6. A sheet containing 3 stamps similar to No. 1068Bc exists, sold as part of a series of sheets sold with a book for $39.90.
Size of Nos. 1066-1067: 33x28mm. No. 1068B sold for $6.

Aircraft A261

No. 1069 — Military aircraft: a, Alouette III helicopter. b, E-2C Hawkeye. c, Hawker Hunter. d, Super Puma AS-332M helicopter. e, Hercules C-130H. f, F-16 C/D Fighting Falcon. g, AH-64D Apache helicopter. h, KC-135R Stratotanker. i, Cessna 172. j, F-5E Tiger II.
No. 1070 — Civil aircraft: a, Airbus 340-500. b, Boeing 747-400. c, Boeing 777-200. d, Boeing 747-400 Freighter. e, Airbus 320. f, Concorde. g, Boeing 737-100. h, Comet IV. i, Viscount. j, Airspeed Consul.

2003, Sept. 3   Perf. 13¼x13½
1069		Sheet of 10	3.50 3.50
a.-j.		A261 (22c) Any single	.35 .35
1070		Sheet of 10	3.50 3.50
a.-j.		A261 (22c) Any single	.35 .35
k.		Sheet of 20, #1069a-1069j, 1070a-1070j	6.00 6.00

Self-Adhesive
Serpentine Die Cut 12½
1071		Sheet of 10	5.00
a.-j.		A261 (22c) Any single	.50 .50
1072		Sheet of 10	5.00
a.-j.		A261 (22c) Any single	.50 .50

Inscribed "For local addresses only." Powered flight, cent.; Singapore Air Force, 35th anniv.

Singapore, A Garden City — A262

Designs: Nos. 1073, 1077, (22c), Singapore Botanic Gardens. 60c, Fort Canning Park. No. 1075, $1, Marina City Park. No. 1076, $1, Sungei Buloh Wetland Reserve.

2003, Oct. 22   Litho.   Perf. 13½
1073-1076	A262	Set of 4	4.50 4.50

Booklet Stamp
Self-Adhesive
Serpentine Die Cut 10x9½
1077	A262	(22c) multi	.60 .60
a.		Booklet pane of 10	6.00 6.00

Nos. 1073, 1077 are inscribed "For Local Addresses Only."
A sheet containing Nos. 1075, 1076, 2 No. 1074 and 2 stamps similar to No. 1073 inscribed "1st Local" + 6 non-personalizable labels sold for $9.90.

New Year 2004 (Year of the Monkey) A263

Designs: (22c), Monkey and heart. $2, Two monkeys.

2004, Jan. 9   Perf. 14x13¼
1078-1079	A263	Set of 2	3.50 3.50
1079a		Sheet, 9 each #1078-1079	32.50 32.50
1079b		Souvenir sheet, #1078-1079, with Hong Kong 2004 Stamp Expo margin	3.50 3.50

No. 1078 is inscribed "For Local Addresses Only." No. 1079a is reserved.

Paintings A264

Nos. 1080, 1082 — Paintings of Liu Kang: a, Farmer's House. b, Artist and Model. c, Lanterns Galore. d, Enjoying a Smoke, Kashmir. e, Life by the River. f, Tenth Trip Up to Huangshan. g, My Young Wife, vert. h, Kek Lok Si, Penang, vert. i, Souri, vert. j, Siesta in Bali, vert.
Nos. 1081, 1083 — Paintings of Ong Kim Seng: a, Kampong Tengah, Singapore. b, Gyantse Market. c, Sebatu Spring, Bali. d, Jetty, Bangkok. e, Resort, Bali. f, Dance Studio, Bali. g, Telok Ayer Market. h, Kathmandu, Nepal. i, Portofino, Italy, vert. j, Boats at Rest, vert.

Perf. 13¼x13½, 13½x13¼ (Vert. stamps)

2004, Feb. 18
1080		Sheet of 10	3.75 3.75
a.-j.		A264 (23c) Any single	.35 .35
1081		Sheet of 10	3.75 3.75
a.-j.		A264 (23c) Any single	.35 .35

Self-Adhesive
Serpentine Die Cut 12½x12¼, 12¼x12½ (Vert. stamps)
1082		Sheet of 10	4.50 4.50
a.-j.		A264 (23c) Any single	.45 .45
1083		Sheet of 10	4.50 4.50
a.-j.		A264 (23c) Any single	.45 .45
		Nos. 1080-1083 (4)	16.50 16.50

Inscribed "For local addresses only."

Suzhou, China Industrial Park, 10th Anniv. A265

2004, Mar. 1   Litho.   Perf. 13x13½
1084	A265	60c multi	1.25 1.25
a.		Sheet of 8	10.00 10.00

Singapore Skyline A266

Designs: (23c), Buildings as seen from street level. 60c, Fountain. 70c, Buildings as seen from distance.
$1, Singapore, circa 1900. $5, Singapore, 2004.

Perf. 14¼x14½   Litho.
1085-1087	A266	Set of 3	2.50 2.50
1087a		Sheet, 3 #1086, 2 #1087, + 10 labels, perf. 12¾x13 ('05)	8.75 8.75

Souvenir Sheets
Perf. 14¼x14
1088	A266	$1 multi	1.75 1.75

Litho. & Engr.
1089	A266	$5 multi	8.00 8.00

No. 1085 is inscribed "1st Local." Nos. 1088 and 1089 each contain one 95x35mm stamp. No. 1087a issued 5/1/05. No. 1087a sold for $6.

Singapore, A Global City — A267

No. 1090: a, Cargo containers. b, Gas tanks.

2004   Litho.   Perf. 14½x14¼
1090		Horiz. pair with central label	6.50 6.50
a.-b.		A267 $2 Either single	3.25 3.25
c.		Souvenir sheet, #1090a-1090b + AIA label	6.50 6.50
d.		As "c," with GlaxoSmithKline label	6.50 6.50
e.		As "c," with HSBC label	6.50 6.50
f.		As "c," with Shell Oil label	6.50 6.50
g.		As "c," with Sony label	6.50 6.50
h.		As "c," ovptd. in margin with World Stamp Championship emblem in silver	6.50 6.50
i.		As "d," ovptd. in margin with World Stamp Championship emblem in silver	6.50 6.50
j.		As "e," ovptd. in margin with World Stamp Championship emblem in silver	6.50 6.50
k.		As "f," ovptd. in margin with World Stamp Championship emblem in silver	6.50 6.50
l.		As "g," ovptd. in margin with World Stamp Championship emblem in silver	6.50 6.50
m.		Souvenir sheet, #1043a, 1043b, 1058a, 1058b, 1090a, 1090b	19.00 19.00

Issued: Nos. 1090, 1090c-1090g, 4/21; 1090h-1090l, 6/23; No. 1090m, 8/28. Nos. 1090h-1090l sold for $4.53 each. No. 1090m sold for $12.60 and exists imperf.

FIFA (Fédération Internationale de Football Association), Cent. — A268

FIFA emblem and: 30c, Soccer field. 60c, Soccer ball. $1, Player's shirt. $2, World map.

Litho. & Embossed
2004, May 21   *Perf. 13*
Flocked Paper
1091-1094 A268   Set of 4   6.25 6.25

Festivals and Holidays — A269

Designs: Nos. 1095, 1103, (23c), Santa Claus, reindeer (Christmas). Nos. 1096, 1104, (23c), Flowers, fruit (Chinese New Year). Nos. 1097, 1105, (23c), Candles (Deepavali). Nos. 1098, 1106, Candle (Eid ul-Fitr). No. 1099, 50c, Carolers (Christmas). No. 1100, 50c, Woman (Chinese New Year). No. 1101, 50c, Woman and candle (Deepavali). No. 1102, 50c, Child with sparkler (Eid ul-Fitr).

2004, July 7   **Litho.**   *Perf. 13*
1095-1102 A269   Set of 8   4.75 4.75
1095a   Perf. 12¾x13 + label   .35 .35
1099a   Perf. 12¾x13 + label   .80 .80
1102a   Sheet, #1099-1102, + 8 labels, perf. 12¾x13   8.25 8.25

Self-Adhesive
Serpentine Die Cut 12½
1103-1106 A269   Set of 4   3.50 3.50

Nos. 1103-1106 were each printed in sheets of 10. Nos. 1095-1098, 1103-1106 are inscribed "1st Local."

Nos. 1095a, 1099a issued 11/7/05. Nos. 1095a, 1099a issued in sheets of 8 + 8 labels.

No. 1102a issued 5/1/05. No. 1102a sold for $6.

National Monuments — A270

No. 1107, (23c): a, Column, City Hall. b, City Hall.
No. 1108, 30c: a, Tower, Victoria Theater and Concert Hall. b, Victoria Theater and Concert Hall.
No. 1109, 60c: a, Dome, Supreme Court. b, Supreme Court.
No. 1110, $1: a, Decoration, Istana (President's residence). b, Istana.
Sizes: Nos. 1107a-1110a, 41x46mm. Nos. 1107b-1110b, 41x27mm.

2004, Aug. 9   *Perf. 13¼x13¾*
Vert. Pairs, #a-b
1107-1110 A270   Set of 4   6.75 6.75
1110c   Souvenir sheet, #1107b, 1108b, 1109b, 1110b   3.50 3.50

No. 1107 is inscribed "1st Local."

2004 Summer Olympics, Athens A271

Carved rocks with stylized: (23c), Runners. 30c, Swimmers. $1, Weight lifter. $2, Sailor.

2004, Aug. 13   *Perf. 13¾*
1111-1114 A271   Set of 4   5.75 5.75

No. 1111 is inscribed "1st Local."

Use of Postage Stamps in Singapore, 150th Anniv. — A272

Cancels, buildings, stamp vignettes and: (23c), Singapore #27, 49, 1067. 60c, Straits Settlements #N27, 271, Singapore #11. $1, Straits Settlements #124, 167, 251. $2, India #6, Straits Settlements #1, 18.

2004, Aug. 28   *Perf. 12¼x11¾*
1115-1118 A272   Set of 4   6.00 6.00
1115a   Sheet of 15 + 15 labels   9.50 9.50
1118a   Souvenir sheet, #1115-1118   6.00 6.00

No. 1115a sold for $6 and labels could be personalized for an additional fee.

Joy and Caring Type of 2003 Inscribed "1st Local"

Designs: No. 1119, Flower (Beauty of a Caring Heart). No. 1120, Hearts (Togetherness). No. 1121, Teddy bear (Joy).

2004   **Litho.**   *Perf. 14½*
1119 A258 (23c) multi + label   1.75 1.75
1120 A258 (23c) multi + label   .50 .50
a.   Pair, #1119-1120 + 2 labels   3.50 3.50
1121 A258 (23c) multi + label   .50 .50
a.   Pair, #1120-1121 + 2 labels   1.00 1.00
   Nos. 1119-1121 (3)   2.75 2.75

Issued: Nos. 1119, 1120, 8/28; No. 1121, 8/30. Nos. 1119 and 1120 were printed in a sheet containing five of each stamp and ten labels that sold for $15. Nos. 1120 and 1121 were printed in a sheet containing ten of each stamp and 20 labels that sold for $8, and a sheet containing 8 No. 1120 and 6 No. 1121 and 18 labels that sold for $20.

Three sheets containing 4 smaller-sized versions of No. 1120 + 4 labels (each sheet with different label and margin) sold for $5 per sheet.

A sheet with 6 No. 1120 with smaller "1st Local" inscriptions and 6 non-personalizable labels sold for $9.90. A similar sheet later sold as part of a set of 8 sheets with various face values for $8.50 per sheet. A similar set of sheets with various face values containing similar sheets containing 6 No. 1120 and 6 non-personalizable labels later sold for $9 per sheet.

Care For Nature — A273

Designs: Nos. 1122a, 1123 Seashore nutmeg. Nos. 1122b, 1124, Oriental pied hornbill. No. 1122c, Knobby sea star. No. 1122d, Common seahorse.

2004, Oct. 20   *Perf. 14*
1122   Horiz. strip of 4   4.00 4.00
a.-b.   A273 (23c) Either single   .35 .35
c.-d.   A273 $1 Either single   1.60 1.60

Booklet Stamps
Self-Adhesive
Serpentine Die Cut 10¼x9½
1123 A273 (23c) multi   .45 .45
1124 A273 (23c) multi   .45 .45
a.   Booklet pane, 5 each #1123-1124   4.50

Nos. 1122a-1122b, 1123-1124 are inscribed "1st Local."

New Year 2005 (Year of the Rooster) A274

Designs: (23c), Rooster. $2, Rooster and hen.

2005, Jan. 14   *Perf. 13¼x13½*
1125-1126 A274   Set of 2   3.75 3.75
1126a   Sheet, 9 each #1125-1126   32.50 32.50
1126b   Souvenir sheet, #1125-1126, perf. 12¾, with Pacific Explorer emblem in margin   3.75 3.75
1126c   Souvenir sheet, #1125-1126, perf. 12¾, with Taipei 2005 emblem in margin   3.75 3.75

No. 1125 is inscribed "1st Local."
No. 1126b issued 4/21; No. 1126c, 8/19.

Greetings A275

Designs: Nos. 1127a, 1132, Balloon animal. Nos. 1127a, 1131, Orchid. Nos. 1127c, 1130, Gift. Nos. 1127d, 1129, Flowers and teddy bears. Nos. 1127e, 1128, Candle and goblets.

2005, Feb. 23   *Perf. 13½x13¾*
1127   Vert. strip of 5   2.00 2.00
a.-e.   A275 (23c) Any single   .40 .40

Booklet Stamps
Self-Adhesive
Serpentine Die Cut 11¼
1128 A275 (23c) multi   .40 .40
1129 A275 (23c) multi   .40 .40
1130 A275 (23c) multi   .40 .40
1131 A275 (23c) multi   .40 .40
1132 A275 (23c) multi   .40 .40
a.   Booklet pane, 2 each #1128-1132   4.00

Inscribed "1st Local." Two sheets, each containing 4 each of Nos. 1127c and 1127d and 5 non-personalizable labels sold for $10. The labels on these sheets could be personalized for an additional fee.

Hans Christian Andersen (1805-75), Author A276

Stories: (23c), Thumbelina. 60c, The Ugly Duckling. $1, The Emperor's New Clothes. $2, The Little Mermaid.

2005, Mar. 30   **Litho.**   *Perf. 13x12¾*
1133-1136 A276   Set of 4   6.00 6.00
1136a   Souvenir sheet, #1133-1136   6.00 6.00

No. 1133 is inscribed "1st Local."

University Education in Singapore, Cent. — A277

Designs: (23c), Global knowledge enterprise. 60c, Quality education. 70c, Artistic and cultural hub. $1, Research excellence.

2005, Apr. 20   *Perf. 12¼*
1137-1140 A277   Set of 4   4.00 4.00

No. 1137 is inscribed "1st Local."

A278   A279

A280   A281

"Uniquely Singapore" — A282

2005, May 1   *Perf. 12¾*
1141   Miniature sheet of 5 + 10 labels   8.00 8.00
a.   A278 $1 multi   1.60 1.60
b.   A279 $1 multi   1.60 1.60
c.   A280 $1 multi   1.60 1.60
d.   A281 $1 multi   1.60 1.60
e.   A282 $1 multi   1.60 1.60

No. 1141 sold for $6. Labels could be personalized.

Sheets containing one each of stamps similar to Nos. 1141a-1141e, lacking "Uniquely" and containing 5 or 10 non-personalizable labels sold for a variety of prices. A sheet of three stamps similar to No. 1141a, lacking "Uniquely" and containing three non-personalizable labels sold for $8.50.

Numerous sheets containing $1.10 stamps of types A278-A282 and two similar types showing other geometric designs, all lacking "Uniquely," and with different colors, exist. Various combinations and quantities of stamps exist on such sheets and all such sheets have non-personalizable labels in various quantities. All of these sheets sold for prices well above face value. Some sheets were sold only together with a variety of other non-philatelic products.

Malay Heritage Center A283

Designs: (31c), Building, drummers. 60c, Fountain pen, seal, manuscript. $1, Stringed instrument, man and woman. $2, Sailor, boat.

2005, May 31   *Perf. 13¾*
1142-1145 A283   Set of 4   6.25 6.25

No. 1142 is inscribed "2nd Local."

Admiral Zheng He's Voyages, 600th Anniv. A284

Map and: No. 1146, (23c), Admiral Zheng He, ship. No. 1147 (23c), Ships. 60c, Ships, diff. $1, Ships, diff.

2005, June 28   *Perf. 13¼x13½*
1146-1149 A284   Set of 4   3.25 3.25
1147a   Sheet, 5 each #1146-1147,
     perf. 12¾   3.75 3.75

Nos. 1146 and 1147 are inscribed "1st Local."

117th International Olympic Committee Session, Singapore — A285

Emblem, world map showing Singapore and candidates for hosting 2012 Olympics and: (23c), Cycling, running, table tennis. 50c, Running, basketball, tennis. 60c, Soccer, tennis, javelin. $1, Gymnastics, weight lifting.

2005, July 5   *Perf. 14¼*
      Size: 44x25mm
1150-1153 A285   Set of 4   3.75 3.75
       Perf. 12¼
1154   Miniature sheet, #1154a-
     1154b, 2 each #1154c-
     1154d, + 6 labels   7.25 7.25
  a.   A285 (23c) multi, 44x28mm   .45 .45
  b.   A285 50c multi, 44x28mm   .95 .95
  c.   A285 60c multi, 44x28mm   1.10 1.10
  d.   A285 $1 multi, 44x28mm   1.75 1.75

Nos. 1150, 1154a are inscribed "1st Local." No. 1154 sold for $6, and labels could be personalized.

A286

A287

National Day — A288

Nos. 1155 and 1157 — Patchwork quilt blocks depicting: a, Stylized people, nine hearts. b, Hearts in a block of nine. c, Flower with face. d, Tower and hearts. e, Red orchid on green patterned background. f, Sun and rainbow. g, "Peace." h, Crescent and heart on Singapore map. i, White and purple orchid. j, Heart with red lace border. k, "Happy Birthday." l, Hands, "One Singapore," and "United We Stand." m, Cats and dog, "Singapore Is Our Home Too." n, Five stars around large star. o, Clothes on line, "One Nation Many Colors." p, Airplane, clouds. q, Love, star, dove, smiling face, "Love, Hope, Peace, Joy." r, Plate of food. s, Hearts and "Many Hearts One Nation." t, Stylized buildings and trees.

Nos. 1156 and 1158 — Patchwork quilt blocks depicting: a, "1" and flowers. b, Children with arms raised, "Home. . . Everyone Fits In!" c, Heads around flag. d, Rainbow and clouds. e, Person looking up, butterflies. f, Sun, butterflies, flowers, "Love Singapore." g, "One People, One Nation, One S'pore." h, Heart and durian. i, Frog on lily pad. j, Bird kites and flowers, "Flying High, My Singapore." k, Hands and heart. l, Singapore skyline, "Singapore My Home." m, Yellow, purple and green orchid on red background. n, Tree, hearts, "Racial Harmony." o, "I" heart, map of Singapore. p, Hand with buttons, child. q, Heart, stars, "Singapore." r, Four hearts in squares. s, Stars, hearts, stylized people in block of four. t, The Pledge.
$1, Entire quilt.

2005, Aug. 9   *Perf. 14¼x14½*
1155 A286 (23c) Sheet of 20, #a-
     t, + label   7.25 7.25
1156 A287 (23c) Sheet of 20, #a-
     t, + label   7.25 7.25
    Self-Adhesive (#1157-1158)
   Serpentine Die Cut 10x9½
1157 A286 (23c) Sheet of 20, #a-
     t, + label   8.00 8.00
1158 A287 (23c) Sheet of 20, #a-
     t, + label   8.00 8.00
      Souvenir Sheet
       Perf. 14
1159 A288 $1 multi   1.75 1.75
  a.   Sheet of 4 #1159   9.25 9.25

Each stamp on Nos. 1155-1158 inscribed "1st Local." No. 1159a sold for $5.50.
A sheet containing 2 each Nos. 1155b, 1155c, 1155j, 1155n, 1156d, 1156r, and 12 labels that could not be personalized sold for $6. This sheet was available with personalized labels for an additional fee. Three different sheets of 6 Nos. 1155n, 1156d or 1156r, and 6 non-personalizable labels each sold as part of a set of 8 sheets with various face values for $8.50 per sheet. A sheet containing 3 each of Nos. 1156d and 1156r and 5 non-personalizable labels sold for $10.50.

Buildings in Belgium and Singapore
A289

Designs: (23c), Belgian Center for Comic Strip Art, Brussels. 60c, Shop on Kandahar Street, Singapore. $1, Shops on Bukit Pasoh Road, Singapore. $2, Museum of Musical Instruments, Brussels.

2005, Sept. 9   *Perf. 12¾*
1160-1163 A289   Set of 4   6.00 6.00
1160a   Perf. 13½x13¼ + label   .80 .80
1161a   Perf. 13½x13¼ + label   1.25 1.25
1162a   Perf. 13½x13¼ + label   1.90 1.90
1163a   Souvenir sheet, #1160-1163   5.75 5.75

No. 1160 is inscribed "1st Local." See Belgium Nos. 2104-2107.
Nos. 1160a, 1161a, 1162a issued 11/7/05. Nos. 1160a issued in sheets of 8 + 8 labels that sold for $5. Nos. 1161a and 1162a were issued in sheets containing four of each stamp + eight labels that sold for $9.

HSBC Tree Top Walk — A290

No. 1164: a, (23c), Colugo. b, 60c, Adenia. c, $1, Red-crowned barbet. d, $1, Common tree nymph butterfly.

2005, Oct. 19   *Perf. 14*
1164 A290   Horiz. strip of 4, #a-d   4.50 4.50
     Booklet Stamp
     Self-Adhesive
   Serpentine Die Cut 10x9½
1165 A290 (23c) Like #1164a   .60 .60
  a.   Booklet pane of 10   5.00 5.00

New Year 2006 (Year of the Dog) A291

Designs: (23c), Dog. $2, Two dogs.

2006, Jan. 6   Litho.   *Perf. 13x13¼*
1167-1168 A291   Set of 2   3.50 3.50
1167a   Perf. 13x12¾, + label   .35 .35
1168a   Sheet, 9 each #1167-
     1168   32.50 32.50
1168b   Souvenir sheet, #1167-
     1168, with Washington
     2006 World Philatelic
     Exhibition emblem in
     sheet margin   3.50 3.50
1168c   Souvenir sheet, #1167-
     1168, with Belgica '06
     emblem in sheet mar-
     gin   3.50 3.50

Issued: Nos. 1167-1168, 1167a, 1168a, 1/6; No. 1168b, 5/27; No. 1168c, 11/16. No. 1167a printed in sheets of 10 + 10 labels. No. 1167 is inscribed "1st Local."

Art by Tan Swie Hian
A292

No. 1169: a, White Cloud. b, Ganges. c, Soaring over the Flower Field. d, Kuta is a Song. e, The Winged Steed.
No. 1170, vert.: a, Black Panther (Pine). b, Ginkgo (Male). c, White Elephant. d, Summer Lotus. e, Water Dhyana.
$2, Calligraphy, vert.

2006, Feb. 22   *Perf. 12*
1169   Horiz. strip of 5   2.00 2.00
  a.-e.   A292 (23c) Any single   .40 .40
       Perf. 12¾
     Size: 27x57mm
1170   Horiz. strip of 5   4.50 4.50
  a.-e.   A292 50c Any single   .90 .90
     Souvenir Sheet
1171 A292 $2 multi   3.50 3.50

Nos. 1169a-1169e are inscribed "1st Local." No. 1171 contains one 40x60mm stamp.

Marine Mammals — A293

Designs: (23c), Indo-Pacific bottlenose dolphin. (31c), Indo-Pacific humpbacked dolphin. $1, Finless porpoise. $2, Dugong.

2006, Mar. 22   *Perf. 13¼*
1172-1175 A293   Set of 4   5.50 5.50
1175a   Souvenir sheet #1172-1175   5.50 5.50
     Self-Adhesive
1175B A293 (23c) Like #1172   .35 .35

Nos. 1172 and 1175B are inscribed "1st Local;" No. 1173, "2nd Local."

A294   Festivals and Holidays — A295

Designs: Nos. 1176, 1184, (23c), Dove (Christmas). Nos. 1177, 1185, (23c), Fruit (Chinese New Year). Nos. 1178, 1186, (23c), Candle (Deepavali). Nos. 1179, 1187 (23c), Crescent and star (Eid ul-Fitr).
No. 1180, 50c, Dove (Christmas), diff. No. 1181, 50c, Fruit (Chinese New Year), diff. No. 1182, 50c, Candle (Deepavali), diff. No. 1183, 50c, Crescent and star (Eid ul-Fitr), diff.

2006, Apr. 19   *Perf. 14½x14*
1176-1179 A294   Set of 4   1.50 1.50
1180-1183 A295   Set of 4   3.25 3.25
     Self-Adhesive
   Die Cut Perf. 14½x14
1184-1187 A294   Set of 4   1.75 1.75

Nos. 1176-1179, 1184-1187 are inscribed "1st Local." Nos. 1184-1187 were each issued in sheets of 10.

Traveler's Palm — A296

2006, May 2   Litho.   *Perf. 12¾*
1188   Vert. strip of 5 + 5 la-
     bels   2.40 2.40
  a.   A296 (23c) beige & multi + label   .40 .40
  b.   A296 (23c) light green & multi +
     label   .40 .40
  c.   A296 (23c) yellow & multi + label   .40 .40
  d.   A296 (23c) lt blue & multi + label   .40 .40
  e.   A296 (23c) pale rose & multi +
     label   .40 .40

No. 1188 was printed in sheets containing 2 strips of stamps and labels. The sheet sold for $3. Nos. 1188a-1188e are inscribed "1st Local." Two sheets containing 4 examples of Nos. 1188c and 1188d, each with four non-personalizable labels sold as part of a set of eight sheets with various face values that sold for $9 each.

Orchid — A297

2006, May 2
1189   Vert. strip of 4 + 4 la-
     bels   3.25 3.25
  a.   A297 50c black, red & pink + la-
     bel   .80 .80
  b.   A297 50c lilac, black & purple +
     label   .80 .80
  c.   A297 50c org yel, black & brown
     + label   .80 .80
  d.   A297 50c lt grn, black & dark grn
     + label   .80 .80

No. 1189 was printed in sheets containing 2 strips of stamps and labels. Two sheets, differing in label and marginal image, were created. Each sheet sold for $5.
Sheets containing five No. 1189a or five No. 1189c, and five non-personalizable labels sold for $8.50 per sheet. A sheet containing 2 each of Nos. 1189b, 1189c, and 1189d and 6 non-personalizable labels sold as part of a set of 8 sheets with various face values for $8.50 per sheet. A sheet containing two each of Nos. 1189c and 1189d and 4 non-personalizable labels sold as part of a set of 8 sheets with various face values that sold for $9 per sheet.

Vanishing Occupations A298

Designs: Nos. 1190, 1200, (23c), Clog maker. Nos. 1191, 1201, (23c), Wooden bucket maker. Nos. 1192, 1202, (23c), Spice grinder. Nos. 1193, 1203, (23c), Snake charmer. Nos. 1194, 1204, (23c), Satay man. No. 1195, 80c, Mama store worker. No. 1196, 80c, Roti man. No. 1197, 80c, Backlane barber. No. 1198, 80c, Chinese medicinal tea shop worker. No. 1199, 80c, Tin bucket maker.

2006, May 24   *Perf. 13*
1190-1199 A298   Set of 10   8.25 8.25

Self-Adhesive
Serpentine Die Cut 10
1200-1204 A298   Set of 5   2.00 2.00

Nos. 1190-1194, 1200-1204 are inscribed "1st Local."

National Computerization Program, 25th Anniv. — A299

Use of computer technology in: (23c), Government. 60c, Trade. 80c, Education. $1, Telecommunications.

2006, June 20   *Perf. 12¾*
1205-1208 A299   Set of 4   4.25 4.25

No. 1205 is inscribed "1st Local."

Singapore Chinese Chamber of Commerce and Industry, Cent. — A300

Map, centenary emblem, Chinese characters and: (23c), Chamber building. (31c), Orchids. 80c, Emblem of World Chinese Entrepreneurs Convention. $1, Nanyang University Administration Building. $2, War Memorial and Sun Yat-sen Nanyang Memorial Hall.

2006, July 19   *Perf. 12¾x12*
1209-1213 A300   Set of 5   7.00 7.00
1213a   Souvenir sheet, #1209-
          1213   7.00 7.00

No. 1209 is inscribed "1st Local;" No. 1210 is inscribed "2nd Local."

National Day — A301

Globe and: (23c), Buildings (partial globe). 60c, People. 80c, Shipping containers. $1, Entertainers and fireworks. $2, Buildings (full globe).

2006, Aug. 9   *Perf. 12¾*
1214-1217 A301   Set of 4   4.25 4.25
Souvenir Sheet
Perf. 12¾x13
1218 A301 $2 multi   3.50 3.50

No. 1214 is inscribed "1st Local." No. 1218 contains one 49x49mm stamp. A sheet containing 3 #1214 exists, sold as part of a series of sheets sold with a book for $39.90.

Singapore Biennale 2006 — A302

2006, Sept. 13   *Perf. 14¼x14*
1219 A302 $2 multi   3.25 3.25

Intl. Monetary Fund World Bank Group Board of Governors Annual Meeting A304

Designs: 50c, Orchids. 80c, Esplanade Performing Arts Center. No. 1222, Buildings. No. 1223, Coin depicting orchid. $5, Coin depicting traveler's palm.

Perf. 13½x13¾
2006, Sept. 13   *Litho.*
1220 A303   50c multi   .95   .95
1221 A303   80c multi   1.50 1.50
1222 A303 $1 multi   1.90 1.90
a.   Miniature sheet, 4 each
       #1220, 1222, perf.
       13½x13¼, + 4 labels 15.00 15.00
Litho. With Foil Application
Perf. 13¼
1223 A304 $1 gold & blk   1.90 1.90
1224 A304 $5 silver & blk 9.75 9.75
       Nos. 1220-1224 (5)   16.00 16.00

Orchids and Paintings — A305

Designs: Nos. 1225, 1231a, (23c), Vanda Mimi Palmer orchid. Nos. 1226, 1231b, (23c), Renanthera Singaporean orchid. Nos. 1227, 1231c, 70c, Vanda Miss Joaquim orchid. Nos. 1228, 1231d, 70c, Mokara Lion's Gold orchid. $1, Hollyhocks and Egret, by Hoitsu Sakai, horiz. (49x34mm). Nos. 1230, 1231e, $2, Irises and Moorhens, by Sakai, horiz. (49x34mm).

2006, Oct. 3   *Litho.*   *Perf. 14¼*
1225-1230 A305   Set of 6   7.75 7.75
1230a   Miniature sheet, #1229-
          1230, 3 each #1227-
          1228, perf. 13½x13¼,
          + 6 labels   10.00 10.00
Litho. With Foil Application (#1231a-1231e)
Perf. 14¼
1231 A305   Miniature sheet,
             #1229, 1231a-
             1231e   7.75 7.75

Nos. 1225-1226, 1231a-1231e are inscribed "1st Local." No. 1230a sold for $8; No. 1231 sold for $5.10. See Japan No. 2966.

A sheet containing 3 perf. 13¼ examples of No. 1230 and three labels that could not be personalized sold for $8.50.

Diplomatic Relations Between Singapore and Vatican City, 25th Anniv. — A306

Designs: 50c, Merlion and St. Peter's Basilica. $2, Flags of Singapore and Vatican City.

2006, Oct. 12   Litho.   Perf. 13½x13¼
1232-1233 A306   Set of 2   4.00 4.00
1233a   Souvenir sheet, #1232-
          1233, perf. 12¾   4.00 4.00

See Vatican City Nos. 1336-1337.

Care for Nature — A307

Designs: Nos. 1234a, 1235, Common palm civet. Nos. 1234b, 1236, Common flying dragon. No. 1234c, Black-spotted sticky frog. No. 1234d, Common tiger butterfly.

2006, Oct. 31   *Perf. 13x13¼*
1234 A307   Block of 4   4.00 4.00
a.-b.   (23c) Either single .35   .35
c.-d. $1 Either single   1.60 1.60
Booklet Stamps
Self-Adhesive
Serpentine Die Cut 11x11¼
1235 A307   (23c) multi   .50   .50
1236 A307   (23c) multi   .50   .50
a.   Booklet pane, 5 each #1235-
       1236   5.00

Nos. 1234a, 1234b, 1235 and 1236 are inscribed "1st Local."

New Year 2007 (Year of the Pig) — A308

Designs: (25c), One pig. $2, Two pigs.

2007, Jan. 19   *Perf. 13½x13¼*
1237-1238 A308   Set of 2   3.50 3.50
1238a   Miniature sheet, 9 each
          #1237-1238, perf. 12¾ 32.50 32.50
1238b   Souvenir sheet, #1237-
          1238, perf. 12¾   3.50 3.50

No. 1237 is inscribed "1st Local." Bangkok 2007 World Stamp Exhibition (#1238b).

Kindness Movement, 10th Anniv. — A309

Children's drawings: Nos. 1239a, 1240a, Boy in wheelchair, children with joined hands. Nos. 1239b, 1240b, Child opening elevator door. Nos. 1239c, 1240c, Girl assisting fallen girl, horiz. Nos. 1239d, 1240h, Red Cross volunteers helping people, horiz. Nos. 1239e, 1240g, Four people under open umbrella,

horiz. Nos. 1239f, 1240f, Children visiting people at hospital, horiz. Nos. 1239g, 1240j, People in subway car, horiz. Nos. 1239h, 1240e, Boy assisting person slipping in rain, horiz. Nos. 1239i, 1240i, Boy helping blind man, horiz. Nos. 1239j, 1240d, People in crosswalk, horiz.

Perf. 13¼x13, 13x13¼ (horiz. stamps)
2007, Feb. 8
1239   Sheet of 10   4.00 4.00
a.-j.   A309 (25c) Any single .40   .40
Booklet Stamps
Self-Adhesive
Serpentine Die Cut 10x10½, 10½x10 (horiz. stamps)
1240   Booklet pane of 10 4.00
a.-j.   A309 (25c) Any single .40   .40

Each stamp is inscribed "1st Local."

Traditional Wedding Costumes A310

No. 1241: a, Korean (mountains in background). b, Korean (flowers in background). c, Chinese. d, Indian. e, Malay. f, Eurasian. g, Korean (flowers in background). h, Korean (ducks in background).

Perf. 13½x13¼
2007, Mar. 30   *Litho.*
1241   Block of 8   8.50 8.50
a.-b.   A310 (25c) Either single .40   .40
c.-f.   A310 65c Any single 1.05 1.05
g.-h.   A310 $1.10 Either single 1.75 1.75
i.   Souvenir sheet, #1241 8.50 8.50

Nos. 1241a-1241b are inscribed "1st Local." See South Korea No. 2250.

Cultural Dances — A311

Dancers from: (25c), Chinese culture. (31c), Indian culture. $1.10, Eurasian and Western cultures. $2, Malay culture.

2007, May 16   *Perf. 15x14¾*
1242-1245 A311   Set of 4   6.00 6.00

No. 1242 is inscribed "1st Local;" No. 1243, "2nd Local."

Birds A312

Flowers — A313

Mammals — A314

Designs: 5c, Crimson sunbird. 20c, Yellow-rumped flycatcher. (25c), Frangipani. 30c, Blue-throated bee-eater. (31c), Torch ginger. 45c, Yellow wagtail. 50c, Stork-billed kingfisher. 55c, Blue-crowned hanging parrot. 65c, Common goldenback. 80c, Jambu fruit dove. $1.10, Large Indian civet. $2, Banded leaf monkey. $5, Malayan pangolin. $10, Cream-colored giant squirrel.

2007, June 6		**Litho.**		**Perf. 14**
1246	A312	5c multi	.25	.25
a.		Dated "2007B"	.25	.25
b.		Dated "2007C"	.25	.25
1247	A312	20c multi	.30	.30
a.		Dated "2007B"	.30	.30
b.		Dated "2007C"	.30	.30
c.		Dated "2007D"	.30	.30
d.		Dated "2007E"	.25	.25
e.		Dated "2007F"	.25	.25
f.		Dated "2007G"	.25	.25
1248	A313	(25c) multi	.40	.40
1249	A312	30c multi	.45	.45
a.		Dated "2007B"	.45	.45
b.		Dated "2007C"	.35	.35
c.		Dated "2007D"	.35	.35
d.		Dated "2007E"	.35	.35
1250	A313	(31c) multi	.50	.50
a.		Dated "2007B"	.50	.50
b.		Dated "2007C"	.50	.50
c.		Dated "2007D"	.50	.50
d.		Dated "2007E"	.40	.40
1251	A312	45c multi	.70	.70
a.		Dated "2007B"	.70	.70
b.		Dated "2007C"	.70	.70
c.		Dated "2007D"	.70	.70
d.		Dated "2007E"	.60	.60
e.		Dated "2007F"	.60	.60
f.		Dated "2007G"	.60	.60
1252	A312	50c multi	.80	.80
a.		Dated "2007B"	.80	.80
b.		Dated "2007C"	.80	.80
c.		Dated "2007D"	.65	.65
d.		Dated "2007E"	.65	.65
e.		Dated "2007F"	.65	.65
f.		Dated "2007G"	.65	.65
1253	A312	55c multi	.90	.90
a.		Dated "2007B"	.90	.90
b.		Dated "2007C"	.70	.70
c.		Dated "2007D"	.70	.70
1254	A312	65c multi	1.05	1.05
a.		Dated "2007B"	1.05	1.05
b.		Dated "2007C"	1.05	1.05
c.		Dated "2007D"	1.05	1.05
d.		Dated "2007E"	.85	.85
e.		Dated "2007F"	.85	.85
1255	A312	80c multi	1.25	1.25
a.		Dated "2007B"	1.25	1.25
b.		Dated "2007C"	1.25	1.25
c.		Dated "2007D"	1.00	1.00
d.		Dated "2007E"	1.00	1.00
e.		Dated "2007F"	1.00	1.00
f.		Dated "2007G"	1.00	1.00
		Perf. 15x14¾		
1256	A314	$1.10 multi	1.75	1.75
a.		Dated "2007B"	1.75	1.75
b.		Dated "2007C"	1.75	1.75
c.		Dated "2007D"	1.40	1.40
d.		Dated "2007E"	1.40	1.40
1257	A314	$2 multi	3.25	3.25
1258	A314	$5 multi	8.00	8.00
a.		Dated "2007B"	8.00	8.00
b.		Dated "2007C"	8.00	8.00
c.		Dated "2007D"	6.50	6.50
1259	A314	$10 multi	16.00	16.00
a.		Miniature sheet, #1246-1259	40.00	40.00
b.		Dated "2007C"	16.00	16.00
c.		Dated "2007C"	16.00	16.00
d.		Dated "2007D"	13.00	13.00
		Nos. 1246-1259 (14)	35.60	35.60

Serpentine Die Cut 9½x10
Self-Adhesive

1260	A313	(25c) multi	.40	.40
a.		Booklet pane of 10	4.00	
b.		Dated "2007B"	.40	.40
c.		Dated "2007C"	.40	.40
d.		Dated "2007D"	.40	.40
e.		Dated "2007E"	.30	.30
f.		Booklet pane of 10 #1260e	3.00	

Nos. 1248 and 1260 are inscribed "1st Local;" No. 1250, "2nd Local." No. 1260a sold for $2.55. No. 1259a sold for $28.

See Nos. 1370-1374, 1439-1441.

National Service Act, 40th Anniv. — A315

Designs: (26c), Enlistees taking oath of allegiance. (32c), Soldiers in basic training. $1.10, Soldiers in drill. $2, Soldiers in action.

2007, July 2			**Perf. 14½x14**	
1261-1264	A315	Set of 4	6.00	6.00

No. 1261 is inscribed "1st Local;" No. 1262, "2nd Local."

Miniature Sheet

Association of South East Asian Nations (ASEAN), 40th Anniv. — A316

No. 1265: a, Secretariat Building, Bandar Seri Begawan, Brunei. b, National Museum of Cambodia. c, Fatahillah Museum, Jakarta, Indonesia. d, Typical house, Laos. e, Malayan Railway Headquarters Building, Kuala Lumpur, Malaysia. f, Yangon Post Office, Myanmar (Burma). g, Malacañang Palace, Philippines. h, National Museum of Singapore. i, Vimanmek Mansion, Bangkok, Thailand. j, Presidential Palace, Hanoi, Viet Nam.

2007, Aug. 8			**Perf. 13¼**	
1265	A316	(26c) Sheet of 10, #a-j	4.00	4.00

Each stamp on No. 1265 is inscribed "1st Local." No. 1265 sold for $2.55.

See Brunei No. 607, Burma No. 370, Cambodia No. 2339, Indonesia No. 2120-2121, Laos Nos. 1717-1718, Malaysia No. 1170, Philippines Nos. 3103-3105, Thailand No. 2315, and Viet Nam Nos. 3302-3311.

Tourist Attractions — A317

Designs: (26c), Chinatown. 65c, Kampong Glam. 80c, Little India. $1.10, Orchard Road. $5, Merlion, vert.

2007, Aug. 9		**Litho.**	**Perf. 12¼**	
1266-1269	A317	Set of 4	4.50	4.50

Souvenir Sheet
Litho. & Embossed

1270	A317	$5 multi	8.00	8.00

No. 1266 is inscribed "1st Local."

Uniforms of Youth Organizations A318

Organization: No. 1271, (32c), National Cadet Corps. No. 1272, (32c), Singapore Scout Association. No. 1273, (32c), Girl Guides Singapore. No. 1274, (32c), Girls' Brigade Singapore. No. 1275, (32c), Boys' Brigade in Singapore. No. 1276, (32c), St. John Ambulance Brigade Singapore. No. 1277, (32c), Red Cross Youth. No. 1278, (32c),

National Police Cadet Corps. No. 1279, (32c), National Civil Defense Cadet Corps.

2007, Sept. 19		**Litho.**	**Perf. 13¼x13**	
1271-1279	A318	Set of 9	4.50	4.50

Nos. 1271-1279 are each inscribed "2nd Local."

Coral Reef Inhabitants A319

Designs: Nos. 1280a, 1281, False clown anemonefish, Sea anemone. Nos. 1280b, 1282, Singapore goby, Blind shrimp. No. 1280c, Hawksbill turtle, Remora. No. 1280d, Razorfish, Sea urchin.

2007, Oct. 17			**Perf. 13x13¼**	
1280		Block of 4	4.50	4.50
a.-b.	A319	(26c) Either single	.40	.40
c.-d.	A319	$1.10 Either single	1.75	1.75

Booklet Stamps
Self-Adhesive

1281	A319	(26c) multi	.40	.40
1282	A319	(26c) multi	.40	.40
a.		Booklet pane of 10, 5 each #1281-1282	4.25	

Nos. 1280a, 1280b, 1281, 1282 are each inscribed "1st Local."

National Library Board A320

Slogans: (26c), Libraries Spark Imagination. 80c, Libraries Bring Knowledge Alive. $1.10, Libraries Create Possibilities. $2, Libraries for Life, Knowledge for Success.

2007, Nov. 12				
1283-1286	A320	Set of 4	6.75	6.75

No. 1283 is inscribed "1st Local."

Opening of Changi Airport Terminal 3 — A321

Designs: (26c), Clouds, Interior of Terminal 3. 65c, Exterior of Terminal 3, Airbus A380. $1.10, Plant leaves, Terminal 3 Vertical Garden. $2, Airplane in flight, Airport control tower, baggage handlers outside Terminal 3.

2008, Jan. 9			**Perf. 14¼x14**	
1287-1290	A321	Set of 4	6.50	6.50

No. 1287 is inscribed "1st Local."

New Year 2008 (Year of the Rat) A322

Designs: (26c), Rat. 65c, Rat and tangerine. $1.10, Two rats, vert.

No. 1294: a, Rat (pig hologram). b, Rat and tangerine (ox hologram).

2008, Jan. 18		**Litho.**	**Perf. 14**	
1291	A322	(26c) multi	.40	.40
a.		Perf. 13¼x13¼	.40	.40
1292	A322	65c multi	1.05	1.05
a.		Perf. 13½x13¼	1.05	1.05

Size: 35x45mm
Perf. 14¼x14½

1293	A322	$1.10 multi	1.75	1.75
a.		Souvenir sheet, #1291a, 1292a, 1293, with Taiwan 2008 emblem in sheet margin	3.25	3.25
b.		As "a," with Olympex 2008 sheet margin	3.25	3.25
c.		As "a," with Jakarta 2008 emblem in sheet margin	3.25	3.25
		Nos. 1291-1293 (3)	3.20	3.20

Souvenir Sheet
Litho. With Transparent Holographic Film
Perf. 13x13¼

1294		Sheet of 2	24.00	24.00
a.	A322	$5 multi	8.00	8.00
b.	A322	$10 multi	16.00	16.00

Litho.
Self-Adhesive
Serpentine Die Cut 10

1295	A322	(26c) multi	.40	.40

Nos. 1291 and 1295 are inscribed "1st Local."

Issued: Nos. 1291a, 1292a, 1293a, 3/7; No. 1293b, 8/18; No. 1293c, 10/23.

Festivals — A323

Designs: Nos. 1296, 1308, (26c), Christmas. Nos. 1297, 1309, (26c), Chinese New Year. Nos. 1298, 1310, (26c), Deepavali. Nos. 1299, 1311, (26c), Eid ul-Fitr. No. 1300, (32c), Easter. No. 1301, (32c), Mid-autumn festival. No. 1302, (32c), Pongal. No. 1303, (32c), Hari Raya Haji. No. 1304, 55c, Christmas, diff. No. 1305, 55c, Chinese New Year, diff. No. 1306, 55c, Deepavali, diff. No. 1307, 55c, Eid ul-Fitr, diff.

2008, Feb. 29		**Litho.**	**Perf. 14x14½**	
1296-1307	A323	Set of 12	7.00	7.00

Self-Adhesive
Die Cut Perf. 14x14½

1308-1311	A323	Set of 4	1.60	1.60

Nos. 1296-1299, 1308-1311 are inscribed "1st Local;" Nos. 1300-1303, "2nd Local."

Embroidery, Beadwork and Porcelain Designs of Peranakan Culture — A324

No. 1312, (26c) — Various designs with bottom panel color of: a, Orange. b, Red.

No. 1313, (32c) — Various designs with bottom panel color of: a, Red violet. b, Green.

No. 1314, 65c — Various designs with bottom panel color of: a, Green. b, Blue.

No. 1315, $1.10 — Various designs with bottom panel color of: a, Olive green. b, Dark red.

$5, Deer with red violet top panel.

2008, Apr. 8		**Litho.**	**Perf. 13x13½**	
		Horiz. Pairs, #a-b		
1312-1315	A324	Set of 4	7.00	7.00

Souvenir Sheet
Litho. With Beads Applied
Perf. 13¾

1316	A324	$5 multi	12.00	12.00

Nos. 1312a-1312b each inscribed "1st Local;" Nos. 1313a-1313b each inscribed "2nd Local." No. 1316 sold for $8 and contains one 44x44mm stamp.

Selection of Singapore as Host of 2010 Youth Olympic Games — A325

No. 1317: a, (26c), People celebrating. b, $2, People, flag, building.

2008, June 25   Litho.   Perf. 12¾
1317   A325   Horiz. pair, #a-b   3.50 3.50
No. 1317a is inscribed "1st Local."

Native Cuisine of Singapore and Macao — A326

No. 1318, (26c) — Macao dishes: a, Carne de porco à Alentejana. b, Lombo de bacalhau braseado em lascas. c, Yangzhou fried rice. d, Crispy fried chicken.
No. 1319, 65c — Singapore dishes: a, Roti Prata. b, Hainanese chicken rice. c, Laksa. d, Satay.
No. 1320, vert.: a, Clay pot rice, Macao. b, Chili crab, Singapore.

2008, July 4   Perf. 14x13¼
Blocks of 4, #a-d
1318-1319   A326   Set of 2   6.00 6.00
Souvenir Sheet
Perf. 13¼x14
1320   A326 $2 Sheet of 2, #a-b   6.50 6.50
Nos. 1318a-1318d are each inscribed "1st Local." See Macao Nos. 1248-1249.

2008 Summer Olympics, Beijing — A327

Designs: (26c), Table tennis. (32c), Sailing. No. 1323, $1.10, Shooting. No. 1324, $1.10, Badminton.

2008, Aug. 8   Perf. 13
1321-1324   A327   Set of 4   4.50 4.50
No. 1321 is inscribed "1st Local;" No. 1322, "2nd Local."

National Day — A328

Various photographs of buildings and Singapore daily life by: No. 1325, (26c), No. 1330, 50c, David Tay Poey Cher. No. 1326, (26c), No. 1331, 50c, Tan Lip Seng. No. 1327, (26c), No. 1332, 50c, Chua Soo Bin. No. 1328, (26c), No. 1333, 50c, Foo Tee Jun. No. 1329, (26c), No. 1334, 50c, Teo Bee Yen.
$2, Photographs by the various photographers.

2008, Aug. 9   Perf. 14¼
1325-1334   A328   Set of 10   6.00 6.00
Souvenir Sheet
Perf. 14½
1335   A328 $2 multi   3.25 3.25
Nos. 1325-1329 each are inscribed "1st Local." No. 1335 contains one 61x61mm stamp.

Singapore Air Force, 40th Anniv. A329

Designs: (26c), Pilots, airplane, helicopter. (32c), Weapon systems officers, plane. 65c, Unmanned aerial vehicle pilot, drone. 80c, Air engineering officer, Senior technician, helicopter. $1.10, Weapons system officers, missiles.

2008, Aug. 28   Perf. 14
1336-1340   A329   Set of 5   5.00 5.00
No. 1336 is inscribed "1st Local;" No. 1337, "2nd Local."

2008 Formula 1 Singapore Grand Prix — A330

No. 1341 — Formula 1 race car and: a, Singapore skyline. b, Checkered flag.

2008, Sept. 26   Perf. 13½
1341   A330 $2 Horiz. pair, #a-b   6.50 6.50
No. 1341 exists imperf.

Singapore Post Office, 150th Anniv. — A331

Postman: (26c), On scooter, 2008. (32c), And scooter, c. 1980. 50c, And bicycle, c. 1970. 80c, And mailbox, c. 1950. $1.10, And post office, c. 1910.

2008, Oct. 29   Perf. 12¾x13¼
1342-1346   A331   Set of 5   4.75 4.75
No. 1342 is inscribed "1st Local;" No. 1343, "2nd Local."

Cash Crops — A332

Designs: (26c), Pepper. 65c, Tapioca. $1.10, Rubber. $2, Nutmeg.

2008, Nov. 12   Perf. 13½
1347-1350   A332   Set of 4   6.50 6.50
Booklet Stamp
Self-Adhesive
Serpentine Die Cut 10x9½
1351   A332   (26c) multi   .40 .40
a.   Booklet pane of 10   4.00
Nos. 1347 and 1351 are inscribed "1st Local."

Fruit — A333

Designs: 65c, Dragon fruit. $1.10, Durian.

2008, Nov. 18   Perf. 13¾
1352-1353   A333   Set of 2   2.75 2.75
1353a   Souvenir sheet, #1352-1353   2.75 2.75
See Viet Nam Nos. 3345-3346.

New Year 2009 (Year of the Ox) A334

Designs: Nos. 1354, 1357a, 1358, Ox facing right. Nos. 1355, 1357b, Ox facing left. $1.10, Two oxen, vert. (35x45mm).

2009, Jan. 9   Litho.   Perf. 13x13¼
1354   A334   (26c) multi   .40 .40
1355   A334   65c multi   1.05 1.05
Perf. 13
1356   A334 $1.10 multi   1.75 1.75
a.   Souvenir sheet, #1354-1356, with China 2009 emblem in sheet margin   3.25 3.25
b.   As "a," with Hong Kong 2009 emblem in sheet margin   3.25 3.25
Nos. 1354-1356 (3)   3.20 3.20
Souvenir Sheet
Litho. With Hologram
Perf. 13x13¼
1357   Sheet of 2   24.00 24.00
a.   A334 $5 multi   8.00 8.00
b.   A334 $10 multi   16.00 16.00
Self-Adhesive
Litho.
Serpentine Die Cut 12
1358   A334   (26c) multi   .40 .40
Nos. 1354 and 1358 are inscribed "1st Local."
Issued: No. 1356a, 4/10; No. 1356b, 5/14.

Greetings A335

Designs: Nos. 1359a, 1364, Man and woman kissing, bowl and umbrella. Nos. 1359b, 1360, Girl blowing out candles. Nos. 1359c, 1361, Boy and girl in frame. Nos. 1359d, 1362, Girl, teddy bear, gift boxes. Nos. 1359e, 1363, Boy with balloons.

2009, Feb. 11   Litho.   Perf. 14x14½
1359   Horiz. strip of 5   2.10 2.10
a.-e.   A335 (26c) Any single   .40 .40
Booklet Stamps
Self-Adhesive
Serpentine Die Cut 11¼x10½
1360   A335   (26c) multi   .40 .40
1361   A335   (26c) multi   .40 .40
1362   A335   (26c) multi   .40 .40
1363   A335   (26c) multi   .40 .40
1364   A335   (26c) multi   .40 .40
a.   Booklet pane of 10, 2 each #1360-1364   4.00
Nos. 1360-1364 (5)   2.00 2.00
Nos. 1359a-1359e, 1360-1364 are each inscribed "1st Local."

Old Movie Theaters A336

Designs: (26c), Cathay Theater, 1939. 50c, Majestic Theater, 1928. 80c, Capitol Theater,

1933. No. 1368, $1.10, Queens Theater, c. 1920. No. 1369, $1.10, Rex Theater, 1946.

2009, Mar. 20   Litho.   Perf. 14¼
1365-1369   A336   Set of 5   6.00 6.00
No. 1365 is inscribed "1st Local."

Flower Type of 2007
Designs: Nos. 1370, 1373, Blue pea vine. Nos. 1371, 1372, 1374, Pigeon orchid.

2009, May 6   Litho.   Perf. 14
1370   A313   (26c) multi   .40 .40
1371   A313   (26c) multi   .40 .40
Souvenir Sheet
Litho. With Embroidered Flower Affixed
1372   A313 $5 multi   11.00 11.00
Self-Adhesive
Litho.
Serpentine Die Cut 9¾x10
1373   A313   (26c) multi   .40 .40
a.   Booklet pane of 10   4.00
b.   Dated "2009B"   .40 .40
c.   Booklet pane of 10 #1373b   4.00
d.   Dated "2009C"   .35 .35
e.   Booklet pane of 10 #1373d   3.50
1374   A313   (26c) multi   .40 .40
a.   Booklet pane of 10   4.00
b.   Dated "2009B"   .35 .35
c.   Booklet pane of 10 #1374b   3.50
d.   Dated "2009C"   .35 .35
e.   Booklet pane of 10 #1374d   3.50
Nos. 1370-1371, 1373-1374 are inscribed "1st Local." No. 1372 sold for $8.

Opening of First Stations on Singapore Mass Rapid Transit Circle Line — A337

Designs: (26c), Map of Singapore and Circle Line. 80c, People in station. $1.10, Circle Line train. $2, People in operation control center.

2009, May 28   Litho.   Perf. 13¾
1375-1378   A337   Set of 4   6.75 6.75
No. 1375 is inscribed "1st Local." Values are for stamps with surrounding selvage.

Singapore Botanic Gardens, 150th Anniv. A338

No. 1379: a, Visitor Center. b, Bandstand. c, Burkill Hall, Girl on a Swing sculpture. d, Swans in flight, bridge.
$2, Swans on lake, bridge

2009, June 19   Perf. 14
1379   Horiz. strip of 4   4.50 4.50
a.-b.   A338 (26c) Either single   .40 .40
c.-d.   A338 $1.10 Either single   1.75 1.75
Souvenir Sheet
Perf. 15x14½
1380   A338 $2 multi   3.25 3.25
Nos. 1379a-1379b are inscribed "1st Local." No. 1380 contains one 48x48mm stamp.

Desserts — A339

Designs: (26c), Ice kacang. (32c), Ondeh-ondeh. 65c, Ang ku kueh. 80c, Lapis sagu. $1.10, Mithai.

2009, July 17   *Perf. 12¾*
1381-1385 A339   Set of 5   5.00 5.00

No. 1381 is inscribed "1st Local;" No. 1382, "2nd Local."

Sculpture — A340

Works by: No. 1386, 50c, Teo Eng Seng. No. 1387, 50c, Anthony Poon. No. 1388, 50c, Han Sai Por. No. 1389, 50c, Wee Beng Chong. No. 1390, 50c, Ng Eng Teng, horiz. No. 1391, 50c, Brother Joseph McNally, horiz. No. 1392, 50c, Tay Chee Toh.
$2, All 7 sculptures, horiz.

Perf. 13¼x13¾, 13¾x13¼
2009, Aug. 9
1386-1392 A340   Set of 7   5.50 5.50
Souvenir Sheet
Perf. 14¾x14
1393 A340 $2 multi   3.25 3.25

No. 1393 contains one 96x37mm stamp.

2010 Youth Olympic Games, Singapore — A341

Designs: (26c), Diver. 65c, Two women athletes. $1.10, Four men. $2, Hurdler.

2009, Aug. 14   *Perf. 13¼*
1394-1397 A341   Set of 4   6.50 6.50

No. 1394 is inscribed "1st Local."

Diplomatic Relations Between Singapore and the Philippines, 40th Anniv. — A342

Bridges: (26c), Bamban Bridge, Philippines. 65c, Cavenagh Bridge, Singapore. 80c, Henderson Waves and Alexandra Arch Bridges, Singapore. $1.10, Marcelo B. Fernan Bridge, Philippines.

2009, Aug. 28   *Perf. 12¾*
1398-1401 A342   Set of 4   4.50 4.50
1401a   Souvenir sheet, #1398-1401   4.50 4.50

No. 1398 is inscribed "1st Local." See Philippines No. 3231.

Tourist Sites in Singapore and Indonesia A343

Designs: (26c), Singaraja Statue, Indonesia. 65c, Merlion, Singapore. 80c, Taman Mini Indonesia Indah (Beautiful Indonesia Miniature Park). $1.10, Sentosa, Singapore.

2009, Oct. 28   *Perf. 14x13½*
1402-1405 A343   Set of 4   4.50 4.50
1405a   Souvenir sheet, #1402-1405   4.50 4.50

No. 1402 is inscribed "1st Local." See Indonesia Nos. 2213-2216.

Asia-Pacific Economic Cooperation 2009 Meetings, Singapore — A344

No. 1406: a, Singapore skyline. b, Port of Singapore.
No. 1407: a, Singapore at night. b, Singapore Airport.

2009, Nov. 9   *Perf. 14x14½*
1406   Horiz. pair, #a-b, + central label   3.75 3.75
   a.   A344 (26c) multi   .40 .40
   b.   A344 $2 multi   3.25 3.25
1407   Horiz. pair, #a-b, + central label   3.25 3.25
   a.   A344 80c multi   1.25 1.25
   b.   A344 $1.10 multi   1.75 1.75

No. 1406a is inscribed "1st Local."

New Year 2010 (Year of the Tiger) A345

Designs: (26c), $5, Tiger, yellow green and yellow background. 65c, $10, Tiger, pink and rose background. $1.10, Two tigers, vert. (35x40mm).

2010, Jan. 8   *Litho.*   *Perf. 13½*
1408 A345 (26c) multi   .40 .40
1409 A345 65c multi   1.05 1.05
       Perf. 13x13¼
1410 A345 $1.10 multi   1.75 1.75
   a.   Souvenir sheet of 3, #1408-1410, with London 2010 emblem in sheet margin   3.00 3.00
   b.   Souvenir sheet of 3, #1408-1410, with Bangkok 2010 emblem in sheet margin   3.00 3.00
    Nos. 1408-1410 (3)   3.20 3.20

Souvenir Sheet
Litho. With Transparent Holographic Film
1411   Sheet of 2   24.00 24.00
   a.   A345 $5 multi   8.00 8.00
   b.   A345 $10 multi   16.00 16.00

Self-Adhesive
Litho.
Serpentine Die Cut 9¾x10½
1412 A345 (26c) multi   .40 .40

Nos. 1408 and 1412 are inscribed "1st Local."
Issued: No. 1410a, 5/8; No. 1410b, 8/4.

Anniversaries A346

Designs: No. 1413, 50c, Housing and Development Board, 50th anniv. No. 1414, 50c, People's Association, 50th anniv. No. 1415, $1, Customs Department, cent., horiz. No. 1416, $1, Singapore Scout Association, cent., horiz.

2010, Jan. 26   *Litho.*   *Perf. 13*
1413-1416 A346   Set of 4   4.75 4.75

Playgrounds — A347

Various playgrounds in Singapore: (26c), 50c, 65c, 80c, $1.10, $2.

2010, Mar. 9   *Perf. 13½*
1417-1422 A347   Set of 6   8.50 8.50

No. 1417 is inscribed "1st Local."

Butterflies A348

Designs: Nos. 1423, 1427, (26c), Common birdwing. 80c, Tailed jay. $1.10, Common posy. $2, Blue glassy tiger.

2010, Apr. 21   *Litho.*   *Perf. 14*
1423-1426 A348   6.75 6.75
Booklet Stamp
Self-Adhesive
Serpentine Die Cut 9½x10
1427 A348 (26c) multi   .40 .40
   a.   Booklet pane of 10   4.00

Trees A349

Designs: Nos. 1428, 1438a, (26c), Saga tree. Nos. 1429, 1438b, (26c), Rain tree. Nos. 1430, 1438c, (26c), Yellow flame tree. Nos. 1431, 1438d, (26c), Tembusu tree. Nos. 1432, 1438e, (26c), Angsana tree, vert. Nos. 1433, 1438f, (26c), Sea almond tree, vert. Nos. 1434, 1438g, (26c), Broad-leafed mahogany tree, vert. Nos. 1435, 1438h, (26c), Sea apple tree, vert. Nos. 1436, 1438i, (26c), Senegal mahogany tree, vert. Nos. 1437, 1438j, (26c), Trumpet tree, vert.

Perf. 14x14¼, 14¼x14
2010, May 26   *Litho.*
1428-1437 A349   Set of 10   3.75 3.75
Booklet Stamps
Self-Adhesive
Serpentine Die Cut 9½x10, 10x9½
1438   Booklet pane of 10   3.75
   a.-j.   A349 (26c) Any single   .35 .35

Nos. 1428-1437, 1438a-1438j are inscribed "1st Local."

Flower Type of 2007
Designs: (26c), Simpoh air. (32c), Singapore rhododendron.

2010, June 23   *Perf. 14*
1439 A313 (26c) multi   .40 .40
1440 A313 (32c) multi   .50 .50
   a.   Dated "2010B"   .50 .50
   b.   Dated "2010C"   .50 .50

Self-Adhesive
Serpentine Die Cut 9¾x10
1441 A313 (26c) multi   .40 .40
   a.   Booklet pane of 10   4.00
   b.   Dated "2010B"   .40 .40
   c.   Booklet pane of 10 #1441b   4.00

Nos. 1439, 1441 are inscribed "1st Local." No. 1440 is inscribed "2nd Local."

National Monuments — A350

Buildings and their architectural features: (26c), Bowyer Block. (32c), College of Medicine Building. 55c, Command House. 65c, Hwa-Chong Institution Clock Tower. 80c, Former Raffles College. $1.10, Tan Teck Guan Building.
$2, Architectural features of the aforementioned buildings.

2010, Aug. 4   *Perf. 13½x13¾*
1442-1447 A350   Set of 6   5.50 5.50
Souvenir Sheet
Perf. 14x13¼
1448 A350 $2 multi   3.00 3.00

No. 1442 is inscribed "1st Local." No. 1443 is inscribed "2nd Local."

2010 Youth Olympics, Singapore — A351

Lyo and Merly, Youth Olympics Mascots: (26c) Sitting on globe. 65c, Sitting under palm tree. $1.10, Merly swimming. $2, Lyo playing basketball.

2010, Aug. 14   *Perf. 13½x13¾*
1449-1452 A351   Set of 4   6.00 6.00
1452a   Sheet of 4, #1449-1452, + 2 labels, perf. 13½x13¼   23.00 23.00

No. 1449 is inscribed "1st Local." No. 1452a with personalized labels sold for $15.50, and for $19.90 with generic labels depicting the 2010 Youth Olympics emblem and mascots.

Heritage Trail and Kent Ridge Park Trail A352

No. 1453: a, Flowers, Bukit Chandu War Museum, sculpture of soldiers. b, Bird, flowers, elevated walkway. c, Flowers, sheltered walkway, eagle. d, Flowers, gazebo.

2010, Sept. 22   *Perf. 12¾*
1453   Horiz. strip of 4   4.50 4.50
   a.   A352 (32c) multi   .50 .50
   b.   A352 65c multi   1.00 1.00
   c.   A352 80c multi   1.25 1.25
   d.   A352 $1.10 multi   1.75 1.75

No. 1453a is inscribed "2nd Local."

Festivals — A353

Designs: Nos. 1454, 1463, (26c), Lion and fish (Chinese New Year). Nos. 1455, 1464, (26c), Candles (Christmas). Nos. 1456, 1465, (26c), Oil lamps (Eid ul-Fitr). Nos. 1457, 1466, (26c), Peacocks (Deepavali). Nos. 1458, 1462a, 55c, Chinese characters, fruit (Chinese New Year). Nos. 1459, 1462b, 55c, Ornaments (Christmas). Nos. 1460, 1462c, 55c, Crescent moon and star, diamonds (Eid ul-Fitr). Nos. 1461, 1462d, 55c, Oil lamp (Deepavali). No. 1462e, Lion, fish, Chinese character, flowers (Chinese New Year). No. 1462f, Ornaments and stars (Christmas). No.

1462g, Oil lamps (Eid ul-Fitr). No. 1462h,
Peacocks (Deepavali).

2010, Oct. 20　Litho.　Perf. 14½
Stamps With White Frames
1454-1461　A353　Set of 8　5.00　5.00
Litho. With Foil Application
Stamps Without White Frames
1462　　Sheet of 8　　17.00　17.00
　a.-d.　A353 55c Any single　1.40　1.40
　e.-h.　A353 $1.10 Any single　2.75　2.75
Litho.
Booklet Stamps
Self-Adhesive
Stamps With White Frames
Serpentine Die Cut 10x9¾
1463　A353　(26c) multi　　.40　.40
　a.　　Booklet pane of 10　4.00
1464　A353　(26c) multi　　.40　.40
　a.　　Booklet pane of 10　4.00
1465　A353　(26c) multi　　.40　.40
　a.　　Booklet pane of 10　4.00
1466　A353　(26c) multi　　.40　.40
　a.　　Booklet pane of 10　4.00
　　　　Nos. 1463-1466 (4)　1.60　1.60

　Nos. 1454-1457, 1463-1466 are inscribed
"1st Local." No. 1462 sold for $10.80.

New Year
2011 (Year
of the
Rabbit)
A354

Designs: (26c), $5, Rabbit facing right. 65c,
$10, Rabbit facing left. $1.10, Two rabbits,
vert. (35x40mm).

2011　　Litho.　　Perf. 13½
1467　A354　(26c) multi　　.40·　.40
1468　A354　65c multi　　1.00　1.00
Perf. 13x13¼
1469　A354　$1.10 multi　　1.75　1.75
　a.　Souvenir sheet of 3, #1467-
　　　1469, with Indipex 2011
　　　emblem in sheet margin　3.25　3.25
　b.　As "a," with PhilaNippon '11
　　　emblem in sheet margin　3.50　3.50
　c.　As "a," with China 2011 ex-
　　　hibition emblem in sheet
　　　margin　　　　　3.25　3.25
　　　　Nos. 1467-1469 (3)　3.15　3.15

Souvenir Sheet
Litho. With Transparent Holographic
Film
1470　　Sheet of 2　　24.00　24.00
　a.　A354 $5 multi　　8.00　8.00
　b.　A354 $10 multi　　16.00　16.00
Self-Adhesive
Litho.
Serpentine Die Cut 9¾x10½
1471　A354　(26c) multi　　.40　.40
　Nos. 1467 and 1471 are inscribed "1st
Local." Issued: No. 1469a, 2/12; No. 1469b,
7/28; No. 1469c, 11/11; others, 1/7.

Spirit of Giving — A355

Children's art with panel at bottom in: $1.10,
Blue. $2, Purple.

2011, Jan. 24　Litho.　Perf. 12¾x13¼
1472-1473　A355　Set of 2　5.00 5.00
　Intl. Association of Volunteer Efforts World
Volunteer Conference, Singapore.

Pond Life
A356

　Flora and fauna: 5c, White-collared kingfisher. 20c, Diving beetle. (26c), Water lily
(30x27mm). 30c, Common redbolt. (32c),
Water hyacinth (30x27mm). 45c, Ornate
coraltail. 50c, Black marsh terrapin. 55c,
White-breated waterhen. 65c, Common green-
back. 80c, Common toad. $1.10, Common
tilapia (50x30mm). $2, Pond wolf spider
(50x30mm). $5, Water strider (50x30mm).
$10, Water scorpion (50x30mm).

Perf. 13x13¼ Syncopated, 13¼
Syncopated (#1476, 1478, 1484-
1487)
2011　　　　　　　　　　Photo.
1474　A356　5c multi　　.25　.25
1475　A356　20c multi　　.35　.35
1476　A356　(26c) multi　　.45　.45
1477　A356　30c multi　　.50　.50
1478　A356　(32c) multi　　.55　.55
1479　A356　45c multi　　.75　.75
1480　A356　50c multi　　.80　.80
1481　A356　55c multi　　.90　.90
1482　A356　65c multi　　1.10　1.10
1483　A356　80c multi　　1.25　1.25
1484　A356　$1.10 multi　　1.75　1.75
1485　A356　$2 multi　　3.25　3.25
1486　A356　$5 multi　　8.00　8.00
1487　A356　$10 multi　　16.00　16.00
　a.　Miniature sheet of 14,
　　　#1474-1487　　36.00　36.00
　　Nos. 1474-1487 (14)　35.90　35.90
Booklet Stamp
Self-Adhesive
Die Cut Perf. 13¼ Syncopated
1488　A356　(26c) multi　　.45　.45
　a.　Booklet pane of 10　4.50
　Nos. 1476 and 1488 are inscribed "1st
Local." No. 1478 is inscribed "2nd Local."
Issued: Nos. 1484-1487, 2/16; others, 4/13.
See Nos. 1532-1534.

Aviation in
Singapore,
Cent.
A357

　Silhouettes of people with airplanes and airports: (26c), Bristol Box Kite airplane, Old
Racecourse. 45c, Fokker F7-A, Seletar Airport. 65c, Airspeed Consul, Kallang Airport.
80c, F-15SG, Paya Lebar Air Base. $1.10,
Airbus A380, Singapore Changi Airport.

2011, Mar. 16　Litho.　Perf. 13¼
1489-1493　A357　Set of 5　5.25 5.25
　No. 1489 is inscribed "1st Local."

Hawker
Centers
A358

　Hawker centers: No. 1494, 80c, Lau Pa Sat.
No. 1495, 80c, East Coast. No. 1496, 80c,
Maxwell. No. 1497, 80c, Newton.

2011, May 18　　　　Perf. 13x13¼
1494-1497　A358　Set of 4　5.25 5.25

Oriental Small-
clawed
Otter — A359

　No. 1498 — Otter: a, Underwater. b, On log
with crab. c, Pair looking at dragonfly. d, Head.

2011, June 3　　　　Perf. 12¾
1498　　Horiz. strip of 4　5.25 5.25
　a.-b.　A359 50c Either single　.80　.80
　c.-d.　A359 $1.10 Either single　1.75　1.75

Spices and
Dishes They Are
In — A360

　Designs: (26c), Cinnamon, Masala teh.
(32c), Coriander, Satay. 65c, Star anise,
Braised duck. 80c, Tamarind, Assam prawns.
$1.10, Turmeric, Fish head curry.

2011, July 15　　　　Perf. 14
1499-1503　A360　Set of 5　5.25 5.25
　No. 1499 is inscribed "1st Local." No. 1500
is inscribed "2nd Local."

Economic
Development
in Singapore,
50th
Anniv — A361

　Designs: (26c), "HOME." $2, Stylized tree.

2011, Aug. 1　　　　Perf. 12¾x13
1504-1505　A361　Set of 2　3.75 3.75
　No. 1504 is inscribed "1st Local."

Historic Areas of Singapore — A362

　Designs: No. 1506, 50c, Joo Chiat. No.
1507, 50c, Taman Jurong. No. 1508, $1.10,
Old Joo Chiat. No. 1509, $1.10, Old Taman
Jurong.
　$2, Old and new Joo Chiat and Taman
Jurong.

2011, Aug. 8　　　　Perf. 13¼
1506-1509　A362　Set of 4　5.50 5.50
Souvenir Sheet
1510　A362　$2 multi　　3.50 3.50
　No. 1510 contains one 72x51mm stamp.

A363

A364

A365

A366

A367

A368

A369

A370

A371

Your
Singapore
A372

2011, Sept. 14　　　　Perf. 12¾
1511　　Sheet of 10　　4.50　4.50
　a.　A363 (26c) multi　　.45　.45
　b.　A364 (26c) multi　　.45　.45
　c.　A365 (26c) multi　　.45　.45
　d.　A366 (26c) multi　　.45　.45
　e.　A367 (26c) multi　　.45　.45
　f.　A368 (26c) multi　　.45　.45
　g.　A369 (26c) multi　　.45　.45
　h.　A370 (26c) multi　　.45　.45
　i.　A371 (26c) multi　　.45　.45
　j.　A372 (26c) multi　　.45　.45
Self-Adhesive
Serpentine Die Cut 13½x13¼
1512　　Booklet pane of 10　4.50
　a.　A363 (26c) multi　　.45　.45
　b.　A364 (26c) multi　　.45　.45
　c.　A365 (26c) multi　　.45　.45
　d.　A366 (26c) multi　　.45　.45
　e.　A367 (26c) multi　　.45　.45
　f.　A368 (26c) multi　　.45　.45
　g.　A369 (26c) multi　　.45　.45

h.	A370 (26c) multi	.45	.45
i.	A371 (26c) multi	.45	.45
j.	A372 (26c) multi	.45	.45

Nos. 1511a-1511j, 1512a-1512j each are inscribed "1st Local."

Rivers — A373

Designs: $1.10, Singapore River. $2, Nile River.

2011, Oct. 17   **Perf. 13¼**
Size: 163x30mm

1513	A373	$1.10 multi	1.75	1.75
1514	A373	$2 multi	3.25	3.25

Souvenir Sheet
Perf. 12¾

1515	A373	Sheet of 2	5.00	5.00
a.		$1.10 multi, 120x22mm	1.75	1.75
b.		$2 multi, 120x22mm	3.25	3.25

See Egypt Nos.

20th World Orchid Conference, Singapore A374

Orchid varieties: (26c), Vanda Miss Joaquim. 45c, Renanthera 20th WOC Singapore 2011. 65c, Dendrobium World Peace. 80c, Cyrtocidium goldiana. $2, Grammatophyllum speciosum.
$5, Grammatophyllum speciosum, Renanthera 20th WOC Singapore, 2011, Dendrobium World Peace, Vanda Miss Joaquim, Cyrtocidiuim goldiana, horiz.

2011, Nov. 12   **Litho.**   **Perf. 14**

1516-1520	A374	Set of 5	6.50	6.50

Souvenir Sheet
Perf. 14½

1521	A374	$5 multi	7.75	7.75

No. 1516 is inscribed "1st Local." No. 1521 contains one 78x40mm stamp.

New Year 2012 (Year of the Dragon) A375

Designs: (26c), $5, Dragon facing right. 65c, $10, Dragon facing left. $1.10, Two dragons, vert. (35x45mm).

2012, Jan. 5   **Perf. 13½**

1522	A375	(26c) multi	.45	.45
1523	A375	65c multi	1.10	1.10

Perf. 13x13¼

1524	A375	$1.10 multi	1.75	1.75
		Nos. 1522-1524 (3)	3.30	3.30

Souvenir Sheet

1525		Sheet of 2	25.00	25.00
a.		A375 $5 multi	8.50	8.50
b.		A375 $10 multi	16.50	16.50

Self-Adhesive
Serpentine Die Cut 9¾x10½

1526	A375	(26c) multi	.45	.45

Nos. 1522 and 1526 are inscribed "1st Local." No. 1525 sold for $15.70.

Local Tea Time Snacks — A376

Designs: Nos. 1527, 1531, (26c), Lapis Sagu (nine-layered kueh). 50c, Kueh Dadar (coconut pancake). 80c, Bao (Chinee buns). $1.10, Kueh Tutu.

2012, Feb. 8   **Perf. 13¼x13½**

1527-1530	A376	Set of 4	4.25	4.25

Booklet Stamp
Self-Adhesive
Serpentine Die Cut 10x9½

1531	A376	(26c) multi	.45	.45
a.		Booklet pane of 10	4.50	

Nos. 1527 and 1531 each are inscribed "1st Local."

Pond Life Type of 2011

Designs: (26c), Yellow burhead flower (30x27mm). (32c), Water lettuce (30x27mm).

Perf. 13¼ Syncopated
2012, Mar. 12   **Photo.**

1532	A356	(26c) multi	.45	.45
1533	A356	(32c) multi	.50	.50

Booklet Stamp
Self-Adhesive
Die Cut Perf. 13¼ Syncopated

1534	A356	(26c) multi	.45	.45
a.		Booklet pane of 10	4.50	

Nos. 1532 and 1534 are inscribed "1st Local." No. 1533 is inscribed "2nd Local."

Reservoirs — A377

Designs: No. 1535, (26c), Serangoon Reservoir. No. 1536, (26c), Marina Reservoir. No. 1537, (26c), Lower Selatar Reservoir. No. 1538, (26c), Punggol Reservoir. No. 1539, (26c), Jurong Lake. No. 1540, 50c, Upper Selatar Reservoir. No. 1541, 50c, Pandan Reservoir. No. 1542, 50c, Bedok Reservoir. No. 1543, 50c, MacRitchie Reservoir. No. 1544, 50c, Lower Peirce Reservoir.

2012, Mar. 22   **Litho.**   **Perf. 14¼x14**

1535-1544	A377	Set of 10	6.00	6.00

Nos. 1535-1539 are each inscribed "1st Local."

A378

A379

A380

Local Markets A381

2012, Apr. 18   **Perf. 14x13¼**

1545	A378	80c multi	1.40	1.40
1546	A379	80c multi	1.40	1.40
1547	A380	80c multi	1.40	1.40
1548	A381	80c multi	1.40	1.40
		Nos. 1545-1548 (4)	5.60	5.60

POSTAGE DUE STAMPS

D1

Wmk. 314
1968, Feb. 1   **Litho.**   **Perf. 9**

J1	D1	1c emerald	.40	.40
J2	D1	2c red org	.70	.70
J3	D1	4c yel org	1.25	1.25
J4	D1	8c brown	1.60	1.60
J5	D1	10c rose mag	4.00	4.00
J6	D1	12c dl vio	2.25	2.25
J7	D1	20c brt bl	4.75	4.75
J8	D1	50c gray grn	11.50	11.50
		Nos. J1-J8 (8)	26.45	26.45

1973-77   **Perf. 13x13½**

J1a	D1	1c Unwmkd. ('77)	87.50	87.50
J3a	D1	4c Unwmkd. ('77)	87.50	87.50
J5a	D1	10c	2.00	2.00
b.		Unwmkd. ('77)	92.50	92.50
J7a	D1	20c Unwmkd. ('77)	100.00	100.00
J8a	D1	50c	17.00	17.00
b.		Unwmkd. ('77)	125.00	125.00

D2

1981   **Unwmk.**   **Perf. 12x11½**

J9	D2	1c emerald	.35	.35
J10	D2	4c orange	.35	.35
J11	D2	10c carmine	3.00	3.00
J12	D2	20c light blue	3.00	3.00
J13	D2	50c light yellow green	4.00	4.00
		Nos. J9-J13 (5)	10.70	10.70

1978, Sept. 25   **Perf. 13x13½**

J9a	D2	1c	1.50	1.50
J10a	D2	4c	1.50	1.50
J11a	D2	10c	1.60	1.60
J12a	D2	20c	1.90	1.90
J13a	D2	50c	3.50	3.50
		Nos. J9a-J13a (5)	10.00	10.00

D3

1989, July 12   **Litho.**   **Perf. 13x13½**

J14	D3	5c red lilac	.25	.25
J15	D3	10c red	.25	.25
J16	D3	20c light blue	1.00	1.00
J17	D3	50c yellow green	3.00	3.00
J18	D3	$1 brown	6.25	6.25
		Nos. J14-J18 (5)	10.75	10.75

Issued: $1, 4/30/93; others, 7/12/89.

1997, Nov. 7   **Litho.**   **Perf. 13x13½**

J19	D3	1c green	65.00	—
J20	D3	4c brown orange	90.00	—

A small quantity of Nos. J19-J20 were produced, which was sold locally only, in late 1997. Postage due stamps were replaced by machine-generated labels on Dec. 31, 1997.

SLOVAKIA

slō-'vä-kē-ə

LOCATION — Central Europe
GOVT. — Republic
AREA — 18,932 sq. mi.
POP. — 5,396,193 (1999 est.)
CAPITAL — Bratislava

Formerly a province of Czechoslovakia, Slovakia declared its independence in Mar., 1939. A treaty was immediately concluded with Germany guaranteeing Slovakian independence but providing for German "protection" for 25 years.
In 1945 the republic ended and Slovakia again became a part of Czechoslovakia.
On January 1, 1993, Czechoslovakia split into the Czech Republic and Slovakia.

100 Halierov = 1 Koruna

> Catalogue values for unused stamps in this country are for never hinged items, beginning with Scott 26 in the regular postage section, Scott B1 in the semipostal section, Scott C1 in the airmail section, Scott EX1 in the personal delivery section, Scott J1 in the postage due section, and Scott P10 in the newspaper section.

Watermark

Wmk. 263 —
Double-Barred
Cross Multiple

Stamps of Czechoslovakia, 1928-39, Overprinted in Red or Blue

1939   **Perf. 10, 12½, 12x12½**

2	A29	5h dk ultra	1.50	1.40
3	A29	10h brown	.25	.25
4	A29	20h red (Bl)	.25	.25
5	A29	25h green	6.00	5.00
6	A29	30h red violet (Bl)	.25	.25
7	A61a	40h dark blue	.25	.25
8	A73	50h deep green	.25	.25
9	A63	50h deep green	.25	.25
10	A63	60h dull violet	.25	.25
11	A63	60h dull blue	9.50	10.25
12	A60	1k rose lake (Bl) (On No. 212)	.25	.25

Overprinted Diagonally

13	A64	1.20k rose lilac (Bl)	1.25	1.25
14	A65	1.50k carmine (Bl)	1.25	1.25
15	A79	1.60k olive grn (Bl)	2.00	2.75
16	A66	2k dk blue green	2.00	2.75
17	A67	2.50k dark blue	1.25	1.25
18	A68	3k brown	1.25	1.25
19	A69	3.50k dk violet	27.50	27.50
20	A69	3.50k dk violet (Bl)	40.00	40.00
21	A70	4k dk violet	17.50	17.50
22	A71	5k green	22.50	22.50
23	A72	10k blue	200.00	175.00
		Nos. 2-23 (22)	335.50	311.65

Excellent counterfeit overprints exist.

Stefánik Type of Czechoslovakia

Gen. Milan Stefánik

1939, Mar. 30   Engr.   Perf. 12½
23A A63 60h dark blue   45.00 37.50

Prepared by Czechoslovakia prior to the German occupation March 15, 1939. Subsequently issued for use in Slovakia.

Andrej Hlinka
A1   A2
Overprinted in Red or Blue
Perf. 12½

1939, Apr.   Unwmk.   Photo.
24 A1 50h dark green
                          (R)   .70   .70
a.   Perf. 10½   5.00 2.50
b.   Perf. 10½x12½   25.00 12.50
25 A1 1k dk car rose
                          (Bl)   .75   .65
a.   Perf. 10½   1,200. 1,000.
     Never hinged   1,800.
b.   Perf. 10½x12½   30.00 17.50

> Catalogue values for unused stamps in this section, from this point to the end of the section, are for Never Hinged items.

1939   Unwmk.   Perf. 12½
26 A2 5h brt ultra   .55   .45
27 A2 10h olive green   .90   .70
a.   Perf. 10½x12½   110.00 50.00
b.   Perf. 10½   600.00 80.00
28 A2 20h orange red   .90   .70
a.   Imperf.   .85   .80
29 A2 30h dp violet   .90   .70
a.   Imperf.   1.00 1.25
b.   Perf. 10½x12½   20.00 10.00
c.   Perf. 10½   50.00 12.00
30 A2 50h dk green   .90   .70
31 A2 1k dk carmine rose   1.25   .70
32 A2 2.50k brt blue   1.25   .30
a.   Perf. 10½x12½   150.00 70.00
33 A2 3k black brown   3.00   .50
a.   Perf. 10½x12½   15.00 5.00
b.   Perf. 10½   15.00 1.50
     Nos. 26-33 (8)   9.65 4.75

On Nos. 32 and 33 a pearl frame surrounds the medallion. See Nos. 55-57, 69.

General Stefánik
and Memorial
Tomb — A3

1939, May   Perf. 12½
Size: 25x20mm
34 A3 40h dark blue   1.10
35 A3 60h slate green   1.10
36 A3 1k gray violet   1.10
Size: 30x23¾mm
37 A3 2k bl vio & sepia   1.25
     Nos. 34-37 (4)   4.55

20th anniv. of the death of Gen. Milan Stefánik, but not issued.

Rev. Josef Murgas
and Radio
Towers — A4

1939   Unwmk.
38 A4 60h purple   .30   .30
39 A4 1.20k slate black   .75   .25

10th anniv. of the death of Rev. Josef Murgas. See No. 65.

Girl
Embroidering   Woodcutter
A5   A6

Girl at
Spring — A7

1939-44   Wmk. 263   Perf. 12½
40 A5 2k dk blue green   6.25   .50
41 A6 4k copper brown   1.40 1.00
42 A7 5k orange red   1.00   .50
a.   Perf. 10 ('44)   1.25 1.00
     Nos. 40-42 (3)   8.65 2.00

Dr. Josef   Presidential
Tiso — A8   Residence — A9

1939-44   Wmk. 263   Perf. 12½
43 A8 50h slate green   .45   .30
43A A8 70h dk red brn ('42) .35   .25
b.   Perf. 10½ ('44)   .50   .35

See No. 88.

1940, Mar. 14
44 A9 10k deep blue   1.00   .75

Tatra   Krivan Peak
Mountains   A11
A10

Edelweiss in   Chamois
the Tatra   A13
Mountains
A12

Church at
Javorina — A14

1940-43   Wmk. 263   Perf. 12½
Size: 17x21mm
45 A10 5h dk olive grn   .30   .25
46 A11 10h deep brown   .25   .25
47 A12 20h blue black   .25   .25
48 A13 25h olive brown   .55   .25
49 A14 30h chestnut brown   .35   .25
a.   Perf. 10½ ('43)   2.50 1.00
     Nos. 45-49 (5)   1.70 1.25

See Nos. 84-87, 103-107.

Hlinka Type of 1939

1940-42   Wmk. 263   Perf. 12½
55 A2 1k dk car rose   .90   .60
56 A2 2.50k brt blue ('42) 1.25   .75
a.   Perf. 10½   .60   .60
57 A2 3k black brn ('41)   2.00 1.00
a.   Perf. 10½   2.00   .90

On Nos. 56 and 57 a pearl frame surrounds the medallion.

Stiavnica   Lietava
A15   A16

Spissky   Bojnice — A18
Hrad — A17

1941   Perf. 12½
58 A15 1.20k rose lake   .25   .25
59 A16 1.50k rose pink   .25   .25
60 A17 1.60k royal blue   .25   .25
61 A18 2k dk gray green   .25   .25
     Nos. 58-61 (4)   1.00 1.00

Slovakian Castles.

S. M. Daxner
and Stefan
Moyses
A19

1941, May 26   Photo.   Wmk. 263
62 A19 50h olive green   2.25 1.50
63 A19 1k slate blue   7.50 6.25
64 A19 2k black   6.00 5.00
     Nos. 62-64 (3)   15.75 12.75

80th anniv. of the Memorandum of the Slovak Nation.

Murgas Type of 1939

1941   Wmk. 263
65 A4 60h purple   .40   .25

Andrej Hlinka — A20

1942
69 A20 1.30k dark purple   .45   .25

Post Horn and
Miniature
Stamp — A21

Philatelist — A22

Philatelist — A23

1942, May 23
70 A21 30h dark green   1.10   .95
71 A22 70h dk car rose   1.10   .95
72 A23 80h purple   1.10   .95
73 A21 1.30k dark brown   1.10   .95
     Nos. 70-73 (4)   4.40 3.80

Natl. Philatelic Exhibition at Bratislava. On No. 70 the miniature stamp bears the coat-of-arms of Bratislava; on No. 73 it shows the National arms of Slovakia.

St. Stephen's
Cathedral,
Vienna — A24

1942, Oct. 12   Perf. 14
74 A24 70h blue green   .75   .75
75 A24 1.30k olive green   1.50 1.50
76 A24 2k sapphire   2.50 2.50
     Nos. 74-76 (3)   4.75 4.75

European Postal Congress held in Vienna.

Slovakian Educational Society — A25

1942, Dec. 14
77 A25 70h black   .25   .25
78 A25 1k rose red   .30   .25
79 A25 1.30k sapphire   .30   .25
80 A25 2k chestnut brown   .35   .25
81 A25 3k dark green   .50   .30
82 A25 4k dull purple   .50   .30
     Nos. 77-82 (6)   2.20 1.60

Slovakian Educational Soc., 150th anniv.

Andrej Hlinka — A26

1943   Wmk. 263
83 A26 1.30k brt ultra   .75   .35

See Nos. 93-94A.

Types of 1939-40

1943   Unwmk.   Perf. 12½
84 A11 10h deep brown   .25   .25
85 A12 20h blue black   .70   .50
86 A13 25h olive brown   .70   .50
87 A14 30h chestnut brown   .50   .35
88 A8   70h dk red brown   .85   .95
     Nos. 84-88 (5)   3.00 2.55

Presov
Church — A27

Locomotive
A28

Railway Tunnel
A29

Viaduct — A30

1943, Sept. 5   **Perf. 14**
89	A27	70h dk rose violet	.60	.50
90	A28	80h sapphire	.60	.50
91	A29	1.30k black	.60	.50
92	A30	2k dk violet brn	.60	.50
		Nos. 89-92 (4)	2.40	2.00

Inauguration of the new railroad line between Presov and Strazske.

Hlinka Type of 1943 and

Ludovit
Stur — A31

Martin
Razus — A32

1944   **Unwmk.**
93	A31	80h slate green	.35	.25
94	A32	1k brown red	.35	.25
94A	A26	1.30k brt ultra	.50	.25
		Nos. 93-94A (3)	1.20	.75

Prince
Pribina — A33

Designs: 70h, Prince Mojmir. 80h, Prince Ratislav. 1.30k, King Svatopluk. 2k, Prince Kocel. 3k, Prince Mojmir II. 5k, Prince Svatopluk II. 10k, Prince Braslav.

1944, Mar. 14
95	A33	50h dark green	.25	.25
96	A33	70h lilac rose	.25	.25
97	A33	80h red brown	.25	.25
98	A33	1.30k brt ultra	.30	.25
99	A33	2k Prus blue	.30	.25
100	A33	3k dark brown	.45	.30
101	A33	5k violet	.95	.70
102	A33	10k black	2.50	2.00
		Nos. 95-102 (8)	5.25	4.25

Scenic Types of 1940

1944, Apr. 1   **Perf. 14**
Size: 18x23mm
103	A11	10h bright carmine	.25	.30
104	A12	20h bright blue	.25	.30
105	A13	25h brown red	.25	.30
106	A14	30h red violet	.25	.30
107	A10	50h deep green	.25	.30
		Nos. 103-107 (5)	1.25	1.50

5th anniv. of Slovakia's independence.
See Nos. B25-B26.

Symbolic of
National
Protection
A41

1944, Oct. 6   **Wmk. 263**
108	A41	2k green	.50	.60
109	A41	3.80k red violet	.50	.90

President Josef
Tiso — A42

1945   **Unwmk.**
110	A42	1k orange	.55	.40
111	A42	1.50k brown	.30	.25
112	A42	2k green	.30	.40
113	A42	4k rose red	.90	.55
114	A42	5k sapphire	.80	.40

Wmk. 263
115	A42	10k red violet	.75	.40
		Nos. 110-115 (6)	3.60	2.40

6th anniv. of the Republic of Slovakia's declaration of independence, Mar. 14, 1939.

Natl. Arms — A50

1993   **Photo. & Engr.**   **Perf. 11½**
150	A50	3k multicolored	.60	.30

Engr.
Perf. 12
Size: 30x44mm
151	A50	8k multicolored	6.00	4.00

Issued: 3k, Jan. 2; 8k, Jan. 1. No. 151 does not have black frameline.
No. 151 was issued in sheets of 6.

Castles &
Churches — A51

Nos. 152-155 are churches, Nos. 156-157 castles.

Perf. 11½x12, 12x11½
1993-95   **Photo. & Engr.**
152	A51	2k Nitra	.25	.25
153	A51	3k Banska Bystrica	.30	.25
154	A51	5k Ruzomberok, horiz.	.50	.25
155	A51	10k Kosice	.90	.45
156	A51	30k Zvolen, horiz.	3.00	1.50
157	A51	50k Bratislava	6.50	3.25
		Nos. 152-157 (6)	11.45	5.95

Issued: 5k, 10k, 1993; 30k, 9/12/93; 50k, 12/31/93; 3k, 11/15/94; 2k, 3/15/95.
See Nos. 218-227.

St. John
Nepomuk,
600th Death
Anniv.
A57

Photo. & Engr.
1993, Mar. 11   **Perf. 12x11½**
158	A57	8k multicolored	1.10	.50

See Czech Republic #2880; Germany #1776.

A58   A59

President Michal Kovac

1993   **Engr.**   **Perf. 12x11½**
159	A58	2k dark gray blue	.25	.25
159A	A58	3k red brown & red	.30	.25

Issued: 2k, 3/2/93; 3k, 11/3/93.

Photo. & Engr.
1993, May 14   **Perf. 11½**
Trees.
160	A59	3k Quercus robur	.65	.25
161	A59	4k Carpinus betulus	.65	.30
162	A59	10k Pinus silvestris	.85	.50
		Nos. 160-162 (3)	2.15	1.05

A60   A61

Famous Men: 5k, Jan Levoslav Bella (1843-1936), composer. 8k, Alexander Dubcek (1921-92), politician. 20k, Jan Kollar (1793-1852), writer.

Photo. & Engr.
1993, May 20   **Perf. 12x11½**
163	A60	5k red brown & blue	.75	.40
164	A60	8k brown & lilac red	1.25	.60
165	A60	20k gray blue & orange	3.00	1.50
		Nos. 163-165 (3)	5.00	2.50

1993, May 31   **Engr.**   **Perf. 12**
Woman with Pitcher, by Marian Cunderlik.
166	A61	14k multicolored	6.00	5.00

Europa. Issued in sheets of 4.

Literary
Slovak
Language,
150th Anniv.
A62

Design: 8k, Arrival of St. Cyril and St. Methodius, 1130th Anniv.

Photo. & Engr.
1993, June 22   **Perf. 12x11½**
167	A62	2k multicolored	.25	.25
168	A62	8k multicolored	.90	.50

See Czech Republic No. 2886.

A63   A64

Arms of Dubnica nad Vahom.

Photo. & Engr.
1993, July 8   **Perf. 12x11½**
169	A63	1k multicolored	.25	.25

Photo. & Engr.
1993, Sept. 2   **Perf. 11½**
The Big Pets, by Lane Smith.
170	A64	5k multicolored	.50	.25

Bratislava Biennial of Illustrators.

Gavcikovo Dam — A65

Photo. & Engr.
1993, Nov. 12   **Perf. 11½**
172	A65	10k multicolored	1.25	.60

No. 172 issued se-tenant with label.

Madonna and Child,
by J. B. Klemens
(1817-83) — A66

Photo. & Engr.
1993, Dec. 1   **Perf. 11½**
173	A66	2k multicolored	.30	.25

Christmas.

Souvenir Sheet

Monument to Gen. Milan
Stefanik — A67

1993, Dec. 17   **Engr.**   **Perf. 11½x12**
174	A67	16k multicolored	2.75	1.25

Art from Bratislava Natl.
Gallery — A68

Sculpture: 9k, Plough of Springtime, by Josef Kostka.

1993, Dec. 31
175	A68	9k multicolored	2.25	2.00

Issued in sheets of 4.
See Nos. 199-200, 237-238, 255.

A69   A70

Photo. & Engr.
1994, Jan. 26   **Perf. 11x11½**
176	A69	2k multicolored	.50	.25
		Complete booklet, 10 #176	6.00	

1994 Winter Olympics, Lillehammer.

Photo. & Engr.
1994, Apr. 29   **Perf. 11x11½**
177	A70	3k multicolored	.35	.25
		Complete booklet, 5 #177	2.75	

Intl. Year of the Family.

Jan Andrej Segner (1704-77), Physicist — A71

Design: 9k, Antoine de Saint-Exupery (1900-44), aviator, author.

Photo. & Engr.
1994, May 25 *Perf. 11½x11*
178 A71 8k red brown & blue 1.00 .45
179 A71 9k black, blue & pink 1.00 .45
See Nos. 196-198.

Josef Murgas (1864-1929), Inventor of Radio Transmitters — A72

1994, May 27 **Engr.** *Perf. 11½*
180 A72 28k multicolored 3.25 2.50
Europa. Issued in sheets of 4

A73

A74

Photo. & Engr.
1994, May 31 *Perf. 11½x11*
181 A73 3k multicolored .30 .25
Intl. Stop Smoking Day.

Photo. & Engr.
1994, June 10 *Perf. 11½*
182 A74 2k blue, black & green .35 .25
1994 World Cup Soccer Championships, US.

Intl. Olympic Committee, Cent. — A75

Photo. & Engr.
1994, June 23 *Perf. 12x11½*
183 A75 3k multicolored .40 .25
No. 183 issued with se-tenant label.

Raptors — A76

Photo. & Engr.
1994, July 4 *Perf. 11½x12*
184 A76 4k Aquila chrysaetos .65 .25
185 A76 5k Falco peregrinus .75 .25
186 A76 7k Bubo bubo .95 .40
Nos. 184-186 (3) 2.35 .90

Prince Svatopluk of Moravia (870-894) — A77

1994, July 20 **Engr.** *Perf. 12*
187 A77 12k red brn, buff & blk 1.60 1.00
Issued in sheets of 4.

UPU, 120th Anniv. — A78

Photo. & Engr.
1994, Aug. 1 *Perf. 11½x12*
188 A78 8k multicolored .90 .45

Slovak Uprising, 50th Anniv. — A79

Design: 6k, Gen. Rudolf Viest, Gen. Jan. Golian. 8k, French Volunteers' Memorial, Strecno hill.

Photo. & Engr.
1994, Aug. 27 *Perf. 12x11½*
189 A79 6k multicolored .75 .40
190 A79 8k multicolored .75 .40
Nos. 189-190 printed with se-tenant label.

Souvenir Sheet

Janko Matuska, Lyricist, 150th Death Anniv. — A80

Design: 34k, Matuska, woman with pitcher, verse of "A Well She Dug."

Photo. & Engr.
1994, Sept. 1 *Perf. 12x11½*
191 A80 34k multicolored 3.50 1.75

Comenius University, 75th Anniv. — A81

Photo. & Engr.
1994, Oct. 18 *Perf. 11½x12*
192 A81 12k multicolored 1.25 .60

Mojmirovce Horse Race, 180th Anniv. A82

1994, Oct. 25 *Perf. 12x11½*
193 A82 2k multicolored .40 .25

St. George's Church, Kostotany pod Tribecom — A83

1994, Nov. 8 *Perf. 11*
194 A83 20k multicolored 2.00 1.00

Christmas — A84

1994, Nov. 29 *Perf. 11½*
195 A84 2k multicolored .35 .25

Personalities Type of 1994

Designs: 5k, Chatam Sofer (1762-1839), rabbi. 6k, Wolfgang Kempelen (1734-1804), polytechnician. 10k, Stefan Banic (1870-1941), inventor of aviation parachute.

1994, Dec. 12 *Perf. 11½x11*
196 A71 5k multicolored .60 .30
 Complete booklet, 5 #196 8.00
197 A71 6k multicolored .70 .35
198 A71 8k multicolored 1.25 .60
 Nos. 196-198 (3) 2.55 1.25

Bratislava Art Type of 1993

Designs: 7k, Girls, by Janko Alexy, horiz. 14k, The Bulls, by Vincent Hloznik.

Perf. 12x11½, 11½x12
1994, Dec. 15 **Engr.**
199 A68 7k multicolored 1.00 .75
200 A68 14k multicolored 2.00 1.50

Ships — A85

5k, Cargo ship, NL EMS. 8k, Cargo ship, Ryn. 10k, 400-passenger cruise ship.

Photo. & Engr.
1994, Dec. 30 *Perf. 12x11½*
201 A85 5k multicolored .55 .30
202 A85 8k multicolored 1.00 .60
203 A85 10k multicolored 1.00 .60
 Nos. 201-203 (3) 2.55 1.50

Samuel Jurkovic, Founder of of Landlords Assoc., 1845 — A86

Photo. & Engr.
1995, Feb. 8 *Perf. 11½*
204 A86 9k multicolored 1.10 .45

European Nature Conservation Year — A87

Protected plants: 2k, Ciminalis clusii. 3k, Pulsatilla slavica. 8k, Onosma tornense.

1995, Feb. 28
205 A87 2k multicolored .55 .25
 Complete booklet, 10 #205 10.00
206 A87 3k multicolored .55 .25
 Complete booklet, 5 #206 10.00
207 A87 8k multicolored 1.10 .50
 Nos. 205-207 (3) 2.20 1.00

Slovak Natl. Theatre, 75th Anniv. A88

1995, Feb. 28 *Perf. 12x11½*
208 A88 10k multicolored 1.10 .45

1995 Group B World Cup Ice Hockey Championships, Bratislava — A89

1995, Mar. 29 *Perf. 11½*
209 A89 5k blue & yellow .55 .25

Bela Bartok (1881-1945), Composer A90

6k, Jan Bahyl (1856-1916), inventor.

Photo. & Engr.
1995, Apr. 20 *Perf. 12x11½*
210 A90 3k multicolored .35 .25
211 A90 6k multicolored .75 .35

Souvenir Sheet

Ludovit Stur (1815-56), Writer — A91

1995, Apr. 20 *Perf. 11½*
212 A91 16k multicolored 1.75 .85

Europa
A92

1995, May 5   Engr.   Perf. 12
213 A92 8k multicolored   1.40 1.10

Liberation of the
Concentration
Camps, 50th
Anniv. — A93

Photo. & Engr.
1995, May 5   Perf. 11
214 A93 12k multicolored   1.25 .60

Slovak
Scouting — A94

1995, May 18   Perf. 11½x11
215 A94 5k multicolored   1.00 .30

Visit of Pope
John Paul
II — A95

1995, May 29   Engr.
216 A95 3k red   .35   .25
     Complete booklet, 10 #216   9.00

Organized Philately in Slovakia,
Cent. — A96

Photo. & Engr.
1995, June 1   Perf. 11½x12
217 A96 3k blue, black & gray   .60   .35
  a.   Souv. sheet of 2   2.25 1.50
     Dunafila '95.

Castles &
Churches — A100

Perf. 11¾x11¼, 11¼x11¾ (#218, 225-226)
1995-2001   Photo. & Engr.
218 A100 50h Bardejov, horiz.   .25   .25
219 A100 4k Nova Bana   .50   .25
220 A100 4k Presov   .40   .25
221 A100 5k Trnava   .50   .25
222 A100 7k Martin   .65   .30
223 A100 8k Trencin Castle   1.25   .60
224 A100 9k Zelina   .85   .40
225 A100 20k Roznava, horiz.   1.90   .95
226 A100 40k Piestany, horiz.   4.00 2.00
227 A100 50k Komarno   5.00 2.50
     Nos. 218-227 (10)   15.30 7.75

Issued: 4k (#219), 6/15/95; 8k, 9/12/95. 9k,
4/15/97. 7k, 7/17/97. 5k. 9/12/98. 4k (#220),
11/3/98. 50h, 2/1/00. 20k, 7/26/00. 40k,
5/25/01. 50k, 4/26/01.
See Nos. 401-402, 424-425, 447.

UNESCO
World
Heritage
Sites
A107

Perf. 11½x12, 12x11½
1995, July 19   Photo. & Engr.
228 A107 7k Banska Stiavnica,
                vert.   .70   .35
229 A107 10k Spissky Hrad   1.00   .50
230 A107 15k Vlkolinec   1.60   .80
     Nos. 228-230 (3)   3.30 1.65

Volleyball,
Cent. — A108

1995, Aug. 16   Perf. 11½
231 A108 9k multicolored   1.25   .70

A109   A110

Bratislava Biennial of Illustrators: 2k, Clown,
by Lorenzo Mattotti, Italy. 3k, Two characters,
by Dusan Kallay, Slovakia.

Photo. & Engr.
1995, Sept. 5   Perf. 11½
232 A109 2k multicolored   .25   .25
     Complete booklet, 10 #232 2.50
233 A109 3k multicolored   .30   .25
     Complete booklet, 10 #233 3.50

1995, Sept. 14
234 A110 4k multicolored   .45   .25
     St. Adalbert Assoc.

The
Cleveland
Agreement,
80th Anniv.
A111

Photo. & Engr.
1995, Oct. 20   Perf. 12x11½
235 A111 5k multicolored   .55   .25

UN, 50th
Anniv.
A112

1995, Oct. 24   Engr.   Perf. 11½x12
235A A112 8k multicolored   1.10   .55
     Issued in sheets of 8 + 2 labels.

Christmas
A113

Photo. & Engr.
1995, Oct. 27   Perf. 11½
236 A113 2k multicolored   .25   .25

Bratislava Art Type of 1993
Designs: 8k, The Hlohovec Nativity. 16k,
Two Women, by Mikulás Galanda.

Photo. & Engr.
1995, Nov. 30   Perf. 11½x12
237 A68 8k multicolored   .80   .40
238 A68 16k multicolored   1.75   .85
     Issued in sheets of 4 + 2 labels.

Jozef Cíger-   Olympic
Hronsky (1896-   Games, Cent.
1960)   A115
A114

4k, Jozef L'udovít Holuby (1836-1923).

Photo. & Engr.
1996, Feb. 15   Perf. 11½
239 A114 3k multicolored   .40   .25
240 A114 4k multicolored   .60   .35
     See Nos. 293-295, 320-322.

1996, Feb. 15
241 A115 9k multicolored   1.25   .50

Folk
Traditions — A116

Easter tradition of dousing women with
water

Photo. & Engr.
1996, Mar. 15   Perf. 11½
242 A116 2k multicolored   .35   .25
     Complete booklet, 10 #242 3.50

Souvenir Sheet

Year for the Eradication of
Poverty — A117

1996, Apr. 15   Engr.   Perf. 12
243 A117 7k multicolored   1.25   .90

A118

Europa: a, Holding thistle, carduus textori-
anus marg. b, Portrait, daphne cneorum.

1996, May 3   Engr.   Perf. 11½
244 A118 8k Pair, #a.-b.   1.75   .85

Izabela Textorisová (1866-1949), Slovakia's
1st female botanist. Issued in sheets of 4.

Souvenir Sheet

A119

Motion Pictures, Cent.: Two frames from
1936 film, Jánosík.

1996, May 15   Perf. 11½x12
245 A119 16k multicolored   2.00 2.00
     Printed se-tenant with label.

Round Slovakia
Cycle
Race — A120

1996, May 30   Engr.   Perf. 11½
246 A120 3k multicolored   .45   .25
     Complete booklet, 10 #246 5.50

Slovak
Perspectives,
150th
Anniv. — A121

1996, May 30
247 A121 18k multicolored   2.00 1.00

A122   A123

Photo. & Engr.
1996, June 14   Perf. 12x11½
248 A122 6k Coat of arms   .65   .35
     Town of Senica.

1996, July 16   Perf. 11½x12
Nature protection: No. 249, Ovis musimon.
No. 250, Bison bonasus. No. 251, Rupicapra
rupicapra.

249 A123 4k multicolored   .50   .25
     Complete booklet, 10 #249 5.50
250 A123 4k multicolored   .50   .25
     Complete booklet, 10 #250 5.50
251 A123 4k multicolored   .50   .25
     Complete booklet, 10 #251 5.50
     Nos. 249-251 (3)   1.50   .75

Splendors of
Homeland — A124

Photo. & Engr.
1996, Sept. 25   *Perf. 11½x12*
252 A124 4k Popradské Lake .40 .25
253 A124 8k Skalnaté Lake .75 .35
254 A124 12k Strbské Lake 1.10 .55
   Nos. 252-254 (3) 2.25 1.15

Bratislava Art Type of 1993
The Baroque Chair, by Endre Nemes (1909-85).

1996, Oct. 5   **Engr.**   *Perf. 11½x12*
255 A68 14k multicolored 2.00 2.00
See Czech Republic #2995, Sweden #2199. Issued in sheets of 4 + label.

Technological Advances A125

4k, Bratislava-Trnava horse-drawn railway.
6k, Andrej Kvasz's (1883-1974) airplane.

Photo. & Engr.
1996, Oct. 15   *Perf. 11*
256 A125 4k multicolored .45 .25
   Complete booklet, 10 #256 6.00
257 A125 6k multicolored .70 .30
   Complete booklet, 10 #257 8.00

Queen Ntombi Twala, by Andy Warhol (1928-87) — A126

Design: 10k, Suppressed Laughter, by Franz Xaver Messerschmidt (1736-83).

1996   **Engr.**   *Perf. 11½*
258 A126 7k multicolored .85 .70
259 A126 10k multicolored 1.25 1.00
   Each issued in sheets of 4.
   Issued: 7k, 11/13/96; 10k, 10/5/96.
See #284-286, 311, 314-315, 340-341, 366-367, 389-391, 417-418, 430, 443-445, 465-466, 488-489, 508-509, 530-531, 555-556, 584-585, 605-606, 628.

Christmas, Kysuce Village — A127

Photo. & Engr.
1996, Nov. 5   *Perf. 11½*
260 A127 2k multicolored .25 .25

Michael Martikén, Olympic Gold Medalist, Canoeing A128

Photo. & Engr.
1996, Dec. 18   *Perf. 12x11½*
261 A128 3k brown & yellow .50 .25

Stamp Day — A129

Designs: Unexecuted 1938 stamp design of a woman with patriarchal cross, dove, Martin Benka, stamp designer.

1996, Dec. 18
262 A129 3k violet & buff .45 .45
   Complete booklet, 9 #262 9.00
No. 262 was printed se-tenant with label.

Bishop Stefan Moyses (1797-1869) — A130

Design: 4k, Svetozar Hurban Vajansky (1847-1916), politician.

Photo. & Engr.
1997, Jan. 16   *Perf. 11½*
263 A130 3k multicolored .30 .25
264 A130 4k multicolored .35 .25

A131   A132

Photo. & Engr.
1997, Jan. 31   *Perf. 11½*
265 A131 6k multicolored .55 .25
1997 World Biathlon Championships, Osrblie.

Photo. & Engr.
1997, Feb. 15   *Perf. 11½*
266 A132 3k multicolored .35 .25
   Complete booklet, 10 #266 3.50
Folk Tradition of collecting dew.

Franciscan Church, Bratislava, 700th Anniv. — A133

Photo. & Engr.
1997, Mar. 25   *Perf. 11½x12*
267 A133 16k multicolored 1.50 .75

Radio, Cent. A135

1997, Apr. 15   *Perf. 12x11½*
269 A135 10k multicolored .95 .45

A136   A137

Europa (Stories and Legends): Miraculous rain near Hron.

1997, May 5   **Engr.**   *Perf. 12x11½*
270 A136 9k multicolored 1.10 .55
Issued in sheets of 7 + 3 labels.

1997, June 12   **Engr.**   *Perf. 12x11½*
Limestone Formations: 6k, Domica Cavern, Silická. 8k, Aragonit Cavern, Octiná.
271 A137 6k multicolored .55 .25
272 A137 8k multicolored .75 .35
Nos. 271-272 issued in sheets of 8 + label.

Souvenir Sheet

Folklore Festival, Vychodná — A138

1997, June 12   **Photo. & Engr.**
273 A138 11k multicolored 1.10 .90

Triennale of Naive Art, Bratislava A139

Photo. & Engr.
1996, June 26   *Perf. 12x11½*
274 A139 3k multicolored .35 .25
   Complete booklet, 10 #274 3.50

World Year of Slovaks A140   Bratislava Biennale of Illustrators A141

1997, July 17   *Perf. 11½*
276 A140 9k multicolored .75 .40

Photo. & Engr.
1997, Aug. 5   *Perf. 11½*
277 A141 3k multicolored .30 .25
   Complete booklet, 10 #277 3.25

Water Mill, Jelka — A142

1997, Aug. 5
278 A142 4k multicolored .40 .25
   Complete booklet, 10 #278 4.00

A143   A144

Photo. & Engr.
1997, Sept. 1   *Perf. 11½*
279 A143 4k multicolored .40 .25
Constitution, 5th anniv.

1997, Sept. 17
280 A144 9k multicolored .85 .40
6th Half Marathon World Championships, Kosice.

Mushrooms — A145

Designs: #281, Boletus aereus. #282, Morchella esculenta. #283, Catathelasma imperiale.

1997, Sept. 17   *Perf. 12*
281 A145 9k multicolored 1.10 .80
282 A145 9k multicolored 1.10 .80
283 A145 9k multicolored 1.10 .80
   a. Souvenir sheet, #281-283 3.50 3.00
   Nos. 281-283 (3) 3.30 2.40

Art Type of 1996
Designs: 9k, Self-portrait, by Ján Kupecky (1667-1740). 10k, Bojnice Altar, St. Peter and St. Lucia, by Nardo Di Cione, 14th cent., horiz. 12k, Towards the Goal (The Miners), by Koloman Sokol (b. 1902).

1997, Oct. 15   **Engr.**   *Perf. 11½*
284 A126 9k multicolored .90 .45
285 A126 10k multicolored 1.10 .55
286 A126 12k multicolored 1.40 .70
   Nos. 284-286 (3) 3.40 1.70

Cernova 1907 A146   Christmas A147

Photo. & Engr.
1997, Oct. 24   *Perf. 11½x12*
287 A146 4k Lamenting woman, church .40 .25

1997, Nov. 3   *Perf. 11½*
288 A147 3k Nativity .30 .25

Ondrej Nepala, Figure Skater — A148   A149

1997, Nov. 3
289 A148 5k multicolored .60 .30

Photo. & Engr.

1997, Dec. 1 **Perf. 11½**
290 A149 4k Resurrection of
Christ .40 .25
Complete booklet, 10 #290 4.00

Spiritual renewal. See #301, 327.

Stamp
Day — A150

1997, Dec. 18
291 A150 4k dark brown & blue .55 .25
Complete booklet, 9 #291 + 12
labels 7.00

No. 291 was printed se-tenant with label.

Slovak Republic, 5th Anniv. — A151

Photo. & Engr.

1998, Jan. 1 **Perf. 11½**
292 A151 4k multicolored .40 .25
Complete booklet, 10 #292 6.00

Personality Type of 1996

Writers: No. 293, Martin Rázus (1888-
1937), politician. No. 294, Ján Smrek (1898-
1982), poet. No. 295, Jozef Skultéty (1853-
1948), linguist, editor.

1998, Jan. 19
293 A114 4k multicolored .40 .25
294 A114 4k multicolored .40 .25
295 A114 4k multicolored .40 .25
Nos. 293-295 (3) 1.20 .75

1998 Winter
Olympic
Games,
Nagano
A152

1998, Jan. 19 **Perf. 12x11½**
296 A152 19k Hockey player 1.75 .70

Folk Tradition,
Banishing of
Winter — A153

Photo. & Engr.

1998, Mar. 3 **Perf. 11½**
297 A153 3k multicolored .30 .25
Complete booklet, 10 #297 4.00

Castles
A154

1998, Mar. 3
298 A154 6k Budatin .60 .35
299 A154 11k Krásna Horka 1.25 .55

Souvenir Sheet

300 A154 18k Nitra 2.00 1.50

Spiritual Renewal Type of 1997

Design: Descent of the Holy Spirit, flames
above peoples' heads.

Photo. & Engr.

1998, May 5 **Perf. 11½**
301 A149 4k multicolored .40 .25
Complete booklet, 10 #301 4.00

Folklore
Festivals — A155

1998, May 5
302 A155 12k Tekov wedding 1.25 .60

Europa. Issued in sheet of 8 + label.

A156 A157

Photo. & Engr.

1998, June 1 **Perf. 11½**
303 A156 3k Child's drawing .45 .25
Complete booklet, 10 #303 4.50

The Children's Center, Ruzomberok.

1998, June 1

Design: Viktor Kolibik (1890-1918),
wireworker, leader of revolt.

304 A157 3k multicolored .30 .25

Mutiny at Kragujevac, 80th anniv.

Slovak
Uprising of
1848-49
A158

1998, June 1
305 A158 4k multi, with 1 or 2 labels 2.00 .40

Railways in Slovakia,
Cent. — A159

Designs: 4k, Bihar steam locomotive. 10k,
Lubochna-Mocidla electrified narrow-gauge
trolley. 15k, Diesel locomotive.

Photo. & Engr.

1998, Aug. 20 **Perf. 11½**
306 A159 4k multicolored .50 .25
307 A159 10k multicolored .95 .45
308 A159 15k multicolored 1.40 .70
Nos. 306-308 (3) 2.85 1.40

Fish
A160

Designs: a, 4k, Umbra krameri. b, 11k,
Zingel zingel. c, 16k, Cyprinus carpio.

1998, Sept. 7
Sheet of 3
309 A160 #a.-c. + label 3.25 2.75

Art Type of 1996

1564 Wooden "Pieta" statue, by unknown
artist, Sastín.

1998, Sept. 14 **Perf. 11½x12**
311 A126 18k multicolored 2.25 2.00

Issued in sheets of 4.

"No" to Drugs — A161

Photo. & Engr.

1998, Oct. 5 **Perf. 11x11½**
312 A161 3k multicolored .30 .25

Ektopfilm, Ecology-Related Film
Festival, 25th Anniv. — A162

1998, Oct. 5 **Perf. 11**
313 A162 4k multicolored .40 .25
Complete booklet, 10 #313 5.00

Art Type of 1996

Designs: 10k, Terchova Landscape, by Martin Benka (1888-1971). 12k, Fishermen, by
L'udovít Fulla (1902-80).

1998, Oct. 15 **Engr.** **Perf. 11½x12**
314 A126 10k multicolored .85 .75
315 A126 12k multicolored 1.25 1.00

Adoration of the
Magi — A163

1998, Nov. 3 **Perf. 11x11½**
317 A163 3k Christmas .30 .25
Complete booklet, 10 #317 3.50

Stamp Day — A164

Photo. & Engr.

1998, Dec. 18 **Perf. 12x11½**
318 A164 4k multi, with 1 or 2 labels .75 .25
Complete booklet, 9 #318 + 12
labels 9.00

19th World Winter Universiad Games,
4th European Youth Olympic
Days — A165

Photo. & Engr.

1999, Jan. 12 **Perf. 12x11½**
319 A165 12k multicolored 2.50 .40

No. 319 is printed se-tenant with 2 labels.

Personality Type of 1996

Designs: 3k, Matej Bel (1684-1749),
teacher, pastor. 4k, Juraj Haulik (1788-1869),
1st cardinal of Croatia. 11k, Pavol Országh-
Hviezdoslav (1849-1921), poet, dramatist.

1999, Jan. 28 **Perf. 11½**
320 A114 3k multicolored .30 .25
321 A114 4k multicolored .40 .25
322 A114 11k multicolored 1.00 .40
Nos. 320-322 (3) 1.70 .90

See Croatia 388.

UPU, 125th A167
Anniv. — A166

Photo. & Engr.

1999, Mar. 12 **Perf. 11½**
323 A166 4k multicolored .40 .25
Complete booklet, 10 #323 4.00

Litho. & Engr.

1999, Mar. 12 **Perf. 11½x12**
Traditional bonnets.

324 A167 4k Cajkov .40 .30
325 A167 15k Helpa 1.25 1.00
326 A167 18k Madunice 1.50 1.10
Nos. 324-326 (3) 3.15 2.40

Nos. 324-326 were each issued in sheets of
10.

Spiritual Renewal Type of 1997

Design: "Transfiguration," by Vincent
Hloznik, depicting ascension of Christ.

Photo. & Engr.

1999, May 5 **Perf. 11½**
327 A149 5k multicolored .50 .25
Complete booklet, 10 #327 5.00

Tatra
National
Park
A168

1999, May 5 **Engr.** **Perf. 11½**
328 A168 9k shown .90 .55
329 A168 11k Mountains, diff. 1.10 .75
a. Pair, #328-329 2.25 2.25

Europa. No. 329a is a continuous design.
Issued in sheets of 8 + label.

Council of
Europe,
50th Anniv.
A169

1999, May 5 **Engr.** **Perf. 12x11½**
330 A169 16k multicolored 1.50 1.50
a. Souvenir sheet of 1 2.00 2.00

A170 A171

Photo. & Engr.

1999, June 15 **Perf. 11½x11¾**
331 A170 4k multicolored .35 .25

Slovak Philharmonic Orchestra, 50th anniv.

1999, June 15 **Perf. 11½**
332 A171 5k multicolored .60 .30

Intl. Year of Older Persons.

Souvenir Sheet

Astronaut Ivan Bella, First Slovak in
Space — A172

1999, June 15   *Perf. 11¾x11½*
333 A172 12k multicolored   1.25 .90

UPU, 125th
Anniv. — A173

Photo. & Engr.
1999, July 15   *Perf. 11½*
334 A173 12k Zilina University   1.00 .50
335 A173 16k Globe   1.25 .60

A174   A175

Photo. & Engr.
1999, Sept. 3   *Perf. 11¼x11¾*
336 A174 4k multicolored   .35 .25

Bratislava Univ. of Fine Arts, 50th anniv.

1999, Sept. 3   *Perf. 11¼x11½*
337 A175 5k multicolored   .50 .30
Complete booklet, 10 #337   5.00

Bratislava Biennale of Illustrators.

Mine Water
Pump Invented
By Jozef Hell
(1713-89)
A176

1999, Sept. 21   *Perf. 11x11¼*
338 A176 7k sepia & yellow   .95 .25

Souvenir Sheet

Birds — A177

a, 14k, Panurus biarmicus. b, 15k, Lanius
collurio. c, 16k, Phoenicurus phoenicurus.

Litho. & Engr.
1999, Sept. 21   *Perf. 11¾*
339 A177 Sheet of 3, #a.-c.   4.75 4.00

Art Type of 1996

Designs: 13k, Malatiná, by Milos Alexander
Bazovsky (1899-1968), horiz. 14k, Study of
the Blacksmith, by Dominik Skutecky.

1999, Oct. 5   Engr.   *Perf. 11¾*
340 A126 13k multicolored   1.25 1.00
341 A126 14k multicolored   1.25 1.00

Each issued in sheets of 4.

Christmas — A178

Photo. & Engr.
1999, Nov. 3   *Perf. 11¾x11¼*
342 A178 4k multicolored   .35 .25
Complete booklet, 10 #342   3.50

Czechoslovakia's "Velvet Revolution,"
10th Anniv. — A179

1999, Nov. 17   *Perf. 12x11¼*
343 A179 5k multicolored   .80 .25

Ceramic Urns, Museum of Jewish
Culture — A180

Litho. & Engr.
1999, Nov. 23   *Perf. 11¾*
344   12k 1776 urn   1.10 .55
345   18k 1734 urn   1.75 .85
a. A180 Pair, #344-345   3.00 1.50

Issued in sheets of 8.
See Israel #1380-1381.

Albín
Brunovsky
(1935-97),
Stamp
Designer
A181

Photo. & Engr.
1999, Dec. 18   *Perf. 12x11¼*
346 A181 5k multi   .60 .25
Complete booklet, 9 #346   8.00

Stamp Day. Issued se-tenant with label.

Rivers and Gaps — A182

Designs: a, 10k, Dunajec. b, 12k, Váh.

Litho. & Engr.
2000, Jan. 1   *Perf. 11¾*
347 A182 Pair, #a.-b.   2.25 1.75
Issued in sheets of 8.

Famous
People — A183

4k, Hana Melickova (1900-78), actress. 5k,
Stefan Anián Jedlik (1800-95), inventor.

Photo. & Engr.
2000, Jan. 11   *Perf. 11½x11¼*
348 A183 4k multi   .40 .25
349 A183 5k multi   .60 .25

Basketball — A184

Photo. & Engr.
2000, Feb. 15   *Perf. 11¼x11½*
351 A184 4k multi   .40 .25

Ruzomberok team, 1999 European
Women's Basketball League champions.

World Mathematics Year — A185

2000, Feb. 15   *Perf. 11¾x11¼*
352 A185 5k multi   .55 .25

Juraj Hronec (1881-1959), Stefan Schwarz
(1914-96), mathematicians.

Easter — A186

2000, Feb. 15   Engr.   *Perf. 11¼x11½*
353 A186 4k brown   .40 .25
Complete booklet, 10 #353   4.00

Ján Holly
(1785-1849),
Poet — A187

Photo. & Engr.
2000, Mar. 24   *Perf. 11½x11¼*
354 A187 5.50k multi   .55 .25

Europa, 2000
Common Design Type
Litho. & Engr.
2000, May 9   *Perf. 11¾*
355 CD17 12k multi   1.10 .55

UNICEF
A188

Photo. & Engr.
2000, June 1   *Perf. 11½x11¼*
356 A188 5.50k multi   .55 .25

A189   A190

Postman and Austria design A1.

Photo. & Engr.
2000, June 1   *Perf. 11¼x11¾*
357 A189 10k multi   1.10 .45

First postage stamp used in Slovakia, 150th
anniv.

     Perf. 11¾x11¼
2000, June 15   Engr.
358 A190 5.50k Pres. Rudolf
       Schuster   .80 .25

See also No. 421.

2000 Summer Olympics,
Sydney — A191

Photo. & Engr.
2000, June 27   *Perf. 11¼x11½*
359 A191 18k multi + label   2.50 2.00

Organization for
Security and
Cooperation in
Europe, 25th
Anniv. — A192

2000, Aug. 18   *Perf. 11½x11¼*
361 A192 4k black & blue   .40 .25

Wooden
Bridge,
Kluknava
A193

2000, Sept. 14   *Perf. 11¼*
362 A193 6k multi   .60 .30

Souvenir Sheet

Berries — A194

No. 363: a, 11k, Rubus idaeus. b, 13k, Fragaria vesca. c, 15k, Vaccinium myrtillus.

Litho. & Engr.
2000, Sept. 14   *Perf. 11¾*
363 A194 Sheet of 3, #a-c   3.75 2.75

Holy Year
2000 — A195

Photo. & Engr.
2000, Oct. 5   *Perf. 11¼x11½*
364 A195 4k multi   .40 .25
    Booklet, 10 #364   4.00

Postal Agreement
with Sovereign
Military Order of
Malta — A196

2000, Oct. 13   *Perf. 11¼x11¾*
365 A196 10k multi   1.10 .45

Art Type of 1996
Designs: 18k, Nativity, from church in
Spisska Stara Ves. 20k, Crucifixion, from
church in Kocelovce, horiz.

Perf. 11½x11¾, 11¾x11½
2000, Oct. 17   **Engr.**
366-367 A126   Set of 2   3.50 2.50

Stamp Day — A197

Photo. & Engr.
2000, Dec. 18   *Perf. 11¾x11½*
368 A197 5.50k multi + label   1.10 .25
    Booklet, 9 #368   11.00

POFIS, 50th Anniv.

History of
Postal
Law
A198

2000, Dec. 18   **Engr.**   *Perf. 11¾*
369 A198 20k multi   2.75 2.00

Issued in sheets of 4.

Mantel Clock, c.   Janko Blaho
1780 — A199   (1901-81),
               Singer — A200

Photo. & Engr.
2001, Jan. 1   *Perf. 11¼x11½*
370 A199 13k multi   1.25 .60

2001, Jan. 15
371 A200 5.50k multi   .55 .25

2001 European
Figure Skating
Championships,
Bratislava — A201

2001, Jan. 16
372 A201 16k multi   1.40 .70

Agricultural Control Institute, 50th
Anniv. — A202

2001, Feb. 22   *Perf. 11¾x11¼*
373 A202 12k multi   1.10 .55

Traditional
Costumes — A203

Designs: 5.50k, Man from Detva. 6k,
Woman and child from Detva.

2001, Feb. 22   *Perf. 11¼x11½*
374 A203 5.50k multi   .50 .25
    Booklet, 10 #374   5.00
375 A203   6k multi   .60 .30
    Booklet, 10 #375   6.50

Archaeological Sites — A204

No. 376: a, 12k. Havránok. b, 15k, Ducové.

2001, Apr. 10   **Engr.**   *Perf. 11¾*
376 A204   Horiz. pair, #a-b   2.10 1.75
Issued in sheets of 4 pairs + 1 label.

Europa
A205

2001, May 5   **Engr.**   *Perf. 11¾*
379 A205 18k multi   1.40 .85

Issued in sheets of 10.

Souvenir Sheet

Princes of Great Moravia — A206

No. 380: a, 6k, Pribina. b, 9k, Rastislav. c,
11k, Kocel. d, 14k, Svatopluk.

Litho. & Engr.
2001, July 4   *Perf. 11¾*
380 A206   Sheet of 4, #a-d   3.25 3.00

Souvenir Sheet

Wild Animals — A207

No. 381: a, 14k, Ursus arctos. b, 15k, Canis
lupus. c, 16k, Lynx lynx.

2001, July 10   *Perf. 11¾x11½*
381 A207   Sheet of 3, #a-c   4.25 4.25

Dobro Resonator Guitar and US
Map — A208

Photo. & Engr.
2001, Aug. 1   *Perf. 11¾x11¼*
382 A208 19k multi   1.75 .85

Bratislava
Biennale of
Illustrators
A209

2001, Aug. 15   *Perf. 11½x11¼*
383 A209 7k multi   .65 .30
    Booklet, 10 #383   6.50

The
Righteous
Among
Nations
A210

2001, Sept. 9   *Perf. 11¾x11¼*
384 A210 14k multi   1.25 .60

Souvenir Sheet

Alexander Dubcek (1921-92),
Czechoslovakian Communist
Leader — A211

Litho. & Engr.
2001, Sept. 18   *Perf. 11¾*
385 A211 18k multi   1.60 1.25

Banská Bystrica   Remembrance
Postal Museum   of Political Trial
A212   Victims
                     A213

Photo. & Engr.
2001, Oct. 9   *Perf. 11¼x11½*
386 A212 6k multi   .55 .25

2001, Oct. 9
387 A213 10k multi   1.10 .45

Maria Valeria Bridge
Reconstruction — A214

2001, Oct. 11   *Perf. 11¾x11¼*
388 A214 10k multi   1.10 .45

See Hungary No. 3776.

Art Type of 1996
Designs: 16k, Raftsman's Dream, by Imrich
Weiner-Král'. 18k, Light of the Soul, by Albín
Brunovsky. 20k, St. Michael the Archangel
with Saints, by unknown artist.

2001, Oct. 15   **Engr.**   *Perf. 11¾*
389-391 A126   Set of 3   4.50 3.50

Christmas
A215

Photo. & Engr.
2001, Oct. 15   *Perf. 11½x11¼*
392 A215 5.50k multi   .55   .25
      Booklet, 10 #392   5.50

Famous
Men — A216

Designs: 10k, Juraj Papánek (1738-1802),
historian. 14k, Bjornsterne Bjornson (1832-
1910), 1903 Nobel laureate for Literature.

2002, Jan. 15
393-394 A216   Set of 2   2.25 1.00

2002
Winter
Olympics,
Salt Lake
City
A217

2002, Jan. 25   *Perf. 11¾x11¼*
395 A217 18k multi   1.60   .80

European Dog
Sled
Championships
A218

Easter
A219

2002, Feb. 8   *Perf. 11¼x11½*
396 A218 6k multi   .55   .25

2002, Feb. 15
397 A219 5.50k multi   .55   .25
      Booklet, 10 #397   5.50

First Slovakian
High
Schools — A220

Designs: 12k, Martin, 1866. 13k, Revuca,
1862. 15k, Klástor pod Znievom, 1869.

2002, Mar. 20   *Perf. 11½x11¼*
398-400 A220   Set of 3   3.50 1.50

Castles and Churches Type of 1995
        Perf. 11¾x11¼, 11¼x11¾
2002   **Photo. & Engr.**
401 A100 10k Kezmarok   1.25   .55
402 A100 16k Levoca, horiz.   1.50   .75
      Issued: 10k, 5/6; 16k, 4/18.

Europa — A221

2002, May 6   **Engr.**   *Perf. 11¾*
403 A221 18k multi   1.75   .85
      Issued in sheets of 8.

Wine Production — A222

Designs: 7k, Barrels. 9k, Wine press.

Photo. & Engr.
2002, June 24   *Perf. 11¾x11¼*
Stamps + labels
404-405 A222   Set of 2   1.60 1.00

Souvenir Sheet

Butterflies — A223

No. 406: a, 10k, Zerynthia polyxena. b, 16k,
Inachis io. c, 25k, Papilio machaon.

Litho. & Engr.
2002, June 26   *Perf. 11¾*
406 A223   Sheet of 3, #a-c, + 4
             labels   8.00 5.00

Souvenir Sheet

Alexander Cardinal Rudnay (1760-
1831) — A224

2002, July 4   **Engr.**
407 A224 17k multi   2.25 2.00

Doves and Roses — A225

Photo. & Engr.
2002, July 4   *Perf. 11¾x11¼*
408 A225 6k multi + label   .90   .55
      Issued in sheets of 12 stamps + 12 labels
which could be personalized.

Victory at 2002 World Ice Hockey
Championships — A226

2002, July 4
409 A226 10k multi   1.10   .45

Architecture in Slovakia and
China — A227

No. 410: a, 6k, Handan Congtai Pavilion,
People's Republic of China. b, 12k, Bojnice
Castle, Slovakia.

2002, Oct. 12   *Perf. 11¾x11½*
410 A227   Horiz. pair, #a-b   1.75   .85
      Issued in sheets of 4 pairs.
      See People's Republic of China No. 3239.

Kosice
Technological
University, 50th
Anniv.
A228

Christmas
A229

Photo. & Engr.
2002, Oct. 17   *Perf. 11¼x11½*
411 A228 6k multi   .55   .25

2002, Nov. 8
412 A229 5.50k multi   .55   .25
      Complete booklet, 10 #412   6.00

Churches — A230

Designs: 7k, St. Michael's Church, Klizske
Hradiste. 14k, St. George's Rotunda, Skalica.
22k, St. Martin's Cathedral, Spisska Kapitula.

2002, Nov. 15   **Engr.**   *Perf. 11¾x11½*
413-415 A230   Set of 3   4.00 2.00
      Issued in sheets of 10.

Miniature Sheet

Astronaut Eugene Cernan and Lunar
Rover — A231

Photo. & Engr.
2002, Dec. 6   *Perf. 11¾x11¼*
416 A231 20k multi + label   2.25 1.75
      Apollo 17 mission, 30th anniv.

Art Type of 1996

Designs: 20k, The Beheading of St. John
the Baptist, by Master Pavol of Levoca. 23k, In
the Studio, by Koloman Sokol.

2002   **Engr.**   *Perf. 11¾*
417-418 A126   Set of 2   4.00 2.00
      Nos. 417-418 issued in sheets of 4.
      Issued: 20k, 12/18; 23k, 12/12.

Stamp Day — A232

Photo. & Engr.
2002, Dec. 18   *Perf. 11¾x11¼*
419 A232 10k multi + 2 labels 1.10   .45
      Nitrafila Stamp Exhibition, Nitra.

Independent
Slovakia, 10th
Anniv. — A233

        Perf. 11¾x11½
2003, Jan. 1   **Litho. & Engr.**
420 A233 20k multi   1.75   .85
      Issued in sheets of 6.

Pres. Schuster Type of 2000
2003, Feb. 5   **Engr.**   *Perf. 11¾x11¼*
421 A190 7k blue   .65   .30

Roses — A234

Photo. & Engr.
2003, Feb. 14   *Perf. 11½x11¼*
422 A234 7k multi   .65   .30
    a.   Sheet of 8 + 8 labels 12.00 6.00
      No. 422a issued 4/30. Labels on No. 422a
could be personalized.

Easter — A235

2003, Mar. 10   *Perf. 11¼x11½*
423 A235 7k multi   .65 .30
    Booklet, 10 #423   6.50

Churches and Castles Type of 1995-2001
Photo. & Engr.
2003   *Perf. 11¾x11¼*
424 A100 18k Kremnica   1.35 .75
425 A100 100k Pezinok   7.75 3.75

    Issued: 18k, 3/20, 100k, 9/18.

Souvenir Sheet

Saints Cyril and Methodius — A236

    No. 426: a, 17k, St. Cyril. b, 22k, St. Methodius.

Litho. & Engr.
2003, Apr. 6   *Perf. 11¾*
426 A236   Sheet of 2, #a-b, + 2   3.75 3.00
      labels

Ludwig van Beethoven (1770-1827), Composer A237

Photo. & Engr.
2003, Apr. 24   *Perf. 11½x11¼*
427 A237 15k multi   1.25 .60

Milan Stefánik (1880-1919), Czechoslovakian General — A238

Litho. & Engr.
2003, May 3   *Perf. 11¾*
428 A238 14k multi   1.40 .75

    Issued in sheets of 8.
    See France No. 2942.

Europa — A239

2003, May 9
429 A239 14k multi   1.25 .60
    Issued in sheets of 10.

Art Type of 1996
Design: The Brook, by Ladislav Mednansky, horiz.

2003, May 9   Engr.   *Perf. 11¾*
430 A126 18k multi   1.60 .80
    Issued in sheets of 4.

Sts. Benedict and Andrej Svorad — A240

Photo. & Engr.
2003, May 16   *Perf. 11½x11¼*
431 A240 13k multi   1.25 .60

Third Place Finish of Slovakian Ice Hockey Team at World Championships, Finland — A241

2003, May 30   Litho.   *Perf. 13½*
432 A241 20k multi   1.90 .95
    Issued in sheets of 4.

Matko and Kubko — A242

Photo. & Engr.
2003, June 1   *Perf. 11¼x11½*
433 A242 7k multi   .65 .30
    Complete booklet, 10 #433   6.50
    Intl. Children's Day.

Worldwide Fund for Nature (WWF) — A243

    Various views of Felis silvestris silvestris: a, 13k. b, 14k. c, 16k. d, 18k.

Litho. & Engr.
2003, June 25   *Perf. 11¾*
434 A243   Sheet of 4, #a-d   5.75 3.50

World Swimming Championships, Barcelona A244

Photo. & Engr.
2003, July 7   *Perf. 11½x11¼*
435 A244 11k multi   1.10 .50

Banska Stiavnica Reservoirs — A245

    No. 436: a, 9k, Lake Klinger. b, 12k, Rozgrund Reservoir.

2003, July 15   Engr.   *Perf. 11¾*
436 A245   Pair, #a-b   2.00 1.00
    Issued in sheets of 4 pairs + 1 label.

Bratislava Biennale of Illustrators — A246

Photo. & Engr.
2003, Aug. 15   *Perf. 11¼x11½*
437 A246 12k multi   1.10 .55
    Complete booklet, 10 # 437   11.00

Visit of Pope John Paul II — A247

Die Cut Perf. 14¾x14½
2003, Sept. 7   Litho.
Self-Adhesive
438 A247 12k violet   1.10 .55
    Issued in sheets of 4.

Father Ján Baltazár Magin (1681-1734), Poet — A248

Photo. & Engr.
2003, Sept. 17   *Perf. 11½x11¼*
439 A248 8k multi   .75 .35

Christmas A249

2003, Oct. 30
440 A249 7k multi   .65 .30
    Complete booklet, 10 #440   6.50

Bronze Buttons, Sword Hilt and Cross A250

2003, Nov. 17   *Perf. 11¾x11¼*
441 A250 18k multi   1.75 .85
    "Travel of History" exhibit of archaeological treasures.

Powered Flight, Cent. — A251

2003, Nov. 17   *Perf. 11½x11¼*
442 A251 18k multi   1.75 .85

Art Type of 1996
Designs: 14k, St. Catherine, by Simon Vouet. 16k, Bagpipes, by Rudolf Krivos, horiz. 21k, The Annunciation, by Master Jan.

2003, Nov. 28   Engr.   *Perf. 11¾*
443-445 A126   Set of 3   4.50 2.25
    Nos. 443-445 issued in sheets of 4.

Marginal Design from Czechoslovakia No. 2517 Sheet, by Josef Baláz — A252

Photo. & Engr.
2003, Nov. 28   *Perf. 11¾x11¼*
446 A252 12k multi + label   1.10 .55
    Stamp Day.

Castles and Churches Type of 1995-2001
2004, Jan. 30   Litho.   *Perf. 14¼x14*
447 A100 9k Liptovsky Mikulás,   .85 .40
      horiz.

St. Valentine's Day — A253

Litho. & Embossed
2004, Jan. 30   *Perf. 11¾*
448 A253 8k multi   .75 .35

Lilium Royal Parade — A254

Perf. 14¾x14½ Syncopated
2004, Feb. 12   Litho.
449 A254 8k multi   .75 .35

Tulip Kaufmanniana — A255

2004, Feb. 12   *Perf. 13¼*
450 A255 9k multi + label   .85 .40

    Printed in sheets of 8 + 8 labels which could be personalized. Value (any label picture), mint $8, used $6.

Easter Egg — A256

2004, Mar. 10   *Die Cut Perf. 14½*
Self-Adhesive
451 A256 8k multi   1.25 .80
 a.   Booklet pane of 10   12.50

Wedding Clothing From Pata — A257

Designs: 15k, Groom. 28k, Bride.

2004, Apr. 16   *Perf. 13¼*
452-453 A257   Set of 2   4.00 2.00

Europa — A258

Perf. 14x14¼ Syncopated
2004, Apr. 23
454 A258 20k multi   1.90 .95

Issued in sheets of 10.

Admission Into European Union A259

2004, May 1   *Perf. 13½*
455 A259 18k multi   1.75 .85

Issued in sheets of 10.

Admission Into NATO — A260

2004, May 1   *Perf. 14*
456 A260 60k multi   5.00 2.50

Grandfather, From Evening Tales Television Program — A261

2004, May 21   *Perf. 13¼*
Granite Paper
457 A261 8k multi   1.00 .35

2004 Paralympics, Athens — A262

2004, May 31   *Perf. 13¼x13½*
458 A262 34k multi   3.00 1.50

Pres. Ivan Gasparovic — A263

2004, June 15   *Perf. 13*
Granite Paper
459 A263 8k multi   .90 .35

Dobroc Forest A264

2004, June 17   *Perf. 14*
Granite Paper
460 A264 12k multi   1.10 .55

Tatra Omnibus, 1904-06 A265

2004, June 30   *Perf. 13¼x13½*
Granite Paper
461 A265 14k multi   1.25 .60

Issued in sheets of 8.

Spania Valley Mining Water System A266

2004, June 30   **Granite Paper**
462 A266 24k multi   2.25 1.10

Issued in sheets of 8.

Dunajec River Raftsmen — A267

2004, Sept. 3   *Perf. 13¼x13*
463 A267 21k multi   2.00 1.00

See Poland No. 3752.

Roman Legions in Trencin — A268

2004, Oct. 15   *Perf. 13*
464 A268 26k multi   2.25 1.10

Art Type of 1996

Designs. 33k, Cock Fight, by Jakub Bogdan, horiz. 35k, Don Quixote, by Július Jakoby.

Litho. & Engr.
2004, Oct. 20   *Perf. 11¾*
465-466 A126   Set of 2   6.50 5.50

Nos. 465-466 issued in sheets of 4.

Christmas A269

2004, Nov. 5   **Litho.**   *Perf. 13*
467 A269 8k multi   .75 .35
   Complete booklet, 10 #467   7.50

Medalists at 2004 Summer Olympics — A270

No. 468: a, Jozef Gonci, air rifle bronze medalist. b, Kayak 1000-meter fours team, bronze medalists. c, Jozef Krnac, 66-kilogram judo silver medalist. d, Michal Martikán, men's canoe slalom silver medalist. e, Elena Kaliská,

women's canoe slalom gold medalist. f, Pavol and Peter Hochschornerovci, canoe slalom doubles gold medalists.

Serpentine Die Cut 12½
2004, Nov. 5   **Litho.**
Self-Adhesive
468   Booklet of 6   10.00
a.-b.   A270 8k Either single   1.00 .75
c.-d.   A270 14k Either single   1.25 .85
e.-f.   A270 20k Either single   2.50 1.10

Stamp Day — A271

2004, Dec. 18   *Perf. 13*
469 A271 9k multi   1.00 .40

St. Valentine's Day — A272   Family — A273

2005, Jan. 31   **Litho.**   *Perf. 13½*
470 A272 9k multi   1.00 .40

2005, Feb. 14   *Perf. 13½x13*
471 A273 9k multi   1.00 .40

Banska Bystrica, 750th Anniv. A274

2005, Feb. 14   *Perf. 13½*
472 A274 16k multi   1.50 .75

Summit Meeting of Presidents George W. Bush and Vladimir Putin A275

2005, Feb. 24   *Perf. 13*
473 A275 25k multi   2.40 1.25

Easter — A276

2005, Mar. 10   **Litho.**   *Perf. 13½*
474 A276 9k multi   .85 .40
   Complete booklet, 10 #474   8.50

Beatification of Sister Zdenka Schelingová — A277

2005, Mar. 10   *Perf. 13x13¼*
475 A277 34k multi   3.25 3.75

Cycling for the Handicapped A278

2005, Mar. 30   *Perf. 13½*
476 A278 22k multi   2.00 .95

Poor Mother, by Frantisek Studeny — A279

Perf. 11¾x11½
2005, Mar. 30   **Litho. & Engr.**
477 A279 25k blk & lt grn   2.25 1.50

Issued in sheets of 8.
An unstated portion of the receipts were donated to UNICEF for relief works for the Dec. 26, 2004 tsunami.

Europa A280

2005, Apr. 22   **Litho.**   *Perf. 13¾*
478 A280 19k multi   1.75 .85

Issued in sheets of 8.

Peace of Bratislava (Pressburg), Bicent. — A281

2005, Apr. 29   *Perf. 13½*
479 A281 23k multi   2.00 1.00

Intl. Year of
Physics
A282

2005, May 16   Litho.   *Perf. 13½*
480 A282 18k multi   1.90   .85

Fish — A283

2005, May 23   Litho.   *Perf. 13½*
481 A283 9k multi   .85   .40
Complete booklet, 10 #481   13.00

Biennale of
Children's Book
Illustrations,
Bratislava — A284

2005, May 23
482 A284 30k multi   2.75 1.40

Holic and Town   Pres. Ivan
Arms   Gasparovic
A285   A286

2005, June 3   Litho.   *Perf. 13¼x13*
483 A285 22k multi   2.10 1.00

Perf. 11¾x11¼
2005, June 15   Litho. & Engr.
484 A286 9k brn & buff   .85   .40

Souvenir Sheet

Horses — A287

No. 485: a, 29k, Lippizaners, carriage. b,
31k, Slovak warm-bloods, rider.

2005, June 30   *Perf. 11¾*
485 A287 Sheet of 2, #a.-b. 7.00 4.50

Locomotives — A288

Designs: 24k, Ciernohronska Railroad. 33k,
Vychylovka.

Litho. & Engr.
2005, Sept. 22   *Perf. 11¾*
486-487 A288 Set of 2   8.00 5.00
Nos. 486-487 issued in sheets of 8 + 1 label.

Art Type of 1996
Designs: 28k, Supper at Emmaus, by Rem-
brandt. 35k, Magic of Still Life Paintings V, by
Karol Baron, horiz.

2005, Oct. 20   Engr.
488-489 A126 Set of 2   5.50 2.75
Nos. 488-489 issued in sheets of 4.

Christmas — A289

2005, Nov. 16   Litho.   *Perf. 13¼*
490 A289 9k multi   1.00   .40
Complete booklet, 10 #490   10.00

Stamp Day — A290

2005, Nov. 25   *Perf. 13¼x13½*
491 A290 15k multi + label 2.00   .70

Karol Kuzmány
(1806-66),
Writer — A291

2006, Feb. 3   *Perf. 13½*
492 A291 16k multi   1.10   .75

2006, Feb. 3   *Perf. 13¼x13½*
493 A292 21k multi + label 5.00 3.00

2006 Winter Olympics, Turin — A292

Poprad and Town
Arms — A293

2006, Feb. 3   *Perf. 13¼*
494 A293 23k multi   1.60 1.10

Narcissus — A294

2006, Mar. 24   Litho.   *Perf. 13¼*
495 A294 10k multi   .85   .55

Easter — A295

2006, Mar. 31   *Perf. 13½*
496 A295 10k multi   .75   .55
Complete booklet, 10 #496   8.00

Souvenir Sheet

Geological Formations — A296

No. 497: a, 32k, Sandberg. b, 35k,
Somoska.

Litho. & Engr.
2006, Apr. 21   *Perf. 11¾*
497 A296 Sheet of 2, #a-b 7.50 6.00

Europa
A297

Litho. & Embossed
2006, May 5   *Perf. 13¼x13*
498 A297 18k multi   1.75   .85
Issued in sheets of 10.

Belfries — A298

Designs: 27k, Kezmarok. 29k, Podolinec.

Photo. & Engr.
2006, May 19   *Perf. 11½x11¾*
499-500 A298 Set of 2   4.50 3.50

Children's   Shepherd's
Art — A299   Pipe — A300

2006, May 31   Litho.   *Perf. 11¼*
501 A299 10k multi   1.00   .55
Complete booklet, 10 #501   10.00

2006, June 9   *Perf. 11¼x12¼*
502 A300 25k multi   2.00 1.50

Devín Castle — A301

2006, June 9   Litho.   *Perf. 12¾x12¼*
503 A301 10k multi + label 3.00 2.00
Printed in sheets of 8 + 8 labels which could
be personalized.

Objects in
Museums — A302

Designs: 28k, Blue cobalt glass goblet, 16th
cent. 31k, Copper measuring cup, 1576.

Litho. & Engr.
2006, June 23   *Perf. 11¾*
504-505 A302 Set of 2   5.25 4.00
Nos. 504-505 issued in sheets of 8 containing 4 of each stamp.

Puppets — A303

Designs: 22k, Indonesian puppet. 25k,
Slovakian marionette.

2006, July 27   Litho.   *Perf. 13¼x13*
506-507 A303 Set of 2   4.00 3.00
Nos. 506-507 issued in sheets of 6 containing 3 of each stamp.
See Indonesia No. 2092.

Art Type of 1996
Designs: 37k, Krivy Jarok, by Dezider Milly,
horiz. 38k, Moravian Venus sculpture
fragment.

2006, Oct. 20   Engr.   *Perf. 11¾*
508-509 A126 Set of 2   7.00 4.25
Nos. 508-509 issued in sheets of 4.

Christmas
A304

2006, Nov. 10   Litho.   *Perf. 11*
510 A304 10k multi   .75   .50
Complete booklet, 10 #510   8.00

Jozef Cincík (1909-92), Stamp
Designer — A305

2006, Nov. 24   *Perf. 13¼x12½*
511 A305 19k multi   1.75   .85
Stamp Day.

Modra and Town
Arms — A306

2007, Feb. 7   Litho.   Perf. 12¼x11½
512 A306 14k multi   1.25   .75

Terézia Vansová
(1857-1942),
Writer — A307

2007, Feb. 7   Perf. 11
513 A307 19k multi   1.60   .80

Flowers   Easter
A308   A309

2007, Feb. 14   Perf. 12x11½
514 A308 (10k) multi   1.00   .55

2007, Mar. 15   Perf. 11x11¼
515 A309 10k multi   1.00   .50
    Complete booklet, 10 #515   12.00

Women's
Tennis — A310

2007, Mar. 21   Perf. 11
516 A310 16k multi   1.30   .80

Souvenir Sheet

Dogs — A311

No. 517: a, Slovakian cuvac. b, Slovakian
kopov.

Litho. & Engr.
2007, Apr. 18   Perf. 11¾
517 A311 31k Sheet of 2, #a-b   10.00 10.00

Slovak League
of America,
Cent. — A312

2007, May 15 Litho. Perf. 11¾x11½
518 A312 22k multi   1.60 1.10

Janko Hrasko, by
Stefan
Cpin — A313

2007, May 30   Perf. 13½
519 A313 10k multi   1.25   .55
    Complete booklet, 10 #519   13.00

Europa
A314

2007, May 30   Perf. 13¾
520 A314 18k multi   1.60   .80
    Issued in sheets of 10.

Monasteries
A315

Designs: 30k, Jasov Monastery. 34k, Hronsky Benadik Monastery.

Photo. & Engr.
2007, June 6   Perf. 11¼x11¾
521-522 A315 Set of 2   7.50 4.75

Biennale of
Children's Book
Illllustrations,
Bratislava — A316

2007, June 27   Litho.   Perf. 13½
523 A316 25k multi   2.25 1.75

Souvenir Sheet

Bratislava Castle — A317

Litho. & Engr.
2007, June 27   Perf. 11¾x12
524 A317 37k multi   10.00 3.00

Castles — A318

No. 525: a, Rocca, San Marino. b, Orava
Castle, Slovakia.

2007, Aug. 24   Perf. 11¾
525 A318 21k Horiz. pair, #a-b   6.00 4.00

No. 525 was printed in sheets containing
four pairs. See San Marino No. 1729.

Jozef Miloslav
Hurban (1817-88),
Nationalist
Leader — A319

2007, Sept. 1 Litho. Perf. 11¼x11¾
526 A319 31k multi   2.25 1.75

Král'ova
Bridge,
Senec
A320

Photo. & Engr.
2007, Sept. 5   Perf. 11¼
527 A320 29k multi   3.00 1.75

Gospel Book of
Nitra — A321

2007, Sept. 22   Perf. 11¼x11¾
528 A321 15k multi   1.10   .75

Robert William
Seton-Watson
(1879-1951),
Historian
A322

2007, Oct. 26 Litho. Perf. 11¾x11¼
529 A322 24k multi   1.90 1.50

Art Type of 1996
Designs: No. 530, 33k, St. Elizabeth of Hungary, by Frantisek X. K. Palko. No. 531, 33k,
Bouquet of Chrysanthemums, by Ján Zelib-
sky, horiz.

2007, Nov. 14   Engr.   Perf. 11¾
530-531 A126 Set of 2   6.00 4.25
    Each stamp printed in sheets of 4.

Christmas — A323

Perf. 11¼x11¾
2007, Nov. 14   Litho.
532 A323 10k multi   1.00   .50
    Complete booklet, 10 #532   12.00

Field Post — A324

2007, Nov. 28   Perf. 11¾x11¼
533 A324 28k multi + label   3.00 1.75
    Stamp Day.

Independence, 15th Anniv. — A325

2008, Jan. 1   Litho.   Perf. 11¾x11¼
534 A325 (16k) multi   1.40   .70

Easter — A326

2008, Feb. 28   Perf. 11¼x11¾
535 A326 (10k) multi   .75   .55
    Complete booklet, 10 #535   8.00

Krupina Arms and
Church — A327

2008, Mar. 6   Perf. 11¾x11¼
536 A327 (14k) multi   1.25   .80

Dahlias — A328

2008, Mar. 20
537 A328 (10k) multi + label   2.50 1.50

Printed in sheets of 8 stamps + 8 labels that
could be personalized.

Constitutional
Court, 15th
Anniv. — A329

2008, Apr. 3   Perf. 11¼x11¾
538 A329 25k multi   2.50 1.75

Eugen Suchon
(1908-93),
Composer — A330

2008, Apr. 17
539 A330 (15k) multi   1.50 1.10

Masa
Hal'amová
(1908-86),
Poet — A331

2008, Apr. 17   Perf. 11¾x11¼
540 A331 (18k) multi   1.75 1.25

1872
Smekal
Fire
Pumper
A332

1880 Seltenhofer Fire Pumper — A333

2008, Apr. 30   Litho. & Engr.
541 A332 (19k) multi   1.50 1.10
542 A333 (31k) multi   2.50 2.00

Europa — A334

2008, May 5   Litho.   Perf. 11¼x11¾
543 A334 21k multi   2.50 2.00

Multi-headed
Dragon from
Stories by Pavol
Dobsinsky — A335

2008, May 29   Perf. 11¼x11½
544 A335 (10k) multi   .75 .55
  Complete booklet, 10 #544   7.50

2008 Summer Olympics,
Beijing — A336

2008, June 4   Perf. 11¾x11¼
545 A336 25k multi   4.00 1.50

2008 Paralympics, Beijing — A337

2008, June 6
546 A337 30k multi   4.00 2.00

9th Cent. Copper
Plaque Found at
Bojná — A338

Litho. & Engr.
2008, June 30   Perf. 11¾
547 A338 33k multi + label   5.00 3.00
  Printed in sheets of 3 stamps + 3 labels.

Souvenir Sheet

Karol Plicka (1894-1987),
Photographer — A339

2008, Sept. 12
548 A339 40k multi + 2 labels 4.50 3.00
  See Czech Republic No. 3397.

Coronation
of King
Matthias
Corvinus,
550th Anniv.
A340

2008, Sept. 25   Litho.   Perf. 11¼
549 A340 (16k) multi   1.50 .75

Wooden Churches — A341

No. 550 — Church in: a, Hervartov. b, Dobroslava.

Litho. & Engr.
2008, Oct. 9   Perf. 11¾
550 A341 (18k) Horiz. pair, #a-b,
  + central label   6.00 5.00
  Printed in sheets containing two of each stamp + 2 labels.

Orchids
A342

Designs: (14k), Cypripedium calceolus. (15k), Ophrys apifera.

Photo. & Engr.
2008, Oct. 23   Perf. 12x11¼
551-552 A342   Set of 2   4.00 3.00
  No. 551 is inscribed "T2 100g;" No. 552, "T2 500g."

Christmas — A343

Perf. 11¼x11¾
2008, Nov. 13   Litho.
553 A343 (10k) multi   .85 .40
  Complete booklet, 10 #553   8.50

Post Rider For Bratislava-Ruzomberok-
Kosice Mail Route — A344

2008, Nov. 27   Perf. 11¾x11¼
554 A344 (16k) multi + label 1.90 .70
  Stamp Day.

Art Type of 1996

Designs: (31k), Illustration by Josef Baláz, from book *The Seven-colored Flower*. (37k), A Girl in White with Factory Chimneys and Flowers, by Zoltán Palugyay.

2008, Nov. 27   Engr.   Perf. 11¾
555-556 A126   Set of 2   5.75 3.00
  Nos. 555-556 each were printed in sheets of 4. No. 555 is inscribed "T2 1000g"; No. 556, "T1 1000g."

100 Cents = 1 Euro

Euro Symbol and
Map of
Slovakia — A345

Perf. 11¾x11½
2009, Jan. 1   Litho. & Engr.
557 A345 €1 multi   2.75 1.40
  Introduction of Euro currency.

A346

Churches and Their
Decorations — A347

Designs: 1c, Chapel of St. Margaret, Kopcany. 2c, Sculpture from Church of the Virgin Mary, Boldog. 5c, Rotunda of Church of St. Margaret, Sivetice. 10c, Altar from Church of St. John the Baptist, Pominovce. 20c, Church, Svätuse. 33c, Church, Cierny Brod. 50c, Sculpture of lion from Church of St. Martin, Spisská Kapitula, horiz. 66c, Columns, Church of St. Egidius, Ilija, vert. 83c, Mural from Church of St. Stephen the King, Zilina-Zavodie, vert. €1, Capital from Church of the Virgin Mary, Bina. €2, Church of St. Michael the Archangel, Drazovce.
€1.33, Church of the Holy Cross, Hamuliakovo.

Photo. & Engr., Litho. (33c, 66c, 83c)
Perf. 11¾x11¼, 11¼x11¾
2009, Jan. 2
558 A346   1c multi   .25 .25
559 A346   2c multi   .25 .25
560 A346   5c multi   .25 .25
561 A346   10c multi   .30 .25
562 A346   20c multi   .55 .25
563 A347   33c multi   .95 .45
564 A346   50c multi   1.40 .70
565 A347   66c multi   1.90 .95
566 A347   83c multi   2.40 1.25
567 A346   €1 multi   2.75 1.40
568 A346   €2 multi   5.50 2.75
  Nos. 558-568 (11)   16.50 8.75

Souvenir Sheet
Perf. 11¾
569 A346 €1.33 multi   3.75 1.90
  See Nos. 587, 610, 631.

Easter — A348

Perf. 11¾x11¼
2009, Feb. 27   Litho.
570 A348 33c multi   2.50 .40
Serpentine Die Cut 16½x15
Booklet Stamp
Self-Adhesive
570A A348 33c multi   3.00 .40
  b.   Booklet pane of 10   30.00

Karate — A349

2009, Mar. 13   Perf. 11¼x11¾
571 A349 60c multi   1.60 .80

Aurel Stodola
(1859-1942),
Engineer
A350

2009, Apr. 17   Perf. 11¾x11¼
572 A350 33c multi   .90 .45

Union of Slovak Philatelists, 40th
Anniv. — A351

Perf. 11½x11¼
2009, Apr. 29 **Litho. & Engr.**
573 A351 (33c) multi + label .90 .45

Supreme Audit
Office, 40th
Anniv. — A352

Photo. & Engr.
2009, May 7 **Perf. 11½x11¼**
574 A352 80c multi 2.25 1.10

Europa
A353

2009, May 28 **Litho.** **Perf. 11¾x11¼**
575 A353 90c multi 2.50 1.25
Intl. Year of Astronomy.

Souvenir Sheet

Zofia Bosniaková (1609-44), Founder
of Poorhouse — A354

Litho. & Engr.
2009, June 2 **Perf. 11¾**
576 A354 80c multi 2.25 1.10

Souvenir Sheet

Pres. Ivan Gasparovic — A355

Litho. With Foil Application
2009, June 15 **Perf. 11¾x12**
577 A355 €1 gold + 2 labels 3.00 1.50

2009 Biennale of
Illustrations,
Bratislava — A356

2009, Aug. 14 **Engr.** **Perf. 11¼x11¾**
578 A356 (33c) brown .95 .45

Souvenir Sheet

Archaeological Excavations of Roman
Military Camps — A357

No. 579: a, Carnuntum. b, Gerulata.

Perf. 11½x11¾
2009, Sept. 11 **Litho. & Engr.**
579 A357 60c Sheet of 2, #a-b 3.50 1.75
See Austria No. 2220.

Nature
Preservation
A358

Designs: No. 580, €1.10, Salamandra salamandra. No. 581, €1.10, Emys orbicularis.

2009, Oct. 23 **Perf. 11¾x11½**
580-581 A358 Set of 2 6.50 3.25
Nos. 580-581 were printed in sheets of 6
containing 3 of each stamp.

Christmas — A359

Perf. 11¼x11¾
2009, Nov. 11 **Litho.**
582 A359 40c multi 1.25 .60
Booklet Stamp
Self-Adhesive
Serpentine Die Cut 15x16½
583 A359 40c multi 2.00 .60
a. Booklet pane of 10 20.00

Art Type of 1996
Designs: No. 584, €1.20, Madonna with
Black Nimbus, by Ján Mudroch. No. 585,
€1.20, Don Quixote, by Cyprián Majerník.

2009, Nov. 27 **Engr.** **Perf. 11¾**
584-585 A126 Set of 2 7.25 3.75
Nos. 584-585 were each printed in sheets of
4 + 2 labels.

Louis Braille (1809-52), Educator of
the Blind — A360

2009, Dec. 4 **Litho.** **Perf. 11¾x11¼**
586 A360 70c multi + label 2.10 1.10
Stamp Day.

**Church Art and Architecture Type of
2009**
Design: Cross, Church of the Assumption of
the Virgin Mary, Spisská Nová Ves.

Photo. & Engr.
2010, Jan. 4 **Perf. 11¾x11¼**
587 A346 60c multi 1.75 .85

2010 Winter Olympics,
Vancouver — A361

2010, Jan. 15 **Litho.**
588 A361 €1 multi 2.75 1.40

Pres. Ivan
Gasparovic — A362

2010, Jan. 29 **Photo. & Engr.**
589 A362 40c multi 1.10 .55

Easter — A363

Perf. 11¼x11¾
2010, Feb. 26 **Litho.**
590 A363 40c multi 1.10 .55
Serpentine Die Cut 15x16½
Booklet Stamp
Self-Adhesive
591 A363 40c multi 1.10 .55
a. Booklet pane of 10 11.00

Count
Matthew
Csák of
Trencin (c.
1260-1321),
Palatine
A364

2010, Mar. 12 **Litho.** **Perf. 11¼**
592 A364 70c multi 1.90 .95

Souvenir Sheet

Zilina Synod, 400th Anniv. — A365

Litho. & Engr.
2010, Mar. 30 **Perf. 11¾**
593 A365 €1.10 multi 3.00 1.50

Milan Hodza
(1878-1944),
Journalist
A366

2010, Apr. 16 **Litho.** **Perf. 11¾x11¼**
594 A366 40c multi 1.10 .55

Europa — A367

2010, May 4 **Perf. 11¼x11¾**
595 A367 90c multi 2.40 1.25

Souvenir Sheet

2010 World Cup Soccer
Championships, South Africa — A368

**Litho. With Three-Dimensional
Plastic Affixed**
2010, June 8 **Die Cut**
Self-Adhesive
596 A368 Sheet of 2 11.00 5.50
a. €2.30 Single stamp 5.50 2.75

Topol'cianky Castle — A369

Betliar
Castle
A370

Photo. & Engr.
2010, June 18   *Perf. 11¾x11¼*
597   A369   40c multi   1.00   .50
598   A370   40c multi   1.00   .50

Miniature Sheet

Saints — A371

No. 599: a, St. Gorazd. b. St. Clement.

2010, July 16   *Perf. 11¾*
599   A371   Sheet of 5, 3
      #599a, 2 #599b, +
      5 labels   8.00 4.00
a.-b.   60c Either single   1.60   .80

Topol'cany Castle — A372

Perf. 11¾x11¼
2010, Sept. 17   **Litho.**
600   A372   40c multi + label   1.10   .55
   Printed in sheets of 8 stamps + 8 labels that could be personalized.

Egyptian Alabaster
Canopic
Jar — A373

2010, Oct. 8   **Litho. & Engr.**
601   A373   €1 multi   2.75 1.40
     See Egypt No.

Miniature Sheet

Protected Flowers of the Muránska
Plain — A374

No. 602: a, Primula auricula. b, Daphne
arbuscula.

2010, Oct. 15   *Perf. 11½x11¾*
602   A374   Sheet of 4, 2 each
      #a-b, + 2 labels   9.00 4.50
a.-b.   80c Either single   2.25 1.10

Christmas — A375

Perf. 11¼x11¾
2010, Nov. 12   **Litho.**
603   A375   40c multi   1.10   .55

Self-Adhesive
Booklet Stamp
Serpentine Die Cut 15x16½
604   A375   40c multi   1.10   .55
a.   Booklet pane of 10   11.00

Art Type of 1996
   Designs: No. 605, €1.20, Coronation of
Charles I of Hungary (Charles Robert), by
unknown artist, St. Martin Cathedral, Spisská
Kapitula (denomination in black). No. 606,
€1.20, Madonna and Child, statue by Master
Paul of Levoca, Assumption of the Virgin Mary
Church, L'ubica (denomination in blue).

2010, Nov. 26   **Engr.**   *Perf. 11¾*
605-606   A126   Set of 2   6.50 3.25
   Nos. 605-606 each were printed in sheets of
4 + 2 labels

Campaign
Against
AIDS — A376

2010, Dec. 1   **Litho.**   *Perf. 11¼*
607   A376   40c multi   1.10   .55
   No. 607 has a die cut cross-shaped hole at
lower left.

Karol Ondreicka (1944-2003), Stamp
Designer — A377

Perf. 11¾x11¼
2010, Dec. 3   **Litho. & Engr.**
608   A377   70c multi + label   1.90   .95
     Stamp Day.

Intl. Year of Chemistry — A378

2011, Jan. 17   **Litho.**   *Perf. 11¾x11¼*
609   A378   80c multi + label   2.25 1.10

Churches and Their Decorations
Type of 2009
   Designs: Sculpture of St. George Killing
Dragon, Church of St. George, Svaty Jur.

2011, Jan. 28   **Photo. & Engr.**
610   A346   70c multi   1.90   .95

Visegrád Group, 20th Anniv. — A379

2011, Feb. 11   **Litho.**
611   A379   90c multi   2.50 1.25
   See Czech Republic No. 3490, Hungary No.
4183, Poland No. 4001.

Meringue
Lamb — A380

2011, Mar. 4   *Perf. 11¾x11¼*
612   A380   40c multi   1.10   .55
     Easter.

2011 World Ice Hockey
Championships, Slovakia — A381

   No. 614: a, 40c, Slovakian player Pavol
Demitra (1974-2011). b, 50c, Russian
goaltender.

Perf. 11¼x11¾
2011, Mar. 25   **Litho.**
614   A381   Horiz. pair, #a-b   2.60 1.25

Dobsinská Ice
Cave UNESCO
World Heritage
Site — A382

Perf. 11¾x11½
2011, Apr. 15   **Litho. & Engr.**
615   A382   €1.10 multi   3.25 1.60

Beatification of
Pope John Paul
II — A383

2011, Apr. 29   *Perf. 11¾*
616   A383   40c multi   1.25   .60
   Pritned in sheets of 4 + label.

Europa — A384

2011, May 6
617   A384   90c multi   2.60 1.25
     Intl. Year of Forests.

Flower — A385

2011, June 3   **Litho.**   *Perf. 11¼x11¾*
618   A385   (40c) multi + label   1.25   .60
   Printed in sheets of 8 stamps + 8 labels that
could be personalized.

Souvenir Sheet

Memorandum of the Slovak Nation,
150th Anniv. — A386

Litho. & Engr.   *Perf. 11¾*
2011, June 6
619   A386   €1.20 multi   3.50 1.75

Old Automobiles — A387

Designs: 40c, Aero 30. 80c, Tatra 87.

Photo. & Engr.
2011, July 1   *Perf. 11¾x11¼*
620-621   A387   Set of 2   3.50 1.75

Ján Cikker
(1911-89),
Composer
A388

2011, July 29   **Litho.**
622   A388   50c multi   1.50   .75

2011 Biennale of Illustrations, Bratislava — A389

2011, Sept. 2   *Perf. 11¼x11¾*
623 A389 40c multi   1.10 .55

Michal Miloslav Hodza (1811-70), Nationalist Leader and Poet — A390

Photo. & Engr.
2011, Sept. 22   *Perf. 11½x11¼*
624 A390 40c multi   1.10 .55

Otis Tarda — A391

Litho. & Engr.
2011, Oct. 14   *Perf. 11¾*
625 A391 €1.10 multi   3.00 1.50
Printed in sheets of 4 + 2 labels.

Fish-shaped Honey Cake — A392

Perf. 11¾x11¼
2011, Nov. 11   **Litho.**
626 A392 40c multi   1.10 .55
Christmas. No. 626 is impregnated with a cinnamon scent.

Art Type of 1996
Design: Woodcut of Historian Ján Sambucus (1534-81), by Tobias Stimmer.

Litho. & Engr.
2011, Nov. 25   *Perf. 11¾*
628 A126 €1.20 blk & beige   3.25 1.60

Mailbox and Postrider — A393

2011, Dec. 2 Litho. *Perf. 11¾x11¼*
629 A393 50c multi + label   1.40 .70
Stamp Day.

Souvenir Sheet

Virgin and Child with St. Anne (Roznava Metercia), by Unknown Artist — A394

Litho. & Engr.
2011, Dec. 13   *Perf. 11¾*
630 A394 €1.60 multi   4.25 2.10

Churches and Their Decorations Type of 2009
Design: Angel, Piarist Church, Prievidza.

Photo. & Engr.
2012, Jan. 27   *Perf. 11¾x11¼*
631 A346 80c multi   2.10 1.10

Jonás Záborsky (1812-76), Writer — A395

2012, Feb. 3   **Litho.**
632 A395 40c multi   1.10 .55

Samo Chalupka (1812-83), Poet — A396

2012, Feb. 27
633 A396 50c multi   1.40 .70

Christ Carrying the Cross, by Hans von Aachen — A397

2012, Mar. 9   *Perf. 11¾x11¼*
634 A397 40c multi   1.10 .55

Booklet Stamp
Self-Adhesive
Serpentine Die Cut 16½x15
635 A397 40c multi   1.10 .55
  a.   Booklet pane of 10   11.00

SEMI-POSTAL STAMPS

Josef Tiso — SP1

Wmk. 263
1939, Nov. 6   Photo.   *Perf. 12½*
B1 SP1 2.50k + 2.50k royal blue 3.75 *4.00*
The surtax was used for Child Welfare.

Medical Corpsman and Wounded Soldier — SP2

1941, Nov. 10
B2 SP2 50h + 50h dull green   .60 .60
B3 SP2 1k + 1k rose lake   .60 .60
B4 SP2 2k + 1k brt blue   1.90 1.50
   Nos. B2-B4 (3)   3.10 2.70

Mother and Child — SP3

1941, Dec. 10
B5 SP3 50h + 50h dull green   1.00 .90
B6 SP3 1k + 1k brown   1.00 .90
B7 SP3 2k + 1k violet   1.00 .90
   Nos. B5-B7 (3)   3.00 2.70
Surtax for the benefit of child welfare.

Soldier and Hlinka Youth — SP4

1942, Mar. 14
B8   SP4 70h + 1k brown org   .50 .30
B9   SP4 1.30k + 1k brt blue   .50 .30
B10 SP4 2k + 1k rose red   1.50 1.10
   Nos. B8-B10 (3)   2.50 1.70
The surtax aided the Hlinka Youth Society "Hlinkova Mladez."

SP5

SP6

National Costumes — SP7

1943   *Perf. 14*
B11 SP5 50h + 50h dk slate grn   .30 .25
B12 SP6 70h + 1k dp carmine   .30 .25
B13 SP7 80h + 2k dark blue   .40 .40
   Nos. B11-B13 (3)   1.00 .90
The surtax was for the benefit of children, the Red Cross and winter relief of the Slovakian popular party.

Infantrymen — SP8

Aviator — SP9

Tank and Gun Crew SP10

1943, July 28
B14 SP8   70h + 2k rose brown   .80 *.95*
B15 SP9   1.30k + 2k sapphire   .80 *.95*
B16 SP10 2k + 2k olive green   .80 *.95*
   Nos. B14-B16 (3)   2.40 2.85
The surtax was for soldiers' welfare.

"The Slovak Language Is Our Life" — L. Stur — SP11

Slovakian National Museum SP12

Slovakian Foundation SP13

Slovakian Peasant — SP14

1943, Oct. 16
B17 SP11 30h + 1k brown red   .50 .35
B18 SP12 70h + 1k slate green   .50 .35
B19 SP13 80h + 2k slate blue   .50 .35
B20 SP14 1.30k + 2k dull brown   .50 .35
   Nos. B17-B20 (4)   2.00 1.40
The surtax was for the benefit of Slovakian cultural institutions.

Soccer Player — SP15

Skier — SP16   Diver — SP17

Relay
Race — SP18

1944, Apr. 30   **Unwmk.**

B21	SP15	70h + 70h slate grn	.75	.90
B22	SP16	1k + 1k violet	.75	.90
B23	SP17	1.30k + 1.30k Prus bl	.75	.90
B24	SP18	2k + 2k chnt brn	.75	.90
	Nos. B21-B24 (4)		3.00	3.60

Symbolic of
National
Protection
SP19

1944, Oct. 6   **Wmk. 263**

B25	SP19	70h + 4h sapphire	.90	1.00
B26	SP19	1.30k + 4k red brown	.90	1.00

The surtax was for the benefit of social
institutions.

Children — SP20

1944, Dec. 18

B27	SP20	2k + 4k light blue	3.00	4.00
a.		Sheet of 8 + Label	50.00	70.00

The surtax was to aid social work for Slovak
youth.

Red Cross — SP21

Photo. & Engr.

1993, Nov. 15   *Perf. 11x11½*

B28	SP21	3k +1k red & gray blue	.40	.40

Souvenir Sheet

1996 Summer Olympics,
Atlanta — SP22

Photo. & Engr.

1996, May 15   *Perf. 12x11½*

B29	SP22	12k +2k multi	1.50	1.50

Surcharge for Slovak Olympic Committee.

AIR POST STAMPS

Planes over Tatra Mountains
AP1   AP2

Perf. 12½

1939, Nov. 20   Photo.   Unwmk.

C1	AP1	30h violet	.40	.40
C2	AP1	50h dark green	.40	.40
C3	AP1	1k vermilion	.40	.40
C4	AP2	2k grnsh black	.65	.65
C5	AP2	3k dark brown	1.00	1.00
C6	AP2	4k slate blue	1.90	1.90
	Nos. C1-C6 (6)		4.75	4.75

See No. C10.

Plane in
Flight — AP3

1940, Nov. 30   Wmk. 263   *Perf. 12½*

C7	AP3	5k dk violet brn	1.50	1.50
C8	AP3	10k gray black	1.75	1.75
C9	AP3	20k myrtle green	2.25	2.25
	Nos. C7-C9 (3)		5.50	5.50

Type of 1939

1944, Sept. 15   **Wmk. 263**

C10	AP1	1k vermilion	1.50	1.50

PERSONAL DELIVERY STAMPS

PD1

1940   Wmk. 263   Photo.   *Imperf.*

EX1	PD1	50h indigo & blue	1.00	1.75
EX2	PD1	50h carmine & rose	1.00	1.75

POSTAGE DUE STAMPS

D1

1939   Unwmk.   Photo.   *Perf. 12½*

J1	D1	5h bright blue	1.00	.55
J2	D1	10h bright blue	.50	.55
J3	D1	20h bright blue	.50	.55
J4	D1	30h bright blue	3.00	1.00
J5	D1	40h bright blue	.70	.75
J6	D1	50h bright blue	2.50	.80
J7	D1	60h bright blue	2.00	.80
J8	D1	1k dark carmine	14.00	8.25
J9	D1	2k dark carmine	14.00	2.50
J10	D1	5k dark carmine	8.00	2.50
J11	D1	10k dark carmine	55.00	7.50
J12	D1	20k dark carmine	18.00	9.25
	Nos. J1-J12 (12)		119.20	35.00

1940-41   **Wmk. 263**

J13	D1	5h bright blue ('41)	.75	.55
J14	D1	10h bright blue ('41)	.30	.30
J15	D1	20h bright blue ('41)	.30	.30
J16	D1	30h bright blue ('41)	4.00	2.00
J17	D1	40h bright blue ('41)	.60	.55
J18	D1	50h bright blue ('41)	.75	.95
J19	D1	60h bright blue	.90	.95
J20	D1	1k dark carmine ('41)	.90	1.10
J21	D1	2k dark carmine ('41)	20.00	9.00
J22	D1	5k dark carmine ('41)	4.00	2.75
J23	D1	10k dark carmine ('41)	3.00	3.25
	Nos. J13-J23 (11)		35.70	21.70

Letter, Post
Horn — D2

1942   Unwmk.   *Perf. 14*

J24	D2	10h deep brown	.25	.25
J25	D2	20h deep brown	.25	.25
J26	D2	40h deep brown	.25	.25
J27	D2	50h deep brown	1.00	.60
J28	D2	60h deep brown	.25	.25
J29	D2	80h deep brown	.30	.25
J30	D2	1k rose red	.35	.25
J31	D2	1.10k rose red	.70	.60
J32	D2	1.30k rose red	.50	.25
J33	D2	1.60k rose red	.50	.25
J34	D2	2k rose red	1.00	.25
J35	D2	2.60k rose red	1.50	1.25
J36	D2	3.50k rose red	11.00	9.00
J37	D2	5k rose red	3.00	2.25
J38	D2	10k rose red	4.00	3.25
	Nos. J24-J38 (15)		24.85	19.20

NEWSPAPER STAMPS

 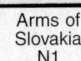

Newspaper Stamps of
Czechoslovakia, 1937,
Overprinted in Red or
Blue

1939, Apr.   Unwmk.   *Imperf.*

P1	N2	2h bister brn (Bl)	.50	.40
P2	N2	5h dull blue (R)	.50	.40
P3	N2	7h red org (Bl)	.50	.40
P4	N2	9h emerald (R)	.50	.40
P5	N2	10h henna brn (Bl)	.50	.40
P6	N2	12h ultra (R)	.50	.40
P7	N2	20h dk green (R)	1.10	.95
P8	N2	50h dk brown (Bl)	3.00	2.50
P9	N2	1k grnsh gray (R)	11.00	10.00
	Nos. P1-P9 (9)		18.10	15.85

Excellent counterfeits exist of Nos. P1-P9.

Arms of
Slovakia
N1

Type Block "N"
(for "Noviny" -
Newspaper)
N2

1939   **Typo.**

P10	N1	2h ocher	.30	.25
P11	N1	5h ultra	.45	.40
P12	N1	7h red orange	.35	.30
P13	N1	9h emerald	.35	.30
P14	N1	10h henna brown	1.60	1.10
P15	N1	12h dk ultra	.40	.35
P16	N1	20h dark green	1.60	1.10
P17	N1	50h red brown	1.90	1.25
P18	N1	1k grnsh gray	1.60	1.10
	Nos. P10-P18 (9)		8.55	6.15

1940-41   **Wmk. 263**

P20	N1	5h ultra	.25	.25
P23	N1	10h henna brown	.25	.25
P24	N1	15h brt purple ('41)	.30	.25
P25	N1	20h dark green	.60	.50
P26	N1	25h lt blue ('41)	.60	.50
P27	N1	40h red org ('41)	.60	.50
P28	N1	50h chocolate	1.10	.75
P29	N1	1k grnsh gray ('41)	1.10	.75
P30	N1	2k emerald ('41)	2.25	1.60
	Nos. P20-P30 (9)		7.05	5.35

1943   Photo.   Unwmk.

P31	N2	10h green	.25	.25
P32	N2	15h dark brown	.25	.25
P33	N2	20h ultra	.35	.35
P34	N2	50h rose red	.35	.35
P35	N2	1k slate green	.45	.45
P36	N2	2k intense blue	.65	.65
	Nos. P31-P36 (6)		2.30	2.30

SLOVENIA

slō-'vē-nē-ə

LOCATION — Southeastern Europe
GOVT. — Independent state
AREA — 7,819 sq. mi.
POP. — 1,970,570 (1999 est.)
CAPITAL — Ljubljana

A constitutent republic of Yugoslavia
since 1945, Slovenia declared its independence on June 25, 1991.

100 Paras = 1 Dinar
100 Stotin = 1 Tolar
100 Cents = 1 Euro (2007)

Declaration of
Independence
A18

1991, June 26   Litho.   *Perf. 10½*

100	A18	5d Parliament building	1.10	1.10

National Arms
A19   A20

1991-92   *Perf. 14*

Background Color

101	A19	1t brown	.35	.35
102	A20	1t brown	.35	.35
103	A20	2t lilac rose	.35	.35
104	A19	4t green	.35	.35
105	A20	4t green	.35	.35
106	A19	5t salmon	.35	.35
107	A20	5t salmon	.35	.35
108	A20	6t yellow	.50	.50
109	A19	11t orange	.70	.70
110	A20	11t orange	.50	.50
111	A20	15t blue	.50	.50

112 A20 20t purple   1.10 1.10
113 A20 50t dark green   1.60 1.60
114 A20 100t gray   2.60 2.60
    Nos. 101-114 (14)   9.95 9.95

Issued: #107, 3/6/91; #101, 104, 106, 109, 12/26/91; #102, 6t, 20t, 50t, 100t, 2/12/92; 2t, 15t, #105, 110, 3/16/92.

1992 Winter Olympics,
Albertville — A21

a, 30t, Ski jumper. b, 50t, Alpine skier.

1992, Feb. 8
134 A21 Pair, #a.-b., + 1 or 2 la-
          bels   7.50 7.50

Rhomboid stamps issued in sheets of 3 #134 plus 4 labels. See No. 143.

Ljubljana
Opera
House,
Cent.
A22

1992, Mar. 31
135 A22 20t multicolored   1.40 1.40

Giuseppe Tartini
(1692-1770),
Italian Violinist
and Composer
A23

1992, Apr. 8
136 A23 27t multicolored   1.50 1.50

Discovery
of
America,
500th
Anniv.
A24

Designs: a, 27t, Map of northwestern Mexico and Gulf of California, Marko Anton Kappus preaching to natives. b, 47t, Map of parts of North and South America, sailing ship.

1992, Apr. 21
137 A24 Pair, #a.-b.   8.00 8.00

Issued in sheets containing 6 No. 137.

Intl. Conference of Interior Designers,
Ljubljana — A25

1992, May 17
138 A25 41t multicolored   1.50 1.50

A. M. Slomsek   Mountain Rescue
(1800-1862),   Service, 80th
Bishop of   Anniv. — A27
Maribor — A26

1992, May 29
139 A26 6t multicolored   .65   .65

1992, June 12
140 A27 41t multicolored   1.50 1.50

A28

1992, June 20
141 A28 6t multicolored   .40   .40

Ljubljana Boatmen's Competition, 900th anniv.

A29

1992, June 25
142 A29 41t multicolored   1.50 1.50

Independence, 1st anniv.

Olympic Type of 1992

a, 40t, Leon Stukelj, triple medalist in 1924, 1928. b, 46t, Olympic rings, three heads of Apollo.

1992, July 25
143 A21 Pair, #a.-b. +1 or 2 la-
          bels   3.75 3.75

1992 Summer Olympics, Barcelona. Rhomboid stamps issued in sheets of 3 #143 plus 4 labels.

World
Championship of
Registered
Dogs,
Ljubljana — A30

1992, Sept. 4
144 A30 40t Slovenian sheep dog 1.50 1.50

Marij Kogoj
(1892-1956),
Composer
A31

1992, Sept. 30
145 A31 40t multicolored   1.50 1.50

Self-Portrait, by
Matevz Langus
(1792-1855),
Painter — A32

1992, Oct. 30
146 A32 40t multicolored   1.50 1.50

Christmas
A33

Designs: 6t, 7t, Nativity Scene, Ljubljana. 41t, Stained glass window of Madonna and Child, St. Mary's Church, Bovec, vert.

1992
147   A33 6t multicolored   .25   .25
147A A33 7t multicolored   .50   .50
148   A33 41t multicolored   1.25 1.25
     Nos. 147-148 (3)   2.00 2.00

Issued: 6t, 41t, Nov. 20. 7t, Dec. 15.

Herman Potocnik, Theoretician of
Geosynchronous Satellite Orbit, Birth
Cent. — A34

1992, Nov. 27   Litho.   Perf. 14
149 A34 46t multicolored   1.50 1.50

Prezihov Voranc (1893-1950),
Writer — A35

1993, Jan. 22   Litho.   Perf. 14
150 A35 7t multicolored   .35   .35

Rihard Jakopic (1869-1943),
Painter — A36

1993, Jan. 22
151 A36 44t multicolored   1.25 1.25

Jozef
Stefan
(1835-93),
Physicist
A37

1993, Jan. 22
152 A37 51t multicolored   1.40 1.40

A38

Designs: 1t, Early cake. 2t, Pan pipes. 5t, Kozolec. 6t, Early building. 7t, Zither. 8t, Water mill. 9t, Sled. 10t, Lonceni bajs. 11t, Kraski kos. 12t, Statue of boy on horseback, Ribnica. 20t, Cross-section of house. 44t, Stone building. 50t, Wind-powered pump. 100t, Potica.

1993-94
153   A38 1t multicolored   .35   .35
154   A38 2t multicolored   .35   .35
155   A38 5t multicolored   .35   .35
156   A38 6t multicolored   .35   .35
157   A38 7t multicolored   .35   .35
158   A38 8t multicolored   .35   .35
159   A38 9t multicolored   .35   .35
160   A38 10t multicolored   .35   .35
160A A38 11t multicolored   .35   .35
160B A38 12t multicolored   .35   .35
161   A38 20t multicolored   .45   .45
162   A38 44t multicolored   .70   .70
163   A38 50t multicolored   .95   .95
164   A38 100t multicolored   1.75 1.75
     Nos. 153-164 (14)   7.35 7.35

Issued: 1t, 6t, 7t, 44t, 2/18/93; 2t, 5t, 10t, 20t, 50t, 5/14/93; 8t, 9t, 8/25/93; 11t, 12t, 7/8/94.

See #208A-220, 370, 373-379, 616-623. For surcharge see #371.

Mountain
Climbers
A39

1993, Feb. 27
165 A39 7t shown   .30   .30
166 A39 44t Route map, moun-
          tain   1.10 1.10

Slovenian Alpine Club, centennial (#165). Joza Cop (1893-1975), mountain climber (#166).

A40

1993, Mar. 19
167 A40 7t multicolored   .30   .30

Slovenian Post Office, 75th anniv.

A41

7t, Altarpiece, by Tintoretto. 44t, Coat of arms.

1993, Apr. 9   Litho.   *Perf. 14*
168 A41 7t multicolored   .30   .30
169 A41 44t multicolored   1.10   1.10

Collegiate Church of Novo Mesto, 500th anniv.

Contemporary Art — A42

Europa: 44t, Round Table of Pompeii, by Marij Pregelj (1913-1967). 159t, Little Girl at Play, by Gabrijel Stupica (1913-1990).

1993, Apr. 29   Litho.   *Perf. 14*
170   44t multicolored   *1.50   1.50*
171   159t multicolored   *3.75   3.75*
  a. A42 Pair, #170-171   *6.00   6.00*

Schwagerina Carniolica — A43

1993, May 7
172 A43 44t multicolored   1.10   1.10

Admission of Slovenia to UN, 1st Anniv. A44

1993, May 21   Litho.   *Perf. 14*
173 A44 62t multicolored   1.50   1.50

Mediterranean Youth Games, Agde, France — A45

1993, June 8
174 A45 36t multicolored   1.00   1.00

Battle of Sisak, 400th Anniv. A46

1993, June 22   Litho.   *Perf. 14*
175 A46 49t multicolored   1.40   1.40

Aphaenopidius Kamnikensis — A47

Designs: 7t, Monolistra spinosissima. 55t, Proteus anguinus. 65t, Zospeum spelaeum.

1993, July 12   Litho.   *Perf. 14*
176 A47 7t multicolored   .30   .30
177 A47 40t multicolored   .80   .80
178 A47 55t multicolored   1.25   1.25
179 A47 65t multicolored   1.60   1.60
  Nos. 176-179 (4)   *3.95   3.95*

A48

1993, July 30
180 A48 65t multicolored   1.50   1.50

World dressage competition.

A49

Coats of Arms: 9t, Janez Vajkard Valvasor. 65t, Citizen's Academy of Ljubljana.

1993, Oct. 29   Litho.   *Perf. 14*
181 A49 9t multicolored   .30   .30
182 A49 65t multicolored   1.40   1.40

Christmas A50

Designs: 9t, Slovenian Family Viewing Nativity, by Maxim Gaspari (1883-1980). 65t, Archbishop Joze Pogacnik (1902-80), writer.

1993, Nov. 15
183 A50 9t multicolored   .30   .30
184 A50 65t multicolored   1.40   1.40

Famous People — A51

Works by: 8t, Josip Jurcic (1844-81), writer. 9t, Simon Gregorcic (1844-1906), poet. 55t, Stanislav Skrabec (1844-1918), linguist. 65t, Jernej Kopitar (1780-1844), linguist.

1994, Jan. 14   Litho.   *Perf. 14*
185 A51 8t multicolored   .30   .30
186 A51 9t multicolored   .30   .30
187 A51 55t multicolored   1.25   1.25
188 A51 65t multicolored   1.40   1.40
  Nos. 185-188 (4)   *3.25   3.25*

Love — A52

1994, Jan. 25
189 A52 9t multicolored   .35   .35

1994 Winter Olympics, Lillehammer — A53

1994, Feb. 4
190 A53 9t Cross-country skiing .25   .25
191 A53 65t Slalom skiing   1.25   1.25
  a. Pair, #190-191   1.50   1.50

World Ski Jumping Championships, Planica — A54

1994, Mar. 11   Litho.   *Perf. 14*
192 A54 70t multicolored   1.60   1.60

City of Ljubljana, 850th Anniv. A55

1994, Mar. 25   Litho.   *Perf. 14*
193 A55 9t multicolored   .25   .25

Europa — A56

70t, Janez Puhar, camera. 215t, Moon, Jurij Vega.

1994, Apr. 22
194 A56 70t multicolored   1.10   1.10
195 A56 215t multicolored   3.75   3.75
  a. Pair, #194-195   5.00   5.00

Miniature Sheet

Flowers of Slovenia — A57

Designs: a, 9t, Primula carniolica. b, 44t, Hladnikia pastinacifolia. c, 60t, Daphne blagayana. d, 70t, Campanula zoysii.

1994, May 20   Litho.   *Perf. 14*
196 A57 Sheet of 4 + 2 labels   4.25   4.25

1994 World Cup Soccer Championships, U.S. — A58

1994, June 10
197 A58 44t multicolored   .90   .90

Intl. Olympic Committee, Cent. A59

1994, June 10
198 A59 100t multicolored   2.25   2.25

Mt. Ojstrica — A60   Max Pletersnik, Professors — A61

1994, July 1   Litho.   *Perf. 14*
199 A60 12t multicolored   .40   .40

1994, July 22
200 A61 70t multicolored   1.50   1.50

First Slovenian-German dictionary published by Max Pletersnik (1840-1932), cent.

Battle of the Frigidus, 1600th Anniv. A62

1994, Sept. 1   Litho.   *Perf. 14*
201 A62 60t multicolored   1.50   1.50

Maribor Post Office, Cent. A63

1994, Sept. 23   Litho.   *Perf. 14*
202 A63 70t multicolored   1.50   1.50

Ljubljana-Novo Mesto Railway, Cent. — A64

1994, Sept. 24   Litho.   *Perf. 14*
203 A64 70t Locomotive 5722,
            1893   1.50   1.50

See Nos. 233, 243, 291, 325, 363.

Philharmonic Assoc., Bicent. — A65

Designs: 12t, Building, Ljubljana. 70t, Beethoven, Brahms, Dvorak, Haydn, Paganini.

1994, Oct. 20
204 A65 12t multicolored .30 .30
205 A65 70t multicolored 1.40 1.40

Black Madonna of Loreto, 700th Anniv. — A66

1994, Nov. 18
206 A66 70t multicolored 1.50 1.50

Christmas — A67   Intl. Year of the Family — A68

1994, Nov. 18
207 A67 12t multicolored .30 .30

1994, Nov. 18
208 A68 70t multicolored 1.40 1.40

Type of 1993

13t, Wind rattle, Prlekija. 14t, Sentjernej pottery cock. 15t, Blast furnace, Zelezniki. 16t, Windmill, Stara Gora. 17t, Corn storage building. 55t, Easter eggs, Bela Krajina. 65t, Cobbler's lamp with glass spheres, Trzic. 70t, Snow skis. 75t, 1812 Iron window lattice, Srednja vas, Bohinj. 80t, Palm Sunday bundle. 90t, Beehive. 200t, "Zajec," insect-shaped bootjack, Dvor. 300t, Slamnati doznjek. 400t, Wine press. 500t, Kumer family's table, Koprivna, Carinthia.

1994-99   Litho.   Perf. 14
Size 25x34mm
208A A38 13t multicolored .50 .25
208B A38 14t multicolored .25 .25
209 A38 15t multicolored .25 .25
210 A38 16t multicolored .25 .25
210A A38 17t multicolored .25 .25
211 A38 55t multicolored .60 .60
212 A38 65t multicolored .80 .80
213 A38 70t multicolored 1.00 1.00
214 A38 75t multicolored 1.00 1.00
215 A38 80t multicolored 1.25 1.25
216 A38 90t multicolored 1.40 1.40
217 A38 200t multicolored 2.50 2.50
218 A38 300t brown 5.00 5.00
219 A38 400t brown & lake 7.25 7.25
220 A38 500t multicolored 7.00 7.00
Nos. 208A-220 (15) 29.30 29.05

Issued: 300t, 400t, 11/7/94; 70t, 11/16/95; 55t, 65t, 75t, 3/22/96; 80t, 3/20/97; 13t, 14t, 8/8/97; 90t, 5/30/97; 15t, 6/23/98; 200t, 500t, 11/12/98; 16t, 2/5/99; 17t, 5/7/99.

Ljubljana University, 75th Anniv. A69

Design: 70t, Provincial palace buildings, founders, I. Hribar, M. Rostohar, D. Majaron.

1994, Dec. 3   Litho.   Perf. 14
221 A69 70t multicolored 1.50 1.50

Postal Service Emblem — A70

1995, Jan. 27
222 A70 13t multicolored .40 .40

Love — A71

1995, Feb. 7
223 A71 20t multicolored .50 .50

Famous People — A72

Works by: 20t, Anton Tomaz Linhart (1756-95), playwright, horiz. No. 225, Ivan Vurnik (1884-1971), architect. No. 226, Lili Novy (1885-1958), poet, horiz.

1995, Feb. 7
224 A72 20t multicolored .50 .50
225 A72 70t multicolored 1.50 1.50
226 A72 70t multicolored 1.50 1.50
Nos. 224-226 (3) 3.50 3.50

A73

1995, Mar. 29   Litho.   Perf. 14
227 A73 13t multicolored .45 .45
End of World War II, 50th anniv.

A74

1995, Mar. 29
228 A74 70t Karavankina schellwieni 1.60 1.60

Liberation of the Concentration Camps, 50th Anniv. — A75

Europa: 60t, Skeleton of Death lying on bride. 70t, Nike going from dark to light.

1995, Mar. 29
229 A75 60t multicolored 1.50 1.50
230 A75 70t multicolored 1.50 1.50
a. Pair, #229-230 4.00 4.00

#230a was issued in sheets of 4.

European Nature Conservation Year — A76

1995, Mar. 29
231 A76 70t Triglav Natl. Park 1.60 1.60

Town of Radovljica, 500th Anniv. A77

1995, June 8   Litho.   Perf. 14
232 A77 44t multicolored 1.00 1.00

Railways Type of 1994
Design: 70t, Locomotive KRB 37, Podnart.

1995, June 8
233 A64 70t multicolored 1.50 1.50
Ljubljana-Jesenice Line, 125th anniv.

Aljaz Tower, Cent. — A78

1995, June 8   Perf. 13½
234 A78 100t multicolored 2.10 2.10
Portions of the design on No. 234 were applied by a thermogrphic process producing a shiny, raised effect.

Endangered Birds — A79

Designs: a, 13t, Falco naumanni. b, 60t, Coracias garrulus. c, 70t, Lanius minor. d, 215t, Emberiza melanocephala.

1995, June 8   Perf. 14
235 A79 Block of 4, #a.-d. 7.00 7.00

Slovenian Boy Scouts A80

1995, Sept. 26   Litho.   Perf. 14
236 A80 70t multicolored 1.50 1.50

Comtemporary Art, by France Kralj — A81

1995, Sept. 26
237 A81 60t Death of a Genius, 1921 1.40 1.40
238 A81 70t Family of Horses, 1959 1.60 1.60
a. Pair, #237-238 3.00 3.00

A82

UN, FAO, 50th Anniv.: No. 239, Stylized pictures of food products, faces of people from many nations. No. 240, Black & white figures touching hands, faces of people from many nations.

1995, Sept. 26
239 A82 70t multicolored 1.50 1.50
240 A82 70t multicolored 1.50 1.50
a. Pair, #239-240 3.25 3.25

Issued in miniature sheets of 4 stamps.

A83

Christmas (Paintings): 13t, Winter, by Marlenka Stupica. 70t, St. Mary of Succour, Brezje, by Leopold Layer.

1995, Nov. 16
241 A83 13t multicolored .30 .30
a. Booklet pane of 10 + 2 labels 3.50 3.50
Complete booklet 3.50 3.50
242 A83 70t multicolored 1.50 1.50
a. Booklet pane of 10 + 2 labels 16.00 16.00
Complete booklet 16.00 16.00

Railways Type of 1994
Design: 70t, Locomotive "Aussee."

1996, Jan. 31   Litho.   Perf. 14
243 A64 70t multicolored 1.50 1.50
The Graz-Celje Line, 150th anniv.

St. Gregory's Day — A84

1996, Jan. 31   Litho.   Perf. 14
244 A84 13t multicolored .50 .50

Carnival Costumes A85

1996, Jan. 31
245 A85 13t Ptujsko region .30 .30
246 A85 70t Dravsko region 1.50 1.50
See Nos. 281-282, 384-385.

Emys Orbicularis A86

World Wildlife Fund: a, 13t, Peeking head out of water. b, 50t, Two young. c, 60t, Adult crawling though water. d, 70t, Laying eggs.

1996, Jan. 31
247 A86 Strip of 4, #a.-d. 4.25 4.25
No. 247 printed in sheets of 4 vertical or horizontal strips, each having a different order.

Fran Saleski Finzgar (1871-1962), Writer, Priest — A87

1996, Apr. 18 Litho. Perf. 14
248 A87 13t multicolored .30 .30

A88

1996, Apr. 18
249 A88 65t multicolored 1.40 1.40
UNICEF, 50th anniv.

A89

Paintings: 65t, Children on Grass (detail). 75t, Bouquet of Dahlias.

1996, Apr. 18
250 65t multicolored 1.50 1.50
251 75t multicolored 1.50 1.50
a. A89 Pair, Nos. 250-251 3.00 3.00
Ivana Kobilca (1861-1926), painter. Issued in sheets of 8 stamps. Europa.

Ita Rina (1907-79), Film Actress A90

1996, Apr. 18
252 A90 100t multicolored 1.60 1.60

Visit of Pope John Paul II, May 17-19 — A91

1996, Apr. 18
253 A91 75t multicolored 1.50 1.50
Souvenir Sheet
254 A91 200t multicolored 3.75 3.75

City of Zagorje ob Savi, 700th Anniv. A92

1996, June 6 Litho. Perf. 14
255 A92 24t Gallenberg Castle .50 .50

World Junior Cycling Championships, Novo Mesto — A93

1996, June 6
256 A93 55t multicolored 1.00 1.00

Independence, 5th Anniv. — A94

1996, June 6
257 A94 75t multicolored 1.50 1.50

Mushrooms — A95

Designs: a, 65t, Cantharellus cibarius. b, 75t, Boletus aestivalis.

1996, June 6
258 A95 Sheet of 2, #a.-b. 3.00 3.00

Modern Olympic Games, Cent., 1996 Summer Olympics, Atlanta — A96

Designs: 75t, Iztok Cop, rower; Fredja Marsic, kayaker. 100t, Britta Bilac, high jumper; Brigita Bukovec, hurdler.

1996, June 6
259 A96 75t multicolored 1.50 1.50
260 A96 100t multicolored 2.00 2.00
a. Pair, #259-260+label 3.75 3.75
No. 260a issued in sheets of 6 stamps + 3 labels.
Two versions of the sheet exist. One with white, red & blue flag, the other with white, blue & red flag.

A97 A98

A99 A100

Idrijan Lace
A101 A102

1996, June 21 Litho. Perf. 14
261 A97 1t shown .25 .25
262 A97 1t olive gray, diff. .25 .25
a. Pair, #261-262 .50 .50
263 A98 2t shown .25 .25
264 A98 2t carmine, diff. .25 .25
a. Pair, #263-264 .50 .50
265 A99 5t shown .25 .25
266 A99 5t square .25 .25
a. Pair, #265-266 .50 .50
267 A100 12t shown .25 .25
268 A100 12t diamond .25 .25
a. Pair, #267-268 .50 .50
269 A101 13t shown .25 .25
270 A101 13t red, diff. .25 .25
a. Pair, #269-270 .50 .50
271 A102 50t shown .55 .55
272 A102 50t lilac, diff. .55 .55
a. Pair, #272-272 1.10 1.10
Nos. 261-272 (12) 3.60 3.60

Nos. 261-272 were originally issued with a background containing "1996," posthorn, and security lettering that appear under UV light, values as shown above. In 1997 Nos. 261-270 were reissued, with date within fluorescent inscription changed to "1997." Value, set, $150.
In their final form, Nos. 261-272 were issued later in 1997 without fluorescent inscription. Value same as for 1996 issue.
See Nos. 297-304.

Modern Cardiology, Cent. — A103

1996, Sept. 6 Litho. Perf. 14
273 A103 12t multicolored .40 .40

Grammar School, Novo Mesto, 250th Anniv. A104

1996, Sept. 6
274 A104 55t multicolored 1.00 .55

Skocjan Caves, Karst Region, UNESCO World Heritage Site A105

1996, Sept. 6
275 A105 55t multicolored 1.00 .55

Moscon Family Portrait, by Jozef Tominc (1790-1866) — A106

1996, Sept. 6
276 A106 65t multicolored 1.40 .90

A107

1996, Oct. 18 Litho. Perf. 14
277 A107 100t multicolored 1.75 .75
Post Office, Ljubljana, cent.

A108

1996, Oct. 20
278 A108 12t multicolored .40 .40
Introduction of automatic letter sorting machines, Maribor.

A109

Christmas
A110

1996, Nov. 20   Litho.   Perf. 14
279 A109 12t Children sled-
ding   .25   .25
  a. Booklet pane of 10   3.00   *3.00*
    Complete booklet, #279a   3.00
280 A110 65t Nativity   1.25   1.25
  a. Booklet pane of 10   15.00 *15.00*
    Complete booklet, #280a   15.00

Carnival Costumes Type of 1996

From Cerkno region: 20t, "Ta terjast." 80t,
"Pust."

1997, Jan. 21   Litho.   Perf. 14
281 A85 20t multicolored   .25   .25
282 A85 80t multicolored   1.25   1.25

Love
A111

1997, Jan. 21   Litho.   Perf. 14
283 A111 15t multicolored   .30   .30

Sneznik
Mountain
A112

1997, Jan. 21
284 A112 20t multicolored   .60   .60

A113

1997, Mar. 27   Litho.   Perf. 14
285 A113 80t Legend of the
Goldenhorn   3.50   3.50
Europa.

A114

1997, Mar. 27
286 A114 80t Wulfenite   1.25   .75

Endangered Fish — A115

1997, Mar. 27
287 A115 12t Salmo marmoratus   .35   .35
288 A115 13t Zingel streber   .60   .60
289 A115 80t Vimba vimba   1.40   1.40
290 A115 90t Umbra krameri   2.00   2.00
    Nos. 287-290 (4)   4.35   4.35
Miniature Sheet

A115a — 290A

290A A115a Sheet of 4, #a-d   5.00   5.00
  a. 12t Salmo marmoratus   .35   .35
  b. 13t Zingel streber   .60   .60
  c. 80t Vimba vimba   1.40   1.40
  d. 90t Umbra krameri   2.00   2.00

Railways Type of 1994

Design: 80t, Locomotive SZ 03-002,
Ljubljana-Trieste Railway Line, 140th anniv.

1997, May 30   Litho.   Perf. 14
291 A64 80t multicolored   1.40   .80

A116

1997, May 30
292 A116 70t multicolored   1.25   .70

Volunteer fire fighting brigades in Slovenia.

A117

Famous People: 13t, Matija Cop (1797-
1835), literary expert. 24t, Sigismundus Zois
(1747-1819), economist, natural scientist. 80t,
Bishop Frederic Baraga (1797-1868), missionary, linguist.

1997, May 30
293 A117 13t multicolored   .25   .25
294 A117 24t multicolored   .55   .25
295 A117 80t multicolored   1.25   .75
    Nos. 293-295 (3)   2.05   1.25

Souvenir Sheet

4th Meeting of the Presidents of
Central European Countries,
Piran — A118

Designs: a, 100t, Tartini Square. b, 200t,
Coats of arms from eight countries.

1997, June 6
296 A118   Sheet of 2, #a.-b.   5.25   5.25

Idrijan Lace Type of 1996

Shape of lace: No. 297, Flower in center of
oval. No. 298, Circular outside with swirl at
bottom. No. 299, Butterfly. No. 300, Diamond.
No. 301, Square. No. 302, Circle. No. 303,
Leaves. No. 304, Tulip.

1997, June 20   Litho.   Perf. 14
297 A97 10t magenta   .30   .30
298 A97 10t magenta   .30   .30
  a. Pair, #297-298   .65   .65
299 A97 20t violet   .35   .35
300 A97 20t violet   .35   .35
  a. Pair, #299-300   .75   .75
301 A97 44t bright blue   .75   .50
302 A97 44t bright blue   .75   .50
  a. Pair, #301-302   1.75   1.75
303 A97 100t gray brown   1.60   1.60
304 A97 100t gray brown   1.60   1.60
  a. Pair, #303-304   3.50   3.50
    Nos. 297-304 (8)   6.00   5.50

A119

1997, Sept. 9
305 A119 14t multicolored   .40   .25
Children's Week.

A120

1997, Sept. 9
306 A120 50t multicolored   .80   .50
Return of Primorska, 50th anniv.

France Gorse (1897-1986),
Sculptor — A121

1997, Sept. 9
307 A121 70t "Bashful Armor"   1.00   1.00
308 A121 80t "Peasant Woman"   1.25   1.25
  a. Pair, #307-308   2.50   2.50

A122   A123

1997, Sept. 9
309 A122 90t multicolored   1.50   1.50
MEJP '97, European Youth Judo
Championship.

1997, Nov. 18   Litho.   Perf. 14
310 A123 90t multicolored   1.25   .80
Golden Fox World Cup Ski Competition for
Women, 35th anniv.

Christmas
& New Year
A124

Designs: 14t, Children watching birds and
snow outside window. 90t, Sculptured Nativity
scene, by Liza Hribar (1913-96).

1997, Nov. 18
311 A124 14t multicolored   .25   .25
312 A124 90t multicolored   1.50   1.00
  a. Booklet pane of 8, 5 #311, 3
    #312   6.25
    Complete booklet, #312a   6.25

New Mail Center,
Ljubljana — A125

1997, Nov. 28
313 A125 30t multicolored   .50   .25

Borovo Gostüvanje (Pine
Wedding) — A126

20t, Participating "players," tree. 80t, Participants, "bride & groom," top of pine tree.

1998, Jan. 22   Litho.   Perf. 14
314 A126 20t multicolored   .35   .25
315 A126 80t multicolored   .95   .75
  a. Pair, #314-315   1.50   1.50

See Nos. 338-339.

1998
Winter
Olympic
Games,
Nagano
A127

1998, Jan. 22
316 A127 70t Woman skater   .75   .50
317 A127 90t Biathlete   1.25   .75
  a. Vert. pair, #316-317 + label 3.00   3.00

Issued in sheets of 6 stamps + 3 labels.

EUROCONTROL (European
Organization for Safety of Air
Navigation), 35th Anniv. — A128

1998, Jan. 22
318 A128 90t multicolored   1.40   .80

Louis Adamic (1898-1951),
Writer — A129

90t, Francesco Robba (1698-1757),
sculptor.

1998, Mar. 25   Litho.   Perf. 14
319 A129 26t multicolored   .30   .25
320 A129 90t multicolored   1.40   .90

Jurjevanje
(Green
George's
Festival)
A130

1998, Mar. 25
321 A130 90t multicolored   3.00   1.75

Europa.

Comic Strip
Characters, by
Miki
Muster — A131

1998, Mar. 25
322 A131 14t Fox   .50   .50
323 A131 105t Turtle   1.75   1.75
324 A131 118t Wolf   2.25   2.25
a.   Sheet, 2 each #322-324   8.00   8.00
       Nos. 322-324 (3)   4.50   4.50

Railways Type of 1994
Design: Steam locomotive SZ 06-018.

1998, June 10   Litho.   Perf. 14
325 A64 80t multicolored   1.25   .75

Boc Mountain,
Pulsatilla
Grandis — A132

1998, June 10
326 A132 14t multicolored   .40   .25

A133

Conifers: a, 14t, Juniperus communis. b,
15t, Picea abies. c, 80t, Pinus nigra. d, 90t,
Larix decidua.

1998, June 10
327 A133   Sheet of 4, #a.-d.   4.75   4.75

A134

1998, June 23   Litho.   Perf. 14
328 A134 15t multicolored   .40   .25
Committee for the Protection of Human
Rights, 10th anniv.

United
Slovenia,
150th
Anniv.
A135

1998, June 23
329 A135 80t multicolored   1.25   .75

Cistercian
Order,
900th
Anniv. and
Sticna
Revival,
Cent.
A136

1998, Sept. 11   Litho.   Perf. 14
330 A136 14t multicolored   .40   .25

Radio
Ljubljana,
70th Anniv.
A137

1998, Sept. 11
331 A137 50t Cuckoo   .80   .50

Avgust
Cernigoj
(1898-1985),
Artist — A138

Designs: 70t, Abstract painting, "Banker."
80t, Sculpture, "El."

1998, Sept. 11
332 A138 70t multicolored   .90   .60
333 A138 80t multicolored   1.00   .70
a.   Pair, #332-333   2.25   2.25

Universal
Declaration of
Human Rights,
50th
Anniv. — A139

1998, Sept. 11
334 A139 100t multicolored   1.50   1.00

Christmas
A140

Designs: 15t, Children walking through
snow, candle. 90t, Fresco of "Bow of the Three
Wise Men of the East," Church of St. Nicholas,
Mace, 1476.

1998, Nov. 12   Litho.   Perf. 14
335 A140 15t multicolored   .30   .25
a.   Booklet pane of 10   3.25   3.25
       Complete booklet, #335a   3.25
336 A140 90t multicolored   1.40   .80
a.   Bklt. pane, 6 #335, 4 #336   7.50   7.50
       Complete booklet, #336a   7.50

Leon Stukelj,
Olympic
Gymnastics
Champion, 100th
Birthday — A141

Designs: a, Portrait. b, As a gymnast. c,
With IOC Pres. Juan Antonio Samaranch,
horiz. (58x40mm).

1998, Nov. 12
337 A141 100t Sheet of 3, #a.-c. 4.75   4.75

Wedding, Festival Type of 1998
Skoromati carnival mask characters: 20t,
Wearing tall hats, Skopit character in black.
80t, Skopit character blowing horn.

1999, Jan. 22   Litho.   Perf. 14
338 A126 20t multicolored   .25   .25
339 A126 80t multicolored   1.00   .65
a.   Pair, #338-339   1.60   1.60

Greetings
A142

1999, Jan. 22
340 A142 15t multicolored   .40   .25

Famous Men — A143

14t, Peter Kozler (1824-79), geographer.
15t, Bozidar Lavric (1899-1961), surgeon. 70t,
Rudolf Maister (1874-1934), general, poet.
80t, France Preseren (1800-49), poet.

1999, Jan. 22
341 A143 14t multicolored   .40   .25
342 A143 15t multicolored   .40   .25
343 A143 70t multicolored   1.10   .55
344 A143 80t multicolored   1.40   .70
       Nos. 341-344 (4)   3.30   1.75

Golica
Mountain,
Narcissus
Flowers
A144

1999, Mar. 23   Litho.   Perf. 14
345 A144 15t multicolored   .40   .25

Slovenian Philatelic Assoc., 50th
Anniv. — A145

1999, Mar. 23
346 A145 16t Yugoslavia #3L5 &
              #305   .40   .25

Mercury &
Cinnabar,
Idrija Mine
A146

1999, Mar. 23
347 A146 80t multicolored   1.25   .60

Council of
Europe,
50th Anniv.
A147

1999, Mar. 23
348 A147 80t multicolored   1.25   .60

Triglav
Natl. Park
A148

1999, Mar. 23
349 A148 90t multicolored   2.50   1.25

Europa.

5th Rescue Dog World
Championships — A149

1999, May 21   Litho.   Perf. 14
350 A149 80t multicolored   1.25   .60

UPU, 125th
Anniv. — A150

Designs: 30t, Early postman with backpack.
90t, Astronaut on moon with backpack.

1999, May 21

351	A150	30t multicolored	.60	.30
352	A150	90t multicolored	1.00	.50
a.		Pair, #351-352	1.60	.80

Horses
A151

Designs: 60t, Slovenian cold-blooded horse. 70t, Ljutomer trotter. 120t, Slovenian warm-blooded horse (show jumper). 350t, Lipizzaner.

1999, May 21

353	A151	60t multicolored	.95	.45
354	A151	70t multicolored	1.10	.55
355	A151	120t multicolored	1.75	.85
356	A151	350t multicolored	5.50	2.75
a.		Sheet of 4, #353-356	11.00	7.00
		Nos. 353-356 (4)	9.30	4.60

Towards A New Millennium — A152

Designs: 20t, Balanced objects. 70t, Roadway, earth. 80t, Cogwheels. 90t, Tree.

1999, Sept. 16   Litho.   Perf. 13¾

357	A152	20t multicolored	.25	.25
358	A152	70t multicolored	.90	.45
359	A152	80t multicolored	1.00	.50
360	A152	90t multicolored	1.25	.60
a.		Block of 4, #357-360	3.50	1.75

Bozidar Jakac (1899-1989),
Painter — A153

Self-portraits and: 70t, Girl drawing curtain. 80t, Landscape.

1999, Sept. 16

361	A153	70t multicolored	.95	.45
362	A153	80t multicolored	1.10	.55
a.		Pair, #361-362	2.25	1.10

Railway Type of 1994

1999, Sept. 16

363	A64	80t multicolored	1.25	.60

Rail Line to Ljubljana, 150th anniv.

Bishop Anton M.
Slomsek (1800-
62) — A154

1999, Sept. 16

364	A154	90t multicolored	1.40	.70

Millennium
A155

Christmas — A156

1999, Nov. 18   Litho.   Perf. 14

365	A155	17t multicolored	.55	.55
a.		Booklet pane of 10	5.50	
		Complete booklet, #365a	5.50	
366	A155	18t multicolored	.55	.55
367	A156	80t multicolored	2.25	1.10
a.		Booklet pane, 5 #365, 3 #367 + 2 labels	9.50	
		Complete booklet, #367a	9.50	
368	A156	90t multicolored	2.50	1.25
		Nos. 365-368 (4)	5.85	3.45

#365 and 367 were issued only in booklets.

Types of 1993-94
and No. 210A
Surcharged

Design: 18t, Accordion. 19t on 17t, Corn storage building. A, Post office door, Zgornji Otok. No. 373, Easter eggs. No. 374, Fishing boat. No. 375, Miner's house, Trbovlje. C, Scythe. No. 377, Ljubljana Palm Sunday bundle. No. 378, Horse collar comb. No. 379, Fishing boat and oars.

1999-2004   Litho.   Perf. 14
Size 25x34mm

370	A38	18t multi	.45	.25
371	A38	19t on 17t multi	.45	.25
372	A38	A multi	.95	.45
373	A38	B multi	.60	.30
374	A38	B multi	1.10	.55
375	A38	B multi	1.25	.60
376	A38	C multi	2.50	1.25
377	A38	D multi	2.50	1.25
378	A38	D multi	3.00	1.50
379	A38	D multi	3.00	1.50
		Nos. 370-379 (10)	15.80	7.90

Issued: 18t, 12/17/99. No. 371, 4/20/2000. Nos. 373, 377, 2/28/02. Nos. 372, 374, 376, 378, 11/19/03. No. 375, 7/3/04. No. 379, 9/22/04.

Nos. 373 and 377 sold for 31t and 107t respectively on day of issue. Nos. 372, 374, 376 and 378 sold for 38t, 44t, 95t and 107t respectively on day of issue. No. 375 sold for 48t on day of issue. No. 379 sold for 107t on day of issue.

Issued: No. 371, 4/20/00.

Love — A158

2000, Jan. 20   Litho.   Perf. 14

383	A158	34t multi	.60	.30

Carnival Costume Type of 1996

Pustovi masks: 34t, Two masks, horiz. 80t, Four masks, horiz.

2000, Jan. 20

384	A85	34t multi	.60	.30
385	A85	80t multi	1.40	.70

A159

2000, Jan. 20

386	A159	64t multi	1.00	.50

Tone Seliskar (1900-69), poet.

A160

2000, Jan. 20

387	A160	120t multi	2.00	1.00

Elvira Kralj (1900-78), actress.

Postal Service in
Slovenia, 500th
Anniv. — A161

2000, Jan. 20

388	A161	500t multi	9.00	7.00

Mt. Storzic
A162

2000, Mar. 21   Litho.   Perf. 14

389	A162	18t multi	.70	.35

Return of
World War
II Exiles
A163

2000, Mar. 21

390	A163	25t multi	.70	.35

Characters from
Children's
Books — A164

#391, 394, Pedenjped. #392, 395, Mojca Pokrajculja. #393, 396, Macek Muri.

2000, Mar. 21   Perf. 14

391	A164	20t multi	1.50	.75
392	A164	20t multi	1.50	.75
393	A164	20t multi	1.50	.75

Booklet Stamps
Self-Adhesive
Serpentine Die Cut 7½

394	A164	20t multi	1.25	.55
395	A164	20t multi	1.25	.55
396	A164	20t multi	1.25	.55
a.		Booklet pane, 3 each #394-396 + 9 labels	12.00	
		Nos. 391-396 (6)	8.25	3.90

No. 396a is a complete booklet.

Fossils and
Minerals
A165

2000, Mar. 21   Perf. 14

397	A165	80t Trilobite	1.60	.80
398	A165	90t Dravite	1.60	.80

See Nos. 453-454, 517.

Souvenir Sheet

Holy Year 2000 — A166

2000, Mar. 21

399	A166	2000t multi	35.00	22.50

Castles — A167

2000-04   Litho.   Perf. 14
Size 23x32mm

400	A167	1t Predjama	.35	.25
401	A167	1t Velenje	.35	.25
a.		Pair, #400-401	.70	.35
404	A167	A Ptuj	.60	.30
405	A167	A Otocec	.60	.30
a.		Pair, #404-405	1.25	.90
406	A167	B Zuzemberk	.60	.30
407	A167	B Turjak	.60	.30
a.		Pair, #406-407	1.25	.90
410	A167	C Dobrovo	1.50	.75
411	A167	C Breziski	1.50	.75
a.		Pair, #410-411	3.00	1.75
411B	A167	C Gewerkenegg	1.50	.75
412	A167	100t Podsreda	1.50	.75
413	A167	100t Bled	1.50	.75
a.		Pair, #412-413	3.00	1.75
414	A167	D Olimje	1.50	.75
415	A167	D Murska Sobota	1.50	.75
a.		Pair, #414-415	3.00	1.75

Size: 38x26mm

415B	A167	1000t Kamen	15.00	7.25
		Nos. 400-415B (14)	28.60	14.20

Nos. 404-405 each sold for 20t; Nos. 406-407 for 21t; Nos. 410-411 for 95t; No. 411B sold for 95t on day of issue; Nos. 414-415 for 107t on day of issue.

Issued: Nos. 1t, 100t, 4/20; A, B, 6/23; Nos. 410-411, 414-415, 10/4/01. 1000t, 3/24/03. No. 411B, 11/18/04.
See Nos. 624-628.

Fruits, Blossoms and
Insects — A168

Designs: No. 416, Apple blossom weevil.
No. 417, Apple blossom. No. 418, Apple.

2000, Apr. 20   Litho.   Perf. 13¾
Vignette Frame Size 20x26½mm
416 A168 10t multi   .25   .25
417 A168 10t multi   .25   .25
418 A168 10t multi   .25   .25
a.   Strip, #416-418   .75   .35

Printed in sheets of 15 stamps + 5 labels.
See Nos. 426-428, 464-466, 502-504, 528-
530, 568-570, 606-608, 629-646, 676-678.

Amateur
Radio
A169

2000, May 9   Litho.   Perf. 14
419 A169 20t multi   1.75   .85

Slovenian Team
Qualification for
European Soccer
Championships
A170

2000, May 9
420 A170 40t multi   1.50   .75

2000
Summer
Olympics,
Sydney
A171

2000, May 9
421 A171 80t Sailboats   2.50   1.25
422 A171 90t Sydney Opera
         House   2.50   1.25
a.   Pair, #421-422   5.00   2.50

World Environment Day — A172

2000, May 9
423 A172 90t multi   30.00   15.00

Issued in sheets of 10 + 5 labels.

Europa, 2000
Common Design Type
2000, May 9   Litho.   Perf. 14
424 CD17 90t multi   3.25   1.60

Issued in sheets of 8 + 1 label.

Meteorology
A173

2000, May 9   Perf. 13¾
425 A173 150t multi   30.00   15.00

Issued in sheets of 9 + 1 label.

Fruits, Blossoms and Insects Type
of 2000

#426, Cherry blossom. #427, European
cherry fruit fly. #428, Cherries.

2000, June 23   Litho.   Perf. 13¾
Vignette Frame Size 20x26½mm
426 A168 5t multi   .25   .25
427 A168 5t multi   .25   .25
428 A168 5t multi   .25   .25
a.   Strip, #426-428   .75   .35

Printed in sheets of 15 stamps + 5 labels.

Paintings by Tone Kralj (1900-
75) — A174

2000, Sept. 15   Litho.   Perf. 14
429   Horiz. pair   3.00   1.25
a.   A174 70t multi   1.25   .50
b.   A174 80t multi, diff.   1.40   .60

Grape
Varieties — A175

Designs: 20t, Zelen. 40t, Ranfol. 80t,
Zametovka. 130t, Rumeni Plavec.

2000, Sept. 15
430-433 A175   Set of 4   6.00   3.00
a.   Souvenir sheet, #430-433   6.00   3.00

Gold
Medalists
at 2000
Summer
Olympics
A176

Winners and events: No. 434, 21t, Iztok
Cop, Luka Spik, double sculls. No. 435, 21t,
Rajmond Debevec, Men's three-position rifle.

2000, Oct. 16
434-435 A176   Set of 2   .80   .40

First Book Printed
in Slovenian,
450th
Anniv. — A177

2000, Nov. 21
436 A177 50t multi   .90   .45

Christmas
A178

Designs: B, Children in snow. 90t, Christ in
manger.

2000, Nov. 21
437 A178   B multicolored   .50   .25
438 A178   90t multicolored   2.00   1.00

Booklet Stamps
Self-Adhesive
Serpentine Die Cut 7¼
439 A178   B multi   .60   .30
a.   Booklet of 10 + 2 labels   6.00
440 A178   90t multi   2.40   1.25
a.   Booklet, 6 #439, 4 #440 + 2 la-
      bels   13.50
      Nos. 437-440 (4)   5.50   2.80

Nos. 437 and 439 sold for 21t on day of
issue.

Advent of New Millennium — A179

2000, Nov. 21   Litho.   Perf. 14
441 A179 40t multi   .80   .40

Wedding
Greetings
A180

2001, Jan. 19   Litho.   Perf. 14
442 A180 B multi   .60   .30

No. 442 sold for 25t on day of issue.

Carnival Masks, Dobrepolje — A181

Mask wearers including: 50t, Woman with
flowers. 95t, Woman in box on cart.

2001, Jan. 19
443-444 A181   Set of 2   2.25   1.10

Writers — A182

Objects symbolic of writer's works: A,
Bucket (Dragotin Kette, 1876-99). 95t, Flowers
in jar (Ivan Tavcar, 1851-1923). 107t, Coffee
cup (Ivan Cankar, 1876-1918).

2001, Jan. 19
445-447 A182   Set of 3   4.00   1.60

No. 445 sold for 24t on day of issue.

Mt. Jalovec and
Triglav
Flowers — A183

2001, Mar. 21   Litho.   Perf. 14
448 A183 B multi   1.00   .50

No. 448 sold for 25t on day of issue.

Comic Strip
Characters by
Bozo Kos — A184

Designs: Nos. 449, 451, Cowboy. Nos. 450,
452, Indian.

2001, Mar. 21
449 A184 B multicolored   1.00   .50
450 A184 B multicolored   1.00   .50

Booklet Stamps
Self-Adhesive
Serpentine Die Cut 7¼
451 A184 B multicolored   1.25   .60
452 A184 B multicolored   1.25   .60
a.   Booklet, 4 each #451-452   9.50
      Nos. 449-452 (4)   4.50   2.20

Nos. 449-452 each sold for 25t on day of
issue.

Fossil and Mineral Type of 2000

No. 453 — Stereoscopic image of fluorite
crystal with arrow at: a, Right. b, Left.
107t, Starfish fossil.

2001, Mar. 21   Litho.   Perf. 14
453   Horiz. pair   3.25   1.60
a.-b.   A165 95t Any single   1.60   .80
454 A165 107t Starfish fossil   1.60   .80

Europe
Day
A185

2001, Mar. 21
455 A185 221t multi   3.50   1.75

Solkan, 1000th Anniv. — A186

2001, Mar. 21
456 A186 261t multi   4.00 2.25

Formation of Liberation Front, 60th Anniv. — A187

2001, Apr. 24   Litho.   Perf. 14
457 A187 24t multi   .95 .45

Independence, 10th Anniv. — A188

2001, May 23
458 A188 100t multi   3.50 2.00
Issued in sheets of 10 + 2 labels.

Europa — A189

2001, May 23
459 A189 107t multi   3.50 1.75
Issued in sheets of 8 + 1 label.

Ljubljana Tram System, Cent. A190

2001, May 23
460 A190 113t multi   2.10 .85

6th World Maxi Basketball Championships, Ljubljana — A191

2001, May 23
461 A191 261t multi   4.00 1.75

Souvenir Sheet

Apiculture — A192

No. 462: a, 24t, Bee on flower. b, 48t, Queen and drones. c, 95t, Worker bees. d, 170t, Hive and apiary.

2001, May 23
462 A192   Sheet of 4, #a-d   6.25 4.00

Flags of US and Russia, Dragon Bridge, Ljubljana — A193

2001, June 14
463 A193 107t multi   1.75 .85
a.   Souvenir sheet of 1   2.25 1.10
First meeting of US Pres. George W. Bush and Russian Pres. Vladimir Putin, Brdo Castle, June 16.

Fruit, Blossoms and Insects Type of 2000
Designs: No. 464, Peach blossom. No. 465, Green peach aphid. No. 466, Peach.

2001, July 21   Perf. 13¾
Vignette Frame Size 20x26mm
464 A168 50t multi   .70 .35
465 A168 50t multi   .70 .35
466 A168 50t multi   .70 .35
a.   Strip, #464-466   2.10 1.00
Printed in sheets of 15 strips + 5 labels.

Mohorjeve Druzbe Publishing House, 150th Anniv. — A194

2001, Sept. 4   Perf. 14
467 A194 B multi   .70 .35
No. 467 sold for 27t on day of issue.

Foundation of First Technical High School, Cent. A195

2001, Sept. 21
468 A195 A multi   .70 .35
No. 468 sold for 26t on day of issue.

World Animal Day — A196

2001, Sept. 21
469 A196 107t multi   2.00 1.00

Year of Dialogue Among Civilizations A197

2001, Sept. 21   Litho.   Perf. 14
470 A197 107t multi   2.50 1.25

Composers — A198

Designs: 95t, Blaz Arnic (1901-70). 107t, Lucijan Marija Skerjanc (1900-73).

2001, Sept. 21   Litho.   Perf. 14
471-472 A198   Set of 2   3.25 1.60

New Year's Greetings A199 ／ Christmas A200

2001, Nov. 16   Litho.   Perf. 14
473 A199 B multi   .35 .25
474 A200 D multi   1.90 .95

Self-Adhesive
Booklet Stamps
Serpentine Die Cut 7¼
475 A199 B multi   .35 .25
a.   Booklet pane of 12   4.25
476 A200 D multi   2.10 1.00
a.   Booklet pane, 6 each #475-476 15.00
Nos. 473 and 475 sold for 31t , Nos. 474 and 476 for 107t on day of issue.

Love — A201

2002, Jan. 23   Litho.   Perf. 14
477 A201 B multi   .70 .35
No. 477 sold for 31t on day of issue.

Masks — A202

Designs: 56t, Rusa. 95t, Picek.

2002, Jan. 23
478-479 A202   Set of 2   2.25 1.10

Famous Slovenians — A203

Designs: 95t, Joze Plecnik (1872-1957), architect. 107t, Janko Kersnik (1852-97), poet.

2002, Jan. 23
480-481 A203   Set of 2   2.75 1.40

2002 Winter Olympics, Salt Lake City — A204

No. 482: a, 95t, Sledder. b, 107t, Skier.

2002, Jan. 23
482 A204   Horiz. pair, #a-b, +
      label   3.25 1.60
No. 482 printed in sheets of three pairs. Labels, which have different designs, appear at left and center in other pairs on the sheet.

Insect Fossil A205

2002, Mar. 21
485 A205 C multi   1.75 .85
No. 485 sold for 95t on day of issue.

Kostanjevica on the Krka, 750th Anniv. A206

2002, Mar. 21
486 A206 D multi   1.75 .85
No. 486 sold for 107t on day of issue.

Intl. Year of Mountains A207

Flowers and mountains: A, Clematis alpina and Martuljek Group. D, Lilium carniolicum and Mt. Spik.

2002, Mar. 21
487-488 A207   Set of 2   3.00 1.50
Nos. 487-488 sold for 30t and 107t respectively on day of issue.

Martin Krpan from Vrh, by Fran Levstik — A208

Designs: No. 489, B, Krpan carrying horse. No. 490, B, Krpan at blacksmith's shop. No. 491, B, Krpan in Ljubljana. No. 492, B, Like #489. No. 493, B, Like #490. No. 494, B, Like No. 491.

2002, Mar. 21   *Perf. 14*
489-491 A208   Set of 3   2.50 1.25
Self-Adhesive
Booklet Stamps
Serpentine Die Cut 7¼
492-494 A208   Set of 3   2.50 1.25
494a   Booklet pane, 3 each #492-
         494   7.00
Nos. 489-494 each sold for 31t on day of issue.

Europa — A209

2002, May 22   *Perf. 14*
495 A209 D multi   15.00 7.50
No. 495 sold for 107t on day of issue.

2002 World Cup Soccer Championships, Japan and Korea — A210

2002, May 22
496 A210 D multi   1.75 .85
No. 496 sold for 107t on day of issue.

Medicinal Plants — A211

Designs: A, Rosa canina. B, Chamomilla recutita. C, Valeriana officinalis. D, Viola odorata.

2002, May 22
497-499 A211   Set of 3   4.00 2.00
Souvenir Sheet
500 A211 D multi   1.75 .85
Nos. 497-500 each sold for 30t, 31t, 95t and 107t respectively on day of issue.

Souvenir Sheet

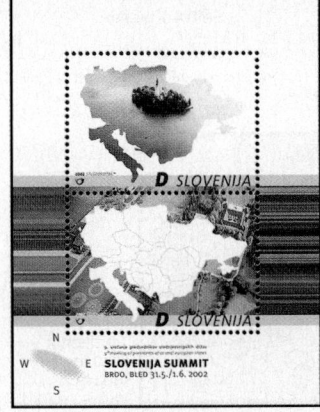

9th Summit of Presidents of Central European States, Bled — A212

No. 501: a, D, Bled Island in map of Europe. b, D, Map of Europe, Brdo Castle.

2002, May 22
501 A212   Sheet of 2, #a-b   3.50 1.75
Nos. 501a and 501b each sold for 107t on day of issue.

Fruit, Blossoms and Insects Type of 2000

Designs: No. 502, Bilberry blossoms. No. 503, Winter moth. No. 504, Bilberries.

2002, July 19   *Perf. 13¾*
Vignette Frame Size 20x26mm
502 A168 150t multi   2.25 1.10
503 A168 150t multi   2.25 1.10
504 A168 150t multi   2.25 1.10
a.   Horiz. strip, #502-504   6.75 3.50

Paintings by Matija Jama (1872-1947) — A213

Designs: 95t, Kolo — A National Dance. 214t, A Village in Winter.

2002, Sept. 19   *Perf. 14*
505-506 A213   Set of 2   4.50 2.25

Souvenir Sheet

35th Chess Olympiad, Bled — A214

No. 507: a, C, Horse, Bled Castle. b, D, Fields in checkerboard pattern.

2002, Sept. 19
507 A214   Sheet of 2, #a-b   4.00 2.00
Nos. 507a and 507b each sold for 95t and 107t respectively on day of issue.

Screw Propeller Invented by Josef Ressel (1793-1857) — A215

2002, Nov. 15   Litho.   *Perf. 13¾*
508 A215 C multi   2.10 1.00
No. 508 sold for 95t on day of issue. Values are for stamps with surrounding selvage.

Christmas and New Year's Greetings — A216

Designs: Nos. 509, 511, Snowman. Nos. 510, 512, Girl with evergreen branch.

2002, Nov. 15   Litho.   *Perf. 14*
509 A216 B multi   .70 .35
510 A216 D multi   1.90 .95
Booklet Stamps
Self-Adhesive
Serpentine Die Cut 7¼
511 A216 B multi   .75 .35
512 A216 D multi   2.25 1.10
a.   Booklet, 6 each #511-512   18.00
       Nos. 509-512 (4)   5.60 2.75
Nos. 509 and 511 each sold for 36t, and Nos. 510 and 512 each sold for 107t on day of issue.

Traditional Istrian Clothing A217

2003, Jan. 21   Litho.   *Perf. 14*
513 A217 A multi   1.10 .55
No. 513 sold for 38t on day of issue.

Love A218

2003, Jan. 21   *Perf. 11*
514 A218 180t multi   2.75 1.40
No. 514 is impregnated with a rose scent. Values are for examples with surrounding selvage.

Famous Men A219

Designs: 107t, Ferdinand Avgustin Hallerstein (1703-74), astronomer and Chinese missionary. 221t, Alfonz Paulin (1853-1942), director of Ljubljana Botanical Gardens.

2003, Jan. 21
515-516 A219   Set of 2   4.50 2.25

Mineral Type of 2000

2003, Mar. 24
517 A165 D Barite   1.60 .80
No. 517 sold for 107t on day of issue.

Vilenica Cave — A220

2003, Mar. 24
518 A220 D multi   1.60 .80
No. 518 sold for 107t on day of issue.

Fairy Tales A221

Designs: No. 519, B, The Three Vixens. No. 520, B, The Golden Bird, vert.

2003, Mar. 24   *Perf. 14*
519-520 A221   Set of 2   1.60 .80
Serpentine Die Cut 7¼
Booklet Stamps
Self-Adhesive
521 A221 B Like #519   1.00 .50
522 A221 B Like #520   1.00 .50
a.   Booklet, 4 each #521-522   8.50
Nos. 519-522 each sold for 44t on day of issue.

Europa — A222

2003, May 22   Litho.   *Perf. 14*
523 A222 D multi   1.75 .85
No. 523 sold for 107t on day of issue. Printed in sheets of 8 + 1 label.

Kresnik, Mythological Character — A223

2003, May 22
524 A223 110t multi   1.75 .85

Souvenir Sheet

Slavko and Vilko Avsenik,
Musicians — A224

2003, May 22
525　A224　180t multi　　　　　3.00　1.50

European Water
Polo
Championships,
Kranj and
Ljubljana — A225

2003, May 22
526　A225　180t multi　　　　　3.00　1.50

Painted
Beehive
Panel
A226

2003, May 22
527　A226　218t multi　　　　　3.25　1.60

Fruit, Blossom and Insect Type of 2000

Designs: No. 528, Olive blossom. No. 529, Olive fruit fly. No. 530, Olives on branch.

2003, Sept. 18　　　　　**Perf. 13¾x14**
Vignette Frame Size 20x26½mm
528　A168　B multi　　　　　　.75　.35
529　A168　B multi　　　　　　.75　.35
530　A168　B multi　　　　　　.75　.35
　a.　Horiz. strip, #528-530　　2.25　1.10

Nos. 528-530 each sold for 44t on day of issue.

Stampless
Covers,
1830
A227

2003, Sept. 18　　　　　**Perf. 14**
531　A227　A multi　　　　　　.90　.45

No. 531 sold for 38t on day of issue.

Illustration from the Tournament Book
of Gasper Lamberger — A228

Jousting contest: a, 76t, Riderless horse. b, 570t, Horse with rider.

2003, Sept. 18　　　　　**Perf. 13¾**
532　A228　Horiz. pair, #a-b　9.00　4.75

Farm
Animals
A229

Designs: 95t, Krsko Polje pig. 107t, Cika cattle. 148t, Jezersko-Solcava sheep. 368t, Styrian hen and rooster, vert.

2003, Sept. 18　　　　　**Perf. 14**
533-535　A229　Set of 3　　5.00　2.50
Souvenir Sheet
536　A229　368t multi　　　　5.00　2.50

Opening of
Mail Sorting
and
Logistics
Center,
Maribor
A230

Litho. with Hologram Applied
2003, Nov. 11　　　**Perf. 13¾x14¼**
537　A230　221t multi　　　　3.00　1.50

Franja
Partisan
Hospital,
60th Anniv.
A231

2003, Nov. 19　　　**Litho.**　**Perf. 14**
538　A231　76t brown & bronze　1.25　.60

Wooden
Cart
A232

2003, Nov. 19
539　A232　221t multi　　　　3.25　1.60

Christmas
A233

2003, Nov. 19　　　　　**Perf. 14**
540　A233　D multi　　　　　1.50　.75
Serpentine Die Cut 7¼
Booklet Stamp
Self-Adhesive
541　A233　D multi　　　　　2.00　1.00
　a.　Booklet pane of 12　　24.00

No. 540 and 541 each sold for 107t on day of issue.

New Year's
Greetings
A234

2003, Nov. 19　　　**Litho.**　**Perf. 14**
542　A234　B multi　　　　　1.00　.50

Serpentine Die Cut 7¼
Booklet Stamp
Self-Adhesive
543　A234　B multi　　　　　1.25　.60
　a.　Booklet pane of 12　　15.00

No. 542 and 543 each sold for 44t on day of issue.

Traditional
Clothing from
Vipava
Valley — A235

2004, Jan. 22　**Litho.**　**Perf. 13¾**
544　A235　A multi　　　　　.75　.35

No. 544 sold for 38t on day of issue.

March of
the 14th
Division to
the Styria,
60th Anniv.
A236

2004, Jan. 22　　　　　**Perf. 14**
545　A236　B multi　　　　　.75　.35

Edvard
Kocbek
(1904-81),
Writer
A237

2004, Jan. 22
546　A237　D multi　　　　　1.40　.70

No. 546 sold for 107t on day of issue.

Love
A238

2004, Jan. 22　　　　　**Perf. 11**
547　A238　180t multi　　　　3.00　1.50

Values are for examples with surrounding selvage.

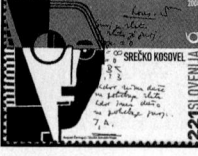

Srecko
Kosovel
(1904-26),
Writer
A239

2004, Jan. 22　　　　　**Perf. 14**
548　A239　221t black & red　3.25　1.60

Sixth Men's
European Handball
Championships
A240

2004, Jan. 22
549　A240　221t multi　　　　3.25　1.60

Fossil Type of 2000
2004, Mar. 24　**Litho.**　**Perf. 14**
550　A165　D Fish　　　　　1.40　.70

No. 541 sold for 107t on day of issue.

European Men's Gymnastic
Championships, Ljubljana — A241

2004, Mar. 24
551　A241　D multi　　　　　1.50　.75

No. 551 sold for 107t on day of issue.

Bled, 1000th
Anniv. — A242

2004, Mar. 24
552　A242　218t multi　　　　3.25　1.60

Kekec, the
Shepherd Boy, by
Josip
Vandot — A243

Designs: No. 553, B, Kekec. No. 554, B, Pehta. No. 555, B, Kosobrin. No. 556, B, Kekec. No. 557, B, Pehta. No. 558, B, Kosobrin.

2004, Mar. 24　　　　　**Perf. 14**
553-555　A243　Set of 3　　2.00　1.00
Serpentine Die Cut 7¼
Booklet Stamps
556-558　A243　Set of 3　　2.00　1.00
　558a　Booklet pane, 3 each #556-
　　　　558　　　　　　　　6.00

Nos. 553-558 each sold for 44t on day of issue.

Admission
to NATO
A244

2004, Apr. 2　**Litho.**　**Perf. 14**
559　A244　D multi　　　　　1.50　.75

No. 559 sold for 107t on day of issue.

Admission to the European Union — A245

2004, May 1
560 A245 95t multi   1.25 .60

Laurenz Koschier (1804-79), Proposer of Postage Stamps A246

2004, May 21
561 A246 B multi   .70 .35

No. 561 sold for 48t on day of issue.

Posthorns — A247

Serpentine Die Cut 12½
2004, May 21
Booklet Stamp
Self-Adhesive
562 A247 B multi   .75 .35
  a.   Booklet pane of 8   6.00

No. 562 sold for 48t on day of issue. See Nos. 583-583A.

Europa — A248

2004, May 21   ***Perf. 14***
563 A248 D multi   1.50 .75

No. 563 sold for 107t on day of issue.

Puch Bicycle, Chainwheel and Chain — A249

2004, May 21
564 A249 110t multi   1.25 .60

Painted Beehive Panel and Bee A250

2004, May 21
565 A250 218t multi   3.00 1.50

See also No. 600.

2004 Summer Olympics, Athens — A251

No. 566: a, C, Discus thrower, silhouette of gymnast. b, Long jumper, silhouette of pole vaulter.

2004, May 21
566 A251 Horiz. pair, #a-b   2.75 1.40

No. 566a sold for 95t; No. 566b sold for 107t on day of issue.

Souvenir Sheet

Opening of Crni Kal Viaduct — A252

2004, Sept. 15   **Litho.**   ***Perf. 14***
567 A252 95t multi   1.25 .60

Fruit, Blossoms and Insect Type of 2000

Designs: No. 568, Pear blossom. No. 569, Pear psylla. No. 570, Pear.

2004, Sept. 22   ***Perf. 13¾***
Vignette Frame Size 19x26½mm
568 A168 A multi   .65 .30
569 A168 A multi   .65 .30
570 A168 A multi   .65 .30
  a.   Horiz. strip, #568-570   2.00 1.00

Nos. 568-570 each sold for 45t on day of issue.

First Mention of Town of Maribor in Document, 750th Anniv. A253

2004, Sept. 22   ***Perf. 13***
571 A253 C multi   1.25 .60

No. 571 sold for 95t on day of issue.

Orchids A254

Designs: B, Epipactis palustris. D, Ophrys holosericea.

2004, Sept. 22   ***Perf. 14***
572 A254 B multi   1.00 .50
Souvenir Sheet
573 A254 D multi   1.75 .85

Nos. 572 and 573 sold for 52t and 107t respectively on day of issue.
See also Nos. 609-610.

Illuminated Manuscripts — A255

No. 574: a, Illuminated "P." b, Illuminated "Q."

2004, Sept. 22
574 A255 107t Pair, #a-b   2.75 1.40

Souvenir Sheet

Signing of Second London Memorandum, 50th Anniv. — A256

2004, Sept. 22
575 A256 221t multi   3.25 1.60

Christmas A257

2004, Nov. 18   ***Perf. 14***
576 A257 C multi   1.50 .75
Booklet Stamp
Self-Adhesive
Serpentine Die Cut 7¼
577 A257 C multi   1.75 .85
  a.   Booklet pane of 12   21.00

Nos. 576 and 577 each sold for 95t on day of issue.

New Year's Greetings — A258

2004, Nov. 18   ***Perf. 14***
578 A258 A multi   .70 .35
Booklet Stamp
Self-Adhesive
Serpentine Die Cut 7¼
579 A258 A multi   .80 .40
  a.   Booklet pane of 12   9.50

Nos. 578 and 579 each sold for 45t on day of issue.

Native Dishes — A259

No. 580 — Map and cuisine of the Prekmurje region: a, Prekmurska gibanica

(pie). b, Bograc, butja repa (goulash, pickled turnips).

2004, Nov. 18   ***Perf. 13¾***
580 A259 52t Pair, #a-b   1.75 .85

Birth Fairies Rojenice and Sojenice — A260

2004, Nov. 18   ***Perf. 14***
581 A260 180t multi   2.75 1.40

Traditional Clothing From Pohorje and Kobansko Areas A261

2005, Jan. 21   ***Perf. 11¾x11¼***
582 A261 A multi   .75 .35

No. 582 sold for 45t on day of issue.

Posthorn Type of 2004
2005   ***Perf. 14, 11¼x11¾ (#583A)***
583 A247 83t multi   1.40 .70
583A A247 83t multi   1.40 .70

Issued: No. 583, 1/21; No. 583A, 4/2. Size of No. 583: 25x34mm.

Janez Sigismund Valentin Popovic (1705-74), Linguist, Scientist — A262

2005, Jan. 21   ***Perf. 11¼x11¾***
584 A262 107t multi   1.40 .70

Love A263

2005, Jan. 21   ***Perf. 11***
585 A263 180t multi   2.50 1.25

Values are for stamps with surrounding selvage.

Janez Trdina (1830-1905), Writer — A264

2005, Jan. 21   *Perf. 11¼x11¾*
586 A264 221t multi   3.50 1.75

Return of Slovenian Exiles, 60th Anniv. A265

2005, Mar. 18   *Perf. 11¾x11¼*
587 A265 A multi   .80   .40
No. 587 sold for 49t on day of issue.

Victory in World War II, 60th Anniv. A266

2005, Mar. 18
588 A266 B multi   .90   .50
No. 588 sold for 57t on day of issue.

Souvenir Sheet

National Tourist Association, Cent. — A267

2005, Mar. 18   *Perf. 11¼*
589 A267 100t multi   1.50   .75

Zoisite A268

2005, Mar. 18   *Perf. 11¾x11¼*
590 A268 D multi   1.50   .75
No. 590 sold for 107t on day of issue.

Folk Tales — A269

Designs: No. 591, A, The Golden Fish. No. 592, A, The Grateful Bear.

2005, Mar. 18   *Perf. 11¼x11¾*
591-592 A269 Set of 2   1.50   .75
Nos. 591 and 592 each sold for 49t on day of issue.

Folk Tales Type of 2005
Serpentine Die Cut 7¼
2005, Mar. 18   Litho.
Booklet Stamps
Self-Adhesive
593 A269 A Like #591   .75   .30
594 A269 A Like #592   .75   .30
  a. Booklet pane, 4 each #593, 594   6.00
Nos. 593 and 594 each sold for 49t on day of issue.

Child and Sunflower — A270

Die Cut Perf. 12½x12¼
2005, May 20   Litho.
Self-Adhesive
595 A270 A multi   .75   .35
  a. Serpentine die cut 13¾x14½   .65   .35
No. 595 sold for 49t on day of issue.
No. 595a sold for 23c when issued in 2008.

1910 Puch Motorcycle A271

2005, May 20   *Perf. 11¾x11¼*
596 A271 98t multi   1.40   .70

Europa A272

2005, May 20
597 A272 D multi   1.50   .75
No. 597 sold for 107t on day of issue.

Postal Wagon and Mail Box — A273

2005, May 20
598 A273 107t multi   1.50   .75

Vesna, Goddess of Spring — A274

2005, May 20   *Perf. 11¼x11¾*
599 A274 180t multi   2.40 1.25

Painted Beehive Panel Type of 2004
2005, May 20   *Perf. 11¾x11¼*
600 A250 221t Hunter and bird   3.25 1.60

Bishop Anton Jeglic and St. Stanislav's Institute A275

2005, May 20
601 A275 221t multi   3.00 1.50
St. Stanislav's Institute, cent.

European Philatelic Cooperation, 50th Anniv. (in 2006) — A276

Magnifying glass and details from Slovenian stamps: No. 602, 60t, #495 (circus elephant). No. 603, 60t, #285 (ram), and stamp tongs. No. 604, 60t, #349 (river). #605, 60t, #195 (Jurij Vega).

2005, May 20   *Perf. 14x13½*
602-605 A276   Set of 4   3.50 1.75
605a   Souvenir sheet, #602-605,
            perf. 14   3.50 1.75

Fruit, Blossoms and Insects Type of 2000
Designs: No. 606, Apricot blossom. No. 607, Apricots on branch. No. 608, San José scale on branch.

2005, July 5   *Perf. 11¾x11¼*
Size 19x23mm
606 A168 D multi   1.50   .75
607 A168 D multi   1.50   .75
608 A168 D multi   1.50   .75
  a. Horiz. strip, #606-608   4.50 2.25
Nos. 606-608 each sold for 107t on day of issue.

Orchids Type of 2004
Designs: B, Dactylorhiza sambucina. D, Platanithera bifolia.

2005, Sept. 23   *Perf. 11¾x11¼*
Size: 37x26mm
609 A254 B multi   .90   .45
Souvenir Sheet
610 A254 D multi   1.60   .80
No. 609 sold for 57t and No. 610 sold for 107t on day of issue. No. 610 contains one 41x28mm stamp.

Dance of Death Fresco, by Janez of Kastav — A277

No. 611: a, Denomination in gray. b, Denomination in brown.

Litho. & Embossed
2005, Sept. 23   *Perf. 13½x13¾*
611 A277 107t Horiz. pair, #a-b 3.25 1.60

Dogs A278

Designs: A, Posavec hound. B, Istrian rough-coated hound. C, Slovenian mountain hound.
D, Istrian smooth-coated hound, vert.

2005, Sept. 23   *Perf. 11¾x11¼*
612-614 A278   Set of 3   3.00 1.50

Souvenir Sheet
Perf. 11¼
615 A278 D multi   1.60   .80
On day of issue, No. 612 sold for 49t, No. 613, 57t, No. 614, 95t, and No. 615, 107t. No. 615 contains one 28x41mm stamp.

Types of 1993 Redrawn
2005 Litho. *Perf. 11¼x11¾*
Size: 26x36mm
616 A38 A Like #374   .60   .30
617 A38 B Like #373   .70   .35
618 A38 B Like #375   .70   .35
619 A38 B Like #375A   .70   .35
620 A38 90t Like #216   1.25   .60
621 A38 C Like #376   1.25   .60
622 A38 D Like #378   1.50   .75
623 A38 D Like #379   1.50   .75
  Nos. 616-623 (8)   8.20 4.05
Issued: Nos. 616-617, 3/18; Nos. 618, 622, 4/2; Nos. 619-621, 623, 5/4. On day of issue No. 616 sold for 49t, Nos. 618-619 each sold for 57t, No. 621 sold for 95t, and Nos. 622-623 each sold for 107t.
Size of Nos. 216, 373-375, 375A, 376, 378-379: 25x34mm.

Castles Type of 2000-04 Redrawn
2005 Litho. *Perf. 11¼x11¾*
Size: 24x34mm
624 A167 1t Predjama   .25   .25
625 A167 1t Velenje   .25   .25
  a. Pair, #624-625   .50   .50
626 A167 C Gewerkenegg   1.25   .60
627 A167 100t Podsreda   1.25   .60
628 A167 100t Bled   1.25   .60
  a. Pair, #626-627   2.50 1.25
  Nos. 624-628 (5)   4.25 2.30
Issued: Nos. 626, 4/2; others 5/4. No. 626 sold for 95t on day of issue.
Size of Nos. 400-401, 411B, 412-413: 23x32mm.

Fruits, Blossoms and Insects Type of 2000 Redrawn
2005 Litho. *Perf. 11¾x11¼*
Vignette Frame Size: 19x23mm
629 A168 5t Like #426   .25   .25
630 A168 5t Like #427   .25   .25
631 A168 5t Like #428   .25   .25
  a. Strip of 3, #629-631   .50   .25
632 A168 10t Like #416   .25   .25
633 A168 10t Like #417   .25   .25
634 A168 10t Like #418   .25   .25
  a. Strip of 3, #632-634   .50   .25
635 A168 A Like #568   .60   .30
636 A168 A Like #569   .60   .30
637 A168 A Like #570   .60   .30
  a. Strip of 3, #635-637   1.75   .90
638 A168 50t Like #464   .65   .30
639 A168 50t Like #465   .65   .30
640 A168 50t Like #466   .65   .30
  a. Strip of 3, #638-640   2.00   .90
641 A168 B Like #528   .80   .40
642 A168 B Like #529   .80   .40
643 A168 B Like #530   .80   .40
  a. Strip of 3, #641-643   2.40 1.20
644 A168 150t Like #502   1.75   .85
645 A168 150t Like #503   1.75   .85
646 A168 150t Like #504   1.75   .85
  a. Strip of 3, #644-646   5.25 2.50
  Nos. 029-040 (18)   12.90 7.05
Issued: Nos. 629-631, 638-640, 5/4; Nos. 632-634, 4/2; Nos. 635-637, 7/22; Nos. 641-643, 6/30; Nos. 644-646, 7/5. On day of issue Nos. 635-637 each sold for 49t; Nos. 641-643 each sold for 57t.
Sizes of vignette frames of Nos. 426-428, 416-418, 568-570, 464-466, 528-530, and 502-504 vary from 19 to 20x26 to 26½mm. Some designs extend beyond vignette frames.

Slovenian Chairmanship of Organization for Security and Cooperation in Europe — A279

2005, Nov. 18   *Perf. 11¼x11¾*
647 A279 107t multi   1.60   .80

Traditional Foods — A280

No. 648: a, Prleska Gibanica and Ajdov Krapec. b, Prleska Tunka (bread, meat, lard and onion on wooden barrel).

2005, Nov. 18
648 A280 107t Pair, #a-b   3.25 1.60

New Year's Day — A281

2005, Nov. 18   Perf. 11¾x11¼
649 A281 A multi   .85 .40

Size: 40x28mm
Self-Adhesive
Serpentine Die Cut 7¼
650 A281 A multi   .85 .40
a.   Booklet pane of 12   10.50
Nos. 649-650 each sold for 49t on day of issue.

Christmas A282

2005, Nov. 18   Perf. 11¾x11¼
651 A282 C multi   1.40 .70

Size: 40x28mm
Self-Adhesive
Serpentine Die Cut 7¼
652 A282 C multi   1.40 .70
a.   Booklet pane of 12   17.00
Nos. 651-652 each sold for 95t on day of issue.

Traditional Carinthian Clothing A283

2006, Jan. 20   Perf. 14
653 A283 A multi   .75 .35
No. 653 sold for 49t on day of issue.

Love A284

2006, Jan. 20   Perf. 11
654 A284 B multi   .90 .45
No. 654 sold for 57t on day of issue. Values are for stamps with surrounding selvage.

Dr. Anton Trstenjak (1906-96), Psychologist — A285

2006, Jan. 20   Perf. 14
655 A285 B multi   .80 .40
No. 655 sold for 57t on day of issue.

Ponikve Carnival — A286

2006, Jan. 20
656 A286 420t multi   5.00 2.50

2006 Winter Olympics, Turin — A287

No. 657: a, 95t, Ski jumper. b, 107t, Snowboarder.

2006, Jan. 20
657 A287   Horiz. pair, #a-b, + label at right   3.00 1.50
Printed in sheets containing 3 pairs and labels.

Pericnik Waterfall — A288

2006, Mar. 24
658 A288 D multi   1.60 .80
No. 658 sold for 107t on day of issue.

Pereiraea Gervaisi Fossil — A289

2006, Mar. 24
659 A289 D multi   1.60 .80
No. 659 sold for 107t on day of issue.

Butterflies A290

Designs: B, Erannis ankeraria. D, Erebia calcaria.

2006, Mar. 24   Perf. 14
660 A290 B multi   .80 .40

Souvenir Sheet
Perf. 14x14x13x14
661 A290 D multi   1.60 .80
On day of issue No. 660 sold for 57t; No. 661 for 107t.

Children's Book Characters A291

Designs: Nos. 662, 664, A, Zvezdica Zaspanka, by Frane Milicinski Jezek. No. 663, 665, A, Zogica Nogica, by Jan Malik.

2006, Mar. 24   Litho.   Perf. 14
662-663 A291   Set of 2   1.40 .70

Booklet Stamps
Self-Adhesive
Serpentine Die Cut 7¼
664-665 A291   Set of 2   2.00 1.00
a.   Booklet pane, 4 each #664-665   8.00
On day of issue Nos. 662-663, 664-665 each sold for 49t.

World Junior Slalom Kayaking Championships, Solkan — A292

2006, May 19   Perf. 14
666 A292 C multi   1.50 .75
No. 666 sold for 95t on day of issue.

Greetings — A293

Serpentine Die Cut 9¼x9
2006, May 19
Self-Adhesive
667 A293 C multi   1.50 .75
No. 667 sold for 95t on day of issue.

Painted Beehive Type of 2004
2006, May 19   Perf. 14
668 A250 D Hay rake fighters   1.60 .80
No. 668 sold for 107t on day of issue.

Europa — A294

2006, May 19
669 A294 D multi   1.60 .80
No. 669 sold for 107t on day of issue. Printed in sheets of 8 + label.

Svarog, Slavic Sun God — A295

2006, May 19
670 A295 D multi   1.75 .85
No. 670 sold for 107t on day of issue.

Souvenir Sheet

Slovenian Air Traffic Control, 15th Anniv. — A296

2006, June 25   Perf. 13¼x14
671 A296 C multi   1.50 .75
No. 671 sold for 95t on day of issue.

Ox-drawn Farm Wagon A297

2006, Sept. 22   Perf. 14
672 A297 D multi   1.75 .85
No. 672 sold for 107t on day of issue.

Souvenir Sheet

Ceiling Painting, Celje Mansion — A298

No. 673 — Text "Masa Kozjek, Tomaz Lauko" at: a, LL. b, LR. c, UL. d, UR.

2006, Sept. 22
673 A298 D Sheet of 4, #a-d   5.25 2.50
Nos. 673a-673d each sold for 107t on day of issue.

Aquatic Plants — A299

Designs: A, Salvinia natans and silhouette of frog. D, Marsilea quadrifolia and silhouette of dragonfly.

2006, Sept. 22
674 A299 A multi .85 .40
Souvenir Sheet
675 A299 D multi 1.75 .85
On day of issue No. 674 sold for 49t and No. 675 sold for 107t.

Fruit, Blossoms and Insects Type of 2000
Designs: No. 676, Persimmon blossom (cvet kakija). No. 677, Persimmon (kaki). No. 678, Citrus flatid planthopper (Medeci skrzat).

2006, Nov. 17 **Perf. 11¾x11¼**
Vignette Size: 19x23mm
676 A168 D multi 1.50 .75
677 A168 D multi 1.50 .75
678 A168 D multi 1.50 .75
a. Horiz. strip of 3, #676-678 4.50 2.25
On day of issue Nos. 676-678 each sold for 107t.

Partisan Couriers of World War II — A300

2006, Nov. 17 **Perf. 14**
679 A300 C multi 1.50 .75
No. 679 sold for 95t on day of issue.

Traditional Foods — A301

No. 680: a, Roast turkey, bread, corn, apple. b, Yeast cake (kvaseníca).

2006, Nov. 17
680 A301 D Horiz. pair, #a-b 2.75 1.40
On day of issue Nos. 680a-680b each sold for 107t.

Souvenir Sheet

Father Simon Asic (1906-92), Herbalist — A302

2006, Nov. 17
681 A302 D multi 1.50 .75
No. 681 sold for 107t on day of issue.

Christmas — A303

Designs: A, Snowman and bird. C, Carolers.

2006, Nov. 17 **Perf. 14**
682 A303 A multi .70 .35
683 A303 C multi 1.40 .70

Booklet Stamps
Self-Adhesive
Serpentine Die Cut 7¼
684 A303 A multi .70 .35
a. Booklet pane of 12 8.50
685 A303 C multi 1.40 .70
a. Booklet pane of 12 17.00
Nos. 682-685 (4) 4.20 2.10
On day of issue Nos. 682 and 684 each sold for 49t, and Nos. 683 and 685 each sold for 95t.

100 Cents = 1 Euro

Flora — A304

Designs: 1c, Asplenium adulterinum. 2c, Moehringia tommasinii. 5c, Himantoglossum adriaticum. 10c, Pulsatilla grandis. 20c, Primula carniolica. A, Campanula zoysii. B, Cypripedium calceolus. 25c, Gladiolus palustris. 35c, Cerastium dinaricum. C, Serratula lycopifolia. D, Genisia holopetala. 48c, Adenophora liliifolia. 50c, Aquilegia bertolonii. 75c, Liparis loeselii. 92c, Scilla litardierei. €1, Eryngium alpinum. €2, Rhododendron luteum.

2007, Jan. 1 **Litho.** **Perf. 11¼x11¾**
686 A304 1c multi .25 .25
687 A304 2c multi .25 .25
688 A304 5c multi .25 .25
689 A304 10c multi .35 .25
690 A304 20c multi .65 .30
691 A304 A multi .65 .30
692 A304 B multi .75 .35
693 A304 25c multi .80 .35
694 A304 35c multi 1.10 .50
695 A304 C multi 1.40 .60
696 A304 D multi 1.50 .70
697 A304 48c multi 1.50 .70
698 A304 50c multi 1.60 .75
699 A304 75c multi 2.40 1.10
700 A304 92c multi 3.00 1.90
701 A304 €1 multi 3.25 1.50
702 A304 €2 multi 6.50 3.00
Nos. 686-702 (17) 26.20 13.05
On day of issue No. 691 sold for 20c; No. 692 for 24c; No. 695 for 40c; No. 696 for 45c. See Nos. 787-797, 881-882.

Souvenir Sheet

Introduction of Euro Currency — A305

Perf. 13¼x13 Syncopated
2007, Jan. 1
703 A305 €1 multi 3.50 1.75

Traditional Clothing From Smlednik A306

2007, Jan. 24 **Perf. 11¾x11¼**
704 A306 20c multi .70 .35

Bride and Groom A307

2007, Jan. 24 **Perf. 11**
705 A307 24c multi .85 .40
Values are for stamps with surrounding selvage.

Vasja Pirc (1907-80), Chess Grandmaster — A308

2007, Jan. 24 **Perf. 14**
706 A308 48c multi 1.60 .80

 A309

 A310

 A311

Generic Personalized Stamps A312

Serpentine Die Cut 12x11½, 11½x12
2007, Jan. 24
Self-Adhesive
707 A309 A multi .75 .35
708 A310 A multi .75 .35
709 A311 A multi .75 .35
710 A312 A multi .75 .35
Nos. 707-710 (4) 3.00 1.40
On day of issue Nos. 707-710 each sold for 20c. Images within the frames shown above are generic images and were the only stamps with these frames sold at 20c. Stamps with these frames and other images are personalized stamps, created starting on Mar. 8, which sold in sheets of 20 for €12.51 per sheet.

Aragonite A313

2007, Mar. 23 **Perf. 11¾x11¼**
711 A313 45c multi 1.60 .80

Mt. Mangart and Geum Reptans A314

2007, Mar. 23 **Perf. 14**
712 A314 45c multi 1.60 .80

Europa A315

2007, Mar. 23
713 A315 50c multi 4.25 1.75
Scouting, cent. Printed in sheets of 8 + label.

Worldwide Fund for Nature (WWF) A316

Sciurus vulgaris: Nos. 714, 718a, 48c, Adult. Nos. 715, 718b, 48c, Adult eating acorn. Nos. 716, 718c, 48c, Two adults. Nos. 717, 718d, 48c, Adult and young.

2007, Mar. 23 **Perf. 11¾x11¼**
Size: 33x24mm
714-717 A316 Set of 4 5.75 2.75
Miniature Sheet
Perf. 13x13¼
Size: 36x26mm
718 A316 48c Sheet, 2 each #a-d 11.50 5.75

Elves — A317

2007, May 25 **Litho.** **Perf. 14**
719 A317 45c multi 1.50 .75

Treaty of Rome, 50th Anniv. — A318

2007, May 25 **Perf. 11¼x11¾**
720 A318 45c multi 1.50 .75

Horse-drawn Wagon — A319

2007, May 25   *Perf. 14*
721 A319 92c multi   2.75 1.40

Butterflies A320

Designs: 24c, Callimorpha quadripunctaria. 45c, Colias myrmidone, vert.

2007, May 25
722 A320 24c multi   .75 .35
Souvenir Sheet
723 A320 45c multi   1.50 .75

Souvenir Sheet

Year of the Bible — A321

2007, May 25
724 A321 75c multi   2.50 1.25

Lent Festival, Maribor A322

2007, June 22   *Perf. 14x13¼*
725 A322 €1 multi   3.25 1.60
Printed in sheets of 6 + 3 labels.

Wall Climbing A323

2007, Sept. 26   *Perf. 14*
726 A323 48c multi   1.50 .75
Printed in sheets of 6 + 3 labels.

Ceiling Fresco, Church of St. Nicholas, Ljubljana, by Giulio Quaglio A324

2007, Sept. 26   *Perf. 11¾x11¼*
727 A324 92c multi   2.75 1.40

Aquatic Flowers — A325

Designs: 20c, Nuphar luteum. 24c, Hydrocharis morsus-ranae. 40c, Nymphoides peltata. 45c, Nymphaea alba, horiz.

2007, Sept. 26   *Perf. 14*
728-730 A325 Set of 3   2.75 1.40
Souvenir Sheet
731 A325 45c multi   1.50 .75

Slovenian Entry Into Schengen Border-Free Zone — A326

2007, Nov. 23   *Perf. 11¾x11¼*
732 A326 45c multi   1.50 .75

Slovenian Food — A327

No. 733: a, Stajerska sour soup, Pohorski stew. b, Pohorje omelet.

2007, Nov. 23   *Perf. 11¼x11¾*
733 A327 45c Horiz. pair, #a-b   3.00 1.50

Souvenir Sheet

Bear Bone Flute From Divje Babe I Archaeological Site — A328

2007, Nov. 23   *Perf. 14*
734 A328 92c multi   3.00 1.50

A329

A330

A331

Personalized Stamps A332

Serpentine Die Cut 12x11½, 11½x12
2007, Nov. 23   **Litho.**
735 A329 A green & org   .65 .30
736 A330 A green & org   .60 .30
737 A331 C gray & org   1.40 .70
738 A332 C gray & org   1.40 .70
   Nos. 735-738 (4)   4.05 2.00

On day of issue, Nos. 735-736 each sold for 20c, and Nos. 737-738 each sold for 40c. Images within the frames shown above are generic images and were the only stamps sold at these prices. Stamps with these frames and other images are personalized stamps, which sold for more.

Christmas — A333

Perf. 13½x13¼
2007, Nov. 23   **Litho.**
739 A333 C multi   1.25 .60
No. 739 sold for 40c on day of issue.

New Year 2008 — A334

2007, Nov. 23   *Perf. 13x13¼*
740 A334 A multi   .60 .30
No. 740 sold for 20c on day of issue.

Slovenian postal authorities have declared illegal two sheetlets of six stamps with a denomination of "45" and bearing the name of "Slovenia" in Cyrillic lettering depicting Marilyn Monroe.

Souvenir Sheet

Slovenian Presidency of the European Union Council of Ministers — A335

Litho. With Foil Application
2008, Jan. 1   *Perf. 14x13½*
741 A335 €2.38 multi   7.00 3.50

Traditional Clothing From Pesnica and Scavnica A336

2008, Jan. 29 Litho.   *Perf. 11¾x11½*
742 A336 20c multi   .70 .35

Love A337

2008, Jan. 29   *Perf. 11*
743 A337 24c multi   .75 .35
Values are for stamps with surrounding selvage.

Primoz Trubar (1508-86), Writer A338

2008, Jan. 29   *Perf. 14*
744 A338 48c multi   1.50 .75

Vrbica Carnival Masks — A339

2008, Jan. 29   *Perf. 11¼x11¾*
745 A339 €1.75 multi   5.25 2.60

Dr. Julius Kugy (1858-1944), Botanist,
and Scabiosa Trenta — A340

2008, Mar. 28   **Litho.**   *Perf. 14*
746 A340 45c multi   1.40 .70

Flowers — A341

Designs: 20c, Paeonia officinalis. 24c, Pulsatilla montana. 40c, Iris illyrica.
45c, Gentiana tergestina.

2008, Mar. 28
747-749 A341   Set of 3   2.75 1.40
Souvenir Sheet
750 A341 45c multi   1.40 .70

Slovenian
Academy
of Arts and
Sciences,
70th Anniv.
A342

2008, May 29   **Litho.**   *Perf. 14*
751 A342 40c multi   1.25 1.25

Mokos, Slavic
Goddess — A343

2008, May 29
752 A343 45c multi   1.50 1.50

Europa
A344

Designs: 45c, Winged letters, postal card,
parcel. 92c, Letters as townspeople.

2008, May 29   *Perf. 11¾x11¼*
753-754 A344   Set of 2   4.50 4.50

Nos. 753-754 were each printed in sheets of
8 + label.

2008 Summer Olympics,
Beijing — A345

No. 755: a, 40c, Combat sports. b, 45c,
Sailing.

2008, May 29
755 A345   Horiz. pair, #a-b   2.75 2.75

Stamp Day — A346

2008, Sept. 29   *Perf. 11¼x11¾*
756 A346 23c multi   .65 .65

Dr. Alojzij Sustar (1920-2007),
Archbishop of Ljubljana — A347

2008, Sept. 29   *Perf. 14*
757 A347 45c multi   1.25 1.25

Rococo Decorations, Gruber
Palace — A348

2008, Sept. 29   *Perf. 11¼x11¾*
758 A348 92c multi   2.60 2.60

Horse-drawn Sledge — A349

2008, Sept. 29   *Perf. 14*
759 A349 92c multi   2.60 2.60

Souvenir Sheet

Slovenian Radio, 80th Anniv. and
Slovenian Television, 50th
Anniv. — A350

Perf. 13¼x14¼ Syncopated
2008, Sept. 29
760 A350 92c multi   2.60 2.60

Amphibians and Reptiles — A351

Designs: 23c, Rana latastei. 27c, Bombina
bombina. 40c, Trituris carnifex.

45c, Elaphe quatuorlineata.

2008, Sept. 29   *Perf. 14*
761-763 A351   Set of 3   2.50 2.50
Souvenir Sheet
764 A351 45c multi   1.25 1.25

Primoz Kozmus, 2008 Hammer Throw
Olympic Gold Medalist
A352

2008, Oct. 14   **Litho.**
765 A352 45c multi   1.25 1.25

Introduction of the
Euro, 10th Anniv.
(in 2009) — A353

2008, Nov. 27
766 A353 45c multi   1.25 1.25

End of
World War
I, 90th
Anniv.
A354

2008, Nov. 27
767 A354 92c multi   2.40 2.40

Souvenir Sheet

Wheel and Axle, c. 3200
B. C. — A355

2008, Nov. 27
768 A355 92c multi   2.40 2.40

Traditional Foods — A356

No. 769: a, Zgornjesavinjski zelodec (dried
sausage), bread. b, Ubrnenik (dumpling), Solcavski sirnek (spiced cheese).

2008, Nov. 27   *Perf. 11¼x11¾*
769 A356 45c Horiz. pair, #a-b   2.40 2.40

A357

Christmas
A358

2008, Nov. 27   *Perf. 11¼x11¾*
770 A357 A multi   .60 .60
            Perf. 11¾x11¼
771 A358 C multi   1.00 1.00

On day of issue, Nos. 770 and 771 sold for
23c and 40c, respectively.

Traditional
Clothing
From Bela
Krajina
A359

2009, Jan. 30   *Perf. 11¾x11¼*
772 A359 23c multi   .60 .60

Love
A360

2009, Jan. 30   *Perf. 11*
773 A360 27c multi   .70 .70

Values are for stamps with surrounding
selvage.

Alojz Knafelc
(1859-1937),
Mountain
Cartographer
A361

2009, Jan. 30   *Perf. 13¼x13*
774 A361 45c multi   1.25 1.25

Jozef Mrak
(1709-86),
Geodesist
A362

2009, Jan. 30   *Perf. 13x13¼*
775 A362 92c multi   2.40 2.40

Selma Carnival Costumes — A363

2009, Jan. 30   *Perf. 11¼x11¾*
776 A363 €1.60 multi   4.25 4.25

Souvenir Sheet

Eye and Braille Letters — A364

Litho. & Embossed
2009, Jan. 30   *Perf. 13x13¼*
777 A364 €2.38 multi   6.25 6.25
Louis Braille (1809-52), educator of the blind.

Essay for
First Stamps
of Slovenia
A365

Perf. 11¾x11½
2009, Mar. 27   **Litho.**
778 A365 23c multi   .65 .65
First Slovenian stamps (Yugoslavia Nos. 3L1-3L8), 90th anniv.

Lovrenc
Lakes
A366

2009, Mar. 27   *Perf. 13x13¼*
779 A366 35c multi   .95 .95

Zice Charterhouse — A367

2009, Mar. 27
780 A367 92c multi   2.50 2.50

Flowers
A368

Designs: 23c, Centaurea cyanus. 27c, Papaver rhoeas. 40c, Agrostemma githago. 45c, Ranunculus arvensis.

2009, Mar. 27   *Perf. 13x13¼*
781-783 A368   Set of 3   2.50 2.50

Souvenir Sheet
Perf. 14x13½
784 A368 45c multi   1.25 1.25

Souvenir Sheet

Preservation of Polar Regions and
Glaciers — A369

No. 785: a, Polar bear and puffins. b, Killer whale and polar bears.

2009, Mar. 27   *Perf. 13x13¼*
785 A369 45c Sheet of 2, #a-b   2.50 2.50

Council of
Europe, 60th
Anniv.
A370

2009, May 8   *Perf. 11¾x11¼*
786 A370 45c multi   1.25 1.25

Flora Type of 2007
Designs as before.

Serpentine Die Cut 14x15
2009, May 29   **Litho.**
Size: 23x30mm
Self-Adhesive
787 A304   1c multi   .25 .25
788 A304   10c multi   .30 .30
789 A304   20c multi   .55 .55
790 A304   25c multi   .70 .70
791 A304   A multi   .75 .75
792 A304   B multi   .85 .85
793 A304   35c multi   1.00 1.00
794 A304   C multi   1.10 1.10
795 A304   D multi   1.25 1.25
796 A304   75c multi   2.10 2.10
797 A304   €1 multi   2.75 2.75
   Nos. 787-797 (11)   11.60 11.60

On day of issue, No. 791 sold for 26c; No. 792, 30c; No. 794, 40c; No. 795, 45c.

Bread in Heart-
shaped Loaf — A371

Serpentine Die Cut 14x15
2009, May 29
Self-Adhesive
798 A371 C multi   1.10 1.10

World Track and
Field
Championships,
Berlin — A372

2009, May 29   *Perf. 13¼x13*
799 A372 45c multi   1.25 1.25
Printed in sheets of 6 + 3 labels.

World Plowing Championships,
Tesanovci — A373

2009, May 29   *Perf. 13x13¼*
800 A373 45c multi   1.25 1.25

Werewolf
A374

2009, May 29   *Perf. 13¼x13*
801 A374 70c multi   2.00 2.00

Ljubljana Jazz Festival, 50th
Anniv. — A375

2009, May 29   *Perf. 11½x11¾*
802 A375 92c black & yellow   2.60 2.60

Europa
A376

Designs: 45c, Stargazers. 92c, Observatory.

2009, May 29   *Perf. 13x13¼*
803-804 A376   Set of 2   4.00 4.00
Intl. Year of Astronomy. Nos. 803-804 were each printed in sheets of 8 + label.

Trolleybus,
Piran
A377

2009, Sept. 25   **Litho.**
805 A377 92c multi   2.75 2.75

Transfer of Seat of the Lavant
Diocese, 150th Anniv. — A378

2009, Sept. 25   *Perf. 11½x11¾*
806 A378 92c multi   2.75 2.75

Bohinj Lake, by Anton
Karinger — A379

2009, Sept. 25
807 A379 €1.50 multi   4.50 4.50

Beetles
A380

Designs: 26c, Lucanus cervus. 30c, Rosalia alpina. 40c, Osmoderma eremita. 45c, Carabus variolosus.

2009, Sept. 25   *Perf. 13x13¼*
808-810 A380   Set of 3   3.00 3.00
Souvenir Sheet
811 A380 45c multi   1.40 1.40

Souvenir Sheet

Stone Buildings — A381

No. 812 — Stone buildings in: a, Pazin, Croatia. b, Kopriva na Krasu, Slovenia.

2009, Sept. 25   *Perf. 13 Syncopated*
812 A381 92c Sheet of 2, #a-b   5.50 5.50
See Croatia No. 743.

Souvenir Sheet

Bronze Age Dagger — A382

2009, Nov. 27   *Perf. 13x14*
813 A382 92c multi   2.75 2.75

Traditional Foods — A383

No. 814: a, Funsterc ali knapovsko sonce (omelet) and Grenadirmars (potatoes and pasta). b, Zasavska jetrnica (sausage).

2009, Nov. 27   *Perf. 11½x11¾*
814 A383 45c Horiz. pair, #a-b   2.75 2.75

Christmas
A384   A385

2009, Nov. 27   *Perf. 11½x11¾*
815 A384 A multi   .80 .80
816 A385 C multi   1.25 1.25

Booklet Stamps
Self-Adhesive
Serpentine Die Cut 12¾
817 A384 A multi   .80 .80
   a.   Booklet pane of 12   9.75
818 A385 C multi   1.25 1.25
   a.   Booklet pane of 12   15.00

On day of issue, Nos. 815 and 817 each sold for 26c, and Nos. 816 and 818 each sold for 40c.

Vertical
Orientation,
Plain Frame
A386

Vertical
Orientation,
Candles in
Frame
A387

Vertical
Orientation,
Flower in
Frame
A388

Vertical
Orientation,
Book in
Frame
A389

Horizontal Orientation, Plain
Frame — A390

Horizontal Orientation, Candles in
Frame — A391

Horizontal Orientation, Flower in
Frame — A392

Horizontal Orientation, Book in
Frame — A393

Vertical
Orientation,
Heart in
Frame
A394

Vertical
Orientation,
Envleopes in
Frame
A395

Horizontal Orientation, Heart in
Frame — A396

Horizontal Orientation, Envelopes in
Frame — A397

Serpentine Die Cut 11½x11¾ (#819, 821), 11¾x11½ (#820, 822)
2009, Nov. 27   Litho.
Self-Adhesive

819	Sheet of 20	22.00	
a.	A386 A red frame	.80	.80
b.	A387 A green frame	.80	.80
c.	A386 A white frame	.80	.80
d.	A388 A purple frame	.80	.80
e.	A389 A orange frame	.80	.80
f.	A386 B white frame	.90	.90
g.	A389 B orange frame	.90	.90
h.	A386 B red frame	.90	.90
i.	A388 B purple frame	.90	.90
j.	A387 B green frame	.90	.90
k.	A386 C red frame	1.25	1.25
l.	A389 C orange frame	1.25	1.25
m.	A386 C white frame	1.25	1.25
n.	A387 C green frame	1.25	1.25
o.	A388 C purple frame	1.25	1.25
p.	A389 D orange frame	1.40	1.40
q.	A387 D green frame	1.40	1.40
r.	A388 D purple frame	1.40	1.40
s.	A386 D white frame	1.40	1.40
t.	A386 D red frame	1.40	1.40
820	Sheet of 20	22.00	
a.	A390 A white frame	.80	.80
b.	A392 A purple frame	.80	.80
c.	A393 A orange frame	.80	.80
d.	A391 A green frame	.80	.80
e.	A390 A red frame	.80	.80
f.	A390 B white frame	.90	.90
g.	A390 B red frame	.90	.90
h.	A391 B green frame	.90	.90
i.	A392 B purple frame	.90	.90
j.	A393 B orange frame	.90	.90
k.	A390 C red frame	1.25	1.25
l.	A393 C orange frame	1.25	1.25
m.	A392 C purple frame	1.25	1.25
n.	A391 C green frame	1.25	1.25
o.	A390 C white frame	1.25	1.25
p.	A391 D green frame	1.40	1.40
q.	A393 D orange frame	1.40	1.40
r.	A392 D purple frame	1.40	1.40
s.	A390 D white frame	1.40	1.40
t.	A390 D red frame	1.40	1.40
821	Sheet of 20	22.50	
a.	A394 A red frame	.80	.80
b.	A386 A gray frame	.80	.80
c.	A395 A blue frame	.80	.80
d.	A386 B dark blue frame	.90	.90
e.	A386 B orange frame	.90	.90
f.	A386 B green frame	.90	.90
g.	A395 B blue frame	.90	.90
h.	A386 B gray frame	.90	.90
i.	A394 B red frame	.90	.90
j.	A386 C orange frame	1.25	1.25
k.	A386 C green frame	1.25	1.25
l.	A395 C blue frame	1.25	1.25
m.	A386 C dark blue frame	1.25	1.25
n.	A394 C red frame	1.25	1.25
o.	A394 D red frame	1.40	1.40
p.	A386 D green frame	1.40	1.40
q.	A386 D dark blue frame	1.40	1.40
r.	A386 D orange frame	1.40	1.40
s.	A386 D gray frame	1.40	1.40
t.	A395 D blue frame	1.40	1.40
822	Sheet of 20	22.50	
a.	A390 A gray frame	.80	.80
b.	A397 A blue frame	.80	.80
c.	A396 A red frame	.80	.80
d.	A390 B green frame	.90	.00
e.	A396 B red frame	.90	.90
f.	A390 B dark blue frame	.90	.90
g.	A390 B gray frame	.90	.90
h.	A390 B orange frame	.90	.90
i.	A397 B blue frame	.90	.90
j.	A397 C blue frame	1.25	1.25
k.	A390 C orange frame	1.25	1.25
l.	A390 C green frame	1.25	1.25
m.	A396 C red frame	1.25	1.25
n.	A390 C dark blue frame	1.25	1.25
o.	A396 D red frame	1.40	1.40
p.	A390 D dark blue frame	1.40	1.40
q.	A397 D blue frame	1.40	1.40
r.	A390 D gray frame	1.40	1.40
s.	A390 D green frame	1.40	1.40
t.	A390 D orange frame	1.40	1.40
	Nos. 819-822 (4)	89.00	

On day of issue, stamps inscribed "A" sold for 26c; "B" sold for 30c; "C" sold for 40c; and "D" sold for 45c. Each vignette on Nos. 819-822 is in sepia. All sepia vignettes are different on the four sheets and are generic images found only on those sheets. Stamps can be personalized, printed in sheets of 20 stamps that have one type of frame and frame color and one personalized image in the vignette area.

Traditional
Clothing From
Prekmurje
A398

2010, Jan. 29   Litho.   *Perf. 13¾*
823 A398 26c multi   .75 .75

Love
A399

2010, Jan. 29   *Perf. 11*
824 A399 30c multi   .85 .85

Values are for stamps with surrounding selvage.

Arrows — A400

Serpentine Die Cut 15x14
2010, Jan. 29
Self-Adhesive
825 A400   D multi   2.40 2.40

No. 825 sold for 85c on day of issue and is for international priority mail.

New Year
2010 (Year
of the
Tiger)
A401

2010, Jan. 29   *Perf. 12¾x13*
826 A401 92c multi   2.60 2.60

Stanko Vraz
(1810-51),
Poet — A402

2010, Jan. 29   *Perf. 13x12¾*
827 A402 €1.10 multi   3.25 3.25

Pustnaki Procession, Mozirje — A403

2010, Jan. 29   *Perf. 13½x13¾*
828 A403 €1.60 multi   4.50 4.50

2010 Winter Olympics, Vancouver
A404

2010, Jan. 29 ***Perf. 12¾x13***

829	Horiz. pair + label	2.40	2.40
a.	A404 40c Ski flags	1.10	1.10
b.	A404 45c Hockey puck and stick	1.25	1.25

Braided Palm Branches
A406 A407

Serpentine Die Cut 14x15

2010, Mar. 18

Self-Adhesive

830	A406	B multi	.80	.80
831	A407	D multi	1.25	1.25

On day of issue, No. 830 sold for 30c and No. 831 sold for 45c.

Souvenir Sheet

World Ski Jumping Championships, Planica — A408

2010, Mar. 18 ***Perf. 13½x13¾***

832 A408 €2.38 multi 6.50 6.50

No. 832 has holes in the sheet margin reading "Planica 2010."

Izola
A409

2010, Mar. 26 ***Perf. 12¾x13***

833 A409 92c multi 2.50 2.50

Jurkloster Monastery
A410

2010, Mar. 26 **Litho.**

834 A410 92c multi 2.50 2.50

Peonies
A411

Designs: 45c, Paeonia officinalis. 92c, Paeonia rockii.

2010, Mar. 26 ***Perf. 12¾x13***

835	A411 45c multi	1.25	1.25
a.	Perf. 14¼x13¾	1.25	1.25
836	A411 92c multi	2.50	2.50
a.	Perf. 14¼x13¾	2.50	2.50
b.	Souvenir sheet, #835a-836a	3.75	3.75

Flowers
A412

Designs: 26c, Dianthus sanguineus. 30c, Dianthus sternbergii. 40c, Dianthus deltoides. 92c, Dianthus carthusianorum.

2010, Mar. 26 ***Perf. 12¾x13***

837-839 A412 Set of 3 2.60 2.60

Souvenir Sheet

Perf. 14¼x13¾

840 A412 92c multi 2.50 2.50

Carved Wooden Pigeon — A413

Serpentine Die Cut 14x15

2010, May 28

Self-Adhesive

841 A413 D multi 1.10 1.10

No. 841 sold for 45c on day of issue.

Kurent, Slovenian Deity — A414

2010, May 28 ***Perf. 13x12¾***

842 A414 70c multi 1.75 1.75

Sports World Championships — A415

Designs: No. 843, 92c, Soccer player, 2010 World Cup Soccer Championships, South Africa. No. 844, 92c, Basketball player, 2010 World Basketball Championships, Turkey.

2010, May 28 ***Perf. 13¾***

843-844 A415 Set of 2 4.50 4.50

Values are for stamps with surrounding selvage. Nos. 843-844 were printed in sheets containing four of each stamp and 2 central labels.

Europa
A416

Designs: D, Boy reading book. 92c, Girl reading book.

2010, May 28 ***Perf. 13x13¼***

845-846 A416 Set of 2 3.25 3.25

No. 845 sold for 45c on day of issue. Nos. 845-846 each were printed in sheets of 8 + label.

Puppets — A417

Designs: No. 847, 92c, Martin Krpan puppet made by Matjaz Schmidt. No. 848, 92c, Pavilha puppet made by Mara Kralj. No. 849, 92c, Gaspercek puppet made by Milan Klemencic. No. 850, 92c, Desetnica puppet made by Alenka Sotler. No. 851, 92c, Tincek Petelincek puppet made by Matej Vogrincic.

2010, May 28 ***Perf. 13½x13¾***

847-851 A417 Set of 5 11.00 11.00

Souvenir Sheet

Medalists at 2010 Winter Olympics, Vancouver — A418

No. 852: a, Tina Maze, Giant Slalom and Super-G skiing silver medalist. b, Petra Majdic, Individual Sprint Classic cross-country skiing bronze medalist

2010, June 24 ***Perf. 13¾x14¼***

852 A418 70c Sheet of 2, #a-b 3.50 3.50

Design of First UNICEF Greeting Card — A419

Die Cut Perf. 10¼x10

2010, Sept. 24

Self-Adhesive

853 A419 A multi .80 .80

No. 853 sold for 29c on day of issue.

Ljubljana Trolleybus
A420

2010, Sept. 24 ***Perf. 12¾x13***

854 A420 €1.50 multi 4.25 4.25

The Letter, by Janez Subic — A421

2010, Sept. 24 ***Perf. 13½x13¾***

855 A421 €1.50 multi 4.25 4.25

Snakes
A422

Designs: A, Vipera aspis. B, Coronella austriaca. C, Natrix natrix.
92c, Vipera ammodytes, vert.

2010, Sept. 24 ***Perf. 12¾x13***

856-858 A422 Set of 3 3.00 3.00

Souvenir Sheet

Perf. 13¾x14¼

859 A422 92c multi 2.60 2.60

On day of issue, Nos. 856-858 sold for 29c, 33c and 44c, respectively.

Souvenir Sheet

Glass Bead Necklace From Early Iron Age — A423

2010, Nov. 26 **Litho.** ***Perf. 13x14***

860 A423 92c multi 2.50 2.50

Traditional Foods — A424

No. 861: a, Mezerli (chopped pork ball). b, Koroska skuta (cottage cheese with onions and pumpkin seed oil).

2010, Nov. 26 ***Perf. 13½***

861 A424 49c Horiz. pair, #a-b 2.75 2.75

Christmas
A425 A426

2010, Nov. 26 ***Perf. 11¼x11¾***

862	A425	A multi	.80	.80
863	A426	C multi	1.25	1.25

Booklet Stamps
Self-Adhesive

Serpentine Die Cut 12¾

864	A425 A multi	.80	.80
a.	Booklet pane of 12	9.75	
865	A426 C multi	1.25	1.25
a.	Booklet pane of 12	15.00	

On day of issue, Nos. 862 and 864 each sold for 29c and Nos. 863 and 865 each sold for 44c.

Traditional Clothing From Notranjska
A427

2011, Jan. 28 ***Perf. 13½x14***

866 A427 A multi .65 .65

No. 866 sold for 24c on day of issue.

Lips
A428

2011, Jan. 28   *Perf. 13¼*
867 A428 B multi   .80 .80

No. 867 sold for 28c on day of issue. Values are for stamp with surrounding selvage.

Dr. Matija Murko (1861-1952), Ethnologist — A429

2011, Jan. 28   *Perf. 14x13¼*
868 A429 41c multi   1.10 1.10

New Year 2011 (Year of the Rabbit) A430

2011, Jan. 28   *Perf. 14x13¼*
869 A430 77c multi   2.10 2.10

Lieutenant General Franc Rozman (Commander Stane) (1911-43) — A431

2011, Jan. 28   *Litho.*
870 A431 92c multi   2.50 2.50

Godlar Stirring Pot, Sencur A432

2011, Jan. 28   *Perf. 13¼x14*
871 A432 €1.33 multi   3.75 3.75

Souvenir Sheet

Maribor Post Office Brass Band, 80th Anniv. — A433

2011, Mar. 25   *Perf. 14*
872 A433 B multi   .90 .90

No. 872 sold for 31c on day of issue.

Easter Egg — A434

Serpentine Die Cut 14x15
2011, Mar. 25
Self-Adhesive
873 A434 D multi   1.25 1.25

No. 434 sold for 44c on day of issue.

Church of the Holy Spirit, Javorca A435

2011, Mar. 25   *Perf. 14x13½*
874 A435 44c multi   1.25 1.25

Carthusian Monastery, Bistra A436

2011, Mar. 25   *Litho.*
875 A436 92c multi   2.75 2.75

Treaty of Paris, 60th Anniv. — A437

2011, Mar. 25   *Perf. 13¼x12¾*
876 A437 92c multi   2.75 2.75

Marsh Plants A438

Designs: A, Drosera rotundifolia. B, Oxycoccus palustris. C, Eriophorum vaginatum. 92c, Andromeda polifolia.

2011, Mar. 25   *Perf. 14x13½*
877-879 A438   Set of 3   3.00 3.00

Souvenir Sheet
Perf. 13x13¼
880 A438 92c multi   2.75 2.75

On day of issue, Nos. 877-879 sold for 27c, 31c and 40c, respectively.

Flowers Type of 2007
Designs as before.

Serpentine Die Cut 14x15
2011, Mar. 31   *Litho.*
Self-Adhesive
Size: 23x30mm
881 A304 2c multi   .25 .25
882 A304 5c multi   .25 .25

First Slovenian Motion Picture, 80th Anniv. A439

2011, May 27   *Perf. 14¼x13¾*
883 A439 44c multi   1.25 1.25

Organization for Economic Cooperation and Development, 50th Anniv. — A440

2011, May 27   *Perf. 14x13½*
884 A440 D multi   1.25 1.25

No. 884 sold for 44c on day of issue.

Water Man — A441

2011, May 27   *Perf. 13¼x14*
885 A441 77c multi   2.25 2.25

2011 World Rowing Championships, Bled — A442

2011, May 27   *Perf. 13¾x14¼*
886 A442 92c multi   2.75 2.75

Printed in sheets of 6 + 3 labels.

Postman Pavli — A443

Postman Pavli: A, Riding bicycle. B, Inserting letter into mailbox.

Serpentine Die Cut 14x15
2011, May 27
Self-Adhesive
887 A443 A multi   .80 .80
888 A443 B multi   .90 .90

On day of issue, No. 887 sold for 27c and No. 888 sold for 31c.
See Nos. 934-935.

Europa A444

Designs: D, Fagus sylvatica. 92c, Tallest pine tree in central Europe.

2011, May 27   *Perf. 13x13¼*
889-890 A444   Set of 2   4.00 4.00

Intl. Year of Forests. No. 889 sold for 44c on day of issue. Nos. 889-890 each were printed in sheets of 8 + label.

Souvenir Sheet

Johann Gerstner (1851-1939), Violinist — A445

Litho. & Engr.
2011, May 27   *Perf. 13¼*
891 A445 €1.33 multi   4.00 4.00

See Czech Republic No. 3501.

Souvenir Sheet

Independence, 20th Anniv. — A446

Litho. & Embossed With Foil Application
2011, June 25   *Perf. 13½x13¾*
892 A446 €3.11 multi   8.75 8.75

First University Chair for Slovene Studies, Bicent. A447

2011, Sept. 23 Litho.   *Perf. 14x13¼*
893 A447 C multi   1.10 1.10

No. 893 sold for 40c on day of issue.

Tomos
Colibri T
12 Moped
A448

2011, Sept. 23
894 A448 €1.33 multi   3.75 3.75

The Green
Veil, by
Rihard
Jakopic
(1896-1943)
A449

2011, Sept. 23   **Perf. 13¼x14**
895 A449 €1.33 multi   3.75 3.75

Worldwide Fund for Nature
(WWF) — A450

No. 896 — Various depictions of Austro-
potamobius torrentium: a, A. b, B. c, C. d, D.

2011, Sept. 23   **Perf. 13¼x13**
896 A450 Block of 4, 3a-d   4.00 4.00
On day of issue, Nos. 896a-896d sold for
27c, 31c, 40c and 44c, respectively.

Birds — A451

Designs: A, Numenius arquata. B, Dendrocopos leucotos. C, Emberiza hortulana.
92c, Ciconia ciconia.

2011, Sept. 23   **Perf. 13¼x14**
897-899 A451   Set of 3   2.75 2.75
Souvenir Sheet
Perf. 13¼x13
900 A451 92c multi   2.50 2.50
On day of issue, Nos. 897-899 sold for 27c,
31c and 40c, respectively.

MKS-Exclusive Microphone, Designed,
by Marko Turk (1920-99) — A452

2011, Nov. 25   **Perf. 14¼x13¾**
901 A452 58c multi   1.60 1.60

Traditional Foods — A453

No. 902: a, Loska smojka (stuffed turnips).
b, Blejska kremna rezina (Bled cream slice).

2011, Nov. 25   **Perf. 14x13¼**
902 A453 D Horiz. pair, #a-b   2.40 2.40
On day of issue Nos. 902a-902b each sold
for 44c.

Souvenir Sheet

Secovlje Salina Nature Park — A454

2011, Nov. 25   **Perf. 13x13¼**
903 A454 77c multi   2.10 2.10

Souvenir Sheet

Bronze Belt Plate With Hunting Motif,
7th-4th Cent. B.C. — A455

2011, Nov. 25   **Litho.**   **Perf. 14**
904 A455 92c multi   2.50 2.50

Personalized Stamps — A456

Frame designs: Nos. 905-912, Christmas
gifts, ornaments, bells, crackers and holly.
Nos. 913-920, Holly and ribbon.

Serpentine Die Cut 12x11¾, 11¾x12
2011, Nov. 25
Self-Adhesive
Country Name in Red
Horizontal Stamps

905 A456 A multi   .75   .75
906 A456 B multi   .85   .85
907 A456 C multi   1.10 1.10

908 A456 D multi   1.25 1.25
  a.   Horiz. strip of 4, #905-908 4.00
Vertical Stamps
909 A456 A multi   .75   .75
910 A456 B multi   .85   .85
911 A456 C multi   1.10 1.10
912 A456 D multi   1.25 1.25
  a.   Vert. strip of 4, #909-912   4.00
Country Name in Green
Horizontal Stamps
913 A456 A multi   .75   .75
914 A456 B multi   .85   .85
915 A456 C multi   1.10 1.10
916 A456 D multi   1.25 1.25
  a.   Horiz. strip of 4, #913-916 4.00
Vertical Stamps
917 A456 A multi   .75   .75
918 A456 B multi   .85   .85
919 A456 C multi   1.10 1.10
920 A456 D multi   1.25 1.25
  a.   Vert. strip of 4, #917-920   4.00
   Nos. 905-920 (16)   15.80 15.80
On day of issue, stamps inscribed "A" each
sold for 27c; stamps inscribed "B" each sold
for 31c; stamps inscribed "C" each sold for
40c; and stamps inscribed "D" each sold for
44c. The generic images for each stamp, an
example of which is shown, depicts a different
work of children's art, with stamps with the
same color of country name and orientation
issued in sheets of 20 containing five of each
type. The vignettes of these stamps could be
personalized, being printed in sheets of 20
containing the same denomination, frame and
orientation.

Christmas   Four-leaf
Bread — A457   Clover — A458

Serpentine Die Cut 14x15
2011, Nov. 25   **Litho.**
Self-Adhesive
921 A457 A multi   .75   .75
922 A457 C multi   1.10 1.10
Booklet Stamps
Size: 26x35mm
Serpentine Die Cut 12¾
923 A457 A multi   .75   .75
924 A457 C multi   1.10 1.10
  a.   Booklet pane of 12, 8 #923, 4
       #924   10.50
Christmas. On day of issue, Nos. 921 and
923 each sold for 27c, and Nos. 922 and 924
each sold for 40c.

Serpentine Die Cut 14x15
2011, Nov. 25
Self-Adhesive
925 A458 A multi   .75   .75
926 A458 C multi   1.10 1.10
Booklet Stamps
Size: 26x35mm
Serpentine Die Cut 12¾
927 A458 A multi   .75   .75
928 A458 C multi   1.10 1.10
  a.   Booklet pane of 12, 8 #927, 4
       #928   10.50
New Year 2012. On day of issue, Nos. 925
and 927 each sold for 27c, and Nos. 926 and
928 each sold for 40c.

Traditional
Clothing
From Bohinj
A459

2012, Jan. 27   **Perf. 11¾x11¼**
929 A459 27c multi   .70   .70

Heart
Carved
in Tree
A460

2012, Jan. 27   **Perf. 13x13¼**
930 A460 31c multi   .85   .85
Values are for stamps with surrounding
selvage.

New Year
2012
(Year of
the
Dragon)
A461

2012, Jan. 27   **Perf. 14¼x13¾**
931 A461 92c multi   2.50 2.50

Mira Mihelic
(1912-85),
Writer — A462

2012, Jan. 27   **Perf. 13¾x14¼**
932 A462 €1.25 multi   3.25 3.25

Souvenir Sheet

Enclosure of Ljubljana Inside Barbed
Wire Fence, 70th Anniv. — A463

2012, Jan. 27   **Perf. 14¼x13¾**
933 A463 €1.33 multi   3.50 3.50

Postman Pavli Type of 2011

Postman Pavli: C, With children at school.
D, With dog and bicycle.

Serpentine Die Cut 14x15
2012, Mar. 30
Self-Adhesive
934 A443 C multi   1.10 1.10
935 A443 D multi   1.25 1.25
On day of issue, No. 934 sold for 40c and
No. 935 sold for 44c.

Heart-shaped Honey
Biscuit — A464

2012, Mar. 30   **Litho.**
Self-Adhesive
936 A464 A multi   .75   .75
No. 936 sold for 27c on day of issue.

Valleys, Solcavsko District A465

2012, Mar. 30   **Perf. 14¼x13¾**
937 A465 €1.25 multi   3.50 3.50

Sts. Peter and Paul Minorite Monastery, Ptuj — A466

2012, Mar. 30
938 A466 €1.33 multi   3.50 3.50

Europa A467

Abstract design with: 44c, Spiral. 92c, Atomic orbits.

2012, Mar. 30   **Perf. 11¾x11¼**
939-940 A467 Set of 2   3.75 3.75

Maribor, 2012 European Capital of Culture. Nos. 939-940 each were printed in sheets of 8 + label.

Flowers in Ljubljana Botanical Gardens A468

Designs: 40c, Pastinaca sativa var. fleischmanni. 44c, Primula x venusta. 77c, Scabiosa hladnikiana. 92c, Scopolia carniolica f. hladnikiana.

2012, Mar. 30   **Perf. 14¼x13¾**
941-943 A468 Set of 3   4.25 4.25
Souvenir Sheet
944 A468 92c multi   2.50 2.50

2012 Summer Olympics, London — A469

No. 945: a, 77c, Judo, sailing. b, 92c, Swimming, handball.

2012, May 25 Litho. Perf. 14¼x13¾
945 A469 Horiz. pair, #a-b   4.25 4.25

Souvenir Sheet

Maribofila 2012 Philatelic Exhibition, Maribor — A470

2012, May 25
946 A470 D multi   1.10 1.10

No. 946 sold for 44c on day of issue.

Souvenir Sheet

Goricko Regional Park — A471

2012, May 25
947 A471 €1.25 multi   3.25 3.25

Souvenir Sheet

Smokehouses and Pottery — A472

No. 948: a, Felsoszölnök, Hungary smokehouse at left, pitcher, two lidded jars. b, Filovci, Slovenia smokehouse at right, jug, colander.

2012, May 25   **Perf. 14x13¼**
948 A472 92c Sheet of 2, #a-b   4.75 4.75

See Hungary No.

POSTAL TAX STAMPS

Catalogue values for unused stamps in this section are for Never Hinged items.

Red Cross — PT1

1992, May 8   **Litho.**   **Perf. 14**
RA1 PT1   3t blue, black & red   1.00 1.00

PT2   PT3

1992, June 2   **Perf. 14½x14**
RA2 PT2 3t multicolored   .60 .60
Red Cross, Solidarity.

1992, Sept. 14   **Litho.**   **Perf. 14**
RA3 PT3 3t multicolored   .50 .50
Stop Smoking Week, Sept. 14-21.

Red Cross — PT4

1993, May 8   **Litho.**   **Perf. 14**
RA4 PT4 3.50t blue, black & red   .50 .50

Rescue Team — PT5

1993, June 1
RA5 PT5 3.50t multicolored   .40 .40

Anti-Smoking Campaign PT6

1993, Sept. 14   **Litho.**   **Perf. 14**
RA6 PT6 4.50t multicolored   .40 .40

PT7

1994, May 8   **Litho.**   **Perf. 14**
RA7 PT7 4.50t multicolored   .40 .40
Obligatory on mail May 8-15.

Red Cross Worker, Child — PT8

1994, June 1
RA8 PT8 4.50t multicolored   .40 .40
Obligatory on mail June 1-7.

PT9

1995, May 8   **Litho.**   **Perf. 14**
RA9 PT9 6.50t multicolored   .50 .50
Obligatory on mail May 8-15.

Red Cross, Solidarity PT10

1995, June 1   **Litho.**   **Perf. 14**
RA10 PT10 6.50t multicolored   .50 .50
Obligatory on mail June 1-7.

Red Cross, Solidarity — PT11

1996, May 8   **Litho.**   **Perf. 14**
RA11 PT11 7t multicolored   .45 .45
Obligatory on mail May 8-15.

Red Cross, Solidarity PT12

1996, June 1   **Litho.**   **Perf. 14**
RA12 PT12 7t multicolored   .45 .45
Obligatory on mail June 1-7.

Red Cross, Solidarity PT13

1997, May 8   **Litho.**   **Perf. 14**
RA13 PT13 7t multicolored   .45 .45
Obligatory on mail May 8-14.

Red Cross, Solidarity PT14

1997, June 1   **Litho.**   **Perf. 14**
RA14 PT14 7t multicolored   .45 .45
Obligatory on mail June 1-7.

Red Cross Week — PT36

No. RA37: a, Girl in water, fish. b, Boy in water, ship.

2008, May 8   Litho.   Perf. 14
RA37 PT36 10c Horiz. pair, #a-b   .65   .65
Obligatory on mail May 8-15.

Fire Prevention Week — PT37

2008, Oct. 6
RA38 PT37 12c multi   .35   .35
Obligatory on mail Oct. 6-11.

Red Cross Solidarity Week — PT38

2008, Nov. 1   Litho.   Perf. 14
RA39 PT38 12c multi   .30   .30
Obligatory on mail Nov. 1-7.

Battle of Solferino, 150th Anniv. — PT39

2009, May 8
RA40 PT39 13c multi   .40   .40
Red Cross Week. Obligatory on mail May 8-15.

Fire Prevention Week — PT40

2009, Oct. 5
RA41 PT40 14c multi   .45   .45
Obligatory on mail Oct. 5-10.

Red Cross Solidarity Week — PT41

2009, Nov. 1
RA42 PT41 13c multi   .40   .40
Obligatory on mail Nov. 1-7.

Red Cross Week — PT42

2010, May 8   Perf. 14
RA43 PT42 13c multi   .35   .35
Obligatory on mail May 8-15.

Fire Prevention Week — PT43

2010, Oct. 4
RA44 PT43 14c multi   .40   .40
Obligatory on mail Oct. 4-9.

Henri Dunant (1828-1910), Founder of the Red Cross — PT44

2010, Nov. 1
RA45 PT44 13c multi   .40   .40
Obligatory on mail Nov. 1-7.

Red Cross Week PT45

2011, May 8
RA46 PT45 15c multi   .45   .45
Obligatory on mail May 8-15.

Fire Prevention Week — PT46

2011, Oct. 3   Perf. 11¼x12
RA47 PT46 15c multi   .45   .45
Obligatory on mail Oct. 3-8.

Red Cross Solidarity Week PT47

2011, Nov. 1   Perf. 14
RA48 PT47 15c multi   .45   .45
Obligatory on mail Nov. 1-7.

SOLOMON ISLANDS

ˈsä-lə-mən ˈī-ləndz

British Solomon Islands

LOCATION — West Pacific Ocean, east of Papua
GOVT. — Independent state in British Commonwealth
AREA — 10,954 sq. mi.
POP. — 455,429 (1999 est.)
CAPITAL — Honiara

The Solomons include 10 large islands and four groups of small islands extending over an area of 375,000 square miles.
The British protectorate of British Solomon Islands changed its name to Solomon Islands in 1975 and achieved independence July 7, 1978.

12 Pence = 1 Shilling
20 Shillings = 1 Pound
100 Cents = 1 Dollar (1966)

> **Catalogue values for unused stamps in this country are for Never Hinged items, beginning with Scott 80 in the regular postage section and Scott B1 in the semi-postal section.**

War Canoe — A1

Unwmk.

1907, Feb. 14		**Litho.**	**Perf. 11**	
1	A1	½p ultra	11.00	16.00
2	A1	1p red	27.50	30.00
3	A1	2p dull blue	37.50	36.00
a.		Horiz. pair, imperf. btwn.	15,000.	
4	A1	2½p orange	38.50	50.00
a.		Vert. pair, imperf. btwn.	7,000.	
b.		Horiz. pair, imperf. btwn.	10,000.	7,000.
5	A1	5p yellow green	67.50	80.00
6	A1	6p chocolate	75.00	77.50
a.		Vertical pair, imperf. btwn.	6,500.	
7	A1	1sh violet	97.50	110.00
		Nos. 1-7 (7)	354.50	399.50

Imperf. between varieties should be accompanied by certificates of authenticity issued by competent authorities. Excellent counterfeits are plentiful.

War Canoe A2

George V A3

Wmk. Multiple Crown and CA (3)

1908-11		**Engr.**	**Perf. 14**	
8	A2	½p green	1.75	1.25
9	A2	1p carmine	1.50	1.25
10	A2	2p gray	1.50	1.25
11	A2	2½p ultra	4.25	2.50
12	A2	4p red, yel ('11)	3.75	13.50
13	A2	5p olive green	10.50	8.75
14	A2	6p claret	11.50	8.25
15	A2	1sh black, green	9.75	9.25
16	A2	2sh vio, bl ('10)	47.50	70.00
17	A2	2sh6p red, bl ('10)	62.50	95.00
18	A2	5sh bl, yel ('10)	115.00	140.00
		Nos. 8-18 (11)	269.50	351.00

Inscribed "POSTAGE - POSTAGE"

1913-24			**Typo.**	
19	A3	½p green	.95	4.00
20	A3	1p carmine	3.25	16.50
21	A3	3p violet, yel	1.00	4.75
a.		3p violet, orange buff	9.25	27.50
22	A3	11p dull violet & red	5.75	14.00

Wmk. 4

23	A3	1½p scarlet ('24)	2.50	.80
		Nos. 19-23 (5)	13.45	40.05

Inscribed "POSTAGE - REVENUE"

1914-23			**Wmk. 3**	
28	A3	½p green	1.10	13.50
a.		½p yellow green ('17)	5.25	21.00
29	A3	1p carmine	1.75	1.50
a.		1p scarlet ('17)	5.50	7.50
30	A3	2p gray	3.50	10.50

31	A3	2½p ultra	4.00	5.75
		Chalky Paper		
32	A3	3p violet, yel ('23)	24.00	110.00
33	A3	4p blk & red, yel	2.25	3.00
34	A3	5p dull vio & ol grn	22.50	35.00
a.		5p brown purple & olive green	22.50	35.00
35	A3	6p dull vio & red vio	7.00	16.00
36	A3	1sh blk, green	5.50	8.00
a.		1sh blk, bl grn, ol back	8.50	27.50
37	A3	2sh dull vio & ultra, bl	8.00	11.50
38	A3	2sh6p blk & red, bl	11.00	22.50
39	A3	5sh grn & red, yel	42.50	55.00
a.		5sh green & red, orange buff	52.50	80.00
40	A3	10sh grn & red, grn	97.50	100.00
41	A3	£1 vio & blk, red	300.00	150.00
		Nos. 28-41 (14)	530.60	542.25

Inscribed "POSTAGE - REVENUE"

1922-31			**Wmk. 4**	
43	A3	½p green	.40	4.00
44	A3	1p carmine ('23)	12.50	12.50
45	A3	1p violet ('27)	1.10	8.50
46	A3	2p gray ('23)	5.25	17.00
47	A3	3p ultra ('23)	.85	5.25
		Chalky Paper		
48	A3	4p blk & red, yel ('27)	4.25	26.00
49	A3	4½p red brn ('31)	3.75	22.50
50	A3	5p dull vio & ol grn	3.75	32.50
51	A3	6p dull vio & red vio	4.50	32.50
52	A3	1sh black, emer	5.00	15.00
53	A3	2sh dull vio & ultra, bl ('27)	16.00	45.00
54	A3	2sh6p blk & red, bl	8.75	52.50
55	A3	5sh grn & red, yel	32.50	65.00
56	A3	10sh grn & red, emer ('25)	120.00	130.00
		Nos. 43-56 (14)	218.60	468.25

No. 49 is on ordinary paper.

Common Design Types pictured following the introduction.

Silver Jubilee Issue
Common Design Type

1935, May 6		**Engr.**	**Perf. 13½x14**	
60	CD301	1½p car & dk bl	1.50	1.50
61	CD301	3p blue & brown	5.00	7.75
62	CD301	6p ol grn & lt bl	13.50	14.00
63	CD301	1sh brt vio & ind	7.50	15.00
		Nos. 60-63 (4)	27.50	38.25
		Set, never hinged	47.50	

Coronation Issue
Common Design Type

1937, May 13			**Perf. 11x11½**	
64	CD302	1p dark purple	.25	.60
65	CD302	1½p dark carmine	.25	.50
66	CD302	3p deep ultra	.40	.40
		Nos. 64-66 (3)	.90	1.50
		Set, never hinged	1.40	

Spears and Shield — A4

Policeman and Chief — A5

Artificial Island, Malaita — A6

Canoe House, New Georgia A7

Roviana War Canoe — A8

View of Munda Point — A9

Meeting House, Reef Islands A10

Coconut Plantation A11

Breadfruit A12

Tinakula Volcano, Santa Cruz Islands A13

Scrub Fowl — A14

Malaita Canoe — A15

Perf. 12½, 13½ (A7, A13, A14)

			1939-51		**Wmk. 4**
67	A4	½p deep grn & ultra		.25	1.10
68	A5	1p dk pur & choc		.25	1.75
69	A6	1½p car & sl grn		.30	1.50
70	A7	2p blk & org brn		.35	1.60
a.		2p black & red brown ('43)		.35	1.75
		Never hinged		.65	
b.		Perf. 12 ('51)		.25	1.60
		Never hinged		.35	
71	A8	2½p ol grn & rose vio		1.25	2.75
a.		Vert. pair, imperf. horiz.		12,000.	
72	A9	3p ultra & blk, perf. 13½		.60	2.00
a.		Perf. 12 ('51)		.85	3.00
		Never hinged		2.00	
73	A10	4½p dk brn & yel grn		3.25	13.00
74	A11	6p rose lil & dk pur		.40	1.25
75	A12	1sh blk & grn		.80	1.25
76	A13	2sh dp org & blk		4.75	6.00
a.		2sh dp org & vio blk ('43)		4.75	6.50
		Never hinged		12.00	

77	A14	2sh6p dull vio & blk	17.50	5.00
78	A15	5sh red & brt bl grn	20.00	11.00
79	A10	10sh red lil & ol ('42)	4.00	8.00
		Nos. 67-79 (13)	53.70	56.20
		Set, never hinged	110.00	

> **Catalogue values for unused stamps in this section, from this point to the end of the section, are for Never Hinged items.**

Peace Issue
Common Design Type
Perf. 13½x14

			1946, Oct. 15		**Wmk. 4**	**Engr.**
80	CD303	1½p carmine			.25	.90
81	CD303	3p deep blue			.25	.30

Silver Wedding Issue
Common Design Types

1949, Mar. 14   Photo.   Perf. 14x14½

82	CD304	2p black	.40	.40

Perf. 11½x11
Engr.; Name Typo.

83	CD305	10sh red violet	13.00	13.00

UPU Issue
Common Design Types
Engr.; Name Typo. on 3p and 5p
Perf. 13½, 11x11½

			1949, Oct. 10		**Wmk. 4**
84	CD306	2p red brown		1.00	.85
85	CD307	3p indigo		2.40	.85
86	CD308	5p green		1.00	1.25
87	CD309	1sh slate		1.00	.85
		Nos. 84-87 (4)		5.40	3.80

Coronation Issue
Common Design Type

1953, June 2   Engr.   Perf. 13½x13

88	CD312 2p gray & black	1.10	1.10

Ysabel Canoe A16

Prow of Roviana Canoe — A17

Designs: 1p, Roviana canoe. 1½p, Artificial Island, Malaita. 2p, Canoe house. 3p, Malaita canoe. 5p, 1sh3p, Map. 6p, Trading schooner. 8p, 9p, Henderson Field, Guadalcanal. 1sh, Chart of Solomons and H.M.S. Swallow, recalling Capt. Philip Carteret's voyage of 1767. 2sh, Tinakula Volcano. 2sh6p, Meeting house, Reef Islands. 5sh, Alvaro de Mendana de Neyra and Caravel. 10sh, Constable and Chief. £1, Coat of Arms.

Perf. 11½x11, 11x11½, 12, 13

			1956-60		**Engr.**	**Wmk. 4**
89	A16	½p lilac & orange			.25	.55
90	A16	1p red brn & ol grn			.25	.25
91	A16	1½p dk car & sl bl			.25	1.10
92	A16	2p gray grn & choc			.35	.30
93	A17	2½p gray bl & blk			.90	.90
94	A16	3p dull red & grn			.80	.25
95	A16	5p blue & black			.30	.65
96	A16	6p bluish grn & blk			.65	.30
97	A16	8p black & ultra			.45	.25
98	A16	9p black & brt grn			3.50	1.00
99	A16	1sh brn org & sl bl			1.75	.75
100	A16	1sh3p blue & black			6.50	2.00
101	A16	2sh car rose & blk			13.50	3.00
102	A17	2sh6p rose lil & emer			7.50	.55
103	A16	5sh red brown			16.00	5.50
104	A17	10sh black brown			25.00	7.25
105	A16	£1 lt blue & blk			32.50	35.00
		Nos. 89-105 (17)			110.45	59.60

Issued: £1, 11/5/58; 9p, 1sh3p, 1/28/60; others, 3/1/56.
See Nos. 113-125.

Great Frigate Bird — A18

Perf. 13x12½

			1961, Jan. 19		**Litho.**	**Wmk. 314**
106	A18	2p blue green & black			.25	.25
107	A18	3p rose red & black			.25	.25
108	A18	9p lilac & black			.35	.40
		Nos. 106-108 (3)			.85	.90

New constitution, brought into operation Oct. 18, 1960. The watermark is sideways and may be found facing both left and right.

Freedom from Hunger Issue
Common Design Type

1963, June 4   Photo.   Perf. 14x14½

109	CD314 1sh3p ultra	3.50	1.50

Red Cross Centenary Issue
Common Design Type

1963, Sept. 2   Litho.   Perf. 13

110	CD315	2p black & red	.40	.25
111	CD315	9p ultra & red	2.00	1.75

Types of 1956-60
Perf. 12, 13, 11½x11

			1963-64		**Engr.**	**Wmk. 314**
113	A16	1p red brn & ol grn			.40	.45
114	A16	1½p dk car & sl bl			1.00	.80
115	A16	2p gray grn & choc			.30	.25
117	A16	3p dull red & grn			.80	.25
119	A16	6p bluish grn & blk			1.00	.65
121	A16	9p black & brt grn			1.10	.55
123	A16	1sh3p blue & blk			1.25	1.75
124	A16	2sh car rose & blk			3.00	7.50
125	A17	2sh6p rose lil & emer			19.00	17.50
		Nos. 113-125 (9)			27.85	29.70

Issued: 3p, 11/16; 6p, 9p, 1sh3p, 7/7/64; 1p, 1½p, 2p, 2sh, 2sh6p, 7/9/64.

ITU Issue
Common Design Type
Perf. 11x11½

			1965, June 28		**Litho.**	**Wmk. 314**
126	CD317	2p ver & grnsh blue			.35	.25
127	CD317	3p grnsh bl & ol bis			.55	.40

Makira Food Bowl — A19

Designs: 1p, 1sh, 1sh3p, Various orchids. 1½p, Scorpion shell. 2p, Papuan hornbill. 2½p, Ysabel shield. 3p, Rennellese club. 6p, Moorish idol (fish). 9p, Great frigate bird. 2sh, Sanford's sea eagle. 2sh6p, Malaita belt. 5sh, Ornithoptera Victoreae (butterfly). 10sh, White cockatoo. £1, Figurehead, western canoe.

Perf. 13x12½

			1965, May 24		**Wmk. 314**

Design Subject in Black

128	A19	½p sl blue & lt bl		.25	1.50
129	A19	1p orange & yel		.45	.60
130	A19	1½p blue & grn		.25	1.25
131	A19	2p vio bl & lt bl		.35	1.60
132	A19	2½p red brn & buff		.25	1.25
133	A19	3p grn & lt grn		.25	.25
134	A19	6p brt car rose & org		.25	.85
135	A19	9p slate grn & buff		.50	.25
136	A19	1sh dp cl & rose		1.10	.25
137	A19	1sh3p ver & buff		4.75	2.50
138	A19	2sh dp mag & lil		9.00	3.00
139	A19	2sh6p ol brn & buff		1.10	.75
140	A19	5sh dk vio bl & lil		13.50	4.75
141	A19	10sh ol grn & yel		16.50	3.75
142	A19	£1 purple & red		10.00	4.75
		Nos. 128-142 (15)		58.50	27.30

For surcharges see Nos. 149-166.

Intl. Cooperation Year Issue
Common Design Type

1965, Oct. 25   Litho.   Perf. 14½

143	CD318	1p bl grn & cl	.25	.25
144	CD318	2sh6p lt violet & grn	1.10	.90

Churchill Memorial Issue
Common Design Type

			1966, Jan. 24		**Photo.**	**Perf. 14**
145	CD319	2p multicolored			.25	.30
146	CD319	9p multicolored			.45	.30
147	CD319	1sh3p multicolored			.60	.30
148	CD319	2sh6p multicolored			.70	.85
		Nos. 145-148 (4)			2.00	1.75

Nos. 128-142 Surcharged with New Value and Three Bars in Black or Red

Perf. 13x12½

			1966-67		**Litho.**	**Wmk. 314**
149	A19	1c on ½p multi			.25	.25
150	A19	2c on 1p multi			.25	.25
151	A19	3c on 1½p multi			.25	.25
152	A19	4c on 2p multi			.25	.25
153	A19	5c on 6p multi			.25	.25
154	A19	6c on 2½p multi			.25	.25
155	A19	7c on 3p multi			.30	.35
156	A19	8c on 9p multi			.35	.35
b.		"8" inverted			40.00	22.50
157	A19	10c on 1sh			.45	.45
158	A19	12c on 1sh3p multi			.80	.45
159	A19	13c on 1sh3p multi			2.75	.50
160	A19	14c on 3p multi			.65	.50
161	A19	20c on 2sh multi			2.75	.85
162	A19	25c on 2sh6p multi			1.00	.75
163	A19	35c on 2p multi			2.75	.40
164	A19	50c on 5sh multi (R)			5.00	1.75
165	A19	$1 on 10sh multi			2.50	1.50
166	A19	$2 on £1 multi			2.25	3.00
		Nos. 149-166 (18)			23.05	12.30

The 12c, 14c, 35c have watermark sideways.
Issued: 12c, 14c, 35c, 3/1/67; others, 2/14/66.

			1966		**Wmk. 314 Sideways**
149a	A19	1c on ½p		.25	.25
150a	A19	2c on 1p		.25	.25
151a	A19	3c on 1½p		.25	.25
152a	A19	4c on 2p		.25	.25
153a	A19	5c on 6p		.30	.30
154a	A19	6c on 2½p		.35	.35
155a	A19	7c on 3p		.40	.40
156a	A19	8c on 9p		.45	.45
157a	A19	10c on 1sh		.60	.60
158a	A19	13c on 1sh3p		4.50	2.75
161a	A19	20c on 2sh		3.25	.35
162a	A19	25c on 2sh6p		2.50	.35
164a	A19	50c on 5sh (R)		10.00	4.75
165a	A19	$1 on 10sh		7.50	2.00
166a	A19	$2 on £1		6.50	3.00
		Nos. 149a-166a (15)		37.35	16.30

World Cup Soccer Issue
Common Design Type

			1966, July 1		**Litho.**	**Perf. 14**
167	CD321	8c multicolored			.30	.30
168	CD321	35c multicolored			1.10	1.10

WHO Headquarters Issue
Common Design Type

			1966, Sept. 20		**Litho.**	**Perf. 14**
169	CD322	3c multicolored			.25	.25
170	CD322	50c multicolored			1.60	1.60

UNESCO Anniversary Issue
Common Design Type

			1966, Dec. 1		**Litho.**	**Perf. 14**
171	CD323	3c "Education"			.40	.25
172	CD323	25c "Science"			.95	.40
173	CD323	$1 "Culture"			2.40	1.90
		Nos. 171-173 (3)			3.75	2.55

Henderson Field, Guadalcanal — A20

Design: 35c, US Marines landing, Red Beach, Guadalcanal, 1942.

Perf. 14x14½

			1967, Aug. 28		**Photo.**	**Wmk. 314**
174	A20	8c multi & silver			.25	.25
175	A20	35c multi & gold			.75	.75

Guadalcanal campaign in WW II, 25th anniv.

Mendana's Ship Off Puerta de la Cruz (Honiara), Guadalcanal, 1568 — A21

Designs: 8c, Arrival of Missionaries. 35c, Naval battle during World War II. $1, Honor guard raising Union Jack during proclamation of Protectorate.

1968, Feb. 2   Photo.   Perf. 14½
176	A21	3c pink & multi	.40	.25
177	A21	8c emerald & multi	.40	.25
178	A21	35c multicolored	.85	.25
179	A21	$1 blue & multi	1.10	2.25
		Nos. 176-179 (4)	2.75	3.00

400th anniv. of the discovery of the British Solomon Islands by the Spanish navigator Alvaro de Mendana de Neyra.

Vine Fishing A22

Designs: 2c, Kite fishing. 3c, Platform fishing. 4c, Net fishing. 6c, Gold lip shell diving. 8c, Night fishing. 12c, Boat building. 14c, Cocoa harvest. 15c, Road building. 20c, Geological survey by plane. 24c, Hauling timber. 35c, Copra. 45c, Harvesting rice. $1, Honiara Port. $2, Map of the Islands, plane and route of Internal Air Service.

Wmk. 314
1968, May 20   Photo.   Perf. 14½
180	A22	1c aqua, brn & blk	.25	.25
181	A22	2c lt yel grn, brn & blk	.25	.25
182	A22	3c brt grn, dk grn & blk	.25	.25
183	A22	4c brt rose lil, brn & blk	.25	.25
184	A22	6c multicolored	.30	.25
185	A22	8c dp ultra, org & blk	.25	.30
186	A22	12c bister, red & blk	.85	.35
187	A22	14c red org, brn & blk	2.75	2.25
188	A22	15c multicolored	.90	.70
189	A22	20c ultra, red & blk	4.50	3.25
190	A22	24c scarlet, yel & blk	2.50	3.75
191	A22	35c multicolored	2.50	.45
192	A22	45c yellow, red & blk	2.00	.45
193	A22	$1 vio bl, emer & blk	3.00	1.75
194	A22	$2 multicolored	7.50	4.00
		Nos. 180-194 (15)	28.05	18.50

Map of South Pacific and University Degrees — A23

Perf. 12½x12
1969, Feb. 10   Litho.   Unwmk.
195	A23	3c multicolored	.25	.25
196	A23	12c multicolored	.25	.25
197	A23	35c multicolored	.55	.50
		Nos. 195-197 (3)	1.05	1.00

Inauguration of the University of the South Pacific in 1969, at the Royal New Zealand Air Force Seaplane Station, Laucala Bay, Fiji.

Field Ball and Games' Emblem — A24

Perf. 14½x14
1969, Aug. 13   Photo.   Wmk. 314
198	A24	3c shown	.25	.25
199	A24	8c Soccer	.25	.25
200	A24	14c Running	.35	.30
201	A24	45c Rugby	1.10	.95
a.		Souvenir sheet of 4, #198-201	6.50	6.50
		Nos. 198-201 (4)	1.95	1.75

3rd S. Pacific Games, Port Moresby, Aug. 13-23.

In No. 201a, shading was added below athlete's foot on 14c, and strengthened on 8c and 45c.

Stained Glass Window with Melanesian Peace Symbol — A25

Christmas: 8c, South Sea Islands scene with palms and Star of Bethlehem.

1969, Nov. 21   Photo.   Wmk. 314
202	A25	8c vio, grnsh bl & blk	.25	.25
203	A25	35c black & multi	.60	.60

C. M. Woodford and Stamp of 1907 — A26

Designs: 7c, British Solomon Islands 1906 handstamp and cancellation, and New South Wales No. 99. 18c, British Solomon Islands No. 18 and 1913 Tulagi cancellation. 23c, New General Post Office, Honiara.

1970, Apr. 15   Litho.   Perf. 13
204	A26	7c lilac rose & black	.25	.25
205	A26	14c lt olive & black	.35	.35
206	A26	18c orange, yel & blk	.45	.45
207	A26	23c multicolored	.65	.65
		Nos. 204-207 (4)	1.70	1.70

Issued to publicize the opening of the new General Post Office in Honiara.

Map of Solomon Islands A27

18c, British Solomon Islands coat of arms, vert.

Perf. 14½x14, 14x14½
1970, June 15   Litho.   Wmk. 314
208	A27	18c multicolored	.55	.55
209	A27	35c multicolored	1.00	1.00

Adoption of the new 1970 Constitution.

Red Cross Headquarters, Honiara — A28

35c, Map of British Solomon Islands showing Red Cross stations, wheelchair.

1970, Aug. 17   Perf. 14½x14
210	A28	3c multicolored	.25	.25
211	A28	35c multicolored	.95	.85

Centenary of British Red Cross Society.

Carved Angel and Southern Cross — A29

Reredos: Symbols of Trinity and Light at St. Luke's Church, Kia — A30

Perf. 14x13½, 13½x14
1970, Oct. 19   Litho.   Wmk. 314
212	A29	8c violet & bister brn	.25	.25
213	A30	45c multicolored	1.00	1.00

Christmas 1970.

Count de La Pérouse and "La Boussole" — A31

4c, Astrolabe, Polynesian reed map. 12c, Abel Tasman, sailing ship Heemskerk, 1643. 35c, Te Puki canoe, Santa Cruz.

1971, Jan. 28   Perf. 14½x14
214	A31	3c multicolored	1.00	.50
215	A31	4c multicolored	1.00	.50
216	A31	12c multicolored	1.25	.75
217	A31	35c multicolored	1.50	1.25
		Nos. 214-217 (4)	4.75	3.00

In honor of famous explorers and ships.
See Nos. 228-231, 250-253.

Bishop Patteson, J. Atkin and S. Taroniara — A32

Designs: 4c, Last landing of the "Southern Cross" at Nukapu. 14c, Memorial for Bishop Patteson and map of Nukapu, vert. 45c, Ceremonial leaf tag (had been attached to Bishop's body), vert.

Perf. 14½x14, 14x14½
1971, Apr. 5   Litho.   Wmk. 314
218	A32	2c lt green & multi	.25	.25
219	A32	4c blue green & multi	.25	.25
220	A32	14c brt pink & multi	.25	.25
221	A32	45c brown & multi	.50	.50
		Nos. 218-221 (4)	1.25	1.25

Bishop John Coleridge Patteson (1827-71), head of the Melanesian mission.

Boxing, Games Emblem A33

8c, Soccer. 12c, Running. 35c, Spear fishing.

1971, Aug. 9   Perf. 14½x14
222	A33	3c orange & multi	.30	.30
223	A33	8c emerald & multi	.30	.30
224	A33	12c yellow & multi	.30	.30
225	A33	35c blue & multi	.50	.50
		Nos. 222-225 (4)	1.40	1.40

4th South Pacific Games, Papeete, French Polynesia, Sept. 8-19.

Melanesian Lectern (wood carving) — A34

Christmas: 45c, Stylized birds, painted by school girl Margarita Bara.

1971, Nov. 15   Litho.   Wmk. 314
226	A34	9c orange & multi	.25	.25
227	A34	45c blue & multi	1.10	1.10

Explorer Type of 1971

4c, Louis Antoine de Bougainville, La Boudeuse, 1776. 9c, Horizontal planisphere, 1574, ivory backstaff, 1695. 15c, Philip Carteret, H.M.S. Swallow, 1707. 45c, Small canoe of Malaita.

1972, Feb. 1   Perf. 14½
228	A31	4c brown & multi	.45	.25
229	A31	9c green & multi	.65	.25
230	A31	15c lt blue & multi	1.10	.50
231	A31	45c blue & multi	2.40	2.50
		Nos. 228-231 (4)	4.60	3.50

Cupha Woodfordi A35

Designs: 1c, 2c, 3c, 4c, $2, Butterflies. 5c, 8c, 9c, 15c, $1. Fishes. 12c, 20c, 25c, 35c, 45c, Orchids. $5, Birds.

1972-73   Perf. 14
232	A35	1c shown	.25	.25
233	A35	2c Ornithoptera priamus	.30	.30
234	A35	3c Vindula sapor	.30	.30
235	A35	4c Papilio orssippus	.30	.30
236	A35	5c Great trevally	.40	.40
237	A35	8c Little bonito	.50	.50
238	A35	9c Sapphire demoiselle	.60	.70
239	A35	12c Costus speciosus	1.50	.80
240	A35	15c Orange anemone	1.50	1.00
241	A35	20c Spathoglottis plicata	3.50	1.25
242	A35	25c Ephemerantha comata	3.50	1.50
243	A35	35c Dendrobium cuthbertsonii	3.75	2.00
244	A35	45c Heliconia salomonica	3.00	3.00
245	A35	$1 Blue-finned triggerfish	3.75	5.00
246	A35	$2 Ornithoptera allotti	11.00	17.50
247	A35	$5 Great frigate bird	18.50	19.50
		Nos. 232-247 (16)	52.65	54.30

Issued: $5, 7/2/73; others, 7/2/72.
For overprints see Nos. 300-311.

Silver Wedding Issue, 1972
Common Design Type

Design: Queen Elizabeth II, Prince Philip, scroll and message drum on woven mat.

1972, Nov. 20   Photo.   Perf. 14x14½
248	CD324	8c car rose & multi	.25	.25
249	CD324	45c olive & multi	.50	.50

Explorer Type of 1971

Designs: 4c, Antoine R. J. d'Entrecasteaux and "The Recherche," 1791. 9c, Ship's hourglass, 17th century, and chronometer, 1761. 15c, Lieutenant Shortland and "The Alexander," 1788. 35c, Tomoko (war canoe).

Wmk. 314
1973, Mar. 9   Litho.   Perf. 14½
250	A31	4c blue & multi	.25	.25
251	A31	9c blue & multi	.55	.55
252	A31	15c blue & multi	1.00	1.00
253	A31	35c blue & multi	3.25	3.25
		Nos. 250-253 (4)	5.05	5.05

Pan Pipes A36

Musical Instruments: 9c, Castanets. 15c, Bamboo flute. 35c, Bauro gongs. 45c, Bamboo band.

1973, Oct. 1   **Perf. 13½x14**
254	A36	4c brick red & multi	.25	.25
255	A36	9c yellow bis & multi	.25	.25
256	A36	15c pink & multi	.40	.40
257	A36	35c blue green & multi	.90	.90
258	A36	45c multicolored	1.25	1.25
		Nos. 254-258 (5)	3.05	3.05

Princess Anne's Wedding Issue
Common Design Type
1973, Nov. 14   **Perf. 14**
259	CD325	4c slate & multi	.30	.30
260	CD325	35c multicolored	.70	.70

Adoration of the Kings, by Jan Brueghel A37

Adoration of the Kings by: 22c, Peter Brueghel, vert. 45c, Botticelli.

1973, Nov. 26   **Litho.**   **Perf. 14**
Size: 39x25mm, 25x39mm
261	A37	8c pink & multi	.25	.25
262	A37	22c lilac & multi	.50	.50

Perf. 13½
Size: 47x35mm
263	A37	45c gray & multi	1.25	1.25
		Nos. 261-263 (3)	2.00	2.00

Christmas 1973.

Map of Solomon Islands — A38

1974, Feb. 18   **Litho.**   **Perf. 13½**
264	A38	4c blue & multi	.25	.25
265	A38	9c citron & multi	.25	.25
266	A38	15c violet gray & multi	.45	.45
267	A38	35c emerald & multi	1.50	1.50
		Nos. 264-267 (4)	2.45	2.45

Visit of British Royal Family.

First Resident Commissioner Landing at Tulagi — A39

Designs: 9c, Marine radar and scanner unit, map of Islands. 15c, Islanders taken to "Blackbirder" ship. 45c, John F. Kennedy's P.T. 109 off Lumbari Island, 1943.

1974, May 15   **Litho.**   **Perf. 14½**
268	A39	4c multicolored	.25	.25
269	A39	9c multicolored	.45	.45
270	A39	15c multicolored	.60	.60
271	A39	45c multicolored	2.75	2.75
		Nos. 268-271 (4)	4.05	4.05

Ships and navigators.

Mailman, Map of Islands — A40

9c, Carrier pigeon, horiz. 15c, Angel Gabriel. 45c, Pegasus, horiz. Designs based on origami (folded paper) figures.

1974, Aug. 29   **Wmk. 314**   **Perf. 14**
272	A40	4c brt green & multi	.25	.25
273	A40	9c lemon & multi	.30	.25
274	A40	15c multicolored	.45	.35
275	A40	45c blue & multi	1.25	1.10
		Nos. 272-275 (4)	2.25	1.95

Centenary of Universal Postal Union.

Solomon Islands No. 208 A41

1974, Dec. 16   **Litho.**   **Perf. 14½**
276	A41	4c shown	.25	.25
277	A41	9c No. 107	.30	.30
278	A41	15c same	.50	.50
279	A41	35c like 4c	1.10	1.10
a.		Souvenir sheet of 4, #276-279	5.00	5.00
		Nos. 276-279 (4)	2.15	2.15

New Constitution, inaugurated Oct. 18, 1960.

Golden Whistler A42

Birds: 2c, River kingfisher. 3c, Red-throated fruit dove. 4c, Button quail. $2, Duchess lorikeet.

1975, Apr. 7   **Wmk. 314**   **Perf. 14**
280	A42	1c yellow grn & multi	.60	.75
281	A42	2c lt blue & multi	.70	1.00
282	A42	3c brt pink & multi	.80	1.00
283	A42	4c orange & multi	.90	.80
284	A42	$2 dp orange & multi	15.00	15.00
		Nos. 280-284 (5)	18.00	18.55

See Nos. 316-320, 323, 330-331. For overprints see Nos. 296-299, 310.

Motor Vessel Walande A43

1975, May 29   **Perf. 13½**
285	A43	4c shown	.60	.50
286	A43	9c M. V. Melanesian	.80	.25
287	A43	15c Ship Marsina, house flag	1.10	.25
288	A43	45c S. S. Himalaya	2.00	1.50
		Nos. 285-288 (4)	4.50	2.25

Runner, 800-meters — A44

1975, Aug. 4   **Litho.**   **Perf. 13½**
289	A44	4c shown	.25	.25
290	A44	9c Long jump	.25	.25
291	A44	15c Javelin	.35	.35

292	A44	45c Soccer	1.00	1.00
a.		Souvenir sheet of 4, #289-292	5.25	5.25
		Nos. 289-292 (4)	1.85	1.85

5th South Pacific Games, Guam, Aug. 1-10.

Nativity and Candles A45

Christmas: 35c, Angels, shepherds and candles. 45c, Three Kings approaching Bethlehem, and candles.

1975, Oct. 13   **Wmk. 373**   **Perf. 14**
293	A45	15c multicolored	.35	.35
294	A45	35c multicolored	.80	.80
295	A45	45c multicolored	1.10	1.10
a.		Souvenir sheet of 3, #293-295	6.00	6.00
		Nos. 293-295 (3)	2.25	2.25

Nos. 236-245, 247, 280-284
Overprinted with Bar Obliterating
"British" in Black or Silver
1975, Nov. 12   **Litho.**   **Wmk. 314**
296	A42	1c multicolored	.85	.70
297	A42	2c multicolored	1.50	.70
298	A42	3c multicolored	.95	.70
299	A42	4c multicolored	1.50	.70
300	A35	5c multicolored	.75	.70
301	A35	8c multicolored	.75	.70
302	A35	9c multicolored	.75	.70
303	A35	12c multicolored	2.50	1.25
304	A35	15c multicolored	2.50	1.75
305	A35	20c multicolored	3.00	2.25
306	A35	25c multicolored	3.00	2.25
307	A35	35c multicolored	3.25	2.25
308	A35	45c multicolored	3.00	2.75
309	A35	$1 multicolored	2.50	4.00
310	A42	$2 multicolored	7.50	9.00
311	A35	$5 multicolored (S)	7.25	18.00
		Nos. 296-311 (16)	41.55	48.15

Ceremonial Food Bowl — A46

Artifacts: 15c, Barava, chief's money. 35c, Nguzu-nguzu, canoe protector spirit, vert. 45c, Nguzu-nguzu on canoe prow.

Wmk. 314
1976, Jan. 12   **Litho.**   **Perf. 14**
312	A46	4c scarlet & black	.25	.25
313	A46	15c lt violet & multi	.25	.25
314	A46	35c multicolored	.75	.75
315	A46	45c multicolored	.90	.90
		Nos. 312-315 (4)	2.15	2.15

Type of 1975 Inscribed "Solomon
Islands" and

Golden Cowries A47

1c, Golden whistler. 2c, River kingfisher. 3c, Red-throated fruit dove. 4c, Button quail. 5c, Willie wagtail. 10c, Glory-of-the-sea cones. 12c, Rainbow lory. 15c, Pearly nautilus. 20c, Venus comb murex. 25c, Commercial trochus. 35c, Melon or baler shell. 45c, Orange spider conch. $1, Pacific triton. $2, Duchess lorikeet. $5, Great frigate bird.

1976   **Wmk. 373**   **Perf. 14**
316	A42	1c yel grn & multi	.40	.35
317	A42	2c lt blue & multi	1.00	.70
318	A42	3c pink & multi	.45	.35
319	A42	4c orange & multi	.45	.40
320	A42	5c red brown & multi	1.00	.70
321	A47	6c rose & multi	.60	.50
322	A47	10c multicolored	.60	.50
323	A42	12c yel grn & multi	1.00	.80
324	A47	15c lilac & multi	.55	.35
325	A47	20c ultra & multi	1.00	.75
326	A47	25c dull grn & multi	.80	.65
327	A47	35c bister & multi	.95	.95
328	A47	45c fawn & multi	1.10	1.10
329	A47	$1 olive & multi	2.50	2.50

330	A42	$2 multicolored	5.00	5.00
331	A42	$5 multicolored	9.75	9.75
		Nos. 316-331 (16)	27.15	25.35

Issue dates: $5, Dec. 6; others Mar. 8.

Coast Watchers, World War II A48

American Bicentennial: 20c, "Amagiri" ramming "P.T.109" and Lt. John F. Kennedy. 35c, Plane on Henderson Airfield. 45c, Map showing landing of US forces on Guadalcanal.

1976, May 24   **Perf. 14**
333	A48	6c black & multi	.40	.25
334	A48	20c black & multi	1.10	.55
335	A48	35c black & multi	1.50	.90
336	A48	45c black & multi	1.50	1.10
a.		Souvenir sheet of 4, #333-336	8.25	8.25
		Nos. 333-336 (4)	4.50	2.80

Alexander Graham Bell — A49

Designs: 20c, Radio-telephone and satellite. 35c, Ericsson's magneto telephone. 45c, Telephone, 1876, and stick telephone.

1976, July 26   **Litho.**   **Perf. 14½x14**
337	A49	6c lt ultra & multi	.25	.25
338	A49	20c multicolored	.45	.45
339	A49	35c orange & multi	.70	.70
340	A49	45c bister & multi	1.00	1.00
		Nos. 337-340 (4)	2.40	2.40

Centenary of first telephone call by Alexander Graham Bell, Mar. 10, 1876.

One-Eleven BAC — A50

Planes: 20c, Solair Britten Norman Islander. 35c, DC-3 Dakota. 45c, De Havilland DH50A.

1976, Sept. 13   **Wmk. 373**   **Perf. 14**
341	A50	6c black & multi	.25	.25
342	A50	20c black & multi	.65	.65
343	A50	35c black & multi	1.10	1.10
344	A50	45c black & multi	1.40	1.40
		Nos. 341-344 (4)	3.40	3.40

1st flight to Solomon Islands, 50th anniv.

Queen Receiving Lei, 1974 Visit — A51

35c, Communion plate, cup. 45c, Communion.

1977, Feb. 7   **Litho.**   **Perf. 14x13½**
345	A51	6c multicolored	.25	.25
346	A51	35c multicolored	.50	.50
347	A51	45c multicolored	.65	.65
		Nos. 345-347 (3)	1.40	1.40

25th anniv. of the reign of Elizabeth II.

Carved Wooden
Figure — A52

Artifacts: 20c, Sea adaro or spirit. 35c, Shark-headed man. 45c, Seated man.

1977, May 9			**Perf. 14**	
348	A52	6c yellow & multi	.25	.25
349	A52	20c blue & multi	.25	.25
350	A52	35c rose & multi	.55	.55
351	A52	45c multicolored	.70	.70
		Nos. 348-351 (4)	1.75	1.75

Man Spraying House, Anopheles
Mosquito — A53

Designs: 20c, Taking blood samples. 35c, Microscope, map of Solomon Islands, Malaria Eradication Program emblem. 45c, Messenger delivering medicine to malaria patient.

1977, July 27		**Litho.**	**Wmk. 373**	
352	A53	6c multicolored	.25	.25
353	A53	20c multicolored	.40	.40
354	A53	35c multicolored	.55	.55
355	A53	45c multicolored	.80	.80
		Nos. 352-355 (4)	2.00	2.00

Malaria eradication.

Adoration of the
Shepherds — A54

Christmas: 20c, Nativity. 35c, Adoration of the Kings. 45c, Flight into Egypt.

			Wmk. 373	
1977, Sept. 12		**Litho.**	**Perf. 14**	
356	A54	6c multicolored	.25	.25
357	A54	20c multicolored	.40	.40
358	A54	35c multicolored	.55	.55
359	A54	45c multicolored	.80	.80
		Nos. 356-359 (4)	2.00	2.00

Traditional Feather Money — A55

Designs: No. 361, New coins. No. 362, Banknotes. No. 363, Traditional shell money.

1977, Oct. 24		**Litho.**	**Perf. 14x14½**	
360		6c brt green & multi	.25	.25
361		6c brt green & multi	.25	.25
a.	A55	Pair, #360-361	.30	.30
362		45c buff & multi	1.00	1.00
363		45c buff & multi	1.00	1.00
a.	A55	Pair, #362-363	2.00	2.00
		Nos. 360-363 (4)	2.50	2.50

New coinage.

Shortland Islands
Figure — A56

Artifacts: 20c, Ceremonial shield. 35c, Santa Cruz ritual figure. 45c, Decorative combs.

1978, Jan. 11			**Perf. 14**	
364	A56	6c multicolored	.25	.25
365	A56	20c multicolored	.45	.45
366	A56	35c multicolored	.80	.80
367	A56	45c multicolored	1.00	1.00
		Nos. 364-367 (4)	2.50	2.50

Elizabeth II Coronation Anniversary Issue
Common Design Types
Souvenir Sheet
Unwmk.

1978, Apr. 21		**Litho.**	**Perf. 15**	
368		Sheet of 6	3.50	3.50
a.	CD326	45c King's dragon	.50	.50
b.	CD327	45c Elizabeth II	.50	.50
c.	CD328	45c Sandford eagle	.50	.50

No. 368 contains 2 se-tenant strips of Nos. 368a-368c, separated by horizontal gutter with commemorative and descriptive inscriptions and showing central part of coronation procession with coach.

National
Flag — A57

Apostles by
Dürer — A58

Independence: 15c, Governor General's flag. 35c, Cenotaph, Honiara, flags of U.S., Great Britain, New Zealand and Australia. 45c, Coat of Arms.

		Wmk. 373		
1978, July 7		**Litho.**	**Perf. 14**	
369	A57	6c multicolored	.25	.25
370	A57	15c multicolored	.30	.30
371	A57	35c multicolored	.70	.70
372	A57	45c multicolored	.95	.95
		Nos. 369-372 (4)	2.20	2.20

1978, Oct. 4		**Litho.**	**Perf. 14**	
373	A58	6c John	.25	.25
374	A58	20c Peter	.40	.40
375	A58	35c Paul	.70	.70
376	A58	45c Mark	.90	.90
		Nos. 373-376 (4)	2.25	2.25

Albrecht Dürer (1471-1528), German painter, 450th death anniversary.

Scouts
Making
Fire — A59

Designs: 20c, Camping. 35c, Solomon Islands Scouts. 45c, Canoeing.

1978, Nov. 15		**Litho.**	**Perf. 14**	
377	A59	6c multicolored	.25	.25
378	A59	20c multicolored	.30	.30
379	A59	35c multicolored	.55	.55
380	A59	45c multicolored	.70	.70
		Nos. 377-380 (4)	1.80	1.80

50 years of Scouting in Solomon Islands.

Discovery
A60

Designs: 18c, Capt. Cook, 1776, painting by Nathaniel Dance. 35c, Sextant. 45c, Capt. Cook after Flaxman / Wedgwood medallion.

		Wmk. 373		
1979, Jan. 16		**Litho.**	**Perf. 11**	
381	A60	8c multicolored	.25	.25
382	A60	18c multicolored	.40	.40
383	A60	35c multicolored	.80	.80

		Litho.; Embossed		
384	A60	45c multicolored	1.00	1.00
		Nos. 381-384 (4)	2.45	2.45

Capt. Cook's voyages.

Fish Net
Float
A61

Artifacts: 20c, Armband made of shell money, vert. 35c, Ceremonial food bowl. 45c, Forehead ornament, vert.

1979, Mar. 21		**Litho.**	**Perf. 14**	
385	A61	8c multicolored	.30	.30
386	A61	20c multicolored	.30	.30
387	A61	35c multicolored	.45	.45
388	A61	45c multicolored	.60	.60
		Nos. 385-388 (4)	1.65	1.65

6th South
Pacific
Games
A62

1979, June 4		**Litho.**	**Wmk. 373**	
389	A62	8c Running	.25	.25
390	A62	20c Hurdles	.25	.25
391	A62	35c Soccer	.30	.30
392	A62	45c Swimming	.50	.50
		Nos. 389-392 (4)	1.30	1.30

Solomon Islands
No. 14 — A63

Sea
Snake — A64

Designs (Rowland Hill and): 20c, Great Britain No. 27. 35c, Solomon Islands No. 372. 45c, Solomon Islands No. 40.

1979, Aug. 16		**Litho.**	**Perf. 14**	
393	A63	8c multicolored	.25	.25
394	A63	20c multicolored	.40	.40
395	A63	35c multicolored	.65	.65
		Nos. 393-395 (3)	1.30	1.30

Souvenir Sheet

396	A63	45c multicolored	1.25	1.25

Sir Rowland Hill (1795-1879), originator of penny postage.

		Perf. 13½x13		
1979-83		**Litho.**	**Wmk. 373**	
397	A64	1c Sea snake	.25	.50
398	A64	3c Red-banded tree snake	.25	.75
399	A64	4c Whip snake	.25	.75
400	A64	6c Pacific boa	.25	.75
401	A64	8c Skink	.25	.45
402	A64	10c Gecko	.25	.50
403	A64	12c Monitor	.30	.75
404	A64	15c Angelhead	.30	.75
405	A64	20c Giant toad	.40	.35
406	A64	25c Marsh frog	.45	.60
407	A64	30c Horned frog	1.50	.60
408	A64	35c Tree frog	.50	.60
408A	A64	40c Burrowing snake	1.50	1.40
409	A64	45c Guppy's snake	.65	.85
409A	A64	50c Tree gecko	1.50	.85
410	A64	$1 Large skink	2.00	1.25
411	A64	$2 Guppy's frog	2.50	2.50
412	A64	$5 Estuarine crocodile	6.50	6.50
412A	A64	$10 Hawksbill turtle	13.00	13.00
		Nos. 397-412A (19)	32.60	33.45

Issued: $10, 9/20/82; 40c, 50c, 1/24/83; others, 9/1979 (undated).

Nos. 403, 406, 410, 412 reissued inscribed "1982." No. 407, "1983."

Madonna and
Child, by
Morando — A65

IYC Emblem and Madonna and Child: 20c, Bernardino Luini. 35c, Bellini. 50c, Raphael.

1979, Nov. 15			**Perf. 14½**	
413	A65	4c multicolored	.25	.25
414	A65	20c multicolored	.25	.25
415	A65	35c multicolored	.40	.40
416	A65	50c multicolored	.65	.65
a.		Souvenir sheet of 4, #413-416	2.00	2.00
		Nos. 413-416 (4)	1.55	1.55

Christmas 1979, Intl. Year of the Child.

Curacoa
and Crest
A66

Ships and Crests: 20c, Herald, 1854. 35c, Royalist, 1889. 45c, Beagle, 1878.

		Wmk. 373		
1980, Jan. 23		**Litho.**	**Perf. 14**	
417	A66	8c multicolored	.25	.25
418	A66	20c multicolored	.45	.45
419	A66	35c multicolored	.70	.70
420	A66	45c multicolored	.95	.95
		Nos. 417-420 (4)	2.35	2.35

See Nos. 435-438.

Steel Fishery Training Ship — A67

1980, Mar. 27		**Litho.**	**Perf. 13½**	
421	A67	8c shown	.25	.25
422	A67	20c Fishery training ship	.25	.25
423	A67	45c Refrigerated carrier	.45	.40
424	A67	80c Research ship	.85	1.75
		Nos. 421-424 (4)	1.80	2.65

"Comliebank," Tulag Cancel — A68

1980, May 6   Litho.   Perf. 14½
425		Sheet of 4	2.00	2.00
a.	A68	45c shown	.50	.50
b.	A68	45c Douglas C-47	.50	.50
c.	A68	45c BAC 1-11, Honiara cancel	.50	.50
d.	A68	45c "Corabank," Auki cancel	.50	.50

London 1980 Intl. Stamp Exhib., May 6-14.

Queen Mother Elizabeth Birthday Issue
Common Design Type
Wmk. 373

1980, Aug. 4   Litho.   Perf. 14
426	CD330	45c multicolored	.50	.50

Angel with Trumpet — A69

Christmas: 20c, Angel with violin. 45c, Angel with trumpet. 80c, Angel with lute.

Wmk. 373

1980, Sept. 2   Litho.   Perf. 14½
427	A69	8c multicolored	.25	.25
428	A69	20c multicolored	.25	.25
429	A69	45c multicolored	.40	.40
430	A69	80c multicolored	.70	.70
		Nos. 427-430 (4)	1.60	1.60

Parthenos Sylvia — A70

Wmk. 373

1980, Nov. 12   Litho.   Perf. 13½
431	A70	8c shown	.75	.45
432	A70	20c *Delias schoenbergi*	1.00	.65
433	A70	45c *Jamides cephion*	1.75	1.25
434	A70	80c *Ornithoptera victoriae*	3.00	3.00
		Nos. 431-434 (4)	6.50	5.35

See Nos. 461-464.

Ship & Crest Type of 1980

8c, Mounts Bay, 1959. 20c, Charybdis, 1970. 45c, Hydra, 1972-73. $1, Britannia, 1974.

1981, Jan. 14
435	A66	8c multicolored	.25	.25
436	A66	20c multicolored	.25	.25
437	A66	45c multicolored	.45	.45
438	A66	$1 multicolored	1.25	1.25
		Nos. 435-438 (4)	2.20	2.20

Maurelle's Map, 1742 — A71

Wmk. 373

1981, Mar. 23   Litho.   Perf. 14
439	A71	8c Francisco Maurelle, vert.	.25	.25
440	A71	10c shown	.25	.25
441	A71	45c La Princesa	.60	.60
442	A71	$1 Compass cards, vert.	1.00	1.00
		Nos. 439-442 (4)	2.10	2.10

Souvenir Sheet
443		Sheet of 4	1.60	1.60
a.	A71	25c any single	.35	.35

Bicent. of arrival of Francisco Antonio Maurelle and of charts of mapmaker Jean Nicholas Buache (1741-1825). No. 443 contains 4 44x28mm stamps, perf. 14½.

Women's Basketball — A72

Wmk. 373

1981, July 7   Litho.   Perf. 12
444	A72	8c shown	.25	.25
445	A72	10c Tennis	.25	.25
446	A72	25c Women's running	.35	.35
447	A72	30c Soccer	.35	.35
448	A72	45c Boxing	.50	.50
		Nos. 444-448 (5)	1.70	1.70

Souvenir Sheet
449	A72	$1 Emblem	1.25	1.25

Mini South Pacific Games, July.

Royal Wedding Issue
Common Design Type

1981, July 22   Perf. 13½x13
450	CD331	8c Bouquet	.25	.25
451	CD331	45c Charles	.30	.30
452	CD331	$1 Couple	1.00	1.00
		Nos. 450-452 (3)	1.55	1.55

For surcharge see No. B1.

Duke of Edinburgh's Awards, 25th Anniv. — A73

Wmk. 373

1981, Sept. 28   Litho.   Perf. 14
453	A73	8c Music	.25	.25
454	A73	25c Handicrafts	.25	.25
455	A73	45c Canoeing	.35	.35
456	A73	$1 Duke of Edinburgh	.90	.90
		Nos. 453-456 (4)	1.75	1.75

Holy Cross Cathedral, Honiara — A74

Christmas: 8c, 25c, Old churches, diff. 10c, St. Barnabas Anglican Cathedral, Honiara.

1981, Oct. 12
457	A74	8c multicolored	.30	.30
458	A74	10c multicolored	.30	.30
459	A74	25c multicolored	.40	.40
460	A74	$2 multicolored	1.50	1.50
		Nos. 457-460 (4)	2.50	2.50

Butterfly Type of 1980
Wmk. 373

1982, Jan. 5   Litho.   Perf. 13½
461	A70	10c *Doleschallia bisaltide*	.75	.40
462	A70	25c *Papilio bridgei hecataeus*	1.00	.75
463	A70	35c *Taenaris phorcas*	1.50	1.25
464	A70	$1 *Graphium sarpedon*	3.75	3.75
		Nos. 461-464 (4)	7.00	6.15

Sanford's Eagle — A75

1982, May 15   Litho.   Perf. 14
465	A75	12c Pair facing left	.60	.60
466	A75	12c Chick	.60	.60
467	A75	12c Mother feeding chicks	.60	.60
468	A75	12c Pair facing right	.60	.60
469	A75	12c Male flying	.60	.60
470	A75	12c Pair flying	.60	.60
		Nos. 465-470 (6)	3.60	3.60

Se-tenant in sheets of 24. Value of complete sheet, $20. The center horiz. row consists of 4 No. 470 + label. No block of 6 contains all 6 designs.

Princess Diana Issue
Common Design Type
Perf. 14½x14

1982, July 1   Litho.   Wmk. 373
471	CD333	12c Arms	.25	.25
472	CD333	40c Diana	.65	.65
473	CD333	50c Wedding	.90	.90
474	CD333	$1 Portrait	1.75	1.75
		Nos. 471-474 (4)	3.55	3.55

A76

1982, Oct. 11   Litho.   Perf. 14
475	A76	25c Running	.40	.40
476	A76	25c Boxing	.40	.40

Souvenir Sheet
477		Sheet of 3, #475-476, 477a	3.75	3.75
a.	A76	$1 Britannia facing left	2.75	2.75

12th Commonwealth Games, Brisbane, Australia, Sept. 30-Oct. 9.

1982, Oct. 11
478	A76	12c Royal couple	.25	.25
479	A76	12c Flags	.25	.25

Souvenir Sheet
480		Sheet of 3, #478-479, 480a	4.00	4.00
a.	A76	$1 Britannia facing right	3.50	3.50

Visit of Queen Elizabeth II and Prince Philip.

Scouting Year A78

Designs: Nos. 481, 485, Scout patroller. Nos. 482, 486, Brigade bugler. Nos. 483, 487, Baden-Powell. Nos. 484, 488, William Smith.

1982, Nov. 30
481	A78	12c dark blue & multi	.25	.25
482	A78	12c brown & multi	.25	.25
483	A78	25c dark blue & multi	.30	.30
484	A78	25c brown & multi	.30	.30
485	A78	35c green & multi	.30	.30
486	A78	35c red & multi	.30	.30
487	A78	50c green & multi	.50	.50
488	A78	50c red & multi	.50	.50
		Nos. 481-488 (8)	2.70	2.70

Turtles A79

1983, Jan. 5   Perf. 14
489	A79	18c Leatherback	.65	.65
490	A79	35c Loggerhead	.90	.90
491	A79	45c Pacific Ridley	1.25	1.25
492	A79	50c Green	1.25	1.25
		Nos. 489-492 (4)	4.05	4.05

Commonwealth Day — A80

1983, Mar. 14
493	A80	12c Oliva vidum, conus generalis, murex tribulus	.25	.25
494	A80	35c Romu, kurila, kakadu, money belt	.55	.55
495	A80	45c Shells, bride necklaces	.70	.70
496	A80	50c Trochus niloticus, natural, polished	.75	.75
		Nos. 493-496 (4)	2.25	2.25

Manned Flight Bicentenary — A81

Wmk. 373

1983, June 30   Litho.   Perf. 14
497	A81	30c Montgolfliere, 1783	.45	.45
498	A81	35c Lockheed Hercules	.50	.50
499	A81	40c Wright Brothers' Flyer III, 1905	.55	.55
500	A81	45c Columbia space shuttle	.60	.60
501	A81	50c Beechcraft Baron-Solair	.75	.75
		Nos. 497-501 (5)	2.85	2.85

Christmas 1983 — A82

1983, Aug. 25
502	A82	12c Weto dance	.25	.25
503	A82	15c Custom wrestling	.25	.25
504	A82	18c Girl dancers	.25	.25
505	A82	20c Devil dancers	.30	.30
506	A82	25c Bamboo band	.35	.35
507	A82	35c Gilbertese dancers	.50	.50
508	A82	40c Pan pipers	.60	.60
509	A82	45c Afufu girl dancers	.65	.65
510	A82	50c Cross, flowers	.75	.75
a.		Souvenir sheet of 9, #502-510	4.00	4.00
		Nos. 502-510 (9)	3.90	3.90

Stamps in #510a do not have "Christmas 1983."
For overprints see Nos. 519-520.

World Communications Year — A83

Wmk. 373

1983, Dec. 19   Litho.   Perf. 14
511	A83	12c Telephone Exchange building	.25	.25
512	A83	18c Ham radio operator	.25	.25
513	A83	25c No. 11	.35	.35
514	A83	$1 No. 14	1.25	1.25
a.		Souvenir sheet of 1	2.00	2.00
		Nos. 511-514 (4)	2.10	2.10

No. 514a is inscribed "1908-1983." See No. 525 for sheet inscribed "1907-1984."

Local
Fungi — A84

1984, Jan. 30 **Perf. 13½**
515 A84 6c Calvatia gardneri .30 .30
516 A84 18c Marasmiellus in-
oderma .50 .50
517 A84 35c Pycnoporus
sanguineus .75 .75
518 A84 $2 Filoboletus manipu-
laris 3.25 3.25
Nos. 515-518 (4) 4.80 4.80

Type of No. 510 overprinted "VISIT OF
POPE JOHN PAUL II May 9th, 1984"

1984, Apr. 16 **Wmk. 373**
519 A82 12c multicolored .25 .25
520 A82 50c multicolored .70 .70

Lloyd's List Issue
Common Design Type
1984, Apr. 21 Litho. Perf. 14½x14
521 CD335 12c Olivebank, 1892 .75 .25
522 CD335 15c Tinhow, 1906 1.00 .75
523 CD335 18c Oriana, Point
Cruz 1.10 1.00
524 CD335 $1 Point Cruz view 2.75 2.75
Nos. 521-524 (4) 5.60 4.75

WCY Type of 1983
Souvenir Sheet
Wmk. 373
1984, June 18 Litho. Perf. 14
525 A83 $1 multicolored 2.25 2.25
UPU Congress. No. 514a is inscribed
"1908-1983," No. 525 inscribed "1907-1984."

Asia-Pacific Broadcasting Union, 20th
Anniv. — A86

1984, July 2 **Perf. 13½**
526 A86 12c Village drums .25 .25
527 A86 45c Radio City Guadalcanal .60 .60
528 A86 60c Broadcasting studio .80 .80
529 A86 $1 Broadcasting station 1.40 1.40
Nos. 526-529 (4) 3.05 3.05

1984 Summer Olympics — A87

Perf. 13½x14
1984, Aug. 4 Litho. Wmk. 373
530 A87 12c Flag, vert. .25 .25
531 A87 25c Lawson Tama Stadium, Honiara .45 .45
532 A87 50c Honiara Community
Center .85 .85
a. Booklet pane, 2 ea #531-532 3.25
533 A87 $1 Olympic Stadium 1.75 1.75
Nos. 530-533 (4) 3.30 3.30

Souvenir Sheet
534 A87 95c Bronte Baths 8.50 8.50
Solomon Islds. first olympic participation.
No. 534 available in booklet only. Margin
shows swimmer A. Wickham (1886-1976).

Little Pied
Cormorant
(Ausipex '84)
A88

Wmk. 373
1984, Sept. 21 Litho. Perf. 14½
535 A88 12c shown .75 .75
536 A88 18c Australian grey
duck 1.00 1.00
537 A88 35c Nankeen night-
heron 1.50 1.50
538 A88 $1 Dollarbird 2.50 2.50
a. Souvenir sheet of 4, #535-538 6.50 6.50
Nos. 535-538 (4) 5.75 5.75

EXPO
'85,
Tsukuba,
Japan
A89

Designs: 12c, Japanese Memorial Shrine,
Mt. Austen, Guadalcanal. 25c, Digital telephone exchange equipment. 45c, Soltai No. 7
fishing vessel. 85c, Coastal village.

Wmk. 373
1985, June 28 Litho. Perf. 14
539 A89 12c multicolored .25 .25
540 A89 25c multicolored .35 .35
541 A89 45c multicolored .60 .60
542 A89 85c multicolored 1.25 1.25
Nos. 539-542 (4) 2.45 2.45

Queen Mother 85th Birthday
Common Design Type
Perf. 14½x14
1985, June 7 Litho. Wmk. 384
543 CD336 12c VE Day, 1945 .25 .25
544 CD336 25c With Margaret .30 .30
545 CD336 35c St. Patrick's
Day celebra-
tion .40 .40
546 CD336 $1 Holding Prince
Henry 1.25 1.25
Nos. 543-546 (4) 2.20 2.20

Souvenir Sheet
547 CD336 $1.50 In a gondola,
Venice 2.25 2.25
For surcharge see No. B2.

Christmas — A90

1985, Aug. 30 Wmk. 373 Perf. 14½
548 A90 12c Titiana Village .25 .25
549 A90 25c Sigana, Santa Isabel .35 .35
550 A90 35c Artificial Island, Lan-
ga Lagoon .45 .45
Nos. 548-550 (3) 1.05 1.05

A $1 stamp is known to exist, but it was not
issued by the Solomon Islands Postal
Administration.

Intl. Youth
Year — A91

12c, Girl Guide activities. 15c, Stop Polio
Campaign. 25c, Relay runners, views of the

islands. 35c, Relay runners, views of Australia.
45c, Saluting natl. flag, badges.

1985, Sept. 30 **Perf. 14**
551 A91 12c multicolored .90 .25
552 A91 15c multicolored 1.00 .60
553 A91 25c multicolored 1.25 .90
554 A91 35c multicolored 1.40 1.00
a. Souvenir sheet of 2, #553-554 2.25 2.25
555 A91 45c multicolored 2.50 1.50
Nos. 551-555 (5) 7.05 4.25

Girl Guides 75th anniv., 12c, 45c; IYY,
others.

Souvenir Sheet

Audubon Birth Bicent. — A92

Bird illustration by Audubon.

1985, Nov. 25 **Wmk. 384**
556 A92 Sheet of 3, 45c, 2
50c 6.50 6.50
a. Portrait 1.75 1.75
b. Osprey 2.25 2.25

Souvenir Sheet

Mini Hydro-Electric Project, Iriri
Village — A93

Designs: 30c, Water-driven generator. 60c,
Illuminated village house.

1986, Jan. 24 **Perf. 14**
557 A93 Sheet of 2 3.00 3.00
a. 30c multicolored 1.00 1.00
b. 60c multicolored 1.75 1.75

Halley's
Comet
A94

Operation Raleigh, 1986: 18c, Construction
of Red Cross Center, Gizo. 30c, Exploring rain
forest. 60c, Observing Halley's Comet. $1,
Ships Sir Walter Raleigh and Zebu.

Perf. 14½x14
1986, Mar. 27 **Wmk. 373**
558 A94 18c multicolored 1.00 .25
559 A94 30c multicolored 1.75 .50
560 A94 60c multicolored 3.00 1.50
561 A94 $1 multicolored 3.50 2.25
Nos. 558-561 (4) 9.25 4.50

Queen Elizabeth II 60th Birthday
Common Design Type
Designs: 5c, Visiting Clydebank Town Hall
with Prince Philip, 1947. 18c, At Queen

Mother's 80th birthday, St. Paul's Cathedral,
1980. 22c, Walking among children of the
islands, Pacific tour, 1982. 55c, 50th birthday,
Windsor Castle, 1976. $2, Visiting Crown
Agents' offices, 1983.

1986, Apr. 21 Wmk. 384 Perf. 14½
562 CD337 5c scarlet, blk & sil .25 .25
563 CD337 18c ultra & multi .25 .25
564 CD337 22c green & multi .25 .25
565 CD337 55c violet & multi .50 .50
566 CD337 $2 rose vio & multi 1.90 1.90
Nos. 562-566 (5) 3.15 3.15

Royal Wedding Issue, 1986
Common Design Type
Designs: 55c, Informal portrait. 60c, Andrew
aboard royal navy vessel.

Wmk. 384
1986, July 23 Litho. Perf. 14
567 CD338 55c multicolored .50 .50
568 CD338 60c multicolored .60 .60

Souvenir Sheet

AMERIPEX '86 — A95

55c, U.S. Memorial, Henderson Field,
Guadalcanal. $1.65, Peace Corps emblem,
Statue of Liberty, Pres. John F. Kennedy.

1986, May 22 Litho. Perf. 13½
569 A95 Sheet of 2 2.50 2.50
a. 55c multicolored .60 .60
b. $1.65 multicolored 1.75 1.75

Intl. Peace Year, Peace Corps 25th anniv.
For surcharge see No. B3.

1987 America's
Cup — A96

Previous winners, challengers, maps and
club emblems: No. 570a, America, US, 1851.
b, Magic, US, 1870. c, Madeleine, US, 1876.
d, Mischief, US, 1881. e, Columbia, US, 1871.
f, British Cup course, 1851. g, America II, US,
1987. h, America's Cup. i, Heart of America,
US, 1987. j, French Kiss, France, 1987.
No. 571a, Puritan, US, 1885. b, Mayflower,
US, 1886. c, Defender, US, 1895. d, Vigilant,
US, 1893. e, Volunteer, US, 1887. f, America
Cup course, Newport, 1930-1962. g, South
Australia, Australia, 1987. h, KA14, Australia,
1987. i, New Zealand II, New Zealand, 1987. j,
St. Francis IX, US, 1987.
No. 572a, Columbia, US, 1899. b, Colum-
bia, US, 1901. c, Enterprise, US, 1930. d,
Resolute, US, 1920. e, Reliance, US, 1903. f,
America Cup course, 1964-1983. g, Kooka-
burra, Australia, 1987. h, Eagle, US, 1987. i,
True North, Canada, 1987. j, Italia, Italy, 1987.
No. 573a, Rainbow, US, 1934. b, Ranger,
US, 1937. c, Constellation, US, 1964. d,
Weatherly, US, 1962. e, Columbia, US, 1958.
f, Western Australia Cup course, 1987. g,
Secret Cove, syndicate, 1987. h, Courageous
III, US, 1987. i, France, France, 1987. j,
Azzurra, Italy, 1987.
No. 574a, Intrepid, US, 1967. b, Intrepid,
US, 1970. c, Freedom, US, 1980. d, Coura-
geous, US, 1977. e, Courageous, US, 1974. f,
Australia II, Australia, 1983. g, Crusader,
Great Britain, 1987. h, Sail America, US,
1987. i, Australia III, Australia, 1987. j, Royal
Perth Yacht Club/America's Cup '87 emblem,
1987.

1986, Aug. 22 Litho. Perf. 14½
570 Strip of 10 + label 6.50 6.50
a.-d. A96 18c any single .25 .25
e.-f. A96 30c any single .35 .35
g.-j. A96 $1 any single 1.00 1.00
571 Strip of 10 + label 6.50 6.50
a.-d. A96 18c any single .25 .25
e.-f. A96 30c any single .35 .35
g.-j. A96 $1 any single 1.00 1.00

572		Strip of 10 + label	6.50	6.50
a.-d.	A96	18c any single	.25	.25
e.-f.	A96	30c any single	.35	.35
g.-j.	A96	$1 any single	1.00	1.00
573		Strip of 10 + label	6.50	6.50
a.-d.	A96	18c any single	.25	.25
e.-f.	A96	30c any single	.35	.35
g.-j.	A96	$1 any single	1.00	1.00
574		Strip of 10 + label	6.50	6.50
a.-d.	A96	18c any single	.25	.25
e.-f.	A96	30c any single	.35	.35
g.-j.	A96	$1 any single	1.00	1.00
		Nos. 570-574 (5)	32.50	32.50

Nos. 570-574 printed se-tenant with center labels picturing natl. arms, 1987 America's Cup emblem and trophy in sheets of 50.

Souvenir Sheet
1987, Feb. 4   Litho.   Perf. 14½

575	A96	$5 Stars and Stripes, U.S., victor	5.50	5.50

Coral — A97

Perf. 14½x14
1987, Feb. 11   Litho.   Wmk. 384

576	A97	18c Dendrophyllia gracilis	.50	.25
577	A97	45c Dendronephthya	.95	.50
578	A97	60c Clavularia	1.25	1.25
579	A97	$1.50 Melithaea squamata	2.75	2.75
		Nos. 576-579 (4)	5.45	4.75

Flowering Plants — A98

1987-88

580	A98	1c Cassia fistula	.25	.25
581	A98	5c Allamanda cathartica	.25	.25
582	A98	10c Catharanthus roseus	.25	.25
583	A98	18c Mimosa pudica	.40	.25
584	A98	20c Hibiscus rosa-sinensis	.40	.25
585	A98	22c Clerodendrum thomsonae	.45	.25
586	A98	25c Bauhinia variegata	.50	.30
587	A98	28c Gloriosa rothschildiana	.55	.30
588	A98	30c Heliconia solomonensis	.60	.35
589	A98	40c Episcia hybrid	.70	.45
590	A98	45c Bougainvillea hybrid	.75	.50
591	A98	50c Alpinia purpurata	.80	.60
592	A98	55c Plumeria rubra	.90	.60
593	A98	60c Acacia farnesiana	1.00	.70
594	A98	$1 Ipomea purpurea	2.50	1.10
595	A98	$2 Dianella ensifolia	3.50	3.50
596	A98	$5 Passiflora foetida	5.75	5.75
596A	A98	$10 Hemigraphis specie ('88)	9.00	9.00
		Nos. 580-596A (18)	28.55	24.65

Issue dates: $10, Mar. 1; others, May 12.

Mangrove Kingfisher — A99   Orchids — A100

Designs: a, Perched on root. b, Diving. c, Landing in water. d, Emerging with fish.

Perf. 14x14½
1987, July 15   Wmk. 373

597		Strip of 4	18.00	18.00
a.-d.	A99	60c any single	4.00	4.00

No. 597 has a continuous design.

Perf. 13½x13
1987, Sept. 23   Wmk. 384

598	A100	18c Dendrobium conanthum	1.50	.35
599	A100	30c Spathoglottis plicata	3.00	.40
600	A100	55c Dendrobium gouldii	3.50	1.00
601	A100	$1.50 Dendrobium goldfinchii	6.50	6.50
		Nos. 598-601 (4)	14.50	8.25

Christmas 1987.

Transportation and Communications Decade — A101

Designs: 18c, Telecommunications link. 30c, Express mail service. 60c, Guadalcanal Road Improvement Project. $2, Beechcraft Queen Air, Henderson Airfield control tower.

1987, Oct. 31   Litho.   Unwmk.

602	A101	18c multicolored	.35	.25
603	A101	30c multicolored	.65	.35
604	A101	60c multicolored	.85	.85
605	A101	$2 multicolored	3.50	3.50
		Nos. 602-605 (4)	5.35	4.95

Queen Victoria's Birdwing Butterfly — A102

Designs: No. 606a, Male. No. 606b, Larva. No. 606c, Pupa. No. 606d, Female.

1987, Nov. 25   Wmk. 384   Perf. 14½

606		Strip of 4	23.50	23.50
a.-d.	A102	45c any single	5.00	5.00

Intl. Fund for Agricultural Development (IFAD), 10th Anniv. — A103

Natl. colors and: No. 607, Student, Natl. Agricultural Training Institute (NATI) farm and emblem (left stamp). No. 608, Students in working in NATI field and emblem (right stamp). No. 609, Flatbed truck transporting produce and emblem (left stamp). No. 610, Canoes, seagulls and emblem (right stamp).

Wmk. 384
1988, Feb. 12   Litho.   Perf. 14½

607		50c multicolored	.80	.80
608	120	61 multicolored	.80	.80
a.	A103	Pair, #607-608	1.75	1.75
609		$1 multicolored	1.00	1.00
610		$1 multicolored	1.00	1.00
a.	A103	Pair, #609-610	2.25	2.25
		Nos. 607-610 (4)	3.60	3.60

EXPO '88, Brisbane, Apr. 30-Oct. 30 — A104

Designs: 22c, Yacht in dry dock. 80c, Canoe. $1.50, Huts.

Perf. 13½x14
1988, Apr. 30   Unwmk.

611	A104	22c multicolored	.25	.25
612	A104	80c multicolored	.85	.85
613	A104	$1.50 multicolored	1.75	1.75
a.		Souv. sheet of 3, #611-613	3.00	3.00
b.		As "a," surcharged $3.50 in margin ('90)	12.00	12.00
		Nos. 611-613 (3)	2.85	2.85

National Independence, 10th Anniv. — A105

Perf. 13x13½
1988, July 7   Litho.   Wmk. 373

614	A105	22c *Capitana* in Estrella Bay	1.25	.25
615	A105	55c Flag raising, 1893	2.00	.60
616	A105	80c Supreme Court	1.75	1.50
617	A105	$1 Traditional celebration	2.00	2.00
		Nos. 614-617 (4)	7.00	4.35

Australia Bicentennial — A106

Ships: 35c, M.V. *Papuan Chief.* 60c, M.V. *Nimos.* 70c, S.S. *Malaita.* $1.30, S.S. *Makambo.*

1988, July 30   Wmk. 384   Perf. 14

618	A106	35c multicolored	1.25	.35
619	A106	60c multicolored	1.60	.55
620	A106	70c multicolored	1.60	.85
621	A106	$1.30 multicolored	2.10	2.10
a.		Souvenir sheet of 4, #618-621	5.00	5.00
		Nos. 618-621 (4)	6.55	3.85

A107   Orchids — A108

Wmk. 384
1988, Aug. 5   Litho.   Perf. 14½

622	A107	22c Archery	1.00	.25
623	A107	55c Weight lifting	1.25	.65
624	A107	70c Running	1.50	1.25
625	A107	80c Boxing	1.75	1.50
		Nos. 622-625 (4)	5.50	3.65

Souvenir Sheet
Wmk. 373

626	A107	$2 Olympic Stadium, horiz.	3.50	3.50

1988 Summer Olympics, Seoul.

Lloyds of London, 300th Anniv.
Common Design Type

Designs: 22c, King George V and Queen Mary at Lloyd's ground-breaking ceremony, 1925. 50c, *Forthbank,* horiz. 65c, Soltel Satellite Ground Station, horiz. $2, *Empress of China.*

1988, Oct. 31   Perf. 14

627	CD341	22c multicolored	.75	.25
628	CD341	50c multicolored	2.25	.45
629	CD341	65c multicolored	2.50	.75
630	CD341	$2 multicolored	4.50	3.00
		Nos. 627-630 (4)	10.00	4.45

Perf. 13½x13
1989, Jan. 20   Litho.   Wmk. 373

631	A108	22c *Bulbophyllum dennisii*	1.25	.30
632	A108	35c *Calanthe langei*	1.50	.55
633	A108	55c *Bulbophyllum blumei*	2.00	1.25
634	A108	$2 *Grammatophyllum speciosum*	3.75	3.75
		Nos. 631-634 (4)	8.50	5.85

Intl. Red Cross, 125th Anniv. — A109

Perf. 14x14½
1989, May 16   Wmk. 384

635		35c Disabled children	.75	.75
636		35c Children's Center minibus	.75	.75
a.	A109	Pair, #635-636	1.75	1.75
637		$1.50 Patient abed	3.00	3.00
638		$1.50 Physical therapy	3.00	3.00
a.	A109	Pair, #637-638	6.50	6.50
		Nos. 635-638 (4)	7.50	7.50

Sea Slugs — A110

1989, June 30   Wmk. 373   Perf. 14½

639	A110	22c *Phyllidia varicosa*	1.50	.30
640	A110	70c *Chromodoris bullocki*	3.25	1.75
641	A110	80c *Chromodoris leopardus*	3.50	2.50
642	A110	$1.50 *Phidiana indica*	5.00	5.00
		Nos. 639-642 (4)	13.25	9.55

Moon Landing, 20th Anniv.
Common Design Type

Apollo 16: 22c, Splashdown. 35c, Launch. 70c, Mission emblem. 80c, Ultraviolet color enhancement of Earth. $4, The Moon, as photographed during the *Apollo 11* mission.

1989, July 20   Wmk. 384   Perf. 14
Size of Nos. 644-645: 29x29mm

643	CD342	22c multicolored	.75	.30
644	CD342	35c multicolored	1.25	.55
645	CD342	70c multicolored	2.00	2.00
646	CD342	80c multicolored	2.25	2.25
		Nos. 643-646 (4)	6.25	5.10

Souvenir Sheet

647	CD342	$4 multicolored	7.00	7.00

Blowing Soap Bubbles A111

Children's games.

1989, Nov. 17   Wmk. 384

648	A111	5c Five stones catch, vert.	.30	.55
649	A111	67c shown	2.00	2.00
650	A111	73c Coconut shell empire	2.00	2.00
651	A111	$1 Seed wind sound, vert.	3.00	3.00
		Nos. 648-651 (4)	7.30	7.55

Souvenir Sheet
Wmk. 373

652	A111	$3 Baseball, softball, vert.	11.00	11.00

World Stamp Expo '89.

Christmas — A112

1989, Nov. 30   Wmk. 384
653	A112	18c Butterfly, fishermen	.75	.30
654	A112	25c Nativity	1.00	.35
655	A112	45c Hospital ward	1.75	.50
656	A112	$1.50 Tug of war	4.00	4.00
		Nos. 653-656 (4)	7.50	5.15

Personal Ornaments A113

1990, Feb. 14   Litho.   Wmk. 373
657	A113	5c shown	.50	1.00
658	A113	12c Necklace	.90	.45
659	A113	18c Islander, diff.	1.00	.60
660	A113	$2 Head ornament	9.00	9.00
		Nos. 657-660 (4)	11.40	11.05

Cowrie Shells A114

1990, July 23
666	A114	4c Spindle cowrie	.50	1.00
667	A114	20c Map cowrie	1.50	.40
668	A114	35c Sieve cowrie	1.75	.50
669	A114	50c Egg cowrie	2.75	2.75
670	A114	$1 Prince cowrie	5.00	5.00
		Nos. 666-670 (5)	11.50	9.65

Queen Mother, 90th Birthday
Common Design Types

25c, Queen Mother, 1987. $5, Inspecting damage to Buckingham Palace, 1940.

1990, Aug. 4   Wmk. 384   Perf. 14x15
671	CD343	25c multicolored	1.25	.40

Perf. 14½
672	CD344	$5 brown & blk	5.25	6.00

First Postage Stamp, 150th Anniv. A115

Designs: 35c, Postman, mail van. 45c, Solomon Islands Post Office. 50c, Solomon Islands No. 1. 55c, Young philatelist. 60c, Solomon Islands No. 20, Penny Black.

1990, Oct. 15   Wmk. 373   Perf. 14
673	A115	35c multicolored	2.00	.50
674	A115	45c multicolored	2.00	.55
675	A115	50c multicolored	2.25	1.75
676	A115	55c multicolored	2.25	2.25
677	A115	60c multicolored	3.00	3.00
		Nos. 673-677 (5)	11.50	8.05

Birds A116

1990, Dec. 5
678	A116	10c Purple swamphen	1.25	1.00
679	A116	25c Rufous brown pheasant dove	2.00	.70
680	A116	30c Superb fruit dove	2.50	.75
681	A116	45c Cardinal honey-eater	2.75	.90
682	A116	$2 Pigmy parrot	7.00	7.00
		Nos. 678-682 (5)	15.50	10.35

Birdpex '90, 20th Intl. Ornithological Congress, New Zealand.

Crop Pests — A117

Perf. 14x13½
1991, Jan. 16   Litho.   Wmk. 373
683	A117	7c Sweet potato weevil	1.00	.50
684	A117	25c Melon fly	1.50	.35
685	A117	40c Taro beetle	2.00	.65
686	A117	90c Cocoa weevil borer	3.00	3.00
687	A117	$1.50 Rhinoceros beetle	4.50	4.50
		Nos. 683-687 (5)	12.00	9.00

For No. 683 overprinted, see No. 884A.

Elizabeth & Philip, Birthdays
Common Design Types
Wmk. 384
1991, June 17   Litho.   Perf. 14½
688	CD346	90c multicolored	1.40	1.40
689	CD345	$2 multicolored	3.00	3.00
a.		Pair, #688-689 + label	4.50	4.50

No. 689a exists with two different labels.

Nutritional Foods — A118

1991, June 24   Wmk. 373   Perf. 14
690	A118	5c Coconut water	.35	.50
691	A118	75c Feed your child	2.00	2.00
692	A118	80c Mother's milk	2.25	2.25
693	A118	90c Local food	3.00	3.00
		Nos. 690-693 (4)	7.60	7.75

A 65c value, depicting healthy and unhealthy foods, was prepared but not issued. Value $300.

9th South Pacific Games — A119

Wmk. 384
1991, Aug. 8   Litho.   Perf. 14
694	A119	25c Volleyball	1.50	.35
695	A119	40c Judo	2.00	.75
696	A119	65c Squash	2.75	2.75
697	A119	90c Lawn bowling	3.00	3.00
		Nos. 694-697 (4)	9.25	6.85

Souvenir Sheet
698	A119	$2 Games emblem	8.75	8.75

Christmas — A120

Wmk. 373
1991, Oct. 28   Litho.   Perf. 14
699	A120	10c Food preparation	.55	.25
700	A120	25c Church service	1.00	.25
701	A120	65c Feast	2.75	1.00
702	A120	$2 Cricket match	5.75	5.75
a.		Souvenir sheet of 4, #699-702	10.50	10.50
		Nos. 699-702 (4)	10.05	7.25

Phila Nippon '91 — A121

Tuna fishing: 5c, Yellowfin tuna. 30c, Boat for pole and line tuna fishing. 80c, Pole and line tuna fishing. $2, Arabushi processing. No. 707a, Food made from tuna, tori nanban. b, Aka miso soup.

Wmk. 384
1991, Nov. 16   Litho.   Perf. 14
703	A121	5c multicolored	.40	.25
704	A121	30c multicolored	1.25	.50
705	A121	80c multicolored	3.00	3.00
706	A121	$2 multicolored	5.50	5.50
		Nos. 703-706 (4)	10.15	9.25

Souvenir Sheet
707	A121	80c Sheet of 2, #a.-		
		b.	4.00	4.00

No. 707 contains two 28x45mm stamps.

Queen Elizabeth II's Accession to the Throne, 40th Anniv.
Common Design Type
Wmk. 384 (5c, 60c), 373
1992, Feb. 6   Litho.   Perf. 14
708	CD349	5c multicolored	.35	.60
709	CD349	20c multicolored	.65	.25
710	CD349	40c multicolored	.95	.45
711	CD349	60c multicolored	1.00	1.00
712	CD349	$5 multicolored	5.00	5.00
		Nos. 708-712 (5)	7.95	7.30

Alvaro Mendana de Niera (1541-1595), Discoveries in the Solomon Islands — A122

Granada '92: 10c, Thousand Ships Bay. 65c, Route to the Solomon Islands. 80c, Alvaro Mendana de Niera. $1, Graciosa Bay settlement. $5, Sailing ships.

Perf. 15x14½
1992, Apr. 24   Litho.   Wmk. 373
713	A122	10c multicolored	1.00	.45
714	A122	65c multicolored	1.75	.70
715	A122	80c multicolored	1.90	1.90
716	A122	$1 multicolored	2.50	2.50
717	A122	$5 multicolored	5.50	5.50
		Nos. 713-717 (5)	12.65	11.05

A123

Perf. 14x13½
1992, May 3   Litho.   Wmk. 373
718	A123	25c Early portrait	.75	.40
719	A123	70c Wearing USMC fatigues	1.50	1.50
720	A123	90c Wearing uniform, cap	1.50	1.50
a.		Booklet pane, 2 ea #718, 720	4.50	
721	A123	$2 Statue	2.25	2.25
a.		Booklet pane, 2 ea #719, 721	7.50	
		Nos. 718-721 (4)	6.00	5.65

Souvenir Sheet
722	A123	$4 In dress uniform	9.50	9.50
a.		Booklet pane of 1	7.50	
		Complete booklet, one each #720a, 721a, 722a	17.00	

Sergeant Major Jacob Vouza (1891-1984). One margin of Nos. 720a, 721a, and 722a is rouletted 8.

A124

World Columbian Stamp Expo '92, Chicago: 25c, Solomon Airlines domestic routes. 80c, Boeing 737-400 airplanes. $1.50, Solomon Airlines international routes. $5, Columbus and Santa Maria.

1992, May 22
723	A124	25c multicolored	1.00	.25
724	A124	80c multicolored	2.75	2.00
725	A124	$1.50 multicolored	3.75	3.75
726	A124	$5 multicolored	7.50	7.50
a.		Souvenir sheet of 4, #723-726	15.00	15.00
b.		As "a," ovptd. with Taipei '93 emblem in sheet margin	8.00	8.00
		Nos. 723-726 (4)	15.00	13.50

No. 726b issued Aug. 14, 1993.

Miniature Sheets

Battle of Guadalcanal, 50th Anniv. A125

Scenes from battle of Guadalcanal: No. 727a, Japanese landing at Esperance. b, US landings. c, Australian Navy cruiser. d, US Navy post office. e, Royal New Zealand Air Force PBY Catalina.

No. 728a, US Marine Wildcat fighters. b, Henderson Field under construction and attack. c, Heavy cruiser USS Quincy. d, Australian Navy heavy cruiser Canberra. e, US Marines land on Guadalcanal. f, Japanese aircraft carrier Ryujo. g, Japanese Zeke fighters attack US positions. h, Japanese bombers attack American beachhead. i, Japanese destroyers of Tokyo Express. j, Japanese heavy cruiser Chokai.

Wmk. 384
1992, Aug. 7   Litho.   Perf. 14
727	A125	30c Sheet of 5, #a.- e. + label	5.00	5.00
728	A125	80c Sheet of 10, #a.-j. + label	20.00	20.00

See No. 889.

Orchids A126

Perf. 14½x14
1992, Dec. 14   Litho.   Wmk. 373
729	A126	15c Dendrobium hybrid	1.00	.30
730	A126	70c Vanda "Amy Laycock"	2.00	1.25
731	A126	95c Dendrobium mirbelianum	2.50	2.50
732	A126	$2.50 Dendrobium macrophyllum	4.00	4.00
		Nos. 729-732 (4)	9.50	8.05

See Nos. 752-755.

Crabs
A127

Wmk. 373

1993, Jan. 15		**Litho.**		**Perf. 13**
733	A127	5c Stalk-eyed ghost	.25	.55
734	A127	10c Red-spotted	.25	.55
735	A127	25c Flat	.25	.55
736	A127	30c Land hermit	.25	.25
737	A127	40c Grapsid	.30	.30
738	A127	45c Red & white painted	.30	.30
739	A127	55c Swift-footed	.35	.35
740	A127	60c Spanner	.40	.35
741	A127	70c Red hermit	.50	.45
742	A127	80c Red-eyed	.55	.50
743	A127	90c Rathbun red	.60	.55
744	A127	$1 Coconut	.65	.60
745	A127	$1.10 Red-spotted white	.70	.70
746	A127	$4 Ghost	2.25	3.00
a.		Souvenir sheet of 1, perf. 14	4.00	4.00
747	A127	$10 Mangrove fiddler	6.25	6.25
		Nos. 733-747 (15)	13.85	15.25

No. 746a for Hong Kong '97. Issued: #733-747, 1/15/93; #746a, 2/3/97.

World War II, 50th Anniv. A128

Designs: 30c, US War Memorial, Skyline Ridge. 80c, Country flags, Guadalcanal. 95c, Major General Alexander A. Vandegrift, map. $4, WWII Scouts, Gizo Islands.

Wmk. 373

1993, Apr. 19		**Litho.**		**Perf. 14**
748	A128	30c multicolored	.55	.35
749	A128	80c multicolored	1.75	1.40
750	A128	95c multicolored	2.00	1.75
751	A128	$4 multicolored	6.25	6.25
		Nos. 748-751 (4)	10.55	9.75

Orchid Type of 1992
Perf. 14½x14

1993		**Litho.**		**Wmk. 373**
752	A126	20c like #729	1.00	.40
753	A126	85c like #730	2.50	2.50
754	A126	$1.15 like #731	3.00	2.75
755	A126	$3 like #732	5.00	5.00
		Nos. 752-755 (4)	11.50	10.40

Nos. 752, 755 are inscribed "World Orchid Conference." Nos. 753-754 are inscribed "Indopex '93 Exhibition."
Issued: #752, 755, 4/24; #753-754, 4/29.

Sinking of PT 109, 50th Anniv. A129

Designs: 30c, PT 109 about to be rammed. 50c, Native, Lt. John F. Kennedy. 95c, Message for help written on coconut, natives in canoe. $1.10, Kennedy, Navy and Marine Corps Medal. $5, PT 109.

Wmk. 373

1993, July 30		**Litho.**		**Perf. 13**
756	A129	30c multicolored	.75	.50
757	A129	50c multicolored	1.00	.70
758	A129	95c multicolored	1.25	1.25
759	A129	$1.10 multicolored	2.50	2.50
		Nos. 756-759 (4)	5.50	4.95

Souvenir Sheet
Perf. 13x13½

760	A129	$5 multicolored	8.50	8.50

Nicobar Pigeon — A130

Wmk. 373

1993, Sept. 21		**Litho.**		**Perf. 14**
761	A130	30c shown	1.50	1.00
762	A130	50c One on ground	2.00	1.25
763	A130	65c Two on branches	2.50	1.75
764	A130	70c One on branch	3.50	2.50
765	A130	$1.10 One on berry branch	1.50	1.50
766	A130	$3 Two in flight	2.75	2.75
		Nos. 761-766 (6)	13.75	10.75

World Wildlife Fund.

Dogs A131

Wmk. 373

1994, Feb. 18		**Litho.**		**Perf. 14½**
767	A131	30c Dachshund	1.00	.35
768	A131	80c German shepherd	1.50	1.50
769	A131	95c Dobermann pinscher	1.75	1.75
770	A131	$1.10 Australian cattle dog	2.00	2.00
		Nos. 767-770 (4)	6.25	5.60

Souvenir Sheet

771	A131	$4 Boxer	10.00	10.00

Hong Kong '94.
No. 771 overprinted "19-25 Aug. Jakarta '95 Surcharge $2-00." was available only at the exhibition. Value, $14.

Dolphins A132

Wmk. 373

1994, May 9		**Litho.**		**Perf. 14**
772	A132	75c Striped	1.25	.90
773	A132	85c Risso's	1.40	1.25
774	A132	$1.15 Common	2.00	2.00
775	A132	$2.50 Spinner	4.25	4.25
776	A132	$3 Bottlenose	4.75	4.75
		Nos. 772-776 (5)	13.65	13.15

Miniature Sheet

Butterflies A133

Designs: a, Vindula sapor. b, Papilio aegeus. c, Graphium hicetaon. d, Graphium mendana. e, PHILAKOREA '94 emblem. f, Graphium meeki. g, Danaus schenkii. h, Papilio ptolychus. i, Phaedyma fissizonata.

Wmk. 373

1994, Aug. 16		**Litho.**		**Perf. 13½**
777	A133	70c Sheet of 9, #a.-i.	8.50	8.50

For overprint see No. 842.

Intl. Year of the Family — A134

Designs: a, Girl writing letter in Brisbane, Australia, family reading letter on Santa Isabel, Solomon Islands. b, Boeing 737-400, Brisbane Intl. Airport, Australia. c, Boeing 737-400, Henderson Airfield, Guadalcanal, DHC 6-Twin Otter. d, Fera Airfield, Buala, Santa Isabel. e, Family.

1994, Aug. 18				**Perf. 13**
778	A134	$1.10 Strip of 5, #a.-e.	6.75	6.75
f.		Sheet of 1, #778	7.25	7.25

Volcanoes of the Solomon Islands A135

Designs: 30c, Cook Island Volcano erupting under sea, 1967. 70c, Kavachi Volcano erupting from sea, 1977. 80c, Kavachi Volcano forming temporary island, 1978. 90c, Tinakulu Volcano, permanent island.
No. 783: a, Map of Solomon Island volcanoes. b, Diagram illustrating formation of volcanic island archipelago.

Wmk. 373

1994, Oct. 24		**Litho.**		**Perf. 14**
779	A135	30c multicolored	1.00	.50
780	A135	70c multicolored	1.25	1.25
781	A135	80c multicolored	1.50	1.50
782	A135	90c multicolored	2.25	2.00
		Nos. 779-782 (4)	6.00	5.25

Souvenir Sheet

783	A135	$2 Sheet of 2, #a.-b.	6.00	6.00

La Perouse Expedition, 210th Anniv. A136

Designs: 30c, La Perouse, King Louis XVI. 80c, Map of Ile de La Perouse. 95c, L'Astrolabe. $1.10, La Boussole. $3, L'Astrolabe foundering on reef.

Wmk. 384

1994, Dec. 16		**Litho.**		**Perf. 14**
784	A136	30c multicolored	.75	.35
785	A136	80c multicolored	1.50	1.50
786	A136	95c multicolored	2.00	2.00
787	A136	$1.10 multicolored	2.25	2.25
788	A136	$3 multicolored	3.50	3.50
		Nos. 784-788 (5)	10.00	9.60

Visit South Pacific Year A137

30c, Tourists watching traditional dance, land hermit crab. 50c, Dendrobium rennellii, milkweed butterfly. 95c, Diver, moorish idol, fish. $1.15, Boats at shore, grapsid crab. $4, Flower, yellow-bibbed lorry.

Perf. 15x14½

1995, Feb. 17		**Litho.**		**Wmk. 373**
789	A137	30c multicolored	.35	.35
790	A137	50c multicolored	.85	.85
791	A137	95c multicolored	.95	.95
792	A137	$1.15 multicolored	1.10	1.10
		Nos. 789-792 (4)	3.25	3.25

Souvenir Sheet

793	A137	$4 multicolored	9.00	9.00

FAO, 50th Anniv. A138

1995, Apr. 5				**Perf. 12**
794	A138	70c Banana	1.10	.90
795	A138	75c Paw paw	1.10	.90
796	A138	95c Pomelo	1.50	1.40
797	A138	$2 Star fruit	2.75	2.75
		Nos. 794-797 (4)	6.45	5.95

Souvenir Sheet

798	A138	$3 Mango	4.00	4.00

End of World War II, 50th Anniv.
Common Design Types

Admirals, aircraft carriers: 95c, Vice Adm. Chuichi Nagumo, Akagi. $1, Rear Adm. Frank J. Fletcher, USS Yorktown. $2, Vice Adm. Robert L. Ghormley, USS Wasp. $3, Vice Adm. William F. Halsey, USS Enterprise. $5, Reverse of War Medal 1939-45.

1995, May 8				**Perf. 13½**
799	CD351	95c multicolored	1.75	1.75
800	CD351	$1 multicolored	1.75	1.75
801	CD351	$2 multicolored	3.25	3.25
802	CD351	$3 multicolored	4.25	4.25
		Nos. 799-802 (4)	11.00	11.00

Souvenir Sheet
Perf. 14

803	CD352	$5 multicolored	6.50	6.50

Orchids — A139

Designs: 45c, Calanthe triplicata. 75c, Dendrobium mohlianum. 85c, Flickingeria comata. $1.15, Dendrobium spectabile. $4, Coelogyne asperata.

Wmk. 373

1995, Sept. 1		**Litho.**		**Perf. 14**
804	A139	45c multicolored	1.75	.35
805	A139	75c multicolored	2.00	1.10
806	A139	85c multicolored	2.00	1.50
807	A139	$1.15 multicolored	2.50	2.50
		Nos. 804-807 (4)	8.25	5.45

Souvenir Sheet

808	A139	$4 multicolored	6.00	6.00

Singapore '95 (#808).

Christmas — A140

Designs: 90c, Start of canoe race. $1.05, Pan pipers, Christmas tree. $1.25, Picnic on beach. $1.45, Local church, nativity.

1995, Nov. 6				**Perf. 13x13½**
810	A140	90c multicolored	1.00	.80
811	A140	$1.05 multicolored	1.00	.85
812	A140	$1.25 multicolored	1.25	1.10
813	A140	$1.45 multicolored	1.75	1.50
		Nos. 810-813 (4)	5.00	4.25

Guglielmo Marconi (1847-1937), Radio, Cent. — A141

Designs: $1.05, Demonstration, Salisbury Plain, 1896. $1.20, Birth of maritime radio,

1900. $1.35, First ground air transmitter, Croydon, 1920. $1.45, Marconi visiting Japan on world tour, 1933-34.

1996, Feb. 28   Litho.   Wmk. 373
Perf. 14½x14

814	A141 $1.05 multicolored	1.00	1.00
815	A141 $1.20 multicolored	1.25	1.25
816	A141 $1.35 multicolored	1.50	1.50
817	A141 $1.45 multicolored	1.75	1.75
	Nos. 814-817 (4)	5.50	5.50

Lories
A142

1996, Apr. 10   Litho.   Perf. 14

818	A142 75c Palm lorikeet	1.50	.60
819	A142 $1.05 Duchess lorikeet	1.60	.80
820	A142 $1.20 Yellow-bibbed lory	1.75	1.50
821	A142 $1.35 Cardinal lory	2.50	2.50
822	A142 $1.45 Meek's lorikeet	2.50	2.50
	Nos. 818-822 (5)	9.85	7.90

Souvenir Sheet

823	A142 $3 Rainbow lorikeet	5.75	5.75

CAPEX
'96 — A143

Island scenes: 40c, Dug-out canoe. 90c, Man, bicycle. $1.20, Mobile Post Office bus. $1.45, "Tulagi Express."
$4, "Tepuke," traditional canoe from Temotu Province.

Wmk. 384
1996, June 8   Litho.   Perf. 13

824	A143 40c multicolored	.60	.45
825	A143 90c multicolored	1.50	1.00
826	A143 $1.20 multicolored	1.60	1.60
827	A143 $1.45 multicolored	2.75	2.75
	Nos. 824-827 (4)	6.45	5.80

Souvenir Sheet

828	A143 $4 multicolored	4.50	4.50

1996 Summer
Olympic Games,
Atlanta — A144

Olympic posters: 90c, Tokyo, 1964. $1.20, Los Angeles, 1932. $1.35, Paris, 1924. $2.50, London, 1908.

Wmk. 384
1996, June 30   Litho.   Perf. 14

829	A144 90c multicolored	.75	.60
830	A144 $1.20 multicolored	.95	.95
831	A144 $1.35 multicolored	1.10	1.10
832	A144 $2.50 multicolored	1.75	1.75
	Nos. 829-832 (4)	4.55	4.40

First Christian Mission, 150th
Anniv. — A145

Designs: 40c, Suiesi, Makira Bay, 1846-47.
65c, Original sketches by Rev. L. Verguet,

1846, Surimahe. $1.35, Bishop Epalle's grave, Isabel, 1845. $1.45, Makira Mission, Jean Claude Colin, Marist founder.

Wmk. 373
1996, Sept. 12   Litho.   Perf. 14

833	A145 40c multicolored	.45	.25
834	A145 65c multicolored	.55	.55
835	A145 $1.35 multicolored	.90	.85
836	A145 $1.45 multicolored	1.10	1.10
	Nos. 833-836 (4)	3.00	2.75

Souvenir Sheet

Taipei '96 — A146

1996, Oct. 21

837	A146 $1.50 Sandford's eagle	2.50	2.50

UNICEF,
50th
Anniv.
A147

Wmk. 373
1996, Nov. 21   Litho.   Perf. 14½

838	A147 40c Food	.40	.30
839	A147 $1.05 Recreation	.80	.80
840	A147 $1.35 Medicine	1.10	1.10
841	A147 $2.50 Education	1.75	1.75
	Nos. 838-841 (4)	4.05	3.95

For surcharge see No. B4.

No. 777 Ovptd. in Red with SINGPEX
'97 Emblem

Wmk. 373
1997, Feb. 21   Litho.   Perf. 13½

842	A133 70c Sheet of 9, #a.-i.	8.50	8.50

Overprint is centered over entire sheet with each stamp containing portion of SINGPEX '97 emblem.
Overprint exists in black from a limited printing.

Northern
Common
Cuscus
A148

15c, In tree. 60c, Eating berries. $2.50, In tree, climbing right. $3, Two in branches.

Wmk. 373
1997, Apr. 21   Litho.   Perf. 12

843	A148 15c multicolored	.25	.25
844	A148 60c multicolored	.35	.35
845	A148 $2.50 multicolored	1.25	1.25
846	A148 $3 multicolored	1.50	1.50
	Nos. 843-846 (4)	3.35	3.35

Whales — A149

a, Whale, calf, vert. b, Whale breaching.

Wmk. 373
1997, May 29   Litho.   Perf. 14½

847	A149 $2 Sheet of 2, #a.-b.	3.50	3.50

PACIFIC 97.

Queen Elizabeth II & Prince Philip,
50th Wedding Anniv. — A150

#848, Queen with two horses. #849, Prince. #850, Prince on polo pony. #851, Queen. #852, Queen, Prince at Royal Ascot.

1997, July 10   Perf. 13

848	$3 multicolored	3.25	3.25
849	$3 multicolored	3.25	3.25
a.	A150 Pair, #848-849	7.00	7.00
850	$3 multicolored	3.25	3.25
851	$3 multicolored	3.25	3.25
a.	A150 Pair, #850-851	7.00	7.00
	Nos. 848-851 (4)	13.00	13.00

Souvenir Sheet

852	A150 $3 multicolored	4.50	4.50

South Pacific Commission, 50th
Anniv. — A151

Chelonia mydas: 50c, Laying eggs. 90c, Young turtles entering water. $1.50, Group swimming under water. $2, Two adults under water.

Wmk. 384
1997, Sept. 29   Litho.   Perf. 14

853	A151 50c multicolored	.65	.40
854	A151 90c multicolored	.95	.85
855	A151 $1.50 multicolored	1.40	1.40
856	A151 $2 multicolored	1.60	1.60
	Nos. 853-856 (4)	4.60	4.25

Christmas
A152

Designs: $1.10, Oni mako. $1.40, Ysabel dancing women with bamboo sticks. $1.50, Pan pipers from Small Malaita. $1.70, Western bamboo band.
No. 861, vert.: a, Pachycephala pectoralis. b, Papilio aegeus, graphium meeki.

Wmk. 373
1997, Nov. 24   Litho.   Perf. 13½

857	A152 $1.10 multicolored	.85	.85
858	A152 $1.40 multicolored	1.00	1.00
859	A152 $1.50 multicolored	1.10	1.10
860	A152 $1.70 multicolored	1.50	1.50
	Nos. 857-860 (4)	4.45	4.45

Souvenir Sheet of 2
Perf. 14

861	A152 $1.50 #a.-b.	4.50	4.50

China Stamp Exhibition, Bangkok '97 (#861).
Issued: #857-860, 11/24; #861, 12/5.

Game
Fish — A153

50c, Black marlin. $1.20, Shortbill swordfish. $1.40, Swordfish. $2, Indo-Pacific sailfish.

Perf. 14½
1998, Feb. 27   Litho.   Unwmk.

862	A153 50c multicolored	.85	.45
863	A153 $1.20 multicolored	1.40	1.10
864	A153 $1.40 multicolored	1.75	1.75
865	A153 $2 multicolored	2.00	2.00
a.	Souv. sheet of 1, wmk. triangles	2.50	2.50
	Nos. 862-865 (4)	6.00	5.30

Singpex '98 (#865a). No. 865a issued 7/23 and sold for $3.

Diana, Princess of Wales (1961-97)
Common Design Type

$2, Wearing white dress (without hat). #867: a, Up close. b, Wearing white hat, dress. c, Wearing evening dress, black background. d, Taking flowers from children.

Perf. 14½x14
1998, Mar. 31   Wmk. 373

866	CD355 $2 multicolored	1.10	1.10
	Complete booklet, 10 #866	11.00	

Sheet of 4

867	CD355 $2.50 #a.-d.	7.00	7.00

No. 867 sold for $10 + 50c, with surtax from international sales being donated to the Princess Diana Memorial Fund and surtax from national sales being donated to designated local charity.
For overprint see No. 1095.; for surcharge see No. B5.

Technical
Cooperation
Between
Solomon
Islands and
Republic of
China
A154

Designs: 50c, Harvesting watermelons. $1.50, Harvesting rice.
No. 870: a, 80c, Growing cucumbers. b, $1.20, Growing tomatoes.

Wmk. 373
1998, May 29   Litho.   Perf. 13

868	A154 50c multicolored	.50	.50
869	A154 $1.50 multicolored	1.25	1.25

Souvenir Sheet

870	A154 Sheet of 2, #a.-b.	2.50	2.50

Melanesian Trade and Culture
Show — A155

a, Group raising arms during traditional dance. b, Men with bows and arrow. c, Man smiling in front of water. d, Four men with poles in traditional dance. e, Masked man kneeling down with bow and arrow. f, Man in traditional garb, flowers. g, Group carrying poles. h, Man with spear and shield. i, Man in traditional garb, sun over water.

1998, July 3   Perf. 13½

871	Sheet of 9	7.50	7.50
a.-c.	A155 50c any single	.45	.45
d.-f.	A155 $1.20 any single	.55	.55
g.-i.	A155 $1.50 any single	.75	.75

Souvenir Sheet

New Natl. Parliament Building — A156

1998, July 7
872 A156 $4 multicolored   3.50 3.50
Independence, 20th anniv.

Souvenir Sheet

Australia '99 World Stamp Expo — A157

Designs: a, HMS Endeavour, 1770. b, Los Reyes being careened at Guadalcanal, 1568.

1999, Mar. 19   Perf. 13¼x13¾
873 A157 $10 Sheet of 2, #a.-
         b.   13.00 13.00

PhilexFrance '99, World Philatelic Exhibition. A158

Marine Life: a, Beach. b, Great frigate bird. c, Coconut crab. d, Green turtle. e, Royal Spanish dancer nudibranch. f, Sun moon and stars butterflyfish. g, Striped Sweetlips. h, Saddle-back butterflyfish. i, Cuttlefish. j, Giant clam. k, Lionfish. l, Spiny lobster.

1999, July 2   Perf. 13¼
874 A158 $1 Sheet of 12, #a.-l.   9.00 9.00

1st Manned Moon Landing, 30th Anniv.
Common Design Type

Designs: 50c, Lift-off. $1.50, Lunar module above moon's surface. $2.50, Aldrin beside US flag. $3.40, Splashdown. $4, Earth as seen from moon.

Perf. 14x13¾
1999, July 20   Litho.   Wmk. 384
875 CD357 50c multicolored   .50   .35
876 CD357 $1.50 multicolored 1.00 1.00
877 CD357 $2.50 multicolored 2.00 2.00
878 CD357 $3.40 multicolored 2.50 2.50
         Nos. 875-878 (4)   6.00 5.85

Souvenir Sheet
Perf. 14
879 CD357 $4 multicolored   4.00 4.00
  a   Ovptd. in margin in red   4.50 4.50

No. 879 contains one circular stamp 40mm in diameter.
Issued 7/7/2000, overprint on No. 879a reads "WORLD STAMP EXPO - USA VALUE $5.00." Sold for $5.

Queen Mother's Century
Common Design Type

Queen Mother: $1, Inspecting bomb damage at Portsmouth, 1941. $1.50, At the Derby, 1983. $2.30, Receiving birthday wishes. $4.90, As colonel-in-chief of Royal Army Medical Corps.
$3, With King George VI, Winston Churchill, V-E Day, 1945.

1999, Aug. 16   Perf. 13½
880 CD358 $1 multicolored   .90   .50
881 CD358 $1.50 multicolored 1.10 .95
882 CD358 $2.30 multicolored 1.50 1.50
883 CD358 $4.90 multicolored 2.50 2.50
         Nos. 880-883 (4)   6.00 5.45

Souvenir Sheet
884 CD358 $5 black   4.00 4.00

No. 683 overprinted "China '99" in red for international stamp exhibition, Beijing.

1999, Aug. 21
884A A117 7c Sweet potato weevil   1.75 1.75

Ferrari Racing Cars A159

1999, Sept. 27   Wmk. 373   Perf. 14
885 A159 $1 212E   .85   .55
886 A159 $1.50 250TR   1.00 .75
887 A159 $3.30 250LM   1.75 1.75
888 A159 $4.20 612 Can-Am   3.00 3.00
         Nos. 885-888 (4)   6.60 6.05

Guadalcanal Type of 1992

Designs: a, Flags at half staff. b, Cenotaph, Honiara. c, Solomon Peace Memorial Park. d, US War Memorial, Skyline Ridge. e, Reunion ship Ocean Pearl.

1999, Aug. 16   Wmk. 384
889 A125 30c Sheet of 5, #a.-e,
             + label   2.75 2.75
  f Sheet of 10, #727a-727e, 889a-
       889e + label   8.50 8.50

Melanesian Mission, 150th Anniv. — A160

Christmas: a, $1, Bishop George Augustus Selwyndd. b, $1, Bishop John Coleridge Patteson. c, $3.30, Text. d, $1.50, Stained glass. e, $1.50, Southern Cross.

1999, Nov. 12   Unwmk.
890 A160 Strip of 5, #a.-e.   4.50 4.50
         See Norfolk Islands #693.

Millennium A161

Designs: Nos. 891, 893a, $1 Munda lighthouse, war canoe. Nos. 892, 893b, $4, Tulagi lighthouse, security boat.

2000, Apr. 27   Perf. 13½x13¼
891 A161 $1 multi   1.50 1.00
892 A161 $4 multi   5.00 5.00

Souvenir Sheet
893 A161   Sheet of 2, #a.-b. 7.50 7.50

Nos. 893a, 893b have red violet margins.

Souvenir Sheet

Commonwealth Youth Minister's Meeting — A162

2000, May 22   Litho.   Perf. 13½x13¼
894 A162 $6 multi   9.50 9.50

Year of the Dragon A163

Dragon head facing: $1, Front. $3.90, Left.

Perf. 11¾x11½
2000, Nov. 13   Litho.   Unwmk.
895-896 A163 Set of 2   4.00 4.00
  896a   Souvenir sheet, #895-896 4.00 4.00

East Rennell Island World Heritage Site A164

Map and: 50c, Rennell Island. $3.40, Lake Tegano. $4, Rennell shrikebill. $4.90, Endemic orchid.

Perf. 11¾x11½
2000, Nov. 30   Litho.
897-900 A164 Set of 4   11.00 11.00

2000 Summer Olympics and Olymphilex, Sydney — A165

Runners in: $1, 100-meter race. $4.50, 1500-meter race.

2000, Dec. 11   Perf. 14
901-902 A165 Set of 2   5.50 5.50
  a   Souvenir sheet, #901-902 5.50 5.50

Birds A166

Designs: 5c, Yellow-throated white eye. 20c, Purple swamphen. 50c, Blyth's hornbill. 80c, Yellow-faced myna. 90c, Blue-faced parrotfinch. $1, Crested tern. $2, Rainbow lorikeet. $3, Eclectus parrot. $4, Dwarf kingfisher. $10, Beach thick-knee. $20, Brahminy kite. $50, Superb fruit dove.

2001   Wmk. 373   Perf. 14¼x14½
903 A166 5c multi   .25   .25
904 A166 20c multi   .25   .25
905 A166 50c multi   .30   .30
906 A166 80c multi   .40   .40
907 A166 90c multi   .50   .50
908 A166 $1 multi   .60   .60
909 A166 $2 multi   1.00 1.00
910 A166 $3 multi   1.50 1.50
911 A166 $4 multi   2.00 2.00
912 A166 $10 multi   4.00 4.00

Size: 48x38mm
Perf. 13¾x13½
913 A166 $20 multi   8.75 8.75
913A A166 $50 multi   25.00 25.00
         Nos. 903-913 (11)   19.55 19.55

Issued: Nos. 5c-$20, 2/1/01; $50, 6/1/01.

East Rennell Island Type of 2000 and

Hong Kong 2001 Stamp Exhibition A167

Snake color: $1.70, Yellow and brown. $2.30, Green and yellow.

2001, Feb. 1   Litho.   Perf. 11¾x11½
914-915 A167 Set of 2   3.50 3.50

Souvenir Sheet
916 A164 $5 Like #900   5.50 5.50

UN High Commissioner for Refugees, 50th Anniv. — A168

Designs: 50c, Refugees. $1, Food and medical supplies. $1.90, Shelter. $2.30, Education.

Perf. 14¼
2001, July 28   Litho.   Unwmk.
917-920 A168 Set of 4   4.00 4.00

Souvenir Sheet

New Year 2001 (Year of the Snake) — A168a

No. 920A: b, Red-banded tree snake. c, Whip snake. d, Pacific boa. e, Guppy's snake.
920A A168a $1 Sheet of 4, #b-e 4.50 4.50

Reef Fish A169

Designs: 70c, Amphiprion chrysopterus. 90c, Amphiprion perideraion. $1, Premnas biaculeatus. $1.50, Amphiprion melanopus. $2.10, Amphiprion clarkii. $4.50, Dascyllus trimaculatus.

Wmk. 373
2001, Dec. 27   Litho.   Perf. 14
921-926 A169 Set of 6   6.50 6.50
  926a Souvenir sheet, #921-926 7.50 7.50

Worldwide Fund for Nature (WWF) A170

Various depictions of gray cuscus: $1, $1.70, $2.30, $5.

2002, Jan. 31
927-930 A170 Set of 4   5.75 5.75
  a   Horiz. strip of 4   6.25 6.25

Reign Of Queen Elizabeth II, 50th Anniv. Issue
Common Design Type

Designs: Nos. 931, 935a, $1, Princess Elizabeth with baby carriage, 1933. Nos. 932, 935b, $1.90, Wearing sunglasses. Nos. 933, 935c, $2.10, In 1955. Nos. 934, 935d, $2.30, Wearing hat. No. 935e, $10, 1955 portrait by Annigoni (38x50mm).

Perf. 14¼x14½, 13¾ (#935e)
2002, Feb. 6   Litho.   Wmk. 373
With Gold Frames
931-934 CD360   Set of 4   6.00 6.00
Souvenir Sheet
Without Gold Frames
935 CD360   Sheet of 5, #a-e   10.00 10.00

Methodist Mission, Cent. A172

Designs: $1, Typical old school building, Western Solomons. $1.70, Mrs. J. F. Goldie and companions. $2.10, Tandanya, first mission schooner. $2.30, Rev. J. F. Goldie and Solomon Islands chiefs.
$5, Rev. Goldie and Sam Aqarao, vert.

2002, May 23   Unwmk.   Perf. 14¼
937-940 A172   Set of 4   7.50 7.50
Souvenir Sheet
941 A172 $5 multi   3.00 3.00

United We Stand — A173

Perf. 13½x13¼
2002, June 17   Unwmk.
942 A173 $2.10 multi   3.50 3.50
Souvenir Sheet

New Year 2002 (Year of the Horse) — A173a

No. 942A: b, Horse. c, Horse, horiz.

Perf. 13½x13¾, 13¾x13½
2002, July 7   Litho.
942A A173a $4 Sheet of 2, #a-b   7.50 7.50
No. 942 was printed in sheets of 4.

Cowrie Shells — A174

No. 943: a, $1, Sieve cowrie. b, $1, Kitten cowrie. c, $1, Stolid cowrie, eroded cowrie. d, $1.90, Tapering cowrie. e, $1.90, Tiger cowrie. f, $1.90, Lynx cowrie. g, $2.30, Map cowrie, h, $2.30, Pacific deer cowrie. i, $2.30, Tortoise cowrie.
$10, Golden cowrie.

Perf. 14¼x14½
2002, Aug. 2   Wmk. 373
943 A174   Sheet of 9, #a-i   14.00 14.00
Souvenir Sheet
944 A174 $10 multi   12.00 12.00
Phila Korea 2002 World Stamp Exhibition, Seoul.

Queen Mother Elizabeth (1900-2002)
Common Design Type

Designs: No. 945, $1, Without hat (sepia photograph). No. 946, $2.30, Wearing blue hat.
No. 947: a, $5, Wearing tiara (black and white photograph). b, $5, Wearing green blue hat.

Wmk. 373
2002, Aug. 5   Litho.   Perf. 14¼
With Purple Frames
945-946 CD361   Set of 2   4.00 4.00
Souvenir Sheet
Without Purple Frames
Perf. 14½x14¼
947 CD361   Sheet of 2, #a-b   7.00 7.00

Battle of Guadalcanal, 60th Anniv. — A175

US servicemen: $1, No. 952d, Coast Guard signalman First Class Douglas Munro. $1.90, No. 952b, Marine Corps Capt. Joe Foss. $2.10, No. 952c, Marine Corps Platoon Sergeant Mitchell Paige. $2.30, No. 952a, Navy Rear Admiral Norman Scott.

2002, Aug. 7   Unwmk.   Perf. 14
948-951 A175   Set of 4   7.00 7.00
Souvenir Sheet
952 A175 $5 Sheet of 4, #a-d   11.00 11.00

Christmas — A176

Paintings: $1, Christmas Night, by Lucas Cranach, the Elder. $2.10, Madonna and Child, by Giovanni Bellini. $2.30, Nativity, by Perugino, horiz. $5, Madonna and Child, by Simone Martini.

2002, Nov. 25   Litho.   Perf. 14
953-956 A176   Set of 4   7.50 7.50

New Year 2003 (Year of the Ram) A177

Perf. 14¼x14½
2003, Apr. 15   Litho.   Unwmk.
957 A177 $3 multi   3.00 3.00
Issued in sheets of 4.

U. S. Medals of Honor — A178

Designs: $1, Air Force Medal of Honor. $1.90, Navy Medal of Honor. $2.10, Army Medal of Honor. $2.30, Medal of Honor ribbon.

2003, June 6   Perf. 14
958-961 A178   Set of 4   8.00 8.00

Prince William, 21st Birthday — A179

No. 962: a, In gray suit. b, In red shirt. c, In black suit.
$15, In blue shirt.

2003, June 21
962 A179 $9 Sheet of 3, #a-c   14.00 14.00
Souvenir Sheet
963 A179 $15 multi   12.00 12.00

Solomon Islands — Republic of China Diplomatic Relations, 20th Anniv. A180

Designs: $1.50, Rice farmers. $2.10, Hospital.

2003, July 8   Perf. 14¼
964-965 A180   Set of 2   5.00 5.00

Coronation of Queen Elizabeth II, 50th Anniv. — A181

No. 966: a, Wearing tiara. b, Wearing green hat. c, Wearing blue hat.
$15, Wearing tiara, diff.

2003, June 2   Litho.   Perf. 14
966 A181 $9 Sheet of 3, #a-c   15.00 15.00
Souvenir Sheet
967 A181 $15 multi   14.00 14.00

Powered Flight, Cent. — A182

No. 968: a, Boeing 747. b, Boeing 707. c, Lockheed Model 649. d, Boeing Model 247D. e, Fokker F.VII. f, Orville and Wilbur Wright. $15, Concorde.

2003, Dec. 17
968 A182 $4 Sheet of 6, #a-f   14.00 14.00
Souvenir Sheet
969 A182 $15 multi   10.00 10.00

Souvenir Sheet

Visit of Pope John Paul II, 20th Anniv. — A183

No. 970: a, $5, Pope waving. b, $10, Pope with crucifix.

2004, Aug. 6   Litho.   Perf. 14
970 A183   Sheet of 2, #a-b   7.00 7.00
For No. 970 overprinted, see No. 1025.

2004 Summer Olympics, Athens — A184

Designs: $1.50, Runner at starting blocks. $2, Runner in full stride. $2.20, Runner at finish line. $10, Solomon Islands flag, Olympic rings.

2004, Aug. 13   Perf. 14
971-974 A184   Set of 4   7.00 7.00

Orchids A185

No. 975: a, Calanthe triplicata. b, Dendrobium johnsoniae. c, Dendrobium capituliflorum. d, Spathoglottis plicata. e, Dendrobium mirbelianum. f, Dendrobium polysema. g, Paphiopedilum bougainvilleanum. h, Coelogyne asperata. i, Dendrobium macrophyllum. j, Dendrobium spectabile.

2004, Aug. 28   Perf. 13½
975   Block of 10   15.00 15.00
a.-e.   A185 $2.60 Any single   .90 .90
f.-j.   A185 $5 Any single   1.75 1.75

Pres. Ronald Reagan (1911-2004) — A186

2004, Sept. 30   Litho.   *Perf. 14*
976 A186 $5 multi   9.00 9.00
Printed in sheets of 4.

Merchant Ships A187

Designs: $1.50, MV Bilikiki. $2.20, MV Spirit of Solomons. $3, SS Oceana. $20, RMS Queen Elizabeth 2.

2004, Oct. 11   *Perf. 13¼*
977-980 A187   Set of 4   12.00 12.00

FIFA (Fédération Internationale de Football Association), Cent. — A188

No. 981, $2.10: a, Player and ball. b, Players.
No. 982, $10: a, Players. b, Player and ball.

2004, Nov. 1   *Perf. 14*
Horiz. Pairs, #a-b
981-982 A188   Set of 2   10.00 10.00

Bird Life International — A189

No. 983, $2.10: a, Rufous-tailed waterhen. b, Buff-banded rail. c, Purple swamphen. d, Woodford's rail e, Roviana rail. f, Makira moorhen.
No. 984, $5: a, Solomon Islands hawk-owl (denomination at LR). b, White-throated eared nightjar (denomination at LR). c, Solomon Islands hawk-owl (denomination at LL). d, White-throated eared nightjar (denomination at UR). e, Marbled frogmouth. f, Fearful owl.
No. 985, $7.50: a, Beach kingfisher. b, Collared kingfisher. c, Ultramarine kingfisher. d, Moustached kingfisher. e, Little kingfisher. f, Variable kingfisher.

2004, Nov. 15   *Perf. 13¾*
Sheets of 6, #a-f
983-985 A189   Set of 3   36.00 36.00

Christmas — A190

Paintings: 10c, Adoration of the Magi, by Peter Paul Rubens. 50c, Madonna della Tenda, by Raphael, vert. $1.50, Madonna and Child, by Titian, vert. $2.60, Madonna by the Arch, by Albrecht Dürer, vert. $3, Holy Family, by Frans Floris. $10, Madonna and Child, by unknown artist.

2004, Dec. 8   *Perf. 14*
986-991 A190   Set of 6   7.00 7.00

Battle of Trafalgar, Bicent. — A191

No. 992, $1.90: a, Vice-Admiral Horatio Lord Nelson. b, HMS Victory. c, Sir Thomas Masterman Hardy. d, The first engagement. e, Breaking the line. f, The death of Nelson.
No. 993, $2.60: a, Lord Cuthbert Collingwood. b, Napoleon Bonaparte. c, Destruction of the Bucentaure. d, Race and chase, 1805. e, The Nelson Touch — Band of Brothers. f, The Nelson Touch.
No. 994, $5: a, Nelson and Hardy on deck. b, Nelson sends the signal "England expects." c, Attempted siege of HMS Victory. d, Neptune tows Victory to Gibraltar. e, Funeral procession on Thames. f, Nelson's Column.
No. 995, $10: a, Nelson's early years. b, The letters of Nelson. c, Siege of Calvi — Nelson loses the sight of his eye. d, Santa Cruz de Tenerife — Nelson loses his arm. e, The Battle of Cape St. Vincent. f, The Battle of the Nile.

2005, Jan. 3   *Perf. 13¼*
Sheets of 6, #a-f
992-995 A191   Set of 4   50.00 50.00

Baha'is in Solomon Islands, 50th Anniv. — A192

Designs: $1.50, Geometric design. $3, Globe, hands, laurel branches. $5, Alvin and Gertrude Blum, horiz.

2005, Mar. 21   Litho.   *Perf. 14¼*
996-998 A192   Set of 3   4.00 4.00

End of World War II, 60th Anniv. — A193

No. 999: a, $2.50, Japanese forces land at Tulagi. b, $2.50, USS Lexington under air attack during Battle of the Coral Sea. c, $2.50, Coastwatcher and Solomon Island scouts. d, $2.50, US forces land at Tulagi and Guadalcanal virtually unopposed. e, $2.50, HMAS Canberra sinking at Iron Bottom Sound. f, $5, Cactus Air Force in action over Henderson Airfield. g, $5, "Tokyo Express" nightly bombardments by Japanese warships. h, $5, P-38 Lightnings shoot down Admiral Yamamoto. i, $5, Lt. John F. Kennedy's PT-109 sank after collision with Japanese warship Amagiri. j, $5, Sgt. Maj. Vouza and medals.
No. 1000, RAN coastwatchers sending enemy intelligence reports by teleradio.

2005, Apr. 21   *Perf. 13¾*
999 A193   Sheet of 10, #a-j   16.00 16.00
Souvenir Sheet
1000 A193 $5 multi   3.50 3.50
Pacific Explorer 2005 World Stamp Expo, Sydney (#1000).

Europa Stamps, 50th Anniv. (in 2006) A194

No. 1001: a, Spain #1262. b, Netherlands #417.

No. 1002: a, Andorra (French) #174. b, Belgium #573.
No. 1003: a, Belgium #496. b, Spain #1567.
No. 1004: a, Austria #657. b, San Marino #701.
No. 1005: a, Netherlands #494. b, Norway #842.
No. 1006: a, Germany #749. b, Italy #750.

2005, May 16   *Perf. 13½x13¾*

1001	Horiz. pair		1.25	1.25
a.-b.	A194 $1 Either single		.55	.55
c.	Souvenir sheet, #1001		1.25	1.25
1002	Horiz. pair		2.50	2.50
a.-b.	A194 $2.10 Either single		1.10	1.10
c.	Souvenir sheet, #1002		2.50	2.50
1003	Horiz. pair		2.75	2.75
a.-b.	A194 $2.50 Either single		1.25	1.25
c.	Souvenir sheet, #1003		2.75	2.75
1004	Horiz. pair		4.75	4.75
a.-b.	A194 $5 Either single		2.00	2.00
c.	Souvenir sheet, #1004		4.75	4.75
1005	Horiz. pair		9.00	9.00
a.-b.	A194 $10 Either single		4.25	4.25
c.	Souvenir sheet, #1005		9.00	9.00
1006	Horiz. pair		16.00	16.00
a.-b.	A194 $15 Either single		7.50	7.50
c.	Souvenir sheet, #1006		16.00	16.00
	Nos. 1001-1006 (6)		36.25	36.25

Queen Elizabeth II's Royal Year — A195

No. 1007, $1: a, Order of the Garter. b, Trooping the Color.
No. 1008, $2.10: a, Royal Ascot. b, Garden party.
No. 1009, $2.50: a, Royal visits. b, State visits.
No. 1010, $5: a, State Opening of Parliament. b, Remembrance Day.
No. 1011, $10: a, Investitures. b, Christmas broadcast.
No. 1012, $15: a, Maundy service. b, Chelsea Flower Show.

2005, June 3   *Perf. 14½*
Horiz. Pairs, #a-b
1007-1012 A195   Set of 6   36.00 36.00

A196

A197

A198

Pope John Paul II (1920-2005) A199

BirdLife International — A200

No. 1021, $2.10: a, Finsch's pygmy parrot. b, Cardinal lory. c, Solomon's cockatoo. d, Eclectus parrot. e, Rainbow lory. f, Song parrot.
No. 1022, $5: a, Red-knobbed imperial pigeon. b, Yellow-bibbed fruit dove. c, Claret-breasted fruit dove. d, Nicobar pigeon. e, Stephan's ground dove. f, Crested cuckoo dove.
No. 1023, $7.50: a, Pied goshawk. b, Imitator sparrowhawk. c, Buff-headed coucal. d, Black-faced pitta. e, Melanesian megapode. f, Blyth's hornbill.

2005, Sept. 1   Litho.   *Perf. 14½x14¾*
Sheets of 6, #a-f
1021-1023 A200   Set of 3   36.00 36.00

Rotary International, Cent. — A201

2005, Sept. 12   *Perf. 14½*
1024 A201 $2.50 multi   1.50 1.50

Embossed on Metal
2005, July   *Die Cut Perf. 12½*
Self-Adhesive

1013	A196	$1.20 shown	.70	.70
1014	A196	$1.20 Pope, diff.	.70	.70
1015	A197	$2.60 shown	1.40	1.40
1016	A197	$2.60 Pope, diff.	1.40	1.40
1017	A198	$5 shown	2.75	2.75
1018	A198	$5 Pope, diff.	2.75	2.75
1019	A199	$10 shown	5.75	5.75
1020	A199	$10 Pope, diff.	5.75	5.75
		Nos. 1013-1020 (8)	21.20	21.20

No. 970 Overprinted

No. 1025: a, $5. b, $10.

2005, Oct. 3   *Perf. 14*
1025 A183   Sheet of 2, #a-b   7.00 7.00

Christmas — A202

Stories by Hans Christian Andersen (1805-75): $1, The Little Fir Tree. $2.10, The Nightingale. $2.50, The Emperor's New Clothes. $5, The Phoenix. $10, The Tinderbox. $15, The Red Shoes.

2005, Oct. 10
1026-1031 A202   Set of 6   17.00 17.00

Battle of Trafalgar, Bicent. — A203

Designs: $5, HMS Victory. $10, Ship in battle, horiz. $20, Admiral Horatio Nelson.

2005, Oct. 18   **Perf. 13¼**
1032-1034　A203　Set of 3   17.00 17.00

Worldwide Fund for Nature (WWF) — A204

Various views of prehensile-tailed skink: $1.50, $2.60, $3, $10.

2005, Dec. 7   **Perf. 14½**
1035-1038　A204　Set of 4   5.25 5.25
1038a   Sheet, 2 each # 1035-1038   11.50 11.50

Queen Elizabeth II, 80th Birthday A205

Queen Elizabeth II: $2.10, As young girl. $2.50, As woman. $5, Holding camera. $20, Wearing red hat.
No. 1043: a, $10, Like $2.50. b, $15, Like $5.

2006, Apr. 21   **Litho.**   **Perf. 14**
Stamps With White Frames
1039-1042　A205　Set of 4   12.00 12.00
Souvenir Sheet
Stamps Without Frames
1043　A205　Sheet of 2, #a-b   10.00 10.00

Anniversaries — A206

No. 1044, $2.20: a, Great Eastern. b, Isambard Kingdom Brunel (1806-59), engineer.
No. 1045, $2.50: a, Charles Darwin. b, Green turtle.
No. 1046: $5: a, Diving bell. b, Edmond Halley (1656-1742), astronomer.
No. 1047, $10: a, Locomotive "Rocket." b, George Stephenson (1781-1848), inventor.

2006, Apr. 30   **Perf. 14¾x14½**
Horiz. Pairs, #a-b
1044-1047　A206　Set of 4   14.00 14.00
Darwin's voyage on the Beagle, 175th anniv. (#1045).

Christopher Columbus (1451-1506), Explorer — A207

Designs: $1.90, Niña. $2.20, Pinta. $2.60, Santa Maria. $10, Arms of Columbus. $20, Columbus.

2006, May 22   **Perf. 13¼x13**
1048-1051　A207　Set of 4   6.50 6.50
Souvenir Sheet
1051A　A207　$20 multi   8.00 8.00
Washington 2006 World Philatelic Exhibition.

2006 World Cup Soccer Championships, Germany — A208

Match scenes from: $4, 1954 West Germany finals victory. $5, 1966 England finals victory. $10, 1998 France finals victory. $20, 2006 Solomon Islands vs. Australia playoff.

2006, June 9   **Perf. 14**
1052-1055　A208　Set of 4   13.00 13.00

Victoria Cross, 150th Anniv. A209

Victoria Cross and: $1, Captured Russian gun used to cast the Victoria Cross. $2.20, Midshipman Charles Lucas, first recipient of Victoria Cross. $2.50, Queen Victoria awarding first Victoria Crosses. $5, Corporal Sukanaivalu, Fijian infantryman at Bougainville, 1944. $10, Corporal Rattey, Australian infantryman at Bougainville, 1945. $15, Private Partridge, Australian infantryman at Bougainville, 1945.

2006, June 26   **Perf. 14x14½**
1056-1061　A209　Set of 6   13.00 13.00

Prehistoric Animals — A210

Designs: 5c, Baryonyx. 10c, Diplodocus. $1.50, Pteranodon. $2.15, Argentinosaurus. $2.40, Centrosaurus. $3, Allosaurus. $10, Ankylosaurus. $20, Iguanodon.

2006, Aug. 14   **Perf. 13¼x13¾**
1062-1069　A210　Set of 8   15.00 15.00

Intl. Coconut Day — A210a

Designs: $1.50, First grade copra drier. $2.40, Standard copra drier. $3, Coconut oil expeller. $5, Coconuts, palm tree, ship, truck on dock, bird.

2006, Sept. 2   **Litho.**   **Perf. 14¼**
1069A-1069D　A210a　Set of 4   3.25 3.25

Cone Shells — A211

Designs: 5c, Conus marmoreus. 10c, Conus auratinus. 20c, Conus ferrugineus. 50c, Conus consors. 80c, Conus magdalenae. 90c, Conus sulcatus brettinghami. $1, Conus tmetus. $1.50, Conus aureus. $2, Conus corallinus. $3, Conus floccatus. $4, Conus punniculus. $10, Conus pohlianus. $20, Conus proximus. $50, Conus canonicus.

2006, Oct. 31   **Perf. 13x12½**
1070	A211	5c multi	.25	.30
1071	A211	10c multi	.25	.30
1072	A211	20c multi	.25	.30
1073	A211	50c multi	.40	.25
1074	A211	80c multi	.30	.25
1075	A211	90c multi	.50	.30
1076	A211	$1 multi	.75	.40
1077	A211	$1.50 multi	.90	.60
1078	A211	$2 multi	1.00	.75
1079	A211	$3 multi	1.00	1.25
1080	A211	$4 multi	1.25	1.75
1081	A211	$10 multi	3.50	3.50
1082	A211	$20 multi	6.75	6.75
1083	A211	$50 multi	17.50	17.50
	Nos. 1070-1083 (14)		34.60	34.20

Tales of Beatrix Potter — A212

Designs: $1.50, The Tale of Peter Rabbit. $1.90, The Tale of Squirrel Nutkin. $2.15, The Tailor of Gloucester. $2.40, The Tale of Benjamin Bunny. $2.65, The Tale of Two Bad Mice. $5, The Tale of Mrs. Tiggy-Winkle.

2006, Dec. 4   **Perf. 13x13½**
1084-1089　A212　Set of 6   6.00 6.00
1089a   Miniature sheet, #1084-1089   6.00 6.00

Wedding of Queen Elizabeth II and Prince Philip, 60th Anniv. — A213

Designs: $2.10, Couple looking straight ahead. $2.50, Couple looking at each other. $5, Wedding ceremony. No. 1093, $20, Elizabeth with flowers. No. 1094, $20, Wedding party.

2007, Jan. 31   **Perf. 13¾**
1090-1093　A213　Set of 4   11.00 11.00
Souvenir Sheet
Perf. 14
1094　A213　$20 multi   7.00 7.00
No. 1094 contains one 42x56mm stamp.

No. 867 Overprinted "1997-2007" in Metallic Blue
Method, Perf. and Watermark As Before
2007, Aug. 3
1095　CD355　$2.50 Sheet of 4, #a-d   3.00 3.00
No. 1095 sold for $10.50 and is additionally overprinted "10th Anniversary / in Memorium" in sheet margin at upper left and upper right.

Princess Diana (1961-97) A214

Various photographs of Princess Diana: $2.10, $2.50, $5, $20.

Perf. 13x12½
2007, Dec. 8   **Litho.**   **Unwmk.**
1096-1099　A214　Set of 4   8.25 8.25

A215

Royal Air Force, 90th Anniv. — A216

Designs: No. 1100, $4, Sir Hugh Trenchard (1873-1956), founder of Royal Air Force. No. 1101, $4, Wing Commander Guy Gibson (1918-44), leader of Dambusters raid. No. 1102, $4, Sir Charles Portal (1893-1971), Marshal. No. 1103, $4, Sir William Sholto Douglas (1893-1969), Marshal. No. 1104, $4, Sir Hugh Dowding (1882-1970), Marshal. $20, Battle of Britain.

Perf. 14¼x14
2008, Apr. 30   **Wmk. 373**
1100-1104　A215　Set of 5   5.25 5.25
Souvenir Sheet
1105　A216　$20 multi   5.25 5.25

British Monarchs — A217

Designs: No. 1106, $2, William I (1027-87). No. 1107, $2, Henry II (1133-89). No. 1108, $2, Henry IV (1366-1413). No. 1109, $2, Henry VI (1421-71). No. 1110, $2, Richard III (1452-1485). No. 1111, $2, Elizabeth I (1533-1603). No. 1112, $2, James I (1566-1625). No. 1113, $2, Edward VII (1841-1910).

Perf. 13x12½
2008, July 15   **Unwmk.**
1106-1113　A217　Set of 8   4.25 4.25
See also Nos. 1122-1129.

2008 Summer Olympics, Beijing A218

Designs: $2.15, Field hockey, bamboo. $3, Pole vault, dragon. $4, Table tennis, lantern. $5, Runner, fish.

2008, Aug. 8   *Perf. 13¼*
1114-1117 A218   Set of 4   3.75 3.75

Police
A219

Inscriptions: $1.90, Restoration of law and order. $2.15, Freedom of movement. $2.40, Children relaxing. $2.65, Community policing, vert.

2008, Aug. 20   *Perf. 13¾*
1118-1121 A219   Set of 4   2.40 2.40

British Monarchs Type of 2008
Designs: No. 1122, $2, William II (c. 1056-1100). No. 1123, $2, Richard I (1157-99). No. 1124, $2, Edward III (1312-77). No. 1125, $2, Edward IV (1442-83). No. 1126, $2, Henry VIII (1491-1547). No. 1127, $2, Charles I (1600-49). No. 1128, $2, George I (1660-1727). No. 1129, $2, George V (1865-1936).

2009, Apr. 21   Litho.   Unwmk.
    Perf. 13x12½
1122-1129 A217   Set of 8   4.00 4.00

Nos. 1122-1129 each were printed in sheets of 8 + central label.

Ships
A220

Alvaro de Mendaña de Neira (1541-95), Discoverer of Solomon Islands — A221

Designs: $3, Discovery. $4, HMS Bounty. $5, Mayflower. $6, USS North Carolina. $10, Boussole and Astrolabe. $20, USS Saratoga.

2009, May 25   Wmk. 406   *Perf. 14*
1130-1135 A220   Set of 6   12.50 12.50
    Souvenir Sheet
1136 A221 $15 multi   4.00 4.00

Naval Aviation, Cent. A222

Designs: $2, Grumman Hellcat. $2.50, Blackburn Skua. $3.50, Fairey Albacore. $10, Gloster Sea Gladiator. $20, Short 184 Seaplane.

2009, June 25
1137-1140 A222   Set of 4   4.75 4.75
    Souvenir Sheet
1141 A222 $20 multi   5.25 5.25

Nos. 1137-1140 each were printed in sheets of 8 + central label.

Wedding of Prince William and Catherine Middleton — A223

No. 1142: a, Couple, hand visible, "L" in "Islands" over pale yellow background. b, Couple, hand not visible, first "S" in "Islands" over pale yellow background. c, As "a," "L" in "Islands" over gray background. d, As "b," first "S" in "Islands" over gray background.
No. 1143: a, Prince William. b, Catherine Middleton.

    Perf. 13 Syncopated
2011, May 15   Litho.
1142 A223 $7.50 Sheet of 4, #a-d   7.75 7.75
    Souvenir Sheet
1143 A223 $15 Sheet of 2, #a-b   7.75 7.75

SEMI-POSTAL STAMPS

> **Catalogue values for unused stamps in this section are for Never Hinged items.**

No. 452 Overprinted in Red: "+ 50c SURCHARGE / CYCLONE RELIEF FUND / 1982"
    Perf. 13½x13
1982, May 3   Litho.   Wmk. 373
B1 CD331 $1 + 50c multi   2.25 2.25

Nos. 546 and 569 Surcharged "Cyclone Relief Fund 1986" and New Value in Scarlet
    Perf. 14½x14
1986, Sept. 23   Litho.   Wmk. 384
B2 CD336 $1 + 50c multi   1.75 1.75
    Souvenir Sheet
    Perf. 13½
B3   Sheet of 2   7.50 7.50
   a.   A95 55c + 25c multi   2.25 2.25
   b.   A95 $1.65 + 75c multi   4.50 4.50

No. 840 Surcharged in Red

    Wmk. 373
2003, Feb. 8   Litho.   *Perf. 14½*
B4 A147 $1.35 +$3 multi   6.00 6.00
World AIDS Day.

No. 866 Surcharged in Red

    Perf. 14½x14
2003, Mar. 17   Wmk. 373
B5 CD355 $2 +$5 multi   6.50 6.50
Surtax for Cyclones Zoe and Beni Relief Fund.

POSTAGE DUE STAMPS

D1

    Perf. 12
1940, Sept. 1   Typo.   Wmk. 4

J1	D1	1p emerald	4.50	8.00
J2	D1	2p dark red	4.75	8.00
J3	D1	3p chocolate	4.75	13.00
J4	D1	4p dark blue	7.25	13.00
J5	D1	5p deep green	8.00	27.50
J6	D1	6p brt red vio	8.00	20.00
J7	D1	1sh dull violet	10.00	32.50
J8	D1	1sh6p turq green	17.50	60.00

Nos. J1-J8 (8)   64.75 182.00
Set, never hinged   120.00

SOMALIA

sō-'mä-lē-ə

(Somali Democratic Republic)

(Italian Somaliland)

(Benadir)

LOCATION — Eastern Africa, bordering on the Indian Ocean and the Gulf of Aden
GOVT. — Probably none
AREA — 246,201 sq. mi.
POP. — 7,140,643 (1999 est.)
CAPITAL — Mogadishu

The former Italian colony which included the territory west of the Juba River became known as Oltre Giuba (Trans-Juba), was absorbed into Italian East Africa in 1936. Somalia stamps continued in use in Italian East Africa for several years. It was under British military administration from 1941-49. Italian trusteeship took effect in 1950, with a UN Advisory Council helping the administrator. On July 1, 1960, the former Italian colony merged with Somaliland Protectorate (British) to form the independent Republic of Somalia.

4 Besas = 1 Anna
16 Annas = 1 Rupee
100 Besas = 1 Rupee (1922)
100 Centesimi = 1 Lira (1905, 1925)
100 Centesimi = 1 Somalo (1950)
100 Centesimi = 1 Somali Shilling (1961)

> **Catalogue values for unused stamps in this country are for Never Hinged items, beginning with Scott 170 in the regular postage section, Scott B52 in the semipostal section, Scott C17 in the airpost section, Scott CB11 in the airpost semi-postal section, Scott CE1 in the airpost special delivery section, Scott E8 in the special delivery section, Scott J55 in the postage due section, and Scott Q56 in the parcel post section.**

> **Used values in italics are for postally used Italian Somalia stamps. CTO's or stamps with fake cancels sell for about the same as unused, hinged stamps.**

Wmk. 140 — Crown

Italian Somaliland

Elephant — A1   Lion — A2

    Wmk. 140
1903, Oct. 12   Typo.   *Perf. 14*

1	A1	1b brown	110.00	24.00
2	A1	2b blue green	1.60	14.50
3	A2	1a claret	1.60	17.50
4	A2	2a orange brown	2.00	32.50
5	A2	2½a blue	1.60	32.50
6	A2	5a orange	2.00	65.00
7	A2	10a lilac	2.00	65.00

Nos. 1-7 (7)   120.80 251.00
For surcharges see Nos. 8-27, 40-50, 70-77.

Surcharged

1905, Dec. 29
8   A2 15c on 5a orange   3,500. 1,300.
9   A2 40c on 10a lilac   1,000. 450.00

Surcharged

1906-07
10   A1 2c on 1b brown   6.50 19.00
11   A1 5c on 2b blue grn   6.50 14.00
  a.   Double surcharge   350.00
  b.   Double surcharge, one invtd.   4,750.
  c.   Pair, one without surcharge   4,750.

Surcharges on No. 11c are virtually on top of each other. Certificates are necessary.

Surcharged

12   A2 10c on 1a claret   6.50 14.00
13   A2 15c on 2a brn org ('06)   6.50 14.00
14   A2 25c on 2½a blue   16.00 14.00
15   A2 50c on 5a yellow   32.50 35.00

Surcharged

16   A2 1 l on 10a lilac   32.50 47.50
Nos. 10-16 (7)   107.00 157.50

Nos. 15 and 16 with
bars over former
Surcharge and

1916, Apr.
18 A2 5c on 50c on 5a
         yel   47.50   52.50
a.   Double surcharge, one
     invtd.   3,750.
19 A2 20c on 1 l on 10a
         dl lil   9.50   35.00

No. 4 Surcharged

20 A2 20c on 2a org brn   24.00   16.00
         Nos. 18-20 (3)   81.00   103.50

Nos. 11-16 Surcharged

a   b

1922, Feb. 1
22 A1(a) 3b on 5c on 2b   13.00   24.00
23 A2(b) 6c on 10c on 1a   24.00   19.00
24 A2(b) 9b on 15c on 2a   24.00   24.00
25 A2(b) 15b on 25c on
            2½a   24.00   18.00
26 A2(b) 30b on 50c on 5a   26.00   52.50
27 A2(b) 60b on 1 l on 10a   26.00   87.50
          Nos. 22-27 (6)   137.00   225.00

Victory Issue

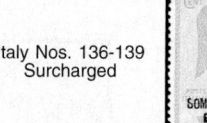

Italy Nos. 136-139
Surcharged

1922, Apr.
28 A64 3b on 5c olive grn   2.00   7.25
29 A64 6b on 10c red   2.00   7.25
30 A64 9b on 15c slate grn   2.00   11.00
31 A64 15b on 25c ultra   2.00   11.00
          Nos. 28-31 (4)   8.00   36.50

Nos. 10-16 Surcharged with Bars and

c   d

1923, July 1
40 A1   1b brown   9.50   37.50
41 A1(c) 2b on 2c on 1b   9.50   37.50
42 A1(c) 3b on 2c on 1b   9.50   18.00
43 A2(d) 5b on 50c on 5a   9.50   19.00
44 A1(c) 6b on 5c on 2b   17.50   19.00
45 A2(d) 18b on 10c on 1a   17.50   19.00
46 A2(d) 20b on 15c on 2a   21.00   19.00
47 A2(d) 25b on 15c on 2a   21.00   19.00
48 A2(d) 30b on 25c on
            2½a   24.00   24.00
49 A2(d) 60b on 1 l on 10a 24.00   52.50
50 A2(d) 1r on 1 l on 10a   65.00   65.00
          Nos. 40-50 (11)   228.00   329.50

No. 40 is No. 10 with bars over the 1907
surcharge.

Propagation of the Faith Issue
Italy Nos. 143-146 Surcharged

1923, Oct. 24   **Wmk. 140**
51 A68 6b on 20c ol grn &
          brn org   11.00   47.50
52 A68 13b on 30c cl & brn
          org   11.00   47.50
53 A68 20b on 50c vio &
          brn org   5.50   55.00
54 A68 30b on 1 l bl & brn
          org   5.50   75.00
          Nos. 51-54 (4)   33.00   225.00

Fascisti Issue

Italy Nos. 159-164
Surcharged in Red or
Black

1923, Oct. 29   Unwmk.   Perf. 14
55 A69 3b on 10c dk grn
          (R)   13.00   16.00
56 A69 13b on 30c dk vio
          (R)   13.00   16.00
57 A69 20b on 50c brn car 13.00   20.00
                          Wmk. 140
58 A70 30b on 1 l blue   13.00   45.00
59 A70 1r on 2 l brown   13.00   52.50
60 A71 3r on 5 l blk & bl
          (R)   13.00   75.00
          Nos. 55-60 (6)   78.00   224.50

Manzoni Issue
Italy Nos. 165-170 Surcharged in Red

1924, Apr. 1
61 A72 6b on 10c brn red &
          blk   12.00   65.00
62 A72 9b on 15c bl grn &
          blk   12.00   65.00
63 A72 13b on 30c blk & sl 12.00   65.00
64 A72 20b on 50c org brn &
          blk   12.00   65.00

Surcharged

65 A72 30b on 1 l bl &
          blk   72.50   350.00
66 A72 3r on 5 l vio &
          blk   475.00 2,750.
          Nos. 61-66 (6)   595.50 3,360.

Victor Emmanuel Issue

Italy Nos. 175-177
Overprinted

1925-26   Unwmk.   Perf. 13½, 11
67 A78 60c brown car   1.60   11.00
a.   Perf. 11   145.00   275.00
68 A78 1 l dk bl, perf.
          11   2.40   17.50
a.   Perf. 13½   9.50   52.50

69 A78 1.25 l dk blue
          ('26)   1.60   27.50
a.   Perf. 11   950.00 1,450.
          Nos. 67-69 (3)   5.60   56.00

Stamps of 1907-16 with Bars over Original Values

1926, Mar. 1   Wmk. 140   Perf. 14
70 A1   2c on 1b brown   27.50   55.00
71 A1   5c on 2b blue grn   19.00   27.50
72 A2   10c on 1a rose red 13.00   11.00
73 A2   15c on 2a org brn   13.00   14.50
74 A2   20c on 2a org brn   14.50   14.50
75 A2   25c on 2½a blue   14.50   19.00
76 A2   50c on 5a yellow   19.00   35.00
77 A2   1 l on 10a dull lil 27.50   47.50
          Nos. 70-77 (8)   148.00   224.00

Saint Francis of Assisi Issue

Italy Nos.
178-180
Overprinted

1926, Apr. 12   Perf. 14
78 A79 20c gray green   2.40   13.00
79 A80 40c dark violet   2.40   13.00
80 A81 60c red brown   2.40   22.50

Italy Nos. 182 and Type of 1926 Overprinted in Red

                          Unwmk.   Perf. 11
81 A82 1.25 l dark blue   2.40   32.50
                          Perf. 14
82 A83 5 l + 2.50 l ol grn 6.50   65.00
          Nos. 78-82 (5)   16.10   146.00

Italian Stamps of 1901-26 Overprinted

1926-30   Wmk. 140
83 A43 2c orange
          brown   4.00   6.50
84 A48 5c green   4.00   6.50
85 A48 10c claret   3.25   .40
86 A49 20c violet brown   3.25   2.40
87 A46 25c grn & pale
          grn   3.25   1.60
88 A49 30c gray ('30)   20.00   47.50
89 A49 60c brown or-
          ange   0.00   12.00
a.   Double overprint   4,000.
90 A46 75c dk red &
          rose   130.00   47.50
91 A46 1 l brown & grn   8.00   .80
92 A46 1.25 l blue & ultra 16.00   2.40
93 A46 2 l dk grn & org   40.00   16.00
94 A46 2.50 l dk grn & org 40.00   24.00
95 A46 5 l blue & rose   87.50   55.00
96 A51 10 l gray grn &
          red   87.50   95.00
          Nos. 83-96 (14)   454.75   317.60

Volta Issue

Type of Italy, 1927,
Overprinted

1927, Oct. 10
97 A84 20c purple   7.00   40.00
98 A84 50c deep orange   12.00   30.00
a.   Double overprint   175.00
99 A84 1.25 l brt blue   17.00   77.50
          Nos. 97-99 (3)   36.00   147.50

Italian Stamps of 1927-28 Overprinted in Black or Red

1928-30
100 A86 7½c lt brown   27.50   72.50
a.   Double overprint   525.00
101 A85 50c brn & sl (R)   27.50   10.00
102 A86 50c brt violet
          ('30)   47.50   80.00
                          Perf. 11
                          Unwmk.
103 A85 1.75 l deep brown 95.00   20.00
          Nos. 100-103 (4) 197.50   182.50

Monte Cassino Issue

Monte
Cassino
Issue of
Italy
Overprinted
in Red or
Blue

1929, Oct. 14   Wmk. 140   Perf. 14
104 A96 20c dk green (R)   5.50   20.00
105 A96 25c red org (Bl)   5.50   20.00
106 A98 50c + 10c crim (Bl) 5.50   22.50
107 A98 75c + 15c ol brn
          (R)   5.50   22.50
108 A96 1.25 l + 25c dk vio
          (R)   13.00   40.00
109 A98 5 l + 1 l saph (R) 13.00   45.00

Overprinted in Red

                          Unwmk.
110 A100 10 l + 2 l gray brn 13.00   65.00
          Nos. 104-110 (7)   61.00   235.00

Royal Wedding Issue

Type of
Italian
Royal
Wedding
Stamps of
1930
Overprinted

1930, Mar. 17   Wmk. 140
111 A101 20c yellow green   1.60   4.75
112 A101 50c + 10c dp org   1.20   8.00
113 A101 1.25 l + 25c rose
          red   1.20   16.00
          Nos. 111-113 (3)   4.00   28.75

Ferrucci Issue

Types of
Italian
Stamps of
1930
Overprinted
in Red or
Blue

1930, July 26
114 A102 20c violet (R)   5.50   5.50
115 A103 25c dark green
          (R)   5.50   5.50
116 A103 50c black (R)   5.50   11.00
117 A103 1.25 l deep blue
          (R)   5.50   20.00
118 A104 5 l + 2 l dp car
          (bl)   11.00   35.00
          Nos. 114-118 (5)   33.00   77.00

Virgil Issue

Types of
Italian
Stamps of
1930
Overprinted
in Red or
Blue

1930, Dec. 4   Photo.   Wmk. 140

119	A106	15c violet blue	1.20	9.50
120	A106	20c orange brown	1.20	4.00
121	A106	25c dark green	1.20	4.00
122	A106	30c lt brown	1.20	4.00
123	A106	50c dull violet	1.20	4.00
124	A106	75c rose red	1.20	8.00
125	A106	1.25 l gray blue	1.20	9.50

Engr. Unwmk.

126	A106	5 l + 1.50 l dk vio	3.50	45.00
127	A106	10 l + 2.50 l ol brn	3.50	67.50
		Nos. 119-127 (9)	15.40	155.50

Saint Anthony of Padua Issue

Types of Italian Stamps of 1931 Overprinted in Blue or Red

1931, May 7   Photo.   Wmk. 140

129	A116	20c brown (Bl)	1.60	20.00
130	A116	25c green (R)	1.60	6.50
131	A118	30c gray brn (Bl)	1.60	6.50
132	A118	50c dull vio (R)	1.60	6.50
133	A120	1.25 l slate bl (R)	1.60	35.00

Overprinted in Red or Black

Engr. Unwmk.

134	A121	75c black (R)	1.60	20.00
135	A122	5 l + 2.50 l dk brn (Bk)	8.00	72.50
		Nos. 129-135 (7)	17.60	167.00

Italy Nos. 218, 221 Overprinted in Red

1931   Wmk. 140

136	A94	25c dk green (R)	14.50	24.00
137	A95	50c purple (R)	14.50	4.50

Lighthouse at Cape Guardafui — A3

Tower at Mnara Ciromo — A4   Governor's Palace at Mogadishu — A5

Termite Nest — A6   Ostrich — A7

Hippopotamus — A8   Greater Kudu — A9

Lion — A10

1932   Wmk. 140   Photo.   Perf. 12

138	A3	5c deep brown	12.00	14.50
139	A3	7½c violet	17.50	32.50
140	A3	10c gray black	24.00	.40
141	A3	15c olive green	9.50	1.20
142	A4	20c carmine	400.00	.40
143	A4	25c deep green	9.50	.40
144	A4	30c dark brown	95.00	1.20
145	A5	35c dark blue	11.00	22.50
146	A5	50c violet	475.00	.40
147	A5	75c carmine	11.00	.80
148	A6	1.25 l dark blue	35.00	.80
149	A6	1.75 l red orange	22.50	.80
150	A6	2 l carmine	11.00	.40
151	A7	2.55 l indigo	55.00	120.00
152	A7	5 l carmine	32.50	14.50
153	A8	10 l violet	47.50	32.50
154	A9	20 l dark green	110.00	145.00
155	A10	25 l dark blue	110.00	275.00
		Nos. 138-155 (18)	1,488.	663.30
		Set, never hinged	3,600.	

1934-37   Perf. 14

138a	A3	5c deep brown	3.25	.80
139a	A3	7½c violet	3.25	40.00
140a	A3	10c gray black	3.25	.40
141a	A3	15c olive green	3.25	2.40
142a	A4	20c carmine	3.25	.25
143a	A4	25c deep green	3.25	.40
144a	A4	30c dark brown	6.50	.40
145a	A5	35c dark blue	12.00	47.50
146a	A5	50c violet	40.00	.40
147a	A5	75c carmine	65.00	.40
148a	A6	1.25 l dark blue	110.00	1.20
149a	A6	1.75 l red orange	275.00	32.50
150a	A6	2 l carmine	72.50	.80
151a	A7	2.55 l indigo	325.00	800.00
152a	A7	5 l carmine	32.50	3.25
153a	A8	10 l violet	240.00	45.00
154a	A9	20 l dark green	15,000.	2,250.
155a	A10	25 l dark blue	950.00	675.00
		Nos. 138a-153a,155a (17)	2,148.	1,650.
		Set, never hinged	5,000.	

Eleven denominations in the foregoing series exist perf. 12x14, 14x12 or compound 12 and 14. See the *Scott Classic Specialized Catalogue of Stamps & Covers* for detailed listings.

Types of 1932 Issue Overprinted in Black or Red

1934, May   Perf. 14

156	A3	10c brown (Bk)	14.50	35.00
157	A4	25c green	14.50	35.00
158	A5	50c dull vio (Bk)	14.50	35.00
159	A6	1.25 l blue	14.50	35.00
160	A7	5 l brown black	14.50	35.00
161	A8	10 l car rose (Bk)	14.50	67.50
162	A9	20 l dull blue	14.50	67.50
163	A10	25 l dark green	14.50	67.50
		Nos. 156-163 (8)	116.00	377.50
		Set, never hinged	240.00	

Duke of the Abruzzi (Luigi Amadeo, 1873-1933).

Mother and Child — A11

1934, Oct.

164	A11	5c ol grn & brn	4.00	20.00
165	A11	10c yel brn & blk	4.00	20.00
166	A11	20c scarlet & blk	4.00	16.00
167	A11	50c dk violet & brn	4.00	16.00
168	A11	60c org brn & blk	4.00	24.00
169	A11	1.25 l dk blue & grn	4.00	40.00
		Nos. 164-169,C1-C6 (12)	48.00	272.00
		Nos. 164-169, never hinged	60.00	

Second Colonial Arts Exhibition, Naples.

> **Catalogue values for unused stamps in this section, from this point to the end of the section, are for Never Hinged items.**

Somalia

Tower at Mnara Ciromo — A12   Governor's Palace, Mogadishu — A13

Design: 5c, 20c, 60c, Ostrich.

Wmk. 277
1950, Mar. 24   Photo.   Perf. 14

170	A12	1c gray black	4.75	9.50
171	A12	5c carmine rose	.25	.25
172	A13	6c violet	2.40	4.00
173	A12	8c Prus green	2.40	4.00
174	A13	10c dark green	.25	.25
175	A12	20c blue green	.25	.25
176	A12	35c red	8.00	9.50
177	A13	55c brt blue	4.00	.80
178	A12	60c purple	4.00	.80
179	A12	65c brown	9.50	4.75
180	A13	1s deep orange	16.00	4.75
		Nos. 170-180,E8-E9 (13)	83.80	66.85

Council in Session A14

1951, Oct. 4

181	A14	20c dk green & brn	3.25	2.00
182	A14	55c brown & violet	8.75	10.00
		Nos. 181-182,C27A-C27B (4)	24.00	22.00

Meeting of First Territorial Council.

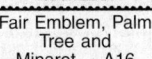

Fair Emblem, Palm Tree and Minaret — A16   Mother and Child — A17

1952, Sept. 14   Wmk. 277   Perf. 14

185	A16	25c red & dk brown	3.50	3.75
186	A16	55c blue & dk brown	3.50	5.00
		Nos. 185-186,C28 (3)	12.00	14.50

1st Somali Fair, Mogadishu, Sept. 14-28.

1953, May 27
Center in Dark Brown

187	A17	5c rose violet	1.00	2.50
188	A17	25c rose	1.00	2.50
189	A17	50c blue	1.25	2.50
		Nos. 187-189,C29 (4)	6.50	12.50

Anti-tuberculosis campaign.

Laborer at Fair Entrance A18

1953, Sept. 28   Unwmk.   Perf. 11½

190	A18	25c dk green & gray	.65	1.00
191	A18	60c blue & gray	1.60	2.25
		Nos. 190-191,C30-C31 (4)	4.50	6.40

2nd Somali Fair, Mogadishu, 9/28-10/12.

Map and Stamps of 1903 A19

Perf. 13x13½
1953, Dec. 16   Engr.   Wmk. 277
"Stamps" in Brown and Rose Carmine

192	A19	25c deep magenta	1.25	2.50
193	A19	35c dark green	1.25	2.50
194	A19	60c orange	1.25	5.00
		Nos. 192-194,C32-C33 (5)	6.25	20.00

50th anniv. of the 1st Somali postage stamps.

Somalia Brushwood A20

Perf. 12½x13½
1954, June 1   Photo.   Unwmk.

195	A20	25c dp blue & dk gray	.90	1.75
196	A20	60c orange brn & brown	.90	1.75
		Nos. 195-196,C37-C38 (4)	4.50	7.15

Convention of Nov. 11, 1953, with the Sovereign Military Order of Malta, providing for the care of lepers.

Somali Flag A21   Adenium Somalense A22

Perf. 13½x13
1954, Oct. 12   Litho.   Wmk. 277

197	A21	25c blk, grn, bl, red & yel	.50	.55

Adoption of a Somali flag. See No. C39.

1955, Feb.   Photo.   Perf. 13

Flowers: 5c, Haemanthus multiflorus martyn. 10c, Grinum scabrum. 25c, Poinciana elata. 60c, Calatropis procera. 1s, Pancratium. 1.20s, Sesamothamnus bussernus.

198	A22	1c bl, dp rose & dk ol brn	.30	.30
199	A22	5c bl, rose lil & grn	.30	.30
200	A22	10c lilac & green	1.10	.30
201	A22	25c vio brn, yel & grn	2.50	1.40
202	A22	60c blk, car & grn	.30	.30
203	A22	1s red brn & grn	.30	1.40
204	A22	1.20s dk brn, yel & grn	.65	2.75
		Nos. 198-204,E10-E11 (9)	7.95	11.25

See #216-220. For overprint see #242.

Weaver at Loom A23

Design: 30c, Cattle fording stream.

Perf. 13½x14

1955, Sept. 24   Wmk. 303
205 A23 25c dark brown   1.25 1.60
206 A23 30c dark green   1.25 1.60
Nos. 205-206,C46-C47 (4)   4.50 6.40

3rd Somali Fair, Mogadishu, Sept. 1955.

Casting   Arms of
Ballots — A24   Somalia — A25

1956, Apr. 30   Perf. 14
207 A24 5c brown & gray grn   .40   .40
208 A24 10c brown & ol bis   .40   .40
209 A24 25c brown & brn red   .40   .85
Nos. 207-209,C48-C49 (5)   2.90 4.15

Opening of the territory's first democratically
elected Legislative Assembly.

1957, May 6   Wmk. 303   Perf. 13½
**Coat of Arms in Dull Yellow, Blue
and Black**
210 A25 5c lt red brown   .45 1.40
211 A25 25c carmine   .45 1.40
212 A25 60c bluish violet   .45 1.90
Nos. 210-212,C50-C51 (5)   3.25 7.50

Issued in honor of the new coat of arms.

Dam at
Falcheiro
A26

10c, Juba River Bridge. 25c, Silos at
Margherita.

1957, Sept. 28   Photo.   Perf. 14
213 A26 5c brown & purple   .25   .25
214 A26 10c bister & bl grn   .25   .25
215 A26 25c carmine & blue   .25 1.25
Nos. 213-215,C52-C53 (5)   3.25 4.25

Fourth Somali Fair and Film Festival.

Flower Type of 1955

Flowers: 1c, Adenium Somalense. 10c,
Grinum scabrum. 15c, Adansonia digitata.
25c, Poinciana elata. 50c, Gloriosa
virescens.

1956-59 Wmk. 303 Photo. Perf. 13
216 A22 1c bl, dp rose & dk ol
          brn   .50   .50
217 A22 10c lil, grn & yel ('59)   .25   .25
218 A22 15c red, grn & yel ('58)   .80   .60
219 A22 15c dull lil, grn & yel
          ('59)   .25   .80
220 A22 50c bl, grn, red & yel
          ('58)   .80 1.25
Nos. 216-220 (5)   2.60 3.40

Fencer — A27

Soccer
Player
A28

Designs: 5c, Discus thrower. 6c, Motorcyclist. 8c, Fencer. 10c, Archer. 25c, Boxers.

1958, Apr. 28   Wmk. 303   Perf. 14
221 A27 2c violet   .25   .25
222 A28 4c green   .25   .25
223 A27 5c vermilion   .25   .25
224 A28 6c gray   .25   .25
225 A27 8c violet blue   .25   .25
226 A28 10c orange   .25   .25
227 A28 25c dark green   .25   .25
Nos. 221-227,C54-C56 (10)   2.50 3.00

Book and
Assembly
Palace — A29

1959, June 19
228 A29 5c green & ultra   .25   .25
229 A29 25c ocher & ultra   .25   .25
Nos. 228-229,C59-C60 (4)   2.70 3.00

Opening of Somalia's Constituent Assembly.
See No. C60a.

White
Stork — A30

Birds: 10c, Saddle-billed stork. 15c, Sacred
ibis. 25c, Pink-backed pelican.

1959, Sept. 4   Photo.   Perf. 14
230 A30 5c yellow, blk & red   .35   .25
231 A30 10c brown, red & yel   .35   .25
232 A30 15c orange & black   .35   .25
233 A30 25c dk car, blk & org   .35   .25
Nos. 230-233,C61-C62 (6)   3.60 2.10

Incense
Bush — A31

Design: 60c, Girl burning incense.

1959, Sept. 28   Wmk. 303
234 A31 20c orange & black   .25   .30
235 A31 60c blk, org & dk red   .25   .30
Nos. 234-235,C63-C64 (4)   2.60 2.75

5th Somali Fair, Mogadishu.

Arms of
University
Institute — A32

Designs: 50c, Map of Africa and arms,
horiz. 80c, Arms of University Institute.

1960, Jan. 14   Photo.   Perf. 14
236 A32 5c brown & salmon   .25   .25
237 A32 50c lt vio bl, brn & blk   .25   .25
238 A32 80c brt red & blk   .35   .35
Nos. 236-238,C65-C66 (5)   1.75 1.85

Opening of the University Institute of
Somalia.

Globe and
Uprooted
Oak
Emblem
A33

Palm — A34

Design: 60c, Like 10c but with inscription
and emblem rearranged.

1960, Apr. 7   Perf. 14
239 A33 10c yel brn, grn & blk   .25   .25
240 A33 60c dp bister & blk   .25   .25
241 A34 80c pink, grn & blk   .25   .25
Nos. 239-241,C67 (4)   2.25 2.35

World Refugee Year, 7/1/59-6/30/60.

Republic

No. 217 Overprinted

Wmk. 303
1960, June 26   Photo.   Perf. 13
242 A22 10c lilac, grn & yel   19.00 24.00
Nos. 242,C68-C69 (3)   88.00 96.50

Independence of British Somaliland, which
became part of the Republic of Somalia.

Gazelle and Map
of Africa — A36

25c, NYC skyline, UN Building and UN flag.

1960, July 1   Perf. 14
243 A36 10c lilac & brown   .40   .40
244 A36 25c blue   .45   .45
Nos. 243-244,C70-C71 (4)   4.90 4.90

Somalia independence.

Boy
Drawing
Giraffe
A37

1960, Nov. 24
245 A37 10c shown   .30   .30
246 A37 15c Zebra   .40   .40
247 A37 25c Black rhinoceros   .45   .45
Nos. 245-247,C72 (4)   5.65 5.65

Olympic Torch,   Girl Harvesting
Somalia   Papaya — A39
Flag — A38

10c, Runners, flag and Olympic rings.

1960   Wmk. 303   Perf. 14
248 A38 5c green & blue   .25   .25
249 A38 10c yellow & blue   .25   .25
Nos. 248-249,C73-C74 (4)   3.10 3.10

17th Olympic Games, Rome, 8/25-9/11.

1961, July 5   Photo.

Girl harvesting: 10c, Durrah (sorghum). 20c,
Cotton. 25c, Sesame. 40c, Sugar cane. 50c,
Bananas. 75c, Peanuts, horiz. 80c, Grapefruit,
horiz.

250 A39 5c multicolored   .25   .25
251 A39 10c multicolored   .25   .25
252 A39 20c multicolored   .25   .25
253 A39 25c multicolored   .25   .25
254 A39 40c multicolored   .30   .25
255 A39 50c multicolored   .50   .40
256 A39 75c multicolored   .80   .80
257 A39 80c multicolored   2.75 2.75
Nos. 250-257 (8)   5.35 5.20

Shield, Bow and
Quiver — A40

Design: 45c, Pottery and incense jug.

1961, Sept. 28
258 A40 25c blk, car & ocher   .25   .25
259 A40 45c blk, bl grn & ocher   .25   .25
Nos. 258-259,C82-C83 (4)   3.15 3.15

6th Somali Fair, Mogadishu.

Pomacanthus
Semicirculatus
A41

Fish: 15c, Girl embroidering fish on cloth.
40c, Novaculichthys taeniourus.

1962, Apr. 26   Photo.
260 A41 15c brown, blk & pink   .50   .50
261 A41 25c orange, blk & ultra   .50   .50
262 A41 40c green, blk & rose   1.00 1.00
Nos. 260-262,C84 (4)   5.50 5.50

Mosquito
Trapped by
Sprays
A42

Design: 25c, Man with spray gun and malaria eradication emblem, vert.

1962, Oct. 25   Wmk. 303   Perf. 14
263 A42 10c orange red & grn   .45   .45
264 A42 25c rose lilac, brn & blk .45   .45
Nos. 263-264,C85-C86 (4)   4.50 4.50

WHO drive to eradicate malaria.

Police
Auxiliary
Woman
A43

10c, Army auxiliary woman. 25c, Radio
police car. 75c, First aid army auxiliary, vert.

1963, May 15   Wmk. 303   Perf. 14
265 A43   5c multicolored   .25   .25
266 A43   10c black & orange   .25   .25
267 A43   25c multicolored   .25   .25
268 A43   75c multicolored   .55   .55
   Nos. 265-268,C87-C88 (6)   4.90 4.90
   Women's auxiliary forces.

Carved
Fork and
Spoon and
Wheat
Emblem
A44

1963, June 25   Photo.
269 A44 75c green & red brown   .65   .65
   FAO "Freedom from Hunger" campaign. See
No. C89.

Pres. Aden
Abdulla
Osman — A45

1963, Sept. 15   Wmk. 303   Perf. 14
270 A45 25c bl, dk brn, org & lt
   bl   .45   .45
   Nos. 270,C90-C91 (3)   3.05 3.05
   3rd anniv. of independence.

Dunes
Theater
A46

55c, African Merchants' and Artisans'
Exhibit.

1963, Sept. 28   Photo.
271 A46 25c blue green   .45   .45
272 A46 55c carmine rose   1.00 1.00
   Nos. 271-272,C92 (3)   4.20 4.20
   7th Somali Fair, Mogadishu.

Somali
Credit
Bank
Building
A47

1964, May 16   Wmk. 303   Perf. 14
273 A47 60c indigo, red lil & yel   .85   .85
   Nos. 273,C93-C94 (3)   5.35 5.35
   10th anniv. of the Somali Credit Bank.

Running — A48   ITU Emblem and
                    Map of
                    Africa — A50

DC-3
A49

1964, Oct. 10   Wmk. 303   Perf. 14
274 A48 10c shown   .25   .25
275 A48 25c High jump   .25   .25
   Nos. 274-275,C95-C96 (4)   4.10 4.10
   18th Olympic Games, Tokyo, Oct. 10-25.
See also Nos. C95-C96.

1964, Nov. 8   Photo.   Perf. 14
Design: 20c, Passengers leaving DC-3.
276 A49   5c dk blue & lil rose   .45   .45
277 A49 20c blue & orange   .95   .95
   Nos. 276-277,C97-C98 (4)   9.55 9.55
   Establishment of Somali Air Lines.

1965, May 17   Wmk. 303   Perf. 14
278 A50 25c dp blue & dp org   .55   .30
   Nos. 278,C99-C100 (3)   3.50 2.35
   ITU centenary.

Tanning
Industry
A51

25c, Meat industry; cannery, cattle. 35c,
Fishing industry; cannery, fishing boats.

1965, Sept. 28   Photo.   Perf. 14
279 A51 10c sepia & buff   .25   .25
280 A51 25c sepia & pink   .25   .25
281 A51 35c sepia & lt blue   .35   .25
   Nos. 279-281,C101-C102 (5)   4.55 3.40
   8th Somali Fair, Mogadishu.

Hottentot
Fig and
Gazelle
A52

Designs: 60c, African tulip and giraffes. 1sh,
Ninfea and flamingos. 1.30sh, Pervincia and
ostriches. 1.80sh, Bignonia and zebras.

1965, Nov. 1   Wmk. 303   Perf. 14
Flowers in Natural Colors
282 A52 20c blk & brt bl   .25   .25
283 A52 60c blk & dk gray   .25   .25
284 A52 1sh blk, sl grn & ol
   grn   .70   .55
285 A52 1.30sh blk & dp grn   1.60 1.40
286 A52 1.80sh blk & brt bl   4.50 4.00
   Nos. 282-286 (5)   7.30 6.45

Narina's
Trogon
A53

Birds: 35c, Bateleur eagle, vert. 50c, Vulture. 1.30sh, European roller. 2sh, Vulturine
guinea fowl, vert.

1966, June 1   Photo.   Wmk. 303
287 A53 25c multicolored   .30   .30
288 A53 35c brt blue &
   multi   .30   .30
289 A53 50c multicolored   .50   .50
290 A53 1.30sh multicolored   2.40 2.40
291 A53 2sh multicolored   4.00 4.00
   Nos. 287-291 (5)   7.50 7.50

Globe and UN
Emblem
A54

UN emblem and: 1sh, Map of Africa. 1.50sh,
Map of Somalia.

1966, Oct. 24   Litho.   Perf. 13x12½
292 A54 35c bl, pur & brt bl   .60   .25
293 A54 1sh brn, yel & brick
   red   .60   .25
294 A54 1.50sh grn, blk, bl & yel   1.20   .60
   Nos. 292-294 (3)   2.40 1.05
   21st anniversary of United Nations.

Woman
Sitting on
Crocodile
A55

Paintings: 1sh, Woman and warrior. 1.50sh,
Boy leading camel. 2sh, Women pounding
grain.

Wmk. 303
1966, Dec. 1   Photo.   Perf. 14
295 A55   25c multicolored   .25   .25
296 A55   1sh multicolored   .35   .25
297 A55 1.50sh multicolored   .70   .25
298 A55   2sh multicolored   2.00   .95
   Nos. 295-298 (4)   3.30 1.70
   Somali art, exhibited in the Garesa
Museum, Mogadishu.

UNESCO
Emblem
A56

1966, Dec. 20   Wmk. 303   Perf. 14
299 A56   35c blk, dk red &
   gray   .25   .25
300 A56   1sh blk, emer & yel   .25   .25
301 A56 1.80sh blk, ultra & red   1.75 1.75
   Nos. 299-301 (3)   2.25 2.25
   UNESCO, 20th anniv.

Haggard's
Oribi — A57

Gazelles: 60c, Long-snouted dik-dik. 1sh,
Gerenuk. 1.80sh, Soemmering's gazelle.

1967, Feb. 20   Photo.   Perf. 14
302 A57   35c blk, ultra & bis   .25   .25
303 A57   60c blk, org & brn   .25   .25
304 A57   1sh blk, red & brn   .40   .40
305 A57 1.80sh blk, yel grn & brn   2.75 2.75
   Nos. 302-305 (4)   3.65 3.65

Unwmk.
1967, July 15   Litho.   Perf. 13
Designs: Various Folk Dances.
306 A58   25c multicolored   .25   .25
307 A58   50c multicolored   .25   .25
308 A58 1.30sh multicolored   .25   .25
309 A58   2sh multicolored   2.10 2.10
   Nos. 306-309 (4)   2.85 2.85

Boy Scout
Giving Scout
Sign — A59

Designs: 50c, Boy Scouts with flags. 1sh,
Boy Scout cooking and tent. 1.80sh, Jamboree emblem.

1967, Aug. 15
310 A59   35c multicolored   .25   .25
311 A59   50c multicolored   .25   .25
312 A59   1sh multicolored   .55   .55
313 A59 1.80sh multicolored   2.10 2.10
   Nos. 310-313 (4)   3.15 3.15
   12th Boy Scout World Jamboree, Farragut
State Park, Idaho, Aug. 1-9.

Pres. Abdirascid Ali Scermarche and
King Faisal — A60

Designs: 1sh, Clasped hands, flags of
Somalia and Saudi Arabia.

Wmk. 303
1967, Sept. 21   Photo.   Perf. 14
314 A60 50c black & lt blue   .25   .25
315 A60 1sh multicolored   .55   .55
   Nos. 314-315,C103 (3)   2.90 2.90
   Visit of King Faisal of Saudi Arabia.

Gaterin
Gaterinus
A61

Tropical Fish: 50c, Chaetodon semilar-
vatus. 1sh, Priacanthus hamrur. 1.80sh,
Epinephelus summana.

1967, Nov. 15   Litho.   Perf. 14
316 A61   35c dk bl, yel & blk   .50   .50
317 A61   50c brt bl, ocher &
   blk   .50   .50
318 A61   1sh emer, org, brn &
   blk   1.75 1.75
319 A61 1.80sh pur, yel & blk   3.25 3.25
   Nos. 316-319 (4)   6.00 6.00

Physician Treating   Waterbuck
Infant   A64
A62

Woman and
Basket with
Lemons
A63

WHO, 20th anniv.: 1sh, Physician examining boy, and nurse. 1.80sh, Physician and nurse treating patient.

Wmk. 303
1968, Mar. 20   Photo.   Perf. 14
320 A62   35c blk, scar, bl & brn   .30   .30
321 A62   1sh blk, grn & brn   .30   .30
322 A62   1.80sh blk, org & brn   1.75   1.75
   Nos. 320-322 (3)   2.35   2.35

1968   Litho.   Perf. 11½
Designs: 10c, Oranges. 25c, Coconuts. 35c, Papayas. 40c, Limes. 50c, Grapefruit. 1sh, Bananas. 1.30sh, Cotton bolls. 1.80sh, Speke's gazelle. 2sh, Lesser kudu. 5sh, Hunter's hartebeest. 10sh, Clark's gazelle (dibatag).
323 A63   5c lt blue & multi   .25   .25
324 A63   10c yellow & multi   .25   .25
325 A63   25c lt lilac & multi   .25   .25
326 A63   35c salmon & multi   .25   .25
327 A63   40c buff & multi   .25   .25
328 A63   50c multicolored   .25   .25
329 A63   1sh lt blue & multi   .85   .85
330 A63   1.30sh gray & multi   2.50   2.50
331 A64   1.50sh lt blue & multi   .45   .45
332 A64   1.80sh multicolored   .45   .45
333 A64   2sh pink & multi   1.40   1.40
334 A64   5sh multicolored   2.75   2.75
335 A64   10sh multicolored   10.00   10.00
   Nos. 323-335 (13)   19.90   19.90

Issued: #323-330, 4/25; #331-335, 5/10.

Javelin — A65   Statuette — A66

Wmk. 303
1968, Oct. 12   Photo.   Perf. 14
336 A65   35c shown   .25   .25
337 A65   50c Running   .25   .25
338 A65   80c High jump   .25   .25
339 A65   1.50sh Basketball   1.90   1.20
   a.   Souvenir sheet of 4, #336-339   6.75   6.75
   Nos. 336-339 (4)   2.65   1.95

19th Olympic Games, Mexico City, Oct. 12-27. No. 339a sold for 3.65sh.

Perf. 11½x12
1968, Dec. 1   Litho.   Unwmk.
Statuettes: 25c, Woman grinding grain. 35c, Woman potter. 2.80sh, Woman mat maker.
340 A66   25c rose lil, blk & brn   .25   .25
341 A66   35c brick red, blk & brn   .25   .25
342 A66   2.80sh green, blk & brn   1.90   1.20
   Nos. 340-342 (3)   2.40   1.70

Cornflower and Rhinoceros A67

80c, Sunflower & elephant. 1sh, Oleander & antelopes. 1.80sh, Chrysanthemums & storks.

Perf. 13x12½
1969, Mar. 25   Litho.   Unwmk.
343 A67   40c red & multi   .25   .25
344 A67   80c violet & multi   .25   .25
345 A67   1sh blue & multi   .55   .55
346 A67   1.80sh yellow & multi   2.90   2.90
   Nos. 343-346 (4)   3.95   3.95

ILO Emblem and Blacksmiths — A68

Designs: 1sh, Oxdrawn plow. 1.80sh, Drawing water from well.

Wmk. 303
1969, May 10   Photo.   Perf. 14
347 A68   25c dk red, dp bis & blk   .25   .25
348 A68   1sh car rose, brn & blk   .25   .25
349 A68   1.80sh multicolored   1.75   1.75
   Nos. 347-349 (3)   2.25   2.25

ILO, 50th anniversary.

Mahatma Gandhi — A69

Designs: 1.50sh, Gandhi, globe and hands releasing dove, horiz. 1.80sh, Gandhi seated.

Unwmk.
1969, Oct. 2   Photo.   Perf. 13
   Size: 25x35½mm
350 A69   35c brown violet   .40   .40
   Perf. 14½x14
   Size: 37½x20mm
351 A69   1.50sh bister brn   .60   .60
   Perf. 13
   Size: 25x35½mm
352 A69   1.80sh olive gray   4.00   4.00
   Nos. 350-352 (3)   5.00   5.00

Mohandas K. Gandhi (1869-1948), leader in India's fight for independence.

1970
US Space Explorations. Set of seven. 60, 80c, 1, 1.50, 1.80, 2, 2.80sh. Souv. sheet, 14sh, issued Feb. 14. Nos. 7001-7008. Values: set, $6; souvenir sheet, $32.50.

Nivprale Vevanes A70

Butterflies: 50c, Leschenault. 1.50sh, Papilio (ornytoptera) aeacus. 2sh, Urania riphaeus.

Perf. 12½x13
1970, Mar. 25   Litho.   Unwmk.
353 A70   25c multicolored   .30   .30
354 A70   50c multicolored   .30   .30
355 A70   1.50sh orange & multi   .80   .80
356 A70   2sh yellow & multi   3.00   3.00
   Nos. 353-356 (4)   4.40   4.40

Somali Democratic Republic

Lenin Addressing Crowd — A71

Designs: 25c, Lenin walking with children. 1.80sh, Lenin in his study, horiz.

Perf. 12x12½, 12½x12
1970, Apr. 22   Litho.   Unwmk.
357 A71   25c multicolored   .25   .25
358 A71   1sh multicolored   .45   .45
359 A71   1.80sh multicolored   2.10   2.10
   Nos. 357-359 (3)   2.80   2.80

Lenin (1870-1924), Russian communist leader.

Bird Feeding Young A72

35c, Monument & Battle of Dagahtur. 1sh, Arms of Somalia, UN emblem, vert. 2.80sh, Boy milking camel, & star, vert.

Perf. 14x13½, 13½x14
1970, July 28   Photo.   Wmk. 303
360 A72   25c blue & multi   .25   .25
361 A72   35c slate & multi   .25   .25
362 A72   1sh violet & multi   .55   .55
363 A72   2.80sh blue & multi   2.00   2.00
   Nos. 360-363 (4)   3.05   3.05

10th anniversary of independence.

"Agriculture" — A73

40c, Soldier and flag. 1sh, Hand on open book. 1.80sh, Grain, scales of justice and dove.

Perf. 14x13½
1970, Oct. 21   Photo.   Wmk. 303
364 A73   35c green & multi   .25   .25
365 A73   40c ultra & blk   .40   .40
366 A73   1sh red brown & blk   .45   .45
367 A73   1.80sh multicolored   1.25   1.25
   Nos. 364-367 (4)   2.35   2.35

First anniversary of Oct. 21st Revolution.

Snake Strangling Black Man, Map of South Africa A74

Design: 1.80sh, Concentration camp and symbols of justice holding scales.

Perf. 14x13½
1971, June 20   Photo.   Wmk. 303
368 A74   1.30sh multicolored   .70   .70
369 A74   1.80sh gray, red & blk   2.50   2.50

Against racial discrimination in South Africa.

Waves A75

Design: 2.80sh, Waves and globe.

1971, June 30
370 A75   25c black & blue   .40   .40
371 A75   2.80sh blk, grn & bl   2.10   2.10

3rd World Telecommunications Day, May 17.

Map of Africa and Telecommunications System — A76

Design: 1.50sh, Map of Africa and telecommunications system, diff.

1971, July 25
372 A76   1sh blk, lt bl & grn   .55   .55
373 A76   1.50sh black & yellow   1.75   1.75

Pan-African Telecommunications system.

White Rhinoceros A77

Wild Animals: 1sh, Cheetahs. 1.30sh, Zebras. 1.80sh, Lion attacking camel.

1971, Aug. 25
374 A77   35c ocher & multi   .40   .40
375 A77   1sh violet & multi   .95   .95
376 A77   1.30sh violet & multi   2.25   2.25
377 A77   1.80sh multicolored   4.50   4.50
   Nos. 374-377 (4)   8.10   8.10

Headquarters, Mogadishu, Flag, Map of Africa — A78

Design: 1.30sh, Desert Fort.

1971, Oct. 18
378 A78   1.30sh blk & red org   .85   .85
379 A78   1.50sh blk, blue & yel   1.75   1.75

East and Central African Summit Conf.

Revolution Monument A79

1sh, Field workers. 1.35sh, Building workers.

1971, Oct. 21
380 A79   10c black & blue   .25   .25
381 A79   1sh blk, yel brn & grn   .55   .55
382 A79   1.35sh blk, dp brn & yel   1.75   1.75
   Nos. 380-382 (3)   2.55   2.55

2nd anniversary of 1969 revolution.

Vaccination of Cow — A80

1.80sh, Veterinarian vaccinating cow.

Perf. 14x13½
1971, Nov. 28   Photo.   Wmk. 303
383 A80   40c blk, red & bl   .40   .25
384 A80   1.80sh lt green & multi   1.75   1.75

Rinderpest campaign.

Postal Union Emblem, Dove and Letter A81

1972, Jan. 25   **Unwmk.**
385 A81 1.50sh multicolored   1.75 1.75
10th anniv. of APU. See No. C108.

Children and UNICEF Emblem A82

Design: 50c, Mother and child, vert.

1972, Mar. 30   **Perf. 13x14, 14x13**
386 A82   50c blk, bis brn & dk brn   .25 .25
387 A82 2.80sh lt blue & multi   2.10 2.10
UNICEF, 25th anniv. (in 1971).

Camel A83

Designs: 10c, Cattle and cargo ship. 20c, Bull. 40c, Sheep. 1.70sh, Goat.

1972, Apr. 10   **Perf. 14x13**
388 A83 5c green & multi   .25 .25
389 A83 10c multicolored   .30 .30
390 A83 20c multicolored   .30 .30
391 A83 40c orange red & blk   .30 .30
392 A83 1.70sh dull grn & blk   3.50 3.50
    Nos. 388-392 (5)   4.65 4.65

Hands Holding Infant A84

1sh, Youth Corps emblem, marchers with flags. 1.50sh, Woman, man, tent, tractor.

1972, Oct. 21   **Photo.**   **Perf. 14x13½**
393 A84 70c yellow & multi   .25 .25
394 A84 1sh red & multi   .40 .40
395 A84 1.50sh lt blue & multi   1.60 1.60
    Nos. 393-395 (3)   2.25 2.25
3rd anniversary of October 21 Revolution.

Folk Dance A85

Folk Dances: 40c, Man and woman, vert. 1sh, Group dance, vert. 2sh, Two men and a woman.

1973   **Photo.**   **Perf. 14x13½, 13½x14**
396 A85 5c dull blue & multi   .25 .25
397 A85 40c brown & multi   .25 .25
398 A85 1sh yellow & multi   .55 .55
399 A85 2sh brick red & multi   1.90 1.90
    Nos. 396-399 (4)   2.95 2.95

Hand Writing Somali Script A86

40c, Flame and "FAR SOMALI" inscription, vert. 1sh, Woman and sunburst with Somali script.

Perf. 13½x14, 14x13½
1973, Oct. 21   **Photo.**
400 A86 40c red & multi   .25 .25
401 A86 1sh blue & multi   .35 .35
402 A86 2sh yellow & multi   1.90 1.90
    Nos. 400-402 (3)   2.50 2.50
Publicity for use of Somali script.

Map of Africa and Emblem — A87

Map of Africa with Target on Somalia — A88

1974, June 12   **Perf. 13½x14**
403 A87 40c multicolored   .40 .40
404 A88 2sh multicolored   2.00 2.00
OAU Meeting, Mogadishu.

Hurdler A89

1sh, Runners. 1.40sh, Netball, vert.

1974, Aug. 1   **Perf. 14x13, 13x14**
405 A89 50c black & orange   .25 .25
406 A89 1sh black & green   .40 .40
407 A89 1.40sh black & olive   2.00 2.00
    Nos. 405-407 (3)   2.65 2.65

Victory Pioneers — A90

Pioneers Helping Woman — A91

1974, Aug. 25   **Photo.**   **Perf. 13x14**
408 A90 40c multicolored   .25 .25
409 A91 2sh multicolored   1.90 1.90
Victory Pioneers, founded Aug. 24, 1972, to defend Socialist Revolution.

Map of Arab Countries A92

Flags of Arab Countries A93

1974, Sept. 1   **Perf. 14x13**
410 A92 1.50sh multicolored   .95 .95
411 A93 1.70sh multicolored   3.00 3.00
Somalia's admission to the Arab League, Feb. 14, 1974.

Tank Tracks in Desert A94

Somalis Reading Books — A95

Perf. 14x13½, 13½x14
1974, Oct. 21   **Litho.**
412 A94 40c multicolored   .25 .25
413 A95 2sh multicolored   1.75 1.75
5th anniversary of the Oct. 21st Revolution.

Carrier Pigeons A96

1975, Feb. 15   **Litho.**   **Perf. 14x13½**
414 A96 50c blue & multi   .25 .25
415 A96 3sh multicolored   1.75 1.75
UPU centenary (in 1974).

Africa A97

Design: 1.50sh, Carrier pigeons.

1975, Apr. 10
416 A97 1sh multicolored   .30 .30
417 A97 1.50sh multicolored   1.90 1.90
African Postal Union.

Somali Warrior — A98

Designs: Traditional costumes of Somali men (1sh, 10sh) and women (40c, 50c, 5sh).

1975, Oct. 27   **Photo.**   **Perf. 13½**
418 A98 10c yellow & multi   .25 .25
419 A98 40c lt blue & multi   .25 .25
420 A98 50c multicolored   .25 .25
421 A98 1sh green & multi   .25 .25
422 A98 5sh claret & multi   2.40 .80
423 A98 10sh rose & multi   6.50 2.40
    Nos. 418-423 (6)   9.90 4.20

Monument — A99

IWY Emblem A100

1975, Dec. 10   **Litho.**   **Perf. 13½x14**
424 A99 50c blk & red org   .25 .25
425 A100 2.30sh blk, pink & mag   2.40 2.40
International Women's Year.

Abdulla Hassan Monument A101

Abdulla Hassan with Warriors — A102

1.50sh, Abdulla Hassan speaking to his men. 2.30sh, Attacking horsemen, horiz.

Perf. 14x13½, 13½x14
1976, Nov. 30   **Photo.**
426 A101 50c multicolored   .25 .25
427 A102 60c multicolored   .25 .25
428 A102 1.50sh multicolored   .85 .85
429 A102 2.30sh multicolored   2.50 2.50
    Nos. 426-429 (4)   3.85 3.85
Sayid Mohammed Abdulla Hassan (1864-1920), poet and military leader.

Cypraea Gracilis A103

Sea Shells: 75c, Charonia bardayi. 1sh, Chlamys townsendi. 2sh, Cymatium ranzanii. 2.75sh, Conus argillaceus. 2.90sh, Strombus oldi.

1976, Dec. 15   Photo.   Perf. 14x13½

430	A103	50c blue & multi	.35	.35
431	A103	75c blue & multi	.35	.35
432	A103	1sh blue & multi	.75	.75
433	A103	2sh blue & multi	3.00	3.00
434	A103	2.75sh blue & multi	8.00	8.00
435	A103	2.90sh blue & multi	11.50	11.50
a.		Souvenir sheet of 6, #430-435	40.00	40.00
		Nos. 430-435 (6)	23.95	23.95

No. 435a sold for 11sh.

Benin Head and Hunters — A104

Benin Head and: 75c, Handicrafts. 2sh, Dancers. 2.90sh, Musicians.

1977, Aug. 30   Photo.   Perf. 14x13½

436	A104	50c multicolored	.25	.25
437	A104	75c multicolored	.25	.25
438	A104	2sh multicolored	.95	.95
439	A104	2.90sh multicolored	3.00	3.00
		Nos. 436-439 (4)	4.45	4.45

2nd World Black and African Festival, FESTAC '77, Lagos, Nigeria, Jan. 15-Feb. 12.

Arms of Somalia A105

Designs: 75c, Somali flags, vert. 1.50sh, Pres. Mohammed Siad Barre and globe. 2sh, Arms over rising sun and flags, vert.

Perf. 13½x14, 14x13½

1977, Sept. 30   **Photo.**

440	A105	75c multicolored	.25	.25
441	A105	1sh multicolored	.95	.95
442	A105	1.50sh multicolored	1.20	1.20
443	A105	2sh multicolored	2.40	2.40
		Nos. 440-443 (4)	4.80	4.80

Somali Socialist Revolutionary Party, established July 1, 1976.

Licaon Pictus A106

Protected Animals: 75c, Bush baby. 1sh, Somali ass. 1.50sh, Aardwolf. 2sh, Greater kudu. 3sh, Giraffe.

1977, Nov. 25   Photo.   Perf. 14x13½

444	A106	50c multicolored	.40	.40
445	A106	75c multicolored	.40	.40
446	A106	1sh multicolored	1.25	1.25
447	A106	1.50sh multicolored	1.90	1.90
448	A106	2sh multicolored	3.00	3.00
449	A106	3sh multicolored	7.75	7.75
a.		Souvenir sheet of 6, #444-449	26.00	26.00
		Nos. 444-449 (6)	14.70	14.70

Leonardo da Vinci's Flying Machine A107

ICAO Emblem and: 1.50sh, Montgolfier's balloon. 2sh, Wright brothers' plane. 2.90sh, Somali Airlines turbojet.

1977, Dec. 23   Photo.   Perf. 14x13½

450	A107	1sh multicolored	.25	.25
451	A107	1.50sh multicolored	.55	.55
452	A107	2sh multicolored	1.20	1.20

453	A107	2.90sh multicolored	2.40	2.40
a.		Souvenir sheet of 4, #450-453	16.00	16.00
		Nos. 450-453 (4)	4.40	4.40

ICAO, 30th anniv. No. 453a sold for 10sh.

Dome of the Rock — A108

Lithographed and Engraved
1978, Apr. 30   **Perf. 13x14**

454	A108	75c multicolored	.25	.25
455	A108	2sh multicolored	1.75	1.75

Palestinian fighters and their families.

Stadium and Soccer Player — A109

Designs: 4.90sh, Stadium and goalkeeper. 5.50sh, Stadium and player.

1978, Aug. 5   **Litho.**   **Perf. 14x13½**

456	A109	1.50sh multicolored	.80	.80
457	A109	4.90sh multicolored	2.40	2.40
458	A109	5.50sh multicolored	4.00	4.00
a.		Souvenir sheet of 3, #456-458	17.50	17.50
		Nos. 456-458 (3)	7.20	7.20

11th World Cup Soccer Championship, Argentina, June 1-25. No. 458a sold for 14sh.

Acacia Tortilis — A110

Trees: 50c, Ficus sycomorus, vert. 75c, Terminalia catapa, vert. 2.90sh, Baobab.

1978, Sept. 5   **Photo.**   **Perf. 14**

459	A110	40c multicolored	.25	.25
460	A110	50c multicolored	.25	.25
461	A110	75c multicolored	.25	.25
462	A110	2.90sh multicolored	3.25	3.25
		Nos. 459-462 (4)	4.00	4.00

Forest conservation.

Hibiscus — A111

Flowers of Somalia: 1sh, Cassia baccarinii. 1.50sh, Kigelia somalensis. 2.30sh, Dichrostachys glomerata.

1978, Dec. 15   Photo.   Perf. 13½x14

463	A111	50c multicolored	.25	.25
464	A111	1sh multicolored	.55	.55
465	A111	1.50sh multicolored	1.60	1.60
466	A111	2.30sh multicolored	2.40	2.40
a.		Souv. sheet, #463-466, perf. 14	12.00	12.00
		Nos. 463-466 (4)	4.80	4.80

Huri and Siganus Rivulatus A112

Fishery Development: 80c, Sail huri, gaterin gaterinus. 2.30sh, Fishing boats, hypacanthus amia. 2.50sh, Motorized fishing boat, mackerel.

1979, Sept. 1   Photo.   Perf. 14x13½

467	A112	75c multicolored	.55	.55
468	A112	80c multicolored	.55	.55
469	A112	2.30sh multicolored	1.60	1.60
470	A112	2.50sh multicolored	3.75	3.75
		Nos. 467-470 (4)	6.45	6.45

Sailing, IYC Emblem — A113

IYC Emblem, Children's Drawings: 50c, 90c, Schoolboy. 1.50sh, 2.50sh, Houses. 3sh, 4sh, Bird and flower. 1sh, as 75c.

1979, Sept. 10   Photo.   Perf. 13½x14

471	A113	50c multicolored	.30	.30
472	A113	75c multicolored	.30	.30
473	A113	1.50sh multicolored	.80	.80
474	A113	3sh multicolored	2.50	2.50
		Nos. 471-474 (4)	3.90	3.90

Souvenir Sheet of 4

474A	A113	#b.-e.	14.00	14.00

Intl. Year of the Child. No. 474A contains 90c, 1sh, 2.50sh, 4sh stamps and sold for 10sh.

University Students, Outdoor Classrooms — A114

Flower and: 50c, Housing construction. 75c, Children's recreation. 1sh, Doctor examining child, woman and man carrying grain and fish. 2.40sh, Woman and children carrying produce over dam. 3sh, Dish antenna.

1979, Nov. 30   Litho.   Perf. 14x13½

475	A114	20c multicolored	.30	.30
476	A114	50c multicolored	.30	.30
477	A114	75c multicolored	.65	.65
478	A114	1sh multicolored	.65	.65
479	A114	2.40sh multicolored	1.90	1.90
480	A114	3sh multicolored	2.40	2.40
		Nos. 475-480 (6)	6.20	6.20

Oct. 21 revolution, 10th anniversary.

Barbopsis Devecchii A115

Freshwater Fish: 90c, Phreatichthys andruzzii. 1sh, Uegitglanis zammaranoi. 2.50sh, Pardi's catfish.

1979, Dec. 12

481	A115	50c multicolored	.80	.80
482	A115	90c multicolored	.80	.80
483	A115	1sh multicolored	2.25	2.25
484	A115	2.50sh multicolored	2.25	2.25
a.		Souvenir sheet of 4, #481-484	12.00	12.00
		Nos. 481-484 (4)	6.10	6.10

No. 484a sold for 10sh.

Taleh Fortress, Congress Emblem — A116

1980, June 1   Photo.   Perf. 14x13½

485	A116	2.25sh multicolored	1.20	1.20
486	A116	3.50sh multicolored	2.40	2.40

1st International Congress of Somalian Studies, Mogadishu, July 6-13.

View of Marka — A117

1980, July 1   Litho.   Perf. 14

487	A117	75c shown	.30	.30
488	A117	1sh Gandershe + label	1.00	1.00
489	A117	2.30sh Afgooye + label	1.00	1.00
490	A117	3.50sh Muqdisho + label	4.00	4.00
		Nos. 487-490 (4)	6.30	6.30

See Nos. 502-505, 527-530.

A118

1980, July 30   Photo.   Perf. 13½x14

491	A118	1sh Batis perkeo	.70	.70
492	A118	2.25sh Rynchostruthus socotranus louisae	1.75	1.75
493	A118	5sh Laniarius ruficeps	4.00	4.00
a.		Souvenir sheet of 3, #491-493	13.00	13.00
		Nos. 491-493 (3)	6.45	6.45

A119

Perf. 13½x14, 14x13½
1981, Oct. 16   **Litho.**

494	A119	75c Globe, grain	.30	.30
495	A119	3.25sh Emblem, horiz.	1.50	1.50
496	A119	5.50sh like No. 494	3.00	3.00
		Nos. 494-496 (3)	4.80	4.80

World Food Day.

13th World Telecommunications Day — A120

1981, Oct. 10 **Perf. 13½x14**
497 A120 1sh Shepherdess, sheep, dish antenna .80 .80
498 A120 3sh Emblems 1.60 1.60
499 A120 4.60sh like No. 498 3.25 3.25
Nos. 497-499 (3) 5.65 5.65

Hegira, 1500th Anniv. — A121

1981, Oct. Photo. Perf. 13½x14
500 A121 1.50sh multicolored .55 .55
501 A121 3.80sh multicolored 1.90 1.90

View Type of 1980
1982, May 31 Litho. Perf. 13½x14
502 A117 2.25sh Balcad 1.20 1.20
503 A117 4sh Jowhar 1.60 1.60
504 A117 5.50sh Golaleey 2.40 2.40
505 A117 8.30sh Muqdisho 2.75 2.75
Nos. 502-505 (4) 7.95 7.95

Nos. 502-505 were each printed in sheets of 10 stamps and 5 labels showing regional map. Value for stamps with attached label: +25%.

1982 World Cup — A122

Designs: Various soccer players.

1982, June 13
506 A122 1sh multicolored .55 .55
507 A122 1.50sh multicolored 1.25 1.25
508 A122 3.25sh multicolored 3.00 3.00
a. Souvenir sheet of 3, #506-508 13.00 13.00
Nos. 506-508 (3) 4.80 4.80

ITU Plenipotentiaries Conference, Nairobi, Sept. — A123

1982, Oct. 15 Photo. Perf. 14x13½
509 A123 75c green & multi .25 .25
510 A123 3.25sh orange & multi 1.40 1.40
511 A123 5.50sh blue & multi 3.50 3.50
Nos. 509-511 (3) 5.15 5.15

Local Snakes — A124

2.80sh, Bitis arietans. 3.20sh, Psammophis punctulatus. 4.60sh, Rhamphiophis oxyrhynchus. 8.60sh, Sphalerosophis josephscorteccii.

1982, Dec. 20 Photo. Perf. 14
512 A124 2.80sh multicolored 1.60 1.60
513 A124 3.20sh multicolored 3.25 3.25
514 A124 4.60sh multicolored 4.75 4.75
Nos. 512-514 (3) 9.60 9.60
Souvenir Sheet
515 A124 8.60sh multicolored 21.00 21.00

Somali Woman — A125   A126

1982, Dec. 30 Perf. 14x13½
516 A125 1sh yel & multi .30 .30
517 A125 5.20sh lilac & multi 1.75 1.75
518 A125 5.80sh org & multi 1.90 1.90
519 A125 6.40sh blue & multi 2.10 2.10
520 A125 9.40sh lt brn & multi 3.25 3.25
521 A125 25sh green & multi 8.00 8.00
Nos. 516-521 (6) 17.30 17.30

1983, July 20 Perf. 13½x14
522 A126 5.20sh multicolored 1.40 1.40
523 A126 6.40sh multicolored 2.40 2.40

World Communications Year.

2nd Intl. Congress of Somali Studies, Hamburg — A127

Various views of Hamburg.

1983, Aug. 1 Perf. 14
524 A127 5.20sh multicolored .85 .85
525 A127 6.40sh multicolored 3.25 3.25

Military Uniforms — A128

Designs: a, Air Force. b, Women's Auxiliary Corps. c, Border Police. d, People's Militia. e, Army Infantry. f, Custodial Corps. g, Police. h, Navy.

1983, Oct. 21 Litho. Perf. 13½x14
526 Strip of 8 9.50 9.50
a.-h. A128 3.20sh, any single 1.20 1.20

View Type of 1980
1983
527 A117 2.80sh Barawe .80 .80
528 A117 3.20sh Bur Hakaba .80 .80
529 A117 5.50sh Baydhabo 1.60 1.60
530 A117 8.60sh Dooy Nuunaay 4.00 4.00
Nos. 527-530 (4) 7.20 7.20

Nos. 527-530 were each printed in sheets of 10 stamps and 5 decorative labels. Value for stamps with attached label: +25%.

Sea Shells A129

1984, Feb. 15 Litho. Perf. 14x13½
531 A129 2.80sh Volutocorbis rosavittoriae .80 .80
532 A129 3.20sh Phalium bi-tuberculosum 2.25 2.25

533 A129 5.50sh Conus milneed-warsi 5.75 5.75
Nos. 531-533 (3) 8.80 8.80
Souvenir Sheet
Perf. 14
534 A129 15sh Cypraea broderipi 13.00 13.00

Olympics 1984 — A130

1984, Sept. Litho. Perf. 13½x14
535 A130 1.50sh Runners .55 .55
536 A130 3sh Discus 1.20 1.20
537 A130 8sh Pole vaulting 3.50 3.50
a. Souvenir sheet of 3, #535-537 8.00 8.00
Nos. 535-537 (3) 5.25 5.25

No. 537a sold for 15sh.

Riccione Fair — A131

1984, Sept. Litho. Perf. 13½x14
538 A131 5.20sh multicolored 1.75 1.75
539 A131 6.40sh multicolored 4.50 4.50

Animals A132

1984, Sept. Litho. Perf. 14x13½
540 A132 1sh Hystrix cris-tata .35 .35
541 A132 1.50sh Ichneumia al-bicauda .35 .35
542 A132 2sh Mungos mungo 1.75 1.75
543 A132 4sh Mellivora capensis 3.00 3.00
a. Souvenir sheet of 4, #540-543 11.00 11.00
Nos. 540-543 (4) 5.45 5.45

No. 543a sold for 10sh.

Intl. Civil Aviation Org., 40th Anniv. — A133

1984, Nov. 20 Litho. Perf. 14
544 A133 3sh multicolored 1.20 1.20
545 A133 6.40sh multicolored 2.40 2.40
Souvenir Sheet
546 Sheet of 2 8.00 8.00
a. A133 3sh like No. 544 1.20 1.20
b. A133 6.40sh like No. 545 2.40 2.40

No. 546 contains 2 49½x46mm stamps. Sold for 10sh.

Dove — A134

Constellations from the Book of Fixed Stars, by Abd al-Rahman al-Sufi.

1985, Aug. 10 Litho. Perf. 13½x14
547 A134 4.30sh shown 1.20 1.20
548 A134 11sh Bull 2.40 2.40
549 A134 12.50sh Rams 2.40 2.40
550 A134 13.80sh Archer 2.90 2.90
Nos. 547-550 (4) 8.90 8.90

Architecture — A135

1985, Sept. Litho. Perf. 13½x14
551 A135 2sh Ras Kiambone .25 .25
552 A135 6.60sh Hannassa .40 .40
553 A135 10sh Mnarani 1.20 1.20
554 A135 18.60sh as #551, diff. 4.75 4.75
Nos. 551-554 (4) 6.60 6.60

Nos. 551-554 were each printed in sheets of 10 stamps and 5 decorative labels. Value for stamps with attached label: +10%.
See Nos. 572-575.

Lady Somalia Seated in Posthorn A136

1985, Oct. Perf. 14x14½
555 A136 2sh multicolored .95 .95
556 A136 20sh multicolored 4.00 4.00
a. Souvenir sheet of 2, #555-556, perf. 13½ 10.00 10.00

ITALIA '85, Rome. No. 556a sold for 30sh.

Bats A137

1985, Dec. 25 Litho. Perf. 14x13½
557 A137 2.50sh Triaenops persicus 1.00 1.00
558 A137 4.50sh Cardioderma cor 1.40 1.40
559 A137 16sh Tadarida con-dylura 4.00 4.00
560 A137 18sh Coleura afra 5.25 5.25
Nos. 557-560 (4) 11.65 11.65
Souvenir Sheet
561 Sheet of 4 16.00 16.00
a. A137 2.50sh like #552 1.00 1.00
b. A137 4.50sh like #553 1.40 1.40
c. A137 16sh like #554 4.00 4.00
d. A137 18sh like #555 5.25 5.25

Nos. 561a-561d printed in continuous design. No. 561 sold for 50sh.

Economic Trade Agreement with
Kenya — A138

Design: Presidents Arap Moi and Barre, satellite communications.

1986, Feb. 15   **Perf. 14**
562 A138   9sh multi   1.75 1.75
563 A138   14.50sh multi   2.75 2.75

EUROFLORA
Flower Exhibition,
Genoa — A139

1986, Apr. 25   **Perf. 13½x14**
564 A139   10sh Flower arrangement   .80   .80
565 A139   15sh Arrangement, diff.   2.40 2.40
  a.   Souvenir sheet of 2, #564-565   5.25 5.25

No. 565a sold for 30sh.

3rd Intl. Congress
on Somali
Studies — A140

1986, May 26
566 A140   11.35sh multi   .80   .80
567 A140   20sh multi   2.40 2.40

1986 World Cup Soccer
Championships, Mexico — A141

Various soccer plays.

1986, June   **Perf. 14x13½**
568 A141   3.60sh multi   .55   .55
569 A141   4.80sh multi   .55   .55
570 A141   6.80sh multi   1.75 1.75
571 A141   22.60sh multi   2.40 2.40
  a.   Souvenir sheet of 4, #568-571   10.00 10.00
  Nos. 568-571 (4)   5.25 5.25

No. 571a sold for 50sh.

Architecture Type of 1985
1986   **Litho.**   **Perf. 13½x14**
572 A135   10sh Bulaxaar   .40   .40
573 A135   15sh Saylac   .40   .40
574 A135   20sh Saylac, diff.   .80   .80
575 A135   31sh Jasiiradaha
            Jawaay   4.75 4.75
  Nos. 572-575 (4)   6.35 6.35

Nos. 572-575 were each printed in sheets of 10 stamps and 5 decorative labels. Value for stamps with attached label: +10%.

Red Crescent — Red Cross
Rehabilitation Center,
Mogadishu — A143

1987, May 8   Litho.   Perf. 13½x13
576 A143   56sh multi   6.75 6.75
Souvenir Sheet
577 A143   56sh multi, diff.   8.75 8.75

No. 577 sold for 60sh. See Norway No. 908.

A144

1987, Sept. 27   Litho.   Perf. 13½x14
578 A144   20sh Running   2.10 2.10
579 A144   48sh Javelin   4.75 4.75
  a.   Souvenir sheet of 2, #578-
       579   10.00 10.00

OLYMPHILEX '87, Rome. No. 579a sold for 75sh.

A145

1987, Oct. 5   Photo.   Perf. 13½x14½
580 A145   53sh multicolored   2.40 2.40
581 A145   72sh multicolored   4.00 4.00

Intl. Year of Shelter for the Homeless.

GEOSOM
'87 — A146

Maps: 10sh, 160,000,000 years ago. 20sh, 60,000,000 years ago. 40sh, 15,000,000 years ago. 50sh, Today.

1987, Nov. 24   Litho.   Perf. 13½x14
582 A146   10sh multi   1.25 1.25
583 A146   20sh multi, diff.   2.40 2.40
584 A146   40sh multi, diff.   4.75 4.75
585 A146   50sh multi, diff.   6.50 6.50
  a.   Souv. sheet of 2, #583, 585   35.00 35.00
  Nos. 582-585 (4)   14.90 14.90

Symposium on the Geology of Somalia, Mogadishu, 11/24-12/1. #585a sold for 130sh.

A147

1988, Dec. 31   Litho.   Perf. 13½x14
586 A147   50sh multicolored   .80   .80
587 A147   168sh multicolored   4.00 4.00

World Health Organization, 40th anniv.

Wildlife
A148

Perf. 13½x14, 14x13½
1989, Oct. 20   **Litho.**
588 A148   75sh *Lepus
            somaliensis*   .55   .55
589 A148   198sh *Syncerus caffer*   1.90 1.90
590 A148   200sh *Papio
            hamadryas*   3.25 3.25
591 A148   216sh *Hippopotamus
            amphibius*   4.00 4.00
  a.   Souvenir sheet of 2, #590-
       591   13.00 13.00
  Nos. 588-591 (4)   9.70 9.70

No. 591a contains 2 labels like #588-589. Sold for 700sh.

Somali
Revolution,
20th Anniv.
A149

Flowers, children's games: 70sh, Kick ball. 100sh, Swinging. 150sh, Teeter-totter. 300sh, Jumping rope, stick and hoop.

1989, Dec. 12   Litho.   Perf. 14x13½
592 A149   70sh multicolored   1.40 1.40
593 A149   100sh multicolored   2.00 2.00
594 A149   150sh multicolored   3.00 3.00
595 A149   300sh multicolored   6.00 6.00
  Nos. 592-595 (4)   12.40 12.40

A150

Liberation: Nos. 599-600, Dove breaking chains, horiz.

1991   Litho.   Perf. 13½x14, 14x13½
596 A150   70sh lilac & multi   .65   .65
597 A150   100sh grn bl & multi   .90   .90
598 A150   150sh brt blue &
            multi   1.40 1.40
599 A150   150sh yellow & multi   1.40 1.40
600 A150   300sh yel grn & mul-
            ti   2.75 2.75
601 A150   300sh yel grn & mul-
            ti   2.75 2.00
  Nos. 596-601 (6)   9.85 9.10

Issued: Nos. 599-600, July 2; others, July 4.

No. 599 Ovptd. in Blue

1991   Litho.   Perf. 14x13½
602 A150   150sh yellow & multi   4.00 4.00

A151

Various minarets.

1991   Litho.   Perf. 14
603 A151   30sh multicolored   .30   .30
604 A151   40sh multicolored   .45   .45
605 A151   50sh multicolored   .55   .55
606 A151   150sh multicolored   1.75 1.75
  Nos. 603-606 (4)   3.05 3.05

Relief efforts have demonstrated the breakdown of government services in Somalia. It is unclear which faction has control of the Postal Service, if any is operating. The status of Scott Nos. 607-638 will be reviewed once more information is available.

Gazelles
A152

1992   **Perf. 14x13½**
Inscribed in Black
607 A152   500sh Two Speke's   3.25
608 A152   700sh One Speke's   4.50
609 A152   800sh One Soem-
            mering's   6.00
610 A152   1000sh Two Soem-
            mering's   7.25
  Nos. 607-610 (4)   21.00

World Wildlife Fund.

Without WWF Emblem
Inscribed in red lilac
611 A152   100sh like #607   .85
612 A152   200sh like #608   1.75
613 A152   300sh like #609   2.40
614 A152   400sh like #610   3.50

Inscribed in black
615 A152   1500sh Baboons   13.00
616 A152   2500sh Hippopota-
            mus   20.00
617 A152   3000sh Giraffes   25.00
618 A152   5000sh Leopard   40.00
  Nos. 607-618 (12)   127.50

Nos. 607-618 are part of an expanding set. Numbers may change.
For overprints see No. 629-632.

Nos. 607-610 Ovptd. in Orange

1992 Litho. Perf. 14x13½

629	A152	500sh on #607	5.00
630	A152	700sh on #608	7.50
631	A152	800sh on #609	10.00
632	A152	1000sh on #610	12.50
	Nos. 629-632 (4)		35.00

Discovery of America, 500th Anniv. A153

Designs: 100sh, Sighting land from crow's nest. 200sh, Three men pointing from ship. 300sh, Columbus in his cabin. 400sh, Claiming land. 2000sh, Building fort in New World.
No. 638: a, 800sh, like #634. b, 900sh, like #635. c, 1300sh, like #633.

1992

633	A153	100sh multicolored	.55
634	A153	200sh multicolored	1.10
635	A153	300sh multicolored	1.60
636	A153	400sh multicolored	2.25
637	A153	2000sh multicolored	11.00
	Nos. 633-637 (5)		16.50

Souvenir Sheet

638	A153	Sheet of 3, #a.-c.	16.50

Nos. 638a-638c do not have white border. No. 638 exists imperf.

SEMI-POSTAL STAMPS

Italy Nos. B1-B4 Overprinted

1916 Wmk. 140 Perf. 14

B1	SP1	10c + 5c rose	16.00	45.00
B2	SP2	15c + 5c slate	55.00	52.50
B3	SP2	20c + 5c orange	16.00	52.50
B4	SP2	20c on 15c + 5c slate	55.00	95.00
	Nos. B1-B4 (4)		142.00	245.00

Holy Year Issue
Italy Nos. B20-B25 Surcharged in Black or Red

1925, June 1 Perf. 12

B5	SP4	6b + 3b on 20c + 10c	3.25	22.50
B6	SP4	13b + 6b on 30c + 15c	3.25	24.00
B7	SP4	15b + 8b on 50c + 25c	3.25	22.50
B8	SP4	18b + 9b on 60c + 30c	3.25	27.50
B9	SP8	30b + 15b on 1 l +50c (R)	3.25	35.00
B10	SP8	1r + 50b on 5 l +2.50 l (R)	3.25	52.50
	Nos. B5-B10 (6)		19.50	184.00

Colonial Institute Issue

"Peace" Substituting Spade for Sword — SP10

1926, June 1 Typo. Perf. 14

B11	SP10	5c + 5c brown	.95	9.50
B12	SP10	10c + 5c olive grn	.95	9.50
B13	SP10	20c + 5c blue grn	.95	9.50
B14	SP10	40c + 5c brown red	.95	9.50
B15	SP10	60c + 5c orange	.95	9.50
B16	SP10	1 l + 5c blue	.95	20.00
	Nos. B11-B16 (6)		5.70	67.50

The surtax was for the Italian Colonial Institute.

Types of Italian Semi-Postal Stamps of 1926 Overprinted

1927, Apr. 21 Unwmk. Perf. 11½

B17	SP10	40c + 20c dk brn & blk	2.40	35.00
B18	SP10	60c + 30c brn red & ol brn	2.40	35.00
B19	SP10	1.25 l + 60c dp bl & blk	2.40	55.00
B20	SP10	5 l + 2.50 l dk grn & blk	4.00	80.00
	Nos. B17-B20 (4)		11.20	205.00

The surtax was for the charitable work of the Voluntary Militia for Italian National Defense.

Allegory of Fascism and Victory — SP11

1928, Oct. 15 Wmk. 140 Perf. 14

B21	SP11	20c + 5c blue grn	3.25	13.00
B22	SP11	30c + 5c red	3.25	13.00
B23	SP11	50c + 10c purple	3.25	22.50
B24	SP11	1.25 l + 20c dk blue	4.00	27.50
	Nos. B21-B24 (4)		13.75	76.00

46th anniv. of the Societa Africana d'Italia. The surtax aided that society.

Types of Italian Semi-Postal Stamps of 1928 Overprinted

1929, Mar. 4 Unwmk. Perf. 11

B25	SP10	30c + 10c red & blk	4.50	22.50
B26	SP10	50c + 20c vio & blk	4.50	26.00
B27	SP10	1.25 l + 50c brn & bl	5.50	45.00
B28	SP10	5 l + 2 l ol grn & blk	5.50	80.00
	Nos. B25-B28 (4)		20.00	173.50

The surtax was for the charitable work of the Voluntary Militia for Italian National Defense.

Types of Italian Semi-Postal Stamps of 1926 Overprinted in Black or Red

1930, Oct. 20 Perf. 14

B29	SP10	30c + 10c dk grn & bl grn (Bk)	27.50	47.50
B30	SP10	50c + 10c dk grn & vio (R)	27.50	65.00
B31	SP10	1.25 l + 30c ol brn & red brn (R)	27.50	80.00
B32	SP10	5 l + 1.50 l ind & grn (R)	87.50	225.00
	Nos. B29-B32 (4)		170.00	417.50

The surtax was for the charitable work of the Voluntary Militia for Italian National Defense.

Irrigation Canal SP14

1930, Nov. 27 Photo. Wmk. 140

B33	SP14	50c + 20c olive brn	4.00	22.50
B34	S414	1.25 l + 20c dp blue	4.00	22.50
B35	SP14	1.75 l + 20c green	4.00	26.00
B36	SP14	2.55 l + 50c purple	8.00	40.00
B37	SP14	5 l + 1 l dp car	8.00	60.00
	Nos. B33-B37 (5)		28.00	171.00

25th anniv. of the Italian Colonial Agricultural Institute. The surtax was for the aid of that institution.

SP15

King Victor Emmanuel III — SP16

1935, Jan. 1

B38	SP15	5c + 5c blk brn	4.75	32.50
B39	SP15	7½c + 7½c vio	4.75	32.50
B40	SP15	15c + 10c ol blk	4.75	32.50
B41	SP15	20c + 10c rose red	4.75	32.50
B42	SP15	25c + 10c dp grn	4.75	32.50
B43	SP15	30c + 10c brn	4.75	32.50
B44	SP15	50c + 10c pur	4.75	32.50
B45	SP15	75c + 15c rose car	4.75	32.50
B46	SP15	1.25 l + 15c dp bl	4.75	32.50
B47	SP15	1.75 l + 25c red org	4.75	32.50
B48	SP15	2.75 l + 25c gray	32.50	130.00
B49	SP15	5 l + 1 l dp cl	32.50	130.00
B50	SP15	10 l + 1.80 l red brn	32.50	130.00
B51	SP16	25 l + 2.75 l brn & red	200.00	475.00
	Nos. B38-B51 (14)		345.00	1,190.
	Set, never hinged		800.00	

Visit of King Victor Emmanuel III.

> **Catalogue values for unused stamps in this section, from this point to the end of the section, are for Never Hinged items.**

Somalia

Nurse Holding Infant — SP17

1957, Nov. 30 Wmk. 303 Perf. 14

B52	SP17	10c + 10c red & brn	.85	.85
B53	SP17	25c + 10c grn & brn	.85	.85
	Nos. B52-B53,CB11-CB12 (4)		3.40	4.20

The surtax was for the fight against tuberculosis.

Republic

Refugees SP18

1964, Dec. 12 Photo. Perf. 14

B54	SP18	25c + 10c vio bl & red	.55	.30
	Nos. B54,CB13-CB14 (3)		3.90	2.35

The surtax was to help refugees.

Red Cross Nurse Feeding Child — SP19

Famine Relief: 80c+20c, Nomad in parched land, horiz. 2.40sh+10c, Family with fish and produce. 2.90sh+10c, Physician and Aid Society emblem, horiz.

1976, Dec. 10 Perf. 13x14, 14x13

B55	SP19	75c + 25c multi	.55	.55
B56	SP19	80c + 20c multi	.55	.55
B57	SP19	2.40sh + 10c multi	1.75	1.75
B58	SP19	2.90sh + 10c multi	2.40	2.40
	Nos. B55-B58 (4)		5.25	5.25

Refugees SP20

1981, Dec. 15 Photo. Perf. 13½x14

B59	SP20	2sh + 50c multi	.85	.85
B60	SP20	6.80sh + 50c multi	4.00	4.00
a.	Souvenir sheet of 2, #B59-B60		8.00	8.00

TB Bacillus Centenary — SP31

1982, Dec. 30 Photo. Perf. 14

B61	SP31	4.60sh + 60c multi	2.00	2.00
B62	SP31	5.80sh + 60c multi	2.50	2.50

AIR POST STAMPS

View of Coast AP1

Cheetahs
AP2

Wmk. 140

1934, Oct.		Photo.		Perf. 14

C1 AP1 25c sl bl & red org   4.00   20.00
C2 AP1 50c dk grn & blk   4.00   16.00
C3 AP1 75c brn & red org   4.00   16.00
  a.   Imperf.   2,500.
C4 AP2 80c org brn & blk   4.00   20.00
C5 AP2 1 l scar & blk   4.00   24.00
C6 AP2 2 l dk bl & brn   4.00   40.00
    Nos. C1-C6 (6)   24.00 136.00
    Set, never hinged   110.00

2nd Colonial Arts Exhibition, Naples.
For overprint see No. CO1.

Banana
Tree and
Airplane
AP3

Designs: 25c, 1.50 l, Banana tree and
plane. 50c, 2 l, Plane over cotton field. 60c, 5 l,
Plane over orchard. 75c, 10 l, Plane over field
workers. 1 l, 3 l, Small girl watching plane.

1936				Photo.

C7   AP3 25c slate green   2.40   8.00
C8   AP3 50c brown   1.60   .25
C9   AP3 60c red orange   3.25   12.00
C10 AP3 75c orange brn   2.40   2.40
C11 AP3 1 l deep blue   1.60   .25
C12 AP3 1.50 l purple   2.40   .80
C13 AP3 2 l slate blue   6.50   1.20
C14 AP3 3 l copper red   24.00   14.50
C15 AP3 5 l yellow green 27.50   17.50
C16 AP3 10 l dp rose red 35.00   32.50
    Nos. C7-C16 (10)   106.65 89.40
    Set, never hinged   240.00

**Catalogue values for unused
stamps in this section, from this
point to the end of the section, are
for Never Hinged items.**

Somalia

AP8

1950-51			Wmk. 277

C17 AP8 30c yellow brn   8.00   3.25
C18 AP8 45c dk carmine   8.00   3.25
C19 AP8 65c dk blue vio   8.00   3.25
C20 AP8 70c dull blue   8.00   6.50
C21 AP8 90c olive brn   8.00   6.50
C22 AP8 1s lilac rose   9.50   3.25
C23 AP8 1.35s violet   14.50   8.00
C24 AP8 1.50s blue green   14.50   9.50
C25 AP8 3s blue   65.00   35.00
C26 AP8 5s chocolate   65.00   35.00
C27 AP8 10s red org ('51)   120.00   24.00
    Nos. C17-C27 (11)   328.50 137.50

Scene in
Mogadishu
AP8a

1951, Oct. 4

C27A AP8a 1s vio & Prus bl   3.25   1.25
C27B AP8a 1.50s ol grn & chnt
                     brn   8.75   8.75

First Territorial Council meeting.

Plane, Palm Tree
and Minaret — AP9

Mother and
Child — AP10

1952, Sept. 14

C28 AP9 1.20s ol bis & dp bl   5.00   5.75

1st Somali Fair, Mogadishu, Sept. 14-28.

1953, May 27

C29 AP10 1.20s dk grn & dk brn   3.25   5.00

Somali anti-tuberculosis campaign.

Fair
Entrance
AP11

1953, Sept. 28		Unwmk.	Perf. 11½

C30 AP11 1.20s brn car & pink   1.00   1.25
C31 AP11 1.50s yel brn & buff   1.25   1.90

2nd Somali Fair, Mogadishu, Sept. 28-Oct.
12, 1953.

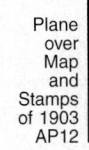

Plane
over
Map
and
Stamps
of 1903
AP12

Perf. 13x13½

1953, Dec. 16		Engr.	Wmk. 277

Early Stamps in Brn and Rose Car

C32 AP12 60c orange brown   1.25   4.00
C33 AP12 1s greenish black   1.25   6.00

1st Somali postage stamps, 50th anniv.

"UPU" among Constellations — AP13

Perf. 11½

1953, Dec. 16		Photo.	Unwmk.

C34 AP13 1.20s red & cream   1.25   3.75
C35 AP13 1.50s brown & cream   2.75   7.75
C36 AP13 2s green & lt blue   2.75   7.75
    Nos. C34-C36 (3)   6.75 19.25

UPU, 75th anniv. (in 1949).

Alexander
Island Juba
River — AP14

Somali
Flag — AP15

1954, June 1		Perf. 13½x12½

C37 AP14 1.20s dk grn & brn   1.10   1.40
C38 AP14 2s dk carmine &
                   pur   1.60   2.25

See note after No. 196.

Perf. 13½x13

1954, Oct. 12		Litho.	Wmk. 277

C39 AP15 1.20s multicolored   .50   .65

Adoption of Somali flag.

Haggard's
Oribi — AP16

Designs: 45c, Phillip's dik-dik. 50c, Speke's
gazelle. 75c, Gerenuk. 1.20s, Soemmering's
gazelle. 1.50s, Waterbuck.

Wmk. 277

1955, Apr. 12		Photo.		Perf. 13½

Antelopes in Natural Colors
Size: 22x33mm

C40 AP16 35c gray grn & blk   .35   .80
C41 AP16 45c lilac & blk   6.50   2.40
C42 AP16 50c rose lil & blk   .40   .80
C43 AP16 75c red   4.00   .80
C44 AP16 1.20s dk gray grn   4.00   5.50
C45 AP16 1.50s bright blue   6.50   9.50
    Nos. C40-C45 (6)   21.75 19.80

See Nos. C57-C58.

Caravan at
Water Hole
AP17

Design: 1.20s, Village well.

Perf. 13½x14

1955, Sept. 24			Wmk. 303

C46 AP17 45c brown & orange   .75   1.60
C47 AP17 1.20s sapphire & pink 1.25   1.60

3rd Somali Fair, Mogadishu, Sept. 1955.

Ballot Type of Regular Issue

1956, Apr. 30		Photo.	Perf. 14

C48 A24 60c brown & ultra   .85   1.25
C49 A24 1.20s brown & org   .85   1.25

Opening of the territory's first democratically
elected Legislative Assembly.

Arms Type of Regular Issue

1957, May 6	Wmk. 303	Perf. 13½

**Coat of Arms in Dull Yellow, Blue
and Black**

C50 A25 45c blue   .95   1.40
C51 A25 1.20s bluish green   .95   1.40

Issued in honor of the new coat of arms.

Type of Regular Issue, 1957 and

Oil Well — AP18

Design: 60c, Irrigation canal construction.

1957, Sept. 28			Perf. 14

C52 A26   60c blue & brown   1.25   1.25
C53 AP18 1.20s black & ver   1.25   1.25

Fourth Somali Fair and Film Festival.

Sport Type of Regular Issue

60c, Runner. 1.20s, Bicyclist. 1.50s, Basketball player.

1958, Apr. 28	Wmk. 303		Perf. 14

C54 A27 60c brown   .25   .25
C55 A27 1.20s blue   .25   .50
C56 A27 1.50s rose carmine   .25   .50
    Nos. C54-C56 (3)   .75   1.25

Animal Type of 1955

3s, Lesser kudu. 5s, Hunter's hartebeest.

1958-59   **Photo.**
Size: 20½x36½mm

C57 AP16 3s ocher & sepia   2.75   3.25
C58 AP16 5s gray, blk & yel ('59) 2.75 3.25

See No. CE1.

Police
Bugler
AP19

1959, June 19			Photo.

C59 AP19 1.20s ocher & ultra   1.10   1.25
C60 AP19 1.50s olive grn & ultra 1.10 1.25
  a. Souv. sheet of 4, #228-229,
         C59-C60   6.00   8.00

Opening of the Constituent Assembly of
Somalia.

Marabou
AP20

1959, Sept. 4			Wmk. 303

C61 AP20 1.20s shown   1.10   .55
C62 AP20 2s Great egret   1.10   .55

Incense
Shipment,
15th
Century
B.C.
AP21

Design: 2s, Incense burner and view of
Mogadishu harbor.

1959, Sept. 28			Perf. 14

C63 AP21 1.20s red & blk   .70   .75
C64 AP21 2s blue, blk & org   1.40   1.40

5th Somali Fair, Mogadishu.

University
Institute
and Arms
AP22

Design: 1.20s, Front view of Institute.

1960, Jan. 14

C65 AP22 45c grn, blk & org
                   brn   .35   .35
C66 AP22 1.20s blue, ultra & blk .55 .65

Opening of the University Institute of
Somalia.

Stork and
Uprooted Oak
Emblem — AP23

1960, Apr. 7	Wmk. 303	Perf. 14

C67 AP23 1.50s lt grn, bl & red 1.50 1.60

World Refugee Year, 7/1/59-6/30/60.

Republic
#C42, C44 Overprinted Like #242
Wmk. 277
1960, June 26   Photo.   Perf. 13½
Antelopes in Natural Colors
C68	AP16	50c rose lil & blk	40.00	40.00
C69	AP16	1.20s dk gray grn	29.00	32.50

See note after No. 242.

Parliament and Italian Flag AP25

1.80s, Somali flag and assembly building.

1960, July 1   Wmk. 303   Perf. 14
C70	AP25	1s org red, grn & red	.80	.80
C71	AP25	1.80s red org, ultra & blk	3.25	3.25

Somalia's independence.

Animal Type of Regular Issue
1960, Nov. 24
C72	A37	3s Leopard	4.50	4.50

Olympic Games Type
45c, Runner, flag, Olympic rings. 1.80s, Long distance runner, flag, Olympic rings.

1960, Nov. 24
C73	A38	45c lilac & blue	.85	.85
C74	A38	1.80s org ver & bl	1.75	1.75

17th Olympic Games, Rome, 8/25-9/11.

Amauris Fenestrata and Jet Plane AP26

Various Butterflies.

1961, Sept. 9
C75	AP26	60c blue, brn & yel	.40	.40
C76	AP26	90c yel, blk & grn	.50	.50
C77	AP26	1s multicolored	2.40	.35
C78	AP26	1.80s org, blk & red	1.10	1.10
C79	AP26	3s multicolored	2.40	2.40
C80	AP26	5s ver, blk & brt bl	8.00	3.50
C81	AP26	10s multicolored	12.50	6.50
		Nos. C75-C81 (7)	27.30	14.75

Wooden Headrest, Comb and Cap AP27

Design: 1.80sh, Camel, metal sculpture.

1961, Sept. 28   Wmk. 303   Perf. 14
C82	AP27	1sh blk, ultra & ocher	.40	.40
C83	AP27	1.80sh blk, yel & brn	2.25	2.25

6th Somali Fair, Mogadishu.

Fish Type
Fish: 2.70sh, Lutianus sebae.

1962, Apr. 26
C84	A41	2.70sh ultra, brn & rose brn	3.50	3.50

Mosquitoes and Malaria Eradication Emblem — AP28

Wmk. 303
1962, Oct. 25   Photo.   Perf. 14
C85	AP28	1sh bis brn & blk	.85	.85
C86	AP28	1.80sh lt green & blk	2.75	2.75

WHO drive to eradicate malaria.

Police Auxiliary Women — AP29

Women's Auxiliary Forces: 1.80sh, Army auxiliary women with flag.

1963, May 15   Wmk. 303   Perf. 14
C87	AP29	1sh dk bl, yel & org	.85	.85
C88	AP29	1.80sh multicolored	2.75	2.75

Freedom from Hunger Type
Design: 1sh, Sower and wheat.

1963, June 25
C89	A44	1sh dk brn, yel & bl	2.75	2.75

President Osman Type
1963, Sept. 15   Wmk. 303   Perf. 14
C90	A45	1sh multicolored	.85	.85
C91	A45	1.80sh multicolored	1.75	1.75

Somali Fair Type
Design: 1.80sh, Government Pavilion.

1963, Sept. 28   Photo.
C92	A46	1.80sh blue	2.75	2.75

Map of Somalia, Animals and Globe AP30

1.80sh, Somali Credit Bank emblem.

1964, May 16   Wmk. 303   Perf. 14
C93	AP30	1sh multicolored	1.75	1.75
C94	AP30	1.80sh blk, bl & yel	2.75	2.75

10th anniversary of Somali Credit Bank.

Olympic Type
1964, Oct. 10   Photo.
C95	A48	90c Diving	.85	.85
C96	A48	1.80sh Soccer	2.75	2.75
a.		Souvenir sheet, #274-275, C95-C96	40.00	

No. C96a sold for 3.55sh.

Elephants and DC-3 AP31

Design: 1.80sh, Plane over Mogadishu.

1964, Nov. 8   Photo.   Perf. 14
C97	AP31	1sh brown & green	2.90	2.90
C98	AP31	1.80sh black & blue	5.25	5.25

Establishment of Somali Air Lines.

ITU Type
1965, May 17   Wmk. 303   Perf. 14
C99	A50	1sh dp grn & blk	.85	.65
C100	A50	1.80sh rose lil & brn	2.10	1.40

Somali Fair Type
Designs: 1.50sh, Sugar industry; harvesting sugar cane and refinery. 2sh, Dairy industry; bottling plant and milk cow.

1965, Sept. 28   Photo.   Perf. 14
C101	A51	1.50sh sepia & pale bl	1.20	.55
C102	A51	2sh sepia & rose	2.50	2.10

Faisal Type
Design: 1.80sh, Ka'aba, Mecca, Pres. Abdirascid Ali Scermarche and King Faisal.

1967, Sept. 21   Wmk. 303   Perf. 14
C103	A60	1.80sh blk, dp rose & org	2.10	2.10

Egret — AP32

Birds: 1sh, Southern carmine bee-eater. 1.30sh, Bruce's green pigeon. 1.80sh, Broad-tailed paradise whydah.

Perf. 11½
1968, Nov. 1		**Unwmk.**	**Litho.**	
C104	AP32	35c blue & multi	.35	.25
C105	AP32	1sh green & multi	.45	.25
C106	AP32	1.30sh vio bl & multi	1.10	.95
C107	AP32	1.80sh yellow & multi	2.75	2.50
		Nos. C104-C107 (4)	4.65	3.95

Somali Democratic Republic
Postal Union Type

1.30sh, Postal Union emblem and letter.

Perf. 14x13½
1972, Jan. 25		**Photo.**	**Unwmk.**	
C108	A81	1.30sh multicolored	1.75	1.75

AIR POST SEMI-POSTAL STAMPS

King Victor Emmanuel III — SPAP1

Wmk. 140
1934, Nov. 5   Photo.   Perf. 14
CB1	SPAP1	25c + 10c gray grn	6.50	24.00
CB2	SPAP1	50c + 10c brn	6.50	24.00
CB3	SPAP1	75c + 15c rose red	6.50	24.00
CB4	SPAP1	80c + 15c blk brn	6.50	24.00
CB5	SPAP1	1 l + 20c red brn	6.50	24.00
CB6	SPAP1	2 l + 20c brt bl	6.50	24.00
CB7	SPAP1	3 l + 25c pur	24.00	120.00
CB8	SPAP1	5 l + 25c org	24.00	120.00
CB9	SPAP1	10 l + 30c rose vio	24.00	120.00
CB10	SPAP1	25 l + 2 l dp grn	24.00	120.00
		Nos. CB1-CB10 (10)	135.00	624.00
		Set, never hinged	370.00	

65th birthday of King Victor Emmanuel III; non-stop flight from Rome to Mogadishu. For overprint see No. CBO1.

> **Catalogue values for unused stamps in this section, from this point to the end of the section, are for Never Hinged items.**

Somalia
Type of Semi-Postal Stamps, 1957
1957, Nov. 30   Wmk. 303   Perf. 14
CB11	SP17	55c + 20c dk bl & brn	.85	1.25
CB12	SP17	1.20s + 20c vio & brn	.85	1.25

The surtax was for the fight against tuberculosis.

Type of Semi-Postal Issue, 1964
Designs: 75c+20c, Destroyed Somali village. 1.80sh+50c, Soldier aiding children, and map of Somalia, vert.

1964, Dec. 12   Photo.   Perf. 14
CB13	SP18	75c + 20c blk, org red & brn	.85	.65
CB14	SP18	1.80sh + 50c blk, ol bis & slate	2.50	1.40

AIR POST SPECIAL DELIVERY STAMP

> **Catalogue value for the stamp in this section is for a Never Hinged item.**

Antelopes APSD1

Wmk. 303
1958, Oct. 4   Photo.   Perf. 14
CE1	APSD1	1.70s org ver & blk	2.75	2.25

AIR POST OFFICIAL STAMP

No. C1 Overprinted

Wmk. 140
1934, Nov. 11   Photo.   Perf. 14
CO1	AP1	25c sl bl & red org	2,800.	4,750.
		Never hinged	4,750.	

Forgeries of this overprint exist.

AIR POST SEMI-POSTAL OFFICIAL STAMP

Air Post Semi-Postal Stamps of 1934 Overprinted in Black

1934, Nov. 5   Wmk. 140   Perf. 14
CBO1	SPAP1	25 l + 2 l cop red	2,950.	5,250.
		Never hinged	5,250.	

SPECIAL DELIVERY STAMPS

Italy No. E3 Surcharged

1923, July 16 **Wmk. 140** **Perf. 14**
E1 SD1 30b on 60c dl red 32.50 29.00

Italy, Type of 1908 Special Delivery Stamp Surcharged

E2 SD2 60b on 1.20 l bl & red 47.50 57.50

"Italia" SD3

1924, June **Engr.** **Unwmk.**
E3 SD3 30b dk red & brn 13.00 24.00
E4 SD3 60b dk blue & red 24.00 35.00

Nos. E3-E4 Surcharged in Black or Red

1926, Oct.
E5 SD3 70c on 30b (Bk) 14.50 21.00
E6 SD3 2.50 l on 60b (R) 17.00 26.50
a. Imperf., pair 1,140.

Same Surcharge on No. E3

1927 **Perf. 11**
E7 SD3 1.25 l on 30b 16.00 16.00
a. Perf. 14 250.00 800.00
b. Imperf., pair 1,050.

Catalogue values for unused stamps in this point to the end of the section, are for Never Hinged items.

Somalia

Bananas, Grant's Gazelles SD4

Wmk. 277
1950, Apr. 24 **Photo.** **Perf. 14**
E8 SD4 40c blue green 14.50 12.00
E9 SD4 80c violet 17.50 16.00

Gardenias SD5

Design: 1s, Eryrhina melanocantha.

1955, Feb. **Perf. 13**
E10 SD5 50c lilac & green .90 1.75
E11 SD5 1s bl, rose brn & grn 1.60 2.75

AUTHORIZED DELIVERY STAMP

Italy No. EY2 Overprinted in Black

1939 **Wmk. 140** **Perf. 14**
EY1 AD2 10c brown 80.00

No. EY1 has yellowish gum. A 1941 printing in grayish brown, with white gum, was not issued. Value: unused, 80 cents; never hinged, $2.00.

POSTAGE DUE STAMPS

Values for Nos. J1-J41 are for examples with perforations touching or cutting into the design on at least one side. Examples with perforations clear of the design on all four sides are scarce and command considerable premiums.

Postage Due Stamps of Italy Overprinted

1906-08 **Wmk. 140** **Perf. 14**
J1 D3 5c buff & magenta 24.00 52.50
J2 D3 10c buff & magenta 72.50 72.50
J3 D3 20c org & magenta 47.50 87.50
J4 D3 30c buff & magenta 47.50 95.00
J5 D3 40c buff & magenta 350.00 95.00
J6 D3 50c buff & magenta 80.00 110.00
J7 D3 60c buff & mag ('08) 72.50 110.00
J8 D3 1 l blue & magenta 1,450. 525.00
J9 D3 2 l blue & magenta 1,450. 525.00
J10 D3 5 l blue & magenta 1,450. 525.00
J11 D3 10 l blue & magenta 275.00 475.00
Nos. J1-J11 (11) 5,319. 2,672.

Postage Due Stamps of Italy Overprinted at Top of Stamps

1909-19
J12 D3 5c buff & magenta 9.50 27.50
J13 D3 10c buff & magenta 9.50 27.50
J14 D3 20c buff & magenta 20.00 55.00
J15 D3 30c buff & magenta 55.00 55.00
J16 D3 40c buff & magenta 55.00 72.50
J17 D3 50c buff & magenta 55.00 95.00
J18 D3 60c buff & mag ('19) 72.50 87.50
J19 D3 1 l blue & magenta 160.00 95.00
J20 D3 2 l blue & magenta 240.00 240.00
J21 D3 5 l blue & magenta 275.00 300.00
J22 D3 10 l blue & magenta 55.00 95.00
Nos. J12-J22 (11) 1,006. 1,150.

Same with Overprint at Bottom of Stamps

1920
J12a D3 5c buff & magenta 145.00 225.00
b. Double overprint 550.00
J13a D3 10c buff & magenta 145.00 225.00
J14a D3 20c buff & magenta 210.00 145.00
J15a D3 30c buff & magenta 210.00 145.00
J16a D3 40c buff & magenta 210.00 225.00
J17a D3 50c buff & magenta 210.00 185.00
J18a D3 60c buff & magenta 210.00 185.00
J19a D3 1 l blue & magenta 210.00 275.00
J20a D3 2 l blue & magenta 210.00 275.00
J21a D3 5 l blue & magenta 210.00 350.00
Nos. J12a-J21a (10) 1,970. 2,235.

D4

1923, July 1
J23 D4 1b buff & black 2.40 9.50
J24 D4 2b buff & black 2.40 9.50
a. Inverted numeral and ovpt. 550.00
J25 D4 3b buff & black 2.40 9.50
J26 D4 5b buff & black 4.00 9.50
J27 D4 10b buff & black 4.00 9.50
J28 D4 20b buff & black 4.00 9.50
J29 D4 40b buff & black 4.00 9.50
J30 D4 1r blue & black 4.50 55.00
Nos. J23-J30 (8) 27.70 121.50

Type of Postage Due Stamps of Italy Overprinted

1926, Mar. 1
J31 D3 5c buff & black 27.50 35.00
J32 D3 10c buff & black 27.50 26.00
J33 D3 20c buff & black 27.50 40.00
J34 D3 30c buff & black 27.50 26.00
J35 D3 40c buff & black 27.50 26.00
J36 D3 50c buff & black 40.00 26.00
J37 D3 60c buff & black 40.00 26.00
J38 D3 1 l blue & black 60.00 40.00
J39 D3 2 l blue & black 95.00 40.00
J40 D3 5 l blue & black 110.00 55.00
J41 D3 10 l blue & black 130.00 80.00
Nos. J31-J41 (11) 612.50 420.00

Numerals and Ovpt. Invtd.
J32a D3 10c 240.00
J33a D3 20c 800.00
J34a D3 30c 240.00
J35a D3 40c 240.00
J36a D3 50c 240.00
J37a D3 60c 240.00

Postage Due Stamps of Italy, 1934, Overprinted in Black

1934, May 12
J42 D6 5c brown .80 6.50
J43 D6 10c blue .80 6.50
J44 D6 20c rose red 4.00 13.00
J45 D6 25c green 4.00 13.00
J46 D6 30c red orange 12.00 17.50
J47 D6 40c black brown 12.00 26.00
J48 D6 50c violet 20.00 8.00
J49 D6 60c black 20.00 45.00
J50 D7 1 l red orange 27.50 19.00
J51 D7 2 l green 47.50 45.00
J52 D7 5 l violet 52.50 87.50
J53 D7 10 l blue 52.50 95.00
J54 D7 20 l carmine 60.00 130.00
Nos. J42-J54 (13) 313.60 512.00

Catalogue values for unused stamps in this section, from this point to the end of the section, are for Never Hinged items.

Somalia

D5

1950 **Wmk. 277** **Photo.** **Perf. 14**
J55 D5 1c dark gray violet 4.00 4.00
J56 D5 2c deep blue 4.00 4.00
J57 D5 5c blue green 4.00 4.00
J58 D5 10c rose lilac 4.00 4.00
J59 D5 40c violet 14.50 14.50
J60 D5 1s dark brown 20.00 20.00
Nos. J55-J60 (6) 50.50 50.50

PARCEL POST STAMPS

These stamps were used by affixing them to the way bill so that one half remained on it following the parcel, the other half staying on the receipt given the sender. Most used halves are right halves. Complete stamps were and are obtainable canceled, probably to order. Both unused and used values are for complete stamps.

Parcel Post Stamps of Italy, 1914-17, Overprinted

1917-19 **Wmk. 140** **Perf. 13½**
Q1 PP2 5c brown 8.00 67.50
a. Double overprint 475.00 —
Q2 PP2 10c blue 9.50 45.00
Q3 PP2 20c black ('19) 350.00 190.00
Q4 PP2 25c red 16.00 80.00
a. Double overprint
Q5 PP2 50c orange 160.00 95.00
Q6 PP2 1 l lilac 52.50 95.00
Q7 PP2 2 l green 72.50 95.00
Q8 PP2 3 l bister 80.00 160.00
Q9 PP2 4 l slate 87.50 160.00
Nos. Q1-Q9 (9) 836.00 987.50

Halves Used
Q1 1.60
Q2 1.60
Q3 7.25
Q4 3.50
Q5 6.00
Q6 4.75
Q7 4.75
Q8 4.75
Q9 4.75

Nos. Q5-Q9 were overprinted in 1922 with a slightly different type in which the final "A" of SOMALIA is directly over the final "A" of ITAL-IANA. They were not regularly issued. Value for set: unused $1,600; never hinged $2,400.

Parcel Post Stamps of Italy, 1914-17, Overprinted

1923
Q10 PP2 25c red 72.50 160.00
Q11 PP2 50c orange 110.00 160.00
Q12 PP2 1 l violet 125.00 250.00
Q13 PP2 2 l green 125.00 250.00
Q14 PP2 3 l bister 200.00 250.00
Q15 PP2 4 l slate 200.00 250.00
Nos. Q10-Q15 (6) 832.50 1,320.

Halves Used
Q10 4.75
Q11 4.75
Q12 3.00
Q13 3.00
Q14 4.75
Q15 5.50

Parcel Post Stamps of Italy, 1914-17, Surcharged

1923
Q16 PP2 3b on 5c brown 27.50 35.00
Q17 PP2 5b on 5c brown 27.50 35.00
Q18 PP2 10b on 10c blue 27.50 32.50
Q19 PP2 25b on 25c red 27.50 52.50
Q20 PP2 50b on 50c org 35.00 75.00
Q21 PP2 1r on 1 l lilac 47.50 75.00
Q22 PP2 2r on 2 l green 80.00 120.00
Q23 PP2 3r on 3 l bister 80.00 120.00
Q24 PP2 4r on 4 l slate 95.00 120.00
Nos. Q16-Q24 (9) 447.50 665.00

Halves Used
Q16 1.60
Q17 1.60
Q18 1.60
Q19 3.25
Q20 3.25
Q21 3.25
Q22 3.25
Q23 3.25
Q24 3.25

No. Q16 has the numeral "3" at the left also.

Parcel Post Stamps of Italy, 1914-22 Overprinted

1926-31 **Red Overprint**
Q25 PP2 5c brown 32.50 80.00
Q26 PP2 10c blue 32.50 80.00
Q27 PP2 20c black 72.50 80.00
Q28 PP2 25c red 72.50 80.00
Q29 PP2 50c orange 72.50 80.00
Q30 PP2 1 l violet 95.00 80.00
Q31 PP2 2 l green 160.00 80.00
Q32 PP2 3 l yellow 27.50 80.00
Q33 PP2 4 l slate 27.50 80.00
Q34 PP2 10 l vio brn ('30) 55.00 105.00
Q35 PP2 12 l red brn ('31) 55.00 105.00
Q36 PP2 15 l olive ('31) 55.00 190.00
Q37 PP2 20 l dull vio ('31) 55.00 190.00
Nos. Q25-Q37 (13) 812.50 1,310.

Halves Used
Q25 2.00
Q26 2.00
Q27 3.25
Q28 3.25
Q29 3.25
Q30 3.25
Q31 3.25
Q32 3.25

Q33			3.25
Q34			4.00
Q35			4.00
Q36			4.00
Q37			4.00

Nos. Q25-Q31 come with two types of overprint: I — The first "I" and last "A" of ITALIANA extend slightly at both sides of SOMALIA. II — Only the I" extends. These seven stamps with type I overprint were not regularly issued, and Nos. Q27-Q31 (type I) sell for less than with type II overprint.

Black Overprint

Q38	PP2	10 l violet brown	80.00	87.50
Q39	PP2	12 l red brown	55.00	87.50
Q40	PP2	15 l olive	55.00	87.50
Q41	PP2	20 l dull violet	55.00	87.50
	Nos. Q38-Q41 (4)		245.00	350.00

Halves Used

Q38	4.00
Q39	4.00
Q40	4.00
Q41	4.00

Same Overprint on Parcel Post Stamps of Italy, 1927-38

1928-39   **Black Overprint**

Q42	PP3	25c red, type I ('31)	40.00	47.50
		Never hinged	160.00	
Q43	PP3	30c ultra	3.25	4.75
Q43A	PP3	50c orange	12,750.	
Q44	PP3	60c red	3.25	8.00
Q45	PP3	1 l lilac brn, type II ('31)	40.00	52.50
Q46	PP3	2 l green, type II ('31)	40.00	52.50
Q47	PP3	3 l bister	6.50	20.00
Q48	PP3	4 l gray black	6.50	20.00
Q49	PP3	10 l rose lil	475.00	550.00
Q50	PP3	20 l lil brn ('34)	475.00	600.00
	Nos. Q42-Q43, Q44-Q50 (9)		1,089.	1,355.

Halves Used

Q42	8.75
Q43	.45
Q43A	160.00
Q44	.45
Q45	2.75
Q46	2.75
Q47	.80
Q48	.80
Q49	20.00
Q50	20.00

The 25c, 1 l and 2 l come with both types of overprint (see note below No. Q37). Both types were regularly issued. Values are for type I on 25c, type II on 1 l and 2 l.

Red Overprint

Q51	PP3	5c brown ('39)	16.00	
Q52	PP3	3 l bister ('30)	32.50	80.00
		Half stamp		2.00
Q53	PP3	4 l gray black ('30)	32.50	80.00
		Half stamp		2.00
	Nos. Q51-Q53 (3)		81.00	

Same Overprint in Black on Italy Nos. Q24-Q25

1940   **Perf. 13**

Q54	PP3	5c brown	3.25	11.00
		Half stamp		.50
Q55	PP3	10c deep blue	4.00	11.00
		Half stamp		.50

> **Catalogue values for unused stamps in this section, from this point to the end of the section, are for Never Hinged items.**

Somalia

PP1

1950   **Wmk. 277**   **Photo.**   **Perf. 14**

Q56	PP1	1c cerise	9.50	9.50
Q57	PP1	3c dark gray violet	9.50	9.50
Q58	PP1	5c rose lilac	9.50	9.50
Q59	PP1	10c red orange	9.50	9.50
Q60	PP1	20c dark brown	9.50	9.50
Q61	PP1	50c blue green	24.00	24.00
Q62	PP1	1s violet	65.00	65.00
Q63	PP1	2s brown	80.00	80.00
Q64	PP1	3s blue	120.00	120.00
	Nos. Q56-Q64 (9)		336.50	336.50

Halves Used

Q56	.20
Q57	.20
Q58	.20
Q59	.20
Q60	.20
Q61	.25

Q62		1.60
Q63		2.00
Q64		3.25

SOMALI COAST

sō-'mä-lē 'kōst

(Djibouti)

LOCATION — Eastern Africa, bordering on the Gulf of Aden
GOVT. — French Overseas Territory
AREA — 8,500 sq. mi.
POP. — 86,000 (est. 1963)
CAPITAL — Djibouti (Jibuti)

The port of Obock, which issued postage stamps in 1892-1894, was included in the territory and began to use stamps of Somali Coast in 1902. See Obock in Vol. 4.

On Mar. 19, 1967, the territory changed its name to the French Territory of the Afars and Issas. The Republic of Djibouti was proclaimed June 27, 1977.

100 Centimes = 1 Franc

> **Catalogue values for unused stamps in this country are for Never Hinged items, beginning with Scott 224 in the regular postage section, Scott B13 in the semipostal section, Scott C1 in the airpost section, Scott CB1 in the airpost semi-postal section, and Scott J39 in the postage due section.**

Navigation and Commerce
A1   A2

A3

Camel and Rider
A4

Obock Nos. 32-33, 35, 45 with Overprint or Surcharge Handstamped in Black, Blue or Red

1894   **Unwmk.**   **Perf. 14x13½**

1	A1	5c grn & red, *grnsh* (with bar)	190.00	160.00
a.		Without bar	1,400.	925.00
2	A2	25c on 2c brn & bl, *buff* (Bl & Bk)	400.00	250.00
a.		"25" omitted	1,150.	950.00
b.		"25" double	1,850.	
c.		"DJIBOUTI" omitted	1,150.	950.00
d.		"DJIBOUTI" inverted	1,300.	1,100.
e.		"DJIBOUTI" double	1,850.	1,400.
3	A3	50c on 1c blk & red, *bl* (R & Bl)	400.00	275.00
a.		"5" instead of "50"	1,800.	1,300.
b.		"0" instead of "50"	1,800.	1,300.
c.		"DJIBOUTI" omitted	1,800.	1,400.

Imperf

4	A4	1fr on 5fr car	725.00	575.00
a.		"DJIBOUTI" omitted	5,000.	
b.		"DJIBOUTI" double	2,200.	1,900.
c.		"1" double	2,200.	1,900.
5	A4	5fr carmine	2,200.	1,500.

Counterfeits exist of Nos. 4-5.

View of Djibouti, Somali Warriors — A5

French Gunboat
A7

Crossing Desert (Size: 66mm wide, including simulated perfs.) — A8

Designs: 15c, 25c, 30c, 40c, 50c, 75c, Different views of Djibouti. 1fr, 2fr, Djibouti quay.

Imperf. (Simulated Perforations in Frame Color)

1894-1902   **Typo.**
Quadrille Lines Printed on Paper

6	A5	1c blk & claret	4.00	3.25
7	A5	2c claret & blk	4.00	3.25
8	A5	4c vio brn & bl	16.00	9.50
9	A5	5c bl grn & red	16.00	7.25
10	A5	5c grn & yel grn ('02)	12.00	8.75
11	A5	10c brown & grn	20.00	8.75
a.		Half used as 5c on cover		200.00
12	A5	15c violet & grn	20.00	8.75
13	A5	25c rose & blue	32.50	11.00
14	A5	30c gray brn & rose	20.00	12.00
a.		Half used as 15c on cover		600.00
15	A5	40c org & bl ('00)	60.00	40.00
a.		Half used as 20c on cover		950.00
16	A5	50c blue & rose	32.50	20.00
a.		Half used as 25c on cover		2,000.
17	A5	75c violet & org	55.00	45.00
18	A5	1fr ol grn & blk	28.00	20.00
19	A5	2fr gray brn & rose	105.00	80.00
a.		Half used as 1fr on cover		2,400.
20	A7	5fr rose & blue	210.00	150.00
21	A8	25fr rose & blue	1,050.	1,100.
22	A8	50fr blue & rose	675.00	750.00
	Nos. 6-20 (15)		635.00	427.50

High values are found with the overprint "S" (Specimen) erased and, usually, a cancellation added.
Values for bisects are for complete covers, newspapers or other printed matter.
For surcharges see Nos. 24-27B.

A9

1899   **Black Surcharge**

23	A9	40c on 4c brn & bl	3,400.	35.00
a.		Double surcharge	6,500.	1,600.
b.		Pair, one without surcharge		4,750.
c.		Inverted surcharge		1,800.
d.		Double surcharge, both inverted		3,400.

Nos. 17-20 Surcharged

1902   **Blue Surcharge**

24	A5	0.05c on 75c	80.00	47.50
a.		Inverted surcharge	650.00	575.00
b.		Double surcharge	650.00	575.00
c.		Pair, one without surcharge	2,800.	
25	A5	0.10c on 1fr	92.50	72.50
a.		Inverted surcharge	575.00	450.00
b.		Double surcharge	575.00	450.00
26	A5	0.40c on 2fr	650.00	450.00
a.		Double surcharge	2,250.	2,100.

Black Surcharge

27	A7	0.75c on 5fr	650.00	450.00
a.		Inverted surcharge	3,000.	2,400.
b.		Double surcharge	3,000.	2,400.

Obock No. 57 Surcharged in Blue

27B	A7	0.05c on 75c gray lil & org	1,700.	1,200.

A10

Nos. 15-16 Surcharged in Black

28	A10	5c on 40c	8.75	5.50
a.		Double surcharge	150.00	150.00
29	A10	10c on 50c	32.50	32.50
a.		Inverted surcharge	575.00	550.00
b.		Double surcharge	675.00	

Surcharged on Stamps of Obock

Group of Warriors
A11

Black Surcharge

30	A11	5c on 30c bis & yel grn	20.00	12.00
a.		Inverted surcharge	325.00	325.00
b.		Double surcharge	350.00	325.00
c.		Triple surcharge	1,700.	

A12

Red Surcharge

31	A12	10c on 25c blk & bl	20.00	14.50
a.		Inverted surcharge	325.00	325.00
b.		Double surcharge	350.00	350.00
c.		Triple surcharge	1,850.	1,850.
d.		"Djibouti" omitted	1,000.	1,400.

A13

Black Surcharge

32	A13	10c on 10fr org & red vio	45.00	35.00
a.		Double surcharge	275.00	225.00
b.		Double surch., one invtd.	2,500.	2,400.
c.		Triple surcharge	1,700.	1,700.
d.		"Djibouti" omitted	130.00	92.50

Black Surcharge

33	A14	10c on 2fr dl vio & org	72.50	60.00
a.	Double surcharge		525.00	500.00
b.	Double surcharge, one inverted		2,500.	2,500.
c.	Triplr surcharge, one inverted		3,100.	3,100.
d.	"DJIBOUTI" inverted		275.00	260.00
e.	Large "0" in "10"		160.00	130.00

Same Surcharge on Obock No. 53 in Red

33D	A7	10c on 25c blk & bl	35,000.	25,000.

A14a

Black Surcharge on Obock Nos. 63-64

33E	A14a	5c on 25fr brn & bl	67.50	60.00
33F	A14a	10c on 50fr red vio & grn	92.50	67.50
g.	"01" instead of "10"		260.00	240.00
h.	"CENTIMES" inverted		3,250.	3,250.
i.	Double surcharge		2,800.	2,400.
k.	Double surcharge, one inverted		2,800.	2,600.

Tadjoura Mosque A15

Somalis on Camel A16

Warriors — A17

1902		Engr.	Perf. 11½	
34	A15	1c brn vio & org	1.20	1.20
35	A15	2c yel brn & yel grn	1.60	1.60
36	A15	4c bl & carmine	2.75	2.40
37	A15	5c bl grn & yel grn	3.25	2.00
38	A15	10c car & red org	7.25	4.75
39	A15	15c brn org & bl	7.25	4.75
40	A16	20c vio & green	17.00	8.75
41	A16	25c blue	26.00	14.50
a.	25c indigo & blue ('03)		28.00	16.00
42	A16	30c red & black	7.25	5.50
43	A16	40c orange & blue	17.50	10.50
44	A16	50c grn & red org	52.50	45.00
45	A16	75c orange & vio	12.00	7.25
46	A17	1fr red org & vio	32.50	20.00
47	A17	2fr yel grn & car	47.50	35.00
a.	Without names of designer and engraver at bottom		160.00	160.00
48	A17	5fr orange & blue	32.50	28.00
	Nos. 34-48 (15)		268.05	191.20

1903				
49	A15	1c brn vio & blk	1.20	1.20
50	A15	2c yel brn & blk	1.60	1.20
51	A15	4c lake & blk	2.00	2.00
a.	4c red & black		3.25	2.75
52	A15	5c bl grn & blk	4.75	3.50
53	A15	10c carmine & blk	9.50	4.50

54	A15	15c org brn & blk	21.00	11.00
a.	15c brown & black		21.00	11.00
55	A16	20c dl vio & blk	27.50	20.00
56	A16	25c ultra & blk	16.00	11.00
58	A16	40c orange & blk	12.00	12.00
a.	40c bister & black		26.00	26.00
59	A16	50c green & blk	27.50	17.00
60	A16	75c buff & blk	14.50	13.00
a.	75c brown orange & black		87.50	87.50
61	A17	1fr orange & blk	24.00	26.00
62	A17	2fr yel grn & blk	13.50	10.50
a.	Without names of designer and engraver at bottom		55.00	55.00
63	A17	5fr red org & blk	28.00	24.00
a.	5fr ocher & black		40.00	35.00
	Nos. 49-63 (14)		203.05	156.90

Imperforates, transposed colors and inverted centers exist in the 1902 and 1903 issues. Most of these were issued from Paris and some are said to have been fraudulently printed.

Tadjoura Mosque A18

Somalis on Camel — A19

Warriors — A20

1909		Typo.	Perf. 14x13½	
64	A18	1c maroon & brn	1.20	1.20
65	A18	2c vio & ol gray	1.20	1.20
66	A18	4c ol gray & bl	1.60	1.20
67	A18	5c grn & gray grn	2.00	1.20
68	A18	10c car & ver	5.25	2.00
69	A18	20c blk & red brn	8.00	6.50
70	A19	25c bl & pale bl	5.50	4.50
71	A19	30c brn & scar	8.75	6.50
72	A19	35c vio & grn	11.00	8.00
73	A19	40c rose & vio	10.50	7.25
74	A19	45c brn & bl grn	10.50	7.25
75	A19	50c maroon & brn	10.50	8.00
76	A19	75c scarlet & grn	24.00	16.00
77	A20	1fr vio & brn	28.00	26.00
78	A20	2fr brn & rose	45.00	35.00
79	A20	5fr vio brn & bl grn	72.50	52.50
	Nos. 64-79 (16)		245.50	184.30

Drummer A21

Somali Girl A22

Djibouti-Addis Ababa Railroad Bridge — A23

1915-33			Perf. 13½x14	
		Chalky Paper		
80	A21	1c brt vio & red brn	.25	.30
81	A21	2c ocher & ind	.25	.25
82	A21	4c dk brn & red	.30	.40
83	A21	5c yel grn & grn	1.20	1.20
84	A21	5c org & dl red ('22)	.80	.80
85	A22	10c car & dk red	2.10	1.90
86	A22	10c ap grn & grn ('22)	1.20	1.20
87	A22	10c ver & grn ('25)	.50	.55
88	A22	15c brn vio & car ('18)	1.20	.80
89	A22	20c org & blk brn	.40	.40
90	A22	20c dp grn & bl grn ('25)	.40	.40

91	A22	20c dk grn & red ('27)	.55	.55
92	A22	25c ultra & dl bl	1.20	.95
93	A22	25c blk & bl grn ('22)	1.20	1.20
94	A22	30c blk & bl grn	2.40	2.40
95	A22	30c rose & red brn ('22)	1.60	1.60
96	A22	30c vio & ol grn ('25)	.50	.55
97	A22	30c grn & dl grn ('27)	.55	.55
98	A22	35c lt grn & dl rose	.80	.80
99	A22	40c bl & brn vio	1.20	.80
100	A22	45c red brn & dk bl	1.20	.80
101	A22	50c car rose & blk	12.00	8.00
102	A22	50c ultra & ind ('24)	1.60	1.60
103	A22	50c dk brn & red ('25)	.90	.65
104	A22	60c ol grn & red vio ('25)	.65	.65
105	A22	65c car rose & ol grn ('25)	.80	.80
106	A22	75c dl vio & choc ('25)	.80	.80
107	A22	75c ind & ultra ('25)	.70	.80
108	A22	75c brt vio & ol brn ('27)	2.10	1.75
109	A22	85c vio brn & bl grn ('25)	1.20	1.20
110	A22	90c brn red & brt red ('30)	8.75	6.50
111	A23	1fr bis brn & red ('28)	2.40	1.60
112	A23	1.10fr lt brn & ultra ('28)	4.75	6.50
113	A23	1.25fr dk bl & blk brn ('33)	10.50	8.75
114	A23	1.50fr lt bl & dk bl ('30)	1.60	1.60
115	A23	1.75fr gray grn & lt red ('33)	8.75	5.50
116	A23	2fr bl vio & blk	4.00	3.25
117	A23	3fr red vio ('30)	12.00	4.50
118	A23	5fr rose red & blk	7.25	4.75
	Nos. 80-118 (39)		100.55	76.90

No. 99 is on ordinary paper.
For surcharges and overprints see Nos. 119-134, 183-193.

Nos. 83, 92 Surcharged in Green or Blue

1922				
119	A21	10c on 5c (G)	.80	.80
a.	Double surcharge		125.00	
120	A22	50c on 25c (Bl)	.80	.80

Type of 1915 Surcharged in Various Colors

1922				
121	A22	0,01c on 15c vio & rose (Bk)	.30	.50
122	A22	0,02c on 15c vio & rose (Bl)	.50	.70
123	A22	0,04c on 15c vio & rose (G)	.80	.80
124	A22	0,05c on 15c vio & rose (R)	.80	.80
	Nos. 121-124 (4)		2.40	2.80

Nos. 88, 99 and Type of 1915 Surcharged

1923-27				
125	A22	60c on 75c ol grn & vio	.80	.80
126	A22	65c on 15c ('25)	2.75	3.25
127	A22	85c on 40c ('25)	2.00	2.40
128	A22	90c on 75c brn red & red ('27)	5.50	6.50
	Nos. 125-128 (4)		11.05	12.95

No. 118 and Type of 1915-17 Surcharged with New Value and Bars in Black or Red

1924-27				
129	A23	25c on 5fr	1.60	1.60
130	A23	1.25fr on 1fr dk bl & ultra (R) ('26)	1.20	1.20
131	A23	1.50fr on 1fr lt bl & dk bl ('27)	1.20	1.60
132	A23	3fr on 5fr ver & red vio ('27)	5.50	6.50
133	A23	10fr on 5fr brn red & ol brn ('27)	9.50	11.00
134	A23	20fr on 5fr gray grn & lil rose ('27)	15.00	18.50
	Nos. 129-134 (6)		34.00	40.40

Common Design Types
pictured following the introduction.

Colonial Exposition Issue
Common Design Types
Engr., Name of Country Typo. in Black

1931			Perf. 12½	
135	CD70	40c deep green	6.50	6.50
136	CD71	50c violet	6.50	6.50
137	CD72	90c red orange	6.50	6.50
138	CD73	1.50fr dull blue	6.50	6.50
	Nos. 135-138 (4)		26.00	26.00

Paris International Exposition Issue
Common Design Types

1937		Engr.	Perf. 13	
139	CD74	20c deep violet	2.10	2.10
140	CD75	30c dark green	2.10	2.10
141	CD76	40c carmine rose	2.10	2.10
142	CD77	50c dk brn & bl	2.25	2.25
143	CD78	90c red	2.00	2.00
144	CD79	1.50fr ultra	2.40	2.40
	Nos. 139-144 (6)		12.95	12.95

Colonial Arts Exhibition Issue
Souvenir Sheet
Common Design Type

1937			Imperf.	
145	CD75	3fr dull violet	13.00	15.00

Mosque of Djibouti — A24

Somali Warriors — A25

Governor Léonce Lagarde — A26

View of Djibouti — A27

1938-40			Perf. 12x12½, 12½	
146	A24	2c dull red vio	.25	.25
147	A24	3c slate grn ('40)	.25	.25
148	A24	4c dull red brn	.25	.25
149	A24	5c carmine	.25	.25
150	A24	10c blue gray	.25	.25
151	A24	15c slate black	.30	.30

152	A24	20c dark orange	.30	.30
153	A25	25c dark brown	.90	.70
154	A25	30c dark blue	.40	.40
155	A25	35c olive grn	1.05	.80
156	A24	40c org brn ('40)	.25	.25
157	A24	45c dull grn ('40)	.35	.35
158	A25	50c red	.70	.55
159	A25	55c dull red vio	1.05	.80
160	A25	60c black ('40)	.70	.70
161	A25	65c orange brown	1.10	.95
162	A25	70c lt violet ('40)	1.45	1.45
163	A26	80c gray blk	2.75	2.10
164	A26	90c rose vio ('39)	1.60	1.60
165	A26	1fr carmine	3.50	2.40
166	A26	1fr black ('40)	.55	.55
167	A26	1.25fr magenta	1.30	1.30
168	A26	1.40fr pck bl ('40)	1.20	1.20
169	A26	1.50fr dull green	1.20	1.20
170	A26	1.60fr brn car ('40)	1.20	1.20
171	A26	1.75fr ultra	1.60	1.20
172	A26	2fr dk orange	1.20	1.20
173	A26	2.25fr ultra ('39)	2.00	2.00
174	A26	2.50fr org brn ('40)	2.10	2.10
175	A26	3fr dull violet	1.20	1.20
176	A27	5fr brn & pale cl	2.40	2.40
177	A27	10fr ind & pale bl	2.75	2.75
178	A27	20fr car lake & gray	2.75	2.75
		Nos. 146-178 (33)	39.10	35.95

For types A24-A26 without "RF," see Nos. 237A-237C.
For overprints and surcharge see Nos. 194-223.

New York World's Fair Issue
Common Design Type

1939		**Engr.**	**Perf. 12½x12**	
179	CD82	1.25fr car lake	1.40	1.40
180	CD82	2.25fr ultra	1.50	1.50

Mosque of Djibouti and Marshal Pétain — A28

1941, Nov. 10	**Engr.**	**Perf. 12x12½**	
181	A28	1fr yellow brown	.80
182	A28	2.50fr blue	.80

Nos. 181-182 were issued by the Vichy government in France, but were not placed on sale in Somali Coast.
For surcharges, see Nos. B11-B12.

Nos. 80-82, 84, 88, 91, 97, 103, 105, 114-115 Overprinted in Black or Red

Perf. 13½x14, 14x13½

1943			**Unwmk.**	
183	A21	1c	3.25	3.25
184	A21	2c	3.25	3.25
185	A21	4c	30.00	30.00
186	A21	5c	3.25	3.25
187	A22	15c	10.50	10.50
188	A22	20c	3.25	3.25
189	A22	30c	3.25	3.25
190	A22	50c	3.25	3.25
191	A22	65c	3.25	3.25
192	A23	1.50fr (R)	3.25	3.25
193	A23	1.75fr	13.50	13.50
		Nos. 183-193 (11)	80.00	80.00

Stamps of 1938-40 Overprinted in Black or Red

On A24   On A25

On A26

On A27

1943		**Perf. 12x12½, 12½**		
194	A24	2c dl red vio	4.00	4.00
195	A24	3c sl grn (R)	4.00	4.00
196	A24	4c dl red brn	4.00	4.00
197	A24	5c carmine	4.00	4.00
198	A24	10c bl gray (R)	1.20	1.20
199	A24	15c sl blk (R)	4.00	4.00
200	A24	20c dk org	4.00	4.00
201	A25	25c dk brn (R)	4.00	4.00
202	A25	30c dk bl (R)	1.20	1.20
203	A25	35c olive (R)	4.75	4.75
204	A24	40c brn org	1.20	1.20
205	A25	45c dl grn (R)	4.75	4.75
206	A25	55c dl red vio (R)	4.00	4.00
207	A25	60c blk (R)	1.20	1.20
208	A25	70c lt vio (R)	1.20	1.20
a.		Inverted overprint	275.00	275.00
b.		Double overprint	325.00	325.00
209	A26	80c gray blk (R)	1.60	1.60
210	A26	90c rose vio (R)	1.20	1.20
211	A26	1.25fr magenta	2.40	2.40
212	A26	1.40fr pck bl (R)	1.20	1.20
213	A26	1.50fr dl grn	2.40	2.40
214	A26	1.60fr brn car	2.40	2.40
215	A26	1.75fr ultra (R)	12.00	12.00
216	A26	2fr dk org	1.60	1.60
217	A26	2.25fr ultra (R)	2.40	2.40
218	A26	2.50fr chestnut	2.00	2.00
219	A26	3fr dl vio (R)	2.40	2.40
220	A27	5fr brn & pale cl	15.00	15.00
221	A27	10fr ind & pale bl	180.00	180.00
222	A27	20fr car lake & gray	12.00	12.00

The space between overprint on Nos. 206 and 208 measures 10½mm.

No. 161 Surcharged in Black

223	A25	50c on 65c org brn	1.60	1.60
		Nos. 194-223 (30)	287.70	287.70

Catalogue values for unused stamps in this section, from this point to the end of the section, are for Never Hinged items.

Locomotive and Palms — A29

1943		**Unwmk. Photo.**	**Perf. 14½x14**	
224	A29	5c royal blue	.40	.25
225	A29	10c pink	.40	.25
226	A29	25c emerald	.70	.55
227	A29	30c gray blk	.70	.55
228	A29	40c violet	.70	.55
229	A29	80c red brn	.70	.55
230	A29	1fr aqua	.70	.55
231	A29	1.50fr scarlet	.70	.55
232	A29	2fr brown	.70	.55
233	A29	2.50fr ultra	1.10	.90
234	A29	4fr brt org	1.45	1.10
235	A29	5fr dp rose lil	1.45	1.10
236	A29	10fr lt ultra	1.60	1.30
237	A29	20fr green	2.10	1.60
		Nos. 224-237 (14)	13.40	10.35

For surcharges see Nos. 240-247.

Types of 1938-40 Without "RF"

1944, Apr. 3		**Engr.**	**Perf. 12½**	
237A	A24	40c org brn		1.25
237B	A25	50c red		1.60
237C	A26	1.50fr dull green		2.40
		Nos. 237A-237C (3)		5.25

Nos. 237A-237C were issued by the Vichy government in France, but were not placed on sale in Somali Coast.

Eboue Issue
Common Design Type

1945		**Engr.**	**Perf. 13**	
238	CD91	2fr black	1.25	1.25
239	CD91	25fr Prus grn	2.00	2.00

Nos. 238 and 239 exist imperforate.

Nos. 224, 226 and 233 Surcharged in Carmine or Black

1945			**Perf. 14½x14**	
240	A29	50c on 5c (C)	.80	.65
a.		Inverted surcharge	350.00	
b.		Double surcharge	275.00	
241	A29	60c on 5c (C)	.80	.65
a.		Inverted surcharge	260.00	
b.		Double surcharge	210.00	
242	A29	70c on 5c (C)	.80	.65
a.		Inverted surcharge	252.00	
b.		Double surcharge, one inverted	375.00	
243	A29	1.20fr on 5c (C)	.95	.70
a.		Double surcharge, one inverted	375.00	
244	A29	2.40fr on 25c	1.30	.95
a.		Inverted surcharge	275.00	
b.		Double surcharge	250.00	
c.		Bars doubly surcharged	140.00	
245	A29	3fr on 25c	1.30	.95
a.		Double surcharge, one inverted	425.00	
246	A29	4.50fr on 25c	1.45	1.00
a.		Inverted surcharge	250.00	
247	A29	15fr on 2.50fr (C)	2.25	1.60
a.		Surcharge bars omitted	210.00	
b.		Value doubly surcharged	275.00	
		Nos. 240-247 (8)	9.65	7.15

Danakil Tent — A30

Khor-Angar Outpost A31

Obock-Tadjouran Road — A32

Somali Woman A33

Somali Village A34

Djibouti Mosque A35

1947		**Unwmk. Photo.**	**Perf. 13**	
248	A30	10c vio bl & org	.30	.25
249	A30	30c ol brn & org	.30	.25
250	A30	40c dp plum & org	.30	.25
251	A31	50c bl grn & org	.50	.30
252	A31	60c choc & dp yel	.50	.30
253	A31	80c vio bl & org	.50	.30
254	A32	1fr bl & choc	.50	.30
255	A32	1.20fr bl grn & ol grn	1.30	.95
256	A32	1.50fr org & vio bl	.65	.30
257	A33	2fr red lil & bl gray	.95	.65
258	A33	3fr dp bl & brn org	1.45	.95
259	A33	3.60fr car rose & cop red	2.50	2.00
260	A33	4fr choc & bl gray	1.90	1.25
261	A34	5fr org & choc	1.25	.80
262	A34	6fr gray bl & int bl	2.00	.95
263	A34	10fr gray bl & red lil	2.00	1.05
264	A35	15fr choc, gray bl & pink	2.40	1.25
265	A35	20fr dk bl, gray bl & org	3.25	1.60
266	A35	25fr vio brn, lil rose & gray bl	7.25	4.00
		Nos. 248-266 (19)	29.80	17.70

Military Medal Issue
Common Design Type

1952		**Engraved and Typographed**		
267	CD101	15fr blk, grn, yel & dk pur	10.50	8.75

Imperforates
Most stamps of Somali Coast from 1956 onward exist imperforate in issued and trial colors, and also in small presentation sheets in issued colors.

FIDES Issue
Common Design Type and

Lighthouse, Ras-Bir — A36

15fr, Loading ship and map, Djibouti.

1956		**Unwmk. Engr.**	**Perf. 13**	
268	CD103	15fr purple	2.40	1.60
269	A36	40fr dp ultra & gray	3.50	2.00

Flower Issue
Common Design Type

Design: 10fr, Haemanthus, horiz.

1958		**Photo.**	**Perf. 12½x12**	
270	CD104	10fr grn, red & yel	4.00	1.60

Wart Hog — A37

40c, Cheetah. 50c, Gerenuk, vert.

1958		**Engr.**	**Perf. 13**	
271	A37	30c red brn & sepia	.80	.40
272	A37	40c brn & olive	.80	.40
273	A37	50c brn, grn & gray	1.25	.80
		Nos. 271-273,C21 (4)	13.85	7.10

Human Rights Issue
Common Design Type

1958, Dec. 10			**Unwmk.**	
274	CD105	20fr brt pur & dk bl	3.25	2.40

Universal Declaration of Human Rights, 10th anniv.

Parrotfish
A38

Designs: Various Tropical Fish.

1959		Engr.	Perf. 13	
275	A38	1fr brt bl, brn & red org	.95	.55
276	A38	2fr blk, lt bl, yel & grn	.95	.55
277	A38	3fr vio & blk brn	.95	.55
278	A38	4fr brt grnsh bl, org & lt brn	1.25	.80
279	A38	5fr brt grnsh bl & blk	2.00	1.00
280	A38	20fr brt bl, dl bred brn & rose	3.50	2.25
281	A38	25fr red, grn & ultra	5.50	2.75
282	A38	60fr bl & dk grn	13.00	5.50
		Nos. 275-282 (8)	28.10	13.95

No. 276 is vertical.

Flamingo — A39

Birds: 15fr, Bee-eater, horiz. 30fr, Sacred ibis, horiz. 75fr, Pink-backed pelican.

1960		Unwmk.	Perf. 13	
283	A39	10fr bluish grn, bis & cl	3.25	1.60
284	A39	15fr rose lil, grn & yel	4.00	1.60
285	A39	30fr bl, blk, org & brn	8.75	4.75
286	A39	75fr grn, sl grn & yel	13.50	8.00
		Nos. 283-286 (4)	29.50	15.95

Dragon Tree — A40

Klipspringer A41

Meleagrina Margaritifera A42

Designs: 4fr, Cony. 6fr, Large flatfish. 25fr, Fennecs. 40fr, Griffon vulture.

1962, Mar. 24		Engr.	Perf. 13	
287	A40	2fr grn, yel, org & brn	2.40	1.60
288	A40	4fr ocher & choc	2.40	1.60
289	A40	6fr brn, mar, grn & yel	4.75	3.25
290	A40	25fr red brn, ocher & grn	5.50	5.50
291	A40	40fr dk bl, brn & gray	13.00	8.00
292	A41	50fr bis, bl & lil	13.00	9.50
		Nos. 287-292 (6)	45.05	29.45

1962, Nov. 24   **Photo.**

Sea Shells: 10fr, Tridacna squamosa, horiz. 25fr, Strombus tricornis, horiz. 30fr, Trochus dentatus.

Shells in Natural Colors

293	A42	8fr red & blk	2.00	1.00
294	A42	10fr car rose & blk	2.00	1.25
295	A42	25fr dp bl & brn	4.50	1.75
296	A42	30fr rose lil & brn	4.50	2.25
		Nos. 293-296 (4)	13.00	6.25

See Nos. C28-C29.

Red Cross Centenary Issue
Common Design Type

1963, Sept. 2		Engr.	Perf. 13	
297	CD113	50fr org brn, gray & car	7.25	7.25

Astraea Coral — A43

Design: 6fr, Organ-pipe coral.

1963, Nov. 30		Photo.	Perf. 13x13½	
298	A43	5fr multi	2.40	1.60
299	A43	6fr multi	2.40	1.60

See Nos. C26-C27, C30.

Human Rights Issue
Common Design Type

1963, Dec. 20		Engr.	Perf. 13	
300	CD117	70fr dk brn & ultra	9.50	9.50

Philatec Issue
Common Design Type

1964, Apr. 7		Unwmk.	Perf. 13	
301	CD118	80fr dp lil rose, grn & brn	8.75	8.75

Houri (Somali Sailboats) A44

Design: 25fr, Sambouk (Somali sailboats).

1964, June 9		Engr.		
302	A44	15fr multi	2.00	1.10
303	A44	25fr multi	2.75	1.75

View of Dadwayya and Map of Somali Coast A45

Design: 20fr, View of Tadjourah and map of Somali Coast.

1965, Oct. 20		Engr.	Perf. 13	
304	A45	6fr ultra, sl grn & red brn	1.25	.80
305	A45	20fr ultra, org brn & brt grn	1.25	1.25

Senna — A46

1966		Engr.	Perf. 13	
306	A46	5fr shown	1.60	1.25
307	A46	8fr Poinciana	1.60	1.25
308	A46	25fr Aloe	2.00	2.00
		Nos. 306-308,C41 (4)	10.70	8.00

Desert Monitor A47

1967, May 8		Engr.	Perf. 13	
309	A47	20fr red brn, ocher & sepia	6.50	4.75

Stamps of Somali Coast were replaced in 1967 by those of the French Territory of the Afars and Issas.

SEMI-POSTAL STAMPS

Somali Girl — SP1

1915		Unwmk.	Perf. 13½x14	
		Chalky Paper		
B1	SP1	10c + 5c car & dk red	10.50	9.50

Curie Issue
Common Design Type

1938		Engr.	Perf. 13	
B2	CD80	1.75fr + 50c brt ultra	8.75	8.75

French Revolution Issue
Common Design Type

Photo., Name and Value Typo. in Black

1939				
B3	CD83	45c + 25c green	10.50	10.50
B4	CD83	70c + 30c brown	10.50	10.50
B5	CD83	90c + 35c red org	10.50	10.50
B6	CD83	1.25fr + 1fr rose pink	10.50	10.50
B7	CD83	2.25fr + 2fr blue	10.50	10.50
		Nos. B3-B7 (5)	52.50	52.50

Common Design Type and

Somali Guard SP2

Local Police — SP3

1941		Photo.	Perf. 13½	
B8	SP2	1fr + 1fr red		1.60
B9	CD86	1.50fr + 3fr maroon		1.60
B10	SP3	2.50fr + 1fr blue		1.60
		Nos. B8-B10 (3)		4.80

Nos. B8-B10 were issued by the Vichy government in France, but were not placed on sale in Somali Coast.

Nos. 181-182 Surcharged in Black or Red

1944		Engr.	Perf. 12x12½	
B11		50c + 1.50fr on 2.50fr deep blue (R)		.95
B12		+ 2.50fr on 1fr yellow brown		1.00

Colonial Development Fund.

Nos. B11-B12 were issued by the Vichy government in France, but were not placed on sale in Somali Coast.

Catalogue values for unused stamps in this section, from this point to the end of the section, are for Never Hinged items.

Red Cross Issue
Common Design Type
Inscribed "Djibouti"

1944			Perf. 14½x14	
B13	CD90	5fr + 20fr emerald	2.40	2.00

The surtax was for the French Red Cross and national relief.

Tropical Medicine Issue
Common Design Type

1950		Engr.	Perf. 13	
B14	CD100	10fr + 2fr red brn & red	8.75	7.25

The surtax was for charitable work.

Anti-Malaria Issue
Common Design Type

1962, Apr. 7		Unwmk.	Perf. 13	
B15	CD108	25fr + 5fr aqua	7.25	7.25

Infant, Sun, Chest and Skulls SP4

1965, Dec. 10		Engr.	Perf. 13	
B16	SP4	25fr + 5fr ocher, sl & brt grn	2.75	2.75

Campaign against tuberculosis.

AIR POST STAMPS

Catalogue values for unused stamps in this section are for Never Hinged items.

Common Design Type
Inscribed "Djibouti"

1941		Unwmk.	Photo.	Perf. 14½x14	
C1	CD87	1fr dk orange		1.10	.90
C2	CD87	1.50fr brt red		1.20	.95
C3	CD87	5fr brown red		1.50	1.20
C4	CD87	10fr black		1.75	1.40
C5	CD87	25fr ultra		3.25	2.40
C6	CD87	50fr dark green		3.25	2.40
C7	CD87	100fr plum		4.75	3.50
		Nos. C1-C7 (7)		16.80	12.75

Obock & Djibouti

1943, June 21		Engr.	Perf. 13	
C7A		1.50fr red brown		1.25
C7B		4fr ultramarine		1.25

50th Ann. of transfer of capital from Obock to Djibouti.

Nos. C7A-C7B were issued by the Vichy government in France, but were not placed on sale in Somali Coast.

Victory Issue
Common Design Type

1946			Perf. 12½	
C8	CD92	8fr deep blue	2.00	1.60

Chad to Rhine Issue
Common Design Types
1946

C9	CD93	5fr gray black	2.40	1.90
C10	CD94	10fr dp orange	2.40	1.90
C11	CD95	15fr violet brn	2.40	1.90
C12	CD96	20fr brt violet	2.40	1.90
C13	CD97	25fr blue green	4.75	3.50
C14	CD98	50fr lt ultra	5.00	3.50
	Nos. C9-C14 (6)		19.35	14.60

Somali Gazing Skyward — AP1

Frontier Post, Loyada — AP2

Governor's Mansion, Djibouti — AP3

Perf. 12½x13, 13x12½
1947   Photo.   Unwmk.

C15	AP1	50fr gray bl & choc	7.25	1.60
C16	AP2	100fr multicolored	8.75	3.25
C17	AP3	200fr multicolored	12.00	4.75
	Nos. C15-C17 (3)		28.00	9.60

UPU Issue
Common Design Type
1949   Engr.   Perf. 13

C18	CD99	30fr bl, dp bl, brn red & grn	13.50	11.00

Liberation Issue
Common Design Type
1954, June 6

C19	CD102	15fr indigo & purple	12.00	9.50

Somali Woman and Map of Djibouti — AP4

1956, Feb. 20   Unwmk.

C20	AP4	500fr dk vio & rose vio	67.50	55.00

Mountain Reedbucks — AP5

1958, July 7   Engr.   Perf. 13

C21	AP5	100fr ultra, lt grn & dk red brn	11.00	5.50

Albert Bernard, Flag and Troops — AP6

1960, Jan. 18

C22	AP6	55fr ultra, sepia & car	2.75	2.00

25th death anniv. of Administrator Albert Bernard at Moraito.

Great Bustard — AP7

1960, Oct. 24   Unwmk.   Perf. 13

C23	AP7	200fr brn, org & slate	26.00	17.50

Salt Dealers' Caravan at Assal Lake — AP8

1962, Jan. 6   Engr.   Perf. 13

C24	AP8	500fr dk bl, red brn, pink & blk	27.50	17.50

Obock — AP9

1962, Mar. 11   Unwmk.   Perf. 13

C25	AP9	100fr blue & org brn	5.50	4.00

Centenary of the founding of Obock.

Rostellaria Magna — AP10

40fr, Millepore coral. 55fr, Brain coral. 100fr, Lambis bryonia (seashell). 200fr, Branch coral.

1962-63   Photo.   Perf. 13½x12½

C26	AP10	40fr multi ('63)	4.00	1.60
C27	AP10	55fr multi ('63)	5.50	4.00
C28	AP10	60fr multi	7.25	3.25
C29	AP10	100fr multi	11.00	5.50
C30	AP10	200fr multi ('63)	14.00	8.00
	Nos. C26-C30 (5)		41.75	22.35

Telstar Issue
Common Design Type
1963, Feb. 9   Engr.   Perf. 13

C31	CD111	20fr dp claret & dk grn	1.00	1.00

Zaroug (Somali Sailboats) — AP11

Designs: 50fr, Sambouk (boat) building. 300fr, Zeima sailboat.

1964-65   Engr.   Perf. 13

C32	AP11	50fr blue, ocher & choc	4.75	2.40
C33	AP11	85fr dk Prus grn, dk brn & mag	6.50	3.25
C34	AP11	300fr brn, lt brn & bl grn ('65)	17.50	8.75
	Nos. C32-C34 (3)		28.75	14.40

Discus Thrower — AP12

1964, Oct. 10   Engr.

C35	AP12	90fr rose lil, red brn & blk	11.00	8.75

18th Olympic Games, Tokyo, Oct. 10-25.

ITU Issue
Common Design Type
1965, May 17

C36	CD120	95fr lil rose, brt bl & lt brn	17.50	10.50

Camels in Ghoubet Kharab and Map of Somali Coast — AP13

1965   Engr.   Perf. 13

C37	AP13	45fr Abbe Lake	3.50	2.00
C38	AP13	65fr shown	4.50	2.00

Issue dates: 45fr, Oct. 20; 65fr, July 16.

French Satellite A-1 Issue
Common Design Type

Designs: 25fr, Diamant rocket and launching installations. 30fr, A-1 satellite.

1966, Jan. 28   Engr.   Perf. 13

C39	CD121	25fr redsh brn, ol brn & dl red	3.50	3.50
C40	CD121	30fr ol brn, dl red & redsh brn	3.50	3.50
a.		Strip of 2, #C39-C40 + label	9.00	9.00

Each sheet contains 16 triptychs (2x8).

Stapelia — AP14

1966   Engr.   Perf. 13

C41	AP14	55fr sl grn, dl mag & emer	5.50	3.50

Feather Starfish and Coral — AP15

Fish: 25fr, Regal angelfish. 40fr, Pomocanthops filamentosus. 50fr, Amphiprion ephippium. 70fr, Squirrelfish. 80fr, Surgeonfish. 100fr, Pterois lunulatus.

1966   Photo.   Perf. 13

C42	AP15	8fr multicolored	2.40	2.40
C43	AP15	25fr multicolored	4.75	4.75
C44	AP15	40fr multicolored	7.25	7.25
C45	AP15	50fr multicolored	9.50	9.50
C46	AP15	70fr multicolored	15.00	15.00
C47	AP15	80fr multicolored	17.50	17.50
C48	AP15	100fr multicolored	23.00	23.00
	Nos. C42-C48 (7)		79.40	79.40

French Satellite D-1 Issue
Common Design Type
1966, June 10   Engr.   Perf. 13

C49	CD122	48fr dk brn, brt bl & grn	4.75	3.25

AIR POST SEMI-POSTAL STAMPS

> Catalogue values for unused stamps in this section are for Never Hinged items.

SPAP1

**   Unwmk.**
1942, June 22   Engr.   Perf. 13

CB1	SPAP1	1.50fr + 3.50fr green		1.75
CB2	SPAP1	2fr + 6fr brown		1.75

Native children's welfare fund. Nos. CB1-CB2 were issued by the Vichy government in France, but were not placed on sale in Somali Coast

Colonial Education Fund
Common Design Type
1942, June 22

CB3	CD86a	1.20fr + 1.80fr blue & red		1.75

No. CB3 was issued by the Vichy government in France, but was not placed on sale in Somali Coast.

Pharaoh Sacrificing before Horus and Hathor — SPAP2

**   Unwmk.**
1964, Aug. 28   Engr.   Perf. 13

CB4	SPAP2	25fr + 5fr multi	10.50	8.75

UNESCO world campaign to save historic monuments in Nubia.

POSTAGE DUE STAMPS

D1

1915 Unwmk. Typo. Perf. 14x13½
Chalky Paper

J1	D1	5c deep ultra	.40	.65
J2	D1	10c brown red	.65	.80
J3	D1	15c black	.95	1.40
J4	D1	20c purple	2.00	2.40
J5	D1	30c orange	2.00	2.40
J6	D1	50c maroon	3.25	3.50
J7	D1	60c green	4.75	5.50
J8	D1	1fr dark blue	6.00	7.25
		Nos. J1-J8 (8)	20.00	23.90

See Nos. J11-J20.

Type of 1915 Issue
Surcharged

2F.

1927
J9	D1	2fr on 1fr light red	9.50	10.50
J10	D1	3fr on 1fr lilac rose	9.50	10.50

Type of 1915
1938 Engr. Perf. 12½x13
J11	D1	5c light ultra	.25	.30
J12	D1	10c dark carmine	.25	.30
J13	D1	15c brown black	.30	.40
J14	D1	20c violet	.30	.40
J15	D1	30c orange yellow	1.10	1.20
J16	D1	50c brown	.70	.80
J17	D1	60c emerald	1.10	1.20
J18	D1	1fr indigo	2.25	2.25
J19	D1	2fr red	1.00	1.10
J20	D1	3fr dark brown	1.40	1.50
		Nos. J11-J20 (10)	8.65	9.45
		Set, never hinged	13.00	

Inscribed "Inst de Grav" below design.

Postage Due Stamps of
1915 Overprinted in
Red or Black

1943 Unwmk. Perf. 14x13½
J21	D1	5c ultra (R)	2.40	2.40
J22	D1	10c brown red	2.40	2.40
J23	D1	15c black (R)	2.40	2.40
J24	D1	20c purple	2.40	2.40
J25	D1	30c orange	2.40	2.40
J26	D1	50c maroon	2.40	2.40
J27	D1	60c green	2.40	2.40
J28	D1	1fr dark blue (R)	8.75	8.75
		Nos. J21-J28 (8)	25.55	25.55
		Set, never hinged	40.00	

Postage Due Stamps
of 1938 Overprinted in
Red or Black

1943 Perf. 12½x13
J29	d1	5c lt ultra (R)	2.40	2.40
J30	D1	10c dark car	2.40	2.40
J31	D1	15c brn blk (R)	2.40	2.40
J32	D1	20c violet	2.40	2.40
J33	d1	30c org yel	2.40	2.40
J34	D1	50c brown	2.40	2.40
J35	D1	60c emerald	2.40	2.40
J36	D1	1fr indigo (R)	2.40	2.40
J37	D1	2fr red	9.50	9.50
J38	D1	3fr dk brn (R)	11.00	11.00
		Nos. J29-J38 (10)	39.70	39.70
		Set, never hinged	65.00	

For type D1 without "RF," see Nos. J38A-J38E.

Type D1 Without "RF"
Engraved, Values Typo
1944, Apr. 3
J38A	D1	30c org yel	.30
J38B	D1	50c yel brn	.30
J38C	D1	60c org	.65
J38D	D1	2fr red	.70
J38E	D1	3fr sepia	1.20
		Nos. J38A-J38E (5)	3.15

Nos. J38A-J38E were issued by the Vichy government in France, but were not placed on sale in Somali Coast.

Catalogue values for unused stamps in this section, from this point to the end of the section, are for Never Hinged items.

D2

1947 Photo. Perf. 13½x13
J39	D2	10c purple	.40	.25
J40	D2	30c brown	.40	.25
J41	D2	50c green	.70	.55
J42	D2	1fr deep orange	.70	.55
J43	D2	2fr lilac rose	1.00	.90
J44	D2	3fr dk org brn	1.00	.90
J45	D2	4fr blue	1.25	1.00
J46	D2	5fr orange red	1.25	1.00
J47	D2	10fr olive green	1.25	1.00
J48	D2	20fr blue violet	3.00	2.40
		Nos. J39-J48 (10)	10.95	8.80

SOMALILAND PROTECTORATE

sō-'mä-lē-ˌland

prə-'tek-t̩ə-ˌrət

LOCATION — Eastern Africa, bordering on the Gulf of Aden
GOVT. — British Protectorate
AREA — 68,000 sq. mi.
POP. — 640,000 (estimated)
CAPITAL — Hargeisa

Formerly administered by the Indian Government, the territory was taken over by the British Foreign Office in 1898 and transferred to the Colonial Office in 1905.
Somaliland Protectorate became part of independent Somalia in 1960.

16 Annas = 1 Rupee
100 Cents = 1 Shilling (1951)

Catalogue values for unused stamps in this country are for Never Hinged items, beginning with Scott 108.

Stamps of India, 1882-1900, Overprinted at Top of Stamp

1903 Wmk. 39 Perf. 14
1	A17	½a light green	3.00	4.50
2	A19	1a carmine rose	3.00	4.00
3	A21	2a violet	2.50	1.60
a.		Double overprint	800.00	
4	A28	2½a ultra	2.25	1.90
5	A22	3a brown orange	3.50	3.50
6	A23	4a olive green	4.00	3.00
7	A25	8a red violet	4.25	5.50
8	A26	12a brown, red	4.50	8.00
a.		Inverted overprint		1,200.
9	A29	1r car rose & grn	7.50	11.00
10	A30	2r yel brn & car rose	38.00	52.50
11	A30	3r green & brown	36.00	62.50
12	A30	5r violet & blue	59.00	72.50

Wmk. Elephant's Head (38)
13	A14	6a bister	6.50	5.25
		Nos. 1-13 (13)	174.00	235.75

Nos. 1-5 exist without the 2nd "I" of "BRITISH."

Same, but Overprinted at Bottom of Stamp

1903 Wmk. 39
14	A28	2½a ultra	4.75	8.50
15	A26	12a violet, red	13.00	14.00
16	A29	1r car rose & grn	7.00	17.50
17	A30	2r yel brn & car rose	120.00	190.00
18	A30	3r green & brn	130.00	190.00
a.		Double overprint, both inverted, one albino	850.00	
19	A30	5r violet & blue	120.00	170.00

Wmk. 38
20	A14	6a bister	8.50	8.00
		Nos. 14-20 (7)	403.25	598.00

Stamps of India, 1902-03, Ovptd.

1903 Wmk. 39
21	A33	½a light green	3.25	.60
22	A34	1a car rose	1.40	.35
23	A35	2a violet	1.90	2.75
24	A37	3a brown orange	2.75	2.75
25	A38	4a olive green	1.60	4.50
26	A40	8a red violet	1.90	2.50
		Nos. 21-26 (6)	12.80	13.45

The above overprints vary in length, also in the relative positions of the letters. Nos. 21-23 exist without the second "I" of "British."

A1

King Edward
VII — A2

1904 Wmk. 2 Typo.
27	A1	½a dl grn & grn	2.25	4.50
28	A1	1a carmine & blk	17.00	3.50
29	A1	2a red vio & dull vio	2.25	2.40
30	A1	2½a ultramarine	8.00	4.00
31	A1	3a gray grn & vio brn	2.50	3.75
32	A1	4a black & gray grn	3.50	6.00
33	A1	6a vio & gray grn	8.00	18.00
34	A1	8a pale blue & blk	7.00	7.50
35	A1	12a ocher & blk	10.00	11.50

Wmk. Crown and C C (1)
36	A2	1r gray grn	16.00	47.50
37	A2	2r red vio & dull vio	60.00	90.00
38	A2	3r blk & gray grn	60.00	120.00
39	A2	5r carmine & blk	02.50	120.00
		Nos. 27-39 (13)	259.00	438.65

1905 Wmk. 3
40	A1	½a dl grn & grn	2.00	8.00
41	A1	1a carmine & blk	17.50	1.75
42	A1	2a red vio & dull vio	8.25	10.00
43	A1	2½a ultramarine	4.50	11.00
44	A1	3a gray grn & vio brn	2.50	16.00
45	A1	4a black & gray grn	5.00	20.00
46	A1	6a violet & gray grn	6.00	27.50
47	A1	8a pale blue & blk	8.00	11.00
48	A1	12a ocher & black	7.25	11.00
		Nos. 40-48 (9)	61.00	116.25

Nos. 41, 42, 44-48 are on both ordinary and chalky paper.

1909
49	A1	½a bluish green	35.00	35.00
50	A1	1a carmine	3.00	2.25

For overprints see Nos. O11-O16.

A3

King George
V — A4

The ½, 1 and 2½a of type A3 are on ordinary paper, the other values of types A3 and A4 are on chalky paper.

1912-19
51	A3	½a green	.90	9.25
52	A3	1a carmine	3.00	.60
53	A3	2a red vio & dull vio	4.25	16.00
54	A3	2½a ultramarine	1.25	9.75
55	A3	3a gray grn & vio brn	2.75	7.50
56	A3	4a blk & grn ('13)	3.00	11.50
57	A3	6a violet & green	3.00	7.00
58	A3	8a lt blue & blk	4.25	17.50
59	A3	12a ocher & blk	4.00	24.00
60	A4	1r dull grn & grn	17.50	21.00
61	A4	2r red vio & dull vio ('19)	28.00	80.00
62	A4	3r blk & gray grn ('19)	75.00	150.00
63	A4	5r car & blk ('19)	75.00	190.00
		Nos. 51-63 (13)	221.90	544.10

1921 Wmk. 4
64	A3	½a blue green	3.75	15.00
65	A3	1a scarlet	4.25	.80
66	A3	2a vio & dull vio	5.00	1.10
67	A3	2½a ultramarine	1.25	8.00
68	A3	3a gray grn & vio brown	3.00	8.50
69	A3	4a black & grn	3.00	10.00
70	A3	6a violet & grn	2.00	15.00
71	A3	8a lt blue & blk	2.50	6.25
72	A3	12a ocher & blk	11.00	17.50
73	A4	1r dull grn & grn	10.00	55.00
74	A4	2r vio & dull vio	30.00	62.50
75	A4	3r blk & gray grn	42.50	125.00
76	A4	5r scarlet & blk	82.50	200.00
		Nos. 64-76 (13)	200.75	524.65

Common Design Types
pictured following the introduction.

Silver Jubilee Issue
Common Design Type
1935, May 6 Engr. Perf. 11x12
77	CD301	1a car & dk blue	2.75	4.00
78	CD301	2a black & ultra	3.25	4.00
79	CD301	3a ultra & brown	2.75	18.00
80	CD301	1r brown vio & ind	9.00	20.00
		Nos. 77-80 (4)	17.75	46.00
		Set, never hinged	32.50	

Coronation Issue
Common Design Type
1937, May 13 Perf. 13½x14
81	CD302	1a carmine	.25	.40
82	CD302	2a black	.35	2.00
83	CD302	3a bright ultra	.50	1.00
		Nos. 81-83 (3)	1.10	3.40
		Set, never hinged	2.25	

Blackhead
Sheep — A5

Greater
Kudu — A6

Map of
Somaliland
Protectorate
A7

1938, May 10 Wmk. 4 Perf. 12½
84	A5	½a green	.80	5.75
85	A5	1a carmine	.60	1.75
86	A5	2a deep claret	2.00	4.00
87	A5	3a ultra	10.00	17.50
88	A6	4a dark brown	4.00	11.00
89	A6	6a purple	8.50	13.00
90	A6	8a gray black	3.75	13.50
91	A6	12a orange	10.00	30.00
92	A7	1r green	8.75	72.50
93	A7	2r rose violet	16.00	72.50
94	A7	3r ultramarine	14.00	45.00
95	A7	5r black	20.00	45.00
a.		Horiz. pair, imperf. btwn.	25,000.	
		Nos. 84-95 (12)	98.40	331.50
		Set, never hinged	155.00	

A8

A9

A10

Camel Carrying
Somali House
A11

Askari
Militiaman
A12

Designs: 35c, 2sh, Rock Pigeon. 50c, 5sh, Martial eagle. 1sh, Blackhead sheep. 1sh30c, Tomb of Sheik Isaaq, Mait. 10sh, Taleh Fort.

1942, Apr. 22

96	A8	½a green	.25	.50
97	A8	1a carmine	.25	.25
98	A8	2a deep claret	.40	.25
99	A8	3a ultramarine	1.50	.25
100	A9	4a dark brown	2.00	.25
101	A9	6a purple	2.00	.25
102	A9	8a gray	2.50	.25
103	A9	12a orange	2.25	1.25
104	A10	1r green	1.75	2.50
105	A10	2r rose violet	2.75	8.50
106	A10	3r ultra	5.50	15.00
107	A10	5r black	9.00	11.00
		Nos. 96-107 (12)	30.15	40.25
		Set, never hinged	47.50	

For surcharges see Nos. 116-126.

Catalogue values for unused stamps in this section, from this point to the end of the section, are for Never Hinged items.

Peace Issue
Common Design Type
Perf. 13¾x14

1946, Oct. 15		Engr.	Wmk. 4	
108	CD303	1a carmine	.25	.25
a.		Perf. 13½	16.00	65.00
109	CD303	3a deep blue	.25	.25

Silver Wedding Issue
Common Design Types
1949, Jan. 28 Photo. Perf. 14x14½

110	CD304	1a scarlet	.25	.25

Engraved; Name Typographed
Perf. 11½x11

111	CD305	5r gray black	6.75	8.00

UPU Issue
Common Design Types
Surcharged in Black or Carmine with New Values in Annas
Engr.; Name Typo. on 3a, 6a
1949, Oct. 10   Perf. 13½, 11x11½

112	CD306	1a on 10c rose car	.25	.35
113	CD307	3a on 30c ind (C)	1.25	1.50
114	CD308	6a on 50c rose vio	.35	1.25
115	CD309	12a on 1sh red org	.60	.60
		Nos. 112-115 (4)	2.45	3.70

Nos. 96 and 98 to 107 Surcharged with New Value in Black or Carmine

1951, Apr. 2	Wmk. 4		Perf. 12½	
116	A8	5c on ½a green	.40	2.25
117	A8	10c on 2a deep claret	.40	.75
118	A8	15c on 3a ultramarine	1.75	2.25
119	A9	20c on 4a dark brown	2.40	1.00
120	A9	30c on 6a purple	2.00	1.00
121	A9	50c on 8a gray	2.75	.25
122	A9	70c on 12a red	4.25	8.00
123	A10	1sh on 1r green	2.50	1.50
124	A10	2sh on 2r rose violet	5.50	20.00
125	A10	2sh on 3r ultra	11.00	9.00
126	A10	5sh on 5r black (C)	19.00	14.50
		Nos. 116-126 (11)	51.95	59.75

Coronation Issue
Common Design Type

1953, June 2	Engr.		Perf. 13½x13	
127	CD312	15c dark green & blk	.40	.25

1953-58		Engr.	Perf. 12½	
128	A11	5c gray	.25	.60
129	A12	10c red orange	2.50	.60
130	A11	15c blue green	.70	.70
131	A11	20c rose red	.70	.40
132	A12	30c lt chocolate	2.50	.40
133	A11	35c blue	5.75	2.00
134	A11	50c lil rose & brn	6.50	.55
135	A11	1sh grnsh blue	1.25	.30
136	A11	1sh30c dark gray & ultra ('58)	17.50	3.75
137	A11	2sh violet & brn	27.50	7.50
138	A11	5sh emer & brn	32.50	9.00
139	A11	10sh rose lilac & brn	25.00	30.00
		Nos. 128-139 (12)	122.65	55.80

Nos. 131 and 135 Overprinted:
"Opening of the Legislative Council 1957"

1957, May 21

140	A11	20c rose red	.25	.25
141	A11	1sh greenish blue	.35	.30

Nos. 131 and 136 Overprinted:
"Legislative Council Unofficial Majority, 1960"

1960, Apr. 5

142	A11	20c rose red	.25	.25
143	A11	1sh30c dk gray & ultra	1.50	.30

Changes in the Legislative Council.

Three stamps of Somalia were overprinted "Somaliland Independence 26 June 1960" and issued in Hargeisa on that day. Somaliland Protectorate became part of Somalia on July 1, 1960. These three stamps are listed in Vol. 5 as Somalia Nos. 242, C68-C69.

Stamps of Somaliland Protectorate were replaced by those of Somalia in 1960.

OFFICIAL STAMPS

Official Stamps of India,
1883-1900, Overprinted

1903, June 1	Wmk. 39		Perf. 14	
O1	A17	½a light green	7.50	55.00
O2	A19	1a carmine rose	17.50	12.50
O3	A21	2a violet	12.00	55.00
O4	A25	8a red violet	14.00	450.00
O5	A29	1r car rose & grn	15.00	750.00
		Nos. O1-O5 (5)	66.00	1,322.

India Nos. 61-63, 68, 49
Overprinted

1903

O6	A33	½a green		.75
O7	A34	1a carmine rose		.75
O8	A35	2a violet		1.25
O9	A40	8a red violet		6.50
O10	A29	1r car rose & grn		20.00
		Nos. O6-O10 (5)		29.25

Nos. O6-O10 were not regularly issued, although used examples are known.

Regular Issue of 1904
Overprinted

1904		Wmk. Crown and C A (2)		
O11	A1	½a gray green	7.00	55.00
O12	A1	1a carmine & blk	3.75	8.00
O13	A1	2a red vio & dull vio	250.00	70.00
O14	A1	8a pale blue & blk	70.00	150.00
		Nos. O11-O14 (4)	330.75	283.00

		Wmk. Crown and C C (1)		
O15	A2	1r gray green	850.00	

Same Overprint on No. 42

1905		Wmk. 3		
O16	A1	2a red vio & dull vio	110.00	1,100.

The period after "M" may be found missing on Nos. O11-O14 and O16.

SOUTH AFRICA

sauth ˈa-fri-kə

LOCATION — Southern Africa
GOVT. — Republic
AREA — 472,730 sq. mi.
POP. — 43,426,386 (1999 est.)
CAPITAL — Pretoria (administrative); Cape Town (legislative); Bloemfontein (Judicial)

The union was formed on May 31, 1910, comprising the former British colonies of Cape of Good Hope, Natal, Transvaal and the Orange Free State, which became provinces. The union became a republic in 1961.

For previous listings, see individual headings.

12 Pence = 1 Shilling
20 Shillings = 1 Pound
100 Cents = 1 Rand (1961)

Catalogue values for unused stamps in this country are for Never Hinged items, beginning with Scott 74 in the regular postage section, Scott B1 in the semipostal section, Scott J30 in the postage due section, and Scott O21 in the officials section.

Watermarks

Wmk. 47 —
Multiple Rosette

Wmk. 177 —
Springbok's Head

Wmk. 201 — Multiple Springbok's
Head

Wmk. 330 —
Coat of Arms,
Multiple

Wmk. 348 — RSA in Triangle, Multiple

Wmk. 359 — RSA in Triangle, Tete
Beche

From Aug. 19, 1910, through December 31, 1937, the stamps of the provinces (Cape of Good Hope, Natal, Orange River Colony and Transvaal) were valid for postage throughout South Africa. They were demonetized effective Jan. 1, 1938.

Union of South Africa

George V
A1   A2

1910	**Engr.**	**Wmk. 47**	**Perf. 14**	
1	A1	2½p blue	3.00	1.75

Union Parliament opening, Nov. 4, 1910.

Type A2 stamps have very small margins at top and bottom. Values are for examples with perfs close to, or touching the frame.

1913-24		**Typo.**	**Wmk. 177**	
2	A2	½p green	1.50	.30
a.		Double impression	15,000.	
e.		Printed on gummed side	825.00	
3	A2	1p rose red	1.75	.25
d.		Printed on gummed side	925.00	
4	A2	1½p org brn ('20)	.80	.25
a.		Tête bêche pair	2.00	18.00
c.		Printed on gummed side	1,000.	
5	A2	2p dull violet	2.25	.25
d.		Printed on gummed side	1,000.	
6	A2	2½p ultra	5.50	1.60
7	A2	3p brn org & blk	13.00	.55
8	A2	3p ultra ('22)	4.75	1.75
9	A2	4p ol grn & org	11.00	.55
10	A2	6p violet & black	9.50	.70
11	A2	1sh orange	20.00	.90
12	A2	1sh3p violet ('20)	17.50	11.00
13	A2	2sh6p green & cl	70.00	5.50
14	A2	5sh blue & claret	140.00	9.00
15	A2	10sh ol grn & blue	350.00	14.50
16	A2	£1 red & dp grn ('16)	850.00	1,600.
a.		£1 lt red & gray green ('24)	1,100.	1,200.
		Nos. 2-16 (15)	1,497.	1,647.

The ½p, 1p and 1½p have the words "Revenue" and "Inkomst" on the stamps. On other stamps of this type these words are replaced by short vertical lines.

All values exist in many shades. No. 4a exists with and without gutter between.

Unwatermarked copies of the 1p are the result of misplaced watermarks.

All values except the 2sh6p and £1 exist with watermark inverted. No. 4 exists with watermark sideways.

For overprint see No. O1.

Coil Stamps
Perf. 14 Horizontally

17	A2	½p green	9.25	1.90
18	A2	1p rose red ('14)	15.00	6.25
19	A2	1½p org brown ('20)	17.00	27.50
20	A2	2p dull violet ('21)	18.00	5.00
		Nos. 17-20 (4)	59.25	40.65

"Hope" — A3

Design: No. 22, inscribed SUIDAFRIKA.

1926	**Engr.**	**Wmk. 201**	**Imperf.**	
21	A3	4p blue gray	2.00	1.40
22	A3	4p blue gray	2.00	1.40

Nos. 21 and 22 were privately rouletted and perforated, but such varieties were not officially made.

No. 21 (English inscription) was printed in a separate sheet from No. 22 (Afrikaans inscription).

English-Afrikaans Se-Tenant

Stamps with English inscriptions and with Afrikaans inscriptions were printed alternately in the same sheets, starting with No. 23. Major-number listings and values are for horizontal pairs (vertical pairs sell for about one-third less) of such stamps consisting of one English and one Afrikaans-inscribed stamp, unless otherwise described.

Values are for pairs with no fold marks between stamps and no perf separations.

Beware of pairs that have been rejoined.

Springbok
A5

Jan van Riebeek's Ship,
Drommedaris — A6

Orange
Tree — A7

1926	**Typo.**	**Perf. 14½x14**		
23	A5	½p dk grn & blk, pair	3.00	4.00
a.		Single, English	.25	.25
b.		Single, Afrikaans	.25	.25
c.		Tete beche pair ('27)	1,500.	
d.		Center omitted	2,000.	
e.		Booklet pane of 6	225.00	
f.		As "e," perf. 14	350.00	
g.		Missing "1" in "1/2" (Afrikaans only)	2,000.	
h.		Perf 13½x14 ('27)	85.00	85.00
i.		As "h," single, English		4.00
j.		As "h," single, Afrikaans		4.00
24	A6	1p car & blk, pair	3.00	3.00
a.		Single, English	.25	.25
b.		Single, Afrikaans	.25	.25
c.		Imperf., pair	1,350.	
d.		Tete beche pair ('27)	1,750.	
f.		Booklet pane of 6	200.00	
g.		As "f," perf. 14	300.00	
h.		Imperf on three sides, vert. pair	700.00	800.00
i.		Perf 13½x14 ('27)	110.00	85.00
j.		As "h," single, English		4.00
k.		As "h," single, Afrikaans		4.00
25	A7	6p org & grn, pair	42.50	47.50
a.		Single, English	3.00	2.25
b.		Single, Afrikaans	3.00	2.25
		Nos. 23-25 (3)	48.50	54.50

Nos. 23c and 24d are from uncut sheets printed for the perf. 14 booklet panes of 1928, Nos. 23f and 24g.

See Nos. 33-35, 42, 45-50, 59-61, 98-99. For overprints see Nos. O2-O4, O6-O9, O12-O15, O18, O21-O25, O30-O32, O42-O45, O48.

Government Buildings, Pretoria — A8

"Groote Schuur," Rhodes's Home — A9

Native Kraal — A10

Gnu — A11

Trekking — A12

Ox Wagon — A13

Cape Town and Table Mountain — A14

Perf. 14, 14x13½

1927-28		**Engr.**	**Wmk. 201**	
26	A8	2p vio brn & gray, pair	13.50	26.00
a.		Single, English	2.50	1.40
b.		Single, Afrikaans	2.50	1.40
c.		Perf. 14x13½, pair	32.50	32.50
d.		As "c," single, English	6.00	.75
e.		As "c," single, Afrikaans	6.00	.75
27	A9	3p red & blk, pair	24.00	37.50
a.		Single, English	2.10	1.40
b.		Single, Afrikaans	2.10	1.40
c.		Perf. 14x13½, pair	67.50	82.50
d.		As "c," single, English	3.25	2.75
e.		As "c," single, Afrikaans	3.25	2.75
28	A10	4p brown, pair ('28)	32.50	67.50
a.		Single, English	3.25	1.90
b.		Single, Afrikaans	3.25	1.90
c.		Perf. 14x13½, pair	67.50	82.50
d.		As "c," single, English	3.25	2.75
e.		As "c," single, Afrikaans	3.25	2.75
29	A11	1sh dp bl & bis brn, pair	47.50	87.50
a.		Single, English	7.50	2.75
b.		Single, Afrikaans	7.50	2.75
c.		Perf. 14x13½, pair ('30)	50.00	60.00
d.		As "c," single, English	7.50	1.25
e.		As "c," single, Afrikaans	7.50	1.25
30	A12	2sh6p brn & bl grn, pair	140.00	400.00
a.		Single, English	20.00	24.00
b.		Single, Afrikaans	20.00	24.00
c.		Perf. 14x13½, pair	475.00	675.00
d.		As "c," single, English	32.50	37.50
e.		As "c," single, Afrikaans	32.50	37.50
31	A13	5sh dp grn & blk, pair	275.00	650.00
a.		Single, English	30.00	40.00
b.		Single, Afrikaans	30.00	40.00
c.		Perf. 14x13½, pair	525.00	850.00
d.		As "c," single, English	47.50	52.50
e.		As "c," single, Afrikaans	47.50	52.50
32	A14	10sh ol grn & bl, pair	200.00	200.00
a.		Single, English	20.00	16.00
b.		Single, Afrikaans	20.00	16.00
c.		Perf. 14x13½, pair	275.00	375.00
d.		As "c," single, English	25.00	20.00
e.		As "c," single, Afrikaans	25.00	20.00
f.		Center inverted, single, English ('28)	12,500.	
g.		Center inverted, single, Afrikaans ('28)	12,500.	
h.		As "c," center inverted	57,500.	
		Nos. 26-32 (7)	732.50	1,468.

See Nos. 36-41, 43-44, 53-54, 58, 62-66. For overprints see Nos. O5, O10-O111, O16-O17, O19-O20, O28, O33-O35, O39, O41, O49-O53.

Types of 1926-28 Redrawn
"SUIDAFRIKA" (No Hyphen) on Afrikaans Stamps

The photogravure, unhyphenated stamps of 1930-45 are distinguished from the 1926-28 typographed or engraved stamps (also unhyphenated) by the following characteristics:

1/2p, 1p, 6p. Leg of "R" in AFRICA or AFRIKA ends in a straight line in the photogravure set; in a curved line in the typographed. No. 35 differs from No. 34, having 2mm space between POSSEEL—INKOMSTE instead of 1mm.

2p. A memorial statue has been added just above and leftward of the "2" in value tablet on Nos. 36-37 (photogravure).

3p. Top frame on No. 38 consists of 3 heavy lines. On No. 27 it has 3 heavy and 2 very thin lines.

4p. On Nos. 40-41 the background in upper corners is solid. On No. 28 it consists of horizontal and vertical lines. No. 41 has pretzel-shaped scroll endings at bottom. On No. 40 these scroll endings enclose a solid mass of color.

1sh. No. 43 has no fine shading lines projecting from the curved top of the left inner frame, as No. 29 has. On No. 43 the shading of the last "A" of the country name partly covers the flower below it.

2sh6p. On No. 44 the shading below the country name is solid or shows signs of wear. On No. 30 it is composed of fine lines.

The engraved pictorials are much more finely executed and show details more clearly than the photogravure.

Perf. 15x14 (½p, 1p, 6p), 14

1930-45		**Photo.**	**Wmk. 201**	
33	A5	½p bl grn & blk, pair	3.75	3.50
a.		Single, English	.25	.25
b.		Single, Afrikaans	.25	.25
c.		Tete-beche single	1,250.	
d.		As "c," gutter between	1,750.	
e.		Booklet pane of 6	50.00	50.00
f.		Vert. pair, monolingual	40.00	—
34	A6	1p car & blk, pair	4.75	3.50
a.		Single, English	.25	.25
b.		Single, Afrikaans	.25	.25
c.		Center omitted	4,500.	
d.		Frame omitted	2,500.	
e.		Tete-beche pair	1,800.	
f.		As "e," gutter between	1,500.	
g.		Booklet pane of 6	20.00	20.00
35	A6	1p rose & blk, pair ('32)	47.50	4.50
a.		Single, English	1.00	.25
b.		Single, Afrikaans	1.00	.25
c.		Center omitted	750.00	
36	A8	2p vio & gray, pair ('31)	24.00	22.50
a.		Single, English	2.00	.40
b.		Single, Afrikaans	2.00	.40
c.		Frame omitted, single stamp (English)	3,000.	
d.		Frame omitted, single stamp (Afrikaans)	3,000.	
e.		Tete-beche pair	6,500.	
f.		Booklet pane of 4	240.00	240.00
37	A8	2p vio & ind, pair ('38)	250.00	100.00
a.		Single, English	12.50	7.25
b.		Single, Afrikaans	12.50	7.25
38	A9	3p red & blk, pair ('31)	72.50	95.00
a.		Single, English	6.75	6.75
b.		Single, Afrikaans	6.75	6.75
39	A9	3p ultra & bl, pair ('33)	22.50	10.00
a.		Single, English	2.00	1.00
b.		Single, Afrikaans	2.00	1.00
c.		Center omitted	30,000.	
40	A10	4p redsh brn, pair ('32)	250.00	210.00
a.		Single, English	25.00	11.00
b.		Single, Afrikaans	25.00	11.00
41	A10	4p brn, pair ('36)	6.50	5.00
a.		Single, English	1.10	.45
b.		Single, Afrikaans	1.10	.45
42	A7	6p org & grn, pair ('31)	20.00	6.50
a.		Single, English	1.10	.45
b.		Single, Afrikaans	1.10	.45
43	A11	1sh dl bl & yel brn, pair	140.00	57.50
a.		Single, English	9.00	2.00
b.		Single, Afrikaans	9.00	2.00
c.		1sh dp bl & brn, pair ('32)	72.50	32.50
d.		As "c," single, English	5.25	.40
e.		As "c," single, Afrikaans	5.25	.40
44	A12	2sh 6p brn & bl, pair ('45)	29.00	19.00
a.		Single, English	1.75	.70
b.		Single, Afrikaans	1.75	.70
c.		2sh6p brn & sl grn ('36), pair	250.00	300.00
d.		As "c," single, English	18.00	8.00
e.		As "c," single, Afrikaans	18.00	8.00
f.		2sh6p choc & dp grn ('37), pair	205.00	190.00
g.		As "f," single, English	14.00	6.50
h.		As "f," single, Afrikaans	14.00	6.50
i.		2sh6p red brn & grn, pair ('32)	210.00	200.00
j.		As "i," single, English	17.50	6.50
k.		As "i," single, Afrikaans	17.50	6.50
		Nos. 33-44 (12)	870.50	537.00

No. 34 unwatermarked, or watermarked multiple clover leaf, is a proof.

Types of 1926-28 with "SUID-AFRIKA" Hyphenated on Afrikaans Stamps, and

Gold Mine — A15

Government Buildings, Pretoria — A16

Government Buildings, Pretoria — A16a

Groote Schuur — A17

Groot Constantia — A18

½p. No. 45 shading in leaves and ornaments strengthened; 40 lines in center background. Size: 18½x22½mm.

No. 46 has 28 heavy horizontal shading lines in center background and similar thicker lines in frame. Top and bottom green bars are scored by a white horizontal line. Size: 18½x22½mm.

No. 47 is smaller, 18x22mm.

1p. No. 48, size 18½x22½mm.

No. 49, size 18x22mm.

No. 50. Size: 17½x21½mm.

2p. On Nos. 53-54, S's in SOUTH and POSTAGE are narrower than on Nos. 36-37.

6p. Die I, "SUID-AFRIKA" 16½mm. Shading in leaves framing oval very faint and broken. Size: 18½x22½mm.

Die II, "SUID-AFRIKA" 17mm. Leaves strongly shaded. Heavy lines of shading in background of tree. Size: 18½x22½mm.

Die III, "question mark" scrolls below top panel are cleanly defined without intrusion of background shading. Size: 18x22mm.

Nos. 45-67 were printed in many shades. Some denominations in some printings were partly or wholly screened. Except for No. 47, the screened stamps were issued after 1947.

5sh. No. 65. Type I, letters "U" and "A" in SOUTH AFRICA have projections. Size: 27x21½mm.

No. 66. Type II, letters "U" and "A" redrawn to eliminate projections. Size: 26½x21½mm.

Perf. 15x14 (½p, 1p, 6p), 14
1933-54   Photo.   Wmk. 201

45	A5	½p grn & gray, pair ('36)	4.00	2.00
a.		Single, English	.25	.25
b.		Single, Afrikaans	.25	.25
c.		Bklt. pane of 6, marginal ads	30.00	30.00
d.		Perf. 13½x14 (coil), pair	40.00	65.00
e.		As "d," single, English	1.75	1.25
f.		As "d," single, Afrikaans	1.75	1.25
46	A5	½p grn & gray, redrawn, pair ('37)	10.00	.40
a.		Single, English	.25	.25
b.		Single, Afrikaans	.25	.25
c.		Booklet pane of 6	45.00	36.00
d.		Booklet pane of 2	10.00	1.25
e.		As "c," 4 blank margins	42.50	42.50
f.		Perf. 14½x14 (coil), pair	12.50	7.25
g.		As "f," single, English	2.25	.80
h.		As "f," single, Afrikaans	2.25	.80
47	A5	½p grn & gray, pair ('47)	1.50	4.00
a.		Single, English	.25	.25
b.		Single, Afrikaans	.25	.25
c.		Bklt. pane of 6, marginal ads	4.75	4.25
d.		As "c," no horiz. margins	6.00	3.50
48	A6	1p car & gray, pair ('34)	1.75	2.00
a.		Single, English	.25	.25
b.		Single, Afrikaans	.25	.25
c.		Booklet pane of 6	45.00	45.00
d.		Booklet pane of 2	3.50	1.50
e.		Perf. 13½x14 (coil), pair	85.00	125.00
f.		As "e," single, English	1.40	2.75
g.		As "e," single, Afrikaans	1.40	2.75
h.		Center omitted, pair	325.00	
j.		Bklt. pane of 6, marginal ads	32.50	32.50
k.		As "j," 4 blank margins	36.00	36.00
m.		Perf. 14½x14 (coil), pair	11.00	11.00
n.		As "m," single, English	1.40	1.40
p.		As "m," single, Afrikaans	1.40	1.40

49	A6	1p rose car & gray blk, pair ('40)	1.50	.30
a.		Single, English	.25	.25
b.		Single, Afrikaans	.25	.25
c.		Unwmkd., pair	325.00	325.00
d.		Booklet pane of 6	4.50	3.25
e.		Perf. 14½x14 (coil), pair	4.00	6.00
f.		As "e," single, English	1.40	.90
g.		As "e," single, Afrikaans	1.40	.90
h.		As "d," marginal ads	6.00	5.00
50	A6	1p car & blk, pair ('51)	1.50	4.00
a.		Single, English	.25	.25
b.		Single, Afrikaans	.25	.25
51	A15	1½p dk grn & gold, 27x21½mm, pair ('36)	2.25	2.25
a.		Single, English	.25	.25
b.		Single, Afrikaans	.25	.25
c.		Booklet pane of 4	11.00	9.50
d.		Center omitted, pair	1,000.	
52	A15	1½p sl grn & och, 22x18mm, pair ('41)	2.25	1.50
a.		Single, English	.25	.25
b.		Single, Afrikaans	.25	.25
c.		Center omitted, pair	7,500.	5,500.
d.		Booklet pane of 6	8.00	5.50
53	A16	2p bl vio & dl bl, pair ('38)	55.00	37.50
a.		Single, English	3.00	1.25
b.		Single, Afrikaans	3.00	1.25
54	A16	2p dl vio & gray, pair ('41)	45.00	85.00
a.		Single, English	1.00	1.50
b.		Single, Afrikaans	1.00	1.50
55	A16a	2p dp reddish vio & sl, 27x21½mm, pair ('45)	1.50	4.00
a.		Single, English	.25	.25
b.		Single, Afrikaans	.25	.25
56	A16a	2p pur & sl bl, 21½ x 17¼mm, pair ('50)	2.75	11.00
a.		Single, English	.25	.25
b.		Single, Afrikaans	.25	.25
c.		Booklet pane of 6 ('51)	4.50	4.50
57	A17	3p ultra, pair ('40)	9.50	3.25
a.		Single, English	.25	.25
b.		Single, Afrikaans	.25	.25
c.		3p bl, pair ('49)	2.00	6.00
d.		As "c," single, English	.25	.25
e.		As "c," single, Afrikaans	.25	.25
58	A10	4p choc brn, pair ('52)	3.50	11.00
a.		Single, English	.25	.25
b.		Single, Afrikaans	.25	.25
59	A7	6p org & bl grn, I, pair ('37)	55.00	35.00
a.		Single, English	3.75	1.10
b.		Single, Afrikaans	3.75	1.10
60	A7	6p org & grn, II, pair ('38)	29.00	3.00
a.		Single, English	1.50	.25
b.		Single, Afrikaans	1.50	.25
61	A7	6p red org & bl grn, III ('50), pair	2.50	1.00
a.		Single, English	.25	.25
b.		Single, Afrikaans	.25	.25
c.		6p org & grn, III, pair ('46)	14.50	1.90
d.		As "c," single, English	1.00	.25
e.		As "c," single, Afrikaans	1.00	.25
62	A11	1sh chlky bl & lt brn ('50), pair	9.00	10.00
a.		As "f," single, English	.55	.25
b.		As "f," single, Afrikaans	.55	.25
c.		1sh lt bl & ol brn, pair ('39)	40.00	15.00
d.		As "c," single, English	1.00	.25
e.		As "c," single, Afrikaans	1.00	.25
f.		1sh vio bl & brnsh blk, pair	16.00	15.00
g.		Single, English	.50	.30
h.		Single, Afrikaans	.50	.30
63	A12	2sh6p brn & brt grn, pair ('49)	7.50	30.00
a.		Single, English	1.25	1.00
b.		Single, Afrikaans	1.25	1.00
64	A13	5sh grn & blk, I, pair	45.00	75.00
a.		Single, English	2.50	2.00
b.		Single, Afrikaans	2.50	2.00
65	A13	5sh bl grn & blk, I, pair ('49)	42.50	75.00
a.		Single, English	4.00	3.50
b.		Single, Afrikaans	4.00	3.50
66	A13	5sh grn & blk, II, pair ('54)	40.00	95.00
a.		Single, English	4.00	4.00
b.		Single, Afrikaans	4.00	4.00
67	A18	10sh ol blk & bl, pair ('39)	50.00	17.50
a.		Single, English	3.00	1.00
b.		Single, Afrikaans	3.00	1.00
		Nos. 45-67 (23)	422.50	509.70

See Nos. 98-99. For overprints see Nos. O26-O27, O29, O36-O38, O40, O46-O47, O54.

George V and Springboks — A19

1935, May 1   Wmk. 201   Perf. 15x14

68	A19	½p Prus grn & blk, pair	5.00	12.00
a.		Single, English top	.25	.25
b.		Single, Afrikaans top	.25	.25

69	A19	1p car rose & blk, pair	5.00	10.00
a.		Single, English top	.25	.25
b.		Single, Afrikaans top	.25	.25
70	A19	3p bl & dk bl, pair	17.50	55.00
a.		Single, English top	1.40	2.75
b.		Single, Afrikaans top	1.40	2.75
71	A19	6p org & grn, pair	35.00	90.00
a.		Single, English top	2.10	3.25
b.		Single, Afrikaans top	2.10	3.25
		Nos. 68-71 (4)	62.50	167.00
		Set, never hinged	105.00	

25th anniv. of the reign of George V. English and Afrikaans inscriptions are transposed on alternate stamps. On the ½p, 3p and 6p with "SOUTH AFRICA" at top, "SILVER JUBILEUM" is at left of medallion, but on 1p with English at top, it is at the right.

Johannesburg International Philatelic Exhibition Issue
Souvenir Sheets

A20

A21

Black Overprint, "JIPEX 1936"
1936, Nov. 2   Perf. 15x14

72	A20	Sheet of 6 (½p)	6.00	9.50
73	A21	Sheet of 6 (1p)	5.75	6.50
		Set, never hinged	25.00	

Sheets made by overprinting booklet panes Nos. 45c and 48j. Sheets exist with and without horizontal perforations through right margin. Sheet size: 81x72.

Catalogue values for unused stamps in this section, from this point to the end of the section, are for Never Hinged items.

George VI — A22

"KRONING SUID-AFRIKA" on alternate stamps.

1937, May 12   Perf. 14

74	A22	½p grn & ol blk, pair	.80	1.25
a.		Single, English	.25	.25
b.		Single, Afrikaans	.25	.25
75	A22	1p car & ol blk, pair	.85	1.00
a.		Single, English	.25	.25
b.		Single, Afrikaans	.25	.25
76	A22	1½p Prus grn & org, pair	.85	.80
a.		Single, English	.25	.25
b.		Single, Afrikaans	.25	.25
77	A22	3p bl & ultra, pair	1.75	3.00
a.		Single, English	.25	.25
b.		Single, Afrikaans	.25	.25
78	A22	1sh Prus bl & org brn, pair	5.00	5.00
a.		Single, English	.50	.25
b.		Single, Afrikaans	.50	.25
		Nos. 74-78 (5)	9.25	11.05

Coronation of George VI and Queen Elizabeth.

Wagon Wheel A23

Voortrekker Family A24

Alternate stamps inscribed "SOUTH AFRICA," "SUID-AFRIKA."

1938, Dec. 14   Perf. 15x14

79	A23	1p rose & slate, pair	7.00	5.50
a.		Single, English	.30	.30
b.		Single, Afrikaans	.30	.30
80	A24	1½p red brn & Prus bl, pair	8.00	6.50
a.		Single, English	.30	.35
b.		Single, Afrikaans	.30	.35

Issued to commemorate the Voortrekkers.

Infantry A25

Nurse and Ambulance A26

Airman and Spitfires (Flight Lt. Robert Kershaw) A27

Sailor A28

Women's Services A29

Artillery — A30

Welder — A31

Tank Corps A32

Signal Corps — A33

Bilingual inscriptions on 2p and 1sh.

Perf. 14 (2p, 4p, 6p), 15x14
1941-43   Photo.   Wmk. 201

81	A25	½p dp bl grn, pair	1.50	3.25
a.		Single, English	.25	.25
b.		Single, Afrikaans	.25	.25
82	A26	1p brt rose, pair	2.00	3.25
a.		Single, English	.25	.25
b.		Single, Afrikaans	.25	.25

83	A27	1½p Prus grn, pair ('42)	1.50	3.00
a.		Single, English	.25	.25
b.		Single, Afrikaans	.25	.25
84	A28	2p dk violet	1.00	.75
85	A29	3p dp blue, pair	22.50	40.00
a.		Single, English	1.00	.75
b.		Single, Afrikaans	1.00	.75
86	A30	4p org brn, pair	22.50	25.00
a.		Single, English	1.00	.25
b.		Single, Afrikaans	1.00	.25
c.		4p red brown, pair	35.00	37.50
d.		As "c," single, English	1.50	1.25
e.		As "c," single, Afrikaans	1.50	1.25
87	A31	6p brt red org, pair	11.75	14.00
a.		Single, English	.50	.25
b.		Single, Afrikaans	.50	.25
88	A32	1sh dark brown	2.25	1.00
89	A33	1sh3p dk ol brn, pair ('43)	13.00	11.00
a.		Single, English	.50	.30
b.		Single, Afrikaans	.50	.30
c.		1sh3p dark brown, pair	6.00	8.00
d.		As "c," single, English	.50	.30
e.		As "c," single, Afrikaans	.50	.30
		Nos. 81-89 (9)	78.00	101.25

Infantry
A34

Nurse
A35

Airman — A36

Sailor — A37

Women's
Services — A38

Artillery — A39

Welder — A40   Tank
Corps — A41

Bilingual inscriptions on 4p and 1sh.

*Pairs: Perf. 14, Roul. 6½ btwn.
Strips of 3: Perf. 15x14, Roul. 6½
btwn.*

			Photo.	Wmk. 201
1942-43				
90	A34	½p Horiz. strip of 3	2.00	1.50
a.		Single, English	.25	.25
b.		Single, Afrikaans	.25	.25
c.		As #90, imperf. between	900.00	650.00
91	A35	1p Horiz. strip of 3 ('43)	1.50	1.50
a.		Single, English	.25	.25
b.		Single, Afrikaans	.25	.25
c.		As #91, imperf. between	725.00	725.00
92	A36	1½p Horiz. pair	.70	2.50
a.		Single, English	.25	.25
b.		Single, Afrikaans	.25	.25
c.		As #92, roul. 13	4.50	4.50
d.		As #92, imperf. btwn.	350.00	375.00

93	A37	2p Horiz. pair ('43)	1.00	2.50
a.		Single, English	.25	.25
b.		Single, Afrikaans	.25	.25
c.		As #93, imperf. btwn.	800.00	675.00
94	A38	3p Vert strip of 3	7.00	18.00
a.		Single, English	.25	.25
b.		Single, Afrikaans	.25	.25
95	A39	4p Vert. strip of 3	18.00	11.00
a.		Single	.25	.25
96	A40	6p Horiz. pair	3.00	2.75
a.		Single, English	.25	.25
b.		Single, Afrikaans	.25	.25
97	A41	1sh Vert. pair	15.00	4.00
a.		Single	.25	.25
		Nos. 90-97 (8)	48.20	43.75

Because of the rouletting these are collected as pairs or strips of three, even on the bilingual stamps.

Types of 1926 Redrawn
"SUID-AFRIKA" Hyphenated
Coil Stamps

			Photo.	Perf. 15x14
1943				
98	A5	½p myrtle grn, vert. pair	3.00	5.00
a.		Single, English	.25	.25
b.		Single, Afrikaans	.25	.25
99	A6	1p rose pink, vert. pair	3.50	4.00
a.		Single, English	.25	.25
b.		Single, Afrikaans	.25	.25

"Victory" — A42

"Peace" — A43

Design: 3p, Profiles of couple ("Hope").

			Photo.	Perf. 14
1945, Dec. 3				
100	A42	1p rose pink & choc, pair	.35	1.25
a.		Single, English	.25	.25
b.		Single, Afrikaans	.25	.25
101	A43	2p vio & sl bl, pair	.35	1.25
a.		Single, English	.25	.25
b.		Single, Afrikaans	.25	.25
102	A43	3p ultra & dp ultra, pair	.50	1.50
a.		Single, English	.25	.25
b.		Single, Afrikaans	.25	.25
		Nos. 100-102 (3)	1.20	4.00

World War II victory of the Allies.

George VI — A44

King
George VI
and Queen
Elizabeth
A45

Princesses
Margaret
Rose and
Elizabeth
A46

Perf. 15x14

			Feb. 17	Wmk. 201
1947,				
103	A44	1p cer & gray, pair	.30	.40
a.		Single, English	.25	.25
b.		Single, Afrikaans	.25	.25
104	A45	2p purple, pair	.30	.60
a.		Single, English	.25	.25
b.		Single, Afrikaans	.25	.25
105	A46	3p dk blue, pair	.40	.75
a.		Single, English	.25	.25
b.		Single, Afrikaans	.25	.25
		Nos. 103-105 (3)	1.00	1.75

Visit of the British Royal Family, Mar.-Apr., 1947.

George VI,
Elizabeth — A47   Gold
Mine — A48

			Photo.	Perf. 14
1948, Apr. 26				
106	A47	3p dp chlky bl & sil, pair	.70	1.25
a.		Single, English	.25	.25
b.		Single, Afrikaans	.25	.25

25th anniv. of the marriage of George VI and Queen Elizabeth.

*Vertical Pairs Perf. 14 all around,
Rouletted 6½ between*

1948, Apr.				
107	A48	1½p sl & och, vert. pair	3.25	5.00
a.		Single, English	.25	.25
b.		Single, Afrikaans	.25	.25

"Wanderer"
in Port
Natal
A49

			Photo.	Perf. 15x14
1949, May 2				
108	A49	1½p red brown, pair	.60	.60
a.		Single, English	.25	.25
b.		Single, Afrikaans	.25	.25

Mercury and
Globe — A50

				Perf. 14x15
1949, Oct. 1				
109	A50	½p dk green, pair	.60	.60
a.		Single, English	.25	.25
b.		Single, Afrikaans	.25	.25
110	A50	1½p dk red, pair	.90	.90
a.		Single, English	.25	.25
b.		Single, Afrikaans	.25	.25
111	A50	3p ultra, pair	1.50	1.50
a.		Single, English	.25	.25
b.		Single, Afrikaans	.25	.25
		Nos. 109-111 (3)	3.00	3.00

75th anniv. of the UPU.

Except for Nos. 216, 310-313, 518a, 669a this is the end of bi-lingual multiples in the postage section.

Voortrekkers en Route to Natal — A51

Voortrekker
Monument,
Pretoria
A52

Voortrekkers Looking Toward Natal,
and Open Bible — A53

				Perf. 15x14
1949, Dec. 1				
112	A51	1p magenta	.25	.25
113	A52	1½p dull green	.25	.25
114	A53	3p dark blue	.75	.75
		Nos. 112-114 (3)	.75	.75

Inauguration of the Voortrekker Monument at Pretoria.

Riebeeck's
Seal and
Dutch East
India
Company
Monogram
A54

Maria de la
Quellerie — A55

2p, van Riebeeck's Ships. 4½p, Jan van Riebeeck. 1sh, Landing of van Riebeeck.

Perf. 15x14, 14x15

			Mar. 14	Wmk. 201
1952,				
115	A54	½p dk brn & red vio	.25	.25
116	A55	1p dark green	.25	.25
117	A54	2p dark purple	.25	.25
118	A55	4½p dark blue	.25	.25
119	A54	1sh brown	.55	.50
		Nos. 115-119 (5)	1.55	1.50

300th anniv. of the landing of Jan van Riebeeck at the Cape of Good Hope.

Nos. 116-117 Overprinted "SATISE" (1p) and "SADIPU" (2p)

1952, Mar. 26				
120	A55	1p dark green	.30	.55
121	A54	2p dark purple	.35	.70

South African Tercentenary Intl. Stamp Exhib., Cape Town, Mar. 26-Apr. 5, 1952.

Coronation Issue

Queen
Elizabeth II — A97

				Perf. 14x15
1953, June 3				
192	A97	2p violet blue	.30	.25

Cape
Triangle of
1853
A98

				Perf. 15x14
1953, Sept. 1				
193	A98	1p red & dk brown	.25	.25
194	A98	4p blue & indigo	.25	.25

Cent. of the introduction of postage stamps in South Africa.

Merino Ram and
Sheep — A99

				Perf. 14
1953, Oct. 1				
195	A99	4½p shown	.50	.25
196	A99	1sh3p Springbok	1.25	.25
197	A99	1sh6p Aloes	1.25	.40
		Nos. 195-197 (3)	3.00	.90

Arms of Orange Free State, Pen and Scroll A100

1954, Feb. 23   *Perf. 15x14*
198 A100   2p red org & dk brown   .25   .25
199 A100   4½p gray & rose violet   .25   .25
    Orange Free State centenary.

Wart Hog A101

White Rhinoceros A102

Lion — A103

1954, Oct. 14   *Perf. 15x14*
200 A101   ½p shown   .25   .25
201 A101   1p Gnu   .25   .25
202 A101   1½p Leopard   .25   .25
203 A101   2p Zebra   .25   .25

Perf. 14
204 A102   3p shown   .25   .25
205 A102   4p Elephant   .45   .25
206 A102   4½p Hippopotamus   .55   .80
207 A103   6p shown   .50   .25
208 A102   1sh Kudu   3.00   .25
209 A103   1sh3p Springbok   2.00   .35
210 A102   1sh6p Gemsbok   1.75   .50
211 A102   2sh6p Nyala   4.25   .30
212 A102   5sh Giraffe   10.50   1.60
213 A102   10sh Sable antelope   16.00   3.75
    Nos. 200-213 (14)   40.25   9.30

    See Nos. 221-228, 241-244, 247, 250-253.

Paul Kruger — A104

    Portrait: 6p, Martinus Wessels Pretorius.

Perf. 14x15
1955, Oct. 21   Photo.   Wmk. 201
214 A104   3p slate green   .30   .25
215 A104   6p brown violet   .60   .30
    Centenary of Pretoria.

Andries Pretorius, Church of the Vow and Flag of Natalia — A105

    Inscribed alternately in English and Afrikaans.

1955, Dec. 1   *Perf. 14*
216 A105   2p ultra & cer, pair   .80   4.00
    a.   Single, English   .25   .25
    b.   Single, Afrikaans   .25   .25
    Union Covenant Celebrations, Pietermaritzburg, Dec. 13-18, 1955.

German Wagon and House — A106

1958, July 1   *Perf. 14*
218 A106 2p pale lilac & brown   .30   .30
    Cent. of the arrival of German settlers.

Seal of Academy A107

Perf. 15x14
1959, May 1   Photo.   Wmk. 201
219 A107   3p brt blue & dk blue   .30   .30
    a.   Dark blue omitted   2,250.
    50th anniv. of the South African Academy of Science and Art, Pretoria.

Globe Showing Antarctica and South Africa — A108

Perf. 14x15
1959, Nov. 16   Wmk. 330
220 A108 3p blue grn, brn & org   .30   .25
    South African Natl. Antarctic Expedition.

Animal Types of 1954

1959-60   Wmk. 330   *Perf. 15x14*
221 A101   ½p Wart hog ('60)   .35   3.00
222 A101   1p Gnu   .25   .25
    a.   Redrawn   .40   .25

Perf. 14
223 A102   3p White rhino   .30   .25
224 A102   4p Elephant   .75   .30
225 A103   6p Lion   1.50   1.50
226 A102   1sh Kudu   4.50   .75
227 A102   2sh6p Nyala   4.50   3.00
228 A102   5sh Giraffe ('60)   12.00   25.00
    Nos. 221-228 (8)   24.15   34.05

    On No. 222a, the numeral "1" is centered above "S." On No. 222, "1" is slightly to right of "S."

Prime Ministers Botha, Smuts, Hertzog, Malan, Strydom and Verwoerd A109

Flag and Notes from National Anthem — A110

Pushing Wheel Uphill A111

    6p, Arms of the Union and of four provinces.
    1sh6p, Official Union festival emblem.

Map, Old and New Locomotives — A112

Perf. 14x15, 15x14
1960   Photo.   Wmk. 330
235 A109   3p chocolate   .25   .25
236 A110   4p lt blue & red org   .25   .25
237 A110   6p yel grn, red & brn   .25   .25
238 A111   1sh yel, dk bl & blk   .50   .25
239 A111   1sh6p lt blue & blk   1.60   1.00
    Nos. 235-239 (5)   2.85   2.00
    50th anniv. of the founding of the Union. See Nos. 245-246, 248-249.

1960, May 2   *Perf. 15x14*
240 A112 1sh3p dark blue   1.25   1.25
    Centenary of railways in South Africa.

Types of 1954 and 1960

    Designs: ½c, Wart hog. 1c, Gnu. 1½c, Leopard. 2c, Zebra. 2½c, Prime Ministers. 3½c, Flag and music notes. 5c, Lion. 7½c, Arms of Union and four provinces. 10c, Pushing wheel uphill. 12½c, Springbok. 20c, Gemsbok. 50c, Giraffe. 1r, Sable antelope.

Perf. 15x14, 14x15, 14 (A102, A103)
1961, Feb. 14   Photo.   Wmk. 330
241 A101   ½c dk bluish grn   .25   .25
242 A101   1c rose brown   .25   .25
243 A101   1½c sepia   .25   .25
244 A101   2c purple   .25   .25
245 A109   2½c chocolate   .25   .25
246 A110   3½c lt bl & red org   .30   .25
247 A103   5c org & dk brn   .35   .25
248 A110   7½c yel grn, red & brn   .40   1.00
249 A111   10c yel, dk bl & blk   .50   .40
250 A103   12½c dull grn & dk brn   1.25   1.25
251 A102   20c pink & dk brn   2.50   2.50
252 A102   50c org yel & blk   5.50   8.25
253 A102   1r blue & black   15.00   15.00
    Nos. 241-253 (13)   27.05   30.15

Republic

Natal Pigmy Kingfisher A112a

Coral Tree Flower A112b

Pouring Gold A113

Groot Constantia A114

    Designs: 1½c, Afrikander bull. 3c, Crimson-breasted shrike. 5c, Baobab tree. 7½c, Corn. 10c, Castle entrance, Cape Town. 12½c, Protea flower. 20c, Secretary bird. 50c, Cape Town, harbor. 1r, Bird of Paradise flower.
    Two types of 2½c:
    Type I — Lines of building faint.
    Type II — Lines of building very strong; strong line between bottom of building and top of name panel.

Perf. 14x15, 15x14
1961, May 31   Photo.   Wmk. 330
254 A112a   ½c blue, mag & brn   .25   .25
    a.   Perf. 14x13½ ('63)   .25   .25
255 A112a   1c gray & red   .25   .25
256 A112a   1½c brown carmine   .25   .25

Perf. 14
257 A113   2c ultra & orange   .25   .25
258 A114   2½c violet & grn (I)   .30   .25
    a.   Type II   .40   .25
259 A113   3c pink, dk bl & red   .30   .25
260 A114   5c grnsh bl & yel   .35   .25
261 A114   7½c emerald & brn   .60   .25
    a.   Brown omitted
262 A114   10c emer & dk brn   .80   .25
263 A114   12½c dk grn, red & yel   2.25   .30
    a.   Yellow omitted   1,000.
264 A114   20c sal, sl bl & pink   3.75   .30
265 A113   50c ultra & blk   22.50   2.25
266 A113   1r blue, org & grn   15.00   2.25
    Nos. 254-266 (13)   46.85   7.35

1961-63   Unwmk.   *Perf. 15x14*
269 A112b 1c gray & red   .25   .25

Perf. 14
270 A113   2c ultra & org ('63)   8.00   .35
271 A114   2½c violet & grn (II)   .30   .25
272 A113   3c pink, dk bl & red   .60   .25
273 A114   5c grnsh blue & yel   .75   .25
274 A114   7½c emer & brn ('62)   1.10   .50
275 A114   10c green & dk brn   1.25   .70
276 A114   20c sal, sl bl & pink ('63)   14.00   4.50
277 A113   50c ultra & blk ('62)   18.00   4.75
    Nos. 269-277 (9)   44.25   11.80

    See Nos. 289-298, 317-322, 324, 326-338, 340-342, 376-377, 379-382, 383-385 and designs A135-A136.

Boeing 707 and Blériot Monoplane A115

Folk Dancers A116

Perf. 14x15
1961, Dec. 1   Photo.   Wmk. 330
280 A115 3c blue & red   .40   .25
    50th anniv. of South Africa's 1st air mail.

1962, Mar. 1
281 A116 2½c lt brn, choc & red org   .35   .25
    50th anniv. of folk dancing in South Africa.

"Chapman" Arriving in 1820 A117

Perf. 15x14
1962, Aug. 20   Photo.   Wmk. 330
282 A117   2½c dp plum & bl grn   .40   .25
283 A117   12½c choc & blue   3.00   1.60
    Unveiling of the precinct stone of the British Settlers Monument at Grahamstown.

Red Disa Orchid, Castle Rock, Kirstenbosch Botanic Gardens — A118

1963, Mar. 14   *Perf. 14*
284 A118 2½c multicolored   .40   .25
    50th anniv. of the Kirstenbosch Botanic Gardens, Cape Town.

Centenary Emblem and Nurse — A119

12½c, Centenary emblem and globe, horiz.

1963, Aug. 30   Wmk. 348   Perf. 14
285 A119 2½c rose claret,
            blk & red   .35   .25

Perf. 15x14
286 A119 12½c dk bl gray &
            red   3.50 1.60
  a.   Red Cross omitted   1,600.

Centenary of the International Red Cross.

Assembly
Seat,
Bunga
Building,
Umtata
A120

Perf. 14½x14
287 A120 2½c dk brn & lt grn   Wmk. 348   .30 .25
  a.   Light green omitted   1,600.

Transkei Legislative Assembly, 1st meeting.

Types of 1961
Perf. 15x14, 14x15
1963-67   Photo.   Wmk. 348
Colors as Before
289 A112b   1c   .25   .25
290 A112a   1½c ('67)   2.25 1.00

Perf. 14
291 A113   2c ('64)   .25   .25
292 A114   2½c (II) ('64)   .50   .25
293 A114   5c ('66)   1.50 .25
294 A114   7½c ('66)   10.00 6.00
295 A114   10c ('64)   1.25 .25
296 A114   20c ('64)   1.50 .45
297 A113   50c ('66)   35.00 7.50
298 A113   1r ('64)   62.50 37.50
  Nos. 289-298 (10)   115.00 53.70

Rugby Board   John
Emblem,   Calvin — A122
Springbok and
Ball — A121

Design: 12½c, Rugby player diving over goal line, horiz.

Perf. 14x15, 15x14
1964, May 8   Photo.   Wmk. 348
301 A121 2½c dk green &
            brn   .50   .25
302 A121 12½c yellow grn &
            blk   4.50 3.00

South African Rugby Board, 75th anniv.

1964, July 10   Perf. 14
303 A122 2½c choc, brt car & vio   .35 .25

John Calvin (1509-64), French theologian and leader of the Reformation.

Nurse's
Lamp — A123

Design: 12½c, Nurse holding lamp, horiz.

Perf. 14x15, 15x14
1964, Oct. 12   Photo.   Wmk. 348
304 A123 2½c gold & ultra   .50   .25
305 A123 12½c ultra & gold   3.50 3.50
  a.   Gold omitted   1,500.

South African Nursing Assoc., 50th anniv.

ITU
Emblem
and
Satellites
A124

Design: 12½c, ITU emblem, old and new communication equipment.

1965, May 17   Perf. 15x14
306 A124 2½c brt blue & org   .40   .25
307 A124 12½c green & claret   2.75 2.25

Cent. of the ITU.

Pulpit, Groote Kerk, Cape Town — A125

Design: 12½c, Emblem of Dutch Reformed Church of South Africa, horiz.

Perf. 14x15, 15x14
1965, Oct. 21   Photo.   Wmk. 348
308 A125 2½c dp brown & yel   .25   .25
309 A125 12½c lt ultra, ocher &
            blk   1.25 1.10

Tercentenary of the Dutch Reformed Church in South Africa.

Diamond — A126

2½c, Flying bird, symbol of freedom & the future, horiz. 3c, Corn. 7½c, Table Mountain, horiz. Inscribed alternately in English & Afrikaans.

1966, May 31   Perf. 14
310 A126 1c blk, yel, dk & lt
            grn, pair   .50   .50
  a.   Single, English   .25   .25
  b.   Single, Afrikaans   .25   .25
311 A126 2½c dk bl, ultra &
            yel grn, pair   1.25 1.25
  a.   Single, English   .25   .25
  b.   Single, Afrikaans   .25   .25

Perf. 14x15, 15x14
312 A126 3c red brn, red &
            yel, pair   2.50 2.50
  a.   Single, English   .25   .25
  b.   Single, Afrikaans   .25   .25
313 A126 7½c ultra, vio bl, och
            & blk, pair   7.50 7.50
  a.   Single, English   .50   .40
  b.   Single, Afrikaans   .50   .40
  Nos. 310-313 (4)   11.75 11.75

5th anniversary of the Republic.

Nos. 310-313 with watermark 359 are reprints made for U.P.U. presentation booklets.

Hendrik F.
Verwoerd
and Union
Buildings,
Pretoria
A127

Designs: 3c, Verwoerd's portrait, vert. 12½c, Verwoerd and map of South Africa.

Perf. 15x14, 14x15
1966, Dec. 6   Photo.   Wmk. 348
314 A127 2½c grnsh blue & blk   .25   .25
315 A127 3c yellow grn & blk   .25   .25
316 A127 12½c dull blue & blk   .75   .65
  Nos. 314-316 (3)   1.25 1.15

Dr. Verwoerd (1901-1966), Prime Minister.

Types of 1961 Redrawn and

Industry — A128

(Inscriptions in larger, bolder type)

½c, 1½c and 1r

On the 1r, the "N" of "VAN" is over the final "A" of "AFRIKA." On Nos. 266 and 298, the "N" is over "KA."

1c, 7½c and 12½c

2½c, 5c, 10c and 20c

2c, 3c and 50c (similar)

Perf. 14x15, 15x14
1964-68   Photo.   Wmk. 348
Colors as Before
317 A112a   ½c   .25   .25
  a.   Imperf., pair   400.00
318 A112b   1c   .40   .25

Perf. 14
319 A113   2c ('68)   .40   .25
320 A114   2½c   .45   .25
321 A113   3c   .75   .25
322 A113   12½c   2.75 .25
323 A128   15c ('67)   6.00 .25
324 A113   1r   19.00 3.00
  Nos. 317-324 (8)   30.00 4.75

See No. 339.

Redrawn Types of 1964-68
4c, Groot Constantia (like 2½c). 6c, Corn (like 7½c). 9c, Protea flower (like 12½c).

1967-71   Photo.   Wmk. 359
326 A112a   ½c   .25   .25
327 A112b   1c   .25   .25
328 A112a   1½c   .25   .25
329 A113   2c ('68)   2.00 .25
330 A114   2½c   .25   .25
331 A113   3c   .25   .25
332 A114   4c ('71)   .40   .25
333 A114   5c ('68)   .25   .25
334 A114   6c ('71)   1.10 .25
335 A114   7½c   1.90 .25
336 A114   9c ('71)   1.40 .25
337 A114   10c ('68)   4.25 .30
338 A114   12½c ('70)   3.50 .65
339 A128   15c ('69)   6.50 .50
340 A114   20c ('68)   8.00 .65

341 A113   50c ('68)   8.75 1.00
342 A113   1r ('68)   12.00 2.10
  Nos. 326-342 (17)   51.30 7.95

Luminescence
Starting in 1969, South Africa began to add phosphorescent "frames" to its definitive stamps.
In 1971, stamps began to appear with the phosphorescent element throughout the paper.
Phosphorescent commemoratives include Nos. 357, 359 et cetera.

Martin   Door of
Luther — A129   Wittenberg
                    Church — A130

Perf. 14x15
1967, Oct. 31   Litho.   Wmk. 348
343 A129 2½c pink & black   .25   .25
Wmk. 359
344 A130 12½c black & orange   1.75 1.60

450th anniversary of the Reformation.

Pres. J. J.   James B. M.
Fouché — A133   Hertzog
                    Statue — A134

Design: 12½c, Full-face portrait.

Perf. 14x15
1968, Apr. 10   Photo.   Wmk. 348
345 A133 2½c lt rose brn & dk
            brn   .25   .25
346 A133 12½c grysh bl & vio bl   .45   .40
Wmk. 359
347 A133 12½c grysh bl & vio bl   .50   .40
  Nos. 345-347 (3)   1.20 1.05

Pres. Jacobus Johannes Fouché, inauguration.

Perf. 13½x14, 14x13½
1968, Sept. 21   Photo.   Wmk. 359
Designs: 2½c, Hertzog in 1902, with hat, horiz. 3c, Hertzog in 1924, horiz.
348 A134 2½c dk brn, lem & blk   .25   .25
Wmk. 348
349 A134 3c multicolored   .25   .25
350 A134 12½c org brn, org &
            blk   1.50 1.40
  Nos. 348-350 (3)   2.00 1.90

Unveiling of a monument in Bloemfontein honoring James Barry Munnik Hertzog (1866-1942), Boer general, prime minister of South Africa (1924-39).

Natal Pigmy   Kaffir Boom
Kingfisher   Flower
A135   A136

1969   Wmk. 359   Photo.   Perf. 14
351 A135 ½c blue & multi   .25 .25
a.   Perf. 14x14½ (coil)   1.50 .25
352 A136 1c grysh brown & multi   .25 .25
See Nos. 374-375.

Springbok, Torch and
Rings — A137

1969, Mar. 15   Perf. 14x13½
353 A137 2½c olive, ind & red   .25 .25
354 A137 12½c bister, ind & red   .95 .85
South African Natl. Games, Bloemfontein,
Mar. 15-Apr. 19.

Groote
Schuur
Hospital
and Dr.
Barnard
A138

Hands
Holding
Heart
A139

Perf. 13½x14
1969, July 7   Photo.   Wmk. 348
355 A138 2½c dp rose, pink & plum .25 .25

Perf. 15x14
Wmk. 359
356 A139 12½c dp bl & dp car   2.00 1.60
1st heart transplant operation (by Dr. Chris-
tiaan Barnard) and opening of the 47th South
African Medical Cong., Pretoria.

Stagecoach of 1869 — A140

Transvaal
No. 1 — A141

Perf. 13½x14, 14x13½
1969, Oct. 6   Photo.   Wmk. 359
357 A140 2½c ocher, Prus bl &
             yel   .35 .25
358 A141 12½c sal, grn & gold   3.25 2.25
Centenary of South African postage stamps.

Water Drop and
Flower — A142

Design: 3c, Waves, horiz.

1970, Feb. 14   Perf. 14
359 A142 2½c brn, brt bl & grn   .25 .25
360 A142 3c pale gray, bl & ind   .50 .25
Issued to publicize the Water 70 campaign
of the Department of Water Affairs.

Sower — A143

"BIBLIA"
A144

1970, Aug. 24   Photo.   Perf. 14
361 A143 2½c multicolored   .30 .25

Photo; Gold Impressed
362 A144 12½c ultra, blk & gold 2.25 1.90
150th anniv. of the South African Bible Soc.

Strijdom Tower,
Johannes G.
Strijdom — A145

Map of
Antarctica
A146

Perf. 14x13½, 13½x14
1971, May 22   Photo.   Wmk. 359
363 A145 5c blue, yel & blk   .50 .25
364 A146 12½c grnsh bl, vio bl &
             red   2.25 2.25

Wmk. 330
365 A145 5c blue, yel & blk   2.25 1.00
       Nos. 363-365 (3)   5.00 3.50
Intl. Stamp Exhib. (INTERSTEX), Cape
Town, May 22-31. No. 364 also for the 10th
anniv. of the Antarctic Treaty pledging peaceful uses of and scientific cooperation in
Antarctica.

Landing of
British
Settlers,
1820, by
Thomas
Baines
A147

Martinus Steyn, Paul
Kruger, Unification
Monument — A148

1971, May 31   Wmk. 359
366 A147 2c magenta & rose red   .25 .25
367 A148 4c blue green & blk   .30 .25
10th anniv. of the Republic of South Africa.

Hendrik
Verwoerd
Dam
A149

1972, Mar. 4   Photo.   Perf. 14
Size: 37x22mm
368 A149 4c shown   .25 .25
369 A149 5c Aerial view of dam .45 .25
Size: 57x22mm
370 A149 10c Dam, reservoir and
             Verwoerd   1.50 .90
       Nos. 368-370 (3)   2.20 1.40
Inauguration of the Hendrik F. Verwoerd
Dam of the Orange River Project.

Ram's Head and
Wool
Mark — A150

Lamb and Wool
Mark — A151

1972, May 15   Wmk. 359   Perf. 14
371 A150 4c blue & multi   .25 .25
372 A151 15c dull bl & dk bl   1.75 .40
South African wool industry. Issued in
sheets of 100 with advertisements in margin.
See Nos. 378-378A, 382A.

Cats — A152

1972, Sept. 19   Wmk. 359
373 A152 5c multicolored   1.50 .40
Centenary of the SPCA.

**Redrawn Types of 1964-69 and
Types of 1972**
**Perf. 14x15 (½c), 14 (1c, #382A),
12½**
1972-74   Photo.   Unwmk.
374 A135 ½c blue & multi   8.00 8.75
375 A136 1c grysh brn &
             red   .25 .25
376 A113 2c brt blue & org   .55 .25
377 A113 3c rose red &
             bluish black   .60 .70
378 A150 4c blue & multi   1.00 .25
378A A150 4c brown & multi   .45 .25
379 A114 5c grnsh bl & yel   1.25 .30
380 A114 6c emerald & brn   2.75 4.25
381 A114 9c dk grn, red &
             yel   2.50 .85
382 A114 10c emer & dk brn   2.75 .50
382A A151 15c dull bl & dk bl   3.00 4.00
383 A114 20c sal, sl bl &
             pink   3.00 .65
384 A113 50c ultra & black   7.75 2.00
385 A113 1r bl, org & grn   21.00 4.00
       Nos. 374-385 (14)   54.85 27.00
Issued: 2c, 1972; 6c, 15c, 1974: others,
1973.

Pylon — A153

Designs: 4c, Electrical usage, pylon, power
plant, horiz. 15c, Smokestacks.

1973, Feb. 1   Photo.   Perf. 12x12½
Size: 37½x20mm
386 A153 4c blue & multi   .25 .25
Size: 20x27mm
Perf. 12½
387 A153 5c blue & black   .35 .25
388 A153 15c ocher & multi   3.75 1.50
       Nos. 386-388 (3)   4.35 2.00
Electricity Supply Commission, 50th anniv.

Arms of
University
A154

Old University,
Cape Town
A156

New
University,
Pretoria
A155

1973, Apr. 2   Unwmk.   Perf. 12½
389 A154 4c blue & multi   .25 .25

Perf. 12x12½
Wmk. 359
390 A155 5c gold & multi   .35 .25

Unwmk.   Perf. 12½
391 A156 15c gold & blk   3.25 1.65
Cent. of the Univ. of South Africa (UNISA).

Woltemade, Sailor and Horse — A157

Designs: 5c, Sinking ship in storm. 15c, "De
Jonge Thomas" sinking.

1973, June 2   Photo.   Perf. 12x12½
392 A157 4c brown red, ol & blk .25 .25
393 A157 5c olive, blk & citron .45 .25
394 A157 15c brown, blk & ocher 5.50 4.50
       Nos. 392-394 (3)   6.20 5.00
Bicentenary of Wolraad Woltemade's hero-
ism in saving 14 people from the ship "De
Jonge Thomas" in Table Bay.

C. J. Langenhoven and
Anthem — A158

4c, 5c, vert., Portrait and signature.

1973, Aug. 1   Perf. 12½
Size: 27x20mm
395 A158 4c orange, blk & ultra .75 .25
Perf. 12½x12, 12x12½
Size: 21x38mm, 37x21mm
396 A158 5c orange, blk & ultra .90 .25
397 A158 15c orange, blk & ultra 4.50 1.50
       Nos. 395-397 (3)   6.15 2.00
Cornelis Jacob Langenhoven (1873-1932),
lawyer, writer, who worked for recognition of
Afrikaans language.

World Map and Communications
Network — A159

Perf. 12½
1973, Oct. 1   Photo.   Unwmk.
398 A159 15c ultra & multi   .60 .50
 a.   Wmk. 359   1.50 1.25
International Telecommunications Day.

Restored Houses,
Tulbagh — A160

Design: 5c, Church Street, Tulbagh.

1974, Mar. 14   Unwmk.   Perf. 12½
Size: 27x21mm
400 A160 4c Prus green & multi   .25 .25
Size: 57x20mm
401 A160 5c ocher & multi   .35 .25
Restoration of historic Church Street in
Tulbagh after 1969 earthquake.

Burgerspond   Prime Minister
A161   D. F. Malan
                     A162

1974, Apr. 7   Litho.   Perf. 12½x12
402 A161 9c multicolored   .55 .40
Centenary of the first official coin struck in
South Africa, 1874. The £1 gold coin shows
portrait of Pres. Thomas Francois Burger.

1974, May 22   Photo.   Unwmk.
403 A162 4c lt ultra & dk blue   .70 .35
Centenary of the birth of Daniel F. Malan
(1874-1959), prime minister of South Africa.

Congress
Emblem
A163

1974, June 13   Perf. 12x12½
404 A163 15c silver & dk blue   .70 .35
15th World Sugar Cong., Durban, 6/13-30.

"50"
A164

1974, July 13   Photo.   Unwmk.
405 A164 4c red & black   .40 .25
50th anniversary of radio in South Africa.

Cultural Center, Grahamstown — A165

1974, July 13   Perf. 12x12½
406 A165 5c red & black   .35 .25
Natl. Monument to British settlers of 1820.

Natal No. 78, Transvaal No. 145, Cape
of Good Hope No. 28 and Orange
River Colony No. 4 — A166

1974, Oct. 9   Photo.   Perf. 12½
407 A166 15c multicolored   .75 .65
Centenary of Universal Postal Union.

Wild   Cape
Iris — A167   Gannet — A168

Galjoen — A169

Bokmakierie (Shrike) — A170

Designs: 2c, Heather. 3c, Geranium. 4c,
Calla lily. 7c, Zebrafish. 9c, Angelfish. 10c,
Moorish idol. 14c, Roman fish. 15c, Greater
double-collared sunbird. 20c, Yellow-billed
hornbill. 25c, Barberton daisy. 50c, Blue
cranes. 1r, Bateleur eagles.

Photo. and Engr.
1974, Nov. 11   Unwmk.   Perf. 12½
408 A167   1c pink & multi   .25 .25
409 A167   2c yellow & multi   .25 .25
410 A167   3c multicolored   .25 .25
411 A167   4c multicolored   .25 .25
412 A168   5c dull blue & multi   .25 .25
413 A169   6c multicolored   .25 .25
414 A169   7c lilac & multi   .30 .25
415 A169   9c buff & multi   .35 .25
416 A169 10c lt blue & multi   .40 .25
417 A169 14c salmon & multi   .60 .25
418 A168 15c gray & multi   .60 .25
419 A168 20c yellow & multi   .80 .30
420 A167 25c dk brown & multi   1.10 .35
Perf. 12x12½
421 A170 30c gray & multi   4.50 .75
422 A170 50c citron & multi   4.00 1.00
423 A170   1r multicolored   7.50 2.00
       Nos. 408-423 (16)   21.65 7.15
The coils that follow are two colors while the
above sheet stamps are multicolored.

1974   Photo.   Perf. 12½
Coil Stamps
430 A167   1c pink & violet   .45 .40
431 A167   2c yellow & grn   .90 .45
432 A168   5c dull blue & blk   2.00 .75
433 A169 10c lt blue & indigo   5.00 5.00
       Nos. 430-433 (4)   8.35 6.60
See note on color that follows No. 423.

1975-76   Perf. 14
Same Designs
430a A167   1c   .55 .25
431a A167   2c ('76)   .45 .25
433a A169 10c ('76)   5.00 5.50
       Nos. 430a-433a (3)   6.00 6.00
No. 430a has black control number on back
of every fifth stamp.

Voortrekker Monument and
Encampment — A171

1974, Dec. 6   Unwmk.   Perf. 12½
438 A171 4c multicolored   .35 .25
Voortrekker Monument, 25th anniversary.

Sasolburg
Refinery
A172

Perf. 12x12½, 12½
1975, Feb. 26   Litho.
439 A172 15c red & multi   .75 .65
25th anniversary of South Africa Coal, Oil
and Gas Corp., Ltd. (SASOL).

Pres. Nicolaes   Jan C. Smuts
Diederichs   A174
A173

Litho. and Engr.
1975, Apr. 19   Perf. 12½x12
440 A173 4c brown & gold   .25 .25
Litho.
441 A173 15c ultra & gold   .40 .40
Installation of Dr. Nicolaes Diederichs as
third State President.

Litho. and Engraved
1975, May 24
442 A174 4c black   .30 .25
Smuts (1870-1950), lawyer, gen., statesman.

Dutch East
Indiaman,
by Baines
A175

Designs: Paintings by John Thomas Baines.

1975, June 18   Photo.   Perf. 12x12½
443 A175   5c gold & multi   .25 .25
444 A175   9c gold & multi   .25 .25
445 A175 15c gold & multi   .30 .25
446 A175 30c gold & multi   .55 .55
 a.   Souvenir sheet of 4   1.25 1.25
       Nos. 443-446 (4)   1.35 1.30
John Thomas Baines (1820-75), painter.
#446a contains 4 litho. stamps similar to #443-
446.

Gideon Malherbe
House,
Paarl — A176

Photo. and Engr.
1975, Aug. 14   Perf. 12½
447 A176 4c multicolored   .30 .25
Society of Real Afrikanders (Genootskap of
Regte Afrikaanders), cent.

Automatic Letter
Sorting — A177

1975, Sept. 11   Photo.   Perf. 12½x12
448 A177 4c brt blue & multi   .30 .25
Postal automation.

Title Page, First   Afrikaans
Afrikaans   Monument,
Paper — A178   Paarl — A179

1975, Oct. 10   Litho.   Perf. 12½x12
449 A178 4c black & orange   .25 .25
450 A179 5c multicolored   .25 .25
Inauguration of Afrikaans Language
Monument.

Table Mountain — A180

1975, Nov. 13   Litho.   Perf. 12½
451 A180 15c shown   2.75 1.75
452 A180 15c Johannesburg   2.75 1.75
453 A180 15c Cape vineyards   2.75 1.75
454 A180 15c Lions, Kruger
            Natl. Park   2.75 1.75
 a.   Block of 4, #451-454   11.00 11.00
Tourist publicity.

Satellites, Radar and Africa on
Globe — A181

1975, Dec. 3   Litho.   Perf. 12½
455 A181 15c dk vio blue & multi .30 .25
Satellite communications.

Lawn Bowler — A182

#457, Cricket batsman. #458, Polo player.
#459, Golfer (Gary Player).

1976   Photo.   Perf. 12½x12
456 A182 15c green & blk   .45 .25
457 A182 15c yellow grn & blk   .45 .25
458 A182 15c olive & blk   .45 .25
459 A182 15c brt green & blk   .45 .25
 a.   Miniature sheet of 4, #456-459 2.00 1.90
       Nos. 456-459 (4)   1.80 1.00
3rd World Bowling Championships, Zoo
Lake Club, Johannesburg, Feb. 1976 (No.
456); cent. of cricket in South Africa (No. 457);

intl. polo (No. 458); Gary Player, South African golf champion (No. 459).

Issue dates: #456, Feb. 18. #457, Mar. 12. #458, Aug. 16. #459, 459a, Dec. 2.

No. 456 Overprinted in Gold

1976, Apr. 6   Photo.   Perf. 12½x12
460 A182 15c green & black   .45   .45
  Victory of South Africa in 3rd World Bowling championships.

Picnic under Baobab Tree A183

Paintings by Erich Mayer: 10c, Wagons at Foot of Blauberg, Transvaal. 15c, Hartbeesspoort Dam, near Pretoria. 20c, Street in Doornfontein.

1976, Apr. 20   Photo.   Perf. 12x12½
461 A183 4c ocher & multi   .25   .25
462 A183 10c dk green & multi   .25   .25
463 A183 15c multicolored   .35   .30
464 A183 20c multicolored   .60   .55
  a. Souvenir sheet of 4, #461-464   1.75 1.75
    Nos. 461-464 (4)   1.45 1.35

Erich Mayer (1876-1960), painter. Artist's signature in horizontal gutter between 2 se-tenant pairs.

Wildlife Protection A184

1976, June 5   Litho.   Perf. 12x12½
465 A184 3c Cheetah   .25   .25
466 A184 10c Black rhinoceros   .30   .25
467 A184 15c Blesbok   .60   .35
468 A184 20c Zebra   .75   .50
    Nos. 465-468 (4)   1.90 1.35

All values exist on yellow toned paper. Value, twice that of stamps on white paper.

Emily Hobhouse, by Johan Hoekstra — A185

1976, June 8   Photo.   Perf. 12½x12
469 A185 4c multicolored   .30 .25
  Emily Hobhouse (1860-1926), the "Angel of Mercy" during Anglo-Boer War.

S.S. Dunrobin Castle, 1876 A186

1976, Oct. 5   Litho.   Perf. 12x12½
470 A186 10c multicolored   .75 .30
  Ocean Mail Service contract, centenary.

Family with Globe — A187

1976, Nov. 6   Photo.   Perf. 12½x12
471 A187 4c salmon & dull red   .30 .25
  Family planning.

Wine Glasses A188   Jacob Daniel du Toit A189

1977, Feb. 14   Litho.   Perf. 12½x12
472 A188 15c multicolored   .50 .25
  a. Word "Die" omitted from left
       inscription   16.00 20.00
  Quality of the Vintage Symposium, Cape Town, Feb. 14-21.

1977, Feb. 21   Photo.
473 A189 4c multicolored   .30 .25
  Dr. Jacob Daniel du Toit (Totius; 1877-1953), theologian, educator, poet.

Transvaal Supreme Court A190

1977, May 18   Photo.   Perf. 12x12½
474 A190 4c red brown   .30 .25
  Transvaal Supreme Court, centenary.

Sugarbush (Protea Repens) — A191

Photo. (1-5, 8, 10, 15, 20c); Litho. (others)
1977, May 27   Perf. 12½
475 A191 1c shown   .25 .25
476 A191 2c P. punctata   .25 .25
477 A191 3c P. neriifolia   .25 .25
478 A191 4c P. longifolia   .25 .25
479 A191 5c P. cynaroides   .25 .25
480 A191 6c P. canaliculata   .25 .25
481 A191 7c P. lorea   .25 .25
482 A191 8c P. mundii   .25 .25
483 A191 9c P. roupelliae   .25 .25
484 A191 10c P. aristata   .25 .25
485 A191 15c P. eximia   .25 .25
486 A191 20c P. magnifica   .25 .25
487 A191 25c P. grandiceps   .30 .25
488 A191 30c P. amplexicaulis   .45 .25
489 A191 50c Leucospermum
             cordifolium   .60 .30
490 A191 1r Paranomus
             reflexus   1.60 .90
491 A191 2r Orothamnus
             zeyheri   3.50 1.75
    Nos. 475-491 (17)   9.45 6.45

Perf. 14
477a A191 3c Litho.   .25 .25
479a A191 5c   .25 .25
480a A191 6c   .25 .25
481a A191 7c   .25 .25
482a A191 8c   .25 .25
483a A191 9c   .25 .25
484a A191 10c   .25 .25
486a A191 20c Litho.   .85 .35
487a A191 25c   .65 .35
488a A191 30c   .80 .30

489a A191 50c   1.50 .50
490a A191 1r   3.00 .95
491a A191 2r   5.75 1.75
    Nos. 477a-491a (13)   14.30 5.85

Perf. 14 Vertically
Photo.   Coil Stamps
492 A191 1c Silver tree   .30 .25
493 A191 2c Bottle brush   .30 .25
494 A191 5c Blushing bride   .30 .25
495 A191 10c Leucadendrom
             sessile   .30 .25
    Nos. 492-495 (4)   1.20 1.00
  Some printings have control number on back of every fifth stamp.

Gymnastics — A192

1977, Aug. 15   Litho.   Perf. 12½x12
496 A192 15c multicolored   .40 .30
  8th Intl. Cong. of Physical Education and Sports for Girls and Women, Cape Town, Aug. 14-20.

World Map and "M" A193

1977, Sept. 15   Litho.   Perf. 12x12½
497 A193 15c multicolored   .40 .30
  Introduction of international metric system.

Nuclear Power Plant and Uranium Atom A194

1977, Oct. 8
498 A194 15c multicolored   .40 .30
  Uranium development.

Flag of South Africa A195

1977, Nov. 11
499 A195 5c multicolored   .25 .25
  50th anniversary of national flag.

Walvis Bay, 1878 — A196

1978, Mar. 10   Litho.   Perf. 12½
500 A196 15c multicolored   .55 .40
  Centenary of Walvis Bay annexation.

Dr. Andrew Murray — A197

1978, May 9   Perf. 12½x12
501 A197 4c multicolored   .25 .25
  Dr. Andrew Murray, pioneer theologian, 150th birth anniversary.

Railroad Rail and ISCOR Emblem — A198

1978, June 5   Litho.   Perf. 12
502 A198 15c multicolored   .45 .40
  50th anniversary of ISCOR (Iron and Steel Industrial Corporation).

Saldanha Bay — A199

Design: No. 504, Richard's Bay.

1978, July 21   Litho.   Perf. 12½
503 A199 15c multicolored   .55 .55
504 A199 15c multicolored   .55 .55
  a. Pair, #503-504   1.10 1.10
  Opening of new harbors on east and west coasts of South Africa.

Landscape by Volschenk — A200

Designs: Landscapes by J. E. A. Volschenk.

1978, Aug. 21
505 A200 10c multicolored   .25 .25
506 A200 15c multicolored   .25 .25
507 A200 20c multicolored   .35 .35
508 A200 25c multicolored   .45 .45
  a. Souvenir sheet of 4, #505-508   1.90 1.90
    Nos. 505-508 (4)   1.30 1.30

Jan Ernst Abraham Volschenk (1853-1936), first South African professional artist.

B. J. Vorster — A201

1978, Oct. 10   Litho.   Perf. 12½x12
509 A201 4c maroon & gold   .25 .25
  a. Perf. 14½x14   .75 .30

Perf. 14½x14
510 A201 15c violet & gold   .40 .30
  Inauguration of Balthazar John Vorster as president of South Africa.

Golden Gate Highlands National
Park — A202

Designs: 15c, Blyde River Canyon, Transvaal. 20c, Amphitheater, Natal National Park.
25c, Cango Caves, Cape Province.

1978, Nov. 13   *Perf. 12½*
511 A202 10c multicolored   .25   .25
512 A202 15c multicolored   .25   .25
513 A202 20c multicolored   .35   .35
514 A202 25c multicolored   .55   .55
     Nos. 511-514 (4)   1.40 1.40
          Tourist publicity.

Tellurometer and Dr. I. R.
Wadley — A203

1979, Feb. 12   Litho.   *Perf. 12½*
515 A203 15c multicolored   .30   .25

15th anniversary of the invention of the tellurometer (to measure radio distances).

South
Africa
No.
C5
A204

1979, Mar. 30   Litho.   *Perf. 14½x14*
516 A204 15c multicolored   .35   .30

First stamp printed by South African Government Printer, 50th anniversary.

"Save Fuel"
A205

Fuel Economy: No. 518, Language inscriptions reversed.

1979, Apr. 2   Photo.   *Perf. 12x12½*
517 A205 4c red & black   .25   .25
518 A205 4c red & black   .25   .25
a.   Pair, #517-518   .40   .40

Battle of Isandlwana, by Melton
Prior — A206

15c, Battle of Ulundi, by Louis Creswicke.
20c, Battle of Rorke's Drift, by Lt. Col.
Crealock.

1979, May 25   Litho.   *Perf. 14x13½*
519 A206 4c red & black   .25   .25
520 A206 15c red & black   .40   .35
521 A206 20c red & black   .50   .40
a.   Souv. sheet, #519-521 + label 3.00 3.00
         Nos. 519-521 (3)   1.15 1.00
          Centenary of Zulu War.

"Health Care and
Service" — A207

1979, June 19   Litho.   *Perf. 12½x12*
522 A207 4c multicolored   .25   .25
a.   Perf. 14¼x14   .30   .30
          Health Year.

Boy and Girl Watching Candle — A208

1979, Sept. 13   Litho.   *Perf. 14½x14*
523 A208 4c multicolored   .25   .25

South African Christmas Stamp Fund, 50th
anniversary.

Cape Town University, 150th
Anniversary — A209

1979, Oct. 1   Litho.   *Perf. 14x14½*
524 A209 4c multicolored   .25   .25
a.   Perf. 12x12½   .30   .30

Southern Sun
Rose — A210

Designs: Roses.

1979, Oct. 4   Litho.   *Perf. 14½x14*
525 A210 4c multicolored   .25   .25
526 A210 15c multicolored   .35   .30
527 A210 20c multicolored   .45   .40
528 A210 25c multicolored   .65   .55
a.   Souvenir sheet of 4, #525-528 2.25 2.25
         Nos. 525-528 (4)   1.70 1.50

Rosafari 1979, 4th World Rose Convention,
Pretoria, October.

Stellenbosch University — A211

1979, Nov. 8
529 A211 4c shown   .25   .25
530 A211 15c Rhenish Church   .30   .25

Stellenbosch (oldest town in South Africa),
300th anniversary.

A212

A213

1979, Dec. 18   Photo.   *Perf. 12½x12*
531 A212 4c multicolored   .25   .25

Federation of Afrikaans Cultural Societies,
50th anniv.

1980, May 6   Litho.   *Perf. 14½x14*
Paintings by Pieter Wenning (1873-1921):
5c, Still Life with Sweet Peas. 25c, House in
the Suburbs, Cape Town.

532 A213 5c multicolored   .25   .25
          Size: 45x37mm
533 A213 25c multicolored   .40   .30
a.   Souvenir sheet of 2, #532-533 .90   .65

Great Star of
Africa
Diamond — A214

1980, May 12   Litho.   *Perf. 14x14½*
534 A214 15c shown   .65   .50
535 A214 20c Cullinan II dia-
           mond   .75   .65
       World Diamond Congress.

A215

A216

1980, Sept. 3   Litho.   *Perf. 14½x14*
536 A215 5c multicolored   .25   .25

Christian Louis Leipoldt (1880-1947), writer
and physician.

1980, Oct. 9   Litho.
537 A216 5c multicolored   .25   .25

University of Pretoria, 50th anniv.

Marine With Ships, by Willem van de
Velde — A217

Paintings: 10c, Firetail and Trainer, by
George Stubbs. 15c, Lavinia, by Thomas
Gainsborough, vert. 20c, Landscape, by Pieter
Post.

1980, Nov. 3   *Perf. 14½x14*
538 A217 5c multicolored   .25   .25
539 A217 10c multicolored   .25   .25
540 A217 15c multicolored   .25   .25
541 A217 20c multicolored   .30   .30
a.   Souvenir sheet of 4, #538-541 1.00 1.00
         Nos. 538-541 (4)   1.05 1.05
          Natl. Gallery, 50th anniv.

P.J. Joubert, Paul Kruger, M.W.
Pretorius (First Leaders of Triumvirate
Government) — A218

Design: 10c, Monument, flag of South African Republic, 1880, vert.

1980, Dec. 15   *Perf. 14x14½ 14½x14*
542 A218 5c multicolored   .25   .25
543 A218 10c multicolored   .25   .25

Paardekraal Monument (built on site of
founding of triumverate government)
centennial.

British Troops in Battle of
Amajuba — A219

1981, Feb. 27   Litho.   *Perf. 14x14½*
544 A219 5c Boer snipers, vert.   .25   .25
545 A219 15c shown   .35   .30

Battle of Amajuba centenary (led to independence of Orange Free State).

Scene
from
Verdi's
Aida
A220

1981, May 23   Litho.   *Perf. 14½x14*
546 A220 20c Raka ballet scene   .35   .30
547 A220 25c shown   .45   .35
a.   Souvenir sheet of 2, #546-547 1.25 1.00

Opening of State Theater, Pretoria.

Pres. Marais
Viljoen — A221

Deaf Girl
Learning to
Speak — A222

1981, May 30   *Perf. 14x14½*
          Size: 57x21mm
548 A221 5c Former presidents   .25   .25
549 A221 15c shown   .30   .25

1981, June 12   *Perf. 14½x14*
550 A222 5c shown   .25   .25
551 A222 15c Man reading braille   .30   .25

Institute for the Deaf and Blind, Worcester,
centenary.

Natl. Cancer Assn.
50th Anniv. — A223

1981, July 10
552 A223 5c multicolored   .25   .25

Calanthe Natalensis A224

Voortrekker Movement, 50th Anniv. A225

1981, Sept. 11   **Litho.**
553 A224 5c shown .25 .25
554 A224 15c Eulophia speciosa .30 .25
555 A224 20c Disperis fanniniae .40 .25
556 A224 25c Disa uniflora .50 .35
a. Souvenir sheet of 4, #553-556 2.00 1.90
Nos. 553-556 (4) 1.45 1.10

10th World Orchid Conf., Durban, 9/11-17.

1981, Sept. 30   **Perf. 14x14½**
557 A225 5c multicolored .25 .25

Scouting Year A226   TB Bacillus Centenary A227

1982, Feb. 22   Litho.   Perf. 14½x14
558 A226 15c Baden-Powell .40 .25

1982, Mar. 24   Litho.
559 A227 20c multicolored .40 .25

Return of Simonstown Naval Base, 25th Anniv. — A228

1982, Apr. 2   Perf. 14½x14
560 A228 8c Submarine .25 .25
561 A228 15c Strike craft .25 .25
562 A228 20c Mine sweeper .25 .25
563 A228 25c Harbor patrol boats .35 .25
a. Souvenir sheet of 4, #560-563 2.75 2.25
Nos. 560-563 (4) 1.10 1.00

Old Provost, Grahamstown A229

Design: 2c, Tuynhuys, Kaapstad (Cape Town). 3c, Appelhof, Bloemfontein. 4c, Raadsaal, Pretoria. 5c, Die Kasteel, Kaapstad. 6c, Goewermentsgebou, Bloemfontein. 7c, Drostdy, Graaf-Reinet. 8c, Leeuwenhof, Cape Town. 9c, Libertas, Pretoria. 10c, City Hall, Pietermaritzburg. 11c, City Hall, Kimberley. 12c, City Hall, Port Elizabeth. 14c, Johannesburg City Hall. 15c, Hotel Milner, Matjesfontein. 16c, Durban City Hall. 20c, Post Office, Durban. 25c, Melrose House, Pretoria. 30c, Old Legislative Assembly Building, Pietermaritzburg. 50c, Raadsaal, Bloemfontein. 1r, Houses of Parliament, Cape Town. 2r, Uniegebou, Pretoria.
Coils have different designs.

1982-87   Litho.   Perf. 14x14½
564 A229 1c brown ('84) .25 .25
565 A229 2c apple green .25 .25
566 A229 2c green .75 .25
567 A229 2c slate grn ('85) .25 .25
568 A229 3c purple ('85) 1.25 .25
569 A229 4c olive grn ('85) .25 .25
570 A229 5c carmine .25 .25
571 A229 6c brt green .25 .25
572 A229 7c gray green .25 .25
573 A229 8c blue .25 .25
574 A229 8c intense bl ('83) .25 .25
575 A229 9c brt rose lilac .25 .25
576 A229 10c lt red brown .25 .25
577 A229 10c violet brn ('83) .30 .25
578 A229 11c cerise ('84) .25 .25
579 A229 12c dp ultra ('85) .35 .25
580 A229 14c rose brn ('86) .50 .25
581 A229 16c red ('87) .60 .25
582 A229 20c vermilion .25 .25
583 A229 20c black ('85) .60 .25
584 A229 25c bister .25 .25

Size: 45x27mm

Perf. 14½x14
586 A229 30c brown ('86) 1.50 .25
587 A229 50c Prus blue ('86) 2.25 .25
588 A229 1r violet blue ('86) 2.50 .25
589 A229 2r cerise ('85) 5.00 .25
Nos. 564-589 (25) 19.10 6.25

For surcharge see No. B12.

Engr.
590 A229 1c dark brown .25 .25
591 A229 2c slate grn ('83) .25 .25
592 A229 3c violet .25 .25
593 A229 4c olive green .25 .25
594 A229 5c dark lake ('83) .25 .25
595 A229 6c green blk ('84) .25 .35
596 A229 15c blue .25 .25
597 A229 20c black ('83) .50 .25
598 A229 30c violet brown .45 .25
599 A229 50c Prus blue .70 .25
600 A229 1r violet blue 1.50 .25
601 A229 2r rose carmine 3.00 .30
Nos. 590-601 (12) 7.90 3.15

In some cases there are slight design differences from litho. stamp.

Perf. 14 Horiz.

	Photo.	Coil Stamps
602 A229 1c Residence, Swellendam .25 .25
603 A229 2c City Hall, East London .40 .25
604 A229 5c Rissik St. PO, Johannesburg .45 .25
605 A229 10c Morgenster, Somerset West .70 .25
Nos. 602-605 (4) 1.80 1.00

Bradysaurus A230

Prehistoric Animals (Karoo Fossils).

1982, Dec. 1   Litho.   Perf. 14x14½
606 A230 8c shown .25 .25
607 A230 15c Lystrosaurus .45 .24
608 A230 20c Euparkeria .60 .25
609 A230 25c Thrinaxodon .90 .35
a. Souvenir sheet of 4, #606-609 1.75 1.75
Nos. 606-609 (4) 2.20 1.10

Weather Station, Gough Island A231

1983, Jan. 19   Litho.
610 A231 8c shown .25 .25
611 A231 20c Marion Isld. station .30 .25
612 A231 25c Reading instruments .40 .25
613 A231 40c Weather balloon, Antarctica .60 .40
Nos. 610-613 (4) 1.55 1.15

Steam Locomotives — A232

1983, Apr. 27   Litho.
614 A232 10c Class 82, 1952 .25 .25
615 A232 20c Class 16E, 1935 .45 .35
616 A232 25c Class 6H, 1901 .60 .45
617 A232 40c Class 15F, 1939 1.00 .70
Nos. 614-617 (4) 2.30 1.75

Soccer — A233

Perf. 14½x14 (10c, 25c), 14x14½ (20c, 40c)

1983, July 20   Litho.
618 A233 10c Rugby, vert. .25 .25
619 A233 20c shown .25 .25
620 A233 25c Sailing, vert. .35 .25
621 A233 40c Equestrian .45 .30
Nos. 618-621 (4) 1.30 1.05

Plettenberg Bay — A234

1983, Oct. 12   Litho.   Perf. 14½x14
622 A234 10c shown .25 .25
623 A234 20c Durban Beach .25 .25
624 A234 25c West Coast beach .25 .25
625 A234 40c Clifton beach scene .40 .30
a. Souvenir sheet of 4, #622-625 1.50 1.40
Nos. 622-625 (4) 1.15 1.05

English Writers of South Africa — A235

Designs: 10c, Thomas Pringle (1789-1834). 20c, Pauline Smith (1882-1959). 25c, Olive Schreiner (1855-1920). 40c, Percy FitzPatrick (1862-1931).

1984, Feb. 24   Litho.   Perf. 14½x14
626 A235 10c multicolored .25 .25
627 A235 20c multicolored .25 .25
628 A235 25c multicolored .25 .25
629 A235 40c multicolored .45 .25
Nos. 626-629 (4) 1.20 1.00

Manganese — A236

1984, June 8   Litho.   Perf. 14x14½
630 A236 11c shown .30 .25
631 A236 20c Chromium .55 .25
632 A236 25c Vanadium .75 .25
633 A236 30c Titanium .85 .30
Nos. 630-633 (4) 2.45 1.05

Bloukrans River Bridge A237

1984, Aug. 24
634 A237 11c shown .25 .25
635 A237 25c Durban 4-level Bridge Interchange .50 .25
636 A237 30c Mfolozi Railroad Bridge .60 .25
637 A237 45c Gouritz River Bridge .90 .40
Nos. 634-637 (4) 2.25 1.15

New Constitution A238   Military Medals A239

1984, Sept. 3   Litho.   Perf. 14x14½
638 A238 11c Preamble (English) .35 .25
639 A238 11c Preamble (Africaans) .35 .25
a. Pair, #638-639 .70 .35
640 A238 25c Symbolic pillars, anthem .75 .40
641 A238 30c Arms .85 .45
Nos. 638-641 (4) 2.30 1.35

1984, Nov. 9   Perf. 14½x14
642 A239 11c Pro Patria .25 .25
643 A239 25c De Wet .25 .25
644 A239 30c John Chard Decoration .40 .25
645 A239 45c Honoris Crux .55 .30
a. Miniature sheet of 4, #642-645 1.25 1.10
Nos. 642-645 (4) 1.45 1.05

Pres. Pieter Willem Botha (b. 1916) — A240

1984, Nov. 2   Litho.   Perf. 14x14½
646 A240 11c multicolored .30 .25
647 A240 25c multicolored .60 .30

Frans David Oerder, Painter (1867-1944) A241

1985, Feb. 22   Litho.   Perf. 14½x14
648 A241 11c Reflections .25 .25
649 A241 25c Ladies in a Garden .25 .25
650 A241 30c Still-Life with Lobster .30 .25
651 A241 50c Still-Life with Marigolds .45 .25
a. Souvenir sheet of 4, #648-651 1.50 1.50
Nos. 648-651 (4) 1.25 1.00

Cape Parliament Cent. A242

1985, May 15   Litho.
652 A242 12c Parliament .25 .25
653 A242 25c Speaker's chair .30 .25
654 A242 30c The National Convention, by Edward Roworth .35 .25
655 A242 50c South African arms .65 .30
Nos. 652-655 (4) 1.55 1.05

Indigenous
Flowers
A243

Cape Silver
A244

1985, Aug. 23   Litho.   *Perf. 14½x14*
656 A243 12c Freesia   .25 .25
657 A243 25c Nerine   .35 .25
658 A243 30c Ixia   .40 .25
659 A243 50c Gladiolus   .70 .45
      Nos. 656-659 (4)   1.70 1.20

1985, Nov. 5   *Perf. 14½x14, 14x14½*
660 A244 12c Sugar bowl, horiz.   .25 .25
661 A244 25c Tea pot, horiz.   .40 .25
662 A244 30c Goblet   .50 .25
663 A244 50c Coffee pot   .90 .35
      Nos. 660-663 (4)   2.05 1.10

Blood
Transfusion
Services
A245

1986, Feb. 20   *Perf. 14½x14*
664 A245 12c Blood donation   .30 .25
665 A245 20c Transfusion   .70 .25
666 A245 25c Surgery   .90 .25
667 A245 30c Emergency aid   1.10 .35
      Nos. 664-667 (4)   3.00 1.10

Republic of
South
Africa, 25th
Anniv.
A246

1986, May 30   Litho.   *Perf. 14x14½*
668 A246 14c Text in Afrikaans   .75 .25
669 A246 14c Text in English   .75 .25
  a. Pair, #668-669   2.00 2.00

Cultural Heritage — A247

Restoration projects: 14c, Drostdyhof, Free
Street, Graaff-Reinet, 19th cent. 20c, Pilgrim's
Rest, Eastern Transvaal, 1873. 25c, J.T.
Strapp and Son importers, c. 1893, Bethle-
hem. 30c, Palmdene, c. 1897,
Pietermaritzburg.

1986, Aug. 14   *Perf. 14½x14*
670 A247 14c multicolored   .40 .25
671 A247 20c multicolored   .60 .30
672 A247 25c multicolored   .70 .35
673 A247 30c multicolored   .85 .40
      Nos. 670-673 (4)   2.55 1.30

Johannesburg, Cent. — A248

Discovery of Gold
in Roodepoort,
Cent. — A249

1986, Sept. 25   *Perf. 14x14½*
674 A248 14c Johannesburg,
              1886   .65 .25
675 A249 20c Gold mine   .95 .35
676 A248 25c Johannesburg,
              1986   1.10 .40
677 A249 30c Gold   1.40 .50
  a. Souvenir sheet of 1   1.90 1.90
      Nos. 674-677 (4)   4.10 1.50

No. 677a for Johannesburg stamp exhibition. Sold for 50c.

Pearl
Mountain — A250

1986, Nov. 20   Litho.   *Perf. 14x14½*
678 A250 14c shown   .50 .50
679 A250 20c The Column,
              Drakensburg   .70 .70
680 A250 25c Maltese Cross,
              Cedarberg   .90 .90
681 A250 30c Bourke's Luck
              Potholes   1.10 1.10
      Nos. 678-681 (4)   3.20 3.20

Beetles — A251

1987, Mar. 6   Litho.   *Perf. 14x14½*
690 A251 14c *Chaetodera regalis* .50 .50
691 A251 20c *Trichostetha fas-*
              cicularis   .70 .70
692 A251 25c *Julodis viridipes* .90 .90
693 A251 30c *Ceroplesis militaris* 1.10 1.10
      Nos. 690-693 (4)   3.20 3.20

Petroglyphs
A252

1987, June 4   *Perf. 14½x14*
694 A252 16c Eland, Sebaaieni
              Cave   .65 .65
695 A252 20c Leaping lion,
              Clocolan   .90 .90
696 A252 25c Black wildebeest,
              uMhlwazini Valley 1.10 1.10
697 A252 30c San dance,
              Floukraal   1.40 1.40
      Nos. 694-697 (4)   4.05 4.05

Paarl,
300th
Anniv.
A253

1987, Sept. 3
698 A253 16c Oude Pastorie   .35 .35
699 A253 20c Winegrowing   .40 .40
700 A253 25c Wagon-building   .50 .50
701 A253 30c KWV Cathedral
              Cellar   1.10 1.10
      Nos. 698-701 (4)   2.35 2.35

A souvenir sheet of one, No. 701, has decorative margin picturing emblem of the natl.
philatelic exhibition at Paarl, Sept. 16-19. Sold
for 50c. Value $3.

Map, "The Bible" in 76
Languages — A254

Religious
Paintings by
Rembrandt
A255

Designs: 30c, *Belshazzar's Feast*. 50c, *St.
Matthew and the Angel*, vert.

Perf. 14x14½, 14½x14 (30c)
1987, Nov. 19
702 A254 16c shown   .35 .35
703 A255 30c shown   .65 .65
704 A255 50c multicolored   1.10 1.10
      Nos. 702-704 (3)   2.10 2.10

Bible Society of South Africa.
A 40c stamp was prepared and sent to post
offices, but was not issued. Some were sold
contrary to the withdrawal order, and used
examples are known.
For surcharge see No. B13.

Discovery of
the Cape of
Good Hope
by
Bartolomeu
Dias — A256

Designs: 16c, Dias, astrolabe, Cape of
Good Hope. 30c, Kwaaihoek Memorial. 40c,
Caravels, 1488. 50c, Martellus Map, c. 1489.

1988, Feb. 3   *Perf. 14½x14*
706 A256 16c multicolored   .55 .55
707 A256 30c multicolored   1.00 1.00
708 A256 40c multicolored   1.25 1.25
709 A256 50c multicolored   1.60 1.60
      Nos. 706-709 (4)   4.40 4.40

A souvenir sheet of one, No. 709, has decorative margin picturing emblem of the natl.
philatelic exhibition held at Pietermaritzburg,
Nov. 22-27. Sold for 70c. Value $3.50.
For surcharge see No. B14.

French Huguenot
Settlement of the
Cape, 300th
Anniv. — A257

1988, Apr. 13   *Perf. 14x14½*
710 A257 16c Memorial, Frans-
              chhoek   .40 .40
711 A257 30c Map of France   .75 .75
712 A257 40c French-Dutch Bi-
              ble, 1672   1.10 1.10
713 A257 50c St. Bartholomew's
              Day Massacre,
              1572   1.50 1.50
      Nos. 710-713 (4)   3.75 3.75

For surcharges see Nos. B15-B18.

Lighthouses
A258

1988, June 9   *Perf. 14½x14*
714 A258 16c Pelican Point, 1932 .65 .65
715 A258 30c Groenpunt, 1824   1.25 1.25
716 A258 40c Agulhas, 1849   1.60 1.60
717 A258 50c Umhlanga Rocks,
              1954   2.00 2.00
  a. Souvenir sheet of 4, #714-717 7.00 7.00
      Nos. 714-717 (4)   5.50 5.50

"Standardised Mail"
"STANDARD POSTAGE"
Stamps inscribed thus were sold
for the amount shown in ( ) on date
of issue.

Succulents
A259

1988-93   Litho.   *Perf. 14x14½*
735 A259 1c *Huernia*
              zebrina   .25 .25
736 A259 2c *Euphorbia*
              symmetrica   .25 .25
737 A259 5c *Lithops*
              dorotheae   .25 .25
738 A259 7c *Gibbaeum*
              newbrownii   .25 .25
739 A259 10c *Didymaotus*
              lapidiformis   .25 .25
740 A259 16c *Vanheerdea*
              divergens   .25 .25
741 A259 18c *Faucaria*
              tigrina   .25 .25
742 A259 20c *Conophytum*
              mundum   .25 .25
743 A259 21c *Gasteria arm-*
              strongii   .25 .25
744 A259 25c *Cheiridopsis*
              pecularis   .25 .25
745 A259 30c *Tavaresia bark-*
              lyi   .25 .25
  a. Strip, 2 ea 1c, 2c, 5c, 7c, 30c 6.00
746 A259 35c *Dinteranthus*
              wilmotianus   .35 .25
747 A259 40c *Frithia pulchra*   .40 .25
748 A259 (45c) *Stapelia*
              grandiflora   .40 .25
749 A259 50c *Lapidaria mar-*
              garetae   .50 .50
750 A259 90c *Dioscorea ele-*
              phantipes   .80 .50
751 A259 1r *Trichocaulon*
              cactiforme   1.00 .70
752 A259 2r *Crassula*
              columnaris   2.00 1.00
753 A259 5r *Anacampseros*
              albissima   7.50 3.00
      Nos. 735-753 (19)   15.70 9.20

Coil Stamps
Photo.
Perf. 14 Horiz.
754 A259 1c *Adromischus*
              marianiae   1.75 1.75
755 A259 2c *Titanopsis cal-*
              carea   .45 .45
756 A259 5c *Dactylopsis*
              digitata   .45 .45
757 A259 10c *Pleiospilos bo-*
              lusii   .85 .85
      Nos. 754-757 (4)   3.50 3.50

Issued: 18c, 4/1/89; 5r, 3/1/90; 21c, 4/2/90;
#748, 4/1/93; others, 9/1/88.

Map and
Settlers — A260

Exodus, Tapestry by W.H. Coetzer
Studio — A261

Crossing the Drakensburg, Tapestry by
Coetzer Studio — A262

Church of the Vow,
Pietermaritzburg — A263

Perf. 14x14½, 14½x14 (50c)
1988, Nov. 21 Litho.
758 A260 16c multicolored .65 .40
759 A261 30c multicolored 1.10 .70
760 A262 40c multicolored 1.50 .95
761 A263 50c multicolored 1.75 1.25
  Nos. 758-761 (4) 5.00 3.30
  The Great Trek, 150th anniv.

Discovery of
a Living
Specimen of
the
Coelacanth,
50th Anniv.
A264

Designs: 16c, *Latimeria chalumnae*. 30c, J.
L. B. Smith, Margaret Courtenay-Latimer. 40c,
Smith Institute of Ichthyology, Grahamstown.
50c, Fish, GEO two-man research submarine.

1989, Feb. 9 **Perf. 14½x14**
762 A264 16c multicolored .80 .80
763 A264 30c multicolored 1.40 1.40
764 A264 40c multicolored 2.00 2.00
765 A264 50c multicolored 2.50 2.50
  a. Souvenir sheet of 1 7.00 7.00
  b. Souvenir sheet of 2 1.25 1.25
  Nos. 762-765 (4) 6.70 6.70

No. 765a has decorative margin picturing
emblem of the natl. philatelic exhibition WAN-
DERERS 101, held Sept. 6-9. Sold for 1.50r.
No. 765b was issued 6/97, sold for 1r and is
inscribed for Old Mutual Environmental Education Center in sheet margin.

Soil Conservation Campaign of the
Natl. Grazing Strategy — A265

1989, May 3 **Perf. 14x14½**
766 A265 18c Desertification .50 .50
767 A265 30c Eroded gullies .80 .80
768 A265 40c Barrage 1.10 1.10
769 A265 50c Verdant plain 1.40 1.40
  Nos. 766-769 (4) 3.80 3.80

Natl.
Rugby
Board,
Cent.
A266

Springboks, foreign team emblems, match
scenes.

1989, June 22
770 A266 18c France, 1980 .60 .45
771 A266 30c Australia, 1963 1.10 .80
772 A266 40c New Zealand,
       1937 1.50 1.10
773 A266 50c British Isles, 1896 1.90 1.40
  Nos. 770-773 (4) 5.10 3.75

Paintings by
Jacob
Hendrik
Pierneef
(1886-1957)
A267

1989, Aug. 3 **Perf. 14½x14**
774 A267 18c *Composition in
       Blue*, 1928 .40 .25
775 A267 30c *Zanzibar*, 1926 .75 .30
776 A267 40c *The Bushveld*,
       1949 1.10 .40
777 A267 50c *Cape Homestead*,
       1942 1.25 .50
  a. Souvenir sheet of 4, #774-777 3.50 3.50
  Nos. 774-777 (4) 3.50 1.45

Election of Pres.
Frederik Willem de
Klerk, Aug.
15 — A268

1989, Sept. 20 **Perf. 14x14½**
778 A268 18c shown .40 .25
779 A268 45c Portrait, diff. 1.00 .55

Fossil
Fuels,
Nuclear
and
Thermal
Power
A269

18c, SOEKOR gas project, Mossel Bay.
30c, SASOL coal conversion plant. 40c,
Koeberg nuclear power plant. 50c, ESKOM
thermal power station.

1989, Oct. 19
780 A269 18c multicolored .45 .25
781 A269 30c multicolored .80 .45
782 A269 40c multicolored .95 .50
783 A269 50c multicolored 1.25 .60
  Nos. 780-783 (4) 3.45 1.80

Cooperation in Southern
Africa — A270

Maps and: 18c, Cahora Bassa hydroelectric
power project. 30c, Railway network. 40c,
Lesotho Highlands water project. 50c, Veterinary care.

1990, Feb. 15 **Perf. 14½x14**
Size of 18c, 40c: 68x26mm
784 A270 18c multicolored .65 .35
785 A270 30c multicolored 1.10 .60
786 A270 40c multicolored 1.25 .75
787 A270 50c multicolored 1.75 .85
  a. Miniature sheet of 4, #784-787 4.75 4.75
  Nos. 784-787 (4) 4.75 2.55

Stamp
Day — A271

Stamps on stamps: a, Great Britain #1. b,
Cape of Good Hope #2. c, Natal #4. d, Orange
River Colony #10. e, Transvaal #3.

1990, May 12 Litho.
788 Strip of 5 2.75 2.75
  a.-e. A271 21c any single .50 .50
  Penny Black, 150th anniv.

Birds — A272

Designs: 21c, *Tauraco corythaix*. 35c, *Cos-
sypha natalensis*. 40c, *Mirafra africana*. 50c,
Telophorus zeylonus.

1990, Aug. 2 Litho. **Perf. 14x14½**
789 A272 21c multicolored .65 .40
790 A272 35c multicolored 1.00 .70
791 A272 40c multicolored 1.25 .90
792 A272 50c multicolored 1.50 .95
  Nos. 789-792 (4) 4.40 2.95

A souvenir sheet of 1 #792 was sold by the
Philatelic Foundation of South Africa. Value
$5.

Karoo
Landscape,
Near
Britstown
A273

Tourism: #794, Camps Bay, Cape Peninsula. #795, Giraffes, Kruger Natl. Park. #796,
Boschendal homestead, Drakenstein.

1990, Nov. 1 **Perf. 14½x14**
793 A273 50c multicolored 1.00 1.00
794 A273 50c multicolored 1.00 1.00
795 A273 50c multicolored 1.00 1.00
796 A273 50c multicolored 1.00 1.00
  a. Block of 4, #793-796 4.25 4.25

A274

National Decorations: No. 797, Woltemade
Cross for Bravery. No. 798, Order of the
Southern Cross. No. 799, Order of the Star of
South Africa. No. 800, Order for Meritorious
Service. No. 801, Order of Good Hope.

1990, Dec. 6
797 A274 21c multicolored .40 .30
798 A274 21c multicolored .40 .30
799 A274 21c multicolored .40 .30
800 A274 21c multicolored .40 .30
801 A274 21c multicolored .40 .30
  a. Souv. sheet of 5, #797-801 2.50 2.50
  b. Strip of 5, #797-801 2.00 2.00

A275

Animal Breeding: a, Boer horse. b, Bonsmara cattle. c, Dorper sheep. d, Ridgeback
dog. e, Putterie racing pigeon.

1991, Feb. 21 Litho.
802 A275 21c Strip of 5, #a.-e. 3.75 3.00

Achievements — A276

Designs: 25c, First heart transplant, vert.
40c, Matimba power plant. 50c, Dolos break-
water blocks. 60c, Western Deep Levels Gold
Mine, world's deepest mine, vert.

**Perf. 14½x14 (25c, 60c), 14x14½
(40c, 50c, #806a)**
1991, May 30 Litho.
803 A276 25c multicolored .40 .25
804 A276 40c multicolored .60 .30
805 A276 50c multicolored .70 .35
806 A276 60c multicolored .55 .40
  a. Souvenir sheet of 1 3.75 3.75
  Nos. 803-806 (4) 2.25 1.30

30th anniv. of Republic of South Africa.

1st Registration of
Nurses &
Midwives,
Cent. — A277

1991, Aug. 15 Litho. **Perf. 14x14½**
807 A277 60c multicolored .85 .85

Creation of South
African Post
Office
Ltd. — A278

1991, Oct. 1 Litho.
808 27c Post office .40 .25
809 27c Telkom SA Ltd. .40 .25
  a. A278 Pair, #808-809 1.00 1.00

South
African
Scientists
A279

Designs: 27c, Sir Arnold Theiler (1867-
1936), veterinarian. 45c, Sir Basil Schonland
(1896-1972), physicist. 65c, Dr. Robert Broom
(1866-1951), paleontologist. 85c, Dr. Alexander L. du Toit (1878-1948), geologist.

1991, Oct. 9 **Perf. 14½x14**
810 A279 27c multicolored .50 .25
811 A279 45c multicolored .80 .50
812 A279 65c multicolored 1.25 .65
813 A279 85c multicolored 1.50 .80
  Nos. 810-813 (4) 4.05 2.20

Antarctic
Treaty, 30th
Anniv.
A280

1991, Dec. 5 Litho.
814 A280 27c SA Agulhas, pen-
       guins .85 .25
815 A280 65c Meteorological
       chart 2.10 .95

Conservation — A281

1992, Feb. 6   Litho.   Perf. 14x14½
816	A281	27c Prevent erosion	.55	.25
817	A281	65c Water pollution	1.50	.90
818	A281	85c Air pollution	1.90	1.10
		Nos. 816-818 (3)	3.95	2.25

A souvenir sheet of 1 #817 was sold by Intersapa. Value $5.

A282

Designs depicting history of postal stones: No. 819, Sailing ships at Table Bay. No. 820, Sailors going ashore at Aguada de Saldanha. No. 821, Sailors discovering postal stone near Versse River. No. 822, Finding letters under postal stones. No. 823, Reading news from other mariners.

1992, May 9   Litho.   Perf. 14x14½
819	A282	35c multicolored	.60	.50
820	A282	35c multicolored	.60	.50
821	A282	35c multicolored	.60	.50
822	A282	35c multicolored	.60	.50
823	A282	35c multicolored	.60	.50
a.		Strip of 5, #819-823	3.25	3.25

Stamp Day.

A283

Antique Cape Furniture: No. 824, Queen Anne settee, c. 1750-70. No. 825, Stinkwood settee, c. 1800. No. 826, Canopy bed, c. 1800, vert. No. 827, Rocking cradle, 19th cent. No. 828, Waterbutt, c. 1800, vert. No. 829, Flemish style cabinet, c. 1700, vert. No. 830, Armoire, c. 1780-1790, vert. No. 831, Church chair, late 17th cent, vert. No. 832, Tub chair, c. 1770-1790, vert. No. 833, Bible desk, c. 1770, vert.

Perf. 14½x14, 14x14½
824	A283	35c multicolored	.65	.55
825	A283	35c multicolored	.65	.55
826	A283	35c multicolored	.65	.55
827	A283	35c multicolored	.65	.55
828	A283	35c multicolored	.65	.55
829	A283	35c multicolored	.65	.55
830	A283	35c multicolored	.65	.55
831	A283	35c multicolored	.65	.55
832	A283	35c multicolored	.65	.55
833	A283	35c multicolored	.65	.55
a.		Miniature sheet of 10, #824-833	6.50	6.50

Sports
A284

1992, July 24   Perf. 14x14½
834	A284	35c Formula 1 Grand Prix	.40	.30
835	A284	35c Soccer	.40	.30
836	A284	55c Paris-le Cap Rally	.65	.50
837	A284	70c Track	.80	.65
838	A284	90c Rugby	1.00	.85
839	A284	1.05r Cricket	1.50	1.25
a.		Souvenir sheet of 6, #834-839	4.75	4.75
		Nos. 834-839 (6)	4.75	3.85

A285

1992, Oct. 8   Litho.   Perf. 14½x14
840	A285	35c Women's Monument	.35	.35
841	A285	70c Sekupu Player	.90	.75
842	A285	90c The Hunter	1.25	.95

843	A285	1.05r Postman Lehman	1.50	.85
a.		Souvenir sheet of 4, #840-843	4.00	4.00
		Nos. 840-843 (4)	4.00	2.90

Sculptures by Anton van Wouw (1862-1945). No. 843a sold for 3.30r.

A286

South African Harbors.

1993, Jan. 28   Litho.
844	A286	35c Walvis Bay	.35	.30
845	A286	55c East London	.65	.45
846	A286	70c Port Elizabeth	.85	.60
847	A286	90c Cape Town	1.00	.80
848	A286	1.05r Durban	1.25	.90
a.		Souv. sheet, #844-848 + label	4.25	4.25
		Nos. 844-848 (5)	4.10	3.05

No. 848a sold for 3.90r.

A287

Aircraft: a, Bristol Boxkite, 1907. b, Voisin, 1909. c, Bleriot XI, 1911. d, Paterson No. 2 biplane, 1913. e, Henri Farman F.27, 1915. f, BE2e, 1918. g, Vickers Vimy Silver Queen, 1920. h, SE-5a, 1921. i, Avro 504K, 1921. j, Armstrong-Whitworth Atalanta, 1930. k, DH66 Hercules, 1931. l, Westland Wapiti, 1931. m, Junkers F.13, 1932. n, Handley Page HP-42, 1933. o, Junkers Ju52/3m, 1934. p, Junkers Ju86, 1936. q, Hawker Hartbees, 1936. r, Short Empire flying boat Canopus, 1937. s, Miles Master II and Airspeed AS-10 Oxford, 1940. t, Harvard Mk IIa, 1942. u, Short Sunderland, 1945. v, Avro York, 1946. w, Douglas DC-7B, 1955. x, Sikorsky S-55C, 1956. y, Boeing 707-344, 1959.

Miniature Sheet of 25
1993, May 7   Litho.   Perf. 14x14½
849	A287	45c #a.-y.	18.00	18.00

A souvenir sheet containing #849a, 849y was sold by the Philatelic Foundation of South Africa.

A288

Endangered Fauna: 1c, Heleophryne rosei. 2c, Bradypodion taeniabronchum. 5c, Cordylus giganteus. 10c, Psammobates geometricus. 20c, Atelerix frontalis. 40c, Bunolagus monticularis. (45c), Diceros bicornis. 50c, Cercopithecus mitis. 55c, Proteles cristatus. 60c, Lycaon pictus. 70c, Hippotragus equinus. 75c, Poecilogale albinucha. 80c, Otis kori. 85c, Serinus citrinipectus. 90c, Spheniscus demersus. 1r, Grus carunculatus. 2r, Hirundo atrocaerulea. 5r, Polemaetus bellicosus. 10r, Terathopius ecaudatus.

Inscriptions in Latin
1993-95   Litho.   Perf. 14x14½
850	A288	1c multicolored	.25	.25
851	A288	2c multicolored	.25	.25
852	A288	5c multicolored	.25	.25
853	A288	10c multicolored	.25	.25
854	A288	20c multicolored	.25	.25
a.		Strip, 1c, 2 ea 2c, 20c	1.00	
b.		Strip, 20c, 2 ea 5c, 10c	1.00	
c.		Strip, 20c, 2 each 5c, 10c, perf. 14½ vert.	1.00	
855	A288	40c multicolored	.30	.25
856	A288	(45c) multicolored	.35	.25
857	A288	50c multicolored	.35	.25
a.		Strip, #850, 852, 857, 2 #851, perf. 14½ vert.	1.10	
858	A288	55c multicolored	.35	.25
859	A288	60c multicolored	.40	.25
860	A288	70c multicolored	.45	.25
861	A288	75c multicolored	.50	.25
862	A288	80c multicolored	.60	.25
862A	A288	80c multicolored	.60	.30
863	A288	90c multicolored	.65	.25
a.		Booklet pane of 10	—	
		Complete booklet, #863a	—	
864	A288	1r multicolored	.75	.25
865	A288	2r multicolored	1.75	.25

866	A288	5r multicolored	4.00	.50
867	A288	10r multicolored	7.50	1.50
		Nos. 850-867 (19)	19.80	6.30

#857a exists with tab showing Reader's Digest emblem in either red or black; also in different order with emblem in blue.
Issued: #854b, 8/24/94; #854c, 10/94; #857a, 9/1/95; 85c, 10/2/95; #863a, 1995; others, 9/3/93.
See designs A336 and A343 (no frames).

Wildlife Type with English Inscriptions

Designs: 1c, Table Mountain ghost frog. 2c, Smith's dwarf chameleon. 10c, Geometric tortoise. 20c, Southern African hedgehog. 40c, Riverine rabbit. (45c), Black rhinoceros. 50c, Samango monkey. 60c, Cape hunting dog. 70c, Roan antelope. 90c, Jackass penguin. 1r, Wattled crane. 2r, Blue swallow. 5r, Martial eagle. 20r, Fish Eagle.

Perf. 14x14¼, 14 Vert. on 1 or 2 sides (1c, 2c, 10c, 55c), 13x14½ (#867F)
867A	A288	1c multicolored	.25	.25
867B	A288	2c multicolored	.25	.25
867C	A288	10c multicolored	.25	.25
867D	A288	20c multicolored	.25	.25
867E	A288	40c multicolored	.25	.25
867F	A288	(45c) multicolored	.40	.25
n.		Booklet pane of 10	3.00	
		Complete booklet, #867Fn	3.00	
o.		Souvenir sheet of 1	.55	.55
867G	A288	50c multicolored	.25	.25
867H	A288	55c multicolored	.60	.60
p.		Strip of 5, 10c, 55c, 2 2c, perf 14 vert.	1.10	
867I	A288	70c multicolored	.25	.25
867J	A288	90c multicolored	.45	.25
867K	A288	1r multicolored	.45	.25
867L	A288	2r multicolored	1.00	.25
867M	A288	5r multicolored	2.00	.90

Perf. 14x14¼ Syncopated
867Q	A288	20c multicolored	.25	.25
867R	A288	(45c) multicolored	.60	.45
867S	A288	50c multicolored	.50	.25
867T	A288	60c multicolored	.25	.25
867U	A288	1r multicolored	3.50	.40

Size: 34x25mm
Perf. 14¾ Syncopated
867V	A288	20r multicolored	9.50	4.75

No. 867Fn is inscribed in sheet margin for ExpoScience Internationale '97, and sold for 1r.
No. 867Hp has tab showing Reader's Digest emblem and release date in either green or orange.
Issued: #867Hp, 8/1; #867F, 7/7/97.

First Postal Services in South Africa, 190th Anniv.
A289

Designs: 45c, Dragoons, Cape Town-False Bay Route. 65c, Ox train, Cape Town-Stellenbosch. 85c, Khoi-Khoin runners. 1.05r, Post riders, Cape Town-eastern districts.

1993, Oct. 8   Perf. 14x14½
868	A289	45c multicolored	.55	.55
869	A289	65c multicolored	.85	.75
870	A289	85c multicolored	1.00	.95
871	A289	1.05r multicolored	1.25	1.25
		Nos. 868-871 (4)	3.65	3.50

Tourism
A290

a, Namaqualand. b, North Beach, Durban. c, Lion. d, Apple Express. e, Oryx gazella.

1993, Nov. 12   Litho.   Perf. 14½x14
872	A290	85c Strip of 5, #a.-e.	3.50	3.50

Export Fruits
A291

1994, Jan. 28   Litho.   Perf. 14½x14
873	A291	85c Grapes	.65	.55
874	A291	90c Apples	.70	.60
875	A291	1.05r Plums	.85	.70
876	A291	1.25r Oranges	1.10	.95
877	A291	1.40r Avocados	1.25	.95
		Nos. 873-877 (5)	4.55	3.65

A souvenir sheet of 1 #873 was sold for 3r by the Philatelic Foundation of South Africa. Value $3.50.

Peace and Goodwill — A292

Childrens' drawings: 45c, Smiling faces, by Nicole Davies. 70c, Dove flying toward olive tree, by Robynne Lawrie. 95c, Three girls, dove, scattered cartridge cases, by Batami Nothmann. 1.15r, Faces surrounding "peace," by Karen Uys.

1994, Apr. 8   Litho.   Perf. 14½x14
878	A292	45c multicolored	.40	.40
879	A292	70c multicolored	.60	.55
880	A292	95c multicolored	.75	.80
881	A292	1.15r multicolored	.95	.85
a.		Souvenir sheet of 1	3.00	3.00
		Nos. 878-881 (4)	2.70	2.60

No. 881a was issued 8/97, sold for 1.15r and is inscribed "Chernobyl's Children, a decade later 1986-1996" in margin.

Inauguration of Pres. Nelson Mandela — A293

Perf. 14x14½, 14½x14
1994, May 10   Litho.
882	A293	45c shown	.70	.60
883	A293	70c Anthems, horiz.	1.10	.90
884	A293	95c Flag, horiz.	1.60	1.25
885	A293	1.15r Union Bldgs., horiz.	2.00	1.50
		Nos. 882-885 (4)	5.40	4.25

Tugboats — A294

1994, May 13   Perf. 14½x14
886	A294	45c TS McEwen	.50	.40
887	A294	70c Sir William Hoy	.70	.65
888	A294	95c Sir Charles Elliott	.95	.90
889	A294	1.15r Eland	1.25	1.00
890	A294	1.35r Pioneer	1.40	1.25
a.		Souvenir sheet of 5, #886-890	5.50	5.50
		Nos. 886-890 (5)	4.80	4.20

Our Family — A295

Children's paintings: a, Mother Hands Out Work (C1.5). b, My Friends and I at Play (C2.5). c, Family Life (C3.5). d, Sunday in Church (C4.5). e, I Visit My Brother in the Hospital (C5.5).

1994, July 10   Litho.   Perf. 14x14½
891 A295 45c Strip of 5, #a.-e.   2.50 2.50

Stamp Day — A296

1994, Sept. 30   Litho.   Perf. 14
892 A296 50c Bulk mail   .40 .40
893 A296 70c Proof of delivery   .55 .55
894 A296 95c Registered mail   .75 .75
895 A296 1.15r Express delivery   .85 .85
     Nos. 892-895 (4)   2.55 2.55

Heather — A297

Designs: a, Erica tenuifolia. b, Erica urnaviridis. c, Erica decora. d, Erica aristata. e, Erica dichrus.

1994, Nov. 18   Litho.   Perf. 14
896 A297 95c Strip of 5, #a.-e.   4.50 4.50

Tourism — A298

#897, Phacochoerus aethiopicus, Eastern, Transvaal Province. #898, Lost City, Sun City, North West Province. #899, Ceratotherium simum, KwaZulu/Natal Province. #900, Waterfront, Cape Town, Western Cape Province. #901, Adansonia digitata, Northern Transvaal Province. #902, Highland Route, Free State. #903, Augrabies Falls, Northern Cape Province. #904, Addo Elephant Natl. Park, Eastern Cape Province. #905, Union Buildings, Pretoria, Gauteng.

1995-97   Litho.   Perf. 14
897 A298 50c multicolored   .60 .60
898 A298 50c multicolored   .60 .60
899 A298 60c multicolored   .70 .70
900 A298 60c multicolored   .70 .70
901 A298 60c multicolored   .70 .70
a.   #901 + label, perf. 14 on one side   1.25 1.25
b.   Souvenir sheet of 1   3.50 3.50
902 A298 60c multicolored   .70 .70
903 A298 60c multicolored   .70 .70
904 A298 60c multicolored   .70 .70
905 A298 60c multicolored   .70 .70
a.   Strip of 5, #901-905   3.75 3.75
     Nos. 897-905 (9)   6.10 6.10

#901a sold for 70c; #901b for 1.10r on date of issue.
Issued: #897, 1/18; #898, 2/15; #899, 4/28; #900, 5/12; #901-905, 6/30; #901a, 2/97; #901b 8/97.

South African Airforce, 75th Anniv. — A299

DeHavilland DH-9 biplane, Cheetah D fighter.

1995, Feb. 1   Litho.   Perf. 14
906 A299 50c multicolored   1.75 1.75

First Trans-Africa Flight, 75th Anniv. — A300

Vickers Vimy bomber Silver Queen, map of route.

1995, Feb. 1
907 A300 95c multicolored   .55 .55

South Africa, 1995 Rugby World Cup Champions A301

Designs: No. 908, Shown. No. 909, Player running with ball, vert. No. 910, Player holding trophy, vert. No. 911, Like #908, World Champions. No. 912, Scrum, two players.

1995   Litho.   Perf. 14
908 A301 60c multicolored   .30 .30
a.   Perf. 14 horiz.   .30
909 A301 60c multicolored   .30 .30
a.   Souvenir sheet of 1   1.25 1.25
b.   Perf. 14 vert.   .30 .30
c.   Booklet pane, 5 each #908a, 909b   5.25
     Complete booklet, #909c   5.25
d.   Booklet pane, 10 #909b   5.25
     Complete booklet, #909d   5.25
910 A301 60c multicolored   .30 .30
911 A301 60c multicolored   .30 .30

Size: 68x26mm
912 A301 1.15r multicolored   .55 .55
     Nos. 908-912 (5)   1.75 1.75
     Issued: #910-911, 6/28; others 5/25.

CSIR (Council for Scientific and Industrial Research), 50th Anniv. A302

1995, June 15
913 A302 (60c) Purifying water   .60 .60

Marine Science in South Africa, Cent. A303

1995, Aug. 25   Litho.   Perf. 14
914 A303 (60c) Dr. JDF Gilchrist   .60 .60

Souvenir Sheet

Singapore '95 — A304

1995, Sept. 1
915 A304 (60c) multicolored   1.00 1.00

Masakhane Campaign A305

1995   Perf. 14x14¼
916 A305 (60c) multicolored   .60 .60
a.   Booklet pane of 10   6.00
     Complete booklet, No. 916a   6.00

Booklet Stamp
Size: 29x20mm
916B A305 (60c) multicolored   .60 .60
c.   Booklet pane of 10   6.00
     Complete booklet, #916c   6.00
     Issued: #916, 9/16; #916B, 12/1.

Visit of Pope John Paul II — A306   Mahatma Gandhi — A307

1995, Sept. 16   Perf. 14
917 A306 (60c) multicolored   .90 .90

1995, Oct. 2
Designs: (60c), 1906 Photograph. 1.40r, Ghandhi in later years.
918 A307 (60c) blue   .85 .85
a.   Souvenir sheet of 1   1.25 1.25
919 A307 1.40r brown   1.90 1.90
a.   Souvenir sheet of 1   2.40 2.40

No. 918a is inscribed in sheet margin for 50th anniv. of Congress Alliance for Democratic South Africa. Issued July 1997.
Design on stamp in No. 919a extends to perforations.
See India Nos. 1534-1535.

World Post Day — A308

1995
920 A308 (60c) multicolored   .70 .70

Size: 65x60mm
Imperf
921 A308 5r multicolored   2.75 2.75
     Stampex '95.
     Issued: (60c), 10/9; 5r, 10/19.

UN, 50th Anniv. A309

1995, Oct. 24   Litho.   Perf. 14
922 A309 (60c) multicolored   .50 .50

Souvenir Sheet

UNESCO, 50th Anniv. — A310

1995, Oct. 24
923 A310 (60c) multicolored   .50 .50

Shells — A311   A312

1995, Nov. 24
924 A311 (60c) Afrivoluta priglei   .55 .55
925 A311 (60c) Lyria africana   .55 .55
926 A311 (60c) Marginella mosaica   .55 .55
927 A311 (60c) Conus pictus   .55 .55
928 A311 (60c) Gypreaea fultoni   .55 .55
a.   Strip of 5, #924-928   2.75 2.75

1996, Jan. 8   Litho.   Perf. 14
1996 African Cup of Nations Soccer Championships: Nos. 929-933, Various soccer plays, map of Africa. No. 934, Player in traditional uniform.

Color of "RSA"
929 A312 (60c) blue   .60 .60
930 A312 (60c) yellow   .60 .60
931 A312 (60c) red   .60 .60
932 A312 (60c) gray   .60 .60
933 A312 (60c) green   .60 .60
a.   Strip of 5, Nos. 929-933   3.00 3.00

Souvenir Sheet
934 A312 (1.15r) multicolored   .70 .70

South African Victory in African Nations Soccer Championship A312a

1996, Feb. 8   Litho.   Perf. 14½x14
934A A312a (60c) multicolored   .70 .70

City of Bloemfontein, 150th Anniv. — A313

1996, Mar. 28   Litho.   Perf. 14
935 A313 (60c) multicolored   .80 .80

Souvenir Sheet

New Year 1996 (Year of the Rat) — A313a

1996, May 18　　Litho.　　Perf. 14
940D　A313a 60c multicolored　　1.00 1.00
CHINA '96.

Man in a Donkey Cart, by Gerard Sekoto (1913-93) — A314

Paintings: #942, 2r, Song of the Pick. #943, 2r, Yellow Houses, Sophiatown, 1940, vert.

1996, June 1　　Litho.　　Perf. 14
941　A314 1r multicolored　　.60 .60
942　A314 2r multicolored　　1.25 1.25

Souvenir Sheet
943　A314 2r multicolored　　1.50 1.50

Youth Day — A315

1996, June 8
944　A315 (60c) multicolored　　.50 .50

Comrades Marathon, 75th Anniv. — A316

1996, June 8　　Litho.　　Perf. 14
945　A316 (60c) multicolored　　.50 .50

Souvenir Sheet

Parliament Building, Toronto — A316a

1996, June 8　　Litho.　　Perf. 14
945A　A316a 2r multicolored　　1.50 1.50
CAPEX '96.

A317　　　　　A318

1996 Summer Olympic Games, Atlanta: No. 946: a, Cycling. b, Swimming. c, Boxing. d, Running. e, Pole vault.
1.40r, South African Olympic emblem.

1996, July 5　　Litho.　　Perf. 14½x14
946　A317 (70c) Strip of 5, #a.-e.　2.40 2.40
Perf. 14
947　A317 1.40r multicolored　　.85 .85
No. 946 was issued in sheets of 10 stamps.

1996, Aug. 1　　Litho.　　Perf. 14
Background color: a, Vermilion & multi. b, Deep blue & multi. c, Deep yellow & multi. d, Bright blue & multi. e, Red & multi.
948　　Strip of 5　　2.50 2.50
　a.-e. A318 (70c) any single　　.50 .50
New Democratic Constitution.

South African Merchant Marine, 50th Anniv. — A319

Paintings of ships, by Peter Bilas: No. 949: a, Sea Pioneer. b, SA Winterberg.
No. 950: a, Langloof. b, SA Vaal.
2r, Constantia.

1996, Aug. 5　　Litho.　　Perf. 14
949　　Pair　　1.25 1.25
　a.-b. A319 (70c) any single　　.60 .60
950　　Pair　　2.75 2.75
　a.-b. A319 1.40r any single　　1.25 1.25
Souvenir Sheet
950C　A319　　2r multicolored　　1.50 1.50
No. 950C contains one 72x30mm stamp.

A320

1996, Aug. 9　　Litho.　　Perf. 14
951　A320 70c multicolored　　.50 .50
Natl. Women's Day.

A321

1996, Oct. 9
952　A321 70c multicolored　　.50 .50
World Post Day.

Christmas — A322

1996, Oct. 9
953　A322 70c multicolored　　.50 .50
No. 953 exists in a privately produced souvenir, sold at 2r for charitable purposes.

Souvenir Sheet

Bloemfontein, 150th Natl. Stamp Show — A323

1996, Oct. 9　　Litho.　　Perf. 14½x14
954　A323 2r multicolored　　1.50 1.50

South African Nobel Laureates, Death Cent. of Alfred Nobel — A324

a, Max Theiler, medicine, 1951. b, Albert Luthuli, peace, 1960. c, Alfred Nobel (1833-96). d, Allan Cormack, medicine, 1979. e, Aaron Klug, chemistry, 1982. f, Desmond Tutu, peace, 1984. g, Nadine Gordimer, literature, 1991. h, Symbol for Nobel Prizes 1901-96. i, Nelson R. Mandela, peace, 1993. j, F.W. de Klerk, peace, 1993.

1996, Nov. 4
955　A324 (70c) Sheet of 10, #a.-
　j.　　　　　　　　　　4.75 4.75
　k.　Souvenir sheet, #955c　　.60 .60

First Motor Car in South Africa, Cent. — A325

1997, Jan. 4　　Litho.　　Perf. 14
956　A325 (70c) multicolored　　1.00 1.00

Souvenir Sheet

Hong Kong '97 — A326

Perf. 14 Syncopated
1997, Feb. 12　　　　　　Litho.
957　A326 3r multicolored　　2.50 2.50

Natl. Water Week and Water Day — A328

Save water for: No. 959, Farming. No. 960, Gardening. No. 961, Health. No. 962, Housing. No. 963, For all.

Perf. 14 Syncopated on 2 or 3 Sides
1997, Mar. 22　　　　　Litho.
Booklet Stamps
959　A328 (70c) multicolored　　.60 .60
960　A328 (70c) multicolored　　.60 .60
961　A328 (70c) multicolored　　.60 .60
962　A328 (70c) multicolored　　.60 .60
963　A328 (70c) multicolored　　.60 .60
　a.　Booklet pane, 2 each #959-963　6.00 6.00
　　　Complete booklet　　6.00 6.00

Perf. 14x14¼ on 2 or 3 Sides
1997, Mar.　　　　　Litho.
Booklet Stamps
963B　A328 (70c) Like #959　　.60 .60
963C　A328 (70c) Like #960　　.60 .60
963D　A328 (70c) Like #961　　.60 .60
963E　A328 (70c) Like #962　　.60 .60
963F　A328 (70c) Like #963　　.60 .60
　g.　Bkt. pane, 2 ea #963B-963F　6.00 6.00
　　　Complete booklet, #963Fg　6.00 6.00

South African Navy, 75th Anniv. — A329

Warships: No. 964, Strike craft SAS Kobie Coetsee. No. 965, Survey ship SAS Protea. No. 966, Mine counter-measures ship SAS Umkomaas. No. 967, Submarine Emily Hobhouse, anti-submarine frigate SAS President Pretorius.

1997, Apr. 1　　　Perf. 14 Syncopated
964　A329 (70c) multicolored　　.60 .60
965　A329 (70c) multicolored　　.60 .60
966　A329 (70c) multicolored　　.60 .60
967　A329 (70c) multicolored　　.60 .60
　a.　Block of 4, #964-967　　2.40 2.40

First Democratic Elections, 5th Anniv. — A330

People voting, signs saying: No. 968, "Election Day, 27, April, 1994." No. 969, "Polling Station." No. 970, "Register Here." No. 971, "Vote Here." No. 972, "Ballot Box."

Perf. 14 Syncopated
1997, Apr. 26　　　　　Litho.
968　A330 (70c) black & red　　.50 .50
969　A330 (70c) black & red　　.50 .50
970　A330 (70c) black & red　　.50 .50
971　A330 (70c) black & red　　.50 .50
972　A330 (70c) black & red　　.50 .50
　b.　Strip of 5, #968-972　　2.50 2.50

Souvenir Sheet

New Year 1997 (Year of the Ox) — A330a

1997, May 2　　Litho.　　Perf. 14
972A　A330a 4.50r multicolored　　2.25 2.25
SAPDA '97.

A331

Cultural Artifacts.

1997, May 18 **Perf. 14**
973 A331 (70c) Zulu baskets .50 .50
974 A331 (70c) S. Sotho figure .50 .50
975 A331 (70c) S. Ndebele figure .50 .50
976 A331 (70c) Venda door .50 .50
977 A331 (70c) Tsonga medicine
        gourd .50 .50
978 A331 (70c) Wooden pot, N.
        cape .50 .50
979 A331 (70c) Khoi walking stick .50 .50
980 A331 (70c) Tswana knife
        handle .50 .50
981 A331 (70c) Xhosa pipe .50 .50
982 A331 (70c) Swazi vessel .50 .50
  a.   Sheet of 10, #973-982 5.00 5.00

1997, Dec. **Perf. 14x15**
973a   Zulu baskets .60 .60
974a   S. Sotho figure .60 .60
975a   S. Ndebele figure .60 .60
976a   Venda door .60 .60
977a   Tsonga medicine gourd .60 .60
978a   Wooden pot, N. cape .60 .60
979a   Khoi walking stick .60 .60
980a   Tswana knife handle .60 .60
981a   Xhosa pipe .60 .60
982a   Swazi vessel .60 .60
982b   Bklt. pane, #973a-981a,
          982b 6.00
982c   Complete booklet, 2 #982c 12.00

A332

Birds.

1997, June 5 **Perf. 14**
983 A332 (70c) White-breasted
        cormorant .50 .50
984 A332 (70c) Hammerkop .50 .50
985 A332 (70c) Pied kingfisher .50 .50
986 A332 (70c) Purple heron .50 .50
987 A332 (70c) Black-headed
        heron .50 .50
988 A332 (70c) Darter .50 .50
989 A332 (70c) Green-backed
        heron .50 .50
990 A332 (70c) White-faced
        duck .50 .50
  a.   Souvenir sheet of 1 1.25 1.25
991 A332 (70c) Saddle-billed
        stork .50 .50
992 A332 (70c) Water dikkop .50 .50
  a.   Sheet of 10, #983-992 5.00 5.00
  b.   Booklet pane of 10, #983-992,
          perf. 14x14¾ 5.00 5.00
          Complete booklet, 2 #992b 10.00

Birds look bluer and browner on some stamps from No. 992b. No. 992a has Ilsapex 98 emblem in margin, which is not found on No. 992b.

No. 990a, issued 7/11/97, is inscribed in sheet margin for JUNASS '97, and sold for 2r.

Grocott's, Muirhead & Gowie
Buildings, Grahamstown — A333

1997, May 29 **Litho.** **Perf. 14**
993 A333 5r multicolored 1.90 1.90
        PACIFIC 97.

Indigenous
Cattle
A335

Perf. 14½ Syncopated
1997, Aug. 10
999 A335 (70c) Nguni .60 .60
1000 A335 (70c) Bonsmara .60 .60
1001 A335 (70c) Afrikander .60 .60
1002 A335 (70c) Drakensberger .60 .60
  a.   Block of 4, #999-1002 2.40 2.40

Antarctic
Wildlife
A336

1997, Aug. 27 **Litho.** **Perf. 14**
1003 A336 (70c) Leopard seal .50 .50
1004 A336 1.20r Antarctic skua .85 .85
1005 A336 1.70r King penguin 1.25 1.25
        Nos. 1003-1005 (3) 2.60 2.60

Enoch Sontonga (1873-1905), Author
of Africa's Natl. Anthem — A337

Perf. 14 Syncopated
1997, Sept. 24 **Litho.**
1006 A337 (70c) shown .50 .50
1007 A337 (70c) "Nkosi Sikelel
        iAfrika" .50 .50
  a.   Pair, #1006-1007 1.00 1.00

Heritage Day.

Souvenir Sheet

Cape Town '97 Natl. Stamp
Show — A338

1997, Oct. 8 **Perf. 14**
1008 A338 4.50r multicolored 2.25 2.25

Souvenir Sheet

World Post Day — A339

1997, Oct. 9 **Perf. 14 Syncopated**
1009 A339 (70c) multicolored .70 .70

No. 1009 sold for 1r on day of issue.

SANTA (South
African Natl.
Tuberculosis Assoc.,
50th Anniv. — A340

Designs featuring former Christmas seals: No. 1010, Bethlehem. No. 1011, Candles on each side of Cross of Lorraine. No. 1012, Candles, angels, Cross. No. 1013, Cross, angel kneeling. No. 1014, Santa carrying Cross. No. 1015, Madonna and Child, Cross. No. 1016, Christmas trees. No. 1017, Magi. No. 1018, Bell, stained glass window. No. 1019, Native African kneeling, flag.

1997, Nov. 3 **Perf. 14 Syncopated**
1010 A340 (70c) multicolored .50 .50
1011 A340 (70c) multicolored .50 .50
1012 A340 (70c) multicolored .50 .50
1013 A340 (70c) multicolored .50 .50
1014 A340 (70c) multicolored .50 .50
1015 A340 (70c) multicolored .50 .50
1016 A340 (70c) multicolored .50 .50
1017 A340 (70c) multicolored .50 .50
1018 A340 (70c) multicolored .50 .50
1019 A340 (70c) multicolored .50 .50
  a.   Sheet of 10, #1010-1019 5.00 5.00

Souvenir Sheet

New Year 1998 (Year of the
Tiger) — A341

1998, Jan. 28 **Litho.** **Perf. 14x14½**
1020 A341 5r multicolored 2.50 2.50

Natl. Sea
Rescue
Institute
A342

1998, Feb. 11 **Perf. 14 Syncopated**
1021 A342 (70c) multicolored .90 .90

Fauna (no
frame) — A343

5c, Giant girdle-tailed lizard. 10c, Geometric tortoise. 20c, Southern African hedgehog. 30c, Spotted hyena. 40c, Riverine rabbit. 50c, Samango monkey. 60c, Cape hunting dog. 70c, Roan antelope. 80c, Kori bustard. 90c, Jackass penguin. 1r, Wattled crane. #1032, Impala. #1033, Waterbuck. #1034, Blue wildebeest. #1035, Eland. #1036, Kudu. #1037, Black rhinoceros. #1038, White rhinoceros. #1039, Buffalo. #1040, Lion. #1041, Leopard. #1042, African elephant. #1044, Giraffe. 1.50r, Tawny eagle, vert. 2r, Blue swallow. 2.30r, Cape vulture, vert. 5r, Martial eagle. 10r, Bateleur. 20r, Fish eagle.

Perf. 14x14¼, 14x14¼, 14¼x14 Syncopated (#1043), 14x14¼ Syncopated on 2 or 3 Sides (#1036B-1036F, 1042B-1042F)
1998-2000 **Litho.**
1021A A343 5c multi .25 .25
1022 A343 10c multi .25 .25
1023 A343 20c multi .25 .25
1024 A343 30c multi .25 .25
1025 A343 40c multi .25 .25
1026 A343 50c multi .25 .25
1027 A343 60c multi .25 .25
1028 A343 70c multi .25 .25
1029 A343 80c multi .35 .35
1030 A343 90c multi .35 .35
1031 A343 1r multi .35 .35
1032 A343 (1.10r) multi, vert. .65 .65
1033 A343 (1.10r) multi, vert. .65 .65
1034 A343 (1.10r) multi, vert. .65 .65
1035 A343 (1.10r) multi, vert. .65 .65
1036 A343 (1.10r) multi, vert. .65 .65
  a.   Strip of 5, #1032-1036 3.25 3.25
  h.   Booklet pane, 2 each
          #1032-1036, "Standard"
          5mm long 6.50
          Booklet, #1036h 6.50
1036B A343 (1.10r) Like #1034 .40 .40
1036C A343 (1.10r) Like #1035 .40 .40
1036D A343 (1.10r) Like #1036 .40 .40
1036E A343 (1.10r) Like #1032 .40 .40
1036F A343 (1.10r) Like #1033 .40 .40
  g.   Booklet pane, 2 each
          #1036B-1036F 4.00
          Booklet, #1036Fg 4.00
1037 A343 (1.10r) multi .40 .40
  a.   Booklet pane of 10 4.00
          Complete bklt., #1037a 4.00
1038 A343 (1.30r) multi .50 .50
1039 A343 (1.30r) multi .50 .50
1040 A343 (1.30r) multi .50 .50
1041 A343 (1.30r) multi .50 .50
1042 A343 (1.30r) multi .50 .50
  g.   Booklet pane, 2 ea #1038-
          1042 5.00
          Complete bklt., #1042a 5.00
1042B A343 (1.30r) Like #1038 .50 .50
1042C A343 (1.30r) Like #1039 .50 .50
1042D A343 (1.30r) Like #1040 .50 .50
1042E A343 (1.30r) Like #1041 .50 .50
1042F A343 (1.30r) Like #1042 .50 .50
  g.   Booklet pane, 2 each
          #1042B-1042F 5.00
          Complete bklt., #1042Fg 5.00
1043 A343 2r multi .80 .80
1043A A343 2r multi .80 .80
1044 A343 3r multi 1.25 1.25
1045 A343 5r multi 2.25 2.25

Size: 20x38mm
Perf. 14¼x13¾
1045A A343 1.50r multi .60 .60
1045B A343 2.30r multi .90 .90

Size: 35x25mm
Perf. 14¼x14
1046 A343 10r multi 4.00 4.00
  a.   Perf. 14¾ 4.00 4.00

Perf. 14¾ Syncopated
1047 A343 20r multi 7.75 7.75
        Nos. 1021A-1047 (40) 32.05 32.05

Self-adhesive
1048 A343 (1.10r) like #1033 .65 .65
1049 A343 (1.10r) like #1032 .65 .65
1050 A343 (1.10r) like #1036 .65 .65
1051 A343 (1.10r) like #1035 .65 .65
1052 A343 (1.10r) like #1034 .65 .65
  a.   Strip of 5, #1048-1052 3.25
  h.   Booklet, 2 each #1048-1052 6.50

Booklet Stamps
Self-Adhesive
Serpentine Die Cut 11x11¼
1052B A343 (1.30r) Like #1035 .45 .45
1052C A343 (1.30r) Like #1036 .45 .45
1052D A343 (1.30r) Like #1032 .45 .45
1052E A343 (1.30r) Like #1034 .45 .45
1052F A343 (1.30r) Like #1033 .45 .45
  g.   Booklet pane, 2 each
          #1052B-1052F 4.50

Nos. 1038-1042F are inscribed "Airmail Postcard."
"Standard" on Nos. 1032-1036, 1036a is 5½mm long.
Nos. 1042B-1042F are booklet stamps. No. 1052Fg is a complete booklet. Nos. 1036B-1036F were issued in a booklet.
Issued: #1037, 1/98; 10c, 40c, 50c, 70c, 90c, 1r, 1/16/98; #1038-1042, 4/98; #1036B-1036F, 5/18/98; 3r, 6/24/98; 20c, 6/25/98; #1032-1036, 1048-1052, 5/18/98; 10r, 9/21/98; #1046a, 10/28/98; #1043A, 1/9/99; #1052B-1052F, 12/99; 1.50r, 2.30r, 6/5/00; 5c, 7/4/00.

Souvenir Sheet

Leopard — A344

1998, May 1   *Perf. 14*
1053 A344 5r multicolored   2.50 2.50
SAPDA '98 Stamp Show, Johannesburg.

A345   A346

1998, June 8
1054 A345 (1.10r) multicolored   .80 .80
1998 World Cup Soccer Championships, France. No. 1054 was issued in sheets of 10.

1998, June 28   *Perf. 14x14½*
Early South African History: #1055, Early stone age hand axe. #1056, Musuku. #1057, San rock engravings. #1058, Early iron age pots. #1059, Khoekhoe pot. #1060, Florisbad skull. #1061, San rock art. #1062, Mapungubwe gold. #1063, Lydenburg head. #1064, Taung child.

1055	A346	(1.10r) multicolored	.55	.55
1056	A346	(1.10r) multicolored	.55	.55
1057	A346	(1.10r) multicolored	.55	.55
1058	A346	(1.10r) multicolored	.55	.55
1059	A346	(1.10r) multicolored	.55	.55
1060	A346	(1.10r) multicolored	.55	.55
1061	A346	(1.10r) multicolored	.55	.55
1062	A346	(1.10r) multicolored	.55	.55
1063	A346	(1.10r) multicolored	.55	.55
1064	A346	(1.10r) multicolored	.55	.55
a.		Sheet of 10, #1055-1064	5.50	5.50
		Booklet, 2 #1064a	11.00	

Raptors — A347

Designs: No. 1065, Pale chanting goshawk. No. 1066, Jackal buzzard. No. 1067, Lanner falcon. No. 1068, Bearded vulture. No. 1069, Black harrier. No. 1070, Cape vulture. No. 1071, Bateleur. No. 1072, Spotted eagle owl. No. 1073, White-headed vulture. No. 1074, African fish eagle.

1998, Aug. 16   *Perf. 14x15*
1065	A347	(1.10r) multicolored	.65	.65
1066	A347	(1.10r) multicolored	.65	.65
1067	A347	(1.10r) multicolored	.65	.65
1068	A347	(1.10r) multicolored	.65	.65
1069	A347	(1.10r) multicolored	.65	.65
1070	A347	(1.10r) multicolored	.65	.65
1071	A347	(1.10r) multicolored	.65	.65
1072	A347	(1.10r) multicolored	.65	.65
1073	A347	(1.10r) multicolored	.65	.65

1074	A347	(1.10r) multicolored	.65	.65
a.		Sheet of 10, #1065-1074	6.50	6.50
b.		Booklet pane, #1065-1074	6.50	
		Complete booklet, 2 #1074b		
		+ 2 prepaid postcards	14.00	

Vert. and horiz. perforations extend to top, bottom and right edges of sheet on No. 1074a, but do not on No. 1074b.

Natl. Arbor Week A348

Trees: No. 1075, Baobab. No. 1076, Umbrella thorn. No. 1077, Shepherd's tree. No. 1078, Karee.

1998, Sept. 4   *Perf. 13¾x14*
1075	A348	(1.10r) multi	.75	.75
1076	A348	(1.10r) multi	.75	.75
1077	A348	(1.10r) multi	.75	.75
1078	A348	(1.10r) multi	.75	.75
a.		Block of 4, #1075-1078	3.00	3.00

Christmas — A349

1998, Oct. 9   *Perf. 14x15*
1079	A349	(1.10r) Angel	.80	.80
1080	A349	(1.10r) Bell	.80	.80
1081	A349	(1.10r) Package	.80	.80
1082	A349	(1.10r) Christmas tree	.80	.80
1083	A349	(1.10r) Star	.80	.80
a.		Strip of 5, #1079-1083	4.00	4.00

Souvenir Sheet

World Post Day — A351

1998, Oct. 9   *Perf. 14x14½*
1089 A351 5r multicolored   2.50 2.50

Souvenir Sheet

ILSAPEX 1998, Midrand, South Africa — A352

Designs of unissued stamps created for 1927 definitive series in colors of: a, Red and green. b, Green and black.

1998, Oct. 20   *Litho.*   *Perf. 14½x14¼*
1090 A352 5r Sheet of 2, #a.-b.   4.00 4.00

Souvenir Sheet

Whales — A354

1998, Oct. 23   *Litho.*   *Perf. 13½x14*
1095 A354 5r multicolored   3.00 3.00
See Namibia #919, Norfolk Island #665.

Souvenir Sheet

Clover SA Limited, 100th Anniv. — A354a

1998, Nov. 15   *Litho.*   *Perf. 14¼x14*
1095A A354a (1.10r) multicolored 2.25 2.25

Universal Declaration of Human Rights, 50th Anniv. — A355

1998, Dec. 9   *Perf. 14¼*
1096 A355 (1.10r) multicolored   1.00 1.00

UPU, 125th Anniv. A356

Designs: No. 1097, Dennis Royal Mail vehicle, 1913. No. 1098, Ford V8 Mail van, 1935. No. 1099, Mobile post office, 1937. No. 1100, Trojan post office van, 1927.

1999, Feb. 15   *Litho.*   *Perf. 13¾x14*
1097	A356	(1.10r) multi	.75	.75
1098	A356	(1.10r) multi	.75	.75
1099	A356	(1.10r) multi	.75	.75
1100	A356	(1.10r) multi	.75	.75
a.		Block of 4, #1097-1100	3.00	3.00

New Year 1999 (Year of the Rabbit) — A357

1999, Feb. 16   *Litho.*   *Perf. 14x13½*
1101 A357 5r multicolored   2.50 2.50

Ships of the Southern Oceans — A358

1999, Mar. 19   *Litho.*   *Perf. 13¾x14*
1102	A358	(1.10r) Endeavour	.75	.75
1103	A358	(1.10r) HMS Beagle	.75	.75
1104	A358	(1.10r) Discovery	.75	.75
1105	A358	(1.10r) Heemskerck	.75	.75
a.		Block of 4, #1102-1105	3.00	3.00

Souvenir Sheet
Perf. 13¾
1106 A358   5r Lawhill, vert.   2.25 2.25
Australia 99 World Stamp Expo (No. 1106).

AIDS Awareness — A359

Perf. 14¼x14 on 3 sides
1999, Apr. 1
1107	A359	(1.20r) purple & multi	.60	.60
1108	A359	(1.20r) green & multi	.60	.60
a.		Booklet pane, 5 each #1107-1108	6.00	
		Complete booklet, #1108a	6.00	

Souvenir Sheets

IBRA '99, Nuremberg, Germany — A360

1999, Apr. 27   *Perf. 14¼x14*
1109 A360 5r multi   3.00 3.00

SAPDA '99, Johannesburg — A361

1999, Apr. 30   *Perf. 13¾*
1110 A361 5r multi   2.75 2.75

A362   A363

1999, May 1   *Perf. 14x14¾*
1111	A362	(1.20r) Nurse	.70	.70
1112	A362	(1.20r) Washerwoman	.70	.70
1113	A362	(1.20r) Lumberjack	.70	.70
1114	A362	(1.20r) Tree planter	.70	.70
1115	A362	(1.20r) Cook	.70	.70
1116	A362	(1.20r) Fisherman	.70	.70

1117 A362 (1.20r) Construction
      worker .70 .70
1118 A362 (1.20r) Miner .70 .70
1119 A362 (1.20r) Mailman .70 .70
1120 A362 (1.20r) Jackhammerer .70 .70
   a.   Sheet of 10, #1111-1120 7.00 7.00
      Labor Day.

1999, June 16   Perf. 14x14¼
1121 A363 (1.20r) multi 1.00 1.00
   Inauguration of Pres. Thabo Mbeki.

Souvenir Sheet

Order of St. John, 900th
Anniv. — A364

1999, June 23   Perf. 14x14¾
1122 A364 2r multi 1.50 1.50

Standard Bank
Arts Festival, 25th
Anniv. — A365

1999, June 29   Perf. 14x14¼
1123 A365 (1.20r) shown .90 .90
1124 A365 (1.20r) Film .90 .90
1125 A365 (1.20r) Music .90 .90
1126 A365 (1.20r) Mask, diff. .90 .90
1127 A365 (1.20r) Painter .90 .90
   a.   Strip of 5, #1123-1127 4.50 4.50

Traditional
Wall
Art — A366

1999, Aug. 8   Perf. 13¼x13¾
1128 A366 (1.20r) North Ndebele .80 .80
1129 A366 (1.20r) South Ndebele .80 .80
1130 A366 (1.20r) Swazi .80 .80
1131 A366 (1.20r) Venda .80 .80
1132 A366 (1.20r) South Sotho .80 .80
1133 A366 (1.20r) Xhosa .80 .80
1134 A366 (1.20r) North Sotho .80 .80
1135 A366 (1.20r) Tsonga .80 .80
1136 A366 (1.20r) Zulu .80 .80
1137 A366 (1.20r) Tswana .80 .80
   a.   Sheet of 10, #1128-1137 8.00 8.00

Souvenir Sheet

China 1999 World Philatelic
Exhibition — A367

1999, Aug. 21   Perf. 14x13¼
1138 A367 5r multi 3.00 3.00

Souvenir Sheet

JOPEX '99 — A368

1999, Sept. 8 Litho.   Perf. 14¼x14½
1139 A368 5r Strelitzia flower 3.25 3.25

Migratory
Animals — A369

1999, Oct. 4   Litho.   Perf. 14x14¾
1140 A369 (1.20r) Barn swallow .80 .80
1141 A369 (1.20r) Great white
      shark .80 .80
1142 A369 (1.20r) Lesser kes-
      trel .80 .80
1143 A369 (1.20r) Common
      dolphin .80 .80
1144 A369 (1.20r) European
      bee-eater .80 .80
1145 A369 (1.20r) Loggerhead
      turtle .80 .80
1146 A369 (1.20r) Curlew sand-
      piper .80 .80
1147 A369 (1.20r) Wandering
      albatross .80 .80
1148 A369 (1.20r) Springbok .80 .80
1149 A369 (1.20r) Lesser fla-
      mingo .80 .80
   a.   Sheet of 10, #1140-1149 8.00 8.00
      Complete booklet, 2 #1149a
      (stitched in) + 2 postal
      cards 20.00
   Complete booklet sold for 29r.

Boer
War,
Cent.
A370

1999, Oct. 11   Litho.   Perf. 13¾
1150 A370 (1.20r) Boer men, wo-
      man 1.25 1.25
1151 A370 (1.20r) Soldiers, ship 1.25 1.25
   a.   Pair, #1150-1151 2.50 2.50
   b.   Booklet pane, #1150-1151,
      perf. 13¼x13¾ ('02) 2.75 —
   Issued: No. 1151b, 5/31/02. See note after
   No. 1282.

Millennium — A371

2000, Jan. 1   Litho.   Perf. 13¼x13¾
1152 A371 (1.20r) multi 1.10 1.10

Start of
National
Lottery
A372

2000, Mar. 2   Litho.   Perf. 13¼x13¾
1153 A372 (1.20r) multi 1.00 1.00

Family
Day — A373

2000, Apr. 5   Litho.   Perf. 13¼
1154 A373 (1.30r) multi 1.00 1.00

Souvenir Sheet

The Stamp Show 2000,
London — A374

2000, May 20   Litho.   Perf. 13¼
1155 A374 4.60r multi 2.75 2.75

Frogs and
Toads — A375

   No. 1156: a, Banded stream frog. b, Yellow-
striped reed frog. c, Natal leaf-folding frog. d,
Paradise toad. e, Table Mountain ghost frog. f,
Banded rubber frog. g, Dwarf grass frog. h,
Long-toed tree frog. i, Namaqua rain frog. j,
Bubbling kassina.
   4.60r, Forest tree frog.

Perf. 13¼x13¾
2000, June 23   Litho.
1156   Sheet of 10 7.00 7.00
   a.-j. A375 1.30r Any single .70 .70
Souvenir Sheet
Perf. 13¼
1157 A375 4.60r multi 2.75 2.75
   Junass 2000, Boksburg (No. 1157). No.
1157 contains one 48x30mm stamp.

Medicinal
Plants — A376

   No. 1158: a, Stalked bulbine. b, Wild dagga.
c, Wild garlic. d, Pig's ear. e, Wild ginger.
   No. 1159: a, Red paintbrush. b, Cancer
bush. c, Yellow star flower. d, Bitter aloe. e,
Sour fig.

2000, Aug. 1   Perf. 13¾x13¼
1158   Horiz. strip of 5 2.50 2.50
   a.-e. A376 1.30r Any single .50 .50
1159   Horiz. strip of 5 4.00 4.00
   a.-e. A376 2.30r Any single .80 .80

2000 Summer
Olympics,
Sydney — A377

   Olympic rings and: 1.30r, Flagbearer. 1.50r,
Elena Meyer of South Africa and Derartu Tulu
of Ethiopia. 2.20r, Joshua Thugwane. 2.30r,
South African flag. 6.30r, Penny Heyns.

2000, Sept. 1   Perf. 13¼x13¾
1160-1164 A377 Set of 5 5.00 5.00

Intl. Year for
the Culture
of Peace
A378

2000, Sept. 19   Litho.   Perf. 13¼
1165 A378 1.30r multi .70 .70

World Heritage Sites — A379

   Designs: No. 1166, 1.30r, Robben Island.
No. 1167, 1.30r, Greater St. Lucia Wetland
Park. No. 1168, 1.30r, Sterkfontein Fossil
Hominid Complex.

2000, Sept. 22   Perf. 13¼x13¾
1166-1168 A379 Set of 3 2.00 2.00

World Post
Day — A380

2000 Litho. Perf. 13¼x13
1169 A380 1.30r multi .70 .70
  a. Perf. 13¾x13 + label .75 .75

Issued: No. 1169, 10/9; No. 1169a, 11/8. No. 1169a was issued in sheets of 20 stamps + 20 different labels depicting characters on the MTN Gladiators 3 television show that sold for 35r.

Souvenir Sheet

Year of the Dragon — A381

2000, Oct. 9 Litho. Perf. 13½x13
1170 A381 4.60r multi 2.10 2.10

Writers of the Boer War Era — A382

Medals and: 1.30r, Sol Plaatje, Johanna Brandt. 4.40r, Sir Arthur Conan Doyle, Sir Winston Churchill.

2000, Oct. 25 Litho. Perf. 13¼x13¾
1171-1172 A382 Set of 2 2.75 2.75
  a. Booklet pane, #1171-1172 3.25 —

Issued: No. 1172a, 5/31/02. See note after No. 1282.

A383

Fish, Flowers, Butterflies and Birds — A384

Designs: 5c, Palette surgeonfish. 10c, Blue-banded surgeonfish. 20c, Royal angelfish. 30c, Emperor angelfish. 40c, Blackbar triggerfish. 50c, Coral rockcod. 60c, Powder-blue surgeonfish. 70c, Threadfin butterflyfish. 80c, Longhorn cowfish. 90c, Longnose butterflyfish. 1r, Coral beauty. Nos. 1184, 1199B, 1199G, 1200, 1205, 1210, 1215, 1219A, 1220, 1225, Botterblom, vert. Nos. 1185, 1199C, 1199H, 1201, 1206, 1211, 1216, 1219B, 1221, 1226, Blue marguerite, vert. Nos. 1186, 1199D, 1199I, 1202, 1207, 1212, 1217, 1219C, 1222, 1227, Karoo violet, vert. Nos. 1187, 1199E, 1199J, 1203, 1208, 1213, 1218, 1219D, 1223, 1228, Tree pelargonium, vert. Nos. 1188, 1199F, 1199K, 1204, 1209, 1214, 1219, 1219E, 1224, 1229, Black-eyed susy, vert. 1.40r, Gold-banded forester. 1.50r, Brenton blue. 1.60r, Yellow pansy butterfly. No. 1191, Silver-barred charaxes. No. 1231, Large-spotted acraea butterfly. 2r, Lilac-breasted roller, vert. 2.10r, Koppie charaxes butterfly. 2.30r, Citrus swallowtail. 2.50r, Common grass-yellow butterfly. 3r, Woodland kingfisher, vert. 5r, White-fronted bee-eater, vert. 6.30r, Green-banded swallowtail. 7r, Southern milkweed butterfly. 10r, African green pigeon, vert. 12.60r, False dotted-border. 14r, Lilac tip butterfly. 20r, Purple-crested lourie, vert.

Non-English country name inscriptions at top: Nos. 1199B, 1199F, 1199I, 1200, 1204, 1207, 1211, 1219A, 1219E, 1220, 1224, 1227, Afrika Borwa. Nos. 1199C, 1199J, 1201, 1208, 1218, 1219B, 1221, 1228, Ningizimu Afrika. Nos. 1199D, 1202, 1219C, 1222, Suid-Afrika. Nos. 1199E, 1203, 1219D, 1223, Afrika Tshipembe. Nos. 1199G, 1205, 1215, 1225, Afrika Dzonga. Nos. 1199H, 1206, 1216,

---

1226, Afrika Sewula. Nos. 1199K, 1209, 1219, 1229, Mzantsi Afrika.

Perf. 14½x14¾, 14¾x14½
2000, Nov. 15 Litho.
1173 A383 5c multi .25 .25
  a. Perf. 13 .25 .25
1174 A383 10c multi .25 .25
  a. Perf. 13 .25 .25
1175 A383 20c multi .25 .25
  a. Perf. 13 .25 .25
  b. Perf. 14x13¾ .25 .25
1176 A383 30c multi .25 .25
  a. Perf. 13 .25 .25
1177 A383 40c multi .25 .25
  a. Perf. 13 .25 .25
1178 A383 50c multi .25 .25
  a. Perf. 13 .25 .25
1179 A383 60c multi .25 .25
  a. Perf. 13 .25 .25
1180 A383 70c multi .25 .25
  a. Perf. 13 .25 .25
  b. Perf. 14x13¾ .25 .25
1181 A383 80c multi .30 .30
  a. Perf. 13 .30 .30
1182 A383 90c multi .35 .35
  a. Perf. 13 .30 .30
1183 A383 1r multi .35 .35
  a. Perf. 13 .35 .35
1184 A383 1.30r multi .50 .50
1185 A383 1.30r multi .50 .50
1186 A383 1.30r multi .50 .50
1187 A383 1.30r multi .50 .50
1188 A383 1.30r multi .50 .50
  a. Horiz. strip of 5, #1184-1188 2.50 2.50
1189 A383 1.40r multi .55 .55
1190 A383 1.50r multi .60 .60
1191 A383 1.90r multi .70 .70
1192 A383 2r multi .80 .80
  a. Perf. 13 .80 .80
1193 A383 2.30r multi .85 .85
1194 A383 3r multi 1.10 1.10
  a. Perf. 13 1.10 1.10
1195 A383 5r multi 2.10 2.10
  a. Perf. 13 2.10 2.10
1196 A383 6.30r multi 2.75 2.75
1197 A383 10r multi 4.00 4.00
  a. Perf. 13 ('01) 4.00 4.00
1198 A383 12.60r multi 5.50 5.50
  a. Perf. 13 ('01) 6.00 6.00
1199 A383 20r multi 8.00 8.00
  a. Perf. 13 6.50 6.50
  m. Perf. 13¾x14 5.25 5.25

Issued: Nos. 1197a, 1199a, 10/1/01. No. 1179a, 10/1/01. Nos. 1178a, 1192a, 1194a, 1195a, 2002. No. 1173a, 4/2/03; No. 1174a, 5/22/03; Nos. 1175a, 1181a, 9/22/03; Nos. 1176a, 1182a, 1199a, 2/27/03; Nos. 1177a, 1180a, 1183a, 9/23/03. Nos. 1175b, 1180b, 2/24/10; No. 1199m, 2/1/10.

Coil Stamps
Self-Adhesive
Serpentine Die Cut 13¼x13½
2000, Nov. 1 Litho.
1199B A384 1.30r multi — —
1199C A384 1.30r multi — —
1199D A384 1.30r multi — —
1199E A384 1.30r multi — —
1199F A384 1.30r multi — —
1199G A384 1.30r multi — —
1199H A384 1.30r multi — —
1199I A384 1.30r multi — —
1199J A384 1.30r multi — —
1199K A384 1.30r multi — —

Booklet Stamps
Self-Adhesive
Die Cut Perf. 13x12½ on 2 or 3 Sides
2000, Nov. 15 Litho.
1200 A384 1.30r multi .50 .50
1201 A384 1.30r multi .50 .50
1202 A384 1.30r multi .50 .50
1203 A384 1.30r multi .50 .50
1204 A384 1.30r multi .50 .50
1205 A384 1.30r multi .50 .50
1206 A384 1.30r multi .50 .50
1207 A384 1.30r multi .50 .50
1208 A384 1.30r multi .50 .50
1209 A384 1.30r multi .50 .50
  a. Booklet, #1200-1209 5.00

2001, May 16 Litho. Perf. 13
1210 A383 1.40r multi .55 .55
1211 A383 1.40r multi .55 .55
1212 A383 1.40r multi .55 .55
1213 A383 1.40r multi .55 .55
1214 A383 1.40r multi .55 .55
  a. Horiz. strip of 5, #1210-1214 2.75 2.75

"Standard Postage" in Thin Letters
Coil Stamps
Self-Adhesive
Photo.
Serpentine Die Cut 13½
1215 A384 (1.40r) multi .55 .55
1216 A384 (1.40r) multi .55 .55
1217 A384 (1.40r) multi .55 .55
1218 A384 (1.40r) multi .55 .55
1219 A384 (1.40r) multi .55 .55
1219A A384 (1.40r) multi .55 .55
1219B A384 (1.40r) multi .55 .55
1219C A384 (1.40r) multi .55 .55
1219D A384 (1.40r) multi .55 .55

1219E A384 (1.40r) multi .55 .55
  f. Strip of 10, #1215-1219E 5.50

Booklet Stamps
Photo.
"Standard Postage" in Thin Letters
Die Cut Perf. 13x12½ on 2 or 3 Sides
1220 A384 (1.40r) multi .55 .55
1221 A384 (1.40r) multi .55 .55
1222 A384 (1.40r) multi .55 .55
1223 A384 (1.40r) multi .55 .55
1224 A384 (1.40r) multi .55 .55
1225 A384 (1.40r) multi .55 .55
1226 A384 (1.40r) multi .55 .55
1227 A384 (1.40r) multi .55 .55
1228 A384 (1.40r) multi .55 .55
1229 A384 (1.40r) multi .55 .55
  a. Booklet, #1220-1229 5.50
  Nos. 1173-1229 (66) 51.20 51.20

Designs: Nos. 1229B, 1229G, 1229M, 1229R, Botterblom, vert. Nos. 1229C, 1229H, 1229N, 1229S, Blue marguerite, vert. Nos. 1229D, 1229I, 1229O, 1229T, Karoo violet, vert. Nos. 1229E, 1229J, 1229P, 1229U, Tree pelargonium, vert. Nos. 1229F, 1229K, 1229Q, 1229V, Black-eyed susy, vert.
Non-English country name inscriptions at top: Nos. 1229B, 1229F, 1229I, 1229M, 1229Q, 1229T, Afrika Borwa. Nos. 1229C, 1229J, 1229N, 1229U, Ningizimu Afrika. Nos. 1229D, 1229O, Suid-Afrika. Nos. 1229E, 1229P, Afrika Tshipembe. Nos. 1229G, 1229R, Afrika Dzonga. Nos. 1229H, 1229S, Afrika Sewula. Nos. 1229K, 1229U, Mzantsi Afrika.

With "Standard Postage" in Thick Letters
Coil Stamps
Self-Adhesive
Serpentine Die Cut 13½x12¾
2001, May 30 Litho.
1229B A384 (1.40r) multi — —
1229C A384 (1.40r) multi — —
1229D A384 (1.40r) multi — —
1229E A384 (1.40r) multi — —
1229F A384 (1.40r) multi — —
1229G A384 (1.40r) multi — —
1229H A384 (1.40r) multi — —
1229I A384 (1.40r) multi — —
1229J A384 (1.40r) multi — —
1229K A384 (1.40r) multi — —

Booklet Stamps
Die Cut Perf. 13x12½ on 2 or 3 Sides
1229M A384 (1.40r) multi — —
1229N A384 (1.40r) multi — —
1229O A384 (1.40r) multi — —
1229P A384 (1.40r) multi — —
1229Q A384 (1.40r) multi — —
1229R A384 (1.40r) multi — —
1229S A384 (1.40r) multi — —
1229T A384 (1.40r) multi — —
1229U A384 (1.40r) multi — —
1229V A384 (1.40r) multi — —
  w. Booklet pane of 10, #1229M-1229V

Nos. 1215-1229 have "Standard Postage" in thin letters.

Type of 2000
2001, June 16 Litho. Perf. 13
1230 A383 1.60r multi .60 .60
1231 A383 1.90r multi .75 .75
1232 A383 2r multi .80 .80
1233 A383 2.50r multi 1.00 1.00
1234 A383 7r multi 2.75 2.75
1235 A383 14r multi 6.00 6.00
  Nos. 1230-1235 (6) 11.90 11.90

Myths and Legends — A385

Designs: 1.30r, The Rain Bull. 1.50r, The Treasure of the Grosvenor. 2.20r, Seven Magic Birds. 2.30r, The Hole in the Wall. 6.30r, Van Hunks and the Devil.

2001, Jan. 24 Litho. Perf. 13¾
1236-1240 A385 Set of 5 4.50 4.50

Souvenir Sheet

Hong Kong 2001 Stamp Exhibition — A386

2001, Feb. 1 Perf. 14½x14
1241 A386 4.60r Tree snake 2.75 2.75

Sports Stars A387

Designs: No. 1242, 1.40r, Ernie Els, golfer. No. 1243, 1.40r, Terence Parkin, swimmer. No. 1244, 1.40r, Hezekiel Sepeng, runner. No. 1245, 1.40r, Rosina Magola, netball player. No. 1246, 1.40r, Francois Pienaar, rugby player. No. 1247, 1.40r, Zanele Situ, javelin thrower. No. 1248, 1.40r, Hestrie Cloete, high jumper. No. 1249, 1.40r, Lucas Radebe, soccer player. No. 1250, 1.40r, Vuyani Bungu, boxer. No. 1251, 1.40r, Jonty Rhodes, cricket player.

2001, Feb. 28 Perf. 13¾x14
1242-1251 A387 Set of 10 6.00 6.00
1251a Sheet of 15 #1251 +15 labels, perf. 14½x14 8.50

Labels on No. 1251a depict players from the 2000-01 South African World Cup Cricket team.

Kgalagadi Transfrontier Park — A388

Designs: 1.40r, Gemsboks, flags of South Africa and Botswana. 2.50r, Cheetahs. 2.90r, Sociable weaver birds. 3.60r, Meerkats.

2001, May 12 Litho. Perf. 13x13¼
1252-1255 A388 Set of 4 4.50 4.50
1254a Souvenir sheet, #1253-1254 3.00 3.00

See Botswana Nos. 714-717.

Campaign Against Child Abuse — A389

2001, May 16 Perf. 13¾
1256 A389 1.40r multi .50 .50

Soweto Uprising, 25th Anniv. — A390

2001, June 16		Litho.	Perf. 13¾	
1257	A390	1.40r multi	.50	.50

Bats — A391

No. 1258: a, Cape horseshoe bat. b, Welwitsch's hairy bat. c, Schreiber's long-fingered bat. d, Wahlberg's epauletted fruit bat. e, Short-eared trident bat. f, Common slit-faced bat. g, Egyptian fruit bat. h, Egyptian free-tailed bat, vert. i, De Winton's long-eared bat. j, Large-eared free-tailed bat.

Serpentine Die Cut 11¼
2001, June 22
Self-Adhesive

1258	A391	Sheet of 10, #a-j	4.50	4.50
a.-j.		1.40r Any single	.45	.45

Boer War, Cent. — A392

Designs: 1.40r, Rev. J. D. Kestell. 3r, Capt. Thomas Crean.

2001, Aug. 1			Perf. 13¼	
1259-1260	A392	Set of 2	2.00	2.00
a.		Booklet pane, #1259-1260, perf. 13¼x13¾	2.25	

Issued: No. 1260a, 5/31/02. See note after No. 1282.

World Conference Against Racism, Durban — A393

No. 1262: a, Kgotlelelo le pharologantsho. b, Kubeketelelana kanye nekwehlukana. c, Verdraagsaamheid en diversiteit. d, U kondelelana na u fhambana. e, Kutlwisiso ka mefutafuta. f, Ku va ni mbilu yo leha ni kuhambana-hambana. g, Ibekezelelwano nehlukahlukano. h, Kgothlelelo le pharologano. i, Ukubekezelelana nokungafani. j, Ukunyamezelana nokungafani.

2001, Aug. 1			Perf. 13¾x13½	
1261	A393	2.10r shown	.75	.75
1262		Sheet of 10	6.00	6.00
a.-j.		A393 1.40r Any single	.60	.60

See Brazil No. 2809.

Musical Instruments — A394

Designs: 1.40r, Concertina. 1.90r, Trumpet. 2.50r, Electric guitar. 3r, African drum. 7r, Cello.

Litho. with Foil Application

2001, Aug. 23			Perf. 13¼x14	
1263-1267	A394	Set of 5	5.25	5.25

Christmas A395

Designs: 2r, Tree. 3r, Angel.

2001, Oct. 1		Litho.	Perf. 13¼	
1268-1269	A395	Set of 2	1.90	1.90

Frame — A396

2001, Oct. 1		Serpentine Die Cut	
		Self-Adhesive	
1270	A396	(1.40r) multi	.60 .60
a.		Double-sided pane of 10 + 40 labels	6.00

Volvo Round-the-World Yacht Race — A397

Designs: 1.40r, Yacht. 6r, Yacht, horiz.

2001, Oct. 23			Perf. 13	
1271	A397	1.40r multi	.75	.75

Souvenir Sheet
Perf. 14x13¼

1272	A397	6r multi	1.25	1.25

No. 1272 contains one 40x30mm stamp.

2003 ICC Cricket World Cup, South Africa — A398

2001, Nov. 1		Perf. 14x13¾	
1273	A398	(1.40r) multi	.85 .85

Souvenir Sheet

New Year 2002 (Year of the Horse) — A399

2001, Nov. 2			Perf. 14x13¼	
1274	A399	6r multi	2.25	2.25

Marine Life — A400

No. 1275: a, Hammerhead shark. b, Loggerhead turtle, vert. c, Clown triggerfish, vert. d, Cape fur seal, vert. e, Bottlenosed dolphins. f, Crowned seahorse, vert. g, Blue-spotted ribbontail ray, vert. h, Moorish idol. i, Common octopus. j, Coral rock cod.

Serpentine Die Cut 12¾
2001, Nov. 2
Self-Adhesive

1275	A400	Sheet of 10	4.50	4.50
a.-j.		(1.40r) Any single	.45	.45

Johannesburg World Summit on Sustainable Development — A401

Designs: Nos. 1276a, 1281c, Prosperity, vert. Nos. 1276b, 1281a, People, vert. Nos. 1276c, 1281b, Planet, vert. (1.50r), Water, sanitation and energy for all. No. 1278, Buildings, globe. No. 1279, Clean environment for health. (3.30r), Food security for all.
Sizes: Nos. 1276a-1276c, 22x32mm, Nos. 1281a-1281c, 21x26mm.

Perf. 13¾x13¼, 13¼x13 (#1277, 1279, 1280), 13¼x13¾ (#1278)

2002			Litho.	
1276	A401	(1.40r) Strip of 3, #a-c	1.40	1.40
1277	A401	(1.50r) multi	.50	.50
1278	A401	(3r) multi	.95	.95
1279	A401	(3r) multi	.95	.95
1280	A401	(3.30r) multi	1.00	1.00

Booklet Stamps
Self-Adhesive
Serpentine Die Cut on 2 or 3 Sides

1281	A401	(1.40r) Strip of 3, #a-c	1.40	1.40
d.		Booklet pane, 4 #1281a, 3 #1281b-1281c	4.50	4.50
		Nos. 1276-1281 (6)	6.20	6.20

Issued: Nos. 1276, 1278, 1281, 4/17. Nos. 1277, 1279, 1280, 8/25. No. 1279 is airmail.

Souvenir Sheet

End of Boer War, Cent. — A402

No. 1282: a, 1.50r, Army officer. b, 3.30r, Government official.

2002, May 31			Perf. 13¼x13¾	
1282	A402	Sheet of 2, #a-b	1.50	1.50
c.		Booklet pane, #1282	1.90	—
		Complete booklet, #1151b, 1172a, 1260a, 1282c + 2 postal cards	10.50	

No. 1282c has rouletting between margin of No. 1282 and the booklet pane margin. Complete booklet sold for 45r.

African Union Summit A403

2002, June 25			Perf. 13½	
1283	A403	1.50r multi	.90	.90

Values are for stamps with surrounding selvage.

Type of 2000

Designs: 1.80r, Emperor moth. 2.20r, Peach moth. 2.80r, Snouted tiger moth. 9r, False tiger moth. 16r, Moon moth.

2002, Sept. 20		Litho.	Perf. 13	
1284	A383	1.80r multi	.55	.55
1285	A383	2.20r multi	.70	.70
1286	A383	2.80r multi	.85	.85
1287	A383	9r multi	2.75	2.75
1288	A383	16r multi	5.00	5.00
		Nos. 1284-1288 (5)	9.85	9.85

A404   A405

A406   A407

ICC Cricket World Cup
A408   A409

2002			Perf. 12½x12¾	
1289	A404	(1.50r) multi	.50	.50
1290	A405	(1.50r) multi	.50	.50
1291	A407	(1.50r) multi	.50	.50
1292	A409	(1.50r) multi	.50	.50

SOUTH AFRICA

306

1293 A406 (1.50r) multi .50 .50
1294 A408 (1.50r) multi .50 .50
Nos. 1289-1294 (6) 3.00 3.00

Issued: Nos. 1289, 1290, 9/23; 1292, 1294, 11/1; Nos. 1291, 1293, 12/21.

Souvenir Sheet

Steve Biko (1946-77), Anti-apartheid Leader — A410

2002, Oct. 9 Perf. 14¾x14½
1295 A410 4.75r multi 1.50 1.50

See note under No. 1321.

Souvenir Sheet

World Post Day — A411

2002, Oct. 9 Perf. 13¼x13½
1296 A411 4.75r multi 1.50 1.50

Christmas — A412

Stained glass patterns: 1.50r, 3r.

2002, Oct. 23 Perf. 14x14¾
1297-1298 A412 Set of 2 1.40 1.40

Souvenir Sheets

Sawfish — A413

Designs: No. 1299, 7r, Pristis pectinata. No. 1300, 7r, Pristis microdon.

2002, Oct. 23 Perf. 13¾
1299-1300 A413 Set of 2 4.50 4.50

JUNASS Philatelic Exhibition (#1299); Algoapex Philatelic Exhibition (#1300).

Souvenir Sheet

New Year 2003 (Year of the Ram) — A414

2002, Nov. 1 Perf. 14½
1301 A414 7r multi 2.25 2.25

AIDS Prevention — A415

No. 1302 — AIDS prevention ribbon and: a, Man with sunglasses, male symbol. b, Woman with open mouth. c, Woman with sunglasses, female symbol. d, Hand holding candle, "Stop." e, Woman, candle. f, Hand holding candle, "Be safe." g, Candle, hand pointing at ribbon. h, Open hand. i, Face in droplet. j, Open hand, pills.

Serpentine Die Cut 11¾
2002, Nov. 29
Self-Adhesive
1302 Booklet of 10 5.25 5.25
a.-j. A415 (1.50r) Any single .50 .50

Souvenir Sheet

Solar Eclipse of Dec. 4, 2002 — A416

2002, Dec. 4 Perf. 14½
1303 A416 4.75r multi 1.50 1.50

ICC Cricket World Cup — A417

No. 1304: a, Huts with windmill blades. b, Horseman. c, Cricket players with bats. d, Bus with people on roof. e, Mother and child. f, Double-decker bus.

2003, Feb. 28 Perf. 14¼x13¾
1304 A417 (1.50r) Sheet of 6, #a-f 2.75 2.75

Tembisile (Chris) Hani (1942-93), African National Congress Leader — A418

2003, Apr. 27 Litho. Perf. 14¾
1305 A418 (1.65r) multi .60 .60

See note after No. 1321.

Life in Informal Settlements — A419

No. 1306: a, Women carrying water jugs on head. b, Man with guitar. c, Man with rake. d, Woman using sewing machine. e, Two children. f, Drink vendor. g, Shoemakers. h, Woman with green cap. i, Young woman with cap and tire. j, Woman with child.

2003, May 16 Perf. 14x13¾
1306 A419 (1.65r) Sheet of 10, #a-j 5.25 5.25

Souvenir Sheet

Africa Day — A420

2003, May 25 Perf. 14¾
1307 A420 11.70r multi 3.75 3.75

Souvenir Sheet

Oliver Reginald Tambo (1917-93), African National Congress President — A421

2003, May 29
1308 A421 (1.65r) multi 1.25 1.25

See note after No. 1321.

Ballroom Dancing — A422

Designs: 1.65r, Salsa. 2.20r, Rumba. 2.80r, Waltz. 3.30r, Foxtrot. 3.80r, Tango.

2003, July 23 Perf. 13¼x13¾
1309-1313 A422 Set of 5 4.75 4.75

Dogs — A423

No. 1314: a, Africanis. b, Rhodesian Ridgeback. c, Boerboel. d, Basenji.

2003, Aug. 1 Perf. 14½
1314 A423 (1.65r) Sheet of 4, #a-d 2.75 2.75

Type of 2000

Designs: No. 1315, Botterblom, vert. No. 1316, Blue marguerite, vert. No. 1317, Karoo violet, vert. No. 1318, Tree pelargonium, vert. No. 1319, Black-eyed susy, vert.

2003, Sept. 15 Litho. Perf. 13
1315 A383 (1.65r) multi .60 .60
a. (2.40r) Perf. 14x13¾ .65 .65
b. (2.40r) Perf. 14¾x14½ .65 .65
1316 A383 (1.65r) multi .60 .60
a. (2.40r) Perf. 14x13¾ .65 .65
b. (2.40r) Perf. 14¾x14½ .65 .65
1317 A383 (1.65r) multi .60 .60
a. (2.40r) Perf. 14x13¾ .65 .65
b. (2.40r) Perf. 14¾x14½ .65 .65
1318 A383 (1.65r) multi .60 .60
a. (2.40r) Perf. 14x13¾ .65 .65
b. (2.40r) Perf. 14¾x14½ .65 .65
1319 A383 (1.65r) multi .60 .60
a. Horiz. strip of 5, #1315-1319 3.00 3.00
b. (2.40r) Perf. 14x13¾ .65 .65
c. Horiz. strip of 5, #1315a, 1316a, 1317a, 1318a, 1319b 3.25 3.25
d. (2.40r) Perf. 14¾x14½ .65 .65
e. Horiz. strip of 5, #1315b, 1316b, 1317b, 1318b, 1319d 3.25 3.25

Issued: Nos. 1315a, 1316a, 1317a, 1318a, 1319b, 2/1/10; Nos. 1315b, 1316b, 1317b, 1318b, 1319d, 2/24/10.

Souvenir Sheet

Walter Max Ulyate Sisulu (1912-2003), African National Congress Deputy President — A424

2003, Sept. 24 Perf. 14¾
1320 A424 11.70r multi 4.75 4.75

See note after No. 1321.

Souvenir Sheet

Robert Mangaliso Sobukwe (1924-1978), Pan Africanist Congress President — A425

2003, Sept. 24 Perf. 14¾
1321 A425 11.70r multi 4.75 4.75

Nos. 1295, 1305, 1308, 1320 and 1321 were sold in, but unattached to, a commemorative booklet that sold for 60r.

Stamp of Fortune Television Show — A426

2003, Sept. 29   *Perf. 14¼x14*
1322 A426 (1.65r) multi   .60 .60

Engineering and Postal Communication — A427

No. 1323, (3.30r): a, Shongweni Dam (60x23mm). b, Kimberley Microwave Tower (30x47mm). c, Northern Cape Legislature Building (30x23mm). d, Durban Westville highway interchange (30x47mm). e, Postal truck on Community Bridge, Limpopo (30x23mm). f, Nelson Mandela Bridge, Johannesburg (60x23mm).

2003, Oct. 9   *Perf. 14x14¼*
1323 A427   Sheet of 6, #a-f   8.00 8.00
   g.   Like No. 1323, with PIARC World Road Congress inscription in margin   8.00 8.00

Souvenir Sheet

South Africa - India Diplomatic Relations, 10th Anniv. — A428

2003, Oct. 16   *Perf. 14¾*
1324 A428 3.35r multi   1.40 1.40

Bid for Hosting 2010 World Cup Soccer Championships — A429

Emblem, soccer fan with painted face and: No. 1325, (3.80r), Map of Africa. No. 1326, (4.25r), Soccer players.

2003, Oct. 23
1325-1326 A429   Set of 2   2.40 2.40
   No. 1325 is airmail.

Cape of Good Hope Triangle Stamps, 150th Anniv. A430

2003, Oct. 23 Litho.   *Perf. 12½x12¾*
1327 A430 (1.65r) blue   .60 .60
   Printed in sheets of 4.

A431

Christmas — A432

No. 1328: a, Joseph, Mary on donkey. b, Angels. c, Magi. d, Madonna and Child. e, Dove.

2003, Nov. 3 Litho.   *Perf. 14x14¼*
1328   Horiz. strip of 5   3.00 3.00
   a.-e.   A431 (1.65r) Any single   .55 .55
            Perf. 14¾
1329 A432 3.80r shown   1.50 1.50

Elephants — A433

No. 1330: a, African elephants. b, Asian elephant.

2003, Dec. 9   *Perf. 14¼x14*
1330 A433 3.35r Horiz. pair, #a-b 3.25 3.25
   South Africa — Thailand diplomatic relations, 10th anniv. See Thailand No. 2105.

Powered Flight, Cent. — A434

No. 1331: a, Paterson Biplane. b, "Silver Queen" Vickers Vimy. c, Wapiti. d, De Havilland DH-9. e, Junkers Ju52/53. f, Sikorsky S-55 helicopter. g, Boeing 707. h, Rooivalk helicopter. i, SUNSAT Microsatellite. j, Mark Shuttleworth, first African in space, and Space Station.

2003, Dec. 17   *Perf. 14¼x14*
1331 A434 (1.65r) Sheet of 10, #a-j   7.00 7.00

Souvenir Sheet

New Year 2004 (Year of the Monkey) — A435

2004, Jan. 22   *Perf. 13¾*
1332 A435 11.70r multi   4.50 4.50

Road Safety — A436

No. 1333 — Inscriptions: a, Be visible. b, Don't drink and drive. c, Maintain your vehicle. d, Slow down. e, Don't drive when tired.

       Perf. 13¼x13¾
2004, Mar. 24   **Litho.**
1333   Vert. strip of 5   3.00 3.00
   a.-e.   A436 (1.70r) Any single   .60 .60

End of Apartheid, 10th Anniv. — A437

No. 1334: a, Dove, map of Africa. b, People voting. c, Women and child. d, Sports fans holding flag and trophies. e, Woman with handicrafts.

2004, Apr. 27 Litho.   *Perf. 13¼*
1334   Vert. strip of 5   3.00 3.00
   a.-e.   A437 (1.70r) Any single   .60 .60

Miniature Sheet

Legacy of Slaves — A438

No. 1335, (1.70r): a, Slave bell, Vergelegen, and slave lodge, Cape Town. b, Hidayat al-Islam, first book in Arabic-Afrikaans. c, Chair and cupboard. d, Traditional foods. e, Indian workers in sugar cane fields. f, Chinese mine workers.

2005, May 1
1335 A438   Sheet of 6, #a-f   4.25 4.25

Souvenir Sheet

FIFA (Fédération Internationale de Football Association), Cent. — A439

2004, Apr. 30 Litho.   *Perf. 14¾*
1336 A439 4.35r multi   2.00 2.00

Spiders — A440

No. 1337: a, Hedgehog spider. b, Golden orb-web spider, vert. c, Lynx spider, vert. d, Black button spider, vert. e, Ladybird spider. f, Flower crab spider. g, Rain spider, vert. h, Horn baboon spider. i, Trap door spider. j, Spotted crab spider.

Serpentine Die Cut 9½x9, 9x9½
2004, July 30
         Self-Adhesive
1337 A440   Sheet of 10, #a-j   7.50 7.50
   a.-j.   (1.70r) Any single   .75 .75

Volunteers — A441

No. 1338: a, Environmental helpers. b, Caring for the elderly. c, Education. d, Medical and ambulance services. e, Surf life saving. f, Helping abandoned pets. g, Caring for orphans. h, Fire fighters. i, Community gardens. j, Tape aids for the blind.

2004, Aug. 9   *Perf. 13½x13¾*
1338 A441 (1.70r) Sheet of 10, #a-j   7.00 7.00

Sports — A442

No. 1339: a, Archery. b, Track. c, Equestrian. d, Cycling. e, Rhythmic gymnastics. f, Canoeing. g, Soccer. h, Swimming. i, Boxing. j, Tennis.

2004, Aug. 13   *Perf. 13¾x13½*
1339 A442 (1.70r) Sheet of 10, #a-j   7.00 7.00

Christmas A443

Icons: (1.70r), Madonna and Child. (4r), Jesus Christ, Pantocrator.

2004, Oct. 1
1340-1341 A443　Set of 2　　　2.00 2.00

No. 1341 is inscribed "International Airmail Letter."

Birds — A444

No. 1342: a, African fish eagles, national bird of Namibia. b, African fish eagles, national bird of Zimbabwe. c, Peregrine falcons, national bird of Angola. d, Cattle egrets, national bird of Botswana. e, Purple-crested louries, national bird of Swaziland. f, Blue cranes, national bird of South Africa. g, Bar-tailed trogons, national bird of Zambia. h, African fish eagles, national bird of Zambia.

2004, Oct. 9　　　　　　**Perf. 14**
1342 A444　12.05r Sheet of 8,
　　#a-h　　　　　　　　　32.50 32.50

See Botswana Nos. 792-793, Malawi No. , Namibia No. 1052, Swaziland Nos. 727-735, Zambia No. 1033, and Zimbabwe No. 975.

Souvenir Sheet

Regular Air Mail Service in South Africa, 75th Anniv. — A445

Litho. with Hologram
2004, Oct. 9　　　　　　**Perf. 13¾**
1343 A445　12.05r multi　　　4.25 4.25

South African Police Service, 10th Anniv. — A446

No. 1344: a, South African Police Service badge, South African flag. b, Fighting drugs. c, Police air wing. d, Fingerprint and forensic science. e, Special task force. f, Protecting women and children. g, Sector policing. h, The Dignified Blue. i, SAPS mounted unit. j, Dog unit.

Serpentine Die Cut 13½x13
2004, Nov. 23　　　　　　**Litho.**
Self-Adhesive
1344 A446　Sheet of 10　　　7.00 7.00
a.-j.　(1.70r) Any single　　　.70 .70

South African Large Telescope A447

No. 1345: a, Exterior of building. b, Cut-away view of building. c, Building aperture, top of telescope, Southern Cross constellation. d, Telescope. e, Building aperture, entire telescope.

2004, Dec. 1　　　　　**Perf. 13¾x13½**
1345　Horiz. strip of 5　　　8.00 8.00
a.-e.　A447 4r Any single　　　1.60 1.60

Souvenir Sheet

New Year 2005 (Year of the Rooster) — A448

2005, Feb. 9　　　　　**Perf. 14¾x14½**
1346 A448　12.05r multi　　　4.50 4.50

Souvenir Sheet

Freedom Charter, 50th Anniv. — A449

No. 1347: a, "Freedom Charter" in mirror image. b, "Freedom Charter" and "50."

2005, June 24　　　　　**Perf. 14¼x13¾**
1347 A449　(1.77r) Sheet of 2, #a-
　　b　　　　　　　　　　1.40 1.40

Miniature Sheet

THE LORE OF SOUTH AFRICAN LORE AND LEGENDS

Legends — A450

No. 1348: a, Honeyguide's Revenge. b, How Ostrich Got His Long Neck. c, How Serval Got His Spots. d, How Zebra Got His Stripes. e, Jackal, the Tiger Eater. f, Jackal and Wolf. g, King Lion and King Eagle. h, Mantis and the Moon. i, Words as Sweet as Honey from Sankhambi. j, When Lion Could Fly.

2005, July 1
1348 A450 B5　Sheet of 10, #a-
　　j　　　　　　　　　　12.00 12.00

Nos. 1348a-11348j each sold for 3.75r on day of issue.

Miniature Sheet

Small Mammals — A451

No. 1349: a, Lesser bushbaby (24x60mm). b, Riverine rabbit (24x30mm). c, African wild-cat (48x30mm). d, Yellow mongoose (24x60mm). e, Steenbok (48x30mm). f, Cape fox (24x30mm).

2005, July 15　　　　　**Perf. 14**
1349 A451　(1.77r) Sheet of 6, #a-
　　f　　　　　　　　　　4.25 4.25

Energy Sources — A452

2005, Sept. 26　　　　　**Perf. 14x14¼**
1350 A452　(1.77r) Wave　　　.70 .70
1351 A452　(3.65r) Wind　　　1.40 1.40
1352 A452　(4.25r) Sun　　　1.75 1.75
　Nos. 1350-1352 (3)　　　3.85 3.85

Inscription on No. 1350, Standard Postage; No. 1351, International Airmail Postcard; No. 1352, International Airmail Letter.

Christmas A453

Wire and bead sculptures: (1.77r), Candle, Christmas tree, heart. (4.25r), Angel and dove.

2005, Oct. 3
1353 A453　(1.77r) multi　　　.70 .70
1354 A453　(4.25r) multi　　　1.60 1.60

Inscription on No. 1353, Standard Postage; No. 1354, International Airmail Letter.

Prevention of Blindness — A454

Litho. & Embossed
2005, Oct. 13　　　　　**Perf. 14¼x14**
1355 A454　(1.77r) org brn & gray　.70 .70

Souvenir Sheet

New Year 2006 (Year of the Dog) — A455

No. 1356: a, Seeing-eye dog. b, Drug-sniffing dog and luggage. c, Bird-chasing dog at airport.

2006, Jan. 26　　　　　**Perf. 13¼x13**
1356 A455 B5　Sheet of 3, #a-c　4.25 4.25

Nos. 1356a-1356c each sold for 3.75r on day of issue.

Rock Art — A456

No. 1357: a, Detail of Linton Panel, Iziko South African Museum. b, Reedbuck, South African Museum of Rock Art (inscription at LR). c, San ritual specialist, South African Museum of Rock Art (inscription at LL). d, Rhinoceros, Wildebeest Kuil rock art site. e, Eland, Game Pass rock art site.

2006, Feb. 15
1357　Horiz. strip of 5　　　3.50 3.50
a.-e.　A456 (1.77r) Any single　.70 .70

Miniature Sheet

Rural Medical Outreach — A457

No. 1358: a, Helicopter and rescuer (24x60mm). b, Doctors clasping hands (24x30mm). c, Airplane, paramedics tending to man on stretcher, horiz. (48x30mm). d, Motorcycle ambulance, paramedic assisting man (24x30mm). e, Phelophepa Health Train, doctor examining woman, horiz. (72x30mm). f, Ambulance, attendants moving patient on gurney (24x30mm).

2006, May 2　　**Litho.**　　**Perf. 13¼**
1358 A457　(1.85r) Sheet of 6, #a-
　　f　　　　　　　　　　4.25 4.25

Chief Bhambatha Zondi, Leader of 1906 Rebellion — A458

2006, June 9　　　　　**Perf. 14x13½**
1359 A458　(1.85r) multi　　　.65 .65

Red Cross War Memorial Children's Hospital, 50th Anniv. — A459

Designs: (1.85r), Nurse and ill child. (4.40r), Hospital building, horiz.

Perf. 13¾x13½, 13½x13¾
2006, June 18
1360-1361 A459　Set of 2　　　2.25 2.25

Inscription on No. 1360 reads "Standard Postage;" on No. 1361, "International Letter."

Souvenir Sheet

Women's Anti-Apartheid March to the Union Building, Pretoria, 50th Anniv. — A460

2006, Aug. 9   *Perf. 14¾x14*
1362   A460 B5 multi   1.40   1.40
    No. 1362 sold for 3.75r on day of issue.

Miniature Sheet

Clivia Flowers — A461

   No. 1363, (1.85r): a, Clivia nobilis. b, Clivia miniata. c, Clivia gardenii. d, Clivia caulescens. e, Clivia mirabilis. f, Clivia robusta.

2006, Sept. 6   *Perf. 13x13¼*
1363   A461 Sheet of 6, #a-f   3.25   3.25

Animal, Text and Tracks A462

Animal, Herd and Tracks A463

   No. 1364: a, Buffalo. b, Elephant. c, Blue wildebeest. d, Hippopotamus. e, Black rhinoceros. f, Giraffe. g, Spotted hyena. h, Leopard. i, Warthog. j, Zebra.

Litho. & Embossed

2006, Sept. 15   *Perf. 13¾x13¼*
1364   Sheet of 10   6.00   6.00
  a.-e.   A462 (1.85r) Any single   .60   .60
  f.-j.   A463 (1.85r) Any single   .60   .60

Christmas — A464

   No. 1365: a, Antelope. b, Warthog. c, Zebra. d, Hippopotamus. e, Lion, as Santa, in sleigh. (4.40r), Lion as Santa.

2006, Oct. 2   Litho.   *Perf. 13½x13*
1365   Horiz. strip of 5   2.50   2.50
  a.-e.   A464 (1.85r) Any single   .50   .50
1366   A464 (4.40r) multi   1.40   1.40
   Inscriptions on Nos. 1365a-1365e read "Standard Postage;" on No. 1366, "International Airmail Letter."

World Post Day — A465

   No. 1367 — Boy and slogan: a, "Start an Adventure." b, "Be Cool." c, "Learn More." d, "Have Fun." e, "Travel the World."

2006, Oct. 9   *Perf. 13x13¼*
1367   Horiz. strip of 5   2.50   2.50
  a.-e.   A465 (1.85r) Any single   .50   .50

Owls — A466

   No. 1368: a, Barn owl. b, Cape eagle owl. c, African barred owlet. d, Verreaux's eagle owl. e, Pel's fishing owl.

2007, Aug. 3   Litho.   *Perf. 14½*
1368   Horiz. strip of 5   6.50   6.50
  a.-e.   A466 (4.64r) Any single   1.25   1.25

Souvenir Sheet

Scouting, Cent. — A467

   No. 1369: a, Scout saluting. b, Scouting fleur-de-lis.

2007, Aug. 22
1369   A467 (3.90r) Sheet of 2, #a-b   2.25   2.25

Souvenir Sheet

New Year 2007 (Year of the Pig) — A468

Litho. & Embossed With Foil Application

2007, Sept. 7
1370   A468 (4.89r) green & gold   2.75   2.75

World Post Day — A469

2007, Oct. 9   Litho.   *Perf. 14x14¼*
1371   A469 (3.90r) multi   1.25   1.25
   First telephone exchange in South Africa, 125th anniv.

Cheetah A470

Ostrich A471

2007, Oct. 19   *Perf. 14*
1372   A470 (3.90r) multi   1.25   1.25
1373   A471 (4.89r) multi   1.50   1.50
  a.   Perf. 14¾x14½   1.60   1.60
    Issued: No. 1373a, 9/3/09.

Miniature Sheet

Intl. Polar and Heliophysical Year — A472

   No. 1374: a, King penguins (24x30mm). b, Scientists at SANAE IV Base, Antarctica (72x30mm). c, Wandering albatross (24x60mm). d, Adélie penguins (24x30mm). e, Killer whale (48x30mm). f, Weddell seal (24x30mm).

2007, Oct. 31
1374   A472 (1.93r) Sheet of 6, #a-f   3.50   3.50

Mills — A473

   No. 1375: a, Mostert's Mill, Cape Town. b, La Cotte Watermill, Franschhoek. c, Witpoort Watermill, Stoffberg. d, Dwars Rivier Watermill, Cederberg. e, Colesberg Horse and Mill, Colesberg.

2007, Nov. 9   *Perf. 14½*
1375   Vert. strip of 5   7.00   7.00
  a.-e.   A473 (4.64r) Any single   1.40   1.40

Union Castle Line Ships A474

   No. 1376: a, Dane. b, Kildonan Castle. c, SA Vaal. d, Edinburgh Castle. e, Windsor Castle.

2007, Dec. 5
1376   Vert. strip of 5   6.25   6.25
  a.-e.   A474 (4.01r) Any single   1.25   1.25

118th Inter-Parliamentary Union Assembly, Cape Town — A475

2008, Apr. 13   Litho.   *Perf. 13¾*
1377   A475 (2.05r) multi   .55   .55

Diplomatic Relations Between South Africa and People's Republic of China — A476

   No. 1378 — Flags of South Africa and People's Republic of China: a, Within circle of text. b, Above text.

2008, Apr. 24
1378   A476   Sheet of 2   1.90   1.90
  a.   (2.05r) multi   .55   .55
  b.   (4.90r) multi   1.25   1.25
   No. 1378a is inscribed "Standard Postage"; No. 1378b, "International Airmail Small Letter."

Miniature Sheet

Constitutional Court Buildings — A477

   No. 1379: a, Part of building, looking up from street level (56x26mm). b, Covered entranceway (26x26mm). c, Plaza between buildings (56x26mm). d, Chambers (26x26mm). e, Rectangular and cylindrical towers (86x26mm). f, Three-storied buildings and plaza (26x26mm). g, Shadows on interior column (26x26mm). h, Wall with multicolored words (26x26mm). i, Curved wall (26x26mm). j, Building and street (56x26mm).

2008, June 25   *Perf. 14x13¼*
1379   A477   Sheet of 10   5.25   5.25
  a.-j.   (2.05r) Any single   .50   .50
   Nos. 1379a-1379j are each inscribed "Standard Postage."

Souvenir Sheets

A478

Pres. Nelson Mandela, 90th
Birthday — A479

2008, July 15   **Perf. 13¼**
1380 A478 (2.05r) multi   .60   .60
1381 A479 (4.90r) multi   1.40 1.40
        No. 1381 is airmail.

Souvenir Sheet

Alma Ata Declaration on Primary
Health Care, 30th Anniv. — A480

2008, Sept. 6 Litho. Perf. 13¼x14
1382 A480 (2.05r) multi   .50   .50

Souvenir Sheet

Onderstepoort, Cent. — A481

Litho. With Foil Application
2008, Oct. 8   **Perf. 13¾x13¼**
1383 A481 (2.05r) multi   .45   .45

World Post
Day — A482

No. 1384: a, Aberdeen Post Office. b, West
Bank Post Office, East London. c, Main Post
Office, Durban. d, Church Square Post Office,
Pretoria. e, Frankfort Post Office.

2008, Oct. 9 Litho. Perf. 13¼x13¾
1384   Horiz. strip of 5   2.25 2.25
  a.-e.   (2.05r) Any single   .45   .45
  Nos. 1384a-1384e are each inscribed
"Standard Postage."

Miniature Sheets

A483

South African Airways, 75th
Anniv. — A484

No. 1385 — Captain's cap and uniform
insignia, with cap insignia at top: a, With
"S.A.A./S.A.L" in crest. b, With large crown
over winged springbok flying left. c, With coat
of arms above winged springbok flying left. d,
With coat of arms above winged springbok flying right. e, With winged springbok in red circle. f, With crest having colors of South African
flag.
No. 1386 — Airline emblem on tail of: a,
Junkers Ju53/3m. b, Douglas DC-4. c, Boeing
707. d, Boeing 747 (winged springbok). e,
Airbus A300. f, Boeing 747 (colors of South
African flag).

**Litho. & Embossed With Foil
Application**
2009, Jan. 30   **Perf. 13¼**
1385 A483 Sheet of 6   2.40 2.40
  a.-f.   (2.05r) Any single   .40   .40

Litho.
1386 A484 Sheet of 6   5.75 5.75
  a.-f.   (4.90r) Any single   .95   .95
  Nos. 1385a-1385f are inscribed "Standard
Postage"; Nos. 1386a-1386f, "International
Airmail Small Letter."

Rose
Varieties
A485

Serpentine Die Cut
2009, Feb. 13   **Litho.**
Self-Adhesive
1387 A485 (2.05r) Johannesburg
                        Sun   .40   .40
1388 A485 (2.05r) Rina Hugo   .40   .40
1389 A485 (2.05r) Beauty From
                        Within   .40   .40
1390 A485 (2.05r) Bewitched   .40   .40
1391 A485 (2.05r) Cotlands Rose .40   .40
  a.   Miniature sheet, 2 each #1387-
                        1391   4.00
        Nos. 1387-1391 (5)   2.00 2.00
  Nos. 1387-1391 are each inscribed "Standard Postage."

Souvenir Sheet

Intl. Polar Year — A486

2009, Mar. 2   **Perf. 13¼x13¾**
1392 A486 Sheet of 2   1.40 1.40
  a.   (2.05r) Sooty albatrosses   .40   .40
  b.   (4.90r) Jellyfish   1.00 1.00
  No. 1392a is inscribed "Standard Postage";
No. 1392b, "International Small Letter."

Pres.
Kgalema
Motlanthe
A487

2009, Mar. 19   **Perf. 14½**
1393 A487 (2.05r) multi   .45   .45

Occupational Health — A488

No. 1394 — Inscriptions: a, Ergonomics in
the office. b, Medical surveillance. c, Personal
protective equipment. d, Ensure a safe work
place. e, Training in the work place.

2009, Mar. 20   **Perf. 13¾x13¼**
1394   Vert. strip of 5   2.25 2.25
  a.-e.   A488 (2.05r) Any single   .45   .45

Miniature Sheet

Artwork in the Constitutional
Court — A489

No. 1395: a, The Benefit of the Doubt 2,
tapestry by Marlene Dumas (26x35mm). b,
Forgotten Family 1, by Penny Siopis
(52x35mm). c, Bass Player, by Dumile Feni
(26x35mm). d, Head, by William Kentridge
(26x35mm). e, Hotel with Landscape (Spy), by
Robert Hodgins (52x35mm). f, Hotlands, by
Andrew Verster (26x70mm). g, Discussion,
tapestry by Willie Bester (52x35mm). h, The
Smoker, by Gerard Sekoto (52x35mm). i,
Tethered Monkey, by Albert Adams
(26x35mm). j, Blue Dress 3, by Judith Mason
(26x35mm).

2009, June 5 Litho. Perf. 14½
1395 A489 Sheet of 10   5.50 5.50
  a.-j.   (2.25r) Any single   .55   .55
  Nos. 1395a-1395j are inscribed "Standard
Postage."

Artifacts From Mapungubwe
Archaeological Site — A490

No. 1396: a, Gold bowl. b, Spouted pots. c,
Gold rhinoceros. d, Terra cotta bowl. e, Gold
scepter.

2009, Sept. 23
1396   Horiz. strip of 5   7.50 7.50
  a.-e.   A490 (5.40r) Any single 1.50 1.50
  Nos. 1396a-1396e are inscribed "International Small Letter."

Souvenir Sheets

South Africa No. 1 — A491

Show Emblem — A492

2009, Oct. 9   **Perf. 13¾**
1397 A491 (2.25r) multi   .60   .60
1398 A492 (5.40r) multi   1.50 1.50
  Joburg 2010 Intl. Stamp Show, Johannesburg. No. 1397 is inscribed "Standard Postage," and No. 1398, "International Small
Letter."

Souvenir Sheet

Solomon Kalushi Mahlangu (1956-79),
Executed African National Congress
Member — A493

2009, Oct. 15   **Perf. 13¼x13¾**
1399 A493 (2.25r) multi   .60   .60
  No. 1399 is inscribed "Standard Postage."

Pres.
Jacob
Zuma
A494

2009, Nov. 10   **Perf. 13¼**
1400 A494 (2.25r) multi   .60   .60

Miniature Sheet

Bridging the Digital Divide — A495

No. 1401: a, People, cellular phone, open
letter (56x28mm triangle). b, City, cellular
phones, envelope (28x28mm square). c,
Envelope and letter (80x40mm triangle). d,
Letter box and digital code (20x60mm rhomboid). e, Computer, boat, hot-air balloons,
paper airplane (80x40mm triangle).

Litho. With Foil Application
2010, Jan. 18   **Perf. 13¾**
1401 A495 Sheet of 5 + label   5.50 5.50
  a.-e.   (4.05r) Any single   1.10 1.10
  Nos. 1401a-1401e are inscribed "Southern
Africa Small Letter."

Hand Signs for Calling Taxis
A496

No. 1402: a, Randberg to Tembisa. b, Tembisa to Sebenza. c, Turffontein to Mulbarton. d, Gauteng to Johannesburg Central Business District. e, Germiston to Katlehong. f, Johannesburg to Sandton. g, Alexandra to Randburg. h, Emdeni to Highgate. i, Local to the area. j, Johannesburg to Phola Park.

2010, Jan. 29 Litho. Perf. 13¾x13¼

1402		Sheet of 10	6.00 6.00
a.-j.	A496 (2.25r) Any single		.60 .60

Nos. 1402a-1402j are inscribed "Standard Postage." Portions of the designs were applied by a thermographic process producing a shiny, raised effect. Sand grains were added to the thermographic ink.

Miniature Sheet

2010 World Cup Soccer Championships, South Africa — A497

No. 1403 — Soccer players, ball, 2010 World Cup mascot and flag of: a, Namibia. b, South Africa. c, Zimbabwe. d, Malawi. e, Swaziland. f, Botswana. g, Mauritius. h, Lesotho. i, Zambia.

2010, Apr. 9 Perf. 13¾

1403	A497	Sheet of 9	14.50 14.50
a.-i.		5.75r Any single	1.60 1.60

See Botswana Nos. 896-905, Lesotho No. , Malawi No. , Mauritius No. , Namibia No. 1188, Swaziland Nos. 794-803, Zambia Nos. 1115-1118, and Zimbabwe Nos. 1112-1121.

Miniature Sheet

History of Constitution Hill — A498

No. 1404 — Photographs of Old Fort prison complex that housed famous political prisoners: a, Cellblock Number Four (48x40mm). b, Atrium of Women's Jail (24x40mm). c, Awaiting-Trial Block (48x40mm). d, Flogging frame in Cell 3 of Cellblock Number Four (48x40mm). e, Remaining stairwells of Awaiting-Trial Block (24x40mm). f, Cells in the Fort (24x40mm). g, Isolation cells in Cellblock Number Four (80x24mm). h, Guard house in front of isolation cells (24x40mm). i, Entrance to the Fort (48x40mm). j, Ramparts (96x40mm).

2010, May 28 Perf. 13½

1404	A498	Sheet of 10 + central label	6.75 6.75
a.-j.		2.40r Any single	.60 .60

A499

2010 World Cup Soccer Championships, South Africa — A500

Zakumi, official mascot of 2010 World Cup Soccer Championships: No. 1405, Holding soccer ball. No. 1406, Dribbling soccer ball, ball at right. No. 1407, Holding flag of South Africa. No. 1408, Running with soccer ball. No. 1409, With arms raised.
Designs: No. 1410, Emblem of 2010 World Cup Soccer Championships. No. 1411, Official soccer ball. No. 1412, World Cup Trophy.

2010, June 11 Die Cut

Self-Adhesive

1405	A499	2.40r multi	.65 .65
1406	A499	2.40r multi	.65 .65
1407	A499	2.40r multi	.65 .65
1408	A499	2.40r multi	.65 .65
1409	A499	2.40r multi	.65 .65
a.	Horiz. strip of 5, #1405-1409		3.25

Serpentine Die Cut

1410	A500	4.90r multi	1.25 1.25
1411	A500	4.90r multi	1.25 1.25
1412	A500	4.90r multi	1.25 1.25
a.	Sheet of 6, 2 each #1410-1412		7.50
	Nos. 1405-1412 (8)		7.00 7.00

Miniature Sheet

South African Railways, 150th Anniv. — A501

No. 1413: a, Natal 0-4-0, 1860. b, Class NGC 16 Garratt 2-6-2+2-6-2, 1937. c, Class 24 2-8-4, 1948. d, Class 25 4-8-4, 1953. e, Class GMA/M Garratt 4-8-2+2-8-4, 1954. f, Class 35 Co-Co Diesel-electric locomotive, 1974. g, Class 9E Co-Co electric locomotive, 1978. h, Class 26 4-8-4, 1981. i, Class 19E Bo-Bo dual voltage electric locomotive, 2009. j, Gautrain Electrostar Bo-Bo, 2010.

2010, June 25 Perf. 13½x12¾

1413	A501	Sheet of 10	6.25 6.25
a.-j.		2.40r Any single	.60 .60

Miniature Sheet

Stadiums Used for 2010 World Cup Soccer Championships — A502

No. 1414: a, Nelson Mandela Bay Stadium, Port Elizabeth. b, Ellis Park Stadium, Johannesburg. c, Free State Stadium, Bloemfontein. d, Cape Town Stadium, Cape Town. e, Moses Mabhida Stadium, Durban. f, Loftus Versfeld Stadium, Tshwane/Pretoria. g, Peter Mokaba Stadium, Polokwane. h, Mbombela Stadium, Nelspruit. i, Soccer City Stadium, Johannesburg. j, Royal Bafokeng Stadium, Rustenburg.

2010, July 19 Perf. 13¼x13

1414	A502	Sheet of 10	6.75 6.75
a.-j.		2.40r Any single	.65 .65

Birds — A503

No. 1415: a, Blue korhaan. b, Buff-streaked chat. c, White-bellied korhaan. d, White-winged flufftail. e, Yellow-breasted pipit.

2010, Aug. 6 Litho.

1415		Horiz. strip of 5	8.00 8.00
a.-e.	A503 5.75r Any single		1.60 1.60

See No. 1464.

Richtersveld UNESCO World Heritage Site — A504

No. 1416: a, Namaqua chameleon. b, Namaqua sandgrouse. c, Bastard quiver tree. d, Nama tribesman. e, Gray rhebok.

2010, Sept. 23 Perf. 13¾x13¼

1416		Horiz. strip of 5	3.50 3.50
a.-e.	A504 2.40r Any single		.70 .70

Miniature Sheet

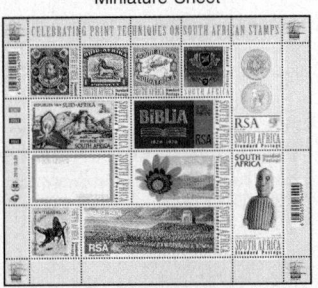

South African Stamps, Cent. — A505

No. 1417 — Stamps of South Africa with original denominations distorted: a, #1 (30x30mm). b, #43b (30x30mm). c, #C5 (30x30mm). d, #1385f (30x30mm). e, #402 (30x60mm). f, #284 (60x30mm). g, #362 (30x60mm). h, #1355 (60x30mm). i, #C87g (60x30mm). j, #980 (30x60mm). k, #C98i (30x30mm). l, #438 (90x30mm).

2010, Oct. 9 Perf. 13¼

1417	A505	Sheet of 12	8.50 8.50
a.-l.		(2.40r) Any single	.70 .70

World Post Day. Nos. 1417a-1417 are inscribed "Standard Postage."

Beadwork A506

Designs: 5c, Ladybug. 10c, Bird. 20c, Llama. 30c, Cell phone. 40c, Hammerhead bird. 50c, Airplane. 60c, Angel. 70c, Nguni cow. 80c, Boxer. 90c, Zebra. 1r, Miner. 2r, Tsonga fertility figure. Nos. 1430, 1445, 1452, Zulu neckpiece, vert. Nos. 1431, 1446, 1453, Ndebele neckpiece, vert. Nos. 1432, 1447, 1454, Xhosa neckpiece, vert. Nos. 1433, 1448, 1455, Swazi necklace, vert. Nos. 1434, 1449, 1456, Tsonga love token pin, vert. 3r, Ndebele married woman's apron. (4.80r) Tsonga neckpiece. (4.90r) Zulu neckpieces, diff. 5r, Mfengu tobacco bag. (5.75r), Bhaca neckpiece. No. 1440, Bhaca neckpiece, diff. 10r, South Sotho ceremonial whisk. (16.90r), Bhaca neckpiece, diff. (19.35r), Vendan pin. 20r, Zulu neckpiece of lion's claws. Nos. 1451, 1458, Bhaca neckpiece, vert.

2010, Oct. 27 Perf. 14½

1418	A506	5c multi	.25 .25
1419	A506	10c multi	.25 .25
1420	A506	20c multi	.25 .25
1421	A506	30c multi	.25 .25
1422	A506	40c multi	.25 .25
1423	A506	50c multi	.25 .25
1424	A506	60c multi	.25 .25
1425	A506	70c multi	.25 .25
1426	A506	80c multi	.25 .25
1427	A506	90c multi	.25 .25
1428	A506	1r multi	.30 .30
1429	A506	2r multi	.60 .60
1430	A506	(2.40r) multi	.70 .70
1431	A506	(2.40r) multi	.70 .70
1432	A506	(2.40r) multi	.70 .70
1433	A506	(2.40r) multi	.70 .70
1434	A506	(2.40r) multi	.70 .70
a.	Horiz. strip of 5, #1430-1434		3.50 3.50
1435	A506	3r multi	.90 .90
1436	A506	(4.80r) multi	1.40 1.40
1437	A506	(4.90r) multi	1.50 1.50
1438	A506	5r multi	1.50 1.50
1439	A506	(5.75r) multi	1.75 1.75
1440	A506	(6r) multi	1.75 1.75
1441	A506	10r multi	3.00 3.00
1442	A506	(16.90r) multi	5.00 5.00
1443	A506	(19.35r) multi	5.75 5.75
1444	A506	20r multi	6.00 6.00
	Nos. 1418-1444 (27)		35.45 35.45

Self-Adhesive
Size: 20x27mm
Serpentine Die Cut 13¼x12¾

1445	A506	(2.40r) multi	.70 .70
1446	A506	(2.40r) multi	.70 .70
1447	A506	(2.40r) multi	.70 .70
1448	A506	(2.40r) multi	.70 .70
1449	A506	(2.40r) multi	.70 .70
a.	Horiz. or vert. strip of 5, #1445-1449		3.50
1451	A506	(6r) multi	1.75 1.75
	Nos. 1445-1451 (6)		5.25 5.25

Booklet Stamps
Die Cut Perf. 12½x12¼ on 2 or 3 Sides

1452	A506	(2.40r) multi	.70 .70
1453	A506	(2.40r) multi	.70 .70
1454	A506	(2.40r) multi	.70 .70
1455	A506	(2.40r) multi	.70 .70
1456	A506	(2.40r) multi	.70 .70
a.	Booklet pane of 10, 2 each #1452-1456		7.00
1458	A506	(6r) multi	1.75 1.75
a.	Booklet pane of 10		17.50
	Nos. 1452-1458 (6)		5.25 5.25

Nos. 1430-1434, 1445-1449 and 1452-1456 are inscribed "Standard Postage." No. 1436 is inscribed "B5." No. 1437 is inscribed "Airmail Postcard." No. 1439 is inscribed "International Small Letter." Nos. 1440, 1451 and 1458 are inscribed "B4." No. 1442 is inscribed "Registered letter small." No. 1443 is inscribed "Registered letter medium."

Nos. 1436, 1440, 1441, 1442, 1443 and 1444 each have two perforations below the line of horizontal perforations at top and two perforations above the line of horizontal perforations at bottom. Nos. 1445-1449 were printed in foldable sheets of 100 containing 20 of each stamp. No. 1451 was printed in a foldable sheet of 50.

Miniature Sheet

National Arms — A507

No. 1459 — Arms used from: a, 1910-30 (antelope standing on ribbon). b, 1930-32 (antelopes on wide grass field without flowers). c, 1932-2000 (antelopes on narrow grass field with flowers). d, 2000-present (bird at top).

2010, Oct. 29   Litho.   Perf. 13½
1459 A507   Sheet of 4   2.80 2.80
a.-d.   (2.40r) Any single   .70   .70

Nos. 1459a-1459d are each inscribed "Standard Postage."

Quiz of South African History A508

No. 1460 — Inscriptions: a, First SA film that won an Academy Award for best foreign language film of the year. b, Number of UNESCO World Heritage Sites in SA. c, Which SA invention has been to the moon? d, Which fish is known as a living fossil. e, Indian spiritual and political leader whose career started in SA. f, When were SA's gold and diamond deposits formed? g, Animal used by Dr. Chris Barnard in trials preceding the first heart transplant. h, Telescope strong enough to see candlelight on the moon. i, The largest bird in the world occurring in SA. j, Where in SA was gold first mined?

2010, Nov. 5   Perf. 13¾x13¼
1460   Sheet of 10   15.00 15.00
a.-j.   A508 4.90r Any single   1.50 1.50

Each stamp on sheet has a scratch-off panel that covers the answer to the question on that stamp. Unused values are for stamps with unscratched panels. Values for used stamps are for stamps with panels unscratched or scratched.

SumbandilaSAT — A509

No. 1461 — Inscriptions: a, Engineering SumbandilaSAT. b, SumbandilaSAT in orbit. c, 12m S-band antenna at Hartebeeshoek. d, Soyuz 2.1b on launch platform. e, SumbandilaSAT, vert.

2011, Apr. 1   Perf. 13¼
1461   Sheet of 10, 2 each
            #a-e   7.50 7.50
a.-e.   A509 (2.50r) Any single   .75   .75

Nos. 1461a-1461e are each inscribed "Standard Postage."

Souvenir Sheet

South African Constitution, 15th Anniv. — A510

2011, May 23   Perf. 13
1462 A510 2.50r multi   .75   .75

African Musical Instruments A511

No. 1463: a, //Gwasi. b, Ramkie. c, Sansa. d, Drums. e, Bullroarer. f, Horns. g, Flute. h, Xylophone. i, Rattles. j, Bows.

2011, June 30   Perf. 13¼
1463   Sheet of 10   17.50 17.50
a.-j.   A511 6r Any single   1.75 1.75

Birds Type of 2010

No. 1464: a, Green twinspot. b, Olive bushshrike. c, Cape parrot. d, Knysna turaco. e, African crowned eagle.

2011, July 15   Perf. 13¼x13¾
1464   Horiz. strip of 5   8.75 8.75
a.-e.   A503 6r Any single   1.75 1.75

Miniature Sheet

Vegetables — A512

No. 1465: a, Spinach. b, Tomatoes. c, Beet. d, Carrots. e, Cabbage. f, Butternut squash.

2011, Aug. 12   Perf. 13¼
1465 A512 Sheet of 6   10.50 10.50
a.-f.   (6.25r) Any single   1.75 1.75

Nos. 1465a-1465f are each inscribed "B4."

Miniature Sheet

Emblems of South African National Rugby Team — A513

No. 1466 — Emblem used from: a, 1906-33. b, 1935-72. c, 1937-62. d, 1963-64. e, 1965-89. f, 1966-91. g, 1992-95. h, 1996-2003. i, 2004-08. j, 2009-11.

Litho. With Foil Application
2011, Aug. 19   Perf. 14½
1466 A513 Sheet of 10   16.00 16.00
a.-j.   (6r) Any single   1.60 1.60

Nos. 1466a-1466j are each inscribed "International Small Letter."

Miniature Sheet

Flora and Fauna of Cape Floral Region — A514

No. 1467: a, Cape ghost frog. b, Fish eagle, vert. c, Cape vulture. d, Cape clawless otter, vert. e, Caracal. f, Strelitzia. g, Cape sugar bird, vert. h, Cape aloe, vert. i, Erica, vert. j, King protea.

Serpentine Die Cut 20
2011, Sept. 23   Litho.
Self-Adhesive
1467 A514   Sheet of 10   12.50
a.-j.   (5r) Any single   1.25 1.25

Nos. 1467a-1467j are each inscribed "B5."

Souvenir Sheet

Sixth Intl. Astronautical Congress, Cape Town — A515

2011, Oct. 3   Perf. 13¾x13½
1468 A515 (2.50r) multi   .65   .65

No. 1468 is inscribed "Standard Postage."

South African Historical Links With Indonesia A516

No. 1469: a, Bo-Kaap Museum, Cape Town. b, Ghoema drum maker. c, Toerang hat and Kaparang sandals. d, Minstrel group. e, Sheikh Yusuf (1626-99), establisher of Islam in South Africa.

2011, Oct. 15   Perf. 13¾x13¼
1469   Vert. strip of 5   3.25 3.25
a.-e.   A516 (2.50r) Any single   .65   .65

Nos. 1469a-1469e are each inscribed "Standard Postage." See Indonesia No.

Souvenir Sheets

A517

Miniature Sheet

Arrival of Indians in South Africa, 150th Anniv. — A518

Designs: No. 1470, SS Truro.
No. 1471 — Indian indentured workers: a, Cutting sugar cane. b, Arriving at Durban harbor.

2011   Perf. 14x14¼
1470 A517 (2.50r) multi   .65   .65
1471 A518 (2.50r) Sheet of 2, #a-
            b   1.25 1.25

Issued: No. 1470, 10/21; No. 1471, 11/25. Nos. 1470, 1471a and 1471b are each inscribed "Standard Postage."

A519

Albert Luthuli (c. 1898-1967), President of African National Congress — A520

Designs: No. 1472, Bronze sculpture of Luthuli. No. 1473, Luthuli with beard. No. 1474, Luthuli without beard.

2011, Dec. 9   Perf. 13¼x13¾
1472 A519 (2.50r) copper & blk   .65   .65
1473 A520 (2.50r) copper & blk   .65   .65
1474 A520 (2.50r) copper & blk   .65   .65
            Nos. 1472-1474 (3)   1.95 1.95

Nos. 1472-1474 are each inscribed "Standard Postage," and were printed in sheets of 10 containing 2 No. 1472 and 4 each Nos. 1473-1474.

South African Native National Congress, Cent. — A521

2012, Jan. 6   Perf. 13¼x13¾
1475 A521 (2.50r) multi   .65   .65

No. 1475 is inscribed "Standard Postage."

SEMI-POSTAL STAMPS

Catalogue values for unused stamps in this section are for Never Hinged items.

English-Afrikaans Se-Tenant
Stamps with English inscriptions and with Afrikaans inscriptions of Nos. B1-B11 were printed alternately in the same sheets. Major-number listings and values are for pairs consisting of one English and one Afrikaans-inscribed stamp.

Church of the Vow — SP1

Cradock's Pass — SP2

Voortrekker — SP3

Voortrekker Woman — SP4

1933-36 Photo. Wmk. 201 Perf. 14

B1	SP1 ½p + ½p grn & blk, pair ('36)		11.00	5.50
a.	Single, English		.55	.55
b.	Single, Afrikaans		.55	.55
B2	SP2 1p + ½p rose & blk, pair		7.25	3.75
a.	Single, English		.45	.35
b.	Single, Afrikaans		.45	.35
B3	SP3 2p + 1p dull vio & gray, pair		12.00	6.00
a.	Single, English		.55	.60
b.	Single, Afrikaans		.55	.60
B4	SP4 3p + 1½p dp blue & gray, pair		18.00	9.50
a.	Single, English		1.50	1.10
b.	Single, Afrikaans		1.50	1.10
	Nos. B1-B4 (4)		48.25	24.75

Issued to commemorate the Voortrekkers. Surtax went to the National Memorial Fund for a national Voortrekker monument.

Voortrekker Plowing — SP5

Crossing the Drakensberg — SP6

Signing Dingaan-Retief Treaty — SP7

Proposed Monument — SP8

1938, Dec. 14 Perf. 14

B5	SP5 ½p + ½p dl grn & ind, pair		7.00	6.75
a.	Single, English		1.00	.60
b.	Single, Afrikaans		1.00	.60
B6	SP6 1p + 1p rose & sl, pair		17.00	7.75
a.	Single, English		1.00	.70
b.	Single, Afrikaans		1.00	.70

Perf. 15x14

B7	SP7 1½p + ½p Prus grn & choc, pair		22.50	13.50
a.	Single, English		1.40	1.40
b.	Single, Afrikaans		1.40	1.40
B8	SP8 3p + 3p chlky bl, pair		26.00	16.00
a.	Single, English		1.75	2.00
b.	Single, Afrikaans		1.75	2.00
	Nos. B5-B8 (4)		72.50	44.00

Voortrekker centenary. Surtax went to the Natl. Memorial Fund for a Voortrekker monument.

"The Old Vicarage," Huguenot Museum — SP9

Rising Sun and Cross — SP10

Huguenot Dwelling, Drakenstein Mountain Valley — SP11

1939, July 17 Photo. Perf. 14

B9	SP9 ½p + ½p Prus grn & gray brn, pair		11.00	8.00
a.	Single, English		1.00	.85
b.	Single, Afrikaans		1.00	.85
B10	SP10 1p + 1p rose car & Prus grn, pair		13.00	10.00
a.	Single, English		1.00	1.00
b.	Single, Afrikaans		1.00	1.00

Perf. 15x14

B11	SP11 1½p + 1½p, pair		27.50	15.00
a.	Single, English		1.60	1.60
b.	Single, Afrikaans		1.60	1.60
	Nos. B9-B11 (3)		51.50	33.00

250th anniv. of the landing of the Huguenots in South Africa. Surtax went to a fund to build a Huguenot memorial at Paarl.

No. 581 Surcharged in English or Afrikaans

a

b

c

d

1987, Nov. 16 Litho. Perf. 14x14½

B12	Pair		1.00	1.00
a.	A229(a) 16c +10c red		.50	.50
b.	A229(b) 16c +10c red		.50	.50

Surcharge for flood relief.

No. 702 Surcharged in English or Afrikaans

1987, Dec. 1

B13	Pair		1.00	1.00
a.	A254(a) 16c +10c multicolored		.50	.50
b.	A254(b) 16c +10c multicolored		.50	.50

"+10c" is overprinted below text on Nos. B13a-B13b. Surcharge for flood relief.

No. 706 Surcharged in English or Afrikaans

1988, Mar. 1 Perf. 14½x14

B14	Pair		1.00	1.00
a.	A256(a) 16c +10c multicolored		.50	.50
b.	A256(b) 16c +10c multicolored		.50	.50

Surcharge for flood relief.

Nos. 710-713 Surcharged in English or Afrikaans

1988, Apr. 13 Perf. 14x14½

B15	Pair		.85	.85
a.	A257(c) 16c +10c multicolored		.40	.40
b.	A257(c) 16c +10c multicolored		.40	.40
B16	Pair		1.60	1.60
a.	A257(c) 30c +10c multicolored		.80	.80
b.	A257(d) 30c +10c multicolored		.80	.80
B17	Pair		2.25	2.25
a.	A257(c) 40c +10c multicolored		1.10	1.10
b.	A257(d) 40c +10c multicolored		1.10	1.10
B18	Pair		2.75	2.75
a.	A257(d) 50c +10c multicolored		1.25	1.25
b.	A257(d) 50c +10c multicolored		1.25	1.25
	Nos. B12-B18 (7)		10.45	10.45

Surcharge for flood relief.
On Nos. B16a, B16b, the "+ 10" is in upper left corner.

AIR POST STAMPS

Mail	Biplane in
Plane — AP1	Flight — AP2

Unwmk.

1925, Feb. 26 Litho. Perf. 12

C1	AP1 1p red		4.50	10.00
C2	AP1 3p ultramarine		10.00	13.00
C3	AP1 6p violet		17.50	24.00
C4	AP1 9p gray green		29.00	32.50
	Nos. C1-C4 (4)		61.00	79.50
	Set, never hinged		150.00	

Forgeries exist.

1929, Aug. 16 Typo. Perf. 14x13½

C5	AP2 4p blue green		8.50	2.75
C6	AP2 1sh orange		27.50	21.00
	Set, never hinged		75.00	

Catalogue values for unused stamps in this section, from this point to the end of the section, are for Never Hinged items.

"AIRMAIL POSTCARD" "AIRMAIL POSTCARD RATE"

Stamps inscribed thus were sold for the amount shown in ( ) on date of issue.
See Nos. 1038-1042F for stamps included with postage sets.

Endangered Fauna Type of 1993
1996, May 8 Litho. Perf. 14x14½

C6A	A288 (1r) White rhinoceros		.70	.70
C6B	A288 (1r) Buffalo		.70	.70
C6C	A288 (1r) Lion		.70	.70
f.	Souvenir sheet of 1 + label		.80	.80
C6D	A288 (1r) Leopard		.70	.70
C6E	A288 (1r) African elephant		.70	.70
g.	Strip of 5, #936-940		3.50	
h.	Sheet of 10, 2 each #936-940		7.00	
i.	Booklet pane of 5, #936-940 + 5 labels		4.00	
	Complete booklet, #940c		4.00	

No. C6Cf is inscribed in sheet margin for Coach House, and sold for 1r.
Issued: #C6Cf, 2/97; #C6Ei, 7/27/97.

Inauguration of Blue Train — AP3

Designs: No. C7, Double-headed Class 6E 1, electric locomotives, Cape Town to Beaufort West. No. C8, Double-headed Class 6E 1 electric locomotives, Hex River Valley. No. C9, 1960's Steam powered locomotives between Three Sisters and Huchinson. No. C10, Diesel locomotives, Modder River Bridge near Kimberly. No. C11, Diesel locomotives, Northern Transvaal.

1997, Aug. 1 Perf. 14 Syncopated

C7	AP3 (1r) multicolored		.70	.70
a.	Souv. sheet of 1, perf. 14		.70	.70
C8	AP3 (1r) multicolored		.70	.70
C9	AP3 (1r) multicolored		.70	.70
a.	Souvenir sheet of 1, perf. 14		.70	.70
C10	AP3 (1r) multicolored		.70	.70
C11	AP3 (1r) multicolored		.70	.70
a.	Strip of 5, #C7-C11		3.50	3.50

No. C7a is inscribed in sheet margin for The Cape Stamp Show and Harmers of London stamp auctioneers.
No. C9a was issued 11/97, sold for 1.30r and is inscribed for Eastgate Universal Stamps & Coins in sheet margin.

1998, Nov. Litho. Perf. 14¾x14
Booklet Stamps

C12	AP3 (1r) Like #C7		.70	.70
C13	AP3 (1r) Like #C8		.70	.70
C14	AP3 (1r) Like #C9		.70	.70
C15	AP3 (1r) Like #C10		.70	.70
C16	AP3 (1r) Like #C11		.70	.70
a.	Bklt. pane, 2 ea #C12-C16		7.00	
	Complete booklet, #C16a		7.00	
	Nos. C12-C16 (5)		3.50	3.50

Tourism AP4

Western Cape of South Africa: No. C7, Sandstone Cliffs. No. C8, Robben Island. No. C9, Pinehurst Homestead. No. C10, Waterfront, Capetown. No. C11, Boschendal Wine Estate.

1998, Sept. 28 Litho. Perf. 14½x14
Booklet Stamps

C17	AP4 (1.30r) multicolored		.60	.60
C18	AP4 (1.30r) multicolored		.60	.60
C19	AP4 (1.30r) multicolored		.60	.60
C20	AP4 (1.30r) multicolored		.60	.60
C21	AP4 (1.30r) multicolored		.60	.60
a.	Bklt. pane, 2 ea #C17-C21 + label		6.00	
	Complete booklet, #C21a		6.00	
	Nos. C17-C21 (5)		3.00	3.00

Perf. 14¾x14 on 3 sides
1998, Sept. 28   **Litho.**

KwaZulu-Natal: No. C22, Drakensberge. No. C23, Zulu women and huts. No. C24, Rhinoceros and pelicans. No. C25, Rickshaw driver. No. C26, Indian dancers.

C22	AP4	(1.30r) multicolored	.60	.60
C23	AP4	(1.30r) multicolored	.60	.60
C24	AP4	(1.30r) multicolored	.60	.60
C25	AP4	(1.30r) multicolored	.60	.60
C26	AP4	(1.30r) multicolored	.60	.60
a.		Booklet pane, 2 ea #C22-C26	6.00	
		Complete booklet, #C26a	6.00	

Worldwide Fund for Nature AP5

1998, Oct. 23   **Litho.**   *Perf. 14¾x14*

C27	AP5	(1.30r) Cuvier's beak-ed whale	1.00	1.00
C28	AP5	(1.30r) Minke whale	1.00	1.00
C29	AP5	(1.30r) Bryde's whale	1.00	1.00
C30	AP5	(1.30r) Pygmy right whale	1.00	1.00
a.		Block of 4, #C27-C30	4.00	4.00
b.		Booklet pane, 3 each #C27-C28, 2 each #C29-C30	10.00	
		Complete booklet	10.00	
		Complete booklet, 2 #C30b + 2 postal cards	30.00	

No. C30b exists with and without perfs running through side and bottom pane margins.

Tourism Type of 1998
Mpumalanga and Northern Province: No. C31, Blyde River Canyon. No. C32, Lone Creek Falls. No. C33, Ndebele women. No. C34, Pilgrim's Rest historical town. No. C35, Elephants, Thulamela, Kruger National Park.

1999, Aug.   **Litho.**   *Perf. 14¾x14*

C31	AP4	(1.30r) multi	.50	.50
C32	AP4	(1.30r) multi	.50	.50
C33	AP4	(1.30r) multi	.50	.50
C34	AP4	(1.30r) multi	.50	.50
C35	AP4	(1.30r) multi	.50	.50
a.		Booklet pane, 2 each #C31-C35	5.00	
		Complete booklet, #C35a	5.00	

Big Game Animals — AP6

Designs: Nos. C36, C45, Elephant. Nos. C37, C44, Lion. Nos. C38, C43, Rhinoceros. Nos. C39, C42, Leopard. Nos. C40, C41, Buffalo.

Perf. 14¾x14½ on 3 or 4 Sides
2001, Apr. 25   **Litho.**
Booklet Stamps

C36	AP6	(1.90r) multi	.70	.70
C37	AP6	(1.90r) multi	.70	.70
C38	AP6	(1.90r) multi	.70	.70
C39	AP6	(1.90r) multi	.70	.70
C40	AP6	(1.90r) multi	.70	.70
a.		Booklet pane, 2 each #C36-C40	7.00	
		Booklet, 2 #C40a + 2 postal cards	14.00	

Self-Adhesive
Size: 30x24mm
Serpentine Die Cut 12x11½ on 2 or 3 Sides

C41	AP6	(1.90r) multi	.70	.70
C42	AP6	(1.90r) multi	.70	.70
C43	AP6	(1.90r) multi	.70	.70
C44	AP6	(1.90r) multi	.70	.70
C45	AP6	(1.90r) multi	.70	.70
a.		Booklet, 2 each #C41-C45	7.00	

See Nos. C65-C69.

Tourism — AP7

Designs: No. C46, (2.10r), Cango Caves. No. C47, (2.10r), Table Mountain. No. C48, (2.10r), West Coast. No. C49, (2.10r), Snow-

---

covered mountains near Elliot. No. C50, (2.10r), Augrabies Waterfall. No. C51, (2.10r), Stellenbosch vineyard country. No. C52, (2.10r), Flowers, Namaqualand. No. C53, (2.10r), Tsitsikamma Forest. No. C54, (2.10r), Cape Mountain zebras. No. C55, (2.10r), Richtersveld Desert.

2001, Sept. 6   **Litho.**   *Perf. 13¼x13¾*

C46-C55	AP7	Set of 10	7.00	7.00

Pres. Nelson Mandela — AP8

Various photographs. Color of country name and size of stamps: a, Lilac, 31x48mm. b, Red and lilac, 50x38mm. c, Orange, 31x48mm. d, Orange, 31x31mm. e, Orange, 38x50mm. f, White, 38x50mm. g, White, 50x38mm. h, White, 31x48mm. i, Lilac, 38x50mm. j, Red, 31x31mm.

2001, Nov. 26   *Perf. 14¾x14, 13¾*

C56		Booklet	9.00	
a.-j.		AP8 (2.10r) Any booklet pane	.90	.90

No. C56 sold for 45r and included two postal cards.

Shaka (1785-1828), Zulu King — AP9

2003, Sept. 24   **Litho.**   *Perf. 13x13¼*

C57	AP9	(3.30r) multi	1.10	1.10

Miniature Sheet

Flora and Fauna of Table Mountain — AP10

No. C58: a, Cape sugarbird, vert. b, Dark opal butterflies. c, King protea. d, Cape rock hyrax. e, Cuckoo wasp. f, Table Mountain ghost frog. g, Table Mountain cockroaches. h, Staavia dodii, vert. i, Spotted skaapsteker. j, Duvalia immaculata.

Serpentine Die Cut 9x9½, 9½x9
2004, Sept. 1   **Litho.**
Self-Adhesive

C58	AP10	Sheet of 10	17.50	17.50
a.-j.		(10r) Any single	1.75	1.75

World Post Day — AP11

2004, Sept. 23   *Perf. 14*

C59	AP11	(3.45r) multi	1.25	1.25

Rotary International, Cent. — AP12

No. C60: a, Doctor listening to boy's heartbeat, infant receiving oral vaccination. b, Child at computer, welder.

2005, Feb. 23   *Perf. 14¼x14*

C60		Horiz. pair	3.25	3.25
a.-b.		AP12 (4r) Either single	1.50	1.50

Miniature Sheet

National Orders — AP13

No. C61: a, Order of Mapungubwe. b, Order of Merit for Bravery. c, Order of the Baobab. d, Order of Luthuli. e, Order of Ikhamanga. f, Order of the Companions of O. R. Tambo.

Litho. & Embossed with Foil Application
2005, Nov. 26   *Perf. 14¾x14¼*

C61	AP13	(4.25r) Sheet of 6, #a-f	9.00	9.00

Miniature Sheet

Art — AP14

No. C62: a, Boland Winter, by Eric Laubscher. b, Table Mountain, by Maggie Laubser. c, Fishermen Drawing Nets, by Walter Battis. d, Oh, South Africa, You've Turned My World Completely Upside Down, by Lallitha Jawahirlal. e, Untitled, by Lucky Sibiya. f, Untitled, by Sophie Masiza. g, Azibuye Emasisweni, by Trevor Makhoba. h, Kontantwinkel Riebeck-Wes, by John Kramer. i, Houses in the Hills, by Gladys Mgudlandlu. j, Sequence City, by Usha Seejarim.

2005, May 6   **Litho.**   *Perf. 14¼x14¾*

C62	AP14	(3.65r) Sheet of 10, #a-j	13.50	13.50

Intl. Year of Physics — AP15

2005, July 7   *Perf. 14½*

C63	AP15	(3.65r) multi	1.40	1.40

Miniature Sheet

"Hello" in Various Languages and Flag — AP16

No. C64: a, Hallo! b, Hi! c, Sawubona. d, Ndi Masiari! e, Lotjha!. f, Avuxeni. g, Dumela. h, Molo!

2005, Oct. 9

C64	AP16	(3.65r) Sheet of 8, #a-h	9.50	9.50

Big Game Animals Type of 2001
Serpentine Die Cut 12¼x12¾ on 2 or 3 Sides
2005, Oct. 10
Self-Adhesive
Booklet Stamps
Size: 30x24mm

C65	AP6	(3.65r) Buffalo	1.25	1.25
C66	AP6	(3.65r) Leopard	1.25	1.25
C67	AP6	(3.65r) Rhinoceros	1.25	1.25
C68	AP6	(3.65r) Lion	1.25	1.25
C69	AP6	(3.65r) Elephant	1.25	1.25
a.		Booklet, 2 each # C65-C69	12.50	

Big Game Animals — AP17

Serpentine Die Cut 12½x13½
2006, Feb. 24
Self-Adhesive
Booklet Stamps

C70	AP17	(3.65r) Lion	1.25	1.25
C71	AP17	(3.65r) Buffalo	1.25	1.25
C72	AP17	(3.65r) Elephant	1.25	1.25
C73	AP17	(3.65r) Rhinoceros	1.25	1.25
C74	AP17	(3.65r) Leopard	1.25	1.25
a.		Booklet, 2 each #C70-C74	12.50	

Cyclists — AP18

2006, Mar. 6   *Perf. 13¼x13¾*

C75	AP18	(4.25r) multi	1.50	1.50

Souvenir Sheet

2010 World Cup Soccer
Championships, South Africa — AP19

2006, July 7 Litho. Perf. 14¾x14½
C76 AP19 (4.40r) multi   1.40 1.40

Miniature Sheet

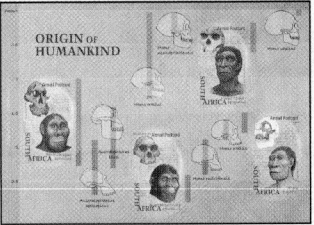

Origins of Humans — AP20

No. C77: a, Paranthropus robustus. b, Australopithecus africanus. c, Homo heidelbergensis. d, Homo ergaster.

Serpentine Die Cut 11½x11¾
2006, Nov. 10
Self-Adhesive
C77 AP20 (3.80r) Sheet of 4, #a-d   4.75 4.75

Big Game
Animals — AP21

Serpentine Die Cut 13½x13¾ on 2 or 3 Sides
2007, Aug. 17 Litho.
Booklet Stamps
Self-Adhesive
C78 AP21 (4.01r) Elephant   1.10 1.10
C79 AP21 (4.01r) Leopard   1.10 1.10
C80 AP21 (4.01r) Buffalo   1.10 1.10
C81 AP21 (4.01r) Lion   1.10 1.10
C82 AP21 (4.01r) Rhinoceros   1.10 1.10
a.   Booklet pane, 2 each #C78-C82   11.00
  Nos. C78-C82 (5)   5.50 5.50

Souvenir Sheet

24th UPU Congress, Nairobi — AP22

2007, Oct. 9 Perf. 13¾
C83 AP22 (4.64r) multi   1.40 1.40

Souvenir Sheet

2010 World Cup Soccer
Championships, South Africa — AP23

2007, Nov. 23 Perf. 13¼x13½
C84 AP23 (4.64r) multi   1.40 1.40

Birds — AP24

No. C85: a, Southern ground hornbill. b, Kori bustard. c, Common ostrich. d, Blue crane. e, Bearded vulture.

2008, July 1 Litho. Perf. 13¼x13¾
C85   Horiz. strip of 5   6.50 6.50
a.-e.   AP24 (4.90r) Any single   1.25 1.25

Nos. C85a-C85e are each inscribed "International Airmail Small Letter."

Intl. Congress of Entomology Conference, Durban — AP25

2008, July 4 Perf. 13¾x13¼
C86 AP25 (4.20r) multi   1.10 1.10

Miniature Sheet

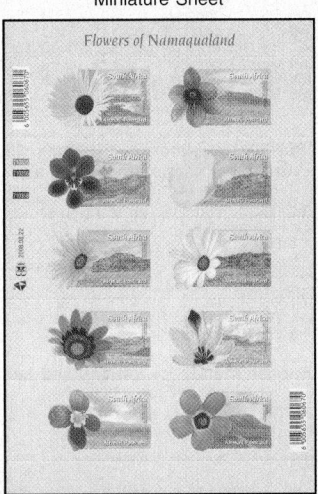

Flowers — AP26

No. C87: a, Common bokbaaivygie. b, Bokkeveld pride. c, Springbok painted petals. d, White-eyed duiker-root. e, Namaqualand daisy. f, Satin boneseed. g, Karoo gazania. h, Harlequin hesperantha. i, Showy sunflax. j, Red-eye sorrel.

2008, Aug. 22 Die Cut
Self-Adhesive
C87   AP26   Sheet of 10   11.00
a.-j.   (4.20r) Any single   1.10 1.10

Nos. C87a-C87j are each inscribed "Airmail Postcard."

Souvenir Sheet

2010 World Cup Soccer
Championships, South Africa — AP27

2008, Sept. 5 Perf. 13¼x13¾
C88 AP27 (3.70r) multi   .95 .95

Miniature Sheet

uKhahlamba-Drakensberg
Park — AP28

No. C89: a, View overlooking Eastern Buttress with Devils Tooth. b, View from the Sentinel overlooking the Eastern Buttress. c, Amphitheater from the Royal Natal National Park. d, View of the Sentinel and Amphitheater.

2008, Sept. 23 Perf. 13¼x13¾
C89   AP28   Sheet of 4   4.75 4.75
a.-d.   (4.90r) Any single   1.10 1.10

Nos. C89a-C89d are each inscribed "International Airmail Small Letter."

Big Game
Animals — AP29

Serpentine Die Cut 12¼x12¾ on 2 or 3 Sides
2008, Nov. 14
Booklet Stamps
Self-Adhesive
C90 AP29 (4.20r) Elephant   .80 .80
C91 AP29 (4.20r) Lion   .80 .80
C92 AP29 (4.20r) Leopard   .80 .80
C93 AP29 (4.20r) Buffalo   .80 .80
C94 AP29 (4.20r) Rhinoceros   .80 .80
a.   Booklet pane of 10, 2 each #C90-C94   8.25
  Nos. C90-C94 (5)   4.00 4.00

Nos. C90-C94 are each inscribed "Airmail Postcard."

Souvenir Sheet

2010 World Cup Soccer
Championships, South Africa — AP30

Perf. 13¼x13¾
2009, June 14 Litho.
C95 AP30 (5.40r) multi   1.40 1.40

No. C95 is inscribed "International Airmail Small Letter."

Miniature Sheet

Gemstones — AP31

No. C96: a, Garnet. b, Sugilite. c, Rhodocrosite. d, Jasper.

Litho. With Foil Application
2009, July 10 Perf. 13½
C96   AP31   Sheet of 4   4.50 4.50
a.-d.   (4.60r) Any single   1.10 1.10

Nos. C96a-C96d are inscribed "Airmail Postcard."

Birds — AP32

No. C97: a, Jackass penguins. b, Black oyster catchers. c, Common cape gannets. d, Cape cormorants. e, Black-backed sea gull.

2009, Aug. 3 Litho. Perf. 14¾x14½
C97   Horiz. strip of 5   7.00 7.00
a.-e.   AP32 (5.40r) Any single   1.40 1.40

Nos. C97a-C97e are each inscribed "International Airmail Small Letter."

Miniature Sheet

Dinosaurs — AP33

No. C98: a, Afrovenator. b, Afrovenator skeleton. c, Ouranosaurus. d, Ouranosaurus skeleton. e, Heterodontosaurus, vert. f, Heterodontosaurus skeleton, vert. g, Jobaria, vert. h, Jobaria skeleton, vert. i, Suchomimus, vert. j, Suchomimus skeleton, vert.

Perf. 13¼x13, 13x13¼ (#C98e-C98j)
2009, Nov. 2
C98   AP33   Sheet of 10   12.50 12.50
a.-j.   (4.60r) Any single   1.25 1.25

Nos. C98a-C98j are inscribed "International Airmail Postcard." The stamp designs, when viewed through red and blue glasses, become three-dimensional.

Miniature Sheet

Life of Fishermen — AP34

No. C99: a, Fish on net, boats ashore. b, Men pushing boat in shallow water. c, Sun, house, men near boat. d, Fishemen in boat on water. e, Fishermen, boat ashore near rocks. f, Fishing community. g, Men in boat, house. h, Boat ashore, fisherman with rod. i, Fish, houses, boat. j, Man hanging fish to dry.

2010, Feb. 19 Perf. 13¼x13
C99   AP34   Sheet of 10   14.00 14.00
a.-j.   (5.40r) Any single   1.40 1.40

Nos. C99a-C99j are inscribed "International Airmail Small Letter."

Big Game
Animals — AP35

Die Cut Perf. 12¾x12½ on 2 or 3 Sides
2010, May 5
Booklet Stamps
Self-Adhesive
C100 AP35 (4.90r) Elephant   1.40 1.40
C101 AP35 (4.90r) Lion   1.40 1.40
C102 AP35 (4.90r) Buffalo   1.40 1.40
C103 AP35 (4.90r) Leopard   1.40 1.40

C104 AP35 (4.90r) Rhinoceros 1.40 1.40
  a. Booklet pane of 10, 2 each 14.00
    #C100-C104
    Nos. C100-C104 (5) 7.00 7.00

Nos. C100-C104 are inscribed "Airmail Postcard."

Cats — AP36

No. C105: a, African wild cat (60x60mm). b, Serval (30x30mm). c, Caracal (30x30mm). d, Black-footed cat (30x30mm). e, African golden cat (30x30mm).

2011, Feb. 4   *Perf. 13¼*
C105 AP36 Block of 5 6.25 6.25
  a.-e. (4.30r) Any single 1.25 1.25

Nos. C105a-C015e are each inscribed "Africa Airmail." Perforations trace around the cat's head on No. C105a.

Souvenir Sheet

First South African Air Mail Flight, Cent. — AP37

2011, Oct. 7   *Perf. 13x13¼*
C106 AP37 (5.10r) multi 1.40 1.40

No. C106 is inscribed "Airmail Postcard."

REGISTRATION STAMPS

Miniature Sheet

Intl. Year of Biodiversity — R1

No. F1: a, Giant African mantis, Common lionfish. b, Black rhinoceros. c, Common chameleon, African reed frog. d, Lilac-breasted roller, Baobab tree.

      Perf. 13¼x13¾
2010, Mar. 12   Litho.
F1 R1 Sheet of 4 18.00 18.00
  a.-d. (15.85r) Any single 4.50 4.50

Nos. F1a-F1d are inscribed "Small Registered Letter."

POSTAGE DUE STAMPS

D1   D2

Wmk. Springbok's Head (177)
1914-15   Typo.   *Perf. 14*
J1 D1 ½p green & blk 2.50 4.25
J2 D1 1p red & blk 2.50 1.25
J3 D1 2p vio & blk ('14) 7.50 .80
J4 D1 3p ultra & blk 2.50 .80
J5 D1 5p brown & blk 4.50 30.00
J6 D1 6p gray & blk 11.00 30.00
J7 D1 1sh black & red 77.50 160.00
    Nos. J1-J7 (7) 108.00 226.10

1922 Unwmk. Litho. *Rouletted 7-8*
J8 D1 ½p blue grn & blk 1.60 15.00
J9 D1 1p dull red & blk 1.75 1.25
J10 D1 1½p yellow brn & blk 2.00 2.40
    Nos. J8-J10 (3) 5.35 18.65

1922-26   *Perf. 14*
J11 D1 ½p blue grn & blk .85 1.75
J12 D1 1p rose & blk ('23) .90 .25
J13 D1 1½p yel brn & blk 1.60 1.25
    ('24)
J14 D1 2p vio & blk ('23) 1.40 .80
  a. Imperf. pair 300.00 400.00
J15 D1 3p blue & blk ('26) 8.00 22.50
J16 D1 6p gray & blue ('23) 16.00 8.00
    Nos. J11-J16 (6) 28.75 34.55

1927-28   Typo.
J17 D2 ½p blue green & blk 1.00 1.50
J18 D2 1p rose & black 1.40 .80
J19 D2 2p violet & black 1.40 1.25
J20 D2 3p ultra & black 13.00 25.00
J21 D2 6p gray & black 24.00 20.00
    Nos. J17-J21 (5) 40.80 50.55

Type of 1927-28 Redrawn
      Perf. 15x14
1932-40   Photo.   Wmk. 201
J22 D2 ½p blue grn & blk 2.75 1.75
    ('34)
J23 D2 1p rose car & blk 2.50 .95
    ('34)
J24 D2 2p blk violet & blk 15.00 2.50
  a. 2p dark purple & black ('40) 32.50 .25
J25 D2 3p dp blue & blk 27.50 14.00
J26 D2 3p ultra & dk bl ('35) 8.00 .40
J27 D2 3p blue & dk bl ('40) 85.00 3.50
J28 D2 6p brn org & grn 25.00 6.00
    ('33)
J29 D2 6p red org & grn 15.00 3.50
    ('38)
    Nos. J22-J29 (8) 180.75 32.60

The ½p No. J22 photogravure has larger but thinner numeral and the "d" is taller and thinner than on No. J17.

The 1p No. J23 photogravure has numeral with parallel sides. The "d" is taller and thicker than on No. J18.

On Nos. J25 and J27 the numeral is followed by a large "d" with thick lines and a large round period below it.

Nos. J22, J24 and J25 have frame in photogravure, value typographed.

> Catalogue values for unused stamps in this section, from this point to the end of the section, are for Never Hinged items.

See "English-Afrikaans Se-tenant" note preceding No. 23.

D3

Horiz. strips of Three, Perf. 15x14 All Around, Rouletted 6½ Between
1943-44   Photo.   Wmk. 201
J30 D3 ½p Prus green ('44) 15.00 50.00
  a. Single .25 .25
J31 D3 1p brt carmine 11.00 5.50
  a. Single .25 .25
J32 D3 2p dark purple 9.00 12.00
  a. Single .25 .25
J33 D3 3p dark blue 55.00 85.00
  a. Single .25 1.25
    Nos. J30-J33 (4) 90.00 152.50

Catalogued as strips of 3 because of the perforations.

Type of 1932-38 Redrawn
Thick Numerals, Capital "D"
1948-49   *Perf. 15x14*
J34 D2 ½p blue green & blk 9.00 13.50
J35 D2 1p deep rose & blk 16.00 6.00
J36 D2 2p dk pur & blk ('49) 17.50 9.00
J37 D2 3p ultra & dk blue 16.00 17.50
J38 D2 6p dp org & grn ('49) 37.50 8.00
    Nos. J34-J38 (5) 96.00 54.00

Redrawn Type of 1948-49
Hyphen between Suid-Afrika
1950-58   *Perf. 15x14*
J40 D2 1p car rose & blk 1.25 .45
J41 D2 2p dk pur & blk ('51) .85 .30
J42 D2 3p ultra & dk blue 6.25 2.50
J43 D2 4p emer & dk grn 14.50 15.00
    ('58)
J44 D2 6p dp org & grn 11.50 11.50
    ('52)
J45 D2 1sh brn red & dk brn 17.50 16.00
    ('58)
    Nos. J40-J45 (6) 51.85 45.75

D4   D5

      Perf. 15x14
1961, Feb. 14   Photo.   Wmk. 330
J46 D4 1c cerise & blk .25 2.50
J47 D4 2c purple & blk .25 2.50
J48 D4 4c brt & dk green 1.10 6.00
J49 D4 5c chalky bl & slate 2.00 6.50
J50 D4 6p yellow grn & grn 8.00 7.00
J51 D4 10c maroon & dk brn 8.50 10.00
    Nos. J46-J51 (6) 20.10 34.50

Republic
1961-69   *Perf. 15x14*
Afrikaans Inscription on Top and Left Side
J52 D5 1c cerise & blk .50 .50
J53 D5 4c brt & dk green 4.25 3.00
J54 D5 6c vermilion & dk grn 8.50 7.25
English Inscription on Top and Left Side
J55 D5 1c cerise & blk ('62) .30 3.50
J56 D5 2c purple & blk .40 .40
J57 D5 4c brt & dk grn ('69) 12.00 17.00
J58 D5 5c chlky bl & dk bl 2.40 3.00
J59 D5 5c chlky bl & blk ('62) 2.75 11.00
J60 D5 10c maroon & dk brn 4.75 3.00
    Nos. J52-J60 (9) 35.85 48.65

1967-70   Photo.   Wmk. 359
Afrikaans Inscription on Top and Left Side
J61 D5 1c carmine rose & .25 .25
    blk
J62 D5 2c brt purple & blk .25 .25
  a. Perf. 14 ('71) 25.00 25.00
J63 D5 4c lt grn & blk ('71) 27.50 25.00
  a. 4c bright & dark green ('70) 110.00 110.00
J64 D5 5c dk blue & blk .85 .85
J65 D5 6c orange & dk grn 4.25 9.75
J66 D5 10c dk rose brown & 3.50 2.10
    blk
English Inscription on Top and Left Side
J67 D5 1c car rose & blk .25 .25
J68 D5 2c brt purple & blk .40 .40
  a. Perf. 14 ('71) 25.00 25.00
J69 D5 4c lt green & blk 27.50 25.00
    ('71)
  a. 4c bright & dark green ('70) 35.00 35.00
  b. As "a," perf. 14 ('71) 6.00 6.00
J70 D5 5c dk blue & blk .85 .85
J71 D5 6c orange & dk grn 4.25 9.75
J72 D5 10c dk rose brown & 3.50 2.10
    blk
    Nos. J61-J72 (12) 73.35 76.55

D6

1972, Mar. 22   *Perf. 14x13½*
J73 D6 1c brt yellow green .55 1.75
J74 D6 2c orange .80 3.00
J75 D6 4c dull purple 2.00 3.00
J76 D6 6c yellow 2.00 5.50
J77 D6 8c bright blue 3.50 5.50
J78 D6 10c rose red 6.00 8.50
    Nos. J73-J78 (6) 14.85 27.25

On the 2c, 6c and 10c "TO PAY" in first row at left.

OFFICIAL STAMPS

Type A2 stamps have very small margins at top and bottom. Values are for examples with perfs close to, or touching the frame.

Regular Issues Overprinted in Black, Periods in Overprint On No. 5

1926   Wmk. 177   *Perf. 14*
O1 A2 2p dull violet 22.50 2.00

See "English-Afrikaans Se-tenant" note preceding No. 23.

On Nos. 23-25
     Perf. 14½x14
       Wmk. 201
O2 A5 ½p dk grn & blk, 8.00 18.00
    pair
  a. Single, English .75 1.50
  b. Single, Afrikaans .75 1.50
O3 A6 1p car & blk, pair 4.00 8.50
  a. Single, English .25 .50
  b. Single, Afrikaans .25 .50
O4 A7 6p org & grn, pair 550.00 80.00
  a. Single, English 25.00 11.00
  b. Single, Afrikaans 25.00 11.00

Nos. 26 and 25 Overprinted, No Periods in Overprint — b

(Reading Up)
1928-29   *Perf. 14, 14½x14*
Space between words 19mm
O5 A8 2p vio brn & gray, pair 7.50 20.00
    ('29)
  a. Single, English .50 1.50
  b. Single, Afrikaans .50 1.50
  c. Space 17½mm, pair 6.00 24.00
  d. As "c," single, English .50 2.00
  e. As "c," single, Afrikaans .50 2.00
Space between words 11½mm
O6 A7 6p org & grn, pair 22.50 47.50
  a. Single, English 2.75 2.75
  b. Single, Afrikaans 2.75 2.75

#23-25 Ovptd. type "b" Reading Down
Space between words 13½-14mm
1929   *Perf. 14½x14*
O7 A5 ½p grn & blk, pair 2.50 4.75
  a. Single, English .25 .35
  b. Single, Afrikaans .25 .35
  c. Period after "OFFISIEEL" on 5.00 5.00
    English stamp
  d. Pair, "c" + normal ½p 45.00 45.00
  e. Period after "OFFISIEEL." on 5.00 5.00
    Afrikaans stamp
  f. Pair, "e" + normal ½p 55.00 65.00
O8 A6 1p car & blk, pair 3.00 6.00
  a. Single, English .30 .50
  b. Single, Afrikaans .30 .50
O9 A7 6p org & grn, pair 8.00 40.00
  a. Single, English 1.25 3.50
  b. Single, Afrikaans 1.25 3.50
  c. Period after "OFFISIEEL." on 10.00 10.00
    English stamp
  d. Pair, "c" + normal 6p 75.00 150.00
  e. Period after "OFFISIEEL." on 12.00 12.00
    Afrikaans stamp
  f. Pair, "e" + normal 6p 90.00 160.00
    Nos. O7-O9 (3) 13.50 50.75

#29-30 Ovptd. type "b" Reading Down
Space between words 17½-19mm
1931   Engr.   *Perf. 14, 14x13½*
O10 A11 1sh dp bl & bis 40.00 90.00
    brn, pair
  a. Single, English 3.00 10.00
  b. Single, Afrikaans 3.00 10.00
  c. Period after "OFFICIAL." 50.00 50.00
    on Afrikaans stamp
  d. Pair, "c" + normal 1sh 115.00 240.00
O11 A12 2sh6p brn & bl 65.00 150.00
    grn, pair
  a. Single, English 10.00 19.00
  b. Single, Afrikaans 10.00 19.00
  c. Period after "OFFICIAL." 72.50 100.00
    on English stamp
  d. Pair, "c" + normal 2sh6p 300.00 550.00

Regular Issues of 1930-45 Overprinted type "b" Reading Down ("SUIDAFRIKA" on Afrikaans stamps)
  Perf. 15x14 (½p, 1p, 6p), 14
1930-47   Photo.   Wmk. 201
Space between words 9½-12mm
(Various spacings occur in same setting)
O12 A5 ½p bl grn & blk 2.25 5.00
    (#33), pair
    ('31)
  a. Single, English .25 .40
  b. Single, Afrikaans .25 .40
  c. Period after "OFFISIEEL." 5.00 5.00
    on English stamp
  d. Pair, "c" + normal ½p 37.50 60.00

e.	Period after "OFFISIEEL." on Afrikaans stamp		5.00	5.00
f.	Pair, "e" + normal ½p		27.50	50.00

Space between words 12½-13½mm

O13	A5	½p bl grn & blk, pair (#33)		3.00	4.00
a.		Single, English		.25	.50
b.		Single, Afrikaans		.25	.50
O14	A6	1p car & blk, pair (#34)		6.00	6.00
a.		Single, English		.50	.60
b.		Single, Afrikaans		.50	.60
c.		Period after "OFFISIEEL." on English stamp		5.00	5.00
d.		Pair, "c" + normal 1p		50.00	75.00
e.		Period after "OFFISIEEL." on Afrikaans stamp		5.00	5.00
f.		Pair, "e" + normal ½p		35.00	55.00
O15	A6	1p rose & blk, pair (#35) ('33)		15.00	9.00
a.		Single, English		1.00	1.00
b.		Single, Afrikaans		1.00	1.00
c.		Double ovpt., pair		275.00	400.00
d.		As "c," English		—	—
e.		As "c," Afrikaans		—	—

Space between words 20½-22mm

O16	A8	2p vio & gray, pair (#36) ('31)		8.00	11.00
a.		Single, English		.80	1.50
b.		Single, Afrikaans		.80	1.50
O17	A8	2p vio & ind, pair (#37)		150.00	100.00
a.		Single, English		10.00	10.00
b.		Single, Afrikaans		10.00	10.00

Space between words 12½-13½mm

O18	A7	6p org & grn, pair (#42)		8.50	8.50
a.		Single, English		.75	1.00
b.		Single, Afrikaans		.75	1.00
c.		Period after "OFFISIEEL." on English stamp		7.00	7.00
d.		Pair, "c" + normal 6p		90.00	100.00
e.		Period after "OFFISIEEL." on Afrikaans stamp		5.50	5.50
f.		Pair, "e" + normal 6p		75.00	90.00

Space between words 21mm

O19	A11	1sh dp bl & brn, pair (#43c) ('32)		60.00	90.00
a.		Single, English		7.50	7.50
b.		Single, Afrikaans		7.50	7.50
c.		1sh dk bl & yel brn (#43), 19mm, pair		50.00	90.00
d.		As "c," single, English		8.50	7.50
e.		As "c," single, Afrikaans		8.50	7.50
f.		As "c," spaced 21mm, pair		42.50	65.00
g.		As "f," single, English		6.00	7.50
h.		As "f," single, Afrikaans		6.00	7.50

Space between words 17½-18½mm

O20	A12	2sh6p brn & sl grn (#44c) ('37), pair		80.00	140.00
a.		Single, English		15.00	15.00
b.		Single, Afrikaans		15.00	15.00
c.		Spaced 21mm, pair		75.00	75.00
d.		As "c," single, English		4.50	8.00
e.		As "c," single, Afrikaans		4.50	8.00
f.		2sh6p red brn & grn, pair (#44i) ('33)		50.00	90.00
g.		As "f," single, English		5.00	8.50
h.		As "f," single, Afrikaans		5.00	8.50
j.		2sh6p brn & bl, 19-20mm (#44) ('47), pair		30.00	60.00
k.		As "j," single, English		3.00	5.00
m.		As "j," single, Afrikaans		3.00	5.00
		Nos. O12-O20 (9)		332.75	373.50

> **Catalogue values for unused stamps in this section, from this point to the end of the section, are for Never Hinged items.**

Regular Issue of 1933-54 Overprinted type "b" Reading Down ("SUID-AFRIKA" Hyphenated)

1935-50   Photo.   Perf. 15x14, 14
Space between words given with each listing

O21	A5	½p grn & gray (#45), 12½-13mm, pair ('36)		7.00	30.00
a.		Single, English		.25	1.75
b.		Single, Afrikaans		.25	1.75
O22	A5	½p grn & gray, (#46), 11½-13mm, pair ('38)		12.00	12.50
a.		Single, English		.50	1.25
b.		Single, Afrikaans		.50	1.25
O23	A5	½p grn & gray (#47), 11½mm, pair ('48)		1.25	5.00
a.		Single, English		.25	.70
b.		Single, Afrikaans		.25	.70
O24	A6	1p car & gray (#48), 11-13mm, pair		4.00	3.00
a.		Single, English		.25	.25
b.		Single, Afrikaans		.25	.25
O25	A6	1p rose car & gray blk (#49), 11½-12mm, pair ('41)		1.00	.50
a.		Single, English		.25	.25
b.		Single, Afrikaans		.25	.25
O26	A15	1½p dk grn & gold (#51), 19-21mm, pair ('37)		30.00	25.00
a.		Single, English		2.25	1.75
b.		Single, Afrikaans		2.25	1.75

O27	A15	1½p sl grn & ocher (#52), 16mm, pair ('44)		50.00	11.50
a.		Single, English		1.25	1.25
b.		Single, Afrikaans		1.25	1.25
c.		Ovpt. spaced 14-14½mm, pair		3.00	10.00
d.		As "c," single, English		.25	.80
e.		As "c," single, Afrikaans		.25	.80
O28	A8	2p bl vio & dl bl (#53), 20-21mm, pair ('39)		150.00	40.00
a.		Single, English		7.50	2.50
b.		Single, Afrikaans		7.50	2.50
O29	A16	2p pur & sl (#55), 19-21mm, pair ('48)		5.75	25.00
a.		Single, English		.25	2.00
b.		Single, Afrikaans		.25	2.00
O30	A7	6p org & bl grn, I (#59), 12-13mm, pair ('38)		80.00	45.00
a.		Single, English		6.50	3.75
b.		Single, Afrikaans		6.50	3.75
O31	A7	6p org & grn, II (#60), 12-13mm, pair ('39)		14.00	10.00
a.		Single, English		1.25	1.25
b.		Single, Afrikaans		1.25	1.25
O32	A7	6p org & grn III (#61), 11½-12mm, pair ('47)		5.00	11.00
a.		Single, English		.85	1.25
b.		Single, Afrikaans		.85	1.25
O33	A11	1sh lt bl & ol brn (#62c), 19-21mm, pair ('40)		80.00	50.00
a.		Single, English		4.50	2.50
b.		Single, Afrikaans		4.50	2.50
c.		"OFFICIAL" on both sides		3,000.	
d.		"OFFISIEEL" on both sides		3,000.	
e.		1sh chlky bl & lt brn (#62) ('50), pair		11.00	30.00
f.		As "e," single, English		2.00	2.50
g.		As "e," single, Afrikaans		2.00	2.50
h.		1sh vio bl & brnsh blk (#62f), 18-19mm, pair		65.00	27.50
j.		As "h," single, English		4.50	2.00
k.		As "h," single, Afrikaans		4.50	2.00
O34	A13	5sh grn & blk (#64) 19-20mm, pair		65.00	160.00
a.		Single, English		3.50	13.50
b.		Single, Afrikaans		3.50	13.50
O35	A13	5sh bl grn & blk (#65), 20mm, pair		40.00	110.00
a.		Single, English		3.50	12.50
b.		Single, Afrikaans		3.50	12.50
O36	A18	10sh ol blk & bl (#67), 19½-20mm, pair ('48)		100.00	275.00
a.		Single, English		10.00	24.00
b.		Single, Afrikaans		10.00	24.00
		Nos. O21-O36 (16)		645.00	813.50

Nos. 52 and 56 Overprinted type "b" Reading Up
Space between words 16mm

1949-50   Size: 22x18mm   Perf. 14

O37	A15	1½p sl grn & ocher, pair		85.00	85.00
a.		Single, English		5.00	4.00
b.		Single, Afrikaans		5.00	4.00

Size: 21½x17½mm

O38	A16	2p pur & sl bl, pair ('50)		3,250.	3,750.
a.		Single, English		200.	275.
b.		Single, Afrikaans		200.	275.

Nos. 64, 67 Overprinted

c

Space between words 18-19mm

1940   Perf. 14

O39	A13	5sh grn & blk, pair		125.00	140.00
a.		Single, English		12.00	12.50
b.		Single, Afrikaans		12.00	12.50
O40	A18	10sh ol brn & bl, pair		500.00	525.00
a.		Single, English		32.50	37.50
b.		Single, Afrikaans		32.50	37.50

No. 54 Overprinted type "c" Reading Up
Space between words 19mm

1945   Perf. 14

O41	A8	2p dl vio & gray, pair		11.00	32.50
a.		Single, English		1.00	2.25
b.		Single, Afrikaans		1.00	2.25

No. 47 Overprinted

1947   Perf. 15x14

O42	A5	½p grn & gray, pair		22.50	20.00
a.		Single, English		1.00	2.00
b.		Single, Afrikaans		1.00	2.00

Stamps of 1937-54 Overprinted

1950-54   Perf. 15x14, 14
Space between words 10mm

O43	A5	½p grn & gray, pair (#47)		.90	1.50
a.		Single, English		.25	.25
b.		Single, Afrikaans		.25	.25
O44	A6	1p rose car & gray blk, pair (#49)		1.00	6.00
a.		Single, English		.25	.25
b.		Single, Afrikaans		.25	.25
O45	A6	1p car & blk, pair (#50)		1.00	3.50
a.		Single, English		.25	.25
b.		Single, Afrikaans		.25	.25

Space between words 14½mm

O46	A15	1½p sl grn & ocher, pair (#52)		2.00	5.00
a.		Single, English		.25	.35
b.		Single, Afrikaans		.25	.35
O47	A16	2p pur & sl bl, pair (#56)		1.00	2.00
a.		Single, English		.25	.25
b.		Single, Afrikaans		.25	.25
c.		Ovpt. reading up, pair			

Space between words 10mm

O48	A7	6p red org & bl grn, III, pair (#61c)		2.00	4.00
a.		Single, English		.35	.35
b.		Single, Afrikaans		.35	.35

Space between words 19mm

O49	A11	1sh chlky bl & lt brn, pair (#62)		6.75	18.00
a.		Single, English		.50	2.00
b.		Single, Afrikaans		.50	2.00
c.		1sh vio bl & brnsh blk (#62f), pair		175.00	200.00
d.		As "c," single, English		12.50	17.50
e.		As "c," single, Afrikaans		12.50	17.50
O50	A12	2sh6p brn & brt grn, pair (#63)		10.00	37.50
a.		Single, English		1.00	3.50
b.		Single, Afrikaans		1.00	3.50
O51	A13	5sh bl grn & blk, pair (#64)		190.00	125.00
a.		Single, English		10.00	10.00
b.		Single, Afrikaans		10.00	10.00
O52	A13	5sh pale bl grn & blk, I, pair (#65)		65.00	85.00
a.		Single, English		5.00	6.50
b.		Single, Afrikaans		5.00	6.50
O53	A13	5sh dp yel grn & blk, II, pair (#66)		80.00	100.00
a.		Single, English		8.00	9.00
b.		Single, Afrikaans		8.00	9.00
O54	A18	10sh ol blk & bl, pair (#67)		80.00	250.00
a.		Single, English		9.00	22.50
b.		Single, Afrikaans		9.00	22.50
		Nos. O43-O54 (12)		439.65	637.50

BOPHUTHATSWANA

ˌbō-ˌpü-tät-'swä-nə

LOCATION — Noncontiguous enclaves, Republic of South Africa
GOVT. — Self-governing tribal homeland
AREA — 27,340 sq. mi.
POP. — 1,660,000 (1985)
CAPITAL — Mmabatho

> **Catalogue values for all unused stamps in this country are for Never Hinged items.**

Independence from South Africa — A1

Perf. 12½
1977, Dec. 6   Litho.   Unwmk.

1	A1	4c Hands, dove released	.60	.60
2	A1	10c Leopard (state emblem)	1.10	.85
3	A1	15c Coat of arms	2.40	1.75
4	A1	20c Flag	3.25	2.40
		Nos. 1-4 (4)	7.35	5.60

An imperf. souvenir sheet exists containing Nos. 1-4 printed in one color (blue). Not valid for postage.

Tribal Totems — A2

Designs: 1c, African buffalo (Malete, Hwaduba). 2c, Bush pig (Kolobeng). 3c, Chacma baboon (Hurutshe, Thlaro). 4c, Leopard (state emblem). 5c, Crocodile (Kwena-Fokeng). 6c, Savanna monkey (Kgatla). 7c, Lion (Taung). 8c, Spotted hyena (Phiring). 9c, Cape porcupine (Rokologadi). 10c, Aardvark (Tlokwa). 15c, Fish (Tlhaping). 20c, Hunting dog (Tlhalerwa). 25c, Common duiker (Mfatlha). 30c, African elephant (Tlhako, Tloung). 50c, Python (Nogeng). 1r, Hippopotamus (Kubung). 2r, Greater kudu (Rolong).

1977, Dec. 6

5	A2	1c multicolored	.25	.25
6	A2	2c multicolored	.25	.25
7	A2	3c multicolored	.25	.25
8	A2	4c multicolored	4.00	1.90
9	A2	5c on 4c multi	1.10	.60
10	A2	6c multicolored	.25	.25
11	A2	7c multicolored	1.00	1.00
12	A2	8c multicolored	.25	.25
13	A2	9c multicolored	.35	.25
14	A2	10c multicolored	.25	.25
15	A2	15c multicolored	.35	.25
16	A2	20c multicolored	.35	.25
17	A2	25c multicolored	.40	.25
18	A2	30c multicolored	.45	.25
19	A2	50c multicolored	.65	.40
20	A2	1r multicolored	1.40	1.10
21	A2	2r multicolored	2.50	2.50
		Nos. 5-21 (17)	14.05	10.25

No. 9 was printed as a 4c stamp. Grass was printed over the 4c at upper right and 5c printed at upper left. Copies exist without the surcharge. No. 9A does not have the 4c.

Perf. 14

5a	A2	1c	.55	.55
6a	A2	2c	.55	.55
7a	A2	3c	.55	.55
8a	A2	4c	.55	.55
9A	A2	5c multicolored	.55	.55
11a	A2	7c	.55	.55
12a	A2	8c	.60	.60
14a	A2	10c	.60	.60
		Nos. 5a-14a (8)	4.50	4.50

World Hypertension Month — A3

1978, Apr. 7   Perf. 12x12½

22	A3	4c Avoid kidney infections	.55	.55
23	A3	10c Lower salt intake	.95	.95
24	A3	15c Overeating is dangerous	1.40	1.40
		Nos. 22-24 (3)	2.90	2.90

Road Safety — A4

1978, July 12

25	A4	4c Don't drink and drive	.55	.35
26	A4	10c Keep children off roads	.80	.50
27	A4	15c Pedestrians observe crossing signals	1.00	.60
28	A4	20c Observe stop signs	1.60	.80
		Nos. 25-28 (4)	3.95	2.25

Cutting and Polishing Semi-precious Stones — A5

1978, Oct. 3

29	A5	4c Cutting slabs of travertine	.50	.25
30	A5	10c Polishing travertine	1.00	.70
31	A5	15c Sorting stones	1.60	1.00
32	A5	20c Factory at Taung	2.00	1.25
		Nos. 29-32 (4)	5.10	3.20

1st Airplane Flight, 75th Anniv. — A6

1978, Dec. 1 — Perf. 12½

33	A6	10c Wright Flyer	1.50	1.50
34	A6	15c Orville and Wilbur Wright	2.00	2.00

Pres. Lucas M. Mangope — A7

1978, Dec. 6

35	A7	4c Profile	.40	.40
36	A7	15c Portrait	.85	.85

Sorghum Beer Production A8

1979, Feb. 28 — Perf. 14x14½

37	A8	4c Drying germinated wheat	.30	.30
38	A8	15c Cooking ground grain	.80	.80
39	A8	20c Straining the liquid	1.00	1.00
40	A8	25c Drinking beer	1.40	1.40
		Nos. 37-40 (4)	3.50	3.50

Tate-Knoetze Boxing Match — A9

1979, June 2

41	A9	15c John Tate	.70	.70
42	A9	15c Kallie Knoetze	.70	.70
a.		Pair, #41-42	2.00	2.00

Intl. Children's Year — A10

Illustrations by local youths: 4c, Boy dazzled by sun, from a folk tale, by Hendrick Sebapo. 15c, Africans and animal silhouettes, by Daisy Morapedi. 20c, Man in profile and landscape, by Peter Tladi. 25c, Old man, boy and mule, by Sebapo.

1979, June 7 — Perf. 14½x14

43	A10	4c multicolored	.25	.25
44	A10	15c multicolored	.25	.25
45	A10	20c multicolored	.40	.40
46	A10	25c multicolored	.50	.50
		Nos. 43-46 (4)	1.40	1.40

Platinum Industry A11

Designs: 4c, Pouring molten metal. 15c, Platinum in industrial use. 20c, Telecommunications satellite in orbit. 25c, Jewelry.

1979, Aug. 15 — Perf. 14x14½

47	A11	4c multicolored	.25	.25
48	A11	15c multicolored	.25	.25
49	A11	20c multicolored	.35	.35
50	A11	25c multicolored	.55	.55
		Nos. 47-50 (4)	1.40	1.40

Agriculture A12

1979, Oct. 25

51	A12	5c Cattle	.25	.25
52	A12	15c Picking cotton	.25	.25
53	A12	20c Researcher in corn field	.40	.40
54	A12	25c Fish in net	.45	.45
		Nos. 51-54 (4)	1.35	1.35

Stop Smoking Campaign A13

Edible Wild Fruit A14

1980, Mar. 5 — Perf. 14½x14

55	A13	5c multicolored	.65	.65

1980, June 4

56	A14	5c Landolphia capensis	.25	.25
57	A14	10c Vangueria infausta	.40	.40
58	A14	15c Bequaertiodendron magalismontanum	.60	.60
59	A14	20c Sclerocarya caffra	.80	.80
		Nos. 56-59 (4)	2.05	2.05

Birds — A15

1980, Sept. 10

60	A15	5c Pied babbler	.25	.25
61	A15	10c Carmine bee-eater	.40	.40
62	A15	15c Shaft-tailed whydah	.60	.60
63	A15	20c Meyer's parrot	.75	.75
		Nos. 60-63 (4)	2.00	2.00

Sun City Tourist Attractions A16

1980, Dec. 5 — Perf. 14x14½

64	A16	5c Hotel, casino, country club	.25	.25
65	A16	10c Golfer at Gary Player Country Club	.25	.25

66	A16	15c Casino interior	.40	.40
67	A16	20c Night club dancers	.50	.50
		Nos. 64-67 (4)	1.40	1.40

Intl. Year for the Disabled — A17

1981, Jan. 30 — Perf. 14½x14

68	A17	5c shown	.25	.25
69	A17	15c Blind boy	.25	.25
70	A17	20c Archer in wheelchair	.40	.40
71	A17	25c X-ray (tuberculosis)	.45	.45
		Nos. 68-71 (4)	1.35	1.35

Easter A18

Bible quotes and: 5c, Lamb, sunset. 15c, Bread. 20c, Man holding lamb. 25c, Wheat field.

1981, Apr. 1 — Perf. 14x14½

72	A18	5c multicolored	.25	.25
73	A18	15c multicolored	.25	.25
74	A18	20c multicolored	.40	.40
75	A18	25c multicolored	.45	.45
		Nos. 72-75 (4)	1.35	1.35

Telephones A19

Grasses A20

5c, Siemens & Halske wall telephone, 1885. 15c, Ericsson table model, 1895. 20c, Hasler table model, 1900. 25c, Mix & Genest wall model, 1904.

1981, July 31 — Perf. 14½x14

76	A19	5c multicolored	.25	.25
77	A19	15c multicolored	.30	.30
78	A19	20c multicolored	.35	.35
79	A19	25c multicolored	.45	.45
		Nos. 76-79 (4)	1.35	1.35

1981, Nov. 25

80	A20	5c Themeda triandra	.25	.25
81	A20	15c Rhynchelytrum repens	.30	.30
82	A20	20c Eragrostis capensis	.35	.35
83	A20	25c Monocymbium ceresiiforme	.45	.45
		Nos. 80-83 (4)	1.35	1.35

Boy Scouts, 75th Anniv. — A21

Easter — A22

1982, Jan. 29

84	A21	5c Scout, 1982	.25	.25
85	A21	15c Mafeking Siege stamps	.35	.35
86	A21	20c Scout cadet, 1907	.45	.45
87	A21	25c Lord Baden-Powell	.55	.55
		Nos. 84-87 (4)	1.60	1.60

1982, Apr. 1

88	A22	15c John 12:1	.25	.25
89	A22	20c Matthew 21:1-2	.25	.25
90	A22	25c Mark 11:5-6	.50	.50
91	A22	30c Matthew 21:7	.60	.60
		Nos. 88-91 (4)	1.60	1.60

Table Telephones — A23

1982, Sept. 3

92	A23	8c Ericsson, 1878	.25	.25
93	A23	15c Ericsson, 1885	.25	.25
94	A23	20c Ericsson, 1893	.30	.30
95	A23	25c Siemens & Halske, 1898	.35	.35
		Nos. 92-95 (4)	1.15	1.15

Independence, 5th Anniv. — A24

8c, Old parliament building. 15c, New government offices. 20c, University, Mmabatho. 25c, Civic Center, Mmabatho.

1982, Dec. 6 — Perf. 14x14½

96	A24	8c multicolored	.25	.25
97	A24	15c multicolored	.25	.25
98	A24	20c multicolored	.30	.30
99	A24	25c multicolored	.35	.35
		Nos. 96-99 (4)	1.15	1.15

Pilanesberg Nature Reserve — A25

1983, Jan. 5

100	A25	8c Ceratotherium simum	.25	.25
101	A25	20c Equus burchelli	.45	.45
102	A25	25c Hippotragus niger	.55	.55
103	A25	40c Alcelaphus caama	.80	.80
		Nos. 100-103 (4)	2.05	2.05

Easter A26

1983, Mar. 30 — Perf. 14½x14

104	A26	8c Matthew 21:7	.25	.25
105	A26	20c Mark 11:7	.35	.35
106	A26	25c Matthew 21:8	.40	.40
107	A26	40c Mark 11:9	.65	.65
		Nos. 104-107 (4)	1.65	1.65

Telephones A27

Birds of the Veld A28

10c, ATM table model, c. 1920. 20c, A/S Elektrisk wall model, c. 1900. 25c, Ericsson wall model, c. 1900. 40c, Ericsson wall model, c. 1900, diff.

1983, June 22
108 A27 10c multicolored .25 .25
109 A27 20c multicolored .35 .35
110 A27 25c multicolored .45 .45
111 A27 40c multicolored .70 .70
  Nos. 108-111 (4) 1.75 1.75

1983, Sept. 14
112 A28 10c Kori bustard .25 .25
113 A28 20c Black korhaan .45 .45
114 A28 25c Red-crested
  korhaan .60 .60
115 A28 40c Stanley bustard 1.00 1.00
  Nos. 112-115 (4) 2.30 2.30

Grasses — A29

1984, Jan. 20
116 A29 10c Panicum maximum .25 .25
117 A29 20c Hyparrhenia drege-
  ana .30 .30
118 A29 25c Cenchrus ciliaris .35 .35
119 A29 40c Urochloa brachyura .50 .50
  Nos. 116-119 (4) 1.40 1.40

Easter
A30

1984, Mar. 23 **Perf. 14½x14**
120 A30 10c Mark 11:11 .25 .25
121 A30 20c Mark 11:15 .30 .30
122 A30 25c Matthew 21:19 .40 .40
123 A30 40c Matthew 21:19, diff. .65 .65
  Nos. 120-123 (4) 1.60 1.60

  See Nos. 165-168, 173-176.

Mining
Industry
A31

1984, Apr. 2 **Perf. 14½x14**
124 A31 11c multicolored .70 .70

Telephones — A32

11c, Shuchhardt table model, c. 1905. 20c, Siemens wall model, c. 1925. 25c, Ericsson table model, c. 1900. 30c, Oki table model, c. 1930.

1984, July 20
125 A32 11c multicolored .25 .25
126 A32 20c multicolored .30 .30
127 A32 25c multicolored .40 .40
128 A32 30c multicolored .45 .45
  Nos. 125-128 (4) 1.40 1.40

Lizards
A33

Designs: 11c, Yellow-throated plated lizard. 25c, Transvaal girdled lizard. 30c, Ocellated sand lizard. 45c, Bibron's thick-toed gecko.

1984, Sept. 25 **Perf. 14x14½**
129 A33 11c multicolored .25 .25
130 A33 25c multicolored .30 .30
131 A33 30c multicolored .35 .35
132 A33 45c multicolored .50 .50
  Nos. 129-132 (4) 1.40 1.40

Child Health   Mafeking,
Care — A34   Cent. — A35

1985, Jan. 25
133 A34 11c Stop Polio .25 .25
134 A34 25c Stop Measles .35 .35
135 A34 30c Stop Diphtheria .45 .45
136 A34 50c Stop Whooping
  Cough .80 .80
  Nos. 133-136 (4) 1.85 1.85

1985, Mar. 11
  Portraits: 11c, Montshiwa (1814-1896), chief of the Barolong booRatshidi. 25c, Sir Charles Warren (1840-1927), army commander who established the Crown Colony and laid out the town of Mafeking.
137 A35 11c multicolored .25 .25
138 A35 25c multicolored .60 .60

Industries
A36

Designs: 1c, Textile mill, Bophuthatswana. 2c, Sewing cloth sacks, Selosesha. 3c, Ceramic tile production line. 4c, Processing sheepskin. 5c, Manufacture of crossbows. 6c, Automobile parts. 7c, Hosiery factory, Babelegi. 8c, Specialized bicycle factory. 9c, Lawn mower assembly line. 10c, Dress factory, Thaba Nchu. 12c, Automobile upholstery factory. 14c, Milling industry, Mafeking. 15c, Manufacturing of plastic bags. 16c, Brickworks, Mmabatho. 18c, Manufacturing of cutlery. 20c, Men's clothing factory. 25c, Chromium plating baby carriage parts. 30c, Spray-painting metal beds. 50c, Milk processing plant. 1r, Printing works. 2r, Industrial complex, Babelegi.

1985-89 **Perf. 14½x14**
139 A36 1c multicolored .25 .25
140 A36 2c multicolored .25 .25
141 A36 3c multicolored .25 .25
142 A36 4c multicolored .25 .25
143 A36 5c multicolored .25 .25
144 A36 6c multicolored .25 .25
145 A36 7c multicolored .25 .25
146 A36 8c multicolored .25 .25
147 A36 9c multicolored .25 .25
148 A36 10c multicolored .25 .25
149 A36 12c multicolored .25 .25
150 A36 14c multicolored .30 .30
151 A36 15c multicolored .35 .35
152 A36 16c multicolored .35 .35
153 A36 18c multicolored .40 .40
154 A36 20c multicolored .45 .45
155 A36 25c multicolored .60 .60
156 A36 30c multicolored .70 .70
157 A36 50c multicolored 1.10 1.10
158 A36 1r multicolored 2.25 2.25
159 A36 2r multicolored 4.75 4.75
  Nos. 139-159 (21) 14.00 14.00

  Issued: 1c-10c, 15c, 20c, 25c, 30c-2r, 10/25/85; 12c, 4/1/85; 14c, 4/1/86; 16c, 4/1/87; 18c, 7/3/89.

Easter Type of 1984

1985, Apr. 2
165 A30 12c Matthew 21:14 .25 .25
166 A30 25c Matthew 21:14, diff. .30 .30
167 A30 30c Matthew 21:15 .35 .35
168 A30 50c Matthew 21:15-16 .55 .55
  Nos. 165-168 (4) 1.45 1.45

Tree Conservation
A37

1985, July 4 **Perf. 14x14½**
169 A37 12c Fourea saligna .25 .25
170 A37 25c Boscia albitrunca .35 .35
171 A37 30c Erythrina lysistemon .40 .40
172 A37 50c Bequaertiodendron
  magalismontanum .65 .65
  Nos. 169-172 (4) 1.65 1.65

Easter Type of 1984

1986, Mar. 6 **Perf. 14½x14**
173 A30 12c John 12:2 .25 .25
174 A30 20c John 12:3 .35 .35
175 A30 25c John 12:3, diff. .45 .45
176 A30 30c Matthew 26:7 .60 .60
  Nos. 173-176 (4) 1.65 1.65

Paintings of Thaba Nchu in the
Africana Museum,
Johannesburg — A38

14c, Wesleyan Mission Station and Residence of Moroka, Chief of the Barolong, 1834, by Charles Davidson Bell. 20c, James Archbell's Congregation, 1834, by Bell. 25c, Mission Station at Thaba Nchu, 1850, by Thomas Baines (1822-75).

1986, May 15 **Perf. 14x14½**
177 A38 14c multicolored .25 .25
178 A38 20c multicolored .30 .30
179 A38 25c multicolored .45 .45
  Nos. 177-179 (3) 1.00 1.00

  Incorporation of Thaba Nchu and Bophuthatswana, Oct. 1, 1983.
  A souvenir sheet of one No. 179 has decorative margin continuing the painting and picturing the emblem of the philatelic exhibition held at Johannesburg, Oct. 6-11. Sold for 50c. Value $1.

Temisano
Development
Projects
A39

1986, Aug. 6 **Perf. 14½x14**
180 A39 14c Agricultural production .25 .25
181 A39 20c Community development .30 .30
182 A39 25c Vocational training .40 .40
183 A39 30c Secondary industries .45 .45
  Nos. 180-183 (4) 1.40 1.40

BOP
Airways,
5th Anniv.
A40

1986, Oct. 16 **Perf. 14x14½**
184 A40 14c Airline personnel,
  aircraft .25 .25
185 A40 20c Passengers .40 .40
186 A40 25c Mmabatho Intl. Airport .50 .50
187 A40 30c Cessna Citation .55 .55
  Nos. 184-187 (4) 1.70 1.70

Sports — A41

1987, Jan. 22
188 A41 14c Netball .25 .25
189 A41 20c Tennis .30 .30
190 A41 25c Soccer .35 .35
191 A41 30c Running .45 .45
  Nos. 188-191 (4) 1.35 1.35

Wildflowers — A42

1987, Apr. 23
192 A42 16c Berkheya zeyheri .30 .30
193 A42 20c Plumbago auriculata .35 .35
194 A42 25c Pterodiscus speciosus .45 .45
195 A42 30c Gazania krebsiana .50 .50
  Nos. 192-195 (4) 1.60 1.60

  A souvenir sheet of one No. 194 has decorative black and white inscribed margin picturing the emblem of the natl. philatelic exhibition held at Paarl, Sept. 16-19. Sold for 70c. Value $1.50.

Education — A43

Designs: 16c, E.M. Mokgoko Farmer Training Center, Ramatlabama. 20c, Main lecture block, University of Bophuthatswana, Mmabatho. 25c, Manpower Center. 30c, Hotel training school, Odi.

1987, Aug. 6 **Perf. 14½x14**
196 A43 16c multicolored .25 .25
197 A43 20c multicolored .30 .30
198 A43 25c multicolored .35 .35
199 A43 30c multicolored .45 .45
  Nos. 196-199 (4) 1.35 1.35

Independence, 10th Anniv. — A44

Communications.

1987, Dec. 4
200 A44 16c Postal service .25 .25
201 A44 30c Telephone .30 .30
202 A44 40c Radio .40 .40
203 A44 50c Television .50 .50
  Nos. 200-203 (4) 1.45 1.45

Easter
A45

1988, Mar. 31
204 A45 16c John 12:12-14 .25 .25
205 A45 30c Mark 14:10-11 .30 .30
206 A45 40c John 13:5 .40 .40
207 A45 50c John 13:26 .45 .45
  Nos. 204-207 (4) 1.40 1.40

Natl. Parks Board Activities — A46

1988, June 23   *Perf. 14½x14*
208	A46	16c	Environmental education	.25 .25
209	A46	30c	Conservation	.40 .40
210	A46	40c	Catering	.50 .50
211	A46	50c	Tourism	.65 .65
		Nos. 208-211 (4)		1.80 1.80

A souvenir sheet of one No. 211 has black and white decorative margin picturing the emblem of the natl. philatelic exhibition held at Pietermaritzburg, Nov. 22-27. Sold for 70c. Value $3.

Crops A47

1988, Sept. 15   *Perf. 14½x14*
212	A47	16c	Sunflowers	.25 .25
213	A47	30c	Peanuts	.40 .40
214	A47	40c	Cotton	.55 .55
215	A47	50c	Cabbages	.65 .65
		Nos. 212-215 (4)		1.85 1.85

Dams — A48

1988, Nov. 17
216	A48	16c	Ngotwane	.30 .30
217	A48	30c	Groothoek	.55 .55
218	A48	40c	Sehujwane	.85 .85
219	A48	50c	Molatedi	.90 .90
		Nos. 216-219 (4)		2.60 2.60

Easter A49

1989, Mar. 9
220	A49	16c	Mark 26:26	.30 .30
221	A49	30c	Matthew 26:39	.55 .55
222	A49	40c	Mark 14:45	.85 .85
223	A49	50c	John 18:10	1.00 1.00
		Nos. 220-223 (4)		2.70 2.70

Children's Art — A50

Designs: 18c, "Rooster," by Thembi Atong. 30c, "Thatched Hut in Rural Setting," by Muhammad Mahri. 40c, "Modern World," by Tshepo Mashokwe. 50c, "Cityscape," by Miles Brown.

1989, May 11
224	A50	18c	multicolored	.25 .25
225	A50	30c	multicolored	.40 .40
226	A50	40c	multicolored	.55 .55
227	A50	50c	multicolored	.70 .70
		Nos. 224-227 (4)		1.90 1.90

Birds of Prey — A51

1989, Sept. 1   *Perf. 14x14½*
228	A51	18c	*Elanus caeruleus*	.70 .70
229	A51	30c	*Melierax canorus*	1.10 1.10
230	A51	40c	*Falco naumanni*	1.50 1.50
231	A51	50c	*Circaetus gallicus*	1.90 1.90
a.		Souvenir sheet of 1		4.75 4.75
		Nos. 228-231 (4)		5.20 5.20

No. 231a has multicolored decorative margin picturing emblem of the WANDERERS 101 natl. philatelic exhibition held Sept. 6-9. Sold for 1.50r.

Traditional Thatched Dwellings A52

1989, Nov. 28   *Perf. 14½x14*
232	A52	18c	shown	.25 .25
233	A52	30c	multi, diff.	.40 .40
234	A52	40c	multi, diff.	.45 .45
235	A52	50c	multi, diff.	.55 .55
		Nos. 232-235 (4)		1.65 1.65

Community Services A53

1990, Jan. 11
236	A53	18c	Playground	.25 .25
237	A53	30c	Immunization clinic	.35 .35
238	A53	40c	Library	.50 .50
239	A53	50c	Hospital	.60 .60
		Nos. 236-239 (4)		1.70 1.70

Wildlife (Small Mammals) A54

1990, Apr. 11   Litho.   *Perf. 14½x14*
240	A54	21c	*Dendromus mystacalis*	.40 .40
241	A54	30c	*Ictonyx striatus*	.55 .55
242	A54	40c	*Elephantulus myurus*	.70 .70
243	A54	50c	*Procavia capensis*	.90 .90
a.		Souvenir sheet of 1		2.75 2.75
		Nos. 240-243 (4)		2.55 2.55

No. 243a has multicolored inscribed margin; text publicizes the natl. philatelic exhibition. Sold for 1.50r.

Sandgrouses — A55

1990, July 12   Litho.   *Perf. 14x14½*
244	A55	21c	*Pterocles burchelli*	.75 .75
245	A55	35c	*Pterocles bicinctus*	1.40 1.40
246	A55	40c	*Pterocles namaqua*	1.50 1.50
247	A55	50c	*Pterocles gutturalis*	1.90 1.90
		Nos. 244-247 (4)		5.55 5.55

Bus Manufacturing — A56

a, Chassis welding. b, Mounting the engine. c, Body construction. d, Spray painting. e, Completed models and bare chassis.

1990, Aug. 3   *Perf. 14½x14*
248		Strip of 5	4.50 4.50
a.-e.	A56	21c any single	.90 .90

Traditional Activities — A57

1990, Oct. 4   *Perf. 14x14½*
249	A57	21c	Basketry	.40 .40
250	A57	35c	Tanning	.60 .60
251	A57	40c	Beer making	.70 .70
252	A57	50c	Pottery making	1.00 1.00
		Nos. 249-252 (4)		2.70 2.70

Bophuthatswana Air Force, 10th Anniv. — A58

Helicopters: a, Alouette III. b, BK117. Airplanes: c, Pilatus Trainer PC-7. d, Pilatus Porter PC-6. e, Casa 212.

1990, Dec. 12   *Perf. 14½x14*
253		Strip of 5	6.00 6.00
a.-e.	A58	21c any single	1.40 1.40

Edible Wild Fruit — A59

1991, Jan. 24   Litho.   *Perf. 14x14½*
254	A59	21c	Annona senegalensis	.40 .40
255	A59	35c	Strychnos pungens	.65 .65
256	A59	40c	Ficus sycomorus	.85 .85
257	A59	50c	Dovyalis caffra	1.00 1.00
		Nos. 254-257 (4)		2.90 2.90

Easter A60

1991, Mar. 21   Litho.   *Perf. 14½x14*
258	A60	21c	Mark 14:46	.45 .45
259	A60	35c	Mark 14:53	.65 .65
260	A60	40c	Mark 14:65	.85 .85
261	A60	50c	Mark 14:67	.95 .95
		Nos. 258-261 (4)		2.90 2.90

Locomotives A61

1991, July 4   Litho.
    Size: 72x25mm (25c, 50c)
262	A61	25c	Class 6A	.85 .85
263	A61	40c	Class 7A	1.40 1.40
264	A61	50c	Class 6Z	1.75 1.75
265	A61	60c	Class 8	2.40 2.40
		Nos. 262-265 (4)		6.40 6.40

A souvenir sheet of 1 #265 was sold by the Philatelic Foundation of South Africa. Value $6.
See Nos. 291-294.

Maps of Africa — A62

1991, Sept. 12   Litho.   *Perf. 14x14½*
266	A62	25c	Caneiro chart, 1502	.90 .90
267	A62	40c	Cantino chart, 1502	1.50 1.50
268	A62	50c	Contarini map, 1506	1.90 1.90
269	A62	60c	Waldseemuller map, 1507	2.50 2.50
		Nos. 266-269 (4)		6.80 6.80

Maps of Africa A63

1992, Jan. 9   Litho.   *Perf. 14½x14*
270	A63	27c	Fracanzano, 1508	.90 .90
271	A63	45c	Waldseemuller, 1513	1.50 1.50
272	A63	65c	Waldseemuller, 1516	1.90 1.90
273	A63	85c	Laurent Fries, 1522	2.50 2.50
		Nos. 270-273 (4)		6.80 6.80

Easter A64

1992, Apr. 1   Litho.
274	A64	27c	Mark 15:1	.25 .25
275	A64	45c	Mark 15:15	.45 .45
276	A64	65c	Mark 15:17-18	.60 .60
277	A64	85c	Mark 15:19	.80 .80
		Nos. 274-277 (4)		2.10 2.10

Acacia Trees — A65

1992, Sept. 17   Litho.
278	A65	35c	Karroo	.30 .30
279	A65	70c	Erioloba	.65 .65
280	A65	90c	Tortilis	.75 .75
281	A65	1.05r	Mellifera	.85 .85
		Nos. 278-281 (4)		2.55 2.55

A souvenir sheet of 1 #279 exists. Sold for 2.50r. Value $3.75.

Lost City Hotel Complex, Sun City — A66

a, View from lake. b, Palace. c, Porte cochere. d, Lobby of Palace. e, Tusk bar.

1992, Nov. 19   Litho.   *Perf. 14x14½*
282		Strip of 5	2.00 2.00
a.-e.	A66	35c any single	.50 .50

Chickens
A67

1993, Feb. 12   Litho.   Perf. 14½x14
283 A67 35c Light Sussex   .45   .45
284 A67 70c Rhode Island red   .90   .90
285 A67 90c Brown leghorn   1.25 1.25
286 A67 1.05r White leghorn   1.40 1.40
        Nos. 283-286 (4)   4.00 4.00

A souvenir sheet of 1 #284 exists. Sold for 3r. Value $5.

Easter
A68

1993, Mar. 5
287 A68 35c Luke 23:25   .60   .60
288 A68 70c John 19:17   1.25 1.25
289 A68 90c Mark 15:21   1.60 1.60
290 A68 1.05r Mark 15:23   1.90 1.90
        Nos. 287-290 (4)   5.35 5.35

Trains Type of 1991

Designs: 45c, Mafeking locomotive shed, c. 1933, RR classes 10, 8, & 12. 65c, Locomotive No. 5. 85c, 1934 Royal visit, White Train, SAR Class 16B. 1.05r, SAR class 19D.

1993, June 18   Litho.
Size: 72x25mm (45c, 85c)
291 A61 45c multicolored   .75   .75
292 A61 65c multicolored   1.10 1.10
293 A61 85c multicolored   1.40 1.40
294 A61 1.05r multicolored   1.75 1.75
a.   Souvenir sheet of 4, #291-294   5.00 5.00
        Nos. 291-294 (4)   5.00 5.00

Maps of Africa
A69

Name of cartographer, year published: 45c, Sebastian Munster, 1540. 65c, Jacopo Gastaldi, 1564. 85c, Gerardus Mercator the Younger, 1595. 1.05r, Abraham Ortelius, 1570.

1993, Aug. 20   Litho.
295 A69 45c multicolored   .60   .60
296 A69 65c multicolored   .90   .90
297 A69 85c multicolored   1.25 1.25
298 A69 1.05r multicolored   1.50 1.50
        Nos. 295-298 (4)   4.25 4.25

Easter
A70

1994, Mar. 25   Litho.   Perf. 14½x14
299 A70 35c Luke 22:33   .65   .65
300 A70 65c Luke 23:35-36   1.25 1.25
301 A70 85c Luke 23:36   1.60 1.60
302 A70 1.05r Luke 23:38   1.90 1.90
        Nos. 299-302 (4)   5.40 5.40

Bophuthatswana ceased to exist 4/27/94.

CISKEI

ˈsis-ˌkī

LOCATION — Enclave, Republic of South Africa
GOVT. — Self-governing tribal homeland
AREA — 5,592 sq. mi.
POP. — 1,000,000

CAPITAL — Bisho

> Catalogue values for all unused stamps in this country are for Never Hinged Items.

Independence from South Africa — A1

Perf. 14x14½
1981, Dec. 4   Litho.   Unwmk.
1 A1 5c Pres. Sebe   .25   .25
2 A1 15c Coat of arms   .25   .25
3 A1 20c Flag   .30   .30
4 A1 25c Mace   .35   .35
     Nos. 1-4 (4)   1.15 1.15

An imperf. souvenir sheet exists containing Nos. 1-4 printed in one color (black). Not valid for postage.

Birds
A2   A3

1981-90   Perf. 14½x14
5   A2   1c Tauraco corythaix   .25   .25
6   A2   2c Motacilla capensis   .25   .25
7   A2   3c Centropus
             superciliosus   .25   .25
8   A2   4c Nectarinia famosa   .25   .25
9   A2   5c Anthropoides
             paradisea   .25   .25
10 A2   6c Onychognathus
             morio   .25   .25
11 A2   7c Ceryle maxima   .25   .25
12 A2   8c Bostrychia
             hagedash   .25   .25
13 A2   9c Cuculus clamosus   .25   .25
14 A2 10c Lybius torquatus   .25   .25
15 A2 11c Oriolus larvatus   .55   .25
16 A2 12c Alcedo cristata   .55   .25
17 A2 14c Upupa epops   .65   .25
18 A2 15c Haliaeetus vocifer   .25   .25
19 A2 16c Batis capensis   .65   .25
20 A2 18c Euplectes progne   1.00   .25
21 A2 20c Macronyx capensis   .35   .25
22 A2 21c Aplopelia larvata   3.25   .25
23 A2 25c Burhinus capensis   .40   .25
24 A2 30c Treron calva   .55   .35
25 A2 50c Poicephalus robus-
             tus   .90   .60
26 A2   1r Apaloderma narina   1.50 1.10
27 A2   2r Bubo capensis   3.25 2.25
     Nos. 5-27 (23)   16.35 9.05

Issued: 11c, 4/4/82; 12c, 4/1/85; 14c, 4/1/86; 16c, 4/1/87; 18c, 7/3/89; 21c, 7/3/90; others, 12/4/81.

Nursing
A4

1982, Apr. 30   Perf. 14½x14, 14x14½
34 A4   8c Cecilia Makiwane,
             vert.   .25   .25
35 A4 15c Surgery, vert.   .30   .30
36 A4 20c Nurses pledge to
             serve   .45   .45
37 A4 25c Hospital care   .55   .55
     Nos. 34-37 (4)   1.55 1.55

Pineapple Industry
A5

1982, Aug. 20   Perf. 14x14½
38 A5   8c Spraying   .25   .25
39 A5 15c Harvesting   .25   .25
40 A5 20c Transporting fruit to
             cannery   .25   .25
41 A5 30c Packing   .40   .40
     Nos. 38-41 (4)   1.15 1.15

Small Mammals
A6

1982, Oct. 29
42 A6   8c Lepus capensis   .25   .25
43 A6 15c Vulpes chama   .35   .35
44 A6 20c Xerus inaurus   .40   .40
45 A6 25c Felis caracal   .45   .45
     Nos. 42-45 (4)   1.45 1.45

Trees — A7

1983, Feb. 2   Perf. 14½x14
46 A7   8c Cussonia spicata   .25   .25
47 A7 20c Curtisia dentata   .30   .30
48 A7 25c Calodendrum capense   .35   .35
49 A7 40c Podocarpus falcatus   .60   .60
     Nos. 46-49 (4)   1.50 1.50

1984, Jan. 6
50 A7 10c Rhus chirindensis   .25   .25
51 A7 20c Phoenix reclinata   .30   .30
52 A7 25c Ptaeroxylon obliquum   .35   .35
53 A7 40c Apodytes dimidiata   .60   .60
     Nos. 50-53 (4)   1.50 1.50

Sharks — A8

1983, Apr. 13   Perf. 14x14½
54 A8   8c Dusky   .25   .25
55 A8 20c Ragged-tooth   .35   .35
Size: 57x21mm
56 A8 25c Tiger   .40   .40
57 A8 30c Scalloped hammer-
             head   .50   .50
58 A8 40c Great white   .60   .60
     Nos. 54-58 (5)   2.10 2.10

Educational Institutions — A9

1983, July 6
59 A9 10c Lovedale   .25   .25
60 A9 20c Fort Hare   .25   .25
61 A9 30c Healdtown   .30   .30
62 A9 40c Lennox Sebe   .40   .40
     Nos. 59-62 (4)   1.20 1.20

Military Uniforms — A10

6th Foot, 1st Warwickshire Regiment, 1821-27 (No. 63): a, White drill uniform (D1.5). b, Light Company privates (D2.5). c, Grenadier Company sergeants (D3.5). d, Light Co.

Officers (D4.5). e, Officer and field officer (D5.5).
    Cape Mounted Rifles, 1827-35 (No. 64): a, Trooper and sergeant, 1830 (D1.5). b, Trooper and sergeant in full dress, 1835 (D2.5). c, Officers, 1830 (D3.5). d, Officers in full dress, 1827-34 (D4.5). e, Officers in full dress, 1834 (D5.5).

1983, Sept. 28   Perf. 14½x14
63   Strip of 5   2.25 2.25
a.-e. A10 20c any single   .45   .45

1984, Oct. 26
64   Strip of 5   2.50 2.25
a.-e. A10 25c any single   .50   .40

Sheets of 10 containing two strips of five.

Coastal Angling
A11

Bait.

1984, Apr. 12   Perf. 14x14½
65 A11 11c Sand prawn   .25   .25
66 A11 20c Coral worm   .25   .25
67 A11 25c Bloodworm   .45   .45
68 A11 30c Red-bait   .55   .55
     Nos. 65-68 (4)   1.50 1.50

1985, Mar. 7
Game fish.
69 A11 11c Lithognathus
             lithognathus   .25   .25
70 A11 25c Pachymetopon
             grande   .45   .30
71 A11 30c Argyrosomus
             hololepidotus   .55   .35
72 A11 50c Pomadasys commer-
             sonni   .90   .60
     Nos. 69-72 (4)   2.15 1.50

Migratory Birds and Maps — A12

1984, Aug. 17   Perf. 14½x14
73 A12 11c Banded sand martin   .25   .25
74 A12 25c House martin   .45   .45
75 A12 30c Greater striped swal-
             low   .50   .50
76 A12 45c European swallow   .75   .75
     Nos. 73-76 (4)   1.95 1.95

Brownies
A13

1985, May 3
77 A13 12c shown   .25   .25
78 A13 25c Rangers planting
             saplings   .25   .25
79 A13 30c Guide color guard   .30   .30
80 A13 50c Camping   .55   .55
     Nos. 77-80 (4)   1.35 1.35

Intl. Year of the Child, 75th anniv. of the Girl Guide movement.

Small Businesses
A14

1985, Aug. 8   Perf. 14x14½
81 A14 12c Furniture   .25   .25
82 A14 25c Dress making   .30   .30
83 A14 30c Welding   .40   .40
84 A14 50c Basketry   .70   .70
     Nos. 81-84 (4)   1.65 1.65

Troop Ships — A15

1985, Nov. 15   **Perf. 14½x14**
85 A15 12c Antelope   .25   .25
86 A15 25c Pilot   .40   .40
87 A15 30c Salisbury   .45   .45
88 A15 50c Olive Branch   .85   .85
        Nos. 85-88 (4)   1.95 1.95

Miniature Sheet

Halley's Comet — A16

Comet streaking through the solar system: a, A1.10. b, A2.10. c, A3.10. d, A4.10. e, A5.10. f, A6.10. g, A7.10. h, A8.10. i, A9.10. j, A10.10.

1986, Mar. 20
89 A16 Sheet of 10   8.00 8.00
a.-j. 12c any single   1.00 1.00

Military Uniforms — A17

98th Foot Regiment: 14c, Fifer in winter. 20c, Private in summer. 25c, Grenadier Company sergeant in summer. 30c, Sergeant-major in winter.

1986, June 12
90 A17 14c multicolored   .25   .25
91 A17 20c multicolored   .35   .35
92 A17 25c multicolored   .45   .45
93 A17 30c multicolored   .50   .50
a.   Souvenir sheet of 1   2.00 2.00
        Nos. 90-93 (4)   1.55 1.55

No. 93a for the natl. philatelic exhibition held at Johannesberg, Oct. 6-11. Sold for 50c.

Bicycle Factory, Dimbaza A18

1986, Sept. 18
94 A18 14c Welding frames   .25   .25
95 A18 20c Painting   .35   .35
96 A18 25c Spoke installation .40   .40
97 A18 30c Assembly   .50   .50
        Nos. 94-97 (4)   1.50 1.50

Independence, 5th Anniv. — A19

14c, Pres. Sebe. 20c, Natl. shrine, Ntaba kaNdoda. 25c, Legislative Assembly, Bisho. 30c, Automatic telephone exchange, Bisho.

1986, Dec. 4   **Perf. 14x14½**
98   A19 14c multicolored   .25   .25
99   A19 20c multicolored   .30   .30
100 A19 25c multicolored   .35   .35
101 A19 30c multicolored   .45   .45
        Nos. 98-101 (4)   1.35 1.35

Edible Mushrooms A20

1987, Mar. 19
102 A20 14c Boletus edulis   .35   .35
103 A20 20c Macrolepiota
               zyheri   .45   .45
a.   Souvenir sheet of 1   3.75 3.75
104 A20 25c Termitomyces   .50   .50
105 A20 30c Russula capensis .65   .65
        Nos. 102-105 (4)   1.95 1.95

No. 103a has fawn and black decorative margin picturing emblem of the natl. philatelic exhibition held at Paarl, Sept. 16-19. Sold for 50c.

Nkone Cattle A21

1987, June 18   **Perf. 14½x14**
106 A21 16c Cow and calf   .25   .25
107 A21 20c Cow   .30   .30
108 A21 25c Bull   .35   .35
109 A21 30c Herd   .45   .45
        Nos. 106-109 (4)   1.35 1.35

Toys — A22

Perf. 14x14½, 14½x14
1987, Sept. 17
110 A22 16c Windmill, vert.   .25   .25
111 A22 20c Rag doll, vert.   .30   .30
112 A22 25c Clay horse   .35   .35
113 A22 30c Wire vehicle   .45   .45
        Nos. 110-113 (4)   1.35 1.35

Folklore A23

Legend of Sikulume: 16c, Seven birds. 20c, Sikulume escapes cannibals. 25c, Fights sea monster. 30c, Elopes and is pursued by bride's father.

1987, Nov. 6   **Perf. 14½x14**
114 A23 16c multicolored   .25   .25
115 A23 20c multicolored   .30   .30
116 A23 25c multicolored   .35   .35
117 A23 30c multicolored   .45   .45
        Nos. 114-117 (4)   1.35 1.35

See Nos. 122, 139-142, 147-150.

Endangered and Protected Plant Species — A24

1988, Mar. 17   **Perf. 14x14½**
118 A24 16c Clivia nobilis   .25   .25
119 A24 30c Dierama pulcher-
               rimum   .45   .45
120 A24 40c Moraea reticulata .55   .55

---

121 A24 50c Crinum campanu-
               latum   .70   .70
a.   Souvenir sheet of 1   2.50 2.50
        Nos. 118-121 (4)   1.95 1.95

No. 121a margin pictures the emblem of the natl. philatelic exhibition held at Pietermaritzburg, Nov. 22-27. Sold for 1r.

Folklore Type of 1987
Miniature Sheet

Legend of Mbulukazi: a, Two wives (B1.10). b, Two doves appear to Numbakatali (B2.10). c, Birth of Mbulukazi and brother (B3.10). d, Mbulukazi and brother at river (B4.10). e, Chief's son announces marriage (B5.10). f, Chief's son presents wives Mbulukazi and Mahlunguluza with huts (B6.10). g, Mahlunguluza drowns Mbulukazi (B7.10). h, Ox tears down Mahlunguluza's hut (B8.10). i, Mbulukazi revived (B9.10). j, Chief's son embraces Mbulukazi, banishes Mahlunguluza (B10.10).

1988, Aug. 26
Size of Nos. 122a-122j: 36x20mm
122   Sheet of 10   2.50 2.50
a.-j. A23 16c any single   .30   .30

Citrus Farming A25

1988, Sept. 29
123 A25 16c Nursery   .25   .25
124 A25 30c Grafting   .40   .40
125 A25 40c Picking fruit   .50   .50
126 A25 50c Grading   .65   .65
        Nos. 123-126 (4)   1.80 1.80

Poisonous Mushrooms A26

1988, Dec. 1
127 A26 16c Amanita phalloides .75 .75
128 A26 30c Chlorophyllum
               molybdites   1.50 1.50
129 A26 40c Amanita muscaria 1.90 1.90
130 A26 50c Amanita pantherina 2.40 2.40
        Nos. 127-130 (4)   6.55 6.55

Dams — A27

1989, Mar. 2   **Perf. 14½x14**
131 A27 16c Kat River   .25   .25
132 A27 30c Cata   .50   .50
133 A27 40c Binfield Park   .60   .60
134 A27 50c Sandile   .70   .70
        Nos. 131-134 (4)   2.05 2.05

Trout Hatcheries A28

Artificial fertilization: 18c, Obtaining eggs from trout. 30c, Fertilized ova, alevins. 40c, Rainbow trout at 5 weeks. 40c, Adult male rainbow trout.

1989, June 8
135 A28 18c multicolored   .30   .30
136 A28 30c multicolored   .45   .45
137 A28 40c multicolored   .65   .65

---

138 A28 50c multicolored   .70   .70
a.   Souvenir sheet of 1   4.00 4.00
        Nos. 135-138 (4)   2.10 2.10

No. 138a margin pictures emblem of the natl. philatelic exhibition WANDERERS 101, held Sept. 6-9. Sold for 1.50r.

Folklore Type of 1987

Legend of the Little Jackal and the Lion: 18c, Lion and Jackal hunt large eland. 30c, Jackal and offspring climbing to lair. 40c, Lion roaring, jackal under rock. 50c, Lion falling.

1989, Sept. 21
139 A23 18c multicolored   .25   .25
140 A23 30c multicolored   .30   .30
141 A23 40c multicolored   .40   .40
142 A23 50c multicolored   .50   .50
        Nos. 139-142 (4)   1.45 1.45

Early Transportation A29

1989, Dec. 7   **Perf. 14x14½**
143 A29 18c Cape cart   .25   .25
144 A29 30c Jubilee Spider   .40   .40
145 A29 40c Transport wagon   .45   .45
146 A29 50c Voortrekker wagon .60   .60
        Nos. 143-146 (4)   1.70 1.70

Folklore Type of 1987

The Legend of Five Heads: 18c, Mpunzikazi presenting offering to Makanda Mahlanu, the 5-headed snake chief. 30c, Snake chief kills Mpunzikazi. 40c, Mpunzanyan presents offering to snake chief. 50c, Snake chief transformed into a man and marries Mpunzanyan.

1990, Mar. 15   **Perf. 14½x14**
147 A23 18c multicolored   .25   .25
148 A23 30c multicolored   .30   .30
149 A23 40c multicolored   .40   .40
150 A23 50c multicolored   .55   .55
        Nos. 147-150 (4)   1.50 1.50

Handmade Carpets — A30

1990, June 14 Litho. Perf. 14x14½
151 A30 21c Hand weaving   .30   .30
152 A30 35c Spinning   .45   .45
153 A30 40c Dyeing yarn   .55   .55
154 A30 50c Hand weaving, diff. .65 .65
a.   Souvenir sheet of 1   2.25 2.25
        Nos. 151-154 (4)   1.95 1.95

No. 154a for the 150th anniv. of the Penny Black. Sold for 1.50r.

Plows — A31

1990, Sept. 6 Litho. Perf. 14½x14
155 A31 21c Wooden beam, c.
               1855   .25   .25
156 A31 35c Triple disc, c. 1895 .40 .40
157 A31 40c Reversible disc, c.
               1895   .50   .50
158 A31 50c "Het Volk", c. 1910 .60 .60
        Nos. 155-158 (4)   1.75 1.75

Prickly Pear — A32

1990, Nov. 29   **Litho.**
159 A32 21c Vendor   .45   .45
160 A32 35c Prickly pear bush .70   .70
161 A32 40c shown   .80   .80

162 A32 50c Flowering prickly
pear   1.00 1.00
Nos. 159-162 (4)   2.95 2.95

Owls — A33

1991, Feb. 2   Litho.   Perf. 14x14½
163 A33 21c Marsh owl   .95 .95
164 A33 35c Scops owl   1.50 1.50
165 A33 40c Barn owl   1.90 1.90
166 A33 50c Wood owl   2.10 2.10
   a.   Miniature sheet of 1   7.00 7.00
      Nos. 163-166 (4)   6.45 6.45

First Letter From
South
Africa — A34

Designs: a, Map showing location of Sao
Bras (Mossel Bay), 1500. b, Storm-damaged
ship off Cabo Tormentoso, 1500. c, Pedro
d'Ataide lands at Sao Bras, 1501. d, D'Ataide
leaves letter in boot, 1501. e, Joao da Nova
finds letter, 1501.

1991, May 11   Litho.
167 A34 25c Strip of 5, #a.-e.   4.50 4.50

Inscriptions on #167a & 167b are reversed.

Solar
System
A35

1991, Aug. 1   Litho.   Perf. 14½x14
168 A35 1c Comet nucleus   .25 .25
169 A35 2c Trojan asteroids   .25 .25
170 A35 5c Meteoroid   .25 .25
171 A35 7c Pluto   .25 .25
172 A35 10c Neptune   .25 .25
173 A35 20c Uranus   .25 .25
174 A35 25c Saturn   .30 .30
175 A35 30c Jupiter   .35 .35
176 A35 35c Asteroid belt   .40 .40
177 A35 40c Mars   .50 .50
178 A35 50c Earth's moon   .60 .60
179 A35 60c Earth   .70 .70
180 A35 1r Venus   1.25 1.25
181 A35 2r Mercury   2.75 2.75
182 A35 5r Sun   6.50 6.50
   a.   Min. sheet of 15, #168-182 17.50 17.50
      Nos. 168-182 (15)   14.85 14.85

Frontier
Forts
A36

Designs: 27c, Xhosa warrior, Fort Arm-
strong. 45c, Sir George Grey, Keiskamma
Hoek Post. 65c, Chief Sandile, Fort Hare. 85c,
Cavalryman, Cavalry Barracks, Peddie.

1991, Nov. 7   Litho.   Perf. 14x14½
183 A36 27c multicolored   .25 .25
184 A36 45c multicolored   .35 .35
185 A36 65c multicolored   .45 .45
186 A36 85c multicolored   .70 .70
      Nos. 183-186 (4)   1.75 1.75

Cloud
Formations — A37

1992, Mar. 19   Litho.
187 A37 27c Cumulonimbus   .30 .30
188 A37 45c Altocumulus   .60 .60
189 A37 65c Cirrus   .75 .75
190 A37 85c Cumulus   1.10 1.10
      Nos. 187-190 (4)   2.75 2.75

Satellites
A38

1992, June 4   Litho.   Perf. 14½x14
191 A38 35c Intelsat VI   .60 .60
192 A38 70c GPS Navstar   1.10 1.10
193 A38 90c Meteosat   1.40 1.40
194 A38 1.05r Landsat VI   1.60 1.60
      Nos. 191-194 (4)   4.70 4.70

A souvenir sheet of one No. 192 exists. Sold
for 2.50r. Value $2.50.

Farm
Implements
A39

35c, John Deere universal disc-harrow, c.
1914. 70c, John Deere clod crusher & pulver-
izer, c. 1914. 90c, Self-dump hay rake, c.
1910. 1.05r, McCormick hay tedder, c. 1900.

1992, Aug. 20   Litho.
195 A39 35c multicolored   .60 .60
196 A39 70c multicolored   1.10 1.10
197 A39 90c multicolored   1.40 1.40
198 A39 1.05r multicolored   1.60 1.60
      Nos. 195-198 (4)   4.70 4.70

Hotels
A40

Designs: 35c, Mpekweni Sun Marine
Resort. 70c, Katberg Protea Hotel. 90c, Fish
River Sun Hotel. 1.05r, Amatola Sun Hotel.

1992, Nov. 5   Litho.
199 A40 35c multicolored   .60 .60
200 A40 70c multicolored   1.10 1.10
201 A40 90c multicolored   1.40 1.40
202 A40 1.05r multicolored   1.60 1.60
      Nos. 199-202 (4)   4.70 4.70

Famous
Explorers
A41

Map of voyage, sailing ship, and explorer:
45c, San Gabriel, 1497-98, Vasco da Gama.
65c, Endeavour, 1768-71, James Cook. 85c,
Victoria, 1519, Ferdinand Magellan. 90c,
Golden Hinde, 1577-80, Sir Francis Drake.
1.05r, Heemskerck, 1642, Abel Tasman.

1993, May 19   Litho.
203 A41 45c multicolored   .70 .70
204 A41 65c multicolored   1.25 1.25
205 A41 85c multicolored   1.80 1.40
206 A41 90c multicolored   1.50 1.50
207 A41 1.05r multicolored   1.75 1.75
      Nos. 203-207 (5)   7.00 6.60

Small Cage
Birds — A42

Designs: 45c, Serinus canarius domesticus.
65c, Melopsittacus undulatus. 85c, Agapornis
roseicollis. 90c, Nymphicus hollandicus. 1.05r,
Chloebia gouldiae.

1993, July 16   Litho.
208 A42 45c multicolored   .60 .60
209 A42 65c multicolored   1.10 1.10
210 A42 85c multicolored   1.25 1.25
211 A42 90c multicolored   1.40 1.40
212 A42 1.50r multicolored   1.50 1.50
      Nos. 208-212 (5)   5.85 5.85

A souvenir sheet of one No. 210 has inscription for National Philatelic Exhibition. Sold for
3r. Value $5.75.

Churches
A43

45c, Goshen Mission Church. 65c, Kamas-
tone Mission Church. 85c, Richie Thompson
Memorial Church. 1.05r, Bryce Ross Memorial
Church.

1993, Sept. 17   Litho.
213 A43 45c black, buff & red   .50 .50
214 A43 65c black, blue & red   .70 .70
215 A43 85c black, tan & red   .95 .95
216 A43 1.05r blk, lt yel & red   1.25 1.25
      Nos. 213-216 (4)   3.40 3.40

Invader
Plants — A44

1993, Nov. 5   Litho.   Perf. 14x14½
217 A44 45c Opuntia aurantiaca   .60 .60
218 A44 65c Datura stramonium   .80 .80
219 A44 85c Sesbania punicea   1.10 1.10
220 A44 1.05r Nicotiana glauca   1.40 1.40
   a.   Souvenir sheet, #217-220   3.75 3.75
      Nos. 217-220 (4)   3.90 3.90

Shipwrecks
A45

1994, Feb. 18   Litho.   Perf. 14½x14
221 A45 45c SS Losna, 1921   .85 .85
222 A45 65c Catherine, 1846   1.25 1.25
223 A45 85c Bennebroek, 1713   1.50 1.50
224 A45 1.05r Sao Joao Bapista,
1622   2.10 2.10
      Nos. 221-224 (4)   5.70 5.70

Roses
A46

1994, Apr. 15   Litho.   Perf. 14½x14
225 A46 45c Herman Steyn   .45 .45
226 A46 70c Esther
Geldenhuys   .75 .75
227 A46 95c Margaret Was-
serfall   .90 .90

228 A46 1.15r Prof. Fred Ziady   1.25 1.25
   a.   Souvenir sheet of 4, #225-228 3.50 3.50
      Nos. 225-228 (4)   3.35 3.35

Ciskei ceased to exist April 27, 1994.

TRANSKEI

ˌtranˌtsˈki

LOCATION — Enclave, East Cape
   Province, Republic of South Africa
GOVT. — Self-governing tribal
   homeland
AREA — 16,910 sq. mi.
POP. — 2,876,122 (1985)
CAPITAL — Umtata

| Catalogue values for all unused
stamps in this country are for
Never Hinged items. |

Independence from
South Africa — A1

1976, Oct. 26   Litho.   Unwmk.
1 A1 4c Paramount Chief
K.D. Matanzima   .40 .40
2 A1 10c Mace, flag   .90 .90
3 A1 15c Matanzima, diff.   1.50 1.50
4 A1 20c Coat of arms   2.00 2.00
      Nos. 1-4 (4)   4.80 4.80

An imperf. souvenir sheet exists containing
Nos. 1-4 printed in one color (black). Not valid
for postage.

Lubisi
Dam — A2

1976, Oct. 26   Perf. 12x12½
5 A2 1c shown   .25 .25
6 A2 2c Soil cultivation   .25 .25
7 A2 3c Threshing sor-
ghum   .25 .25
8 A2 4c Transkei matron   2.75 .30
9 A2 5c Grinding corn   2.75 .30
10 A2 6c Cutting *Phormium
tenax*   .25 .25
11 A2 7c Shepherd boy   .25 .25
12 A2 8c Felling timber   .25 .25
13 A2 9c Agricultural school   .25 .25
14 A2 10c Picking tea   .25 .25
15 A2 15c Wood gathering   .30 .25
16 A2 20c Weaving industry   .30 .25
17 A2 25c Improving cattle
breeds   .35 .25
18 A2 30c Sledge transportation   .60 .50
19 A2 50c Map, coat of arms   .55 .50
20 A2 1r Administrative
Building, Umtata   1.25 1.25
21 A2 2r The Bunga, flag   2.00 1.90
      Nos. 5-21 (17)   12.85 7.50

Perf. 14
5a A2 1c   .25 .25
6a A2 2c   .25 .25
7a A2 3c   .25 .25
8a A2 4c   .25 .25
9a A2 5c   .25 .25
10a A2 6c   .25 .25
12a A2 8c   .25 .25
13a A2 9c   .25 .25
14a A2 10c   .40 .40
15a A2 15c   .50 .50
16a A2 20c   .70 .70
17a A2 25c   1.00 1.00
18a A2 30c   1.25 1.25
19a A2 50c   2.00 2.00
      Nos. 5a-19a (14)   7.85 7.85

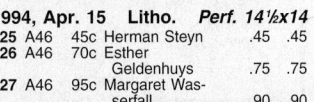

Transkei Airways Inaugural Flight,
Umtata-Johannesburg — A3

1977, Feb. 11
22	A3	4c Aircraft	.60	.60
23	A3	15c Aircraft, terminal	2.40	2.40

Artemesia affra — A4

Medicinal plants.

1977, May 16　　Perf. 12½x12
24	A4	4c shown	.40	.40
25	A4	10c *Bulbine natalensis*	1.60	1.60
26	A4	15c *Melianthus major*	2.40	2.40
27	A4	20c *Cotyledon orbiculata*	3.25	3.25
		Nos. 24-27 (4)	7.65	7.65

1978, Sept. 25

Edible fruit.
28	A4	4c *Carissa bispinosa*	.25	.25
29	A4	10c *Dovyalis caffra*	.35	.35
30	A4	15c *Harpephyllum caffrum*	.50	.50
31	A4	20c *Syzygium cordatum*	.70	.70
		Nos. 28-31 (4)	1.80	1.80

1981, Apr. 15

Medicinal plants.
32	A4	5c *Leonotis leonurus*	.25	.25
33	A4	15c *Euphorbia bupleurifolia*	.25	.25
34	A4	20c *Pelargonium reniforme*	.35	.35
35	A4	25c *Hibiscus trionum*	.50	.50
		Nos. 32-35 (4)	1.35	1.35

Transkei Radio, 1st Anniv. A5

1977, Oct. 26　　Perf. 12x12½
36	A5	4c Disc jockey	.40	.40
37	A5	15c Announcer	1.00	1.00

"Help the Blind" — A6

1977, Nov. 18　　Perf. 12½x12
38	A6	4c Basket weaver	.25	.25
39	A6	15c Reading Braille	.60	.60
40	A6	20c Spinning wool	.80	.80
		Nos. 38-40 (3)	1.65	1.65

1978, Nov. 30

"Care for Cripples."
41	A6	4c Leg brace on boy	.25	.25
42	A6	10c Man in wheelchair	.60	.60
43	A6	15c Nurse examining boy	.85	.85
		Nos. 41-43 (3)	1.70	1.70

Men's Pipes A7

1978, Mar. 1　　Perf. 12x12½
44	A7	4c shown	.40	.40
45	A7	10c multi, diff.	.60	.60
46	A7	15c multi, diff.	1.00	1.00
47	A7	20c Woman's and witch doctor's pipes	1.10	1.10
		Nos. 44-47 (4)	3.10	3.10

Weaving Industry A8

1978, June 9
48	A8	4c Angora goat	.25	.25
49	A8	10c Spinning mohair	.60	.60
50	A8	15c Dyeing mohair	1.00	1.00
51	A8	20c Weaving mohair rug	1.25	1.25
		Nos. 48-51 (4)	3.10	3.10

Initiation Ceremony of Xhosa Men — A9

1979, Jan. 30　　Perf. 12½
52	A9	4c Chi Cha youth	.40	.40
53	A9	10c Youths in seclusion	.40	.40
54	A9	15c Umtshilo dance	1.00	1.00
55	A9	20c Leaving the Sutu	1.10	1.10
		Nos. 52-55 (4)	3.10	3.10

Chief Matanzima A10　　Water Resources A11

1979, Feb. 20　　Perf. 14½x14
56	A10	4c brn car & gold	.25	.25
57	A10	15c olive grn & gold	.40	.40

Inauguration of Matanzima, second state president.

1979, Mar. 13　Perf. 14½x14, 14x14½
58	A11	4c Windmill	.25	.25
59	A11	10c Woman filling water jar	.25	.25
60	A11	15c Irrigation, Indwe River, horiz.	.35	.35
61	A11	20c Ncora dam, horiz.	.45	.45
		Nos. 58-61 (4)	1.30	1.30

Waterfalls A12　　Child Healh Care A13

1979, Sept. 4
62	A12	4c Magwa Falls	.25	.25
63	A12	10c Bawa Falls	.25	.25
64	A12	15c Waterfall Bluff, horiz.	.30	.30
65	A12	20c Tsitsa Falls, horiz.	.40	.40
		Nos. 62-65 (4)	1.20	1.20

1979, Dec. 3　　Perf. 14½x14
66	A13	5c Pre-natal nourishment	.25	.25
67	A13	15c Primary feeding	.45	.45
68	A13	20c Immunization	.65	.65
		Nos. 66-68 (3)	1.35	1.35

Fishing Flies — A14

a, Durham ranger. b, Colonel Bates. c, Black gnat. d, Zug bug. e, March brown.

1980, Jan. 15　　Perf. 14x14½
69		Strip of 5	1.25	1.25
	a.-e.	A14 5c any single	.25	.25

1981, Jan. 15

Designs: a, Kent's lightning. b, Wickham's fancy. c, Jock Scott. d, Green highlander. e, Tan nymph.
70		Strip of 5	1.50	1.50
	a.-e.	A14 10c any single	.30	.30

1982, Jan. 6

a, Royal coachman. b, Light spruce. c, Montana nymph. d, Butcher. e, Blue charm.
71		Strip of 5	2.00	2.00
	a.-e.	A14 10c any single	.40	.40

1983, Mar. 2

Designs: a, Alexandra. b, Kent's marbled sedge. c, White marabou. d, Mayfly nymph. e, Silver Wilkinson.
72		Strip of 5	2.00	2.00
	a.-e.	A14 20c any single	.40	.40

1984, Feb. 10

Designs: a, Silver gray. b, Ginger quill. c, Hardy's favorite. d, March brown nymph. e, Kent's spectrum Mohawk.
73		Strip of 5	2.50	2.50
	a.-e.	A14 20c any single	.50	.50

Rotary Intl., 75th Anniv. — A15　　Cycads — A16

1980, Feb. 22　　Perf. 14½x14
74	A15	15c blk, ultra & gold	.30	.30

1980, Apr. 30
75	A16	5c *Encephalartos altensteinii*	.25	.25
76	A16	10c *Encephalartos princeps*	.25	.25
77	A16	15c *Encephalartos vilosus*	.30	.30
78	A16	20c *Encephalartos friderici-guilielmi*	.45	.45
		Nos. 75-78 (4)	1.25	1.25

Birds — A17

1980, July 30
79	A17	5c *Cuculus solitarius*	.25	.25
80	A17	10c *Batis capensis*	.55	.55
81	A17	15c *Balearica pavonina*	.85	.85
82	A17	20c *Ploceus ocularius*	1.10	1.10
		Nos. 79-82 (4)	2.75	2.75

Tourism — A18

1980, Oct. 26
83	A18	5c Hole in the Wall	.25	.25
84	A18	10c Port St. Johns	.25	.25
85	A18	15c The Citadel	.40	.40
86	A18	20c The Archway	.45	.45
		Nos. 83-86 (4)	1.35	1.35

Xhosa Women's Headdresses — A19

1981, Aug. 28
87	A19	5c Eyamakhwenkwe	.25	.25
88	A19	15c Eyabafana	.25	.25
89	A19	20c Umfazana	.30	.30
90	A19	25c Ixhegokazi	.40	.40
	a.	Souvenir sheet of 4, #87-90	1.00	1.00
		Nos. 87-90 (4)	1.20	1.20

Independence, 5th Anniv. — A20

1981, Oct. 26　　Perf. 14x14½
91	A20	5c State House	.30	.30
92	A20	15c University	.50	.50

Boy Scout Movement, 75th Anniv. A21　　Great Medical Pioneers A22

1982, May 14　　Perf. 14½x14
93	A21	8c Salute	.25	.25
94	A21	10c Planting tree	.25	.25
95	A21	20c Rafting	.30	.30
96	A21	25c Nature hike with dog	.40	.40
		Nos. 93-96 (4)	1.20	1.20

1982, Oct. 5
97	A22	15c Hippocrates	.25	.25
98	A22	20c Anton van Leeuwenhoek	.25	.25
99	A22	25c William Harvey	.30	.30
100	A22	35c Joseph Lister	.35	.35
		Nos. 97-100 (4)	1.15	1.15

1983, Aug. 17
101	A22	10c Edward Jenner	.25	.25
102	A22	20c Gregor Mendel	.25	.25
103	A22	25c Louis Pasteur	.30	.30
104	A22	40c Florence Nightingale	.40	.40
		Nos. 101-104 (4)	1.20	1.20

1984, Oct. 12
105	A22	11c Nicholas of Cusa	.25	.25
106	A22	25c William Morton	.25	.25
107	A22	30c Wilhelm Roentgen	.30	.30
108	A22	45c Karl Landsteiner	.45	.45
		Nos. 105-108 (4)	1.25	1.25

1985, Sept. 20
109	A22	12c Andreas Vesalius	.25	.25
110	A22	25c Marcello Malpighi	.30	.30
111	A22	30c Francois Magendie	.40	.40
112	A22	50c William Stewart Halsted	.60	.60
		Nos. 109-112 (4)	1.55	1.55
		Nos. 97-112 (16)	4.95	4.95

Umtata, Cent. A23

Architecture: 8c, City Hall. 15c, The Bunga. 20c, Botha Sigcau Building. 25c, Palace of Justice, Matanzima Building.

1982, Nov. 10　　Perf. 14x14½
113	A23	8c multicolored	.25	.25
114	A23	15c multicolored	.25	.25
115	A23	20c multicolored	.25	.25
116	A23	25c multicolored	.30	.30
		Nos. 113-116 (4)	1.05	1.05

Wildcoast Holiday Resort, Mzamba A24

1983, May 25
117	A24	10c	Hotel complex	.25	.25
118	A24	20c	Beach scene	.30	.30
119	A24	25c	Casino	.40	.40
120	A24	40c	Carousel	.55	.55
			Nos. 117-120 (4)	1.50	1.50

Post Offices A25

1983, Nov. 9   **Perf. 14½x14**
121	A25	10c	Lady Frere	.25	.25
122	A25	20c	Idutywa	.25	.25
123	A25	25c	Lusikisiki	.25	.25
124	A25	40c	Cala	.35	.35
			Nos. 121-124 (4)	1.10	1.10

1984, May 11
125	A25	11c	Umzimkulu	.25	.25
126	A25	20c	Mount Fletcher	.25	.25
127	A25	25c	Qumbu	.25	.25
128	A25	30c	Umtata	.35	.35
			Nos. 125-128 (4)	1.10	1.10

Xhosa Lifestyle A26

1984-90
129	A26	1c	Amagqira	.25	.25
130	A26	2c	Horsemen	.25	.25
131	A26	3c	Mat maker	.25	.25
132	A26	4c	Xhosa dancers	.25	.25
133	A26	5c	Man, donkeys	.25	.25
134	A26	6c	Musicians	.25	.25
135	A26	7c	Fingo brides	.25	.25
136	A26	8c	Tasting beer	.25	.25
137	A26	9c	Thinning corn	.25	.25
138	A26	10c	Dance demonstration	.25	.25
139	A26	11c	Carrying water from the river	.25	.25
140	A26	12c	Meal preparation	.25	.25
141	A26	14c	Weeding	.25	.25
142	A26	15c	Stick fighting	.25	.25
143	A26	16c	Morning pasture	.25	.25
144	A26	20c	Abakhwetha dancers	.30	.30
145	A26	21c	Building initiation hut	.30	.30
146	A26	25c	Tribesmen singing	.35	.35
147	A26	30c	Matrons	.35	.35
148	A26	50c	Pipe maker	.70	.70
149	A26	1r	Intonjane women	1.40	1.40
150	A26	2r	Abakhwetha	3.00	3.00
			Nos. 129-150 (22)	10.15	10.15

Issued: 11c, 4/2/84; 12c, 4/1/85; 14c, 4/1/86; 16c, 4/1/87; 21c, 7/3/90; others, 7/6/84.

Soil Conservation A27

Designs: 11c, Erosion from over-grazing. 25c, Wall construction to collect sediment. 30c, Regeneration of vegetation. 50c, Cattle grazing on verdant plain.

1985, Feb. 7
155	A27	11c	shown	.25	.25
156	A27	25c	multicolored	.25	.25
157	A27	30c	multicolored	.30	.30
158	A27	50c	multicolored	.45	.45
			Nos. 155-158 (4)	1.25	1.25

Bridges A28

1985, Apr. 18
159	A28	12c	Tsitsa	.25	.25
160	A28	25c	White Kei	.30	.30
161	A28	30c	Mitchell	.35	.35
162	A28	50c	Umzimvubu	.55	.55
			Nos. 159-162 (4)	1.45	1.45

Match Industry — A29

1985, July 25   **Perf. 14½x14**
163	A29	12c	Peeling logs	.25	.25
164	A29	25c	Splint chopping	.25	.25
165	A29	30c	VPO machine	.25	.25
166	A29	50c	Filling boxes	.40	.40
			Nos. 163-166 (4)	1.15	1.15

Port St. Johns A30

Designs: 12c, Early street scene. 20c, Coaster *Umzimvubu* at the Old Jetty. 25c, Unloading corn from wagons at the Jetty. 30c, View of the town, 1890's.

1986, Feb. 6
167	A30	12c	multicolored	.25	.25
168	A30	20c	multicolored	.40	.40
169	A30	25c	multicolored	.45	.45
170	A30	30c	multicolored	.50	.50
a.			Souvenir sheet of 4, #167-170	1.25	1.25
			Nos. 167-170 (4)	1.60	1.60

Aloes — A31

1986, May 1
171	A31	14c	*Aloe ferox*	.25	.25
172	A31	20c	*Aloe arborescens*	.30	.30
173	A31	25c	*Aloe maculata*	.40	.40
174	A31	30c	*Aloe ecklonis*	.50	.50
a.			Souvenir sheet of 4	1.40	1.40
			Nos. 171-174 (4)	1.45	1.45

No. 174a margin pictures emblem of the natl. philatelic exhibition held at Johannesburg, Oct. 6-11. Sold for 50c.

Hydroelectric Power Stations A32

14c, First Falls, Umtata River. 20c, Second Falls, Umtata River. 25c, Ncora, Qumanco River. 30c, Collywobbles, Mbashe River.

1986, July 24
175	A32	14c	shown	.25	.25
176	A32	20c	multicolored	.25	.25
177	A32	25c	multicolored	.30	.30
178	A32	30c	multicolored	.40	.40
			Nos. 175-178 (4)	1.20	1.20

Independence, 10th Anniv. — A33

Designs: 14c, Prime Minister G. M. Matanzima. 20c, Technical College, Umtata. 25c, University of Transkei, Umtata. 30c, Palace of Justice, Umtata.

1986, Oct. 26
179	A33	14c	multicolored	.25	.25
180	A33	20c	multicolored	.25	.25
181	A33	25c	multicolored	.30	.30
182	A33	30c	multicolored	.35	.35
			Nos. 179-182 (4)	1.15	1.15

Transkei Airways, 10th Anniv. — A34

1987, Feb. 5
183	A34	14c	shown	.25	.25
184	A34	20c	Aircraft tail	.40	.40
185	A34	25c	Nose, propellers	.50	.50
186	A34	30c	Plane, control tower	.60	.60
			Nos. 183-186 (4)	1.75	1.75

Beadwork — A35

1987, May 22   **Perf. 14x14½**
187	A35	16c	Pondo girl	.25	.25
188	A35	20c	Bomvana woman	.30	.30
189	A35	25c	Xessibe woman	.35	.35
a.			Souvenir sheet of 1	1.60	1.60
190	A35	30c	Xhosa man	.65	.65
			Nos. 187-190 (4)	1.55	1.55

No. 189a has blue and black decorative margin picturing the emblem of the natl. philatelic exhibition held at Paarl, Sept. 16-19. Sold for 50c.

Spiders — A36

1987, Aug. 24
191	A36	16c	*Latrodectus indistinctus*	.25	.25
192	A36	20c	*Nephila pilipes fenestrata*	.35	.35
193	A36	25c	*Lycosidae*	.40	.40
194	A36	30c	*Argiope nigrovittata*	.50	.50
			Nos. 191-194 (4)	1.50	1.50

Domestic Animals A37

1987, Oct. 22
195	A37	16c	Black pigs	.25	.25
196	A37	30c	Goats	.30	.30
197	A37	40c	Merino sheep	.40	.40
198	A37	50c	Cattle	.50	.50
			Nos. 195-198 (4)	1.45	1.45

Seaweed — A38

1988, Feb. 18
199	A38	16c	*Plocamium corallorhiza*	.25	.25
200	A38	30c	*Gelidium amanzil*	.30	.30
201	A38	40c	*Ecklonia biruncinata*	.40	.40
202	A38	50c	*Halimeda cuneata*	.50	.50
			Nos. 199-202 (4)	1.45	1.45

Blanket Factory, Butterworth A39

1988, May 5   **Perf. 14½x14**
203	A39	16c	Spinning machines	.25	.25
204	A39	30c	Warping machine	.25	.25
205	A39	40c	Weaving machine	.30	.30
206	A39	50c	Raising the nap	.40	.40
			Nos. 203-206 (4)	1.20	1.20

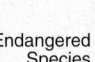

Wreck of the *Grosvenor*, 1782 — A40

Designs: 16c, Ship, map. 30c, *The Wreck of the Grosvenor*, by R. Smirke. 40c, Dirk hilt, compass and coins salvaged. 50c, *African Hospitality*, by G. Morland.

1988, Aug. 4
207	A40	16c	multicolored	.35	.35
208	A40	30c	multicolored	.60	.60
209	A40	40c	multicolored	.80	.80
210	A40	50c	multicolored	1.00	1.00
a.			Souvenir sheet of 1	3.25	3.25
			Nos. 207-210 (4)	2.75	2.75

No. 210a margin pictures emblem of the natl. philatelic exhibition at Pietermaritzburg, Nov. 22-27. Sold for 1r.

Endangered Species A41

1988, Oct. 20
211	A41	16c	*Felis nigripes*	.40	.40
212	A41	30c	*Philantomba monticola*	.75	.75
213	A41	40c	*Ourebia ourebi*	1.00	1.00
214	A41	50c	*Lycaon pictus*	1.25	1.25
			Nos. 211-214 (4)	3.40	3.40

Locomotive, Trains and Bridges — A42

Designs: 16c, Class 14 CRB locomotive. 30c, CRB pulling train over Toleni-Halt Bridge. 40c, Train on the Great Kei River Bridge, vert. 50c, Train in the Kei Valley.

1989, Jan. 19   Perf. 14x14½, 14½x14

215	A42	16c	multi	.30	.30
216	A42	30c	multi	.55	.55
217	A42	40c	multi	.85	.85
218	A42	50c	multi, vert.	.95	.95
		Nos. 215-218 (4)		2.65	2.65

A souvenir sheet of one No. 218 has margin picturing the emblem of the natl. philatelic exhibition WANDERERS 101, held Sept. 6-9. Sold for 1.50r. Value $5.

Basketry
A43

1989, Apr. 20   Perf. 14½x14

219	A43	18c	shown	.25	.25
220	A43	30c	multi, diff.	.35	.35
221	A43	40c	multi, diff.	.40	.40
222	A43	50c	multi, diff.	.55	.55
		Nos. 219-222 (4)		1.55	1.55

Mackerel
A44

1989, July 20

223	A44	18c	shown	.55	.55
224	A44	30c	Squid	.90	.90
225	A44	40c	Brown mussel	1.10	1.10
226	A44	50c	Rock lobster	1.50	1.50
		Nos. 223-226 (4)		4.05	4.05

Trees
A45

1989, Oct. 5   Perf. 14x14½

227	A45	18c	Broom cluster fig	.50	.50
228	A45	30c	Natal fig	.90	.90
229	A45	40c	Broad-leaved coral	1.10	1.10
230	A45	50c	Cabbage tree	1.50	1.50
		Nos. 227-230 (4)		4.00	4.00

Fossils
A46

1990, Jan. 18

231	A46	18c	*Ginkgo koningensis*	.65	.65
232	A46	30c	*Pseudoctenis spatulata*	1.25	1.25
233	A46	40c	*Rissikia media*	1.60	1.60
234	A46	50c	*Taeniopteris anavolans*	2.25	2.25
		Nos. 231-234 (4)		5.75	5.75

Great Medical
Pioneers — A47

1990, Mar. 29   Perf. 14x14½

235	A47	18c	Aretaeus	.65	.65
236	A47	30c	Claude Bernard	1.10	1.10
237	A47	40c	Oscar Minkowski	1.50	1.50
238	A47	50c	Frederick Banting	2.00	2.00
		Nos. 235-238 (4)		5.25	5.25

Diviners — A48

1990, June 28   Litho.   Perf. 14x14½

239	A48	21c	Dancing to the Drum	.65	.65
240	A48	35c	Lecturing Imichetywa	1.10	1.10
241	A48	40c	Initiation ceremony	1.25	1.25
242	A48	50c	Induction ceremony	1.50	1.50
a.		Souvenir sheet of 1		5.00	5.00
		Nos. 239-242 (4)		4.50	4.50

No. 242a for the 150th anniv. of the Penny Black. Sold for 1.50r.

Flowers — A49

1990, Sept. 20   Litho.   Perf. 14x14½

243	A49	21c	*Cyrtanthus obliquus*	.70	.70
244	A49	35c	*Disa crassicornis*	1.10	1.10
245	A49	40c	*Sandersonia aurantiaca*	1.40	1.40
246	A49	50c	*Podranea ricasoliana*	1.50	1.50
		Nos. 243-246 (4)		4.70	4.70

Parasitic
Plants — A50

1991, Jan. 10   Litho.

247	A50	21c	*Harveya pulchra*	.65	.65
248	A50	35c	*Harveya speciosa*	1.10	1.10
249	A50	40c	*Alectra sessiliflora*	1.25	1.25
250	A50	50c	*Hydnora africana*	1.60	1.60
		Nos. 247-250 (4)		4.60	4.60

Dolphins
A51

1991, Apr. 4   Litho.   Perf. 14½x14

251	A51	25c	*Delphinus delphis*	.95	.95
252	A51	40c	*Tursiops truncatus*	1.50	1.50
253	A51	50c	*Sousa plumbea*	1.90	1.90
254	A51	60c	*Grampus griseus*	2.25	2.25
		Nos. 251-254 (4)		6.60	6.60

Birds — A52

1991, June 20   Litho.

255	A52	25c	*Balearica regulorum*	.80	.80
256	A52	40c	*Gyps coprotheres*	1.25	1.25
257	A52	50c	*Grus carunculata*	1.50	1.50
258	A52	60c	*Neophron percnopterus*	1.75	1.75
a.		Souvenir sheet of 1		5.50	5.50
		Nos. 255-258 (4)		5.30	5.30

Medical
Pioneers — A53

Developers of vaccines: 25c, Emil von Behring (1854-1917) and Shibasaburo Kitasato (1852-1931), diphtheria. 40c, Leon Albert Calmette (1863-1933) and Camille Guerin (1872-1961), tuberculosis. 50c, Jonas Salk (b. 1914), polio. 60c, John Franklin Enders (1897-1985), measles.

1991, Sept. 26   Litho.   Perf. 14x14½

259	A53	25c	multicolored	.85	.85
260	A53	40c	multicolored	1.50	1.50
261	A53	50c	multicolored	1.75	1.75
262	A53	60c	multicolored	2.40	2.40
		Nos. 259-262 (4)		6.50	6.50

Orchids — A54

1992, Feb. 20   Litho.

263	A54	27c	*Eulophia speciosa*	.30	.30
264	A54	45c	*Satyrium sphaerocarpum*	.50	.50
265	A54	65c	*Disa scullyi*	.75	.75
266	A54	85c	*Disa tysonii*	.95	.95
		Nos. 263-266 (4)		2.50	2.50

Medical
Pioneers
A55

27c, Thomas Huckle Weller (b. 1915), developer of rubella vaccine. 45c, Ignaz Philipp Semmelweis (1818-65), diagnosed septicaemia. 65c, Sir James Young Simpson (1811-70), 1st to use chloroform in obstetrics. 85c, Rene Theophile Hyacinthe Laennec (1781-1826), inventor of stethoscope.

1992, Apr. 1   Litho.   Perf. 14½x14

267	A55	27c	multicolored	.70	.70
268	A55	45c	multicolored	1.25	1.25
269	A55	65c	multicolored	1.75	1.75
270	A55	85c	multicolored	2.25	2.25
		Nos. 267-270 (4)		5.95	5.95

Waterfowl — A56

1992, July 16   Litho.   Perf. 14x14½

271	A56	35c	*Anas erythrorhyncha*	.60	.60
272	A56	35c	*Anas hottentota*	.60	.60
a.		Pair, #271-272		1.25	1.25
273	A56	70c	*Oxyura punctata*	1.25	1.25
274	A56	70c	*Thalassornis leuconotus*	1.25	1.25
a.		Pair, #273-274		2.50	2.50
275	A56	90c	*Anas sparsa*	1.60	1.60
276	A56	90c	*Alopochen aegyptiacus*	1.60	1.60
a.		Pair, #275-276		3.25	3.25
277	A56	1.05r	*Anas smithi*	1.60	1.60
278	A56	1.05r	*Anas capensis*	1.60	1.60
a.		Pair, #277-278		3.25	3.25
		Nos. 271-278 (8)		10.10	10.10

A souvenir sheet of 1 #273 was sold by the Philatelic Foundation of South Africa. Value $5.

Fossils
A57

Designs: 35c, Pseudomelania sutherlandi. 70c, Gaudryceras denseplicatum. 90c, Neithea quinquecostata. 1.05r, Pugilina (Mayeria) acuticarinatus.

1992, Sept. 17   Litho.   Perf. 14½x14

279	A57	35c	multicolored	.75	.75
280	A57	70c	multicolored	1.50	1.50
281	A57	90c	multicolored	2.00	2.00
282	A57	1.05r	multicolored	2.25	2.25
		Nos. 279-282 (4)		6.50	6.50

Dogs — A58

1993, Feb. 12   Litho.

283	A58	35c	Papillon	.55	.55
284	A58	70c	Pekingese	1.10	1.10
285	A58	90c	Chihuahua	1.50	1.50
286	A58	1.05r	Dachshund	1.75	1.75
		Nos. 283-286 (4)		4.90	4.90

A souvenir sheet of one No. 284 exists. Sold for 3r. Value $6.

Prehistoric
Animals
A59

1993, June 18   Litho.

287	A59	45c	Fabrosaurus	1.00	1.00
288	A59	65c	Diictodon	1.40	1.40
289	A59	85c	Chasmatosaurus	1.75	1.75
290	A59	1.05r	Rubidgea	2.25	2.25
		Nos. 287-290 (4)		6.40	6.40

Medical
Pioneers
A60

Designs: 45c, Sir Alexander Fleming (1881-1955), discovered penicillin and Lord Howard Walter Florey (1898-1968), purified penicillin for general use. 65c, Alexis Carrel (1873-1944), developed Carrel-Dakin fluid and method to suture blood vessels. 85c, James Lind (1716-1794), recommended citrus fruit to combat scurvy. 1.05r, Santiago Ramon y Cajal (1852-1934), established neuron as basic unit of nervous structure.

1993, Aug. 20   Litho.

291	A60	45c	multicolored	1.00	1.00
292	A60	65c	multicolored	1.25	1.25
293	A60	85c	multicolored	1.60	1.60
294	A60	1.05r	multicolored	2.00	2.00
		Nos. 291-294 (4)		5.85	5.85

Doves — A61

Designs: 45c, Streptopelia senegalensis. 65c, Turtur tympanistria. 85c, Turtur chalcospilos. 1.05r, Oena capensis.

1993, Oct. 15   Litho.   Perf. 14x14½

295	A61	45c	multicolored	.90	.90
296	A61	65c	multicolored	1.25	1.25
297	A61	85c	multicolored	1.60	1.60
298	A61	1.05r	multicolored	1.90	1.90
a.		Souvenir sheet of 4, #295-298		5.50	5.50
		Nos. 295-298 (4)		5.65	5.65

No. 298a sold for 3.50r.

Modern
Shipwrecks
A62

1994, Mar. 18   Litho.   Perf. 14½x14
299	A62	45c Clan Lindsay, 1898	1.10	1.10
300	A62	65c Horizon, 1967	1.75	1.75
301	A62	85c Oceanos, 1991	2.40	2.40
302	A62	1.05r Forresbank, 1958	2.75	2.75
		Nos. 299-302 (4)	8.00	8.00

A souvenir sheet of 1 #301 exists. Sold for 3r. Value $8.

Transkei ceased to exist April 27, 1994.

VENDA

ˈven-də

LOCATION — Enclave, Republic of South Africa
GOVT. — Self-governing tribal homeland
AREA — 4,040 sq. mi.
POP. — 343,480 (1980)
CAPITAL — Thohoyandou

Catalogue values for all unused stamps in this country are for Never Hinged items.

Independence from South Africa — A1

Designs: 4c, Mace, flag. 15c, Administrative buildings. 20c, P.R. Mphephu, paramount chief and president. 25c, Coat of arms.

Perf. 14½x14
1979, Sept. 13   Litho.   Unwmk.
1	A1	4c multicolored	.35	.35
2	A1	15c multicolored	.90	.90
3	A1	20c multicolored	1.25	1.25
4	A1	25c multicolored	1.60	1.60
		Nos. 1-4 (4)	4.10	4.10

Flowers — A2   Wood Carvings — A3

1979-85   Perf. 12½, 14 (11c, 12c)
5	A2	1c *Tecomaria capensis*	.25	.25
6	A2	2c *Catophractes alexandri*	.25	.25
7	A2	3c *Tricliceras longipedunculatum*	.25	.25
8	A2	4c *Dissotis princeps*	.25	.25
9	A2	5c *Gerbera jamesonii*	1.60	.60
10	A2	6c *Hibiscus mastersianus*	.25	.25
11	A2	7c *Nymphaea caerulaea*	.25	.25
12	A2	8c *Crinum lugardiae*	.30	.25
13	A2	9c *Xerophyta retinervis*	.25	.25
14	A2	10c *Hypoxis angustifolia*	.25	.25
15	A2	11c *Combretum microphyllum*	.25	.25
16	A2	12c *Clivia caulescens*	.35	.25
17	A2	15c *Pycnostachys urticifolia*	.25	.25
18	A2	20c *Zantedeschia jucunda*	.25	.25
19	A2	25c *Leonotis mollis*	2.00	.75
20	A2	30c *Littonia modesta*	.35	.25
21	A2	50c *Protea caffra*	.60	.25
22	A2	1r *Adenium multiflorum*	.80	.40
23	A2	2r *Strelitzia caudata*	1.75	1.00
		Nos. 5-23 (19)	10.50	6.50

Issue dates: 11c, Apr. 2, 1984; 12c, Apr. 1, 1985; others, Sept. 13, 1979.

Perf. 14
5a	A2	1c	.25	.25
6a	A2	2c	.25	.25
7a	A2	3c	.25	.25
9a	A2	5c	.25	.25
12a	A2	8c	.25	.25
14a	A2	10c	.40	.25
19a	A2	25c	1.25	.60
21a	A2	50c	2.75	1.25
		Nos. 5a-21a (8)	5.65	3.35

1980, Feb. 13   Perf. 14½x14, 14x14½

Designs: 5c, Man with cup. 10c, Woman with corn, bowl and spoon. 15c, King Nebuchadnezzar, horiz. 20c, Python killing woman, horiz.
24	A3	5c multicolored	.25	.25
25	A3	10c multicolored	.35	.35
26	A3	15c multicolored	.50	.50
27	A3	20c multicolored	.65	.65
		Nos. 24-27 (4)	1.75	1.75

Tea Cultivation A4

1980, May 14   Perf. 14x14½
28	A4	5c Plants in nursery	.25	.25
29	A4	10c Harvest	.25	.25
30	A4	15c Withering	.35	.35
31	A4	20c Cut, twist, curl unit	.50	.50
		Nos. 28-31 (4)	1.35	1.35

Banana Industry A5

1980, Aug. 13
32	A5	5c Plants	.25	.25
33	A5	10c Cutting "hands"	.25	.25
34	A5	15c Sorting	.35	.35
35	A5	20c Packing	.50	.50
		Nos. 32-35 (4)	1.35	1.35

Butterflies A6   Sunbirds A7

1980, Nov. 13   Perf. 14½x14
36	A6	5c *Precis tugela*	.25	.25
37	A6	10c *Charaxes bohemani*	.25	.25
38	A6	15c *Catacroptera cloanthe*	.50	.50
39	A6	20c *Papilio dardanus*	.60	.60
		Nos. 36-39 (4)	1.60	1.60

1981, Feb. 16
40	A7	5c *Anthreptes collaris*	.25	.25
41	A7	15c *Nectarinia mariquensis*	.35	.35
42	A7	20c *Nectarinia talatala*	.45	.45
43	A7	25c *Nectarinia senegalensis*	.55	.55
		Nos. 40-43 (4)	1.60	1.60

Nwanedi Dam — A8

1981, May 6
44	A8	5c shown	.25	.25
45	A8	15c Mahovhohovho Falls	.25	.25
46	A8	20c Phiphidi Falls	.30	.30
47	A8	25c Lake Fundudzi	.40	.40
		Nos. 44-47 (4)	1.20	1.20

Orchids — A9   Musical Instruments — A10

1981, Sept. 11
48	A9	5c *Cynorkis kassnerana*	.25	.25
49	A9	15c *Eulophia fridericii*	.25	.25
50	A9	20c *Bonatea densiflora*	.40	.40
51	A9	25c *Mystacidium brayboniae*	.45	.45
a.		Souvenir sheet of 4, #48-51	.90	.90
		Nos. 48-51 (4)	1.35	1.35

1981, Nov. 13   Perf. 14x14½
52	A10	5c Mbila	.25	.25
53	A10	15c Phalaphala	.25	.25
54	A10	20c Tshizambi	.25	.25
55	A10	25c Ngoma	.40	.40
		Nos. 52-55 (4)	1.15	1.15

Sisal Cultivation A11

1982, Feb. 26
56	A11	5c Harvesting	.25	.25
57	A11	10c Drying	.25	.25
58	A11	20c Grading	.35	.35
59	A11	25c Baling	.45	.45
		Nos. 56-59 (4)	1.30	1.30

History of Writing — A12

Designs: 8c, Bison, petroglyph, Atlamira, Spain. 15c, Animal, petroglyph, eastern California. 20c, Pictographic script on a Sumerian tablet. 25c, Bushman burial stone, Humansdorp, South Africa.

1982, June 15   Perf. 14½x14
60	A12	8c multicolored	.25	.25
61	A12	15c multicolored	.25	.25
62	A12	20c multicolored	.35	.35
63	A12	25c multicolored	.45	.45
		Nos. 60-63 (4)	1.30	1.30

1983, May 11   Size: 21x37mm

10c, Indus Valley script, 3000 B.C. 20c, Sumerian cuneiform, 2000 B.C. 25c, Egyptian hieroglyphics, 1300 B.C. 40c, Chinese handscroll, A.D. 1100.
64	A12	10c multicolored	.25	.25
65	A12	20c multicolored	.30	.30
66	A12	25c multicolored	.35	.35
67	A12	40c multicolored	.40	.40
		Nos. 64-67 (4)	1.30	1.30

1984, Feb. 17   Perf. 14x14½
Size: 37½x20½mm

Designs: 10c, Evolution of the cuneiform sign. 20c, Evolution of the Chinese character. 25c, Development of Cretan hieroglyphics. 40c, Development of Egyptian hieroglyphics.
68	A12	10c multicolored	.25	.25
69	A12	20c multicolored	.30	.30
70	A12	25c multicolored	.35	.35
71	A12	40c multicolored	.60	.60
		Nos. 68-71 (4)	1.50	1.50

1985, Mar. 21   Perf. 14½x14
Size: 34x24½mm

Designs: 11c, Southern Arabic characters. 25c, Phoenician characters. 30c, Aramaic characters. 50c, Canaanite characters.
72	A12	11c multicolored	.25	.25
73	A12	25c multicolored	.30	.30
74	A12	30c multicolored	.35	.35
75	A12	50c multicolored	.60	.60
		Nos. 72-75 (4)	1.50	1.50

1986, Apr. 10   Perf. 14x14½
Size: 24½x34mm
76	A12	14c Etruscan	.25	.25
77	A12	20c Greek	.40	.40
78	A12	25c Roman	.45	.45
79	A12	30c Cyrillic	.55	.55
		Nos. 76-79 (4)	1.65	1.65

1988, Apr. 28   Perf. 14½x14
Size: 34x26mm
80	A12	16c Chinese	.25	.25
81	A12	30c Hindi	.30	.30
82	A12	40c Russian	.40	.40
83	A12	50c Arabic	.45	.45
		Nos. 80-83 (4)	1.40	1.40
		Nos. 60-83 (24)	8.40	8.40

See Nos. 209-212.

Trees A13

1982, Sept. 17
84	A13	8c *Euphorbia ingens*	.25	.25
85	A13	15c *Pterocarpus angolensis*	.25	.25
86	A13	20c *Ficus ingens*	.35	.35
87	A13	25c *Adansonia digitata*	.45	.45
		Nos. 84-87 (4)	1.30	1.30

1983, Aug. 3
88	A13	10c *Gardenia spatulifolia*	.25	.25
89	A13	20c *Hyphaene natalensis*	.30	.30
90	A13	25c *Albizia adianthifolia*	.30	.30
91	A13	40c *Sesamothamnus lugardii*	.55	.55
		Nos. 88-91 (4)	1.40	1.40

1984, June 21
92	A13	11c *Afzelia quanzensis*	.25	.25
93	A13	20c *Peltophorum africanum*	.30	.30
94	A13	25c *Gyrocarpus americanus*	.35	.35
95	A13	30c *Acacia sieberana*	.40	.40
		Nos. 92-95 (4)	1.30	1.30
		Nos. 84-95 (12)	3.85	3.85

Frogs — A14

1982, Nov. 26   Perf. 14x14½
96	A14	8c *Rana angolensis*	.25	.25
97	A14	15c *Chiromantis xerampelina*	.30	.30
98	A14	20c *Leptopelis*	.35	.35
99	A14	25c *Ptychadena anchietae*	.45	.45
		Nos. 96-99 (4)	1.35	1.35

Migratory Birds and Maps — A15

1983, Feb. 16   Perf. 14½x14
100	A15	8c European bee-eater	.25	.25
101	A15	20c Steppe eagle	.40	.40
102	A15	25c Plum-colored starling	.50	.50
103	A15	40c White-bellied stork	.85	.85
		Nos. 100-103 (4)	2.00	2.00

Subtropical
Fruit
A16

1983, Oct. 26   Perf. 14x14½
104 A16 10c Avocado   .25 .25
105 A16 20c Mango   .25 .25
106 A16 25c Papaya   .30 .30
107 A16 40c Litchi   .50 .50
Nos. 104-107 (4)   1.30 1.30

Migratory
Birds — A17

1984, Apr. 26   Perf. 14½x14
108 A17 11c White stork   .30 .30
109 A17 20c Paradise flycatcher   .55 .55
110 A17 25c Yellow-billed kite   .65 .65
111 A17 30c Wood sandpiper   .85 .85
Nos. 108-111 (4)   2.35 2.35

Independence, 5th Anniv. — A18

1984, Sept. 13   Perf. 14½x14
112 A18 11c Dzata Ruins   .25 .25
113 A18 25c Traditional hut   .25 .25
114 A18 30c Low-income housing   .30 .30
115 A18 45c Modern home   .45 .45
Nos. 112-115 (4)   1.25 1.25

Songbirds   Food of the Veld
A19   A20

1985, Jan. 10
116 A19 11c Heuglin's robin   .25 .25
117 A19 25c Black-collared bar-
          bet   .40 .40
118 A19 30c Black-headed oriole   .50 .50
119 A19 50c Kurrichane thrush   .85 .85
Nos. 116-119 (4)   2.00 2.00

1985, June 21   Perf. 14x14½
120 A20 12c Mimusops zeyheri   .25 .25
121 A20 25c Ziziphus mucronata   .25 .25
122 A20 30c Citrullus lanatus   .30 .30
123 A20 50c Berchemia discolor   .50 .50
Nos. 120-123 (4)   1.30 1.30

See Nos. 173-176.

Ferns — A21

1985, Sept. 5   Perf. 14½x14
124 A21 12c *Pellaea dura*   .25 .25
125 A21 25c *Actiniopteris radiata*   .25 .25
126 A21 30c *Adiantum his-
          pidulum*   .30 .30

127 A21 50c *Polypodium poly-
          podioides*   .50 .50
Nos. 124-127 (4)   1.30 1.30

Reptiles
A22

1986-90   Perf. 14x14½
128 A22 1c *Psammophylax
          tritaeniatus*   .25 .25
129 A22 2c *Pseudaspis cana*   .25 .25
130 A22 3c *Nucras taeniolata
          ornata*   .25 .25
131 A22 4c *Bitis arietans*   .25 .25
132 A22 5c *Mabuya capensis*   .25 .25
133 A22 6c *Naja haje annu-
          lifera*   .25 .25
134 A22 7c *Mabuya quin-
          quetaeniata
          margaritifer*   .25 .25
135 A22 8c *Philothamnus
          semivariegatus*   .25 .25
136 A22 9c *Gerrhosaurus
          flavigularis*   .25 .25
137 A22 10c *Prosymna sun-
          devallii lineata*   .25 .25
138 A22 14c *Platysaurus in-
          termedius*   .30 .30
139 A22 15c *Lacerta rupicola*   .30 .30
140 A22 16c *Varanus niloticus*   .35 .35
141 A22 18c *Dendroaspis
          polylepis*   .40 .40
142 A22 20c *Afroedura trans-
          vaalica*   .45 .45
143 A22 21c *Chamaeleo dilep-
          sis*   .45 .45
144 A22 25c *Elapsoidea sun-
          devallii longi-
          cauda*   .55 .55
145 A22 30c *Pachydactylus
          tigrinus*   .65 .65
146 A22 50c *Mehelya capensis*   1.10 1.10
147 A22 1r *Cordylus warreni
          depressus*   2.25 2.25
148 A22 2r *Python sebae
          natalensis*   4.50 4.50
Nos. 128-148 (21)   13.80 13.80

Issued: 14c, 4/1/86; 16c, 4/1/87; 18c, 7/3/89; 21c, 8/3/90; others, 1/16/86.

Forestry
A23

Designs: 14c, Planting pine seedlings. 20c, Felling and extracting saw timber. 25c, Unloading timber at sawmill. 30c, Construction workers using pre-cut lumber.

1986, June 26   Perf. 14x14½
153 A23 14c multicolored   .25 .25
154 A23 20c multicolored   .40 .40
155 A23 25c multicolored   .45 .45
156 A23 30c multicolored   .55 .55
Nos. 153-156 (4)   1.65 1.65

FIVA World Classic Car Rally — A24

1986, Sept. 4   Perf. 14½x14
157 A24 14c 1910 Maxwell   .25 .25
158 A24 20c 1929 Bentley 4½ l   .25 .25
159 A24 25c 1933 Plymouth
          Coupe   .35 .35
160 A24 30c 1958 Mercedes
          Cabriolet   .40 .40
a.   Souvenir sheet of 1   1.40 1.40
Nos. 157-160 (4)   1.25 1.25

No. 160a for the natl. philatelic exhibition held at Johannesburg, Oct. 6-11. Sold for 50c.

Waterfowl   Wood Carvings
A25   A26

1987, Jan. 8   Perf. 14x14½, 14½x14
161 A25 14c *Sarkidiornis mela-
          notos*   .90 .90
162 A25 20c *Dendrocygna vidu-
          ata*   1.40 1.40
163 A25 25c *Plectropterus
          gambensis*   1.60 1.60
a.   Souvenir sheet of 1   4.50 4.50
164 A25 30c *Alopochen aegyp-
          tiacus*   2.10 2.10
Nos. 161-164 (4)   6.00 6.00

Nos. 163-164 are horiz. No. 163a margin pictures emblem of the natl. philatelic exhibition held at Paarl, Sept. 16-19. Sold for 50c.

1987, Apr. 9   Perf. 14½x14
165 A26 16c *Iron Master*   .35 .35
166 A26 20c *Distant Drums*   .40 .40
167 A26 25c *Sunrise*   .55 .55
168 A26 30c *Obedience*   .70 .70
Nos. 165-168 (4)   2.00 2.00

Freshwater
Fish — A27

1987, July 2   Perf. 14x14½
169 A27 16c *Hydrocynus vittatus*   .30 .30
170 A27 20c *Opsardium
          zambezense*   .35 .35
171 A27 25c *Oreochromis mos-
          sambicus*   .40 .40
172 A27 30c *Clarias gariepinus*   .55 .55
Nos. 169-172 (4)   1.60 1.60

Food of the Veld Type

1987, Oct. 2
173 A20 16c *Grewia occidentalis*   .25 .25
174 A20 30c *Phoenix reclinata*   .30 .30
175 A20 40c *Halleria lucida*   .45 .45
176 A20 50c *Cucumis africanus*   .55 .55
Nos. 173-176 (4)   1.55 1.55

Coffee
Industry
A28

1988, Jan. 21   Perf. 14½x14
177 A28 16c Harvesting   .25 .25
178 A28 30c Weighing   .30 .30
179 A28 40c Sun drying   .40 .40
180 A28 50c Roasting   .50 .50
Nos. 177-180 (4)   1.45 1.45

Nurse's
Training
College,
Shayandima
A29

1988, Aug. 18
181 A29 16c shown   .25 .25
182 A29 30c Microscopy   .30 .30
183 A29 40c Anatomy lecture   .40 .40
184 A29 50c Clinical training   .50 .50
Nos. 181-184 (4)   1.45 1.45

Watercolors
by Kenneth
Thabo
A30

1988, Oct. 6
185 A30 16c Fetching Water   .25 .25
186 A30 30c Grinding Maize   .30 .30
187 A30 40c Offering Food   .40 .40
188 A30 50c Kindling the Fire   .50 .50
a.   Souvenir sheet of 1   1.90 1.90
Nos. 185-188 (4)   1.45 1.45

No. 188a for the natl. philatelic exhibition held at Pietermaritzburg, Nov. 22-27. Sold for 1.50r.
See Nos. 193-196.

Traditional
Kitchenware
A31

1989, Jan. 5
189 A31 16c Ndongwana   .25 .25
190 A31 30c Ndilo   .30 .30
191 A31 40c Mufaro   .40 .40
192 A31 50c Muthatha   .50 .50
Nos. 189-192 (4)   1.45 1.45

Art Type of 1988

Traditional dances: watercolors by Kenneth Thabo.

1989, Apr. 5
193 A30 18c Domba   .25 .25
194 A30 30c Tshinzerere   .30 .30
195 A30 40c Malende   .40 .40
196 A30 50c Malombo   .50 .50
Nos. 193-196 (4)   1.45 1.45

Endangered Bird
Species — A32

1989, June 27
197 A32 18c *Bucorvus
          leadbeateri*   .90 .90
198 A32 30c *Torgos tracheliotus*   1.25 1.25
199 A32 40c *Terathopius
          ecaudatus*   1.60 1.60
200 A32 50c *Polemaetus bel-
          licosus*   2.25 2.25
a.   Souvenir sheet of 1   4.00 4.00
Nos. 197-200 (4)   6.00 6.00

No. 200a for the natl. philatelic exhibition WANDERERS 101, held Sept. 6-9. Sold for 1.50r.

Independence, 10th Anniv. — A33

1989, Sept. 13
201 A33 18c Pres. Ravele   .25 .25
202 A33 30c Presidential office   .30 .30
203 A33 40c Presidential resi-
          dence   .40 .40
204 A33 50c Thohoyandou Stadi-
          um   .45 .45
Nos. 201-204 (4)   1.40 1.40

Wildlife Conservation, Nwanedi Natl. Park — A34

1990, Mar. 1
205	A34	18c	*Panthera leo*	.50 .50
206	A34	30c	*Equus burchelli*	.90 .90
207	A34	40c	*Acinonyx jubatus*	1.10 1.10
208	A34	50c	*Ceratotherium simum*	1.25 1.25
a.		Souvenir sheet of 1		4.00 4.00
		Nos. 205-208 (4)		3.75 3.75

No. 208a for the natl. philatelic exhibition. Sold for 1.50r.

History of Writing Type

Designs: 21c, Calligraphy. 30c, Musical notation, Beethoven's *Moonlight Sonata*. 40c, Computer characters. 50c, Black-and-white television picture transmitted across interstellar distances by the Arecibo radio telescope.

1990, May 23   Litho.   Perf. 14½x14
209	A12	21c multicolored	.25 .25
210	A12	30c multicolored	.35 .35
211	A12	40c multicolored	.45 .45
212	A12	50c multicolored	.65 .65
		Nos. 209-212 (4)	1.70 1.70

Aloe Plants — A35   Butterflies — A36

1990, Aug. 23   Litho.   Perf. 14½x14
213	A35	21c Aloe globuligemma	.40 .40
214	A35	35c Aloe aculeata	.60 .60
215	A35	40c Aloe lutescens	.70 .70
216	A35	50c Aloe angelica	.85 .85
		Nos. 213-216 (4)	2.55 2.55

1990, Nov. 15   Perf. 14x14½
217	A36	21c Pseudacraea boisduvalii	.60 .60
218	A36	35c Papilio nireus	1.10 1.10
219	A36	40c Charaxes jasius	1.25 1.25
220	A36	50c Aeropetes tulbaghia	1.40 1.40
		Nos. 217-220 (4)	4.35 4.35

Birds A37

1991, Mar. 7   Litho.   Perf. 14½x14
221	A37	21c Batis capensis	.55 .55
222	A37	35c Cossypha natalensis	.85 .85
223	A37	40c Anthreptes collaris	1.00 1.00
224	A37	50c Phyllastrephus flavostriatus	1.25 1.25
		Nos. 221-224 (4)	3.65 3.65

A38

Chinese inventions.

1991, June 6   Litho.   Perf. 14½x14
225	A38	25c Paper made from pulp	.90 .90
226	A38	40c Magnetic compass	1.40 1.40
227	A38	50c Abacus	1.75 1.75

228	A38	60c Gunpowder	2.00 2.00
a.		Souvenir sheet of 1	3.25 3.25
		Nos. 225-228 (4)	6.05 6.05

Hotels A39

1991, Aug. 29   Litho.
229	A39	25c Venda Sun	.50 .50
230	A39	40c Mphephu Resort	.90 .90
231	A39	50c Sagole Spa	1.10 1.10
232	A39	60c Luphephe-Nwanedi Resort	1.50 1.50
		Nos. 229-232 (4)	4.00 4.00

Trees A40

1991, Nov. 21   Litho.
233	A40	27c Acacia xanthophloea	.55 .55
234	A40	45c Faurea saligna	1.00 1.00
235	A40	65c Strelitzia caudata	1.40 1.40
236	A40	85c Kigelia africana	1.75 1.75
		Nos. 233-236 (4)	4.70 4.70

Clothing Factory A41

1992, Mar. 5   Litho.
237	A41	27c Setting the web	.35 .35
238	A41	45c Knitting a pattern	.80 .80
239	A41	65c Using sewing machine	1.10 1.10
240	A41	85c Testing for flaws	1.40 1.40
		Nos. 237-240 (4)	3.65 3.65

Bees A42

1992, May 21   Litho.
241	A42	35c Honey bee	.80 .80
242	A42	70c Carder bee	1.60 1.60
243	A42	90c Leafcutter bee	1.75 1.75
244	A42	1.05r Carpenter bee	2.25 2.25
		Nos. 241-244 (4)	6.40 6.40

A souvenir sheet of 1 #242 was sold by the Philatelic Foundation of South Africa. Value $3.75.

Inventions A43

Designs: 35c, Plow, Egypt 1259 B.C. 70c, Wheel, Mesopotamia, 3200 B.C. 90c, Brickmaking, Egypt, 3000 B.C. 1.05r, Sailing ship, Egypt, 1600 B.C.

1992, Aug. 13
245	A43	35c multicolored	.70 .70
246	A43	70c multicolored	1.40 1.40
247	A43	90c multicolored	1.50 1.50
248	A43	1.05r multicolored	2.00 2.00
		Nos. 245-248 (4)	5.60 5.60

Crocodile Farming A44

1992, Oct. 15   Litho.
249	A44	35c Emerging from water	.70 .70
250	A44	70c Egg laying	1.40 1.40
251	A44	90c Hatchlings	1.50 1.50
252	A44	1.05r Maternal care	2.00 2.00
		Nos. 249-252 (4)	5.60 5.60

Domestic Cats — A45

1993, Mar. 19   Litho.
253	A45	45c Burmese	.90 .90
254	A45	65c Tabby	1.75 1.75
255	A45	85c Siamese	1.90 1.90
256	A45	1.05r Persian	2.50 2.50
		Nos. 253-256 (4)	7.05 7.05

A souvenir sheet of one No. 254 has inscription for National Philatelic Exhibition. Sold for 3r. Value $6.50.

Herons A46

Designs: 45c, Butorides striatus. 65c, Nycticorax nycticorax. 85c, Ardea purpurea. 1.05r, Ardea melanocephala.

1993, July 16   Litho.   Perf. 14½x14
257	A46	45c multicolored	1.00 1.00
258	A46	65c multicolored	1.50 1.50
259	A46	85c multicolored	1.75 1.75
260	A46	1.05r multicolored	2.25 2.25
a.		Souvenir sheet of 4, #257-260	6.50 6.50
		Nos. 257-260 (4)	6.50 6.50

Shoe Factory — A47

1993, Sept. 17   Litho.   Perf. 14x14½
261	A47	45c Punching out sole lining	.45 .45
262	A47	65c Shaping heel	.60 .60
263	A47	85c Joining upper to inner sole	.70 .70
264	A47	1.05r Forming sole	1.00 1.00
		Nos. 261-264 (4)	2.75 2.75

Inventions A48

1993, Nov. 5   Litho.   Perf. 14x14½
265	A48	45c Axe	.60 .60
266	A48	65c Armor	.90 .90
267	A48	85c Arch	1.10 1.10
268	A48	1.05r Aqueduct	1.40 1.40
		Nos. 265-268 (4)	4.00 4.00

Dogs A49

1994, Jan. 14   Litho.   Perf. 14½x14
269	A49	45c Cocker spaniel	1.00 1.00
270	A49	65c Maltese	1.60 1.60
271	A49	85c Scottish terrier	1.90 1.90
272	A49	1.05r Miniature schnauzer	2.50 2.50
		Nos. 269-272 (4)	7.00 7.00

A souvenir sheet of 1 #271 was sold for 3r by the Philatelic Foundation of Southern Africa and sold for 1.50r. Value $7.

Monkeys A50

Designs: 45c, Cercopithecus aethiops. 65c, Galago moholi. 85c, Cercopithecus mitis. 1.05r, Otolemur crassicaudatus.

1994, Mar. 4   Litho.   Perf. 14½x14
273	A50	45c multicolored	.90 .90
274	A50	65c multicolored	1.40 1.40
275	A50	85c multicolored	1.60 1.60
276	A50	1.05r multicolored	2.10 2.10
a.		Souvenir sheet of 4, #273-276	6.00 6.00
		Nos. 273-276 (4)	6.00 6.00

Starlings A51

45c, Lamprotornis nitens. 70c, Cinnyricinclus leucogaster. 95c, Onychognathus morio. 1.15r, Creatophora cinerea.

1994, Apr. 29   Litho.   Perf. 14½x14
277	A51	45c multicolored	1.10 1.10
278	A51	70c multicolored	1.75 1.75
279	A51	95c multicolored	2.25 2.25
280	A51	1.15r multicolored	2.75 2.75
		Nos. 277-280 (4)	7.85 7.85

Venda ceased to exist April 27, 1994. The Venda postal service continued to operate until 1996.

SOUTH ARABIA

sauth ə-'rā-bē-ə

LOCATION — Southern Arabia
GOVT. — Federation; British
　dependency
AREA — 61,890 sq. mi.
POP. — 771,000 (est. 1966)
CAPITAL — Al Ittihad

The Federation of South Arabia was established in 1959 and consists of 14 states including Aden colony and part of Aden protectorate. When the Federation became independent, Nov. 30, 1967, it became the People's Republic of Southern Yemen. See People's Democratic Republic of Yemen, Vol. 6.

100 Cents = 1 Shilling
1000 Fils = 1 Dinar (1965)

Catalogue values for all unused stamps in this country are for Never Hinged items.

Common Design Types pictured following the introduction.

Red Cross Centenary Issue
Common Design Type

Wmk. 314

1963, Nov. 25		Litho.		Perf. 13
1	CD315	15c black & red	.40	.40
2	CD315	1sh25c ultra & red	.85	.85

Arms of
Federation of
South
Arabia — A1

Flag of Federation — A2

Perf. 14½x14

1965, Apr. 1		Photo.		Unwmk.
3	A1	5f blue	.25	.25
4	A1	10f light violet blue	.25	.25
5	A1	15f blue green	.25	.25
6	A1	20f green	.25	.25
7	A1	25f orange brown	.25	.25
8	A1	30f lemon	.30	.25
9	A1	35f red brown	.30	.25
10	A1	50f rose red	.30	.25
11	A1	65f light yellow green	.35	.25
12	A1	75f rose carmine	.40	.25

Perf. 14½

Flag in Black, Yellow, Green and Blue

13	A2	100f reddish brown	.55	.25
14	A2	250f dark blue	5.50	1.75
15	A2	500f dark red	10.00	2.00
16	A2	1d violet	17.50	15.00
		Nos. 3-16 (14)	36.45	21.50

Intl. Cooperation Year Issue
Common Design Type with Coat of Arms Replacing Queen's Portrait

Wmk. 314

1965, Oct. 24		Litho.		Perf. 14½
17	CD318	5f blue grn & claret	.30	.25
18	CD318	65f lt violet & green	.90	.25

Churchill Memorial Issue
Common Design Type with Coat of Arms Replacing Queen's Portrait

Unwmk.

1966, Jan. 24		Photo.		Perf. 14

Design in Black, Gold and Carmine Rose

19	CD319	5f bright blue	.25	.25
20	CD319	10f green	.55	.25
21	CD319	65f brown	1.25	.50
22	CD319	125f violet	1.75	1.50
		Nos. 19-22 (4)	3.80	2.50

World Cup Soccer Issue
Common Design Type with Coat of Arms Replacing Queen's Portrait

1966, July 1		Litho.		Perf. 14
23	CD321	10f multicolored	.40	.25
24	CD321	50f multicolored	1.50	.30

WHO Headquarters Issue
Common Design Type with Coat of Arms Replacing Queen's Portrait

1966, Sept. 20		Litho.		Unwmk.
25	CD322	10f multicolored	.60	.25
26	CD322	75f multicolored	1.50	.45

UNESCO Anniversary Issue
Common Design Type with Coat of Arms Replacing Queen's Portrait

1966, Dec. 15		Litho.		Perf. 14
27	CD323	10f "Education"	.40	.30
28	CD323	65f "Science"	1.50	1.25
29	CD323	125f "Culture"	3.75	4.75
		Nos. 27-29 (3)	5.65	6.30

SOUTHERN NIGERIA

'sə-thərn nī-'jir-ē-ə

LOCATION — In western Africa bordering on the Gulf of Guinea
GOVT. — British Crown Colony and Protectorate
AREA — 90,896 sq. mi.
POP. — 8,590,545
CAPITAL — Lagos

The Protectorate of Southern Nigeria, formed in 1900, absorbed in that year the Niger Coast Protectorate. In 1906 it united with Lagos and became the Colony and Protectorate of Southern Nigeria. An amalgamation was effected in 1914 between Northern and Southern Nigeria to form the Colony and Protectorate of Nigeria. See Nigeria, Northern Nigeria, Niger Coast Protectorate and Lagos.

12 Pence = 1 Shilling
20 Shillings = 1 Pound

Victoria
A1

Edward VII
A2

Wmk. Crown and C A (2)

1901, Mar.		Typo.		Perf. 14
1	A1	½p yel grn & blk	2.00	2.50
a.		½p yel grn & sepia ('02)	2.50	3.00
2	A1	1p car rose & blk	1.75	1.75
a.		1p carmine rose & sepia ('02)	2.50	2.00
3	A1	2p org brn & blk	3.75	4.50
4	A1	4p ol grn & blk	3.25	24.00
5	A1	6p red vio & blk	3.25	8.00
6	A1	1sh blk & gray grn	9.75	30.00
7	A1	2sh6p brn & blk	57.50	92.50
8	A1	5sh yellow & blk	60.00	120.00
9	A1	10sh vio & blk, yel	120.00	225.00
		Nos. 1-9 (9)	261.25	508.25

1903-04

10	A2	½p yel grn & blk	1.10	.35
11	A2	1p car rose & blk	1.50	.80
12	A2	2p org brn & blk	11.00	1.75
13	A2	2½p ultra & blk ('04)	2.25	1.00
14	A2	4p ol grn & blk	3.25	6.25
15	A2	6p red vio & blk	7.00	9.25
16	A2	1sh blk & gray grn	40.00	22.50
17	A2	2sh6p brown & blk	37.50	70.00
18	A2	5sh yellow & blk	90.00	190.00
19	A2	10sh vio & blk, yel	42.50	130.00
20	A2	£1 pur & gray grn	425.00	900.00
		Nos. 10-20 (11)	661.10	1,331.

1904-07

Chalky Paper

Wmk. 3

21	A2	½p yel grn & blk	.75	.25
22	A2	1p carmine & blk	14.00	.25
23	A2	2p org brn & blk	3.00	.50
24	A2	2½p ultra & blk	1.25	1.10

24A	A2	3p vio & org brn ('07)	11.00	1.50
25	A2	4p ol grn & blk ('05)	16.00	29.00
26	A2	6p red vio & blk	14.50	5.00
27	A2	1sh blk & gray grn	3.75	4.00
28	A2	2sh6p brn & blk ('05)	27.50	21.00
29	A2	5sh yellow & blk	47.50	85.00
30	A2	10sh vio & blk, yel ('08)	150.00	210.00
31	A2	£1 pur & gray grn ('05)	325.00	400.00
		Nos. 21-31 (12)	614.25	757.60

#23 and 24 are on ordinary paper, #24A and 25 on chalky, and the other values on both papers.

1907-10

Ordinary Paper

32	A2	½p green ('08)	2.25	.25
33	A2	1p carmine	4.00	.70
34	A2	2p gray	3.00	.80
35	A2	2½p ultra	4.00	4.25

Chalky Paper

36	A2	3p violet, yel	2.25	.35
37	A2	4p scar & blk, yel	2.50	.90
38	A2	6p red vio & dl vio	29.00	3.75
39	A2	1sh black, green	8.00	.50
40	A2	2sh6p car & blk, bl	9.50	1.75
41	A2	5sh scar & grn, yel	45.00	55.00
42	A2	10sh red & grn, grn	90.00	130.00
43	A2	£1 blk & vio, red	250.00	300.00
		Nos. 32-43 (12)	449.50	498.25

1910 Ordinary Paper Redrawn

44	A2	1p carmine	1.10	.25

In the redrawn stamp the "1" of "1d" is not as thick as in No. 33 but the "d" is taller and broader.

King George V — A3

1912

45	A3	½p green	3.00	.25
46	A3	1p carmine	3.00	.25
47	A3	2p gray	1.00	.95
48	A3	2½p ultra	4.00	3.25
49	A3	3p violet, yel	1.25	.35
50	A3	4p scar & blk, yel	1.60	2.40
51	A3	6p red vio & dl vio	2.50	1.50
52	A3	1sh black, green	3.50	1.00
53	A3	2sh6p red & blk, bl	10.00	42.50
54	A3	5sh red & grn, yel	26.00	87.50
55	A3	10sh red & grn, grn	60.00	110.00
56	A3	£1 blk & vio, red	225.00	275.00
		Nos. 45-56 (12)	340.85	524.95

Stamps of Southern Nigeria were replaced in 1914 by those of Nigeria.

SOUTHERN RHODESIA

'sə-thərn rō-'dē-zh,ē-ə

LOCATION — Southeastern Africa between Northern Rhodesia and Mozambique
GOVT. — British Colony
AREA — 150,333 sq. mi.
POP. — 4,010,000 (est. 1963)
CAPITAL — Salisbury

Prior to 1923 this territory was administered by the British South Africa Company. The colony was created in that year by the British Government at the request of the inhabitants. In 1953, Southern Rhodesia joined Northern Rhodesia and Nyasaland to form the Federation of Rhodesia and Nyasaland. When the Federation dissolved at the end of 1963, Southern Rhodesia again

---

became an internally self-governing colony. See Rhodesia and Northern Rhodesia.

12 Pence = 1 Shilling
20 Shillings = 1 Pound

Catalogue values for unused stamps in this country are for Never Hinged items, beginning with Scott 56 in the regular postage section and Scott J1 in the postage due section.

King George V — A1

1924-30 Unwmk. Engr. Perf. 14

1	A1	½p dark green	5.00	.25
a.		Vert. pair, imperf. btwn.	950.00	1,100.
b.		Horiz. pair, imperf. btwn.	950.00	1,100.
c.		Perf. pair, imperf. vert.	1,100.	
2	A1	1p scarlet	2.00	.25
a.		Horiz. pair, imperf. btwn.	850.00	950.00
b.		Perf. 12½ (coil) ('30)	3.25	92.50
c.		Vert. pair, imperf. btwn.	1,500.	
d.		Vert. pair, imperf. horiz.	950.00	
3	A1	1½p bister brown	2.50	.90
a.		Horiz. pair, imperf. btwn.	11,000.	
b.		Vert. pair, imperf. btwn.	6,500.	
4	A1	2p vio blk & blk	4.50	1.50
a.		Horiz. pair, imperf. btwn.	13,000.	
5	A1	3p deep blue	3.50	4.00
6	A1	4p org red & blk	3.25	3.25
7	A1	6p lilac & blk	2.50	6.00
a.		Horiz. pair, imperf. btwn.	40,000.	
8	A1	8p gray grn & vio	12.50	50.00
9	A1	10p rose red & bl	16.00	57.50
10	A1	1sh turq bl & blk	6.00	9.00
11	A1	1sh6p yellow & blk	22.50	37.50
12	A1	2sh brown & blk	20.00	20.00
13	A1	2sh6p blk brn & bl	37.50	70.00
14	A1	5sh bl grn & blk	75.00	175.00
		Nos. 1-14 (14)	212.75	435.15

Values for imperf between pairs are for stamps from the same pane. Stamps separated by wide margins are cross-gutter pairs and sell for much lower prices.

George V
A2

Victoria Falls
A3

1931-37 Perf. 11½, 14 (1p)

16	A2	½p dp green ('33)	.75	.25
a.		Bklt. pane of 8 ('32)	150.00	
b.		Perf. 12	1.50	1.10
c.		Perf. 14 ('35)	1.90	.35
17	A2	1p scarlet ('35)	.60	.25
a.		Bklt. pane of 6 ('32)	150.00	
b.		Perf. 11½ ('33)	2.25	.25
c.		Perf. 12	1.10	.80
18	A2	1½p dp brown ('32)	3.00	.90
a.		Bklt. pane of 6 ('32)	600.00	
b.		Perf. 11½ ('33)	62.50	47.50

Typo. Perf. 14½x14

19	A3	2p blk brn & blk	5.50	1.75
20	A3	3p dark blue	11.50	12.50

Perf. 12, 11½ (2sh6p)

Engr.

21	A2	4p org red & blk	1.50	1.75
a.		Perf. 14 ('37)	37.50	60.00
b.		Perf. 11½ ('35)	20.00	5.75
22	A2	6p rose lilac & blk	2.50	3.50
a.		Perf. 14 ('37)	8.00	1.00
b.		Perf. 11½ ('33)	17.50	1.75
23	A2	8p green & violet	2.00	3.75
a.		Perf. 11½ ('34)	20.00	37.50
24	A2	9p gray grn & ver ('34)	7.25	10.50
25	A2	10p car & ultra	8.50	2.75
a.		Perf. 11½ ('33)	7.50	15.00
26	A2	1sh turq bl & blk	2.25	3.00
a.		Perf. 11½ ('36)	125.00	160.00
b.		Perf. 14 ('37)	250.00	160.00
27	A2	1sh6p ocher & blk	12.00	22.50
a.		Perf. 11½ ('36)	60.00	130.00
28	A2	2sh dk brn & blk	25.00	7.50
a.		Perf. 11½ ('33)	42.50	42.50
29	A2	2sh6p ol brn & ultra ('33)	35.00	35.00
a.		Perf. 12	40.00	42.50
30	A2	5sh bl grn & ultra	60.00	57.50
		Nos. 16-30 (15)	177.35	163.40

Victoria Falls — A4

1932, May   *Perf. 12½*
31	A4	2p dark brn & grn	7.00	1.25
32	A4	3p dark blue	7.00	2.10
a.		Vert. pair, imperf. horiz.	10,000.	13,000.
b.		Vert. pair, imperf. btwn.	28,000.	
		Set, never hinged	22.50	

See Nos. 37-37A.

Silver Jubilee Issue

Victoria Falls and George V A5

1935, May 6   *Perf. 11x12*
33	A5	1p car rose & olive	4.25	3.25
34	A5	2p blk brn & lt grn	7.50	8.50
35	A5	3p blue & violet	6.25	11.00
36	A5	6p dp violet & blk	11.00	22.50
		Nos. 33-36 (4)	29.00	45.25
		Set, never hinged	42.50	

25th anniv. of the reign of George V.

"Postage and Revenue" A6

1935-41   *Perf. 14*
37	A6	2p dk brn & grn ('41)	1.75	.25
b.		Perf. 12½	5.00	16.00
37A	A6	3p deep blue ('38)	2.75	1.25
		Set, never hinged	17.00	

Queen Elizabeth, George VI — A7

1937, May 12   *Perf. 12½*
38	A7	1p carmine & gray grn	.45	1.00
39	A7	2p brown & green	.45	1.75
40	A7	3p lt blue & violet	2.00	9.50
41	A7	6p red violet & blk	1.10	4.00
		Nos. 38-41 (4)	4.00	16.25
		Set, never hinged	7.50	

Coronation of George VI & Elizabeth.

King George VI — A8

1937, Nov. 25   *Perf. 14*
42	A8	½p yellow green	.40	.25
43	A8	1p red	.40	.25
44	A8	1½p red brown	.75	.35
45	A8	4p orange red	1.00	.25
46	A8	6p dark gray	1.00	.60
47	A8	8p blue green	1.50	4.00
48	A8	9p blue	1.25	1.10
49	A8	10p violet	1.75	3.50
50	A8	1sh green & blk	1.50	.25
51	A8	1sh6p ocher & blk	9.50	3.00
52	A8	2sh brown & blk	16.00	.70
53	A8	2sh6p violet & blue	8.00	8.00
54	A8	5sh green & blue	15.00	3.50
		Nos. 42-54 (13)	58.05	25.75
		Set, never hinged	85.00	

> Catalogue values for unused stamps in this section, from this point to the end of the section, are for Never Hinged items.

Seal of British South Africa Co. — A9

Fort Salisbury, 1890 — A10

Cecil John Rhodes — A11

Pioneer Fort and Mail Coach A12

Rhodes Makes Peace, 1896 — A13

Victoria Falls Bridge — A14

Sir Charles Coghlan — A15

Queen Victoria, George VI, Lobengula's Kraal and Government House A16

Unwmk.
1940, June 3   Engr.   *Perf. 14*
56	A9	½p dp grn & dull vio	.25	.65
57	A10	1p red & vio blue	.25	.25
58	A11	1½p cop brn & blk	.25	.80
59	A12	2p pur & brt grn	.50	.40
60	A13	3p dk blue & blk	.80	1.00
61	A14	4p brn & bl grn	2.00	3.00
62	A15	6p sepia & dull grn	1.50	3.00
63	A16	1sh dk bl & brt grn	1.50	2.00
		Nos. 56-63 (8)	7.05	11.10

50th anniv. of the founding of Southern Rhodesia by Cecil John Rhodes.

Pioneer — A17

1943, Nov. 1   Photo.   Wmk. 201
64	A17	2p Prus grn & choc	.35	.50

50th anniv. of Matabeleland under British control.

Princess Elizabeth and Princess Margaret Rose A18

King George VI and Queen Elizabeth A19

Unwmk.
1947, Apr. 1   Engr.   *Perf. 14*
65	A18	½p dk green & blk	.30	.60
66	A19	1p carmine & blk	.30	.60

Visit of the British Royal Family, Apr., 1947.

Victory Issue

Queen Elizabeth A20

George VI A21

Princess Elizabeth A22

Princess Margaret Rose A23

1947, May 8
67	A20	1p deep carmine	.25	.25
68	A21	2p slate black	.25	.25
69	A22	3p deep blue	.60	.50
70	A23	6p red orange	.30	.75
		Nos. 67-70 (4)	1.40	1.75

Victory of the Allied Nations in WW II.

Common Design Types pictured following the introduction.

UPU Issue
Common Design Types
Engr.; Name Typo.
1949, Oct. 10   Wmk. 4   *Perf. 11x11½*
71	CD307	2p slate black	.70	.50
72	CD308	3p slate blue	1.25	1.75

75th anniv. of the UPU.

Queen Victoria and King George VI A24

Unwmk.
1950, Sept. 12   Engr.   *Perf. 14*
73	A24	2p choc & blue grn	.90	1.10

60th anniversary of Rhodesia.

Hospital, Doctor and Natives A25

Designs: 1p, African Scene. 2p, Native Houses, Modern City and Cecil Rhodes. 4½p, Dam and Natives. 1sh, Transportation.

1953, Apr. 15
74	A25	½p dk brown & blue	.25	.40
75	A25	1p blue grn & fawn	.25	.25
76	A25	2p vio & dk bl grn	.35	.25
77	A25	4½p dk bl & bl grn	1.50	2.75
78	A25	1sh chestnut & blk	3.25	1.75
		Nos. 74-78 (5)	5.60	5.40

#77 is inscribed Matabeleland Diamond Jubilee.

Type of Nyasaland Prot., 1953
1953, May 30   *Perf. 14x13½*
79	A17	6p purple	.35	.35

Nos. 74-79 were issued to commemorate the Central African Cecil Rhodes Centenary Exhibition.

Coronation Issue

Elizabeth II — A26

1953, June 1   *Perf. 12x12½*
80	A26	2sh6p cerise	7.25	7.25

Sable Antelope A27

Rhodes' Grave A28

Flame Lily — A29

Designs: 1p, Tobacco planter. 3p, Farm Worker. 4½p, Victoria Falls. 6p, Baobab tree. 9p, Lion. 1sh, Zimbabwe ruins. 2sh, Birchenough Bridge. 2sh6p, Kariba Gorge. 5sh, Basket maker. 10sh, Balancing rocks. £1, Arms.

Perf. 14x13½, 13½x14
1953, Aug. 31
Portrait in Various Positions
81	A27	½p rose lake & dk ol grn	.35	.45
82	A27	1p choc & grn	.35	.25
83	A28	2p rose vio & org brn	.35	.25

Size: 28x22½mm
84	A29	3p car & sep	.70	1.50
85	A29	4p gray, brn, car & grn	3.50	.40
86	A29	4½p ultra & blk	3.00	4.50
87	A28	6p aqua & olive	4.25	1.50
88	A29	9p org brn & dp bl	4.00	4.00
89	A29	1sh grnsh bl & rose vio	1.75	.25
90	A29	2sh red & rose vio	15.00	6.50
91	A29	2sh6p org brn & ol grn	8.00	8.00
92	A28	5s dk grn & org brn	11.00	9.00

Size: 37x27mm

93	A29	10sh ol grn & red brn		19.00	27.50
94	A29	£1 dk gray & car		25.00	32.50
		Nos. 81-94 (14)		96.25	96.60

Ansellia Orchid — A30

1964, Feb. 19　Photo.　Perf. 14½
Size: 23x19mm

95	A30	½p Corn	.25	2.00
96	A30	1p Cape buffalo	.25	.25
a.		Purple omitted	3,250.	
97	A30	2p Tobacco	.60	.25
98	A30	3p Kudu	.25	.25
99	A30	4p Oranges	.30	.25

Perf. 13½x13
Size: 27x23mm

100	A30	6p Flame lily	.50	.25
101	A30	9p shown	2.75	1.25
102	A30	1sh Emeralds	3.75	.25
a.		Green omitted	4,000.	
103	A30	1sh3p Aloe	3.00	.25
104	A30	2sh Lake Kyle	2.50	2.50
105	A30	2sh6p Tiger fish	4.00	1.00
a.		Red omitted	4,500.	
b.		Ultra omitted	13,000.	

Perf. 14½x14
Size: 32x27mm

106	A30	5sh Cattle	4.00	2.75
107	A30	10sh Guinea fowl	11.50	8.50
108	A30	£1 Arms	14.00	18.00
		Nos. 95-108 (14)	47.65	37.75

#95-108 with overprint "Independence 11th November 1965" are listed as Rhodesia #208-221.

Stamps of Southern Rhodesia were replaced in 1965 by those of Rhodesia (formerly Southern Rhodesia).

POSTAGE DUE STAMPS

Catalogue values for unused stamps in this section are for Never Hinged items.

Great Britain Postage Due Stamps of 1938-51 Overprinted in Black

1951　Wmk. 251　Perf. 14x14½

J1	D1	½p emerald	3.75	17.50
J2	D1	1p violet blue	3.50	2.75
J3	D1	2p black brown	3.00	2.25
J4	D1	3p violet	3.25	3.00
J5	D1	4p brt blue	2.25	4.00
		4p slate green	275.00	600.00
J6	D1	1sh blue	3.00	4.50
		Nos. J1-J6 (6)	18.75	34.00

SOUTH GEORGIA

ˈsauth ˈjor-jə

LOCATION — Island in South Atlantic Ocean, 1,100 mi. east of Tierra del Fuego

GOVT. — Dependency of Falkland Islands

AREA — 1,450 sq. mi.

POP. — Military and biological staff only.

CAPITAL — Grytviken Harbor (military garrison)

South Georgia remained a dependency of the Falkland Islands in 1962 when three other dependencies became Antarctic Territory, a separate colony. In 1985 South Georgia and the

---

South Sandwich Islands became a separate colony. See Falkland Islands Dependencies Nos. 3L1-3L8.

12 Pence = 1 Shilling
20 Shillings = 1 Pound
100 Pence = 1 Pound (1971)

Catalogue values for all unused stamps in this country are for Never Hinged items.

Reindeer A1

Sperm Whale — A2

Designs: 1p, South Sandwich Islands map. 2½p, Penguins. 3p, Fur seals. 4p, Finback whale and ship. 5½p, Elephant seals. 6p, Sooty albatross. 9p, Whaling ship. 1sh, Leopard seal. 2sh, Shackleton's cross. 2sh6p, Wandering albatross. 5sh, Elephant and fur seals. 10sh, Plankton and krill (shrimp). No. 15, Blue whale. No. 16, King penguins.

Wmk. 314 Upright

1963-69		Engr.	Perf. 15	
1	A1	½p dull red	.55	1.00
a.		Perf. 14x15 ('67)	1.00	1.60
b.		Watermark sideways ('70)	1.60	4.00
2	A2	1p violet blue	1.75	1.25
3	A2	2p blue green	1.40	1.00
4	A1	2½p black	6.00	2.25
5	A2	3p olive	3.00	.35
6	A1	4p green	5.50	.75
7	A1	5½p dull violet	2.75	.40
8	A2	6p orange	.80	.45
9	A2	9p blue	7.50	1.75
10	A1	1sh lilac	.90	.30
11	A1	2sh cit & lt blue	27.50	6.00
12	A1	2sh6p blue	25.00	4.50
13	A1	5sh ocher	22.00	4.50
14	A2	10sh rose claret	40.00	12.50
15	A1	£1 ultra	110.00	62.50
16	A2	£1 slate green	12.00	17.50
		Nos. 1-16 (16)	266.65	117.00
		Set, hinged	135.00	

Issued: No. 16, 12/1/69; others 7/10/63.

Stamps and Type of 1963 Surcharged with New Value (Decimal Currency) and 3 Bars

Wmk. 314 Upright; Sideways on ½p

1971-72			Perf. 15	
17	A1	½p on ½p dull red	1.25	.75
a.		Wmk. upright ('73)	4.00	3.50
18	A2	1p on 1p vio blue	2.00	.90
a.		Wmk. sideways ('76)	.75	3.25
19	A1	1½p on 5½p dull vio	1.50	1.50
20	A2	2p on 2p blue grn	.90	.50
21	A1	2½p on 2½p black	2.50	.70
22	A2	3p on 3p olive	1.25	.75
23	A1	4p on 4p green	1.25	.90
24	A2	5p on 6p orange	2.25	.90
25	A1	6p on 9p blue	1.75	.55
26	A1	7½p on 1sh lilac	2.50	1.50
27	A1	10p on 2sh cit & lt bl	35.00	13.00
28	A1	15p on 2sh6p blue	13.00	9.00
29	A1	25p on 5sh ocher	10.00	7.50
30	A2	50p on 10sh rose claret, glazed paper ('72)	8.50	15.00
a.		Wmk. sideways ('76)	17.50	30.00
c.		Ordinary paper	40.00	20.00
		Nos. 17-30 (14)	83.65	53.45

Two types of surcharge are found on ½p, 1p, 1½p and 50p.
Issued: Nos. 17-29, 30b, 2/15/71. No. 30, 12/1/72. No. 30a, 3/9/76.

Wmk. 373 Sideways; Upright on 3p, 50p; Inverted on 1p, 5p

1977				
17b	A1	½p on ½p dull red	1.75	2.00
18b	A2	1p on 1p vio blue	1.00	2.00
19b	A1	1½p on 5½p dl vio	1.25	2.00
21b	A1	2½p on 2½p black	14.00	3.25
22b	A2	3p on 3p olive	7.00	3.25
23b	A1	4p on 4p green	20.00	14.00

24b	A2	5p on 6p orange	4.00	2.75
26b	A1	7½p on 1sh lilac	2.00	5.00
27b	A1	10p on 2sh cit & lt bl	1.50	6.50
28b	A1	15p on 2sh6p blue	2.75	5.50
29b	A1	25p on 5sh ocher	2.00	6.00
30b	A2	50p on 10sh lil rosc ('70)	2.00	6.00
		Nos. 17b-30b (12)	59.25	58.25

Ernest Shackleton and "Quest" — A3

1½p, "Endurance" in ice of Weddell Sea. 5p, Launching of sailboat "James Caird." 10p, Route of "James Caird" to South Georgia.

1972, Jan. 5　Litho.　Perf. 13½

31	A3	1½p vio bl, blk & yel	1.25	1.50
32	A3	5p bl grn, blk & yel	1.50	1.75
33	A3	10p lt blue & blk	1.75	2.00
34	A3	20p multicolored	2.25	2.25
		Nos. 31-34 (4)	6.75	7.50

Sir Ernest Shackleton (1874-1922), explorer of Antarctica.

Common Design Types pictured following the introduction.

Silver Wedding Issue, 1972
Common Design Type

Design: Queen Elizabeth II, Prince Philip, elephant seal and king penguins.

1972, Nov. 20　Photo.　Perf. 14x14½

35	CD324	5p slate grn & multi	.50	.50
36	CD324	10p violet & multi	.90	.90

Princess Anne's Wedding Issue
Common Design Type

1973, Dec. 1　Litho.　Perf. 14

37	CD325	5p citron & multi	.25	.25
38	CD325	15p slate & multi	.50	.50

Churchill, Parliament and Big Ben — A4

Design: 25p, Churchill and battleship.

1974, Dec. 14　Litho.　Perf. 14½

39	A4	15p vio blue & multi	1.25	1.00
40	A4	25p orange & multi	2.00	1.25
a.		Souvenir sheet of 2, #39-40	7.50	7.50

Sir Winston Churchill (1874-1965).

Capt. James Cook — A5

Cook's "Possession" — A6

Design: 16p, Possession Bay.

1975, Apr. 26　Wmk. 314

41	A5	2p multicolored	2.25	1.25
42	A6	8p multicolored	3.50	1.75
43	A6	16p multicolored	3.75	2.50
		Nos. 41-43 (3)	9.50	5.50

Bicentenary of Capt. Cook's discovery of South Georgia.

"Discovery" and Biological Laboratory — A7

Designs: 8p, "William Scoresby" and Nansen-Pettersson water sampling bottles. 11p, "Discovery II" and plankton net. 25p, Biological station and krill (shrimp).

Wmk. 373

1976, Dec. 21　Litho.　Perf. 14

44	A7	2p multicolored	1.50	.65
45	A7	8p multicolored	1.75	1.10
46	A7	11p multicolored	2.00	1.25
47	A7	25p multicolored	3.25	1.50
		Nos. 44-47 (4)	8.50	4.50

50th anniversary of the biological investigations of the "Discovery."

Queen with Regalia and Westminster Abbey — A8

6p, Prince Philip visiting Shackleton Memorial, 1957. 33p, Queen in procession after coronation.

1977, Feb. 7　Perf. 13½x14

48	A8	6p multicolored	.25	.25
49	A8	11p multicolored	.40	.30
50	A8	33p multicolored	.90	.90
		Nos. 48-50 (3)	1.55	1.45

25th anniv. of the reign of Elizabeth II.

Elizabeth II Coronation Anniversary Issue
Common Design Types
Souvenir Sheet
Unwmk.

1978, June 2　Litho.　Perf. 15

51		Sheet of 6	3.00	3.00
a.	CD326	25p Panther of Henry VI	.80	.65
b.	CD327	25p Elizabeth II	.80	.65
c.	CD328	25p Fur seal	.80	.65

No. 51 contains 2 se-tenant strips of Nos. 51a-51c, separated by horizontal gutter with commemorative and descriptive inscriptions and showing central part of coronation procession with coach.

Resolution A9

Cook's voyages: 6p, Map of South Georgia and South Sandwich Islands with Cook's route. 11p, King penguin, drawing by Forster. 25p, Cook after Flaxman/Wedgwood medallion.

1979, Feb. 14　Litho.　Perf. 11

52	A9	3p multicolored	1.50	1.00
53	A9	6p multicolored	1.50	.90
54	A9	11p multicolored	2.00	1.25

Lithographed; Embossed

55	A9	25p multicolored	2.75 1.75
		Nos. 52-55 (4)	7.75 4.90

Capt. Cook's voyages.

SOUTH GEORGIA and SOUTH SANDWICH ISLANDS
Queen Elizabeth II 60th Birthday
Common Design Type

Designs: 10p, With King George and Queen Mary at christening of Prince Charles, 1948. 24p, Engagement of Prince Charles and Lady Diana, Buckingham Palace Music Room, 1981. 29p, Order of the British Empire, service at St. Paul's Cathedral, London, 1974. 45p, Banquet for Canadian Prime Minister Trudeau during the 1976 Olympics. 58p, Visiting Crown Agents' offices, 1983.

1986, Apr. 21   Wmk. 384   Perf. 14½

101	CD337	10p multicolored	.40 .40
102	CD337	24p multicolored	.60 .60
103	CD337	29p multicolored	.70 .70
104	CD337	45p multicolored	.85 .85
105	CD337	58p multicolored	1.00 1.00
		Nos. 101-105 (5)	3.55 3.55

Wedding of Prince Andrew and Sarah Ferguson — A12

1986, Nov. 10   Litho.   Perf. 14½

106	A12	17p Couple at Ascot	.85 1.10
107	A12	22p Wedding	.95 1.40
108	A12	29p Andrew, helicopter	1.75 1.75
		Nos. 106-108 (3)	3.55 4.25

Birds A13

1987, Apr. 24   Litho.   Wmk. 384

109	A13	1p Dominican gull	1.50 1.75
110	A13	2p Blue-eyed cormorant	1.75 2.00
111	A13	3p Wattled sheathbill	2.25 2.25
112	A13	4p Brown skua	2.00 2.25
113	A13	5p Cape pigeon	2.00 2.25
114	A13	6p South Georgia diving petrel	2.00 2.25
115	A13	7p South Georgia pipit	2.25 2.25
116	A13	8p South Georgia pintail	2.25 2.25
117	A13	9p Fairy prion	2.25 2.25
118	A13	10p Chinstrap penguin	2.50 2.25
119	A13	20p Macaroni penguin	2.75 2.50
120	A13	25p Light-mantled sooty albatross	2.75 2.50
121	A13	50p Southern giant petrel	3.00 2.75
122	A13	£1 Wandering albatross	3.50 4.00
123	A13	£3 King penguin	7.50 8.00
		Nos. 109-123 (15)	40.25 41.50

3, 4, 7, 8, 20, 25, 50p and £3 vert.

Intl. Geophysical Year, 30th Anniv. — A14

1987, Dec. 5   Litho.   Perf. 14½

124	A14	24p shown	.90 .65
125	A14	29p Grytviken Whaling Station	1.00 .75
126	A14	58p Glaciologist	1.75 1.25
		Nos. 124-126 (3)	3.65 2.65

Sea Shells A15

1988, Feb. 26   Wmk. 384   Perf. 14½

127	A15	10p Gaimardia trapesina	.75 .35
128	A15	24p Margarella tropidophoroides	1.50 .65
129	A15	29p Trophon scotianus	1.75 .70
130	A15	58p Chlanidota densesculpta	3.00 1.50
		Nos. 127-130 (4)	7.00 3.20

Lloyds of London, 300th Anniv.
Common Design Type

10p, Queen Mother at the official opening of the Lloyds Building, Lime Street, 1957. 24p, Lindblad Explorer, horiz. 29p, Leith Harbor whaling station, horiz. 58p, Whale oil tanker Horatio on fire.

1988, Sept. 17   Perf. 14

131	CD341	10p multicolored	.80 .40
132	CD341	24p multicolored	1.25 .80
133	CD341	29p multicolored	1.75 .90
134	CD341	58p multicolored	2.50 1.60
		Nos. 131-134 (4)	6.30 3.70

Glacier Formations — A16

1989, July 31

135	A16	10p Glacier headwall	.70 .50
136	A16	24p Accumulation area	1.10 .90
137	A16	29p Ablation area	1.25 1.00
138	A16	58p Calving front	2.50 1.50
		Nos. 135-138 (4)	5.55 3.90

Combined Services Expedition, 1964-65 A17

1989, Nov. 28   Perf. 14x14½

139	A17	10p "Last ordeal" of the trek	.70 .50
140	A17	24p Survey of Royal Bay	1.10 .90
141	A17	29p HMS *Protector*	1.25 1.00
142	A17	58p 1st Ascent of Mt. Paget	2.50 1.50
		Nos. 139-142 (4)	5.55 3.90

Queen Mother, 90th Birthday
Common Design Types

Designs: 26p, Queen Mother. £1, King, Queen & Air Raid Wardens, 1940.

Perf. 14x15

1990, Sept. 15   Wmk. 384

143	CD343	26p multicolored	1.00 1.00

Perf. 14½

144	CD344	£1 blue & black	4.75 4.75

Shipwrecks A18

Wmk. 384

1990, Dec. 22   Litho.   Perf. 14

145	A18	12p Brutus	.65 .50
146	A18	26p Bayard	1.25 1.00
147	A18	31p Karrakatta	1.50 1.10
148	A18	62p Louise	2.75 2.00
		Nos. 145-148 (4)	6.15 4.60

Elizabeth & Philip, Birthdays
Common Design Types

1991, July 2   Perf. 14½

149	CD345	31p multicolored	2.75 2.75
150	CD346	31p multicolored	2.75 2.75
a.		Pair, #149-150 + label	7.00 7.00

No. 150a exists with two different labels.

Elephant Seals A19

1991, Nov. 2   Wmk. 373   Perf. 14

151	A19	12p Two bulls	.85 .85
152	A19	26p One bull	1.50 1.50
153	A19	29p Using sand as sunscreen	1.75 1.75
154	A19	31p Bull, close up	1.75 1.75
155	A19	34p Harem on beach	2.00 2.00
156	A19	62p Cow and pup	3.25 2.50
		Nos. 151-156 (6)	11.10 10.35

Queen Elizabeth II's Accession to the Throne, 40th Anniv.
Common Design Type

1992, Feb. 6

157	CD349	7p multicolored	.50 .45
158	CD349	14p multicolored	.75 .70
159	CD349	29p multicolored	1.10 1.10
160	CD349	34p multicolored	1.25 1.25
161	CD349	68p multicolored	2.25 2.25
		Nos. 157-161 (5)	5.85 5.75

South Georgia Teal A20

1992, Mar. 22   Wmk. 384

162	A20	2p Adult, young	.75 .40
163	A20	6p Adult, nest of eggs	1.00 .70
164	A20	12p Four swimming	1.60 1.60
165	A20	20p Adult, two chicks	2.10 2.00
		Nos. 162-165 (4)	5.45 4.70

World Wildlife Fund.

South Georgia Whaling Museum A21

Designs: 15p, Abandoned factory, Grytviken. 31p, Whaler's lighter, bones. 36p, King Edward Cove. 72p, Museum Building.

Wmk. 373

1993, June 29   Litho.   Perf. 13½

166-169	A21	Set of 4	8.50 8.50

Macaroni Penguins A22

16p, Swimming underwater. 34p, Part of rookery. 39p, Two juveniles. 78p, Two adults.

Perf. 14x14½

1993, Dec. 10   Litho.   Wmk. 373

170-173	A22	Set of 4	8.25 8.25

Ovptd. with Hong Kong '94 Emblem

1994, Feb. 18

174-177	A22	Set of 4	8.25 8.25

Whales and Dolphins A23

Designs: 1p, Hourglass dolphin. 2p, Southern right whale dolphin. 5p, Long-finned pilot whale. 8p, Southern bottlenose whale. 9p, Killer whale. 10p, Minke whale. 20p, Sei whale. 25p, Humpback whale. 50p, Southern right whale. £1, Sperm whale. £3, Fin whale. £5, Blue whale.

Wmk. 373

1994, Jan. 24   Litho.   Perf. 14

178	A23	1p multicolored	1.50 1.10
179	A23	2p multicolored	2.00 1.75
180	A23	5p multicolored	2.50 2.00
181	A23	8p multicolored	2.75 2.00
182	A23	9p multicolored	2.75 2.00
183	A23	10p multicolored	2.75 2.00
184	A23	20p multicolored	4.00 3.00
185	A23	25p multicolored	4.00 3.00
186	A23	50p multicolored	5.00 3.25
187	A23	£1 multicolored	6.25 3.75
188	A23	£3 multicolored	11.50 7.00
189	A23	£5 multicolored	18.50 11.00
		Nos. 178-189 (12)	63.50 41.85

Native Wildlife A24

Wmk. 384

1994, Sept. 28   Litho.   Perf. 14

190	A24	17p Bull elephant seals	1.00 1.00
191	A24	35p Fur seal, vert.	2.00 2.00
192	A24	40p Gray-headed albatrosses	2.25 2.25
193	A24	65p King penguins, vert.	3.25 3.25
		Nos. 190-193 (4)	8.50 8.50

Capt. C. A. Larsen's First Voyage to South Georgia A25

1994, Dec. 1

194	A25	17p Map of Jason Harbor	.75 .75
195	A25	35p Castor, 1886	1.75 1.75
196	A25	40p Hertha, 1884	2.00 2.00
197	A25	65p Jason, 1881	3.25 3.25
		Nos. 194-197 (4)	7.75 7.75

End of World War II, 50th Anniv.
Common Design Types

#198, HMS Queen of Bermuda moored at Leith Harbor. #199, 4-inch gun, Hansen Point, four men of Norwegian Defense Force. £1, Reverse of War Medal 1939-45.

Wmk. 384

1995, May 8   Litho.   Perf. 14

198	CD351	50p multicolored	3.50 3.50
199	CD351	50p multicolored	3.50 3.50
a.		Pair, #198-199	7.75 7.75

Souvenir Sheet
Wmk. 373

200	CD352	£1 multicolored	7.00 7.00

No. 199a is a continuous design.

Yachts — A26

Wmk. 373
1995, Nov. 16		**Litho.**	**Perf. 14½**	
201	A26	35p Damien II	1.75	1.75
202	A26	40p Curlew	2.25	2.25
203	A26	76p Mischief	3.75	3.75
	Nos. 201-203 (3)		7.75	7.75

Sir Ernest Shackleton's King Haakon Bay-Stromness Trek, 80th Anniv. — A27

Designs: 15p, Shackleton, Ridge 2493 Point of No Return. 20p, Frank Worsley, King Haakon Bay from Shackleton Gap. 30p, Map of Shackleton's route. 65p, Tom Crean, Manager's Villa, Stromness Whaling Station.

Wmk. 384
1996, May 20		**Litho.**	**Perf. 14**	
204	A27	15p multicolored	.85	.85
205	A27	20p multicolored	1.50	1.50
206	A27	30p multicolored	2.00	2.00
207	A27	65p multicolored	3.75	3.75
	Nos. 204-207 (4)		8.10	8.10

Chinstrap Penguins — A28

Perf. 14½x14
1996, Nov. 8		**Litho.**	**Wmk. 373**	
208	A28	17p Swimming	1.00	1.00
209	A28	35p Male, female	1.50	1.50
210	A28	40p Feeding chicks	2.00	2.00
211	A28	76p Feeding on krill	4.00	4.00
a.	Souvenir sheet of 1, perf. 14x14½		4.75	4.75
	Nos. 208-211 (4)		8.50	8.50

Return of Hong Kong to China (#211a).

Queen Elizabeth and Prince Philip, 50th Wedding Anniv. — A29

#212, Queen. #213, Prince driving team of horses. #214, Queen looking at horses. #215, Prince. #216, Princess Anne on horseback, Queen. #217, Prince, child on horseback. £1.50, Queen, Prince in open carriage, horiz.

Perf. 14½x14
1997, July 10		**Litho.**	**Wmk. 384**	
212		15p multicolored	.90	.90
213		15p multicolored	.90	.90
a.	A29	Pair, #212-213	2.25	2.25
214		17p multicolored	1.00	1.00
215		17p multicolored	1.00	1.00
a.	A29	Pair, #214-215	2.75	2.75
216		40p multicolored	2.50	2.50
217		40p multicolored	2.50	2.50
a.	A29	Pair, #216-217	6.00	6.00
	Nos. 212-217 (6)		8.80	8.80

Souvenir Sheet
218	A29	£1.50 multicolored	8.50	8.50

Flora and Fauna A30

---

a, Reindeer. b, Antarctic tern. c, Gray-headed albatross. d, King penguin. e, Prickly burr. f, Fur seal.

Perf. 14½x14
1998, Mar. 16		**Litho.**	**Wmk. 373**	
219	A30	35p Sheet of 6, #a.-f.	10.00	10.00

Diana, Princess of Wales (1961-97)
Common Design Type

Designs: a, Looking left. b, In white evening dress. c, In red dress. d, In white.

1998, Mar. 31				
220	CD355	35p Sheet of 4, #a.-d.	5.25	5.25

No. 220 sold for £1.40 + 20p, with surtax and 50% of the profits from the issue being donated to the Princess Diana Memorial Fund.

Tourism A31

Designs: 30p, MS Explorer. 35p, Wandering albatross. 40p, Elephant seal. 65p, Post Office, King Edward Point.

Wmk. 373
1998, Sept. 28		**Litho.**	**Perf. 14½**	
221	A31	30p multicolored	2.50	1.50
222	A31	35p multicolored	2.75	1.75
223	A31	40p multicolored	3.00	2.00
224	A31	65p multicolored	3.75	3.25
	Nos. 221-224 (4)		12.00	8.50

Island Views A32

Designs: 9p, Grytviken and Sugartop Mountain. 17p, Old sealing ships, Grytviken. 35p, King Edward Point. 40p, Arrival at South Georgia. 65p, Church, Grytviken.

Wmk. 384
1999, Jan. 4		**Litho.**	**Perf. 14**	
225	A32	9p multicolored	2.00	.85
226	A32	17p multicolored	2.75	1.25
227	A32	35p multicolored	4.00	1.75
228	A32	40p multicolored	4.25	1.75
229	A32	65p multicolored	5.25	2.00
	Nos. 225-229 (5)		18.25	7.60

Souvenir Sheet

Capt. James Cook's Ship HMS Resolution, 1773 — A33

1999, Mar. 5			**Perf. 13½**	
230	A33	£1.50 multicolored	18.50	18.50

Australia '99, World Stamp Expo.

Queen Mother's Century
Common Design Type

Queen Mother: 25p, At air raid shelter, 1940. 30p, With Prince Edward, Lady Sarah Armstrong-Jones, Viscount Linley, 70th birthday. 35p, With Prince William, 94th birthday. 40p, As colonel-in-chief of Royal Anglian Regiment. £1, Funeral procession for Queen Victoria, portrait of Victoria.

Wmk. 384
1999, Aug. 18		**Litho.**	**Perf. 13½**	
231	CD358	25p multicolored	3.00	2.75
232	CD358	30p black	3.25	3.50
233	CD358	35p multicolored	4.25	4.00
234	CD358	40p multicolored	4.75	4.50
	Nos. 231-234 (4)		15.25	14.75

Souvenir Sheet
235	CD358	£1 black	15.00	15.00

Birds — A34

Designs: 1p, Chinstrap penguin, vert. 2p, White chinned petrel. 5p, Gray backed storm petrel, vert. 10p, South Georgia pipit, vert. 11p, Gray headed albatross. 30p, Blue petrel, vert. 35p, Black browed albatross. 40p, South Georgia diving petrel. 50p, Macaroni penguin, vert. £1, Light mantled sooty albatross. £3, South Georgia pintail. £5, King penguin, vert.

Wmk. 384
1999, Nov. 15		**Litho.**	**Perf. 14**	
236	A34	1p multicolored	1.00	1.40
237	A34	2p multicolored	1.25	1.40
238	A34	5p multicolored	1.50	1.50
239	A34	10p multicolored	1.75	1.75
240	A34	11p multicolored	1.90	1.90
241	A34	30p multicolored	2.75	3.00
242	A34	35p multicolored	3.00	3.00
243	A34	40p multicolored	3.25	3.00
244	A34	50p multicolored	3.75	3.75
245	A34	£1 multicolored	6.25	6.25
246	A34	£3 multicolored	14.00	15.00
247	A34	£5 multicolored	20.00	21.00
	Nos. 236-247 (12)		60.40	62.95

Millennium — A35

Perf. 14½x14¼
1999, Dec. 18		**Litho.**	**Wmk. 384**	
248	A35	11p Sunrise	2.00	2.00
249	A35	11p Church	2.00	2.00
250	A35	11p Albatrosses	2.00	2.00
251	A35	35p Penguins	3.00	3.00
252	A35	35p Reindeer	3.00	3.00
253	A35	35p Sunset	3.00	3.00
	Nos. 248-253 (6)		15.00	15.00

Sir Ernest Shackleton (1874-1922), Polar Explorer — A36

Designs: 35p, Voyage across Scotia Sea, 1916. 40p, Shackleton, Thomas Crean and Frank Worsley crossing South Georgia. 65p, Shackleton's grave.

Perf. 14
2000, Feb. 20		**Litho.**	**Wmk. 373**	
254	A36	35p multi	6.00	6.00
255	A36	40p multi	6.25	6.25
256	A36	65p multi	7.50	7.50
	Nos. 254-256 (3)		19.75	19.75

See British Antarctic Territory Nos. 285-287, Falkland Islands Nos. 758-760.

Prince William, 18th Birthday
Common Design Type

William: 25p, In suit, carrying bag, vert. 30p, With ski equipment, vert. 35p, Wearing suit and wearing sweater. 40p, In suit, waving. 50p, In beret, saluting.

Perf. 13¾x14¼, 14¼x13¾
2000, June 21		**Litho.**	**Wmk. 373**	
Stamps With White Border				
257	CD359	25p multi	2.75	2.75
258	CD359	30p multi	3.00	3.00
259	CD359	35p multi	3.25	3.25
260	CD359	40p multi	4.00	4.00
	Nos. 257-260 (4)		13.00	13.00

Souvenir Sheet
Stamps Without White Border
Perf. 14¼
261		Sheet of 5	16.00	16.00
a.	CD359	25p multi	2.25	2.25
b.	CD359	30p multi	2.50	2.50
c.	CD359	35p multi	2.75	2.75
d.	CD359	40p multi	3.00	3.00
e.	CD359	50p multi	3.25	3.25

King Penguins — A37

#262, 37p, Penguins at sea. #263, 37p, Adult & creche. #264, 43p, Advertisement walk & courtship. #265, 43p, Nesting.

Perf. 14¾x14
2000, Oct. 16		**Litho.**	**Wmk. 373**	
262-265	A37	Set of 4	20.00	20.00

Royal Fleet Auxiliary Vessels A38

Designs: No. 266, 37p, RFA Sir Percivale. No. 267, 37p, RFA Tidespring. No. 268, 43p, RFA Diligence. No. 269, 43p, RFA Gold Rover.

Wmk. 373
2001, May 28		**Litho.**	**Perf. 14**	
266-269	A38	Set of 4	20.00	20.00

Marine Life — A39

Designs: 33p, Icefish. No. 271, 37p, Spiny back crab. No. 272, 37p, Krill, vert. 43p, Toothfish, vert.

Wmk. 373
2001, Oct. 22		**Litho.**	**Perf. 13¾**	
270-273	A39	Set of 4	20.00	20.00

Reign Of Queen Elizabeth II, 50th Anniv. Issue
Common Design Type

Designs: Nos. 274, 278a, 20p, With dog, 1952. Nos. 275, 278b, 37p, With Prince Philip, 1997. Nos. 276, 278c, 43p, Examining royal stamp collection, 1946. Nos. 277, 278d, 50p, Wearing blue hat, 1999. No. 278e, 50p, 1955 portrait by Annigoni (38x50mm).

Perf. 14¼x14½, 13¾ (#278e)
2002, Feb. 6		**Litho.**	**Wmk. 373**	
With Gold Frames				
274-277	CD360	Set of 4	12.00	12.00

Souvenir Sheet
Without Gold Frames
278	CD360	Sheet of 5, #a-e	16.50	16.50

World Record Animals — A40

No. 279: a, 10p, Fin whale. b, 10p, Blue whale. c, 20p, Sperm whale. d, 37p, Leopard seal with mouth open. e, 37p, Leopard seal on ice. f, 43p, Elephant seal. £1.50, Elephant seal, diff.

2002, Mar. 2   Litho.   *Perf. 13¾*
279 A40   Sheet of 6, #a-f   18.50 18.50

Souvenir Sheet
280 A40   £1.50 multi   18.50 18.50

Queen Mother Elizabeth (1900-2002)
Common Design Type

Designs: 22p, Wearing hat (black and white photograph). 40p, Wearing tiara. Nos. 283, 285a, 45p, Holding dog (black and white photograph). Nos. 284, 285b, 95p, Wearing white stole.

Perf. 14¼, 13¾x14¼ (#283-284)
2002, Aug. 5   Litho.   Wmk. 373
With Purple Frames
281-284 CD361   Set of 4   11.00 11.00

Souvenir Sheet
Without Purple Frames
Perf. 14½x14¼
285 CD361   Sheet of 2, #a-b   9.00 9.00

Antarctic Fur Seals — A41

Designs: No. 286, 40p, Seal in water. No. 287, 40p, Two seals on ice. No. 288, 45p, Six seals. No. 289, 45p, One seal.

Wmk. 373
2002, Oct. 25   Litho.   *Perf. 13¾*
286-289 A41   Set of 4   21.00 21.00

Worldwide Fund for Nature (WWF) — A42

Gray-headed albatross: 40p, Adults at nesting ground. No. 291, 45p, Adult and chick (WWF emblem at LL). No. 292, 45p, Two adults (WWF emblem at UL). 70p, Bird's head.

Wmk. 373
2003, Jan. 7   Litho.   *Perf. 14*
290-293 A42   Set of 4   10.00 10.00
293a   Strip of 4   11.00 11.00

Head of Queen Elizabeth II
Common Design Type
Wmk. 373
2003, June 2   Litho.   *Perf. 13¾*
294 CD362   £2 multi   9.00 9.00

Prince William, 21st Birthday
Common Design Type

No. 295: a, Color photograph at right. b, Color photograph at left.

Wmk. 373
2003, June 21   Litho.   *Perf. 14¼*
295   Horiz. pair   9.00 9.00
a.-b.   CD364 70p Either single   4.00 4.00

History of South Georgia — A43

No. 296: a, HMS Sappho visits Grytviken, 1906. b, Norwegian reindeer introduced, 1911. c, Largest blue whale landed, 1912. d, Shackleton's island crossing, 1916. e, Shackleton Memorial Cross, 1922. f, Discovery investigations, 1925. g, First powered flight over South Georgia, 1938. h, Operation Tabarin, 1943. i, Duke of Edinburgh visits, 1957. j, Bird Island Research Station, 1958. k, Mt. Paget climbed, 1964. l, Liberation of the island, 1982. m, Royal charter and crest, 1985. n, Museum inaugurated, 1992. o, Applied fishery research, 2001. p, Grytviken remedial work, 2003.

Wmk. 373
2004, Feb. 6   Litho.   *Perf. 13¼*
296 A43   40p Sheet of 16, #a-p   40.00 40.00

Royal Navy Ships A44

Designs: 10p, HMS Ajax. 25p, HMS Amazon. 45p, HMS Dartmouth. 50p, HMS Penelope. 70p, HMS St. Austell Bay. £1, HMS Plymouth.

Wmk. 373
2004, Apr. 26   Litho.   *Perf. 14*
297-302 A44   Set of 6   18.50 18.50

Merchant Ships A45

Designs: No. 303, 42p, RMS Queen Elizabeth 2. No. 304, 42p, MS Endeavour. 50p, MS Lindblad Explorer. 75p, SS Canberra.

Perf. 13¼x13½
2004, Nov. 10   Litho.
303-306 A45   Set of 4   15.50 15.50

Animal Juveniles — A46

Designs: 1p, Skua. 2p, Reindeer. 3p, Antarctic prion, horiz. 5p, Humpback whale, horiz. 10p, Gentoo penguins. 25p, Antarctic fur seal. 50p, South Georgia pintail, horiz. 75p, Light-mantled sooty albatross. £1, Weddell seal, horiz. £2, King penguin, horiz. £3, Southern right whale, horiz. £5, Wandering albatross.
(42p), Elephant seal, horiz.

Perf. 13½x13¼, 13¼x13½
2004, Nov. 15   Wmk. 373
307 A46   1p multi   .25 .25
308 A46   2p multi   .40 .40
309 A46   3p multi   .50 .50
310 A46   5p multi   .65 .65
311 A46   10p multi   .80 .80
312 A46   25p multi   1.10 1.10
313 A46   50p multi   2.40 2.40
314 A46   75p multi   3.50 3.50
315 A46   £1 multi   4.75 4.75
316 A46   £2 multi   8.50 8.50
317 A46   £3 multi   12.00 12.00
318 A46   £5 multi   19.00 19.00
        Nos. 307-318 (12)   53.85 53.85

Booklet Stamp
Self-Adhesive
Unwmk.
Serpentine Die Cut 12½
319 A46   (42p) multi   2.50 2.50
a.   Booklet pane of 4   10.00
        Complete booklet, 2 #319a   20.00

No. 319 is inscribed "Airmail Postcard."

Grytviken, Cent. — A47

Designs: 24p, Capt. Carl Anton Larsen, founder of Grytviken. 42p, Grytviken from Mount Hodges. 50p, Whale catcher Fortuna. £1, Ski jumper.

2004, Dec. 10   Wmk. 373   *Perf. 13¾*
320-323 A47   Set of 4   11.50 11.50

Duncan Carse (1913-2004), Survey Expedition Leader — A48

Designs: No. 324, 50p, Carse. No. 325, 50p, Map of South Georgia, surveyors. 75p, Carse as radio broadcaster. £1, AMOW, Carse's hut, Undine South.

Wmk. 373
2005, Sept. 26   Litho.   *Perf. 13¾*
324-327 A48   Set of 4   14.00 14.00

A49

A50

A51

A52

A53

Penguins A54

2005, Nov. 1   *Perf. 14*
328 A49   45p multi   3.00 3.00
329 A50   45p multi   3.00 3.00
330 A51   45p multi   3.00 3.00
331 A52   45p multi   3.00 3.00
332 A53   45p multi   3.00 3.00
333 A54   45p multi   3.00 3.00
        Nos. 328-333 (6)   18.00 18.00

Queen Elizabeth II, 80th Birthday A55

Queen: No. 334, 50p, As child, with dog. Nos. 335, 338a, 50p, As young woman. Nos. 336, 338b, 75p, As older woman. £1, Wearing hat.

2006, Apr. 21   Litho.   *Perf. 14*
With White Frames
334-337 A55   Set of 4   11.00 11.00

Souvenir Sheet
Without White Frames
338 A55   Sheet of 2, #a-b   9.00 9.00

BirdLife International A56

Birds: 24p, Black-browed albatross. 45p, Southern giant petrel. 50p, White-chinned petrel. 75p, Wandering albatross.
No. 343: a, Black-browed albatross, diff. b, White-chinned petrel, diff.

Wmk. 373
2006, Oct. 18   Litho.   *Perf. 13¾*
339-342 A56   Set of 4   12.00 12.00

Souvenir Sheet
343 A56   £1 Sheet of 2, #a-b   13.00 13.00

Communications — A57

Designs: 25p, Mail drop from Royal Air Force Hercules plane. 50p, Radio/wireless room. 60p, MV Sigma. £1.05, SS Fleurus.

Perf. 14¼x14
2006, Nov. 30   Litho.   Wmk. 373
344-347 A57   Set of 4   14.50 14.50

Mapping — A58

No. 348, 50p: a, Map of Neumayer Glacier, 1958. b, Map of Neumayer Glacier, 2003.

No. 349, 60p: a, Kern DKM1 theodolite and map. b, Landsat 7 satellite.

2007, Jan. 5   **Perf. 13¾**
Horiz. Pairs, #a-b
348-349 A58   Set of 2   14.50 14.50

Falkland Islands War, 25th Anniv. — A59

Designs: 25p, Ellerbeck Peak, Wasp helicopter. 50p, Stanley Peak, Wessex 3 helicopter. 60p, Sheridan Peak, Royal Marines Commandos. £1.05, Mills Peak, Royal Marines.

Perf. 12½x13
2007, Apr. 25   **Litho.**   **Wmk. 373**
350-353 A59   Set of 4   14.50 14.50
353a   Souvenir sheet, #350-353   14.50 14.50

On No. 353a, the bottom perforations of Nos. 352-353 measure 13¼.

Scouting, Cent. — A60

Designs: 25p, Cover of Oct. 8, 1921 *Young Britain* magazine. 50p, Scouts James Marr and Norman Mooney raising flag on the Quest. 60p, Marr and Mooney with Sir Ernest Shackleton. 85p, Autographed postcard depicting Marr. £1.05, The Quest locked in ice.

Perf. 14¼
2007, Oct. 15   **Litho.**   **Unwmk.**
354-358 A60   Set of 5   19.00 19.00

Intl. Polar Year A61

Designs: 50p, Zoological Building, Moltke Base. 60p, Meteorological Station, King Edward Point. 85p, Zooplankton. £1.05, Leopard seals.

2008, Jan. 25   **Litho.**   **Perf. 14¼x14**
359-362 A61   Set of 4   16.00 16.00

Marine Stewardship Council — A62

Ships and marine life: 50p, Longliner, Patagonian toothfish. 60p, Trawler, Mackerel icefish. 85p, Krill trawler and refrigerator ship, Krill. £1.05, Fishery Patrol Vessel Pharos SG.

Perf. 14¼
2008, May 1   **Litho.**   **Unwmk.**
363-366 A62   Set of 4   16.50 16.50

Worldwide Fund for Nature (WWF) — A63

Chinstrap penguins: No. 367, 55p, Three adults. No. 368, 55p, Two adults and a chick. 65p, Three adults in water. 90p, Two adults.

2008, July 10   **Litho.**   **Perf. 14**
367-370 A63   Set of 4   13.00 13.00
370a   Souvenir sheet of 4,   #367-370   13.50 13.50

Falkland Islands Dependencies Letter Patent, Cent. — A64

Designs: 27p, H.M.S. Sappho. 65p, Magistrate's Residence, Grytviken. 90k, James Innes Wilson, 1909-1914 Magistrate. £1.10, S.S. Coronda.

2008, Nov. 30   **Litho.**   **Perf. 14**
371-374 A64   Set of 4   14.50 14.50

Souvenir Sheet

Preservation of Polar Regions — A65

No. 375 — Antarctic ozone map of: a, September 2008. b, September 1979.

Serpentine Die Cut
2009, Apr. 2   **Litho.**
Self-Adhesive
375 A65   £1.10 Sheet of 2,   #a-b   11.50 11.50

Naval Aviation, Cent. A66

Royal Navy aircraft and ships: 27p, Supermarine Walrus, HMS Exeter. 65p, Westland Wasp HASI helicopter, HMS Plymouth. 90p, Westland Whirlwind HARI helicopter, HMS Protector. £1.10, Agusta Westland AW101 Merlin helicopter, HMS Lancaster.

2009, May 27   **Litho.**   **Perf. 14**
376-379 A66   Set of 4   13.00 13.00

Ernest H. Shackleton (1874-1922), Explorer — A67

Designs: 1p, Shackleton at age 11. 2p, Shackleton at age 16. 5p, Shackleton on Discovery Expedition, 1902. 10p, Shackleton's wife, Emily, and children, Raymond, Cecily and Edward. 27p, Shackleton, Frank Wild, Dr. Eric Marshall and Jameson Adams aboard the *Nimrod*, 1909. 55p, *Endurance* trapped in ice. 65p, Launching the lifeboat *James Caird*, horiz. 90p, Shackleton, Frank Worsley and Tom Crean after crossing South Georgia, horiz. £1, Shackleton as Major. £2, Ship *Quest*. £3, Shackleton's grave, horiz. £5, Shackleton at desk, horiz.

2009, Aug. 14   **Litho.**   **Perf. 14**
380 A67   1p multi   .25 .25
381 A67   2p multi   .30 .30
382 A67   5p multi   .40 .40
383 A67   10p multi   .50 .50
384 A67   27p multi   1.00 1.00
385 A67   55p multi   2.00 2.00
386 A67   65p multi   2.50 2.30
387 A67   90p multi   3.25 3.25
388 A67   £1 multi   3.50 3.50
389 A67   £2 multi   7.50 7.50
390 A67   £3 multi   11.00 11.00
391 A67   £5 multi   17.50 17.50
    Nos. 380-391 (12)   49.70 49.50

Corals — A68

Designs: 55p, Thouarella sp. 65p, Paragorgia sp. 90p, Stylaster sp. £1.40, Thouarella sp., diff.

2009, Nov. 9   **Litho.**   **Perf. 13¼**
392-395 A68   Set of 4   13.00 13.00

South Georgia Post Office, Cent. — A69

No. 396, 65p: a, SS Cachelote, first mail ship. b, Old postal hut.
No. 397, 90p: a, Post Office, 2009. b, FPV Pharos SG, current mail ship.

2009, Dec. 23   **Litho.**   **Perf. 14**
Horiz. Pairs, #a-b
396-397 A69   Set of 2   12.00 12.00

Cephalopods A70

Designs: 27p, Galiteuthis glacialis. 65p, Psychroteuthis glacialis. 90p, Thaumeledone gunteri. £1.10, Stauroteuthis gilchristi.
£2, Mesonychoteuthis hamiltoni, Physeter macrocephalus.

2010, Apr. 7   **Perf. 13¼**
398-401 A70   Set of 4   9.25 9.25
Souvenir Sheet
402 A70   £2 multi   6.50 6.50

No. 402 contains one 51x51mm stamp.

Miniature Sheet

London 2010 Festival of Stamps — A71

No. 403: a, South Georgia essay depicting King George V. b, Falkland Islands #52. c, Bisect of Falkland Islands #56. d, Falkland Islands Dependencies #3L8. e, Falkland Islands Dependencies #1L18. f, South Georgia #13. g, South Georgia #42. h, Falkland Islands Dependencies #1LB1. i, South Georgia & South Sandwich Islands #165. j, South Georgia & South Sandwich Islands #391.

2010, Apr. 12   **Perf. 14x14¾**
403 A71   65p Sheet of 10, #a-j,   + 2 labels   22.00 22.00

Shipwrecks and Hulks — A72

Designs: 60p, Bayard. 70p, Dias, Albatros. 95p, Karrakatta. £1.15, Petrel.

2010, June 25   **Perf. 14x14¾**
404-407 A72   Set of 4   12.00 12.00

William Hodges (1744-97), Artist on Second Pacific Expedition of Capt. James Cook — A73

Artwork by Hodges depicting: No. 408, 70p, The Resolution. No. 409, 70p, Monuments on Easter Island, horiz. 95p, Capt. Cook. £1.15, Possession Bay, South Georgia, horiz.

2010, Sept. 30   **Perf. 13¾**
408-411 A73   Set of 4   12.00 12.00

Flora — A74

Designs: 27p, Small fern. 70p, Water blinks. 95p, Antarctic pearlwort. £1.15, Adder's tongue.

2010, Dec. 15   **Perf. 13x13¼**
412-415 A74   Set of 4   13.00 13.00

Pets — A75

Designs: 45p, Vervet monkey. 60p, Anne-Marie Sorlle with puppies. 70p, Whalers with dog and fox. 95p, Nan Brown with penguin, Stugie. £1.15, Perce Blackborow and cat, Mrs. Chippy. £1.20, Sir Ernest Shackleton and puppy, Query.

2011, Feb. 15   **Perf. 13¼**
416-421   A75   Set of 6   18.50   18.50

Sir Alister Hardy (1896-1985), Marine Biologist — A76

Hardy and: 60p, Continuous plankton recorder type II. 70p, Microscope. 95p, Whaling Station, Grytviken. £1.15, RRS Discovery.

2011, Mar. 15   **Perf. 13¼x13½**
422-425   A76   Set of 4   11.50   11.50

Wedding of Prince William and Catherine Middleton — A77

Couple: 70p, Laughing at rugby match. 95p, In St. James's Palace. £1.15, At wedding ceremony. £2, Wedding portrait, vert.

2011, July 25   **Litho.**   **Perf. 14**
426-428   A77   Set of 3   9.50   9.50
Souvenir Sheet
Perf. 14¾x14
429   A77   £2 multi   6.75   6.75

No. 429 contains one 32x48mm stamp.

Paintings of Petrels by John Gale — A78

Designs: 60p, Southern Giant Petrel. 70p, Snow Petrels. 95p, Cape Petrel. £1.15, South Georgia Diving Petrels.

2011, Aug. 10   **Perf. 13½**
430-433   A78   Set of 4   11.50   11.50

Filming in South Georgia of *Frozen Planet* Television Series A79

Designs: 60p, Elephant seals. 70p, Wandering albatross on ground. 95p, Blonde fur seal pup. £1.15, King penguin and juveniles. £2.50, Wandering albatross in flight.

2011, Sept. 15   **Perf. 13¼x13¾**
434-437   A79   Set of 4   11.00   11.00
Souvenir Sheet
438   A79   £2.50 multi   8.00   8.00

Polar Explorers — A80

No. 439, 60p: a, Frank Wild (1873-1939), expedition ship Discovery and Polar Medal. b, Capt. Robert Falcon Scott (1868-1912) and Discovery.

No. 440, 70p: a, Wild, members of Nimrod expedition, British flag and Polar Medal. b, Ernest Shackleton (1874-1922) and expedition ship Nimrod.
No. 441, 95p: a, Wild, members of Aurora expedition and Polar Medal. b, Douglas Mawson (1882-1958) and expedition ship Aurora.
No. 442, £1.15: a, Wild, members of Endurance expedition and Polar Medal. c, Shackleton and expedition ship Endurance.

2011, Nov. 23   **Perf. 14¼**
Horiz. Pairs, #a-b
439-442   A80   Set of 4   21.50   21.50

Miniature Sheet

Marine Life — A81

No. 443: a, Ten-legged sea spider. b, Pink cushion seastar. c, White-tipped nudibranch. d, Branching sea cucumber. e, Giant Antarctic isopod. f, South Georgia top shell.

2012, Jan. 1   **Perf. 13¼**
443   A81   70p   Sheet of 6, #a-f   13.50   13.50

Worldwide Fund for Nature (WWF) — A82

Birds: Nos. 444, 448a, 60p, Imperial shags. Nos. 445, 448b, 70p, Antarctic terns. Nos. 446, 448c, 95p, Southern skuas. Nos. 447, 448d, £1.15, Kelp gulls. £3.50, Southern skua and chicks.

2012, Mar. 10   **Perf. 14**
Stamps With White Frames
444-447   A82   Set of 4   11.00   11.00
Stamps Without White Frame
448   A82   Strip of 4, #a-d   11.00   11.00
Souvenir Sheet
449   A82   £3.50 multi   11.50   11.50

No. 448 was printed in sheets of 16 containing four each Nos. 448a-448d.

SEMI-POSTAL STAMPS

Liberation of South Georgia, 10th Anniv. — SP1

Designs: 14p+6p, King Edward Point, Winter 1982. 29p+11p, Queen Elizabeth 2 in Cumberland Bay. 34p+16p, Royal Marines on South Sandwich Islands. 68p+32p, HMS Endurance and Wasp Helicopter.

Wmk. 384
1992, June 20   **Litho.**   **Perf. 14**
B1   SP1   14p +6p multicolored   1.00   1.00
B2   SP1   29p +11p multicolored   1.75   1.75
B3   SP1   34p +16p multicolored   2.00   2.00
B4   SP1   68p +32p multicolored   4.00   4.00
  a.   Souvenir sheet of 4, #B1-B4   12.50   12.50
   Nos. B1-B4 (4)   8.75   8.75

Surtax for Soldiers', Sailors' and Airmen's Families Association.

AIR POST STAMPS

Penguins — AP1

Designs: No. C1, (60p), King penguins and chick. No. C2, (60p), Macaroni penguin. No. C3, (60p), Chinstrap penguins. No. C4, (60p), Gentoo penguin and juveniles.

2010, Oct. 25   **Litho.**   **Perf. 13¾**
C1-C4   AP1   Set of 4   8.00   8.00
C4a   Sheet of 8, 2 each #C1-C4   16.50   16.50

SOUTH KASAI

This part of a Congo province declared itself an autonomous state and in 1961 issued several series of stamps, some of which were overprints on Congo (ex-Belgian) stamps. Established nations did not recognize South Kasai as an independent state.

SOUTH MOLUCCAS
(Republik Maluku Selatan)

It appears that stamps of the so-called republic of South Moluccas were privately issued and had no postal use. Accordingly, they are not recognized as postage stamps.

SOUTH RUSSIA

sauth 'rəsh-ə

LOCATION — An area in southern Russia bordering on the Caspian and Black Seas.

A provisional government set up and maintained by General Denikin in opposition to the Bolshevik forces in Russia following the downfall of the Empire. The stamps were used in the field postal service established for carrying on communication between the various armies united in the revolt. These armies included the Don Cossacks, the Kuban Cossacks, and also the neighboring southern Russian people in favor of the counter-revolution against the Bolsheviks.

100 Kopecks = 1 Ruble

Values for used stamps are for canceled to order examples. Postally used stamps sell for considerably more.

Watermark

Wmk. 171 — Diamonds

Don Government (Novocherkassk) Rostov Issue

Russian Stamps of 1909-17 Surcharged

1918   **Unwmk.**   **Perf. 14x14½**
1   A14   25k on 1k dl org yel   2.00   1.90
  a.   Inverted surcharge   100.00   100.00
2   A14   25k on 2k dl grn   .50   .60
  a.   Inverted surcharge   100.00   75.00
3   A14   25k on 3k car   .75   .75
  a.   Double surcharge   75.00   75.00
4   A15   25k on 4k car   2.50   3.50
  a.   Inverted surcharge   100.00   100.00
5   A14   50k on 7k blue   5.00   6.50
Imperf
6   A14   25k on 1k orange   .60   1.25
  a.   Inverted surcharge   75.00   100.00
7   A14   25k on 2k gray grn   7.50   12.50
8   A14   25k on 3k red   4.75   3.00
  a.   Inverted surcharge   100.00
   Nos. 1-8 (8)   23.60   30.00

Counterfeits exist of Nos. 1-8.

Ermak, Cossack Leader — A1

Inscription on Back
1919   **Perf. 11½**
10   A1   20k green   50.00   85.00

This stamp was available for both postage and currency.

Novocherkassk Issue

25   1P.   1P.

Russian stamps with these surcharges are bogus.

Kuban Government Ekaterinodar Issues
Russian Stamps of 1909-17 Surcharged

d

e

f

g

h

i

1918-20   **Unwmk.**   **Perf. 14x14½**
20   A14(d)   25k on 1k dl org yel   .50   .65
  a.   Inverted surcharge   75.00   40.00
  b.   Dbl. surch., one inverted   75.00   25.00
21   A14(d)   50k on 2k dl grn   6.00   6.00
  a.   Inverted surcharge   50.00   27.50
  b.   Double surcharge   100.00   20.00
  c.   Dbl. surcharge inverted   75.00   20.00
22   A14(e)   70k on 5k dk cl   2.40   6.00
23   A14(f)   1r on 3k car   5.00   5.00
  a.   Inverted surcharge   50.00   20.00
  b.   Double surcharge   50.00   15.00
  c.   Pair, one without surch.   50.00   15.00

24	A14(g)	1r on 3k car		.65	*1.00*
a.		Inverted surcharge		50.00	*20.00*
b.		Double surcharge		100.00	*20.00*
c.		Pair, one without surcharge		100.00	*20.00*
25	A15(h)	3r on 4k rose		12.00	*18.00*
b.		Inverted surcharge		100.00	*50.00*
c.		Double surcharge		100.00	*60.00*
d.		Dbl. surcharge inverted		100.00	*60.00*
26	A15(i)	10r on 4k rose		15.00	*5.00*
a.		10r on 4k carmine		12.00	*13.00*
b.		Inverted surcharge		75.00	*55.00*
27	A11(i)	10r on 15k red brn & dp bl		1.25	*2.00*
a.		Surchd. on face & back		40.00	*15.00*
b.		Dbl. surch., one inverted		75.00	*60.00*
28	A14(i)	25r on 3k car		10.00	*3.00*
a.		Inverted surcharge		100.00	*20.00*
29	A14(i)	25r on 7k bl		30.00	*50.00*
a.		Inverted surcharge		100.00	*100.00*
30	A11(i)	25r on 14k bl & car		75.00	*80.00*
a.		Inverted surcharge		100.00	*100.00*
31	A11(i)	25r on 25k dl grn & dk vio		30.00	*60.00*
a.		Inverted surcharge		100.00	*70.00*
		Nos. 20-31 (12)		187.80	236.65

Imperf

35	A14(d)	25d on 1k org		5.00	*2.50*
36	A14(d)	50k on 2k gray grn		2.00	*.60*
a.		Inverted surcharge		50.00	*25.00*
b.		Double surcharge		50.00	*25.00*
c.		Pair, one without surch.		50.00	*30.00*
37	A14(e)	70k on 5k claret		2.50	*3.25*
38	A14(f)	1r on 3k red		1.40	*2.00*
a.		Inverted surcharge		40.00	*20.00*
b.		Double surcharge		30.00	*15.00*
c.		Pair, one without surch.		30.00	*15.00*
d.		Double surcharge, both inverted		100.00	*—*
39	A14(g)	1r on 3k red		1.00	*1.00*
a.		Double surcharge		20.00	*20.00*
b.		Pair, one without surch.		20.00	*20.00*
c.		As "a," inverted		40.00	*45.00*
d.		Inverted surcharge		100.00	*—*
40	A11(i)	10r on 15k red brn & dp bl		4.75	*6.00*
41	A14(i)	25r on 3k red		6.00	*10.00*
a.		Inverted surcharge		100.00	
		Nos. 35-41 (7)		22.65	25.35

Russian Stamps of 1909-17 Surcharged

1919   **Perf. 14, 14½x15**

45	A14	70k on 1k dl org yel		1.25	1.00
a.		Inverted surcharge		100.00	

Imperf

46	A14	70k on 1k orange		1.25	*2.40*
a.		Inverted surcharge		100.00	*20.00*
b.		Double surch., one inverted		100.00	*25.00*

The 1k postal savings stamp with this surcharge inverted is a proof. Value, $500. Counterfeits exist of Nos. 20-46.

On Russia Nos. AR1-AR3

A2

1919   **Wmk. 171**   **Perf. 14½x15**

47	A2	10r on 1k red, buff		50.00	60.00
a.		Inverted surcharge		75.00	
48	A2	10r on 5k grn, buff		50.00	60.00
a.		Double surcharge		250.00	
49	A2	10r on 10k brn, buff		120.00	150.00
		Nos. 47-49 (3)		220.00	270.00

Counterfeits exist of Nos. 47-49.

Crimea

Russian Stamp of 1917 Surcharged

35 коп.

1919   **Unwmk.**   **Imperf.**

51	A14	35k on 1k orange		2.00	*3.00*
a.		Comma, instead of period in surcharge		2.00	

A3

Paper with Buff Network Inscription on Back

1919   **Imperf.**

52	A3	50k brown		37.50	*85.00*

Available for both postage and currency.

Russia Nos. 77, 82, 123, 73, 119 Surcharged

Nos. 53-57   Nos. 58-59

1920   **Perf. 14x14½**

53	A14	5r on 5k dk claret		1.25	*2.40*
a.		Inverted surcharge		100.00	
b.		Double surcharge		100.00	
54	A8	5r on 20k dl bl & dk car		1.25	*2.40*
a.		Inverted surcharge		100.00	
b.		Double surcharge		100.00	
c.		"5" omitted		75.00	

Imperf

55	A14	5r on 5k claret		1.25	*2.40*
a.		Double surcharge		25.00	

Same Surcharge on Stamp of Denikin Issue, No. 64

57	A5	5r on 35k lt bl		12.00	*14.00*
a.		Double surcharge		80.00	
		Nos. 53-57 (4)		15.75	21.20

1920   **Perf. 14x14½**

58	A14	100r on 1k dl org yel		5.00	
a.		"10" in place of "100"		150.00	
b.		Inverted surcharge		150.00	
c.		Double surcharge		150.00	

Imperf

59	A14	100r on 1k orange		2.75	

Nos. 53-57 were issued at Sevastopol during the occupation by General Wrangel's army. Nos. 58-59 were prepared but not used.

Denikin Issue

A5   St. George — A6

1919   **Unwmk.**   **Imperf.**

61	A5	5k orange		.25	*.25*
62	A5	10k green		.25	*.25*
63	A5	15k red		.25	*.35*
64	A5	35k light blue		.25	*.25*
65	A5	70k dark blue		.25	*.35*
a.		Tête bêche pair		90.00	
66	A6	1r brown & red		.90	*.90*
67	A6	2r gray vio & yellow		1.50	*1.60*
68	A6	3r dl rose & green		1.00	*1.25*
69	A6	5r slate & violet		1.25	*1.00*
70	A6	7r gray grn & rose		2.25	*3.25*
71	A6	10r red & gray		2.00	*2.50*
		Nos. 61-71 (11)		10.15	12.35

Perf. 11½

68a	A6	3r dull rose & green		3.00	*10.00*
69a	A6	5r slate & violet		4.00	*10.00*
71a	A6	10r red & gray		3.00	*10.00*
		Nos. 68a-71a (3)		10.00	30.00

Nos. 61-71 were issued at Ekaterinodar and used in all parts of South Russia that were occupied by the People's Volunteer Army under Gen. Anton Ivanovich Denikin. The inscription on the stamps reads "United Russia."

Stamps of type A6 with rosettes instead of numerals in the small circles at the sides may be essays. Perforated examples of Nos. 61-67 and 70 are of private origin.

For surcharges see Russia, Offices in Turkish Empire Nos. 303-319.

SOUTH WEST AFRICA

sauth 'west 'a-fri-kə

(Namibia)

LOCATION — Southwestern Africa between Angola, Botswana and South Africa, bordering on the Atlantic Ocean

GOVT. — Administered by the Republic of South Africa under a mandate of the League of Nations

AREA — 318,261 sq. mi.

POP. — 1,039,800 (1982)

CAPITAL — Windhoek

Formerly a German possession, South West Africa was occupied by South African forces in 1915 and by the Treaty of Versailles was mandated to the Union of South Africa. On March 20, 1990 it became Namibia.

12 Pence = 1 Shilling
20 Shillings = 1 Pound
100 Cents = 1 Rand (1961)

Catalogue values for unused stamps in this country are for Never Hinged items, beginning with Scott 125 in the regular postage section, Scott B1 in the semi-postal section, Scott J86 in the postage due section, and Scott O13 in the officials section.

Watermarks

Watermarks 177, 201, 330, 348 and 359 can be found at the beginning of South Africa.

Stamps of South Africa, Nos. 2-3, 5 and 9-16, Overprinted in English or Afrikaans alternately throughout the sheets.

Major-number listings and values of Nos. 1-40 and 85-93 are for pairs with both overprints.

Setting I

"South West" 14½mm wide
"Zuid-West" 13mm wide
Overprint Spaced 14mm

1923, Jan. 2   Wmk. 177   Perf. 14

1	A2	½p green, pair	3.00	10.50
a.		Single, Dutch	1.10	1.10
2	A2	1p red, pair	4.00	10.50
a.		Single, Dutch	1.10	1.10
b.		Inverted overprint, pair	550.00	
c.		As "b," single, English	125.00	
d.		As "b," single, Dutch	125.00	
e.		As #2, English "Af.rica"	175.00	275.00
f.		Double overprint, pair	1,000.	
g.		As "f," single, English	500.00	
h.		As "f," single, Dutch	500.00	
3	A2	2p dull vio, pair	6.50	14.00
a.		Single, Dutch	1.75	1.75
b.		Inverted overprint, pair	700.00	800.00
c.		As "b," single, English	150.00	
d.		As "b," single, Dutch	150.00	
4	A2	3p ultra, pair	9.00	19.00
a.		Single, Dutch	3.25	3.25
5	A2	4p ol grn & org, pair	15.00	52.50
a.		Single, Dutch	4.50	4.50
6	A2	6p vio & blk, pair	9.25	50.00
a.		Single, Dutch	4.75	4.75

7	A2	1sh orange, pair	27.50	55.00
a.		Single, Dutch	5.75	5.75
b.		As #7, without period after "Afrika"	7,500.	
8	A2	1sh3p violet, pair	37.50	62.50
a.		Single, Dutch	6.50	6.50
b.		Inverted overprint, pair	400.00	
c.		As "b," single, English	75.00	
d.		As "b," single, Dutch	75.00	
9	A2	2sh6p grn & cl, pair	70.00	150.00
a.		Single, Dutch	22.50	22.50
10	A2	5sh blue & cl, pair	200.00	375.00
a.		Single, Dutch	57.50	57.50
11	A2	10sh ol grn & bl, pair	1,500.	2,900.
a.		Single, Dutch	475.00	500.00
12	A2	£1 red & dp grn, pair	800.00	2,000.
a.		Single, Dutch	300.00	300.00
		Nos. 1-12 (12)	2,681.	5,699.

Most values exist with "t" of "West" partly or totally missing. Vertical displacement in overprinting accounts for the stamps with only one line of overprint.

For English from setting I "a," see note after No. 27.

Setting II

Words Same Width as Setting I
Overprint Spaced 9½-10mm

1923, Apr.

13	A2	5sh blue & cl, pair	160.00	300.00
a.		Single, English	52.50	52.50
b.		Single, Dutch	52.50	52.50
c.		As #13, without period after "Afrika"	1,200.	1,400.
d.		As "b," without period after "Afrika"	225.00	225.00
14	A2	10sh ol grn & bl, pair	575.00	1,000.
a.		Single, English	160.00	160.00
b.		Single, Dutch	160.00	160.00
c.		As #14, without period after "Afrika"	2,600.	3,250.
d.		As "b," without period after "Afrika"	550.00	550.00
15	A2	£1 red & green, pair	1,150.	1,700.
a.		Single, English	225.00	225.00
b.		Single, Dutch	225.00	225.00
c.		As #15, without period after "Afrika"	6,000.	5,750.
d.		As "b," without period after "Afrika"	1,000.	1,000.

Setting III

English as in Setting I
"Zuidwest" 11mm wide, No Hyphen
Overprint Spaced 14mm

1923-24

16	A2	½p grn, pair ('24)	9.00	40.00
a.		Single, English	.75	4.25
b.		Single, Dutch	.75	4.25
17	A2	1p red, pair	6.25	10.50
a.		Single, English	.30	1.60
b.		Single, Dutch	.30	1.60
18	A2	2p dull vio, pair	9.00	11.00
a.		Single, English	.50	1.50
b.		Single, Dutch	.50	1.50
c.		Dbl. ovpt., pair	1,200.	
d.		As "c," single, English	150.00	
e.		As "c," single, Dutch	150.00	
19	A2	3p ultra, pair	5.75	11.50
a.		Single, English	.70	1.50
b.		Single, Dutch	.70	1.50
20	A2	4p ol grn & org, pair	7.00	24.00
a.		Single, English	.75	3.25
b.		Single, Dutch	.75	3.25
21	A2	6p vio & blk, pair	14.00	47.50
a.		Single, English	1.00	5.50
b.		Single, Dutch	1.00	5.50
22	A2	1sh orange, pair	16.00	52.50
a.		Single, English	1.50	5.75
b.		Single, Dutch	1.50	5.75
23	A2	1sh3p violet, pair	32.50	52.50
a.		Single, English	2.25	6.25
b.		Single, Dutch	2.25	6.25
24	A2	2sh6p grn & cl, pair	52.50	92.50
a.		Single, English	7.00	11.50
b.		Single, Dutch	7.00	11.50
25	A2	5sh blue & cl, pair	70.00	150.00
a.		Single, English	11.00	21.00
b.		Single, Dutch	11.00	21.00

26	A2	10sh ol grn & bl, pair	190.00	300.00
a.		Single, English	35.00	47.50
b.		Single, Dutch	35.00	47.50
27	A2	£1 red & green, pair	350.00	450.00
a.		Single, English	55.00	70.00
b.		Single, Dutch	55.00	70.00
		Nos. 16-27 (12)	762.00	1,242.

The English overprint of Setting III is the same as that of Setting I.

Setting IV

Type g (on left), Type h (on right)

"South West" 16mm wide
"Zuidwest" 12mm wide
Overprint Spaced 14mm

1924, July

28	A2	2sh6p grn & cl, pair	92.50	175.00
a.		Single, English	15.00	32.50
b.		Single, Dutch	15.00	32.50

Setting VI

"South West" 16, 16½mm wide
"Zuidwest" 12½mm wide
Overprint Spaced 9½mm

1924, Dec.

29	A2	½p green, pair	8.00	45.00
a.		Single, English	.50	5.75
b.		Single, Dutch	.50	5.75
30	A2	1p red, pair	3.75	11.50
a.		Single, English	.25	1.60
b.		Single, Dutch	.25	1.60
31	A2	2p dull vio, pair	5.75	25.00
a.		Single, English	.30	2.00
b.		Single, Dutch	.30	2.00
32	A2	3p ultra, pair	5.25	32.50
a.		Single, English	.50	3.25
b.		Single, Dutch	.50	3.25
33	A2	4p ol grn & org, pair	7.50	52.50
a.		Single, English	.70	4.50
b.		Single, Dutch	.70	4.50
34	A2	6p vio & blk, pair	10.50	55.00
a.		Single, English	.75	5.75
b.		Single, Dutch	.75	5.75
35	A2	1sh orange, pair	12.50	55.00
a.		Single, English	.90	5.75
b.		Single, Dutch	.90	5.75
36	A2	1sh3p violet, pair	17.50	55.00
a.		Single, English	1.25	5.75
b.		Single, Dutch	1.25	5.75
37	A2	2sh6p grn & cl, pair	37.50	80.00
a.		Single, English	5.00	11.50
b.		Single, Dutch	5.00	11.50
38	A2	5sh blue & cl, pair	52.50	140.00
a.		Single, English	8.50	16.00
b.		Single, Dutch	8.50	16.00
39	A2	10sh ol grn & bl, pair	92.50	180.00
a.		Single, English	13.00	22.50
b.		Single, Dutch	13.00	22.50
40	A2	£1 red & grn, pair	290.00	475.00
a.		Single, English	50.00	75.00
b.		Single, Dutch	50.00	75.00
		Nos. 29-40 (12)	543.25	1,206.

Setting VII

South Africa Nos. 21-22 Overprinted:

m

n

o

1926-27   Wmk. 201   Imperf.

81	A3 (m)	4p blue gray	.85	3.50
82	A3 (n)	4p blue gray	.85	3.50
83	A3 (o)	4p blue gray ('27)	7.00	22.50
		Nos. 81-83 (3)	8.70	29.50

Nos. 81-83 were not officially perforated, but firms and individuals applied various forms of perforation and rouletting for their own convenience. Perf. 11 examples of Nos. 81-82 were made by John Meinert, Ltd., Windhoek, same values.

Setting VIII

South Africa Nos. 23-25 Overprinted Alternately with type "p" on English-inscribed Stamps and type "q" on Afrikaans-inscribed Stamps

p

q

"South West" 16½mm wide
"Suidwes" 11mm wide
Overprint Spaced 11½mm

1926   Typo.   Perf. 14½x14

85	A5	½p dk grn & blk, pair	4.25	9.00
a.		Single, English	.75	1.00
b.		Single, Afrikaans	.75	1.00
c.		Ovpt. "q" on English stamp	.75	1.00
d.		Ovpt. "p" on Afrikaans stamp	.75	1.00
e.		Pair, "c" + "d"	2.25	9.00
f.		As "e," without period after "Africa"	175.00	
86	A6	1p car & blk, pair	3.50	8.00
a.		Single, English	.50	.80
b.		Single, Afrikaans	.50	.80
c.		Ovpt. "q" on English stamp	.50	.50
d.		Ovpt. "p" on Afrikaans stamp	.50	.50
e.		Pair, "c" + "d"	3.50	3.50
f.		As "e," without period after "Africa"	350.00	
87	A7	6p org & grn, pair	24.00	50.00
a.		Single, English	7.00	8.50
b.		Single, Afrikaans	7.00	8.50
c.		Ovpt. "q" on English stamp	3.00	3.50
d.		Ovpt. "p" on Afrikaans stamp	3.00	3.50
e.		Pair, "c" + "d"	10.00	35.00
f.		As "e," without period after "Africa"	210.00	
		Nos. 85-87 (3)	31.75	67.00

For overprints see Nos. O1-O3.

Setting IX

South Africa Nos. 26-27, 29-32 Overprinted in Blue with types "p" and "q" Spaced 16mm

1927   Engr.   Perf. 14

88	A8	2p vio brn & gray, pair	5.50	17.50
a.		Single, English	.60	2.00
b.		Single, Afrikaans	.60	2.00
89	A9	3p red & blk, pair	5.50	32.50
a.		Single, English	.75	3.00
b.		Single, Afrikaans	.75	3.00
90	A11	1sh dp bl & bis brn, pair	17.50	37.50
a.		Single, English	1.75	4.50
b.		Single, Afrikaans	1.75	4.50
91	A12	2sh6p brn & bl grn, pair	40.00	110.00
a.		Single, English	8.00	15.00
b.		Single, Afrikaans	8.00	15.00
92	A13	5sh dp grn & blk, pair	85.00	225.00
a.		Single, English	17.50	22.50
b.		Single, Afrikaans	17.50	22.50
93	A14	10sh ol brn & bl, pair	75.00	180.00
a.		Single, English	12.00	22.50
b.		Single, Afrikaans	12.00	22.50
		Nos. 88-93 (6)	228.50	602.50

South Africa Nos. 12 and 16a Overprinted at Foot

1927	Typo.		Wmk. 177	
94	A2	1sh3p violet	1.50	7.50
a.	Without period after "A"		110.00	
95	A2	£1 lt red & gray grn	110.00	190.00
a.	Without period after "A"		1,750.	2,600.

South Africa Nos. 23-25 Overprinted type "r" at Foot

1927		Wmk. 201	Perf. 14½x14	
96	A5	½p green & blk, pair	2.75	8.00
a.	Single, English		.25	.90
b.	Single, Afrikaans		.25	.90
c.	As #96, without period after "A" on one stamp		47.50	85.00
97	A6	1p car & blk, pair	1.50	3.75
a.	Single, English		.25	.65
b.	Single, Afrikaans		.25	.65
c.	As #97, without period after "A" on one stamp		47.50	85.00
d.	Ovpt. at top, pair ('30)		2.00	16.00
e.	As "d," single, English		.35	1.90
f.	As "d," single, Afrikaans		.35	1.90
98	A7	6p org & grn, pair	11.00	28.00
a.	Single, English		1.75	3.25
b.	Single, Afrikaans		1.75	3.25
c.	As #98, without period after "A" on one stamp		125.00	
		Nos. 96-98 (3)	15.25	39.75

For overprints see Nos. O5-O7.

South Africa Nos. 26-32 Overprinted type "r" at Top

1927-28		Engr.	Perf. 14	
99	A8	2p vio brn & gray, pair	10.50	32.50
a.	Single, English		1.25	1.75
b.	Single, Afrikaans		1.25	1.75
c.	As #99, without period after "A" on one stamp		85.00	140.00
d.	Double ovpt., one inverted		800.00	1,050.
100	A9	3p red & blk, pair	7.00	26.00
a.	Single, English		1.00	3.75
b.	Single, Afrikaans		1.00	3.75
c.	As #100, without period after "A" on one stamp		92.50	150.00
101	A10	4p brn, pair ('28)	17.50	45.00
a.	Single, English		1.75	8.00
b.	Single, Afrikaans		1.75	8.00
c.	As #101, without period after "A" on one stamp		97.50	150.00
102	A11	1sh dp bl & bis brn, pair	22.50	55.00
a.	Single, English		1.75	5.75
b.	Single, Afrikaans		1.75	5.75
c.	As #102, without period after "A" on one stamp		1,500.	1,800.
103	A12	2sh6p brn & bl grn, pair	47.50	97.50
a.	Single, English		6.50	14.00
b.	Single, Afrikaans		6.50	14.00
c.	As #103, without period after "A" on one stamp		250.00	400.00
104	A13	5sh dp grn & blk, pair	70.00	140.00
a.	Single, English		9.50	21.00
b.	Single, Afrikaans		9.50	21.00
c.	As #104, without period after "A" on one stamp		325.00	475.00
105	A14	10sh bl brn & bl, pair	110.00	225.00
a.	Single, English		20.00	32.50
b.	Single, Afrikaans		20.00	32.50
c.	As #105, without period after "A" on one stamp		425.00	675.00
		Nos. 99-105 (7)	285.00	621.00

Nos. 99-102 exist perf 14x13½. Values about two times those shown.
For overprint see No. O8.

South Africa Nos. 33-34 Overprinted type "r" at Foot

1930		Photo.	Perf. 15x14	
106	A5	½p bl grn & blk, pair	15.00	37.50
a.	Single, English		1.50	3.25
b.	Single, Afrikaans		1.50	3.25
107	A6	1p car rose & blk, pair	10.00	30.00
a.	Single, English		1.25	3.25
b.	Single, Afrikaans		1.25	3.25

Kori Bustard — A15

Cape Cross — A16

Mail Transport — A17

Bogenfels — A18

Windhoek — A19

Waterberg — A20

Lüderitz Bay — A21

Bush Scene — A22

Elands — A23

Zebras and Brindled Gnus — A24

Herero Houses — A25

Welwitschia Plant — A26

Okuwahakan Falls — A27

			Perf. 14x13½	
1931-37		Wmk. 201		Engr.
108	A15	½p grn & blk, pair	3.25	3.00
a.	Single, English		.25	.25
b.	Single, Afrikaans		.25	.25
109	A16	1p red & ind, pair	2.75	3.00
a.	Single, English		.25	.25
b.	Single, Afrikaans		.25	.25
110	A17	1½p vio brn, pair ('37)	27.50	4.25
a.	Single, English		1.00	.35
b.	Single, Afrikaans		1.00	.35
111	A18	2p dk brn & dk bl, pair	.80	6.50
a.	Single, English		.25	.25
b.	Single, Afrikaans		.25	.25
112	A19	3p dp bl & gray blk, pair	.80	5.00
a.	Single, English		.25	.25
b.	Single, Afrikaans		.25	.25
113	A20	4p brn vio & grn, pair	2.10	8.00
a.	Single, English		.30	.25
b.	Single, Afrikaans		.30	.25
114	A21	6p ol brn & bl, pair	1.75	11.00
a.	Single, English		.30	.25
b.	Single, Afrikaans		.30	.25
115	A22	1sh bl & vio brn, pair	3.00	15.00
a.	Single, English		.50	.30
b.	Single, Afrikaans		.50	.30
116	A23	1sh3p ocher & pur, pair	8.75	12.50
a.	Single, English		.60	.60
b.	Single, Afrikaans		.60	.60
117	A24	2sh6p dk gray & rose, pair	24.00	27.50
a.	Single, English		2.75	2.00
b.	Single, Afrikaans		2.75	2.00
118	A25	5sh vio brn & ol grn, pair	19.00	45.00
a.	Single, English		3.50	3.25
b.	Single, Afrikaans		3.50	3.25
119	A26	10sh grn & brn, pair	52.50	57.50
a.	Single, English		9.50	7.00
b.	Single, Afrikaans		9.50	7.00
120	A27	20sh bl grn & mar, pair	85.00	95.00
a.	Single, English		12.50	12.50
b.	Single, Afrikaans		12.50	12.50
		Nos. 108-120 (13)	231.20	293.25

For overprints see Nos. O13-O27.

George V — A28

1935, May 6			Perf. 14x13½	
121	A28	1p carmine & blk	1.25	.30
122	A28	2p dk brown & blk	1.25	.30
123	A28	3p blue & blk	8.00	22.50
124	A28	6p violet & blk	4.00	13.00
		Nos. 121-124 (4)	14.50	36.10
		Set, never hinged	30.00	

25th anniv. of the reign of George V.

Catalogue values for unused stamps in this section, from this point to the end of the section, are for Never Hinged items.

Coronation Issue

Inscribed alternately in English and Afrikaans

George VI — A29

1937, May 12		Engr.	Perf. 13½x14	
125	A29	½p emer & blk, pair	.45	.25
a.	Single, English		.25	.25
b.	Single, Afrikaans		.25	.25
126	A29	1p car & blk, pair	.45	.25
a.	Single, English		.25	.25
b.	Single, Afrikaans		.25	.25
127	A29	1½p org & blk, pair	.45	.25
a.	Single, English		.25	.25
b.	Single, Afrikaans		.25	.25
128	A29	2p dk brn & blk, pair	.45	.30
a.	Single, English		.25	.25
b.	Single, Afrikaans		.25	.25
129	A29	3p brt bl & blk, pair	.55	.30
a.	Single, English		.25	.25
b.	Single, Afrikaans		.25	.25
130	A29	4p dk vio & blk, pair	.55	.35
a.	Single, English		.25	.25
b.	Single, Afrikaans		.25	.25
131	A29	6p yel & blk, pair	.60	3.25
a.	Single, English		.25	.30
b.	Single, Afrikaans		.25	.30
132	A29	1sh gray & blk, pair	2.00	3.50
a.	Single, English		.75	.75
b.	Single, Afrikaans		.75	.75
		Nos. 125-132 (8)	5.50	8.45

George VI & Queen Elizabeth coronation.

Voortrekker Issue

South Africa Nos. 79-80 Overprinted type "r"

1938, Dec. 14		Photo.	Perf. 15x14	
133	A23	1p rose & sl, pair	14.00	22.50
a.	Single, English		1.50	1.75
b.	Single, Afrikaans		1.50	1.75
134	A24	1½p red brn & Prus bl, pair	21.00	27.50
a.	Single, English		2.00	2.25
b.	Single, Afrikaans		2.00	2.25

Issued to commemorate the Voortrekkers.

South Africa Nos. 81-89 Overprinted — s

1941-43			Wmk. 201	
135	A25	½p dp blue grn, pair	1.75	2.75
a.	Single, English		.25	.25
b.	Single, Afrikaans		.25	.25
136	A26	1p brt rose, pair	2.00	3.75
a.	Single, English		.25	.25
b.	Single, Afrikaans		.25	.25
137	A27	1½p Prus grn, pair ('42)	3.00	4.00
a.	Single, English		.25	.25
b.	Single, Afrikaans		.25	.25
138	A28	2p dk violet	.60	1.75
139	A29	3p dp blue, pair	24.50	26.00
a.	Single, English		1.00	1.25
b.	Single, Afrikaans		1.00	1.25
140	A30	4p brown, pair	7.50	20.00
a.	Single, English		.80	1.00
b.	Single, Afrikaans		.80	1.00
141	A31	6p brt red org, pair	8.00	9.00
a.	Single, English		.75	1.00
b.	Single, Afrikaans		.75	1.00
142	A32	1sh dk brown	1.60	2.00
143	A33	1sh3p dk ol brn, pair ('43)	15.00	24.50
a.	Single, English		1.25	1.50
b.	Single, Afrikaans		1.25	1.50
		Nos. 135-143 (9)	63.95	93.75

South Africa Nos. 90-97 Overprinted

t   u

Pairs or Strips of 3 Perf. 14 or 15x14 all around, Rouletted 6½ or 13 btwn.

1942-45			Wmk. 201	
144	A34(t)	½p dp grn, horiz. strip of 3	.75	7.00
a.	Single, English		.25	.25
b.	Single, Afrikaans		.25	.25
c.	½p dp bl grn, horiz. strip of 3		4.25	7.50
d.	As "c," single, English		.25	.25
e.	As "c," single, Afrikaans		.25	.25
145	A35(t)	1p brt car, horiz. strip of 3	3.50	7.00
a.	Single, English		.25	.25
b.	Single, Afrikaans		.25	.25
c.	1p rose car, horiz. strip of 3		4.00	7.00
d.	As "c," single, English		.25	.25
e.	As "c," single, Afrikaans		.25	.25
146	A36(u)	1½p cop brn, horiz. pair	.75	1.75
a.	Single, English		.25	.25
b.	Single, Afrikaans		.25	.25
147	A37(t)	2p dk vio, horiz. pair	8.50	5.50
a.	Single, English		.25	.25
b.	Single, Afrikaans		.25	.25
148	A38(t)	3p dp bl, vert. strip of 3	4.00	22.50
a.	Single, English		.25	.65
b.	Single, Afrikaans		.25	.65
149	A39(t)	4p sl grn, vert. strip of 3	5.00	22.50
a.	Single		.30	.35
b.	As "c," single, English		55.00	60.00
c.	Invtd. ovpt., strip of 3		850.00	550.00
150	A40(t)	6p brt red org, horiz. pair	7.00	3.00
a.	Single, English		.30	.35
b.	Single, Afrikaans		.30	.35
c.	Inverted overprint, pair		650.00	
d.	As "c," single, English		60.00	60.00
e.	As "c," single, Afrikaans		60.00	60.00
151	A41(u)	1sh dk brn, vert. pair	15.00	29.00
a.	Single		1.25	2.00
b.	As "c," single		85.00	
c.	Inverted overprint, pair		700.00	375.00

152 A41(t) 1sh dk brn, vert.
	pair	5.00	6.50
a.	Single	.30	.35
b.	As "c," single	55.00	40.00
c.	Invtd. ovpt., vert. pair	600.00	350.00

Nos. 144-152 (9)   49.50 104.75

Issue years: #144-145, 147-151, 1943; #152, 1944; #144c, 145c, 149c, 1945.

Peace Issue

South Africa Nos. 100-102 Overprinted Type "w"

1945, Dec. 3   Wmk. 201   Perf. 14

153	A42	1p rose pink & choc, pair	.40	.75
a.		Single, English	.25	.25
b.		Single, Afrikaans	.25	.25
c.		Inverted overprint, pair	400.00	425.00
d.		As "c," single, English	40.00	
e.		As "c," single, Afrikaans	40.00	
154	A43	2p vio & sl bl, pair	.40	.75
a.		Single, English	.25	.25
b.		Single, Afrikaans	.25	.25
155	A43	3p ultra & dp ultra, pair	1.75	2.00
a.		Single, English	.30	.25
b.		Single, Afrikaans	.30	.25

Nos. 153-155 (3)   2.55   3.50

WW II victory of the Allies.

Royal Visit Issue

South Africa Nos. 103-105 Overprinted

1947, Feb. 17   Perf. 15x14

156	A44	1p cerise & gray, pair	.30	.25
a.		Single, English	.25	.25
b.		Single, Afrikaans	.25	.25
157	A45	2p purple, pair	.30	.60
a.		Single, English	.25	.25
b.		Single, Afrikaans	.25	.25
158	A46	3p dk blue, pair	.40	.45
a.		Single, English	.25	.25
b.		Single, Afrikaans	.25	.25

Nos. 156-158 (3)   1.00 1.30

Visit of the British Royal Family, Mar.-Apr., 1947.

South Africa No. 106 Overprinted

1948, Apr. 26   Perf. 14

159	A47	3p dp chalky bl & sil, pair	1.25	.35
a.		Single, English	.25	.25
b.		Single, Afrikaans	.25	.25

25th anniv. of the marriage of George VI and Queen Elizabeth.

UPU Issue

South Africa Nos. 109-111 Overprinted type "w" 13mm wide

1949, Oct. 1   Perf. 14x15

160	A50	½p dk green, pair	1.10	2.25
a.		Single, English	.25	.30
b.		Single, Afrikaans	.25	.30
161	A50	1½p dk red, pair	1.10	1.75
a.		Single, English	.25	.25
b.		Single, Afrikaans	.25	.25
162	A50	3p ultra, pair	1.75	2.00
a.		Single, English	.25	.30
b.		Single, Afrikaans	.25	.30

Nos. 160-162 (3)   3.95 6.00

75th anniv. of the UPU.

This ends the bi-lingual multiples in the postage section.

Voortrekker Monument Issue

South Africa Nos. 112-114 Ovptd.

1949, Dec. 1   Perf. 15x14

163	A51	1p magenta	.25	.25
164	A52	1½p dull green	.25	.25
165	A53	3p dark blue	.30	.30

Nos. 163-165 (3)   .80   .80

Inauguration of the Voortrekker Monument at Pretoria.

South Africa Nos. 115-119 Overprinted

w

x

1952, Mar. 14   Perf. 15x14, 14x15

166	A54(w)	½p dk brown & red vio	.40	.50
167	A55(x)	1p dark green	.40	.40
168	A54(w)	2p dark purple	.85	.40
169	A55(x)	4½p dark blue	.85	2.00
170	A54(w)	1sh brown	1.75	1.00

Nos. 166-170 (5)   4.25 4.30

300th anniv. of the landing of Jan van Riebeeck at the Cape of Good Hope.

Coronation Issue

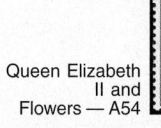

Queen Elizabeth II and Flowers — A54

Various flowers.

1953, June 2   Photo.   Perf. 14

244	A54	1p carmine rose	.55	.30
245	A54	2p dark green	.55	.30
246	A54	4p deep magenta	1.10	.65
247	A54	6p deep blue	1.10	1.00
248	A54	1sh chestnut brown	1.60	1.25

Nos. 244-248 (5)   4.90 3.50

Rock Painting of Two Bucks — A55

Rhinoceros Hunt — A56

Designs: 2p, "White Lady" (rock painting). 4p, Elephant and giraffe (rock painting). 4½p, Karakul lamb. 6p, Owambo blowing Kudu horn. 1sh, Ukuanjama woman. 1sh3p, Herero woman. 1sh6p, Ukuanjama girl. 2sh6p, Lioness. 5sh, Cape Oryx. 10sh, Elephant.

1954, Nov. 15   Wmk. 201   Perf. 14

249	A55	1p rose brown	.55	.25
250	A55	2p dk brown	.55	.25
251	A56	3p brown vio	1.40	.25
252	A56	4p olive gray	1.75	.25
253	A55	4½p blue vio	1.10	.25
254	A55	6p gray green	1.50	.40
255	A55	1sh magenta	2.10	.50
256	A55	1sh3p rose pink	4.00	1.25
257	A55	1sh6p dull purple	4.50	1.10
258	A55	2sh6p yel brown	8.50	2.50
259	A55	5sh blue	19.00	6.00
260	A55	10sh dk green	37.50	16.00

Nos. 249-260 (12)   82.45 29.00

1960   Wmk. 330   Perf. 14

261	A55	1p rose brown	1.50	.60
262	A55	2p dark brown	1.75	.80
263	A56	3p brown vio	2.40	1.50
264	A56	4p olive gray	5.50	6.25
265	A55	1sh6p dull purple	26.00	21.00

Nos. 261-265 (5)   37.15 30.15

General Post Office, Windhoek — A57

Fishing Industry — A58

Designs: 1c, Finger Rock, Asab. 1½c, Monument, Mounted Soldier. 2c, Quivertree (aloe dichotoma Masson). 2½c, Administrator's residence. 3c, Swakopmund Lighthouse and flamingoes. 5c, Flamingo. 7½c, Christchurch. 10c, Diamonds. 12½c, Fort Namutoni. 15c, Hardap Dam. 20c, Topaz. 50c, Tourmaline. 1r, Heliodor.

1961-63   Wmk. 330   Photo.   Perf. 14

266	A58	½c blue & brown	.70	.35
267	A58	1c pale lil & brn	.35	.30
268	A58	1½c sal & dk pur	.35	.30
269	A58	2c yel & green	1.00	1.40
270	A57	2½c lt bl & red brn	.75	.35
271	A58	3c dp rose & vio bl	5.50	1.25
272	A58	3½c blue grn & ind	1.00	.40
273	A58	5c bluish gray & red	8.00	2.10
274	A58	7½c yellow & brn	.90	.90
275	A58	10c brt blue & yel	1.75	.55
276	A57	12½c yellow & ind	2.75	2.75
277	A57	15c dp brn & blue	16.00	5.75
278	A58	20c sal, brn & blk	5.50	2.10
279	A58	50c org yel & Prus grn	7.75	5.50
280	A58	1r brt blue, mar & yel	10.00	12.00

Nos. 266-280 (15)   62.30 36.00

Issued: 3c, 10/1/62; 15c, 3/16/63; others, 2/14/61.

1962-73   Unwmk.

281	A57	½c blue & brn	.60	2.25
282	A58	1½c sal & dk pur ('63)	6.75	.55
283	A58	2c yellow & grn	5.25	5.00
284	A57	2½c lt bl & red brn ('64)	9.00	7.00
285	A58	3c dp rose & vio bl ('73)	2.50	1.50
286	A58	3½c bl grn & ind ('66)	12.00	5.50
287	A58	5c bluish gray & red	7.75	3.25

Nos. 281-287 (7)   43.85 25.05

See Nos. 304-308, 314-328.

Hardap Dam and Development A59

Centenary Emblem and S.W.A. Map A60

1963, Mar. 16   Wmk. 330

294	A59	3c sepia green	.90	.90

Opening of Hardap Dam near Mariental.

1963, Aug. 30   Unwmk.   Perf. 14

Design: 15c, Emblem and globe.

295	A60	7½c blue, blk & red	5.75	5.00
296	A60	15c brn org, blk & red	12.00	8.00

Centenary of the International Red Cross.

Assembly Hall — A61

John Calvin — A62

1964, May 14   Photo.   Wmk. 330

297	A61	3c salmon pink & vio bl	.90	.75

Issued to commemorate the opening of the new hall of the Legislative Assembly.

1964, Oct. 1   Unwmk.   Perf. 14

298	A62	2½c magenta & gold	.50	.55
299	A62	15c green & gold	3.75	3.75

John Calvin (1509-64), French theologian and leader of the Reformation.

Mail Runner, 1890 — A63

Kurt von François — A64

Wmk. 348

1965, Oct. 18   Photo.   Perf. 14

300	A63	3c red & deep brown	.55	.30
301	A64	15c green & deep brn	2.75	1.75

75th anniversary of Windhoek.

Dr. H. H. Vedder, Missionary, Educator and Senator, 90th Birthday — A65

1966, July 4   Perf. 14

302	A65	3c black & salmon	.40	.30
303	A65	15c black & light blue	2.50	2.25

Types of 1961-62

1966-67   Wmk. 348   Photo.   Perf. 14
Chalky Paper

304	A57	½c lt blue & brn	2.00	.50
304A	A58	1c pale lil & brn	.75	.25
305	A58	2c brt yel & dp grn	.75	.25
306	A57	2½c gray blue & red brn	1.00	.25
307	A58	3½c pale grn & vio bl	4.25	2.00
308	A58	7½c brt yel & brn	4.00	.80

Nos. 304-308 (6)   12.75 4.05

The watermark on Nos. 304, 305-308 is very faint, and these stamps can be distinguished by the shades and by the thick chalky paper. The watermark on No. 304A is clear.
Issued: 2c, 2½c, 1966; others, 1967.

Camelthorn Tree — A66

Verwoerd A67

Swart A68

Design: 3c, Waves breaking against rock.

Perf. 14, 14x15 (15c)

1967, Jan. 6   Litho.   Wmk. 348

309	A66	2½c green & black	.30	.25
310	A67	3c brt blue & brown	.40	.25
311	A67	15c rose lilac & black	2.75	2.50

Nos. 309-311 (3)   3.45 3.00

Dr. Hendrik F. Verwoerd (1901-1966), Prime Minister of South Africa.

Perf. 14x15

1968, Jan. 2   Photo.   Wmk. 359

15c, President and Mrs. C. R. Swart.

312		Strip of 3	4.00	4.00
a.	A68	3c Single, English	.45	.30
b.	A68	3c Single, Afrikaans	.45	.30
c.	A68	3c Single, German	.45	.30

313		Strip of 3	11.00	11.00
a.	A68 15c	Single, English	2.75	2.00
b.	A68 15c	Single, Afrikaans	2.75	2.00
c.	A68 15c	Single, German	2.75	2.00

Charles Robberts Swart, 1st president of South Africa, (1961-67).

Types of 1961-62

Designs: 4c, like 2½c. 6c, Christchurch. 9c, Fort Namutoni.

1968-72 Wmk. 359 Photo. Perf. 14

314	A57	½c blue & brown	1.25	.25
315	A57	½c blue & brn, redrawn ('70)	2.50	1.00
316	A58	1c pale lilac & brn ('70)	1.00	.25
317	A58	1½c salmon & dk pur	1.25	.35
318	A58	1½c sal & dk pur, redrawn ('71)	15.00	17.50
319	A58	2c yel & grn, redrawn ('70)	4.00	.35
320	A57	2½c lt bl & red brn ('70)	2.00	.30
321	A58	3c dp rose & vio bl ('70)	8.50	1.75
322	A57	4c lt bl & red brn ('71)	2.00	1.50
323	A58	5c bluish gray & red	4.25	.45
324	A58	6c yel & brn ('71)	8.75	7.50
325	A57	9c yel & ind ('71)	10.00	9.00
326	A58	10c brt bl & yel ('70)	18.00	2.50
327	A57	15c dp brn & bl ('72)	25.00	7.00
328	A58	20c org, brn & blk	19.00	2.00
		Nos. 314-328 (15)	122.50	51.70

Nos. 315, 318-319 are without inscription "Posgeld Incomste Postage Revenue" and the numerals have been enlarged. The ½c (#315), 2c and 10c were also issued as coils.

Water Type of South Africa, 1970

2½c, Water drop and flower. 3c, Waves, horiz.

1970, Feb. 14 Perf. 14

| 329 | A142 | 2½c brown, brt bl & grn | .80 | .50 |
| 330 | A142 | 3c pale gray, bl & indigo | 1.00 | .60 |

Water '70 campaign of the South African Department of Water Affairs.

Bible Society Types of South Africa

Designs: 2½c, Sower, stained glass window. 12½c, "BIBLIA" and open book.

1970, Aug. 24 Photo. Perf. 14

| 331 | A143 | 2½c multicolored | 1.10 | .55 |

Photo.; Gold Impressed

| 332 | A144 | 12½c ultra, blk & gold | 11.00 | 8.00 |

South African Bible Soc., 150th anniv.

Stamp Exhibition Types of South Africa

Perf. 14x13½, 13½x14

1971, May 31 Photo. Wmk. 359

| 333 | A145 | 5c blue, yel & blk | 4.00 | 3.25 |
| 334 | A146 | 12½c grnsh bl, vio bl & red | 47.50 | 27.50 |

Intl. Stamp Exhib. (INTERSTEX), Cape Town, May 22-31. No. 334 also for the 10th anniv. of the Antarctic Treaty pledging peaceful uses of and scientific cooperation in Antarctica.

Republic Anniversary Types of South Africa

1971, May 31 Perf. 14

| 335 | A147 | 2c mag, rose red & buff | 2.00 | 1.25 |
| 336 | A148 | 4c blue green & black | 4.25 | 1.50 |

10th anniv. of the Republic of South Africa.

Cat Type of South Africa

1972, Sept. 19 Perf. 14

| 337 | A152 | 5c multicolored | 3.75 | 2.75 |

Cent. of the SPCA.

Landscape, by Adolph Jentsch — A69

Designs: Various landscapes by Adolph Jentsch (1888-1977). 10c, 15c, vert.

1973, Apr. 28 Litho. Perf. 11½x12½

338	A69	2c multicolored	.85	.85
339	A69	4c multicolored	1.40	1.40
340	A69	5c multicolored	1.75	1.75
341	A69	10c multicolored	3.00	3.00
342	A69	15c multicolored	5.00	5.00
		Nos. 338-342 (5)	12.00	12.00

Sarcocaulon Rigidum A70

Pachypodium Namaqua-num A71

Designs: 1c-50c, Various succulent plants. 1r, Welwitschia. 30c, 1r, horiz.

1973, Sept. 1 Litho. Perf. 12½
Plants in Natural Colors

343	A70	1c light blue	.25	.25
344	A70	2c yellow	.25	.25
345	A70	3c salmon pink	.25	.25
346	A70	4c gray	.30	.25
347	A70	5c blue	.50	.25
348	A70	6c greenish gray	2.50	3.00
349	A70	7c bright yellow	1.50	2.00
350	A70	9c dull yellow	1.00	1.75
351	A70	10c blue green	.60	.25
352	A70	14c yellow green	2.00	2.25
353	A70	15c light brown	1.50	.50
354	A70	20c light olive	5.00	3.50
355	A70	25c orange	5.00	4.00

Perf. 12x12½, 12½x12

356	A71	30c dull yellow	1.25	1.00
357	A71	50c light green	1.75	1.50
358	A71	1r blue green	2.00	5.00
		Nos. 343-358 (16)	25.65	26.00

1979 Same Designs Perf. 14

344a	A70	2c	.70	.35
345a	A70	3c	.70	.35
347a	A70	5c	1.00	.50
351a	A70	10c	1.00	.50
356a	A70	30c	1.75	.75
357a	A70	50c	3.00	.90
		Nos. 344a-357a (6)	8.15	3.35

Coil Stamps

1973, Sept. 1 Photo. Perf. 14

359	A70	1c brt pink & black	1.00	.70
360	A70	2c yellow & black	.75	.60
361	A70	5c red & black	1.75	.80

1978 Perf. 14 Vertically

361A	A70	1c brt pink & black	5.00	4.00
362	A70	2c yellow & black	1.50	.50
362A	A70	5c red & black	1.50	.65
		Nos. 359-362A (6)	11.50	7.25

For overprints, see Nos. 423-428.

NOTE: coil stamps, Nos. 359-362A, are printed in two colors, sheet stamps are multicolored.

Chat-shrike — A72

Designs: Rare birds.

Perf. 12½x11½

1974, Feb. 13 Litho.

363	A72	4c shown	3.25	2.00
364	A72	5c Rosy-faced love-birds	4.50	2.50
365	A72	10c Damara rockjumper	11.00	8.50
366	A72	15c Ruppell's parrot	18.50	15.00
		Nos. 363-366 (4)	37.25	28.00

Rock Carvings, Twyfelfontein A73

Mining A74

1974, Apr. 10 Litho. Perf. 12½

| 367 | A73 | 4c Giraffe & horse | 1.50 | .85 |
| 368 | A73 | 5c Elephant | 2.25 | 1.10 |

Perf. 12x12½
Size: 37x21½mm

| 369 | A73 | 15c Deer, horiz. | 9.50 | 5.25 |
| | | Nos. 367-369 (3) | 13.25 | 7.20 |

1974, Sept. 30 Perf. 12½x11½

| 370 | A74 | 10c Diamonds | 5.50 | 3.75 |
| 371 | A74 | 15c Diamond open pit mining | 6.75 | 4.75 |

Map Showing Route, Covered Wagons A75

Perf. 11½x12

1974, Nov. 13 Unwmk.

| 372 | A75 | 4c yellow & multi | 1.10 | .90 |

Centenary of "Thirstland Trek" from Transvaal through Kalahari Desert to Angola.

Peregrine Falcon — A76

Designs: Protected Birds of Prey.

1975, Mar. 19 Perf. 12½x11½

373	A76	4c shown	2.75	1.50
374	A76	5c Black eagle	3.25	1.75
375	A76	10c Martial eagle	7.00	4.50
376	A76	15c Egyptian vulture	9.50	7.50
		Nos. 373-376 (4)	22.50	15.25

Kolmanskop, Ghost Diamond Mining Town — A77

Designs: 9c, German steam traction engine, 1896. 15c, Old Fort, Windhoek and statue of Colonial German trooper on horseback.

1975, July 23 Litho. Perf. 12x12½

377	A77	5c violet & multi	.30	.30
378	A77	9c ocher & multi	.70	.70
379	A77	15c yellow & multi	1.10	1.10
		Nos. 377-379 (3)	2.10	2.10

Historic monuments.

Paintings by Otto Schröder (1913-75) A78

1975, Oct. 15 Litho. Perf. 12x12½

380	A78	15c Luderitz	1.00	1.00
381	A78	15c Swakopmund	1.00	1.00
382	A78	15c Unloading freighters	1.00	1.00

383	A78	15c Ships at anchor, Walvis Bay	1.00	1.00
a.		Souvenir sheet of 4, #380-383	5.00	5.00
b.		Block of 4, #380-383	4.50	4.50

No. 383a has a horizontal gutter with black inscription on silver panel.

Elephants A79

Pre-historic Rock Paintings: 10c, Rhinoceros. 15c, Antelope and hunter. 20c, Hunter with bow and arrow.

1976, Mar. 12 Litho. Perf. 12x12½

384	A79	4c red brown & multi	.25	.25
385	A79	10c red brown & multi	.55	.55
386	A79	15c red brown & multi	.85	.85
387	A79	20c red brown & multi	1.40	1.40
a.		Souvenir sheet of 4, #384-387	3.75	3.75
		Nos. 384-387 (4)	3.05	3.05

Schloss Duwisib A80

Castles Built by German Settlers: 10c, Schwerinsburg. 20c, Heynitzburg.

1976, May 14 Litho. Perf. 12x12½

388	A80	10c multicolored	.55	.55
389	A80	15c multicolored	.85	.85
390	A80	20c multicolored	1.10	1.10
		Nos. 388-390 (3)	2.50	2.50

Nature Protection A81

1976, July 16 Litho. Perf. 11½x12½

391	A81	4c Daman	.40	.40
392	A81	10c Dik-diks	1.00	1.25
393	A81	15c Tree squirrel	1.50	1.50
		Nos. 391-393 (3)	2.90	3.15

Augustineum Training Institute, Windhoek — A82

20c, Katutura State Hospital, Windhoek.

1976, Sept. 17 Litho. Perf. 12x12½

| 394 | A82 | 15c ocher & black | .55 | .55 |
| 395 | A82 | 20c citron & black | .75 | .75 |

Owambo Canal System A83

20c, Ruacana Dam and hydroelectric station.

1976, Nov. 19 Litho. Perf. 12x12½

| 396 | A83 | 15c multicolored | .55 | .55 |
| 397 | A83 | 20c multicolored | .75 | .75 |

Water and electricity supply.

Sinking Ship off Namib Shore — A84

Designs: Namib Desert, various views.

1977, Mar. 29   Litho.   Perf. 12½

398	A84	4c multicolored	.25	.25
399	A84	10c multicolored	.45	.45
400	A84	15c multicolored	.70	.65
401	A84	20c multicolored	1.00	.95
		Nos. 398-401 (4)	2.40	2.30

Owambo Kraal — A85

Designs: 10c, Giant grain baskets. 15c, Women pounding corn. 20c, Body painting.

1977, July 15   Litho.   Perf. 12x12½

402	A85	4c multicolored	.25	.25
403	A85	10c multicolored	.35	.35
404	A85	15c multicolored	.50	.50
405	A85	20c multicolored	.80	.80
		Nos. 402-405 (4)	1.90	1.90

Traditions of the Wambo people.

J. G. Strijdom Airport, Windhoek — A86

1977, Aug. 22   Perf. 12½

406	A86	20c multicolored	.55	.45

Drostdy, Lüderitz, 1910 A87

Historic Houses: 10c, Woermannhaus, Swakopmund, 1895. 15c, Neu-Heusis, Windhoek. 20c, Schmelenhaus, Bethanie, 1814.

1977, Nov. 4   Litho.   Perf. 12x12½

407	A87	5c multicolored	.25	.25
408	A87	10c multicolored	.35	.35
409	A87	15c multicolored	.55	.55
410	A87	20c multicolored	.75	.75
a.		Souvenir sheet of 4, #407-410	2.25	2.25
		Nos. 407-410 (4)	1.90	1.90

Side-winding Adder — A88

Small Animals of the Namib Desert: 10c, Golden sand mole. 15c, Palmato gecko. 20c, Namaqua chameleon.

1978, Feb. 6   Litho.   Perf. 12½

411	A88	4c multicolored	.25	.25
412	A88	10c multicolored	.40	.40
413	A88	15c multicolored	.60	.60
414	A88	20c multicolored	.85	.85
		Nos. 411-414 (4)	2.10	2.10

Bushman Hunter Disguised as Ostrich A89

Bushmen: 10c, Woman carrying ostrich eggs on back. 15c, Making fire. 20c, Family sitting in front of hut.

1978, Apr. 14   Litho.   Perf. 12x12½

415	A89	4c brown, buff & blk	.25	.25
416	A89	10c brown, buff & blk	.30	.30
417	A89	15c brown, buff & blk	.50	.50
418	A89	20c brown, buff & blk	.65	.65
		Nos. 415-418 (4)	1.70	1.70

Lutheran Church, Windhoek — A90

Designs: 10c, Lutheran Church, Swakopmund. 15c, Rhenish Mission Church, Otjimbingwe. 20c, Rhenish Mission Church, Keetmanshoop.

1978, June 16   Litho.   Perf. 12½

419	A90	4c ol bister & blk	.25	.25
420	A90	10c bister & blk	.30	.30
421	A90	15c pale red brn & blk	.50	.50
422	A90	20c blue gray & blk	.65	.65
a.		Souvenir sheet of 4, #419-422	1.75	1.75
		Nos. 419-422 (4)	1.70	1.70

Type of 1973 Inscribed in English, German or Afrikaans:

a, UNIVERSAL / SUFFRAGE
b, ALLGEMEINES / WAHLRECHT
c, ALGEMENE / STEMREG

1978, Nov. 1   Litho.   Perf. 12½

423		Strip of 3	.25	.25
a.-c.	A70	4c any single	.25	.25
424		Strip of 3	.30	.30
a.-c.	A70	5c any single	.25	.25
425		Strip of 3	.60	.60
a.-c.	A70	10c any single	.25	.25
426		Strip of 3	.90	.90
a.-c.	A70	15c any single	.25	.25
427		Strip of 3	1.20	1.20
a.-c.	A70	20c any single	.35	.35
428		Strip of 3	1.60	1.60
a.-c.	A70	25c any single	.50	.50
		Nos. 423-428 (6)	4.85	4.85

General suffrage. Printed se-tenant with inscriptions alternating horizontally and vertically in sheets of 30 (3x10).

Greater Flamingoes A91

Water Birds: 15c, White-breasted cormorants. 20c, Chestnut-banded plovers. 25c, White pelicans.

1979, Apr. 5   Litho.   Perf. 14x14½

429	A91	4c multicolored	.25	.25
430	A91	15c multicolored	.40	.40
431	A91	20c multicolored	.55	.55
432	A91	25c multicolored	.70	.70
		Nos. 429-432 (4)	1.90	1.90

Silver Topaz A92

1979, Nov. 26   Litho.   Perf. 14x14½

433	A92	4c shown	.30	.30
434	A92	15c Aquamarine	.50	.50
435	A92	20c Malachite	.80	.80
436	A92	25c Amethyst	.95	.95
		Nos. 433-436 (4)	2.55	2.55

Killer Whale — A93

1980, Mar. 25   Litho.   Perf. 14x14½

437	A93	4c shown	.35	.30

Size: 37½x21mm

438	A93	5c Humpback whale	.40	.30
439	A93	10c Southern right whale	.75	.55

Size: 57½x21mm

440	A93	15c Sperm whale, giant squid	1.25	.85
441	A93	20c Fin whale	1.75	1.10

Size: 87½x21mm

442	A93	25c Blue whale, diver	1.90	1.25
a.		Souvenir sheet of 6, #437-442	7.00	7.00
		Nos. 437-442 (6)	6.40	4.35

Impala A94

1980, June 25   Litho.   Perf. 14½x14

443	A94	5c shown	.25	.25
444	A94	10c Tsessebe	.30	.30
445	A94	15c Roan antelope	.40	.40
446	A94	20c Sable antelope	.55	.55
		Nos. 443-446 (4)	1.50	1.50

Cape Hunting Dog — A95

1980-85   Litho.   Perf. 14½x14

447	A95	1c Black backed jackal	.25	.25
448	A95	2c shown	.25	.25
449	A95	3c Hyena	.25	.25
450	A95	4c Dorcas antelope	.25	.25
451	A95	5c Oryx	.25	.25
452	A95	6c Greater kudu	.25	.25

Perf. 14x14¼

453	A95	7c Zebra, horiz.	.25	.25
454	A95	8c Porcupine, horiz.	.25	.25
455	A95	9c Honey badger, horiz.	.25	.25
456	A95	10c Cheetah, horiz.	.25	.25
456A	A95	11c Blue wildebeest ('84)	.85	.85
456B	A95	12c Syncerus caffer, horiz. ('85)	.55	.30
c.		Booklet pane of 10	5.50	
457	A95	15c Hippopotamus, horiz.	.30	.30
458	A95	20c Taurotragus oryx, horiz.	.45	.45
459	A95	25c Rhinoceros, horiz.	.55	.55
460	A95	30c Lion, horiz.	.65	.65

Perf. 14½x14

461	A95	50c Giraffe	1.00	1.00
462	A95	1r Leopard	1.75	1.75
463	A95	2r Elephant	3.75	3.25
		Nos. 447-463 (19)	12.35	11.10

Coil Stamps

1980, Oct. 1   Litho.   Perf. 14 Vert.

464	A95	1c Suricate suricata	.40	.40
465	A95	2c Guenon	.40	.40
466	A95	5c South African chacma	.40	.40
		Nos. 464-466 (3)	1.20	1.20

See Nos. 556-557.

Von Bach Dam, Swakop River — A96

1980, Nov. 25   Litho.   Perf. 14x14½

467	A96	5c shown	.25	.25
468	A96	10c Swakoppoort Dam	.25	.25
469	A96	15c Naute Dam	.25	.25
470	A96	20c Hardap Dam	.35	.35
		Nos. 467-470 (4)	1.10	1.10

Water conservation in the desert.

Fish River Canyon — A97

Designs: Views of Fish River Canyon.

1981, Mar. 20   Litho.   Perf. 14½x14

471	A97	5c multicolored	.25	.25
472	A97	15c multicolored	.25	.25
473	A97	20c multicolored	.25	.25
474	A97	25c multicolored	.30	.30
		Nos. 471-474 (4)	1.05	1.05

Aloe Erinacea — A98

1981, Aug. 14

475	A98	5c shown	.25	.25
476	A98	15c Aloe viridiflora	.25	.25
477	A98	20c Aloe pearsonii	.30	.30
478	A98	25c Aloe littoralis	.30	.30
		Nos. 475-478 (4)	1.10	1.10

Paul Weiss-Haus Building, 1909, Luderitz — A99

Designs: Historic buildings in Luderitz.

1981, Oct. 16

479	A99	5c shown	.25	.25
480	A99	15c Deutsche Afrika Bank, 1906	.25	.25
481	A99	20c Schroederhaus, 1911	.30	.30
482	A99	25c Imperial P.O., 1908	.40	.40
a.		Souvenir sheet of 4, #479-482	1.25	1.25
		Nos. 479-482 (4)	1.20	1.20

Salt Making A100

1981, Dec. 4   Litho.   Perf. 14x14½

483	A100	5c Salt pan	.25	.25
484	A100	15c Dumping and washing	.25	.25
485	A100	20c Stockpiling	.25	.25
486	A100	25c Loading	.30	.30
		Nos. 483-486 (4)	1.05	1.05

Kalahari Starred Tortoise A101

1982, Mar. 12

487	A101	5c shown	.25	.25
488	A101	15c Leopard tortoise	.25	.25
489	A101	20c Angulated tortoise	.45	.45
490	A101	25c Speckled padloper	.55	.55
		Nos. 487-490 (4)	1.50	1.50

Discoverers of South-West Africa — A102

1982, May 28   Litho.   Perf. 14½x14
491 A102 15c Archbishop Olaus Magnus, sea monster .25 .25
492 A102 20c Bartolomeu Dias, ships, map .40 .30
493 A102 25c Caravel .65 .40
494 A102 30c Dias erecting cross, Angra das Voltas .70 .50
    Nos. 491-494 (4) 2.00 1.45

The Needle, Upper Brandberg A103

Designs: Mountain peaks.

1982, Aug. 3   Litho.   Perf. 14x14½
495 A103 6c Brandberg .25 .25
496 A103 15c Omatako twin peaks .25 .25
497 A103 20c shown .25 .25
498 A103 25c Spitzkuppe, Karakul sheep .35 .35
    Nos. 495-498 (4) 1.10 1.10

Traditional Headdress, Herero Tribe — A104

1982, Oct. 15   Litho.   Perf. 14x14½
499 A104 6c shown .25 .25
500 A104 15c Himba .25 .25
501 A104 20c Ngandjera .30 .30
502 A104 25c Kwanyama .40 .40
    Nos. 499-502 (4) 1.20 1.20

See Nos. 524-527.

Fort Vogelsang A105

Bethany Chief Joseph Fredericks — A106

Perf. 14x14½ (6c, 25c), 14½x14 (20c, 30-40c)

1983, Mar. 16
503 A105 6c shown .25 .25
504 A106 20c shown .25 .25
505 A105 25c Angra Pequena Bay .35 .35
506 A106 30c Explorer Heinrich Vogelsang .40 .40
507 A106 40c Adolf Luderitz (1834-1886) .60 .60
    Nos. 503-507 (5) 1.85 1.85

City of Luderitz centenary (1982).

Diamond Field, 1908 A107

Ernest Oppenheimer (1880-1957), Diamond Industry Leader — A108

Perf. 14x14½ (10-20c), 14½x14 (25-40c)

1983, June 8   Litho.
508 A107 10c shown .25 .25
509 A107 20c Field, diff. .35 .35
510 A108 25c shown .45 .45
511 A108 40c August Stauch, prospector .75 .75
    Nos. 508-511 (4) 1.80 1.80

75th anniv. of discovery of diamonds at Luderitz.

Zebras Drinking, by J.J. van Ellinckhuijzen (b. 1940) — A109

Paintings: 20c, Rossing Mountain, by Herman H.-J. Henckert (b. 1906). 25c, Stampeding Buffalo, by Fritz Krampe (1913-1966). 40c, Erongo Mountains, by Johann Blatt (1905-1973).

1983, Sept. 1   Perf. 14x14½
512 A109 10c multicolored .25 .25
513 A109 20c multicolored .30 .30
514 A109 25c multicolored .40 .40
515 A109 40c multicolored .65 .65
    Nos. 512-515 (4) 1.60 1.60

Lobster Industry A110

1983, Nov. 23   Perf. 13½x14
516 A110 10c Lobsters .25 .25
517 A110 20c Dinghies .30 .30
518 A110 25c Raising trap .40 .40
519 A110 40c Packaging .65 .65
    Nos. 516-519 (4) 1.60 1.60

Historic Buildings, Swakopmund — A111

1984, Mar. 8   Litho.   Perf. 14x13½
520 A111 10c Hohenzollern House .25 .25
521 A111 20c Railway Station .35 .35
522 A111 25c Imperial District Bureau .45 .45
523 A111 30c Ritterburg .55 .55
    Nos. 520-523 (4) 1.60 1.60

Headdress Type of 1982

1984, May 25   Litho.
524 A104 11c Kwambi .25 .25
525 A104 20c Bushman .35 .35
526 A104 25c Kwaluudhi .45 .45
527 A104 30c Mbukushu .55 .55
    Nos. 524-527 (4) 1.60 1.60

German Colonization Centenary — A112

1984, Aug. 7   Litho.   Perf. 13½x14
528 A112 11c Map, flag .40 .40
529 A112 25c Flag raising .70 .70
530 A112 30c Land marker .75 .75
531 A112 45c Corvettes Elisabeth & Leipzig 1.75 1.75
    Nos. 528-531 (4) 3.60 3.60

Spring Flowers — A113

1984, Nov. 22   Litho.   Perf. 14½x14
532 A113 11c Sweet thorn .25 .25
533 A113 25c Camel thorn .45 .45
534 A113 30c Hook thorn .55 .55
535 A113 45c Candle-pod acacia .85 .85
    Nos. 532-535 (4) 2.10 2.10

Ostrich A114

1985, Mar. 15
536 A114 11c Head of bird .35 .35
537 A114 25c Female nesting .70 .70
538 A114 30c Chick, eggs .80 .80
539 A114 50c Male mating dance 1.25 1.25
    Nos. 536-539 (4) 3.10 3.10

Historic Buildings, 1900-1912, Windhoek — A115

1985, June 6
540 A115 12c Erkrath, Gathemann Buildings, Kaiser Street .25 .25
541 A115 25c Gymnasium .30 .30
542 A115 30c Supreme Court .40 .40
543 A115 50c Railway Station .55 .55
    Nos. 540-543 (4) 1.50 1.50

600mm Narrow-gauge Locomotives — A116

1985, Aug. 2
544 A116 12c Zwilling Schmalspur, 1898 .35 .35
545 A116 25c Feldspur Side-Tank .70 .70
546 A116 30c 0-6-2 Side-Tank, 1904 .80 .80
547 A116 50c Henschel hd Smalspoor, 1912 1.50 1.50
    Nos. 544-547 (4) 3.35 3.35

Swakopmund-Tsumeb Railway line, 79th anniv.

Endemic Musical Instruments A117

1985, Oct. 17
548 A117 12c Lidumu-dumu .25 .25
549 A117 25c Ngoma .25 .25
550 A117 30c Okambulum bumbwa .30 .30
551 A117 50c Gwashi .55 .55
    Nos. 548-551 (4) 1.35 1.35

Diogo Cao, Portuguese Explorer, 1486 Visit to SWA A118

1986, Jan. 24   Perf. 14½x14
552 A118 12c Erecting padroes on shore .35 .35
553 A118 20c Cao coat of arms .55 .55
554 A118 25c Caravel .75 .75
555 A118 30c Portrait .95 .95
    Nos. 552-555 (4) 2.60 2.60

Wildlife Type of 1980
1986-87   Litho.   Perf. 14x14½
556 A95 14c Caracal, horiz. 4.25 4.25
557 A95 16c Warthog, horiz. 2.50 2.50

Issue dates: 14c, Apr. 1; 16c, Apr. 1, 1987.

Rock Formations A119

Designs: 14c, Granite bornhardt, Erongo. 20c, Vingerklip, Outjo. 25c, Aeolian sandstone, Kuiseb River. 30c, Columnar dolerite, Twyfelfontein.

1986, Apr. 24   Perf. 14½x14
566 A119 14c multicolored .30 .30
567 A119 20c multicolored .50 .50
568 A119 25c multicolored .65 .65
569 A119 30c multicolored .95 .95
    Nos. 566-569 (4) 2.40 2.40

Karakul Wool (Swakara) Industry — A120

1986, July 10   Perf. 14x14½
570 A120 14c Model .30 .30
571 A120 20c Hand loom .45 .45
572 A120 25c Sheep .65 .65
573 A120 30c Rams .75 .75
    a.   Souvenir sheet of 1 3.00 3.00
    Nos. 570-573 (4) 2.15 2.15

No. 573a margin pictures design of No. 570 and Johannesburg stamp exhib. emblem. Sold for 50c to benefit stamp exhib.

Caprivi Strip — A121

1986, Nov. 6   Litho.   Perf. 14½x14
574 A121 14c Lake Liambezi .35 .35
575 A121 20c Stock and crop farming .60 .60
576 A121 25c Settlement .75 .75
577 A121 30c Map 1.20 1.20
    Nos. 574-577 (4) 2.90 2.90

Paintings by
Thomas
Baines
(1820-1875)
A122

Designs: 14c, *Rhenish Mission Church at Gababis*, 1863. 20c, *Outspan in October*, 1861. 25c, *Outspan Under Oomahaama Tree*, 1862. 30c, *Swa-Kop River S.W. Africa*, 1861.

1987, Feb. 19   Litho.   Perf. 14½x14
578	A122	14c multicolored	.45	.45
579	A122	20c multicolored	.75	.75
580	A122	25c multicolored	.85	.85
a.		Souvenir sheet of 1	3.25	3.25
581	A122	30c multicolored	1.00	1.00
		Nos. 578-581 (4)	3.05	3.05

No. 580a for the natl. philatelic exhibition at Paarl, Sept. 16-19. Sold for 50c.

Insects
A123

1987, May 7
582	A123	16c *Garreta nitens*	.75	.75
583	A123	20c *Alcimus stenurus*	.95	.95
584	A123	25c *Anthophora caerulea*	1.25	1.25
585	A123	30c *Hemiempusa capensis*	1.40	1.40
		Nos. 582-585 (4)	4.35	4.35

Resorts — A124

1987, July 23
586	A124	16c Okaukuejo, Etosha Natl. Park	.40	.40
587	A124	20c Daan Viljoen Game Park	.55	.55
588	A124	25c Ai-Ais Hot Springs	.65	.65
589	A124	30c Hardap, Mariental	.80	.80
		Nos. 586-589 (4)	2.40	2.40

Shipwrecks
A125

1987, Oct. 15
590	A125	16c *Hope*, 1804	.70	.70
591	A125	30c *Tilly*, 1885	1.20	1.20
592	A125	40c *Eduard Bohlen*, 1909	1.60	1.60
593	A125	50c *Dunedin Star*, 1942	2.10	2.10
		Nos. 590-593 (4)	5.60	5.60

Discovery of the
Cape of Good
Hope by
Bartolomeu Dias,
500th
Anniv. — A126

1988, Jan. 7   Perf. 14x14½
594	A126	16c shown	.40	.40
595	A126	30c Caravel	.70	.70
596	A126	40c The Cantino Map, 1502	1.00	1.00
597	A126	50c King John II	1.25	1.25
		Nos. 594-597 (4)	3.35	3.35

Historic
Sites
A127

1988, Mar. 3   Perf. 14½x14
598	A127	16c Sossusvlei Clay Pans	.35	.35
599	A127	30c Sesriem Canyon	.60	.60
600	A127	40c Hoaruseb clay castles	.85	.85
601	A127	50c Hoba meteorite	1.40	1.40
		Nos. 598-601 (4)	3.20	3.20

Postal
Service,
Cent.
A128

1988, July 7   Perf. 14x14½
602	A128	16c Otyimbingue P.O., 1888	.40	.40
603	A128	30c Windhoek P.O., 1904	.85	.85
604	A128	40c Mail runner, 1888	1.20	1.20
605	A128	50c Camel post, 1904	1.40	1.40
a.		Souvenir sheet of 1	4.00	4.00
		Nos. 602-605 (4)	3.85	3.85

No. 605a for the natl. philatelic exhibition held at Windhoek, July 7-9. Sold for 1r.

Birds — A129

1988, Nov. 3
606	A129	16c *Namibornis hereo*	1.10	1.10
607	A129	30c *Ammomanes grayi*	1.60	1.60
608	A129	40c *Eupodotis rueppel-lii*	1.90	1.90
609	A129	50c *Tockus monteiri*	2.10	2.10
		Nos. 606-609 (4)	6.70	6.70

Missionaries and Mission
Stations — A130

16c, Carl Hahn (1818-95) & Gross-Barmen Mission. 30c, Johann Kronlein (1826-92) & Berseba Mission. 40c, Franz Kleinschmidt (1812-64) & Rehoboth Mission. 50c, Johann Schmelen (1777-1848) & Bethanien Mission.

1989, Feb. 16
610	A130	16c multicolored	.40	.40
611	A130	30c multicolored	.75	.75
612	A130	40c multicolored	1.20	1.20
613	A130	50c multicolored	1.40	1.40
		Nos. 610-613 (4)	3.75	3.75

Aviation
Industry,
75th Anniv.
A131

Maps and aircraft.

1989, May 18   Perf. 14½x14
614	A131	18c Beechcraft 1900	.85	.85
615	A131	30c Ryan Navion, 1948	1.20	1.20
616	A131	40c Junkers F13, 1930	1.60	1.60
617	A131	50c Pfalz Otto biplane, 1914	2.10	2.10
a.		Souvenir sheet of 1	5.00	5.00
		Nos. 614-617 (4)	5.75	5.75

No. 617a has decorative bright blue and black inscribed margin picturing emblem of

---

Namib Desert Sand Dunes — A132

1989, Aug. 14   Perf. 14x14½
Size of 30c, 50c: 31x21½mm
618	A132	18c Barchan dunes	.25	.25
619	A132	30c Star dunes	.50	.50
620	A132	40c Transverse dunes	.75	.75
621	A132	50c Crescent dunes	.95	.95
		Nos. 618-621 (4)	2.45	2.45

Suffrage, UN
Resolution
435 — A133

1989, Aug. 24
622	A133	18c dull org & gray vio	.25	.25
623	A133	35c green & blue	.50	.50
624	A133	45c yellow & purple	.80	.80
625	A133	60c golden brn & gray grn	1.20	1.20
		Nos. 622-625 (4)	2.75	2.75

Minerals — A134

Mines
A135

1989-90   Perf. 14½x14
626	A134	1c Gypsum	.25	.25
627	A134	2c Fluorite	.25	.25
628	A134	5c Mimetite	.25	.25
629	A134	7c Cuprite	.25	.25
630	A134	10c Azurite	.25	.25
631	A134	18c Boltwoodite	.30	.30
631A	A134	18c see footnote	14.00	8.00
632	A134	20c Dioptase	.30	.30
633	A135	25c Alluvial diamond field, Oranjemund	.35	.35
634	A135	30c Lead, copper & zinc mine, Tsumeb	.40	.40
635	A135	35c Zinc mine, Rosh Pinah	.50	.50
636	A134	40c Diamonds	.55	.55
637	A134	45c Wulfenite	.65	.65
638	A135	50c Tin mine, Uis	.70	.70
639	A135	1r Uranium mine, Rossing	1.50	1.50
640	A134	2r Gold	3.00	3.00
		Nos. 626-640 (16)	23.50	17.50

#631 has formula, K(H3O)(UO2)(SiO4); #631A K2(UO2)2(SiO3)2(OH)2.5H2O. Issued: #631A, 10/25/90; others, 11/16/89. This set remained in use until Namibia issued a definitive set Jan. 2, 1991.

Flora — A136

1990, Feb. 1   Perf. 14½x14
641	A136	18c *Adenium boehmianum*	.40	.40
642	A136	35c *Adansonia digitata*	.80	.80
643	A136	45c *Kigelia africana*	1.00	1.00
644	A136	60c *Harpagophytum procumbens*	1.25	1.25
a.		Souvenir sheet of 1	5.00	5.00
		Nos. 641-644 (4)	3.45	3.45

No. 644a margin publicizes the natl. phil. exhib. Sold for 1.50r.

SEMI-POSTAL STAMPS

> Catalogue values for unused stamps in this section are for Never Hinged items.

Voortrekker Monument Issue

South Africa Nos. B1-B4 Overprinted

1935-36   Wmk. 201   Perf. 14
B1	SP1	½p + ½p grn & blk, pair	3.00	7.00
a.		Single, English	.40	.85
b.		Single, Afrikaans	.40	.85
B2	SP2	1p + ½p rose & blk, pair	4.00	4.00
a.		Single, English	.45	.45
b.		Single, Afrikaans	.45	.45
B3	SP3	2p + 1p dl vio & gray, pair	17.50	10.00
a.		Single, English	1.75	1.25
b.		Single, Afrikaans	1.75	1.25
B4	SP4	3p + 1 ½p dp bl & gray, pair	30.00	40.00
a.		Single, English	3.25	4.50
b.		Single, Afrikaans	3.25	4.50
		Nos. B1-B4 (4)	54.50	61.00

Voortrekker Centenary Issue
South Africa Nos. B5-B8 Overprinted

1938, Dec. 14   Perf. 14
B5	SP5	½p + ½p dl grn & indigo, pair	11.00	25.00
a.		Single, English	1.00	2.25
b.		Single, Afrikaans	1.00	2.25
		Perf. 15x14		
B6	SP6	1p + 1p rose & sl, pair	27.50	20.00
a.		Single, English	1.50	1.50
b.		Single, Afrikaans	1.50	1.50
B7	SP7	1 ½p + 1 ½p Prus grn & choc, pair	29.00	35.00
a.		Single, English	2.00	3.25
b.		Single, Afrikaans	2.00	3.25
B8	SP8	3p + 3p chlky bl, pair	55.00	85.00
a.		Single, English	4.50	8.50
b.		Single, Afrikaans	4.50	8.50
		Nos. B5-B8 (4)	122.50	165.00

Same Overprint on South Africa Nos. B9-B11

1939, July 17   Perf. 14
B9	SP9	½p + ½p Prus grn & gray brn, pair	14.00	16.00
a.		Single, English	1.00	1.25
b.		Single, Afrikaans	1.00	1.25
B10	SP10	1p + 1p rose car & Prus grn, pair	21.00	16.00
a.		Single, English	1.25	1.25
b.		Single, Afrikaans	1.25	1.25
		Perf. 15x14		
B11	SP11	1 ½p + 1 ½p rose vio, dk vio & Prus grn, pair	34.00	20.00
a.		Single, English	2.00	1.75
b.		Single, Afrikaans	2.00	1.75
		Nos. B9-B11 (3)	69.00	52.00

250th anniv. of the landing of the Huguenots in South Africa. Surtax went to a fund to build a Huguenot memorial at Paarl.

AIR POST STAMPS

South Africa
Nos. C5-C6
Overprinted

1930		**Unwmk.**		**Perf. 14x13½**
C1	AP2	4p blue green	10.00	32.50
a.		Without period after "A"	80.00	150.00
C2	AP2	1sh orange	16.00	57.50
a.		Without period after "A"	500.00	750.00

Overprinted

C3	AP2	4p blue green	1.50	7.00
a.		Double overprint	200.00	
b.		Inverted overprint	200.00	
c.		Small "I" in "AIR"	6.00	
C4	AP2	1sh orange	4.25	17.50
a.		Double overprint	575.00	

Monoplane over Windhoek — AP3

Biplane over Windhoek — AP4

Wmk. 201

1931, Mar. 5		**Engr.**		**Perf. 14**
C5	AP3	3p blue & dk brn, pair	40.00	45.00
a.		Single, English	3.00	3.00
b.		Single, Afrikaans	3.00	3.00
C6	AP4	10p brn vio & blk, pair	85.00	85.00
a.		Single, English	7.00	7.00
b.		Single, Afrikaans	7.00	7.00

POSTAGE DUE STAMPS

Postage Due Stamps of South Africa and Transvaal Overprinted like Regular Issues.

Setting I
On South Africa Nos. J11, J14
Perf. 14 Unwmk.

1923				
J1	D1	½p blue grn & blk, pair	6.75	30.00
a.		Single, English	.75	5.50
b.		Single, Dutch	.75	5.50
c.		As #J1, without period after "Afrika"	130.00	
d.		Inverted ovpt., pair	600.00	
J2	D1	2p violet & blk, pair	4.00	28.00
a.		Single, English	.50	5.00
b.		Single, Dutch	.50	5.00
c.		As #J2, without period after "Afrika"	170.00	170.00

On South Africa Nos. J9-J10
Rouletted 7-8

J3	D1	1p dull red & blk, pair	8.00	30.00
a.		Single, English	.90	5.50
b.		Single, Dutch	.90	5.50
c.		As #J3, without period after "Afrika"	150.00	150.00
d.		Pair, imperf. between	1,800.	
J4	D1	1 ½p yel brn & blk, pair	1.50	16.00
a.		Single, English	.25	2.75
b.		Single, Dutch	.25	2.75
c.		As #J4, without period after "Afrika"	110.00	110.00

On South Africa Nos. J3-J4, J6
Perf. 14
Wmk. 177

J5	D1	2p violet & blk, pair	42.50	55.00
a.		Single, English	3.00	10.00
b.		Single, Dutch	3.00	10.00
c.		As #J5, without period after "Afrika"	275.00	
d.		"Wes" for "West"	325.00	
J6	D1	3p ultra & blk, pair	21.00	55.00
a.		Single, English	1.50	10.00
b.		Single, Dutch	1.50	10.00
J7	D1	6p gray & blk, pair	40.00	65.00
a.		Single, English	4.00	13.00
b.		Single, Dutch	4.00	13.00
		Nos. J5-J7 (3)	103.50	175.00

On Transvaal Nos. J5-J6
Wmk. Multiple Crown and C A (3)

J8	D1	5p violet & blk, pair	4.50	55.00
a.		Single, English	.75	11.00
b.		Single, Dutch	.75	11.00
c.		As #J8, without period after "Afrika"	130.00	130.00
J9	D1	6p red brn & blk, pair	19.00	55.00
a.		Single, English	2.50	11.00
b.		As #J9, without period after "Afrika"	275.00	

For No. J9 single in English see No. J17a and note after No. 27.
The "t" of "West" may be found partly or entirely missing on Nos. J1, J3-J6, J8-J9.

Setting II
On South Africa No. J9
Rouletted
Unwmk.

J10	D1	1p dull red & blk, pair	14,000.	
a.		Single, English	800.00	1,600.
b.		Single, Dutch	800.00	1,600.

On South Africa Nos. J3-J4
Perf. 14
Wmk. 177

J11	D1	2p violet & blk, pair	19.00	50.00
a.		Single, English	1.75	9.00
b.		Single, Dutch	1.75	9.00
c.		As #J11, without period after "Afrika"	275.00	250.00
J12	D1	3p ultra & blk, pair	8.50	32.50
a.		Single, English	1.00	5.50
b.		Single, Dutch	1.00	5.50
c.		As #J12, without period after "Afrika"	130.00	150.00

On Transvaal No. J5
Wmk. Multiple Crown and C A (3)

J13	D1	5p violet & blk, pair	75.00	200.00
a.		Single, English	15.00	20.00
b.		Single, Dutch	15.00	20.00

Setting III
On South Africa Nos. J11, J12, J9
Unwmk.

J14	D1	½p blue grn & blk, pair	17.50	37.50
a.		Single, Dutch	1.50	5.50
J15	D1	1p rose & black, pair	27.50	37.50
a.		Single, English	1.50	6.00
b.		Single, Dutch	1.50	6.00

Rouletted 7

J16	D1	1p dull red & blk, pair	9.50	37.50
a.		Single, English	1.00	6.00

For Nos. J14 and J16 singles in English see Nos. J1a and J3a and note after No. 27.

On Transvaal No. J6
Perf. 14
Wmk. 3

J17	D1	6p red brown & blk, pair	23.50	100.00
a.		Single, English	2.50	20.00
b.		Single, Dutch	2.50	20.00

See note below No. 27.

Setting IV
On South Africa Nos. J11-J12, J16

1924				**Unwmk.**
J18	D1	½p blue grn & blk, pair	8.50	35.00
a.		Single, English	.75	5.50
b.		Single, Dutch	.75	5.50
J19	D1	1p rose & blk, pair	8.50	32.50
a.		Single, English	.60	5.50
b.		Single, Dutch	.60	5.50
J20	D1	6p gray & blk, pair	3.00	45.00
a.		Single, English	.30	9.00
b.		Single, Dutch	.30	9.00

On Transvaal No. J5
Wmk. Multiple Crown and C A (3)

J21	D1	5p violet & blk, pair	800.00	1,200.
a.		Single, English	140.00	175.00
b.		Single, Dutch	140.00	175.00

Setting V

i   j

"South West" 16mm wide
"Zuidwest" 12mm wide
Overprint Spaced 12mm

On South Africa Nos. J4, J11, J13

1924				**Unwmk.**
J22	D1	½p green & blk, pair	3.50	32.50
a.		Single, English	.25	6.50
b.		Single, Dutch	.25	6.50
J23	D1	1 ½p yel brown & blk	5.75	47.50
a.		Single, English	.50	7.50
b.		Single, Dutch	.50	7.50

Wmk. Springbok's Head (177)

J24	D1	3p ultra & black, pair	16.00	60.00
a.		Single, English	1.75	11.00
b.		Single, Dutch	1.75	11.00

On Transvaal No. J5
Wmk. Multiple Crown and C A (3)

J25	D1	5p violet & blk, pair	3.00	25.00
a.		Single, English	.40	7.50
b.		Single, Dutch	.40	7.50

Setting VI
On South Africa Nos. J4, J11-J16

1924, Dec.				**Unwmk.**
J26	D1	½p blue grn & blk, pair	14.00	40.00
a.		Single, English	1.00	7.50
b.		Single, Dutch	1.00	7.50
J27	D1	1p rose & black, pair	2.25	14.00
a.		Single, English	.25	1.75
b.		Single, Dutch	.25	1.75
c.		As #J27, without period after "Africa"	100.00	
J28	D1	1 ½p yel brown & blk, pair	5.00	35.00
a.		Single, English	.30	6.50
b.		Single, Dutch	.30	6.50
c.		As #J28, without period after "Africa"	110.00	
J29	D1	2p violet & blk, pair	3.00	19.00
a.		Single, English	.35	3.50
b.		Single, Dutch	.35	3.50
c.		As #J29, without period after "Africa"	85.00	
J30	D1	3p blue & black, pair	5.25	20.00
a.		Single, English	.85	3.75
b.		Single, Dutch	.85	3.75
c.		As #J30, without period after "Africa"	92.50	
J31	D1	6p gray & blk, pair	16.00	57.50
a.		Single, English	2.00	14.00
b.		Single, Dutch	2.00	14.00
c.		As #J31, without period after "Africa"	180.00	
		Nos. J26-J31 (6)	45.50	185.50

Wmk. Springbok's Head (177)

J32	D1	3p ultra & black, pair	10.00	65.00
a.		Single, English	1.75	11.00
b.		Single, Dutch	1.75	11.00

On Transvaal No. J5
Wmk. 3

J33	D1	5p violet & blk, pair	3.25	22.50
a.		Single, English	.25	3.50
b.		Single, Dutch	.25	3.50
c.		As #J33, without period after "Africa"	92.50	75.00

Setting VIII
On South Africa Nos. J18, J13-J16

1927				**Unwmk.**
J34	D2	1p rose & black, pair	1.25	13.00
a.		Single, English	.25	2.25
b.		Single, Afrikaans	.25	2.25
c.		As #J34, without period after "Africa"	10.50	17.50
J35	D1	1 ½p yel brown & blk, pair	1.25	22.50
a.		Single, English	.25	3.50
b.		Single, Afrikaans	.25	3.50
c.		As #J35, without period after "Africa"	50.00	60.00
J36	D1	2p violet & blk, pair	6.00	18.00
a.		Single, English	.30	3.25
b.		Single, Afrikaans	.30	3.25
c.		As #J36, without period after "Africa"	50.00	60.00

J37	D1	3p blue & black, pair	16.00	50.00
a.		Single, English	1.75	11.00
b.		Single, Afrikaans	1.75	11.00
c.		As #J37, without period after "Africa"	70.00	70.00
J38	D1	6p gray & black, pair	12.00	40.00
a.		Single, English	1.50	8.50
b.		Single, Afrikaans	1.50	8.50
c.		As #J38, without period after "Africa"	100.00	115.00
		Nos. J34-J38 (5)	36.50	143.50

On Transvaal No. J5
Wmk. Multiple Crown and C A (3)

J39	D1	5p violet & blk, pair	22.50	97.50
a.		Single, English	3.00	22.50
b.		Single, Afrikaans	3.00	22.50

South Africa Nos. J15-J16 Overprinted

1928				**Unwmk.**
J79	D1	3p blue & black	1.65	12.00
a.		Without period after "A"	42.50	45.00
J80	D1	6p gray & black	7.50	32.50
a.		Without period after "A"	150.00	

Same Overprint on South Africa Nos. J17-J21

J81	D2	½p blue grn & blk	.65	9.50
J82	D2	1p rose & black	.65	4.00
a.		Without period after "A"	45.00	50.00
J83	D2	2p violet & black	.65	5.00
a.		Without period after "A"	62.50	
J84	D2	3p ultra & black	2.75	30.00
a.		Without period after "A"	1.75	22.50
J85	D2	6p gray & black	1.75	22.50
a.		Without period after "A"	62.50	225.00
		Nos. J81-J85 (5)	6.45	71.00

Catalogue values for unused stamps in this section, from this point to the end of the section, are for Never Hinged items.

D3   D4

Wmk. 201

1931, Feb. 23		**Litho.**		**Perf. 12**
		Size: 19x22mm		
J86	D3	½p yel green & blk	2.00	8.50
J87	D3	1p rose & black	2.00	1.65
J88	D3	2p violet & black	2.50	3.25
J89	D3	3p blue & black	5.00	15.00
J90	D3	6p gray & black	17.50	30.00
		Nos. J86-J90 (5)	29.00	58.40

Cover values are for properly franked commercial items. Philatelic usages also exist and sell for less.

Photo. (Frame) & Typo. (Center)

1959				**Perf. 14½x14**
		Size: 17x21mm		
J91	D3	1p rose & black	2.25	15.00
J92	D3	2p violet & black	2.25	15.00
J93	D3	3p blue & black	2.25	15.00
		Nos. J91-J93 (3)	6.75	45.00

1960				**Wmk. 330**
		Size: 17x21mm		
J94	D3	1p rose & black	3.75	4.50
J95	D3	3p blue & black	3.75	6.00

1961, Feb.		**Photo.**		**Perf. 14½x14**
J96	D4	1c green & black	1.00	4.25
J97	D4	2c red & black	1.00	4.25
J98	D4	4c lilac & black	1.00	6.00
J99	D4	5c blue & black	1.75	5.25
J100	D4	6c emerald & black	2.00	7.50
J101	D4	10c yellow & black	4.50	11.00
		Nos. J96-J101 (6)	11.25	38.25

Type of South Africa, 1972

1972		**Wmk. 359**		**Perf. 14x13½**
J102	D6	1c bright green	1.10	8.00
J103	D6	8c violet blue	3.75	8.50

OFFICIAL STAMPS

Nos. 85-87 (Setting VIII) Overprinted at top with type "c" on English-inscribed Stamps and type "d" on Afrikaans-inscribed Stamps

c   d

Without Periods after Words

1927	**Wmk. 201**	**Perf. 14½x14**		
O1	A5	½p dk green & blk, pair	95.00	200.00
a.		Single, English	12.50	30.00
b.		Single, Afrikaans	12.50	30.00
O2	A6	1p car & blk, pair	95.00	200.00
a.		Single, English	12.50	30.00
b.		Single, Afrikaans	12.50	30.00
O3	A7	6p org & grn, pair	120.00	225.00
a.		Single, English	15.00	30.00
b.		Single, Afrikaans	15.00	30.00

South Africa No. 5 Overprinted As Nos. 85-87 plus "c" and "d"

Perf. 14
Wmk. 177

O4	A2	2p dull violet	225.00	375.00
a.		Single, English	35.00	45.00
b.		Single, Afrikaans	35.00	45.00

Nos. 96-98 Overprinted like Nos. J79-J85 at foot, Overprinted Types "c" and "d" at Top

1929	**Wmk. 201**	**Perf. 14½x14**		
O5	A5	½p green & blk, pair	1.25	17.50
a.		Single, English	.25	2.75
b.		Single, Afrikaans	.25	2.75
O6	A6	1p car & blk, pair	2.00	23.00
a.		Single, English	.25	2.75
b.		Single, Afrikaans	.25	2.75
O7	A7	6p org & grn, pair	4.50	23.00
a.		Single, English	.75	3.75
b.		Single, Afrikaans	.75	3.75
		Nos. O5-O7 (3)	7.75	63.50

No. 99 Overprinted in Black

With Periods after Words
Perf. 14

O8	A8	2p vio brn & gray, pair	2.50	22.50
a.		Single, English	.35	3.75
b.		Single, Afrikaans	.35	3.75
c.		Without period after "OFFI-CIAL"	7.00	50.00
d.		Pair, "c" + normal 2p	17.00	95.00
e.		Without period after "OF-FISIEEL"	7.00	50.00
f.		Pair, "e" + normal 2p	17.00	95.00
g.		Pair, "c" + "e"	22.00	95.00

In each sheet of 120 stamps there were 12 No. O8c and 10 No. O8e.

South Africa Nos. 23-25 Overprinted

Without Periods after Words

1929	**Wmk. 201**	**Perf. 14½x14**		
O9	A5	½p green & blk, pair	.85	16.00
a.		Single, English	.25	2.75
b.		Single, Afrikaans	.25	2.75
O10	A6	1p car & blk, pair	1.25	17.50
a.		Single, English	.25	3.25
b.		Single, Afrikaans	.25	3.25
O11	A7	6p org & grn, pair	3.00	27.50
a.		Single, English	.40	6.50
b.		Single, Afrikaans	.40	6.50
		Nos. O9-O11 (3)	5.10	61.00

South Africa No. 26 Overprinted

With Periods after Words
Perf. 14

O12	A8	2p vio brn & gray, pair	1.50	22.00
a.		Single, English	.25	3.50
b.		Single, Afrikaans	.25	3.50
c.		Without period after "OFFI-CIAL"	3.75	45.00
d.		Pair, "c" + normal 2p	17.00	95.00
e.		Without period after "OF-FISIEEL"	6.50	50.00
f.		Pair, "e" + normal 2p	17.00	95.00
g.		Pair, "c" + "e"	22.00	95.00

> **Catalogue values for unused stamps in this section, from this point to the end of the section, are for Never Hinged items.**

Nos. 108-109, 111 and 114 Overprinted in Red

1931

O13	A15	½p green & blk, pair	15.00	22.00
a.		Single, English	1.25	3.75
b.		Single, Afrikaans	1.25	3.75
O14	A16	1p red & indigo, pair	1.50	19.00
a.		Single, English	.25	3.50
b.		Single, Afrikaans	.25	3.50
O15	A18	2p dk brn & dk bl, pair	3.75	11.00
a.		Single, English	.40	2.25
b.		Single, Afrikaans	.40	2.25
O16	A21	6p ol brn & bl, pair	5.75	15.00
a.		Single, English	.50	3.25
b.		Single, Afrikaans	.50	3.25
		Nos. O13-O16 (4)	26.00	67.00

No. 110 Overprinted in Red

1938, July 1			**Wmk. 201**	
O17	A17	1½p violet brn, pair	36.50	50.00
a.		Single, English	3.50	6.00
b.		Single, Afrikaans	3.50	6.00

Nos. 108-111, 114 Ovptd. in Red

1945-50	**Wmk. 201**	**Perf. 14x13½**		
O18	A15	½p green & blk, pair	14.00	35.00
a.		Single, English	1.50	5.00
b.		Single, Afrikaans	1.50	5.00
O19	A16	1p red & ind, pair ('50)	14.00	20.00
a.		Single, English	.85	3.25
b.		Single, Afrikaans	.85	3.25
O20	A17	1½p vio brown, pair	40.00	55.00
a.		Single, English	5.00	7.00
b.		Single, Afrikaans	5.00	7.00
O21	A18	2p dk brn & dk bl, pair ('47)	675.00	875.00
a.		Single, English	100.00	100.00
b.		Single, Afrikaans	100.00	100.00
O22	A21	6p ol brn & bl, pair	30.00	70.00
a.		Single, English	2.00	8.00
b.		Single, Afrikaans	2.00	8.00
		Nos. O18-O20,O22 (4)	98.00	180.00

Nos. 108-111, 114 Ovptd. in Red

1951-52

O23	A15	½p grn & blk, pair ('52)	19.00	25.00
a.		Single, English	2.00	4.50
b.		Single, Afrikaans	2.00	4.50
O24	A16	1p red & ind, pair	6.00	22.50
a.		Single, English	.40	2.00
b.		Single, Afrikaans	.40	2.00
c.		Ovpt. transposed, pair	110.00	250.00
d.		As "c," single, English ovpt.	10.00	
e.		As "c," single, Afrikaans ovpt.	10.00	
O25	A17	1½p violet brn, pair	30.00	32.50
a.		Single, English	3.00	5.00
b.		Single, Afrikaans	3.00	5.00
c.		Ovpt. transposed, pair	80.00	95.00
d.		As "c," single, English ovpt.	7.50	
e.		As "c," single, Afrikaans ovpt.	7.50	
O26	A18	2p dk brn & dk bl, pair	4.00	26.00
a.		Single, English	.45	3.50
b.		Single, Afrikaans	.45	3.50
c.		Ovpt. transposed, pair	75.00	250.00
d.		As "c," single, English ovpt.	4.50	
e.		As "c," single, Afrikaans ovpt.	4.50	
O27	A21	6p ol brn & blue, pair	4.00	55.00
a.		Single, English	.50	7.50
b.		Single, Afrikaans	.50	7.50
c.		Ovpt. transposed, pair	28.00	170.00
d.		As "c," single, English ovpt.	4.00	
e.		As "c," single, Afrikaans ovpt.	4.00	
		Nos. O23-O27 (5)	63.00	161.00

"Overprint transposed" means English inscription on Afrikaans stamp, or vice versa. Use of official stamps ceased in Jan. 1955.

SPAIN

'spän

LOCATION — Southwestern Europe, Iberian Peninsula
GOVT. — Monarchy

AREA — 194,884 sq. mi.
POP. — 39,167,744 (1999 est.)
CAPITAL — Madrid

Spain was a monarchy until about 1931, when a republic was established. After the Civil War (1936-39), the Spanish State of Gen. Francisco Franco was recognized. The monarchy was restored in 1975.

32 Maravedis = 8 Cuartos = 1 Real
1000 Milesimas = 100 Centimos = 1 Escudo (1866)
100 Milesimas = 1 Real
4 Reales = 1 Peseta
100 Centimos = 1 Peseta (1872)
100 Cents = 1 Euro (2002)

> **Catalogue values for unused stamps in this country are for Never Hinged items, beginning with Scott 909 in the regular postage section, Scott B139 in the semi-postal section, Scott C159 in the airpost section, and Scott E21 in the special delivery section.**

Watermarks

Wmk. 104 — Loops   Wmk. 105 — Crossed Lines

Wmk. 116 — Crosses and Circles   Wmk. 178 — Castle

Stamps punched with a small round hole have done telegraph service. In this condition most of them sell for 20 cents to $20.

Stamps of 1854 to 1882 canceled with three parallel horizontal bars or two thin lines are remainders. Most of these are valued through No. 101.

For additional shades see the *Scott Classic Catalogue.*

Kingdom

Queen Isabella II
A1   A2

A2a   A2b

A2c

6 CUARTOS:
Type I — "T" and "O" of CUARTOS separated.
Type II — "T" and "O" joined.

Unwmk.
1850, Jan. 1　　Litho.　　Imperf.

1	A1	6c blk, thin paper (II)	700.00	17.00
a.		Thick paper (II)	700.00	25.00
b.		Thick paper (I)	850.00	20.00
c.		Thin paper (I)	850.00	32.50
2	A2	12c lilac	3,000.	250.00
a.		Thin paper	4,500.	325.00
3	A2a	5r red	3,000.	250.00
4	A2b	6r blue	3,750.	850.00
5	A2c	10r green	5,850.	2,000.

Stamps of types A2, A3, A4, A6, A7a and A8 are inscribed "FRANCO" on the cuarto values and "CERTIFICADO," "CERTIFO" or "CERT DO" on the reales values.

A3

A4

1851, Jan. 1　　　　　　Typo.
Thin Paper

6	A3	6c black	375.00	3.50
a.		Thick paper	825.00	20.00
7	A3	12c lilac	6,000.	200.00
8	A3	2r red	26,000.	8,000.
9	A3	5r rose	3,000.	225.00
a.		5r red brown (error)	22,000.	—
10	A3	6r blue	5,250.	900.00
a.		Cliche of 2r in plate of 6r	—	125,000.
11	A3	10r green	3,750.	550.00

1852, Jan. 1　　　　Thick Paper

12	A4	6c rose	500.00	3.50
a.		Thin paper	625.00	5.50
13	A4	12c lilac	2,600.	150.00
14	A4	2r pale red	19,000.	5,000.
15	A4	5r yellowish green	2,950.	125.00
16	A4	6r grnsh blue	4,600.	525.00

Arms of Madrid — A5

Isabella II — A6

1853, Jan. 1　　　　Thin Paper

17	A5	1c bronze	3,300.	500.00
18	A5	3c bronze	19,000.	8,000.
19	A6	6c carmine rose	750.00	2.25
a.		Thick paper	975.00	16.00
b.		Thick bluish paper	1,300.	22.50
20	A6	12c reddish purple	2,750.	135.00
21	A6	2r vermilion	15,000.	3,000.
22	A6	5r lt green	3,000.	130.00
23	A6	6r deep blue	4,100.	450.00

Nos. 17-18 were issued for use on Madrid city mail only. *They were reprinted on this white paper in duller colors.*

A7

A7a

Coat of Arms of Spain — A8

1854　　　　　Thin White Paper

24	A7	2c green	2,650.	525.00
c.		Thick paper	3,650.	525.00

25	A7a	4c carmine	525.00	2.10
a.		Thick paper	675.00	17.50
26	A8	6c carmine	450.00	1.60
27	A7a	1r indigo	4,500.	350.00
		Bar cancellation		21.00
28	A8	2r scarlet	2,100.	120.00
		Bar cancellation		10.00
c.		Thick paper	—	250.00
29	A8	5r green	2,000.	110.00
		Bar cancellation		16.00
30	A8	6r blue	4,000.	325.00
		Bar cancellation		25.00

See boxed note on bar cancellation before #1.

Thick Bluish Paper

31	A7	2c green	*17,500.*	*2,100.*
b.		Thin paper	18,500.	2,400.
32	A7a	4c carmine	525.00	5.50
c.		Thin paper	600.00	17.50
32A	A8	6c carmine	1,050.	19.00
d.		Thin paper	—	100.00
33	A7a	1r pale blue		*8,250.*
a.		Thin paper		9,500.
34	A8	2r dull red	*8,500.*	825.00
		Thin paper	8,500.	825.00

Full margins = ¾mm.

The 2c with watermark 104 is a proof.

Isabella II — A9

1855, Apr. 1　　　　Wmk. 104
Blue Paper

36	A9	2c green	*3,650.*	140.00
a.		2c yellow green	4,500.	175.00
		Bar cancellation, #36 or 36a		10.00
37	A9	4c brown red	350.00	1.00
a.		4c carmine	440.00	2.50
b.		4c lake	350.00	.90
		Bar cancellation, #37, 37a or 37b		2.50
		Bar cancellation		2.50
38	A9	1r green blue	1,550.	15.00
a.		1r blue	1,600.	20.00
		Bar cancellation, #38 or 38a		5.00
b.		Cliché of 2r in plate of 1r	25,000.	3,250.
		Bar cancellation, #38b		850.00
39	A9	2r reddish purple	1,050.	15.00
a.		2r deep violet	1,450.	20.00
		Bar cancellation, #39, 39a or 39b		13.50

1856, Jan. 1　　　　Wmk. 105
Rough Yellowish Paper

40	A9	2c green	*4,400.*	275.00
		Bar cancellation		15.00
41	A9	4c rose	13.50	2.25
		Bar cancellation		2.50
42	A9	1r grnsh blue	*4,500.*	200.00
a.		1r dull blue	5,750.	275.00
		Bar cancellation, #42 or 42a		8.50
43	A9	2r brown purple	625.00	25.00
a.		2r dark reddish purple	775.00	45.00
		Bar cancellation, #43, 43a		7.50

1856, Apr. 11　　　　Unwmk.
White Smooth Paper

44	A9	2c blue green	700.00	42.50
a.		2c yellow green	825.00	50.00
		Bar cancellation, #44 or 44a		7.50
45	A9	4c rose	5.75	.35
a.		4c carmine ('59)	9.25	20.00
46	A9	1r blue	27.50	25.00
a.		1r pale greenish blue	40.00	32.50
		Bar cancellation, #46 or 46a		4.00
47	A9	2r brown lilac	90.00	29.00
a.		2r dull lilac	100.00	35.00
		Bar cancellation, #47 or 47a		10.00

Three types of No. 45.

1859

48	A9	12c dark orange	200.00	
		Bar cancellation		55.00
a.		Tete-beche pair (#48)	5,750.	
		Bar cancellation		150.00

Nos. 48-48b were never put in use. *Reprints exist.*

A10

A11

1860-61　　　　　Tinted Paper

49	A10	2c green, *grn*	400.00	19.00
		Bar cancellation		2.50
50	A10	4c orange, *grn*	55.00	.80
51	A10	12c car, *buff*	400.00	14.00
		Bar cancellation		8.75
52	A10	19c brn, *buff* ('61)	3,000.	1,500.
53	A10	1r blue, *grn*	360.00	12.50
		Bar cancellation		4.50
54	A10	2r lilac, *lil*	450.00	11.00
		Bar cancellation		4.50

1862, July 16

55	A11	2c dp bl, *yel*	37.50	11.00
56	A11	4c dk brn, *redsh buff*	2.40	.70
a.		4c brown, *white*	24.00	7.00
		Bar cancellation		2.50
57	A11	12c blue, *pnksh*	42.50	8.50
		Bar cancellation		3.25
58	A11	19c car, *lil*	200.00	225.00
a.		19c carmine, *white*	300.00	275.00
		Bar cancellation, #58 or 58a		175.00
59	A11	1r brown, *yel*	57.50	17.50
		Bar cancellation		3.50
60	A11	2r green, *pnksh*	37.50	11.00
		Bar cancellation		3.25
		Nos. 55-60 (6)	377.40	273.70

A12

A13

1864, Jan. 1

61	A12	2c dk bl, *lil*	50.00	20.00
62	A12	4c rose, *redsh buff*	2.50	1.00
a.		4c carmine, *reddish buff*	22.50	7.50
		Bar cancellation, #62 or 62a		2.50
63	A12	12c green, *pnksh*	42.50	14.50
64	A12	19c violet, *pnksh*	210.00	190.00
65	A12	1r brown, *grn*	190.00	75.00
		Bar cancellation		5.00
66	A12	2r blue, *pnksh*	45.00	12.00
		Bar cancellation, #66 or 66a		5.00
		Nos. 61-66 (6)	540.00	312.50

1865, Jan. 1　　Litho.　　Imperf.

67	A13	2c rose	325.00	35.00
68	A13	4c blue	2,750.	
69	A13	12c blue & rose	425.00	19.00
		Bar cancellation		5.25
a.		Frame inverted	13,500.	1,000.
		Bar cancellation		100.00
70	A13	19c brown & rose	1,300.	700.00
		Bar cancellation		100.00
71	A13	1r yellow grn	425.00	65.00
		Bar cancellation		17.50
72	A13	2r red lilac	425.00	35.00
		Bar cancellation		16.00
73	A13	2r rose	550.00	65.00
		Bar cancellation		17.50
a.		2r salmon	475.00	70.00
		Bar cancellation		50.00

No. 68 is without gum and was never put in use.

A majority of the perforated stamps from 1865 to about 1950 are rather poorly centered. The very fine examples that are valued will be fairly well centered. Poorly centered stamps sell for less. Stamps of some issues are almost always badly centered, and our values will be for examples with fine centering. Such issues will be noted.

1865, Jan. 1　　　　　Perf. 14

74	A13	2c rose red	600.00	130.00
		Bar cancellation		13.50
75	A13	4c blue	50.00	1.00
76	A13	12c blue & rose	700.00	60.00
		Bar cancellation		10.50
a.		Frame inverted	20,000.	2,650.
		As "a," bar cancel		50.00
77	A13	19c brown & rose	3,750.	2,500.
78	A13	1r yellow grn	1,800.	525.00
		Bar cancellation		26.50
79	A13	2r violet	1,500.	250.00
		Bar cancellation		24.00
80	A13	2r rose	1,400.	350.00
a.		2r salmon	1,400.	350.00
b.		2r dull orange	1,400.	350.00
		Bar cancellation, #80, 80a or 80b		35.00

Values for Nos. 74-80 are for stamps with perforations touching the frame on at least one side.

A14

A14a

1866, Jan. 1

81	A14	2c rose	250.00	32.50
		Bar cancellation		5.50
82	A14	4c blue	42.50	.80
83	A14	12c orange	260.00	12.75
a.		12c orange yellow	350.00	25.00
84	A14	19c brown	1,250.	525.00
		Bar cancellation		50.00
		Nos. 81-84 (4)	1,802.	571.05

1866

85	A14	10c green	300.00	27.50
		Bar cancellation		4.00
86	A14	20c lilac	200.00	21.00
		Bar cancellation		4.00
87	A14a	20c dull lilac	1,250.	75.00
		Bar cancellation		3.00
		Nos. 85-87 (3)	1,750.	123.50

For the Type A14a 20c in green, see Cuba No. 25.

A15

A15a

A15b

A15c

1867-68

88	A15	2c yell brn	450.00	47.50
89	A15a	4c blue	27.50	1.00
90	A15b	12c org yell	250.00	8.00
a.		12c dark orange	300.00	12.00
b.		12c red orange ('68)	925.00	40.00
91	A15c	19c rose	1,450.	425.00
		Bar cancellation		40.00

See Nos. 100-102. For overprints see Nos. 114-115a, 124-128, 124a-128a, 124c-124c, 124e-126e.

A15d

A15e

92	A15d	10c blue green	275.00	24.50
		Bar cancellation		2.50
93	A15e	20c lilac	130.00	10.50
		Bar cancellation		2.50

For overprints see Nos. 116-117, 116a-117a, 116c-117c, 117d, 117e, 117f.

A16

A17

A18

A19

94	A16	5m green	47.50	17.50
		Bar cancellation		2.50
95	A17	10m brown	47.50	17.50
a.		Tête bêche pair	20,000.	
96	A18	25m blue & rose	225.00	24.00
		Bar cancellation		5.00
a.		Frame inverted		*50,000.*

97	A18	50m bister brown	22.00	.80
		Bar cancellation		2.50
		Nos. 94-97 (4)	342.00	59.80

See No. 98. For overprints see Nos. 118-122, 118a-122a, 120c-122c, 122d, 120e, 122e, 119f, 122f.

1868-69

98	A18	25m blue	275.00	17.00
		Bar cancellation		3.50
99	A19	50m violet	29.00	.60
		Bar cancellation		2.50
100	A15b	100m brown	550.00	75.00
		Bar cancellation		2.50
101	A15c	200m green	210.00	14.00
		Bar cancellation		2.50
102	A15c	19c brown	2,500.	525.00

For overprints see #123, 123a, 123c, 123e.

Provisional Government

Excellent counterfeits exist of the provisional and provincial overprints.

For Madrid

Regular Issues
Handstamped in Black

1868-69

116	A15d	10c green	30.00	16.00
117	A15e	20c lilac	25.00	12.00
118	A16	5m green	20.00	5.50
119	A17	10m brown	15.00	5.50
120	A18	25m blue & rose	40.00	14.50
g.		Frame inverted	15,000.	
121	A18	25m blue	40.00	12.00
g.		Double overprint (black & red)		75.00
122	A18	50m bister brn	10.00	5.00
123	A19	50m violet	10.00	5.00
124	A15b	100m brown	100.00	28.50
125	A15c	200m green	37.50	9.00
126	A15b	12c orange yellow (#90)	40.00	11.00
127	A15c	19c rose	400.00	140.00
128	A15c	19c brown	850.00	165.00
		Nos. 116-128 (13)	1,617.	429.00

Nos. 116-128 exist with handstamp in blue, a few in red. These sell for more.

For Andalusian Provinces

Regular Issues
Handstamped Vertically
in Blue

114a	A15	2c brown	87.50	36.00
115a	A15a	4c blue	45.00	25.00
116a	A15b	10c green	45.00	15.00
117a	A15e	20c lilac	32.50	16.00
118a	A16	5m green	22.50	8.25
119a	A17	10m brown	16.50	6.00
120a	A18	25m blue & rose	50.00	15.00
b.		Frame inverted	22,000.	
121a	A18	25m blue	50.00	15.50
122a	A18	50m bister brown	11.00	5.50
123a	A19	50m violet	11.00	5.50
124a	A15b	100m brown	110.00	32.50
125a	A15c	200m green	35.00	12.00
126a	A15b	12c org yel (#90)	37.50	13.50
127a	A15c	19c rose	475.00	210.00
128a	A15c	19c brown	950.00	275.00
		Nos. 114a-128a (15)	1,978.	690.75

For Valladolid Province

Regular Issues
Handstamped in Black

(Two types of overprint)

116c	A15d	10c green	45.00	16.50
117c	A15e	20c lilac	42.50	19.00
120c	A18	25m blue & rose	65.00	15.00
121c	A18	25m blue	65.00	21.00
122c	A18	50m bister brown	18.00	9.25
123c	A19	50m violet	18.00	7.75
124c	A15b	100m brown	130.00	38.00
125c	A15c	200m green	45.00	15.00
126c	A15b	12c orange	45.00	12.50
127c	A15c	19c rose	450.00	175.00
128c	A15c	19c brown	1,150.	240.00
		Nos. 116c-126c (9)	473.50	154.00

For Asturias Province
Llanes (Oviedo)

Regular Issues
Handstamped in Black

117d	A15e	20c lilac	210.00	125.00
122d	A18	50m bister brown	230.00	125.00

For Teruel Province

Regular Issues
Handstamped in Black

117e	A15e	20c lilac	90.00	55.00
120e	A18	25m blue & rose	110.00	55.00
122e	A18	50m bister brown	85.00	32.50
123e	A19	50m violet	85.00	32.50
124e	A15b	100m brown	185.00	75.00
125e	A15c	200m green	135.00	45.00
126e	A15b	12c orange	110.00	60.00
		Nos. 117e-126e (7)	800.00	355.00

For Salamanca Province

Regular Issues
Handstamped in Blue

117f	A15e	20c lilac	90.00	55.00
119f	A17	10m brown	80.00	42.00
122f	A18	50m bister brown	90.00	50.00
		Nos. 117f-122f (3)	260.00	147.00

Duke de la Torre Regency

"España" — A20

1870, Jan. 1   Typo.

159	A20	1m brn lil, *buff*	6.50	6.50
		Bar cancellation		2.00
b.		1m brown lilac, *pinkish buff*	7.00	7.75
161	A20	2m blk, *pinkish*	7.75	8.00
a.		2m black, *buff*	8.75	9.00
163	A20	4m bister brn	16.00	13.50
164	A20	10m rose	19.00	6.00
a.		10m carmine	21.00	7.50
165	A20	25m lilac	52.50	6.50
		Bar cancellation		2.00
a.		25m gray lilac	55.00	6.50
b.		25m aniline violet	85.00	8.25
166	A20	50m ultra	11.50	.35
a.		50m dull blue	125.00	5.00
167	A20	100m red brown	35.00	5.25
		Bar cancellation		1.40
a.		100m claret	35.00	6.25
b.		100m orange brown	35.00	5.50
168	A20	200m pale brown	32.50	5.25
		Bar cancellation		2.00
169	A20	400m green	325.00	25.00
		Bar cancellation		3.00
170	A20	1e600m dull lilac	1,700.	850.00
		Bar cancellation		27.50
171	A20	2e blue	1,400.	525.00
		Bar cancellation		27.50
172	A20	12c red brown	325.00	7.25
173	A20	19c yellow green	425.00	225.00

The 12c carmine rose and 12c blue on pink paper were not put in use. Value $1,000. and $1,250., respectively.

Kingdom

A21

A22

King Amadeo
A23   A24

1872, Oct. 1   *Imperf.*

174	A21	¼c ultra	2.25	2.25
a.		Complete 1c (block of 4 ¼c)	120.00	90.00
		Bar cancellation		5.00
b.		As "a," one cliche inverted	1,800.	1,750.

See No. 221A.

1872-73   *Perf. 14*

176	A22	2c gray lilac	20.00	8.00
a.		2c violet	32.50	18.00
b.		Imperf.		75.00
177	A22	5c green	130.00	62.50
a.		Imperf.	170.00	
178	A23	5c rose ('73)	27.50	5.75
179	A23	6c blue	160.00	39.00
180	A23	10c brown lilac	375.00	240.00
181	A23	10c ultra ('73)	10.00	.55
182	A23	12c gray lilac	27.50	3.00
		Bar cancellation		3.10
183	A23	20c gray vio ('73)	140.00	80.00
		Bar cancellation		5.25
184	A23	25c brown	90.00	12.00
		Bar cancellation		2.10
185	A23	40c pale red brn	65.00	10.50
		Bar cancellation		2.10
186	A23	50c deep green	105.00	11.00
		Bar cancellation		2.10
187	A24	1p lilac	115.00	55.00
		Bar cancellation		3.50
188	A24	4p red brown	750.00	625.00
		Bar cancellation		8.00
189	A24	10p deep green	2,300.	2,400.
		Bar cancellation		260.00

First Republic

Mural Crown
A25

"España"
A26

1873, July 1   *Imperf.*

190	A25	¼c green	1.00	1.00
a.		Complete 1c (block of 4 ¼c)	37.50	20.00
		As "a," bar cancellation		2.50
d.		As "a," ultra (error)	210.00	160.00

1873, July 1   *Perf. 14*

191	A26	2c orange	13.50	6.00
192	A26	5c claret	30.00	6.00
		Bar cancellation		2.00
193	A26	10c green	6.75	.35
		Bar cancellation		2.00
a.		Tête bêche pair		32,500.
194	A26	20c black	95.00	25.00
		Bar cancellation		3.75
195	A26	25c deep brown	35.00	6.00
		Bar cancellation		2.00
196	A26	40c brown vio	42.50	6.00
		Bar cancellation		2.00
197	A26	50c ultra	21.00	6.75
		Bar cancellation		2.00
198	A26	1p lilac	72.50	32.50
		Bar cancellation		2.00
199	A26	4p red brown	750.00	475.00
		Bar cancellation		12.50
200	A26	10p violet brn	2,100.	1,750.
		Bar cancellation		17.50

Only one example of No. 193a is known, and it is in a block of six stamps.

"Justice"
A27

Coat of Arms
A28

1874, July 1

201	A27	2c yellow	22.50	8.50
		Bar cancellation		2.10
202	A27	5c violet	45.00	10.00
		Bar cancellation		2.10
a.		5c red violet	32.50	10.00
203	A27	10c ultra	12.50	.40
a.		Imperf.	13.50	
204	A27	20c dark green	200.00	45.00
		Bar cancellation		4.00

205	A27	25c red brown	50.00	6.75
		Bar cancellation		2.10
a.		25c lilac (error)	325.00	
		As "a," bar cancellation		30.00
b.		Imperf.		57.50
206	A27	40c violet	400.00	8.00
		Bar cancellation		2.10
a.		40c brown (error)	250.00	
b.		Imperf.	190.00	
207	A27	50c yellow	105.00	8.25
		Bar cancellation		2.10
a.		Imperf.	120.00	
208	A27	1p yellow green	100.00	34.00
		Bar cancellation		2.10
a.		1p emerald	92.50	47.50
b.		Imperf.	175.00	
209	A27	4p rose	750.00	410.00
		Bar cancellation		8.00
a.		4p carmine	800.00	600.00
210	A27	10p black	3,500.	1,900.
		Bar cancellation		10.50

1874, Oct. 1

211	A28	10c red brown	25.00	.70
		Bar cancellation		1.60
a.		10c brown	42.50	3.50
b.		Imperf.	90.00	

Kingdom

Nos. 212-221 are almost always badly centered and are often irregularly perforated. Values are for stamps with complete perforations and fine centering. Sound stamps with average centering are worth about 50% of these values. Stamps with very fine centering sell for more.

King Alfonso XII — A29

1875, Aug. 1
Blue Framed Numbers on Back,
1-100 on Each Sheet

212	A29	2c orange brown	22.50	11.00
a.		2c chocolate brown	30.00	15.00
b.		Imperf.	45.00	45.00

213	A29 5c lilac	95.00	13.00
a.	Imperf.	95.00	87.50
214	A29 10c blue	8.25	.40
	Bar cancellation		2.00
a.	Imperf.	22.50	22.50
215	A29 20c brown orange	300.00	125.00
216	A29 25c rose	72.50	8.00
	Bar cancellation		2.00
217	A29 40c deep brown	125.00	37.50
	Bar cancellation		4.50
a.	Imperf.	140.00	140.00
218	A29 50c gray lilac	175.00	42.50
	Bar cancellation		5.25
219	A29 1p black	225.00	80.00
	Bar cancellation		3.00
220	A29 4p dark green	550.00	525.00
221	A29 10p ultra	1,800.	1,750.

1876, June 1   *Imperf.*

221A	A21 ¼c green	.25	.25
b.	Complete 1c (block 4 ¼c)	1.10	.30
	As "b," on cover		30.00
c.	As "b," two ¼c sideways, 1p color invtd.	110.00	110.00
d.	As "b," both upper ¼c invtd.	140.00	140.00
e.	As "b," upper left ¼c invtd.	1,000.	500.00
f.	As "b," both lower ¼c invtd.	140.00	140.00

No. 221Ac has one stamp upright, one inverted, one facing right and one facing left.

Nos. 222-230 are almost always badly centered. Values are for stamps with fine centering, fresh color and, in the case of mint stamps, full original gum. Sound stamps with average centering are worth about 50% of these values. Stamps with very fine centering sell for more.

King Alfonso XII
A30   A31

ONE PESETA:
Type I — Thin figures of value and "PESETA" in thick letters.
Type II — Thick figures of value and "PESETA" in thin letters.

Wmk. 178
1876, June 1   Engr.   Perf. 14

222	A30 5c yellow brown	15.50	3.75
223	A30 10c blue	3.75	.45
	Bar cancellation		50.00
224	A30 20c bronze green	19.00	13.00
225	A30 25c brown	8.50	5.50
226	A30 40c black brown	80.00	100.00
227	A30 50c green	15.00	6.75
228	A30 1p dp blue, I	20.00	9.00
a.	1p ultra, II	27.50	13.00
229	A30 4p brown violet	55.00	57.50
230	A30 10p vermilion	125.00	125.00
	Nos. 222-230 (9)	341.75	320.95

Imperf

222a	A30 5c	11.50	
223a	A30 10c	5.75	
225a	A30 25c	12.50	
227a	A30 50c	18.00	
228b	A30 1p	26.00	
229a	A30 4p	92.50	
230a	A30 10p	200.00	

Two plates each were used for the 5c, 10c, 25c, 50c, 1p and 10p. The 1p plates are most easily distinguished.
The 20c value also exists imperf. Value $500.

Unwmk.
1878, July 1   Typo.   Perf. 14

232	A31 2c mauve	32.50	11.00
a.	Imperf.	60.00	
233	A31 5c orange	45.00	14.00
234	A31 10c brown	8.25	.50
	Bar cancellation		3.00
235	A31 20c black	175.00	125.00
a.	Imperf.	275.00	
236	A31 25c olive bister	25.00	2.75
	Bar cancellation		6.25
237	A31 40c red brown	190.00	140.00
238	A31 50c blue green	120.00	11.00
	Bar cancellation		2.00
239	A31 1p gray	100.00	21.00
	Bar cancellation		2.00
240	A31 4p violet	200.00	125.00
241	A31 10p blue	450.00	350.00
a.	Imperf.	475.00	
	Nos. 232-241 (10)	1,345.	800.25

A32   A33

1879, May 1

242	A32 2c black	9.50	4.50
	Bar cancellation		3.00
243	A32 5c gray green	15.00	1.10
	Bar cancellation		3.00
244	A32 10c rose	15.00	.45
	Bar cancellation		2.00
245	A32 20c red brown	145.00	15.00
	Bar cancellation		2.00
246	A32 25c bluish gray	15.50	.45
	Bar cancellation		2.00
247	A32 40c brown	29.00	5.50
	Bar cancellation		2.00
248	A32 50c dull buff	130.00	5.00
	Bar cancellation		2.00
a.	50c yellow	190.00	7.00
249	A32 1p brt rose	150.00	2.25
	Bar cancellation		2.00
250	A32 4p lilac gray	600.00	32.50
	Bar cancellation		3.00
251	A32 10p olive bister	2,200.	175.00
	Bar cancellation		6.25

1882, Jan. 1

252	A33 15c salmon	10.50	.25
	Bar cancellation		2.00
a.	15c reddish orange	35.00	.45
253	A33 30c red lilac	310.00	5.25
	Bar cancellation		2.00
254	A33 75c gray lilac	210.00	4.75
	Bar cancellation		2.00
a.	Imperf.	300.00	

Nos. 255-270 are usually poorly centered and often exhibit defective perforations. Values are for fine to very fine examples, well centered but not very fine, fresh and without perforation faults. Average examples sell for about half these values.

King Alfonso XIII
A34   A35

1889-99

255	A34 2c blue green	6.00	.45
256	A34 2c black ('99)	35.00	7.25
257	A34 5c blue	12.50	.25
258	A34 5c blue grn ('99)	145.00	1.40
259	A34 10c yellow brown	16.50	.25
260	A34 10c red ('99)	240.00	4.50
261	A34 15c violet brown	4.75	.25
262	A34 20c yellow green	50.00	4.75
263	A34 25c blue	20.00	.25
264	A34 30c olive gray	82.50	5.25
265	A34 40c brown	87.50	3.00
266	A34 50c rose	80.00	2.10
267	A34 75c orange	210.00	4.25
268	A34 1p dark violet	55.00	.45
a.	1p carmine rose (error)	350.00	
269	A34 4p carmine rose	650.00	47.50
270	A34 10p orange red	1,050.	110.00

The 15c yellow, type A34 is an official stamp listed as No. O9.
Several values exist imperf.

Nos. 272-286 are almost always badly centered. Values are for stamps with fine centering, fresh color and, if unused, full original gum. Sound stamps with average centering sell for about half these values. Very fine stamps sell more more.

Control Number on Back
1901-05   Engr.   Unwmk.

272	A35 2c bister brown	3.25	.25
273	A35 5c dark green	5.75	.25
274	A35 10c rose red	9.50	.25
275	A35 15c blue black	17.00	.25
276	A35 15c dull lilac ('02)	13.00	.25
277	A35 15c purple ('05)	6.25	.25
278	A35 20c grnsh black	32.50	2.75
279	A35 25c blue	6.25	.40
280	A35 30c deep green	42.50	.35
281	A35 40c olive bister	125.00	5.00
282	A35 40c rose ('05)	300.00	4.50
283	A35 50c slate blue	32.50	.55
b.	50c blue green (error)	2,250.	1,100.

284	A35 1p lake	30.00	.80
285	A35 4p dk violet	250.00	22.50
286	A35 10p brown orange	225.00	72.50
	Nos. 272-286 (15)	1,098.	110.85
	Set, never hinged	1,800.	

There are numerous shades and unissued colors for this issue.

Imperf

272a	A35 2c	57.50	
273a	A35 5c	25.00	
274a	A35 10c	25.00	
275a	A35 15c	110.00	
276a	A35 15c	22.50	
277a	A35 15c	17.00	
278a	A35 20c	90.00	
279a	A35 25c	17.00	
280b	A35 30c	110.00	
282a	A35 40c	300.00	
283a	A35 50c	125.00	
284a	A35 1p	57.50	
285a	A35 4p	200.00	
286a	A35 10p	190.00	

The 15c in red brown (value $850), 30c blue ($950), 1p olive ($1,000), 1p blue green ($900) and 1p dark violet ($900) were prepared but not issued.

Nos. 287-296 are almost always badly centered. Values are for stamps with fine centering, fresh color and, if unused, full original gum. Sound stamps with average centering sell for about half these values. Very fine stamps sell for more.

Don Quixote Starts Forth A36

10c, Don Quixote attacks windmill. 15c, Meets country girls. 25c, Sancho Panza tossed in blanket. 30c, Don Quixote knighted. 40c, Tilting at sheep. 50c, On Wooden horse. 1p, Adventure with lions. 4p, In bullock cart, 10p, The Enchanted Lady.

Control Number on Back
1905, May 1   Typo.

287	A36 5c dark green	1.25	1.10
a.	Imperf.	50.00	
288	A36 10c orange red	2.50	1.75
289	A36 15c violet	2.50	1.75
a.	Imperf.	80.00	
290	A36 25c dark blue	7.50	3.50
291	A36 30c dk blue green	60.00	10.00
292	A36 40c bright rose	85.00	32.50
293	A36 50c slate	25.00	7.00
294	A36 1p rose red	260.00	90.00
295	A36 4p dk violet	125.00	90.00
296	A36 10p brown orange	200.00	135.00
	Nos. 287-296 (10)	768.75	372.60
	Set, never hinged	2,000.	

300th anniversary of the publication of Cervantes' "Don Quixote."
Counterfeits exist of Nos. 287-296.
For surcharges see Nos. 586-588, C91.

Six stamps picturing King Alfonso XIII and Queen Victoria Eugenia were put on sale Oct. 1, 1907, at the Madrid Industrial Exhibition. They were not valid for postage. Value, unused $40, mint never hinged $60.
The original labels were engraved and perf 11½. Examples printed by other methods or with other perfs are reprints. Value $2.

Alfonso XIII — A46   A47

Blue Control Number on Back
Perf. 13x12½, 13, 13½x13, 14
1909-22   Engr.

297	A46 2c dark brown	.55	.55
a.	No control number	.55	.25
	Never hinged	1.00	
298	A46 5c green	2.00	.25
299	A46 10c carmine	3.00	.25
300	A46 15c violet	9.50	.25
301	A46 20c olive green	50.00	.90
302	A46 25c deep blue	4.75	.25

303	A46 30c blue green	9.75	.25
304	A46 40c rose	15.50	.65
305	A46 50c blue ('22)	11.50	.40
a.	50c slate blue	12.50	.40
	Never hinged	18.50	
306	A46 1p lake	32.50	.40
307	A46 4p deep violet	80.00	12.00
309	A46 10p orange	100.00	26.00
	Nos. 297-309 (12)	319.05	42.15
	Set, never hinged	1,000.	

Nos. 297-309 exist imperforate. Value $500.
The 5c exists in carmine; the 10c in yellow orange (value $400); the 15c in blue (value $400); the 4p in lake (value $1,000). The 5c and 15c are unissued trial colors, privately perforated and back-numbered. The 4p lake is known only with perfin "B.H.A." (Banco Hispano-Americano). 100 examples of the 4p exist, most poorly centered.
See Nos. 310, 315-317. For overprints see Nos. C1-C5, C58-C61.
Counterfeits exist.

Control Number on Back in Red or Orange
1917

310	A46 15c yellow ocher	3.50	.35
	Never hinged	6.00	
a.	Control number in blue	14.50	1.10

Control Number on Back in Blue
1918

313	A46 40c light red	82.50	5.75
	Never hinged	150.00	

1920   Typo.   Imperf.

314	A47 1c blue green	.25	.25
	Never hinged	.30	

Perf. 13x12½,
Litho.

315	A46 2c bister	5.00	.25
316	A46 20c violet	42.50	.25
	Nos. 314-316 (3)	47.75	.75
	Set, Never Hinged	145.00	

Nos. 314-315 have no control number on back.
For overprints and surcharge see Nos. 358, 449, 457, 468, 10L1, 11LB1.

1921   Engr.

317	A46 20c violet	30.00	.25
	Never hinged	52.50	

Madrid Post Office — A48

1920, Oct. 1 Typo.   Perf. 13½
Center and Portrait in Black

318	A48 1c blue green	.25	.25
319	A48 2c olive bister	.25	.25

Control Number on Back

320	A48 5c green	1.00	1.10
321	A48 10c red	1.00	1.10
322	A48 15c yellow	1.60	1.40
323	A48 20c violet	1.90	1.75
324	A48 25c gray blue	3.00	3.00
325	A48 30c dark green	7.00	5.50
326	A48 40c rose	29.00	7.25
327	A48 50c brt blue	32.50	20.00
328	A48 1p brown red	32.50	16.50
329	A48 4p brown violet	100.00	70.00
330	A48 10p orange	200.00	145.00
	Nos. 318-330 (13)	410.00	273.10
	Set, never hinged	1,200.	

King Alfonso XIII
A49   A49a

Type I   Type II

Type I   Type II

FIFTEEN CENTIMOS:
Die I — Narrow "5."
Die II — Wide "5."

TWENTY FIVE CENTIMOS:
Die I — "25" is 2¾mm high. Vertical stroke of "5" is 1mm long.
Die II — "25" is 3mm high. Vertical stroke of "5" is 1½mm long.

Perf. 11 to 14, Compound
1922-26   Engr.   Unwmk.

331	A49	2c olive green	.85	.25
a.		2c deep orange (error)	87.50	210.00
		Never hinged	110.00	

Control Number on Back

332	A49	5c red violet	4.00	.25
333	A49	5c claret	1.60	.25
334	A49	10c carmine	1.60	1.10
335	A49	10c yellow green	1.50	.25
a.		10c blue green ('23)	2.25	.25
		Never hinged	6.00	
336	A49	15c slate bl (I)	8.00	.25
a.		15c black green (II)	27.50	2.25
		Never hinged	52.50	
337	A49	20c violet	3.50	.25
		Never hinged	11.50	
338	A49	25c carmine (I)	3.50	.25
a.		25c rose red (II)	5.50	1.00
		Never hinged	12.00	
b.		25c lilac rose (error)	100.00	160.00
		Never hinged	190.00	
339	A49	30c black brn ('26)	15.00	.25
		Never hinged	35.00	
340	A49	40c deep blue	4.00	.25
341	A49	50c orange	19.50	.25
a.		50c orange red	77.50	1.90
		Never hinged	120.00	
342	A49	1p blue black	18.00	.25
343	A49a	4p lake	85.00	4.00
344	A49a	10p brown	40.00	13.50
		Nos. 331-344 (14)	206.05	21.35
		Set, never hinged	525.00	

Nos. 331, 334, 336-344 exist imperf.
The 5c exists in vermilion (value $110); the 25c in dark blue (value $200). The 50c exists in red brown, the 4p in brown and 10p in lake; value, each $90. These five were not regularly issued.
For overprints see Nos. 359-370, 467.

"Santa Maria" and View of Seville A50

Herald of Barcelona — A51

Exposition Buildings — A52

King Alfonso XIII and View of Barcelona A53

1929, Feb. 15   Perf. 11

345	A50	1c grnsh blue	2.50	2.50
346	A51	2c pale yel grn	.30	.30
347	A52	5c rose lake	.50	.50

Control Number on Back

348	A53	10c green	.50	.50
349	A50	15c Prus blue	.85	.85
350	A51	20c purple	.55	.55
351	A50	25c brt rose	.55	.55
352	A52	30c black brn	4.00	4.75
353	A53	40c dark blue	7.75	7.75
354	A51	50c deep orange	7.75	4.75
355	A52	1p blue black	11.50	12.00
356	A53	4p deep rose	25.00	25.00
357	A53	10p brown	65.00	70.00
		Nos. 345-357,E2 (14)	146.25	152.50
		Set, never hinged	340.00	

Perf. 14

345a	A50	1c greenish blue	.70	.70
348a	A53	10c green	20.00	37.50
349a	A50	15c Prus blue	22.50	22.50
350a	A51	20c purple	26.00	37.50
351a	A50	25c bright rose	32.50	37.50
352a	A52	30c black brown	32.50	37.50
353a	A53	40c dark blue	70.00	90.00
354a	A51	50c deep orange	32.50	37.50
355a	A52	1p blue black	32.50	37.50
356a	A53	4p deep rose	25.00	25.00
357a	A53	10p brown	110.00	140.00
		Nos. 345a-357a,E2a (12)	436.70	540.70
		Set, never hinged	725.00	

Seville and Barcelona Exhibitions.
Nos. 345-357 exist imperf. Value, $85 each.
See note after No. 432.

Sociedad de las Naciones
LV reunión del Consejo
Madrid

Nos. 314, 331, 333, 335-344 Overprinted in Red or Blue

1929, June 10   Imperf.

358	A47	1c blue green	.50	.80

Perf. 13½x12½

359	A49	2c olive green	.55	1.00
360	A49	5c claret (Bl)	.55	1.00
361	A49	10c yellow green	.55	1.00
362	A49	15c slate blue	.55	1.00
363	A49	20c violet	.55	1.00
364	A49	25c carmine (Bl)	.55	1.00
365	A49	30c black brown	2.25	4.00
366	A49	40c deep blue	2.25	4.00
367	A49	50c orange (Bl)	2.25	4.00
368	A49a	1p blue black	11.00	19.00
369	A49a	4p lake (Bl)	11.00	21.00
370	A49a	10p brown (Bl)	40.00	70.00
		Nos. 358-370,E4 (14)	84.55	153.80
		Set, never hinged	200.00	

55th assembly of League of Nations at Madrid June 10-16. The stamps were available for postal use only on those days.
Nos. 359-370 values are for off-center copies. Well centered stamps seel for about 4 times these values.

Exposition Building — A54

1930   Litho.   Perf. 11

371	A54	5c dk blue & salmon	6.25	5.00
372	A54	5c dk violet & blue	6.25	5.00
		Set, Never Hinged	22.50	

Barcelona Philatelic Congress and Exhibition. "C. F. y E. F." are the initials of "Congreso Filatelico y Exposicion Filatelica." For each admission ticket, costing 2.75 pesetas, the holder was allowed to buy one of each of these stamps.

A55

Locomotives A56

1930, May 10   Perf. 14

373	A55	1c light blue	.95	.95
374	A55	2c apple green	.95	.95

Control Number on Back

375	A55	5c lake	.95	.95
376	A55	10c yellow green	.95	.95
377	A55	15c bluish gray	.95	.95
378	A55	20c purple	.95	.95
379	A55	25c brt rose	.95	.95
380	A55	30c olive gray	2.25	2.00
381	A55	40c dark blue	2.25	2.00
382	A55	50c dk orange	7.50	7.50
383	A56	1p dark gray	7.50	7.50
384	A56	4p deep rose	90.00	70.00
385	A56	10p bister brn	350.00	350.00
		Nos. 373-385,C12-C17,E6 (20)	631.65	598.15
		Set, never hinged	1,500.	

11th Intl. Railway Congress, Madrid, 1930.
These stamps were on sale May 10-21, 1930, exclusively at the Palace of the Senate in Madrid and at the Barcelona and Seville expositions.
Forgeries are plentiful.

Francisco de Goya at Age 80
("1746 1828") ("1828 1928")
A57   A59

"La Maja Desnuda" — A58

1930, June 15   Litho.   Perf. 12½
Inscribed "Correos Espana"

386	A57	1c yellow	.25	.25
387	A57	2c bister brn	.25	.25
388	A57	5c lilac rose	.25	.25
389	A57	10c green	.25	.25

Engr.

390	A57	15c lt blue	.30	.25
391	A57	20c brown violet	.30	.25
392	A57	25c red	.30	.25
393	A57	30c brown	4.25	4.00
394	A57	40c dark blue	4.25	4.00
395	A57	50c vermilion	4.25	4.00
396	A57	1p black	5.00	4.75
397	A58	1p dark violet	1.25	.75
398	A58	4p slate gray	.90	.55
399	A58	10p red brown	12.50	7.00

Inscribed "1828 Goya 1928"
Litho.

400	A59	2c olive green	.25	.25
401	A59	5c gray violet	.25	.25

Engr.

402	A59	25c rose carmine	.40	.35
		Nos. 386-402,C18-C30,CE1,E7 (32)	49.40	41.90
		Set, never hinged	72.50	

To commemorate the death of Francisco de Goya y Lucientes, painter and engraver.
Nos. 386-399 were issued in connection with the Spanish-American Exposition at Seville.
Nos. 386-402 exist imperf. Value, set $300.
See note after No. 432.

King Alfonso XIII — A61

Two types of the 40c:

Type I   Type II

1930   Perf. 11½, 12x11½

406	A61	2c red brown	.25	.25

Control Number on Back

407	A61	5c black brown	.70	.25
408	A61	10c green	3.25	.25
409	A61	15c slate green	11.00	.25
410	A61	20c dark violet	6.00	.70
411	A61	25c carmine	.70	.25
412	A61	30c brown lake	15.50	1.75
413	A61	40c dk blue (I)	21.00	1.10
a.		Type II	27.50	1.10
		Never hinged	60.00	
414	A61	50c orange	19.00	1.90
		Nos. 406-414 (9)	77.40	6.70
		Set, never hinged	240.00	

Nos. 406-414 exist imperf. Value for set, $350.
For overprints see #450-455, 458-466, 469-487.

Bow of "Santa Maria" — A63

Stern of "Santa Maria" — A64

"Santa Maria," "Niña," "Pinta" — A65

Columbus Leaving Palos — A66

Columbus Arriving in America — A67

1930, Sept. 29 Litho. Perf. 12½

418	A63	1c olive gray	.25	.25
419	A64	2c olive green	.25	.25
420	A63	2c olive green	.25	.25
421	A64	5c red brown	.25	.25
422	A63	5c red brown	.25	.25
423	A64	10c blue green	.85	.70
424	A63	15c ultra	.85	.90
425	A64	20c violet	1.25	1.10

Engr.

426	A65	25c dark red	1.25	1.10
427	A66	30c bis brn, bl & blk brn	5.50	5.50
428	A65	40c ultra	5.00	5.00
429	A66	50c dk vio, bl & vio brn	7.00	5.75
430	A65	1p black	7.00	5.75
431	A67	4p blk & dk blue	8.75	6.50
432	A67	10p red brn & dk brn	30.00	30.00
		Nos. 418-432,E8 (16)	70.60	65.45
		Set, never hinged	135.00	

Christopher Columbus tribute.

Nos. 418 to 432 were privately produced. Their promoters presented a certain quantity of these labels to the Spanish Postal Authorities, who placed them on sale and allowed them to be used for three days, retaining the money obtained from the sale.

This note will also apply to Nos. 345-357, 386-402, 433-448, 557-571, B1-B105, C18-C57, C73-C87, CB1-CB5, CE1, E2, E7-E9, E15 and EB1.

Many so-called "errors" of color and perforation are known.

Nos. 418-432 exist imperf. Value, set $450. stamps.

See Nos. 2671, B194.

Arms of Spain, Bolivia, Paraguay A68

Pavilion and Map of Central America — A69

Exhibition Pavilion of Ecuador — A70

Colombia Pavilion — A71

Dominican Republic Pavilion A72

Uruguay Pavilion A73

Argentina Pavilion A74

Chile Pavilion A75

Brazil Pavilion A76

Mexico Pavilion A77

Cuba Pavilion A78

Peru Pavilion A79

U.S. Pavilion A80

King Alfonso XIII and Queen Victoria — A82

Exhibition Pavilion of Portugal — A81

Unwmk.

1930, Oct. 10 Photo. Perf. 14

433	A68	1c blue green	.25	.25
434	A69	2c bister brown	.25	.25
435	A70	5c olive brown	.25	.25
436	A71	10c dark green	.35	.35
437	A72	15c indigo	.35	.35
438	A73	20c violet	.35	.35
439	A74	25c car rose	.35	.35
440	A75	25c car rose	.35	.35
441	A76	30c rose lilac	1.75	1.75
442	A77	40c slate blue	1.00	1.00
443	A78	40c slate blue	1.00	1.00
444	A79	50c brown org	1.75	1.75
445	A80	1p ultra	2.50	2.50
446	A81	4p brown violet	30.00	27.50
447	A82	10p brown	2.10	2.10

Perf. 11, 14

Engr.

448	A82	10p dk reddish brn	47.50	47.50
		Nos. 433-448,C50-C57,E9 (25)	112.30	103.85
		Set, never hinged	325.00	

Spanish-American Union Exhibition, Seville. The note after No. 432 will also apply to Nos. 433-448. All values exist imperforate. Value, set: hinged $250; never hinged $350.

Reprints of Nos. 433-448 have blurred colors, yellowish paper and an inferior, almost invisible gum. They sell for about one-tenth the value of originals.

**Revolutionary Issues
Madrid Issue**

Regular Issues of 1920-30 Overprinted in Black, Green or Red

On No. 314

1931 Imperf.

449	A47	1c blue green	.25	.25

On Nos. 406-411

Perf. 11½

450	A61	2c red brown (G)	.30	.25
451	A61	5c black brn (R)	.40	.40
452	A61	10c green	.70	.70
453	A61	15c slate grn (R)	1.40	1.50
454	A61	20c dk violet (R)	1.40	1.50
455	A61	25c carmine (R)	1.90	2.25
		Nos. 449-455,E10 (8)	11.35	11.85
		Set, never hinged	22.50	

The status of Nos. 449-455, E10 has been questioned.

First Barcelona Issue

Regular Issues of 1920-30 Overprinted in Black or Red

On No. 314

1931 Imperf.

457	A47	1c blue green	.25	.25

On Nos. 406-414

Perf. 11½

458	A61	2c red brown	.25	.25
459	A61	5c black brown	.25	.25
460	A61	10c green	.55	.55
461	A61	15c slate grn (R)	.60	.60
462	A61	20c dk violet (R)	.60	.60
463	A61	25c carmine	.60	.60
464	A61	30c brown lake	4.50	4.50
465	A61	40c dk blue (R)	1.25	1.25
466	A61	50c orange	1.25	1.25

On Stamp of 1922-26

467	A49a	1p blue blk (R)	7.50	6.25
		Nos. 457-467,E11 (12)	23.10	21.85
		Set, never hinged	45.00	

Nos. 457-467 are known both with and without accent over "U."

The status of Nos. 457-467, E11 has been questioned.

Second Barcelona Issue

Regular Issues of 1920-30 Overprinted in Black or Red

On No. 314

Imperf

468	A47	1c blue green	.25	.25

On Nos. 406-414

Perf. 11½

469	A61	2c red brown	.25	.25
470	A61	5c black brown (R)	.25	.25
471	A61	10c green	.25	.25
472	A61	15c slate grn (R)	1.40	1.25
473	A61	20c dark violet (R)	.40	.45
474	A61	25c carmine	.40	.45
475	A61	30c brown lake	5.75	5.75
476	A61	40c dark blue (R)	1.25	1.25
477	A61	50c orange	4.50	3.50
		Nos. 468-477 (10)	14.70	13.65
		Set, never hinged	27.50	

The status of Nos. 469-477, C58-C61 has been questioned.

General Issue of the Republic

Nos. 406-414, 342 Overprinted in Blue or Red

1931, May 27

478	A61	2c red brown	.25	.25
479	A61	5c black brn (R)	.25	.25
480	A61	10c green (R)	.30	.25
481	A61	15c slate grn (R)	3.50	.25
482	A61	20c dk violet (R)	1.50	1.00
483	A61	25c carmine	.50	.25
484	A61	30c brown lake	4.50	1.00
485	A61	40c dk blue (R)	4.50	.55
486	A61	50c orange	7.75	.55
487	A49a	1p blue blk (R)	57.50	1.00
		Nos. 478-487,E12 (11)	87.05	6.60
		Set, never hinged	210.00	

The setting contained 18 repetitions of "Republica Espanola" for each vertical row of 10 stamps. According to its sheet position, a stamp received different parts of the overprinted words.

Overprint position varieties include: reading down on 25c, 30c, 40c and 50c; double on 1p; double, both reading down, on 25c, 40c and 50c.

"Republica Espanola"

Stamps of various Spanish colonies overprinted "Republica Espanola" are listed with the colonies.

Fountain of Lions, The Alhambra, Granada A84

Interior of Mosque, Córdoba — A85

Alcántara Bridge and Alcazar, Toledo A86

Francisco
García y
Santos
A87

Puerta del
Sol, Madrid,
on April 14,
1931 as
Republic
Was
Proclaimed
A88

Perf. 12½

1931, Oct. 10	Unwmk.	Engr.	
491	A84	5c violet brown	.25	.25
492	A85	10c blue green	.35	.35
493	A86	15c dark violet	.35	.35
494	A85	25c deep red	.35	.35
495	A87	30c olive green	.35	.35
496	A84	40c indigo	.90	.90
497	A85	50c orange red	.90	.90
498	A86	1p black	1.60	1.60
499	A88	4p red violet	8.00	8.00
500	A88	10p red brown	25.00	25.00

Nos. 491-500,C62-C67,CO1-
CO6,O20-O29 (32)   100.25   99.35
Set, never hinged   130.00

3rd Pan-American Postal Union Cong.,
Madrid.
Nos. 491-500 exist imperforate. Value, set:
hinged $150; never hinged $250.

Symbolical of
Montserrat Cut
With a
Saw — A89

Abbott Oliva and
Monastery
Workman — A90

"Black Virgin"
A91   A92

Montserrat
Monastery — A93

1931, Dec. 9		Perf. 11, 14	
501	A89	1c myrtle green	1.25	1.50
a.		Perf. 14	21.00	21.00
		Never hinged	40.00	
502	A89	2c red brown	.70	1.10
a.		Perf. 14	15.00	16.00

Control Number on Back

503	A89	5c black brown	.85	1.40
a.		Perf. 14	15.00	16.00
		Never hinged	30.00	

504	A89	10c yellow green	.95	1.40
a.		Perf. 14	15.00	19.00
		Never hinged	30.00	
505	A90	15c myrtle green	1.25	1.75
a.		Perf. 14	21.00	25.00
		Never hinged	40.00	
506	A91	20c dark violet	2.50	2.50
a.		Perf. 11	110.00	150.00
		Never hinged	210.00	
507	A92	25c lake	3.50	3.50
a.		Perf. 11	6.25	7.25
		Never hinged	12.50	
508	A91	30c deep red	38.50	36.00
a.		Perf. 14	45.00	45.00
		Never hinged	87.50	
509	A93	40c dull blue	22.00	19.00
a.		Perf. 14	150.00	175.00
		Never hinged	310.00	
510	A90	50c dark orange	50.00	47.50
a.		Perf. 14	70.00	80.00
		Never hinged	140.00	
511	A92	1p gray black	50.00	47.50
a.		Perf. 11	87.50	110.00
		Never hinged	175.00	
512	A93	4p lilac rose	500.00	500.00
a.		Perf. 14	575.00	900.00
		Never hinged	1,000.	
513	A92	10p deep brown	375.00	325.00
a.		Perf. 14	800.00	950.00
		Never hinged	1,500.	

Nos. 501-511,C68-C72,E13
(17)   270.55   262.20
Set, never hinged   410.00
Nos. 501-513,C68-C72,E13
(19)   1,145.   1,087.
Set, never hinged   2,200.

Commemorative of the building of the old
Monastery at Montserrat, started in 1031, and
of the image of the Black Virgin (said to have
been carved by St. Luke) which was crowned
by Pope Leo XIII in 1881.
Nos. 501-513 exist imperforate. Value, set
$4,000.
For surcharges see Nos. 589, C92-C96.

Francisco Pi y
Margall — A95   Joaquín
                     Costa — A96

Nicolás
Salmerón
A97   Pablo Iglesias
           A99

Emilio Castelar — A100

1931-32		Perf. 11½	
Control Number on Back			
516	A95	5c brnsh black	3.00	.30
517	A96	10c yellow green	7.25	.30
518	A97	15c slate green	4.75	.25
520	A99	25c lake	22.50	.70
b.		Imperf.	175.00	
		Never hinged	225.00	
521	A99	30c carmine rose	7.25	.25
c.		Imperf.	82.50	
		Never hinged	125.00	
522	A100	40c dark blue	42.50	4.50
523	A97	50c orange	52.50	7.75
		Never hinged	165.00	

Nos. 516-523 (7)   139.75   14.05
Set, never hinged   425.00

Without Control Number

516a	A95	5c brownish blk ('32)	4.50	.25
517a	A96	10c yellow green ('32)	4.00	.25
518a	A97	15c slate green ('32)	.60	.25
520a	A99	25c lake	32.50	.25
521a	A99	30c carmine rose	1.90	.25
522a	A100	40c dark blue ('32)	.25	.25
523a	A97	50c orange ('32)	26.00	.50

Nos. 516a-523a (7)   69.75   2.00
Set, never hinged   150.00

Without Control Number, Imperf.

516b	A95	5c	6.50
517b	A96	10c	11.00
518b	A97	15c	6.25
520c	A99	25c	110.00
521b	A99	30c	5.50

522b	A100	40c	14.00
523b	A97	50c	125.00

Nos. 516b-523b (7)   278.25
Set, Never Hinged   550.00

See Nos. 532, 538, 550, 579, 579a.
For overprints and surcharges see Nos.
7LC12-7LC13, 7LC15-7LC16, 7LC18, 7LE4,
8LB6, 8LB9-8LB10, 9LC17-9LC18, 10L7,
10L10-10L12, 10L16-10L18, 10L22-10L23,
11L7, 11L10-11L12, 11LB8, 12L4, 12L8,
12L11-12L12, 13L8, 14L6, 14L10-14L12,
14L18, 14L22-14L24.

Blasco Ibáñez
A103   Manuel Ruiz-
            Zorrilla
            A104

Without Control Number

1931-34		Perf. 11½	
526	A103	2c red brown ('33)	.25	.25
528	A103	5c chocolate ('34)	.25	.25
532	A95	20c dark violet	.25	.25
534	A104	25c lake ('34)	.45	.25
538	A100	60c apple green ('32)	.25	.25

Nos. 526-538 (5)   1.45   1.25
Set, never hinged   2.50

Imperf

526a	A103	2c	14.00
528a	A103	5c	2.75
532a	A95	20c	6.25
534a	A104	25c	5.25
538a	A100	60c	6.25

Nos. 526a-538a (5)   34.50
Set, never hinged   70.00

For overprints and surcharges see Nos.
8LB3, 8LB7, 9LC3, 9LC8-9LC9, 9LC14, 10L6,
10L13, 11L4, 11L8, 11LB5, 11LB9, 12L5,
12L9, 13L5, 13L7, 14L3, 14L7, 14L15, 14L19.

Cliff Houses,
Cuenca — A105   Alcázar of
                     Segovia — A106

Gate of the Sun at
Toledo — A107

1932-38		Perf. 10	
539	A105	1p gray black ('38)	.25	.25
540	A106	4p magenta ('38)	.30	.40
541	A107	10p deep brown ('38)	.65	.70

Nos. 539-541 (3)   1.20   1.35
Set, never hinged   2.75

Imperf

539a	A105	1p	5.25	2.75
540a	A106	4p	9.00	6.50
541a	A107	10p	6.50	6.00

Nos. 539a-541a (3)   20.75   15.25
Set, never hinged   45.00

Perf. 11½

539b	A105	1p	.25	.25
540b	A106	4p	.70	.85
541b	A107	10p	1.90	3.00

Nos. 539b-541b (3)   2.85   4.10
Set, never hinged   5.00

For overprints and surcharge see Nos.
9LC19, 10L19, 13L9, 14L25, 14L27-14L28.

Numeral
A108   Santiago
            Ramón y
            Cajal
            A109

1933	Unwmk.	Typo.	Imperf.	
542	A108	1c blue green	.25	.25

Perf. 11½

543	A108	2c buff	.25	.25
a.		Perf. 13½x13	.65	.65
		Never hinged	1.40	
Set, never hinged			.65	

See Nos. 592-597. For surcharges and
overprints see Nos. 590-590A, 634A-634D,
8LB1-8LB2, 9LC1-9LC2, 9LC4-9LC7, 9LC11-
9LC12, 9LC20, 9LC26, 10L2-10L4, 11L1-
11L2, 11LB2-11LB3, 12L1-12L2, 13L1-13L3,
14L1, 14L13.

1934	Engr.	Perf. 11½x11	
545	A109	30c black brown	6.00	1.10
		Never hinged	16.00	
a.		Perf. 14	22.50	30.00
		Never hinged	42.50	
b.		Imperf.	32.50	
		Never hinged	55.00	

Type of 1931 and

Mariana
Pineda
A110   Concepción
            Arenal
            A111

Gumersindo
de Azcarate
A112   Gaspar
            Melchor de
            Jovellanos
            A113

1935				
546	A110	10c green	.25	.25
b.		10c blue green ('36)	.25	.25
547	A111	15c green	.25	.25
b.		15c yellow green ('36)	.25	.25
548	A112	30c carmine rose	7.25	.25
549	A113	30c rose red	.25	.25
550	A97	50c dark blue	1.00	.30

Nos. 546-550 (5)   9.00   1.30
Set, never hinged   22.00

Imperf

546a	A110	10c	1.60
547a	A111	15c	5.25
548a	A112	30c	26.00
549a	A113	30c	1.90
550a	A97	50c	225.00

Nos. 546a-550a (5)   259.75
Set, never hinged   500.00

Shades exist.
For overprints and surcharges see Nos.
7LE3, 8LB4-8LB5, 8LB8, 10L8-10L9, 10L14,
10L20-10L21, 11L5-11L6, 11L9, 11LB6-
11LB7, 11LB10, 12L6-12L7, 12L10, 13L6,
14L4-14L5, 14L8, 14L16-14L17, 14L20.

Lope's
Bookplate
A116   Lope de
            Vega
            A117

Alcántara
and Alcázar,
Toledo
A118

1935, Oct. 12	Perf. 11½x11, 11x11½		
552	A116	15c myrtle green	6.25	.30
553	A117	30c rose red	2.75	.30
554	A117	50c dark blue	12.00	3.00
555	A118	1p blue black	23.00	2.00

Nos. 552-555 (4)   44.00   5.60
Set, never hinged   100.00

Imperf

552a	A116	15c	450.00
553a	A117	30c	16.00
554a	A117	50c	70.00
555a	A118	1p	65.00
	Nos. 552a-555a (4)		601.00
	Set, never hinged		1,100.

Perf. 14

553b	A117	30c	6.50	14.50
554b	A117	50c	29.00	45.00
555b	A118	1p	32.50	50.00
	Nos. 553b-555b (3)		68.00	109.50
	Set, never hinged		150.00	

Lope Felix de Vega Carpio (1562-1635), Spanish dramatist and poet.
For surcharge see No. 11LB11.

Map of Amazon by Bartolomeo Oliva, 16th Century A119

1935, Oct. 12   Perf. 11½

556	A119	30c rose red	2.10	.95
	Never hinged		5.50	
a.	Perf. 14		26.00	
	Never hinged		54.00	
b.	Imperf.		37.50	
	Never hinged		72.50	

Proposed Iglesias Amazon Expedition.

Miguel Moya — A120   Torcuato Luca de Tena — A121

José Francos Rodríguez A122   Alejandro Lerroux A123

Nazareth School and Rotary Press — A124

1936, Feb. 14   Photo.   Perf. 12½
Size: 22x26mm

557	A120	1c crimson	.25	.25
558	A121	2c orange brown	.25	.25
559	A122	5c black brown	.25	.25
560	A123	10c emerald	.25	.25

Size: 24x28½mm

561	A120	15c blue green	.25	.25
562	A121	20c violet	.25	.25
563	A122	25c red violet	.25	.25
564	A123	30c crimson	.25	.25

Size: 25½x30½mm

565	A120	40c orange	.55	.40
566	A121	50c ultra	.25	.25
567	A122	60c olive green	.55	.40
568	A123	1p gray black	.55	.40
569	A124	2p lt blue	7.25	3.25
570	A124	4p lilac rose	7.25	6.50
571	A124	10p red brown	18.50	15.50
	Nos. 557-571,E15 (16)		37.15	29.00
	Set, never hinged		70.00	
	Nos. 557-571,C73-C87,E15 (31)		68.30	47.90
	Set, never hinged		130.00	

Madrid Press Association, 40th anniversary.
Nos. 557-571 exist imperf. Values about 7 times those of perf. stamps.
See note after No. 432. See Nos. C73-C87.

Arms of Madrid — A125

1936, Apr. 2   Engr.   Imperf.

572	A125	10c brown black	47.50	47.50
573	A125	15c dark green	47.50	47.50
	Set, never hinged		135.00	

1st National Philatelic Exhibition which opened in Madrid, Apr. 2, 1936.
For overprints see Nos. C88-C89.

"Republica Espanola" A126   Gregorio Fernández A127

1936   Litho.   Perf. 11½, 13½x13

574	A126	2c orange brown	.25	.25
	Never hinged		.35	

For surcharges & overprints see #591, 9LC24, 10L5, 11L3, 11LB4, 12L3, 13L4, 14L2, 14L14.

1936, Mar. 10   Engr.   Perf. 11½

576	A127	30c carmine	1.10	.85
	Never hinged		2.25	
a.	Perf. 14		9.00	8.25
	Never hinged		17.50	
b.	Imperf.		15.00	
	Never hinged		22.50	

Tercentenary of the death of Gregorio Fernandez, sculptor.
For overprints see Nos. 7LC20-7LC21.

Type of 1931 and

Pablo Iglesias A128   A129

Velázquez A130   Fermín Salvoechea A131

1936-38   Perf. 11, 11½, 11½x11

577	A128	30c rose red	.25	.25
578	A129	30c car rose	1.10	.50
579	A100	40c car rose ('37)	1.10	.50
580	A129	45c carmine ('37)	.25	.25
581	A130	50c dark blue	.25	.25
582	A131	60c indigo ('37)	.75	.90
583	A131	60c dp orange ('38)	6.00	5.00
	Nos. 577-583 (7)		9.70	7.65
	Set, never hinged		26.00	

Perf. 14

577a	A128	30c rose red	6.50
578a	A129	30c carmine rose	6.75
579a	A100	40c carmine rose	6.50
580a	A129	45c carmine	6.00
582a	A131	60c indigo	6.00
583a	A131	60c deep orange	9.50
	Nos. 577a-583a (6)		41.25
	Set, never hinged		90.00

Nos. 577-583 exist imperf. Value, set $70, never hinged $150.
For overprints see Nos. C90, 7LC17, 7LC22-7LC23, 10L15, 14L21.

Statue of Liberty, Spanish and US Flags — A132

1938, June 1   Photo.   Perf. 11½

585	A132	1p multicolored	16.50	17.50
	Never hinged		32.50	
a.	Imperf., pair		82.50	55.00
	Never hinged		110.00	
b.	Horiz. pair, imperf. vert.		62.50	82.50
	Never hinged		92.50	
c.	Souvenir sheet of 1		27.50	32.50
	Never hinged		44.00	
d.	As "c," imperf.		350.00	250.00
	Never hinged		600.00	

150th anniv. of the US Constitution.
For surcharge see No. C97.

No. 289 Surcharged in Black

1938   Perf. 14

586	A36	45c on 15c violet	15.50	15.50
	Never hinged		19.00	

7th anniversary of the Republic.
Values are for examples with perforations nearly touching the design on one or two sides.

No. 289 Surcharged in Black

a

b

1938, May 1

587	A36	45c on 15c violet	3.00	3.00
588	A36	1p on 15c violet	5.25	5.25
	Set, never hinged		12.00	

Issued to commemorate Labor Day.
Values are for examples with perforations nearly touching the design on one or two sides.

No. 507 Surcharged in Black

1938, Nov. 10   Perf. 11½

589	A92	2.50p on 25c lake	.25	.25
	Never hinged		.20	
b.	Perf. 14		3.50	6.00
	Never hinged		6.00	

Types of 1933-36 Surcharged in Blue or Red

1938   Perf. 10, 11, 13½x13, 13x14

590	A108	45c on 1c grn (R)	.40	.25
b.	Imperf.		6.00	5.00
	Never hinged		10.00	
590A	A108	45c on 2c buff (Bl)	17.00	14.00
591	A126	45c on 2c org brn (Bl)	.25	.25
	Nos. 590-591 (3)		17.65	14.50
	Set, never hinged		29.00	

Many overprint varieties exist.

Numeral Type of 1933

1938-39   Litho.   Perf. 11½, 13
White or Gray Paper

592	A108	5c gray brown	.25	.25
593	A108	10c yellow green	.25	.25
594	A108	15c slate green	.25	.25
595	A108	20c vio, gray paper	.25	.25
596	A108	25c red violet	.25	.25
597	A108	30c scarlet	.25	.25
	Nos. 592-597 (6)		1.50	1.50
	Set, never hinged		1.40	

"Republic" — A133

1938   Perf. 11½

598	A133	40c rose red	.25	.25
599	A133	45c car rose	.25	.25
a.	Printed on both sides		11.00	11.00
	Never hinged		27.50	
600	A133	50c ultra	.25	.25
601	A133	60c dp ultra	.50	.30
	Nos. 598-601 (4)			1.05
	Set, never hinged		1.10	

Nos. 598-601 exist imperf. Value for set $22.50

Machine Gunners A134

Infantry — A135

Perf. 11½x11, 11x11½, Imperf.
1938, Sept. 1   Photo.

602	A134	25c dark green	9.25	9.25
603	A135	45c red brown	9.25	9.25
	Set, never hinged		60.00	

43rd Division of the Republican Army. Sold only at the Philatelic Agency and for foreign exchange.

Blast Furnace A136   Steel Mill and Sculpture, "Defenders of Numantia" A137

1938, Aug. 9   Perf. 16

604	A136	45c black	.25	.25
605	A137	1.25p dark blue	.25	.25
	Set, never hinged			

Issued in honor of the workers of Sagunto.

Submarine — A137a

Designs: 1p, 15p, U-Boat D1. 2p, 6p, U-Boat A1. 4p, 10p, U-Boat B2.

1938, Aug. 11   **Perf. 16**

605A	A137a	1p blue	6.00	6.00
605B	A137a	2p red brown	11.00	11.00
605C	A137a	4p red orange	13.00	13.00
605D	A137a	6p deep blue	30.00	30.00
605E	A137a	10p magenta	50.00	50.00
605F	A137a	15p dp gray green	450.00	450.00
	Nos. 605A-605F (6)		560.00	560.00
	Set, never hinged		750.00	

Souvenir Sheet
Perf. 10½

605G	A137a	Sheet of 3	600.00	600.00
	Never hinged		775.00	
a.	4p carmine & gray black		140.00	140.00
b.	6p dull blue & gray black		140.00	140.00
c.	15p green & gray black		140.00	140.00

Nos. 605A-605G were issued for use on a proposed submarine mail service between Barcelona and Mahon, Minorca. One voyage was made on this mail route, carrying 300 agency-prepared covers. The stamps were also valid for ordinary mail.

Nos. 605A-605G were sold only at the Philatelic Agency in Barcelona, for double their face value.

Nos. 605A-605G exist imperf. Value: set of 6 stamps, $775 unused, $1,000 never hinged; souvenir sheet, $2,250 unused, $2,900, never hinged.

Riflemen
A138

Machine Gunners
A139

Bomb Throwing — A140

1938, Nov. 25   Engr.   Perf. 10

606	A138	5c sepia	3.50	3.50
607	A138	10c dp violet	3.50	3.50
608	A138	25c blue green	3.50	3.50
609	A139	45c rose red	3.50	3.50
610	A139	60c dark blue	6.25	6.25
611	A139	1.20p black	125.00	125.00
612	A140	2p orange	37.50	37.50
613	A140	5p dark brown	200.00	200.00
614	A140	10p dk blue grn	40.00	40.00
	Nos. 606-614 (9)		422.75	422.75
	Set, never hinged		800.00	

Honoring the Militia. Sold only at the Philatelic Agency and for foreign exchange. Exist imperf. Value unused $1,200, never hinged $1,800.

Spanish State

Arms of Spain — A141

1936   Litho.   Imperf.
Thin Transparent Paper

615	A141	30c blue	250.00

616	A141	30c pale green	250.00

Perf. 11
Thick Wove Paper

617	A141	30c dark blue	550.00	150.00
	Set, never hinged		1,300.	

Issued in Granada during siege. After the city was liberated, these stamps were used throughout the province of Granada.

Well-centered copies of No. 617 are worth twice as much as the values above.

Many forgeries exist.

A143

Cathedral of Burgos — A145

University of Salamanca
A146

Cathedral del Pilar, Zaragoza — A147

"La Giralda," Seville — A148

Xavier Castle, Navarre — A149

Court of Lions, Alhambra at Granada
A150

Mosque, Córdoba
A151

Alcántara Bridge and Alcázar, Toledo — A152

Soldier Carrying Flag — A153

Troops Landing at Algeciras
A154

Type II

Two types of 30c:
Type I — Imprint 12mm long; "3" does not touch frame.

Type II — Imprint 8mm long; "3" touches frame.

1936   Unwmk.   Litho.   Imperf.

623	A143	1c green	6.00	4.50

Perf. 11½

624	A143	2c orange brown	.60	.45
625	A145	5c gray brown	.60	.55
626	A146	10c green	.60	.45
627	A147	15c dull green	.60	.45
628	A148	25c rose lake	.85	.45
629	A149	30c carmine (I)	.60	.45
a.	Type II		.70	.55
	Never hinged		1.60	
630	A150	50c deep blue	14.00	8.75
631	A151	60c yellow green	.95	.70
632	A152	1p black	5.25	3.75
633	A153	4p rose vio, red & yel	52.50	29.00
634	A154	10p light brown	52.50	29.00
	Nos. 623-634 (12)		135.05	78.50
	Set, never hinged		290.00	

Nos. 624-634 exist imperf. Value, set $275. Numerous forgeries exist for Nos. 623-634.
Nos. 625-631, 633-634 were privately overprinted "VIA AEREA" and plane, supposedly for use in Ifni.
For surcharges see Nos. 9LC21, 9LC23.

Nos. 542-543 Surcharged "Habilitado 0'05 ptas." in Two Lines

1936   Imperf., Perf. 11½

634A	A108	5c on 1c bl grn	2.25	3.00
634B	A108	5c on 2c buff	2.25	3.00
634C	A108	10c on 1c bl grn	2.25	3.00
634D	A108	15c on 2c buff	2.25	3.00
	Nos. 634A-634D (4)		9.00	12.00
	Set, never hinged		15.00	

Issued in the Balearic Islands to meet a shortage of these values. Nos. 634A and 634C are imperf., Nos. 634B and 634D are perf. 11½.

St. James of Compostela — A155

St. James Cathedral
A156

Pórtico de la Gloria
A157

Two types of 30c:
I — No dots in "1937."
II — Dot before and after "1937."

1937   Perf. 11½, 11x11½

635	A155	15c violet brown	.95	1.25
636	A156	30c rose red (I)	5.00	.55
a.	Type II		17.50	14.00
	Never hinged		37.50	
637	A157	1p blue & orange	14.50	3.25
a.	Center inverted		275.00	250.00
	Never hinged		425.00	
	Nos. 635-637 (3)		20.45	5.05
	Set, never hinged		52.50	

Holy Year of Compostela. Nos. 635-637 exist imperf. Value for set $150.

"Estado Espanol"
A159   A160

"El Cid" — A161

Isabella I — A162

Two types of 5c, 30c and 10p:
5 Centimos: Type I Imprint 9½mm long. Type II Imprint 14mm long.
30 Centimos: Type I Imprint, "Hija De B. Fournier Burgos." Type II Imprint, "Fournier Burgos".
10 Pesetas: Type I "10" 2½mm high. Type II "10" 3mm high.

With Imprint

1936-40   Imperf.

638	A159	1c green	.25	.25

Perf. 11

640	A160	2c brown	.25	.25

Perf. 11, 11½, 11½x11, 11½x10½

641	A161	5c brown (I)	.45	.25
642	A161	5c brown (II)	.25	.25
643	A161	10c green	.25	.25

Perf. 11, 11x11½

644	A162	15c gray black	.25	.25
645	A162	20c dark violet	.40	.25
646	A162	25c brown lake	.25	.25
647	A162	30c rose (I)	.50	.25
648	A162	30c rose (II)	17.50	2.10
649	A162	40c orange	1.60	.25
650	A162	50c dark blue	1.60	.25
651	A162	60c yellow	.30	.25
652	A162	1p blue	16.50	.50
653	A162	4p magenta	21.00	5.25
654	A161	10p dk bl (I) ('37)	75.00	40.00
655	A161	10p dp bl (II) ('40)	32.50	15.00
	Nos. 638-655 (17)		168.85	65.85
	Set, never hinged		375.00	

No. 638 was privately perforated. See Nos. 662-667. For overprint and surcharges see Nos. E18, 9LC10, 9LC13, 9LC15-9LC16, 9LC22, 9LC25, 9LC27-9LC30, 9LC34-9LC53.

Ferdinand the Catholic
A163

Emblem of the Falange
A164

1938   Perf. 10½, 11½x11
Imprint: "Lit Fournier Vitoria"

656	A163	15c deep green	1.40	.25
657	A163	30c deep red	4.00	.25

Imprint: "Fournier Vitoria"
Perf. 10

658	A163	15c deep green	1.40	.25
659	A163	20c purple	9.00	1.40
660	A163	25c brown car	.65	.25
661	A163	30c deep red	4.00	.25
	Nos. 656-661 (6)		20.45	2.65
	Set, never hinged		80.00	

Nos. 656-661 exist imperf.; value for set, $150. Part-perf. varieties exist.
For overprints see Nos. C98-C99.

Without Imprint

1938-48   Perf. 11, 13½

Two types of the 15 Centimos:
Type I — Medieval style numerals with diagonal line through "5."
Type II — Modern numerals. Narrower "5" without diagonal line.

662	A159	1c green, imperf.	.25	.25
663	A160	2c brn (18½x22mm; '40)	.25	.25
a.	2c bis brn (17¼x21mm; '48)		.25	.25
	Never hinged		.20	
664	A161	5c gray brn ('39)	.25	.25
a.	Perf. 13½x13¼ ('49)		.25	.25
665	A161	10c dk carmine	.25	.25
a.	10c rose		.35	.25
	Never hinged		.75	
b.	Perf. 13½x13¼ ('49)		.25	.25
666	A161	15c dk green (I)	.90	.25
666A	A161	15c dk green (II)	.60	.25
b.	Perf 13½x13¼ ('50)		.65	.25
667	A162	70c dk blue ('39)	.75	.25
	Nos. 662-667 (7)		3.25	1.75
	Set, never hinged		4.25	

1938, July 17   **Perf. 10**
668	A164	15c bl grn & lt grn	4.25	3.75
669	A164	25c rose red & rose	4.25	3.75
670	A164	30c bl & lt bl	2.25	2.50
671	A164	1p brown & yellow	90.00	80.00
		Nos. 668-671 (4)	100.75	90.00
		Set, never hinged	250.00	

Second anniversary of the Civil War.
Nos. 678-681 exist imperforate. Value, set $725 hinged, $950 never hinged.

Isabella I
A165

Gen. Francisco Franco
A166

1938-39   **Litho.**   **Perf. 10**
672	A165	20c brt violet ('39)	.60	.25
673	A165	25c brown carmine	6.00	.60
674	A165	30c rose red	.25	.25
675	A165	40c dull violet	.30	.25
676	A165	50c indigo ('39)	27.50	2.50
677	A165	1p deep blue	9.00	.90
		Nos. 672-677 (6)	43.65	4.75
		Set, never hinged	120.00	

Nos. 672-677 exist imperf. Value set, $225 hinged, $350 never hinged.

Imprint: "Sanchez Toda"

1939-40   **Perf. 10**
678	A166	20c brt violet	.35	.25
679	A166	25c rose lake	.35	.25
680	A166	30c rose carmine	.30	.25
681	A166	40c slate green	.25	.25
682	A166	45c vermilion ('40)	1.75	1.75
683	A166	50c indigo	.30	.25
684	A166	60c orange	2.75	2.75
685	A166	70c blue	.40	.25
686	A166	1p black	11.00	.25
687	A166	2p dark brown	15.00	1.25
688	A166	4p dark violet	85.00	17.50
689	A166	10p light brown	40.00	44.00
		Nos. 678-689 (12)	157.45	69.00
		Set, never hinged	300.00	

#686-689 have value & "Pta." on 1 line while #702-705 have value & "Pta." on 2 lines.
Nos. 678-689 exist imperf. Value set, $525 hinged, $700 never hinged.

Without Imprint
Perf. 9½x10½

1939-47   **Litho.**   **Unwmk.**
690	A166	5c dull brn vio	.50	.25
691	A166	10c brown orange	2.25	.65
692	A166	15c lt green	.55	.25
693	A166	20c brt violet ('40)	.55	.25
694	A166	25c dp claret ('40)	.55	.25
695	A166	30c blue ('40)	.55	.25
697	A166	40c Prus grn ('40)	.55	.25
a.		40c greenish black	.65	.25
		Never hinged	1.10	
698	A166	45c ultra ('41)	.55	.25
699	A166	50c indigo ('40)	.50	.25
a.		Perf. 11½ ('47)	32.50	3.00
		Never hinged	55.00	
700	A166	60c dull org ('40)	.70	.25
701	A166	70c blue ('40)	.85	.25
702	A166	1p gray blk ('40)	7.50	.25
703	A166	2p dull brn ('41)	8.75	.25
704	A166	4p dull rose ('40)	32.50	.25
705	A166	10p lt brown ('40)	160.00	2.75
		Nos. 690-705 (15)	216.85	6.65
		Set, never hinged	425.00	

Perf. 13x13¼

1949-53   **Litho.**   **Unwmk.**
693a	A166	20c brt violet	.25	.25
694a	A166	25c dp claret	.25	.25
695a	A166	30c blue	.25	.25
696	A166	35c aqua ('51)	.25	.25
697b	A166	40c Prus grn ('50)	.25	.25
698a	A166	45c ultra ('52)	.25	.25
699b	A166	50c indigo	.25	.25
700a	A166	60c dull org	.25	.25
701a	A166	70c blue ('53)	16.00	.25
702a	A166	1p gray blk ('51)	8.25	.25
703a	A166	2p dull brn ('50)	3.00	.25
704a	A166	4p dull red	5.00	.25
705a	A166	10p lt brown ('53)	1.10	.30
		Nos. 693a-705a (13)	35.35	3.30
		Set, never hinged	80.00	

The 40c exists in three types, with variations in the value tablet: I. "CTS" does not touch bottom line. II. Light background in tablet. "CTS" touches bottom line. III. As type I, but with well defined lines of white and color around rectangle.

The 60c exists in two types: I. Top and left side of value tablet touch rest of design. II. Tablet separated from rest of design by white lines.

Five values exist with perf. 10: 5c, 10c, 45c, 4p and 10p.
Nos. 690-704 exist imperf. Values, set: mint, never hinged, $1,600; unused, $1,200.
The imperforate 10c dull claret, type A166, without imprint, is a postal tax stamp, RA14.

1944   **Redrawn**
706	A166	1p gray	50.00	.65
		Never hinged	110.00	

"PTS" instead of "PTA" as No. 702.
Nos. 690-704 and 706 exist imperforate. Value, set $925.

The value reads "PTAS" instead of "PTS"

1944   **Unwmk.**   **Perf. 9½x10½, 13**
709	A166	10p brown	14.00	.30
		Never hinged	20.00	

General Franco — A167

St. John of the Cross — A168

1942-48   **Engr.**   **Perf. 12½x13**
712	A167	40c chestnut	.40	.25
713	A167	75c dk bl, perf. 9½x10½ ('46)	3.50	.40
714	A167	90c dk green ('48)	.30	.25
a.		Perf. 9½x10½ ('47)	1.40	.25
715	A167	1.35p purple ('48)	.90	.25
a.		Perf. 9½x10½ ('46)	2.00	.40
		Nos. 712-715 (4)	5.10	1.15
		Set, never hinged	8.50	

1942   **Litho.**   **Perf. 9½x10½**
721	A168	20c violet	.55	.25
722	A168	40c salmon	1.25	.60
723	A168	75c ultra	1.50	1.75
		Nos. 721-723 (3)	3.30	2.60
		Set, never hinged	4.00	

St. John of the Cross (1542-1591).
Nos. 721-723 exist imperforate. Value, $65 hinged, $80 never hinged.

Holy Year Issues

Statue in St. James Cathedral
A169

St. James of Compostela
A170

Incense Burner — A171

Carvings in St. James Cathedral
A172   A174

St. James — A173   St. James' Casket — A175

East Portal of Cathedral
A176

St. James Cathedral
A177

Perf. 9½x10½

1943, Oct.   **Litho.**   **Unwmk.**
724	A169	20c deep blue	.25	.25
725	A170	40c dk red brown	.50	.25
726	A171	75c deep blue	2.10	2.10

Nos. 725 and 727 exist imperforate. Value, $550.

1943-44   **Perf. 9½x10½, 10½x9½**
727	A172	20c rose red ('44)	.25	.25
728	A173	40c dull green	.50	.25
729	A174	75c dk blue ('44)	2.75	2.25

1944
730	A175	20c red violet	.25	.25
731	A176	40c dull brown	.70	.25
732	A177	75c bright blue	30.00	32.00
		Nos. 724-732 (9)	37.30	37.85
		Set, never hinged	92.50	

Millenium of Castile Issues

Arms of Soria — A178

Arms of Castile — A179

Arms of Avila
A180

Fortress
A181

Arms of Segovia
A182

Arms of Fernan González
A183

Arms of Burgos
A185

Arms of Santander
A186

1944   **Litho.**   **Perf. 9½x10½**
733	A178	20c violet	.30	.25
734	A179	40c dull brown	3.00	.50
735	A180	75c blue	3.00	3.00

1944
736	A181	20c rose violet	.25	.25
737	A182	40c dull brown	2.75	.50
738	A183	75c dull blue	2.60	2.75

1944
739	A180	20c red violet	.25	.25
740	A185	40c dull brown	2.10	.50
741	A186	75c blue	3.00	3.25
		Nos. 733-741 (9)	17.25	11.25
		Set, never hinged	32.50	

Nos. 733, 738 and 741 exist imperforate. Value, $650. Value never hinged, $900.
No. 739 exists imperforate on grayish paper.

Francisco Gomez de Quevedo y Villegas (1580-1645), Writer — A187

1945, Sept. 8   **Engr.**   **Perf. 10**
742	A187	40c dark brown	.65	.55
		Never hinged	1.10	

Exists imperf. Value $80.

Type of Semi-Postal Stamp, 1940 Without Imprint at Lower Left and Right

1946, Jan. 1   **Litho.**   **Perf. 11**
743	SP20	50c (40c + 10c) sl grn & rose vio	1.40	.25
		Never hinged	2.40	

No. 743 was used as an ordinary postage stamp of 50c denomination.
Exists imperf. Value $80.

Elio Antonio de Nebrija — A188

University of Salamanca and Signature of Francisco de Vitoria — A189

1946, Oct. 12   **Engr.**   **Perf. 9½x10**
744	A188	50c deep plum	.40	.30
745	A189	75c deep blue	.50	.45
		Nos. 744-745,C121 (3)	2.80	3.25
		Set, never hinged	5.25	

Stamp Day and the Day of the Race, Oct. 12, 1946.
Nos. 744-745 and C121 exist imperforate. Value set, $160 hinged, $240 never hinged.

Francisco de Goya
A190

Benito Jeronimo Feijoo y Montenegro
A191

1946, Oct 26
746	A190	25c deep plum	.25	.25
747	A190	50c green	.25	.25
748	A190	75c dark blue	.60	.75
		Nos. 746-748 (3)		1.25
		Set, never hinged	1.00	

Francisco de Goya, birth bicentenary.
Nos. 746-748 exist imperforate. Value set, $25 hinged, $32.50 never hinged.

1947, June 1   **Unwmk.**
749	A191	50c deep green	.45	.35
		Never hinged	.65	

No. 749 exists imperforate. Value, $35.

Don Quixote Reading
A192

"Don Quixote" by Zuloaga
A193

1947, Oct. 9   **Engr.**   **Perf. 9½x10½**
750	A192	50c sepia	.25	.25
751	A193	75c dark blue	.40	.45
		Nos. 750-751,C122 (3)	5.15	5.20
		Set, never hinged	7.75	

Stamp Day and the 400th anniv. of the birth of Miguel de Cervantes Saavedra.

Nos. 750-751 and C122 exist imperforate. Value set, $550 hinged, $650 never hinged.

General Franco
A194   A195

1948   Litho.   Perf. 12½x13
752 A194 15c green   .25 .25
753 A195 50c violet   .80 .25
Set, never hinged   1.25

Nos. 752 and 753 exist imperforate. Value set, $400 hinged, $550 never hinged.
See Nos. 760-768, 780, 801-803. For surcharges see Nos. B137-B138.

Hernando Cortez — A196   Mateo Aleman — A197

1948, June 15   Engr.   Perf. 12½x13
754 A196 35c black   .25 .25

Perf. 9½x10½
755 A197 70c dk violet brn   1.40 2.00
a.   Perf. 12½x13   25.00 25.00
Set, never hinged   2.25

No. 754 exists imperforate. Value set, $100 hinged, $125 never hinged.

Ferdinand III (The Saint) — A198   Grandson of Adm. Ramon de Bonifaz — A199

1948, Sept. 20   Litho.   Perf. 12½x13
756 A198 25c rose violet   .25 .25
757 A199 30c scarlet   .25 .25
Set, never hinged   .50

700th anniversary of the Spanish navy and of the capture of Seville by Ferdinand the Saint.

José de Salamanca y Mayol — A200   Train Crossing Pancorbo Viaduct — A201

Perf. 12½x13, 13x12½
1948, Oct. 9   Unwmk.
758 A200 50c brown   .50 .25
759 A201 5p deep green   1.40 .60
Nos. 758-759,C125 (3)   3.40 2.00
Set, never hinged   6.00

Centenary of Spanish railroads.

Franco Types of 1948
1948-49   Litho.   Perf. 12½x13
760 A194 5c brown   .30 .25
761 A195 25c vermilion   .30 .25
762 A195 35c blue green   .30 .25
763 A195 40c red brown   .65 .25
764 A195 45c car rose ('49) .40 .25
765 A194 50c bister   1.10 .25
766 A195 70c purple ('49)   1.90 .30

767 A195 75c dk vio blue   1.60 .30
768 A195 1p rose pink   5.00 .25
Nos. 760-768 (9)   11.55 2.35
Set, never hinged   17.50

Imperforates exist of Nos. 761 ($100), 762 ($300), 764 ($300) and 768 ($500).

Symbols of UPU
A202

1949, Oct. 9
769 A202 50c red brown   .35 .25
770 A202 75c violet blue   .35 .55
Nos. 769-770,C126 (3)   .95 1.25
Set, never hinged   2.25

75th anniv. of the UPU.

St. John of God — A203   Pedro Calderon de la Barca — A204

1950, Mar. 8   Engr.   Unwmk.
771 A203 1p dark violet   7.00 4.50
Never hinged   12.50

400th anniversary of the death of St. John of God, humanitarian.

1950-53   Photo.   Perf. 12½
Designs: 10c Lope de Vega. 15c, Tirso de Molina. 20c, Juan Ruiz de Alarcon, dramatist. 50c, St. Antonio Maria Claret y Clara.

772 A204 5c brown ('51)   .25 .25
773 A204 10c dp rose brn ('51) .25 .25
773A A204 15c dk sl grn ('53) .25 .25
774 A204 20c violet   .25 .25

Perf. 12½x13
Engr.
775 A204 50c dp bluish gray ('51) 2.50 1.50
Nos. 772-775 (5)   3.50 2.50
Set, never hinged   4.35

No. 774 exists imperforate. Value, $250.

Stamp of 1850 — A205   Queen Isabella I — A206

1950, Oct. 12   Engr.   Imperf.
776 A205 50c purple   4.75 6.50
777 A205 75c ultra   4.75 6.50
778 A205 10p dk slate grn 85.00 87.50
779 A205 15p red   85.00 87.50
Nos. 776-779,C127-C130 (8) 348.50 376.00
Set, never hinged   625.00

Centenary of Spain's stamps.

Franco Type of 1948
1950   Litho.   Perf. 12½x13
780 A195 45c red   .60 .25
Never hinged   .90

1951, Apr. 22   Photo.   Perf. 12½
781 A206 50c brown   .50 .35
782 A206 75c blue   .60 .35
783 A206 90c rose brown   .35 .25
784 A206 1.50p orange   7.50 7.50
785 A206 2.80p olive grn   18.00 20.00
Nos. 781-785 (5)   26.95 28.45
Set, never hinged   47.50

500th anniversary of the birth of Queen Isabella I. See Nos. C132-C136.

Ferdinand, the Catholic A210   Maria Michaela Dermaisiéres A211

1952, May 10   Photo.   Perf. 13
787 A210 50c green   .45 .30
788 A210 75c indigo   2.25 1.25
789 A210 90c rose brown   .40 .35
790 A210 1.50p orange   6.50 6.50
791 A210 2.80p brown   11.50 13.50
Nos. 787-791 (5)   21.10 21.90
Set, never hinged   40.00

500th anniversary of the birth of Ferdinand the Catholic of Spain. See Nos. C139-C143.

1952, May 26   Perf. 12½x13
792 A211 90c claret   .25 .25
Never hinged   .30

35th International Eucharistic Congress, Barcelona, 1952. See No. C137.

Dr. Santiago Ramon y Cajal — A212

Portrait: 4.50p, Dr. Jaime Ferran y Clua.

1952, July 8   Photo.
793 A212 2p bright blue   10.00 .50
794 A212 4.50p red brown   .50 .80
Set, never hinged   25.00

Centenary of the births of Dr. Santiago Ramon y Cajal and Dr. Jaime Ferran y Clua.

University Seal — A213   Luis de Leon — A214

Cathedral of Salamanca A215

1953, Oct. 12   Perf. 12½x13, 13x12½
795 A213 50c deep magenta   .50 .35
796 A214 90c dark olive gray 1.60 1.60
797 A215 2p brown   11.00 3.50
Nos. 795-797 (3)   13.10 5.45
Set, never hinged   21.00

Stamp Day, 10/12/53, and 700th anniv. of the founding of the University of Salamanca.

The Magdalene — A216

1954, Jan. 10   Perf. 12½x13
798 A216 1.25p deep magenta .25 .25
Never hinged   .30

José de Ribera, painter, 300th death anniv.

St. James of Compostela A217   St. James Cathedral A218

1954, Mar. 1
799 A217 50c dark brown   .25 .25
800 A218 3p blue   25.00 4.00
Set, never hinged   47.50

Holy year of Compostela, 1954.

Franco Types of 1948
1954   Litho.   Perf. 12½x13
801 A194 5c olive gray   .25 .25
802 A195 30c deep green   .25 .25
803 A194 80c dull car rose 1.50 .25
Nos. 801-803 (3)   2.00 .75
Set, never hinged   4.75

Virgin by Alonso Cano — A219   Marcelino Menendez y Pelayo — A220

Virgins: 15c, Begoña. 25c, Of the Abandoned. 30c, Black. 50c, Of the Pillar. 60c, Covadonga. 80c, Kings'. 1p, Almudena. 2p, Africa. 3p, Guadalupe.

1954, July 18   Photo.   Perf. 12½x13
804 A219 10c dk car rose   .25 .25
805 A219 15c olive green   .25 .25
806 A219 25c purple   .25 .25
807 A219 30c brown   .25 .25
808 A219 50c brown olive   .50 .25
809 A219 60c gray   .25 .25
810 A219 80c grnsh gray   2.25 .25
811 A219 1p lilac gray   2.25 .25
812 A219 2p red brown   .70 .25
813 A219 3p bright blue   .60 .60
Nos. 804-813 (10)   7.55 2.85
Set, never hinged   11.00

Issued to publicize the Marian Year.

1954, Oct. 12
814 A220 80c dk gray grn   5.25 .35
Never hinged   9.50

Stamp Day, October 12, 1954.

Gen. Franco — A221

Imprint: "F.N.M.T."

1954-56   Perf. 12½x13
815 A221 10c dk car lake   .25 .25
816 A221 15c bister   .25 .25
817 A221 20c dk ol grn ('55) .25 .25
818 A221 25c blue violet   .25 .25
819 A221 30c brown   .25 .25
820 A221 40c rose vio ('55) .25 .25
821 A221 50c dk brn olive   .25 .25
822 A221 60c dk vio brown   .25 .25
823 A221 70c dk green   .25 .25
824 A221 80c dk blue grn   .25 .25
825 A221 1p dp orange   .25 .25
826 A221 1.40p lil rose ('56) .25 .25
827 A221 1.50p lt bl grn ('56) .25 .25
828 A221 1.80p emerald ('56) .25 .25
829 A221 2p red   12.00 1.25
830 A221 2p red lilac ('56) .25 .25
831 A221 3p Prus blue   .25 .25
832 A221 5p dk red brn   .25 .25
833 A221 6p dk gray ('55)   .25 .25
834 A221 8p brt vio ('56)   .25 .25
835 A221 10p yel grn ('55)   .25 .25
Nos. 815-835 (21)   17.00 6.25
Set, never hinged   20.00

Coils: The 1.50p, No. 830, the 3p and the 6p were issued in coils in brighter tones (the 3p in 1974, others in 1973). Every fifth stamp has a black control number on the back.
See Nos. 937-938, 1852-1855.

St. Ignatius of Loyola — A222

St. Ignatius and Loyola Palace A223

Perf. 13x12½, 12½x13

1955, Oct. 12	**Photo.**		**Unwmk.**	
836	A222	25c dull purple	.25	.25
837	A223	60c bister	.40	.30
838	A222	80c Prus green	1.65	.25
		Nos. 836-838 (3)	2.30	.80
		Set, never hinged	4.25	

4th cent. of the death of St. Ignatius of Loyola, founder of the Jesuit Order, and Day of the Stamp.

Symbols of Telegraph and Radio Communication A224

St. Vincent Ferrer A225

1955, Dec. 8			**Perf. 13x12½**	
839	A224	15c dk olive bis	.30	.25
840	A224	80c Prus green	4.25	.25
841	A224	3p bright blue	8.00	1.25
		Nos. 839-841 (3)	12.55	1.75
		Set, never hinged	27.50	

Spanish telegraph system centenary.

1955, Dec. 20			**Perf. 13**	
842	A225	15c olive bister	.35	.25
		Never hinged	.60	

Canonization of St. Vincent Ferrer, 5th cent.

"Holy Family" by El Greco — A226

Marching Soldiers and Dove — A227

1955, Dec. 24			**Perf. 13x12½**	
843	A226	80c dark green	3.25	.65
		Never hinged	6.00	

1956, July 17			**Unwmk.**	
844	A227	15c olive bis & brn	.25	.25
845	A227	50c lt ol grn & ol	.50	.30
846	A227	80c mag & grnsh blk	4.25	.25
847	A227	3p ultra & dp blue	4.25	1.40
		Nos. 844-847 (4)	9.25	2.20
		Set, never hinged	19.00	

20th anniversary of Civil War.

Ciudad de Toledo A228

1956, Aug. 3			**Perf. 12½x13**	
848	A228	3p blue	3.25	2.00
		Never hinged	5.75	

Issued to publicize the voyage of the S. S. Ciudad de Toledo to Central and South America carrying the First Floating (Industrial) Exposition.

Black Virgin of Montserrat A229

Archangel Gabriel by Fra Angelico A230

Design: 60c, Monastery of Montserrat, mountains and crucifix.

1956, Sept. 11			**Perf. 13x12½**	
849	A229	15c bister	.25	.25
850	A229	60c violet black	.25	.25
851	A229	80c blue green	.30	.40
		Nos. 849-851 (3)	.80	.90
		Set, never hinged	.85	

75th anniv. of the coronation of the Black Virgin of Montserrat.

1956, Oct. 12			**Engr.**	
852	A230	80c dull green	.75	.35
		Never hinged	1.00	

Stamp Day, Oct. 12.

Statistical Chart A231

1956, Nov. 3			**Perf. 12½x13**	
853	A231	15c dk olive bis	.30	.30
854	A231	80c orange	2.75	.60
855	A231	1p red orange	2.75	.60
		Nos. 853-855 (3)	5.80	1.50
		Set, never hinged	10.00	

Centenary of Spanish Statistics.

Hermitage and Monument A232

1956, Dec. 4				
856	A232	80c dull blue grn	2.00	.25
		Never hinged	5.50	

20th anniversary of the nomination of Gen. Franco as chief of state and commander in chief of the army.

Hungarian Children A233

St. Marguerite Alacoque's Vision of Jesus A234

1956, Dec. 17			**Perf. 13x12½**	
857	A233	10c brown lake	.25	.25
858	A233	15c dk bister	.25	.25
859	A233	50c olive gray	.30	.25
860	A233	80c dk blue grn	2.00	.25

861	A233	1p red orange	2.25	.25
862	A233	3p brt blue	6.00	2.25
		Nos. 857-862 (6)	11.05	3.50
		Set, never hinged	19.00	

Issued in sympathy to the children of Hungary.

1957, Oct. 12	**Photo.**		**Unwmk.**	
863	A234	15c dk olive bis	.25	.25
864	A234	60c violet blk	.25	.25
865	A234	80c dk blue grn	.30	.25
		Nos. 863-865 (3)	.80	.75
		Set, never hinged	.90	

Centenary of the feast of the Sacred Heart of Jesus and for Stamp Day 1957.

Gonzalo de Cordoba — A235

1958, Feb. 28	**Engr.**		**Perf. 13x12½**	
866	A235	1.80p yellow green	.25	.25
		Never hinged	.30	

Issued in honor of El Gran Capitan, 15th century military leader.

"The Parasol," by Goya — A236

"Wife of the Bookseller of Carretas Street" — A237

Goya Paintings: 50c, Duke of Fernan-Nunez. 60c, The Crockery Seller. 70c, Isabel Cobos de Porcel. 80c, Goya by Vicente Lopez. 1p, "El Pelele" (Carnival Doll). 1.80p, Goya's grandson Marianito. 2p, The Vintage. 3p, The Drinker.

1958, Mar. 24	**Photo.**		**Perf. 13**	
		Gold Frame		
867	A236	15c bister	.25	.25
868	A237	40c plum	.25	.25
869	A237	50c olive gray	.25	.25
870	A237	60c violet gray	.25	.25
871	A237	70c dp yellow grn	.25	.25
872	A237	80c dk slate grn	.25	.25
873	A237	1p orange red	.25	.25
874	A237	1.80p brt green	.25	.25
875	A237	2p red lilac	.30	.30
876	A236	3p brt blue	.50	.50
		Nos. 867-876 (10)	2.80	2.80
		Set, never hinged	2.40	

Issued to honor Francisco Jose de Goya and for the "Day of the Stamp," Mar. 24.

See Nos. 1111-1114. For other art types see A240a, A246a, A257, A272, A285a, A300, A310, A324, A340-A341, A360, A371 and footnote following No. 1606.

Exhibition Emblem and Globe — A238

1958, June 7			**Perf. 13x12½**	
877	A238	80c car, dk brn & gray	.25	.25
a.		Souvenir sheet, imperf.	17.50	17.50
878	A238	3p car, vio blk & bl	.85	.85
a.		Souvenir sheet, imperf.	17.50	17.50

	Set, never hinged	2.00	
	#877a-878a never hinged	55.00	

No. 877a sold for 2p, No. 878a for 5p. Universal and Intl. Exposition at Brussels.

Charles V — A239

Various Portraits of Charles V: 50c, 1.80p, with helmet. 70c, 2p, facing left. 80c, 3p, with beret.

1958, July 30	**Photo.**		**Perf. 13**	
879	A239	15c buff & brown	.25	.25
880	A239	50c lt grn & ol brn	.25	.25
881	A239	70c gray, grn & blk	.25	.25
882	A239	80c pale brn & Prus grn	.25	.25
883	A239	1p bis & brick red	.25	.25
884	A239	1.80p pale grn & brt grn	.25	.25
885	A239	2p gray & lilac	.30	.30
886	A239	3p pale brn & brt bl	.75	.60
		Nos. 879-886 (8)	2.55	2.40
		Set, never hinged	3.25	

400th anniv. of the death of Charles V (Carlos I of Spain.)

Escorial and Streamlined Train — A240

Designs: 60c, 2p, Railroad bridge at Despeñaperros, vert. 80c, 3p, Train and Castle de La Mota.

1958, Sept. 29			**Perf. 12½x13**	
887	A240	15c dk olive bis	.25	.25
888	A240	60c dk purple	.25	.25
889	A240	80c dk blue grn	.25	.25
890	A240	1p red orange	.25	.25
891	A240	2p red lilac	.25	.25
892	A240	3p blue	.70	.40
		Nos. 887-892 (6)	1.95	1.65
		Set, never hinged	3.00	

Intl. Railroad Cong., Madrid, Sept. 28-Oct. 7.

Velazquez Self-portrait A240a

Velazquez Paintings: 15c, The Drinkers, horiz. 40c, The Spinners. 50c, Surrender of Breda. 60c, The Little Princesses. 70c, Prince Balthazar. 1p, The Coronation of Our Lady. 1.80p, Aesop. 2p, Vulcan's Forge. 3p, Menippus.

1959, Mar. 24	**Photo.**		**Perf. 13**	
		Gold Frame		
893	A240a	15c dk brown	.25	.25
894	A240a	40c rose violet	.25	.25
895	A240a	50c olive	.25	.25
896	A240a	60c black brown	.25	.25
897	A240a	70c dp yellow grn	.25	.25
898	A240a	80c dk slate grn	.25	.25
899	A240a	1p orange red	.25	.25
900	A240a	1.80p emerald	.25	.25
901	A240a	2p red lilac	.25	.25
902	A240a	3p brt blue	.35	.45
		Nos. 893-902 (10)	2.60	2.70
		Set, never hinged		

Issued to honor Diego de Silva Velazquez (1599-1660) and for Stamp Day, Mar. 24.

For other art types see A236-A237, A246a, A257, A272, A285a, A300, A310, A324, A340-A341, A360, A371 and footnote following No. 1606.

Civil War Memorial — A241

1959, Apr 1. Litho. Unwmk.
903 A241 80c yel grn & dk sl grn .25 .25
   Never hinged .30

Inauguration of the war memorial at the monastery of the Holy Cross in the Valley of the Fallen.

Louis XIV and Philip IV — A242

1959, Oct. 24 Photo. Perf. 13x12½
904 A242 1p gold & rose brn .25 .25
   Never hinged .30

300th anniv. of the signing of the Treaty of the Pyrenees. Design shows the French-Spanish meeting at Isle des Faisans in 1659, as pictured in the Lebrun Tapestry, Versailles.

Monastery of Guadalupe A243

80c, Monastery, different view. 1p, Portals.

1959, Nov. 16 Engr. Perf. 12½x13
905 A243 15c lt red brown .25 .25
906 A243 80c slate .25 .25
907 A243 1p rose red .25 .25
   Nos. 905-907 (3) .75
   Set, never hinged .60

Entrance of the Franciscan Brothers into Guadalupe monastery, 50th anniv.

Holy Family, by Goya — A244

1959, Dec. 10 Photo. Perf. 13x12½
908 A244 1p orange brown .25 .25
   Never hinged .35

Catalogue values for unused stamps in this section, from this point to the end of the section, are for Never Hinged items.

Lidian Bull A245

Bullfighter, 19th Century — A246

Designs: 20c, Rounding up bulls. 25c, Running with the bulls, Pamplona. 30c, Bull entering arena. 50c, Bullfighting with cape. 70c, Bullfighting with banderillas. 80c, 1p, 1.40p, 1.50p, Fighting with muleta, various poses. 1.80p, Mounted bullfighter placing banderillas.

Perf. 12½x13, 13x12½
1960, Feb. 29 Engr. Unwmk.
909 A245 15c sepia & bis .25 .25
910 A245 20c vio & bl vio .25 .25
911 A246 25c gray .25 .25
912 A246 30c sepia & bister .25 .25
913 A246 50c dull vio & sep .25 .25
914 A246 70c sepia & sl grn .25 .25
915 A246 80c blue grn & grn .25 .25
916 A246 1p red & brn .25 .25
917 A246 1.40p brown & lake .25 .25
918 A246 1.50p grnsh bl & grn .25 .25
919 A245 1.80p grn & dk grn .25 .25
920 A246 5p brn & brn car .55 .45
   Nos. 909-920,C159-C162 (16) 4.60 4.35

Murillo Self-portrait A246a

Christ of Lepanto A247

Murillo Paintings: 25c, The Good Shepherd. 40c, Rebecca and Eliezer. 50c, Virgin of the Rosary. 70c, Immaculate Conception. 80c, Children with Shell. 1.50p, Holy Family with Bird, horiz. 2.50p, Children Playing Dice. 3p, Children Eating. 5p, Children counting Money.

1960, Mar. 24 Photo. Perf. 13
Gold Frame
921 A246a 25c dull violet .25 .25
922 A246a 40c plum .25 .25
923 A246a 50c olive gray .25 .25
924 A246a 70c dp yel grn .25 .25
925 A246a 80c deep green .25 .25
926 A246a 1p violet brown .25 .25
927 A246a 1.50p blue green .25 .25
928 A246a 2.50p rose car .25 .25
929 A246a 3p brt blue 1.25 .60
930 A246a 5p deep red brn .35 .25
   Nos. 921-930 (10) 3.60 2.85

Issued to honor Bartolome Esteban Murillo (1617-1682) and for Stamp Day, Mar. 24.
For other art types see A236-A237, A240a, A257, A272, A285a, A300, A310, A324, A340-A341, A360, A371 and footnote following No. 1606.

1960, Mar. 27 Perf. 13x12½
80c, 2.50p, 10p, Holy Family Church, Barcelona.

931 A247 70c brn car & grn 1.60 1.25
932 A247 80c blk & ol grn 1.60 1.25
933 A247 1p cl & brt red 1.60 1.25
934 A247 2.50p brt vio & gray vio 1.60 1.25
935 A247 5p sepia & bister 1.60 1.25
936 A247 10p sepia & bister 1.60 1.25
   Nos. 931-936,C163-C166 (10) 28.60 20.50

First International Congress of Philately, Barcelona, March 26-Apr. 5. Nos. 931-936 could be bought at the exhibition upon presentation of 5p entrance ticket.

Franco Type of 1954-56
Imprint: "F.N.M.T.-B"
1960, Mar. 31 Photo. Perf. 13
937 A221 1p deep orange 1.40 .60
938 A221 5p dark red brown 1.40 .60

Printed and issued at the International Congress of Philately in Barcelona.

St. Juan de Ribera — A248

St. Vincent de Paul — A249

1960, Aug. 16 Photo. Perf. 13
939 A248 1p orange red .25 .25
940 A248 2.50p lilac rose .25 .25

Canonization of St. Juan de Ribera.

Common Design Types pictured following the introduction.

Europa Issue, 1960
Common Design Type
1960, Sept. 19 Perf. 12½x13
Size: 38½x21½mm
941 CD3 1p sl grn & ol bis .75 .25
942 CD3 5p choc & salmon .75 .50

1960, Sept. 27 Unwmk. Perf. 13
943 A249 25c violet .25 .25
944 A249 1p orange red .40 .25

3rd centenary of the death of St. Vincent de Paul.

Pedro Menendez de Aviles — A250

Runner — A251

70c, 2.50p, Hernando de Soto. 80c, 3p, Ponce de Leon. 1p, 5p, Alvar Nunez Cabeza de Vaca.

1960, Oct. 12 Perf. 13x12½
945 A250 25c vio bl, bl .25 .25
946 A250 70c slate grn, pink .25 .25
947 A250 80c dk grn, pale brn .25 .25
948 A250 1p org brn, yel .25 .25
949 A250 2p dk car rose, pink .30 .25
950 A250 2.50p lil rose, buff .60 .25
951 A250 3p dk blue, grnsh 2.75 .50
952 A250 5p dk brown, cit 2.25 .85
   Nos. 945-952 (8) 6.90 2.85

Florida's discovery & colonization, 4th cent.

Perf. 13x12½, 12½x13
1960, Oct. 31 Photo.
Sports: 40c, 2p, Bicycling, horiz. 70c, 2.50p, Soccer, horiz. 80c, 3p, Athlete with rings. 1p, 5p, Hockey on roller skates, horiz.

953 A251 25c dk vio, brn & blk .25 .25
954 A251 40c purple, org & blk .25 .25
955 A251 70c brt green & red .30 .25
956 A251 80c dp grn, car & blk .25 .25
957 A251 1p red org, brt grn & blk .55 .25
958 A251 1.50p Prus grn, brn & blk .40 .25
959 A251 2p red lil, emer & blk 1.10 .25
960 A251 2.50p lil rose & green .40 .25
961 A251 3p ultra, red & blk .75 .25
962 A251 5p red brn, bl & blk .75 .35
   Nos. 953-962,C167-C170 (14) 7.80 4.20

Isaac Albeniz — A252

1960, Nov. 7 Perf. 13
963 A252 25c dark gray .25 .25
964 A252 1p orange red .25 .25

Isaac Albeniz, composer, birth centenary.

Courtyard of Samos Monastery A253

1p, Fountain, vert. 5p, Facade, vert.

Perf. 12½x13, 13x12½
1960, Nov. 21 Engr.
965 A253 80c bl grn & Prus grn .25 .25
966 A253 1p org brn & car rose 1.10 .25
967 A253 5p sepia & ocher 1.10 .45
   Nos. 965-967 (3) 2.45 .95

Issued in honor of the reconstructed Benedictine monastery at Samos, Lugo.

Adoration, by Velazquez — A254

1960, Dec. 1 Photo. Perf. 13x12½
968 A254 1p orange red .30 .25

Flight into Egypt by Francisco Bayeu A255

1961, Jan. 23 Perf. 12½x13
969 A255 1p copper red .25 .25
970 A255 5p dull red brown .45 .30

World Refugee Year.

Leandro F. de Moratin, by Goya — A256

St. Peter by El Greco — A257

1961, Feb. 13 Perf. 13
971 A256 1p henna brown .25 .25
972 A256 1.50p dk blue green .25 .25

Leandro Fernandez de Moratin (1760-1828), poet and dramatist, 200th birth anniv.

1961, Mar. 24 Perf. 13
El Greco Paintings: 40c, Virgin Mary. 70c, Head of Christ. 80c, Knight with Hand on Chest. 1p, Self-portrait. 1.50p, Baptism of Christ. 2.50p, Holy Trinity. 3p, Burial of Count Orgaz. 5p, Christ Stripped of His Garments. 10p, St. Mauritius and the Theban Legion.

Gold Frame
973 A257 25c violet black .25 .25
974 A257 40c lilac .25 .25
975 A257 70c green .30 .25
976 A257 80c Prus green .30 .25
977 A257 1p chocolate 2.50 .25
978 A257 1.50p grnsh blue .30 .25
979 A257 2.50p dk car rose .50 .25
980 A257 3p bright blue 1.25 .45
981 A257 5p black brown 3.50 1.40
982 A257 10p purple .60 .30
   Nos. 973-982 (10) 9.75 3.90

El Greco and Stamp Day, March 24.
For other art types see A236-A237, A240a, A246a, A272, A285a, A300, A310, A324, A340-A341, A360, A371 and footnote following No. 1606.

Diego
Velazquez — A258

Canceled
Stamp — A259

Velazquez Paintings: 1p, Duke de Olivares. 2.50p, Infanta Margarita. 10p, Detail from The Spinners, horiz.

Unwmk.

1961, Apr. 17		**Engr.**	**Perf. 13**	
983	A258	80c dk blue & sl grn	2.00	.75
a.		Souvenir sheet	8.00	8.50
984	A258	1p brn red & choc	6.00	.75
a.		Souvenir sheet	8.50	8.50
985	A258	2.50p vio bl & bl	1.50	1.00
a.		Souvenir sheet	8.50	8.50
986	A258	10p grn & yel grn	7.00	2.50
a.		Souvenir sheet	8.50	8.50
		Nos. 983-986 (4)	16.50	5.00

300th anniversary (in 1960) of the death of Velazquez, painter.

Each souvenir sheet contains one imperf. stamp. The colors of the stamps have been changed: 80c, red brown & slate; 1p, blue & violet; 2.50p, green & blue; 10p, slate blue & greenish blue. The sheets were sold at a premium.

1961, May 6		**Photo.**	**Perf. 13x12½**	
987	A259	25c gray & red	.25	.25
988	A259	1p orange & blk	1.10	.25
989	A259	10p olive grn & brn	1.10	.60
		Nos. 987-989 (3)	2.45	1.10

Issued for International Stamp Day.

Juan Vazquez de Mella — A260

Flag, Angel and Peace Doves — A261

1961, June 8		**Unwmk.**	**Perf. 13**	
990	A260	1p henna brown	.45	.25
991	A260	2.30p red lilac	.25	.25

Birth centenary of Juan Vazquez de Mella y Fanjul, politician and writer.

1961, July 10

Designs: 80c, Ships and Strait of Gibraltar. 1p, Alcazar and horseman. 1.50p, Ruins and triumphal arch. 2p, Horseman over Ebro. 2.30p, Victory parade. 2.50p, Ship building. 3p, Steel industry. 5p, Map of Spanish irrigation dams and statue, horiz. 6p, Dama de Elche statue and power station. 8p, Mining development. 10p, General Franco.

992	A261	70c multicolored	.25	.25
993	A261	80c multicolored	.25	.25
994	A261	1p multicolored	.25	.25
995	A261	1.50p gold, pink & brn	.25	.25
996	A261	2p gold, gray & bl	.25	.25
997	A261	2.30p multicolored	.25	.25
998	A261	2.50p multicolored	.25	.25
999	A261	3p gold, red & dk gray	.35	.25
1000	A261	5p bl grn, ol gray & pink	2.25	1.10
1001	A261	6p multicolored	1.10	.25
1002	A261	8p gold, ol & sep	.70	.55
1003	A261	10p gold, gray & grn	.70	.55
		Nos. 992-1003 (12)	6.85	4.95

25th anniversary of national uprising.

Christ, San Clemente, Tahull A262

Luis de Argote y Gongora A263

Designs: 25c, Bas-relief, Compostela Cathedral. 1p, Cloister of Silos. 2p, Virgin of Irache.

1961, July 24		**Unwmk.**	**Perf. 13**	
		Gold Frame		
1004	A262	25c blue violet	.40	.25
1005	A262	1p orange brown	.50	.25
1006	A262	2p deep plum	.70	.25
1007	A262	3p grnsh bl, sal & blk	.90	.40
		Nos. 1004-1007 (4)	2.50	1.15

Seventh Exposition of the Council of Europe dedicated to Romanesque art, Barcelona-Santiago de Compostela, July 10-Oct. 10.

1961, Aug. 10		**Photo.**	**Perf. 13**	
1008	A263	25c violet black	.25	.25
1009	A263	1p henna brown	.50	.25

400th anniversary of the birth of Luis de Argote y Gongora, poet.

Europa Issue, 1961
Common Design Type

1961, Sept. 18			**Perf. 12½x13**	
		Size: 37½x21½mm		
1010	CD4	1p brt vermilion	.25	.25
1011	CD4	5p brown	.45	.30

Cathedral at Burgos A264

Sebastian de Belalcazar A265

1961, Oct. 1			**Perf. 13**	
1012	A264	1p gold & olive green	.25	.25

25th anniversary of the nomination of Gen. Francisco Franco as Head of State.

Builders of the New World

Portraits: 70c, 2.50p, Blas de Lezo. 80c, 3p, Rodrigo de Bastidas. 1p, 5p, Nuflo de Chaves.

1961, Oct. 12		**Photo.**	**Perf. 13x12½**	
1013	A265	25c indigo, *grn*	.25	.25
1014	A265	70c grn, *cream*	.25	.25
1015	A265	80c sl grn, *pnksh*	.25	.25
1016	A265	1p dk blue, *sal*	.60	.25
1017	A265	2p dk car, *bluish*	3.75	.25
1018	A265	2.50p lil, *pale lil*	.90	.45
1019	A265	3p blue, *grysh*	1.90	.80
1020	A265	5p brown, *yel*	2.00	.90
		Nos. 1013-1020 (8)	9.90	3.40

Issued to honor the discoverers and conquerors of Colombia and Bolivia.

See Nos. 1131-1138, 1187-1194, 1271-1278, 1316-1323, 1377-1384, 1489-1496, 1548, 1550, 1587-1588, 1632-1633.

Views of Escorial
Monastery — A266

Designs: 70c, Patio of the Kings. 80c, Patio. 1p, Garden of the Monks and Escorial, horiz. 2.50p, Staircase. 5p, General view of Escorial, horiz. 6p, Main altar.

1961, Oct. 31		**Engr.**	**Unwmk.**	
1021	A266	70c bl grn & ol grn	.25	.25
1022	A266	80c Prus grn & ind	.25	.25
1023	A266	1p ocher & dk red	.55	.25
1024	A266	2.50p cl & dull vio	.55	.25
1025	A266	5p bister & dk brn	1.60	.70
1026	A266	6p sl bl & dull pur	2.25	1.50
		Nos. 1021-1026 (6)	5.45	3.20

Alfonso XII Monument, Retiro Park — A267

Designs: 1p, King Philip II. 2p, Town hall, horiz. 2.50p, Cibeles fountain, horiz. 3p, Alcala gate, horiz. 5p, Cervantes memorial, Plaza de Espagna.

Photogravure (25c, 2p, 5p)
Engraved (1p, 2.50p, 3p)

1961, Nov. 13		**Unwmk.**	**Perf. 13**	
1027	A267	25c gray & dull pur	.25	.25
1028	A267	1p bis brn & gray	.30	.25
1029	A267	2p claret & gray	.30	.25
1030	A267	2.50p black & lilac	.25	.25
1031	A267	3p slate & ind	.60	.35
1032	A267	5p Prus grn & beige	1.10	.55
		Nos. 1027-1032 (6)	2.80	1.90

400th anniv. of Madrid as capital of Spain.

Church of St. Mary, Naranco — A268

Designs: 1p, King Fruela I, founder of Oviedo. 2p, Cross of the Angels. 2.50p, King Alfonso II. 3p, King Alfonso III. 5p, Apostles from Oviedo Cathedral (sculpture).

1961, Nov. 27				
1033	A268	25c pur & gray grn	.25	.25
1034	A268	1p bis brn & brn	.30	.25
1035	A268	2p dk brn & pale pur	.65	.25
1036	A268	2.50p claret & ind	.30	.25
1037	A268	3p slate & indigo	.65	.45
1038	A268	5p ol & ol grn	1.25	.55
		Nos. 1033-1038 (6)	3.40	2.00

1200th anniversary of the founding of Oviedo, capital of Asturia.

Nativity Sculptured by José Gines — A269

"La Cierva" Autogiro — A270

1961, Dec. 1		**Photo.**	**Perf. 13x12½**	
1039	A269	1p dull purple	.30	.25

1961, Dec. 11		**Unwmk.**	**Perf. 13**	

2p, Hydroplane "Plus Ultra.," horiz. 3p, "Jesus del Gran Poder," plane of Madrid-Manila flight, horiz. 5p, Bustard hunt by plane. 10p, Madonna of Loretto, patron saint of Spanish airmen.

1040	A270	1p indigo & blue	.25	.25
1041	A270	2p grn, dl pur & blk	.25	.25
1042	A270	3p blk & ol grn	1.25	.35
1043	A270	5p dl pur, gray bl & blk	2.50	.90
1044	A270	10p blk, lt bl & ol gray	1.25	.60
		Nos. 1040-1044 (5)	5.50	2.35

50th anniversary of Spanish aviation.

Provincial Arms Issue

Alava — A271

Arms of Spain — A271a

1962		**Photo.**	**Perf. 13**	
1045	A271	5p Alava	.25	.25
1046	A271	5p Albacete	.25	.25
1047	A271	5p Alicante	.25	.25
1048	A271	5p Almeria	.25	.25
1049	A271	5p Avila	.25	.25
1050	A271	5p Badajoz	.25	.25
1051	A271	5p Baleares	.25	.25
1052	A271	5p Barcelona	.25	.25
1053	A271	5p Burgos	.65	.40
1054	A271	5p Caceres	.35	.25
1055	A271	5p Cadiz	.45	.35
1056	A271	5p Castellon de la Plana	3.50	1.50
		Nos. 1045-1056 (12)	6.95	4.50

1963				
1057	A271	5p Ciudad Real	.45	.35
1058	A271	5p Cordoba	3.50	1.25
1059	A271	5p Coruña	.55	.35
1060	A271	5p Cuenca	.55	.35
1061	A271	5p Fernando Po	.80	.75
1062	A271	5p Gerona	.25	.25
1063	A271	5p Gran Canaria	.25	.25
1064	A271	5p Granada	.25	.25
1065	A271	5p Guadalajara	.55	.35
1066	A271	5p Guipuzcoa	.25	.25
1067	A271	5p Huelva	.25	.25
1068	A271	5p Huesca	.25	.25
		Nos. 1057-1068 (12)	7.90	4.90

1964				
1069	A271	5p Ifni	.25	.25
1070	A271	5p Jaen	.25	.25
1071	A271	5p Leon	.25	.25
1072	A271	5p Lerida	.25	.25
1073	A271	5p Logrono	.25	.25
1074	A271	5p Lugo	.25	.25
1075	A271	5p Madrid	.25	.25
1076	A271	5p Malaga	.25	.25
1077	A271	5p Murcia	.25	.25
1078	A271	5p Navarra	.25	.25
1079	A271	5p Orense	.25	.25
1080	A271	5p Oviedo	.25	.25
		Nos. 1069-1080 (12)	3.00	3.00

1965				
1081	A271	5p Palencia	.25	.25
1082	A271	5p Pontevedra	.25	.25
1083	A271	5p Rio Muni	.25	.25
1084	A271	5p Sahara	.25	.25
1085	A271	5p Salamanca	.25	.25
1086	A271	5p Santander	.25	.25
1087	A271	5p Segovia	.25	.25
1088	A271	5p Seville	.25	.25
1089	A271	5p Soria	.25	.25
1090	A271	5p Tarragona	.25	.25
1091	A271	5p Tenerife	.25	.25
1092	A271	5p Teruel	.25	.25
		Nos. 1081-1092 (12)	3.00	3.00

1966				
1093	A271	5p Toledo	.25	.25
1094A	A271	5p Valencia	.25	.25
1094B	A271	5p Valladolid	.25	.25
1094C	A271	5p Vizcaya	.25	.25
1094D	A271	5p Zamora	.25	.25
1094E	A271	5p Zaragoza	.25	.25
1094F	A271	5p Ceuta	.25	.25
1094G	A271a	10p Spain	.25	.25
		Nos. 1093-1094G (9)	2.25	2.25
		Nos. 1045-1094G (57)	20.95	15.35

Zurbaran Self-portrait
A272

Zurbaran Paintings: 25c, Martyr, horiz. 40c, Burial of St. Catherine. 70c, St. Casilda. 80c, Jesus crowning St. Joseph. 1.50p, St. Jerome. 2.50p, Virgin of Grace. 3p, The Apotheosis of St. Thomas Aquinas. 5p, The Virgin as a child. 10p, The Immaculate Virgin.

Unwmk.
1962, Mar. 24   Photo.   *Perf. 13*
Gold Frame
1095	A272	25c olive gray	.40	.25
1096	A272	40c purple	.40	.25
1097	A272	70c green	.50	.25
1098	A272	80c Prus green	.40	.25
1099	A272	1p chocolate	7.50	.25
1100	A272	1.50p brt blue grn	.90	.25
1101	A272	2.50p dk car rose	.90	.25
1102	A272	3p bright blue	1.00	.35
1103	A272	5p deep brown	2.50	.75
1104	A272	10p olive green	2.50	.75
	Nos. 1095-1104 (10)		17.00	3.60

Issued to honor Francisco de Zurbaran (1598-1664) and for Stamp Day, March 24.
For other art types see A236-A237, A240a, A246a, A257, A285a, A300, A310, A324, A340-A341, A360, A371 and footnote following No. 1606.

San Jose
Convent, Avila
A272a

St. Theresa (by Velázquez?)
A273

Design: 1p, St. Theresa by Bernini.

1962, Apr. 10   *Perf. 13*
1105	A272a	25c bluish blk	.25	.25
1106	A272a	1p brown	.25	.25

Perf. 13x12½
1107	A273	3p bright blue	1.25	.40
	Nos. 1105-1107 (3)		1.75	.90

4th centenary of St. Theresa's reform of the Carmelite order.

Mercury — A274

1962, May 7
1108	A274	25c vio, rose & mag	.25	.25
1109	A274	1p brn, org & lt brn	.25	.25
1110	A274	10p dp grn, ol grn & brt grn	1.75	.80
	Nos. 1108-1110 (3)		2.25	1.30

International Stamp Day, May 7.

Painting Type of 1958
Rubens Paintings: 25c, Ferdinand of Austria. 1p, Self-portrait. 3p, Philip II. 10p, Duke of Lerma on horseback.

1962, May 28   *Perf. 13*
Gold Frame
Size: 25x30mm
1111	A237	25c violet black	.65	.30
1112	A237	1p chocolate	5.75	.30
1113	A237	3p blue	5.25	2.00

Perf. 13x12½
Size: 26x38mm
1114	A237	10p slate green	4.00	2.75
	Nos. 1111-1114 (4)		15.65	5.35

St. Benedict
A275

El Cid, Statue by Cristobal
A276

Berruguete Sculptures: 80c, Apostle. 1p, St. Peter. 2p, St. Christopher carrying Christ Child. 3p, Ecce Homo (Christ). 10p, St. Sebastian.

1962, July 9   *Perf. 13x12½*
1115	A275	25c lt blue & plum	.25	.25
1116	A275	80c sal & ol gray	.35	.25
1117	A275	1p gray & red	.45	.25
1118	A275	2p gray & magenta	3.50	.25
1119	A275	3p brn pink & dk bl	1.50	.85
1120	A275	10p rose & brown	1.50	.50
	Nos. 1115-1120 (6)		7.55	2.35

Alonso Berruguete (1486-1561), architect, sculptor and painter.

Perf. 13x12½, 12½x13
1962, July 30   Engr.

2p, Equestrian statue by Anna Huntington. 3p, El Cid's treasure chest, horiz. 10p, Oath-taking ceremony at Santa Gadea, horiz.
1121	A276	1p lt green & gray	.25	.25
1122	A276	2p brown & choc	1.40	.25
1123	A276	3p blue & sl grn	4.25	1.10
1124	A276	10p lt grn & sl grn	2.75	.60
	Nos. 1121-1124 (4)		8.65	2.20

El Cid Campeador (Rodrigo Diaz de Vivar, 1040-99), Spain's national hero.

Europa Issue, 1962

Bee and Honeycomb — A277

1962, Sept. 13   Photo.   *Perf. 12½x13*
1125	A277	1p deep rose	.25	.25
1126	A277	5p dull green	*1.00*	*.40*

Discus Thrower
A278

UPAE Emblem
A279

80c, Runner. 1p, Hurdler. 3p, Sprinter at start.

1962, Oct. 7   *Perf. 13x12½*
1127	A278	25c pale pink & vio blk	.25	.25
1128	A278	80c pale yel & dk grn	.25	.25
1129	A278	1p pale rose & brn	.25	.25
1130	A278	3p pale bl & dk bl	.25	.30
	Nos. 1127-1130 (4)		1.00	1.05

Second Spanish-American Games, Madrid, Oct. 7-12.

Builders of the New World
Portrait Type of 1961

Portraits: 25c, 2p, Alonso de Mendoza. 70c, 2.50p, Jiménez de Quesada. 80c, 3p, Juan de Garay. 1p, 5p, Pedro de la Gasca.

1962, Oct. 12   Unwmk.
1131	A265	25c rose lil, *gray*	.25	.25
1132	A265	70c grn, *pale pink*	1.00	.25
1133	A265	80c dk grn, *pale yel*	.70	.25
1134	A265	1p red brn, *gray*	1.40	.25
1135	A265	2p car, *lt bl*	3.25	.25
1136	A265	2.50p dk vio, *pnksh*	.70	.25
1137	A265	3p dp bl, *pale pink*	7.00	1.25
1138	A265	5p brn, *pale yel*	3.50	1.50
	Nos. 1131-1138 (8)		17.80	4.25

1962, Oct. 20   Engr.   *Perf. 13*
1139	A279	1p sepia & green	.25	.25

50th anniv. of the founding of the Postal Union of the Americas and Spain, UPAE.

The Annunciation, by Murillo — A280

Holy Family by Pedro de Mena — A281

Mysteries of the Rosary: 70c, The Visitation, Correa. 80c, Nativity, Murillo. 1p, The Presentation, Pedro de Campaña. 1.50p, The Finding in the Temple, (unknown painter). 2p, The Agony in the Garden, Gianquinto. 2.50p, The Scourging at the Pillar, Alonso Cano. 3p, The Crowning with Thorns, Tiepolo. 5p, Carrying of the Cross, El Greco. 8p, The Crucifixion, Murillo. 10p, The Resurrection, Murillo.

1962, Oct. 26
1140	A280	25c lilac & brown	.25	.25
1141	A280	70c grn & dk bl grn	.25	.25
1142	A280	80c ol & dk bl grn	.25	.25
1143	A280	1p green & gray	4.00	.70
1144	A280	1.50p green & dk bl	.25	.25
1145	A280	2p brown & violet	1.10	.50
1146	A280	2.50p dk brn & rose claret	.40	.25
1147	A280	3p lilac & gray	.40	.25
1148	A280	5p brn & dk car	.60	.35
1149	A280	8p vio brn & blk	.60	.25
1150	A280	10p grn & yel grn	.95	.25
	Nos. 1140-1150,C171-C174 (15)		11.65	4.80

1962, Dec. 6   Photo.   *Perf. 13x12½*
1151	A281	1p olive gray	.35	.25

Malaria Eradication Emblem
A282

1962, Dec. 21   *Perf. 12½x13*
1152	A282	1p blk, yel grn & yel	.25	.25

WHO drive to eradicate malaria.

Pope John XXIII and St. Peter's, Rome
A283

1962, Dec. 29   Engr.
1153	A283	1p dp plum & blk	.25	.25

Vatican II, the 21st Ecumenical Council of the Roman Catholic Church. See No. 1199.

St. Paul, by El Greco
A284

Courtyard, Poblet Monastery
A285

1963, Jan. 25   *Perf. 13*
1154	A284	1p brn, blk & olive	.30	.25

St. Paul's visit to Spain, 1,900th anniv.

Perf. 12½x13, 13x12½
1963, Feb. 25   Unwmk.

Designs: 1p, Royal sepulcher. 3p, View of monastery, horiz. 5p, Gothic arch.
1155	A285	25c choc & slate grn	.25	.25
1156	A285	1p org ver & rose car	.35	.25

1157	A285	3p vio bl & dk bl	1.10	.25
1158	A285	5p brown & ocher	2.40	.90
	Nos. 1155-1158 (4)		4.10	1.65

Issued in honor of the Cistercian monastery of Santa Maria de Poblet.

José de Ribera, Self-portrait
A285a

Coach
A286

Ribera Paintings: 25c, Archimedes. 40c, Jacob's Flock. 70c, Triumph of Bacchus. 80c, St. Christopher. 1.50p, St. Andrew. 2.50p, St. John the Baptist. 3p, St. Onofre. 5p, St. Peter. 10p, The Immaculate Virgin.

Unwmk.
1963, Mar. 24   Photo.   *Perf. 13*
Gold Frame
1159	A285a	25c violet	.35	.25
1160	A285a	40c red lilac	.40	.25
1161	A285a	70c green	1.00	.25
1162	A285a	80c dark green	1.00	.25
1163	A285a	1p brown	1.00	.25
1164	A285a	1.50p blue green	1.00	.25
1165	A285a	2.50p car rose	2.75	.25
1166	A285a	3p dark blue	3.00	.50
1167	A285a	5p olive	10.50	2.25
1168	A285a	10p dull red brn	4.00	1.40
	Nos. 1159-1168 (10)		25.00	5.90

Issued to honor José de Ribera (1588-1652) and for Stamp Day, Mar. 24.
For other art types see A236-A237, A246a, A257, A272, A300, A310, A324, A340-A341, A360, A371 and footnote following No. 1606.

1963, May 3   *Perf. 13x12½*
1169	A286	1p multicolored	.25	.25

First Intl. Postal Conference, Paris, 1863.

Globe
A287

1963, May 8   *Perf. 12½x13*
1170	A287	25c multicolored	.25	.25
1171	A287	1p multicolored	.25	.25
1172	A287	10p multicolored	1.10	.65
	Nos. 1170-1172 (3)		1.60	1.15

Issued for International Stamp Day, 1963.

"Give us this Day our Daily Bread..."
A288

1963, June 1   Unwmk.
1173	A288	1p multicolored	.25	.25

FAO "Freedom from Hunger" campaign.

"Pillars of Hercules" and Globes — A289

Designs: 80c, Fleet of Columbus. 1p, Columbus and compass rose.

1963, June 4   **Perf. 13**
1174	A289	25c multicolored	.25	.25
1175	A289	80c brn, lt grn & gold	.25	.25
1176	A289	1p sl grn, sepia & gold	.25	.25
		Nos. 1174-1176 (3)	.75	.75

Cong. of Institutions of Spanish Culture, June 5-15.

Seal of Council of San Sebastian
A290

80c, Burning of city, 1813. 1p, View, 1836.

1963, June 27   **Photo.**
1177	A290	25c vio, grn & blk	.25	.25
1178	A290	80c dk brn, gray & red	.25	.25
1179	A290	1p dk grn, grn & ol	.30	.25
		Nos. 1177-1179 (3)	.80	.75

Rebuilding of San Sebastian, 150th anniv.

Europa Issue, 1963

Our Lady of Europe — A291

1963, Sept. 16   **Engr.**   **Perf. 13x12½**
| 1180 | A291 | 1p bis brn & choc | .25 | .25 |
| 1181 | A291 | 5p bluish grn & blk | .55 | .40 |

Arms of Order of Mercy — A292

King James I — A293

Designs: 1p, Our Lady of Mercy. 1.50p, St. Pedro Nolasco. 3p, St. Raimundo de Penafort.

1963, Sept. 24   **Photo.**
| 1182 | A292 | 25c blk, car rose & gold | .25 | .25 |

Engr.
1183	A293	80c sepia & green	.25	.25
1184	A293	1p gray vio & brn vio	.25	.25
1185	A293	1.50p dull bl & blk	.25	.25
1186	A293	3p gray & black	.25	.25
		Nos. 1182-1186 (5)	1.25	1.25

Coronation of Our Lady of Mercy, 75th anniv.

Builders of the New World
Portrait Type of 1961

25c, 2p, Father Junipero Serra. 70c, 2.50p, Vasco Nuñez de Balboa. 80c, 3p, José de Galvez. 1p, 5p, Diego Garcia de Paredes.

1963, Oct. 12   **Perf. 13x12½**
1187	A265	25c vio bl, bl	.25	.25
1188	A265	70c grn, pale rose	.25	.25
1189	A265	80c dk grn, yel	.50	.25
1190	A265	1p dk bl, pale rose	.60	.25
1191	A265	2p magenta, lt bl	1.75	.25
1192	A265	2.50p vio blk, dl rose	1.10	.25
1193	A265	3p brt bl, pink	2.40	1.00
1194	A265	5p brown, yel	3.00	2.25
		Nos. 1187-1194 (8)	9.85	4.75

The Good Samaritan — A294

1963, Oct. 28   **Unwmk.**
| 1195 | A294 | 1p gold, pur & brt car | .25 | .25 |

Centenary of International Red Cross.

Holy Family by Alonso Berruguete (1486-1561)
A295

Father Raymond Lully
A296

1963, Dec. 2   **Photo.**   **Perf. 13x12½**
| 1196 | A295 | 1p dark green | .25 | .25 |

Christmas 1963. See No. 1279.

1963, Dec. 5   **Engr.**
Portrait: 1.50p, Cardinal Luis Antonio de Belluga (1662-1743).
1197	A296	1p dk violet & blk	.25	.25
1198	A296	1.50p sepia & dull vio	.25	.25
		Nos. 1197-1198,C175-C176 (4)	3.50	1.45

Papal Type of 1962

Design: 1p, Pope Paul VI and St. Peter's, Rome.

1963, Dec. 30   **Perf. 12½x13**
| 1199 | A283 | 1p dk green & blk | .25 | .25 |

Second session of Vatican II, the 21st Ecumenical Council of the Roman Catholic Church.

Alcazar, Segovia
A297

...

Dragon Caves, Majorca — A298

Tourism: 40c, Potes, Santander. 50c, Leon Cathedral. No. 1202, Crypt of San Isidro at Leon. No. 1203, Costa Brava. 80c, Christ of the Lanterns, Cordova. No. 1206, Court of Lions, Alhambra, Granada. No. 1208, Interior of La Mezquita, Cordova. 1.50p, View of Gerona.

1964   **Engr.**   **Perf. 13**
1200	A297	40c sepia & blue	.25	.25
1201	A298	50c gray & sepia	.25	.25
1202	A298	70c ind & dk bl grn	.25	.25
1203	A298	70c violet & brown	.25	.25
1204	A298	80c dp ultra & blk	.25	.25
1205	A297	1p vio bl & pur	.25	.25
1206	A297	1p rose red & dl pur	.25	.25
1207	A298	1p dk green & blk	.25	.25
1208	A298	1p brn vio & rose	.25	.25
1209	A297	1.50p gray grn, brn & blk	.25	.25
		Nos. 1200-1209 (10)	2.50	2.50

See Nos. 1280-1289.

Santa Maria de Huerta Monastery
A299

Joaquin Sorolla, Self-portrait
A300

Designs: 1p, Great Hall. 5p, View of monastery with apse, horiz.

1964, Feb. 24   **Perf. 13x12½, 12½x13**
1212	A299	1p gray grn & grn	.25	.25
1213	A299	2p grnsh blue & sepia	.25	.25
1214	A299	5p dark blue	1.50	.75
		Nos. 1212-1214 (3)	2.00	1.25

Santa Maria Monastery, Huerta, 8th cent.

1964, Mar. 24   **Photo.**   **Perf. 13**
Sorolla Paintings: 25c, The Jug (woman and child). 40c, Oxen and Driver, horiz. 70c, Man and Woman from La Mancha. 80c, Fisher Woman of Valencia. 1p, Self-portrait. 1.50p, Round up, horiz. 2.50p, Fishermen, horiz. 3p, Children at the Beach, horiz. 5p, Unloading the Boat. 10p, Man and Woman on Horseback, Valencia.

Gold Frame
1215	A300	25c violet	.25	.25
1216	A300	40c purple	.25	.25
1217	A300	70c dp yellow grn	.25	.25
1218	A300	80c bluish grn	.25	.25
1219	A300	1p brown	.25	.25
1220	A300	1.50p Prus blue	.25	.25
1221	A300	2.50p dk car rose	.25	.25
1222	A300	3p violet blue	.45	.45
1223	A300	5p chocolate	1.40	1.00
1224	A300	10p deep green	.65	.35
		Nos. 1215-1224 (10)	4.25	3.55

Issued to honor Joaquin Sorolla y Bastida (1863-1923) and for Stamp Day, March 24.
For other art types see A236-A237, A240a, A246a, A257, A272, A285a, A310, A324, A340-A341, A360, A371 and footnote following No. 1606.

"Peace" A301

"Sport" — A302

Designs: 40c, Radio and television. 50c, New apartments. 70c, Agriculture. 80c, Reforestation. 1p, Economic development. 1.50p, Modern architecture. 2p, Transportation. 2.50p, Hydroelectric development. 3p, Electrification. 5p, Scientific achievements. 6p, Buildings, tourism. 10p, Generalissimo Franco.

1964, Apr. 1
1225	A301	25c blk, emer & gold	.25	.25
1226	A302	30c blk, bl & sal pink	.25	.25
1227	A301	40c gold & blk	.25	.25
1228	A302	50c multicolored	.25	.25
1229	A301	70c multicolored	.25	.25
1230	A301	80c multicolored	.25	.25
1231	A302	1p multicolored	.25	.25
1232	A302	1.50p multicolored	.25	.25
1233	A301	2p multicolored	.25	.25
1234	A302	2.50p multicolored	.25	.25
1235	A301	3p gold, blk & red	.90	.90
1236	A302	5p gold, grn & red	.30	.30
1237	A301	6p multicolored	.45	.45
1238	A302	10p multicolored	.55	.55
		Nos. 1225-1238 (14)	4.70	4.70

Issued to commemorate 25 years of peace.

Bullfight and Unisphere
A303

Stamp of 1850 and Modern Stamps
A304

Designs: 1p, Spanish pavilion, horiz. 2.50p, La Mota castle, Medina de Campo. 5p, Spanish dancer. 50p, Jai alai.

Perf. 12½x13, 13x12½

1964, Apr. 23   **Engr.**
1239	A303	1p bl grn & yel grn	.25	.25
1240	A303	1.50p carmine & brn	.25	.25
1241	A303	2.50p dk bl & sl grn	.25	.25
1242	A303	5p car & dk car rose	.30	.30
1243	A303	50p vio bl & dk bl	.85	.40
		Nos. 1239-1243 (5)	1.90	1.45

New York World's Fair, 1964-65.

1964, May 6   **Perf. 13x12½**
1244	A304	25c dk car rose & dl pur	.25	.25
1245	A304	1p yel grn & dk bl	.25	.25
1246	A304	10p orange & rose red	.40	.35
		Nos. 1244-1246 (3)	.90	.85

Issued for International Stamp Day, 1964.

Virgin of Hope — A305

1964, May 31   **Photo.**   **Perf. 13x12½**
| 1247 | A305 | 1p dark green | .25 | .25 |

Canonical coronation of the Virgin of Hope (La Macarena) in St. Gil's Church, Seville, May 31.

Santa Maria — A306

Designs (ships): 15c, 13th cent. ship of King Alfonso X, from medieval manuscript, vert. 25c, Carrack, from 15th cent. engraving, vert. 50c, Galley. 70c, Galleon. 80c, Xebec. 1p, Warship, Santisima Trinidad, vert. 1.50p, 18th cent. corvette, Atrevida, vert. 2p, Steamer, Isabel II. 2.50p, Frigate, Numancia, Spain's 1st armored ship. 3p, Destroyer. 5p, Submarine of Isaac Peral. 6p, Cruiser, Baleares. 10p, Training ship, Juan Sebastian Elcano.

1964, July 16   **Perf. 13**
1248	A306	15c dp rose & vio blk	.25	.25
1249	A306	25c org yel & gray grn	.25	.25
1250	A306	40c ultra & dk bl	.25	.25
1251	A306	50c slate grn & dk bl	.25	.25
1252	A306	70c vio & dk bl	.25	.25
1253	A306	80c dl bl grn & ultra	.25	.25
1254	A306	1p org & vio brn	.25	.25
1255	A306	1.50p car & sepia	.25	.25
1256	A306	2p blk & slate grn	.75	.25
1257	A306	2.50p rose car & dl vio	.25	.25
1258	A306	3p sepia & indigo	.25	.25
1259	A306	5p dk bl, lt grn & vio	.90	.90
1260	A306	6p lt green & vio	.80	.80
1261	A306	10p org yel & rose red	.35	.25
		Nos. 1248-1261 (14)	5.30	4.70

Issued to honor the Spanish Navy.

Europa Issue, 1964
Common Design Type
1964, Sept. 14 **Photo.** *Perf. 12½x13*
Size: 21½x39mm
1262	CD7	1p bis, red & grn	.30	.25
1263	CD7	5p brt bl, mag & grn	1.00	.55

Madonna of Alcazar — A307   Shot Put — A308

1964, Oct. 9 **Photo.** *Perf. 13*
1264	A307	25c bister & brn	.25	.25
1265	A307	1p gray & indigo	.25	.25

Reconquest of Jerez de la Frontera, 700th anniv.

1964, Oct. 10
Gold Olympic Rings
1266	A308	25c shown	.25	.25
1267	A308	80c Broad jump	.25	.25
1268	A308	1p Slalom	.25	.25
1269	A308	3p Judo	.25	.25
1270	A308	5p Discus	.25	.25
		Nos. 1266-1270 (5)	1.25	1.25

1964 Olympic Games.

Builders of the New World
Portrait Type of 1961

25c, 2p, Diego de Almagro. 70c, 2.50p, Francisco de Toledo. 80c, 3p, Archbishop Toribio de Mogrovejo. 1p, 5p, Francisco Pizarro.

1964, Oct. 12 *Perf. 13x12½*
1271	A265	25c pale grn & vio	.25	.25
1272	A265	70c pink & ol gray	.25	.25
1273	A265	80c buff & Prus grn	.30	.25
1274	A265	1p buff & gray vio	.30	.25
1275	A265	2p pale bl & ol gray	.30	.25
1276	A265	2.50p pale grn & cl	.25	.25
1277	A265	3p gray & dk bl	3.00	1.00
1278	A265	5p yellow & brown	1.75	1.25
		Nos. 1271-1278 (8)	6.40	3.75

Christmas Type of 1963

Nativity by Francisco de Zurbaran (1598-1664).

1964, Dec. 4 **Photo.**
1279	A295	1p olive black	.25	.25

Tourism Types of 1964

Designs: 25c, Columbus monument, Barcelona. 30s, Facade of Santa Maria, Burgos. 50c, Santa Maria la Blanca (medieval synagogue), Toledo. 70c, Bridge, Zamora. 80c, La Giralda (tower) and Cathedral of Seville. 1p, Boat and nets in Cudillero harbor. No. 1286, Cathedral of Burgos, interior. No. 1287, View of Mogrovejo, Santander. 3p, Bridge, Cambados, Pontevedra. 6p, Silk merchants' hall (Lonja), Valencia, interior.

1965 **Engr.** *Perf. 13*
1280	A298	25c dk blue & blk	.25	.25
1281	A298	30c dull grn & sep	.25	.25
1282	A298	50c cl & rose car	.25	.25
1283	A297	70c vio bl & ind	.25	.25
1284	A298	80c rose cl & dk pur	.25	.25
1285	A298	1p dp cl, car & blk	.25	.25
1286	A298	2.50p brn vio & bis	.25	.25
1287	A297	2.50p dull bl & gray	.25	.25
1288	A298	3p rose car & dk brn	.25	.25
1289	A298	6p slate & black	.25	.25
		Nos. 1280-1289 (10)	2.50	2.50

Alfonso X, the Wise (1232-84) A309   Julio Romero de Torres, Self-portrait A310

25c, Juan Donoso-Cortes (1809-53). 2.50p, Gaspar M. Jovellanos (1744-1810). 5p, St. Dominic de Guzman (1170-1221).

1965, Feb. 25 **Engr.** *Perf. 13x12½*
1292	A309	25c slate bl & blk	.25	.25
1293	A309	70c blue & indigo	.25	.25
1294	A309	2.50p slate grn & sep	.25	.25
1295	A309	5p dull grn & sl grn	.25	.25
		Nos. 1292-1295 (4)	1.00	1.00

1965, Mar. 24 **Photo.** *Perf. 13*

De Torres Paintings: 25c, Girl with Jar. 40c, "The Song" (girl with guitar). 70c, Madonna of the Lanterns. 80c, Girl with guitar. 1.50p, "The Poem of Cordova" (pensive woman). 2.50p, Martha and Mary. 3p, "The Poem of Cordova" (two women holding statue of angel). 5p, Girl with the Charcoal. 10p, Back of woman's head.

Gold Frame
1296	A310	25c dull purple	.25	.25
1297	A310	40c purple	.25	.25
1298	A310	70c olive green	.25	.25
1299	A310	80c slate green	.25	.25
1300	A310	1p dk red brn	.25	.25
1301	A310	1.50p blue green	.25	.25
1302	A310	2.50p lilac rose	.25	.25
1303	A310	3p dark blue	.35	.25
1304	A310	5p brown	.35	.25
1305	A310	10p slate green	.50	.30
		Nos. 1296-1305 (10)	2.95	2.55

Issued to honor Julio Romero de Torres (1880-1930) and for Stamp Day, March 24.

For other art types see A236-A237, A240a, A246a, A257, A272, A285a, A300, A324, A340-A341, A360, A371 and footnote following No. 1606.

Bull and Symbolic Stamps — A311

1965, May 6 *Perf. 13x12½*
1306	A311	25c multicolored	.25	.25
1307	A311	1p orange & multi	.25	.25
1308	A311	10p multicolored	.50	.30
		Nos. 1306-1308 (3)	1.00	.80

Issued for International Stamp Day, 1965.

ITU Emblem, Old and New Communication Equipment — A312

1965, May 17 *Perf. 12½x13*
1309	A312	1p salmon, blk & red	.25	.25

International Telecommunication Union, cent.

Pilgrim — A313   Explorer, Royal Flag of Spain and Ships — A314

Design: 2p, Pilgrim (profile).

1965, July 25 **Photo.** *Perf. 13*
1310	A313	1p multicolored	.25	.25
1311	A313	2p multicolored	.25	.25

Issued to commemorate the Holy Year of St. James of Compostela, patron saint of Spain.

1965, Aug. 28 *Perf. 13x12½*
1312	A314	3p red, blk & yel	.25	.25

400th anniv. of the settlement of Florida, and the 1st permanent European settlement in the continental US, St. Augustine, Fla. See US No. 1271.

St. Benedict — A315

Europa Issue, 1965
1965, Sept. 27 **Engr.** *Perf. 13x12½*
1313	A315	1p yel grn & sl grn	.25	.25
1314	A315	5p lilac & violet	.40	.25

Sports Palace, Madrid — A316

1965, Oct. 9 **Photo.** *Perf. 13*
1315	A316	1p gray, gold & dk brn	.25	.25

Issued to commemorate the meeting of the International Olympic Committee in Madrid.

Builders of the New World
Portrait Type of 1961

25c, 2p, Don Fadrique de Toledo. 70c, 2.50p, Father José de Anchieta. 80c, 3p, Francisco de Orellana. 1p, 5p, St. Luis Beltran.

1965, Oct. 12 **Photo.** *Perf. 13x12½*
1316	A265	25c pale grn & dp pur	.25	.25
1317	A265	70c pink & brown	.25	.25
1318	A265	80c cream & Prus grn	.25	.25
1319	A265	1p buff & dk vio	.25	.25
1320	A265	2p lt bl & dk ol grn	.25	.25
1321	A265	2.50p lt blue & pur	.25	.25
1322	A265	3p gray & dk bl	1.00	.35
1323	A265	5p yellow & brn	1.00	.30
		Nos. 1316-1323 (8)	3.50	2.15

Chamber of Charles V, Yuste Monastery A317   Stamp of 1865 (No. 78) A318

Yuste Monastery: 1p, Courtyard, horiz. 5p, View of monastery, horiz.

Perf. 12½x13, 13x12½
1965, Nov. 15 **Engr.**
1324	A317	1p bl gray & blk	.25	.25
1325	A317	2p red brn & brn blk	.25	.25
1326	A317	5p grayish bl & grn	.75	.75
		Nos. 1324-1326 (3)		

Monastery of Yuste, Estremadura.

1965, Nov. 22 *Perf. 13x12½*

Designs: 1p, Stamp of 1865 (No. 77). 5p, Stamp of 1865 (No. 80).
1327	A318	80c blk & yel grn	.25	.25
1328	A318	1p plum, brn & rose	.25	.25
1329	A318	5p sepia & org brn	.25	.25
		Nos. 1327-1329 (3)	.75	.75

Cent. of the 1st Spanish perforated postage stamps.

Nativity A319

1965, Dec. 1 **Photo.** *Perf. 12½x13*
1330	A319	1p bright green	.25	.25

Virgin of Peace, Antipolo A320   Globe and Four Beasts of Apocalypse A321

Design: 3p, Father Andres de Urdaneta.

1965, Dec. 3 *Perf. 13x12½*
1331	A320	1p pale sal & ol brn	.25	.25
1332	A320	3p gray & dp blue	.25	.25

Christianization of the Philippines, 400th anniv.

1965, Dec. 29 **Photo.** *Perf. 13x12½*
1333	A321	1p grnsh bl, yel & brn	.25	.25

Vatican II, the 21st Ecumenical Council of the Roman Catholic Church, 10/11/62-12/8/65.

Adm. Alvaro de Bazan (1526-88) A322   Exhibition Emblem; Type Block "P" A323

2p, Daza de Valdes, scientist, 17th cent.

1966, Feb. 26　Engr.　Perf. 13x12½
1334 A322 25c dull blue & gray　.25　.25
1335 A322　2p magenta & violet　.25　.25
See Nos. C177-C178.

1966, Mar. 4　Photo.　Perf. 13
1336 A323 1p red, grn & vio bl　.25　.25
Graphic Arts and Advertising Packaging Exhibition "Graphispack," Barcelona, 3/4-13.

José Maria Sert,
Self-portrait
A324

Sert Paintings: 25c, The Magic Ball. 40c, Evocation of Toledo, horiz. 70c, Christ on the Cross. 80c, Parachutists. 1.50p, "Audacity." 2.50p, "Justice." 3p, Jacob Wrestling with the Angel. 5p, "The Five Continents." 10p, Sts. Peter and Paul.

1966, Mar. 24
Gold Frame
1337 A324　25c dk purple　.25　.25
1338 A324　40c dp magenta　.25　.25
1339 A324　70c green　.25　.25
1340 A324　80c dk ol grn　.25　.25
1341 A324　1p claret brn　.25　.25
1342 A324 1.50p dull blue　.25　.25
1343 A324 2.50p dk red　.25　.25
1344 A324　3p deep blue　.25　.25
1345 A324　5p sepia　.25　.25
1346 A324　10p grnsh blk　.25　.25
Nos. 1337-1346 (10)　2.50 2.50
Issued to honor José Maria Sert (1876-1945) and for Stamp Day, Mar. 24.
For other art types see A236-A237, A240a, A246a, A257, A272, A285a, A300, A310, A340-A341, A360, A371 and footnote following No. 1606.

Santa Maria
Church,
Guernica — A325

Designs: 1p, Arms of Guernica and Luno. 3p, Tree of Guernica.

1966, Apr. 28　Photo.　Perf. 13
1347 A325 80c bl, sepia & grn　.25　.25
1348 A325　1p yel grn & multi　.25　.25
1349 A325　3p bl, grn & vio brn　.25　.25
Nos. 1347-1349 (3)　.75　.75
Founding of Guernica and Luno, 6th cent.

Cover with
Stamp of
1850 (#1)
A326

Designs (covers): 1p, 5r (#3). 10p, 10r (#5).

1966, May 6　　　Perf. 12½x13
1350 A326 25c rose vio, blk & red　.25　.25
1351 A326　1p red brn, org & blk　.25　.25
1352 A326 10p ol grn, grn & org　.25　.25
Nos. 1350-1352 (3)　.75　.75
Issued for International Stamp Day, 1966.

Bohi
Valley — A327

Torla, Huesca
A328

Tourism: 40c, Portal of Sigena Monastery, Huesca. 50c, Santo Domingo Church, Soria. 80c, Torre del Oro, Seville. 1p, Palm and view, Pico de Teyde, Santa Cruz de Tenerife. 1.50p, Monastery of Guadalupe, Caceres. 2p, Alcala de Henares University. 3p, Seo Cathedral, Lerida. 10p, Courtyard of St. Gregorio, Valladolid.

1966　　　　　Engr.　　　Perf. 13
1353 A327　10c gray grn & bl grn　.25　.25
1354 A328　15c gray grn & brn　.25　.25
1355 A327　40c bis brn & brn　.25　.25
1356 A327　50c car rose & dp cl　.25　.25
1357 A327　80c lilac & rose vio　.25　.25
1358 A327　1p vio bl & bl grn　.25　.25
1359 A328 1.50p dk bl & blk　.25　.25
1360 A328　2p sl bl & sepia　.25　.25
1361 A328　3p ultra & blk　.25　.25
1362 A327　10p brt bl & grnsh bl　.25　.25
Nos. 1353-1362 (10)　2.50 2.50

Tree and
Globe
A329

1966, June 6　Photo.　Perf. 12½x13
1363 A329 1p brn & dk grn　.25　.25
6th Intl. Forestry Cong., Madrid, June 6-18.

Navy
Emblem — A330

1966, July 1　Photo.　Perf. 13
1364 A330 1p gray & dk bl　.25　.25
Naval Week, Barcelona, July 1-8.

Guadamur
Castle — A331

Castles: 25c, Alcazar, Segovia. 40c, La Mota. 50c, Olite. 70c, Monteagudo. 80c, Butron, vert. 1p, Manzanares. 3p, Almansa, vert.

1966, Aug. 13　Engr.　Perf. 13
1365 A331　10c grysh bl & sep　.25　.25
1366 A331　25c violet & purple　.25　.25
1367 A331　40c grnsh bl & bl grn　.25　.25
1368 A331　50c grnsh bl & ultra　.25　.25
1369 A331　70c vio bl & ind　.25　.25
1370 A331　80c vio & sl grn　.25　.25
1371 A331　1p ol bis & gray　.25　.25
1372 A331　3p rose & red lil　.25　.25
Nos. 1365-1372 (8)　2.00 2.00

Don Quixote, Dulcinea and Aldonza
Lorenzo — A332

1966, Sept. 5　Photo.　Perf. 13
1373 A332 1.50p sal, lt grn & blk　.25　.25
4th World Congress of Psychiatry, Madrid.

Europa Issue, 1966

The Rape
of Europa
A333

1966, Sept. 28　Photo.　Perf. 12½x13
1374 A333 1p multicolored　.25　.25
1375 A333 5p multicolored　.25　.25

Don Quixote
and Sancho
Panza on
Clavileno
A334

Title Page of
"Dotrina
Christiana"
A335

1966, Oct. 9　　　Perf. 13x12½
1376 A334 1.50p sl bl, red brn & dk brn　.25　.25
17th Cong. of the Intl. Astronautical Federation.

Builders of the New World
Types of 1961 and A335

30c, Antonio de Mendoza. 1p, José A. Manso de Velasco. 1.20p, Coins of Lima, 1699. 1.50p, Manuel de Castro y Padilla. 3p, Portal of Oruro Convent, Bolivia. 3.50p, Manuel de Amat. 6p, Inca courier, El Chasqui.

1966, Oct. 12
1377 A265　30c pale pink & brn　.25　.25
1378 A335　50c pale bis & brn　.25　.25
1379 A265　1p gray & vio　.25　.25
1380 A335 1.20p gray & slate　.25　.25
1381 A265 1.50p pale grn & dp grn　.25　.25
1382 A335　3p pale gray & dp bl　.25　.25
1383 A265 3.50p pale lil & pur　.25　.25
1384 A265　6p buff & sepia　.25　.25
Nos. 1377-1384 (8)　2.00 2.00

Ramon del Valle
Inclan — A336

Portraits: 3p, Carlos Arniches. 6p, Jacinto Benavente y Martinez.

1966, Nov. 7　Photo.　Perf. 13
1385 A336 1.50p blk & green　.25　.25
1386 A336　3p blk & gray vio　.25　.25
1387 A336　6p blk & slate　.25　.25
Nos. 1385-1387 (3)　.75　.75
Issued to honor Spanish writers.
See design A355.

Carthusian
Monastery,
Jerez
A337

St. Mary Carthusian Monastery: 1p, Portal, vert. 5p, Entrance gate.

Perf. 13x12½, 12½x13
1966, Nov. 24　　　　　Engr.
1388 A337 1p grnsh bl & sl bl　.25　.25
1389 A337 2p green & yel grn　.25　.25
1390 A337 5p lilac & claret　.25　.25
Nos. 1388-1390 (3)　.75　.75

Nativity,
Sculpture
by Pedro
Duque
Cornejo
A338

1966, Dec. 5　Photo.　Perf. 12½x13
1391 A338 1.50p multicolored　.25　.25

Regional Costumes Issue

Woman from
Alava — A339

1967　　　　Photo.　　Perf. 13
1392 A339 6p shown　.25　.25
1393 A339 6p Albacete　.25　.25
1394 A339 6p Alicante　.25　.25
1395 A339 6p Almeria　.25　.25
1396 A339 6p Avila　.25　.25
1397 A339 6p Badajoz　.25　.25
1398 A339 6p Baleares　.25　.25
1399 A339 6p Barcelona　.25　.25
1400 A339 6p Burgos　.25　.25
1401 A339 6p Caceres　.25　.25
1402 A339 6p Cadiz　.25　.25
1403 A339 6p Castellon de la Plana　.25　.25
Nos. 1392-1403 (12)　3.00 3.00
1968
1404 A339 6p Ciudad Real　.25　.25
1405 A339 6p Cordoba　.25　.25
1406 A339 6p Coruna　.25　.25
1407 A339 6p Cuenca　.25　.25
1408 A339 6p Fernando Po　.25　.25
1409 A339 6p Gerona　.25　.25
1410 A339 6p Gran Canaria, Las Palmas　.25　.25
1411 A339 6p Granada　.25　.25
1412 A339 6p Guadalajara　.25　.25
1413 A339 6p Guipuzcoa　.25　.25
1414 A339 6p Huelva　.25　.25
1415 A339 6p Huesca　.25　.25
Nos. 1404-1415 (12)　3.00 3.00
1969
1416 A339 6p Ifni　.25　.25
1417 A339 6p Jaen　.25　.25
1418 A339 6p Leon　.25　.25
1419 A339 6p Lerida　.25　.25
1420 A339 6p Logroño　.25　.25
1421 A339 6p Lugo　.25　.25
1422 A339 6p Madrid　.25　.25
1423 A339 6p Malaga　.25　.25
1424 A339 6p Murcia　.25　.25
1425 A339 6p Navarra　.25　.25
1426 A339 6p Orense　.25　.25
1427 A339 6p Oviedo　.25　.25
Nos. 1416-1427 (12)　3.00 3.00
1970
1428 A339 6p Palencia　.25　.25
1429 A339 6p Pontevedra　.25　.25
1430 A339 6p Sahara　.25　.25
1431 A339 6p Salamanca　.25　.25
1432 A339 6p Santa Cruz de Tenerife　.25　.25
1433 A339 6p Santander　.25　.25
1434 A339 6p Segovia　.25　.25
1435 A339 6p Seville　.25　.25
1436 A339 6p Soria　.25　.25
1437 A339 6p Tarragona　.25　.25
1438 A339 6p Teruel　.25　.25
1439 A339 6p Toledo　.25　.25
Nos. 1428-1439 (12)　3.00 3.00
1971
1440 A339 6p Valencia　.25　.25
1441 A339 8p Valladolid　.25　.25
1442 A339 8p Vizcaya　.25　.25

1443	A339	8p Zamora	.25	.25
1444	A339	8p Zaragoza	.25	.25
		Nos. 1440-1444 (5)	1.25	1.25
		Nos. 1392-1444 (53)	10.60	10.60

Archers
A340

Ornament — A341

50c, Boar hunt. 1.20p, Bison. 1.50p, Hands. 2p, Warrior. 2.50p, Deer. 3.50p, Archers. 4p, Hunters & gazelle. 6p, Hunters & deer herd.

1967, Mar. 27   Photo.   Perf. 13
Gold Frame

1449	A340	40c ocher & car rose	.25	.25
1450	A340	50c gray & dk red	.25	.25
1451	A341	1p ocher & org ver	.25	.25
1452	A340	1.20p gray & rose brn	.25	.25
1453	A340	1.50p gray & red	.25	.25
1454	A341	2p lt brn & dk car rose	.25	.25
1455	A341	2.50p sky bl & rose brn	.25	.25
1456	A340	3.50p yellow & blk	.25	.25
1457	A341	4p citron & red	.25	.25
1458	A341	6p olive & red	.25	.25
		Nos. 1449-1458 (10)	2.50	2.50

Issued for Stamp Day, 1967. The designs are from paleolithic and mesolithic wall paintings found in Spanish caves.
For other art types see A236-A237, A240a, A246a, A257, A272, A285a, A300, A310, A324, A360, A371 and footnote following No. 1606.

Palma Cathedral and Conference Emblem — A342

1967, Mar. 28
1459	A342	1.50p brt blue grn	.25	.25

Issued to publicize the Congress of the Interparliamentary Union, Palma de Mallorca.

W. K. Röntgen, X-ray Tube and Atom — A343

1967, Apr. 3   Photo.   Perf. 13
1460	A343	1.50p green	.25	.25

7th Cong. of Latin Radiologists and 1st Cong. of European Radiologists, Barcelona, Apr. 2-8.

Averroes (1120-1198), Physician and Philosopher — A344

Portraits: 3.50p, José de Acosta (1539-1600), Jesuit, historian, poet. 4p, Moses ben Maimonides (1135-1204), Jewish philosopher and physician. 25p, Andres Laguna, 16th century physician.

1967, Apr. 6   Engr.   Perf. 13x12½
1461	A344	1.20p lil & dl vio	.25	.25
1462	A344	3.50p mag & dl pur	.25	.25
1463	A344	4p brn & sep	.25	.25
1464	A344	25p dl bl & blk	.25	.25
		Nos. 1461-1464 (4)	1.00	1.00

Europa Issue, 1967
Common Design Type

1967, May 2   Photo.   Perf. 13
Size: 25x31mm

1465	CD10	1.50p sl grn, red brn & dl red	.25	.25
1466	CD10	6p vio, brt bl & brn	.25	.25

Exhibition Building and Fountain, Valencia — A345

1967, May 3
1467	A345	1.50p gray grn	.25	.25

International Fair at Valencia, 50th anniv.

Numeral Postmark No. 3 of 1850 — A346

Designs: 1.50p, No. 2, 12c stamp of 1850 with crowned M postmark of Madrid. 6p, No. 4, 6r stamp of 1850 with 1r postmark.

1967, May 6
1468	A346	40c brn org, dl bl & blk	.25	.25
1469	A346	1.50p brn, grn & blk	.25	.25
1470	A346	6p bl, red & blk	.25	.25
		Nos. 1468-1470 (3)	.75	.75

Intl. Stamp Day, 1967. See #1527-1528.

Guardian Angel Over Indigent Sleeper — A347

1967, May 16   Perf. 13
1471	A347	1.50p bl, blk, brn & red	.25	.25

Issued for National Caritas Day to honor Caritas, Catholic welfare organization.

Betanzos Church, Coruña — A348

International Tourist Year Emblem A349

Tourism: 1p, Tower of St. Miguel Church, Palencia. 1.50p, Human pyramid (Castellers). 2.50p, Columbus monument, Huelva. 5p, The

Enchanted City, Cuenca. 6p, Church of Our Lady, Sanlucar, Cadiz.

1967, July 26   Engr.   Perf. 13
1472	A348	10c ultra & blk	.25	.25
1473	A348	1p dl bl & blk	.25	.25
1474	A348	1.50p lt brn & blk	.25	.25
1475	A348	2.50p grnsh bl & dk bl	.25	.25
1476	A349	3.50p dl pur & dk bl	.25	.25
1477	A348	5p yel grn & dk grn	.25	.25
1478	A348	6p red lil & dl lil	.25	.25
		Nos. 1472-1478 (7)	1.75	1.75

Balsareny Castle — A350

Castles: 1p, Jaradilla. 1.50p, Almodovar. 2p, Ponferrada, vert. 2.50p, Peniscola. 5p, Coca. 6p, Loarre. 10p, Belmonte.

1967, Aug. 11   Engr.
1479	A350	50c gray & lt brn	.25	.25
1480	A350	1p bl gray & dl pur	.25	.25
1481	A350	1.50p bl gray & sage grn	.25	.25
1482	A350	2p brick red & bis brn	.25	.25
1483	A350	2.50p grnsh bl & sep	.25	.25
1484	A350	5p rose vio & vio bl	.25	.25
1485	A350	6p bis brn & gray brn	.25	.25
1486	A350	10p aqua & slate	.25	.25
		Nos. 1479-1486 (8)	2.00	2.00

Globe, Snowflake and Thermometer A351

1967, Aug. 30   Photo.
1487	A351	1.50p bright blue	.25	.25

12th Intl. Refrigeration Cong., Madrid, Sept. 4-8.

Galleon, Map of Americas, Spain and Philippines A352

1967, Oct. 10   Photo.   Perf. 13
1488	A352	1.50p red lilac	.25	.25

4th Congress of Spanish, Portuguese, American & Philippine Municipalities, Barcelona, Oct. 6-12.

Builders of the New World
Type of 1961 and

Nootka Settlement A353

Designs: 40c, Francisco de la Bodega. 50c, Old map of Nootka coast, vert. 1p, Francisco Antonio Mourelle. 1.50p, Esteban José Martinez. 3p, Old maps of coast of Northern California. 3.50p, Cayetano Valdes. 6p, Ships, San Elias, Alaska.

1967, Oct. 12
1489	A265	40c pink & grnsh gray	.25	.25
1490	A353	50c dk brn	.25	.25
1491	A265	1p pale bl & red lil	.25	.25
1492	A353	1.20p dk ol grn	.25	.25
1493	A265	1.50p pale pink & bl grn	.25	.25
1494	A353	3p buff & vio blk	.25	.25
1495	A265	3.50p pale pink & bl	.25	.25
1496	A353	6p red brn, bluish	.25	.25
		Nos. 1489-1496 (8)	2.00	2.00

Issued to honor the explorers of the Northwest coast of North America.

Roman Statue and Gate
A354

José Bethencourt
A355

Designs: 3.50p, Ancient plower with ox team, horiz. 6p, Roman coins of Caceres.

1967, Oct. 31   Photo.   Perf. 13
1497	A354	1.50p multi	.25	.25
1498	A354	3.50p multi	.25	.25
1499	A354	6p multi	.25	.25
		Nos. 1497-1499 (3)	.75	.75

Founding of Caceres by the Romans, 2000th anniv.

1967, Nov. 15

1.50p, Enrique Granados (composer). 3.50p, Ruben Dario (poet). 6p, St. Ildefonso.

1500	A355	1.20p gray & red brn	.25	.25
1501	A355	1.50p blk & grn	.25	.25
1502	A355	3.50p brn & pur	.25	.25
1503	A355	6p blk & slate	.25	.25
		Nos. 1500-1503 (4)	1.00	1.00

Issued to honor famous Spanish men. See design A336.

Santa Maria de Veruela Monastery
A356

St. José Receiving Last Unction, by Goya
A357

Designs: 3.50p, Aerial view of monastery, horiz. 6p, Inside view, horiz.

1967, Nov. 24   Engr.   Perf. 13
1504	A356	1.50p ultra & ind	.25	.25
1505	A356	3.50p grn & blk	.25	.25
1506	A356	6p rose vio & bis brn	.25	.25
		Nos. 1504-1506 (3)	.75	.75

1967, Nov. 27   Photo.
1507	A357	1.50p multi	.25	.25

200th anniversary of the canonization of St. José de Calasanz (1556-1648), founder of the first Christian Schools in Rome.

Nativity, by Francisco Salzillo — A358

1967, Dec. 5
1508	A358	1.50p multi	.25	.25

Christmas, 1967.

Slalom
A359

3.50p, Bobsled, vert. 6p, Ice hockey.

1968, Feb. 6   Photo.   Perf. 13
1509 A359 1.50p multi   .25   .25
1510 A359 3.50p multi   .25   .25
1511 A359 6p multi   .25   .25
    Nos. 1509-1511 (3)   .75   .75

Issued to commemorate the 10th Winter Olympic Games, Grenoble, France, Feb. 6-18.

Mariano Fortuny, Self-portrait
A360

Fortuny Paintings: 40c, The Vicariate, horiz. 50c, "Fantasy" (pianist). 1p, "Idyll" (piper and sheep). 1.20p, The Print Collector, horiz. 2p, Old Man in the Sun. 2.50p, Calabrian Man. 3.50p, Lady with Fan. 4p, Battle of Tetuan, 1860. 6p, Queen Christina in Carriage, horiz.

1968, Mar. 25   Photo.   Perf. 13
Gold Frame
1512 A360 40c dp red lil   .25   .25
1513 A360 50c dk bl grn   .25   .25
1514 A360 1p brown   .25   .25
1515 A360 1.20p dp vio   .25   .25
1516 A360 1.50p dp grn   .25   .25
1517 A360 2p org brn   .25   .25
1518 A360 2.50p car rose   .25   .25
1519 A360 3.50p dk red brn   .25   .25
1520 A360 4p dk ol   .25   .25
1521 A360 6p brt bl   .25   .25
    Nos. 1512-1521 (10)   2.50 2.50

Issued to honor Mariano Fortuny y Carbo (1838-74), and for Stamp Day.
For other art types see A236-A237, A240a, A246a, A257, A272, A285a, A300, A310, A324, A340-A341, A371 and footnote following No. 1606.

Beatriz Galindo
A361

Famous Women: 1.50p, Agustina de Aragon. 3.50p, Maria Pacheco. 6p, Rosalia de Castro.

1968, Apr. 8   Engr.   Perf. 12½x13
1522 A361 1.20p yel brn & blk
     brn   .25   .25
1523 A361 1.50p blk grn & dk bl   .25   .25
1524 A361 3.50p lt vio & dk vio   .25   .25
1525 A361 6p gray bl & blk   .25   .25
    Nos. 1522-1525 (4)   1.00 1.00

Europa Issue, 1968
Common Design Type
1968, Apr. 29   Photo.   Perf. 13
Size: 38x22mm
1526 CD11 3.50p brt bl, gold &
     brn   .25   .25

Spain No. 1 with Galicia Puebla Postmark — A362

Stamp Day: 3.50p, Spain No. 4 with Serena postmark.

1968, May 6   Photo.   Perf. 13
1527 A362 1.50p blk, bl & ocher   .25   .25
1528 A362 3.50p bl, dk grn & blk .25   .25
    See Nos. 1568-1569, 1608, 1677, 1754.

Map of León and Seal — A363

Designs: 1.50p, Roman legionary. 3.50p, Emperor Galba coin, horiz.

Perf. 13x12½, 12½x13
1968, June 15   Photo.
Size: 25x38½mm
1529 A363 1p lil, red brn & yel   .25   .25
Size: 25x47½mm
1530 A363 1.50p brn, dk brn &
     buff   .25   .25
Size: 37½x26mm
1531 A363 3.50p ocher & sl grn   .25   .25
    Nos. 1529-1531 (3)   .75   .75

1900th anniversary of the founding of León by the Roman Legion VII Gemina.

Human Rights Emblem
A364

Benavente Palace, Baeza
A365

1968, June 25 Photo. Perf. 13x12½
1532 A364 3.50p bl, red & grn   .25   .25
International Human Rights Year, 1968.

1968, July 15   Engr.   Perf. 13
Tourism: 1.20p, View of Salamanca with Tormes River Bridge, horiz. 1.50p, Statuary group from St. Vincent's Church, Avila (The Adoration of the Magi). 2p, Tomb of Martin Vazquez de Arce, Cathedral of Sigüenza, horiz. 3.50p, Portal of St. Mary's Church, Sangüesa, Navarre.

1533 A365 50c dp rose & brn   .25   .25
1534 A365 1.20p emer & sl grn   .25   .25
1535 A365 1.50p dp grn & ind   .25   .25
1536 A365 2p lil rose & blk   .25   .25
1537 A365 3.50p brt lil & rose lil .25   .25
    Nos. 1533-1537 (5)   1.25 1.25

Escalona Castle, Toledo — A366

Castles: 1.20p, Fuensaldaña, Valladolid. 1.50p, Peñafiel, Valladolid. 2.50p, Villasobroso, Pontevedra. 6p, Frias, Burgos, vert.

1968, July 29   Engr.   Perf. 13
1538 A366 40c dk bl & sepia   .25   .25
1539 A366 1.20p vio brn & vio
     blk   .25   .25
1540 A366 1.50p ol & blk   .25   .25
1541 A366 2.50p ol grn & blk   .25   .25
1542 A366 6p vio bl & bl grn   .25   .25
    Nos. 1538-1542 (5)   1.25 1.25

Rifle Shooting
A367

Designs: 1.50p, Horse jumping. 3.50p, Bicycling. 6p, Sailing, vert.

Perf. 12½x13, 13x12½
1968, Sept. 24   Photo.
1543 A367 1p multi   .25   .25
1544 A367 1.50p multi   .25   .25
1545 A367 3.50p multi   .25   .25
1546 A367 6p multi   .25   .25
    Nos. 1543-1546 (4)   1.00 1.00

19th Olympic Games, Mexico City, 10/12-27.

Builders of the New World
Type of 1961 and

Map of Capuchin Missions along Orinoco River, 1732 — A368

1p, Diego de Losada. 1.50p, Losada family coat of arms. 3.50p, Diego de Henares. 6p, Map of Caracas, drawn by Diego de Henares, 1578, horiz.

1968, Oct. 12   Photo.   Perf. 13
1547 A368 40c grnsh bl, *bluish* .25   .25
1548 A265 1p red lil, *gray*   .25   .25
1549 A368 1.50p sl, *pale rose*   .25   .25
1550 A265 3.50p dk bl, *pnksh*   .25   .25
1551 A368 6p dk ol bis   .25   .25
    Nos. 1547-1551 (5)   1.25 1.25

Christianization of Venezuela and the founding of Caracas.

St. Maria del Parral Monastery, Segovia — A369

3.50p, Monastery, inside view. 6p, Madonna & Child, statue from main altar.

1968, Nov. 25   Engr.   Perf. 13
1552 A369 1.50p gray bl & rose
     vio   .25   .25
1553 A369 3.50p brn & red brn   .25   .25
1554 A369 6p rose claret &
     brn   .25   .25
    Nos. 1552-1554 (3)   .75   .75

Nativity, by Federico Fiori da Urbino — A370

1968, Dec. 2 Photo. Perf. 13x12½
1555 A370 1.50p gold & multi   .25   .25
Christmas, 1968.

Alonso Cano by Velázquez
A371

Cano Paintings: 40c, St. Agnes. 50c, St. John. 1p, Jesus and Angel. 2p, Holy Family. 2.50p, Circumcision of Jesus. 3p, Jesus and the Samaritan Woman. 3.50p, Madonna and Child. 4p, Sts. John Capistrano and Bernardino, horiz. 6p, Vision of St. John the Baptist.

Gold Frame
1969, Mar. 24   Photo.   Perf. 13
1556 A371 40c deep plum   .25   .25
1557 A371 50c green   .25   .25
1558 A371 1p sepia   .25   .25
1559 A371 1.50p slate grn   .25   .25
1560 A371 2p red brown   .25   .25
1561 A371 2.50p dp red lil   .25   .25
1562 A371 3p ultra   .25   .25
1563 A371 3.50p dk rose brn   .25   .25
1564 A371 4p dull lilac   .25   .25
1565 A371 6p slate blue   .25   .25
    Nos. 1556-1565 (10)   2.50 2.50

Alonso Cano (1601-1667), and Stamp Day. For other art types see A236-A237, A240a, A246a, A257, A272, A285a, A300, A310, A324, A340-A341, A360 and footnote following No. 1606.

DNA (Genetic Code) Molecule and Chart
A372

1969, Apr. 7   Photo.   Perf. 13
1566 A372 1.50p gray & multi   .25   .25

Issued to publicize the 6th European Congress of Biochemistry, Madrid, Apr. 7-11.

Europa Issue, 1969
Common Design Type
1969, Apr. 28
Size: 38x22mm
1567 CD12 3.50p multi   .25   .25

Stamp Day Type of 1968
1.50p, Spain #6 with crowned M and "AL.3/1851" postmark. 3.50p, Spain #11 with Corvera postmark.

1969, May 6   Photo.   Perf. 13
1568 A362 1.50p blk, red & grn   .25   .25
1569 A362 3.50p grn, bl & red   .25   .25

Issued for Stamp Day, 1969.

Spectrum
A373

1969, May 26
1570 A373 1.50p blk & multi   .25   .25

Issued to publicize the 15th International Spectroscopy Colloquium, Madrid, May 26-30.

World Map, Red Crescent, Cross, Lion and Sun Emblems
A374

1969, May 30
1571 A374 1.50p multi   .25   .25

League of Red Cross Societies, 50th anniv.

Last Supper, Finial from Lugo Cathedral — A375

1969, June 4
1572 A375 1.50p grn, brn & blk   .25   .25

300th anniversary of the dedication of Galicia Province to the reign of Jesus.

Turegano Castle, Segovia A376

Castles: 1.50p, Villalonso, Zamora. 2.50p, Velez Blanco, Almeria. 3.50p, Castilnovo, Segovia. 6p, Torrelobaton, Valladolid.

1969, June 24   Engr.   Perf. 13
1573	A376	1p dl grn & sl	.25	.25
1574	A376	1.50p bluish lil & dk bl	.25	.25
1575	A376	2.50p bl vio & bluish lil	.25	.25
1576	A376	3.50p red brn & ol grn	.25	.25
1577	A376	6p gray grn & dl brn	.25	.25
		Nos. 1573-1577 (5)	1.25	1.25

Father Junipero Serra — A377

1969, July 16   Photo.   Perf. 13
1578	A377	1.50p multi	.25	.25

Bicentenary of San Diego, Calif.

Rock of Gibraltar — A378

2p, View of Gibraltar across the Bay of Algeciras.

1969, July 18
1579	A378	1.50p bl grn	.25	.25
1580	A378	2p brt rose lil	.25	.25

Dama de Elche — A379

Tourism: 1.50p, Alcañiz Castle, Teruel, horiz. 3p, Murcia Cathedral. 6p, St. Maria de la Redonda, Logrono.

1969, July 23   Engr.   Perf. 13
1581	A379	1.50p dl grn & blk	.25	.25
1582	A379	3p yel grn & bl grn	.25	.25
1583	A379	3.50p gray bl & dk bl	.25	.25
1584	A379	6p yel grn & vio blk	.25	.25
		Nos. 1581-1584 (4)	1.00	1.00

Builders of the New World
Type of 1961 and

Santo Domingo Church, Santiago, Chile — A380

1.50p, Casa de Moneda de Chile, horiz. 2p, Ambrosio O'Higgins. 3.50p, Pedro de Valdivia. 6p, First large bridge over Mapocho River, horiz.

1969, Oct. 12   Photo.   Perf. 13
1585	A380	40c lt bl & dk red brn	.25	.25
1586	A380	1.50p pale rose & dk vio	.25	.25
1587	A265	2p pale pink & ol	.25	.25
1588	A265	3.50p pale yel & dk Prus grn	.35	.30
1589	A380	6p pale yel & blk brn	.25	.25
		Nos. 1585-1589 (5)	1.35	1.30

Exploration and development of Chile. See Nos. 1630-1631, 1634.

Adoration of the Magi, by Juan Bautista Mayno — A381

Christmas: 2p, Nativity, bas-relief from altar of Cathedral of Gerona.

1969, Nov. 3
1590	A381	1.50p multi	.25	.25
1591	A381	2p multi	.25	.25

Tomb of Alfonso VIII and Wife, Las Huelgas Monastery, Burgos — A382

Designs: 1.50p, Las Huelgas Monastery. 6p, Inside view, vert.

1969, Nov. 22   Engr.
1592	A382	1.50p lt bl grn & indigo	.25	.25
1593	A382	3.50p ultra & vio bl	.40	.35
1594	A382	6p olive & yel grn	.25	.25
		Nos. 1592-1594 (3)	.90	.85

See Nos. 1639-1641.

St. Juan de Avila, by El Greco — A383   St. Stephen, by Luis de Morales — A384

Design: 50p, Bishop Rodrigo Ximenez de Rada, Juan de Borgona mural.

1970, Feb. 25   Engr.   Perf. 13
1595	A383	25p pale pur & ind	4.00	.25
1596	A383	50p brn org & brn	1.60	.25

1970, Mar. 24   Photo.   Perf. 13

Morales Paintings: 1p, Annunciation. 1.50p, Madonna and Child with St. John. 2p, Madonna and Child. 3p, Presentation at the Temple. 3.50p, St. Jerome. 4p, St. John de Ribera. 5p, Ecce Homo. 6p, Pieta. 10p, St. Francis of Assisi.

1597	A384	50c gold & multi	.25	.25
1598	A384	1p gold & multi	.25	.25
1599	A384	1.50p gold & multi	.25	.25
1600	A384	2p gold & multi	.25	.25
1601	A384	3p gold & multi	.25	.25
1602	A384	3.50p gold & multi	.25	.25
1603	A384	4p gold & multi	.25	.25
1604	A384	5p gold & multi	.25	.25
1605	A384	6p gold & multi	.25	.25
1606	A384	10p gold & multi	.25	.25
		Nos. 1597-1606 (10)	2.50	2.50

Issued to honor Luis de Morales, "El Divino" (1509-1586), and for Stamp Day.
For other art types see A397, A410, A431, A448, A501, A522, A538, A558 and footnote following No. 876.

Europa Issue, 1970
Common Design Type

1970, May 4   Photo.   Perf. 13x12½
Size: 37½x22mm
1607	CD13	3.50p brt bl & gold	.25	.25

Stamp Day Type of 1968

Stamp Day: 2p, Spain No. 51 with "Ferro Carril de Langreo" postmark.

1970, May 4   Perf. 13x12½
1608	A362	2p dl red, grn & blk	.25	.25

Barcelona Fair Building A385

1970, May 27   Perf. 13
1609	A385	15p multi	.25	.25

Barcelona Trade Fair, 50th anniversary.

Miguel Primo de Rivera — A386

1970, June 6   Photo.   Perf. 13
1610	A386	2p buff, brn & ol grn	.25	.25

Gen. Miguel Primo de Rivera (1870-1930), Spanish dictator, 1923-1930.

Valencia de Don Juan Castle — A387

Castles: 1.20p, Monterrey. 3.50p, Mombeltran. 6p, Sadaba. 10p, Bellver.

1970, June 24   Engr.
1611	A387	1p blk & dl bl	.35	.25
1612	A387	1.20p lt grnsh bl & vio	.25	.25
1613	A387	3.50p pale grn & brn	.25	.25
1614	A387	6p sep & dl pur	.25	.25
1615	A387	10p fawn & sepia	.80	.25
		Nos. 1611-1615 (5)	1.90	1.25

Alcazaba Castle, Almeria A388

Tourism: 1p, Malaga Cathedral. 1.50p, St. Mary of the Assumption, Lequemo, vert. 2p, Cloister of St. Francis of Orense. 3.50p, Market (Lonja), Zaragoza, vert. 5p, The Gate of Vitoria, vert.

1970, July 23   Engr.   Perf. 13
1616	A388	50c bluish gray & dl pur	.25	.25
1617	A388	1p red brn & ocher	.25	.25
1618	A388	1.50p bluish gray & sl grn	.25	.25
1619	A388	2p sl & dk bl	.40	.25
1620	A388	3.50p pur & vio bl	.25	.25
1621	A388	5p gray grn & red brn	.80	.25
		Nos. 1616-1621 (6)	2.20	1.50

Tailor, from Book Published in Madrid, 1589 A389

1970, Aug. 18   Photo.   Perf. 13
1622	A389	2p mag, brn & dl vio	.25	.25

14th Intl. Tailoring Congress, Madrid.

Diver and Map of Europe A390

1970, Aug. 25
1623	A390	2p grn & brt bl	.25	.25

12th European Championships in Swimming, Diving and Water Polo, Barcelona.

Concha Espina — A391

1p, Guillen de Castro. 1.50p, Juan Ramon Jimenez. 2p, Gustavo Adolfo Becquer. 2.50p, Miguel de Unamuno. 3.50p, José M. Gabriel y Galan.

1970, Sept. 21   Photo.   Perf. 13x12½
1624	A391	50c brn, vio bl & pale rose	.25	.25
1625	A391	1p sl grn, dp rose lil & gray	.25	.25
1626	A391	1.50p dk bl, brt grn & gray	.25	.25
1627	A391	2p grn, dk ol & buff	.25	.25
1628	A391	2.50p pur, rose lake & buff	.25	.25
1629	A391	3.50p brn, dk red & gray	.25	.25
		Nos. 1624-1629 (6)	1.50	1.50

Issued to honor Spanish writers.

Builders of the New World
Portrait Type of 1961 and Building Type of 1969

40c, Ecala House, Queretaro, Mexico. 1.50p, Mexico Cathedral, horiz. 2p, Vasco de Quiroga. 3.50p, Brother Juan de Zumarraga. 6p, Cathedral Towers, Morelia, Mexico.

1970, Oct. 12   Photo.   Perf. 13
1630	A380	40c lt bl & ol gray	.25	.25
1631	A380	1.50p lt bl & brn	.25	.25
1632	A265	2p buff & dk vio	.50	.25
1633	A265	3.50p pale grn & dk grn	.25	.25
1634	A380	6p pale pink & Prus bl	.25	.25
		Nos. 1630-1634 (5)	1.50	1.25

Exploration and development of Mexico.

Map of Western Mediterranean — A392

1970, Oct. 20   Photo.   Perf. 13
1635	A392	2p multi	.25	.25

Geographical and Statistical Institute, cent.

Adoration of the Shepherds, by El Greco — A393

Christmas: 2p, Adoration of the Shepherds, by Murillo.

1970, Oct. 30
1636 A393 1.50p multi   .25 .25
1637 A393 2p multi   .25 .25

UN Emblem and Headquarters — A394

1970, Nov. 3
1638 A394 8p multi   .25 .25

25th anniversary of the United Nations.

Monastery Type of 1969
Ripoll Monastery: 2p, Portal. 3.50p, View of monastery. 5p, Inside court.

1970, Nov. 12   **Engr.**
1639 A382 2p vio & pur   .45 .25
1640 A382 3.50p org & mar   .25 .25
1641 A382 5p Prus grn & yel grn   .90 .25
        Nos. 1639-1641 (3)   1.60 .75

Map with Main European Pilgrimage Routes — A395

Cathedral of St. David, Wales A396

#1643, Map of main pilgrimage routes. #1644, St. Bridget statue, Vadstena, Sweden. #1645, Santiago Cathedral. #1646, Tower of St. Jacques, Paris. #1647, Pilgrim before entering Santiago de Compostela. #1648, St. James statue, Pistoia, Italy. #1649, Lugo Cathedral. 2.50p, Villafranca del Bierzo church. #1652, Astorga Cathedral. 3.50p, San Marcos de León. #1654, Charlemagne, bas-relief, Aachen Cathedral, Germany. #1655, San Tirso de Sahagun. 5p, San Martín de Fromista. 6p, Bas-relief, King's Hospital, Burgos. 7p, Portal of Santo Domingo de la Calzada. 7.50p, Cloister, Najera. 8p, Puente de la Reina (Christ on the Cross and portal). 9p, Santa Maria de Eunate. 10p, Cross of Roncesvalles.

1971   **Engr.**   **Perf. 13**
1642 A395 50c grnsh bl & sep   .25 .25
1643 A396 50c bl & dl vio   .25 .25
1644 A395 1p brn & sl grn   .25 .25
1645 A396 1p grn & sl grn   .25 .25
1646 A395 1.50p dl grn & dp plum   .25 .25
1647 A396 1.50p vio bl & lil   .25 .25
1648 A395 2p dk pur & blk   .25 .25
1649 A395 2p sl grn & dk bl   .80 .25
1650 A396 2.50p vio brn & dl vio   .25 .25
1651 A396 3p ultra & dk bl   .25 .25
1652 A395 3p dl red & rose lil   .40 .25
1653 A396 3.50p dp org & gray grn   .25 .25
1654 A395 4p ol grn   .35 .25
1655 A395 4p grnsh bl & brn   .25 .25
1656 A395 5p lt grn & blk   .35 .25
1657 A395 5p ultra   .25 .25
1658 A395 7p lil & dl vio   .45 .25

1659 A396 7.50p car lake & dl vio   .25 .25
1660 A395 8p grn & vio blk   .25 .25
1661 A396 9p grn & vio   .25 .25
1662 A395 10p grn & brn   .40 .25
        Nos. 1642-1662 (21)   6.50 5.25

Holy Year of Compostela, 1971.

Ignacio Zuloaga, Self-portrait A397

Zuloaga Paintings: 50c, "My Uncle Daniel." 1p, View of Segovia, horiz. 1.50p, Countess of Alba. 3p, Juan Belmonte. 4p, Countess of Noailles. 5p, Pablo Uranga. 8p, Cobblers' Houses at Lerma, horiz.

1971, Mar. 24   Photo.   Perf. 13
1663 A397 50c gold & multi   .25 .25
1664 A397 1p gold & multi   .25 .25
1665 A397 1.50p gold & multi   .25 .25
1666 A397 2p gold & multi   .25 .25
1667 A397 3p gold & multi   .25 .25
1668 A397 4p gold & multi   .25 .25
1669 A397 5p gold & multi   .25 .25
1670 A397 8p gold & multi   .25 .25
        Nos. 1663-1670 (8)   2.00 2.00

Ignacio Zuloaga (1870-1945). Stamp Day.
For other art types see A384, A410, A431, A448, A473, A501, A522, A538, A558 and footnote following No. 876.

Amadeo Vives, Composer A398

2p, St. Teresa de Avila. 8p, Benito Perez Galdos, writer. 15p, Ramon Menendez Pidal, writer.

1971, Apr. 20
1671 A398 1p multicolored   .25 .25
1672 A398 2p multicolored   .25 .25
1673 A398 8p multicolored   .25 .25
1674 A398 15p multicolored   .25 .25
        Nos. 1671-1674 (4)   1.00 1.00

Europa Issue, 1971
Common Design Type
1971, Apr. 29   Photo.   Perf. 13
Size: 37x26mm
1675 CD14 2p lt bl, brn & vio bl   .45 .25
1676 CD14 8p lt grn, dk brn & dk grn   .30 .30

Stamp Day Type of 1968
Spain No. 1 with blue "A" cancellation.

1971, May 6
1677 A362 2p black, bl & olive   .25 .25

Gymnast — A399

Design: 2p, Gymnast on bar.

1971, May 14
1678 A399 1p ocher & multi   .25 .25
1679 A399 2p lt blue & multi   .25 .25

9th European Gymnastic Championships for Men, Madrid, May 14-15.

Great Bustard A400

Designs: 2p, Pardine lynx. 3p, Brown bear. 5p, Red-legged partridge, vert. 8p, Spanish ibex, vert.

1971, May 24
1680 A400 1p multicolored   .25 .25
1681 A400 2p multicolored   .25 .25
1682 A400 3p multicolored   .25 .25
1683 A400 5p multicolored   .35 .35
1684 A400 8p multicolored   .35 .35
        Nos. 1680-1684 (5)   1.45 1.35

Legionnaires — A401

2p, Legionnaires on dress parade. 5p, Memorial service. 8p, Desert fighter and tank column.

1971, June 21   Photo.   Perf. 13
1685 A401 1p multicolored   .25 .25
1686 A401 2p multicolored   .25 .25
1687 A401 5p multicolored   .25 .25
1688 A401 8p multicolored   .30 .30
        Nos. 1685-1688 (4)   1.05 1.05

50th anniversary of the Legion, a voluntary military organization.

UNICEF Emblem, Children of Various Races — A402

1971, Sept. 10
1689 A402 8p multicolored   .25 .25

25th anniv. of UNICEF.

Don Juan of Austria, Fleet Commander A403

Designs: 5p, Battle of Lepanto, horiz. 8p, Holy League banner in Cathedral.

1971, Oct. 7   Engr.   Perf. 13
1690 A403 2p sepia & slate grn   .40 .25
1691 A403 5p chocolate   .75 .25
1692 A403 8p rose car & vio bl   .60 .60
        Nos. 1690-1692 (3)   1.75 1.10

400th anniversary of the Battle of Lepanto against the Turks.

Hockey Players, Hockey League and Games Emblems — A404

1971, Oct. 15   Photo.
1693 A404 5p multicolored   .50 .25

First World Hockey Cup, Barcelona, Oct. 15-24.

De Havilland DH-9 over Seville A405

Design: 15p, Boeing 747 over Plaza de la Cibeles, Madrid.

1971, Oct. 25
1694 A405 2p multicolored   .25 .25
1695 A405 15p multicolored   .25 .25

50th anniversary of Spanish air mail service.

Nativity, Avia Altarpiece A406

Christmas: 8p, Nativity, Sagas altarpiece.

1971, Nov. 4   Perf. 12½x13
1696 A406 2p multicolored   .25 .25
1697 A406 8p multicolored   .25 .25

Emilia Pardo Bazan — A407

Portraits: 25p, José de Espronceda. 50p, King Fernan Gonzalez.

1972, Jan. 27   Engr.   Perf. 13
1698 A407 15p brown & slate grn   .25 .25
1699 A407 25p lt grn & slate grn   .25 .25
1700 A407 50p claret & dp brn   .55 .25
        Nos. 1698-1700 (3)   1.05 .75

Honoring Emilia Pardo Bazan (1852-1921), novelist (15p); José de Espronceda (1808-1842), poet (25p); Fernan Gonzalez (910-970), first King of Castile (50p).

Figure Skating — A408

Don Quixote Title Page, 1605 — A409

Design: 2p, Ski jump and Sapporo Olympic emblem, horiz.

1972, Feb. 10   **Photo.**
1701 A408 2p gray & multi   .35 .25
1702 A408 15p blue & multi   .25 .25

11th Winter Olympic Games, Sapporo, Japan, Feb. 3-13.

1972, Feb. 24   **Engr.**   **Perf. 13x12½**
1703 A409 2p brown & claret   .25 .25

International Book Year 1972.

A410

Gutierrez Solana Paintings: 1p, Clowns, horiz. 2p, José Gutierrez Solana with wife and child. 3p, Balladier. 4p, Fisherman. 5p, Mask makers. 7p, The book collector. 10p, Merchant marine captain. 15p, Afterdinner speaker, horiz.

1972, Mar. 24   **Photo.**   **Perf. 13**
1704 A410 1p gold & multi   .25 .25
1705 A410 2p gold & multi   .35 .25
1706 A410 3p gold & multi   .40 .25
1707 A410 4p gold & multi   .25 .25
1708 A410 5p gold & multi   1.25 .35
1709 A410 7p gold & multi   .55 .25
1710 A410 10p gold & multi   .55 .25
1711 A410 15p gold & multi   .55 .25
    Nos. 1704-1711 (8)   4.15 2.10

José Gutierrez Solana (1886-1945). Stamp Day 1972.
For other art types see A384, A397, A431, A448, A473, A501, A522, A538, A558 and footnote following No. 876.

A411

1972, Apr. 21
1712 A411 1p Fir   .25 .25
1713 A411 2p Strawberry tree   .35 .25
1714 A411 3p Cluster pine   .40 .25
1715 A411 5p Evergreen oak   .55 .25
1716 A411 10p Juniper   .35 .30
    Nos. 1712-1716 (5)   1.90 1.30

Europa, 1972
Common Design Type and Type A412

Europeans Interlocking
A412

1972, May 2
1717 A412 2p dull grn & ocher   1.40 .25
    Size: 25x38mm
1718 CD15 8p multicolored   .50 .40

Pre-stamp Cordoba Postmark (1824-42)
A413

1972, May 6   **Perf. 12½x13**
1719 A413 2p dull yel, blk & car   .25 .25

Stamp Day 1972.

Santa Catalina Castle, Jaen — A414

Castles: 1p, Sajazarra, Rioja, vert. 3p, Biar, Alicante. 5p, San Servando, Toledo. 10p, Pedraza, Segovia.

1972, June 22   **Engr.**   **Perf. 13**
1720 A414 1p dull bl grn & brn   .45 .35
1721 A414 2p gray olive & grn   .85 .25
1722 A414 3p rose car & red brn   .85 .25
1723 A414 5p vio bl & dull grn   .85 .25
1724 A414 10p slate & lilac   2.50 .25
    Nos. 1720-1724 (5)   5.50 1.35

Weight Lifting, Olympic Emblems — A415

1972, Aug. 26   **Photo.**   **Perf. 13**
1725 A415 1p Olympic emblems, fencing, horiz.   .25 .25
1726 A415 2p shown   .25 .25
1727 A415 5p Sculling   .25 .25
1728 A415 8p Pole vaulting   .25 .25
    Nos. 1725-1728 (4)   1.00 1.00

20th Olympic Games, Munich, 8/26-9/11.

Egyptian Mongoose
A416

1972, Sept. 14
1729 A416 1p Aquatic mole, vert.   .25 .25
1730 A416 2p Chamois   .25 .25
1731 A416 3p Wolf   .25 .25
1732 A416 5p shown   .50 .25
1733 A416 7p Spotted genet   .40 .25
    Nos. 1729-1733 (5)   1.65 1.25

Brigadier M.A. de Ustariz — A417

San Juan, 1870
A418

1972, Oct. 12   **Photo.**   **Perf. 13**
1734 A417 1p shown   .25 .25
1735 A418 2p shown   .25 .25
1736 A418 5p San Juan, 1625   .40 .25
1737 A418 8p Map of Plaza and Bay, 1792   .40 .30
    Nos. 1734-1737 (4)   1.30 1.05

450th anniversary of San Juan.

St. Tomas Monastery, Avila — A419

8p, Inside view. 15p, Cloister, horiz.

1972, Oct. 26   **Engr.**
1738 A419 2p Prus bl & gray grn   .80 .25
1739 A419 8p gray & claret   .65 .30
1740 A419 15p violet & red lil   .50 .25
    Nos. 1738-1740 (3)   1.95 .80

Teatro del Liceo, Barcelona
A420

1972, Nov. 7   **Perf. 12½x13**
1741 A420 8p ultra & sepia   .25 .25

125th anniversary of the Gran Teatro del Liceo in Barcelona.

Annunciation — A421

Christmas: 8p, Angel and shepherds. Designs are from Romanesque murals in the Collegiate Basilica of San Isidro, Leon.

1972, Nov. 14   **Photo.**   **Perf. 13**
1742 A421 2p gold & multi   .25 .25
1743 A421 8p gold & multi   .25 .25

Juan de Herrera and Escorial
A422

Great Spanish Architects: 10p, Juan de Villanueva and Prado. 15p, Ventura Rodriguez and Apollo Fountain.

1973, Jan. 29   **Engr.**   **Perf. 12½x13**
1744 A422 8p sepia & slate grn   .50 .25
1745 A422 10p blk brn & bluish blk   1.60 .25
1746 A422 15p brt green & indigo   .40 .25
    Nos. 1744-1746 (3)   2.50 .75

Myrica Faya — A423

Europa, Roman Mosaic — A424

Designs: Flora of Canary Islands.

1973, Mar. 21   **Photo.**   **Perf. 13**
1747 A423 1p Apollonias canariensis, horiz.   .25 .25
1748 A423 2p shown   .55 .25
1749 A423 4p Palms   .25 .25
1750 A423 5p Holly   .55 .25
1751 A423 15p Dracaena draco   .30 .25
    Nos. 1747-1751 (5)   1.90 1.25

Europa Issue
Common Design Type and A424

1973, Apr. 30   **Photo.**   **Perf. 13**
1752 A424 2p multicolored   .40 .25
    Size: 37x26mm
1753 CD16 8p lt blue, blk & red   .35 .25

Stamp Day Type of 1968
Stamp Day: 2p, Spain No. 23 with red Madrid, 1853, cancellation.

1973, May 5
1754 A362 2p black, blue & red   .25 .25

Iznajar Dam on Genil River — A425

1973, June 9   **Photo.**   **Perf. 12½x13**
1755 A425 8p multicolored   .25 .25

11th Congress of the International Commission on High Dams, Madrid, June 11-15.

Oñate University, Guipuzcoa
A426

Designs: 2p, Plaza del Campo and fountain, Lugo. 3p, Plaza de Llerena and fountain, Badajoz, vert. 5p, House of Columbus, Las Palmas. 8p, Windmills, La Mancha.

1973, June 11   **Engr.**   **Perf. 13**
1756 A426 1p gray & sepia   .25 .25
1757 A426 2p brt grn & sl grn   .55 .25
1758 A426 3p dk brn & org brn   .55 .25
1759 A426 5p dk gray & vio blk   1.40 .25
1760 A426 8p dk gray & car   .60 .25
    Nos. 1756-1760 (5)   3.35 1.25

Azure-winged Magpie — A427

Birds: 1p, Black-bellied sand grouse, horiz. 2p, Black stork, horiz. 7p, Imperial eagle, horiz. 15p, Red-crested pochard.

1973, July 3   **Perf. 13**
1761 A427 1p multicolored   .25 .25
1762 A427 2p multicolored   .35 .25
1763 A427 5p multicolored   .50 .40
1764 A427 7p multicolored   .60 .25
1765 A427 15p multicolored   .25 .25
    Nos. 1761-1765 (5)   1.95 1.40

Knight, Holy Fraternity of Castile, 1488 — A428

Uniforms: 2p, Knight, Castile, 1493, horiz. 3p, Harquebusier, 1534. 7p, Mounted rifleman, 1560. 8p, Infantry sergeants, 1567.

1973, July 17
1766 A428 1p multicolored   .25 .25
1767 A428 2p multicolored   .50 .25
1768 A428 3p multicolored   .50 .25

1769 A428 7p multicolored   .40   .25
1770 A428 8p multicolored   .40   .25
      Nos. 1766-1770 (5)   2.05 1.25

See Nos. 1794-1798, 1824-1828, 1869-1873, 1902-1906, 1989-1993, 2020-2024, 2051-2055, 2078-2082.

Fish in Net
A429

1973, Sept. 12   Photo.   Perf. 13
1771 A429 2p multicolored   .25   .25
6th Intl. Fishing Exhibition, Vigo, Sept. 12-19.

Conference Hall — A430

1973, Sept. 14
1772 A430 8p multicolored   .25   .25
Plenipotentiary Conf. of the Intl. Telecommunications Union, Torremolinos, Sept. 1973.

Vicente López,
Self-portrait
A431

Stamp Day (Paintings by Vicente López y Portana (1772-1850)): 1p, King Ferdinand VII. 3p, Señora de Carvallo. 4p, Marshal Castelldosrrius. 5p, Queen Isabella II. 7p, Francisco Goya. 10p, Maria Amalia de Sajonia. 15p, The organist Felix López.

1973, Sept. 29   Photo.   Perf. 13
1773 A431 1p gold & multi   .25   .25
1774 A431 2p gold & multi   .25   .25
1775 A431 3p gold & multi   .25   .25
1776 A431 4p gold & multi   .25   .25
1777 A431 5p gold & multi   .25   .25
1778 A431 7p gold & multi   .25   .25
1779 A431 10p gold & multi   .25   .25
1780 A431 15p gold & multi   .25   .25
      Nos. 1773-1780 (8)   2.00 2.00

For other art types see A384, A397, A410, A448, A473, A501, A522, A538, A558 and footnote following No. 876.

Leon
Cathedral,
Nicaragua
A432

Designs: 2p, Subtiava Church. 5p, Portal of Governor's House, vert. 8p, Rio San Juan Castle.

1973, Oct. 12
1781 A432 1p multicolored   .25   .25
1782 A432 2p multicolored   .30   .25
1783 A432 5p multicolored   .50   .25
1784 A432 8p multicolored   .50   .25
      Nos. 1781-1784 (4)   1.55 1.00
Hispanic-American buildings in Nicaragua.

Pope Gregory XI
and Pedro
Fernandez
Pecha — A433

1973, Oct. 26
1785 A433 2p multicolored   .25   .25
600th anniversary of the founding of the Order of the Hermites of St. Jerome by Pedro Fernandez Pecha.

St. Domingo de
Silos Monastery
A434

Nativity, Column
Capital, Silos
Church
A435

Designs: 8p, Cloister walk, horiz. 15p, Three saints, sculpture.

Perf. 13x12½, 12½x13
1973, Oct. 26   Engr.
1786 A434 2p brn & rose mag   .45   .25
1787 A434 8p dk blue & purple   .25   .25
1788 A434 15p Prus grn & indigo   .25   .25
      Nos. 1786-1788 (3)   .95   .75
St. Domingo de Silos Monastery, Burgos.

1973, Nov. 6   Photo.   Perf. 13
Christmas: 8p, Adoration of the Kings, Butrera Church, horiz.
1789 A435 2p multicolored   .25   .25
1790 A435 8p multicolored   .25   .25

Map of
Spain and
Americas
with Dates
of First
Printings
A436

500 years of Spanish Printing: 7p, Teacher and Pupils, woodcut from "Libros de los Suenos," Valencia, 1474, vert. 15p, Title page from "Los Sinodales," Segovia, 1472.

1973, Dec. 11   Engr.   Perf. 13
1791 A436 1p ind & slate grn   .30   .25
1792 A436 7p violet bl & purple   .25   .25
1793 A436 15p purple & black   .25   .25
      Nos. 1791-1793 (3)   .80   .75

Uniform Type of 1973

Uniforms: 1p, Harquebusier on horseback, 1603. 2p, Harquebusiers, 1632. 3p, Cuirassier, 1635. 5p, Mounted drummer of the Dragoons, 1677. 9p, Two Musketeers, 1694.

1974, Jan. 5   Photo.   Perf. 13
1794 A428 1p multicolored   .25   .25
1795 A428 2p multicolored   .50   .25
1796 A428 3p multicolored   .70   .25
1797 A428 5p multicolored   .90   .25
1798 A428 9p multicolored   .25   .25
      Nos. 1794-1798 (5)   2.60 1.25

Nautical Chart of
Western Europe
and North
Africa — A437

1974, Jan. 26
1799 A437 2p multicolored   .25   .25
50th anniv. of the Superior Geographical Council of Spain. The chart is from a 14th cent. Catalan atlas.

M. Biada
and Steam
Engine
A438

1974, Apr. 2   Photo.   Perf. 13
1800 A438 2p multicolored   .25   .25
Barcelona-Mataro Railroad, 125th anniv.

Young
Collector,
Album,
Magnifier
A439

Exhibition Emblem — A440

Design: 8p, Emblem, globe and arrows.

1974, Apr. 4   Perf. 13
1801 A439 2p lilac rose & multi   .25   .25
           Perf. 12½
1802 A440 5p buff, blk & dull bl   .35   .30
1803 A440 8p dull green & multi   .30   .25
      Nos. 1801-1803 (3)   .90   .80
Espana 75, International Philatelic Exhibition, Madrid, Apr. 4-13, 1975.

Woman with
Offering — A441

Europa: 8p, Woman from Baza, painted sculpture.

1974, Apr. 29   Photo.   Perf. 13
1804 A441 2p multicolored   .45   .25
1805 A441 8p multicolored   .25   .25

No. 28 and
1854
Seville
Cancel
A442

1974, May 6
1806 A442 2p black, blue & red   .25   .25
World Stamp Day.

Father
Jaime
Balmes
A443

Designs: 10p, Father Pedro Poveda. 15p, Jorge Juan y Santacilla.

1974, May 28   Engr.   Perf. 13
1807 A443 8p blue gray & sepia   .25   .25
1808 A443 10p red brn & dk brn   .60   .25
1809 A443 15p brown & slate   .25   .25
      Nos. 1807-1809 (3)   1.10   .75
Famous Spaniards: Jaime Balmes (1810-1848), mathematician; death centenary of Pedro Poveda, pedagogue; Don Jorge Juan (1712-1773), explorer and writer.

Templeto, by
Bramante,
Rome — A444

1974, June 4   Photo.
1810 A444 5p multicolored   .25   .25
Cent. of the Spanish Academy of Fine Arts, Rome.

Aqueduct,
Segovia
A445

Designs: 2p, Tajo Bridge, Alcantara. 3p, Marcus Valerius Martial lecturing. 4p, Triumphal Arch, Tarragona, vert. 5p, Theater, Merida. 7p, Bishop Ossius of Cordoba preaching. 8p, Tribunal Arch, Talavera Forum, vert. 9p, Emperor Trajan, vert.

1974, June 25   Engr.
1811 A445 1p brown & black   .25   .25
1812 A445 2p gray grn & sepia   .30   .25
1813 A445 3p lt & dk brown   .25   .25
1814 A445 4p green & indigo   .25   .25
1815 A445 5p gray bl & choc   .25   .25
1816 A445 7p gray grn & lilac   .25   .25
1817 A445 8p dk brown & green   .25   .25
1818 A445 9p brt red lil & cl   .25   .25
      Nos. 1811-1818 (8)   2.05 2.00
Roman architecture and history in Spain.

Greek
Tortoise
A446

Reptiles: 2p, Common chameleon. 5p, Wall gecko. 7p, Emerald lizard. 15p, Blunt-nosed viper.

1974, July 3   Photo.
1819 A446 1p multicolored   .25   .25
1820 A446 2p multicolored   .30   .25
1821 A446 5p multicolored   .60   .50
1822 A446 7p multicolored   .40   .25
1823 A446 15p multicolored   .25   .25
      Nos. 1819-1823 (5)   1.80 1.50

Uniform Type of 1973

Uniforms: 1p, Hussar and horse, 1705. 2p, Artillery officers, 1710. 3p, Piper and drummer, Granada Regiment, 1734. 7p, Mounted standard-bearer, Numancia Dragoons, 1737. 8p, Standard-bearer and soldier, Zamora Regiment, 1739.

1974, July 17

1824	A428	1p multicolored	.25	.25
1825	A428	2p multicolored	.40	.25
1826	A428	3p multicolored	.40	.25
1827	A428	7p multicolored	.30	.25
1828	A428	8p multicolored	.25	.25
		Nos. 1824-1828 (5)	1.60	1.25

Life Saving A447

1974, Sept. 5   Photo.   Perf. 13

1829	A447	2p multicolored	.25	.25

18th World Life Saving Championships, Barcelona, Sept. 1974.

Eduardo Rosales, by Federico Madrazo — A448

Stamp Day (Eduardo Rosales, 1836-73, Paintings): 1p, Tobias and the Angel. 3p, The Last Will of Isabella the Catholic. 4p, Nena (little girl). 5p, Presentation of John of Austria to Charles I. 7p, The First Step. 10p, St. John the Evangelist. 15p, St. Matthew.

1974, Sept. 29   Photo.   Perf. 13

1830	A448	1p gold & multi	.25	.25
1831	A448	2p gold & multi	.25	.25
1832	A448	3p gold & multi, horiz.	.25	.25
1833	A448	4p gold & multi	.25	.25
1834	A448	5p gold & multi, horiz.	.25	.25
1835	A448	7p gold & multi, horiz.	.25	.25
1836	A448	10p gold & multi	.30	.25
1837	A448	15p gold & multi	.25	.25
		Nos. 1830-1837 (8)	2.05	2.00

For other art types see A384, A397, A410, A431, A473, A501, A522, A538, A558 and footnote following No. 876.

"International Mail" — A449

UPU Monument, Bern — A450

1974, Oct. 9

1838	A449	2p dark blue & multi	.25	.25
1839	A450	8p red & multi	.25	.25

Centenary of Universal Postal Union.

Sobremonte House, Cordoba, Argentina — A451

Ruins of San Ignacio de Mini, 18th Century — A452

The Gaucho Martin Fierro — A453

Design: 2p, Municipal Council Building, Buenos Aires, 1829.

1974, Oct. 12

1840	A451	1p multicolored	.25	.25
1841	A451	2p multicolored	.40	.25
1842	A452	5p multicolored	.30	.25
1843	A453	10p multicolored	.25	.25
		Nos. 1840-1843 (4)	1.20	1.00

Cultural ties with Latin America.

Nativity, Valdavia Church A454

Adoration of the Kings, Valcobero Church — A455

1974   Photo.   Perf. 13

1844	A454	2p multicolored	.25	.25
1845	A455	3p lt blue & multi	.25	.25
1846	A455	8p olive & multi	.25	.25
		Nos. 1844-1846 (3)	.75	.75

Christmas 1974.
Issue dates: 2p, 8p, Nov. 4; 3p, Dec. 2.

Teucriun Lanigerum A456

Flowers: 2p, Hypericum ericoides. 4p, Thymus longiflorus. 5p, Anthyllis onobrychioides. 8p, Helianthemun paniculatum.

1974, Nov. 8

1847	A456	1p multicolored	.25	.25
1848	A456	2p multicolored	.25	.25
1849	A456	4p multicolored	.25	.25

1850	A456	5p multicolored	.25	.25
1851	A456	8p multicolored	.25	.25
		Nos. 1847-1851 (5)	1.25	1.25

Franco Type of 1954-56
Imprint: "F.N.M.T."

1974-75   Photo.   Perf. 12½x13

1852	A221	4p rose car ('75)	.25	.25
1853	A221	7p brt ultra	.25	.25
1854	A221	12p blue green	.25	.25
1855	A221	20p rose carmine	.25	.25
		Nos. 1852-1855 (4)	1.00	1.00

Leyre Monastery A457

8p, Column and bas-relief, vert. 15p, Crypt.

1974, Dec. 10   Engr.   Perf. 12½x13

1862	A457	2p slate grn & bl gray	.45	.25
1863	A457	8p carmine	.25	.25
1864	A457	15p grnsh black	.35	.25
		Nos. 1862-1864 (3)	1.05	.75

Leyre Monastery, Navarre.

Spain Nos. 1 and 1802 — A458

Mail Coach, 1850 A459

Designs: 8p, Mail ship of Indian Service. 10p, Chapel of St. Mark.

Perf. 12½x13, 13x12½

1975, Jan. 2   Engr.

1865	A458	2p slate blue	.35	.30
1866	A459	3p olive & brown	.45	.40
1867	A459	8p lilac & slate bl	1.00	.50
1868	A458	10p brn & slate grn	.50	.40
		Nos. 1865-1868 (4)	2.30	1.60

125th anniversary of Spanish postage stamps.

Uniform Type of 1973

1p, Sergeant and grenadier, Toledo Regiment, 1750. 2p, Royal Artillery, 1762. 3p, Queen's Regiment, 1763. 5p, Fusiliers, Vitoria Regiment, 1766. 10p, Dragoon, Sagunto Regiment, 1775.

1975, Jan. 7   Photo.   Perf. 13

1869	A428	1p multicolored	.25	.25
1870	A428	2p multicolored	.25	.25
1871	A428	3p multicolored	1.60	.25
1872	A428	5p multicolored	.50	.25
1873	A428	10p multicolored	1.40	.25
		Nos. 1869-1873 (5)	4.00	1.25

Antonio Gaudi A460

Designs: 10p, Antonio Palacios and Casa Guell, Barcelona. 15p, Secundino Zuazo.

1975, Feb. 25   Engr.   Perf. 13

1874	A460	8p green & black	.25	.25
1875	A460	10p carmine & dp claret	.40	.25
1876	A460	15p brown & black	.25	.25
		Nos. 1874-1876 (3)	.90	.75

Contemporary Spanish architects.

Souvenir Sheets

Spanish Goldsmiths' Works — A461

Designs: 2p, Agate box, 9th cent. 3p, Votive crown of Recesvinto. 8p, Cover of Evangelistary, Roncesvalles Collegiate Church, 12th cent. 10p, Chalice of Infanta Donna Urraca, 11th cent. 12p, Processional monstrance, St. Domingo de Silos, 16th cent. 15p, Sword of Boabdil, 15th cent. 25p, Sword and head of Charles V (Carlos I of Spain). 50p, Earring and bracelet from Aliseda, 6th-4th centuries B.C. 3p, 10p, 12p, 25p vertical (No. 1878).

1975, Apr. 4   Engr.   Perf. 13

1877	A461	Sheet of 4	8.00	8.00
a.		2p gray & Prussian blue	2.00	2.00
b.		8p brown & Prus blue	2.00	2.00
c.		15p gray & dark carmine	2.00	2.00
d.		50p dark carmine & gray	2.00	2.00
1878	A461	Sheet of 4	8.00	8.00
a.		3p slate green & gray	2.00	2.00
b.		10p sepia & slate	2.00	2.00
c.		12p gray & bluish black	2.00	2.00
d.		25p sepia & bluish black	2.00	2.00

Espana 75 Intl. Phil. Exhib., Madrid, 4/4-13.

Pomegranates A462

1975, Apr. 21   Photo.

1879	A462	1p Almonds, nuts and blossoms, horiz.	.25	.25
1880	A462	2p shown	.25	.25
1881	A462	3p Oranges	.25	.25
1882	A462	4p Chestnuts	.25	.25
1883	A462	5p Apples	.25	.25
		Nos. 1879-1883 (5)	1.25	1.25

Woman Gathering Honey, Arana Cave — A463

Europa: 12p, Horse, wall painting from Tito Bustillo Cave, horiz.

1975, Apr. 28   Photo.   Perf. 13

1884	A463	3p brown & multi	.25	.25
1885	A463	12p brown & multi	.35	.25

Pre-stamp León Cancellation A464

1975, May 6   Perf. 12½x13

1886	A464	3p multicolored	.25	.25

World Stamp Day.

World Tourism Organization
Emblem — A465

1975, May 12   Photo.   Perf. 13
1887 A465 3p dark blue   .25 .25
First General Assembly of the World Tourism Organization, Madrid, May 1975.

Fair Emblem,
Agricultural
Symbols — A466

1975, May 14
1888 A466 3p multicolored   .25 .25
25th Agricultural Fair.

Equality
Between
Men and
Women
A467

1975, June 3
1889 A467 3p multicolored   .25 .25
International Women's Year.

Virgin of
Cabeza
Sanctuary
A468

1975, June 18   Photo.   Perf. 13
1890 A468 3p multicolored   .25 .25
Virgin of Cabeza Sanctuary, site of siege during Civil War, 1937.

Cervantes'
Prison Cell,
Argamasilla de
Álba — A469

Tourism: 2p, Bridge of St. Martin, Toledo. 3p, Church of St. Peter, Tarrasa. 4p, Arch, Alhambra, Granada, vert. 5p, Street, Mijas, Malaga, vert. 7p, Church of St. Mary, Tarrasa, vert.

1975, June 25   Engr.   Perf. 13
1891 A469 1p purple & black   .25 .25
1892 A469 2p red brn & brn   .25 .25
1893 A469 3p slate & sepia   .25 .25
1894 A469 4p orange & claret   .25 .25
1895 A469 5p slate grn & indigo   .25 .25
1896 A469 7p violet bl & indigo   .40 .25
        Nos. 1891-1896 (6)   1.65 1.50

Salamander — A470

1975, July 9   Photo.   Perf. 13
1897 A470 1p shown   .25 .25
1898 A470 2p Newt   .25 .25
1899 A470 3p Tree toad   .25 .25
1900 A470 6p Midwife toad   .25 .25
1901 A470 7p Leaf frog   .25 .25
        Nos. 1897-1901 (5)   1.25 1.25

Uniform Type of 1973

1p, Cavalry officer, 1788. 2p, Fusilier, Asturias Regiment, 1789. 3p, Infantry Colonel, 1802. 4p, Artillery standard-bearer, 1803. 7p, Sapper, 1809.

1975, July 17
1902 A428 1p multicolored   .25 .25
1903 A428 2p multicolored   .50 .25
1904 A428 3p multicolored   .25 .25
1905 A428 4p multicolored   .25 .25
1906 A428 7p multicolored   .25 .25
        Nos. 1902-1906 (5)   1.50 1.25

Infant and
Children
Playing
A471

1975, Sept. 9   Photo.   Perf. 13
1907 A471 3p multicolored   .25 .25
"Defend Life."

Scroll and
Emblem
A472

1975, Sept. 25
1908 A472 3p multicolored   .25 .25
13th International Congress of Latin Notaries, Barcelona, Sept. 26-Oct. 4.

Blessing of
the Birds
A473

Scenes from Apocalypse: 2p, Angel at River of Life. 3p, Angel Guarding Gate of Paradise. 4p, Fox carrying cock. 6p, Daniel with wild bulls. 7p, The Last Judgment. 10p, Four horsemen of the Apocalypse. 12p, Bird holding snake.

1975, Sept. 29
1909 A473 1p gold & multi   .25 .25
1910 A473 2p gold & multi, vert.   .25 .25
1911 A473 3p gold & multi, vert.   .25 .25
1912 A473 4p gold & multi   .25 .25
1913 A473 6p gold & multi   .25 .25
1914 A473 7p gold & multi, vert.   .25 .25
1915 A473 10p gold & multi, vert.   .25 .25
1916 A473 12p gold & multi, vert.   .25 .25
        Nos. 1909-1916 (8)   2.00 2.00

Millenium Gerona Cathedral.
For other art types see A384, A397, A410, A431, A448, A501, A522, A538, A558 and footnote following No. 876.

Symbols of
Industry
A474

1975, Oct. 7   Engr.   Perf. 13
1917 A474 3p violet & lilac   .25 .25
Spanish industrialization.

Pioneers'
Covered
Wagon
A475

Designs: 1p, El Cabildo, meeting house of 1st Uruguayan Government. 3p, Fort St. Theresa over River Plate. 8p, Montevideo Cathedral, vert.

1975, Oct. 12   Photo.
1918 A475 1p multicolored   .25 .25
1919 A475 2p multicolored   .25 .25
1920 A475 3p multicolored   .25 .25
1921 A475 8p multicolored   .25 .25
        Nos. 1918-1921 (4)   1.00 1.00
Cultural ties with Latin America; sesquicentennial of Uruguay's independence.

Ruined Columns,
San Juan de la
Peña — A476

3p, Monastery, horiz. 8p, Cloister, horiz.

Perf. 13x12½, 12½x13
1975, Oct. 28   Engr.
1922 A476 3p slate grn & brn   .30 .25
1923 A476 8p violet & brt lil   .25 .25
1924 A476 10p dp magenta &
                 car   .25 .25
        Nos. 1922-1924 (3)   .80 .75
San Juan de la Pena Monastery.

Madonna, Mosaic,
Navarra
Cathedral — A477

Christmas: 12p, Flight into Egypt, carved capital, Navarra Cathedral, horiz.

1975, Nov. 4   Photo.   Perf. 13
1925 A477 3p multicolored   .25 .25
1926 A477 12p multicolored   .25 .25

King Juan Carlos
I — A478

Queen Sofia
and
King — A479

Designs: No. 1928, Queen Sofia.

1975, Dec. 29 Photo. Perf. 13x12½
1927 A478 3p multicolored   .25 .25
1928 A478 3p multicolored   .25 .25

Perf. 12½
1929 A479 3p multicolored   .25 .25
1930 A479 12p multicolored   .25 .25
        Nos. 1927-1930 (4)   1.00 1.00
King Juan Carlos I, accession to the throne.

Pilgrim Virgin,
Pontevedra
A480

Mountains and
Center Emblem
A481

1976, Jan. 2   Engr.   Perf. 13
1931 A480 3p rose & brown   .25 .25
Holy Year of St. James of Compostela, patron saint of Spain.

1976, Feb. 10   Photo.
1932 A481 6p multicolored   .25 .25
Catalunya Excursion Center, centenary.

Cosme Damian
Churruca — A482

Navigators: 12p, Luis de Requesens. 50p, Juan Sebastian Elcano, horiz.

1976, Mar. 1   Engr.   Perf. 13
1933 A482 7p vio brn & grnsh
                 blk   1.50 .25
1934 A482 12p lt blue & violet   .25 .25
1935 A482 50p dp brn & gray ol   .55 .25
        Nos. 1933-1935 (3)   2.30 .75

A. G. Bell,
Radar and
Telephone
A483

1976, Mar. 10   Photo.
1936 A483 3p multicolored   .25 .25
Centenary of first telephone call by Alexander Graham Bell, March 10, 1876.

"Watch at
Street
Crossings"
A484

Road Safety: 3p, "Don't pass when in doubt," vert. 5p, "Wear seat belts."

1976, Apr. 6   Photo.   Perf. 13
1937 A484 1p orange & multi   .25 .25
1938 A484 3p gray & multi   .35 .25
1939 A484 5p lilac & multi   .25 .25
        Nos. 1937-1939 (3)   .85 .75

St.
George,
Alcoy
Cathedral
A485

1976, Apr. 23
1940 A485 3p multicolored   .25 .25
7th centenary of the apparition of St. George in Alcoy.

Talavera Pottery A486

Europa: 12p, Lace making.

1976, May 3   **Photo.**   *Perf. 13*
1941 A486   3p multicolored   .65 .25
1942 A486   12p multicolored   .80 .30

17th Conference of European Postal and Telecommunications Administrations.

6r Stamp of 1851 with Coruna Cancel — A487

1976, May 6
1943 A487   3p blue, org & blk   .25 .25

World Stamp Day.

Coin of Caesar Augustus A488

7p, Map of Roman camp on banks of Ebro, and coin. 25p, Orpheus, mosaic from Roman era, vert.

1976, May 26   **Engr.**   *Perf. 13*
1944 A488   3p dk brn & mar   1.90 .25
1945 A488   7p dk brown & blue   1.00 .30
1946 A488   25p brown & black   .50 .25
   Nos. 1944-1946 (3)   3.40 .80

Founding of Saragossa, 2000th anniv,

Spanish-made Rifle, 1757 — A489

Designs (Bicentennial Emblem and): 3p, Bernardo de Galvez, Spanish governor. 5p, Dollar bank note, Richmond, 1861. 12p, Spanish capture of Pensacola from English.

1976, May 29
1947 A489   1p dk brn & vio bl   .25 .25
1948 A489   3p sl grn & dk brn   .90 .25
1949 A489   5p dk grn & sl grn   .40 .25
1950 A489   12p grn & dk brn   .40 .30
   Nos. 1947-1950 (4)   1.95 1.05

American Bicentennial.

Old Customs House, Cadiz A490

Customs Houses: 3p, Madrid. 7p, Barcelona.

1976, June 9
1951 A490   1p black & maroon   .25 .25
1952 A490   3p sepia & green   .55 .25
1953 A490   7p red brn & vio brn   1.10 .35
   Nos. 1951-1953 (3)   1.90 .85

Postal Savings Box with Symbols — A491

Railroad Post Office — A492

Rural Mailman in Winter A493

Postal Service: 10p, Automatic letter sorting machine.

1976, June 16   **Photo.**
1954 A491   1p multicolored   .25 .25
1955 A492   3p multicolored   .35 .25
1956 A493   6p multicolored   .25 .25
1957 A493   10p multicolored   .25 .25
   Nos. 1954-1957 (4)   1.10 1.00

King and Queen, Map of Americas A494

1976, June 25
1958 A494   12p multicolored   .25 .25

Visit of King Juan Carlos I and Queen Sofia to the Americas, June 1976.

San Marcos, León — A495

Tourism (Famous Hotels): 2p, Las Cañadas, Tenerife. 3p, Portal of R. R. Catolicos, Santiago, vert. 4p, Cruz de Tejeda, Las Palmas. 7p, Gredos, Avila. 12p, La Arruzafa, Cordoba.

1976, June 30   **Engr.**   *Perf. 13*
1959 A495   1p slate & sepia   .25 .25
1960 A495   2p green & indigo   .65 .25
1961 A495   3p brn & red brn   .45 .25
1962 A495   4p sepia & slate   .25 .25
1963 A495   7p slate & sepia   .85 .35
1964 A495   12p rose brn & pur   1.00 .25
   Nos. 1959-1964 (6)   3.45 1.60

Greco-Roman Wrestling — A496

Montreal Olympic Emblem and: 1p, Men's rowing, horiz. 2p, Boxing, horiz. 12p, Basketball.

1976, July 9   **Photo.**
1965 A496   1p multicolored   .25 .25
1966 A496   2p lilac & multi   .35 .25
1967 A496   3p multicolored   .25 .25
1968 A496   12p multicolored   .25 .25
   Nos. 1965-1968 (4)   1.10 1.00

21st Olympic Games, Montreal, Canada, July 17-Aug. 1.

King Juan Carlos I — A497

1976-77   **Photo.**   *Perf. 13*
1969 A497   10c orange ('77)   .25 .25
1970 A497   25c apple grn ('77)   .25 .25
1971 A497   30c dp blue ('77)   .25 .25
1972 A497   50c purple ('77)   .25 .25
1973 A497   1p emerald ('77)   .25 .25
1974 A497   1.50p scarlet   .25 .25
1975 A497   2p dp blue   .25 .25
1976 A497   3p dp green   .25 .25
1977 A497   4p blue grn ('77)   .25 .25
1978 A497   5p dp car rose   .25 .25
1979 A497   6p brt green ('77)   .25 .25
1980 A497   7p olive   .25 .25
1982 A497   8p brt blue ('77)   .25 .25
1983 A497   10p lilac rose ('77)   .25 .25
1984 A497   12p golden brown   .25 .25
1985 A497   15p vio blue ('77)   .30 .25
1986 A497   20p brt red lil ('77)   .35 .25
   Nos. 1969-1986 (17)   4.40 4.25

Nos. 1976, 1978-1980, 1982-1983 also issued as coils with number on back of every fifth stamp.
See Nos. 2185-2194, 2268-2270.
Nos. 1969-1970, 1972-1973, 1975-1983, 1985-1986, 2185-2194 and 2268-2270 also printed on prephosphored paper. Value, mint set of 27 values, $40.

Uniform Type of 1973

Uniforms: 1p, Trumpeter, Alcantara Regiment, 1815. 2p, Sapper, 1821. 3p, Engineer in dress uniform, 1825. 7p, Artillery infantry, 1828. 25p, Infantry riflemen, 1830.

1976, July 17
1989 A428   1p multicolored   .25 .25
1990 A428   2p multicolored   .80 .25
1991 A428   3p multicolored   .30 .25
1992 A428   7p multicolored   .25 .25
1993 A428   25p multicolored   .30 .25
   Nos. 1989-1993 (5)   1.90 1.25

Blood Donors A498

Mosaic, Batitales A499

1976, Sept. 7   **Engr.**   *Perf. 13*
1994 A498   3p carmine & black   .25 .25

Give blood, save a life!

1976, Sept. 22

Designs: 3p, Lugo city wall. 7p, Obverse and reverse of Roman 1st Legion coin.

1995 A499   1p black & purple   .25 .25
1996 A499   3p black & dp brn   .25 .25
1997 A499   7p green & magenta   .45 .25
   Nos. 1995-1997 (3)   .95 .75

2000th anniversary of Lugo City.

Parliament, Madrid A500

1976, Sept. 23
1998 A500   12p green & sepia   .25 .25

63rd Conference of Inter-parliamentary Union, Madrid.

Still Life, by L. E. Menendez — A501

Luis Eugenio Menendez Paintings: 2p, Peaches and jar. 3p, Pears, melon and barrel. 4p, Brace of pigeons and basket. 6p, Sea bream and oranges, horiz. 7p, Water melon and bread, horiz. 10p, Figs, bread and jug, horiz. 12p, Various fruits, horiz.

1976, Sept. 29   **Photo.**   *Perf. 13*
1999 A501   1p gold & multi   .25 .25
2000 A501   2p gold & multi   .25 .25
2001 A501   3p gold & multi   .25 .25
2002 A501   4p gold & multi   .25 .25
2003 A501   6p gold & multi   .25 .25
2004 A501   7p gold & multi   .30 .25
2005 A501   10p gold & multi   .25 .25
2006 A501   12p gold & multi   .30 .25
   Nos. 1999-2006 (8)   2.10 2.00

Luis Eugenio Menendez (1716-1780). Stamp Day 1976.
For other art types see A384, A397, A410, A431, A448, A473, A522, A538, A558 and footnote following No. 876.

St. Christopher Carrying Christ Child — A502

Christmas: 3p, Nativity, horiz. Both designs after painted wood carvings.

1976, Oct. 8
2007 A502   3p multicolored   .75 .25
2008 A502   12p multicolored   1.50 .50

Nicoya Church, Costa Rica — A503

Juan Vazquez de Coronado — A504

Designs: 3p, Orosi Mission, Costa Rica, horiz. 12p, Tomas de Acosta.

1976, Oct. 12
2009	A503	1p multicolored	.25	.25
2010	A504	2p multicolored	.25	.25
2011	A503	3p multicolored	.25	.25
2012	A504	12p multicolored	.25	.25
		Nos. 2009-2012 (4)	1.00	1.00

Spain's link with Costa Rica.

Map of South and Central America,
Santa Maria, King and Queen
A505

1976, Oct. 12
2013	A505	12p multicolored	.25	.25

Visit of King Juan Carlos I and Queen Sofia
to Latin America.

St. Peter
of
Alcantara
Monastery
A506

Tomb of Peter of
Alcantara
A507

St. Peter of
Alcantara
A508

1976, Oct. 29   Engr.   Perf. 13
2014	A506	3p dp brown & sepia	.30	.25
2015	A507	7p dk purple & blk	.25	.25
2016	A508	20p brown & dk brown	.30	.25
		Nos. 2014-2016 (3)	.85	.75

St. Peter of Alcantara (1499-1562), Franciscan reformer.

Hand
Releasing
Doves
A509

1976, Nov. 23   Litho.   Perf. 13
2017	A509	3p multicolored	.25	.25

11th Philatelic Exhibition of the National
Association of the Handicapped.

Casals and
Cello
A510

Design: 5p, Manuel de Falla and Fire Dance
from El Amor Brujo.

1976, Dec. 29   Engr.   Perf. 13
2018	A510	3p black & vio bl	.25	.25
2019	A510	5p slate grn & car	.25	.25

Birth centenaries of Pablo Casals (1876-
1973), cellist and composer, and of Manuel de
Falla (1876-1946), composer.

Uniform Type of 1973

Uniforms: 1p, Outrider, Calatrava Lancers,
1844. 2p, Sapper, 1850. 3p, Corporal, Light
Infantry, 1860. 4p, Drum Major, 1861. 20p,
Artillery Captain, Mounted, 1862.

1977, Jan. 5   Photo.   Perf. 13
2020	A428	1p multicolored	.25	.25
2021	A428	2p multicolored	.35	.25
2022	A428	3p multicolored	.25	.25
2023	A428	4p multicolored	.25	.25
2024	A428	20p multicolored	.25	.25
		Nos. 2020-2024 (5)	1.35	1.25

King
James
I
A511

1977, Feb. 10   Engr.   Perf. 13
2025	A511	4p purple & ocher	.25	.25

James I, El Conquistador (1208-1276), King
of Aragon, 700th death anniversary.

Jacinto
Verdaguer — A512

Portraits: 7p, Miguel Servet. 12p, Pablo
Sarasate. 50p, Francisco Tarrega.

1977, Feb. 22
2026	A512	5p purple & dk red	.25	.25
2027	A512	7p olive & slate grn	.25	.25
2028	A512	12p dk blue & bl grn	.25	.25
2029	A512	50p lt green & brown	.55	.25
		Nos. 2026-2029 (4)	1.30	1.00

Honoring Jacinto Verdaguer (1845-1902),
Catalan poet; Miguel Servet (1511-1553), physician and theologian; Pablo Sarasate (1844-
1908), violinist and composer; Francisco Tarrega (1854-1909), creator of modern Spanish
guitar music.

Marquis de Penaflorida — A513

1977, Feb. 24   Engr.   Perf. 13
2030	A513	4p dull green & brn	.25	.25

Bicentenary of the Economic Society of the
Friends of the Land (agricultural
improvements).

Trout
A514

1977, Mar. 8   Photo.
2031	A514	1p Salmon, vert.	.25	.25
2032	A514	2p shown	.25	.25
2033	A514	3p Eel	.25	.25
2034	A514	4p Carp	.25	.25
2035	A514	6p Barbel	.25	.25
		Nos. 2031-2035 (5)	1.25	1.25

Slalom
A515

1977, Mar. 24   Engr.   Perf. 13
2036	A515	5p multicolored	.25	.25

World Ski Championships, Granada, Sierra
Nevada, Mar. 24-27.

La Cuadra,
1900
A516

Spanish Pioneer Automobiles: 4p, Hispano
Suiza, 1916. 5p, Elizalde, 1915. 7p, Abadal,
1914.

1977, Apr. 23   Photo.   Perf. 13
2037	A516	2p multicolored	.25	.25
2038	A516	4p multicolored	.25	.25
2039	A516	5p multicolored	.25	.25
2040	A516	7p multicolored	.25	.25
		Nos. 2037-2040 (4)	1.00	1.00

Ordesa
National
Park
A517

Europa: 3p, Tree in Doñana National Park.

1977, May 2   Litho.
2041	A517	3p multicolored	.25	.25
2042	A517	12p multicolored	.25	.25

Plaza
Mayor,
Spanish
Stamps,
Tongs
A518

1977, May 7   Engr.   Perf. 13
2043	A518	3p multicolored	.25	.25

50th anniversary of Philatelic Market on
Plaza Mayor, Madrid.

Enrique de
Osso, St.
Theresa
and Book
A519

1977, June 7   Photo.   Perf. 13
2044	A519	8p multicolored	.25	.25

Centenary of the founding by Enrique de
Osso of the Society of St. Theresa of Jesus.

Toledo Gate,
Ciudad
Real — A520

Tourism: 2p, Roman aqueduct, Almuñecar.
3p, Cathedral, Jaen, vert. 4p, Ronda Gorge,
Malaga, vert. 7p, Ampudia Castle, Palencia.
12p, Bisagra Gate, Toledo.

1977, June 24   Engr.   Perf. 13
2045	A520	1p orange & brown	.25	.25
2046	A520	2p sepia & slate	.25	.25
2047	A520	3p violet & purple	.25	.25
2048	A520	4p brt & dk green	.25	.25
2049	A520	7p brown & black	.25	.25
2050	A520	12p vio & org brn	.25	.25
		Nos. 2045-2050 (6)	1.50	1.50

Uniform Type of 1973

Uniforms: 1p, Military Administration official,
1875. 2p, Cavalry lancers, 1883. 3p, General
Staff Commander, 1884. 7p, Trumpeter, Divisional Artillery, 1887. 25p, Medical Corps official, 1895.

1977, July 16   Photo.
2051	A428	1p multicolored	.25	.25
2052	A428	2p multicolored	.25	.25
2053	A428	3p multicolored	.25	.25
2054	A428	7p multicolored	.25	.25
2055	A428	25p multicolored	.30	.25
		Nos. 2051-2055 (5)	1.30	1.25

A521

St. Emilian Cuculatus and earliest known
Catalan manuscript.

1977, Sept. 9   Engr.   Perf. 13
2056	A521	5p violet, grn & brn	.25	.25

Millennium of Catalan language.

A522

Federico Madrazo (1815-94) Portraits: 1p,
The Boy Florez. 2p, Duke of San Miguel. 3p,
Senora Coronado. 4p, Campoamor. 6p, Marquesa de Montelo. 7p, Rivadeneyra. 10p,
Countess de Vilches. 15p, Senora Gomez de
Avellaneda.

1977, Sept. 29   Photo.   Perf. 13
2057	A522	1p gold & multi	.25	.25
2058	A522	2p gold & multi	.25	.25
2059	A522	3p gold & multi	.25	.25
2060	A522	4p gold & multi	.25	.25
2061	A522	6p gold & multi	.25	.25
2062	A522	7p gold & multi	.25	.25
2063	A522	10p gold & multi	.25	.25
2064	A522	15p gold & multi	.25	.25
		Nos. 2057-2064 (8)	2.00	2.00

For other art types see A384, A397, A410,
A431, A448, A473, A501, A538, A558 and
footnote following No. 876.

Sailing Ship and Mail Routes, 18th
Century — A523

1977, Oct. 7   Engr.
2065	A523	15p black, brn & grn	.30	.30

ESPAMER '77 Philatelic Exhibition, Barcelona, Oct. 7-13, and for the Bicentenary for
regular mail routes to the Indies (Central and
South America). No. 2065 issued in sheets of
8 stamps and 8 labels showing exhibition
emblem.

Church of St. Francis, Guatemala City A524

Designs (Guatemala City): 3p, Modern buildings. 7p, Government Palace. 12p, Columbus Square and monument.

1977, Oct. 12   **Photo.**   *Perf. 13*
2066	A524	1p multicolored	.25	.25
2067	A524	3p multicolored	.25	.25
2068	A524	7p multicolored	.25	.25
2069	A524	12p multicolored	.25	.25
		Nos. 2066-2069 (4)	1.00	1.00

Spain's link with Guatemala.

San Pedro Monastery, Cardeña A525

Designs: 7p, Cloister. 20p, Tomb of El Cid and Dona Gimena.

1977, Oct. 28   **Engr.**
2070	A525	3p vio blue & slate	.25	.25
2071	A525	7p brown & maroon	.25	.25
2072	A525	20p green & slate	.25	.25
		Nos. 2070-2072 (3)	.75	.75

San Pedro Monastery, Cardena, Burgos.

Adoration of the Kings A526

Christmas: 12p, Flight into Egypt, vert. Designs from Romanesque paintings in Jaca Cathedral Museum.

1977, Nov. 3   **Photo.**
2073	A526	5p multicolored	.25	.25
2074	A526	12p multicolored	.25	.25

Old and New Iberia Planes A527

1977, Nov. 3
2075	A527	12p multicolored	.25	.25

IBERIA, Spanish Airlines, 50th anniversary.

Felipe de Borbon, Prince of Asturias — A528

1977, Dec. 22   **Photo.**   *Perf. 13*
2076	A528	5p multicolored	.25	.25

Felipe de Borbon, Spanish crown prince.

Judo, Games Emblem — A529

1977, Dec. 29
2077	A529	3p multicolored	.25	.25

10th World Judo Championships, Taiwan.

Uniform Type of 1973

Uniforms: 1p, Flag bearer, 1908. 2p, Lieutenant Colonel, Hussar, 1909. 3p, Mounted artillery lieutenant, 1912. 5p, Engineers' captain, 1921. 12p, Captain General, 1925.

1978, Jan. 5
2078	A428	1p multicolored	.25	.25
2079	A428	2p multicolored	.25	.25
2080	A428	3p multicolored	.25	.25
2081	A428	5p multicolored	.25	.25
2082	A428	12p multicolored	.25	.25
		Nos. 2078-2082 (5)	1.25	1.25

Hilarión Eslava and Score A530

8p, José Clara and sculpture. 25p, Pio Baroja and farm. 50p, Antonio Machado Ruiz and castle.

1978, Feb. 20   **Engr.**   *Perf. 13*
2083	A530	5p black & dk pur	.25	.25
2084	A530	8p blue grn & blk	.25	.25
2085	A530	25p yel grn & blk	.30	.25
2086	A530	50p dk pur & dk brn	.55	.25
		Nos. 2083-2086 (4)	1.35	1.00

Miguel Hilarión Eslava (1807-1878), composer; José Clara, sculptor; Pio Baroja (1872-1956), author and physician; Antonio Machado Ruiz (1875-1939), poet and playwright.

Burial of Christ, by de Juni — A531

Detail from Burial of Christ — A532

Designs: No. 2089, Juan de Juni. No. 2090, Rape of Sabine Women, by Rubens. No. 2091, Rape (detail) and Rubens portrait. No. 2092, Rubens signature and palette. No. 2093, Judgment of Paris, by Titian. No. 2094, Judgment and Titian portrait. No. 2095, Initial "TF" and palette.

1978, Mar. 28   **Engr.**   *Perf. 12½x13*
2087	A532	3p multicolored	.25	.25
2088	A531	3p multicolored	.25	.25
2089	A532	3p multicolored	.25	.25
a.		Strip of 3, #2087-2089	.25	.25
2090	A532	5p multicolored	.25	.25
2091	A531	5p multicolored	.25	.25
2092	A532	5p multicolored	.25	.25
a.		Strip of 3, #2090-2092	.25	.25
2093	A532	8p multicolored	.25	.25
2094	A531	8p multicolored	.25	.25
2095	A532	8p multicolored	.25	.25
a.		Strip of 3, #2093-2095	.25	.25

Juan de Juni (1507-77), sculptor, (3p); Peter Paul Rubens (1577-1640), painter, (5p); Titian (1477-1576), painter, (8p).

Edelweiss in Pyrenees — A533

Designs: 5p, Fish and duck, wetlands. 7p, Forest, and forest destroyed by fire. 12p, Waves, oil rig, tanker and city. 20p, Sea gulls and seals, vert.

1978, Apr. 4   **Photo.**   *Perf. 13*
2096	A533	3p multicolored	.25	.25
2097	A533	5p multicolored	.25	.25
2098	A533	7p multicolored	.25	.25
2099	A533	12p multicolored	.25	.25
2100	A533	20p multicolored	.25	.25
		Nos. 2096-2100 (5)	1.25	1.25

Protection of the environment.

Palace of Charles V, Granada A534

Europa: 12p, The Lonja, Seville.

1978, May 2   **Engr.**   *Perf. 13*
2101	A534	5p dull grn & sl grn	.25	.25
2102	A534	12p dull grn & car rose	.25	.25

"España" — A535

1978, May 5   **Photo.**   *Perf. 12½*
2103	A535	12p multicolored	.25	.25

Spain's admission to the Council of Europe.

Symbols and Emblems of Postal Service A536

1978, June 27   **Engr.**   *Perf. 13*
2104	A536	5p slate green	.25	.25

Stamp Day.

Map of Las Palmas, 16th Century A537

5p, Hermitage of Columbus Church, vert. 12p, View of Las Palmas, 16th century.

1978, June 23   **Photo.**
2105	A537	3p multicolored	.25	.25
2106	A537	5p multicolored	.25	.25
2107	A537	12p multicolored	.25	.25
		Nos. 2105-2107 (3)	.75	.75

Founding of Las Palmas, 500th anniv.

Pablo Picasso, Self-portrait A538

Picasso Paintings: 3p, Señora Canals. 8p, Jaime Sabartes. 10p, End of the Act (actress). 12p, Science and Charity (woman patient, doctor, nurse and child), horiz. 15p, "Las Mennas" (blue period), horiz. 20p, The Sparrows. 25p, The Painter and his Model, horiz.

1978, Sept. 29   **Photo.**   *Perf. 13*
2108	A538	3p gold & multi	.25	.25
2109	A538	5p gold & multi	.25	.25
2110	A538	8p gold & multi	.25	.25
2111	A538	10p gold & multi	.25	.25
2112	A538	12p gold & multi	.25	.25
2113	A538	15p gold & multi	.25	.25
2114	A538	20p gold & multi	.25	.25
2115	A538	25p gold & multi	.30	.25
		Nos. 2108-2115 (8)	2.05	2.00

Pablo Picasso (1881-1973). Stamp Day 1978.
A 7p stamp like No. 2111 was not issued.
For other art types see A384, A397, A410, A431, A448, A473, A501, A522, A558 and footnote following No. 876.

José de San Martin A539

Design: 12p, Simon Bolivar.

1978, Oct. 12   **Engr.**   *Perf. 13*
2116	A539	7p sepia & car	.25	.25
2117	A539	12p violet & car	.25	.25

José de San Martin (1778-1850) and Simon Bolivar (1783-1830), South American liberators.

Flight into Egypt, Capital from St. Mary de Nieva A540

Christmas: 12p, Annunciation, capital from St. Mary de Nieva.

1978, Nov. 3   **Photo.**   *Perf. 13*
2118	A540	5p multicolored	.25	.25
2119	A540	12p multicolored	.25	.25

Mexican Calendar Stone A541

Designs (King Juan Carlos I, Queen Sofia and): No. 2121, Machu Picchu. No. 2122, Calchaqui jars from Tucuman and Angalgala.

1978
2120	A541	5p multicolored	.25	.25
2121	A541	5p multicolored	.25	.25
2122	A541	5p multicolored	.25	.25
		Nos. 2120-2122 (3)	.75	.75

Royal visits to Mexico, Peru and Argentina. Issued: #2120 (Mexico), Nov. 17; #2121 (Peru), Nov. 22; #2122 (Argentina), Nov. 26.

King Philip
V — A542

Rulers of Spain: No. 2124, Louis I. 8p, Ferdinand VI. 10p, Carlos III. 12p, Carlos IV. 15p, Ferdinand VII. 20p, Isabella II. 25p, Alfonso XII. 50p, Alfonso XIII. 100p, Juan Carlos I.

1978, Nov. 22	Engr.		Perf. 13	
2123	A542	5p dk blue & rose red	.25	.25
2124	A542	5p olive & dull grn	.25	.25
2125	A542	8p vio bl & red brn	.25	.25
2126	A542	10p blue grn & blk	.25	.25
2127	A542	12p brown & mar	.25	.25
2128	A542	15p black & indigo	.25	.25
2129	A542	20p olive & indigo	.25	.25
2130	A542	25p ultra & vio brn	.30	.25
2131	A542	50p vermilion & brn	.55	.25
2132	A542	100p ultra & vio blk	1.10	.35
	Nos. 2123-2132 (10)		3.70	2.60

Spanish Flag, Preamble to
Constitution, Parliament — A543

1978, Dec.   Photo.   Perf. 13
2133 A543 5p multicolored   .25 .25
Proclamation of New Constitution.

Illuminated Pages from Bible and
Codex — A544

1978, Dec. 27
2134 A544 5p multicolored   .25 .25
Millennium of the consecration of the Basilica of Santa Maria de Ripoll.

Car and Drop of
Oil — A545

Designs: 8p, Insulated house and thermometer. 10p, Hand pulling plug.

1979, Jan. 24   Photo.   Perf. 13
2135 A545 5p multicolored   .25 .25
2136 A545 8p multicolored   .25 .25
2137 A545 10p multicolored   .25 .25
Nos. 2135-2137 (3)   .75 .75
Energy conservation.

De La
Salle,
Students
A546

1979, Feb. 14   Photo.   Perf. 13
2138 A546 5p multicolored   .25 .25
Institute of Christian Brothers, founded by Jean-Baptiste de la Salle, centenary.

Jorge
Manrique — A547

Portraits: 8p, Fernan Caballero (pen name of Cecilia Böhl de Faber). 10p, Francisco Villaespesa. 20p, Gregorio Marañon.

1979, Feb. 28   Engr.
2139 A547 5p green & brown   .25 .25
2140 A547 8p dark red & blue   .25 .25
2141 A547 10p brown & purple   .25 .25
2142 A547 20p green & olive   .25 .25
Nos. 2139-2142 (4)   1.00 1.00

Jorge Manrique, poet, 500th death anniversary; Fernan Caballero, Francisco Villaespesa, and Gregorio Marañon, writers, birth centenaries.

Running
and
Jumping
A548

Sport for All: 8p, Children kicking ball and skipping rope, jogging and bicycling. 10p, Family jogging, and dog.

1979, Mar. 14   Photo.   Perf. 13
2143 A548 5p multicolored   .25 .25
2144 A548 8p multicolored   .25 .25
2145 A548 10p multicolored   .25 .25
Nos. 2143-2145 (3)   .75 .75

Children in
Library
A549

1979, Apr. 27   Photo.   Perf. 13
2146 A549 5p multicolored   .25 .25
International Year of the Child.

Manuel Ysasi (1810-1855) Postal
Reformer — A550

Europa: 5p, Mounted messenger and postilion, 1761 engraving, vert.

1979, Apr. 30   Engr.
2147 A550 5p brown & sepia   .25 .25
2148 A550 12p red brn & sl grn   .25 .25

Radar and
Satellite
A551

5p, Symbolic people and cables, vert.

1979, May 17   Photo.   Perf. 13
2149 A551 5p multicolored   .25 .25
2150 A551 8p multicolored   .25 .25
World Telecommunications Day, May 17.

Bulgaria No. 1, Sofia Opera House,
Housing Development — A552

1979, May 18
2151 A552 12p multicolored   .25 .25
Philaserdica '79, International Philatelic Exhibition, Sofia, Bulgaria, May 18-27.

Tank, Jet
and
Destroyer
A553

1979, May 25
2152 A553 5p multicolored   .25 .25
Armed Forces Day.

Messenger Handing Letter to
King — A554

1979, June 15   Litho. & Engr.
2153 A554 5p multicolored   .25 .25
Stamp Day 1979.

Daroca Gate,
Zaragoza — A555

Architecture: 8p, Gerona Cathedral. 10p, Interior, Carthusian Monastery Church, Granada. 20p, Portal, Palace of the Marques de Dos Aguas, Valencia.

1979, June 27   Engr.
2154 A555 5p vio bl & lilac brn   .25 .25
2155 A555 8p dk blue & sepia   .25 .25
2156 A555 10p black & green   .25 .25
2157 A555 20p brown & sepia   .25 .25
Nos. 2154-2157 (4)   1.00 1.00

Turkey
Sponge
A556

Fauna: 7p, Crayfish. 8p, Scorpion. 20p, Starfish. 25p, Sea anemone.

1979, July 11   Photo.   Perf. 13
2158 A556 5p multicolored   .25 .25
2159 A556 7p multicolored   .25 .25
2160 A556 8p multicolored   .25 .25
2161 A556 20p multicolored   .25 .25
2162 A556 25p multicolored   .30 .25
Nos. 2158-2162 (5)   1.30 1.25

Gen.
Antonio
Gutierrez
and Battle
A557

1979, Aug.   Engr.
2163 A557 5p multicolored   .25 .25
Naval defense of Tenerife, 18th century.

A558

Juan de Juanes Paintings: 8p, Immaculate Conception. 10p, Holy Family. 15p, Ecce Homo. 20p, St. Stephen in the Synagogue. 25p, The Last Supper, horiz. 50p, Adoration of the Mystic Lamb, horiz.

1979, Sept. 28   Photo.   Perf. 13x13½
2164 A558 8p multicolored   .25 .25
2165 A558 10p multicolored   .25 .25
2166 A558 15p multicolored   .25 .25
2167 A558 20p multicolored   .25 .25
2168 A558 25p multicolored   .30 .25
2169 A558 50p multicolored   .55 .25
Nos. 2164-2169 (6)   1.85 1.50

For other art types see A384, A397, A410, A431, A448, A473, A501, A522, A538 and footnote following No. 876.

A559

Zaragoza Cathedral, Mother and Child statue.

1979, Oct. 3   Photo.   Perf. 13x13½
2170 A559 5p multicolored   .25 .25
8th Mariology and 15th International Marianist Congresses, Zaragoza, Oct. 3-12.

Felipe de
Borbon,
Hospital
A560

1979, Oct.   Perf. 13½x13
2171 A560 5p multicolored   .25 .25
Hospital of the Child Jesus, centenary.

St. Bartholomew College,
Bogota — A561

Hispanidad 79: 12p, University of St. Mark, Lima, coat of arms.

1979, Oct. 12   Engr.   Perf. 13
2172 A561 7p multicolored   .25 .25
2173 A561 12p multicolored   .25 .25

Clasped Hands, Badge, Governor's Palace A562

Design: No. 2175, Statute book, vert.

Lithographed and Engraved
1979, Oct. 27   *Perf. 13*
2174 A562 8p multicolored .25 .25
2175 A562 8p multicolored .25 .25

Catalonian and Basque autonomy statute.

Type A54, Barcelona Coat of Arms A563

Photogravure and Engraved
1979, Nov. 6   *Perf. 13½x13*
2176 A563 5p multicolored .25 .25

Barcelona Philatelic Congress and Exhibition, 50th anniversary.

Nativity, Capital from St. Peter the Elder A564

Christmas 1979: 19p, Flight into Egypt, column from St. Peter the Elder, Huesca.

1979, Nov. 14   **Photo.**
2177 A564 8p multicolored .25 .25
2178 A564 19p multicolored .25 .25

Carlos I, Coat of Arms A565

Kings of the House of Austria (Hapsburg Dynasty): 20p, Philip II. 25p, Philip III. 50c, Philip IV. 100p, Carlos II.

1979, Nov. 22   **Engr.**   *Perf. 13*
2179 A565 15p sl grn & dk bl .25 .25
2180 A565 20p dk blue & mag .25 .25
2181 A565 25p violet & yel bis .30 .25
2182 A565 50p brown & sl grn .55 .25
2183 A565 100p magenta & brn 1.10 .30
    Nos. 2179-2183 (5) 2.45 1.30

2nd International Olive Oil Year — A566

1979, Dec. 4   **Photo.**   *Perf. 13½x13*
2184 A566 8p multicolored .25 .25

King Juan Carlos I Type of 1976
1980-84   **Photo.**   *Perf. 13*
2185 A497 13p dk red brn ('81) .25 .25
2186 A497 14p red orange ('82) .25 .25
2187 A497 16p sepia .30 .25
2188 A497 17p bluish gray ('84) .25 .25
2189 A497 19p orange .35 .25
2190 A497 30p dk green ('81) .40 .25
2191 A497 50p org ver ('81) .90 .25
2192 A497 60p blue ('81) .80 .25
2193 A497 75p brt yel grn ('81) 1.00 .30
2194 A497 85p gray ('81) 1.25 .45
    Nos. 2185-2194 (10) 5.75 2.75

No. 2186 and 2187 also issued as coil with number on back of every fifth stamp.

Train and People A567

1980, Feb. 20   **Engr.**   *Perf. 13½*
2200 A567 3p shown .25 .25
2201 A567 4p Bus .25 .25
2202 A567 5p Subway .25 .25
    Nos. 2200-2202 (3) .75 .75

Public transportation.

Steel Export A568

1980, Mar. 15   **Photo.**   *Perf. 13½x13*
2203 A568 5p shown .25 .25
2204 A568 8p Ships .25 .25
2205 A568 13p Shoes .25 .25
2206 A568 19p Machinery .25 .25
2207 A568 25p Technology .30 .25
    Nos. 2203-2207 (5) 1.30 1.25

Federico Garcia Lorca (1899-1936) — A569

Europa: 19p, José Ortega y Gasset (1883-1955), philosopher and statesman.

1980, Apr. 28   **Engr.**   *Perf. 13½*
2208 A569 8p violet & ol grn .25 .25
2209 A569 19p brown & dk grn .25 .25

Armed Forces Day A570

1980, May 24   **Photo.**   *Perf. 13½x13*
2210 A570 8p multicolored .25 .25

Soccer Players A571

1980, May 23
2211 A571 8p shown .25 .25
2212 A571 19p Soccer ball, flags .25 .25

World Soccer Cup 1982.

Bourbon Arms, Ministry of Finance A572

1980, June 9   **Engr.**   *Perf. 13½*
2213 A572 8p dark brown .25 .25

Public Finances in Bourbon Spain Exhibition.

Helen Keller, Sign Language A573

1980, June 27
2214 A573 19p dk yel grn & rose lake .25 .25

Helen Keller (1880-1968), deaf mute writer and lecturer.

Mounted Postman, 12th Century Panel, Barcelona — A574

Lithographed and Engraved
1980, June 28   *Perf. 13x12½*
2215 A574 8p multicolored .25 .25

Stamp Day.

King Alfonso and Count of Maceda at 1930 National Exhibition A575

1980, July 1   **Photo.**   *Perf. 13½*
2216 A575 8p multicolored .25 .25

1st Natl. Stamp Exhibition, Barcelona, 50th anniv.

A576

Altar of the Virgin, La Palma Cathedral.

1980, July 12   **Engr.**   *Perf. 13*
2217 A576 8p black & brown .25 .25

Appearance of the Virgin of the Snow at La Palma, 300th anniversary.

A577

1980, Aug. 9   **Engr.**   *Perf. 13*
2218 A577 100p slate & sepia 1.10 .25

Ramon Perez de Ayala (1881-1962), novelist and diplomat.

La Atlantida Ruins, Mexican Bonampak Musicians — A578

Designs: b, Sun Gate, Tiahuanaco; Roman arch, Medinaceli. c, Alonso de Ercilla, Garcilaso de la Vega; title pages from La Arauca and Commentario Reales. d, Virgin of Quito, Virgin of Seafarers.

1980, Oct. 3   **Engr.**   *Perf. 13*
2219 A578 Sheet of 4 + 2 labels 2.25 2.25
  a. 25p multicolored .30 .30
  b. 25p multicolored .30 .30
  c. 50p multicolored .55 .45
  d. 100p multicolored 1.10 .85

ESPAMER '80 Stamp Exhib., Madrid, Oct. 3-12.

400th Anniversary of Buenos Aires — A579

1980, Oct. 24
2220 A579 19p multicolored .25 .25

Miniature Sheet

The Creation, Tapestry, Gerona Cathedral — A580

1980, Nov.   **Litho.**   *Perf. 13½x13*
2221 A580 Sheet of 6 2.50 2.00
  a.-c. 25p, any single .25 .25
  d.-f. 50p, any single .55 .25

Conference Building, Flags of Participants A581

1980, Nov. 11   **Photo.**   *Perf. 13½*
2222 A581 22p multicolored .25 .25

Holy Family Church of Santa Maria, Cuina — A582

Christmas 1980, 22p, Adoration of the Kings, portal, Church of Santa Maria, Cuina, horiz.

1980, Nov. 12
2223 A582 10p multicolored .25 .25
2224 A582 22p multicolored .25 .25

Pedro Vives and His Airplane A583

Designs: Aviation pioneers.

1980, Dec. 10
2225 A583 5p shown .25 .25
2226 A583 10p Benito Loygorri .25 .25
2227 A583 15p Alfonso De Orleans .25 .25
2228 A583 22p Alfredo Kindelan .25 .25
　　Nos. 2225-2228 (4) 1.00 1.00

Winter University Games A584

1981, Mar. 4　　Perf. 13½x13
2229 A584 30p multicolored .35 .25

Picasso's Birth Centenary Emblem, by Joan Miro — A585

1981, Mar. 27　　Perf. 13
2230 A585 100p multicolored 1.00 .25
　　Pablo Picasso (1881-1973).

Galician Autonomy — A586

1981, Mar. 27　Photo.　Perf. 13
2231 A586 12p multicolored .25 .25

Homage to the Press A587

1981, Apr. 8　Photo.　Perf. 13½x13
2232 A587 12p multicolored .25 .25

International Year of the Disabled — A588

1981, Apr. 29　　　　Litho.
2233 A588 30p multicolored .35 .25

Soccer Players A589

1981, May 2　　　　Photo.
2234 A589 12p Soccer players, diff., vert. .25 .25
2235 A589 30p shown .35 .25
　　1982 World Cup Soccer.

Europa Issue 1981

La Jota Folkdance A590

1981, May 4　　　　Engr.
2236 A590 12p shown .25 .25
2237 A590 30p Virgin of Rocio procession .35 .25

Armed Forces Day — A591

1981, May 29　Photo.　Perf. 13x13½
2238 A591 12p multicolored .25 .25

Gabriel Miro (1879-1930), Writer — A592

Famous Men: 12p, Francisco de Quevedo (1580-1645), writer. 30p, St. Benedict (480-543), patron saint of Europe.

1981, June 17　　　　Engr.
2239 A592 6p purple & dk grn .25 .25
2240 A592 12p brown & purple .25 .25
2241 A592 30p dk green & brown .35 .25
　　Nos. 2239-2241 (3) .85 .75

Mail Messenger, 14th Cent., Woodcut A593

Photogravure and Engraved
1981, June 19　　Perf. 12½x13
2242 A593 12p multicolored .25 .25
　　Stamp Day.

Map of Balearic Islands, Diego Homem's Atlas, 1563 — A594

1981, July 8　Photo.　Perf. 13x12½
2243 A594 7p shown .25 .25
2244 A594 12p Canary Islds., Prunes map, 1563 .25 .25

Kings Alfonso XII and Juan Carlos, Advocates Arms A595

1981, July 27　Engr.　Perf. 13½x13
2245 A595 50p multicolored .55 .25
　　Chamber of Advocates of State (Public Prosecutor) centenary.

King Sancius VI of Navarre with City Charter, 12th Cent. Miniature A596

1981, Aug. 5　Photo.　Perf. 12½x13
2246 A596 12p multicolored .25 .25
　　Vitoria, 800th anniv.

Exports A597

1981, Sept. 30　Photo.　Perf. 13½x13
2247 A597 6p Fruit .25 .25
2248 A597 12p Wine .25 .25
2249 A597 30p Vehicles .35 .25
　　Nos. 2247-2249 (3) .85 .75

Congress Palace, Buenos Aires A598

1981, Oct. 12　Engr.　Perf. 13½x13
2250 A598 12p dk bl & car rose .25 .25
　　ESPAMER '81 Intl. Stamp Exhibition, Buenos Aires, Nov. 13-22.

World Food Day A599

1981, Oct. 16
2251 A599 30p multicolored .35 .25

Souvenir Sheet

Guernica, by Pablo Picasso (1881-1973) — A600

1981, Oct. 25　　　　Photo.
2252 A600 200p multicolored 2.25 2.25
　　Control number comes in two types.

A601

Christmas 1981: 12p, Adoration of the Kings, Cervera de Pisuerga, Palencia. 30p, Nativity, Paredes de Nava.

1981, Nov. 18　Litho.　Perf. 13
2253 A601 12p shown .25 .25
2254 A601 30p multicolored .35 .25

A602

King Juan Carlos I.

1981, Oct. 21　Engr.　Perf. 13x12½
2268 A602 100p brown 1.25 .25
2269 A602 200p dark green 2.60 .25
2270 A602 500p dark blue 6.25 .55
　　Nos. 2268-2270 (3) 10.10 1.05

Postal Museum, Madrid A603

1981, Nov. 30　Engr.　Perf. 13
2273 A603 7p Telegrapher .25 .25
2274 A603 12p Coach .25 .25
Souvenir Sheet
2275　　Sheet of 4 1.90 1.90
c.　A603 50p Emblem .55 .50
d.　A603 100p Cap, posthorn, pouch 1.10 1.00
　　No. 2275 also contains Nos. 2273, 2274.

Royal Mint Building, Seville A604

1981, Dec. 4　Engr.　Perf. 13
2276 A604 12p black & brown .25 .25
　　Spanish Administration of the Bourbons in the Indies.

A605

12p, Iparraguirre (1820-81). 30p, Juan Ramon Jimenez (1881-1958), writer. 50p, Pedro Calderon (1600-81), playwright.

1981-82
2277	A605	12p black & dk bl	.25	.25
2278	A605	30p dk bl & dk grn	.35	.25
2279	A605	50p black & violet	.55	.25
		Nos. 2277-2279 (3)	1.15	.75

Issued: 12p, 12/16; 30p, 50p, 3/10/82.

A606

1982, Feb. 24   **Photo.**
2280	A606	14p Poster by Joan Miro	.25	.25
2281	A606	33p Cup, emblem	.40	.25

Espana '82 World Cup Soccer.

A607   A608

1982, Mar. 10   **Engr.**
2282	A607	30p grn & dk grn	.35	.25

Andres Bello (1782-1865), writer.

1982, Mar. 31   **Photo.**   *Perf. 13*
2283	A608	14p St. John of Compostelo	.25	.25

Holy Year of Compostelo.

A609-A610

Operetta composers and scenes from their works: #2284, Manuel Fernandez Caballero (1835-1906). #2285, Gigantes and Cabezudos. #2286, Amadeo Vives Roig (1871-1932). #2287, Dona Francisquita. #2288, Tomas Breton Hernandez (1850-1923). #2289, Verbena of Paloma.

Lithographed and Engraved
1982, Apr. 28   *Perf. 13*
2284	A609	3p multicolored	.25	.25
2285	A610	3p multicolored	.25	.25
a.		Pair, #2284-2285	.25	.25
2286	A609	6p multicolored	.25	.25
2287	A610	6p multicolored	.25	.25
a.		Pair, #2284-2285	.25	.25
2288	A609	8p multicolored	.25	.25
2289	A610	8p multicolored	.25	.25
a.		Pair, #2284-2285	.25	.25

See Nos. 2319-2324, 2378-2383.

Europa 1982 — A611

1982, May 3   **Engr.**   *Perf. 12½*
2290	A611	14p Unification, 1512	.25	.25
2291	A611	33p Discovery of New World, 1492	.40	.25

Armed Forces Day — A612

1982, May 28   **Photo.**   *Perf. 13*
2292	A612	14p multicolored	.25	.25

1982 World Cup A613

Designs: Soccer players.

1982, June 13   *Perf. 13*
2293	A613	14p multicolored	.25	.25
2294	A613	33p multicolored	.40	.25

Souvenir Sheets
2295		Sheets of 4, #2293-2294, 9p, 100p, each	1.75	1.75
a.	A613	9p Captains' handshake	.25	.25
b.	A613	100p Player holding cup	1.10	1.10

#2295 has two types of margin, each showing 7 arms of the 14 host cities. One sheet has 3 blue coats of arms, the other has 2.

Stamp Day — A614

1982, July 16   **Litho.**   *Perf. 12½*
2296	A614	14p Map, postal code	.25	.25

Organ Transplants A615

1982, July 28   **Photo.**   *Perf. 13*
2297	A615	14p Symbolic organs	.25	.25

Storks and Express Train — A616

Locomotive, 1850 — A617

Perf. 12½, 13 (A617)
1982, Sept. 27   **Photo.**
2298	A616	9p shown	.25	.25
2299	A617	14p shown	.25	.25
2300	A617	33p Santa Fe locomotive	.40	.25
		Nos. 2298-2300 (3)	.90	.75

23rd Intl. Railways Congress, Malaga.

ESPAMER '82 Intl. Stamp Exhibition, San Juan, Oct. 12-17 A618

1982, Oct. 12   **Engr.**   *Perf. 13½x13*
2301	A618	33p dk blue & pur	.40	.25

St. Teresa of Avila (1515-1582) — A619

1982, Oct. 15
2302	A619	33p Statue by Gregorio Hernandez	.40	.25

Visit of Pope John Paul II, Oct. 31-Nov. 9 — A620

1982, Oct. 31   **Engr.**   *Perf. 12½*
2303	A620	14p multicolored	.25	.25

Water Wheel, Alcantarilla A621

Landscapes and Monuments: 6p, Bank of Spain, 19th cent., horiz. 9p, Crucifixion. 14p, St. Martin's Tower, Teruel. 33p, St. Andrew's Gate, Zamora.

1982, Nov. 5   *Perf. 13x12½, 12½x13*
2304	A621	4p gray & dk blue	.25	.25
2305	A621	6p dk blue & gray	.25	.25
2306	A621	9p brt blue & vio	.25	.25
2307	A621	14p brt blue & vio	.25	.25
2308	A621	33p claret & brown	.40	.25
		Nos. 2304-2308 (5)	1.40	1.25

Christmas 1982 A622

1982, Nov. 17   **Photo.**   *Perf. 13½*
2309	A622	14p Nativity, wood carving, by Gil de Siloe	.25	.25
2310	A622	33p Flight into Egypt	.40	.25

Pablo Gargallo, Sculptor, Birth Centenary A623

1982, Dec. 9   **Engr.**   *Perf. 13*
2311	A623	14p blue & dk grn	.25	.25

Salesian Fathers in Spain, Centenary A624

1982, Dec. 16   **Photo.**   *Perf. 12½x13*
2312	A624	14p multicolored	.25	.25

Arms of King Juan Carlos I A625

1983, Feb. 9   **Photo.**   *Perf. 12½*
2313	A625	14p multicolored	.25	.25

Andalusia Autonomy Statute A626

1983   **Litho.**   *Perf. 13½*
2314	A626	14p shown	.25	.25
2315	A626	14p Cantabria	.25	.25

Issued: #2314, Feb. 28; #2315, Mar. 15.

State Security Forces A627

1983, Mar. 23   **Photo.**
2316	A627	9p	Natl. Police Force	.25	.25
2317	A627	14p	Civil Guard	.25	.25
2318	A627	33p	Superior Police Corps	.40	.25

Operetta Type of 1982

Designs: #2319, Scene from La Parranda. Francisco Alonso Lopez (1887-1948). #2320, Francisco Alonso Lopez (1887-1948). #2321, Jacinto Guerrero y Torres (1895-1951). #2322, Scene from La Rosa del Azafran. #2323, Jesus de Guridi Bidaola (1886-1961). #2324, Scene from El Caserio.

Lithographed and Engraved
1983, Apr. 22   **Perf. 13**
2319	A610	4p	multicolored	.25	.25
2320	A609	4p	multicolored	.25	.25
a.			Pair, #2319-2320	.25	.25
2321	A609	6p	multicolored	.25	.25
2322	A610	6p	multicolored	.25	.25
a.			Pair, #2321-2322	.25	.25
2323	A609	9p	multicolored	.25	.25
2324	A610	9p	multicolored	.25	.25
a.			Pair, #2323-2324	.35	.35

Europa 1983 — A628

Designs: 16p, Scene from Don Quixote, by Miguel Cervantes. 38p, L. Torres Quevaedo's Niagara Spanish aerocar.

1983, May 5   **Engr.**   **Perf. 13x12½**
Granite Paper
2325	A628	16p	dk grn & brn red	.25	.25
2326	A628	38p	brown	.45	.25

Francisco Salzillo Alvarez (1707-83), Painter — A629

Designs: 38p, Antonio Soler Ramos (1729-1783), composer. 50p, Joaquin Turina Perez (1882-1949), composer. 100p, St. Isidro Labrador (1082-1170), patron saint of Madrid.

1983, May 14   **Perf. 13**
2327	A629	16p	purple & dk grn	.25	.25
2328	A629	38p	blue & brown	.45	.25
2329	A629	50p	bl grn & dk brn	.55	.25
2330	A629	100p	red brn & pur	1.10	.25
			Nos. 2327-2330 (4)	2.35	1.00

World Communications Year — A630

1983, May 17   **Photo.**   **Perf. 13**
2331	A630	38p	multicolored	.45	.25

Rioja Autonomous Region — A631

Lithographed and Engraved
1983, May 25   **Perf. 13**
2332	A631	16p	multicolored	.25	.25

Armed Forces Day — A632

1983, May 26   **Photo.**
2333	A632	16p	multicolored	.25	.25

Intl. Canine Exhibition, Madrid, June 1984 A633

Lithographed and Engraved
1983, June 8   **Perf. 13½**
2334	A633	10p	Pointer	.25	.25
2335	A633	16p	Mastiff	.25	.25
2336	A633	26p	Iberian hound	.35	.25
2337	A633	38p	Navarro pointer	.50	.25
			Nos. 2334-2337 (4)	1.35	1.00

Discovery of Tungsten Bicentenary — A634

Scouting Year A635

400th Anniv. of University of Zaragoza A636

1983, June 22   **Photo.**   **Perf. 13**
2338	A634	16p	Elhuyar brothers	.25	.25
2339	A635	38p	multicolored	.45	.25
2340	A636	50p	multicolored	.60	.25
			Nos. 2338-2340 (3)	1.30	.75

Murcia Autonomous Region — A637

Photogravure and Engraved
1983, July 8   **Perf. 13½**
2341	A637	16p	Arms	.25	.25

Asturias Autonomous Region — A638

Lithographed and Engraved
1983, Sept. 8   **Perf. 13**
2342	A638	14p	Victory Cross, Covadonga Basilica	.25	.25

Intl. Institute of Statistics, 44th Congress, Madrid, Sept. 12-22 A639

1983, Sept. 12   **Photo.**   **Perf. 13**
2343	A639	38p	Institute building	.45	.25

Stamp Day — A640

Lithographed and Engraved
1983, Oct. 8   **Perf. 13x12½**
2344	A640	16p	Roman mail cart	.35	.30

No. 2344 se-tenant with label publicizing ESPANA '84 Philatelic Exhibition, April 27-May 6, 1984.

Valencia Autonomy Statute, 1st Anniv. A641

1983, Oct. 10   **Perf. 13**
2345	A641	16p	multicolored	.25	.25

View of Seville, 16th cent. — A642

1983, Oct. 12   **Engr.**   **Perf. 12½x13**
2346	A642	38p	multicolored	.45	.25

Spanish-American trade in 17th century.

Stained-glass Windows A643

Designs: 10p, King, Leon Cathedral. 16p, Epiphany, Gerona Cathedral. 38p, Apostle Santiago, Royal Hospital Chapel, Santiago.

Lithographed and Engraved
1983, Oct. 28   **Perf. 12½x13**
2347	A643	10p	multicolored	.25	.25
2348	A643	16p	multicolored	.25	.25
2349	A643	38p	multicolored	.45	.25
			Nos. 2347-2349 (3)	.95	.75

Church at Llivia, Gerona — A644

Designs: 6p, Temple, Santa Maria del Mar, Barcelona. 16p, Cathedral, Ceuta. 38p, Gate of the Santiago Bridge, Melilla. 50p, Charity Hospital, Seville.

1983, Nov. 9   **Engr.**   **Perf. 13x12½**
2350	A644	3p	dk bl gray & grn	.25	.25
2351	A644	6p	dark blue gray	.25	.25
2352	A644	16p	red brn & dull vio	.25	.25
2353	A644	38p	bis brn & rose car	.45	.25
2354	A644	50p	brown & org red	.55	.25
			Nos. 2350-2354 (5)	1.75	1.25

Christmas 1983 — A645

1983, Nov. 23   **Photo.**   **Perf. 13x13½**
2355	A645	16p	The Nativity, Tortosa	.25	.25
2356	A645	38p	The Adoration, Vich	.45	.25

Indalecio Prieto (1883-1962), Patriot — A646

1983, Dec. 14   **Engr.**   **Perf. 13**
2357	A646	16p	red brn & blk	.25	.25

Industrial Accident Prevention A647

1984, Jan. 25   **Photo.**   **Perf. 13½**
2358	A647	7p	Construction worker	.25	.25
2359	A647	10p	Fire	.25	.25
2360	A647	16p	Electrical plug, pliers	.25	.25
			Nos. 2358-2360 (3)	.75	.75

Extremadura Statute of Autonomy, First Anniv. — A648

Lithographed and Engraved
1984, Feb. 25   **Perf. 13**
2361	A648	16p	multicolored	.25	.25

1500th Anniv. of City of Burgos A649

1984, Mar. 1   Engr.
2362 A649 16p multicolored   .25 .25

Carnivals A650

1984   Photo.   *Perf. 13½x13*
2363 A650 16p Santa Cruz de Tenerife   .25 .25
2364 A650 16p Valencia Fallas   .25 .25

Issued: #2363, Mar. 5; #2364, Mar. 16.

Man and the Biosphere A651

1984, Apr. 11
2365 A651 38p da Vinci's Study of Man   .45 .25

Aragon Statute of Autonomy, 2nd Anniv. A652

Lithographed and Engraved
1984, Apr. 23   *Perf. 13x13½*
2366 A652 16p Map   .25 .25

Souvenir Sheet

Juan Carlos — A653

Espana '84 (Spanish Royal Family): b, Sofia of Greece. c, Cristina de Borbon. d, Prince of Asturias Felipe de Borbon. e, Elene de Borbon.

1984, Apr. 27   *Perf. 12½x13*
2367 A653 Sheet of 5   3.25 3.25
   a.-e.   38p, any single   .65 .65

Congress Emblem — A654

1984, May 3   Engr.   *Perf. 13x13½*
2368 A654 38p purple & red   .45 .25

World Philatelic Federation, 53rd Congress, Madrid, May 7-9.

Europa (1959-84) A655

1984, May 5
2369 A655 16p orange   .25 .25
2370 A655 38p dark blue   .45 .25

Armed Forces Day A656

Design: 17p, Monument to Hunters Regiment of Caceres, by Mariano Benlliure.

1984, May 19   Photo.   *Perf. 13½x13*
2371 A656 17p multicolored   .25 .25

Canary Islds. Statute of Autonomy — A657

Lithographed and Engraved
1984, May 29   *Perf. 13*
2372 A657 16p Arms, map   .25 .25

Castilla-La Mancha Statute of Autonomy — A658

1984, May 31   *Perf. 13*
2373 A658 17p Arms   .25 .25

King Alfonso X (1252-84) A659

Design: 38p, Ignacio Barroquer (1884-1965), ophthalmologist

1984, June 20   Engr.   *Perf. 13*
2374 A659 16p multicolored   .25 .25
2375 A659 38p multicolored   .45 .25

Balearic Islands Statute of Autonomy — A660

1984, June 29   Litho. & Engr.
2376 A660 17p multicolored   .25 .25

Feast of San Fermin of Pamplona A661

1984, July 5   Photo.
2377 A661 17p Bull runners   .25 .25

Operetta Type of 1982
#2378, El Nino Judio. #2379, Pablo Luna (1880-1942). #2380, Ruperto Chapi (1851-1909). #2381, La Revoltosa. #2382, La Reina Mora. #2383, Jose Serrano (1873-1941).

Lithographed and Engraved
1984, July 20   *Perf. 13*
2378 A610   6p multicolored   .25 .25
2379 A609   6p multicolored   .25 .25
   a.   Pair, #2378-2379   .25 .25
2380 A609   7p multicolored   .25 .25
2381 A610   7p multicolored   .25 .25
   a.   Pair, #2380-2381   .25 .25
2382 A610 10p multicolored   .25 .25
2383 A609 10p multicolored   .25 .25
   a.   Pair, #2382-2383   .30 .30

1984 Summer Olympics A662

Greek or Roman sculptures.

1984, July 27   Photo.
2384 A662 1p Chariot race   .25 .25
2385 A662 2p Diving, vert.   .25 .25
2386 A662 5p Wrestling   .25 .25
2387 A662 8p Discus, vert.   .25 .25
   Nos. 2384-2387 (4)   1.00 1.00

Navarra Statute of Autonomy A663

Lithographed and Engraved
1984, Aug. 16   *Perf. 13*
2388 A663 17p multicolored   .25 .25

Intl. Bicycling Championship, Barcelona, Aug. 27-Sept. 2 — A664

1984, Aug. 27   Photo.
2389 A664 17p multicolored   .25 .25

Castilla and Leon Statute of Autonomy A665

1984, Sept. 5   Litho. & Engr.
2390 A665 17p multicolored   .25 .25

Jerez Vintage Feast — A666

1984, Sept. 20   Photo.   *Perf. 13*
2391 A666 17p Women picking grapes   .25 .25

Journey to the Holy Land by Sister Egeria, 1600th Anniv. — A667

1984, Sept. 26
2392 A667 40p Map, Sister Egeria   .45 .25

Stamp Day — A668

1984, Oct. 5   Litho. & Engr.
2393 A668 17p Arab postrider   .25 .25

Father Junipero Serra (1713-84), Mission Founder in California A669

1984, Oct. 12   Engr.   *Perf. 13*
2394 A669 40p Map, Serra, mission   .45 .25

Christmas 1984 A670

1984, Nov. 21   Photo.
2395 A670 17p Nativity   .25 .25
2396 A670 40p Adoration of the Kings, vert.   .45 .25

Madrid Autonomy Statue A671

1984, Nov. 28   Litho. & Engr.
2397 A671 17p Arms, buildings   .25 .25

Andean Pact, 15th Anniv. A672

Condor, Flags of Bolivia, Colombia, Ecuador, Peru and Venezuela.

1985, Jan. 16   Photo.   Perf. 13
2398 A672 17p multicolored   .25 .25

The Virgin of Louvain, by Jan Gossaert (c. 1478-1536) A673

1985, Jan. 21   Perf. 13½
2399 A673 40p multicolored   .45 .25
EUROPALIA '85. See Belgium No. 1185.

Santa Cruz College, Valladolid University, 500th Anniv. — A674

1985, Feb. 20   Litho. & Engr.
2400 A674 17p Main gateway   .25 .25

OLYMPHILEX '85, Lausanne, Switz. — A675

1985, Mar. 18   Photo.
2401 A675 40p multicolored   .45 .25

ESPAMER '85, Cuba A676

1985, Mar. 20   Engr.
2402 A676 40p Cathedral, Havana   .45 .25

Fairs A677

Perf. 13½, 13½x14 (#2405)
1985   Photo.
2403 A677 17p Seville   .25 .25
2404 A677 17p Alcoy   .25 .25
2405 A677 17p Arriondas-Ribadesella .25 .25
2406 A677 18p Toledo, vert.   .25 .25
      Nos. 2403-2406 (4)   1.00 1.00

Issued: #2403, Apr. 16; #2404, Apr. 22; #2405, Aug. 2; #2406, June 6.

Intl. Youth Year — A678

1985, Apr. 17   Engr.   Perf. 13½
2407 A678 17p blk, hn brn & dk grn .25 .25

Europa '85 A680

Designs: 18p, Antonio de Cabezon (1510-1566), organist and composer, court Musician to Felipe II. 45p, Natl. Youth Orchestra.

1985, May 3   Engr.
2408 A680 18p dk bl, dk red & blk, buff .25 .25
2409 A680 45p ol grn, dk red & blk, buff .45 .25

Armed Forces Day A681

1985, May 24   Photo.
2410 A681 18p multicolored   .25 .25

Natl. Flag Bicent. — A682

#2411, Arms of King Carlos III, text of 1785 Decree, sailing ship Santisima Trinidad. #2412, Natl. arms, Article No. 4 from 1978 Constitution, lion ornament from Chamber of Deputies Building.

Lithographed and Engraved
1985, May 28   Perf. 13x13½
2411 18p multicolored   .25 .25
2412 18p multicolored   .25 .25
   a. A682 Pair, #2411-2412   .50 .45

Intl. Environment Day — A683

1985, June 5   Photo.
2413 A683 17p multicolored   .25 .25

Juan Carlos — A684

1985-92   Photo.   Perf. 14
2414 A684 10c indigo   .25 .25
2415 A684 50c lt blue green   .25 .25
2416 A684 1p brt blue   .25 .25
2417 A684 2p dark green   .25 .25
2418 A684 3p chestnut brn   .25 .25
2419 A684 4p olive green   .25 .25
2420 A684 5p brt rose lilac   .25 .25
2421 A684 6p brown black   .25 .25
2422 A684 7p brt violet   .25 .25
2423 A684 7p apple grn   .25 .25
2424 A684 8p gray black   .25 .25
2425 A684 10p lake   .25 .25
2426 A684 12p red   .25 .25
2427 A684 13p Prus blue   .25 .25
2428 A684 15p emerald   .25 .25
2429 A684 17p yellow bis   .25 .25
2430 A684 18p brt grnsh bl   .25 .25
2431 A684 19p violet brn   .25 .25
   a. Booklet pane of 6   1.50
2432 A684 20p brt pink   .25 .25
2433 A684 25p olive green   .30 .25
2434 A684 27p deep rose lil   .35 .25
2435 A684 30p ultra   .35 .25
2436 A684 45p brt green   .50 .25
2437 A684 50p violet blue   .55 .25
2438 A684 55p black brown   .60 .25
2439 A684 60p dark orange   .65 .25
2440 A684 75p deep rose lil   .80 .30
      Nos. 2414-2440 (27)   8.85 6.80

Issued: 1p, 5p, 8p, 12p, 18p, 45p, 6/12; #2422, 17p, 7/16; #2423, 1/86; 2p, 3p, 4p, 10p, 4/3/86; 19p, 9/27/86; 6p, 20p, 30p, 1/26/87; 50p, 60p, 75p, 4/24/89; 10c, 50c, 13p, 15p, 5/16/89; 25p, 55p, 12/14/90; 27p, 2/92.

Astrophysical Observatory Opening, La Palma, Canary Islands — A685

1985, June 25   Photo.   Perf. 14
2441 A685 45p multicolored   .50 .25

European Music Year — A686

Designs: 12p, Ataulfo Argenta, conductor. 17p, Tomas Luis de Victoria, composer. 45p, Fernando Sor, composer.

Litho. & Engr.
1985, June 26   Perf. 13
2442 A686 12p multicolored   .25 .25
2443 A686 17p multicolored   .25 .25
2444 A686 45p multicolored   .50 .25
      Nos. 2442-2444 (3)   1.00 .75

Bernal Diaz del Castillo (1492-1585), Historian — A687

Famous men: 12p, Esteban Terradas (1883-1950), mathematician. 17p, Vicente Aleixandre (1898-1984), 1977 Nobel laureate in literature. 45p, Leon Felipe Camino (1884-1968), poet.

1985, July 24   Engr.   Perf. 13½
2445 A687 7p dk red, blk & dk grn, buff .25 .25
2446 A687 12p brt ver, dk bl & blk, buff .25 .25
2447 A687 17p blk, dk grn & dk red, buff .25 .25
2448 A687 45p bis, blk & dk grn, buff .55 .25
      Nos. 2445-2448 (4)   1.30 1.00

Monastic Mail Delivery, 1122 — A688

Lithographed and Engraved
1985, Sept. 27   Perf. 13
2449 A688 17p multicolored   .25 .25
Stamp Day 1985.

12th Rhythmic Gymnastics World Championships, Valladolid — A689

1985, Oct. 9   Photo.   Perf. 13x13½
2450 A689 17p Ribbon exercise   .25 .25
2451 A689 45p Hoop exercise   .50 .25

Souvenir Sheet

Prado Museum, La Alcachofa Fountain — A690

Lithographed and Engraved
1985, Oct. 18   Perf. 13
2452 A690 17p multicolored   .50 .50
EXFILNA '85, Madrid, Oct. 18-27.

Virgin and Child, Seville Cathedral A691

Stained glass windows: 12p, Monk, by Peter Boniface, Toledo Cathedral. 17p, King Henry II of Castile, Alcazar of Segovia.

1985, Oct. 24   Perf. 12½x13
2453 A691 7p multicolored   .25 .25
2454 A691 12p multicolored   .25 .25
2455 A691 17p multicolored   .25 .25
      Nos. 2453-2455 (3)   .75 .75

Christmas 1985 A692

14th-15th century paintings in the Episcopal Museum, Vich: 17p, Nativity, Guimera Altarpiece retable, 14th cent., by Ramon de Mur. 45p, Epiphany, from an embroidered frontal, 15th cent.

1985, Nov. 27   Photo.   Perf. 13½
2456 A692 17p multicolored   .25 .25
2457 A692 45p multicolored   .50 .25

Birds — A693

1985, Dec. 4   Litho. & Engr.
2458 A693 6p Sylvia cantillans   .25 .25
2459 A693 7p Monticola saxa-
       tilis   .25 .25
2460 A693 12p Sturnus unicolor   .25 .25
2461 A693 17p Panurus
       biarmicus   .35 .25
    Nos. 2458-2461 (4)   1.10 1.00
Wildlife conservation.

Count of Penaflorida (1729-
1785) — A694

1985, Dec. 11   Engr.   Perf. 13½
2462 A694 17p dark blue   .25 .25
Francisco Javier de Munibe e Idiaquez,
founded Natl. Economic Society of Friends in
1765.

Government Palace, Madrid, and
Accession Agreement Text — A695

17p, Map and flags of EEC countries. 30p,
Hall of Columns, Royal Palace. 45p, Member
flags.

1986, Jan. 7   Litho.   Perf. 13½x13
2463 A695 7p multicolored   .25 .25
2464 A695 17p multicolored   .25 .25
2465 A695 30p multicolored   .35 .25
2466 A695 45p multicolored   .60 .25
  a.   Bklt. pane of 4, #2463-2466   3.25
    Nos. 2463-2466 (4)   1.45 1.00
Admission of Spain and Portugal to European Economic Community. See Portugal
Nos. 1661-1662.

Tourism — A696

Historic sites: 12p, Inner courtyard, La Lupi-
ana Monastery, Guadalajara. 35p, Balcony of
Europe, Nerja.

1986, Jan. 20   Engr.   Perf. 13x12½
2467 A696 12p dk rose, brn & gray
       brn   .25 .25
2468 A696 35p brt blue & sep   .45 .25

2nd World Conference on Merino
Sheep — A697

1986, Jan. 27   Photo.   Perf. 13½
2469 A697 45p multicolored   .50 .25

Masquerade, 19th Cent., by F.
Hohenleiter — A698

1986, Feb. 5
2470 A698 17p multicolored   .25 .25
Cadiz Carnival.

Intl. Peace Year — A699

Lithographed and Engraved
1986, Feb. 12   Perf. 13x13½
2471 A699 45p multicolored   .50 .25

Festival of
Religious
Music,
Cuenca
A700

1986, Mar. 26   Photo.   Perf. 13½
2472 A700 17p multicolored   .25 .25

Chamber of Commerce, Cent. — A701

Painting detail: Swearing in of the Regent,
Queen Maria Christina, Before the Spanish
Parliament, 1886, by Francisco Jover and Joa-
quin Sorolla y Bastida, Senate Palace, Madrid.

1986, Apr. 9   Engr.   Perf. 13½
2473 A701 17p sage grn & grnsh
       blk   .25 .25

Emigration of
Spaniards — A702

1986, Apr. 22   Photo.
2474 A702 45p multicolored   .50 .25

Europa 1986 — A703

Lithographed and Engraved
1986, May 5   Perf. 13x13½
2475 A703 17p Youth feeding birds   .25 .25
2476 A703 45p Girl watering tree   .55 .25

Our Lady
of the Dew
Festival, Almonte
A704

1986, May 14   Photo.   Perf. 13½x13
2477 A704 17p multicolored   .25 .25

Army Day
A705

Captains-General Building, Canary Islands.

1986, May 16   Engr.   Perf. 13½
2478 A705 17p pale yel brn, sep &
       red   .25 .25

Rodrigo City
Cathedral
A706

Design: 35p, Calella Lighthouse.

1986, June 16   Perf. 12½x13½
2479 A706 12p blue & black   .25 .25
2480 A706 35p multicolored   .55 .25

10th World Basketball Championships,
July 5-20 — A707

1986, July 4   Photo.   Perf. 12½
2481 A707 45p multicolored   .50 .25

Famous
Men — A708

1986, July 16   Engr.   Perf. 13
2482 A708 7p olive grn & bl   .25 .25
2483 A708 11p brt rose & blk   .25 .25
2484 A708 17p dk brn vio & blk   .25 .25
2485 A708 45p org, red vio & blk   .50 .25
    Nos. 2482-2485 (4)   1.25 1.00

Mystery of the
Virgin's Death
Festival
Elche — A709

Designs: 7p, Francisco Loscos Bernal
(1823-1886), botanist. 11p, Salvador Espriu
(1913-1985), author. 17p, Jose Martinez Ruiz
(Azorin, 1873-1967), writer. 45p, Jose Vitori-
ano Gonzalez (Juan Gris, 1887-1927), painter.

1986, Aug. 11   Photo.   Perf. 13½x13½
2486 A709 17p Angels carrying
       soul   .25 .25

5th World Swimming, Water Polo,
Diving and Synchronized Swimming
Championships — A710

1986, Aug. 13   Engr.   Perf. 13½
2487 A710 45p multicolored   .50 .25

10th World Pelota
Championships — A711

1986, Sept. 12
2488 A711 17p multicolored   .25 .25

Stamp Day — A712

Messenger, The Husband's Return, Song
63, TI1 Codex, 1979 edition, Spanish Royal
Academy.

1986, Sept. 27   Litho.   Perf. 13x12½
2489 A712 17p multicolored   .25 .25

Souvenir Sheet

EXFILNA '86, Cordova, Oct. 9-
18 — A713

1986, Oct. 7   Litho. & Engr.
2490 A713 17p Man, Cordova
       "Mosque"   .25 .25

Discovery of America, 500th Anniv. (in 1992) — A714

Men and text: 7p, Aristotle, text from De Cielo et Mundo. 12p, Seneca, text from Medea. 17p, San Isidoro, text from Etimologias. 30p, Pedro de Ailly, text from Imago Mundi. 35p, Mayan, prophesy from Libros de Chilam Balam. 45p, European, prophesy from Libros de Chilam Balam.

Lithographed and Engraved

1986, Oct. 15		**Perf. 13x13½**	
2491	A714	7p multicolored	.25 .25
2492	A714	12p multicolored	.25 .25
2493	A714	17p multicolored	.25 .25
2494	A714	30p multicolored	.35 .25
2495	A714	35p multicolored	.40 .25
2496	A714	45p multicolored	.50 .25
a.		Bklt. pane of 6, #2491-2496	1.90
		Nos. 2491-2496 (6)	2.00 1.50

Caspar de Portola y Rovira (1717-1786), Pioneer of California — A715

1986, Nov. 6		**Perf. 13½**	
2497	A715	22p multicolored	.25 .25

Christmas A716

Wood carving details: 19p, The Holy Family, by Diego de Siloe (c. 1495-1563), Natl. Sculpture Museum, Valladolid, vert. 48p, Nativity, Toledo Cathedral altarpiece, by Felipe de Borgona (c. 1475-1543).

1986, Nov. 19	**Photo.**	**Perf. 13½**	
2498	A716	19p multicolored	.25 .25
2499	A716	48p multicolored	.55 .25

Spanish-Islamic Cultural Heritage — A717

Famous men: 7p, Abd Al Rahman II (792-852), 4th independent emir of Cordoba. 12p, Ibn Hazm (994-1064), scholar. 17p, Al-Zarqali (1061-1100), astronomer. 45p, Alfonso VII, scholar, Toledo School of Translators.

1986, Dec. 3		**Engr.**	
2500	A717	7p org red & dk red brn	.25 .25
2501	A717	12p brn blk & red org	.25 .25
2502	A717	17p black & dk blue	.25 .25
2503	A717	45p green & black	.50 .25
		Nos. 2500-2503 (4)	1.25 1.00

Alfonso R. Castelao (1886-1950), Artist, Writer — A718

Lithographed and Engraved

1986, Dec. 11		**Perf. 13x13½**	
2504	A718	32p El Buen Cura, 1917	.40 .25

Globe, Chateau de la Muette A719

1987, Jan. 14		**Perf. 14**	
2505	A719	48p multicolored	.55 .25

Organization for Economic Cooperation and Development, OECD, 25th anniv.

EXPO '92, Seville A720

1987, Jan. 21		**Photo.**	
2506	A720	19p Geometric shapes	.35 .25
2507	A720	48p Earth, Moon's surface	.95 .25

See Nos. 2540-2541, 2550-2551.

Portrait of Vitoria, by Vera Fajardo A721

1987, Feb. 11		**Engr.**	
2508	A721	48p dark rose brown	.55 .25

Francisco de Vitoria (c. 1486-1546), theologian, teacher and a founder of intl. law.

Marine Corps, 450th Anniv. A722

Design: 18th Cent. 74-gun man-of-war, period standard bearer, corps insignia.

1987, Feb. 25			
2509	A722	19p multicolored	.25 .25

Deusto University, Cent. — A723

1987, Feb. 26	**Engr.**	**Perf. 14x13½**	
2510	A723	19p blk, hn brn & dk grn	.25 .25

UN Child Survival Campaign A724

1987, Mar. 4		**Perf. 13½x14**	
2511	A724	19p red brown & blk	.25 .25

Constitution of Cadiz, 175th Anniv. — A725

Nos. 2512a-2512c in a continuous design: The Promulgation of 1812, by Salvador Viniegra. No. 2512d, Anniv. emblem.

1987, Mar. 18		**Litho.**	**Perf. 13½**
2512		Strip of 4	1.25 1.25
a.-d.	A725	25p, any single	.30 .25

Ceramicware A726

Designs: 7p, Pharmaceutical jar, 15th cent., Manises of Valencia. 14p, Abstract figurine, 20th cent., Sargadelos of Galicia. 19p, Neo-classical lidded urn, 18th cent., Buen Retiro of Madrid. 32p, Water jar, 20th cent., Salvatierra of Extremadura. 40p, Pitcher, 18th cent., Talavera of Toledo. 48p, Pitcher, 18th-19th cent., Granada of Andalucia.

Lithographed and Engraved

1987, Mar. 20		**Perf. 12½x13**	
2513		Block of 6 + 3 labels	2.25 2.25
a.	A726	7p multicolored	.25 .25
b.	A726	14p multicolored	.25 .25
c.	A726	19p multicolored	.30 .25
d.	A726	32p multicolored	.45 .30
e.	A726	40p multicolored	.50 .30
f.	A726	48p multicolored	.60 .30

See No. 2552.

Passion Week in Zamora and Seville A727

Paintings: 19p, The Amanecer Procession, by Gallego Marquina, vert. 48p, Jesus Carrying the Cross, by Martinez Montanes, and the Gate of Forgiveness, Seville Cathedral.

1987, Apr. 13	**Photo.**	**Perf. 14x13½**	
2514	A727	19p multicolored	.25 .25
2515	A727	48p multicolored	.55 .25

Tourism A728

14p, Rock of Ifach, Calpe. 19p, Nave of Santa Marina d'Ozo Church, Pontevedra, before restoration. 40p, Sonanes Palace, Villacarriedo. 48p, Monastery of St. Joan de les Abadesses, Gerona, vert.

1987		**Engr.**	**Perf. 12½x13**
2515A	A728	14p dp bl & sage grn	.25 .25
2516	A728	19p dp grn & grnsh blk	.30 .25
2516A	A728	40p dp claret	.50 .25
2517	A728	48p black	.60 .25
		Nos. 2515A-2517 (4)	1.65 1.00

Issued: 19p, 48p, 4/21; 14p, 40p, 6/10.

Europa 1987 A729

Modern architecture: 19p, Bilbao Bank, Madrid, designed by Saenz de Oiza, vert. 48p, Natl. Museum of Roman Art, Merida, designed by Rafael Moneo.

Lithographed and Engraved

1987, May 4		**Perf. 14x13½**	
2518	A729	19p multicolored	.25 .25
2519	A729	48p multicolored	.55 .25

Horse Fair, Jerez de La Frontera A730

1987, May 6	**Photo.**	**Perf. 13½x14**	
2520	A730	19p multicolored	.25 .25

Ramon Carande (1887-1986), Historian — A731

1987, May 29		**Engr.**	
2521	A731	40p blk & dk vio brn	.45 .25

Postal Code Inauguration — A732

1987, June 1	**Litho.**	**Perf. 14**	
2522	A732	19p multicolored	.25 .25

Eibar Weaponry School, 75th Anniv. A733

1987, July 2	**Litho.**	**Perf. 14**	
2523	A733	20p multicolored	.25 .25

1992 Summer Olympics, Barcelona A734

1987, July 15		**Photo.**	
2524	A734	32p Casa de Battlo masonry	.50 .25
2525	A734	65p Athletes	1.00 .25

25th Folk Festival of the Pyrenees, Jaca — A735

1987, July 22
2526 A735 50p multicolored   .55   .25

Monturiol and Submarine Designs A736

1987, Sept. 9   Engr.   Perf. 13½x14
2527 A736 20p black brown   .25   .25

Narcis Monturiol (d. 1887), builder of the submarine Ictineos.

Stamp Day — A737

Illuminated codex from *Constitutiones Jacobi II Regis Majoricum*, 14th cent., King Albert I Royal Library, Brussels.

Litho & Engr.
1987, Sept. 16   Perf. 13
2528 A737 20p multicolored   .25   .25

Postal service of Mallorca under James II.

ESPAMER '87 — A738

Designs: 8p, Handstamped letter that traveled from La Coruna to Havana, Cuba, 18th cent. 12p, La Coruna Harbor, 19th cent., engraving. 20p, Illustration of Havana harbor from *Viaje Alrededor da La Isla de Cuba*, by Francisco Mialche, 18th cent. 50p, West Indies packets.

1987, Oct. 2   Litho. & Engr.   Perf. 13
2529 A738   Sheet of 4   3.25   3.25
  a.   8p blk, brt blue & red   .30   .30
  b.   12p brt blue, red & blk   .45   .45
  c.   20p blk, brt blue & red   .75   .75
  d.   50p blk, brt blue & red   1.75   1.75

No. 2529 printed se-tenant (rouletted between) with ESPAMER entrance ticket. Sold for 180p. Size: 150x83mm (including ticket).

Souvenir Sheet

EXFILNA '87, Gerona, Oct. 24-Nov. 1 — A739

Greek statue, Emporion, Olympic torch-bearer.

1987, Oct. 24   Photo.   Perf. 13x12½
2530 A739 20p multicolored   .25   .25

Discovery of America, 500th Anniv. (in 1992) — A740

Ships and: 14p, Amerigo Vespucci (1454-1512), Italian navigator. 20p, Ferdinand and Isabella. 32p, Friar Juan Perez, Queen's confessor. 40p, Juan de la Cosa (c. 1460-1510), master of the Santa Maria, cartographer who made first map of the New World. 50p, Christopher Columbus. 65p, Vicente Yanez Pinzon (c. 1460-1523) and Martin Alonso Pinzon (c. 1441-1493), brothers, navigators and ship owners, accompanied Columbus on voyage.

Litho. & Engr.
1987, Oct. 30   Perf. 13
2531 A740 14p multicolored   .25   .25
2532 A740 20p multicolored   .25   .25
2533 A740 32p multicolored   .40   .25
2534 A740 40p multicolored   .45   .25
2535 A740 55p multicolored   .55   .25
2536 A740 65p multicolored   .75   .30
  a.   Bklt. pane of 6, #2531-2536   3.00
  Nos. 2531-2536 (6)   2.65   1.55

Christmas — A741

1987, Nov. 17   Photo.   Perf. 14x13½
2537 A741 20p Ornaments   .30   .25
2538 A741 50p Zambomba, tambourine   .60   .25

Self-portrait, Sculpture by Victorio Macho (1887-1966) A742

1987, Dec. 23   Engr.
2539 A742 50p brown black   .55   .25

EXPO '92 Type of 1987
1987, Dec. 29   Photo.   Perf. 13½x14
2540 A720 8p like No. 2506   .30   .25
2541 A720 20p like No. 2507   .55   .25

HRH Sofia and Juan Carlos, 50th Birth Annivs. — A743

1988, Jan. 5   Perf. 13x13½
2542 A743 20p Sofia   .30   .25
2543 A743 20p Juan Carlos   .30   .25
  a.   Pair, #2542-2543 + label   .60   .50

Clara Campoamor (b. 1888), Suffragette — A744

1988, Feb. 12   Photo.   Perf. 14
2544 A744 20p multicolored   .25   .25

1988 Winter Olympics, Calgary — A745

1988, Feb. 15   Perf. 14
2545 A745 45p Speed skater   .60   .25

Passion Week in Valladolid and Malaga — A746

Designs: 20p, Valladolid Cathedral and 17th cent. statue of Christ at the column by Gregorio Fernandez. 50p, Christ carrying the cross along Malaga procession route.

1988, Mar. 30   Photo.   Perf. 14
2546 A746 20p multicolored   .30   .25
2547 A746 50p multicolored   .60   .25

Tourism A747

1988, Apr. 7
2548 A747 18p Paella pan, ingredients   .25   .25
2549 A747 45p Covadonga Natl. Park   .50   .25

EXPO '92 Type of 1987
Era of Discoveries: 8p, Road to globe, rays of light, vert. 45p, Compass rose, globe.

1988, Apr. 12
2550 A720 8p multicolored   .25   .25
2551 A720 45p multicolored   .50   .25

Art Type of 1987
Glassware: a, Chalice, Valencia, 18th cent. b, Cadalso de los Vidrios, Madrid, 18th cent. c, Candy dish, La Granja de San Ildefonso, 18th cent. d, Castril double-handled jar, Andalucia, 18th cent. e, Jug, Catalina, 17th cent. f, Bottle, Baleares, 20th cent.

Litho. & Engr.
1988, Apr. 13   Perf. 12½x13
2552   Block of 6 + 6 labels   1.75   1.75
  a.-f.   A726 20p any single   .25   .25

Stamp Day 1988 — A748

Francis of Taxis, postmaster by royal appointment (1505) in charge of establishing communications between Spain, France, Germany, Rome, Naples.

1988, Apr. 29   Engr.   Perf. 12½x13
2553 A748 20p dk violet & dk brn   .25   .25

General Workers' Union (UGT), Cent. A749

Emblem and Pablo Iglesias, union pioneer.

1988, May 1   Photo.   Perf. 14
2554 A749 20p multicolored   .25   .25

Europa 1988 — A750

Transport and communication: 20p, Locomotive made in Spain and operated in Cuba, 1837. 50p, Spanish telegraph in the Philippines linking Plaza de Manila and Bagumbayan Camp, 1818.

1988, May 5   Engr.   Perf. 13
2555 A750 20p black & dk red   .25   .25
2556 A750 50p black & dk grn   .50   .25

Jean Monnet (1888-1979), Economist A751

1988, May 9   Perf. 14x13½
2557 A751 45p blue black   .50   .25

Universal Exposition, Barcelona, Cent. A752

1988, May 31   Photo.   Perf. 13½x14
2558 A752 50p multicolored   .55   .25

Intl. Music and
Dance Festival,
Granada — A753

1988, June 1   *Perf. 14x13½*
2559 A753 50p multicolored   .55   .25

World
Expo '88,
Brisbane,
Australia
A754

1988, June 14   *Perf. 13½x14*
2560 A754 50p Bull   .55   .25

Coronation of the
Virgin of
Hope — A755

1988, June 18   *Perf. 14x13½*
2561 A755 20p multicolored   .25   .25
Holy Week in Malaga.

Souvenir Sheet

EXFILNA '88, June 25-July 3,
Madrid — A756

1988, June 25   *Perf. 13x12½*
2562 A756 20p Ciudadela For-
tress floor plan   .25   .25

Tourism
A757

1988, July 11   Engr.   Perf. 13½x14
2563 A757 18p Cantabrian Coast
storehouse   .30   .25
2564 A757 45p Dulzaina (wind
instrument)   .60   .25

28th World Roller Hockey
Championships, La Coruna — A758

1988, Sept. 7   Photo.   Perf. 13½x14
2565 A758 20p multicolored   .25   .25

1st World Cong. of
Spanish Regional
Shelters — A759

1988, Sept. 9   *Perf. 14*
2566 A759 20p multicolored   .25   .25

1988 Summer
Olympics,
Seoul — A760

1988, Sept. 10   Litho.
2567 A760 50p Yachting   .55   .25

Catalonia Millennium — A761

1988, Sept. 21   Photo.   Perf. 12½
2568 A761 20p multicolored   .25   .25

1st Call to
Session of the
Leon Court,
800th
Anniv. — A762

Illumination & seal of Alfonso IX, King of
Leon.

1988, Sept. 26   Photo.   Perf. 12½x13
2569 A762 20p multicolored   .25   .25

Federation
of Spanish
Philatelic
Societies,
25th Anniv.
A763

1988, Sept. 27   *Perf. 14x13½*
2570 A763 20p multicolored   .25   .25

1992
Summer
Olympics,
Barcelona
A764

1988, Oct. 3   Photo.   Perf. 14
2571 A764 8p multicolored   .25   .25
See Nos. B139-B141.

A765

Design: Castle in Valencia and royal seal of
James I, 13th cent.

1988, Oct. 7   *Perf. 14x13½*
2572 A765 20p multicolored   .25   .25
Reconquest of Valencia by King James I,
750th anniv.

A766

1988, Oct. 10   *Perf. 13x13½*
2573 A766 20p multicolored   .25   .25
Civil Law, cent.

Discovery of America (in 1992), 500th
Anniv. — A767

Conquerors, exporers and symbols: No.
2574, Hernando Cortez, conqueror of Mexico,
and serpent Quetzalcoatl. No. 2575, Vasco
Nunez de Balboa, discoverer of the Pacific
Ocean, and sun setting over sea. No. 2576,
Francisco Pizarro, conqueror of Peru, and
llama. No. 2577, Portuguese navigator Ferdinand Magellan, Juan de Elcano (c. 1476-
1526) and globe symbolizing circumnavigation
of the world. No. 2578, Alvar Nunez Cabeza
de Vaca (c. 1490-1560), explorer, and sunrise.
No. 2579, Andres de Urdaneta (1498-1568),
and symbol of the west-to-east route between
the Philippines and America that he
discovered.

1988, Oct. 13   Engr.   Perf. 13x13½
2574 A767 10p multicolored   .25   .25
2575 A767 10p multicolored   .25   .25
2576 A767 20p multicolored   .25   .25
2577 A767 20p multicolored   .25   .25
2578 A767 50p multicolored   .55   .25
2579 A767 50p multicolored   .55   .25
a.   Bklt. pane of 6, #2574-2579   2.25
     Nos. 2574-2579 (6)   2.10 1.50

Henry III of Castile, 1st Prince of
Asturias — A768

1988, Oct. 26   Photo.   Perf. 13
2580 A768 20p multicolored   .25   .25
1st Bestowal of the title Prince of Asturias,
600th anniv., guaranteeing that the throne
would continue to be inherited according to
primogeniture.

Christmas — A769

1988, Nov. 24   Photo.   Perf. 14
2581 A769 20p Snowflakes,
horiz.   .25   .25
2582 A769 50p Shepherd   .55   .25

Sites and Cities Appearing on the
UNESCO World Heritage List — A770

1988, Dec. 1   Engr.   Perf. 12½x13
2583 A770 18p Mosque de Cor-
doba, vert.   .25   .25
2584 A770 20p Burgos Cathedral, vert.   .30   .25
2585 A770 45p El Escorial
Monastery   .55   .25
2586 A770 50p The Alhambra,
Granada   .65   .25
     Nos. 2583-2586 (4)   1.75 1.00

Natl. Constitution, 10th Anniv. — A771

1988, Dec. 7   Photo.   Perf. 14
2587 A771 20p multicolored   .25   .25

Souvenir Sheet

Charles III (1759-1788) and the
Enlightenment — A772

1988, Dec. 14   Engr.   Perf. 13x12½
2588 A772 45p black & dk grn   .55   .55

Natl. Organization for the Blind, 50th
Anniv. — A773

1988, Dec. 27   Photo.   Perf. 14
2589 A773 20p multicolored   .25   .25

Fr. Luis de Granada (1504-1588) A774

1988, Dec. 31
2590 A774 20p multicolored .25 .25

1992 Summer Olympics, Barcelona A775

1989, Jan. 3
2591 A775 20p multicolored .25 .25

Stamp Collecting — A776

1989, Jan. 3
2592 A776 20p multicolored .25 .25

French Revolution, Bicent. — A777

1989, Jan. 24 Photo. Perf. 13
2593 A777 45p multicolored .50 .25

Maria de Maeztu (b. 1882), Educator A778

1989, Feb. 7 Photo. Perf. 14x13½
2594 A778 20p multicolored .25 .25

Postal Service, Cent. A779

Litho. & Engr.
1989, Mar. 11 Perf. 13½x14
2595 A779 20p Uniform, 1889 .25 .25

Stamp Day — A780

Design: Intl. postal treaty negotiated with France and Italy by Franz von Taxis, 1601.

1989, Apr. 4 Engr. Perf. 13
2596 A780 20p black .25 .25

A781

1989, Apr. 22 Perf. 14x13½
2597 A781 20p black .25 .25

Casa del Cordon, Burgos.

A782

Europa: Children's toys.

1989, May 5 Photo. Perf. 13x13½
2598 A782 40p shown .40 .25
2599 A782 50p Top .50 .25

Spain's Presidency of the European Economic Community A783

1989, May 9 Perf. 13½x14
2600 A783 45p multicolored .50 .25

Souvenir Sheet

Holy Family with St. Anne, by El Greco — A784

1989, May 20 Litho. Perf. 14x13½
2601 A784 20p multicolored .25 .25

EXFILNA '89. Exists imperf in different colors.

Gabriela Mistral (1889-1957), Chilean Poet Awarded 1945 Nobel Prize for Literature — A785

Litho. & Engr.
1989, June 1 Perf. 14x13½
2602 A785 50p multicolored .60 .25

European Parliament 3rd Elections — A786

1989, June 12 Photo. Perf. 13x13½
2603 A786 45p multicolored .50 .25

Lace A787

Lace produced in: a, Catalonia. b, Andalusia. c, Extremadura. d, Canary Isls. e, Castile-La Mancha. f, Galicia.

Litho. & Engr.
1989, June 20 Perf. 13x12½
2604 Block of 6 + 3 labels 1.40 1.40
a.-f. A787 20p any single .25 .25

Three center labels printed in a continuous design and picture lace-making.

Pope John Paul II at the Intl. Catholic Youth Forum, Santiago — A788

1989, Aug. 19 Engr. Perf. 13x12½
2605 A788 50p myrtle grn, dk red brn & blk .55 .25

Athletics World Cup, Barcelona A789

1989, Sept. 1 Photo. Perf. 13½x14
2606 A789 50p multicolored .55 .25

A790

Litho. & Engr.
1989, Sept. 19 Perf. 14x13½
2607 A790 50p multicolored .55 .25

Charlie Chaplin (1889-1977), English comedian and actor.

Type A34 — A791

1989, Oct. 2 Photo. Perf. 14x13½
2608 A791 50p gray, ver & blk .55 .25

Cent. of the 1st Alfonso XIII issue.

A792

Fr. Andres Manjon (d. 1923), teacher.

1989, Oct. 13
2609 A792 20p multicolored .25 .25

Founding of the Ave Maria Schools by Fr. Manjon, cent.

A793

UPAE emblem and "Irrigating Corn Field in November, 17th Cent.," an illustration from the *New Chronicle and Good Government,* by Guaman Poma de Ayala.

1989, Nov. 7 Litho. & Engr.
2610 A793 50p multicolored .55 .25

America issue.

Christmas A794

Perf. 14x13½, 13½x14
1989, Nov. 29 Photo.
2611 A794 20p Star, "NAVIdAd 89," vert. .25 .25
2612 A794 45p shown .50 .25

Sites on the UNESCO World Heritage List — A795

Litho. & Engr.
1989, Dec. 5   *Perf. 13x12½*
2613 A795 20p Altamira Caverns .25 .25
2614 A795 20p Santiago de
            Compostela .25 .25
2615 A795 20p Roman aqueduct,
            Segovia .25 .25
2616 A795 20p Guell Park and
            palace, Mila
            House .25 .25
     Nos. 2613-2616 (4) 1.00 1.00

Souvenir Sheet

Sites on the World Heritage
List — A796

Royal palaces: a, El Escorial. b, Aranjuez. c,
Summer palace, La Granja, San Ildefonso. e,
Madrid.

1989, Dec. 20   **Engr.**   *Perf. 13x13½*
2617   Sheet of 4 2.00 2.00
   a.-d. A796 45p any single .30 .30

Illustration by
Daniel Garcia
Perez, Winner of
the 2nd Youth
Stamp Design
Contest — A797

1990, Jan. 29   **Photo.**   *Perf. 14x13½*
2618 A797 20p multicolored .25 .25
1992 Summer Olympics, Barcelona.

A798

1990, Feb. 2
2619 A798 20p multicolored .25 .25
World Cycle Cross Championship, Getzu.

A799

1990, Feb. 12   **Engr.**
2620 A799 20p dark purple .25 .25
Victoria Kent (1897-1987), prisons directer,
reformer.

Honorary Postman Rafael Alvarez
Sereix and Cancel — A800

Litho. & Engr.
1990, Apr. 18   *Perf. 13*
2621 A800 20p sepia, buff & dull
            grn .25 .25
Stamp Day.

Europa
1990
A801

Post offices.

     Perf. 13½x14, 14x13½
1990, May 4   **Photo.**
2622 A801 20p Vitoria .25 .25
2623 A801 50p Malaga, vert. .50 .25

Intl. Telecommunications Union, 125th
Anniv. — A802

1990, May 17   *Perf. 13½x14*
2624 A802 8p multicolored .25 .25

Wrought
Iron — A803

Designs: a, 15th Cent. door knocker. b, 16th
cent. lyre-shaped door knocker. c, 17th Cent.
pistol. d, 17th-18th Cent. door knocker. e, 19th
Cent. lock. f, Fire iron.

Litho. & Engr.
1990, May 18   *Perf. 12½*
2625   Block of 6 + 3 labels 1.75 1.75
   a.-f. A803 20p any single .25 .25
Nos. 2625a-2625f printed se-tenant in a
continuous design. Three labels continue the
design and contain text or picture a forge.

Souvenir Sheet

Patio de La Infanta, Zaporta Palace,
Zaragoza — A804

1990, May 25   **Engr.**   *Perf. 14x13½*
2626 A804 20p red brown .25 .25
EXFILNA '90.

Charity, by
Lopez
Alonso — A805

1990, June 19   **Litho.**   *Perf. 13½x13*
2627 A805 8p multicolored .25 .25
Daughters of Charity in Spain, bicentennial.

Jose Padilla, Composer, Birth
Centenary — A806

1990, June 19   **Photo.**   *Perf. 13x12½*
2628 A806 20p multicolored .30 .25

Town of Estella, 900th Anniv. — A807

1990, June 19   **Litho. & Engr.**
2629 A807 45p multicolored .60 .25

Novel, "Tirant lo
Blanch," 500th
Anniv. — A808

1990, June 19   *Perf. 12½x13*
2630 A808 50p multicolored .65 .25

Souvenir Sheet

Crypt, Palencia Cathedral — A809

1990, June 22   **Engr.**   *Perf. 13½x14*
2631 A809 20p red brown .25 .25
Topical philatelic exposition.

A810

1990, Aug. 27   **Photo.**   *Perf. 14x13½*
2632 A810 50p multicolored .55 .25
17th Intl. Congress of Historical Sciences.

A811

America Issue: UPAE emblem and Car-
ribean fauna.

Litho. & Engr.
1990, Nov. 14   *Perf. 14*
2633 A811 50p multicolored .55 .25

A812

Christmas: Scenes from the film "Cosmic
Poem" by Jose Antonio Sistiaga.

1990, Nov. 22   **Photo.**
2634 A812 25p multicolored .30 .25
2635 A812 45p multi, horiz. .50 .25

A813

Tapestries in Monastery of San Lorenzo: a,
The Crucifixion by Jan van Roome and Ber-
nard van Orley. b, Flamenco Soldiers by Philip
Wouvermans. c, Shipwreck of the Telemac by
Miguel Angel Houasse. d, Flowers by Fran-
cisco Goya.

Litho. & Engr.
1990, Nov. 28   *Perf. 13*
2636   Sheet of 4 1.00 1.00
   a.-d. A813 20p any single .25 .25

European Tourism
Year — A814

1990, Dec. 1   **Photo.**   *Perf. 14*
2637 A814 45p multicolored .50 .25

World Heritage List — A815

Designs: No. 2638, Church of San Vicente, Avila. No. 2639, Tower of San Pedro, Teruel, vert. No. 2640, Church of San Miguel de Lillo, Oviedo, vert. No. 2641, Tower of Bujaco, Caceres.

Litho. & Engr.
1990, Dec. 10   **Perf. 13**
2638 A815 20p multicolored   .30 .25
2639 A815 20p multicolored   .30 .25
2640 A815 20p multicolored   .30 .25
2641 A815 20p multicolored   .30 .25
    Nos. 2638-2641 (4)   1.20 1.00

Natl. Orchestra of Spain A816

1990, Dec. 20 Photo. Perf. 13½x14
2642 A816 25p grn, yel grn & blk .30 .25

Maria Moliner (1900-1981), Spanish Linguist — A817

1991, Jan. 21 Photo. Perf. 14x13½
2643 A817 25p multicolored   .35 .25

Souvenir Sheet

Santa Fe, 500th Anniv. — A818

Litho. & Engr.
1991, Apr. 19   Perf. 13½x14
2644 A818 25p brown & purple   .35 .35
World Philatelic Exhibition, Granada '92.

Child's Drawing — A819

1991, Apr. 12 Photo. Perf. 14x13½
2645 A819 25p Olympic rings, sailboats   .35 .25

Juan de Tassis y Peralta (1582-1622), Postal Reformer A820

1991, Apr. 26   Engr.   Perf. 12½
2646 A820 25p black   .35 .25
Stamp Day.

Souvenir Sheet

Porcelain and Ceramics — A821

a, Apothecary jar, 17th cent. b, Figurine, 18th cent. c, Vase, 19th cent. d, Plate, 19th cent.

1991, May 3 Litho. & Engr. Perf. 13
2647 A821 25p Sheet of 4, #a.-d. 1.50 1.50
a.-d. Any single   .30 .25
    See No. 2692.

Europa A822

1991, May 28 Litho. Perf. 13½x14
2648 A822 25p INTA-NASA ground station .35 .25
2649 A822 45p Olympus I satellite .55 .25

St. John of the Cross (1651-1695), Mystic — A823

Anniversaries: No. 2651, Fr. Luis de Leon (1527-1591), Augustinian writer, vert. No. 2652, Abd Al Rahman III (891-961), Moslem caliph, vert. No. 2653, St. Ignatius of Loyola (1451-1556), founder of Society of Jesus, vert.

Perf. 13½x14, 14x13½
1991, June 6   Litho.
2650 A823 15p multicolored   .25 .25
2651 A823 15p multicolored   .25 .25
2652 A823 25p multicolored   .35 .25
2653 A823 25p multicolored   .35 .25
    Nos. 2650-2653 (4)   1.20 1.00

Antique Furniture A824

Designs: a, Wedge top armoire, 18th cent. b, Hutch cabinet, c. 19th cent. c, Ladder-back cane chair, c. 19th cent. d, Baby cradle, 19th cent. e, Round-top trunk, c. 19th cent. f, Ornate chest, c. 18th cent.

Litho. & Engr.
1991, Sept. 9   Perf. 12½x13
2654 Block of 6 + 3 labels 1.90 1.90
a.-f. A824 25p any single   .30 .25

Orfeo Catala (Catalan Choral Society), Cent. — A825

1991, Sept. 6 Litho. Perf. 14x13½
2655 A825 25p multicolored   .35 .25

Intl. Fishing Exposition, Vigo — A826

1991, Sept. 10
2656 A826 55p multicolored   .65 .25

America Issue — A827

Litho. & Engr.
1991, Nov. 4   Perf. 14x13½
2657 A827 55p Nocturlabe   .65 .25

Christmas — A828

25p, The Nativity, illustration from 17th cent. book. 45p, The Birth of Christ, 16th cent. icon.

1991, Nov. 22 Photo. Perf. 14x13½
2658 A828 25p multicolored   .35 .25
2659 A828 45p multicolored   .55 .25

Souvenir Sheet

The Meadowlands of St. Isidro by Goya — A829

Litho. & Engr.
1991, Dec. 12   Perf. 13½x14
2660 A829 25p multicolored   .35 .35
EXFILNA '91, Madrid.

Sites on UNESCO World Heritage List — A830

#2661, Giralda bell tower, Seville Cathedral. #2662, Alcantara Gate, Toledo, vert. #2663, Casa de las Conchas, Salamanca, vert. #2664, Garajonay Natl. Park, Gomera, Canary Islands.

Perf. 12½x13, 13x12½
1991, Dec. 16   Engr.
2661 A830 25p brown & blue   .40 .25
2662 A830 25p red brn & brn   .40 .25
2663 A830 25p red brn & blk   .40 .25
2664 A830 25p violet & dk grn .40 .25
    Nos. 2661-2664 (4)   1.60 1.00
    See Nos. 2756, 2830.

Carlos Ibanez de Ibero (1825-1891), Cartographer A831

Antarctic Treaty, Research Ship A52 — A832

1991, Dec. 27 Litho. Perf. 14x13½
2665 A831 25p multicolored   .35 .25
2666 A832 55p multicolored   .65 .25

Margarita Xirgu (1889-1969), Actress — A833

1992, Jan. 20   Perf. 14
2667 A833 25p lake & gold   .35 .25

Child's Drawing A834

1992, Feb. 14   *Perf. 13½x14*
2668 A834 25p multicolored .35 .25
EXPO 92.

Pedro Rodriguez Campomanes (1723-1802), Historian, Postal Administrator — A835

1992, Feb. 21   *Perf. 13x12½*
2669 A835 27p multicolored .45 .25

Expo '92, Seville A836

1992, Feb. 28   *Perf. 13½x14*
2670 A836 27p gray, blk & brn .40 .25

Columbus Types of 1930
Souvenir Sheet
1992, Apr. 24   **Engr.**   *Perf. 14*
2671   Sheet of 2   10.00 10.00
   a. A65 250p black   4.50 2.50
   b. A67 250p brown   4.50 2.50
Intl. Philatelic Exhibition, Granada '92.

Miniature Sheets

Expo '92, Seville — A837

#2672: a, Expo '92 World Trade Center. b, Aerial tram. c, Avenue 4. d, Barqueta Gate. e, Nature pavilion. f, Biosphere. g, Alamillo Bridge. h, Press center. i, 15th Century pavilion. j, Expo harbor. k, Tourist train. l, One day entrance ticket.
#2673: a, Cartuja Monastery. b, Arena. c, Monorail train. d, Europe Avenue. e, Discovery pavilion. f, Auditorium. g, Avenue 1. h, Plaza of the Future. i, Gate to Italy's exhibit. j, Terminal. k, Expo theater. l, Expo Mascot, Curro.

1992, Apr. 21   **Litho.**   *Perf. 13½x14*
2672 A837 Sheet of 12 + 4 labels   5.00 5.00
   a.-l. 17p any single   .40 .25
2673 A837 Sheet of 12 + 4 labels   8.50 8.50
   a.-l. 27p any single   .60 .30
See No. B195.

1992 Paralympics, Barcelona — A838

1992, Apr. 22   **Photo.**   *Perf. 14*
2674 A838 27p multicolored .60 .25

Discovery of America, 500th Anniv. A839

Europa: 17p, Preparation Before Departing from Palos, by R. Espejo. 45p, Globe, ships, and buildings at La Rabida.

1992, May 5   **Photo.**   *Perf. 14*
2675 A839 17p multicolored .75 .25
2676 A839 45p multicolored 1.50 .25

Souvenir Sheets

Voyages of Columbus — A840

#2677, Columbus in sight of land. #2678, Landing of Columbus. #2679, Columbus soliciting aid from Isabella. #2680, Columbus welcomed at Barcelona. #2681, Columbus presenting natives. #2682, Columbus.
Borders on Nos. 2677-2682 are lithographed. Nos. 2677-2682 are similar in design to US Nos. 230-231, 234-235, 237, 245.

Litho. & Engr.
1992, May 22   *Perf. 14*
2677 A840 60p blue 1.25 1.10
2678 A840 60p brown violet 1.25 1.10
2679 A840 60p chocolate 1.25 1.10
2680 A840 60p purple 1.25 1.10
2681 A840 60p black brown 1.25 1.10
2682 A840 60p black 1.25 1.10
Nos. 2677-2682 (6) 7.50 6.60
See US Nos. 2624-2629, Italy Nos. 1883-1888 and Portugal Nos. 1918-1923.

1992 Winter & Summer Olympics, Albertville & Barcelona A841

1992, June 19   **Photo.**   *Perf. 14*
2683 A841 45p multicolored .60 .25

A842   A843

1992, June 5   **Photo.**   *Perf. 14x13½*
2684 A842 27p blue & yellow .40 .25
World Environment Day.

1992, Oct. 29   **Litho.**   *Perf. 14x13½*
2685 A843 17p multicolored .25 .25
Juan Luis Vives (1492-1540), Philosopher.

Pamplona Choir, Cent. A844

1992, Oct. 29   *Perf. 13½x14*
2686 A844 27p multicolored .35 .25

Unified Europe — A845

1992, Nov. 4   **Photo.**   *Perf. 14x13½*
2687 A845 45p multicolored .60 .25

Christmas A846

1992, Nov. 5   *Perf. 13½x14*
2688 A846 27p multicolored .40 .25

1992 Special Olympics, Madrid A847

1992, Sept. 7   **Photo.**   *Perf. 13½x14*
2689 A847 27p brown & blue .35 .25

Souvenir Sheet

St. Paul's Church, Valladolid — A848

Litho. & Engr.
1992, Oct. 9   *Perf. 14x13½*
2690 A848 27p multicolored .35 .35
Exfilna '92, Natl. Philatelic Exhibition, Valladolid.

Discovery of America, 500th Anniv. A849

1992, Oct. 15   *Perf. 13½x14*
2691 A849 60p dk brn, lt brn & bis .75 .25

Natl. Heritage Type of 1991
Miniature Sheet
Codices: a, Veitia, 18th cent. b, Trujillo of Peru, 18th cent. c, The Chess Book, 13th cent. d, General History of New Spain, 16th cent.

Litho. & Engr.
1992, Dec. 10   *Perf. 13*
2692 A821 27p Sheet of 4, #a.-d. 1.75 1.40

Road Safety A850   Environmental Protection A851

Health and Sanitation — A852

1993   **Photo.**   *Perf. 14x13½*
2693 A850 17p green & red .35 .25
2694 A851 28p green & blue .40 .25
2695 A852 65p blue & green .90 .25
Nos. 2693-2695 (3) 1.65 .75
Issued: 17p, 4/20; 28p, 1/4; 65p, 2/12.

Maria Zambrano (1904-1991), Writer — A854

1993, Jan. 18   **Photo.**   *Perf. 14*
2697 A854 45p buff, lil rose & brn .65 .25

Andres Segovia (1893-1987), Guitarist — A855

1993, Feb. 19   **Engr.**   *Perf. 14x13½*
2698 A855 65p black & brown .90 .25

1908 Mailbox, Madrid Postal Museum A856

Litho. & Engr.
1993, Mar. 12   *Perf. 13½x14*
2699 A856 28p multicolored .45 .25
Stamp Day.

Mushrooms — A857

1993, Mar. 18   Photo.   Perf. 14
2700 A857 17p Amanita caesa-
                rea   .35   .25
2701 A857 17p Lepiota procera   .35   .25
2702 A857 28p Lactarius
                sanguifluus   .40   .25
2703 A857 28p Russula cyanox-
                antha   .40   .25
    Nos. 2700-2703 (4)   1.50 1.00
        See Nos. 2759-2762.

Souvenir Sheet

Holy Week Celebration — A858

1993, Apr. 2   Litho.   Perf. 14x13½
2704 A858 100p multicolored   1.40 1.40
    Exfilna '93, Alcaniz. Margin of No. 2704 is
Litho. & Engr.

Fusees, by
Joan Miro
A859

    Europa: 65p, La Bague d'Aurore, by Miro,
vert.

Perf. 13½x14, 14x13½
1993, May 5   Litho.
2705 A859 45p blue & black   .90   .25
Litho. & Engr.
2706 A859 65p multicolored   1.40   .25

Year of St.
James
A860

    Designs: 17p, Transfer of St. James' body
by boat. 28p, Discovery of tomb of St. James.
45p, St. James on horseback.

1993, May 13   Photo.   Perf. 13½x14
2707 A860 17p multicolored   .35   .25
2708 A860 28p multicolored   .40   .25
2709 A860 45p multicolored   .60   .25
    Nos. 2707-2709 (3)   1.35   .75

World Telecommunications
Day — A861

1993, May 17
2710 A861 28p multicolored   .40   .25

Compostela '93 — A862

    Stylized designs: 28p, Pilgrims paying hom-
age to Saint James. 100p, Pilgrim under star
tree while on way to Santiago de Campostela,
vert.

1993, May 18   Photo.   Perf. 13½x14
2711 A862 28p multicolored   .45   .25
Souvenir Sheet
Perf. 14x13½
2712 A862 100p multicolored   3.00 1.75

World
Environment
Day — A863

1993, June 4   Litho.   Perf. 14x13½
2713 A863 28p multicolored   .40   .25

King Juan Carlos — A864a
A864

1993-98   Photo.   Perf. 14x13½
A864 Gold and:
2714 A864 1p prussian bl   .25   .25
2715 A864 2p green   .25   .25
2716 A864 10p magenta   .25   .25
2717 A864 15p green   .25   .25
2718 A864 16p brn lake   .25   .25
2719 A864 17p yel org   .25   .25
2720 A864 18p grn bl   .25   .25
2721 A864 19p brown   .25   .25
2722 A864 20p lil rose   .25   .25
2723 A864 21p dark grn   .25   .25
2724 A864 28p vio brn   .35   .25
2725 A864 29p olive   .40   .25
2726 A864 30p ultramarine   .40   .25
2727 A864 32p green   .45   .25
2728 A864 35p red   .40   .25
2729 A864 45p bluish grn   .55   .25
2730 A864 55p sepia   3.00   .50
  a.   Block of 4, #2714, 2720,
         2725, 2730 + 2 labels   3.00   .50
2731 A864 60p org brn   1.00   .50
  a.   Block of 4, #2716, 2721,
         2726, 2731 + 2 labels   2.50 1.25
2732 A864 65p red org   .70   .25
  a.   Block of 4, #2719, 2724,
         2729, 2732 + 2 labels   2.50 2.00
2733 A864 70p vermilion   .90   .45
Engr.
2734 A864a 100p brown   2.50   .30
2735 A864a 200p green   6.25   .60
2736 A864a 300p maroon   11.00   .90
2737 A864a 500p blue   17.50 1.50
2738 A864a 1000p vio blk   35.00 4.00
    Nos. 2714-2738 (25)   82.90 13.00

    Issued: 17p, 28p, 45p, 65p, 5/21/93; 1p,
18p, 29p, 1/31/94; 19p, 30p, 1994; 19p, 30p,
1/3/95; 10p, 60p, 6/5/95; 1000p, 11/24/95;
100p, 200p, 300p, 500p, 12/12/96; 21p, 32p,
1/27/97; 2p, 16p, 5/19/97; 15p, 3/6/98; 35p,
2/13/98; 70p, 1/30/98. 20p, 11/20/00.

Don Juan de
Borbon (1913-
1993), Count of
Barcelona — A865

1993, June 20 Photo. Perf. 14x13½
2744 A865 28p multicolored   .35   .25

Igualada-Martorell Railway,
Cent. — A866

1993, July 4   Engr.   Perf. 13½x14
2745 A866 45p black & green   .60   .25

Natl. Mint
(F.N.M.T.),
Cent.
A867

1993, Sept. 13
2746 A867 65p dark blue   .90   .25

Explorers
A868

    Designs: 45p, Alejandro Malaspina (1754-
1809), Italian explorer of South America. 65p,
Jose Celestino Mutis (1732-1808), Spanish
naturalist in the Americas, vert.

Perf. 13½x14, 14x13½
1993, Sept 20   Litho.
2747 A868 45p multicolored   .60   .25
2748 A868 65p multicolored   .90   .25

Ciconia
Nigra
A869

    Endangered birds: No. 2750, Gypaetus
barbatus (Quebrantahuesos).

Litho. & Engr.
1993, Oct. 11   Perf. 13½x14
2749 A869 65p pink & black   .90   .25
2750 A869 65p orange & black   .90   .25

Child's
Painting — A870

1993, Oct. 2   Litho.   Perf. 14x13½
2751 A870 45p multicolored   .60   .25

European
Year of the
Elderly
A871

1993, Oct. 29   Photo.   Perf. 14
2752 A871 45p multicolored   .60   .25

A872

Christmas — A873

Perf. 13½x14, 14x13½
1993, Nov. 23   Photo.
2753 A872 17p multicolored   .25   .25
Litho., Photo. & Engr.
2754 A873 28p multicolored   .40   .25

Jorge Guillen
(1893-1984),
Poet — A874

1993, Nov. 29 Engr. Perf. 14x13½
2755 A874 28p green   .40   .25

**UNESCO World Heritage Type of
1991**

    Design: 50p, Monastery of Santa Maria of
Poblet, Tarragona.

1993, Dec. 3   Engr.   Perf. 13x12½
2756 A830 50p multicolored   .65   .25

Spanish
Film
Industry
A875

    29p, Luis Bunuel (1900-83), director. 55p,
Segundo de Chomon (1871-1929), film
pioneer.

1994, Jan. 28   Photo.   Perf. 14
2757 A875 29p multicolored   .40   .25
2758 A875 55p multicolored   .75   .25

Mushroom Type of 1993
1994, Feb. 18   Photo.   Perf. 14
2759 A857 18p Boletus satanas   .25   .25
2760 A857 18p Boletus edulis   .25   .25
2761 A857 29p Amanita phal-
                loides   .35   .25
2762 A857 29p Lactarius delici-
                osus   .35   .25
    Nos. 2759-2762 (4)   1.20 1.00

Minerals
A876

a, Cinnabar. b, Sphalerite. c, Pyrite. d, Galena.

1994, Feb. 25
2763 A876 29p Block of 4, #a.-d.,
+ 2 labels   2.75 2.00

Barrister's
Mailbox
A877

Litho. & Engr.
1994, Mar. 9   *Perf. 13½x14*
2764 A877 29p light & dark brn   .40 .25
Stamp Day.

ILO, 75th
Anniv.
A878

1994, Apr. 7   Photo.   *Perf. 13½x14*
2765 A878 65p multicolored   .85 .25

Art of
Salvador
Dali (1904-
89)
A879

Paintings: #2766, Retrato de Gala. #2767, Poesia de America. #2768, El Gran Masturbador. #2769, Port Alguer. #2770, Self portrait. #2771, Cesta del Pan. #2772, El Enigma Sin Fin. #2173, Galatea de las Esferas.

1994, Apr. 22   *Perf. 13½x14, 14x13½*
2766 A879 18p multi   .25 .25
2767 A879 18p multi, vert.   .25 .25
2768 A879 29p multi   .40 .25
2769 A879 29p multi, vert.   .40 .25
2770 A879 55p multi, vert.   .80 .25
2771 A879 55p multi   .80 .25
2772 A879 65p multi   1.00 .25
2773 A879 65p multi, vert.   1.00 .25
   Nos. 2766-2773 (8)   4.90 2.00

Josep Pla (1897-1981), Writer — A880

1994, Apr. 23   Engr.   *Perf. 13½x14*
2774 A880 65p dark grn & lake   .85 .25

A881

Painting: Martyrdom of St. Andrew, by Rubens.

1994, Apr. 29   Photo.   *Perf. 14*
2775 A881 55p multicolored   .70 .25
Carlos de Amberes Foundation, 400th anniv.

A882

A883

1994, May 3   Photo.
2776 A882 18p multicolored   .25 .25
Litho., Photo. & Engr.
2777 A883 29p multicolored   .40 .25
Santa Cruz de Tenerife, 400th anniv. (#2776). Complutense University of Madrid, 700th Anniv. (#2777).

Europa
A884

Designs: 55p, Severo Ochoa (1905-93), 1959 Nobel Laureate in Medicine. 65p, Miguel Angel Catalan (1894-1957), physicist.

1994, May 5   Litho. & Engr.
2778 A884 55p multicolored   .65 .25
2779 A884 65p multicolored   .80 .25

Spanish
Literature
A885

Novels by Camilo Jose Cela: 18p, The Family of Pascual Duarte. 29p, Journey to Alcarria.

1994, May 11   Photo.
2780 A885 18p multicolored   .25 .25
2781 A885 29p multicolored   .55 .25

King Sancho
Ramirez, 900th
Death
Anniv. — A886

Treaty of Tordesillas, 500th
Anniv. — A887

Design: 55p, Natl. Archives, Simancas.

Litho. & Engr.
1994, June 7   *Perf. 14*
2782 A886 18p multicolored   .25 .25
2783 A887 29p multicolored   .35 .25
2784 A887 55p multicolored   .70 .25
   Nos. 2782-2784 (3)   1.30 .75

Souvenir Sheet

Cathedral of St. Anne, Las Palmas,
Grand Canary Island — A888

1994, July 1   *Perf. 13½x14*
2785 A888 100p multicolored   2.00 1.50
Exfilna '94, Natl. Philatelic Exhibition, Grand Canary Island.

Yachts — A889

1994, July 15   Photo.   *Perf. 14x13½*
2786 A889 16p Giralda   .25 .25
2787 A889 29p Saltillo   .35 .25

Roman City of Augusta Emerita
(Merida), Badajoz — A890

Litho. & Engr.
1994, Sept. 8   *Perf. 13*
2788 A890 55p lake, brn & buff   .80 .25
UNESCO World Heritage list.

Museum of Cards,
Alava — A891

Antique cards: 18p, Horse of Spades. 29p, Jack of Diamonds. 55p, King of Hearts. 65p, War god, Mars, of Diamonds.

1994, Sept. 20   Photo.   *Perf. 14x13½*
2789 A891 18p multicolored   .25 .25
2790 A891 29p multicolored   .35 .25
2791 A891 55p multicolored   .70 .25
2792 A891 65p multicolored   .90 .25
   Nos. 2789-2792 (4)   2.20 1.00

Postal Transportation — A892

1994, Oct. 11   Litho.   *Perf. 13½*
2793 A892 65p DC-8   .90 .25

Public Transit — A893

Civil Guard
A894

1994, Oct. 17   Photo.   *Perf. 14x13½*
2794 A893 18p multicolored   .25 .25
        Perf. 13½x14
2795 A894 29p multicolored   .40 .25

Western
European
Union
A895

1994, Oct. 21   *Perf. 13½x14*
2796 A895 55p multicolored   .75 .25

Olympic
Venues
A896

Designs: a, Track. b, Skiing. c, Equestrian. d, Wrestling. e, Archery. f, Cycling. g, Soccer. h, Field hockey. i, Swimming. j, Sailing.

1994, Oct. 27
2797   Block of 10 + 10 labels   6.00 5.00
   a.-j. A896 29p any single   .50   .40
Labels inscribed with names of Spanish gold medalists and Intl. Olympic Committee cent.
See Nos. 2822, 2850.

Christmas — A897

1994, Nov. 18   *Perf. 14x13½*
2798 A897 29p multicolored   .40 .25

Spanish
Motion
Pictures
A898

Designs: 30p, Belle Epoque, by Fernando Trueba. 60p Volver A Empezar (Begin the Beguine), by Jose Luis Garci.

1995, Jan. 20   **Photo.**   *Perf. 14*
2799 A898 30p multicolored   .40 .25
2800 A898 60p multicolored   .85 .25

City of Logrono, 900th Anniv. A899

1995, Jan. 25
2801 A899 30p multicolored   .40 .25

Souvenir Sheet

SIERRA NEVADA '95, Granada — A900

1995, Jan. 30
2802 A900 130p White star flower   1.75 1.75

World Alpine Skiing Championships.

Mushrooms — A901

1995, Feb. 9   **Photo.**   *Perf. 13½x14*
2803 A901 19p Coprinus comatus   .25 .25
2804 A901 30p Dermocybe cinnamomea   .40 .25

Minerals A902

Designs: a, Dolomite. b, Technical School for Mining Engineers, Madrid. c, Aragonite.

1995, Feb. 24
2805   Strip of 3   1.25 1.25
   a.-c.   A902 30p any single   .40 .25

Stamp Day A903

1995, Mar. 9   **Engr.**
2806 A903 30p Bronze lion's head   .40 .25

Alejandro Goicoechea Omar, TALGO Train — A904

Design: 60p, Young Omar, early train.

1995, Mar. 17   **Photo.**   *Perf. 14*
2807 A904 30p multicolored   .40 .25
2808 A904 60p multicolored   .85 .25

A905   A906

1995, Apr. 6
2809 A905 60p multicolored   .85 .25

Nature conservation in Europe.

Litho. & Engr.
1995, Apr. 7   *Perf. 14*
18th Century Sailing Ships: 19p, San Juan Nepomuceno. 30p, San Telmo.

2810 A906 19p multicolored   .30 .25
   a.   Miniature sheet of 4   1.20 1.20
2811 A906 30p multicolored   .70 .25
   a.   Miniature sheet of 4   2.80 2.80

See also Nos. 2847-2848.

Lebaniego Celebration Year — A907

60p, Mountains, St. Toribio Monastery.

1995, Apr. 21   **Photo.**   *Perf. 12½*
2812 A907 30p multicolored   .40 .25
2813 A907 60p multicolored   .85 .25

Spanish Literature A908

Designs: 19p, El Nino Yuntero, by Miguel Hernandez (1910-42). 30p, Juanita la Larga, by Juan Valera (1824-1905), vert.

Litho. & Engr.
1995, Apr. 27   *Perf. 14*
2814 A908 19p multicolored   .25 .25
Engr.
2815 A908 30p green & blue   .40 .25

Jose Marti (1853-95), Cuban Writer A909

1995, Apr. 28   **Photo.**
2816 A909 60p multicolored   .85 .25

Spanish Cartoon Characters A910

1995, May 4   **Photo.**   *Perf. 14*
2817 A910 30p Captain Trueno   .45 .25
2818 A910 60p Carpanta, vert.   .90 .25

See Nos. 2854-2855.

Europa A911

1995, May 5
2819 A911 60p multicolored   .90 .25

Motion Pictures, Cent. A912

19p, Auguste and Louis Lumiere, early camera.

1995, May 12   **Engr.**   *Perf. 14*
2820 A912 19p brownish black   .25 .25

Press Assoc. of Madrid, Cent. A913

1995, May 12   **Litho.**
2821 A913 30p multicolored   .45 .25

Olympic Venue Type of 1994

Designs: a, Track. b, Basketball. c, Boxing. d, Soccer. e, Gymnastics. f, Equestrian. g, Field hockey. h, Canoeing. i, Polo. j, Two-man rowing. k, Tennis. l, Shooting. m, Sailing. n, Water polo.

1995, June 2   **Photo.**   *Perf. 14*
2822   Block of 14 + 6 labels   6.25 6.25
   a.-n.   A896 30p any single   .45 .25

Labels are inscribed with names of Spanish silver medallists.

UN, 50th Anniv. A914

FAO, 50th Anniv. — A915

World Tourism Organization, 20th Anniv. — A916

1995, June 26
2823 A914 60p multicolored   .90 .25
2824 A915 60p multicolored   .90 .25
2825 A916 60p multicolored   .90 .25
   Nos. 2823-2825 (3)   2.70 .75

A917

1995, July 1
2826 A917 60p multicolored   .90 .25

Spanish Presidentcy of the European Community Council of Ministers.

A918

1995, Sept. 4   **Photo.**   *Perf. 14*
2827 A918 60p multicolored   .90 .25

4th World Conference on Women, Beijing.

Souvenir Sheet

17th Intl. Conference of Cartography, Barcelona — A919

1995, Sept. 5
2828 A919 130p multicolored   2.75 2.25

Santiago de Compostela University, 500th Anniv. — A920

1995, Sept. 15
2829 A920 30p multicolored   .45 .25

UNESCO World Heritage Type of 1991 and

A921

#2830, Royal Monastery of Santa Maria de Guadalupe, vert. #2831, Map of Santiago de Compostela's 9th cent. route through northern Spain.

1995, Sept. 29   **Engr.**   *Perf. 12½*
2830 A830 60p dark brown   1.00 .25
Photo. & Engr.
2831 A921 60p multicolored   1.00 .25

Ecological Protection System, Lagunas Manchegas — A922

Ducks: 60p, Anade real, pato colorado.

1995, Oct. 11   **Photo.**   **Perf. 14**
2832 A922 60p multicolored   .90   .25
America Issue.

Souvenir Sheet

EXFILNA '95, Nat. Philatelic Exhibition, Malaga — A923

Litho. & Engr.
1995, Oct. 6   **Perf. 14x13½**
2833 A923 130p dark green   2.00 2.00

Archaeology — A924

#2834, Cave of Menga, Antequera, Malaga. #2835, Ruins of Torralba, Minorca.

1995, Oct. 20   **Photo.**
2834 A924 30p multicolored   .50   .25
2835 A924 30p multicolored   .50   .25

Souvenir Sheet

The Contemporary Poets, by Antonio Maria Esquivel (1806-57) — A925

Group of poets: a, Seated at left. b, One reading from paper. c, Four standing. d, Standing, seated at right.

1995, Oct. 27
2836 A925 Sheet of 4   3.25 3.25
 a.   19p multicolored   .30   .25
 b.   30p multicolored   .55   .45
 c.-d.   60p any single   1.25   .90

Christmas A926

Design: 30p, Capital sculpture of "Adoration of the Magi," Collegiate Church of San Martin de Elines, Cantabria.

1995, Nov. 17   **Photo.**   **Perf. 14**
2837 A926 30p multicolored   .45   .25

Espamer '96, Aviation & Space Philatelic Exhibitions, Seville — A927

#2838, Sevilla-Plaza de Armas Railway Station. #2839, Lorenzo Galindez de Carvajal, Master Courier, King Fernando's Court, vert.

1995, Dec. 20   **Photo.**   **Perf. 13**
2838 A927 60p multicolored   .90   .25
2839 A927 60p multicolored   .90   .25

Spanish Motion Pictures, Cent. A928

Designs: 30p, Scene from first Spanish motion picture, "Salida de los Fieles del Pilar de Zaragoza." 60p, Poster for 1952 motion picture, "Bienvenido, Mister Marshall."

1996, Jan. 30   **Photo.**   **Perf. 14**
2840 A928 30p multicolored   .45   .25
2841 A928 60p multicolored   .90   .25

Spanish Mining — A929

Designs: 30p, Miner's lamp from Museum of Mining and Industry, mine shaft. 60p, Fluorite.

1996, Feb. 7
2842 A929 30p multicolored   .45   .25
2843 A929 60p multicolored   .90   .25

Madrid-Irun Visual Telegraph Line, 150th Anniv. — A930

1996, Mar. 8   **Engr.**   **Perf. 14**
2844 A930 60p lake & gray grn   .90   .25
Stamp Day.

Barcelona, 10th Anniv. of Urban Transformation — A931

1996, Mar. 22
2845 A931 30p multicolored   .45   .25

Endangered Wildlife — A932

1996, Mar. 27   **Photo.**
2846 A932 30p Ursus arctos   .45   .25

18th Cent. Sailing Ship Type of 1995
Designs: 30p, King Phillip. 60p, Catalán.

Litho. & Engr.
1996, Apr. 19   **Perf. 14x13½**
2847 A906 30p multicolored   .50   .25
 a.   Miniature sheet of 4   2.50 2.50
2848 A906 60p multicolored   1.00   .25
 a.   Miniature sheet of 4   4.50 4.50

Nos. 2847-2848 printed in miniature sheets of 4.

Madrid Bar Assoc., 400th Anniv. A933

1996, Apr. 23   **Photo.**   **Perf. 14**
2849 A933 19p multicolored   .30   .25

Olympic Venue Type of 1994
Symbols of Olympic venues, bronze ribbon: a, like #2797a. b, like #2822c. c, like #2797b. d, like 2797h. e, like #2797i. f, like 2822h. g, like #2822k. h, like #2822 l. i, like #2797j.

1996, Apr. 26   **Photo.**   **Perf. 14**
2850   Block of 9 + 6 labels   5.00 4.50
 a.-i.   A896 30p Any single   .50   .25

Labels are inscribed with names of Spanish bronze medalists.

Souvenir Sheets

A934

Royal Family — A935

Espamer '96 Philatelic Exhibition, World Aviation and Space Exposition: No. 2851a, Map of Seville-Larache Air Route, 1921. b, Zeppelin cover, Seville, 1930. c, Rocket launch. d, Hispano HA 200 SAETA aircraft.

1996, May 4
2851   Sheet of 4   7.00 6.50
 a.-d.   A934 100p any single   1.60 1.40
2852 A935 400p multicolored   7.00 6.50

Carmen Amaya, Flamenco Dancer — A936

1996, May 6   **Perf. 14x13½**
2853 A936 60p multicolored   .90   .25
Europa.

Cartoon Characters Type of 1995
1996, May 10   **Perf. 14x13½, 13½x14**
2854 A910 19p El Jabato, vert.   .35   .25
2855 A910 30p El Reporter Tribulete   .65   .25

Paintings by Francisco de Goya Y Lucientes (1746-1828) — A937

19p, Gen. Don Antonio Ricardos, vert. 30p, Dairymaid of Bordeaux, vert. 60p, Boys with a Mastiff. 130p, The 3rd of May, 1808.

1996, May 31   **Photo.**   **Perf. 14x13½**
2856 A937 19p multicolored   .35   .25
2857 A937 30p multicolored   .60   .25

Perf. 13½x14
2858 A937 60p multicolored   1.10   .25
2859 A937 130p multicolored   2.00   .40
 Nos. 2856-2859 (4)   4.05 1.15

Philatelic Service, 50th Anniv. A938

1996, June 4   **Perf. 13½x14**
2860 A938 30p multicolored   .65   .25

Popular Personalities — A939

Designs: 19p, José Monge Cruz, singer, vert. 30p, Lola Flores, movie star.

Perf. 14x13½, 13½x14
1996, June 14
2861 A939 19p multicolored   .25   .25
2862 A939 30p multicolored   .45   .25

Lanuza Central Market, Zaragoza A940

1996, July 5   **Photo.**   **Perf. 13½x14**
2863 A940 30p multicolored   .65   .25
19th Intl. Congress of Architects, Barcelona.

Gerardo Diego (1896-1987),
Poet — A941

Joaquín Costa (1846-1911), Lawyer,
Teacher — A942

1996, Sept. 13   **Engr.**
2864 A941 19p red, black & vio   .30   .25
     Litho. & Engr.
2865 A942 30p multicolored   .60   .25

UNICEF, 50th
Anniv. — A943

1996, Sept. 13   **Photo.**
2866 A943 60p blue, black & red 1.00   .25

Archaeological Finds — A944

Designs: No. 2867, Naveta Des Tudons,
tomb, 2000-1500BC. No. 2868, Cabezo de
Alcala, reamains of Roman temple, 54-49BC.

1996, Sept. 27   **Photo.**
2867 A944 30p multicolored   .50   .25
2868 A944 30p multicolored   .50   .25

           Souvenir Sheet

Exfilna '96, Natl. Philatelic Exhibition,
Vitoria-Gasteiz — A945

Painting of Vitoria-Gasteiz, capital of Alava
Province, by Ignacio Diaz Ruiz de Olano
(1860-1937).

1996, Oct. 11   **Engr.**   **Perf. 14x13½**
2869 A945 130p rose carmine   2.25 2.00
     Sheet margin is litho.

America
Issue — A946

Traditional costume of Charro Region,
Salamanca.

1996, Oct. 15   **Photo.**   **Perf. 14**
2870 A946 60p multicolored   .85   .25

Sites on UNESCO World Heritage
List — A947

Designs: 19p, Albaicin, old Muslim quarter,
Granada, vert. 30p, Gateway to Tiberiades
Square, statue of Maimonides. 60p, Deer, De
Donana Natl. Park, Huelva province, vert.

     Perf. 12½x13, 13x12½
1996, Oct. 25   **Engr.**
2871 A947 19p dark blue violet   .35   .25
2872 A947 30p deep claret   .55   .25
2873 A947 60p dark blue   1.10   .25
    Nos. 2871-2873 (3)   2.00   .75

Spanish
Literature
A948

Designs: 30p, "La Regenta," by Leopoldo
Garcia-Alas Ureña (1852-1901), vert. 60p,
Don Juan Tenorio, by José Zorrilla Moral
(1817-93).

     Perf. 14x13½, 13½x14
1996, Nov. 13   **Engr.**
2874 A948 30p bl, dep mag & dp
          vio   .40   .25
2875 A948 60p dp blue & dp brn   .80   .25

Christmas — A949

Birth of Christ, by Fernando Gallego.

1996, Nov. 22   **Photo.**   **Perf. 14**
2876 A949 30p multicolored   .40   .25

           Souvenir Sheet

Official Map of Spain and Its
Provinces — A950

1996, Dec. 5
2877 A950 130p multicolored   2.25 2.00

A951

Endangered species.

1997, Jan. 30 Photo.   **Perf. 14x13½**
2878 A951 32p Genetta genetta   .45   .25
     See Nos. 2928, 2978-2980.

A952

1997, Feb. 28 Photo.   **Perf. 14x13½**
2879 A952 32p multicolored   .40   .25
    Juvenia '97, Natl. Juvenile Philatelic
Exhibition.

Stamp
Day
A953

1997, Mar. 7   **Engr.**   **Perf. 14**
2880 A953 65p Antique letter box 1.00   .25

Spanish Motion
Pictures — A954

1997, Mar. 12   **Photo.**
2881 A954 21p "Trip to Nowhere"   .25   .25
2882 A954 32p "The South"   .40   .25

World Day of
Water — A955

1997, Mar. 22   **Perf. 14x13½**
2883 A955 65p multicolored   .80   .25

19th Cent. Sailing
Ships — A956

1997, Apr. 16   **Litho. & Engr.**
2884 A956 21p Frigate Asturias   .40   .25
   a.   Miniature sheet of 4   1.50 1.50

2885 A956 32p Spanish Brigan-
            tine   .60   .25
   a.   Miniature sheet of 4   3.00 3.00

Bilbao School of Engineering,
Cent., — A957

194p, Atocha Station, High-Speed Spanish
Train (AVE), 5th Anniv.

1997, Apr. 22 Photo.   **Perf. 14x13½**
2886 A957 32p multicolored   .75   .25
2887 A957 194p multicolored   3.00   .70

Dr. Josep Trueta (1897-1977),
Orthopedic Surgeon — A958

1997, Apr. 30   **Perf. 14**
2888 A958 32p multicolored   .40   .25

Stories and
Legends — A959

Europa: Princess, Prince, gnome, castle.

1997, May 5 Photo.   **Perf. 14x13½**
2889 A959 65p multicolored   1.25   .25

Fictional
Characters
A960

Designs: 21p, "El Lazarillo de Tormes," vert.
32p, "El Séneca," by José María Pemán.

1997, May 8   **Engr.**   **Perf. 14**
2890 A960 21p green & black   .30   .25
2891 A960 32p black & blue   .60   .25

Anxel Fole
(1903-86),
Poet,
Writer
A961

1997, May 17   **Photo.**
2892 A961 65p multicolored   1.00   .25

Comics
A962

1997, May 30
2893 A962 21p The Ulysses
           Family   .30   .25
2894 A962 32p The Masked War-
           rior   .65   .25

Popular Personalities — A963

32p, Manuel Rodríguez Sánchez (Manolete) (1917-47), bullfighter. 65p, Charlie Rivel (Josep Andreu i Lasserre) (1896-1983), circus clown.

1997, June 5   Photo.
2895 A963 32p multicolored   .50 .25
2896 A963 65p multicolored   1.25 .25

A964

"The Age of Man" Cultural Exhibition: a, 21p, Painting, "The Annunciation," from Church of Nuestra Señora de la Peña, Agreda. b, 32p, Cathedral of El Burgo de Osma. c, 65p, Miniature from Codex titled "Commentary on the Apocalypse," by Beatus of Liebana, 786AD. d, 140p, Statue of Santo Domingo de Silos.

1997, June 13   Perf. 13
2897 A964 Sheet of 4, #a.-d.   4.50 4.00

A965

1997, June 24   Perf. 14
2898 A965 65p multicolored   .80 .25
30th European Men's Basketball Championships.

NATO Summit, Madrid — A966

1997, July 8   Perf. 13
2899 A966 65p multicolored   1.25 .25

A967

Design: Natl. monument to honor grape harvesting, Requena.

1997, July 11   Litho.   Perf. 14
2900 A967 32p multicolored   .40 .25

A968

Anniversaries: 21p, Don Antonio Canovas del Castillo (1828-97), politician. 32p, Roman colony of Elche, 2000th anniv. 65p, Naval defense of Tenerife, bicent.

1997, July 24   Photo.
2901 A968 21p multicolored   .25 .25
2902 A968 32p multicolored   .40 .25
2903 A968 65p multicolored   .80 .25
     Nos. 2901-2903 (3)   1.45 .75

Peace in Basque Region — A969

1997, July 30   Photo.   Perf. 14
2904 A969 32p multicolored   .35 .25

Spanish Artists — A970

Designs: 32p, Mariano Benlliure Gil (1862-1947), sculptor. 65p, Photograph of Remero Vasco, by José Ortíz Echagüe (1886-1980).

1997, Sept. 12
2905 A970 32p multicolored   .50 .25
2906 A970 65p black & beige   1.00 .25

VIGO '97, World Exposition on Fisheries A971

1997, Sept. 17   Litho.
2907 A971 32p multicolored   .35 .25

Anniversaries — A972

21p, City of Melilla, 500th anniv., vert. 32p, Declaration of St. Pascual Baylon as patron saint of World Eucharistic Congress, cent., vert. 65p, Ausias March (1397-1459), writer.

1997, Sept. 24   Photo.
2908 A972 21p multicolored   .25 .25
2909 A972 32p multicolored   .50 .25
                 Engr.
2910 A972 65p multicolored   1.00 .25
     Nos. 2908-2910 (3)   1.75 .75

Sites on UNESCO World Heritage List — A973

Churches in Oviedo: 21p, San Julian de los Prados. 32p, Santa Cristina de Lena.

1997, Sept. 26   Engr.   Perf. 13
2911 A973 21p multicolored   .50 .25
2912 A973 32p multicolored   .75 .25

29th Intl. Congress of Transport and Communications Museums, Madrid — A974

1997, Oct. 1   Litho.   Perf. 14x13½
2913 A974 140p multicolored   2.00 .65

Souvenir Sheet

Monument to Don Pelayo, Revillagigedo Palace, Gijón — A975

1997, Oct. 4   Litho. & Engr.   Perf. 14
2914 A975 140p multicolored   2.50 2.00
Exfilna '97, Natl. Stamp Exhibition, Gijón, Asturias

Opening of Royal Theater, Madrid — A976

Designs: 21p, Miguel Fleta (1897-1938), opera singer. 32p, Outside view of theater.

1997, Oct. 11   Engr.   Perf. 14x13½
2915 A976 21p violet brown   .25 .25
2916 A976 32p gray brown   .40 .25

America Issue — A977

1997, Oct. 10   Photo.
2917 A977 65p Postman   .80 .30

Foundation of St. Cristobal de La Laguna, 500th Anniv. — A978

1997, Oct. 17   Litho. & Engr.
2918 A978 32p multicolored   .40 .25

6th World Conference on Down Syndrome, Madrid — A979

1997, Oct. 23   Photo.   Perf. 13½x14
2919 A979 65p blue & yellow   .80 .30

Veterinary College, Cordoba, 150th Anniv. A980

1997, Nov. 14   Engr.   Perf. 14
2920 A980 21p green & blue   .25 .25

Christmas — A981

Painting, Adoration of the Kings, by Pedro Berruguete.

1997, Nov. 20   Photo.
2921 A981 32p multicolored   .40 .25

Jewish Heritage in Spain A982

Designs: 21p, Porta Nova, Ourense. No. 2923, Women's Gallery, Cordoba Synagogue. No. 2924, Jewish quarter, Caceres, 15th cent. 65p, Jewish Museum, Girona.

1997, Nov. 28   Engr.   Perf. 13½x14
2922 A982 21p black & brown   .30 .25
2923 A982 32p black & violet   .50 .25
2924 A982 32p black & brown   .50 .25
2925 A982 65p black & violet 1.00 .30
  a. Strip of 4, #2922-2925 3.00 1.25

See Nos. 2969-2972.

Spanish Sports Accomplishments — A983

1997, Dec. 5   Photo.
2926 A983 32p multicolored   1.25 .25

XACOBEO 99 — A984

1998, Jan. 12 Photo. Perf. 14x13½
2927 A984 35p blk, org & gray .60 .25

Endangered Fauna — A985

1998, Feb. 5
2928 A985 35p Lynx pardina .90 .25

Bilbao Athletic Club, Cent. — A986

1998, Feb. 10 Perf. 13½x14
2929 A986 35p multicolored .45 .25

Comic Book Characters A987

Designs: 35p, Mortadelo and Filemón, by Ibáñez, vert. 70p, Zipi & Zape, by Escobar.

Perf. 14x13½, 13½x14
1998, Feb. 26 Photo.
2930 A987 35p multicolored .50 .25
2931 A987 70p multicolored 1.10 .45

See Nos. 2998-2999.

Gredos State Hotel A988

1998, Mar. 12 Photo. Perf. 13½x14
2932 A988 35p multicolored .45 .25

Self-Government Statutes for Melilla and Ceuta — A989

1998, Mar. 16 Perf. 13½x14, 14x13½
2933 A989 150p Melilla 1.90 1.00
2934 A989 150p Ceuta, vert. 1.90 1.00

"Generation of '98" Authors — A990

Design: Azorín (José Martinez Ruiz) (1873-1967), Pío Baroja (1872-1956), Miguel de Unamuno (1864-1936), Ramiro de Maetzu (1874-1936), Antonio Machado (1875-1939), Ramon Valle Inclán (1866-1936).

1998, Apr. 3 Photo. Perf. 14
2935 A990 70p multicolored 1.10 .45

A991

Design: Pedro Abarca de Bolea, Count of Aranda (1719-98), soldier, politician.

1998, Apr. 17
2936 A991 35p multicolored .45 .25

A992

Literary characters from: 35p, Fernando de Rojas' "Le Celestina." 70p, Benito Perez Galdos' "Fortunata and Jacinta."

1998, Apr. 29 Engr. Perf. 14x13½
2937 A992 35p multicolored .55 .25
2938 A992 70p multicolored 1.10 .45

Ships A993

1998, Apr. 30 Litho. Perf. 14
2939 A993 35p Embarcación real .45 .25
2940 A993 70p Jabeque tajo .90 .45

Popular Festivals — A994

1998, May 5 Photo.
2941 A994 70p Bonfire of St. John .90 .45

Europa.

College of Medicine, Madrid, Cent. A995

Dr. D. Carlos Jiménez Díaz (1898-1967).

1998, May 18 Perf. 13½x14
2942 A995 35p multicolored .45 .25

Popular Personalities — A996

35p, Félix Rodríguez de la Fuente (b. 1928), wildlife activist. 70p, Alfonso Aragón Bermúdez ("Fofó") (1923-76), circus comic, vert.

1998, May 28 Perf. 13½x14, 14x13½
2943 A996 35p multicolored .55 .25
2944 A996 70p multicolored 1.10 .45

A997

Design: King Philip II (1527-98).

1998, June 1 Photo. Perf. 14x13½
2945 A997 35p multicolored .45 .25

A998

Fedrico Garcia Lorca (1898-1936), poet, dramatist.

1998, June 2 Litho. & Engr.
2946 A998 35p multicolored .85 .25

Spanish Stamp Engravers A999

35p, Antonio Manso (1934-93), Spain #2129. 70p, J.L.L. Sánchez Toda (1901-), Spain #546.

1998, June 5 Perf. 14
2947 A999 35p multicolored .45 .25
2948 A999 70p multicolored .90 .45

Philippine Independence, Cent. — A1000

Design: Spanish flag, Basilica of Cebu, Holy Child of Cebu, Philippine flag.

1998, June 12 Photo. Perf. 13½x14
2949 A1000 70p multicolored .95 .50

See Philippines No. 2539.

Sculpture, "Foster Brothers," by Aniceto Marinas (1866-1953) A1000a

1998, July 10 Photo. Perf. 14
2949A A1000a 35p multi .50 .25

Expo '98, Lisbon A1001

1998, Sept. 4
2950 A1001 70p multicolored 1.00 .50

Letter Writing — A1002

Scenes from "Don Quixote" — #2951: a, "En un lugas de la Mancha." b, "Llenósele la fantasía." c, "Armado caballero." d, "La del alba sería." e, "Le molió como cibera." f, "El donoso escrutinio." g, "Has de saber, amigo Sancho." h, "Los gigantes." i, "Viole bajar y subir con tanta gracia." j, "El escuadrón de ovejas." k, "Los galeotes." l, "Los cueros."
No. 2952: a, "El encantamiento." b, "Oh princesa del toboso." c, "El caballero de los espejos." d, "El leon." e, "La cueva de montesinos." f, "Clavileño." g, "Sancho gobernador." h, "Doña Rodríguez." i, "Compañero mío." j, "Parecioles espaciosísimo." k, "El caballero de la blanca luna." l, "La vuelta a casa."

1998, Sept. 25 Perf. 13
2951 Sheet of 12 4.50 4.50
  a.-l. A1002 20p any single .30 .25
2952 Sheet of 12 4.50 4.50
  a.-l. A1002 20p any single .30 .25

See #3016, 3053-3954, 3121, 3175.

20th Intl. Conference on Data Protection, Santiago de Compostela — A1003

1998, Sept. 16 Litho. Perf. 14
2953 A1003 70p multicolored .90 .45

Souvenir Sheet

EXFILNA '98 Natl. Philatelic Exhibition — A1004

Litho. & Engr.
1998, Sept. 18 Perf. 14
2954 A1004 150p Cathedral of Barcelona 2.75 2.25

UNESCO World Heritage
Sites — A1005

Designs: 35p, Walled city of Cuenca. 70p,
Silk Exchange, Valencia.

1998, Sept. 19   Engr.   Perf. 13
2955 A1005 35p blue & brown   .60   .25
2956 A1005 70p red & brown   1.40   .45

Angel
Ganivet
(1865-98),
Writer
A1006

1998, Oct. 6   Engr.   Perf. 14
2957 A1006 35p brown & purple   .50   .25

A1007

1998, Oct. 6
2958 A1007 70p multicolored   1.00   .50
The Giralda of Seville, 800th Anniv.

A1008

1998, Oct. 8   Engr.   Perf. 14
2959 A1008 35p brn & yel grn   .50   .25
Aga Khan Architecture Award, Alhambra of
Granada.

Stamp Day
A1009

1998, Oct. 9   Photo.
2960 A1009 70p multicolored   1.00   .50

María Guerrero (1867-1928), Theater
Actress — A1010

1998, Oct. 13
2961 A1010 70p multicolored   1.00   .50
America Issue.

Spanish
Railroads,
150th
Anniv.
A1011

1998, Oct. 28   Engr.
2962 A1011 35p multicolored   .50   .25

Juan
Carlos I
Antarctic
Base
A1012

1998, Nov. 6   Photo.
2963 A1012 35p multicolored   .50   .25

A1013

Christmas (Works of art): 35p, Chestnut
Seller, by Rafael Seco. 70p, Marriage of the
Virgin and St. Joseph, Cathedral of Oviedo.

1998, Nov. 13
2964 A1013 35p multicolored   .50   .25
2965 A1013 70p multicolored   1.00   .50

Souvenir Sheet

A1014

The Cathedral of San Salvador, Zaragoza
(Details from Altarpiece: a, Holding cross,
angel. b, Holy family.

1998, Nov. 11   Photo.   Perf. 14
2966 A1014 35p Sheet of 2, a.-b. 1.50 1.25

Founding
of New
Mexico,
400th
Anniv.
A1015

Designs: 35p, Expedition of Juan de Oñate.
70p, Early map of Nueva Espana (Mexico) and
Nuevo Mexico.

1998, Nov. 20
2967 A1015 35p multicolored   .50   .25
2968 A1015 70p multicolored   1.00   .50

**Jewish Heritage in Spain Type of
1997**

Designs: No. 2969, Bust of Benjamin de
Tudela, Tudela Commune, Navarre. No. 2970,
Residence, Hervás Community, Cáceres. No.
2971, Courtyard, Corpus Christi Church,
Segovia. No. 2972, Santa Maria la Blanca
Synagogue, Toledo.

1998, Nov. 23   Engr.
2969 A982 35p dp blue & dp ol   .60   .25
2970 A982 35p dp blue & dp cl   .60   .25
2971 A982 70p dp blue & dp ol   1.10   .50
2972 A982 70p dp blue & dp ol   1.10   .50
  a.   Strip of 4, #2969-2972   4.00 4.00
  Nos. 2969, 2971 have Star of David. Nos.
2970, 2972 have menorah.

UNESCO
Biosphere
Reserve,
Minorca
A1016

1998, Dec. 2   Photo.
2973 A1016 35p multicolored   .50   .25

Spanish
Olympic
Academy,
30th Anniv.
A1017

1998, Dec. 9
2974 A1017 70p Bust of Plato,
                amphora   1.00   .50

Universal Declaration of Human
Rights, 50th Anniv.
A1018   A1019

Designs: 35p, Angel Sanz Briz (1910-80),
Spanish ambassador. 70p, Fingerprints.

1998, Dec. 10
2975 A1018 35p multicolored   .50   .25
2976 A1019 70p multicolored   1.00   .50

Carthusian Horses — A1020

Designs: a, 100p, Mare standing with colt. b,
185p, Two with heads together. c, 35p, Adult
standing in grass. d, 150p, Adult standing in
flowers. e, 20p, Colt lying down, mare eating
grass. f, 70p, Head of adult, silhouette.

1998, Dec. 29
2977 A1020 Block of 6, #a.-f. 25.00 25.00

España 2000, Intl. Philatelic Exhibition.
  Issued in sheets of two blocks, the lower
one in a different order. Two of the devices
shown on the coat of arms appear on each
block at the intersection of the perfs. On the
top block the crown is on a.-b., d.-e., while the
"H" is on b.-c., e.-f. On the bottom block the
location of these devices is reversed, giving all
the stamps in the sheet a slightly different
design.
  See #3019, 3052.

Gallotia
simonyi
machadoi
A1020a

Pandion haliaetus
A1020b

Puffinus
puffinus —
A1020c

1999, Jan. 28   Photo.   Perf. 14
2978 A1020a   35p multicolored   .50   .25
2979 A1020b   70p multicolored   1.00   .50
2980 A1020c 100p multicolored   1.40   .70
  Nos. 2978-2980 (3)   2.90 1.45
       Endangered fauna.

Xacobeo
'99
A1021

Designs: 35p, Stone cross of Paradela, vert.
70p, Sculpture of St. James, door on Church of
St. James, Sangüesa. 100p, Stone cross,
Cizur Bridge, Pamplona, vert. 185p, Jurisdic-
tional stone pillar, Boadilla del Camino, vert.

**   Litho. & Engr.**
1999, Feb. 22   Perf. 13¾
2981 A1021   35p multicolored   .60   .25
2982 A1021   70p multicolored   1.25   .45
2983 A1021 100p multicolored   1.50   .65
2984 A1021 185p multicolored   2.75 1.10
  Nos. 2981-2984 (4)   6.10 2.45

Barcelona Soccer
Club,
Cent. — A1022

1999, Mar. 11   Photo.   Perf. 14
2985 A1022 35p multicolored   .45   .25

Juvenia
'99, Natl.
Junior
Philatelic
Exhibition
A1023

1999, Mar. 12   Litho.   Perf. 14
2986 A1023 35p multicolored   .50   .25

Spanish
Police
Force,
175th
Anniv.
A1024

1999, Mar. 26
2987 A1024 35p multicolored   .50   .25

Souvenir Sheet

Palace of Alfonso I el Batallador,
Zaragoza — A1025

Litho. & Engr.
1999, Apr. 9   *Perf. 14x13½*
2988 A1025 185p multicolored   3.00 2.75
Exfilna '99, Zaragoza.

Spanish
Amateur
Radio
Union,
50th Anniv.
A1026

1999, Apr. 16   **Photo.**   *Perf. 14*
2989 A1026 70p multicolored   .95 .50

7th World Track &
Field
Championships,
Seville — A1027

1999, Apr. 30   **Photo.**   *Perf. 14x13½*
2990 A1027 70p multicolored   .90 .45

Monfragüe
Nature
Park
A1028

Litho. & Engr.
1999, May 5   *Perf. 13½x14*
2991 A1028 70p multicolored   .90 .45
Europa.

Barcelona
Subway
System,
75th Anniv.
A1029

1999, May 7   **Photo.**   *Perf. 14*
2992 A1029 70p multicolored   .90 .45

Spanish
Art — A1030

Designs: 35p, Portrait of King Solomon.
70p, Artifact from cathedral, Palencia.

1999, May 14
2993 A1030 35p multicolored   .50 .25
2994 A1030 70p multicolored   1.00 .45

Introduction of the Euro — A1031

Design: a, European Union flag.
Maps: b, Germany. c, Austria. d, Belgium e,
Spain. f, Finland. g, France. h, Netherlands. i,
Ireland. j, Italy. k, Luxembourg. l, Portugal.

1999, May 28   *Perf. 13½x14*
2995 A1031 166p Sheet of 12,
        #a.-l.   35.00 30.00
Denomination is shown in both pesetas and
euros. Each stamp shows the equivilent of 1
euro in the currency of the represented
country.

Royal
Recreation
Club of
Huelva
A1032

1999, June 7
2996 A1032 35p multicolored   .45 .25

Souvenir Sheet

Palma '99, Natl. Topical Philatelic
Exhibition — A1033

1999, June 18   *Perf. 14x13½*
2997 A1033 185p multicolored   3.00 3.00

Comic Book Character Type
35p, Dona Urraca, by Jorge, vert. 70p, El
Coyote, by José Mallorquí Figuerola, vert.

1999, June 11   **Photo.**   *Perf. 13¾*
2998 A987 35p multicolored   .50 .25
2999 A987 70p multicolored   1.00 .45

Defense of Las Palmas de Gran
Canaria, 400th Anniv. — A1034

1999, June 25   **Litho. & Engr.**
3000 A1034 70p multicolored   .90 .45

A1035

1999, July 2   **Photo.**   *Perf. 13¾*
3001 A1035 35p multicolored   .45 .25
San Pedro de Villanueva Benedictine
Monastery.

A1036

1999, July 12
3002 A1036 35p multicolored   .45 .25
Village of Balmaseda, 800th anniv.

Carlos
Buigas (b.
1898),
Graphic
Designer
A1037

1999, July 12
3003 A1037 70p multicolored   .90 .45

General Society
of Authors and
Editors,
Cent. — A1038

1999, July 12
3004 A1038 70p multicolored   .90 .45

Spanish
Mining
Institute,
150th
Anniv.
A1039

1999, July 12
3005 A1039 150p multicolored   1.90 .95

El Cid (Rodrigo
Diaz de Vivar)
(1040-99)
A1040

1999, July 16   **Photo.**   *Perf. 13¾*
3006 A1040 35p multicolored   .45 .25

Paintings
by Jose
Vela
Zanetti
(1913-99)
A1041

70p, "Winter." 150p, "The Harvest."

1999, Sept. 10   **Photo.**   *Perf. 13¾*
3007 A1041 70p multi   1.25 .45
3008 A1041 150p multi, vert.   2.25 .95

Diego Velazquez
(1599-1660),
Painter — A1042

Paintings: 35p, Sebastián de Morra. 70p,
Sibyl.

1999, Sept. 24
3009 A1042 35p multicolored   .45 .25
3010 A1042 70p multicolored   .90 .45

Intl. Year
of Older
Persons
A1043

1999, Sept. 30
3011 A1043 35p multicolored   .45 .25

Oix
Castle,
Lower
Pyrenees
A1044

1999, Oct. 1   **Engr.**   *Perf. 13½x14*
3012 A1044 70p blue & vio brn   .90 .45

World Heritage Sites — A1045

Designs: 35p, San Millán de Yuso Monastery. 70p, San Millán de Suso Monastery.

1999, Oct. 8   *Perf. 13x12½*
3013 A1045 35p multicolored   .75 .25
3014 A1045 70p multicolored   1.50 .45

UPU,
125th
Anniv.
A1046

1999, Oct. 9   **Photo.**   *Perf. 13¾*
3015 A1046 70p multicolored   .90 .45

Letter Writing Type of 1998
Designs: a, "Cumplimos 150 años." b,
"Recorremos el mundo." c, "Llegamos juntos."
d, "Escríbeme." e, "Ama la lectura." f, "Vive la
naturaleza." g, "Te mostramos el patrimonio."
h, "Te acercamos a la pintura." i, "Jugamos
contigo." j, "Sentimos la musica." k, "Y además
nos coleccionan." l, "Os esperamos."

400

SPAIN

1999, Oct. 13 Photo. *Perf. 13x12½*
3016   Sheet of 12   4.50 4.50
a.-l. A1002 20p any single   .30 .25

America Issue, A new Millennium Without Arms — A1047

1999, Oct. 15   *Perf. 13¾*
3017 A1047 70p multicolored   .90 .45

Intl. Congress of Money Museums, Madrid — A1048

1999, Oct. 18 Engr. *Perf. 13x12½*
3018 A1048 70p blue & brown   .90 .45

Carthusian Horse Type of 1998

Designs: a, 185p, White horse, six men. b, 70p, Espana Intl. Philatelic Exhibition emblem. c, 100p, Two white horses. d, 150p, Two white horses, one with leg raised. e, 35p, Emblem, exhibition dates. f, 20p, Horse, handler.

1999, Nov. 3 Photo. *Perf. 13¾*
3019 A1020 Block of 6, #a.-f. 14.00 14.00

See footnote following No. 2977.

Christmas A1049

35p, Adoration of the Magi, Toledo Cathedral retable. 70p, Child, statue, candles.

1999, Nov. 5
3020 A1049 35p multi, vert.   .60 .25
3021 A1049 70p multi   1.25 .45

Spanish Postage Stamps, 150th Anniv. A1050

a, King Juan Carlos, altered 12c design A2. b, King, altered 6c design A1. c, King, altered 5r design A2. d, King, altered 6r design A2. e, 150th anniv. emblem, altered 6c design A1. f, King, altered 10r design A2. g, King, coat of arms.

Litho. & Engr.
2000, Jan. 3   *Perf. 13¾x14*
3022   Sheet of 12   7.00 6.50
a.-g. A1050 35p any single   .60 .25

#3022 contains 2 ea #3022a-3022d, 3022f, 1 ea #3022e, 3022g.

Endangered Butterflies — A1051

Designs: 35p, Parnassius apollo. 70p, Agriades zullichi.

2000, Jan. 31 Photo. *Perf. 13¾*
3023 A1051 35p multi   .60 .25
3024 A1051 70p multi   1.25 .45

First Printing at Montserrat Monastery, 500th Anniv. — A1052

2000, Feb. 4 Photo. *Perf. 13¾*
3025 A1052 35p multi   .45 .25

Holy Roman Emperor Charles V (1500-58) A1053

2000, Feb. 24   *Perf. 12¾x13*
3026 A1053 35p shown   .60 .25
3027 A1053 70p At age 40 1.25 .45

Souvenir Sheet
Perf. 13¼x12¾
3028 A1053 150p In armor 2.75 1.75

No. 3028 contains one 40x49mm stamp. See Belgium Nos. 1791-1793.

"Age of Man" Exhibition, Astorga — A1054

Designs: 70p, Carving of the Virgin Mary. 100p, Cross, Arab perfume bottle.

2000, Mar. 24 Photo. *Perf. 14x13¾*
3029 A1054 70p multi   .75 .40
3030 A1054 100p multi 1.10 .55

Ferdinand of Aragon Inn, Sos A1055

2000, Apr. 7   *Perf. 13¾x14*
3031 A1055 35p multi   .60 .25

University Anniversaries — A1056

35p, Lleida, 700th anniv. 70p, Valencia, 500th anniv. (in 1999).

2000, Apr. 12 Engr. *Perf. 13¾x14*
3032 A1056 35p red lil & brown .50 .25
3033 A1056 70p blue & choc   1.00 .40

A1057

2000, Apr. 28 Photo. *Perf. 14x13¾*
3034 A1057 35p multi   .60 .25

Royal Barcelona Sports Club, soccer team, cent.

A1058

2000, May 4
3035 A1058 35p multi   .60 .25

María de las Mercedes de Borbón y Orleáns (1910-2000), mother of King Juan Carlos.

Europa Issue
Common Design Type
2000, May 9
3036 CD17 70p multi   .75 .40

Royal Academy of Medicine, Seville, 300th Anniv. A1060

Julio Rey Pastor (1888-1962), Mathematician — A1061

Pharmacy College of Granada, 150th Anniv. — A1062

Valencia, City of Arts and Sciences A1063

2000, May 25 *Perf. 13¾x14, 14x13¾*
3037 A1060 35p multi   .60 .25
3038 A1061 70p multi   1.00 .40
3039 A1062 100p multi 1.50 .55
3040 A1063 185p multi 3.00 1.00
  Nos. 3037-3040 (4)   6.10 2.20

Intl. Mathematics Year (No. 3038).

Comic Strips A1064

Designs: 35p, Las Hermanas Gilda, by Manuel Vázquez. 70p, Roberto Alcázar y Pedrín, by Eduardo Vañó, vert.

2000, May 26 *Perf. 13¾x14, 14x13¾*
3041 A1064 35p multi   .60 .25
3042 A1064 70p multi   1.25 .40

Guggenheim Museum, Bilbao — A1065

2000, June 2 Photo. *Perf. 13¾x14*
3043 A1065 70p multi   1.00 .40

Bilbao, 700th anniv.

Angel From Prayer in the Garden, Sculpture by Francisco Salzillo (1707-73) A1066

2000, June 9 Photo. *Perf. 14x13¼*
3044 A1066 70p multi   1.10 .40

Souvenir Sheet

Fountains of San Francisco, Aviles — A1067

Litho. & Engr.
2000, June 16   *Perf. 14x13¾*
3045 A1067 185p multi 3.50 2.50

Exfilna 2000 Philatelic Exhibition, Aviles.

Trees A1068

Designs: 70p, Pinus sylvestris. 150p, Quercus ilex (encina).

Perf. 12¾x12½
2000, June 19   Photo.
3046-3047 A1068 Set of 2 3.50 1.10

Local Festivals
A1069

Designs: 35p, Fire Walking Festival, San Pedro Manrique. 70p, Chivalry Festival of San Juan, Ciudadela.

2000, June 23   *Perf. 13¾x14*
3048-3049   A1069   Set of 2   1.60   .55

Josemaria Escrivá de Balaguer (1902-75), Founder of Opus Dei. A1070

2000, June 26   Litho. & Engr.   *Perf. 13¾x14*
3050   A1070   70p black & orange   1.10   .40

Souvenir Sheet

World Map of Juan de la Cosa, 500th Anniv. — A1071

2000, July 14   Photo.   *Perf. 13¾x14*
3051   A1071   150p multi   2.50   1.50

Carthusian Horses Type of 1998

No. 3052: a, 20p, Head of horse, five horses. b, 35p, White horse, sun partially obscured by clouds. c, 70p, Horse's head, two horses galloping. d, 100p, Heads of two horses. e, 150p, Horse's head, horse in lilac. f, 185p, Horse with bridle.

2000, July 28
3052   A1020   Block of 6, #a-f   13.00   13.00
     See note following No. 2977.

Letter Writing Type of 1998

No. 3053: a, Atapuerca Man, 800,000 B.C. b, Cave paintings of Altamira, 12,000 B.C. c, Phoenecians, 1100 B.C. d, Tartessians, 800 B.C. e, Iberians and Celts, 500 B.C. f, Lady of Elche, Iberian statue, 480 B.C. g, Carthaginians, 237 B.C. h, Roman Spain, 197 B.C. i, Viriathus, Lusitanian war leader against Romans, 147 B.C. j, Siege of Numantia, 133 B.C. k, Segovia aqueduct, A.D. 50. l, Vandals, Suebis, and Alanis, 409.

No. 3054: a, Visigoths, 415. b, Conversion of Recared to Catholicism, 589. c, Arabs, 711. d, Victory over Arabs by Asturian King, Pelayo, 722. e, Discovery of alleged tomb of St. James, 813. f, Collapse of the caliphate, 1031. g, Death of El Cid, 1099. h, Alfonso VIII's victory at Las Navas de Tolosa, 1212. i, Alfonso X (the Wise) becomes King, 1252. j, Trastámara Dynasty, 1369. k, Spanish Inquisition, 1478. l, Union of Aragon and Castile, 1479.

2000, Sept. 22   *Perf. 13x12¾*
3053   Sheet of 12   2.50   2.50
   a.-l. A1002 20p Any single   .25   .25
3054   Sheet of 12   2.50   2.50
   a.-l. A1002 20p Any single   .25   .25

World Heritage Sites — A1072

Designs: 35p, Las Médulas. 70p, Pyrénées — Mt. Perdido, vert. 150p, Catalan Music Palace, Barcelona.

Perf. 13x12¾(35p), 12¾
2000, Sept. 21   Litho. (35p), Engr.
3055-3057   A1072   Set of 3   2.75   1.40

Souvenir Sheets

España 2000 Intl. Philatelic Exhibition — A1073

Designs: No. 3058, Hand of Julio Iglesias, singer. No. 3059, Signature of Alejandro Sanz, singer. No. 3060, Signature of Antonio Banderas, movie star. No. 3061, Mannequin, signature of Jesús del Pozo, fashion designer. No. 3062, Signature of Miguel Induráin, cyclist. No. 3063, Soccer ball, signature of Raúl González, soccer player. No. 3064, Hands of Joaquín Cortés, dancer. No. 3065, Feet of Sara Baras, dancer. No. 3066, Emblem of TVE 1 television network. No. 3067, Radio and antenna. No. 3068, Newspaper mastheads.
Illustration reduced.

Perf. 13 (round stamps), 13¾x14
2000   Photo.
3058-3068   A1073   200p Set of
      11   35.00   35.00
   150th anniv. of Spanish stamps, #3066.
   Nos. 3060-3061, 3064-3068 each contain one 41x28mm rectangular stamp.
   Exist imperf. Value $65.
   Issued: #3058-3059, 10/6; #3060, 10/7; #3061, 10/8; #3062-3063, 10/9; #3064-3065, 10/10; #3066, 10/11; #3067, 10/12; #3068, 10/13.

Alfredo Kraus (1927-99), Operatic Tenor — A1074

2000, Oct. 27   *Perf. 14x13¾*
3069   A1074   70p multi   1.00   .40

America Issue, Fight Against AIDS — A1075

2000, Oct. 19   Photo.   *Perf. 14x13¾*
3070   A1075   70p multi   1.00   .40

Christmas A1076

Designs: 35p, Nativity scene. 70p, Birth of Christ, by Conrad von Soest.

2000, Nov. 9   *Perf. 12¾*
3071-3072   A1076   Set of 2   1.50   .55
     See Germany No. B878-B879.

Santa María la Real Church, Aranda de Duero — A1077

2000, Nov. 10   Engr.   *Perf. 14x13¾*
3073   A1077   35p brown   .50   .25

Spanish Literature A1078

Designs: 35p, Entre Naranjos, by Vicente Blasco Ibáñez. 70p, La Venganza de Don Mendo, by Pedro Muñoz Seca. 100p, El Alcalde Zalamea, by Pedro Calderón de la Barca.

Photo., Engr. (100p)
2000, Nov. 17   *Perf. 13¾x14*
3074-3076   A1078   Set of 3   3.25   1.50

Commercial Agents College, 75th Anniv. — A1079

2001, Jan. 8   Photo.   *Perf. 14x13¾*
3077   A1079   40p multi   .60   .25

Fire Fighters — A1080

2001, Jan. 19
3078   A1080   75p multi   1.10   .45

Infantry College, Toledo, 150th Anniv. A1081

2001, Feb. 16   *Perf. 13¾x14*
3079   A1081   120p multi   2.00   .65

Intl. Campaign Against Domestic Violence — A1082

2001, Feb. 22   *Perf. 14x13¾*
3080   A1082   155p multi   2.25   .85

First Spanish Mail Box, Mayorga A1083

2001, Mar. 2   Engr.   *Perf. 13¾x14*
3081   A1083   155p black   2.25   .85
     Stamp Day.

Juvenia 2001, Natl. Youth Philatelic Exhibition A1084

2001, Mar. 9   Photo.
3082   A1084   120p multi   1.75   .70

Placencia Inn — A1084a

2001, Mar. 16   *Perf. 14x13¾*
3083   A1084a   40p multicolored   .60   .25

Famous People A1085

Designs: 40p, Joaquín Rodrigo (1901-99), musician. 75p, Rafael Alberti (1902-99), writer.

2001, Mar. 22   Engr.   *Perf. 13¾x14*
3084-3085   A1085   Set of 2   1.75   .60

Castles A1086

Designs: 40p, Zuda, Tortosa, vert. 75p, Cid, Jadraque. 155p, San Fernando, Figueres. 260p, Montesquiu, Montesquiu.

2001, Apr. 20   *Perf. 14x13¾, 13¾x14*
3086-3089   A1086   Set of 4   8.00   3.00

Book Day — A1087

2001, Apr. 23   Photo.   *Perf. 14x13¾*
3090   A1087   40p multi   .60   .25

Souvenir Sheet

First Flights, 75th Anniv. — A1088

No. 3091: a, 40p, Spain-Argentina. b, 75p, Spain-Philippines. c, 155p, Spain-Equatorial Guinea. d, 260p, Commemorative flight.

2001, Apr. 26   **Perf. 13¾x14**
3091 A1088   Sheet of 4, #a-d   8.00 3.00

Grand Theater, Liceu — A1089

2001, Apr. 27   **Perf. 14x13¾**
3092 A1089 120p multi   1.75 .65

King Juan Carlos — A1091

2001   **Photo.**   **Perf. 12¾x13¼**
3093 A1091   5p sil & lil rose   .25 .25
3094 A1091   40p sil & yel grn   .60 .25
3095 A1091   75p sil & bl vio   1.10 .40
3096 A1091   100psil & lt red brn   1.50 .55
    Nos. 3093-3096 (4)   3.45 1.45

Issued: 40p, 5/4; 5p, 75p, 6/28; 100p, 7/15. See also Nos. 3133-3140, 3271-3274, 3337-3343, 3387-3391.

Europa — A1092

2001, May 9   **Photo.**   **Perf. 14x13¾**
3097 A1092 75p multi   .80 .40

Architecture A1093

Designs: 40p, San Martiño Church, Noia. 75p, Santa Maria Cathedral, Tui. 155p, Villaconcha dovecote, Frechilla.

Engr., Photo. (75p)
2001, May 17   **Perf. 14x13¾**
3098-3100 A1093   Set of 3   4.00 1.50

Luarca Harbor A1094

2001, May 26   **Photo.**   **Perf. 13¾x14**
3101 A1094 40p multi   .60 .25

Cardinal Rodrigo de Castro (1523-1600) — A1095

2001, June 1
3102 A1095 40p multi   .60 .25

Leopoldo Alas, "Clarín," (1852-1901), Writer — A1096

2001, June 13
3103 A1096 75p multi   1.10 .40

Trees A1097

Designs: 40p, Olive. 75p, Beech.

2001, June 22   **Perf. 12¾**
3104-3105 A1097   Set of 2   1.75 .60

King's Soccer Cup, 25th Anniv. A1098

2001, July 6   **Litho.**   **Perf. 13¾x14**
3106 A1098 40p multi   .60 .25
   Issued in sheets of 8 + 4 labels.

Local Festivals A1099

Designs: 40p, Cipotegato, Tarazona. 120p, Giants of Pí, Barcelona, vert.

Perf. 13¾x14, 14x13¾
2001, July 10   **Photo.**
3107-3108 A1099   Set of 2   2.40 .80

Baltasar Gracian (1601-58), Writer A1100

2001, July 13   **Perf. 13¾x14**
3109 A1100 120p multi   1.75 .60

"Age of Man" Exhibition — A1101

Designs: 120p, Our Lady of La Calva. 155p, Cathedral dome, Zamora.

2001, July 20   **Engr.**   **Perf. 14x13¾**
3110-3111 A1101   Set of 2   4.00 1.50

Grandparent's Day — A1102

Siervas de Jesús de la Caridad A1103

Perf. 14x13¾, 13¾x14
2001, July 26   **Photo.**
3112 A1102 40p multi   .60 .25
3113 A1103 75p multi   1.10 .40

Salamanca, European City of Culture — A1104

2001, Sept. 5   **Photo.**   **Perf. 13x13¼**
3114 A1104 75p multi   1.10 .40

Covadonga Basilica, Cent. of Consecration — A1105

2001, Sept. 7   **Perf. 13¾x14**
3115 A1105 40p multi   .60 .25

Emblem of Privatized Postal System A1106

2001, Sept. 15
3116 A1106 40p multi   .60 .25

Souvenir Sheet

Exfilna 2001 Natl. Philatelic Exhibition, Vigo — A1107

Engr. (Litho. Margin)
2001, Sept. 21
3117 A1107 260p multi   4.00 4.00

St. Dominic of Silos (c. 1000-73) — A1108

Litho. & Engr.
2001, Oct. 4   **Perf. 14x13¾**
3118 A1108 40p multi   .60 .25
   a.   Souvenir sheet of 1 with margin like stamp design   .60 .60
   b.   Souvenir sheet of 1 with margin differing   .60 .60

Year of Dialogue Among Civilizations A1109

2001, Oct. 9   **Photo.**
3119 A1109 120p multi   1.75 .70
   Stamp Day.

Posidonia Oceanica, Ses Salines Nature Reserve A1110

2001, Oct. 15   **Perf. 13¾x14**
3120 A1110 155p multi   2.25 .85
   America issue — UNESCO World Heritage Sites.

Letter Writing Type of 1998

No. 3121: a, Christopher Columbus, 1492. b, Treaty of Tordesillas, 1494. c, Election of King Charles I as Holy Roman Emperor Charles V, 1519. d, Conquest of Mexico by Hernán Cortés, 1519. e, Circumnavigation by Juan Sebastián Elcano, 1522. f, Campaign against Incas by Francisco Pizarro, 1532. g, Ascension to throne of King Philip II, 1556. h, Start of construction of El Escorial Monastery, 1563. i, Battle of Lepanto, 1571. j, Saints John of the Cross, Teresa of Jesus and painter El Greco, 1580. k, First play by Lope de Vega, 1593. l, Ascension to throne of King Philip III, 1598.

2001, Oct. 19   **Perf. 13x12½**
3121   Sheet of 12   5.25 5.25
   a.-l.   A1002 25p Any single   .40 .25

Souvenir Sheet

Bullfighter Curro Romero — A1111

2001, Oct. 25   *Perf. 14x13¾*
3122 A1111 260p multi   4.00 4.00

Christmas
A1112

Designs: 40p, Virgin With Child, by Alfredo Roldan. 75p, Adoration of the Shepherds, by José Ribera.

2001, Nov. 8   *Perf. 12¾*
3123-3124 A1112   Set of 2   1.75   .60
    a. Souvenir sheet, # 3123-3124, Germany #B895-B896, litho., perf. 13¼   5.50 5.50

    See Germany No. B896a.

Score of "El Sombrero de Tres Picos," by Manuel de Falla (1876-1946) — A1113

2001, Nov. 14 Photo.   *Perf. 13¾x14*
3125 A1113 75p multi   1.10   .40

Comic Strips
A1114

Designs: 40p, Cartoon by Josep Coll i Coll. 75p, Rompetechos, by Francisco Ibañez.

2001, Nov. 20
3126-3127 A1114   Set of 2   1.75   .60

Carlos Cano (1946-2000), Singer — A1115

2001, Nov. 23   *Perf. 14x13¾*
3128 A1115 40p black   .60   .25

Intl. Volunteer Day for Economic and Social Development
A1116

2001, Nov. 27
3129 A1116 120p multi   1.75   .70

World Heritage Sites — A1117

No. 3130: a, Catalan Romanesque Churches of the Vall de Boí. b, The Mystery of Elx (Elche). c, Hospital de Sant Pau, Barcelona. d, San Cristóbal de La Laguna. e, Archaeological Site of Atapuerca. f, Palmeral of Elche. g, Monuments of Oviedo. h, Roman Walls of Lugo. i, Rock Art of the Mediterranean Basin. j, Ibiza, Biodiversity and Culture. k, Archaeological Ensemble of Tarraco. l, University and Historic Precinct of Alcalá de Henares.

2001, Nov. 30   *Perf. 12¾*
3130   Sheet of 12   7.00 7.00
    a.-l. A1117 40p Any single   .60   .25

Souvenir Sheet

Ministry of Development, 150th Anniv. — A1118

No. 3131 — Maps showing: a, 40p, Automated postal centers. b, 75p, Ports. c, 120p, High-speed train lines. d, 155p, Airports. e, 260p, Highways.

2001, Dec. 11
3131 A1118   Sheet of 5, #a-e, + label   11.00 10.00

Souvenir Sheet

King Juan Carlos, 25th Anniv. of Reign — A1119

No. 3132: a, 40p, Crown Prince Felipe. b, 40p, Princess Elena (patterned dress). c, 40p, Royal arms. d, 40p, Princess Cristina (black dress). e, 75p, King Juan Carlos. f, 75p, Queen Sofia. g, 260p, Royal palace, Madrid (49x28mm).

2001, Dec. 14   *Perf. 12¾x13¼*
3132 A1119   Sheet of 7, #a-g   10.00 10.00

100 Cents = 1 Euro (€)
King Juan Carlos Type of 2001 With Euro Denominations Only

2002, Jan. 2 Photo.   *Perf. 13½x14*
3133 A1091   1c sil & black   .25   .25
3134 A1091   5c sil & brt blue   .25   .25
3135 A1091   10c sil & gray blue   .25   .25
3136 A1091   25c sil & claret   .60   .25
3137 A1091   50c sil & gray   1.25   .35

3138 A1091 75c sil & red lil   1.90   .55
    Perf. 12¾x13¼
3139 A1091   €1 sil & green   2.50   .75
3140 A1091   €2 sil & ver   5.00 1.50
    Nos. 3133-3140 (8)   12.00 4.15

Spain's Presidency of European Union
A1120

Color of star at UR: 25c, Orange. 50c, White.

2002, Jan. 2 Photo.   *Perf. 13¾x14*
3141-3142 A1120   Set of 2   1.90   .65

Trees
A1121

Designs: 50c, Savin (sabina). 75c, Elm (olmo).

2002, Jan. 25   *Perf. 12¾*
3143-3144 A1121   Set of 2   3.00 1.10

A1122   A1123

A1124   A1125

A1126   A1127

Flowers
A1128   A1129

    Die Cut Perf. 13
2002, Feb. 20   **Litho.**
    Self-Adhesive
3145   Booklet of 8   5.50
    a. A1122 25c multi   .60   .25
    b. A1123 25c multi   .60   .25
    c. A1124 25c multi   .60   .25
    d. A1125 25c multi   .60   .25
    e. A1126 25c multi   .60   .25
    f. A1127 25c multi   .60   .25
    g. A1128 25c multi   .60   .25
    h. A1129 25c multi   .60   .25

España 2002 Youth Philatelic Exhibition, Salamanca
A1130

Designs: 50c, Exhibition emblem. €1.80, Emblem and New Cathedral, vert.

2002, Feb. 22 Photo.   *Perf. 13¾x14*
3146 A1130   50c multi   1.25   .45
    Souvenir Sheet
    Perf. 14x13¾
3147 A1130   €1.80 multi   5.00 4.50
    See No. 3183.

Father Francisco Piquer, Founder of Pawn Brokerage
A1131

2002, Feb. 25 Litho.   *Perf. 14x13¾*
3148 A1131   25c multi   .60   .25

Caja Madrid Savings Bank, 300th anniv.

Real Madrid Soccer Team, Cent.
A1132

2002, Feb. 25   *Perf. 13¾x14*
3149 A1132   75c yel & gray   1.90   .65

Souvenir Sheet

Tarazona Town Hall Portico — A1133

2002, Feb. 26
3150 A1133   €2.10 multi   5.25 5.25

Philaiberia '02, Tarazona.

Alejandro Mon (1801-82), Politician — A1134

2002, Feb. 27   *Perf. 14x13¾*
3151 A1134   25c multi   .60   .25

Retirement of Peseta Currency — A1135

2002, Feb. 28   **Litho.**
3152 A1135 25c multi   .60   .25

Sil Canyons, Ribiera Sacra — A1136

Cabo de Gata Natl. Park A1137

2002, Mar. 8   **Perf. 14x13¾, 13¾x14**
3153 A1136   75c multi   2.00   .65
3154 A1137 €2.10 multi   5.50   2.75

Zaragoza Military Academy, 75th Anniv. — A1138

2002, Mar. 15   **Perf. 14x13¾**
3155 A1138 25c multi   .60   .25

Real Unión Soccer Team, Cent. — A1139

2002, Mar. 22
3156 A1139 50c multi   1.25   .45

Stamp Day A1140

2002, Mar. 25   **Perf. 13¾x14**
3157 A1140 25c multi   .60   .25

Castle Type of 2001

Designs: 25c, Banyeres de Mariola. 50c, Soutomaior. 75c, Catalorao.

2002, Apr. 8   **Engr.**   **Perf. 13¾x14**
3158-3160 A1086   Set of 3   3.75   1.40

Tudela, 1200th Anniv. A1141

2002, Apr. 12   **Photo.**
3161 A1141 75c multi   1.90   .70

Monastery of Sant Cugat, 1000th Anniv. A1142

2002, Apr. 12
3162 A1142 €1.80 multi   4.50   2.25

Luis Cernuda (1902-63), Poet A1143

2002, May 8
3163 A1143 50c multi   .90   .45

Dr. Federico Rubio (1827-1902) — A1144

2002, May 8
3164 A1144 50c multi   1.25   .45

Europa A1145

2002, May 9
3165 A1145 50c multi   1.25   .45

Reincorporation of Menorca to Spanish Crown, Bicent. — A1146

2002, May 10
3166 A1146 50c multi   1.25   .45

World Equestrian Games — A1147

No. 3167: a, Carriage driving. b, Endurance (Raid). c, Dressage (Doma). d, Reining. e, Vaulting (Volteo). f, Jumping (Saltos). g, Three-day event (Completo).

2002, May 11   **Perf. 12¾x13¼**
3167   Sheet of 7 + 2 labels   9.50   9.50
   a.-e. A1147 25c Any single   .60   .25
   f. A1147 75c multi   1.90   .70
   g. A1147 €1.80 multi   4.50   2.25

Dolores Peinado (1819-94), Character From Folk Song "La Dolores" A1148

2002, May 31   **Perf. 13¾x14**
3168 A1148 50c multi   1.25   .50

Souvenir Sheet

Exfilna 2002 Natl. Philatelic Exhibition, Salamanca — A1149

No. 3169 — Plaza Mayor, Salamanca: a, 25c, West facade. b, 25c, City Hall. c, 25c, Royal Pavilion. d, €1.80, Aerial view.

Engr. (#a-c), Litho. (#d, margin)
2002, July 7   **Perf. 13¾x14**
3169 A1149   Sheet of 4, #a-d   6.25   6.25

Iberian Airlines, 75th Anniv. A1150

Airplanes: 25c, Rohrbach R-VIII Roland. 50c, Boeing 747.

2002, June 10 Photo.   Perf. 13¾x14
3170-3171 A1150   Set of 2   1.90   .75

Wine Producing Regions — A1151

Grapes and map of: 25c, Rias Baixas region. 50c, Rioja region. 75c, Manzanilla — Sanlúcar de Barrameda region.

2002   **Perf. 14x13¼**
3172-3174 A1151   Set of 3   3.75   1.50
   Issued: 25c, 7/27; 50c, 75c, 9/20.

Letter Writing Type of 1998

No. 3175: a, Publication of *Don Quixote*, by Miguel de Cervantes, 1605. b, Accession to throne of King Philip IV and rise in power of Conde-Duque de Olivares, 1621. c, Rivalry of poets Francisco de Quevedo and Luis de Góngora, 1620. d, Painting of "Las Meninas" by Diego Velázquez, 1656. e, Accession to throne of King Charles II, 1665. f, Accession to throne of King Philip V, 1701. g, Accesstion to throne of King Ferdinand VI, 1746. h, Accession to throne of King Charles III, 1759. i, Squillaci Riots, 1766. j, Gaspar Melchor de Jovellanos, 1787. k, Accession to throne of King Charles IV, 1788. l, Appointment of Manuel de Godoy as prime minister, 1792.

2002, Sept. 27   **Perf. 12¾**
3175   Sheet of 12   4.50   4.50
   a.-l. A1002 10c Any single   .30   .25

Expiatory Temple of the Holy Family, by Architect Antonio Gaudí (1852-1926) A1152

2002, Sept. 27 Litho.   Perf. 14x13¾
3176 A1152 50c blue & black   1.25   .50

A1153

A1154

A1155

A1156

A1157

A1158

A1159

Paintings With Musical Instruments by Goyo Domínguez A1160

2002, Sept. 30   **Die Cut Perf. 13**
Self-Adhesive

3177   Booklet pane of 8   5.00
   a. A1153 25c multi   .60   .25
   b. A1154 25c multi   .60   .25
   c. A1155 25c multi   .60   .25
   d. A1156 25c multi   .60   .25
   e. A1157 25c multi   .60   .25
   f. A1158 25c multi   .60   .25
   g. A1159 25c multi   .60   .25
   h. A1160 25c multi   .60   .25

America Issue — Youth, Education and Literacy A1161

2002, Oct. 14   Photo.   Perf. 13¾x14
3178 A1161 75c multi   1.90   .75

Almanzor (Muhammad ibn Abu Amir al-Mansur, c. 938-1002), Caliph of Córdoba — A1162

2002, Oct. 25
3179 A1162 75c multi   1.90   .75

Dijous Bó Fair, Mallorca — A1163

2002, Nov. 4   Perf. 14x13¾
3180 A1163 75c multi   1.90   .75

UNESCO World Heritage Sites — A1164

No. 3181 — Architectural details of: a, Aranjuez. b, Santa Maria Church, Calatayud. c, San Martin Church, Teruel. d, Santa Maria Church, Tobed. e, Santa Tecla Church, Cervera de la Cañada. f, San Pablo Church, Zaragoza.

2002, Nov. 8
3181 A1164 Sheet of 7, #a-d, f, 2 #e, + 5 labels   19.00 19.00
a.-b. 25c Either single   .60   .25
c.   50c multi   1.25   .50
d.   75c multi   1.90   .75
e.   €1.80 multi   4.50 2.25
f.   €2.10 multi   2.75 2.75

The two examples of No. 3181e are tete-beche in the sheet.

Alcañiz Inn — A1164a

2002, Nov. 15   Perf. 13¾x14
3182 A1164a 25c multicolored   .60   .25

España 2002 Youth Philatelic Exhibition, Salamanca — A1165

Designs: No. 3183a, 50c, Like #3146. Nos. 3183b, 3190, 75c, Character from comic Strip "El Capitan Alatriste," by Arturo Pérez-Reverte. Nos. 3183c, 3185, 75c, Television and names of television shows. Nos. 3183d, 3189, 75c, Hand and compact disc. Nos. 3183e, 3187, 75c, Radio, musical notes and logos of Spanish radio stations. Nos. 3183f, 3188, 75c, Skier, race car, soccer ball, bicyclist and names of Spanish sports stars. Nos. 3183g, 3186, 75c, Photojournalist. Nos. 3183h, 3184, 75c, Clapboard and names of Spanish film personalities. No. 3183i, €1.80, Like #3147, vert.

2002   Litho.   Die Cut Perf. 13
Self-Adhesive (#3183)
3183 A1165 Sheet of 9   19.00 19.00
a.   50c multi   1.25   .50
b.-h. 75c Any single   1.90   .75
i.   €1.80 multi   4.50 2.25

Souvenir Sheets
Perf. 13¾x14
3184-3190 A1165 Set of 7   11.50 11.50

Issued: No. 3183, 11/17; No. 3184, 11/18; No. 3185, 11/19; No. 3186, 11/20; No. 3187, 11/21; No. 3188, 11/22; No. 3189, 11/23; No. 3190, 11/24.
No. 3183 exists with at least three different pictures on backing paper.

San Jorge Church, Alcoy — A1166

Litho. & Engr.
2002, Nov. 25   Perf. 14x13¾
3191 A1166 75c multi   1.90   .75

Compludo Forge, León A1167

2002, Nov. 27   Perf. 13¾x14
3192 A1167 50c multi   1.25   .50

Stained Glass Window, Santa Maria Cathedral, Vitoria-Gasteiz — A1168

2002, Nov. 27   Perf. 14x13¾
3193 A1168 50c multi   1.50 1.00

Crucifix, Hío — A1169

2002, Nov. 29
3194 A1169 25c multi   .60   .25

Christmas A1170

Designs: 25c, Adoration of the Magi, from church altarpiece, Calzadilla de los Barros. 50c, Maternity, by Goyo Dominguez.

2002, Nov. 29   Photo.
3195-3196 A1170 Set of 2   1.90   .75

Opening of Somport Tunnel A1171

2003, Jan. 17   Photo.   Perf. 13¾x14
3197 A1171 51c multi   1.10   .55

Traditional Dress from Ansó Valley — A1172

2003, Jan. 20   Perf. 14x13¾
3198 A1172 76c multi   1.75   .85

World Leprosy Day, 50th Anniv. — A1173

2003, Jan. 21
3199 A1173 26c multi   .55   .30

Pedro Rodríguez de Campomanes (1723-1802), Jurist — A1174

2003, Feb. 14
3200 A1174 26c multi   .55   .30

Juvenia 2003 Natl. Youth Philatelic Exhibition, Benissa A1175

2003, Feb. 21   Perf. 13¾x14
3201 A1175 51c multi   1.10   .55

Práxedes Mateo Sagasta (1825-1903), Politician — A1176

2003, Mar. 11
3202 A1176 26c multi   .55   .30

ABC Newspaper, Cent. A1177

2003, Mar. 17
3203 A1177 €2.15 multi   4.50 2.25

Nobel Prize Winners For Physiology or Medicine From Spain — A1178

No. 3204: a, Santiago Ramón y Cajal, 1906. b, Severo Ochoa, 1959.

Litho. & Engr.
2003, Mar. 20   Perf. 13x12¾
3204 A1178 Horiz. pair   3.25 3.25
a.   51c multi   1.25   .55
b.   76c multi   1.90   .80

See Sweden No. 2460.

School of Civil Engineering, Madrid, Bicent. — A1179

Designs: 26c, Tui Bridge.
No. 3206: a, Estrecho de Puentes Dam. b, El Musel Port.

2003, Mar. 21   Photo.   Perf. 13¾x14
3205 A1179 26c multi   .55   .30

Souvenir Sheet
3206 Sheet of 3, #3205, 3206a, 3206b   4.00 2.00
a.   A1179 51c multi   1.25   .55
b.   A1179 76c multi   1.75   .80

La Verdad Newspaper, Cent. A1180

2003, Mar. 26
3207 A1180 26c multi   .55 .30

Paintings by Chico Montilla A1181

No. 3208: a, La Hoz de Priego. b, Fields of Gold. c, Desfiladero de los Tornos. d, Campos de Pastrana. e, Campos de Armilla. f, Nenúfar. g, De qué Color es el Vento? h, Flores Tempranas.

Die Cut Perf. 13
2003, Mar. 28   **Litho.**
Self-Adhesive
3208   Booklet pane of 8   4.50
a.-h. A1181 26c Any single   .55 .30

Ramón José Sender (1901-82), Writer A1182

Litho. & Engr.
2003, Mar. 31   ***Perf. 13½x14***
3209 A1182 €2.15 multi   4.75 2.40

Rural Schools A1183

2003, Apr. 3   Photo.   Perf. 13¾x14
3210 A1183 26c multi   .55 .30

Souvenir Sheet

EXFILNA 2003 Natl. Philatelic Exhibition, Granada — A1184

Litho. (margin) & Engr. (stamp)
2003, Apr. 7
3211 A1184 €2.15 multi   4.75 2.40

Aviles, 1000th Anniv. A1185

2003, Apr. 11   **Photo.**
3212 A1185 51c multi   1.10 .55

Stamp Day A1186

2003, Apr. 11
3213 A1186 €1.85 multi   4.00 2.00

Europa A1187

2003, Apr. 24
3214 A1187 76c multi   1.75 .85

Atlético de Madrid Soccer Team, Cent. — A1188

2003, Apr. 25   ***Perf. 14x13¾***
3215 A1188 26c red & blue   .60 .30

Roman Theater, Zaragoza A1189

2003, May 5   ***Perf. 13¾x14***
3216 A1189 €1.85 multi   4.25 2.10

European Year of the Disabled A1190

2003, May 8   Photo. & Embossed
3217 A1190 76c multi   1.75 .85

Castles A1191

Designs: 26c, San Felipe Castle, Ferrol. 51c, Cuellar Castle, Segovia. 76c, Montilla Castle, Córdoba.

2003, May 17   Engr.   Perf. 13¾x14
3218-3220 A1191 Set of 3   3.75 1.90

Battles of Ceriñola and Garellano, 500th anniv. (No. 3220).

World Swimming Championships, Barcelona — A1192

2003, May 23 Photo.   Perf. 14x13¾
3221 A1192   Sheet of 5 + label   13.00 6.50
a. 26c Breaststroke   .60 .30
b. 51c Diving   1.25 .60
c. 76c Synchronized swimming 1.75 .85
d. €1.85 Freestyle   4.25 2.10
e. €2.15 Water polo   5.00 2.50

Max Aub (1903-72), Writer — A1193

2003, June 2   **Engr.**
3222 A1193 76c black & red   1.75 .85

Sabadell Soccer Team, Cent. — A1194

2003, June 4   **Photo.**
3223 A1194 76c multi   1.75 .85

Juan Bravo Murillo (1803-73), Prime Minister — A1195

2003, June 9
3224 A1195 51c multi   1.25 .60

Diario de Cadiz Newspaper, 136th Anniv. — A1196

2003, June 16
3225 A1196 26c multi   .60 .30

Souvenir Sheet

Royal Automobile Club of Spain, Cent. — A1197

2003, June 27   ***Perf. 13¾x14***
3226 A1197 Sheet of 4   7.75 4.00
a. 26c 1967 Dodge Dart Barreiros   .60 .30
b. 51c 1957-73 Seat 600   1.10 .55
c. 76c 1907 Hispano-Suiza 20/30 HP   1.75 .85
d. €1.85 1953 Pegaso Z-102 Berlinetta   4.25 2.10

Chilean Postage Stamps, 150th Anniv. — A1198

2003, July 1   Photo.   Perf. 14x13¾
3227 A1198 76c Chile Type A1 1.75 .85

El Diario Montañés Newspaper, Cent. — A1199

2003, July 4
3228 A1199 26c multi   .60 .30

Santa Catalina Inn, Jaén — A1200

2003, July 9   ***Perf. 13x13¼***
3229 A1200 76c multi + label 1.75 .85

Diario de Navarra Newspaper, Cent. — A1201

2003, July 11   ***Perf. 13¾x14***
3230 A1201 26c multi   .60 .30

Seu Vella, Lleida, 800th Anniv. A1202

2003, July 22 Engr.   Perf. 13¾x14
3231 A1202 €1.85 pur & brn blk 4.25 2.10

El Adelanto de Salamanca Newspaper, 120th Anniv. — A1203

2003, July 24 Photo. Perf. 14x13¾
3232 A1203 26c multi .60 .30

A1204 A1205

A1206 A1207

A1208 A1209

A1210 A1211

Paintings by Alfredo Roldán A1210 A1211

Die Cut Perf. 13
2003, July 28 Litho.
Self-Adhesive
3233 Booklet pane of 8 5.00
a. A1204 A multi .60 .30
b. A1205 A multi .60 .30
c. A1206 A multi .60 .30
d. A1207 A multi .60 .30
e. A1208 A multi .60 .30
f. A1209 A multi .60 .30
g. A1210 A multi .60 .30
h. A1211 A multi .60 .30

Nos. 3233a-3233g each sold for 26c on day of issue.

El Correo Gallego Newspaper, 125th Anniv. — A1212

2003, Aug. 1 Photo. Perf. 13¾x14
3234 A1212 26c multi .60 .30

El Comercio de Gijón Newspaper, 125th Anniv. — A1213

2003, Sept. 2
3235 A1213 26c multi .60 .30

Holy Cross of Caravaca A1214

2003, Sept. 4 Perf. 14x13¾
3236 A1214 76c multi 1.75 .85
Holy Year 2003.

World Sailing Championships, Gulf of Cádiz — A1215

2003, Sept. 9 Perf. 13¾x14
3237 A1215 76c multi 1.75 .85

Wine of Penedés Region — A1216

Wine of Montilla-Moriles Region — A1217

Wine of Valdepeñas Region — A1218

Wine of Bierzo Region — A1219

2003 Perf. 14x13¾
3238 A1216 26c multi .60 .30
3239 A1217 51c multi 1.25 .60
3240 A1218 76c multi 1.75 .90
3241 A1219 €1.85 multi 4.50 2.25
Nos. 3238-3241 (4) 8.10 4.05
Issued: 26c, 10/30; others, 9/22.

Academy of Military Engineering, Bicent. — A1220

2003, Sept. 24 Perf. 13¾x14
3242 A1220 51c multi 1.25 .60

Souvenir Sheet

Santa María Cathedral, León, 700th Anniv — A1221

2003, Sept. 26 Litho. & Engr.
3243 A1221 76c multi 2.00 1.00

Souvenir Sheet

Royal Geographical Society, Cent. — A1222

2003, Oct. 1
3244 A1222 €1.85 multi 4.75 2.50

Trees — A1223

Designs: 26c, Ficus macrophylla. 51c, Quercus rober.

2003, Oct. 3 Photo. Perf. 14x13¾
3245-3246 A1223 Set of 2 1.90 .95

School of Aeronautical Engineering, Madrid, 75th Anniv. — A1224

2003, Oct. 6 Perf. 13¾x14
3247 A1224 51c multi 1.25 .60

America Issue - Rail Transport A1225

2003, Oct. 14
3248 A1225 76c multi 1.75 .90

El Viejo y el Pájaro, by Luis Seoane (1910-79) A1226

2003, Oct. 17 Perf. 14x13¾
3249 A1226 €1.85 multi 4.50 2.25

El Correo de Andalucia Newspaper, Cent. — A1227

Faro de Vigo Newspaper, 150th Anniv. — A1228

La Voz de Galicia Newspaper, 121st Anniv. — A1229

2003, Nov. 3 Perf. 13¾x14
3250 A1227 26c multi .60 .30
3251 A1228 26c multi .60 .30
3252 A1229 26c multi .60 .30
Nos. 3250-3252 (3) 1.80 .90

Camilo José Cela (1916-2002), 1989 Nobel Laureate in Literature A1230

2003, Nov. 10 Perf. 14x13¾
3253 A1230 26c multi .65 .30

Parade of the Magi — A1231

Nativity, by Raquel Fariñas — A1232

2003, Nov. 10
3254	A1231	26c multi	.65	.30
3255	A1232	51c multi	1.25	.60

Christmas.

España 2004 Intl. Philatelic Exhibition A1233

Designs: 76c, Exhibition emblem. €1.85, Exhibition venue, Valencia.

2003, Nov. 14   Perf. 13¾x14
3256	A1233	76c multi	1.90	.95

Souvenir Sheet
3257	A1233	€1.85 multi	4.50	2.25

Organos de Montoro A1234

2003, Nov. 17
3258	A1234	51c multi	1.25	.60

Souvenir Sheet

Completion of National Geological Map — A1235

2003, Nov. 24
3259	A1235	26c multi	.65	.30

Souvenir Sheets

Constitution, 25th Anniv. — A1236

Various photos or paintings with inscriptions in lower left corner of: No. 3260, 26c, RCM-FNMT. No. 3261, 26c, Miguel Torner. No. 3262, 26c, R. Seco. No. 3263, 26c, Araceli Alarcón. No. 3264, 26c, Galicia. No. 3265, 26c, Fesanpe. No. 3266, 26c, J. Carrero. No. 3267, 26c, J. Carrero, vert. No. 3268, 26c, Goyo Domínguez, vert. No. 3269, 26c, Juan Bautista Nieto, vert.

2003, Dec. 5   Perf. 13¾x14, 14x13¾
3260-3269	A1236	Set of 10	6.50	3.25

Powered Flight, Cent. A1237

2003, Dec. 17   Engr.   Perf. 13¾x14
3270	A1237	76c blue & brown	1.90	.95

King Juan Carlos Type of 2001 With Euro Denominations Only

2004, Jan. 2   Photo.   Perf. 12¾x13¼
3271	A1091	2c sil & brt pink	.25	.25
3272	A1091	27c sil & blue	.70	.35
a.		Sheet of 4 + label	2.80	2.80
3273	A1091	52c sil & bister brn	1.25	.65
3274	A1091	77c sil & dull grn	1.90	.95
		Nos. 3271-3274 (4)	4.10	2.20

No. 3272a issued 5/25.

Roman Art of Jaca — A1238

No. 3275: a, Grate. b, Huesca Cathedral Bible page. c, Painting of two apostles. d, Cloister, Monastery of San Juan de la Peña. e, Coins. f, Capital, Church of Santiago de Jaca. g, Detail of sarcophagus of Doña Sancha. h, Wooden carved crucifix.

Serpentine Die Cut 13
2004, Jan. 16   Litho.
Self-Adhesive
3275		Booklet pane of 8	5.75	
a.-h.	A1238	A Any single	.70	.70

Nos. 3275a-3275h each sold for 27c on day of issue.

Souvenir Sheets

Paintings of Women Reading by Fabio Hurtado (1960-) — A1239

No. 3276: a, 27c, Woman reading book in rowboat. b, 52c, Woman with head on hand reading book. c, 77c, Woman reading newspaper.
No. 3277: a, 27c, Woman with legs crossed reading book. b, 52c, Woman on back reading book. c, 77c, Woman with black hat reading book.

2004, Jan. 23   Photo.   Perf. 13¾x14
Sheets of 3, #a-c, + label
3276-3277	A1239	Set of 2	8.00	4.50

Campaign Against Cancer A1240

2004, Feb. 2
3278	A1240	27c multi	.70	.35

"La Terrona" Oak Tree, Zarza de Montánchez A1241

2004, Feb. 6   Perf. 14x13¾
3279	A1241	52c multi	1.40	.70

World Rowing Championships, Banyoles — A1242

2004, Feb. 9   Perf. 13¾x14
3280	A1242	77c multi	1.90	.95

School Letter Writing Campaign — A1243

No. 3281 — Scenes from comic strip Trazo de Tiza, by Miguelanxo Prado: a, Woman on cliff. b, Sailboat. c, Woman near injured gull. d, Aerial view of lighthouse.

2004, Feb. 10
3281	A1243	27c Sheet of 4, #a-d, + 12 labels	2.75	1.40

Souvenir Sheet

Santa María de Carracedo Monastery, Bierzo — A1244

2004, Mar. 8   Perf. 14x13¾
3282	A1244	€1.90 multi	4.75	2.40

36th Chess Olympiad A1245

2004, Mar. 18   Perf. 13¾x14
3283	A1245	77c multi	1.90	.95

Clocks — A1246

No. 3284: a, 27c, Clock with Muse Calliope, 19th cent. b, 52c, Clock with Cupid, 18th cent. c, 77c, Clock with Empress María Luisa, child and harp, 19th cent. d, €1.90, Clock with Venus and Cupid, 18th cent.

Perf. 13¼x12¾
2004, Mar. 31   Litho. & Engr.
3284	A1246	Sheet of 4, #a-d	8.50	4.25

Diario de Burgos Newspaper, 113th Anniv. — A1247

2004, Apr. 1   Photo.   Perf. 14x13¾
3285	A1247	27c multi	.65	.35

March 11, 2004 Terrorist Attacks — A1248

2004, Apr. 2   Litho.   Perf. 14x13¾
3286	A1248	27c black & gray	.65	.35

Booklet Stamp
Self-Adhesive
Size: 22x33mm
Serpentine Die Cut 13
3287	A1248	A black & gray	.65	.35
a.		Booklet pane of 8	5.25	

No. 3287 sold for 27c on day of issue.

Egg Painting Festival, Pola de Siero A1249

2004, Apr. 5   Photo.   Perf. 13¾
3288	A1249	27c multi	.65	.35

Miniature Sheet

Paintings of Shawls, by Soledad
Fernández — A1250

2004, Apr. 7   **Perf. 14x13¾**
3289 A1250   Sheet of 4   8.50 8.50
  a.   27c Shawl, shell   .65   .35
  b.   52c Shawl, hands   1.25   .65
  c.   77c Shawl, flowers   1.90   .95
  d.   €1.90 Shawl on chair 4.50 2.25

Department of Technical Engineering
of Public Works, 150th
Anniv. — A1251

2004, Apr. 15   **Perf. 13¾x14**
3290 A1251 52c multi   1.25   .60

Cable Inglés Loading Pier,
Almadrabillas, Cent. — A1252

2004, Apr. 27
3291 A1252 52c multi   1.25   .60

Europa — A1253

2004, Apr. 29   **Perf. 14x13¾**
3292 A1253 77c multi   1.90   .95

Expansion
of the
European
Union
A1254

2004, May 3   **Perf. 13¾x14**
3293 A1254 52c multi   1.25   .60

Self-Portrait with the Neck of Rafael,
by Salvador Dali (1904-89) — A1255

2004, May 11   **Photo.**
3294 A1255 77c multi   1.90   .95

FIFA (Fédération Internationale de
Football Association), Cent. — A1256

2004, May 21
3295 A1256 77c multi   1.90   .95

Wedding of Prince Felipe and Letizia
Ortiz Rocasolano — A1257

2004, May 22
3296 A1257 27c multi   .65   .30

España 2004 Intl. Philatelic
Exhibition — A1258

No. 3297 — Music: a, Vicente Martín y
Soler (1754-1806), opera composer. b, Band
instruments.

2004, May 23 Photo.   Perf. 13¾x14
3297 A1258   Horiz. pair + cen-
             tral label   1.90 1.90
  a.   27c multi   .65   .30
  b.   52c multi   1.25   .60

Miniature Sheet

España 2004 Intl. Philatelic
Exhibition — A1259

No. 3298 — Royalty: a, Prince Felipe and
Letizia Ortiz Rocasolano. b, Prince Felipe. c,
King Juan Carlos and Queen Sofia.

Litho., Litho. & Engr. (#3298c)
2004, May 24   **Perf. 13¾x14**
3298 A1259   Sheet of 3 + 3
             labels   17.00 17.00
  a.   27c multi   .65   .30
  b.   77c multi   1.90   .95
  c.   €6 multi   14.00 7.00

España 2004 Intl. Philatelic
Exhibition — A1260

No. 3299 — Festival of the Bulls, Valencia:
a, Running of the bulls. b, Bullfighter.

2004, May 26 Photo.   Perf. 13¾x14
3299 A1260   Horiz. pair + cen-
             tral label   2.50 2.50
  a.   27c multi   .60   .30
  b.   77c multi   1.90   .95

Miniature Sheet

España 2004 Intl. Philatelic
Exhibition — A1261

No. 3300 — Sports: a, Tennis. b, Motorcycle
racing. c, Golf.

2004, May 27   **Perf. 12¾x13**
3300 A1261   Sheet of 3 + 3 la-
             bels   7.00 7.00
  a.   35c multi   .85   .40
  b.   52c multi   1.25   .65
  c.   €1.90 multi   4.50 2.25

España 2004 Intl. Philatelic
Exhibition — A1262

No. 3301 — The Sea: a, Yacht Bravo
España. b, Valencia skyline.

2004, May 28 Photo.   Perf. 13¾x14
3301 A1262   Horiz. pair + cen-
             tral label   3.25 3.25
  a.   52c multi   1.25   .65
  b.   77c multi   1.90   .95

Diario de Valencia Newspaper, 214th
Anniv. — A1263

2004, May 29
3302 A1263 27c multi   .65   .30

Jacobean Holy Year — A1264

2004, June 11   **Perf. 14x13¾**
3303 A1264 52c multi   1.25   .65

Lerma Inn
A1265

2004, July 18   **Perf. 13¾x14**
3304 A1265 52c multi   1.25   .65

Castles
A1266

Designs: 27c, Granadilla Fortress, Granadilla. 52c, Aguas Mansas Castle, Agoncillo.

77c, Mota Fortress, Alcalá la Real. €1.90, Villafuerte de Esgueva Castle, Villafuerte de
Esgueva, vert.

2004 Engr.   Perf. 13¾x14, 14x13¾
3305-3308 A1266   Set of 4   8.50 4.25
  Issued: 27c, 77c, 7/1; 52c, €1.90, 7/19.

Anchor Museum,
Salinas — A1267

2004, July 16 Photo.   Perf. 14x13¾
3309 A1267 €1.90 multi   4.75 2.40

Ceramics in
Paintings by Antonio
Miguel
González — A1268

No. 3310: a, Jar with two handles and lid,
oranges. b, Goblet, amphora and jar. c,
Pitcher with handle at top, bread, garlic. d,
Decorated pitcher with side handle. e, Pitcher
with handle at top, pentagonal dodecahedron,
bread, tomatoes. f, Vase. g, Pitcher with side
handle, plate of pears, grapes. h, Jar with
flower design and lid.

Serpentine Die Cut 13
2004, July 22   **Litho.**
          Self-Adhesive
3310   Booklet pane of 8   5.25
  a.-h. A1268 A Any single   .65   .35
  Nos. 3310a-3310h sold for 27c on day of
issue.

Círculo
Oscense
Building,
Huesca,
Cent.
A1269

2004, July 23 Photo.   Perf. 13¾x14
3311 A1269 52c multi   1.25   .65

Our Lady of the
Snows Festival,
Vitoria-Gasteiz,
50th
Anniv. — A1270

2004, July 30   **Perf. 14x13¾**
3312 A1270 27c multi   .65   .30

Ribeiro Wine
Grapes — A1271

Wine of
Malaga — A1272

2004, Sept. 1 *Perf. 14x13¾*
3313 A1271 27c multi .70 .35
3314 A1272 52c multi 1.25 .65

First Philippines Stamp, 150th
Anniv. — A1273

2004, Sept. 6 *Perf. 13¾x14*
3315 A1273 77c Philippines #1 1.90 .95

Heraldo de
Aragón
Newspaper, 109th
Anniv. — A1274

2004, Sept. 20 *Perf. 14x13¾*
3316 A1274 27c multi .70 .35

Nautical Astronomy, 250th
Anniv. — A1275

2004, Sept. 24 *Perf. 13¾x14*
3317 A1275 €1.90 multi 4.75 2.40

Souvenir Sheet

EXFILNA 2004 National Philatelic
Exhibition, Valladolid — A1276

Litho. & Engr.
2004, Oct. 1 *Perf. 14x13¾*
3318 A1276 €1.90 multi 4.75 4.75

Buildings in China
and
Spain — A1277

Designs: 52c, Park Guell, Barcelona. 77c,
Jinmao Tower, Shanghai.

2004, Oct. 8 *Photo.*
3319-3320 A1277 Set of 2 3.25 1.60
See People's Republic of China Nos. 3406-
3407.

America Issue — Environmental
Protection — A1278

2004, Oct. 14 *Perf. 13¾x14*
3321 A1278 77c multi 2.00 1.00

CERN (European Organization for
Nuclear Research), 50th
Anniv. — A1279

2004, Oct. 19
3322 A1279 €1.90 multi 5.00 2.50

Nature — A1280

Designs: 27c, Cíes Islands. 52c, Ebro Delta
Natural Park, horiz. 77c, Taburiente Caldera
National Park, horiz.

2004, Oct. 21 *Perf. 14x13¾, 13¾x14*
3323-3325 A1280 Set of 3 4.25 2.10
Taburiente Caldera National Park, 50th
anniv. (#3325).

First Registered Letter, 400th
Anniv. — A1281

2004, Oct. 22 *Perf. 13¾x14*
3326 A1281 77c multi 2.00 1.00
Stamp Day.

Ebre Observatory, Cent. — A1282

2004, Nov. 5
3327 A1282 €1.90 multi 5.00 2.50

Start of Reign of
Alfonso I, King of
Aragon, 900th
Anniv. — A1283

Litho. & Engr.
2004, Nov. 12 *Perf. 14x13¾*
3328 A1283 €1.90 multi 5.00 2.50

Christmas
A1284

Designs: 27c, Birth of Christ, 18th cent.
Neapolitan nativity scene. 52c, Nativity, by
Juan Manuel Cossío.

2004, Nov. 17 *Photo.*
3329-3330 A1284 Set of 2 2.25 1.10

Queen Isabella I
(1451-1504)
A1285

2004, Nov. 26
3331 A1285 €2.19 multi 6.00 3.00

Royal Expedition for Smallpox
Vaccination in Latin America and
Philippines, Bicent. — A1286

2004, Nov. 30 *Engr.* *Perf. 13¾x14*
3332 A1286 77c brown 2.10 1.10

Souvenir Sheet

Stained Glass, Toledo
Cathedral — A1287

Litho. & Engr.
2004, Dec. 3 *Perf. 14x13¾*
3333 A1287 €1.90 multi 5.25 5.25

Arms of
the Prince
of
Asturias
A1288

2004, Dec. 23 Photo. *Perf. 13¾x14*
3334 A1288 27c multi .75 .40
Best wishes for Prince Felipe's marriage to
Letizia Ortiz Rocasolano on May 22, 2004.

A1289 A1290

A1291 A1292

A1293 A1294

Paintings of Circus Performers by
Manolo Elices
A1295 A1296

2005, Jan. 3 Litho. *Die Cut Perf. 13*
Self-Adhesive

3335 Booklet pane of 8 6.00
a. A1289 A multi .75 .35
b. A1290 A multi .75 .35
c. A1291 A multi .75 .35
d. A1292 A multi .75 .35
e. A1293 A multi .75 .35
f. A1294 A multi .75 .35
g. A1295 A multi .75 .35
h. A1296 A multi .75 .35

Nos. 3335a-3335h each sold for 28c on day
of issue.

Signing of European Union
Constitutional Treaty — A1297

2005, Jan. 12   Photo.   Perf. 13¾x14
3336 A1297 28c multi   .75   .35

**King Juan Carlos Type of 2001 With
Euro Denominations Only**
Perf. 12¾x13¼
2005, Jan. 14   Photo.
3337 A1091 28c sil & ol grn   .75   .35
3338 A1091 35c sil & orange   .90   .45
3339 A1091 40c sil & blue
                        gray   1.00   .50
3340 A1091 53c sil & dull
                        pur   1.40   .70
3341 A1091 78c sil & red   2.00 1.00
3342 A1091 €1.95 sil & yel brn   5.00 2.50
3343 A1091 €2.21 sil & ol brn   5.75 2.75
       Nos. 3337-3343 (7)   16.80 8.25

Ahuehuete Tree,
Retiro Park,
Madrid — A1298

2005, Jan. 17   Photo.   Perf. 14x13¾
3344 A1298 78c multi   2.00 1.00

Road
Safety
A1299

Blood
Donation
A1300

2005, Jan. 26   Perf. 13¾x14
3345 A1299 28c multi   .75   .35
3346 A1300 53c multi   1.40   .70

University of
Seville, 500th
Anniv. — A1301

2005, Feb. 3   Engr.   Perf. 14x13¾
3347 A1301 28c brn & claret   .75   .35

First Royal
Spanish
Pharmacopoeia,
500th
Anniv. — A1302

2005, Feb. 3   Litho. & Engr.
3348 A1302 28c multi   .75   .35

Miniature Sheet

Children's Songs and Stories — A1303

No. 3349: a, Al Levantar una Lancha. b,
Aquí te Espero. c, Estaba la Pájara Pinta. d,
Cuatro Esquinitas. e, El Patio de mi Casa. f,
Pero Mira Cómo Beben. g, Los Pollitos
Cantan. h, Para Entrar en Clase.

2005, Feb. 14   Photo.
3349 A1303 Sheet of 8   11.00 11.00
a.-c.   28c Any single   .75   .40
d.-f.   53c Any single   1.40   .70
g.-h.   78c Either single   2.10 1.10

Juvenia 2005
Youth Stamp
Exhibition,
Tordera — A1304

2005, Feb. 25   Perf. 14x13¾
3350 A1304 28c multi   .75   .35

Sevilla FC
(Seville
Soccer
Team), Cent.
A1305

Real Sporting de
Gijón Soccer
Team,
Cent. — A1306

15th Mediterranean
Games,
Almería — A1307

2005, Mar. 1   Perf. 13¾x14
3351 A1305 35c red   .95   .45

                              Perf. 14x13¾
3352 A1306 40c multi   1.10   .55
3353 A1307 78c multi   2.10 1.10
       Nos. 3351-3353 (3)   4.15 2.10

Europa
A1308

2005, Apr. 15   Perf. 13¾x14
3354 A1308 53c multi   1.40   .70

Juan Valera
(1824-1905),
Writer and
Diplomat
A1309

2005, Apr. 18   Engr.   Perf. 14x13¾
3355 A1309 €2.21 vio brn &
                        blue   5.75 2.75

Souvenir Sheet

Publication of Don Quixote, 400th
Anniv. — A1310

Various scenes from book.

2005, Apr. 22
3356 A1310 Sheet of 4   10.00 10.00
a.   28c black   .75   .35
b.   53c black   1.40   .70
c.   78c black   2.00 1.00
d.   €2.21 black   5.75 2.75

Telegraphy in Spain, 150th
Anniv. — A1311

2005, Apr. 26   Photo.   Perf. 13¾x14
3357 A1311 28c multi   .75   .35

Intl. Year of
Physics — A1312

Die Cut Perf. 13¼
2005, Apr. 28   Litho.
Self-Adhesive
3358 A1312 28c multi   .75   .35

Souvenir Sheet

Fans — A1313

No. 3359 — Fan depicting: a, Flowers. b,
Madrid street scene. c, Nymphs.

2005, May 9   Photo.   Perf. 13¾
3359 A1313 Sheet of 3 + label   4.00 4.00
a.   28c multi   .70   .35
b.   53c multi   1.40   .70
c.   78c multi   1.90   .95

Diario Palentino
Newspaper, 124th
Anniv. — A1314

Ultima Hora Newspaper, 112th
Anniv. — A1315

Diario de Ibiza Newspaper, 112th
Anniv. — A1316

2005, May 16   Perf. 14x13¾
3360 A1314 78c multi   1.90   .95
                              Perf. 13¾x14
3361 A1315 €1.95 multi   4.75 2.40
3362 A1316 €2.21 multi   5.50 2.75
       Nos. 3360-3362 (3)   12.15 6.10

Inn,
Oropesa
A1317

2005, June 13   Engr.   Perf. 13¾x14
3363 A1317 €1.95 brown   4.75 2.40

Souvenir Sheet

EXFILNA 2005, Alicante — A1318

Litho. & Engr.
2005, June 20   **Perf. 14x13¾**
3364   A1318   €2.21 multi   5.50   2.75

Castles
A1319

Designs: 78c, Alcaudete Castle. €1.95, Valderrobres Castle. €2.21, Molina de Aragón Castle.

2005, July 4   **Engr.**   **Perf. 13¾x14**
3365-3367   A1319   Set of 3   12.00   6.00

Fingerprint Registration for Newborns — A1320

2005, July 11   **Photo.**
3368   A1320   28c multi   .70   .35

Stamp Day — A1321

Die Cut Perf. 13
2005, Sept. 1   **Litho.**
Self-Adhesive
3369   A1321   28c multi   .70   .35

Nuestra Señora de la Asuncion Church, Pont de Suert
A1322

2005, Sept. 7   **Photo.**   **Perf. 13¾x14**
3370   A1322   28c multi   .70   .35

Lunnispark Building   Lucho
A1323   A1324

Lupita in Bed — A1325

Die Cut Perf. 13
2005, Sept. 16   **Litho.**
Self-Adhesive
3371   Booklet pane of 8   5.75
   a.   A1323 28c shown   .70   .35
   b.   A1324 28c shown   .70   .35
   c.   A1323 28c Green building   .70   .35
   d.   A1324 28c Lulila   .70   .35
   e.   A1324 28c Lupita   .70   .35
   f.   A1325 28c shown   .70   .35
   g.   A1324 28c Lublú   .70   .35
   h.   A1323 28c Orange building   .70   .35

Los Lunnis children's television show.

World Cycling Championships, Madrid — A1326

2005, Sept. 20   **Photo.**   **Perf. 13¾x14**
3372   A1326   78c multi   1.90   .95

España 2006 World Philatelic Exhibition, Malaga
A1327

2005   **Photo.**   **Perf. 13¾x14**
3373   A1327   53c multi   1.40   .70

Gardens
A1328

No. 3374: a, Gardens of La Granja de San Ildefonso, Segovia. b, Bagh-e-Shahzadeh Garden, Kerman, Iran.

2005, Oct. 10
3374   Horiz. pair + central label   7.25   3.75
   a.   A1328 78c multi   1.90   .95
   b.   A1328 €2.21 multi   5.25   2.60

See Iran No. 2912.

15th Iberoamerican Summit, Salamanca — A1329

2005, Oct. 13
3375   A1329   78c multi   1.90   .95

America Issue, Fight Against Poverty
A1330

2005, Oct. 14   **Perf. 12¾**
3376   A1330   78c multi   1.90   .95

La Orotava, 500th Anniv. — A1331

2005, Oct. 20   **Perf. 14x13¾**
3377   A1331   €2.21 multi   5.50   2.75

Colonial Postage Stamps for Cuba and Philippines, 150th Anniv. — A1332

2005, Oct. 20   **Perf. 13¾x14**
3378   A1332   €2.21 multi   5.50   2.75

Prince of Asturias Awards, 25th Anniv. — A1333

2005, Oct. 20   **Perf. 13¼x13**
3379   A1333   28c multi + label   .70   .35

Printed in sheets of 8 stamps + 8 different labels.

Miniature Sheet

Scenes from Television Show "Al Filo de lo Imposible" — A1334

No. 3380: a, Underwater cave explorers. b, Hot-air balloon with man on rope outside of gondola. c, Man pulling sled. d, Kayaker. e, Climber on snowy mountain. f, Rock climber.

2005, Oct. 24   **Perf. 14x13¾**
3380   A1334   Sheet of 6 + 6 labels   4.25   2.10
   a.-f.   28c Any single   .70   .35

See No. 3398.

A1335

Christmas
A1336

2005, Oct. 31
3381   A1335   28c multi   .70   .35
3382   A1336   53c multi   1.25   .65

Souvenir Sheet

Stained Glass Window, Avila Cathedral — A1337

2005, Nov. 2   **Litho. & Engr.**
3383   A1337   €2.21 multi   5.25   2.60

Euromediterranean Summit,
Barcelona — A1338

2005, Nov. 3 Photo. Perf. 13¾x14
3384 A1338 53c multi   1.25   .65

Queen Juana of
Castile (1479-
1555)
A1339

2005, Nov. 4   Perf. 14x13¾
3385 A1339 28c multi   .70   .35

Parliament of Toro, 500th anniv.

Toys — A1340

No. 3386: a, Marionettes. b, Tops. c, Toy car. d, Toy truck. e, Doll. f, Container of marbles. g, Toy horse and cart. h, Toy motorcycle.

2006, Jan. 2 Litho. Die Cut Perf. 13
Self-Adhesive
3386 Booklet pane of 8   5.50
a.-h. A1340 A Any single   .65   .35

Nos. 3386a-3386h each sold for 28c on day of issue.

King Juan Carlos Type of 2001 With Euro Denominations Only

2006   Photo.   Perf. 12¾x13¼
3387 A1091 29c sil & brown   .70   .35
3388 A1091 57c sil & org   1.40   .70
3389 A1091 €2.26 sil & pur   5.50 2.75
3390 A1091 €2.33 sil & claret 5.50 2.75
3391 A1091 €2.39 sil & dull
             grn   5.75 2.75
Nos. 3387-3391 (5)   18.85 9.30

Issued: 29c, 57c, 2/1; €2.26, 1/5; €2.33, €2.39, 2/13.

Carnation — A1341

Die Cut Perf. 13
2006, Jan. 20   Litho.
Self-Adhesive
3392 A1341 28c multi   .70   .35

No. 3392 was printed in sheets of 10, which were bound in booklets of 10 sheets.

Bank of Spain,
150th
Anniv. — A1342

2006, Jan. 27 Engr.   Perf. 14x13¾
3393 A1342 78c brown & black 1.90   .95

Cypress Tree, La
Anunciada
Convent,
Villafranca del
Bierzo — A1343

2006, Jan. 30   Photo.
3394 A1343 53c multi   1.40   .70

Sparrow — A1344

Die Cut Perf. 13
2006, Feb. 1   Litho.
Self-Adhesive
3395 A1344 A multi   .70   .35

No. 3395 sold for 29p on day of issue, and was printed in sheets of 10 which were bound in booklets of 10 sheets.

Intl. Year of Deserts and
Desertification — A1345

2006, Feb. 6 Photo. Perf. 13¾x14
3396 A1345 29c multi   .70   .35

Woman
Suffrage,
75th Anniv.
A1346

2006, Mar. 8
3397 A1346 29c blue & sepia   .70   .35

"Al Filo de lo Imposible" Type of 2005

No. 3398: a, Cyclists. b, Man in desert. c, Parachutist. d, Kayakers. e, Rafters. f, Waterfall rock climbers.

2006, Mar. 22   Perf. 14x13¾
3398 A1334 Sheet of 6 + 6 labels   12.00 6.00
a.   29c multi   .70   .35
b.   38c multi   .95   .45
c.   41c multi   1.00   .50
d.   57c multi   1.40   .70
e.   78c multi   1.90   .95
f.   €2.39 multi   6.00 3.00

Goldfinch
A1347

Strelitzia Flower
A1348

2006, Apr. 1 Litho. Die Cut Perf. 13
3399 A1347 29c multi   .70   .35
3400 A1348 38c multi   .95   .45

Nos. 3399-3400 were each printed in sheets of 10, which were bound in booklets of 10 sheets.

Civic
Values — A1349

Designs: No. 3401, 29c, Water conservation. No. 3402, 29c, Man with "No Drugs" balloons. 38c, Social Security and Labor inspectors, cent., horiz. 57c, Fight against human trafficking, horiz.

Perf. 14x13¾, 13¾x14
2006, Apr. 4   Photo.
3401-3404 A1349 Set of 4   3.75 1.90

Diario de Pontevedra Newspaper,
117th Anniv. — A1350

Diario de Léon
Newspaper,
Cent. — A1351

Diario de Avila
Newspaper, 108th
Anniv. — A1352

El Norte de
Castilla
Newspaper, 150th
Anniv. — A1353

Levante-El Mercantil Valenciano
Newspaper, 134th Anniv. — A1354

2006, Apr. 20 Perf. 13¾x14, 14x13¾
3405 A1350 41c multi   1.10   .55
3406 A1351 41c multi   1.10   .55
3407 A1352 41c multi   1.10   .55
3408 A1353 41c red & blk   1.10   .55
3409 A1354 41c multi   1.10   .55
Nos. 3405-3409 (5)   5.50 2.75

Souvenir Sheet

Christopher Columbus (1451-1506),
Explorer — A1355

2006, Apr. 24   Perf. 14x13¾
3410 A1355 €2.39 multi   6.25 3.00

Coronation of
Santa Maria de
Los Remedios
Icon,
Cent. — A1356

2006, Apr. 27
3411 A1356 €2.33 multi   6.00 3.00

Souvenir Sheet

Exfilna 2006 Philatelic Exhibition,
Algeciras — A1357

Litho. & Engr.
2006, May 5   Perf. 13¾x14
3412 A1357 €2.39 multi   6.25 3.00

Inauguration of Taxis Family Postal
System in Spain, 500th
Anniv. — A1358

2006, May 9   Photo.
3413 A1358 29c multi   .75   .35

Internet Day A1359

25th Intl. Mathematics Conference, Madrid — A1360

Die Cut Perf. 13

2006, May 17   **Litho.**
3414 A1359 29c multi   .75   .35
3515 A1360 57c multi   1.50   .75

Socialist Youth In Spain, Cent. A1361

2006, May 23   **Photo.**   **Perf. 13¾x14**
3416 A1361 78c multi   2.00 1.00

Souvenir Sheet

España 06 Intl. Philatelic Exhibition, Málaga — A1362

2006, May 29
3417 A1362 78c multi   2.00 1.00

San Pedro and San Marcial Festivals, Irún — A1363

2006, June 5   **Perf. 14x13¾**
3418 A1363 29c multi   .75   .35

Architecture A1364

Designs: 29c, Casa Battló, Barcelona. 38c, Vapor Aymerich, Amt y Jover, Terrassa. 41c, Depósitos del Sol Library, Albacete. 57c, Campos Eliseos Theater, Bilbao. 78c, Alfredo Kraus Auditorium, Las Palmas, horiz. €2.33, Bus station, Casar de Cáceres, horiz.

Engr., Photo. (41c, 78c, €2.33)
2006, June 8   **Perf. 14x13¾, 13¾x14**
3419-3424 A1364   Set of 6   12.00 6.00

Al-Idrisi (c. 1100-65), Geographer A1365

2006, June 15   **Photo.**   **Perf. 14x13¾**
3425 A1365 78c multi   2.00 1.00

Greenfinch   Iris
A1366   A1367

2006, July 5   **Litho.**   **Die Cut Perf. 13**
Self-Adhesive
3426 A1366 29c multi   .75   .35
3427 A1367 41c multi   1.10   .55

Nos. 3426-3427 were each printed in sheets of 10 which were bound in booklets of 10 sheets.

Sanlúcar de Barrameda Horse Race A1368

2006, July 6   **Photo.**   **Perf. 13¾x14**
3428 A1368 €2.33 multi   6.00 3.00

Archaeology A1369

Designs: 29c, Los Millares archaeological site. 57c, Art on vase from L'Alcudia archaeological site, horiz. 78c Moixent Warrior, bronze sculpture.

2006, July 6   **Perf. 14x13¾, 13¾x14**
3429-3431 A1369   Set of 3   4.25 2.10

Earth Sciences A1370

Designs: No. 3432, 29c, Derived cartography. No. 3433, 29c, Vulcanology and seismology.

2006, July 13   **Perf. 13¾x14**
3432-3433 A1370   Set of 2   1.50   .75

Benavides Thursday Market, Orbigo, 700th Anniv. A1371

Aragon-Cataluña Canal, Cent. — A1372

2006, July 20
3434 A1371 38c multi   1.00   .50
3435 A1372 38c multi   1.00   .50

Diplomatic Relations Between Spain and Israel, 20th Anniv. A1373

2006, Sept. 1
3436 A1373 78c multi   2.00 1.00

Castles A1374

Designs: 29c, Baños de la Encina Castle. €2.39, Torroella de Montgri.

2006, Sept. 8   **Engr.**
3437-3438 A1374   Set of 2   6.75 3.50

A1375

Europa — A1376

2006, Sept. 12   **Photo.**   **Perf. 14x13¾**
3439 A1375 29c multi   .75   .35
3440 A1376 57c multi   1.50   .75

Bridges Between Spain and Portugal — A1377

No. 3441: a, Ayamonte International Bridge (Vila Real de Santo António). b, Alcántara Bridge.

2006, Sept. 14   **Perf. 13x13¼**
3441   Horiz. pair   2.25 1.10
   a. A1377 29c multi   .75   .35
   b. A1377 57c multi   1.50   .75

See Portugal Nos. 2855-2856.

Rioja Grape Harvest Festival A1378

2006, Sept. 21   **Perf. 13¾x14**
3442 A1378 29c multi   .75   .35

Real Club Deportivo La Coruna Soccer Team, Cent. A1379

2006, Sept. 25
3443 A1379 57c multi   1.50   .75

Souvenir Sheet

Victory of Spanish Team at 2006 World Basketball Championships — A1380

2006, Oct. 2   **Photo.**   **Perf. 13¾x14**
3444 A1380 29c multi   .75   .35

Swallow   Poinsettia
A1381   A1382

2006, Oct. 4   **Litho.**   **Die Cut Perf. 13**
Self-Adhesive
3445 A1381 29c multi   .75   .35
3446 A1382 29c multi   .75   .35

Souvenir Sheets

España 06 World Philatelic Exhibition, Malaga — A1383

Exhibition emblem and: No. 3447, €2.33, Emblem of Vitorio & Lucchino, fashion designers. No. 3448, €2.33, Silhouette of hat and hand (cinema), vert. No. 3449, €2.33, Musical notes and staff. No. 3450, €2.33, Guitarist, vert. No. 3451, €2.33, Hand (flamenco dancing). No. 3452, €2.33, Tennis racquet and basketball, vert. No. 3453, €2.33, Pablo Picasso (1881-1973), artist.

2006 Photo. Perf. 13¾x14, 14x13¾
3447-3453 A1383 Set of 7 42.00 21.00
Issued: No. 3447, 10/8; No. 3448, 10/9; Nos. 3449-3450, 10/10; No. 3451, 10/11; No. 3452, 10/12; No. 3453, 10/13.

America Issue, Energy Conservation — A1384

2006, Oct. 14 Perf. 13¾
3454 A1384 78c multi 2.00 1.00

Appointment of First Spanish Postmen, 250th Anniv. — A1385

Die Cut Perf. 13
2006, Oct. 25 Litho.
Self-Adhesive
3455 A1385 29c multi .75 .35
Stamp Day.

Ramón Rubial (1906-99), Politician A1386

2006, Oct. 27 Engr. Perf. 14x13¾
3456 A1386 57c multi 1.50 .75

A1387

Christmas A1388

Die Cut Perf. 13
2006, Nov. 2 Litho.
Self-Adhesive
3457 A1387 29c multi .75 .35
3458 A1388 57c multi 1.50 .75

Souvenir Sheet

Stained Glass Window, School of Architecture, Polytechnic University of Madrid — A1389

Litho. & Engr.
2006, Nov. 3 Perf. 14x13¾
3459 A1389 €2.39 multi 6.25 3.25

St. Francis Xavier (1506-52) A1390

2006, Nov. 7 Perf. 13¾x14
3460 A1390 29c multi .80 .40

Television Broadcasting in Spain, 50th Anniv. — A1391

2006, Nov. 8 Photo.
3461 A1391 29c multi .80 .40

La Vanguardia Newspaper, 125th Anniv. — A1392

2006, Nov. 9 Perf. 14x13¾
3462 A1392 29c multi .80 .40

Pío Baroja (1872-1956), Writer — A1393

2006, Nov. 23
3463 A1393 29c multi .80 .40

Revision of Spanish Coat of Arms, 25th Anniv. — A1394

2006, Nov. 23
3464 A1394 29c multi .80 .40

A1395

Historical Memory Year A1396

2006, Nov. 30 Perf. 13¾x14
3465 A1395 29c multi .80 .40
3466 A1396 29c multi .80 .40

Toys — A1397

No. 3467: a, Tricycle. b, Bus. c, Train. d, Bowling game. e, Baby carriage. f, Seaplane. g, Printing kit. h, Firetruck.

2007, Jan. 2 Litho. Die Cut Perf. 13
Self-Adhesive
3467 Booklet pane of 8 6.50
a.-h. A1397 A Any single .80 .40
Nos. 3467a-3467h each sold for 30c on day of issue.

King Juan Carlos — A1398

Perf. 12¾x13¼
2007, Jan. 13 Photo.
Color of Portrait
3468 A1398 30c blue .80 .40
3469 A1398 58c olive grn 1.50 .75
3470 A1398 €2.43 org brn 6.25 3.25
3471 A1398 €2.49 rose pink 6.50 3.25
Nos. 3468-3471 (4) 15.05 7.65
See Nos. 3532-3539, 3615-3618, 3688-3691, 3774-3777.

Hoopoe A1399

Red Rose A1400

Die Cut Perf. 13
2007, Jan. 20 Litho.
Self-Adhesive
3472 A1399 30c multi .80 .40
3473 A1400 39c multi 1.00 .50
Nos. 3472-3473 each were printed in sheets of 10, which were bound in booklets of 10 sheets.

Teacher and Pupils A1401

2007, Jan. 23
Self-Adhesive
3474 A1401 58c multi 1.50 .75

Las Provincias Newspaper, 140th Anniv. (in 2006) — A1402

2007, Jan. 31 Photo. Perf. 13¾x14
3475 A1402 42c multi 1.10 .55

Stylized Periodic Table of Elements A1403

Gregorian Calendar, 425th Anniv. — A1404

Die Cut Perf. 13
2007, Feb. 2 Litho.
Self-Adhesive
3476 A1403 30c multi .80 .40
3477 A1404 42c multi 1.10 .55

Institute of Catalan Studies, Cent. A1405

2007, Feb. 5 Photo. Perf. 13¾x14
3478 A1405 30c multi .80 .40

2007 America's Cup Challenger Races — A1406

2007, Feb. 8
3479 A1406 30c multi .80 .40

Earth and Space Sciences A1407

Designs: 30c, Map (cartography). 78c, Yebes Astronomical Center radio telescope.

Die Cut Perf. 13
2007, Feb. 16 Litho.
Self-Adhesive
3480-3481 A1407 Set of 2 3.00 1.50

Fuentepiña Pine Tree — A1408

2007, Mar. 5   Photo.   Perf. 13¾x14
3482 A1408 78c multi   2.10 1.10

Mosaic from Roman Villa, Pedrosa de la Vega A1409

Roman Baths, Campo Valdés A1410

2007, Mar. 8
3483 A1409 30c multi   .80   .40
3484 A1410 30c multi   .80   .40

European Economic Community, 50th Anniv. — A1411

2007, Mar. 23   Perf. 14x13¾
3485 A1411 58c multi   1.60   .80

Canary A1412

Violet A1413

2007, Apr. 2 Litho. Die Cut Perf. 13
Self-Adhesive
3486 A1412 30c multi   .80   .40
3487 A1413 42c multi   1.25   .60

Souvenir Sheet

Madrid Movement, 25th Anniv. — A1414

2007, Apr. 13   Photo.   Perf. 13¾x14
3488 A1414 30c multi   .85   .40

Souvenir Sheet

Mallorca Cathedral — A1415

Engr., Litho. Margin
2007, Apr. 16
3489 A1415 €2.43 blue   6.75 3.25
Exfilna 2007 National Philatelic Exhibition,
Palma de Mallorca.

Europa — A1416

2007, Apr. 23   Photo.   Perf. 14x13¾
3490 A1416 58c multi   1.60   .80
Scouting, cent.

Architecture A1417

Designs: 30c, Valleacerón Chapel, Almadenejos. 39c, El Capricho, Comillas. 42c, Santa Caterina Market, Barcelona. 58c, Vizcaya Bridge, Las Arenas, horiz. 78c, Barajas Airport, Madrid. €2.49, Casa Lis, Salamanca, horiz.

Photo., Engr. (39c, 58c)
2007, Apr. 26   Perf. 14x13¾, 13¾x14
3491-3496 A1417 Set of 6   13.50 6.75

Juvenia 2007 Natl. Youth Philatelic Exhibition, Calahorra A1418

2007, Apr. 28   Photo.   Perf. 13¾x14
3497 A1418 30c multi   .85   .40

Stamp Day — A1419

2007, May 7 Litho. Die Cut Perf. 13
Self-Adhesive
3498 A1419 30c multi   .80   .40

Song of the Cid, 800th Anniv. A1420

2007, May 9   Die Cut Perf. 13
Self-Adhesive
3499 A1420 30c multi   .80   .40

Law of the Court of Auditors, 25th Anniv. — A1421

2007, May 12   Photo.   Perf. 14x13¾
3500 A1421 30c multi   .80   .40

Civic Values — A1422

Designs: 30c, Racial integration. 39c, No school violence. 58c, Organ donation. 78c, Equality of the sexes.

2007, May 16
3501-3504 A1422 Set of 4   5.50 2.75

Mushrooms A1423

Designs: 30c, Tricholoma equestre. 78c, Amanita muscaria.

2007, June 1
3505-3506 A1423 Set of 2   3.00 1.50

Carmen Conde (1907-96), Writer A1424

Rosa Chacel (1898-1994), Writer — A1425

2007, June 4   Engr.   Perf. 13¾x14
3507 A1424 €2.49 red & blk   6.75 3.50
3508 A1425 €2.49 org & blk   6.75 3.50

Real Betis Balompié Soccer Team, Cent. A1426

2007, June 14 Photo.   Perf. 13¾x14
3509 A1426 78c multi   2.10 1.10

Canonical Coronation of Blessed Mary of the O — A1427

2007, June 16   Perf. 14x13¾
3510 A1427 30c multi   .85   .40

Nightingale A1428

Hyacinth A1429

2007, July 2 Litho. Die Cut Perf. 13
Self-Adhesive
3511 A1428 30c multi   .85   .40
3512 A1429 30c multi   .85   .40

Spanish Armed Forces Peace Missions — A1430

2007, July 4   Photo.   Perf. 13x13¼
3513 A1430 30c multi   .85   .40

Expo Zaragoza 2008 A1431

2007, July 5 Litho. *Die Cut Perf. 13*
Self-Adhesive
3514 A1431 58c multi   1.60   .80

Miniature Sheet

Scenes From Television Show "Al Filo de lo Imposible" — A1432

No. 3515: a, Diver under ice shelf. b, Skier. c, People pulling sleds. d, Sailboat in Antarctic waters. e, Kayaker in fjord. f, Iditarod dog sled team.

2007, July 12 Photo. *Perf. 14x13¾*
3515 A1432 Sheet of 6 + 6
         labels   13.50 13.50
  a. 30c multi   .85   .40
  b. 39c multi   1.00   .50
  c. 42c multi   1.10   .55
  d. 58c multi   1.60   .80
  e. 78c multi   2.10   1.10
  f. €2.43 multi   6.75   3.25

Nature Parks A1433

Designs: No. 3516, 30c, Albufera Nature Park. No. 3517, 30c, Lagunas de Ruidera Nature Park.

2007, July 19   *Perf. 13¾x14*
3516-3517 A1433 Set of 2   1.75   .85

Miniature Sheet

Lighthouses — A1434

No. 3518: a, Punta del Hidalgo Lighthouse, Tenerife. b, Cabo Mayor Lighthouse, Cantabria. c, Punta Almina Lighthouse, Ceuta. d, Melilla Lighthouse, Melilla. e, Cabo de Palos Lighthouse, Murcia. f, Gorliz Lighthouse, Vizcaya.

2007, Sept. 6
3518 A1434 Sheet of 6 + 6
         labels   13.50 13.50
  a. 30c multi   .85   .40
  b. 39c multi   1.00   .50
  c. 42c multi   1.10   .55
  d. 58c multi   1.60   .80
  e. 78c multi   2.10   1.10
  f. €2.43 multi   6.75   3.25

Castles A1435

Designs: No. 3519, €2.49, Almenar Castle. No. 3520, €2.49, Villena Castle.

2007, Sept. 10 Engr. *Perf. 13¾x14*
3519-3520 A1435 Set of 2   14.00 7.00

Souvenir Sheet

Statues of Asclepius, Greek God of Medicine — A1436

No. 3521: a, Statue from Museum of Ampurias, Spain. b, Statue from National Archaeological Museum, Athens.

2007, Sept. 13 Photo. *Perf. 12¾x13*
3521 A1436 Sheet of 2   2.50 2.50
  a. 30c multi   .85   .40
  b. 58c multi   1.60   .80

See Greece No. 2319.

Dupont Lark — A1437   Daisy — A1438

2007, Oct. 1 Litho. *Die Cut Perf. 13*
Self-Adhesive
3522 A1437 30c multi   .85   .40
3523 A1438 30c multi   .85   .40

El Adelantado de Segovia Newspaper, 106th Anniv. — A1439

2007, Oct. 4 Photo. *Perf. 13¾x14*
3524 A1439 78c multi   2.25 1.10

America Issue, Education For All A1440

2007, Oct. 11
3525 A1440 78c multi   2.25 1.10

Miniature Sheet

Women's Clothing by Balenciaga In Costume Museum, Madrid — A1441

No. 3526: a, Ivory chantily lace and taffeta dress, 1948-50. b, Red silk satin two-piece party dress, 1960. c, Red morning coat and dress, 1960s. d, Yellow linen dress.

2007, Oct. 18 Photo. *Perf. 13¼x13*
3526 A1441 Sheet of 4   6.25 6.25
  a. 39c multi   1.10   .55
  b. 42c multi   1.25   .60
  c. 58c multi   1.60   .80
  d. 78c multi   2.25 1.10

Altarpiece Sculpture Depicting Epiphany, by Damián Forment A1442

Children in Envelope A1443

Die Cut Perf. 13
2007, Oct. 31   **Litho.**
Self-Adhesive
3527 A1442 30c multi   .90   .45
3528 A1443 58c multi   1.75   .85

Christmas.

Self-Portraits A1444

Self-portraits of: 39c, Pedro Berruguete. 42c, Mariano Salvador Maella.

2007, Nov. 5 Photo. *Perf. 14x13¾*
3529-3530 A1444 Set of 2   2.40 1.25

Miniature Sheet

Stained-Glass Window by Alberto Martorell — A1445

Litho. & Engr.
2007, Nov. 9   *Perf. 13¾x14*
3531 A1445 €2.43 multi   7.25 3.75

King Juan Carlos Type of 2007
2008, Jan. 2 Photo. *Perf. 12¾x13¼*
Color of Portrait
3532 A1398 1c black   .25   .25
3533 A1398 2c lilac rose   .25   .25
3534 A1398 5c blue   .25   .25
3535 A1398 10c greenish
            blue   .30   .25
3536 A1398 31c brown   .90   .45
3537 A1398 60c violet blue   1.75   .90
3538 A1398 78c rose   2.40 1.25
3539 A1398 €2.60 slate green 7.75 3.50
       Nos. 3532-3539 (8)   13.85 7.10

Toys — A1446

No. 3540: a, Steamship with wheels. b, Bean bag target with clown's face. c, Three sand pails. d, Stagecoach. e, Wafer container. f, Diabolo. g, Building blocks. h, Submarine.

2008, Jan. 2 Litho. *Die Cut Perf. 13*
Self-Adhesive
3540   Booklet pane of 8   7.50
 a.-h. A1446 A Any single   .90   .45
  Nos. 3540a-3540h each sold for 31c on day of issue.

Green Woodpecker A1447   Camellia A1448

2008, Jan. 10   *Die Cut Perf. 13*
Self-Adhesive
3541 A1447 31c multi   .90   .45
3542 A1448 60c multi   1.75   .90

Sciences A1449

Designs: 39c, Medicine. 43c, Meteorology.

2008, Jan. 17   **Litho.**
Self-Adhesive
3543-3544 A1449 Set of 2   2.40 1.25
  See also Nos. 3613-3614.

La Voz de Avilés Newspaper,
Cent. — A1450

2008, Jan. 30 Photo. *Perf. 13¾x14*
3545 A1450 31c multi   .95 .45

International Years — A1451

Designs: 78c, Intl. Polar Year. €2.60, Intl.
Year of Planet Earth.

Die Cut Perf. 13
2008, Feb. 4   Litho.
Self-Adhesive
3546-3547 A1451 Set of 2   10.50 5.25

Hand and
Phone
Number
for
Abused
Women's
Hotline
A1452

2008, Feb. 11   *Die Cut Perf. 13*
Self-Adhesive
3548 A1452 31c multi   .95 .45

Black Poplar of
Horcajuelo
A1453

2008, Feb. 18 Photo. *Perf. 14x13¾*
3549 A1453 €2.44 multi   7.50 3.75

Expo
Zaragoza
2008
A1454

Die Cut Perf. 13
2008, Feb. 22   Litho.
Self-Adhesive
3550 A1454 31c multi   .95 .45

Civic
Values
A1455

Designs: 31c, Fight against child exploitation. 39c, Intergenerational solidarity. 43c, Cultural diversity.

2008, Feb. 29 Photo. *Perf. 13¾x14*
3551-3553 A1455 Set of 3   3.50 1.75

Archaeology — A1456

Designs: No. 3554, 31c, Bicha of Balazote.
No. 3555, 31c, Funerary urn of Apophis I.

2008, Mar. 3
3554-3555 A1456 Set of 2   1.90 .95

Landscapes — A1457

Designs: No. 3556, 31c, Hoces del Rio
Duratón Nature Park. No. 3557, 31c, Montes
de Toledo.

2008, Mar. 10
3556-3557 A1457 Set of 2   2.00 1.00

Maritime
Rescue
Craft
A1458

Die Cut Perf. 13
2008, Mar. 12   Litho.
Self-Adhesive
3558 A1458 31c multi   1.00 .50

University
of Oviedo,
400th
Anniv.
A1459

2008, Mar. 14 Photo. *Perf. 13¾x14*
3559 A1459 31c multi   1.00 .50

European Parliament, 50th
Anniv. — A1460

2008, Mar. 19
3560 A1460 60c multi   1.90 .95

Common   Tulips — A1462
Kestrel — A1461

2008, Apr. 1 Litho. *Die Cut Perf. 13*
Self-Adhesive
3561 A1461 31c multi   1.00 .50
3562 A1462 43c multi   1.40 .70

Palacio de
Longoria,
Madrid
A1463

Casa Vicens,
Barcelona
A1464

Agbar Tower,
Barcelona
A1465

Tenerife Auditorium, Tenerife — A1466

Torrespaña,
Madrid — A1467

Montjuic
Communications
Tower, Barcelona
A1468

2008, Apr. 2 Engr. *Perf. 13¾x14*
3563 A1463 31c multi   1.00 .50
          Perf. 14x13¾
3564 A1464 31c multi   1.00 .50
          Photo.
3565 A1465 31c multi   1.00 .50
          Perf. 13¾x14
3566 A1466 31c multi   1.00 .50

          Perf. 13¼x13
3567 A1467 31c multi   1.00 .50
3568 A1468 31c multi   1.00 .50
     Nos. 3563-3568 (6)   6.00 3.00

Traditional
Sports
and
Games
A1469

Designs: No. 3569, Court handball (Pelota
Valenciana). No. 3570, Handball (Pelota
Vasca), vert. No. 3571, Stone carrying
(Levantamiento de piedras), vert. No. 3572,
Bar throwing (Lanzamiento de barra), vert. No.
3573, Sling hurling (Tiro con honda), vert.
 No. 3574, Rowing race (regatas de
traineras). No. 3575, Human tower (castillos
humanos), vert.
 No. 3576 — Bowling: a, Bolo leonés. b, Bolo
palma. c, Bolo asturiano.
 No. 3577, vert. — Martial arts: a, Stick fight-
ing (palo canario). b, Wrestling (lucha
leonesa). c, Wrestling (lucha canaria).
 No. 3578 — Throwing games: a, Chito. b,
Chave. c, Calva.

2008 Photo. *Perf. 13¾x14, 14x13¾*
3569 A1469 43c multi + label   1.40 .70
3570 A1469 43c multi + label   1.40 .70
3571 A1469 43c multi + label   1.40 .70
3572 A1469 43c multi + label   1.40 .70
3573 A1469 43c multi + label   1.40 .70
3574 A1469 43c multi + label   1.40 .70
3575 A1469 43c multi + label   1.25 .60
     Nos. 3569-3575 (7)   9.65 4.80
          Miniature Sheets
3576   Sheet of 3 + 3 labels   4.25 2.10
 a.-c. A1469 43c Any single   1.40 .70
3577   Sheet of 3 + 5 labels   4.25 2.10
 a.-c. A1469 43c Any single   1.40 .70
3578   Sheet of 3 + 3 labels   3.50 1.75
 a.-c. A1469 43c Any single   1.10 .55

 Issued: Nos. 3569-3570, 4/16; No. 3571,
5/16; Nos. 3572-3573, 5/30. Nos. 3574, 3577,
7/16; No. 3575, 10/9; No. 3576, 6/5; No. 3578,
10/27.

          Souvenir Sheet

Europa — A1470

2008, Apr. 23   *Perf. 13¼x12¾*
3579 A1470 60c multi   1.90 .95

Souvenir Sheet

Cross of Victory, San Salvador
Cathedral, Oviedo — A1471

2008. Apr. 28   **Perf. 14x13¾**
3580 A1471 €2.44 multi   7.50 3.75
Exfilna 2008 (National Philatelic Exhibition),
Oviedo.

Royal Decree of
the Maritime
Post — A1472

2008, May 5 Litho. Die Cut Perf. 13
Self-Adhesive
3581 A1472 39c black & brown   1.25 .60
Stamp Day.

El Progreso Newspaper, Lugo,
Cent. — A1473

2008, May 9 Photo. Perf. 13¾x14
3582 A1473 31c multi   1.00 .50

Joan Oró (1923-
2004), Biochemist
A1474

Zenobia
Camprubí (1887-
1956), Literary
Translator
A1475

María Lejárraga (1874-1974),
Writer — A1476

Design: No. 3586, Carmen Martín Gaite
(1925-2000), writer.

2008, June 2 Engr. Perf. 14x13¾
3583 A1474 31c black   1.00 .50
3584 A1475 31c ver & black   1.00 .50
3585 A1476 31c black & ver   1.00 .50
3586 A1476 31c black & ver   1.00 .50
Nos. 3583-3586 (4)   4.00 2.00

Souvenir Sheets

Francisco de Goya Monument,
Zaragoza — A1477

Model of Expo Zaragoza
Grounds — A1478

Engr. (Litho. Margin)
2008 Perf. 14x13¾
3587 A1477 €2.60 Prus blue   8.00 4.00
Photo.
Perf. 13¾x14
3588 A1478 Sheet of 3   11.50 5.75
a. 31c Expo buildings   1.00 .50
b. 78c Buildings, diff.   2.40 1.25
c. €2.60 Bridge Pavilion   8.00 4.00
Issued: No. 3587, 6/13; No. 3588, 7/4.

European Bee-
eater
A1479

Dahlia
A1480

2008, July 1 Litho. Die Cut Perf. 13
Self-Adhesive
3589 A1479 31c multi   1.00 .50
3590 A1480 60c multi   1.90 .95

2008
Summer
Olympics,
Beijing
A1481

2008, July 8 Perf. 13¾x14
3591 A1481 31c multi   1.00 .50

Souvenir Sheet

Spain, UEFA 2008 Soccer
Champions — A1482

2008, July 24 Photo.
3592 A1482 €1 multi   3.25 1.60

Souvenir Sheets

Tapestries — A1483

Tapestries of works by Francisco de Goya:
60c, The Swing. €2.60, The Blind Man and
the Guitar.

2008, July 29 Perf. 12¾
3593-3594 A1483 Set of 2   10.00 5.00

Miniature Sheet

Lighthouses — A1484

No. 3595: a, Barbaria Lighthouse, Isla de
Formantera. b, Irta Lighthouse, Castelón. c,
Pechiguera Lighthouse, Isla de Lanzarote. d,
Silleiro Lighthouse, Pontevedra. e, Tor-
redembarra Lighthouse, Tarragona. f, Punta
Orchilla Lighthouse, Isla de la Hierro.

2008, Sept. 2 Photo. Perf. 14x13¾
3595 A1484 Sheet of 6   10.50 5.25
a.-f. 60c Any single   1.75 .85

Self-Portraits
A1485

Self-portrait of: No. 3596, 31c, Antonio
Maria Esquivel (1806-57). No. 3597, 43c,
Darío de Regoyos (1857-1913).

2008, Sept. 8
3596-3597 A1485 Set of 2   2.10 1.10

Royal Spanish
Tennis Federation,
Cent. — A1486

2008, Sept. 19 Litho.
3598 A1486 31c red & orange   .90 .45

Jay
A1487

Daffodil
A1488

2008, Oct. 1 Die Cut Perf. 13
Self-Adhesive
3599 A1487 31c multi   .90 .45
3600 A1488 31c multi   .90 .45

Mushrooms — A1489

Designs: No. 3601, 31c, Lepista nuda. No.
3602, 31c, Boletus regius.

2008, Oct. 10 Photo. Perf. 13¾x14
3601-3602 A1489 Set of 2   1.75 .85

America
Issue,
National
Day
A1490

2008, Oct. 13
3603 A1490 78c multi   2.00 1.00

Castles
A1491

Designs: No. 3604, €2.60, Maqueda Castle,
Toledo. No. 3605, €2.60, La Calahorra Castle,
Granada.

2008, Oct. 16 Engr.
3604-3605 A1491 Set of 2   13.50 6.75

Miniature Sheet

Women's Clothing by Pedro Rodriguez
In Costume Museum, Madrid — A1492

No. 3606: a, Red ball gown, 1968-70. b,
Strapless dress, c. 1947. c, V-neck chiffon
dress, 1960s. d, Pink crepe dress with
embroidery.

Photo. & Embossed
2008, Oct. 23　　　　　　**Perf. 13¼x13**
3606　A1492　Sheet of 4　　　3.25　1.60
　a.-d.　　31c Any single　　　　.80　.40

Creche
Figures
A1493

Maternity, by J.
Carrero — A1494

Die Cut Perf. 13
2008, Nov. 3　　　　　　　　**Litho.**
Self-Adhesive
3607　A1493　31c multi　　　　.80　.40
3608　A1494　60c multi　　　　1.60　.80

Souvenir Sheet

Dancers — A1495

No. 3609: a, Flamenco dancer, Spain. b,
Irish dancer, Ireland.

2008, Nov. 7　Photo.　Perf. 13¼x13
3609　A1495　Sheet of 2　　　3.50　1.75
　a.　60c multi　　　　　　　1.50　.75
　b.　78c multi　　　　　　　2.00　1.00

See Ireland Nos. 1809-1810.

Souvenir Sheet

Stained-Glass Window, by Dragant de
Burdeos — A1496

Photo., Litho. & Engr.
2008, Nov. 14　　　　　**Perf. 13¾x14**
3610　A1496　€2.60 multi　　6.75　3.50

Symbols of
Nation and
Autonomous
Communities
A1497

No. 3611: a, Flag of Spain. b, Flag and map
of Asturias. c, Flag and map of Galicia. d, Flag
and map of Cantabria. e, Arms of Spain. f,
Flag and map of Cataluña. g, Flag and map of
Basque Country (Euzkadi). h, Flag and map of
Andalusia.

2009, Jan. 2　Litho.　Die Cut Perf. 13
Self-Adhesive
3611　　Booklet pane of 8　　7.25
　a.-h.　A1497 A Any single　　.90　.45

On day of issue, Nos. 3611a-3611h each
sold for 32c.
See Nos. 3682, 3762.

Fan and
Manila
Shawl
A1498

2009, Jan. 2　　Die Cut Perf. 13
Self-Adhesive
3612　A1498　B multi　　　　1.75　.85

Sold for 62c on day of issue.

Sciences Type of 2008
Designs: 39c, Botany. 43c, Genetics.

2009, Jan. 12　　Die Cut Perf. 13
Self-Adhesive
3613-3614　A1449　Set of 2　　2.25　1.10

King Juan Carlos Type of 2007
Perf. 12¾x13¼
2009, Jan. 14　　　　　　　**Photo.**
Color of Portrait
3615　A1398　32c red　　　　.85　.40
3616　A1398　62c gray　　　　1.60　.80
3617　A1398　€2.47 olive green　6.50　3.25
3618　A1398　€2.70 blue　　　7.00　3.50
　　　Nos. 3615-3618 (4)　　15.95　7.95

La Rioja Newspaper, 120th
Anniv. — A1499

2009, Jan. 15　Photo.　Perf. 13¾x14
3619　A1499　32c multi　　　　.85　.40

Great Tit
A1500

Hydrangea
A1501

Die Cut Perf. 13
2009, Jan. 20　　　　　　　**Litho.**
Self-Adhesive
3620　A1500　32c multi　　　.85　.40
3621　A1501　62c multi　　　1.60　.80

Archaeology — A1502

Roman mosaics: No. 3622, €2.70, Ocea-
nus, from Carranque archaeological site,
Toledo. No. 3623, €2.70, Oriens, from Casa
del Mitreo, Mérida.

2009, Feb. 10　Photo.　Perf. 13¾x14
3622-3623　A1502　Set of 2　14.00　7.00

Civic
Values
A1503

Designs: 32c, Planting for the Planet. 62c,
Balancing of work and family life. 78c, Reduction of carbon dioxide output.

2009, Feb. 17　　　　　　　**Litho.**
3624-3626　A1503　Set of 3　4.50　2.25

Renewable
Energy
A1504

Millennium
Development
Goals
A1505

Designs: 32c, Hydroelectric energy. 43c,
Wind energy. 62c, Solar energy. 78c, Geothermal energy.

2009, Feb. 20　Photo.　Perf. 13
3627-3630　A1504　Set of 4　5.50　2.75

2009, Mar. 2
3631　A1505　32c multi　　　.85　.40

Nature
Parks
A1506

Designs: No. 3632, 43c, Cañón Río Lobos
Nature Park. No. 3633, 43c, Izki Nature Park.

2009, Mar. 9　　　　　　**Perf. 13¾x14**
3632-3633　A1506　Set of 2　2.40　1.25

Gladiolus
A1507

Capercaillie
A1508

2009, Apr. 1　Litho.　Die Cut Perf. 13
Self-Adhesive
3634　A1507　32c multi　　　.90　.45
3635　A1508　43c multi　　　1.25　.60

Council of
Europe,
60th Anniv.
A1509

2009, Apr. 6　　　　　　**Perf. 13¾x14**
3636　A1509　62c multi　　　1.75　.85

Miniature Sheet

Lighthouses — A1510

No. 3637: a, Porto Colom Lighthouse, Mallorca. b, Higuera Lighthouse, Huelva. c, Igeldo
Lighthouse, Guipúzcoa. d, Arinaga Lighthouse, Grand Canary Island. e, Tower of Hercules Lighthouse, La Coruña. f, Torrox Lighthouse, Málaga.

2009, Apr. 15　Photo.　Perf. 14x13¾
3637　A1510　Sheet of 6　10.50　5.25
　a.-f.　　62c Any single　　1.75　.85

Europa
A1511

2009, Apr. 23　Litho.　Perf. 13¾x14
3638　A1511　62c multi　　　1.75　.85

Intl. Year of Astronomy.

Traditional Dances — A1512

Designs: No. 3639, Isa. No. 3640, Mateixa.
No. 3641, Bolero. No. 3642, Rueda
(75x29mm). No. 3643, Aurresku, vert.
(29x75mm). No. 3644, Muñeira, vert. No.
3645, Fandango, vert. No. 3646, Candil, vert.
No. 3647, Seguidillas, vert.
No. 3649, Sevillanas, vert. (29x41mm).

2009　　　**Photo.　Perf. 13x12¾**
3639　A1512　43c multi　　　1.25　.60
3640　A1512　43c multi　　　1.25　.60
3641　A1512　43c multi + label　1.25　.60
Perf. 12¾x13¼
3642　A1512　43c multi　　　1.25　.60

Perf. 13¼x12¾
3643 A1512 43c multi   1.25   .60
Perf. 12¾x13
3644 A1512 43c multi + label   1.25   .60
3645 A1512 43c multi + label   1.25   .60
3646 A1512 43c multi + label   1.25   .60
3647 A1512 43c multi + label   1.25   .60
Perf. 13x12¾
3648 A1512 43c multi + label   1.25   .60
      Nos. 3639-3648 (10)   12.50   6.00
Souvenir Sheet
Perf. 14x13¾
3649 A1512 43c multi   1.25   .60
3650 A1512 43c multi   1.25   .60

Issued: Nos. 3639, 3649, 4/27; Nos. 3640-
3641, 5/14; Nos. 3642-3643, 6/4; Nos. 3644-
3645, 7/22; Nos. 3646-3647, 9/14. Nos. 3648,
3650, 10/15.

King Alfonso VI of
León and Castile
(c. 1040-1109)
A1513

2009, May 7 Photo.   Perf. 14x13¾
3651 A1513 39c multi   1.10   .55

St. Dominic de la
Calzada (1019-
1109)
A1514

2009, May 7
3652 A1514 62c multi   1.75   .85

Souvenir Sheet

Stained-Glass Window of Spanish
National Mint Paper Factory,
Burgos — A1515

2009, May 29   Litho. & Engr.
3653 A1515 €2.70 multi   7.75   3.75

Miniature Sheet

Women's Clothing Designed by
Manuel Piña (1944-94) — A1516

No. 3654: a, Linen dress and hat. b, Knitted
wool suit. c, Linen dress with hoops. d, Silk
wedding dress.

Photo. & Embossed
2009, June 15   Perf. 13¼x13
3654 A1516 Sheet of 4   3.75   1.90
   a.-d.   32c Any single   .90   .45

Graellsia   Geranium
Isabelae   A1518
A1517

2009, July 1 Litho.   Die Cut Perf. 13
Self-Adhesive
3655 A1517 32c multi   .90   .45
3656 A1518 62c multi   1.75   .85

Souvenir Sheet

Tapestries — A1519

No. 3657 — Tapestries of sports scenes
taken from painting: a, By Francisco de Goya
(El Juego de Pelota a Pala). b, By Antonio
González Velázquez (Juego de Bolos).

2009, July 6   Photo.   Perf. 12¾
3657 A1519 Sheet of 2   9.75   5.00
   a.   78c multi   2.25   1.10
   b.   €2.70 multi   7.50   3.75

Souvenir Sheet

Introduction of the Euro, 10th
Anniv. — A1520

Litho. & Engr.
2009, July 10   Perf. 14x13¾
3658 A1520 €1 multi   2.75   1.40

Traffic
Safety — A1521

2009, July 14 Photo.   Perf. 13x13¼
3659 A1521 32c multi   .90   .45

Famous
Men — A1522

Designs: No. 3660, 32c, Claudio Moyano
(1809-90), explorer. No. 3661, 32c, Charles
Darwin (1809-82), naturalist. No. 3662, 32c,
Louis Braille (1809-52), educator of the blind.

Engr., Litho. & Engr. (#3662)
2009, July 15   Perf. 14x13¾
3660-3662 A1522   Set of 3   2.75   1.40
Braille dots on No. 3662 were applied by a
thermographic process.

First
Powered
Flight in
Spain,
Cent.
A1523

2009, Sept. 5   Photo.   Perf. 13¾x14
3663 A1523 32c multi   .95   .45

Real
Sociedad
Soccer
Team,
Cent.
A1524

2009, Sept. 7   Litho.
3664 A1524 32c multi   .95   .45

Canal of
Castile
A1525

Los Tilos
Bridge, La
Palma
Island
A1526

Four Towers Business Area,
Madrid — A1527

No. 3667: a, Crystal Tower (with white area
above top floors). b, Caja Madrid Tower (3
separate blocks in rectangular frame). c,
Space Tower (with helical sides). d, Sacyr Val-
lehermoso Tower (with black area above top
floors).

2009, Sept. 9   Photo.   Perf. 13¾x14
3665 A1525 32c multi   .95   .45
3666 A1526 32c multi   .95   .45
Souvenir Sheet
Perf. 14x13¾
3667 A1527 Sheet of 4   4.00   2.00
   a.-d.   32c Any single   .95   .45

Arévalo
Castle,
Avila
A1528

Javier
Castle,
Navarre
A1529

2009, Sept. 21 Engr.   Perf. 13¾x14
3668 A1528 €2.70 brn & blk   8.00   4.00
3669 A1529 €2.70 black   8.00   4.00

Hyphoraia
Dejeani
A1530

Pansies — A1531

2009, Oct. 1 Litho.   Die Cut Perf. 13
Self-Adhesive
3670 A1530 32c multi   .95   .45
3671 A1531 32c multi   .95   .45

Souvenir Sheet

Isla de los Faisanes, Engraving by
Adam Perelle — A1532

2009, Oct. 6   Photo.   Perf. 13¾x14
3672 A1532 €2.47 multi   7.50 3.75
Exfilna 2009 Stamp Exhibition, Irún.

America
Issue,
Spanish
Playing
Cards
A1533

2009, Oct. 8
3673 A1533 78c multi   2.40 1.25

Royal Spanish
Soccer Federation,
Cent. — A1534

2009, Oct. 14   Litho.   Perf. 14x13¾
3674 A1534 32c multi   .95 .50

Mushrooms — A1535

Designs: No. 3675, 32c, Cantharellus
cibarius. No. 3676, 32c, Boletus pinophilus.

2009, Oct. 16   Photo.   Perf. 13¾x14
3675-3676 A1535 Set of 2   1.90 .95
Compare with Type A1489.

Souvenir Sheet

Paintings by Diego
Velázquez — A1536

No. 3677: a, The Royal Family of Felipe IV.
b, The Infanta Margarita Teresa in a Blue
Dress.

2009, Oct. 29   Perf. 14x13¾
3677 A1536 Sheet of 2   4.25 2.10
a.   62c multi   1.90 .95
b.   78c multi   2.25 1.10
See Austria No. 2228.

A1537

A1538

Christmas
A1539

No. 3678 — Details from Adoration of the
Shepherds and Landscape with Lady in Red,
by J. Carrero: a, Holy Family. b, Adoration of
the Shepherds.
32c, Maternity, by Carrero. 62c, The Coming of the Three Wise Men, by Carrero.

Perf. 13¼x12¾
2009, Oct. 31   Litho. & Engr.
3678 A1537 Sheet of 2   15.00 7.50
a.-b.   €2.47 Either single   7.50 3.75
Litho.
Self-Adhesive
Die Cut Perf. 13
3679 A1538 32c multi   .95 .50
3680 A1539 62c multi   1.90 .95

Juvenia 2009
Youth Philately
Exhibition,
Mieres — A1540

2009, Nov. 6   Litho.   Perf. 14x13¾
3681 A1540 39c multi   1.25 .60

Symbols of Nation and Autonomous Communities Type of 2009

No. 3682 — a, Arms and building of the
Congress of Deputies. b, Flag and map of La
Rioja. c, Flag and map of Castilla-La Mancha.
d, Flag and map of Valencia. e, Arms and
building of the Senate. f, Flag and map of the
Canary Islands. g, Flag and map of Murcia. h,
Flag and map of Aragon.

2010, Jan. 2   Die Cut Perf. 13
Self-Adhesive
3682   Booklet pane of 8   7.75
a.-h.   A1497 A Any single   .95 .45
On day of issue, Nos. 3682a-3682h each
sold for 34c.

Tourism
A1541

2010, Jan. 2   Litho.
Self-Adhesive
3683 A1541 B multi   1.90 .95
No. 3683 sold for 64c on day of issue.

Butterflies
A1542

Designs: No. 3684, Artimelia latreillei. No.
3685, Euphydryas aurinia. No. 3686, Zygaena
rhadamanthus. No. 3687, Zerynthia rumina.

2010   Litho.   Die Cut Perf. 13
Self-Adhesive
3684 A1542 34c multi   .95 .45
3685 A1542 34c multi   .95 .45
3686 A1542 64c multi   1.90 .95
3687 A1542 64c multi   1.75 .85
Nos. 3684-3687 (4)   5.55 2.70
Issued: Nos. 3684, 3686, 1/20; Nos. 3685,
3687, 4/1.

King Juan Carlos Type of 2007
2010, Feb. 5   Photo.   Perf. 12¾x13¼
Color of Portrait
3688 A1398   34c dark blue   .95 .45
3689 A1398   45c olive green   1.25 .60
3690 A1398   64c bister   1.75 .85
3691 A1398   €2.75 brt rose lil 7.50 3.75
Nos. 3688-3691 (4)   11.45 5.65

Civic
Values
A1543

Designs: €1, Trash recycling. €2, Responsible consumption of goods (jar with lock).

2010, Feb. 11   Litho.   Perf. 13¾x14
3692-3693 A1543 Set of 2   8.25 4.00

Ceramics — A1544

No. 3694 — Items from Ruiz de Luna
Museum, Talavera: a, Plate from 1970 at left,
amphora from 20th cent. at right. b, Amphora
at left, inkwell from 18th cent. at right. c, Inkwell at left, pitcher from 18th cent. at right. d,
Pitcher at left, plate at right.

Perf. 13¼x13¾
2010, Feb. 18   Photo.
3694 A1544 Horiz. strip of 4   3.75 1.90
a.-d.   34c Any single   .90 .45

Spanish Presidency of the European
Union — A1545

Background color: 34c, Red. 64c, Gray.

Die Cut Perf. 13
2010, Feb. 22   Litho.
Self-Adhesive
3695-3696 A1545 Set of 2   2.75 1.40

Musical
Instruments
A1546

Design: No. 3697, Trumpet (trompeta). No.
3698, Euphonium (bombardino). 45c, Tenor
saxophone. 64c, French horn.

2010   Litho.   Die Cut Perf. 13
Self-Adhesive
3697 A1546 34c multi   .95 .45
3698 A1546 34c multi   .95 .45
3699 A1546 45c multi   1.25 .60
3700 A1546 64c multi   1.60 .80
Nos. 3697-3700 (4)   4.75 2.30
Issued: No. 3697, 4/9; No. 3698, 10/5; No.
3699, 2/24; No. 3700, 7/1.

Constituent
Assembly,
Bicent. — A1547

2010, Mar. 1   Litho.   Perf. 14x13¾
3701 A1547 34c multi   .95 .45

Souvenir Sheet

Cathedrals of Plasencia — A1548

2010, Mar. 4   Litho. & Engr.
3702 A1548 €2.75 brown & blue 7.50 3.75

Goya
Award,
Poster for
Film
"Celda
211"
A1549

2010, Mar. 9   Litho.   Perf. 13¾x14
3703 A1549 34c multi   .95 .45

Seven
Goya
Awards,
Poster for
Film
"Agora"
A1550

2010, Apr. 5   Litho.   Perf. 13¾x13¼
3704 A1550 34c multi   .95 .45

Latin American Independence,
Bicent. — A1551

2010, Apr. 7   **Photo.**
3705 A1551 €2.49 multi   6.75 3.50

UNESCO World Heritage
Sites — A1552

Designs: No. 3706, 45c, Patio of Casa de
las Torres, Ubeda. No. 3707, 45c, Jabalquinto
Palace, Baeza.

2010, Apr. 15   **Perf. 12¾**
3706-3707 A1552 Set of 2   2.40 1.25

Urban
Planners
A1553

Designs: No. 3708, 34c, Carlos María de
Castro (1810-93), and map of Madrid. No.
3709, 34c, Ildefonso Cerdá (1815-76), and
map of Barcelona.

2010   **Photo.**   **Perf. 13¾x13¼**
3708-3709 A1553 Set of 2   1.90 .95
Issued: No. 3708, 4/20; No. 3709, 10/14.

Gran Via, Madrid,
Cent. — A1554

2010, Apr. 21   **Litho.**   **Perf. 13¼x13¾**
3710 A1554 34c blur & yellow   .90 .45

Souvenir Sheet

Spanish Pavilion at Expo 2010,
Shanghai — A1555

Perf. 13¾x13¼
2010, Apr. 21   **Photo.**
3711 A1555 €2.49 multi   6.75 3.50

Levante U.
D. Soccer
Team,
Cent. (in
2009)
A1556

2010, Apr. 23
3712 A1556 34c multi   .90 .45

El Correo
Newspaper,
Bilbao,
Cent. — A1557

2010, Apr. 30   **Perf. 13¼x13¾**
3713 A1557 34c multi   .90 .45

Europa
A1558

2010, May 6   **Perf. 13¾x13¼**
3714 A1558 64c multi   1.75 .85

Souvenir Sheet

Kingdom of León, 1100th
Anniv. — A1559

**Photo. & Embossed With Foil
Application**
Perf. 13x12¼x12¼x13x12¾
Syncopated
2010, May 6
3715 A1559 €2.49 multi   6.50 3.25

Compostela
Jubilee
Year — A1560

Die Cut Perf. 13
2010, May 13   **Litho.**
Self-Adhesive
3716 A1560 34c multi   .85 .40

Parks — A1561

Flora or fauna and scenery from: No. 3717,
45c, Sierras de Cazoria, Segura y Las Villas
Nature Park. No. 3718, 45c, Doñana National
Park. No. 3719, 45c, Garajonay National Park.
No. 3720, 45c, Picos de Europa National Park.
No. 3721, 45c, Monfragüe National Park. No.
3722, 45c, Sierra Nevada National Park. No.
3723, 45c, Ordesa y Monte Perdido National
Park. No. 3724, 45c, Lago de Sanabria Nature
Park. No. 3725, 45c, Teide National Park. No.
3726, 45c, Cabrera Archipelago National
Park. No. 3727, 45c, Aigüestortes y Lago de
San Mauricio National Park. No. 3728, 45c,
Cabo de Gata Nijar Nature Park.

2010   **Photo.**   **Perf. 13¼x13¾**
3717-3728 A1561   Set of 12   14.50 7.25
   Issued: Nos. 3717-3719, 5/20; Nos. 3720-
3722, 7/19; Nos. 3723-3725, 9/15; Nos. 3726-
3728, 10/2.

2010 Ibero-
American Athletics
Championships,
San Fernando
A1562

2010 European
Athletics
Championships,
Barcelona
A1563

2010 World Cup
Soccer
Championships,
South
Africa — A1564

2010, June 4
3729 A1562 34c multi   .85 .40
3730 A1563 64c multi   1.60 .80
3731 A1564 78c multi   1.90 .95
   Nos. 3729-3731 (3)   4.35 2.15

Gregorio Marañón (1887-1960),
Founder of Institute of Medical
Pathology — A1565

Julián Arcas
(1832-82),
Guitarist — A1566

2010, June 11   **Perf. 13¾x13¼**
3732 A1565 34c multi   .85 .40
         Perf. 13¼x13¾
3733 A1566 34c pur & orange   .85 .40

Entry Into
European
Community, 25th
Anniv. — A1567

Die Cut Perf. 13
2010, June 12   **Litho.**
3734 A1567 34c multi   .85 .45

Souvenir Sheet

Oscar Niemeyer International Cultural
Center, Asturias — A1568

2010, June 19   **Perf. 13¾x13¼**
3735 A1568 €2.49 multi   6.25 3.25
   Filatem 2010 Thematic Philatelic Exhibition,
Asturias.

José Luis López
Vázquez (1922-
2009),
Actor — A1569

2010, July 6   **Photo.**   **Perf. 13¼x13¾**
3736 A1569 45c multi   1.25 .60

Souvenir Sheet

Zenobia and Emperor Aurelian,
tapestry by Gerard Peemas — A1570

2010, July 12
3737 A1570 78c multi   2.10 1.10

Souvenir Sheet

Segovia Cathedral — A1571

Litho. & Engr.

2010, July 15   **Perf. 14x13¾**
3738 A1571   €2.75 blue & brn   7.25 3.75

Renewable Energy — A1572

Designs: No. 3739, 78c, Biomass energy. No. 3740, 78c, Tidal energy (mareomotriz). No. 3741, 78c, Wave energy (undimotriz).

2010, Sept. 3   Photo.   Perf. 13¼x13
3739-3741 A1572   Set of 3   6.00 3.00

World Alzheimer's Disease Day — A1573

2010, Sept. 9   **Perf. 13¾x13¼**
3742 A1573 34c multi   .90 .45

Cádiz Soccer Team, Cent. A1574

2010, Sept. 10
3743 A1574 34c multi   .90 .45

Roman Walls of Lugo UNESCO World Heritage Site — A1575

Mosque-Cathedral of Cordoba UNESCO World Heritage Site — A1576

2010, Sept. 17   Photo.   Perf. 13x12¾
3744 A1575 34c multi   .95 .45

Souvenir Sheet
Litho. & Engr.
Perf.
3745 A1576   €2 multi   5.50 2.75

Miniature Sheet

Lighthouses — A1577

No. 3746: a, Avilés Lighthouse, San Juan de Nieva, Asturias. b, Ciutadella de Menorca Lighthouse, Menorca Island. c, Cabo de Huertas Lighthouse, Alicante. d, Punta de la Polacra Lighthouse, Nijar, Almería. e, San Cibrao Lighthouse, Cervo, Lugo. f, Punta Cumplida Lighthouse, Barlovento, La Palma Island.

     Perf. 13¼x13¾
2010, Sept. 20   **Photo.**
3746 A1577   Sheet of 6   10.50 5.25
  a.-f.   64c Any single   1.75 .85

Famous Men — A1578

Designs: No. 3747, 34c, Francisco Ayala (1906-2009), writer. No. 3748, 34c, Gonzalo Torrente Ballester (1910-99), writer. No. 3749, 34c, Vicente Ferrer (1920-2009), humanitarian.

Litho. & Engr.
2010, Oct. 8   **Perf. 14x13¾**
3747-3749 A1578   Set of 3   3.00 1.50

America Issue, Spanish Arms — A1579

     Perf. 13¼x13¾
2010, Oct. 11   **Photo.**
3750 A1579 78c multi   2.25 1.10

People, Flags of Bicentennial Group Countries — A1580

2010, Oct. 11   **Perf. 13¾x13¼**
3751 A1580 78c multi   2.25 1.10

The Bicentennial Group countries are Spain and nine Ibero-American countries (Argentina, Bolivia, Chile, Colombia, Ecuador, El Salvador, Mexico, Paraguay, and Venezuela) that achieved their independence from Spain 200 years ago.

El Día Newspaper, Santa Cruz de Tenerife, Cent. — A1581

2010, Oct. 15
3752 A1581 34c multi   1.00 .50

Miniature Sheet

Women's Clothing Designed by Manuel Pertegaz — A1582

No. 3753: a, Silk wedding dress. b, Taffeta suit and skirt. c, Taffeta cocktail dress with floral print. d, Black lace and white satin cocktail dress.

Photo. & Embossed
2010, Oct. 15   **Perf. 13¼x13**
3753 A1582   Sheet of 4   4.00 2.00
  a.-d.   34c Any single   1.00 .50

Souvenir Sheet

Spain #18 and Cliché — A1583

2010, Oct. 18   Litho.   Perf. 13¼x13¾
3754 A1583   €2.49 multi   7.00 3.50

Exfilna 2010 National Philatelic Exhibition, Madrid.

Souvenir Sheet

Religious Buildings in Spain and Turkey — A1584

No. 3755: a, Santa María de la Mayor Collegiate Church, Toro, Spain. b, Örtaköy Mosque, Istanbul, Turkey.

     Perf. 13¾x13¼
2010, Oct. 18   **Photo.**
3755 A1584   Sheet of 2   3.50 1.75
  a.-b.   64c Either single   1.75 .85

See Turkey No. 3240.

Souvenir Sheet

Victory of Spanish Team at 2010 World Cup Soccer Championships — A1585

Photo. & Embossed With Foil Application
2010, Oct. 21   **Perf. 13¼x13¾**
3756 A1585   €2 multi   5.75 3.00

Christmas A1586

Designs: 34c, Mother holding baby. 64c, Columns, arms holding baby.

Die Cut Perf. 13
2010, Nov. 3   **Litho.**
Self-Adhesive
3757-3758 A1586   Set of 2   2.75 1.40

Souvenir Sheet

Sculpture From San Salvador Monastery, Oña — A1587

2010, Nov. 5 Photo. Perf. 13¼x13¾
3759 A1587 78c multi 2.25 1.10
San Salvador Monastery, 1000th anniv.

Souvenir Sheet

Bilbao Cathedral — A1588

Litho. & Engr.
2010, Nov. 8 Perf. 14x13¾
3760 A1588 €2.75 multi 7.50 3.75

Tourism A1589

2011, Jan. 3 Litho. Die Cut Perf. 13
Self-Adhesive
3761 A1589 B multi 1.75 .85
No. 3761 sold for 65c on day of issue.

Symbols of Nation and Autonomous Communities Type of 2009

No. 3762: a, Constitutional Court Building. b, Flag and map of Ceuta. c, Flag and map of Extremadura. d, Flag and map of Melilla. e, Flag and map of Balearic Islands. f, Flag and map of Madrid. g, Flag and map of Castilla y León. h, Flag and map of Navarra.

2011, Jan. 3 Die Cut Perf. 13
Self-Adhesive
3762 Booklet pane of 8 7.50
a.-h. A1497 A Any single .90 .45
On day of issue, Nos. 3762a-3762h each sold for 35c.

Butterflies A1590

Designs: No. 3763, 65c, Melanargia ines. No. 3764, 65c, Charaxes jasius. No. 3765,

65c, Papilio machaon. No. 3766, 65c, Argynnis adippe.

2011, Jan. 12 Litho.
Self-Adhesive
3763-3766 A1590 Set of 4 7.00 3.50

St. Sebastian Festival, El Pont de Suert, 425th Anniv. — A1591

2011, Jan. 20 Perf. 14x13¾
3767 A1591 35c multi .95 .45

2010 Malaspina Oceanographic Expedition — A1592

2011, Jan. 20 Die Cut Perf. 13
Self-Adhesive
3768 A1592 50c multi 1.40 .70

Stringed Instruments A1593

Designs: No. 3769, 35c, Guitar. No. 3770, 35c, Violin. No. 3771, 35c, Lute. No. 3772, 35c, Mandolin.

2011, Jan. 24 Litho.
Self-Adhesive
3769-3772 A1593 Set of 4 3.75 1.90

Almería Railway Station A1594

2011, Jan. 27 Perf. 13¾x14
3773 A1594 35c multi .95 .50

King Juan Carlos Type of 2007
2011, Feb. 4 Photo. Perf. 12¾x13¼
Color of Portrait
3774 A1398 35c lilac .95 .50
3775 A1398 50c bright blue 1.40 .70
3776 A1398 80c brt blue grn 2.25 1.10
3777 A1398 €2.84 blue violet 7.75 4.00
Nos. 3774-3777 (4) 12.35 6.30

Marie Curie (1867-1934), Chemist — A1595

Litho. & Engr.
2011, Feb. 7 Perf. 13¾x14
3778 A1595 35c multi .95 .45
Intl. Year of Chemistry.

Property Act, 150th Anniv. A1596

2011, Feb. 8 Litho.
3779 A1596 65c multi 1.75 .90

Civic Values A1597

Designs: No. 3780, 35c, Respect on the Internet. No. 3781, 35c, Protect people with disabilities. No. 3782, 35c, Clean up and dispose of dog droppings. No. 3783, 35c, Use safety belts.

2011, Feb. 18 Die Cut Perf. 13
Self-Adhesive
3780-3783 A1597 Set of 4 4.00 2.00

Souvenir Sheet

Sigüenza Cathedral — A1598

Litho. & Engr.
2011, Mar. 4 Perf. 13¾x14
3784 A1598 €2.84 multi 8.00 4.00

Intl. Women's Day A1599

Die Cut Perf. 13
2011, Mar. 8 Litho.
Self-Adhesive
3785 A1599 80c multi 2.25 1.10

Europa — A1600

2011, Apr. 4 Photo. Perf. 13¼x13¾
3786 A1600 65c multi 1.90 .95
Intl. Year of Forests.

Jubilee Year of the Holy Cross of Canjáyar A1601

2011, Apr. 11 Litho. Perf. 14x13¾
3787 A1601 65c multi 1.90 .95

Miniature Sheet

Lighthouses — A1602

No. 3788: a, Calella Lighthouse, Barcelona. b, Chipiona Lighthouse, Cádiz. c, Punta La Entallada Lighthouse, Fuerteventura Island. d, Cap Sant Sebastià Lighthoue, Girona. e, Castell de Ferro Lighthouse, Granada. f, Valencia Lighthouse, Valencia.

Perf. 13¼x13¾
2011, Apr. 11 Photo.
3788 A1602 Sheet of 6 11.50 5.75
a.-f. 65c Any single 1.90 .95

Juvenia 2011 National Youth Philatelic Exhibition, Santa Fe — A1603

2011, Apr. 12 Litho. Perf. 14x13¾
3789 A1603 65c multi 1.90 .95

Movie Poster for Pa Negre, Winner of 2010 Goya Award for Best Film A1604

Goya Award — A1605

2011, Apr. 26 Litho. Perf. 13¾x14
3790 A1604 35c multi 1.00 .50
Souvenir Sheet
Photo.
Perf. 13¾x13¼
3791 A1605 €2.84 multi 8.25 4.25
Goya Awards, 25th anniv.

Souvenir Sheet

Alhambra of Granada UNESCO World Heritage Site — A1606

2011, May 12   Litho. & Engr.   Perf.
3792 A1606 €2 multi   5.75 3.00

Souvenir Sheet

Dido Bids Farewell to Aeneas, 17th Cent. Tapestry — A1607

Perf. 13¼x13¾
2011, May 16   Photo.
3793 A1607 €2.84 multi   8.25 4.25

Miniature Sheet

Military Aviation in Spain, Cent. — A1608

No. 3794: a, Aerospatiale SA-332 Super Puma helicopter (41x29mm). r. b, Two CASA-101 Aviojets (41x29mm). c, Lockheed C-130 Hercules (41x29mm). d, Eurofighter EF-2000 Typhoon (123x29mm).

2011, May 31   Perf. 13¾x13¼
3794 A1608 Sheet of 4   7.75 4.00
a.-d.   65c Any single   1.90   .95

Conversion of Abandoned Railroad Lines to Greenways — A1609

2011, June 13 Litho. Perf. 13¾x14
3795 A1609 35c multi   1.00   .50

Corps of Architects of the Treasury, 105th Anniv. A1610

2011, June 17
3796 A1610 80c multi   2.25 1.10

World Youth Day — A1611

2011, July 1   Perf. 14x13¾
3797 A1611 80c multi   2.25 1.10
See Vatican City No. 1472.

Souvenir Sheet

Albarracín Cathedral — A1612

2011, July 15   Litho. & Engr.
3798 A1612 €2.84 blue & green 8.25 4.25

Film Personalities A1613

Designs: No. 3799, 80c, Luis García Berlanga (1921-2010), director. No. 3800, 80c, Rafael Azcona (1926-2008), screenwriter.

2011, July 22   Litho.
3799-3800 A1613 Set of 2   4.75 2.40

Ceramics From Manises — A1614

No. 3801: a, Pitcher with lid and handle. b, Vase. c, Plate. d, Bottle.

Perf. 13¼x13¾
2011, Sept. 5   Photo.
3801 A1614 Horiz. strip of 4   9.00 4.50
a.-d.   80c Any single   2.25 1.10

Miniature Sheet

Art by Antoni Tàpies (1923-2012) — A1615

No. 3802 — Unnamed works depicting: a, Face and flags on blue background. b, Horizontal line across brown area. c, Chair on gray background. d, Abstract on red background.

2011, Sept. 12
3802 A1615   Sheet of 4   9.00 4.50
a.-d.   80c Any single   2.25 1.10

Miniature Sheets

Spanish National Soccer Team — A1616

No. 3803 — Soccer players from 1900-70 with Spanish text in black capitals: a, Pichichi (41x56mm). b, Zamora Parando (41x56mm). c, El Gol de Zarra (41x56mm). d, Una Excelente Delantera (82x28mm). e, El Gol de Marcelino (82x28mm).
No. 3804 — Soccer players from 1970-2010 with Spanish text in black capitals: a, Celebración del Gol Clasificatorio para Argentina 78 (41x56mm). b, Mundial España 82 (41x56mm). c, Victoria de la Selección en los Juegos Olímpicos 92 (82x28mm). d, El Gol de Torres en la Eurocopa 2008 (41x56mm). e, El Gol de Iniesta en el Mundial 2010 (82x28mm).

2011, Sept. 19   Perf. 13¾x13¼
3803 A1616   Sheet of 5 + label 11.50 5.50
a.-e.   80c Any single   2.25 1.10
3804 A1616   Sheet of 5 + label 11.50 5.50
a.-e.   80c Any single   2.25 1.10

Souvenir Sheet

Exfilna 2011 National Philatelic Exposition, Valladolid — A1617

2011, Oct. 1   Litho.   Perf. 13¾x14
3805 A1617 €2.84 multi   7.75 4.00

Awarding of 2010 Nobel Prize in Literature to Mario Vargas Llosa — A1618

Litho. (Litho & Engr. Label)
2011, Oct. 3   Perf. 14x13¾
3806 A1618 80c multi   2.25 1.10

Miguel Delibes (1920-2010), Writer — A1619

Gaspar Melchor de Jovellanos (1744-1811), Statesman and Writer — A1620

Luis Rosales (1910-92), Poet A1621

Miguel Servet (1511-53), Physician and Theologian — A1622

Litho. & Engr.
2011, Oct. 3   Perf. 14x13¾
3807 A1619 80c multi   2.25 1.10
Perf. 13¾x14
3808 A1620 80c multi   2.25 1.10
Litho.
3809 A1621 80c multi   2.25 1.10
3810 A1622 80c multi   2.25 1.10
Nos. 3807-3810 (4)   9.00 4.40

America Issue, Mailbox — A1623

Perf. 13¼x13¾
2011, Oct. 11   Photo.
3811 A1623 80c multi   2.25 1.10

Miniature Sheet

Women's Clothing Designed by Elio
Berhanyer — A1624

No. 3812: a, Black and white strapless ball
gown. b, Green and white striped dress. c,
Coat and dress. d, Black and white polka dot
ball gown.

Photo. & Embossed
2011, Oct. 20 *Perf. 13¼x13*
3812 A1624 Sheet of 4 9.00 4.50
a.-d. 80c Any single 2.25 1.10

Holy
Family
with Baby
Jesus,
Sculpture
by Luisa
Roldán
A1625

Holy
Family — A1626

Die Cut Perf. 13
2011, Nov. 3 **Litho.**
Self-Adhesive
3813 A1625 35c multi 1.00 .50
3814 A1626 65c multi 1.90 .95

Christmas.

National
Library,
300th
Anniv.
A1627

2011, Nov. 4 *Perf. 13¾x14*
3815 A1627 80c multi 2.25 1.10

Barcelona Boat
Show, 50th
Anniv. — A1628

2011, Nov. 5 *Perf. 14x13¾*
3816 A1628 80c multi 2.25 1.10

Souvenir Sheet

Tarazona Cathedral — A1629

2011, Nov. 8 **Litho. & Engr.**
3817 A1629 €2.84 blue & green 7.75 4.00

Year of
Russia in
Spain and
Year of
Spain in
Russia
A1630

2011, Nov. 10 **Litho.** *Perf. 13¾x14*
3818 A1630 80c multi 2.25 1.10

Arches and
Gates
A1631

No. 3819: a, Macarena Arch, Seville. b,
Alcalá Gate, Madrid. c, Santa María Arch, Bur-
gos. d, Serrano Gate, Valencia. e, Triumphal
Arch, Barcelona. f, Palmas Gate, Badajoz. g,
Bisagra Gate, Toledo. h, Bará Arch,
Tarragona.

2012, Jan. 2 *Die Cut Perf. 13*
Self-Adhesive
3819 Booklet pane of 8 7.75
a.-h. A1631 A Any single .95 .45
Nos. 3819a-3819h each sold for 36c on day
of issue.

Tourism
A1632

2012, Jan. 2 **Litho.**
Self-Adhesive
3820 A1632 B multi 1.90 .95
No. 3820 sold for 70c on day of issue.

Lorca
Tourist
Attractions
A1633

Designs: No. 3821, 36c, Virgin of the
Orchards Sanctuary (Santuario de la Virgen
de las Huertas). No. 3822, 36c, Castle (Castillo). No. 3823, 36c, Town Hall (Ayuntami-
ento). No. 3824, 36c, Guevara Palace (Palacio
de Guevara). No. 3825, 36c, St. Patrick's Collegiate Church (Colegiata de San Patricio).

2012, Jan. 2 *Die Cut Perf. 13*
Self-Adhesive
3821-3825 A1633 Set of 5 4.75 2.40

Civic
Values
A1634

Designs: 36c, No pollution. 51c, Follow
speed limits. 70c, Avoid distractions while
driving.

2012, Jan. 9 **Litho.**
Self-Adhesive
3826-3828 A1634 Set of 3 4.25 2.10

Intl. Year of Sustainable Energy for
All — A1635

2012, Feb. 27 *Die Cut Perf. 13*
Self-Adhesive
3829 A1635 70c multi 1.90 .95

King Juan
Carlos — A1636

Perf. 12¾x13¼
2012, Feb. 27 **Photo.**
Color of Portrait
3830 A1636 36c red .95 .50
3831 A1636 51c green 1.40 .70
3832 A1636 85c blue 2.25 1.10
3833 A1636 €2.90 dk rose brn 7.75 4.00
Nos. 3830-3833 (4) 12.35 6.30

Tourism
A1637

Die Cut Perf. 13
2012, Feb. 28 **Litho.**
Self-Adhesive
3834 A1637 70c multi 1.90 .95

Military
Anniversaries
A1638

Designs: No. 3835, 85c, Battle of Navas de
Tolosa, 800th anniv. No. 3836, 85c, Conquest
of Navarre, 500th anniv.

2012, Feb. 29 *Perf. 14x13¾*
3835-3836 A1638 Set of 2 4.50 2.25

Souvenir Sheet

Matron and Warrior in Boat, Tapestry
by Gerard Peemans — A1639

2012, Mar. 8 **Photo.** *Perf. 13¼x13¾*
3837 A1639 €2.90 multi 7.75 4.00

Royal and Military
Order of San
Fernando, 200th
Anniv. — A1640

2012, Mar. 12 **Litho.** *Perf. 14x13¾*
3838 A1640 85c multi 2.25 1.10

1812
Constitution,
Bicent.
A1641

2012, Mar. 16 **Photo.** *Perf. 12¾*
3839 A1641 36c multi .95 .45

Souvenir Sheet

Spanish Coin Depicting Burgos
Cathedral — A1642

2012, Mar. 16 **Litho. & Engr.** *Perf.*
3840 A1642 €2 multi 5.25 2.60
Burgos Cathedral UNESCO World Heritage
Site.

SEMI-POSTAL STAMPS

Red Cross Issue

Princesses María Cristina and Beatrice SP1

Queen as a Nurse — SP2 | Queen Victoria Eugénia — SP3

Prince of Asturias — SP4 | King Alfonso XIII — SP5

Perf. 12½

1926, Sept. 15   Unwmk.   Engr.

B1	SP1	1c black	2.50 2.25
B2	SP2	2c ultra	2.50 2.25
B3	SP3	5c violet brn	5.50 4.00
B4	SP1	10c green	4.50 4.00
B5	SP1	15c indigo	1.75 1.50
B6	SP4	20c dull violet	1.75 1.50
a.		20c violet brown (error)	500.00 375.00
B7	SP5	25c rose red	.30 .30
B8	SP1	30c blue green	42.50 40.00
B9	SP3	40c dark blue	24.00 21.00
B10	SP2	50c red orange	24.00 21.00
B11	SP4	1p slate	1.75 1.10
B12	SP3	4p magenta	1.40 .80
B13	SP5	10p brown	1.40 1.10
	Nos. B1-B13,EB1 (14)		122.60 109.55
	Set, never hinged		260.00

The 20c was printed in violet brown for use in the colonies (Cape Juby, Spanish Guinea, Spanish Morocco and Spanish Sahara). No. B6a, the missing overprint error, is listed here because it is not known to which colony it belongs.

For overprints see Nos. B19-B46.

Airplane and Map of Madrid-Manila Flight — SP6

1926, Sept. 15

B14	SP6	15c dp ultra & org	.40 .40
B15	SP6	20c car & yel grn	.40 .40
B16	SP6	30c dk brn & ultra	.40 .40
B17	SP6	40c dk grn & brn org	.40 .40
B18	SP6	4p magenta & yel	100.00 100.00
	Nos. B14-B18,CB1-CB5 (10)		109.10 109.10
	Set, never hinged		210.00

Madrid to Manila flight of Captains Eduardo G. Gallarza and Joaquim Loriga y Taboada.

Nos. B1-B18, CB1-CB5 and EB1 were used for regular postage on Sept. 15, 16, 17, 1926. Subsequently the unsold stamps were given to the Spanish Red Cross Society, by which they were sold uncanceled but they then had no franking power.

For overprints see Nos. B47-B53.

Coronation Silver Jubilee Issue
Red Cross Stamps of 1926 Overprinted "ALFONSO XIII," Dates and Ornaments in Various Colors

1927, May 27

B19	SP1	1c black (R)	5.25 5.25
B20	SP2	2c ultra (Bl)	9.00 9.00
B21	SP3	5c vio brn (R)	2.25 2.25
a.		Double overprint	37.50
B22	SP4	10c green (Bl)	62.50 62.50
B23	SP1	15c indigo (R)	1.90 1.90
B24	SP4	20c dull vio (Bl)	3.50 3.50
B25	SP5	25c rose red (Bl)	.50 .50
B26	SP1	30c blue grn (Bl)	.95 .95
B27	SP3	40c dk blue (R)	.95 .95
B28	SP2	50c red org (Bl)	.95 .95
B29	SP4	1p slate (R)	1.90 1.90
B30	SP3	4p magenta (Bl)	9.50 9.50
B31	SP5	10p brown (G)	37.50 37.50
	Nos. B19-B31 (13)		136.65 136.65
	Set, never hinged		350.00

Same with Additional Surcharges of New Values

B32	SP2	3c on 2c (G)	9.50 9.50
B33	SP2	4c on 2c (Bk)	9.50 9.50
B34	SP5	10c on 25c (Bk)	.55 .55
B35	SP5	25c on 25c (Bl)	.55 .55
B36	SP2	55c on 2c (R)	1.00 1.00
B37	SP4	55c on 10c (Bk)	55.00 55.00
B38	SP4	55c on 20c (Bk)	55.00 55.00
B39	SP1	75c on 15c (R)	.70 .70
B40	SP1	75c on 30c (R)	140.00 140.00
B41	SP3	80c on 5c (R)	52.50 50.00
B42	SP3	2p on 40c (R)	1.00 1.00
B43	SP1	2p on 1p (R)	1.00 1.00
B44	SP2	5p on 50c (G)	1.90 1.90
B45	SP3	5p on 4p (Bk)	3.25 3.25
B46	SP5	10p on 10p (G)	27.50 27.50
	Nos. B32-B46 (15)		358.95 356.45
	Set, never hinged		800.00

Nos. B14-B18 Overprinted

B47	SP6	15c (Br)	.50 .40
a.		Double overprint	30.00
B48	SP6	20c (Bl)	.50 .40
a.		Brown overprint (error)	65.00
b.		Inverted overprint	30.00
B50	SP6	30c (R)	.50 .40
a.		Blue overprint (error)	65.00
b.		Double overprint	30.00
B52	SP6	40c (Br)	.50 .40
a.		Inverted overprint	30.00
b.		Double ovpt. (Bl + Br)	95.00
B53	SP6	4p (Bl)	100.00 95.00
a.		Inverted overprint	160.00

Semi-Postal Special Delivery Stamp Overprinted "ALFONSO XIII," Dates and Ornaments in Violet

B54	SPSD1	20c	5.50 5.50
	Nos. B47-B54 (6)		107.50 102.10

Nos. CB1-CB5 Overprinted in Various Colors

B55	SPAP1	5c (R)	1.90 1.60
a.		Inverted overprint	30.00
B56	SPAP1	10c (R)	2.25 2.25
a.		Inverted overprint	30.00
B57	SPAP1	25c (Bl)	.40 .40
B58	SPAP1	50c (R)	.40 .40
a.		Double ovpt., one invtd.	72.50
B59	SPAP1	1p (R)	2.50 2.50
a.		Inverted overprint	95.00

Same with Additional Surcharges of New Values

B60	SPAP1	75c on 5c (R)	4.50 3.25
a.		Inverted surcharge	30.00
B61	SPAP1	75c on 10c (R)	17.00 13.00
a.		Inverted surcharge	30.00
B62	SPAP1	75c on 25c (Bl)	32.50 27.50
a.		Double surcharge	55.00
B63	SPAP1	75c on 50c (Bl)	15.00 13.00
	Nos. B55-B63 (9)		76.45 63.90
	Set, never hinged		275.00

Nos. B54-B63 were available for ordinary postage.

Stamps of Spanish Offices in Morocco and Spanish Colonies, 1926 (Spain Types SP3, SP5) Surcharged in Various Colors

On Spanish Morocco

B64	SP3	55c on 4p bis (Bl)	25.00 21.00
B65	SP5	80c on 10p vio (Br)	25.00 21.00

On Spanish Tangier

B66	SP5	1p on 10p vio (Br)	135.00 110.00
B67	SP3	4p bis (G)	45.00 40.00

On Cape Juby

B68	SP3	5p on 4p bis (R)	85.00 70.00
B69	SP5	10p on 10p vio (R)	40.00 40.00

On Spanish Guinea

B70	SP5	1p on 10p vio (Bl)	25.00 21.00
B71	SP3	2p on 4p bis (G)	25.00 21.00

On Spanish Sahara

B72	SP5	80c on 10p vio (R)	40.00 32.50
B73	SP3	2p on 4p bis (R)	25.00 21.00
	Nos. B64-B73 (10)		475.00 397.50
	Set, never hinged		1,100.

Nos. B64-B73 were available for postage in Spain only.

Nos. B19-B73 were for the 25th year of the reign of King Alfonso XIII.

Counterfeits of Nos. B64-B73 abound.

Catacombs Restoration Issues

Pope Pius XI and King Alfonso XIII SP7

1928, Dec. 23   Engr.   Perf. 12½

Santiago Issue

B74	SP7	2c violet & blk	.30 .30
B75	SP7	2c lake & blk	.35 .35
B76	SP7	3c bl blk & vio	.30 .30
B77	SP7	3c dl bl & vio	.35 .35
B78	SP7	5c ol grn & vio	.75 .75
B79	SP7	10c yel grn & blk	1.40 1.40
B80	SP7	15c bl grn & vio	4.50 4.50
B81	SP7	25c dp rose & vio	4.50 4.50
B82	SP7	40c ultra & blk	.30 .30
B83	SP7	55c ol brn & vio	.30 .30
B84	SP7	80c red & blk	.30 .30
B85	SP7	1p gray blk & vio	.30 .30
B86	SP7	2p red brn & blk	6.25 6.25
B87	SP7	3p pale rose & vio	6.25 6.25
B88	SP7	4p vio brn & blk	6.25 6.25
B89	SP7	5p grnsh blk & vio	6.25 6.25

Toledo Issue

B90	SP7	2c bl blk & car	.30 .30
B91	SP7	2c ultra & car	.35 .35
B92	SP7	3c bis brn & ul-tra	.30 .30
B93	SP7	3c ol grn & ultra	.35 .35
B94	SP7	5c red vio & car	.75 .75
B95	SP7	10c yel grn & ul-tra	1.40 1.40
B96	SP7	15c slate bl & car	4.50 4.50
B97	SP7	25c red brn & ul-tra	4.50 4.50
B98	SP7	40c ultra & car	.30 .30
B99	SP7	55c dk brn & ultra	.30 .30
B100	SP7	80c black & car	.30 .30
B101	SP7	1p yellow & car	.30 .30
B102	SP7	2p dk gray & ul-tra	6.25 6.25
B103	SP7	3p violet & car	6.25 6.25
B104	SP7	4p vio brn & car	6.25 6.25
B105	SP7	5p bister & ultra	6.25 6.25
	Nos. B74-B105 (32)		77.30 77.30
	Set, never hinged		140.00

Nos. B74-B105 replaced regular stamps from Dec. 23, 1928 to Jan. 6, 1929. The proceeds from their sale were given to a fund to restore the catacombs of Saint Damasus and Saint Praetextatus at Rome.

Nos. B74-B105 exist imperf. Value set, $325 hinged, $400 never hinged.

Issues of the Republic

SP13

1938, Apr. 15   Perf. 11½

B106	SP13	45c + 2p bl & grnsh bl	.90 .75
a.		Imperf., pair	17.50 14.50
b.		Souv. sheet of 1	26.00 26.00
c.		Souv. sheet of 1, im-perf.	725.00 650.00
		Never hinged	1,000.

Surtax for the defenders of Madrid.
For overprint and surcharge see Nos. B108, CB6.

Nurse and Orderly Carrying Wounded Soldier — SP14

1938, June 1   Engr.   Perf. 10

B107	SP14	45c + 5p cop red	.55 .55
a.		Imperf., pair	220.00

For surcharge see No. CB7.

No. B106 Overprinted in Black

1938, Nov. 7   Perf. 11½

B108	SP13	45c + 2p	3.25 3.25
		Never hinged	5.00

Defense of Madrid, 2nd anniversary.
A similar but larger overprint was applied to cover blocks of four. Value, $15 hinged, $30 never hinged.

Values for souvenir sheets of 1937-38 are for examples with some faults. Undamaged sheets are very hard to find.

Spanish State
Souvenir Sheets

Alcazar, Toledo SP15

Design: No. B108C, A patio of Alcazar after Civil War fighting.

1937   Unwmk.   Photo.   Perf. 11½
Control Numbers on Back

B108A	SP15	2p org brn	22.00 22.00
b.		Imperf.	450.00 450.00
B108C	SP15	2p dark green	22.00 22.00
d.		Imperf.	450.00 450.00
		Never hinged	95.00
	Set, never hinged		125.00
	Set, B108Ab, B108Cd, never hinged		1,300.

Nos. B108A-B108C sold for 4p each.

SP16

Designs: 20c, Covadongas Cathedral. 30c, Palma Cathedral, Majorca. 50c, Alcazar of Segovia. 1p, Leon Cathedral.

1938, Unwmk. Photo. Perf. 12½
Control Numbers on Back

B108E	SP16	Sheet of 4	42.50	42.50
f.		20c dull violet	5.00	5.00
g.		30c rose red	5.00	5.00
h.		50c bright blue	5.00	5.00
i.		1p greenish gray	5.00	5.00
j.		Imperf. sheet	72.50	65.00
		Never hinged	125.00	

Each sheet sold for 4p.

SP17

Designs, alternating in sheet: Flag bearer. Battleship "Admiral Cervera." Soldiers in trenches. Moorish guard.

1938, July 1 Unwmk. Perf. 13
Control Numbers on Back

B108K	SP17	Sheet of 20	40.00	40.00
		Never hinged	52.50	
l.		Imperf. sheet	185.00	185.00
		Never hinged	240.00	

Sheet measures 175x132mm. Consists of five vertical rows of four 2c violet, 3c deep blue, 5c olive gray, 10c deep green and 30c red orange, with each denomination appearing in two different designs. Marginal inscription: "Homenaje al Ejercito y a la Marina" (Honoring the Army and Navy). Sold for 4p, or double face value.

Souvenir Sheets

Don Juan of Austria — SP18

Battle of Lepanto SP19

Perf. 12½
1938, Dec. 15 Unwmk. Engr.
Control Numbers on Back

B108M	SP18	30c dk car	22.50	22.50
B108N	SP19	50c blue black	22.50	22.50
		Nos. B108M-B108N (2)	45.00	45.00
		Set, never hinged	77.50	

Imperf

B108O	SP18	30c black vio	450.00	550.00
B108P	SP19	50c dk sl grn	450.00	550.00
		Nos. B108O-B108P (2)	900.00	1,100.
		Set, never hinged	1,300.	

Victory over the Turks in the Battle of Lepanto, 1571.
Nos. B108M-B108N contain one stamp. The dates "1571-1938" appear in the lower sheet margin. Size: 89x74mm. Sold for 10p a pair.

LOCAL CHARITY STAMPS

Hundreds of different charity stamps were issued by local organizations and cities during the Civil War, 1936-39. Some had limited franking value, but most were simply charity labels. They are of three kinds: 1. Local semipostals. 2. Obligatory surtax stamps. 3. Propaganda or charity labels.

Ruins of Belchite SP20

Miracle of Calanda — SP21

Designs: 10c+5c, 70c+20c, Ruins of Belchite. 15c+10c, 80c+20c, The Rosary. 20c+10c, 1.50+50c, El Pilar Cathedral. 25c+10c, 1p+30c, Mother Raffols praying. 40c+10c, 2.50p+50c, The Little Chamber. 45c+15c, 1.40p+40c, Oath of the Besieged. 10p+4p, The Apparition.

Perf. 10½, 11½x10½, 11½
1940, Jan. 29 Litho. Unwmk.
Design SP20

B109		10c + 5c dp bl & vio brn	.25	.25
B110		15c + 10c rose vio & dk grn	.25	.25
B111		20c + 10c vio & dp bl	.25	.25
B112		25c + 10c dp rose & vio brn	.25	.25
B113		40c + 10c sl grn & rose vio	.25	.25
B114		45c + 15c vio & dp rose	.30	.30
B115		70c + 20c multi	.30	.30
B116		80c + 20c dp rose & vio	.40	.40
B117		1p + 30c dk sl grn & pur	.40	.40
B118		1.40p + 40c pur & gray blk	40.00	40.00
B119		1.50p + 50c lt bl & brn vio	.50	.50
B120		2.50p + 50c choc & bl	.50	.50

Design SP21

B121		4p + 1p rose lil & sl grn	12.00	12.00
B122		10p + 4p ultra & chnt	190.00	190.00
		Nos. B109-B122,CB8-CB17,EB2 (25)	457.20	457.10
		Set, never hinged	950.00	

19th centenary of the Virgin of the Pillar. The surtax was used to help restore the Cathedral at Zaragoza, damaged during the Civil War.
No. B121 exists in violet & slate green, No. B122 in ultramarine & brown violet. Value, $42.50 each.
Nos. B109-B122 exist imperf. Value, $750.
See No. 743, CB8-CB17.

General Franco — SP23

Knight and Lorraine Cross — SP24

1940, Dec. 23 Unwmk. Perf. 10

B123	SP23	20c + 5c dk grn & red	.65	.65
B124	SP23	40c + 10c dk bl & red	.90	.40
		Set, never hinged	3.50	

The surtax was for the tuberculosis fund. See Nos. RA15, RAC1.

Stamps of 10c denomination, types SP23 to SP28, are postal tax issues.

1941, Dec. 23

B125	SP24	20c + 5c bl vio & red	.50	.30
B126	SP24	40c + 10c sl grn & red	.50	.25
		Set, never hinged	1.40	

The surtax was used to fight tuberculosis. See Nos. RA16, RAC2.

Cross of Lorraine
SP25   SP26

1942, Dec. 23 Litho.

B127	SP25	20c + 5c pale brn & rose red	1.40	1.25
B128	SP25	40c + 10c lt bluish grn & rose red	.80	.45
		Set, never hinged	4.00	

The surtax was used to fight tuberculosis. See Nos. RA17, RAC3.

1943, Dec. 23 Photo. Perf. 11½

B129	SP26	20c + 5c dl sl grn & dl red	3.25	1.40
B130	SP26	40c + 10c brt bl & dl red	.80	1.10
		Set, never hinged	12.00	

The surtax was used to fight tuberculosis. See Nos. RA18, RAC4.

Dragon Slaying — SP27

St. George Slaying the Dragon — SP28

Perf. 9½x10
1944, Dec. 23 Litho. Unwmk.

B131	SP27	20c + 5c sl grn & red	.25	.25
B132	SP27	40c + 10c dl vio & red	.50	.50
B133	SP27	80c + 10c ultra & rose	7.75	7.75
		Nos. B131-B133 (3)	8.50	8.50
		Set, never hinged	16.00	

The surtax was used to fight tuberculosis. See Nos. RA19, RAC5.

1945, Dec. 23
Lorraine Cross in Red

B134	SP28	20c + 5c dl gray grn	.25	.25
B135	SP28	40c + 10c vio	.30	.25
B136	SP28	80c + 10c ultra	8.00	7.50
		Nos. B134-B136 (3)	8.55	8.00
		Set, never hinged	14.00	

The surtax was used to fight tuberculosis. See Nos. RA20, RAC6.

Nos. 753 and 768 Surcharged in Blue

1950, Oct. 23

B137	A195	50c + 10c	32.50	32.50
a.		"Caudillo" 14¾mm wide	95.00	97.50
B138	A195	1p + 10c	32.50	32.50
a.		"Caudillo" 14¾mm wide	95.00	97.50
#B137a-B138a, never hinged			300.00	
			120.00	

Visit of General Franco to Canary Islands. First printing, brighter colors and pale blue surcharge, was issued in Canary Islands. Value, $200 hinged, $300 never hinged, $200

used. Second printing was issued in Madrid Feb. 22, 1951. See No. CB18.

Catalogue values for unused stamps in this section, from this point to the end of the section, are for Never Hinged items.

1992 Summer Olympics, Barcelona SP29

1988, Oct. 3 Photo. Perf. 14

B139	SP29	20p +5p Track and field	.35	.35
B140	SP29	45p +5p Badminton	.60	.60
B141	SP29	50p +5p Basketball	.70	.70
		Nos. B139-B141 (3)	1.65	1.65

See Nos. B146-B152, B163-B168, B177-B179, B184-B186, B191-B193.

EXPO '92, Seville — SP30

Globes and sites of previous exhibitions: No. B142, Crystal Palace, London, 1851. No. B143, Eiffel Tower, Paris, 1889. No. B144, "The Atom," Brussels, 1958. No. B145, Monument, Osaka, 1970.

1989, Feb. 9 Photo. Perf. 14x13½

B142	SP30	8p +5p multi	.25	.25
B143	SP30	8p +5p multi	.25	.25
B144	SP30	20p +5p multi	.30	.30
B145	SP30	20p +5p multi	.30	.30
		Nos. B142-B145 (4)	1.10	1.10

Summer Olympics Type of 1988

1989, Mar. 7 Photo. Perf. 14

B146	SP29	8p +5p Handball	.25	.25
B147	SP29	18p +5p Boxing	.35	.35
B148	SP29	20p +5p Cycling	.35	.35
B149	SP29	45p +5p Equestrian	.60	.60
		Nos. B146-B149 (4)	1.55	1.55

1989, Oct. 3 Photo. Perf. 13½x14

B150	SP29	18p +5p Fencing	.65	.65
B151	SP29	20p +5p Soccer	.65	.65
B152	SP29	45p +5p Pommel horse	1.25	1.25
		Nos. B150-B152 (3)	2.55	2.55

500th Anniv. Emblem and Produce or Fauna Indigenous to the Americas — SP31

1989, Oct. 16 Litho. Perf. 13x13½

B153	SP31	8p +5p Cocoa	.25	.25
B154	SP31	8p +5p Corn	.25	.25
B155	SP31	20p +5p Tomato	.30	.30
B156	SP31	20p +5p Horse	.30	.30
B157	SP31	50p +5p Potato	.60	.60
B158	SP31	50p +5p Turkey	.60	.60
a.		Bklt. pane of 6, #B153-B158	2.25	
		Nos. B153-B158 (6)	2.30	2.30

Discovery of America, 500th anniv.

EXPO '92, Seville SP32

Curro, the character trademark, and symbols of development in Spain.

1990, Feb. 22   Photo.   Perf. 14
B159 SP32   8p +5p multi   .25   .25
B160 SP32 20p +5p multi, diff.   .30   .30
B161 SP32 45p +5p multi, diff.   .60   .60
B162 SP32 50p +5p multi, diff.   .70   .70
     Nos. B159-B162 (4)   1.85 1.85

Summer Olympics Type of 1988
1990, Mar. 7   Photo.   Perf. 13½x14
B163 SP29 18p +5p Weight lifting   .30   .30
B164 SP29 20p +5p Field hockey   .30   .30
B165 SP29 45p +5p Judo   .55   .55
     Nos. B163-B165 (3)   1.15 1.15

1990, Oct. 3   Photo.   Perf. 13½x14
B166 SP29   8p +5p Wrestling   .25   .25
B167 SP29 18p +5p Swimming   .40   .40
B168 SP29 20p +5p Baseball   .50   .50
     Nos. B166-B168 (3)   1.15 1.15

Discovery of America, 500th Anniv. (in 1992) — SP33

Drawings of sailing ships.

1990, Oct. 15   Litho.   Perf. 13
B169 SP33   8p +5p "Viajes-A"   .25   .25
B170 SP33   8p +5p "Viajes-B"   .25   .25
B171 SP33 20p +5p "Viajes-C"   .30   .30
B172 SP33 20p +5p "Viajes-D"   .30   .30
  a.   Bklt. pane of 4, #B169-B172   1.00
     Nos. B169-B172 (4)   1.10 1.10

Expo '92, Seville SP34

Designs: 15p+5p, La Cartuja, Monastery of Santa Maria de las Cuevas. 25p+5p, Amphitheater. 45p+5p, La Cartuja Bridge. 55p+5p, La Bargueta Bridge.

Litho. & Engr.
1991, Feb. 12   Perf. 14
B173 SP34 15p +5p multi   .30   .30
B174 SP34 25p +5p multi   .40   .40
B175 SP34 45p +5p multi   .65   .65
B176 SP34 55p +5p multi   .80   .80
     Nos. B173-B176 (4)   2.15 2.15

Summer Olympics Type of 1988
1991, Mar. 7   Litho.   Perf. 13½x14
B177 SP29 15p + 5p Five athletes   .30   .30
B178 SP29 25p + 5p Kayaking   .40   .40
B179 SP29 45p + 5p Rowing   .65   .65
     Nos. B177-B179 (3)   1.35 1.35

Madrid, European City of Culture, 1992 SP35

Designs: 15p+5p, Fountain of Apollo. 25p+5p, Statue of Alvaro de Bazan. 45p+5p, Bank of Spain. 55p+5p, St. Isidore's Institute.

1991, July 29   Photo.   Perf. 13½x14
B180 SP35 15p + 5p multi   .30   .30
B181 SP35 25p + 5p multi   .40   .40
B182 SP35 45p + 5p multi   .60   .60
B183 SP35 55p + 5p multi   .75   .75
     Nos. B180-B183 (4)   2.05 2.05

Summer Olympics Type of 1988
1991, Oct. 3   Litho.   Perf. 14
B184 SP29 15p +5p Tennis   .45   .45
B185 SP29 25p +5p Table tennis   .60   .60
B186 SP29 55p +5p Shooting   1.25 1.25
     Nos. B184-B186 (3)   2.30 2.30

Discovery of America, 500th Anniv., 1992 — SP36

15p+5p, Garcilaso Gomez Suarez de Figueroa, the Inca, poet. 25p+5p, Pope Alexander VI. 45p+5p, Luis de Santangel, banker. 55p+5p, Friar Toribio de Paredes, monk.

1991, Oct. 15   Photo.   Perf. 13x13½
B187 SP36 15p +5p multi   .30   .30
B188 SP36 25p +5p multi   .40   .40
B189 SP36 45p +5p multi   .60   .60
B190 SP36 55p +5p multi   .75   .75
  a.   Bklt. pane of 4, #B187-B190   2.00
     Nos. B187-B190 (4)   2.05 2.05

Summer Olympics Type of 1988
1992, Mar. 6   Photo.   Perf. 13½x14
B191 SP29 15p +5p Archery   .40   .40
B192 SP29 25p +5p Sailing   .55   .55
B193 SP29 55p +5p Volleyball   1.10 1.10
     Nos. B191-B193 (3)   2.05 2.05

Columbus Type of 1930
Souvenir Sheet
1992, Mar. 31   Engr.   Perf. 14
B194 Sheet of 3   1.00 1.00
  a.   A65 17p +5p dark red   .30   .30
  b.   A65 17p +5p ultramarine   .30   .30
  c.   A65 17p +5p black   .30   .30

    Discovery of America, 500th anniv.

Expo '92 Type
Design: No. B195, Seville, 16th cent.

1992, Apr. 21   Litho.   Perf. 13½x14
Souvenir Sheet
B195 A837 17p +5p multi   .35   .35

1992 Summer Olympics, Barcelona — SP37

Perf. 14x13½, 13½x14
1992, July 16   Photo.
B196 SP37 17p +5p Mascot COBI   .40   .40
B197 SP37 17p +5p Hand holding torch, horiz. .40   .40
B198 SP37 17p +5p "25 Jul"   .40   .40
     Nos. B196-B198 (3)   1.20 1.20

1992 Summer Olympics, Barcelona SP38

Designs: a, Olympic Stadium. b, San Jordi Sports Palace. c, INEF Sports University.

1992, July 25   Perf. 13½x14
B199 SP38 27p +5p Triptych, #a.-c.   1.40 1.40

1992 Summer Olympics, Barcelona
SP39   SP40

#B200, Olympic mascot as stamp collector.
#B201, Sagrada Family Church, Barcelona.

1992, July 29   Photo.   Perf. 14x13½
B200 SP39 17p +5p multi   .35   .35
B201 SP40 17p +5p multi   .35   .35

    Olymphilex '92 (#B201).

Madrid, European City of Culture — SP41

#B202, Municipal Museum. #B203, Royal Theater. #B204, The Prado Museum. #B205, Queen Sofia Natl. Center for the Arts.

1992, Nov. 24   Photo.   Perf. 14x13½
B202 SP41 17p +5p multi   .35   .30
B203 SP41 17p +5p multi   .35   .30
B204 SP41 17p +5p multi   .35   .30
B205 SP41 17p +5p multi   .35   .30
     Nos. B202-B205 (4)   1.40 1.20

AIR POST STAMPS

Regular Issue of 1909-10 Overprinted in Red or Black

Perf. 13x12½, 14
1920, Apr. 4   Unwmk.
C1 A46   5c green (R)   1.50   1.00
  a.   Imperf., pair   105.00 105.00
  b.   Double overprint   35.00   35.00
  c.   Inverted overprint   90.00   90.00
  d.   Double ovpt., one invtd.   35.00   35.00
  e.   Triple overprint   35.00   35.00
C2 A46 10c car (Bk)   1.75   1.25
  a.   Imperf., pair   105.00 105.00
  b.   Double overprint   35.00   35.00
  d.   Double ovpt., one invtd.   35.00   35.00
C3 A46 25c dp blue (R)   3.25   1.75
  a.   Inverted overprint   90.00   90.00
  b.   Double overprint   35.00   35.00
C4 A46 50c sl blue (R)   13.00   6.00
  a.   Imperf., pair   105.00 105.00
C5 A46   1p lake (Bk)   42.50   22.50
  a.   Imperf., pair   385.00 385.00
     Nos. C1-C5 (5)   62.00   32.50
     Set, never hinged   170.00

Dangerous counterfeits are plentiful.
A 30c green was authorized, but not issued. Value: hinged $550; never hinged $750.
For overprints see Nos. C58-C61.

"Spirit of St. Louis" over Coast of Europe - AP1   Plane and Congress Seal — AP2

Seville-Barcelona Exposition Issue
Control Numbers on Back
1929, Feb. 15   Engr.   Perf. 11
C6   AP1   5c brown   5.00   5.00
C7   AP1 10c rose   5.00   5.00
C8   AP1 25c dark blue   5.50   5.50
C9   AP1 50c purple   5.75   5.75
C10 AP1   1p green   30.00   20.00
C11 AP1   4p black   21.00   20.00
     Nos. C6-C11 (6)   72.25   66.25
     Set, never hinged   270.00

Nos. C6 to C11 exist imperforate. Value set, $675.

The so-called errors of color of Nos. C10, C18-C21, C23-C24, C28-C31, C37, C40, C42, C44, C46, C48, C50, C52, C55, C62-C67 are believed to have been irregularly produced.

Railway Congress Issue
Control Numbers on Back
1930, May 10   Litho.   Perf. 14
C12 AP2   5c bister brn   6.00   7.50
C13 AP2 10c rose   6.00   7.50
C14 AP2 25c dark blue   6.00   7.50
C15 AP2 50c purple   17.50   15.00
  a.   Vert. pair, imperf. between 300.00
         Never hinged   600.00
C16 AP2   1p yellow green   37.50   30.00
C17 AP2   4p black   37.50   30.00
     Nos. C12-C17 (6)   92.25   92.25
     Set, never hinged   300.00

The note after No. 385 will apply here also. Dangerous counterfeits exist.

Goya Issue

Fantasy of Flight AP3

Asmodeus and Cleofas — AP4

Fantasy of Flight AP5

Fantasy of Flight AP6

1930, June 15   Engr.   Perf. 12½
C18 AP3   5c brn red & yel   .25   .25
C19 AP3 15c blk & red org   .25   .25
C20 AP3 25c brn car & dp red   .25   .25
C21 AP4   5c ol grn & grnsh bl   .25   .25
C22 AP4 10c sl grn & yel grn   .25   .25
C23 AP4 20c ultra & rose red   .25   .25
C24 AP4 40c vio bl & lt bl   .30   .30
C25 AP5 30c brown & vio   .30   .30
C26 AP5 50c ver & grn   .30   .30
C27 AP5   4p brn car & blk   2.00   2.00
C28 AP6   1p vio brn & vio   .30   .30
C29 AP6   4p bl blk & sl grn   2.00   2.00
C30 AP6 10p blk brn & bis brn   7.00   7.00
     Nos. C18-C30,CE1 (14)   13.95 13.95
     Set, never hinged   30.00

Nos. C18-C30 exist imperf. Value for set, $150.

Christopher Columbus Issue

La Rábida Monastery — AP7

Martín Alonso
Pinzón — AP8

Vicente Yanez
Pinzón — AP9

Columbus in His Cabin — AP10

1930, Sept. 29   **Litho.**
C31	AP7	5c lt red brn	.25	.25
C32	AP7	5c olive bister	.25	.25
C33	AP7	10c blue green	.25	.25
C34	AP7	15c dark violet	.25	.25
C35	AP7	20c ultra	.25	.25

Engr.
C36	AP8	25c carmine rose	.25	.25
C37	AP9	30c dp red brn	2.00	2.00
C38	AP8	40c indigo	2.00	2.00
C39	AP9	50c orange	2.00	2.00
C40	AP8	1p dull violet	2.00	2.00
C41	AP10	4p olive green	2.00	2.00
C42	AP10	10p light brown	11.00	12.00
	Nos. C31-C42 (12)		22.50	23.50
	Set, never hinged		35.00	

Nos. C31-C42 exist imperf. Value for set, $190.

Spanish-American Issue

AP11

Columbus
AP12

Columbus
and Pinzón
Brothers
AP13

1930, Sept. 29   **Litho.**
C43	AP11	5c lt red	.25	.25
C44	AP11	10c dull green	.25	.25

Engr.
C45	AP12	25c scarlet	.25	.25
C46	AP12	50c slate gray	2.50	2.10
C47	AP12	1p fawn	2.50	2.10
C48	AP13	4p slate blue	2.50	2.10
C49	AP13	10p brown violet	11.00	10.00
	Nos. C43-C49 (7)		19.25	17.05
	Set, never hinged		35.00	

Nos. C43-C49 exist imperf. Value for set, $200.

Spanish-American Exhibition Issue

Santos-Dumont and First Flight of His
Airplane — AP14

Teodoro
Fels and
His
Airplane
AP15

Dagoberto Godoy and Pass over
Andes — AP16

Sacadura
Cabral
and Gago
Coutinho
and Their
Airplane
AP17

Sidar of Mexico
and Map of
South
America — AP18

Ignacio Jiménez
and Francisco
Iglesias — AP19

Charles A.
Lindbergh,
Statue of
Liberty,
Spirit of
St. Louis
and Cat
AP20

Santa
Maria,
Plane and
Torre del
Oro,
Seville
AP21

1930, Oct. 10   **Photo.**   **Perf. 14**
C50	AP14	5c gray black	.90	.55
C51	AP15	10c dk olive grn	.90	.55
C52	AP16	25c ultra	.90	.55
C53	AP17	50c blue gray	1.90	1.40
C54	AP18	50c black	1.90	1.40
C55	AP19	1p car lake	4.00	3.00
a.		1p brown violet	75.00	75.00
		Never hinged	175.00	

C56	AP20	1p deep green	4.00	3.00
C57	AP21	4p slate blue	7.25	5.50
	Nos. C50-C57 (8)		21.75	15.95
	Set, never hinged		90.00	

Exist imperf. Value, set $110.
Note after No. 432 also applies to Nos. C31-C57.
Reprints of Nos. C50-C57 have blurred impressions, yellowish paper. Value: one-tenth of originals.

Nos. C1-C4
Overprinted in Red or
Black

1931   **Perf. 13x12½**
C58	A46	5c green (R)	12.50	11.50
C59	A46	10c carmine (Bk)	12.50	11.50
C60	A46	25c deep blue (R)	17.50	16.50
C61	A46	50c slate blue (R)	35.00	26.00
	Nos. C58-C61 (4)		77.50	65.50
	Set, never hinged		160.00	

Counterfeits of overprint exist.
The status of Nos. C58-C61 has been questioned.

Plane
and
Royal
Palace,
Madrid
AP22

Madrid
Post
Office
and
Cibeles
Fountain
AP23

Plane
over
Calle de
Alcalá,
Madrid
AP24

1931, Oct. 10   **Engr.**   **Perf. 12**
C62	AP22	5c brown violet	.25	.30
C63	AP22	10c deep green	.25	.30
C64	AP22	25c dull red	.25	.30
C65	AP23	50c deep blue	.45	.50
C66	AP23	1p deep violet	.65	.60
C67	AP24	4p black	9.00	9.00
	Nos. C62-C67 (6)		10.85	11.00
	Set, never hinged		15.00	

3rd Pan-American Postal Union Congress, Madrid.
Exist imperf. Value, set $45.
For overprints see Nos. CO1-CO6.

Montserrat Issue

Plane over
Montserrat
Pass — AP25

1931, Dec. 9   **Perf. 11½**
Control Number on Back
C68	AP25	5c black brown	.55	.55
C69	AP25	10c yellow green	2.50	2.50
C70	AP25	25c deep rose	10.00	10.00
C71	AP25	50c orange	36.00	36.00
C72	AP25	1p gray black	25.00	25.00
	Nos. C68-C72 (5)		74.05	74.05
	Set, never hinged		100.00	

Perf. 14
C68a	AP25	5c	7.50	14.50
C69a	AP25	10c	40.00	45.00
C70a	AP25	25c	72.50	72.50

C71a	AP25	50c	72.50	72.50
C72f	AP25	1p	72.50	72.50
	Nos. C68a-C72f (5)		265.00	277.00
	Set, never hinged		275.00	

900th anniv. of Montserrat Monastery.
Nos. C68-C72 exist imperf. Value set, $525.

Autogiro over
Seville — AP26

1935-39   **Perf. 11½**
C72A	AP26	2p gray blue	22.50	4.50
g.		Imperf., pair	350.00	

Re-engraved
C72B	AP26	2p dk blue ('38)	.75	.25
c.		Imperf., pair	20.00	
d.		Perf. 10 ('39)	1.50	1.10
	Set, #C72A-C72B, never hinged		45.00	

The sky has heavy horizontal lines of shading. Entire design is more heavily shaded than No. C72A.
No. C72B exists privately perforated 14. Value, $9 unused, $9 used.
For overprints see Nos. 7LC14, 7LC19, 14L26.

Eagle and Newspapers — AP27

Press Building,
Madrid — AP28

Don Quixote and Sancho Panza Flying
on the Wooden Horse — AP29

Design: 15c, 30c, 50c, 1p, Autogiro over House of Nazareth.

1936, Mar. 11   **Photo.**   **Perf. 12½**
C73	AP27	1c rose car	.25	.25
C74	AP28	2c dark brown	.25	.25
C75	AP27	5c black brown	.25	.25
C76	AP28	10c dk yellow grn	.25	.25
C77	AP28	15c Prus blue	.25	.25
C78	AP27	20c violet	.25	.25
C79	AP28	25c magenta	.25	.25
C80	AP28	30c red orange	.25	.25
C81	AP27	40c orange	.50	.25
C82	AP28	50c light blue	.30	.25
C83	AP28	60c olive green	.65	.40
C84	AP28	1p brnsh black	.65	.45
C85	AP29	2p brt ultra	5.75	2.25
C86	AP29	4p lilac rose	5.75	2.75
C87	AP29	10p violet brown	16.00	11.00
	Nos. C73-C87 (15)		31.20	18.85
	Set, never hinged		42.50	

Madrid Press Association, 40th anniv.
Exist imperf. Value, set $250 hinged, and $325 never hinged.
See note after No. 432.

Types of Regular Postage of 1936 Overprinted in Blue or Red

1936 *Imperf.*
C88 A125 10c dk red (Bl) 150.00 150.00
C89 A125 15c dk blue (R) 150.00 150.00
Set, never hinged 450.00

1st National Philatelic Exhibition which opened in Madrid, Apr. 2, 1936.

No. 577 Overprinted in Black

1936, Aug. 1 *Perf. 11½*
C90 A128 30c rose red 3.00 3.75
Never hinged 7.75
b. Imperf., pair 140.00

Issued in commemoration of the flight of aviators Antonio Arnaiz and Juan Calvo from Manila to Spain.
Counterfeit overprints exist.
Exists privately perforated 14. Value, $50 unused, $50 used.

No. 288 Surcharged in Black

1938, Apr. 13 *Perf. 14*
C91 A36 2.50p on 10c 90.00 80.00
Never hinged 175.00

7th anniversary of the Republic.
Values are for examples with perforations nearly touching the design on one or two sides.

No. 507 Surcharged in Various Colors

1938, Aug. *Perf. 11½*
C92 A92 50c on 25c (Bk) 29.00 29.00
C93 A92 1p on 25c (G) 2.25 1.50
C94 A92 1.25p on 25c (R) 2.25 1.50
C95 A92 1.50p on 25c (Bl) 2.25 1.50
C96 A92 2p on 25c (Bk & R) 40.00 34.00
Nos. C92-C96 (5) 75.75 67.50
Set, never hinged 125.00

No. 585 Surcharged

1938, June 1 *Perf. 11*
C97 A132 5p on 1p multi 275. 275.
Never hinged 425.
a. Imperf., pair 550. 550.
b. Inverted surcharge 350. 350.
c. Souvenir sheet 2,000. 2,000.
2,500.

d. As "c," imperf. 6,500. 6,500.
e. As "c," inverted surcharge 6,000. 6,000.
Counterfeit surcharges exist.

Type of 1938-39 Overprinted in Red or Carmine

1938, May *Perf. 10, 10½*
C98 A163 50c indigo (R) .70 .55
C99 A163 1p dk blue (C) 3.00 .70
Set, never hinged 4.50

Exist imperf. Value, each $100.
Examples without overprint are proofs.

Juan de la Cierva and his Autogiro over Madrid AP30

1939, Jan. Unwmk. Litho. *Perf. 11*
C100 AP30 20c red orange .60 .40
C101 AP30 25c dk carmine .45 .25
C102 AP30 35c brt violet .65 .40
C103 AP30 50c dk brown .65 .25
C105 AP30 1p blue .65 .25
C107 AP30 2p green 3.25 1.75
C108 AP30 4p dull blue 5.00 2.75
Nos. C100-C108 (7) 11.25 6.05
Set, never hinged 19.00

Exist imperf. Value, set $325.

1941-47 *Perf. 10*
C109 AP30 20c dk red orange .25 .25
C110 AP30 25c redsh brown .25 .25
C111 AP30 35c lilac rose 1.60 .50
C112 AP30 50c brown .45 .25
C113 AP30 1p chalky blue 1.40 .25
C114 AP30 2p lt gray grn 1.60 .25
C115 AP30 4p gray blue 5.00 .30
C116 AP30 10p brt purple ('47) 3.75 .65
Nos. C109-C116 (8) 14.30 2.70
Set, never hinged 26.00

Issued in honor of Juan de la Cierva (1895-1936), inventor of the autogiro.
Nos. C109-C115 exist imperf. Value, set $300.
The overprint "EXPOSICION NACIONAL DE FILATELIA 1948 SAN SEBASTIAN" multiple, in parallel horizontal lines, on Nos. C109 to C113 and other airmail stamps, was privately applied.

Correo Aéreo **Correo Aéreo**

Correo Aéreo Mariano Pardo de Figueroa (Dr. Thebussem) AP31

Nos. 625-634, 660, 676 and 677 with either of these overprints have not been established as issues of the Spanish government.

1944, Oct. 12 Engr. *Perf. 10*
C117 AP31 5p brt ultra 15.00 13.00
Never hinged 23.00

"Stamp Day" and "Day of the Race," Oct. 12, 1944. Valid for franking air mail correspondence one day only.

Mail Coach, Plane and Count of St. Louis AP32

1945, Oct. 12 *Unwmk.*
C118 AP32 10p yellow green 17.50 19.00
Never hinged 25.00

"Stamp Day" and "Day of the Race," Oct. 12, 1945, and to honor Luis José Sartorius, Count of St. Louis, who issued the decree for Spain's 1st postage stamps. No. C118 was valid for franking air mail correspondence one day only.
C118 exists imperf. Value, $1,000.

Maj. Joaquin Garcia Morato AP33

1945, Nov. 27
C119 AP33 10p deep claret 13.50 5.50
Never hinged 35.00

C119 exists imperf. Value, $300 hinged, $475 never hinged.

Capt. Carlos Haya Gonzalez AP34

Bartolomé de las Casas AP35

1945, Dec. 14
C120 AP34 4p red 5.50 4.50
Never hinged 12.50

C120 exists imperf. Value, $400 hinged and $600 never hinged.

1946, Oct. 12 *Perf. 11½x11*
C121 AP35 5.50p green 1.90 2.50
3.00

Stamp Day and Day of the Race. Exists imperf. Value $16.

Don Quixote and Sancho Panza Astride Clavileno AP36

1947, Oct. 9 *Perf. 10*
C122 AP36 5.50p purple 4.50 4.50
Never hinged 6.75

Stamp Day and the 400th anniversary of the birth of Miguel de Cervantes Saavedra.
C122 exists imperf. Value, $800.

Manuel de Falla — AP37

Ignacio Zuloaga — AP38

1947, Dec. 1 *Perf. 9½x10½*
Control Number on Back
C123 AP37 25p dk vio brn 27.50 15.00
C124 AP38 50p dk carmine 110.00 40.00
Set, never hinged 275.00

For overprint see No. CB18.
C124 exists imperf. Value, $925.

Train and Plane — AP39

1948, Oct. 9 Litho. *Perf. 13x12½*
C125 AP39 2p scarlet 1.50 1.50
Never hinged 2.25

Cent. of Spanish railroads and Stamp Day.

UPU Type of Regular Issue with Pedestal and Propeller Added
1949, Oct. 9 *Perf. 12½x13*
C126 A202 4p dk olive green .25 .45
Never hinged .40

Stamp Day and the 75th anniv. of the UPU.

Stamp of 1850 AP40

Map of Western Hemisphere AP41

1950, Oct. 12 Engr. *Imperf.*
C127 AP40 1p rose brn 4.50 6.50
C128 AP40 2.50p brown org 4.50 6.50
C129 AP40 20p dark blue 80.00 87.50
C130 AP40 25p green 80.00 87.50
Nos. C127-C130 (4) 169.00 188.00
Set, never hinged 325.00

Centenary of Spanish postage stamps.

1951, Apr. 16 Photo. *Perf. 12½*
C131 AP41 1p blue 4.50 2.25
Never hinged 6.25

6th Congress of the Postal Union of the Americas and Spain.

Isabella I AP42

1951, Oct. 12 Engr. *Perf. 13*
C132 AP42 60c dk gray grn 6.50 .40
C133 AP42 90c orange .80 .55
C134 AP42 1.30p plum 5.00 4.00
C135 AP42 1.90p sepia 4.50 4.00
C136 AP42 2.30p dk blue 2.75 2.75
Nos. C132-C136 (5) 19.55 11.70
Set, never hinged 27.50

Stamp Day and 500th anniv. of the birth of Queen Isabella I.

"The Eucharist" by Tiepolo — AP43

St. Francis Xavier — AP44

1952, May 26 Photo. *Perf. 12½x13*
C137 AP43 1p gray green 3.00 .60
Never hinged 3.50

35th International Eucharistic Congress, Barcelona, 1952.

1952, July 3 *Engr.*
C138 AP44 2p deep blue 30.00 14.00
Never hinged 55.00

400th anniv. of the death of St. Francis Xavier.

Ferdinand the Catholic and Columbus Presenting Natives AP45

1952, Oct. 12

C139	AP45	60c dull green	.25	.25
C140	AP45	90c orange	.25	.25
C141	AP45	1.30p plum	.45	.30
C142	AP45	1.90p sepia	2.00	2.00
C143	AP45	2.30p deep blue	10.00	9.50
		Nos. C139-C143 (5)	12.95	12.30
		Set, never hinged	17.50	

500th anniversary of the birth of Ferdinand the Catholic and to publicize Stamp Day.

Joaquin Sorolla y Bastida AP46

Miguel Lopez de Legazpi AP47

1953, Oct. 9   *Perf. 13x12½*

C144	AP46	50p dark violet	250.00	22.50
		Never hinged	600.00	

Issued to honor Joaquin Sorolla y Bastida (1863-1923), impressionist painter.

1953, Nov. 5

C145	AP47	25p gray black	50.00	27.50
		Never hinged	100.00	

Spanish-Philippine Postal Convention of 1951.

Leonardo Torres Quevedo (1852-1939), Mathematician and Inventor — AP48

Perf. 13x12½

1955, Sept. 6   Engr.   Unwmk.

C146	AP48	50p bluish gray & blk	5.00	.90
		Never hinged	11.00	

Plane and Caravel AP49

1955-56   Photo.   *Perf. 12½x13*

C147	AP49	20c gray grn ('56)	.25	.25
C148	AP49	25c gray violet	.25	.25
C149	AP49	50c ol gray ('56)	.25	.25
C150	AP49	1p red orange	.25	.25
C151	AP49	1.10p emer ('56)	.25	.25
C152	AP49	1.40p rose car	.25	.25
C153	AP49	3p brt blue ('56)	.25	.25
C154	AP49	4.80p yellow	.25	.25
C155	AP49	5p redsh brown	1.50	.25
C156	AP49	7p lilac ('56)	.45	.25
C157	AP49	10p lt ol grn ('56)	.50	.25
		Nos. C147-C157 (11)		2.75
		Set, never hinged	4.00	

Mariano Fortuny y Carbo (1838-1874), Painter — AP50

1956, Jan. 10   Engr.   *Perf. 13x12½*

C158	AP50	25p grnsh black	14.00	.90
		Never hinged	30.00	

> **Catalogue values for unused stamps in this section, from this point to the end of the section, are for Never Hinged items.**

Bullfight Type of Regular Issue

25c, Small town arena. 50c, Fighting with cape. 1p, Dedication of the bull. 5p, Bull ring.

Perf. 13x12½, 12½x13

1960, Feb. 29   Engr.   Unwmk.

C159	A246	25c brn car & dl lil	.25	.25
C160	A245	50c blue	.25	.25
C161	A246	1p red & dull red	.25	.25
C162	A245	5p red lilac & vio	.55	.40
		Nos. C159-C162 (4)	1.15	1.00

Jai Alai AP51

1960, Mar. 27   Photo.   *Perf. 12½x13*

C163	AP51	1p brt red & dk brn	4.75	3.25
C164	AP51	5p dull brn & mag	4.75	3.25
C165	AP51	6p vio blk & mag	4.75	3.25
C166	AP51	10p grn, mag & dk brn	4.75	3.25
		Nos. C163-C166 (4)	19.00	13.00

1st Intl. Cong. of Philately, Barcelona, Mar. 26-Apr. 5. Nos. C163-C166 could be bought at the exhibition upon presentation of 5p entrance ticket.

Sport Type of Regular Issue

Sports: 1.25p, 6p, Steeplechase, horiz. 1.50p, 10p, Basque ball game.

Perf. 12½x13, 13x12½

1960, Oct. 31   Unwmk.

C167	A251	1.25p choc & car	.30	.25
C168	A251	1.50p pur, brn & blk	.30	.25
C169	A251	6p vio blk & car	.95	.55
C170	A251	10p ol grn, red & blk	1.25	.55
		Nos. C167-C170 (4)	2.80	1.50

Rosary Type of Regular Issue

Mysteries of the Rosary: 25c, The Ascension, Bayeu. 1p, The Descent of the Holy Ghost, El Greco. 5p, The Assumption, Mateo Cerezo. 10p, The Coronation of the Virgin Mary, El Greco.

1962, Oct. 26   Engr.   *Perf. 13*

C171	A280	25c vio & dl gray vio	.25	.25
C172	A280	1p olive & brown	.35	.25
C173	A280	5p brn & rose cl	.60	.25
C174	A280	10p bluish grn & yel grn	1.40	.50
		Nos. C171-C174 (4)	2.60	1.15

Recaredo I, Visigothic King, 586-601 — AP52

Portrait: 50p, Francisco Cardinal Jimenez de Cisneros (1436-1517).

1963, Dec. 5   Engr.   *Perf. 13x12½*

C175	AP52	25p dull purple	1.10	.40
C176	AP52	50p green & black	1.90	.55

1966, Feb. 26

Portraits: 25p, Seneca (4 B.C.-65 A.D.). 50p, Pope St. Damasus I (304?-384).

C177	AP52	25p yel grn & dk grn	1.75	.25
C178	AP52	50p sky bl & gray bl	2.75	.55

Plaza de Espana, Seville AP53

1981, Nov. 26   Engr.   *Perf. 13*

C179	AP53	13p shown	.25	.25
C180	AP53	20p Rande River Bridge, Pontevedra	.25	.25

St. Thomas, by El Greco — AP54

1982, July 7   Photo.   *Perf. 13*

C181	AP54	13p Sts. Andrew and Francis	.25	.25
C182	AP54	20p shown	.25	.25

Bowling AP55

1983, Apr. 13   Photo.   *Perf. 13*

C183	AP55	13p Bicycling, vert.	.25	.25
C184	AP55	20p shown	.25	.25

AIR POST SEMI-POSTAL STAMPS

Red Cross Issue

Ramon Franco's Plane Plus Ultra SPAP1

Perf. 12½, 13

1926, Sept. 15   Engr.   Unwmk.

CB1	SPAP1	5c black & vio	1.40	1.40
CB2	SPAP1	10c ultra & blk	3.00	3.00
CB3	SPAP1	25c carmine & blk	.30	.30
CB4	SPAP1	50c red org & blk	.30	.30
CB5	SPAP1	1p black & green	2.50	2.50
		Nos. CB1-CB5 (5)	7.50	7.50
		Set, never hinged	10.00	

For overprints and surcharges see Nos. B55-B63.

No. B106 Surcharged in Black

1938, Apr. 15   *Perf. 11½*

CB6	SP13	45c + 2p + 5p	250.	225.
		Never hinged	600.	
a.		Imperf., pair	1,150.	900.
b.		Souvenir sheet of 1	3,000.	4,500.
		Never hinged	5,500.	
c.		Souvenir sheet, imperf.	6,000.	6,000.
d.		Souv. sheet, surch. invtd.	6,500.	5,750.

The surtax was used to benefit the defenders of Madrid.

This issue has been extensively counterfeited.

No. B107 Surcharged

1938, June 1   *Perf. 10*

CB7	SP14	45c + 5p + 3p	10.00	9.75
		Never hinged	17.50	

Monument SPAP2

Dome Fresco by Goya, Cathedral of Zaragoza SPAP3

#CB9, CB14, Caravel Santa Maria. #CB10, CB12, The Ascension. #CB13, The Coronation. #CB17, Bombardment of Cathedral of Zaragoza.

Perf. 10½, 11½x10½, 11½

1940, Jan. 29   Litho.   Unwmk.

Bicolored

CB8	SPAP2	25c + 5c	.25	.25
CB9	SPAP2	50c + 5c	.25	.25
CB10	SPAP2	65c + 15c	.25	.25
CB11	SPAP2	70c + 15c	.25	.25
CB12	SPAP2	90c + 20c	.25	.25
CB13	SPAP2	1.20p + 30c	.25	.25
CB14	SPAP2	1.40p + 40c	.50	.50
CB15	SPAP2	2p + 50c	.40	.40
CB16	SPAP3	4p + 1p sl grn & rose lil	8.75	8.75
CB17	SPAP3	10p + 4p chnt & ultra	200.00	200.00
		Nos. CB8-CB17 (10)	211.15	211.15
		Set, never hinged	375.00	

19th centenary of the Pillar Virgin. The surtax was used to help restore the Cathedral at Zaragoza, damaged during the Civil War.

No. CB16 exists in slate green & violet, No. CB17 in red violet & ultramarine. Value, $32.50 each.

Nos. CB8-CB17 exist imperf. Value, set $350.

No. C123 Surcharged in Black

1950-51   *Perf. 9½x10½*

Control Number on Back

CB18	AP37	25p + 10c	300.00	250.00
		Never hinged	600.00	
a.		Without control number	3,250.	1,500.
		Without control number, never hinged	5,000.	

Visit of Gen. Franco to the Canary Islands, Oct., 1950.

The control number was printed on the gum, and regummed copies of No. CB18 are frequently offered as No. CB18a.

Counterfeit surcharges exist.

Issued: #CB18a, 10/23/50; #CB18 2/22/51.

434   SPAIN

AIR POST SPECIAL DELIVERY STAMP

Goya Commemorative Issue

Type of Air Post
Stamp of 1930
Overprinted

1930   Unwmk.   Perf. 12½
CE1 AP4 20c bl blk & lt brn
    (Bk)   .25   .25
    Never hinged   .25
  a. Blue overprint   15.00   7.75
    Never hinged   21.00
  b. Overprint omitted   15.00   22.50
    Never hinged   25.00

    See note after No. 432.

AIR POST OFFICIAL STAMPS

Pan-American Postal Union Congress Issue
Types of Air Post Stamps of 1931
Overprinted in Red or Blue

1931   Unwmk.   Perf. 12
CO1 AP22 5c red brown (R)   .25   .25
CO2 AP22 10c blue grn (Bl)   .25   .25
CO3 AP22 25c rose (Bl)   .25   .25
CO4 AP23 50c lt blue (R)   .25   .25
CO5 AP23 1p violet (R)   .25   .25
CO6 AP24 4p gray blk (R)   3.50   3.50
    Nos. CO1-CO6 (6)   4.75   4.75
    Set, never hinged   7.00

    Shades exist.
Nos. CO1-CO6 exist imperf. Value, set
$22.50

SPECIAL DELIVERY STAMPS

Pegasus and Coat of Arms — SD1

1905-25   Unwmk.   Typo.   Perf. 14
Control Number on Back
E1 SD1 20c deep red   45.00   .30
    Never hinged   100.00
  a. 20c rose red, litho. ('25) 38.00   .30
    Never hinged   70.00
  b. Imperf., pair   300.00
  c. As "a," imperf., pair   300.00

Gazelle
SD2

1929   Engr.   Perf. 11
Control Number on Back
E2 SD2 20c dull red   19.50   22.50
    Never hinged   37.50
  a. Perf. 14   32.50   37.50
    Never hinged   60.00

Seville and Barcelona Exhibitions. See note
after No. 432.

Pegasus — SD3

1929-32   Perf. 13½x12½, 11½
Control Number on Back
E3 SD3 20c red   21.00   4.00
    Never hinged   40.00
  a. Imperf., pair   400.00
  b. Without control number, perf.
    11½ ('32)   60.00   1.50
    Never hinged   97.50
  c. As "b," imperf., pair   950.00

No. E3 Overprinted like Nos. 358-370
E4 SD3 20c red (Bl)   12.00   25.00
    Never hinged   25.00

    League of Nations 55th assembly.
For overprints see Nos. E5, E10-E12.

No. E3 Overprinted in Blue

1930   Perf. 13½x12½, 11½
E5 SD3 20c red   13.50   .75
    Never hinged   40.00

Railway Congress Issue

Electric Locomotive — SD4

1930, May 10   Litho.   Perf. 14
Control Number on Back
E6 SD4 20c brown orange   55.00   55.00
    Never hinged   105.00

    See note after No. 385.

Goya Issue

Type of Regular
Issue of 1930
Overprinted

1930   Perf. 12½
E7 A57 20c lilac rose   .25   .30
    Never hinged   .45

Christopher Columbus Issue

Type of Regular
Issue of 1930
Overprinted

1930 Sept. 29
E8 A64 20c brown violet   1.90   1.90
    Never hinged   3.00

    See note after No. 432.

Spanish-American Exhibition Issue

View of Seville Exhibition — SD5

1930, Oct. 10   Photo.   Perf. 14
E9 SD5 20c orange   .45   .30
    Never hinged   .60

    See note after No. 432.

Madrid Issue

No. E5 Overprinted in
Green

1931   Perf. 11½
E10 SD3 20c red   5.00   5.00
    Never hinged   8.00
The status of No. E10 has been questioned.

Barcelona Issue

No. E3 Overprinted

E11 SD3 20c red   5.50   5.50
    Never hinged   12.00
No. E11 also exists with accent over "U."
The status of No. E11 has been questioned.

No. E3 Overprinted in
Blue

E12 SD3 20c red   6.50   1.25
    Never hinged   21.00

Montserrat Issue

Pegasus — SD6

1931   Engr.   Perf. 11
Control Number on Back
E13 SD6 20c vermilion   25.00   25.00
    Never hinged   38.00
  a. Perf. 14   55.00   60.00

SD7

1934   Perf. 10
E14 SD7 20c vermilion   .25   .25
    Never hinged   .20
  a. Imperf., pair   32.50

For overprints see #10LE1, 11LE1-11LE4,
14LE1.

Newsboy — SD8

1936   Photo.   Perf. 12½
E15 SD8 20c rose carmine   .25   .30
    Never hinged   .50

40th anniversary of the Madrid Press
Association.
    See note after No. 432.

Pegasus
SD9

Spanish State
1937-38   Unwmk.   Litho.   Perf. 11
**With imprint "Hija. deB Fournier-
Burgos"**
E16 SD9 20c violet brn   7.75   4.50
    Never hinged   11.00
  a. Imperf., pair   77.50

Without Imprint
E17 SD9 20c dk vio brn ('38) 1.50   .30
    Never hinged   3.00
  a. Imperf., pair   50.00

No. 645 Overprinted
in Black

1937
E18 A162 20c dark violet   11.00   11.00
    Never hinged   14.50

Pegasus
SD10

1939-42   Perf. 10½
Imprint: "SANCHEZ TODA"
E19 SD10 25c carmine   4.50   .70
    Never hinged   6.25
  a. Imperf., pair   50.00

Without Imprint
Perf. 10
E20 SD10 25c carmine ('42)   .25   .25
    Never hinged   .30
  a. Imperf., pair   8.50

> Catalogue values for unused
> stamps in this section, from this
> point to the end of the section, are
> for Never Hinged items.

"Flight"
SD11

Centaur — SD12

Perf. 12½x13, 13x12½

1956, Feb. 12   Photo.   Unwmk.
E21 SD11 2p scarlet   .25 .25
E22 SD12 4p black & magenta   .25 .25

1965-66
E23 SD11 3p dp car   .25 .25
E24 SD12 5p dp org ('66)   .25 .25
E25 SD12 6.50p dk vio & rose
              brn ('66)   .25 .25
Nos. E21-E25 (5)   1.25 1.25

Chariot
SD13

Mail Circling
Globe — SD14

1971, June 1   Photo.   Perf. 13
E26 SD13 10p red & yel grn   .25 .25
E27 SD14 15p red, bl & blk   .25 .25

Communications — SD15

1993, Apr. 20 Photo. Perf. 14x13½
E28 SD15 180p red & yellow   2.50 .35

SEMI-POSTAL SPECIAL DELIVERY STAMPS

Red Cross Issue

Royal Family
Group
SPSD1

1926 Unwmk. Engr. Perf. 12½, 13
EB1 SPSD1 20c red vio & vio
              brn   8.75 8.75
     Never hinged   17.00

See notes after Nos. 432 and B18.
For overprint see No. B54.

Motorcyclist
and
Zaragoza
Cathedral
SPSD2

1940   Litho.   Perf. 11½
EB2 SPSD2 25c + 5c rose red &
              buff   .40 .30

19th cent. of the Pillar Virgin. The surtax was used to help restore the Cathedral at Zaragoza, damaged during the Civil War.

DELIVERY TAX STAMPS

D1

1931   Unwmk.   Litho.   Perf. 11½
ER1 D1 5c black   7.25 .25
     Never hinged   12.00

For overprints see Nos. ER2-ER3, 7LE5-7LE6.

No. ER1 Overprinted in
Red

1931
ER2 D1 5c black   1.25 1.40
     Never hinged   2.25

No. ER2 also exists with accent over "U."

No. ER1 Overprinted in
Red

ER3 D1 5c black   3.00 3.00
     Never hinged   5.50

These stamps were originally issued for Postage Due purpose but were later used as regular postage stamps.

WAR TAX STAMPS

These stamps did not pay postage but represented a fiscal tax on mail matter in addition to the postal fees. Their use was obligatory.

Coat of Arms
WT1   WT2

Unwmk.
1874, Jan. 1   Typo.   Perf. 14
MR1 WT1 5c black   11.00 .95
  a. Imperf. pair   14.00
MR2 WT1 10c pale blue   12.00 1.60
  a. Imperf., pair   62.50

1875, Jan. 1
MR3 WT2 5c green   6.00 .60
  a. Imperf., pair   27.50
MR4 WT2 10c lilac   12.00 2.75
  a. Imperf., pair   55.00

King Alfonso XII
WT3   WT4

1876, June 1
MR5 WT3 5c pale green   7.50 1.00
MR6 WT3 10c blue   7.50 1.00
  a. Cliche of 5c in plate of
         10c   125.00
MR7 WT3 25c black   50.00 17.00
MR8 WT3 1p lilac   475.00 110.00
MR9 WT3 5p rose   775.00 300.00

Nos. MR5-MR9 exist imperforate. Value, $1,100.

1877, Sept. 1
MR10 WT4 15c claret   27.50 1.00
  a. Imperf., pair   100.00
MR11 WT4 50c yellow   775.00 110.00

WT5   WT6

1879
MR12 WT5 5c blue   45.00
MR13 WT5 10c rose   27.50
MR14 WT5 15c violet   17.00
MR15 WT5 25c brown   27.50
MR16 WT5 50c olive green   17.00
MR17 WT5 1p bister   27.50
MR18 WT5 5p gray   100.00
Nos. MR12-MR18 (7)   261.50

Nos. MR12-MR18 were never placed in use. Nos. MR17 and MR18 exist imperforate. Value, $225.

Inscribed "1897 A 1898"

1897   Perf. 14
MR19 WT6 5c green   3.25 2.10
MR20 WT6 10c green   3.25 2.10
MR21 WT6 15c green   600.00 210.00
MR22 WT6 20c green   8.25 3.25

Nos. MR19-MR22 exist imperf. Value for set $825.

Inscribed "1898-99"

1898
MR23 WT6 5c black   2.25 1.75
MR24 WT6 10c black   2.25 1.75
MR25 WT6 15c black   50.00 9.50
MR26 WT6 20c black   3.50 3.00
Nos. MR23-MR26 (4)   58.00 16.00

Nos. MR23-MR26 exist imperf. Value about $275 a pair.

King Alfonso
XIII — WT7

1898
MR27 WT7 5c black   9.00 .60
  a. Imperf., pair   85.00

OFFICIAL STAMPS

Coat of Arms
O1   O2

Unwmk.
1854, July 1   Typo.   Imperf.
O1 O1 ½o blk, *yellow*   2.10 2.75
O2 O1 1o blk, *rose*   2.75 3.25
  a. 1o black, *blue*   29.00
O3 O1 4o blk, *green*   7.50 9.25
O4 O1 1 l blk, *blue*   52.50 60.00
Nos. O1-O4 (4)   64.85 75.25

1855-63
O5 O2 ½o blk, *yellow*   1.50 1.75
  a. ½o black, *straw* ('63)   1.75 1.90
O6 O2 1o blk, *rose*   1.50 1.75
  a. 1o black, *salmon rose*   3.25 1.90
O7 O2 4o blk, *green*   3.25 1.90
  a. 4o black, *yellow green*   8.75 1.90
O8 O2 1 l blk, *gray blue*   14.50 17.50
Nos. O5-O8 (4)   20.75 22.90

The "value indication" on Nos. O1-O8 actually is the weight of the mail in onzas (ounces, "o") and libras (pounds, "l") for which they were valid.

Type of Regular Issue of 1889

1895   Perf. 14
O9 A34 15c yellow   11.00 6.00
  a. Imperf., pair   250.00

Coat of Arms — O5

1896-98
O10 O5 rose   5.25 1.75
  a. Imperf., pair   87.50
O11 O5 dk blue ('98)   19.00 6.00

Cervantes Issue

Chamber of
Deputies
O6

Statue of
Cervantes — O7

Cervantes — O9

National
Library
O8

1916, Apr. 22   Engr.   Perf. 12
For the Senate
O12 O6 green & blk   1.10 .90
O13 O7 brown & blk   1.10 .90
O14 O8 carmine & blk   1.10 .90
O15 O9 brown & blk   1.10 .90
For the Chamber of Deputies
O16 O6 violet & blk   1.10 .90
O17 O7 carmine & blk   1.10 .90
O18 O8 green & blk   1.10 .90
O19 O9 violet & blk   1.10 .90
Nos. O12-O19 (8)   8.80 7.20

Exist imperf. Value set of pairs, $110.
Exist with centers inverted. Value for set, $87.50

Pan-American Postal Union Congress Issue

Types of
Regular Issue
of 1931
Overprinted in
Red or Blue

1931   Perf. 12½
O20 A84 5c dk brown (R)   .50 .25
O21 A85 10c brt green (Bl)   .50 .25
O22 A86 15c dull violet (R)   .50 .25
O23 A85 25c deep rose (Bl)   .50 .25
O24 A87 30c olive green (R)   .50 .25
O25 A84 40c ultra (R)   .70 .60
O26 A85 50c deep orange (Bl)   .70 .60
O27 A86 1p blue black (R)   .70 .60
O28 A88 4p magenta (Bl)   14.00 14.00
O29 A88 10p lt brown (R)   25.00 25.00
Nos. O20-O29 (10)   43.60 42.05
Set, never hinged   70.00

Nos. O22-O29 exist imperf. Values about 3 times those quoted.

Mail Coach
O30

Decorative Mailbox Opening
O10

Mail Pouch
O11

Bicycle for Mail Delivery
O12

1999   Photo.   Perf. 13¾x14
O30 O9   multi   —
O31 O10 multi   —
O32 O11 multi   —
O33 O12 multi   —
  a.   Horiz. strip, #O30-O33   —

For use by the Philatelic Service to any address. Not normally available unused.

POSTAL TAX STAMPS

PT5

PT6

Perf. 10½x11½
1937, Dec. 23   Litho.
RA11 PT5 10c blk, pale bl & red   8.00 5.00
      Never hinged   21.00
  a.   Imperf. pair   80.00
      Never hinged   120.00

The tax was for the tuberculosis fund.

1938, Dec. 23   Perf. 11½
RA12 PT6 10c multicolored   4.50 1.75
      Never hinged   10.00
  a.   Imperf. pair   45.00
      Never hinged   55.00

The tax was for the tuberculosis fund.

"Spain" Holding Wreath of Peace over Marching Soldiers
PT7

1939, July 18   Perf. 11
RA13 PT7 10c blue   .25   .25
      Never hinged   .25
  a.   Imperf. pair   65.00
      Never hinged   82.50

Type of Regular Issue, 1939
Without Imprint
Unwmk.
1939, Dec. 23   Litho.   Imperf.
RA14 A166 10c dull claret   .25   .25
      Never hinged   .25

Tuberculosis Fund Issue
Types of Corresponding Semi-Postal Stamps

1940, Dec. 23   Perf. 10
RA15 SP23 10c violet & red   .25   .25
      Never hinged   .25

1941, Dec. 23
RA16 SP24 10c black & red   .25   .25
      Never hinged   .25

1942, Dec. 23
RA17 SP25 10c dl sal & rose red   .25   .25
      Never hinged   .25

1943, Dec. 23   Photo.   Perf. 11
RA18 SP26 10c purple & dl red   .30   .25
      Never hinged   .50

Perf. 9½x10
1944, Dec. 23   Litho.   Unwmk.
RA19 SP27 10c salmon & rose   .25   .25
      Never hinged   .25

1945, Dec. 23
RA20 SP28 10c salmon & car   .25   .25
      Never hinged   .25

Mother and Child — PT8

1946, Dec. 22 Litho. Perf. 9½x10½
RA21 PT8 5c violet & red   .25   .25
RA22 PT8 10c green & red   .25   .25
      Set, never hinged   .40

See No. RAC7.

Lorraine Cross
PT9

Tuberculosis Sanatorium
PT10

Perf. 9½x10½
1947, Dec. 22   Unwmk.
RA23 PT9 5c dk brown & red   .25   .25
RA24 PT10 10c vio bl & red   .25   .25
      Set, never hinged   .40

See No. RAC8.

Aesculapius
PT11

"El Cid"
PT11a

Photogravure; Cross Engraved
1948, Dec. 22 Unwmk. Perf. 12½
RA25 PT11 5c brown & car   .25   .25
RA26 PT11 10c dp green & car   .25   .25
      Set, never hinged   .40

The tax on Nos. RA15-RA26 was used to fight tuberculosis. See Nos. RAB1, RAC9.

1949, Feb. 1 Litho. Perf. 10½x9½
RA27 PT11a 5c violet   .25   .25
      Never hinged   .25

The tax aided displaced children. Valid for ordinary postage after Dec. 24, 1949.

Tuberculosis Fund Issues

Galleon and Lorraine Cross — PT12

Pine Branch and Candle — PT13

Photogravure; Cross Engraved
1949, Dec. 22   Perf. 12½
RA28 PT12 5c violet & red   .25   .25
RA29 PT12 10c yel grn & red   .25   .25
      Set, never hinged   .40

See Nos. RAB2, RAC10.

1950, Dec. 22   Cross in Carmine
RA30 PT13 5c rose violet   .25   .25
RA31 PT13 10c deep green   .25   .25
      Set, never hinged   .35

See Nos. RAB3, RAC11.

Children at Seashore
PT14

Nurse and Baby
PT15

1951, Oct. 1   Cross in Carmine
RA32 PT14 5c rose brown   .25   .25
RA33 PT14 10c dull green   .35   .25
      Set, never hinged   .75

See No. RAC12.

1953, Oct. 1
Cross in Carmine
RA34 PT15 5c carmine lake   .30   .25
RA35 PT15 10c gray blue   .80   .25
      Set, never hinged   2.25

The tax on RA28-RA35 was used to fight tuberculosis. See No. RAC13.

POSTAL TAX SEMI-POSTAL STAMPS

Types of Corresponding Postal Tax Stamps
Photogravure; Cross Engraved
1948   Unwmk.   Perf. 12½
RAB1 PT11 50c + 10c red brn & car .80   .75
      Never hinged   1.25

1949
RAB2 PT12 50c + 10c dk ol bis & red .50 .25
      Never hinged   .80

1950
RAB3 PT13 50c + 10c brn & car   1.25 1.25
      Never hinged   2.25

The surtax on Nos. RAB1-RAB3 was used to fight tuberculosis. Combines domestic letter rate and tax obligatory Dec. 22-Jan. 3.

POSTAL TAX AIR POST STAMPS

Tuberculosis Fund Issues
Franco Type of Semi-Postal Stamps
Unwmk.
1940, Dec. 23   Litho.   Perf. 10
RAC1 SP23 10c bright pink & red   .90   .90
      Never hinged   2.50

Knight and Lorraine Cross — PTAP2

1941, Dec. 23
RAC2 PTAP2 10c blue & red   .25   .25
      Never hinged   .50

Lorraine Cross and Doves
PTAP3

1942, Dec. 23
RAC3 PTAP3 10c dl sal & rose   .80   .50
      Never hinged   1.25

Cross of Lorraine — PTAP4

1943, Dec. 23   Photo.   Perf. 11
RAC4 PTAP4 10c vio & dl red   .90 1.00
      Never hinged   1.60

Tuberculosis Sanatorium
PTAP5

1944, Dec. 23   Litho.   Perf. 10x9½
RAC5 PTAP5 25c salmon & rose   3.75 3.75
      Never hinged   5.50

Lorraine Cross and Eagle — PTAP6

1945, Dec. 23   Perf. 10
RAC6 PTAP6 25c red & car   1.40 1.25
      Never hinged   1.75

Eagle — PTAP7

1946, Dec. 22
RAC7 PTAP7 25c red & car   .25   .25
      Never hinged   .40

Tuberculosis Sanatorium
PTAP8

1947, Dec. 22   Perf. 11½
RAC8 PTAP8 25c red vio   .25   .25
      Never hinged   .40

Plane over Sanatorium PTAP9

Photogravure; Cross Engraved

1948, Dec. 22 *Perf. 12½*
RAC9 PTAP9 25c ultra & car .30 .25
Never hinged .60

Bell and Lorraine Cross PTAP10

Dove and Flowers PTAP11

1949, Dec. 22
RAC10 PTAP10 25c maroon & red .25 .25
Never hinged .25

1950, Dec. 22
RAC11 PTAP11 25c dk bl & car .30 .30
Never hinged .60

Mother and Child PTAP12

Tobias and Archangel PTAP13

1951, Oct. 1
RAC12 PTAP12 25c brn & car .50 .25
Never hinged .80

1953, Oct. 1
RAC13 PTAP13 25c brn & car 3.50 5.50
6.50

FRANCHISE STAMPS

F1 F2

1869 **Unwmk.** **Litho.** *Imperf.*
S1 F1 blue 52.50 38.00
a. Tête bêche pair 135.00 120.00

The franchise of No. S1 was granted to Diego Castell to use in distributing his publications on Spanish postal history.

1881
S2 F2 black, *buff* 36.00 15.50

The franchise of No. S2 was granted to Antonio Fernandez Duro for his book, "Resena histórico-descriptiva de los sellos correos de Espana."
Reprints of No. S2 have been made on carmine, blue, gray, fawn and yellow paper.

CARLIST STAMPS

From the beginning of the Civil War (April 21, 1872) until separate stamps were issued on July 1, 1873, stamps of France were used on all mail from the provinces under Carlist rule.

King Carlos VII — A1

Tilde on N — A1a

1873, July 1 **Unwmk.** **Litho.** *Imperf.*
X1 A1 1r blue 550.00
X2 A1a 1r blue 450.00 300.00

These stamps were reprinted three times in 1881 and once in 1887. The originals have 23 white lines and dots in the lower right spandrel. They are thin and of even width and spacing. The first reprint has 17 to 20 lines in the spandrel, most of them thick and of irregular width and length. The second and third reprints have 21 very thin lines, the second from the bottom being almost invisible. In the fourth reprint the lower right spandrel is an almost solid spot of color.
Originals of type A1 have the curved line above "ESPANA" broken at the left of the "E." All reprints of this type have the curved line continuous.
The reprints exist in various shades of blue, rose, red, violet and black.

King Carlos VII
A2 A3

A4 A5

1874
X3 A2 1r violet 275.00 275.00
X4 A3 16m rose 5.50 72.50
X5 A4 ½r rose 115.00 100.00

Nos. X3 and X6-X7 were for use in the Basque Provinces and Navarra; No. X4 in Catalonia, and No. X5 in Valencia.
Two types of No. X5, alternating in each sheet.
No. X4 with favor cancellation (lozenge of dots) sells for same price as unused.

1875 **White Paper**
X6 A5 50c green 8.00 82.50
a. 50c blue green 25.00 100.00
b. Bluish paper 50.00
X7 A5 1r brown 8.00 82.50
a. Bluish paper 50.00
Set, #X6-X7, never hinged 24.00

Fake cancellations exist on Nos. X1-X7.

REVOLUTIONARY OVERPRINTS

Issued by the Nationalist (Revolutionary) Forces

Many districts or cities made use of the stamps of the Republic overprinted in various forms. Most such overprinting was authorized by military or postal officials but some were without official sanction. These overprints were applied in patriotic celebration and partly as a protection from the use of unoverprinted stamps seized or stolen by soldiers.

BURGOS AIR POST STAMPS

RAP1

Revenue Stamps Overprinted in Red, Blue or Black

1936, Dec. 1 **Unwmk.** *Perf. 11½*
Control Number on Face of Stamp
7LC1 RAP1 25c gray grn & blk (R) 47.50 47.50
a. Blue overprint 47.50 47.50
7LC2 RAP1 1.50p bl & blk (R) 6.00 6.00
7LC3 RAP1 3p rose & blk (Bl) 6.00 6.00
Nos. 7LC1-7LC3 (3) 59.50 59.50
Set, never hinged 105.00

RAP2 RAP4

Perf. 13½
Blue Control Number on Back
7LC4 RAP2 15c green (R) 3.75 3.75
7LC5 RAP2 25c blue (R) 27.50 27.50
Set, never hinged 45.00

Perf. 11½
Without Control Number
Overprint in Black
7LC6 RAP4 1.50p dk blue 6.50 6.50
7LC7 RAP4 3p carmine 6.50 6.50
Set, never hinged 21.00

RAP5 RAP6

Overprint in Black
Perf. 13½, 11½
7LC8 RAP5 1.20p green 25.00 25.00
Never hinged 37.50

Perf. 14
Control Number on Back
7LC9 RAP6 1.20p green 25.00 25.00
7LC10 RAP6 2.40p green 25.00 25.00
Set #7LC9-7LC10, never hinged 70.00

No. 7LC9 is inscribed "CLASE 8a."

RAP7

1937 **Unwmk.** *Perf. 11½*
Control Number on Back
7LC11 RAP7 25c ultra (R) 225.00 225.00

Stamps of Spain, 1931-36, Overprinted in Red or Black (10p)

Perf. 11, 11½, 11x11½
1937 **Unwmk.**
Overprint 13mm high
7LC12 A100 40c blue 1.10 1.10
a. Ovpt. 15mm high 1.10 1.10
7LC13 A97 50c dark blue 1.40 1.40
a. Ovpt. 15mm high 1.40 1.40
7LC14 A130 50c dark blue 1.75 1.75
a. Ovpt. 15mm high 1.75 1.75
7LC15 A100 60c apple green 2.50 2.50
a. Ovpt. 15mm high 2.50 2.50
7LC16 AP26 2p gray blue 32.50 32.50
a. Ovpt. 15mm high 32.50 32.50
7LC17 A49a 10p brown 82.50 82.50
a. Ovpt. 15mm high 82.50 82.50
Nos. 7LC12-7LC17 (6) 121.75 121.75

Issue dates: Nos. 7LC12-7LC17, 4/1. Nos. 7LC12a-7LC17a, 5/1.

Spain Nos. 576, 578 and 541b overprinted in Blue or Black

Nos. 7LC18, 7LC19

Nos. 7LC20, 7LC21

Perfs as on Basic Stamps
1937, May
7LC18 A127 30c carmine (Bk) 1.40 1.40
7LC19 A127 30c carmine (Bl) .70 .70
7LC20 A129 30c car rose (Bk) 1.40 1.40
7LC21 A129 30c car rose (Bl) .70 .70
7LC22 A107 10p dp brn (Bk) 11.00 11.00
Nos. 7LC18-7LC22 (5) 15.20 15.20

Spain Nos. 539b and 540b, the 1p and 4p values, were prepared with this overprint in January, 1938, but were not issued. Value, each $4.50.

BURGOS ISSUE SPECIAL DELIVERY STAMPS

Pair of Spain No. 546 Overprinted in Black

1936 **Unwmk.** *Perf. 11½x11*
7LE3 A110 20c (10c+10c) em-er 4.50 4.50
Never hinged 9.00
a. Overprint inverted 14.00

Type of Regular Stamp of 1931 Overprinted in Red

7LE4 A95 20c dark violet 10.00 10.00

Type of Delivery Tax Stamp of 1931 Overprinted in Red on Block of 4

Perf. 11½

7LE5 D1 20c black   8.75 8.00
Never hinged   13.50

Same Overprinted in Red on Block of 4

7LE6 D1 20c black   30.00 25.00
Never hinged   50.00

SD1

1936   Unwmk.   Perf. 11½

7LE7 SD1 20c green & blk   7.25 5.50
7LE8 SD1 20c green & red   7.25 5.50
Set, never hinged   25.00

Nos. 7LE7-7LE8 exist with control number on back. Value $42.50 each.

CADIZ ISSUE SEMI-POSTAL STAMPS

Stamps of Spain, 1931-36, Surcharged in Black or Red

1936   Unwmk.   Imperf.

8LB1 A108 1c + 5c blue grn   .25 .25

Perf. 11½x11, 11½

8LB2 A108 2c + 5c orange
                    brn   .25 .25
8LB3 A103 5c + 5c choc (R)   .45 .45
8LB4 A110 10c + 5c green   .45 .45
8LB5 A111 15c + 5c Prus grn
                    (R)   2.75 2.75
8LB6 A95   20c + 5c dk vio
                    (R)   3.25 3.25
8LB7 A104 25c + 5c lake   2.50 2.50
8LB8 A113 30c + 5c rose red   1.40 1.40
8LB9 A100 40c + 5c dk blue
                    (R)   3.25 3.25
8LB10 A97   50c + 5c dk blue
                    (R)   6.50 6.50
Nos. 8LB1-8LB10 (10)   21.05 21.05

CANARY ISLANDS AIR POST STAMPS

Issued for Use via the Lufthansa Service

Stamps of Spain, 1932-34, Surcharged in Blue

1936, Oct. 27   Unwmk.   Imperf.

9LC1 A108 50c on 1c bl grn   27.50 17.50

Perf. 11½x11

9LC2 A108 80c on 2c buff   14.50 6.50
9LC3 A103 1.25p on 5c choc   30.00 17.50
Nos. 9LC1-9LC3 (3)   72.00 41.50
Set, never hinged   82.50

The date July 18, 1936, in the overprints of Nos. 9LC1-9LC22 marks the beginning of the Franco insurrection.

Spain Nos. 542, 543, 528 and 641 Surcharged in Black, Red or Green

The surcharge on Nos. 9LC4 and 9LC6 exists in two types: Type I, 2½-3mm space between numerals and "Cts." Type II, 1½-2mm space between numerals and "Cts."

1936-37   Imperf.

9LC4 A108 50c on 1c bl
                  grn (I)   4.50 2.75
  a.   Overprint type II   11.00 7.75
9LC5 A108 50c on 1c bl
                  grn (R)
                  ('37)   4.50 2.75

Perf. 11, 11½x11

9LC6 A108 80c on 2c buff
                  (I)   2.25 1.60
  a.   Overprint type II   5.50 3.25
9LC7 A108 80c on 2c buff
                  (G) ('37)   3.25 1.60
9LC8 A103 1.25 Pts on 5c
                  choc (R)   6.25 4.50
9LC9 A103 Pts 1.25 on 5c
                  choc (R)
                  ('37)   17.00 11.00
9LC10 A161 1.25p on 5c brn
                  (G) ('37)   3.25 1.40
Nos. 9LC4-9LC10 (7)   41.00 25.60
Set, never hinged   65.00

Issued: Nos. 9LC4, 9LC6, 11/28/36; No. 9LC8, 1/7/37; Nos. 9LC4a, 9LC6a, 9LC9, 2/12/37; Nos. 9LC5, 9LC7, 9LC10, 3/2/37.

Spain Nos. 542, 543 and 641 Surcharged in Blue

The surcharge on Nos. 9LC11-9LC13 exists in two types: Type I, 18mm tall. Type II, 20mm tall.

1937, Mar. 31   Imperf.

9LC11 A108 50c on 1c bl
                  grn (I)   11.00 5.50
  a.   Overprint type II   4.50 2.25

Perf. 11

9LC12 A108 80c on 2c buff
                  (I)   11.00 4.50
  a.   Overprint type II   2.75 1.10
9LC13 A161 1.25p on 5c
                  brown (I)   3.25 1.10
Nos. 9LC11-9LC13 (3)   25.25 11.10
Set, never hinged   40.00

Type II overprints issued 4/17/37.

Stamps of Spain, 1931-1936, Surcharged in Blue or Red (#9LC17, 9LC19)

The surcharge on Nos. 9LC15 and 9LC18 exists in two types: Type I, 2mm space between "+" and denomination. Type II, "+"

abuts surcharged denomination. Other values are Type I.

1937

9LC14 A104 25c + 50c lake   55.00 10.00
9LC15 A162 30c + 80c rose   19.50 7.75
  a.   Overprint type II   19.50 7.75
9LC16 A162 30c + 1.25p
                  rose   25.00 8.25
9LC17 A97   50c + 1.25p dp
                  bl   32.50 11.00
9LC18 A100 60c + 80c ap
                  grn   25.00 8.75
  a.   Overprint type II   27.50 10.00
9LC19 A105 1p + 1.25p bl
                  blk   80.00 22.50
Nos. 9LC14-9LC19 (6)   237.00 68.25
Set, never hinged   350.00

The surcharge represents the airmail rate and the basic stamp the postage rate.
Issued: 9LC15a, 9LC18a, 4/15. 9LC14-9LC19, 5/5.

Spain Nos. 542, 624 and 641 Surcharged in Black

1937, May 25   Unwmk.   Imperf.

9LC20 A108 50c on 1c bl
                  grn   7.75 4.50

Perf. 11½, 11½x11

9LC21 A143 80c on 2c org
                  brn   6.50 2.25
9LC22 A161 1.25p on 5c gray
                  brn   6.50 2.25
Nos. 9LC20-9LC22 (3)   20.75 9.00
Set, never hinged   30.00

Stamps and Type of Spain, 1933-36, Surcharged in Black

1937, July   Perf. 13½x13, 11, 11½

9LC23 A143 50c on 2c
                  org brn   3.50 2.25
9LC24 A126 80c on 2c
                  org brn   300.00 180.00
9LC25 A161 80c on 5c
                  gray brn   3.50 2.25
9LC26 A108 1.25p on 1c bl
                  grn   4.25 2.25
9LC27 A161 2.50p on 10c
                  grn   16.00 8.75

Spain Nos. 647, 650 and 652 Surcharged in Black or Red

Perf. 11

9LC28 A162 30c + 80c rose   3.00 1.40
9LC29 A162 50c + 1.25p dk
                  bl (R)   10.50 5.00
9LC30 A162 1p + 1.25p bl
                  (R)   16.00 8.75
Nos. 9LC23-9LC30 (8)   356.75 210.65
Set, never hinged   550.00

See note after No. 9LC19.

AP1

Perf. 14x13½

1937, July 16   Wmk. 116

Surcharge in Various Colors

9LC31 AP1   50c on 5c ultra
                  (Br)   2.75 2.50
9LC32 AP1   80c on 5c ultra
                  (G)   1.90 1.75
9LC33 AP1   1.25p on 5c ultra
                  (V)   2.25 2.25
Nos. 9LC31-9LC33 (3)   6.90 6.50
Set, never hinged   10.00

Spain Nos. 641, 643 and 640 Surcharged in Green or Orange

1937, Oct. 29   Unwmk.   Perf. 11

9LC34 A161 50c on 5c (G)   9.25 3.75
9LC35 A161 80c on 10c (O)   5.75 2.75
9LC36 A160 1.25p on 2c (G) 10.50 7.25
Nos. 9LC34-9LC36 (3)   25.50 13.75
Set, never hinged   40.00

Spain Nos. 638, 640 and 643 Surcharged in Red, Blue or Violet

1937, Dec. 23   Imperf.

9LC37 A159 50c on 1c (R)   10.50 4.50

Perf. 11, 11x11½

9LC38 A160 80c on 2c (Bl)   4.25 2.75
9LC39 A161 1.25p on 10c (V) 9.25 3.50
Nos. 9LC37-9LC39 (3)   24.00 10.75
Set, never hinged   37.50

Spain Nos. 647, 650 to 652 Surcharged in Black, Green or Brown

1937, Dec. 29

9LC40 A162 30c + 30c rose
                  bl (G)   4.50 3.75
9LC41 A162 50c + 2.50p dk
                  bl (G)   29.00 21.00
9LC42 A162 60c + 2.30p yel
                  (G)   29.00 21.00
9LC43 A162 1p + 5p bl (Br) 35.00 21.00
Nos. 9LC40-9LC43 (4)   97.50 66.75
Set, never hinged   110.00

See note after No. 9LC19.

Stamps of Spain, 1936, Surcharged in Black, Green, Blue or Red

1938, Feb. 2   Perf. 11, 11½, 11x11½

9LC44 A160 50c on 2c brn   5.00 3.75
9LC45 A161 80c on 5c brn
                  (G)   3.75 3.25
9LC46 A162 80c on 30c rose
                  (Bl)   4.50 2.50
9LC47 A161 1.25p on 10c grn
                  (Bl)   4.50 3.25
9LC48 A162 1.25p on 50c dk
                  bl (R)   4.50 2.75
Nos. 9LC44-9LC48 (5)   22.25 15.50
Set, never hinged   27.50

Spain Nos. 645, 646 and 649 Surcharged in Brown, Green or Violet

1938, Feb. 14

9LC51 A162 2.50p on 20c
                  (Br)   50.00 25.00
9LC52 A162 5p on 25c
                  (G)   50.00 25.00
9LC53 A162 10p on 40c (V)   50.00 25.00
Nos. 9LC51-9LC53 (3)   150.00 75.00
Set, never hinged   175.00

MALAGA ISSUE

Stamps of 1920-36 Overprinted in Black or Red

1937 Unwmk. Imperf.

10L1	A47	1c blue green	.25	.25
10L2	A108	1c blue green	.25	.25
10L3	A108	1c lt green (R)	.25	.25

Perf. 13½, 13½x13, 11, 11½x11

10L4	A108	2c orange brn	14.50	14.50
10L5	A126	2c orange brn	.25	.25
10L6	A103	5c chocolate (R)	.25	.25
10L7	A96	10c yellow green	12.00	12.00
10L8	A110	10c emerald	.30	.30
10L9	A111	15c Prus grn (R)	.55	.55
10L10	A97	15c blue grn (R)	.55	.55
10L11	A95	20c dk violet (R)	.50	.50
10L12	A99	25c lake	1.50	1.50
10L13	A104	25c lake	.50	.50
10L14	A113	30c carmine	.50	.50
10L15	A129	30c carmine rose	2.50	2.50
10L16	A100	40c blue (R)	.45	.45
10L17	A97	50c dk blue (R)	2.50	2.50
10L18	A100	60c apple green	1.40	1.40
10L19	A105	1p black (R)	2.75	2.75
	Nos. 10L1-10L19 (19)		41.75	41.75

Stamps of 1932-35 Overprinted in Red or Black in panes of 25, reading down. "8.2.37" and "¡Arriba Espana!" form the lower half of all overprints. The upper half varies.

Overprint a (1st and 2nd rows): "MALAGA AGRADECIDA A TRANQUILLO-BIANCHI"
Overprint b (3rd row): "MALAGA A SU SALVADOR QUEIPO DE LLANO"
Overprint c (4th and 5th rows): "MALAGA A SU CAUDILLO FRANCO"
Values are for vertical strips of 3 containing examples of each overprint type.

1937 Perf. 11½

10L20	A111	15c Prus grn (R)	5.50	5.50
a.		15c single stamp, ovpt. a	.85	.85
b.		15c single stamp, ovpt. b	1.60	1.60
c.		15c single stamp, ovpt. c	.85	.85
10L21	A113	30c rose red (Bk)	5.50	5.50
a.		30c single stamp, ovpt. a	.85	.85
b.		30c single stamp, ovpt. b	1.60	1.60
c.		30c single stamp, ovpt. c	.85	.85
10L22	A97	50c dk blue (R)	8.75	8.75
a.		50c single stamp, ovpt. a	1.60	1.60
b.		50c single stamp, ovpt. b	3.25	3.25
c.		50c single stamp, ovpt. c	1.60	1.60
10L23	A100	60c apple grn (Bk)	11.00	11.00
a.		60c single stamp, ovpt. a	1.60	1.60
b.		60c single stamp, ovpt. b	3.25	3.25
c.		60c single stamp, ovpt. c	1.60	1.60
	Nos. 10L20-10L23 (4)		30.75	30.75

SPECIAL DELIVERY STAMP

Overprinted like Nos. 10L1-10L19 on Type of Special Delivery Stamp of 1934

1937 Perf. 10

10LE1	SD7	20c rose red (Bk)	.45	.45

ORENSE ISSUE

Stamps of 1931-36 Overprinted in Red, Blue or Black

1936 Imperf.

11L1	A108	1c blue grn (Bl)	.45	.45
a.		Red overprint	1.10	1.10

Perf. 11½, 13½x13

11L2	A108	2c org brn (Bk)	3.50	3.25
11L3	A126	2c org brn (R)	.65	.65
11L4	A103	5c brown (R)	1.50	1.50
11L5	A110	10c lt green (Bl)	2.25	2.25
a.		Red overprint	11.00	11.00
11L6	A111	15c Prus grn (R)	3.25	3.25
11L7	A95	20c violet (Bl)	3.25	3.25
11L8	A104	25c lake (Bk)	3.75	3.75
11L9	A113	30c rose red (Bl)	2.75	2.75
a.		Black overprint	5.50	5.50
11L10	A100	40c blue (R)	3.75	3.75
a.		Imperf, pair	50.00	
11L11	A97	50c dark blue (R)	6.50	6.50
11L12	A100	60c apple grn (Bk)	4.75	4.75
a.		Red overprint	17.00	17.00
b.		As "a," Imperf, pair	50.00	
	Nos. 11L1-11L12 (12)		36.35	36.10

SEMI-POSTAL STAMPS

Stamps of Spain, 1931-36, Surcharged in Blue on front and on back of stamp

1936-37 Unwmk. Imperf.

11LB1	A47	1c + 5c bl grn	2.25	2.25
11LB2	A108	1c + 5c green	.40	.40

Perf. 13½x13, 11½, 11½x11

11LB3	A108	2c + 5c org brn	.45	.45
11LB4	A126	2c + 5c red brn	.45	.45
11LB5	A103	5c + 5c choc	.65	.65
11LB6	A110	10c + 5c emer	.65	.65
11LB7	A111	15c + 5c Prus grn	.95	.95
11LB8	A95	20c + 5c violet	.65	.65
11LB9	A104	25c + 5c lake	.95	.95
11LB10	A113	30c + 5c rose red	2.75	2.75
11LB11	A117	30c + 5c rose red	42.50	42.50
11LB12	A100	60c + 5c apple grn	250.00	190.00
	Nos. 11LB1-11LB12 (12)		302.65	242.65

SPECIAL DELIVERY STAMPS

Type of Special Delivery Stamp of 1934 Overprinted "¡VIVA ESPANA!" in Blue or Black

1936 Perf. 10

11LE1	SD7	20c rose red (Bl)	1.90	1.90
11LE2	SD7	20c rose red (Bk)	4.25	4.25

Same with Surcharge "+ 5 cts."

11LE3	SD7	20c + 5c rose red	1.00	1.00

Same Surcharge, Overprint Repeated at Right

11LE4	SD7	20c + 5c rose red	1.10	1.10
	Nos. 11LE1-11LE4 (4)		8.25	8.25

SAN SEBASTIAN ISSUE

For Use in Province of Guipuzcoa

Stamps of 1931-36 Overprinted in Red or Blue

1937 Unwmk. Imperf.

12L1	A108	1c bl grn (R)	.65	.65

Perf. 11, 13½

12L2	A108	2c buff (Bl)	1.00	1.50
12L3	A126	2c org brn (Bl)	2.10	2.10
12L4	A95	5c chocolate (R)	5.00	5.00
12L5	A103	5c chocolate (R)	1.75	1.75
12L6	A110	10c emerald (R)	1.75	1.75
12L7	A111	15c Prus grn (R)	2.10	2.10
12L8	A95	20c dk violet (R)	2.75	2.75
12L9	A104	25c car lake (Bl)	2.75	2.75
12L10	A113	30c rose red (Bl)	2.75	2.75
12L11	A100	40c blue (R)	5.50	5.50
12L12	A97	50c dark blue (R)	5.50	5.50
	Nos. 12L1-12L12 (12)		33.60	34.10

SANTA CRUZ DE TENERIFE ISSUE

Stamps of Spain, 1931-36 Overprinted in Black or Red

1936 Unwmk. Imperf.

13L1	A108	1c bl grn (R)	.75	.75
13L2	A108	1c bl grn (Bk)	2.75	2.75

Perf. 11, 13½

13L3	A108	2c buff (Bk)	5.50	5.50
13L4	A126	2c org brn (Bk)	.95	.95
13L5	A103	5c choc (R)	3.00	3.00
13L6	A110	10c green (R)	3.00	3.00
13L7	A104	25c lake (Bk)	11.00	11.00
13L8	A100	40c dk blue (R)	3.25	3.25
13L9	A107	10p dp brn (Bk)	275.00	225.00
	Nos. 13L1-13L9 (9)		305.20	255.20

Many forgeries of #13L9 exist.

SEVILLE ISSUE

Stamps of Spain, 1931-36, Overprinted in Black or Red

1936 Imperf.

14L1	A108	1c blue grn (Bk)	.30	.30

Perf. 13½x13, 11, 11½x11

14L2	A126	2c org brn (Bk)	.35	.35
14L3	A103	5c chocolate (R)	.45	.45
14L4	A110	10c emerald (Bk)	.55	.55
14L5	A111	15c Prus grn (R)	1.40	1.40
14L6	A95	20c violet (R)	1.40	1.40
14L7	A104	25c lake (Bk)	1.40	1.40
14L8	A113	30c carmine (Bk)	1.40	1.40
14L9	A128	30c rose red (Bk)	8.25	8.25
14L10	A100	40c blue (R)	5.50	5.50
14L11	A97	50c dk blue (R)	5.50	5.50
14L12	A100	60c apple grn (Bk)	6.75	6.75
	Nos. 14L1-14L12 (12)		33.25	33.25

Stamps of Spain, 1931-36, Handstamped in Black

Imperf

14L13	A108	1c blue grn	.30	.30

Perf. 13½x13, 11, 11x11½, 11½x11

14L14	A126	2c orange brn	.45	.45
14L15	A103	5c chocolate	.45	.45
14L16	A110	10c emerald	.45	.45
14L17	A111	15c Prus green	.55	.55
14L18	A95	20c violet	.55	.55
14L19	A104	25c lake	.55	.55
14L20	A113	30c carmine	.55	.55
14L21	A128	30c rose red	3.00	3.00
14L22	A100	40c blue	1.10	1.10
14L23	A97	50c dk blue	3.00	3.00
14L24	A100	60c apple grn	1.00	1.00
14L25	A105	1p black	3.00	3.00
14L26	AP26	2p gray blue	13.50	13.50
14L27	A106	4p magenta	7.25	7.25
14L28	A107	10p deep brown	10.50	10.50
	Nos. 14L13-14L28,14LE1 (17)		47.95	47.95

The date "Julio-1936" in the overprints of Nos. 14L1-14L28 and 14LE1 marks the beginning of the Franco insurrection.

SPECIAL DELIVERY STAMP

Overprinted like Nos. 14L13-14L25 on Type of Special Delivery Stamp of 1934

1936 Perf. 10

14LE1	SD7	20c rose red	1.75	1.75

SPANISH GUINEA

'spa-nish 'gi-nē

LOCATION — In western Africa, bordering on the Gulf of Guinea
GOVT. — Spanish Colony
AREA — 10,852 sq. mi.
POP. — 212,000 (est. 1957)
CAPITAL — Santa Isabel

Spanish Guinea 1-84 were issued for and used only in the continental area later called Rio Muni. From 1909 to 1960, Spanish Guinea also included Fernando Po, Elobey, Annobon and Corisco.

Fernando Po and Rio Muni united in 1968 to become the Republic of Equatorial Guinea.

100 Centimos = 1 Peseta

> Catalogue values for unused stamps in this country are for Never Hinged items, beginning with Scott 319 in the regular postage section, Scott B13 in the semi-postal section, and Scott C13 in the airpost section.

King Alfonso XIII
A1   A2

1902   **Unwmk.**   **Typo.**   *Perf. 14*
Blue Control Numbers on Back

1	A1	5c dark green	12.50	6.25
2	A1	10c indigo	12.50	6.25
3	A1	25c claret	92.50	47.50
4	A1	50c deep brown	92.50	47.50
5	A1	75c violet	92.50	47.50
6	A1	1p carmine rose	140.00	47.50
7	A1	2p olive green	180.00	100.00
8	A1	5p dull red	275.00	175.00
		Nos. 1-8 (8)	897.50	477.50
		Set, never hinged	1,800.	

Exists imperf, value set $2,000.

Revenue Stamps Surcharged

1903   *Imperf.*
Blue or Black Control Numbers on Back

8A		10c on 25c blk (R)	550.00	240.00
8B		10c on 50c org (Bl)	140.00	40.00
8D		10c on 1p 25c car (Bk)	750.00	400.00
8F		10c on 2p cl (Bk)	800.00	600.00
g.		Blue surcharge	1,450.	800.00
8H		10c on 2p 50c red brn (Bl)	1,100.	725.00
8J		10c on 5p ol blk (R)	1,500.	525.00

Nos. 8A-8J are surcharged on stamps inscribed "Posesiones Espanolas de Africa Occidental" and "1903", with arms at left.
This surcharge was also applied to revenue stamps of 10, 15, 25, 50, 75 and 100 pesetas and in other colors.
See Nos. 98-101C.

1903   **Typo.**   *Perf. 14*
Blue Control Numbers on Back

9	A2	¼c black	1.50	.85
10	A2	½c blue green	1.50	.85
11	A2	1c claret	1.50	.70
12	A2	2c dark olive	1.50	.70
13	A2	3c dark brown	1.50	.70
14	A2	4c vermilion	1.50	.70
15	A2	5c black brown	1.50	.70
16	A2	10c red brown	2.50	.85
17	A2	15c dark blue	8.50	6.25
18	A2	25c orange buff	8.50	6.25

19	A2	50c carmine lake	16.00	14.00
20	A2	75c violet	21.00	14.00
21	A2	1p blue green	35.00	22.00
22	A2	2p dark green	35.00	22.00
23	A2	3p scarlet	95.00	28.50
24	A2	4p dull blue	110.00	50.00
25	A2	5p dark violet	210.00	72.50
26	A2	10p carmine rose	300.00	100.00
		Nos. 9-26 (18)	852.00	341.55
		Set, never hinged	1,500.	

1905

Same, Dated "1905"
Blue Control Numbers on Back

27	A2	1c black	.30	.25
28	A2	2c blue grn	.30	.25
29	A2	3c claret	.30	.25
30	A2	4c bronze grn	.30	.25
31	A2	5c dark brown	.30	.25
32	A2	10c red	1.60	.85
33	A2	15c black brown	4.50	2.75
34	A2	25c chocolate	4.50	2.75
35	A2	50c dark blue	9.75	6.25
36	A2	75c orange buff	11.00	6.25
37	A2	1p carmine rose	11.00	6.25
38	A2	2p violet	26.00	13.00
39	A2	3p blue green	67.50	27.50
40	A2	4p dark green	67.50	39.00
40A	A2	5p vermilion	110.00	42.00
41	A2	10p dull blue	200.00	130.00
		Nos. 27-41 (16)	514.85	277.85
		Set, never hinged	900.00	

Stamps of Elobey, 1905, Overprinted in Violet or Blue

1906

42	A1	1c rose	4.00	2.25
43	A1	2c deep violet	4.00	2.25
44	A1	3c black	4.00	2.25
45	A1	4c orange red	4.00	2.25
46	A1	5c deep green	4.00	2.25
47	A1	10c blue green	9.25	5.25
48	A1	15c violet	16.00	9.00
49	A1	25c rose lake	16.00	9.00
50	A1	50c orange buff	22.50	13.00
51	A1	75c dark blue	26.00	15.00
52	A1	1p red brown	47.50	25.00
53	A1	2p black brown	67.50	37.50
54	A1	3p vermilion	97.50	55.00
55	A1	4p dark brown	475.00	250.00
56	A1	5p bronze green	475.00	250.00
57	A1	10p claret	2,000.	1,100.
		Nos. 42-54 (13)	322.25	180.00

King Alfonso XIII
A3   A4

1907   **Typo.**
Blue Control Numbers on Back

58	A3	1c dark green	.75	.25
59	A3	2c dull blue	.75	.25
60	A3	3c violet	.75	.25
61	A3	4c yellow grn	.75	.25
62	A3	5c carmine lake	.75	.25
63	A3	10c orange	4.00	1.25
64	A3	15c brown	3.00	.80
65	A3	25c dark blue	3.00	.80
66	A3	50c black brown	3.00	.80
67	A3	75c blue green	3.00	.80
68	A3	1p red	6.00	1.40
69	A3	2p dark brown	9.00	6.25
70	A3	3p olive gray	9.00	6.25
71	A3	4p maroon	13.00	6.25
72	A3	5p green	13.50	9.50
73	A3	10p red violet	20.00	12.00
		Nos. 58-73 (16)	90.25	47.35
		Set, never hinged	210.00	

Issue of 1907
Surcharged in Black or Red

1908-09

74	A3	05c on 1c dk grn (R)	3.00	1.50
75	A3	05c on 2c blue (R)	3.00	1.50
76	A3	05c on 3c violet	3.00	1.50
77	A3	05c on 4c yel grn	3.00	1.50

78	A3	05c on 10c orange	3.00	1.50
a.		Red surcharge	5.25	2.75
84	A3	15c on 10c orange	14.00	9.00
		Nos. 74-84 (6)	29.00	16.50

Many stamps of this issue are found with the surcharge inverted, sideways, double and in both black and red. Other stamps of the 1907 issue are known with this surcharge but are not believed to have been put in use. Value, each $17.

1909   **Typo.**   *Perf. 14½*
Blue Control Numbers on Back

85	A4	1c orange brown	.25	.25
86	A4	2c rose	.25	.25
87	A4	5c dark green	1.40	.25
88	A4	10c vermilion	.40	.25
89	A4	15c dark brown	.40	.25
90	A4	20c violet	.65	.35
91	A4	25c dull blue	.65	.35
92	A4	30c chocolate	.85	.30
93	A4	40c lake	.50	.30
94	A4	50c dark violet	.50	.30
95	A4	1p blue green	13.50	7.00
96	A4	4p orange	3.50	4.25
97	A4	10p red	3.50	4.25
		Nos. 85-97 (13)	26.35	18.35
		Set, never hinged	50.00	

For overprints see Nos. 102-114.

Revenue Stamps Surcharged like Nos. 8A-8J in Black

1909   *Imperf.*
With or Without Control Numbers on Back

98	10c on 50c bl grn	87.50	57.50
a.	Red or violet surcharge	110.00	80.00
99	10c on 1p 25c violet	110.00	80.00
100	10c on 2p dk brn	600.00	350.00
100A	10c on 5p dk vio	600.00	350.00
101	10c on 25p red brn	800.00	575.00
101A	10c on 50p brn lil	2,750.	1,600.
101B	10c on 75p carmine	2,750.	1,600.
101C	10c on 100p orange	2,750.	1,600.

Nos. 98-101C are surcharged on undated stamps, arms centered. Stamps inscribed: "Territorios Espanoles del Africa Occidental." Basic revenue stamps similar to Rio de Oro type A3.

Stamps of 1909 Overprinted with Handstamp in Black, Blue, Green or Red

1911

102	A4	1c orange brn (Bl)	.40	.35
103	A4	2c rose (G)	.40	.35
104	A4	5c dk green (R)	2.00	.35
105	A4	10c vermilion	1.15	.45
106	A4	15c dk brown (R)	2.00	.75
107	A4	20c violet	2.50	1.15
108	A4	25c dull blue (R)	3.00	2.40
109	A4	30c choc (Bl)	3.75	3.50
110	A4	40c lake (Bl)	4.00	3.50
111	A4	50c dark violet	6.75	5.00
112	A4	1p blue grn (R)	55.00	40.00
113	A4	4p orange (R)	29.00	23.00
114	A4	10p red (G)	37.50	40.00
		Nos. 102-114 (13)	147.45	120.80
		Set, never hinged	300.00	

The date "1911" is missing from the overprint on the first stamp in each row, or ten times in each sheet of 100 stamps. This variety occurs on all stamps of the series. Value, set $550.

King Alfonso XIII
A5   A6

1912   **Typo.**   *Perf. 13½*
Blue Control Numbers on Back

115	A5	1c black	.30	.30
116	A5	2c dark brown	.30	.30
117	A5	5c deep green	.30	.30
118	A5	10c red	.30	.30
119	A5	15c claret	.30	.30
120	A5	20c red	.30	.30
121	A5	25c dull blue	.30	.30
122	A5	30c lake	3.50	2.00
123	A5	40c car rose	2.10	1.00
124	A5	50c brown org	2.00	.35

125	A5	1p dark violet	2.25	1.25
126	A5	4p lilac	5.00	2.50
127	A5	10p blue green	10.50	9.50
		Nos. 115-127 (13)	27.45	18.70
		Set, never hinged	42.50	

For overprints and surcharges see Nos. 141-157.

1914   *Perf. 13*
Blue Control Numbers on Back

128	A6	1c dull violet	.35	.30
129	A6	2c car rose	.35	.30
130	A6	5c deep green	.35	.30
131	A6	10c vermilion	.35	.30
132	A6	15c dark violet	.35	.30
133	A6	20c dark brown	1.05	.55
134	A6	25c dark blue	.45	.35
135	A6	30c brown orange	1.60	.55
136	A6	40c blue green	1.60	.55
137	A6	50c dp claret	.75	.30
138	A6	1p vermilion	2.00	2.25
139	A6	4p maroon	7.00	4.50
140	A6	10p olive black	7.75	8.50
		Nos. 128-140 (13)	23.95	19.10
		Set, never hinged	40.00	

Stamps with these or similar overprints are unauthorized and fraudulent.

Stamps of 1912 Overprinted

1917   *Perf. 13½*

141	A5	1c black	125.00	85.00
142	A5	2c dark brown	125.00	85.00
143	A5	5c deep green	.40	.35
144	A5	10c red	.40	.35
145	A5	15c claret	.40	.35
146	A5	20c red	.40	.35
147	A5	25c dull blue	.40	.35
148	A5	30c lake	.40	.35
149	A5	40c carmine rose	.75	.40
150	A5	50c brown orange	.40	.35
151	A5	1p dark violet	.75	.40
152	A5	4p lilac	8.25	4.00
153	A5	10p blue green	8.25	4.00
		Nos. 141-153 (13)	270.80	181.25
		Set, never hinged	370.00	

Nos. 143-153 exist with overprint double, inverted, in dark blue, reading "9117" and in pairs one without overprint.

Stamps of 1917 Surcharged

1918

154	A5	5c on 40c car rose	36.00	14.50
155	A5	10c on 4p lilac	36.00	14.50
156	A5	15c on 20c red	65.00	25.00
157	A5	25c on 10p bl grn	65.00	25.00
a.		"52" for "25"	500.00	425.00
		Nos. 154-157 (4)	202.00	79.00
		Set, never hinged	345.00	

The varieties "Gents" and "Censt" occur on Nos. 154-157. Values 50 percent more.

King Alfonso XIII
A7   A8

1919   Typo.   Perf. 13
Blue Control Numbers on Back

158	A7	1c lilac	1.00	.30
159	A7	2c rose	1.00	.30
160	A7	5c vermilion	1.00	.30
161	A7	10c violet	1.75	.30
162	A7	15c brown	1.75	.55
163	A7	20c blue	1.75	.80
164	A7	25c green	1.75	.80
a.		25c blue (error)	62.50	
165	A7	30c orange	2.25	.80
166	A7	40c orange	4.50	.80
167	A7	50c red	4.50	.80
168	A7	1p light green	4.50	1.50
169	A7	4p claret	10.00	10.50
170	A7	10p brown	20.00	19.00
		Nos. 158-170 (13)	55.75	38.00
		Set, never hinged	82.50	

1920
Blue Control Numbers on Back

171	A8	1c brown	.35	.30
172	A8	2c dull rose	.35	.30
173	A8	5c gray green	.35	.30
174	A8	10c dull rose	.35	.30
175	A8	15c orange	.35	.30
176	A8	20c yellow	.35	.35
177	A8	25c dull blue	1.15	.35
178	A8	30c greenish blue	42.50	25.00
179	A8	40c lt brown	2.00	.35
180	A8	50c lilac	2.40	.35
181	A8	1p light red	2.40	.35
182	A8	4p bright rose	6.50	6.25
183	A8	10p gray lilac	10.00	12.50
		Nos. 171-183 (13)	69.05	47.00
		Set, never hinged	110.00	

A9

Nipa House — A10

1922
Blue Control Numbers on Back

184	A9	1c dark brown	.70	.25
185	A9	2c claret	.70	.25
186	A9	5c blue green	.70	.25
187	A9	10c pale red	4.75	1.15
188	A9	15c orange	.70	.30
189	A9	20c lilac	3.00	1.05
190	A9	25c dark blue	4.75	1.40
191	A9	30c violet	4.50	1.50
192	A9	40c turq blue	3.25	.75
193	A9	50c deep rose	3.25	.75
194	A9	1p myrtle green	3.25	.75
195	A9	4p red brown	13.00	13.00
196	A9	10p yellow	26.00	25.00
		Nos. 184-196 (13)	68.55	46.40
		Set, never hinged	120.00	

1924
Blue Control Numbers on Back

197	A10	5c choc & bl	.25	.25
198	A10	10c gray grn & bl	.25	.25
199	A10	15c rose & blk	.25	.25
200	A10	20c violet & blk	.25	.25
201	A10	25c org red & blk	.40	.25
202	A10	30c orange & blk	.40	.25
203	A10	40c dl bl & blk	.40	.25
204	A10	50c claret & blk	.40	.25
205	A10	60c red brn & blk	.40	.25
206	A10	1p dk vio & blk	1.60	.25
a.		Center inverted	850.00	140.00
207	A10	4p brt bl & blk	3.75	2.25
208	A10	10p bl grn & blk	8.75	4.50
		Nos. 197-208 (12)	17.10	9.25
		Set, never hinged	25.00	

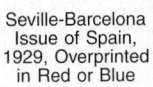

Seville-Barcelona Issue of Spain, 1929, Overprinted in Red or Blue

1929   Perf. 11

209	A52	5c rose lake	.35	.40
210	A53	10c green (R)	.35	.40
211	A50	15c Prus bl (R)	.35	.40
212	A51	20c purple (R)	.35	.40
213	A50	25c brt rose	.35	.40
214	A50	30c black brn	.35	.40
215	A53	40c dk blue (R)	.70	.65
216	A51	50c dp orange	.70	.65
217	A52	1p blue blk (R)	11.50	6.00
218	A53	4p deep rose	22.00	11.50
219	A53	10p brown	42.50	23.00
		Nos. 209-219 (11)	79.50	44.20
		Set, never hinged	160.00	

Porter A11

Drummers A12

King Alfonso XIII and Queen Victoria — A13

1931   Engr.   Perf. 14

220	A11	1c blue green	.30	.25
221	A11	2c red brown	.30	.25

Blue Control Numbers on Back

222	A11	5c brown black	.30	.25
223	A11	10c light green	.30	.25
224	A11	15c dark green	.30	.25
225	A11	20c deep violet	.30	.25
226	A12	25c carmine	.30	.25
227	A12	30c lake	.40	.25
228	A12	40c dark blue	.90	.65
229	A12	50c red orange	1.75	1.25
230	A12	80c blue violet	3.25	1.90
231	A13	1p black	5.75	5.25
232	A13	4p violet rose	37.50	20.00
233	A13	5p dark brown	17.50	14.00
		Nos. 220-233 (14)	69.15	45.05
		Set, never hinged	150.00	

Exist imperf. Value for set, $300.
See Nos. 262-271. For overprints and surcharges see Nos. 234-277, 282-283, 298.

Stamps of 1931 Overprinted

1931

234	A11	1c blue green	.30	.30
235	A11	2c red brown	.30	.30
236	A11	5c brown black	.30	.30
237	A11	10c light green	.30	.30
238	A11	15c dark green	.30	.30
239	A11	20c deep violet	.30	.30
240	A12	25c carmine	.30	.30
241	A12	30c lake	.30	.30
242	A12	40c dark blue	2.25	.65
243	A12	50c red orange	14.50	7.75
244	A13	80c blue violet	4.50	2.50
245	A13	1p black	14.50	5.00
246	A13	4p violet rose	25.00	14.50
247	A13	5p dark brown	25.00	14.50
		Nos. 234-247 (14)	88.15	47.30
		Set, never hinged	160.00	

Stamps of 1931 Overprinted in Red or Blue

1933

248	A11	1c blue grn (R)	.30	.25
249	A11	2c red brown (Bl)	.30	.25
250	A11	5c brown blk (R)	.30	.25
251	A11	10c lt green (Bl)	.30	.25
252	A11	15c dk green (R)	.30	.25
253	A11	20c dp violet (R)	.30	.25
254	A12	25c carmine (Bl)	.30	.25
255	A12	30c lake (Bl)	.30	.25
256	A12	40c dk blue (R)	3.50	.95
257	A12	50c red orange (Bl)	22.00	4.75
258	A13	80c blue vio (R)	7.25	4.25
259	A13	1p black (R)	25.00	4.50
260	A13	4p violet rose (Bl)	47.50	20.00
261	A13	5p dk brown (Bl)	47.50	20.00
		Nos. 248-261 (14)	155.15	56.45
		Set, never hinged	250.00	

Types of 1931
Without Control Number
1934-35   Engr.   Perf. 10

262	A11	1c blue green ('35)	11.50	.25
263	A11	2c red brown ('35)	11.50	.25
264	A11	5c black brn	2.25	.25
265	A11	10c light green	2.25	.25
266	A11	15c dark green	3.50	.25
267	A12	30c rose red	4.50	.35
268	A12	50c indigo ('35)	9.75	1.10
		Nos. 262-268 (7)	45.25	2.70
		Set, never hinged	62.50	

Types of 1931
1941   Litho.   Unwmk.

269	A11	5c olive gray	2.40	.25
270	A11	20c violet	2.40	.25
271	A12	40c gray green	.95	.25
		Nos. 269-271 (3)	5.75	.75
		Set, never hinged	7.00	

Stamps of 1931-33 Surcharged in Black

1936-37   Perf. 10, 14

272	A12	30c on 40c (#228)	5.50	3.50
273	A12	30c on 40c (#242)	22.00	5.25
274	A12	30c on 40c (#256)	80.00	25.00
		Nos. 272-274 (3)	107.50	33.75
		Set, never hinged	150.00	

The surcharge on Nos. 272-274 exists in two types, differing in the "3" which is scarcer in italic.

No. 268 Surcharged in Red

275	A12	1p on 50c indigo	30.00	
276	A12	4p on 50c indigo	90.00	
277	A12	5p on 50c indigo	55.00	
		Nos. 275-277 (3)	175.00	

Nos. 275-277 were not issued.

Stamps of Spain, 1936, Overprinted in Black or Carmine

1938   Perf. 11

278	A161	10c gray green	1.75	.55
279	A162	15c gray black (C)	1.75	.55
280	A162	20c dark violet	4.25	1.75
281	A162	25c brown lake	4.25	1.75
		Nos. 278-281 (4)	12.00	4.60
		Set, never hinged	16.00	

Nos. 278-281 exist imperf. Value $175.

Stamps of 1931-33, Surcharged in Black

1939

282	A13	40c on 80c (#244)	12.00	8.00
283	A13	40c on 80c (#258)	12.00	5.00
		Set, never hinged	32.50	

A14   A15

Revenue Stamps Surcharged in Black
1940-41   Perf. 11½

284	A14	5c on 35c pale grn	6.00	2.10
285	A14	25c on 60c org brn	6.25	2.50
286	A14	50c on 75c blk brn	8.75	2.75
		Nos. 284-286 (3)	21.00	7.35

Red Surcharge

287	A15	10c on 75c blk brn	8.75	2.75
288	A15	15c on 1.50p lt vio	6.25	2.50
289	A15	25c on 60c org brn	11.00	3.50
		Nos. 287-289 (3)	26.00	8.75

A16   A17

Black or Carmine Surcharge

290	A16	1p on 17p deep red	52.50	15.50
291	A17	1p on 40p yel grn (C)	12.50	4.00

See No. C1

A18   A19

Black Surcharge
Perf. 11, 13x12½

292	A18	5c carmine	5.25	1.40
293	A19	1p yellow	87.50	32.50

A20   General Francisco Franco — A21

Black Surcharge

294	A20	1p on 15c gray grn	9.50	3.25

1940   Perf. 11½, 13½

295	A21	5c olive brown	3.75	.50
296	A21	40c blue	5.50	.50
297	A21	50c brown	6.75	.50
a.		50c greenish gray	40.00	9.00
		Nos. 295-297 (3)	16.00	1.50
		Set, never hinged	45.00	

Nos. 295-297 exist imperf. Values $50.

No. 270 Surcharged in Black

1942

298	A11	3p on 20c vio	10.00	1.40

Spain, Nos. 702 and 704 Overprinted in Carmine or Black

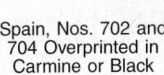

1942　　　　　　　　　**Perf. 9½x10½**
299 A166 1p gray blk (C)　　.55　.25
300 A166 4p dl rose (Bk)　　7.50　.75

The overprint on No. 299 exists in two types: Spacing between lines of 2mm, and spacing of 3mm. The 3mm spacing sells for about twice as much.

For surcharges and overprint see #302-303, C3.

Spain, No. 703
Overprinted in
Carmine

1943
301 A166 2p dull brown　　.85　.25

Nos. 299 and 301
Surcharged in Green

Habilitado
para quince
cts.

1949　　**Unwmk.**　　**Perf. 9½x10½**
302 A166 5c (cinco) on 1p gray
　　blk　　　　　　　　.25　.25
303 A166 15c on 2p dl brn　　.25　.25

The two types of No. 299, described in footnote, also exist on No. 302.

Men Poling
Canoe
A22

1949, Oct. 9　Litho.　**Perf. 12½x13**
304 A22 4p dk vio　　　　.85　.65
　　Never hinged　　　　1.25

UPU, 75th anniversary.

San Carlos
Bay — A23

Designs: Various Views

1949-50　　　　　　　**Perf. 12½x13**
305 A23　2c brown　　　　.25　.25
306 A23　5c rose vio　　　.25　.25
307 A23　10c Prussian bl　.25　.25
308 A23　15c dp ol gray　.25　.25
309 A23　25c red brown　.25　.25
309A A23　30c brt yel ('50)　.25　.25
310 A23　40c olive gray　.30　.25
311 A23　45c rose lake　.30　.25
312 A23　50c brn orange　.30　.25
312A A23　75c ultra ('50)　.30　.25
313 A23　90c dl bl grn　.35　.25
314 A23　1p gray　　　　1.10　.25
315 A23　1.35p violet　　4.00　1.10
316 A23　2p sepia　　　11.00　2.25
317 A23　5p lilac rose　14.00　5.75
318 A23　10p light brn　60.00　23.00
　　Nos. 305-318 (16)　93.15　35.10
　　Set, never hinged　165.00

Catalogue values for unused
stamps in this section, from this
point to the end of the section, are
for Never Hinged items.

Surveyor
A24

1951, Dec. 5
319 A24 50c orange　　　.40　.25
320 A24 5p indigo　　　7.50　1.25

Intl. Conference of West Africans, 1951.

Drummer
A25

1952, Mar. 10
321 A25　5c red brown　　.25　.25
322 A25　50c olive gray　.40　.25
323 A25　5p violet　　　2.40　.25
　　Nos. 321-323 (3)　　3.05　.75

Musician
A26

Design: 60c, Musician facing right.

1953, July 1　　　　　**Photo.**
324 A26 15c sepia　　　.25　.25
325 A26 60c brown　　　.30　.25
　　Nos. 324-325,B25-B26 (4)　1.10　1.00

Woman and
Dove
A27

Drummer
A28

1953, Sept. 5　　　　**Perf. 13x12½**
326 A27　5c orange　　　.25　.25
327 A27　10c brt lilac rose　.25　.25
328 A27　60c brown　　　.25　.25
329 A28　1p dull purple　1.60　.35
330 A28　1.90p greenish blk　2.50　.35
　　Nos. 326-330 (5)　　4.85　1.35

Tragocephala
Nobilis — A29

Butterfly: 60c, Papilio antimachus.

1953, Nov. 23
331 A29 15c dark green　.35　.25
332 A29 60c brown　　　.60　.25
　　Nos. 331-332,B27-B28 (4)　1.35　1.00

Colonial Stamp Day.

Hunter
A30

Design: 60c, Hunter and elephant.

1954, June 10　　　　**Perf. 12½x13**
333 A30 15c dark gray green　.35　.25
334 A30 60c dark brown　.50　.25
　　Nos. 333-334,B29-B30 (4)　1.40　1.00

Swimming
Turtle
A31

1954, Nov. 23
335 A31 15c shown　　　.30　.25
336 A31 60c Shark　　　.75　.25
　　Nos. 335-336,B31-B32 (4)　1.65　1.00

Colonial Stamp Day.

Manuel
Iradier y
Bulfy, Birth
Cent. (in
1954)
A32

1955, Jan. 18
337 A32 60c orange brown　.50　.25
338 A32 1p dark violet　3.25　.30

Priest Saying
Mass — A33

1955, June 1　Photo.　Perf. 13x12½
339 A33 50c olive gray　.30　.25
　　Nos. 339,B33-B34 (3)　.95　.75

Centenary of the establishment of an Apostolic Prefecture at Fernando Po.

Palace of
Pardo
A34

1955, July 18　　　　**Perf. 12½x13**
340 A34　5c ol brn　　　.30　.25
341 A34　15c brn lake　.30　.25
342 A34　80c Prus grn　.35　.25
　　Nos. 340-342 (3)　　.95　.75

Treaty of Pardo, 1778.

Red-eared
Guenons — A35

Orchid — A36

1955, Nov. 23　　　　**Perf. 13x12½**
343 A35 70c gray grn & bl　.60　.25
　　Nos. 343,B35-B36 (3)　1.15　.75

Colonial Stamp Day.

1956, June 1　　　　　**Unwmk.**

Flower: 50c, Strophantus Kombe.

344 A36 20c bluish green　.25　.25
345 A36 50c brown　　　.30　.25
　　Nos. 344-345,B37-B38 (4)　1.10　1.00

See Nos. 360-361, B53-B54.

Arms of Santa
Isabel — A37

African Gray
Parrot — A38

1956, Nov. 23　　　　**Perf. 13x12½**
346 A37 70c light olive green　.25　.25
　　Nos. 346,B39-B40 (3)　.75　.75

Colonial Stamp Day.

1957, June 1　　　　　**Photo.**
347 A38 70c olive green　.40　.25
　　Nos. 347,B41-B42 (3)　.95　.75

Elephants
A39

Design: 70c, Elephant, vert.

Perf. 12½x13, 13x12½
1957, Nov. 23
348 A39 20c blue green　.35　.25
349 A39 70c emerald　　.45　.25
　　Nos. 348-349,B43-B44 (4)　1.45　1.00

Colonial Stamp Day.

Boxing
A40

Basketball
A41

Preaching
Missionary
A42

Various Sports: 15c, 2.30p, Jumping. 80c, 3p, Runner at finish line.

1958, Apr. 10　**Photo.**　**Unwmk.**
350 A40　5c violet brn　.25　.25
351 A41　10c orange brn　.25　.25
352 A40　15c brown　　.25　.25
353 A41　80c green　　.25　.25
354 A40　1p orange red　.25　.25
355 A41　2p rose lilac　.35　.25
356 A40　2.30p dl violet　.40　.25
357 A41　3p brt blue　　.45　.25
　　Nos. 350-357 (8)　2.15　2.00

1958, June 1　　　　**Perf. 13x12½**

Design: 70c, Crucifix and missal.

358 A42 20c blue green　.30　.25
359 A42 70c green　　　.40　.25
　　Nos. 358-359,B48-B49 (4)　1.25　1.00

Catholic missions in Spanish Guinea, 75th anniv.

Type of 1956 Inscribed: "Pro-Infancia 1959"

1959, June 1　　　　**Perf. 13x12½**
360 A36 20c Castor bean　.25　.25
361 A36 70c Digitalis　　.30　.25
　　Nos. 360-361,B53-B54 (4)　1.10　1.00

Promoting child welfare.

Stamps of Spanish Guinea were succeeded by those of Fernando Po and Rio Muni in 1960.

SEMI-POSTAL STAMPS

Red Cross Issue

Types of Semi-Postal Stamps of Spain, 1926, Ovptd. in Black or Blue

1926	**Unwmk.**	**Perf. 12½, 13**	
B1	SP3	5c black brown	11.00 7.00
B2	SP4	10c dark green	11.00 7.00
B3	SP1	15c dark vio (Bl)	2.50 1.75
B4	SP4	20c violet brown	2.50 1.75
B5	SP5	25c deep carmine	2.50 1.75
B6	SP3	30c olive green	2.50 1.75
B7	SP3	40c ultra	.55 .25
B8	SP2	50c red brown	.55 .25
B9	SP6	60c myrtle green	.55 .25
B10	SP4	1p vermilion	.55 .25
B11	SP3	4p bister	2.25 1.50
B12	SP5	10p light violet	7.50 5.00
		Nos. B1-B12 (12)	43.95 28.50
		Set, never hinged	60.00

See Spain No. B6a for No. B4 without overprint. For surcharges see Spain Nos. B70-B71.

Catalogue values for unused stamps in this section, from this point to the end of the section, are for Never Hinged items.

Allegory — SP1   Leopard — SP2

1950, Dec. 1		**Photo.**	**Perf. 13x12½**
B13	SP1	50c + 10c ultra	.35 .30
B14	SP2	1p + 25c dk grn	12.00 4.00
B15	SP1	6.50p + 1.65p dp org	3.00 2.00
		Nos. B13-B15 (3)	15.35 6.30

The surtax was to help the native population.

1951, Nov. 23			
B16	SP2	5c + 5c brown	.25 .25
B17	SP2	10c + 5c red orange	.25 .25
B18	SP2	60c + 15c olive brn	.35 .25
		Nos. B16-B18 (3)	.85 .75

Colonial Stamp Day, Nov. 23.

Love Lily — SP3   Brown-cheeked Hornbill — SP4

1952, June 1			
B19	SP3	5c + 5c brown	.25 .25
B20	SP3	50c + 10c gray	.25 .25
B21	SP3	2p + 30c blue	1.50 1.00
		Nos. B19-B21 (3)	2.00 1.50

The surtax was to help the native population.

1952, Nov. 23			**Perf. 12½**
B22	SP4	5c + 5c brown	.25 .25
B23	SP4	10c + 5c brown car	.25 .25
B24	SP4	60c + 15c dk green	.45 .30
		Nos. B22-B24 (3)	.95 .80

Colonial Stamp Day, Nov. 23.

Music Type of Regular Issue

1953, July 1			**Perf. 12½x13**
B25	A26	5c + 5c like #324	.25 .25
B26	A26	10c + 5c like #325	.30 .25

The surtax was to help the native population.

Insect Type of Regular Issue

1953, Nov. 23			**Perf. 13x12½**
B27	A29	5c + 5c like #331	.25 .25
B28	A29	10c + 5c like #332	.30 .25

Hunter Type of Regular Issue

1954, June 10			**Perf. 12½x13**
B29	A30	5c + 5c like #333	.25 .25
B30	A30	10c + 5c like #334	.30 .25

The surtax was to help the native population.

Type of Regular Issue

1954, Nov. 23			
B31	A31	5c + 5c like #335	.30 .25
B32	A31	10c + 5c like #336	.30 .25

Type of Regular Issue and

Baptism — SP5

			Perf. 13x12½
1955, June 1		**Photo.**	**Unwmk.**
B33	A33	10c + 5c like #339	.30 .25
B34	SP5	25c + 10c shown	.35 .25

Type of Regular Issue and

Red-eared Guenons SP6

		Perf. 13x12½, 12½x13	
1955, Nov. 23			
B35	A35	5c + 5c like #343	.25 .25
B36	SP6	15c + 5c shown	.30 .25

Flower Type of Regular Issue

1956, June 1			**Perf. 13x12½**
B37	A36	5c + 5c like #344	.25 .25
B38	A36	15c + 5c like #345	.30 .25

The tax was for native welfare work.

Type of Regular Issue and

Drummers and Arms of Bata SP7

		Perf. 13x12½, 12½x13	
1956, Nov. 23			
B39	A37	5c + 5c like #346	.25 .25
B40	SP7	15c + 5c shown	.25 .25

Type of Regular Issue and

African Gray Parrot SP8

		Perf. 13x12½, 12½x13	
1957, June 1		**Photo.**	**Unwmk.**
B41	A38	5c + 5c like #347	.25 .25
B42	SP8	15c + 5c shown	.30 .25

The surtax was for child welfare.

Type of Regular Issue, 1957

		Perf. 12½x13, 13x12½	
1957, Nov. 23			
B43	A39	10c + 5c like #348	.30 .25
B44	A39	15c + 5c like #349	.35 .25

Pigeons and Arms of Valencia and Santa Isabel SP9

1958, Mar. 6			**Perf. 12½x13**
B45	SP9	10c + 5c org brn	.25 .25
B46	SP9	15c + 10c bister	.25 .25
B47	SP9	50c + 10c ol gray	.25 .25
		Nos. B45-B47 (3)	.75 .75

The surtax was to aid the victims of the Valencia flood, Oct., 1957.

Type of Regular Issue, 1958

1958, June 1		**Photo.**	**Perf. 13x12½**
B48	A42	10c + 5c like #358	.30 .25
B49	A42	15c + 5c like #359	.35 .25

The surtax was to help the native population.

Butterflies SP10   Early Bicycle SP11

Stamp Day: Various butterflies.

1958, Nov. 23			**Unwmk.**
B50	SP10	10c + 5c brown red	.35 .25
B51	SP10	25c + 10c brt pur	.35 .25
B52	SP10	50c + 10c gray olive	.40 .25
		Nos. B50-B52 (3)	1.10 .75

Type of Regular Issue 1956 Inscribed: "Pro-Infancia 1959"

1959, June 1		**Photo.**	**Perf. 13x12½**
B53	A36	10c + 5c like #361	.25 .25
B54	A36	15c + 5c like #360	.30 .25

The surtax was for child welfare.

1959, Nov. 23

Designs: 20c+5c, Bicycle race. 50c+20c, Bicyclist winning race.

B55	SP11	10c + 5c lt rose brn	.25 .25
B56	SP11	20c + 5c turq blue	.25 .25
B57	SP11	50c + 20c olive gray	.30 .25
		Nos. B55-B57 (3)	.80 .75

Stamp Day.

AIR POST STAMPS

AP1

Revenue Stamp Surcharged

Type I — "Correo Aereo," 20½mm.
Type II — "Correo Aereo," 22mm.

1941		**Unwmk.**	**Perf. 11**
C1	AP1	1p on 17p dp red, I	35.00 8.00
a.		Type II	45.00 11.00

Spain No. C113 Overprinted in Red

1942, June 23			
C2	AP30	1p chalky blue	1.90 .35

No. 300 Overprinted in Green

1948, Jan. 15			**Perf. 10½x9½**
C3	A166	4p dull rose	9.00 2.75
		Never hinged	15.00

The overprint exists in two types: I — The numeral 1's are lower case L's. II — The numeral 1's are actual ones.

Count of Argelejo and Frigate Catalina at Fernando Po, 1778 AP2

1949, Nov. 23		**Photo.**	**Perf. 12½x13**
C4	AP2	5p dark slate green	1.00 .75
		Never hinged	1.50

Stamp Day, Nov. 23, 1949.

Manuel Iradier and Native Products — AP3

1950, Nov. 23		**Unwmk.**	**Perf. 12½**
C5	AP3	5p dk brn	2.50 1.00
		Never hinged	3.50

Stamp Day, Nov. 23, 1950.

Benito Rapids AP4

Various views.

1951, Mar. 1		**Litho.**	**Perf. 12½x13**
C6	AP4	25c ocher	.25 .25
C7	AP4	50c lilac rose	.25 .25
C8	AP4	1p green	.25 .25
C9	AP4	2p bright blue	.25 .25
C10	AP4	3.25p rose lilac	.50 .25
C11	AP4	5p gray brown	4.00 1.75
C12	AP4	10p rose red	15.50 6.25
		Nos. C6-C12 (7)	21.00 9.25
		Set, never hinged	37.50

Catalogue values for unused stamps in this section, from this point to the end of the section, are for Never Hinged items.

Woman Holding
Dove — AP5

1951, Apr. 22   Engr.   Perf. 10
C13 AP5 5p dark blue   21.00 2.75
  500th birth anniv. of Queen Isabella I.

Ferdinand the
Catholic — AP6

Soccer
Players — AP7

1952, July 18 Photo. Perf. 13x12½
C14 AP6 5p red brown   25.00 6.00
  500th birth anniv. of Ferdinand the Catholic
  of Spain.

1955-56   Unwmk.
C15 AP7 25c blue vio ('56)   .30 .25
C16 AP7 50c olive ('56)   .30 .25
C17 AP7 1.50p brown ('56)   1.05 .25
C18 AP7 4p rose car ('56)   3.25 .45
C19 AP7 10p yellow grn   1.75 .45
    Nos. C15-C19 (5)   6.65 1.65

Planes and Arm
Holding
Spear — AP8

1957, Sept. 19   Perf. 13x12½
C20 AP8 25p bister & sepia   8.25 .95
  30th anniv. of the Atlantida Squadron flight
  to Spanish Guinea.

SPECIAL DELIVERY STAMP

View of
Fernando
Po — SD1

Perf. 12½x13
1951, Mar. 1 Litho. Unwmk.
E1 SD1 25c rose carmine   .35 .25
    Never hinged   .50

SPANISH MOROCCO

ˈspa-nish mə-ˈrä-ˌkō

LOCATION — Northwest coast of Africa
GOVT. — Spanish Protectorate
AREA — 17,398 sq. mi. (approx.)
POP. — 1,010,117 (1950)
CAPITAL — Tetuán

Spanish authority in northern Morocco was established after Spain's invasion of the area in 1859. Spanish Morocco was a Spanish Protectorate

until 1956 when it, along with the French and Tangier zones of Morocco, became the independent country, Morocco.

100 Centimos = 1 Peseta

> **Catalogue values for unused stamps in this country are for Never Hinged items, beginning with Scott 280 in the regular postage section, Scott B27 in the semi-postal section, Scott C24 in the airpost section, and Scott E11 in special delivery section.**

Unoverprinted Spanish stamps were used in Spanish Morocco from 1860 until the appearance of separate issues for the territory in 1903. Spain No. E1 was used as a regular postage stamp in April 1914.

Spanish Offices in Morocco

Spain No. 221A
Overprinted in Carmine

1903-09   Unwmk.   Imperf.
1 A21 ¼c blue green   .55 .25
  a. Complete 1c (block 4 ¼c)   2.25 1.50
    See Nos. 26, 39, 52, Tetuan 1, 7.

Stamps of Spain
Overprinted in Carmine
or Blue — a

On Stamps of 1900
Perf. 14
2 A35 2c bister brown   1.75 1.40
3 A35 5c green   2.10   .80
4 A35 10c rose red (Bl)   2.25   .35
5 A35 15c brt violet   3.25   .80
6 A35 20c grnsh black   13.00 3.50
7 A35 25c blue   1.00   .85
8 A35 30c blue green   7.50 3.50
9 A35 40c rose (Bl)   13.00 6.00
10 A35 50c slate grn   7.75 5.75
11 A35 1p lake (Bl)   16.00 8.00
12 A35 4p dull violet   42.50 14.00
13 A35 10p brown org (Bl)   42.50 35.00
    Nos. 1-13 (13)   153.15 80.20
Set, never hinged   225.00

Many varieties of overprint exist. Nos. 7-13 exist imperf. Value, $500.
See Tetuan Nos. 2-6, 8-15.

On Stamps of 1909-10
1909-10   Perf. 13x12½, 14
14 A46 2c dark brown   .75 .25
15 A46 5c green   3.75 .30
16 A46 10c carmine (Bl)   4.25 .30
17 A46 15c violet   10.50 .65
18 A46 20c olive green   26.00 1.25
19 A46 25c deep blue   95.00
20 A46 30c blue green   8.50 .65
21 A46 40c rose (Bl)   8.50 .65
22 A46 50c slate blue   14.50 14.00
23 A46 1p lake (Bl)   34.50 29.00
24 A46 4p deep violet   95.00
25 A46 10p orange (Bl)   95.00
    Nos. 14-18,20-23 (9)   111.25 47.05
Set, never hinged   155.00
    Nos. 14-25 (12)   396.25

The stamps overprinted "Correo Espanol Marruecos" were used in all Morocco until the year 1914. After the issue of special stamps for the Protectorate the "Correo Espanol" stamps were continued in use solely in the city of Tangier.
Many varieties of overprint exist.
Nos. 19, 24 and 25 were not regularly issued.
See Nos. 27-38, 40-51, 53-67, 75-76, 78.

Spanish Morocco

Spain No. 221A
Overprinted in Carmine

1914   Imperf.
26 A21 ¼c green   .25 .25
  a. Complete 1c (block 4 ¼c)   1.25 .90

Stamps of Spain 1909-
10 Overprinted in
Carmine or Blue

Perf. 13x12½, 14
27 A46 2c dark brown (C)   .35 .25
28 A46 5c green (C)   .35 .25
29 A46 10c carmine (Bl)   .35 .25
30 A46 15c violet (C)   1.50 .90
31 A46 20c olive grn (C)   3.00 1.90
32 A46 25c deep blue (C)   3.00 1.50
33 A46 30c blue grn (C)   5.75 2.75
34 A46 40c rose (Bl)   13.00 3.75
35 A46 50c slate blue (C)   6.50 2.75
36 A46 1p lake (Bl)   6.50 3.75
37 A46 4p dp violet (C)   33.00 24.00
38 A46 10p orange (Bl)   50.00 32.00
    Nos. 26-38,E1 (14)   129.30 76.90
Set, never hinged   225.00

Many varieties of overprint exist, including inverted.
#27-38 exist imperf. Value for set, $525.

Stamps of Spain 1876
and 1909-10
Overprinted in Red or
Blue

1915   Imperf.
39 A21 ¼c blue grn (R)   .25 .25
  a. Complete 1c (block 4 ¼c)   1.50 1.50

Perf. 13x12½, 14
40 A46 2c dk brown (R)   .30 .30
41 A46 5c green (R)   .35 .35
42 A46 10c carmine (Bl)   .35 .35
43 A46 15c violet (R)   .35 .35
44 A46 20c olive grn (R)   1.25 .35
45 A46 25c deep blue (R)   1.25 .55
46 A46 30c blue grn (R)   1.40 .60
47 A46 40c rose (Bl)   3.75 .60
48 A46 50c slate blue (R)   6.25 .55
49 A46 1p lake (Bl)   6.25 .60
50 A46 4p deep violet (R)   42.50 26.00
51 A46 10p orange (Bl)   60.00 29.00
    Nos. 39-51,E2 (14)   127.25 61.45
Set, never hinged   240.00

One stamp in the setting on Nos. 39-51 has the first "R" of "PROTECTORADO" inverted. Many other varieties of overprint exist, including double and inverted.
Nos. 40-51 exist imperf. Value, set $650.

Stamps of Spain 1877
and 1909-10
Overprinted in Red or
Blue — b

1916-18   Imperf.
52 A21 ¼c blue grn (R)   1.25 .25
  a. Complete 1c (block 4 ¼c)   2.00 1.40

Perf. 13x12½, 14
53 A46 2c dk brown (R)   1.25 .25
54 A46 5c green (R)   5.50 .25
55 A46 10c carmine (Bl)   6.00 .25
56 A46 15c violet (R)   140.00
57 A46 20c olive grn (R)   140.00
58 A46 25c dp blue (R)   21.00 3.25
59 A46 30c blue grn (R)   27.50 22.00
60 A46 40c rose (Bl)   28.50 .50
61 A46 50c slate blue (R)   13.50 .25
62 A46 1p lake (Bl)   33.00 2.40
63 A46 4p dp violet (R)   55.00 32.50
64 A46 10p orange (Bl)   110.00 72.50
    Nos. 53-55,58-64 (11)   302.50 134.40
Set, never hinged   440.00
    Nos. 52-64 (13)   582.50
Set, never hinged   1,100.

Nos. 56-57 were not regularly issued.
Varieties of overprint, including double and inverted, exist for several denominations.
The 5c exists in olive brown. Value $525.

Same Overprint on Spain No. 310
1920
65 A46 15c ocher (Bl)   5.50 .30

Exists imperf.; also with overprint inverted.

Nos. 44, 46 Perforated through the middle and each half Surcharged "10 céntimos" in Red
1920
66 A46 10c on half of 20c   5.00 1.90
67 A46 15c on half of 30c   11.00 7.25

No. E2 Divided and Surcharged in Black
68 SD1 10c on half of 20c   12.00 7.75
  a. "10/cts." surcharge added 160.00 50.00
    Nos. 66-68 (3)   28.00 16.90

Values of Nos. 66-68 are for pairs, both halves of the stamp. Varieties were probably made deliberately.

"Justice" — A1

Revenue Stamps Perforated through
the Middle and each half Surcharged
in Red or Green

1920   Perf. 11½
69 A1 5c on 5p lt bl   11.50 2.40
70 A1 5c on 10p green   .50 .25
71 A1 10c on 25p dk grn   .50 .25
  a. Inverted surcharge   13.50 12.00
72 A1 10c on 50p indigo   .55 .40
73 A1 10c on 100p red (G)   .55 .40
74 A1 15c on 500p cl (G)   15.50 8.00
    Set, never hinged (6)   29.10 11.70
    Set, never hinged   47.50

Values of Nos. 69-74 are for pairs, both halves of the stamp.

Stamps of Spain 1917-20
Overprinted Type "a" in Blue or Red
1921-24   Perf. 13
75 A46 15c ocher (Bl)   1.50 .25
76 A46 20c violet (R)   2.25 .25

Stamps of Spain 1920-21
Overprinted Type "b" in Red
Imperf
77 A47 1c blue green   1.50 .25
Engr.
Perf. 13
78 A46 20c violet   11.00 .25

See No. 92.

Stamps of Spain, 1922 Overprinted
Type "a" in Red or Blue
1923-28   Perf. 13½x12½
79 A49 2c olive green (R)   4.25 .25
80 A49 5c red violet (Bl)   4.25 .25
81 A49 10c yellow green (R)   5.00 .25
82 A49 20c violet (R)   7.00 1.10
    Nos. 79-82 (4)   20.50 1.85

Same Overprinted Type "b"
1923-25
83 A49 2c olive green (R)   .75 .25
84 A49 5c red violet (Bl)   .75 .25
85 A49 10c yellow grn (R)   3.00 .25
86 A49 15c blue (R)   3.00 .25
87 A49 20c violet (R)   6.50 .25
88 A49 25c carmine (Bl)   13.00 1.50
89 A49 40c deep blue (R)   13.50 5.00
90 A49 50c orange (Bl)   35.00 8.50
91 A49a 1p blue black (R)   55.00 10.00
    Nos. 83-91,E3 (10)   142.50 31.00
Set, never hinged   230.00

Spain No. 314 Overprinted Type "a"
in Red
1927   Imperf.
92 A47 1c blue green   .25 .25

Mosque of
Alcazarquivir
A2

Moorish
Gateway at
Larache
A3

Well at Alhucemas
A4

View of Xauen — A5

View of Tetuan — A6

1928-32   Engr.   Perf. 14, 14½

93	A2	1c red ("Cs")	.25	.25
94	A2	1c car rose ("Ct") ('32)	.50	.40
95	A2	2c dark violet	.30	.25
96	A2	5c deep blue	.35	.25
97	A2	10c dark green	.35	.25
98	A2	15c orange brown	.75	.35
99	A3	20c olive green	.75	.35
100	A3	25c copper red	.80	.35
102	A3	30c black brown	2.60	.40
103	A3	40c dull blue	3.25	.40
104	A3	50c brown violet	6.75	.40
105	A4	1p yellow green	8.25	.45
106	A5	2.50p red violet	32.50	10.00
107	A6	4p ultra	24.00	7.50
		Nos. 93-107,E4 (15)	86.40	23.20
		Set, never hinged	130.00	

For surcharges see Nos. 164-167.

Seville-Barcelona Issue of Spain, 1929, Ovptd. in Red or Blue

1929   Perf. 11, 14

108	A50	1c greenish blue	.40	.30
109	A51	2c pale yel grn (R)	.40	.30
110	A52	5c rose lake (Bl)	.40	.30
111	A53	10c green	.40	.30
112	A50	15c Prussian blue	.40	.30
113	A51	20c purple	.40	.30
114	A50	25c bright rose (Bl)	.40	.30
115	A52	30c black brown (bl)	1.00	.75
116	A51	40c dark blue	1.00	.75
117	A51	50c deep orange (Bl)	1.00	.75
118	A52	1p blue black	8.00	5.75
119	A53	4p deep rose (Bl)	18.00	12.50
120	A53	10p brown (Bl)	40.00	29.00
		Nos. 108-120 (13)	71.80	51.60
		Set, never hinged	115.00	

See Nos. L1-L11.

Stamps of Spain, 1922-31, Overprinted Type "a" in Black, Blue or Red

1929-34   Perf. 11½, 13x12½

121	A49	5c claret (Bk)	3.50	.25
122	A61	10c green (R)	3.00	.45
123	A61	15c slate grn (R)	110.00	1.10
124	A61	20c violet (R)	3.00	.50
125	A61	30c brown lake (Bl)	3.25	1.10
126	A61	40c dark blue (R)	12.00	5.50
127	A49	50c orange (R)	30.00	5.25
128	A49a	10p brown (Bl)	3.00	5.75
		Nos. 121-128 (8)	167.75	19.90
		Set, never hinged	230.00	

Stamps of Spain, 1922-26, overprinted diagonally as above, and with no control number, or with "A000,000" on back, were not issued but were presented to the delegates at the 1929 UPU Congress in London. Value of complete set of 16, $3,250.

Stamps of Spain 1931-32, Overprinted in Black

1933-34   Imperf.

130	A108	1c blue green	.25	.25

Perf. 11½

131	A108	2c buff	.25	.25
132	A95	5c brnsh black	.25	.25
133	A96	10c yellow green	.25	.25
134	A97	15c slate green	.25	.25
135	A95	20c dark violet	.30	.25
136	A104	25c lake	.30	.25
137	A99	30c carmine rose	60.00	6.00
138	A100	40c dark blue	.65	.25
139	A97	50c orange	1.25	.30
140	A100	60c apple green	1.25	.30
141	A105	1p blue black	1.25	.50
142	A106	4p magenta	2.75	2.50
143	A107	10p deep brown	3.50	5.50
		Nos. 130-143,E7 (15)	74.00	17.35
		Set, never hinged	110.00	

Street Scene in Tangier — A7

View of Xauen — A8

Gate in Town Wall, Arzila — A9

Street Scene in Tangier A10

Mosque of Alcazarquivir A11

Caliph and His Guard A12

View of Tangier A13

Green Control Numbers Printed on Gum

1933-35   Photo.   Perf. 14, 13½

144	A7	1c brt rose	.35	.25
145	A8	2c green ('35)	.35	.25
146	A9	5c magenta ('35)	.35	.25
147	A10	10c dark green	.45	
148	A11	15c yellow ('35)	3.00	.30
149	A7	20c slate green	1.25	.30
150	A12	25c crimson ('35)	29.00	.30
151	A10	30c red brown	8.00	.35
152	A13	40c deep blue	12.50	.35
153	A13	50c red orange	42.50	5.00
154	A8	1p slate blk ('35)	18.00	.45
155	A9	2.50p brown ('35)	32.50	5.00
156	A11	4p yel grn ('35)	42.50	5.00
157	A12	5p black ('35)	42.50	5.25
		Nos. 144-157,E5 (15)	234.40	23.45
		Set, never hinged	340.00	

For surcharge see No. CB1.

Mosque — A14

Landscape A15

Green Control Numbers Printed on Gum

1935

158	A14	25c violet	1.25	.25
159	A15	30c crimson	16.50	.25
160	A14	40c orange	8.50	.25
161	A15	50c bright blue	8.50	.30
162	A14	60c dk blue green	8.50	.35
163	A15	2p brown lake	42.50	6.00
		Nos. 158-163 (6)	85.75	7.40
		Set, never hinged	120.00	

See No. 174.

Regular Issue and Special Delivery Stamp of 1928, Surcharged in Blue, Green or Red with New Values and Ornaments

1936

164	A6	1c on 4p ultra (Bl)	.35	.25
165	A5	2c on 2.50p red vio (G)	.35	.25
166	A3	5c on 25c cop red (R)	.35	.25
167	A4	10c on 1p yel grn (G)	10.00	4.00
168	SD2	15c on 20c blk (Bl)	7.75	2.10
		Nos. 164-168 (5)	18.80	6.85
		Set, never hinged	24.50	

Caliph and Viziers — A16

View of Bokoia A17

View of Alcazarquivir — A18

Sidi Saida Mosque A19

Caliph and Procession A20

Without Control Numbers

1937   Photo.   Perf. 13½

169	A16	1c green	.30	.25
170	A17	2c red violet	.30	.25
171	A18	5c orange	.30	.25
172	A16	15c violet	.30	.25
173	A19	30c red	.85	.25
a.		Souvenir sheet of 4, #170-173	22.00	12.00

174	A14	1p ultra	7.50	.30
a.		Souv. sheet of 4, #169-171, 174	22.00	12.00
175	A20	10p brown	60.00	17.50
		Nos. 169-175 (7)	69.55	19.05
		Set, never hinged	100.00	

Nos. 173a, 174a for 1st year of the Spanish Civil War.

Nos. 173a, 174a were privately overprinted "TANGER" in black on each stamp in the sheet for "use" in the International City of Tangier, and "GUINEA" for "use" in Spanish Guinea.

Harkeno Rifleman — A21

Troops Marching A22

Designs: 2c, Legionnaires. 5c, Cavalryman leading his mount. 10c, Moroccan phalanx. 15c, Legion flag-bearer. 20c, Colonial soldier. 25c, Ifni sharpshooters. 30c, Mounted trumpeters. 40c, Cape Juby Dromedary Corps. 50c, Regular infantry. 60c, Caliphate guards. 1p, Orderly on guard. 2p, Sentry. 2.50p, Regular cavalry. 4p, Orderly.

1937   Perf. 13½

176	A21	1c dull blue	.35	.25
177	A21	2c orange brn	.35	.25
178	A21	5c cerise	.35	.25
179	A21	10c emerald	.35	.25
180	A21	15c brt blue	.35	.25
181	A21	20c red brown	.35	.25
182	A21	25c magenta	.35	.30
183	A21	30c red orange	.35	.30
184	A21	40c orange	.35	.35
185	A21	50c ultra	.35	.35
186	A21	60c yellow grn	.35	.35
187	A21	1p blue violet	.35	.35
188	A21	2p Prus blue	11.50	5.00
189	A21	2.50p gray black	11.50	5.00
190	A21	4p dark brown	11.50	5.00
191	A22	10p black	11.50	5.00
		Nos. 176-191,E6 (17)	50.45	23.75
		Set, never hinged	82.50	

First Year of Spanish Civil War.
Exists imperf. Value, set $250.
For overprints see Nos. 214-229.

Spanish Quarter — A25

Designs: 10c, Moroccan quarter. 15c, Street scene, Larache. 20c, Tetuan.

1939   Unwmk.   Photo.   Perf. 13½

194	A25	5c orange	.30	.25
195	A25	10c brt blue grn	.30	.25
196	A25	15c golden brown	.50	.30
197	A25	20c brt ultra	.50	.30
		Nos. 194-197 (4)	1.60	1.10

Postman — A26

Mail Box — A27

Landscape
A28

Street Scene,
Alcazarquivir
A29

View of
Xauen — A30

Sentry
Guarding
Palace at
Sat — A31

The
Chieftain — A32

Market Place,
Larache — A33

Tetuán — A34

Ancient
Gateway at
Xauen — A35

Scene in
Alcazarquivir
A36

Post Office
A37

Spanish War
Veterans — A38

Victory Flag
Bearers — A39

Cavalry — A40

Day of
Court — A41

1940 Unwmk. Photo.   Perf. 11½x11

198	A26	1c dark brown	.35	.30
199	A27	2c olive grn	.35	.30
200	A28	5c dk blue	.35	.30
201	A29	10c dk red lilac	.35	.30
202	A30	15c dk green	.45	.35
203	A31	20c purple	.35	.35
204	A32	25c black brown	.35	.35
205	A33	30c brt green	.35	.35
206	A34	40c slate green	2.75	.35
207	A35	45c orange ver	1.10	.35
208	A36	50c brown orange	1.10	.35
209	A37	70c sapphire	1.10	.35
210	A38	1p indigo & brn	3.25	.35
211	A39	2.50p choc & dk grn	18.00	4.75
212	A40	5p dk cerise & sep	3.50	.45
213	A41	10p dk ol grn & brn org	32.50	8.00
		Nos. 198-213,E8 (17)	67.05	17.90
		Set, never hinged	120.00	

"ZONA" printed in black on back.
Exists imperf. Value, set $325.

Stamps of 1937
Overprinted in
Various Colors

1940   Unwmk.   Perf. 13½

214	A21	1c dull blue (Bk)	.95	.70
215	A21	2c org brn (Bk)	.95	.70
216	A21	5c cerise (Bk)	.95	.70
217	A21	10c emerald (Bk)	.95	.70
218	A21	15c brt blue (Bk)	.95	.70
219	A21	20c red brn (Bk)	.95	.70
220	A21	25c mag (Bk)	.95	.70
221	A21	30c red org (V)	.95	.70
222	A21	40c orange (V)	1.60	1.40
223	A21	50c ultra (Bk)	1.60	1.40
224	A21	60c yel grn (Bk)	1.60	1.40
225	A21	1p blue vio (V)	1.60	1.40
226	A21	2p Prus bl (Bl)	50.00	50.00
227	A21	2.50p gray blk (V)	50.00	50.00
228	A21	4p dk brn (Bl)	50.00	50.00
229	A22	10p black (R)	50.00	50.00
		Nos. 214-229,E10 (17)	226.00	220.70
		Set, never hinged	450.00	

4th anniversary of Spanish Civil War.

Larache
A42

Alcazarquivir
A43

Market Place,
Larache — A44

Tangier
A45   A46

1941   Unwmk. Photo.   Perf. 10½

230	A42	5c dk brn & brn	.25	.25
231	A43	10c dp rose & ver	.25	.25
232	A44	15c sl grn & yel grn	.25	.25
233	A45	20c vio bl & dp bl	.55	.25
234	A46	40c dp plum & claret	1.50	.25
		Nos. 230-234 (5)	2.80	1.25
		Set, never hinged	5.00	

Exists imperf. Value, set $150.

1943   Perf. 12x12½

234A	A43	5c dark blue	.25	.25
235	A44	40c dull violet brn	55.00	.25

Plowing
A47

Harvesting
A48

Returning
from Work
A49

Transporting Wheat — A50

Vegetable
Garden
A51

Picking
Oranges
A52

Goat
Herd — A53

1944   Unwmk. Photo.   Perf. 12½

236	A47	1c choc & lt bl	.25	.25
237	A48	2c sl grn & lt grn	.25	.25
238	A49	5c choc & grnsh blk	.25	.25
239	A50	10c brt ultra & red org	.25	.25
240	A51	15c sl grn & lt grn	.25	.25
241	A52	20c dp cl & blk	.25	.25
242	A53	25c lt bl & choc	.25	.25
243	A47	30c yel grn & brt ultra	.25	.25
244	A48	40c choc & red vio	.25	.25
245	A49	50c brt ultra & red brn	.65	.25
246	A50	75c yel grn & brt ultra	.90	.25
247	A51	1p brt ultra & choc	.90	.25

248	A52	2.50p blk & brt ultra	7.75	1.75
249	A53	10p sal & gray blk	11.50	3.75
		Nos. 236-249 (14)	23.95	8.50
		Set, never hinged	42.50	

Exists imperf. Value, set $100.

Potters
A54

Dyers
A55

Blacksmiths
A56

Cobblers
A57

Weavers
A58

Metal
Workers
A59

1946 Unwmk. Litho. Perf. 10½x10

250	A54	1c purple & brn	.25	.25
251	A55	2c dk Prus grn & vio blk	.25	.25
252	A54	10c dp org & vio bl	.25	.25
253	A55	15c dk bl & bl grn	.25	.25
254	A54	25c yel grn & ultra	.25	.25
255	A56	40c dk bl & brn, perf. 12½	.25	.25
256	A55	45c black & rose	.50	.25
257	A57	1p dk Prus grn & dp bl	.60	.25
258	A58	2.50p dp org & gray	1.75	.65
259	A59	10p dk bl & gray	3.00	1.50
		Nos. 250-259 (10)	7.35	4.15
		Set, never hinged	9.50	

Control letter "Z" in circle in black on back.
Exists imperf. Value, set $85.

A60

Sanitorium — A61

1946, Sept. 1 Perf. 11½x10½, 10½
260 A60 10c crim & bl grn .25 .25
261 A61 25c crimson & brn .25 .25
Nos. 260-261,B14-B16 (5) 1.80 1.25

Issued to aid anti-tuberculosis work.

A62   A63

1947 Perf. 10
262 A62 10c carmine & blue .25 .25
263 A63 25c red & chocolate .25 .25
Nos. 262-263,B17-B19 (5) 1.90 1.55

Issued to aid anti-tuberculosis work.

Commerce by Railroad A64

Commerce by Truck A65

Urban Market A66

Country Market A67

Caravan A68

Maritime Commerce A69

1948 Litho. Perf. 10, 10x10½
264 A64 2c purple & brn .25 .25
265 A65 5c dp cl & vio .25 .25
266 A66 15c brt ultra & bl grn .25 .25
267 A67 25c blk & Prus grn .25 .25
268 A65 35c brt ultra & gray blk .25 .25
269 A68 50c red & violet .25 .25
270 A66 70c dk gray grn & ultra .25 .25
271 A67 90c cer & dk gray grn .25 .25
272 A68 1p brt ultra & vio .60 .25
273 A64 2.50p vio brn & sl grn 1.50 .45
274 A69 10p blk & dp ultra 2.75 1.25
Nos. 264-274 (11) 6.85 3.95
Set, never hinged 11.00

Exists imperf. Value, set $90.

Emblem of Tuberculosis Association
A70   A71

Design: 25c, Plane over sanatorium.

1948, Oct. 1 Perf. 10
275 A70 10c car & green .25 .25
276 A70 25c car & grnsh gray 1.75 .65
Nos. 275-276,B20-B23 (6) 29.85 10.15

See No. B39.
Exists imperf. Value, set $75.

1949
10c, Road of Health. 25c, Minaret and Palm.

Black Control Number on Back
277 A71 5c car & green .25 .25
278 A71 10c car & dk vio .25 .25
279 A71 25c car & black .90 .30
Nos. 277-279,B25-B26 (5) 3.35 1.50

> Catalogue values for unused stamps in this section, from this point to the end of the section, are for Never Hinged items.

Mail Transport, 1890 — A72   Herald — A73

Designs: 5c, 50c, 90c, Mail transport, 1890. 10c, 45c, 1p, Mail transport, 1906. 15c, 1.50p, Mail transport, 1913. 35c, 75c, 5p, Mail transport, 1914. 10p, Mail transport, 1918.

1950 Litho. Perf. 10½
280 A72 5c choc & vio bl .25 .25
281 A72 10c deep bl & sep .25 .25
282 A72 15c grnsh blk & emer .25 .25
283 A72 35c pur & gray blk .25 .25
284 A72 45c dp car & rose lil .25 .25
285 A72 50c emer & dk brn .25 .25
286 A72 75c dk vio bl & bl .25 .25
287 A72 90c grnsh blk & rose car .25 .25
288 A72 1p blk brn & gray .25 .25
289 A72 1.50p carmine & blue .70 .25
290 A72 5p black & vio brn 1.25 .25
291 A72 10p purple & blue 26.00 10.00
Nos. 280-291,E11 (13) 57.70 22.75

UPU, 75th anniv. (in 1949).
Nos. 280-291 exist imperf. Value $400.

1950 Unwmk. Perf. 10
Frame and Device in Carmine
Black Control Number on Back
292 A73 5c gray black .25 .25
293 A73 10c Old fort .25 .25
294 A73 25c Sanatorium 1.00 .50
Nos. 292-294,B27-B28 (5) 3.15 1.85

Boar Hunt A74

10c, 1p, Hunters and hounds. 50c, Boar hunt. 5p, Fishermen. 10p, Moorish fishing boat.

1950, Dec. 30 Perf. 10½x10
Black Control Number on Back
295 A74 5c dk brn & rose vio .25 .25
296 A74 10c carmine & gray .25 .25
297 A74 50c green & sepia .25 .25

298 A74 1p bl vio & claret .45 .25
299 A74 5p dp claret & bl vio .70 .25
300 A74 10p grnsh blk & dp cl 2.25 .40
Nos. 295-300 (6) 4.15 1.65

Emblem — A75

10c, Patients expressing gratitude. 25c, Plane in the Clouds.

Dated "1951"
Frame and Device in Carmine
Black Control Number on Back
1951 A75 Litho. Perf. 12
301 A75 5c green .25 .25
302 A75 10c blue violet .25 .25
303 A75 25c gray black .85 .30
Nos. 301-303,B29-B32 (7) 15.00 5.65

Issued to aid anti-tuberculosis work.

Armed Attack A76

Designs: 10c, Horses on parade. 15c, Holiday procession. 20c, Road to market. 25c, "Brother-hoods." 35c, "Offering." 45c, Soldiers. 50c, On the rooftop. 75c, Teahouse. 90c, Wedding. 1p, Pilgrimage. 5p, Storyteller. 10p, Market corner.

Black Control Number on Back
1952 Perf. 11
304 A76 5c dk blue & brn .25 .25
305 A76 10c dk brn & lil rose .25 .25
306 A76 15c black & emer .25 .25
307 A76 20c ol grn & red vio .25 .25
308 A76 25c red & lt blue .25 .25
309 A76 35c olive & orange .25 .25
310 A76 45c red & rose red .25 .25
311 A76 50c rose car & gray grn .25 .25
312 A76 75c purple & ultra .25 .25
313 A76 90c dk bl & rose vio .25 .25
314 A76 1p dk bl & red brn .25 .25
315 A76 5p red & blue 1.25 .25
316 A76 10p dk grn & gray blk 1.75 .40
Nos. 304-316,E12 (14) 6.00 3.65

Worship — A77

10c, Distributing alms. 25c, Prickly pear.

Black Control Number on Back
1952, Oct. 1 Dated "1952"
317 A77 5c car & dk ol grn .25 .25
318 A77 10c car & dk brown .25 .25
319 A77 25c car & dp blue .35 .25
Nos. 317-319,B33-B37 (8) 10.45 4.35

Semi-Postal Types of 1948-49 Dated "1953"
1953 Litho. Perf. 10
Black Control Number on Back
320 SP7 5c shown .25 .25
321 SP9 10c like #B26 .25 .25
322 SP7 25c like #B23 .85 .35
Nos. 320-322,B38-B42 (8) 18.45 6.50

Issued to aid anti-tuberculosis work.

A78

1953, Nov. 15
Black Control Number on Back
323 A78 5c red .25 .25
324 A78 10c gray green .25 .25

Mountain Women — A79   Zauia — A80

50c and 2.50p, Water carrier. 90c and 2p, Mountaineers and donkey. 1p and 4.50p, Moorish women and child. 10p, Mounted dignitary.

1953, Dec. 15 Photo.
Black Control Number on Back
334 A79 35c grn & rose vio .25 .25
335 A79 50c red & green .25 .25
336 A79 90c dk bl & org .25 .25
337 A79 1p dk brn & grn .25 .25
338 A79 1.25p dk grn & car rose .25 .25
339 A79 2p dk rose vio & bl .25 .25
340 A79 2.50p black & orange .65 .25
341 A79 4.50p brt car rose & dk grn 3.25 .35
342 A79 10p green & black 4.25 .65
Nos. 334-342,E13 (10) 9.90 3.00

25th anniv. of Spanish Morocco's first definitive postage stamps.

1954, Nov. 1 Dated "1954"
10c, "The Family." 25c, Plane, Spanish coast.

Black Control Number on Back
343 A80 5c car & bl grn .25 .25
344 A80 10c car & dk brn .25 .25
345 A80 25c car & blue .25 .25
Nos. 343-345,B43-B45 (6) 8.55 4.90

Queen's Gate — A81   Honor Guard — A82

1955 Litho. Perf. 11
Black Control Number on Back
Frames in Black
346 A81 15c shown .25 .25
347 A81 25c Saida .25 .25
348 A81 80c like #346 .25 .25
349 A81 1p like #347 .25 .25
350 A81 15p Ceuta 3.00 .65
Nos. 346-350,E14 (6) 4.25 1.90

Perf. 13x12½
1955, Nov. 8 Photo. Unwmk.
Designs: 25c, 80c, 3p, Caliph Moulay Hassen ben el-Medi. 30c, 1p, 5p, Caliph and procession. 15p, Coat of arms.

351 A82 15c ol brn & ol .25 .25
352 A82 25c lil & dp rose .25 .25
353 A82 30c brn blk & Prus grn .25 .25
354 A82 70c Prus grn & yel grn .25 .25
355 A82 80c ol & ol brn .25 .25
356 A82 1p dk bl & redsh brn .25 .25
357 A82 1.80p black & bl vio .25 .25
358 A82 3p blue & gray .25 .25
359 A82 5p dk grn & brn 1.25 .45

Engr.

360 A82 15p red brn & yel grn 2.75 1.65
Nos. 351-360 (10) 6.00 4.10

30th anniv. of accession to throne by Caliph Moulay Hassan ben el-Medi ben Ismail.
Succeeding issues, released under the Kingdom, are listed under Morocco.

SEMI-POSTAL STAMPS

Types of Semi-Postal Stamps of Spain, 1926, Ovptd. in Black or Blue

1926   Unwmk.   Perf. 12½, 13

B1	SP1	1c orange	8.50	5.50
B2	SP2	2c rose	12.00	10.00
B3	SP3	5c black brn	4.50	3.50
B4	SP4	10c dark grn	4.50	3.50
B5	SP1	15c dk violet (Bl)	.80	.65
B6	SP2	20c violet brn	.80	.65
B7	SP5	25c deep carmine	.80	.65
B8	SP1	30c olive grn	.80	.65
B9	SP4	40c ultra	.25	.25
B10	SP2	50c red brown	.25	.25
B11	SP4	1p vermilion	.25	.25
B12	SP3	4p bister	.80	.65
B13	SP5	10p light violet	3.50	2.75
		Nos. B1-B13,EB1 (14)	40.50	31.65
		Set, never hinged	70.00	

See Spain No. B6a for No. B6 without overprint. For surcharges see Spain Nos. B64-B65.

Tuberculosis Fund Issues

SP1

SP2

SP3

Perf. 10½, 11½x10½

1946, Sept. 1   Litho.   Unwmk.

B14	SP1	25c + 5c crim & rose vio	.25	.25
B15	SP2	50c + 10c crim & blue	.30	.25
B16	SP3	90c + 10c crim & gray brn	.75	.25
		Nos. B14-B16 (3)	1.25	.65

Medical Center — SP4

Nurse and Children — SP5

"Protection" SP6

Herald SP7

1947   Perf. 10

B17	SP4	25c + 5c red & violet	.25	.25
B18	SP5	50c + 10c red & blue	.35	.25
B19	SP6	90c + 10c red & sepia	.80	.55
		Nos. B17-B19 (3)	1.35	.95

1948, Oct. 1

Designs: No. B21, Protection. No. B22, Sun bath. No. B23, Plane over Ben Karrich.

B20	SP7	50c + 10c car & dk vio	.35	.25
B21	SP7	90c + 10c car & dk gray	1.50	.50
B22	SP7	2.50p + 50c car & brn	10.00	3.25
B23	SP7	5p + 1p car & vio bl	16.00	5.25
		Nos. B20-B23 (4)	27.85	9.25

See Nos. 320, 322.

Moulay Hassan ben el-Medi ben Ismail — SP8

Flag — SP9

1949, May 15

B24 SP8 50c + 10c lilac rose 1.10 .45

Wedding of the Caliph at Tetuan, June 5.

Tuberculosis Fund Issues

Design: No. B26, Fight with dragon.

1949
Black Control Numbers on Back

B25	SP9	50c + 10 car & brown	.35	.30
B26	SP9	90c + 10 car & grnsh gray	1.60	.40

See No. 321.

> Catalogue values for unused stamps in this section, from this point to the end of the section, are for Never Hinged items.

Crowd at Fountain of Life — SP10

Warrior — SP11

90c+10c, Mohammedan hermit's tomb.

1950, Oct. 1   Litho.   Perf. 10
Black Control Numbers on Back
Frame and Cross in Carmine

B27	SP10	50 + 10c dk brown	.40	.30
B28	SP10	90 + 10c dk green	1.25	.55

1951   Unwmk.   Perf. 12

Designs: 90c+10c, Fort. 1p+5p, Port of Salvation. 1.10p+25c, Road to market.

Black Control Numbers on Back

B29	SP11	50c + 10c car & brn	.25	.25
B30	SP11	90c + 10c car & bl	.40	.25
B31	SP11	1p + 5p car & gray	8.25	2.75
B32	SP11	1.10p + 25c car & gray	4.75	1.60
		Nos. B29-B32 (4)	13.60	4.80

See No. B40.

Pilgrimage SP12

Armed Horseman in Action SP13

Designs: 60c+25c, Palmettos. 90c+10c, Fort. 1.10p+25c, Agave. 5p+2p, Warrior.

1952   Perf. 11
Black Control Numbers on Back

B33	SP12	50 + 10c car & gray	.25	.25
B34	SP12	60 + 25c car & dk grn	.80	.40
B35	SP12	90 + 10c car & vio brn	.80	.40
B36	SP12	1.10p + 25c car & pur	2.25	.80
B37	SP12	5p + 2p car & gray	5.50	1.75
		Nos. B33-B37 (5)	9.55	3.55

1953   Perf. 10

#B39, As #276. #B42, Plane & clouds.

Black Control Numbers on Back

B38	SP13	50c + 10c car & vio	.30	.25
B39	A70	60c + 25c car & brn	2.50	.80
B40	SP11	90c + 10c car & blk	.80	.35
B41	SP13	1.10p + 25c car & vio brn	4.00	1.25
B42	A73	5p + 2p car & bl	9.50	3.00
		Nos. B38-B42 (5)	17.10	5.60

Stork — SP14

50c+10c, Father & Child. 5p+2p, Tomb.

1954   Photo.
Black Control Numbers on Back

B43	SP14	5c + 5c car & rose vio	.25	.25
B44	SP14	50c + 10c car & gray grn	.80	.40
B45	SP14	5p + 2p car & gray	6.75	3.50
		Nos. B43-B45 (3)	7.75	4.10

AIR POST STAMPS

Mosque de Baja and Plane — AP1

View of Tetuán and Plane AP2

10c, Stork of Alcazar. 25c, Shore scene, plane. 40c, Desert tribesmen watching plane. 75c, View of shoreline at Larache. 1p, Arab mailman, plane above. 1.50p, Arab farmers, stork. 2p, Plane at twilight. 3p, Shadow of plane over city.

1938   Unwmk.   Photo.   Perf. 13½

C1	AP1	5c red brown	.25	.25
C2	AP1	10c emerald	.25	.25
C3	AP1	25c crimson	.25	.25
C4	AP1	40c dull blue	2.00	.50
C5	AP2	50c cerise	.25	.25
C6	AP2	75c ultra	.25	.25
C7	AP1	1p dark brown	.25	.25
C8	AP1	1.50p purple	.65	.35
C9	AP1	2p brown lake	.40	.25
C10	AP1	3p gray black	1.75	.25
		Nos. C1-C10 (10)	6.30	2.85
		Set, Never Hinged	11.00	

Nos. C1-C10 exist imperf. Value of set, $100. For surcharge see No. C32.

Landscape, Ketama — AP3

Mosque, Tangier — AP4

Velez — AP5

Sanjurjo — AP6

Strait of Gibraltar
AP7   AP8

1942   Perf. 12½

C11	AP3	5c deep blue	.25	.25
C12	AP4	10c orange brn	.25	.25
C13	AP5	15c grnsh black	.25	.25
C14	AP6	90c dark rose	.25	.25
C15	AP7	5p black	1.50	.85
		Nos. C11-C15 (5)	2.50	1.85
		Set, never hinged	3.25	

Exist imperf. Value, set $55.

1949   Litho.   Perf. 10

Designs: 5c, 1.75p, Strait of Gibraltar. 10c, 3p, Market day. 30c, 4p, Kebira Fortress. 6.50p, Airmail arrival. 8p, Horseman.

C16	AP8	5c vio brn & brt grn	.25	.25
C17	AP8	10c blk & rose lilac	.25	.25
C18	AP8	30c dk vio bl & grnsh gray	.25	.25
C19	AP8	1.75p car & bl vio	.25	.25
C20	AP8	3p dk blue & gray	.25	.25
C21	AP8	4p grnsh blk & car rose	.30	.25

C22	AP8	6.50p brt grn & brn	.95	.25
C23	AP8	8p rose lil & bl vio	1.60	.40

Nos. C16-C23 (8) 4.10 2.15
Set, never hinged 5.50

Exist imperf. Value, set $80.

> Catalogue values for unused stamps in this section, from this point to the end of the section, are for Never Hinged items.

Road to Tetuan — AP9

Designs: 4p, Arrival of mail from Spain. 8p, Greeting plane. 16p, Shadow of plane.

1952 *Perf. 11*
Black Frames and Inscriptions
Black Control Numbers on Back

C24	AP9	2p brt blue	.25	.25
C25	AP9	4p scarlet	.30	.25
C26	AP9	8p dk olive green	.45	.25
C27	AP9	16p violet brown	2.25	.95

Nos. C24-C27 (4) 3.25 1.70

Part of the proceeds was used toward the establishment of a postal museum at Tetuan.

Plane over Boat — AP10

Designs: 60c, Mosques, Sidi Saidi. 1.10p, Plowing. 4.50p, Fortress, Xauen.

1953 *Perf. 10*

C28	AP10	35c dp bl & car rose	.25	.25
C29	AP10	60c dk car & sl grn	.25	.25
C30	AP10	1.10p dp blue & blk	.30	.25
C31	AP10	4.50p dk car & dk brn	1.25	.40

Nos. C28-C31 (4) 2.05 1.15

Exist imperf. Value, set $75.

No. C6 Surcharged in Black

Type I

Type II

1953 *Perf. 13½*
C32	AP2	50c on 75c ultra (I)	.50	.25
a.		50c on 75c ultra (II)	.50	.25
b.		Vert. gutter pair, types I and II	2.75	

Sheets of 2 panes, 25 stamps each, with gutter between. Upper pane surcharged type I, lower type II.

AIR POST SEMI-POSTAL STAMPS

No. 150 Surcharged in Black

1936 **Unwmk.** *Perf. 14*
CB1	A12	25c + 2p on 25c	14.00	5.75
		Never hinged	32.50	
a.		Bars at right omitted	57.50	42.50
b.		Blue surcharge	45.00	15.00

25c was for postage, 2p for air post.

Nos. C1-C10 surcharged "Lucha Antituberculosa," a Lorraine cross and surtax are stated to be bogus.

Crowd at Palace — SPAP1

1949, May 15 **Unwmk.** *Perf. 10*
CB2	SPAP1	1p + 10c gray black	.75	.35

Wedding of the Caliph at Tetuan, June 5.

SPECIAL DELIVERY STAMPS

Special Delivery Stamp of Spain Overprinted in Blue

1914 **Unwmk.** *Perf. 14*
E1	SD1	20c red	5.75	2.60

Special Delivery Stamp of Spain Overprinted in Blue

1915
E2	SD1	20c red	3.00	1.60

For bisected surcharge see No. 68.

Special Delivery Stamp of Spain Overprinted in Blue

1923
E3	SD1	20c red	12.00	9.75

Mounted Courier SD2

1928 **Engr.** *Perf. 14, 14½*
E4	SD2	20c black	5.00	1.60

For surcharge see No. 168.

Moorish Postman — SD3

Mounted Courier — SD4

1935 **Photo.** *Perf. 14*
Green Control Number on Back
E5	SD3	20c vermilion	1.15	.25

See No. E9.

1937 *Perf. 13½*
E6	SD4	20c bright carmine	.25	.25

1st Year of the Spanish Civil War.
For surcharge see No. E10.

Spain No. E14 Overprinted in Black

1938 *Perf. 10*
E7	SD7	20c vermilion	1.50	.25

Arab Postman SD5

Airmail 1935 SD6

1940 **Photo.** *Perf. 11½x11*
E8	SD5	25c scarlet	.85	.35

"ZONA" printed on back in black.

Type of 1935
1940 **Litho.** *Perf. 10*
E9	SD3	20c black brown	2.60	

No. E9 was prepared but not issued.
Exists imperf. Value, $10.

No. E6 Surcharged with New Value, Bars and

1940 *Perf. 13½*
E10	SD4	25c on 20c brt car	12.00	9.50

4th anniversary of Spanish Civil War.

> Catalogue values for unused stamps in this section, from this point to the end of the section, are for Never Hinged items.

1950 **Unwmk.** **Litho.** *Perf. 10½*
E11	SD6	25c carmine & gray	27.50	10.00

UPU, 75th anniv. (in 1949).

Moorish Postrider SD7

1952 *Perf. 11*
Black Control Number on Back
E12	SD7	25c car & rose car	.25	.25

Rider with Special Delivery Mail — SD8

Gate of Tangier — SD9

1953 **Photo.** *Perf. 10*
Black Control Number on Back
E13	SD8	25c dk bl & car rose	.25	.25

25th anniv. of Spanish Morocco's first definitive postage stamps.

1955 **Litho.** *Perf. 11*
Black Control Number on Back
E14	SD9	2p violet & black	.25	.25

SEMI-POSTAL SPECIAL DELIVERY STAMP

Type of Semi-Postal Special Delivery Stamp of Spain, 1926, Overprinted like #B1-B13

1926 **Unwmk.** *Perf. 12½, 13*
EB1	SPSD1	20c ultra & black	2.75	2.40

POSTAL TAX STAMPS

General Francisco Franco — PT1

1937-39 Unwmk. Photo. *Perf. 12½*
RA1	PT1	10c sepia	.50	.25
a.		Sheet of 4, imperf.	4.50	1.75
RA2	PT1	10c copper brn ('38)	.50	.25
a.		Sheet of 4, imperf.	4.50	1.75
RA3	PT1	10c blue ('39)	.50	.25
a.		Sheet of 4, imperf.	4.50	1.75

Nos. RA1-RA3 (3) 1.50 .75
Set, never hinged 3.50
Set, RA1a-RA3a 13.50

The tax was used for the disabled soldiers in North Africa.

Soldiers PT2

1941 **Litho.** *Perf. 13½*
RA4	PT2	10c brt grn	4.00	.25
RA5	PT2	10c rose pink	4.00	.25
RA6	PT2	10c henna brn	4.00	.25
RA7	PT2	10c blue	4.00	.25

Nos. RA4-RA7 (4) 16.00 1.00
Set, never hinged 25.00

The tax was used for the disabled soldiers in North Africa.
Exist imperf. Value, set $60.

General Francisco
Franco — PT3

1943   **Photo.**   *Perf. 10*
RA8 PT3 10c chalky blue   9.00 .25
RA9 PT3 10c slate blue   9.00 .25
RA10 PT3 10c dl gray brn   9.00 .25
RA11 PT3 10c blue violet   9.00 .25
   Nos. RA8-RA11 (4)   36.00 1.00
   Set, never hinged   52.50

Exists imperf. Value, set $125.

1944   *Perf. 12*
RA12 PT3 10c dp mag & brn   6.00 .25
RA13 PT3 10c dp org & dk grn   6.00 .25
   Set, never hinged   16.00

Exists imperf. Value, set $45.00.

1946   Litho.
RA14 PT3 10c ultra & brown   6.75 .25
RA15 PT3 10c gray blk & rose lil   6.75 .25
   Set, never hinged   17.50

Exists imperf. Value, set $45.00.

TANGIER

For the International City of Tangier
Seville-Barcelona Issue of Spain,
1929, Ovptd. in Blue or Red

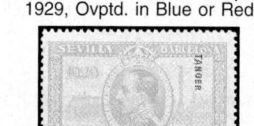

1929   *Perf. 11*
L1 A52 5c rose lake   .30 .30
L2 A53 10c green (R)   .30 .30
L3 A50 15c Prus blue (R)   .30 .30
L4 A51 20c purple (R)   .30 .30
L5 A50 25c brt rose   .30 .30
L6 A52 30c black brn   .30 .30
L7 A53 40c dk blue (R)   .75 .75
L8 A51 50c deep org   .75 .75
L9 A52 1p blue blk (R)   7.75 7.75
L10 A53 4p deep rose   21.00 21.00
L11 A53 10p brown   30.00 30.00
   Nos. L1-L11 (11)   62.05 62.05
   Set, never hinged   105.00

Overprints of 1937-39
The following overprints on stamps
of Spain exist in black or in red:
"TANGER" vertically on Nos. 517-
518, 522-523, 528, 532, 534, 539-
543, 549.
"Correo Espanol Tanger" horizontally or vertically in three lines on
Nos. 540, 592-597 (gray paper), 598-
601.
"Tanger" horizontally on Nos. 539-
541, 592-601.
"Correo Tanger" horizontally in two
lines on five consular stamps.

Woman — A1   Palm Tree — A2

Man — A3   Old map of
Tangier — A4

Tangier
Street — A5   Moroccan
Women — A6

Head of Moor — A7

Perf. 9½x10½, 12½x13 (1c, 2c, 10c, 20c)

1948-51   **Photo.**   Unwmk.
L12 A1 1c blue grn ('51)   .25 .25
L13 A1 2c red org ('51)   .25 .25
     Engr.
L14 A2 5c vio brn ('49)   .25 .25
L15 A3 10c deep blue ('51)   .25 .25
L16 A3 20c gray ('51)   .25 .25
L17 A2 25c green ('51)   .25 .25
L18 A4 30c dk slate grn   .35 .25
L19 A5 45c car rose   .35 .25
L20 A6 50c dp claret   .35 .25
L21 A7 75c deep blue   .70 .25
L22 A7 90c green   .60 .25
L23 A4 1.35p org ver   2.10 .35
L24 A6 2p purple   3.75 .35
L25 A5 10p dk grnsh bl ('49)   4.25 .65
   Nos. L12-L25,LE1 (15)   14.80 4.45
   Set, never hinged   25.00

Nos. L18-L25, LE1 exist imperf. Value, set $400.

TANGIER SEMI-POSTAL STAMPS

Types of
Semi-Postal
Stamps of
Spain, 1926,
Overprinted

1926   *Perf. 12½, 13*
LB1 SP1 1c orange   7.50 8.00
LB2 SP2 2c rose   7.50 8.00
LB3 SP3 5c black brn   3.75 3.75
LB4 SP4 10c dk green   3.75 3.75
LB5 SP1 15c dk violet   1.25 1.60
LB6 SP4 20c violet brn   1.25 1.60
LB7 SP5 25c dp carmine   1.25 1.60
LB8 SP1 30c olive grn   1.25 1.60
LB9 SP3 40c ultra   .35 .35
LB10 SP2 50c red brn   .35 .35
LB11 SP1 1p vermilion   .75 .75
LB12 SP3 4p bister   .75 .75
LB13 SP5 10p lt violet   3.25 3.25
   Nos. LB1-LB13,LE1 (14)   35.95 38.35
   Set, never hinged   65.00

For overprints & surcharges see Spain Nos. B66-B67.

TANGIER AIR POST STAMPS

Overprints of 1939
The following overprints on stamps
of Spain exist in black or in red:
"Correo Aereo Tanger" in two lines
on Nos. 539-541, 596 (gray paper),
600, C72B.
"Via Aerea Tanger" in three lines
on Nos. 539-540, 592-597 (gray
paper), 599, 601, E14.
"Correo Aereo Tanger" in three
lines on four consular stamps.
"Correo Espanol Tanger" in three
lines on No. C72B.
"Tanger" on No. C72B.

Plane over
Shore — AP1

Twin-Engine
Plane — AP2

Passenger Plane
in Flight — AP3

Perf. 11x11½, 11½

1949-50   **Engr.**   Unwmk.
LC1 AP1 20c violet brn ('50)   .25 .25
LC2 AP2 25c bright red   .25 .25
LC3 AP3 35c dull green   .25 .25
LC4 AP1 1p violet ('50)   .80 .25
LC5 AP2 2p deep blue   1.50 .25
LC6 AP3 10p brown violet   2.75 1.00
   Nos. LC1-LC6 (6)   5.80 2.25
   Set, never hinged   9.50

Nos. LC1, LC4-LC6 exist imperf. Value $100 each.

TANGIER SPECIAL DELIVERY STAMP

Arab
Postrider — SD1

1949   Unwmk.   Engr.   *Perf. 13*
LE1 SD1 25c red   .85 .35
   Never hinged   1.40

TANGIER SEMI-POSTAL SPECIAL DELIVERY STAMP

Types of Semi-Postal Special Delivery
Stamp of Spain, 1926, Overprinted like
#LB1-LB13

1926   Unwmk.   *Perf. 12½, 13*
LEB1 SPSD1 20c ultra & black   3.00 3.00
   Never hinged   5.00

TETUAN

Stamps of Spanish
Offices in Morocco,
1903-09, Handstamped
in Black, Blue or Violet

1908   Unwmk.   *Imperf.*
1 A21 ¼c blue green   13.00 10.00
     Perf. 14
2 A35 2c bister brown   150.00 60.00
3 A35 5c green   140.00 35.00
4 A35 10c rose red   140.00 35.00
5 A35 20c grnsh black   300.00 125.00
6 A35 25c blue   100.00 35.00
   Nos. 1-6 (6)   843.00 300.00

Same Handstamp On Stamps of
Spain, 1876 and 1900-05, in Black,
Blue or Violet

1908   *Imperf.*
7 A21 ¼c deep green   7.50 3.25
     Perf. 14
8 A35 2c bister brn   40.00 13.00
9 A35 5c dark green   55.00 22.50
10 A35 10c rose red   52.50 22.50
11 A35 15c purple   52.50 25.00
12 A35 20c grnsh black   150.00 110.00

---

13 A35 25c blue   80.00 35.00
14 A35 30c blue green   175.00 60.00
15 A35 40c olive bister   225.00 110.00
   Nos. 7-15 (9)   837.50 401.25

Counterfeits of this overprint are plentiful.

SPANISH SAHARA

'spa-nish sə-'har-ə

(Spanish Western Sahara)

LOCATION — Northwest Africa, bor-
dering on the Atlantic Ocean.
GOVT. — Spanish possession
AREA — 102,703 sq. mi.
POP. — 76,425 (1970)
CAPITAL — Aaiún

Spanish Sahara was a subdivision of
Spanish West Africa. It included the colony of Rio de Oro and the territory of
Saguiet el Hamra. Spanish Sahara was
formerly known as Spanish Western
Sahara, which superseded the older
title of Rio de Oro.
In 1976, Spanish Sahara was divided
between Morocco and Mauritania.

100 Centimos = 1 Peseta

> Catalogue values for unused
> stamps in this country are for
> Never Hinged items, beginning
> with Scott 51 in the regular post-
> age section, Scott B13 in the semi-
> postal section, Scott C8 in the air-
> post section, and Scott E1 in the
> special delivery section.

Tuareg and
Camel — A1

1924   Unwmk.   Typo.   *Perf. 13*
     Control Number on Back
1 A1 5c blue green   3.00 .90
2 A1 10c gray green   3.00 .90
3 A1 15c turq blue   3.00 .90
4 A1 20c dark violet   3.00 1.25
5 A1 25c red   3.00 1.25
6 A1 30c red brown   3.00 1.25
7 A1 40c dark blue   3.00 1.25
8 A1 50c orange   3.00 1.25
9 A1 60c violet   3.00 1.25
10 A1 1p rose   16.00 6.50
11 A1 4p chocolate   70.00 33.00
12 A1 10p claret   170.00 105.00
   Nos. 1-12 (12)   283.00 154.70
   Set, never hinged   375.00

#1-12 were for use in La Aguera & Rio de
Oro.
An unissued set of 10, similar to Nos. 3-12,
exists perf. 10 or imperf, and no control num-
ber except on 50c. The set also exists perf 14.
Value, $200.
Nos. 1-12 also exist perf 14. Value, unused
$300.
For overprints see Nos. 24-35.

Seville-Barcelona
Issue of Spain,
1929 Overprinted
in Blue or Red

1929   *Perf. 11*
13 A52 5c rose lake   .30 .30
14 A53 10c green (R)   .30 .30
15 A50 15c Prus blue (R)   .30 .30
16 A51 20c purple (R)   .40 .30
17 A50 25c bright rose   .40 .30
18 A52 30c black brown   .40 .30
19 A53 40c dark blue (R)   .90 .45
20 A51 50c deep orange   .90 .45
21 A52 1p blue black (R)   3.50 1.90

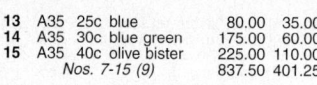

22	A53	4p deep rose	27.50	17.50
23	A53	10p brown	52.50	35.00
		Nos. 13-23 (11)	87.40	57.10
		Set, never hinged	125.00	

**Stamps of 1924
Overprinted in Red or
Blue**

1931			**Perf. 13**	
24	A1	5c blue grn (R)	.95	.65
25	A1	10c gray grn (R)	.95	.65
26	A1	15c turq blue (R)	.95	.65
27	A1	20c dark violet (R)	.95	.65
28	A1	25c red	.95	.65
29	A1	30c red brown	.95	.65
30	A1	40c dark blue (R)	4.50	.90
31	A1	50c orange	4.50	2.25
32	A1	60c violet	4.50	2.25
33	A1	1p rose	4.50	2.25
34	A1	4p chocolate	45.00	16.00
35	A1	10p claret	92.50	50.00
		Nos. 24-35 (12)	161.20	83.55
		Set, never hinged	240.00	

The stamps of the 1931 issue exist with the
overprint reading upward, downward, or horizontally. Some values also exist with double
overprint, double overprint, one inverted and
diagonal overprint.

**Stamps of Spain,
1936-40, Overprinted
in Carmine or Blue**

1941-46		**Unwmk.**	**Imperf.**	
36	A159	1c green	2.25	1.50
		Perf. 10 to 11		
37	A160	2c org brn (Bl)	2.25	1.50
38	A161	5c gray brown	.70	.45
39	A161	10c dk car (Bl)	2.25	1.50
40	A161	15c dark green	.70	.45
41	A166	20c bright violet	.70	.45
42	A166	25c deep claret	1.75	.90
43	A166	30c light blue	1.75	1.10
44	A166	40c Prus grn	.70	.45
45	A166	50c indigo	20.00	1.25
46	A166	70c blue	13.50	1.90
47	A166	1p gray black	26.50	2.75
48	A166	2p dull brown	150.00	75.00
49	A166	4p dull rose (Bl)	425.00	225.00
50	A166	10p lt brown	1,250.	325.00
		Nos. 36-50 (15)	1,898.	639.20
		Set, never hinged	3,000.	

The stamps of this issue are normally poorly
centered and are valued thus.
Counterfeit overprints exist.

> **Catalogue values for unused
> stamps in this section, from this
> point to the end of the section, are
> for Never Hinged items.**

Dorcas
Gazelles — A2

Designs: 2c, 20c, 45c, 3p, Caravan. 5c, 75c,
10p, Camel troops.

1943		**Unwmk.**	**Perf. 12½**	
51	A2	1c brown & lil rose	.25	.25
52	A2	2c yel grn & sl bl	.30	.25
53	A2	5c magenta & vio	.35	.25
54	A2	15c slate grn & grn	.35	.25
55	A2	20c violet & red brn	.40	.25
56	A2	40c rose vio & vio	.40	.25
57	A2	45c brn vio & red	.60	.30
58	A2	75c indigo & blue	.60	.30
59	A2	1p red & brown	2.00	.90
60	A2	3p bl vio & sl grn	4.00	1.60
61	A2	10p black brn & blk	60.00	25.00
		Nos. 51-61,E1 (12)	71.00	30.55

Nos. 51-61, E1 exist imperf. Value for set,
$90.

Gen.
Franco and
Desert
Scene
A5

1951		**Photo.**	**Perf. 12½x13**	
62	A5	50c deep orange	.25	.25
63	A5	1p chocolate	.35	.30
64	A5	5p blue green	30.00	12.00
		Nos. 62-64 (3)	30.60	12.55

Visit of Gen. Francisco Franco, 1950.

Allegorical
Figure and
Globe — A6

Woman
Musician — A7

1953, Mar. 2			**Perf. 13x12½**	
65	A6	5c red orange	.25	.25
66	A6	35c dk slate green	.25	.25
67	A6	60c brown	.35	.25
		Nos. 65-67 (3)	.85	.75

75th anniv. of the founding of the Royal
Geographical Society.

1953, June 1

Design: 60c, Man musician.

68	A7	15c olive gray	.25	.25
69	A7	60c brown	.25	.25
		Nos. 68-69,B25-B26 (4)	1.00	1.00

Orange Scorpionfish — A8

Fish: 60c, Banded sargo.

1953, Nov. 23			**Perf. 12½x13**	
70	A8	15c dk olive green	.25	.25
71	A8	60c orange	.40	.25
		Nos. 70-71,B27-B28 (4)	1.15	1.00

Colonial Stamp Day.

Hurdlers
A9

Runner — A10

1954, June 1		**Perf. 12½x13, 13x12½**		
72	A9	15c gray green	.25	.25
73	A10	60c brown	.30	.25
		Nos. 72-73,B29-B30 (4)	1.05	1.00

Atlantic
Flyingfish
A11

1954, Nov. 23			**Perf. 12½x13**	
74	A11	15c shown	.25	.25
75	A11	60c Gilthead	.40	.25
		Nos. 74-75,B31-B32 (4)	1.15	1.00

Colonial Stamp Day.

Emilio
Bonelli
A12

1955, June 1		**Photo.**	**Unwmk.**	
76	A12	50c olive gray	.25	.25
		Nos. 76,B33-B34 (3)	.75	.75

Birth cent. of Emilio Bonelli, explorer.

Scimitar-horned Oryx — A13

1955, Nov. 23				
77	A13	70c green	.25	.25
		Nos. 77,B35-B36 (3)	.75	.75

Colonial Stamp Day.

Antirrhinum
Romosissimum
A14

Design: 50c, Sesiviun portulacastrum.

1956, June 1		**Perf. 13x12½**		
78	A14	20c bluish green	.25	.25
79	A14	50c brown	.35	.25
		Nos. 78-79,B37-B38 (4)	1.10	1.00

Arms of
Aaiun and
Camel
Rider
A15

1956, Nov. 23		**Perf. 12½x13**		
80	A15	70c olive grn & sepia	.25	.25
		Nos. 80,B39-B40 (3)	.75	.75

Colonial Stamp Day.

Dromedaries
A16

Golden Eagle
A17

15c, 80c, Ostrich. 50c, 1.80p, Mountain
gazelle.

1957, Apr. 10		**Perf. 13x12½**		
81	A16	5c purple	.25	.25
82	A16	15c bister	.25	.25
83	A16	50c dark olive	.25	.25
84	A16	70c yellow green	.70	.25
85	A16	80c blue green	.75	.25
86	A16	1.80p lilac rose	.75	.25
		Nos. 81-86 (6)	2.95	1.50

1957, June 1		**Photo.**	**Unwmk.**	
87	A17	70c dark green	.25	.25
		Nos. 87,B41-B42 (3)	.75	.75

Striped
Hyena — A18

Design: 70c, Striped Hyena, horiz.

Perf. 13x12½, 12½x13

1957, Nov. 23				
88	A18	20c slate green	.25	.25
89	A18	70c yellowish green	.25	.25
		Nos. 88-89,B43-B44 (4)	1.00	1.00

Stamp Day.

Don
Quixote
and the
Lion
A19

Cervantes
A20

Gray Heron
A21

1958, June 1		**Perf. 12½x13, 13x12½**		
90	A19	20c bister brn & grn	.25	.25
91	A20	70c dk grn & yel grn	.30	.25
		Nos. 90-91,B48-B49 (4)	1.05	1.00

Cervantes Type of 1958

Designs: 20c, Actor as "Peribanez," by Lope
de Vega. 70c, Lope de Vega.

1959, June		**Photo.**	**Perf. 13x12½**	
92	A20	20c lt green & brn	.25	.25
93	A20	70c yel grn & slate grn	.30	.25
		Nos. 92-93,B53-B54 (4)	1.05	1.00

Promoting child welfare.

1959, Oct. 15			**Perf. 13x12½**	

Birds: 50c, 1.50p, 5p, Sparrowhawk. 75c,
2p, 10p, Sea gull.

94	A21	25c dull violet	.25	.25
95	A21	50c dark olive	.25	.25
96	A21	75c dark brown	.25	.25
97	A21	1p red orange	.30	.25
98	A21	1.50p brt green	.35	.25
99	A21	2p brt red lilac	1.00	.30
100	A21	3p blue	1.05	.30
101	A21	5p red brown	1.90	.35
102	A21	10p olive green	11.00	4.75
		Nos. 94-102 (9)	16.35	6.95

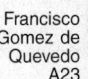

Scene from "The
Pilferer Don Pablos"
by Quevedo — A22

Francisco
Gomez de
Quevedo
A23

1960, June		**Perf. 13x12½, 12½x13**		
103	A22	35c slate green	.25	.25
104	A23	80c Prussian green	.25	.25
		Nos. 103-104,B58-B59 (4)	1.00	1.00

Francisco Gomez de Quevedo, writer.

Houbara
Bustard — A24

Map of Spanish
Sahara — A25

Gen.
Franco and
Camel
Rider
A26

Design: 50c, 1p, 2p, 5p, Doves.

1961, Apr. 18 Photo.   Perf. 13x12½
105 A24   25c blue violet   .25   .25
106 A24   50c olive gray   .25   .25
107 A24   75c brown violet   .25   .25
108 A24   1p orange ver   .25   .25
109 A24   1.50p blue green   .25   .25
110 A24   2p magenta   .80   .25
111 A24   3p dark blue   .95   .25
112 A24   5p red brown   1.10   .35
113 A24   10p olive   3.00 1.50
        Nos. 105-113 (9)   7.10 3.60

1961, Oct. 1   Perf. 13x12½, 12½x13
Design: 70c, Chapel of Aaiun.

114 A25   25c gray violet   .25   .25
115 A26   50c olive brown   .25   .25
116 A25   70c brt green   .25   .25
117 A26   1p red orange   .25   .25
        Nos. 114-117 (4)   1.00 1.00

25th anniv. of the nomination of Gen. Francisco Franco as Chief of State.

Neurada
Procumbres
A27

Clock Fish
A28

50c, 1.50p, 10p, Anabasis articulata, flower. 70c, 2p, Euphorbia resinifera, cactus.

1962, Feb. 26   Perf. 13x12½
118 A27   25c black violet   .25   .25
119 A27   50c dark brown   .25   .25
120 A27   70c brt green   .25   .25
121 A27   1p orange ver   .30   .25
122 A27   1.50p blue green   .40   .25
123 A27   2p red lilac   1.25   .25
124 A27   3p slate   2.00   .30
125 A27   10p olive   4.75 1.50
        Nos. 118-125 (8)   9.45 3.30

**   Perf. 13x12½, 12½x13**
1962, July 10   Photo.
Design: 50c, Avia fish, horiz.

126 A28   25c violet black   .25   .25
127 A28   50c dark green   .25   .25
128 A28   1p orange brown   .30   .25
        Nos. 126-128 (3)   .80   .75

Goats
A29

Stamp Day: 35c, Sheep.

1962, Nov. 23   Perf. 12½x13
129 A29   15c yellow green   .25   .25
130 A29   35c magenta   .25   .25
131 A29   1p orange brown   .25   .25
        Nos. 129-131 (3)   .75   .75

Seville Cathedral
Tower — A30

1963, Jan. 29   Perf. 13x12½
132 A30   50c olive   .25   .25
133 A30   1p brown orange   .25   .25
        Issued to help Seville flood victims.

Camel
Riders — A31

Hands
Releasing Dove
and
Arms — A32

Design: 50c, Tuareg and camel.

1963, June 1   Unwmk.
134 A31   25c deep violet   .25   .25
135 A31   50c gray   .25   .25
136 A31   1p orange red   .25   .25
        Nos. 134-136 (3)   .75   .75

Issued for child welfare.

1963, July 12
137 A32   50c Prussian green   .25   .25
138 A32   1p orange brown   .25   .25

Issued for Barcelona flood relief.

John Dory
A33

Fish: 50c, Plain bonito, vert.

**   Perf. 12½x13, 13x12½**
1964, Mar. 6   Photo.
139 A33   25c purple   .25   .25
140 A33   50c olive green   .25   .25
141 A33   1p brown red   .45   .25
        Nos. 139-141 (3)   .95   .75

Issued for Stamp Day 1963.

Moth and
Flowers
A34

Design: 50c, Two moths, vert.

**   Perf. 12½x13, 13x12½**
1964, June 1   Unwmk.
142 A34   25c dull violet   .25   .25
143 A34   50c brown black   .25   .25
144 A34   1p orange red   .45   .25
        Nos. 142-144 (3)   .95   .75

Issued for child welfare.

Camel Rider
and Microphone
A35

Squirrel
A36

Designs: 50c, 1.50p, 3p, Boy with flute and camels. 70c, 2p, 10p, Woman with drum.

1964, Sept. Photo. Perf. 13x12½
145 A35   25c dull purple   .25   .25
146 A35   50c olive   .25   .25
147 A35   70c green   .25   .25
148 A35   1p dull red brn   .30   .25
149 A35   1.50p bright green   .30   .25
150 A35   2p Prus green   .35   .30
151 A35   3p dark blue   .40   .30
152 A35   10p carmine lake   1.50   .70
        Nos. 145-152 (8)   3.60 2.55

1964, Nov. 23   Unwmk.
Stamp Day: 1p, Squirrel's head, horiz.

153 A36   50c olive gray   .25   .25
154 A36   1p brown carmine   .25   .25
155 A36   1.50p green   .25   .25
        Nos. 153-155 (3)   .75   .75

Tuareg
Girl — A37

Wellhead and
Camel
Rider — A38

25 Years of Peace: 1p, Physician examining patient, horiz.

**   Perf. 13x12½, 12½x13**
1965, Feb. 22   Photo.
156 A37   50c black brown   .25   .25
157 A38   1p dark red   .25   .25
158 A38   1.50p deep blue   .25   .25
        Nos. 156-158 (3)   .75   .75

Anthia Sexmaculata — A39

1p, 3p, Blepharopsis mendica, vert.

**   Perf. 12½x13, 13x12½**
1965, June 1   Unwmk.
159 A39   50c slate blue   .25   .25
160 A39   1p blue green   .30   .25
161 A39   1.50p brown   .35   .30
162 A39   3p dark blue   1.40   .60
        Nos. 159-162 (4)   2.30 1.40

Issued for child welfare.

Basketball
A40

Arms and
Camels
A41

1965, Nov. 23   Perf. 13x12½
163 A40   50c rose claret   .25   .25
164 A41   1p deep magenta   .25   .25
165 A40   1.50p slate blue   .25   .25
        Nos. 163-165 (3)   .75   .75

Issued for Stamp Day.

Ship "Rio
de Oro"
A42

Design: 1.50p, S.S. Fuerte Ventura.

1966, June 1 Photo. Perf. 12½x13
166 A42   50c olive   .25   .25
167 A42   1p dark red brown   .25   .25
168 A42   1.50p blue green   .30   .25
        Nos. 166-168 (3)   .80   .75

Issued for child welfare.

Ocean
Sunfish — A43

Designs: 10c, 1.50p, Bigeye tuna, horiz.

1966, Nov. 23   Photo.   Perf. 13
169 A43   10c bl gray & cit   .25   .25
170 A43   40c slate & pink   .25   .25
171 A43   1.50p brown & olive   .30   .25
172 A43   4p rose vio & gray   .45   .25
        Nos. 169-172 (4)   1.25 1.00

Issued for Stamp Day.

A44

Designs: 40c, 4p, Flower and leaves.

1967, June 1   Photo.   Perf. 13
173 A44   10c blk, ocher & gray
                grn   .25   .25
174 A44   40c emerald & lilac   .25   .25
175 A44   1.50p dk grn & yel grn   .25   .25
176 A44   4p brt blue & org   .30   .25
        Nos. 173-176 (4)   1.05 1.00

Issued for child welfare.

Aaiun
Harbor
A45

Design: 4p, Villa Cisneros Harbor.

1967, Sept. 28 Photo. Perf. 12½x13
177 A45   1.50p brt bl & red brn   .25   .25
178 A45   4p brt bl & bis brn   .25   .25

Modernization of harbor installations.

Ruddy
Sheldrake
A46

Stamp Day: 1.50p, Flamingo, vert. 3.50p, Rufous bush robin.

1967, Nov. 23   Photo.   *Perf. 13*

179	A46	1p bister brn & grn	.25	.25
180	A46	1.50p brt rose & gray	.30	.25
181	A46	3.50p brn red & sep	.45	.25
		Nos. 179-181 (3)	1.00	.75

Scorpio — A47

Zodiac Issue

1.50p, Aries. 2.50p, Virgo.

1968, Apr. 25   Photo.   *Perf. 13*

182	A47	1p brt mag, *lt yel*	.25	.25
183	A47	1.50p brown, *pink*	.25	.25
184	A47	2.50p dk vio, *yel*	.40	.25
		Nos. 182-184 (3)	.90	.75

Issued for child welfare.

Mailman — A48

Stamp Day: 1p, Post horn, pigeon, letter and Spain No. 1. 1.50p, Letter, canceller and various stamps of Spain and Ifni.

1968, Nov.   Photo.   *Perf. 13x12½*

185	A48	1p dp lil rose & dk bl	.25	.25
186	A48	1.50p green & sl grn	.30	.25
187	A48	2.50p dp org & dk bl	.45	.25
		Nos. 185-187 (3)	1.00	.75

Dorcas Gazelle — A49

Designs: 1.50p, Doe and fawn. 2.50p, Gazelle and camel. 6p, Leaping gazelle.

1969, June 1   Photo.   *Perf. 13*

188	A49	1p gldn brn & blk	.25	.25
189	A49	1.50p gldn brn & blk	.30	.25
190	A49	2.50p gldn brn & blk	.35	.25
191	A49	6p gldn brn & blk	.55	.35
		Nos. 188-191 (4)	1.45	1.15

Child welfare. See Nos. 196-199, 209-212.

Woman Playing
Drum — A50

Stamp Day: 1.50p, Man with flute. 2p, Drum and camel rider, horiz. 25p, Flute, horiz.

1969, Nov. 23   Photo.   *Perf. 13*

192	A50	50c brn red & lt ol	.25	.25
193	A50	1.50p dk bl grn & grnsh gray	.25	.25
194	A50	2p indigo & bis brn	.30	.25
195	A50	25p brn & lt bl grn	1.00	.30
		Nos. 192-195 (4)	1.80	1.05

Animal Type of 1969

Fennec: 50c, Sitting. 2p, Running. 2.50p, Head. 6p, Vixen and pups.

1970, June 1   Photo.   *Perf. 13*

196	A49	50c dp bister & blk	.25	.25
197	A49	2p org brn & blk	.25	.25
198	A49	2.50p dp bister & blk	.30	.25
199	A49	6p dp bister & blk	.50	.25
		Nos. 196-199 (4)	1.30	1.00

Issued for child welfare.

Grammodes Boisdeffrei — A51

Designs: 1p, like 50c. 2p, 5p, Danaus chrysippus. 8p, Celerio euphorbiae.

1970, Nov. 23   Photo.   *Perf. 12½*

200	A51	50c red & multi	.25	.25
201	A51	1p carmine & multi	.30	.25
202	A51	2p green & multi	.35	.25
203	A51	5p Prus bl & multi	.45	.30
204	A51	8p dk blue & multi	.75	.40
		Nos. 200-204 (5)	2.10	1.45

Issued for Stamp Day. See Nos. 233-234.

Gazelle, Arms of   Smara
Aaiun — A52   Mosque — A53

Designs: 2p, Inn, horiz. 5p, Assembly building, Aaiun, horiz.

Perf. 12½x13, 13x12½

1971, June 1   Photo.

205	A52	1p multicolored	.25	.25
206	A53	2p gray grn & ol	.25	.25
207	A53	5p lt bl & lt red brn	.30	.25
208	A53	25p lt bl & grnsh gray	.90	.35
		Nos. 205-208 (4)	1.70	1.10

Issued for child welfare.

Animal Type of 1969

Birds: 1.50p, 2p, Trumpeter bullfinch. 5p, Cream-colored courser. 24p, Lanner (falcon).

1971, Nov. 23   Photo.   *Perf. 12½*

209	A49	1.50p black & multi	.25	.25
210	A49	2p blue & multi	.25	.25
211	A49	5p green & multi	.30	.25
212	A49	24p black & multi	.85	.35
		Nos. 209-212 (4)	1.65	1.10

Stamp Day.

Saharan
Woman — A55

1.50p, 2p, Saharan man. 8p, 10p, Man's head. 12p, Woman. 15p, Soldier. 24p, Dancer.

1972, Feb. 18   Photo.   *Perf. 13*

213	A55	1p blue, pink & brn	.25	.25
214	A55	1.50p brn, lil & blk	.25	.25
215	A55	2p green, buff & sep	.25	.25
216	A55	5p green, pur & vio brn	.25	.25
217	A55	8p black, lt grn & vio	.30	.25
218	A55	10p black, gray & Prus bl	.35	.30
219	A55	12p multicolored	.40	.35

220	A55	15p multicolored	.50	.45
221	A55	24p multicolored	1.00	.60
		Nos. 213-221 (9)	3.55	2.95

Tuareg
Woman — A56

1972, June 1   Photo.   *Perf. 13*

222	A56	8p shown	.30	.25
223	A56	12p Tuareg man	.40	.25

Child welfare.

Mother and
Child — A57

1972, Nov. 23   Photo.   *Perf. 13*

224	A57	4p shown	.25	.25
225	A57	15p Saharan man	.45	.25

Stamp Day. See No. 229.

Dunes
A58

Design: 7p, Old Market and Gate, Aaiun.

1973, June 1   Photo.   *Perf. 13*

226	A58	2p multicolored	.25	.25
227	A58	7p multicolored	.30	.25

Child welfare.

Type of 1972 and

View of
Villa
Cisneros
A59

1973, Nov. 23   Photo.   *Perf. 13*

228	A59	2p shown	.25	.25
229	A57	7p Tuareg man	.30	.25

Stamp Day.

UPU Monument,
Bern — A60

1974, May   Photo.   *Perf. 13*

230	A60	15p multicolored	.55	.25

Centenary of the Universal Postal Union.

Gate, Smara
Mosque — A61

2p, Court and Minaret, Villa Cisneros Mosque.

1974, May

231	A61	1p multicolored	.25	.25
232	A61	2p multicolored	.25	.25

Child welfare.

Animal Type of 1970

1974, Nov.   Photo.   *Perf. 13*

233	A51	2p Desert eagle owl	.25	.25
234	A51	5p Lappet-faced vulture	.25	.25

Stamp Day.

Espana 75
Emblem, Spain
No. 1084 — A63

1975, Apr. 4   Photo.   *Perf. 13*

235	A63	8p olive, blk & bl	.25	.25

Espana 75 Intl. Phil. Exhib., Madrid, 4/4-13.

Children
A64

1975   Photo.   *Perf. 13*

236	A64	1.50p shown	.25	.25
237	A64	3p Children's village	.25	.25

Child welfare.

Old Man — A65

1975, Nov. 7   Photo.   *Perf. 13*

238	A65	3p blk, lt grn & mar	.25	.25

SEMI-POSTAL STAMPS

Red Cross Issue

Types of Semi-
Postal Stamps of
Spain, 1926,
Overprinted

1926   Unwmk.   *Perf. 12½, 13*

B1	SP3	5c black brown	8.75	8.75
B2	SP4	10c dark green	8.75	8.75
B3	SP1	15c dark violet	2.75	2.75
B4	SP4	20c violet brown	2.75	2.75

B5	SP5	25c deep carmine	2.75	2.75
B6	SP1	30c olive green	2.75	2.75
B7	SP3	40c ultra	.25	.25
B8	SP2	50c red brown	.25	.25
B9	SP5	60c myrtle green	.25	.25
B10	SP4	1p vermilion	.25	.25
B11	SP3	4p bister	2.75	2.10
B12	SP3	10p light violet	7.25	6.00
		Nos. B1-B12 (12)	39.50	37.60
		Set, never hinged	57.50	

See Spain No. B6a for No. B4 without overprint. For surcharges see Spain #B72-B73.

> Catalogue values for unused stamps in this section, from this point to the end of the section, are for Never Hinged items.

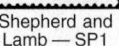
Shepherd and Lamb — SP1

Dromedary and Calf — SP2

1950, Oct. 20   Photo.   Perf. 13x12½

B13	SP1	50c + 10c brown	.40	.25
B14	SP1	1p + 25c rose brn	16.50	7.25
B15	SP1	6.50p + 1.65p dk gray grn	8.50	2.25
		Nos. B13-B15 (3)	25.40	9.75

The surtax was for child welfare.

1951, Nov. 23

B16	SP2	5c + 5c brown	.25	.25
B17	SP2	10c + 5 red org	.25	.25
B18	SP2	60c + 15c olive brn	.50	.30
		Nos. B16-B18 (3)	1.00	.80

Colonial Stamp Day, Nov. 23.

Child and Protector SP3

Ostrich SP4

1952, June 1

B19	SP3	5c + 5c brown	.30	.25
B20	SP3	50c + 10c gray	.35	.35
B21	SP3	2p + 30c blue	1.75	1.25
		Nos. B19-B21 (3)	2.40	1.85

The surtax was for child welfare.

1952, Nov. 23   Perf. 12½

B22	SP4	5c + 5c brn	.25	.25
B23	SP4	10c + 5c brn car	.35	.25
B24	SP4	60c + 15c dk grn	.45	.30
		Nos. B22-B24 (3)	1.05	.80

Colonial Stamp Day, Nov. 23.

Musician Type of Regular Issue

1953, June 1   Perf. 13x12½

B25	A7	5c + 5c like #68	.25	.25
B26	A7	10c + 5c like #69	.25	.25

The surtax was for child welfare.

Fish Type of Regular Issue

1953, Nov. 23   Perf. 12½x13

B27	A8	5c + 5c like #70	.25	.25
B28	A8	10c + 5c like #71	.25	.25

Athlete Types of Regular Issue

1954, June 1   Perf. 12½x13, 13x12½

B29	A9	5c + 5c brn org	.25	.25
B30	A10	10c + 5c purple	.25	.25

The surtax was to help the native population.

Fish Type of Regular Issue

1954, Nov. 23   Perf. 12½x13

B31	A11	5c + 5c like #74	.25	.25
B32	A11	10c + 5c like #75	.25	.25

Type of Regular Issue and

Emilio Bonelli SP5

1955, June 1   Photo.   Unwmk.

B33	A12	10c + 5c red vio	.25	.25
B34	SP5	25c + 10c violet	.25	.25

The surtax was for child welfare.

Antelope Type of Regular Issue

15c+5c, Head of scimitar-horned oryx.

1955, Nov. 23   Perf. 12½x13

B35	A13	5c + 5c org brn	.25	.25
B36	A13	15c + 5c olive bister	.25	.25

Flower Type of Regular Issue

1956, June 1   Perf. 13x12½

B37	A14	5c + 5c like #78	.25	.25
B38	A14	15c + 5c like #79	.25	.25

The tax was for the children.

Aaiun Type of Regular Issue and

Arms of Villa Cisneros and Man — SP6

Perf. 12½x13, 13x12½

1956, Nov. 23   Unwmk.

B39	A15	5c + 5c pur & blk	.25	.25
B40	SP6	15c + 5c bis & grn	.25	.25

Eagle Type of Regular Issue

15c+5c, Lesser spotted eagle in flight.

1957, June 1   Perf. 13x12½

B41	A17	5c + 5c red brown	.25	.25
B42	A17	15c + 5c golden brn	.25	.25

The surtax was for child welfare.

Hyena Type of Regular Issue
Perf. 13x12½, 12½x13

1957, Nov. 23

B43	A18	10c + 5c like #88	.25	.25
B44	A18	15c + 5c like #89	.25	.25

Stork and Arms of Valencia and Aaiun SP7

1958, Mar. 6   Photo.   Perf. 12½x13

B45	SP7	10c + 5c org brn	.25	.25
B46	SP7	15c + 10c bister	.25	.25
B47	SP7	50c + 10c brn olive	.25	.25
		Nos. B45-B47 (3)	.75	.75

The surtax was to aid the victims of the Valencia flood, Oct. 1957.

Cervantes Type of Regular Issue

15c+5c, Don Quixote & Sancho Panza.

1958, June 1   Perf. 13x12½

B48	A20	10c + 5c hn brn & chnt brn	.25	.25
B49	A20	15c + 5c dp org & slate grn	.25	.25

The surtax was for child welfare.

Hoopoe Lark — SP8

Mailman — SP9

25c+10c, Hoopoe larks, horiz. 50c+10c, Bird.

Perf. 13x12½, 12½x13

1958, Nov. 23   Photo.   Unwmk.

B50	SP8	10c + 5c brn red	.25	.25
B51	SP8	25c + 10c brt pur	.25	.25
B52	SP8	50c + 10c olive	.30	.25
		Nos. B50-B52 (3)	.80	.75

Cervantes Type of Regular Issue

10c+5c, Lope de Vega. 15c+5c, Actress from "Star of Seville," by Lope de Vega.

1959, June   Perf. 13x12½

B53	A20	10c + 5c org brn & ol gray	.25	.25
B54	A20	15c + 5c dp ocher & choc	.25	.25

The surtax was for child welfare.

1959, Nov. 23   Photo.

Stamp Day: 20c+5c, Mailman. 50c+20c, Mailman on camel.

B55	SP9	10c + 5c rose & brn	.25	.25
B56	SP9	20c + 5c lt grn & brn	.25	.25
B57	SP9	50c + 20c ol gray & slate	.25	.25
		Nos. B55-B57 (3)	.75	.75

Quevedo Type of Regular Issue

Designs: 10c+5c, Francisco Gomez de Quevedo. 15c+5c, Winged wheel and hourglass, symbolic of "Hora de Todas."

1960, June 1   Perf. 12½x13, 13x12½

B58	A23	10c + 5c maroon	.25	.25
B59	A22	15c + 5c bister brown	.25	.25

The surtax was for child welfare.

Leopard SP10

Alonso Fernandez de Lugo SP11

Stamp Day: 20c+5c, Desert fox. 30c+10c, Eagle and leopard. 50c+20c, Sand fox.

1960, Nov. 23   Photo.   Perf. 13x12½

B60	SP10	10c + 5c rose lilac	.25	.25
B61	SP10	20c + 5c dk slate grn	.25	.25
B62	SP10	30c + 10c chocolate	.30	.25
B63	SP10	50c + 20c olive gray	.40	.30
		Nos. B60-B63 (4)	1.20	1.05

**Animal Type of 1961 inscribed:
"Pro-Infancia 1961"**

Designs: Various Mountain Gazelles.

1961, June 21   Unwmk.

B64	SP10	10c + 5c rose brn	.25	.25
B65	SP10	25c + 10c gray vio	.25	.25
B66	SP10	80c + 20c dk grn	.35	.25
		Nos. B64-B66 (3)	.85	.75

The surtax was for child welfare.

1961, Nov. 23   Perf. 13x12½

Stamp Day: #B68, B70, Diego de Herrera.

B67	SP11	10c + 5c org red	.25	.25
B68	SP11	25c + 10c dk pur	.25	.25
B69	SP11	30c + 10c dk red brn	.25	.25
B70	SP11	1p + 10c red org	.35	.25
		Nos. B67-B70 (4)	1.10	1.00

AIR POST STAMPS

> In 1942, seven air post stamps of Spain, Nos. C100-C108, were overprinted "SAHARA ESPAÑOL", but satisfactory information regarding their status is not available.

> Catalogue values for unused stamps in this section are for Never Hinged items.

Ostriches — AP1

Desert Scene — AP2

1943   Unwmk.   Litho.   Perf. 12½

C8	AP1	5c cer & vio brn	.25	.25
C9	AP2	25c yel grn & ol grn	.25	.25
C10	AP1	50c ind & turq grn	.25	.25
C11	AP2	1p pur & grnsh bl	.30	.25
C12	AP1	1.40p gray grn & bl	.35	.25
C13	AP2	2p mag & org brn	2.50	1.40
C14	AP1	5p brown & purple	3.25	1.40
C15	AP2	6p brt bl & gray grn	62.50	25.00
		Nos. C8-C15 (8)	69.65	29.05

Nos. C8-C15 exist imperf. Value of set $90.

Diego Garcia de Herrera AP3

1950, Nov. 23   Photo.

C16	AP3	5p rose violet	2.75	1.10

Stamp Day.

Woman Holding Dove — AP4

1951, Apr. 22   Engr.   Perf. 10

C17	AP4	5p deep green	25.00	7.25

500th birth anniv. of Queen Isabella I.
No. C17 is valued in the grade of fine.

Helmet and Trappings AP5

Plane and Camel Rider AP6

1952, July 18   Photo.   Perf. 13x12½

C18	AP5	5p brown	27.50	6.50

500th birth anniv. of Ferdinand the Catholic, of Spain.

1961, May 16   Unwmk.

C19	AP6	25p gray brown	3.00	1.00

SPECIAL DELIVERY STAMPS

Catalogue value for unused stamps in this section are for Never Hinged items.

Type A2 Inscribed "URGENTE"

1943   Unwmk.   Perf. 12½
E1 A2 25c Camel troops   1.75 .95

Messenger on Motorcycle — SD1

Unwmk.
1971, Sept. 6   Photo.   Perf. 13
E2 SD1 10p bright rose & olive   .85 .40

SPANISH WEST AFRICA

'spa-nish 'west 'a-fri-kə

LOCATION — Northwest Africa bordering on the Atlantic Ocean
GOVT. — Spanish administration
AREA — 117,000 sq. mi.
POP. — 95,000 (1950)
CAPITAL — Sidi Ifni

Spanish West Africa was the major political division of Spanish areas in northwest Africa. It included Spanish Sahara (Rio de Oro and Saguiet el Hamra) Ifni and, for administrative purposes, Southern Morocco. Separate stamp issues have been used for Rio de Oro, Ifni and La Aguera.

Catalogue values for all unused stamps in this country are for Never Hinged items.

Native — A1

Perf. 13x12½
1949, Oct.   Litho.   Unwmk.
1 A1 4p dark gray green   3.00 1.10
UPU, 75th anniversary.

Nomad Camp A2

5c, 30c, 75c, 2p, Tinzgarrentz Oasis. 10c, 40c, 90c, 5p, Desert well. 15c, 45c, 1p, Caravan.

1950, June 5   Perf. 12½x13
2 A2 2c brown   .25 .25
3 A2 5c rose violet   .25 .25
4 A2 10c Prussian blue   .25 .25
5 A2 15c deep olive
       gray   .25 .25
6 A2 25c red brown   .25 .25
7 A2 30c bright yellow   .25 .25
8 A2 40c olive gray   .25 .25
9 A2 45c rose lake   .25 .25
10 A2 50c brown orange   .30 .25

11 A2 75c ultramarine   .30 .25
12 A2 90c dull blue grn   .35 .25
13 A2 1p gray   .35 .25
14 A2 1.35p violet   .95 .55
15 A2 2p sepia   1.75 1.15
16 A2 5p lilac rose   14.50 4.25
17 A2 10p light brown   33.50 23.00
       Nos. 2-17 (16)   54.00 31.95

AIR POST STAMPS

Isabella the Catholic, Queen of Castile — AP1

Perf. 13x12½
1949, Nov. 23   Photo.   Unwmk.
C1 AP1 5p yellow brown   2.25 1.00
Stamp Day, Nov. 23, 1949.

Desert Camp AP2

Designs: Various Desert Scenes.

1951, Mar. 1   Litho.   Perf. 12½x13
C2 AP2 25c ocher   .40 .25
C3 AP2 50c lilac rose   .40 .25
C4 AP2 1p green   .45 .25
C5 AP2 2p bright blue   .95 .25
C6 AP2 3.25p rose lilac   1.75 .85
C7 AP2 5p gray brown   17.50 3.90
C8 AP2 10p rose red   30.00 19.00
       Nos. C2-C8 (7)   51.45 23.85

SPECIAL DELIVERY STAMP

Tilimenzo Pass and Franco SD1

Perf. 12½x13
1951, Mar. 1   Litho.   Unwmk.
E1 SD1 25c rose carmine   .45 .30

SRI LANKA

ˌsrē 'läŋ-kə

LOCATION — Indian Ocean south of India
GOVT. — Democratic Socialist Republic
AREA — 26,244 sq. mi.
POP. — 19,144,875 (1999 est.)
CAPITAL — Colombo

Sri Lanka was named Ceylon until May 22, 1972. Issues inscribed "Ceylon" are listed under that name in Volume 2.

100 Cents = 1 Rupee

Catalogue values for all unused stamps in this country are for Never Hinged items.

Watermark

Wmk. 385 — CARTOR

Wmk. 233 — "Harrison & Sons, London" in Script

Wmk. 388 — Multiple "SPM"

Wmk. 408

Lotus and Sunrise over Adam's Peak — A162

1972, May 22   Litho.   Perf. 13½x13
470 A162 15c blue & multi   .85 .60
Inauguration of Ceylon as Republic of Sri Lanka.

A162a

Overprinted "1972" in Red
1972, May 26   Perf. 14x13½
471 A162a 5c orange brn & multi   .45 .60
World Fellowship of Buddhists, Sri Lanka, May 22-28.
Supposedly not issued without overprint, copies sell for 25-cents.

Book Year Emblem, Oil Lamp — A163

1972, Sept. 8   Photo.   Perf. 13
472 A163 20c yellow & dk brn   .40 .50
International Book Year 1972.

Imperial Angelfish A164

Tropical Fish: 3c, Green chromide. 30c, Skipjack bonito. 2r, Black ruby barbs.

Perf. 14x13½
1972, Oct. 12   Litho.   Unwmk.
473 A164 2c ultra & multi   .25 1.25
474 A164 3c dp orange &
       multi   .25 1.25
475 A164 30c brt green & mul-
       ti   2.25 .40
476 A164 2r dp green & multi   6.50 6.00
       Nos. 473-476 (4)   9.25 8.90
3rd Session of Indian Ocean Fisheries Commission, Colombo, Oct. 9-14.

Bandaranaike Memorial Hall — A165

1973, May 17   Litho.   Perf. 14
477 A165 15c lt ultra & vio blue   .40 .40
Opening of Bandaranaike Memorial International Conference Hall.

Women Holding Lotus A166

Rock and Temple Paintings: 35c, King giving away his children, Degaldoruwa Temple, near Kandy, 18th cent. 50c, Prince and gravedigger, Polonaruwa, 12th cent. 90c, Holy man holding lotus, Polonaruwa, 12th cent. Design of 1.55r is from Sigiriya, 5th cent.

1973, Sept. 3   Perf. 13½x14
478 A166 35c lt gray & multi   .45 .25
479 A166 50c gray & multi   .60 .25
480 A166 90c slate & multi   .85 .85
481 A166 1.55r brown & multi   1.00 1.75
a. Souvenir sheet of 4, #478-481   5.25 5.25
       Nos. 478-481 (4)   2.90 3.10

For surcharges see Nos. 538-540.

Bandaranaike Conference Hall — A167

1974, Sept. 6   Litho.   Perf. 14
482 A167 85c multicolored   .50 .50
20th Commonwealth Parliamentary Conference, Sri Lanka, Sept. 1-15.

S.W.R.D. Bandaranaike A168

1974, Sept. 25   Photo.   Perf. 14½
486 A168 15c ultra & multi   .40 .40
For surcharge see No. 541.

"UPU," "100" and UPU Emblem A170

1974, Oct. 9   Litho.   Perf. 13
490 A170 50c multicolored   1.75 1.25

Parliament, Colombo A171

1975, Apr. 1   Litho.   Perf. 13½
491 A171 1r multicolored   .40 .40

Interparliamentary Union, Spring Meeting at Bandaranaike Memorial International Conference Hall, Sri Lanka, Mar. 31-Apr. 5.

Ponnambalam Ramanathan A172

D. J. Wimalasurendra A173

1975, Sept. 4   Litho.   Perf. 13½
492 A172 75c multicolored   .45 .70

Sir Ponnambalam Ramanathan (1851-1930), lawyer and educator.

1975, Sept. 17
493 A173 75c ultra & blue blk   .45 .70

Devapura Jayasena Wimalasurendra (1874-1953), engineer and irrigation specialist.

Map, Mrs. Bandaranaike, Dove — A174

1975, Dec. 22   Litho.   Perf. 13½
494 A174 1.15r blue & multi   3.75 1.90

International Women's Year 1975.
For surcharge, see No. 1579.

Rhododendron Zeylanicum A175

Flowers: 50c, Exacum trinerve. 75c, Daffodil orchid. 10r, Wormia triquetra.

1976, Jan. 1   Litho.   Perf. 13
495 A175 25c blue & multi   .25 .25
496 A175 50c ocher & multi   .25 .25
497 A175 75c black & multi   .25 .25
498 A175 10r black & multi   4.00 4.50
  a.   Souvenir sheet of 4, #495-498   20.00 20.00
        Nos. 495-498 (4)   4.75 5.25

Mahaveli-ganga Sluice — A176

1976, Jan. 8   Litho.   Perf. 13x12½
499 A176 85c lt blue, lt grn & lil   .45 1.00

Mahaveli-ganga River diversion.

Radar Station — A177

1976, May 6   Litho.   Perf. 14
500 A177 1r blue & multi   1.00 1.25

Opening of Satellite Earth Station, Padukka.

Prince Siddhartha as White Elephant and Sleeping Queen — A178

Birth of Buddha: 10c, King consulting astrologers. 1.50r, King entertaining astrologers at banquet. 2r, Queen taken in procession to her parents. 2.25r, Flag bearers, musicians in procession. 5r, Queen giving birth to Prince Siddhartha, the Buddha. Designs taken from 18th cent. wall paintings in Dambawa Vihara Temple.

1976, May 7   Litho.   Perf. 13½
501 A178 5c blue & multi   .25 .75
502 A178 10c blue & multi   .25 .75
503 A178 1.50r blue & multi   .85 1.00
504 A178 2r blue & multi   .85 1.00
505 A178 2.25r blue & multi   1.75 2.00
506 A178 5r blue & multi   4.00 5.00
  a.   Souvenir sheet of 6, #501-506   14.00 14.00
        Nos. 501-506 (6)   7.95 10.50

Blue Sapphire A179

Gems of Sri Lanka: 1.15r, Cat's-eye. 2r, Star sapphire. 5r, Ruby.

1976, June 16   Perf. 12x12½
507 A179 60c multicolored   6.50 .40
508 A179 1.15r multicolored   10.50 2.40
509 A179 2r multicolored   12.00 5.00
510 A179 5r multicolored   16.00 16.00
  a.   Souv. sheet of 4, #507-510   65.00 45.00
        Nos. 507-510 (4)   45.00 23.80

Prime Minister Sirimavo Bandaranaike A180

Statue of Liberty A181

1976, Aug. 3   Photo.   Perf. 14¼x14½
511 A180 1.15r pink & multi   .40 .40
512 A180 2r pink & multi   .70 .70

5th Summit Conference of Non-aligned Countries, Colombo, Aug. 9-19.

For surcharges, see Nos. 1347-1348.

1976, Nov. 29   Litho.   Perf. 14
513 A181 2.25r lt blue & indigo   .85 1.25

American Bicentennial.

A. G. Bell, Telephone and Telephone Line A182

Maitreya Bodhisattva A183

1976, Dec. 21   Litho.   Perf. 13x13½
514 A182 1r orange & multi   .90 .35

Centenary of first telephone call by Alexander Graham Bell, Mar. 10, 1876.

1977, Jan. 1   Litho.   Perf. 12½x13
Bronze Statues: 1r, Sundara Murti Swami, 11th century. 5r, Goddess Tara.
515 A183 50c multicolored   .45 .45
516 A183 1r multicolored   .45 .45
517 A183 5r multicolored   4.00 4.50
        Nos. 515-517 (3)   4.90 5.40

Colombo Museum, centenary.

Kandyan Crown, 1737-1815 A184

2r, Kandyan throne and footstool, 1693-1815.

1977, Jan. 18
518 A184 1r multicolored   .60 .60
519 A184 2r multicolored   1.90 2.50

Rahula Thero — A185

No. 521, Ponnambalam Arunachalam.

1977   Litho.   Perf. 13½
520 A185 1r multicolored   1.10 1.10
521 A185 1r multicolored   .70 .70

Sri Rahula Thero, 15th cent. poet and scholar, and Sir Ponnambalam Arunachalam (1851-1930), 1st president of Ceylon University Assoc., member of Congress.
Issue dates: #520, Feb. 23; #521, Mar. 10.

Brass Lamps — A186

Handicrafts: 25c, Jewelry box and jewelry. 50c, Caparisoned ivory elephant. 5r, Sinhala wooden mask.

1977, Apr. 7   Perf. 13
522 A186 20c multicolored   .25 .25
523 A186 25c multicolored   .25 .25
524 A186 50c multicolored   .45 .45

525 A186 5r multicolored   2.50 2.75
  a.   Souvenir sheet of 4, #522-525   5.75 5.75
        Nos. 522-525 (4)   3.45 3.70

Mohammed Cassim Siddi Lebbe — A187

1977, June 11   Litho.   Perf. 13
526 A187 1r multicolored   .50 .80

Lebbe (1838-98), lawyer, educator and Moslem journalist.

Girl Guide A188

1977, Dec. 13   Litho.   Perf. 15
527 A188 75c multicolored   1.25 .50

60th anniversary of Sri Lanka Girl Guides.

Parliament and Wheel of Life — A189

1978, Feb. 4   Photo.   Perf. 12x12½
528 A189 15c green & gold   .40 .25

J.R. Jayewardene, first elected president, assumption of office.
See Nos. 559, 611-611A, 847. For surcharges see Nos. 542, 572, 698A-698B.

Runners — A190

1978, Apr. 27   Litho.   Perf. 15
529 A190 15c multicolored   .40 .60

National Youth Service Council.
For surcharge see No. 543.

Bodhisattva in Royal Attire in Lotus Position A191

Vesak Festival: 50c, Bodhisattva without royal attire cutting off his hair with sword. Both designs from rock carvings in Borobudur Temple, Java.

1978, May 16   Perf. 13
530 A191 15c multicolored   1.10 1.10
531 A191 50c multicolored   1.50 1.50

Veera Puran
Appu and his
Flag — A192

Birdwing
Butterfly — A193

1978, Aug. 8   Litho.   Perf. 13
532 A192 15c multicolored   .40 .30
Veera Puran Appu (1848-1908), revolutionist, 130th birth anniversary.

1978, Nov. 28   Litho.   Perf. 14x13½
Butterflies: 50c, Tamil lacewing. 5r, Blue oakleaf. 10r, Blue mormon.
534 A193 25c multicolored   .90   .25
535 A193 50c multicolored   1.50   .25
536 A193 5r multicolored   2.75 1.75
537 A193 10r multicolored   2.75 2.75
  a.   Souvenir sheet of 4, #534-
        537   20.00 16.00
        Nos. 534-537 (4)   7.90 5.00

Nos. 478, 480-481 Surcharged with
New Value and Bar
1978   Litho.   Perf. 13½x14
538 A166 5c on 90c multi   10.50 10.50
539 A166 10c on 35c multi   3.50 3.50
540 A166 1r on 1.55r multi   7.00 7.00
        Nos. 538-540 (3)   21.00 21.00

Nos. 486, 528 Surcharged with New
Value and 2 Bars; No. 529 with New
Value on Pink Panel
Perf. 14½, 12x12½, 15
1979, Jan.   Litho.; Engr.
541 A168 25c on 15c multi   7.00 7.00
542 A189 25c on 15c multi   7.00 7.00
543 A190 25c on 15c multi   7.00 7.00
        Nos. 541-543 (3)   21.00 21.00

Ceylon No. 390 Overprinted Vertically
"SRI LANKA" in Green and
Surcharged in Black
1979, Mar. 22   Photo.   Perf. 11½
Granite Paper
544 A118 15c on 10c brt green   4.50 3.00

Arrival of Sacred
Tooth — A194

Wrestlers — A195

Wall Paintings from Kelaniya Temple: 25c, Prince Danta and Princess Hema Mala bringing Sacred Tooth from Kalinga, 4th century A.D. 1r, Princess Theri Sanghamitta bringing, by ship, the bodhi tree branch, 3rd century B.C. 10r, King Kirti offering fan of authority to supreme patriarch, 18th century.

1979, May 3   Litho.   Perf. 13½
546 A194 25c multicolored   .25   .25
547 A194 1r multicolored   .25   .25
548 A194 10r multicolored   2.00 2.00
  a.   Souvenir sheet of 3, #546-548 4.25 4.25
        Nos. 546-548 (3)   2.50 2.50
        2523rd Vesak Festival, May 11.

1979, May 18   Litho.   Perf. 14
Design: 50r, Dancer. Woodcarvings from Embekke Temple.
549 A195 20r multicolored   1.75 1.25
550 A195 50r multicolored   4.25 3.50

Piyadasa Sirisena
A196

Dudley S.
Senanayake
A197

1979, May 22   Perf. 13x13½
551 A196 1.25r deep green   .60   .60
Piyadasa Sirisena (1875-1946), patriot, journalist, novelist and poet.

1979, June 19   Photo.
552 A197 1.25r deep green   .40   .40
27th death anniversary of Prime Minister Dudley S. Senanayake.

Mother
Feeding Child,
IYC Emblem
A198

Designs: 3r, Faces and IYC emblem. 5r, Children with rope and ball, IYC emblem.

1979, July 31   Litho.   Perf. 12½
553 A198 5c multicolored   .25   .25
554 A198 3r multicolored   .40   .90
555 A198 5r multicolored   .45 1.10
        Nos. 553-555 (3)   1.10 2.25
International Year of the Child.

Ceylon No. 2,
Rowland
Hill — A199

1979, Aug. 27   Litho.   Perf. 13½
556 A199 3r multicolored   .60 1.00
Sir Rowland Hill (1795-1879), originator of penny postage.

Airlanka
Emblem — A200

1979, Sept. 1   Litho.   Perf. 12½
557 A200 3r red, dk grn & blk   1.25 1.60
Airlanka National Airline, inaugural flight, Colombo-Bangkok.

Coconut
Palm — A201

1979, Oct. 9   Litho.   Perf. 13½
558 A201 2r multicolored   1.50 1.50
Asian and Pacific Coconut Community, 10th anniversary.

No. 528 Redrawn Without Date
1979, Oct. 9   Photo.   Perf. 13
Size: 20x24mm
559 A189 25c green & gold   .65   .25

Family in
Cogwheel,
Parliament
A202

1979, Oct.   Litho.   Perf. 13½
560 A202 2r multicolored   1.25 1.50
Intl. Conf. of Parliamentarians on Population & Development, Colombo, Aug. 28-Sept. 1.

Swami Vipulananda
(1892-1947),
Philosopher &
Theologian — A203

1979, Nov. 18   Perf. 12½
561 A203 1.25r multicolored   .40   .50

Text and
Crescent
A204

1979, Nov. 22
562 A204 3.75r multicolored   .60 1.50
Hegira (pilgrimage year).

Institute
Emblem
A205

Blue Magpie
A206

1979, Nov. 29   Perf. 13
563 A205 15c multicolored   .40   .60
Ayurveda Medical Institute, 50th anniversary.

1979, Dec. 13   Litho.   Perf. 14
564 A206 10c shown   .25   .25
565 A206 15c Lorikeet   .25   .25
566 A206 75c Arrenga   .25   .25
567 A206 1r Spurfowl   .25   .25
568 A206 5r Yellow-fronted
            barbet   1.50 1.50
569 A206 10r Yellow-eared
            bulbul   1.90 1.90
  a.   Souvenir sheet of 6, #564-
        569   11.00 11.00
        Nos. 564-569 (6)   4.40 4.40
For surcharges, see Nos. 1062B, 1512.

Rotary
Emblem,
Map of Sri
Lanka
A207

1979, Dec. 27   Litho.   Perf. 14½
570 A207 1.50r multicolored   1.10 1.50
Rotary International, 75th anniversary.

A. Ratnayake,
Educator and Pres.
of Senate — A208

1980, Jan. 7   Photo.   Perf. 14x13½
571 A208 1.25r slate green   .40   .40

No. 559 Surcharged
1980, Mar. 17   Photo.   Perf. 13
572 A189 35c on 25c multi   .50   .40
One position has ".33" instead of ".35."

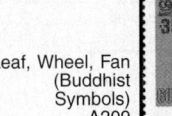

Leaf, Wheel, Fan
(Buddhist
Symbols)
A209

1980, Mar. 25   Photo.   Perf. 13½x14
573 A209 10c Steeple   .50 1.25
574 A209 35c shown   .50   .40
All Ceylon Buddhist Cong., 60th anniv.

Col. Henry
Olcott, Buddhist
Emblem — A210

1980, May 17   Litho.   Perf. 14
575 A210 2r multicolored   1.25 1.50
Col. Henry S. Olcott (1832-1907), American theosophist and Buddhist lecturer, centenary of arrival in Sri Lanka.

Journey of
Patachara,
Temple
Painting — A211

Vesak Festival (Paintings, life of Buddha): 1.60r, Patachara crossing river.

1980, May 23   Perf. 13½x14
576 A211 35c multicolored   .40   .40
577 A211 1.60r multicolored   1.90 2.10

George E. De
Silva — A212

1980, June 8   Perf. 13x13½
578 A212 1.60r multicolored   .50   .50
George E. de Silva (1879-1950), politician.

Siva Temples, Polonnaruwa — A213

1980, Aug. 25   Litho.   Perf. 13½
579 A213 35c shown   .25   .40
580 A213 35c Cave Temples,
            Dambulla   .25   .40
581 A213 35c Sacred Tooth
            Temple, Kandy   .25   .40
582 A213 1.60r Abhayagiri Hill   .80 1.25

583 A213 1.60r Jetavanarama
Hill .80 *1.25*
584 A213 1.60r Sigiri .80 *1.25*
a. Souvenir sheet of 6, #579-584 4.00 4.00
Nos. 579-584 (6) 3.15 *4.95*

UNESCO "Cultural Triangle" Project.

Department of
Cooperative
Development,
50th Anniversary
A214

1980, Oct. 1 **Litho.** **Perf. 13½**
585 A214 20c multicolored .40 .50

Women's
Movement
Emblem
A215

1980, Oct. 16 **Photo.** **Perf. 14x13½**
586 A215 35c multicolored .40 .50

Mahila Samiti (Rural Women's Movement),
50th anniversary.

Nativity — A216

1980, Nov. 20 **Litho.** **Perf. 13½**
587 A216 35c shown .30 .30
588 A216 3.75r Three kings .80 .90
a. Souvenir sheet of 2, #587-588 2.00 2.00

Christmas 1980/Year of the family.

Colombo
Public
Library
Opening
A217

1980, Dec. 17 **Perf. 12x12½**
589 A217 35c multicolored .40 .40

Peacock
Banner
A218

Designs: Ancient flags.

1980, Dec. 18 **Perf. 13**
590 A218 10c shown .25 .25
591 A218 25c Elephant banner .25 .25
592 A218 1.60r Sinhalese royal
flag .25 .25
593 A218 20r Kings Civil Standard 1.75 2.10
a. Souvenir sheet of 4, #590-593 2.50 2.50
Nos. 590-593 (4) 2.50 2.85

For surcharge on No. 592, see No. 1550.

Fishing
Cat — A219

1981, Feb. 10 **Litho.** **Perf. 14**
594 A219 2.50r on 1.60r, shown .55 .25
595 A219 3r on 1.50r, Golden
palm cat .55 .25
596 A219 4r on 2r, Mouse
deer .55 .45
597 A219 5r on 3.75r, Rusty-
spotted cat .85 .60
a. Souvenir sheet of 4, #594-597 3.00 3.00
Nos. 594-597 (4) 2.50 1.55

See #728-730A, 928. For surcharge see
#731.

Population and
Housing
Census — A220

1981, Mar. 2 **Litho.** **Perf. 12½x12**
598 A220 50c multicolored 1.00 1.25

Ceylon Light
Infantry
Centenary
A221

1981, Apr. 1 **Litho.** **Perf. 12**
599 A221 2r multicolored 1.60 1.60

The Death of
Buddha, Carved
Panel, 1st
Cent. — A222

1981, May 5 **Perf. 13x13½**
600 A222 35c shown .25 .25
601 A222 50c Silk banner .25 .25
602 A222 7r Statuette 2.00 3.25
a. Souvenir sheet of 3, #600-602 5.75 5.75
Nos. 600-602 (3) 2.50 3.75

Vesak Festival.

St. John
Baptist de
la Salle
A223

1981, May 15 **Litho.** **Perf. 12½x12**
603 A223 2r multicolored 2.25 2.25

De la Salle Brothers Order, 300th anniv.

Polwatte Sri
Buddadatta
A224

Intl. Year of the
Disabled — A225

Famous Men: No. 605, Mohottiwatte Guna-
nanda, Buddhist leader. No. 606, Gnanapra
Kasar, Catholic missionary. No. 607, Al-Haj
T.B. Jayah, Muslim teacher. No. 608, James
Peiris. No. 609, N.M. Perera, founded first
Marxist Party in Sri Lanka, 1935.

1981 **Photo.** **Perf. 12**
604 A224 50c olive bister .75 1.00
605 A224 50c dull red brown .75 1.00
606 A224 50c lilac .75 1.00
607 A224 50c gray green .75 1.00
608 A224 50c brown .75 1.00
609 A224 50c crimson rose .75 1.00
Nos. 604-609 (6) 4.50 6.00

Issued: #604-606, 5/22; #607, 5/31; #609,
6/6; #608, 12/20.
See #623-624, 640-642, 646, 672-676, 713-
717.

1981, June 19 **Litho.** **Perf. 12½x12**
610 A225 2r multicolored 1.50 1.75

**No. 528 Redrawn with Denomination
in Upper Right Corner**
1981-83 **Photo.** **Perf. 13**
Size: 20x24mm
611 A189 50c green & gold 3.00 .25
611A A189 60c green & gold 11.00 1.75

Issued: 50c, June 6; 60c, Dec. 30, 1983.
For surcharges see Nos. 698A-698B.

Hand
Putting
Ballot in
Box
A226

Perf. 12½x12, 12x12½
1981, July 7 **Litho.**
612 A226 50c shown .30 .30
613 A226 7r Ballot box on map,
vert. 2.40 3.00

Universal Franchise, 50th anniv.

Rhys
Davids
(Society
Founder)
A227

1981, July 14 **Perf. 12½x12**
614 A227 35c multicolored 1.25 .65

All Ceylon
Buddhist
Students'
Federation,
25th Anniv.
A228

1981, July 21 **Litho.** **Perf. 13½**
615 A228 2r multicolored 1.50 1.50

Family
Planning — A229

1981, Sept. 25
616 A229 50c multicolored 1.50 1.50

7th World
Acupuncture
Cong. — A230

1981, Oct. 20 **Litho.** **Perf. 12x12½**
617 A230 2r multicolored 4.25 4.25

Visit of
Queen
Elizabeth
II, Oct.
A231

Designs: Flags of Gt. Britain and Sri Lanka.

1981, Oct. 21 **Perf. 14**
618 A231 50c multicolored .75 .75
619 A231 5r multicolored 2.25 2.25
a. Souvenir sheet of 2, #618-619 3.50 4.00

Forest
Conservation
A232

1981, Nov. 27 **Perf. 13½x13**
620 A232 35c Forest .25 .25
621 A232 50c Tree planting .30 .30
622 A232 5r Jack tree 2.50 2.75
a. Souvenir sheet of 3, #620-622,
perf. 14x13 2.75 3.75
Nos. 620-622 (3) 3.05 3.30

Famous Men Type of 1981

Designs: No. 623, F.R. Senanayaka (1882-
1926), lawyer and politician. No. 624, Philip
Gunawardhane, politician, 10th death anniv.

1982 **Litho.** **Perf. 14**
623 A224 50c brown 1.00 1.00
624 A224 50c bright rose 1.00 1.00

Issue dates: #623, Jan. 1; #624, Jan. 11.

Dept. of Inland
Revenue, 50th
Anniv.
A233

Natl. Television
Inauguration
A234

1982, Feb. 9 **Litho.** **Perf. 14**
625 A233 50c multicolored 1.00 1.00

1982, Feb. 15
626 A234 2.50r multicolored 3.75 3.75

Sesquicentennial of Cricket Introduction and Centenary of Sri Lanka vs. England Match — A235

1982, Feb. 17
627 A235 2.50r multicolored   9.00 9.00

Osbeckia Wightiana A236

1982, Apr. 1   *Perf. 12*
628 A236 35c shown   .25   .25
629 A236 2r Mesua nagas-
            sarium   .35   .25
630 A236 7r Rhodomyrtus to-
            mentosa   .80   .85
631 A236 20r Phaius tancarvil-
            leae   2.25 2.25
 a.   Souvenir sheet of 4, #628-
       631   10.50 10.50
       Nos. 628-631 (4)   3.65 3.60

Food and Nutrition Planning A237

1982, Apr. 6   Litho.   Perf. 13
632 A237 50c multicolored   2.40 2.40

World Hindu Conference A238

1982, Apr. 21   Perf. 14x14½
633 A238 50c multicolored   1.60 1.60

Vesak Festival 1982 A239

Scenes from Jataka Story (Pre-incarnation of Buddha), Cloth Painting, 3rd cent. B.C., Hanguranketa Temple (King Vessantara and): 35c, Giving away white elephant. 50c, Giving away his children to a Brahmin. 5r, Royal family in chariot.

1982, Apr. 23   Perf. 14
634 A239 35c multicolored   .80   .25
635 A239 50c multicolored   .95   .25
636 A239 2.50r multicolored   3.25 2.75
637 A239 5r multicolored   4.25 4.25
 a.   Souvenir sheet of 4, #634-
       637   13.50 13.50
       Nos. 634-637 (4)   9.25 7.50

New Parliament Building Opening A240

1982, Apr. 29
638 A240 50c multicolored   1.40 1.40

Scouting Year A241

1982, May 24   Litho. Perf. 12½x12
639 A241 50c multicolored   2.50 2.25

Famous Men Type of 1981
1982   *Perf. 12x12½*
640 A224 50c C.W.W. Kannan-
            gara   1.50 1.50
641 A224 50c G.P. Malalasekara   1.50 1.50
642 A224 50c John Kotelawala   1.50 1.50
       Nos. 640-642 (3)   4.50 4.50
Issued: #640, 5/22; #641, 5/26; #642, 6/8.

World Buddhist Leaders Conference — A242

1982, June 10   Perf. 12½x12
643 A242 50c multicolored   1.50 1.50

World Environment Day — A243

1982, June 5
644 A243 50c multicolored   2.50 2.10

YMCA Centenary — A244

1982, June 24   Photo.   Perf. 11½
645 A244 2.50r multicolored   5.00 5.00

Famous Men Type of 1981
1982, June 14   Litho.   Perf. 12x12½
646 A224 50c Waitialingam
            Duraiswamy   1.50 1.50

Weliwita Saranankara Sangharaja A245

1982, July 5
647 A245 50c orange & black   1.50 1.50

25th Anniv. of Sasana Sevaka Samithiya A246

1982, Aug. 8
648 A246 50c multicolored   2.25 2.25

TB Bacillus Centenary A247

1982, Sept. 21
649 A247 50c Koch, microscope,
            bacillus   3.00 2.50

Eye Donation Society — A248

1982, Nov. 16   Litho.   Perf. 12x12½
650 A248 2.50r Emblems, map   4.50 4.75

125th Anniv. of Ceylon Postage Stamps — A249

1982, Dec. 1   Litho.   Perf. 13½
651 A249 50c Ceylon #5, 302   .65   .65
652 A249 2.50r Ceylon #12, #611   2.50 2.50
 a.   Souv. sheet, #651-652, perf. 12   4.00 4.00
       Natl. Stamp Exhibition.

Sir Oliver Goonetilleke A250

1982, Dec. 17   Litho.   Perf. 12x12½
653 A250 50c black & brown   .80 1.10

25th Anniv. of Sarvodaya Social Movement A251

1983, Jan. 1   Perf. 13½
654 A251 50c multicolored   1.50 1.50

55th Anniv. of Amateur Radio Society A252

1983, Jan. 17
655 A252 2.50r multicolored   4.50 4.50

Customs Cooperation Council and First Intl. Customs Day — A253

1983, Jan. 26   Litho.   Perf. 12
656 A253 50c orange & multi   .80   .80
657 A253 5r green & multi   5.25 6.00

Bottlenose Dolphin A254

1983, Feb. 22   Perf. 14½x14
658 A254 50c shown   1.00   .25
659 A254 2r Dugongs   1.60 1.00
660 A254 2.50r Humpback
            whale   4.75 2.50
661 A254 10r Great sperm
            whale   10.50 8.75
       Nos. 658-661 (4)   17.85 12.50

Ceylon Shipping Corp. A255

1983, Mar. 1   Perf. 12x12½
662 A255 50c Container ship   .40   .25
663 A255 2.50r Liner services
            map   1.50   .90
664 A255 5r Conventional ship   2.25 2.10
665 A255 20r Oil tanker   3.50 5.50
       Nos. 662-665 (4)   7.65 8.75

Intl. Women's Day — A256

1983, Mar. 8   Perf. 13½
666 A256 50c Woman, flag   .40   .25
667 A256 5r Woman, map   1.50 2.25

Commonwealth Day — A257

1983, Mar. 14
668 A257 50c Waterfall   .25   .25
669 A257 2.50r Tea picking   .25   .25
670 A257 5r Harvesting   .35   .50
671 A257 20r Cultural pageant   1.40 1.75
       Nos. 668-671 (4)   2.25 2.75

Famous Men Type of 1981

1983 **Litho.** **Perf. 12**
672 A224 50c Henry W.
Amarasuriya .45 .75

Size: 29x40mm

673 A224 50c Charles A. Lorenz .45 .75
674 A224 50c Simon G. Perera .45 .75
675 A224 50c Nordeen H.M. Abdul Cader .45 .75
676 A224 50c C.W. Tamotherampillai 1.25 1.25
Nos. 672-676 (5) 3.05 4.25

No. 676 shows Tamotherampillai looking towards the right of the stamp. A version that was to be issued May 22, showed someone labeled C. W. Tamotherampillai looking straight ahead.
Issued: No. 676, Oct. 1; others, May 22.

25th Anniv. of Lions Club A258

1983, May 7 **Litho.** **Perf. 14**
677 A258 2.50r multicolored 4.25 2.75

Vesak Festival 1983 — A259

Various Colombo murals.

1983, May 13 **Perf. 12½x12**
678 A259 35c multicolored .25 .25
679 A259 50c multicolored .25 .25
680 A259 5r multicolored 1.10 1.10
681 A259 10r multicolored 1.90 1.90
a. Souvenir sheet of 4, #678-681 3.75 4.25
Nos. 678-681 (4) 3.50 3.50

125th Anniv. of Telecommunication Service — A260

1983, May 17 **Perf. 12x12½**
682 A260 2r shown 1.00 .80
683 A260 10r World Communications Year 3.00 4.25

Gam Udawa Village Re-awakening Movement — A261

1983, June 23 **Litho.** **Perf. 12x12½**
684 A261 50c Family .25 .30
685 A261 5r Village .75 1.75

Cattle Transport A262

1983, Aug. 1 **Litho.** **Perf. 12**
686 A262 35c shown .30 .30
687 A262 2r Train 3.25 3.25
688 A262 2.50r Cattle cart 1.75 1.75
689 A262 5r Model T Ford 3.50 3.50
Nos. 686-689 (4) 8.80 8.80

Sir Tikiri Banda Panabokke, 20th Death Anniv. — A263

1983, Sept. 2 **Litho.** **Perf. 13½x14**
690 A263 50c dark red 1.50 1.50

Ceylon Wood Pigeon A264

1983, Dec. 1 **Litho.** **Perf. 14½**
691 A264 25c shown 1.20 1.20
692 A264 35c Ceylon white-eye 1.20 1.20
693 A264 2r Dusky-blue flycatcher 1.75 1.75
694 A264 20r Ceylon coucal 2.75 2.75
a. Souvenir sheet of 4, #691-694 7.00 7.00
Nos. 691-694 (4) 6.90 6.90

See No. 877. For surcharge see No. 780A.

Christmas, Stone Carvings — A265

1983, Dec. 5 **Litho.** **Perf. 12½x13**
695 A265 50c multicolored .25 .25
696 A265 5r ultra & bister .50 1.75
a. Souv. sheet, #695-696+label 1.10 2.25

A266

1983, Nov. 25 **Litho.** **Perf. 14x15**
697 A266 50c brown 2.25 2.25
Rev. Pelene Thero (1878-1955), Buddhist leader.

A267

1983 **Litho.** **Perf. 13½**
698 A267 50c Ahamed Orabi Al-
Misri 1.50 1.50

#611 Surcharged with Four Bars, #611A with Three Bars and New Denomination in Black or Green

1983-85 **Photo.** **Perf. 13**
698A A189 60c on 50c ('83) 17.00 4.00

Size: 20x24mm

698B A189 75c on 60c (G) ('85) 1.00 .40

Ovpt. on No. 698A also exists with two bars. Value, $20.
Issue dates: both Dec. 1.

World Food Day (Oct. 16) A268

1984, Jan. 2 **Perf. 12½x12**
699 A268 3r Rice paddy .70 1.75

Colombo Tea Auctions Centenary A269

1984, Jan. 31
700 A269 1r Auction House .25 .25
701 A269 2r Emblem .50 .50
702 A269 5r Tea picker 1.25 1.75
703 A269 10r Auction 2.50 3.50
Nos. 700-703 (4) 4.50 6.00

Mahapola Anniversary (Educational System) — A270

1984, Feb. 10 **Perf. 12**
704 A270 60c Students .25 .25
705 A270 1r Classroom .25 .25
706 A270 5.50r Student in library,
lab .35 1.50
707 A270 6r Emblem .40 1.50
Nos. 704-707 (4) 1.25 3.50

Vesak Festival 1984 A271

Wooden Casket Paintings, Temple Godapitiya Rajamaha Vihara, Akuressa: Scenes from Daham Sonda Jathaka legend.

1984, Apr. 27 **Litho.** **Perf. 14**
708 A271 35c multicolored .25 .25
709 A271 60c multicolored .80 .70
710 A271 5r multicolored 2.75 2.75
711 A271 10r multicolored 3.25 3.25
a. Souv. sheet of 4, #708-711, perf.
13x13½ 4.50 4.50
Nos. 708-711 (4) 7.05 6.95

Lions Club Intl., District 306A — A272

1984, May 5 **Litho.** **Perf. 14x14½**
712 A272 60c multicolored 2.10 1.50

Famous Men Type of 1981

Designs: No. 713, K. Balasingham, lawyer. No. 714, Mohamed Macan Markar (1879-1952), Muslim politician. No. 715, W. Arthur de Silva (d. 1942), industrialist. No. 716, Tissa Mahanayake Thero (1826-1907), Buddhist educator. No. 717, G.P. Wickremarachchi, medical pioneer.

1984, May 22 **Litho.** **Perf. 12x12½**
713 A224 60c brown .45 .80
714 A224 60c green .45 .80
715 A224 60c orange red .45 .80
716 A224 60c bister .45 .80
717 A224 60c yellow green .45 .80
Nos. 713-717 (5) 2.25 4.00

Public Service Mutual Provident Assoc. Centenary A273

1984, June 16 **Perf. 13x13½**
718 A273 4.60r Emblem 1.00 2.00

Village Re-awakening Movement A274

1984, June 23 **Perf. 12x12½**
719 A274 60c "One Million Houses" .60 .80

Asia-Pacific Broadcasting Union, 20th Anniv. — A275

1984, June 30 **Perf. 12½x12**
720 A275 7r Map 3.00 3.25

For surcharge see No. 776.

Cultural Pageant A276

Procession: a, Drummers, elephant. b, Torch bearers, 3 elephants (green or red masks). c, Torch bearers, 3 elephants (orange or yellow masks). d, Dancers. Continuous design.

1984, Aug. 11 **Litho.** **Perf. 12½x12**
721 Strip of 4 7.00 7.00
a.-d. A276 4.60r any single 1.50 1.50
e. Souvenir sheet of 4 7.50 7.50

Orchid Circle of Sri Lanka, 50th Anniversary A277

1984, Aug. 31 **Perf. 14**
722 A277 60c Vanda
memoria 1.60 1.60
723 A277 4.60r Acanthephippi-
um bicolor 3.25 3.25

724	A277	5r Vanda Tessel-		
		lata	2.25	2.25
725	A277	10r Anoectochillus		
		setaceus	7.00	7.00
a.		Souvenir sheet of 4, #722-		
		725	13.00	13.00
		Nos. 722-725 (4)	14.10	14.10

Wildlife Type of 1981

1982-89   Litho.   Perf. 14

728	A219	2.50r Felis viverrina	.40	.30
729	A219	3r Paradoxurus		
		zeylonensis	5.50	5.50
730	A219	4r Tragulus		
		meminna	.40	.40
730A	A219	5r Felis rubiginosa		
		('89)	.50	.40
		Nos. 728-730A (4)	6.80	6.60

No. 729 has brown inscriptions. See No. 928 for black inscriptions.
No. 728 is unwatermarked.
Issued: 2.50r, 6/1/83; 3r, 6/21/83; 4r, 11/16/82; 5r, 12/1/89.

No. 728 Surcharged in Brown

1985, Dec. 1   Litho.   Perf. 14

731	A219	5.75r on 2.50r multi	5.25	2.75

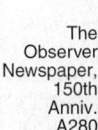

The Observer Newspaper, 150th Anniv. A280

1984, Aug. 31   Litho.   Perf. 13x13½

732	A280	4.60r Publisher, Colombo	3.50	4.00

Natl. School Games — A281

1984, Oct. 5   Perf. 13½x13

733	A281	60c blue, gray & blk	2.75	2.25

D. S. Senanayake (1884-1952), Prime Minister — A282

1984, Oct. 20   Perf. 14½x14

734	A282	35c Irrigated field	.25	.25
735	A282	60c Statue	.25	.25
736	A282	4.60r Reservoir	.45	.55
737	A282	6r Parliament House, Colombo	.65	.75
		Nos. 734-737 (4)	1.60	1.80

World Food Program — A284   Baari Arabic College, Weligama, Cent. — A285

1984, Dec. 10   Litho.   Perf. 13x13½

738	A284	7r Globe, Sri Lankans working field	2.40	1.60

1984, Dec. 24   Perf. 13x12½

739	A285	4.60r dull bl grn & blk	2.25	2.75

Intl. Youth Year — A286

1985, Jan. 1   Perf. 12½x13

740	A286	4.60r multicolored	.80	.60
741	A286	20r multicolored	3.00	3.50

For surcharge see No. 790.

World Religion Day — A287

Design: Emblems of World religions.

1985, Jan. 20   Perf. 12

742	A287	4.60r multicolored	3.50	3.50

Royal College, Colombo, 150th Anniv. — A288   Mahapola Scholarship Program for Development & Education, 5th Anniv. — A289

1985, Jan. 29   Perf. 13x12½

743	A288	60c College crest	.25	.30
744	A288	7r Campus	3.00	3.75

1985, Feb. 7   Perf. 14

745	A289	60c Diplomas, freighter, office buildings	1.40	1.75

Wariyapola Sri Sumangala Thero, Leader of the 1818 Great Uva Rebellion — A290

1985, Mar. 2   Perf. 13x13½

746	A290	60c brown & yellow	1.10	1.25

Victoria Project A291

Perf. 12½x12, 12x12½

1985, Apr. 12   Litho.

747	A291	60c Victoria Dam	1.25	1.25
748	A291	7r Dam, map, vert.	7.50	7.50

Vesak Festival 1985 — A292   Natl. Heroes — A293

Designs: 35c, Frontispiece of the Buddhist Annual golden jubilee issue. 60c, Women worshiping at temple, Vesak Poya Holiday cent.

6r, Bauddha Mandiraya, Colombo. 9r, Buddhist flag cent.

1985, Apr. 26   Perf. 13x12½

749	A292	35c multicolored	.25	.25
750	A292	60c multicolored	.25	.25
751	A292	6r multicolored	.85	.85
752	A292	9r multicolored	1.75	1.75
a.		Souvenir sheet of 4, #749-752	7.25	7.25
		Nos. 749-752 (4)	3.10	3.10

1985, May 22   Perf. 13x12½

#753,753, Waskaduwe Sri Subhuthi Thero (1835-1917), Pali scholar, philologist responsible for the Sinhala dictionary. #754, Rev. Fr. Peter A. Pillai (1904-64), educational & social reformer. #755, Dr. Senarath Paranavitane (c. 1900-72), epigraphist. #756, A.M. Wapche Marikar (1829-1925), educational reformer, architect.

Pale Yellow Orange and

753	A293	60c tan	.45	.70
754	A293	60c brt rose lilac	.45	.70
755	A293	60c brown	.45	.70
756	A293	60c emerald	.45	.70
		Nos. 753-756 (4)	1.80	2.80

Gam Udawa — Yovur Udanaya Village Reformation Movement A294

1985, June 23   Perf. 13½x13

757	A294	60c multicolored	1.60	1.60

Colombo Young Poets Assoc., 50th Anniv. — A295

1985, June 25   Perf. 14

758	A295	60c Emblem	1.75	1.75

Kothmale Project Commission — A296

1985, Aug. 24

759	A296	60c Dam, lake	1.00	1.00
760	A296	6r Hydro-electric power station	5.00	5.00

A297

Child Survival: 35c, Mother breastfeeding. 60c, Infant, oral inoculant. 6r, Weighing toddler. 9r, Infant, intravenous inoculant.

1985, Sept. 1   Wmk. 385   Perf. 13½

761	A297	35c multicolored	.45	.25
762	A297	60c multicolored	.65	.40
763	A297	6r multicolored	2.50	2.75
764	A297	9r multicolored	3.25	3.50
a.		Souvenir sheet of 4, #761-764	7.50	7.50
		Nos. 761-764 (4)	6.85	6.90

A298

1985, Sept. 2   Unwmk.   Perf. 14

765	A298	7r Womb, infant	5.50	5.50

10th Asian & Oceanic Congress of Obstetrics & Gynecology.

World Tourism Org., 10th Anniv. A299

1985, Sept. 27   Litho.   Perf. 14

766	A299	1r Conch shell horn	.55	.25
767	A299	6r Parliament complex	1.50	1.50
768	A299	7r Tea plantation	2.25	2.25
769	A299	10r Buddhist monastery, Ruwanveliseya	2.75	2.75
a.		Souv. sheet of 4, #766-769, perf. 13½	9.00	9.00
		Nos. 766-769 (4)	7.05	6.75

Land Development Ordinance, 50th Anniv. — A300

1985, Oct. 15   Perf. 14x15

770	A300	4.60r Deeds presentation	3.50	3.75

Sinhal Translation, Koran — A301

1985, Oct. 17   Wmk. 385   Perf. 13½

771	A301	60c violet & gold	3.25	2.50

Christmas — A302

1985, Nov. 5   Perf. 12

772	A302	60c Our Lady of Matara	.40	.25
773	A302	9r Our Lady of Madhu	2.00	2.25
a.		Souvenir sheet of 2, #772-773	9.25	10.00

SAARC 1st Summit, Dec. 7-8 A303

1985, Dec. 8   *Perf. 14½x14*
774 A303 60c shown   6.00 7.00
775 A303 5.50r Flags on UN
     emblem   6.00 6.00

No. 720 Surcharged in Intense Blue
1986, Jan. 20   *Perf. 12½x12*
776 A275 1r on 7r Map   12.00 4.50

Viceroy
Special
Train
A304

1986, Feb. 2   *Perf. 12½x13*
777 A304 1r multicolored   1.75 1.50

Colombo-Kandy line inauguration.

Students
A305

1986, Feb. 14   *Perf. 14*
778 A305 75c multicolored   .80 1.10

Mahapola Scholarship Program for development and education, 6th anniv.

Don Richard
Wijewardene
(1886-1950),
Newspaper
Publisher — A306

Welitara
Gnanatillake
Mahanayake
Thero (1858-
1941),
Scientist — A307

1986, Feb. 23   *Perf. 14x15*
779 A306 75c sage grn & brn   .40 1.00

1986, Feb. 26   Wmk. 385   *Perf. 13½*
780 A307 75c multicolored   1.00 1.10

No. 692 Surcharged
1986, Mar. 10   Litho.   *Perf. 14½*
780A A264 7r on 35c   8.00 1.50

Natl. Red
Cross
Society, 50th
Anniv.
A308

1986, Mar. 31   *Perf. 12½x13*
781 A308 75c multicolored   3.25 2.50

Halley's
Comet
A309

1986, Apr. 5   *Perf. 12½*
782 A309 50c Comet is not an
     omen   .25 .25
783 A309 75c Constellations   .25 .25
784 A309 6.50r Trajectory dia-
     grams   .40 1.25
785 A309 8.50r Edmond Halley   .55 2.00
  a.   Souvenir sheet of 4, #782-785,
     perf. 12½x13   8.50 10.50
     Nos. 782-785 (4)   1.45 3.75

Sinhalese and
Tamil New
Year — A310

Designs: 50c, Woman lighting lamp. 75c, Woman, holiday foods. 6.50r, Women celebrating around table. 8.50r, Food preparation, feast, anointment ritual.

1986, Apr. 10
786 A310 50c multicolored   .25 .25
787 A310 75c multicolored   .25 .25
788 A310 6.50r multicolored   .50 1.75
789 A310 8.50r multicolored   .80 2.00
  a.   Souvenir sheet of 4, #786-789,
     perf. 13x12½   5.00 5.50
     Nos. 786-789 (4)   1.80 4.25

No. 740 Surcharged
1986, Apr. 29   *Perf. 12½x13*
790 A286 1r on 4.60r multi   9.00 4.50

Vesak
Festival
A311

Jathaka Story frescoes from the house Samudragiri Vihara, Mirissa, recounting the life of Siddhartha (583-463 B.C.): 50c, King Kurudhamma Jathakaya gives elephant to the brahman. 75c, Vasavarthi heaven. 5r, Sujatha's milk rice offering. 10d, Thapassu and Bhalluka's parched corn and honey offering.

1986, May 16
791 A311 50c multicolored   .25 .25
792 A311 75c multicolored   .25 .25
793 A311 5d multicolored   .60 2.00
794 A311 10d multicolored   .70 3.00
     Nos. 791-794 (4)   1.80 5.50

Natl.
Heroes — A312

#795, Kalukondayave Sri Prajnasekhara Mahanayaka Thero (1895-1977), theologian. #796, Brahmachari Walisinghe Harischandra (1876-1913), historian, social reformer. #797, Martin Wickramasinghe (1890-1970), author. #798, Ganapathipillai Gangaser Ponnambalam (1901-72), diplomat. #799, Aboobucker Mohammed Abdul Azeez (1911-73), scholar.

1986, May 22   *Perf. 13x12½*
795 A312 75c multicolored   .25 .70
796 A312 75c multicolored   .25 .70
797 A312 75c multicolored   .25 .70
798 A312 75c multicolored   .25 .70
799 A312 75c multicolored   .25 .70
     Nos. 795-799 (5)   1.25 3.50

Natl. Cooperative
Movement, 75th
Anniv. — A313

1986, June 23
800 A313 1r multicolored   1.60 2.00

Gam Udawa,
Intl. Year of
Housing
A314

1986, June 23   *Perf. 13½x13*
801 A314 75c multicolored   2.10 2.10

Arthur V.
Dias — A315

1986, July 31   *Perf. 14x15*
802 A315 1r multicolored   2.50 2.50

World
Wildlife
Fund
A316

Elephants: a, Adult with tusks. b, Adult, calf. c, Adult. d, Family in river.

1986, Aug. 5   *Perf. 15x14*
803   Strip of 4   70.00 40.00
  a.-d.   A316 5r any single   15.00 10.00

2nd Indo-Pacific
Congress on
Legal Medicine
and Forensic
Sciences — A317

1986, Aug. 14   *Perf. 13½x13*
804 A317 8.50r multicolored   4.00 4.00

Submarine Cable — A318

1986, Sept. 8   *Perf. 13½x14*
805 A318 5.75r Handset, map   7.75 4.75
South-East Asia, Middle East, Western Europe Submarine Cable System.

Dag
Hammarskjold
Award — A320

1986, Sept. 20   Litho.   *Perf. 13x12½*
808 A320 2r multicolored   1.90 1.50

Second Natl.
School Games,
Sept. 22-
27 — A321

1986, Sept. 22   *Perf. 12*
809 A321 1r multicolored   4.75 2.40

Natl. Surveyor's
Institute, 60th
Anniv. — A322

1986, Sept. 27   *Perf. 13½x13*
810 A322 75c multicolored   1.00 1.25

Ananda
College,
Cent.
A323

College crest and: 75c, College. 5r, Athletic field. 5.75r, Founders Migettuwatte Gunananda, Hikkaduwe Sumangala and Col. H.S. Olcott, Buddhist flag and College, 1886, 1986. 6r, Crest on flag.

1986, Nov. 1   *Perf. 12*
811 A323 75c multicolored   .25 .25
812 A323 5r multicolored   .50 .80
813 A323 5.75r multicolored   .55 .80
814 A323 6r multicolored   .65 1.00
     Nos. 811-814 (4)   1.95 2.85

Wildlife Conservation — A324

1986, Nov. 11
815 A324 35c Mangrove
     habitat   1.25 1.25
816 A324 50c Rhizophora
     apiculata   1.40 1.40
817 A324 75c Germinating
     flower   1.50 1.50
818 A324 6r Fiddler crab   11.00 11.00
     Nos. 815-818 (4)   15.15 15.15

Preservation of mangrove habitats.
For surcharges on Nos. 815 and 818, see Nos. 1513 and 1516.

Intl. Year of
Shelter for
the
Homeless
A325

1987, Jan. 1   Litho.   *Perf. 13x13½*
819 A325 75c multicolored   3.00 .95

A.I. Thero, 19th
Cent. Theologian
A326

1987, Jan. 29   *Perf. 12*
820 A326 5.75r multicolored   4.50 1.25

Proctor John De
Silva (b. 1854),
Lawyer and
Playwright
A327

1987, Jan. 31
821 A327 5.75r multicolored   1.10 1.10

Mahapola Educational Plan, 7th
Anniv. — A328

1987, Feb. 6
822 A328 75c multicolored   1.25 1.25

Dr. R.L. Brohier,
Historian — A329

1987, Feb. 14
823 A329 5.75r multicolored   3.75 1.75

Sri Lanka
Tire
Corp.,
25th
Anniv.
A330

1987, Mar. 23   *Perf. 14*
824 A330 5.75r multicolored   .80 .80

Sri Lanka
Medical
Assoc.,
Cent.
A331

1987, Mar. 24   *Perf. 13x13½*
825 A331 5.75r multicolored   3.25 3.50

Farmers' Pension
and Social
Security
Plan — A332

1987, Mar. 29   *Perf. 14*
826 A332 75c multicolored   1.60 1.60

AGRO
MAHAWELI '87
Agricultural
Exposition
A333

1987, Apr. 2   *Perf. 12*
827 A333 75c multicolored   .60 .60

Child Immunization Program — A334

1987, Apr. 7   *Perf. 13½*
828 A334 1r multicolored   4.25 1.50
World Health Day.

Sinhalese and
Tamil New
Year — A335

1987, Apr. 9   *Perf. 12*
829 A335 75c Three girls, swing   .25 .25
830 A335 5r Lamp, women   .80 .80

Vesak
Festival
Lanterns
A336

1987, May 4   *Perf. 12*
831 A336 50c Lotus   .25 .25
832 A336 75c Octagonal   .25 .25
833 A336 5r Star   .45 .45
834 A336 10r Gok   .65 .65
   a. Souvenir sheet of 4, #831-834   1.75 1.75
    Nos. 831-834 (4)   1.60 1.60

Natl. Olympic Committee, 50th
Anniv. — A337

1987, May 8   *Perf. 13½*
835 A337 10r multicolored   3.75 1.60

Birds
A338

1987, May 18   *Perf. 14*
836 A338 50c Layard's parakeet   .70 .25
837 A338 1r Legge's
     flowerpecker   1.10 .25
   a. Dated "1989"   1.10 .25
838 A338 5r Sri Lanka white-
     headed starling   1.60 1.75
839 A338 10r Sri Lanka rufous
     babbler   2.10 2.25
   a. Souvenir sheet of 4, #836-839   9.75 9.75
   b. As #839, dated "1990"   2.25 2.25
    Nos. 836-839 (4)   5.50 4.50

Natl.
Heroes — A339

#840, Heenatiyana Sri Dhammaloka Thero,
20th cent. theologian. #841, P. de S.
Kularatne, educator. #842, M.C. Abdul
Rahuman, politician.

1987, May 22   *Perf. 12*
840 A339 75c multicolored   .60 .40
841 A339 75c multicolored   .60 .40
842 A339 75c multicolored   .60 .40
    Nos. 840-842 (3)   1.80 1.20

Gam
Udawa
A340

1987, June 23
843 A340 75c multicolored   .50 .50
Village reformation movement.

Natl.
Forestry
Agency,
Cent.
A341

1987, June 25
844 A341 75c Mesua nagassari-
     um   .30 .30
845 A341 5r Elephants in forest 2.00 2.00

Founder
H.S. Olcott
and
College
A342

1987, June 30
846 A342 75c multicolored   4.00 .55
Dharmaraja College, cent.

**No. 528 Redrawn with Denomination
in Upper Right Corner**
1987, July 1   Photo.   *Perf. 13x13½*
    Size: 20x24mm
847 A189 75c green & gold   .40 .25

Youth
Services
Emblem
A343

1987, July 15   Litho.   *Perf. 12*
848 A343 75c multicolored   .40 .40
Natl. Youth Services Act, 20th anniv.

Mahaweli
Games — A344

1987, Sept. 5   Litho.   *Perf. 12*
849 A344 75c multicolored   5.25 2.75

Ceylon Bible
Society, 175th
Anniv. — A345

1987, Oct. 2
850 A345 5.75r multicolored   .80 .80

Kandy Friend-in-Need Society, 150th
Anniv. — A346

1987, Nov. 4   *Perf. 13½x13*
851 A346 75c multicolored   .40 .40

Christmas
1987 — A347

Sir Ernest de Silva
(1887-1957),
Banker,
Philatelist — A348

1987, Nov. 25   Litho.   Perf. 12
852 A347 75c Mother and Child   .25   .25
853 A347 10r Infant, star, dove   .50   .50
a.   Souvenir sheet of 2, #852-853   1.60   1.60

1987, Nov. 25   Perf. 13x13½
854 A348 75c multicolored   .40   .40

1st Convocation
Ceremony at
Buddhist and Pali
University — A349

1987, Dec. 14   Perf. 12
855 A349 75c yel, lake & org yel   .40   .40

Missionary Work
of Fr. Joseph Vaz
(1651-1711),
300th
Anniv. — A350

1987, Dec. 15
856 A350 75c multicolored   .40   .40

Buddhist
Publication Soc.,
Kandy, 30th
Anniv. — A351

Design: Wheel of Life, dagaba (temple
cupola) and Bo (Tree of Life) leaf.

1988, Jan. 1   Litho.   Perf. 12
857 A351 75c multicolored   .50   .50

Mahapola
Dharmayatra,
5th Anniv.
A352

1988, Jan. 4   Perf. 13½x13
858 A352 75c multicolored   .60   .60

Ceylon Arts Soc.,
Cent. — A353

1988, Jan. 8   Perf. 12
859 A353 75c multicolored   1.00   .90

Opening of
the Natl.
Youth Center,
Maharagama
A354

1988, Jan. 31   Perf. 13½x13
860 A354 1r multicolored   5.50   .80

Natl.
Independence,
40th
Anniv. — A355

1988, Feb. 4   Perf. 12
861 A355 75c shown   .25   .25
862 A355 8.50r Heraldic lion, "40" 1.10   1.10

Mahapola
Movement, 8th
Anniv. — A356

1988, Feb. 11
863 A356 75c Youth Education
               Services   .40   .40

Transportation Board, 30th
Anniv. — A357

1988, Feb. 19
864 A357 5.75r multicolored   .80   .80

Weligama Sri
Sumangala Maha
Nayake Thero
(1825-1905),
Buddhist Monk,
Sanskrit
Scholar — A358

1988, Mar. 13
865 A358 75c multicolored   .40   .40

Artillery
Regiment,
Cent.
A359

1988, Apr. 20
866 A359 5.75r multicolored   4.25   1.25

Chevalier I.X.
Pereira (1888-
1951),
Politician — A360

1988, Apr. 26   Litho.   Perf. 12
867 A360 5.75r multicolored   .50   .50

Vesak
Festival
A361

Paintings in Suriyagoda Sri Naren-
draramaya Viharaya temple, Kandy District:
50c, Buddha inviting deities and brahmas to
be born into the world as Buddhists. 75c, Buddha walking seven steps on seven lotus flowers, followers paying homage.

1988, May 13   Perf. 12½x12
868 A361 50c multicolored   .40   .40
869 A361 75c multicolored   .40   .40
a.   Souvenir sheet of 2, #868-869   2.40   2.40

Natl.
Heroes — A362

Designs: No. 870, Rev.-Father Ferdinand
Bonnel (1873-1945), Jesuit priest who
founded St. Michael's College, Batticaloa. No.
871, Sir Razik Fareed (1893-1984), political
and social reformer. No. 872, W.F.
Gunawardhana (b. 1861), founder of the Oriental Studies Soc. No. 873, Edward Alexander
Nugawela (1898-1972), politician. No. 874, Sir
Edwin Arthur Lewis Wijeyewardene (b. 1887),
first Ceylonese chief justice, attorney general.

1988, May 22   Perf. 12x12½
870 A362 75c multicolored   .25   .25
871 A362 75c multicolored   .25   .25
872 A362 75c multicolored   .25   .25
873 A362 75c multicolored   .25   .25
874 A362 75c multicolored   .25   .25
        Nos. 870-874 (5)   1.25   1.25

Gam
Udawa,
10th Anniv.
A363

1988, June 23   Litho.   Perf. 12
875 A363 75c multicolored   .60   .30

Village reformation movement.

Maliyadeva
College,
Cent. — A364

1988, June 30   Perf. 13½x13
876 A364 75c multicolored   .60   .30

Bird Type of 1983
1988, Sept. 28   Litho.   Perf. 14½
877 A264 7r like No. 692   1.00   1.00

Mohamed J.M. Lafir (1929-1980),
World Amateur Billiards
Champion — A365

1988, July 5   Litho.   Perf. 12½x12
878 A365 5.75r multicolored   1.00   .60

Australia Bicentennial — A366

1988, July 19   Litho.   Perf. 12
879 A366 8.50r multicolored   1.00   .75

A367

1988, Aug. 11   Perf. 12x12½
880 A367 75c multicolored   .50   .30

Gunaratna Maha Nayake Thero (1752-
1832), Buddhist and Sinhalese language
scholar.

A368

1988, Sept. 3   Perf. 12
881 A368 75c multicolored   .50   .30

Mahaweli games.

1988 Summer
Olympics,
Seoul — A369

1988, Sept. 6   Perf. 12x12½
882 A369   75c Running   .25   .25
883 A369   1r Swimming   .25   .25
884 A369 5.75r Boxing   .55   .55
885 A369 8.50r Handshake, map,
                emblems   .95   .95
a.   Souvenir sheet of 4, #882-885   2.25   2.25
        Nos. 882-885 (4)   2.00   2.00

WHO, 40th
Anniv. — A370

1988, Sept. 12   Perf. 12
886 A370 75c multicolored   .50   .50

3rd Natl. School Games, Sept. 20-25 A371

1988, Sept. 20
887 A371 1r multicolored 4.25 .60

Mahatma Gandhi — A372

1988, Oct. 2 *Perf. 12*
888 A372 75c multicolored 3.50 1.00

Transportation and Communication Decade, 1978-88 — A373

Modes of transportation and: 75c, Globe. 5.75r, Communication tower.

1988, Oct. 24 Litho. *Perf. 12½x12*
889 A373 75c multicolored .75 .25
890 A373 5.75r multicolored 4.00 2.40
For surcharge, see No. 1580.

Randenigala Project — A374

1988, Oct. 31 *Perf. 12*
891 A374 75c Woman, dam, power station .35 .35
892 A374 5.75r Hydrelectric dam 1.05 1.05
Some stamps were distributed at the time the set was originally planned to be issued in 1986.

A375

1988, Nov. 17 Litho. *Perf. 13½*
893 A375 75c multicolored .50 .50
Opening of Gramodaya Folk Art Center.

Christmas — A376

1988, Nov. 25 *Perf. 12x12½*
894 A376 75c shown .25 .25
895 A376 8.50r Shepherds see star 1.00 1.00
a. Souvenir sheet of 2, #894-895 3.00 3.00

A377

1988, Dec. 28 *Perf. 12*
896 A377 75c multicolored .50 .50
E.W. Adikaram (1905-85), educator.

Waterfalls — A378

1989, Aug. 11 Litho. *Perf. 12*
897 A378 75c Dunhinda .30 .30
898 A378 1r Rawana .30 .30
899 A378 5.75r Laxapana 1.25 1.25
900 A378 8.50r Diyaluma 1.75 1.75
Nos. 897-900 (4) 3.60 3.60

Free Distribution of School Text Books, 10th Anniv. A379

1989, Jan. 23 Litho. *Perf. 13½x13*
901 A379 75c multicolored .40 .40

Poets — A380

1989, Jan. 27 *Perf. 13*
902 A380 75c Wimalaratne Kumaragama .25 .25
903 A380 75c G.H. Perera .25 .25
904 A380 75c Sagara Palan- suriya .25 .25
905 A380 75c P.B. Alwis Perera .25 .25
Nos. 902-905 (4) 1.00 1.00

Mahapola Educational Plan, 8th Anniv. — A381

1989, Feb. *Perf. 13½*
906 A381 75c multicolored .40 .25

Chamber of Commerce, 150th Anniv. — A382

1989, Mar. 25 Litho. *Perf. 12*
907 A382 75c multicolored .40 .25

AGRO Mahaweli A383

1989, Sept. 2 Litho. *Perf. 12*
908 A383 75c multicolored .65 .30

Famous Men A384

1989, May 22
909 A384 75c Simon Casie Chitty .35 .35
910 A384 75c Parawahera Sri Vajiragnana Thero .35 .35
911 A384 75c Fr. Maurice Le Goc .35 .35
912 A384 75c Hemapala Munidasa .35 .35
913 A384 75c Ananda Samarakoon .35 .35
Nos. 909-913 (5) 1.75 1.75
Nos. 910-913 vert.

Hartley College, 150th Anniv. (in 1988) — A385

1989, June 5
914 A385 75c multicolored .40 .25

Vesak Festival A386

Various paintings in Medawala Viharaya, Harispattuwa.

1989, May 15 Litho. *Perf. 12½x12*
915 A386 50c multicolored .25 .25
916 A386 75c multicolored .25 .25
917 A386 5r multicolored .55 .40
918 A386 5.75r multicolored .65 .50
a. Souvenir sheet of 4, #915-918 2.10 2.10
Nos. 915-918 (4) 1.70 1.40
For surcharge see No. 953A.

Pres. Premadasa's Declaration Establishing the Ministry of Buddha Sasana — A387

1989, June 18 Litho. *Perf. 12½x12*
919 A387 75c multicolored .40 .40

Gam Udawa, 11th Anniv. A388

1989, June 23
920 A388 75c multicolored .50 .40
Village reformation movement.

French Revolution, Bicent. A389

1989, Aug. 26 Litho. *Perf. 13½x13*
921 A389 8.50r rose & deep blue 1.75 1.75

Bank of Ceylon, 50th Anniv. A390

1989, Aug. 31
922 A390 75c Old, new head- quarters .25 .25
923 A390 5r Emblem, flowers .80 .65

Jana Saviya Grants A391

1989, June 23 Litho. *Perf. 12x11½*
924 A391 75c multicolored .70 .70
Development program to eliminate poverty and improve the standard of living through education and by providing food, health care, shelter and clothing.
See No. 953. For surcharge see No. 955.

Baptist Mission, 177th Anniv. A392

1989, Aug. 19 *Perf. 12½x12*
925 A392 5.75r James Chater, church, 1812 1.00 1.00
For surcharge, see No. 1405.

State Literary
Festival — A393

1989, Sept. 22   *Perf. 12x11½*
926 A393 75c multicolored   .50   .40

Wilhelm
Geiger — A394

1989, Sept. 30   *Perf. 13x13½*
927 A394 75c multicolored   .50   .40
  Wilhelm Geiger (1856-1943), German philologist who studied Sinhalese.

Wildlife Type of 1981
1989, Oct. 11   *Perf. 14*
928 A219 3r like No. 595   4.00   .40
  No. 928 has black inscriptions and is dated
"1989." See No. 729 for brown inscriptions.

Famous
Lawyers — A395

1989, Oct. 16   *Perf. 12x11½*
929 A395 75c H.V. Perera (1890-
                1969)   .25   .25
930 A395 75c Sir Ivor Jennings
                (1903-1965)   .25   .25

Sir Cyril de
Zoysa — A396

1989, Oct. 26   *Perf. 13x13½*
931 A396 75c multicolored   .50   .40
  Sir Cyril de Zoysa (1896-1978), key figure in
the Buddhist cultural reformation.

Asia-Pacific
Telecommunity,
10th
Anniv. — A397

1989, Nov. 1   *Perf. 12x12½*
932 A397 5.75r multicolored   .90   .60
  For surcharge, see No. 1574.

Sri
Sucharitha
Viyaparaya
Oratory
Children's
Soc., 50th
Anniv.
A398

1989, Nov. 9   *Perf. 13*
933 A398 75c multicolored   .60   .60

1st Moon
Landing, 20th
Anniv. — A399

1989, Nov. 10   *Perf. 12x12½*
934 A399 75c Apollo 11 liftoff,
                crew   .25   .25
935 A399 1r Astronaut de-
                scending ladder   .25   .25
936 A399 2r Astronaut on lu-
                nar surface   .45   .40
937 A399 5.75r Lunar surface,
                view of Earth   1.25 .70
  a.   Souvenir sheet of 4, #934-937 3.25 3.25
       Nos. 934-937 (4)   2.20 1.60
  For No. 937 surcharged, see No. 1515.

Christmas — A400

1989, Nov. 21   *Perf. 13½*
938 A400 75c Adoration of the
                Shepherds   .25   .25
939 A400 8.50r Adoration of the
                Magi   .80   .80
  a.   Souvenir sheet of 2, #938-939 2.25 2.25

Devananda
Nayake
Thero — Á401

1989, Nov. 25   *Perf. 12x11½*
940 A401 75c multicolored   .50   .50
  Devananda Nayake Thero (1921-1983),
religious scholar, educator, reformer.

Rev. William
Ault, College
and Crest
A402

1989, Nov. 29   *Perf. 11½x12*
941 A402 75c multicolored   .50   .40
  Batticaloa Methodist Central College, 175th
anniv.

Nuwara
Eliya Golf
Club, Cent.
A403

1989, Dec. 8   *Perf. 14x13½*
942 A403 75c shown   4.50   .50
943 A403 8.50r Course, golf
                house   12.00 9.50

Raja — A404

1989, Dec. 12   *Perf. 13x13½*
944 A404 75c multicolored   7.50 1.25
  Raja (1913-1988), the royal tusker of the Sri
Dalada Maligawa that carried the relic casket
in the Kandy Esala Procession.

Gampaha Wickamarachchi Ayurveda
Medical College, 60th Anniv. — A405

1989, Dec. 14   *Perf. 13½x13*
945 A405 75c Founder, institute   .70   .40

Udunuwara Sri
Sarananda
Mahanayake
Thero (1867-
1947),
Educator — A406

1989, Dec. 20   *Perf. 12x12½*
946 A406 75c multicolored   .50   .35

Railway
Dept., 125th
Anniv.
A407

1989, Dec. 27   *Perf. 11½x12, 13 (3r)*
947 A407 75c Train, viaduct   1.00   .30
948 A407 2r Train, light signal,
                Maradana Sta-
                tion   2.40   .50
949 A407 3r Steam locomo-
                tive, semaphore
                signal   2.40   .85
950 A407 7r 1st train in Sri
                Lanka   4.75 2.00
       Nos. 947-950 (4)   10.55 3.65

A408

1989, Dec. 28   *Perf. 13x13½*
951 A408 75c multicolored   2.25   .35
  Thomas Cooray (1901-88), 1st native Sri
Lankan Cardinal.

A409

1990, Jan. 14   *Perf. 12x12½*
952 A409 1r multicolored   3.25   .35
  Justin Wijayawardena (1904-82), educator,
politician.

Jana Saviya Grants Type of 1989
1990, Jan. 31   Litho.   *Perf. 12x11½*
953 A391 1r multicolored   .75   .40

No. 918 Surcharged

1990, Feb. 16   Litho.   *Perf. 12½x12*
953A A386 25c on 5.75r multi   1.40   .30

Induruwe
Uttarananda
Mahanayake
Thero — Á411

1990, Mar. 15   Litho.   *Perf. 12*
954 A411 1r multicolored   2.25 1.40

No. 924
Surcharged

1990, Mar. 22   Litho.   *Perf. 12x11½*
955 A391 1r on 75c multi   3.00 1.75

Silver
Jubilee of
Laksala
A413

Traditional handicrafts.

1990, Apr. 2   Litho.   Perf. 12
956 A413 1r Drums   .40   .25
957 A413 2r Silverware   .55   .25
958 A413 3r Lacquerware   .90   .30
959 A413 8r Dumbara mats   2.40   2.75
   Nos. 956-959 (4)   4.25   3.55

Vesak
Festival
A414

Various paintings in Wewurukannala
Buduraja Maha Viharaya.

1990, May 2   Perf. 12½x12
960 A414 75c multicolored   .25   .25
961 A414 1r multicolored   .25   .25
962 A414 2r multicolored   .30   .30
963 A414 8r multicolored   1.10   1.10
   a. Souvenir sheet of 4, #960-963   2.25   2.25
   Nos. 960-963 (4)   1.90   1.90

A415

Famous
Men — A416

1990, May 22   Perf. 12
964 A415 1r Rev. T.M.F. Long   .60   .35
        Size: 25x39mm
        Perf. 12x12½
965 A416 1r D.P.A. Wijewardene   .60   .35
966 A416 1r L.T.P. Manjusri   .60   .35
967 A416 1r M.D. Ratnasuriya   .60   .35
   Nos. 964-967 (4)   2.40   1.40

Gam
Udawa
Program,
12th
Anniv.
A417

1990, June 23   Perf. 12½x12
968 A417 1r multicolored   2.50   .60

Dept. of
Archaeology,
Cent. — A418

1r, Gold reliquary from Delivala Temple, c.
200 B.C. 2r, Statuette of Ganesha (the Elephant God) from Polonnaruwa. 3r, Terrace of
the Bodhi-tree at Isurumuni Vihara. 8r, Stone
seat with inscription of King Nissankamalle,
12th cent. A.D.

1990, July 7   Perf. 12
969 A418 1r black & orange   .40   .25
970 A418 2r black & gray   .70   .25
971 A418 3r black, yel grn & gold   1.00   .40
972 A418 8r black & gold   2.40   1.50
   Nos. 969-972 (4)   4.50   2.40

Sri Lanka
Tennis
Assoc.,
75th Anniv.
A419

1990, Aug. 14   Perf. 13½
973 A419 1r Player ready to vol-
              ley   1.00   1.00
974 A419 1r Player receiving vol-
              ley   1.00   1.00
   a. Pair, #973-974   2.25   2.25
975 A419 8r Men players   3.50   3.50
976 A419 8r Women players   3.50   3.50
   a. Pair, #975-976   7.75   7.75
   Nos. 973-976 (4)   9.00   9.00

Fish — A420

1990, Sept. 14   Perf. 11½
977 A420 25c Spotted loach   .30   .30
978 A420   2r Ornate paradise
              fish   .45   .45
979 A420   8r Mountain labeo   1.25   1.25
980 A420 20r Cherry barb   2.50   2.50
   a. Souvenir sheet of 4, #977-980   5.50   5.50
   Nos. 977-980 (4)   4.50   4.50

For No. 979 surcharged, see No. 1303A.

A421

1990, Dec. 26   Perf. 12
981 A421   1r Letter box, 1904   .85   .60
982 A421   2r Mail runner, 1815   1.60   .85
983 A421   5r Mail coach, 1832   3.25   2.75
984 A421 10r Nuwara-Eliya Post
              Office, 1894   4.25   4.25
   Nos. 981-984 (4)   9.95   8.45

Sri Lanka Postal Service, 175th anniv.

A422

1990, Oct. 28   Litho.   Perf. 12
985 A422 1r multicolored   6.25   1.75

Rukmani Devi (1923-78), actress.

Christmas
A423

1990, Nov. 28   Perf. 13
986 A423   1r Mary, Joseph at
              inn   .75   .45
987 A423 10r Adoration of the
              Magi   5.25   4.75
   a. Souv. sheet of 2, #986-987, perf.
       12   7.00   7.00

World
AIDS Day
A424

1990, Nov. 30
988 A424 1r multicolored   1.50   .25
989 A424 8r AIDS Virus   5.50   4.00

A425

1990, Dec. 8   Perf. 12
990 A425 1r multicolored   3.50   1.60

Dharmapala College, 50th anniv.

A426

1990, Dec. 14   Litho.   Perf. 12
991 A426 1r olive green & brown 4.25   1.50
   Peri Sunderam (b. 1890), political & social
reformer.

Ceylon Institute
of Chemistry,
50th
anniv. — A427

1991, Jan. 25   Litho.   Perf. 12
992 A427 1r multicolored   4.25   1.50

Vesak
Festival
A428

Various scenes from Buddha's life.

1991, May 17   Litho.   Perf. 12
993 A428 75c multicolored   .45   .25
994 A428   1r multicolored   .45   .25
995 A428   2r multicolored   .85   .40
996 A428 11r multicolored   3.75   3.25
   a. Souvenir sheet of 4, #993-996   6.50   6.50
   Nos. 993-996 (4)   5.50   4.15

A429

1991, May 31   Perf. 12
997 A429 1r multicolored   2.00   1.10

Mahabodhi Society, cent.

A430

Famous men.

1991, May 22   Litho.   Perf. 12x12½
998 A430 1r Narada Thero   .75   .65
999 A430 1r Sir Muttu
              Coomaraswamy   .75   .65
1000 A430 1r Dr. Andreas Nell   .75   .65
1001 A430 1r W.A. Silva   .75   .65
   Nos. 998-1001 (4)   3.00   2.60

Gam
Udawa,
13th
Anniv.
A431

1991, June 23   Litho.   Perf. 12½
1002 A431 1r multicolored   3.25   .90

Henpitagedera
Gnanaseeha
Nayake Thero
(1909-1981),
Religious
Leader — A432

1991, Aug. 1
1003 A432 1r multicolored   2.50   .95

Colombo
Plan, 40th
Anniv.
A433

1991, July 1   Litho.   Perf. 12
1004 A433 1r multicolored   3.75   1.40

Survey
Dept.,
190th
Anniv.
A434

1991, Aug. 2   Perf. 12½
1005 A434 1r multicolored   3.50   1.25

Police
Service,
125th
Anniv.
A435

1991, Sept. 3   Litho.   Perf. 12½
1006 A435 1r multicolored   1.75 .70

6th
SAARC
Summit
A436

1991, Dec. 21   Litho.   Perf. 12½
1007 A436 1r shown   .25 .25
1008 A436 8r Flags encircling
            bldg.   .70 1.25

Kingswood College, Cent. — A437

1991, Oct. 26   Perf. 12½x12
1009 A437 1r multicolored   1.00 .50

Christmas — A439

1991, Nov. 19   Litho.   Perf. 12½
1014 A439 1r The Annunciation   .40 .25
1015 A439 10r Nativity scene   1.50 2.00
  a.   Sheet of 2, #1014-1015   2.50 2.50

A440

Telecommunications: 1r, Early telephone
network. 2r, Switchboard operations. 8r, Satellite transmitters, cable network. 10r, Telephone, fiber optic cable, computer, cordless
telephone, FAX machine.

1991, Nov. 23
1016 A440 1r multicolored   .25 .25
1017 A440 2r multicolored   .30 .25
1018 A440 8r multicolored   .90 1.10
1019 A440 10r multicolored   .90 1.10
       Nos. 1016-1019 (4)   2.35 2.70

5th South
Asian
Federation
Games
A441

1991, Dec. 22   Perf. 14
1020 A441 1r Mascot   .30 .25
1021 A441 2r Emblem   .60 .25
1022 A441 4r Stadium, Colom-
            bo   1.10 1.25
1023 A441 11r Globe and flags   2.50 3.50
       Nos. 1020-1023 (4)   4.50 5.25

Year of
Exports
A442

1992, Jan. 13   Litho.   Perf. 11½x12
1024 A442 1r multicolored   3.00 1.00

Mahinda
College,
Cent.
A443

1992, Mar. 2   Litho.   Perf. 11½x12
1025 A443 1r multicolored   .40 .40

General Ranjan
Wijeratne (1931-
1991)
A444

1992, Mar. 2   Litho.   Perf. 12x12½
1026 A444 1r multicolored   .60 .25

Tea
Production,
125th Anniv.
A445

Field of tea and: 1r, Tea picker. 2r, Family,
cup and glass of tea. 5r, Package of tea. 10r,
James Taylor.

1992, Feb. 12   Perf. 13½
1027 A445 1r multicolored   .70 .25
1028 A445 2r multicolored   1.40 .30
1029 A445 5r multicolored   3.25 2.50
1030 A445 10r multicolored   4.75 4.00
       Nos. 1027-1030 (4)   10.10 7.05

Newstead
College,
175th
Anniv. (in
1991)
A446

1992, Mar. 13   Litho.   Perf. 11½x12
1031 A446 1r multicolored   .40 .40
       Dated 1991.

Mahapola
Scholarship Fund,
11th
Anniv. — A447

1992, Mar. 30   Perf. 12
1032 A447 1r multicolored   .40 .40

Vesak
Festival
A448

Mural paintings from Kottimbulwala
Rajamaha Vihara: 75c, Dukula and Parika
retiring to forest. 1r, Sama and parents living in
forest. 8r, Sama directing blind parents to hermitage. 11r, Sama's parents approach
wounded son.

1992, May 5   Litho.   Perf. 11½x12
1033 A448 75c multicolored   .25 .25
1034 A448 1r multicolored   .35 .25
1035 A448 8r multicolored   1.75 1.75
1036 A448 11r multicolored   2.50 2.50
  a.   Souvenir sheet, #1033-1036   5.50 5.50
       Nos. 1033-1036 (4)   4.85 4.75

A449

National Heroes: No. 1037, Wadeebhasinha
Dewamottawe Amarawansa Thero. No. 1038,
R. A. Mirando. No. 1039, Gate Mudaliyar N.
Canaganayagam. No. 1040, I.L.M. Abdul
Azeez.

1992, May 22   Perf. 14
1037 A449 1r multicolored   .25 .25
1038 A449 1r multicolored   .25 .25
1039 A449 1r multicolored   .25 .25
1040 A449 1r multicolored   .25 .25
       Nos. 1037-1040 (4)   1.00 1.00

A450

1992, June 14   Litho.   Perf. 12x12½
1041 A450 1r multicolored   .70 .45

Introduction of Buddhism on Sri Lanka by
Anubudu Mihindu Jayanthi, 2300th anniv.

Gam Udawa,
14th Anniv.
A451

1992, June 23   Perf. 12
1042 A451 1r multicolored   .90 .45

Postal
Excellence
Service
Awards
A452

Designs: 1r, Award presentation, postal
work. 10r, Award of excellence medals, No.
1043 canceled on envelope.

1992, July 11   Litho.   Perf. 14
1043 A452 1r multicolored   .75 .75
1044 A452 10r multicolored   4.50 4.50

A453

Masks of Sri Lanka.

1992, Aug. 19   Litho.   Perf. 13
1045 A453 1r Narilata   .40 .25
1046 A453 2r Mudali   .50 .40
1047 A453 5r Queen   1.00 .75
1048 A453 10r King   1.75 1.75
  a.   Souvenir sheet, #1045-1048   4.50 4.50
       Nos. 1045-1048 (4)   3.65 3.15

A454

1992, Sept. 15   Litho.   Perf. 14
1049 A454 1r Running   .35 .25
1050 A454 11r Rifle shooting   2.50 2.50
1051 A454 13r Swimming   3.00 3.00
1052 A454 15r Weight lifting   3.25 3.25
  a.   Souvenir sheet #1049-1052   11.00 11.00
       Nos. 1049-1052 (4)   9.10 9.00

1992 Summer Olympics, Barcelona.

Cricket in
Sri Lanka,
160th
Anniv.
A455

1992, Sept. 8   Litho.   Perf. 13
1053 A455 5r multicolored   5.50 3.25

Vijaya
Kumaratunga,
Entertainer and
Political Leader,
Birth
Anniv. — A456

1992, Oct. 9
1054 A456 1r multicolored   .80 .50

Al-Bahjathul Ibraheemiyyah Arabic
College, Cent. — A457

1992, Oct. 24   Perf. 12
1055 A457 1r multicolored   .60 .50

1992, Oct. 25   Litho.   Perf. 12x11½
1056 A458 1r multicolored   2.25 .75
Dutch Reformed Church in Sri Lanka, 350th
anniv.

Christmas
A459

1992, Nov. 17   Litho.   Perf. 12x11½
1057 A459 1r Holy Family   .50 .25
1058 A459 9r Church, family   2.50 2.50
a.   Souvenir sheet, #1057-1058   3.50 3.50

Discovery
of
America,
500th
Anniv.
A460

Designs: 1r, Ships at sea, Aug. 1492. 11r,
First landing in the Americas, Oct. 1492. 13r,
Santa Maria aground, Dec. 1492. 15r, Return
to Spain, Apr. 1493.

1992, Dec. 1   Perf. 14
1059 A460 1r multicolored   1.00 .35
1060 A460 11r multicolored   2.00 2.00
1061 A460 13r multicolored   2.75 2.75
1062 A460 15r multicolored   3.00 3.00
a.   Souvenir sheet, #1059-1062   9.50 9.50
Nos. 1059-1062 (4)   8.75 8.10

No. 564
Surcharged

1992, Dec. 1   Litho.   Perf. 14
1062B A206 2r on 10c multi   8.25 1.00

Dambagasare Sri Sumedhankara
Maha Nayake Thero (1892-1984),
Buddhist Monk — A461

1992, Dec. 10   Litho.   Perf. 12
1063 A461 1r multicolored   .40 .40

University
Education
in Sri
Lanka
A462

1992, Dec. 12   Litho.   Perf. 12
1064 A462 1r multicolored   .40 .40
No. 1064 was not available until Dec. 1993.

University
of
Colombo,
50th Anniv.
(in 1992)
A463

1993, Mar. 23   Litho.   Perf. 13
1065 A463 1r multicolored   1.10 .35

Zahira
College,
Cent.
A464

1993, Apr. 7
1066 A464 1r multicolored   1.25 .40

Vesak
Festival — A465

Designs based on verses from the Dham-
mapada (sermons of Buddha): 75c,
Magandiya being presented to Buddha. 1r,
Kisa Gotami carrying dead child. 3r,
Patachara, dead family members. 10r, Con-
version of Angulimala, the murderer.

1993, Apr. 30   Perf. 12x12½
1067 A465 75c multicolored   .25 .25
1068 A465 1r multicolored   .35 .35
1069 A465 3r multicolored   .75 .75
1070 A465 10r multicolored   1.50 1.50
a.   Souvenir sheet, #1067-1070   3.50 3.50
Nos. 1067-1070 (4)   2.85 2.85

A466

1993, May 10   Perf. 12
1071 A466 1r Guide, tent, em-
      blem   .80 .35
1072 A466 5r Activities, map   2.40 2.10
Girl Guides in Sri Lanka, 75th Anniv. (in
1992).

A467

National Heroes: No. 1073, Yagirala Sri
Pagnananda Maha Nayaka Thero. No. 1074,
C.P. De Silva. No. 1075, Wilmot A. Perera. No.
1076, N.D.H. Abdul Caffoor.

1993, May 22   Perf. 14
1073 A467 1r multicolored   .45 .50
1074 A467 1r multicolored   .45 .50
1075 A467 1r multicolored   .45 .50
1076 A467 1r multicolored   .45 .50
Nos. 1073-1076 (4)   1.80 2.00

Gam
Udawa,
15th Anniv.
A468

1993, June 23   Litho.   Perf. 12½
1077 A468 1r multicolored   1.90 .50

Co-operative Consumer Service, 50th
Anniv. — A469

1993, July 3   Perf. 13
1078 A469 1r multicolored   2.25 .50

Birds
A470

Designs: 3r, Ashy-headed laughing thrush.
4r, Ceylon brown-capped babbler. 5r, Red-
faced malkoha. 10r, Ceylon hill-mynah.

1993, July 14   Perf. 12½x12
1079 A470 3r multicolored   .60 .60
1080 A470 4r multicolored   .60 .60
1081 A470 5r multicolored   1.00 1.00
1082 A470 10r multicolored   2.00 2.00
a.   Souvenir sheet, #1079-1082   5.00 5.00
Nos. 1079-1082 (4)   4.20 4.20

Talawila
Church,
150th
Anniv.
A471

1993, July 26   Perf. 13
1083 A471 1r multicolored   1.50 .50

Postal Excellence
Service
Awards — A472

1993, Aug. 22
1084 A472 1r multicolored   1.50 .50

Technical
Education
in Sri
Lanka,
Cent.
A473

1993, Dec. 17
1085 A473 1r multicolored   1.50 .50

Musaeus College,
Cent. — A474

1993, Nov. 15
1086 A474 1r multicolored   2.75 .50

Christmas
A475

Designs: 1r, Presentation of infant Jesus in
Temple of Jerusalem. 17r, Boy Jesus in
Temple.

1993, Nov. 30   Litho.   Perf. 14x13½
1087 A475 1r multicolored   .30 .25
1088 A475 17r multicolored   1.60 1.60
a.   Souvenir sheet, #1087-1088   2.25 2.25

Youth and Health — A476

1993, Dec. 16   Perf. 14
1089 A476 1r multicolored   .80 .40

Old Boy's Assoc.,
Trinity College,
Kandy,
Cent. — A478

1994, Feb. 11   Litho.   Perf. 12½
1091 A478 1r multicolored   .50 .45

St.
Thomas
College,
Matara,
150th
Anniv.
A479

1994, Mar. 10   Litho.   Perf. 13
1092 A479 1r multicolored   .50 .45

St. Joseph's College, 125th Anniv. A480

1994, Apr. 4　Litho.　*Perf. 12½*
1093　A480　1r multicolored　　.60　.35

Siyambalangamuwe Sri Gunaratana Thero — A481

1994, Apr. 2　Litho.　*Perf. 13*
1094　A481　1r multicolored　2.50　.45

ILO, 75th Anniv. — A482

1994, May. 12
1095　A482　1r multicolored　1.75　.45

Vesak Festival A483

Designs show actions by Bodhisatva in four of ten perfections: 1r, Dana, displaying generosity. 2r, Sila, morality. 5r, Nekkhamma, ascetic surrounded by worshippers. 17r, Panna, wisdom dispensed by Bodhisatva to others.

1994, May 7　Litho.　*Perf. 12½*
1096　A483　1r multicolored　　.25　.25
1097　A483　2r multicolored　1.25　1.25
1098　A483　5r multicolored　1.25　1.25
1099　A483　17r multicolored　2.25　2.25
　a.　Souvenir sheet, #1096-1099　5.50　5.50
　　Nos. 1096-1099 (4)　5.00　5.00

Famous People A484

Designs: No. 1100, Pres. Ranasinghe Premadasa. No. 1101, Ven. Mihiripanne Dhammaratana Thero. No. 1102, E. Periyathambipillai, poet. No. 1103, Dr. Colvin R. De Silva, politician.

1994, May 22　Litho.　*Perf. 14*
1100　A484　1r multicolored　　.35　.40
1101　A484　1r multicolored　　.35　.40
1102　A484　1r multicolored　　.35　.40
1103　A484　1r multicolored　　.35　.40
　　Nos. 1100-1103 (4)　1.40　1.60

World Conference of Intl. Federation of Social Workers, Colombo A485

1994, July 9　Litho.　*Perf. 12½*
1104　A485　8r blue, lt blue & blk　4.25　4.25

Bellanwila Sri Somaratana Nayake Thero — A486

1994, Aug. 2　Litho.　*Perf. 12½*
1105　A486　1r multicolored　2.60　.40

Infotel Lanka '94 A487

1994, Sept. 8
1106　A487　10r multicolored　3.25　3.25

Intl. Year of Indigenous People — A488

Designs: 1r, Veddah man making bow. 17r, Veddah man seated by rock art paintings.

1994, Sept. 12　Litho.　*Perf. 12*
1107　A488　1r multicolored　　.55　.50
1108　A488　17r multicolored　5.00　5.00

Natl. Wildlife & Nature Protection Society, Cent. A489

1994, Nov. 24　Litho.　*Perf. 12½*
1109　A489　1r Emblem　　.50　.25
1110　A489　2r Rhino-horned lizard　.90　.90
1111　A489　10r Giant squirrel　2.50　2.50
1112　A489　17r Sloth bear　3.75　3.75
　a.　Souvenir sheet, #1109-1112　8.00　8.00
　　Nos. 1109-1112 (4)　7.65　7.40

Gam Udawa, 16th Anniv. A490

1994, Sept.　Litho.　*Perf. 13*
1113　A490　1r multicolored　1.00　.25

A491　　　　A492

1994, Oct. 11　Litho.　*Perf. 12½*
1114　A491　1r multicolored　2.75　.90

Double entry bookkeeping, 500th anniv.

1995, Feb. 22　　　*Perf. 14*
1115　A492　1r Water lily　1.25　.25

Richmond College Old Boys Assoc., Cent. A493

1994　　　　*Perf. 12½*
1116　A493　1r multicolored　　.40　.25

ICAO, 50th Anniv. A494

1994, Dec. 7　Litho.　*Perf. 13*
1117　A494　10r multicolored　4.75　3.00

Christmas A495

Designs: 1r, Nativity. 17r, Jesus growing up, at home with Joseph and Mary.

1994, Dec. 8　Litho.　*Perf. 13*
1118　A495　1r multicolored　　.30　.25
1119　A495　17r multicolored　3.75　3.75
　a.　Souvenir sheet, #1118-1119　4.50　4.50

Assoc. for Advancement of Science, 50th Anniv. — A496

1994, Dec. 19　Litho.　*Perf. 13*
1120　A496　1r multicolored　3.25　.60

Orchid Circle of Ceylon, 60th Anniv. — A498

Orchids: 50c, Dendrobium maccarthiae. 1r, Cottonia peduncularis. 5r, Bulbophyllum wightii. 17r, Habenaria crinifera.

1994, Dec. 27　Litho.　*Perf. 13*
1122　A498　50c multicolored　　.35　.25
1123　A498　1r multicolored　　.50　.40
1124　A498　5r multicolored　　.90　.90
1125　A498　17r multicolored　1.75　3.00
　a.　Souvenir sheet, #1122-1125　6.00　6.00
　　Nos. 1122-1125 (4)　3.50　4.55

Visit of Pope John Paul II, Beatification of Fr. Joseph Vaz — A499

1995, Jan. 20
1126　A499　1r multicolored　5.00　1.00

St. Joseph's College, Colombo, Cent. A500

1995, Mar. 2　Litho.　*Perf. 13*
1127　A500　1r multicolored　1.60　.50

Royal Asiatic Society of Sri Lanka, 150th Anniv. — A501

1995, Apr. 4
1128　A501　1r multicolored　3.50　.90

Sirimavo Bandaranaike, World's First Woman Prime Minister — A502

1995, Apr. 17　Litho.　*Perf. 12*
1129　A502　2r multicolored　2.25　1.10

A503

Vesak Festival (Designs show actions by a Bodhisatva in four of ten perfections): 1r, Endeavor, standing on shore. 2r, Forebearance, one holding another. 10r, Veracity, two people listening to truths. 17r, Resolution, man holding hoe.

1995, May 5　　　*Perf. 12x12½*
1130　A503　1r multicolored　　.35　.25
1131　A503　2r multicolored　　.45　.25
1132　A503　10r multicolored　1.40　1.10
1133　A503　17r multicolored　2.50　2.25
　a.　Souvenir sheet, #1130-1133　5.50　5.50
　　Nos. 1130-1133 (4)　4.70　3.85

A504

1995, June 3   *Perf. 11*
1134 A504 2r M. C. Abdul Cader   2.50   1.25

St. Aloysius College, Galle, Cent. A506

1995, June 21   Litho.   *Perf. 12½x12*
1136 A506 2r multicolored   2.50   1.25

T.B. Ilangaratna (1913-92), Politician A507

1995, July 7   Litho.   *Perf. 13*
1137 A507 2r multicolored   2.50   1.25

Dhamma School, Cent. A508

1995, Aug. 3
1138 A508 2r multicolored   2.50   1.25

General Post Office, Colombo, Cent. A509

1995, Aug. 22   Litho.   *Perf. 13½*
1139 A509 1r multicolored   1.75   .45

Help the Elderly — A510

1995, Oct. 1   Litho.   *Perf. 14x13½*
1140 A510 2r multicolored   2.50   1.10

41st Commonwealth Parliamentary Conference — A511

1995, Oct. 9   Litho.   *Perf. 14x13½*
1141 A511 2r multicolored   2.50   1.10

UN, 50th Anniv. — A512

1995, Oct. 24   *Perf. 13½x14*
1142 A512 2r multicolored   2.50   1.10

World Thrift Day — A513

1995, Oct. 15
1143 A513 2r multicolored   2.50   1.10

Christmas A514

Designs: 2r, Arms of Colombo and Kurunegla, Persian cross from Anuradhapura, Christian church. 20r, Clasping arms, nativity scene.

1995, Nov. 10   Litho.   *Perf. 13*
1144 A514 2r multicolored   .50   .25
1145 A514 20r multicolored   3.00   2.40
   a.   Souvenir sheet, #1144-1145   4.00   4.00

A515   A516

1995, Dec. 8
1146 A515 2r multicolored   3.50   1.25

SAARC, 10th anniv.

1996, Jan. 22   Litho.   *Perf. 12*
1147 A516 50c Little Basses   .75   .50
1148 A516 75c Great Basses   .75   .50
1149 A516 2r Devinuwara   1.75   1.00
1149A A516 2.50r like #1149   .75   .50
1150 A516 20r Galle   5.00   2.75
   a.   Souv. sheet, #1147-1149, 1150   10.00   10.00
    Nos. 1147-1150 (5)   9.00   5.25

Lighthouses of Sri Lanka.
For surcharges see Nos. 1191-1193, 1282A.

Vincent High School, Batticaloa, 175th Anniv. — A517

1996, Jan. 17   Litho.   *Perf. 13*
1151 A517 2r multicolored   2.50   1.10

Handicrafts A518

1996, Mar. 13   *Perf. 12*
1152 A518 25c Traditional sesath   .25   .25
1153 A518 8.50r Pottery   .50   .45
1154 A518 10.50r Mats   .80   .70
1155 A518 17r Lace   1.10   1.10
   a.   Souvenir sheet, #1152-1155   4.25   4.25
    Nos. 1152-1155 (4)   2.65   2.50

For surcharges see Nos. 1189-1190, 1548, 1575.

A519

1996, Mar. 21
1156 A519 2r multicolored   3.00   1.10

Chundikuli Girls' College, Jaffna, cent.

A520

Vesak Festival: 1r, Capa cradling her son, teasing her husband. 2r, Dantika, mahout, elephant. 5r, Subha holding her eye in her hand, man of low morals. 10r, Punna explaining purification by water to Brahmin.

1996, Apr. 30   Litho.   *Perf. 12*
1157 A520 1r multicolored   .25   .25
1158 A520 2r multicolored   .50   .50
1159 A520 5r multicolored   .65   .65
1160 A520 10r multicolored   1.25   1.25
   a.   Souvenir sheet, #1157-1160   3.00   3.00
    Nos. 1157-1160 (4)   2.65   2.65

1996 Summer Olympic Games, Atlanta A521

1996, July 22   Litho.   *Perf. 13½*
1161 A521 1r Diving, vert.   .30   .25
1162 A521 2r Volleyball, vert.   1.25   .55
1163 A521 5r Shooting   1.50   1.50
1164 A521 17r Running   3.00   3.00
    Nos. 1161-1164 (4)   6.05   5.30

Sri Lanka, 1996 World Cup Cricket Champions — A522

1996, Aug. 18
1165 A522 2r Bowler   .55   .55
1166 A522 10.50r Wicketkeeper   1.10   1.10
1167 A522 17r Batsman   1.60   1.60
1168 A522 20r Trophy   1.75   1.75
   a.   Souvenir sheet, #1165-1168   5.50   5.50
    Nos. 1165-1168 (4)   5.00   5.00

No. 1168a contains two se-tenant pairs.

Jaffna Central College, 180th Anniv. A523

1996, Sept. 7   Litho.   *Perf. 13½*
1169 A523 2r multicolored   2.75   1.10

A524

1996, Nov. 4   Litho.   *Perf. 13½x14*
1170 A524 2r multicolored   3.00   1.25

UNESCO, 50th anniv.

A525

Christmas (Scenes of parables from murals, Trinity College Chapel): 2r, Washing of the feet. 17r, Good Samaritan.

1996, Dec. 2   *Perf. 13½x13*
1171 A525 2r multicolored   .35   .25
1172 A525 17r multicolored   1.90   1.60
   a.   Souvenir sheet, #1171-1172   2.25   2.25

UNICEF, 50th Anniv. — A526

1996, Dec. 12   Litho.   *Perf. 13½x14*
1173 A526 5r multicolored   1.10   .90

Swami Vivekananda A527

1997, Jan. 15   *Perf. 13½x13*
1174 A527 2.50r multicolored   1.50   .90

Personalities A528

Designs: No. 1175, Lt. Gen. Denzil Kob-bekaduwa. No. 1176, Ven. Welivitiye Serata Thero. No. 1177, Dr. S.A. Wickremasinghe.

1997, Apr. 4   Litho.   Perf. 13½x13
1175	A528	2r multicolored	.60	.60
1176	A528	2r multicolored	.60	.60
1177	A528	2r multicolored	.60	.60
		Nos. 1175-1177 (3)	1.80	1.80

Vesak Festival — A529

Cemeteries, monuments to the dead: 1r, Thuparama. 2.50r, Ruwanvalisaya. 3r, Abhayagiri Dagaba. 17r, Jetavana Dagaba.

1997, May 7   Perf. 12x12½
1178	A529	1r multicolored	.25	.25
1179	A529	2.50r multicolored	.25	.25
1180	A529	3r multicolored	.25	.25
1181	A529	17r multicolored	1.25	1.25
a.		Souvenir Sheet of 4, #1178-1181	2.75	2.75
		Nos. 1178-1181 (4)	2.00	2.00

D.J. Kumarage, Birth Cent. — A530

1997, Apr. 4   Litho.   Perf. 13½x14
1182	A530	2.50r multicolored	1.75	.90

Medicinal Herbs — A531

2.40r, Munronia pinnata. 14r, Rauvolfia serpentina.

1997, July 22   Litho.   Perf. 13½x14
1183	A531	2.50r multicolored	.30	.25
1184	A531	14r multicolored	1.50	1.50

Tourism A532

1997, Sept. 11   Perf. 12
1185	A532	20r multicolored	3.50	3.00

St. Servatius College, Matara, Cent. A533

1997, Nov. 1   Perf. 12½x12
1186	A533	2.50r multicolored	.90	.30

Mahagama Sekera — A534

1997, Apr. 4   Litho.   Perf. 13½x13
1187	A534	2r multicolored	.85	.40

Asterisks obliterate portions of Mahagama Sekera's name.

Sri Jayawardenapura Vidalaya, Kotte, 175th Anniv. — A535

1997, Jan. 28   Perf. 12½
1188	A535	2.50r multicolored	.60	.30

Nos. 1153-1154 Srchd.

1997, May 6   Litho.   Perf. 12
1189	A518	1r on 8.50r, #1153	8.00	1.00
1190	A518	11r on 10.50r, #1154 (a)	6.50	6.50
a.		Surcharge type b	6.50	6.50

Surcharge Type a on #1190 is 2½mm high. Type b surcharge is 3mm high.

No. 1149 Surcharged

c   d

e

1997, Feb. 12   Litho.   Perf. 12
1191	A516(c)	2.50r on 2r	6.00	6.00
1192	A516(d)	2.50r on 2r	6.00	6.00
1193	A516(e)	2.50r on 2r	6.00	6.00
		Nos. 1191-1193 (3)	18.00	18.00

A number has been reserved additional surcharge on No. 1149.

Reptiles A537

2.50r, Lyre head lizard. 5r, Boie's roughside. 17r, Common Lanka skink. 20r, Great forest gecko.

1997, Oct. 18   Litho.   Perf. 12
1195	A537	2.50r multicolored	.30	.30
1196	A537	5r multicolored	.45	.45
1197	A537	17r multicolored	.85	.85
1198	A537	20r multicolored	.95	.95
a.		Souvenir sheet, #1195-1198	3.00	3.00
		Nos. 1195-1198 (4)	2.55	2.55

A538

Christmas: 2.50r, Holy Family. 20r, Adoration of the Magi.

1997, Nov. 20   Perf. 12½x13
1199	A538	2.50r multicolored	.30	.25
1200	A538	20r multicolored	1.50	.90
a.		Souvenir sheet, #1199-1200	1.90	1.90

A539

Personalities: #1201, Hegoda Sri Indasara Thero (1932-87), religious leader. #1202, Abdul Aziz (d. 1990), politician. #1203, Subramaniam Vithiananthan (b. 1924), teacher, writer. #1204, Vivienne Goonewardene (1916-96), politician.

1997, Nov. 11   Litho.   Perf. 12½
1201	A539	2.50r multicolored	.30	.30
1202	A539	2.50r multicolored	.30	.30
1203	A539	2.50r multicolored	.30	.30
1204	A539	2.50r multicolored	.30	.30
a.		Block of 4, #1201-1204	1.40	1.40

Young Men's Buddhist Assoc., Colombo, Cent. A540

1998, Jan. 1   Litho.   Perf. 12½
1205	A540	2.50r multicolored	.70	.35

Traditional Jewelry and Crafts — A541

Designs: 2.50r, Chunam box. 5r, Necklace of agate. 10r, Bangle and hairpin. 17r, Sigiri earrings.

1998, Apr. 24   Litho.   Perf. 13½
1206	A541	2.50r multicolored	.45	.25
1207	A541	5r multicolored	.70	.30
1208	A541	10r multicolored	1.25	1.25
1209	A541	17r multicolored	2.00	2.00
a.		Souvenir sheet, #1206-1209	5.00	5.00
		Nos. 1206-1209 (4)	4.40	3.80

Independence, 50th Anniv. — A542

Natl. flag and: 2r, People holding up arms, letters and symbols. No. 1211, Ceylon #300. No. 1212, People standing, images of industry and technology. 5r, People playing musical instruments, book, pen, television, musical instruments. 10r, People holding up items, symbols of religion, government.

Perf. 13, 13½ (#1211)
1998, Feb. 4   Litho.
1210	A542	2r multicolored	.60	.25
1211	A542	2.50r multicolored	.85	.60
1212	A542	2.50r multicolored	.85	.60
1213	A542	5r multicolored	.85	.70
1214	A542	10r multicolored	1.75	1.50
		Nos. 1210-1214 (5)	4.90	3.65

No. 1211 is 28x38mm.

William Gopallawa, 1st President A543

1998   Litho.   Perf. 13½
1215	A543	2.50r multicolored	.60	.25

5th Natl. Scout Jamboree A544

Designs: 2.50r, Scouts holding flag, emblem, campground. 17r, Campground, flag, emblems, scout saluting.

1998, Feb. 18
1216	A544	2.50r multicolored	1.25	1.00
1217	A544	17r multicolored	3.50	2.75

World Health Organization, 50th Anniv. — A545

1998, Apr. 7   Litho.   Perf. 13x12½
1218	A545	2.50r multicolored	.80	.25

St. John's College, Jaffna, 175th Anniv. — A546

1998, May 7   Litho.   Perf. 14½x14
1219	A546	2.50r multicolored	.40	.25

Elephas Maximus Ceylonensis — A547

Designs: 2.50r, Wading in lake. 10r, Female, calf. 17r, Three standing in plains. 50r, Large bull.

1998, May 28 **Perf. 13**
1220	A547	2.50r multicolored	1.00	.70
1221	A547	10r multicolored	1.50	1.10
1222	A547	17r multicolored	2.10	1.40
1223	A547	50r multicolored	3.50	2.75
a.		Souvenir sheet, #1220-1223	9.00	9.00
		Nos. 1220-1223 (4)	8.10	5.95

Vesak Festival — A548

Kelaniya Rajamaha Vihara paintings: 1r, Waterfalls, tree. 2.50r, Procession of people, elephant with rider. 4r, Looking at mother with newborn baby. 17r, Presenting child for ceremony, laying stone.

1998, Apr. 30 **Litho.** **Perf. 12½**
1224	A548	1r multicolored	.40	.25
1225	A548	2.50r multicolored	.40	.25
1226	A548	4r multicolored	.75	.35
1227	A548	17r multicolored	1.75	1.00
a.		Souvenir sheet, #1224-1228	2.75	2.75
		Nos. 1224-1227 (4)	3.30	1.85

SAARC Summit, Colombo — A549

1998 **Litho.** **Perf. 14½x14**
1228	A549	2.50r multicolored	1.10	.35

1998, Year of Information Technology A550

1998 **Litho.** **Perf. 13½**
1229	A550	2.50r multicolored	.90	.25

Personalities A551

#1230, Ven. Pannakitti Nayake Thero. #1231, Sir Nicholas Attygalle. #1232, Dr. Samuel Fisk Green. #1233, Prof. Ediriweera Sarachchandra.

1998 **Perf. 13**
1230	A551	2.50r multicolored	.50	.35
1231	A551	2.50r multicolored	.50	.35
1232	A551	2.50r multicolored	.50	.35
1233	A551	2.50r multicolored	.50	.35
		Nos. 1230-1233 (4)	2.00	1.40

Meteorological Dept., 50th Anniv. — A552

1998 **Litho.** **Perf. 14x13½**
1234	A552	2.50r multicolored	1.75	.55

26th Forum of South Asia, Africa & Middle East Lions Clubs Intl. — A553

1998, Nov. 20 **Litho.** **Perf. 14x14½**
1235	A553	2.50r multicolored	3.00	1.25

Christmas A554

1998, Dec. 10 **Perf. 13½x14**
1236	A554	2.50r Nativity	.35	.25
1237	A554	20r Annunciation	1.60	1.50
a.		Souvenir sheet, #1236-1237	2.00	2.00

A555

S.W.R.D. Bandaranaike, Birth Cent.: No. 1238, Wearing white scarf. No. 1239, Wearing blue scarf.

1999, Jan. 8 **Litho.** **Perf. 12**
1238	A555	3.50r multicolored	1.00	1.00
1239	A555	3.50r multicolored	1.00	1.00
a.		Souvenir sheet, #1238-1239, perf. 12½	2.25	2.25

Kandyan Dancer — A556

1999, Feb. 3 **Photo.** **Perf. 12**
1240	A556	1r brown	.25	.25
1241	A556	2r green blue	.25	.25
1242	A556	3r plum	.25	.25
1243	A556	3.50r blue	.25	.25
1244	A556	4r dark red	.25	.25

Size: 21x26mm
1245	A556	5r green	.25	.25
1246	A556	10r violet	.35	.30
1247	A556	13.50r bright red	.45	.40
1248	A556	17r blue green	.55	.45
1249	A556	20r olive bister	.65	.55
		Nos. 1240-1249 (10)	3.50	3.20

Telecommunications, 50th Anniv. — A557

Portraits of Sir Arthur C. Clarke, diagrams of Orbital Concept: a, Rocket launch, satellites, space shuttle. b, Satellites, earth from outer space, space capsule.

1999, Feb. 10 **Litho.** **Perf. 12**
1250	A557	3.50r Pair, #a.-b.	2.25	2.25

Dated 1998.

Salvation Army, 116th Anniv. A558

1999, Apr. 28 **Litho.** **Perf. 11¾x12**
1251	A558	3.50r multicolored	1.00	.70

British Council, 50th Anniv. — A559

1999, May 20 **Perf. 12**
1252	A559	3.50r multicolored	.80	.45

Sumithrayo Organization Suicide Hot Line, 25th Anniv. — A560

1999, June 14 **Perf. 12½**
1253	A560	3.50r multicolored	1.00	.50

Vesak Festival — A561

Designs: 2r, Flowers. 3.50r, Leaf, wheel. 13.50r, Nut, flower. 17r, Young people with traditional lanterns.

Unwmk.
1999, May 25 **Litho.** **Perf. 12**
1254	A561	2r multicolored	.25	.25
1255	A561	3.50r multicolored	.25	.25
1256	A561	13.50r multicolored	.80	.80
1257	A561	17r multicolored	1.00	1.00
		Nos. 1254-1257 (4)	2.30	2.30

Souvenir Sheet
Wmk. 388
Perf. 12½
1258		Sheet of 4	2.75	2.75
a.	A561	2r like #1254	.25	.25
b.	A561	3.50r like #1255	.25	.25
c.	A561	13.50r like #1256	.80	.80
d.	A561	17r like #1257	1.00	1.00

Independent Television Network, 20th Anniv. — A562

1999, June 5 **Unwmk.** **Perf. 12¾**
1259	A562	3.50r multicolored	.70	.40

Vidyodaya Pirivena, 125th Anniv. — A563

Perf. 12¾
1999, Sept. 17 **Litho.** **Unwmk.**
1260	A563	3.50r multicolored	.60	.30

Sri Lankan Cinema, 50th Anniv. — A564

1999, Sept. 17 **Litho.** **Perf. 12¾**
1261	A564	3.50r Handaya, 1979	.25	.25
1262	A564	4r Nidhanaya, 1972	.35	.30
1263	A564	10r Gam Peraliya, 1963	.55	.40
1264	A564	17r Kadawunu Poronduwa, 1947	1.50	1.25
a.		Souvenir sheet, #1261-1264	3.00	3.00
		Nos. 1261-1264 (4)	2.65	2.20

Bhakthi Prabodanaya Magazine, Cent. — A565

1999, Sept. **Litho.** **Perf. 12x12¼**
1265	A565	3.50r multicolored	.60	.30

Hector Kobbekaduwa, Politician — A566

Perf. 12¾x12½
1999, Sept. 19 **Wmk. 388** **Litho.**
1266	A566	3.50r multicolored	.60	.30

National Army,
50th
Anniv. — A567

1999, Oct. 10   **Unwmk.**   **Perf. 12¾**
1267 A567 3.50r multicolored   .80 .40

Convention on
the Rights of the
Child, 10th
Anniv. — A568

1999, Nov. 20   **Perf. 12¾x12½**
1268 A568 3.50r multicolored   1.25 .70

A569

1999, Nov. 26   **Perf. 12¾**
1269 A569 3.50r multicolored   .60 .30

Balangoda Ananda Maitreya Mahanyake
Thero (b. 1895), Buddhist priest.

A570

Paintings.

1999, Dec. 12   **Perf. 12¾**
1270 A570 3.50r By David
      Paynter   .40 .25
1271 A570 4r By Justin
      Daraniyagala   .40 .25
1272 A570 17r By Ivan Peries   .80 .80
1273 A570 20r By Solias
      Mendis   1.25 1.25
   a.   Souvenir sheet of 4, #1270-
      1273   4.00 4.00
     Nos. 1270-1273 (4)   2.85 2.55

Athletic Accomplishments — A571

Designs: 1r, Kumar Anandan's swim across
Palk Strait. 3.50r, World champions in cricket.
13.50r, International fame in track and field.

1999   **Perf. 12¾**
1274 A571   1r multicolored   .35 .25
1275 A571   3.50r multicolored   .80 .75
1276 A571   13.50r multicolored   1.60 2.00
     Nos. 1274-1276 (3)   2.75 3.00

Natl. Commission
for UNESCO,
50th
Anniv. — A572

Perf. 12¾x12½
1999, Nov. 16   **Litho.**   **Wmk. 388**
1277 A572 13.50r multi   3.50 2.75

Christmas
A573

1999, Nov. 30   **Perf. 12½x12¾**
1278 A573 3.50r shown   .30 .25
1279 A573 20r Magi   1.10 .80
   a.   Souvenir sheet, #1278-1279   2.50 2.50

Famous
People — A574

Designs: No. 1280, Dr. Pandithamani S.
Kanapathipillai, Tamil scholar. No. 1281, Sunil
Santha, musician. No. 1282, Dr. Al Haj Badi-
udin Mahmud, Education minister.

1999, Dec. 3   **Perf. 12¾x12½**
1280 A574 3.50r multi   1.25 .70
1281 A574 3.50r multi   2.00 .90
1282 A574 3.50r multi   1.25 .70
     Nos. 1280-1282 (3)   4.50 2.30

No. 1149A
Surcharged

1999, Dec. 3   **Litho.**   **Perf. 12**
1282A A516 2r on 2.50r multi   11.00 1.40

Butterflies — A575

Designs: 3.50r, Striped albatross. 13.50r,
Ceylon tiger. 17r, Three-spot grass yellow.
20r, Great orange tip.

Perf. 12x11¾
1999, Dec. 30   **Unwmk.**
Granite Paper
1283 A575 3.50r multi   .50 .30
1284 A575 13.50r multi   1.10 .85
1285 A575 17r multi   1.50 1.25
1286 A575 20r multi   1.75 1.40
   a.   Souvenir sheet, #1283-1286   5.00 5.00
     Nos. 1283-1286 (4)   4.85 3.80

Corals
A576

1999, Dec. 30   **Perf. 11¾x12**
Granite Paper
1287 A576 3.50r Boulder   .35 .40
1288 A576 13.50r Blue-tipped   1.50 1.10
1289 A576 14r Brain-boulder   1.50 1.10
1290 A576 22r Elkhorn   1.75 1.40
   a.   Souvenir sheet, #1287-1290   5.75 5.75
     Nos. 1287-1290 (4)   5.10 4.00

For surcharge, see No. 1581.

Auditor General's Department,
Bicent. — A576a

Perf. 12½x12¾
1999, Dec.   **Litho.**   **Unwmk.**
1290B A576a 3.50r multi   .80 .60

Year 2000 — A577

Satellite and: 10r, Birds, religious symbols.
No. 1292, Scales, girl, Red Cross, computer.
No. 1293, airplane, satellite dish, man at computer. No. 1294, Hands, symbols of women's
equality, crippled and blind.

2000, Jan. 1   **Perf. 11¾**
Granite Paper
1291 A577 10r multi   .30 .30
1292 A577 100r multi   4.25 4.25
1293 A577 100r multi   4.25 4.25
1294 A577 100r multi   4.25 4.25
   a.   Souvenir sheet, #1291-1294   13.50 13.50
     Nos. 1291-1294 (4)   13.05 13.05

Kurunagala
Diocese,
50th Anniv.
A578

Unwmk.
2000, Feb. 2   **Litho.**   **Perf. 12**
1295 A578 13.50r multi   1.50 1.75

Wesley
College,
Colombo,
125th
Anniv.
A579

2000, Mar. 2   **Perf. 11¾x12**
1296 A579 3.50r multi   .60 .30

Panadura Pinwatte Saddharmakara
Vidyayathana Pirivena, Cent. — A580

2000, Mar. 12
1297 A580 3.50r multi   .60 .30

Vesak
Festival — A581

2r, Arrival of Jaya Sri Maha Bodhi sapling.
3.50r, King Devanampiyatissa carrying sapling
on his head. 10r, Venerating sapling. 13.50r,
Royal tree planting, Anuradhapura.

2000, Apr. 28   **Litho.**   **Perf. 12¾x12½**
1298-1301 A581   Set of 4   2.50 2.00
  1301a   Souvenir sheet, #1298-1301   4.50 4.50

Sri Lanka Bar Association, 25th Anniv.
(in 1999) — A582

2000, June 10   **Perf. 12**
1302 A582 3.50r multi   .60 .30

Co-operative Wholesale
Establishment, 50th Anniv. — A583

2000, July 1   **Perf. 12¾**
1303 A583 3.50r multi   .60 .30

No. 979
Surcharged

2000, July 21   **Litho.**   **Perf. 11½**
1303A A420 50c on 8r multi   7.50 3.25

St.
Patrick's
College,
Jaffna,
150th
Anniv.
A584

2000, July 21
1304 A584 3.50r multi   1.25 .70

Survey Dept., 200th Anniv. A585

2000, Aug. 2
1305 A585 3.50r multi .65 .30

Central Bank of Sri Lanka, 50th Anniv. — A586

2000, Aug. 27   **Perf. 13¼**
1306 A586 3.50r multi .60 .30

Dr. Maria Montessori (1870-1952), Educator — A587

2000, Aug. 31   **Perf. 11¾**
1307 A587 3.50r multi .65 .30

2000 Summer Olympics, Sydney — A588

Sydney Olympic Games emblem and: a, Hurdler, map. b, Shooter, runners. c, Runners. d, Hurdlers, swimmer.

2000, Sept. 7
1308   A588 10r Horiz. strip of 4, #a-d   3.00 3.00
   e.   Souvenir sheet, #1308   3.75 3.75

All Ceylon Young Men's Muslim Association Conference, 50th Anniv. — A589

2000, Sept. 16
1309 A589 3.50r multi .60 .30

Hotel Industry, 25th Anniv. A590

2000, Sept. 18   **Perf. 12¾**
1310 A590 10r multi 3.00 1.75

Immigration and Emigration Dept., 50th Anniv. A591

2000, Oct. 2   **Perf. 11¾**
1311 A591 3.50r multi 1.00 .70

Traditional Dancer — A592

Perf. 13½x13 Syncopated
2000, Oct. 5   **Litho.**
1312 A592 50r multi   1.75 1.75
1313 A592 100r multi   3.50 3.50
1314 A592 200r multi   6.75 6.75
   Nos. 1312-1314 (3)   12.00 12.00

All-Ceylon Buddhist Congress Natl. Awards Ceremony A593

2000, Aug. 27   **Litho.**   **Perf. 12¾**
1315 A593 3.50r multi 1.00 .70

Saumiyamoorthy Thondaman, Government Minister — A594

2000, Oct. 30
1316 A594 3.50r multi .70 .40

Famous People — A595

Designs: No. 1317, 3.50r, Most Ven. Baddegama Siri Piyaratana Nayake Thero, educator. No. 1318, 3.50r, Aluthgamage Simon de Silva (1874-1920), writer. No. 1319, 3.50r, Desigar Ramanujam (1907-68), politician.

Perf. 12x12¼ (#1317), 12¾x12½
2000, Nov. 14
1317-1319 A595   Set of 3   1.25 1.00

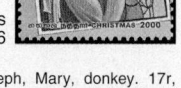

Christmas A596

Designs: 2r, Joseph, Mary, donkey. 17r, Holy family.

Lalith Athulathmudali (1936-93), Politician — A597

2000, Nov. 30   **Perf. 12½x12¾**
1322 A597 3.50r multi .60 .30

Medicina Alternativa Medical Society, 38th Anniv. A598

2000, Dec. 1   **Perf. 12¾**
1323 A598 13.50r multi 2.25 1.50

Ladies' College, Cent. — A599

2000, Dec. 7
1324 A599 3.50r multi .75 .30

Navy, 50th Anniv. A600

2000, Dec. 9
1325 A600 3.50r multi 1.00 .50

Peliyagoda Vidyalankara Pirivena, 125th Anniv. — A601

2000, Dec. 30   **Perf. 12x12¼**
1326 A601 3.50r multi .60 .30

Bishop's College, 125th Anniv. A602

2001, Jan. 19   **Litho.**
1327 A602 3.50r multi .60 .30

2000, Nov. 23   **Perf. 12¾x12½**
1320-1321 A596   Set of 2   2.25 1.75
  1321a   Souvenir sheet, #1320-1321, perf. 12   2.50 2.50

St. Thomas' College, 150th Anniv. A603

2001, Feb. 3   **Perf. 12¾**
1328 A603 3.50r multi .60 .30

Lanka Mahila Samiti Women's Training Society, 70th Anniv. A604

2001, Feb. 15
1329 A604 3.50r multi .60 .30

Air Force, 50th Anniv. A605

2001, Mar. 9
1330 A605 3.50r multi 1.20 .50

St. Lawrence's School, Cent. A606

2001, Mar. 15
1331 A606 3.50r multi .60 .30

Bernard Soysa (1914-97), Politician — A607

2001, Mar. 20   **Perf. 12¾**
1332 A607 3.50r multi .60 .30

Vesak Festival — A608

Designs: 2r, Sri Nagadeepa Chaithya, Jaffna. 3,50r, Muthiyangana Chaithya, Badulla. 13.50r, Kirivehera, Kataragama. 17r, Sri Dalada Maligawa, Kandy.

2001, Apr. 7   **Litho.**   **Perf. 13½x13¾**
1333 A608 2r multi   .25 .25
   a.   Perf. 14¼   .25 .25
        Perf. 14¼
1334 A608 3.50r multi   .25 .25
   a.   Perf. 13½x13¾   .25 .25
1335 A608 13.50r multi   .90 .90
1336 A608 17r multi   1.25 1.25
   a.   Souvenir sheet, #1333a, 1334-1336   2.75 2.75

Hansa Jataka, by George Keyt (1901-93) — A609

2001, Apr. 24   *Perf. 13¼*
1337 A609 13.50r multi   1.60 2.00

Coins
A610

Designs: 3.50r, Kahavanu gold coin, 9th cent. 13.50r, Vijayabahu I silver coin, 1055-1111. 17r, Sethu copper coin, 13th-14th cent. 20r, Buddha Jayanthi 5r commemorative silver coin, 1957.

Perf. 13¾x13½, 14¼ (17r)
2001, June 18
1338 A610 3.50r multi   .25 .25
1339 A610 13.50r multi   .90 .90
1340 A610 17r multi   1.25 1.25
   a.   Perf. 13¾x13½x14¼x13½   1.25 1.25
1341 A610 20r multi   1.60 1.60
   a.   Perf. 13¾x13½x14¼x13½   1.60 1.60
   b.   Souvenir sheet, #1338-1339, 1340a, 1341a   4.50 4.50

Colombo Plan, 50th Anniv. — A611

2001, July 2   *Perf. 13½x13¾*
1342 A611 10r multi   1.00 1.00

US-Sri Lankan Diplomatic Relations, 150th Anniv. A612

2001, July 3   *Perf. 12¾*
1343 A612 10r multi   1.25 1.00

Lance Corporal Gamini Kularatne (1966-91), Military Hero — A613

2001, July 14   *Perf. 13¾x13½*
1344 A613 3.50r multi   .60 .30

Prince and Princess of Wales College, Moratuwa, 125th Anniv. A614

2001, Sept. 14   *Perf. 13¼*
1345 A614 3.50r multi   .60 .30

Year of Dialogue Among Civilizations A615

2001, Oct. 9   *Perf. 13x13½*
1346 A615 10r multi   1.30 1.00

No. 511 Surcharged

2001, July 9 Photo.   *Perf. 14¼x14½*
1347 A180 5r on 1.15r multi   5.00 4.00
1348 A180 10r on 1.15r multi   7.00 5.00

An additional surcharge was released in this set. The editors would like to examine it.

13th Meeting of Parties to the Montreal Protocol — A616

2001, Oct. 18 Litho.   *Perf. 13x13¼*
1349 A616 13.50r multi   .75 1.10

Ramakrishna Mission Students' Home, Batticaloa, 75th Anniv. — A617

2001, Oct. 19   *Perf. 12¾*
1350 A617 3.50r multi   .60 .30

Drummer — A618

Drummer from: 1r, 2r, 3r, 3.50r, Daul. 4r, 5r, 10r, Kandy. 13.50r, 17r, 20r, Low country.

2001, Nov. 8 Litho.   *Perf. 12½x13¼*
1351 A618   1r rose   .25 .25
1352 A618   2r emerald   .25 .25
1353 A618   3r fawn   .25 .25
1354 A618   3.50r dark blue   .25 .25
    Size: 23x28mm
    Perf. 13¼x12½
1355 A618   4r pink   .35 .25
1356 A618   5r orange   .35 .25
1357 A618   10r violet   .75 .30
1358 A618   13.50r dull purple   1.00 .45
1359 A618   17r yel orange   1.25 .50
1360 A618   20r Prus blue   1.50 .60
    Nos. 1351-1360 (10)   6.20 3.35

See Nos. 1389A, 1410. For surcharges, see Nos. 1409, 1514, 1549, 1582.

S.W.R.D. Bandaranaike Natl. Memorial Foundation, 25th Anniv. — A619

2001, Nov. 27   *Perf. 13¾x13¼*
1361 A619 3.50r multi   .60 .30

Christmas A620

Designs: 3.50r, Jesus and children. 17r, The Annunciation.

2001, Nov. 28   *Perf. 13*
1362-1363 A620 Set of 2   1.00 .75
   1363a   Souvenir sheet, #1362-1363   1.25 1.25

Frogs A621

Designs: 3.50r, Conical wart pygmy tree frog. 13.50r, Sharp-snout saddle tree frog. 17r, Round-snout pygmy tree frog. 20r, Sri Lanka wood frog.

2001, Dec. 3   *Perf. 13¼x13*
1364-1367 A621 Set of 4   3.50 2.75
   1367a   Souvenir sheet, #1364-1367   3.75 3.75

St. Bridget's Convent, Cent. A622

2002, Feb. 1
1368 A622 3.50r multi   .60 .30

Ceylon Government Gazette, 200th Anniv. — A623

2002, Mar. 15 Litho.   *Perf. 13¾x14*
1369 A623 3.50r multi   .60 .30

D. S. Senanayake (1884-1952), Prime Minister — A624

2002, Mar. 22   *Perf. 14x13¾*
1370 A624 3.50r multi   .60 .30

Gamini Dissanayake (1942-94), Assassinated Government Minister — A625

2002, Mar. 27   *Perf. 13¾x14*
1371 A625 3.50r multi   .60 .30

Lester James Peries (b. 1919), Film Director A626

2002, Apr. 5   *Perf. 13¼x13*
1372 A626 3.50r multi   .60 .30

Natural Beauty of Sri Lanka — A627

Designs: 5r, Sinharaja Forest Reserve. 10r, Horton Plains National Park. 13.50r, Knuckles Range. 20r, Rumassala Cliff and Bonavista Coral Reef.

2002, Apr. 10   *Perf. 13x13¼*
1373-1376 A627 Set of 4   2.00 2.00

Pres. Ranasinghe Premadasa (1924-93) A628

2002, Apr. 29   *Perf. 13¾x14*
1377 A628 4.50r multi   .60 .25

Sri Lanka - Japan Diplomatic Relations, 50th Anniv. — A629

2002, Apr. 29   *Perf. 14x13¾*
1378 A629 16.50r multi   1.00 .75

Vesak Festival A630

Dambulla Raja Maha Vihara rock paintings: 3r, Queen Mahamaya's dream. 4.50r, Birth of Prince Siddhartha. 16.50r, Siddhartha's exhibition of archery talents. 23r, Ordination of Prince Siddhartha.

2002, May 17   *Perf. 13¾x14*
1379-1382 A630 Set of 4   2.00 1.50
   1382a   Souvenir sheet, #1379-1382   2.25 2.25

Most Venerable Madihe Pannasiha Maha Nayaka Thera, Religious Leader, 90th Birthday — A631

2002, June 23   *Perf. 14x13¾*
1383 A631 4.50r multi   .60   .25

Sri Lanka Oriental Studies Society, Cent. A632

2002, July 24   *Perf. 13¾x14*
1384 A632 4.50r multi   .75   .25

Rifai Thareeq Association, 125th Anniv. — A633

2002, July 26
1385 A633 4.50r multi   .75   .25

14th Asian Track and Field Championships, Colombo — A634

Designs: 4.50r, Discus thrower. 16.50r, Sprinter. 23r, Hurdler. 26r, Long jumper.

2002, Aug. 8
1386-1389 A634   Set of 4   3.00   3.00

Daul Drummer Type of 2001
Perf. 12½x13¼
2002, Aug. 16   **Litho.**
1389A A618 4.50r blue violet   —
    For surcharge, see No. 1785.

National Museum, 125th Anniv. — A635

No. 1390: a, Carved lion (sitting). b, Carved lion (standing with head turned).

2002, Aug. 27
1390 A635 4.50r Horiz. pair, #a-b 2.00 2.00

Woman's Hand Holding Flower — A636

2002, Aug. 28   *Perf. 14x13¾*
1391 A636 10r multi   1.10   .65
    Tourism promotion.

Dr. A. C. S. Hameed (1929-99), Government Minister — A637

2002, Sept. 3
1392 A637 4.50r multi   .70   .25

Freemasons' Hall, Colombo, Cent. — A638

2002, Sept. 5   *Perf. 13¾x14*
1393 A638 4.50r multi   .90   .50

Holy Cross College, Kalutara, Cent. A639

2002, Sept. 13
1394 A639 4.50r multi   .70   .25

German Dharmaduta Society, 50th Anniv. — A640

2002, Sept. 21   *Perf. 14x13¾*
1395 A640 4.50r multi   1.00   .25

Intl. Children's Day — A641

2002, Oct. 1
1396 A641 4.50r multi   .70   .25

Dr. M. C. M. Kaleel (1899-1995), Government Minister — A642

2002, Oct. 18
1397 A642 4.50r green   .70   .25

Uduppiddy American Mission College, 150th Anniv. A643

2002, Oct. 19   Litho.   Perf. 13¾x14
1398 A643 4.50r multi   1.50   1.50

Dr. Wijayananda Dahanayake (1902-97), Prime Minister — A644

2002, Oct. 22   Litho.   Perf. 14x13¾
1399 A644 4.50r brown   .70   .25

Sri Lanka - Netherlands Relations, 400th Anniv. — A645

2002, Nov. 22   *Perf. 13¾x14*
1400 A645 16.50r multi   1.50   1.00

Christmas — A646

Designs: 4.50r, Madonna and Child. 26r, Holy Family.

2002, Dec. 15   *Perf. 13x13¼*
1401-1402 A646   Set of 2   2.00   1.60
  1402a   Souvenir sheet, #1401-1402   2.00   2.00

Sri Lanka - China Rubber and Rice Pact, 50th Anniv. A647

2002, Dec. 20   *Perf. 13¾x14*
1403 A647 4.50r multi   .75   .25

Kopay Christian College, 150th Anniv. A648

2002, Dec. 28
1404 A648 4.50r multi   .70   .25

No. 925 Srchd.

2002 ?   Litho.   Perf. 12½x12
1405 A392 25c on 5.75r multi   —

No. 1354 Surcharged

2002 ?   Litho.   Perf. 12½x13¼
1406 A618 4.50r on 3.50r dk bl   —   —

Teachers' College, Maharagama, Cent. — A649

2003, Jan. 21   *Perf. 13¾x14*
1407 A649 4.50r multi   .70   .25

Holy Family Convent, Bambalapitiya, Cent. — A650

2003, Feb. 3   *Perf. 14x13¾*
1408 A650 4.50r multi   .80   .25

Drummer Type of 2001 and

No. 1359 Surcharged

Drummer from: 16.50r, Low country.

Perf. 13¼x12½
2003, Feb. 17   **Litho.**
1409 A618 50c on 5r org yel   .50   .35
1410 A618 16.50r purple   1.30   .90

M. D. Banda (1914-74), Government Minister — A651

2003, Mar. 14   *Perf. 13¾x14*
1411 A651 4.50r multi   .80   .25

Balagalle Saraswati Maha Pirivena, Cent. A652

2003, Apr. 3
1412 A652 4.50r multi   .80   .25

D. B. Welagedara,
Politician — A653

2003, Apr. 22   *Perf. 14x13¾*
1413 A653 4.50r multi   .80 .25

Vesak
Festival — A654

Designs: 2.50r, Paying obeisance to parents. 3r, Dhamma school. 4.50r, Going on alms round. 23r, Meditation.

2003, Apr. 26
1414-1417 A654 Set of 4   2.00 1.50
1417a   Souvenir sheet, #1414-1417   2.25 2.25

Dagoba
Construction
Features — A655

Designs: 4.50r, Stupa. 16.50r, Guard stone, horiz. (58x28mm). 50r, Moonstone, horiz.

2003, Apr. 28 *Perf. 13x13¼, 13¼x13*
1418-1420 A655 Set of 3   3.50 2.50
1420a   Souvenir sheet, #1418-1420   4.00 4.00

Second World
Hindu Conference,
Colombo — A656

2003, May 2   *Perf. 14x13¾*
1421 A656 4.50r multi   .90 .25

International
Nursing
Day — A657

2003, May 12   *Perf. 13¾x14*
1422 A657 4.50r multi   .90 .25

Sirimavo Bandaranaike Memorial
Exhibition Center — A658

2003, May 17   *Perf. 13¼x12*
1423 A658 4.50r multi   .90 .25

Al-Haj H. S. Ismail
(1901-73),
Parliament
Speaker — A659

2003, May 18   *Perf. 14x13¾*
1424 A659 4.50r multi   .65 .25

Board of Investment, 25th
Anniv. — A660

2003, May 21   *Perf. 13¾x12*
1425 A660 4.50r multi   .65 .25

World Biodiversity Day — A661

Designs: 4r, Pidurutalagal Mountain Range. 4.50r, Seven Maidens Mountain Range. 16.50r, Kirigalpoththa Mountain. 23r, Ritigala Mountain.

2003, May 22   *Perf. 13¾x12*
1426-1429 A661 Set of 4   3.00 1.75

Saralankara College, Gonapinuwala,
Cent. — A662

2003, June 6   *Perf. 13¾x14*
1430 A662 4.50r multi   .65 .25

A663   A664

First Arab settlement, Beruwala: 4.50r, Masjidul Abrar. 23r, Masjidul Abrar, horiz. (57x22mm).

Perf. 14x13¾, 13¼x12 (23r)
2003, June 8
1431-1432 A663 Set of 2   1.50 1.10

2003, June 23   *Perf. 14x13¾*
1433 A664 4.50r multi   .65 .25
Anti-narcotics Week.

Syamopali
Maha
Nikaya,
250th
Anniv.
A665

Designs: No. 1434, 4.50r, Asgiri Maha Viharaya. No. 1435, 4.50r, Malwathu Maha Viharaya.

2003, July 13   *Perf. 13¾x14*
1434-1435 A665 Set of 2   1.10 .75

Lanka Philex Intl. Stamp Exhibition,
Colombo — A666

2003, July 31   *Perf. 13¼x12*
1436 A666 16.50r multi   1.25 .75
a.   Souvenir sheet of 1   2.25 2.25

Dr. Ananda Tissa de Alwis,
Government Minister — A667

2003, Aug. 21   *Perf. 13¾x14*
1437 A667 4.50r multi   .70 .35

Panadura
Controversy, 130th
Anniv. — A668

2003, Aug. 24   *Perf. 14x13¾*
1438 A668 4.50r multi   .70 .35

Venerable
Haldanduwana
Dhammarakkitha
Thero — A669

2003, Sept. 3   *Litho.*
1439 A669 4.50r multi   .70 .35

Ragama
Walpola
Poson
Maha
Perahara,
75th Anniv.
A670

2003, Sept. 10   *Perf. 13¾x14*
1440 A670 4.50r multi   .90 .45

M. H. M. Ashraff
(1948-2000),
Government
Minister — A671

2003, Sept. 18   *Perf. 14x13¾*
1441 A671 4.50r multi   .75 .35

Sisters of
the Holy
Angels,
Cent.
A672

2003, Sept. 27   *Perf. 13¾x14*
1442 A672 4.50r multi   .75 .35

Birds — A673

No. 1443: a, Black-necked stork. b, Purple swamphen. c, Gray heron. d, White-throated kingfisher. e, Black-crowned night heron. f, Scarlet minivet. g, White-rumped shama. h, Malabar trogon. i, Asian paradise flycatcher. j, Little green bee-eater. k, Brown wood owl. l, Crested serpent eagle. m, Crested goshawk. n, Jungle owlet. o, Rufous-bellied eagle. p, Black-headed munia. q, Pompadour green pigeon. r, Plum-headed parakeet. s, Coppersmith barbet. t, Emerald dove. u, Blue-faced malkoha. v, Scimitar babbler. w, Painted francolin. x, Red-backed woodpecker. y, Malabar pied hornbill.

2003, Sept. 27   *Perf. 14x13¾*
1443 A673 4.50r Sheet of 25,
                #a-y   19.50 19.50

World
Habitat
Day — A674

2003, Oct. 6   *Perf. 13*
1444 A674 4.50r multi   .70 .25

World Post Day   Blue
A675   Sapphire
                        A676

2003, Oct. 9   *Perf. 14x13¾*
1445 A675 23r multi   2.25 1.50

2003, Oct. 21   *Perf. 12x13½*
1446 A676 4.50r multi   .70 .25
See also No. 1497.

Pontificate of Pope John Paul II, 25th Anniv. — A677

2003, Oct. 22 *Perf. 13*
1447 A677 4.50r multi 1.75 .40

Deepavali Festival — A678

2003, Oct. 23
1448 A678 4.50r multi .70 .25

Pinnawala Elephant Orphanage A679

Designs: 4.50r, Two adult and two young elephants. 16.50r, Elephants and caretaker. 23r, Two adult elephants. 26r, Elephants in water.

2003, July 13 Litho. *Perf. 13½x13*
1449-1452 A679 Set of 4 5.50 3.50
1452a Souvenir sheet, #1449-1452 6.00 6.00

For surcharge, see No. 1576.

Waterfalls — A680

Designs: 2.50r, Ramboda. 4.50r, Saint Clair. 23r, Bopath Ella. 50r, Devon.

2003, Nov. 11 *Perf. 14x13¾*
1453-1456 A680 Set of 4 4.00 2.75

Ukku Banda Wanninayake (1905-73), Finance Minister — A681

2003, Nov. 23 *Perf. 13*
1457 A681 4.50r multi .65 .25

Christmas A682

Designs: 4.50r, Church. 16.50r, Shepherds and angel, vert.

2003, Nov. 30
1458-1459 A682 Set of 2 .80 .70

Pandith W. D. Amaradeva, Musician, 76th Birthday — A683

2003, Dec. 5
1460 A683 4.50r multi 1.00 .35

Gangarama Seemamalakaya — A684

2003, Dec. 20
1461 A684 4.50r multi .65 .25

Daham Pahana, Sri Pushparamaya, Malegoda — A685

2003, Dec. 31
1462 A685 4.50r multi .65 .25

Shazuliyathul Fassiya Tharika — A686

2004, Jan. 6
1463 A686 18r multi 1.00 .70

Chavakachcheri Hindu College, Cent. — A687

2004, Jan. 30 *Perf. 12x13½*
1464 A687 4.50r multi 1.00 .25

Royal-Thomian Cricket Match, 125th Anniv. — A688

2004, Jan. 30 *Perf. 13*
1465 A688 4.50r multi 1.10 .40

Pres. Dingiri Banda Wijetunga A689

2004, Feb. 15 Litho. *Perf. 13*
1466 A689 4.50r multi .75 .25

Planters Association of Ceylon, 150th Anniv. — A690

2004, Feb. 17 *Perf. 13¾x14*
1467 A690 4.50r multi .75 .40

Kalashuri Most Venerable Mapalagama Vipulasara Thero, Religious Leader — A691

Maithripala Senanayeke A692

Cathiravelu Sittampalam (1898-1964), First Posts and Telecommunications Minister — A693

M. G. Mendis, Communist Leader — A694

2004, Feb. 28 *Perf. 13x13¼*
1468 A691 3.50r multi .50 .25
1469 A692 3.50r multi .50 .25
1470 A693 3.50r multi .50 .25
1471 A694 3.50r multi .50 .25
Nos. 1468-1471 (4) 2.00 1.00

Nos. 1468-1471 are dated 2002. They were made available then, but not issued.

75th Ananda-Nalanda Cricket Match — A695

2004, Mar. 7 *Perf. 12x13¼*
1472 A695 4.50r multi 1.20 .50

St. Anthony's College, Kandy, 150th Anniv. — A696

2004, Mar. 12 *Perf. 13½x12*
1473 A696 4.50r multi .65 .25

Vesak Festival — A697

Various scenes of Sittara painting on wooden casket (with white borders on top and bottom): 4r, 4.50r, 16.50r, 20r.
26r, Scene of Sittara painting (no white borders).

2004, Apr. 30
1474-1477 A697 Set of 4 2.00 2.00
Souvenir Sheet
1478 A697 26r multi 1.50 1.50

Gongalegoda Banda (1809-49), Leader of 1848 Rebellion — A698

2004, May 22 *Perf. 14x13¾*
1479 A698 4.50r multi .65 .25

World Blood Donor Day — A699

2004, June 15 *Perf. 13*
1480 A699 4.50r multi .75 .25

2004 Summer Olympics,
Athens — A700

Designs: 4.50r, Swimming. 16.50r,
Women's track. 17r, Shooting. 20r, Men's
track.

2004, Aug. 6   **Litho.**
1481-1484 A700 Set of 4   2.40 2.40

Sri Siddhartha
Buddharakkhita,
18th Cent.
Religious
Leader — A701

2004, Aug. 16
1485 A701 4.50r brown   .65   .25

Robert
Gunawardena,
Communist
Leader — A702

2004, Aug. 23   **Perf. 14x13¾**
1486 A702 4.50r multi   .65   .25

Pres. Junius
Richard
Jayewardene
(1906-96)
A703

2004, Sept. 27   **Perf. 13**
1487 A703 4.50r multi   .65   .25

Intl. Day of
Peace — A704

2004, Sept. 21
1488 A704 4.50r multi   .65   .25

Sri Chandrarathna
Manawasinghe,
Writer — A705

2004, Oct. 6   **Perf. 12x13¼**
1489 A705 4.50r multi   .65   .25

Government Service Buddhist
Association, 50th Anniv. — A706

2004, Oct. 7   **Perf. 13**
1490 A706 4.50r multi   .65   .25

World Post
Day — A707

2004, Oct. 9   **Perf. 12x13½**
1491 A707 4.50r multi   1.00   .25

Raddelle Sri
Pannaloka
Anunayaka Thero,
Religious
Leader — A708

2004, Oct. 20   **Perf. 13**
1492 A708 4.50r multi   .65   .25

Christmas
A709

2004, Nov. 27   **Perf. 14x13¾**
1493 A709 5r multi   .65   .25

Fathers Jacome Gonsalves and
Edmond Peiris — A710

2004, Nov. 27   **Perf. 13¼x12**
1494 A710 20r multi   .90   .90

Information and Communication
Technology Week — A711

2004, Nov. 29   **Perf. 13¾x14**
1495 A711 5r multi   .90   .25

De Soysa Hospital for Women,
Colombo, 125th Anniv.
A712

2004, Dec. 11   **Perf. 13½x14**
1496 A712 5r multi   .65   .25

Blue Sapphire Type of 2003
2004, Dec. 14   Litho.   Perf. 12x13½
1497 A676 5r multi   1.00   .25

Most Venerable
Talalle Siri
Dhammananda
Maha Nayaka
Thero,
Educator — A713

2005, Mar. 13   **Perf. 14x13¾**
1498 A713 5r multi   .65   .25

Most Venerable
Hammalawa
Saddhatissa
Nayaka Maha
Thero (1914-90),
Monk — A714

2005, Mar. 22
1499 A714 5r multi   .65   .25

T. B. Tennakoon,
Politician — A715

2005, Mar. 25
1500 A715 5r multi   .65   .25

D. A.
Rajapaksa
(1905-67),
Politician
A716

2005, Mar. 25   **Perf. 13¾x14**
1501 A716 5r multi   .65   .25

Vesak
Festival — A717

Designs: 4.50r, Ambulatory meditation. 5r,
Spiritual bliss through Buddhism. 10r, Meditation in standing posture. 50r, Sedentary
meditation.

2005, May 12   **Perf. 14x13¾**
1502-1505 A717 Set of 4   3.00 3.00
1505a   Sheet, #1502-1505   3.25 3.25
          Compare with Type A723.

Rev.
Marcelline
Jayakody
(1902-98)
A718

2005, June 3   **Perf. 13**
1506 A718 20r multi   1.25 1.25

Rana Viru
Day — A719

2005, June 7   **Perf. 14x13¾**
1507 A719 50r multi   1.50 1.50

Deshamanya M.
A. Bakeer Markar
(1917-96),
Parliament
Speaker — A720

2005, July 20
1508 A720 5r multi   .60   .25

Most Venerable
Matara Kithalagama
Sri Seelalankara
Nayaka
Thero — A721

2005, July 21
1509 A721 25r multi   .70   .70

South Asia Tourism Year — A722

2005, July 29   *Perf. 13*
1510 A722 100r multi   3.00 3.00

Kalutara Bodhi Trust A723

2005, Aug. 6   *Perf. 13¾x14*
1511 A723 5r multi   .50 .25

Nos. 564, 815, 818, 937 and 1352 Surcharged

Methods and Perfs As Before
2005
1512 A206 50c on 10c #564   1.25 1.25
1513 A324 50c on 35c #815   1.25 1.25
1514 A618 50c on 2r #1352   1.25 1.25
1515 A399 50c on 5.75r #937   1.25 1.25
1516 A324 50c on 6r #818   1.25 1.25
    Nos. 1512-1516 (5)   6.25 6.25

Issued: No. 1514, 9/16; others, 3/21.

Postal Headquarters — A725

2005, Sept. 12   **Litho.**   *Perf. 13½x14*
1518 A725 5r multi   .40 .25

Ampitiya National Seminary A726

2005, Oct. 1
1519 A726 10r multi   .40 .25

World Post Day A727

2005, Oct. 9
1520 A727 5r multi   .40 .25

General Sir John Kotelawala Defense Academy, 25th Anniv. — A728

2005, Oct. 11   **Litho.**   *Perf. 13*
1521 A728 5r multi   .50 .25

Christmas A729

Cross of Blessed Joseph Vaz, Madonna and Child and: 5r, Angel. 30r, Star of Bethlehem.

2005, Dec. 3   **Litho.**   *Perf. 13¾x14*
1522-1523 A729 Set of 2   1.10 1.10
1523a   Souvenir sheet, #1522-1523   1.20 1.20

Admission to the UN, 50th Anniv. — A730

2005, Dec. 13   **Litho.**   *Perf. 14x13½*
1524 A730 20r multi   .90 .90

Amarapura Maha Nikaya, Bicent. A731

2005, Dec. 20   *Perf. 13½x14*
1525 A731 10r multi   .50 .50

Ancient Sri Lanka — A732

Designs: 5r, Minhagalkanda and stone tools. 20r, Extinct animals in Ratnapura gem gravels and rhinoceros and hippopotamus bone fragments. 25r, Kuruwita, Batadomba-lena and human skull from Bellan-bandi Palassa. 30r, Agriculture on the Horton Plains, fossilized barley pollen grain.

2005, Dec. 21   *Perf. 13¼x12*
1526-1529 A732 Set of 4   2.75 2.75

Damage From Dec. 26, 2004 Tsunami A733

Designs: 5r, Damaged Kalmunai Post Office, vehicles. 20r, Train derailed near Telwatte. 30r, Giant wave breaking along coast. 33r, Lighthouse and tsunami wave.

2005, Dec. 26   **Litho.**   *Perf. 13¾x14*
1530-1533 A733 Set of 4   1.75 1.75
1533a   Souvenir sheet, #1530-1533   1.75 1.75

Animals of Wilpattu National Park — A734

Designs: 5r, Barking deer. 10r, White-bellied sea eagle. 20r, Sloth bear. 50r, Leopard.

2006, Jan. 4   **Litho.**   *Perf. 13½x12*
1534 A734 5r multi   .60 .60
   a.   Souvenir sheet of 1   .60 .60
1535 A734 10r multi   .60 .60
   a.   Souvenir sheet of 1   .60 .60
1536 A734 20r multi   .95 .95
   a.   Souvenir sheet of 1   .95 .95
1537 A734 50r multi   2.40 2.40
   a.   Souvenir sheet of 1   2.40 2.40
    Nos. 1534-1537 (4)   4.55 4.55

Institution of Engineers Sri Lanka, Cent. — A735

2006, Jan. 6   **Litho.**   *Perf. 12x13¼*
1538 A735 5r black & blue   .35 .25

Europa Stamps, 50th Anniv. — A736

Sri Lanka flag and: 100r, Ceylon #336. 500r, Ship, maps of Europe and Sri Lanka.

2006, Feb. 2   *Perf. 12¾x13¼*
1539-1540 A736 Set of 2   13.50 13.50
1540a   Souvenir sheet, #1539-1540   13.50 13.50

Most Venerable Madithiyawala Vijithasena Anunayake Thero — A737

2006, Mar. 5   **Litho.**   *Perf. 14x13¾*
1541 A737 17r multi   .75 .75

100th Kingswood-Dharmaraja Cricket Match — A738

2006, Mar. 24   *Perf. 13¾x14*
1542 A738 4.50r multi   .50 .50

Vesak — A739

No. 1543: a, Wall painting depicting a plea to the Master to descend from heaven, Tivamka Image House, Polonnaruva (1/50). b, Bas-relief of Queen Mahamaya on her way to visit her parents, Jetavana Vihara, Anuradhapura (2/50). c, Wall painting depicting birth of Prince Siddhartha, Shailabimbarama Vihara, Dodanduwa (3/50). d, Wall painting of royal teacher Asita visiting Prince Siddhartha, Purwarama Viharaya, Kataluva (4/50). e, Bas-relief of Great Renunciation, Girihandu Vihara, Ambalantota (5/50). f, Rock painting depicting defeat of evils by the Master, Hindagala Vihara, Hindagala (6/50). g, Rock painting depicting first sermon of Dhammachakka, Rangiri Dambulu Vihara, Dambulla (7/50). h, Wall painting depicting conversion of Alavaka, Sapugoda Vihara, Beruvala (8/50). i, Wall painting depicting funeral pyre of the Master, Veheragalla Samudragiri Vihara, Mirissa (9/50). j, Tapassu and Bhalluka arriving in Sri Lanka with relics of the Master, Girihandu Seya, Tiriyaya (10/50). k, Wall painting depicting perfection of generosity, Bodhirukkharama Vihara, Eluvapitiya (11/50). l, Rock painting depicting perfection of wisdom, Kaballelena Vihara, Wariyapola (12/50). m, Wall painting depicting perfection of reunification, Degaldoruva Vihara, Kandy (13/50). n, Wall painting depicting perfection of equanimity, Paramakanda Vihara, Anamaduwa (14/50). o, Wall painting depicting perfection of loving kindness, Sunandarama Vihara, Ambalangoda (15/50). p, Recitation of Chullahastpadopama Sutta by Arhat Mahinda, Stupa, Mihintale (16/50). q, Establishment of Buddhism in Sri Lanka, Rajagiri Lena, Mihintale (17/50). r, Sri Maha Bodhi entering city, Sri Maha Bodhi, Anuradhapura (18/50). s, Writing Dhamma on ola leaves, Alu Vihara, Matale (19/50). t, Arrival of tooth relic of the Master, Lankapattana, Trincomalee (20/50). u, Practice of aranyaka, Situlpavuva Vihara (21/50). v, Symbols of three traditions, Lovamahapaya, Abhayagiri Vihara, Vajra symbol and lotus (22/50). w, Emergence of katikavatas, Vatadage, Polonnaruva (23/50). x, Buddhist discourse between Sri Lanka and Southeast Asia, Tooth Relic Temple, Kandy (24/50). y, Translation of the Tripitaka into Sinhala, Buddhajayanti Vihara, Colombo (25/50). z, Vesak festival scene, Deepaduttarama Vihara, Kotahena (26/50). aa, Serving of food to Buddhist clergy, Refectory at Abhayagiriya, Anuradhapura (27/50). ab, Chanting Paritta, Nishshanka Lata Mandapa, Polonnaruva (28/50). ac, Combination with village, temple tank and stupa, Tissamaharama Stupa (29/50). ad, Veneration of Bodhi tree, Bodhighara, Nillakgama (30/50). ae, Hatthikuchchi Vihara, Galgamuva, Padhanaghara, Anuradhapura (31/50). af, Ritual performance for tooth relic, Atadage, Polonnaruva (32/50). ag, Perahara, Subodharma Vihara, Karagampitiya (33/50). ah, Wall painting of a street market, Mulgirigala Vihara, local coin (34/50). ai, Sanctity of the temple, Namal Uyana, Ranava (35/50). aj, Ruvanvalisaya and Thuparama Stupas, Anuradhapura (36/50). ak, Kirivehera Stupa, Kataragama, Seruvila Stupa (37/50). al, Mahiyangana and Nagadipa Stupas, Jaffna (38/50). am, Kelaniya Stupa and Samantakuta (39/50). an, Mutiyangana Stupa, Badulla, and Deeghavapi Stupa (40/50). ao, Painted stupa, Hanguranketa Raja Maha Vihara, ancient stupas at Kandarodai, Jaffna (41/50). ap, Facade of Mihintale Stupa, bas-relief of Bahiravas (42/50). aq, Twin pond, Anuradhapura, Punkalasa lotus pond, Polonnaruva (43/50). ar, Moonstone, Mangul Maha Vihara, Lahugala (44/50). as, Bodhisattva Avalokiteshvara, Muhudumaha Vihara, Potuvil (45/50). at, Nalanda Gedige, Naula, Satmahal Prasada, Polonnaruva (46/50). au, Bas-relief of Vimana, Lankatilaka Vihara, Polonnaruva (47/50). av, Thuparama Image House, Polonnaruva, Tampita Vihara, Menikkadawara (48/50). aw, Wall painting depicting Buddhist cosmos, Omalpe Vihara, Kolonne (49/50). ax, Depiction of time in the motif of Makara, Madanvala Vihara, Hanguranketa (50/50).

2006, May 5   **Litho.**   *Perf. 13¼x12*
1543   Sheet of 50   21.00 21.00
   a.-j.   A739 2.50r Any single   .25 .25
   k.-t.   A739 4.50r Any single   .30 .30
   u.-ad.   A739 5r Any single   .30 .30
   ae.-an.   A739 10r Any single   .50 .50
   ao.-ax.   A739 17r Any single   .75 .75

Sinhala Bauddhaya Newspaper,
Cent. — A740

2006, May 7   *Perf. 13¾x14*
1544 A740 5r multi   .40 .25

Natl. Cadet Corps,
125th
Anniv. — A741

2006, May 18   *Perf. 12x13¼*
1545 A741 2r multi   .40 .25

Kotte Sri Kalyani Samagridharma
Maha Sanga Sabha, 150th
Anniv. — A742

2006, June 25   *Perf. 13¾x14*
1546 A742 4.50r multi   .40 .25

Sri Lanka
Ramanna Maha
Nikaya — A743

2006, June 29   *Perf. 14x13¾*
1547 A743 4.50r multi   .40 .25

Nos. 592, 1154, and 1353 Surcharged

Methods and Perfs As Before
2006
1548 A518 10r on 10.50r #1154   1.00 1.00
1549 A618 20r on 3r #1353   1.50 1.50
1550 A218 50r on 1.60r #592   3.50 3.50
Nos. 1548-1550 (3)   6.00 6.00

Size, location and style of surcharges vary.

St. Vincent Boys
Home, Maggona,
125th
Anniv. — A744

2006, July 15   **Litho.**   *Perf. 14x13¾*
1551 A744 10r multi   .50 .50

Lakshman
Kadiragamar
(1932-2005),
Foreign
Minister — A745

2006, Aug. 10
1552 A745 10r multi   .50 .50

St. John Dal Bastone Church,
Talangama, 125th Anniv. — A746

2006, Aug. 13   *Perf. 13¾x14*
1553 A746 5r multi   .40 .25

St. John Ambulance, Cent. — A747

2006, Aug. 15
1554 A747 5r multi   .50 .30

Tenth
South
Asian
Games
A748

Designs: 10r, High jump. 100r, Cycling.

2006, Aug. 17
1555-1556 A748   Set of 2   4.00 4.00

St. Joseph's Church, Wennappuwa,
125th Anniv. — A749

2006, Aug. 23
1557 A749 2r multi   .35 .25

Senaka Bibile (1920-
77), Pharmacologist
A750

2006, Sept. 29   *Perf. 12x13½*
1558 A750 10r multi   .50 .50

World
Children's
Day
A751

2006, Oct. 1   *Perf. 13¾x14*
1559 A751 5r multi   .35 .25

Flowers — A752

Designs: No. 1560, Indian laburnum. No.
1561, Sacred lotus. No. 1562, Foxtail orchid.
No. 1563, Orange jessamine.

2006, Oct. 2   *Perf. 14x13¾*
1560 A752 4.50r multi   .30 .30
1561 A752 4.50r multi   .30 .30
1562 A752 50r multi   1.25 1.25
    a.   Miniature sheet of 8, 4 each
      #1560, 1562   7.25 7.25
1563 A752 50r multi   1.25 1.25
    a.   Miniature sheet of 8, 4 each
      #1561, 1563   7.25 7.25
    Nos. 1560-1563 (4)   3.10 3.10

World
Post Day
A753

2006, Oct. 9   *Perf. 13¾x14*
1564 A753 40r multi   1.50 1.50

Christmas
A754

2006, Nov. 13   *Perf. 14x13¾*
1565 A754 5r multi   .35 .25

St.
Anthony's
Shrine,
Wahakotte
A755

2006, Nov. 13   *Perf. 13¾x14*
1566 A755 20r multi   .60 .60

Rugby in Sri Lanka, 125th Anniv. (in
2003) — A756

2006, Dec. 8   *Perf. 13*
1567 A756 4.50r multi   .75 .30

D. M. Rajapaksa,
Politician — A757

2006, Dec. 14   *Perf. 14x13¾*
1568 A757 5r multi   .35 .25

Vee Bissakara
Govijana Chaityaya,
Ambuluwawa
A758

Biodiversity Complex,
Ambuluwawa — A759

2006, Dec. 18   *Perf. 12x13½*
1569 A758 5r multi   .35 .25
                Perf. 13¾x14
1570 A759 25r multi   .75 .75

Kande
Viharaya
A760

2007, Jan. 6   *Perf. 13¾x14*
1571 A760 5r multi   .35 .25

Ceylon Nos. 351,
352, 397, 403, and
Sri Lanka Nos. 494,
890, 932, 1153,
1290, 1355, and
1452 Srchd.

Methods and Perfs As Before

2007

1572	A86	50c on 35c Ceylon #351	.75	.75
1573	A124	50c on 60c Ceylon #403	.75	.75
1574	A397	50c on 5.75r #932	.75	.75
1575	A518	50c on 8.50r #1153	.75	.75
1576	A679	50c on 26r #1452	.75	.75
1577	A91	4.50r on 50c Ceylon #352	1.00	.75
1578	A122	4.50r on 50c Ceylon #397	1.00	.75
1579	A174	4.50r on 1.15r #494	1.00	.75
1580	A373	4.50r on 5.75r #890	1.00	.75
1581	A576	4.50r on 22r #1290	1.00	.75
1582	A618	5r on 4r #1355	1.00	.75
		Nos. 1572-1582 (11)	9.75	8.25

Issued: Nos. 1572-1576, 1582, 2/13; Nos. 1577-1581, 1/29.

Diplomatic Relations Between Sri Lanka and People's Republic of China, 50th Anniv. — A761

2007, Feb. 7   Litho.   Perf. 13¼x12
1583 A761 50r multi   2.50 2.50

ICC Cricket World Cup — A762

Flags of participating nations, Sri Lanka Cricket emblem and: 5r, Batsman and players. 50r, Players, Sri Lanka flag.

2007, Feb. 23   Perf. 13
1584-1585 A762 Set of 2   1.50 1.50

I. M. R. A. Iriyagolle (1907-73), Education and Cultural Affairs Minister — A763

2007, Mar. 20   Litho.   Perf. 14x13¾
1586 A763 5r multi   .35 .30

First Ceylon Postage Stamps, 150th Anniv. A764

Designs: 5r, Steamship, Ceylon #2. 10r, Mail runner, Ceylon #6, 10, 11. 20r, Mail canoe, Ceylon #3, 4. 45r, Mail coach, Ceylon #15.

2007, Apr. 1   Litho.   Perf. 13¾x14
1587-1590 A764 Set of 4   2.25 2.25
1590a   Souvenir sheet, #1587-1590 2.50 2.50

Wall Paintings of Thelpatta Jataka — A765

No. 1591, 5r: a, House at right. b, House at center.
No. 1592, 20r: a, Flag bearer at right. b, King on throne at right.

2007, Apr. 20   Litho.   Perf. 13¾x14
Horiz. Pairs, #a-b
1591-1592 A765   Set of 2   3.00 3.00
1592c   Souvenir sheet, #1591-1592, perf. 13¾x13¼ 3.00 3.00

Sri Lankan Cricket Team, Runners-up in 2007 ICC Cricket World Cup — A766

Designs: No. 1593, 15r, Team, stadium. No. 1594, 15r, Players on field, faces of players.

2007, Apr. 30   Perf. 13¾x14
1593-1594 A766 Set of 2   2.75 2.75

Shells A767

Designs: 5r, Textile cone. 12r, Aquatile hairy triton. 15r, Rose-branched murex. 45r, Trapezium horse conch.

2007, May 22   Litho.   Perf. 13¾x14
1595-1598 A767   Set of 4   5.50 5.50
1598a   Souvenir sheet, #1595-1598 5.75 5.75

Scouting, Cent. — A768

2007, May 26   Perf. 13½x12
1599 A768 5r multi   .35 .25

Sri Sangamitta Balika Maha Vidyalaya, Cent. — A769

2007, June 17   Perf. 12x13¼
1600 A769 5r multi   .35 .25

Sri Lanka-Japan Friendship Society, 50th Anniv. — A770

2007, June 26   Litho.   Perf. 13¼x12
1601 A770 15r multi   1.10 1.10

Ceylon Baithulmal Fund, 50th Anniv. — A771

2007, July 3   Litho.   Perf. 12x13¼
1602 A771 5r multi   .35 .25

Prisons Day — A772

2007, July 16   Perf. 14x13¾
1603 A772 5r multi   .40 .25

Jabbar Central College, Galagedara, 104th Anniv. — A773

2007, July 27   Perf. 13¼x12
1604 A773 5r multi   .35 .25

First Sri Lankan Buddhist Mission to Germany, 50th Anniv. — A774

2007, Aug. 22   Perf. 13
1605 A774 5r multi   .35 .25

Diplomatic Relations Between Sri Lanka and Nepal, 50th Anniv. — A775

2007, Sept. 1   Litho.   Perf. 13
1606 A775 15r multi   1.10 1.10

Shrine of Our Lady of Matara, Cent. A776

2007, Sept. 9   Litho.   Perf. 13
1607 A776 5r multi   .35 .25

World Tourism Day A777

2007, Sept. 27
1608 A777 5r multi   .40 .25

Lions International in Sri Lanka, 50th Anniv. — A778

2007, Oct. 6   Perf. 12x13¼
1609 A778 5r multi   .40 .25

World Post Day — A779

2007, Oct. 9   Perf. 13¼x12
1610 A779 5r multi   .50 .25

Constellations — A780

2007, Oct. 9   Litho.   Perf. 13x12¾
Size: 20x25mm

1611	A780	50c Aries	.35	.35
1612	A780	1r Taurus	.35	.35
1613	A780	2r Gemini	.35	.35
1614	A780	3r Cancer	.35	.35
1615	A780	4r Leo	.35	.35
1616	A780	4.50r Virgo	.35	.35
1617	A780	5r Libra	.35	.35
1618	A780	10r Scorpius	.35	.35
1619	A780	12r Sagittarius	.35	.35
1620	A780	15r Capricornus	.40	.40
1621	A780	20r Aquarius	.45	.45
1622	A780	25r Pisces	.60	.60
a.		Sheet of 12, #1611-1622	2.50	2.50

Size: 25x30mm
Perf. 12x13½

1623	A780	30r Centaurus	.70	.70
1624	A780	35r Ursa Major	.80	.80
1625	A780	40r Ophiuchus	.90	.90
1626	A780	45r Orion	1.05	1.05
a.		Sheet of 4, #1623-1626	3.75	3.75
		Nos. 1611-1626 (16)	8.05	8.05

National Farmer's Day — A781

2007, Oct. 16   Litho.   Perf. 13
1627 A781 5r multi   .35 .25

Fauna of Udawalawe National Park A782

Designs: 5r, Water buffalos. 15r, Herd of elephants. 40r, Ruddy mongoose. 45r, Common langurs.

2007, Oct. 31   Perf. 13
1628-1631 A782   Set of 4   3.00 3.00
1630a   Souvenir sheet, #1629-1630, perf. 13¾x14 3.00 3.00
1631a   Souvenir sheet, #1628, 1631, perf. 13¾x14 3.00 3.00

Leslie Goonewardene (1909-83), Governmental Minister — A783

2007, Nov. 6   Litho.   Perf. 13
1632 A783 5r multi   .70 .70

Commonwealth Games Federation General Assembly, Colombo — A784

Emblem and: 5r, Man blowing into conch shell. 45r, Winged figures.

2007, Nov. 7   Litho.   Perf. 13
1633-1634 A784 Set of 2   1.50 1.50

St. Henry's College, Ilavalai, Cent. A785

2007, Nov. 10
1635 A785 5r multi   .35 .25

Christmas A786

2007, Nov. 18
1636 A786 5r multi   .35 .25

St. James' Church, Mutwal A787

2007, Nov. 18
1637 A787 30r multi   .75 .75

Muthiah Muralidaran, Cricket Player — A788

2007, Dec. 3   Perf. 13¾
Granite Paper
1638 A788 5r multi   .50 .30
   a.   Sheet of 12 + 3 labels   6.00 6.00
Values are for stamps with surrounding selvage.

Children's Stories — A789

No. 1639 — Scenes from the Race Between the Hare and Tortoise: a, Hare and tortoise before race (green panels). b, Hare sleeping (pink panels). c, Hare leaping (blue panels).

2007, Dec. 9   Perf. 12x13¼
1639   Horiz. strip of 3   .75 .75
   a.-c. A789 5r Any single   .25 .25

St. Mary's Church, Maggona, 150th Anniv. A790

2007, Dec. 9   Perf. 13
1640 A790 5r multi   .35 .25

Intl. Anti-Corruption Day — A791

2007, Dec. 10   Litho.
Granite Paper
1641 A791 5r multi   .35 .25

Global Knowledge to the Village — A792

2008, Jan. 4   Perf. 13¼x12
1642 A792 5r multi   .40 .25
Opening of 500th Nenasala Center.

Most Venerable Halgasthota Sri Devananda Mahanayaka Thero — A793

2008, Jan. 30   Perf. 14x13¾
1643 A793 5r multi   .35 .25

Independence, 60th Anniv. — A794

2008, Feb. 4   Perf. 12x13¼
1644 A794 5r multi   .35 .25

Deshamanya N. U. Jayawardena (1908-2002), Governor of Central Bank — A795

2008, Feb. 25   Perf. 13½x14
1645 A795 5r multi   .35 .25

7th Commonwealth Youth Ministers Meeting, Colombo — A796

Perf. 13¼x12¾ Syncopated
2008, Apr. 26
1646 A796 5r multi   .35 .25

St. Mary's Convent, Matara, Cent. A797

Perf. 12¾x13¼ Syncopated
2008, Apr. 29
1647 A797 5r multi   .35 .25

Ancient Sri Lanka — A798

Designs: 5r, Megalithic cist, bead necklace, Ibbankatuwa, 600-400 B.C. 10r, Basawakku-lama Veva (reservoir), 3rd cent. B.C. 12r, Inscribed Vallipuram gold plate, 1st cent. 15r, Alakolavela iron furnace, 1st-2nd cent. 30r, Gajalakshmi coin, 1st cent. B.C.-A.D. 4th cent., punch mark coin, 3rd cent. B.C.-A.D. 4th cent. 40r, Sigiri painting, 5th cent.

2008, Apr. 30   Perf. 12x13¼
1648-1653 A798 Set of 6   3.50 3.50

Vesak A799

Various Dahamsonda Jataka wall paintings from Reswehere Raja Maha Vihara, Kudakatnoruwa: 4.50r, 5r, 15r, 40r.

2008, May 9   Perf. 13¾x14
1654-1657 A799 Set of 4   2.50 2.50
1657a   Souvenir sheet, #1654-1657,
           perf. 13¾x13½   3.00 3.00

2008 Summer Olympics, Beijing — A800

Designs: 5r, Shooting. 15r, Javelin. 40r, Boxing. 45r, Running.

2008, July 23   Perf. 12¾x13
1658-1661 A800 Set of 4   3.25 3.25
1658a   Tete-beche pair   .40 .40
1659a   Tete-beche pair   1.00 1.00
1660a   Tete-beche pair   2.50 2.50
1661a   Tete-beche pair   3.00 3.00

15th South Asian Association for Regional Cooperation Summit, Colombo — A801

2008, Aug. 2   Perf. 13
Granite Paper
1662 A801 15r multi   .75 .75

Takiko Yoshida, Philantropist A802

Perf. 13¼x12¾ Syncopated
2008, Aug. 16
1663 A802 5r multi   .35 .25

Employees' Provident Fund, 50th Anniv. — A803

2008, Sept. 11   Perf. 14x13¾
1664 A803 5r multi   .35 .25

Ancient Sri Lanka — A804

Designs: 5r, Gold ingot, coin and mold, 8th-10th cents. 10r, Medirigiriya Vatadage ruins and conjectural drawing of structure, 7th cent. 15r, Urinal stone from Western monastery, Anuradhapura, cross section of sanitary system, 7th-8th cents. 20r, Jewelry, 6th-9th cents. 30r, Bodhisattva Vajrapani, Avalokithesvara, and sculpture of royal family, Isurumuniya, 8th-9th cents.

2008, Sept. 16   *Perf. 13¼x12*
1665-1669 A804   Set of 5   3.00 3.00

Lion — A805

Perf. 12½ Syncopated
2008, Sept. 24   **Photo. & Engr.**
Granite Paper
Color of Denomination

1670	A805	50r red violet	1.05	1.05
1671	A805	70r blue	1.60	1.60
1672	A805	100r olive green	2.10	2.10
1673	A805	500r orange	10.00	10.00
1674	A805	1000r purple	21.00	21.00
1675	A805	2000r blue green	42.50	42.50
		Nos. 1670-1675 (6)	78.25	78.25

World Post Day
A806

2008, Oct. 9   **Litho.**   *Perf. 13½x14*
1676 A806 5r multi   .35 .25

Dutch Burgher Union of Ceylon, Cent. A807

2008, Oct. 22
1677 A807 5r multi   .35 .25

Anton Jayasuriya (1930-2005), Acupuncturist A808

Perf. 13¼x12¾ Syncopated
2008, Nov. 7
1678 A808 5r multi   .35 .25

Pieter Keuneman (1917-97), Politician — A809

2008, Dec. 1
1679 A809 5r multi   .35 .25

The Two Men and the Bear — A810

Perf. 12¾x13¼ Syncopated
2008, Dec. 5
1680 A810 5r multi   .35 .25

Most Venerable Weweldeniye Medhalankara Mahanayake Mahathero A811

Perf. 13¼x12¾ Syncopated
2008, Dec. 7
1681 A811 5r multi   .35 .25

Christmas A812

Perf. 12¾x13¼ Syncopated
2008, Dec. 9
1682 A812 5r multi   .35 .25

St. Mary's Cathedral, Kaluwella A813

Perf. 13¼x12¾ Syncopated
2008, Dec. 9
1683 A813 30r multi   .75 .75

Universal Declaration of Human Rights, 60th Anniv. A814

2008, Dec. 10   *Perf. 13¾x14*
1684 A814 5r multi   .40 .25

Sri Lanka Transport Board, 50th Anniv. — A815

2008, Dec. 30   *Perf. 13¼x12*
1685 A815 5r multi   .35 .25

Madu Ganga Wetlands A816

Designs: 5r, Lumnitzera littorea flowers, river. 25r, Mangroves and river.

2009, Feb. 2   **Litho.**   *Perf. 13¾x14*
1686-1687 A816   Set of 2   .80 .80

Year of English and Information Technology A817

2009, Feb. 13   *Perf. 14x13¾*
1688 A817 5r multi   .35 .25

University of Sri Jayewardenepura, Nugegoda, 50th Anniv. — A818

2009, Feb. 18   *Perf. 13¾x14*
1689 A818 5r multi   .35 .25

F. R. Jayasuriya (1909-84), Economics Professor at Kelaniya University — A819

2009, Feb. 25   *Perf. 14x13¾*
1690 A819 5r multi   .35 .25

A. P. de Zoysa (1890-1968), Buddhist Scholar — A820

2009, Mar. 5   *Perf. 13¾x14*
1691 A820 5r multi   .35 .25

Moors Sports Club (Cricket Team), Cent. A821

Perf. 12¾x13¼ Syncopated
2009, Mar. 5
1692 A821 5r multi   .35 .25

Sri Lanka Railway Running Shed, Dematagoda, Cent. — A822

2009, Mar. 9   **Litho.**
1693 A822 5r multi   .35 .25

Mahmoud Shamsuddeen Kariapper, Politician — A823

2009, Mar. 13   *Perf. 12x13¼*
1694 A823 5r multi   .35 .25

University of Vocational Technology A824

Perf. 13¼x12¾ Syncopated
2009, Mar. 31
1695 A824 5r multi   .35 .25

Natural Rubber Research and Development in Sri Lanka, Cent. — A825

Perf. 12¾x13¼ Syncopated
2009, Apr. 2
1696 A825 5r multi   .35 .25

Jeyaraj Fernandopulle (1953-2008), Politician — A826

Perf. 13¼x12¾ Syncopated
2009, Apr. 7
1697 A826 5r multi   .35 .25

SRI LANKA

Leprosy Hospital, Hendala, 300th Anniv. (in 2008) A827

2009, Apr. 23   *Perf. 13¾x14*
1698 A827 5r multi   .35 .25

Sri Sumangala College, Panadura, Cent. A828

Perf. 12¾x13¼ Syncopated
2009, Apr. 23
1699 A828 5r multi   .35 .25

Handupelpola Sri Punnaratana Nayaka Maha Thero, Politician — A829

Perf. 13¼x12¾ Syncopated
2009, May 2
1700 A829 5r multi   .35 .25

Most Venerable Welithara Sri Gnanawimala Tissa Mahanayake Thero (1766-1833), Religious Leader — A830

2009, May 5
1701 A830 5r multi   .35 .25

Vesak Festival A831

Designs 4r, Visit to the temple. 5r, Meditation.

2009, May 5   *Perf. 13¾x14*
1702 A831 4r multi   .45 .45
Perf. 12¾x13¼ Syncopated
1703 A831 5r multi   .55 .55

Nimal S. de Silva, President of 2009-10 World Health Assembly A832

2009, June 8   *Perf. 13¾x14*
1704 A832 5r multi   .35 .25

Polonnaruwa Era — A833

Designs: 5r, Galpotha inscription of King Nissankamalla, obverse and reverse of coin of Queen Leelawathi. 10r, Siva Temple and adornments.15r, Parakrama Samudra Reservoir and statue of King Parakramabahu or of a sage. 25r, Palace of King Parakramabahu and Audience Hall of King Nissankamalla. 30r, Ancient hospital, medical trough, surgical instrument and grinding stone. 40r, Scupltures of Siva, Uma, and Saiva Saint Karaikkal Ammaiyar.

Perf. 12¾x13¼ Syncopated
2009, June 23
1705-1710 A833 Set of 6   3.25 3.25

Mahmood Hasarath, Educator — A834

2009, July 25   *Perf. 14x13¾*
1711 A834 5r slate blue   .35 .25

Hameed Al Husseinie College Colombo, 125th Anniv. A835

2009, July 30   *Perf. 13¾x14*
1712 A835 5r multi   .35 .25

University of Kelaniya, 50th Anniv. — A836

2009, July 31   *Perf. 13¼x12*
1713 A836 5r multi   .35 .25

Bank of Ceylon, 70th Anniv. — A837

2009, Aug. 3   *Perf. 14x13¾*
1714 A837 5r multi   .35 .25

Retirement of Colombo Archbishop Oswald Gomis — A838

2009, Aug. 10   *Litho.*
1715 A838 15r multi   .60 .60

Sri Lanka Customs, 200th Anniv. A839

Perf. 12¾x13¼ Syncopated
2009, Aug. 25
1716 A839 15r multi   .70 .70

Sree Narayana Gurudev (1856-1924), Religious Leader — A840

2009, Sept. 4   *Perf. 14x13¾*
1717 A840 5r multi   .35 .25

Sivali Central College, Ratnapura, Cent. — A841

2009, Sept. 25   *Perf. 13¼x12*
1718 A841 15r multi   .70 .70

World Post Day — A842

2009, Oct. 9   *Perf. 14x13¾*
1719 A842 15r multi   .80 .80

Sri Lanka Army, 60th Anniv. A843

2009, Oct. 10   *Perf. 13*
1720 A843 15r multi   .70 .70

Humane Eradication of Rabies — A844

2009, Nov. 5   *Perf. 14x13¾*
1721 A844 15r multi   .70 .70

A845

Christmas A846

2009, Nov. 8   *Perf. 14x13¾*
1722 A845 5r multi   .35 .25
  a.   Souvenir sheet of 2   .50 .50
          Perf. 13¾x14
1723 A846 15r multi   .65 .65
  a.   Souvenir sheet of 2   1.00 1.00

No. 1722a sold for 20r; No. 1723a for 40r.

Diplomatic Relations Between Sri Lanka and Cuba, 50th Anniv. — A847

2009, Nov. 9   *Perf. 12x13¼*
1724 A847 5r multi   .45 .25

Intl. Day of Persons With Disabilities A848

2009, Dec. 3   *Perf. 13¾x14*
1725 A848 10r multi   .50 .50

Voet Lights Society, 110th Anniv. A849

2009, Dec. 4
1726 A849 15r multi   .60 .60

Peduru Hewage William de Silva (1908-88), Politician — A850

Perf. 13¼x12¾ Syncopated
2009, Dec. 15   *Litho.*
1727 A850 10r multi   .50 .50

Dr. Hudson Silva
(1929-99),
Founder of Intl.
Eye Bank — A851

2009, Dec. 21   *Perf. 14x13¾*
1728 A851 10r multi   .50 .50

D. M. Dasanayake
(1953-2008),
Politician — A852

2010, Jan. 8   *Perf. 14x13¾*
1729 A852 10r multi   .50 .50

Thurstan College, Colombo, 60th
Anniv. — A853

2010, Jan. 11   *Perf. 13¼x12*
1730 A853 10r multi   .50 .50

Ceylon-German Technical Training
Institute, 50th Anniv. — A855

2010, Feb. 15   Litho.   *Perf. 13¾x14*
1733 A855 10r multi   .50 .50

Government Officers' Benefit
Association, Cent. (in 2009) — A856

2010, Feb. 24
1734 A856 5r multi   .35 .25

Rotary International in
Sri Lanka, 80th Anniv. (in
2009) — A857

2010, Mar. 18   *Perf. 14x13¾*
1735 A857 10r muti   .50 .50

M. J. C. Fernando (1885-1939),
Buddhist Leader — A858

2010, Mar. 27   *Perf. 13¾x14*
1736 A858 10r multi   .50 .50

Buddhist Flag,
125th
Anniv. — A859

2010, Apr. 28   *Perf. 14x13¾*
1737 A859 5r multi   .35 .25

Vesak
Festival — A860

Designs: 4r, Arrival of Lord Buddha at
Mahiyanganaya. 5r, Mahiyangana Stupa. 10r,
Mirisawetiya Stupa, Anuradhapura, horiz. 30r,
Jetawana Stupa, Anuradhapura, horiz.

2010, May 24   *Perf. 14x13¾, 13¾x14*
1738-1741 A860 Set of 4   2.00 2.00
1741a   Souvenir sheet of 4,
   #1738-1741   2.00 2.00

St. Anthony's
Shrine,
Kochchikade,
175th
Anniv. — A861

2010, June 12   *Perf. 14x13¾*
1742 A861 5r multi   .35 .25

Sri Kalyaniwansa Nikaya Buddhist
Order, 200th Anniv. — A862

2010, June 17   *Perf. 13¾x14*
1743 A862 10r multi   .50 .50

Mahajana
College,
Tellippalai,
Cent.
A863

2010, June 18   Litho.
1744 A863 10r multi   .50 .50

Pepiliyana Sunethra Mahadevi Piriven
Rajamaha Viharaya, 600th
Anniv. — A864

2010, June 20   *Perf. 13¼x12*
1745 A864 5r multi   .35 .25

Victory and
Peace — A865

2010, July 6   *Perf. 14x13¾*
1746 A865 5r multi   .35 .25

Postal History — A866

No. 1747: a, National Postal Museum. b,
Philatelic Exhibition Center.

2010, July 6   *Perf. 13¾x14*
1747 A866 5r Horiz. pair, #a-b   .50 .50

A souvenir sheet containing Nos. 1747a-
1747b sold for 60r.

Anuradhapura Teaching Hospital, 50th
Anniv. — A867

2010, July 10
1748 A867 5r multi   .35 .25

Royal
College,
Colombo,
175th
Anniv.
A868

2010, July 16   Litho.
1749 A868 10r multi   .50 .50

Kokuvil
Hindu
College,
Cent.
A869

2010, July 22
1750 A869 10r multi   .50 .50

M. P. De Zoysa,
Politician, Cent. of
Birth — A870

2010, Aug. 9   *Perf. 14x13¾*
1751 A870 10r multi   .50 .50

2010 Youth Olympics,
Singapore — A871

Perf. 12¾x13¼ Syncopated
2010, Aug. 12
1752 A871 10r multi   .50 .50

World Indigenous People's
Day — A872

No. 1753: a, Indigenous people. b, Art by
indigenous people.

2010, Aug. 25   *Perf. 13¾x14*
1753 A872 5r Horiz. pair, #a-b   .50 .50

A souvenir sheet containing Nos. 1753a-
1753b sold for 60r.

Central Bank of Sri Lanka, 60th
Anniv. — A873

2010, Aug. 27   *Perf. 13¼x12*
1754 A873 10r multi   .50 .50

Beaches — A874

Designs: 15r, Pasikudah Beach. 25r,
Trincomalee Beach. 40r, Arugam Bay Beach.

2010, Sept. 7   *Perf. 13¼*
1755-1757 A874 Set of 3   2.50 2.50

Souvenir sheets of 1 of Nos. 1755-1757
each sold for 100r.

Horton Plains National Park — A875

Designs: 5r, Sri Lanka whistling thrush. 15r, Sambur, horiz. 25r, Rhinohorn lizard, horiz. 40r, Purple-faced leaf monkey.

2010, Sept. 7   *Perf. 13¼*
1758-1761 A875 Set of 4   3.00 3.00

Four souvenir sheets each containing one of Nos. 1758-1761 sold for 15r, 25r, 35r and 50r, respectively.

University of Peradeniya Faculty of Engineering, 60th Anniv. — A876

2010, Sept. 9   *Litho.*   *Perf. 13¾x14*
1762 A876 15r multi   .60 .60

Vienna Convention for Ozone Layer Protection, 25th Anniv. — A877

2010, Sept. 16   *Perf. 14x13¾*
1763 A877 5r multi   .35 .25

St. Michael's Church, Koralawella, 150th Anniv. — A878

2010, Sept. 29
1764 A878 5r multi   .35 .25

World Children's Day — A879

2010, Oct. 3   *Perf. 13*
1765 A879 5r multi   .35 .25

Children's Story, "The Story of How the Tortoise Flew" — A880

2010, Oct. 3   *Perf. 13¾x14*
1766 A880 5r multi   .35 .25

World Post Day A881

2010, Oct. 9   *Litho.*
1767 A881 5r multi   .35 .25

Rankot Viharaya, Panadura, 200th Anniv. A882

2010, Oct. 10
1768 A882 5r multi   .35 .25

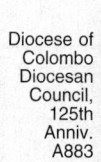

Diocese of Colombo Diocesan Council, 125th Anniv. A883

2010, Oct. 14
1769 A883 5r multi   .35 .25

Louis Braille (1809-52), Educator of the Blind A884

2010, Oct. 15
1770 A884 5r multi   .35 .25

World Fellowship of Buddhists, 60th Anniv. — A885

2010, Nov. 14   *Litho.*   *Perf. 13½x12*
1771 A885 5r multi   .25 .25

Magam Ruhunupura Rajapaksa Port — A886

2010, Nov. 18   *Perf. 13¾x14*
1772 A886 5r multi   .25 .25

Christmas A887

Designs: 5r, People around Christmas tree. 15r, St. Mary's Church, Kegalle.

2010, Nov. 28
1773-1774 A887 Set of 2   .35 .35
1774a   Souvenir sheet of 2, #1773-1774   .65 .65

No. 1774a sold for 35r.

Sri Lanka Navy, 60th Anniv. A888

2010, Dec. 9   *Perf. 13*
1775 A888 5r multi   .25 .25

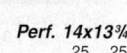

Holy Emmanuel Church, Moratuwa, 150th Anniv. — A889

2010, Dec. 27   *Perf. 14x13¾*
1776 A889 5r multi   .25 .25

Labugama Reservoir, 125th Anniv. — A890

2011, Jan. 18   *Perf. 13½x12*
1777 A890 5r multi   .25 .25

Dr. P. R. Anthonis (1911-2009), University of Colombo Chancellor A891

2011, Jan. 21   *Perf. 14x13¾*
1778 A891 5r multi   .25 .25

Intl. Year of Chemistry A892

2011, Jan. 30   *Perf. 12x13½*
1779 A892 5r multi   .25 .25

Trains A893

No. 1780: a, Viceroy Special steam locomotive BB 240. b, Viceroy Special locomotive B2 213. c, Sentinel Camel steam rail car V2 331. d, Narrow gauge steam locomotive JI 220. 45r, Viceroy Special steam train B1 251.

Perf. 12¾x13½ Syncopated
2011, Feb. 2
    Granite Paper
1780   Horiz. strip of 4   .40 .40
a.-d.   A893 5r Any single   .25 .25
    Souvenir Sheet
    Perf. 13¾x14
1781 A893 45r multi   1.10 1.10

Viceroy Special steam train, 25th anniv. No. 1781 contains one 123x30mm stamp and sold for 60r.

St. Mary's Church, Dehiwala, 175th Anniv. A894

2011, Feb. 6   *Perf. 13¾x14*
1782 A894 5r multi   .25 .25

Southlands College, Galle, 125th Anniv. — A895

2011, Feb. 18   *Perf. 13½x12*
1783 A895 5r multi   .25 .25

Sri Lanka Air Force, 60th Anniv. A896

2011, Mar. 2   Perf. 13¾x14
1784 A896 5r multi   .25 .25

No. 1389A Surcharged

Method and Perf As Before
2011, Apr. 1
1785 A618 15r on 4.50r #1389A   .30 .30

First Man in Space, 50th Anniv. A897

2011, Apr. 26   Litho.   Perf. 13¾
1787 A897 5r multi   .25 .25
Values are for stamp with surrounding selvage.

Sambuddhatva Jayanthi (Enlightenment of Buddha) Festival, 2600th Anniv. — A898

No. 1788 — Inscriptions at bottom: a, Buddhism is a universal doctrine. b, Let us practice Buddhist principles. c, Let us take care of our parents and respect them. d, Let us help the sick. e, Person who practices Buddhism illuminates the entire world. f, Let us build an antinarcotic society.

2011, Apr. 29   Perf. 13½x12
Granite Paper
1788 A898 5r Block of 6, #a-f   .55 .55

Rabindranath Tagore (1861-1941), Poet — A899

2011, May 7   Perf. 14x13¾
1789 A899 5r multi   .25 .25

Vesak Festival — A900

No. 1790 — Map of India and Sri Lanka, Sambuddhatva Jayanthi Festival 2600th anniversary emblem and Buddhist temples at: a, Lumbini, Nepal. b, Buddhagaya, India. c, Baranesa Isipathanarama, India. d, Kusinara, India.

2011, May 14   Perf. 14x13¾
1790 A900 5r Block of 4, #a-d   .40 .40
  e.   Souvenir sheet, #1790a-1790d   .65 .65
No. 1790e sold for 35r.

Bridges — A901

No. 1791: a, Ancient stone bridge, Mahakanadarawa. b, Suspension bridge, Peradeniya.
No. 1792: a, Wooden bridge, Bogoda. b, Steel arch bridge, Ruwanwella.

2011, May 27   Perf. 13½x12
1791 A901 10r Vert. pair, #a-b   .40 .40
1792 A901 15r Vert. pair, #a-b   .55 .55
  c.   Souvenir sheet of 2, #1791a, 1792a, perf. 13½   .75 .75
  d.   Souvenir sheet of 2, #1791b, 1792b, perf. 13½   .75 .75

Nos. 1792c and 1792d each sold for 40r.

People's Bank, 50th Anniv. A902

Perf. 12¾x13½ Syncopated
2011, July 1
1793 A902 5r multi   .25 .25

Radampala Sri Sumangala Central College, Cent. — A903

2011, July 15   Perf. 13¾x14
1794 A903 5r multi   .25 .25

Non-aligned Movement, 50th Anniv. — A904

Perf. 13½x12¾ Syncopated
2011, July 21
1795 A904 5r multi   .25 .25

World Tourism Day A905

Designs: No. 1796, 5r, Buddhist stupa ("Heritage" at left). No. 1797, 5r, Sigiriya Rock ("Heritage" at right). No. 1798, 5r, Dancers and drummers. No. 1799, 5r, Sri Lankan women and flag. No. 1800, 15r, Woman bathing under floating flowers. No. 1801, 15r, Waterfall. 30r, Elephants. 35r, Leopard. 40r, Sailboat near shore. 45r, Whitewater rafters.

2011, Sept. 27   Litho.   Perf. 13
1796-1805 A905   Set of 10   3.75 3.75
1805a   Souvenir sheet of 10, #1796-1805, + 2 central labels   3.75 3.75

World Children's Day — A906

Perf. 13½x12¾ Syncopated
2011, Oct. 1
1806 A906 5r multi   .25 .25

World Post Day A907

Perf. 12¾x13½ Syncopated
2011, Oct. 9
1807 A907 5r multi   .25 .25

First South Asian Beach Games, Hambantota — A908

2011, Oct. 11   Perf. 13¾x14
1808 A908 5r multi   .25 .25

Dudley Senanayake (1911-73), Prime Minister — A909

Perf. 13½x12¾ Syncopated
2011, Oct. 14
1809 A909 5r black & brown   .25 .25

Telephone and Number for Government Information Center — A910

Perf. 12¾x13½ Syncopated
2011, Oct. 17
1810 A910 5r multi   .25 .25

POSTAL-FISCAL STAMP

The editors believe that six additional revenue stamps were authorized for postal use during 1979-98 and would like to examine them.

Coat of Arms Type of 1983
Perf. 13x12
1979, May 28   Engr.   Wmk. 233
AR2 PF1 20r dark green
No. AR2 was issued in 1974 for revenue purposes, and was usable on mail starting on May 28, 1979.

National Coat of Arms With Sinhalese Characters at Left and Right — PF1

Perf. 13x12
1983, Oct. 14   Engr.   Wmk. 233
AR4 PF1 100r carmine   26.00 32.00

National Coat of Arms — PF2

1984   Engr.   Perf. 14½x14
AR6 PF2 50r vermilion   2.00 2.00
AR7 PF2 100r deep claret   3.75 3.75
A lithographed 500r value exists but was not authorized for postal use.

Arms Type of 1984
Perf. 14½x14¼
1998, Dec. 16   Engr.   Wmk. 408
AR9 PF2 100r chocolate   —
An additional stamp was issued in this set. The editors would like to examine it.

National Coat of
Arms — PF3

Perf. 12½ Syncopated
2002, May 28   **Litho. & Engr.**
Granite Paper
Color of Denomination

AR10 PF3 50r brown   —

Stamps of type PF3 with denominations of
500r and 1000r were not valid for postage.
An additional stamp was issued in this set.
The editors would like to examine it.

National Coat of
Arms — PF4

Perf. 12¾x12½ Syncopated
2007, Nov. 23   **Photo. & Engr.**
Granite Paper
Color of Denomination

AR13	PF4	50r blue	1.15 1.15
AR14	PF4	100r gray green	2.50 2.50
AR15	PF4	200r lilac	5.00 5.00
		Nos. AR13-AR15 (3)	8.65 8.65

STELLALAND

'ste-lə-ˌland

LOCATION — South Africa
GOVT. — Republic
AREA — 5,000 sq. mi. (approx.)
CAPITAL — Vryburg

This short-lived republic was set up
by the Boers in an effort to annex territory ruled by the Bechuana chiefs.
Great Britain refused to recognize it and
in 1885 sent an expeditionary force
which ended the political career of the
country.
Stellaland was annexed by Great Britain in 1885 and became a part of British
Bechuanaland.

12 Pence = 1 Shilling

A1

1884, Feb. Unwmk. Litho. Perf. 12

1	A1	1p red	225.00	375.00
a.	Horiz. pair, imperf. vert.		4,250.	
b.	Vert. pair, imperf. horiz.		4,600.	
2	A1	3p orange	28.00	375.00
a.	Horiz. pair, imperf. vert.		850.00	
b.	Vert. pair, imperf. horiz.		1,700.	
3	A1	4p gray	26.00	400.00
a.	Horiz. pair, imperf. vert.		750.00	
b.	Vert. pair, imperf. horiz.		2,100.	
4	A1	6p lilac	28.00	400.00
a.	Horiz. pair, imperf. vert.		1,500.	
b.	Vert. pair, imperf. horiz.		1,750.	
5	A1	1sh green	67.50	750.00
		Nos. 1-5 (5)	374.50	2,300.

Imperf. varieties are believed to be proofs.

No. 3
Handstamped in
Blackish Violet

1885

6	A1	2p on 4p gray	4,000.

The status of No. 6 has long been
questioned.

STRAITS SETTLEMENTS

ˈstrāts ˈse-təl-mənts

LOCATION — Malay Peninsula in
southeastern Asia
GOVT. — British Colony
AREA — 1,356 sq. mi.
POP. — 1,435,895 (estimated)
CAPITAL — Singapore

The colony comprised the settlements of Malacca, Singapore and
Penang, which were incorporated under
one government in 1826 and the admin-
istration transferred from India to the
Secretary of State for the Colonies in
1867.
The colony was dissolved in 1946
when Singapore became a separate
crown colony. Malacca and Penang
were incorporated into the Malayan
Union, which became the Federation of
Malaya in 1948.
Stamps of India were used in
Malacca, Penang and Singapore, 1854-
67.
See Malaya for stamps of the Feder-
ated Malay States, the Federation of
Malaya, Johore, Kedah, Kelantan,
Malacca, Negri Sembilan, Pahang,
Penang, Perak, Perlis, Selangor, Sun-
gei Ujong and Trengganu.

100 Cents = 1 Dollar

Stamps of India Surcharged in Red,
Blue, Black Violet or Green

Nos. 1-7   Nos. 8-9

1867, Sept. 1   Wmk. 38   Perf. 14

1	A7	1½c on ½a bl (R)	100.00	200.00
2	A7	2c on 1a brn (R)	160.00	85.00
3	A7	3c on 1a brn (Bl)	150.00	90.00
4	A7	4c on 1a brn (Bk)	275.00	275.00
5	A7	6c on 2a yel (V)	650.00	250.00
6	A7	8c on 2a yel (G)	225.00	42.50
7	A9	12c on 4a grn (R)	1,050.	325.00
a.	Double surcharge		3,250.	
8	A7	24c on 8a rose (Bl)	500.00	90.00
9	A7	32c on 2a yel (Bk)	375.00	95.00

Manuscript Surcharge, Pen Bar
Across "THREE HALF" of No. 1

9A	A7	2(c) on 1½c on ½a	10,500.	5,000.

Values for Nos. 1-9A are for stamps with
perforations touching the frame line on one or
two sides. Used values for Nos. 1-9 are for
stamps with company chops in addition to
postal cancellations. Examples with postal
cancels only sell for somewhat higher prices.
For detailed listings, see the Scott Classic
Specialized catalogue.

A2   A3

A4   A5

1867-72   Typo.   Wmk. 1   Perf. 14

10	A2	2c bister brown	42.50	6.00
11	A2	4c rose	75.00	10.00
12	A2	6c violet	110.00	20.00
13	A3	8c yellow	200.00	15.00
a.	8c orange	240.00	20.00
14	A3	12c blue	160.00	10.00
15	A3	24c green	140.00	6.50
16	A4	30c claret ('72)	325.00	14.00
17	A5	32c pale red	550.00	75.00
18	A5	96c olive gray	325.00	50.00
		Nos. 10-18 (9)	1,927.	206.50

Corner ornaments of types A2, A3 and A5
differ for each value.
See Nos. 19, 40-44, 48-50, 52-57. For
surcharges see Nos. 20-35, 58-59, 61-66, 73-
82, 91. For overprints see Malaya, Johore No.
1, Perak Nos. 1, O1-O2, Selangor Nos. 1-2,
Sungei Ujong Nos. 2-3.
See the Scott Classic Catalogue for other
shades.

Stamps of Straits Settlements,
1867-82, overprinted "B" are listed
under Bangkok.

1871   Perf. 12½

19	A5	96c olive gray	2,300.	275.00

Stamps of 1867-72 Surcharged

1879, May   Perf. 14

20	A3	5c on 8c yellow	120.00	180.00
a.	No period after "CENTS"	950.00	1,100.
21	A5	7c on 32c pale red	150.00	190.00
a.	No period after "CENTS"	1,500.	1,800.

No. 16 Surcharged

e   f

g   k

m

1010
j   h

1880

22	A4(e)	10c on 30c	225.00	55.00
23	A4(f)	10c on 30c	700.00	125.00
24	A4(g)	10c on 30c	250.00	55.00
25	A4(h)	10c on 30c	—	
25A	A4(j)	10c on 30c	5,500.	925.00
25B	A4(k)	10c on 30c	5,500.	925.00
25C	A4(m)	10c on 30c	5,500.	925.00

Surcharges e & f and g, h, j & m are virtually
identical. These must have an expert certifi-
cate identifying them. Values can be suspect
because of misidentifications.
Unused examples are valued without gum.

With Additional
Surcharge

26	A4(e)	10c on 30c	450.	85.
27	A4(f)	10c on 30c	8,500.	850.
27A	A4(g)	10c on 30c	5,000.	500.
28	A4(h)	10c on 30c	14,000.	1,800.
28A	A4(j)	10c on 30c	14,000.	1,800.
28B	A4(k)	10c on 30c	14,000.	1,800.
28C	A4(m)	10c on 30c	14,000.	1,800.

Unused examples are valued without gum.

No. 13 Surcharged

n   p

1880

29	A3(n)	5c on 8c yellow	150.00	180.00
30	A3(o)	5c on 8c yellow	550.00	700.00
31	A3(p)	5c on 8c yellow	160.00	190.00

No. 11 Surcharged

1882, Jan.

32	A2	5c on 4c rose	275.00	300.00

Nos. 12, 14a, 16
Surcharged

1880-81

33	A2	10c on 6c violet ('81)	70.00	7.50
a.	Double surcharge	—	2,750.
34	A3	10c on 12c blue ('81)	55.00	16.00
35	A4	10c on 30c claret	400.00	97.50
		Nos. 33-35 (3)	525.00	121.00

A6   A7

1882, Jan.   Typo.   Perf. 14

38	A6	5c violet brown	100.00	110.00
39	A7	10c slate	450.00	70.00

See Nos. 45-47, 51. For surcharges see
Nos. 60, 67-72, 89-92.

1882-99   Wmk. Crown and C A (2)

40	A2	2c bister brown	300.00	47.50
41	A2	2c car rose ('83)	10.00	1.00
a.	2c rose	45.00	4.50
42	A2	4c rose	130.00	9.00
43	A2	4c car rose ('99)	5.25	1.40
44	A2	4c bister brn ('83)	27.50	1.50
45	A6	5c ultra ('83)	16.00	1.10
46	A6	5c brown ('94)	5.50	1.10
47	A6	5c magenta ('99)	2.75	2.40
48	A2	6c violet	2.25	4.00
49	A3	8c orange	4.00	1.10
50	A3	8c ultra ('94)	5.25	.60
51	A7	10c slate	9.00	1.50
52	A3	12c vio brn ('83)	75.00	12.00
53	A3	12c claret ('94)	12.00	9.75
54	A3	24c blue grn ('83)	7.50	4.50
a.	24c yellow green ('84)	77.50	9.00
55	A4	30c claret ('91)	17.00	11.00
56	A5	32c red org ('87)	3.50	15.00
57	A5	96c olive gray ('88)	82.50	55.00
		Nos. 40-57 (18)	722.50	167.45

For overprints see Malaya, Perak Nos. O3-
O9, Selangor Nos. 3-4, Sungei Ujong Nos. 6-
7, 11.

Preceding Issues Surcharged

Surcharged Vertically

1883-84 **Wmk. 2, 1**
58	A3	2c on 8c orange	125.00	77.50
a.		Double surcharge	2,750.	1,100.
59	A5	2c on 32c pale red	650.00	190.00
a.		Double surcharge		
60	A6	2c on 5c ultra ('84)	130.00	140.00
a.		Pair, one without surcharge		
b.		Double surcharge		
		Nos. 58-60 (3)	905.00	407.50

Five types of surcharge on No. 58, two types on No. 59 and three types on No. 60.

Surcharged in Black

1883 **Wmk. 2**
61	A2	2c on 4c rose	85.00	97.50
b.		"s" of "Cents." inverted	1,325.	1,425.

Wmk. 1
62	A3	2c on 12c blue	275.00	140.00
a.		"s" of "Cents." inverted	4,000.	2,000.

Surcharged in Black or Blue

1884
63	A3	8c on 12c blue	475.00	130.00

Wmk. 2
64	A3	8c on 12c vio brn	325.00	130.00

With Additional Surcharge Handstamped in Red

65	A3	8c on 8c on 12c vio brn (R + Bk)	275.00	300.00
66	A3	8c on 8c on 12c vio brn (R + Bl)	7,250.	

Surcharged in Black or Red

1884
67	A6	4c on 5c ultra (Bk)	3,250.	4,250.
68	A6	4c on 5c ultra (R)	125.00	110.00

No. 68 Surcharged in Red

4

69	A6	4c on 4c on 5c ultra		24,000.

No. 69 may be a trial printing. "Usage" seems to been restricted to less than 10 letters known sent from the Postmaster General to his wife.

Surcharged in Black

3 CENTS

1885-87
70	A6	3c on 5c ultra	125.00	250.00
a.		Double surcharge	2,500.	

Surcharged in Black

3 cents

71	A6	3c on 5c vio brn ('86)	210.00	225.00

Surcharged

2 Cents.

72	A6	2c on 5c ultra ('87)	25.00	70.00
a.		Double surcharge	1,200.	1,100.
b.		"C" omitted		3,000.

In the surcharged issues of 1883 to 1887, Nos. 59, 62, 63 and 71 are on stamps watermarked Crown and C C, the others are watermarked Crown and C A.

Surcharged

THREE CENTS

1885-94 **Wmk. Crown and C A (2)**
73	A5	3c on 32c magenta	1.50	1.10
74	A5	3c on 32c rose ('94)	2.75	.85
a.		Without surcharge	4,000.	

No. 74a value is for a stamp with perfs touching frame line.

Surcharged

10 CENTS

1891
75	A3	10c on 24c green	3.50	1.40
a.		Narrow "0" in "10"	32.50	32.50

Surcharged

THIRTY CENTS

76	A5	30c on 32c red orange	8.25	4.25

Surcharged

ONE CENT

1892
77	A2	1c on 2c rose	2.25	4.25
78	A2	1c on 4c bister brn	5.75	6.25
a.		Double surcharge	1,300.	
79	A2	1c on 6c violet	1.60	5.50
a.		Dbl. surch., one invtd.	1,425.	1,325.
80	A3	1c on 8c orange	1.25	1.50
81	A3	1c on 12c vio brown	5.75	10.50
		Nos. 77-81 (5)	16.60	28.00

Surcharged

ONE CENT

82	A3	1c on 8c gray green	1.10	1.75

Queen Victoria — A13

1892-99				**Typo.**
83	A13	1c gray green	3.75	.80
84	A13	3c car rose ('95)	12.50	.55
85	A13	3c brown ('99)	6.50	.70
86	A13	25c dk vio & grn	32.50	7.50
87	A13	50c ol grn & car	22.50	3.00
88	A13	$5 org & car ('98)	500.00	275.00
		Nos. 83-88 (6)	577.75	287.55

Denomination of $5, is in color on plain tablet.

Stamps of 1883-94 Surcharged

4 cents.

1899
89	A6	4c on 5c ultra	4.00	15.00
a.		Double surcharge		1,400.
90	A6	4c on 5c brown	3.25	5.25
91	A3	4c on 8c brt blue	1.50	1.25
a.		4c on 8c ultra	1.00	3.25
b.		Double surcharge	1,100.	1,000.
		Nos. 89-91 (3)	8.75	21.50

Type of 1882 Issue Surcharged

FOUR CENTS

92	A6	4c on 5c rose	.85	.40
a.		Without surcharge	30,000.	

King Edward VII — A14

Numerals of 5c, 8c, 10c, 30c, $1 and $5, type A14, are in color on plain tablet.

1902			**Wmk. 2**	**Typo.**
93	A14	1c green	3.25	3.50
94	A14	3c vio & org	4.00	.25
95	A14	4c violet, red	5.50	.35
96	A14	5c violet	6.25	.95
97	A14	8c violet, blue	4.50	.30
98	A14	10c vio & blk, yel	29.00	1.75
99	A14	25c violet & grn	14.00	7.00
100	A14	30c gray & car rose	21.00	9.25
101	A14	50c grn & car rose	22.50	22.50
102	A14	$1 green & blk	25.00	75.00
103	A14	$2 violet & blk	80.00	80.00
104	A14	$5 grn & brn org	225.00	190.00

104A	A14	$100 dl vio & grn, yel	11,000.	
		Nos. 93-104 (12)	440.00	390.85

High values of the 1902 and 1904 issues with revenue cancellations are of minimal value. No. 104A is inscribed "Postage & Revenue" but the limit of weight probably precluded its use postally.

See Nos. 113, 115-128B, 133.

A15

A16

A17

A18

1903-04
105	A15	1c gray green	2.00	9.25
106	A16	3c dull violet	12.50	5.25
107	A17	4c violet, red	5.50	.35
108	A18	8c violet, blue	55.00	1.50
		Nos. 105-108 (4)	75.00	16.35

See Nos. 109-112, 114, 129-132, 134.

1904-11		**Chalky Paper**	**Wmk. 3**	
109	A15	1c gray green	3.25	.25
110	A16	3c dull violet	2.75	.35
111	A17	4c violet, red	11.50	.85
112	A17	4c dull vio ('08)	6.25	.25
113	A14	5c violet ('06)	12.50	2.75
114	A18	8c violet, bl	32.50	1.75
115	A14	10c vio & blk, yel	9.25	.90
116	A14	10c vio, yel ('08)	8.50	1.10
117	A14	25c vio & grn	37.50	24.00
118	A14	25c violet ('09)	16.00	8.00
119	A14	30c gray & car rose	55.00	3.00
120	A14	30c vio & org ('09)	45.00	4.50
121	A14	50c grn & car rose	62.50	17.50
122	A14	50c blk, grn ('10)	5.75	5.50
123	A14	$1 green & blk	62.50	21.00
124	A14	$1 blk & red, bl ('11)	17.00	5.75
125	A14	$2 violet & blk	110.00	97.50
		Revenue cancel		12.00
126	A14	$2 grn & red, yel ('09)	27.50	27.50
127	A14	$5 grn & brn org	225.00	160.00
128	A14	$5 grn & red, grn ('10)	140.00	85.00
		Revenue cancel		5.00
128A	A14	$25 green & blk	1,725.	1,600.
		Revenue cancel		55.00
128B	A14	$100 dl vio & grn, yel	12,650.	
		Revenue cancel		200.00
		Nos. 109-128 (20)	890.25	467.45

Nos. 125, 128A and 128B are on chalky paper, the other values are on both ordinary and chalky. The note about No. 104A will apply to No. 128B.

1906-11   Ordinary Paper
129	A15	1c blue grn ('10)	26.00	1.25
130	A16	3c carmine ('08)	3.75	.25
131	A17	4c carmine ('07)	6.25	3.00
132	A17	4c lake ('11)	2.25	.95
133	A14	5c orange ('09)	3.25	2.25
134	A18	8c ultra ('06)	4.00	.60
		Nos. 129-134 (6)	45.50	8.30

Stamps of Labuan 1902-03, Overprinted or Surcharged in Red or Black

a   b

c

Perf. 12½ to 16 and Compound
1907   Unwmk.
134A	A38(a)	1c violet & blk	70.00	200.00
135	A38(a)	2c grn & blk	350.00	350.00
136	A38(a)	3c brn & blk	22.50	97.50
137	A38(a)	4c on 12c yel & blk	2.75	7.00
a.		No period after "CENTS"	350.00	—
138	A38(c)	4c on 16c org brn & grn (Bk)	5.25	9.25
a.		With additional name in red	750.00	800.00
139	A38(c)	4c on 18c bis & blk	3.25	7.50
a.		No period after "CENTS." & bar	325.00	—
b.		"FOUR CENTS." & bar double	8,650.	
140	A38(a)	8c orange & blk	3.50	9.25
141	A38(b)	10c sl bl & brn	8.50	8.00
a.		No period after "Settlements"	375.00	
142	A38(a)	25c grnsh bl & grn	17.00	45.00
143	A38(a)	50c gray lil & vio	18.00	80.00
144	A38(a)	$1 org & red brn	52.50	125.00
		Nos. 134A-144 (11)	553.25	938.50

A19   A20

1908-11   Typo.   Wmk. 3   Perf. 14
Chalky Paper
145	A19	$25 bl & vio, bl ('11)	1,600.	1,250.
146	A19	$500 violet & org	92,000.	
		Revenue cancel		275.

No. 146 is inscribed "Postage-Revenue" but was probably used only for revenue. Excellent forgeries of No. 146 exist.

1910   Chalky Paper
147	A20	21c maroon & vio	7.50	40.00
148	A20	45c black, green	3.00	4.50

King George V
A21   A22

A23   A24

A25   A26

Die I (Type A24)

For description of dies I and II see front section of the Catalogue.

The 25c, 50c and $2 denominations of type A24 show the numeral on horizontally-lined tablet.

1912-18   Chalky Paper   Wmk. 3
149	A21	1c green	7.00	1.50
150	A21	1c black ('18)	1.75	1.10
151	A25	2c dp green ('18)	1.10	.60
152	A22	3c scarlet	2.50	.40
a.		3c carmine	3.25	1.00
153	A23	4c gray violet	1.75	.40
154	A23	4c scarlet ('18)	2.75	.25
a.		Booklet pane of 1		
b.		Booklet pane of 12		
c.		4c carmine ('18)	2.75	.25
155	A24	5c orange	2.00	.60
156	A25	6c claret ('18)	2.00	.60
157	A25	8c ultra	2.25	.90
158	A24	10c violet, yel	1.75	.60
159	A24	10c ultra ('18)	7.00	.60
160	A26	21c maroon & vio	5.75	11.00
161	A24	25c vio & red vio	14.00	9.75
162	A24	30c vio & org ('14)	9.25	2.25
163	A26	45c blk, bl grn, ol back ('14)	3.75	22.50
a.		45c black, emerald ('17)	3.75	15.00
164	A24	50c black, grn ('14)	6.50	3.25
a.		50c black, bl grn, olive back	21.00	8.50
b.		50c black, emerald	14.00	11.00
c.		Die II	3.50	4.50
165	A24	$1 blk & red, bl ('14)	10.50	9.75
166	A24	$2 grn & red, yel ('15)	11.50	50.00
167	A24	$5 grn & red, grn ('15)	92.50	70.00
a.		$5 grn & red, bl grn, ol back	175.00	97.50
b.		$5 grn & red, emer ('15)	92.50	110.00
c.		Die II	110.00	75.00
		Nos. 149-167 (19)	185.60	186.05

The 1c, 3c, 5c and 8c are on ordinary paper.

Surface-colored Paper
168	A24	10c violet, yel	1.75	1.10
169	A26	45c black, grn ('14)	7.50	21.00
170	A24	$2 grn & red, yel ('14)	9.75	50.00
171	A24	$5 grn & red, grn ('14)	92.50	50.00
		Nos. 168-171 (4)	111.50	122.10

See Nos. 179-201. For surcharges see Nos. B1-B2.

A27

1915
172	A27	$25 bl & vio, bl	1,600.	500.00
		Revenue cancel		5.75
173	A27	$100 red & blk, bl	5,750.	
		Revenue cancel		90.00
174	A27	$500 org & dl vio	46,000.	
		Revenue cancel		200.00

Although Nos. 173 and 174 were available for postage, it is probable that they were used only for fiscal purposes. See Nos. 202-204, AR1.

Die II (Type A24)
1921-32   Ordinary Paper   Wmk. 4
179	A21	1c black	.60	.25
180	A25	2c green	.60	.25
181	A25	2c brown	8.00	3.00
182	A22	3c green	1.75	.90
183	A23	4c scarlet	2.25	4.75
184	A23	4c dp violet ('25)	.70	.25
185	A23	4c orange ('29)	1.10	.25
186	A25	5c orange ('23)	2.75	1.50
a.		Die I	1.75	.25
187	A24	5c dk brown ('32)	3.25	.25
		Die I ('32)	5.75	.25
188	A25	6c claret	2.25	.25
189	A25	6c scarlet ('27)	3.00	.25
a.		6c rose red ('25)	22.50	11.00
190	A24	10c ultra (I)	2.00	3.00

Chalky Paper
191	A24	10c vio, yel ('27)	2.25	.35
a.		Die I ('25)	3.00	7.50
192	A25	12c ultra	1.10	.25
193	A26	21c maroon & vio	7.00	55.00
194	A24	25c vio & red vio	5.75	2.00
a.		Die I	32.50	80.00
195	A24	30c violet & org	2.25	1.50
a.		Die I	26.00	40.00
196	A26	35c orange & vio	14.00	7.00
197	A26	35c vio & car ('31)	11.50	8.00
198	A24	50c blk, emerald	2.00	.45
199	A24	$1 blk & red, bl	7.00	.75
200	A24	$2 grn & red, yel	11.50	9.25
201	A24	$5 grn & red, grn	100.00	37.50
202	A27	$25 bl & vio, bl	1,100.	140.00
203	A27	$100 red & blk, bl		1,900.
204	A27	$500 org & dl vio	37,000.	
		Nos. 179-201 (23)	192.60	136.95

No. 192 is on ordinary paper.

Nos. 203 and 204 were probably used only for fiscal purposes.

Stamps of 1912-21 Overprinted in Black

1922   Wmk. 3
151d	A25	2c deep green	32.50	85.00
154d	A23	4c scarlet	8.50	26.00
155d	A24	5c orange	5.75	22.50
157d	A25	8c ultra	2.00	8.50
161d	A24	25c vio & red vio	3.75	35.00
163d	A26	45c blk, bl grn, ol back	3.50	30.00
165d	A24	$1 blk & red, bl	225.00	800.00
166d	A24	$2 grn & red, yel	30.00	125.00
167d	A24	$5 grn & red, grn	275.00	450.00

Wmk. 4
179d	A21	1c black	3.50	14.00
180d	A25	2c green	2.75	16.00
183d	A23	4c scarlet	4.00	30.00
186d	A25	5c orange (II)	3.25	45.00
190d	A24	10c ultra	2.75	29.00
199d	A24	$1 blk & red, bl	22.50	140.00
		Nos. 151d-199d (15)	624.75	1,856.

Industrial fair at Singapore, Mar. 31-Apr. 15, 1922.

Common Design Types
pictured following the introduction.

Silver Jubilee Issue
Common Design Type
1935, May 6   Engr.   Perf. 11x12
213	CD301	5c black & ultra	3.50	.35
214	CD301	8c indigo & green	3.75	3.50
215	CD301	12c ultra & brown	3.75	4.25
216	CD301	25c brown vio & ind	4.00	5.75
		Nos. 213-216 (4)	15.00	13.85
		Set, never hinged	24.00	

George V — A28

1936-37   Typo.   Perf. 14
Chalky Paper
217	A28	1c black ('37)	.90	.25
218	A28	2c green	1.00	.80
220	A28	4c orange brn	2.00	.80
221	A28	5c brown	.80	.35
222	A28	6c rose red	1.10	1.25
223	A28	8c gray	1.50	.80
224	A28	10c dull vio	1.75	.70
225	A28	12c ultra	2.00	3.00
226	A28	25c rose red & vio	1.60	.60
227	A28	30c org & dk vio	1.10	3.50
229	A28	40c dk vio & car	1.10	2.75
230	A28	50c blk, emerald	4.00	1.40
232	A28	$1 red & blk, blue	17.00	1.90
233	A28	$2 rose red & gray grn	37.50	11.50
234	A28	$5 grn & red, grn ('37)	80.00	11.50
		Nos. 217-234 (15)	153.35	41.10
		Set, never hinged	290.00	

Coronation Issue
Common Design Type
1937, May 12   Engr.   Perf. 13½x14
235	CD302	4c deep orange	.25	.25
236	CD302	8c gray black	.30	.25
237	CD302	12c bright ultra	.50	.65
		Nos. 235-237 (3)	1.05	1.15
		Set, never hinged	2.00	

George VI — Die I — A29

Two Dies

Die I. Printed in two operations. Lines of background touch outside of central oval. Foliage of palms touches outer frame line. Palm frond in front of King's eye has two points.

Die II. Printed from a single plate. Lines of background separated from central oval by a white line. Foliage of palms does not touch outer frame line. Palm frond in front of King's eye has one point.

1937-41   Typo.   Perf. 14
238	A29	1c black (I)	2.75	.25
239	A29	2c green (I)	9.00	.25
c.		Die II ('38)	35.00	.45
239A	A29	2c brown org ('41) (II)	1.25	5.00
239B	A29	3c green ('41) (II)	2.25	3.00
240	A29	4c brown org (I)	8.00	.25
a.		Die II ('38)	50.00	.35
241	A29	5c brown (I)	10.00	.35
a.		Die II ('39)	27.50	.25
242	A29	6c rose red ('38) (I)	5.50	.50
243	A29	8c gray ('38) (I)	19.00	.25
244	A29	10c dull vio (I)	4.00	.25
245	A29	12c ultra ('38) (I)	8.00	.35
245A	A29	15c ultra ('41) (II)	3.25	6.25
246	A29	25c rose red & vio (I)	40.00	1.10
247	A29	30c org & vio (I)	25.00	2.00
248	A29	40c dk vio & rose red (I)	10.00	2.25
249	A29	50c blk, emer ('38) (I)	10.00	.45
250	A29	$1 red & blk, bl ('38) (I)	15.00	.40
251	A29	$2 rose red & gray grn ('38) (I)	30.00	4.25
252	A29	$5 grn & red, grn ('38) (I)	25.00	4.50
		Nos. 238-252 (18)	228.00	31.65
		Set, never hinged	375.00	

For overprints see #256-271, N1-N29 and Malaya, Malacca #N1-N14, Penang #N1-N26.

Stamps and Type of 1937-41 Overprinted in Red or Black

1945-48
256	A29	1c black (R)	.25	.25
257	A29	2c brown org (II)	.25	.25
a.		Die I ('46)	7.50	3.75
258	A29	3c green	.25	.25
259	A29	5c brown	.75	.60
260	A29	6c gray	.25	.25
261	A29	8c rose red	.25	.25
262	A29	10c dull vio (I)	.30	.25
a.		10c claret (II) ('48)	10.00	1.25
263	A29	12c ultra	1.75	3.25
264	A29	15c ultra (Bk)	2.25	4.75
265	A29	15c ultra (R)	.25	.25
266	A29	25c rose red & vio	1.40	.25
a.		Double overprint	400.00	
267	A29	50c blk, emer (R)	.60	.25
268	A29	$1 rose red & blk	2.00	.25
269	A29	$2 rose red & gray grn	2.50	.65
270	A29	$5 grn & red, grn	72.50	72.50
271	A29	$5 brn org & vio	3.75	2.75
		Nos. 256-271 (16)	89.30	87.00
		Set, never hinged	140.00	

The letters "B M A" are initials of "British Military Administration".

An 8c gray with BMA overprint was prepared but not issued. Value $5.

The 6c gray, 8c rose red and $5 brown orange & violet exist without BMA overprint but were issued only with it.

No. 262a does not exist without overprint.

No. 262 exists in at least three shades.

POSTAL-FISCAL STAMP

Type of 1915 with head George VI
Inscribed "REVENUE" at each side

1938
AR1 A27 $25 Blue & pur-
ple, *blue* 490.00 375.00

Although documentation authorizing its postal use has not been found, No. AR1 was frequently used as a postage stamp throughout 1941.

SEMI-POSTAL STAMPS

Nos. 152-153
Surcharged

1917 Wmk. 3 Perf. 14
B1 A22 3c + 2c scarlet 3.00 29.00
  a. No period after "C" 375.00 575.00
B2 A23 4c + 2c gray violet 4.00 29.00
  a. No period after "C" 400.00 575.00

POSTAGE DUE STAMPS

D1

1924-26 Typo. Wmk. 4 Perf. 14
J1 D1 1c violet 5.75 7.50
J2 D1 2c black 3.75 1.50
J3 D1 4c green ('26) 2.25 5.50
J4 D1 8c red 5.25 .60
J5 D1 10c orange 7.00 .95
J6 D1 12c ultramarine 8.00 .75
  Nos. J1-J6 (6) 32.00 16.80
  Set never hinged 55.00

OCCUPATION STAMPS

Issued Under Japanese Occupation

Nos. 238, 239A, 239B,
243 and 245A
Handstamped in Red

1942, Mar. 16 Wmk. 4 Perf. 14
N1 A29 1c black 16.00 20.00
N2 A29 2c brown orange 16.00 16.00
N3 A29 3c green 70.00 85.00
N4 A29 8c gray 27.50 22.50
N5 A29 15c ultra 20.00 20.00
  Nos. N1-N5 (5) 149.50 163.50
  Set, never hinged 200.00

Other denominations with this handstamp are believed to be proofs.
The handstamp reads: "Seal of Post Office of Malayan Military Department."

Stamps of 1937-41,
Handstamped in Red,
Black, Violet or Brown

1942, Apr. 3
N6 A29 1c black 4.00 4.00
N6A A29 2c green (V) 2,875. 500.00
N7 A29 2c brown org 3.50 3.50
N8 A29 3c green 3.25 3.50
N9 A29 5c brown 25.00 30.00
N10 A29 8c gray 5.00 3.50
N11 A29 10c dull violet 55.00 45.00
N12 A29 12c ultra 92.50 90.00
N13 A29 15c ultra 4.50 4.00
N14 A29 30c orange & vio 2,200. 350.00
N15 A29 40c dk vio & rose
red 100.00 125.00

N16 A29 50c blk, *emerald* 60.00 60.00
N17 A29 $1 red & blk, *bl* 87.50 80.00
N18 A29 $2 rose red &
gray grn 150.00 150.00
N19 A29 $5 grn & red,
grn 200.00 165.00

Nos. N6-N7, N9, N11-N12, N15-N19 with red handstamp were used in Sumatra. The 2c green with red handstamp was not regularly issued.

Straits Settlements Nos.
239A, 239B, 243 and
245A Ovptd. in Black

1942
N20 A29 2c brown orange 2.00 6.00
  a. Inverted overprint 14.50 21.00
  b. Dbl. ovpt., one invtd. 55.00 70.00
N21 A29 3c green 62.50 75.00
N22 A29 8c gray 5.75 2.75
  a. Inverted overprint 17.00 32.50
N23 A29 15c ultra 15.00 9.25
  Nos. N20-N23 (4) 85.25 93.00
  Set never hinged 100.00

Straits Settlements Nos.
239A and 243
Overprinted in Black

1942, Nov. 3
N24 A29 2c brown orange 14.00 25.00
  a. Inverted overprint 375.00 375.00
N25 A29 8c gray 15.00 20.00
  a. Inverted overprint 375.00 375.00

Agricultural-Horticultural Exhibition held at Kuala Lumpur, Selangor, Nov. 1-2, 1942. Sold only at a temporary post office at the exhibition.

Straits Settlements Nos.
243, 245 and 248
Ovptd. in Black or Red

1943
N26 A29 8c gray (Bk) 1.60 .60
  a. Inverted overprint 52.50 62.50
N27 A29 8c gray (R) 2.50 3.00
N28 A29 12c ultramarine 1.40 10.50
N29 A29 40c dk vio & rose red 2.00 4.50
  Nos. N26-N29 (4) 7.50 18.60
  Set never hinged 10.00

The Japanese characters read: "Japanese Postal Service."

SUDAN

sü-'dan

LOCATION — Northeastern Africa, south of Egypt
GOVT. — Republic
AREA — 967,500 sq. mi.
POP. — 27,953,000 (1997 est.)
CAPITAL — Khartoum

10 Milliemes = 1 Piaster
100 Piasters = 1 Egyptian Pound
Dinar (1992)
100 Qirsh = 1 Pound (2007)

Catalogue values for unused stamps in this country are for Never Hinged items, beginning with Scott 79 in the regular postage section, Scott C35 in the air post section, Scott CO1 in the air post official section, Scott J12 in the postage due section, and Scott O28 in the officials section.

Watermarks

Wmk. 71 — Rosette

Wmk. 179 — Multiple Crescent and Star

Wmk. 214 — Multiple S G

Wmk. 334 — Rectangles

Wmk. 345 — Rhinoceros

Egyptian Stamps of 1884-93 Overprinted in Black

1897, Mar. 1 Wmk. 119 Perf. 14
1 A18 1m brown 3.75 2.50
  a. Inverted overprint 300.00
2 A19 2m green 2.50 2.75
3 A20 3m orange 1.75 2.10
4 A22 5m carmine rose 2.50 2.00
  a. Inverted overprint 300.00 275.00
5 A14 1p ultra 9.00 2.50
6 A15 2p orange brown 80.00 19.00
7 A16 5p gray 80.00 22.50
  a. Double overprint 5,500.
8 A23 10p violet 50.00 60.00
  Nos. 1-8 (8) 229.50 113.35

Counterfeits of Nos. 1-8 are plentiful.

Camel Post — A1

1898, Mar. 1 Typo. Wmk. 71
9 A1 1m rose & brn 2.00 3.00
10 A1 2m brown & grn 3.75 3.00
11 A1 3m green & vio 4.00 2.75
12 A1 5m black & rose 3.50 2.00
13 A1 1p yel brn & ultra 8.00 4.75
14 A1 2p ultra & blk 40.00 11.00

15 A1 5p grn & org brn 47.50 21.00
16 A1 10p dp vio & blk 35.00 3.00
  Nos. 9-16 (8) 143.75 50.50

See Nos. 17-27, 43-50. For overprints see Nos. C3, MO1-MO15, O1-O9, O17-O24. For surcharges see Nos. 28, 62, C16.

1902-21 Wmk. 179
17 A1 1m car rose & brn ('05) 1.60 .90
18 A1 2m brown & grn 2.25 .25
19 A1 3m grn & vio ('03) 3.00 .35
20 A1 4m ol brn & bl ('07) 2.00 3.50
21 A1 4m brn & red ('03) 2.00 1.00
22 A1 5m blk & rose red ('03) 2.50 .25
23 A1 1p brn & ultra ('03) 3.00 .40
24 A1 2p ultra & blk ('08) 35.00 2.50
25 A1 2p org & vio brn, chalky paper ('21) 8.00 11.00
26 A1 5p grn & org brn ('08) 35.00 4.00
27 A1 10p dp vio & blk ('11) 35.00 4.75
  Nos. 17-27 (11) 129.35 25.35

No. 15 Surcharged
in Black

1903, Sept. Wmk. 71
28 A1 5m on 5p 10.00 12.00
  a. Inverted surcharge 325.00 275.00

A2

1921-22   Typo.   Wmk. 179

29	A2	1m orange & blk ('22)	1.25	5.25
30	A2	2m dk brn & org ('22)	11.00	13.50
31	A2	3m green & vio ('22)	3.00	11.00
32	A2	4m brown & grn ('22)	8.00	9.00
33	A2	4m blk & ol brn ('22)	3.00	.25
34	A2	10m black & car ('22)	6.00	.25
35	A2	15m org brn & ultra	4.00	1.25
		Nos. 29-35 (7)	36.25	40.50

See Nos. 36-42. For overprints see Nos. C1-C2, O10-O16.

For surcharges see Nos. 60-61.

1927-40   Wmk. 214

36	A2	1m org yel & blk	1.00	.25
37	A2	2m dk brn & org	1.00	.25
38	A2	3m green & violet	1.00	.25
39	A2	4m brown & green	.90	.25
40	A2	5m blk & ol brn	.75	.25
a.		Booklet pane of 4		
41	A2	10m black & car	2.00	.25
42a	A2	15m org brn & ultra	1.60	.25
43	A1	2p orange & vio brn	4.50	.25
44	A1	3p dk bl & red brn ('40)	7.50	.25
45	A1	4p black & ultra ('36)	4.75	.25
46	A1	5p dk grn & org brn ('36)	1.75	.25
47	A1	6p blk & pale bl ('36)	12.00	2.00
48	A1	8p blk & pck grn ('36)	12.00	4.00
49	A1	10p dp vio & blk	9.00	.25
50a	A1	20p bl & lt blue	9.00	.25
		Nos. 36-50a (15)	52.00	7.85

Charles George Gordon — A3

Gordon Memorial College A4

Memorial Service at Khartoum — A5

1935, Jan. 1   Engr.   Perf. 13½x14

51	A3	5m deep green	.75	.25
52	A3	10m brown	1.50	.30
53	A3	13m ultra	1.75	13.50
54	A3	15m carmine	3.00	.30
55	A4	2p deep blue	2.75	.25
56	A4	5p orange	3.00	.50
57	A4	10p dull violet	11.00	10.00
58	A5	20p black	32.50	72.50
59	A5	50p red brown	125.00	155.00
		Nos. 51-59 (9)	181.25	252.60
		Set, never hinged	325.00	

50th anniv. of the death of Gen. Charles George ("Chinese") Gordon (1833-85).

No. 41 Surcharged in Black

5 Mills.

Wmk. Multiple S G (214)

1940, Feb. 25   Typo.   Perf. 14

60	A2	5m on 10m black & car	1.50	1.50

Nos. 40 and 48 Surcharged in Black

a   b

1940-41

61	A2(a)	4½p on 5m ('41)	65.00	12.00
62	A1(b)	4½p on 8p	57.50	14.00

Sudan Landscape A6

Perf. 13½, 14x13½

1941   Litho.   Unwmk.

Size: 21½x17½mm

63	A6	1m orange & slate bl	2.50	6.00
64	A6	2m chocolate & org	2.50	6.00
65	A6	3m grn & rose vio	2.75	.25
66	A6	4m choc & bl grn	.60	.90
67	A6	5m indigo & ol bis	.25	.25
68	A6	10m indigo & rose pink	12.00	4.50
69	A6	15m chestnut & ultra	1.00	.25

Size: 29x25mm

71	A6	2p orange & claret	1.50	.90
72	A6	3p dk blue & fawn	.85	.25
73	A6	4p blk & brt ultra	2.75	.25
74	A6	5p dk grn & brn org	5.00	13.50
75	A6	6p ind & turq bl	15.00	1.25
76	A6	8p black & green	15.00	1.00
77	A6	10p rose vio & gray	57.50	1.10
78	A6	20p dk & lt blue	50.00	45.00
		Nos. 63-78 (15)	172.20	81.40
		Set, never hinged	300.00	

> **Catalogue values for unused stamps in this section, from this point to the end of the section, are for Never Hinged items.**

Types of 1898-1940 with Changed Arabic Wording Below Camel

A7   A8

Wmk. 214

1948, Jan. 1   Typo.   Perf. 14

79	A7	1m dk orange & blk	.45	5.50
80	A7	2m chocolate & org	1.00	5.00
81	A7	3m green & rose lilac	.40	7.50
82	A7	4m choc & sl grn	.65	2.00
83	A7	5m black & ol brn	9.75	2.75
84	A7	10m black & car	6.50	.25
a.		Center inverted		52,500.
85	A7	15m org brn & ultra	6.00	.25
86	A8	2p org yel & vio brn	10.00	3.00
87	A8	3p dk bl & red brn	8.50	.40
88	A8	4p black & ultra	4.50	2.00
89	A8	5p dk grn & org	4.50	6.00
90	A8	6p blk & pale bl	5.00	3.50
91	A8	8p blk & peacock grn	6.25	5.00
92	A8	10p dp rose lil & blk	13.50	5.00
93	A8	20p dk blue & blue	5.25	.75
a.		Perf. 13	60.00	210.00
94	A8	50p ultra & carmine		2.75
		Nos. 79-94 (16)	90.50	51.65

Arabic inscription, types A7 and A8: "Berid es-Sudan"; types A1 and A2; "Postai-Sudaniye."

For overprints see Nos. O28-O43.

Stamp of 1898 — A9

1948, Oct. 1   Perf. 12½x13

95	A9	2p dull blue & gray blk	.50	.25

50th anniv. of Sudan's 1st postage stamp.

A10

1948, Dec. 19   Perf. 13

96	A10	10m black & carmine	.75	.25
97	A10	5p dk green & orange	1.50	1.50

Legislative Assembly opening, Dec., 1948.

Nubian Ibex — A11   Cotton Picking — A12

Camel Post — A13

Designs: 2m, Shoebill. 3m, Giraffe. 4m, Baggara girl. 5m, Shilluk warrior. 10m, Hadendowa. 15m, Sudan policeman. 3p, Ambatch canoe. 3½p, Nuba wrestlers. 4p, Weaving. 5p, Saluka farming. 6p, Gum tapping. 8p, Darfur chief. 10p, Stack laboratory. 20p, Nile lechwe.

1951, Sept. 1   Typo.   Perf. 14
Center in Black (#98-104)

98	A11	1m orange	3.50	1.75
99	A11	2m ultra	3.25	1.50
100	A11	3m dark green	9.75	5.00
101	A11	4m emerald	3.00	5.50
102	A11	5m plum	2.75	.25
103	A11	10m light blue	.40	.25
104	A11	15m dp orange brn	7.00	.25

Perf. 13

105	A12	2p lt blue & dk blue	.35	.25
106	A12	3p vio blue & brn	11.00	.25
107	A12	3½p brown & bl grn	3.00	.25
108	A12	4p black & dp blue	3.75	.25
109	A12	5p emer & org brn	1.00	.25
110	A12	6p black & blue	8.50	2.75
111	A12	8p brown & dp bl	14.00	4.75
112	A12	10p green & black	1.75	1.50
113	A12	20p black & blue grn	10.00	3.75
114	A13	50p black & carmine	17.50	4.00
		Nos. 98-114 (17)	100.50	32.50

See #159. For overprints see #O44-O61, O75.

Camel Post — A14

1954, Jan. 9   Perf. 12½x13

115	A14	15m emerald & brn org	.55	1.00
116	A14	3p black & blue	.65	3.00
117	A14	5p red violet & blk	.80	1.75
		Nos. 115-117 (3)	2.00	5.75

Self-government in the Sudan.

A quantity of these sets inscribed "1953" was sold in London. They were not valid for postage. Value, set $25.

Independent Republic

Map of Sudan and Sun — A15   Rhinoceros Carrying Globe — A16

Wmk. 214

1956, Sept. 15   Engr.   Perf. 14

118	A15	15m rose lilac & org	.40	.40
119	A15	3p dk blue & org	.60	.60
120	A15	5p green & org	.60	.60
		Nos. 118-120 (3)	1.60	1.60

Independence Day, Jan. 1, 1956.

1958, Aug. 2
Center in Orange

121	A16	15m plum	.50	.25
122	A16	3p blue	.75	.35
123	A16	5p green	1.10	.75
		Nos. 121-123 (3)	2.35	1.35

APU Cong., Khartoum, Aug. 2, 1958.

Soldier, Farmer and Map of Nile — A17

Lithographed and Engraved

1959, Nov. 17   Unwmk.   Perf. 14

124	A17	15m brown, yel & ultra	.30	.25
125	A17	3p multicolored	.70	.40
126	A17	55m multicolored	.80	.60
		Nos. 124-126 (3)	1.80	1.25

Sudanese army revolution, 1st anniv.

Arab League Center A17a

Perf. 13x13½

1960, Mar. 22   Photo.   Wmk. 328

127	A17a	15m dull green & blk	.60	.40

Opening of the Arab League Center and the Arab Postal Museum in Cairo.

Uprooted Oak Emblem, Refugee Man and Child — A18

Wmk. 214
1960, Apr. 7   Litho.   Perf. 14
128 A18 15m black, buff & ultra   .25 .25
129 A18 55m black, beige & org   .75 .50
World Refugee Year, 7/1/59-6/30/60.

Soccer
Player — A19

1960, Aug. 25   Wmk. 214   Perf. 14
130 A19 15m ultra, blk & yel   .30 .25
131 A19 3p yellow, blk & grn   .65 .40
132 A19 55m emerald, blk & yel .75 .50
    Nos. 130-132 (3)   1.70 1.15
17th Olympic Games, Rome, 8/25-9/11.

Forest — A20

1960, Sept. 6
133 A20 15m multicolored   .30 .25
134 A20 3p multicolored   .65 .50
135 A20 55m multicolored   .75 .50
    Nos. 133-135 (3)   1.70 1.00
5th World Forestry Cong., Seattle, WA, Aug.
29-Sept. 10.

King Tirhaqah,   Girl with
689-663   Book — A22
B.C. — A21

Unwmk.
1961, Mar. 1   Engr.   Perf. 14
136 A21 15m yellow grn & brown   .30 .25
137 A21 3p salmon & violet   .60 .50
138 A21 55m lt blue & red brown 1.10 .70
    Nos. 136-138 (3)   2.00 1.45
Save historic monuments in Nubia.
An imperf. souvenir sheet exists, not sold at
post offices, containing one each of Nos. 136-
138. Size: 154x97mm. The sheet was not
issued for postal purposes and cancellation
requests are declined. Value $9.

1961, Nov. 17   Litho.   Wmk. 214
139 A22 15m violet, claret & pink   .30 .25
140 A22 3p orange, blk & blue   .65 .40
141 A22 55m gray grn, blk & och   .90 .65
    Nos. 139-141 (3)   1.85 1.30
50 years of girls' education in the Sudan.

Malaria   Arab League
Eradication   Building,
Emblem — A23   Cairo — A24

1962, Apr. 7   Unwmk.   Perf. 14
142 A23 15m black, pur & blue   .55 .25
143 A23 55m dk brown & green   1.10 .65
WHO drive to eradicate malaria.

1962, Apr. 22   Photo.   Perf. 13½x13
144 A24 15m deep orange   .30 .25
145 A24 55m blue green   .70 .50
Arab League Week, Mar. 22-28.

Type of 1951 and

Palace of the   Cotton
Republic,   Picker — A26
Khartoum — A25

Designs: 15m, Straw cover. 35m, 4p, Wild
animals. 55m, 6p, Cattle. 8p, Date palms. 10p,
Sailboat. 20p, Bohein Temple, 1500 B.C. 50p,
Sennar Dam. £1, Camel Post (A13 redrawn).

Perf. 14½x14, 14x14½
1962, Oct. 1   Litho.   Wmk. 345
Size: 23x19mm, 19x23mm
146 A25 5m blue   .25 .25
147 A26 10m blue & lilac   .25 .25
148 A25 15m multicolored   .25 .25
149 A25 2p lt purple   .25 .25
150 A26 3p bl grn, red brn &
            brn   .40 .25
151 A26 35m yel grn, brn & org
            brn   .75 .25
152 A26 4p red, lt bl & lil .75 .25
153 A25 55m gray & yel ol   .75 .30
154 A25 6p brown & lt blue   .90 .30
155 A25 8p green   .90 .30
**Perf. 14x14½, 13x13½, 14x13½,
13½x14**
Size: 24½x30mm, 30x24½mm
156 A26 10p lt bl, red brn &
            blk   1.00 .50
157 A25 20p gray ol & yel grn 2.50 1.10
158 A25 50p dk gray, ol & bl 6.00 1.75
Engr.
159 A13 £1 green & brn org   12.00 6.50
  b.   Wmk 334
    Nos. 146-159 (14)   26.95 12.50
The frame of No. 159 has been altered with
Arabic inscription on top and English at
bottom.
See Nos. 420, 427-428. For surcharge and
overprints see Nos. 430, O62-O74, O92, O99-
O100.

1975-79   Unwmk.
**Perfs, Sizes and Printing Methods
as Before**
146a A25 5m ('76)   .25 .25
147a A26 10m ('76)   .25 .25
148a A25 15m   .25 .25
149a A25 2p   .25 .25
150a A26 3p ('76)   .30 .25
151a A26 35m   .50 .25
152a A26 4p   .50 .25
153a A25 55m ('79)   .50 .25
154a A25 6p   .60 .25
155a A25 8p ('77)   .75 .25
156a A26 10p   1.00 .40
157a A25 20p   2.00 .90
158a A25 50p   5.50 1.25
159a A13 £1   —   6.00
    Nos. 146a-158a (13) 12.65 5.05

Corn and
Millet — A27

1963, Mar. 21   Litho.   Wmk. 345
160 A27 15m. emerald, gray &
            brn   .30 .25
161 A27 55m violet, lt & dk blue .70 .40
FAO "Freedom from Hunger" campaign.

Centenary
Emblem and
Medals — A28

1963, Oct. 1   Perf. 14
162 A28 15m blk, red, gray &
            gold   .50 .25
163 A28 55m grn, gray, red &
            gold   1.00 .50
Centenary of the International Red Cross.

Melchior — A29

Designs: 30m, St. Joseph seated, with
cross and manuscript, horiz. 55m, Archangel
with cross. Designs from frescoes in excavated Faras Church.

1964, Mar. 8   Litho.   Perf. 14
164 A29 15m multicolored   .40 .25
165 A29 30m red brn, blk & brn .55 .30
166 A29 55m red brn, blk & brn 1.25 .65
    Nos. 164-166 (3)   2.20 1.20
UNESCO world campaign to save historic
monuments in Nubia.

Khashm El
Girba
Dam — A30

New York World's Fair, 1964-65: 3p, Pavilion. 55m, Illustrated map of Sudan, vert.

Perf. 14x14½, 14½x14
1964, Apr. 22   Wmk. 345
167 A30 15m lt vio bl & vio brn .25 .25
168 A30 3p multicolored   .30 .30
169 A30 55m multicolored   .80 .35
    Nos. 167-169 (3)   1.35 .90

Eleanor Roosevelt
and People
Breaking
Chains — A31

1964, Dec. 10   Perf. 14
170 A31 15m grnsh blue & blk   .25 .25
171 A31 3p violet & black   .40 .25
172 A31 55m orange brn & blk   .65 .65
    Nos. 170-172 (3)   1.30 1.15
Eleanor Roosevelt (1884-1962), on the 16th
anniv. of the Universal Declaration of Human
Rights.

Arab Postal
Union
Emblem — A32

1964, Dec. 30   Litho.
173 A32 15m brick red, blk &
            gold   .25 .25
174 A32 3p gray green, blk &
            gold   .40 .30
175 A32 55m violet, blk & gold .85 .50
    Nos. 173-175 (3)   1.50 1.05
10th anniv. of the Permanent Office of the
Arab Postal Union.

ITU Emblem, Old and New
Communication Equipment — A33

1965, May 17   Wmk. 345   Perf. 13½
176 A33 15m brown & gold   .30 .25
177 A33 3p black & gold   .65 .30
178 A33 55m green & gold   2.25 .60
    Nos. 176-178 (3)   3.20 1.15
Cent. of the ITU.

"Gurashi" and Revolutionists — A34

1965, Nov. 10   Litho.   Perf. 12
179 A34 15m deep ocher & black .30 .25
180 A34 3p bright red & black .40 .25
181 A34 55m dark gray & black   .85 .50
    Nos. 179-181 (3)   1.55 1.00
1st anniv. of the October 21st Revolution
and to honor "Gurashi," one of its heroes.

ICY
Emblem — A35

Perf. 14½x14
1965, Dec. 10   Wmk. 345
182 A35 15m violet & blk   .45 .25
183 A35 3p yellow green & blk   .55 .30
184 A35 55m vermilion & blk   1.75 .55
    Nos. 182-184 (3)   2.75 1.10
International Cooperation Year, 1965.

El Siddig el
Mahdi — A36

1966, Jan. 1   Perf. 13
185 A36 15m lt blue & vio blue   .50 .25
186 A36 3p orange & brown   .75 .50
187 A36 55m gray & red brown   1.75 .90
    Nos. 185-187 (3)   3.00 1.45
El Siddig el Mahdi (1911-61), imam of Ansar
region and political leader.

Mubarak
Zaroug
A37

1966, Jan. 1   Litho.
188 A37 15m pink & lt olive grn   .50 .25
189 A37 3p brt yel grn & dk grn .75 .50
190 A37 55m orange brn & dk
            brn   1.40 .85
    Nos. 188-190 (3)   2.65 1.60
Issued in memory of Mubarak Zaroug
(1917-65), lawyer and political leader.

WHO Headquarters, Geneva — A38

1966, June 11 Photo.   Perf. 11½x11
191 A38 15m blue   .30 .25
192 A38 3p magenta   .40 .30
193 A38 55m brown   1.25 .50
    Nos. 191-193 (3)   1.95 1.05

Inauguration of WHO Headquarters, Geneva.

Map of Sudan and Crests of Upper Nile, Blue Nile and Kassala Provinces — A39

Designs: 3p, Map of Sudan and crests of Equatoria, Kordofan and Khartoum Provinces. 55m, Map of Sudan and crests of Bahr El Gazal, Darfur and Northern Provinces.

1967, Apr. 1 Litho.   Perf. 14
194 A39 15m org, pur & lt blue grn   .25 .25
195 A39 3p dp org, vio & lt blue   .50 .35
196 A39 55m yel, dp claret & yel grn 1.10 .60
    Nos. 194-196 (3)   1.85 1.20

Month of the South.

Giraffe and ITY Emblem — A40

Clasped Hands and Arab League Emblem — A41

Perf. 12½x13
1967, Aug. 15 Litho.   Wmk. 345
197 A40 15m multicolored   .40 .25
198 A40 3p multicolored   1.00 .35
199 A40 55m multicolored   2.25 .60
    Nos. 197-199 (3)   3.65 1.20

International Tourist Year 1967.

Perf. 11x11½
1967, Aug. 29 Photo.   Unwmk.
200 A41 15m orange & ultra   .30 .25
201 A41 3p brown org & emer   .35 .35
202 A41 55m lemon & violet   .60 .40
    Nos. 200-202 (3)   1.25 1.00

Arab League Summit Conference.

Emblem of Palestine Liberation Organization — A42

1967, Aug. 29   Perf. 11½x11
203 A42 15m olive, car & yel   .50 .30
204 A42 3p green, car & yel   1.25 .40
205 A42 55m brt green, car & yel 1.50 .50
    Nos. 203-205 (3)   3.25 1.20

Palestine Liberation Organization.

Abdullahi el Fadil el Mahdi A43

Perf. 11½x11
1968, Feb. 15 Photo.   Unwmk.
206 A43 15m ultra & brt purple   .40 .25
207 A43 3p dp ultra & brt grn   .55 .30
208 A43 55m orange & green   1.20 .55
    Nos. 206-208 (3)   2.15 1.10

Issued in memory of Abdullahi el Fadil el Mahdi (1892-1966), political leader.

Mohammed Nur el Din — A44

1968, Feb. 15
209 A44 15m sl blue & apple grn   .40 .25
210 A44 3p blue & olive   .55 .30
211 A44 55m blue & violet blue   1.20 .50
    Nos. 209-211 (3)   2.15 1.05

Issued in memory of Mohammed Nur el Din (1898-1964), political leader.

Ahmed Yousif Hashim A45

Perf. 11½x11
1968, Mar. 5 Photo.   Unwmk.
212 A45 15m green & brown   .40 .25
213 A45 3p brt blue & sepia   .55 .30
214 A45 55m indigo & violet   1.20 .50
    Nos. 212-214 (3)   2.15 1.05

Ahmed Yousif Hashim (1906-1958), journalist.

Mohammed Ahmed el Mardi (1905-1966), Political Leader — A46

Perf. 11x11½
1968, Mar. 5 Photo.   Unwmk.
215 A46 15m Prus bl & vio bl   .50 .30
216 A46 3p ultra, och & dl rose   .75 .50
217 A46 55m dk blue & brown   1.40 .60
    Nos. 215-217 (3)   2.65 1.40

DC-3 A47

20th anniv. of Sudan Airways: 2p, De Havilland Dove. 3p, Fokker Friendship. 55m, De Havilland Comet 4C.

1968, Dec. 15 Litho.   Perf. 13½x13
218 A47 15m multicolored   .50 .25
219 A47 2p multicolored   1.00 .25
220 A47 3p multicolored   1.25 .30
221 A47 35m multicolored   1.75 .50
    Nos. 218-221 (4)   4.50 1.30

African Development Bank Emblem (right) — A48

Wmk. Rectangles (334)
1969, Dec. 20 Photo.   Perf. 13
222 A48 2p black, gray & gold   .35 .25
223 A48 4p dark red & gold   .50 .30
224 A48 65m green & gold   1.00 .35
    Nos. 222-224 (3)   1.85 .90

5th anniv. of the African Development Bank.

ILO Emblem A49

Unwmk.
1969, Dec. 27 Litho.   Perf. 14
225 A49 2p blue, blk & pink   .35 .25
226 A49 4p yellow, blk & silver   .45 .30
227 A49 65m green, blk & lilac   .90 .35
    Nos. 225-227 (3)   1.70 .90

50th anniv. of the ILO.

Citizens A50

1970, May 25   Perf. 11½x11
228   A50 2p multicolored
228A A50 4p multicolored
228B A50 65m multicolored
       Set, 228-228B   90.00

First anniv. of May 25th Revolution.
    This set was withdrawn on day of issue; 1721 sets of the 2p, 4p and 65m stamps in same design were sold through the Philatelic service. A few copies of No. 228 were sold at Post offices. Nos. 229-231 were issued in October to replace this set.

Citizens A51

1970, Oct. 21 Photo.   Perf. 11½x11
229 A51 2p brown, olive & red   .35 .25
230 A51 4p lt blue, olive & red   .55 .30
231 A51 65m olive, dk blue & red   .90 .40
    Nos. 229-231 (3)   1.80 .95

1st anniv. of the May 25th Revolution.

Map and Flags of UAR, Libya, Sudan A52

1971, Jan. 2 Unwmk.   Perf. 11½
232 A52 2p lt green, car & blk   .50 .25

Signing of the Charter of Tripoli affirming the unity of UAR, Libya and the Sudan, Dec. 27, 1970.

Education Year Emblem — A53

Emblem — A54

1971, May 2 Photo.   Perf. 11x11½
233 A53 2p blue, blk & brn   .30 .25
234 A53 4p carmine, blk & brn   .45 .30
235 A53 65m vio brn, blk & brn   .85 .40
    Nos. 233-235 (3)   1.60 .95

International Education Year.

1971, Nov. 10   Perf. 11x11½
236 A54 2p yellow, grn & blk   .35 .25
237 A54 4p blue, grn & blk   .75 .35
238 A54 10½p gray, grn & blk   2.00 .55
    Nos. 236-238 (3)   3.10 1.15

2nd anniversary of May 25th Revolution.

Arab League and Sudanese Emblems — A55

UN Emblem — A56

1972, Feb. 10 Photo.   Perf. 11x11½
239 A55 2p yellow, grn & blk   .40 .25
240 A55 4p orange, bl & blk   .70 .30
241 A55 10½p orange, brn & blk   1.75 .55
    Nos. 239-241 (3)   2.85 1.10

25th anniv. (in 1971) of the Arab League.

1972, Mar. 12 Photo.   Perf. 11x11½
242 A56 2p emer, rose red & org   .40 .25
243 A56 4p ultra, rose red & org   .70 .30
244 A56 10½p blk, rose red & org 1.75 .55
    Nos. 242-244 (3)   2.85 1.10

25th anniv. (in 1970) of the UN.

Emblems and Measure A57

1972, Apr. 22 Photo.   Perf. 11½x11
245 A57 2p multicolored   .40 .25
246 A57 4p lt blue & multi   .70 .30
247 A57 10½p pink & multi   1.75 .55
    Nos. 245-247 (3)   2.85 1.10

World Standards Day, Oct. 14, 1970.

Pres. Nimeiry and Arms of Sudan A58

1972, May 2 Litho.   Perf. 13x13½
248 A58 2p vio bl, blk & gold   .40 .25
249 A58 4p dp org, blk & gold   .70 .30
250 A58 10½p ol grn, blk & gold   1.75 .55
    Nos. 248-250 (3)   2.85 1.05

Election of Gaafar al-Nimeiry as President, Oct. 1971.

Arms of Sudan and Congress Emblem A59

1972, Oct. 15 Photo. Perf. 11½x11
251 A59 2p blue & multi .30 .25
252 A59 4p multicolored .60 .35
253 A59 10½p lt olive & multi 1.75 .45
Nos. 251-253 (3) 2.65 1.05
Founding Congress of the Sudanese Socialist Union.

Letter and African Postal Union Emblem A60

1972, Dec. 16
254 A60 2p yellow & multi .30 .25
255 A60 4p multicolored .55 .30
256 A60 10½p blue & multi 1.75 .45
Nos. 254-256 (3) 2.60 1.00
10th anniv. (in 1971) of the APU.

Emblems of Sudanese Provinces A61

Designs: 4p, Governing Council of Sudan. 10½p, Nat'l Coat of Arms and Unity emblem, vert.

1973, Jan. 1 Litho. Perf. 13
257 A61 2p gold & multi .30 .25
258 A61 4p dk red brn & blk .40 .25
259 A61 10½p silver, org & grn 2.00 .40
Nos. 257-259 (3) 2.70 .90
National Unity Day, March 3, 1972.

Emperor Haile Selassie — A62

1973, June 25 Unwmk. Perf. 13
260 A62 2p tan & multi .60 .30
261 A62 4p silver & multi 1.00 .40
262 A62 10½p gold & multi 2.00 .60
Nos. 260-262 (3) 3.60 1.30
80th birthday of Haile Selassie, Emperor of Ethiopia.

Nasser and Crowd A63

1973, July 15 Photo. Perf. 11½x11
263 A63 2p black .50 .25
264 A63 4p pale green & blk .75 .25
265 A63 10½p lilac & blk 1.75 .45
Nos. 263-265 (3) 3.00 .95
Gamal Abdel Nasser (1918-70), President of Egypt.

UN and FAO Emblems, Portal and Map of Resettlement Project — A64

1973, Dec. 30 Litho. Perf. 13
266 A64 2p multicolored .30 .25
267 A64 4p multicolored .60 .25
268 A64 10½p multicolored 2.25 .50
Nos. 266-268 (3) 3.15 1.00
World Food Program, 10th anniversary.

Scout Emblem, Knotted Rope and Stave — A65

1974, Jan. 15
269 A65 2p multicolored .60 .25
270 A65 4p multicolored .75 .35
271 A65 10½p multicolored 2.10 .65
Nos. 269-271 (3) 3.45 1.25
24th World Boy Scout Conference.

INTERPOL Emblem A66

1974, Feb. 16 Litho. Perf. 13x13½
272 A66 2p orange & multi .70 .25
273 A66 4p gray & multi 1.00 .25
274 A66 10½p lt blue & multi 1.75 .50
Nos. 272-274 (3) 3.45 1.00
50th anniv. of Intl. Criminal Police Organ.

K.S.M. Building A67

1974, July 1 Litho. Perf. 13x13½
275 A67 2p lilac rose & multi .50 .25
276 A67 4p lt green & multi .75 .25
277 A67 10½p vermilion & multi 2.50 .55
Nos. 275-277 (3) 3.75 1.05
50th anniversary of the Faculty of Medicine, University of Khartoum.

African Postal Union and UPU Emblems — A68

4p, Letters, Arab Postal Union and UPU emblems. 10½p, Letters, UPU and African Postal Union emblems.

1974, Sept. 9 Litho. Perf. 13½
278 A68 2p multicolored .25 .25
279 A68 4p lt blue & multi .40 .30
280 A68 10½p lilac & multi 1.25 .45
Nos. 278-280 (3) 1.90 1.00
Centenary of Universal Postal Union.

Ali Abdel Latif, Abdel Fadil Elmaz, Revolutionary Flag and Nile — A69

1975, July 26 Litho. Perf. 14x13½
281 A69 2½p green & vio blue .25 .25
282 A69 4p rose & vio blue .40 .25
283 A69 10½p sepia & vio blue 1.00 .50
Nos. 281-283 (3) 1.65 1.00
50th anniversary of 1924 revolution. Portraits show political and military leaders of the revolution.

ADB Emblem with Map of Africa A70

1975, July 26
284 A70 2½p multicolored .25 .25
285 A70 4p multicolored .40 .25
286 A70 10½p multicolored 1.00 .50
Nos. 284-286 (3) 1.65 1.00
African Development Bank, 10th anniv.

Radar Station and Camel Rider — A71

1976, Feb. 2 Litho. Perf. 13½x14
287 A71 2½p lt green & multi .25 .25
288 A71 4p lilac & multi .40 .25
289 A71 10½p vio blue & multi 1.25 .50
Nos. 287-289 (3) 1.90 1.00
Umm Haraz Satellite Station.

IWY Emblem, Flag and Woman A72

1976, May 10 Litho. Perf. 14x13½
290 A72 2½p multicolored .25 .25
291 A72 4p multicolored .35 .25
292 A72 10½p dk blue & multi .90 .50
Nos. 290-292 (3) 1.50 1.00
International Women's Year 1975.

Arms of Sudan, Olympic Rings, Track — A73

1976, July 17 Litho. Perf. 13½x14
293 A73 2½p green & multi .35 .25
294 A73 4p green & multi .50 .30
295 A73 10½p green & multi 1.25 .60
Nos. 293-295 (3) 2.10 1.15
21st Olympic Games, Montreal, Canada, July 17-Aug. 1.

Education, Engineering, Forestry, Agriculture and Defense — A74

1977, July 20 Litho. Perf. 13½x14
296 A74 2½p multicolored .25 .25
297 A74 4p multicolored .25 .35
298 A74 10½p multicolored .85 .35
Nos. 296-298 (3) 1.35 .95
5th anniversary of national unity.

Archbishop Capucci — A75

1977, Oct. 22 Photo. Perf. 11x11½
299 A75 2½p black .75 .25
300 A75 4p black & green 1.00 .35
301 A75 10½p black & red 2.00 .60
Nos. 299-301 (3) 3.75 1.20
Palestinian Archbishop Hilarion Capucci, jailed by Israel in 1974.

Fair Emblem, Sudanese Flag A76

Perf. 11½x 11
1978, Jan. 19 Photo. Wmk. 342
302 A76 3p multicolored .25 .25
303 A76 4p multicolored .40 .25
304 A76 10½p multicolored .65 .40
Nos. 302-304 (3) 1.30 .90
International Khartoum Fair, Jan. 19-27.

APU Emblem A77

1978, Mar. 8 Litho. Perf. 14x13½
305 A77 3p black, car & sil .25 .25
306 A77 4p dk green, blk & sil .30 .25
307 A77 10½p ultra, blk & sil .75 .40
Nos. 305-307 (3) 1.30 .90
APU, 25th anniv. (in 1977).

Jinnah and Sudanese Flag A78

1978, May 6 Litho. *Perf. 13*
308 A78 3p multicolored .25 .25
309 A78 4p multicolored .40 .25
310 A78 10½p multicolored .70 .40
Nos. 308-310 (3) 1.35 .90

Mohammed Ali Jinnah (1876-1948), first Governor General of Pakistan.

Desert A79

1978, May 6 *Perf. 14x13½*
311 A79 3p multicolored .25 .25
312 A79 4p multicolored .45 .25
313 A79 10½p multicolored 1.25 .65
Nos. 311-313 (3) 1.95 1.15

UN Desertification Conference.

Lion God Apedemek, African Unity Emblems — A80

1978, July 18 Litho. *Perf. 13½x14*
314 A80 3p multicolored .25 .25
315 A80 4p multicolored .50 .25
316 A80 10½p multicolored 1.10 .40
Nos. 314-316 (3) 1.85 .90

15th African Summit Conference, Khartoum, July 18-21.

A81

1979, Oct. 1 Litho. *Perf. 13½x14*
317 A81 3½p multicolored .25 .25
318 A81 6p multicolored .40 .25
319 A81 13p multicolored .85 .45
Nos. 317-319 (3) 1.50 .95

May Revolution, 10th Anniversary.

A82

1980, Jan. 19 Litho. *Perf. 13½x14*
320 A82 4½p orange & black .25 .25
321 A82 8p olive green & blk .40 .35
322 A82 15½p blue & black .85 .50
Nos. 320-322 (3) 1.50 1.10

UNESCO emblem, children holding globe.

IYC Emblem, Hands Protecting Child A83

1980, Mar. 15 *Perf. 14x13½*
323 A83 4½p multicolored .30 .25
324 A83 8p multicolored .40 .40
325 A83 15½p multicolored 1.50 .50
Nos. 323-325 (3) 2.20 1.15

International Year of the Child (1979).

25th Anniv. of Independence — A84

1982, Mar. 4 Photo. *Perf. 11½*
326 A84 60m multicolored .50 .25
327 A84 120m multicolored 1.00 .30
328 A84 250m multicolored 1.75 .75
Nos. 326-328 (3) 3.25 1.30

World Food Day, Oct. 16, 1981 A85

1983, Jan. 15 Photo. *Perf. 11½*
329 A85 60m Emblem on map, reaching hands .35 .25
330 A85 120m Produce .60 .30
331 A85 250m Map, grain 1.25 .60
Nos. 329-331 (3) 2.20 1.15

A86

1984, Feb. 20 Litho. *Perf. 13½*
332 A86 10p pink & silver .25 .25
333 A86 25p lt blue & silver .55 .40
334 A86 40p green & silver 1.00 .75
Nos. 332-334 (3) 1.80 1.40

25th Anniv. of Economic Commission for Africa (1983).

A87

1984, June 16 Litho. *Perf. 14*
335 A87 10p multicolored .30 .25
336 A87 25p multicolored .70 .50
337 A87 40p multicolored 1.25 .65
Nos. 335-337 (3) 2.25 1.40

Cent. of Shaykan Battle, Kordofan (1983).

Olympic Week A88

Sudan-Egypt Integration Charter, 2nd Anniv. — A89

Bakht Erruda, Teacher Training Institute — A90

1984, Dec. 1 Litho. *Perf. 14*
338 A88 10p multicolored .40 .25
339 A88 25p multicolored .75 .40
340 A88 40p multicolored 1.40 .65
Nos. 338-340 (3) 2.55 1.30

1985, Mar. 16 Photo. *Perf. 13½x13*
341 A89 10p multicolored .35 .25
342 A89 25p multicolored .70 .50
343 A89 40p multicolored 1.40 .65
Nos. 341-343 (3) 2.45 1.40

1985, Apr. 1
344 A90 10p multicolored .30 .25
345 A90 25p multicolored .70 .50
346 A90 40p multicolored 1.10 .65
Nos. 344-346 (3) 2.10 1.40

April 6 Uprising, 1st Anniv. A91

1986, Apr. 1 Litho. *Perf. 14*
347 A91 5p multicolored .25 .25
348 A91 25p multicolored .65 .35
349 A91 40p multicolored 1.25 .65
Nos. 347-349 (3) 2.15 1.25

World Food Day 1986 A92

Perf. 13x13½, 13½x13 (30p), 14 (50p)

1988, Jan. 1 Litho.
350 A92 25p Net fishermen .45 .25
351 A92 30p Two fish, vert. .40 .25
352 A92 50p Globe .65 .45
353 A92 75p Stylized fish on wave 1.00 .60
354 A92 300p Fish in sea 3.50 1.75
Nos. 350-354 (5) 6.00 3.30

Souvenir Sheet
Imperf
354A A92 75p like 25p 2.75 2.75

Child Survival — A93

Perf. 14, Imperf. (No. 357)

1988, Mar. 15 Litho.
355 A93 50p Breast-feeding, vert. .50 .30
356 A93 75p Oral rehydration 1.00 .40
357 A93 75p like 50p, vert. 1.75 1.75
358 A93 100p Oral vaccine 1.00 .60
359 A93 150p Growth monitoring 2.10 .90
Nos. 355-359 (5) 6.75 3.95

No. 357 issued without gum. Size: 63x84mm.

Red Crescent in Sudan, 30th Anniv. (in 1987) — A94

Designs: 100p, Crescent, candle. 150p, Crescent, stylized figure of a man.

1988, Oct. 31 Litho. *Perf. 14*
360 A94 40p org yel, blk & dk red .50 .30
361 A94 100p blk, blue grn & dk red 1.25 .60
362 A94 150p blk, brt blue & dk red 1.75 .90
Nos. 360-362 (3) 3.50 1.80

Nos. 361-362 horiz.

World Food Day, Oct. 16, 1987, and the Small Farmer — A95

FAO emblem and: 40p, Early farming tools, horiz. 100p, Ox-drawn plow. 150p, Crude public water supply.

1988, Oct. 31 *Perf. 13x13½, 13½x13*
363 A95 40p multicolored .40 .30
364 A95 100p shown 1.20 .60
365 A95 150p multicolored 1.60 .90
Nos. 363-365 (3) 3.20 1.80

Khartoum Bank, 75th Anniv. A96

Designs: 40p, Anniv. emblem. 100p, Spheres, emblem, medallion on ribbon. 150p, Text, emblem.

1988, Oct. 31 *Perf. 14*
366 A96 40p multicolored .50 .30
367 A96 100p multicolored 1.20 .60
368 A96 150p multicolored 1.60 .90
Nos. 366-368 (3) 3.30 1.80

Declaration of Palestinian State, 1st Anniv. — A97

#370, 372, 374, Crowd of demonstrators.

1989, Dec. 10 Litho. *Perf. 14*
369 A97 100p yellow grn & multi 1.75 .50
370 A97 100p buff & multi 2.00 .50
371 A97 150p lt vio & multi 2.50 1.00
372 A97 150p lt blue & multi 2.75 1.00
373 A97 200p pink & multi 3.50 1.25
374 A97 200p lt green & multi 3.50 1.25
Nos. 369-374 (6) 16.00 5.50

Palestinian Uprising (Nos. 370, 372, 374).

African Development Bank, 25th Anniv. — A99

1989, Dec. 28   *Perf. 13x13½*
375 A99 100p yel grn, blk & sil   1.50   .50
376 A99 150p blue, blk & sil   2.50   .75
377 A99 200p plum, blk & sil   3.25 1.00
Nos. 375-377 (3)   7.25 2.25

Independence, 33rd Anniv. (in 1989) — A100

1990, Jan. 22   Litho.   *Perf. 13½x13*
378 A100 50p blue & yellow   .50   .25
379 A100 100p deep claret & yel   1.25   .60
380 A100 150p brt rose & yel   1.75   .60
381 A100 200p dp rose lil & yel   2.50   .90
Nos. 378-381 (4)   6.00 2.15

Mammals A101

1990, Feb. 20   *Perf. 13x13½*
382 A101 25p Leopard   .80   .25
383 A101 50p Elephant   1.25   .50
    Perf. 14
384 A101 75p Giraffe, vert.   2.00   .75
385 A101 100p White rhinoceros   2.50 1.00
386 A101 125p Addax, vert.   3.50 1.25
Nos. 382-386 (5)   10.05 3.75

No. 385 inscribed "Rino."

Birds — A102

1990, Mar. 25   *Perf. 13½x13*
387 A102 25p Zande hornbill   .75   .25
388 A102 50p Marabou stork   1.40   .50
389 A102 75p Buff-crested bustard   2.00   .80
390 A102 100p Saddle-bill   2.75 1.00
    Perf. 14
391 A102 150p Bald-headed ibis   3.50 1.25
Nos. 387-391 (5)   10.40 3.80

Traditional Dances A103

Perf. 13x13½, 13½x13
1990, May 10   *Litho.*
392 A103 25p Mardoum   .45   .30
393 A103 50p Zandi, vert.   1.00   .40
394 A103 75p Kambala, vert.   1.50   .60
395 A103 100p Nubian, vert.   1.75   .75
396 A103 125p Sword   2.25   .95
Nos. 392-396 (5)   6.95 3.00

Natl. Salvation Revolution, 1st Anniv. — A104

1991, Apr. 14   Litho.   *Perf. 13*
399 A104 150p multicolored   1.25   .75
400 A104 200p multicolored   1.75 1.00
401 A104 250p multicolored   2.00 1.25
402 A104 £5 multicolored   3.75 2.50
403 A104 £10 multicolored   7.50 4.75
Nos. 399-403 (5)   16.25 10.25

For surcharge see No. 438.

Type of 1962 and

Shoebill A105   Camel Postman A109

1991, July 1   *Perf. 13½x13*
404 A105 25p shown   .25   .25
405 A105 50p Sunflower   .40   .40
406 A105 75p Gum Arabic   .60   .40
407 A105 100p Cotton   .80   .50
408 A105 125p Crowned crane   1.00   .55

Size: 30x24mm
Perf. 14x14½, 13½x14
409 A105 150p Kenana Sugar Co., horiz.   1.25   .75
410 A105 175p Secretary bird   1.50   .85
411 A105 £2 Atbara cement factory, horiz.   2.00   .95

Size: 26x37mm
Perf. 14
412 A105 250p King Taharqa statue   2.50 1.25
413 A105 £3 Republican palace   3.00 1.50

Size: 24x30mm
Perf. 13½x14
414 A105 £4 Hug jar   3.50 2.00
415 A105 £5 Gabana coffee pot   4.25 2.40

Size: 36x27mm
Litho. & Engr.
Perf. 14
Wmk. 334
416 A109 £8 Pterois volitans, horiz.   6.00 4.00
417 A109 £10 Animal wealth, horiz.   7.50 4.75
418 A109 £15 Nubian ibex   11.00 7.00
419 A109 £20 shown   16.00 9.50
Nos. 404-419 (16)   61.55 36.90

For surcharges on No. 416, see Nos. 605-606.

1992   Litho.   Unwmk.   *Perf. 14½x14*
420 A25 25p Cattle   .25   .25

1990   Unwmk.   *Perf. 14x13½*
427 A25 £5 Bohein Temple   14.50 10.00
   Perf. 13½x14
428 A26 £10 Sailboat   24.00 15.00

See Nos. O76-O100. For surcharges see Nos. 430, 436-453, O104-O111.

No. 156a Handstamp Surcharged in Blue Violet

1990, Sept.   *Perf. 13½x14*
430 A26 £1 on 10p #156a   65.00 8.50

Surcharge on No. 430 is often incomplete.

Pan-African Rinderpest Campaign A114

   Perf. 13½x13
1991, July 27   Litho.   Unwmk.
431 A114 £1 black & brt grn   1.25   .50
432 A114 £2 dp violet & emer   2.50 1.75
433 A114 £5 orange & blue grn   6.50 2.50
Nos. 431-433 (3)   10.25 4.75

Nos. 404, 407, 411, 413-414 Srchd. in Black or Blue Violet

Nos. 406, 409, 420 Surcharged

Nos. 405//420 Surcharged

No. 441 Surcharged   No. 409 Surcharged in Black

No. 406 Surcharged in Black   No. 412 Surcharged in Red

No. 451 Surcharged in Black

No. 408 Surcharged

1992?-97
Perfs. & Printing Methods as Before
436 A105 1d on 100p #407 (Blk)   5.00 2.50
437 A105 2d on £2 #411   9.00 4.75
438 A104 2.50d on 25p #404   12.50 5.75
438A A105 2.50d on 25p #420   2.50 1.75
439 A105 3d on £3 #413   15.00 7.00
440 A105 4d on £4 #414   17.50 9.50
441 A105 5d on 50p #405   2.75   .90
443 A105 7.50d on 75p #406   7.50 5.00
446 A105 1.50d on 150p #409   1.50 1.00
447 A105 15d on 150p #409   4.00   —
448 A105 25d on 25p #406   —   —
449 A105 25d on 250p #412   7.00 4.00
451 A105 35d on £8 #416   8.00 5.00
   a. Inverted surcharge
452 A105 100d on 125p #408   5.75 5.75
453 A105 100d on 125p #408 (R)   *50.00*   —
Nos. 436-453 (15)   148.00 52.90

Intl. Human Rights Day — A115

Designs: £5, Chain links, rainbow of colors, horiz. 750p, Trellis, rose, inscription.

1993, Dec. 20   Litho.   *Perf. 14*
454 A115 £4 multicolored   1.00   .65
455 A115 £5 multicolored   1.25   .90
456 A115 750p multicolored   1.75 1.25
Nos. 454-456 (3)   4.00 2.80

Fung Sultanate, 5th Cent. — A116

Designs: £5, Inscription on tablet. 750p, Inscription in circle, helmet, horiz.

1993, Dec. 20
457 A116 £4 multicolored   1.00   .65
458 A116 £5 multicolored   1.25   .90
459 A116 750p multicolored   1.75 1.25
Nos. 457-459 (3)   4.00 2.80

Wild Ass — A117

1994, July 15   Litho.   *Perf. 14½*
460 A117 4d With young   1.00   .50
461 A117 8d Standing   1.50 1.00
462 A117 10d Running   1.75 1.25
463 A117 15d Up close   2.50 2.00
Nos. 460-463 (4)   6.75 4.75

A118

1994, Aug. 1   Litho.   Perf. 14
464 A118   5d vermilion & multi   .50   .40
465 A118   7d green & multi   1.00   .55
466 A118 15d gray & multi   2.00   1.10
    Nos. 464-466 (3)   3.50   2.05

Intl. Olympic Committee, cent.

A119

1994, Dec. 7   Litho.   Perf. 13½
467 A119   5d lilac & multi   .35   .25
468 A119   7d brown & multi   .60   .45
469 A119 15d blue & multi   1.25   .95
    Nos. 467-469 (3)   2.20   1.65

ICAO, 50th anniv.

A120

1994 World Cup Soccer Championships, US: 4d, Goalie, green vest. 5d, Like 4d, blue vest. 7d, Player about to kick ball, green shirt. 8d, Like 7d, brown shirt. 10d, Player, long-sleeved shirt. 15d, Player, yellow shirt. 20d, Player, magenta & blue background. 25d, Player, white shirt & pants. 35d, Like 20d, blue & green background.
75d, Goalie, orange shirt, horiz. 100d, Player kicking ball, horiz.

1995, July 15   Litho.   Perf. 14
470 A120   4d multicolored   .40   .25
471 A120   5d multicolored   .40   .25
472 A120   7d multicolored   .60   .35
473 A120   8d multicolored   .70   .35
474 A120 10d multicolored   .85   .50
475 A120 15d multicolored   1.00   .50
476 A120 20d multicolored   1.75   1.00
477 A120 25d multicolored   2.00   1.25
478 A120 35d multicolored   3.00   1.50
    Nos. 470-478 (9)   10.70   5.95

Souvenir Sheets
479 A120 75d multicolored   7.50   7.50
480 A120 100d multicolored   11.50 11.50

A121

1995, Dec. 16   Litho.   Perf. 13½
481 A121 15d apple grn & blk   1.50   1.00
482 A121 25d blue & black   2.75   1.50
483 A121 30d purple & black   3.25   2.00
    Nos. 481-483 (3)   7.50   4.50

Arab League, 50th anniv.

A122

1996, May 4   Litho.   Perf. 13½
484 A122 15d orange & multi   1.50   1.00
485 A122 25d apple grn & multi   2.75   1.50
486 A122 30d purple & multi   3.50   2.00
    Nos. 484-486 (3)   7.75   4.50

Common Market for East and South Africa (COMESA).

A123

A124

1997, Jan. 22   Photo.   Perf. 13½
487 A123 25d black & violet   2.00   1.75
488 A123 35d black & red brown   3.25   2.00
489 A123 50d black & brown   4.25   3.00
    Nos. 487-489 (3)   9.50   6.75

Abdel Rahman el Mahdi (1885-1959).

1997, June 1   Photo.   Perf. 13½x13
490 A124   5d multicolored   .75   .40

Waiting For Peace.

A125

A126

1997, Oct. 15   Photo.   Perf. 13½
491 A125 25d lilac & multi   2.00   1.75
492 A125 35d apple grn &
    multi   3.00   2.75
493 A125 50d green, black &
    sil   4.00   3.50
    Nos. 491-493 (3)   9.00   8.00

Police Commanders, Arab Security Conference, 25th anniv.

1997, Nov. 1

Al-Shaykh Qaribulla's Mosque:Various views of mosque.
494 A126 25d blue & multi   1.50   1.25
495 A126 35d yellow & multi   2.50   1.75
496 A126 50d buff & multi, vert.   3.50   2.50
    Nos. 494-496 (3)   7.50   5.50

A127

1998, Jan. 18   Litho.   Perf. 13½
497 A127 25d multicolored   1.75   1.25
498 A127 35d violet & multi   2.75   2.25
499 A127 50d multicolored   3.50   2.75
    Nos. 497-499 (3)   8.00   6.25

Pan African Postal Union, 18th anniv.

A128

Sudanese Archeology: No. 500, Kerma pottery, 2500 BC. No. 501, Fresco, Faras church, 11th cent. No. 502, Close-up of fresco, Faras Church, 11th cent. 60d, C Group pottery, 2000 BC. No. 504, Meroe pottery, 4000 BC. No. 505, Tomb of Natakamani Meroitic king, 1st cent. BC, vert. 100d, C Group pottery, 2000 BC, diff.

1998, Jan. 25   Perf. 13½x13, 13x13½
500 A128 50d multicolored   2.25   2.00
501 A128 50d multicolored   2.25   2.00
502 A128 50d multicolored   2.25   2.00
503 A128 60d multicolored   2.50   2.25
504 A128 75d multicolored   3.25   2.50
505 A128 75d multicolored   3.25   2.50
506 A128 100d multicolored   4.25   3.50
    Nos. 500-506 (7)   20.00 16.75

A129

1998, Mar. 1   Perf. 13x13½
507 A129 100d Ruins, Camel
    Post rider   7.00   6.00

First Sudanese Postage Stamp, cent.

A130

1999, May 15   Litho.   Perf. 13¼x13½
508 A130 75d multicolored   4.50   3.75
509 A130 100d green & multi   6.00   5.50
510 A130 150d blue & multi   9.00   8.00
    Nos. 508-510 (3)   19.50 17.25

Battle of Kerreri, cent.

American Bombing of Elshifa Pharmaceuticals Factory, Aug. 20, 1998 — A131

75d, Bomb damage. 100d, Company emblem, falling bombs. 150d, Casualties.

Perf. 13¾x13½, 13¾x13¼
1999, July 1   Litho.
511 A131 75d multi   4.50   3.75
512 A131 100d multi, vert.   6.00   5.50
513 A131 150d multi   9.00   8.00
    Nos. 511-513 (3)   19.50 17.25

A132

A133

Perf. 13¼x13½, 13½x13¼
1999, Oct. 20   Litho.
514 A132 75d shown   4.50   3.75
515 A133 100d shown   6.00   5.50
516 A132 150d 7 people   9.00   8.00
    Nos. 514-516 (3)   19.50 17.25

Intl. Year of the Elderly.

SOS Children's Villages, 50th Anniv. — A134

1999, Oct. 31   Perf. 13½x13¼
517 A134 75d brn & multi   4.50   3.75
518 A134 100d grn & multi   6.00   5.50
519 A134 150d blue & multi   9.00   8.00
    Nos. 517-519 (3)   19.50 17.25

UPU, 125th Anniv. (in 1999) — A134a

2000, Mar. 1   Litho.   Perf. 13½x13¼
Denomination   Color
519A A134a 75d red   5.00   4.50
519B A134a 100d violet   6.00   5.25
519C A134a 150d black   10.00   8.00
    Nos. 519A-519C (3)   21.00 17.75

Common Market for Eastern and Southern Africa Free Trade Area — A135

Panel color: 100d, White. 150d, Pink. 200d, Yellow.

2000, Oct. 31   Litho.   Perf. 13¼x13¾
520-522 A135   Set of 3   27.50 27.50

UN High Commissioner for Refugees, 50th Anniv. — A136

Frame color: 100d, Green. 150d, Red. 200d, Violet.

Perf. 13¼x13½
2001, Aug. 15   Litho.
523-525 A136   Set of 3   27.50 27.50

Al-Zubair Prize for Innovation and Scientific Excellence A137

Frame color: 100d, Yellow. 150d, Red. 200d, Green.

2002, Feb. 14   Perf. 13¼
526-528 A137   Set of 3   30.00 30.00

Association for the Promotion of Scientific Innovation — A138

Frame color: 100d, Black. 150d, Red. 200d, Green.

2002, Feb. 14
529-531 A138   Set of 3   30.00 30.00

Year of Dialogue Among Civilizations A139

Country name in: 100d, Red. 150d, Orange. 200d, Black.

2002, Jan. 28   Litho.   Perf. 13¼x13¾
532-534 A139   Set of 3   32.50 32.50

Guinea Worm Eradication Campaign A140

Designs: 100d, Infested foot, campaign emblem. 150d, Campaign emblem. 200d, Child, campaign emblem.

2002, Mar. 3   Litho.   Perf. 13¼
535-537 A140   Set of 3   27.50 27.50

Palestinian Intifada — A141

Country name in: 100d, Green. 150d, Red. 200d, Black.

Perf. 13½x13¼
2002, Feb. 14   Litho.
538-540 A141   Set of 3   30.00 30.00

Sudanese postal officials have declared as illegal the following items:
Sheets of six stamps depicting Pope John Paul II (2 different).
Miniature sheet of two stamps depicting Pope John Paul II (2 different).

Association of African Banknote and Security Document Printers 11th Annual Conference — A142

Conference emblem and: 100d, Association emblem, circular design. 150d, Banknote rosettes. 200d, Archaeological ruins.

2003, May 10 Litho. Perf. 13½x13¼
541-543 A142   Set of 3   37.50 37.50

Mango — A143   Nile Perch — A144

Cattle — A145   Soldiers — A146

Muhammad Ahmad (Al-Mahdi, 1844-85), Religious Leader — A147   Butterflyfish — A148

Temple of Amun Ra — A149   Baobab Tree — A150

Doum Palm Tree — A151   Sheep — A152

Grapefruit A153   Oil Rigs A154

Tomb of Sheikh El-Mursi A155   Camel Postman A156

Perf. 13½x13¼, 13¼x13½
2003, July 15
544 A143 50d multi   .75   .75
545 A144 50d multi   .75   .75
546 A145 75d multi   1.25   1.25
547 A146 100d multi 1.50   1.50
548 A147 100d multi 1.50   1.50
549 A148 125d multi 2.00   2.00
550 A149 150d multi 2.25   2.25
551 A150 150d multi 2.25   2.25
552 A151 150d multi 2.25   2.25
553 A152 150d multi 2.25   2.25
554 A153 200d multi 3.00   3.00
555 A154 200d multi 3.00   3.00
556 A155 300d multi 4.50   4.50
557 A156 500d multi 7.50   7.50
a. Souvenir sheet, #544-557, imperf.   35.00 35.00
Nos. 544-557 (14)   34.75 34.75

Parliament, 50th Anniv. — A157

Panel colors: 100d, Lilac. 200d, Yellow orange. 250d, Pink.

2004, Jan. 5   Perf. 13½x13¼
558-560 A157   Set of 3   9.25 9.25

General Secretariat for Council of Ministers, 50th Anniv. — A158

Panel colors: 100d, Light blue. 200d, Yellow. 250d, Pink.

2004, Jan. 8
561-563 A158   Set of 3   9.25 9.25

Rural Women's Innovation — A159

Panel colors: 100d, Light blue. 200d, Yellow. 250d, Lilac.

2004, Jan. 26
564-566 A159   Set of 3   9.25 9.25

Armed Forces, 50th Anniv. — A160

Background color: 100d, Orange. 200d, Red. 250d, Purple.

Perf. 13¼x13½
2004, Aug. 14   Litho.
567-569 A160   Set of 3   12.00 12.00

Peace — A161

Background color: 200d, Dark blue. 300d, Green and yellow, 400d, Light blue.

2005, Jan. 9   Perf. 13½x13¼
570-572 A161   Set of 3   15.50 15.50

7th Conference of Sudanese Women's General Union — A162

Panel color: 200d, White. 300d, Lilac. 400d, Light blue.

Perf. 13½x13¼
2005, June 29   Litho.
573-575 A162   Set of 3   14.00 14.00

Merowe Dam Project — A163

Background color: 200d, Light blue. 300d, Light green. 400d, Lilac.

2005, June 30
576-578 A163   Set of 3   13.00 13.00

World Summit on the Information Society, Tunis — A164

Background color: 200d, Yellow green. 300d, Blue. 400d, Yellow orange.

2005, Sept. 24
579-581 A164   Set of 3   13.00 13.00

Merowe Dam Housing Rehabilitation Projects — A165

Denomination in: 200d, Black. 300d, Green. 400d, Red.

2005, Oct. 1   Litho.   Perf. 13¼x13¾
582-584 A165   Set of 3   12.50 12.50

Merowe Dam Archaeology Project — A166

Map and clay pot: 200d, Shown. 300d, With blue panel. 400d, With peach panel.

2005, Dec. 20   Perf. 13¾x13¼
585-587 A166   Set of 3   12.50 12.50

A167

A168

Independence, 50th Anniv. — A169

Perf. 13¼x13¾, 13¾x13¼
2006, Jan. 15
588 A167 200d multi 3.25   3.25
589 A168 300d multi 4.75   4.75
590 A169 400d multi 6.25   6.25
a. Souvenir sheet, #588-590, imperf.   35.00 35.00
Nos. 588-590 (3)   14.25 14.25

OPEC Intl. Development Fund, 30th Anniv. — A170

Background color: 200d, Red. 300d, Green. 400d, Blue.

2006, Oct. 12 Litho. Perf. 13¾x13½
591-593 A170 Set of 3 　　11.50 11.50

100 qirsh = 1 pound

African Soccer Confederation, 50th Anniv. — A171

Background colors; £2, Pink. £3.50, Pale yellow. £4.50, White.

Perf. 13¾x13½
2007, Feb. 11　　　　　　Litho.
594-596 A171 Set of 3 　　14.00 14.00

10th Meeting of Regional African Satellite Communications Organization A172

Background colors: £1, Lilac. £2, Light green. £3.50, Yellow. £4.50, Blue.

2007　　　　　Perf. 13½x13¾
597-600 A172 Set of 4 　　15.00 15.00

24th Universal Postal Union Congress, Nairobi — A173

Panel color: £1, Lilac. £2, Brown. £3.50, Blue. £4.50, Ocher.

2008　　　　　Perf. 13¾x13½
601-604 A173 Set of 4 　　15.00 15.00
Due to political unrest in Kenya, the UPU Congress was moved to Geneva, Switzerland.

No. 416 Srchd. in Black or Red

Methods, Perfs and Watermarks As Before
2008
605 A109 £2 on £8 #416 (Bk) 12.00 12.00
606 A109 £2 on £8 #416 (R) 7.00 7.00

Comprehensive Peace Agreement, 3rd Anniv. — A174

Panel color in: £1, Blue. £2, Black. £3.50, Green. £4.50, Brown.

Perf. 13¾x13½
2008, Jan. 22 Litho. Unwmk.
607-610 A174 Set of 4 　17.50 17.50

Population and Housing Census — A175

Background colors: £1, Blue. £2, Yellow. £3.50, Lilac. £4.50, Green.

2008, Jan. 22 Litho. Perf. 13¾x13½
611-614 A175 Set of 4 　17.00 17.00

Arab Postal Day — A176

Emblem and: £2, Camel caravan. £3.50, World map, pigeon.

2008, Aug. 3
615-616 A176 Set of 2 　　8.75 8.75

Diplomatic Relations Between Sudan and People's Republic of China, 50th Anniv. — A177

Background color: £2.50, Pink. £5, Pale green. £6, Gray.

Perf. 13¾x13½
2009, Feb. 19　　　　　　Litho.
617-619 A177 Set of 3 　17.50 17.50

Merowe Dam Transmission Lines — A178

Background color: £2.50, Purple. £5, Green. £6, Blue.

2009
620-622 A178 Set of 3 　15.50 15.50

Inauguration of Merowe Dam — A179

Panel color: £2.50, Pink. £5, Light blue. £6, Buff.

2009
623-625 A179 Set of 3 　15.50 15.50

Completion of Merowe Dam — A180

Frame color: £3, Blue. £5.50, Orange brown. £7, Green.

2010, Apr. 7
626-628 A180 Set of 3 　18.00 18.00

Solidarity — A181

Color of country name: £3, Green. £5.50, Yellow. £7, Orange brown.

2010, Sept. 7　　　Perf. 13½x13¾
629-631 A181 Set of 3 　15.50 15.50

Sudan Radio — A182

Background color: £3, Green. £5.50, Blue. £7, Red.

2010, Sept. 26　　　Perf. 13¾x13½
632-634 A182 Set of 3 　15.50 15.50

Sudan E-Government A183

Frame color: £3, Red. £5.50, Blue. £7, Blue green.

2011, July 27 Litho. Perf. 13½x13¾
635-637 A183 Set of 3 　15.50 15.50

AIR POST STAMPS

Nos. 40-41, 43 Overprinted in Black

Nos. C1-C2　　　　No. C3

1931 Wmk. 214 Perf. 11½x12½, 14
C1 A2 5m blk & olive brown 1.00 1.00
C2 A2 10m blk & carmine 1.75 4.00
C3 A1 2p org & vio brown 2.50 3.50
　　Nos. C1-C3 (3) 5.25 8.50

Statue of Gen. C. G. Gordon AP3

1931-35　　　Engr.　　Perf. 14
C4 AP3 3m dk brn & grn ('33) 3.50 7.25
C5 AP3 5m grn & blk 1.50 .25
C6 AP3 10m car rose & blk 1.50 .25
C7 AP3 15m dk brn & brn .75 .25
C8 AP3 2p org & blk .65 .25
C9 AP3 2½p bl & red vio ('33) 4.75 .25
C10 AP3 3p gray & blk 1.00 .25
C11 AP3 3½p dl vio & blk 2.25 .90
C12 AP3 4½p gray & brn 12.50 16.50
C13 AP3 5p ultra & blk 1.75 .35
C14 AP3 7½p pck grn & dk grn ('35) 12.00 6.00
C15 AP3 10p peacock bl & sep ('35) 11.50 2.00
　Nos. C4-C15 (12) 53.65 34.50
See Nos. C23-C30. For surcharges see Nos. C17-C22, C31-C34.

No. 43 Surcharged in Black

1932, July 18　　　　Typo.
C16 A1 2½p on 2p 2.50 4.00

Nos. C6, C4-C5, C12 Surcharged

1935　　　Engr.　　Perf. 14
C17 AP3 15m on 10m .60 .25
　a. Double surcharge 950.00 1,100.
　b. Arabic characters omitted 750.00
C18 AP3 2½p on 3m 1.25 6.00
　a. "½" 2¼mm high instead of 3mm 4.50 20.00
　b. Second Arabic character of surcharge omitted 65.00 125.00
C19 AP3 2½p on 5m .85 1.75
　a. "½" 2¼mm high instead of 3mm 4.75 9.00
　b. Second Arabic character of surcharge omitted 40.00 60.00
　c. Inverted surcharge 1,000. 1,200.
　d. As "a," inverted 2,500. 20,000.
　e. As "b," inverted 1,500. 1,600.
　f. Pair, C19c and C19d 35,000.
C20 AP3 3p on 4½p 2.50 18.50
C21 AP3 7½p on 4½p 9.00 52.50
　a. "7¼" instead of "7½"
C22 AP3 10p on 4½p 9.00 52.50
　Nos. C17-C22 (6) 23.20 131.50

Type of 1931-35

1936-37　　　Perf. 11½x12½
C23 AP3 15m dk brn & brn ('37) 4.75 .25
C24 AP3 2p org & blk ('37) 5.25 18.00
C25 AP3 2½p bl & red vio ('37) 3.00 .25
C26 AP3 3p gray & blk ('37) 1.00 .40
C27 AP3 3½p dl vio & blk ('37) 2.50 15.00
C28 AP3 5p ultra & blk ('37) 4.25 .40
C29 AP3 7½p pck grn & dk grn ('37) 4.75 11.00
C30 AP3 10p pck bl & sep ('37) 7.00 27.50
　Nos. C23-C30 (8) 32.50 72.80

Nos. C25, C11, C14 and C15 Srchd. as in 1935

1938 Wmk. 214 Perf. 11½x12½, 14
C31 AP3 5m on 2½p 3.50 .25
C32 AP3 3p on 3½p 42.50 60.00
　a. On No. C27 700.00 750.00
C33 AP3 3p on 7½p 7.50 7.25
　a. On No. C29 700.00 750.00

C34	AP3	5p on 10p	1.75	5.50
a.		On No. C30	700.00	750.00
		Nos. C31-C34 (4)	55.25	73.00

Catalogue values for unused stamps in this section, from this point to the end of the section, are for Never Hinged items.

Bridge Over Blue Nile, Khartoum AP4

Designs: 2½p, Kassala Jebel. 3p, Water wheel. 3½p, Port Sudan. 4p, Gordon Memorial College. 4½p, Nile post boat. 6p, Suakin. 20p, General Post Office, Khartoum.

1950, July 1   Engr.   Perf. 12

C35	AP4	2p dk bl grn & blk	5.75	1.75
C36	AP4	2½p red org & bl	1.00	1.50
C37	AP4	3p dp bl & plum	4.50	1.50
C38	AP4	3½p chnt & choc	4.50	5.00
C39	AP4	4p bl & brn	1.75	3.50
C40	AP4	4½p ultra & blk	3.00	5.00
C41	AP4	6p car & blk	3.50	4.00
C42	AP4	20p plum & blk	3.00	6.75
		Nos. C35-C42 (8)	27.00	29.00

For overprints see Nos. CO1-CO8.

AIR POST OFFICIAL

Catalogue values for unused stamps in this section are for Never Hinged items.

Nos. C35 to C42 Overprinted in Carmine or Black

1950, July 1   Wmk. 214   Perf. 12

CO1	AP4	2p dk bl grn & blk (C)	18.50	3.75
CO2	AP4	2½p red org & bl	1.75	2.00
CO3	AP4	3p dp bl & plum	1.00	1.25
CO4	AP4	3½p chnt & choc	1.00	10.00
CO5	AP4	4p bl & brn	1.00	9.50
CO6	AP4	4½p ultra & blk (C)	5.00	21.00
CO7	AP4	6p car & blk (C)	1.25	5.50
CO8	AP4	20p plum & blk (C)	5.50	15.00
		Nos. CO1-CO8 (8)	35.00	68.00

POSTAGE DUE STAMPS

Postage Due Stamps of Egypt, 1889, Overprinted in Black

1897   Wmk. 119   Perf. 14

J1	D3	2m green	2.50	6.00
J2	D3	4m maroon	2.50	6.00
J3	D3	1p ultra	14.00	5.00
J4	D3	2p orange	14.00	10.00
		Nos. J1-J4 (4)	33.00	27.00

Steamboat on Nile River — D1

1901   Typo.   Wmk. 179

J5	D1	2m orange brn & blk	1.00	.85
J6	D1	4m blue green & brn	3.25	1.25
J7	D1	10m blue vio & blue grn	8.00	5.00
J8	D1	20m car rose & ultra	4.75	4.75
		Nos. J5-J8 (4)	17.00	11.85

1927-30   Wmk. Multiple S G (214)

J9	D1	2m org brn & blk ('30)	4.50	3.00
J10	D1	4m blue grn & brn	1.75	1.00
J11	D1	10m violet & blue grn	2.75	2.00
		Nos. J9-J11 (3)	9.00	6.00

Catalogue values for unused stamps in this section, from this point to the end of the section, are for Never Hinged items.

Redrawn

Bottom inscription altered — D2

1948, Jan. 1

J12	D2	2m dp orange & blk	2.75	50.00
J13	D2	4m blue grn & choc	4.50	37.50
J14	D2	10m rose lil & bl grn	26.50	19.00
a.		Wmk. 345 ('71?)		
J15	D2	20m brt car rose & ul-tra	28.50	30.00
a.		Wmk. 345 ('73)		
		Nos. J12-J15 (4)	62.25	136.50

ARMY OFFICIAL STAMPS

Regular Issues of 1898 and 1902-08 Overprinted in Black

Nos. MO1, MO3 and MO2, MO4

1905   Wmk. 71   Perf. 14

MO1	A1	1m rose & brown	190.00	200.00
a.		"OFFICIAL"	4,750.	3,250.
b.		Pair, #MO1 and #MO2	4,500.	
MO2	A1	1m rose & brown	3,000.	3,000.

**   Wmk. 179**

MO3	A1	1m car rose & brn	6.50	3.00
a.		"OFFICIAL"	80.00	47.50
b.		Inverted overprint	70.00	60.00
c.		Horizontal overprint	450.00	
MO4	A1	1m car rose & brn	60.00	30.00
a.		Inverted overprint	350.00	375.00

Regular Issues of 1902-11 Overprinted in Black

1906-11

MO5	A1	1m car rose & brn	2.50	.30
a.		"Army" and "Service" 14mm apart	550.00	400.00
b.		Inverted overprint	650.00	700.00
c.		Pair, one without ovpt.		7,000.
d.		Double overprint		1,750.
e.		"Service" omitted		4,500.
MO6	A1	2m brn & grn	22.50	1.25
a.		Pair, one without ovpt.	4,000.	
b.		"Army" omitted	4,200.	4,200.
MO7	A1	3m green & violet	22.50	.50
a.		Inverted overprint	2,200.	
MO8	A1	5m blk & rose red	3.50	.25
a.		Inverted overprint		375.00
b.		Double overprint	325.00	250.00
c.		Double ovpt., one invtd.	1,500.	550.00
MO9	A1	1p yel brn & ultra	22.50	.40
a.		"Army" omitted	3,250.	3,250.
MO10	A1	2p ultra & blk ('09)	85.00	15.00
a.		Double overprint		3,400.
MO11	A1	5p grn & org brn ('08)	175.00	75.00
MO12	A1	10p dp vio & blk ('11)	625.00	750.00
		Nos. MO5-MO12 (8)	958.50	842.70

Same Overprint On Regular Issue of 1898

Wmk. 71

MO13	A1	2p ultra & black	90.00	11.50
a.		Inverted overprint		
MO14	A1	5p grn & org brn	130.00	250.00
MO15	A1	10p dp vio & blk	175.00	475.00

There are two types of this overprint which may be distinguished by the size and shape of the "y."

OFFICIAL STAMPS

Regular Issue of 1898 Overprinted in Black

O.S.G.S.

1902-06   Wmk. 71   Perf. 14

O1	A1	1m rose & brown	3.50	11.00
a.		Inverted overprint	325.00	450.00
b.		Round periods	8.00	45.00
c.		Double overprint	650.00	
d.		Oval "O" in overprint	90.00	
e.		As "d," inverted overprint	5,500.	
O2	A1	10p dp vio & blk ('06)	16.00	27.50

Same Ovpt. on Stamps of 1902-11

1903-12   Wmk. 179

O3	A1	1m car rose & brn ('04)	.60	.25
a.		Double overprint		
O4	A1	3m grn & vio ('04)	3.25	.25
O5	A1	5m blk & rose red	3.25	.25
O6	A1	1p yel brn & ultra	6.00	.25
O7	A1	2p ultra & blk	30.00	.25
O8	A1	5p grn & org brn	2.75	.40
O9	A1	10p dp vio & blk	5.25	70.00
		Nos. O3-O9 (7)	51.10	71.65

Regular Issue of 1927-40 Overprinted in Black

S.G.

Perf. 14, 13½x 14

1936-46   Wmk. 214

O10	A2	1m dk org & int blk ('46)	2.25	12.50
O11	A2	2m dk brn & dk org ('45)	2.25	8.00
O12	A2	3m green & vio ('37)	2.00	.25
O13	A2	4m brown & green	3.25	4.00
O14	A2	5m blk & ol brn ('40)	3.00	.25
O15	A2	10m blk & car ('46)	.90	.25
O16	A2	15m org brn & ultra ('37)	7.50	.35

Regular Issue of 1927-40 Overprinted in Black

S.G.

O17	A1	2p org & vio brn ('37)	11.50	.25
O18	A1	3p dk bl & red brn ('46)	5.25	3.00
O19	A1	4p blk & ultra ('46)	22.00	5.50
O20	A1	5p dk grn & org brn	8.50	9.00
O21	A1	6p blk & pale bl ('46)	6.00	7.00
O22	A1	8p blk & pck grn ('46)	4.00	22.50
O23	A1	10p dp vio & blk ('37)	37.50	6.50
O24	A1	20p blk & lt bl ('46)	25.00	32.50
		Nos. O10-O24 (15)	140.90	111.85

Catalogue values for unused stamps in this section, from this point to the end of the section, are for Never Hinged items.

#79-85 Overprinted Like #O10-O16

1948, Jan. 1

O28	A7	1m dk org & blk	.50	4.50
O29	A7	2m choc & org	2.00	.25
O30	A7	3m grn & rose lil	5.00	10.00
O31	A7	4m choc & sl grn	4.75	6.00
O32	A7	5m blk & ol brn	4.75	.25
O33	A7	10m blk & car	4.25	1.00
O34	A7	15m org brn & ultra	4.25	.25

Nos. 86-94 Overprinted Like Nos. O17-O24

O35	A8	2p org yel & vio brn	5.00	.25
O36	A8	3p dk bl & red brn	6.00	.25
O37	A8	4p blk & ultra	4.25	.25
a.		Perf. 13	13.00	18.00
O38	A8	5p dk grn & org	6.50	.25
O39	A8	6p blk & pale bl	4.25	.25
O40	A8	8p blk & pck grn	4.25	6.50
O41	A8	10p dp rose lil & blk	7.75	.25
O42	A8	20p dk bl & bl	5.75	1.00
a.		Perf. 13		
O43	A8	50p ultra & car	82.50	70.00
		Nos. O28-O43 (16)	152.50	101.25

Nos. 98-104 Overprinted Liked Nos. O10-O16 in Red

1951, Sept. 1   Wmk. 214   Perf. 14

Center in Black

O44	A11	1m orange	.75	5.00
O45	A11	2m ultra	.75	2.00
O46	A11	3m dk grn	12.00	18.00
O47	A11	4m emerald	.25	6.00
O48	A11	5m plum	.25	.25
O49	A11	10m light blue	.25	.25
O50	A11	15m dp org brn	1.00	.25

Nos. 105-114 Overprinted Like Nos. O17-O24 in Black or Red

Perf. 13

O51	A12	2p lt bl & dk bl	.25	.25
a.		Inverted overprint	1,100.	
O52	A12	3p vio bl & brn	22.50	.25
O53	A12	3½p brn & bl grn	.85	.40
O54	A12	4p blk & dp bl	5.00	.25
O55	A12	5p emer & org brn	.90	.25
O56	A12	6p blk & bl	1.10	4.50
O57	A12	8p brn & dp bl	1.50	.35
O58	A12	10p grn & blk (R)	1.75	.35
O59	A12	20p blk & bl grn	2.75	1.25
a.		Inverted overprint	3,500.	
O60	A13	50p blk & car	8.50	4.00
		Nos. O44-O60 (17)	60.35	43.60

No. 112 Overprinted Like Nos.O17-O24 in Black

1958

O61	A12	10p green & black	22.50	3.75

Nos. 146-159 Overprinted

Perf. 14½x14, 14x14½

1962, Oct. 1   Litho.   Wmk. 345

Size: 23x19mm, 19x23mm

O62	A25	5m blue	.25	.25
O63	A25	10m blue & lilac	.25	.25
O64	A25	15m yel, vio, org & brn	.25	.25
O65	A25	2p lt pur	.30	.25
O66	A26	3p bl grn, red brn & org brn	.55	.25
O67	A26	35m yel grn, brn & org brn	.70	.25
O68	A26	4p red, lt bl & lil	.85	.30
O69	A25	5m gray & yel ol	1.10	.50
O70	A25	6p brn & lt bl	1.10	.50
O71	A25	8p green	1.40	.60

Size: 24½x30mm, 30x24½mm

O72	A26	10p lt bl, red brn & blk	1.75	.65
O73	A25	20p gray ol & yel grn	3.50	1.40
a.		Perf. 13½x12½	2.75	1.10
b.		Perf. 13½x14	.80	1.90
O74	A25	50p dk gray, ol & bl	8.00	3.50
a.		Perf. 13½x14	6.50	3.25

Engr.

O75	A13	£1 grn & brn org	20.00	12.50
		Nos. O62-O75 (14)	40.00	21.45

The overprint measures 12x4½mm on Nos. O62-O71; 16x6mm on Nos. O72-O75.

1975-79   Unwmk.

Same Perfs., Sizes and Printing Methods as Before

O62a	A25	5m	.25	.25
O63a	A26	10m ('76)	.25	.25
O64a	A25	15m	.25	.25
O65a	A25	2p	.25	.25
O66a	A26	3p	.35	.25
O67a	A26	35m	.40	.25
O68a	A26	4p	.45	.25

O69a	A25	55m	.75	.45
O70a	A25	6p ('76)	.80	.45
O71a	A25	8p	1.10	.55
O72a	A26	10p	1.50	.70
O73b	A25	20p	2.50	1.25
O74b	A25	50p	2.50	1.25
O75a	A13	£1 ('79)	19.00	12.50
	Nos. O62a-O75a (14)		30.35	18.90

Nos. 404-419
Overprinted

Perf. 13½x13

1991, July 1　Litho.　Unwmk.

O76	A105	25p on #404	.25	.25
O77	A105	50p on #405	.25	.25
O78	A105	75p on #406	.45	.25
O79	A105	100p on #407	.55	.35
O80	A105	125p on #408	.65	.40

Size: 30x24mm
Perf. 14x14½, 13½x14

O81	A105	150p on #409	.75	.45
O82	A105	175p on #410	.90	.55
O83	A105	£2 on #411	1.10	.65

Size: 26x37mm
Perf. 14

O84	A105	250p on #412	1.35	.75
O85	A105	£3 on #413	1.50	.95

Size: 24x30mm
Perf. 13½x14

O86	A105	£4 on #414	2.10	1.25
O87	A105	£5 on #415	2.60	1.50

Size: 36x27mm
Perf. 14
Wmk. 334

O88	A105	£8 on #416	4.25	2.75
O89	A105	£10 on #417	5.00	3.75
O90	A105	£15 on #418	7.50	5.75
O91	A105	£20 on #419	10.00	7.50
	Nos. O76-O91 (16)		39.20	27.35

For surcharges see Nos. O104-O111.

Nos. 420, 427-428
Overprinted

1992　Litho.　Unwmk.　Perf. 14½

O92	A25	25p on #420	.30	.25

Perf. 14x13½, 13½x14

O99	A25	£5 on #427	2.75	1.75
O100	A25	£10 on #428	5.50	3.50
	Nos. O92-O100 (3)		8.55	5.50

Nos. O79,
O81, O83,
O85-O87
Srchd. in Blue
Violet or Black

Perf. 13½x13

1993?　Litho.　Unwmk.

O104	A105	1d on 100p #O79	1.00	.65

Perf. 13½x14

O105	A105	1.50d on 150p #O81	1.50	1.00
O107	A105	2d on £2 #O83	2.00	1.25

Perf. 14

O109	A105	3d on £3 #O85	3.00	2.00

Perf. 14½x14

O110	A105	4d on £4 #O86	4.00	2.75

Perf. 13½x14

O111	A105	5d on £5 #O87 (Blk)	5.00	3.25

Perf. 14
Size: 36x27mm

O112	A109	35d on £8 #O88	14.50	14.50
	Nos. O104-O112 (7)		31.00	25.40

Coat of Arms — O1

2003　Litho.　Perf. 13½x13¼

O113	O1	50d multi	.50	.50
O114	O1	100d multi	.95	.95
O115	O1	200d multi	1.90	1.90
O116	O1	300d multi	3.00	3.00
	Nos. O113-O116 (4)		6.35	6.35

SURINAM

ˈsur-ə-ˌnam

(Dutch Guiana)

LOCATION — On the northeast coast of South America, bordering on the Atlantic Ocean
GOVT. — Republic
AREA — 63,234 sq. mi.
POP. — 431,156 (1999 est.)
CAPITAL — Paramaribo

The Dutch colony of Surinam became an integral part of the Kingdom of the Netherlands under the Constitution of 1954. It became an independent state November 25, 1975.

100 Cents = 1 Gulden (Florin)
100 Cents = 1 Dollar (2004)

Catalogue values for unused stamps in this country are for Never Hinged items, beginning with Scott 168 in the regular postage section, Scott B34 in the semipostal section, Scott C23 in the airpost section, Scott CB1 in the airpost semi-postal section, and Scott J33 in the postage due section.

Watermark

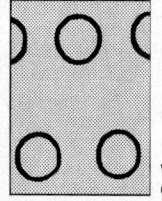

Wmk. 202 —
Circles

Early issues of Surinam were sent to the colony without gum. Many of these were subsequently gummed locally.

King William
III — A1

Numeral of
Value — A2

Perf. 11½, 11½x12, 12½x12, 13½, 14
1873-89　Typo.　Unwmk.
Without Gum

1	A1	1c lil gray ('85)	2.50	3.00
2	A1	2c yellow ('85)	1.75	1.75
3	A1	2½c rose	1.75	1.75
4	A1	3c green	21.00	18.50
5	A1	5c dull violet	20.00	7.00
6	A1	10c bister	4.00	2.75
7	A1	12½c sl bl ('85)	21.00	8.25
8	A1	15c gray ('89)	25.00	8.25
9	A1	20c green ('89)	37.50	35.00
10	A1	25c grnsh blue	85.00	10.00
11	A1	25c ultra	300.00	25.00
12	A1	30c red brn ('88)	35.00	37.50
13	A1	40c dk brn ('89)	32.50	32.50

14	A1	50c brown org	32.50	21.00
15	A1	1g red brn & gray ('89)	52.50	52.50
16	A1	2.50g grn & org ('79)	80.00	70.00
	Nos. 1-16 (16)		752.00	334.75

Perf. 14, Small Holes

3b	A1	2½c rose	12.00	14.00
4b	A1	3c green	22.00	29.00
5b	A1	5c dull violet	22.00	18.00
6b	A1	10c bister	21.00	25.00
11b	A1	25c ultra	300.00	72.50
14b	A1	50c brown org	57.50	50.00
	Nos. 3b-14b (6)		434.50	208.50

The paper of Nos. 3-6, 11 and 14 sometimes has an accidental bluish tinge of varying strength. During its manufacture a chemical whitener (bluing agent) was added in varying quantities. No particular printing was made on bluish paper.

"Small hole" varieties have the spaces between the holes wider than the diameter of the holes.

Nos. 1-16 and 3b-14b exist with gum.
For surcharges see Nos. 23, 31-35, 39-42.

1890　Perf. 11½x11, 12½
Without Gum

17	A2	1c gray	1.90	1.40
18	A2	2c yellow brn	3.00	2.50
19	A2	2½c carmine	2.50	2.00
20	A2	3c green	5.75	4.00
21	A2	5c ultra	27.50	1.50
	Nos. 17-21 (5)		40.65	11.40

Nos. 17-21 exist with gum.
For surcharges see Nos. 63-64.

A3

1892, Aug. 11　Perf. 10½
Without Gum

22	A3	2½c black & org	1.90	1.25
a.	First and fifth vertical words have fancy "F"		27.50	17.50
b.	Imperf.		2.50	
c.	As "a," imperf.		32.50	

No. 14 Surcharged in
Black

1892, Aug. 1　Perf. 14
Without Gum

23	A1	2½c on 50c	250.00	12.00
a.	Perf. 12½x12	375.00	12.00
b.	Perf. 11½x12	425.00	17.50
c.	Double surcharge	375.00	275.00
d.	Perf. 14, small holes	275.00	12.00

Nos. 23-23c were issued without gum.

Queen
Wilhelmina — A5

1892-93　Typo.　Perf. 12½
Without Gum

25	A5	10c bister	42.50	3.25
26	A5	12½c rose lilac	50.00	5.75
27	A5	15c gray	4.00	2.75
28	A5	20c green	4.50	3.25
29	A5	25c blue	10.00	5.75
30	A5	30c red brown	5.75	5.00
	Nos. 25-30 (6)		116.75	25.75

Nos. 25-30 exist with gum.
For surcharges see Nos. 65-66.

Nos. 7-12 Surcharged

1898　Perf. 11½x12, 12½x12, 13½
Without Gum

31	A1	10c on 12½c sl bl	27.50	4.00
32	A1	10c on 15c gray	65.00	55.00
33	A1	10c on 20c green	5.25	4.00
34	A1	10c on 25c grnsh bl	11.00	6.25
c.	Perf. 11½x12			
34A	A1	10c on 25c ultra	575.00	500.00
b.	Perf. 11½x12	675.00	600.00
35	A1	10c on 30c red brn	4.25	4.25
a.	Double surcharge	325.00	

Dangerous counterfeits exist.

Netherlands Nos. 80, 83-84
Surcharged

No. 36 　　　Nos. 37-38

1900, Jan. 8　Perf. 12½
Without Gum

36	A11	50c on 50c	27.50	9.00

Engr.
Perf. 11½x11

37	A12	100c on 1g dk grn	25.00	14.00
38	A12	2.50g on 2½g brn lil	25.00	12.50
	Nos. 36-38 (3)		77.50	35.50

For surcharge see No. 67.

Nos. 13-16 Surcharged

Perf. 11½, 11½x12, 12½x12, 14
1900　Typo.
Without Gum

39	A1	25c on 40c	5.00	3.50
40	A1	25c on 50c	5.00	3.50
a.	Perf. 14, small holes	130.00	140.00
b.	Perf. 11½x12	3.75	3.75
41	A1	50c on 1g	40.00	35.00
42	A1	50c on 2.50g	150.00	175.00
	Nos. 39-42 (4)		200.00	217.00

Counterfeits of No. 42 exist.

A9

Queen Wilhelmina
A10 　　　　A11

1902-08　Typo.　Perf. 12½
Without Gum

44	A9	½c violet	1.00	.90
45	A9	1c olive grn	2.10	1.25
46	A9	2c yellow brn	11.50	4.50
47	A9	2½c blue grn	5.00	.45
48	A9	3c orange	8.25	5.25
49	A9	5c red	8.25	.45
50	A9	7½c gray ('08)	18.00	8.25
51	A10	10c slate	12.00	.95
52	A10	12½c deep blue	4.50	.45
53	A10	15c dp brown	30.00	10.50
54	A10	20c olive grn	27.50	5.25
55	A10	22½c brn & ol grn	24.00	13.00
56	A10	25c violet	20.00	1.25
57	A10	30c orange brn	47.50	15.00
58	A10	50c lake brown	37.50	9.25

Engr.
Perf. 11

59	A11	1g violet	60.00	20.00
60	A11	2½g slate blue	60.00	65.00
	Nos. 44-60 (17)		377.10	161.70

Nos. 44-60 exist with gum.

A12

1909 Typeset Serrate Roulette 13½
Without Gum

61	A12	5c red		13.50	11.50
a.		Tête bêche pair		190.00	175.00

Perf. 11½x10½

62	A12	5c red		14.50	12.00
a.		Tête bêche pair		140.00	140.00

Nos. 17-18, 29-30, 38 Surcharged in Red

Nos. 63-64

Nos. 65-66

No. 67

1911, July 15 Typo. Perf. 12½
Without Gum

63	A2	½c on 1c		1.75	1.10
64	A2	½c on 2c		12.25	9.00
65	A5	15c on 25c		75.00	57.50
66	A5	20c on 30c		14.00	9.50

Engr.
Perf. 11½x11

67	A12	30c on 2.50g on 2½g		125.00	110.00
		Nos. 63-67 (5)		228.00	187.10

A13

1912, July Typeset Perf. 11½
Without Gum

70	A13	½c lilac		.95	.95
a.		Horiz. pair, imperf. btwn.		200.00	
71	A13	2½c dk green		.95	.95
72	A13	5c pale red		8.75	8.75
a.		Vert. pair, imperf. btwn.		240.00	
73	A13	12½c deep blue		11.00	11.00
		Nos. 70-73 (4)		21.65	21.65

Numeral of Value — A14

Queen Wilhelmina
A15 · A16

1913-31 Typo. Perf. 12½

74	A14	½c violet		.40	.25
75	A14	1c olive green		.40	.25
76	A14	1½c blue, perf 11½ ('21)		.40	.25
a.		Perf. 12½ ('32)		1.10	.85
77	A14	2c yellow brn		1.60	1.10
78	A14	2½c green		.95	.25
79	A14	3c yellow		.80	.65
80	A14	3c green ('26)		3.25	2.50
81	A14	4c chlky bl ('26)		8.25	5.00
82	A14	5c rose		1.60	.25

83	A14	5c green ('22)		2.00	1.00
84	A14	5c lilac ('26)		1.60	.25
85	A14	6c bister ('26)		2.75	2.50
86	A14	6c red org ('31)		2.25	.50
87	A14	7½c drab		1.00	.40
a.		Perf. 11x11½		1.40	.65
88	A14	7½c orange ('27)		1.40	.40
89	A14	7½c yellow ('31)		9.25	9.25
90	A14	10c violet ('22)		5.00	5.00
91	A14	10c rose ('26)		4.00	.55
92	A15	10c car rose		1.40	.65
93	A15	12½c blue		1.90	.65
94	A15	12½c red ('22)		2.00	2.25
95	A15	15c olive grn		.55	.70
96	A15	15c lt blue ('26)		7.75	4.75
97	A15	20c green		3.50	3.25
98	A15	20c blue ('22)		2.40	2.00
99	A15	20c ol grn ('26)		3.50	2.75
100	A15	22½c orange		2.50	2.50
101	A15	25c red violet		4.00	.40
102	A15	30c slate		5.00	1.10
103	A15	32½c vio & org ('22)		15.00	17.50
104	A15	35c sl & red ('26)		5.00	5.00

Perf. 11, 11½, 11½x11, 12½

Engr.

105	A16	50c green		4.00	.85
a.		Perf. 12½ ('32)		14.00	1.60
106	A16	1g brown		5.50	.50
a.		Perf. 12½ ('32)		15.00	1.00
107	A16	1½g dp vio ('26)		35.00	35.00
108	A16	2½g carmine ('23)		30.00	26.00
a.		Perf. 11½x11		35.00	32.50
		Nos. 74-108 (35)		175.90	136.20

Nos. 74, 75, 77-79, 82, 87, 105, 106 and 108 were issued both with and without gum.
Early printings of Nos. 74-104 had water soluble ink.
For surcharges see Nos. 116-120, 139.

Queen Wilhelmina — A17

1923, Oct. 5 Perf. 11, 11x11½, 11½

109	A17	5c green		1.10	.70
110	A17	10c car rose		1.75	1.50
111	A17	20c indigo		3.50	3.00
112	A17	50c brown org		19.00	19.00
113	A17	1g brown vio		26.00	17.00
114	A17	2½g gray blk		75.00	200.00
115	A17	5g brown		100.00	240.00
		Nos. 109-115 (7)		226.35	481.20

25th anniv. of the assumption of the government of the Netherlands by Queen Wilhelmina, at age 18.
Values for Nos. 114-115 used are for stamps with postmarks clearly dated before July 15, 1924.

Nos. 83, 93-94, 98 Surcharged in Black or Red

j

k

m

15

1925, Dec. 19 Typo. Perf. 12½

116	A14	3c on 5c green		1.10	1.10
117	A15	10c on 12½c red		2.25	2.25
118	A15	15c on 12½c blue (R)		1.60	1.60
119	A15	15c on 20c blue		1.60	1.60
		Nos. 116-119 (4)		6.55	6.55

No. 100 Surcharged in Blue

1926, Jan. 1

120	A15	12½c on 22½c org		27.50	27.50

Postage Due Stamps Nos. J14 and J29 Surcharged in Blue or Black

o · p

121	D2(o)	12½c on 40c (Bl)		3.25	3.25
122	D2(p)	12½c on 40c (Bk)		30.00	30.00
		Nos. 120-122 (3)		60.75	60.75

No. 121 issued without gum.

Queen Wilhelmina — A21

1927-30 Engr. Perf. 11½

123	A21	10c carmine		1.00	.40
124	A21	12½c red orange		1.75	1.90
125	A21	15c dark blue		2.00	.60
126	A21	20c indigo		2.00	.80
127	A21	21c dk brown ('30)		19.00	19.00
128	A21	22½c brown ('28)		8.00	9.75
129	A21	25c dk violet		3.00	.70
130	A21	30c dk green		3.00	1.10
131	A21	35c black brown		3.00	3.00
		Nos. 123-131 (9)		42.75	37.25

Types of Netherlands Marine Insurance Stamps Inscribed "SURINAME" and Surcharged

1927, Oct. 26

132	MI1	3c on 15c dk grn		.65	.65
133	MI1	10c on 60c car rose		.65	.65
134	MI1	12½c on 75c gray brn		.65	.65
135	MI2	15c on 1.50 dk blue		2.75	2.75
136	MI2	25c on 2.25g org brn		7.25	7.25
137	MI3	30c on 4½g black		9.00	7.25
138	MI3	50c on 7½g red		7.25	7.25
		Nos. 132-138 (7)		28.20	26.45

Nos. 135-137 have "FRANKEERZEGEL" in small capitals in one line. Nos. 135 and 136 have a heavy bar across the top of the stamp.

No. 88 Surcharged

1930, Mar. 1 Typo. Perf. 12½

139	A14	6c on 7½c orange		1.90	1.00

Prince William I (Portrait by Van Key) — A22

1933, Apr. 24 Photo.

141	A22	6c deep orange		6.75	1.90

400th birth anniv. of Prince William I, Count of Nassau and Prince of Orange, frequently referred to as William the Silent.

Van Walbeeck's Ship
A23

Queen Wilhelmina
A24

1936-41 Litho. Perf. 13½x12½

142	A23	½c yellow brn		.30	.30
143	A23	1c lt yellow grn		.40	.25
144	A23	1½c brt blue		.55	.40
145	A23	2c black brown		.60	.25
146	A23	2½c green		.25	.25
a.		Perf. 13 ('41)		9.00	3.25
147	A23	3c dark ultra		.60	.40
148	A23	4c orange		.60	.75
149	A23	5c gray		.60	.25
150	A23	6c red		2.50	2.00
151	A23	7½c red violet		.25	.25
a.		7½c plum, perf. 13 ('41)		3.00	.25

Engr.
Perf. 14, 12½
Size: 20x30mm

152	A24	10c vermilion		.85	.25
a.		Perf. 12½ ('39)		60.00	11.50
153	A24	12½c dull green		3.50	1.25
154	A24	15c dark blue		1.25	.60
155	A24	20c yellow org		2.10	.60
156	A24	21c dk gray		3.25	3.00
a.		Perf. 12½ ('39)		3.75	3.75
157	A24	25c brown lake		2.40	1.00
158	A24	30c brown vio		3.75	1.00
159	A24	35c olive brown		4.00	4.00

Perf. 12½x14
Size: 22x33mm

160	A24	50c dull yel grn		4.00	2.00
161	A24	1g dull blue		8.25	3.00
162	A24	1.50g black brown		22.50	18.00
163	A24	2.50g rose lake		13.50	9.50
		Nos. 142-163 (22)		76.00	49.30

For surcharges see Nos. 181-183, B37-B40.

Queen
Wilhelmina — A25

Perf. 12½x12
1938, Aug. 30   Photo.   Wmk. 202
164	A25	2c dull purple	.50	.30
165	A25	7½c red orange	1.50	1.25
166	A25	15c royal blue	3.00	3.00
		Nos. 164-166 (3)	5.00	4.55

Reign of Queen Wilhelmina, 40th anniv.

> Catalogue values for unused stamps in this section, from this point to the end of the section, are for Never Hinged items.

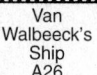

Van Walbeeck's Ship A26

Queen Wilhelmina A27

1941   Unwmk.   Typo.   Perf. 12
168	A26	1c lt yellow grn	1.00	.25
169	A26	2c black brown	2.50	2.50

Type A26 is similar to type A23 except for the white side frame lines which extend to the base.
For surcharges see No. 180.

1941-46   Photo.   Perf. 13½x12½
Size: 18x22½mm
174	A27	12½c royal blue ('46)	1.50	.25

Perf. 12½
175	A27	15c ultra	22.50	8.25

Royal Family — A28

1943, Nov. 2   Engr.   Perf. 13½x13
176	A28	2½c deep orange	.25	.35
177	A28	7½c red	.25	.25
178	A28	15c black	2.75	2.25
179	A28	40c deep blue	3.25	2.75
		Nos. 176-179 (4)	6.50	5.60

Birth of Princess Margriet Francisca of the Netherlands.

Nos. 168, 151, 152 Surcharged with New Values and Bars in Black
1945   Unwmk.   Perf. 13, 14, 12
180	A26	½c on 1c	.25	.25
181	A23	2½c on 7½c	3.50	3.00
182	A24	5c on 10c	1.25	.70
183	A24	7½c on 10c	1.50	.70
a.		Double surcharge	225.00	190.00
		Nos. 180-183 (4)	6.50	4.65

Bauxite Mine, Moengo A29

Queen Wilhelmina
A30   A31

Designs: 1½c, Bush Negroes on Cottica River near Moengo. 2c, Waterfall in interior. 2½c, Road scene, Coronie District. 3c, Surinam River near Berg en Dahl Plantation. 4c, Government Square, Paramaribo. 5c, Mining gold. 6c, Street in Paramaribo. 7½c, Sugar cane train.

1945, Nov. 5   Engr.   Perf. 12
184	A29	1c rose carmine	.25	.25
185	A29	1½c rose lake	1.25	1.25
186	A29	2c violet	.55	.40
187	A29	2½c olive brn	.55	.40
188	A29	3c dull green	1.25	.70
189	A29	4c brown	1.25	.75
190	A29	5c blue	1.25	.25
191	A29	6c olive	2.25	1.60
192	A29	7½c deep orange	.80	.35
193	A30	10c blue	1.60	.25
194	A30	15c brown	2.00	.25
195	A30	20c dull green	3.25	.25
196	A30	22½c gray	3.75	.90
197	A30	25c carmine	10.00	4.50
198	A30	30c olive green	10.00	.55
199	A30	35c brt blue grn	17.00	7.25
200	A30	40c rose lake	9.75	.25
201	A30	50c red orange	9.75	.25
202	A30	60c violet	9.75	.80
203	A31	1g red brown	12.00	.35
204	A31	1.50g lilac	10.00	.80
205	A31	2.50g olive brn	20.00	.95
206	A31	5g rose carmine	45.00	12.50
207	A31	10g red orange	77.50	19.00
		Nos. 184-207 (24)	250.75	54.80

For surcharges see #240, B41-B46, CB2-CB3.

Nos. 151 and 152 Surcharged with New Value and Bar in Blue or Black
1947   Perf. 13½x12½, 14
209	A23	1½(c) on 7½c (Bl)	.25	.25
a.		Double surcharge	200.00	
210	A24	2½c on 10c (Bk)	1.75	.50

Numeral A32

Queen Wilhelmina A33

Perf. 12½x13½
1948, July 21   Unwmk.   Photo.
211	A32	1c dark red	.25	.25
212	A32	1½c plum	.25	.25
213	A32	2c purple	.25	.25
214	A32	2½c olive grn	1.50	.25
215	A32	3c dark green	.25	.25
216	A32	4c red brown	.25	.25

Perf. 13½x12½
217	A33	5c deep blue	.40	.25
218	A33	6c dark olive	1.00	.75
219	A33	7½c scarlet	.40	.25
220	A33	10c blue	.60	.25
221	A33	12½c dark blue	1.25	1.25
222	A33	15c henna brown	1.75	.45
223	A33	17½c dk vio brn	1.90	1.50
224	A33	20c dk blue grn	1.60	.25
225	A33	22½c slate blue	1.60	.75
226	A33	25c crimson	1.60	.35
227	A33	27½c car lake	1.60	.25
228	A33	30c olive green	1.90	.25
229	A33	37½c olive brn	3.25	2.25
230	A33	40c lilac rose	2.25	.35
231	A33	50c red orange	2.25	.35
232	A33	60c purple	2.50	.45
233	A33	70c black	3.00	.75
		Nos. 211-233 (23)	31.60	12.20

See Nos. 241-242.

Wilhelmina - Juliana
A34   A35

1948, Aug. 30   Engr.   Perf. 12½x14
234	A34	7½c vermilion	1.10	1.10
235	A34	12½c deep blue	1.10	1.10

Reign of Queen Wilhelmina, 50th anniv.

Perf. 14x13
1948, Sept. 10   Wmk. 202   Photo.
236	A35	7½c deep orange	3.50	3.50
237	A35	12½c ultra	3.50	3.50

Investiture of Queen Juliana, Sept. 6, 1948.
For surcharges see Nos. B53-B54.

Post Horns Entwined — A36

1949, Oct. 1   Unwmk.   Perf. 11½x12
238	A36	7½c brown red	7.00	3.75
239	A36	27½c dull blue	7.00	2.75

UPU, 75th anniversary.

No. 192 Surcharged with New Value, Square and Bar in Black
1950, Aug. 9   Perf. 12
240	A29	1c on 7½c dp org	.60	.60

Numeral Type of 1948
1951, Apr. 5   Perf. 12½x13½
241	A32	5c deep blue	1.75	.25
242	A32	7½c deep orange	4.25	2.25

A37

Queen Juliana — A38

1951, Apr. 5   Perf. 13½x13
243	A37	10c blue	.45	.25
244	A37	15c henna brn	1.00	.25
245	A37	20c dk blue grn	2.40	.25
246	A37	25c crimson	1.50	.40
247	A37	27½c carmine lake	1.50	.25
248	A37	30c olive green	1.50	.40
249	A37	35c olive brown	1.90	1.60
250	A37	40c lilac rose	2.10	.40
251	A37	50c red orange	2.50	.45

Engr.
Perf. 12½x12
252	A38	1g red brown	27.50	.50
		Nos. 243-252 (10)	42.35	4.75

For surcharge see No. 271.

Shooting Fish
A39

Fisherman
A40

Designs: 5c, Bauxite mining. 6c, Log raft. 7½c, Plowing with Water Buffalo. 10c, Woman picking fruit. 12½c, Armored catfish. 15c, Macaw. 17½c, Armadillo. 20c, Poling canoe. 25c, Common iguana.

1953-55   Photo.   Perf. 14x13, 13x14
253	A39	2c olive green	.25	.25
254	A40	2½c blue green	.30	.25
255	A40	5c gray	.50	.25
256	A40	6c bright blue	2.50	1.75
257	A40	7½c purple	.25	.25
258	A40	10c bright red	.25	.25
259	A40	12½c dk gray blue	3.25	2.10
260	A40	15c crimson	1.10	.25
261	A40	17½c red brown	5.00	3.00
262	A40	20c Prus green	.90	.25
263	A40	25c olive green	4.50	1.25
a.		Min. sheet of 4, #259-261, 263	90.00	90.00
		Nos. 253-263 (11)	18.80	9.85

Issued: 2c, 7½c, 10c, 20c, 5/9/53; #263a, 2/14/55; others, 12/1/54.

Queen Juliana — A41

1954, Dec. 15   Perf. 13½
264	A41	7½c dark red brown	.90	.90

Charter of the Kingdom, adopted Dec. 15, 1954.

Harvesting Bananas — A46

Designs: 7½c, Pounding rice. 10c, Preparing cassava. 15c, Fishing.

1955, May 12   Perf. 14x13
265	A46	2c dark green	2.10	2.10
266	A46	7½c dull yellow	3.25	3.00
267	A46	10c orange brown	3.25	3.00
268	A46	15c ultra	3.25	3.00
		Nos. 265-268 (4)	11.85	11.10

4th anniv. of the establishment of the Caribbean Tourist Assoc.

Globe and Mercury's Rod
A47

Flags and Map of Caribbean
A48

1955, Sept. 19   Unwmk.   Perf. 13x12
269	A47	5c bright ultra	.50	.45

Paramaribo Trade Fair, Oct. 1955.

1956, Dec. 6   Litho.   Perf. 13x14
270	A48	10c lt blue & red	.40	.35

10th anniv. of Caribbean Commission.

No. 247 Surcharged

1958, Nov. 11   Photo.   Perf. 13½x13
271	A37	8c on 27½c car lake	.25	.25

Queen Juliana — A49

Symbolic Flowers — A50

Perf. 12½x12

1959, Oct. 15   Unwmk.   Litho.
272 A49 1g magenta   2.00 .25
273 A49 1.50g olive bister   3.25 .80
274 A49 2.50g dk carmine   4.75 .50
275 A49 5g dull blue   9.00 .50
       Nos. 272-275 (4)   19.00 2.05

1959, Dec. 15   Photo.   Perf. 12½x13
276 A50 20c multicolored   3.75 2.75

5th anniv. of the constitution. Flowers in design symbolize Netherlands, Surinam and Netherlands Antilles.

Charles Lindbergh's Plane — A51

10c, De Snip plane. 15c, Cessna 170B. 20c, Super Constellation. 40c, Boeing 707 Jet.

1960, Mar. 12   Perf. 12½
277 A51 8c chalky blue   1.25 1.40
278 A51 10c bright green   1.75 2.00
279 A51 15c rose red   1.75 2.00
280 A51 20c pale violet   2.00 2.40
281 A51 40c light brown   3.00 3.25
       Nos. 277-281 (5)   9.75 11.05

Inauguration of Zanderij Airport, Mar. 12. Nos. 277-281 show 25 years of Surinam's civil aviation.

Flag of Surinam and Map — A52

Arms of Surinam — A53

1960, July 1   Litho.   Perf. 12½x13
282 A52 10c multicolored   .70 .70

Perf. 13x12½
283 A53 15c multicolored   .70 .70

Day of Freedom, July 1.

Bananas — A54

1961, Mar. 1   Litho.   Perf. 13½
284 A54 1c shown   .25 .25
285 A54 2c Citrus fruit   .25 .25
286 A54 3c Cacao   .25 .25
287 A54 4c Sugar cane   .25 .25

288 A54 5c Coffee   .25 .25
289 A54 6c Coconuts   .25 .25
290 A54 8c Rice   .25 .25
       Nos. 284-290 (7)   1.75 1.75

Finance Building — A55

Buildings: 15c, Court of Justice. 20c, Concordia Lodge (Masons). 25c, Neve Shalom Synagogue, Paramaribo, horiz. 30c, Old Dutch lock in New Amsterdam. 35c, Government office, horiz. 40c, Governor's palace, horiz. 50c, Legislative Council, horiz. 60c, Old Dutch Reformed Church, horiz. 70c, Zeelandia Fortress, horiz.

1961   Perf. 13½x14, 14x13½
291 A55 10c multi   .25 .25
292 A55 15c multi   .25 .25
293 A55 20c multi   .30 .30
294 A55 25c multi   .65 .65
295 A55 30c multi   1.75 1.75
296 A55 35c multi   1.75 1.75
297 A55 40c multi   .90 .90
298 A55 50c multi   .90 .90
299 A55 60c multi   1.00 1.00
300 A55 70c multi   1.10 1.10
       Nos. 291-300 (10)   8.85 8.85

Issued: 10c, 20c, 25c, 50c, 70c, 4/1; others, 5/15.

Dag Hammarskjold (1905-1961) A56

1962, Jan. 2 Litho. Perf. 11½, 12½
301 A56 10c brt blue & blk   .30 .30
302 A56 20c lilac & blk   .30 .30

Dag Hammarskjold, Secretary General of the United Nations, 1953-61.
Sheets of both perfs. exist either with or without extension of perforations through the margins.

A56a

1962, Feb. 1   Photo.   Perf. 14x13
303 A56a 20c olive green   .50 .50

Silver wedding anniversary of Queen Juliana and Prince Bernhard.

A57

Malaria eradication emblem.

1962, May 2   Litho.   Perf. 13x14
304 A57 8c bright red   .30 .30
305 A57 10c blue   .30 .30

WHO drive to eradicate malaria.

Stoelmans Guesthouse — A58

Design: 15c, Torarica Hotel.

1962, July 4   Perf. 14x13½
306 A58 10c multicolored   .50 .50
307 A58 15c multicolored   .50 .50

Opening of the Torarica Hotel in Paramaribo and Stoelmans Guesthouse on Stoelman Island.

Deaconess Residence and Recreation Area — A59

Design: 20c, Deaconess Hospital.

1962, Nov. 30
308 A59 10c multicolored   .50 .50
309 A59 20c multicolored   .50 .50

Hands Holding Wheat Emblem A60

20c, Farmer harvesting & wheat emblem, vert.

Perf. 14x13, 13x14
1963, Mar. 21   Photo.
310 A60 10c deep carmine   .30 .30
311 A60 20c dark blue   .30 .30

FAO "Freedom from Hunger" campaign.

Broken Chain — A61

1963, June 28   Litho.   Perf. 14x13
312 A61 10c red & blk   .30 .30
313 A61 20c green & blk   .30 .30

Centenary of emancipation of the slaves.

Prince William of Orange Landing at Scheveningen A61a

Faja Lobbi Wreath A62

1963, Nov. 21   Photo.   Perf. 13½x14
Size: 26x26mm
314 A61a 10c dull bl, blk & brn .30 .30

Founding of the Kingdom of the Netherlands, 150th anniv.

1964, Dec. 15   Litho.   Perf. 12½x13
315 A62 25c multicolored   .40 .40

Charter of the Kingdom of the Netherlands, 10th anniv.

Abraham Lincoln (1809-1865) — A63

1965, Apr. 14 Litho. Perf. 12½x13
316 A63 25c olive bister & brn .30 .30

ICY Emblem A64

1965, May 26   Perf. 13x12½
317 A64 10c orange & blue   .30 .30
318 A64 15c red & violet bl   .30 .30

International Cooperation Year.

Bauxite Mine, Moengo A65

Designs: 15c, Alum Pottery Works, Paranam. 20c, Hydroelectric plant, Afobaka. 25c, Aluminum smeltery, Paranam.

1965, Oct. 9   Photo.   Unwmk.
319 A65 10c ocher   .55 .55
320 A65 15c dark green   .55 .55
321 A65 20c dark blue   .55 .55
322 A65 25c carmine   .55 .55
       Nos. 319-322 (4)   2.20 2.20

Opening of the Brokopondo Power Station.

Red-breasted Blackbird — A66

2c, Great kiskadee. 3c, Silver-beaked tanager. 4c, Ruddy ground dove. 5c, Blue-gray tanager. 6c, Glittering-throated emerald (hummingbird). 8c, Turquoise tanager. 10c, Pale-breasted robin.

1966, Feb. 16   Litho.   Perf. 13x14
323 A66 1c brt grn, blk & red .50 .50
324 A66 2c lt ultra, yel & brn .50 .50
325 A66 3c multi   .50 .50
326 A66 4c lt ol grn, red brn & blk .50 .50
327 A66 5c org, ultra & blk   .50 .50
328 A66 6c multi   .50 .50
329 A66 8c gray, vio bl & blk .50 .50
330 A66 10c multi   .50 .50
       Nos. 323-330 (8)   4.00 4.00

Central Hospital A67

Design: 15c, Hospital, side view.

1966, Mar. 9   Litho.   Perf. 13x12½
331 A67 10c multi   .60 .60
332 A67 15c multi   .60 .60

Opening of Central Hospital, Paramaribo.

Father Petrus
Donders — A68

Designs: 10c, Church and parsonage,
Batavia. 15c, Msgr. Joannes B. Swinkels.
25c, Cathedral, Paramaribo.

1966, Mar. 26 Photo. Perf. 12½x13
333 A68 4c org brn & blk   .25 .25
334 A68 10c rose brn & blk   .25 .25
335 A68 15c yel brn & blk   .25 .25
336 A68 25c lt vio & blk   .25 .25
    Nos. 333-336 (4)   1.00 1.00

Centenary of the Redemptorist Mission in
Surinam (Congregation of the Most Holy
Redeemer).

100-Year-Old
Tree — A69

1966, May 9 Litho. Perf. 13x12½
337 A69 25c grn, dp org & blk   .60 .60
338 A69 30c red org, grn & blk   .60 .60

Centenary of the Surinam Parliament.

Television
Transmitter, Eye and
Globe — A70

1966, Oct. 20 Litho. Perf. 12½x13
339 A70 25c dk bl & ver   .60 .60
340 A70 30c brn & ver   .60 .60

Inauguration of television service.

Bauxite
Industry,
1916 — A71

Design: 25c, Bauxite industry, 1966.

1966, Dec. 19 Litho. Perf. 13x12½
341 A71 20c yel, org & blk   .60 .60
342 A71 25c org, bl & blk   .60 .60

50th anniversary of bauxite industry.

Central
Bank,
Paramaribo
A72

Design: 25c, Central Bank, different view.

1967, Apr. 1 Litho. Perf. 13x12½
343 A72 10c dp yel & blk   .30 .30
344 A72 25c lil & blk   .30 .30

Central Bank of Surinam, 10th anniv.

Amelia
Earhart,
Lockheed
Electra and
Paramaribo
A73

Siva Nataraja, God of
Dance, and
Ballerina's
Foot — A74

Design: 25c, Drummer's mask "Bashi Lele,"
and scroll of violin.

1967, June 3 Photo. Perf. 13x12½
345 A73 20c yel & dk car   .40 .40
346 A73 25c yel & grn   .40 .40

30th anniv. of Amelia Earhart's visit to Surinam, June 3-4, 1937.

1967, June 21 Litho. Perf. 12½x13
347 A74 10c yel grn & bl   .30 .30
348 A74 25c yel grn & brn   .30 .30

20th anniv. of the Surinam Cultural Center
Foundation.

New Amsterdam, 1660 (New York
City) — A75

Designs after 17th Century Engravings: 10c,
Fort Zeelandia, Paramaribo, 1670. 25c, Breda
Castle, Netherlands, 1667.

1967, July 31 Litho. Perf. 13½x13
349 A75 10c yel, blk & bl   .40 .40
350 A75 20c red brn, yel & blk   .40 .40
351 A75 25c bl grn, yel & blk   .40 .40
    Nos. 349-351 (3)   1.20 1.20

300th anniv. of the Treaty of Breda between
Britain, France and the Netherlands.

WHO
Emblem
A76

1968, Apr. 7 Litho. Perf. 13x12½
352 A76 10c magenta & dk bl   .25 .25
353 A76 25c bl & dk pur   .50 .50

WHO, 20th anniversary.

Chandelier
and
Christian
Symbols
A77

15c, like 10c, reversed. Brass chandelier
from the Reformed Church, Paramaribo.

1968, May 29 Litho. Perf. 13x12½
354 A77 10c dark blue   .25 .25
355 A77 25c dp yel grn   .50 .50

Reformed Church of Paramaribo, 300th
anniv.

Missionary
Store,
1768 — A78

Designs: 25c, Main Church and store, Paramaribo, 1868. 30c, C. Kersten & Co., 1968.

1968, June 29 Litho. Perf. 13x12½
356 A78 10c yel & blk   .30 .30
357 A78 25c lt grnsh bl & blk   .30 .30
358 A78 30c lilac rose & bl   .30 .30
    Nos. 356-358 (3)   .90 .90

200th anniv. of C. Kersten & Co., which is
partially owned by the Evangelical Brotherhood Missionary Society.

Joden Savanne   Mahatma
Synagogue   Gandhi
A79   A81

Spectacled
Caiman
A80

Designs: 20c, Map of Joden Savanne and
Surinam River. 30c, Gravestone, 1733. The
Hebrew inscriptions are quotations from the
Bible: 20c, Joshua 24:2; 25c, Isaiah 56:7; 30c,
Genesis 31:52.

1968, Aug. 28 Perf. 12½x13
359 A79 20c multi   .35 .35
360 A79 25c multi   .50 .50
361 A79 30c multi   .50 .50
    Nos. 359-361 (3)   1.35 1.35

Founding of the first synagogue in the Western Hemisphere in 1685 in Joden Savanne,
Surinam.

Perf. 13x12½, 12½x13
1969, Aug. 20 Litho.
20c, Squirrel monkey, vert. 25c, Armadillo.
362 A80 10c grn & multi   .90 .90
363 A80 20c bl gray & multi   .90 .75
364 A80 25c vio & multi   .90 .75
    Nos. 362-364 (3)   2.70 2.25

1969, Oct. 2 Litho. Perf. 12½x13
365 A81 25c red & blk   1.00 1.00

Mohandas K. Gandhi (1869-1948), leader in
India's fight for independence.

ILO Emblem
A82

1969, Oct. 29 Litho. Perf. 12½x13
366 A82 10c brt bl grn & blk   .25 .25
367 A82 25c red & blk   .40 .40

ILO, 50th anniversary.

Queen Juliana
and Rising
Sun — A82a

1969, Dec. 15 Photo. Perf. 14x13
368 A82a 25c blue & multi   .50 .50

15th anniv. of the Charter of the Kingdom of
the Netherlands. Phosphorescent paper.

"1950-1970"
A83

1970, Apr. 3 Litho. Perf. 13x12½
369 A83 10c brn, grn & org   .25 .25
370 A83 25c emer, dk bl & org   .40 .40

20th anniv. of secondary education in
Surinam.

Inauguration of UPU Headquarters,
Bern — A84

Design: 25c, UPU Headquarters, sideview
and UPU emblem.

1970, May 20 Litho. Perf. 13x12½
371 A84 10c sky bl & dk pur   .25 .25
372 A84 25c red & blk   .50 .50

"UNO"   Plane over
A85   Paramaribo
               A86

1970, June 26 Litho. Perf. 12½x13
373 A85 10c ocher & yel   .25 .25
374 A85 25c dp bl & ultra   .50 .50

25th anniversary of the United Nations.

1970, July 15
Designs: 20c, Plane over map of Totness,
25c, Plane over Nieuw-Nickerie.
375 A86 10c bl, vio bl & gray   .40 .40
376 A86 20c yel, red & gray   .40 .40
377 A86 25c pink, dk red & gray .40 .40
    Nos. 375-377 (3)   1.20 1.20

40th anniv. of domestic airmail service.

Plan of Soccer Field
and Ball — A87

Plan of soccer field with ball in different
positions.

1970, Oct. 1
378 A87 4c yel, red brn & blk   .25 .25
379 A87 10c pale lem, red brn &
        blk   .25 .25
380 A87 15c lt yel grn, red brn &
        blk   .25 .25
381 A87 25c lt grn, red brn & blk .65 .65
    Nos. 378-381 (4)   1.40 1.40

50th anniv. of the Soccer Assoc. of Surinam.

Cocoi Heron
A88

Birds in Flight: 20c, Flamingo. 25c, Scarlet
macaw.

1971, Feb. 14 Litho. Perf. 13x12½
382 A88 15c gray & multi   .75 .75
383 A88 20c ultra & multi   .75 .75
384 A88 25c pale grn & multi   .75 .75
    Nos. 382-384 (3)   2.25 2.25

25th anniversary of regular air service
between the Netherlands, Surinam and
Netherlands Antilles.

Morse Key — A89

Designs: 20c, Telephone. 25c, Lunar landing module, telescope.

1971, May 17 Photo. Perf. 12½x13
385 A89 15c light green & multi .45 .40
386 A89 20c blue & multi .55 .55
387 A89 25c lilac & multi .75 .60
　Nos. 385-387 (3) 1.75 1.55

3rd World Telecommunications Day.

Prince Bernhard, Fokker F27, Boeing 747B — A89a

Map of Surinam, Population Chart — A90

1971, June 29 Photo. Perf. 13x14
388 A89a 25c multi .60 .50

60th birthday of Prince Bernhard.

1971, July 31 Litho. Perf. 12½x13

Design: 30c, Map of Surinam and individual representing population.

389 A90 15c gray bl, blk & ver .25 .25
390 A90 30c ver, gray bl & blk .50 .50

50th anniv. of the first census; introduction of civil registration in Surinam.

William Mogge's Map of Surinam A91

1971, Oct. 27 Perf. 11½x11
391 A91 30c dull yel & dk brn .80 .85

300th anniv. of the first map of Surinam.

Map of Albina A92

August Kappler — A93

Drop of Water — A94

20c, View of Albina from Maroni River.

1971, Dec. 13 Perf. 13x12½, 12½x13
392 A92 15c sapphire & blk .55 .55
393 A92 20c brt grn & blk .60 .60
394 A93 25c yel & blk .60 .60
　Nos. 392-394 (3) 1.75 1.75

125th anniv. of the founding of Albina by August Kappler (1815-1887).

1972, Feb. 2 Perf. 12½x13

Design: 30c, Faucet and water tower.
395 A94 15c vio & blk .60 .60
396 A94 30c bl & blk .75 .75

Surinam water works, 40th anniversary.

Air Mail Envelope A95

1972, Aug. 2 Litho. Perf. 13x12½
397 A95 15c red & blue .25 .25
398 A95 30c blue & red .50 .50

Arrival of the 1st airmail in Surinam, carried by Capt. Dutertre from French Guiana, 50th anniv.

Giant Tree — A96

Hindu Woman in Rice Field — A97

Designs: 20c, Wood transport by air lift. 30c, Hands tending seedling.

1972, Dec. 20 Photo. Perf. 12½x13
399 A96 15c yel & dk brn .25 .25
400 A96 20c bl & dp brn .25 .25
401 A96 30c brt grn & dp brn .95 .95
　Nos. 399-401 (3) 1.45 1.45

Surinam Forestry Commission, 25th anniv.

1973, June 5 Litho. Perf. 13½x14

25c, J. F. A. Cateau van Rosevelt with map of Surinam, ship "Lalla Rookh." 30c, Symbolic bird, flower, sun, flag, factories.

402 A97 15c purple & yel .45 .45
403 A97 25c maroon & gray .45 .45
404 A97 30c yel & light blue .50 .50
　Nos. 402-404 (3) 1.40 1.20

1st immigrants from India, cent.

Queen Juliana, Surinam and House of Orange Colors A97a

Engr. & Photo.
1973, Sept. 4 Perf. 12½x12
405 A97a 30c sil, blk & org .80 .80

25th anniversary of reign of Queen Juliana.

INTERPOL Emblem — A98

Mailman — A99

Design: 30c, INTERPOL emblem, Surinam visa handstamp.

1973, Nov. 7 Litho. Perf. 14x14½
406 A98 15c vio bl & multi .25 .25
407 A98 30c lt bl, lil & blk .80 .80

50th anniv. of Intl. Criminal Police Org.

1973, Dec. 12 Litho. Perf. 12½x13

15c, Pigeons carrying Letters. 30c, Map of Surinam, plane, ship, train and truck.

408 A99 15c lt yel grn & bl .25 .25
409 A99 25c sal, blk & bl .35 .35
410 A99 30c ver & multi .60 .60
　Nos. 408-410 (3) 1.20 1.20

Centenary of stamps of Surinam.

Patient and Blood Transfusion A100

30c, Cross section of tissue and oscilloscope.

1974, June 1 Litho. Perf. 14½x14
411 A100 15c red brn & multi .25 .25
412 A100 30c lemon & multi .50 .50

75th anniversary of the Medical College.

Crop Dusting A101

1974, July 17 Litho. Perf. 13½
413 A101 15c shown .25 .25
414 A101 30c Fertilizer plant .50 .50

Foundation for Development of Mechanical Agriculture in Surinam, 25th anniv.

Old Title Page — A102

1974, July 31 Perf. 14x14½
415 A102 15c multicolored .25 .25
416 A102 30c multicolored .50 .50

"Weekly Wednesday Surinam Newspaper," bicent. 1st editor was Beeldsnijder Matroos.

Paramaribo Main Post Office A103

Design: 30c, Post Office, different view.

1974, Sept. 11 Litho. Perf. 14½x14
417 A103 15c brown & blk .25 .25
418 A103 30c blue & blk .70 .70

Centenary of Universal Postal Union.

Gold Panner A104

Design: 30c, Modern excavator.

1975, Feb. 5 Litho. Perf. 13x12½
419 A104 15c brown & olive bis .25 .25
420 A104 30c vermilion & maroon .80 .80

Centenary of prospecting policy granting concessions for winning of raw materials.

Symbolic Design A105

1975, June 25 Litho. Perf. 13x12½
421 A105 15c green & multi .55 .55
422 A105 25c blue & multi .60 .60
423 A105 30c red & multi .60 .60
　Nos. 421-423 (3) 1.75 1.75

Cent. of Intl. Meter Convention, Paris, 1875.

Hands Holding Saw — A106

Designs: 50c, Book with notes and letter "a." 75c, Hands holding ball.

1975, Nov. 25 Litho. Perf. 13½x14
424 A106 25c yellow, red & brn .60 .60
425 A106 50c yellow, red & pur 1.40 1.40
426 A106 75c dk bl, org & emer 2.00 2.00
　Nos. 424-426 (3) 4.00 4.00

Independence. Sheets of 10 (5x2) with ornamental margins.

Oncidium Lanceanum A107

Central Bank, Paramaribo A109

Orchids: 2c, Epidendrum stenopetalum. 3c, Brassia lanceana. 4c, Epidendrum ibaguense. 5c, Epidendrum fragrans.

1975-76 Litho. Perf. 14½x13½
427 A107 1c multicolored .35 .35
428 A107 2c multicolored .35 .35
429 A107 3c multicolored .35 .35
430 A107 4c multicolored .35 .35
431 A107 5c multicolored .35 .35
Perf. 14x13½
436 A109 1g rose lil & blk 1.75 .35
437 A109 1½g brn, dp org & blk 3.00 .35
438 A109 2½g red brn, org red & blk 4.50 .35
439 A109 5g grn, yel grn & blk 8.50 .35
440 A109 10g dk vio bl & blk 19.00 .95
　Nos. 427-431,436-440 (10) 38.50 4.10

Issued: #436-439, Nov. 25, 1975; #427-431, Feb. 18, 1976; #440, May 5, 1976.
For surcharges see Nos. 772-774, 810.

Flag of Surinam — A110

Design: 35c, Coat of Arms.

1976, Mar. 3 Perf. 14x13½
445 A110 25c emerald & multi .65 .65
446 A110 35c red orange & multi .85 .85

Sheets of 12 (6x2) with ornamental margins.

Pomacanthus Semicirculatus — A111

Fish: 2c, Adioryx diadema. 3c, Pogonoculius zebra. 4c, Balistes vetula. 5c, Myripristis jacobus.

1976, June 2   Litho.   Perf. 12½x13

447	A111	1c multicolored	.25	.25
448	A111	2c multicolored	.25	.25
449	A111	3c multicolored	.25	.25
450	A111	4c multicolored	.25	.25
451	A111	5c multicolored	.25	.25
	Nos. 447-451,C55-C57 (8)		6.75	4.10

See #471-475, 504-508, C72-C74, C85-C87.

19th Century Switchboard and
Telephone — A112

35c, Satellite, globe and 1976 telephone.

1976, Aug. 5   Litho.   Perf. 13½x14

452	A112	20c yellow & multi	.45	.45
453	A112	35c ultra & multi	.90	.90

Centenary of first telephone call by Alexander Graham Bell, Mar. 10, 1876.

The Story of Anansi Tori, by A.
Baag — A113

Designs: 30c, "Surinam Now" (young people), by R. Chang. 35c, Lamentation, by Nola Hatterman, vert. 50c, Chess Players, by Q. Jan Telting.

Perf. 13½x14, 14x13½

1976, Sept. 29   Photo.

454	A113	20c multicolored	.40	.40
455	A113	30c multicolored	.70	.60
456	A113	30c multicolored	.90	.70
457	A113	50c multicolored	1.25	1.25
	Nos. 454-457 (4)		3.25	2.95

Paintings by Surinam artists.

Franklin's Divided Snake Poster,
1754 — A114

1976, Nov. 10   Litho.   Perf. 13½x14

458	A114	20c green & blk	.65	.65
459	A114	60c orange & blk	2.10	2.10

American Bicentennial.

Ionopsis
Utricularioides
A115

Orchids: 30c, Rodiguezia secunda. 35c, Oncidium pusillum. 55c, Sobralia sessilis. 60c, Octomeria surinamensis.

1977, Jan. 19   Litho.   Perf. 14½x13½

460	A115	20c vermilion & multi	.45	.25
461	A115	30c ultra & multi	.65	.25
462	A115	35c magenta & multi	.65	.50
463	A115	55c yellow & multi	1.25	.90
464	A115	60c green & multi	1.25	1.00
	Nos. 460-464 (5)		4.25	2.90

Surinam
Costume
A116

Various Surinamese women's costumes.

1977, Mar. 2   Litho.   Perf. 14x13½

465	A116	10c brt blue & multi	.35	.35
466	A116	15c green & multi	.35	.35
467	A116	35c violet & multi	.45	.45
468	A116	60c orange & multi	1.00	1.00
469	A116	75c ultra & multi	1.25	1.25
470	A116	1g yellow & multi	1.60	1.60
	Nos. 465-470 (6)		5.00	5.00

Fish Type of 1976

Tropical Fish: 1c, Liopropoma carmabi. 2c, Holacanthus ciliaris. 3c, Opistognathus aurifrons. 4c, Anisotremus virginicus. 5c, Gramma loreto.

1977, June 8   Litho.   Perf. 13x13½

471	A111	1c multicolored	.25	.25
472	A111	2c multicolored	.25	.25
473	A111	3c multicolored	.25	.25
474	A111	4c multicolored	.25	.25
475	A111	5c multicolored	.25	.25
	Nos. 471-475,C72-C74 (8)		6.50	5.05

Edison's Phonograph, 1877 — A117

Design: 60c, Modern turntable.

1977, Aug. 24   Litho.   Perf. 13½x14

476	A117	20c multicolored	.35	.35
477	A117	60c multicolored	.85	.85

Invention of the phonograph, cent.

Packet
Curacao,
1827
A118

Designs: 15c, Hellevoetsluis Harbor and postmark, 1827. 30c, Sea chart and technical details of packet Curacao. 35c, Logbook and compass rose. 60c, Map of Paramaribo harbor and 1852 postmark. 95c, Modern liner Stuyvesant.

1977, Sept. 28   Litho.   Perf. 14x13½

478	A118	5c grnsh bl & dk bl	.25	.25
479	A118	15c orange & mar	.25	.25
480	A118	30c lt brn & blk	.25	.25
481	A118	35c olive & blk	.25	.25

482	A118	60c lilac & blk	.30	.30
483	A118	95c yel grn & dk grn	.70	.70
	Nos. 478-483 (6)		2.00	2.00

Regular steamer connection between the Netherlands and Surinam, 150th anniversary.

Passiflora
Quad-rangularis
A119

Javanese
Costume
A120

Flowers: 30c, Centropogon surinamensis. 55c, Gloxinia perennis. 60c, Hydrocleis nymphoides. 75c, Clusia grandiflora.

1978, Feb. 8   Litho.   Perf. 13x14

484	A119	20c multicolored	.60	.60
485	A119	30c multicolored	.60	.60
486	A119	55c multicolored	.95	.75
487	A119	60c multicolored	1.10	.95
488	A119	75c multicolored	1.25	1.10
	Nos. 484-488 (5)		4.50	4.00

1978, Mar. 1   Litho.   Perf. 13x14

People of Surinam, Costumes: 20c, Forest black. 35c, Chinese. 60c, Creole. 75c, Aborigine Indian. 1g, Hindustani.

489	A120	10c multicolored	.35	.35
490	A120	20c multicolored	.35	.35
491	A120	35c multicolored	.35	.35
492	A120	60c multicolored	.55	.55
493	A120	75c multicolored	.65	.65
494	A120	1g multicolored	1.00	1.00
	Nos. 489-494 (6)		3.25	3.25

Air Post Stamps
of 1972
Surcharged

1977, Nov. 15   Litho.   Perf. 13½x14

495	AP6	1c on 25c #C44	.25	.25
496	AP6	4c on 15c #C42	.25	.25
497	AP6	4c on 30c #C45	.25	.25
498	AP6	5c on 40c #C47	.35	.25
499	AP6	10c on 75c #C54	.45	.25
	Nos. 495-499 (5)		1.55	1.25

"Luchtpost" obliterated with 2 bars.

Old Municipal
Church
A121

Johannes
King — A122

Designs: 55c, New Municipal Church. 60c, Johannes Raillard.

1978, May 31   Litho.   Perf. 14x13

500	A121	10c blue, blk & gray	.30	.30
501	A121	20c gray & blk	.30	.30
502	A121	55c rose lil & blk	.50	.50
503	A122	60c orange & blk	.55	.55
	Nos. 500-503 (4)		1.65	1.65

Evangelical Brothers Community Church, Paramaribo, bicentenary.

Fish Type of 1976

Tropical Fish: 1c, Nannacara Anomala. 2c, Leporinus fasciatus. 3c, Pristella riddlei. 4c, Nannostomus beckfordi. 5c, Rivulus agilae.

1978, June 21   Perf. 12½x13½

504	A111	1c multicolored	.25	.25
505	A111	2c multicolored	.25	.25
506	A111	3c multicolored	.25	.25
507	A111	4c multicolored	.25	.25
508	A111	5c multicolored	.25	.25
	Nos. 504-508,C85-C87 (8)		6.10	4.45

Souvenir Sheet

Commewijne River
Development — A124

Development: 60c, Map of Surinam and dam. 95c, Planes and world map.

1978, Oct. 18   Litho.   Perf. 14x13

509		Sheet of 3	2.75	2.75
a.	A124	20c multi	.25	.25
b.	A124	60c multi	.35	.35
c.	A124	95c multi	.50	.50

Coconuts
A125

Wright Brothers' Flyer 1
A126

1978-85   Litho.   Perf. 13½x13

510	A125	5c shown	.25	.25
a.		Bklt. pane, 4 #510, 3 #511, 5 #515 ('80)	2.00	
511	A125	10c Oranges	.25	.25
512	A125	15c Papayas	.25	.25
a.		Bklt. pane, 5 #512, 6 #514 + label ('79)	2.00	
513	A125	20c Bananas	.25	.25
514	A125	25c Soursop	.25	.25
514A	A125	30c Cocoa beans ('85)	.85	.85
b.		Bklt. pane, 6 #514A, 1 #513 + label ('85)	3.25	3.25
515	A125	35c Watermelon	.55	.55
	Nos. 510-515 (7)		2.65	2.65

Perf. 13x14, 14x13

1978, Dec. 13   Litho.

Designs: 20c, Daedalus and Icarus, vert. 95c, DC 8. 125c, Concorde.

516	A126	20c multicolored	.40	.40
517	A126	60c multicolored	.95	.95
518	A126	95c multicolored	1.40	1.40
519	A126	125c multicolored	1.75	1.75
	Nos. 516-519 (4)		4.50	4.50

75th anniversary of 1st powered flight.

Rodriguezia
Candida
A127

Javanese
Dancer
A128

Flowers: 20c, Stanhopea grandiflora. 35c, Scuticaria steelei. 60c, Bollea violacea.

1979, Feb. 7   Litho.   Perf. 13x14

520	A127	10c multicolored	.45	.45
521	A127	20c multicolored	.45	.45
522	A127	35c multicolored	.85	.60
523	A127	60c multicolored	1.10	.90
	Nos. 520-523 (4)		2.85	2.40

1979, Feb. 28

Dancing Costumes: 10c, Forest Negro. 15c, Chinese. 20c, Creole. 25c, Aborigine Indian. 35c, Hindustani.

524	A128	5c multicolored	.25	.25
525	A128	10c multicolored	.25	.25
526	A128	15c multicolored	.25	.25
527	A128	20c multicolored	.25	.25
528	A128	25c multicolored	.25	.25
529	A128	35c multicolored	.70	.70
	Nos. 524-529 (6)		1.95	1.95

Equetus
Pulchellus
A129

Tropical Fish: 2c, Apogon binotatus. 3c,
Anisotremus virginicus. 5c, Bodianus rufus.
35c, Microspathodon chrysurus.

1979, May 30   Photo.   Perf. 14x13
530 A129 1c multicolored   .25   .25
531 A129 2c multicolored   .25   .25
532 A129 3c multicolored   .25   .25
533 A129 5c multicolored   .25   .25
534 A129 35c multicolored   .45   .30
    Nos. 530-534,C89-C91 (8)   5.20 3.90

See Nos. 557-561, C92-C94.

Javanese
Wooden
Head — A130

Folkart: 35c, Head ornament, Indian. 60c,
Horse's head, Javanese.

1979, Aug. 29   Litho.   Perf. 14x13
535 A130 20c multicolored   .30   .30
536 A130 35c multicolored   .50   .50
537 A130 60c multicolored   .85   .85
    Nos. 535-537 (3)   1.65 1.65

Sir Rowland
Hill — A131

1979, Oct. 3   Litho.   Perf. 13x14
538 A131 1g yellow & olive   1.50 1.00

Sir Rowland Hill (1795-1879), originator of
penny postage.

SOS Emblem,
House
A132

Design: 60c, SOS emblem and buildings.

1979, Oct. 3   Perf. 13x14
539 A132 20c multicolored   .35   .35
540 A132 60c multicolored   .80   .80

Intl. Year of the Child; SOS Children's Villages, 30th anniv.

Javanese Girl's
Costume — A133

1980, Feb. 6   Photo.   Perf. 13x14
541 A133 10c Javanese girl   .40   .40
542 A133 15c Forest Black boy   .40   .40
543 A133 25c Chinese girl   .40   .40
544 A133 60c Creole girl   .95   .65
545 A133 90c Indian girl   1.10   .95
546 A133 1g Hindustani boy   1.25 1.00
    Nos. 541-546 (6)   4.50 3.80

Rotary Intl.,
75th
Anniversary
A134

20c, Handshake, Rotary emblem, vert.

Perf. 13x14, 14x13
1980, Feb. 23   Litho.
547 A134 20c ultra & yellow   .30   .30
548 A134 60c ultra & yellow   .85   .65

Rowland
Hill — A135

Weight
Lifting — A136

1980, May 6   Litho.   Perf. 13x14
549 A135 50c Mailcoach   .50   .50
550 A135 1g shown   1.25 1.25
    a. Souvenir sheet   1.40 1.40
551 A135 2g People mailing let-
           ters   2.75 2.75
    Nos. 549-551 (3)   4.50 4.50

London 1980 Intl. Stamp Exhibition, May 6-
14. No. 550a contains No. 550 in changed
colors. Blue and black margin shows designs
of Nos. 549, 551, London 1980 emblem. (No.
550 in lilac rose and multicolored; stamps of
No. 550a in light green and multicolored).

1980, June 17
552 A136 20c shown   .25   .25
553 A136 30c Diving   .45   .45
554 A136 50c Gymnast   .55   .55
555 A136 75c Basketball   1.00 1.00
556 A136 150c Running   2.00 2.00
    a. Souvenir sheet of 3, #554-556 3.75 3.75
    Nos. 552-556 (5)   4.25 4.25

22nd Summer Olympic Games, Moscow,
July 19-Aug. 3.

Fish Type of 1979

Tropical Fish: 10c, Osteoglossum bicir-
rhosum. 15c, Colossoma species. 25c,
Hemigrammus pulcher. 30c, Petitella
georgiae. 45c, Copeina guttata.

1980, Sept. 10   Photo.   Perf. 14x13
557 A129 10c multicolored   .25   .25
558 A129 15c multicolored   .25   .25
559 A129 25c multicolored   .25   .25
560 A129 30c multicolored   .25   .25
561 A129 45c multicolored   .70   .70
    Nos. 557-561,C92-C94 (8)   5.70 4.75

Souvenir Sheet

Open Hands
(Reflection) — A137

1980, Nov. 19   Litho.   Perf. 13x14
562   Sheet of 3   5.00 5.00
    a. A137 50c shown   .50   .50
    b. A137 1g Shaking hands (coopera-
           tion)   .90   .90
    c. A137 2g Victory sign   1.75 1.75

5th anniv. of independence.

Passiflora
Laurifolia — A138

Designs: Flower paintings by Maria Sibylle
Merian (1647-1717).

1981, Jan. 14   Litho.   Perf. 13x14
563 A138 20c shown   .30   .30
564 A138 30c Aphelandra pec-
           tinata   .40   .40
565 A138 60c Caesalpinia
           pulcherrima   .90   .90
566 A138 75c Hibiscus
           mutabilis   1.00 1.00

567 A138 1.25g Hippeastrum
           puniceum   1.90 1.90
    Nos. 563-567 (5)   4.50 4.50

Renovation of
the Economic
Order
A139

1981, Feb. 25   Perf. 14x13
568 A139 30c shown   .25   .25
569 A139 60c Educational Order   .70   .70
570 A139 75c Social Order   .80   .80
571 A139 1g Political Order   1.10 1.10
    a. Souvenir sheet of 2, #569, 571 3.00 3.00
    Nos. 568-571 (4)   2.85 2.85

Government renovation.

Miniature Sheet

SAMEN NAAR EEN BETERE TOEKOMST

Youths — A140

1981, Apr. 29   Litho.   Perf. 14x13½
572 A140   Sheet of 2   2.75 2.75
    a.   1g shown   .95   .95
    b.   1.50g Youths, diff.   .95   .95

Youth and its future. Entire sheet in continuous design.

Souvenir Sheet

No. 424,
Exhibition
Hall — A141

1981, May 22   Litho.   Perf. 13½x14
573   Sheet of 3   5.00 5.00
    a. A141 50c shown   .55   .60
    b. A141 1g Penny Black   1.10 1.10
    c. A141 2g Austria #5   2.10 2.25

WIPA '81 Intl. Philatelic Exhibition, Vienna,
May 22-31.

Leptodactylus
Pentadactylus
A142

1981, June 24   Photo.   Perf. 14x13
574 A142 40c Phyllomedusa hy-
           pochondrialis   .75   .35
575 A142 50c shown   .95   .50
576 A142 60c Hyla boans   1.10   .65
    Nos. 574-576,C95-C97 (6)   9.00 4.80

Child Wearing
Earphones
A143

1981, Sept. 16   Litho.   Perf. 14x13
580 A143 50c shown   .60   .60
581 A143 100c Child reading
           Braille   1.50 1.50
582 A143 150c Woman in wheel-
           chair   2.40 2.40
    Nos. 580-582 (3)   4.50 4.50

Intl. Year of the Disabled.

Planter's
House on
Parakreek
River — A144

Designs: Illustrations from Voyage to Surinam, by P.I. Benoit.

1981, Oct. 21   Photo.   Perf. 14x13
583 A144 20c shown   .25   .25
584 A144 30c Sarameca St.,
           Paramaribo   .40   .40
585 A144 75c Negro Hamlet,
           Paramaribo   1.00 1.00
586 A144 1g Fish Market, Par-
           amaribo   1.40 1.40
    a. Miniature sheet of 1, perf
        13½x13   1.60 1.60
587 A144 1.25g Blaauwe Berg
           Cascade   2.00 2.00
    Nos. 583-587 (5)   5.05 5.05

Research and
Peaceful Uses
of Space
A145

1982, Jan. 13   Litho.
588 A145 35c Satellites   .60   .60
589 A145 65c Columbia space
           shuttle   1.25 1.25
590 A145 1g Apollo-Soyuz   1.75 1.75
    Nos. 588-590 (3)   3.60 3.60

Caretta
Caretta
A146

1982, Feb. 17   Photo.   Perf. 14x13
591 A146 5c shown   .35   .35
592 A146 10c Chelonia mydas   .35   .35
593 A146 20c Dermochelys
           coriacea   .45   .45
594 A146 25c Eretmochelys im-
           bricata   .60   .60
595 A146 35c Lepidochelys
           olivacea   .80   .80
    Nos. 591-595,C98-C100 (8)   7.05 5.50

25th Anniv. of
Lions Intl. in
Surinam
A147

1982, May 7   Litho.
596 A147 35c multicolored   .65   .65
597 A147 70c multicolored   1.25 1.25

A148   A149

1982, May 18   Litho.   Perf. 13x14
598 A148 35c Helping the sick   1.10 1.10
599 A148 65c Birthplace, map   2.10 2.10
    a. Souvenir sheet   2.00 2.00

Beatification of Father Petrus Donders, May
23.

1982, June 9   Litho.   Perf. 13x14
600 A149 50c Stamp designing   .75   .75
601 A149 100c Printing   1.50 1.50
602 A149 150c Collecting   2.25 2.25
    a. Souvenir sheet of 3, #600-602 5.00 5.00
    Nos. 600-602 (3)   4.50 4.50

PHILEXFRANCE '82 Stamp Exhibition,
Paris, June 11-21. Nos. 600-602 in continuous
design.

TB Bacillus
Centenary
A150

1982, Sept. 15   Litho.   Perf. 14x13
603 A150 35c Text   .40   .40
604 A150 65c Microscope   1.10 1.10
605 A150 150c Bacillus   3.00 3.00
    Nos. 603-605 (3)   4.50 4.50

Marienburg
Sugar Co.
Centenary
A151

1982, Oct. 20
606 A151 35c Mill   .50   .50
607 A151 65c Gathering cane   .90   .90
608 A151 100c Rail transport 1.60 1.60
609 A151 150c Gears   2.50 2.50
    Nos. 606-609 (4)   5.50 5.50

A152   Inga
                Edulis — A153

EBG Missionaries, 250th Anniv. in Caribbean: 35c, Municipal Church, horiz. 65c, St. Thomas Monastery, horiz. 150c, Johan Leonhardt Dober (1706-1766).

Perf. 14x13, 13x14
1982, Dec. 13   Litho.
610 A152 35c multicolored   .50   .50
611 A152 65c multicolored   .95   .95
612 A152 150c multicolored   2.50 2.50
    Nos. 610-612 (3)   3.95 3.95

1983, Jan. 12

Flower Paintings by Maria Sibylle Merian (1647-1717). Nos. 613-618 horiz.

613 A153 1c Erythrina fusca   .25   .25
614 A153 2c Ipomoea
           acuminata   .25   .25
615 A153 3c Heliconia psit-
           tacorum   .25   .25
616 A153 5c Ipomoea   .25   .25
617 A153 10c Herba non de-
           nominata   .25   .25
618 A153 15c Anacardium oc-
           cidentale   .45   .45
619 A153 20c shown   .55   .55
620 A153 25c Abelmoschus mos-
           chatus   .80   .80
621 A153 30c Argemone mexi-
           cana   1.00 1.00
622 A153 35c Costus arabicus 1.10 1.10
623 A153 45c Muellera frutes-
           cens   1.25 1.25
624 A153 65c Punica granatum 2.10 2.10
    Nos. 613-624 (12)   8.50 8.50

 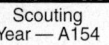

Scouting   500th Birth
Year — A154   Anniv. of
               Raphael — A155

1983, Feb. 22   Litho.   Perf. 13x14
625 A154 40c Anniv. emblem   1.00 1.00
626 A154 65c Baden-Powell   1.50 1.50
627 A154 70c Tent, campfire   1.60 1.60
628 A154 80c Ax in log   1.75 1.75
    Nos. 625-628 (4)   5.85 5.85

1983, Apr. 13   Photo.
Crayon sketches.
629 A155 5c multicolored   .30   .30
630 A155 10c multicolored   .30   .30
631 A155 40c multicolored   .80   .80
632 A155 65c multicolored   1.25 1.25
633 A155 70c multicolored   1.25 1.25
634 A155 80c multicolored   1.50 1.50
    Nos. 629-634 (6)   5.40 5.40

1982 Coins
and
Banknotes
A156

1983, June 1   Litho.   Perf. 14x13
635 A156 5c 1-cent coin   .25   .25
636 A156 10c 5-cent coin   .25   .25
637 A156 40c 10-cent coin   .65   .65
638 A156 65c 25-cent coin   1.10 1.10
639 A156 70c 1g note   1.25 1.25
640 A156 80c 2.50g note   1.50 1.50
    Nos. 635-640 (6)   5.00 5.00

For surcharge & overprints see Nos. 751, J59-J60.

25th Anniv. of Dept. of
Construction — A157

1983, June 15   Litho.   Perf. 13x14
641 A157 25c Map   .55   .55
642 A157 50c Map, bulldozers 1.25 1.25

Local
Butterflies
A158

Drawings by Maria Sibylle Merian (1647-1717). Nos. 643-648 vert.

Perf. 13x14, 14x13
1983, Sept. 14   Litho.
643 A158 1c Papile anchi-
           siades esper   .25   .25
644 A158 2c Urania leilus   .25   .25
645 A158 3c Morpho deida-
           mia   .25   .25
646 A158 5c Thysania aguip-
           pina   .25   .25
647 A158 10c Morpho sp.   .30   .25
648 A158 15c Metamorpha di-
           do   .45   .30
649 A158 20c Morpho menela-
           us   .60   .40
650 A158 25c Manduca rustica 1.00   .65
651 A158 30c Rothschildia sp. 1.25   .65
652 A158 35c Catopsilia ebule 1.50   .95
653 A158 45c Pailio androgeos 1.90 1.90
654 A148 65c Eumorpha vitis 3.00 1.90
    Nos. 643-654 (12) 11.00 7.35

Manned Ballooning,
200th Anniv. — A159

Designs: 5c, 1783, sheep, cock and duck. 10c, first manned flight, d'Arlandes and Pilatre de Rozier. 40c, first hydrogen balloon, Jacques Charles. 65c, 1870, Paris flight, minister Gambetta. 70c, Double Eagle II, transatlantic flight. 80c, Intl. Balloon Festival, Albuquerque.

1983, Oct. 19   Litho.   Perf. 13x14
655 A159 5c multicolored   .25   .25
656 A159 10c multicolored   .25   .25
657 A159 40c multicolored   .95   .95
658 A159 65c multicolored   1.40 1.40
659 A159 70c multicolored   1.50 1.50
660 A159 80c multicolored   2.00 2.00
    Nos. 655-660 (6)   6.35 6.35

Martin Luther, 500th
Birth Anniv. — A160

1983, Dec. 7   Litho.
661 A160 25c Portrait   .50   .50
662 A160 50c Engraving   1.25 1.10

Local Flowers   Local Seashells
A161   A162

1984, Jan. 11   Litho.
663 A161 5c Catasetum discolor .25   .25
664 A161 10c Menadenium labi-
           osum   .25   .25
665 A161 40c Comparettia fal-
           cata   .95   .95
666 A161 50c Rodriquezia
           decora   1.40 1.10
667 A161 70c Oncidium papilio 1.60 1.40
668 A161 75c Epidendrum
           porpax   1.90 1.50
    Nos. 663-668 (6)   6.35 5.60

1984, Feb. 22   Litho.
669 A162 40c Arca zebra   .95   .65
670 A162 65c Trachycardium
           egmontianum   1.60 1.10
671 A162 70c Tellina radiata   1.60 1.10
672 A162 80c Vermicularia knorrii 2.00 1.25
    Nos. 669-672 (4)   6.15 4.10

Intl. Civil
Aviation Org.,
40th Anniv.
A163

1984, May 16   Litho.   Perf. 14x13
673 A163 35c Sea plane   .65   .65
674 A163 65c Surinam Airways
           jet   1.50 1.50

A164   A165

Greek Art and Artifacts: Ancient Games.

1984, June 13   Perf. 13x14
675 A164 2c Running   .25   .25
676 A164 3c Javelin, discus,
           long jump   .25   .25
677 A164 5c Massage   .25   .25
678 A164 10c Ointment massage .25   .25
679 A164 15c Wrestling   .25   .25
680 A164 20c Boxing   .25   .25
681 A164 30c Horse racing   .75   .75
682 A164 35c Chariot racing   .85   .85
683 A164 45c Temple of Olympia 1.00 1.00
684 A164 50c Crypt entrance   1.10 1.10
685 A164 65c Olympia Stadium 1.90 1.90
686 A164 75c Zeus (bust)   1.90 1.90
    a. Min. sheet of 3, #675, 682, 686 3.25 3.25
    Nos. 675-686 (12)   9.00 9.00

1984 Summer Olympics.
For overprint see No. 843.

1984, Sept. 18   Litho.   Perf. 13x14
687 A165 50c Ball, net   1.25 1.10
688 A165 90c Ball in net   2.00 1.90

Intl. Council of Military Sports basketball championship.

World Chess Championship,
Moscow — A166

1984, Oct. 10   Litho.   Perf. 14x13
689 A166 10c Red Square   .40   .40
690 A166 15c Knight, king,
           pawn   .40   .40
691 A166 30c Kasparov   .70   .70
692 A166 50c Board   1.25 1.25
693 A166 75c Karpov   1.90 1.90
    a. Souv. sheet of 3 (30c, 50c,
       75c), perf 13½x13   6.00 6.00
694 A166 90c Game   2.25 2.25
    Nos. 689-694 (6)   6.90 6.90

For overprints see Nos. 742, 796.

World Food
Day, Oct.
16 — A167

1984, Oct. 10
695 A167 50c Children receiving
           milk   1.25 1.25
696 A167 90c Food   2.00 2.00

A168   A169

Cacti.

1985, Jan. 9   Litho.   Perf. 13x14
697 A168 5c Leaf   .25   .25
698 A168 10c Melon   .25   .25
699 A168 30c Pillar   .95   .95
700 A168 50c Fig   1.40 1.40
701 A168 75c Nightqueen   2.25 2.25
702 A168 90c Segment   2.40 2.40
    Nos. 697-702 (6)   7.50 7.50

1985, Feb. 22

Independence, 5th Anniv.: 5c, Star, red stripe from national flag. 30c, Unified labor. 50c, Perpetual flowering plant. 75c, Growth of agriculture. 90c, Peace dove and plant.

703 A169 5c multicolored   .25   .25
704 A169 30c multicolored   .60   .60
705 A169 50c multicolored   1.00 1.00
    a. Min. sheet of 3, 2 #703, #705 3.00
706 A169 75c multicolored   1.60 1.60
707 A169 90c multicolored   2.10 2.10
    Nos. 703-707 (5)   5.55 5.55

Chamber of
Commerce
and Industry,
75th Anniv.
A170

1985, Apr. 17   Litho.   Perf. 14x13
708 A170 50c Chamber emblem .75   .75
709 A170 90c Chamber, factories 1.75 1.75

UN Emblem, Natl.
Coat of
Arms — A171

1985, Apr. 29   Litho.   Perf. 13x14
710 A171 50c multicolored   .85   .85
711 A171 90c multicolored   1.90 1.90

UN, 40th anniv.

Trains — A172

1985, June 5   Litho.   Perf. 13½

712	A172	5c No. 192	.25	.25
713	A172	5c Monaco, No. J50	.25	.25
a.		Pair, #712-713	.40	.40
714	A172	10c Locomotive "Dam"	.25	.25
715	A172	10c Diesel locomotive	.25	.25
a.		Pair, #714-715	.60	.60
716	A172	20c Steam locomotive "No. 3737"	.50	.50
717	A172	20c Netherlands locomotive "IC III"	.50	.50
a.		Pair, #716-717	1.00	1.00
718	A172	30c Stephenson's locomotive "Rocket"	.85	.85
719	A172	30c French Railways high-speed TGV	.85	.85
a.		Pair, #716-717	1.60	1.60
720	A172	50c Stephenson's locomotive "Adler"	1.25	1.25
721	A172	50c French Railways commuter train	1.25	1.25
a.		Pair, #720-721	2.75	2.75
722	A172	75c Locomotive "General"	2.00	2.00
723	A172	75c Japanese bullet train "Shinkansen"	2.00	2.00
a.		Pair, #722-723	4.00	4.00
		Nos. 712-723 (12)	10.20	10.20

For surcharges see Nos. 749-750, 808-809, 928-929.

Birds — A173

1985-95   Litho.   Perf. 14x13

724	A173	10c Toucan	.25	.25
725	A173	1g American purple fowl	1.75	1.75
a.		Miniature sheet of 1	6.00	6.00
726	A173	1.50g Tiger bird	3.25	3.25
727	A173	2.50g Red ibis	5.00	5.00
728	A173	5g Guyana red cockerel	10.00	10.00
729	A173	10g Harpy eagle	16.00	16.00
730	A173	15g Parrot	22.50	22.50
731	A173	25g Owl	35.00	35.00
732	A173	1300g Rose lepelaar	37.50	37.50
733	A173	1780g Toucan	9.25	9.25
734	A173	2225g Hummingbird	11.50	11.50
735	A173	2995g Hoatzin	16.00	16.00
		Nos. 724-735 (12)	168.00	168.00

Nos. 724, 730 inscribed 1990.
Issued: 1g, 1.50g, 2.50g, 8/21; #725a, 5g, 1/2/86; 10g, 10/1/86; 10c, 15g, 1/30/91; 25g, 1/20/93; 1300g, 3/31/94; 1780g, 2225g, 2995g, 9/6/95.
See #1040, 1053-1055, 1108-1111, 1136-1138, 1160, 1194-1195, 1220-1221. For surcharges & overprint see #963-964, J63.

Mailboxes — A174

1985, Oct. 2   Litho.   Perf. 13x14

736	A174	15c Germany, 1900	.35	.35
737	A174	30c France, 1900	.55	.55
738	A174	50c England, 1932	.95	.95
739	A174	90c Netherlands, 1850	1.90	1.90
		Nos. 736-739 (4)	3.75	3.75

Natl. Independence, 10th Anniv. — A175

1985, Nov. 22

740	A175	50c Agriculture	1.25	1.25
741	A175	90c Industry	2.00	2.00
a.		Miniature sheet of 2, #740-741	3.25	3.25

No. 691 Ovptd. in Red

1985, Nov. 22   Litho.   Perf. 14x13

742	A166	30c multi	3.25	3.25

Orchids, World Wildlife Fund — A177

1986, Feb. 19   Litho.   Perf. 14x13

743	A177	5c Epidendrum ciliare	3.00	3.00
744	A177	15c Cycnoches chlorochilon	7.50	7.50
745	A177	30c Epidendrum anceps	15.00	15.00
746	A177	50c Epidendrum vespa	24.00	24.00
		Nos. 743-746 (4)	49.50	49.50

Halley's Comet A178

Designs: 50c, The Bayeux Tapestry, c. 1092, France. 110c, Halley's Comet.

1986, Mar. 5   Litho.   Perf. 14x13

747	A178	50c multi	1.00	1.00
748	A178	110c multi	2.00	2.00

Nos. 720-721 Surcharged in Red

1986, May 28   Litho.   Perf. 13½

749	A172	15c on 50c #720	2.50	2.50
750	A172	15c on 50c #721	2.50	2.50
a.		Pair, #749-750	6.00	6.00

No. 639 Surcharged

1986, June 25   Litho.   Perf. 14x13

751	A156	30c on 70c multi	2.75	2.75

Finance Building, Paramaribo, 150th anniv.

Surinam Shipping Co., 50th Anniv. A179

1986, Sept. 1   Litho.   Perf. 14x13

752	A179	50c Emblem	.70	.70
753	A179	110c Freighter Saramacca	2.00	2.00

Monkeys A180

1987, Jan. 7   Litho.

755	A180	35c Alouatta	.60	.60
756	A180	60c Aotus	1.00	1.00
757	A180	110c Saimiri	2.00	2.00
758	A180	120c Cacajao	2.25	2.25
		Nos. 755-758 (4)	5.85	5.85

Esperanto, Cent. — A181

1987, Feb. 4   Litho.

759	A181	60c shown	1.00	1.00
760	A181	110 World map, doves	1.90	1.90
761	A181	120c L.L. Zamenhof	2.10	2.10
		Nos. 759-761 (3)	5.00	5.00

10th Pan-American Games, Indianapolis, July 23 — A182

Forestry Commission, 40th Anniv. — A183

1987, June 3   Litho.   Perf. 13x14

763	A182	90c Soccer	1.50	1.50
764	A182	110c Swimming	1.75	1.75
765	A182	150c Basketball	2.25	2.25
		Nos. 763-765 (3)	5.50	5.50

1987, July 21   Litho.   Perf. 13x14

766	A183	90c Emblem	1.50	1.50
767	A183	120c Logging	2.00	2.00
768	A183	150c Parrot in virgin forest	2.75	2.75
		Nos. 766-768 (3)	6.25	6.25

Intl. Year of Shelter for the Homeless A184

1987, Sept. 2   Litho.   Perf. 14x13

769	A184	90c Distressed boy, encampment	1.40	1.40
770	A184	120c Man, ghetto	2.10	2.10

Founders Catherine and William Booth — A185

1987, Sept. 2   Perf. 14x13

771	A185	150c multi	2.25	2.25

Salvation Army in the Caribbean, cent.

Nos. 436-438 Surcharged

1986, Dec. 29   Litho.   Perf. 13½x13

772	A109	35c on 1g	2.75	2.75
773	A109	50c on 1.50g	4.25	4.25
774	A109	60c on 2.50g	5.50	5.50
		Nos. 772-774 (3)	12.50	12.50

Fruits — A186

1987, Oct. 14   Litho.   Perf. 13x13½

775	A186	10c Bananas	.25	.25
776	A186	15c Cacao	.25	.25
777	A186	20c Pineapple	.25	.25
778	A186	25c Papaya	.50	.50
779	A186	35c Oranges	.75	.75
		Nos. 775-779 (5)	2.00	2.00

Aircraft and Aircraft on Stamps — A187

1987, Oct. 14   Litho.   Perf. 13½

784	A187	25c Degen, 1808	.25	.25
785	A187	25c Ultra Light	.25	.25
a.		Pair, #784-785	.90	.90
786	A187	35c J.C.H. Ellehammer, 1906	.55	.55
787	A187	35c Concorde jet	.55	.55
a.		Pair, #786-787	1.25	1.25
788	A187	60c Fokker F7, 1924	.90	.90
789	A187	60c Fokker F28 jet	.90	.90
a.		Pair, #788-789	2.10	2.10
790	A187	90c Spin Fokker, 1910	1.40	1.40
791	A187	90c DC-10	1.40	1.40
a.		Pair, #790-791	3.00	3.00
792	A187	110c Orion, 1932	1.75	1.75
793	A187	110c Boeing 747	1.75	1.75
a.		Pair, #792-793	3.75	3.75
794	A187	120c No. 346	1.90	1.90
795	A187	120c No. 518	1.90	1.90
a.		Pair, #794-795	4.00	4.00
		Nos. 784-795 (12)	13.50	13.50

No. 693a Overprinted "3e match sevilla 1987" on Stamps in 3 or 4 Lines and with Bar and "sevilla 1987" in Sheet Margin

1987, Nov. 2   Litho.   Perf. 13½x13
Souvenir Sheet

796		Sheet of 3	32.50
a.	A166	30c Kasparov	3.50
b.	A166	50c Board	6.00
c.	A166	75c Karpov	9.00

Alligators and Crocodiles A188

1988, Jan. 20   Litho.   Perf. 14x13

797	A188	50c Gavialis gangeticus	.80	.80
798	A188	60c Crocodylus niloticus	1.10	1.10
799	A188	90c Melanosuchus niger	1.50	1.50
800	A188	110c Mississippi alligator	2.10	2.10
		Nos. 797-800 (4)	5.50	5.50

Traditional Wedding Costumes — A189

1988, Feb. 24   Litho.   Perf. 13x14

801	A189	35c Javanese	.50	.50
802	A189	60c Bushman	.95	.95
803	A189	80c Chinese	1.10	1.10
804	A189	110c Creole	1.60	1.60

805 A189 120c Indian   1.75 1.75
806 A189 130c Hindustan   2.10 2.10
        Nos. 801-806 (6)   8.00 8.00

Nos. 722-723 and 440 Surcharged in
Black or Silver

No. 808

No. 810

Perf. 13½x13, 13½

1988, Mar. 23   Litho.
808 A172 60c on 75c #722   5.50
809 A172 60c on 75c #723   5.50
  a.   Pair, #808-809   11.00
810 A109 125c on 10g #440 (S)   12.00
        Nos. 808-810 (3)   23.00

1988 Summer   Abolition of
Olympics,   Slavery, 125th
Seoul — A190   Anniv. — A191

1988, May 4   Litho.   Perf. 13x14
812 A190 90c Relay   1.10 1.10
813 A190 110c Soccer   1.75 1.75
814 A190 120c Pole vault   1.90 1.90
  a.   Souvenir sheet of 3, #812-
       814   5.00 5.00
815 A190 250c Women's ten-
           nis   4.25 4.25
        Nos. 812-815 (4)   9.00 9.00

1988, June 29   Litho.
816 A191 50c Abaisa Monu-
           ment   .65   .65
817 A191 110c Kwakoe Monu-
           ment   1.75 1.75
818 A191 120c Home of Anton
           de Kom   2.10 2.10
        Nos. 816-818 (3)   4.50 4.50

See Netherlands Antilles Nos. 597-598.

Intl. Fund for
Agricultural
Development
(IFAD), 10th
Anniv.
A192

1988, Sept. 21   Perf. 14x13
819 A192 105c Crop harvest   1.75 1.75
820 A192 110c Net fishing   1.75 1.75
821 A192 125c Agricultural re-
           search   2.25 2.25
        Nos. 819-821 (3)   5.75 5.75

FILACEPT '88, The
Netherlands, Oct.
18-23 — A193

1988, Oct. 18   Litho.   Perf. 13x14
822 A193 120c Egypt #49   1.50 1.50
823 A193 150c Netherlands
           #334   2.25 2.25
824 A193 250c Surinam #238   3.50 3.50
        Nos. 822-824 (3)   7.25 7.25

Souvenir Sheet
**Same Types, Colors Changed (120c,
150c)**
825   Sheet of 3   10.00 10.00
  a.   A193 120c Egypt Type A23
       (4m green)   1.10 1.10
  b.   A193 150c Netherlands Type
       A81 (10c red brown)   1.40 1.40
  c.   A193 250c Surinam No. 239   2.40 2.40

Stylized
Butterfly
Stroke
A194

1988, Nov. 1   Litho.   Perf. 14x13
826 A194 110c multi   1.60 1.60

Anthony Nesty, swimmer and 1st Olympic
gold medalist from Surinam.

Otters
A195

1989, Jan. 18   Litho.   Perf. 14x13
827 A195 10c Otter   .25   .25
828 A195 20c Two on land   .25   .25
829 A195 25c Two crossing log   .50   .50
830 A195 30c Fishing   .60   .60
        Nos. 827-830,C107 (5)   4.60 4.60

Classic and Modern
Automobiles — A196

1989, June 7   Litho.   Perf. 13½
       Design A196
831   25c 1930 Mercedes
                Tourenwagen   .60   .60
832   25c 1985 Mercedes-
                Benz 300E   .60   .60
  a.   Pair, #831-832   1.00 1.00
833   60c 1897 Daimler   1.25 1.25
834   60c 1986 Jaguar Sover-
                eign   1.25 1.25
  a.   Pair, #833-834   2.50 2.50
835   90c 1898 Renault Voi-
                turette   2.00 2.00
836   90c 1989 Renault 25TX   2.00 2.00
  a.   Pair, #835-836   3.75 3.75
837   105c 1927 Volvo Jacob   2.25 2.25
838   105c 1989 Volvo 440   2.25 2.25
  a.   Pair, #837-838   4.50 4.50
839   110c Left half of Monaco
                #484   2.40 2.40
840   110c Right half of Mona-
                co #484   2.40 2.40
  a.   Pair, #839-840   5.00 5.00
841   120c 1936 Toyota AA   2.75 2.75
842   120c 1988 Toyota Corolla
                sedan   2.75 2.75
  a.   Pair, #841-842   5.75 5.75
        Nos. 831-842 (12)   22.50 22.50

No. 686a Ovptd. "PHILEXFRANCE
7t/m 17 juli 1989" on Margin, with
Exhibition Emblem on Stamps in Gold

1989, July 7   Litho.   Perf. 13x14
       Miniature Sheet
843   Sheet of 3   6.25 6.25
  a.   A164 2c on No. 675   .25   .25
  b.   A164 35c on No. 682   .40   .40
  c.   A164 75c on No. 686   .95   .95

PHILEXFRANCE '89.

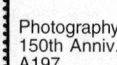

Photography,
150th Anniv.
A197

1989, Sept. 6   Litho.   Perf. 14x13
844 A197 60c Joseph Niepce   1.00 1.00
845 A197 110c Daguerreotype
                camera   1.90 1.90
846 A197 120c Louis Daguerre   2.10 2.10
        Nos. 844-846 (3)   5.00 5.00

America
Issue — A198

UPAE emblem and pre-Columbian amulets.

1989, Oct. 12   Litho.   Perf. 13x14
847 A198 60c Amazon or
                Jade Stones   10.00 10.00
848 A198 110c Bisque fertility
                statue   10.00 10.00

The White
House,
Washington,
DC, and
Stamps on
Stamps
A199

Perf. 13x14, 14x13
1989, Nov. 17   Litho.
849 A199 110c No. 445, vert.   2.00 2.00
850 A199 150c US No. 990   2.50 2.50
851 A199 250c No. 459   4.00 4.00
  a.   Souv. sheet, #849-851, perf
       13x14, 14   8.75 8.75
        Nos. 849-851 (3)   8.50 8.50

World Stamp Expo '89 and 20th UPU Congress, Washington, DC.

UNESCO Intl.   Arya Dewaker
Literacy   Temple, 60th
Year — A200   Anniv. — A201

1990, Jan. 19   Photo.   Perf. 13x14
852 A200 60c shown   1.10 1.10
853 A200 110c Emblems   2.10 2.10
854 A200 120c Emblems, youth
                reading   2.25 2.25
        Nos. 852-854 (3)   5.45 5.45

1990, Feb. 14   Litho.
855 A201 60c dk red brn, blk &
                red   1.10 1.10
856 A201 110c vio blue & blk   2.10 2.10
857 A201 200c emer grn & blk   3.50 3.50
        Nos. 855-857 (3)   6.70 6.70

A202   A203

1990, May 4
858 A202 110c Surinam #C1   1.75 1.75
859 A202 200c Great Britain
                #1   3.00 3.00
860 A202 250c Great Britain
                #208   4.25 4.25
  a.   Souvenir sheet of 3, #858-
       860   11.00 11.00
        Nos. 858-860 (3)   9.00 9.00

Penny Black, 150th anniv. Stamps World
London '90.

1990, Aug. 9
861 A203 60c Couple carrying
                baskets   1.00 1.00
862 A203 110c Woman carrying
                bundle   1.90 1.90
863 A203 120c Man carrying
                baskets   2.10 2.10
        Nos. 861-863 (3)   5.00 5.00

Javanese Immigration, cent.

Flowers — A204

1990, Sept. 5   Perf. 13½
864 A204 25c Punica
                granatum   .45   .45
865 A204 25c Passiflora
                laurifolia   .45   .45
  a.   Pair, #864-865   .80   .80
866 A204 35c Hippeastrum
                puniceum   .55   .55
867 A204 35c Ipomaea
                batatas   .55   .55
  a.   Pair, #866-867   1.10 1.10
868 A204 60c Hibiscus
                syriacus   1.00 1.00
869 A204 60c Jasminum of-
                ficinale   1.00 1.00
  a.   Pair, #868-869   2.10 2.10
870 A204 105c Musa serapion-
                is   1.75 1.75
871 A204 105c Hibiscus
                mutabilis   1.75 1.75
  a.   Pair, #870-871   3.50 3.50
872 A204 110c Plumiria rubra   1.75 1.75
873 A204 110c Hibiscus diver-
                sifolius   1.75 1.75
  a.   Pair, #872-873   3.50 3.50
874 A204 120c Bixa orellana   2.00 2.00
875 A204 120c Ceasalpinia
                pulcherima   2.00 2.00
  a.   Pair, #874-875   4.00 4.00
        Nos. 864-875 (12)   15.00 15.00

America
Issue — A205

1990, Oct. 10   Litho.   Perf. 14x13
876 A205 60c bluish grn & blk   4.75 4.75
877 A205 110c brn & blk   8.75 8.75

Organization
of American
States,
Cent. — A206

1990, Oct. 10
878 A206 110c multicolored   1.60 1.60

Independence, 15th
Anniv. — A207

1990, Nov. 21   Litho.   Perf. 13x14
879 A207 10c shown   .25   .25
880 A207 60c Passion flower   .95   .95
881 A207 110c Dove with olive
                branch   2.10 2.10
        Nos. 879-881 (3)   3.30 3.30

Architecture
A208

Buildings: 35c, Waterfront warehouse. 60c,
Upper class residence. 75c, Labor inspection

building. 105c, Plantation supervisor's residence. 110c, Ministry of Labor. 200c, Small residences.

1991, May 15   Litho.   Perf. 14x13

882	A208	35c multicolored	.80	.80
883	A208	60c multicolored	1.10	1.10
884	A208	75c multicolored	1.50	1.50
885	A208	105c multicolored	2.10	2.10
886	A208	110c multicolored	2.25	2.25
887	A208	200c multicolored	4.00	4.00
		Nos. 882-887 (6)	11.75	11.75

Nos. 714-715, 720-721 Surcharged

Methods and Perfs as Before

1991

888	A172	2c on 10c #714	1.00	1.00
889	A172	2c on 10c #715	1.00	1.00
a.		Pair, #888-889	2.25	2.25
890	A172	3c on 50c #720	1.00	1.00
891	A172	3c on 50c #721	1.00	1.00
a.		Pair, #890-891	2.25	2.25
		Nos. 888-891 (4)	4.00	4.00

Puma
Concolor
A209

Various pictures of pumas.

Perf. 13x14, 14x13

1991, Sept. 12   Litho.

892	A209	10c multi, vert.	.25	.25
893	A209	20c multi, vert.	.25	.25
894	A209	25c multi, vert.	.40	.40
895	A209	30c multi, vert.	.50	.50
896	A209	125c multi	1.90	1.90
897	A209	500c multi	6.75	6.75
		Nos. 892-897 (6)	10.05	10.05

Nos. 896-897 are airmail.

Discovery of America, 500th Anniv. (in 1991) — A210

Diagram showing Columbus' route: 60c, Western Atlantic and Caribbean Sea. 110c, Eastern Atlantic.

1991, Oct. 11   Perf. 13x14

898		60c lt bl, red & blk	2.50	2.50
899		110c lt bl, red & blk	5.50	5.50
a.	A210 Pair, #898-899		11.00	11.00

UPAEP. No. 899a has continous design.

Snakes — A211

#900, Corallus enydris. #901, Corallus caninus. #902, Lachesis muta. #903, Boa constrictor. #904, Micrurus surinamensis. #905, Crotalus durissus. #906, Eunectes murinus. #907, Clelia cloelia. #908, Epicrates cenchris. #909, Chironius carinatus. #910, Oxybelis argenteus. #911, Spilotes pullatus.

1991, Nov. 14   Perf. 13½

900	A211	25c multicolored	.30	.30
901	A211	25c multicolored	.30	.30
a.		Pair, #900-901	.80	.80

902	A211	35c multicolored	.55	.55
903	A211	35c multicolored	.55	.55
a.		Pair, #902-903	1.10	1.10
904	A211	60c multicolored	.90	.90
905	A211	60c multicolored	.90	.90
a.		Pair, #904-905	2.10	2.10
906	A211	75c multicolored	1.25	1.25
907	A211	75c multicolored	1.25	1.25
a.		Pair, #906-907	2.50	2.50
908	A211	110c multicolored	1.75	1.75
909	A211	110c multicolored	1.75	1.75
a.		Pair, #908-909	3.75	3.75
910	A211	200c multicolored	3.25	3.25
911	A211	200c multicolored	3.25	3.25
a.		Pair, #910-911	6.75	6.75
		Nos. 900-911 (12)	16.00	16.00

Orchids — A212

Designs: 50c, Cycnoches haagii. 60c, Lycaste cristata. 75c, Galeandra dives, horiz. 125c, Vanilla mexicana. 150c, Cyrtopodium glutiniferum. 250c, Gongora quinquenervis.

1992, Feb. 12   Perf. 13x14, 14x13

912	A212	50c multicolored	.65	.65
913	A212	60c multicolored	.85	.85
914	A212	75c multicolored	1.00	1.00
915	A212	125c multicolored	2.00	2.00
916	A212	150c multicolored	2.50	2.50
917	A212	250c multicolored	4.00	4.00
		Nos. 912-917 (6)	11.00	11.00

Souvenir Sheet

A213

Designs: a, 75c, #847. b, 125c, #848. c, 150c, #898. d. 250c, #899.

1992, Mar. 24   Litho.   Perf. 13x13½

918	A213	Sheet of 4, #a.-d.	11.00	11.00

Granada '92, Intl. Philatelic Exibition.

1992 Summer
Olympics,
Barcelona — A214

1992, Apr. 8   Litho.   Perf. 13x14

919	A214	35c Basketball	.55	.55
920	A214	60c Volleyball	.95	.95
921	A214	75c Running	1.10	1.10
922	A214	125c Soccer	1.90	1.90
923	A214	150c Cycling	2.25	2.25
924	A214	250c Swimming	4.25	4.25
a.		Souvenir sheet of 3, #921, 922, 924, perf 13x13½	7.50	7.50
		Nos. 919-924 (6)	11.00	11.00

YWCA, 50th
Anniv.
A215

1992, June 12   Litho.   Perf. 14x13

925	A215	60c red brown & multi	1.00	1.00
926	A215	250c purple & multi	4.00	4.00

Expulsion of
Jews from
Spain, 500th
Anniv.
A216

1992, Aug. 17

927	A216	250c multicolored	4.00	4.00

Nos. 712-713 Surcharged

1992, Aug. 17   Perf. 13½

928	A172	1c on 5c multi	1.75	1.75
929	A172	1c on 5c multi	1.75	1.75
a.		Pair, #928-929	4.25	4.25

A217   A218

1992, Sept. 15   Perf. 13x14

930	A217	60c green & multi	1.00	1.00
931	A217	250c pink & multi	4.00	4.00

Jan E. Matzeliger (1852-1889), inventor of shoe lasting machine.

1992, Oct. 12

932	A218	60c blue grn & multi	1.50	1.50
933	A218	250c dp org & multi	6.00	6.00

Discovery of America, 500th anniv.

Christmas — A219

Various abstract designs.

1992, Nov. 15

934	A219	10c multicolored	.50	.50
935	A219	60c multicolored	1.00	1.00
936	A219	250c multicolored	3.50	3.50
937	A219	400c multicolored	6.00	6.00
		Nos. 934-937 (4)	11.00	11.00

Medicinal
Plants
A220

Designs: 50c, Costus arabicus, vert. 75c, Quassia amara, vert. 125c, Combretum rotundifolium. 500c, Bixa orellana.

Perf. 13x14, 14x13

1993, Feb. 3   Litho.

938	A220	50c multicolored	.85	.85
939	A220	75c multicolored	1.40	1.40
940	A220	125c multicolored	2.25	2.25
941	A220	500c multicolored	9.00	9.00
		Nos. 938-941 (4)	13.50	13.50

Beetles and Grasshoppers — A221

Designs: No. 942, Macrodontia cervicornis. No. 943, Acrididae. No. 944, Curculionidae. No. 945, Acrididae, diff. No. 946, Euchroma gigantea. No. 947, Tettigonidae. No. 948, Tettigonidae. No. 949, Phanaeus festivus. No. 950, Gryllidae. No. 951, Phanaeus lancifer. No. 952, Tettigonidae. No. 953, Batus barbicornis.

1993, June 30   Litho.   Perf. 13½

942	A221	25c multicolored	.40	.40
943	A221	25c multicolored	.40	.40
a.		Pair, #942-943	.90	.90
944	A221	35c multicolored	.50	.50
945	A221	35c multicolored	.50	.50
a.		Pair, #944-945	1.60	1.60
946	A221	50c multicolored	.70	.70
947	A221	50c multicolored	.70	.70
a.		Pair, #946-947	2.00	2.00
948	A221	100c multicolored	1.40	1.40
949	A221	100c multicolored	1.40	1.40
a.		Pair, #948-949	3.75	3.75
950	A221	175c multicolored	2.75	2.75
951	A221	175c multicolored	2.75	2.75
a.		Pair, #950-951	6.75	6.75
952	A221	220c multicolored	3.25	3.25
953	A221	220c multicolored	3.25	3.25
a.		Pair, #952-953	8.50	8.00
		Nos. 942-953 (12)	18.00	18.00

A222

#956b, 250c, like #955. #956c, 500c, like #956.

1993, July 30   Perf. 13x14

954	A222	50c Brazil No. 3	.75	.75
955	A222	250c Brazil No. 2	3.75	3.75
956	A222	500c Brazil No. 1	8.00	8.00
		Nos. 954-956 (3)	12.50	12.50

Souvenir Sheet

956A	A222	Sheet of 2, #b.-c.	10.00	10.00

1st Brazilian postage stamps, 150th Anniv. Brasiliana '93 (#956A).
Nos. 956b-956c have purple border.

A223

America issue: Paleosuchus palpebrosus.

1993, Oct. 12   Perf. 14x13

957	A223	50g brown & multi	3.75	3.75
958	A223	100g green & multi	8.00	8.00

Christmas
Angels — A224

25g, African angel with drum. 45g, Asian angel holding lamp. 50g, Oriental angel holding lantern. 150g, American Indian angel holding wand.

1993, Nov. 15   Litho.   Perf. 13x14

959	A224	25g multicolored	1.00	1.00
960	A224	45g multicolored	1.75	1.75
961	A224	50g multicolored	2.00	2.00
962	A224	150g multicolored	6.25	6.25
		Nos. 959-962 (4)	11.00	11.00

The foreign exchange rate of the Surinam florin was allowed to float freely against foreign currencies on Oct. 19, 1994. The florin's value against the dollar has fluctuated dramatically. Stamps may sell for values significantly different from those quoted in the Scott listings.

Nos. 729-730 Surcharged

1993   Litho.   Perf. 14x13
963 A173 5g on 10g Harpy eagle 1.90 .25
964 A173 5g on 15g Parrot   1.90 1.90

Surcharges differ slightly. Issued: #963, 12/16. #964, 12/28.

Traditional Musical Instruments — A225

1994, Feb. 16   Litho.   Perf. 13x14
965 A225 25g Indian drum   1.50 1.50
966 A225 50g Bosland
              Creooise
              drum   3.00 3.00
967 A225 75g Tambourine   5.00 5.00
968 A225 100g Hindu drum   6.50 6.50
       Nos. 965-968 (4)   16.00 16.00

Environmental Protection A226

1994, June 8   Litho.   Perf. 14x13
969 A226 50g Smoke stacks   .75   .75
970 A226 350g Dying fish   6.25 6.25

Intl. Olympic Committee, Cent. — A227

1994, July 4   Litho.   Perf. 14x13
971 A227 250g multicolored   7.75 7.75

1994 World Cup Soccer Championships, U.S. — A228

1994, July 4   Perf. 13x14
972 A228 100g Goalkeeper's
              hands   1.25 1.25
973 A228 250g Soccer shoe   4.25 4.25
974 A228 300g Goal   6.50 6.50
a.   Souvenir sheet of 2, #973-
       974   13.50 13.50
       Nos. 972-974 (3)   12.00 12.00

Butterflies — A229

1994, Sept. 7   Litho.   Perf. 13½
975 A229 25g Dulcedo   .45   .45
976 A229 25g Ithomia   .45   .45
a.   Pair, #975-976   .90   .90
977 A229 30g Danaus   .50   .50
978 A229 30g Danaus, diff.   .50   .50
a.   Pair, #977-978   1.00 1.00
979 A229 45g Echenais   .75   .75
980 A229 45g Bithijs   .75   .75
a.   Pair #979-980   1.50 1.50
981 A229 75g Junonia
              evarette   1.25 1.25
982 A229 75g Anartia ja-
              trophae   1.25 1.25
a.   Pair, #981-982   2.50 2.50
983 A229 250g Heliconius   4.00 4.00
984 A229 250g Heliconius era-
              to   4.00 4.00
a.   Pair, #983-984   8.25 8.25
985 A229 300g Eurytides   5.00 5.00
986 A229 300g Parides   5.00 5.00
a.   Pair, #985-986   10.00 10.00
       Nos. 975-986 (12)   23.90 23.90

For surcharges see #1088-1091.

FEPAPOST '94 — A230

1994, Oct. 1   Litho.   Perf. 14x13
987 A230 250g Netherlands
              #B148   3.50 3.50
988 A230 300g #168   4.00 4.00
a.   Souvenir sheet of 2, #987-
       988, perf. 13½x13   7.50 7.50

America Issue A231

Post vehicles: 50g, Airplane, canoe. 400g, Van, donkey cart.

1994, Oct. 12   Litho.   Perf. 13½
989 A231 50g multicolored   1.40 1.40
990 A231 400g multicolored   12.00 12.00

A232   A233

Christmas: (A), Angel in sky. 250g, Mother reading to children. 625g, Woman kneeling in prayer.

1994, Nov. 22   Perf. 13x14
991 A232 (A) multicolored   .60   .60
992 A232 250g multicolored   1.90 1.90
993 A232 625g multicolored   5.00 5.00
a.   Souvenir sheet, #992-993 9.00 9.00
       Nos. 991-993 (3)   7.50 7.50

No. 991 sold for 37g on day of issue.

1995, Jan. 31
994 A233 375g shown   3.25 3.25
995 A233 650g Volleyballs   5.25 5.50
a.   Souvenir sheet, #994-995 9.00 9.00

Volleyball, cent.

Medicinal Plants — A234

Designs: No. 998, Stachytarpheta jamaicense. No. 999, Ruellia tuberosa. No. 1000, Peperomia pellucida. No. 1001, Ocimum sanctum. No. 1002, Phyllanthus amarus. No.

1003, Portulaca oleracea. No. 1004, Wulffia baccata. No. 1005, Sesamum indicum. No. 1006, Ascelepias curassavica. No. 1007, Heliotropium indicum. No. 1008, Wedelia trilobata. No. 1009, Lantana camara.

1995, Mar. 31   Litho.   Perf. 13½
998 A234 30g multicolored   .35   .35
999 A234 30g multicolored   .35   .35
a.   Pair, #998-999   .50   .50
1000 A234 50g multicolored   .50   .50
1001 A234 50g multicolored   .50   .50
a.   Pair, #1000-1001   .80   .80
1002 A234 75g multicolored   .75   .75
1003 A234 75g multicolored   .75   .75
a.   Pair, #1002-1003   1.40 1.40
1004 A234 250g multicolored 2.40 2.40
1005 A234 250g multicolored 2.40 2.40
a.   Pair, #1004-1005   4.75 4.75
1006 A234 500g multicolored 4.75 4.75
1007 A234 500g multicolored 4.75 4.75
a.   Pair, #1006-1007   9.50 9.50
1008 A234 600g multicolored 5.75 5.75
1009 A234 600g multicolored 5.75 5.75
a.   Pair, #1008-1009   12.00 12.00
       Nos. 998-1009 (12)   29.00 29.00

World Wildlife Fund — A235

25g, Herpailurus yaguarondi. 30g, same up close. 50g, Leopardus tigrinus. 100g, same up close. 1000g, Leopardus wiedi. 1200g, same up close.

1995, May 31   Perf. 14x13
1010 A235 25g multicolored   .90   .40
1011 A235 30g multicolored   .90   .40
1012 A235 50g multicolored   .90   .40
1013 A235 100g multicolored 2.25 1.25
1014 A235 1000g multicolored 5.75 5.75
1015 A235 1200g multicolored 7.00 7.00
       Nos. 1010-1015 (6)   17.70 15.20

Nos. 1014-1015 are airmail and do not contain WWF emblem.

UN, 50th Anniv. — A236

1995, June 26   Litho.   Perf. 13x14
1016 A236 135g green & multi .75   .75
1017 A236 740g blue & multi 5.00 5.00

Surinam Police Force, Cent. — A237

1995, June 21   Perf. 14x13
1018 A237 875g multicolored 6.00 6.00

Nilom Junior Chamber, 25th Anniv. A238

1995, Sept. 6   Litho.   Perf. 14x13
1019 A238 700g multicolored 3.75 3.75

Environmental Protection A239

1995, Oct. 12
1020 A239 135f multicolored 1.00 1.00
1021 A239 1500f multicolored 11.50 11.50

America issue.

A240   A241

Christmas: 70g, Shepherds, star. 135g, Flight into Egypt. 295g, Magi. 1000g, Nativity, horiz.

1995, Nov. 15   Perf. 13x14, 14x13
1022 A240 70g multicolored   .35   .35
1023 A240 135g multicolored   .75   .75
1024 A240 295g multicolored 1.50 1.50
1025 A240 1000g multicolored 6.25 6.25
a.   Souvenir sheet of 1   5.50 5.50
       Nos. 1022-1025 (4)   8.85 8.85

For surcharges see #1065A-1065B.

1995, Dec. 5   Perf. 13x14
Paintings of Jesters, by Corneille.
1026 A241 135f With bird   1.00 1.00
1027 A241 615f With cat   4.75 4.75

Orchids — A242

#1028, Cyrtopodium cristatum. #1029, Epidendrum cristatum. #1030, Otostylis lepida. #1031, Cochleanthes guianensis. #1032, Rudolfiella aurantiaca. #1033, Catasetum longifolium. #1034, Maxillaria splendens. #1035, Encyclia granitica. #1036, Catasetum macrocarpum. #1037, Brassia caudata. #1038, Vanilla grandiflora. #1039, Maxillaria rufescens.

1996, Feb. 29   Litho.   Perf. 13½
1028 A242 10g multicolored   .25   .25
1029 A242 10g multicolored   .25   .25
a.   Pair, #1028-1029   .30   .30
1030 A242 75g multicolored   .50   .50
1031 A242 75g multicolored   .50   .50
a.   Pair, #1030-1031   1.00 1.00
1032 A242 135g multicolored   .85   .85
1033 A242 135g multicolored   .85   .85
a.   Pair, #1032-1033   1.75 1.75
1034 A242 250g multicolored 1.60 1.60
1035 A242 250g multicolored 1.60 1.60
a.   Pair, #1034-1035   3.50 3.50
1036 A242 300g multicolored 2.00 2.00
1037 A242 300g multicolored 2.00 2.00
a.   Pair, #1036-1037   4.50 4.50
1038 A242 750g multicolored 4.75 4.75
1039 A242 750g multicolored 4.75 4.75
a.   Pair, #1038-1039   11.00 11.00
       Nos. 1028-1039 (12)   19.90 19.90

Bird Type of 1985
1996, Apr. 16   Litho.   Perf. 14x13
1040 A173 2000f Kraagpape-
              gaai   14.00 14.00

Ecotourism A243

Designs: No. 1041, Traditional huts. No. 1042, Butterfly in rain forest. No. 1043, Two natives. No. 1044, Native woman.

Perf. 13½x13 on 3 Sides
1996, Apr. 30   Litho.
              Booklet Stamps
1041 A243 70g multicolored   1.50 1.50
1042 A243 70g multicolored   1.50 1.50
1043 A243 135g multicolored 3.00 3.00
1044 A243 135g multicolored 3.00 3.00
a.   Booklet pane of 4, #1041-
       1044   9.00
       Complete booklet, #1044a 10.00

Radio,
Cent. — A244

135g, First wireless radio communication device, vert. 615g, Guglielmo Marconi.

Perf. 13x14, 14x13
1996, May 17   **Litho.**
1045	A244	135g multicolored	1.00	1.00
1046	A244	615g multicolored	5.00	5.00

1996 Summer
Olympic Games,
Atlanta — A245

Olymphilex '96, Atlanta — A245a

Stamp on stamp: b, 135f, #678. c, 865f, #683.

1996, June 27   **Litho.**   **Perf. 13x14**
1047	A245	70g Basketball	.50	.50
1048	A245	135g Athletics	.95	.95
1049	A245	195g Badminton	1.40	1.40
1050	A245	200g Swimming	1.60	1.60
1051	A245	900g Cycling	7.00	7.00
1052	A245	1000g Hurdles	7.50	7.50
		Nos. 1047-1052 (6)	18.95	18.95

Souvenir Sheet
1052A	A245a	Sheet of 2, #b.-c.	9.00	9.00

Bird Type of 1985

Designs: 75f, Fisman. 160f, Fremusu-aka. 1765f, Roodpoot honingzuiger.

1996, Oct. 2   **Litho.**   **Perf. 14x13**
1053	A173	75f multicolored	.45	.45
1054	A173	160f multicolored	1.00	1.00
1055	A173	1765f multicolored	11.00	11.00
		Nos. 1053-1055 (3)	12.45	12.45

A246

Women's Traditional Costumes: Various styles.

1996, Oct. 9   **Litho.**   **Perf. 13x14**
1056	135f multicolored	1.25	1.25
1057	990f multicolored	7.75	7.75
a.	A246 Pair, #1056-1057	10.00	10.00

America issue.

A247

Christmas: Various stylized designs of Madonna and Child.

1996, Oct. 30   **Litho.**   **Perf. 13x14**
1058	A247	10f multicolored	.25	.25
1059	A247	70f multicolored	.50	.50
1060	A247	135f multicolored	.90	.90
1061	A247	285f multicolored	2.40	2.40
1062	A247	775f multicolored	6.00	6.00
a.		Souvenir sheet, #1062	6.25	6.25
		Nos. 1058-1062 (5)	10.05	10.05

A248   A249

Youth Care: Paintings, by Jan Telting: 135f, Brown dog, child. 865f, White dog, child.

1996, Dec. 4   **Litho.**   **Perf. 13x14**
1063	A248	135f multicolored	1.00	1.00
1064	A248	865f multicolored	8.00	8.00

1996, Dec. 13

City of Albina, 150th Anniv.: August Kappler (1815-87), founder.
1065	A249	875f multicolored	7.25	7.25

Nos. 1024, 1025
Surcharged in Black
or Silver

Methods and perfs as before
1996, Dec. 16
1065A	A240	(125g) on 295g	2.40	2.40
1065B	A240	(125g) on 1000g (S)	2.40	2.40

SURALCO
(Surinam
Aluminum
Co.) — A250

10f, Opening of aluminum smelter, Paranam, 1965. 70f, Drilling blasting holes for ore exploration, Moengo, 1947. 130f, Workers' housing, Moengo, 1919. 150f, Dust-free loading of alumina, Paranam dock, 1995. 160f, Constructing dam, power station, 1960. 730f, Schooner Moengo, 1922.

Perf. 13½x13 on 2 or 3 Sides
1996, Dec. 18
Booklet Stamps
1066	A250	10f multicolored	.25	.25
1067	A250	70f multicolored	.70	.70
1068	A250	130f multicolored	1.25	1.25
1069	A250	150f multicolored	1.40	1.40
1070	A250	160f multicolored	1.60	1.60
1071	A250	730f multicolored	7.25	7.25
a.		Booklet pane, #1066-1071 + label	12.50	
		Complete booklet, #1071a	14.00	

Heinrich von
Stephan (1831-
97) — A251

1997, Jan. 31   **Litho.**   **Perf. 13x14**
1072	A251	275f brown & multi	2.75	2.75
1073	A251	475f dk blue & multi	4.00	4.00

Fauna — A252

#1074, Cebus nigrivittatus. #1075, Cebus apella. #1076, Saguinus midas. #1077, Ateles paniscus. #1078, Ateles geoffroyi panamensis. #1079, Ateles geoffroyi frontatus. #1080, Cacajao calvus. #1081, Lagothrix flavicauda. #1082, Saguinus bicolor. #1083, Saguinus oedipus. #1084, Alouatta seniculus. #1085, Saimiri sciureus.

1997, Feb. 12   **Litho.**   **Perf. 13½**
1074	A252	25f multicolored	.25	.25
1075	A252	25f multicolored	.25	.25
a.		Pair, #1074-1075	.40	.40
1076	A252	75f multicolored	.55	.55
1077	A252	75f multicolored	.55	.55
a.		Pair, #1076-1077	1.25	1.25
1078	A252	100f multicolored	.75	.75
1079	A252	100f multicolored	.75	.75
a.		Pair, #1078-1079	1.60	1.60
1080	A252	275f multicolored	2.00	2.00
1081	A252	275f multicolored	2.00	2.00
a.		Pair, #1080-1081	4.50	4.50
1082	A252	300f multicolored	2.50	2.50
1083	A252	300f multicolored	2.50	2.50
a.		Pair, #1082-1083	5.25	5.25
1084	A252	725f multicolored	5.25	5.25
1085	A252	725f multicolored	5.25	5.25
a.		Pair, #1084-1085	12.00	12.00
		Nos. 1074-1085 (12)	22.60	22.60

Retracing and Completion of Amelia Earhart's Trans-Global Flight by Linda Finch — A253

1997, Mar. 30   **Litho.**   **Perf. 14x13**
1086	A253	275f multicolored	2.50	2.50

Surinam
Museum, 50th
Anniv.
A254

1997, Apr. 3
1087	A254	625f multicolored	4.75	4.75

Nos. 983-986 Surcharged in Black or Silver

1996-97   **Litho.**   **Perf. 13½**
1088	A229	50f on 250g #983	1.40	1.40
1089	A229	50f on 250g #984	1.40	1.40
a.		Pair, #1088-1089	6.75	6.75
1090	A229	100f on 300g #985 (S)	2.75	2.75
1091	A229	100f on 300g #986 (S)	2.75	2.75
a.		Pair, #1090-1091	9.00	9.00
		Nos. 1088-1091 (4)	8.30	8.30

Issued; #1089a, 11/1; #1091a, 1/1/97.

Orchids — A255

Designs: 25f, Selenipedium steyermarkii. 50f, Phragmipedium schlimii. 75f, Criosantes

arietina. 200f, Cypripedium margaritaceum. 775f, Paphiopedilum gratrixianum.

1997, Apr. 3   **Litho.**   **Perf. 13x14**
1092	A255	25f multicolored	.25	.25
1093	A255	50f multicolored	.45	.45
1094	A255	75f multicolored	.60	.60
1095	A255	200f multicolored	1.75	1.75
1096	A255	775f multicolored	6.75	6.75
		Nos. 1092-1096 (5)	9.80	9.80

Souvenir Sheet

PACIFIC 97, San Francisco — A256

1997, May 29   **Litho.**   **Perf. 13½x13**
1097	A256	675f #458-459	5.00	5.00

A257   A258

Mosques: 50f, Great Mosque, Isfahan, Iran. 125f, Dome of the Rock, Jerusalem. 175f, Madrasa of Ulugh beg, Samarkand. 225f, Taj Mahal, Agra, India. 275f, Kaiser St. Mosque, Paramaribo. 325f, Sülcjamiye, Istanbul.

1997, July 7   **Perf. 13x14**
Background Color
1098	A257	50f pink	.35	.35
1099	A257	125f olive	.90	.90
1100	A257	175f blue	1.25	1.25
1101	A257	225f purple	1.60	1.60
1102	A257	275f green	2.10	2.10
1103	A257	325f brown	2.50	2.50
a.		Souvenir sheet of 1	2.75	2.75
		Nos. 1098-1103 (6)	8.70	8.70

Perf. 13x13½ on 3 Sides
1997, Aug. 16   **Litho.**

State Oil Co. Refinery, Saramacca: 50f, Pumping station. 125f, Derrick, butterfly. #1106, Storage tanks. #1107, Gauge, testing mechanism.

Booklet Stamps
1104	A258	50f multicolored	.55	.55
1105	A258	125f multicolored	1.60	1.60
1106	A258	275f multicolored	3.75	3.75
1107	A258	275f multicolored	3.75	3.75
a.		Booklet pane, #1104-1107	11.00	
		Complete booklet, #1107a	12.50	

Bird Type of 1985
1997, Sept. 17   **Litho.**   **Perf. 14x13**
1108	A173	50f Krabu-owrukuku	.50	.50
1109	A173	125f Mangrodoifi	1.50	1.50
1110	A173	275f Peprefowru	2.00	2.00
1111	A173	3150f Kroonvink	25.00	25.00
		Nos. 1108-1111 (4)	29.00	29.00

A259   A260

Child Care: 50f, Right side of boy's face. 100f, Left side of boy's face, 175f, Right side of girl's face. 225f, Left side of girl's face. 350f, 675f, Boy's face upside down, girl's face.

1997, Dec. 4   **Litho.**   **Perf. 13x14**
1112	A259	50f multicolored	.40	.40
1113	A259	100f multicolored	.75	.75
1114	A259	175f multicolored	1.25	1.25

1115	A259	225f multicolored	1.75	1.75
1116	A259	350f multicolored	2.75	2.75
		Nos. 1112-1116 (5)	6.90	6.90

Souvenir Sheet

1117	A259	675f multicolored	5.00	5.00

1997, Dec. 4

Christmas: 125f, Madonna and Child. 225f, Children looking at baby. 450f, Angel. 675f, Children singing, horiz.

1118	A260	125f multicolored	1.00	1.00
1119	A260	225f multicolored	1.75	1.75
1120	A260	450f multicolored	3.50	3.50
		Nos. 1118-1120 (3)	6.25	6.25

Souvenir Sheet

1121	A260	675f multicolored	5.00	5.00

America Issue — A261

Designs: 170f, Postal worker, motorcycle. 230f, Postal worker carrying package.

1997, Dec. 10   Litho.   Perf. 13x14

1122	170f multicolored		1.00	1.00
1123	230f multicolored		1.40	1.40
a.	A261 Pair, #1122-1123		4.50	4.50

Moths & Butterflies — A262

1998, Jan. 26   Perf. 13½

1124	A262	50f Alcandor	.30	.30
1125	A262	50f Achilles	.30	.30
a.		Pair, #1124-1125	.85	.85
1126	A262	75f Alphenor	.45	.45
1127	A262	75f Ceres	.45	.45
a.		Pair, #1126-1127	1.50	1.50
1128	A262	100f Cecropia	.60	.60
1129	A262	100f Helenor	.60	.60
a.		Pair, #1128-1129	1.90	1.90
1130	A262	175f Promothea	1.00	1.00
1131	A262	175f Cassiae	1.00	1.00
a.		Pair, #1130-1131	3.25	3.25
1132	A262	275f Ino	2.10	2.10
1133	A262	275f Phidippus	2.10	2.10
a.		Pair, #1132-1133	6.00	6.00
1134	A262	725f Palamedes	5.50	5.50
1135	A262	725f Helenor, diff.	5.50	5.50
a.		Pair, #1134-1135	15.00	15.00
		Nos. 1124-1135 (12)	19.90	19.90

Bird Type of 1985

1998, Mar. 12   Perf. 14x13, 13x14

1136	A173	50f Marjrietje	.40	.40
1137	A173	225f Aka	2.10	2.10
1138	A173	2425f Timmerman, vert.	22.50	22.50
		Nos. 1136-1138 (3)	25.00	25.00

Hindustani Immigration, 125th Anniv. A263

Designs: 175f, Painting showing first immigrants from boat, "Lala Rooch." 200f, Statue of Baba and Mai, first immigrants from India.

1998, June 4   Litho.   Perf. 14x13

1139	A263	175f multicolored	1.60	1.60
1140	A263	200f multicolored	2.10	2.10

Temples A264

Designs: 50f, Sri Lanka. 75f, Golden Pagoda, Burma, vert. 275f, Swayambhunath,

---

Nepal, vert. 325f, Borobudur, Indonesia. 400f, Wat Phra Kaew, Thailand, vert. 450f, Peking Temple, China, vert. 675f, Statue, Borobudur, Indonesia, vert.

Perf. 13½x12½, 12½x13½

1998, June 4

1141	A264	50f multicolored	.40	.40
1142	A264	75f multicolored	.60	.60
1143	A264	275f multicolored	2.25	2.25
1144	A264	325f multicolored	2.75	2.75
1145	A264	400f multicolored	3.00	3.00
1146	A264	450f multicolored	3.75	3.75
		Nos. 1141-1146 (6)	12.75	12.75

Souvenir Sheet

1147	A264	675f multicolored	6.50	6.50

No. 1147 is a continuous design.

Ferry Boat A265

1998, Oct. 31   Perf. 13½x14

1148	A265	275f blue & multi	2.25	2.25
1149	A265	400f sepia & multi	3.25	3.25

America Issue — A266

Outstanding women: 400f, Sophie Redmond (1907-55). 1000f, Grace Ruth Schneiders-Howard (1869-1968).

1998, Oct. 8   Litho.   Perf. 13x14

1150	A266	400f multicolored	3.75	3.75
1151	A266	1000f multicolored	8.25	8.25

World Stamp Exhibition, The Hague, Netherlands A267

Designs: 400f, #245, portions of #174, #141. 800f, #174, portions of #245, #141. 2400f, #141, portions of #245, #174.

1998, Oct.   Litho.   Perf. 14x13

1152	A267	400f multicolored	3.00	3.00
1153	A267	800f multicolored	5.75	5.75

Souvenir Sheet

1154	A267	2400f multicolored	20.00	20.00

A268   A269

Christmas: Various nativity scenes.

1998, Nov. 1   Perf. 13x14

1155	A268	50f multicolored	.40	.40
1156	A268	325f multicolored	1.60	1.60
1157	A268	400f multicolored	2.00	2.00
1158	A268	1225f multicolored	7.00	7.00
		Nos. 1155-1158 (4)	11.00	11.00

Souvenir Sheet

1159	A268	1400f multicolored	8.00	8.00

Bird Type of 1985

1998, Nov. 16   Litho.   Perf. 14x13

1160	A173	3800f Butarides striatus	16.00	16.00

1998, Dec. 4   Litho.   Perf. 13x14

1161	A269	400f Mother, child, foods	2.10	2.10
1162	A269	1000f Mother, child, flower	5.50	5.50

World Health Organization, 50th anniv.

Child Care — A270

1998, Dec. 4   Litho.   Perf. 14x13

1163	A270	375f shown	2.00	2.00
1164	A270	400f Flying kite, diff.	2.00	2.00
1165	A270	1225f Holding kite	7.00	7.00
		Nos. 1163-1165 (3)	11.00	11.00

Heliconia — A271

#1166, Caribaea kawauchi. #1167, Pastazae. #1168, Rostrata. #1169, Sexy pink. #1170, Collinsiana. #1171, Wagneriana. #1172, Bihai-nappi. #1173, Jaded forest. #1174, Golden torch. #1175, Latispatha-red yellow gyro. #1176, Sexy pink, diff. #1177, Nappi yellow.

1999, Jan. 27   Litho.   Perf. 13½

1166	A271	50f multicolored	.25	.25
1167	A271	50f multicolored	.25	.25
a.		Pair, #1166-1167	.30	.30
1168	A271	200f multicolored	.65	.65
1169	A271	200f multicolored	.65	.65
a.		Pair, #1168-1169	1.50	1.50
1170	A271	300f multicolored	1.00	1.00
1171	A271	300f multicolored	1.00	1.00
a.		Pair, #1170-1171	2.50	2.50
1172	A271	400f multicolored	1.25	1.25
1173	A271	400f multicolored	1.25	1.25
a.		Pair, 1172-1173	3.25	3.25
1174	A271	750f multicolored	2.50	2.50
1175	A271	750f multicolored	2.50	2.50
a.		Pair, #1174-1175	6.50	6.50
1176	A271	1300f multicolored	4.25	4.25
1177	A271	1300f multicolored	4.25	4.25
a.		Pair, #1176-1177	11.00	11.00
		Nos. 1166-1177 (12)	19.80	19.80

Old Plantation Houses A272

1999, Mar. 17   Litho.   Perf. 14x13

1178	A272	75f Katwijk	.30	.30
1179	A272	300f Sorgvliet	1.25	1.25
1180	A272	400f Peperpot	1.50	1.50
1181	A272	2225f Spieringshoek	8.75	8.75
		Nos. 1178-1181 (4)	11.80	11.80

Endangered Species — A273

1999, June 30   Litho.   Perf. 13x14

1182	A273	75f Flamingo	.25	.25
1183	A273	375f Orangutan	.75	.75
1184	A273	450f Elephant	.90	.90
1185	A273	500f Whale	.95	.95
1186	A273	850f Frog	1.60	1.60
1187	A273	900f Rhinoceros	1.75	1.75
1188	A273	1600f Giant panda	3.00	3.00
1189	A273	7250f Tiger	14.00	14.00
		Nos. 1182-1189 (8)	23.20	23.20

Coppename Bridge A274

1999, June 30   Perf. 14x13

1190	A274	850f black & green	1.60	1.60
1191	A274	2250f black & blue	4.25	4.25

A275   A276

1999, July 9   Perf. 13x14

1192	A275	850f multicolored	1.40	1.40
1193	A276	2650f multicolored	4.25	4.25
a.		Souvenir sheet, #1192-1193, perf. 13x13½	5.75	5.75

Surinam Conservation Foundation, 30th anniv. (No. 1192), Central Surinam Nature Preserve, 1st anniv. (No. 1193).

Bird Type of 1985-95

1999, Aug. 21   Perf. 14x13

1194	A173	1000f Blauwtje	1.90	1.90
1195	A173	5500f Kepanki	8.75	8.75

A277

1999, Oct. 9   Perf. 13x14

1196	A277	950f Earth	1.75	1.75
1197	A277	1000f Saturn	1.90	1.90

UPU, 125th anniv.

A278

1999, Oct. 9

1198	1000f Gun		1.75	1.75
1199	2250f Flower		3.50	3.50
a.	A278 Pair, #1198-1199		6.00	6.00

America issue, A New Millennium Without Arms.

Christmas — A279

1999, Nov. 3   Perf. 13x14

1200	A279	500f Star, stable	.80	.80
1201	A279	850f Christmas tree	1.40	1.40
1202	A279	900f Angel	1.50	1.50
1203	A279	1000f Candle	1.60	1.60
		Nos. 1200-1203 (4)	5.30	5.30

Souvenir Sheet

1204	A279	2275f Mother and child	4.25	4.25

Children's Pictures
A280

1999, Dec. 3   Litho.   Perf. 14x13
1205	A280	1100f multi	1.75	1.75
1206	A280	1400f multi, diff.	2.25	2.25
1207	A280	1600f multi, diff.	2.50	2.50
a.		Souvenir sheet of 1	2.75	2.75
		Nos. 1205-1207 (3)	6.50	6.50

Children's Drawings
A281

2000, Jan. 3   Litho.   Perf. 14x13
| 1208 | A281 | 1000f By Tahirih van Kanten | 2.00 | 2.00 |
| 1209 | A281 | 2500f By Tirsa Braaf | 5.50 | 5.50 |

See No. 1224.

Traffic Signs — A282

2000   Perf. 13x14
1210	A282	2000f Turn right	4.00	4.00
1211	A282	2000f No passing	4.00	4.00
1212	A282	2000f Sharp turns	4.00	4.00
1213	A282	2000f Traffic circle	4.00	4.00
		Nos. 1210-1213 (4)	16.00	16.00

Issued: #1210, 1/3; #1211, 4/3; #1212, 5/18. #1213, 9/29.
See Nos. 1246-1248, 1267-1268, 1275-1278, 1311-1312.

Fruits
A283

No. 1214, 50f: a, Citrullus vulgaris. b, Carica papaya.
No. 1215, 175f: a, Mangifera indica. b, Garcinia mangostana.
No. 1216, 200f: a, Musa nana. b, Citrus paradisi.
No. 1217, 250f: a, Punika granatum. b, Ananas comosus.
No. 1218, 325f: a, Cocos nucifera. b, Passiflora quadrangularis.
No. 1219, 5000f: a, Citrus sinensis. b, Persea gratissima.

2000, Feb. 29   Litho.   Perf. 13¼
Pairs, #a-b
| 1214-1219 | A283 | Set of 6 | 20.00 | 20.00 |

No. 1219 is airmail.

Bird Type of 1985
Designs: 1100f, Dendrocygna autumnalis. 4425f, Ceryle torquata.

2000, Apr. 3   Perf. 14x13
| 1220 | A173 | 1100f multi | 1.75 | 1.75 |
| 1221 | A173 | 4425f multi | 7.50 | 7.50 |

Surinam River Bridge
A284

Lettering in: 1100f, Red. 1700f, Blue.

2000, May 18
| 1222-1223 | A284 | Set of 2 | 4.75 | 4.75 |

Children's Drawings Type
Souvenir Sheet

2000   Perf. 13¼x13
| 1224 | A281 | 3575f #1208, 1209 | 6.50 | 6.50 |

World Stamp Expo 2000, Anaheim, Stampin' the Future children's stamp design contest.

2000 Summer Olympic, Sydney
A285

No. 1225, 1100f: a, Soccer. b, Track and field.
No. 1226, 3900f: a, Tennis. b, Swimming.
No. 1227: a, Soccer, diff. b, Swimming, diff.

2000, Aug. 8   Litho.   Perf. 13¼
Pairs, #a-b
| 1225-1226 | A285 | Set of 2 | 18.00 | 18.00 |
Souvenir Sheet
| 1227 | A285 | 2500f Sheet of 2, #a-b | 8.25 | 8.25 |

America Issue, Fight Against AIDS — A286

No. 1228: a, 1100f, Foot with condom stamping out AIDS, horiz. b, 6400f, People holding condoms.

2000   Perf. 13x14
| 1228 | A286 | Pair, #a-b | 13.50 | 13.50 |

25th Anniv. of International Agencies Ltd. as Philatelic and Numismatic Agent — A287

Designs: 125f, Paper money. 5900f, Stamps.

2000, Nov. 24
| 1229-1230 | A287 | Set of 2 | 7.00 | 7.00 |
| 1230a | | Souvenir sheet, #1229-1230 | 7.25 | 7.25 |

Children — A288

Child: 1100f, Walking. 3900f, Breastfeeding. 2000f, With umbilical cord, horiz.

2000, Dec. 5   Perf. 13x14
| 1231-1232 | A288 | Set of 2 | 6.00 | 6.00 |
Souvenir Sheet
Perf. 14x13
| 1233 | A288 | 2000f multi | 2.75 | 2.75 |

Fight Against Poverty
A289

Country name in: 1100f, Green. 4900f, Red.

2000   Perf. 14x13
| 1234-1235 | A289 | Set of 2 | 6.00 | 6.00 |

Christmas — A290

Designs: 1100f, Star of Bethlehem. 3900f, Madonna and Child.
3000f, Magi with gifts, horiz.

2000   Perf. 13x14
| 1236-1237 | A290 | Set of 2 | 6.75 | 6.75 |
Souvenir Sheet
Perf. 14x13
| 1238 | A290 | 3000f multi | 4.25 | 4.25 |

No. 945a Surcharged

Methods and Perfs as Before

2000 (?)
1238A		Pair	2.50	2.50
b.		A221 1000f on 25c No. 942	.95	.95
c.		A221 1000f on 25c No. 943	.95	.95
1239		Pair	6.75	6.75
a.		A221 3100f on 35c No. 944	2.50	2.50
b.		A221 3100f on 35c No. 945	2.50	2.50

Birds
A291

No. 1240, 50f: a, Rood zwart vink tagara. b, Tyarman.
No. 1241, 175f: a, Sabaku. b, Kolibrie.
No. 1242, 200f: a, Aka. b, Timmerman.
No. 1243, 250f: a, Paarskeel cotinga. b, Zwarte kraag donfowru.
No. 1244, 825f: a, Kees. b, Stonkuyake.
No. 1245, 7500f: a, Guyanese rood cotinga. b, Butabuta.

2001, Jan. 31   Litho.   Perf. 13¼
Pairs, #a-b
| 1240-1245 | A291 | Set of 6 | 18.00 | 18.00 |

No. 1245 is airmail.

Traffic Signs Type of 2000
2001   Litho.   Perf. 13x14
1246	A282	2000f No parking	4.50	4.50
1247	A282	4000f Drawbridge	5.00	5.00
1248	A282	4000f Tractor, No entry	5.00	5.00

Issued: 2000f, 3/8; No. 1247, 4/25; No. 1248, 9/12.

UN Women's Human Rights Campaign
A292

Youth Philately
A293

Designs: 1400f, Female and male symbols. 4600f, Woman.

2001, Mar. 15   Litho.   Perf. 13x14
| 1249-1250 | A292 | Set of 2 | 6.00 | 6.00 |

2001, Apr. 25
Children's art by: 650f, Bhoelai Surender Kumar. 5350f, Sharon Cameron.
| 1251-1252 | A293 | Set of 2 | 6.00 | 6.00 |

Bird Type of 1985
Designs: 4500f, Charadrius collaris. 9000f, Bubo virginianus.

2001, May 10   Perf. 14x13
| 1253 | A173 | 4500f multi | 5.25 | 5.25 |
| 1254 | A173 | 9000f multi | 10.50 | 10.50 |

Fruit — A294

Designs: 150f, Sapotille. 200f, Noni vrucht. 800fr, Baby bananas. 1200f, Mope. 1700f, Pommerak.

2001, July 20   Litho.   Perf. 12¾x13½
| 1255-1259 | A294 | Set of 5 | 5.25 | 5.25 |

America Issue — A295

Paramaribo buildings: Nos. 1260a, 1261a, 1700f, Bishop's house. Nos. 1260b, 1261b, 7300f, Presidential palace.

2001, Sept. 12   Litho.   Perf. 14x13
Country Name in Red
| 1260 | A295 | Pair, #a-b | 10.50 | 10.50 |
Souvenir Sheet
Country Name in Green
Perf. 13¼x13
| 1261 | A295 | Sheet of 2, #a-b | 10.50 | 10.50 |

Stamp Day — A296

Designs: No. 1262a, 3750f, #648 (green background). No. 1262b, 5250f, #29 (red background).
No. 1263a, 3750f, #648 (red background). No. 1263b, 5250f, #29 (orange background).

2001, Oct. 19   Perf. 13x14
| 1262 | A296 | Pair, #a-b | 10.50 | 10.50 |
Souvenir Sheet
Perf. 13x13¼
| 1263 | A296 | Sheet of 2, #a-b | 10.50 | 10.50 |

Christmas
A297

Children's
Sports — A298

2001, Nov. 2   *Perf. 13¼*
1264 A297 1700f blue & multi   2.25 2.25
     Perf. 14x13
1265 A298 5000f red & multi   6.25 6.25
     Souvenir Sheet
     Perf. 13¼x13
1266   Sheet of 2   8.50 8.50
  a.   A297 1700f green & multi   2.10 2.10
  b.   A298 5000f blue & multi   6.25 6.25

No. 947a
Surcharged
in Gold

2001, Dec. 7   **Litho.**   *Perf. 13½*
1266C   Pair   6.75 6.75
  d.   A221 2500f on 50c No. 946   3.25 3.25
  e.   A221 2500f on 50c No. 947   3.25 3.25

Traffic Signs Type of 2000
2001-02   *Perf. 13x14*
1267 A282 4000f Pedestrian
          crossing   5.00 5.00
1268 A282 4000f Yield   5.00 5.00
  Issued: No. 1267, 12/7/01; No. 1268,
2/13/02.

Parrots
A299

  No. 1269, 150f: a, Deroptyus acciptrinus. b,
Amazona achrocephala.
  No. 1270, 200f: a, Ara manilata. b,
Amazona dufresniana.
  No. 1271, 800f: a, Ara severa. b, Pionites
melanocephala.
  No. 1272, 1200f: a, Ara nobilis. b, Pionus
fiscus.
  No. 1273, 1700f: a, Ara chloroptera. b, Pio-
nopsitta caicca.
  No. 1274, 5325f: a, Ara macao. b, Amazona
farinosa.

2002, Jan. 9   *Perf. 13¼*
     Pairs, #a-b
1269-1274 A299   Set of 6   17.50 17.50
     No. 1274 is airmail.

Traffic Signs Type of 2000
2002-03   **Litho.**   *Perf. 13x14*
1275 A282 4000f U turn   3.75 3.75
     Perf. 12¾x14
1276 A282 4000f Pedestrian
          path   4.50 4.50
1277 A282 4000f Train cross-
          ing without
          barriers   4.50 4.50
1278 A282 4000f Motorcycles   4.50 4.50
     Nos. 1275-1278 (4)   17.25 17.25
  Issued: No. 1275, 4/17/02; No. 1276,
6/19/02; No. 1277, 9/20/02; No. 1278, 2/13/03.

Traffic Signs Type of 2000
2002-03   **Litho.**

Costumes
A300

Birds
A301

  Costumes of: Nos. 1279a, 1279c, 1279e,
1279g, 1279i, 1279k, Various men. Nos.
1279b, 1279d, 1279f, 1279h, 1279j, 1279l,
Various women.

2002, May 15   *Perf. 12¾x13¼*
1279   Horiz. strip of 12   17.00 17.00
  a.-b.   A300 150f Either single   .25 .25
  c.-d.   A300 200f Either single   .25 .25
  e.-f.   A300 800f Either single   .75 .75
  g.-h.   A300 1200f Either single   1.10 1.10
  i.-j.   A300 1700f Either single   1.60 1.60
  k.-l.   A300 4950f Either single   4.50 4.50

2002, June 19   *Perf. 12¾x14*
1280 A301 5000f Royal fly-
          catcher   5.75 5.75
1281 A301 8500f Swampufowru 10.00 10.00

**Amphilex 2002 Intl. Stamp Exhibition,
Amsterdam — A302**

  No. 1282: a, 1700f, Netherlands #244 (yellow background). b, 6800f, Netherlands #103
(maroon background).
  No. 1283: a, 1700f, Like No. 1282a (maroon
background). b, 6800f, Like No. 1282b (yellow
background).

2002, Aug. 30   *Perf. 13¼x12¾*
1282 A302   Horiz. pair, #a-b   8.75 8.75
     Souvenir Sheet
1283 A302   Sheet of 2, #a-b   8.75 8.75

     Souvenir Sheet
   No. 1230a Overprinted in Gold

2002, Aug. 30   **Litho.**   *Perf. 13x14*
1284 A287   Sheet of 2   9.50 9.50
  a.   250f on 125f #1229   .45 .45
  b.   5900f #1230 overprinted   9.25 9.25

**America Issue - Youth, Education and
Literacy — A303**

  No. 1285 — Letters, numbers and: a, 1700f,
Stylized head and question mark. b, 7300f, "X"
in signature box.

2002, Sept. 20   *Perf. 13¼x12¾*
1285 A303   Horiz. pair, #a-b   11.00 11.00

Christmas
A304

  Designs: No. 1286, 1700f, Unclothed Santa
Claus and clothing (light blue background).
No. 1287, 5000f, Christmas tree, decorations
and gifts (green background).
  No. 1288: a, 1700f, Like No. 1286 (yellow
background). b, 5000f, Like No. 1287 (blue
background).

2002, Nov. 6
1286-1287 A304   Set of 2   7.00 7.00
     Souvenir Sheet
1288 A304   Sheet of 2, #a-b   7.00 7.00

  **Nos. 949a, 953a Surcharged Like
    No. 1266C in Gold or Silver**
2002 ?   **Litho.**   *Perf. 13½*
1289   Pair   4.75 4.75
  a.   A221 2500f on 100c #948   2.25 2.25
  b.   A221 2500f on 100c #949   2.25 2.25
1290   Pair   9.00 9.00
  a.   A221 3750f on 220c #952 (S)   4.50 4.50
  b.   A221 3750f on 220c #953 (S)   4.50 4.50

Birds — A305

  No. 1291: a, Falco deiroleucus. b, Lophornis
ornatus. c, Touit purpurata. d, Thanlurania fur-
cata. e, Myrmeciza ferruginea. f, Pteroglossus
aracari. g, Cotinga cotinga. h, Granatellus
pelzelni. i, Euphonia musica. j, Pitangus lictor.
k, Cacicus haemorrhous. l, Columba speciosa.

2003, Jan. 9   *Perf. 13¼x14*
1291   Block of 12   21.00 21.00
  a.-b.   A305 150f Either single   .25 .25
  c.-d.   A305 200f Either single   .25 .25
  e.-f.   A305 800f Either single   .90 .90
  g.-h.   A305 1200f Either single   1.25 1.25
  i.-j.   A305 1700f Either single   1.90 1.90
  k.-l.   A305 4950f Either single   5.50 5.50

  **No. 951a Surcharged in Silver Like
        No. 1266C**
2002, Dec. 30   **Litho.**   *Perf. 13½*
1292   Pair   5.00 5.00
  a.   A221 2750f on 175c #950   2.50 2.50
  b.   A221 2750f on 175c #951   2.50 2.50

Dolls — A306

  No. 1293: a, A. M. 352/1030. b, S&H 1079,
1892. c, Jumeau, 1895 (denomination in
white). d, Jumeau, 1895 (denomination in red).
e, A. M. 390, 1900. f, Minerva, 1900. g, K&R
126, 1905. h, K&R, 1905. i, Handwerck, 1905.
j, SFBJ, 1907. k, A. M. 980, 1920. l, K&R,
1910.

2003, May 12   *Perf. 13½x14*
1293   Block of 12   12.50 12.50
  a.-l.   A306 1000f Any single   1.00 1.00

A307   A308

  Designs: 150f, Izaak Enschedé. 800f, Old
building of Johann Enschedé Printers, horiz.
1700f, Surinam #7. 3850f, First Surinam banknote printed by Enschedé, horiz.
7500f, Like 150f.

    Perf. 12¾x13½, 13½x12¾
2003, June 3
1294-1297 A307   Set of 4   5.25 5.25
     Souvenir Sheet
1298 A307 7500f multi   7.50 7.50
  Johann Enschedé and Sons, printers, 300th
anniv.

2003, Sept. 3   *Perf. 12¾x14*
  Birds: 5400f, Anthracothorax viridigula.
6600f, Campephilus melanoleucos.
1299 A308   5400f multi   6.25 6.25
1300 A308   6600f multi   7.25 7.25

Traffic Signs Type of 2000
2003, Sept. 3   **Litho.**   *Perf. 12¾x14*
1301 A282 4000f 10% grade   4.50 4.50

America Issue - Flora and
Fauna — A309

  No. 1302: a, 1700f, Faya lobi. b, 8500f,
Puma.

2003, Sept. 20   **Litho.**   *Perf. 14x12¾*
1302 A309   Horiz. pair, #a-b   8.25 8.25
  c.   Souvenir sheet, #1302   8.25 8.25

    Nos. 889a, 929a Surcharged

    Methods and Perfs as Before
2003
1303   Pair   7.50 7.50
  a.   A172 3500f on 1c on 5c #928   3.75 3.75
  b.   A172 3500f on 1c on 5c #929   3.75 3.75
1304   Pair   7.50 7.50
  a.   A172 3500f on 2c on 10c #888   3.75 3.75
  b.   A172 3500f on 2c on 10c #889   3.75 3.75
  Issued: No. 1303, 11/1; No. 1304, 12/1.

Christmas — A310

  Designs: 1700f, Children, dog, toy horse.
5300f, Woman holding candle.

2003, Nov. 6   **Litho.**   *Perf. 12¾x14*
1306 A310 1700f multi   1.40 1.40
1307 A310 5300f multi   4.25 4.25
  a.   Horiz. pair, #1306-1307 + central
     label   7.50 7.50
  b.   Souvenir sheet, #1306-1307   7.50 7.50

Powered
Flight, Cent.
A311

  Designs: 1700f, Santos-Dumont 14bis, first
European flight, 1906. 5300f, Replica of 1903
aircraft by Richard Pearse, New Zealand.

2003, Dec. 13   *Perf. 14x12¾*
1308 A311 1700f multi   2.00 2.00
1309 A311 5300f multi   5.50 5.50
  a.   Souvenir sheet, #1308-1309   7.50 7.50

  The Surinam dollar replaced the florin
in January 2004 at an exchange rate of
1000 florins to 1 dollar. Nos. 1310-
1313, though issued after the introduction of the new currency, have denominations expressed in florins.

Butterflies
A312

No. 1310: a, Anartia amathea. b, Vanessa carye. c, Papilio demetrius. d, Precis octavia. e, Papilio blumei. f, Papilio aritodemus ponceanus. g, Zerynthia rumina. h, Parides gundlachianus. i, Ornithoptera priamus. j, Lyropteryx apollonia. k, Agrias narcissus. l, Elzunia bonplandii.

2004, Jan. 12   *Perf. 12¾x14*

1310	Block of 12	22.00	22.00
a.-b.	A312 150f Either single	.25	.25
c.-d.	A312 200f Either single	.25	.25
e.-f.	A312 800f Either single	.65	.65
g.-h.	A312 1200f Either single	.95	.95
i.-j.	A312 1700f Either single	1.40	1.40
k.-l.	A312 L Either single	7.50	7.50

Nos. 1310k-1310l sold for 9500f on day of issue.

Traffic Signs Type of 2000

2004   Litho.   *Perf. 12¾x14*

1311	A282 4000f Horse and rider crossing	7.75	7.75
1312	A282 4000f Large vehicles prohibited	7.75	7.75
a.	Souvenir sheet, #1278, 1301, 1311, 1312	16.50	16.50

Issued: Nos. 1311-1312, 3/31; No. 1312a, 10/1.

Mailboxes of the World — A313

No. 1313: a, Indonesia. b, Brazil. c, Macao. d, Germany. e, Uruguay. f, Republic of Korea. g, Oman. h, Mexico. i, Australia. j, Switzerland. k, Hong Kong. l, United States.

2004, May 6

1313	Block of 12	25.00	25.00
a.-b.	A313 150f Either single	.25	.25
c.-d.	A313 200f Either single	.25	.25
e.-f.	A313 800f Either single	.65	.65
g.-h.	A313 1200f Either single	.95	.95
i.-j.	A313 1700f Either single	1.40	1.40
k.-l.	A313 K Either single	9.00	9.00

Nos. 1313k-1313l each sold for 11,500f ($11.50) on day of issue.

Greek Amphorae — A314

No. 1314 — Inscriptions: a, Athena en Poseidon. b, Wedren. c, Athena Promachus, 363/62 v. C. d, Hippodamia ontvoerd door Pelops, 415 v. C. e, Winnaar muziekconcours, 440-430 v. C. f, Wedren 485-470 v. C. g, Vaashals: speer-en discuswerpers. h, Wedren vier paarden. i, Heracles met leeuw van Nemea, 520 v. C. j, Amfoor, 566 v. C. k, Winnaar muziekconcours (no handles). l, Winnaar muziekconcours (with handles).

No. 1315 — Portions of an amphora: a, $2, Left. b, $3, Center. c, $5, Right.

2004, July 1

1314	Block of 12	28.00	28.00
a.-b.	A314 5c Either single	.25	.25
c.-d.	A314 15c Either single	.25	.25
e.-f.	A314 20c Either single	.25	.25
g.-h.	A314 45c Either single	.35	.35
i.-j.	A314 80c Either single	.60	.60
k.-l.	A314 M Either single	12.50	12.50

Souvenir Sheet

1315	A314 Sheet of 3, #a-c	8.00	8.00

2004 Summer Olympics, Athens (No. 1315). Nos. 1314k-1314l each sold for $16 on day of issue, and are airmail.

America Issue - Birds — A315

Designs: $1.70, Duck. $12, Parrots.

2004, Sept. 16   *Perf. 14x12¾*

1316-1317	A315 Set of 2	11.00	11.00
1317a	Souvenir sheet, #1316-1317	12.00	12.00

Birds — A316

No. 1318: a, Chloroceryle inda. b, Brotogeris chrysopterus. c, Buteo magnisrostris. d, Buteo albicaudatus. e, Calliphlox amethystina (facing left). f, Calliphlox amethystina (facing right). g, Harpagus diodon. h, Aratinga pertinax. i, Chlorocersyle amazona. j, Galbula galbula. k, Buteogallus aequinoctialis. l, Polyborus plancus.

2004, Oct. 21   *Perf. 12¾x14*

1318	Block of 12	28.00	28.00
a.-b.	A316 5c Either single	.25	.25
c.-d.	A316 15c Either single	.25	.25
e.-f.	A316 20c Either single	.25	.25
g.-h.	A316 45c Either single	.35	.35
i.-j.	A316 80c Either single	.60	.60
k.-l.	A316 M Either single	12.50	12.50

Nos. 1318k-1318l each sold for $16 on day of issue, and are airmail.
See Nos. 1329, 1350.

Child Care A317   Christmas A318

2004, Nov. 18   Litho.   *Perf. 12¾x14*

1319	A317 $1.70 multi	1.40	1.40
1320	A318 $7.70 multi	6.25	6.25
a.	Souvenir sheet, #1319-1320	7.75	7.75

Teddy Bears — A319

No. 1321: a, Bing, 1919. b, Steiff "Teddy Clown," 1926. c, Steiff "Teddy Girl," 1905. d, Steiff, 1905. e, Steif "Elliot," 1907. f, Ideal "Aloysius," 1907. g, Steiff, 1936. h, Steif "Zotty," 1951. i, Steiff, 1910. j, Steiff "Titanic," 1912. k, Steiff "Berlin," 1985. l, Aux Nations, 1903.

No. 1322: a, Blue mohair, 1938-52. b, Musical bear, 1937. c, Red mohair, 1908. d, Shaggy beige mohair, 1908. e, Ally bear, 1916. f, National bear, 1917. g, Cowboy, 1940s. h, Coronation bear, 1953. i, Tumbling bear, 1920-30s. j, Messenger bear, 1923. k, Bear on a tricycle, 1958. l, Michi Takahashi, 1999.

2004-05   Litho.   *Perf. 12¾x14*

1321	Block of 12	21.00	21.00
a.-b.	A319 5c Either single	.25	.25
c.-d.	A319 15c Either single	.25	.25
e.-f.	A319 20c Either single	.25	.25
g.-h.	A319 45c Either single	.35	.35
i.-j.	A319 80c Either single	.65	.65
k.-l.	A319 K Either single	9.00	9.00
1322	Block of 12	30.00	30.00
a.-b.	A319 5c Either single	.25	.25
c.-d.	A319 15c Either single	.25	.25
e.-f.	A319 20c Either single	.25	.25
g.-h.	A319 45c Either single	.35	.35
i.-j.	A319 80c Either single	.65	.65
k.-l.	A319 N Either single	13.50	13.50

Issued: No. 1321, 2004; No. 1322, 3/1/05. Nos. 1321k-1321l each sold for $11.50 on day of issue, and are airmail. Nos. 1322k-1322l each sold for $17 on day of issue, and are airmail.

Butterflies — A320

No. 1323: a, Papilio chikae. b, Iphiclides podalirius. c, Paraphnaeus. d, Morpho didius. e, Delias eucharis. f, Parides sesostris. g, Baronia brevicornis. h, Graphium agamemnon. i, Papilio palinurus. j, Ornithoptera meridionalis. k, Battus bhilenor. l, Eurytides bellerophon.

2005, Jan. 5

1323	Block of 12	30.00	30.00
a.-b.	A320 5c Either single	.25	.25
c.-d.	A320 15c Either single	.25	.25
e.-f.	A320 20c Either single	.25	.25
g.-h.	A320 45c Either single	.35	.35
i.-j.	A320 80c Either single	.60	.60
k.-l.	A320 N Either single	13.50	13.50

Nos. 1323k-1323l each sold for $17 on day of issue, and are airmail.

Ships A321

No. 1324: a, Louis Roux, Altana. b, Fanerom Eni. c, Nafsika. d, Aristeidis Glykas. e, G. D'Esposito. f, G. D'Esposito, diff.

2005, May 4   Litho.   *Perf. 14x12¾*

1324	Block of 6	17.00	17.00
a.	A321 5c multi	.25	.25
b.	A321 15c multi	.25	.25
c.	A321 20c multi	.25	.25
d.	A321 80c multi	.60	.60
e.	A321 $1.70 multi	1.40	1.40
f.	A321 P multi	14.00	14.00

No. 1324f is airmail and sold for $18 on day of issue.

Orchids — A322

No. 1325: a, Vanda hybrid. b, Phalaenopsis hybrid, dark pink flowers. c, Dendrobium hybrid, pink flowers. d, Dendrobium hybrid, dark red flowers with foliage in background. e, Vanda hybrid, diff. f, Peristeria elata. g, Spathoglottis hybrid. h, Dendrobium hybrid, yellow orange flowers. i, Vanda sanderiana. j, Phalaenopsis hybrid, peach flowers. k, Phalaenopsis hybrid, pink flowers. l, Phalaenopsis hybrid, white flowers.

2005, June 29   *Perf. 12¾x14*

1325	Block of 12	27.50	27.50
a.-b.	A322 5c Either single	.25	.25
c.-d.	A322 15c Either single	.25	.25
e.-f.	A322 20c Either single	.25	.25
g.-h.	A322 45c Either single	.40	.40
i.-j.	A322 80c Either single	.70	.70
k.-l.	A322 Q Either single	10.00	10.00

Nos. 1325k and 1325 l are airmail and each sold for $12.50 on day of issue. See No. 1337.

America Issue, Fight Against Poverty A323

Designs: $1.70, Teacher and children. $14.50, Farmer, oxen and plow. $14, Teacher and children, diff.

Perf. 14x12¾, 12¾x14

2005, Sept. 14

1326-1327	A323 Set of 2	13.00	13.00

Souvenir Sheet
Perf. 12¾x13¼

1328	A323 $14 multi	11.50	11.50

Birds Type of 2004

No. 1329: a, Porphyrula flavirostris. b, Asio clamator. c, Herpetotheres cashinnans. d, Jacana jacana. e, Touit batavica. f, Dendrocygna autumnalis. g, Coccyzus minor. h, Busarellus nigricollis. i, Lophostrix cristata. j, Otus choliba. k, Chrysolampis mosquitus. l, Pyrrhula picta.

2005, Oct. 19   *Perf. 12¾x14*

1329	Block of 12	35.00	35.00
a.-b.	A316 5c Either single	.25	.25
c.-d.	A316 15c Either single	.25	.25
e.-f.	A316 20c Either single	.25	.25
g.-h.	A316 80c Either single	.65	.65
i.-j.	A316 $1.80 Either single	1.40	1.40
k.-l.	A316 P Either single	14.50	14.50

Nos. 1329k and 1329 l are airmail and each sold for $18 on day of issue.

Children — A324

Designs (country name in red): 80c, Girl jumping rope. $9.50, Boy on swing.
No. 1332 — Country name in white: a, Girl jumping rope, diff. b, Boy on swing, diff.

2005, Nov. 16   *Perf. 12¾x13¼*

1330-1331	A324 Set of 2	8.50	8.50

Souvenir Sheet

1332	A324 $5 Sheet of 2, #a-b	8.50	8.50

No. 891a Surcharged

Methods and Perfs as Before

2005, Dec. 1

1333	Pair	6.50	6.50
a.	A172 $3.50 on 3c on 50c #891a	3.00	3.00
b.	A172 $3.50 on 3c on 50c #891b	3.00	3.00

Europa Stamps, 50th Anniv. — A325

Designs: $1, Netherlands #379. $2, Netherlands #369. $9, Netherlands #375.

2006, Jan. 4   Litho.   *Perf. 12¾x13¼*

1334-1336	A325 Set of 3	8.75	8.75
1336a	Souvenir sheet, #1334-1336	8.75	8.75

Orchids Type of 2005

No. 1337: a, Dendrobium hybrid, yellow flowers. b, Dendrobium hybrid, white flowers. c, Phalaenopsis hybrid, light purple flowers. d, Phalaenopsis hybrid, pink flowers. e, Vanda hybrid, white flowers. f, Vanda hybrid, purple flowers. g, Dendrobium hybrid, purple and white flowers. h, Arachnis hybrid. i, Vanda hybrid, light orange flowers. j, Vanda hybrid, speckled purple flowers. k, Complex hybrid, orange flowers. l, Vanda hybrid, purple and white flowers.

2006, Feb. 15　　　　　**Perf. 12¾x14**
1337	Block of 12	28.00	28.00
a.-b.	A322 5c Either single	.25	.25
c.-d.	A322 15c Either single	.25	.25
e.-f.	A322 20c Either single	.25	.25
g.-h.	A322 45c Either single	.35	.35
i.-j.	A322 80c Either single	.60	.60
k.-l.	A322 Q Either single	12.50	12.50

Nos. 1337k and 1337 l are airmail and each sold for $17.50 on day of issue.

Birds — A326

No. 1338: a, Phaethornis ruber. b, Threnetes leucurus. c, Podager nacunda. d, Columbina passerina. e, Leptotila rufaxilla. f, Claravis pretiosa. g, Campylopterus largipennis. h, Otus choliba. i, Porzana albicollis. j, Amazilia fimbriata. k, Ciccata virgata. l, Nyctidromus albicollis.

2006, May 15　**Litho.**　**Perf. 14x12¾**
1338	Block of 12	28.00	28.00
a.-b.	A326 5c Either single	.25	.25
c.-d.	A326 15c Either single	.25	.25
e.-f.	A326 20c Either single	.25	.25
g.-h.	A326 45c Either single	.30	.30
i.-j.	A326 80c Either single	.55	.55
k.-l.	A326 Q Either single	12.50	12.50

Nos. 1338k-1338l each sold for $17.50, and are airmail.

Nobel Laureates — A327

No. 1339: a, Aung San Suu Kyi, Peace, 1991. b, Milton Friedman, Economics, 1976. c, Marie Curie, Chemistry, 1911. d, Johannes Diderik van der Waals, Physics, 1910. e, Selma Lagerlöf, Literature, 1909. f, Gary S. Becker, Economics, 1992.

2006, June 26　　　　**Perf. 12¾x13¼**
1339	Block of 6	8.50	8.50
a.	A327 20c multi	.25	.25
b.	A327 $1.20 multi	.85	.85
c.	A327 $1.70 multi	1.25	1.25
d.	A327 $2 multi	1.40	1.40
e.	A327 $3 multi	2.25	2.25
f.	A327 $3.50 multi	2.50	2.50

America Issue, Energy Conservation A328

Designs: 80c, Solar-powered airplane. $16.20, Windmill.
No. 1342: a, $3.50, Glider. b, $12.50, Windmills.

2006, Sept. 15　　　　　**Perf. 14**
1340-1341 A328	Set of 2	12.50	12.50

Souvenir Sheet
1342 A328	Sheet of 2, #a-b	12.00	12.00

Fish — A329

No. 1343: a, Crown betta. b, Barbus barilioides. c, Macropodus opercularis. d, Xiphophorus maculatus. e, Acanthurus lineatus. f, Carassius auratus.

2006, Oct. 15　　　　**Perf. 13¼x12¾**
1343	Block of 6	14.50	14.50
a.	A329 $1.20 multi	.85	.85
b.	A329 $1.70 multi	1.25	1.25
c.	A329 $2 multi	1.40	1.40
d.	A329 $3 multi	2.25	2.25
e.	A329 $3.50 multi	2.50	2.50
f.	A329 $8.60 multi	6.25	6.25

Child Care — A330

Christmas A331

2006, Nov. 6　　　　　　**Perf. 14**
1344 A330	$4 shown	3.00	3.00
1345 A331	$9.20 shown	6.75	6.75

Souvenir Sheet
1346	Sheet of 2	5.00	5.00
a.	A330 80c Children with ball	.60	.60
b.	A331 $6 Stained glass, diff.	4.25	4.25

No. 447 Surcharged in Brown

Methods and Perfs As Before
2006, Dec. 1
1347 A111	$3.25 on 1c #447	2.40	2.40
1348 A111	$3.75 on 1c #447	2.75	2.75

Primates — A332

No. 1349: a, Hylobates lar. b, Leontopithecus rosalia. c, Saguinus imperator. d, Callithrix geoffroyi. e, Callithrix argentata. f, Pygathrix nemaeus nemaeus. g, Saimiri sciureus. h, Douc langur. i, Cercopithecus neglectus. j, Alouatta caraya. k, Verreaux sitaka. l, Pan troglodytes.

2006, Dec. 13　　　　**Perf. 12¾x13¼**
1349	Block of 12	24.00	24.00
a.	A332 R multi	.25	.25
b.	A332 20c multi	.25	.25
c.	A332 45c multi	.35	.35
d.	A332 80c multi	.60	.60
e.	A332 $1.20 multi	.90	.90
f.	A332 $1.70 multi	1.25	1.25
g.	A332 $2 multi	1.40	1.40
h.	A332 $3 multi	2.25	2.25
i.	A332 $3.50 multi	2.60	2.60
j.	A332 $4 multi	3.00	3.00
k.	A332 $5 multi	3.75	3.75
l.	A332 $10 multi	7.25	7.25

No. 1349a sold for 15c on day of issue.

Bird Type of 2004
2006, Dec. 20　　　　**Perf. 12¾x14**
1350 A316	$10 Phaethornis superciliosus	7.25	7.25

Printed in sheets of 2 + label.

Orchids — A333

No. 1351: a, Cattleya labiata. b, Vuylstekeara. c, Cymbidium. d, Odontoglossum pestcatorei. e, Odontocidium f, Odontioda. g, Vanda. h, Cattleya. i, Paphiopedilum insigne. j, Phalaenopsis. k, Thunia. l, Oncidium.

2007, Jan. 3　　　　**Perf. 12¾x13¼**
1351	Block of 12	24.00	24.00
a.	A333 S multi	.25	.25
b.	A333 20c multi	.25	.25
c.	A333 45c multi	.35	.35
d.	A333 80c multi	.60	.60
e.	A333 $1.20 multi	.90	.90
f.	A333 $1.70 multi	1.25	1.25
g.	A333 $2 multi	1.40	1.40
h.	A333 $3 multi	2.25	2.25
i.	A333 $3.50 multi	2.50	2.50
j.	A333 $4 multi	3.00	3.00
k.	A333 $5 multi	3.75	3.75
l.	A333 $10 multi	7.25	7.25

No. 1351a sold for 10c on day of issue.

Butterflies A334

No. 1352: a, Great spangled fritillary. b, Peacock pansy. c, Viceroy. d, Unidentified taxco. e, Tropical buckeye. f, Limenitis popul.

2007, Feb. 14　　　　　**Perf. 14**
1352	Block of 6	9.00	9.00
a.	A334 T multi	.25	.25
b.	A334 $1.20 multi	.85	.85
c.	A334 $1.70 multi	1.25	1.25
d.	A334 $2 multi	1.40	1.40
e.	A334 $3 multi	2.25	2.25
f.	A334 $4 multi	3.00	3.00

No. 1352a sold for 5c on day of issue. See No. 1366.

Reptiles A335

No. 1353: a, Terapene carolina. b, Cuora flavomarginata. c, Chelonia mydas. d, Testudo hermanni. e, Uromastyx acanthinura. f, Physignathus cocincinus. g, Iguana iguana. h, Amblyrhynchus cristatus. i, Chamaeleo jacksoni. j, Crocodylus niloticus. k, Caiman crocodilus. l, Varanus komodensis.

Perf. 13¼x12¾
2007, Mar. 21　　　　**Litho.**
1353	Block of 12	24.00	24.00
a.	A335 S multi	.25	.25
b.	A335 20c multi	.25	.25
c.	A335 45c multi	.30	.30
d.	A335 80c multi	.60	.60
e.	A335 $1.20 multi	.90	.90
f.	A335 $1.70 multi	1.25	1.25
g.	A335 $2 multi	1.50	1.50
h.	A335 $3 multi	2.25	2.25
i.	A335 $3.50 multi	2.60	2.60
j.	A335 $4 multi	3.00	3.00
k.	A335 $5 multi	3.75	3.75
l.	A335 $10 multi	7.25	7.25

No. 1353a sold for 10c on day of issue.

Parrots — A336

No. 1354: a, Callocephalon fimbriatum. b, Cacatua ophthalmica. c, Cacatua galerita. d, Cacatua sulphure amazone. e, Calyporhychus magunificus. f, Cacatua sulphure amazone, diff. g, Eolophus rosicapillus. h, Cacatua sulphure amazone, diff. i, Parrot (inscribed "Pan troglodytes" in error).

2007, Apr. 26　　　　　**Perf. 14**
1354	Block of 9	11.50	11.50
a.	A336 T multi	.25	.25
b.	A336 25c multi	.25	.25
c.	A336 55c multi	.40	.40
d.	A336 80c multi	.60	.60
e.	A336 $1.10 multi	.80	.80
f.	A336 $1.20 multi	.90	.90
g.	A336 $2 multi	1.50	1.50
h.	A336 $4 multi	3.00	3.00
i.	A336 $5 multi	3.75	3.75

No. 1354a sold for 5c on day of issue.

Birds — A337

No. 1355: a, Agamia agami. b, Botaurus pinnatus. c, Rallus maculatus. d, Melanerpes cruentatus. e, Piculus chrysochloros. f, Paroaria gularis. g, Gyanicterus cyanicterus. h, Tersina viridis. i, Sicalis floreola.

2007, May 23　　　　**Perf. 12¾x13¼**
1355	Block of 9	18.00	18.00
a.	A337 T multi	.25	.25
b.	A337 20c multi	.25	.25
c.	A337 45c multi	.35	.35
d.	A337 80c multi	.60	.60
e.	A337 $1.20 multi	.90	.90
f.	A337 $2 multi	1.50	1.50
g.	A337 $4 multi	3.00	3.00
h.	A337 $5 multi	3.75	3.75
i.	A337 $10 multi	7.25	7.25

No. 1355a sold for 5c on day of issue. See Nos. 1373, 1388.

Fish — A338

No. 1356: a, Brachydanio rerio. b, Pterois miles. c, Pomacanthus annularis. d, Balsitoides conspicillum. e, Plectorhynchus orientalis. f, Chaetodon auriga.

Perf. 13¼x12¾
2007, June 27　　　　　**Litho.**
1356	Block of 6	15.00	15.00
a.	A338 $1.20 multi	.90	.90
b.	A338 $1.70 multi	1.25	1.25
c.	A338 $2 multi	1.50	1.50
d.	A338 $3 multi	2.25	2.25
e.	A338 $3.50 multi	2.60	2.60
f.	A338 $8.60 multi	6.25	6.25

Ferrari Automobiles A339

No. 1357: a, 1947 125 S. b, 1962 250 GTO. c, 1984 GTO. d, 1999 F399. e, 1983 Mondial Cabriolet. f, 1994 F 333 SP. g, 1971 365 GT4 BB. h, 2006 FXX.

2007, July 11　　　　　**Perf. 14**
1357	Block of 8 + label	9.75	9.75
a.	A339 10c multi	.25	.25
b.	A339 20c multi	.25	.25
c.	A339 50c multi	.35	.35
d.	A339 $1 multi	.75	.75
e.	A339 $1.60 multi	1.10	1.10
f.	A339 $1.75 multi	1.25	1.25
g.	A339 $3 multi	2.25	2.25
h.	A339 $5 multi	3.50	3.50

No. 1357 was issued in sheets containing two blocks, one of which had the label in the lower right corner, and the other with the label in the upper left corner.

Primates — A340

No. 1358: a, Pan troglodytes. b, Cercopithecus neglectus. c, Nasalis larvatus. d, Macaca fascicularis. e, Mandrillus sphinx. f, Rhinopithecus roxellana.

2007, Aug. 15　**Litho.**　**Perf. 14**
1358	Block of 6	15.00	15.00
a.	A340 $1.20 multi	.90	.90
b.	A340 $1.70 multi	1.25	1.25
c.	A340 $2 multi	1.50	1.50
d.	A340 $3 multi	2.25	2.25
e.	A340 $3.50 multi	2.60	2.60
f.	A340 $8.60 multi	6.25	6.25

America
Issue,
Education
A341

Designs: 80c, Children in classroom. $16.20, Children in classroom, diff.
No. 1361: a, $7, Boy at blackboard. b, $9, Two children.

2007, Sept. 19
1359-1360 A341   Set of 2   12.50 12.50
Souvenir Sheet
1361 A341   Sheet of 2, #a-b   12.00 12.00

Christmas — A342

Designs: $4, Four children at desks. $6, Holy Family.
No. 1364: a, 80c, Children, words and letters. b, $9.20, Holy Family, sheep.

2007, Nov. 7
1362-1363 A342   Set of 2   7.25 7.25
Souvenir Sheet
1364 A342   Sheet of 2, #a-b   7.25 7.25

Frogs
A343

No. 1365: a, Agalychnis callidryas. b, Dendrobates pumilio. c, Sphaeramia nematoptera. d, Hoffmanni. e, Sphaeramia nematoptera, diff. f, Dendrobates histrionicus.

2007, Dec. 12   Litho.   Perf. 14x12¾
1365   Block of 6   11.00 11.00
a. A343 T multi   .25   .25
b. A343 $1.20 multi   .85   .85
c. A343 $1.70 multi   1.25   1.25
d. A343 $2 multi   1.40   1.40
e. A343 $3 multi   2.25   2.25
f. A343 $7 multi   5.00   5.00

On day of issue, No. 1365a sold for 5c.

Butterflies Type of 2007
No. 1366: a, Anthocharis bella. b, Satyr angelwing. c, Red lacewing. d, Inachis io. e, Purple sapphire. f, Pearly crescentspot. g, Monarch. h, Marpesia berania. i, Darkmuseum swallowtail. j, Byasa alcinous. k, Brown peacock. l, Brown and orange Mexican.

2008, Jan. 2   Litho.   Perf. 14
1366   Block of 12   24.00 24.00
a. A334 T multi   .25   .25
b. A334 25c multi   .25   .25
c. A334 45c multi   .30   .30
d. A334 80c multi   .60   .60
e. A334 $1.20 multi   .90   .90
f. A334 $1.70 multi   1.25   1.25
g. A334 $2 multi   1.50   1.50
h. A334 $3 multi   2.25   2.25
i. A334 $3.50 multi   2.60   2.60
j. A334 $4 multi   3.00   3.00
k. A334 $5 multi   3.75   3.75
l. A334 $10 multi   7.25   7.25

No. 1366a sold for 5c on day of issue.

Fish — A344

No. 1367: a, Sphaeramia nematoptera. b, Neophrynichthys latus. c, Cheilodipterus isostigmus.

2008, Feb. 13
1367   Horiz. strip of 3   8.75 8.75
a. A344 $1.20 multi   .90   .90
b. A344 $3 multi   2.25   2.25
c. A344 $7.80 multi   5.50   5.50

Children in Native Costumes — A345

Children in various costumes.

2008, Mar. 19   Litho.   Perf. 14
1368 A345   Block of 12   24.00 24.00
a. T multi   .25   .25
b. 25c multi   .25   .25
c. 45c multi   .35   .35
d. 80c multi   .60   .60
e. $1.20 multi   .90   .90
f. $1.70 multi   1.25   1.25
g. $2 multi   1.50   1.50
h. $3 multi   2.25   2.25
i. $3.50 multi   2.60   2.60
j. $4 multi   3.00   3.00
k. $5 multi   3.75   3.75
l. $10 multi   7.25   7.25

No. 1368a sold for 5c on day of issue.

2008 Summer
Olympics,
Beijing — A346

No. 1369: a, Archery. b, Weight lifting. c, Basketball. d, Runner crossing finish line.

2008, Apr. 9   Litho.   Perf. 14
1369   Horiz. strip of 4   5.25 5.25
a. A346 $1 multi   .75   .75
b   A346 $1.50 multi   1.10   1.10
c. A346 $2 multi   1.50   1.50
d. A346 $2.50 multi   1.90   1.90

Stamp Passion
Philatelic Exhibition,
the Netherlands
A347

No. 1370: a, Netherlands #104. b, Surinam #120. c, Netherlands #43. d, Netherlands #103. e, Netherlands #B85. f, Netherlands #C9. g, Netherlands #J27. h, Netherlands #O25. i, Surinam #B10. j, Surinam #C14. k, Netherlands #160. l, Netherlands #96.

2008, Apr. 9   Litho.   Perf. 14
1370   Block of 12   37.50 37.50
a. A347 $1 multi   .75   .75
b. A347 $1.50 multi   1.10   1.10
c. A347 $2 multi   1.50   1.50
d. A347 $2.50 multi   1.90   1.90
e. A347 $3 multi   2.25   2.25
f. A347 $3.50 multi   2.60   2.60
g. A347 $4 multi   3.00   3.00
h. A347 $5 multi   3.75   3.75
i. A347 $5.50 multi   4.00   4.00
j. A347 $6 multi   4.50   4.50
k. A347 $7 multi   5.25   5.25
l. A347 $9 multi   6.75   6.75

Images of some stamps are distorted.

Buildings — A348

No. 1371: a, F.H.R. Lim A Postraat 34A. b, Combékerk. c, Waterkant 10. d, Waterkant 14. e, Waterkant 12. f, Officierswoning 6. g, Grote Combéweg 33. h, Officierswoning 5. i, Officierswoning 9.

2008, Apr. 23
1371   Block of 9   16.50 16.50
a. A348 V multi   .25   .25
b. A348 40c multi   .30   .30
c. A348 50c multi   .35   .35
d. A348 80c multi   .60   .60
e. A348 $1.20 multi   .90   .90
f. A348 $2 multi   1.50   1.50
g. A348 $4 multi   3.00   3.00
h. A348 $5 multi   3.75   3.75
i. A348 $8 multi   5.75   5.75

No. 1371a sold for 15c on day of issue.

Snakes
A349

No. 1372: a, Candoia carinata. b, Viper. c, Yellow Chondropython viridis. d, Red juvenile Chondropython viridis. e, Eyelash viper. f, Green mamba. g, Emerald tree boa. h, Tiger rat snake.

2008, May 21
1372   Block of 8 + label   33.00 33.00
a. A349 $1 multi   .75   .75
b. A349 $1.50 multi   1.10   1.10
c. A349 $2 multi   1.50   1.50
d. A349 $3 multi   2.25   2.25
e. A349 $5 multi   3.75   3.75
f. A349 $7.50 multi   5.25   5.25
g. A349 $10 multi   7.25   7.25
h. A349 $15 multi   11.00   11.00

Bird Type of 2007
No. 1373: a, Ceryle torquata. b, Tangara velia. c, Florisuga mellivora. d, Psarocollus viridis. e, Pionus fuscus. f, Chloroceryle aenea. g, Caryothraustes canadensis. h, Campephilus rubricollis.

Perf. 13¼x13¾
2008, Aug. 15   Litho.
Size: 16x21mm
1373   Horiz. strip of 8   8.00 8.00
a. A337 30c multi   .25   .25
b. A337 45c multi   .30   .30
c. A337 50c multi   .35   .35
d. A337 75c multi   .55   .55
e. A337 90c multi   .65   .65
f. A337 $1.40 multi   1.00   1.00
g. A337 $2.50 multi   1.90   1.90
h. A337 $4 multi   3.00   3.00
i. Souvenir sheet, 2 each #1373e,
     1373f + central label   6.75   6.75

America Issue,
Festivals — A350

No. 1374: a, Two Carifesta participants. b, Surinam flag at Carifesta.
No. 1375: a, $7, Woman in Carnaval costume. b, $15, Woman wearing Carnaval hat.

2008, Sept. 17   Litho.   Perf. 14
1374   Horiz. pair + central
       label   16.00 16.00
a. A350 $9 multi   6.75   6.75
b. A350 $12.50 multi   9.25   9.25
Souvenir Sheet
1375 A350   Sheet of 2, #a-b   16.50 16.50

Birds — A351

No. 1376: a, Ceryle rudis. b, Copsychus saularis. c, Dicaeum cruetatum. d, Garrulax perspicillatus. e, Halcyon smyrnensis. f, Leiothrix lutea.

2008, Oct. 15
1376   Block of 6   11.50 11.50
a. A351 V multi   .25   .25
b. A351 $1.10 multi   .80   .80
c. A351 $1.80 multi   1.40   1.40
d. A351 $3 multi   2.25   2.25
e. A351 $4 multi   3.00   3.00
f. A351 $5 multi   3.75   3.75

No. 1376a sold for 15c on day of issue. Bird names are misspelled on Nos. 1376c and 1376e.

Children and
Adults — A352

No. 1377: a, Woman swinging girl by arms. b, Boy in soap box derby car.
No. 1378: a, $5, Woman and girl with cut flowers. b, $7, Woman and girl painting birdhouse.

2008, Nov. 5
1377   Horiz. pair + central la-
       bel   9.00 9.00
a. A352 80c multi   .60   .60
b. A352 $11.20 multi   8.25   8.25
Souvenir Sheet
1378 A352   Sheet of 2, #a-b   9.00 9.00

Flowers
A353

No. 1379: a, Ixora Nora Grant White. b, Ixora Bonnie Lynn. c, Ixora coccinea. d, Ixora Dwarf Pink. e, Ixora Dwarf Orange. f, Ixora Maui Pink

2008, Dec. 10
1379   Block of 6   15.00 15.00
a. A353 $1.10 multi   .80   .80
b. A353 $1.80 multi   1.40   1.40
c. A353 $2 multi   1.50   1.50
d. A353 $3 multi   2.25   2.25
e. A353 X multi   3.75   3.75
f. A353 $7 multi   5.25   5.25

No. 1379e sold for $5.10 on day of issue.

Souvenir Sheet

Streptopelia Orientalis — A354

2009, Jan. 7   Litho.   Perf. 14
1380 A354 $9.50 multi   7.00 7.00

Frogs
A355

Designs: $1, Ceratophrys cornuta. $2, Bufo marinus. $2.50, Eleutherodactylus counouspeus. $3.50, Gastrotheca monticola. $5, Leptodactylus pentadactylus. $6, Pipa pipa. $7, Pseudis paradoxa.

2009, Feb. 15   Litho.   Perf. 14
1381-1387 A355   Set of 7   20.00 20.00

Nos. 1381-1387 were printed in a sheet containing 2 of each stamp + a central label.

Birds Type of 2007

No. 1388: a, Tinamus major. b, Crypturellus erythropus. c, Crypturellus variegatus. d, Crypturellus cinereus. e, Aburria pipile. f, Bucco capensis. g, Crypturellus soui. h, Ortalis motmot. i, Penelope marail. j, Chelidoptera tenebrosa.

2009, Mar. 18	Litho.	Perf. 14	
1388	Block of 10	33.00	33.00
a.	A337 Z multi	.90	.90
b.	A337 $1.50 multi	1.10	1.10
c.	A337 $2.50 multi	1.75	1.75
d.	A337 $3 multi	2.25	2.25
e.	A337 $3.50 multi	2.50	2.50
f.	A337 $4 multi	3.00	3.00
g.	A337 $5 multi	3.50	3.50
h.	A337 $5.50 multi	4.00	4.00
i.	A337 $7 multi	5.25	5.25
j.	A337 $12 multi	8.75	8.75

No. 1388a sold for $1.25 on day of issue.

Electricity, 200th Anniv. — A356

No. 1389: a, Sir Humphry Davy (1778-1829), chemist. b, Diagram of light bulb. c, Thomas Alva Edison (1847-1931), inventor.

2009, Mar. 21	Litho.	Perf. 14	
1389	Vert. strip of 3	11.00	11.00
a.	A356 $2 blk & red	1.50	1.50
b.	A356 $5 blk & red	3.75	3.75
c.	A356 $8 blk & red	5.75	5.75

Mailboxes From Around the World — A357

2009, May 27	Litho.	Perf. 14	
1390	Block of 10	29.00	29.00
a.	A357 Z Argentina	.90	.90
b.	A357 $2 Canada	1.50	1.50
c.	A357 $2.50 China	1.75	1.75
d.	A357 $3 India	2.25	2.25
e.	A357 $3.25 Ireland	2.40	2.40
f.	A357 $3.75 Russia	2.75	2.75
g.	A357 $5 Turkey	3.50	3.50
h.	A357 $5.50 Venezuela	4.00	4.00
i.	A357 $6.50 Yemen	4.50	4.50
j.	A357 $7 Great Britain	5.25	5.25

No. 1390a sold for $1.25 on day of issue.

Fish — A358

No. 1391: a, Cephalopholis miniata. b, Epinephelus fasciatus. c, Pomacanthus xanthocephalus. d, Anampses meleagrides. e, Chaetodon bennetti. f, Cephalopholis argus. g, Chaetodon xanthocephalus. h, Scarus frenatus. i, Priacanthus hamrur. j, Cephalopholis polieni. k, Pomacanthus semicirculatus. l, Ostracion cubicus.

2009, July 8			
1391	Block of 12	33.50	33.50
a.	A358 Z multi	.90	.90
b.	A358 $1.25 multi	.90	.90
c.	A358 $1.50 multi	1.10	1.10
d.	A358 $2 multi	1.50	1.50
e.	A358 $2.50 multi	1.75	1.75
f.	A358 $3 multi	2.25	2.25
g.	A358 $3.50 multi	2.50	2.50
h.	A358 $4 multi	3.00	3.00
i.	A358 $5.75 multi	4.25	4.25
j.	A358 $6 multi	4.50	4.50
k.	A358 $7 multi	5.25	5.25
l.	A358 $7.50 multi	5.50	5.50

No. 1391a sold for $1.25 on day of issue.

Children at Play — A359

No. 1392: a, $8, Knikkeren (marbles). b, $15, Hoepelen (hoop rolling).
No. 1393: a, $10, Hoelahoep (hula hoop). b, $12, Vijfsteentje (five girls in circle).

2009, Sept. 16			
1392	A359	Horiz. pair, #a-b	17.00 17.00

Souvenir Sheet

1393	A359	Sheet of 2, #a-b	16.00 16.00

Miniature Sheet

Chess Board — A360

No. 1394: a, 10c, Black rook. b, 20c, Black bishop. c, 30c, Black queen. d, 40c, Black rook. e, 50c, Black king. f, 60c, Black pawn. g, 70c, Black pawn. h, 80c, Black pawn. i, 90c, Black pawn. j, $1, Black pawn. k, $1.10, Black knight. l, $1.20, Black pawn. m, $1.30, Black knight. n, $1.40, Black pawn. o, $1.50, White pawn. p, $1.60, White pawn. q, $1.70, White pawn. r, $1.80, White pawn. s, $1.90, White pawn. t, $2, White knight. u, $2.10, White bishop. v, $2.20, White bishop. w, $2.50, White pawn. x, $3, White pawn. y, $4.50, White rook. z, $4.80, White queen. aa, $4.90, White rook. ab, $5, White king.

2009, Oct. 21	Litho.	Perf. 14	
1394	A360	Sheet of 28, #a-ab, + 36 labels	37.00 37.00

No. 1394 shows position of pieces of 1948 match between Paul Keres and Mikhail Botvinnik. Compare with No. 1428.

Endangered Primates — A361

No. 1395: a, $1, Aotus trivirgatus. b, $1.50, Alouatta palliata. c, $2, Cacajao calvus. d, $2.50, Lagothrix lagotricha. e, $3, Pithecia pithecia. f, $5, Callithrix mauesi. g, $7, Alouatta seniculus. h, $8, Gorilla. i, $9, Cercopithecus diana.

2009, Nov. 4			
1395	A361	Block of 9, #a-i	29.00 29.00

Flowers — A362

No. 1396: a, Pulsatilla vernalis. b, Crisanthemum maximum. c, Abronia villosa. d, Aquilegia caerulea. e, Zinnia elegans. f, Bougainvillea glabra. g, Daffodil. h, Victoria cruziana. i, Rosa palustris. j, Nymphaea.

2009, Dec. 9		Perf. 14	
1396	Block of 10	30.00	30.00
a.	A362 Z multi	.90	.90
b.	A362 $2 multi	1.50	1.50
c.	A362 $2.50 multi	1.90	1.90
d.	A362 $3 multi	2.25	2.25
e.	A362 $3.25 multi	2.40	2.40
f.	A362 $3.75 multi	2.75	2.75
g.	A362 $5 multi	3.75	3.75
h.	A362 $5.50 multi	4.00	4.00
i.	A362 $6.50 multi	4.75	4.75
j.	A362 $7 multi	5.25	5.25

No. 1396a sold for $1.25 on day of issue.

Miniature Sheet

Masks — A363

No. 1397: a, 50c, Wadal werdi. b, $1, Bambang painem. c, $2, Demang mones. d, $3, Raden gunung sari. e, $8, Joyo rengangon. f, $15, Demang tirtoyudo.

2009, Dec. 30		Perf. 12¾x13¼	
1397	A363	Sheet of 6, #a-f	22.00 22.00

Shells — A364

No. 1398: a, Cardita megastropha. b, Frangum unedo. c, Galeodea echinophora. d, Architectonica maxima. e, Opeatostoma pseudodon. f, Haliotis queketti. g, Cymatium hepaticum. h, Clanculus pharaonius. i, Harpa harpa. j, Hydatina nobilis.

2010, Jan. 20		Perf. 14	
1398	Block of 10	30.00	30.00
a.	A364 $1 multi	.75	.75
b.	A364 $1.50 multi	1.10	1.10
c.	A364 $2 multi	1.50	1.50
d.	A364 $2.50 multi	1.90	1.90
e.	A364 $3 multi	2.25	2.25
f.	A364 $4 multi	3.00	3.00
g.	A364 $5 multi	3.75	3.75
h.	A364 $6 multi	4.50	4.50
i.	A364 $7 multi	5.25	5.25
j.	A364 $8 multi	6.00	6.00

No. 1398 was printed in a sheet containing two irregular blocks of 10 + a central label.

Souvenir Sheet

Mushrooms — A365

No. 1399: a, $2, Amanita muscaria. b, $5, Boletus edulis. c, $8, Agaricus xanthoderma.

2010, Feb. 24		Perf. 13¼x12¾	
1399	A365	Sheet of 3, #a-c	11.00 11.00

Cuckoo Clocks A366

No. 1400 — Clock from: a, $1.50, 1760. b, $2.50, 1890. c, $3.50, 1900. d, $4.50, 1910. e, $5, 1920. f, $8, 1950.

2010, Mar. 25		Perf. 14	
1400	A366	Block of 6, #a-f	18.50 18.50

Butterflies — A367

No. 1401: a, Maniola jurtina. b, Melanargia galathea. c, Argynnis adippe. d, Apatura iris. e, Lasiommata megera. f, Pararge aegeria. g, Argynnis paphia. h, Vanessa atalanta. i, Limenitis camilla. j, Polyomnatus bcllargus. k, Argynnis aglaja. l, Pyronia tithonus. $12, Apatura ilia, horiz.

2010, Apr. 28			
1401	Block of 12	32.00	32.00
a.	A367 70c multi	.50	.50
b.	A367 $1.25 multi	.90	.90
c.	A367 $1.75 multi	1.25	1.25
d.	A367 $2.50 multi	1.90	1.90
e.	A367 $2.75 multi	2.00	2.00
f.	A367 $3 multi	2.25	2.25
g.	A367 $3.75 multi	2.75	2.75
h.	A367 $4.25 multi	3.00	3.00
i.	A367 $4.50 multi	3.25	3.25
j.	A367 $5 multi	3.75	3.75
k.	A367 $6 multi	4.50	4.50
l.	A367 $7 multi	5.25	5.25

Souvenir Sheet
Perf. 13¼x12¾

1402	A367	$12 multi	8.75 8.75

No. 1402 contains one 34x23mm stamp.

Birds — A368

No. 1403: a, Tangara chilensis. b, Leptopogon amaurocephalus. c, Xolmis cinerea. d, Tangara cayana. e, Conopophaga aurita. f, Megarhynchus pitangua. g, Tangara mexicana. h, Picumnus exilis. i, Hirundinea ferruginea. j, Galbula albirostris. k, Tyrannopsis sulphurea. l, Tangara varia.

2010, May 26		Perf. 14	
1403	Block of 12	37.00	37.00
a.	A368 50c multi	.35	.35
b.	A368 $1 multi	.75	.75
c.	A368 $1.50 multi	1.10	1.10
d.	A368 $2 multi	1.50	1.50
e.	A368 $2.50 multi	1.90	1.90
f.	A368 $3 multi	2.25	2.25
g.	A368 $3.50 multi	2.60	2.60
h.	A368 $4 multi	3.00	3.00
i.	A368 $5 multi	3.75	3.75
j.	A368 $7 multi	5.25	5.25
k.	A368 $9 multi	6.50	6.50
l.	A368 $11 multi	8.00	8.00

Orchids A369

No. 1404: a, Laeliocattleya. b, Coelogyne mooreana. c, Phalaenopsis. d, Calanthe. e, Maxillaria fucata. f, Cymbidium erythrostylum. g, Cymbidium beaumont. h, Cattleya portia. i, Miltoniopsis portelet. j, Sophrolaeliacattleya marion. k, Dendrobium thwaitesii. l, Ascocenda vernon.

2010, July 7

1404		Block of 12	34.00	34.00
a.	A369	A multi	.35	.35
b.	A369	55c multi	.40	.40
c.	A369	$1 multi	.75	.75
d.	A369	$1.50 multi	1.10	1.10
e.	A369	$2 multi	1.50	1.50
f.	A369	$2.50 multi	1.90	1.90
g.	A369	$3 multi	2.25	2.25
h.	A369	$4.50 multi	3.25	3.25
i.	A369	$5 multi	3.75	3.75
j.	A369	$6.50 multi	4.75	4.75
k.	A369	$7 multi	5.25	5.25
l.	A369	$11 multi	8.00	8.00

No. 1404a sold for 45c on day of issue.

America Issue, National Symbols — A370

No. 1406: a, $11, Presidential Palace. b, $13, National anthem.

2010, Sept. 15

1405	A370	Horiz. pair	20.50	20.50
a.		$13 National flag	9.50	9.50
b.		$15 National arms	11.00	11.00

Souvenir Sheet

1406	A370	Sheet of 2, #a-b	17.50	17.50

Fish — A372

No. 1408: a, Amphiprion ocellaris. b, Pomacentrus caeruleus. c, Barbus tetrazona. d, Betta smaragdina. e, Calisa lalia. f, Geophagus brasiliensis. g, Astronotus ocellatus. h, Microgeophagus ramirezi.

2010, Dec. 1   Litho.   Perf. 13¼x12¾

1408		Block of 8	33.00	33.00
a.	A372	A multi	.35	.35
b.	A372	$1.55 multi	1.10	1.10
c.	A372	$3 multi	2.25	2.25
d.	A372	$5 multi	3.75	3.75
e.	A372	$7 multi	5.25	5.25
f.	A372	$8 multi	5.75	5.75
g.	A372	$9 multi	6.50	6.50
h.	A372	$11 multi	8.00	8.00

No. 1408a sold for 45c on day of issue.

Masks — A373

No. 1409: a, Begawan wiro sekti. b, Dewi kilisuci. c, Kartolo. d, Bilung. e, Panji amerdadu. f, Betara kalla.

2010, Dec. 29   Perf. 14

1409		Block of 6	22.00	22.00
a.	A373	50c multi	.35	.35
b.	A373	$1.50 multi	1.10	1.10
c.	A373	$3.50 multi	2.60	2.60
d.	A373	$6 multi	4.50	4.50
e.	A373	$8 multi	5.75	5.75
f.	A373	$10 multi	7.25	7.25

Shells A374

Designs: 50c, Tonicella lineata. $1, Chione paphia. $3.50, Callanaitis disjecta. $5, Angaria tyria. $8, Epitonium pallasi. $9, Strombus pipus. $13, Haliotis marmorata.

2011, Jan. 19   Perf. 13¼x12¾

1410-1416	A374	Set of 7	29.00	29.00

Nos. 1410-1416 were printed in a sheet containing 2 of each stamp + a central label.

Postal Union of the Americas, Spain and Portugal (UPAEP), Cent. — A376

No. 1418 — Arc of circles containing flags of member nations: a, $5. b, $7. c, $9. d, $11.

2011, Mar. 16   Perf. 14

1418	A376	Block of 4, #a-d	19.50	19.50

Peonies — A378

No. 1420: a, Red peony, denomination at LR reading across. b, White peony, denomination at LL reading across. c, Pink peonies, denomination at LL reading up. d, Red and white peonies, denomination at LR reading down.
$7, Pink peony.

2011, Apr. 20   Litho.   Perf. 14

1420	A378	$2 Sheet of 4, #a-d	5.00	5.00

Souvenir Sheet

1421	A378	$7 multi	4.25	4.25

Orchids — A380

No. 1423: a, Pink Phalaenopsis hybrid, bright green background. b, Dendrobium mousmee. c, Dendrobium densiflorum. d, Laelia purpurata. e, Encyclia vitellina. f, Miltoniopsis rozel. g, Yellow Cymbidium hybrid. h, Dendrobium hybrid. i, Ascocenda. j, Red Cymbidium hybrid. k, Laelliocattleya hybrid. l, Pink Phalaenopsis hybrid, olive green background.

2011, June 29   Litho.   Perf. 14

1423		Block of 12	26.00	26.00
a.	A380	A multi	.30	.30
b.	A380	55c multi	.35	.35
c.	A380	$1 multi	.65	.65
d.	A380	$1.50 multi	.95	.95
e.	A380	$2 multi	1.25	1.25
f.	A380	$2.50 multi	1.60	1.60
g.	A380	$3 multi	1.90	1.90
h.	A380	$4 multi	2.50	2.50
i.	A380	$4.50 multi	2.75	2.75
j.	A380	$5.50 multi	3.50	3.50
k.	A380	$7 multi	4.50	4.50
l.	A380	$8 multi	5.00	5.00

No. 1423a sold for 45c on day of issue.

Primates — A381

No. 1424: a, A, Papio hamadryas. b, $2.55, Saguinus oedipus. c, $4, Cebus apella. d, $6, Erythrocebus patas. e, $8, Macaca nemestrina. f, $9, Chlorocebus pygerythrus.

2011, Aug. 10   Perf. 12¾x13¼

1424	A381	Block of 6, #a-f	18.50	18.50

No. 1424a sold for 45c on day of issue.

Azaleas A382

No. 1425: a, Country name at UL, denomination adjacent to vignette. b, Country name adjacent to vignette, denomination at LR.

2011, Sept. 14   Perf. 14¼x13¾

1425	A382	$1.50 Vert. pair, #a-b	1.90	1.90

America Issue, Mailboxes — A383

No. 1426: a, $11, Mailbox on black pedestal near wall. b, $15, Rectangular mailbox.
No. 1427: a, $11, Mailbox on black pedestal. b, $13, Top of mailbox.

2011, Sept. 14   Perf. 14

1426	A383	Horiz. pair, #a-b	17.00	17.00

Souvenir Sheet

1427	A383	Sheet of 2, #a-b	15.00	15.00

Miniature Sheet

Chess Board — A384

No. 1428: a, 10c, Black rook. b, 20c, Black king. c, 30c, Black rook. d, 40c, Black pawn. e, 50c, Black bishop. f, 60c, Black pawn. g, 70c, White bishop. h, 80c, White bishop. i, 90c, Black pawn. j, $1, Black pawn. k, $1.20, Black bishop. l, $1.40, White pawn. m, $1.60, White pawn. n, $1.75, Black queen. o, $1.90, White pawn. p, $2.15, White pawn. q, $3, White

pawn. r, $4.50, White pawn. s, $5, White rook. t, $6, White king.

2011, Oct. 26

1428	A384	Sheet of 20, #a-t,		
		+ 44 labels	21.00	21.00

No. 1428 shows position of pieces at end of 1852 match between Adolf Anderssn and Jean Dufresne. Compare with No. 1394.

Masks — A385

No. 1429: a, $1, Botu terong. b, $2, Demang mundu. c, $3, Emban dawala. d, $7, Jarodeh. e, $8, Kelono baron sakeber. f, $9, Maheso suro.

2011, Dec. 7   Perf. 14

1429	A385	Block of 6, #a-f	18.50	18.50

SEMI-POSTAL STAMPS

SP1   SP2

Green Cross — SP3

Perf. 12½

1927, Aug. 1   Unwmk.   Photo.

B1	SP1	2c (+ 2c) bl blk & grn	1.10	1.00
B2	SP2	5c (+ 3c) vio & grn	1.10	1.00
B3	SP3	10c (+ 3c) ver & grn	2.00	1.75
		Nos. B1-B3 (3)	4.20	3.75
		Set, never hinged	10.50	

Surtax was given to the Green Cross Society, which promotes public health services.

Nurse and Patient   Good Samaritan
SP4   SP5

1928, Dec. 1   Perf. 11½

B4	SP4	1½c (+ 1½c) ultra	4.50	4.50
B5	SP4	2c (+ 2c) bl grn	4.50	4.50
B6	SP4	5c (+ 3c) vio	4.50	4.50
B7	SP4	7½c (+ 2½c) ver	4.50	4.50
		Nos. B4-B7 (4)	18.00	18.00
		Set, never hinged	67.50	

The surtax on these stamps was for a fund to combat indigenous diseases.

1929, Dec. 1   Perf. 12½

B8	SP5	1½c (+ 1½c) grn	6.75	6.75
B9	SP5	2c (+ 2c) scar	6.75	6.75
B10	SP5	5c (+ 3c) ultra	6.75	6.75
B11	SP5	6c (+ 4c) blk	6.75	6.75
		Nos. B8-B11 (4)	27.00	27.00
		Set, never hinged	72.50	

Surtax for the Green Cross Society.

Surinam Mother and
Child — SP6

1931, Dec. 14
B12	SP6	1½c (+ 1½c) blk	4.75	4.75
B13	SP6	2c (+ 2c) car rose	4.75	4.75
B14	SP6	5c (+ 3c) ultra	4.75	4.75
B15	SP6	6c (+ 4c) dp grn	4.75	4.75
	Nos. B12-B15 (4)		19.00	19.00
	Set, never hinged		45.00	

The surtax was for Child Welfare Societies.

Designs Symbolical of the Creed
of the Moravians
SP7　　　　　SP8

1935, Aug. 1　　　*Perf. 13x14*
B16	SP7	1c (+ ½c) dk brn	6.00	6.00
B17	SP7	2c (+ 1c) dp ultra	6.00	6.00
B18	SP8	3c (+ 1½c) grn	7.50	7.50
B19	SP8	4c (+ 2c) red org	7.50	7.50
B20	SP8	5c (+ 2½c) blk brn	9.00	9.00
B21	SP7	10c (+ 5c) car	9.00	9.00
	Nos. B16-B21 (6)		45.00	45.00
	Set, never hinged		90.00	

200th anniv. of the founding of the Moravian
Mission in Surinam.

Surinam
Child — SP9

1936, Dec. 14　　　*Perf. 12½*
B22	SP9	2c (+ 1c) dk grn	2.75	2.75
B23	SP9	3c (+ 1½c) dk bl	2.75	2.75
B24	SP9	5c (+ 2½c) brn blk	4.00	4.00
B25	SP9	10c (+ 5c) lake	4.00	4.00
	Nos. B22-B25 (4)		13.50	13.50
	Set, never hinged		26.50	

Surtax for baby food and the Green Cross
Society.

"Emancipation"　　　Surinam Girl
SP10　　　　　　　SP11

1938, June 1　Litho.　Perf. 12½x12
B26	SP10	2½c (+ 2c) dk bl grn	2.40	1.90

Photo.
B27	SP11	3c (+ 2c) vio blk	2.40	1.90
B28	SP11	5c (+ 3c) dk brn	2.60	2.25
B29	SP11	7½c (+ 5c) indigo	2.60	2.25
	Nos. B26-B29 (4)		10.00	8.30
	Set, never hinged		20.00	

75th anniv. of the abolition of slavery in Surinam. Surtax to Slavery Remembrance
Committee.

Creole　　　　　　Javanese
Woman — SP12　　Woman — SP13

Hindustani　　　　American Indian
Woman — SP14　　Woman — SP15

1940, Jan. 8　Engr.　Perf. 13x14
B30	SP12	2½c (+ 2c) dk grn	3.00	3.00
B31	SP13	3c (+ 2c) red org	3.00	3.00
B32	SP14	5c (+ 3c) dp bl	3.00	3.00
B33	SP15	7½c (+ 5c) henna brn	3.00	3.00
	Nos. B30-B33 (4)		12.00	12.00
	Set, never hinged		25.00	

Surtax to leper care and baby food.

> **Catalogue values for unused
> stamps in this section, from this
> point to the end of the section, are
> for Never Hinged items.**

Netherlands Coat of
Arms and Inscription,
"Netherlands Shall Rise
Again" — SP16

1941, Aug. 30　Litho.　Perf. 12½
B34	SP16	7½c + 7½c dp org, ultra & blk	3.75	3.00
B35	SP16	15c + 15c scar, ultra & blk	3.75	3.00
B36	SP16	1g + 1g gray & ultra	26.00	22.50
	Nos. B34-B36 (3)		33.50	28.50

The surtax was used to buy fighters for
Dutch pilots in the Royal Air Force of Great
Britain.

Nos. 145, 169, 146, 151 Surcharged
in Red

I

II　　III　　IV　　V

1942, Jan. 2
B37	A23	2c + 2c blk brn, I	2.50	2.50
a.		Type II	2.50	2.50
B38	A26	2c + 2c blk brn, I	67.50	67.50
a.		Type II	67.50	67.50
B39	A23	2½c + 2c green, I	2.50	2.50
a.		Type II	2.50	2.50
B40	A23	7½c + 5c red vio, III	2.50	2.50
a.		Type IV	8.00	8.00
b.		Type V	20.00	20.00
	Nos. B37-B40,CB1 (5)		77.50	77.50

The surtax was for the Red Cross.

In type III, the "c" may be "large," as illustrated, or "small," as in type II. Value is the
same.

The distinctive feature of type IV is the
pointed ending of the lower part of the "5."

Types of Regular Issue of 1945
Surcharged in Black

1945, July 23　Unwmk.
Engr.　Perf. 12
B41	A29	7½c + 5c dp org	3.75	2.50
B42	A30	15c + 10c brn	3.00	2.50
B43	A30	20c + 15c dl grn	3.00	2.50
B44	A30	22½c + 20c gray	3.00	2.50
B45	A30	40c + 35c rose lake	3.00	2.50
B46	A30	60c + 50c vio	3.00	2.50
	Nos. B41-B46 (6)		18.75	15.00

Surtax for the National Welfare Fund.

Star — SP17　　　Marie
　　　　　　　　　Curie — SP18

1947, Dec. 16　Photo.　Perf. 13½x13
B47	SP17	7½c + 12½c red org	2.75	2.25
B48	SP17	12½c + 37½c blue	2.75	2.25
	Nos. B47-B48,CB4-CB5 (4)		10.00	8.00

The surtax was used to combat leprosy.

1950, May 15　Perf. 14x13
7½c+22½c, 27½c+12½c, Wm. Roentgen.
B49	SP18	7½c + 7½c	17.50	10.50
B50	SP18	7½c + 22½c	17.50	10.50
B51	SP18	27½c + 12½c	17.50	10.50
B52	SP18	27½c + 97½c	17.50	10.50
	Nos. B49-B52 (4)		70.00	42.00

The surtax was used to combat cancer.

Nos. 236-237
Surcharged in
Black (#B53) or
Red (#B54)

1953, Feb. 18　Wmk. 202
B53	A35	12½c + 7½c on 7½c	2.75	2.75
B54	A35	20c + 10c on 12½c	2.75	2.75

The surtax was for flood relief in the
Netherlands.

Stadium, Paramaribo — SP19

1953, Aug. 29　Unwmk.　Perf. 13½
B55	SP19	10c + 5c claret	11.50	8.25
B56	SP19	15c + 7½c brn	11.50	8.25
B57	SP19	30c + 15c dk grn	11.50	8.25
	Nos. B55-B57 (3)		34.50	24.75

Opening of the new stadium.

Surinam
Children — SP20

1954, Nov. 1　Perf. 13x14
B58	SP20	7½c + 3c sepia	6.00	4.75
B59	SP20	10c + 5c bl grn	6.00	4.75
B60	SP20	15c + 7½c red brn	6.00	4.75
B61	SP20	30c + 15c blue	6.00	4.75
	Nos. B58-B61 (4)		24.00	19.00

Surtax for the youth center of the Moravian
Church.

Doves — SP21

1955, May 5　Perf. 14x13
B62	SP21	7½c + 3½c brt red	2.75	3.00
B63	SP21	15c + 8c ultra	2.75	3.00

The Netherlands' liberation, 10th anniv.

Queen Juliana
and Prince
Bernhard
SP22

1955, Oct. 27　Unwmk.
B64	SP22	7½c + 2½c dk olive	.55	.55

Royal visit to Surinam, 1955. Surtax for the
Royal present.

Theater,
1837 — SP23

Designs: 10c+5c, Theater and car, circa
1920. 15c+7½c, Theater and car, circa 1958.
20c+10c, Theater interior.

1958, Feb. 15　Litho.　Perf. 13x12½
B65	SP23	7½c + 3c lt bl & blk	.45	.45
B66	SP23	10c + 5c rose lil & blk	.45	.45
B67	SP23	15c + 7½c lt grn & blk	.45	.45
B68	SP23	20c + 10c org & blk	.45	.45
	Nos. B65-B68 (4)		1.80	1.80

120th anniv. of the "Thalia" theatrical society.

Carved Eating
Utensils and
Map of South
America
SP24

Native Art (Map of So. America and):
10c+5c, Feather headgear. 15c+7c, Clay pottery. 20c+10c, Carved wooden stool.

1960, Jan. 15
B69	SP24	8c + 4c multi	.90	.90
B70	SP24	10c + 5c salmon, red & bl	.90	.90
B71	SP24	15c + 7c red org, grn & sepia	.90	.90
B72	SP24	20c + 10c lt bl, ultra & bis	.90	.90
	Nos. B69-B72 (4)		3.60	3.60

SP25

SP26

Design: Uprooted Oak emblem of WRY.

1960, Apr. 7   Perf. 13x14
B73	SP25	8c + 4c choc & grn	.25	.25
B74	SP25	10c + 5c vio bl & ol grn	.25	.25

World Refugee Year, July 1, 1959-June 30, 1960. The surtax was for aid to refugees.

1960, Aug. 10   Litho.   Perf. 14x13
B75	SP26	8c + 4c Shot put	.55	.55
B76	SP26	10c + 5c Basketball	.55	.55
B77	SP26	15c + 7c Runner	.85	.85
B78	SP26	20c + 10c Swimmer	.85	.85
B79	SP26	40c + 20c Soccer	.85	.85
		Nos. B75-B79 (5)	3.65	3.65

17th Olympic Games, Rome, 8/25-9/11. Surtax for Olympic Committee.

Girl
Scout
Signaling
SP27

Designs: 10c+3c, Scout Saluting, vert. 15c+4c, Brownies around toadstool. 20c+5c, Scouts around campfire, vert. 25c+6c, Scouts cooking outdoors.

Perf. 14x13, 13x14
1961, Aug. 19   Litho.
Multicolored Designs
B80	SP27	8c + 2c blue	.30	.30
B81	SP27	10c + 3c lilac	.35	.35
B82	SP27	15c + 4c yellow	.35	.35
B83	SP27	20c + 5c brn red	.40	.40
B84	SP27	25c + 6c aqua	.40	.40
		Nos. B80-B84 (5)	1.80	1.80

Caribbean Girl Scout Jamborette. Surtax for various charities.

Hibiscus
SP28

Flowers: 10c+5c, Caesalpinia pulcherrima. 15c+6c, Heliconia psittacorum. 20c+10c, Lochnera rosea. 25c+12c, Ixora macrothyrsa.

1962, Mar. 7   Photo.   Perf. 14x13
Cross in Red
B85	SP28	8c + 4c dk ol & scar	.32	.30
B86	SP28	10c + 5c dk bl & org	.32	.30
B87	SP28	15c + 6c multi	.32	.30
B88	SP28	20c + 10c multi	.32	.30
B89	SP28	25c + 12c dk bl grn, red & yel	.32	.30
		Nos. B85-B89 (5)	1.60	1.50

The surtax was for the Red Cross.

Hands
Protecting
Duck — SP29

American Indian
Girl — SP30

1962, Dec. 15   Litho.   Perf. 13x14
B90	SP29	2c + 1c shown	.25	.25
B91	SP29	8c + 2c Dog	.25	.25
B92	SP29	10c + 3c Donkey	.25	.25
B93	SP29	15c + 4c Horse	.25	.25
		Nos. B90-B93 (4)	1.00	1.00

The surtax was for the Organization for Animal Protection.

1963, Oct. 30   Photo.   Unwmk.

Girls: 10c+4c, Negro. 15c+10c, East Indian. 20c+10c, Indonesian. 40c+20c, Caucasian.
B94	SP30	8c + 3c Prus grn	.25	.25
B95	SP30	10c + 4c red brn	.25	.25
a.		Min. sheet, 2 each #B94-B95	1.25	1.25
B96	SP30	15c + 10c dp blue	.25	.25
B97	SP30	20c + 10c brn red	.25	.25
B98	SP30	40c + 20c red vio	.35	.35
		Nos. B94-B98 (5)	1.35	1.35

The surtax was for Child Welfare.

X-15
SP31

Designs: 8c+4c, Flag of the Aeronautical and Astronautical Foundation. 10c+5c, 20c+10c, Agena B Ranger rocket.

1964, Apr. 15   Perf. 13x12½
B99	SP31	3c + 2c blk & rose lake	.25	.25
B100	SP31	8c + 4c blk, ultra & lt ultra	.25	.25
B101	SP31	10c + 5c blk & grn	.25	.25
B102	SP31	15c + 7c blk & yel brn	.25	.25
B103	SP31	20c + 10c blk & vio	.25	.25
		Nos. B99-B103 (5)	1.25	1.25

Surtax for the Aeronautical and Astronautical Foundation of Surinam.

Stylized Campfire
amid Trees — SP32

1964, July 29   Litho.   Perf. 13x14
B104	SP32	3c + 1c brn ol, yel bis & lem	.25	.25
B105	SP32	8c + 4c bluish blk, vio bl & yel bis	.25	.25
B106	SP32	10c + 5c dk red, red & yel bis	.25	.25
B107	SP32	20c + 10c grnsh bl, ol grn & yel bis	.25	.25
		Nos. B104-B107 (4)	1.00	1.00

Jamborette at Paramaribo, Aug. 20-30, marking the 40th anniv. of the Surinam Boy Scout Association.
Surtax for various charities.

Girls Skipping
Rope — SP33

10c+4c, Children on swings. 15c+9c, Girl on scooter. 20c+10c, Boy rolling hoop.

1964, Nov. 30   Photo.   Perf. 14x13
B108	SP33	8c + 3c dk blue	.25	.25
B109	SP33	10c + 4c red	.25	.25
a.		Min. sheet, 2 each #B108-B109	.55	.55
B110	SP33	15c + 9c olive grn	.25	.25
B111	SP33	20c + 10c magenta	.25	.25
		Nos. B108-B111 (4)	1.00	1.00

Issued for Child Welfare.

Mother and
Child — SP34

Designs: 4c+2c, Pregnant woman. 15c+7c, Child. 25c+12c, Old man.

1965, Feb. 27   Photo.   Perf. 13x14
B112	SP34	4c + 2c green	.25	.25
B113	SP34	10c + 5c brn & grn	.25	.25
B114	SP34	15c + 7c Prus bl & grn	.25	.25
B115	SP34	25c + 12c brt pur & grn	.25	.25
		Nos. B112-B115 (4)	1.00	1.00

50th anniv. of the Green Cross Assoc. which promotes public health services.

Girl with
Leopard and
Spider
SP35

Designs: 10c+5c, Boy with monkey and spider. 15c+7c, Girl with tortoise and spider. 25c+10c, Boy with rabbit and spider.

Perf. 13x12½
1965, Nov. 26   Litho.   Unwmk.
B116	SP35	4c + 4c lt grn & blk	.25	.25
B117	SP35	10c + 5c ocher & blk	.25	.25
B118	SP35	15c + 7c dp org & blk	.25	.25
a.		Min. sheet, 2 each #B116, B118	.55	.55
B119	SP35	25c + 10c lt ultra & blk	.25	.25
		Nos. B116-B119 (4)	1.00	1.00

Issued for Child Welfare.

"Help them to
a safe haven"
SP35a

1966, Jan. 31   Photo.   Perf. 14x13
B120	SP35a	10c + 5c blk & grn	.25	.25
B121	SP35a	25c + 10c blk & rose brn	.25	.25
a.		Min. sheet of 3, 2 #B120, B121	.45	.45

The surtax was for the Intergovernmental Committee for European Migration (ICEM). The message on the stamps was given and signed by Queen Juliana.

Mary
Magdalene,
Disciples and
"Round Table"
Emblem
SP36

"New Year's
Eve" Boys with
Bamboo Gun
SP37

Mary Magdalene (John 20:18), and Service Club Emblems: 15c+8c, Toastmasters Intl. 20c+10c, Junior Chamber, Surinam. 25c+12c, Rotary Intl. 30c+15c, Lions Intl.

1966, Apr. 13   Photo.   Perf. 12½x13
B122	SP36	10c + 5c dp crim, blk & gold	.25	.25
B123	SP36	15c + 8c dp vio, blk & bl	.25	.25
B124	SP36	20c + 10c yel org, blk & ultra	.25	.25
B125	SP36	25c + 12c grn, blk & gold	.25	.25

B126	SP36	30c + 15c ultra, blk & gold	.25	.25
		Nos. B122-B126 (5)	1.25	1.25

Easter charities.

1966, Nov. 25   Litho.   Perf. 12½x13

Designs: 15c+8c, "The End of Lent," boys pouring paint over each other. 20c+10c, "Liberation Day," parading children. 25c+12c, "Queen's Birthday," children on hobbyhorses. 30c+15c, "Christmas," Children decorating room with star.
B127	SP37	10c + 5c multi	.25	.25
B128	SP37	15c + 8c multi	.25	.25
B129	SP37	20c + 10c multi	.25	.25
a.		Min. sheet of 3, 2 #B127, B129	.35	.35
B130	SP37	25c + 12c multi	.25	.25
B131	SP37	30c + 15c multi	.25	.25
		Nos. B127-B131 (5)	1.25	1.25

Child welfare.

Good
Samaritan
Giving His Coat
SP38

Children Stilt-
walking
SP39

The Good Samaritan: 15c+8c, Dressing the wounds. 20c+10c, Feeding the poor man. 25c+12c, Poor man riding Samaritan's horse. 30c+15c, Samaritan taking poor man to the inn.

1967, Mar. 22
B132	SP38	10c + 5c yellow & blk	.25	.25
B133	SP38	15c + 8c lt blue & blk	.25	.25
B134	SP38	20c + 10c buff & blk	.25	.25
B135	SP38	25c + 12c pale rose & blk	.25	.25
B136	SP38	30c + 15c grn & blk	.25	.25
		Nos. B132-B136 (5)	1.25	1.25

Easter charities.

1967, Nov. 21   Litho.   Perf. 12½x13

Children's Games: 15c+8c, Boys playing with marbles. 20c+10c, Girl playing dibs (five stones). 25c+12c, Boy making kite. 30c+15c, Girls play-cooking.
B137	SP39	10c + 5c multi	.25	.25
B138	SP39	15c + 8c multi	.25	.25
B139	SP39	20c + 10c multi	.25	.25
a.		Min. sheet of 3, 2 #B139	.45	.45
B140	SP39	25c + 12c multi	.25	.25
B141	SP39	30c + 15c multi	.25	.25
		Nos. B137-B141 (5)	1.25	1.25

Child welfare.

Cross, Ash
Wednesday
SP40

Hopscotch
SP41

Easter Symbols: 15c+8c, Palms, Palm Sunday. 20c+10c, Bread and Wine, Maundy Thursday. 25c+12c, Cross, Good Friday. 30c+15c, Chrismon, Easter Sunday.

1968, Mar. 27   Litho.   Perf. 12½x13
B142	SP40	10c + 5c lilac & gray	.25	.25
B143	SP40	15c + 8c brick red & grn	.25	.25
B144	SP40	20c + 10c yellow & dk grn	.25	.25
B145	SP40	25c + 12c gray & blk	.25	.25
B146	SP40	30c + 15c brt yel & brn	.25	.25
		Nos. B142-B146 (5)	1.25	1.25

Easter charities.

1968, Nov. 22   Litho.   *Perf. 12½x13*

15c+8c, Balancing pyramid. 20c+10c, Handball. 25c+12c, Handicraft. 30c+15c, Tug-of-war.

B147	SP41	10c + 5c fawn & blk	.25	.25
B148	SP41	15c + 8c lt ultra & blk	.25	.25
B149	SP41	20c + 10c pink & blk	.25	.25
a.		Min. sheet, #B149, 2 #B147	.50	.50
B150	SP41	25c + 12c yel grn & blk	.25	.25
B151	SP41	30c + 15c bluish lil & blk	.30	.30
		Nos. B147-B151 (5)	1.30	1.30

Child welfare.

Globe with Map
of South
America
SP42

Pillow Fight
SP43

1969, Apr. 2   Litho.   *Perf. 12½x13*

B152	SP42	10c + 5c bl & lt bl	.25	.25
B153	SP42	15c + 8c sl grn & yel	.25	.25
B154	SP42	20c + 10c sl grn & gray grn	.25	.25
B155	SP42	25c + 12c brn & bis	.25	.25
B156	SP42	30c + 15c vio & gray	.25	.25
		Nos. B152-B156 (5)	1.25	1.25

Easter charities.

1969, Nov. 21   Litho.   *Perf. 12½x13*

15c+8c, Eating contest. 20c+10c, Pole climbing. 25c+12c, Sack race. 30c+15c, Obstacle race.

B157	SP43	10c + 5c lt ultra & mag	.25	.25
B158	SP43	15c + 8c yel & brn	.25	.25
B159	SP43	20c + 10c gray & dp bl	.25	.25
a.		Min. sheet, #B159, 2 B157	.80	.80
B160	SP43	25c + 12c pink & brt bl	.25	.25
B161	SP43	30c + 15c emer & brn	.25	.25
		Nos. B157-B161 (5)	1.25	1.25

Child welfare.

Butterfly
SP44

Ludwig van
Beethoven,
1786
SP45

Designs: 10c+5c, Flower. 20c+10c, Flying bird. 25c+12c, Sun. 30c+15c, Star.

1970, Mar. 25   Litho.   *Perf. 12½x13*

B162	SP44	10c + 5c multi	.50	.50
B163	SP44	15c + 8c multi	.50	.50
B164	SP44	20c + 10c multi	.50	.50
B165	SP44	25c + 12c multi	.50	.50
B166	SP44	30c + 15c multi	.50	.50
		Nos. B162-B166 (5)	2.50	2.50

Easter.

1970, Nov. 25   Litho.   *Perf. 12½x13*

Various Portraits of Beethoven. 15c + 8c, l...

Donkey and
Palm — SP46

Leapfrog, by Peter
Brueghel — SP47

Easter: 15c+8c, Cock. 20c+10c, Lamb of God. 25c+12c, Cross and Crown of Thorns. 30c+15c, Sun.

1971, Apr. 7   Litho.   *Perf. 12½x13*

B172	SP46	10c + 5c multi	.50	.50
B173	SP46	15c + 8c blue & multi	.50	.50
B174	SP46	20c + 10c multi	.50	.50
B175	SP46	25c + 12c multi	.50	.50
B176	SP46	30c + 15c multi	.50	.50
		Nos. B172-B176 (5)	2.50	2.50

Easter charities.

1971, Nov. 24   Photo.   *Perf. 13x14*

Children's Games, by Peter Brueghel: 15c+8c, Girl strewing flowers. 20c+10c, Spinning the hoop. 25c+12c, Ball players. 30c+15c, Stilt walker.

B177	SP47	10c + 5c multi	.60	.60
B178	SP47	15c + 8c multi	.60	.60
B179	SP47	20c + 10c multi	.60	.60
a.		Min. sheet, #B179, 2 #B177	2.00	2.00
B180	SP47	25c + 12c multi	.60	.60
B181	SP47	30c + 15c multi	.60	.60
		Nos. B177-B181 (5)	3.00	3.00

Child welfare.

Easter
Candle — SP48

Toys — SP49

Easter: 15c+8c, Christ teaching Apostles, and crosses. 20c+10c, Cup and folded hands. 25c+12c, Fish in net. 30c+15c, Judas' bag of silver.

1972, Mar. 29   Litho.   *Perf. 12½x13*

B182	SP48	10c + 5c multi	.45	.45
B183	SP48	15c + 8c multi	.45	.45
B184	SP48	20c + 10c multi	.45	.45
B185	SP48	25c + 12c multi	.45	.45
B186	SP48	30c + 15c multi	.45	.45
		Nos. B182-B186 (5)	2.25	2.25

Easter charities.

1972, Nov. 29   Litho.   *Perf. 12½x13*

Designs: 15c+8c, Abacus and clock. 20c+10c, Pythagorean theorem. 25c+12c, Model of molecule. 30c+15c, Monkey wrench and drill. Each design represents a different stage of education.

B187	SP49	10c + 5c multi	.50	.50
B188	SP49	15c + 8c multi	.50	.50
B189	SP49	20c + 10c multi	.50	.50
a.		Min. sheet, #B189, 2 #B187	1.50	1.50
B190	SP49	25c + 12c multi	.50	.50
B191	SP49	30c + 15c multi	.50	.50
		Nos. B187-B191 (5)	2.50	2.50

Child welfare.

1973, Apr. 4   Litho.   *Perf. 12½x13*

B192	SP50	10c + 5c multi	.45	.45
B193	SP50	15c + 8c multi	.45	.45
B194	SP50	20c + 10c multi	.45	.45
B195	SP50	25c + 12c multi	.45	.45
B196	SP50	30c + 15c multi	.45	.45
		Nos. B192-B196 (5)	2.25	2.25

Easter charities.

Red Cross
and
Florence
Nightingale
SP51

1973, Oct. 3   Litho.   *Perf. 14½x14*

B197	SP51	30c + 10c multi	.90	.90

30th anniversary of Surinam Red Cross.

Flower
SP52

Bitterwood
SP53

1973, Nov. 28   Litho.   *Perf. 14x14½*

B198	SP52	10c + 5c shown	.25	.25
B199	SP52	15c + 8c Tree	.45	.45
B200	SP52	20c + 10c Dog	.40	.40
a.		Min. sheet, #B200, 2 #B198	1.25	1.25
B201	SP52	25c + 12c House	.60	.60
B202	SP52	30c + 15c Girl	.60	.60
		Nos. B198-B202 (5)	2.30	2.30

Child welfare.

1974, Apr. 3   Litho.   *Perf. 14x14½*

Tropical Flowers: 15c+8c, Passion flower. 20c+10c, Wild angelica. 25c+12c, Candlestick senna. 30c+15c, Blood flower.

B203	SP53	10c + 5c multi	.45	.45
B204	SP53	15c + 8c multi	.45	.45
B205	SP53	20c + 10c multi	.45	.45
B206	SP53	25c + 12c multi	.45	.45
B207	SP53	30c + 15c multi	.45	.45
		Nos. B203-B207 (5)	2.25	2.25

Easter charities.

Boy Scout, Tent and
Trees — SP54

Designs: 15c+8c, 5th Caribbean Jamboree emblem. 20c+10c, Scouts and emblem.

1974, Aug. 21   Litho.   *Perf. 14x14½*

B208	SP54	10c + 5c multi	.40	.40
B209	SP54	15c + 8c multi	.40	.40
B210	SP54	20c + 10c multi	.40	.40
		Nos. B208-B210 (3)	1.20	1.20

50th anniversary of Surinam Boy Scouts.

B214	SP55	25c + 12c multi	.55	.55
B215	SP55	30c + 15c multi	.60	.60
		Nos. B211-B215 (5)	2.10	2.10

Child welfare.

The Good
Shepherd
SP56

Woman and
IWY Emblem
SP57

Designs: 20c+10c, Peter's denial. 30c+15c, The Women at the Tomb. 35c+20c, Jesus showing His wounds to Thomas.

1975, Mar. 26   Litho.   *Perf. 12½x13*

B216	SP56	15c + 5c yel grn & grn	.45	.45
B217	SP56	20c + 10c org & dk bl	.60	.60
B218	SP56	30c + 15c yel & red	.60	.60
B219	SP56	35c + 20c bl & pur	.60	.60
		Nos. B216-B219 (4)	2.25	2.25

Easter charities.

1975, May 14   Litho.   *Perf. 12½x13*

B220	SP57	15c + 5c multi	.65	.65
B221	SP57	30c + 15c multi	.65	.65

International Women's Year.

Carib Indian
Water
Jug — SP58

Feeding the
Hungry — SP59

Designs: 20c+10c, 35c+20c, Indian arrow head, diff. 30c+15c, Wayana board with animal figures.

1975, Nov. 12   Litho.   *Perf. 12½x13*

B222	SP58	15c + 5c multi	.25	.25
B223	SP58	20c + 10c multi	.55	.55
a.		Min. sheet, #B223, 2 #B222	1.50	1.50
B224	SP58	30c + 15c multi	.90	.90
B225	SP58	35c + 20c multi	.90	.90
		Nos. B222-B225 (4)	2.60	2.60

Child welfare.

Perf. 14½x13½

1976, Apr. 14   Photo.

Paintings: 25c+15c, Visiting the Sick. 30c+15c, Clothing the Naked. 35c+15c, Burying the Dead. 50c+25c, Giving Water to the Thirsty. Designs after panels in Alkmaar Church, 1504.

B226	SP59	20c + 10c multi	.70	.70
B227	SP59	30c + 15c multi	.85	.85
B228	SP59	30c + 15c multi	1.25	1.25
a.		Souv. sheet, #B228, 2 #B226	3.50	3.50
B229	SP59	35c + 15c multi	1.25	1.25
B230	SP59	50c + 25c multi	1.75	1.75
		Nos. B226-B230 (5)	5.80	5.80

Easter.

25c+10c, German shepherd. 30c+15c, Dachshund. 35c+15c, Retriever. 50c+25c, Terrier.

1976 **Litho.** **Perf. 13½**
B231	SP60	20c + 10c multi	.90	.60
B232	SP60	25c + 10c multi	1.25	.80
B233	SP60	30c + 15c multi	1.50	.95
a.	Min. sheet, #B233, 2 #B231		8.00	6.50
B234	SP60	35c + 15c multi	1.50	1.00
B235	SP60	50c + 25c multi	2.40	1.50
	Nos. B231-B235 (5)		7.55	4.85

Surtax was for child welfare.

St. Veronica's Veil — SP61   Descent from the Cross — SP62

Easter: Religious scenes, side panels, front and back, from triptych by Jan Mostaert (1473-1555).

1977, Apr. 6 **Litho.** **Perf. 13½x14**
B236	SP61	20c + 10c multi	.25	.25
B237	SP61	25c + 15c multi	.50	.50
B238	SP61	30c + 15c multi	.55	.55
B239	SP62	35c + 15c multi	.65	.65
B240	SP61	50c + 25c multi	.80	.80
	Nos. B236-B240 (5)		2.75	2.75

Dog and Girl's Head — SP63   Crosses, Luke 23:43 — SP64

Child's Head and: 25c+15c, Monkey. 30c+15c, Rabbit. 35c+15c, Cat. 50c+25c, Parrot.

1977, Nov. 23 **Litho.** **Perf. 13x14**
B241	SP63	20c + 10c multi	.50	.50
B242	SP63	25c + 15c multi	.60	.60
B243	SP63	30c + 15c multi	.70	.70
a.	Min. sheet, #B243, 2 #B241		1.75	1.75
B244	SP63	35c + 15c multi	.85	.85
B245	SP63	50c + 25c multi	1.25	1.25
	Nos. B241-B245 (5)		3.90	3.90

Surtax was for child welfare.

1978, Mar. 22 **Litho.** **Perf. 12½x14**

Easter: 25c+15c, Serpent and Cross, John 3:14. 30c+15c, Lamb and blood, Exodus 12:13. 35c+15c, Passover plate, chalice and bread. 60c+30c, Cross and solar eclipse.

B246	SP64	20c + 10c multi	.25	.25
B247	SP64	25c + 15c multi	.35	.35
B248	SP64	30c + 15c multi	.40	.40
B249	SP64	35c + 15c multi	.45	.45
B250	SP64	60c + 30c multi	.90	.90
	Nos. B246-B250 (5)		2.35	2.35

Child's Head and White Cat — SP65

Child's head and cats in various positions.

1978, Nov. 22 **Litho.** **Perf. 14x13**
B251	SP65	20c + 10c multi	.30	.30
B252	SP65	25c + 15c multi	.50	.35
B253	SP65	50c + 15c multi	.55	.40
a.	Min. sheet, #B253, 2 #B251		1.65	1.65
B254	SP65	35c + 15c multi	.60	.50
B255	SP65	60c + 30c multi	1.00	.80
	Nos. B251-B255 (5)		2.95	2.35

Surtax was for child welfare.

Church, Cross and Chalice — SP66

Easter: Cross, chalice and various churches.

1979, Apr. 11 **Litho.** **Perf. 13x14**
B256	SP66	20c + 10c multi	.25	.25
B257	SP66	30c + 15c multi	.40	.40
B258	SP66	35c + 15c multi	.55	.55
B259	SP66	40c + 20c multi	.65	.65
B260	SP66	60c + 30c multi	.95	.95
	Nos. B256-B260 (5)		2.80	2.80

Boy, Bird, Red Cross, Blood Transfusion Bottle — SP67

1979, Nov. 21 **Litho.** **Perf. 13x14**
B261	SP67	20c + 10c multi	.25	.25
B262	SP67	30c + 15c multi	.40	.40
B263	SP67	35c + 15c multi	.55	.55
a.	Min. sheet, #B263, 2 #B261		2.25	2.25
B264	SP67	40c + 20c multi	.65	.65
B265	SP67	60c + 30c multi	.95	.95
	Nos. B261-B265 (5)		2.80	2.80

Surtax was for child welfare.

Cross — SP68   Anansi — SP69

Easter: Various symbols.

1980, Mar. 26 **Litho.** **Perf. 13x14**
B266	SP68	20c + 10c multi	.30	.30
B267	SP68	30c + 15c multi	.45	.45
B268	SP68	40c + 20c multi	.55	.55
B269	SP68	50c + 25c multi	.80	.80
B270	SP68	60c + 30c multi	.90	.90
	Nos. B266-B270 (5)		3.00	3.00

1980, Nov. 5 **Litho.** **Perf. 13x14**

Characters from Anansi and His Creditors.

B271	SP69	20c + 10c shown	.30	.30
B272	SP69	25c + 15c Ba Tigri	.45	.45
B273	SP69	30c + 15c Kakafowroe	.50	.50
B274	SP69	35c + 15c Ontiman	.55	.55
B275	SP69	60c + 30c Mat Kalaka	.95	.95
a.	Min. sheet, #B275, 2 #B271		1.75	1.75
	Nos. B271-B275 (5)		2.75	2.75

Surtax was for child welfare.

Woman Reading SP70

1980, Dec. 10 **Perf. 14x13**
B276	SP70	25c + 10c shown	.40	.40
B277	SP70	50c + 15c Gardening	.70	.70
B278	SP70	75c + 20c With grandchildren	1.00	1.00
	Nos. B276-B278 (3)		2.10	2.10

Surtax was for the elderly.

Crucifixion SP71   Indian Girl SP72

Easter: Scenes from the Passion of Christ.

1981, Apr. 8 **Litho.** **Perf. 13x14**
B279	SP71	20c + 10c multi	.25	.25
B280	SP71	30c + 15c multi	.40	.40
B281	SP71	50c + 25c multi	.85	.85
B282	SP71	60c + 30c multi	.90	.90
B283	SP71	75c + 35c multi	1.10	1.10
	Nos. B279-B283 (5)		3.50	3.50

Surtax was for the elderly.

1981, Nov. 26 **Litho.**
B284	SP72	20c + 10c shown	.25	.25
B285	SP72	30c + 15c Black	.45	.45
B286	SP72	50c + 25c Hindustani	.75	.75
B287	SP72	60c + 30c Javanese	.80	.80
B288	SP72	75c + 35c Chinese	.90	.90
a.	Souv. sheet, #B288, 2 #B285		3.00	3.00
	Nos. B284-B288 (5)		3.15	3.15

Surtax was for child welfare.

Easter SP73   Man Pushing Wheelbarrow SP74

Designs: Stained-glass windows, Sts. Peter and Paul Church, Paramaribo.

1982, Apr. 7 **Litho.** **Perf. 13x14**
B289	SP73	20c + 10c multi	.35	.35
B290	SP73	30c + 15c multi	.65	.65
B291	SP73	50c + 25c multi	1.00	1.00
B292	SP73	65c + 30c multi	1.00	1.00
B293	SP73	75c + 35c multi	1.25	1.25
	Nos. B289-B293 (5)		4.25	4.25

1982, Nov. 17 **Litho.**

Children's Drawings of City Cleaning Activities.

B294	SP74	20c + 10c multi	.35	.35
B295	SP74	30c + 15c multi	.65	.65
B296	SP74	50c + 25c multi	1.25	1.25
B297	SP74	65c + 30c multi	1.25	1.25
B298	SP74	75c + 35c multi	1.50	1.50
a.	Souv. sheet, #B298, 2 #B295		3.50	3.50
	Nos. B294-B298 (5)		5.00	5.00

Surtax was for child welfare.

Easter — SP75   Pitcher — SP76

Mosaic Symbols.

1983, Mar. 23 **Litho.** **Perf. 13x14**
B299	SP75	10c + 5c Dove	.25	.25
B300	SP75	15c + 5c Bread	.35	.35
B301	SP75	50c + 10c Fish	.80	.80
B302	SP75	50c + 25c Eye	1.75	1.75
B303	SP75	65c + 30c Wine cup	1.90	1.90
	Nos. B299-B303 (5)		5.05	5.05

1983, Nov. 16 **Litho.** **Perf. 13x14**
B304	SP76	10c + 5c shown	.35	.35
B305	SP76	15c + 5c Headdress	.35	.35
B306	SP76	25c + 10c Medicine rattle	.60	.60
B307	SP76	50c + 25c Sieve	1.75	1.75

B308	SP76	65c + 30c Basket	1.90	1.90
a.	Min. sheet, #B305, B306, B308		3.50	3.50
	Nos. B304-B308 (5)		4.95	4.95

Easter — SP77   SP78

1984, Apr. 4 **Litho.** **Perf. 13x14**
B309	SP77	10c + 5c Cross, rose	.30	.30
B310	SP77	15c + 15c Cemetery	.30	.30
B311	SP77	25c + 10c Candles	.55	.55
B312	SP77	50c + 25c Cross, crown of thorns	1.50	1.50
B313	SP77	65c + 30c Candle	1.75	1.50
	Nos. B309-B313 (5)		4.40	4.15

1984, Aug. 15 **Litho.** **Perf. 13x14**

Boy Scouts in Surinam, 60th Anniv.: 30c+10c, 8th Caribbean Jamboree emblem. 35c+10c, Salute. 50c+10c, Gardening. 90c+10c, Campfire in map of Surinam. Surtax was for Boy Scouts.

B314	SP78	30c + 10c multi	.90	.90
B315	SP78	35c + 10c multi	1.10	1.10
B316	SP78	50c + 10c multi	1.40	1.40
B317	SP78	90c + 10c multi	2.25	2.25
	Nos. B314-B317 (4)		5.65	5.65

Children's Games — SP79   Easter — SP80

1984, Nov. 14 **Litho.** **Perf. 13x14**
B318	SP79	5c + 5c Kites	.30	.30
B319	SP79	10c + 5c Kites, diff.	.30	.30
B320	SP79	30c + 10c Pingi-pingi-kasi	.70	.70
B321	SP79	50c + 25c Cricket	1.40	1.40
a.	Souv. sheet of 3, #B319-B321		2.50	2.50
B322	SP79	90c + 30c Peroen, peroen	2.10	2.10
	Nos. B318-B322 (5)		4.80	4.80

Surtax was for child welfare.

1985, Mar. 27 **Litho.** **Perf. 12½x14**
B323	SP80	5c + 5c multi	.30	.30
B324	SP80	10c + 5c multi	.30	.30
B325	SP80	30c + 15c multi	.80	.80
B326	SP80	50c + 25c multi	1.25	1.25
B327	SP80	90c + 30c multi	2.10	2.10
	Nos. B323-B327 (5)		4.75	4.75

Surtax for child welfare.

Map, Emblem SP81   Literacy SP82

1985, Oct. 22 **Litho.** **Perf. 13x14**
B328	SP81	30c + 10c shown	.75	.75
B329	SP81	50c + 10c Crucifix, missionaries	1.10	1.10
B330	SP81	90c + 20c Scroll	1.90	1.90
	Nos. B328-B330 (3)		3.75	3.75

Evangelical Brotherhood Mission in Surinam, 250th anniv. Surtax for mission medical and social work.

1985, Nov. 6
B331	SP82	5c + 5c Boy reading	.35	.35
B332	SP82	10c + 5c Learning alphabet	.35	.35
B333	SP82	30c + 10c Writing	.60	.60

B334 SP82 50c + 25c Girl read-
　　　　ing   1.25 1.25
　　a. Min. sheet of 3, #B332-B334   2.50 2.50
B335 SP82 90c + 30c Studying   2.25 2.25
　　Nos. B331-B335 (5)   4.80 4.80

Surtax for child welfare.

Easter — SP83 ｜ Sts. Peter and
　　　　　　　　Paul Cathedral,
　　　　　　　　Cent. — SP84

1986, Mar. 19   Litho.   Perf. 13x14
B336 SP83 5c + 5c multi   .25 .25
B337 SP83 10c + 5c multi   .25 .25
B338 SP83 30c + 15c multi   .65 .65
B339 SP83 50c + 25c multi   1.10 1.10
B340 SP83 90c + 30c multi   1.60 1.60
　　Nos. B336-B340 (5)   3.85 3.85

1986, May 28   Litho.
B341 SP84 30c + 10c Exterior   .55 .55
B342 SP84 50c + 10c Saints,
　　　　bas-relief   .80 .80
B343 SP84 110c + 30c Baptismal
　　　　font   2.00 2.00
　　Nos. B341-B343 (3)   3.35 3.35

Ancient Order
of Foresters
Court Charity,
Cent. — SP85

1986, July 29   Litho.   Perf. 14x13
B344 SP85 50c + 20c Foresters
　　　　emblem   .90 .90
B345 SP85 110c + 30c Court
　　　　building   2.00 2.00

Youth
Activities
SP86

1986, Nov. 5   Litho.   Perf. 14x13
B346 SP86   5c + 5c Hopscotch   .30 .30
B347 SP86   5c + 5c Ballet   .30 .30
B348 SP86 30c + 10c Mobile li-
　　　　brary   .60 .60
B349 SP86 50c + 25c Crafts   1.10 1.10
　　a. Min. sheet of 3, #B347-B349   2.75 2.75
B350 SP86 110c + 30c Educa-
　　　　tion   2.40 2.40
　　Nos. B346-B350 (5)   4.70 4.70

Surtax for Children's Charities.

Easter — SP87 ｜ Natl. Girl Guides
　　　　　　　　Movement, 40th
　　　　　　　　Anniv. — SP88

1987, May 7   Litho.
Designs: 15c+10c, Mushroom, Brownie's
emblem. 60c+10c, Clover, Guides' emblem.
110c+10c, Campfire, Rangers' emblem.
120c+10c, Ivy, Captain's emblem.

B356 SP88 15c + 10c multi   .50 .50
B357 SP88 60c + 10c multi   1.10 1.10
B358 SP88 110c + 10c multi   2.00 2.00
B359 SP88 120c + 10c multi   2.25 2.25
　　Nos. B356-B359 (4)   5.85 5.85

Surtax for the Surinam Girl Guides.

Caribbean   Easter — SP90
Manari — SP89

1987, Nov. 4   Litho.   Perf. 13x14
B360 SP89 50c + 25c Herring
　　　　bone   .95 .95
B361 SP89 60c + 30c Tortoise-
　　　　back   1.00 1.00
B362 SP89 110c + 50c Whirlpool
　　　　(squares)   1.90 1.90
　　a. Min. sheet of 2, #B360, B362 2.75 2.75
　　Nos. B360-B362 (3)   3.85 3.85

Surtax to benefit child welfare organizations.

1988, Mar. 23   Perf. 13x13½
B363 SP90 50c + 25c multi   .80 .80
B364 SP90 60c + 30c multi   1.10 1.10
B365 SP90 110c + 50c multi   2.00 2.00
　　Nos. B363-B365 (3)   3.90 3.90

Surtax for annual Easter Charity programs.

Intl. Red Cross and
Red Crescent
Organizations, 125th
Anniv. — SP91

#B367, Anniv. & blood donation emblems.

1988, Oct. 26   Litho.   Perf. 13x14
B366 SP91 60c + 30c multi   1.75 1.75
B367 SP91 120c + 60c multi   2.75 2.75

Children's
Drawings
SP92

1988, Dec. 5   Litho.   Perf. 14x13
B368 SP92 50c + 25c Man and
　　　　animal   1.00 1.00
B369 SP92 60c + 30c Children
　　　　and nature   1.10 1.10
B370 SP92 110c + 50c Stop
　　　　drugs   2.25 2.25
　　a. Souv. sheet of 3, #B368-B370,
　　　　perf 13½x13   4.25 4.25
　　Nos. B368-B370 (3)   4.35 4.35

Surtax to benefit children's charities.

1989, Mar. 21   Litho.   Perf. 13½
Size: No. B372, 28½x36½mm
B371 SP93 60c + 30c multi   1.10 1.10
B372 SP93 105c + 50c multi   2.00 2.00
B373 SP93 110c + 55c multi   2.25 2.25
　　Nos. B371-B373 (3)   5.35 5.35

Surtax for annual East Charity programs.

Children's
Drawings
SP94

No. B374, Helping each other. No. B375,
Child and nature. No. B376, In the school bus.

1989, Dec. 6   Litho.   Perf. 14x13
B374 SP94 60c +30c multi   1.40 1.40
B375 SP94 105c +50c multi   2.40 2.40
B376 SP94 110c +55c multi   2.50 2.50
　　a. Souv. sheet of 2, #B374, B376 3.75 3.75
　　Nos. B374-B376 (3)   6.30 6.30

Surtax for children's charities.

Easter — SP95

Designs: No. B377, Mother holding Christ
child. No. B378, Christ, follower. No. B379,
Mary holding martyred Christ.

1990, Mar. 28   Litho.   Perf. 13x14
B377 SP95 60c +30c multi   1.00 1.00
B378 SP95 105c +50c multi   1.75 1.75
B379 SP95 110c +55c multi   1.90 1.90
　　Nos. B377-B379 (3)   4.65 4.65

Children's
Drawings
SP96

1990, Dec. 4   Litho.   Perf. 14x13
B380 SP96 60c +30c Children,
　　　　hammock   1.25 1.25
B381 SP96 105c +50c Child,
　　　　animal, palm
　　　　tree   2.00 2.00
B382 SP96 110c +55c Child, bird
　　　　in tree   2.25 2.25
　　a. Souv. sheet of 2, #B380,
　　　　B382, perf. 13½x13   4.00 4.00
　　Nos. B380-B382 (3)   5.50 5.50

Easter — SP97   SP98

Easter: 60c+30c, Christ carrying cross.
105c+50c, The Crucifixion. 110c+55c, Woman
cradling Christ's body.

1991, Mar. 20   Litho.   Perf. 13x14
B383 SP97 60c +30c multi   1.25 1.25

SP99   SP100

Easter: 60c+30c, Crucifixion. 105c+50c,
Taking away body of Christ. 110c+55c,
Resurrection.

1992, Mar. 18
B389 SP99 60c +30c multi   1.00 1.00
B390 SP99 105c +50c multi   2.00 2.00
B391 SP99 110c +55c multi   2.25 2.25
　　Nos. B389-B391 (3)   5.25 5.25

1992, Dec. 3   Litho.   Perf. 13x14
Children's Drawings: 60c + 30c, Child as
tree. 105c + 50c, Face as tree. 110c, + 55c,
Boy and girl hanging from tree.
B392 SP100 60c +30c multi   1.00 1.00
B393 SP100 105c +50c multi   1.90 1.90
B394 SP100 110c +55c multi   2.10 2.10
　　a. Souv. sheet of 2, #B392, B394 3.50 3.50
　　Nos. B392-B394 (3)   5.00 5.00

Surtax for Child Welfare.

SP101   SP102

Easter: 60c+30c, Message from Christ.
110c+50c, Crucifixion. 125c+60c,
Resurrection.

1993, Mar. 31   Litho.   Perf. 13x14
B395 SP101 60c +30c multi   1.25 1.25
B396 SP101 110c +50c multi   2.25 2.25
B397 SP101 125c +60c multi   2.50 2.50
　　Nos. B395-B397 (3)   6.00 6.00

1993, Dec. 3
Children Playing Hopscotch: 25c+10c, 2
children. 35c+10c, 3 children. 50c+25c, 8 children. 75c+25c, 7 children.

B398 SP102 25c +10c grn &
　　　　multi   1.10 1.10
B399 SP102 35c +10c bl &
　　　　multi   1.40 1.40
B400 SP102 50c +25c grn &
　　　　multi   2.25 2.25
　　a. Souvenir sheet of 2,
　　　　#B399-B400   4.50 4.50
B401 SP102 75c +25c bl &
　　　　multi   3.00 3.00
　　Nos. B398-B401 (4)   7.75 7.75

Surtax for Child Welfare.
Stamps in No. B400a do not have the 1993
date in lower left corner.

AIR POST STAMPS

Allegory of
Flight — AP1

Perf. 12½

Nos. C1-C7
Overprinted in Black
or Red

1931, Aug. 8

C8	AP1	10c red (Bk)	19.00	15.00
a.		Double overprint	425.00	
C9	AP1	15c ultra (Bk)	19.00	15.00
C10	AP1	20c dull grn (R)	19.00	15.00
C11	AP1	40c orange (Bk)	29.00	22.50
a.		Double overprint	425.00	
C12	AP1	60c brn vio (R)	62.50	52.50
C13	AP1	1g gray blk (R)	72.50	65.00
C14	AP1	1½g deep brn (Bk)	72.50	67.50
	Nos. C8-C14 (7)		293.50	252.50

The variety with period omitted after "Do" occurs twice on each sheet.
Warning: The red overprint may dissolve in water.

Type of 1930
Thick Paper

1941, Sept. 25   Litho.   Perf. 13

C15	AP1	20c lt green	1.25	.90
C16	AP1	40c lt orange	7.50	5.25
C17	AP1	2½g yellow	7.50	12.50
C18	AP1	5g blue green	300.00	350.00
C19	AP1	10g lt bister	17.50	52.50
	Nos. C15-C19 (5)		333.75	421.15

The lines of shading on Nos. C15 and C16 are not as heavy as on Nos. C3 and C4. For surcharges see Nos. C24-C25.

Type of 1930
Redrawn

1941   Engr.   Perf. 12

C20	AP1	10c light red	1.50	.35
C21	AP1	60c dl brn vio	.85	.45
C22	AP1	1g black	19.00	22.50
	Nos. C20-C22 (3)		21.35	23.30

Redrawn stamps have three horizontal lines through post horn and many minor variations. For surcharges see Nos. C23, CB1.

> **Catalogue values for unused stamps in this section, from this point to the end of the section, are for Never Hinged items.**

Nos. C21, C17, C19 Surcharged with
New Values and Bars in Carmine

1945, Mar. 12   Perf. 13, 12

C23	AP1	22½c on 60c	.45	.70
a.		Inverted surcharge	250.00	250.00
C24	AP1	1g on 2½g	15.00	15.00
C25	AP1	5g on 10g	22.50	22.50
	Nos. C23-C25 (3)		37.95	38.20

Women of
Netherlands and
Surinam — AP2

Globe and
Winged Post
Horn — AP3

Perf. 12x12½

1949, May 10   Photo.   Unwmk.

C26	AP2	27½c henna brown		7.50	3.50

Valid only on first flight of Paramaribo-Amsterdam service.

1954, Sept. 25   Perf. 13½x12½

C27	AP3	15c dp ultra & ultra	1.75	1.50

Establishment of airmail service in Surinam, 25th anniv.

Redstone
Mercury
Rocket and
Comdr. Alan
B. Shepard,
Jr. — AP4

15c, Cosmonaut Gagarin in capsule and globe.

1961, July 3   Litho.   Perf. 12

C28	AP4	15c multicolored	.85	.85
C29	AP4	20c multicolored	.85	.85

"Man in Space," Major Yuri A. Gagarin, USSR, and Comdr. Alan B. Shepard, Jr., US. Printed in sheets of 12 (4x3) with ornamental borders and inscriptions. Two printings differ in shades and selvage perforations.

Water
Tower — AP5

Designs: 15c, 65c, Brewery. 20c, Boat on lake. 25c, 75c, Wood industry. 30c, Bauxite mine. 35c, 50c, Poelepantje bridge. 40c, Ship in harbor. 45c, Wharf.

1965, July 31   Photo.   Perf. 14x13½
Size: 25x18mm

C30	AP5	10c olive grn	.25	.25
C31	AP5	15c ocher	.25	.25
C32	AP5	20c slate grn	.25	.25
C33	AP5	25c violet blue	.25	.25
C34	AP5	30c blue green	.25	.25
C35	AP5	35c red orange	.35	.35
C36	AP5	40c orange	.35	.35
C37	AP5	45c dk carmine	.35	.35
C38	AP5	50c vermilion	.35	.35
C39	AP5	55c emerald	.35	.35
C40	AP5	65c bister	.45	.45
C41	AP5	75c blue	.45	.45
	Nos. C30-C41 (12)		3.90	3.90

See Nos. C75-C82.

Eucyane
Bicolor — AP6

1972, July 26   Litho.   Perf. 13½x14

C42	AP6	15c shown	.25	.25
C43	AP6	20c Helicopis cupido	.35	.25
C44	AP6	25c Papilio thoas thoas	.35	.25
C45	AP6	30c Urania leilus	.40	.25
C46	AP6	35c Stalachtis calliope	.40	.50
C47	AP6	40c Stalachtis phlegia	.45	.40
C48	AP6	45c Victorina steneles	.60	.25
C49	AP6	50c Papilio neophilus	.65	.25
C50	AP6	55c Anartia amathea	.80	.85
C51	AP6	60c Adelpha cytherea	.85	1.25
C52	AP6	65c Heliconius doris metharmina	.85	.85
C53	AP6	70c Nessaea obrinus	1.00	1.00
C54	AP6	75c Ageronia feronia	1.00	.80
	Nos. C42-C54 (13)		7.95	7.15

Surinam butterflies. Valid for regular postage also. For surcharges, see Nos. 495-499. #C42, C45 exist perf 14 with redrawn design.

Fish Type of 1976

Fish: 35c, Chaetodon unimaculatus. 60c, Centropyge loriculus. 95c, Caetodon collare.

1976, June 2   Litho.   Perf. 12½x13

C55	A111	35c multicolored	1.00	.55
C56	A111	60c multicolored	1.75	.90
C57	A111	95c multicolored	2.75	1.40
	Nos. C55-C57 (3)		5.50	2.85

Black-headed
Sugarbird
AP7

Birds of Surinam: 20c, Leistes militaris. 30c, Paradise tangara. 40c, Whippoorwill. 45c, Hemitraupis flavicollis. 50c, White-tailed goldthroated hummingbird. 55c, Saberwing. 60c, Blackcap parrot, vert. 65c, Toucan, vert. 70c, Manakin, vert. 75c, Collared parrot, vert. 80c, Cayenne cotinga, vert. 85c, Trogon, vert. 95c, Black-striped tropical tree owl, vert.

1977   Litho.   Perf. 14x13, 13x14

C58	AP7	20c multi	.25	.25
C59	AP7	25c multi	.35	.25
C60	AP7	30c multi	.40	.25
a.		Min. sheet of 4, 2 each #C59-C60, perf. 13½x14	3.75	2.00
C61	AP7	40c multi	.70	.40
C62	AP7	45c multi	.70	.40
C63	AP7	50c multi	.80	.50
C64	AP7	55c multi	.95	.55
C65	AP7	60c multi	1.00	.65

C66	AP7	65c multi	1.10	.70
C67	AP7	70c multi	1.25	.70
C68	AP7	75c multi	1.25	.80
C69	AP7	80c multi	1.25	.80
C70	AP7	85c multi	1.40	.95
C71	AP7	95c multi	1.75	1.10
	Nos. C58-C71 (14)		13.15	8.30

A souv. sheet of 4 with same stamps and perf. as No. C60a has marginal inscription "Amphilex 77" with magnifier over No. 424. Sold in folder at phil. exhib. in Amsterdam May 26-June 5, 1977. Value $5.75.
Issued: 25c, 30c, 50c, 60c, 75c, 80c, 95c, Apr. 27; #C60a, May 26; others, Aug. 24.
See Nos. C88, C101. For surcharges and overprints see Nos. C102-C105, C108-C111, J58, J62.

Tropical Fish Type of 1976

60c, Chaetodon striatus. 90c, Bodianus pulchellus. 120c, Centropyge argi.

1977, June 8   Litho.   Perf. 13x13½

C72	A111	60c multi	1.00	.80
C73	A111	90c multi	1.75	1.10
C74	A111	120c multi	2.50	1.90
	Nos. C72-C74 (3)		5.25	3.80

Type of 1965 Redrawn

Designs: 5c, Brewery. 10c, Water tower. 20c, Boat on lake. 25c, Wood industry. 30c, Bauxite mine. 35c, Poelepantje bridge. 40c, Ship in harbor. 60c, Wharf.

1976-78   Photo.   Perf. 12½x13½
Size: 22x18mm

C75	AP5	5c ocher	.25	.25
a.		Bklt. pane, 4 #C75, 3 #C82 + label	2.50	
C76	AP5	10c olive green	.55	.55
a.		Bklt. pane, 1 #C76, 4 #C80 + label	2.75	
C77	AP5	20c slate green	.25	.25
a.		Bklt. pane, 2 ea #C77-C79	2.75	
b.		Bklt. pane, 6 #C77, 2 #C81	2.50	
C78	AP5	25c vio bl	.55	.55
C79	AP5	30c dl brn	.65	.65
C80	AP5	35c red org	.55	.55
C81	AP5	40c org	.90	.90
C82	AP5	60c dk car	.75	.75
	Nos. C75-C82 (8)		4.45	4.45

Nos. C75-C82 issued in booklets only. Nos. C75a and C77b have inscribed selvage the size of 4 stamps; Nos. C76a and C77a the size of 6 stamps.
Issued: 10c-35c, 12/8; 5c, 40c, 60c, #C77b, 1/11/78.

Tropical Fish Type of 1976

60c, Astyanax species. 90c, Corydoras wotroi. 120c, Gasteropelecus sternicla.

1978, June 21   Litho.   Perf. 13x13½

C85	A111	60c multi	1.00	.95
C86	A111	90c multi	1.60	1.00
C87	A111	120c multi	2.25	1.25
	Nos. C85-C87 (3)		4.85	3.20

Bird Type of 1977

Design: 5g, Crested curassow, vert.

1979, Jan. 10   Engr.   Perf. 13x13½

C88	AP7	5g violet	6.00	3.00

Tropical Fish Type of 1979

60c, Cantherinus macrocerus. 90c, Holocenthrus rufus. 120c, Holacanthus tricolor.

1979, May 30   Photo.   Perf. 14x13

C89	A129	60c multi	.75	.30
C90	A129	90c multi	1.25	.90
C91	A129	120c multi	1.75	1.40
	Nos. C89-C91 (3)		3.75	2.60

Tropical Fish Type of 1979

60c, Symphysodon discus. 75c, Aeqidens curviceps. 90c, Catoprion mento.

1980, Sept. 10   Photo.   Perf. 14x13

C92	A129	60c multi	1.00	.80
C93	A129	75c multi	1.50	1.00
C94	A129	90c multi	1.50	1.25
	Nos. C92-C94 (3)		4.00	3.05

Frog Type of 1981

1981, June 24   Perf. 13x14

C95	A142	75c Phyllomedusa burmeisteri, vert.	1.60	.80
C96	A142	1g Dendrobates tinctorius, vert.	2.10	1.10
C97	A142	1.25g Bufo guttatus, vert.	2.50	1.40
	Nos. C95-C97 (3)		6.20	3.30

Turtle Type of 1982

1982, Feb. 17   Photo.   Perf. 14x13

C98	A146	65c Platemys platycephala	1.00	.65
C99	A146	75c Phrynops gibba	1.25	.80
C100	A146	125c Rhinoclemys punctularia	2.25	1.50
	Nos. C98-C100 (3)		4.50	2.95

Bird Type of 1977

1985, Jan. 9   Litho.   Perf. 13x14

C101	AP7	90c Venezuelan Amazon, vert.	5.25	5.25

For overprint see No. J61.

No. C60 Surcharged

1986, Oct. 1   Litho.   Perf. 14x13

C102	AP7	15c on 30c multi	4.50	4.50

Nos. C70-C71 and
C67 Surcharged

1987, Mar.   Litho.   Perf. 13x14

C103	AP7	10c on 85c No. C70	2.00	2.00
C104	AP7	10c on 95c No. C71	2.00	2.00
C105	AP7	25c on 70c No. C67	6.00	6.00
	Nos. C103-C105 (3)		10.00	10.00

Otter Type of 1989

1989, Jan. 18   Litho.   Perf. 13x14

C107	A195	185c Otters, vert.	3.00	3.00

No. C63
Surcharged

1993, Jan. 20   Litho.   Perf. 14x13

C108	AP7	35c on 50c multi	.40	.40

Nos. C62,
C64-C65
Surcharged

1994, Apr. 11   Perf. 14x13, 13x14

C109	AP7	( ) on 60c #C65	.25	.25
C110	AP7	( ) on 45c #C62	1.00	1.00
C111	AP7	( ) on 55c #C64	1.50	1.50
	Nos. C109-C111 (3)		1.75	1.75

The face value of Nos. C109-C111 fluctuates with postal rate changes. Face values on day of issue were: No. C109, 2.50f; No. C110, 10f; No. C111, 25f. No. C109 paid the additional 5 grams letter rate to the Netherlands. No. C110 paid the basic rate to North and South America and the Caribbean. No. C111 paid the basic 10-gram letter rate to the Netherlands.
Size and location of surcharge varies.

AIR POST SEMI-POSTAL STAMPS

> **Catalogue values for unused stamps in this section are for Never Hinged items.**

No. C20 Surchd. in Red like No. B40.
Unwmk.

1942, Jan. 2   Engr.   Perf. 12

CB1	AP1	10c + 5c lt red, III	2.50	2.50
a.		Type IV	4.25	5.25
b.		Type V	11.50	14.00

The surtax was for the Red Cross.
See note on types III and IV below No. B40.

Nos. 193 and 194
Surcharged in Carmine

1946, Feb. 24   *Perf. 12*
CB2 A30 10c + 40c blue   1.00 1.00
CB3 A30 15c + 60c brown   1.00 1.00

The surtax was for the Red Cross.

Star Type of Semi-Postals
Perf. 13½x12½

1947, Dec. 16   Photo.
CB4 SP17 22½c + 27½c gray   2.25 1.75
CB5 SP17 27½c + 47½c grn   2.25 1.75

POSTAGE DUE STAMPS

D1   D2

Type I — 34 loops. "T" of "BETALEN" over center of loop; top branch of "E" of "TE" shorter than lower branch.
Type II — 33 loops. "T" of "BETALEN" over space between two loops.
Type III — 32 loops. "T" of "BETALEN" slightly to the left of center of loop; top branch of first "E" of "BETALEN" shorter than lower branch.
Type IV — 37 loops and letters of "PORT" larger than in the other 3 types.

Value in Black
Perf. 12½x12

1886-88   Typo.   Unwmk.
Type III

J1	D1	2½c lilac	3.00	3.00
J2	D1	5c lilac	9.00	9.00
J3	D1	10c lilac	100.00	65.00
J4	D1	20c lilac	9.00	9.00
J5	D1	25c lilac	12.50	12.50
J6	D1	30c lilac ('88)	2.50	2.50
J7	D1	40c lilac	6.00	6.00
J8	D1	50c lilac ('88)	3.00	3.00
		Nos. J1-J8 (8)	145.00	110.00

Type I

J1a	D1	2½c	6.00	6.00
J2a	D1	5c	11.00	11.00
J3a	D1	10c	125.00	90.00
J4a	D1	20c	22.50	22.50
J5a	D1	25c	19.00	19.00
J6a	D1	30c	22.50	22.50
J7a	D1	40c	12.50	12.50
J8a	D1	50c	4.00	4.00
		Nos. J1a-J8a (8)	222.50	187.50

Type II

J1b	D1	2½c	5.00	5.00
J2b	D1	5c	10.00	10.00
J3b	D1	10c	1,250.	1,250.
J4b	D1	20c	9.00	9.00
J5b	D1	25c	300.00	300.00
J6b	D1	30c	75.00	75.00
J7b	D1	40c	350.00	350.00
J8b	D1	50c	5.00	5.00

Type IV

J3c	D1	10c	350.00	250.00
J5c	D1	25c	160.00	150.00
J7c	D1	40c	150.00	150.00
		Nos. J3c-J7c (3)	660.00	550.00

Nos. J1-J16 were issued without gum. For surcharges, see Nos. J15-J16.

1892-96   Value in Black   *Perf. 12½*
Type III

J9	D2	2½c lilac	.40	.40
J10	D2	5c lilac	1.25	1.00

Type II

J9b	D2	2½c	.80	.80
J10b	D2	5c	3.00	3.00
J11b	D2	10c	40.00	42.50
J12b	D2	20c	90.00	90.00
J13b	D2	25c	100.00	100.00

For surcharges, see Nos. 121-122.

Stamps of 1888
Surcharged in Red

1911, July 15

J15	D1	10c on 30c lil (III)	80.00	80.00
a.		10c on 30c lilac (I)	200.00	225.00
b.		10c on 30c lilac (II)	1,800.	1,800.
J16	D1	10c on 50c lil (III)	110.00	110.00
a.		10c on 50c lilac (I)	115.00	115.00
b.		10c on 50c lilac (II)	115.00	115.00

D3

Type I
Value in Color of Stamp

1913-31   *Perf. 12½, 13½x12½*

J17	D2	½c lilac ('30)	.25	.25
J18	D2	1c lilac ('31)	.25	.35
J19	D2	2c lilac ('31)	.25	.25
J20	D2	2½c lilac	.25	.25
J21	D2	5c lilac	.25	.25
J22	D2	10c lilac	.25	.25
J23	D2	12c lilac ('31)	.25	.25
J24	D2	12½c lilac ('22)	.25	.25
J25	D2	15c lilac ('26)	.55	.45
J26	D2	20c lilac	.85	.45
J27	D2	25c lilac	.45	.25
J28	D2	30c lilac ('26)	.45	.60
J29	D2	40c lilac	14.50	14.00
J30	D2	50c lilac ('26)	1.25	1.25
J31	D2	75c lilac ('26)	1.50	1.50
J32	D2	1g lilac ('26)	1.75	1.50
		Nos. J17-J32 (16)	23.30	22.10

> **Catalogue values for unused stamps in this section, from this point to the end of the section, are for Never Hinged items.**

D4

1945   Litho.   *Perf. 12*

J33	D4	1c light brown violet	.25	.30
J34	D4	5c light brown violet	3.00	2.50
J35	D4	25c light brown violet	7.00	.50
		Nos. J33-J35 (3)	10.25	3.30

D5   D6

Perf. 13½x12½

1950   Unwmk.   Photo.

J36	D5	1c purple	3.00	2.50
J37	D5	2c purple	4.50	2.25
J38	D5	2½c purple	3.75	2.50
J39	D5	5c purple	5.50	.50

J52	D6	15c purple	.70	.70
J53	D6	20c purple	.70	.70
J54	D6	25c purple	.80	.40
J55	D6	50c purple	2.10	.50
J56	D6	75c purple	2.75	1.60
J57	D6	1g purple	4.00	1.25
		Nos. J47-J57 (11)	13.30	7.20

For surcharges, see Nos. J64-J69.

Stamps of 1977-1985 Overprinted "TE BETALEN"
Perf. 13x14, 14x13

1987, July   Litho.

J58	AP7	65c No. C66	3.00	3.00
J59	A156	65c No. 638	3.00	3.00
J60	A156	80c No. 640	3.75	3.75
J61	AP7	90c No. C101	4.25	4.25
J62	AP7	95c No. C71	5.00	5.00
J63	A173	1g No. 725	5.25	5.25
		Nos. J58-J63 (6)	24.25	24.25

Nos. J47, J50, J55 and J57 Surcharged

Methods and Perfs. As Before
2007, Dec. 3

J64	D6	$1 on 1c #J47	.75	.75
J65	D6	$1.50 on 1g #J57	1.10	1.10
J66	D6	$2 on 5c #J50	1.50	1.50
J67	D6	$3 on 50c #J55	2.25	2.25
J68	D6	$3.50 on 1g #J57	2.60	2.60
J69	D6	$4 on 1g #J57	3.00	3.00
		Nos. J64-J69 (6)	11.20	11.20

SWAZILAND

ˈswə-zē-ˌland

LOCATION — Southeast Africa bordered by the Transvaal and Zululand in South Africa and by Mozambique
GOVT. — Constitutional monarchy
AREA — 6,705 sq. mi.
POP. — 985,335 (1999 est.)
CAPITAL — Mbabane

An independent state in the 19th century, Swaziland was administered by Transvaal from 1894 to 1906, when the administration was transferred to the British High Commissioner for South Africa. In 1934 Swaziland and Bechuanaland Protectorate came under the administration of the British High Commissioner for Basutoland. The issuing of individual postage stamps had been resumed in 1933. Internal self-government was introduced in 1967. Independence was proclaimed September 6, 1968.

12 Pence = 1 Shilling
20 Shillings = 1 Pound
100 Cents = 1 Rand (1961)
100 Cents = 1 Emalangeni (1975)

> **Catalogue values for unused stamps in this country are for Never Hinged items, beginning with Scott 38 in the regular postage section and Scott J1 in the postage due section.**

2	A1	1p rose	20.00	19.00
a.		Inverted overprint	800.00	750.00
3	A1	2p olive bister	20.00	18.00
a.		Inverted overprint	900.00	525.00
b.		"Swazielan"	550.00	475.00
c.		Perf. 12½x12	100.00	25.00
d.		As "c," "Swazielan"	1,250.	725.00
e.		As "d," inverted overprint		1,250.
f.		As "b," inverted overprint	5,100.	4,600.
g.		Double overprint	2,600.	
4	A1	6p gray blue	25.00	50.00
5	A1	1sh green	13.00	16.00
a.		Inverted overprint	1,100.	525.00
6	A1	2sh6p yellow	275.00	325.00
7	A1	5sh slate	175.00	225.00
a.		Inverted overprint	1,900.	2,500.
b.		"Swazielan"	5,250.	
c.		As "b," inverted overprint	5,750.	
8	A1	10sh lt brown	6,500.	4,000.

1892   Red Overprint

9	A1	½p gray	8.50	19.00
a.		Inverted overprint	575.00	
b.		Double overprint	525.00	525.00
c.		Pair, one without overprint		1,900.

Beware of counterfeits.
Reprints have a period after "Swazieland."

Stamps of Swaziland were replaced by those of Transvaal in 1895. Swaziland issues were resumed in 1933.

Perf. 14
1933, Jan. 2   Engr.   Wmk. 4

10	A2	½p green	.40	.35
11	A2	1p carmine	.40	.25
12	A2	2p lt brown	.40	.50
13	A2	3p ultra	.55	3.00
14	A2	4p orange	3.50	3.50
15	A2	6p rose violet	1.60	1.10
16	A2	1sh olive green	1.90	3.25
17	A2	2sh6p violet	19.00	25.00
18	A2	5sh gray	37.50	57.50
19	A2	10sh black brown	100.00	140.00
		Nos. 10-19 (10)	165.25	234.45
		Set, never hinged	375.00	

Common Design Types
pictured following the introduction.

Silver Jubilee Issue
Common Design Type

1935, May 4   *Perf. 11x12*

20	CD301	1p carmine & blue	.70	2.00
21	CD301	2p black & ultra	1.25	2.00
22	CD301	3p ultra & brown	1.00	6.00
23	CD301	6p brown, vio & ind	1.25	3.00
		Nos. 20-23 (4)	4.20	13.00
		Set, never hinged	7.00	

Coronation Issue
Common Design Type

1937, May 12   *Perf. 11x11½*

24	CD302	1p dark carmine	.35	.55
25	CD302	2p brown	.35	.25
26	CD302	3p deep ultra	.35	.55
		Nos. 24-26 (3)	1.05	1.35
		Set, never hinged	1.75	

George VI — A3

1938, Apr. 1   *Perf. 13, 13x13½*

27	A3	½p green	.25	1.50
28	A3	1p rose carmine	.80	1.50
29	A3	1½p light blue	.30	.85
a.		Perf. 14 ('42)	1.40	1.25
30	A3	2p brown	.30	.45
31	A3	3p ultra	2.75	2.00
32	A3	4p red orange	.40	1.60
33	A3	6p rose violet	3.50	1.75
34	A3	1sh olive green	.95	.75
35	A3	2sh6p dark violet	10.50	2.75
36	A3	5sh gray	20.00	15.00
37	A3	10sh black brown	4.75	6.50
		Nos. 27-37 (11)	44.50	34.65
		Set, never hinged	70.00	

Peace Issue

South Africa,
Nos. 100-102
Overprinted

Basic stamps inscribed alternately in English and Afrikaans.

1945, Dec. 3   Wmk. 201   Perf. 14
38	A42	1p rose pink & choc, pair	.80	1.25
a.		Single, English	.25	.25
b.		Single, Afrikaans	.25	.25
39	A43	2p vio & sl blue, pair	.80	1.25
a.		Single, English	.25	.25
b.		Single, Afrikaans	.25	.25
40	A43	3p ultra & dp ultra, pair	.80	4.00
a.		Single, English	.25	.25
b.		Single, Afrikaans	.25	.25
		Nos. 38-40 (3)	2.40	6.50

World War II victory of the Allies.

Royal Visit Issue
Type of Basutoland, 1947
Perf. 12½
1947, Feb. 17   Wmk. 4   Engr.
44	A3	1p red	.25	.25
45	A4	2p green	.25	.25
46	A5	3p ultramarine	.25	.25
47	A6	1sh dark violet	.25	.25
		Nos. 44-47 (4)	1.00	1.00

Visit of the British Royal Family, 3/25/47.

Silver Wedding Issue
Common Design Types
1948, Dec. 1   Photo.   Perf. 14x14½
48	CD304	1½p bright ultra	.30	.25

Perf. 11½x11
Engraved; Name Typographed
49	CD305	10sh violet brown	30.00	40.00

UPU Issue
Common Design Types
Engr.; Name Typo. on 3p, 6p
Perf. 13½, 11x11½
1949, Oct. 10   Wmk. 4
50	CD306	1½p blue	.40	.25
51	CD307	3p indigo	.70	.65
52	CD308	6p red lilac	.90	.65
53	CD309	1sh olive	1.00	.65
		Nos. 50-53 (4)	3.00	2.20

Coronation Issue
Common Design Type
1953, June 3   Engr.   Perf. 13½x13
54	CD312	2p yellow brown & blk	.30	.25

Asbestos Mine — A4

Married Woman — A5

1p, 2sh 6p, Highveld view. 3p, 1sh 3p, Courting couple. 4½p, 5sh, Warrior. 6p, £1, Kudu. 1sh, Asbestos mine. 10sh, Married woman.

Perf. 13x13½, 13½x13
1956, July 2   Engr.   Wmk. 4
Center in Black, except Nos. 63-64
55	A4	½p orange	.25	.25
56	A4	1p emerald	.25	.25
57	A5	2p redsh brown	.40	.25
58	A5	3p rose red	.30	.25
59	A5	4½p ultra	.85	.25
60	A5	6p magenta	.55	.25
61	A4	1sh gray olive	.40	.25
62	A5	1sh3p brown	1.50	10.00
63	A4	2sh6p car & brt grn	1.50	1.50
64	A5	5sh blue gray & vio	9.50	2.75

65	A5	10sh dull violet	20.00	9.00
66	A5	£1 turquoise	47.50	35.00
		Nos. 55-66 (12)	83.00	60.00

Nos. 55-61 and 63-66 Surcharged with New Value

1961
67	A4	½c on ½p	3.50	3.25
a.		Inverted surcharge	525.00	
68	A4	1c on 1p	.25	.25
a.		"1c" at center	35.00	
b.		Double surcharge	525.00	
69	A5	2c on 2p	.25	.25
70	A5	2½c on 2p	.25	.25
71	A5	3c on 3p (I)	.25	.25
a.		Type II	.25	.25
72	A5	3½c on 2p	.25	.25
73	A5	4c on 4½p (II)	.25	.25
a.		Type I	.25	.25
74	A5	5c on 6p (II)	.25	.25
a.		Type I	.25	.25
75	A4	10c on 1sh	27.50	9.25
a.		Double surcharge	575.00	
76	A4	25c on 2sh6p (I)	.40	1.50
a.		Type II, "25c" centered	1.60	1.00
b.		Type II, "25c" at lower left	375.00	240.00
77	A5	50c on 5sh (I)	.40	1.90
a.		Type II	7.75	4.25
b.		Type III	700.00	475.00
78	A5	1r on 10sh (I)	2.25	2.50
a.		Type I	5.25	5.25
b.		Type III	72.50	90.00
79	A5	2r on £1 (II, "R2" at middle left)	10.00	8.00
a.		Type I	15.00	15.00
b.		Type II, "R2" at center bottom	35.00	60.00
		Nos. 67-79 (13)	45.80	28.15

The type II "25c" surcharge is nearly centered in the sky on No. 76a, and is at lower left touching the value tablet on No. 76b. Surcharge types are numbered chronologically.
For surcharges see Nos. J3-J6.

Types of 1956
½c, 10c, Asbestos mine. 1c, 25c, Highveld view. 2c, 1r, Married woman. 2½c, 12½c, Courting couple. 4c, 50c, Warrior. 5c, 2r, Kudu.

Perf. 13x13½, 13½x13
1961   Engr.   Wmk. 4
Center in Black, except Nos. 88-89
80	A4	½c orange	.25	1.10
81	A4	1c emerald	.25	.25
82	A5	2c redsh brown	.25	3.25
83	A5	2½c rose red	.25	.25
84	A5	4c ultra	.25	1.40
85	A5	5c magenta	.50	.25
86	A4	10c gray olive	.25	.25
87	A5	12½c brown	1.75	.60
88	A5	25c car & brt green	3.00	4.00
89	A5	50c blue gray & vio	3.25	2.10
90	A5	1r dull violet	6.25	13.00
91	A5	2r turquoise	14.00	16.00
		Nos. 80-91 (12)	30.25	42.45

Swazi Shields — A6

Train and Railroad Map — A7

Designs: 1c, Battle axe. 2c, Forestry. 2½c, Ceremonial headdress. 3½c, Musical instrument. 4c, Irrigation. 5c, Widow bird. 7½c, Rock paintings. 10c, Secretary bird. 12½c, Pink arum lily. 15c, Married woman. 20c, Malaria control. 25c, Swazi warrior. 50c, Ground hornbill, horiz. 1r, Aloes. 2r, Msinsi (flame tree), horiz.

Perf. 12½x14, 14x12½
1962, Apr. 24   Photo.   Wmk. 314
92	A6	½c ocher, blk & brn	.25	.25
93	A6	1c gray & orange	.25	.25
94	A6	2c lt yel grn, dk grn & blk		1.25
95	A6	2½c vermilion & blk	.25	.25
96	A6	3½c gray & emerald	.25	.70
97	A6	4c aqua & black	.25	.25
98	A6	5c orange red & blk	.90	.25
99	A6	7½c dull ocher & brn	1.00	.40
100	A6	10c lt blue & black	1.60	.25
101	A6	12½c lt olive & dp car	1.25	2.75
102	A6	15c red lilac & blk	1.75	1.25
103	A6	20c emerald & blk	.50	1.50
104	A6	25c ultra & blk	.60	1.25
105	A6	50c rose red & dk brn	11.00	4.75
106	A6	1r bister & emer	3.75	3.00
107	A6	2r ultra & scar	15.00	11.00
		Nos. 92-107 (16)	38.85	29.35

For surcharge & overprints see #138, 143-159.

Freedom from Hunger Issue
Common Design Type
1963, June 4   Perf. 14x14½
108	CD314	15c lilac	.50	.50

Red Cross Centenary Issue
Common Design Type
1963, Sept. 2   Litho.   Perf. 13
109	CD315	2½c black & red	.30	.30
110	CD315	15c ultra & red	.80	.80

Perf. 11½x12
1964, Nov. 5   Engr.   Wmk. 314
111	A7	2½c purple & brt grn	.60	.25
112	A7	3½c dk olive & blue	.65	1.10
113	A7	15c dk brown & orange	.80	.70
114	A7	25c dk blue & yellow	1.00	.80
		Nos. 111-114 (4)	3.05	2.85

Opening of the Swaziland Railroad linking Ka Dake with Lourenco Marques.

ITU Issue
Common Design Type
Perf. 11x11½
1965, May 17   Litho.   Wmk. 314
115	CD317	2½c blue & bister	.25	.25
116	CD317	15c red lil & rose red	.50	.50

Intl. Cooperation Year Issue
Common Design Type
1965, Oct. 25   Perf. 14½
117	CD318	½c bl grn & claret	.25	.25
118	CD318	15c lt violet & grn	.50	.50

Churchill Memorial Issue
Common Design Type
1966, Jan. 24   Photo.   Perf. 14
Design in Black, Gold and Carmine Rose
119	CD319	½c brt blue	.25	.50
120	CD319	2½c green	.30	.25
121	CD319	15c brown	.50	.40
122	CD319	25c violet	.75	.80
		Nos. 119-122 (4)	1.80	1.95

UNESCO Anniversary Issue
Common Design Type
1966, Dec. 1   Litho.   Perf. 14
123	CD323	2½c "Education"	.25	.25
124	CD323	7½c "Science"	.40	.40
125	CD323	15c "Culture"	.80	.80
		Nos. 123-125 (3)	1.45	1.45

King Sobhuza II and Map of Swaziland A8

Design: 7½c, 25c, King Sobhuza II, vert.

Perf. 14½x14, 14x14½
1967, Apr. 25   Photo.   Wmk. 314
126	A8	2½c multicolored	.25	.25
127	A8	7½c multicolored	.25	.25
128	A8	15c multicolored	.25	.25
129	A8	25c multicolored	.40	.40
		Nos. 126-129 (4)	1.15	1.15

Attainment of internal self-government.

King Sobhuza II, University Buildings and Graduates — A9

Perf. 14x14½
1967, Sept. 1   Photo.   Unwmk.
130	A9	2½c yel, sepia & dp bl	.25	.25
131	A9	7½c blue, sepia & dp bl	.25	.25
132	A9	15c dl rose, sepia & dp bl	.25	.25
133	A9	25c lt vio, sepia & dp bl	.40	.40
		Nos. 130-133 (4)	1.15	1.15

1st conferment of degrees by the University of Botswana, Lesotho and Swaziland at Roma, Lesotho.

Swazi Reed Dance (Umhlanga) — A10

Designs: 3c, 15c, Feast of the First Fruits, Incwala (bull, sun and king), horiz.

Perf. 14½x14, 14x14½
1968, Jan. 5   Photo.   Wmk. 314
134	A10	3c red, blk & silver	.25	.25
135	A10	10c brown, blk, org & sil	.25	.25
136	A10	15c red, blk & gold	.25	.25
137	A10	25c brown, blk, org & gold	.40	.40
		Nos. 134-137 (4)	1.15	1.15

No. 98 Surcharged with New Value

1968, May 1   Perf. 12½x14
138	A6	3c on 5c org red & blk	.75	.45

Independent Kingdom

Plowing and King Sobhuza II — A11

Designs: 4½c, Cable lift carrying asbestos. 17½c, Worker cutting sugar cane. 25c, Iron ore mining and map showing Swaziland railroad.

Perf. 14x12½
1968, Sept. 6   Photo.   Wmk. 314
139	A11	3c gold & multi	.25	.25
140	A11	4½c gold & multi	.25	.25
141	A11	17½c gold & multi	.25	.25
142	A11	25c slate & gold	.50	.50
a.		Strip of 4, #139-142	4.00	4.00
		Nos. 139-142 (4)	1.25	1.25

Swaziland's independence.
Nos. 139-142 printed in sheets of 50. No. 142a printed in sheets of 20 (4x5).

Nos. 92-107 Overprinted; No. 96 Surcharged

1968, Sept. 6   Perf. 12½x14, 14x12½
143	A6	½c ocher, blk & brn	.25	.25
144	A6	1c gray & orange	.25	.25
145	A6	2c multicolored	.25	.25
146	A6	2½c vermilion & blk	1.00	2.25
147	A6	3c on 2½c #146	.25	.25
148	A6	3½c gray & emerald	.25	.25
149	A6	4c aqua & black	.25	.25
150	A6	5c org red & blk	4.75	.25
151	A6	7½c dull ocher & brn	.75	.25
152	A6	10c lt blue & blk	5.25	.25
153	A6	12½c lt olive & dp car	.45	.90
154	A6	15c red lilac & blk	.45	1.10

SWAZILAND

Page 534

155	A6	20c emerald & blk	1.25	2.40
156	A6	25c ultra & blk	.60	1.10
157	A6	50c rose red & dk brn	9.75	6.75
a.		Wmk. sideways	4.25	4.25
158	A6	1r bister & emerald	3.50	6.75
159	A6	2r ultra & scarlet	6.75	13.50
a.		Wmk. sideways	7.00	7.00
		Nos. 143-159 (17)	36.00	37.00

Caracal (African Lynx) — A12

Waterbuck — A12a

1c, Cape porcupine. 2c, Crocodile. 3c, Lion. 3½c, African elephants. 5c, Bush pig. 7½c, Impalas. 10c, Chacma baboon. 12½c, Ratel (honey badger). 15c, Leopard. 20c, Blue wildebeest (brindled gnu). 25c, White (square-lipped) rhinoceros. 50c, Burchell's zebra. 2r, Giraffe.

Perf. 13x12½, 12½x13
1969, Aug. 1   Litho.   Wmk. 314
Size: 30½x21½mm

160	A12	½c multicolored	.25	.25
161	A12	1c multicolored	.25	.25
162	A12	2c multicolored	.25	.25

Size: 35x25mm

163	A12	3c multicolored	.50	.25
a.		Wmk. upright ('75)	5.00	5.00
164	A12	3½c multicolored	.70	.25

Size: 30½x21½mm, 21½x30½mm

165	A12	5c multicolored	.35	.25
166	A12	7½c multicolored	.45	.25
167	A12	10c multicolored	.65	.25
168	A12	12½c multicolored	.80	4.25
169	A12	15c multicolored	1.25	.90
170	A12	20c multicolored	1.00	.75
171	A12	25c multicolored	1.60	2.10
172	A12	50c multicolored	2.10	3.50
173	A12a	1r multicolored	5.25	7.50
174	A12a	2r multicolored	11.50	13.00
		Nos. 160-174 (15)	26.90	34.00

See #228-229. For surcharges see #259-260.

King Sobhuza II and Flags — A13

Designs: 7½c, 25c, UN emblem, UN Headquarters, NY, and King Sobhuza II.

1969, Sept. 24   Litho.   Perf. 13½

175	A13	3c dp blue & multi	.25	.25
176	A13	7½c pink & multi	.25	.25
177	A13	12½c yellow & multi	.25	.25
178	A13	15c lt blue & multi	.45	.45
		Nos. 175-178 (4)	1.20	1.20

1st anniv. of admission to the UN.

Perf. 14x14½
1970, July 16   Litho.   Wmk. 314

179	A14	3c red org & multi	.25	.25
180	A14	7½c yellow & multi	.25	.25
181	A14	12½c lt blue & multi	.35	.35
182	A14	25c multicolored	.55	.55
		Nos. 179-182 (4)	1.40	1.40

Issued to publicize the 9th Commonwealth Games, Edinburgh, July 16-25.

Perf. 14x14½
1971, Feb. 1   Litho.   Wmk. 314

Flowers of Swaziland: 10c, Crocosmia aurea. 15c, Gloriosa superba. 25c, Watsonia densiflora.

183	A15	3c bister & multi	.35	.25
184	A15	10c pale salmon & multi	.40	.25
185	A15	15c pale green & multi	.85	.50
186	A15	25c multicolored	1.25	1.25
		Nos. 183-186 (4)	2.85	2.25

King Sobhuza II — A16

Designs (King Sobhuza II): 3½c, In 1971. 7½c, In tribal costume at gathering of chiefs (Incwala). 25c, Opening Swazi parliament.

1971, Dec. 22

187	A16	3c blue & multi	.25	.25
188	A16	3½c gold, blk, bl & brn	.25	.25
189	A16	7½c gold & multi	.25	.25
190	A16	25c lilac & multi	.30	.30
		Nos. 187-190 (4)	1.05	1.05

50th anniv. of the reign of Sobhuza II.

UNICEF Emblem, King Sobhuza II — A17

1972, Apr. 17   Perf. 14½x14

| 191 | A17 | 15c violet & black | .25 | .25 |
| 192 | A17 | 25c olive & black | .50 | .60 |

25th anniv. (in 1971) of UNICEF.

Traditional Reed Dancers — A18

Perf. 13½x14
1972, Sept. 11   Wmk. 314

193	A18	3½c shown	.25	.25
194	A18	7½c Swazi beehive hut	.25	.25
195	A18	15c Ezulwini Valley	.55	.55
196	A18	25c Usutu River fishing	.90	.90
		Nos. 193-196 (4)	1.95	1.95

Tourist publicity.

Mpaka Coal Mines — A20

7½c, Oxen pulling plow. 15c, Weir over Komati River. 25c, Experimental rice plantation.

Perf. 13½x14
1973, June 21   Wmk. 314

199	A20	3½c multicolored	.60	.25
200	A20	7½c multicolored	.30	.25
201	A20	15c multicolored	.40	.25
202	A20	25c multicolored	.60	.60
		Nos. 199-202 (4)	1.90	1.35

Development of natural resources.

Swaziland Coat of Arms — A21

10c, King Sobhuza II in dress uniform. 15c, Parliament. 25c, National Somhlolo Stadium.

1973, Sept. 7   Litho.   Perf. 14

203	A21	3c brick red & black	.25	.25
204	A21	10c dull orange & multi	.25	.25
205	A21	15c blue & multi	.40	.50
206	A21	25c multicolored	.50	1.00
		Nos. 203-206 (4)	1.40	2.00

5th anniversary of independence.

Botswana, Lesotho, Swaziland Flags and Cap — A22

12½c, Kwaluseni Campus. 15c, Map of Africa & location of Botswana, Lesotho & Swaziland. 25c, Shield of University.

1974, Mar. 29   Litho.   Perf. 14

207	A22	7½c orange & multi	.25	.25
208	A22	12½c emerald & multi	.35	.25
209	A22	15c yellow & multi	.40	.30
210	A22	25c ultra & multi	.50	.45
		Nos. 207-210 (4)	1.50	1.25

10th anniversary of the University of Botswana, Lesotho and Swaziland.

Sobhuza as Student at Lovedale College, South Africa — A23

Mail Carried by Overhead Cable A24

1974, Oct. 9   Perf. 14

214	A24	4c Post Office, Lobamba	.25	.25
215	A24	10c Mbabane temporary P.O., 1902	.25	.25
216	A24	15c shown	.45	.45
217	A24	25c Mule-drawn mail coach	.65	.65
		Nos. 214-217 (4)	1.60	1.60

Centenary of Universal Postal Union.

Animal Type of 1969
"E" instead of "R"

Designs as before.

1975, Jan. 2   Litho.   Perf. 12½x13

| 228 | A12a | 1e multicolored | 3.75 | 3.00 |
| 229 | A12a | 2e multicolored | 7.50 | 6.00 |

Girl's Umcwasho Ceremony — A26

Swazi youth: 10c, Butimba, hunting ceremony. 15c, Lusekwane, ceremony of preparation, horiz. 25c, Gcina Regiment marching with flags.

1975, Mar. 20   Wmk. 314   Perf. 14

232	A26	3c lt green & multi	.25	.25
233	A26	10c lt violet & multi	.25	.25
234	A26	15c brown org & multi	.45	.40
235	A26	25c yellow & multi	.65	.65
		Nos. 232-235 (4)	1.60	1.55

Matsapa Airport Control Tower A27

5c, Fire brigade car and staff. 15c, Douglas C-47 Dakota. 25c, Hawker Siddeley 748.

1975, Aug. 18   Litho.   Perf. 14½

236	A27	4c multicolored	.40	.25
237	A27	5c multicolored	.85	.30
238	A27	15c multicolored	2.00	1.75
239	A27	25c multicolored	2.75	2.75
		Nos. 236-239 (4)	6.00	5.05

10th anniversary of internal air service.

Women in Service — A28   Green Pigeon — A29

1976, Jan. 2   Wmk. 373   Perf. 14

Birds: 1c, Black-headed oriole, horiz. 3c, Melba finch, horiz. 4c, Plum-colored starling. 5c, Black-headed heron. 6c, Stonechat. 7c, Chorister robin. 10c, Gorgeous bush shrike. 15c, Black-collared barbet. 20c, Gray heron. 25c, Giant kingfisher. 30c, Black eagle. 50c, Red bishop. 1e, Pin-tailed whydah. 2e, Lilac-breasted roller, horiz.

244	A29	1c orange & multi	.85	1.75
245	A29	2c lilac & multi	.95	1.75
246	A29	3c yel grn & multi	1.40	1.40
247	A29	4c gray blue & multi	.95	1.10
248	A29	5c orange & multi	1.10	1.60
249	A29	6c orange & multi	1.90	2.00
250	A29	7c orange & multi	1.90	2.00
251	A29	10c slate & multi	1.90	2.25
252	A29	15c lt green & multi	3.00	1.25
253	A29	20c ocher & multi	4.25	4.25
254	A29	25c orange & multi	4.50	4.50
255	A29	30c orange & multi	4.50	4.50
256	A29	50c sepia & multi	2.50	3.00
257	A29	1e vermilion & multi	3.00	3.50
258	A29	2e lt blue & multi	5.25	6.50
		Nos. 244-258 (15)	37.95	41.35

Nos. 166 and 168 Surcharged in Ultra or Brown

1976   Wmk. 314   Perf. 13x12½

259	A12	3c on 7½c multi (U)	1.00	1.25
260	A12	6c on 12½c multi (B)	1.75	1.75

Denomination at lower left on No. 260.

Blindness from Malnutrition — A30

Designs (WHO Emblem and): 10c, Retina, "Operation prevents blindness." 20c, Blind eye, "Blindness from trachoma." 25c, Medicine and syringe, "Medicine and rehabilitation."

Wmk. 373

1976, June 15   Litho.   Perf. 14

261	A30	5c multicolored	.25	.25
262	A30	10c multicolored	.35	.25
263	A30	20c multicolored	.65	.60
264	A30	25c multicolored	.70	.70
		Nos. 261-264 (4)	1.95	1.80

World Health Day: Foresight prevents blindness.

Marathon Runner — A31   Soccer — A32

Designs (Olympic Rings and): 6c, Boxing. 20c, Soccer. 25c, Olympic torch and flame.

1976, July 17   Litho.   Wmk. 373

265	A31	5c lt blue & multi	.25	.25
266	A31	6c olive & multi	.25	.25
267	A31	20c lt violet & multi	.50	.50
268	A31	25c dull orange & multi	.70	.70
		Nos. 265-268 (4)	1.70	1.70

21st Olympic Games, Montreal, Canada, July 17-Aug. 1.

1976, Sept. 13   Litho.   Perf. 14½

Designs: 5c, Player heading ball. 20c, Goalkeeper catching ball. 25c, Player kicking ball.

269	A32	4c blue & multi	.25	.25
270	A32	5c olive & multi	.25	.25
271	A32	20c red & multi	.45	.40
272	A32	25c multicolored	.60	.55
		Nos. 269-272 (4)	1.55	1.45

FIFA membership for Swaziland in 1976 (Federation Internationale de Football Associations).

A. G. Bell and 1976 Telephone — A33

Designs (A. G. Bell and Telephone): 5c, 1895. 10c, 1876. 15c, 1877. 20c, 1905.

1976, Nov. 22   Perf. 14

273	A33	4c multicolored	.25	.25
274	A33	5c multicolored	.25	.25
275	A33	10c multicolored	.25	.25
276	A33	15c multicolored	.30	.30
277	A33	20c multicolored	.40	.40
		Nos. 273-277 (5)	1.45	1.45

Centenary of first telephone call by Alexander Graham Bell, Mar. 10, 1876.

Elizabeth II and Sobhuza II — A34

Designs: 25c, Queen's coach at Admiralty Arch. 50c, Queen seated in coach.

1977, Feb. 7   Perf. 13½

278	A34	20c silver & multi	.25	.25
279	A34	25c silver & multi	.30	.30
280	A34	50c silver & multi	.65	.65
		Nos. 278-280 (3)	1.20	1.20

25th anniv. of the reign of Elizabeth II.

Matsapa College A35

10c, Men's & Women's uniforms & jeep. 20c, Police badge. 25c, Dog handler & dog.

1977, May 2   Litho.   Perf. 14

281	A35	5c multi	.35	.35
282	A35	10c multi	.55	.55
283	A35	20c multi, vert.	.85	.85
284	A35	25c multi	1.40	1.25
		Nos. 281-284 (4)	3.15	2.80

50 years of police training in Swaziland.

Various Animals A36

Rock Paintings: 10c, 20c, Groups of men. 15c, Cattle and herdsman.

Perf. 14x14½

1977, Aug. 8   Wmk. 373

285	A36	5c multicolored	.30	.25
286	A36	10c multicolored	.40	.35
287	A36	15c multicolored	.60	.55
288	A36	20c multicolored	.60	.75
a.		Souvenir sheet of 4, #285-288	3.75	3.75
		Nos. 285-288 (4)	2.10	1.90

Rock paintings from Highveld area, c. 1700-1850.

Evergreens, Timber, Map of Highveld — A37

Designs: 10c, Pineapple and map of Middleveld. 15c, Map of Lowveld, orange and lemon. 20c, Map of Lubombo and grazing cattle. No. 293, Map of Swaziland and produce, vert.: UL, Evergreens; UR, Orange and lemon; LL, Pineapple; LR, Cattle.

1977, Oct. 17   Litho.   Perf. 13½

289	A37	5c multicolored	.25	.25
290	A37	10c multicolored	.70	.70
291	A37	15c multicolored	1.00	1.00
292	A37	20c multicolored	1.50	1.50
		Nos. 289-292 (4)	3.45	3.45

Souvenir Sheet

293	Sheet of 4	2.75	2.75
a.-d.	A37 25c single stamp	.65	.65

Nos. 293a-293d are vertical.

Cussonia Spicata Thunb. — A38

Trees: 10c, Sclerocarya birrea. 20c, Pterocarpus angolensis. 25c, Erythrina lysistemon.

1978, Jan. 12   Litho.   Wmk. 373

294	A38	5c multicolored	.25	.25
295	A38	10c multicolored	.35	.25
296	A38	20c multicolored	.60	.55
297	A38	25c multicolored	.75	1.00
		Nos. 294-297 (4)	1.95	2.05

Rural Electrification, Lobamba — A39

Hydroelectric Power: 10c, Edwaleni Power Station. 20c, Switchgear, Maguduza Power Station. 25c, Hydroturbine hall, Edwaleni.

1978, Mar. 6   Litho.   Perf. 13½

298	A39	5c black & ocher	.25	.25
299	A39	10c black & yel grn	.25	.25
300	A39	20c black & blue	.30	.30
301	A39	25c black & rose mag	.55	1.00
		Nos. 298-301 (4)	1.35	1.80

Elizabeth II Coronation Anniversary Issue

Souvenir Sheet

Common Design Types

1978, Apr. 21   Unwmk.   Perf. 15

302	Sheet of 6	2.50	2.50
a.	CD326 25c Queen's lion	.40	.40
b.	CD327 25c Elizabeth II	.40	.40
c.	CD328 25c African Elephant	.40	.40

No. 302 contains 2 se-tenant strips of Nos. 302a-302c, separated by horizontal gutter with commemorative and descriptive inscriptions and showing central part of coronation procession with coach.

Clay Pots A40

Handicrafts: 10c, Basketwork. 20c, Wooden utensils. 30c, Wooden pot with lid.

Wmk. 373

1978, June 26   Litho.   Perf. 13½

303	A40	5c multicolored	.25	.25
304	A40	10c multicolored	.25	.25
305	A40	20c multicolored	.30	.30
306	A40	30c multicolored	.50	.50
		Nos. 303-306 (4)	1.30	1.30

See Nos. 317-320.

Defense Force A41

Designs: 6c, King's Regiment. 10c, Tinkabi tractor and ox-drawn plow. 15c, Laying water pipe. 25c, Adult literacy class. 50c, Fire engine and ambulance.

1978, Sept. 6   Litho.   Perf. 14

307	A41	4c multicolored	.25	.25
308	A41	6c multicolored	.25	.25
309	A41	10c multicolored	.25	.25
310	A41	15c multicolored	.40	.25
311	A41	25c multicolored	.55	.50
312	A41	50c multicolored	1.75	1.00
		Nos. 307-312 (6)	3.45	2.50

10th anniversary of independence.

Angel Appearing to the Shepherds — A42

Christmas: 10c, Adoration of the Kings. 15c, Angel warning Joseph in a dream. 25c, Flight into Egypt.

1978, Dec. 12   Litho.   Perf. 14

313	A42	5c multicolored	.25	.25
314	A42	10c multicolored	.25	.25
315	A42	15c multicolored	.25	.25
316	A42	25c multicolored	.45	.45
		Nos. 313-316 (4)	1.20	1.20

Handicrafts Type of 1978

1979, Jan. 10   Perf. 13½

317	A40	5c Sisal bowls	.25	.25
318	A40	15c Clay pots	.35	.35
319	A40	20c Basketwork	.40	.40
320	A40	30c Hide shield	.60	.60
		Nos. 317-320 (4)	1.60	1.60

Prospecting at Phophonyane A43

15c, Early 3-stamp battery mill. 25c, Cyanide tanks at Piggs Peak. 50c, Pouring off molten gold.

Wmk. 373

1979, Mar. 27   Litho.   Perf. 14

321	A43	5c blue & gold	.35	.30
322	A43	15c brown & gold	.70	.60
323	A43	25c green & gold	.95	.90
324	A43	50c red & gold	1.90	1.90
		Nos. 321-324 (4)	3.90	3.70

Centenary of discovery of gold in Swaziland.

Girls at Piano, 1892, by Renoir A44

Paintings by Renoir: 15c, Madame Charpentier and her Children, 1878. 25c, Girls Picking Flowers, 1889. 50c, Girl with Watering Can, 1876.

1979, May 8   Perf. 13½

325	A44	5c multicolored	.25	.25
326	A44	15c multicolored	.25	.25
327	A44	25c multicolored	.45	.45
328	A44	50c multicolored	.90	.90
a.		Souvenir sheet of 4, #325-328	2.50	2.50
		Nos. 325-328 (4)	1.85	1.85

International Year of the Child.

Swaziland No. 40 and Rowland Hill — A45

Rowland Hill and: 20c, Swaziland #18. 25c, Swaziland #142. 50c, Swaziland #60.

1979, July 17   Litho.   Perf. 14½

329	A45	10c multicolored	.25	.25
330	A45	20c multicolored	.35	.30
331	A45	25c multicolored	.40	.40
		Nos. 329-331 (3)	1.00	.95

Souvenir Sheet

332	A45	50c multicolored	1.25	1.25

Sir Rowland Hill (1795-1879), originator of penny postage.

5c Cupro-Nickel Coin — A46

Coins: 10c, King Sobhuza II and sugar cane. 20c, King and elephant head. 50c, Coat of arms. 1e, Mother and son.

Perf. 13½x14
1979, Sept. 6   Litho.   Wmk. 373

333	A46	5c multicolored	.25	.25
334	A46	10c multicolored	.25	.25
335	A46	20c multicolored	.40	.25
336	A46	50c multicolored	.65	.65
337	A46	1e multicolored	1.25	1.25
		Nos. 333-337 (5)	2.80	2.65

Big Bend Post Office A47

15c, Mount Ntondozi microwave station, vert. 20c, Swaziland #53. 50c, Swaziland #217.

1979, Nov. 22

338	A47	5c multicolored	.25	.25
339	A47	15c multicolored	.25	.25
340	A47	20c multicolored	.25	.25
341	A47	50c multicolored	.55	.55
		Nos. 338-341 (4)	1.30	1.30

25th anniv. of Post and Telecommunications service (5c, 15c); 10th anniv. of UPU membership (20c, 50c).

Rotary International, 75th Anniversary A48

Wmk. 373
1980, Feb. 23   Litho.   Perf. 14

Flowers A49

Designs: 1c, Brunsvigia radulosa, vert. 2c, Aloe suprafoliata, vert. 3c, Haemanthus magificus, vert. 4c, Aloe marlothii, vert. 5c, Dicoma zeyheri, vert. 6c, Aloe kniphofioides, vert. 7c, Cyrtanthus bicolor, vert. 10c, Eucomis autumnalis. 15c, Leucospermum gerrardii. 20c, Haemanthus multiflorus. 30c, Acridocarpus natalitius. 50c, Adenium swazicum. 1e, Protea simplex, vert. 2e, Calodendrum capense, vert. 5e, Gladiolus ecklonii, vert.

1980, Apr. 28   Unwmk.   Perf. 13½
Without Year Inscription

346	A49	1c multicolored	.25	.25
347	A49	2c multicolored	.25	.25
348	A49	3c multicolored	.25	.25
a.		Perf. 12	3.50	3.50
349	A49	4c multicolored	.25	.25
350	A49	5c multicolored	.25	.25
a.		Perf. 12	4.00	2.50
351	A49	6c multicolored	.25	.25
352	A49	7c multicolored	.25	.25
353	A49	10c multicolored	.25	.25
354	A49	15c multicolored	.30	.30
355	A49	20c multicolored	.40	.40
356	A49	30c multicolored	.55	.55
357	A49	50c multicolored	.70	.70

Size: 22x37½mm

358	A49	1e multicolored	1.40	1.40
359	A49	2e multicolored	3.00	3.00
360	A49	5e multicolored	7.00	7.00
		Nos. 346-360 (15)	15.35	15.35

1983   Perf. 12
Inscribed "1983"

346a	A49	1c	1.00	.75
347a	A49	2c	1.00	.75
349a	A49	4c	1.25	1.25
b.		As "a," without date inscription below design	—	
351a	A49	6c	2.00	1.50
353a	A49	10c	2.50	1.00
355a	A49	20c	2.75	1.75
		Nos. 346a-355a (6)	10.50	7.00

For surcharges see Nos. 465-470.

Mail Runner, London 1980 Emblem A50

1980, May 6   Wmk. 373   Perf. 14

361	A50	10c shown	.25	.25
362	A50	20c Mail truck	.30	.25
363	A50	25c Mail sorting	.40	.30
364	A50	50c Mail ropeway	.80	.80
		Nos. 361-364 (4)	1.75	1.60

London 80 Intl. Stamp Exhib., May 6-14.

Yellow Fish A51

1980, Aug. 25   Litho.   Perf. 14

365	A51	5c shown	.50	.25
366	A51	10c Silver barbel	.50	.25
367	A51	15c Tigerfish	.70	.45
368	A51	30c Squeaker fish	.80	.70
369	A51	1e Bream	2.50	2.50
		Nos. 365-369 (5)	5.00	4.15

Bus A53

1981, Jan. 5   Litho.   Perf. 14½

374	A53	5c shown	.25	.25
375	A53	25c Jet	.50	.50
376	A53	30c Truck	.55	.55
377	A53	1e Train	1.90	1.90
		Nos. 374-377 (4)	3.20	3.20

Mantenga Falls — A54

1981, Apr. 16   Litho.   Perf. 14

378	A54	5c shown	.30	.30
379	A54	15c Mananga Yacht Club	.35	.35
380	A54	30c White rhinoceri, Millwane Game Sanctuary	.65	.65
381	A54	1e Gambling	2.00	2.00
		Nos. 378-381 (4)	3.30	3.30

Royal Wedding Issue
Common Design Type
Wmk. 373
1981, July 21   Litho.   Perf. 14

382	CD331	10c Bouquet	.25	.25
383	CD331	25c Charles	.40	.40
384	CD331	1e Couple	1.50	1.50
		Nos. 382-384 (3)	2.15	2.15

Installation of King Sobhuza II, 1921 A55

60th Anniv. of King Sobhuza II's Reign (King and): 10c, Visit of Royal Family, 1947. 15c, Coronation of Queen Elizabeth II, 1953. 25c, Independence ceremony, 1968. 30c, Early portrait. 1e, Parliament buildings.

Wmk. 373
1981, Aug. 24   Litho.   Perf. 14½

385	A55	5c multicolored	.25	.25
386	A55	10c multicolored	.25	.25
387	A55	15c multicolored	.25	.25
388	A55	25c multicolored	.40	.40
389	A55	30c multicolored	.50	.50
390	A55	1e multicolored	1.60	1.60
		Nos. 385-390 (6)	3.25	3.25

Duke of Edinburgh's Awards, 25th Anniv. — A56

Intl. Year of the Disabled — A57

1981, Nov. 5   Litho.   Perf. 14

391	A56	5c Basketball	.25	.25
392	A56	20c Compass reading	.35	.35
393	A56	50c Square	.90	.90
394	A56	1e Duke of Edinburgh	1.75	1.75
		Nos. 391-394 (4)	3.25	3.25

Papilio Demodocus — A58

1982, Jan. 6   Litho.   Perf. 14

399	A58	5c shown	.65	.25
400	A58	10c Charaxes candiope	.70	.35
401	A58	50c Papilio nireus	2.50	2.40
402	A58	1e Eurema desjardinsii	5.00	4.75
		Nos. 399-402 (4)	8.85	7.75

A59   A60

1982, Apr. 27   Litho.   Perf. 14

403	A59	5c Non-smoker, flowers	.75	.70
404	A59	10c Smoker, non-smoker	.90	.85

First Intl. Conference on Smoking and Health, Apr. 25-29

Perf. 13½x13
1982, June 16   Litho.   Wmk. 373

a, Female fishing owl. b, Pair. c, Owl in nest, egg. d, Adult and young owls. e, Male.

405		Strip of 5, multi	125.00	85.00
a.-e.	A60	35c, any single	16.00	10.00

Princess Diana Issue
Common Design Type
1982, July 1   Perf. 14½

406	CD333	5c Arms	.30	.30
407	CD333	20c Diana	.55	.55
408	CD333	50c Wedding	1.40	1.40
409	CD333	1e Portrait	2.75	2.75
		Nos. 406-409 (4)	5.00	5.00

Sugar Industry A61

1982, Sept. 1   Litho.

410	A61	5c Planting sugar cane	.25	.25
411	A61	20c Harvesting cane	.45	.45
412	A61	30c Mhlume Mills	.65	.65
413	A61	1e Rail transport	2.25	2.25
		Nos. 410-413 (4)	3.60	3.60

Baphalali Red Cross Society A62

1982, Nov. 9   Perf. 14

414	A62	5c Immunization	.25	.25
415	A62	20c Red Cross Juniors	.45	.45
416	A62	50c Disaster relief	1.10	1.10
417	A62	1e Red Cross founder Henry Dunant	2.25	2.25
		Nos. 414-417 (4)	4.05	4.05

Perf. 14½x14
1982, Dec. 6　Litho.　Wmk. 373
418	A63	5c Reciting promise	.25	.25
419	A63	10c Hiking	.25	.25
420	A63	25c Community development	.65	.65
421	A63	75c Baden-Powell	1.90	1.90
		Nos. 418-421 (4)	3.05	3.05

Souvenir Sheet
422	A63	1e Emblem	3.25	3.25

A64　　　Bearded Vulture — A65

1983, Mar. 14　Litho.　Perf. 14
423	A64	6c Satellite view	.25	.25
424	A64	10c King Sobhuza II, flag	.25	.25
425	A64	50c Beehive huts, horiz.	1.00	1.00
426	A64	1e Spraying sugar crop, horiz.	2.00	2.00
		Nos. 423-426 (4)	3.50	3.50

Commonwealth Day.

Perf. 13½x13
1983, May 16　Litho.　Wmk. 373

Designs: a, Male. b, Pair. c, Nest, egg. d, Female at nest. e, Adult, fledgling.
427		Strip of 5	25.00	25.00
a.-e.		A65 35c, any single	3.50	3.50

Souvenir Sheets

Soccer Tour of Swaziland 1983 — A66

1983, Aug. 20　Litho.　Perf. 14x13½
428	A66	75c Natl. team	1.50	1.50
429	A66	75c Tottenham Hotspur	1.50	1.50
430	A66	75c Manchester United	1.50	1.50
		Nos. 428-430 (3)	4.50	4.50

Manned Flight Bicentenary A67

1983, Sept. 22　Litho.　Perf. 14
431	A67	5c Montgolfiere, 1783, vert.	.25	.25
432	A67	10c Wright brothers' plane	.25	.25
433	A67	25c Royal Swazi Fokker Fellowship	.50	.50
434	A67	50c Bell X-1 jet	1.00	1.00
		Nos. 431-434 (4)	2.00	2.00

Souvenir Sheet
435	A67	1e Columbia space shuttle take-off, vert.	2.75	2.75

Alfred Nobel, 100th Birth Anniv. A68

1983, Oct. 21
436	A68	6c Albert Schweitzer	2.10	.50
437	A68	10c Dag Hammarskjold	.80	.80

438	A68	50c Albert Einstein	2.50	2.50
439	A68	1e shown	5.50	5.50
		Nos. 436-439 (4)	10.90	9.30

World Food Program A69

1983, Nov. 29
440	A69	6c Maize	.25	.25
441	A69	10c Rice	.40	.40
442	A69	50c Cattle	1.25	1.25
443	A69	1e Tractor	2.10	2.10
		Nos. 440-443 (4)	4.00	4.00

Women's College A70

Wmk. 373
1984, Mar. 12　Litho.　Perf. 14
444	A70	5c shown	.25	.25
445	A70	15c Technical training school	.30	.30
446	A70	50c University	.90	.90
447	A70	1e Primary school	1.75	1.75
		Nos. 444-447 (4)	3.20	3.20

Bald Ibis — A71

Designs: a, Male. b, Male, female. c, Nest, egg. d, Female at nest. e, Adult, fledgeling.

1984, May 18　Litho.　Perf. 13½x13
448		Strip of 5	29.00	29.00
a.-e.		A71 35c, any single	4.50	4.50

1984 UPU Congress — A72

Mail Coaches.

1984, June 15　Litho.　Perf. 14½
449	A72	7c Mule-drawn coach	.45	.25
450	A72	15c Oxen-drawn post wagon	.60	.35
451	A72	50c Mule-drawn, diff.	1.40	1.00
452	A72	1e Bristol-London	2.10	2.10
		Nos. 449-452 (4)	4.55	3.70

1984 Summer Olympics A73

1984, July 28　　　　Perf. 14
453	A73	7c Running	.25	.25
454	A73	10c Swimming	.25	.25
455	A73	50c Shooting	.90	.85
456	A73	1e Boxing	1.75	1.75
a.		Souvenir sheet of 4, #453-456	4.50	4.50
		Nos. 453-456 (4)	3.15	3.10

Local Fungi A74

1984, Sept. 19　Litho.　Perf. 14
457	A74	10c Suillus bovinus	2.25	.45
458	A74	15c Langermannia gigantea, vert.	3.25	.80
459	A74	50c Coriolus versicolor, vert.	3.50	2.50
460	A74	1e Boletus edulis	4.75	4.75
		Nos. 457-460 (4)	13.75	8.50

20th Anniv. of Swazi Railways A75

1984, Nov. 5　Litho.　Wmk. 373
461	A75	10c Opening ceremony	.40	.25
462	A75	25c Type 15A locomotive, Siweni Exchange Yard	.75	.60
463	A75	30c Container loading, Matsapha Station	.90	.75
464	A75	1e No. 268, Alto Tunnel	3.00	2.50
a.		Souvenir sheet of 4, #461-464	6.75	6.75
		Nos. 461-464 (4)	5.05	4.10

Nos. 346a, 346-349, 351-352 Surcharged

1984, Dec. 15　Litho.　Perf. 12
465	A49	10c on 4c #349a	.40	.25
a.		Perf. 13½ (#349)	50.00	50.00
b.		On No. 349b (perf. 12, without date inscription below design)	—	

Perf. 13½, 12 (#469)
466	A49	15c on 7c #352	.50	.30
467	A49	20c on 3c #348	.45	.25
a.		Perf 12	—	
468	A49	25c on 6c #351	.50	.25
469	A49	30c on 1c #346a	.60	.30
470	A49	30c on 2c #347	2.75	2.75
		Nos. 465-470 (6)	5.20	4.10

Rotary Intl., 80th Anniv. A76

1985, Feb. 23　Wmk. 373　Perf. 14
471	A76	10c Rotary emblem, world map	.70	.50
472	A76	15c Training scholarships	1.25	.50
473	A76	50c Two children	1.75	1.75
474	A76	1e Nurse, children	3.25	3.25
		Nos. 471-474 (4)	6.95	6.00

Life Cycle of the Ground Hornbill — A77

Audubon birth bicentenary.

1985, May 15　　　　Wmk. 373
475		Strip of 5	17.50	17.50
a.-e.		A77 25c, any single	2.50	2.50

Queen Mother 85th Birthday
Common Design Type
Perf. 14½x14
1985, June 7　Litho.　Wmk. 384
476	CD336	10c Visit to South Africa, 1947	.40	.25
477	CD336	15c With Elizabeth II and Margaret	.40	.25
478	CD336	50c 75th birthday celebration	1.10	.75
479	CD336	1e Holding Prince Henry	1.50	1.50
		Nos. 476-479 (4)	3.40	2.75

Souvenir Sheet
480	CD336	2e Greeting Prince Andrew	4.25	4.25

Classic Automobiles — A78

Wmk. 373
1985, Sept. 16　Litho.　Perf. 14
481	A78	10c Buick Tourer	.85	.85
482	A78	15c Four-cylinder Rover	.90	.85
483	A78	50c De Dion Bouton	2.10	1.75
484	A78	1e Ford Model-T	3.50	3.50
		Nos. 481-484 (4)	7.35	6.95

Intl. Youth Year A79

1985, Dec. 2
485	A79	10c Bridge-building	.25	.25
486	A79	20c Girl Guides camping	.25	.25
487	A79	50c Recreation	.75	.65
488	A79	1e Guides collecting branches	1.40	1.40
		Nos. 485-488 (4)	2.65	2.55

Girl Guide Movement, 20c, 1e. IYY, 10c, 50c.

Halley's Comet A80

1986, Feb. 27　Wmk. 384　Perf. 14½
489	A80	1.50e multicolored	4.25	4.25

Queen Elizabeth II 60th Birthday
Common Design Type

10c, Princess Anne's christening, 1950. 30c, Wedding of Prince Charles and Lady Diana, 1981. 45c, With George VI, the Duchess of York and Sobhuza II at Nhlangano, 1947. 1e, At Windsor Polo Ground, 1984. 2e, Visiting Crown Agents' offices, 1983.

1986, Apr. 21　　　　Perf. 14x14½
490	CD337	10c scar, blk & sil	.25	.25
491	CD337	30c ultra & multi	.30	.30
492	CD337	45c green, blk & sil	.45	.45
493	CD337	1e violet & multi	.95	.95
494	CD337	2e rose vio & multi	2.00	2.00
		Nos. 490-494 (5)	3.95	3.95

For overprints see Nos. 527-530.

Coronation of Crown Prince Makhosetive A81

10c, Portrait, vert. 20c, Prince and King Sobhuza II at an Incwala ceremony. 25c, Prince at primary school. 30c, At school in England. 40c, Escorted from Matsapha Airport by Guard of Honor. 2e, Dancing the Simemo.

1986, Apr. 25　　　　Perf. 14½
495	A81	10c multicolored	.50	.50
496	A81	20c multicolored	.60	.60
497	A81	25c multicolored	.75	.75
498	A81	30c multicolored	.90	.90
499	A81	40c multicolored	1.75	1.10
500	A81	2e multicolored	5.75	5.75
		Nos. 495-500 (6)	10.25	9.60

Assoc. of Round
Tables in Central
Africa, 50th
Anniv. — A82

Club emblems.

Wmk. 384

1986, Oct. 4		Litho.	Perf. 14	
501	A82	15c Orbis	.40	.25
502	A82	25c Ehlanzeni 51	.50	.45
503	A82	55c Mbabane 30	1.10	.90
504	A82	70c Bulembu 54	1.25	1.25
505	A82	2e Manzini 44	3.25	3.25
		Nos. 501-505 (5)	6.50	6.10

Butterflies — A83

Unwmk.

1987, Mar. 17		Litho.	Perf. 14	
506	A83	10c Yellow pansy	.55	.50
507	A83	15c Guineafowl	.65	.50
508	A83	20c Red forest charaxes	.65	.30
509	A83	25c Paradise skipper	.65	.60
510	A83	30c Broad-bordered acraea	.65	.50
511	A83	35c Veined swallow-tail	.65	.50
512	A83	45c Large striped swordtail	.70	.65
513	A83	50c Eyed pansy	.75	.50
514	A83	55c Zebra white	.75	.50
515	A83	70c Gaudy commodore	1.00	1.25
516	A83	1e Common dotted border	1.50	3.00
517	A83	5e Queen purple tip	4.50	2.00
518	A83	10e Natal barred blue	7.00	5.75
		Nos. 506-518 (13)	20.00	16.55

See Nos. 600-611. For surcharges see Nos. 574-577. Compare with design A101.

White
Rhinoceros
A84

1987, July 1		Wmk. 384	Perf. 14½	
519	A84	15c Two adults	3.00	1.25
520	A84	25c Adult, calf	4.50	2.00
521	A84	45c Adult walking	8.25	5.50
522	A84	70c Adult in mud	10.00	6.25
		Nos. 519-522 (4)	25.75	15.00

World Wildlife Fund.

Nos. 491-494 Ovptd. "40TH
WEDDING ANNIVERSARY" in Silver
Perf. 14x14½

1987, Dec. 9		Litho.	Wmk. 384	
527	CD337	30c ultra & multi	.30	.30
528	CD337	45c green, blk & sil	.45	.45
529	CD337	1e violet & multi	1.00	1.00
530	CD337	2e rose vio & multi	2.00	2.00
		Nos. 527-530 (4)	3.75	3.75

Insects
A86

Wmk. 384

1988, Mar. 14		Litho.	Perf. 14	
531	A86	15c Zabalius aridus	2.00	.30
532	A86	55c Callidea bohemani	3.75	1.25
533	A86	1e Phymateus viridipes	6.50	6.50
534	A86	2e Nomadacris septemfasciata	10.00	11.00
		Nos. 531-534 (4)	22.25	19.05

1988
Summer
Olympics,
Seoul
A87

1988, Aug. 22		Litho.	Wmk. 384	
535	A87	15c Flag-bearer, stadium	1.25	.45
536	A87	35c Tae kwon do	1.75	.95
537	A87	1e Boxing	2.50	2.50
538	A87	2e Tennis	4.50	4.50
		Nos. 535-538 (4)	10.00	8.40

Intl. Tennis Federation, 75th anniv. (2e).

Small
Mammals
A88

Wmk. 384

1989, Jan. 16		Litho.	Perf. 14	
539	A88	35c Green monkey	2.10	.50
540	A88	55c Rock dassie	3.00	.95
541	A88	1e Zorilla	5.50	4.25
542	A88	2e African wildcat	9.50	11.00
		Nos. 539-542 (4)	20.10	16.70

Intl. Red Cross and Red Crescent
Organizations, 125th Annivs. — A89

Wmk. 373

1989, Sept. 21		Litho.	Perf. 12	
543	A89	15c David Hynd	.35	.25
544	A89	60c First aid	.90	.80
545	A89	1e Sigombeni Clinic	1.50	1.50
546	A89	2e Relief work	2.50	2.50
		Nos. 543-546 (4)	5.25	5.05

Perf. 14½x14

1989, Nov. 15			Unwmk.	
547	A90	15c multicolored	.25	.25
548	A90	60c multicolored	.55	.55
549	A90	1e multicolored	.95	.95
550	A90	2e multicolored	1.90	1.90
		Nos. 547-550 (4)	3.65	3.65

African
Development
Bank, 25th
Anniv. — A91

15c, Manzini-Mahamba Road. 60c, Mbabane microwave radio link. 1e, Mbabane Government Hospital. 2e, Ezulwini Power Switching Station.

Perf. 14x14½

1989, Dec. 18			Wmk. 384	
551	A91	15c multicolored	.40	.25
552	A91	60c multicolored	.70	.50
553	A91	1e multicolored	1.25	1.25
554	A91	2e multicolored	2.25	2.25
		Nos. 551-554 (4)	4.60	4.25

Stamp
World
London
'90 — A92

Wmk. 384

1990, May 3		Litho.	Perf. 12½	
555	A92	15c Intl. priority mail	.35	.30
556	A92	60c Facsimile service	.80	.65
557	A92	1e Post office	1.50	1.50
558	A92	2e Ezulwini Earth Satellite Station	2.75	2.75
		Nos. 555-558 (4)	5.40	5.20

Souvenir Sheet

559	A92	2e Mail runner	7.50	7.50

150th anniv. of the Penny Black.

Queen Mother, 90th Birthday
Common Design Types

1990, Aug. 4	Wmk. 384	Perf. 14x15	
565	CD343 75c Queen Mother	.70	.60

Perf. 14½

566	CD344	4e King, Queen visiting Hatfield House	3.50	3.50

Intl.
Literacy
Year
A94

Wmk. 373

1990, Sept. 21		Litho.	Perf. 14	
567	A94	15c shown	.25	.25
568	A94	75c Outdoor class	.65	.65
569	A94	1e Modern instruction	.80	.80
570	A94	2e Receiving diploma	1.60	1.60
		Nos. 567-570 (4)	3.30	3.30

Nos. 509-510, 512, 514 Surcharged

Unwmk.

1990, Dec. 17		Litho.	Perf. 14	
574	A83	10c on 25c multi	.35	.35
575	A83	15c on 30c multi	.75	.75
575A	A83	15c on 45c multi	75.00	75.00
576	A83	20c on 45c multi	.75	.75
577	A83	40c on 55c multi	1.00	1.00

National
Heritage
A96

Perf. 14x14½

1991, Feb. 11			Wmk. 233	
578	A96	15c Lobamba Hot Spring	.50	.25
579	A96	60c Sibebe Rock	1.10	.80
580	A96	1e Jolobela Falls	1.75	1.75
581	A96	2e Mantjolo Sacred Pool	2.75	2.75
		Nos. 578-581 (4)	6.10	5.55

Souvenir Sheet
Perf. 14

581A	A96	2e Usushwana River	6.50	6.50

Coronation
of King
Mswati III,
5th Anniv.
A97

Perf. 14x13½

1991, Apr. 24		Litho.	Wmk. 373	
582	A97	15c King making radio address	.35	.25
583	A97	75c Butimba royal hunt	1.25	.95
584	A97	1e King, schoolmates, 1986	1.25	1.25
585	A97	2e King opening parliament	2.75	2.75
		Nos. 582-585 (4)	5.60	5.20

Elizabeth & Philip, Birthdays
Common Design Types

Wmk. 384

1991, June 17		Litho.	Perf. 14½	
586	CD346	1e multicolored	1.50	1.50
587	CD345	2e multicolored	2.40	2.40
a.		Pair, #586-587 + label	4.25	4.25

Flowers — A98   Christmas — A99

1991, Sept. 30   Wmk. 373   Perf. 14

Reptiles
A100

1992, Feb. 25
596	A100	20c	Lubombo flat lizard	1.25	.25
597	A100	70c	Natal hinged tortoise	3.00	1.60
598	A100	1e	Swazi thick-toed gecko	3.75	3.75
599	A100	2e	Nile monitor	5.25	5.25
		Nos. 596-599 (4)		13.25	10.85

Butterflies
A101

1992-2000   Litho.   Perf. 14
600	A101	5c	Red tip	.25	.25
601	A101	10c	like #506	.25	.25
602	A101	15c	like #507	.25	.25
603	A101	20c	like #508	.25	.25
604	A101	25c	like #509	.25	.25
605	A101	30c	like #510	.30	.25
606	A101	35c	like #511	.35	.30
607	A101	45c	like #512	.40	.35
608	A101	50c	like #513	.45	.40
609	A101	55c	like #514	.50	.45
610	A101	70c	like #515	.55	.55
611	A101	1e	like #516	1.00	1.00
612	A101	5e	Like #517	—	—
613	A101	10e	Like #518	—	—
		Nos. 600-611 (12)		4.80	4.55

Issued: Nos. 600-611, 8/26/92. No. 612, 2000.
Nos. 600-611 dated 1991. Nos. 612 and 613 dated 2000.
Nos. 600-612 have different portrait of King Mswati III from Nos. 506-517.

A102   A103

Designs: 20c, Missionaries with royal family. 1e, Pioneer missionaries.

1992, Dec. 16   Litho.   Perf. 13½x14
614	A102	20c	multicolored	.75	.65
615	A102	1e	multicolored	3.00	3.00

Evangelical Alliance Mission in Swaziland, cent.

1993, Mar. 18   Litho.   Perf. 13½x14

Cooking Utensils: 20c, Calabashes. 70c, Contemporary pottery for cooking. 1e, Wooden bowls. 2e, Quern for grinding seeds.

616	A103	20c	multicolored	.65	.25
617	A103	70c	multicolored	1.50	.95
618	A103	1e	multicolored	2.10	2.10
619	A103	2e	multicolored	3.25	3.25
		Nos. 616-619 (4)		7.50	6.55

A104   A105

King Mswati, 25th Birthday: 25c, King Mswati as baby with mother. 40c, King Mswati III addressing PTA meeting. 1e, King Sobhuza II receiving Instrument of Independence, 1968. 2e, King Mswati III delivering first speech on Coronation Day, 1986.

1993, Sept. 6   Litho.   Perf. 13½x14
620	A104	25c	multicolored	.25	.25
621	A104	40c	multicolored	.35	.25
622	A104	1e	multicolored	.90	.90
623	A104	2e	multicolored	1.75	1.75
		Nos. 620-623 (4)		3.25	3.15

Independence, 25th anniv.

1993, Nov. 25   Perf. 13½

Common Waxbill

624	A105	25c	Male & female	.55	.30
625	A105	40c	Nest & eggs	.85	.35
626	A105	1e	Incubating	1.90	1.90
627	A105	2e	Feeding nestlings	3.25	3.25
		Nos. 624-627 (4)		6.55	5.80

A106   A107

1994, Feb. 22   Litho.   Perf. 13½
628	A106	25c	Education	.35	.25
629	A106	40c	Rural services	.45	.25
630	A106	1e	Swazi culture	1.75	1.75
631	A106	2e	People to people	2.00	2.00
		Nos. 628-631 (4)		4.55	4.25

US Peace Corps, 25th anniv.

1994, Sept. 15   Perf. 13½x14

Mushrooms.

632	A107	30c	Horse mushroom	1.40	.60
633	A107	40c	Penny bun bolete	1.40	.60
634	A107	1e	Rusulla verdigris	3.00	2.00
635	A107	2e	Honey fungus	4.00	4.00
		Nos. 632-635 (4)		9.80	7.20

ICAO, 50th Anniv. A108

1994, Nov. 30   Litho.   Perf. 14
636	A108	30c	Natl. airline	.50	.25
637	A108	40c	Control tower	.55	.30
638	A108	1e	Air rescue service	1.25	1.25
639	A108	2e	Air traffic control	1.75	1.75
		Nos. 636-639 (4)		4.05	3.55

A109   A110

Traditional handicrafts.

1995, Apr. 7   Litho.   Perf. 13½
640	A109	35c	Wooden bowls	.40	.40
641	A109	50c	Chicken nests	.60	.60
642	A109	1e	Leather crafts	1.10	1.10
643	A109	2e	Wood carvings	2.25	2.25
		Nos. 640-643 (4)		4.35	4.35

1995, June 5   Litho.   Perf. 14

FAO, 50th anniv.: 35c, Corn harvest. 50c, Planting vegetables. 1e, Herd of cattle. 2e, Community harvest.

644	A110	35c	multicolored	.25	.25
645	A110	50c	multicolored	.40	.40
646	A110	1e	multicolored	.90	.90
647	A110	2e	multicolored	1.60	1.60
		Nos. 644-647 (4)			

Lourie
A111

1995, Sept. 27   Litho.   Perf. 13½x13
648	A111	35c	Knysna lourie	.65	.30
649	A111	50c	Lourie in flight	.85	.50
650	A111	1e	Purple crested lourie	1.25	1.25
651	A111	2e	Gray lourie	1.75	1.75
		Nos. 648-651 (4)		4.50	3.80

Reptiles
A112

1996, Jan. 17   Litho.   Perf. 13½x13
652	A112	35c	Chameleon	.70	.30
653	A112	50c	Rock monitor	.90	.50
654	A112	1e	African python	1.50	1.50
655	A112	2e	Tree agama	2.25	2.25
		Nos. 652-655 (4)		5.35	4.55

Trees — A113

1996, Apr. 23   Litho.   Perf. 13
656	A113	40c	Waterberry	.40	.25
657	A113	60c	Sycamore fig	.50	.40
658	A113	1e	Stem fruit	.90	.90
659	A113	2e	Wild medlar	1.60	1.60
		Nos. 656-659 (4)		3.40	3.15

Local Landmarks A114

Designs: 40c, First church, Mahamba Methodist. 60c, Colonial Secretariat, Mbabane. 1e, King Sobhuza II Memorial Monument. 2e, First High Court Building, Hlatikulu.

1996, Aug. 26   Litho.   Perf. 13½x13
660	A114	40c	multicolored	.30	.30
661	A114	60c	multicolored	.50	.50
662	A114	1e	multicolored	1.10	1.10
663	A114	2e	multicolored	2.10	2.10
		Nos. 660-663 (4)		4.00	4.00

UNICEF, 50th Anniv. A115

Designs: 40c, Basic education for all. 60c, Universal child immunization, vert. 1e, No more polio, vert. 2e, Children first, vert.

1996, Dec. 31   Litho.   Perf. 13½x14
664	A115	40c	multicolored	.30	.30

Perf. 14x13½
665	A115	60c	multicolored	.60	.60
666	A115	1e	multicolored	.90	.90
667	A115	2e	multicolored	1.75	1.75
		Nos. 664-667 (4)		3.45	3.45

Wild Antelope A116

50c, Klipspringer, vert. 70c, Gray duiker, vert. 1e, Antbear. 2e, Cape clawless otter.

Perf. 14x13½, 13½x14

1997, Sept. 22   Litho.
668	A116	50c	multicolored	.50	.40
669	A116	70c	multicolored	.60	.50
670	A116	1e	multicolored	1.00	1.00
671	A116	2e	multicolored	1.75	1.75
		Nos. 668-671 (4)		3.85	3.65

Traditional Costumes — A117

1997, Dec. 1   Litho.   Perf. 13x13½
672	A117	50c	Umgaco	.30	.30
673	A117	70c	Sigeja	.55	.55
674	A117	1e	Umdada	.75	.75
675	A117	2e	Ligcebesha	1.60	1.60
		Nos. 672-675 (4)		3.20	3.20

Toads and Frogs A118

1998, June 1   Litho.   Perf. 14
676	A118	55c	Olive toad	.45	.25
677	A118	75c	African bullfrog	.60	.35
678	A118	1e	Water lily frog	1.00	1.00
679	A118	2e	Bushveld rain frog	1.90	1.90
		Nos. 676-679 (4)		3.95	3.50

Independence, 30th Anniv., King Mswati III, 30th Birthday — A119

55c, King Sobhuza II Memorial Park. 75c, King Mswati III taking oath. 1e, King Mswati III delivering 1st speech. 2e, King Sobhuza II receiving instrument of independence.

Perf. 13½x14, 14x13½

1998, Sept. 3   Litho.
680	A119	55c	multicolored	.30	.30
681	A119	75c	multicolored	.75	.75
682	A119	1e	multicolored	1.10	1.10
683	A119	2e	multicolored	1.75	1.75
		Nos. 680-683 (4)		3.90	3.90

Traditional Utensils — A120

1999, May 17   Litho.   Perf. 13¾x13¼
684	A120	60c	Grinding stone	.30	.30
685	A120	75c	Stirring sticks	.50	.50
686	A120	80c	Clay pot	.50	.50
687	A120	95c	Swazi spoons	.50	.50
688	A120	1.75e	Beer cup	1.00	1.00
689	A120	2.40e	Mortar and pestle	1.40	1.40
		Nos. 684-689 (6)		4.20	4.20

UPU, 125th Anniv. A121

Perf. 13¾x13½

1999, Oct. 9   Litho.   Unwmk.
690 A121 60c Internet service,
          vert.   .30   .30
691 A121 80c Cellular phone
          service, vert.   .50   .50

Perf. 13½x13¾

692 A121 1e Intl. mail ex-
          change   .65   .65
693 A121 2.40e Training school   1.60 1.60
        Nos. 690-693 (4)   3.05 3.05

Wildlife
A122

Designs: 65c, Lion, vert. 90c, Leopard.
1.50e, Rhinoceros. 2.50e, Buffalo, vert.

Perf. 13½x13¼, 13¼x13½

2000, July 3   Litho.   Unwmk.
694 A122 65c multi   .50   .30
695 A122 90c multi   .80   .40
696 A122 1.50e multi   2.00 2.00
697 A122 2.50e multi   1.75 1.75
        Nos. 694-697 (4)   5.05 4.45

Worldwide Fund for Nature
(WWF) — A123

Designs: 65c, Oribi with young. 90c, Oribi.
1.50e, Klipspringers. 2.50e, Klipspringers, diff.

Wmk. 373

2001, Feb. 1   Litho.   Perf. 14
698-701 A123 Set of 4   3.75 3.75
701a Sheet, 4 each #698-701   14.00 14.00

Environmental Protection — A124

Designs: 70c, Fighting forest fires. 95c, Tree
planting. 2.05e Construction of Maguga Dam.
2.80e, Building embankment.

2001, July 30   Litho.   Perf. 14
702-705 A124 Set of 4   4.00 4.00

**Reign Of Queen Elizabeth II, 50th
Anniv. Issue**
Common Design Type

Designs: Nos. 706, 710a, 70c, Princess
Elizabeth, Princess Anne, Princes Philip and
Charles, 1947. Nos. 707, 710b, 95c, Wearing
purple hat. Nos. 708, 710c, 2.05e, Wearing
crown. Nos. 709, 710d, 2.80e, Wearing yellow
hat, 2001. No. 710e, 22.50e, 1955 portrait by
Annigoni (38x50mm).

Perf. 14¼x14½, 13¾ (#710e)

2002, Feb. 6   Litho.   Wmk. 373
With Gold Frames
706-709 CD360 Set of 4   4.75 4.75

Souvenir Sheet
Without Gold Frames
710 CD360 Sheet of 5, #a-e   7.75 7.75

Tourism
A125

Designs: 75c, Swazi chalets. 1e, King
Mswati III leading lions, vert. 2.05e, Crocodile.
2.80e, Ostriches.

Perf. 13¼x13¾, 13¾x13¼

2002, Dec. 23   Litho.
711-714 A125 Set of 4   4.00 4.00

Musical Instruments — A126

Designs: 80c, Mouth organ, vert. 1.05e,
Rattles. 2.35e, Kudu horn trumpet. 2.80e,
Chordphone, vert.

2003, Aug. 12   Litho.   Perf. 14
715-718 A126 Set of 4   3.25 3.25

AIDS Prevention — A127

Designs: 85c, Community home-based
care. 1.10e, Know your HIV status. 2.45e,
Testing blood samples, vert. 3.35e, Unster-
ilized instruments can transmit HIV and AIDS,
vert.

Perf. 13¼x13¾, 13¾x13¼

2004, Mar. 9   Litho.
719-722 A127 Set of 4   3.25 3.25

Global 2003 Smart
Partnership
International
Dialogue,
Ezulwini — A128

Designs: 85c, King Mswati III, Swaziland
flag, map of Africa. 1.10e, Map of Africa, Swaziland flag, Smart Partnership International
Movement emblems, horiz. 2.45e, Sharing
ideas. 3.35e, Man, woman at microphone.

Perf. 13¾x13¼, 13¼x13¾

2004, June 14   Litho.
723-726 A128 Set of 4   3.25 3.25

Birds
A129

Designs: 85c, Purple-crested louries,
national bird of Swaziland. 1.10e, Blue cranes,
national bird of South Africa. 1.35e, Cattle
egrets, national bird of Botswana. 1.90e, African fish eagles, national bird of Zimbabwe. 2e,
African fish eagles, national bird of Namibia.
2.45e, Bar-tailed trogons. 3e, African fish
eagles, national bird of Zambia. 3.35e, Peregrine falcons, national bird of Angola.
No. 735: a, Cattle egrets, national bird of
Botswana. b, African fish eagles, national bird
of Namibia. c, Bar-tailed trogons. d, African
fish eagles, national bird of Zambia. e, Peregrine falcons, national bird of Angola.

2004, Oct. 11   Litho.   Perf. 14
727-734 A129 Set of 8   6.50 6.50
735   Sheet of 8, #727,
      728, 730, #735a-
      735e   13.50 13.50
  a.-b. A129 1.90e Either single 1.75 1.75
  c. A129 2.25e multi   2.25 2.25
  d.-e. A129 2.30e Either single 2.25 2.25

See Botswana Nos. 792-793, Malawi No.
—, Namibia No. 1052, South Africa —,
Zambia No. 1033.

Road
Safety
Council
A130

Inscriptions: 85c, Stop Killing Them In Traffic. 1.10e, Avoid Accidents. 2.45e, Safe Crossing. 3.35e, No Overloading.

2005, Jan. 25   Litho.   Perf. 13¼x13¾
736-739 A130 Set of 4   3.00 3.00

Snakes
A131

Designs: 85c, Black mamba. 1.10e, Python.
2.45e, Boomslang. 3.35e, Puff adder.

2005, Apr. 5   Litho.   Perf. 13¼x13¾
740-743 A131 Set of 4   3.25 3.25

Pope John Paul II
(1920-2005)
A132

2005, Aug. 18   Litho.   Perf. 14
744 A132 4.50e multi   1.50 1.50

Locusts
A133

Designs: 85c, Schistocerca solitaria. 1.10e,
Red locust. 2.45e, Southern Africa desert
locust. 3.35e, African migratory locust.

2005, Oct. 11   Litho.   Perf. 13¼x13¾
745-748 A133 Set of 4   2.40 2.40

Queen
Mothers — A134

Designs: 85c, Ntombi Tfwala. 1.10e, Dze-
liwe Shongwe. 2e, Lomawa Ndwandwe. 2.45e,
Labotsibeni Mdluli. 3.35e, Tibati Nkambule.

2006, Jan. 10   Perf. 13¾x13¼
749-753 A134 Set of 5   3.25 3.25

Postal
History
A135

Designs: 85c, Hlatikulu Post Office and
wagon. 1.15e, Ox wagon. 2e,
Mdlazempofu Post Office, 1893. 2.55e, Mail
runner, vert. 3.50e, Mbabane Temporary Post
Office, 1902.

Perf. 13¾

2006, May 8   Litho.   Unwmk.
754-758 A135 Set of 5   3.50 3.50

Waterfalls — A136

Designs: 90c, Mgubudla Falls. 1.15e,
Phophonyane Falls. 1.40e, Mantenga Falls,
horiz. 2e, Malolotja Falls. 2.55e, Mabhudlweni
Falls. 3.50e, Manzamnyama Falls.

2006, Sept. 26
759-764 A136 Set of 6   3.00 3.00

Trees
A137

Designs: 70c, Common cabbage tree. 85c,
Broom cluster fig. 90c, Scented thorn. 1.05e,
Natal mahogany. 1.15e, Marula. 1.40e, Stem
fruit tree. 2e, Fever tree. 2.40e, Large-leaved
coral tree. 2.55e, African teak. 3.50e, Red
ivory. 5e, Common coral tree. 10e, Jacket-
plum. 20e, Sausage tree.

2007, Jan. 23   Litho.   Perf. 13¼x13¾
765 A137 70c multi   .25   .25
766 A137 85c multi   .25   .25
767 A137 90c multi   .25   .25
768 A137 1.05e multi   .30   .30
769 A137 1.15e multi   .30   .30
770 A137 1.40e multi   .40   .40
771 A137 2e multi   .55   .55
772 A137 2.40e multi   .65   .65
773 A137 2.55e multi   .70   .70
774 A137 3.50e multi   1.00 1.00
775 A137 5e multi   1.40 1.40
776 A137 10e multi   2.75 2.75
777 A137 20e multi   5.50 5.50
        Nos. 765-777 (13)   14.30 14.30

Community-based Tourism — A138

Designs: 1e, Rock art at Nsangwini Rock
Art Center. 1.20e, Mahamba Gorge Lodge.
2.70e, Shewula Mountain Camp. 3.70e,
Khopo Camp, Ngwempisi Hiking Trails.

2008, Jan. 22   Litho.   Perf. 13½x13¾
778-781 A138 Set of 4   2.40 2.40

Decorations and
Jewelry for
Warriors — A139

Designs: 1e, Shoulder strap. 2.70e, Beaded
necklace, horiz. 3.70e, Anklets, horiz.

Perf. 13¾x13¾

2008, Nov. 10   Litho.
782-784 A139 Set of 3   1.90 1.90

Independence, 40th Anniv. and 40th
Birthday of King Mswati III — A140

Designs: 1e, Transportation infrastructure.
1.05e, King Mswati III receives constitution,
vert. 1.30e, Maguga Dam. 1.60e, Maidens at
reed dance, vert. 2.15e, First lilangeni currency. 2.40e, Health and social welfare. 2.75e,
Information and communications technology.
2.90e, King Mswati III's 40th birthday. 3.95e,
King Sobhuza at Independence ceremony,
1968, vert.

Perf. 13¼x13¾, 13¾x13¼

2008, Oct. 28				**Litho.**
785-793	A140	Set of 9	4.00	4.00

2010 World Cup Soccer
Championships, South Africa — A141

Soccer players, ball, 2010 World Cup mascot and flag of: Nos. 794, 803a, 1e, Zimbabwe.
Nos. 795, 803b, 1.25e, South Africa. Nos. 796,
803c, 1.50e, Mauritius. Nos. 797, 803d, 1.90e,
Namibia. Nos. 798, 803e, 2.50e, Zambia. Nos.
799, 803f, 3.40e, Swaziland. Nos. 800, 803g,
3.80e, Malawi. Nos. 801, 803h, 4.60e, Botswana. Nos. 802, 803i, 4.90e, Lesotho.

2010, Apr. 9			**Perf. 13½**
On Plain Paper With Olive Brown			
Background			
794-802	A141	Set of 9	7.00 7.00
On Gold-faced Paper			
803	A141	Sheet of 9, #a-i	12.50 12.50

No. 803 sold for 45e.
See Botswana Nos. 896-905, Lesotho No. ,
Malawi No. , Mauritius No. , Namibia No.
1188, South Africa No. 1403, Zambia Nos.
1115-1118, and Zimbabwe Nos. 1112-1121.

POSTAGE DUE STAMPS

> Catalogue values for unused
> stamps in this section are for
> Never Hinged items.

D1

1933	**Typo.**	**Wmk. 4**		**Perf. 14**
J1	D1	1p carmine rose	.30	8.25
a.		Wmk. 4a (error)	275.00	
J2	D1	2p violet	2.25	30.00

No. 57 Surcharged

	I			II
1961	**Engr.**			**Perf. 13½x13**
J3	A5	(2d) on 2p, type I	10.00	12.00
a.		Type II		.40

J4	A5	1c on 2p, type I	2.00	3.25
a.		Type II	1.50	1.50
J5	A5	2c on 2p, type I	2.00	3.25
a.		Type II	1.10	1.10
J6	A5	5c on 2p, type I	2.00	3.25
a.		Type II	1.75	1.75
		Nos. J3-J6 (4)	16.00	21.75
		Nos. J3a-J6a (4)	4.75	
		Nos. J4a-J6a (3)	4.35	

No. J3a was surcharged after decimal currency was introduced.

Type of 1933

1961	**Typo.**			**Perf. 14**
J7	D1	1c carmine rose	.25	.85
J8	D1	2c violet	.30	1.25
J9	D1	5c green	.75	1.75
		Nos. J7-J9 (3)	1.30	3.85

D2

Wmk. 314

1971, Feb. 1	**Litho.**			**Perf. 11½**
J10	D2	1c carmine rose	.60	.75
J11	D2	2c dull purple	.80	1.00
J12	D2	5c green	1.40	1.60
		Nos. J10-J12 (3)	2.80	3.35

1977, Jan. 17				**Wmk. 373**
J10a	D2	1c carmine rose	.80	.80
J11a	D2	2c dull purple	1.10	1.10
J12a	D2	5c green	1.90	1.90
		Nos. J10a-J12a (3)	3.80	3.80

1978-91				**Perf. 15x14**
Size: 17½x21mm				
J13	D2	1c carmine lake	.50	.50
J14	D2	2c purple	.50	.50
J15	D2	5c green	.50	.50
J16	D2	10c sky blue	.50	.50
J17	D2	25c brown	.70	.50
		Nos. J13-J17 (5)	2.70	2.50

Nos. J14-J15 reissued dated 1991.
Issued: 1c-5c, 4/20; 10c-25c, 7/17/91.

SWEDEN

'swē-dən

LOCATION — Northern Europe, occupying the eastern half of the Scandinavian Peninsula
GOVT. — Constitutional Monarchy
AREA — 173,341 sq. mi.
POP. — 9,182,927 (2007 est.)
CAPITAL — Stockholm

48 skilling banco = 1 riksdaler banco (until 1858)

100 öre = 1 riksdaler (1858 to 1874)
100 öre = 1 krona (since 1874)

Catalogue values for unused stamps in this country are for Never Hinged items, beginning with Scott 358 in the regular postage section, and Scott B37 in the semi-postal section.

Watermarks

Wmk. 180 — Crown | Wmk. 307 — Crown and 1955

Wmk. 181 — Wavy Lines

Values for unused stamps are for examples with original gum as defined in the catalogue introduction except Nos. 1-5, excluding reprints, and LX1 which are valued without gum.

Coat of Arms
A1 | A2

				Unwmk.	Typo.	Perf. 14
1855						
1	A1	3s blue green		10,000.		5,000.
a.		3s orange (error)				3,000,000.
2	A1	4s lt blue		1,600.		100.00
3	A1	6s gray		10,000.		1,500.
f.		Imperf.				

4	A1	8s red orange		5,500.	600.00
h.		Imperf.			5,000.
5	A1	24s dull red		8,750.	2,200.

Nos. 1-5 were reprinted from new blocks in 1868 (twice), 1871 (No. 1 only) and 1885. The 1868 and 1871 printings were perf 14, and the 1885 printing was perf 13. These later printings were made after Nos. 1-5 were withdrawn, but before being demonetized. The post office did not distinguish between these and earlier printings, although most saw little, if any, postal use. See the Scott Specialized Catalogue of Stamps and Covers 1840-1940 for detailed listings.

			1858-62	Perf. 14
6	A2	5o green	210.00	20.00
a.		5o deep green	575.00	250.00
7	A2	9o violet	425.00	275.00
a.		9o red lilac	625.00	325.00
8	A2	12o blue	225.00	2.00
9	A2	12o ultra ('61)	450.00	12.50
10	A2	24o orange	500.00	35.00
a.		24o yellow	750.00	62.50
11	A2	30o brown	500.00	35.00
a.		30o dark red brown	750.00	87.50
12	A2	50o rose	600.00	100.00
a.		50o carmine	750.00	110.00
		Nos. 6-12 (7)	2,910.	479.50

Nos. 6 and 8 exist with double impressions. No. 8 is known printed on both sides. No. 11 exists imperf.

Nos. 6-8, 10-12 were reprinted in 1885, perf. 13. See the Scott Specialized Catalogue of Stamps and Covers 1840-1940 for detailed listings. Also reprinted in 1963, perf. 13½, with lines in stamp color crossing denominations, and affixed to book page. Value $12.50 each.

Lion and Arms
A3 | A4

			1862-69	
13	A3	3o bister brown	275.00	16.00
a.		Printed on both sides		3,700.
14	A4	17o red violet ('66)	800.00	160.00
15	A4	17o gray ('69)	850.00	800.00
16	A4	20o vermilion ('66)	300.00	20.00
		Nos. 13-16 (4)	2,225.	996.00

Nos. 13-15 were reprinted in 1885, perf. 13. See the Scott Specialized Catalogue of Stamps and Covers 1840-1940 for detailed listings.

Numeral of Value — A5 | Coat of Arms — A6

			1872-77	Perf. 14
17	A5	3o bister brown	80.00	10.00
18	A5	4o gray ('76)	525.00	160.00
19	A5	5o blue green	400.00	5.00
a.		5o emerald	500.00	25.00
20	A5	6o violet	400.00	50.00
a.		6o dark violet	1,000.	250.00
21	A5	6o gray ('74)	1,100.	95.00
22	A5	12o blue	250.00	1.00
23	A5	20o vermilion	1,000.	9.00
a.		20o pale org ('75)	3,500.	40.00
b.		Double impression, dull yel & ver ('76)	4,000.	55.00
24	A5	24o orange	1,000.	42.50
a.		24o yellow	1,000.	42.50
25	A5	30o pale brown	875.00	11.00
a.		30o black brown	875.00	14.00
26	A5	50o rose	925.00	50.00
a.		50o carmine	1,000.	50.00
27	A6	1rd bister & blue	1,150.	95.00
a.		1rd bister & ultra	1,150.	95.00
		Nos. 17-27 (11)	7,705.	528.50

			1877-79	Perf. 13
28	A5	3o yellow brown	125.00	6.00
29	A5	4o gray ('79)	240.00	3.50
30	A5	5o dark green	150.00	1.00
31	A5	6o lilac	175.00	5.00
a.		6o red lilac	375.00	14.00
32	A5	12o blue	35.00	1.00
33	A5	20o vermilion	275.00	1.00
a.		"TRETIO" instead of "TJUGO" ('79)	10,000.	7,000.
34	A5	24o orange ('78)	75.00	30.00
a.		24o lemon yellow ('83)	625.00	55.00
35	A5	30o pale brown	450.00	2.00
a.		30o black brown	875.00	3.00
36	A5	50o carmine ('78)	325.00	9.00
37	A6	1rd bister & blue	2,400.	500.00
38	A6	1k bister & bl ('78)	625.00	20.00
		Nos. 28-36,38 (10)	2,475.	78.50

Imperf., Pairs

28a	A5	3o	1,000.	
29a	A5	4o	1,000.	
30a	A5	5o	1,000.	
31b	A5	6o	1,000.	
32a	A5	12o	1,000.	
33b	A5	20o	1,000.	
34b	A5	24o	1,000.	
35b	A5	30o	1,000.	4,000.
36a	A5	50o	1,000.	
38a	A6	1k	1,000.	

See Nos. 40-44, 46-49. For surcharges see Nos. B1-B10, B22-B31.

No. 37 has been reprinted in yellow brown and dark blue; perforated 13. Value, $325.

King Oscar II — A7

			1885	Typo.
39	A7	10o dull rose	225.00	1.00
a.		Imperf., pair	2,500.	

Numeral Type with Post Horn on Back

			1886-91	
40	A5	2o orange ('91)	2.50	8.00
a.		Period before "FRIMARKE"	12.00	22.50
b.		Imperf., pair	725.00	
41	A5	3o yellow brn ('87)	15.00	25.00
42	A5	4o gray	30.00	2.00
43	A5	5o green	62.50	1.00
44	A5	6o red lilac ('88)	30.00	62.50
a.		6o violet	35.00	62.50
45	A7	10o pink	87.50	.50
a.		10o rose	87.50	.25
b.		Imperf.		3,250.
46	A5	20o vermilion	125.00	1.00
47	A5	30o pale brown	210.00	2.00
48	A5	50o rose	190.00	5.00
49	A6	1k bister & dk bl	100.00	3.00
a.		Imperf., pair	700.00	
		Nos. 40-49 (10)	852.50	110.00

Nos. 32, 34 with Blue Surcharge

			1889, Oct. 1	
50	A5	10o on 12o blue	3.75	5.00
51	A5	10o on 24o orange	11.00	50.00

A9

King Oscar II
A10 | A11

Wmk. 180

			1891-1904	Typo.	Perf. 13
52	A9	1o brown & ultra ('92)	1.40	.65
53	A9	2o blue & yellow org	3.25	.40
54	A9	3o brown & orange ('92)	.60	1.75
55	A9	4o carmine & ultra ('92)	4.75	.50

Engr.

56	A10	5o yellow green	2.75	.30
a.		5o blue green	11.50	.30
d.		5o brown (error)	7,500.	
e.		Booklet pane of 6	140.00	
57	A10	8o red violet ('03)	3.25	1.25
58	A10	10o carmine	4.50	.30
c.		Booklet pane of 6	240.00	
59	A10	15o red brown ('96)	27.50	.50
60	A10	20o blue	28.00	.40
61	A10	25o red orange ('96)	37.50	.50
62	A10	30o brown	55.00	.40
63	A10	50o slate	125.00	.85
64	A10	50o olive gray ('04)	100.00	.85
65	A11	1k car & sl ('00)	175.00	2.25
		Nos. 52-65 (14)	568.50	10.90

Imperf., Pairs

52a	A9	1o	87.50
53a	A9	2o	325.00
54a	A9	3o	325.00
55a	A9	4o	325.00
56b	A10	5o No. 56	85.00
c.		No. 56a	300.00
57a	A10	8o	500.00
58a	A10	10o	52.50
59a	A10	15o	500.00
60a	A10	20o	150.00
61a	A10	25o	600.00
62a	A10	30o	600.00
63a	A10	50o	650.00
64a	A10	50o	500.00
65a	A11	1k	625.00

No. 56d may be a color proof.

A booklet pane of 6 invalid stamps similar to No. 56 but with engraved lines through the denominations was released in 2004 to commemorate the 100th anniversary of the first Swedish booklet. This booklet pane is unwatermarked.

See Nos. 75-76.

Stockholm Post Office — A12

			1903, Oct. 26	
66	A12	5k blue	240.00	27.50
a.		Imperf., pair	2,500.	

Opening of the new General Post Office at Stockholm.

For surcharge see No. B11.

Arms — A13 | Gustaf V — A14

Perf. 13, 13x13½

			1910-14	Typo.	Wmk. 180
67	A13	1o black ('11)	.65	1.50
68	A13	2o orange	1.75	4.00
69	A13	4o violet	2.50	1.10

Engr.

70	A14	5o green ('11)	14.00	29.00
71	A14	10o carmine	10.00	.50
72	A14	1k black, yel ('11)	95.00	.50
73	A14	5k claret, yel ('14)	2.00	3.00
		Nos. 67-73 (7)	125.90	39.60

See #77-98. For surcharges see #99-104, Q1-Q2.

1911 | **Unwmk.**

75	A10	20o blue	22.50	15.00
76	A10	25o red orange	27.50	4.00

1910-19

77	A14	5o green ('11)	3.00	.30
a.		Booklet pane of 10	225.00	
b.		Booklet pane of 4	125.00	
78	A14	7o gray grn ('18)	.30	.30
a.		Booklet pane of 10	8.75	
79	A14	8o magenta ('12)	.30	.30
80	A14	10o carmine ('10)	2.50	.30
a.		Booklet pane of 10	225.00	
b.		Booklet pane of 4	125.00	
81	A14	12o rose lake ('18)	.30	.30
a.		Booklet pane of 10	8.75	
82	A14	15o red brown ('11)	6.50	.30
83	A14	20o deep blue ('11)	9.50	.30
a.		Booklet pane of 10	350.00	
84	A14	25o orange red ('11)	.30	.30
85	A14	27o pale blue ('11)	.40	.90
86	A14	30o claret brn ('11)	20.00	.30
87	A14	35o dk violet ('11)	17.00	.30
88	A14	40o olive green ('17)	25.00	.30
89	A14	50o gray ('12)	50.00	.30
90	A14	55o pale blue ('18)	2,100.	6,500.
91	A14	65o pale ol grn ('18)	.65	2.00
92	A14	80o black ('18)	2,100.	6,500.
93	A14	90o gray green ('18)	.60	.65
94	A14	1k black, yel ('19)	92.50	.30
		Nos. 77-89,91,93-94 (16)	228.85	7.45

Excellent forgeries of Nos. 90 and 92 exist.

1911-19 Typo. Wmk. 181 Perf. 13

95	A13	1o black	.30	.30
96	A13	2o orange	.30	.30
97	A13	3o pale brown ('19)	.30	.30
98	A13	4o pale violet	.30	.30
		Nos. 95-98 (4)	1.20	1.20

Remainders of Nos. 95-98 received various private overprints, mostly as publicity for stamp exhibitions. They were not postally valid.

Unwatermarked Stamps with Watermarks

Stamps of these and later issues through the UPU Congress issue of 1924, are frequently found with watermark showing parts of the words "Kungl Postverket" in double-lined capitals. This watermark is normally located in the margins of the sheets of unwatermarked paper or paper watermarked wavy lines or crown.

Nos. 80, 84, 91, 90, 92 Surcharge

a   b

1918 | **Unwmk.**

99	A14(a)	7o on 10o	.30	.40
100	A14(b)	12o on 25o	1.90	.40
a.		Inverted surcharge	625.00	1,000.
101	A14(a)	12o on 65o	.85	1.40
102	A14(a)	27o on 55o	.75	1.60
103	A14(a)	27o on 65o	1.40	3.50
104	A14(a)	27o on 80o	.85	1.60
		Nos. 99-104 (6)	6.05	8.90

Arms A15

Heraldic Lion Supporting Arms of Sweden A16

Two types each of 5o green, 5o copper red and 10o violet, type A16.

Perf. 10 Vertically

1920-25 Engr. | **Unwmk.**

115	A15	3o copper red	.30	.40
116	A16	5o green ('25)	4.00	.40
117	A16	5o copper red ('21)	5.00	.40
118	A16	10o copper red ('21)	21.00	.40
a.		Tête bêche pair	1,650.	3,250.
119	A16	10o violet ('25)	5.25	.40
120	A16	25o orange ('21)	13.00	.40
121	A16	30o brown	.45	.45

Wmk. 181

122	A16	5o green	2.50	1.30
123	A16	5o copper red ('21)	8.25	1.00
124	A16	10o copper red ('21)	2.50	1.30
125	A16	30o brown	8.25	18.00
		Nos. 115-125 (11)	70.50	24.45

Coil Stamps

Unless part of a booklet pane any stamp perforated only horizontally or vertically is a coil stamp.

1920-26 | **Unwmk.** | **Perf. 10**

126	A16	5o green	4.00	1.00
a.		Booklet pane of 10	80.00	
127	A16	10o green ('21)	11.50	3.50
a.		Booklet pane of 10	225.00	
128	A16	10o violet ('25)	6.50	.85
a.		Booklet pane of 10	180.00	
129	A16	30o brown	32.50	4.00

Wmk. 181

130	A16	5o green	11.50	30.00
131	A16	10o green ('21)	45.00	100.00
a.		Booklet pane of 10	425.00	

Perf. 13 Vertically

Unwmk.

132	A16	5o green ('25)	4.00	1.50
133	A16	5o copper red ('21)	325.00	160.00
134	A16	10o violet ('26)	25.00	37.50

Wmk. 181

135	A16	5o green ('25)	2.00	8.00
136	A16	5o copper red ('22)	2.00	7.00
137	A16	10o green ('24)	9.00	40.00
138	A16	10o violet ('25)	8.00	25.00
		Nos. 126-138 (13)	486.00	418.35

The paper used for the earlier printings of types A16, A17, A18, A18a and A20 is usually tinted by the color of the stamp. Printings of 1934 and later are on white paper in slightly different shades.

King Gustaf V — A17

1920-21 Unwmk. Perf. 10 Vertically

139	A17	10o rose	30.00	.40
140	A17	15o claret	.30	.45
141	A17	20o blue	35.00	.50

Perf. 10

142	A17	10o rose	12.50	6.00
143	A17	20o blue ('21)	29.00	11.00
a.		Booklet pane of 10	550.00	
		Nos. 139-143 (5)	106.80	18.35

Wmk. 181

144	A17	20o blue	4,000.	

A18a

A18
Crown and Post Horn

See note after No. 138 regarding paper. There are 2 types of the 35, 40, 45 and 60o.

1920-34 | **Unwmk.** | **Perf. 10 Vert.**

145	A18	35o yellow ('22)	42.50	.75
146	A18	40o olive green	32.50	.75
147	A18	45o brown ('22)	1.25	.55
148	A18	60o claret	19.00	.40
149	A18	70o red brn ('22)	.60	2.50
150	A18	80o deep green	.40	.40
151	A18	85o myrtle grn ('29)	4.50	.45
152	A18	90o lt blue ('25)	60.00	.30
153	A18a	1kr dp org ('21)	7.75	.40
154	A18	110o ultra	.50	.40
155	A18	115o red brn ('29)	9.00	.45
156	A18	120o gray blk ('25)	60.00	.60

157	A18	120o lil rose ('33)	14.00	.60
158	A18	140o gray black	.90	.30
159	A18	145o brt grn ('30)	8.50	.55

Wmk. 181

160	A18	35o yellow ('23)	60.00	7.50
161	A18	60o red violet	100.00	150.00
162	A18	80o blue green	8.25	15.00
163	A18	110o ultra	3.50	4.50
		Nos. 145-163 (19)	433.15	186.40

The value for #147 is for the 2nd type, issued in 1925.

Gustavus Adolphus A19

King Gustaf V A20

Perf. 10 Vertically

1920, July 28 | **Unwmk.**

164	A19	20o deep blue	2.25	.40

Wmk. 181

165	A19	20o blue	160.00	35.00

Unwmk.

Perf. 10

166	A19	20o blue	6.25	2.25
a.		Booklet pane of 10	130.00	
		Nos. 164-166 (3)	168.50	37.65

Tercentenary of Swedish post which first ran between Stockholm and Hamburg.

1921-36 | **Unwmk.** | **Perf. 10 Vert.**

See note after No. 138 regarding paper. There are two types each of the 15o rose and 40o olive green.

167	A20	15o violet ('22)	17.00	.40
168	A20	15o rose ('28)	5.50	.45
169	A20	15o brown ('36)	4.75	.45
170	A20	20o violet	.25	.30
171	A20	20o rose ('22)	22.50	.60
172	A20	20o orange ('25)	.25	.45
174	A20	25o rose red ('22)	.55	1.50
175	A20	25o dk bl ('25)	17.00	.40
176	A20	25o ultra ('34)	17.00	.80
177	A20	25o yel org ('36)	27.50	.45
178	A20	30o blue ('23)	19.00	.45
179	A20	30o brown ('25)	20.00	.35
180	A20	30o lt blue ('36)	6.00	.70
181	A20	35o red vio ('30)	24.00	.45
182	A20	40o blue	.45	.70
183	A20	40o ol grn ('29)	40.00	2.00
184	A20	45o brown ('29)	5.00	.90
185	A20	50o gray	1.75	1.00
186	A20	85o myrtle grn ('25)	17.00	2.00
187	A20	115o brn red ('25)	11.00	2.00

188	A20	145o apple grn ('25)	8.25	2.00
		Nos. 167-188 (21)	264.75	18.35

Wmk. 181

189	A20	15o violet ('22)	3,500.	1,050.
189A	A20	20o violet		4,750.

Gustavus Vasa — A21

1922-36 | **Unwmk.** | **Perf. 10**

190	A20	15o violet	17.50	.70
a.		Booklet pane of 10	400.00	
191	A20	15o rose red ('25)	22.50	.90
a.		Booklet pane of 10	600.00	
192	A20	15o brown ('36)	5.75	1.25
a.		Booklet pane of 10	175.00	
193	A20	20o violet ('22)	.50	1.50
a.		Booklet pane of 10	10.00	
		Nos. 190-193 (4)	46.25	4.35

1921, June | | Perf. 10 Vertically

194	A21	20o violet	14.00	30.00
195	A21	110o ultra	55.00	8.00
196	A21	140o gray black	30.00	8.00
		Nos. 194-196 (3)	99.00	46.00

400th anniversary of Gustavus Vasa's war of independence from the Danes.

Universal Postal Union Congress

Composite View of Stockholm's Skyline A22

King Gustaf V — A23

1924, July 4 | **Unwmk.** | **Perf. 10**

197	A22	5o red brown	1.60	3.25
198	A22	10o green	1.60	3.25
199	A22	15o dk violet	1.60	2.00
200	A22	20o rose red	12.50	21.00
201	A22	25o dp orange	15.00	21.00
202	A22	30o deep blue	15.00	21.00
a.		30o greenish blue	87.50	125.00
203	A22	35o black	20.00	28.00
204	A22	40o olive green	29.00	32.50
205	A22	45o deep brown	32.50	32.50
206	A22	50o gray	32.50	32.50
207	A22	60o violet brn	47.50	55.00
208	A22	80o myrtle grn	37.50	37.50

209	A23	1k green	57.50	87.50
210	A23	2k rose red	125.00	250.00
211	A23	5k deep blue	275.00	450.00

Wmk. 181

212	A22	10o green	26.00	65.00
		Nos. 197-212 (16)	729.80	1,142.
		Set, never hinged	1,400.	

Postrider Watching Airplane A24

Carrier Pigeon and Globe — A25

1924, Aug. 16   Engr.   Unwmk.

213	A24	5o red brown	2.75	4.50
214	A24	10o green	2.75	5.75
215	A24	15o dk violet	3.00	3.00
216	A24	20o rose red	21.00	32.50
217	A24	25o deep orange	26.00	32.50
218	A24	30o deep blue	26.00	32.50
a.		30o greenish blue	90.00	52.50
219	A24	35o black	32.50	47.50
220	A24	40o olive green	32.50	37.50
221	A24	45o deep brown	37.50	35.00
222	A24	50o gray	50.00	62.50
223	A24	60o violet brown	50.00	77.50
224	A24	80o myrtle green	37.50	37.50
225	A25	1k green	75.00	87.50
226	A25	2k rose red	125.00	75.00
227	A25	5k deep blue	250.00	225.00

Wmk. 181

228	A24	10o green	35.00	65.00
		Nos. 213-228 (16)	806.50	855.75
		Set, never hinged	1,750.	

Universal Postal Union issue.

Royal Palace at Stockholm A26

1931, Nov. 26   Unwmk.   Perf. 10

229	A26	5k dark green	100.00	12.50
		Never hinged	300.00	
a.		Booklet pane of 10	3,100.	

Death of Gustavus Adolphus — A27

1932, Nov. 1

230	A27	10o dark violet	2.50	5.50
a.		Booklet pane of 10	40.00	
231	A27	15o dark red	4.50	2.00
a.		Booklet pane of 10	110.00	

Perf. 10 Vertically

232	A27	10o dark violet	1.90	.40
233	A27	15o dark red	2.50	.40
234	A27	25o dark blue	6.00	.95
235	A27	90o dark green	22.50	2.25
		Nos. 230-235 (6)	39.90	11.50
		Set, never hinged	85.00	

300th anniv. of the death of King Gustavus Adolphus II who was killed on the battlefield of Lützen, Nov. 6, 1632.

Catching Sunlight in Bowl — A28

1933, Dec. 6   Perf. 10

236	A28	5o green	2.50	2.00
a.		Booklet pane of 10	60.00	

There are two types of No. 236.

Perf. 10 Vertically

237	A28	5o green	2.50	.40

Perf. 13 Vertically

238	A28	5o green	3.50	7.25
		Nos. 236-238 (3)	8.50	9.65
		Set, never hinged	17.50	

50th anniv. of the Swedish Postal Savings Bank.

The Old Law Courts — A29

The "Four Estates" and Arms of Engelbrekt A34

Designs: 10o, Stock exchange. 15o, Parish church (Storkyrkan). 25o, House of the Nobility. 35o, House of Parliament.

1935, Jan. 10   Perf. 10

239	A29	5o green	2.25	1.40
a.		Booklet pane of 10	55.00	
240	A29	10o dull violet	4.25	5.75
a.		Booklet pane of 10	60.00	
241	A29	15o carmine	4.75	1.10
a.		Booklet pane of 10	125.00	

Perf. 10 Vertically

242	A29	5o green	1.25	.40
243	A29	10o dull violet	5.75	.40
244	A29	15o carmine	2.25	.40
245	A29	25o ultra	6.00	.60
246	A29	35o deep claret	12.00	2.25
247	A34	60o deep claret	17.50	2.50
		Nos. 239-247 (9)	56.00	14.80
		Set, never hinged	125.00	

500th anniv. of the Swedish Parliament.

Chancellor Axel Oxenstierna A35

Post Runner — A36

Mounted Courier — A37

Old Sailing Packet — A38

Mail Paddle Steamship A39

Mail Coach — A40

1855 Stamp Model — A41

Mail Train — A42

Postmaster General A. W. Roos — A43

Mail Truck and Trailer — A44

Modern Swedish Liner — A45

Junkers Plane with Pontoons — A46

1936, Feb. 20   Engr.   Perf. 10

248	A35	5o green	1.75	.85
a.		Booklet pane of 18	72.50	
249	A36	10o dk violet	2.10	3.00
a.		Booklet pane of 18	95.00	
250	A37	15o dk carmine	3.00	.55
a.		Booklet pane of 18	250.00	

Perf. 10 Vertically

251	A35	5o green	1.75	.25
252	A36	10o dk violet	1.75	.25
253	A37	15o dk carmine	3.25	.25
254	A38	20o lt blue	8.25	5.00
255	A39	25o lt ultra	5.25	.50
256	A40	30o yellow brn	16.00	3.25
257	A41	35o plum	5.50	1.25
258	A42	40o olive grn	5.75	2.75
259	A43	45o myrtle grn	7.75	1.50
260	A44	50o gray	20.00	2.75
261	A45	60o maroon	25.00	.70
262	A46	1k deep blue	8.25	8.50
		Nos. 248-262 (15)	115.35	31.35
		Set, never hinged	320.00	

300th anniv. of the Swedish Postal Service. See Nos. 946-950, B55-B56.

Airplane over Bromma Airport A47

1936, May 23   Perf. 10 Vert.

263	A47	50o ultra	4.00	8.50
		Never hinged	10.50	

Opening of Bromma Airport near Stockholm.

Swedish Booklets

Before 1940, booklets were hand-made and usually held two panes of 10 stamps (2x5). About every third booklet contained one row of stamps with straight edges at right or left side. Se-tenant pairs may be obtained with one stamp perforated on 4 sides and one perforated on 3 sides.

Starting in 1940, booklet stamps have one or more straight edges.

Emanuel Swedenborg — A48

1938, Jan. 29   Perf. 12½

264	A48	10o violet	1.00	.35
a.		Perf. on 3 sides	8.00	4.00
		Never hinged	17.00	
b.		Booklet pane of 10	30.00	

Perf. 12½ Vertically

266	A48	10o violet	.90	.25
267	A48	100o green	2.00	1.40
		Nos. 264-267 (3)	3.90	2.00
		Set, never hinged	14.00	

250th anniv. of the birth of Swedenborg, scientist, philosopher and religious writer.

Johann Printz and Indian Chief — A49

"Kalmar Nyckel" Sailing from Gothenburg A50

Symbolizing the Settlement of New Sweden — A51

Holy Trinity Church, Wilmington, Del. — A52

Queen Christina — A53

1938, Apr. 8   Perf. 12½ Vert.

268	A49	5o green	.40	.30
269	A50	15o brown	.50	.30
270	A51	20o red	.90	.70
271	A52	30o ultra	2.00	.85
272	A53	60o brown lake	2.50	.35

Perf. 12½

273	A49	5o green	1.00	1.00
a.		Perf. on 3 sides	5.00	7.50
		Never hinged	17.00	
b.		Booklet pane of 18	67.50	
274	A50	15o brown	1.50	.70
a.		Perf. on 3 sides	10.00	4.75
		Never hinged	29.00	
b.		Booklet pane of 18	115.00	
		Nos. 268-274 (7)	8.80	4.20
		Set, never hinged	39.00	

Tercentenary of the Swedish settlement at Wilmington, Del. See No. B54.

King Gustaf V — A54

1938, June 16 **Perf. 12½ Vert.**
275 A54 5o green .40 .30
276 A54 15(o) brown .45 .30
277 A54 30(o) ultra 5.00 .75

Perf. 12½
278 A54 5o green .85 .40
a. Perf. on 3 sides 5.00 5.50
    Never hinged 22.50
b. Booklet pane of 10 45.00
279 A54 15(o) brown 1.00 .40
a. Perf. on 3 sides 7.00 1.40
    Never hinged 35.00
b. Booklet pane of 10 37.50
    Nos. 275-279 (5) 7.70 2.15
    Set, never hinged 37.00

80th birthday of King Gustaf V.

King Gustaf V — A55   Three Crowns — A56

1939 **Perf. 12½ Vertically**
280 A55 10o violet .40 .40
281 A55 20o carmine 1.00 .60
282 A56 60o lake .40 .30
283 A56 85o dk green .30 .30
284 A56 90o peacock blue .30 .30
285 A56 1k orange .30 .30
286 A56 1.15k henna brn .30 .30
287 A56 1.20k brt rose vio .80 .30
288 A56 1.45k lt yel grn .85 .80

Perf. 12½
289 A55 10o violet 1.00 4.00
a. Perf. on 3 sides 25.00 65.00
    Never hinged 80.00
b. Bklt. pane of 10, perf. on 4 sides 30.00
    Nos. 280-289 (10) 5.65 7.60
    Set, never hinged 20.00

See Nos. 394-398, 416-417, 425-426, 431, 439-441, 473, 588-591, 656-664.

Per Henrik Ling — A57

1939, Feb. 25 **Perf. 12½ Vert.**
290 A57 5o green .25 .25
291 A57 25(o) brown .40 .40

Perf. 12½
292 A57 5o green .40 .40
a. Perf. on 3 sides 6.00 6.00
    Never hinged 29.00
b. Booklet pane of 10 37.50
    Nos. 290-292 (3) 1.05 1.05
    Set, never hinged 4.00

Centenary of the death of P. H. Ling, father of Swedish gymnastics.

J. J. Berzelius — A58   Carl von Linné — A59

Perf. 12½ Vertically
1939, June 2 **Engr.**
293 A58 10o violet 1.00 .40
294 A59 15o fawn .25 .30
295 A58 30o ultra 6.00 .45
296 A59 50o gray 6.50 1.00

Perf. 12½
297 A58 10o violet .90 .65
a. Perf. on 3 sides 25.00 19.00
    Never hinged 135.00
b. Booklet pane of 10 65.00
298 A59 15o fawn 1.00 .50
a. Perf. on 3 sides 5.00 .45
    Never hinged 20.00

b. Booklet pane of 10 100.00
c. As "a," bklt. pane of 20 450.00
    Nos. 293-298 (6) 15.65 3.30
    Set, never hinged 70.00

200th anniv. of the founding of the Royal Academy of Science at Stockholm.

King Gustaf V — A60

Type A55 Re-engraved
1939-46 **Perf. 12½**
299 A60 5o dp green ('46) .30 .30
b. Perf. on 3 sides ('41) .30 .30
    Never hinged .50
c. As "b," bklt. pane of 20 12.00
300 A60 10(o) violet ('46) .30 .30
a. Bklt. pane of 10, perf. on 4 sides 55.00
    Never hinged .50
c. Perf. on 3 sides 2.00 .30
i. As "c," booklet pane of 20 50.00
300D A60 15(o) chestnut ('46) .30 .30
f. Perf. on 3 sides ('45) .30 .30
    Never hinged .65
j. As "f," booklet pane of 20 7.75
300G A60 20(o) red ('42) .30 .25
b. Booklet pane of 20 6.50
    Nos. 299-300G (4) 1.20 1.15
    Set, never hinged 1.50

No. 300 differs slightly from the original due to deeper engraving. No. 300G was issued only in booklets; all examples have one straight edge.
Nos. 299, 300, 300D exist in booklet panes of 20 made from sheets of stamps. These can be collected as booklets.

1940-42 **Perf. 12½ Vertically**
301 A60 5o dp green ('41) .25 .30
302 A60 10(o) violet .25 .30
302A A60 15(o) chestnut ('42) .25 .30
303 A60 20(o) red .25 .30
304 A60 25(o) orange .40 .30
305 A60 30(o) ultra .40 .30
306 A60 35(o) red vio ('41) .40 .30
307 A60 40(o) olive grn .40 .30
308 A60 45(o) dk brown .40 .30
309 A60 50(o) gray blk ('41) 2.75 .30
    Nos. 301-309 (10) 5.75 3.00
    Set, never hinged 13.00

Numerals measure 4½mm high. Less shading around head gives a lighter effect. Horizontal lines only as background for "SVERIGE."
See Nos. 391-393, 399.

Carl Michael Bellman — A61   Tobias Sergel — A62

1940, Feb. 4 Engr. **Perf. 12½ Vert.**
310 A61 5o green .25 .25
311 A61 35(o) rose red .40 .40

Perf. 12½
312 A61 5o green .50 .60
a. Perf. on 3 sides 2.25 .75
    Never hinged 21.00
b. Booklet pane of 10 50.00
c. As "a," bklt. pane of 20 425.00
    Nos. 310-312 (3) 1.15 1.05
    Set, never hinged 3.75

Bellman (1740-95), lyric poet.

1940, Sept. 5 **Perf. 12½ on 3 Sides**
313 A62 15o lt brown 3.00 .50
a. Booklet pane of 20 275.00

Perf. 12½ Vertically
314 A62 15o lt brown .75 .40
315 A62 50o gray black 5.00 1.40
    Nos. 313-315 (3) 8.75 2.30
    Set, never hinged 70.00

Bicentenary of birth of Johan Tobias von Sergel (1740-1814), sculptor.

Reformers Presenting Bible to Gustavus Vasa A63   View of Skansen A64

1941, May 11 **Perf. 12½ on 3 Sides**
316 A63 15o brown 2.75 .45
a. Booklet pane of 18 90.00

Perf. 12½ Vertically
317 A63 15o brown .30 .25
318 A63 90o ultra 19.00 .95
    Nos. 316-318 (3) 22.05 1.65
    Set, never hinged 50.00

400th anniv. of the 1st authorized version of the Bible in Swedish.

1941, June 18 Perf. 12½ on 3 Sides
319 A64 10o violet 2.50 .65
a. Booklet pane of 20 85.00

Perf. 12½ Vertically
320 A64 10o violet 3.00 .25
321 A64 60o red lilac 8.00 .60
    Nos. 319-321 (3) 13.50 1.50
    Set, never hinged 35.00

50th anniv. of Skansen, an open air extension of the Nordic Museum.

Royal Palace at Stockholm A65   Artur Hazelius A66

1941 **Perf. 12½ on 3 Sides**
322 A65 5k blue 1.50 .25
    Never hinged 2.50
a. Perf. on 4 sides 29.00 1.00
    Never hinged 65.00
b. Bklt. pane of 20, perf. 3 sides 50.00
c. Bklt. pane of 10, perf. 4 sides 575.00

For coil stamp see No. 537.

1941, Aug. 30 Perf. 12½ on 3 Sides
323 A66 5o lt green 2.50 .55
a. Booklet pane of 20 100.00

Perf. 12½ Vertically
324 A66 5o lt green .25 .25
325 A66 1k lt orange 7.00 4.00
    Nos. 323-325 (3) 9.75 4.80
    Set, never hinged 28.00

Issued to honor Artur Hazelius, founder of Skansen, Nordic museum.

St. Bridget of Sweden — A67

Perf. 12½ on 3 Sides
1941, Oct. 7 **Engr.**
326 A67 15o deep brown 1.90 .40
a. Booklet pane of 18 60.00

Perf. 12½ Horiz.
327 A67 15o deep brown .25 .25
328 A67 1.20k red vio 21.00 10.50
    Nos. 326-328 (3) 23.15 11.15
    Set, never hinged 65.00

King Gustavus III — A68

K. G. Tessin, Architect — A69

1942, June 29 Perf. 12½ on 3 Sides
329 A68 20o red 1.25 .45
a. Booklet pane of 20 45.00

Perf. 12½ Vertically
330 A68 20o red .60 .25
331 A69 40o olive green 14.00 1.25
    Nos. 329-331 (3) 15.85 1.95
    Set, never hinged 40.00

Sesquicentennial of the Swedish National Museum, Stockholm.

Torsten Rudenschold and Nils Mansson — A70

1942, July 1 **Perf. 12½ Horiz.**
332 A70 10o magenta .25 .40
a. Booklet pane of 10 3.50

Perf. 12½ Vertically
333 A70 10o magenta .25 .35
334 A70 90o light blue 2.50 6.00
    Nos. 332-334 (3) 3.00 6.75
    Set, never hinged 5.00

Swedish Public School System, 100th anniv.

Carl Wilhelm Scheele A71   King Gustaf V A72

1942, Dec. 9 Perf. 12½ on 3 Sides
335 A71 5o green 1.50 1.00
a. Booklet pane of 20 55.00

Perf. 12½ Vertically
336 A71 5o green .25 .25
337 A71 60o deep magenta 7.00 .60
    Nos. 335-337 (3) 8.75 1.85
    Set, never hinged 17.50

200th anniv. of the birth of Carl Wilhelm Scheele, chemist.

Perf. 12½ Horizontally
1943, June 16
338 A72 20o red .60 .45
339 A72 30o ultra .90 2.50
340 A72 60o brt red vio 1.10 3.25

Perf. 12½ on 3 Sides
341 A72 20o red 4.50 1.10
a. Booklet pane of 20 160.00
    Nos. 338-341 (4) 7.10 7.30
    Set, never hinged 16.00

85th birthday of King Gustaf V, June 16.

Rifle Federation Emblem A73   Oscar Montelius A74

1943, July 22 **Perf. 12½ Vert.**
342 A73 10o rose violet .25 .25
343 A73 90o dp ultra 3.75 .45

Perf. 12½ on 3 Sides
344 A73 10o rose violet .40 .40
a. Booklet pane of 20 12.50
    Nos. 342-344 (3) 4.40 1.10
    Set, never hinged 11.00

50th anniversary of the Swedish Voluntary Rifle Associations.

1943, Sept. 9 Engr. *Perf. 12½ Vert.*
345 A74 5o green .25 .25
346 A74 1.20k brt red vio 6.00 2.50

Perf. 12½ on 3 Sides
347 A74 5o red .55 .40
a. Booklet pane of 20 19.00
Nos. 345-347 (3) 6.80 3.15
Set, never hinged 11.50

Montelius (1843-1921), archaeologist.

Johan Mansson's
Chart of Baltic,
1644 — A75

Perf. 12½ on 3 Sides
1944, Apr. 15 Engr. Unwmk.
348 A75 5o green .60 .80
a. Booklet pane of 20 25.00

Perf. 12½ Vertically
349 A75 5o green .25 .25
350 A75 60o lake 4.25 .80
Nos. 348-350 (3) 5.10 1.85
Set, never hinged 12.00

1st Swedish Marine Chart, tercentenary.

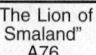

"The Lion of
Smaland"
A76

Clas Fleming
A77

30o, "Kung Karl." 40o, Stern of "Amphion,"
Flagship of Gustavus III. 90o, "Gustaf V."

1944, Oct. 13 *Perf. 12½ Vert.*
351 A76 10o purple .35 .35
352 A77 20o red .30 .25
353 A76 30o blue .50 .80
354 A76 40o olive green .60 1.25
355 A76 90o gray black 6.50 2.25

Perf. 12½ on 3 Sides
356 A76 10o purple .60 2.00
a. Booklet pane of 20 24.00
357 A77 20o red 2.25 .35
a. Booklet pane of 20 90.00
Nos. 351-357 (7) 11.10 7.25
Set, never hinged 30.00

Issued to honor the Swedish Fleet and mark
the tercentenary of the Swedish naval victory
at Femern, 1644.
See Nos. B53, B57-B58.

> Catalogue values for unused
> stamps in this section, from this
> point to the end of the section, are
> for Never Hinged items.

Red
Cross — A81

Torch and
Quill
Pen — A82

1945, Feb. 27 *Perf. 12½ Vert.*
358 A81 20o red .60 .25

Perf. 12½ on 3 Sides
359 A81 20o red 3.00 .40
a. Booklet pane of 20 65.00

Swedish Red Cross Society, 80th anniv.

1945, May 29 *Perf. 12½ Vert.*
360 A82 5o green .25 .25
361 A82 60o carmine rose 7.00 .45

Perf. 12½ on 3 Sides
362 A82 5o green .35 .45
a. Booklet pane of 20 7.75
Nos. 360-362 (3) 7.60 1.15

Tercentenary of Swedish press.

Rydberg
A83

Oak Tree
A84

1945, Sept. 21 *Perf. 12½ Vert.*
363 A83 20o red .35 .25
364 A83 90o blue 7.00 .45

Perf. 12½ on 3 Sides
365 A83 20o red 1.50 .45
a. Booklet pane of 20 32.50
Nos. 363-365 (3) 8.85 1.15

Viktor Rydberg (1828-95), author.

1945, Oct. 27 *Perf. 12½ Vert.*
366 A84 10o violet .25 .35
367 A84 40o olive 1.60 1.25

Perf. 12½ on 3 Sides
368 A84 10o violet .40 .70
a. Booklet pane of 20 10.00
Nos. 366-368 (3) 2.25 2.30

125th anniv. of the Savings Bank movement.

Angel and Lund
Cathedral
A85

View of Lund
Cathedral
A86

Perf. 12½ Vertically
1946, May 28 Unwmk.
369 A85 15o orange brn .70 .55
370 A86 20o red .30 .25
371 A85 90o ultra 9.25 .85

Perf. 12½ on 3 Sides
372 A85 15o orange brn .95 1.10
373 A86 20o red 2.25 .45
a. Booklet pane of 20 45.00
Nos. 369-373 (5) 13.45 3.20

Lund Cathedral, 800th anniversary.

Mare and
Colt — A87

Esaias
Tegner — A88

1946, June 8 *Perf. 12½ Vert.*
374 A87 5o green .25 .25
375 A87 60o carmine rose 8.25 .40

Perf. 12½ on 3 Sides
376 A87 5o green .30 .45
a. Booklet pane of 20 6.50
Nos. 374-376 (3) 8.80 1.10

Centenary of Swedish agricultural shows.

Perf. 12½ Vertically
1946, Nov. 2 Engr. Unwmk.
377 A88 10o deep violet .25 .25
378 A88 40o dk olive grn 1.40 .45

Perf. 12½ on 3 Sides
379 A88 10o dp violet .30 .25
a. Booklet pane of 20 6.00
Nos. 377-379 (3) 1.95 .95

Esaias Tegner (1782-1846), poet.

Nobel — A89

Geijer — A90

1946, Dec. 10 *Perf. 12½ Vert.*
380 A89 20o red .80 .25
381 A89 30o ultra 2.25 .60

Perf. 12½ on 3 Sides
382 A89 20o red 1.90 .55
a. Booklet pane of 20 40.00
Nos. 380-382 (3) 4.95 1.40

50th anniversary of the death of Alfred
Nobel, inventor and philanthropist.

1947, Apr. 23 *Perf. 12½ Vert.*
383 A90 5o dk yellow grn .25 .25
384 A90 90o ultra 5.00 .25

Perf. 12½ on 3 Sides
385 A90 5o dk yellow grn .30 .45
a. Booklet pane of 20 7.00
Nos. 383-385 (3) 5.55 .95

Centenary of the death of Erik Gustaf
Geijer, historian, philosopher and poet.

King Gustaf
V — A91

1947, Dec. 8 Engr. *Perf. 12½ Horiz.*
386 A91 10o deep violet .25 .25
387 A91 20o red .25 .25
388 A91 60o red violet 1.40 1.40

Perf. 12½ on 3 Sides
389 A91 10o deep violet .25 .30
a. Booklet pane of 20 4.00
390 A91 20o red .40 .40
a. Booklet pane of 20 8.00
Nos. 386-390 (5) 2.55 2.60

40th anniv. of the reign of King Gustaf V.

King and 3-Crown Types of 1939
1948 Unwmk. *Perf. 12½ Vertically*
391 A60 5o orange .25 .25
392 A60 10o green .30 .25
393 A60 25o violet 1.50 .25
394 A56 55o orange brown 1.40 .25
395 A56 80o olive green .80 .25
396 A56 1.10k violet 7.00 .25
397 A56 1.40k dk blue green .80 .25
398 A56 1.75k brt grnsh blue 12.50 6.75

Perf. 12½ on 3 Sides
399 A60 10o green .25 .25
a. Booklet pane of 20 6.00
Nos. 391-399 (9) 24.80 8.75

Plowman,
Early and
Modern
Buildings
A92

August
Strindberg
A93

1948, Apr. 26 *Perf. 12½ Vert.*
400 A92 15o orange brown .25 .25
401 A92 30o ultra .50 .55
402 A92 1k orange 1.50 1.25

Perf. 12½ on 3 Sides
403 A92 15o orange brown .40 .50
a. Booklet pane of 20 2.65 2.55
Nos. 400-403 (4)

Centenary of the Swedish pioneers' settlement in the United States.

1949, Jan. 22 *Perf. 12½ Vert.*
404 A93 20o red .45 .25
405 A93 30o blue .80 .75
406 A93 80o olive green 2.75 .45

Perf. 12½ on 3 Sides
407 A93 20o red .80 .35
a. Booklet pane of 20 16.00
Nos. 404-407 (4) 4.80 1.80

Birth centenary of August Strindberg (1849-
1912), author and playwright.

Girl and Boy
Gymnasts — A94

Perf. 12½ Horiz.
1949, July 27 Engr.
408 A94 5o ultra .30 .45
409 A94 15o brown .35 .25

Perf. 12½ on 3 Sides
410 A94 15o brown .45 .45
a. Booklet pane of 20 9.00
Nos. 408-410 (3) 1.10 1.35

2nd Lingiad or World Gymnastics Festival,
Stockholm, July-August 1949.

A95

Symbols of
UPU — A96

1949, Oct. 9 *Perf. 12½ Vert.*
411 A95 10o green .25 .25
412 A95 20o red .30 .25

Perf. 12½ Horizontally
413 A96 30o lt blue .40 .65

Perf. 12½ on 3 sides
414 A95 10o green .25 .25
a. Booklet pane of 20 3.50
415 A95 20o red .25 .25
a. Booklet pane of 20 4.00
Nos. 411-415 (5) 1.45 1.65

75th anniv. of the formation of the UPU.

Three-Crown Type of 1939
Perf. 12½ Vertically
1949, Nov. 11 Unwmk.
416 A56 65o lt yellow grn .75 .30
417 A56 70o peacock blue 4.00 1.40

Gustaf VI
Adolf (Letters
in color)
A97

Christopher
Polhem
A98

1951, June 6 *Perf. 12½ Vert.*
Without Imprint
418 A97 10o dull green .25 .25
419 A97 15o chestnut brown .35 .25
420 A97 20o carmine rose .35 .25
421 A97 25o gray .65 .25
422 A97 30o ultra .45 .25

Perf. 12½ on 3 sides
423 A97 10o dull green .40 .25
a. Booklet pane of 20 8.00
424 A97 25o gray .50 .25
a. Booklet pane of 20 12.00
Nos. 418-424 (7) 2.95 1.75

See Nos. 435-438, 442-443, 456-461, 502,
505-509, 515-517.

Three-Crown Type of 1939
1951, June 1 *Perf. 12½ Vert.*
425 A56 85o orange brown 5.75 1.60
426 A56 1.70k red 1.25 .25

1951, Aug. 30 *Perf. 12½ Vert.*
427 A98 25o gray 1.40 .25
428 A98 45o brown .55 .40

Perf. 12½ on 3 sides
429 A98 25o gray .45 .30
a. Booklet pane of 20 9.00
Nos. 427-429 (3) 2.40 .95

200th anniversary of the death of Christopher Polhem, engineer and technician.

Numeral
(Lettering in
color)
A99

Olaus Petri
Preaching
A100

Type A99 and 3-Crown Type of 1939
1951, Nov.   **Engr.**   *Perf. 12½ Vert.*
430 A99   5o rose carmine   .25   .25
431 A56   1.50k red violet   1.60   1.25

For other stamps similar to type A99, see type A115a, Nos. 503-504, 513-514, 570, 580, 666-667.

1952, Apr. 19   *Perf. 12½ Horiz.*
432 A100   25o gray black   .45   .25
433 A100   1.40k brown   3.00   .80

Perf. 12½ on 3 sides
434 A100   25o gray black   2.00   2.60
  a.   Booklet pane of 20   50.00
    Nos. 432-434 (3)   5.45   3.65

Olaus Petri (1493-1552), Lutheran clergyman, historian and Bible translator.

King and 3-Crown Types of 1951 and 1939
1952   *Perf. 12½ Vertically*
Without Imprint
435 A97   20o gray   .30   .25
436 A97   25o car rose   1.25   .25
437 A97   30o dk brown   .50   .40
438 A97   40o blue   1.00   .40
439 A56   50o gray   1.75   .25
440 A56   75o orange brown   2.75   .80
441 A56   2k red violet   .90   .25

Perf. 12½ on 3 sides
442 A97   20o gray   .55   .60
  a.   Booklet pane of 20   15.00
443 A97   25o carmine rose   1.25   .40
  a.   Booklet pane of 20   27.50
    Nos. 435-443 (9)   10.25   3.60

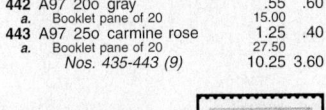

Ski Jump   A101   Ice Hockey   A102

40o, Woman throwing slingball. 1.40kr, Wrestlers.

Perf. 12½ Vert. (V), Horiz. (H)
1953, May 27
444 A101   10o green (V)   .50   .25
445 A102   15o brown (H)   .75   1.10
446 A102   40o deep blue (H)   1.50   1.60
447 A101   1.40k red violet (V)   4.50   1.25

Perf. 12½ on 3 sides
448 A101   10o green   .75   1.10
  a.   Booklet pane of 20   17.50
    Nos. 444-448 (5)   8.00   5.30

50th anniv. of Swedish Athletic Association.

Old Stockholm   A103

Original and Present Seals of Stockholm   A104

1953, June 17   *Perf. 12½ Vert.*
449 A103   25o blue   .40   .25
450 A104   1.70k red   2.75   .75

Perf. 12½ on 3 sides
451 A103   25o blue   .80   .30
  a.   Booklet pane of 20   17.50
    Nos. 449-451 (3)   3.95   1.30

700th anniv. of the founding of Stockholm.

"Telephone" — A105

1953, Nov. 2   *Perf. 12½ Horiz.*
452 A105   25o shown   .30   .25
453 A105   40o "Radio"   1.50   1.60
454 A105   60o "Telegraph"   3.00   2.75

Perf. 12½ on 3 sides
455 A105   25o shown   .85   .50
  a.   Booklet pane of 20   20.00
    Nos. 452-455 (4)   5.65   5.10

Centenary of the foundation of the Swedish Telegraph Service.

King Type of 1951
1954   *Perf. 12½ Vertically*
Without Imprint
456 A97   10o dark brown   .25   .25
457 A97   25o ultra   .25   .25
458 A97   30o red   9.00   .25
459 A97   40o olive green   .60   .25

Perf. 12½ on 3 sides
460 A97   10o dark brown   .25   .25
  a.   Booklet pane of 10   9.00
  b.   Booklet pane of 20   7.50
461 A97   25o ultra   .25   .25
  a.   Booklet pane of 4   10.00   11.00
  b.   Booklet pane of 8   100.00
  c.   Booklet pane of 20   10.00
    Nos. 456-461 (6)   10.60   1.50

The booklet pane of 4 contains two copies of No. 461 which are perforated on two adjoining sides.

Skier   A106   Anna Maria Lenngren   A107

1954, Feb. 13   *Perf. 12½ Vert.*
462 A106   20o shown   .50   .45
463 A106   1k Girl skier   8.50   1.25

Perf. 12½ on 3 sides
464 A106   20o shown   1.25   1.90
  a.   Booklet pane of 20   35.00
    Nos. 462-464 (3)   10.25   3.60

World Ski Championship Matches, 1954.

1954, June 18   *Perf. 12½ Horiz.*
465 A107   20o gray   .30   .30
466 A107   65o dark brown   5.50   3.75

Perf. 12½ on 3 sides
467 A107   20o gray   1.25   1.90
  a.   Booklet pane of 20   35.00
    Nos. 465-467 (3)   7.05   5.95

200th anniversary of the birth of Anna Maria Lenngren, author.

Rock Carvings   A108   Coat of Arms   A109

1954, Nov. 8   *Perf. 12½ Vert.*
468 A108   50o gray   .30   .25
469 A108   60o dp carmine   .50   .25
470 A108   65o dk olive grn   1.25   .25
471 A108   75o dk brown   2.00   .25
472 A108   90o dk blue   .60   .25
    Nos. 468-472 (5)   4.65   1.25

See Nos. 510-512, 655.

Three-Crown Type of 1939
1954, Dec. 10   *Perf. 12½ Vert.*
473 A56   2.10k dp ultra   7.50   .50

1955, May 16   *Perf. 12½ Vert.*
474 A109   25o blue   .25   .25
475 A109   40o green   1.25   .35

Perf. 12½ on 3 sides
476 A109   25o blue   .25   .25
  a.   Booklet pane of 4   9.00   8.50
  b.   Booklet pane of 20   4.00
    Nos. 474-476 (3)   1.75   .85

Centenary of Sweden's 1st postage stamps. The booklet pane of 4 contains two copies of No. 476 which are perforated on two adjoining sides.

Crown and Flag — A110   A111

Perf. 12½
1955, June 6   **Unwmk.**   **Litho.**
477 A110   10o green, bl & yel   .25   .30
478 A110   15o lake, bl & yel   .30   .40

National Flag Day.

Wmk. 307
1955, July 1   **Typo.**   *Perf. 13*
479 A111   3o yellow green   2.25   5.00
480 A111   4o blue   2.25   5.00
481 A111   6o gray   2.25   5.00
482 A111   8o orange yellow   2.25   5.00
483 A111   24o salmon   2.25   5.00
    Nos. 479-483 (5)   11.25   25.00

Cent. of the 1st Swedish postage stamps. Nos. 479-483 were printed in sheets of nine. They were sold in complete sets at the Stockholmia Philatelic Exhibition, July 1-10, 1955. A set cost 45 ore (face value) plus 2k (entrance fee).

Per Atterbom   A112   Greek Horseman   A113

Perf. 12½ Horizontally
1955, July 21   **Engr.**   **Unwmk.**
484 A112   20o dark blue   .40   .30
485 A112   1.40k sepia   4.00   .80

Perf. 12½ on 3 sides
486 A112   20o dark blue   1.25   1.40
  a.   Booklet pane of 20   35.00
    Nos. 484-486 (3)   5.65   2.50

Cent. of the death of Per Daniel Amadeus Atterbom, poet.

1956, Apr. 16   *Perf. 12½ Vert.*
487 A113   20o carmine   .85   .60
488 A113   25o ultra   .85   .25
489 A113   40o gray green   4.00   2.10

Perf. 12½ on 3 sides
490 A113   20o carmine   .40   .70
  a.   Booklet pane of 20   10.00
491 A113   25o ultra   .40   .25
  a.   Booklet pane of 20   10.00
    Nos. 487-491 (5)   6.50   3.90

Issued to publicize the Olympic Equestrian Competitions, Stockholm, June 10-17, 1956.

Northern Countries Issue

Whooper Swans — A113a

Perf. 12½ Vertically
1956, Oct. 30   **Engr.**   **Unwmk.**
492 A113a   25o rose red   .25   .25
493 A113a   40o ultra   .75   .65

See footnote after Norway No. 354.

Railroad Builders — A114

Designs: 25o. First Swedish locomotive and passenger car. 40o. Express train crossing Årsta bridge.

1956, Dec. 1   *Perf. 12½ Vert.*
494 A114   10o olive green   .60   .25
495 A114   25o ultra   .25   .25
496 A114   40o orange   3.00   3.00

Perf. 12½ on 3 sides
497 A114   10o olive green   .45   .45
  a.   Booklet pane of 20   11.00
498 A114   25o ultra   .75   .45
  a.   Booklet pane of 20   18.00
    Nos. 494-498 (5)   5.05   4.40

Centenary of Swedish railroads.

Ship in Distress and Lifeboat — A115

Perf. 12½ Vertically
1957, June 1   **Engr.**   **Unwmk.**
499 A115   30o blue   3.75   .25
500 A115   1.40k deep rose   6.00   1.25

Perf. 12½ on 3 sides
501 A115   30o blue   1.60   1.50
  a.   Booklet pane of 20   45.00
    Nos. 499-501 (3)   11.35   3.00

Swedish Life Saving Society, 50th anniv.

King Type of 1951
1957, June 1   *Perf. 12½ Vert.*
Without Imprint
502 A97   25o dark brown   1.10   1.75

Re-engraved Types of 1951 and 1954 with Imprint, and

Numeral (Letters in white) — A115a

1957-64   *Perf. 12½ Vertically*
503 A115a   5o red ('61)   .25   .25
  a.   5o dark red   .25   .25
504 A115a   10o blue ('61)   .25   .25
  a.   10o dark blue   .30
505 A97   15o dark red   .30   .25
506 A97   20o gray   .25   .25
507 A97   25o brown   .60   .25
508 A97   30o blue   .45   .25
509 A97   40o olive green   1.25   .25
510 A108   55o vermilion   1.25   .25
511 A108   70o orange   .60   .25
512 A108   80o yellow green   .80   .25

Perf. 12½ on 3 sides
513 A115a   5o red ('61)   .25   .25
  a.   Bklt. pane of 20 ('64)   2.00
  b.   5o dark red   5.00   1.00
  c.   Bklt. pane, 5 #513b, 5 #515   22.50
514 A115a   10o blue ('61)   .25   .25
  a.   10o dark blue   20.00   2.50
  b.   Bklt. pane, 5 #514a, 3 #517   37.50   18.00
515 A97   15o dark red   .60   .25
  a.   Bklt. pane of 20   12.00
516 A97   20o gray   1.00   .60
  a.   Bklt. pane of 20   30.00
517 A97   30o blue   .75   .25
  a.   Bklt. pane of 20   35.00
    Nos. 503-517 (15)   8.85   4.10

In the redrawn Numeral type A99, "Sverige, ore" and the "g" tail flourishes are white instead of in color.
Booklet pane including #513 is listed as #581b.
The booklet pane of 4, No. 514b, contains two copies of No. 517 which are imperf. on two adjoining sides. No. 514a was issued only in booklet pane No. 514b.
See Nos. 570, 580, 580a, 581b, 584b, 586b-586c, 666-667, 668a, 669b-669c.

Helicopter Mail Service — A116

Perf. 12½ Vertically
1958, Feb. 10   **Engr.**   **Unwmk.**
518 A116   30o blue   .40   .25
519 A116   1.40k brown   4.50   1.00

Perf. 12½ on 3 sides
520 A116   30o blue   .80   .55
  a.   Booklet pane of 20   20.00
    Nos. 518-520 (3)   1.70   1.80

10th anniversary of helicopter mail service to the Stockholm archipelago, Feb. 10.

Modern and 17th
Century
Vessels — A117

1958, Feb. 10   Perf. 12½ Vert.
521 A117 15o dark red   .40   .25
522 A117 40o gray olive   4.25 3.25
Perf. 12½ on 3 sides
523 A117 15o dark red   .50   .60
a.   Booklet pane of 20   12.00
     Nos. 521-523 (3)   5.15 4.10

3 centuries of transatlantic mail service.

Soccer
Player — A118

1958, May 8   Perf. 12½ Vert.
524 A118 15o vermilion   .85   .25
525 A118 20o yellow green   .50   .25
526 A118 1.20k dark blue   1.90 1.10
Perf. 12½ on 3 sides
527 A118 15o vermilion   .55   .45
a.   Booklet pane of 20   9.00
528 A118 20o yellow green   .50   .65
a.   Booklet pane of 20   12.00
     Nos. 524-528 (5)   4.30 2.70

Issued to publicize the 6th World Soccer
Championships, Stockholm, June 8-29.

Bessemer   Selma Lagerlof
Converter   A120
A119

Perf. 12½ Horizontally
1958, June 18   Engr.   Unwmk.
529 A119 30o gray blue   .35   .25
530 A119 1.70k dull red brown   3.00   .95
Perf. 12½ on 3 sides
531 A119 30o gray blue   .65   .55
a.   Booklet pane of 20   15.00
     Nos. 529-531 (3)   4.00 1.75

Centenary of the first successful Bessemer
blow in Sweden, July 18, 1858.

1958, Nov. 20   Perf. 12½ Horiz.
532 A120 20o dark red   .30   .30
533 A120 30o blue   .40   .25
534 A120 80o olive green   .75   .90
Perf. 12½ on 3 Sides
535 A120 20o dark red   .50   .75
a.   Booklet pane of 20   13.00
536 A120 30o blue   .50   .60
a.   Booklet pane of 20   16.00
     Nos. 532-536 (5)   2.45 2.80

Selma Lagerlof, writer, birth cent.

Palace Type of 1941
1958, Sept. 17   Perf. 12½ Vert.
537 A65 5k blue   2.75   .25

Electric Power   Hydroelectric Plant
Line — A121   and Dam — A122

Perf. 12½ Horiz. (H), Vert. (V)
1959, Jan. 20   Unwmk.
538 A121 30o ultra (H)   .45   .25
539 A122 90o carmine rose (V)   3.25 2.40

Perf. 12½ on 3 sides
540 A121 30o ultra   .50   .50
a.   Booklet pane of 20   14.00
     Nos. 538-540 (3)   4.20 3.15

50th anniv. of the establishment of the State
Power Board.

Verner von   Forest
Heidenstam   A124
A123

Perf. 12½ Horizontally
1959, July 6   Engr.   Unwmk.
541 A123 15o rose carmine   1.00   .35
542 A123 1k slate   3.00   .90
Perf. 12½ on 3 Sides
543 A123 15o rose carmine   .50   .95
a.   Booklet pane of 20   13.00
     Nos. 541-543 (3)   4.50 2.20

Verner von Heidenstam, poet, birth cent.

1959, Sept. 4   Perf. 12½ Horiz.
Design: 1.40k, Felling tree.
544 A124 30o green   1.50   .25
545 A124 1.40k brown red   3.50   .60
Perf. 12½ on 3 sides
546 A124 30o green   1.10 1.10
a.   Booklet pane of 20   29.00
     Nos. 544-546 (3)   6.10 1.95

Administration of crown lands and forests,
cent.

Svante   Anders Zorn
Arrhenius   A126
A125

Perf. 12½ Horizontally
1959, Dec. 10   Engr.   Unwmk.
547 A125 15o dull red brown   .25   .25
548 A125 1.70k dark blue   3.50   .45
Perf. 12½ on 3 sides
549 A125 15o dull red brown   .45   .60
a.   Booklet pane of 20   10.00
     Nos. 547-549 (3)   4.20 1.30

Arrhenius (1859-1927), chemist and
physicist.

1960, Feb. 18   Perf. 12½ Horiz.
550 A126 30o gray   .35   .25
551 A126 80o sepia   3.50 2.25
Perf. 12½ on 3 sides
552 A126 30o gray   1.60   .60
a.   Booklet pane of 20   35.00
     Nos. 550-552 (3)   5.45 3.10

Zorn (1860-1920), painter and sculptor.

Uprooted Oak   People of
Emblem   Various Races,
A127   WRY Emblem
                      A128

Perf. 12½ Vert. (V), Horiz. (H)
1960, Apr. 7   Engr.   Unwmk.
553 A127 20o red brown (V)   .25   .25
554 A128 40o purple (H)   .30   .30

Perf. 12½ on 3 sides
555 A127 20o red brown   .50   .60
a.   Booklet pane of 20   12.00
     Nos. 553-555 (3)   1.05 1.15

World Refugee Year, 7/1/59-6/30/60.

Target Shooting   Gustaf Froding
A129   A130

Design: 90o, Parade of riflemen.

1960, June 30   Perf. 12½ Vert.
556 A129 15o rose carmine   .30   .25
557 A129 90o grnsh blue   2.50 2.00
Perf. 12½ on 3 sides
558 A129 15o rose carmine   .35   .50
a.   Booklet pane of 20   9.00
     Nos. 556-558 (3)   3.15 2.75

Centenary of the founding of the Voluntary
Shooting Organization.

1960, Aug. 22   Perf. 12½ Horiz.
559 A130 30o red brown   .30   .25
560 A130 1.40k slate green   2.60   .45
Perf. 12½ on 3 sides
561 A130 30o red brown   .45   .35
a.   Booklet pane of 20   10.00
     Nos. 559-561 (3)   3.35 1.05

Gustaf Froding (1860-1911), poet.

Common Design Types
pictured following the introduction.

Europa Issue, 1960
Common Design Type
1960, Sept. 19   Perf. 12½ Vert.
Size: 27x21mm
562 CD3 40o blue   .25   .25
563 CD3 1k red   .80   .30

Hjalmar Branting
(1860-1925), Labor
Party Leader and
Prime
Minister — A131

Perf. 12½ Horiz.
1960, Nov. 23   Engr.
564 A131 15o rose carmine   .25   .25
565 A131 1.70k slate blue   3.00   .65
Perf. 12½ on 3 sides
566 A131 15o rose carmine   .45   .35
a.   Booklet pane of 20   4.50
     Nos. 564-566 (3)   3.70 1.25

SAS Issue

DC-8
Airliner — A131a

Perf. 12½ Vertically
1961, Feb. 24   Unwmk.
567 A131a 40o blue   .30   .35
Perf. 12½ on 3 sides
568 A131a 40o blue   1.00 1.25
a.   Booklet pane of 10   10.00

Scandinavian Airlines System, SAS, 10th
anniv.

Numeral Type of 1957, Three-Crown
Type of 1939 and

Gustaf VI   Rune Stone,
Adolf (Letters,   Oland, 11th
numerals in   Century
white)   A133
A132

1961-65   Perf. 12½ Vert.
570 A115a 15o green ('62)   .30   .25
571 A132 15o red   .35   .25
572 A132 20o gray   .35   .25
573 A132 25o brown   .65   .25
574 A132 30o ultra   1.50   .25
575 A132 30o lilac ('62)   .55   .25
576 A132 35o lilac   .55   .25
577 A132 35o ultra ('62)   1.10   .25
578 A132 40o emerald   1.00   .25
579 A132 50o gray grn ('62)   .65   .25
Perf. 12½ on 3 sides
580 A115a 15o grn ('65)   .30   .30
a.   Bklt. pane, 2 each #514, 580,
     583   2.25
581 A132 15o red   .25   .25
a.   Bklt. pane of 20   5.00
b.   Bklt. pane, 5 #513, 5 #581   2.50
582 A132 20o gray   1.25   .85
a.   Bklt. pane of 20   27.50
583 A132 25o brown ('62)   .35   .25
a.   Bklt. pane of 20   15.00
b.   Bklt. pane of 4   2.25
584 A132 30o ultra   .65   .25
a.   Bklt. pane of 20   15.00
b.   Bklt. pane, #514 + 3 #584   4.00
585 A132 30o lilac ('64)   .65   .50
a.   Bklt. pane of 20   14.00
586 A132 35o ultra ('62)   .55   .25
a.   Bklt. pane, 3 #514, 2 #586 +
     blank label   5.00 3.50
c.   As "b," inscribed label   3.50 1.50
Perf. 12½ Vertically
588 A56 1.05k Prus grn ('62)   1.10   .40
589 A56 1.50k brown ('62)   .80   .30
590 A56 2.15k dk sl grn ('62)   4.00   .80
591 A56 2.50k emerald   1.50   .25
Perf. 12½ on 3 sides
592 A133 10k dl red brn   20.00 .65
a.   Bklt. pane of 10 ('68)   250.00
b.   Bklt. pane of 20   850.00
     Nos. 570-592 (22)   38.40 7.55

Booklet panes of 4, 5 or 6 (Nos. 580a, 583b,
584b, 586b, 586c) contain two stamps which
are imperf. on two adjoining sides.

Combination panes (Nos. 580a, 581b, 584b,
586b, 586c) come in different arrangements of
the denominations.

The label of No. 586c is inscribed "ett brev /
betyder / sa / mycket" ("a letter means so
much"). The label inscription "nord 63 / 5-13
oktober / GÖTEBORG" was privately applied
to No. 586b by the Gothenburg Philatelic Society to raise funds for Nord 63 Philatelic Exhibition in Gothenburg. The pane was sold for the
equivalent of $1 US, 5 times face value.

See Nos. 648-654A, 666a, 668-672F.

K.-G. Pilo, Self-   Jonas Alstromer
portrait   A135
A134

1961, Apr. 17   Perf. 12½ Horiz.
594 A134 30o brown   .35   .25
595 A134 1.40k Prus blue   3.50 1.30
Perf. 12½ on 3 sides
596 A134 30o brown   1.10   .45
a.   Booklet pane of 20   30.00
     Nos. 594-596 (3)   4.95 2.00

Karl-Gustaf Pilo (1711-1793), painter. Self-
portrait from "The Coronation of Gustavus III."

1961, June 2   Perf. 12½ Vert.
597 A135 15o dull claret   .25   .25
598 A135 90o grnsh blue   1.60 2.25

Perf. 12½ on 3 sides

599	A135	15o dull claret	.25	.40
a.		Booklet pane of 20	7.00	
		Nos. 597-599 (3)	2.10	2.90

200th anniversary of the birth of Jonas Alstromer, pioneer of agriculture and industry.

17th Century Printer and Student in Library — A136

Perf. 12½ Vert.

1961, Sept. 22   Engr.

600	A136	20o dark red	.30	.30
601	A136	1k blue	7.00	1.60

Perf. 12½ on 3 sides

602	A136	20o dark red	.30	.55
a.		Booklet pane of 20	7.00	
		Nos. 600-602 (3)	7.60	2.45

300th anniversary of the regulation requiring copies of all Swedish printed works to be deposited in the Royal Library.

Roentgen, Prudhomme, von Behring, van't Hoff — A137

1961, Dec. 9   **Perf. 12½ Vertically**

603	A137	20o vermilion	.25	.25
604	A137	40o blue	.25	.25
605	A137	50o green	.50	.25

Perf. 12½ on 3 sides

606	A137	20o vermilion	.25	.25
a.		Booklet pane of 20	6.00	
		Nos. 603-606 (4)	1.25	1.00

Winners of the 1901 Nobel Prize; Wilhelm K. Roentgen, Rene Sully Prudhomme, Emil von Behring, Jacob van't Hoff.
See Nos. 617-619, 637-639, 673-676, 689-692, 710-713, 769-772, 804-807.

A138   A139

Footsteps and postmen's badges.

1962, Jan. 29 Engr. Perf. 12½ Vert.

607	A138	30o lilac	.40	.25
608	A138	1.70k rose red	3.50	.65

Perf. 12½ on 3 sides

609	A138	30o lilac	.50	.50
a.		Booklet pane of 20	11.00	
		Nos. 607-609 (3)	4.40	1.40

Local mail delivery service in Sweden, cent.

1962, Mar. 21   **Perf. 12½ Horiz.**

Voting Tool (Budkavle), Codex of Law and Gavel

610	A139	30o dark blue	.35	.25
611	A139	2k red	4.50	.35

Perf. 12½ on 3 sides

612	A139	30o dark blue	.40	.45
a.		Booklet pane of 20	10.50	
		Nos. 610-612 (3)	5.25	1.05

Centenary of the municipal reform laws.

St. George, Great Church, Stockholm   Skokloster Castle
A140   A141

Perf. 12½ Horiz. (H), Vert. (V)

1962, Sept. 24

613	A140	20o rose lake (H)	.25	.25
614	A141	50o dk slate grn (V)	.55	.35

Perf. 12½ on 3 sides

615	A140	20o rose lake	.25	.30
a.		Booklet pane of 20	6.00	
616	A141	50o dk slate grn	1.00	1.25
a.		Booklet pane of 10	10.00	
		Nos. 613-616 (4)	2.05	2.15

Nobel Prize Winners Type of 1961

Designs: 25o, Theodor Mommsen and Sir Ronald Ross. 50o, Hermann Emil Fischer, Pieter Zeeman and Hendrik Antoon Lorentz.

1962, Dec. 10   **Perf. 12½ Vert.**

617	A137	25o dark red	.30	.30
618	A137	50o blue	.40	.40

Perf. 12½ on 3 sides

619	A142	25o dark red	.40	.65
a.		Booklet pane of 20	10.00	
		Nos. 617-619 (3)	1.10	1.35

Winners of the 1902 Nobel Prize.

Ice Hockey — A143

1963, Feb. 15   **Perf. 12½ Horiz.**

620	A143	25o green	.40	.30
621	A143	1.70k violet bl	3.00	.85

Perf. 12½ on 3 sides

622	A143	25o green	.35	.65
a.		Booklet pane of 20	7.00	
		Nos. 620-622 (3)	3.75	1.80

1963 Ice Hockey World Championships.

Wheat Emblem and Stylized Hands — A144

1963, Mar. 21   **Perf. 12½ Vertically**

623	A144	35o lilac rose	.35	.25
624	A144	50o violet	.30	.25

Perf. 12½ on 3 sides

625	A144	35o lilac rose	.30	.40
a.		Booklet pane of 20	6.00	
		Nos. 623-625 (3)	.95	1.00

FAO "Freedom from Hunger" campaign.

Engineering and Industry Symbols — A145

1963, May 27   **Perf. 12½ Vertically**

626	A145	50o gray	.50	.35
627	A145	1.05k orange	3.25	3.00

Perf. 12½ on 3 sides

628	A145	50o gray	2.60	2.75
a.		Booklet pane of 10	27.50	
		Nos. 626-628 (3)	6.35	6.10

Gregoire François Du Reitz — A146

Perf. 12½ Vertically

1963, Sept. 16   Engr.   Unwmk.

629	A146	25o brown	.40	.45
630	A146	35o dark blue	.30	.25
631	A146	2k dark red	4.00	.55

Perf. 12½ on 3 sides

632	A146	25o brown	.65	.75
a.		Booklet pane of 20	16.00	
633	A146	35o dark blue	.40	.30
a.		Booklet pane of 20	10.00	
		Nos. 629-633 (5)	5.75	2.30

300th anniversary of the Swedish Board of Health. Dr. Du Rietz (1607-1682) was first

president of the "Collegium Medicorum," fore-runner of the Board of Health.

Hammarby, Home of Carl von Linné (Linnaeus) A147

1963, Oct. 25   **Perf. 12½ Vert.**

634	A147	20o orange red	.30	.25
635	A147	50o yellow grn	.30	.25

Perf. 12½ on 3 sides

636	A147	20o orange red	.30	.35
a.		Booklet pane of 20	6.00	
		Nos. 634-636 (3)	.90	.85

Nobel Prize Winners Type of 1961

Designs: 25o, Svante Arrhenius, Niels Finsen, Bjornstjerne Bjornson. 50o, Antoine Henri Becquerel, Pierre and Marie Curie.

Perf. 12½ Vertically

1963, Dec. 10   Engr.   Unwmk.

637	A137	25o gray olive	.75	.70
638	A137	50o chocolate	.40	.50

Perf. 12½ on 3 sides

639	A137	25o gray olive	.75	1.10
a.		Booklet pane of 20	16.00	
		Nos. 637-639 (3)	1.90	2.30

Winners of the 1903 Nobel Prize.

A149   A150

"The Assumption of Elijah."

1964, Feb. 3   **Perf. 12½ Horiz.**

640	A149	35o lt ultra	.65	.25
641	A149	1.05k dull red	3.75	3.75

Perf. 12½ on 3 sides

642	A149	35o lt ultra	.45	.35
a.		Booklet pane of 20	10.00	
		Nos. 640-642 (3)	4.85	4.35

Erik Axel Karlfeldt (1864-1931), poet.

1964, June 12   **Perf. 12½ Horiz.**

Seal of Archbishop Stephen.

643	A150	40o slate green	.30	.30
644	A150	60o orange brown	.30	.35

Perf. 12½ Vertically

645	A150	40o slate green	.30	.30
a.		Booklet pane of 20	3.50	
646	A150	60o orange brown	.35	.55
a.		Booklet pane of 10	4.00	
		Nos. 643-646 (4)	1.25	1.50

800th anniv. of the Archbishopric of Uppsala.

Types of Regular Issues, 1939-61, and

Post Horns — A151   Ship Grave, Skane (Bronze Age) — A152

1964-71   Engr.   **Perf. 12½ Vert.**

647	A151	20o sl bl & org yel ('65)	.25	.25
648	A132	35o gray	.60	.25
649	A132	40o ultra	.60	.25
650	A132	45o orange	.60	.25
651	A132	45o violet bl ('67)	.60	.25
652	A132	50o green ('68)	.55	.25
652A	A132	55o dark red ('69)	.40	.25
653	A132	60o rose car	.65	.65
653A	A132	65o dull grn ('71)	.80	.25
654	A132	70o lil rose ('67)	.50	.25
654A	A132	85o dp cl ('71)	.80	.30
655	A108	95o violet	3.00	4.00

656	A56	1.20k lt blue	3.50	3.50
657	A56	1.80k dk blue ('67)	1.25	.50
658	A56	1.85k blue ('67)	3.00	1.00
659	A56	2k dp car ('69)	.75	.25
660	A56	2.30k choc ('65)	5.50	.25
661	A56	2.55k red	2.10	2.60
662	A56	2.80k red ('67)	1.40	.25
663	A56	2.85k orange ('65)	2.75	4.00
664	A56	3k brt ultra	1.40	.25
665	A152	3.50k grnsh gray ('66)	1.50	.25

Perf. 12½ on 3 Sides

666	A115a	10o brown	.25	.25
a.		Bklt. pane, 2 each #666, 667, 583	3.00	
667	A115a	15o brown	.50	.80
668	A132	30o rose red ('66)	.85	.85
a.		Bklt. pane, 2 each #513, 580, 668	1.40	
b.		Perf. on 3 sides	1.10	1.10

No. 668 is perf. on 2 adjoining sides.

669	A132	40o ultra	.25	.25
a.		Bklt. pane of 20	16.00	
b.		Bklt. pane, 2 ea #514, 669	1.50	
c.		Bklt. pane, 2 each #513-514, 580, 668b-669	4.00	
670	A132	45o org ('67)	.65	.25
a.		Bklt. pane of 20	14.00	
671	A132	45o vio bl ('67)	.70	.25
a.		Bklt. pane of 20	14.00	
672	A132	50o green ('69)	.50	.60
a.		Bklt. pane of 10	5.00	
672B	A132	55o dk red ('69)	.50	.25
a.		Bklt. pane of 10	5.00	
672D	A132	65o dull grn ('71)	.85	.50
a.		Bklt. pane of 10	9.00	
672F	A132	85o dp cl ('71)	.90	1.25
a.		Bklt. pane of 10	9.50	
		Nos. 647-672F (32)	38.45	25.30

Some combination booklet panes of 4, 6 or 10 contain two stamps which are imperf. on two adjoining sides. Combination panes come in different arrangements of the denominations.

Fluorescent Paper

Starting in 1967, fluorescent paper was used in printing both definitive and commemorative issues. Its use was gradually eliminated starting in 1976. Numerous definitives and a few commemoratives were printed on both ordinary and fluorescent paper.

Nobel Prize Winners Type of 1961

30o, José Echegaray y Eizaguirre, Frédéric Mistral and John William Strutt, Lord Rayleigh. 40o, Sir William Ramsey and Ivan Petrovich Pavlov.

Perf. 12½ Vertically

1964, Dec. 10   Engr.

673	A137	30o blue	.45	.45
674	A137	40o red	.70	.25

Perf. 12½ on 3 Sides

675	A137	30o blue	.45	.75
a.		Booklet pane of 20	12.00	
676	A137	40o red	.75	.35
a.		Booklet pane of 20	18.00	
		Nos. 673-676 (4)	2.35	1.80

Winners of the 1904 Nobel Prize.

Visby Town Wall A154   Antenna A155

1965, Apr. 5   **Perf. 12½ Horiz.**

677	A154	30o dk car rose	.30	.25
678	A154	2k brt ultra	4.25	.35

Perf. 12½ on 3 Sides

679	A154	30o dk car rose	.40	.35
a.		Booklet pane of 20	9.00	
		Nos. 677-679 (3)	4.95	.95

1965, May 17   **Perf. 12½ Horiz.**

680	A155	60o lilac	.45	.45
681	A155	1.40k bluish blk	2.25	1.90

Perf. 12½ on 3 Sides

682	A155	60o lilac	1.10	1.60
a.		Booklet pane of 10	12.50	
		Nos. 680-682 (3)	3.80	3.95

Centenary of the ITU.

Prince Eugen — A156

1965, July 5   *Perf. 12½ Horiz.*
683 A156 40o black   .25 .25
684 A156 1k brown   2.10 .35

Perf. 12½ on 3 Sides
685 A156 40o black   .25 .25
a.   Booklet pane of 20   7.00
   Nos. 683-685 (3)   2.60 .85

Prince Eugen (1865-1947), painter and patron of the arts.

Fredrika Bremer (1801-65), Novelist — A157

Perf. 12½ Vertically
1965, Oct. 25   Engr.
686 A157 25o violet   .25 .25
687 A157 3k gray green   4.00 .35

Perf. 12½ on 3 Sides
688 A157 25o violet   .25 .25
a.   Booklet pane of 20   5.00
   Nos. 686-688 (3)   4.50 .85

Nobel Prize Winners Type of 1961
30o, Philipp von Lenard, Adolf von Baeyer. 40o, Robert Koch, Henryk Sienkiewicz.

Perf. 12½ Vertically
1965, Dec. 10   Unwmk.
689 A137 30o ultra   .35 .45
690 A137 40o dark red   .40 .25

Perf. 12½ on 3 Sides
691 A137 30o ultra   .45 .75
a.   Booklet pane of 20   11.00
692 A137 40o dark red   .85 .30
a.   Booklet pane of 20   19.00
   Nos. 689-692 (4)   2.05 1.75

Winners of the 1905 Nobel Prize.

Nathan Soderblom A158   Speed Skater A159

1966, Jan. 15   *Perf. 12½ Horiz.*
693 A158 60o brown   .35 .25
694 A158 80o green   .85 .25

Perf. 12½ on 3 Sides
695 A158 60o brown   .75 .90
a.   Booklet pane of 10   8.00
   Nos. 693-695 (3)   1.95 1.40

Nathan Soderblom (1866-1931), Protestant theologian, who worked for the union of Christian churches and received 1930 Nobel Peace Prize.

Perf. 12½ on 3 Sides
1966, Feb. 18   Engr.
696 A159 5o rose red   .25 .25
697 A159 25o slate green   .25 .25
698 A159 40o dark blue   .35 .70
a.   Bklt. pane, 4 ea #696-697, 2 #698   2.25
   Nos. 696-698 (3)   .85 1.20

World Speed Skating Championships for Men, Gothenburg, Feb. 18-20, and 75th anniversary of World Skating Championships.

National Museum, Staircase, 1866 — A160   Baron Louis Gerhard De Geer — A161

1966, Mar. 26   *Perf. 12½ Vert.*
699 A160 30o violet   .25 .25
a.   Booklet pane of 10   2.50
700 A160 2.30k olive green   1.40 1.75
a.   Booklet pane of 10   13.00

National Gallery, Blasieholmen, Stockholm, cent. The design is from an 1866 woodcut showing the inauguration of the Museum.

1966, May 12   *Perf. 12½ Vertically*
701 A161 40o dark blue   .25 .25
702 A161 3k brown carmine   3.75 .65

Perf. 12½ on 3 Sides
703 A161 40o dark blue   .25 .35
a.   Booklet pane of 20   8.00
   Nos. 701-703 (3)   4.25 1.25

Cent. of the reform of the Representative Assembly under the leadership of Minister of Justice (1858-70) Baron Louis Gerhard De Geer (1818-96).

Stage, Drottningholm Court Theater — A162   Almqvist and Wild Rose — A163

Perf. 12½ on 3 Sides
1966, June 15   Engr.
Salmon Paper
704 A162 5o vermilion   .25 .25
705 A162 25o olive bister   .25 .25
706 A162 40o dark purple   .40 .65
a.   Bklt. pane, 4 ea #704-705, 2 #706   2.00
   Nos. 704-706 (3)   .90 1.15

Drottningholm Court Theater, 200th anniv.

Perf. 12½ Horizontally
1966, Sept. 26   Engr.
707 A163 25o magenta   .25 .25
708 A163 1k green   2.25 .30

Perf. 12½ on 3 Sides
709 A163 25o magenta   .25 .25
a.   Booklet pane of 20   4.75
   Nos. 707-709 (3)   2.75 .80

Carl Jonas Love Almqvist (1793-1866), writer and poet.

Nobel Prize Winner Type of 1961
Designs: 30o, Joseph John Thomson and Giosue Carducci. 40o, Henri Moissan, Camillo Golgi and Santiago Ramon y Cajal.

Perf. 12½ Vertically
1966, Dec. 10   Engr.
710 A137 30o rose lake   .55 .25
711 A137 40o dark green   .50 .25

Perf. 12½ on 3 Sides
712 A137 30o rose lake   .55 .45
a.   Booklet pane of 20   11.00
713 A137 40o dark green   .55 .45
a.   Booklet pane of 20   12.00
   Nos. 710-713 (4)   2.15 1.40

Winners of the 1906 Nobel Prize.

Field Ball Player A164   EFTA Emblem A165

1967, Jan. 12   *Perf. 12½ Horiz.*
714 A164 45o dk violet blue   .25 .25
715 A164 2.70k dp rose lilac   2.75 1.50

Perf. 12½ on 3 Sides
716 A164 45o dk violet blue   .25 .30
a.   Booklet pane of 20   6.00
   Nos. 714-716 (3)   3.25 2.05

World Field Ball Championships, Jan. 12-21.

1967, Feb. 15   *Perf. 12½ Horiz.*
717 A165 70o orange   .45 .40

Perf. 12½ on 3 Sides
718 A165 70o orange   1.10 1.25
a.   Booklet pane of 10   15.00

European Free Trade Association. Tariffs were abolished Dec. 31, 1966, among EFTA members: Austria, Denmark, Finland, Great Britain, Norway, Portugal, Sweden, Switzerland.

"The Fjeld," by Sixten Lundbohm A166   Lion Fortress, Gothenburg A167

Uppsala Cathedral A168   Gripsholm Castle A169

1967   Engr.   *Perf. 12½ Vert.*
719 A166 35o dl bl & blk brn   .25 .25

Perf. 12½ Horiz.
720 A167 3.70k violet   2.10 .25
721 A168 4.50k dull red   2.40 .25

Perf. 12½ Vert.
722 A169 7k vio bl & rose red   3.25 .55

Perf. 12½ on 3 Sides
723 A166 35o dl bl & blk brn   .25 .25
a.   Booklet pane of 10   2.50
   Nos. 719-723 (5)   8.25 1.55

Issued: #719, 721, 723, 3/15; #720, 2/15; #722, 4/11.

Table Tennis — A170

1967, Apr. 11   *Perf. 12½ Horiz.*
724 A170 35o bright magenta   .30 .25
725 A170 90o greenish blue   1.30 .50

Perf. 12½ on 3 Sides
726 A170 35o bright magenta   .35 .40
a.   Booklet pane of 20   7.00
   Nos. 724-726 (3)   1.95 1.15

World Table Tennis Championships, Stockholm.

Man with Axe and Fettered Beast — A171   Double Mortise Corner — A172

Designs: 15o, Man fighting two bears. 30o, Warrior disguised as wolf pursuing enemy. 35o, Two warriors with swords and lances. The designs are taken from 6th century bronze plates (1¾in. x 2½in.) used to decorate helmets; now in Swedish Museum of National Antiquities.

Perf. 12½ on 3 Sides
1967, May 17   Engr.
727 A171 10o dk brown & dp bl   .25 .25
728 A171 15o dp blue & dk brn   .25 .25
729 A171 30o brt pink & dk brn   .25 .25
730 A171 35o dk brown & brt pink   .25 .25
a.   Bklt. pane, 4 #727, 2 ea #728-730   2.10 2.75
   Nos. 727-730 (4)   1.00 1.00

Lithographed and Photogravure
1967, June 16   *Perf. 12½*
731 A172 10o olive & multi   .25 .25
732 A172 35o dk blue multi   .25 .25
a.   Bklt. pane, 6 #731, 4 #732   1.75 2.00

Issued to honor generations of Finnish settlers in Sweden.

Right-hand Driving as Seen Through Windshield — A173

1967, Sept. 2   Engr.   *Perf. 12½ Vert.*
733 A173 35o dp bl, ocher & blk   .30 .35
734 A173 45o yel grn, ocher & blk   .35 .45

Perf. 12½ Horiz.
735 A173 35o dp bl, ocher & blk   .30 .45
a.   Booklet pane of 10   3.00
736 A173 45o yel grn, ocher & blk   .25 .25
a.   Booklet pane of 10   2.50
   Nos. 733-736 (4)   1.20 1.50

Issued to publicize the introduction of right-hand driving in Sweden, Sept. 3, 1967.

Postrider A174   The Prodigal Son, 13th cent., Rada Church A174a

Griffin A174b   Rocky Isles in Bloom, by Harald Lindberg A175

Dalsland Canal — A176

Log roller — A176a

Gothenburg Harbor — A176b

Horse-drawn timber sled — A176c

Nils Holgersson Riding Wild Goose — A176d

Windmills, Ölana Island — A176e

Steamer Storskar and Royal Palace, Stockholm A176f

Elk — A177   Roe deer — A177a

Dancing cranes — A177b

Mail Coach, by Eigil Schwab A177c

Illustration from Lapponia, by Johannes Schefferus — A177d

Blood-money Coins and Old Map of Sweden A177e

Great Seal, 1439 (St. Erik with Banner and Shield) — A177f

10o, Merchant vessel in Oresund, 1661. 20o, St. Stephen as a boy tending horses, medallion from Dädesio Church. #742, Lion, from Grodinge tapestry, 15th cent. 2.55k, Seal of Magnus Ladulas, 1285 (King Magnus Birgersson on throne with lily scepter and orb). 3k, Seal of Duke Erik Magnusson, 1306 (Duke on horseback with standard of Folkunga dynasty). 6k, Gustavus Vasa's silver daler.

1967-72   Perf. 12½ Horiz. or Vert.

737	A174	5o red & blk	.25	.25
738	A174	10o blue & blk	.25	.25
739	A174a	15o sl grn, *grnsh* ('71)	.25	.25
740	A174	20o sep, buff ('70)	.25	.25
741	A174b	25o bis & blk ('71)	.25	.25
742	A174b	25o blk & bis ('71)	.25	.25
a.		Pair, #741-742	.40	.50
743	A175	30o ultra & ver	.25	.25
744	A176	40o blk, dk grn & ultra ('68)	.30	.25
745	A176a	45o bl & brn blk ('70)	.30	.25
746	A176b	55o bl & vio, vert. ('71)	.40	.25
747	A176c	60o black brn ('71)	.30	.25
747A	A176d	65o brt blue ('71)	.30	.25
748	A176e	75o slate grn ('71)	.30	.25
749	A176f	80o blue & blk ('71)	.40	.25
750	A177	90o sep & bl gray	.55	.25
750A	A177a	95o sepia ('72)	.40	.25
751	A177b	1k slate grn ('68)	.55	.25
751A	A177c	1.20k multi ('71)	.65	.25
751B	A177d	1.40k lt bl & red ('72)	.75	.25
752	A177f	2.55k brt blue ('70)	1.25	.65
753	A177f	3k dk gray bl ('70)	1.25	.25
754	A177e	4k black ('71)	1.60	.25
755	A177f	5k Prus grn ('70)	2.00	.25
755A	A177e	6k indigo ('72)	3.00	.25

Perf. 12½ on 3 Sides, 12½ Horiz. (#761)

756	A174	5o red & blk	.25	.25
a.		Booklet pane of 20	.75	
757	A174	10o bl & blk ('69)	.25	.25
a.		Booklet pane of 20	2.10	
758	A175	30o ultra & ver	.30	.30
a.		Booklet pane of 10	3.25	
759	A176	40o blk, dk grn & ultra ('68)	.25	.30
a.		Booklet pane of 10	2.75	
760	A176a	45o bl & brn blk ('70)	.25	.25
a.		Booklet pane of 10	2.75	
761	A176b	55o bl & vio ('71)	.35	.25
a.		Booklet pane of 10	3.50	
762	A176d	65o brt blue ('71)	.40	.40
a.		Booklet pane of 10	4.00	
763	A176e	75o slate grn ('72)	.50	.25
a.		Booklet pane of 10	5.50	
764	A177	90o sepia & bl gray	1.00	1.00
a.		Booklet pane of 10	10.00	
		Nos. 737-764 (33)	19.60	9.65

King Gustaf VI Adolf — A178

Perf. 12½ Horiz.

1967, Nov. 11   Engr.

765	A178	45o lt ultra	.30	.25
766	A178	70o green	.30	.30

Perf. 12½ on 3 Sides

767	A178	45o lt ultra	.25	.25
a.		Booklet pane of 20	4.50	
768	A178	70o green	.65	.95
a.		Booklet pane of 10	6.50	
		Nos. 765-768 (4)	1.50	1.75

85th birthday of King Gustaf VI Adolf.

Nobel Prize Winners Type of 1961

35o, Eduard Buchner (Chemistry), Albert A. Michelson (Physics). 45o, Charles L. A. Laveran (Medicine), Rudyard Kipling (Literature).

1967, Dec. 9   Perf. 12½ Vert.

769	A137	35o vermilion	.65	.50
770	A137	45o dark blue	.55	.25

Perf. 12½ on 3 Sides

771	A142	35o vermilion	.70	.95
a.		Booklet pane of 10	7.50	

772	A142	45o dark blue	.45	.50
a.		Booklet pane of 10	6.50	
		Nos. 769-772 (4)	2.35	2.20

Winners of the 1907 Nobel Prize.

Franz Berwald, Violin and His Music — A179

1968, Apr. 3   Perf. 12½ Horiz.

773	A179	35o black & red	.35	.25
774	A179	2k blk, vio bl & org yel	3.00	.80

Perf. 12½ on 3 Sides

775	A179	35o black & red	.45	.60
a.		Booklet pane of 10	4.50	
		Nos. 773-775 (3)	3.80	1.65

Franz Berwald (1796-1868), composer. Design includes opening bar of overture to his opera, "The Queen of Golconda."

National Bank Seal — A180

Perf. 12½ Vertically

1968, May 15   Engr.

776	A180	45o dull blue	.25	.25
777	A180	70o black, *pink*	.30	.35

Perf. 12½ on 3 Sides

778	A180	45o dull blue	.35	.50
a.		Booklet pane of 10	4.00	
779	A180	70o black, *pink*	.55	.85
a.		Booklet pane of 10	6.50	
		Nos. 776-779 (4)	1.45	1.95

300th anniv. of the National Bank of Sweden. Nos. 777, 779 are on non-fluorescent paper.

Seal of Lund University — A181   Butterfly Orchid — A182

1968, June 4   Perf. 12½ on 3 sides

780	A181	10o deep blue	.25	.25
781	A181	35o red	.30	.50
a.		Bklt. pane, 6 #780, 4 #781	2.25	2.75

300th anniversary of University of Lund.

1968, June 4

Nordic Wild Flowers: No. 783, Wood anemone. No. 784, Dog rose. No. 785, Prune Cherry. No. 786, Lily of the valley.

782	A182	45o slate green	.90	.55
783	A182	45o gray green	.90	.55
784	A182	45o sl grn & rose car	.90	.55
785	A182	45o gray green	.90	.55
786	A182	45o slate green	.90	.55
a.		Bklt. pane, 2 each #782-786	11.00	
		Nos. 782-786 (5)	4.50	2.75

World Council of Churches' Emblem A183   Electron Orbits A184

1968, July 4   Perf. 12½ Horiz.

787	A183	70o plum	.55	.60
788	A183	90o Prus green	1.00	.50

Perf. 12½ on 3 Sides

789	A183	70o plum	.65	.95
a.		Booklet pane of 10	7.50	
		Nos. 787-789 (3)	2.20	2.05

4th General Assembly of the World Council of Churches, Uppsala, July 4-19.

Perf. 12½ Horizontally

1968, Aug. 9   Engr.

790	A184	45o rose carmine	.55	.25
791	A184	2k dark blue	2.90	.40

Perf. 12½ on 3 Sides

792	A184	45o rose carmine	.50	.45
a.		Booklet pane of 10	5.00	
		Nos. 790-792 (3)	3.95	1.10

Establishment of the 1st 3 People's Colleges, cent.

"Orienteer" Finding Way through Forest — A185   "Fingerkrok" by Axel Petersson — A186

Perf. 12½ Horizontally

1968, Sept. 5   Engr.

793	A185	40o violet & red brn	.35	.45
794	A185	2.80k green & violet	3.00	3.00

Perf. 12½ on 3 Sides

795	A185	40o violet & red brn	.40	.65
a.		Booklet pane of 10	5.00	
		Nos. 793-795 (3)	3.75	4.05

Issued to publicize the World Championships in Orienteering, Linkoping, Sept. 28-29.

Perf. 12½ on 3 Sides

1968, Oct. 28   Engr.

796	A186	5o green	.25	.25
797	A186	25o sepia	1.40	1.10
798	A186	45o blk brn & red brn	.25	.25
a.		Bklt. pane, 3 #796, 2 #797, 3 #798	3.00	
		Nos. 796-798 (3)	1.90	1.60

Axel Petersson, called "Doderhultarn" (1868-1925), sculptor.

Black-backed Gull — A187

Designs: No. 799, Varying hare. No. 801, Red fox. No. 802, Hooded crows harassing golden eagle. No. 803, Weasel.

Perf. 12½ on 3 Sides

1968, Nov. 9   Engr.

799	A187	30o blue	.65	.80
800	A187	30o black	.65	.80
801	A187	30o dark brown	.65	.80
802	A187	30o black	.65	.80
803	A187	30o blue	.65	.80
a.		Bklt. pane, 2 each #799-803	6.50	
		Nos. 799-803 (5)	3.25	4.00

See Nos. 873-877.

Nobel Prize Winners Type of 1961

35o, Elie Metchnikoff, Paul Ehrlich, Ernest Rutherford. 45o, Gabriel Lippmann, Rudolf Eucken.

1968, Dec. 10   Perf. 12½ Vertically

804	A137	35o maroon	.55	.50
805	A137	45o dark green	.50	.25

Perf. 12½ on 3 Sides

806	A137	35o maroon	.50	1.15
a.		Booklet pane of 10	6.00	
807	A137	45o dark green	.45	.50
a.		Booklet pane of 10	5.00	
		Nos. 804-807 (4)	2.00	2.40

Nordic Cooperation Issue

Five Ancient Ships — A187a

1969, Feb. 28 Engr. *Perf. 12½ Vert.*
808 A187a 45o dark gray .35 .35
809 A187a 70o blue .55 .90

Perf. 12½ on 3 Sides
810 A187a 45o dark gray .50 .85
a. Booklet pane of 10 11.00
  Nos. 808-810 (3) 1.40 2.10

50th anniv. of the Nordic Society and centenary of postal cooperation among the northern countries. The design is taken from a coin found at the site of Birka, an ancient Swedish town. See also Denmark Nos. 454-455, Finland No. 481, Iceland Nos. 404-405 and Norway Nos. 523-524.

Worker, by Albin Amelin — A188

Perf. 12½ Horiz.
1969, Mar. 31 Engr.
811 A188 55o dk carmine rose .45 .25
812 A188 70o dk blue .70 .65

Perf. 12½ on 3 Sides
813 A188 55o dk carmine rose .35 .25
a. Booklet pane of 10 4.00
  Nos. 811-813 (3) 1.50 1.15

50th anniv. of the ILO.

Europa Issue, 1969
Common Design Type
1969, Apr. 28 Photo. *Perf. 14 Vert.*
Size: 27x22mm
814 CD12 70o orange & multi 1.50 .45
815 CD12 1k vio blue & multi 1.00 .40

Perf. 14 on 3 Sides
816 CD12 70o orange & multi 1.50 2.00
a. Booklet pane of 10 17.50
  Nos. 814-816 (3) 4.00 2.85

Not fluorescent.

Albert Engstrom with Owl, Self-portrait A189

1969, May 12 Engr. *Perf. 12½ Vert.*
817 A189 35o black brown .30 .25
818 A189 55o blue gray .30 .25

Perf. 12½ on 3 Sides
819 A189 35o black brown .35 .55
a. Booklet pane of 10 3.50
820 A189 55o blue gray .30 .30
a. Booklet pane of 10 3.00
  Nos. 817-820 (4) 1.25 1.35

Albert Engstrom (1869-1940), cartoonist.

Souvenir Sheet

Paintings by Ivan Agueli — A190

1969, June 6 Litho. *Perf. 13½*
821 A190 Sheet of 6 2.50 4.25
a. 45o Landscape .40 .45
b. 45o Still life .40 .45
c. 45o Near East town .40 .45
d. 55o Young woman .40 .45
e. 55o Sunny landscape .40 .45
f. 55o Street at night .40 .45

Ivan Agueli (1869-1917), painter. Size: #821a-821c, 35x28mm. #821d-821e, 28x44mm. #821f, 48x44mm. Not fluorescent.

Tjorn Bridges — A191

Designs: 15o, 30o, Various bridges.

Perf. 12½ on 3 Sides
1969, Sept. 3 Engr.
Size: 20x19mm
Bluish Paper
822 A191 15o deep blue 1.10 .45
823 A191 30o dk grn & blk 1.10 .45
Size: 41x19mm
824 A191 55o blk & dp bl 1.10 .45
a. Bklt. pane, 2 each #822-824 8.00
  Nos. 822-824 (3) 3.30 1.35

Tjorn highway bridges connecting the Islands of Orust and Tjorn in the Gothenburg Archipelago with the mainland.

Man's Head, Woodcarving — A192

Warship Wasa, 1628 — A193

Designs: No. 826, Crowned lion. No. 827, Great Swedish coat of arms. No. 828, Lion, front view. No. 829, Man's head (different from No. 825).

1969, Sept. 3 *Perf. 12½ on 3 Sides*
825 A192 55o dark red .40 .25
826 A192 55o brown .40 .25
827 A193 55o dark blue .60 .70
828 A192 55o brown .40 .25
829 A192 55o dark red .40 .25
830 A193 55o dark blue .60 .70
a. Bklt. pane, #827, #830, 2 each #825-826, 828-829 5.50
  Nos. 825-830 (6) 2.80 2.40

Salvaging in 1961 of the warship Wasa, sunk on her maiden voyage, Aug. 10, 1628.

Soderberg A194   Bo Bergman A195

Perf. 12½ Horiz.
1969, Oct. 13 Engr.
831 A194 45o brown, *buff* .40 .30

Perf. 12½ Vert.
832 A195 55o green, *grnsh* .40 .25

Perf. 12½ on 3 Sides
833 A194 45o brown, *buff* .50 .85
a. Booklet pane of 10 5.00
834 A195 55o green, *grnsh* .25 .40
a. Booklet pane of 10 4.00
  Nos. 831-834 (4) 1.55 1.80

Hjalmar Soderberg (1869-1941), writer; Bo Bergman (1869-1967), poet.

Lever Light, Lightship, Landsort and Svenska Lighthouses — A196

Perf. 12½ Vert.
1969, Nov. 17 Photo.
835 A196 30o gray, blk & pink .25 .25
836 A196 55o lt bl, blk & brn .35 .25

300th anniversary of Swedish lighthouses.

Pelle's New Suit — A197

The Adventures of Nils — A198

Swedish Fairy Tales: No. 839, Pippi Longstocking (little girl, horse and monkey). No. 840, Vill-Vallareman (boy blowing horn). No. 841, Kattresan (child riding on back of cat).

Perf. 12½ on 3 Sides
1969, Nov. 17 Engr.
837 A197 35o org, red & dk brn 1.60 1.60
838 A198 35o dark brown 1.60 1.60
839 A197 35o org, red & dk brn 1.60 1.60
840 A198 35o dark brown 1.60 1.60
841 A197 35o org, red & dk brn 1.60 1.60
a. Bklt. pane, 2 each #837-841 20.00 22.50
  Nos. 837-841 (5) 8.00 8.00

Issued for use in Christmas cards.

Dr. Emil T. Kocher and Wilhelm Ostwald — A199

55o, Selma Lagerlof, open book. 70o, Guglielmo Marconi, Carl Ferdinand Braun.

1969, Dec. 10 *Perf. 12½ Vert.*
842 A199 45o dull green .75 .35
843 A199 55o blk, *pale sal* .60 .25
844 A199 70o black .75 1.25

Perf. 12½ on 3 Sides
845 A199 45o dull green .45 .55
a. Booklet pane of 10 5.00
846 A199 55o blk, *pale sal* .40 .30
a. Booklet pane of 10 4.50
  Nos. 842-846 (5) 2.95 2.70

Winners of the 1909 Nobel Prize.

Weather Vane, Soderala Church A200   Door with Iron Fittings, Bjorksta Church, Vastmanland A201

Swedish Art Forgings: 10o, like 5o, facing right. 30o, Memorial cross, Ekshärad churchyard, Varmland.

Perf. 12½ on 3 sides
1970, Feb. 9 Engr.
847 A200 5o slate grn & brn .30 .25
848 A200 10o slate grn & brn .30 .25
849 A200 30o blk & slate grn .30 .25

Perf. 12½ Vert.
850 A201 55o brn & slate grn .30 .25
a. Bklt. pane, 2 each #847-850 2.00 3.75
  Nos. 847-850 (4) 1.20 1.00

Ljusman River Rapids A202

1970, May 11 Engr. *Perf. 12½ Vert.*
851 A202 55o black & multi .30 .25
852 A202 70o black & multi .65 .60

European Nature Conservation Year, 1970.

Skiing — A203

"Around the Arctic Circle": No. 853, View of Kiruna. No. 855, Boat on mountain lake in Stora Sjofellet National Park. No. 856, Reindeer herd and herdsman. No. 857, Rocket probe under northern lights.

Perf. 12½ Horiz.
1970, June 5 Engr.
853 A203 45o sepia .50 .85
854 A203 45o violet blue .50 .85
855 A203 45o dull green .50 .85
856 A203 45o sepia .50 .85
857 A203 45o violet blue .50 .85
a. Bklt. pane, 2 each #853-857 5.50
  Nos. 853-857 (5) 2.50 4.25

China Palace, Drottningholm Park, 1769 — A204

Perf. 12½ Vert.
1970, Aug. 28 Photo.
858 A204 2k yel, grn & pink 1.50 .25

Glimmingehus, Skane Province, 15th Century — A205

Perf. 12½ Horiz.
1970, Aug. 28 Engr.
859 A205 55o gray green .30 .25

Perf. 12½ on 3 Sides
860 A205 55o gray green .35 .35
a. Booklet pane of 10 2.50

Timber Industry A206   Miner A208

Shipping Industry — A207

Designs: No. 863, Heavy industry (propeller). No. 864, Hydroelectric power (dam and diesel). No. 865, Mining (freight train and mine). No. 866, Technical research.

Perf. 12½ on 3 sides
1970, Sept. 28 Engr.
861 A206 70o indigo & lt brn 2.00 *2.50*
862 A207 70o ind, lt brn & dp plum 2.00 *2.50*
863 A206 70o ind & dp plum 2.00 *2.50*

864	A206	70o ind & dp plum	2.00	2.50
865	A207	70o ind & dp plum	2.00	2.50
866	A206	70o dp plum & lt brn	2.00	2.50
a.		Booklet pane of 6, #861-866	12.00	20.00
867	A208	1k black, buff	.40	.35
a.		Booklet pane of 10	4.00	

Perf. 12½ Vertically

868	A208	1k black, buff	.75	.30
		Nos. 861-868 (8)	13.15	15.65

Swedish trade and industry.

"Love, Not War" A209

Design: 70o, Four-leaf clovers symbolizing efforts for equality and brotherhood.

Engraved and Lithographed
1970, Oct. 24   Perf. 12½ Horiz.

869	A209	55o rose red, yel & blk	.25	.40
a.		Booklet pane of 4	1.00	
870	A209	70o emerald, yel & blk	.40	.55
a.		Booklet pane of 4	1.25	

Perf. 12½ Vert.

871	A209	55o rose red, yel & blk	.35	.30
872	A209	70o emerald, yel & blk	.30	.35
		Nos. 869-872 (4)	1.30	1.60

25th anniversary of the United Nations.

Bird Type of 1968

Birds: No. 873, Blackbird. No. 874, Great titmouse. No. 875, Bullfinch. No. 876, Greenfinch. No. 877, Blue titmouse.

Perf. 12½ on 3 Sides
1970, Nov. 20   Photo.

873	A187	30o blue grn & multi	.85	1.00
874	A187	30o bister & multi	.85	1.00
875	A187	30o blue & multi	.85	1.00
876	A187	30o pink & multi	.85	1.00
877	A187	30o org yel & multi	.85	1.00
a.		Bklt. pane, 2 each #873-877	8.00	14.00
		Nos. 873-877 (5)	4.25	5.00

Paul Johann Ludwig Heyse A210

Kerstin Hesselgren A211

Designs: 55o, Otto Wallach and Johannes Diderik van der Waals. 70o, Albrecht Kossel.

Perf. 12½ Horiz.
1970, Dec. 10   Engr.

878	A210	45o violet	.80	.40
879	A210	55o slate blue	.50	.30
880	A210	70o gray	1.10	1.10

Perf. 12½ on 3 Sides

881	A210	45o violet	.60	1.10
a.		Booklet pane of 10	6.50	
882	A210	55o slate blue	.65	.35
a.		Booklet pane of 10	6.50	
		Nos. 878-882 (5)	3.65	3.25

Winners of the 1910 Nobel Prize.

Perf. 12½ Horiz.
1971, Feb. 19   Engr.

883	A211	45o dp claret, gray	.45	.40
884	A211	1k dp brn, buff	.65	.25

Perf. 12½ on 3 Sides

885	A211	45o dp claret, gray	.30	.85
a.		Booklet pane of 10	3.25	
		Nos. 883-885 (3)	1.40	1.50

50th anniv. of woman suffrage; Kerstin Hesselgren, was 1st woman member of Swedish Upper House.

Terns in Flight A212

Abstract Music, by Ingvar Lidholm A213

1971, Mar. 26   Perf. 13½ Vert.

886	A212	40o dark red	.40	.35
887	A212	55o violet blue	.80	.25

Perf. 12½ on 3 Sides

888	A212	55o violet blue	.40	.25
a.		Booklet pane of 10	4.50	
		Nos. 886-888 (3)	1.60	.85

Joint northern campaign for the benefit of refugees.

Perf. 12½ Horiz.
1971, Aug. 27   Engr.

889	A213	55o deep lilac	.40	.25
890	A213	85o green	.45	.30

Perf. 12½ on 3 Sides

891	A213	55o deep lilac	.30	.30
a.		Booklet pane of 10	3.00	
		Nos. 889-891 (3)	1.15	.85

The Three Kings, Grotlingbo Church — A214

Flight into Egypt, Stanga Church A215

Designs: 10o, Adam and Eve, Gammelgarn Church. 55o, Saint on horseback and Samson with the lion, Hogrän Church.

Perf. 12½ on 3 Sides
1971, Sept. 28   Engr.

892	A214	5o violet & brn	.60	.45
893	A214	10o violet & sl grn	.60	.45

Perf. 12½ Horiz.

894	A215	55o slate grn & brn	.60	.40
895	A215	65o brown & vio blk	.30	.25
a.		Bklt. pane, #892-894, 2 #895	2.50	4.50
		Nos. 892-895 (4)	2.10	1.55

Art of medieval stonemasons in Gotland.

Toddler and Automobile Wheel — A216

1971, Oct. 20   Perf. 12½ Vert.

896	A216	35o black & red	.25	.30
897	A216	65o dp blue & multi	.60	.25

Perf. 12½ on 3 Sides

898	A216	65o dp blue & multi	.40	.35
a.		Booklet pane of 10	5.75	
		Nos. 896-898 (3)	1.25	.90

Publicity for road safety.

King Gustavus Vasa's Sword, c. 1500 — A217

Swedish Crown Regalia: No. 900, Scepter. No. 901, Crown (No. 902, Scepter, crown and orb were made in 1561 for Erik XIV). No. 903, Karl IX's anointing horn, 1606.

Perf. 12½ on 3 Sides
1971, Oct. 20   Engr.

899	A217	65o lt blue & multi	.50	.40
900	A217	65o lt ol grn & multi	.50	.40
901	A217	65o dk blue & multi	.50	.40
902	A217	65o lt ol grn & multi	.50	.40
903	A217	65o lt blue & multi	.50	.40
a.		Bklt. pane, 2 each #899-903	5.50	10.00
		Nos. 899-903 (5)	2.50	2.00

Christmas Elf and Goat Bringing Gifts — A218

Christmas Customs (Old Prints): No. 905, Christmas market. No. 906, Dancing children and father playing fiddle. No. 907, Ice-skating on frozen waterways in Stockholm. No. 908, Sleigh ride to church.

1971, Nov. 10

904	A218	35o deep carmine	1.25	1.25
905	A218	35o violet blue	1.25	1.25
906	A218	35o violet brown	1.25	1.25
907	A218	35o violet blue	1.25	1.25
908	A218	35o slate green	1.25	1.25
a.		Bklt. pane, 2 each #904-908	12.50	16.00
		Nos. 904-908 (5)	6.25	6.25

Maurice Maeterlinck A219

Women Athletes A220

Designs: 65o, Wilhelm Wien and Allvar Gullstrand. 85o, Marie Sklodovska Curie.

1971, Dec. 10   Perf. 12½ Horiz.

909	A219	55o orange	.65	.55
910	A219	65o green	.65	.25
911	A219	85o dk carmine	.65	.60

Perf. 12½ on 3 Sides

912	A219	55o orange	.60	.80
a.		Booklet pane of 10	6.00	
913	A219	65o green	.65	.40
a.		Booklet pane of 10	6.50	
		Nos. 909-913 (5)	3.20	2.60

Winners of the 1911 Nobel Prize.

1972, Feb. 23   Perf. 12½ on 3 Sides

914	A220	55o Fencing	.75	.75
915	A220	55o Diving	.75	.75
916	A220	55o Gymnastics	.75	.75
917	A220	55o Tennis	.75	.75
918	A220	55o Figure skating	.75	.75
a.		Bklt. pane, 2 each #914-918	7.75	12.00
		Nos. 914-918 (5)	3.75	3.75

Lars Johan Hierta, by Christian Eriksson — A221

Frans Michael Franzen, by Soderberg and Hultstrom — A222

Hugo Alfven, by Carl Milles — A223

Georg Stiernhielm, by David K. Ehrenstrahl — A224

Photo., Perf 12½ Horiz. (35, 85o); Engr., Perf. 12½ Vert. (50, 65o)
1972 Feb. 23

919	A221	35o multicolored	.30	.25
920	A222	50o violet	.40	.25
921	A223	65o bluish black	.40	.25
922	A224	85o multicolored	.50	.55
		Nos. 919-922 (4)	1.60	1.30

Hierta (1801-72), journalist. Franzen (1772-1847), poet. Alfven (1872-1960), composer. Stiernhielm (1598-1672), poet, writer, scientist.

Lifting Molten Glass A225

Swedish Glassmaking: No. 924, Glass blower. No. 925, Decorating vase. No. 926, Annealing vase. No. 927, Polishing jug.

Perf. 12½ Horiz.
1972, Mar. 22   Engr.

923	A225	65o black	.80	.90
924	A225	65o violet blue	.80	.90
925	A225	65o carmine	.80	.90
926	A225	65o black	.80	.90
927	A225	65o violet blue	.80	.90
a.		Bklt. pane, 2 each #923-927	8.00	
		Nos. 923-927 (5)	4.00	4.50

Horses and Ruin of Borgholm Castle — A226

Designs: No. 929, Oland Island Bridge. No. 930, Kalmar Castle. No. 931, Salmon fishing. No. 932, Schooner Falken, Karlskrona.

1972, May 8   Perf. 12½ Horiz.

928	A226	55o chocolate	.65	.85
929	A226	55o dk violet blue	.65	.85
930	A226	55o chocolate	.65	.85
931	A226	55o blue green	.65	.85
932	A226	55o dk violet blue	.65	.85
a.		Bklt. pane, 2 each #928-932	6.00	
		Nos. 928-932 (5)	3.25	4.25

Tourist attractions in Southeast Sweden.

"Only one Earth" Environment Emblem — A227

"Spring," Bror Hjorth — A228

1972, June 5   Engr.   Perf. 12½ Vert.

933	A227	65o blue & carmine	.30	.25

Perf. 12½ Horiz.

934	A227	65o blue & carmine	.30	.30
a.		Booklet pane of 10	3.00	

Perf. 12½ Vert.

935	A228	85o brown & multi	.45	.30
a.		Booklet pane of 4	1.80	
		Nos. 933-935 (3)	1.05	.85

UN Conference on Human Environment, Stockholm, June 5-16.

Junkers JU52 — A229

Historic Planes: 5o, Junkers F13. 25o, Friedrichshafen FF49. 75o, Douglas DC-3.

1972, Sept. 8   Perf. 12½ on 3 Sides
Size: 20x19mm

936	A229	5o lilac	.25	.25

Size: 44x19mm

937	A229	15o blue	.45	.50
938	A229	25o blue	.45	.50
939	A229	75o gray green	.30	.30
a.		Bklt. pane, #937-938, 2 ea #936, 939	1.60	3.00
		Nos. 936-939 (4)	1.45	1.55

Stockholm from the South, by Johan Fredrik Martin — A230

Amphion Figurehead, by Per Ljung — A231

Lady with Veil, by Alexander Roslin — A232

#941, Anchor Forge, by Pehr Hillestrom. #943, Quadriga, by Johan Tobias von Sergel. #945, (Queen) Sofia Magdalena, by Carl Gustaf Pilo.

1972, Oct. 7   Engr.   Perf. 12½ Horiz.

940	A230	75o greenish black	.40	.60
941	A230	75o dark brown	.40	.60

Perf. 12½ on 3 Sides

942	A231	75o dark carmine	.45	.55
943	A231	75o dark carmine	.45	.55

Perf. 12½ on 2 Sides

944	A232	75o dk brn, blk & dk car	.45	.60
945	A232	75o dk brn, blk & dk car	.45	.60
a.		Booklet pane of 6, #940-945	2.75	4.75

18th century Swedish art.

Types of 1936
Imprint: "1972"

1972, Oct. 7   Perf. 12½ on 3 Sides

946	A36	10o dark carmine	.35	.50
947	A37	15o yellow green	.35	.50
948	A42	40o deep blue	.35	.50
949	A44	50o deep claret	.35	.50
950	A45	60o deep blue	.35	.50
a.		Bklt. pane, 2 each #946-950	3.00	7.00
		Nos. 946-950 (5)	1.75	2.50

Olle Hjortzberg (1872-1959), stamp designer. Booklet sold for 5k of which 1.50k was for Stockholmia 74, Intl. Phil. Exhib., Sept. 21-29, 1973.

Santa Claus — A233

St. Lucia Singers A234

Perf. 14 on 3 Sides
1972, Nov. 6   Photo.

951	A233	45o Candles	.35	.25
952	A233	45o shown	.35	.25
a.		Bklt. pane, 5 each #951-952	3.50	

Perf. 12½ Vert.

953	A234	75o gray & multi	.55	.25
		Nos. 951-953 (3)	1.25	.75

Christmas 1972 (children's drawings).

Horse — A235

Viking Ship — A236

Willows, by Peter A. Persson A237

Trosa, by Reinhold Ljunggren A238

Spring Birches, by Oskar Bergman A239

King Gustaf VI Adolf — A240

Perf. 12½ Horiz. or Vert.
1972-73   Engr.

954	A235	5o maroon ('73)	.25	.25
955	A236	10o dk blue ('73)	.25	.25
956	A237	40o sepia ('73)	.25	.25
957	A238	50o blk & brn ('73)	.30	.25
958	A239	55o yel grn ('73)	.35	.25
959	A240	75o indigo	.40	.25
960	A240	1k dp carmine	.65	.25

1973   Perf. 12½ on 3 Sides

961	A235	5o maroon	.25	.25
a.		Booklet pane of 20	.50	
962	A236	10o dark blue	.25	.25
a.		Booklet pane of 20	.60	
963	A240	75o indigo	.40	.25
a.		Booklet pane of 10	4.00	
		Nos. 954-963 (10)	3.35	2.50

King Gustaf VI Adolf — A245

Chinese Objects — A246

Designs: No. 983, King opening Parliament. No. 984, Etruscan vase and dish. No. 985, King with flowers.

1972, Nov. 11   Perf. 12½ Vert.

981	A245	75o violet blue	1.25	2.75
982	A246	75o slate green	1.25	2.75
983	A245	75o maroon	1.25	2.75

984	A246	75o violet blue	1.25	2.75
985	A245	75o slate green	1.25	2.75
a.		Bklt. pane of 5, #981-985	5.75	15.00

90th birthday of King Gustaf VI Adolf. Booklet sold for 4.75k of which 1k was for the King Gustaf VI Adolf Foundation for Swedish Cultural Activities.

Paul Sabatier and Victor Grignard — A247

Dr. Alexis Carrel — A248

75o, Nils Gustaf Dalen. 1k, Gerhart Hauptmann.

1972, Dec. 8   Engr.   Perf. 12½ Vert.

986	A247	60o olive bister	.60	.40

Perf. 12½ Horiz.

987	A248	65o dark blue	.70	.40
988	A248	75o violet	.90	.25
989	A248	1k redsh brown	1.10	.30
		Nos. 986-989 (4)	3.30	1.35

Winners of the 1912 Nobel Prize.

Mail Coach, 1923 — A249

Design: 70o, Postal autobus, 1972.

Perf. 12½ on 3 Sides
1973, Jan. 18   Engr.

990	A249	60o black, yellow	.30	.25
a.		Booklet pane of 10	3.00	

Perf. 12½ Vert.

991	A249	70o blue, orange & grn	.45	.25

Tintomara, by Lars Johan Werle — A250

Orpheus and Eurydice, by Christoph W. Gluck — A251

1973, Jan. 18   Perf. 12½ Horiz.

992	A250	75o green	.55	.25

Booklet Stamp

993	A251	1k red lilac	.55	.35
a.		Booklet pane of 5	3.00	

Bicentenary of the Royal Theater in Stockholm. The 75o shows a stage setting by Bo-Ruben Hedwall for Tintomara, a new opera, performed for the bicentenary celebration. The 1k shows painting by Pehr Hillestrom of Orpheus and Eurydice, which was first opera performed in Royal Theater.

Vaasa Ski Race, Dalecarlia — A252

Designs: No. 995, "Going to Church in Mora" (church boats), by Anders Zorn. No. 996, Church stables, Rättvik. No. 997, Falun copper mine. No. 998, Midsummer Dance, by Bengt Nordenberg.

1973, Mar. 2   Perf. 12½ Horiz.

994	A252	65o slate green	.40	.40
995	A252	65o slate green	.40	.40
996	A252	65o black	.40	.40
997	A252	65o slate green	.40	.40
998	A252	65o claret	.40	.40
a.		Bklt. pane, 2 each #994-998	4.00	
		Nos. 994-998 (5)	2.00	2.00

Tourist attractions in Dalecarlia.

Worker, Confederation Emblem — A253

1973, Apr. 26   Perf. 12½ Vert.

999	A253	75o dark carmine	.40	.25
1000	A253	1.40k slate blue	.75	.25

75th anniversary of the Swedish Confederation of Trade Unions (LO).

Observer Reading Temperature A254

Design: No. 1002, Clouds, photographed by US weather satellite.

1973, May 24   Engr.   Perf. 12½ Vert.

1001	A254	65o slate green	.75	.65
1002	A254	65o black & ultra	.75	.65
a.		Pair, #1001-1002	1.50	2.50

Cent. of the Swedish Weather Organization and of Intl. Meteorological Cooperation.

Nordic Cooperation Issue 1973

Nordic House, Reykjavik A254a

1973, June 26   Perf. 12½ Vert.

1003	A254a	75o multicolored	.45	.25
1004	A254a	1k multicolored	.65	.25

A century of postal cooperation among Denmark, Finland, Iceland, Norway and Sweden and in connection with the Nordic Postal Conference, Reykjavik, Iceland.

Carl Peter Thunberg (1743-1828) — A255

Swedish Explorers: No. 1006, Anders Sparrman (1748-1820) and Polynesian double canoe. No. 1007, Nils Adolf Erik Nordenskjold (1832-1901) and ship in pack ice. No. 1008, Salomon August Andrée (1854-1897) and balloon on snow field. No. 1009, Sven Hedin (1865-1952) and camel riders.

1973, Sept. 22   Perf. 12½ Horiz.

1005	A255	1k sl grn, bl & brn	.95	1.10
1006	A255	1k bl, sl grn & brn	.95	1.10
1007	A255	1k bl, sl grn & brn	.95	1.10
1008	A255	1k black & multi	.95	1.10
1009	A255	1k black & multi	.95	1.10
a.		Bklt. pane of 5, #1005-1009	5.00	8.25

Plower with Ox Team A256

Designs: No. 1011, Woman working flax brake. No. 1012, Farm couple planting potatoes. No. 1013, Women baking bread. No. 1014, Man with horse-drawn sower.

1973, Oct. 24   **Perf. 12½ Horiz.**
1010 A256 75o grnsh black   1.00   .45
1011 A256 75o red brown   1.00   .45
1012 A256 75o grnsh black   1.00   .45
1013 A256 75o plum   1.00   .45
1014 A256 75o red brown   1.00   .45
    a.   Bklt. pane, 2 ea #1010-1014   10.00
     Nos. 1010-1014 (5)   5.00 2.25

Centenary of Nordic Museum, Stockholm.

Gray Seal — A257

King Gustaf VI Adolf — A258

Protected Animals: 20o, Peregrine falcon. 25o, Lynx. 55o, Otter. 65o, Wolf. 75o, White-tailed sea eagle.

1973, Oct. 24   **Perf. 12½ on 3 Sides**
1015 A257 10o slate green   .25   .25
1016 A257 20o violet   .25   .25
1017 A257 25o Prus green   .25   .25
1018 A257 55o Prus green   .25   .25
1019 A257 65o violet   .25   .25
1020 A257 75o slate green   .35   .35
    a.   Bklt. pane, 2 each #1015-1020   3.00
     Nos. 1015-1020 (6)   1.60 1.60

1973, Oct. 24   **Perf. 12½ Vert.**
1021 A258 75o dk violet blue   .30 .25
1022 A258 1k purple   .50 .25

King Gustaf VI Adolf (1882-1973).

The Three Kings A259

Charles XIV John A260

The Goosegirl, by Josephson A261

#1024, Merry country dance. #1026, Basket with stylized Dalecarlian gourd plant.

Perf. 14 Horiz.
1973, Nov. 12   **Photo.**
1023 A259 45o multicolored   .35 .30
1024 A259 45o multicolored   .35 .30
    a.   Bklt. pane, 5 each #1023-1024   3.50

Coil Stamps
1025 A260 75o multicolored   1.40 .25
1026 A260 75o multicolored   1.40 .25
    a.   Pair, #1025-1026   3.00 5.00
     Nos. 1023-1026 (4)   3.50 1.10

Christmas 1973. Designs are from Swedish peasant paintings.

Perf. 12½ Horiz.
1973, Nov. 12   **Engr.**
1027 A261 10k multicolored   4.50 .35

Ernst Josephson (1851-1906), painter.

Alfred Werner and Heike Kamerlingh-Onnes A262

Charles Robert Richet A263

Design: 1.40k, Rabindranath Tagore.

1973, Dec. 10   **Engr.**   **Perf. 12½ Vert.**
1028 A262 75o dark violet   .55 .25

Perf. 12½ Horiz.
1029 A263 1k dark brown   .55 .30
1030 A263 1.40k green   .65 .25
     Nos. 1028-1030 (3)   1.75 .80

Winners of 1913 Nobel Prize.

Ski Jump A264

Skiing: No. 1032, Cross-country race. No. 1033, Relay race. No. 1034, Slalom. No. 1035, Women's cross-country race.

Perf. 12½ Horiz.
1974, Jan. 23   **Engr.**
1031 A264 65o slate green   .55 .65
1032 A264 65o violet blue   .55 .65
1033 A264 65o slate green   .55 .65
1034 A264 65o dk carmine   .55 .65
1035 A264 65o violet blue   .55 .65
    a.   Bklt. pane, 2 each #1031-1035   11.00
     Nos. 1031-1035 (5)   2.75 3.25

Drawing of First Industrial Digester A265

Hans Järta and Quotation from 1809 — A266

Samuel Owen and 19th Century Factory A267

1974, Mar. 5   **Engr.**   **Perf. 12½ Vert.**
1036 A265 45o sepia   .25   .25
1037 A266 60o green   .30   .30
1038 A267 75o dull red   .45   .25
     Nos. 1036-1038 (3)   1.00 .80

Centenary of sulphite pulp process (45o); Hans Järta (1774-1847), statesman responsible for the Instrument of Government Act of 1809 (60o); Samuel Owen (1774-1854), English-born industrialist who introduced new production methods (75o).

Stora Sjofallet (Great Falls) — A268

Street in Ystad — A269

1974, Apr. 2   **Perf. 12½ Horiz.**
1039 A268 35o blue grn & blk   .45 .25
Perf. 12½ on 3 Sides
1040 A269 75o dull claret   .30 .25
    a.   Booklet pane of 10   3.00

UPU Type of 1924 A270

1974   **Engr.**   **Perf. 12½ on 3 Sides**
1041 A270 20o green   .30 .35
1042 A270 25o ultra   .30 .35
1043 A270 30o dark brown   .30 .35
1044 A270 35o dark red   .30 .35
    a.   Bklt. pane, 2 each #1041-1044   2.50 3.50
     Nos. 1041-1044 (4)   1.20 1.40

Miniature Sheets
Perf. 12½
1045   Sheet of 4   2.00 3.50
    a.   A270 20o ocher, single stamp   .40 .75
1046   Sheet of 4   2.00 3.50
    a.   A270 25o dk vio, single stamp   .40 .75
1047   Sheet of 4   2.00 3.50
    a.   A270 30o dk red, single stamp   .40 .75
1048   Sheet of 4   2.00 3.50
    a.   A270 35o yel grn, single stamp   .40 .75

Stockholmia 74 philatelic exhibition, Stockholm, Sept. 21-29. Booklet sold for 3k with surtax going toward financing the exhibition. Nos. 1045-1048 sold during exhibition in folder with 5k entrance ticket. Issued: #1041-1044, 4/2; #1045-1048, 9/21.

"Man in Storm," by Bror Marklund — A271

Europa: 1k, Sculpture by Picasso, Lake Vanern, Kristinehamm.

Perf. 12½ Horiz.
1974, Apr. 29   **Engr.**
1049 A271 75o violet brown   1.10 .30
1050 A271 1k slate green   1.25 .30

King Carl XVI Gustaf — A272

1974-78   **Engr.**   **Perf. 12½ Vert.**
1068 A272   75o slate grn   .40 .25
1069 A272   90o brt blue ('75)   .35 .25
1070 A272   1k maroon   .45 .25
1071 A272 1.10k rose red ('75)   .40 .25
1072 A272 1.30k green ('76)   .50 .25
1073 A272 1.40k violet bl ('77)   .75 .25
1074 A272 1.50k red lilac ('80)   .60 .25
1075 A272 1.70k orange ('78)   .85 .25
1076 A272   2k dk brown ('80)   .85 .25

Perf. 12½ on 3 Sides
1077 A272   75o slate green   .30 .25
    a.   Booklet pane of 10   3.00
1078 A272   90o brt blue ('75)   .30 .25
    a.   Booklet pane of 10   3.00
1079 A272   1k maroon ('76)   .40 .25
    a.   Booklet pane of 10   4.00
1080 A272 1.10k rose red ('77)   .40 .25
    a.   Booklet pane of 10   4.00
1081 A272 1.30k green ('78)   .50 .25
    a.   Booklet pane of 10   5.00
1082 A272 1.50k red lilac ('80)   .60 .25
    a.   Booklet pane of 10   6.00
     Nos. 1068-1082 (15)   7.65 3.75

Central Post Office, Stockholm A274

Mailman, Northernmost Rural Delivery Route — A275

Perf. 12½ on 3 Sides
1974, June 7   **Engr.**
1084 A273 75o violet brown   .70 .40
1085 A274 75o violet brown   .70 .40
    a.   Bklt. pane, 5 ea #1084-1085   7.00
Perf. 12½ Vert.
1086 A275 1k slate green   .65 .25
     Nos. 1084-1086 (3)   2.05 1.05

Centenary of Universal Postal Union.

Regatta A276

Scenes from Sweden's West Coast: No. 1088, Vinga Lighthouse. No. 1089, Varberg Fortress. No. 1090, Seine fishing. No. 1091, Fishing village Mollosund.

1974, June 7   **Perf. 12½ Horiz.**
1087 A276 65o crimson   .55 .55
1088 A276 65o blue   .55 .55
1089 A276 65o dk olive green   .55 .55
1090 A276 65o slate green   .55 .55
1091 A276 65o brown   .55 .55
    a.   Bklt. pane, 2 each #1087-1091   4.50
     Nos. 1087-1091 (5)   2.75 2.75

Mr. Simmons, by Axel Fridell — A277

Thread and Spool — A278

Perf. 12½ on 3 Sides
1974, Aug. 28   **Engr.**
1092 A277   45o black   .25 .25
    a.   Booklet pane of 10   2.50
Perf. 12½ Horiz.
1093 A277 1.40k deep claret   .75 .25

Swedish Publicists' Club, centenary.

1974, Aug. 28   **Perf. 12½ Horiz.**
#1095, Sewing machines (abstract).
1094 A278 85o deep violet   .40 .30
1095 A278 85o black & org   .40 .30
    a.   Pair, #1094-1095   1.00 .90

Swedish textile and clothing industries.

Tugs in Stockholm Harbor — A279

#1096, Tanker. #1097, Liner "Snow Storm." #1098, Ice breakers Tor and Atle. #1099, Skane Train Ferry, Trelleborg-Sassnitz.

1974, Nov. 16   **Perf. 12½ Horiz.**
1096 A279 1k dark blue   .80 .90
1097 A279 1k dark blue   .80 .90
1098 A279 1k dark blue   .80 .90
1099 A279 1k dark blue   .80 .90
1100 A279 1k dark blue   .80 .90
    a.   Bklt. pane of 5. #1096-1100   4.00 7.00

Swedish shipping industry.

Miniature Sheet

Quilt from Skepptuna Church — A280

Deer, Quilt from Hog Church — A281

Designs are from woolen quilts, 15th-16th centuries. Motifs shown on No. 1101 are stylized deer, griffins, lions, unicorn and horses.

1974, Nov. 16   **Photo.**   **Perf. 14**
1101 A280   Sheet of 10   9.50   13.00
a.-j.   45o, single stamp   .95   1.00

Perf. 13 Horiz.
1102 A281   75o bl blk, red & yel   .45   .25

Max von Laue — A282

Designs: 70o, Theodore William Richards. 1k, Robert Bárány.

1974, Dec. 10   **Engr.**   **Perf. 12½ Vert.**
1103 A282   65o rose red   .35   .25
1104 A282   70o slate   .45   .30
1105 A282   1k indigo   .95   .25
    Nos. 1103-1105 (3)   1.75   .80
Winners of 1914 Nobel Prize.

A283

No. 1106, Sven Jerring's children's program. No. 1107, Televising parliamentary debate.

1974, Dec. 10   **Perf. 12½ Vert.**
1106   75o dk blue & brn   .65   .25
1107   75o brown & dk bl   .65   .25
a.   A283   Pair, #1106-1107   1.25   2.00
Swedish Broadcasting Corp., 50th anniv.

Account Holder's Envelope A285

Photogravure and Engraved
1975, Jan. 21   **Perf. 14 Vert.**
1108 A285   1.40k ocher & blk   .65   .35
Swedish Postal Giro Office, 50th anniv.

Male and Female Architects, New Parliament A286

Jenny Lind (1820-87), by J. O. Sodermark A287

1975, Mar. 25   **Engr.**   **Perf. 12½ Vert.**
1109 A286   75o slate green   .40   .25
Perf. 12½ Horiz.
1110 A287   1k claret   .60   .25
Perf. 12½ on 3 Sides
1111 A286   75o slate green   .35   .25
a.   Booklet pane of 10   3.50
    Nos. 1109-1111 (3)   1.35   .75
International Women's Year 1975.

Horseman, Helmet Decoration A288

"Gold Men" A289

Designs: 15o, Scabbard and hilt. 20o, Shield buckle. 25o, Iron helmet.

1975, Mar. 25   **Perf. 12½ on 3 sides**
1112 A288   10o dull red   .25   .25
1113 A288   15o slate green   .25   .25
1114 A288   20o violet   .25   .25
1115 A288   55o violet brown   .25   .25
a.   Bklt. pane, 2 each #1112-1115   .75   1.60
Perf. 12½ Horiz.
1116 A289   25o deep yellow   .25   .25
    Nos. 1112-1116 (5)   1.25   1.25

Treasures from tombs of the Vendel period (550-800 A.D.), and "gold men" (25o) from Eketorp II excavations (400-700 A.D.).

Europa Issue 1975

New Year's Eve at Skansen, by Eric Hallstrom — A290

Inferno, by August Strindberg — A291

Perf. 12½ Vert.
1975, Apr. 28   **Photo.**
1117 A290   90o multi   .75   .25
Perf. 12½ Horiz.
1118 A291   1.10k multi   .75   .25

Capercaillie A292

Rok Stone, 9th Century A293

1975, May 20   **Engr.**   **Perf. 12½ Vert.**
1119 A292   170o indigo   .70   .25
Perf. 12½ Horiz.
1120 A293   2k deep claret   .85   .25

Metric Tape Measure — A294

Folke Filbyter Statue, by Milles — A296

Hernqvist by Per Krafft the Younger — A295

1975, May 20   **Perf. 12½ Vert.**
1121 A294   55o deep blue   .35   .30
1122 A295   70o yel brn & dk brn   .40   .30
Perf. 12½ Horiz.
1123 A296   75o violet   .40   .25
    Nos. 1121-1123 (3)   1.15   .85

Cent. of Intl. Meter Convention, Paris, 1875; bicent. of Swedish veterinary medicine, founded by Peter Hernqvist (1726-1808); Carl Milles (1875-1955), sculptor.

Officers' Mess, Rommehed, 1798 — A297

No. 1124, Skelleftea Church Village, 17th cent. No. 1125, Foundry and furnace, Engelsberg, 18th cent. No. 1126, Gunpowder Tower, Visby. No. 1127, Falun Mine pithead gear, 1852.

1975, June 13   **Perf. 12½ Horiz.**
1124 A297   75o black   .50   .75
1125 A297   75o dk carmine   .50   .75
1126 A297   75o black   .50   .75
1127 A297   75o dk carmine   .50   .75
1128 A297   75o violet blue   .50   .75
a.   Bklt. pane, 2 each #1124-1128   5.50
    Nos. 1124-1128 (5)   2.50   3.75
European Architectural Heritage Year 1975.

Rescue at Sea: Helicopter over Ice-covered Tanker — A298

Designs: No. 1129, Fire fighters: firemen fighting fire. No. 1130, Customs narcotics service: trained dogs checking cargo. No. 1131, Police: Officer talking to boy on bridge. No. 1132, Hospital Service: patient arriving by ambulance.

1975, Aug. 27   **Perf. 12½ Horiz.**
1129 A298   90o dk car rose   .65   .45
1130 A298   90o dk bl   .65   .45
1131 A298   90o dk car rose   .65   .45
1132 A298   90o dk bl   .65   .45
1133 A298   90o green   .65   .45
a.   Bklt. pane, 2 each #1129-1133   6.50
    Nos. 1129-1133 (5)   3.25   2.25
Public service organizations watching, guarding, helping.

"Fryckstad" A299

"Gotland" A300

Design: 90o, "Prins August."

1975, Aug. 27   **Perf. 12½ on 3 Sides**
    Size: 20x19mm
1134 A299   5o green   .25   .25
1135 A300   5o dark blue   .25   .25
    Size: 45x19mm
1136 A299   90o slate green   .55   .25
a.   Bklt. pane, 2 each #1134-1136   1.75   2.50
    Nos. 1134-1136 (3)   1.05   .75

Scouts — A302

1975, Oct. 11   **Photo.**   **Perf. 14 Vert.**
1137   90o Around campfire   .50   .25
1138   90o In canoes   .50   .25
a.   A301   Pair, #1137-1138   1.25   2.00
Nordjamb 75, 14th World Boy Scout Jamboree, Lillehammer, Norway, July 29-Aug. 7.

Hedgehog A303

Old Man Playing Key Fiddle — A304

Romeo and Juliet Ballet — A305

1975, Oct. 11   **Engr.**   **Perf. 12½ Vert.**
1139 A303   55o black   .30   .25
1140 A304   75o dk red   .55   .25
Perf. 12½ Horiz.
1141 A305   7k blue green   3.25   .25
Perf. 12½ on 3 Sides
1142 A303   55o black   .25   .25
a.   Booklet pane of 10   2.50
    Nos. 1139-1142 (4)   4.35   1.00
    See No. 2642c.

Virgin Mary, 12th Cent. Statue — A306

Chariot of the Sun, from 12th Cent. Altar — A307

Mourning Mary, c. 1280 — A308

Jesse at Foot of Genealogical Tree, c. 1510 — A309

Christmas: #1145, Nativity, from 12th cent. gilt-copper altar. #1148, like #1147.

Perf. 14 Horiz.
1975, Nov. 11   **Photo.**
1143 A306   55o multi   .30   .25
Perf. 12½ on 3 Sides
1144 A307   55o gold & multi   .35   .30
1145 A307   55o gold & multi   .35   .30
a.   Bklt. pane, 5 each #1144-1145   3.00
Perf. 12½ Horiz.
Engr.
1146 A308   90o brown   .50   .25

Perf. 12½ on 3 Sides

1147	A309	90o red	.60 .30
1148	A309	90o blue	.60 .30
a.		Bklt. pane, 5 ea #1147-1148	6.00
		Nos. 1143-1148 (6)	2.70 1.70

No. 1145a was issued with top row of 5 either No. 1144 or No. 1145.

William H. and William L. Bragg — A310

Designs: 90o, Richard Willstätter. 1.10k, Romain Rolland.

1975, Dec. 10   Engr.   Perf. 12½ Vert.
1149	A310	75o claret	.40 .45
1150	A310	90o violet blue	.45 .25
1151	A310	1.10k slate green	.55 .35
		Nos. 1149-1151 (3)	1.40 1.05

Winners of 1915 Nobel Prize.

Cave of the Winds, by Eric Grate — A311

1976, Jan. 27   Perf. 12½ Vert.
1152	A311	1.90k slate green	.90 .25

The sculpture by Eric Grate (b. 1896) stands in front of the Town Hall of Vasteras.

Razor-billed Auks and Black Guillemot A312

Bobbin Lace Maker from Vadstena A313

1976, Mar. 10   Engr.   Perf. 12½ Vert.
1153	A312	85o dark blue	.55 .25

Perf. 12½ Horiz.
1154	A313	1k claret brn	.45 .30

Perf. 12½ on 3 Sides
1155	A312	85o dk bl	.30 .30
a.		Booklet pane of 10	3.00
1156	A313	1k claret brn	.40 .30
a.		Booklet pane of 10	4.00
		Nos. 1153-1156 (4)	1.70 1.15

Old and New Telephones, Relays — A314

1976, Mar. 10   Perf. 12½ Vert.
1157	A314	1.30k brt violet	.75 .25
1158	A314	3.40k red	1.35 .55

Centenary of first telephone call by Alexander Graham Bell, March 10, 1876.

Europa Issue 1976

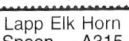

Lapp Elk Horn Spoon — A315

Tile Stove — A316

Perf. 14½ Horiz.

1976, May 3   Photo.
1159	A315	1k multi	.65 .25
1160	A316	1.30k multi	.65 .45

Wheat and Cornflower Seeds — A317

Viable and Nonviable Seedlings A318

1976, May 3   Engr.   Perf. 12½ Vert.
1161	A317	65o brown	.30 .25
1162	A318	65o choc & grn	.30 .25
a.		Pair, #1161-1162	.90 .90

Swedish seed testing centenary.

King Carl XVI Gustaf and Queen Silvia — A319

Perf. 12½ Vert.
1976, June 19   Engr.
1163	A319	1k rose car	.30 .25
1164	A319	1.30k slate grn	.40 .25

Perf. 12½ on 3 Sides
1165	A319	1k rose car	.30 .25
a.		Booklet pane of 10	3.00
		Nos. 1163-1165 (3)	1.00 .75

Wedding of King Carl XVI Gustaf and Silvia Sommerlath.

View from Ringkallen, by Helmer Osslund — A320

Views in Angermanland Province: No. 1167, Tugboat pulling timber. No. 1168, Hay-drying racks. No. 1169, Granvagsnipan slope, Angerman River. No. 1170, Seine fishing.

1976, June 19   Perf. 12½ Horiz.
1166	A320	85o slate grn	.40 .55
1167	A320	85o vio bl	.40 .55
1168	A320	85o dp brn	.40 .55
1169	A320	85o vio bl	.40 .55
1170	A320	85o brn red	.40 .55
a.		Bklt. pane, 2 each #1166-1170	4.50
		Nos. 1166-1170 (5)	2.00 2.75

Roman Cross and Ship's Wheel — A321

1976, June 19   Perf. 12½ Horiz.
1171	A321	85o brt bl & bl	.55 .40

Swedish Seamen's Church, centenary.

Torgny Segerstedt and 1917 Page of Gothenburg Journal — A322

1976, June 19   Perf. 12½ Vert.
1172	A322	1.90k brn & blk	.80 .30

Torgny Segerstedt (1876-1945), editor in chief of the Gothenburg Journal of Commerce and Shipping, birth centenary.

Coiled Snake, Bronze Buckle — A323

Pilgrim's Badge, Adoration of the Magi — A324

Drinking Horn, 14th Century — A325

Chimney Sweep — A326

Girl's Head, by Bror Hjorth, 1922 — A327

Perf. 12½ Horiz., Vert. (30o)
1976, Sept. 8   Engr.
1173	A323	15o bister	.25 .25
1174	A324	20o green	.25 .25
1175	A325	30o dk rose brn	.25 .25
1176	A326	90o indigo	.40 .25
1177	A327	9k yel grn & sl grn	3.50 .25
		Nos. 1173-1177 (5)	4.65 1.25

Inventors A328

#1178, John Ericsson (1803-1889), ship propeller and "Monitor". #1179, Helge Palmcrantz (1842-80) & reaper. #1180, Lars Magnus Ericsson (1846-1926) & switchboard. #1181, Sven Wingquist (1876-1953) & ball bearing. #1182, Gustaf de Laval (1845-1913) & milk separator.

1976, Oct. 9   Engr.   Perf. 12½ Horiz.
1178	A328	1.30k multi	.60 .75
1179	A328	1.30k multi	.60 .75
1180	A328	1.30k multi	.60 .75
1181	A328	1.30k multi	.60 .75
1182	A328	1.30k multi	.60 .75
a.		Bklt. pane of 5, #1178-1182	3.75 6.00

Swedish inventors and their technological inventions.

Hands and Cogwheels A329

1976, Oct. 9   Perf. 12½ Vert.
1183	A329	85o org & dk vio	.40 .25
1184	A329	1k yel grn & brn	.55 .25

Industrial safety.

Verner von Heidenstam, Lake Vattern — A330

1976, Nov. 17   Perf. 12½ Vert.
1185	A330	1k yellow green	.40 .25
1186	A330	1.30k blue	.55 .45

Verner von Heidenstam (1859-1940), Swedish poet, 1916 Nobel Prize winner.

Archangel Michael A331

Virgin Mary Visiting St. Elizabeth A332

Christmas: No. 1189, like No. 1187. No. 1190, St. Nicholas saving 3 children. No. 1191, like No. 1188. No. 1192, Illuminated page, prayer to Virgin Mary. 65o, stamps are from Flemish prayer book, c. 1500. 1k stamps are from Austrian prayer book, late 15th century.

Perf. 12½ Horiz.
1976, Nov. 17   Photo.
1187	A331	65o blue & multi	.30 .25
1188	A332	1k gold & multi	.30 .25

Perf. 12½ on 3 Sides
1189	A331	65o blue & multi	.25 .40
1190	A331	65o blue & multi	.25 .40
a.		Bklt. pane, 5 each #1189-1190	2.50

Perf. 12½ Vert.
1191	A332	1k gold & multi	.30 .25
1192	A332	1k gold & multi	.30 .25
a.		Bklt. pane, 5 each #1191-1192	3.00
		Nos. 1187-1192 (6)	1.70 1.80

Five Water Lilies — A333

Photogravure and Engraved
1977, Feb. 2   Perf. 12½ Horiz.
1193	A333	1k brt grn & multi	.55 .25
1194	A333	1.30k ultra & multi	.65 .55

Nordic countries cooperation for protection of the environment and 25th Session of Nordic Council, Helsinki, Feb. 19.

Tailor — A334

1977, Feb. 24   Perf. 12½ Vert.
1195	A334	2.10k red brn	.95 .25

Longdistance Skating — A335

Perf. 12½ Horiz.

1977, Mar. 24 Engr.
1196 A335 95o shown .45 .55
1197 A335 95o Swimming .45 .55
1198 A335 95o Bicycling .45 .55
1199 A335 95o Jogging .45 .55
1200 A335 95o Badminton .45 .55
a. Bklt. pane, 2 each #1196-1200 4.50
Nos. 1196-1200 (5) 2.25 2.75

Physical fitness.

Politeness, by "OA,"
1905 — A336

1977, Mar. 24 Perf. 12½ on 3 Sides
1201 A336 75o black .35 .25
a. Booklet pane of 10 3.50

Perf. 12½ Horiz.
1202 A336 3.80k red 2.00 .45

Oskar Andersson (1877-1906), cartoonist.

Calle
Schewen
A337

No. 1204, Seagull. No. 1205, Dancers and accordionist. No. 1206, Fishermen in boat. No. 1207, Tree on shore at sunset.
Designs are illustrations for poem The Calle Schewen Waltz, by Evert Taube, and include bars of music of this song.

1977, May 2 Engr. Perf. 12½ Horiz.
1203 A337 95o slate grn .45 .55
1204 A337 95o vio bl .45 .55
1205 A337 95o grn & blk .45 .55
1206 A337 95o dark blue .45 .55
1207 A337 95o red .45 .55
a. Bklt. pane, 2 each #1203-1207 4.50
Nos. 1203-1207 (5) 2.25 2.75

Tourist publicity for Roslagen (archipelago) and to honor Evert Taube (1890-1976), poet.

Gustavianum,
Uppsala
University
A338

1977, May 2 Photo. Perf. 14 Vert.
1208 A338 1.10k multi .55 .25

Perf. 14 on 3 Sides
1209 A338 1.10k multi .35 .25
a. Booklet pane of 10 3.50

Uppsala University, 500th anniversary.

Europa Issue 1977

Forest in
Snow
A339

Rapadalen Valley — A340

1977, May 2 Perf. 14 Vert.
1210 A339 1.10k multi 1.10 .30
1211 A340 1.40k multi 1.10 .65

Owl — A341

Cast-iron Stove
Decoration — A342

Gotland
Ponies
A343

1977, Sept. 8 Engr. Perf. 12½ Vert.
1212 A341 45o dk slate grn .50 .40

Perf. 12½ Horiz.
1213 A342 70o dk vio bl .45 .25

Booklet Stamp
1214 A343 1.40k brown .55 .35
a. Booklet pane of 5 2.75
Nos. 1212-1214 (3) 1.50 1.00

Wild
Berries — A344

Perf. 14 on 3 Sides

1977, Sept. 8 Photo.
1215 A344 75o Blackberry .40 .50
1216 A344 75o Cranberry .40 .50
1217 A344 75o Raspberry .40 .50
1218 A344 75o Whortleberry .40 .50
1219 A344 75o Alpine strawberry .40 .50
a. Bklt. pane, 2 each #1215-1219 4.00 6.50
Nos. 1215-1219 (5) 2.00 2.50

Horse-drawn Trolley — A345

Designs: Public transportation.

1977, Oct. 8 Engr. Perf. 12½ Horiz.
1220 A345 1.10k shown .75 .90
1221 A345 1.10k Electric trolley .75 .90
1222 A345 1.10k Ferry .75 .90
1223 A345 1.10k Tandem bus .75 .90
1224 A345 1.10k Subway .75 .90
a. Bklt. pane of 5, #1220-1224 3.75 6.50

Putting up
Sheaf for the
Birds — A346

Preparing Dried
Soaked
Fish — A347

Traditional Christmas Preparations: No. 1227, Children baking ginger snaps. No. 1228, Bringing in Yule tree. No. 1229, Making straw goat. No. 1230, Candle dipping.

Perf. 12½ Horiz.

1977, Nov. 17 Engr.
1225 A346 75o violet .35 .25
1226 A347 1.10k yel grn .55 .25

Perf. 12½ on 3 Sides
1227 A346 75o ocher .35 .25
1228 A346 75o slate grn .35 .25
a. Bklt. pane, 5 each #1227-1228 2.50

1229 A347 1.10k dk red .40 .25
1230 A347 1.10k dk bl .40 .25
a. Bklt. pane, 5 each #1229-1230 4.00
Nos. 1225-1230 (6) 2.40 1.50

Christmas 1977.

Henrik
Pontoppidan,
Karl Adolph
Gjellerup
A348

Design: 1.40k, Charles Glover Barkla.

1977, Nov. 17 Perf. 12½ Vert.
1231 A348 1.10k red brn .60 .30
1232 A348 1.40k yel grn .65 .65

1917 Nobel Prize winners: Henrik Pontoppidan (1857-1943) and Karl Adolph Gjellerup (1857-1919), Danish writers; Charles Glover Barkla (1877-1944), English X-ray pioneer.

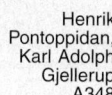

Space Without
Affiliation, by
Arne
Jones — A349

Brown
Bear — A350

1978, Jan. 25 Perf. 12½ Horiz.
1233 A349 2.50k vio bl 1.00 .25

1978, Apr. 11 Perf. 12½ Horiz.
1234 A350 1.15k dark brown .50 .25

Europa Issue 1978

Örebro
Castle — A351

Arch and
Stairs — A352

1978, Apr. 11 Perf. 12½ Vert.
1235 A351 1.30k slate green 1.35 .35

Perf. 12½ Horiz.
1236 A352 1.70k dull red 1.75 .65

Pentecostal
Preacher and
Congregation
A353

Free Churches: No. 1238, Swedish Missionary Society. No. 1239, Evangelical National Missionary Society. No. 1240, Baptist Society. No. 1241, Salvation Army.

1978, Apr. 11 Perf. 12½ on 3 sides
1237 A353 90o purple .50 .50
1238 A353 90o slate .50 .50
1239 A353 90o violet .50 .50
1240 A353 90o slate .50 .50
1241 A353 90o purple .50 .50
a. Bklt. pane, 2 each #1237-1241 5.00 7.50
Nos. 1237-1241 (5) 2.50 2.50

Independent Christian Associations.

Brosarp Hills — A354

Grindstone
Production
A355

Red Limestone
Cliff — A356

Designs: No. 1243, Avocets. No. 1245, Linnaea borealis (Linné's favorite flower.) No. 1247, Linné with Lapp drum, wearing Lapp clothes and Dutch doctor's hat.

Perf. 12½ Horiz.

1978, May 23 Engr.
1242 A354 1.30k gray green .65 .50
1243 A354 1.30k violet blue .65 .50

Perf. 12½ on 3 Sides
1244 A355 1.30k violet brown .65 .60
1245 A355 1.30k brown red .65 .60

Perf. 12½ on 2 Sides
1246 A356 1.30k violet blue .65 .60
1247 A356 1.30k violet brown .65 .60
a. Bklt. pane of 6, #1242-1247 4.25 5.50

Travels of Carl von Linné (1707-1778), botanist.

Cranes, Lake Hornborgasjon — A357

Designs: No. 1248, Gliding School, Alleberg. No. 1250, Skara Church, Lacko Island. No. 1251, Ancient rock tomb, Luttra. No. 1252, Cloth merchants, sculpture by Nils Sjogren.

1978, May 23 Perf. 12½ Horiz.
1248 A357 1.15k dull green .55 .45
1249 A357 1.15k maroon .55 .45
1250 A357 1.15k violet blue .55 .45
1251 A357 1.15k dk gray grn .55 .45
1252 A357 1.15k brn & gray grn .55 .45
a. Bklt. pane, 2 each #1284-1252 5.50
Nos. 1248-1252 (5) 2.75 2.25

Tourist publicity for Vastergotland.

Laurel and
Scroll — A358

1978, May 23 Perf. 12½ Vert.
1253 A358 2.50k gray & sl grn 1.00 .25

Stockholm University, centenary.

Homecoming, by Carl Kylberg — A359

Nude, by Karl Isakson
A360

Self-portrait, by Ivar Arosenius
A361

1978, Sept. 5 Engr. *Perf. 12½ Vert.*
1254 A359 90o multicolored   .40 .40

Perf. 12½ Horiz.
1255 A360 1.15k multi   .55 .30
1256 A361 4.50k multi   1.75 .50
   Nos. 1254-1256 (3)   2.70 1.20

Swedish painters: Carl Kylberg (1878-1952); Karl Isakson (1878-1922); Ivar Arosenius (1878-1909).

North Arrow (Compass Rose), Map, 1769 — A362

1978, Sept. 5   *Perf. 12½ Horiz.*
1257 A362 10k lilac   3.75 .25

Coronation Coach, 1699 — A363

1978, Oct. 7 Engr. *Perf. 12½ Horiz.*
1258 A363 1.70k dk red, *yel*   .80 .45
   a. Booklet pane of 5   4.00

Orange Russula — A364

Designs: Edible mushrooms.

1978, Oct. 7   *Perf. 12½ on 3 Sides*
1259 A364 1.15k shown   .60 .75
1260 A364 1.15k Lycoperdon
                   perlatum   .60 .75
1261 A364 1.15k Macrolepiota
                   procera   .60 .75
1262 A364 1.15k Cantharellus
                   cibarius   .60 .75
1263 A364 1.15k Boletus edulis .60 .75
1264 A364 1.15k Ramaria bo-
                   trytis   .60 .75
   a. Bklt. pane of 6, #1259-1264 4.00 7.50

Toy Ferris Wheel — A365

Rider Drawing Water Cart — A366

Toys: No. 1266, Teddy bear. No. 1267, Dalecarlian wooden horse. No. 1268, Doll. No. 1269, Spinning tops.

Perf. 12½ Horiz.
1978, Nov. 14   Engr.
1265 A365 90o dk red & grn   .45 .25
1266 A365 1.30k brt ultra   .65 .25

Perf. 12½ on 3 Sides
Photo.
1267 A365 90o multicolored   .35 .25
1268 A365 90o multicolored   .35 .25
   a. Bklt. pane, 5 each #1267-1268 3.50
1269 A366 1.30k multicolored   .55 .25
1270 A366 1.30k multicolored   .55 .25
   a. Bklt. pane, 5 each #1269-1270 5.50
   Nos. 1265-1270 (6)   2.90 1.50
         Christmas 1978.

Fritz Haber — A367

Design: 1.70k, Max Planck.

1978, Nov. 14 Engr. *Perf. 12½ Vert.*
1271 A367 1.30k dark brown   .65 .50
1272 A367 1.30k dark violet bl .85 .65

   1918 Nobel Prize winners: Fritz Haber (1868-1934), German chemist; Max Planck (1858-1947), German physicist.
   See #1310-1312, 1341-1344, 1387-1389.

Bandy — A368

1979, Jan. 25 Engr. *Perf. 12½ Vert.*
1273 A368 1.05k violet blue   .45 .40
1274 A368 2.50k orange   1.10 .60

Child Wearing Gas Mask in Heavy Traffic — A369

1979, Mar. 13   *Perf. 12½ Vert.*
1275 A369 1.70k dark blue   1.00 1.00
   International Year of the Child.

Drill-weave Tapestry, c. 1855-1860
A370

Carrier Pigeon, Hand with Quill
A371

1979, Mar. 13   *Perf. 12½ Horiz.*
1276 A370 4k gray & red   1.65 .25

Perf. 14x14½ on 3 Sides
1979, Apr. 2   Photo.
1277 A371 (1k) ultra & yel   1.50 .25
   a. Booklet pane of 20   30.00
         Price of booklet 20k.

DISCOUNT BOOKLETS
   Every Swedish household received during Apr. 1979, 2 coupons for the purchase of 2 discount booklets, #1277a. The stamps were for use on post cards and letters within Sweden. The stamps are inscribed "INRIKES POST."
   The program continued with numerous changes. The Inscription changed to "PRIVATPOST" in 1981, the same year that denominations were added. At some point the stamps could also be used to Denmark, Norway, Finland and Iceland. In 1991 the discount value of the stamps ended July, 1.
   The last stamps inscribed "PRIVAT POST" were issued in 1993.

Mail Service by Boat, Grisslehamn to Echero
A372

Europa: 1.70k, Hand on telegraph.

1979, May 7 Engr. *Perf. 12½ Vert.*
1278 A372 1.30k slate grn & blk 2.25 .50
1279 A372 1.70k ocher & blk   2.25 1.00

Woodcutter, Winter — A373

Designs: No. 1281, Sowing, spring. No. 1282, Grazing cattle, summer. No. 1283, Harvester, summer. No. 1284, Plowing, autumn.

1979, May 7   *Perf. 12½ Horiz.*
1280 A373 1.30k multicolored   .55 .45
1281 A373 1.30k sl grn & dk brn .55 .45
1282 A373 1.30k dk brn & sl grn .55 .45
1283 A373 1.30k sl grn & ocher   .55 .45
1284 A373 1.30k multicolored   .55 .45
   a. Bklt. pane, 2 each #1280-1284 5.75
   Nos. 1280-1284 (5)   2.75 2.25

Tourist Steamer Juno — A374

Roller Bridge, Hajstorp — A375

Sailing Ship — A376

Gota Canal: No. 1286, Borenshult Lock. No. 1288, Hand-drawn gate. No. 1290, Rowboat in Forsvik lock.

1979, May 7   *Perf. 12½ Horiz.*
1285 A374 1.15k violet blue   .55 .75
1286 A374 1.15k slate green   .55 .75

Perf. 12½ on 3 Sides
1287 A375 1.15k dull purple   .55 .85
1288 A375 1.15k carmine   .55 .85

Perf. 12½ on 2 Sides
1289 A376 1.15k violet blue   .55 .85
1290 A376 1.15k slate green   .55 .85
   a. Bklt. pane of 6, #1285-1290 3.50 5.75
   Nos. 1285-1290 (6)   3.30 4.90

Strikers and Sawmill
A377

Temperance Movement Banner — A378

Jons Jacob Berzelius
A379

Johan Olof Wallin
A380

1979, Sept. 6 Engr. *Perf. 12½ Vert.*
1291 A377 90o car & dp brn   .55 *.35*

Perf. 12½ Horiz.
Litho.
1292 A378 1.30k multi   .55 .30
Engr.
1293 A379 1.70k brown & grn   .75 .40
1294 A380 4.50k slate blue   1.75 .50
   Nos. 1291-1294 (4)   3.60 1.55

   Centenaries of Sundsvall strike and Swedish Temperance Movement; birth bicentennials of Jons Jacob Berzelius (1779-1848), physician and chemist; Johan Olof Wallin (1779-1839), Archbishop and poet.

Dragonfly
A381

Green Spotted Toad
A383

Pike
A382

1979, Sept. 6   *Perf. 12½ Horiz.*
1295 A381 60o violet   .40 .40

Perf. 12½ Vert.
1296 A382 65o gray   .50 .35
1297 A383 80o olive green   .50 .55
   Nos. 1295-1297 (3)   1.40 1.30

Souvenir Sheet

Swedish Rococo — A384

Designs: 90o, Potpourri pot. 1.15k, Portrait, by Johan Henrik Scheffel. 1.30k, Silver coffeepot. 1.70k, Bust of Carl Johan Cronstedt.

Engraved and Photogravure
1979, Oct. 6   *Perf. 12x12½*
1298 A384   Sheet of 4   2.40 *3.25*
   a.-d. Any single   .50 .60
   No. 1298 sold for 6k; surtax was for philately.

Herrings, Age Determination — A386

Sea Research: No. 1300, Acoustic survey of sea bottom. No. 1301, Water bloom of algae in Baltic Sea. No. 1302, Computer map of herring distribution in South Baltic Sea. No. 1303, Research ship Argos.

1979, Oct. 6   Engr.   Perf. 12½ Horiz.

1299	A386	1.70k multicolored	.90	1.00
1300	A386	1.70k sepia	.90	1.00
1301	A386	1.70k multicolored	.90	1.00
1302	A386	1.70k sepia	.90	1.00
1303	A386	1.70k multicolored	.90	1.00
a.		Bkt. pane of 5, #1299-1303	4.50	6.50

Brooch from Jamtland A387 | Ljusdal Costume A388

Christmas (Costumes and Jewelry from): #1305, Pendant, Smaland. #1307, Osteraker. #1308, Goinge. #1309, Mora.

Perf. 12½ Horiz.

1979, Nov. 15   Engr.

1304	A387	90o dk Prus blue	.40	.30
1305	A387	1.30k dull red	.40	.25

Perf. 12½ on 3 Sides
Photo.
Size: 22x27mm

1306	A388	90o multicolored	.30	.30
1307	A388	90o multicolored	.30	.30
a.		Bkt. pane, 5 each #1306-1307	3.00	

Perf. 12½ Vert.
Size: 26x44mm

1308	A388	1.30k multicolored	.45	.25
1309	A388	1.30k multicolored	.45	.25
a.		Bkt. pane, 5 each #1308-1309	4.50	
		Nos. 1304-1309 (6)	2.30	1.65

Nobel Prize Winner Type of 1978

1919 Winners: 1.30k, Jules Bordet (1870-1961), Belgian bacteriologist. 1.70k, Johannes Stark (1874-1957), German physicist. 2.50k, Carl Spitteler (1845-1924), Swiss poet.

1979, Nov. 15   Engr.   Perf. 12½ Vert.

1310	A367	1.30k lilac	.70	.35
1311	A367	1.70k ultra	.90	1.00
1312	A367	2.50k olive green	1.25	.45
		Nos. 1310-1312 (3)	2.85	1.80

Wind Power — A389

Renewable Energy Sources: No. 1314, Biodegradable material. No. 1315, Solar energy. No. 1316, Geothermal energy. No. 1317, Hydro power.

1980, Jan. 29   Perf. 12½ on 3 sides

1313	A389	1.15k dark blue	.75	.85
1314	A389	1.15k dk grn & bis	.75	.85
1315	A389	1.15k yellow orange	.75	.85
1316	A389	1.15k dark green	.75	.85
1317	A389	1.15k dk bl & dk grn	.75	.85
a.		Bkt. pane, 2 each #1313-1317	7.50	12.50
		Nos. 1313-1317 (5)	3.75	4.25

Crown Princess Victoria and King Carl XVI Gustaf — A390

1980, Feb. 26   Perf. 12½ on 3 sides

1318	A390	1.30k brt blue	.40	.25
a.		Booklet pane of 10	4.00	

Perf. 12½ Vert.

1319	A390	1.30k brt blue	.55	.25
1320	A390	1.70k carmine rose	.75	.40
		Nos. 1318-1320 (3)	1.70	.90

Child Holding Adult's Hand — A391 | Hand Holding Cane — A392

1980, Apr. 22   Perf. 12½ Horiz.

1321	A391	1.40k red brown	.65	.25
1322	A392	1.60k slate green	.75	.25

Parents' insurance system; care for the elderly.

Squirrel — A393

Perf. 15 on 3 Sides

1980, May 12   Photo.

1323	A393	(1k) ultra & yellow	1.50	.25
a.		Booklet pane of 20	30.00	

See note after No. 1277.

Elise Ottesen-Jensen (1886-1973), Journalist A394

Europa: 1.70k, Joe Hill (1879-1915), member of American Workers' Movement and poet.

1980, June 4   Engr.   Perf. 12½ Vert.

1324	A394	1.30k green	1.10	.25
1325	A394	1.70k red	1.30	1.10

Banga Farm, Alfta, Halsingland Province — A395

Tourism (Halsingland Province): No. 1327, Iron Works, Iggesund. No. 1328, Blaxas Ridge, Forsa. No. 1329, Tybling farm, Tyby. No. 1330, Sunds Canal, Hudiksvall.

1980, June 4   Perf. 12½ Horiz.

1326	A395	1.15k red	.65	.75
1327	A395	1.15k dark blue	.65	.75
1328	A395	1.15k dark green	.65	.75
1329	A395	1.15k chocolate	.65	.75
1330	A395	1.15k dark blue	.65	.75
a.		Bkt. pane, 2 each #1326-1330	6.50	
		Nos. 1326-1330 (5)	3.25	3.75

Chair, Scania, 1831 — A396 | Cradle, North Bothnia, 19th Century — A397

Perf. 12½ Horiz.

1980, Sept. 9   Engr.

1331	A396	1.50k grnsh blue	.65	.25

Perf. 12½ Vert.

1332	A397	2k dk red brown	.95	.45

Norden 80.

Scene from "Diagonal Symphony," 1924 — A398

1980, Sept. 9   Perf. 12½ Horiz.

1333	A398	3k dark blue	1.10	.30

Viking Eggeling (1880-1925), artist and film maker.

Souvenir Sheet

Swedish Automobile History — A399

90o, Gustaf Erikson's carriage. 1.15k, Vabis, 1909. 1.30k, Thulin, 1923. 1.40k, Scania, 1903. 1.50k, Tidaholm, 1917. 1.70k, Volvo, 1927.

Photogravure and Engraved

1980, Oct. 11   Perf. 12½

1334	A399	Sheet of 6	4.00	6.50
a.-f.		Any single	.65	.75

No. 1334 sold for 9k.

Bamse the Bear — A401

Farmer Kronblom — A402

Christmas 1980 (Comic Strip Characters): No. 1336, Mandel Karlsson, vert. No. 1337, Adamson, vert.

1980, Oct. 11   Engr.   Perf. 12½ Vert.

1335	A401	1.15k multicolored	.45	.30

Perf. 12½ on 3 sides
Photo.

1336	A401	1.15k multicolored	.50	.40
a.		Booklet pane of 10	5.00	

Perf. 12½ Horiz.
Engr.

1337	A401	1.50k black	.70	.25

Photo.

1338	A402	1.50k multicolored	.50	.25
a.		Booklet pane of 10	5.00	
		Nos. 1335-1338 (4)	2.15	1.20

Angel Blowing Horn A403 | Necken, by Ernst Josephson A404

Perf. on 3 Sides

1980, Nov. 18   Engr.

1339	A403	1.25k multicolored	.50	.25
a.		Booklet pane of 12	6.00	

Christmas 1980.

1980, Nov. 18   Perf. 12½ Horiz.

1340	A404	8k multicolored	3.25	.25

Nobel Prize Winner Type of 1978

1920 Winners: #1341, Knut Hamsun (1859-1953), Norwegian writer. #1342, August Krogh (1874-1949), Danish Physiologist. #1343, Charles-Edouard Guillaume (1861-1938), French physicist. #1344, Walther Nernst (1864-1941), German chemist.

1980, Nov. 18   Perf. 13 on 3 Sides

1341	A367	1.40k dk blue gray	.65	.40
1342	A367	1.40k red	.65	.40
a.		Bkt. pane, 5 each #1341-1342	6.50	
1343	A367	2k green	.85	.55
1344	A367	2k brown	.85	.55
a.		Bkt. pane, 5 each #1343-1344	8.50	
		Nos. 1341-1344 (4)	3.00	1.90

Ernst Wigforss (1881-1977), Politician & Writer A405 | Freya (Fertility Goddess) A406

1981, Jan. 29   Engr.   Perf. 12½ Vert.

1345	A405	5k rose carmine	2.25	.35

1981, Jan. 29   Perf. 12½ on 3 Sides

Norse Mythological Characters: 10o, Thor (thunder god). 15o, Heimdall (rainbow god). 50o, Frey (god of peace, fertility, weather). 1k, Odin.

1346	A406	10o blue black	.25	.25
1347	A406	15o dk carmine	.25	.25
1348	A406	50o dk carmine	.30	.25
1349	A406	75o deep green	.30	.25
1350	A406	1k blue black	.35	.25
a.		Bkt. pane, 2 each #1346-1350	2.75	
		Nos. 1346-1350 (5)	1.45	1.25

Gyrfalcon A407

1981, Feb. 26   Engr.   Perf. 12½ Vert.

1351	A407	50k multicolored	13.50	.75
a.		Booklet pane of 4	55.00	

Troll Chasing Boy — A408

Europa: 2k, Lady of the Woods.

1981, Apr. 28   Engr.

1352	A408	1.50k dk blue & red	1.40	.50
1353	A408	2k dk green & red	1.40	.60

Intl. Year of the Disabled — A409

1981, Apr. 28

1354	A409	1.50k dk green	.65	.30
1355	A409	3.50k purple	1.60	.70

Arms of Oster-gotland Province A410

Sail Boat, Bohuslan A411

Perf. 14½ on 3 Sides

1981, May 18				Photo.	
1356	A410	1.40k	shown	1.50	.25
1357	A410	1.40k	Jamtland	1.50	.25
1358	A410	1.40k	Dalarna	1.50	.25
1359	A410	1.40k	Bohuslan	1.50	.25
a.			Bklt. pane, 5 each #1356-1359	30.00	
			Nos. 1356-1359 (4)	6.00	1.00

See note after No. 1277. See Nos. 1403-1406, 1456-1459, 1492-1495, 1534-1537, 1592-1595.

Perf. 12½ on 3 Sides

1981, May 26				Engr.	
1360	A411	1.65k	shown	.75	.75
1361	A411	1.65k	Blekinge	.75	.75
1362	A411	1.65k	Norrbotten	.75	.75
1363	A411	1.65k	Halsingland	.75	.75
1364	A411	1.65k	Gotland	.75	.75
1365	A411	1.65k	Skane	.75	.75
a.			Bklt. pane of 6, #1360-1365	5.50	*8.00*

King Carl XVI Gustaf A412

Queen Silvia A413

1981-84				*Perf. 12½ Vert.*	
1366	A412	1.65k	dark green	.65	.25
1367	A413	1.75k	dark blue	.85	.50
1368	A412	1.80k	dark blue ('83)	.85	.25
1369	A412	1.90k	red ('84)	1.00	.25
1370	A412	2.40k	violet brn	1.00	.75
1371	A413	2.40k	grnsh black ('84)	1.00	1.00
1372	A412	2.70k	brt lilac ('83)	1.25	1.10
1373	A413	3.20k	red ('83)	1.40	1.25
			Nos. 1366-1373 (8)	8.00	5.35

Day and Night — A414

Scene from Par Lagerkvist's Autobiography Guest of Reality — A415

Perf. 12½ on 3 Sides

1981, Sept. 9				Engr.	
1376	A414	1.65k	dark blue	.50	.25
a.			Booklet pane of 10	5.00	

1981, Sept. 9				*Perf. 12½ Horiz.*	
1377	A415	1.50k	dark green	.75	.25

Conductor Sixten Ehrling and Opera Singer Birgit Nilsson — A416

Bjorn Borg, Tennis Player A417

Baker's Sign A418

Designs: No. 1378, Electric locomotive. No. 1379, Trucks. No. 1381, Oil rig. No. 1383, Ingemar Stenmark, skier.

Perf. 12½ on 2 (Type A416) or 3 (Type A417) sides

1981, Sept. 9					
1378	A416	2.40k	rose carmine	1.25	1.00
1379	A416	2.40k	red	1.25	1.00
1380	A416	2.40k	rose lilac	1.25	1.00
1381	A416	2.40k	deep violet	1.25	1.00
1382	A417	2.40k	dark blue	1.25	1.00
1383	A417	2.40k	dark blue	1.25	1.00
a.			Bklt. pane of 6, #1378-1383	7.50	12.00

1981, Sept. 9				*Perf. 12½ Vert.*	
1384	A418	2.30k	shown	1.75	.25
1385	A418	2.30k	Pewter shop sign	1.75	.25
a.			Pair, #1384-1385	3.50	1.90

A419

Swedish Films: a, Olof Ahs in The Coachman. b, Ingrid Bergman and Gosta Ekman in Intermezzo. c, Greta Garbo in The Gosta Berling Saga, d, Stig Jarrel and Alf Kjellin in Persecution. e, Kari Sylwan and Harriet Andersson in Cries and Whispers

Photogravure and Engraved

1981, Oct. 10				*Perf. 13½*	
1386	A419		Sheet of 5	3.75	*6.00*
a.-e.			Any single	.75	*.90*

No. 1386 sold for 10k.

Nobel Prize Winner Type of 1978

1921 Winners: 1.35k, Albert Einstein (1879-1955), German physicist. 1.65k, Anatole France (1844-1924), French writer. 2.70k, Frederick Soddy (1877-1956), British chemist.

1981, Nov. 24			Engr.	*Perf. 12½ Vert.*	
1387	A367	1.35k	red	.70	.40
1388	A367	1.65k	green	.90	.30
1389	A367	2.70k	blue	1.25	1.00
			Nos. 1387-1389 (3)	2.85	1.70

Christmas 1981 — A421

Designs: Wooden birds.

1981, Nov. 24				*Perf. 12½ on 3 Sides*	
1390	A421	1.40k	red	.65	.25
1391	A421	1.40k	green	.65	.25
a.			Bklt. pane, 5 each #1390-1391	6.50	

Knight on Horseback, by John Bauer A422

John Bauer (1882-1918), Fairytale Illustrator: No. 1393, "What a Miserable Little Pale-face, said the Troll Mother." No. 1394, Marsh Princess. No. 1395, Now the Dusk of the Night is already Upon Us.

Perf. 12x12½ on 3 sides

1982, Feb. 16				Engr.	
1392	A422	1.65k	multicolored	.75	.75
1393	A422	1.65k	multicolored	.75	.75
1394	A422	1.65k	multicolored	.75	.75
1395	A422	1.65k	multicolored	.75	.75
a.			Bklt. pane of 4, #1392-1395	3.25	*4.75*

Impossible Figures — A423

Designs: Geometric figures.

1982, Feb. 16				*Perf. 12½ Horiz.*	
1396	A423	25o	violet brown	.25	.25
1397	A423	50o	brown olive	.25	.25
1398	A423	75o	dark blue	.30	.25
			Nos. 1396-1398 (3)	.80	.75

Newspaper Distributor, by Svenolov Ehren A424

Graziella, by Carl Larsson A425

1982, Feb. 16					
1399	A424	1.35k	deep violet	.70	.25
1400	A425	5k	violet brown	1.90	.25

Europa Issue 1982

Land Reform, 19th Cent. A426

Anders Celsius (1701-1744), Inventor of Temperature Scale — A427

1982, Apr. 26			Engr.	*Perf. 12½ Vert.*	
1401	A426	1.65k	dk olive grn	2.75	.25

Perf. 12½ on 3 Sides

1402	A427	2.40k	dark green	1.10	.80
a.			Booklet pane of 6	6.50	

Provincial Arms Type of 1981

Perf. 14 on 3 Sides

1982, Apr. 26				Photo.	
1403	A410	1.40k	Dalsland	1.50	.25
1404	A410	1.40k	Oland	1.50	.25
1405	A410	1.40k	Vastmandland	1.50	.25
1406	A410	1.40k	Halsingland	1.50	.25
a.			Bklt. pane, 5 each #1403-1406	30.00	
			Nos. 1403-1406 (4)	6.00	1.00

See note after No. 1277.

Elin Wagner (1882-1949), Writer — A428

Perf. 12½ Horiz.

1982, June 3				Engr.	
1407	A428	1.35k	Sketch by Siri Derkert	.60	.50

Burgher House — A429

Embroidered Lace Ribbon, 19th Cent. — A430

1982, June 3				*Perf. 12½ Vert.*	
1408	A429	1.65k	brown	.75	.25

Perf. 12½ Horiz.

1409	A430	2.70k	bister	1.10	1.10

Cent. of Museum of Cultural History, Lund.

1982 Intl. Buoyage System A431

Designs: Various buoy signals.

1982, June 3				*Perf. 13 Horiz.*	
1410	A431	1.65k	shown	.75	.55
1411	A431	1.65k	Ferry	.75	.55
1412	A431	1.65k	Six sailboats	.75	.55
1413	A431	1.65k	One-globed buoy	.75	.55
1414	A431	1.65k	Two-globed buoy	.75	.55
a.			Bklt. pane, 2 each #1410-1414	7.50	
			Nos. 1410-1414 (5)	3.75	2.75

Vietnamese Workers in Sweden — A432

Living Together: Swedish emigration and immigration.

1982, Aug. 26			Engr.	*Perf. 13 Horiz.*	
1415	A432	1.65k	Leaving Sweden, 1880	.65	.55
1416	A432	1.65k	shown	.65	.55
1417	A432	1.65k	Local voting right	.65	.55
1418	A432	1.65k	Girls	.65	.55
a.			Bklt. pane, 2 each #1415-1418	5.50	
			Nos. 1415-1418 (4)	2.60	2.20

Wild Orchids — A433

Wild Orchids: 1.65k (No. 1419a), Orchis mascula. 1.65k (No. 1419d), Cypripedium calcéolus. 2.40k, Epipactis palustris. 2.70k, Dactylorhiza sambucina.

Photogravure and Engraved

1982, Oct. 9				*Perf. 12x13*	
1419	A433		Sheet of 4	5.00	*6.00*
a.-d.			Any single	1.10	1.30

Sold for 10k for benefit of stamp collecting.

Christmas 1982 — A434

Stained-glass Windows, Church at Lye, Gotland, 14th cent.

Perf. 13 on 3 Sides

			Photo.	
1982, Nov. 24				
1420	A434	1.40k Angel	.65	.40
1421	A434	1.40k Child in the Temple	.65	.40
1422	A434	1.40k Adoration of the Kings	.65	.40
1423	A434	1.40k Tidings to the Shepherds	.65	.40
1424	A434	1.40k Birth of Christ	.65	.40
a.		Bklt. pane, 2 each #1420-1424	6.50	7.50
		Nos. 1420-1424 (5)	3.25	2.00

Signature, Atomic Model — A435

Nobel Prizewinners in Physics (Quantum Mechanics). Various Atomic Models: No. 1425, Niels Bohr, Denmark, 1922. No. 1426, Erwin Schrodinger, Austria, 1933. No. 1427, Louis de Broglie, France, 1929. No. 1428, Paul Dirac, England, 1933. No. 1429, Werner Heisenberg, Germany, 1932.

			Engr.	**Perf. 13 Horiz.**	
1982, Nov. 24					
1425	A435	2.40k multi		1.25	1.10
1426	A435	2.40k multi		1.25	1.10
1427	A435	2.40k multi		1.25	1.10
1428	A435	2.40k multi		1.25	1.10
1429	A435	2.40k multi		1.25	1.10
a.		Bklt. pane of 5, #1425-1429		6.75	8.00
		Nos. 1425-1429 (5)		6.25	5.50

Fruit
A436

Games
A436a

Crown and Posthorn
A436b

King Carl XVI Gustaf
A436c

Queen Silvia
A436d

Games
A436e

			Engr.	**Perf. 12½ Vert.**	
1983-85					
1430	A436	5o Horse chestnut		.25	.25
1431	A436	10o Norway maple		.25	.25
1432	A436	15o Dogrose		.25	.25
1433	A436	20o Sloe		.25	.25
1434	A436a	50o Fox and cheese		.30	.25
1435	A436a	60o Dominoes		.30	.25
1436	A436a	70o Ludo		.30	.30
1437	A436a	80o Chinese checkers		.40	.30
1438	A436a	90o Backgammon		.45	.40
1439	A436b	1.60k deep blue		.75	.25
1440	A436c	2k black		.80	.25
1441	A436b	2.50k bister		1.10	.45
1442	A436c	2.70k dull red brn		1.10	1.00
		Perf. 12½ Horiz.			
1443	A436e	3k Chess		1.40	.25

			Perf. 12½ Vert.	
1444	A436d	3.20k brt blue	1.50	1.60
1445	A436b	4k dp car	1.50	.25
		Nos. 1430-1445 (16)	10.90	6.60

Issued: #1430-1433, 2/10/83; #1434-1438, 1443, 10/12/85; #1439-1442, 1444-1445, 1/24/85.

See Nos. 1567-1580, 1783.

Peace Movement Centenary
A437

1983, Feb. 10				
1446	A437	1.35k blue	.55	.35

Nils Ferlin (1898-1961), Poet — A438

1983, Feb. 10				
1447	A438	6k dk grn	2.50	.25

500th Anniv. of Printing in Sweden
A439

			Perf. 13 Horiz.	
1983, Feb. 10				
1448	A439	1.65k Lead type	.75	.45
1449	A439	1.65k Dialogus Creaturarum, 1483	.75	.45
1450	A439	1.65k Carolus XII Bible, 1703	.75	.45
1451	A439	1.65k ABC Books, 1760s	.75	.45
1452	A439	1.65k Laser photo composition	.75	.45
a.		Bklt. pane, 2 each #1448-1452	8.50	
		Nos. 1448-1452 (5)	3.75	2.25

Sweden-US Relations Bicentenary — A440

1983, Mar. 24				
1453	A440	2.70k Ben Franklin, Swedish Arms	1.25	.65
a.		Booklet pane of 5	6.25	

See US No. 2036.

Nordic Cooperation Issue — A441

			Perf. 12½ Horiz.	
1983, Mar. 24			**Engr.**	
		Size: 21x27mm		
1454	A441	1.65k Bicycling	.75	.35
		Perf. 13 Vert.		
1455	A441	2.40k Sailing	1.25	.85

Provincial Arms Type of 1981

			Photo.	**Perf. 14½x14**	
1983, Apr. 25					
1456	A410	1.60k Vastergotland		1.50	.25
1457	A410	1.60k Medelpad		1.50	.25
1458	A410	1.60k Gotland		1.50	.25
1459	A410	1.60k Gastrikland		1.50	.25
a.		Bklt. pane, 5 each #1456-1459		30.00	
		Nos. 1456-1459 (4)		6.00	1.00

See note after No. 1277.

Europa — A442

			Perf. 12½ Horiz.	
1983, Apr. 25			**Engr.**	
1460	A442	1.65k Swedish Ballet Co.	1.50	.50
1461	A442	2.70k Sliding-jaw wrench	1.50	1.50

A443

Designs: 1k, 3k, 10-ore King Oscar II definitive essays, 1884. 2k, No. 39. 4k, No. 58.

			Perf. 12½	
1983, May 25				
1462	A443	1k blue	.90	.50
1463	A443	2k red	.95	.55
1464	A443	3k blue	1.10	.85
1465	A443	4k green	1.25	1.00
a.		Bklt. pane of 4, #1462-1465	4.75	5.25

STOCKHOLMIA Intl. Stamp Exhibition, Aug. 28-Sept. 7, 1986

Red Cross — A444

Greater Karlso — A445

			Perf. 12½ Horiz.	
1983, Aug. 24				
1466	A444	1.50k red	.75	.25
1467	A445	1.60k dk blue	.75	.25

Planorbis Snail — A446

Arctic Fox — A447

			Perf. 12½ on 3 Sides	
1983, Aug. 24				
1468	A446	1.80k green	.65	.25
a.		Booklet pane of 10	6.50	
		Perf. 12½ Horiz.		
1469	A447	2.10k grnsh blk	1.00	.55

See Nos. 1488-1489, 1526-1527, 1623-1626, 1678-1680, 1762-1763.

Hjalmar Bergman (1883-1931), Writer — A448

			Perf. 13 Horiz.	
1983, Aug. 24				
1470	A448	1.80k Portrait	.75	.25
1471	A448	1.80k Jac the Clown illustration by Nisse Skoog	.75	.25
a.		Pair, #1470-1471	1.50	1.25

View of Helgeandsholmen, Stockholm, by Franz Hogenberg, 1580 — A449

			Perf. 12½ Vert.	
1983, Aug. 24				
1472	A449	2.70k dl pur & dk bl	1.25	.70

A450

Photogravure and Engraved

			Perf. 13½	
1983, Oct. 1				
1473	A450	Sheet of 5	5.25	7.00
a.		1.80k Wilhelm Stenhammar, pianist	.95	.75
b.		1.80k Aniara (opera)	.95	.75
c.		1.80k Lars Gullin, jazz saxophonist	.95	.75
d.		1.80k ABBA, pop music group	.95	.75
e.		2.70k Hins Anders, violinist	1.20	1.20
		Sold for 11.50k.		

Christmas 1983 — A452

Postcard designs: No. 1474, Christmas Gnomes around the tree. No. 1475, on straw goats. No. 1476, Folk children, Christmas porridge and gingerbread. No. 1477, Gnomes carrying Christmas gifts on a pole.

			Perf. 12½x14 on 3 sides	
1983, Nov. 22			**Photo.**	
1474	A452	1.60k multi	.65	.30
1475	A452	1.60k multi	.65	.30
1476	A452	1.60k multi	.65	.30
1477	A452	1.60k multi	.65	.30
a.		Bklt. pane, 3 each #1474-1477	7.50	
		Nos. 1474-1477 (4)	2.60	1.20

Chemistry, Nobel Prize Winners — A453

Designs: No. 1478, Arne Tiselius (1902-1971), Electrophoresis Studies. No. 1479, George De Hevesy (1885-1966), Radioactive isotope tracers. No. 1480 Svante Arrhenius (1859-1927), Theory of Electrolytic Dissociation. No. 1481, Theodor Svedberg (1884-1971), Colloid Studies. No. 1482, Hans Von Euler-Chelpin (1873-1964). Enzyme and Vitamin Structures.

Photogravure and Engraved

			Perf. 12½ Horiz.	
1983, Nov. 22				
1478	A453	2.70k slate	1.25	1.10
1479	A453	2.70k dp bl vio	1.25	1.10
1480	A453	2.70k red lilac	1.25	1.10
1481	A453	2.70k blue blk	1.25	1.10
1482	A453	2.70k grnsh blk	1.25	1.10
a.		Bklt. pane of 5, #1478-1482	6.50	8.50

Postal Savings Centenary — A454

Design: 100o, Three crowns.

1984, Feb. 9   Engr.   *Perf. 12½ Vert.*

1483	A454	100o orange	.45 .35
1484	A454	1.60k purple	.65 .55
1485	A454	1.80k pink	.95 .95
		Nos. 1483-1485 (3)	2.05 1.15

Europa
1984
A455

Symbolic bridge of communications exchange.

1984, Feb. 9   *Perf. 12½ Horiz.*

1486	A455	1.80k red	.75 .25
a.		Booklet pane of 10	7.50

Perf. 13 Vert.

1487	A455	2.70k dp ultra	2.75 1.50

Conservation Type of 1983 and

Angelica — A457

1984, Mar. 27   *Perf. 12½ on 3 Sides*

1488	A447	1.90k Lemmings	.60 .25
1489	A447	1.90k Musk ox	.60 .25
a.		Bklt. pane, 5 each #1488-1489	6.00

Perf. 12½ Horiz.

1490	A457	2k shown	1.00 .25
1491	A457	2.25k Alpine birch	1.10 1.00
		Nos. 1488-1491 (4)	3.30 1.75

Provincial Arms Type of 1981

1984, Apr. 24   Photo.   *Perf. 14½x14*

1492	A410	1.60k Sodermanland	1.50 .25
1493	A410	1.60k Blekinge	1.50 .25
1494	A410	1.60k Vasterbotten	1.50 .25
1495	A410	1.60k Skane	1.50 .25
a.		Bklt. pane, 5 ea #1492-1495	30.00
		Nos. 1492-1495 (4)	6.00 1.00

See note after No. 1277.

A458

Swedish Patent System Centenary: No. 1496, Paraffin stove, F.W. Lindqvist, 1892. No. 1497, Industrial robot ASEA-IRB 6. No. 1498, Fan suction vacuum cleaner, Axel Wennergren, 1912. No. 1499, Inboard-outboard motor, AQ-200, No. 1500, SLIC integrated electronic circuit. No. 1501, Tetrahedron container, 1948, 1951.

Perf. 12½ on 3 Sides

1984, June 6   Engr.

1496	A458	2.70k red	1.25 1.25
1497	A458	2.70k sepia	1.25 1.25
1498	A458	2.70k green	1.25 1.25
1499	A458	2.70k green	1.25 1.25
1500	A458	2.70k sepia	1.25 1.25
1501	A458	2.70k blue	1.25 1.25
a.		Bklt. pane of 6, #1496-1501	7.75 9.50

A459

Stockholmia '86 (Famous Letters): 1k, Erik XIV's marriage proposal to Queen Elizabeth I, 1561. 2k, Erik Dahlbergh to Sten Bielke, 1684. 3k, Feather letter, 1834. 4k, August Strindberg to Harriet Bosse, 1905.

Lithographed and Engraved

1984, June 6   *Perf. 12½*

1502	A459	1k multi	.90 .60
1503	A459	2k multi	.95 .65
1504	A459	3k multi	1.10 .85
1505	A459	4k multi	1.25 1.10
a.		Bklt. pane of 4, #1502-1505	4.75 6.00

Fredrika Bremer Assn. (Women's Rights) Centenary A460

Perf. 12½ Vert.

1984, Aug. 28   Engr.

1506	A460	1.50k pink	.70 .50
1507	A460	6.50k red	2.50 1.10

Medieval Towns A461

Engravings by E. Dahlbergh or M. Karl.

1984, Aug. 28   *Perf. 12½x13*

1508	A461	1.90k Jonkoping	1.00 1.10
1509	A461	1.90k Karlstad	1.00 1.10
1510	A461	1.90k Gavle	1.00 1.10
1511	A461	1.90k Sigtuna	1.00 1.10
1512	A461	1.90k Norrkoping	1.00 1.10
1513	A461	1.90k Vadstena	1.00 1.10
a.		Bklt. pane of 6, #1508-1513	6.25 8.25

Viking Satellite, 1985 A462

1984, Oct. 13   *Perf. 12½ Vert.*

1514	A462	1.90k Satellite	1.00 .50
1515	A462	3.20k Receiving station	1.75 1.75

Souvenir Sheet

Swedish Aviation History — A463

Designs: a, Thulin D Two-Seater, 1915. b, SAAB-90 Scandia, 1946. c, Carl Gustaf Cederstrom (1867-1918, "The Flying Baron"), Bleriot, 1910. d, Tomten, 1927. e, Carl Nyberg's Flugan, 1900.

1984, Oct. 13   *Perf. 12½*

1516	A463	Sheet of 5	5.75 5.75
a.-d.		1.90k, any single	.90 .85
e.		2.70k, multi	1.10 1.00
		Sold for 12k.	

Christmas 1984 — A465

Birds.

Lithographed and Engraved

1984, Nov. 29   *Perf. 12½ on 3 Sides*

1517	A465	1.60k Coccothraustes coccothraustes	.55 .35
1518	A465	1.60k Bombycilla garrulus	.55 .35
1519	A465	1.60k Dendrocopos major	.55 .35

1520	A465	1.60k Sitta europaea	.55 .35
a.		Bklt. pane, 3 each #1517-1520	7.00
		Nos. 1517-1520 (4)	2.20 1.40

Inner Ear A466

Nobel Prize Winners in Physiology or Medicine: No. 1521, Georg von Bekesy, 1961, hearing. No. 1522, John Eccles, Alan Hodgkin & Andrew Huxley, 1963, Nerve cell activation. No. 1523, Julius Axelrod, Bernard Katz & Ulf von Euler, 1970, nerve cell storage and release. No. 1524, Roger Sperry, 1981, brain functions. No. 1525, David Hubel, Torsten Wiesel, 1981, Visual information processing.

Perf. 12½ Horiz.

1984, Nov. 29   Engr.

1521	A466	2.70k shown	1.25 1.25
1522	A466	2.70k Nerve, arrows	1.25 1.25
1523	A466	2.70k Nerve (front, side)	1.25 1.25
1524	A466	2.70k Brain halves	1.25 1.25
1525	A466	2.70k Eye	1.25 1.25
a.		Bklt. pane of 5, #1521-1525	7.00 8.00

Conservation Type of 1983 and

A467

Perf. 13 on 3 Sides

1985, Mar. 14   Engr.

1526	A447	2k Muscardinus avellanarius	1.25 .30
1527	A447	2k Salvelinus salvelinus	1.25 .30
a.		Bklt. pane, 5 each #1526-1527	13.00

World Wildlife Fund.

Perf. 12½ Horiz.

1528	A467	2.20k Nigritella nigra	.75 .40
1529	A467	3.50k Nymphaea alba	1.75 .65
		Nos. 1526-1529 (4)	5.00 1.65

World Table Tennis Championships A468

1985, Mar. 14   *Perf. 12½ Vert.*

1530	A468	2.70k Jan-Ove Waldner, Sweden	1.50 .90
1531	A468	3.20k Cai Zhenhua, China	1.90 1.20

Clavichord — A469

1985, Apr. 24   *Perf. 13 Vert.*

1532	A469	2k bluish blk, *buff*	3.75 .50

Key Harp — A470

Perf. 13 on 3 Sides

1533	A470	2.70k dl red brn, *buff*	.90 .75
a.		Booklet pane of 6	5.50

Europa 1985.

Provincial Arms Type of 1981

Perf. 14½x14 on 3 Sides

1985, Apr. 24   Photo.

1534	A410	1.80k Narke	1.50 .25
1535	A410	1.80k Angermanland	1.50 .25
1536	A410	1.80k Varmland	1.50 .25
1537	A410	1.80k Smaland	1.50 .25
a.		Bklt. pane, 5 ea #1534-1537	30.00
		Nos. 1534-1537 (4)	6.00 1.00

See note after No. 1277.

St. Cnut's Land Grant to Lund Cathedral, 900th Anniv. — A471

Seal of St. Cnut and: No. 1538, Lund Cathedral. No. 1539, City of Helsingborg.

Perf. 12½ on 3 Sides

1985, May 21   Engr.

1538	A471	2k bluish blk & blk	.75 .25
1539	A471	2k blk & dk red	.75 .25
a.		Bklt. pane, 5 each #1538-1539	8.50

See Denmark Nos. 777-778.

Stockholmia '86 — A472

Paintings of old Stockholm: No. 1540, A View of Slussen, by Sigrid Hjerten (1919). No. 1541, Skeppsholmen, Winter, by Gosta Adrian-Nilsson (1919). No. 1542, A Summer's Night by the Riddarholmen, by Hilding Linnqvist (1945). No. 1543, Klara Church Tower, by Otte Skold (1927).

Lithographed and Engraved

1985, May 21   *Perf. 12½*

1540	A472	2k multi	1.10 1.10
1541	A472	2k multi	1.10 1.10
1542	A472	3k multi	1.25 1.25
1543	A472	4k multi	1.40 1.25
a.		Bklt. pane of 4, #1540-1543	5.50 7.50

Swedish Touring Club Cent. — A473

#1544, Touring Club Syl Station (c. 1920). #1545, Af Chapman Hostel, Stockholm.

1985, May 21   Engr.   *Perf. 12½ Vert.*

1544		2k blk & dp bl	.75 .45

Size: 58x23mm

1545		2k dp bl & blk	.75 .60
a.		A473 Pair, #1544-1545	1.75 1.75

Trade Signs — A474

Perf. 12½ on 3 Sides

1985, Aug. 28   Engr.

1546	A474	10o Music Shop, Slottsgatan	.25 .25
1547	A474	20o Furrier, Stockholm	.25 .25
1548	A474	20o Coppersmith, Landskrona	.25 .25
1549	A474	50o Haberdasher, Stockholm	.30 .25
1550	A474	2k Shoemaker, Norrkoping	.70 .25
a.		Bklt. pane, #1546-1549, 2	
		#1550	2.00 3.00
		Nos. 1546-1550 (5)	1.75 1.25

The Dying Spartan Hero, Otryades, 1779, by Johan Tobias Sergel — A475

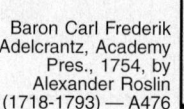

Baron Carl Frederik Adelcrantz, Academy Pres., 1754, by Alexander Roslin (1718-1793) — A476

1985, Aug. 28   *Perf. 12½ Vert.*
1551 A475 2k slate blue   1.00 .30
     Perf. 12½ Horiz.
1552 A476 7k dk red brn   3.00 .70
Royal Academy of Fine Arts, 250th anniv.

Intl. Youth Year — A477

Children's drawings: 2k, Participation, by Marina Karlsson. 2.70k, Development, by Madeleine Andersson. 3.20k, Peace, by Charlotta Ankar.

Lithographed and Engraved
1985, Oct. 12   *Perf. 12½x13*
1553 A477   Sheet of 3   4.25 5.25
a.   2k multi   1.25 .80
b.   2.70k multi   1.25 1.10
c.   3.20k multi   1.50 1.30

Sold for 10k.

Prime Minister Per Albin Hansson (1885-1946) — A478

Birger Sjoberg (1885-1929), Journalist, Novelist, Poet — A479

1985, Oct. 12   *Engr.*   *Perf. 12½ Vert.*
1556 A478 1.60k black & red   .65 .65
     Perf. 12½ Horiz.
1557 A479   4k dk blue grn   1.65 .45

Christmas 1985 — A480

15th cent. religious paintings by Albertus Pictor.

     Perf. 13x12½ on 3 Sides
1985, Nov. 21   *Engr.*
1558 A480 1.80k Annunciation   .85 .50
1559 A480 1.80k Birth of Christ   .85 .50
1560 A480 1.80k Adoration of the Magi   .85 .50

1561 A480 1.80k Mary as the Apocalyptic Virgin   .85 .50
a.   Bklt. pane, 3 each #1558-1561   10.50
   Nos. 1558-1561 (4)   3.40 2.00

Nobel Laureates in Literature — A481

Authors: No. 1562, William Faulkner (1897-1962), 1949, Southern United States. No. 1563, Halldor Kiljan Laxness (b.1902), 1955, Iceland. No. 1564, Miguel Angel Asturias (1899-1974), 1967, Guatemala. No. 1565, Yasunari Kawabata (1899-1972), 1968, Japan. No. 1566, Patrick White (b. 1912), 1973, Australia.

Lithographed and Engraved
1985, Nov. 21   *Perf. 13 Horiz.*
1562 A481 2.70k myr grn   1.25 .95
1563 A481 2.70k dp brn, chlky bl & myr grn   1.25 .95
1564 A481 2.70k myr grn & tan   1.25 .95
1565 A481 2.70k chlky bl & myr grn   1.25 .95
1566 A481 2.70k chlky bl & ocher   1.25 .95
a.   Bklt. pane of 5, #1562-1566   7.50 6.25

Types of 1983-85
Engr., Litho. (1.80k, 3.20k, 6k)
1986-89   *Perf. 12½ Vert.*
1567 A436b 1.70k dk violet   .75 .25
1568 A436b 1.80k brt violet   .85 .25
1569 A436c 2.10k dk blue   1.00 .25
1570 A436c 2.20k int blue   1.00 .25
1571 A436c 2.30k dk ol grn   1.00 .25
1572 A436b 2.80k emerald   1.10 .80
1573 A436c 2.90k dk green   1.40 .60
1574 A436c 3.10k dk brown   1.40 .65
1575 A436b 3.20k yellow brn   1.40 .85
1576 A436c 3.30k dk rose brn   1.40 1.00
1577 A436d 3.40k dk red   1.50 .55
1578 A436d 3.60k green   1.75 .60
1579 A436d 3.90k violet blue   1.75 1.50
1580 A436b 6k blue green   2.00 .95
   Nos. 1567-1580 (14)   18.30 8.15

Issued: 2.10, 2.90, 3.40k, 1/23'; 1.70, 2.80k, 2/20; 1.80, 3.10, 3.20, 3.60, 6k, 1/27/87; 2.20k, 1/29/88; 2.30, 3.30, 3.90k, 4/20/89. See No. 1796.

Waterbirds A484

     Perf. 13 on 2 or 3 Sides
1986, Jan. 23   *Engr.*
1582 A484 2.10k Eider   .75 .25
1583 A484 2.10k Smaspov   .75 .25
a.   Bklt. pane, 5 each #1582-1583   7.50
1584 A484 2.30k Storlom   .85 .35
   Nos. 1582-1584 (3)   2.35 .85

STOCKHOLMIA '86 — A485

Lithographed and Engraved
1986, Jan. 23   *Perf. 13*
1585 A485 2k #33a, cancel   .95 .95
1586 A485 2k Stamp engraver   .95 .95
1587 A485 3k #268, 271, US #836   1.25 1.10
1588 A485 4k Boy soaking stamps   1.50 1.40
a.   Bklt. pane of 4, #1585-1588   4.75 6.50

See US Nos. 2198-2201a.

Swedish PO, 350th Anniv. A486   Sundial A487

Lithographed and Engraved
1986, Feb. 20   *Perf. 13x12½*
1589 A486 2.10k org yel & dk bl   .75 .25
a.   Bklt pane of 8   6.00

1986, Feb. 20   *Engr.*   *Perf. 13 Horiz.*
No. 1591, Motto of the Swedish Academy.
1590 A487 1.70k dk bl & lake, gray   .75 .60
1591 A487 1.70k grn & dk red, gray   .75 .60
a.   Pair, #1590-1591   1.60 1.50
Royal Swedish Academy of Letters, History and Antiquities, and Swedish Academy, bicents.

Provincial Arms Type of 1981
     Perf. 15x14½ on 3 Sides
1986, Apr. 23   *Photo.*
1592 A410 1.90k Harjedalen   1.50 .25
1593 A410 1.90k Uppland   1.50 .25
1594 A410 1.90k Halland   1.50 .25
1595 A410 1.90k Lapland   1.50 .25
a.   Bklt. pane, #1592-1595   30.00
   Nos. 1592-1595 (4)   6.00 1.00

See note after No. 1277.

King Carl XVI Gustaf — A488   Royal Cipher — A489

40th birthday: No. 1598, King presenting Nobel Prize for literature to Czeslaw Milosz, 1980. No. 1600, Royal family at Soldien palace

Lithographed and Engraved
1986, Apr. 23   *Perf. 12 on 3 Sides*
1596 A488 2.10k grnsh blk & pale grn   1.25 .40
1597 A489 2.10k dk bl, pink & gold   1.25 .40
1598 A488 2.10k dk bl & pale bl   1.25 .40
1599 A489 2.10k dk bl, pale grn & gold   1.25 .40
1600 A488 2.10k blk & pale pink   1.25 .40
a.   Bklt. pane, 2 each #1596-1600   13.00 11.00
   Nos. 1596-1600 (5)   6.25 2.00

Olof Palme (1927-1986), Prime Minister — A490

     Perf. 13 on 3 Sides
1986, Apr. 11   *Engr.*
1601 A490 2.10k dk lilac rose   1.10 1.10
1602 A490 2.90k grnsh black   1.25 1.25
a.   Bklt. pane, 5 ea #1601-1602   13.00

Nordic Cooperation Issue — A491

Sister towns.

1986, May 27   *Engr.*   *Perf. 13 Vert.*
1603 A491 2.10k Uppsala   .85 .30
1604 A491 2.90k Eskilstuna   1.25 .90

Europa 1986 — A492

1986, May 27   *Perf. 13 Horiz.*
1605 A492 2.10k Automotive pollutants   2.10 .50
     Perf. 13 on 3 Sides
1606 A492 2.90k Industrial pollutants   1.10 1.25
a.   Booklet pane of 6   6.75

STOCKHOLMIA '86 — A493

Designs: No. 1607, Mail handling terminal, Tomteboda, 1986. No. 1608, Railroad mail car, 19th cent. No. 1609, Post Office, 18th cent. No. 1610, Postman, 17th cent.

Lithographed and Engraved
1986, Aug. 29   *Perf. 13*
1607 A493 2.10k multi   3.00 3.00
1608 A493 2.10k multi   3.00 3.00
1609 A493 2.90k multi   3.00 3.00
1610 A493 2.90k multi   3.00 3.00
a.   Bklt. pane of 4, #1607-1610   12.00 16.00
Bklt. sold for 40k, including 30k ticket to STOCKHOLMIA '86.

     Souvenir Sheet

World Class Athletes in Track and Field — A494

Designs: a, Ann-Louise Skoglund, 400-meter hurdle, 1982. b, Dag Wennlund, 1986, and Eric Lemming, c. 1900, javelin. c, Standing high jumper and Patrik Sjoberg, high jump, 1985. d, Anders Garderud, 300-meter steeplechase record-holder.

1986, Oct. 18   *Engr.*   *Perf. 12½*
1611 A494   Sheet of 4   5.25 7.00
a.-d.   2.10k, any single   1.25 1.25
No. 1611 sold for 11k to benefit philatelic organizations.

Intl. Peace Year — A495

Amnesty Intl., 25th Anniv. — A496

1986, Oct. 18   *Perf. 13 Vert.*
1612 A495 3.40k bluish blk & emer grn   2.25 2.25
1613 A496 3.40k dk red & bluish blk   2.25 2.25
a.   Pair, #1612-1613   4.50 5.00

Christmas — A497

Winter village scenes.

Perf. 13x12½ on 3 Sides

1986, Nov. 25   **Litho. & Engr.**

1614	A497	1.90k Postal van	1.00	.35
1615	A497	1.90k Postman on bicycle	1.00	.35
1616	A497	1.90k Children, sled	1.00	.35
1617	A497	1.90k Child mailing letter	1.00	.35
a.	A497 Block of 4, #1614-1617		4.00	4.00
b.	Bklt. pane of 12, 3 #1617a		12.00	—

Nobel Peace Prize Laureates — A498

#1618, Bertha von Suttner, 1905. #1619, Carl von Ossietzky, 1935. #1620, Albert Luthuli, 1960. #1621, Martin Luther King, Jr., 1964. #1622, Mother Teresa, 1979.

1986, Nov. 25   **Engr.**   *Perf. 13 Horiz.*

1618	A498	2.90k brt bl, blk & hn brn	1.50	1.50
1619	A498	2.90k blk & hn brn	1.50	1.50
1620	A498	2.90k brt bl, blk & brn blk	1.50	1.50
1621	A498	2.90k brn blk & hn brn	1.50	1.50
1622	A498	2.90k blk, brt bl & hn brn	1.50	1.50
a.	Bklt. pane of 5, #1618-1622		9.00	9.50

Conservation Type of 1983

Perf. 13 on 3 Sides

1987, Mar. 10   **Engr.**

1623	A447	2.10k Parnassius mnemosyne	1.00	.25
1624	A447	2.10k Gentianella campestris	1.00	.30
a.	Booklet pane, 5 ea #1623-1624		10.00	

Perf. 13 Horiz.

1625	A447	2.50k Osmoderma eremita	1.10	.25
1626	A447	4.20k Arnica montana	1.75	.50
	Nos. 1623-1626 (4)		4.85	1.30

Swedish Aviation Industry A500

1987, Mar. 10   *Perf. 13 Vert.*

1627	A500	25k Saab SF340	10.00	.40

Europa 1987 — A501

Nos. 1628-1629, City Library, Asplund. No. 1630, Lewerentz Marcus Church.

1987, May 14   **Engr.**   *Perf. 13 Vert.*

1628	A501	2.10k int blk & grn	2.75	.35

Perf. 13 on 3 Sides

1629	A501	3.10k emer grn & red brn	1.10	1.10
1630	A501	3.10k emer grn & sep	1.10	1.10
a.	Bklt. pane, 3 each #1629-1630		7.00	
	Nos. 1628-1630 (3)		4.95	2.55

Illustrations from Children's Novels by Astrid Lindgren (b. 1907) — A502

Perf. 13x12½ on 3 Sides

1987, May 14   **Litho. & Engr.**

1631	A502	1.90k Karlsson Pa Taket	2.00	.25
1632	A502	1.90k Barnen and Bullerbyn	2.00	.25
1633	A502	1.90k Madicken	2.00	.25
1634	A502	1.90k Mio, Min Mio	2.00	.25
1635	A502	1.90k Nils Karlsson-Pyssling	2.00	.25
1636	A502	1.90k Emil and Lonneberga	2.00	.25
1637	A502	1.90k Ronja Rovardotter	2.00	.25
1638	A502	1.90k Pippi Long-stocking	2.00	.25
1639	A502	1.90k Broderna Lejonhjarta	2.00	.25
1640	A502	1.90k Lotta Pa Brakmakargatan	2.00	.25
a.	Bklt. pane, 2 ea #1631-1640		40.00	
	Nos. 1631-1640 (10)		20.00	2.50

See note after No. 1277.

Medieval Towns — A503

#1641, Hans Brask, Bishop of Linkoping, 16th cent. #1642, Nykopingshus Castle.

1987, May 14   **Engr.**   *Perf. 12½ Vert.*

1641	A503	2.10k blk, dk vio & yel bis	.85	.55
1642	A503	2.10k dk vio, blk & yel bis	.85	.55
a.	Pair, #1641-1642		1.75	2.00

Swedes in the Service of Mankind A504

Designs: No. 1643, Raoul Wallenberg, Swedish diplomat in Budapest during World War II. No. 1644, Dag Hammarskjold (1905-1961), UN secretary-general. No. 1645, Folke Bernadotte af Wisborg (1895-1948), organizer of the Red Cross operation that saved thousands from Nazi death camps.

Perf. 12½ Horiz.

1987, Aug. 10   **Engr.**

1643	A504	3.10k blue	1.40	1.10
1644	A504	3.10k green	1.40	1.10
1645	A504	3.10k brown violet	1.40	1.10
a.	Bklt. pane, 2 each #1643-1645		8.50	
	Nos. 1643-1645 (3)		4.20	3.30

Gripsholm Castle, 450th Anniv. — A505

Paintings from the Royal Castle Collection, Gripsholm: No. 1646, King Gustav I Vasa (d. 1560), artist unknown. No. 1647, Blue Tiger, 1673, favorite horse of King Charles XI, by D.K. Ehrenstrahl. No. 1648, Hedvig Charlotta Nordenflycht (1718-1763), poet, by Kopia J.H. Scheffel. No. 1649, Gripsholm Castle Outer Courtyard, 17th Cent., 19th cent. lithograph by C.J. Billmark.

1987, Aug. 10   *Perf. 13 Vert.*

1646	A505	2.10k multi	.85	.40
1647	A505	2.10k multi	.85	.40
1648	A505	2.10k multi	.85	.40
1649	A505	2.10k multi	.85	.40
a.	Bklt. pane of 8, 2 strips of #1646-1649 with gutter btwn.		7.00	
	Nos. 1646-1649 (4)		3.40	1.60

Botanical Gardens A506

Designs: No. 1650, Victoria cruziana (water lily), Victoria House, Bergian Garden, c. 1790, Stockholm University. No. 1651, Layout of baroque palace garden, by Carl Harleman (1700-1753), Uppsala University. No. 1652, White anemones, rock garden, Gothenberg Botanical Gardens, 1923. No. 1653, Tulip tree blossoms, Academy Garden, c. 1860, Lund University.

1987, Oct. 10   **Engr.**   *Perf. 13 Vert.*

1650	A506	2.10k multi	1.00	.55
1651	A506	2.10k multi	1.00	.55
1652	A506	2.10k multi	1.00	.55
1653	A506	2.10k multi	1.00	.55
a.	Bklt. pane, 2 each #1650-1653 with gutter between		8.25	
	Nos. 1650-1653 (4)		4.00	2.20

The Circus in Sweden, Bicent. — A507

Litho. & Engr.

1987, Oct. 10   *Perf. 13*

1654	A507	2.10k Juggler, clown	.95	.95
1655	A507	2.10k High wire	.95	.95
1656	A507	2.10k Equestrian	.95	.95
a.	Bklt. pane of 3, #1654-1656		3.00	4.00

Stamp Day. Sold for 8k.

Christmas A508

Customs: No. 1657, Putting porridge in the stable for the gray Christmas elf. No. 1658, Watering horses at a north-running stream on Boxing Day. No. 1659, Sled-race home from church on Christmas Day. No. 1660, Hanging out sheaves of wheat to foretell a good harvest.

Perf. 13 on 3 Sides

1987, Nov. 25   **Litho.**

1657	A508	2k multi	1.00	.30
1658	A508	2k multi	1.00	.30
1659	A508	2k multi	1.00	.30
1660	A508	2k multi	1.00	.30
a.	Bklt. pane, 3 each #1657-1660		12.50	
	Nos. 1657-1660 (4)		4.00	1.20

Nobel Prize Winners in Physics A509

Space and diagram or formula: No. 1661, Antony Hewish, Great Britain, 1974. No. 1662, Subrahmanyan Chandrasekhar, US, 1983. No. 1663, William Fowler, US, 1983. No. 1664, Arno Penzias and Robert Wilson, US, 1978. No. 1665, Martin Ryle, Great Britain, 1974.

1987, Nov. 25   **Engr.**   *Perf. 13*

1661	A509	2.90k dark blue	1.50	1.50
1662	A509	2.90k blk	1.50	1.50
1663	A509	2.90k dark blue	1.50	1.50
1664	A509	2.90k dark blue	1.50	1.50
1665	A509	2.90k blk	1.50	1.50
a.	Bklt. pane of 5, #1661-1665		8.00	10.00

Inland Boats A510

1988, Jan. 29   **Engr.**   *Perf. 13*

1666	A510	3.10k Skiff, Lake Hjalmaren	1.25	1.25
1667	A510	3.10k Village boat, Lake Vattern	1.25	1.25
1668	A510	3.10k Rowboat, Byske	1.25	1.25
1669	A510	3.10k Flat-bottomed rowboat, As-nen	1.25	1.25
1670	A510	3.10k Ice boat, Lake Vanern	1.25	1.25
1671	A510	3.10k Church boat, Lake Locknesjon	1.25	1.25
a.	Bklt. pane of 6, #1666-1671		8.00	9.50

A511

A512

Settling of New Sweden, 350th Anniv. — A513

Designs: No. 1672, 17th Cent. European settlers negotiating with American Indians, map of New Sweden, the Swedish ships *Kalmar Nyckel* and *Fogel Grip*, based on an 18th cent. illustration from a Swedish book about the American Colonies. No. 1673, Bishop Hill and painter Olof Krans. No. 1674, Carl Sandburg (1878-1967), author, and Jenny Lind (1820-1867), opera singer known as the "Swedish Nightingale." No. 1675, Charles Lindbergh (1902-1974), and *The Spirit of St. Louis*. No. 1676, American astronaut with Swedish Hasselblad camera on the Moon. No. 1677, Swedish players in National Hockey League.

Litho. & Engr., Engr. (#1674-1675)

1988, Mar. 29   *Perf. 13x12½ Horiz*

1672	A511	3.60k multi	1.60	1.60
1673	A511	3.60k multi	1.60	1.60

Perf. 13x12½ on 3 Sides

1674	A512	3.60k brn	1.60	1.60
1675	A512	3.60k dk bl & brn	1.60	1.60

Perf. 13x12½ on 2

1676	A513	3.60k dk bl & yel	1.60	1.60
1677	A513	3.60k dk red, dk bl & blk	1.60	1.60
a.	Bklt. pane of 6, #1672-1677		10.50	12.50

See US No. C117 and Finland No. 768.

Conservation Type of 1983

Species Inhabiting Coastal Waters

Perf. 13 on 3 Sides

1988, Mar. 29				**Engr.**
1678	A447	2.20k	Haliaetus albicilla	1.00 .30
1679	A447	2.20k	Halichoerus grypus	1.00 .30
a.		Bklt. pane, 5 #1678, 5 #1679		10.00

Perf. 13 Horiz.

1680	A446	4.40k	Anguilla anguilla	2.10 .35
		Nos. 1678-1680 (3)		4.10 .95

Midsummer Celebration A515

Skara Township Millennium A516

Perf. 12½ on 3 Sides

1988, May 17				**Litho. & Engr.**
1681	A515	2k	Wildflowers in meadow	1.80 .25
1682	A515	2k	Rowing	1.80 .25
1683	A515	2k	Children making wreaths	1.80 .25
1684	A515	2k	Raising maypole	1.80 .25
1685	A515	2k	Fiddlers	1.80 .25
1686	A515	2k	Ferry	1.80 .25
1687	A515	2k	Dancing	1.80 .25
1688	A515	2k	Accordion player	1.80 .25
1689	A515	2k	Maypole, residence	1.80 .25
1690	A515	2k	Bouquet of flowers	1.80 .25
a.		Bklt. pane, 2 ea #1681-1690		36.00
		Nos. 1681-1690 (10)		18.00 2.50

See note after No. 1277.

1988, May 17　　　　　**Perf. 13 Horiz.**

Design: Detail from Creation, a Skara Cathedral stained-glass window by Bo Beskow, 20th cent.

1691	A516	2.20k	multi	.90 .40

Stora Mining Co., 700th Anniv. — A517

Royal Dramatic Theater, Stockholm, Founded by King Gustav III in 1788 — A518

1988, May 17　　　　　　　　**Engr.**

1692	A517	4.40k	Mine, 18th cent.	1.65 1.25

1988, May 17

Design: Scene from *The Queen's Diamond Ornament*, about the murder of King Gustav III at the Royal Opera in 1792.

1693	A518	8k	grn, red & blk	3.00 2.00

Self-portrait, 1923, by Nils Dardel (1888-1943) A519

Paintings: No. 1695, *Old Age Home in Autumn*, c. 1930, by Vera Nilsson (1888-1979). No. 1696, *Self-portrait*, 1912, by Isaac Grunewald (1899-1979). No. 1697, *Visit of an Eccentric Lady*, 1921, by Dardel. No. 1698,

Soap Bubbles, 1927, by Nilsson. No. 1699, *The Fair*, 1915, by Grunewald.

Perf. 13 on 3 Sides

1988, Aug. 25　　**Litho. & Engr.**
Size: 33x35mm (Nos. 1695, 1698)

1694	A519	2.20k	shown	.95 .90
1695	A519	2.20k	multi	.95 .90
1696	A519	2.20k	multi	.95 .90
1697	A519	2.20k	multi	.95 .90
1698	A519	2.20k	multi	.95 .90
1699	A519	2.20k	multi	.95 .90
a.		Bklt. pane of 6, #1694-1699		5.75 7.50

Europa — A520

Transport and communication.

1988, Aug. 25　**Engr.**　**Perf. 13 Vert.**

1700	A520	2.20k	like No. 1701	2.75 .90

Perf. 13 on 3 Sides

1701	A520	3.10k	X2 high-speed train	1.25 1.25
1702	A520	3.10k	Steam locomotive, 1887	1.25 1.25
a.		Bklt. pane, 3 each #1701-1702		7.50
		Nos. 1700-1702 (3)		5.25 3.40

Common Swift — A521

1988, Aug. 25　　　　**Perf. 12½ Vert.**

1703	A521	20k	brt vio & dk vio	6.50 .35

Dan Andersson (1888-1920), Poet, and Manuscript A522

Forest and Pond, Finnmarken — A523

1988, Oct. 8　**Engr.**　**Perf. 13 Vert.**

1704	A522	2.20k	vio, dk bl & dk bl grn	.90 .45
1705	A523	2.20k	vio, dk bl & dk bl grn	.90 .75
a.		Pair, #1704-1705		1.90 1.75

Soccer — A524

Match scenes: No. 1706, Dribble (Torbjorn Nilsson representing local club matches). No. 1707, Heading the ball (Ralf Edstrom of the national league). No. 1708, Kick (Pia Sundhage, women's soccer).

1988, Oct. 8　**Litho. & Engr.**　**Perf. 13**

1706	A524	2.20k	multi	1.25 1.00
1707	A524	2.20k	multi	1.25 1.00
1708	A524	2.20k	multi	1.25 1.00
a.		Bklt. pane of 3, #1706-1708		3.75 4.25

No. 1708a sold for 8.50k; surtax benefited stamp collecting.

Nobel Laureates in Chemistry A525

Christmas A526

Designs: No. 1709, Willard F. Libby, US, 1960, carbon-14 method of dating artifacts. No. 1710, Karl Ziegler, West Germany, and Guilio Natta, Italy, 1963, catalysts. No. 1711, Aaron Klug, South Africa, 1982, electron microscopy. No. 1712, Ilya Prigogine, Belgium, 1977, proof that molecular order can occur spontaneously out of chaos.

1988, Nov. 29　　　**Perf. 12½ Vert.**

1709	A525	3.10k	multi	1.40 1.25
1710	A525	3.10k	multi	1.40 1.25
1711	A525	3.10k	multi	1.40 1.25
1712	A525	3.10k	multi	1.40 1.25
a.		Bklt. pane, 2 each #1709-1712		12.00
		Nos. 1709-1712 (4)		5.60 5.00

Perf. 12½x13 on 3 Sides
1988, Nov. 29

Story of Christ's birth according to Luke (2:7-20): No. 1713, Angels appear to inform shepherds of Christ's birth. No. 1714, Star of Bethlehem, angel, horse. No. 1715, Birds singing. No. 1716, Magi offering gifts. No. 1717, Holy family. No. 1718, Shepherds with palm offering.

1713	A526	2k	multi	1.00 .75
1714	A526	2k	multi	1.00 .75
1715	A526	2k	multi	1.00 .75
1716	A526	2k	multi	1.00 .75
1717	A526	2k	multi	1.00 .75
1718	A526	2k	multi	1.00 .75
a.		Bklt. pane, 2 each #1713-1718		12.00
		Nos. 1713-1718 (6)		6.00 4.50

Nos. 1713 and 1716, 1714 and 1717, 1715 and 1718 have continuous designs.

Lighthouses A527

Designs: 1.90k, Twin masonry lighthouses, 1832, and concrete lighthouse, 1946, Nidingen, Kattegat Is. 2.70k, Soderarm, Uppland, 1839. 3.80k, Sydostbrotten, Gulf of Bothnia, 1963. 3.90k, Sandhammaren, Skane, c. 1860.

1989, Jan. 31　**Engr.**　**Perf. 13 Vert.**

1719	A527	1.90k	multi	1.00 .50
1720	A527	2.70k	multi	1.50 1.00
1721	A527	3.80k	multi	1.75 1.50
1722	A527	3.90k	multi	2.25 1.75
		Nos. 1719-1722 (4)		6.50 4.75

Endangered Species — A528

1989, Jan. 31　　**Perf. 13 on 3 Sides**

1723	A528	2.30k	*Gulo gulo*	1.00 .25
1724	A528	2.30k	*Strix uralensis*	1.00 .25
a.		Bklt. pane, 5 each #1723-1724		8.50

Perf. 13 Horiz.

1725	A528	2.40k	*Dendrocopos minor*	1.00 .40
1726	A528	2.60k	*Calidris alpina schinzii*	1.50 .85
1727	A528	3.30k	*Hyla arborea*	1.50 1.10
1728	A528	4.60k	*Ficedula parva*	2.25 .50
		Nos. 1723-1728 (6)		8.25 3.35

Opening of The Globe Arena, Stockholm — A529

Perf. 13 Horiz.

1989, Apr. 14				**Litho. & Engr.**
1729	A529	2.30k	Exterior	1.25 .55
1730	A529	2.30k	Ice hockey	1.25 .55
1731	A529	2.30k	Gymnastics	1.25 .55
1732	A529	2.30k	Concert	1.25 .55
a.		Bklt. pane of 4, #1729-1732		5.00

Nordic Cooperation Issue — A530

Folk costumes.

Perf. 13 Horiz.

1989, Apr. 20				**Litho. & Engr.**
1733	A530	2.30k	Woman's wool waist	1.10 .40
1734	A530	3.30k	Belt pouch	1.60 1.10

Natl. Labor Movement, Cent. — A531

1989, May 17　**Engr.**　**Perf. 13 Horiz.**

1735	A531	2.30k	dk red & blk	1.10 .75

Europa 1989 — A532

Children's games: 2.30k, No. 1738, Sailing toy boats. No. 1737, Kick-sledding.

1989, May 17　　　　**Perf. 13 Vert.**

1736	A532	2.30k	car lake	3.25 .75

Perf. 13

1737	A532	3.30k	greenish blue	1.10 1.25
1738	A532	3.30k	lilac	1.10 1.10
a.		Bklt. pane, 3 #1737, 3 #1738		6.60
		Nos. 1736-1738 (3)		5.45 3.25

Summer — A533

Perf. 13 on 3 Sides

1989, May 17				**Litho.**
1739	A533	2.10k	Sailing	1.90 .35
1740	A533	2.10k	Beach ball	1.90 .35
1741	A533	2.10k	Cycling	1.90 .35
1742	A533	2.10k	Canoeing	1.90 .35
1743	A533	2.10k	Angling	1.90 .35
1744	A533	2.10k	Camping	1.90 .35
1745	A533	2.10k	Croquet	1.90 .35
1746	A533	2.10k	Badminton	1.90 .35
1747	A533	2.10k	Gardening	1.90 .35
1748	A533	2.10k	Sand sculpture	1.90 .35
a.		Bklt. pane, 2 ea #1739-1748		38.00
		Nos. 1739-1748 (10)		19.00 3.50

See note after No. 1277.

Polar Exploration
A534

Swedish polar techniques used in the Arctic (Nos. 1749-1751) and Antarctic: No. 1749, Aircraft, temperature experiment. No. 1750, Settlement, Arctic pass. No. 1751, Icebreaker, experiment. No. 1752, Penguins, tall ship and longboat. No. 1753, Antarctic transports, helicopter. No. 1754, Surveying, albatross.

Perf. 13 on 3 Sides
1989, Aug. 22   **Litho. & Engr.**
Size: 40x43mm (Nos. 1750, 1753)

1749	A534	3.30k multi	1.75	1.75
1750	A534	3.30k multi	1.75	1.75
1751	A534	3.30k multi	1.75	1.75
1752	A534	3.30k multi	1.75	1.75
1753	A534	3.30k multi	1.75	1.75
1754	A534	3.30k multi	1.75	1.75
a.		Bklt. pane of 6, #1749-1754	11.00	13.50

Smaland Businesses
A535

Perf. 12½x12 on 3 Sides
1989, Aug. 22   **Engr.**

1755	A535	2.30k Furniture	1.25	1.25
1756	A535	2.30k Assembly equipment	1.25	1.25
1757	A535	2.30k Sewing machines	1.25	1.25
1758	A535	2.30k Glassware	1.25	1.25
1759	A535	2.30k Metal springs	1.25	1.25
1760	A535	2.30k Matchsticks	1.25	1.25
a.		Bklt. pane of 6, #1755-1760	8.00	10.50

Eagle Owl, *Bubo bubo* A536

1989, Aug. 22   **Perf. 13 Vert.**

1761	A536	30k vio, blk & grn blk	10.00	.40

Conservation Type of 1983 and

Birds and Coastline, Bla Jungfrun Natl. Park — A537

Perf. 13x12½ on 3 Sides
1989, Sept. 12   **Engr.**

1762	A447	2.40k *Rhododendron lapponicum*	.90	.25
1763	A447	2.40k *Calypso bulbosa*	.90	.25
a.		Bklt. pane, 5 ea #1762-1763	9.00	

Perf. 12½ Vert.

1764	A537	4.30k dark blue, blk & brn vio	2.10	1.50
		Nos. 1762-1764 (3)	3.90	2.00

See Nos. 1776-1780.

Swedish Kennel Club, Cent. — A538

---

a, Large spitz. b, Fox hound. c, Small spitz.

1989, Oct. 7   **Litho.**   **Perf. 13x12½**

1765	A538	Bklt. pane of 3	3.50	4.50
a.-c.		2.40k any single	1.10	1.00

Sold for 9.50k.

Christmas — A539

Holiday symbols: No. 1766, Top of Christmas tree, wreath. No. 1767, Candelabrum, foods. No. 1768, Star, poinsettia plant, grot pot. No. 1769, Bottom of tree, straw goat, gifts. No. 1770, Gifts, television, girl. No. 1771, Boy, grandfather, girl opening gift.

Perf. 12½x13 on 3 Sides
1989, Nov. 24   **Litho.**

1766	A539	2.10k multi	1.25	.50
1767	A539	2.10k multi	1.25	.50
1768	A539	2.10k multi	1.25	.50
1769	A539	2.10k multi	1.25	.50
1770	A539	2.10k multi	1.25	.50
1771	A539	2.10k multi	1.25	.50
a.		Bklt. pane, 2 each #1766-1771	15.00	
		Nos. 1766-1771 (6)	7.50	3.00

Nobel Laureates in Physiology
A540

Genetics: No. 1772, Thomas Morgan (1866-1945), US, 1933, chromosomal study of fruit flies to determine laws and mechanism of heredity. No. 1773, James Watson, US, and Francis Crick with Maurice Wilkins, Great Britain, 1962, molecular structure of DNA. No. 1774, Werner Arber, Switzerland, Daniel Nathans and Hamilton Smith, US, 1978, enzymatic cutting of nucleotides to create gene hybrids. No. 1775, Barbara McClintock, botanist, US, 1983, corn color studies that led to theory of gene jumping.

Perf. 12½ Vert.
1989, Nov. 24   **Litho. & Engr.**

1772	A540	3.60k multi	1.50	1.10
1773	A540	3.60k multi	1.50	1.10
1774	A540	3.60k multi	1.50	1.10
1775	A540	3.60k multi	1.50	1.10
a.		Bklt. pane, 2 each #1772-1775 with gutter between	12.00	
		Nos. 1772-1775 (4)	6.00	4.40

Natl. Parks Type of 1989

Designs: No. 1776, Campground, sailboat on lake, Angso Park. No. 1777, Hiking, Pieljekaise Park. 3.70k, Three whooper swans over wetlands, Muddus Park. 4.10k, Deer, lake, Padjelanta Park. 4.80k, Bears, forest, Sanfjallet Park.

Perf. 13 on 3 Sides
1990, Jan. 26   **Engr.**

1776	A537	2.50k multicolored	.95	.25
1777	A537	2.50k multicolored	.95	.25
a.		Bklt. pane, 5 each #1776-1777	9.50	

Perf. 13 Vert.

1778	A537	3.70k multicolored	2.00	.30
1779	A537	4.10k multicolored	2.50	2.00
1780	A537	4.80k multicolored	2.50	1.75
		Nos. 1776-1780 (5)	8.90	4.55

King and Queen Types of 1985-86 and

Queen Silvia — A541   King Carl XVI Gustaf — A542

King Carl XVI Gustav A543   Queen Silvia A544

King Carl XVI Gustaf — A545

Perf. 12½ Vert., Horiz. (A541, A542, A545)
1990-97   **Engr.**

1783	A436c	2.50k deep claret	1.00	.25
1784	A542	2.80k dk blue	1.10	.25
1785	A542	2.90k deep green	1.30	.25
1786	A542	3.20k violet	1.50	.25
1787	A543	3.70k dark red brown	1.50	.25
1788	A543	3.85k black	1.75	.30
1789	A436d	4.60k bright org	2.00	1.75
1790	A541	5k deep rose vio	2.00	.40
1791	A545	(5k) deep blue	2.10	.30
1792	A541	6k deep claret	2.25	.60
1793	A544	6k dark green	2.75	1.25
1794	A541	6.50k purple	3.50	2.00
1795	A544	7.50k purple	3.10	1.65
1796	A544	8k brown red	3.10	1.00
		Nos. 1783-1796 (14)	28.95	10.50

Issued: 2.50k, 4.60k, 1/26; 5k, 3/20/91; 2.80k, 11/20/91; 2.90k, #1792, 1/2/93; 3.20k, 1/17/94; 6.50k, 3/18/94; 3.70k, #1793, 1/2/95; 3.85k, 7.50k, 1/2/96; (5k), 8k, 2/28/97. No. 1791 is inscribed "BREV."

Viking Heritage A546

Designs: No. 1801, Viking head of carved bone, dragon carving from a molding found in Birka. No. 1802, Three viking longships. No. 1803, Viking town. No. 1804, Bronze statue of pagan fertility god, silver filigree cross. No. 1805, Bishop's crosier, southern Russian carved statue of a deer. No. 1806, Viking longship (stern). No. 1807, Viking longship (bow), horsemen, woman, warrior, wolf. No. 1808, Sword hilts.

Perf. 12x13 on 3 Sides
1990, Mar. 28   **Litho. & Engr.**

1801	A546	2.50k multicolored	1.10	.85
1802	A546	2.50k multicolored	1.10	.85
1803	A546	2.50k multicolored	1.10	.85
1804	A546	2.50k multicolored	1.10	.85
1805	A546	2.50k multicolored	1.10	.85
1806	A546	2.50k multicolored	1.10	.85
1807	A546	2.50k multicolored	1.10	.85
1808	A546	2.50k multicolored	1.10	.85
a.		Bklt. pane of 8, #1801-1808	9.00	10.00

Nos. 1802-1803, 1806-1807 printed in a continuous design.

Swedish Industrial Safety, Cent. — A547

1990, Mar. 28   **Engr.**   **Perf. 13 Horiz.**

1809	A547	2.50k Lumberjack	1.10	.30

Europa 1990 — A548

Post offices.

1990, Mar. 28   **Perf. 13 Vert.**

1810	A548	2.50k Postal Museum, 1720	3.25	.45

Perf. 13 on 3 Sides

1811	A548	3.80k Sollebrunn, 1985	1.50	1.10
1812	A548	3.80k Vasteras, 1956	1.50	1.10
a.		Bklt. pane, 3 each #1811-1812	9.00	
		Nos. 1810-1812 (3)	6.25	2.65

World Equestrian Games, Stockholm A549

Litho. & Engr.
1990, May 15   **Perf. 12½x13**

1813	A549	3.80k Endurance riding	1.60	1.40
1814	A549	3.80k Combined training	1.60	1.40
1815	A549	3.80k Show jumping	1.60	1.40
1816	A549	3.80k Dressage	1.60	1.40
1817	A549	3.80k Volting	1.60	1.40
1818	A549	3.80k Four-in-hand	1.60	1.40
a.		Bklt. pane of 6, #1813-1818	10.00	11.50

Apiculture — A550

#1819, Worker bee collecting nectar. #1820, Bee, bilberry flower. #1821, Worker bee. #1822, Apiary hive. #1823, Two bees in honeycomb. #1824, Drone, 7 cells, blue green panel. #1825, Queen bee, 7 cells, yellow panel. #1826, Swarm hanging from tree. #1827, Beekeeper. #1828, Honey.

1990, May 15   **Litho.**

1819	A550	2.30k multicolored	1.80	.40
1820	A550	2.30k multicolored	1.80	.40
1821	A550	2.30k multicolored	1.80	.40
1822	A550	2.30k multicolored	1.80	.40
1823	A550	2.30k multicolored	1.80	.40
1824	A550	2.30k multicolored	1.80	.40
1825	A550	2.30k multicolored	1.80	.40
1826	A550	2.30k multicolored	1.80	.40
1827	A550	2.30k multicolored	1.80	.40
1828	A550	2.30k multicolored	1.80	.40
a.		Bklt. pane, 2 ea #1819-1828	36.00	
		Nos. 1819-1828 (10)	18.00	4.00

See note after No. 1277.

Wasa Nautical Museum — A551

Man-of-war *Wasa*: 2.50k, Bow. 4.60k, Stern.

1990, May 15   **Engr.**   **Perf. 13 Vert.**

1829	A551	2.50k org & blk	1.10	.45
1830	A551	4.60k dk bl & org	2.00	1.50

Dearest Brothers, Sisters and Friends — A552

Proud City
A553

Allusions to poetry verses of Carl Michael Bellman (No. 1833) and Evert Taube: No. 1833, Fredmen in the gutter. No. 1834, Happy baker in San Remo. No. 1835, At sea. No. 1836, Violava.

Perf. 13 on 3 Sides
1990, Aug. 8   **Litho. & Engr.**
1831	A552	2.50k multicolored	1.75	1.50
1832	A553	2.50k multicolored	1.75	1.50
1833	A553	2.50k multicolored	1.75	1.50
1834	A552	2.50k multicolored	1.75	1.50
1835	A552	2.50k multicolored	1.75	1.50
1836	A552	2.50k multicolored	1.75	1.50
a.		Bklt. pane of 6, #1831-1836	7.50	12.00

Paper Production
A554

#1837, Paper production c. 1600. #1838, Watermark. #1839, Newspaper mastheads. #1840, Modern paper production.

1990, Aug. 8   **Perf. 12½ Vert.**
1837	A554	2.50k multicolored	1.10	.45
1838	A554	2.50k multicolored	1.10	.45
1839	A554	2.50k multicolored	1.10	.45
1840	A554	2.50k multicolored	1.10	.45
a.		Bklt. pane, 2 each #1837-1840 with gutter between	9.00	
		Nos. 1837-1840 (4)	4.40	1.80

Ovedskloster Palace — A555

1990, Aug. 8   **Engr.**   **Perf. 13 Vert.**
1841	A555	40k multicolored	11.00	.30

See Nos. 1874-1877.

Photography
A556

Litho. & Engr.
1990, Oct. 6   **Perf. 12½**
1842	A556	2.50k Bellows camera	1.10	1.25
1843	A556	2.50k August Strindberg	1.10	1.25
1844	A556	2.50k 35mm camera	1.10	1.25
a.		Bklt. pane of 3, #1842-1844	3.30	5.00

Stamp Day. Booklet of two panes sold for 20k. Surtax benefited stamp collecting.

Clouds — A557   A558

1990, Oct. 6 Engr.   Perf. 12½ Horiz.
1845	A557	4.50k Cumulus	2.00	.45
1846	A557	4.70k Cumulonimbus	2.25	1.25
1847	A557	4.90k Cirrus	2.50	1.25
1848	A557	5.20k Alto cumulus	2.75	1.50
		Nos. 1845-1848 (4)	9.50	4.45

1990, Oct. 6   **Perf. 12½ Vert.**
1849	A558	2.50k shown	1.20	.50
1850	A558	2.50k Women bathing	1.20	.50
a.		Pair, #1849-1850	2.50	2.25

Moa Martinson (1890-1964), author.

Nobel Laureates in Literature — A559

Perf. 13 on 2 Sides
1990, Nov. 27   **Engr.**
1851	A559	3.80k Par Lagerkvist, 1951	1.50	1.40
1852	A559	3.80k Ernest Hemingway, 1954	1.50	1.40
1853	A559	3.80k Albert Camus, 1957	1.50	1.40
1854	A559	3.80k Boris Pasternak, 1958	1.50	1.40
a.		Bklt. pane, 2 each #1851-1854 with gutter between	13.00	
		Nos. 1851-1854 (4)	6.00	5.60

See Nos. 1914-1917.

Christmas — A560

Flowers.

Perf. 13 on 3 Sides
1990, Nov. 27   **Litho.**
1855	A560	2.30k Schlumbergera x buckleyi	1.00	.55
1856	A560	2.30k Helleborus niger	1.00	.55
1857	A560	2.30k Rhododendron simsii	1.00	.55
1858	A560	2.30k Hippeastrum x hortorum	1.00	.55
1859	A560	2.30k Hyacinthus orientalis	1.00	.55
1860	A560	2.30k Euphorbia pulcherrima	1.00	.55
a.		Bklt. pane, 2 each #1855-1860	12.00	
		Nos. 1855-1860 (6)	6.00	3.30

Carta Marina by Olaus Magnus, 1572 — A561

Scandanavia by A. Bureas and J. Blaeus, 1662 — A562

Maps: No. 1863, Celestial globe by Anders Akerman, 1759. No. 1864, Contour map, 1938. No. 1865, Stockholm, 1989. No. 1866, Bedrock Map, Geological Survey, 1984.

Perf. 13 on 3 Sides
1991, Jan. 30   **Litho. & Engr.**
1861	A561	5k multicolored	2.40	1.75
1862	A562	5k multicolored	2.40	1.75
1863	A561	5k multicolored	2.40	1.75
1864	A561	5k multicolored	2.40	1.75
1865	A562	5k multicolored	2.40	1.75
1866	A561	5k multicolored	2.40	1.75
a.		Bklt. pane of 6, #1861-1866	15.00	18.00

Fish — A563

Perf. 13 on 3 Sides
1991, Jan. 30   **Engr.**
1867	A563	2.50k shown	1.25	.35
1868	A563	2.50k Siluris glanis, diff.	1.25	.35
b.		Bklt. pane, 5 each #1867-1868	13.50	

Perf. 13 Vert.
1869	A563	5k Cobitis taenia	1.75	.25
1870	A563	5.40k Gobio gobio	2.75	3.00
1871	A563	5.50k Noemacheilus barbatulus	2.40	.25
1872	A563	5.60k Leucaspius delineatus	2.40	1.75
		Nos. 1867-1872 (6)	11.80	5.95

Palace Type of 1990
Designs: 10k, Stromsholm Castle. 20k, Karlberg Castle. 25k, Drottningholm Palace.

1991-92   **Engr.**   **Perf. 13 Vert.**
1874	A555	10k blk & olive brn	4.00	.25
1876	A555	20k multicolored	6.50	.75

Size: 58x23mm
1877	A555	25k multicolored	7.00	.75
		Nos. 1874-1877 (3)	17.50	1.75

Issued: 10k, 4/27; 25k, 3/20; 20k, 5/21/92.

A564

Perf. 12½x13 on 3 Sides
1991, May 15   **Litho.**
1883	A564	2.40k Seglora church	.95	.25
1884	A564	2.40k Flag above park	.95	.25
1885	A564	2.40k Wedding	.95	.25
1886	A564	2.40k Animals	.95	.25
b.		Bklt. pane, 5 ea #1883-1886	19.00	
		Nos. 1883-1886 (4)	3.80	1.00

Skansen Park, Stockholm, 100th anniv. See note after No. 1277. Complete booklet of 20 stamps sold for 46k.

Kolmarden Zoological Park, Ostergotland
A565

Perf. 12½ Horiz.
1991, May 15   **Engr.**
1887	A565	2.50k Polar bears	1.10	.25
1888	A565	4k Dolphin show	1.75	1.10
		Norden '91.		

A566

Public Parks, cent.: #1890, Dancing in park.

1991, May 15   **Perf. 13 Vert.**
1889	A566	2.50k dark blue	1.10	.50
1890	A566	2.50k dark blue	1.10	.50
a.		Pair, #1889-1890	2.25	2.25

Europa — A567

Litho. & Engr.
1991, May 15   **Perf. 13**
1891	A567	4k Hermes space plane	1.75	1.75
1892	A567	4k Freja satellite	1.75	1.75
1893	A567	4k Tele-X satellite	1.75	1.75
a.		Bklt. pane of 3, #1891-1893	5.50	8.50

Olympic Champions
A568

Designs: No. 1894, Magda Julin, figure skating, Antwerp, 1920. No. 1895, Toini Gustaffson, cross country skiing, Grenoble, 1968. No. 1896, Agneta Andersson, Anna Olsson, two-person kayak, Los Angeles, 1984. No. 1897, Ulrika Knape, diving, Munich, 1972.

Perf. 12x13 on 3 Sides
1991, Aug. 27   **Litho. & Engr.**
1894	A568	2.50k multicolored	1.10	.70
1895	A568	2.50k multicolored	1.10	.70
1896	A568	2.50k multicolored	1.10	.70
1897	A568	2.50k multicolored	1.10	.70
a.		Bklt. pane, 2 each #1894-1897	9.00	
		Nos. 1894-1897 (4)	4.40	2.80

See Nos. 1937-1940, 1953-1956.

Iron Mining — A569

#1898, Spetal Mine, Norberg. #1899, Forsmark Mill. #1900, Ironworks forge. #1901, Forge welding. #1902, Dannemora Mine. #1903, Blast furnace, Pershyttan.

Perf. 13 on 2 or 3 Sides
1991, Aug. 27   **Engr.**
1898	A569	2.50k multicolored	1.25	.85
1899	A569	2.50k multicolored	1.25	.85

Size: 31x26mm
1900	A569	2.50k multicolored	1.25	1.10
1901	A569	2.50k multicolored	1.25	1.10

Size: 31x40mm
1902	A569	2.50k multicolored	1.25	1.10
1903	A569	2.50k multicolored	1.25	1.10
a.		Bklt. pane of 6, #1898-1903	7.50	6.75

Coronation of King Gustavus III, by Carl Gustaf Pilo — A570

Details from painting: No. 1904, King Gustavus III. No. 1905, Gustavus with crown held above head. No. 1906, Chancellor Arvid Horn, Archbishop Mattias Beronius holding crown above Gustavus III.

1991, Oct. 5   Engr.   **Perf. 13**
1904 A570 10k blue   4.00 3.50
1905 A570 10k violet   4.00 3.50
    Size: 76x44mm
1906 A570 10k greenish black   5.00 5.00
  a.   Bklt. pane of 3, #1904-1906   13.00 13.00

Czeslaw Slania, engraver, 70th birthday. No. 1906a sold for 35k to benefit stamp collecting.

Rock Musicians A571

1991, Oct. 5   Litho. & Engr.
1907 A571 2.50k Lena Philipsson 1.75 1.00
1908 A571 2.50k Roxette 1.75 1.00
1909 A571 2.50k Jerry Williams 1.75 1.00
  a.   Bklt. pane of 3, #1907-1909   7.50 5.00

A572   A573

Christmas: No. 1910, Boy with star, girl with snacks. No. 1911, Family dancing around Christmas tree. No. 1912, Cat beside tree. No. 1913, Child beside bed.

Perf. 12½x13 on 3 Sides
1991, Nov. 20   Litho.
1910 A572 2.30k multicolored .95 .45
1911 A572 2.30k multicolored .95 .45
1912 A572 2.30k multicolored .95 .45
1913 A572 2.30k multicolored .95 .45
  b.   Bklt. pane, 3 ea #1910-1913   12.00
   Nos. 1910-1913 (4)   3.80 1.80

Nobel Laureates Type of 1990

Nobel Peace Prize Winners: No. 1914, Jean Henri Dunant, founder of Red Cross. No. 1915, Albert Schweitzer, physician and theologian. No. 1916, Alva Myrdal, disarmament negotiator. No. 1917, Andrei Sakharov, physicist.

1991, Nov. 20   Engr.   **Perf. 13 Horiz.**
1914 A559 4k carmine 1.60 1.60
1915 A559 4k dk green 1.60 1.60
1916 A559 4k dk ultra 1.60 1.60
1917 A559 4k dk violet 1.60 1.60
  a.   Bklt. pane, 2 each #1914-1917 with gutter between   13.00
   Nos. 1914-1917 (4)   6.40 6.40

1992, Jan. 30   Engr.   **Perf. 13 Horiz.**
1918 A573 2.30k red, grn & blk 1.10 .35

Outdoor Life Assoc., cent.

A574   A575

Wild Animals

Perf. 13 on 3 Sides
1992-2009   Engr.
1920 A574 2.80k Capreolus capreolus 1.00 .25
1921 A574 2.80k Capreolus capreolus (with fawn) 1.00 .25
  b.   Bklt. pane, 5 ea #1920-1921   10.00
1922 A574 2.90k Ursus arctos (2 cubs) 1.10 .30
1923 A574 2.90k Ursus arctos (adult) 1.10 .30
  b.   Bklt. pane, 5 ea #1922-1923   11.00
1924 A574 3.85k Mustela erminea 1.00 .25
1925 A574 3.85k Lutra lutra 1.00 .25
  a.   Bklt. pane #1924-1925   16.00
   Complete booklet, 1 #1925a   16.00

Perf. 13 Vert. (A574), Horiz. (A575)
1926 A574 1k Erinaeceus eropaeus .40 .10
1927 A574 2.80k like #1921 .00 .25
1928 A574 2.90k like #1922 1.25 .25
1929 A574 3k Mustela putorius 1.25 .45
1930 A575 3.20k Castor fiber 1.50 1.25
1931 A574 3.85k like #1924 1.50 .35
1932 A575 5.80k Canis lupus 2.75 .40
1933 A575 6k Sciurus vulgaris 2.50 .50
1934 A575 7k Alces alces 3.50 .50
1935 A574 7.70k Vulpes vulpes 3.00 .60
1936 A575 12k Lynx lynx 3.75 .85

Perf. 12 Horiz. Syncopated
1936A A575 12k Lynx lynx 3.25 3.25
   Nos. 1920-1936 (17)   28.60 7.30

Issued: #1920-1921, 1930, 6k, 7k, Jan. 30; #1922-1923, 1928-1929, 1932, 1936, Jan. 28, 1993; 1k, 3.20k, 3.85k, 7.70k, 1/2/96. No. 1936A, 1/1/2009.
See Nos. 2207-2209, 2238.

Olympic Champions Type of 1991

No. 1937, Gunde Svan, cross-country skiing, Sarajevo, 1984. No. 1938, Thomas Wassberg, cross-country skiing, Lake Placid, 1980. No. 1939, Tomas Gustafson, speed skating, Sarajevo, 1984. No. 1940, Ingemar Stenmark, slalom skiing, Lake Placid, 1980.

Perf. 12x13 on 3 Sides
1992, Jan. 30   Litho. & Engr.
1937 A568 2.80k multicolored 1.25 .75
1938 A568 2.80k multicolored 1.25 .75
1939 A568 2.80k multicolored 1.25 .75
1940 A568 2.80k multicolored 1.25 .75
  a.   Bklt. pane, 2 each #1937-1940   10.50
   Nos. 1937-1940 (4)   5.00 3.00

European Soccer Championships, Sweden — A576

1992, Mar. 26   Engr.   **Perf. 13 Vert.**
1941 A576 2.80k shown 1.25 .35
1942 A576 2.80k Two players 1.25 .35
  a.   Pair, #1941-1942   2.50 1.50

Sweden No. 1a A577

Litho. & Engr.
1992, Mar. 26   **Perf. 13**
1943 A577 2.80k No. 1 3.50 3.00
1944 A577 4.50k No. 1 3.50 3.00
1945 A577 5.50k shown 3.00 1.60
  a.   Bklt. pane, #1943-1944, 2 #1945   13.00 11.00
   Nos. 1943-1945 (3)   10.00 7.60

No. 1945a sold for 25k. Surtax benefited stamp collecting.

Sailing Ships — A578

1992, Mar. 26
1946 A578 4.50k Sprengtporten, 1785 2.10 1.50
1947 A578 4.50k Superb, 1855 2.10 1.50
1948 A578 4.50k Big T 2.10 1.50
  a.   Bklt. pane of 3, #1946-1948   6.50 6.50

Europa. Discovery Race, Spain-Florida (No. 1948).

Children's Drawings A579

Perf. 13x12½ on 3 Sides
1992, May 21   Litho.
1949 A579 2.50k Rabbit 1.25 .25
1950 A579 2.50k Horses 1.25 .25
1951 A579 2.50k Cat 1.25 .25
1952 A579 2.50k Elephant 1.25 .25
  a.   Bklt. pane, 5 ea #1949-1952   25.00
   Nos. 1949-1952 (4)   5.00 1.00

See note after No. 1277.

Olympic Champions Type of 1991

Designs: No. 1953, Gunnar Larsson, swimming, 1972. No. 1954, Bernt Johansson, cycling, 1976. No. 1955, Anders Garderud, steeplechase, 1976. No. 1956, Gert Fredriksson, kayaking, 1948-1956.

Perf. 12x13 on 3 Sides
1992, May 21   Litho. & Engr.
1953 A568 5.50k multicolored 2.50 2.50
1954 A568 5.50k multicolored 2.50 2.50
1955 A568 5.50k multicolored 2.50 2.50
1956 A568 5.50k multicolored 2.50 2.50
  a.   Bklt. pane, 2 ea #1953-1956   21.00
   Nos. 1953-1956 (4)   10.00 10.00

Greetings Stamps — A580

Perf. 13x12 on 3 Sides
1992, Aug. 14   Litho.
1957 A580 2.80k Hand with flower 1.10 .85
1958 A580 2.80k Cheese 1.10 .85
1959 A580 2.80k Baby 1.10 .85
1960 A580 2.80k Hand holding pen 1.10 .85
  b.   Bklt. pane, 2 each #1957-1960   9.00
   Nos. 1957-1960 (4)   4.40 3.40

88th Inter-Parliamentary Union Conference, Stockholm — A581

Swedish Patent and Registration Office, Cent. — A582

#1961, Riksdag building. #1962, First automatic lighthouse, Gustaf Dalen's sun valve.

Perf. 12½ Vert.
1992, Aug. 27   Engr.
1961 A581 2.80k violet, tan 1.25 .25
Perf. 13 Horiz.
1962 A582 2.80k blue & black 1.25 .35

Kitchen Maid, by Rembrandt A583

The Triumph of Venus, by Francois Boucher A584

Paintings: No. 1965, Portrait of a Girl, by Albrecht Dürer. No. 1966, Rorstrand Vase, by Erik Wahlberg. No. 1967, Motif from the Seine/The Tree and the River Bend III, by Carl Fredrik Hill. No. 1968, Sergel in his Studio, by Carl Larsson.

Perf. 12½ on 3 Sides
1992, Aug. 27   Litho. & Engr.
1963 A583 5.50k multicolored 3.00 3.00
1964 A583 5.50k multicolored 3.00 3.00
1965 A583 5.50k multicolored 3.00 3.00
1966 A583 5.50k multicolored 3.00 3.00
1967 A584 5.50k multicolored 3.00 3.00
1968 A583 5.50k multicolored 3.00 3.00
  a.   Bklt. pane of 6, #1963-1968   18.50 20.00

National Museum of Fine Arts, 200th anniv.

Prehistoric Animals — A585

Perf. 13x12½ on 3 Sides
1992, Oct. 3   Litho. & Engr.
1969 A585 2.80k Plateosaurus 1.25 .90
1970 A585 2.80k Thoracosaurus scanicus 1.25 .90
1971 A585 2.80k Coelodonta antiquitatis 1.25 .90
1972 A585 2.80k Mammuthus primigenius 1.25 .90
  a.   Bklt. pane, 2 ea #1969-1972   10.40
   Nos. 1969-1972 (4)   5.00 3.60

No. 1972a sold for 27k to benefit stamp collecting.

1950 Automobiles A586

1992, Oct. 3 Engr. *Perf. 12½ Vert.*
1973	A586	4k Saab 92	1.75 1.50
1974	A586	4k Volvo P 831	1.75 1.50
a.		Pair, #1973-1974	3.75 3.50

Birds of the
Baltic
Shores — A587

1992, Oct. 3 Litho. & Engr. *Perf. 13*
1975	A587	4.50k Pandion haliaetus	2.50 1.25
1976	A587	4.50k Limosa limosa	2.50 1.25
1977	A587	4.50k Mergus merganser	2.50 1.25
1978	A587	4.50k Tadorna tadorna	2.50 1.25
a.		Bklt. pane of 4, #1975-1978	10.00 7.50

See Estonia Nos. 231-234, Latvis Nos. 332-335, and Lithuania Nos. 427-430.

A588   A589

A590   A591
Christmas

Icons: No. 1979, Joachim and Anna, 16th cent. No. 1980, Madonna and Child, 14th cent. No. 1981, Archangel Gabriel, 12th cent. No. 1982, St. Nicholas, 16th cent.

Perf. 12½x13 on 3 Sides
1992, Nov. 27   Litho. & Engr.
1979	A588	2.30k multicolored	1.25 .50
1980	A589	2.30k multicolored	1.25 .50
1981	A590	2.30k multicolored	1.25 .50
1982	A591	2.30k multicolored	1.25 .50
a.		Bklt. pane, 3 ea #1979-1982	15.00
		Nos. 1979-1982 (4)	5.00 2.00

See Russia Nos. 6103-6106.

Derek Walcott,
Nobel Laureate
in Literature,
1992 — A592

1992, Nov. 27 Engr. *Perf. 12½ Vert.*
1983	A592	5.50k Text	2.25 1.60
1984	A592	5.50k Portrait	2.25 1.60
a.		Pair, #1983-1984	5.00 5.00

1993 Sports Championships — A593

Perf. 12½x13 on 3 Sides
1993, Jan. 28   Litho. & Engr.
1985	A593	6k Gliding	2.40 1.90
1986	A593	6k Wrestling	2.40 1.90
1987	A593	6k Table tennis	2.40 1.90
1988	A593	6k Bowling	2.40 1.90
1989	A593	6k Team handball	2.40 1.90
1990	A593	6k Cross-country skiing	2.40 1.90
a.		Booklet pane, #1985-1990	14.50 13.50

World Gliding Championships, Borlange (#1985). World Wrestling Championships,

Stockholm (#1986). World Table Tennis Championships, Gothenburg (#1987). European Bowling Championships, Malmo (#1988). World Team Handball Championships, Gothenburg (#1989). World Cross-Country Skiing Championships, Falun (#1990).

Uppsala
Convocation,
400th
Anniversary
A594

Litho. & Engr.
1993, Mar. 25   *Perf. 13 Vert.*
1991	A594	2.90k Stone carving	1.25 .45
1992	A594	2.90k Uppsala Cathedral	1.25 .45
a.		Pair, #1991-1992	2.50 2.00

A595

Tourist Attractions in Gothenburg: No. 1993, Roller coaster Liseberg Loop, Liseburg Amusement Park. No. 1994, Fountain of Poseidon, by Carl Milles.

1993, Mar. 25
1993	A595	3.50k multicolored	1.50 *1.40*
1994	A595	3.50k multicolored	1.50 *1.40*
a.		Pair, #1993-1994	3.25 *3.25*

Fruit
A596   A596a
Perf. 12½ on 3 Sides
1993-95   Engr.
1995	A596	2.40k Ribes uva crispa	1.10 .75
1996	A596	2.40k Pyrus communis	1.10 .75
b.		Bklt. pane, 5 ea #1996-1996	11.00
1997	A596	2.80k Victoria plum	1.25 .60
1998	A596	2.80k Opal plum	1.25 .60
b.		Bklt. pane, 5 ea #1997-1998	12.50
2001	A596a	3.35k Ribes nigrum	1.40 .60
2002	A596a	3.35k Rubus idaeus	1.40 .60
a.		Bklt. pane, 5 ea #2001-2002	13.50
		Complete booklet, #2002a	13.50

Perf. 12½ Vert.
2004	A596	2.40k Prunus avium	1.00 .75
2005	A596	2.80k James Grieve apple	1.40 .50

Perf. 12½ Horiz.
2008	A596a	3.35k Fragaria ananassa	1.40 .60
		Nos. 1995-2008 (9)	11.30 5.75

Issued: #1995-1996, 2004, 3/25/93; #1997-1998, 2005, 1/17/94; #2000-2001, 2008, 1/2/95.
This is an expanding set. Numbers may change.

Oxe-eye
Daisy — A597   Poppy — A598

Buttercup   Bluebell
A599   A600

Perf. 12½x13 on 3 Sides
1993, May 21   Litho.
2013	A597	2.60k multicolored	.95 .35
2014	A598	2.60k multicolored	.95 .35
2015	A599	2.60k multicolored	.95 .35
2016	A600	2.60k multicolored	.95 .35
b.		Bklt. pane, 5 ea #2013-2016	19.00
		Nos. 2013-2016 (4)	3.80 1.40

See note after No. 1277.

Contemporary
Art — A601

Europa: No. 2017, Oguasark, by Olle Baertling (1911-81). No. 2018, Ade-Lidic-Nander II, by Oyvind Fahlstrom (1928-76), horiz. No. 2019, The Cubist Chair, by Otto G. Carlsund (1897-1948).

Litho. & Engr.
1993, May 21   *Perf. 13*
2017	A601	5k multicolored	2.10 1.90
2018	A601	5k multicolored	2.10 1.90
2019	A601	5k multicolored	2.10 1.90
a.		Booklet pane of 3, #2017-2019	6.50 7.50

Butterflies — A602

1993, May 21   *Perf. 12½ Horiz.*
2020	A602	6k Papilio machaon	2.25 2.10
2021	A602	6k Nymphalis antiopa	2.25 2.10
2022	A602	6k Colias palaeno	2.25 2.10
2023	A602	6k Euphydryas maturna	2.25 2.10
a.		Booklet pane, 2 each #2020-2023 with gutter between	19.00
		Nos. 2020-2023 (4)	9.00 8.40

A603   A604

A605   A606
Greetings

Perf. 13 on 3 Sides
1993, Aug. 6   Litho.
2024	A603	2.90k multicolored	1.00 .40
2025	A604	2.90k multicolored	1.25 .75
2026	A605	2.90k multicolored	1.00 .40
2027	A606	2.90k multicolored	1.25 .75
b.		Booklet pane, 3 each #2024, 2026, 2 each #2025, 2027	11.00
		Nos. 2024-2027 (4)	4.50 2.30

Sea
Birds
A607

Perf. 12½ Horiz.
1993, Aug. 26   Engr.
2028	A607	5k Mergus serrator	2.50 2.00
2029	A607	5k Melanitta fusca	2.50 2.00
2030	A607	5k Aythya fuligula	2.50 2.00
2031	A607	5k Somateria mollissima	2.50 2.00
a.		Booklet pane, 2 each #2028-2031 with gutter between	20.00
		Nos. 2028-2031 (4)	10.00 8.00

A608   A609

1993, Oct. 2 Engr. *Perf. 13 Vert.*
2032	A608	2.90k Modern echo sounding	1.20 .35
2033	A608	2.90k 1643 Method	1.20 .35
a.		Pair, #2032-2033	2.90 1.75

Hydrographic survey.

1993, Oct. 2   Engr.   *Perf. 13*
2034	A609	8k King holding flag	5.00 2.75
2035	A609	10k King	5.00 3.50
2036	A609	10k Queen Silvia	5.00 3.50

Size: 75x43mm
2037	A609	12k Royal family	5.50 *5.25*
a.		Booklet pane, #2034-2037	21.00 *15.50*
		Nos. 2034-2037 (4)	20.50 15.00

Reign of King Carl XVI Gustaf, 20th anniv.

Christmas — A610

Perf. 12½ on 3 Sides
1993, Nov. 25   Engr.
2038	A610	2.40k Plaited heart	.95 .40
2039	A610	2.40k Straw goat	.95 .40
b.		Bklt. pane, 5 ea #2038-2039	9.50

Toni Morrison,
Nobel laureate in
Literature,
1993 — A611

#2041, Stockholm City Hall.

1993, Nov. 25 Engr. *Perf. 12½ Vert.*
2040	A611	6k red brown & brown	3.00 1.75
2041	A611	6k multicolored	3.00 1.75
a.		Pair, #2040-2041	6.50 4.25

European
Economic Assoc.
Agreement
A612

1994, Jan. 17   *Perf. 12½ Vert.*
2042	A612	5k Mother Svea	2.25 .65

Domestic Animals — A613

No. 2047, North Sweden horse, vert. No. 2048, Two horses, vert. No. 2049, Red polled cattle, vert. No. 2050, Goat, vert. No. 2054, Swedish dwarf poultry. No. 2055, Gotland sheep. No. 2059, Mountain cow. No. 2060, Scanian goose. No. 2060A, Yellow duck.

1994-95 Engr. Perf. 13 on 3 Sides

2047	A613	3.20k multicolored	1.25	.40
2048	A613	3.20k multicolored	1.25	.40
a.		Bklt. pane, 5 ea #2047-2048	12.50	
2049	A613	3.70k multicolored	1.40	.40
2050	A613	3.70k multicolored	1.40	.40
a.		Bklt. pane, 5 ea #2049-2050	14.00	
		Complete booklet, #2050a	14.00	

Perf. 13 Vert.

2054	A613	3.10k multicolored	1.40	.45
2055	A613	3.70k multicolored	1.50	.30
2059	A613	6.40k multicolored	3.00	.60
2060	A613	7.40k multicolored	3.00	.60
2060A	A613	7.50k multicolored	3.50	2.25
		Nos. 2047-2060A (9)	17.70	5.80

Issued: #2047-2048, 2055, 2059, 1/17/94; #2049-2050, 2054, 1/2/95; 2060-2060A, 3/17/95.
This is an expanding set. Numbers may change.

Cats — A614

Litho. & Engr.

1994, Mar. 18 Perf. 13

2061	A614	4.50k Siamese	2.00	1.75
2062	A614	4.50k Persian	2.00	1.75
2063	A614	4.50k European	2.00	1.75
2064	A614	4.50k Abyssinian	2.00	1.75
a.		Booklet pane of 4, #2061-2064	8.00	9.00

Roman De La Rose — A615

Swedish, French Flags A616

Swedish-French cultural relations: No. 2067, House of the Nobility, designed by Simon and Jean de la Vallee. No. 2068, Household Chores, by Hillestrom. No. 2069, Banquet for Gustavus III at the Trianon, 1784, by Lafrensen. No. 2070, Charles XIV John, by Gerard.

Litho. & Engr., Litho. (#2066)

1994, Mar. 18 Perf. 13 on 3 Sides

2065	A615	5k multicolored	2.25	2.25
2066	A616	5k multicolored	2.25	2.25
2067	A615	5k multicolored	2.25	2.25
2068	A615	5k multicolored	2.25	2.25
2069	A616	5k multicolored	2.25	2.25
2070	A615	5k multicolored	2.25	2.25
a.		Booklet pane of 6, #2065-2070	14.00	15.50

See France Nos. 2410-2415.

Roses — A617

Swedish Design — A618

Perf. 12½x13 on 3 Sides

1994, May 11 Litho.

2071	A617	3.20k Nyponros rosa dumalis	1.10	.45
2072	A617	3.20k Rosa alba maxima	1.10	.45
2073	A617	3.20k Tuscany superb	1.10	.45
2074	A617	3.20k Peace	1.10	.45
2075	A617	3.20k Quatre saisons	1.10	.45
a.		Bklt. pane, 2 ea #2071-2075	11.00	
		Nos. 2071-2075 (5)	5.50	2.25

Perf. 12½ on 3 Sides

1994, May 11 Litho. & Engr.

#2076, Vase with Irises, by Gunnar Wennerberg, 1897. #2077, Table and Chair, by Carl Malmsten; Wallpaper, by Uno Ahren, 1917. #2078, Cabinet, 1940s, and textile, 1920s, by Josef Franck. #2079, Fireworks Bowl, by Edward Hald, 1921. #2080, Silver water jug, by Wiwen Nilsson, 1941. #2081, Towel, by Astrid Sampe; Plate, by Stig Lindberg; Fork and Spoon, by Sigurd Persson, 1955.

2076	A618	6.50k multicolored	2.50	2.50
2077	A618	6.50k multicolored	2.50	2.50
2078	A618	6.50k multicolored	2.50	2.50
2079	A618	6.50k multicolored	2.50	2.50
2080	A618	6.50k multicolored	2.50	2.50
2081	A618	6.50k multicolored	2.50	2.50
a.		Bklt. pane, #2076-2081	15.50	18.50

1994 World Cup Soccer Championships, US — A619

1994, May 11 Engr. Perf. 12½ Vert.

2082	A619	3.20k red & blue	1.60	.50

First Manned Moon Landing, 25th Anniv. A620

1994, May 11

2083	A620	6.50k multicolored	2.50	2.25

Greetings A621

Perf. 12½ on 3 Sides

1994, Aug. 5 Litho.

2084	A621	3.20k Cat	1.10	.40
2085	A621	3.20k Snail	1.10	.40
2086	A621	3.20k Frog	1.20	.70
2087	A621	3.20k Dog	1.20	.70
a.		Booklet pane, 3 each #2084-2085, 2 each #2086-2087	11.50	
		Nos. 2084-2087 (4)	4.60	2.20

Swedish Explorers A622

Europa: No. 2088, Erland Nordenskiold (1877-1932), explored South America. No. 2089, Eric Von Rosen (1879-1948), explored Africa. No. 2090, Sten Bergman (1895-1975), explored Asia and the Pacific.

Litho. & Engr.

1994, Aug. 26 Perf. 12½

2088	A622	5.50k multicolored	2.50	2.00
2089	A622	5.50k multicolored	2.50	2.00
2090	A622	5.50k multicolored	2.50	2.00
a.		Booklet pane of 3, #2088-2090	7.50	8.75

Finland-Sweden Track and Field Meet — A623

#2091, Seppo Raty, Finland, javelin. #2092, Patrick Sjoberg, Sweden, high jump.

1994, Aug. 26 Perf. 12½ on 3 Sides Litho. & Engr.

2091	A623	4.50k multicolored	2.00	2.00
2092	A623	4.50k multicolored	2.00	2.00
a.		Bklt. pane, 2 ea #2091-2092	8.50	8.50

See Finland Nos. 942-943.

Johan Helmich Roman (1694-1758), Composer A624

No. 2094, Opera House, Gothenburg.

Perf. 12½ Vert.

1994, Aug. 26 Engr.

2093	A624	3.20k multicolored	1.25	.25
2094	A624	3.20k multicolored	1.25	.25

Yes & No Stamps — A625

1994, Oct. 1 Litho. Perf. 12½ Vert.

2095	A625	3.20k Ja	1.25	.60
2096	A625	3.20k Nej	1.25	.60

See Nos. 2107-2108.

World Wildlife Fund — A626

#2097, Sterna caspia. #2098, Haliaeetus albicilla. #2099, Dendrocopos leucotos. #2100, Anser erythropus.

Litho. & Engr.

1994, Oct. 1 Perf. 12½

2097	A626	5.50k multicolored	3.00	2.00
2098	A626	5.50k multicolored	3.00	2.00
2099	A626	5.50k multicolored	3.00	2.00
2100	A626	5.50k multicolored	3.00	2.00
a.		Booklet pane of 4, #2097-2100	12.00	10.00

Frans G. Bengtsson (1894-1954), Writer — A627

1994, Oct. 1 Engr. Perf. 12½ Vert.

2101	A627	6.40k multicolored	3.00	2.00

Nobel Laureates in Literature A628

Christmas A629

Designs: 4.50k, Erik Axel Karlfeldt (1864-1931). 5.50k, Eyvind Johnson (1900-76). 6.50k, Harry Martinson (1904-78).

1994, Nov. 11

2102	A628	4.50k multicolored	1.90	1.00
2103	A628	5.50k multicolored	2.25	1.25
2104	A628	6.50k multicolored	2.75	1.40
		Nos. 2102-2104 (3)	6.90	3.65

Perf. 12½x13 on 3 Sides

1994, Nov. 11 Litho. & Engr.

Scenes from medieval altar pieces: No. 2105, Annunciation. No. 2106, Flight to Egypt.

2105	A629	2.80k multicolored	1.25	.40
2106	A629	2.80k multicolored	1.25	.40
a.		Bklt. pane, 5 ea #2105-2106	12.50	

Yes & No Type of 1994

1995, Jan. 2 Litho. Perf. 12½ Vert.

2107	A625	3.70k Ja	1.40	.40
2108	A625	3.70k Nej	1.40	.40

Houses A630

Designs: No. 2109, Country cottage. No. 2110, Soldier's log house. No. 2111, Farmhouse courtyard. No. 2112, Timbered farmhouse. No. 2113, Manor house.

Perf. 14 Horiz.

1995, Mar. 17 Litho. & Engr.

2109	A630	3.70k multicolored	1.60	.65
2110	A630	3.70k multicolored	1.60	.65
2111	A630	3.70k multicolored	1.60	.65
2112	A630	3.70k multicolored	1.60	.65
2113	A630	3.70k multicolored	1.60	.65
a.		Booklet pane of 5, #2109-2113	8.00	8.00
		Complete booklet, #2113a	8.50	

1995 Ice Hockey World Championships — A631

1995 World Track & Field Championships A632

Litho. & Engr.

1995, Mar. 17 Perf. 13 Vert.

2114	A631	3.70k multicolored	3.00	1.25

Perf. 13 Horiz.

2115	A632	3.70k multicolored	1.90	.75

A633

Wood Sculptures, by Bror Hjorth — A634

Europa: Nos. 2116, 2118, Walt Whitman, Christ, Socrates. Nos. 2117, 2119, Patrice Lumumba, Albert Schweitzer, children dancing.

1995, Mar. 17		**Litho.**	**Perf. 13**	
2116	A633	5k multicolored	2.25	1.75
2117	A634	5k multicolored	2.25	1.75
2118	A633	6k multicolored	2.50	2.00
2119	A634	6k multicolored	2.50	2.00
a.		Bklt. pane of 4, #2116-2119	9.50	10.00
		Complete booklet, 2 #2119a	19.00	

Swedish Membership in European Union — A635

1995, Mar. 17			**Perf. 13 Vert.**	
2120	A635	6k multicolored	2.40	1.10

Rock Speedwell A636

Cloudberry A637

Mountain Heath — A638

Alpine Arnica — A639

	Perf. 13 on 3 Sides			
1995, May 12			**Litho.**	
2121	A636	3.70k multicolored	1.25	.45
2122	A637	3.70k multicolored	1.50	.60
2123	A638	3.70k multicolored	1.25	.45
2124	A639	3.70k multicolored	1.50	.60
a.		Booklet pane, 3 each #2121, 2123, 2 each #2122, 2124	13.50	
		Complete booklet, #2124a	13.50	
		Nos. 2121-2124 (4)	5.50	2.10

Tourist Attractions — A640

#2125, Canal boat Wilhelm Tham on Gota Canal. #2126, Sail boat anchored on Lake Vattern.

1995, May 12			**Engr.**	
2125	A640	5k dark green	2.10	1.75
2126	A640	5k dark violet	2.10	1.75
a.		Bklt. pane, 2 ea #2125-2126	8.50	
		Complete booklet, #2126a	8.50	

Trams A641

#2127, Gothenburg, c. 1900. #2128, Norrkoping, 1905. #2129, Helsingborg, 1921. #2130, Kiruna, 1958. #2131, Stockholm, 1967.

1995, May 12			**Perf. 13 Horiz.**	
2127	A641	7.50k rose claret	3.25	3.00
2128	A641	7.50k dp brown vio	3.25	3.00
2129	A641	7.50k dk green	3.25	3.00
2130	A641	7.50k dk gray violet	3.25	3.00
2131	A641	7.50k dk violet blue	3.25	3.00
a.		Bklt. pane of 5, #2127-2131	17.50	18.50
		Complete booklet, #2131a	17.50	

UN, 50th Anniv. A642

1995, Aug. 3		**Engr.**	**Perf. 13 Vert.**	
2132	A642	3.70k multicolored	2.50	.45

Greetings A643

Children's drawings: No. 2133, "The Ball is Yours," by M. Angesjo. No. 2134, Happy man, by E. Sandstrom. No. 2135, Teddy Bear saying "I miss you," by L. Nordenhem. No. 2136, Mussel saying "Hello," by C. Stenbom.

1995, Aug. 3		**Litho.**	**Perf. 13x12½**	
2133	A643	3.70k multicolored	1.40	.55
2134	A643	3.70k multicolored	1.40	.55
2135	A643	3.70k multicolored	1.75	1.00
2136	A643	3.70k multicolored	1.75	1.00
a.		Booklet pane, 3 each #2133-2134, 2 each #2135-2136	15.50	
		Complete booklet, #2136a	15.50	
		Nos. 2133-2136 (4)	6.30	3.10

1995 IAAF World Track & Field Championships, Gothenburg A644

	Perf. 13 Horiz.			
1995, Aug. 3			**Litho. & Engr.**	
2137	A644	7.50k Maria Akraka	3.00	2.25

Motion Picture, Cent. A645

Scenes from films: No. 2138, Soldier Bom, 1948. No. 2139, Sir Arne's Treasure, 1919. No. 2140, Wild Strawberries, 1957. No. 2141, House of Angels, 1992. No. 2142, One Summer of Happiness, 1951. No. 2143, The Apple War, 1971.

1995, Oct. 7		**Litho. & Engr.**	**Perf. 12½x13**	
	Booklet Stamps			
2138	A645	6k multicolored	3.00	2.50
2139	A645	6k multicolored	3.00	2.50
2140	A645	6k multicolored	3.00	2.50
2141	A645	6k multicolored	3.00	2.50
2142	A645	6k multicolored	3.00	2.50
2143	A645	6k multicolored	3.00	2.50
a.		Booklet pane, #2138-2143	18.00	18.00
		Complete booklet, #2143a	19.00	

Fritiof Nilsson (1895-1972), Writer — A646

	Litho. & Engr.			
1995, Oct. 27			**Perf. 13 Vert.**	
2144	A646	3.70k blue & claret	1.75	.40

Ancient Artifacts — A647

Designs: No. 2145, Bronze cult figures of man with beak, nude woman, Bronze Age. No. 2146, Detail of gold collar, Great Migration period. No. 2147, Bracteate pendant picturing figure on horse, Great Migration period. No. 2148, Circular bronze cult object, Bronze Age.

1995, Oct. 27			**Perf. 13**	
2145	A647	3.70k multicolored	1.50	1.25
2146	A647	3.70k multicolored	1.50	1.25
2147	A647	3.70k multicolored	1.50	1.25
2148	A647	3.70k multicolored	1.50	1.25
a.		Booklet pane of 4, #2145-2148	6.00	7.50
		Complete booklet, 2 #2148a	12.00	

A648   A649

Tycho Brache (1546-1601), Astronomer: 5k, Uranienborg Observatory, Ven Island. 6k, Sextant.

	Litho. & Engr.			
1995, Oct. 27			**Perf. 13 Vert.**	
2149	A648	5k multicolored	1.90	1.25
2150	A648	6k multicolored	2.50	2.00
		See Denmark Nos. 1035-1036.		

	Perf. 12½x13 on 3 Sides			
1995, Nov. 9			**Litho.**	
	Christmas candlesticks.			
2151	A649	3.35k Santa	1.10	.45
2152	A649	3.35k Apple	1.50	.80
2153	A649	3.35k Wrought iron	1.50	.45
2154	A649	3.35k Red wooden	1.50	.80
a.		Booklet pane, 3 ea #2151, 2153, 2 ea #2152, 2154	12.50	
		Complete booklet, No. 2151a	12.50	
		Nos. 2151-2154 (4)	5.20	2.50

Nobel Prize Fund Established, Cent. — A650

Designs: No. 2155, Alfred Nobel, last will and testament. No. 2156, Nobel's home, 59 Avenue de Malakoff, Paris. No. 2157, Björkborn Laboratory, Karlkoga. No. 2158, Wilhelm Röntgen receiving the first physics prize, 1901.

	Photo. & Engr.			
1995, Nov. 9			**Perf. 13 Horiz.**	
2155	A650	6k multicolored	2.75	2.50
2156	A650	6k multicolored	2.75	2.50
2157	A650	6k multicolored	2.75	2.50
2158	A650	6k multicolored	2.75	2.50
a.		Booklet pane, #2155-2158	11.00	12.00
		Complete booklet, No. 2158a	11.00	

Holly — A651

Rowan Berries — A652

Rose Hips & Juniper — A653

Lingonberries & Sloe — A654

1996, Jan. 2		**Litho.**	**Perf. 13 Horiz.**	
2159	A651	3.50k multicolored	1.50	.75
2160	A652	7.50k multicolored	3.25	1.60
	Perf. 13 on 3 Sides			
2161	A653	3.50k multicolored	1.25	.55
2162	A654	3.50k multicolored	1.25	.55
a.		Bklt. pane, 5 ea, #2161-2162	12.50	
		Complete booklet, #2162a	12.50	
		Nos. 2159-2162 (4)	7.25	3.45

End of Railway Mail Sorting — A655

1996, Mar. 29		**Engr.**	**Perf. 13 Vert.**	
2163	A655	6k multicolored	3.00	1.25

King Carl XVI Gustaf, 50th Birthday — A656

King Carl XVI Gustaf: No. 2164, In forest. No. 2165, In front of portrait of King Charles XIV John. No. 2166, In carriage with King Albert of Belgium, 1994. 20kr, With family.

	Litho. & Engr.			
1996, Apr. 19			**Perf. 13x12½**	
2164	A656	10k multicolored	5.00	5.00
2165	A656	10k multicolored	5.00	5.00
2166	A656	10k multicolored	5.00	5.00
	Size: 80x48mm			
2167	A656	20k multicolored	10.00	6.50
a.		Booklet pane, #2164-2167	25.00	25.00

Historic Buildings — A657

Designs: No. 2168, Railway station, Halsingland. No. 2169, Motala Assembly Hall, Östergotland. No. 2170, Parish storehouse, Smaland. No. 2171, Half-timbered barn, Vasterbotten. No. 2172, Sheep shelter, Gotland. No. 2173, Old Town Hall, Lidkoping.

	Perf. 13 on 2 or 3 Sides			
1996, Apr. 19				
2168	A657	3.85k multicolored	1.50	.75
2169	A657	3.85k multicolored	1.50	.75
	Size: 28x29mm			
2170	A657	3.85k multicolored	1.50	1.00
2171	A657	3.85k multicolored	1.50	1.00
	Size: 28x38mm			
2172	A657	3.85k multicolored	1.50	1.00
2173	A657	3.85k multicolored	1.50	1.00
a.		Booklet pane of 6, #2168-2173	9.00	11.00

Famous
Women — A658

Europa: No. 2174, Karin Kock (1891-1976), economist. No. 2175, Astrid Lindgren (b. 1907), creator of Pippi Longstocking.

1996, May 3   Engr.   Perf. 13 on 3 Sides

2174	A658	6k multicolored	3.25	2.25
2175	A658	6k multicolored	3.25	2.25
a.		Bklt. pane, 2 ea #2174-2175	9.00	
		Complete booklet, #2175a	9.00	

Summer
Scenes
A659

Paintings by: No. 2176, Sven X:Et Erixson (1899-1970). No. 2177, Roland Svensson (b. 1910). No. 2178, Eric Hallström (1893-1946), No. 2179, Thage Nordholm (1927-90). No. 2180, Ragnar Sandberg (1902-72).

Perf. 13 on 2 Sides

1996, May 24   Litho.

2176	A659	3.85k multicolored	1.50	.40
2177	A659	3.85k multicolored	1.50	.40
2178	A659	3.85k multicolored	1.50	.40
2179	A659	3.85k multicolored	1.50	.40
2180	A659	3.85k multicolored	1.50	.40
a.		Bklt. pane, 2 ea #2176-2180	15.00	
		Complete booklet, #2180a	15.00	
		Nos. 2176-2180 (5)	7.50	2.00

Golf — A660

1996, Aug. 23   Engr.   Perf. 13 Horiz.

2181	A660	3.50k dark green, buff	2.25	1.25

Greetings
Stamps — A661

Designs: No. 2182, Masks of comedy, tragedy, "don't worry, be happy." No. 2183, Hearts, "Var Glad (Be happy)," vert. No. 2184, Posthorn. No. 2185, Hearts, person, "Minns du mig? (Do you remember me?)."

Perf. 13x12½ on 3 Sides

1996, Aug. 23   Litho.

2182	A661	3.85k multicolored	1.40	.40
2183	A661	3.85k multicolored	1.40	.40
2184	A661	3.85k multicolored	1.60	.75
2185	A661	3.85k multicolored	1.60	.75
a.		Booklet pane, 3 each #2182-2183, 2 each #2184-2185	15.00	
		Complete booklet, #2185a	15.00	
		Nos. 2182-2185 (4)	6.00	2.30

Mushrooms — A662

3.85k, Boletus edulis. #2187, Russula integra. #2188, Cantharellus cibarius. #2189, Craterellus cornucopioides. #2190, Coprinus comatus.

Perf. 13 Horiz.

1996, Aug. 23   Litho. & Engr.

2186	A662	3.85k multicolored	1.75	.45

Perf. 12½x13 on 3 Sides

2187	A662	5k multicolored	1.75	1.25
2188	A662	5k multicolored	1.75	1.25
2189	A662	5k multicolored	1.75	1.25
2190	A662	5k multicolored	1.75	1.25
a.		Booklet pane of 4, #2187-2190	7.00	8.50
		Complete booklet, #2190a	7.00	
		Nos. 2186-2190 (5)	8.75	5.45

Ecopark,
Stockholm
A663

Designs: No. 2191, Pelousen, grassy area, Haga Park. No. 2192, Copper tents, Haga Park. No. 2193, Rosendals Palace, roe deer. No. 2194, Isbladskarret, marsh birds.

Litho. & Engr.

1996, Aug. 23   Perf. 12½Vert.

2191	A663	7.50k multicolored	3.00	3.00
2192	A663	7.50k multicolored	3.00	3.00
2193	A663	7.50k multicolored	3.00	3.00
2194	A663	7.50k multicolored	3.00	3.00
a.		Booklet pane of 4, #2191-2194	12.50	15.50
		Complete booklet, #2194a	12.50	

Four Decades
A664

Designs: No. 2195, Errand boy, 1930's. No. 2196, Flower child, 1960's. No. 2197, Zootsuiter, 1940's. No. 2198, Biker, 1950's.

Perf. 12½x13 on 3 Sides

1996, Oct. 5   Litho. & Engr.

2195	A664	3.85k multicolored	1.75	.65
2196	A664	3.85k multicolored	2.25	1.50
2197	A664	3.85k multicolored	1.75	.65
2198	A664	3.85k multicolored	2.25	1.50
a.		Bklt. pane, 3 ea #2195, 2197, 2 ea #2196, 2198	17.50	
		Complete booklet, #2198a	17.50	
		Nos. 2195-2198 (4)	8.00	4.30

The Baroque
Chair, by Endre
Nemes — A665

1996, Oct. 5   Perf. 12½ Horiz.

2199	A665	6k multicolored	2.25	1.60

See Czech Republic #2995, Slovakia #255.

Christmas
A666

Illustrations from Book of Hours (15th cent.): No. 2200, The Annunciation. No. 2201, The Birth. No. 2202, Adoration of the Magi.

Perf. 12½ Vert.

1996, Nov. 8   Litho. & Engr.

2200	A666	3.50k multicolored	1.75	1.00

Perf. 12½x13 on 3 Sides

2201	A666	3.50k multicolored	1.10	.45
2202	A666	3.50k multicolored	1.10	.45
a.		Bklt. pane, 5 ea #2201-2202	11.00	
		Complete booklet, #2202a	11.00	
		Nos. 2200-2202 (3)	3.95	1.90

Nobel Laureates in Physiology or
Medicine — A667

#2203, Sune Bergström (b. 1916), medical chemist. #2204, Bengt Samuelsson (b. 1934), medical chemist. #2205, Hugo Theorell (1903-82), biochemist. #2206, Ragnar Granit (1900-91), neurophysiologist.

Perf. 13x12½ on 3 Sides

1996, Nov. 8   Engr.

2203	A667	5k blue, grn & blk + label	2.00	1.50
2204	A667	5k grn, blue & blk+ label	2.00	1.50
2205	A667	5k blue, grn & blk+ label	2.75	2.25
2206	A667	5k green & black+ label	2.75	2.25
a.		Booklet pane, 3 each #2203-2204, 2 each #2205-2206	23.00	
		Complete booklet, #2206a	23.00	
		Nos. 2203-2206 (4)	9.50	7.50

Wild Animal Types of 1992

1997, Jan. 2   Engr.   Perf. 13 Vert.

2207	A574	3.20k Gulo gulo	1.25	1.10
2208	A574	3.50k Nyclea scandiaca	1.25	.70

Perf. 13 Horiz.

2209	A575	7.70k Ciconia ciconia	4.25	4.25
		Nos. 2207-2209 (3)	6.75	6.05

Churches — A668

Perf. 13 Horiz.

1997, Jan. 2   Litho. & Engr.

2210	A668	3.85k Dalby	1.60	1.60
2211	A668	3.85k Vendel	1.60	1.60

Size: 27x23mm

Perf. 13x12½ on 2 or 3 Sides

2212	A668	3.85k Hagby	1.60	1.60
2213	A668	3.85k Overtornea	1.60	1.60

Size: 27x37mm

2214	A668	3.85k Varnhem	1.60	1.60
2215	A668	3.85k Ostra Amtervik	1.60	1.60
a.		Booklet pane of 6, #2210-2215	9.50	12.50
		Complete booklet, #2215a	9.50	

Kalmar Union, 600th Anniv. — A669

Design: Queen Margareta, Erik of Pomerania, coronation document.

1997, Jan. 2   Engr.   Perf. 12½ Vert.

2216	A669	3.85k dark blue	1.50	.50

Love
Stamps — A670

Perf. 13x12½ on 3 Sides

1997, Jan. 2   Litho.

2217	A670	3.85k gray & multi	1.75	.75
2218	A670	3.85k yellow & multi	1.75	.75
a.		Bklt. pane, 5 ea #2217-2218	17.50	
		Complete booklet, #2218a	17.50	

Stamps that follow, with denominations in parenthesis, are inscribed "Brev," "Ekonomibrev," "Forenings-brev," etc.

Wild
Animals — A671

Perf. 13 on 2 Sides

1997, Feb. 28   Engr.

2219	A671	(4.50k) Alopex lagopus	1.60	.55
2220	A671	(5k) Equus przewalskii	2.50	.35

Perf. 13 on 3 Sides

2221	A671	(5k) Panthera unica, adult	2.00	.35
2222	A671	(5k) same, cubs	2.00	.35
a.		Bklt. pane, 2 ea #2221-2222	12.00	
		Complete booklet, #2222a	12.00	
		Complete booklet, 1 ea #2221-2222	10.00	
		Nos. 2219-2222 (4)	8.10	1.60

No. 2220 is 28x21mm.

Easter
Stamps — A672

Perf. 13x12½ on 3 Sides

1997, Feb. 28   Litho.

2223	A672	(5k) Rooster	2.10	.55
2224	A672	(5k) Daffodils	2.10	.55
a.		Bklt. pane, 3 ea #2223-2224	12.50	
		Complete booklet, #2224a	12.50	

Pheasants
A673

Designs: No. 2225, Phasianus colchicus. No. 2226, Chrysolophus amherstiae.

Perf. 12½ Horiz.

1997, May 9   Litho. & Engr.

2225	A673	2k multicolored	.85	.60
2226	A673	2k multicolored	.85	.60
a.		Pair, #2225-2226	1.75	1.40

See China (PRC) Nos. 2763-2764.

Garden
Flowers — A674

#2227, Iris sibirica. #2228, Lonicera periclymenum. #2229, Aquilegia vulgaris. #2230, Hemerocallis flava. #2231, Viola x wittrokiana.

1997, May 9   Litho.   Perf. 12½x13

2227	A674	(5k) multicolored	2.10	.45
2228	A674	(5k) multicolored	2.10	.45
2229	A674	(5k) multicolored	2.10	.45
2230	A674	(5k) multicolored	2.10	.45
2231	A674	(5k) multicolored	2.10	.45
a.		Bklt. pane, 2 ea #2227-2231	21.00	
		Complete booklet, #2231a	21.00	
		Nos. 2227-2231 (5)	10.50	2.25

A675   A676

6k, Ship's figurehead, 18th cent., Naval Museum, Karlskrona. 7k, Compass rose, 18th cent. atlas. 8k, Compass rose, 1568 atlas.

Perf. 12½ Vert.
1997, May 9　　　　**Litho. & Engr.**
2232 A675 6k multicolored　　　2.50 1.20

Litho.
Perf. 12½ Horiz.
2233 A676 7k multicolored　　　2.50 1.50
2234 A676 8k multicolored　　　3.00 1.90
　Nos. 2232-2234 (3)　　　　8.00 4.60

18th Intl. Cartographic Conf. (#2233-2234).

Gnomes and Trolls — A677

Illustrations from "Among Trolls and Sprites," by John Bauer: No. 2235, Troll looking through treasure chest, gnome. No. 2236, Trolls looking at girl seated on rock. No. 2237, Troll talking with boy.

Litho. & Engr.
1997, May 9　　　　**Perf. 12x13**
2235 A677 7k multicolored　　　2.75 2.00
2236 A677 7k multicolored　　　2.75 2.00
2237 A677 7k multicolored　　　2.75 2.00
　a.　Bkt. pane, 2 ea, #2235-
　　　2237　　　　　　16.50
　　Complete booklet, #2237a　16.50
　Nos. 2235-2237 (3)　　　8.25 6.00

Europa.

Wild Animal Type of 1992
Perf. 12½ Horiz.
1997, Aug. 21　　　　**Engr.**
2238 A575 (3.50k) Ailurus
　　　　　fulgens, vert. 2.00 1.50

Construction of High Coast Bridge — A678

1997, Aug. 21
2239 A678 (5k) multicolored　　2.50 .75

Swedish Elk A679

Designs: No. 2240, Elk as fantasy character. No. 2241, Bar code elk. No. 2242, Swedish elk, yellow bars. No. 2243, Forest elk, green background. No. 2244, Road sign elk, black silhouette against yellow. No. 2245, Old Norse elks, adult & calf.

1997, Aug. 21　Litho.　Perf. 13
2240 A679 (5k) multicolored　　2.50 1.00
2241 A679 (5k) multicolored　　2.50 1.00
2242 A679 (5k) multicolored　　2.50 1.00
2243 A679 (5k) multicolored　　2.50 1.00
2244 A679 (5k) multicolored　　2.50 1.00
2245 A679 (5k) multicolored　　2.50 1.00
　a.　Booklet pane, #2240-2245　15.00 15.00
　　Complete booklet, #2245a　15.00

Perforations at each corner of Nos. 2240-2245 end in a large hole within the pane or semi-circles at the edges of the pane, giving the corners of each stamp a slightly concave appearance.

King Gustav III's Museum of Antiquities, Stockholm Palace — A680

Perf. 13x12½ on 3 Sides
1997, Aug. 21　　　　**Engr.**
2246 A680 8k Muses Gallery　　3.50 2.75
2247 A680 8k Endymion　　　3.50 2.75
　a.　Booklet pane, 2 each #2246-
　　　2247 + 4 labels　　14.00
　　Complete booklet, #2247a　14.00

Classic Cars A681

#2248, 1958 Volvo Duett. #2249, 1955 Chevrolet Bel-Air. #2250, 1959 Porsche 356A Coupé. #2251, 1952, Citroen B11. #2252, 1963 Saab 96. #2253, 1961 E-Type Jaguar.

Perf. 12½x13 on 3 Sides
1997, Oct. 4　　　**Litho. & Engr.**
Booklet Stamps
2248 A681 (5k) multicolored　　2.50 2.50
2249 A681 (5k) multicolored　　2.50 2.50
2250 A681 (5k) multicolored　　2.50 2.50
2251 A681 (5k) multicolored　　2.50 2.50
2252 A681 (5k) multicolored　　2.50 2.50
2253 A681 (5k) multicolored　　2.50 2.50
　a.　Booklet pane, #2248-2253　15.00 18.00
　　Complete booklet, #2253a　15.00

Alfred Nobel (1833-1896), Founder of Nobel Prize — A682

Design: No. 2255, Paul Karrer (1889-1971), winner of Nobel prize for chemistry, 1937.

Perf. 12½x13 on 3 Sides
1997, Nov. 13　　　**Litho. & Engr.**
2254 A682 7k lt pink & black　　3.00 2.50
2255 A682 7k gray & black　　　3.00 2.50
　a.　Bkt. pane, 2 ea #2254-2255　12.00 14.50
　　Complete booklet, #2255a　12.00

See Switzerland Nos. 1004-1005.

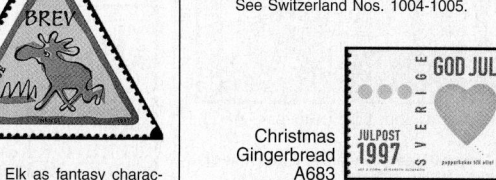

Christmas Gingerbread A683

Perf. 12½ Vert.
1997, Nov. 20　　　　**Litho.**
2256 A683 (3.50k) Heart　　　1.75 1.50
Perf. 12½ on 3 Sides
2257 A683 (3.50k) Animals　　1.50 1.00
2258 A683 (3.50k) People　　　1.50 1.00
　a.　Bkt. pane, 5 ea #2257-2258　15.00
　　Complete booklet, #2258a　15.00

Christmas Angels — A684

Angels from altarpiece, Litslena Church: No. 2259, Playing horn, mandolin. No. 2260, Playing pipes, harp.

1997, Nov. 20　　　**Perf. 13x12½**
2259 A684 6k multicolored　　　3.00 2.00
2260 A684 6k multicolored　　　3.00 2.00
　a.　Booklet pane, 5 each #2259-
　　　2260 + 10 labels　　22.50
　　Complete booklet, #2260a　22.50

Photographer Jan Lindblad (1932-87) and His Tigers — A685

Perf. 12½ Horiz.
1998, Jan. 15　　　**Litho. & Engr.**
2261 A685 (3.50k) shown　　　2.00 1.25
2262 A685 (3.50k) Two tigers on
　　　　　rock　　　　2.00 1.25
　a.　Pair, #2261-2262　　4.25 3.50

New Modern Museum of Art, Stockholm A686

#2263, Fungus Sculpture, by Yves Klein. #2264, Skeppsholmen, by Göran Gidenstam. #2265, Monogram, by Robert Rauschenberg.

1998, Jan. 15　　　**Perf. 12½ Vert.**
2263 A686 (5k) multicolored　　2.25 .65
2264 A686 (5k) multicolored　　2.25 .65
2265 A686 (5k) multicolored　　2.25 .65
　a.　Booklet pane of 3, #2263-
　　　2265　　　　　6.75 7.00
　　Complete booklet, 2 #2265a　13.50

Valentine's Day — A687

Perf. 13 (on 3 Sides)
1998, Jan. 15　　　　**Litho.**
2266 A687 (5k) dp grn & org
　　　　　red　　　　2.00 .70
2267 A687 (5k) dp blue & rose
　　　　　red　　　　2.00 .70
　a.　Bkt. pane, 3 ea #2266-2267　12.00
　　Complete booklet, #2267a　12.00

Swedish Confederation of Trade Unions, Cent. — A688

Perf. 12½ Horiz.
1998, Mar. 19　　　　**Engr.**
2268 A688 (5k) multicolored　　2.10 .50

Public Buildings A689

#2269, Fire station, Gävle. #2270, Shoe shop, Askersund. #2271, Fish halls, Gothenburg. #2272, Rödalvarm (Red Mill) Cinema, Halmstad. #2273, Town Hotel, Eksjö.

1998, Mar. 19　　　**Perf. 12½ Horiz.**
2269 A689 (5k) multicolored　　2.00 .60
2270 A689 (5k) multicolored　　2.00 .60
2271 A689 (5k) multicolored　　2.00 .60
2272 A689 (5k) multicolored　　2.00 .60
2273 A689 (5k) multicolored　　2.00 .60
　a.　Booklet pane, #2269-2273　10.00
　　Complete booklet, #2273a　10.00

Queen Christina, Medallion Commemorating the Peace of Westphalia, 1648 — A690

1998, Mar. 19　Engr.　Perf. 12½ Vert.
2274 A690 7k rose brn & dp grn　3.25 2.00

Handicrafts A691

Designs: (4.50k), Apron from costume, Dalecarlia. (5k), Wrought iron ornamental designs. No. 2277, Lovikka mitten. No. 2278, Boxes made from wood shavings.

1998, Mar. 19　　　**Perf. 13 Vert.**
2275 A691 (4.50k) multicolored　2.00 1.25
2276 A691 (5k) multicolored　　2.00 .40

Perf. 12½ on 3 Sides
2277 A691 8k multicolored　　　3.50 4.00
2278 A691 8k multicolored　　　3.50 4.00
　a.　Bkt. pane, 2 ea #2277-2278　14.00
　　Complete booklet, #2278a +
　　　4 labels　　　　14.00

Wetland Flowers
A692　　　　　　A693

Perf. 13 on 3 Sides
1998, May 14　　　　**Litho.**
2279 A692 (5k) Marsh violet　　2.25 .35
2280 A693 (5k) Great willow-
　　　　　herb　　　　2.25 .35
　a.　Bkt pane, 5 ea #2279-2280　22.50
　　Complete booklet, #2280a　22.50

City of Stockholm — A694

Designs: Nos. 2281, 2287, Stockholm Palace. Nos. 2282, 2288, Skerry boats. No. 2283, Opera House, cent. No. 2284, Sail boats. No. 2285, Langholmen Beach, vert. No. 2286, Fireworks over City Hall, vert.

Perf. 13 on 2 or 3 Sides
1998, May 14　　　**Litho. & Engr.**
2281 A694 (5k) multicolored　　2.10 1.25
2282 A694 (5k) multicolored　　2.10 1.25

Size: 27x22mm
2283 A694 (5k) multicolored　　2.25 1.60
2284 A694 (5k) multicolored　　2.25 1.60

Size: 27x36mm
2285 A694 (5k) multicolored　　2.25 1.60
2286 A694 (5k) multicolored　　2.25 1.60
　a.　Booklet pane, #2281-2286　13.00 14.50
　　Complete booklet, #2286a　13.00 14.50

Size: 58x23mm
2287 A694 7k multicolored　　　2.50 2.50
2288 A694 7k multicolored　　　2.50 2.50
　a.　Bkt. pane, 2 ea #2287-2288　10.50
　　Complete booklet, #2288a　10.50

Cruise Ship Albatros in Stockholm
Harbor — A695

1998, May 14   Perf. 13 Vert.
Coil Stamp

2289 A695 6k multicolored   3.00 2.25

Festivals and
Holidays — A696

Europa: No. 2290, Crayfish party, paper
moon. No. 2291, Dancing around maypole,
Midsummer in June.

Perf. 13 on 3 Sides
1998, May 14   Litho.

2290 A696 7k multicolored   2.75 2.75
2291 A696 7k multicolored   2.75 2.75
 a.   Bklt. pane, 2 ea #2289-2290   11.00 13.00
       Complete booklet, #2291a +
       4 labels   11.00 13.00

King Carl XVI
Gustaf, 25th
Anniv. of
Accession to the
Throne — A697

1998, May 14 Engr. Perf. 13 Vert.

2292 A697 (5k) multicolored   2.25 .50

Vilhelm Moberg (1898-1973),
Writer — A698

Litho. & Engr.
1998, Aug. 20   Perf. 13 Vert.
Coil Stamp

2293 A698 (5k) multicolored   2.50 .80

Pastries
A699

Designs: No. 2294, Princess cake. No.
2295, Gustav Adolf pastry. No. 2296, Napoleon pastry. No. 2297, Mocha cake. No. 2298,
National pastry. No. 2299, Lent bun (semla).

Perf. 13 on 3 Sides
1998, Aug. 20   Litho.

2294 A699 (5k) multicolored   2.25 1.25
2295 A699 (5k) multicolored   2.25 1.25
2296 A699 (5k) multicolored   2.25 1.25
2297 A699 (5k) multicolored   2.25 1.25
2298 A699 (5k) multicolored   2.25 1.25
2299 A699 (5k) multicolored   2.25 1.25
 a.   Booklet pane, #2294-2299   13.50 14.50
       Complete booklet, #2299a   13.50

The Millennium — A700

Swedish developments during 1900's: No.
2300, Painting, "Flowers on the Window Sill,"
by Carl Larsson. No. 2301, Stockholm Stadium, poster for 1912 Olympic Games. No.
2302, Power plant, Porjus, Lapland. No. 2303,
Inventions; zippers, ball bearings, vacuum
cleaners, refrigerators. No. 2304, Johnson
(shipping) Line. No. 2305, AB Radiotjänst,
1924. No. 2306, Jazz music, Charleston
dance. No. 2307, Ellen Key, Kerstin Hesselgren, pioneers for women's rights. No. 2308,
Arne Borg, swimmer, Gillis Grafström, figure
skater, world champions. No. 2309, Ernst Rolf,
entertainer, 1920's.

Perf. 12½ Horiz.
1998, Oct. 3   Litho. & Engr.

2300 A700 (5k) multicolored   2.50 2.50
2301 A700 (5k) multicolored   2.50 2.50
2302 A700 (5k) multicolored   2.50 2.50
2303 A700 (5k) multicolored   2.50 2.50
2304 A700 (5k) multicolored   2.50 2.50
2305 A700 (5k) multicolored   2.50 2.50
2306 A700 (5k) multicolored   2.50 2.50
2307 A700 (5k) multicolored   2.50 2.50
2308 A700 (5k) multicolored   2.50 2.50
2309 A700 (5k) multicolored   2.50 2.50
 a.   Booklet pane, #2300-2309   25.00 30.00
       Complete booklet, #2309a   25.00

See Nos. 2327-2336, 2379-2388.

Nobel Laureates
A701

Perf. 13x12½ on 3 Sides
1998, Oct. 3   Engr.

2310 A701 6k Nadine Gordimer,
              1991   2.25 2.00
2311 A701 6k Sigrid Undset,
              1928   2.25 2.00
 a.   Bklt. pane, 2 ea #2310-2311   9.00
       Complete booklet, #2311a + 4
       labels   9.00

Sigismund
(1566-1632),
King of Sweden
and
Poland — A702

Perf. 12½ Horiz.
1998, Oct. 3   Litho. & Engr.

2312 A702 7k multicolored   3.00 2.50
See Poland No. 3421.

A703   A704

Perf. 12½ Horiz.
1998, Nov. 19   Litho.

2313 A703 (4k) Hyacinth   2.00 1.25

Perf. 12½ on 3 Sides

2314 A703 (4k) Mistletoe   1.60 .50
2315 A703 (4k) Amaryllis   1.60 .50
 a.   Bklt. pane, 5 ea #2314-2315   16.00
       Complete booklet, #2315a   16.00

2316 A703 6k Wreath   2.75 2.00
2317 A703 6k Azalea   2.75 2.00
 a.   Bklt. pane, 5 ea #2316--2317 27.50
       Complete booklet, #2317a   27.50
       Nos. 2313-2317 (5)   10.70 6.25
              Christmas.

1999, Jan. 14 Litho. Perf. 13 Vert.

2318 A704 (5k) multicolored   2.10 .40
       Swedish Cooperative Union, cent.

A705   A706

Swedish Coins: No. 2319, Gustav Vasa
daler. No. 2320, Carl XIV John riksdaler.

1999, Jan. 14 Engr. Perf. 12½ Vert.

2319 A705 (4.50k) dark green   1.60 1.00
2320 A705 (5k) dark blue   2.00 .40

Easter Eggs: No. 2321, Sugar egg. No.
2322, Egg filled with marzipan chicks.

Perf. 12½ on 3 Sides
1999, Jan. 14   Litho.
Panel Color

2321 A706 (5k) green   2.25 1.00
2322 A706 (5k) red   2.25 1.00
 a.   Bklt. pane, 3 ea #2321-2322   13.50
       Complete booklet, #2322a   13.50

"Little Sister
Rabbit," by Ulf
Nilsson — A707

Rabbits: No. 2323, Preparing meal over fireplace. No. 2324, Feeding Little Sister. No.
2325, Dancing to music. No. 2326, Hopping
through thicket.

Perf. 12½ Vert.
1999, Jan. 14   Litho. & Engr.

2323 A707 (5k) multicolored   2.00 1.00
2324 A707 (5k) multicolored   2.00 1.00
2325 A707 (5k) multicolored   2.00 1.00
2326 A707 (5k) multicolored   2.00 1.00
 a.   Booklet pane, #2323-2326   8.00 7.50
       Complete booklet, #2326a   8.00

The Millennium Type of 1998

Sweden in years 1939-1969: No. 2327,
Scene from Bergman's film "Smiles of a Sum-
mer Night," 1955. No. 2328, Vällingby Centre.
No. 2329, Silhouette of soldier, singer Ulla Bil-
quist. No. 2330, Cobra telephone, three-point
seat belt, ASEA high voltage cables and
breakers, Tetra Pak's milk carton. No. 2331,
Scandinavian Airlines System formed, DC-4
over New York City, 1946. No. 2332, "Hyland's
Corner," Carl-Gustaf Lindstedt, Prime Minister
Tage Erlander on television. No. 2333, Protests of the 60's, Hep Stars band. No. 2334,
Volvo Amazon car, family picnic. No. 2335,
Ingemar Johansson, heavy-weight boxing
champion, 1959, Mora-Nisse Karlsson, skiing
champion, Gunder Hägg, running champion,
1941-45. No. 2336, Jazz singer Alice Babs,
opera singer Jussi Björling.

Perf. 12½ Horiz.
1999, Mar. 11   Litho.

2327 A700 (5k) multicolored   2.10 1.25
2328 A700 (5k) multicolored   2.10 1.25
2329 A700 (5k) multicolored   2.10 1.25
2330 A700 (5k) multicolored   2.10 1.25
2331 A700 (5k) multicolored   2.10 1.25
2332 A700 (5k) multicolored   2.10 1.25
2333 A700 (5k) multicolored   2.10 1.25
2334 A700 (5k) multicolored   2.10 1.25
2335 A700 (5k) multicolored   2.10 1.25
2336 A700 (5k) multicolored   2.10 1.25
 a.   Booklet pane, #2327-2336   21.00 21.00
       Complete booklet, #2336a   21.00

Construction of
the Oresund
Bridge — A708

(5k), Swan Pontoon Crane. 6k, Building
bridge.

1999, Mar. 11   Perf. 12½ Vert.

2337 A708 (5k) multicolored   2.00 .40
2338 A708 6k multicolored   2.25 2.00

Swedish
Ships
A709

Perf. 12½x13 on 3 Sides
1999, Mar. 11   Litho. & Engr.

2339 A709 8k East Indiaman   3.50 3.00
2340 A709 8k Mary Anne   3.00 3.00
2341 A709 8k Beatrice   3.00 3.00
2342 A709 8k SS Austalic   3.00 3.00
 a.   Bklt. pane, #2339-2342   14.00 15.00
       Complete booklet, #2342a +
       4 labels   15.00
       Australia '99 World Stamp Expo.

Pyramid   Lady's
Orchid — A710   Slipper — A711

Marsh   Green-Winged
Helleborine   Ordhid
A712   A713

Perf. 12½ on 3 Sides
1999, May 20   Litho.

2343 A710 (5k) multicolored   2.10 .40
2344 A711 (5k) multicolored   2.50 .75
2345 A712 (5k) multicolored   2.10 .40
2346 A713 (5k) multicolored   2.50 .75
 a.   Booklet pane, 3 each #2343,
       2345, 2 each #2344, #2346   22.50
       Complete booket, #2346a   22.50
       Nos. 2343-2346 (4)   9.20 2.30

Council of Europe,
50th Anniv. — A714

1999, May 20   Perf. 12½ Horiz.

2347 A714 7k multicolored   3.00 2.50

Europa — A715

Perf. 12½x13 on 3 Sides
1999, May 20
2348	A715	7k Tyresta Natl.		
		Park	2.50	2.00
2349	A715	7k Gotska Sandön		
		Natl. Park	2.50	2.00
a.		Bklt. pane, 2 ea #2348-2349	10.00	11.00
		Complete bklt., #2349a+4		
		labels	10.00	

Post Bike — A716

Racing Bike — A717

Town Bike — A718

Messenger Bike — A719

Engr., Litho. (#2351)
1999, May 20   **Perf. 12½ Horiz.**
| 2350 | A716 | (3.50k) multicolored | 2.00 | 1.75 |

Perf. 12½ Vert.
2351	A717	(5k) multicolored	2.00	.90
2352	A718	6k multicolored	2.25	1.50
2353	A719	8k multicolored	2.75	2.25
		Nos. 2350-2353 (4)	9.00	6.40

Signs of the Zodiac A720

No. 2354: a, Aquarius. b, Pisces. c, Aries. d, Taurus. e, Gemini. f, Cancer.
No. 2355: a, Leo. b, Virgo. c, Libra. d, Scorpio. e, Sagittarius. f, Capricorn.

Litho. & Engr.
1999, Aug. 12   **Perf. 13**
2354		Booklet pane of 6	15.00	12.00
a.-f.		A720 (5k) any single	2.50	1.75
2355		Booklet pane of 6	15.00	12.00
a.-f.		A720 (5k) any single	2.50	.75
		Complete booklet, #2354-2355		
			30.00	

Perforations at each corner of Nos. 2354a-2354f, 2355a-2355f end in a large hole within the pane or semi-circles at the edges of the pane, giving the corners of each stamp a slightly concave appearance.

Butterflies A721

a, Inachis io. b, Junonia orithya wallacei. c, Hypolimnas bolina. d, Vanessa atalanta.

1999, Aug. 12   **Perf. 12½x13**
2356		Booklet pane of 4	10.00	10.50
a.-d.		A721 6k any single	2.50	1.75
		Complete bklt., #2356 + 4 labels		
			10.00	

See Singapore Nos. 903-907.

Nobel Laureates in Peace — A722

#2357, Auguste Beernaert (1829-1912).
#2358, Henri La Fontaine (1854-1943).

Perf. 13x12½ on 3 sides
1999, Sept. 30   **Litho. & Engr.**
2357	A722	7k gold & blue	2.75	2.25
2358	A722	7k gold & red	2.75	2.25
a.		Bklt. pane, 2 ea #2357-2358	11.00	
		Complete booklet, #2358a + 4 labels		
			11.00	

See Belgium Nos. 1749-1750.

Dance Bands A723

Designs: a, Thorleifs. b, Arvingarna. c, Lotta Engbergs. d, Sten & Stanley.

Litho. & Engr.
1999, Oct. 2   **Perf. 12¾**
2359		Booklet pane of 4	12.00	12.00
a.-d.		A723 (5k) any single	3.25	2.25
		Complete booklet, 2 #2359	24.00	

A724

Christmas A725

Stained glass: No. 2360, Nativity, Klinte Church. No. 2361, Nativity, Hablingbro Church. No. 2362, Three kings, Hablingbro Church.
Madonna and child icons from: No. 2363, Bälinge Church. No. 2364, Skänninge Church.

Perf. 12½ Vert.
1999, Nov. 18   **Litho.**
| 2360 | A724 | (4.50k) multicolored | 1.75 | 1.25 |

Perf. 12¾ on 3 sides
2361	A724	(4.50k) multicolored	1.50	.60
2362	A724	(4.50k) multicolored	1.50	.60
a.		Bklt. pane, 5 ea #2361-2362	15.00	
		Complete booklet, # 2362a	15.00	

Litho. & Engr.
2363	A725	6k multicolored	2.25	2.00
2364	A725	6k multicolored	2.25	2.00
a.		Booklet pane, 5 each #2363-2364 + 10 labels	22.50	
		Complete booklet, #2364a	22.50	
		Nos. 2360-2364 (5)	9.25	6.45

Millennium — A726

Sun rays touching Heligholmen Island: No. 2365, Island rocks. No. 2366, Island map.

Perf. 12¾ Horiz.
1999, Dec. 27   **Litho. & Engr.**
2365	A726	5k multicolored	2.25	1.75
2366	A726	5k multicolored	2.25	1.75
a.		Bklt. pane, 2 ea #2365-2366	9.00	
		Complete booklet, 2 #2366a	18.00	

New Year 2000 (Year of the Dragon) A727

Dragon from children's book "The Dragon with Red Eyes," by Astrid Lindgren: No. 2367, In flight (shown). No. 2368, With basket. No. 2369, In flight, diff.

Perf. 12¾ Horiz.
2000, Jan. 13   **Litho.**
2367	A727	(5k) multi	2.25	1.10
2368	A727	(5k) multi	2.25	1.10
2369	A727	(5k) multi	2.25	1.10
a.		Bklt. pane, 2 ea #2367-2369	13.50	
		Complete booklet #2369a	13.50	

A728   A729

Love.

2000, Jan. 13   **Perf. 12¾ on 3 sides**
2370	A728	(5k) shown	2.00	1.25
2371	A728	(5k) Heart, diff.	2.00	1.25
a.		Bklt. pane, 3 ea #2370-2371	12.00	
		Complete booklet, #2371a	12.00	

2000, Jan. 13   **Engr.**   **Perf. 12½ Vert.**

Watch of King Karl XII, 1701: (4.50k), Works. (5k), Face.
| 2372 | A729 | (4.50k) blue | 1.60 | 1.25 |
| 2373 | A729 | (5k) claret brown | 2.25 | .45 |

Souvenir Sheet

Detail of "Great Deeds by Swedish Kings," by David Ehrenstrahl — A730

Litho. & Engr.
2000, Mar. 17   **Perf. 12¾**
| 2374 | A730 | 50k multi | 11.50 | 14.50 |

Czeslaw Slania's 1000th postage stamp.

Forests — A731

Designs: (3.80k), People in forest. No. 2376, Elk in forest. No. 2377, Bird in forest. 6k, Birch forest.

Perf. 12¾ Vert.
2000, Mar. 17   **Litho.**
2375	A731	(3.80k) multi	2.00	1.75
2376	A731	(5k) multi	1.90	.55
2377	A731	(5k) multi	1.90	.55
a.		Pair, #2376-2377	3.75	3.50
2378	A731	6k multi	2.50	2.00
		Nos. 2375-2378 (4)	8.30	4.85

Millennium Type of 1998
Sweden in the years 1970-99: No. 2379, Art in Stockholm subway stations. No. 2380, Swedish UN forces, postal clerk. No. 2381, Computer, mouse and mobile phone. No. 2382, Cullberg Ballet, Svenska Ord repertory company. No. 2383, Jönköping railway station. No. 2384, Youth with spiked hair, musical group ABBA. No. 2385, European Union flag, map of member countries. No. 2386, Scene from film, "The Apple War." No. 2387, Skiiers Pernilla Wiberg, Ingemar Stenmark, tennis player Björn Borg. No. 2388, Photo of child in womb, taken by Lennart Nilsson.

Perf. 12¾ Horiz.
2000, Mar. 17   **Litho.**
2379	A700	(5k) multi	2.00	1.40
2380	A700	(5k) multi	2.00	1.40
2381	A700	(5k) multi	2.00	1.40
2382	A700	(5k) multi	2.00	1.40
2383	A700	(5k) multi	2.00	1.40
2384	A700	(5k) multi	2.00	1.40
2385	A700	(5k) multi	2.00	1.40
2386	A700	(5k) multi	2.00	1.40
2387	A700	(5k) multi	2.00	1.40
2388	A700	(5k) multi	2.00	1.40
a.		Booklet pane, #2379-2388	20.00	20.00
		Complete booklet, #2388a	20.00	

Art by Philip von Schantz (1928-98) — A732

Designs: No. 2389, A Peck of Apples. No. 2390, A Bowl of Blueberries.

Perf. 12¾ on 3 sides
2000, May 9   **Litho.**
2389	A732	(5k) multi	2.00	.60
2390	A732	(5k) multi	2.00	.60
a.		Bklt. pane, 5 ea #2389-2390	20.00	
		Complete booklet, #2390a	20.00	

A733

Oresund Bridge, Sweden-Denmark — A734

2000, May 9   **Engr.**   **Perf. 12½ Vert.**
| 2391 | A733 | (5k) blue & ultra | 2.25 | .75 |

Litho.
Perf. 12¾ Horiz.
2392	A734	6k shown	2.50	1.75
2393	A734	6k Map	2.50	1.75
a.		Booklet pane, 2 each #2392-2393, + 4 etiquettes	10.00	
		Complete booklet, #2393a	10.00	

See Denmark Nos. 1187-1188.

Europa Issue
Common Design Type
2000, May 9 Litho. Perf. 12¾ Horiz.
2394 CD17 7k multi   3.00 2.25

2000 Summer Olympics,
Sydney — A735

No. 2395: a, Hurdler Ludmila Engquist. b, Archer Magnus Petersson. c, Windsurfer Fredrik Palm. d, Beach volleyball player Lena Malm.

Perf. 12¾x12½ on 3 sides
2000, Aug. 17   Litho.
2395 A735 Booklet pane of 4   11.00 12.50
a.-d.   8k Any single   2.75 2.25
            Booklet, 2 #2395 + 4 eti-
            quettes   11.00

Sky Conditions
A736

No. 2396: a, Clouds and sun. b, Clouds and lightning. c, Clouds and rainstorm. d, Aurora borealis. e, Rainbow. f, Cumulus clouds.

2000, Aug. 17   Die Cut Perf. 9¾x10
Self-Adhesive
2396 Booklet of 6   12.00
a.-f. A736 (5k) Any single   2.00 1.25

King Carl XVI
Gustaf — A737

Design: 8k, Queen Silvia.

Perf. 12¾ Vert.
2000, Aug. 17   Engr.
2397 A737 (5k) blue   2.25 .50
2398 A737 8k red   2.75 2.00
See Nos. 2466-2467.

Nobel Laureates for Literature — A738

a, Wislawa Szymborska. b, Nelly Sachs.

Perf. 12¾x12½ on 3 sides
2000, Oct. 7   Engr.
2399 A738 Pair   5.00 5.00
a.-b.   7k Any single   2.50 2.40
c.   Booklet pane, 2 #2399   10.00
      Booklet, #2399c + 4
      etiquettes   10.00

Toys — A739

No. 2400: a, Doll, tea set, teddy bear. b, Marbles, tin soldier, yo-yo, jump rope. c, Pine cone cow, doll, horse-drawn wagon. d, Cars and policeman. e, Model train, mechanical men. f, Lego car, robot, Furbee.

Perf. 12¾ on 3 sides
2000, Oct. 7   Litho. & Engr.
2400 Booklet of 6   13.50 15.00
a.-f. A739 (5k) Any single   2.25 2.25

Christmas
Songs — A740

Christmas Snowflakes — A741

Designs: No. 2401, Hey, Santas.
No. 2402, vert.: a, It's Christmas Again (four children, tree). b, Three Gingerbread Men. c, The Fox Runs Over the Ice. d, Christmas Has Come to Our House (three children, candles).
No. 2403: a, White background. b, Blue background.

Perf. 12¾ Vert.
2000, Nov. 16   Litho.
2401 A740 (4.30k) multi   1.50 1.00
Perf. 12¾ on 3 sides
2402 Block of 4   6.00 5.50
a.-d. A740 (4.30k) Any single 1.50 .70
e.   Booklet pane, 3 ea #2402a,
      2402c, 2 ea #2402b, 2402d 15.00
      Booklet, #2402e   15.00
2403 A741 Pair   4.50 5.50
a.-b. 6k Any single   2.25 2.25
c.   Booklet pane, 5 #2403 + 10
      etiquettes   22.50
      Booklet, #2403c   22.50
      Nos. 2401-2403 (3)   12.00 12.00

Rock Carvings, Tanum
World Heritage
Site — A742

Swedish
World
Heritage
Site
A743

Designs: (4.50k), Rock carvings of animals and people. (5k), Rock carvings of ships.
No. 2406: a, Gammelstad Church Village. b, Karlskrona Naval Port. c, Theater, Drottningholm Palace. d, Engelsberg Ironworks.

2001, Jan. 31 Engr. Perf. 12½ Vert.
2404 A742 (4.50k) blue, gray   2.00 1.25
2405 A742 (5k) red, gray   2.00 .45
Litho.
Perf. 12½x12¾ on 3 sides
2406 Booklet pane of 4   8.00 10.00
a.-d. A743 6k Any single   2.00 2.00
      Booklet, #2406 - 4 etiquettes 8.00

New Year 2001 (Year of the
Snake) — A744

No. 2407: a, Snake with tongue extended. b, Snake curled up.

Perf. 12¾ on 3 sides
2001, Jan. 31   Litho.
2407 A744 Pair   4.00 2.75
a.-b.   (5k) Any single   2.00 1.00
c.   Booklet pane, 3 #2407   12.00
      Booklet, #2407c   12.00

Dogs — A745

No. 2408: a, Golden retriever. b, German shepherd. c, Labrador retriever. d, Dachshund.

2001, Jan. 31   Perf. 12¾ Vert.
2408 Booklet of 4   8.00 7.50
a.-d. A745 (5k) Any single   2.00 1.00

Birds — A746

Designs: (3.80k), Vanellus vanellus. (5k), Pica pica. 6k, Larus argentatus. 7k, Aegithalos caudatus.

2001, Mar. 22 Engr. Perf. 12¾ Vert.
2409 A746 (3.80k) multi   1.75 1.75
2410 A746 (5k) multi   1.90 .50
2411 A746 6k multi   2.00 1.50
2412 A746 7k multi   2.25 1.75
      Nos. 2409-2412 (4)   7.90 5.00

Europa — A747

No. 2413: a, Waterways of northern Sweden. b, Large ship in Trollhätte Canal, trees. c, Waterways of southern Sweden. d, Ship "Juno" in Trollhätte Canal, duck.

Perf. 12¾ on 3 Sides
2001, Mar. 22   Litho.
2413 A747 Booklet pane of 4 11.00 12.00
a.-d. 7k Any single   2.75 2.25
      Booklet, #2413 + 4 etiquettes 11.00

Easter
A748

No. 2414: a, Orange egg. b, Purple egg. c, Chick.

2001, Mar. 22   Die Cut Perf. 9¾x10
Self-Adhesive
2414 A748 Booklet pane of 3 6.00 6.00
a.-c.   (5k) Any single   1.90 1.60
            Booklet, 2 #2414 12.00

Nobel
Prize,
Cent.
A749

No. 2415: a, Alfred Nobel, Peace medal, obverse of Physics, Chemistry, Physiology or Medicine, Literature medal. b, Reverse of Physiology or Medicine medal. c, Reverse of medal for Physics or Chemistry. d, Reverse of Literature medal.

Perf. 12¾x13½ on 3 Sides
2001, Mar. 22   Litho. & Engr.
2415 Vert. strip of 4   10.00 12.50
a.-d. A749 8k Any single   2.50 2.50
e.   Booklet pane, #2415 + 4 eti-
      quettes + 4 blank labels 10.00
      Booklet, #2415e   10.00
See United States No. 3504.

Ivar Lo-Johansson (1901-90),
Writer — A750

No. 2416: a, Portrait. b, Lo-Johansson, truck.

2001, May 17 Engr. Perf. 12¾ Vert.
2416 A750 Pair   3.75 3.50
a.-b.   (5k) Any single   1.90 .90

Peonies — A751

No. 2417: a, Fernleaf peony (two flowers, one bud). b, Chinese peony "Mons Jules Elie." c, Herbaceous peony (yellow). d, Common peony (flower and bud). e, Tree peony.

Perf. 12¾ on 3 Sides
2001, May 17   Litho.
2417 Horiz. strip of 5   9.25 6.00
a.-e. A751 (5k) Any single   1.90 1.10
f.   Booklet pane, 2 #2417   19.00
      Booklet, #2417f   19.00

Nobel Prize, Cent. — A752

Past winners: a, Doctors Without Borders. b, Red Cross.

Perf. 12¾ Vert.

2001, Aug. 16			Litho.	
2418	A752	Horiz. pair	6.00	6.50
a.-b.		8k Any single	3.00	3.00

Daniel Solander (1733-82), Botanist on Endeavour A753

No. 2419: a, Barringtonia calyptrata and Solander. b, Cochlospermum gillivraei and Endeavour.

Perf. 12½x12¾ on 3 Sides

2001, Aug. 16			Litho. & Engr.	
2419	A753	Vert. pair	5.00	5.50
a.-b.		8k Any single	2.50	2.25
c.		Booklet pane, 2 #2419	10.00	
		Booklet, #2419c + 4 etiquettes	10.00	

See Australia Nos. 1996-1997.

Fish A754

Designs: a, Perca fluviatilis. b, Abramis brama. c, Triglopsis quadricornis.

Die Cut Perf. 13½ Horiz.

2001, Aug. 16			Litho. & Engr.	
Self-Adhesive				
2420	A754	Booklet pane of 3	6.00	5.50
a.-c.		A754 (5k) Any single	2.00	1.20
d.		Booklet, 2 #2420	12.00	

Souvenir Sheet

Aviation — A755

No. 2421: a, Lilienthal glider, 1895. b, Royal Swedish Aero Club. c, Saab J-29, 1962. d, Friedrichshafen FF49. e, Trike ultralight, 1999. f, Douglas DC-3, 1938.

Perf. 12½x12¾

2001, Oct. 6			Litho. & Engr.	
2421	A755	Sheet of 6	18.00	13.50
a.-f.		5k Any single	2.00	1.75

Stamp Design Contest Winners — A756

No. 2422: a, Rollerblader, by Emilie Kilström, Kikebo School, Oskarshamn. b, The Letter, by Thomas Fröhling.

Perf. 12¾ on 3 Sides

2001, Oct. 6			Litho.	
2422	A756	Horiz. pair	4.00	4.50
a.-b.		(5k) Any single	2.00	1.50
c.		Booklet pane, 3 #2422	12.00	
		Booklet, #2422c	12.00	

A757

Christmas — A758

Designs: No. 2423, Christmas tree. No. 2424 — Tree ornaments (26x20mm): a, Star. b, Cracker. c, Angel. d, Heart e, Cone. No. 2425 — Crumpled paper art by Yrjö Edelmann: a, Straw goat. b, Christmas tree.

Perf. 12¾ Vert.

2001, Nov. 21			Litho.	
2423	A757	(4.50k) multi	1.90	1.25

Self-Adhesive

Die Cut Perf. 10¾x11¼

2424		Vert. strip of 5	8.25	8.25
a.-e.		A757 (4.50k) Any single	1.60	.80
		Booklet, 2 #2424	16.50	

Water-Activated Gum

Perf. 12¾ on 3 Sides

2425	A758	Horiz. pair	4.50	5.25
a.-b.		6k Any single	2.25	2.25
c.		Booklet pane, 5 #2425 + 10 etiquettes	22.50	
		Booklet, #2425c	22.50	
		Nos. 2423-2425 (3)	14.65	

World Ice Hockey Championships A759

2002, Jan. 24	Litho.	**Perf. 12¾ Vert.**		
2426	A759	(5k) multi	2.00	1.10

Pandion Haliaetus A760

2002, Jan. 24			Engr.	
2427	A760	10k multi	2.25	1.25

New Year 2002 (Year of the Horse) — A761

No. 2428 — The Stones Family, by Bertil Almqvist: a, Boy and girl on horse. b, Girl on, and boy leading horse, dog running.

Perf. 12¾ on 3 Sides

2002, Jan. 24			Litho.	
2428	A761	Horiz. pair	4.00	2.50
a.-b.		(5k) Any single	2.00	1.00
c.		Booklet pane, 5 #2428	20.00	—
		Booklet, #2428c	20.00	

Love and Miss Terrified, by Joanna Rubin Dranger A762

No. 2429: a, "Det tror. . ." b, "Men jag. . ." c, "Anej!!!"

Die Cut Perf. 13¾ Horiz.

2002, Jan. 24			Litho.	
Self-Adhesive				
2429	A762	Booklet pane of 3	6.00	5.00
a.-c.		(5k) Any single	2.00	1.25
d.		Booklet, 2 #2429	12.00	

Antarctic Expedition of Otto Nordenskjöld, Cent. — A763

No. 2430: a, Scientists, ship, gull. b, Ship, penguin.

Litho. & Engr., Litho. (#2430b)

2002, Jan. 24		**Perf. 12¾ Horiz.**		
2430	A763	Vert. pair	6.00	6.25
a.-b.		10k Any single	3.00	2.75
		Booklet pane, 2 #2430	12.00	—
		Booklet, #2430c + 4 etiquettes	12.00	

Astrid Lindgren (1907-2002), Children's Book Writer — A764

Designs: a, Pippi Langstrump (Pippi Longstocking). b, Karlsson pa Taket. c, Bröderna Lejonhjärta, vert. d, Lindgren (24x29mm), vert. e, Emil i Lönneberga, vert. f, Lotta pa Brakmakargatan. g, Madicken.

2002, Mar. 5	Litho.	**Perf. 13x13¼**		
2431	A764	Booklet pane of 7	14.00	17.50
a.-g.		5k Any single	2.00	2.50
		Booklet, #2431	14.00	

Stockholm, 750th Anniv. — A765

Painting of Stockholm, 1535: (5k), Town and Lake Mälaren. 10k, Close-up view of Cathedral and palace.

2002, Mar. 21	Engr.	**Perf. 12¾ Vert.**		
2432	A765	(5k) shown	1.75	1.10
		Size: 28x28mm		
2433	A765	10k claret	3.00	2.25

A766

Swedish World Heritage Sites A767

Artifacts from Birka archaeological site: (3.80k), Cross. (4.50k), Runic stone. (5k), Man's face. No. 2437 — Scenes from Visby: a, Town and ring wall. b, Wall towers. c, Burmeister building, flowers. d, Square, walls of St. Catherine's Church.

2002, Mar. 21	Engr.	**Perf. 12½ Vert.**		
2434	A766	(3.80k) purple	1.40	1.10
2435	A766	(4.50k) blue	1.75	.75
2436	A766	(5k) brn & claret	1.75	.75
		Nos. 2434-2436 (3)	4.90	2.60

Litho. & Engr.

Perf. 12½x12¾ on 3 Sides

2437		Booklet pane of 4	7.25	8.00
a.-d.	A767	(5k) Any single	1.75	1.40
		Booklet, #2437	7.25	

Kristianstad Sculptures — A768

No. 2438: a, Structure by Takashi Naraha. b, Sprung From, by Pal Svensson.

Perf. 12¾ Vert.

2002, Mar. 23			Litho. & Engr.	
2438	A768	Horiz. pair	5.50	5.50
a.-b.		8k Any single	2.75	2.50

Europa — A769

No. 2439: a, Charlie Rivel (1896-1983), clown. b, Clowns Without Borders (boy and clown). c, Cirkus Cirkör (performer with balloon). d, Cirkus Scott (woman on elephant).

Perf. 12¾ on 3 Sides

		2002, May 2		Litho.
2439	A769	Booklet pane of 4	11.00	12.50
a.-d.		8k Any single	2.75	3.00
		Booklet, #2439 + 4 etiquettes	11.00	

Art From Sweden and New Zealand A770

No. 2440: a, Rain Forest, glass vase blown by Ola Höglund, Sweden. b, Maori basket, by Willa Rogers, New Zealand.

Perf. 12½x12¾ on 3 Sides

		2002, May 2		Litho. & Engr.
2440	A770	Vert. pair	10.00	12.00
a.-b.		10k Any single	5.00	4.50
c.		Booklet pane, 2 #2440	20.00	—
		Booklet, #2440c + 4 etiquettes	20.00	

See New Zealand Nos. 1780, 1786.

A771

Summer in Bohuslän — A772

Designs: No. 2441, Waterfront building.
No. 2442: a, Lighthouse and gull. b, Lighthouse and three birds. c, Bridge, sailboat, waterfront buildings. d, Boat with outboard motor.

		2002, May 10 Engr.	Perf. 12¾ Vert.	
2441	A771	(5k) multi	1.75	1.00

Litho.
Self-Adhesive
Serpentine Die Cut 6¾

2442	A772	Block of 4	7.00	7.50
a.-d.		(5k) Any single	1.75	1.00
e.		Booklet, #2442c-2442d, 2 #2442	17.50	

Grönköpings Veckoblad Satirical Newspaper, Cent. — A773

No. 2443: a, Newspaper and fictitious Postmaster of Grönköping. b, Fictitious police chief and criminal.

Perf. 12¾ Vert.

		2002, Aug. 29	Litho. & Engr.	
2443	A773	Pair	4.00	3.75
a.-b.		(5k) Either single	2.00	1.75

Chefs A774

No. 2444: a, Charles Emil Hagdahl (1809-97) and Cajsa Warg (1703-69). b, Marit "Hiram" Huldt, cook with cauldron and bird, flowers. c, Tore Wretman and medal. d, Leif Mannerström, fish and lobster. e, Gert Klötzke and Swedish Culinary Team. f, Christer Lingström, poultry, peas and apples.

Perf. 12½x12¾ on 3 Sides

		2002, Aug. 29		Litho.
2444		Booklet pane of 6	10.50	10.50
a.-f.		A774 (5k) Any single	1.75	1.25
		Booklet, #2444	10.50	

Royal Palaces A775

No. 2445: a, Sweden. b, Thailand.

Perf. 12½x13 on 3 Sides

		2002, Oct. 5		Litho. & Engr.
2445	A775	Vert. pair	8.00	8.00
a.-b.		5k Either single	4.00	3.50
c.		Booklet pane, 2 #2445	16.00	
		Booklet, #2445c	16.00	

See Thailand Nos. 2040-2041.

Motorcycle Racers — A776

No. 2446: a, Hakan Carlqvist. b, Sten Lundin. c, Anders Eriksson. d, Ulf Karlsson.
No. 2447: a, Ove Fundin. b, Tony Rickardsson. c, Peter Linden. d, Varg-Olle Nygren.

		2002, Oct. 5	Litho.	Perf. 12¾
2446	A776	Booklet pane of 4	6.50	9.00
a.-d.		5k Any single	1.60	2.00

Litho. & Engr.

2447	A776	Booklet pane of 4	6.50	9.00
a.-d.		5k Any single	1.60	2.00
		Booklet, #2446-2447	13.00	

Animated Film Karl-Bertil Jonsson's Christmas A777

Designs: No. 2448, Man with arm on Karl-Bertil's shoulder.
No. 2449: a. Karl-Bertil and mail sack of Christmas parcels. b. Karl-Bertil asleep with Robin Hood hat. c. Karl-Bertil giving parcel to poor man. d. Karl-Bertil with man, woman and child.

Perf. 12¾ Vert.

		2002, Nov. 21		Litho.
2448	A777	(4.50k) multi	1.50	1.50

Self-Adhesive
Serpentine Die Cut 6½x6 on 3 Sides

2449		Block of 4	5.50	6.50
a.-d.		A777 (4.50k) Any single	1.40	1.00
e.		Booklet pane, 3 #2449a-2449b, 2 #2449c-2449d	14.00	

Churches — A778

No. 2450: a, Kiruna Church. b, Habo Church. c, Sundborn Church. d, Tensta Bell Tower.

2002, Nov. 21 Perf. 12¾ on 3 Sides

2450	A778	Block of 4	11.00	11.00
a.-d.		8k Any single	2.50	2.25
e.		Booklet pane, 3 #2450a-2450b, 2 #2450c-2450d	27.50	—
		Booklet, #2450e	27.50	

St. Bridget (1303-73) — A779

2003, Jan. 20 Engr. Perf. 12¾ Vert.

2451	A779	(5.50k) red & brown	1.90	1.25

Swedish Sports Federation, Cent. — A780

No. 2452: a, Woman and child. b, Wheelchair racer. c, Snowboarder and sign language. d, Girl running.

Serpentine Die Cut 8½

		2003, Jan. 20		Litho.
		Self-Adhesive		
2452		Booklet pane, 3 each #2452a, 2452c, 2 each #2452b, 2452d	17.50	
a.-d.		A780 (5.50k) Any single	1.75	1.25

Europa — A781

Posters by: a, Anders Beckman, 1935. b, Georg Magnusson, 1930. c, Owe Gustafson, 1984. d, Carina Länk, 1993.

Perf. 12¾x12½ on 3 Sides

		2003, Jan. 20		
2453	A781	Booklet pane of 4	11.00	12.50
a.-d.		10k Any single	2.75	2.50
		Booklet, #2453 + 4 etiquettes	11.00	

Knots — A782

Various knots.

2003, Jan. 20 Engr. Perf. 12½ Vert.

2454	A782	(4.80k) green	1.40	1.75
2455	A782	(5k) blue	1.50	1.00
2456	A782	(5.50k) red	1.75	.65
		Nos. 2454-2456 (3)	4.65	3.40

Regional Houses — A783

Perf. 12¼ Vert. Syncopated

		2003, Mar. 20		Engr.
2457	A783	2k Närke	.75	.55
2458	A783	4k Bohuslän	1.25	1.10
2459	A783	5k Medelpad	1.50	1.40
		Nos. 2457-2459 (3)	3.50	3.05

Nobel Prize Winners For Physiology or Medicine From Spain — A784

No. 2460: a, Santiago Ramón y Cajal, 1906. b, Severo Ochoa, 1959.

Perf. 12 Vert. Syncopated

		2003, Mar. 20	Litho. & Engr.	
2460	A784	Horiz. pair	5.50	6.00
a.-b.		10k Either single	2.75	2.75

See Spain No. 3204.

Flowers — A785

No. 2461: a, Hepatica nobilis. b, Primula veris. c, Tussilago farfara.

Die Cut Perf. 9¾x10

		2003, Mar. 20		Litho.
		Self-Adhesive		
2461		Booklet pane of 3	4.50	5.50
a.-c.		A785 (5.50k) Any single	1.50	1.25
		Booklet, 2 #2461	9.00	

Oland Moorland, UNESCO World Heritage Site A786

No. 2462: a, Windmills. b, Megaliths and windmill. c, Cow and linear village. d, Sheep and lighthouse.

Perf. 12¾ Horiz.

		2003, Mar. 20	Litho. & Engr.	
2462		Booklet pane of 4	7.75	7.00
a.-d.		A786 (5.50k) Any single	1.90	1.50
		Booklet, #2462	7.75	

A787

Garden
Pavilions
A788

Designs: No. 2463, 1820s pavilion, by Frederik Blom.
No. 2464: a, Pavilion of Emanuel Swedenborg. b, Pavilion of Ebba Brahe. c, Västana farm pavilion, Borensberg. d, Godegard pavilion.

Perf. 12½ Vert. Syncopated
2003, May 16   Engr.
2463 A787 (5.50k) multi   1.75 1.40
Litho.
Self-Adhesive
Serpentine Die Cut 6½ on 3 Sides
2464   Block of 4   7.00 7.50
a.-d.   A788 (5.50k) Any single   1.75 1.25
e.   Booklet pane, 3 #2464a-2464b,
   2 #2464c-2464d   17.50

Souvenir Sheet

St. Bridget (1303-73) — A789

Litho. & Engr.
2003, May 31   Perf. 13
2465 A789 40k multi   10.50 12.50
No. 2465 exists with and without numbers printed in LL and LR corners of the margin.

Royalty Type of 2000
Designs: (5.50k), King Carl XVI Gustaf. 10k, Queen Silvia.

Perf. 13 Vert. Syncopated
2003, Aug. 21   Engr.
2466 A737 (5.50k) red brown   2.00 .75
2467 A737 10k purple   3.50 2.00

Harvest Time — A790

No. 2468: a, Tree, radicchio, parsnip, cucumber, beet, onion. b, Pitchfork, artichoke,

---

pear, gourd, raspberries, apple, plum, pumpkin, eggplant. c, Trowel, garlic, peas, cabbage, tomato, potato, turnip, carrots. d, Strawberries, sunflower, cherries, plums, apple, pear.

Serpentine Die Cut 6½ on 3 Sides
2003, Aug. 21   Litho.
Self-Adhesive
2468 A790   Block of 4   7.25 7.50
a.-d.   (5.50k) Any single   1.75 1.25
e.   Booklet pane, 3 each
    #2468a-2468b, 2 each
    #2468c-2468d   18.00

Birds — A791

No. 2469: a, Recurvirostra avosetta. b, Podiceps auritus. c, Gavia arctica. d, Podiceps cristatus.

Perf. 12½x12¾ on 3 Sides
2003, Oct. 4   Litho. & Engr.
2469 A791   Booklet pane of
       4   12.00 13.50
a.-d.   10k Any single   3.00 2.75
   Complete booklet, #2469 +
     4 etiquettes   12.00
See Hong Kong Nos. 1052-1055.

Building of East Indiaman
"Götheborg" — A792

No. 2470: a, Figurehead (19x23mm). b, Ship under construction (19x23mm). c, Side view of ship, horiz. (23x40mm). d, Ship at sea (39x50mm).

2003, Oct. 4   Perf. 12½x12¾
2470 A792   Booklet pane of
       4   19.00 25.00
a.-b.   5.50k Either single   2.50 2.50
c.   10k multi   3.50 4.00
d.   30k multi   10.00 12.00
   Complete booklet, #2470 +
    label   19.00

Christmas at Sundborn, by Carl
Larsson — A793

No. 2471: a, Martina med Frukostbrickan. b, Kerstis Slädfärd.

Perf. 12¾ on 3 Sides
2003, Nov. 10   Litho.
2471 A793   Horiz. pair   5.25 6.00
a.-b.   9k Either single   2.50 2.25
c.   Booklet pane, 5 #2471 +10
    etiquettes   26.50
   Complete booklet, #2471c   26.50

Christmas
Paintings by Carl
Larsson — A794

Designs: No. 2472, Aftonvarden.
No. 2473, vert.: a, Esbjörn pa Skidor. b, Brita med Julljus. c, Farfar och Esbjörn. d, Garden och Brygghuset.

Perf. 12¾ Vert. Syncopated
2003, Nov. 10
2472 A794 (5k) multi   1.50 1.40
Self-Adhesive
Serpentine Die Cut 6½x6 on 3 Sides
2473 A794   Block of 4   6.50 7.50
a.-d.   (5k) Any single   1.60 1.40
e.   Booklet pane, #2473b,
    2473d, 2 #2473   16.00

Anna Lindh (1957-2003), Murdered
Minister of Foreign Affairs — A795

Perf. 12¾ on 3 Sides
2003, Nov. 11   Engr.
2474 A795   Pair   5.25 5.50
a.   (5.50k) claret   2.00 1.60
b.   10k blue   3.00 2.75
c.   Booklet pane, 2 each #2474a-
    2474b   10.00 —
   Complete booklet, #2474c   10.00
No. 2474c sold for 35k, 4k of which went to the Anna Lindh Memorial Fund.

Woodworking
Tools — A796

Designs: (4.80k), Brace and bit. (5k), Saw. (5.50k), Plane.

Perf. 12 Vert. Syncopated
2004, Jan. 26   Engr.
2475 A796 (4.80k) green   1.40 1.40
2476 A796 (5k) blue   1.40 1.00
2477 A796 (5.50k) claret   1.60 .60
   Nos. 2475-2477 (3)   4.40 3.00

Flowers
A797

No. 2478: a, Tulip. b, Lily. c, Hibiscus. d, Amaryllis. e, Calla lily.

Perf. 12¾ Horiz.
2004, Jan. 26   Litho.
2478   Vert. strip of 5   7.75 7.75
a.-e.   A797 (5.50k) Any single   1.50 1.25
f.   Booklet pane, 2 #2478   15.50
   Complete booklet, #2478f   15.50

Europa
A798

No. 2479 — Views of Lapland: a, Mountain with purple sky. b, Tents near lake.

Perf. 12¾x13½ on 3 Sides
2004, Jan. 26
2479 A798   Pair   5.75 6.50
a.-b.   10k Either single   2.75 2.75
c.   Booklet pane, 2 #2479   11.50
   Complete booklet, #2479c +
    4 etiquettes   11.50

Souvenir Sheet

Norse Mythology — A799

No. 2480 — Return to Valhalla: a, Return of a warrior (denomination at LR). b, Welcoming Valkyrie (denomination at UR).

Litho. & Engr.
2004, Mar. 26   Perf. 12¾
2480 A799   Sheet of 2   5.75 7.00
a.-b.   10k Either single   2.75 3.00

Falun, UNESCO World Heritage
Site — A800

No. 2481: a, Excavation pit, red mine shaft entrance building. b, Yellow green and green copper weighing building, red, white and purple mining operations building. c, Gray mine entrance building. d, Miners and houses.

Perf. 12½x12¾ on 3 Sides
2004, Mar. 26   Litho.
2481 A800   Block of 4   9.50 8.50
a.-d.   (5.50k) Any single   1.75 1.75
e.   Booklet pane, #2481b, 2481d,
    2 each #2481a, 2481c   9.50 —
   Complete booklet, #2481e   9.50

Swedish Soccer
Association,
Cent. — A801

No. 2482: a, Nils Liedholm. b, Hanna Ljungberg. c, Fredrik Ljungberg. d, Henrik Larsson. e, Victoria Svensson. f, Thomas Ravelli.

Serpentine Die Cut 7x6¼ on 3 Sides
2004, Mar. 26
Self-Adhesive
2482   Booklet pane of 6   10.50 13.00
a.-f.   A801 (5.50k) Any single   1.75 1.75

Sunset Scenes — A802

No. 2483: a, Fisherman. b, Lighthouse.

Perf. 12½ Vert. Syncopated
2004, May 13   Engr.
2483 A802   Horiz. pair   3.50 3.00
a.-b.   (5.50k) Either single   1.75 1.25

Stockholm
Archipelago
A803

No. 2484: a, Sailboat, red house, Gillöga. b, Rowboat, houses, Langviksskär. c, Ferry, Stora Nassa. d, Sailboat, lighthouse, Nämdöfjärden.

Serpentine Die Cut 6¾ on 3 Sides
2004, May 13   **Litho.**

Self-Adhesive

2484	Block of 4	7.00	7.50
a.-d.	A803 (5.50k) Any single	1.75	1.50
e.	Booklet pane, 3 #2484a-2484b, 2 #2484c-2484d	15.00	

Cottages
A804

Designs: 3k, Blacksmith's cottage, Uppland. 6k, Dalsland cottage. 8k, Stone cottage, Gotland.

Perf. 12¾ Vert. Syncopated
2004, Aug. 19   **Engr.**

2485	A804 3k multi	.80	.60
2486	A804 6k multi	1.60	.90
2487	A804 8k multi	2.10	1.50
	Nos. 2485-2487 (3)	4.50	3.00

Birds — A805

Designs: (5k), Streptopelia decaocto. (5.50k), Swedish tumbler. 10k, Columba palumbus.

2004, Aug. 19

2488	A805 (5k) multi	1.40	1.25
2489	A805 (5.50k) multi	1.50	.60
2490	A805 10k multi	2.75	2.50
	Nos. 2488-2490 (3)	5.65	4.35

Forest Larder — A806

No. 2491: a, Mushrooms, lingonberries. b, Wild strawberries, butterfly, basket of blueberries. c, Juniper berries, basket of mushrooms. d, Cloudberries, cranberries.

Serpentine Die Cut 6½ on 3 Sides
2004, Aug. 19   **Litho.**

Self-Adhesive

2491	A806 Block of 4	7.25	6.00
a.-d.	(5.50k) Any single	1.75	1.25
e.	Booklet pane, 3 each #2491a-2491b, 2 each #2491c-2491d	15.00	

Nobel Prize Winners for Literature from Ireland — A807

No. 2492: a, William Butler Yeats, 1923. b, George Bernard Shaw, 1925. c, Samuel Beckett, 1969. d, Seamus Heaney, 1995.

Perf. 12½x13½ on 3 Sides
2004, Oct. 1   **Litho. & Engr.**

2492	A807 Booklet pane of 4	11.00	12.50
a.-d.	10k Any single	2.75	2.75
	Complete booklet, #2492 + 4 etiquettes	11.00	

See Ireland Nos. 1576-1579.

Rock Music, 50th Anniv. — A808

No. 2493: a, Jerry Williams (29x39mm). b, Elvis Presley (36x39mm). c, Eva Dahlgren (29x39mm). d, Ulf Lundell (36x39mm). e, Tomas Ledin (29x39mm). f, Pugh Rogefeldt (29x33mm). g, Sahara Hotnights (36x33mm). h, Louise Hoffsten (29x33mm).

Litho., Litho. & Engr. (#2493b, 2493d)
2004, Oct. 2   **Perf. 12x12¾**

2493	Booklet pane of 8 + 2 labels	14.00	16.50
a.-h.	A808 5.50k Any single	1.75	1.75
	Complete booklet, #2493	14.00	
i.	Sheet of 9 #2493b	17.00	—

Labels and margins of Nos. 2493 and 2493i have perforations reading "Rock 54-04." No. 2493i sold for 55k.

Regional Houses Type of 2003 and

Log Cabin — A809   Scanian Farm House — A810

Designs: 1k, Miner's house. 9k, Blekinge cottage.

Perf. 12 Vert. Syncopated
2004, Nov. 11   **Engr.**

2494	A809 50o multi	.30	.25

Perf. 12¼ Vert. Syncopated

2495	A783 1k multi	.35	.30
2496	A810 7k multi	2.00	1.25
2497	A810 9k multi	2.75	2.00
	Nos. 2494-2497 (4)	5.40	3.80

Birds — A811

No. 2498: a, Parus major. b, Emberiza citrinella. c, Pinicola enucleator. d, Pyrrhula pyrrhula.

Perf. 12¾ on 3 Sides
2004, Nov. 11   **Litho.**

2498	A811 Booklet pane of 4	12.00	13.00
a.-d.	10k Any single	3.00	2.75
	Complete booklet, #2498 + 4 etiquettes	12.00	

Christmas
A812

Designs: No. 2499, Gnomes playing leap frog.

No. 2500: a, Three gnomes. b, Gnome with Christmas tree. c, Two gnomes with chair on skis. d, Gnome, birds at mail box.

Perf. 12¼ Vert. Syncopated
2004, Nov. 11

2499	A812 (5k) multi	1.50	1.50

Self-Adhesive
Serpentine Die Cut 6¼x6 on 3 Sides

2500	Block of 4	6.00	6.75
a.-d.	A812 (5k) Any single	1.50	1.50
e.	Booklet pane, 3 each #2500a-2500b, 2 each #2500c-2500d	15.00	

King Carl XVI Gustaf — A813

Queen Silvia — A814

Perf. 12½ Vert. Syncopated
2005, Jan. 27   **Engr.**

2501	A813 (5.50k) multi	1.60	1.00
2502	A814 10k multi	3.00	2.50

See No. 2560.

High Coast, UNESCO World Heritage Site — A815

No. 2503: a, Högbonden Lighthouse, birds on rocks. b, Cliffs and eagles, Storön Nature Reserve. c, Fishing boat at dock, Ulvön. d, Lakes near Häggvik.

Perf. 12¾x13½ on 3 Sides
2005, Jan. 27   **Litho. & Engr.**

2503	A815 Booklet pane of 4	12.00	14.00
a.-d.	10k Any single	3.00	3.00
	Complete booklet, #2503 + 4 etiquettes	12.00	

Swedish Design A816

No. 2504: a, Glassware, by Ingegerd Raman. b, Turn-o-matic number ticket machine, by A/E Design. c, Speedway 9000 welding helmet, by Carl-Göran Crafoord and Hakan Bergkvist. d, Camilla chair and Pilaster shelving unit, by John Kandell. e, Women's watch, by Vivianna Torun Bülow-Hübe. f, Streamliner toy car, by Ulf Hanses.

Die Cut Perf. 12½ Horiz.
2005, Jan. 27

Self-Adhesive

2504	Booklet pane of 6	10.00	10.00
a.-f.	A816 (5.50k) Any single	1.75	1.25

Oriolus Oriolus A817

Perf. 12½ Vert. Syncopated
2005, Mar. 10   **Litho. & Engr.**

2505	A817 11k multi	3.25	2.50

Dag Hammarskjold (1905-61), UN Secretary General — A818

No. 2506: a, Hammarskjold. b, United Nations flag.

2005, Mar. 10	**Horiz. pair**	**Engr.**	
2506	A818	3.25	3.25
a.-b.	(5.50k) Either single	1.60	1.60

Europa A819

No. 2507: a, Lemon, star anise, elderberry marmalade. b, Apples, rosemary, Jerusalem artichokes. c, Chives, goat cheese, beets.

2005, Mar. 10	**Litho.**	**Perf. 12¾**	
2507	A819 Vert. strip of 3	5.00	5.00
a.-c.	(5.50k) Any single	1.75	1.00
d.	Booklet pane, 2 #2507	10.00	—
	Complete booklet, #2507d	10.00	

Spring Flowers A820

No. 2508: a, Convallaria majalis. b, Gagea lutea. c, Pulsatilla vulgaris. d, Anemone nemorosa.

Serpentine Die Cut 10 on 3 Sides
2005, Mar. 10

Self-Adhesive

2508	Block of 4	6.50	6.50
a.-d.	A820 (5.50k) Any single	1.60	1.10
e.	Booklet pane, 3 each #2508a-2508b, 2 each #2508c-2508d	16.00	12.50
f.	As "a," serpentine die cut 6¾ on 3 sides	12.50	6.00
g.	As "b," serpentine die cut 6¾ on 3 sides	12.50	6.00
h.	As "c," serpentine die cut 6¾ on 3 sides	12.50	9.00
i.	As "d," serpentine die cut 6¾ on 3 sides	12.50	9.00
j.	Booklet pane, 3 each #2508f-2508g, 2 each #2508h-2508i	125.00	

Nos. 2508f-2508i issued 9/6.

Mother Svea A821

Perf. 12½ Vert. Syncopated
2005, May 26   **Litho. & Engr.**

2509	A821 15k multi	4.00	4.00

Tumba Bruk, manufacturer of Swedish banknotes, 250th anniv.

A822

Allotment Gardens — A823

No. 2511: a, Girl near shrub, man tending vegetable garden. b, Woman at table. b, Man tending garden, woman with basket of vegetables. c, Man watering garden.

Perf. 12¾ Vert. Syncopated
2005, May 26   Litho.
2510 A822 (5.50k) multi   1.50 1.50

Self-Adhesive
Serpentine Die Cut 10 on 3 Sides
2511 A823   Block of 4   6.00 7.50
a.-d.   (5.50k) Any single   1.50 1.50
e.   Complete booklet, 3 each
        #2511a, 2511c, 2 each
        #2511b, 2511d   15.00

A824

Swedish Postage Stamps, 150th Anniv. — A825

No. 2512 — Details from stamps: a, #944 (1972). b, #430 (1951). c, #250 (1936). d, #1490 (1984).
No. 2513: a, Count Pehr Ambjörn Sparre, #2, printing press. b, Woman reading letter, cover. c, Airplane, train. d, Mailman in van at mailbox.

2005, May 26   Litho.   Perf. 12¾
2512 A824   Booklet pane of 4   6.00 8.50
a.-d.   (5.50k) Any single   1.50 1.50

Litho. & Engr.
2513 A825   Booklet pane of 4   6.00 8.50
a.-d.   (5.50k) Any single   1.50 1.50
e.   Miniature sheet, 9 #2513a 15.00   —
        Complete booklet, #2512-
        2513   12.00

No. 2513e sold for 55k.

Souvenir Sheet

Dissolution of Union of Sweden and Norway, Cent. — A826

No. 2514 — Svinesund Bridge: a, View of roadway with cars. b, View from valley.

Perf. 12½x12¾
2005, May 27   Litho. & Engr.
2514 A826   Sheet of 2   6.50 7.00
a.-b.   10k Either single   3.25 3.25

See Norway Nos. 1430-1431.

Varberg Radio Station World Heritage Site — A827

Skogskyrkogarden Cemetery World Heritage Site — A828

Perf. 12½ Vert. Syncopated
2005, Sept. 23   Engr.
2515 A827 (4.80k) grn & violet   1.40 1.40
2516 A828 (5k) multi   1.60   .50

Greta Garbo (1905-90), Actress — A829

No. 2517: a, Portrait. b, Caricature and "Greta."

Perf. 12¾x12½ on 3 Sides
2005, Sept. 23   Litho. & Engr.
2517 A829   Pair   5.50 6.50
a.-b.   10k Either single   2.75 2.75
c.   Booklet pane, 2 each
        #2517a-2517b   11.00   —
        Complete booklet,
        #2517c + 4 etiquettes   11.00
d.   Souvenir sheet of 4
        #2517a, perf.
        12¾x12½   110.00 125.00

No. 2517d sold for 45k and has a lithographed sheet margin. Single stamps from #2517d are perforated on all four sides. See United States No. 3943.

Juvenile Wild Animals — A830

No. 2518: a, Lynx. b, Bear. c, Wolf. d, Fox.

Serpentine Die Cut 10 on 3 Sides
2005, Sept. 23   Litho.
Self-Adhesive
2518 A830   Block of 4   6.00
a.-d.   (5.50k) Any single   1.60 1.60
e.   Complete booklet, 3 each
        #2518a-2518b, 2 each
        #2518c-2518d   16.00

A831

Mopeds — A832

No. 2519: a, Man, woman, Fram moped. b, Husqvarna moped. c, Kuli moped engine and wheel. d, Two men sitting on mopeds.
No. 2520: a, Man repairing hoisted moped. b, Three-wheeled platform scooter. c, Zundapp moped engine. d, Man riding moped.

Litho., Litho. & Engr. (#2519b, 2519c, 2520b, 2520c)
2005, Sept. 24   Perf. 12¾
2519 A831   Booklet pane of
              4   6.00 7.50
a.-d.   5.50k Any single   1.50 1.50
e.   Sheet of 9 #2519d   14.50 14.50
2520 A832   Booklet pane of
              4   6.00 7.50
a.-d.   5.50k Any single   1.50 1.50
        Complete booklet, #2519-
        2520   12.00

No. 2519e sold for 55k.

Christmas A833

Illustrations from Christmas in a Noisy Village, by Astrid Lindgren: No. 2521, Dog, child on skis.
No. 2522: a, Children near fence. b, Dog, children with sled. c, Girl wrapping gifts. d, Children looking at Christmas tree.

Perf. 12¾ Vert. Syncopated
2005, Nov. 10   Litho.
2521 A833 (5k) multi   1.25 1.25

Self-Adhesive
Serpentine Die Cut 10 on 3 Sides
2522 A833   Block of 4   6.50 6.50
a.-d.   A833 (5k) Any single   1.50 1.25
e.   Booklet pane, 3 each #2522a-
        2522b, 2 each #2522c-2522d 12.50

Angel Musicians, Sculptures by Carl Milles — A834

No. 2523: a, Angel with horn facing right. b, Angel with horn facing left. c, Angel with flute facing right. d, Angel with flute facing forward.

Perf. 12¾ on 3 Sides
2005, Nov. 10   Litho. & Engr.
2523 A834   Booklet pane of
              4   10.00 13.00
a.-d.   10k Any single   2.50 2.50
        Complete booklet, #2523 +
        4 etiquettes   10.00

Swedish Railroads, 150th Anniv. — A835

Designs: 10k, X40 train.
No. 2525: a, Mallet steam locomotive (green). b, Gasoline-powered Rail bus (tan). c, SJ Class D electric locomotive (orange). d, R steam locomotive (black). e, RC electric locomotive (red).

Perf. 12½ Vert. Syncopated
2006, Jan. 26   Litho.
2524 A835 10k multi   2.50 2.50

Litho. & Engr.
Booklet Stamps
Perf. 12½ Horiz.
2525   Vert. strip of 5   8.00 8.00
a.-e.   A835 (5.50k) Any single   1.60 1.50
f.   Booklet pane, 2 #2525   16.00
        Complete booklet, #2525f 16.00

Hearts — A836

No. 2526: a, Tattooed heart. b, Red heart. c, Heart-shaped leaf. d, Heart carved in tree trunk.

Serpentine Die Cut 10 on 3 Sides
2006, Jan. 26   Litho.
Self-Adhesive
2526	A836	Block of 4, #a-d	6.00 5.00
a.-d.		(5.50k) Any single	1.50 1.40
e.		Booklet pane, 2 each #2526c-2526d, 3 each #2526a-2526b	15.00

Souvenir Sheet

Norse Mythology — A837

No. 2527: a, Skogsraet, reindeer, goats and bird. b, Näcken, horse and violin.

Litho. & Engr.
2006, Mar. 29   Perf. 12¾
2527	A837	Sheet of 2	5.25 7.00
a.-b.		10k Either single	2.50 3.00

Souvenir Sheet

King Carl XVI Gustaf, 60th Birthday — A838

2006, Mar. 29   Engr.   Perf. 13x12¾
2528	A838	Sheet, 2 #2528a, 1 #2528b	8.00 10.00
a.		10k black	3.00 4.00
b.		10k blue	2.60 2.60

Coffee — A839

No. 2529: a, Coffee cups stacked on coffeemaker. b, Glass of cappucino. c, Espresso machine and cup, sugar dispenser and spoon. d, Steamed milk dispenser and measuring cup.

Serpentine Die Cut 10 on 3 Sides
2006, Mar. 29   Litho.
Self-Adhesive
2529	A839	Block of 4	6.25 7.00
a.-d.		(5.50k) Any single	1.60 1.25
e.		Booklet pane, 3 each #2529a-2529b, 2 each #2529c-2529d	15.50

Suomenlinna (Sveaborg) Fortress, Helsinki, Finland — A840

No. 2530: a, Ship without oars, flagpole at fortress. b, Ship with oars facing fortress. c, Ship with oars, windmill.

Litho. & Engr.
2006, May 4   Perf. 12¾
2530	A840	Booklet pane of 3	8.25 9.00
a.-c.		10k Any single	2.75 3.25
		Complete booklet, #2530	8.25

See Finland No. 1266.

Track and Field Athletes — A841

Designs: (4.80k), Stefan Holm, high jump. 10k, Christian Olsson, triple jump.
No. 2533: a, Carolina Klüft, heptathlon. b, Kajsa Bergqvist, high jump.

Perf. 13¼ Vert. Syncopated
2006, May 4   Litho.
2531	A841	(4.80k) grn & multi	1.40 1.40
2532	A841	10k gray & multi	3.00 2.75
2533		Horiz. pair	3.00 3.00
a.-b.	A841	(5.50k) Either single	1.50 1.00
		Nos. 2531-2533 (3)	7.40 7.15

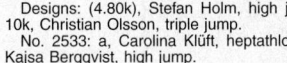

Europa A842

No. 2534 — Children's art by: a, Alexandros Terzis. b, Linda Wong.

Perf. 12¾x12½ on 3 Sides
2006, May 4
2534	A842	Pair	5.50 6.50
a.-b.		10k Either single	2.75 2.75
c.		Booklet pane, 2 each #2534a-2534b	11.00
		Complete booklet, #2534c + 4 etiquettes	11.00

Summer by the Lake — A843

No. 2536: a, Elk and immigrant women's picnic. b, Father and daughter fishing. c, Dog watching swimmers. d, Frog and boaters.

Perf. 12¼ Vert. Syncopated
2006, May 4
2535	A843	(5.50k) shown	1.50 1.50

Self-Adhesive
Size: 34x24mm
2536		Block of 4	6.00 7.00
a.-d.	A843	(5.50k) Any single	1.50 1.00
e.		Booklet pane, 3 each #2536a-2536b, 2 each #2536c-2536d	15.00

Famous Men — A844

Designs: (4.80k,) Carl Michael Bellman (1740-95), poet. (5k), Joseph Martin Kraus (1756-92), composer. (5.50k), Wolfgang Amadeus Mozart (1756-91), composer.

2006, Sept. 7   Engr.   Perf. 12¾
2537	A844	(5.50k) multi	3.00 3.00

Coil Stamps
Perf. 12½ Vert. Syncopated
2538	A844	(4.80k) multi	1.40 1.40
2539	A844	(5k) multi	1.40 1.40
2540	A844	(5.50k) multi	1.50 1.50
		Nos. 2537-2540 (4)	7.30 7.30

No. 2537 was issued in a sheet of 6 stamps that sold for 38k.

Hanseatic League, 650th Anniv. — A845

Designs: No. 2541, Hanseatic cog, 1380. No. 2542, Building and ships, Visby. No. 2543, City seal, shopper and salesman, Stockholm.

Perf. 12½x13½ on 3 Sides
2006, Sept. 7   Litho. & Engr.
2541	A845	10k multi	2.75 2.75
2542	A845	10k multi	2.75 2.75
2543	A845	10k multi	2.75 2.75
a.		Booklet pane, #2542-2543, 2 #2541	11.00
		Complete booklet, #2543a	11.00

Souvenir Sheets

A846

Characters from Swedish Children's Television Shows — A847

No. 2544: a, Andy Pandy (marionette), Humle and Dumle (puppets). b, Anita on Television, Captain Zoom. c, Fablernas Värld (owl), Teskedsgumman (woman). d, Kalles Klätterträd (cartoon), Beppe Wolgers Godnattstunden (man in pajamas).
No. 2545: a, Trazan and Banarne, pink elephant. b, Pippi Longstockings, bear. c, Dinosaur, characters from Tjet och Allram Eest. d, Loophole, Bananas in Pajamas.

Litho. & Engr.
2006, Sept. 30   Perf. 12½x13
2544	A846	Sheet of 4	6.00 6.00
a.-d.		5.50k Any single	1.50 1.50

2545	A847	Sheet of 4	6.00 6.00
a.-d.		5.50k Any single	1.50 1.50
e.		Booklet pane, #2544-2545	12.00
		Complete booklet, #2545e	12.00
f.		Sheet of 9 #2545a	15.00 15.00

No. 2545e has a row of rouletting separating No. 2544 from No. 2545, and has a wider margin where the pane is attached to the booklet cover.

Winter Scenes in Art — A848

No. 2546: a, Bourdelle's Heracles in Snow, by Prince Eugen. b, Lelle-Kalle, by Sven Ljundberg. c, Modification of a Winter Landscape by W. O. Petersen, by Philip von Schantz. d, Rime Frost on Ice, by Gustaf Adolf Fjaestad.

Perf. 12¾ on 3 Sides
2006, Nov. 9   Litho.
2546	A848	Booklet pane of 4	12.00 —
a.-d.		10k Any single	3.00 3.00
		Complete booklet, #2546 + 4 etiquettes	12.00

Christmas A849

Designs: No. 2547, Santa Claus, New Year's ornament, candles.
No. 2548: a, Star ornament. b, Spherical and New Year's ornaments. c, Bird at feeder, poinsettia. d, Candles.

Perf. 12½ Vert. Syncopated
2006, Nov. 9
2547	A849	(5k) multi	1.50 1.50

Self-Adhesive
Size: 25x25mm
Serpentine Die Cut 10 on 3 Sides
2548		Block of 4	6.00
a.-d.	A849	(5k) Any single	1.50 1.50
e.		Booklet pane, 3 each #2548a-2548b, 2 each #2548c-2548d	15.00

Linnaea Borealis — A850

Enneandria and Carl von Linné (1707-78), Creator of Linnaean Taxonomic System — A851

Perf. 12½ Vert. Syncopated
2007, Jan. 25   Engr.
2549	A850	(5.50k) multi	1.60 1.60

Litho. & Engr.
2550	A851	11k multi	3.25 3.25

Spring — A852

No. 2551: a, Birds, heart, musical notes. b, Sun, cloud, person. c, Flower, heart, person. d, Bird, sun, musical notes.

Serpentine Die Cut 10 on 3 Sides

		2007, Jan. 25		Litho.	
2551	A852	Block of 4		6.25	
a.-d.		(5.50k) Any single		1.50	1.50
e.		Booklet pane, 3 each #2551a-2551b, 2 each #2551c-2551d		15.50	

Souvenir Sheet

Intl. Polar Year — A853

No. 2552: a, Stenfragment I, etching by Svenerik Jakobsson. b, Arctic Ocean 2001 88 Degrees North, 145 Degrees East, by Johan Petterson.

Perf. 13, 12¾x13¼ (#2552b)

		2007, Jan. 25		Litho. & Engr.	
2552	A853	Sheet of 2		5.75	6.25
a.-b.		10k Either single		2.75	3.00

Wing of Maculinea Arion Butterfly — A854

Serpentine Die Cut 9 Vert. Syncopated

		2007, Mar. 22		Litho. & Engr.	
		Self-Adhesive			
2553	A854	20k multi		5.75	5.75

Printed in sheets of 40.

Swedish Sea Rescue Society, Cent. — A855

Designs: (4.80k), Rowboat, rescuer on jet-ski. (5k), Helicopter rescue. (5.50k), Nautical chart, rescue boat.

Litho. & Engr., Engr. (#2554, 2557)

		2007, Mar. 22		Perf. 13x12¾	
2554	A855	(5.50k) multi		1.90	1.90
		Perf. 12½ Vert. Syncopated			
2555	A855	(4.80k) multi		1.40	1.40
2556	A855	(5k) multi		1.40	1.40
2557	A855	(5.50k) multi		1.60	1.60
		Nos. 2554-2557 (4)		6.30	6.30

No. 2554 was printed in sheets of 6 that sold for 38k.

Europa A856

No. 2558: a, "Jamboree", globe and airplane. b, Scouts.

Perf. 13½x12¾ on 3 Sides

		2007, Mar. 22		Litho.	
2558	A856	Horiz. or vert. pair		3.25	3.25
a.-b.		(5.50k) Either single		1.60	1.60
c.		Booklet pane, 2 each #2558a-2558b		6.50	

Scouting, cent.

Swedish Inventions — A857

No. 2559: a, Wall anchor for screws, by Oswald Thorsman. b, Allergy globe for flowers, by Elisabeth Gagnemyhr. c, Cooling food cover, by Birgitta Folcker-Sundell. d, Adjustable wrench, by Johan Petter Johansson.

Serpentine Die Cut 9 Horiz.

		2007, Mar. 22			
2559		Horiz. strip or block of 4		5.75	
a.-d.		A857 (5k) Any single		1.40	1.40
e.		Booklet pane of 20, 5 each #2559a-2559d		29.00	

Queen Silvia Type of 2005
Perf. 12½ Vert. Syncopated

		2007, May 10		Engr.	
2560	A814	11k grn & blue		3.25	3.25

Souvenir Sheet

Botanical Illustrations by Georg Dionys Ehret — A858

No. 2561: a, Musa x paradisiaca. b, Podophyllum peltatum.

Litho. & Engr.

		2007, May 10		Perf. 13	
2561	A858	Sheet of 2		6.50	6.50
a.-b.		11k Either single		3.25	3.25

Exists with serial number in margin.

Children Fishing — A859

Designs: No. 2562, Boy fishing in pail. No. 2563: a, Boy on dock. b, Child kissing fish. c, Girls holding caught fish. d, Boys with fishing pole and caught fish.

Perf. 12½ Vert. Syncopated

		2007, May 10		Litho.	
2562	A859	(5.50k) multi		1.60	1.60
		Size: 34x24mm			
		Self-Adhesive			
		Booklet Stamps			
		Serpentine Die Cut 10 on 3 Sides			
2563		Block of 4		6.50	
a.-d.		A859 (5.50k) Any single		1.60	1.60
e.		Booklet pane, 3 each #2563a-2563b, 2 each #2563c-2563d		16.00	

Landscapes — A860

No. 2564: a, Rape field and house, Skane. b, Duck on lake, Muddus National Park. c, Elk in forest, Sveafallen. d, Hay field and Kallsjön Lake, Jämtland.

Perf. 12¾x13½

		2007, May 10		Litho. & Engr.	
2564	A860	Booklet pane of 4		13.00	—
a.-d.		11k Any single		3.25	3.25
		Complete booklet, #2564 + 4 etiquettes		13.00	

Wing of Papilio Machaon A861

Serpentine Die Cut 9¼ Vert. Syncopated

		2007, Sept. 27		Litho. & Engr.	
		Self-Adhesive			
2565	A861	50k multi		15.50	15.50

Chocolate A862

Designs: No. 2566, Chocolate candy. No. 2567: a, Chocolate bonbon with whipped cream and cherry. b, Chocolate-dipped strawberry. c, Cacao pod. d, Cup of cocoa.

Perf. 12½ Vert. Syncopated

		2007, Sept. 27		Litho.	
		Coil Stamp			
2566	A862	(5.50k) multi		1.75	1.75
		Self-Adhesive			
		Booklet Stamps			
		Serpentine Die Cut 10 on 3 Sides			
		Size: 25x26mm			
2567		Block of 4		7.00	
a.-d.		A862 (5.50k) Any single		1.75	1.75
e.		Booklet pane of 10, 3 each #2567a-2567b, 2 each #2567c-2567d		17.50	

Swedish Fashion — A863

No. 2568 — Clothing designs by: a, Lars Wallin. b, Ann-Sofie Back. c, Katja of Sweden. d, Behnaz Aram. e, Gunilla Pontén. f, Carin Rodebjer. g, Rohdi Heintz. h, Nakkna.

Litho. & Engr.

		2007, Sept. 29		Perf. 12½x13	
2568		Booklet pane of 8		14.00	
a.-h.		A863 5.50k Any single		1.75	1.75
		Complete booklet, #2568		14.00	
i.		Miniature sheet, 4 each #2568a, 2568g		15.50	

No. 2568i sold for 49k.

Sami Culture A864

Designs: No. 2569, Reindeer from ceremonial drum, country name in red. No. 2570, Silver button, country name in green. No. 2571, Glass dish, country name in blue.

		2007, Nov. 8		Perf. 12¾x13	
2569	A864	11k multi		4.00	4.00
		Booklet Stamps			
		Perf. 12¾x13 on 3 Sides			
2570	A864	11k multi		3.50	3.50
2571	A864	11k multi		3.50	3.50
a.		Booklet pane of 6, 2 each #2569-2571		21.00	—
		Complete booklet, #2571a		21.00	
		Nos. 2569-2571 (3)		11.00	11.00

No. 2569 was printed in sheets of 4 that sold for 49k. Examples of No. 2569 from booklet pane are perforated on 3 sides like Nos. 2570-2571. No. 2571a sold for 66k.

Souvenir Sheet

Astrid Lindgren (1907-2002), Writer — A865

Litho. & Engr.

		2007, Nov. 8		Perf. 12¾	
2572	A865	11k multi		10.00	10.00

See Germany No. 2462.

Christmas A866

Scenes from children's stories by Astrid Lindgren: No. 2573, Pippi Longstocking rolling gingerbread dough on floor. No. 2574: a, Houses in winter. b, Children in snowball fight. c, Lotta and father roping Christmas tree to sled. d, Children and horse-drawn sleigh.

Perf. 12½ Vert. Syncopated

		2007, Nov. 8		Litho.	
		Coil Stamp			
2573	A866	(5k) multi		1.60	1.60
		Self-Adhesive			
		Booklet Stamps			
		Serpentine Die Cut 10 on 3 Sides			
2574		Block of 4		6.50	
a.-d.		A866 (5k) Any single		1.60	1.60
e.		Booklet pane of 10, 3 each #2574a-2574b, 2 each #2574c-2574d		16.00	

Olof von Dalin (1708-63),
Historian — A867

No. 2575: a, Illuminated letter "D." b, Illustration from first edition of *The Swedish Argus.*

Perf. 13¼ Vert. Syncopated

			Engr.	
2008, Jan. 24				
2575	A867	Horiz. pair	7.00	7.00
a.-b.		11k Either single	3.50	3.50

Ingmar Bergman
(1918-2007), Film
Director — A868

Scene From "Fanny and
Alexander" — A869

Perf. 13 Vert. Syncopated

			Engr.	
2008, Jan. 24				
2576	A868	(5.50k) indigo	1.75	1.75

Souvenir Sheet
Litho. & Engr.
Perf. 12¾x13¼

2577	A869	11k multi	4.00	4.00

A book containing an imperf example of No. 2577, an imperf example of the litho portions of No. 2577 and an imperf example of the engraved portions of No. 2577 sold for 299k.

A870

Insects — A871

Designs: (4.80k), Bombus hypnorum (bee). (5k), Formica rufa (ants). (5.50k), Coccinella (ladybug).

2008, Jan. 24		**Litho.**	**Perf. 13½**	
2578	A870	(5.50k) multi	2.00	2.00

Coil Stamps
Engr.
Perf. 12½ Vert. Syncopated
Size: 27x21mm

2579	A871	(4.80k) multi	1.50	1.50

Size: 28x24mm

2580	A871	(5k) multi	1.60	1.60

Litho.
Perf. 13¼ Vert. Syncopated
Size: 27x28mm

2581	A870	(5.50k) multi	1.75	1.75
		Nos. 2578-2581 (4)	6.85	6.85

Coil Stamp
Perf. 13¼ Horiz. Syncopated

2581A	A870	(5.50k) multi	1.75	1.75

No. 2578 was printed in a sheet of 6 that sold for 38k.

Dogs — A872

No. 2582: a, Lagotto Romagnolo (light green background). b, Saluki (pink background). c, Pug (yellow background). d, Great Dane (light blue background).

Serpentine Die Cut 10 on 3 Sides

2008, Jan. 24			**Litho.**	
2582	A872	Block of 4	7.00	
a.-d.		(5.50k) Any single	1.75	1.75
e.		Booklet pane of 10, 3 each # 2582a, 2582c, 2 each #2582b, 2582d	17.50	

Trees — A873

No. 2583: a, Juniperus communis tree. b, Juniperus communis berries.
No. 2584: a, Betula pendula tree. b, Betula pendula catkins.

Perf. 12 Vert. Syncopated

2008, Mar. 27			**Litho.**	
2583	A873	Horiz. pair	.70	.70
a.-b.		1k Either single	.35	.35
2584	A873	Horiz. pair	1.40	1.40
a.-b.		2k Either single	.70	.70

Eyes and Hearts — A874

No. 2585: a, Eye with heart-shaped pupil. b, Eye with heart on cheek. c, Eye with hearts as eyebrow. d, Eye with hearts as teardrops.

Serpentine Die Cut 10 on 3 Sides
2008, Mar. 27
Self-Adhesive

2585	A874	Block of 4	7.50	
a.-d.		(5.50k) Any single	1.75	1.75
e.		Booklet pane of 10, 3 each #2585a-2585b, 2 each #2585c-2585d	19.00	

Europa — A875

No. 2586: a, Semicolon. b, Comma.

Perf. 12¾ on 3 Sides

2008, Mar. 27			**Litho. & Engr.**	
2586	A875	Pair	7.50	7.50
a.-b.		11k Either single	3.75	3.75
c.		Booklet pane of 4, 2 each #2586a-2586b	15.00	
		Complete booklet, #2586c + 4 etiquettes	15.00	

Souvenir Sheet

Blakulla — A876

No. 2587: a, Woman riding backwards on ram. b, Bats.

2008, Mar. 27 Perf. 12¾

2587	A876	Sheet of 2	7.50	7.50
a.-b.		11k Either single	3.75	3.75

Butterfly
Wings — A877

Wings of: 5k, Argynnis aglaja. 10k, Parnassius apollo.

Serpentine Die Cut 9¼ Vert. Syncopated

2008, May 15			**Litho. & Engr.**	
		Self-Adhesive		
2588	A877	5k multi	1.75	1.25
		Size: 24x34mm		
2589	A877	10k multi	3.50	2.50

Food Served
Outdoors
A878

Designs: No. 2590, Plate of crawfish, glasses of wine.
No. 2591: a, Strawberry cake, potatoes, cheese, pickled herring in sour cream and chives. b, Fish on grill. c, Coffee and pastries. d, Ham, bread, watermelon, tomatoes, wine.

Perf. 12¾ Vert. Syncopated

2008, May 15			**Litho.**	
		Coil Stamp		
2590	A878	(5.50k) multi	1.90	1.90

Booklet Stamps
Self-Adhesive
Size: 34x23mm
Serpentine Die Cut 10 on 3 Sides

2591		Block of 4	7.75	
a.-d.		A878 (5.50k) Any single	1.90	1.90
e.		Booklet pane of 10, 3 each #2591a-2591b, 2 each #2591c-2591d	19.00	

Sailing
Ships
A879

Designs: No. 2592, Tre Kronor af Stockholm.
No. 2593: a, Training ship Gunilla. b, Like #2592. c, Gratitude. d, Gladan and Falken.

Perf. 12½x12¾

2008, May 15			**Litho. & Engr.**	
2592	A879	11k multi	4.25	4.25

Perf. 12½x12¾ on 3 Sides

2593		Booklet pane of 4	15.00	—
a.-d.		A879 11k Any single	3.75	3.75
		Complete booklet, #2593 + 4 etiquettes	15.00	

No. 2592 was printed in sheets of 4 that sold for 49k.

Organic Fruits
and Vegetables
A880

Designs: No. 2594, Apples. 11k, Carrots. No. 2596, vert.: a, Beets. b, Cabbages. c, Pumpkin. d, Potatoes.

Perf. 12½ Vert. Syncopated

2008, Sept. 25			**Litho.**	
		Coil Stamps		
2594	A880	(5.50k) multi	1.75	1.75

Size: 27x21mm

2595	A880	11k multi	3.50	3.50

Booklet Stamps
Self-Adhesive
Serpentine Die Cut 10 on 3 Sides
Size: 23x27mm

2596		Block of 4	7.00	
a.-d.		A880 (5.50k) Any single	1.75	1.75
e.		Booklet pane of 10, 3 each #2596a, 2596c, 2 each #2596b, 2596d	17.50	

A881

Comic Strips — A882

No. 2597: a, Assar, by Ulf Lundkvist. b, Ensamma Mamman, by Cecilia Torudd. c, Arne Anka, by Charlie Christensen. d, Rocky, by Martin Kellerman.
No. 2598: a, Nameless Gloomy Girl, by Nina Hemmingsson. b, Hälge, by Lars Mortimer. c, Socker-Conny, by Joakim Pirinen. d, Swedish Manga, by Asa Ekström.

Litho. & Engr.

2008, Sept. 25			**Perf. 12½x13**	
2597	A881	Sheet of 4	7.00	7.00
a.-d.		5.50k Any single	1.75	1.75
2598	A882	Sheet of 4	7.00	7.00
a.-d.		5.50k Any single	1.75	1.75
e.		Booklet pane, #2597-2598	14.00	14.00
		Complete booklet, #2598e	14.00	
f.		Miniature sheet of 9, 5 #2597a, 4 #2598b	16.50	16.50

No. 2598e has a row of rouletting separating No. 2597 from No. 2598, and has a wider margin where the pane is attached to the booklet cover. No. 2598f sold for 54.50k.

Souvenir Sheet

Dario Fo, 1997 Nobel Laureate for Literature — A883

No. 2599: a, Fo (31x39mm). b, Illustration on Fo's Nobel diploma (34x50mm).

Litho. & Engr.
				Perf. 12¾	
2008, Nov. 13					
2599	A883	Sheet of 2		5.25	5.25
a.-b.		11k Either single		2.60	2.60

Winter Activities A884

No. 2600: a, Child sledding. b, Snowball lantern and house. c, Children making snowman.

2008, Nov. 13　Perf. 12¾ on 3 Sides
Booklet Stamps
2600		Horiz. strip of 3	8.00	8.00
a.-c.	A884	11k Any single	2.60	2.60
d.		Booklet pane of 6, 2 each		
		#2600a-2600c	16.00	—
		Complete booklet, #2600d + 6		
		etiquettes	16.00	

A885

Christmas — A886

No. 2602 — Various wreaths with background color of: a, Green. b, Gray. c, Blue. d, Brown.

Perf. 12¾ Vert. Syncopated
2008, Nov. 13　　　　　Litho.
Coil Stamp
2601	A885	(5k) multi	1.25	1.25

Booklet Stamps
Self-Adhesive
2602	A886	Block of 4	5.00	
a.-d.		(5k) Any single	1.25	1.25
e.		Complete booklet, 3 each		
		#2602a-2602b, 2 each		
		#2602c-2602d	12.50	

A887

Greetings — A888

No. 2604: a, Swans. b, Skaters making hearts in ice. c, White hearts. d, Hearts as flowers.

Perf. 12¾ Vert. Syncopated
2009, Jan. 29　　　Litho. & Engr.
Coil Stamp
2603	A887	(6k) red & pink	1.50	1.50

Booklet Stamps
Self-Adhesive
2604	A888	Block of 4	6.00	
a.-d.		(6k) Any single	1.50	1.50
e.		Booklet pane of 10, 3 each		
		#2604a-2604b, 2 each		
		#2604c-2604d	15.00	

Die cuts and rouletting are found on face of Nos. 2604a-2604d to prevent reuse of stamps.

Europa — A889

No. 2605: a, Polarimeter. b, Star chart of Crab Nebula, balloon.

Perf. 12¾ on 3 Sides
2009, Jan. 29　　　　　Litho.
Booklet Stamps
2605	A889	Horiz. or vert. pair	6.00	6.00
a.-b.		12k Either single	3.00	3.00
c.		Booklet pane of 4, 2 each		
		#2605a-2605b	12.00	—
		Complete booklet, #2605c +		
		4 etiquettes	12.00	

A small star-shaped hole is punched into No. 2605b.

Automobiles — A890

Designs: Nos. 2606, 2608e, Ford Mustang convertible. 12k, Volvo Amazon and trailer. No. 2608: a, Volkswagen 1200. b, Volvo PV 444. c, Cadillac Coupe de Ville. d, Citroen DS 19.

Litho. & Engr.
			Perf. 12¾	
2009, Jan. 29				
2606	A890	(6k) multi	1.75	1.75

Coil Stamp
Engr.
Perf. 12¾ Vert. Syncopated
2607	A890	12k multi	3.00	3.00

Booklet Stamps
Perf. 12¾ Horiz.
2608		Vert. strip of 5	7.50	7.50
a.-e.	A890	(6k) Any single	1.50	1.50
f.		Booklet pane of 10, 2 each		
		#2608a-2608e	15.00	—
		Complete booklet, #2608f	15.00	

No. 2606 was printed in sheets of 6 that sold for 41k.

A891

A892

Birds — A893

Designs: (5k), Pandion haliaetus. (5.50k), Accipiter nisus.
No. 2611: a, Haliaeetus albicilla. b, Asio flammeus.

Perf. 12¾ Vert. Syncopated
2009, Mar. 26　　　　　Engr.
Coil Stamps
2609	A891	(5k) multi	1.25	1.25
2610	A892	(5.50k) multi	1.40	1.40

Perf. 13¼ Vert. Syncopated
2611	A893	Horiz. pair	3.00	3.00
a.-b.		(6k) Either single	1.50	1.50
		Nos. 2609-2611 (3)	5.65	5.65

Creation of the Grand Duchy of Finland, Bicent. — A894

No. 2612 — Text and date: a, 1809. b, 2009.

Perf. 13¼ Vert. Syncopated
2009, Mar. 26　　　　　Litho.
Coil Stamps
2612	A894	Horiz. pair	6.00	6.00
a.-b.		12k Either single	3.00	3.00

Souvenir Sheet

Wheel of Life, by Albertus Pictor (c. 1440-1509) — A895

No. 2613: a, Musician, man riding wheel. b, Man at top of wheel. c, Man falling off wheel, corpse.

Litho. & Engr.
			Perf. 12¾x13	
2009, Mar. 26				
2613	A895	Sheet of 3	9.00	9.00
a.-c.		12k Any single	3.00	3.00

Bananas — A896

No. 2614 — Clay figures: a, Young banana with love letter. b, Banana mother and child. c, Banana holding gift. d, Young banana giving flower to old banana.

Serpentine Die Cut 10 on 3 Sides
2009, Mar. 26　　　　　Litho.
Booklet Stamps
Self-Adhesive
2614	A896	Block of 4	6.00	
a.-d.		(6k) Any single	1.50	1.50
e.		Booklet pane of 10, 3 each		
		#2614a-2614b, 2 each		
		#2614c-2614d	15.00	

Queen Silvia Type of 2005
Perf. 12½ Vert. Syncopated
2009, May 14　　　　　Engr.
Coil Stamp
2615	A814	12k multi	3.00	3.00

Architecture — A897

Designs: No. 2616, Turning Torso, Malmö. No. 2617: a, Kaknäs Tower, Stockholm. b, Lugnet ski jump, Falun. c, Balder roller coaster, Gothenburg. d, Like #2616.

2009, May 14　Engr.　Perf. 12½x12¾
2616	A897	12k dark blue	3.25	3.25

Booklet Stamps
Perf. 12½x12¾ on 3 Sides
2617		Booklet pane of 4	12.00	12.00
a.-d.	A897	12k Any single	3.00	3.00
e.		Complete booklet, #2617 + 4		
		etiquettes	12.00	

No. 2616 was printed in a sheet of 4 stamps that sold for 53k.

Flora and Fauna A898

Designs: No. 2618, Sand star, Kosterhavet Park.
No. 2619: a, Globeflowers, Abisko National Park. b, Tree frog, Stenshuvud National Park. c, Dormouse, Garphyttan National Park. d, Cranberries, Store Mosse National Park.

Perf. 12¼ Vert. Syncopated
2009, May 14　　　　　Litho.
Coil Stamp
2618	A898	(6k) multi	1.50	1.50

Booklet Stamps
Self-Adhesive
Size: 37x26mm
Serpentine Die Cut 10 on 3 Sides
2619		Block of 4	6.00	
a.-d.	A898	(6k) Any single	1.50	1.50
e.		Booklet pane of 10, 3 each		
		#2619a-2619b, 2 each		
		#2619c-2619d	15.00	

Souvenir Sheet

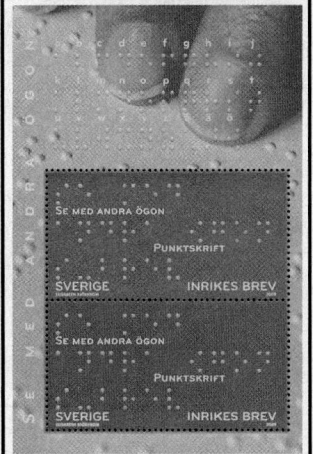

Braille Text — A899

No. 2620 — Text in Swedish and Braille with background color of: a, Red violet. b, Purple.

2009, May 14 Litho. Perf. 12¾x12½
2620 A899 Sheet of 2 3.00 3.00
a.-b. (6k) Either single 1.50 1.50

Louis Braille (1809-52), educator of the blind. Braille dots were applied by a thermographic process.

Christer Fugelsang, First Swede in Space — A900

No. 2621: a, Fugelsang waving (39x33mm). b, Fugelsang and Astronaut Robert Curbeam repairing solar panel (39x33mm). c, Space Shuttle Discovery (39x33mm). d, Fugelsang with helmet on lap (39x33mm). e, Fugelsang on space walk (39x66mm).

Litho. & Engr.
2009, Sept. 24 Perf. 12¾
2621 A900 Block of 5 8.75 8.75
a.-e. 6k Any single 1.75 1.75
f. Booklet pane, 2 #2621 17.50
Complete booklet, #2621f 17.50
g. Sheet of 9 #2621d 17.00 17.00

Star-shaped holes are punched into Nos. 2621a, 2621c and 2621e. No. 2621g sold for 59k.

A901

A902

Spices — A903

Designs: No. 2622, Anethum graveolens (dill). 12k, Allium schoenoprasum (chives).
No. 2624: a, Ocimum basilicum (basil). b, Capsicum (chili peppers). c, Rosmarinus officinalis (rosemary). d, Allium sativum (garlic).

Perf. 12½ Vert. Syncopated
2009, Sept. 24 Engr.
Coil Stamps
2622 A901 (6k) multi 1.75 1.75
2623 A902 12k multi 3.50 3.50

Booklet Stamps
Litho.
Serpentine Die Cut 10 on 3 Sides
2624 A903 Block of 4 7.00
a.-d. (6k) Any single 1.75 1.75
e. Booklet pane of 10, 3 each 17.50
#2624a-2624b, 2 each
#2624c-2624d

White Animals A910

No. 2625: a, Lagopus muta. b, Mustela erminea. c, Lepus timidus.

Perf. 12¾ on 3 Sides
2009, Nov. 19 Engr.
Booklet Stamps
2625 Horiz. strip of 3 10.50 10.50
a.-c. A910 12k Any single 3.50 3.50
d. Booklet pane of 6, 2 each 21.00 —
#2625a-2625c, + 6 etiquettes
Complete booklet, #2625d 21.00

A911

Christmas — A912

No. 2627 — Various wrapped gifts including: a, Lamp and bottle. b, Large ball and saw. c, Teddy bear and rolling pin. d, Toy train and flower.

Perf. 13¼ Vert. Syncopated
2009, Nov. 19 Litho.
Coil Stamp
2626 A911 (5.50k) multi 1.60 1.60

Booklet Stamps
Self-Adhesive
Serpentine Die Cut 10 on 3 Sides
2627 A912 Block of 4 6.40
a.-d. (5.50k) Any single 1.60 1.60
e. Booklet pane of 10, 3 each 16.00
#2627a-2627b, 2 each
#2627c-2627d

A913

Castles and Palaces — A914

Designs: Nos. 2628, 2629d, Läckö Castle. No. 2629a, Vadstena Castle. No. 2629b, Ulriksdal Palace. No. 2629c, Tjolöholm Castle. No. 2629e, Sofiero Palace.

2010, Jan. 28 Engr. Perf. 12¾x12½
2628 A913 12k blue & green 3.75 3.75

Booklet Stamps
Self-Adhesive
Serpentine Die Cut 10 Horiz. (A914),
Serpentine Die Cut 10 on 3 Sides
(A913)
2629 Booklet pane of 5 + 5 16.50
etiquettes
a.-c. A914 12k Any single 3.25 3.25
d.-e. A913 12k Either single 3.25 3.25

No. 2628 was printed in sheets of 4 that sold for 53k.

Europa — A915

No. 2630 — Illustrations from children's books: a, Maja's Alphabet, by Lena Andersson. b, Children of the Forest, by Elsa Beskow.

Perf. 13¼ Vert. Syncopated
2010, Jan. 28 Litho. & Engr.
Coil Stamps
2630 A915 Horiz. pair 6.50 6.50
a.-b. 12k Either single 3.25 3.25

Black Cats — A916

No. 2631 — Cat: a, Drinking from saucer. b, Playing with ball. c, Arching back. d, Stretching.

Serpentine Die Cut 10
2010, Jan. 28 Litho.
Booklet Stamps
Self-Adhesive
2631 A916 Block of 4 6.40
a.-d. (6k) Any single 1.60 1.60
e. Booklet pane of 10, 3 each 16.00
#2631a-2631b, 2 each
#2631c-2631d

King Carl XVI Gustaf — A917

Queen Silvia — A918

Perf. 13¼ Vert. Syncopated
2010, Mar. 24 Engr.
Coil Stamps
2632 A917 (6k) dark green 1.75 1.75
2633 A918 12k dark brown 3.50 3.50

Wedding Rings — A919

Celebrations — A920

No. 2635: a, Cake. b, Birds. c, Hands and hearts. d, Champagne bottle and glasses.

Perf. 13¼ Vert. Syncopated
2010, Mar. 24 Litho.
Coil Stamp
2634 A919 (6k) multi 1.75 1.75
Booklet Stamps
Self-Adhesive
Serpentine Die Cut 10 on 3 Sides
2635 A920 Block of 4 7.00
a.-d. (6k) Any single 1.75 1.75
e. Booklet pane of 10, 3 each 17.50
#2635a-2635b, 2 each
#2635c-2635d

Souvenir Sheet

Life on the Coast — A921

No. 2636: a, Mytilus edulis. b, Fishing boat SD141 Emelie.

Litho. & Engr.

2010, Mar. 24   **Perf. 13x12½**

| 2636 | A921 | Sheet of 2 | 7.00 | 7.00 |
| a.-b. | | 12k Either single | 3.50 | 3.50 |

Karolinska Institutet, Bicent. — A922

No. 2637 — Electron microscope photographs by Lennart Nilsson of: a, Silicon (blue crystals) b, Selenium (red violet crystals).

Perf. 13¼ Vert. Syncopated

2010, May 13   **Engr.**

Coil Stamps

| 2637 | A922 | Horiz. pair | 3.00 | 3.00 |
| a.-b. | | (5.50k) Any single | 1.50 | 1.50 |

Sea Mammals — A923

No. 2638: a, Phocoena phocoena. b, Enhydra lutris. c, Balaenoptera musculus. d, Pusa hispida.

Perf. 13x12¾ on 3 Sides

2010, May 13   **Litho. & Engr.**

Booklet Stamps

2638	A923	Block of 4	13.00	13.00
a.-d.		12k Any single	3.25	3.25
e.		Booklet pane, #2638a-		
		2638d + 4 etiquettes	13.00	
		Complete booklet, #2638e	13.00	

See Canada No. 2387.

A924

Pansies — A925

No. 2640 — Flower color: a, Yellow and red, green petal showing. b, Blue violet. c, Red. d, Purple and red.

Perf. 12½ Vert. Syncopated

2010, May 13   **Litho.**

Coil Stamp

| 2639 | A924 | (6k) multi | 1.60 | 1.60 |

Booklet Stamps
Self-Adhesive

Serpentine Die Cut 10 on 3 Sides

2640	A925	Block of 4	6.40	
a.-d.		(6k) Any single	1.60	1.60
e.		Booklet pane of 10, 3 each		
		#2640a-2640b, 2 each		
		#2640c-2640d	16.00	

Souvenir Sheet

Wedding of Crown Princess Victoria and Daniel Westling — A926

No. 2641: a, Crown Princess Victoria (27x36mm). b, Royal monogram of Crown Princess Victoria (27x36mm). c, Crown Princess Victoria and Daniel Westling (54x40mm).

Perf. 13¼x12¾

2010, May 13   **Litho. & Engr.**

| 2641 | A926 | Sheet of 3 | 5.00 | 5.00 |
| a.-c. | | 6k Any single | 1.60 | 1.60 |

Souvenir Sheet

Art of Engraving — A927

No. 2642: a, Viking era silver bowl, engraved by Martin Mörck. b, Armor of King Erik XIV, engraved by Lars Sjööblom. c, Sweden Type A305, engraved by Czeslaw Slania.

Litho. & Engr.

2010, Aug. 26   **Perf. 12¾**

| 2642 | A927 | Sheet of 3 | 10.50 | 10.50 |
| a.-c. | | 12k Any single | 3.50 | 3.50 |

See Ireland No. 1895.

A928

A929

Swedish Foods — A930

Designs: No. 2643, Waffles and cloudberries. 12k, Crispbread and Västerbotten cheese.

No. 2645: a, Girl eating peppermint stick. b, Hand holding gravlax (marinated salmon). c, Man cutting pyramid cake. d, Man sniffing can of fermented herring.

Perf. 12½ Vert. Syncopated

2010, Aug. 26   **Engr.**

Coil Stamps

| 2643 | A928 | (6k) bis & org | 1.75 | 1.75 |

Perf. 12¾ Vert. Syncopated

| 2644 | A929 | 12k brn & bis | 3.50 | 3.50 |

Booklet Stamps
Litho.

Serpentine Die Cut 10 on 3 Sides
Self-Adhesive

2645	A930	Block of 4	7.00	
a.-d.		(6k) Any single	1.75	1.75
e.		Booklet pane of 10, 3 each		
		#2645a-2645b, 2 each		
		#2645c-2645d	17.50	

Crime Novelists — A931

No. 2646: a, Maj Sjöwall, Per Wahlöö (1926-75), helicopter and handcuffs (66x27mm). b, Henning Mankell, dead body, handcuffs, gavel (66x27mm). c, Liza Marklund and police car (66x27mm). d, Hakan Nesser and pistol (33x30mm). e, Stieg Larsson (1954-2004) and laptop computer (33x30mm).

Litho. & Engr.

2010, Aug. 26   **Perf. 13x12¾**

2646	A931	Block of 5	8.75	8.75
a.-e.		6k Any single	1.75	1.75
f.		Booklet pane, 2 #2646	17.50	—
		Complete booklet, #2646f	17.50	
g.		Sheet of 9 #2646d	16.50	16.50

Nos. 2646a-2646c each have two holes and Nos. 2646d-2646e each have one hole drilled through stamp. No. 2646g sold for 59k.

A932

A933

A934

A935

Snowflakes
A936

Perf. 12¾x12½

2010, Nov. 18   **Litho. & Engr.**

| 2647 | A932 | 12k multi | 4.00 | 4.00 |

Self-Adhesive

Serpentine Die Cut 10 on 3 Sides, Serpentine Die Cut 10 Horiz. (A933)

2648		Booklet pane of 5 + 5		
		etiquettes	17.50	
a.	A933	12k multi	3.50	3.50
b.	A934	12k multi	3.50	3.50
c.	A932	12k multi	3.50	3.50
d.	A935	12k multi	3.50	3.50
e.	A936	12k multi	3.50	3.50

No. 2647 was printed in a sheet of 4 that sold for 53k.

Christmas — A937

No. 2649 — "J" as: a, Candy cane. b, Santa Claus. c, Christmas light. d, Stocking.

Serpentine Die Cut 10 on 3 Sides

2010, Nov. 18   **Litho.**

Booklet Stamps
Self-Adhesive

2649	A937	Block of 4	6.40	
a.-d.		(5.50k) Any single	1.60	1.60
e.		Booklet pane of 10, 3 each		
		#2649a, 2649c, 2 each		
		#2649b, 2649d	16.00	

Fossils — A938

Fossils of: 30k, Molluscs. 40k, Cuttlefish.

SWEDEN

Serpentine Die Cut 9 Horiz.
2011, Jan. 27   Litho. & Engr.
Self-Adhesive
2650 A938 30k multi   9.25 9.25

Serpentine Die Cut 9 Vert.
Size: 28x28mm
2651 A938 40k multi   12.50 12.50

Bicycles and Tricycles A939

No. 2652: a, Tricycle and air pump. b, Bicycle and helmet. c, Bicycle and chain guard. d, Bicycle and chain ring. e, Tricycle and horn.

2011, Jan. 27   Perf. 12¾ Horiz.
Booklet Stamps
2652   Vert. strip of 5   9.50 9.50
a.-e.   A939 (6k) Any single   1.90 1.90
f.   Booklet pane, 2 #2652   19.00   —
         Complete booklet, #2652f 19.00

A940

Flag of Sweden — A941

No. 2654: a, Flag on flagpole. b, People waving flags. c, Flag on person's forehead. d, Flag on vehicle.

2011, Jan. 27 Litho. Perf. 12½ Vert.
Coil Stamp
2653 A940 (6k) multi   1.90 1.90

Booklet Stamps
Self-Adhesive
Serpentine Die Cut 10 on 3 Sides
2654   Block of 4   7.60
a.-d.   (6k) Any single   1.90 1.90
e.   Booklet pane of 10, 3 each
         #2654a-2654b, 2 each
         #2654c-2654d   19.00

Hands and Curved Lines — A942

No. 2655 — Hands and lines in: a, Red. b, Blue.

Perf. 13¼ Vert. Syncopated
2011, Mar. 24   Litho. & Engr.
Coil Stamps
2655 A942 Horiz. pair, #a-b   3.25 3.25
a.-b.   (5k) Either single   1.60 1.60

Europa — A943

No. 2655 — Wood of: a, Betula. b, Pica abies.

2011, Mar. 24
Coil Stamps
2656 A943 Horiz. pair, #a-b   8.00 8.00
a.-b.   12k Either single   4.00 4.00

Intl. Year of Forests.

A944

Renewable Energy — A945

No. 2658: a, Clouds, solar panels. b, Field, wind turbine. c, Trees, bioenergy tank. d, Underwater scene, wave energy converter.

Perf. 13 Vert. Syncopated
2011, Mar. 24   Litho.
Coil Stamp
2657 A944 (6k) multi   2.00 2.00

Booklet Stamps
Self-Adhesive
Serpentine Die Cut 10 on 3 Sides
2658   Block of 4   8.00
a.-d.   (6k) Any single   2.00 2.00
e.   Booklet pane of 10, 3 each
         #2658a-2658b, 2 each
         #2658c-2658d   20.00

Scenes From Industrial Towns — A946

Buildings or workers in: Nos. 2659, 2660e, Mackmyra. No. 2660a, Forsvik, horiz. (58x29mm). No. 2660b, Glasriket. No. 2660c, Avesta. No. 2660d, Jonsered.

2011, Mar. 24 Engr. Perf. 12¾x12½
2659 A946 12k dk brn & brn   4.25 4.25
Self-Adhesive
Serpentine Die Cut 10 on 2 or 3 Sides
2660   Booklet pane of 5 + 5
          etiquettes   20.00
a.-e.   A946 12k Any single   4.00 4.00

No. 2659 was printed in sheets of 4 that sold for 53k.

Souvenir Sheet

Struve Geodetic Arc UNESCO World Heritage Site — A947

No. 2661: a, Theodolite. b, Wilhelm Struve (1793-1864), astronomer.

2011, May 6 Litho. & Engr. Perf. 13
2661 A947 Sheet of 2   8.00 8.00
a.-b.   12k Either single   4.00 4.00

Water Lilies — A948

No. 2662: a, Four red water lilies, one white water lily, dragonfly. b, Four white water lilies, three yellow water lilies, dragonfly. c, Yellow water lily. d, White water lily.

Perf. 12¾ on 3 Sides
2011, May 12   Litho.
Booklet Stamps
2662 A948 Block of 4   15.00 15.00
a.-d.   12k Any single   3.75 3.75
e.   Booklet pane, #2662a-
          2662d + 4 etiquettes   15.00
          Complete booklet, #2662e 15.00

Banana Split A949

Ice Cream — A950

No. 2664: a, Ice cream bar. b, Vanilla ice cream cone. c, Sundae with cherries. d, Chocolate-coated ice cream cone.

Perf. 12½ Vert. Syncopated
2011, May 12   Litho.
Coil Stamp
2663 A949 (6k) multi   1.90 1.90

Booklet Stamps
Self-Adhesive
Serpentine Die Cut 10 on 3 Sides
2664 A950 Block of 4   7.60
a.-d.   (6k) Any single   1.90 1.90
e.   Booklet pane of 10, 3 each
          #2664a-2664b, 2 each
          #2664c-2664d   19.00

Equestrian Sports — A951

Designs: Nos. 2665, 2666a, Harness racing (Stig H. Johannson driving Victory Tilly). No. 2666b, Show jumping (Malin Baryard-Johnsson on Butterfly Flip). No. 2666c, Pony racing (Ebba Stigenberg on Norrskenets Grim). No. 2666d, Dressage (Jan Brink on Briar). No. 2666e, Eventing (Hannes Melin on Gaston KLG).

Perf. 12¾x12½
2011, Aug. 25   Litho. & Engr.
2665 A951 6k multi   2.00 2.00
Booklet Stamps
Perf. 12¾ Horiz.
2666   Vert. strip of 5   9.50 9.50
a.-e.   A951 6k Any single   1.90 1.90
f.   Booklet pane, 2 #2666   19.00
         Complete booklet, #2666f 19.00

No. 2665 was printed in sheets of 9 that sold for 59k.

Poppy, Rye and Barley Seed Capsules A952

Conifer Cones A953

A954

A955

A956

Seed Capsules A957

Perf. 12¼ Vert. Syncopated
2011, Aug. 25   Engr.

Coil Stamps

| 2667 | A952 | (6k) multi | 1.90 | 1.90 |
| 2668 | A953 | 12k multi | 3.75 | 3.75 |

Booklet Stamps
Self-Adhesive
Litho.

Serpentine Die Cut 10 on 3 Sides

2669		Block of 4		7.75
a.	A954	(6k) multi	1.90	1.90
b.	A955	(6k) multi	1.90	1.90
c.	A956	(6k) multi	1.90	1.90
d.	A957	(6k) multi	1.90	1.90
e.		Booklet pane of 10, 3 each		
		#2669a-2669b, 2 each		
		#2669c-2669d		19.00

Winter
Clothing — A958

Designs: Nos. 2670, 2671e, Mittens. No. 2671a, Socks, horiz. (62x32mm). No. 2671b, Hats (31x39mm). No. 2671c, Scarf (31x39mm). No. 2671d, Sweater (31x39mm).

Perf. 12¾x12½
2011, Nov. 17   Litho. & Engr.

| 2670 | A958 | 12k multi | 4.00 | 4.00 |

Booklet Stamps
Self-Adhesive

Serpentine Die Cut 10 on 2 or 3 Sides

| 2671 | | Booklet pane of 5 + 5 etiquettes | | 19.00 |
| a.-e. | A958 | 12k Any single | 3.75 | 3.75 |

No. 2670 was printed in a sheet of 4 that sold for 53k.

Souvenir Sheet

Intl. Year of Chemistry — A959

No. 2672: a, Marie Curie (1867-1934), 1911 Nobel laureate for Chemistry (40x55mm). b, Nobel medal and radium, horiz. (36x28mm).

Perf. 13x12¾ (#2672a), 12¾ (#2672b)
2011, Nov. 17

| 2672 | A959 | Sheet of 2 | 7.50 | 7.50 |
| a.-b. | | 12k Either single | 3.75 | 3.75 |

See Poland No. 4024.

Christmas
Cactus — A960

Poinsettia
A961

Amaryllis
A962

Hellebore
A963

Serpentine Die Cut 10 on 3 Sides
2011, Nov. 17   Litho.

Booklet Stamps

2673		Block of 4		7.00
a.	A960	(5.50k) multi	1.75	1.75
b.	A961	(5.50k) multi	1.75	1.75
c.	A962	(5.50k) multi	1.75	1.75
d.	A963	(5.50k) multi	1.75	1.75
e.		Booklet pane of 10, 3 each		
		#2673a-2673b, 2 each		
		#2673c-2673d		17.50

Christmas.

Europa — A964

No. 2674 —Tourist attractions: a, Dalarna. b, Ericsson Globe Arena, Stockholm.

Perf. 12½ Vert. Syncopated
2012, Jan. 12   Engr.

Coil Stamps

2674	A964	Horiz. pair	7.50	7.50
a.		12k green	3.75	3.75
b.		12k blue	3.75	3.75

A965

Octahedrons
A966   A967

Perf. 12½ Vert. Syncopated
2012, Jan. 12

Coil Stamp

| 2675 | A965 | (5.50k) green | 1.75 | 1.75 |

Booklet Stamps
Self-Adhesive

Serpentine Die Cut 9 Horiz.

2676		Block or horiz. strip of 4		7.00
a.	A966	(5.50k) blue	1.75	1.75
b.	A967	(5.50k) red	1.75	1.75
c.	A967	(5.50k) blue	1.75	1.75
d.	A966	(5.50k) red	1.75	1.75
e.		Booklet pane of 20, 5 each		
		#2676a-2676d		35.00

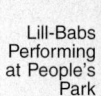

Lill-Babs
Performing
at People's
Park
A968

Entrance to People's Park, Borlänge — A969

Entrance to
People's
Park,
Björneborg
A970

Dance Floor
at People's
Park, Arvika
A971

Chocolate
Wheel at
People's
Park,
Kolsnäs
A972

2012, Jan. 12   Perf. 12¾

| 2677 | A968 | (6k) claret | 2.00 | 2.00 |

Coil Stamp

Perf. 12½ Vert. Syncopated

| 2678 | A969 | (6k) purple | 1.90 | 1.90 |

Booklet Stamps
Self-Adhesive

Serpentine Die Cut 10 on 3 Sides

2679		Block of 4		7.75
a.	A970	(6k) red	1.90	1.90
b.	A971	(6k) blue	1.90	1.90
c.	A968	(6k) blue	1.90	1.90
d.	A972	(6k) red	1.90	1.90
e.		Booklet pane of 10, 3 each		
		#2679a-2679b, 2 each		
		#2679c-2679d		19.00

No. 2677 was printed in a sheet of six that sold for 41k.

Fishing Pole
With
Ambassadeur
Reel — A973

Salmon
Fly — A974

Hi-Lo
Wobbler and
Toby Spoon
Spinner
Lures
A975

Die Cut Perf. 11¾x11½
2012, Mar. 21

Coil Stamps
Self-Adhesive

| 2680 | A973 | 5k multi | 1.50 | 1.50 |

Die Cut Perf. 11¾

2681	A974	10k multi	3.00	3.00
2682	A975	20k multi	6.00	6.00
		Nos. 2680-2682 (3)	10.50	10.50

Art Photography
A976

Designs: (6k), 2680, by Dawid.
No. 2684: a, Dreamer in the Blue House, by Sune Jonsson (man with open book, 58x29mm). b, At Home, by Gunnar Smoliansky (plant cutting in glass, 27x36mm). c, Agneta, Finland, by Denise Grünstein (woman swimming, 27x36mm). d, Attempting to Deal With Time and Space, by Annika von Hausswolff (person squeezing balloon, 27x36mm). e, Paris, by Christer Strömholm (people kissing, 27x36mm).

Perf. 12¼ Vert. Syncopated
2012, Mar. 21   Litho.

Coil Stamp

| 2683 | A976 | (6k) shown | 1.90 | 1.90 |

Serpentine Die Cut 10 Horiz.,
Serpentine Die Cut 10 on 3 Sides
(#2684b-2684d)

| 2684 | | Booklet pane of 5 + 5 etiquettes | | 19.00 |
| a.-e. | A976 | 12k Any single | 3.75 | 3.75 |

Poultry Breeds — A977

No. 2685: a, Hedemora hens (Hedemorahöna). b, Old Swedish dwarf hens (Gammalsvensk dvärghöna). c, Swedish spotted hens (Skansk blommehöna). d, Orust hens (Orusthöna).

Serpentine Die Cut 10 on 3 Sides
2012, Mar. 21

Booklet Stamps
Self-Adhesive

2685	A977	Block of 4		7.75
a.-d.		(6k) Any single	1.90	1.90
e.		Booklet pane of 10, 3 each		
		#2685a-2685b, 2 each		
		#2685c-2685d		19.00

Souvenir Sheet

Life on the Coast — A978

No. 2686: a, Häradskär Lighthouse, Arkö 833 pilot boat. b, Dash 8Q-300 surveillance airplane.

Litho. & Engr.
2012, Mar. 21   Perf. 12¾

| 2686 | A978 | Sheet of 2 | 7.50 | 7.50 |
| a.-b | | 12k Either single | 3.75 | 3.75 |

Type
Fonts — A979

No. 2687: a, Berling Antiqua. b, Indigo Antiqua. c, Sispos. d, Satura. e, Traffic.

Serpentine Die Cut 9 Horiz.
2012, May 10   Engr.
Self-Adhesive

2687	Vert. strip of 5	17.50	
a.-e.	A979 12k Any single	3.50	3.50

A980

Olympic Gold Medalists — A981

Designs: 12k, Eric Lemming (1880-1930), javelin gold medalist, 1912 Olympics.
No. 2689: a, Ragnar Skanaker, pistol shooting gold medalist, 1972 Olympics. b, Carolina Klüft, heptathlon gold medalist, 2004 Olympics.

Litho. & Engr. (12k), Litho.
2012, May 10   *Perf. 12¾*
2688	A980 12k multi	4.00	4.00

Coil Stamps
Perf. 13¼ Vert. Syncopated
2689	A981 Horiz. pair	3.50	3.50
a.-b.	(6k) Either single	1.75	1.75

Perf. 12¾ Vert. Syncopated
2690	A980 12k multi	3.50	3.50

No. 2688 was printed in sheets of 4 that sold for 53k.

 Flowers — A982

Designs: No. 2691: Cowslip, hairy violet, mountain everlasting, meadow saxifrage.
No. 2692: a, Cowslip (gullviva). b, Hairy violet (buskviol). c, Mountain everlasting (kattfot). d, Meadow saxifrage (mandelblomma).

Perf. 13¼ Vert. Syncopated
2012, May 10   Litho.
Coil Stamp
2691	A982 (6k) multi	1.75	1.75

Booklet Stamps
Self-Adhesive
Serpentine Die Cut 10 on 3 Sides
2692	Block of 4	7.00	
a.-d.	A982 (6k) Any single	1.75	1.75
e.	Booklet pane of 10, 3 each #2692a-2692b, 2 each #2692c-2692d	17.50	

Souvenir Sheet

Raoul Wallenberg (1912-47), Diplomat — A983

Litho. & Engr.
2012, May 10   *Perf. 12¾*
2693	A983 12k multi	3.50	3.50

SEMI-POSTAL STAMPS

Type of 1872-91 Issues Surcharged in Dark Blue

Perf. 13x13½
1916, Dec. 21   Wmk. 181
B1	A5	5o + 5o on 2o org	4.75	7.25
B2	A5	5o + 5o on 3o yel brn	4.75	7.25
B3	A5	5o + 5o on 4o gray	4.75	7.25
B4	A5	5o + 5o on 5o grn	4.75	7.25
B5	A5	5o + 5o on 6o lilac	4.75	7.25
B6	A5	10o + 10o on 12o pale bl	4.75	7.25
B7	A5	10o + 10o on 20o red org	4.75	7.25
B8	A5	10o + 10o on 24o yel	4.75	7.25
B9	A5	10o + 10o on 30o brn	4.75	7.25
B10	A5	10o + 10o on 50o rose red	4.75	7.25
	Nos. B1-B10 (10)		47.50	72.50

The surtax on Nos. B1-B31 was for the militia. See note after No. B21.
For surcharges see Nos. B22-B31.

No. 66 Surcharged in Dark Blue

1916, Dec. 21   Wmk. 180   Perf. 13
B11	A12 10o + 4.90k on 5k	150.00	375.00

Nos. J12-J22 Surcharged in Dark Blue

1916, Dec. 21   Unwmk.   Perf. 13
B12	D1	5o + 5o on 1o	25.00	18.00
B13	D1	5o + 5o on 3o	5.00	7.00
B14	D1	5o + 5o on 5o	18.00	7.00
B15	D1	5o + 10o on 6o	5.00	8.00
B16	D1	5o + 15o on 12o	42.50	32.50
B17	D1	10o + 20o on 20o	15.00	25.00
B18	D1	10o + 40o on 24o	55.00	100.00
B19	D1	10o + 20o on 30o	6.50	6.00
B20	D1	10o + 40o on 50o	20.00	42.50
B21	D1	10o + 90o on 1kr	150.00	375.00
	Nos. B12-B21 (10)		342.00	621.00

The surtax on Nos. B12-B21 is indicated not in figures, but in words at bottom of surcharge: Fem, 5; Tio, 10; Femton, 15; Tjugo, 20; Fyrtio, 40; Nittio, 90.

Nos. B1-B10 Surcharged

1918, Dec. 18   Wmk. 181
B22	A5	7o + 3o on #B1	8.00	9.00
B23	A5	7o + 3o on #B2	2.75	1.25
B24	A5	7o + 3o on #B3	2.75	1.25
B25	A5	7o + 3o on #B4	2.75	1.25
B26	A5	7o + 3o on #B5	2.75	1.25
B27	A5	12o + 8o on #B6	2.75	1.25
B28	A5	12o + 8o on #B7	2.75	1.25
B29	A5	12o + 8o on #B8	2.75	1.25
B30	A5	12o + 8o on #B9	2.75	1.25
B31	A5	12o + 8o on #B10	2.75	1.25
	Nos. B22-B31 (10)		32.75	20.25

The 12o+8o surcharge exists on Nos. B1-B5 and the 7o+3o surcharge exists on Nos. B6-B10. Value, each $72.50.
Nos. B24, B26, B28 and B30 exist with surcharge inverted. Value unused, each $140.

King Gustaf V — SP1

Unwmk.
1928, June 16   Engr.   Perf. 10
B32	SP1	5o (+ 5o) yel grn	2.75	6.00
B33	SP1	10o (+ 5o) dk vio	2.75	6.00
B34	SP1	15o (+ 5o) car	2.75	4.50
	Complete booklet, pane of 8 ea. #B32, B33, B34	275.00	
B35	SP1	20o (+ 5o) org	4.75	2.75
B36	SP1	25o (+ 5o) dk bl	4.75	3.25
	Nos. B32-B36 (5)	17.75	22.50
	Set, never hinged	27.50	

70th birthday of King Gustaf V. The surtax was used for anti-cancer work.

> **Catalogue values for unused stamps in this section, from this point to the end of the section, are for Never Hinged items.**

King Gustaf V — SP2

1948, June 16   Perf. 12½ Vertically
B37	SP2	10o + 10o green	.55	.60
B38	SP2	20o + 10o red	.80	.75
B39	SP2	30o + 10o ultra	.55	.60

Perf. 12½ on 3 Sides
B40	SP2	10o + 10o green	.65	.70
a.	Booklet pane of 20	10.00	
B41	SP2	20o + 10o red	.80	.90
a.	Booklet pane of 20	12.00	
	Nos. B37-B41 (5)	3.35	3.55

90th anniv. of the birth of King Gustaf V. The surtax provided aid for Swedish youth.

King Gustaf VI Adolf — SP3   Henri Dunant — SP4

1952, Nov. 11   Perf. 12½ Horiz.
B42	SP3	10o + 10o green	.35	.40
B43	SP3	25o + 10o car rose	.35	.40
B44	SP3	40o + 10o ultra	.65	.60

Perf. 12½ on 3 Sides
B45	SP3	10o + 10o green	.35	.40
a.	Booklet pane of 20	6.50	
B46	SP3	25o + 10o car rose	.35	.40
a.	Booklet pane of 20	7.00	
	Nos. B42-B46 (5)	2.05	2.20

70th birthday of King Gustaf VI Adolf. The surtax was used to promote Swedish culture.

1959, May 8   Perf. 12½ Horizontally
B47	SP4	30o + 10o red	.50	.75

Perf. 12½ on 3 Sides
B48	SP4	30o + 10o red	1.00	1.25
a.	Booklet pane of 20	18.00	

Centenary of the Red Cross idea. The surtax went to the Swedish Red Cross.

King Gustaf VI Adolf — SP5

Perf. 12½ Vertically
1962, Nov. 10   Engr.   Unwmk.
Size: 58x24mm
B49	SP5	20o + 10o brown	.30	.30
B50	SP5	35o + 10o blue	.30	.30

Perf. 12½ Horizontally
B51	SP5	20o + 10o brown	.30	.40
a.	Booklet pane of 10	3.00	
B52	SP5	35o + 10o blue	.30	.40
a.	Booklet pane of 10	3.00	
	Nos. B49-B52 (4)	1.20	1.40

80th birthday of King Gustav VI Adolf. The surtax went to the King Gustav VI Adolf 80th anniv. Foundation for Swedish Cultural Activities.

Ship Types of Regular Issues
Imprint: "1966"

Designs (Ships): 10o, "The Lion of Smaland." 15o, "Kalmar Nyckel." 20o, Old Sailing Packet. 25o, Mail Paddle Steamship. 30o, "Kung Karl." 40o, Stern of "Amphion."

1966, Nov. 15   Perf. 12½ on 3 Sides
B53	A76	10o vermilion	.30	.45
B54	A50	15o vermilion	.30	.45
B55	A38	20o slate grn	.30	.45
B56	A39	25o ultra	.25	.25
B57	A76	30o vermilion	.30	.55
B58	A76	40o vermilion	.30	.55
a.	Bklt. pane. #B53-B54, B57-B58, 2 #B55, 4 #B56	2.75	
	Nos. B53-B58 (6)	1.75	2.70

The booklet sold for 3.50k and the surtax of 1.15k went to the National Cancer Fund.

Save the Children Sweden — SP6

No. B59 — Three children, birds with tree at center and: a, Right. b, Left.

Serpentine Die Cut 10 on 3 Sides
2011, Mar. 24   Litho.
Booklet Stamps
Self-Adhesive
B59	SP6	Horiz. pair	4.50	
a.-b.	(6k+1k) Either single	2.25	2.25
c.	Booklet pane of 10, 5 each #B59a-B59b	22.50	

Surtax for Save the Children Sweden.

Swedish Cancer Society — SP7

No. B60: a, Silhouette of man. b, Abstract design.

2012, Jan. 12
Booklet Stamps
Self-Adhesive
B60	SP7	Horiz. pair	4.25	
a.-b.	(6k+1k) Either single	2.10	2.10
c.	Booklet pane of 10, 5 each #B60a-B60b	21.50	

Surtax for Swedish Cancer Society.

AIR POST STAMPS

Official Stamps Surcharged in Dark Blue

1920, Sept. 17   Wmk. 181   Perf. 13
C1	O3	10o on 3o brn	2.25	7.75
a.	Inverted surcharge	375.00	1,350.
C2	O3	20o on 2o org	3.50	11.00
a.	Inverted surcharge	375.00	1,100.
C3	O3	50o on 4o vio	19.00	25.00
a.	Inverted surcharge	375.00	1,350.
	Nos. C1-C3 (3)	24.75	43.75
	Set, never hinged	62.50	

Wmk. 180
C4	O3	20o on 2o org	3,250.	
C5	O3	50o on 4o vio	190.00	600.00

Airplane over
Stockholm
AP2

Perf. 10 Vertically

1930, May 9 Engr. Unwmk.

C6	AP2	10o deep blue	.25	.60
C7	AP2	50o dark violet	.65	1.75
	Set, never hinged		1.50	

Flying
Swans — AP3

1942-53 Perf. 12½ on 3 Sides

C8	AP3	20k brt ultra ('53)	4.50	.65
	Never hinged		7.00	
a.	Bklt. pane of 20 ('53)		725.00	
b.	Bklt. pane of 10 ('68)		65.00	
c.	Perf. on 4 sides		75.00	13.50
	Never hinged		140.00	
d.	As "c," bklt. pane of 10		1,350.	

Issued: #C8c, May 4, 1942; #C8, July 7.

POSTAGE DUE STAMPS

D1

1874 Unwmk. Typo. Perf. 14

J1	D1	1o black	75.00	40.00
J2	D1	3o rose	75.00	40.00
J3	D1	5o brown	75.00	35.00
J4	D1	6o yellow	150.00	95.00
J5	D1	12o pale red	7.75	6.00
J6	D1	20o blue	80.00	37.50
J7	D1	24o violet	625.00	375.00
J8	D1	24o gray	75.00	52.50
J9	D1	30o dk grn	87.50	40.00
J10	D1	50o brown	275.00	60.00
J11	D1	1k blue & bister	300.00	75.00
	Nos. J1-J11 (11)		1,825.	856.00

1877-86 Perf. 13

J12	D1	1o black ('80)	2.75	4.00
J13	D1	3o rose	6.25	7.25
J14	D1	5o brown	4.50	4.50
J15	D1	6o yellow	4.50	4.50
a.	Printed on both sides		1,600.	
J16	D1	12o pale red ('82)	14.50	17.00
J17	D1	20o pale blue ('78)	5.25	4.50
J18	D1	24o red lilac ('86)	26.00	29.00
a.	24o violet ('84)		26.00	29.00
J19	D1	24o gray lil ('82)	190.00	240.00
J20	D1	30o yellow green	6.50	4.50
J21	D1	50o yellow brown	10.50	5.75
J22	D1	1k blue & bister	30.00	17.50
	Nos. J12-J22 (11)		300.75	338.50

Nos. J12-J17, J19-J22 exist imperf. Value, pairs, each $400.
For surcharges see Nos. B12-B21.

STAMPS FOR CITY POSTAGE

S1

1856-62 Typo. Unwmk. Perf. 14

LX1	S1	(1sk) (3o) blk		
		('58)	1,100.	500.00
LX2	S1	(3o) bis brn		
		('62)	600.00	525.00

From 1856 to 1858 No. LX1 was sold at 1sk, from 1858 to 1862 at 3o. The paper of the 1sk black is thin while the paper of the 3o black is medium thick.

No. LX1 was reprinted three times with perf. 14, once with perf. 13. No. LX2 was reprinted once with each perforation. Value of lowest cost Perf. 14 reprints, $250 each. See the

---

Scott Specialized Catalogue of Stamps and Covers 1840-1940 for detailed listings.

OFFICIAL STAMPS

O1

1874-77 Unwmk. Typo. Perf. 14

O1	O1	3o bister	90.00	42.50
O2	O1	4o gray ('77)	300.00	75.00
O3	O1	5o yel green	140.00	52.50
O4	O1	6o lilac	275.00	65.00
O5	O1	6o gray	525.00	175.00
O6	O1	12o blue	200.00	3.00
O7	O1	20o pale red	1,050.	90.00
O8	O1	24o yellow	1,050.	20.00
a.	24o orange		1,050.	22.50
O9	O1	30o pale brn	425.00	37.50
O10	O1	50o rose	600.00	125.00
O11	O1	1k bl & bis	1,700.	65.00
	Nos. O1-O11 (11)		6,355.	750.50

Imperf., Pairs

O1a	O1	3o	1,500.
O2a	O1	4o	1,500.
O3a	O1	5o	1,500.
O4a	O1	6o	1,500.
O6a	O1	12o	1,500.
O7a	O1	20o	1,500.
O8b	O1	24o	1,500.
O9a	O1	30o	1,500.
O10a	O1	50o	1,500.
O11a	O1	1k	2,500.

1881-95 Perf. 13

O12	O1	2o org ('91)	1.40	2.00
O13	O1	3o bis brn	1.40	2.25
O14	O1	4o gray blk ('93)	2.50	.70
a.	4o gray ('82)		20.00	2.75
O15	O1	5o grn ('84)	5.25	.60
O16	O1	6o red lil ('82)	40.00	60.00
a.	6o lilac ('81)		45.00	65.00
O17	O1	10o car ('95)	3.00	.25
b.	10o rose ('85)		45.00	1.25
O18	O1	12o blue	57.50	22.50
O19	O1	20o ver ('82)	200.00	2.50
O20	O1	20o dk bl ('91)	5.75	.60
O21	O1	24o yellow	72.50	25.00
a.	24o orange		65.00	25.00
O22	O1	30o brown	26.00	.70
O23	O1	50o pale rose	140.00	25.00
O24	O1	50o pale gray ('93)	18.00	3.00
O25	O1	1k dk bl & yel brn	9.00	3.00
	Nos. O12-O25 (14)		582.30	148.10

Imperf., Pairs

O12a	O1	2o	400.00
O17a	O1	10o No. O17	400.00
c.	No. O17b		400.00
O20a	O1	20o	50.00
O24a	O1	50o	400.00

Surcharged
in Dark
Blue

1889

O26	O1	10o on 12o blue	13.00	18.00
a.	Inverted surcharge		2,100.	5,000.
b.	Perf. 14		5,500.	5,500.
O27	O1	10o on 24o yel	16.00	25.00
a.	Inverted surcharge		7,000.	5,500.
b.	Perf. 14		5,500.	5,500.

O3

1910-12 Wmk. 180 Typo.

O28	O3	1o black	.30	.45
O29	O3	2o orange	1.40	4.50
O30	O3	4o pale violet	1.75	4.00
O31	O3	5o green	.50	1.10
O32	O3	8o claret	.40	1.10
O33	O3	10o red	11.00	.70
O34	O3	15o red brown	.80	.80
O35	O3	20o deep blue	7.00	1.75
O36	O3	25o red orange	7.00	2.50
O37	O3	30o chocolate	7.00	3.50
O38	O3	50o gray	7.00	3.50
O39	O3	1k black, yellow	7.75	7.75
O40	O3	5k claret, yellow	10.00	4.00
	Nos. O28-O40 (13)		61.90	35.65

1910-19 Wmk. Wavy Lines (181)

O41	O3	1o black	2.00	3.75
O42	O3	2o orange	.30	.40
O43	O3	3o pale brown	.40	1.00
O44	O3	4o pale violet	.30	.40
O45	O3	5o green	.30	.40
O46	O3	7o gray green	.40	1.25
O47	O3	8o rose	18.00	27.50
O48	O3	10o red	.30	.25
O49	O3	12o rose red	.30	.40
O50	O3	15o org brown	.30	.30
O51	O3	20o deep blue	.45	.30
O52	O3	25o orange	.80	.50
O53	O3	30o chocolate	.55	.55
O54	O3	35o dark violet	.85	1.00
O55	O3	50o gray	3.25	2.25
	Nos. O41-O55 (15)		28.50	40.25

For surcharges see Nos. C1-C5.

Use of official stamps ceased on July 1, 1920.

PARCEL POST STAMPS

Regular Issue of 1914
Surcharged

1917 Wmk. 180 Perf. 13

Q1	A14	1.98k on 5k claret, *yel*	1.40	6.00
Q2	A14	2.12k on 5k claret, *yel*	1.40	6.00

SWITZERLAND

'swit-sər-lənd

(Helvetia)

LOCATION — Central Europe, between France, Germany and Italy
GOVT. — Republic
AREA — 15,943 sq. mi.
POP. — 7,062,400 (1998 est.)
CAPITAL — Bern

100 Rappen or Centimes = 1 Franc

Catalogue values for unused stamps in this country are for Never Hinged items, beginning with Scott 365 in the regular postage section, Scott B272 in the semi-postal section, Scott C46 in the airpost section, Scott CB1 in the airpost semi-postal section, and Scott 3O94, 4O40, 5O26, 7O31, 8O1, 9O1, 10O1, 11O1, 12O1 in the official sections.

Watermarks

Wmk. 182 —
Cross in Oval

Wmk. 183 —
Swiss Cross

Watermark 182 is not a true watermark, having been impressed after the paper was manufactured. There are two types:
Type 1 — width just under 9mm.
Type 2 — width just under 8½mm.
There are many other differences of ⅒mm to ½mm.

CANTONAL ADMINISTRATION

Unused values of Nos. 1L1-3L1 are for stamps without gum.
Counterfeit and repaired copies of Nos. 1L1-3L1 abound.

Zurich

Numerals of
A1   Value — A2

1843   Unwmk.   Litho.   Imperf.
Red Vertical Lines
1L1 A1 4r black   24,000. 21,000.
1L2 A2 6r black   7,750.   2,100.

1846   Red Horizontal Lines
1L3 A1 4r black   21,000. 27,000.
1L4 A2 6r black   2,250.   1,925.

Five varieties of each value.
Reprints of the Zurich stamps show signs of wear and lack the red lines. Values 4r, $6,500; 6r, $2,150.

Coat of Arms — A3

1850   Unwmk.   Imperf.
1L5 A3 2½r black & red   7,750. 4,750.

No. 1L5 has separation designs in the margins between stamps as shown. Values are for stamps showing part of the separation design on all four sides.

Geneva

Coat of Arms — A4

1843   Unwmk.   Litho.   Imperf.
2L1 A4 10c blk, *yel grn*   72,500. 47,500.
  a. Either half   24,000. 11,000.
  b. Stamp composed of right
      half at left & left half at
      right   85,000. 62,500.

A5   A6

1845-48
2L2 A5 5c blk, *yel grn*   3,500. 1,950.
2L3 A6 5c blk, *yel grn* ('46) 2,500. 2,100.
2L4 A6 5c blk, *dk grn* ('48)   5,000. 3,500.

A7   Coat of
            Arms — A8

1849-50
2L5 A7 4c black & red   42,500. 25,000.
2L6 A7 5c blk & red ('50)   3,000.   2,100.

1851
2L7 A8 5c black & red   11,500.   3,500.

ENVELOPE STAMP USED AS ADHESIVE

E1

1847   Unwmk.   Imperf.
2LU1 E1 5c yel grn, see foot-
       note   26,000.

Value is for cut-out stamp used on folded letters. This use was authorized and is known from Feb. 19, 1847. Value of unused envelope cut-out, $500. Value of used cut-out off cover, $3,300.

Basel

Dove of Basel — A9

Typo. & Embossed
1845   Unwmk.   Imperf.
3L1 A1 2½r blk, crim & bl   17,000. 15,000.

FEDERAL ADMINISTRATION

Due to its tendency to damage the paper and/or the color of the stamps, the gum on Nos. 1-40 very often is removed. Unused values for Nos. 1-40 are for stamps without gum. Stamps with original gum sell for about the same prices.

A10   A11

1850   Unwmk.   Litho.   Imperf.
Full Black Frame Around Cross
1   A10 2½r black & red   3,500. 1,950.
2   A11 2½r black & red   3,000. 1,800.

Without Frame Around Cross
3   A10 2½r black & red   7,000. 3,250.
4   A11 2½r blk & red   57,500. 30,000.

Forty types of each.

A12   A13

1850
Full Black Frame Around Cross
5   A12 5r dk bl, blk &
         red   6,000. 1,500.
  a. 5r dk grayish bl, blk &
      red   6,250. 1,500.
6   A13 10r yel, blk &
         red   130,000.

No. 6 used, with only parts of frame around cross showing, value $175 to $900.
Beware of examples of Nos. 7-8 with faked frame added.

Without Frame Around Cross
7   A12 5r lt bl, blk & red   2,100.   600.
  a. 5r dp bl, blk & red   1,700.   650.
  b. 5r pur bl, blk & red   6,500.
  c. 5r grnsh bl, blk & red   2,400.   700.
8   A13 10r yel, blk & red   1,150.   150.
  a. 10r buff, blk & red   1,550.   275.
  b. 10r org yel, blk & red   1,500.   300.
  c. Half used as 5r on cover, 5r
      rate   16,000.

1851
Full Blue Frame Around Cross
9   A12 5r light blue & red   210,000.

No. 9 used, with only parts of frame around cross showing, value $180 to $3,750.
Beware of examples of No. 10 with faked frame added.

Without Frame Around Cross
10 A12 5r lt blue & red   700.   150.00

Forty types of each.

A14   A15

A16

1852
Vermilion Frame Around Cross
11 A14 15r vermilion   18,000.   850.
12 A15 15r vermilion   3,000.   150.
13 A16 15c vermilion   17,000. 1,200.

Ten types of each.
On October 1st, 1854, all stamps of the preceding issues were declared obsolete.

The Sitting Helvetia type (Scott Nos. 14-40) are valued with three margins clear of frame lines, with the fourth margin touching or lightly cutting into the frame line. Stamps with four margins clear of all frame lines are rare and command sustantial premiums.

Helvetia — A17

1854   Embossed.   Unwmk.
Thin Paper, Fine Impressions
Emerald Silk Threads
14 A17 5r orange brn   9,500. 1,950.
15 A17 5r red brown   650.   170.00
16 A17 10r blue   925.00   95.00
17 A17 15r carmine
         rose   1,400.   210.00
  a. 15r pale rose   1,400.   210.00
18 A17 40r pale yel grn 12,000. 1,400.
19 A17 40r yellow grn   1,400.   325.00

1854-55
Emerald Silk Threads
Medium Thick Paper
Fine Impressions
20 A17 5r pale yel brn   775.00 180.00
21 A17 10r blue   1,900.   130.00
22 A17 15r rose   1,100.   120.00
23 A17 20r pale orange   1,700.   210.00

1855-57
Colored ( ) Silk Threads
Medium Thick Paper
Fine to Rough Impressions
24 A17 5r yel brn (yel)   700.00 120.00
25 A17 5r dk brown
         (blk)   400.00   42.50
26 A17 10r mlky bl
         (red)   1,100.   210.00
27 A17 10r blue (car)   350.00   55.00
  a. Thin paper   6,000.   500.00
28 A17 15r rose (bl)   650.00   77.50
29 A17 40r yel grn
         (mar)   1,200.   120.00
30 A17 1fr lav (blk)   1,700.   1,000.
31 A17 1fr lav (yel)   1,700.   1,000.
  a. Thin paper   24,000.   8,750.

1857

Thin (Emergency) Paper
Rough Impressions
Green Silk Threads

32	A17	5r pale gray brn	5,500.	1,200.
32A	A17	10r blue	7,750.	1,000.
33	A17	15r pale dl rose	4,000.	400.
34	A17	20r pale dl org	4,250.	300.

1858-62

Thick Ordinary Paper
Rough Impressions
Green Silk Threads

35	A17	2r gray	300.00	650.00
a.		One and one-half used as 3r on newspaper or wrapper		17,000.
c.		Half used as 1r on cover		
36	A17	5r brown	275.00	26.00
a.		5r black brown	325.00	50.00
b.		5r gray brown	300.00	32.50
c.		Half used as 2r on cover		1,700.
37	A17	10r blue	300.00	26.00
a.		Half used as 5r on cover		8,750.
b.		10r pale blue	325.00	32.50
c.		10r dark blue	300.00	27.00
d.		10r greenish blue	375.00	50.00
38	A17	15r dark rose	450.00	77.50
a.		15r pale rose	475.00	87.50
39	A17	20r dark orange	575.00	85.00
a.		Half used as 10r on cover		21,000.
b.		20r yel orange	600.00	95.00
40	A17	40r green (to dp grn)	550.00	110.00
a.		Half used as 20r on cover		32,500.
e.		40r yellow green	575.00	120.00
		Nos. 35-40 (6)	2,450.	974.50

Helvetia — A18

Double transfer errors, Nos. 43c, 44a, 55b, 60a, 61a, 61b, 67b, have the design impressed twice. These do not refer to the "embossed" watermark.

1862-64 **Wmk. 182** **Perf. 11½**
White Wove Paper

41	A18	2c gray	170.00	5.00
42	A18	3c black	17.50	140.00
43	A18	5c dark brown	4.25	1.10
a.		5c bister brown	130.00	8.00
b.		5c gray brown	130.00	40.00
c.		Dbl. transfer, one invtd.	4,750.	575.00
d.		Dbl. transfer of lower left "5"		1,750.
44	A18	10c blue	875.00	1.10
a.		Dbl. transfer, one invtd.		9,500.
45	A18	20c orange	3.00	3.25
a.		20c yellow orange	425.00	3.50
46	A18	30c vermilion	2,000.	50.00
47	A18	40c green	1,900.	80.00
48	A18	60c bronze	1,750.	210.00
50	A18	1fr gold	25.00	140.00
a.		1fr yellowish bronze ('64)	1,750.	500.00

1867-78

52	A18	2c bister brown	3.50	2.10
a.		2c red brown	800.00	325.00
53	A18	10c carmine	5.00	1.20
54	A18	15c lemon	3.50	500.00
55	A18	25c blue green	2.10	5.00
a.		25c yellow green	72.50	47.50
b.		Dbl. transfer, one invtd.		700.00
56	A18	30c ultra	700.00	12.00
a.		30c blue		2,400. 300.00
58	A18	40c gray	2.10	190.00
59	A18	50c violet	70.00	77.50
		Nos. 52-59 (7)	786.20	787.80

1881 **Granite Paper**

60	A18	2c bister	.85	30.00
a.		Dbl. transfer, one invtd.	425.00	
61	A18	5c brown	.65	15.50
a.		Dbl. transfer, one invtd.	42.50	500.00
b.		Double transfer of lower left "5"		1,500.
62	A18	10c rose	8.50	12.50
63	A18	15c lemon	12.50	575.00
64	A18	20c orange	.85	190.00
65	A18	25c green	.65	125.00
66	A18	40c gray	2.10	4,000.
67	A18	50c deep violet	21.00	700.00
b.		Dbl. transfer, one invtd.	350.00	5,500.
68	A18	1fr gold	21.50	1,300.

The granite paper contains fragments of blue and red silk threads.

Forged or backdated cancellations are found frequently on Nos. 42, 50, 54, 58 and 60-68.

All stamps of the preceding issues were declared obsolete on October 1st, 1883.

Some of the remainders of Nos. 41-68 were overprinted "AUSSER KURS" (Obsolete) diagonally in black.

Numeral — A19

1882-99 **Typo.** **Perf. 11½**
Granite Paper

69	A19	2c bister	2.75	.80
70	A19	3c gray brown	4.25	12.00
a.		3c gray	62.50	62.50
71	A19	5c maroon	26.00	.70
a.		Tête bêche pair		
72	A19	5c deep grn ('99)	11.00	.70
73	A19	10c red	10.00	.70
a.		10c chalky blue	77.50	1.30
b.		10c light rose	350.00	6.00
74	A19	12c ultra	11.00	.70
a.		12c chalky blue	30.00	26.00
b.		12c greenish blue	550.00	
75	A19	15c yellow	200.00	40.00
a.		15c orange	19,500.	4,750.
b.		Tête bêche pair		
76	A19	15c violet ('89)	250.00	24.00
		Nos. 69-76 (8)	515.00	79.60

Nos. 69-74, 76 are watermark type 1. Nos. 70a, 73a-73b, 75-75a are type 2.

1882 **White Paper**

77	A19	2c bister	525.00	425.00
78	A19	5c maroon	1,150.	125.00
79	A19	10c rose	2,800.	85.00
80	A19	12c chalky blue	210.00	32.50
81	A19	15c yellow	300.00	350.00

Watermark type 1.
See Nos. 113-118.

Helvetia (Large numerals) A20	Helvetia (Small numerals) A21

1882-1904 **Engr.** **Perf. 11½ - 11¾**

82	A20	20c orange	210.00	7.00
83	A20	25c green	115.00	3.50
95b	A20	30c brown	—	24,000.
84	A20	40c gray	170.00	55.00
85	A21	40c gray ('04)	50.00	30.00
86	A20	50c blue	170.00	27.50
87	A20	1fr claret	300.00	8.00
88	A20	3fr yellow brn ('91)	250.00	25.00

1888 **Perf. 9½**

89	A20	20c orange	1,050.	125.00
90	A20	25c yellow grn	180.00	21.00
91	A20	40c gray	1,000.	775.00
92	A20	50c blue	1,500.	400.00
93	A20	1fr claret	1,100.	110.00

Values for Nos. 89-93 are for well-centered stamps with slightly uneven perforations. Stamps missing perforations sell for much less.

1891-99 **Perf. 11½x11**

82a	A20	20c orange	80.00	2.10
83a	A20	25c green	13.00	2.10
94	A20	25c blue ('99)	15.00	2.75
95	A20	30c red brn ('92)	42.50	2.75
84a	A20	40c gray	92.50	6.50
86a	A20	50c blue	55.00	15.00
96	A20	50c green ('99)	60.00	30.00
87a	A20	1fr claret	50.00	5.00
97	A20	1fr carmine	110.00	11.00
88a	A20	3fr yellow brown	190.00	32.50

1901-03 **Perf. 11½x12**

82b	A20	20c orange	32.50	2.10
94a	A20	25c blue	17.00	1.50
95a	A20	30c red brown	50.00	2.40
84b	A20	40c gray	110.00	42.50
96a	A20	50c green	85.00	8.50
87b	A20	1fr claret	2,400.	350.00
97a	A20	1fr carmine ('03)	500.00	47.50
88b	A20	3fr yellow brown	250.00	25.00

Numerous retouches and plate flaws exist on all values of this issue.

Nos. 82-88 have wmk. type 1 and are ½mm taller (paper size) than Nos. 82b-88b, which have wmk. type 2.
See Nos. 105-112, 119-125.

UPU Allegory — A22

1900 **Perf. 11½**

98	A22	5c gray green	42.50	2.10
99	A22	10c carmine rose	13.00	2.10
100	A22	25c blue	35.00	40.00
		Nos. 98-100 (3)	90.50	44.20

Re-engraved

101	A22	5c gray green	4.25	1.90
102	A22	10c carmine rose	62.50	50.00
103	A22	25c blue	850.00	13,500.

Universal Postal Union, 25th anniv.

The impression of the re-engraved stamps is much clearer, especially the horizontally lined background. The figures of value are lined instead of being solid.

Helvetia Types of 1882-1904

1905 **Wmk. 183** **Perf. 11½x11**
White Paper

105	A20	20c orange	3.75	2.25
106	A20	25c blue	5.00	9.00
107	A20	30c brown	5.00	2.00
108a	A21	40c gray	90.00	140.00
109	A20	50c green	30.00	7.25
110	A20	1fr carmine	77.50	3.00
111	A20	3fr yellow brn	200.00	110.00

Some clichés in the plates of the 20c, 25c, 30c, 50c and 3fr have been retouched.

1906 **Re-engraved** **Perf. 11½x11**
| 112 | A20 | 25c pale blue | 6.00 | 2.25 |

In the re-engraved stamp the stars are larger and the background below "FRANCO" is of horiz. or horiz. and vert. crossed lines, instead of horiz. and curved lines.

1906 **Perf. 11½**

112a	A20	25c pale blue	85.00	7.50
108	A21	40c gray	27.50	11.00

1907 **Perf. 11½x12**

105a	A20	20c orange	6.00	6.00
109a	A20	50c green	37.50	12.00
110a	A20	1fr carmine	100.00	9.00
111a	A20	3fr yellow brown	240.00	190.00

Numeral Type of 1882-99

1905 **Typo.** **Perf. 11½**
Granite Paper

113	A19	2c dull bister	4.25	1.90
114	A19	3c gray brown	4.50	60.00
115	A19	5c green	4.25	.50
116	A19	10c scarlet	4.25	.50
117	A19	12c ultra	5.50	2.00
118	A19	15c brown vio	60.00	13.50
		Nos. 113-118 (6)	82.75	78.40

Helvetia Types of 1882-1904

1907 **Engr.** **Perf. 11½x12**
Granite Paper

119	A20	20c orange	2.25	3.75
120	A20	25c blue	7.75	10.00
121	A20	30c red brown	6.50	7.00
122	A21	40c gray	21.00	45.00
a.		Helvetia without diadem	300.00	1,050.
123	A20	50c gray green	5.50	5.00
124	A20	1fr carmine	19.00	9.25
125a	A20	3fr yellow brown		10,500.

There are retouches and plate flaws on all values.

Perf. 11½x11

120a	A20	25c deep blue	10.00	6.50
121a	A20	30c red brown	140.00	325.00
122b	A21	40c gray		13,000.
124a	A20	1fr carmine		10,000.
125	A20	3fr yel brn	100.00	65.00

William Tell's Son — A23

Helvetia
A24   A25

1907-25 **Typo.** **Perf. 11½**
Granite Paper

126	A23	2c pale bister	.30	.55
127	A23	3c lilac brn	.25	10.00
128	A23	5c yellow grn	2.25	.50
129	A24	10c rose red	1.50	.50
130	A24	12c ocher	.30	3.50
131	A24	15c red vio	3.00	13.00
132	A25	20c red & yel	2.25	1.00
133	A25	25c dp blue ('08)	1.90	.65
a.		Tête bêche pair	17.00	55.00
134	A25	30c yel brn & pale grn ('08)	1.60	.50
135	A25	35c yel grn & yel ('08)	1.90	1.40
136	A25	40c red vio & yel ('08)	12.50	1.00
a.		Designer's name in full on the rock ('08)	6.00	82.50
137	A25	40c deep blue ('22)	1.75	.50
a.		40c light blue ('21)	5.50	1.90
138	A25	40c red vio & grn ('25)	25.00	.50
139	A25	50c dp grn & pale grn ('08)	11.00	.50
140	A25	60c brn org & buff ('18)	9.25	.65
141	A25	70c dk brn & buff ('08)	55.00	17.00
142	A25	70c vio & buff ('24)	14.50	2.25
143	A25	80c slate & buff ('15)	9.75	1.10
144	A25	1fr dp cl & pale grn ('08)	7.00	.55
145	A25	3fr bis & yel ('08)	275.00	2.10
		Nos. 126-145 (20)	436.00	57.75

No. 136 has two leaves and "CL" below sword hilt. No. 136a has three leaves and designer's full name below hilt.
For surcharges and overprints see Nos. 189, 199, O10-O13, O15, 1O6-1O8, 1O14-1O16, 2O18-2O26, 3O14-3O22.

1933 **With Grilled Gum**

135a	A25	35c yel grn & yel	1.40	12.50
138a	A25	40c red vio & grn	32.50	1.50
139a	A25	50c dp grn & pale grn	9.00	1.50
140a	A25	60c brn org & buff	12.00	1.50
142a	A25	70c vio & buff	17.50	3.75
143a	A25	80c slate & buff	13.00	4.25
144a	A25	1fr dp cl & pale grn	19.00	6.50
		Nos. 135a-144a (7)	104.40	31.50

"Grilled" Gum
In 1930-44 many Swiss stamps were treated with a light grilling process, applied with the gumming to counteract the tendency to curl. It resembles a faint grill of vertical and horizontal ribs covering the entire back of the stamp, and can be seen after the gum has been removed. Listings of the grilled gum varieties begin with No. 135a.

William Tell's Son — A26	Bow-string in front of stock

1909 **Perf. 11½, 12**
Granite Paper

146	A26	2c bister	.25	1.40
a.		Tête bêche pair	3.25	17.50
147	A26	3c dark violet	.25	14.00
148	A26	5c green	3.75	.25
a.		Tête bêche pair	14.00	50.00
		Nos. 146-148 (3)	4.25	15.65

See Nos. 149-163. For surcharges and overprints see Nos. 186, 193-195, 207-208, 1O1-1O3, 1O9-1O11, 2O1-2O7, 3O1-3O5.

First Redrawing

Bow-string behind stock. Thin loop above crossbow. Letters of "HELVETIA" without serifs.

1910-17   Granite Paper
149	A26	2c bister ('10)	8.75	8.00
150	A26	3c dk violet ('10)	.25	.25
a.		Tête bêche pair	2.75	2.75
b.		Booklet pane of 6	12.50	
151	A26	3c brown org ('17)	.25	.25
a.		Tête bêche pair	8.25	11.00
152	A26	5c green ('10)	21.00	6.50
a.		Tête bêche pair	92.50	175.00
		Nos. 149-152 (4)	30.25	15.00

Second Redrawing

Bow-string behind stock. Thick loop above crossbow. Letters of "HELVETIA" have serifs.

7½ CENTIMES:
Type I — Top of "7" is ½mm thick. The "1" of "½" has only traces of serifs. The two base plates of the statue are of even thickness.
Type II — Top of "7" is 1mm thick. The "1" of "½" has distinct serifs. The upper base plate is thinner than the lower.

1911-30   Granite Paper
153	A26	2c bister ('11)	.25	.25
a.		Tête bêche pair	3.25	1.60
154	A26	2½c claret ('18)	.25	1.10
155	A26	2½c ol, buff ('28)	.55	2.10
156	A26	3c ultra, buff ('30)	2.75	6.00
157	A26	5c green ('11)	1.75	.25
a.		Tête bêche pair	5.50	10.00
158	A26	5c org, buff ('21)	.25	.25
a.		Bklt. pane of 6 (5 #158, 168)	14.00	47.50
159	A26	5c gray vio, buff ('24)	.25	.25
a.		Bklt. pane of 6 (5 #159, 168)	6.50	19.00
160	A26	5c red vio, buff ('27)	.25	.25
a.		Bklt. pane 6 (5 #160, 168)	30.00	65.00
161	A26	5c dk grn, buff ('30)	.30	.25
a.		Bklt. pane 6 (5 #161, 169)	27.50	70.00
162	A26	7½c gray (I) ('18)	1.10	.25
a.		Tête bêche pair	13.00	45.00
c.		7½c slate (II)	4.50	2.75
163	A26	7½c dp grn, buff (I) ('28)	.30	3.25
		Nos. 153-163 (11)	8.00	14.20

1933   With Grilled Gum
156a	A26	3c ultra, buff	4.75	17.50
161b	A26	5c dark green, buff	.55	5.00

Helvetia A27   William Tell A28

1909   Granite Paper
164	A27	10c carmine	.60	.40
a.		Tête bêche pair	2.25	6.00
165	A27	12c bister brn	.85	.40
166	A27	15c red violet	26.00	1.10
		Nos. 164-166 (3)	27.45	1.90

For surcharge see No. 187.

1914-30   Granite Paper   Perf. 11½
TEN CENTIMES:
Type I — Bust 16½mm high. "HELVETIA" 15½mm wide. Cross bar of "H" at middle of the letter.
Type II — Bust 15mm high. "HELVETIA" 15mm wide. Cross bar of "H" above middle of the letter.

167	A28	10c red, buff (type II)	.75	.25
a.		10c red, buff (type I)	2.50	26.00
b.		Tête bêche pair	3.25	4.25
d.		Bklt. pane 6 (5 #167, 172)	50.00	160.00
168	A28	10c grn, buff (type II) ('21)	.25	.25
a.		Tête bêche pair	1.10	1.40
168C	A28	10c bl grn, buff (type II) ('28)	.25	.25
d.		Tête bêche pair	2.50	2.50
169	A28	10c vio, buff (type II) ('30)	2.25	.25
a.		Tête bêche pair	9.25	1.40
170	A28	12c brn, buff	.25	3.25
171	A28	13c ol grn, buff ('15)	1.40	.50
172	A28	15c vio, buff	3.50	.25
b.		15c dk vio, buff	32.50	4.25
			87.50	125.00
173	A28	15c brn red, buff ('28)	2.50	2.75
174	A28	20c red vio, buff ('21)	3.25	.25
a.		Tête bêche pair	6.50	7.50
175	A28	20c ver, buff ('24)	1.00	.50
a.		Tête bêche pair	5.75	9.25
176	A28	20c car, buff ('25)	.25	.25
a.		Tête bêche pair	2.50	.55

177	A28	25c ver, buff ('21)	2.25	1.60
178	A28	25c car, buff ('22)	1.10	.85
179	A28	25c brn, buff ('25)	3.25	1.25
180	A28	30c dp bl, buff ('24)	9.25	.50
		Nos. 167-180 (15)	31.50	12.95

1932-33   With Grilled Gum
169c	A28	10c violet, buff	4.50	1.50
173a	A28	15c brn red, buff ('33)	50.00	52.50
176c	A28	20c carmine, buff	7.25	1.50
179a	A28	25c brown, buff ('33)	125.00	35.00
180a	A28	30c deep blue, buff	72.50	2.50
		Nos. 169c-180a (5)	259.25	93.00

For surcharges and overprints see Nos. 188, 196-198, 1O4-1O5, 1O12-1O13, 2O8-2O17, 3O6-3O13.

The Mythen A29

The Rütli — A30

The Jungfrau A31

1914-30   Engr.   Granite Paper
181	A29	3fr dk green	650.00	6.50
182	A29	3fr red ('18)	87.50	1.40
183	A30	5fr dp ultra	35.00	3.00
184	A31	10fr dull violet	100.00	3.25
185	A31	10fr gray grn ('30)	225.00	37.50
		Nos. 181-185 (5)	1,097.	51.65

See No. 206. For overprints see Nos. 2O27-2O30, 3O23-3O26.

Stamps of 1909-14 Surcharged

a

b

c

1915
186	A26(a)	1c on 2c bister	.25	1.25
187	A27(b)	13c on 12c bis brn	.25	9.25
188	A28(c)	13c on 12c brn, buff	.30	.90
		Nos. 186-188 (3)	.80	11.40

No. 141 Surcharged
189	A25	80c on 70c	25.00	17.50

Significant of Peace A32

"Peace" A33

"Dawn of Peace" A34

Perf. 11½
1919, Aug. 1   Typo.   Unwmk.
190	A32	7½c olive drab & blk	.80	2.25
191	A33	10c red & yel	1.10	8.75
192	A34	15c violet & yel	1.90	2.75
		Nos. 190-192 (3)	3.80	13.75

Commemorating Peace after World War I.

Nos. 151, 149, 162, 171-172, 133 Surcharged in Black, Red or Dark Blue

a   b

c

1921   Wmk. 183
193	A26(a)	2½c on 3c (Bl)	.25	1.10
a.		Tête bêche pair	1.10	3.25
b.		Inverted surcharge	800.00	1,550.
c.		Double surcharge	550.00	775.00
194	A26(a)	5c on 2c (R)	.25	4.50
a.		Double surcharge	450.00	450.00
195	A26(a)	5c on 7½c (R)	.25	.55
a.		Tête bêche pair	6.50	55.00
b.		Double surcharge	550.00	550.00
c.		5c on 7½c slate (II)	2,200.	4,500.
196	A28(b)	10c on 13c (R)	.25	2.25
a.		Double surcharge	550.00	550.00
197	A28(c)	20c on 15c (Bk)	.55	2.75
a.		Tête bêche pair	2.50	55.00
198	A28(c)	20c on 15c (Bl)	2.25	5.50
b.		Double surcharge	875.00	875.00
199	A25(c)	20c on 25c dp bl (R)	.25	.55
a.		Tête bêche pair	1.50	4.50
		Nos. 193-199 (7)	4.05	17.20

A36

1924   Typo.   Perf. 11½
Granite Paper, Surface Colored
200	A36	90c grn & red, grn	15.00	2.75
201	A36	1.20fr brn rose & red, rose	5.25	5.25
202	A36	1.50fr bl & red, bl	37.50	6.50
203	A36	2fr gray blk & red, gray	47.50	6.75
		Nos. 200-203 (4)	105.25	21.25
		Set, never hinged	325.00	

1933   With Grilled Gum
200a	A36	90c	17.50	3.25
201a	A36	1.20fr	47.50	5.50
202a	A36	1.50fr	32.50	6.50
203a	A36	2fr	27.50	8.25
		Nos. 200a-203a (4)	125.00	23.50
		Set, never hinged	325.00	

For overprints see Nos. O16-O18, 2O31-2O34, 3O27-3O30.

1940   With Smooth Gum
Ordinary Paper
200b	A36	90c	16.00	80.00
201b	A36	1.20fr	16.00	80.00
202b	A36	1.50fr	16.00	650.00
		Nos. 200b-202b (3)	48.00	810.00
		Set, never hinged	120.00	

Building in Bern, Location of 1st UPU Congress, 1874
A37   A38

1924, Oct. 9   Engr.   Wmk. 183
Granite Paper
204	A37	20c vermilion	.55	1.60
205	A38	30c dull blue	1.10	6.25
		Set, never hinged	3.25	

50th anniv. of the UPU.

Type of 1914 Issue

The Rütli — A39

1928   Re-engraved   Perf. 11½
206	A39	5fr blue	110.00	9.75
		Never hinged	300.00	
a.		Imperf., pair, never hinged	10,000.	

In the re-engraved stamp the picture is clearer and lighter than on No. 183. "HELVETIA" is in smaller letters. The names at foot of the stamp are "Grasset-J. Sprenger" instead of "E. GRASSET-A. BURKHARD."
For overprints see Nos. 2O35, 3O31.

Nos. 155 and 163 Surcharged

1930, June   Perf. 11½
207	A26	3c on 2½c ol grn, buff	.25	2.75
208	A26	5c on 7½c dp grn, buff	.25	8.00
		Set, never hinged	1.10	

The Mythen A40

1931   Engr.   Granite Paper
209	A40	3fr orange brown	65.00	5.25
		Never hinged	150.00	

For overprints see Nos. 2O56, 3O47.

Dove on Broken Sword — A41

"Peace" A42

1932, Feb. 2   Typo.   Perf. 11½
Granite Paper
210	A41	5c peacock blue	.25	.25
211	A41	10c orange	.25	.25
212	A41	20c cerise	.25	.25
213	A41	30c ultra	2.25	1.60
214	A41	60c olive brown	17.50	8.75

Unwmk.
Photo.

215	A42	1fr olive gray & bl	17.50	8.75
		Nos. 210-215 (6)	38.00	19.85
		Set, never hinged	95.00	

Intl. Disarmament Conf., Geneva, Feb. 1932.
For overprints see #2O36-2O41, 3O32-3O37.

Louis Favre — A43

Alfred Escher — A44

Design: 30c, Emil Welti.

Wmk. 183
1932, May 31   **Engr.**   **Perf. 11½**
Granite Paper

216	A43	10c red brown	.25	.25
217	A44	20c vermilion	.25	.25
218	A44	30c deep ultra	.55	2.10
		Nos. 216-218 (3)	1.05	2.60
		Set, never hinged	3.00	

Completion of the St. Gotthard tunnel, 50th anniv.
Nos. 216-218 exist imperforate.

Staubbach Falls A46

Mt. Pilatus A47

Chillon Castle A48

Rhone Glacier A49

St. Gotthard Railroad A50

Via Mala Gorge A51

Rhine Falls — A52

1934, July 2   **Typo.**   **Perf. 11½**
Granite Paper

219	A46	3c olive	.25	3.00
220	A47	5c emerald	.25	.25
221	A48	10c brt violet	.40	3.25
222	A49	15c orange	.50	3.25
223	A50	20c red	.60	.60
224	A51	25c brown	7.75	8.25
225	A52	30c ultra	25.00	2.10
		Nos. 219-225 (7)	34.75	17.70
		Set, never hinged	100.00	

Tête bêche Pairs

220a	A47	5c	1.60	1.60
221a	A48	10c	1.50	.85
222a	A49	15c	1.75	3.00
223a	A50	20c	3.50	2.25

Souvenir Sheet
1934, Sept. 29

226	Sheet of 4	500.00	550.00
	Never hinged	825.00	

No. 226 was issued in connection with the Swiss National Philatelic Exhibition at Zurich, Sept. 29 to Oct. 7, 1934. It contains one each of Nos. 220-223. Size: 62x72mm.

For overprints see Nos. 2O42-2O46, 3O48.

Staubbach Falls A53

Mt. Pilatus A54

Chillon Castle A55

Rhone Glacier A56

St. Gotthard Railroad A57

Via Mala Gorge A58

Rhine Falls — A59

Balsthal Pass — A60

Alpine Lake of Säntis — A61

Type I

Type II

Two types of 10c red violet:
I — Shading inside "0" of 10 has only vertical lines.
II — Shading in "0" includes two diagonal lines.

1936-42   **Unwmk.**   **Engr.**   **Perf. 11½**

227	A53	3c olive	.25	.25
228	A54	5c blue green	.25	.25
229	A55	10c red vio (II)	.85	.25
	b.	Type I	.85	.25
230	A55	10c dk red brn ('39)	.25	.25
230B	A55	10c org brn ('42)	.25	.25
231	A56	15c orange	.40	1.10
232	A57	20c carmine	4.75	.25
233	A58	25c lt brown	.50	1.10
234	A59	30c ultra	.90	.25
235	A60	35c yellow grn	1.10	1.25
236	A61	40c gray	6.00	.25
		Nos. 227-236 (11)	15.50	5.45
		Set, never hinged	37.50	

Two types of the 20c. See Nos. 316-321.
For overprints see Nos. O1-O4, O6-O9, O19-O19-O22, O24-O27, 2O47-2O55, 2O68-2O68A, 2O70-2O73, 2O75-2O78, 3O38-3O46, 3O60-3O60A, 3O62-3O65, 3O67-3O70, 4O1-4O4, 4O6-4O9, 4O23-4O24, 4O27-4O28, 5O1-5O2, 5O5.

Tête bêche Pairs

228a	A54	5c blue green	.45	.30
229a	A55	10c red violet (II)	4.50	5.50
230a	A55	10c dark red brown	1.75	1.10
230d	A55	10c orange brown	.50	.60
232a	A57	20c carmine	25.00	35.00

1936-40   **With Grilled Gum**

227a	A53	3c olive	.65	6.25
228d	A54	5c blue green	.25	.25
229d	A55	10c red violet (II)	.30	.25
	e.	Type I	1.00	.25
230e	A55	10c dark red brown ('40)	1.90	25.00
231a	A56	15c orange	.30	1.10

232c	A57	20c carmine	6.75	.25
233a	A58	25c light brown	1.00	5.00
234a	A59	30c ultra	.95	.25
235a	A60	35c yellow green	1.40	3.25
236a	A61	40c gray	9.25	.25
		Nos. 227a-236a (10)	22.80	42.10
		Set, never hinged	47.50	

Mobile Post Office A62

1937, Sept. 5   **Photo.**
Granite Paper

237	A62	10c black & yellow	.25	.50
		Never hinged	.55	

No. 237 was sold exclusively by the traveling post office. It exists on two kinds of granite paper, black and red fibers or blue and red fibers. See No. 307 for type A62 redrawn.

View of Labor Building from Lake Geneva A63

Palace of League of Nations A64

Main Building, Palace of League of Nations A65

Labor Building and Albert Thomas Monument A66

1938, May 2   **Perf. 11½**
Granite Paper

238	A63	20c red & buff	.25	.25
239	A64	30c blue & lt blue	.45	.25
240	A65	60c brown & buff	1.75	2.25
241	A66	1fr black & buff	7.50	17.00
		Nos. 238-241 (4)	9.95	19.75
		Set, never hinged	37.50	

Opening of Assembly Hall of the Palace of the League of Nations.
For overprints see Nos. 2O57-2O64, 3O49-3O56.

Souvenir Sheet

A67

Engraved and Typographed
1938, Sept. 17   **Unwmk.**   **Perf. 11½**
Granite Paper

242	A67	Sheet of 3	37.50	32.50
		Never hinged	70.00	
	a.	AP4 10c on 65c gray bl & dp bl	19.00	25.00
	b.	A68 20c red	1.10	2.50

Natl. Phil. Exhib. at Aarau, Sept. 17-25, and 25th anniv. of Swiss air mail. No. 242 contains 2 No. 243, but on granite paper, and a 10c on 65c similar to No. C22 but redrawn, with wing tips 1½mm from side frame lines; overall size 37x20½mm; no watermark.
On No. C22, wing tips touch frame lines; size is 36x21½mm; Wmk. 183.

Lake Lugano — A68

First Federal Pact, 1291 A69

Diet of Stans, 1481 A70

Citizens Voting A71

1938, Sept. 17   **Engr.**   **Perf. 11½**

243	A68	20c red	.25	.25
	a.	"c," tête bêche pair	.50	.85
	c.	Grilled gum	.40	.40
	d.	As "c," tête bêche pair	1.40	15.00

Granite Paper

244	A69	3fr brn car, grnsh	11.00	8.75
245	A70	5fr slate bl, grnsh	7.50	6.00
246	A71	10fr grn, grnsh	47.50	35.00
		Nos. 243-246 (4)	66.25	50.00
		Set, never hinged	190.00	

No. 243 is printed on ordinary paper. Nos. 244-246 are on granite surface-colored paper. The greenish surface coating has faded on most examples.
For type A68 in orange brown, see No. 318.
See Nos. 224b, 284-286. For overprints see Nos. O5, O23, 2O65-2O67, 2O69, 2O74, 2O88-2O90, 3O57-3O59, 3O61, 3O66, 3O80-3O82, 4O5, 4O19-4O21, 4O25, 5O3, 5O23-5O25, 7O18-7O20.

Deputation of Trades and Professions — A72

Swiss Family A73

Alpine Scenery A74

Engr., Photo. (30c)
1939, Feb. 1   **Perf. 11½**
Inscribed in French

247	A72	10c dl pur & red	.25	.25
248	A73	20c lake & red	.50	.25

249 A74 30c dp blue & red 2.50 *3.00*

Inscribed in German

250 A72 10c dl pur & red .25 .25
251 A73 20c lake & red .40 .25
252 A74 30c dp blue & red 2.50 8.25

Inscribed in Italian

253 A72 10c dl pur & red .25 .25
254 A73 20c lake & red 1.90 .25
255 A74 30c dp blue & red 2.50 *9.25*
Nos. 247-255 (9) 11.05 22.00
Set, never hinged 35.00

National Exposition of 1939, Zurich.

Tree and
Crossbow — A75

1939, May 6   Photo.   Perf. 11½
Granite Paper
Inscribed in French

256 A75 5c deep green .55 1.60
257 A75 10c gray brown .55 1.90
258 A75 20c brt carmine 1.10 1.60
259 A75 30c violet blue 3.00 8.00

Inscribed in German

260 A75 5c deep green .55 2.50
261 A75 10c gray brown .55 2.50
262 A75 20c brt carmine 1.10 3.50
263 A75 30c violet blue 8.75 9.50

Inscribed in Italian

264 A75 5c deep green .85 4.50
265 A75 10c gray brown .55 3.50
266 A75 20c brt carmine 1.10 4.25
267 A75 30c violet blue 3.25 11.00
Nos. 256-267 (12) 21.90 54.35
Set, never hinged 32.50

National Exposition of 1939.
The 5c, 10c and 20c stamps in the three languages exist se-tenant in coils. On the 10c coil stamp, the inscription "COURVOISIER S.A." beneath is design is smaller, with the "A" just left of the point on the "V" of "HELVETIA." On the sheet stamp, the 'A' is just right of the 'V.' Value about three times that of the sheet stamp.

1939   With Grilled Gum

256a A75 5c deep green .75 2.25
257a A75 10c gray brown .75 2.25
258a A75 20c bright carmine 1.90 3.00
260a A75 5c deep green .75 1.60
262a A75 20c bright carmine 1.90 1.60
264a A75 5c deep green 1.10 3.75
265a A75 10c gray brown 1.00 3.00
266a A75 20c bright carmine 1.90 3.25
Nos. 256a-266a (8) 10.05 20.70

View of
Geneva
A76

Perf. 11½
1939, Aug. 22   Photo.   Unwmk.
Granite Paper

268 A76 20c red, car & buff .25 .25
269 A76 30c blue, car & gray .30 2.75
Set, never hinged 1.40

75th anniv. of the founding of the Intl. Red Cross Society.

"The Three
Swiss" — A77

William
Tell — A78

Fighting
Soldier — A79

Dying
Warrior — A80

Standard
Bearer — A81

Ludwig
Pfyffer — A82

Jürg
Jenatsch — A83

Francois de
Reynold — A84

Joachim
Forrer — A85

1941-59   Engr.   Perf. 11½
Granite Paper

270 A77 50c dp pur, *grnsh* 4.25 .25
271 A78 60c red brn, *buff* 5.50 .25
272 A79 70c rose vio, *pale lil* 2.75 1.00
273 A80 80c blk, *pale gray* 1.10 .25
a. 80c black, *pale lilac* ('58) .80 .50
274 A81 90c dk red, *pale rose* 1.00 .25
a. 90c dark red, *buff* ('59) 1.00 1.25
275 A82 1fr dk grn, *grnsh* 1.00 .25
276 A83 1.20fr red vio, *pale
gray* 1.10 .25
a. 1.20fr red vio, *pale lil* ('58) 1.90 .75
277 A84 1.50fr dk bl, *buff* 1.50 .25
278 A85 2fr mar, *pale rose* 2.25 .25
a. 2fr maroon, *buff* ('59) 2.25 .50
Nos. 270-278 (9) 20.45 3.00
Set, never hinged 47.50

For overprints see Nos. O28-O36, 2O79-2O87, 3O71-3O79, 4O10-4O18, 5O17-5O22, 6O6-6O8, 7O12-7O17.

Farmer
Plowing
A86

1941, Mar. 21   Photo.
Granite Paper

279 A86 10c brown & buff .25 *.50*
Never hinged .20

Natl. Agriculture Development Plan of 1941.

Masons,
Knight and
Bern Coat
of Arms
A87

1941, Sept. 6   Granite Paper

280 A87 10c multicolored .25 *.75*
Never hinged .20

750th anniversary of Bern.

"In order to Endure, Reclaim Used
Materials" Inscribed in French
A88

1942, Mar. 21   Unwmk.   Perf. 11½

281 A88 10c shown .35 .50
282 A88 10c German .40 1.00
283 A88 10c Italian 6.25 4.00
Nos. 281-283 (3) 7.00 5.50
Set, never hinged 14.00
Sheet of 25 550.00

Printed in sheets of 25, containing 8 No. 281, 12 No. 282 and 5 No. 283.

Types of 1938

1955   Engr.
Cream-surfaced Granite Paper

284 A69 3fr brown car 7.00 .75
285 A70 5fr slate blue 5.00 .80
286 A71 10fr green 7.00 3.00
Nos. 284-286 (3) 19.00 4.55
Set, never hinged 27.50

1942   Cream paper

284a A69 3fr 22.50 .50
285a A70 5fr 10.00 .50
286a A71 10fr 32.50 2.00
Nos. 284a-286a (3) 65.00 3.00
Set, never hinged 160.00

The 1955 set is on cream-surfaced granite paper with white back, and blue and red fibers. The 1942 set is on colored-through cream paper with black and red fibers.

Zurich
Stamps of
1843
A91

1943, Feb. 26

287 A91 10c blk & salmon .25 .25
Never hinged .20

Centenary of postage stamps of Switzerland. See Nos. B130-B131.

Apollo Statue — A94

1944, Mar. 21   Photo.
Granite Paper

290 A94 10c org yel & gray blk .25 1.00
291 A94 20c cer & gray blk .30 1.00
292 A94 30c lt bl & gray blk .60 6.00
Nos. 290-292 (3) 1.15 8.00
Set, never hinged 2.50

Olympic Jubilee.

Numeral of
Value — A95

Olive
Branch
A96

Designs: 60c, Keys of peace. 80c, Horn of plenty. 1fr, Dove of peace. 2fr, Plowing. 3fr, Field of crocus. 5fr, Clasped hands. 10fr, Aged couple.

1945, May 9   Unwmk.   Perf. 12
Granite Paper

293 A95 5c gray & green .25 .50
294 A95 10c gray & brown .25 .25
295 A95 20c gray & car
rose .35 .25
296 A95 30c gray & ultra .70 3.00
297 A95 40c gray & orange 2.00 10.00
298 A96 50c dark red 2.75 19.00
299 A96 60c dull gray 2.75 6.75
300 A96 80c slate green 6.25 85.00
301 A96 1fr blue 8.75 95.00
302 A96 2fr red brown 22.50 *160.00*

Engr.

303 A96 3fr dk sl grn, *buff* 30.00 65.00
304 A96 5fr brn lake, *buff* 100.00 325.00
305 A96 10fr rose vio, *buff* 110.00 125.00
Nos. 293-305,B145 (14) 286.85 895.50
Set, never hinged 525.00

End of war in Europe.

Johann Heinrich
Pestalozzi — A104

1946, Jan. 12   Engr.   Perf. 11½
306 A104 10c rose violet .25 .25
Never hinged .50

200th anniversary of the birth of J. H. Pestalozzi, educational reformer.
For overprint see No. 4O22.

Mobile P.O. Type of 1937
Redrawn
1946, July 6   Photo.
Granite Paper

307 A62 10c black & yellow 1.10 .25
Never hinged 3.00

The designer's and printer's names are larger on the redrawn stamp. There are many minor differences in the two designs. Sizes: 1937, 37½x21mm. 1946, 38x22½mm.

First Swiss Steam Locomotive — A105

Modern Steam Locomotive — A106

Electric
Gotthard
Express
A107

Electric
Trains
Passing on
Bridge
A108

1947, Aug. 6   Photo.   Perf. 11½
Granite Paper

308 A105 5c dk grn, blk & yel .40 .50
309 A106 10c dk brn, gray & blk .40 .50
310 A107 20c dk red & red .35 .50
311 A108 30c dk bl & bl gray .90 1.75
Nos. 308-311 (4) 2.05 3.25
Set, never hinged 5.00

Centenary of the opening of the first Swiss railroad, between Zurich and Baden.

Johann Rudolf Wettstein — A109

Castle at Neuchatel A110

"Helvetia" A111

Symbol of Swiss Federal State A112

1948, Feb. 27　　　　Granite Paper

312	A109	5c dp grn	.25	.50
313	A110	10c gray blk	.25	.25
314	A111	20c dk red	.30	.25
315	A112	30c dk bl & red	.45	1.25
		Nos. 312-315 (4)	1.25	2.25
		Set, never hinged	2.00	

Tercentenary of the acknowledgement of independence of the Swiss Confederation, and the centenaries of the Neuchatel Revolution and the Swiss Federal State.

See Nos. B178a and B178b for 10c and 20c denominations, type A109.

Types of 1936-42 and

Grisons National Park — A113

1948, Mar. 1　　　　Engr.

316	A54	5c chocolate	.25	.25
a.		Tête bêche pair	1.25	1.25
317	A55	10c green	.25	.25
a.		Tête bêche pair	1.25	1.50
318	A68	20c org brn	.30	.25
a.		Tête bêche pair	1.65	2.25
319	A113	25c carmine	1.50	1.50
320	A59	30c grnsh bl	6.25	4.00
321	A61	40c ultra	11.00	.75
		Nos. 316-321 (6)	19.55	7.00
		Set, never hinged	42.50	

For overprints see Nos. 4O26, 5O4.

Figures Encircling Globe A114

Designs: 25c, Globe and inscribed ribbon. 40c, Globe and pigeons.

1949, May 16　Perf. 11½
Photo.　　　　Unwmk.

322	A114	10c green	.25	.25
323	A114	25c dark red	.40	6.25
324	A114	40c brt blue	.60	4.00
		Nos. 322-324 (3)	1.25	10.50
		Set, never hinged	2.00	

75th anniv. of the UPU.

Post Horn A115

Horse Drawn Mail Coach A116

Design: 30c, Post bus with trailer.

1949, May 16

325	A115	5c gray, yel & pink	.25	.50
326	A116	20c pur, gray & yel	.25	.30
327	A116	30c dk org brn, gray & yel	.45	6.75
		Nos. 325-327 (3)	.95	7.55
		Set, never hinged	1.50	

Centenary of the establishment of the Federal Post in Switzerland.

High Tension Conductors A117

Viaducts — A118

Mountain Railway — A119

Rotary Snow Plow — A120

Reservoir, Grimsel — A121

Lake Dam — A122

Dam and Power Station — A123

Alpine Postal Road — A124

Harbor of the Rhine — A125

Suspension Railway — A126

Railway Viaduct — A127

Triangulation Point — A128

Two types of 20c:
Type I — Three lines above curved rock.
Type II — Two lines above rock.

Perf. 12x11½

1949, Aug. 1　Engr.　Unwmk.

328	A117	3c gray	1.50	4.00
329	A118	5c orange	.25	.25
a.		Tête bêche pair	.90	.25
330	A119	10c yel grn	.25	.25
a.		Tête bêche pair	.60	.25
331	A120	15c aqua	.25	.50
332	A121	20c brown car (II)	.30	.25
a.		Tête bêche pair	1.75	.75
c.		Type I	2,000.	67.50
		Type I, never hinged	3,750.	
333	A122	25c red	.25	.25
334	A123	30c olive	.25	.25
335	A124	35c red brown	.45	.60
336	A125	40c deep blue	1.40	.25
337	A126	50c slate gray	1.40	.25
338	A127	60c blue green	4.00	.50
339	A128	70c purple	1.10	.30
		Nos. 328-339 (12)	11.40	7.65
		Set, never hinged	22.50	

For use in vending machines, some printings of the 5c, 10c, 20c (II), 25c, 30c and 40c carry a control number on the back of every fifth stamp. The number was applied on top of the gum.

For overprints see Nos. O37-O47, 3O83-3O93, 4O29-4O39, 5O6-5O16, 6O1-6O5, 7O1-7O11.

Symbolical of the Telegraph — A129

10c, Telephone. 20c, Radio. 40c, Television.

1952, Feb. 1　Photo.　Perf. 11½

340	A129	5c org & yel	.25	.50
341	A129	10c brt grn & pink	.30	.25
342	A129	20c dp red lil & gray bl	.45	.25
343	A129	40c dp bl & lt bl	1.40	4.75
		Nos. 340-343 (4)	2.40	5.75
		Set, never hinged	5.25	

"A century of telecommunications."

Zurich Airport and Tail of Plane A130

1953, Aug. 29

| 344 | A130 | 40c blue, red & gray | 3.25 | 10.50 |
| | | Never hinged | 5.50 | |

Opening of Zurich-Kloten airport.

Alpine Post Bus, Winter Background — A131

Design: 20c, Same, summer background.

1953, Oct. 8

345	A131	10c dk grn, grn & yel	.25	.25
346	A131	20c dk red, red brn & yel	.30	.25
		Set, never hinged	1.00	

Sold only on Swiss alpine post buses.

Symbols of Agriculture, Forestry and Horticulture — A132

Map and Nautical Emblems — A133

20c, Winged spoon. 40c, Football and map.

1954, Mar. 15　　　Perf. 11½

347	A132	10c multicolored	.25	.25
348	A132	20c multicolored	.40	.25
349	A133	25c red, dk ol grn & gray	1.00	3.00
350	A132	40c bl, yel & brn	1.60	3.50
		Nos. 347-350 (4)	3.25	7.00
		Set, never hinged	6.00	

Nos. 347-348 were issued to publicize exhibitions at Lucerne and Bern; No. 349, fifty years of navigation on the Rhine; No. 350, the 1954 World Soccer Championships in Switzerland.

Lausanne Cathedral A134

Alphorn Blower — A135

Designs: 10c, Vaud costume hat. 40c, Automobile steering wheel.

1955, Feb. 15　　　Perf. 11½

351	A134	5c multi	.25	.60
352	A134	10c grn, yel & red	.25	.50
a.		Souvenir sheet of 2	60.00	80.00
		Never hinged	90.00	
353	A135	20c red & sepia	.55	.50
354	A134	40c bl, pink & gray	1.25	2.10
		Nos. 351-354 (4)	2.30	3.70
		Set, never hinged	5.50	

No. 352a contains 10c and 20c multicolored, imperf. stamps of Cathedral type A134. Size: 104x52mm.

National Philatelic Exhibition (5c, #352a), Winegrowers' Festival (10c), Alpine Herdsman and Costume Festival (20c) and 25th Intl. Automobile Show (40c).

First Swiss Post Bus — A136

10c, North Gate of Simplon Tunnel and Stockalper Palace. 20c, Children crossing street and road signs. 40c, Planes and emblem of Swissair, vert.

1956, Mar. 1   Photo.
Granite Paper

355	A136	5c ol gray, blk & yel	.25	.50
356	A136	10c brt grn, gray & red	.25	.25
357	A136	20c multi	.45	.50
358	A136	40c blue & red	1.00	1.40
		Nos. 355-358 (4)	1.95	2.65
		Set, never hinged	4.50	

50th anniv. of the Swiss Motor Coach Service (#355); 50th anniv. of the opening of Simplon Tunnel (#356); Accident prevention (#357); 25th anniv. of the founding of Swissair (#358).

Inking Device, Printing Machine A137

10c, Train on southern ramp of Gotthard Railroad. 20c, Shield of civil defense and coat of arms. 40c, Munatius Plancus and view of Basel.

Two types of 10c:
I — "Black" bottom line on train.
II — Brown bottom line.

1957, Feb. 27   Perf. 11½
Granite Paper

359	A137	5c multicolored	.25	.25
360	A137	10c lt bl grn, dk grn & red brn (I)	1.10	.25
a.		Type II	1.00	.50
361	A137	20c red org & gray	.25	.50
362	A137	40c multi	.75	1.25
		Nos. 359-362 (4)	2.35	2.25
		Set, never hinged	4.50	

Intl. Exhibition for Graphic Arts, Lausanne, June 1-16, 1957 (#359). 75th anniv. of St. Gotthard railroad (#360). Civil defense (#361). 2000th anniv. of Basel (#362).

Rope and Symbol of European Unity — A138

1957, July 15   Engr.   Perf. 11½

363	A138	25c lt red	.50	.35
364	A138	40c blue	.80	.35
		Set, never hinged	4.50	

Issued to emphasize European unity.

Catalogue values for unused stamps in this section, from this point to the end of the section, are for Never Hinged items.

Nyon Castle and Corinthian Capital A139

Designs: 10c, Woman's head and ribbons in Swiss colors. 20c, Crossbow emblem. 40c, Salvation Army hat.

1958, Mar. 5   Photo.   Unwmk.
Granite Paper

365	A139	5c ol bis & dl pur	.25	.25
366	A139	10c grn, dk grn & red	.25	.25
367	A139	20c ver, lil & car	.50	.25
368	A139	40c multicolored	1.40	1.25
		Nos. 365-368 (4)	2.40	2.00

2000th anniv. of Nyon (#365). Saffa Exhibition, Zurich, July 17-Sept. 15 (#366). 25th anniv. of Swiss manufacturing emblem (#367). 75th anniv. of the Salvation Army in Switzerland (#368).

Symbol of Nuclear Fission A140

1958, Aug. 25   Perf. 11½
Granite Paper

369	A140	40c blue, yel & red	.60	.60

2nd UN Atomic Conf. for peaceful uses of atomic power, Geneva, Sept. 1958.

"Transportation" — A141

Designs: 10c, Fasces and post horn. 20c, Owl, rabbit and fish. 50c, Jean Calvin, Theodore de Beze and University of Geneva.

1959, Mar. 9   Photo.   Unwmk.
Granite Paper

370	A141	5c multicolored	.25	.25
371	A141	10c emer, yel & lt gray	.30	.25
a.		Souvenir sheet of 2, imperf.	14.00	14.00
372	A141	20c multicolored	.60	.25
373	A141	50c multicolored	1.25	.75
		Nos. 370-373 (4)	2.40	1.50

Opening of the Swiss House of Transport and Communications (5c). Natl. Phil. Exhib., St. Gall, Aug. 21-30 (10c and #371a). Protection of animals (20c). 400th anniv. of the University of Geneva (50c).

No. 371a contains a 10c green, gold and light gray and a 20c deep carmine. Sold for 2fr; the money went for the St. Gall Phil. Exhib.

Chain Symbolizing European Unity — A142

1959, June 22   Engr.   Perf. 11½

374	A142	30c brick red	1.60	.30
375	A142	50c lt ultra	2.75	.45

Issued to emphasize European Unity.

Overprinted "REUNION DES PTT D'EUROPE 1959" in Ultramarine or Red

1959, June 22

376	A142	30c brick red	37.50	6.50
377	A142	50c lt ultra	37.50	6.50

European Conference of PTT Administrations, Montreux, June 22-July 31. Nos. 376-377 were on sale only during the conference at a special P. O. in Montreux.

"Cancer Control" A143

Designs: 20c, Founding charter and scepter of University of Basel. 50c, Uprooted Oak Emblem. 75c, Swissair Jet DC-8.

1960, Apr. 7   Photo.   Perf. 11½
Granite Paper

378	A143	10c brt grn & red	.55	.25
379	A143	20c car rose, gray blk & yel	.55	.25
380	A143	50c ultra & yel	.75	1.25
381	A143	75c lt bl, grn & red	3.50	4.00
		Nos. 378-381 (4)	5.35	5.75

50th anniv. of the Swiss League for Cancer Control (10c). 500th anniv. of the University of Basel (20c). World Refugee Year, July 1, 1959-June 30, 1960 (50c). Swissair's entry into the jet age (75c).

Messenger, Fribourg A144   Cathedral, Lausanne A145

Designs: 10c, Messenger, Schwyz. 15c, Messenger and pack animal. 20c, Postilion on horseback. 30c, Grossmünster (church), Zürich. 35c, 1.30fr, Woodcutters' Guildhall, Biel. 40c, Cathedral, Geneva. 50c, Spalen Gate, Basel. 60c, Clock Tower, Berne. 70c, 2.80fr, Sts. Peter and Stephen Church, Bellinzona (tower omitted on 2.80fr). 75c, Bridge and water tower, Lucerne. 80c, Cathedral, St. Gallen. 90c, Munot tower, Schaffhausen. 1fr, Townhall, Fribourg. 1.20fr, Basel gate, Solothurn. 1.50fr, Reding house, Schwyz. 1.70fr, 2fr, 2.20fr, Church, Einsiedeln.

Two types of 5c, 10c, 20c, 50c:
5 Centimes:
Type I — Four lines on pike at left of hand.
Type II — Three lines.
10 Centimes:
Type I — Dot on pike below head.
Type II — No dot.
20 Centimes:
Type I — Ten dots on horiz. harness strip.
Type II — Nine dots.
50 Centimes:
Type I — 3 shading lines at right above arch.
Type II — 2 shading lines.

1960-63   Engr.   Perf. 11½
1.30fr, 1.70fr, 2.20fr, 2.80fr on Granite Paper, Red and Blue Fibers

382	A144	5c lt ultra (I)	.25	.25
c.		Tête bêche pair	.25	.25
383	A144	10c blue grn (I)	.25	.25
c.		Tête bêche pair	.40	.25
384	A144	15c lt red brn	.25	.25
385	A144	20c rose pink (I)	.30	.25
c.		Tête bêche pair	.90	.45
386	A145	25c emerald	.35	.25
387	A145	30c vermilion	.45	.25
388	A145	35c orange red	.50	.30
389	A145	40c lilac	.60	.25
390	A145	50c lt vio bl (I)	.75	.25
c.		Tête bêche pair	2.75	2.75
391	A145	60c rose red	.90	.25
392	A145	70c orange	1.10	.40
393	A145	75c lt blue	1.20	.25
394	A145	80c dp claret	1.25	.25
395	A145	90c olive green	1.30	.25
396	A144	1fr dull orange	1.50	.25
397	A144	1.20fr dull red	1.75	.30
397A	A145	1.30fr red brn, *pink* ('63)	1.90	.25
398	A144	1.50fr brt green	2.25	.50
398A	A144	1.70fr rose lil, *pink* ('63)	2.50	.25
399	A144	2fr brt blue	3.25	.50
399A	A144	2.20fr bl grn, *grn* ('63)	3.25	.50
399B	A145	2.80fr org, *buff* ('63)	3.75	.40
		Nos. 382-399B (22)	29.60	6.65

See Nos. 440-455.

1963-76
Violet Fibers, Fluorescent Paper

382d	A144	5c lt ultra (I)	.25	.25
g.		Tête bêche pair ('68)	.25	.25
383d	A144	10c bl grn (I)	.25	.25
e.		Bklt. pane of 2 + 2 labels ('68)	.65	.65
g.		Tête bêche pair ('68)	.35	.25
384a	A144	15c lt red brn	.55	.55
385d	A144	20c rose pink (I)	.30	.25
g.		Tête bêche pair ('68)	.70	.45
386a	A145	25c emerald	.35	.25
387a	A145	30c vermilion	.35	.25
c.		Tête bêche pair ('68)	1.00	.75
389a	A145	40c lilac ('67)	.55	.35
c.		Tête bêche pair ('76)	1.25	1.10
390d	A145	50c lt vio bl (I)	.75	.25
391a	A145	60c rose red ('67)	.80	.30
393a	A145	75c lt blue ('68)	1.25	.45
394a	A145	80c dp claret	1.00	.25
395a	A145	90c olive grn ('67)	1.00	.25
396a	A144	1fr dull org ('67)	2.00	.25
397b	A144	1.20fr dl red ('68)	3.00	1.75
398b	A145	1.50fr brt green ('68)	3.00	1.75
		Nos. 382d-398b (15)	15.40	7.40

Coil Stamps

1960   White Paper

382b	A144	5c lt ultra (II)	1.40	1.40
383b	A144	10c blue grn (II)	.85	.85
385b	A144	20c rose pink (II)	.85	.85
390b	A145	50c lt vio bl (II)	4.00	4.00
		Nos. 382b-390b (4)	7.10	7.10

The coil stamps were printed in sheets (available to collectors) and pasted into coils. Every fifth stamp has a control number on the back.

Other denominations issued in coils on white paper are: 40c, 60c, 90c, 1fr, 1.30fr, 1.70fr, 2.20fr and 2.80fr.

Denominations issued in coils on granite paper (red & blue fibers) are: 1.30fr, 1.70fr, 2.20fr and 2.80fr.

Coil Stamps

1965-68
Violet Fibers, Fluorescent Paper

382e	A144	5c lt ultra (II)	1.25	1.25
383e	A144	10c blue grn (II)	.85	.85
385e	A144	20c rose pink (II)	.85	.85
390e	A145	50c lt vio bl (II)	4.00	4.00
		Nos. 382e-390e (4)	6.45	5.85

Other denominations issued in coils on violet-fiber paper are: 40c, 60c, 90c and 1fr.

Common Design Types pictured following the introduction.

Europa Issue, 1960
Common Design Type

1960, Sept. 19   Unwmk.   Perf. 11½
Size: 33x23mm

400	CD3	30c vermilion	.50	.25
401	CD3	50c ultra	.75	.40

Wall under Construction and Globe — A146

Designs: 10c, Symbolic sun (HYSPA Emblem). 20c, Ice hockey stick and puck. 50c, Wiring diagram on map of Switzerland.

1961, Feb. 20   Photo.   Perf. 11½
Granite Paper

402	A146	5c gray, brick red & grnsh bl	.35	.25
403	A146	10c aqua & yel	.35	.25
404	A146	20c multicolored	1.50	.60
405	A146	50c ultra, gray & car rose	1.25	1.00
		Nos. 402-405 (4)	3.45	2.10

Development aid to new nations (5c). HYSPA 1961, Health and Sports Exhibition, Bern, May 18-July 17 (10c). Intl. Ice Hockey Championships, Lausanne and Geneva, Mar. 2-12 (20c). Fully automatic Swiss telephone service (50c).

St. Matthew and Angel — A147

Evangelists: 5fr, St. Mark and winged lion. 10fr, St. Luke and winged ox. 20fr, St. John and eagle.

Perf. 11½

1961, Sept. 18   Unwmk.   Engr.
Granite Paper

406	A147	3fr rose carmine	4.00	.25
407	A147	5fr dark blue	6.50	.25
408	A147	10fr dark brown	8.25	.45
409	A147	20fr red	20.00	3.00
		Nos. 406-409 (4)	38.75	3.95

Designs are after 15th century wood carvings from St. Oswald's church, Zug.

Europa Issue, 1961
Common Design Type

1961, Sept. 18
Size: 26x21mm

410	CD4	30c vermilion	.50	.25
411	CD4	50c blue	.75	.35

Trans-Europe Express A148

10c, Rower. 20c, Jungfrau railroad station and Mönch. 50c, WHO Anti-malaria emblem.

1962, Mar. 19   Photo.   Perf. 11½

412	A148	5c multicolored	.50	.25
413	A148	10c brt grn, lem & lil	.45	.25
414	A148	20c rose lil, pale bl & bis	.90	.25
415	A148	50c ultra, lt grn & rose lil	.90	.60
		Nos. 412-415 (4)	2.75	1.35

Introduction of Swiss electric TEE trains (5c). Rowing world championship, Lucerne, Sept. 6-9 (10c). 50th anniv. of the railroad station on the Jungfrau mountain (20c). WHO Anti-Malaria campaign (50c).

Europa Issue, 1962
Common Design Type

1962, Sept. 17   Unwmk.   Perf. 11½
Size: 33x23mm

416	CD5	30c orange, yel & brn	.65 .40
417	CD5	50c ultra, lt grn & brn	1.00 .60

Boy Scout — A149

Designs: 10c, Swiss Alpine Club emblem. 20c, Luegelkinn viaduct. 30c, Wheat Emblem. No. 426, 428a, Red Cross Jubilee Emblem. No. 427, Post Office Building, Paris, 1863.

1963, Mar. 21   Photo.

422	A149	5c gray, dk red & brn	.55 .25
423	A149	10c dk grn, gray & red	.40 .25
424	A149	20c dk car, brn & gray	1.10 .25
425	A149	30c yel grn, yel & org	1.60 1.60
426	A149	50c blue, sil & red	.85 .80
427	A149	50c ultra, pink, yel & gray	.90 .75
		Nos. 422-427 (6)	5.40 3.90

Souvenir Sheet
Imperf

428		Sheet of 4	7.00 6.00
a.		A149 50c bl, lt bl, sil & red	1.75 1.25

50 years of Swiss Boy Scouts (5c). Cent. of Swiss Alpine Club (10c). 50 years Lötschberg Railroad (20c). FAO "Freedom from Hunger" campaign (30c). Red Cross Cent. (#426, 428). 1st Intl. Postal Conf., Paris 1863 (#427).

No. 428 sold for 3fr.

Europa Issue, 1963
Common Design Type

1963, Sept. 16   Unwmk.   Perf. 11½
Granite Paper
Size: 26x21mm

429	CD6	50c ultra & ocher	.90 .60

EXPO Emblem A150

50c, EXPO emblem on globe & moon ("Outlook"). 75c, EXPO emblem on globe ("Insight").

1963, Sept. 16   Unwmk.   Perf. 11½
Granite Paper

430	A150	10c brt grn & dk grn	.30 .25
431	A150	20c red & maroon	.35 .25
432	A150	50c ultra & red	.65 .40
433	A150	75c purple & red	1.00 .45
		Nos. 430-433 (4)	2.30 1.35

Issued to publicize the Swiss National Exhibition, Lausanne, Apr. 30-Oct. 25, 1964.

Road Tunnel Through Great St. Bernard A151

10c, Symbolic water god & waves. 20c, Soldiers of 1864 & 1964. 50c, Standards of Swiss Confederation & Geneva.

1964, Mar. 9   Photo.
Granite Paper

434	A151	5c ol, ultra & red	.25 .25
435	A151	10c Prus bl & grn	.25 .25
436	A151	20c red, ultra, blk & sal	.45 .25
437	A151	50c ultra, red, yel & blk	1.15 .65
		Nos. 434-437 (4)	2.10 1.40

1st Trans-Alpine Automobile route from Switzerland to Italy (5c). "Pro Aqua" water conservation campaign (10c). Centenary of the Swiss Noncommissioned Officers' Association (20c). Sesqui. of union of Geneva with Swiss Confederation (50c).

Europa Issue, 1964
Common Design Type

1964, Sept. 14   Engr.   Perf. 11½
Size: 21x26mm
Violet Fibers, Fluorescent Paper

438	CD7	20c vermilion	.45 .25
439	CD7	50c ultra	1.15 .25

Type of Regular Issue, 1960-63

Designs: 5c, Lenzburg. 10c, Freuler Mansion, Näfels. 15c, St. Mauritius Church, Appenzell. 20c, Planta House, Samedan. 30c, Gabled houses, Gais. 50c, Castle and Abbey Church, Neuchâtel. 70c, Lussy House, Wolfenschiessen. 1fr, Santa Croce Church, Riva San Vitale. 1.20fr, Abbey Church, Payerne. 1.30fr, Church of St. Pierre de Clages. 1.50fr, La Porte de France, Porrentruy. 1.70fr, Frauenfeld Castle. 2fr, A Pro Castle, Seedorf. 2.20fr, Thomas Tower and Gate. Liestal. 2.50fr, St. Oswald's Church, Zug. 3.50fr, Benedictine Abbey, Engelberg.

1964-68   Engr.   Perf. 11½
Violet Fibers, Fluorescent Paper

440	A144	5c car rose ('68)	.25 .25
441	A144	10c violet bl ('68)	.25 .25
b.		Tête bêche pair	.55 .55
c.		Booklet pane of 2 + 2 labels	.70
442	A144	15c brown red ('68)	.35 .25
b.		Tête bêche pair	.80 .80
443	A144	20c blue grn ('68)	.45 .25
b.		Tête bêche pair	1.10 1.10
444	A144	30c vermilion ('68)	.70 .25
b.		Tête bêche pair	1.60 1.60
445	A145	50c ultra ('68)	1.15 .25
446	A145	70c brown ('67)	1.60 .25
447	A145	1fr dk green ('68)	2.25 .25
448	A145	1.20fr brown red ('68)	2.75 .25
449	A145	1.30fr violet bl ('66)	3.00 .75
450	A145	1.50fr green ('68)	3.50 .40
451	A145	1.70fr brown org ('66)	4.00 1.25
452	A145	2fr orange ('67)	4.50 .40
453	A145	2.20fr green	5.00 .80
454	A145	2.50fr Prus grn ('67)	5.75 .55
455	A145	3.50fr purple ('67)	8.00 .60
		Nos. 440-455 (16)	43.50 7.00

The 15c was issued in coils in 1972 (?) with control number on the back of every fifth stamp.

Nurse and Patient A152

Seated Helvetia, 1854 — A153

Women's Army Auxiliary A154

Intercontinental Communications Map — A155

1965, Mar. 8   Photo.   Perf. 11½
Violet Fibers, Fluorescent Paper

462	A152	5c lt ultra & red	.25 .25
463	A153	10c emer, brn & blk	.25 .25
464	A154	20c red & multi	.45 .25

Granite Paper, Red and Blue Fibers

465	A155	50c dl bl grn & mar	1.15 .50
		Nos. 462-465 (4)	2.10 1.25

Nursing and auxiliary medical professions (5c). Natl. Postage Stamp Exhibition, NABRA, Bern, Aug. 27-Sept. 5, 1965 (10c). 20th anniv. of Women's Army Auxiliary Corps (20c). Cent. of ITU (50c).

See No. B344.

Swiss Arms, Cantonal Emblems of Valais, Neuchatel, Geneva A156

1965, June 1   Unwmk.   Perf. 11½
Granite Paper, Red and Blue Fibers

466	A156	20c multicolored	.45 .25

150th anniversary of the entry of the cantons of Valais, Neuchatel and Geneva in the Swiss Confederation.

Matterhorn A157

30c, like 10c but inscribed in French "Cervin."

1965, June 1   Photo.
Granite Paper, Red and Blue Fibers

467	A157	10c grn, slate & dk red	.25 .25

Violet Fibers, Fluorescent Paper

468	A157	30c dk red, grn & slate	.70 .40

Year of the Alps; the cent. of the 1st wintertime visitors to the Alps and cent. of the 1st ascent of the Matterhorn. Nos. 467-468 on sale only at Swiss Alpine post buses.

Europa Issue, 1965
Common Design Type

1965, Sept. 14   Unwmk.   Perf. 11½
Violet Fibers, Fluorescent Paper

469	CD8	50c bl, dk bl & grn	1.15 .25

Figure Skating A159

1965, Sept. 14   Photo.
Violet Fibers, Fluorescent Paper

470	A159	5c grn, dl bl & blk	.25 .25

Issued to publicize the World Figure Skating Championships, Davos, Feb. 22-27, 1966.

ITU Emblem and Atom Diagram A160

Cent. of the ITU: 30c, Symbol of communications, waves.

1965, Sept. 14
Violet Fibers, Fluorescent Paper

471	A160	10c ultra & multi	.25 .25

Granite Paper, Red and Blue Fibers

472	A160	30c org, red & gray	.70 .40

Violet Fibers, Fluorescent Paper Paper from No. 473 onward is fluorescent and has violet fibers, unless otherwise noted.

Mercury's Helmet and Laurel A162

Flags of 13 Member Nations and Nuclear Fission A163

1966, Feb. 21   Photo.

473	A161	10c emer & multi	.25 .25
474	A162	20c dp mag, red & brt grn	.45 .25
475	A163	50c slate blue & multi	1.15 .40
		Nos. 473-475 (3)	1.85 .90

Intl. Cong. for Conservation "Pro Natura," Lucerne (10c). 50th anniv. of Swiss Trade Fair, Basel, Apr. 16-26 (20c). European Organization for Nuclear Research, CERN (50c).

Emblem of Society of Swiss Abroad — A164

1966, June 1   Photo.   Perf. 11½

476	A164	20c ultra & ver	.45 .25

50th anniv. of the Society of Swiss Abroad.

Europa Issue, 1966
Common Design Type

1966, Sept. 26   Engr.   Perf. 11½
Size: 21x26mm

477	CD9	20c vermilion	.45 .25
478	CD9	50c ultra	1.15 .35

Finsteraarhorn — A165

1966, Sept. 26   Photo.

479	A165	10c lt grnsh bl, dk bl & dk red	.30 .25

Automobile Wheels and White Cane — A166

Flags of EFTA Members A167

1967, Mar. 13   Photo.   Perf. 11½

480	A166	10c bl grn, blk & yel	.25 .25
481	A167	20c multicolored	.45 .25

No. 480 issued to publicize the white cane as a distinguishing mark for blind pedestrians. No. 481 publicizes the European Free Trade Association, EFTA. See note after Norway No. 501.

Europa Issue, 1967
Common Design Type

1967, Mar. 13   Engr.

482	CD10	30c blue gray	.70 .25

European Kingfisher A161

Cogwheel and Swiss Emblem
A169

Hourglass and Sun — A170

San Bernardino, from North — A171

Railroad Wheel A172

1967, Sept. 18   Photo.   Perf. 11½
483 A169 10c multicolored   .25 .25
484 A170 20c red, yel & blk .45 .25
485 A171 30c multicolored   .70 .25
486 A172 50c multicolored 1.15 .50
    Nos. 483-486 (4)   2.55 1.25

50th anniv. of Swiss Week (10c). 50th anniv. of the Foundation for the Aged (20c). Opening of the San Bernardino Road Tunnel (30c). 75th anniv. of the Central Office for Intl. Railroad Transportation (50c).

Mountains and Club's Emblem A173

Golden Key with CEPT Emblem A174

Rook and Chessboard A175

Aircraft Tail and Satellites A176

1968, Mar. 14   Photo.   Perf. 11½
487 A173 10c grn, lt ultra & red .25 .25
488 A174 20c Prus bl, yel & brn   .45 .25
489 A175 30c dk ol bis & vio bl   .70 .25
490 A176 50c dk blue & red   1.15 .35
    Nos. 487-490 (4)   2.55 1.10

50th anniv. of the Swiss Women's Alpine Club (10c). A unified Europe through postal cooperation (20c). 18th Chess Olympics, Lugano, Oct. 17-Nov. 6 (30c). Inauguration of the new Geneva-Cointrin Air Terminal (50c).

Worker's Protective Helmet A177

Double Geneva and Zurich Stamps of 1843 — A178

Map Showing Systematic Planning A179

Flag of Rhine Navigation Committee A180

1968, Sept. 12   Photo.   Perf. 11½
491 A177 10c bl grn & yel   .25 .25
492 A178 20c dp car, blk & yel grn .45 .25
493 A179 30c multicolored   .70 .25
494 A180 50c bl, yel & blk   1.15 .50
    Nos. 491-494 (4)   2.55 1.25

50th anniv. of the Swiss Accident Insurance comp., SUVA (10c). 125th anniv. of 1st Swiss postage stamps (20c). 25th anniv. of the Swiss Society for Territorial Planning (30c). Cent. of the Rhine Navigation Act (50c).

Swiss Girl Scouts' Emblem and Camp — A181

Pegasus Constellation A182

Comptoir Suisse Emblem and Beaulieu Building, Lausanne A183

Gymnaestrada Emblem (Man in Circle) — A184

Swissair DC-8 and DH-3 — A185

1969, Feb. 12   Photo.   Perf. 11½
495 A181 10c multicolored   .25 .25
496 A182 20c dark blue   .45 .25
497 A183 30c red, ocher, grn & gray .70 .25
498 A184 50c vio bl, bl, red, grn & sil 1.15 .50
499 A185 2fr bl, dk bl & red   4.50 2.00
    Nos. 495-499 (5)   7.05 3.25

50th anniv. of Swiss Girl Scouts (10c). Opening of 1st Swiss Planetarium, Lucerne, July 1 (20c). 50th anniv. of the Comptoir Suisse (trade fair, 30c). 5th Gymnaestrada (gymnastic meet), Basel, July 1-5 (50c). 50th anniv. of Swiss airmail service (2fr).

Europa Issue, 1969
Common Design Type
1969, Apr. 28   Size: 32½x23mm
500 CD12 30c brn org & multi   .70 .25
501 CD12 50c chlky bl & multi 1.15 .35

Huldreich Zwingli (1484-1531) A186

Famous Swiss: 20c, Gen. Henri Guisan (1874-1960). 30c, Francesco Borromini, architect (1599-1667). 50c, Othmar Schoeck, musician (1886-1957). 80c, Germaine de Stael, writer (1766-1817).

1969, Sept. 18   Engr.   Perf. 11½
502 A186 10c brt purple   .25 .25
503 A186 20c green   .45 .25
504 A186 30c deep carmine   .70 .25
505 A186 50c deep blue   1.15 .60
506 A186 80c red brown   1.90 1.00
    Nos. 502-506 (5)   4.45 2.35

Kreuzberge, Alpstein Mountains A187

Children Crossing Street — A188

Steelworker A189

1969, Sept. 18   Photo.
507 A187 20c blue & multi   .45 .25
508 A188 30c car & multi   .70 .25
509 A189 50c violet & multi 1.15 .45
    Nos. 507-509 (3)   2.30 .95

No. 508 publicizes the traffic safety campaign; No. 509 for 50th anniv. of the ILO.

Telex Tape — A190

Fireman Rescuing Child — A191

Pro Infirmis Emblem A192

United Nations Emblem A193

New UPU Headquarters A194

1970, Feb. 26   Photo.   Perf. 11½
510 A190 20c dk grn, yel & blk .45 .25
511 A191 30c dk car & multi   .70 .25
512 A192 30c red & multi   .70 .25
513 A193 50c dk bl, lt grnsh bl & sil 1.15 .35
514 A194 80c dk pur, sep & tan 1.90 .70
    Nos. 510-514 (5)   4.90 1.80

75th anniv. of the Swiss Telegraph Agency (20c). Cent. of the Swiss Firemen's Assoc. (No. 511). 50th anniv. of the Pro Infirmis Foundation (No. 512). UN, 5th anniv. (50c). New Headquarters of the UPU in Bern (80c).

Europa Issue, 1970
Common Design Type
1970, May 4   Engr.   Perf. 11½
Size: 21x26mm
515 CD13 30c vermilion   .70 .25
516 CD13 50c brt blue   1.15 .35

Soccer A195

Census Form — A196

Piz Palu, Grisons A197

"Nature Conservation" A198   Numeral A199

1970, Sept. 17   Photo.   Perf. 11½
517 A195 10c green & multi   .40 .25
518 A196 20c dk grn & multi   .45 .25
519 A197 30c slate bl & multi .70 .25
520 A198 50c dk bl & multi   1.15 .65
    Nos. 517-520 (4)   2.70 1.40

75th anniv. of Swiss Soccer Association (10c). Federal Census of 1970 (20c). Swiss Alps (30c). Nature Conservation Year (50c).

Coil Stamps
1970, Sept. 17   Engr.   Perf. 11½
521 A199 10c brown lake   .25 .25
522 A199 20c olive grn   .45 .25
523 A199 50c ultra   1.15 .60
    Nos. 521-523 (3)   1.85 1.10

Control number in stamp's color on back of every fifth stamp. Nos. 521-523 were regularly issued only in coils, but exist in sheets of 50.

Gymnastic Trio — A200

Rose — A201

Switzerland No. 8 — A202

Rising Spiral — A203

Intelsat 4 Satellite A204

NABA 1971 BASEL
Adaptation of 1850 Design — A205

Design: No. 525, Runners (men).

1971, Mar. 11   **Photo.**   *Perf. 11½*
524	A200	10c ol, brn & bl	.25	.30
525	A200	10c gray, brn & yel	.25	.30
a.		Pair, #524-525	.50	.30
526	A201	20c dk grn & multi	.45	.25
527	A202	30c dp car & multi	.70	.30
528	A203	50c dk bl & bis	1.15	.60
529	A204	80c multicolored	1.90	1.00
		Nos. 524-529 (6)	4.70	2.75

Souvenir Sheet
Typo.
Imperf
530	A205	2fr blue & multi	5.40	3.00

New article on gymnastics and sports in Swiss Constitution (10c). Intl. Child Welfare Org. (20c); NABA Natl. Postage Stamp Exhibition, Basel, June 4-13 (30c, 2fr); 2nd decade of development aid (50c); Intl. Space Communications Conf., Geneva, June-July, 1971 (80c).
#525a printed checkerwise. #530 sold for 3fr.

Europa Issue, 1971
Common Design Type

1971, May 3   **Engr.**   *Perf. 11½*
Size: 26x21mm
531	CD14	30c rose car & org	.70	.25
532	CD14	50c blue & org	1.15	.40

Les Diablerets, Vaud — A206

Telecommunications Symbols — A207

1971, Sept. 23   **Photo.**   *Perf. 11½*
533	A206	30c rose lil & bl gray	.70	.30
534	A207	40c ultra, yel & brt pink	.95	.55

No. 534 for the 50th anniv. of Radio-Suisse, which is also in charge of air traffic control.

Alexandre Yersin (1863-1943) Bacteriologist A208

Physicians: 20c, Auguste Forel (1848-1931), psychiatrist. 30c, Jules Gonin (1870-1935), ophthalmologist. 40c, Robert Koch (1843-1910), German bacteriologist. 80c, Frederick G. Banting (1891-1941), Canadian physiologist.

1971, Sept. 23   **Engr.**
535	A208	10c gray olive	.25	.25
536	A208	20c bluish green	.45	.25
537	A208	30c carmine rose	.70	.25
538	A208	40c dark blue	.95	.55
539	A208	80c brt purple	1.90	.90
		Nos. 535-539 (5)	4.25	2.20

Wrench, Road Sign, Club Emblems A209

Electronic Switch Panel — A210

Boy's Head and Radio Waves A211

Symbolic Tree — A212

1972, Feb. 17   **Photo.**   *Perf. 11½*
540	A209	10c multicolored	.25	.25
541	A210	20c olive & multi	.45	.25
542	A211	30c orange & maroon	.70	.30
543	A212	40c blue, grn & pur	.95	.60
		Nos. 540-543 (4)	2.35	1.40

75th anniv. of the touring and automobile clubs of Switzerland (10c). 125th anniv. of Swiss railroads (20c). 50th anniv. of Swiss radio (30c). 50th annual congress of Swiss citizens living abroad, Bern, Aug. 25-27 (40c).

Europa Issue 1972
Common Design Type

1972, May. 2
Size: 21x26mm
544	CD15	30c multicolored	.70	.25
545	CD15	40c multicolored	.95	.35

Alberto Giacometti (1901-66), Painter and Sculptor — A213

Portraits and Signatures: 20c, Charles Ferdinand Ramuz (1878-1947), writer. 30c, Le Corbusier (Charles Edouard Jeanneret; 1887-1965) architect. 40c, Albert Einstein (1879-1955), physicist. 80c, Arthur Honegger (1892-1955), composer.

Engraved & Photogravure
1972, Sept. 21   *Perf. 11½*
546	A213	10c ocher & blk	.25	.25
547	A213	20c lt olive & blk	.45	.25
548	A213	30c pink & blk	.70	.25
549	A213	40c lt blue & blk	.95	.60
550	A213	80c lil rose & blk	1.90	.75
		Nos. 546-550 (5)	4.25	2.10

Civil Defense Emblem A214

Spannörter, Swiss Alps — A215

Red Cross Rescue Helicopter A216

Clean Air, Fire, Earth and Water — A217

1972, Sept. 21   **Photo.**
551	A214	10c org, bl & yel	.25	.25
552	A215	20c bl grn & multi	.45	.30
553	A216	30c lilac, red & indigo	.75	.25
554	A217	40c lt blue & multi	.95	.60
		Nos. 551-554 (4)	2.40	1.40

Earth Satellite Station, Leuk, World Map — A218

Quill Pen and Arrows in Circle — A219

INTERPOL Emblem A220

1973, Feb. 15   **Photo.**   *Perf. 11½*
555	A218	15c gray, yel & bl	.35	.25
556	A219	30c multicolored	.70	.25
557	A220	40c dp bl, lt bl & gray	.95	.50
		Nos. 555-557 (3)	2.00	1.00

Opening of the satellite station at Leuk; Swiss Association of Commercial Employees, cent. (30c); International Criminal Police Organization (INTERPOL), 59th anniv.

Sottoceneri A221

Sign of Inn "Zur Sonne," Toggenburg A222

Villages: 10c, Graubunden. 15c, Central Switzerland. 25c, Jura. 30c, Simme Valley. 35c, Central Switzerland (2 buildings). 40c, Vaud. 50c, Valais. 60c, Engadine. 70c, Sopraceneri. 80c, Eastern Switzerland.
Designs: 1fr, Rose window, Lausanne Cathedral. 1.10fr, Gallus Portal, Basel Cathedral. 1.20fr, Romanesque capital (eagle), St. Jean Baptiste Church, Grandson. 1.50fr, Ceiling medallion (bird feeding nestlings), Stein am Rhein Convent. 1.70fr, Romanesque capital (St. George and dragon), St. Jean Baptiste, Grandson. 1.80fr, Gargoyle, Bern Cathedral. 2fr, Bay window, Schaffhausen. 2.50fr, Cock weather vane, St. Ursus Cathedral, Solothurn. 3fr, Font, St. Maurice Church, Saanen. 3.50fr, Astronomical clock, Bern clock tower.

1973-80   **Engr.**   *Perf. 11½*
Fluorescent, No Violet Fibers
558	A221	5c dl yel & dk bl	.25	.25
559	A221	10c rose lil & ol grn	.25	.25
560	A221	15c org & vio bl	.35	.25
561	A221	25c emer & vio bl	.60	.25
562	A221	30c brick red & dk bl	.70	.25
563	A221	35c red org & brt vio ('75)	.80	.25
564	A221	40c brt bl & blk	.95	.25
565	A221	50c ol grn & org	1.15	.25
566	A221	60c yel brn & gray	1.40	.25
567	A221	70c sep & dk grn	1.60	.25
568	A221	80c brt grn & brick red	1.90	.25

Violet Fibers, Fluorescent Paper
569	A222	1fr pur ('74)	2.25	.25
a.		Without fibers, fluorescent paper ('78)	2.25	1.50
570	A222	1.10fr Prus bl ('75)	2.50	.40
571	A222	1.20fr rose red ('74)	2.75	1.25
572	A222	1.30fr ocher	3.00	.90
573	A222	1.50fr grn ('74)	3.50	1.25
574	A222	1.70fr gray	4.00	.60
575	A222	1.80fr dp org	4.25	.60
576	A222	2fr ultra ('74)	4.75	.40
a.		Without fibers, fluorescent paper ('78)	4.75	3.50
577	A222	2.50fr gldn brn ('75)	5.75	.60
578	A222	3fr dk car ('79)	7.00	1.00
579	A222	3.50fr ol grn ('80)	8.00	1.25
		Nos. 558-579 (22)	57.70	11.25

No. 577 exists without tagging. Value, $60 unused, $30 used.

Europa Issue 1973
Common Design Type

1973, Apr. 30   **Engr. and Photo.**
Size: 38x28mm
580	CD16	25c brown & yel	.60	.25
581	CD16	40c ultra & yel	.95	.35

"Man and Time" — A223

Skier and Championship Emblem A224

Child — A225

1973, Aug. 30   Photo.   Perf. 11½
582 A223 15c multicolored .35 .25
583 A224 30c pink & multi .70 .25
584 A225 40c blue vio & blk .95 .50
 Nos. 582-584 (3) 2.00 1.00

Opening of the Intl. Clock Museum, La Chaux-de-Fonds, 1974 (15c); Intl. Alpine Skiing Championships, St. Moritz, Feb. 2-10, 1974 (30c); "Terre des hommes" children's aid program (40c).

Souvenir Sheet

Medieval Postal Couriers — A226

1974, Jan. 29   Photo.   Perf. 11½
585 A226 Sheet of 4 5.50 5.50
 a. 30c Basel (with staff) 1.10 1.10
 b. 30c Zug (without staff) 1.10 1.10
 c. 60c Uri 1.40 1.10
 d. 80c Schwyz 1.90 1.10

Cent. of UPU and for INTERNABA 74 Intl. Phil. Exhib., Basel, June 7-16. No. 585 sold for 3fr.

Pine and Cabin on Globe — A227

Gymnast and Hurdlers A228

Target and Pistol — A229

1974, Jan. 29
586 A227 15c lt green & multi .35 .25
587 A228 30c red & multi .70 .25
588 A229 40c blue & multi .95 .30
 Nos. 586-588 (3) 2.00 .80

50th anniv. of Swiss Youth Hostels (15c); Cent. of Swiss Workers' Gymnast and Sports Association (SATUS) (30c); World Marksmanship Championships, Thun and Bern, Sept. 1974 (40c).

Old Houses, Parliament RR Station, Bern — A230

Eugéne Borel — A231

Designs: No. 590, Castle, Town Hall, Chauderon Center, Lausanne. 40c, Heinrich von Stephan. 80c, Montgomery Blair.

1974, Mar. 28   Photo.   Perf. 11½
589 A230 30c orange & multi .70 .25
590 A230 30c scarlet & multi .70 .25

Engr.
591 A231 30c rose & blk .70 .25
592 A231 40c gray & blk .95 .50
593 A231 80c lt yel grn & blk 1.90 .75
 Nos. 589-593 (5) 4.95 2.00

Cent. of the UPU. Nos. 589-590 publicize the Cent. Cong., Lausanne, May 22-July 5; Nos. 591-593 honor the founders of the UPU.

"Continuity," by Max Bill — A232

Europa: 40c, "Amazon," bronze sculpture by Carl Burckhardt.

1974, Mar. 28   Photo.
594 A232 30c red & black .70 .25
595 A232 40c ultra & sepia .95 .35

Oath of Allegiance, by Werner Witschi — A233

Sports Foundation Emblem A234

Conveyor Belts, Paths of Mail Transport and Delivery A235

1974, Sept. 19   Photo.   Perf. 11½
596 A233 15c lil, ol & dk ol .35 .25
597 A234 30c silver & multi .70 .25
598 A235 30c plum & multi .70 .25
 Nos. 596-598 (3) 1.75 .75

Centenary of Swiss Constitution (15c); Swiss Sports Foundation (No. 597); 125th anniversary of Swiss Federal Post (No. 598).

Standard Meter, Krypton Spectrum A236

Women of Four Races A237

Red Cross Flag, Barbed Wire — A238

"Ville de Lucerne" Dirigible A239

1975, Feb. 13   Photo.   Perf. 11½
599 A236 15c grn, org & ultra .35 .25
600 A237 30c brown & multi .70 .25
601 A238 60c ultra, blk & red 1.40 .40
602 A239 90c blue & multi 2.10 1.00
 Nos. 599-602 (4) 4.55 1.90

Cent. of Intl. Meter Convention, Paris, 1875 (15c); Intl. Women's Year 1975 (30c); 2nd Session of Diplomatic Conf. on Humanitarian Intl. Law, Geneva, Feb. 1975 (60c); Aviation and Space Travel exhibition in Museum of Transport and Communications, Lucerne (90c).

Mönch, by Ferdinand Hodler — A240

Vineyard Worker, by Maurice Barraud — A241

Europa: 50c, Still Life with Guitar, by René Auberjonois.

1975, Apr. 28   Photo.   Perf. 12x11½
603 A240 30c gray & multi .70 .25
604 A241 50c multicolored 1.15 .50
605 A241 60c bl gray & multi 1.40 .80
 Nos. 603-605 (3) 3.25 1.55

Man Pulling Wheel Chair Upstairs A242

"The Helping Hand" A243

Architectural Heritage Year Emblem A244

Beat Fischer von Reichenbach A245

1975, Sept. 11   Photo.
606 A242 15c lilac, blk & grn .35 .25
607 A243 30c red, blk & car .70 .25
608 A244 50c yel brn & mar 1.15 .60
609 A245 60c blue & multi 1.40 .75
 Nos. 606-609 (4) 3.60 1.85

Special building features for the handicapped (15c); interdenominational telephone pastoral counseling (30c); European Architectural Heritage Year 1975 (50c); Fischer Post, Bern, tercentenary (60c).

Forest A246

Fruits and Vegetables A247

Black Infant — A248

Telephones of 1876 and 1976 — A249

1976, Feb. 12   Photo.   Perf. 11½
Fluorescent, No Violet Fibers
610 A246 20c green & multi .50 .25
611 A247 40c car & multi .95 .25
612 A248 40c lil rose & multi .95 .25

Engr.
Violet Fibers, Fluorescent Paper
613 A249 80c lt bl & dk bl 1.90 1.00
 Nos. 610-613 (4) 4.30 1.75

Centenary of Federal forest laws (20c); healthy nutrition to combat alcoholism (No. 611); fight against leprosy (No. 612); telephone centenary (80c).

Cotton and Gold Lace, St. Gall — A250

Pocket Watch, 18th Century — A251

1976, May 3   Engr.   Perf. 11½
614 A250 40c red brn & multi .95 .25
615 A251 80c black & multi 1.90 .90

Europa. Both 40c and 80c are on fluorescent paper, the 80c having violet fibers.

Fawn, Frog and Swallow A252

"Conserve Energy" A253

St. Gotthard
Mountains
A254

Skater
A255

1976, Sept. 16   Photo.   Perf. 11½
Fluorescent, No Violet Fibers
616	A252	20c multicolored	.75	.30
617	A253	40c multicolored	.95	.25
618	A254	40c multicolored	.95	.30
619	A255	80c multicolored	1.90	.90
		Nos. 616-619 (4)	4.55	1.75

Wildlife protection (20c); energy conservation (No. 617); Pizzo Lucendro to Pizzo Rotondo, seen from Altanca (No. 618); World Men's Skating Championships, Davos, Feb. 5-6, 1977 (80c).

Oskar Bider,
Bleriot
Monoplane
A256

Swiss Aviation Pioneers: 80c, Eduard Spelterini and balloon gondola. 100c, Armand Dufaux and Dufaux plane. 150c, Walter Mittelholzer and Dornier hydroplane.

1977, Jan. 27   Engr.   Perf. 11½
620	A256	40c multicolored	.95	.65
621	A256	80c multicolored	1.90	1.25
622	A256	100c multicolored	2.25	1.00
623	A256	150c multicolored	3.50	1.75
		Nos. 620-623 (4)	8.60	4.65

Blue
Cross — A257

Festival
Emblem
A258

Balloons
Carrying
Letters
A259

1977, Jan. 27   Photo.
624	A257	20c gray, bl & blk	.45	.25
625	A258	40c red, gold & brn	.95	.25
626	A259	80c lt bl & multi	1.90	1.00
		Nos. 624-626 (3)	3.30	1.50

Blue Cross Society (care of alcoholics and fight against alcoholism), centenary (20c); Vintage Festival, Vevey, July 30-Aug. 14 (40c); JUPHILEX 77 Youth Philatelic Exhibition, Bern, Apr. 7-11 (80c).

Fluorescent Paper
From No. 624 onward the paper lacks violet fibers but is fluorescent, unless otherwise noted.

St. Ursanne
on Doubs
River — A260

Europa: 80c, Sils-Baselgia on Inn River.

1977, May 2   Engr.   Perf. 11½
627	A260	40c multicolored	.95	.25
628	A260	80c multicolored	1.90	.70

Worker and
Factories
A261

Ionic Column
and Shield
A262

Swiss Cross,
Arrow and
Butterfly
A263

1977, Aug. 25   Photo.   Perf. 11½
629	A261	20c multicolored	.45	.25
630	A262	40c multicolored	.95	.40
631	A263	80c multicolored	1.90	1.00
		Nos. 629-631 (3)	3.30	1.65

Federal Factories Act, centenary (20c); protection of cultural monuments (40c); Swiss hiking trails (80c).

Star Singer,
Bergün — A264

Folk Customs: 10c, Horse race, Zürich. 20c, New Year's Eve costumes, Herisau. 25c, Chesslete, Solothurn. 30c, Rollelibutzen, Altstatten. 35c, Cutting off the goose, Sursee. 40c, Herald reading proclamation and men scaling wall, Geneva. 45c, Klausjagen, Kussnacht. 50c, Masked men, Laupen. 60c, Schnabelgeissen, Ottenbach. 70c, Procession (horse and masked men), Mendrisio. 80c, Griffins, Basel. 90c, Masked men, Lotschental.

1977-84   Engr.   Perf. 11½
632	A264	5c blue grn	.25	.25
a.		Bklt. pane of 4 ('84)	.45	
633	A264	10c dark red	.25	.25
a.		Bklt. pane of 2 + 2 labels ('79)	.45	
b.		Bklt. pane of 4 ('84)	.95	
634	A264	20c orange	.45	.25
a.		Booklet pane of 4 ('79)	1.90	
635	A264	25c brown	.60	.25
636	A264	30c brt green	.70	.25
637	A264	35c olive	.80	.25
a.		Bklt. pane of 4 ('84)	3.25	
638	A264	40c brown lake	.95	.25
a.		Booklet pane of 4 ('79)	3.75	
b.		Violet fibers, fluorescent paper ('78)	.95	.25
639	A264	45c gray blue	1.00	.30
640	A264	50c red brown	1.15	.25
a.		Bklt. pane of 2+2 labels ('84)	2.25	
b.		Bklt. pane of 4 ('84)	4.50	
641	A264	60c gray brown	1.40	.45
642	A264	70c purple	1.60	.30
643	A264	80c steel blue	1.90	.75
644	A264	90c deep brown	2.10	.90
		Nos. 632-644 (13)	13.15	4.70

Issue dates: 30c, Nov. 25, 1982; 25c, 40c, 60c, Sept. 11, 1984; others, Aug. 25, 1977.

Arms of Vaud
Canton
A265

Old Lucerne
A266

Title Page of
"Melusine"
A267

Stylized Lens
and Bellows
A268

Steamers on Swiss Lakes — A269

1978, Mar. 9   Photo.   Perf. 11½
652	A265	20c multicolored	.45	.25
653	A266	40c multicolored	.95	.25
654	A267	70c multicolored	1.60	.80
655	A268	80c multicolored	1.90	1.00
		Nos. 652-655 (4)	4.90	2.30

Miniature Sheet
656	A269	Sheet of 8	9.50	9.50
a.		20c La Suisse, 1910	.45	.30
b.		20c Il Verbano, 1826	.45	.30
c.		40c MS Gotthard, 1970	.95	.85
d.		40c Ville de Neuchatel, 1972	.95	.85
e.		40c MS Romanshorn, 1958	.95	.85
f.		40c Le Winkelried, 1871	.95	.85
g.		70c DS Loetschberg, 1914	1.60	.90
h.		80c DS Waedenswil, 1895	1.90	1.25

LEMANEX 78 Philatelic Exhibition, Lausanne, May 26-June 4 (#652); Founding of Lucerne, 800th anniv. (#653); printing in Geneva, 500th anniv. (#654); 2nd Intl. Triennial Photography Exhibition, Fribourg, June 17-Oct. 22 (#655).
Size of No. 656: 134x129mm. Sold for 5fr.

Stockalper
Palace,
Brig — A270

Europa: 80c, Diet Hall, Bern.

1978, May 2   Engr.   Perf. 11½
657	A270	40c multicolored	.95	.30
658	A270	80c multicolored	1.90	.75

Machinist
A271

#660, Chemical worker (French inscription).
#661, Construction worker (Italian inscription).

1978, Sept. 14   Photo.   Perf. 11½
659	A271	40c multicolored	.95	.45
660	A271	40c multicolored	.95	.45
661	A271	40c multicolored	.95	.45
a.		Strip of 3, #659-661	2.75	2.75

Industrial safety.

Joseph Bovet (1879-
1951),
Composer — A272

Portraits: 40c, Henri Dunant (1828-1910), founder of Red Cross. 70c, Carl Gustave Jung (1875-1961), psychologist. 80c, Auguste Piccard (1884-1962), physicist and balloonist.

1978, Sept. 14   Engr.
662	A272	20c dull green	.45	.25
663	A272	40c rose lake	.95	.25
664	A272	70c gray	1.60	.75
665	A272	80c blue gray	1.90	.90
		Nos. 662-665 (4)	4.90	2.15

Arms of
Switzerland
and
Jura — A273

1978, Sept. 25   Photo.   Perf. 11½
666	A273	40c buff, red & blk	.95	.35

Admission of Jura as 23rd Canton.

Rainer Maria Rilke
(1875-1926), Poet,
Muzot
Castle — A274

Designs: 40c, Paul Klee (1879-1940), painter and "heroic roses." 70c, Hermann Hesse (1877-1962), writer, and vines. 80c, Thomas Mann (1875-1955), writer, and Lubeck buildings.

1979, Feb. 21   Engr.   Perf. 11½
667	A274	20c gray green	.45	.25
668	A274	40c red	.95	.30
669	A274	70c brown	1.60	.70
670	A274	80c gray blue	1.90	1.00
		Nos. 667-670 (4)	4.90	2.25

O. H. Ammann, Verrazano-Narrows
Bridge, NY — A275

Target Hit with
Pole and
Lucerne
Flag — A276

Hot Air
Balloon
A277

Airport,
Swissair and
Air France
Jets — A278

1979, Feb. 21   Photo.
671	A275	20c multicolored	.45	.25
672	A276	40c multicolored	.95	.25
673	A277	70c multicolored	1.60	.70
674	A278	80c multicolored	1.90	1.00
		Nos. 671-674 (4)	4.90	2.20

Othmar H. Ammann (1879-1965), engineer, bridge builder in US; 50th Federal Riflemen's Festival, Lucerne, July 7-22; World Esperanto Congress, Lucerne; new runway at Basel-Mulhouse Intl. Airport.

Letter Box, 1845, Spalentor, Basel — A279

Europa: 80c, Microwave radio relay station on Jungfraujoch.

1979, Apr. 30   **Engr.**   **Perf. 11½**
675 A279 40c multicolored   .95   .35
676 A279 80c multicolored   1.90   .90

Helvetian Gold Quarter Stater, 2nd Century B.C. — A280

Three-stage Launcher Ariane — A283

Child and Dove — A281

Morse Key and Satellite A282

1979, Sept. 6   **Photo.**
677 A280 20c multicolored   .45   .25
678 A281 40c multicolored   .95   .25
679 A282 70c multicolored   1.60   .70
680 A283 80c multicolored   1.90   .90
    Nos. 677-680 (4)   4.90 2.10

Centenary of Swiss Numismatic Society; International Year of the Child; Union of Swiss Radio Amateurs, 50th anniv.; European Space Agency (ESA).

Tree in Bloom A284

Hand Carved Milk Bucket A285

Winterthur Town Hall — A286

"Pic-Pic," 1930 — A287

1980, Feb. 21   **Photo.**
681 A284 20c multicolored   .45   .25
682 A285 40c multicolored   .95   .25
683 A286 70c multicolored   1.60   .80
684 A287 80c multicolored   1.90 1.00
    Nos. 681-684 (4)   4.90 2.30

Green '80, Swiss Horticultural & Gardening Expo., Basel, 4/12-9/9/12; Swiss Arts Crafts Centers, 50th anniv.; Soc. for Swiss Art History, cent.; 50th Intl. Automobile Show, Geneva, 3/16.

Johann Konrad Kern (1808-1888), Politician A288

Europa: 80c, Gustav Adolf Hasler (1830-1900), communications pioneer.

1980, Apr. 28   **Lith. & Engr.**
Granite Paper
685 A288 40c multicolored   .95   .25
686 A288 80c multicolored   1.90   .90

Postal Giro System A289

Postal Bus System A290

Security Printing Plant, 50th Anniversary A291

Swiss Telephone Service Centenary A292

Photo., Photo. & Engr. (70c)
1980, Sept. 5   **Perf. 12**
687 A289 20c multicolored   .45   .25
688 A290 40c multicolored   .95   .25
689 A291 70c multicolored   1.60   .75
690 A292 80c multicolored   1.90 1.10
    Nos. 687-690 (4)   4.90 2.35

Swiss Meteorological Office Centenary A293

Swiss Trade Union Federation Centenary A294

Opening of St. Gotthard Tunnel for Year-round Traffic — A295

1980, Sept. 5   **Photo.**
691 A293 20c multicolored   .35   .25
692 A294 40c multicolored   .55   .25
693 A295 80c multicolored   1.25 1.00
    Nos. 691-693 (3)   2.15 1.50

Granary, Kiesen, 17th Century A296

International Year of the Disabled A297

The Parish Clerk, by Albert Anker — A298

Theodolite and Rod — A299

DC-9 (50th Anniversary of Swissair) A300

1981, Mar. 9   **Photo.**   **Perf. 11½**
694 A296 20c multicolored   .45   .25
695 A297 40c multicolored   .95   .25
696 A298 70c multicolored   1.60   .80
697 A299 80c multicolored   1.90   .90
698 A300 110c multicolored   2.50 1.10
    Nos. 694-698 (5)   7.40 3.30

Ballenberg Open-air Museum of Rural Architecture, Furnishing and Crafts; Albert Anker (1831-1910), artist (70c); 16th Congress of the International Federation of Surveyors, Montreux, Aug. (80c).

Europa Issue 1981

Couple Dancing in Native Costumes — A301

1981, May 4   **Photo.**   **Perf. 11½**
699 A301 40c shown   .95   .35
700 A301 80c Stone putting   1.90 1.00

Seal of Fribourg A302

1981, Sept. 3   **Photo. & Engr.**
701 A302 40c shown   .95   .25
702 A302 40c Seal of Solothurn   .95   .25
703 A302 80c Old Town Hall, Stans   1.90 1.00
    Nos. 701-703 (3)   3.80 1.50

Diet of Stans, 50th anniv., and entry of Fribourg & Solothurn into the Swiss Confederation.

Voltage Regulator A303

Crossbow Quality Emblem A304

Youths A305

Flower Mosaic, St. Peter's Cathedral, Geneva A306

1981, Sept. 3   **Photo.**
704 A303 20c multi   .45   .25
705 A304 40c multi   .95   .30
706 A305 70c multi   1.60   .75
707 A306 1.10fr multi   2.50 1.25
    Nos. 704-707 (4)   5.50 2.55

Technorama Industrial Fair, Winterthur; Crossbow Quality Emblem, 50th anniv.; Swiss Youth Assoc., 50th anniv.; restoration of St. Peter's Cathedral.

Gotthard Railway Centenary A307

Designs: Locomotives. Nos. 708-709 setenant with label showing workers' monument.

1982, Feb. 18   **Photo.**
708 A307 40c Steam   .95   .30
709 A307 40c Electric   .95   .30

Swiss Hoteliers' Assoc. Centenary A308

Federal Gymnastic Society Sesquicentennial — A309

Intl. Gas Union, 50th Anniv. Convention, Lausanne A310

Bern Museum of Natural History Sesquicentennial — A311

Society of
Chemical
Industries
Centenary
A312

1982, Feb. 18
710 A308 20c multicolored   .45 .25
711 A309 40c multicolored   .95 .30
712 A310 70c multicolored   1.60 .75
713 A311 80c multicolored   1.90 1.00
714 A312 110c multicolored   2.50 1.10
  Nos. 710-714 (5)   7.40 3.40

Europa
1982 — A313

1982, May 3   Photo.   *Perf. 11½*
715 A313 40c Oath of Eternal
              Fealty   .45 .30
716 A313 80c Pact of 1291   1.90 1.00

Virgo, Schwarzee
above
Zermatt — A314

Signs of the Zodiac and City Views.

Photogravure and Engraved
1982-86   *Perf. 11½*
717 A314 1fr   Aquarius,
                 Old Bern   2.25 .30
718 A314 1.10fr Pisces, Nax
                 near Sion   2.50 .30
719 A314 1.20fr Aries,
                 Graustock   2.75 .30
719A A314 1.40fr Gemini, Bis-
                 chofszell   3.25 1.40
720 A314 1.50fr Taurus, Ba-
                 sel Cathe-
                 dral   3.50 .30
721 A314 1.60fr Gemini,
                 Schonen-
                 grund   3.75 1.10
722 A314 1.70fr Cancer, Wet-
                 terhorn,
                 Grindelwald 4.00 .30
723 A314 1.80fr Leo, Areuse
                 Gorge,
                 Neuchatel   4.25 1.00
724 A314 2fr   Virgo, Jung-
                 frau Monch
                 Eiger Mts. 4.50 2.25
725 A314 2fr   shown   4.50 .30
726 A314 2.50fr Libra, Fechy 5.75 .80
727 A314 3fr   Scorpio,
                 Corippo   7.00 1.25
728 A314 4fr   Sagittarius,
                 Glarus   9.25 1.50
728A A314 4.50fr Capricorn,
                 Schuls   10.50 2.00
  Nos. 717-728A (14)   67.75 13.10

Issued: #717-719, 720-721, 8/23/82; #719A,
2/11/86; #722-724, 2/17/83; #725, 11/24/83;
#726-727, 2/19/85; #728-728A, 2/21/84.

Zurich Tram
Centenary
A315

Centenary of
Salvation
Army in
Switzerland
A316

World Dressage Championship,
Lausanne, Aug. 25-29 — A317

Intl. Water
Supply
Assoc., 14th
World
Congress,
Zurich, Sept.
6-10 — A318

1982, Aug. 23   **Photo.**
729 A315 20c multicolored   .45 .25
730 A316 40c multicolored   .95 .30
731 A317 70c multicolored   1.60 .90
732 A318 80c multicolored   1.90 1.00
  Nos. 729-732 (4)   4.90 2.40

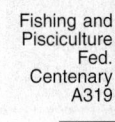

Fishing and
Pisciculture
Fed.
Centenary
A319

Zurich University
Sesquicentennial — A320

Journalists'
Fed.
Centenary
A321

Machine Manufacturers' Assoc.
Centenary — A322

1983, Feb. 17   **Photo.**
Granite Paper
733 A319 20c Perch   .45 .25
734 A320 40c multicolored   .95 .30
735 A321 70c Computer print
              outs   1.60 .90
736 A322 80c Micrometer, cycloi-
              dal computer pat-
              tern   1.90 1.00
  Nos. 733-736 (4)   4.90 2.45

Europa 1983   Basel Seal,
A323   1832-1848
                 A324

Photogravure and Engraved
1983, May 3   *Perf. 11½*
737 A323 40c Celestial globe,
              1594   .95 .25
738 A323 80c Cog railway, 1871 1.90 1.00

1983, May 26   **Photo.**
739 A324 40c multicolored   .95 .35
  Basel Canton sesquicentennial (land
division).

Octodurus
Martigny
Bimillenium
A325

Swiss Kennel
Club
Centenary
A326

Bicycle and
Motorcycle
Federation
Centenary
A327

World Communications Year — A328

1983, Aug. 22   **Photo.**
740 A325 20c multicolored   .45 .25
741 A326 40c multicolored   .95 .25
742 A327 70c multicolored   1.60 .90
743 A328 80c multicolored   1.90 .90
  Nos. 740-743 (4)   4.90 2.30

NABA-ZURI'84 Natl. Stamp Show,
Zurich, June 22-July 1 — A329

1100th Anniv.
of Saint
Imier — A330

Upper City,
Lausanne
A331

1984, Feb. 21   **Photo.**
744 A329 25c multicolored   .60 .25
745 A330 50c multicolored   1.15 .35
746 A331 80c multicolored   1.90 1.10
  Nos. 744-746 (3)   3.65 1.70

Selection of Lausanne as permanent headquarters for the Intl. Olympic Committee (80c).

Europa (1959-
1984)
A332

1984, May 2   Photo.   *Perf. 11½*
747 A332 50c lilac rose   1.15 .50
748 A332 80c ultra   1.90 1.00

Panoramic View of Zurich — A333

1984, May 24
749 A333 Sheet of 4   5.50 5.50
  a.-d. 50c any single   4.50 1.20
NABA-ZURI '84 Stamp Show. Sold for 3fr.

Fire
Prevention
A334

1984, Sept. 11   **Photo.**
750 A334 50c Flames, match   .70 .35

Railway Staff
Association,
Cent. — A335

Rheto-Roman
Culture
Bimillennium
A336

Lake Geneva
Rescue Soc.,
Cent. — A337

Intl. Congress
on Large
Dams,
Lausanne
A338

1985, Feb. 19   Photo.   *Perf. 12x11½*
751 A335 35c Conductor's hat,
              paraphernalia   .80 .25
752 A336 50c Engraved artifact,
              Chur   1.15 .40
753 A337 70c Rescuing drowning
              victim   1.60 .90
754 A338 80c Grande Dizence
              Dam, Canton
              Valais   1.90 1.00
  Nos. 751-754 (4)   5.45 2.50

Europa
1985 — A339

Designs: 50c, Ernest Ansermet (1883-
1969), composer, conductor. 80c, Frank Martin (1890-1974), composer.

1985, May 7   Photo.   *Perf. 11½x12*
755 A339 50c multicolored   1.15 .25
756 A339 80c multicolored   1.90 1.00

Swiss Master Bakers and Confectioners Federation, Bern, Cent. — A340

Swiss Radio Intl., 50th Anniv. A341

Postal, Telegraph & Telephone Intl. Congress, Sept. 16-21, Interlaken A342

1985, Sept. 10   Photo.   Perf. 12x11½

757	A340	50c Baker	1.15	.25
758	A341	70c multi	1.60	.75
759	A342	80c PTTI 75th anniv.	1.90	.90
		Nos. 757-759 (3)	4.65	1.90

Swiss Worker's Relief Org., 50th Anniv. A343

Battle of Sempach, 600th Anniv. A344

Roman Chur Bimillennium A345

Vindonissa Bimillennium A346

Zurich Bimillennium A347

1986, Feb. 11   Photo.   Perf. 12

772	A343	35c Knot	.80	.40
773	A344	50c Military map, 1698	1.15	.25
774	A345	80c Mercury statue	1.90	1.00
775	A346	90c Gallic head	2.10	1.00
776	A347	1.10fr Augustus coin	2.50	1.25
		Nos. 772-776 (5)	8.45	3.80

Europa 1986 A348

Mail Handling A349

1986, Apr. 22   Photo.   Perf. 13½

777	A348	50c Woman	1.15	.30
778	A348	90c Man	2.10	1.25

Photo. & Engr.

1986-89   Perf. 13½x13

779	A349	5c Franz mail van, 1911	.25	.25
780	A349	10c Parcel sorting	.25	.25
781	A349	20c Mule post	.45	.25
782	A349	25c Letter-facing, canceling	.60	.25
783	A349	30c Mail coach, 1735-1960	.70	.90
784	A349	35c Counter service	.80	.40
785	A349	45c Packet steamer, 1837-40	1.00	.45
786	A349	50c Postman, 1986	1.15	.35
a.		Bklt. pane of 10 ('88)	11.50	
787	A349	60c Loading airmail, 1986	1.40	.45
788	A349	75c 17th Cent. courier	1.75	.75
789	A349	80c Postman, ca. 1900	1.90	.80
790	A349	90c Railroad mail car	2.10	1.00
		Nos. 779-790 (12)	12.35	6.10

Issued: 5c, 10c, 25c, 35c, 80c, 90c, 9/9/86; 20c, 30c, 45c, 50c, 60c, 3/10/87; 75c, 3/7/89. For surcharge see No. B535.

Intl. Peace Year — A351

Swiss Winter Relief Fund, 50th Anniv. A352

Berne Convention for the Protection of Literary and Artistic Copyrights, Cent. — A353

25th Intl. Red Cross Conference, Geneva, Oct. 23-31 A354

1986, Sept. 9   Photo.   Perf. 12x11½

799	A351	35c multicolored	.80	.30
800	A352	50c multicolored	1.15	.25
801	A353	80c multicolored	1.90	1.00
802	A354	90c multicolored	2.10	1.10
		Nos. 799-802 (4)	5.95	2.65

Mobile P.O., 50th Anniv. A355

Lausanne University, 450th Anniv. A356

Swiss Engineers & Architects Assoc., Sesquicent. A357

Cointrin Airport-Geneva, Rail Link Opening, June 1, 1987 — A358

Baden Hot Springs, 2000th Anniv. A359

1987, Mar. 10   Photo.

803	A355	35c multicolored	.80	.35
804	A356	50c multicolored	1.15	.25
805	A357	80c multicolored	1.90	1.00
806	A358	90c multicolored	2.10	1.25
807	A359	1.10fr multicolored	2.50	1.50
		Nos. 803-807 (5)	8.45	4.35

Europa 1987 — A360

Sculpture: 50fr, Scarabaeus, 1979, by Bernard Luginbuhl. 90fr, Carnival Fountain, 1977, by Jean Tinguely, Basel Theater.

1987, May 26   Photo.   Perf. 11½

808	A360	50c multicolored	1.15	.30
809	A360	90c multicolored	2.10	1.25

Swiss Master Butchers' Federation, Cent. — A361

Stamp Day, 50th Anniv. A362

Swiss Dairy Assoc., Cent. — A363

1987, Sept. 4   Photo.   Perf. 12x11½

810	A361	35c multicolored	.80	.40
811	A362	50c multicolored	1.15	.40
812	A363	90c Cheesemaker	2.10	1.00
		Nos. 810-812 (3)	4.05	1.80

Tourism Industry, Bicent. — A364

Switzerland's four language regions: 50c, Clock Tower, Zug, German. 80c, Church of San Carlo, Blenio Valley, Italian. 90c, Witches' Tower, Sion Castle, French. 140c, Jorgenberg Castle ruins. Waltensburg/Vuorz. Surselva, Rhaeto-Romansh.

1987, Sept. 4   Perf. 11½

813	A364	50c multicolored	1.15	.40
814	A364	80c multicolored	1.90	.75
815	A364	90c multicolored	2.10	1.00
816	A364	140c multicolored	3.25	1.50
a.		Souvenir sheet of 4, #813-816	9.75	9.75
		Nos. 813-816 (4)	8.40	3.65

Swiss Women's Benevolent Soc., Cent. — A365

Swiss Hairdressers Assoc., Cent. — A366

Battle of Naefels, 600th Anniv. A367

European Campaign to Protect Undeveloped and Developing Lands A368

Intl. Music Festival, Lucerne, 50th Anniv. A369

1988, Mar. 8   Photo.   Perf. 12x11½

817	A365	25c multicolored	.60	.25
818	A366	35c multicolored	.80	.40
819	A367	50c Banner of St. Fridolin, medieval manuscript	1.15	.25
820	A368	80c multicolored	1.90	.90
821	A369	90c Girl playing a shawm	2.10	1.25
		Nos. 817-821 (5)	6.55	3.05

Europa 1988 — A370

1988, May 24   Photo.   Perf. 11½

822	A370	50c Arrows (transport)	1.15	.40
823	A370	90c Circuitry (communication)	2.10	1.25

Swiss Accident Prevention Office, 50th Anniv. A371

Assoc. of Metalworkers and Watchmakers, Cent. — A372

Federal Topography Office, 150th Anniv. A373

Intl. Red Cross Museum, Geneva A374

1988, Sept. 13 Photo. Perf. 12x11½
824	A371	35c multicolored	.80	.40
825	A372	50c multicolored	1.15	.25
826	A373	80c Triangulation pyramid, theodolite, map	1.90	.90
827	A374	90c multicolored	2.10	1.10
		Nos. 824-827 (4)	5.95	2.65

Metamecanique, by Jean Tinguely — A375

1988, Nov. 25 Photo. Perf. 13x12½
828	A375	90c multicolored	2.10	3.00

See France No. 2137.

Military Post, Cent. — A376

Delemont Municipal Charter, 700th Anniv. A377

Public Transport Assoc., Cent. — A378

Rhaetian Railway, Cent. — A379

Great St. Bernard Pass Bimillennium A380

25c, Army postman. 35c, Fontaine du Sauvage & the Porte au Loup, Delemont. 50c, Eye, modes of transportation. 80c, Train, viaduct. 90c, St. Bernard dog, statue of saint, hospice on summit.

1989, Mar. 2 Photo. Perf. 12x11½
829	A376	25c multicolored	.60	.25
830	A377	35c multicolored	.80	.40
831	A378	50c multicolored	1.15	.25
832	A379	80c multicolored	1.90	1.00
833	A380	90c multicolored	2.10	1.10
		Nos. 829-833 (5)	6.55	3.00

Europa — A381

Children's games: 50c, Hopscotch. 90c, Blindman's buff.

1989, May 23 Perf. 11½
834	A381	50c multicolored	1.15	.50
835	A381	90c multicolored	2.10	1.25

Industry — A382

Engr., Litho. & Eng. (2.80, 3, 3.60, 4, 5fr)
1989-94 Perf. 13x13½
842	A382	2.75fr Bricklayer	6.25	2.25
843	A382	2.80fr Cook	6.50	2.40
844	A382	3fr Cabinet maker	7.00	1.75
845	A382	3.60fr Pharmacist	8.25	3.00
846	A382	3.75fr Fisherman	8.75	3.50
847	A382	4fr Wine grower	9.25	3.00
848	A382	5fr Cheesemaker	11.50	4.00
849	A382	5.50fr Dressmaker	12.50	4.00
		Nos. 842-849 (8)	70.00	23.90

Issued: 2.75fr, 5.50fr, 8/29/89; 3.75fr, 3/6/90; 2.80fr, 3.60fr, 1/24/92; 5fr, 9/7/93; 4fr, 3/15/94; 3fr, 7/5/94.

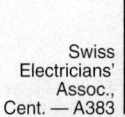

Swiss Electricians' Assoc., Cent. — A383

Swiss Travel Fund, 50th Anniv. A384

Fribourg University, Cent. — A385

Opening of the Natl. Sound-Recording Archives, 1st Anniv. — A386

Interparliamentary Union, Cent. — A387

1989, Aug. 25 Photo. Perf. 11½
851	A383	35c multicolored	.80	.45
852	A384	50c multicolored	1.15	.25
853	A385	80c "Wisdom" and "Science"	1.90	.80
854	A386	90c multicolored	2.10	1.00
855	A387	140c multicolored	3.25	1.25
		Nos. 851-855 (5)	9.20	3.75

Union of Swiss Philatelic Societies, Cent. — A388

Urban Railway System, Zurich A389

Assistance for Mountain Communities, 50th Anniv. A390

1990 World Ice Hockey Championships — A391

1990, Mar. 6
856	A388	25c 5c maroon type A19, 50c stamp type A20	.60	.25
857	A389	35c Locomotives	.80	.40
858	A390	50c Mountain farmer	1.15	.30
859	A391	90c Athletes	2.10	1.00
		Nos. 856-859 (4)	4.65	1.95

Europa 1990 — A393

Post offices.

Litho. & Engr.
1990, May 22 Perf. 13½
861	A393	50c Lucerne	1.15	.25
862	A393	90c Geneva	2.10	1.25

Conrad Ferdinand Meyer (1825-1898), Writer — A394

Designs: 50c, Angelika Kaufmann (1741-1807), painter. 80c, Blaise Cendrars (1887-1961), journalist. 90c, Frank Buchser (1828-1890), artist.

1990, Sept. 5 Litho.
863	A394	35c green & blk	.80	.40
864	A394	50c blue & blk	1.15	.30
865	A394	80c yellow & blk	1.90	.80
866	A394	90c vermilion & blk	2.10	1.10
		Nos. 863-866 (4)	5.95	2.60

Swiss Confederation, 700th Anniv. in 1991 — A395

1990, Sept. 5 Photo. Perf. 11½
867	A395	50c shown	1.15	.40
868	A395	90c multi, diff.	2.10	1.25

Natl. Census A396

1990, Nov. 20
869	A396	50c multicolored	1.15	.40

Animals — A397

1990-95 Litho. & Engr. Perf. 13
870	A397	10c Cow	.30	.25
871	A397	50c House cats	1.15	.30
872	A397	70c Rabbit	1.60	.65
a.		Booklet pane of 10	16.00	
		Complete booklet, #872a	16.00	
873	A397	80c Barn owls	1.90	.60
874	A397	100c Horses	2.25	.80
875	A397	110c Geese	2.50	.60
876	A397	120c Dog	2.75	1.00
877	A397	140c Sheep	3.25	.75
878	A397	150c Goats	3.50	.75
879	A397	160c Turkey	3.75	1.25
880	A397	170c Donkey	4.00	.90
881	A397	200c Chickens	4.50	1.75
		Nos. 870-881 (12)	31.45	9.60

Issued: 50c, 3/6/90; 70c, 80c, 1/15/91; 10c, 160c, 1/24/92; 100c, 120c, 3/16/93; 150c, 200c, 7/5/94; #872a, 110c, 140c, 170c, 11/28/95.

Swiss Confederation, 700th Anniv. — A398

Swiss Parliament, US Capitol A399

1991, Feb. 22 Photo. Perf. 12
884	A398	50c "700 jahre"	1.15	.25
885	A398	50c "700 onns"	1.15	.25
886	A398	50c "700 ans"	1.15	.25
887	A398	50c "700 anni"	1.15	.25
a.		Block of 4, #884-887	4.75	1.00
888	A399	1.60fr multicolored	3.75	.80
		Nos. 884-888 (5)	8.35	1.80

See US No. 2532.

Bern, 800th Anniv. — A400

1991, Feb. 22 Perf. 11½
889	A400	80c multicolored	1.90	.60

Europa — A401

1991, May 14 Litho. Perf. 11½
890	A401	50c Ariane payload fairing	1.15	.25
891	A401	90c Giotto probe	1.75	1.00

Union of Postal, Telephone and Telegraph Officials, Cent. — A402

1991, Sept. 10   Photo.   Perf. 11½
892 A402 80c multicolored   1.90   .70

Bridges A403

Designs: 50c, Stone bridge near Lavertezzo. 70c, Wooden "New Bridge" near Bremgarten. 80c, Railway bridge between Koblenz and Felsenau. 90c, Ganter Bridge, Simplon Pass.

1991, Sept. 10
893 A403 50c multicolored   1.15   .25
894 A403 70c multicolored   1.60   .55
895 A403 80c multicolored   1.90   .75
896 A403 90c multicolored   2.10   .90
       Nos. 893-896 (4)   6.75 2.45

Mountain Lakes — A404

A404a

A404b

Design: 50c, Lago Moesola. 60c, Lac de Tanay. 80c, Melchsee.

Litho., Litho. & Engr. (60c, #908)
1991-95   Perf. 13½x13
904 A404   50c shown   1.15   .25
905 A404   60c blue & multi   1.40   .25
  a.   Booklet pane of 10   14.00
907 A404   80c red & multi   1.90   .50
908 A404a 80c multicolored   1.90   .40
909 A404b 90c multicolored   2.10   .75
  a.   Booklet pane of 10   21.00
       Complete booklet, #909a   21.00
       Nos. 904-909 (5)   8.45 2.15

Issued: 50c, #907, 12/16/91; 60c, #908, 1/19/93; 90c, 11/28/95.
See No. 1102.

Bird Over Rhine River — A405

Faces of Parents, Child — A406

Molecular Formula, Structure and Model A407

1992, Mar. 24   Photo.   Perf. 11½
911 A405 50c multicolored   1.15   .25
912 A406 80c multicolored   1.90   .60
913 A407 90c multicolored   2.10 1.00
       Nos. 911-913 (3)   5.15 1.85

Intl. Rhine Regulation, cent. (No. 911), Pro Familia Switzerland, 50th anniv. (No. 912), Intl. Chemical Nomenclature Conf., Geneva, cent. (No. 913).

A408   A409

Europa: 90c, Columbus, map of voyage.

1992, Mar. 24
914 A408 50c multicolored   1.15   .50
915 A408 90c multicolored   2.10 1.10

Discovery of America, 500th anniv.

1992, May 22   Photo.   Perf. 12
916 A409 90c multicolored   2.10   .90

Protect the Alps.
See Austria No. 1571.

Comic Strips A410

1992, May 22   Perf. 11½
917 A410 50c Cosey   1.15   .30
918 A410 80c Zep   1.90   .60
919 A410 90c Aloys   2.10 1.00
       Nos. 917-919 (3)   5.15 1.90

World of the Circus A411

50c, Clowns on trapeze. 70c, Sea lion, clown. 80c, Clown, elephant. 90c, Lipizzaner, harlequin.

1992, Aug. 25   Photo.   Perf. 12x11½
920 A411 50c multicolored   1.15   .30
921 A411 70c multicolored   1.60   .60
922 A411 80c multicolored   1.90   .60
923 A411 90c multicolored   2.10 1.00
       Nos. 920-923 (4)   6.75 2.50

Central Office for Intl. Carriage by Rail, Cent. (in 1993) — A412

1992, Nov. 24   Photo.   Perf. 11½
924 A412 90c multicolored   2.10   .75

First Swiss Postage Stamps, 150th Anniv. — A413

Designs: 60c, Zurich Types A1, A2, Geneva Type A1. 80c, Stylized canceled stamp. 100c, Stylized stamps on album page.

Paracelsus (1493-1541), Physician A414

Opening of Olympic Museum, Lausanne A415

Intl. Metalworkers' Federation, Cent. — A416

1993, Mar. 16   Photo.   Perf. 11½
925 A413 60c multicolored   1.40   .50
926 A413 80c multicolored   1.90   .60
927 A413 100c multicolored   2.25 1.00
       Nos. 925-927 (3)   5.55 2.10

1993, Mar. 16   Photo.   Perf. 11½
928 A414 60c blue & sepia   1.40   .35
929 A415 80c multicolored   1.90   .60
930 A416 180c multicolored   4.25 1.75
       Nos. 928-930 (3)   7.55 2.85

Lake Constance Steamer Hohentwiel A417

1993, May 5   Photo.   Perf. 11½x12
931 A417 60c multicolored   1.40   .50

See Austria No. 1598, Germany No. 1786.

Contemporary Architecture A418

Europa: 60c, Media House, Villeurbanne, France. 80c, House, Breganzona, Switzerland.

Litho. & Engr.
1993, May 5   Perf. 13½
932 A418 60c multicolored   1.40   .40
933 A418 80c red & black   1.90   .90

Works of Art by Swiss Women A419

Designs: 60c, Work No. 095, by Emma Kunz. 80c, Grande Cantatrice Lilas Goergens, by Aloise Corbaz. 100c, Under the Rain Cloud, by Meret Oppenheim. 120c, Four Spaces in Horizontal Bands, by Sophie Taeuber-Arp.

1993, Sept. 7   Photo.   Perf. 11½
934 A419 60c multicolored   1.40   .40
       Size: 33x33½mm
935 A419 80c multicolored   1.90   .75
936 A419 100c multicolored   2.25 1.00
937 A419 120c multicolored   2.75 1.25
       Nos. 934-937 (4)   8.30 3.40

Swiss Sports School, 50th Anniv. A420

Jakob Bernoulli (1654-1705), Mathematician A421

Swiss Telecom PTT Participation in Unisource A422

ICAO, 50th Anniv. A423

1994, Mar. 15   Photo.   Perf. 11½
938 A420 60c multicolored   1.40   .40
939 A421 80c multicolored   1.90   .45
940 A422 100c multicolored   2.25   .85
941 A423 180c multicolored   4.25 1.25
       Nos. 938-941 (4)   9.80 2.95

Intl. Congress of Mathematicians, Zurich (#939).

"Books and the Press" Exhibition, Geneva A424

1994, Mar. 15
942 A424 60c Early manuscripts 1.40   .40
943 A424 80c Letterpress   1.90   .75
944 A424 100c Electronic publishing 2.25 1.00
       Nos. 942-944 (3)   5.55 2.15

1994 World Cup Soccer Championships, U.S. — A425

1994, Mar. 15
945 A425 80c multicolored   1.90   .65

Research Vehicles of August & Jacques Piccard — A426

Europa: 60c, Bathyscaphe Trieste. 100c, Stratospheric balloon.

1994, May 17   Photo.   Perf. 12
946 A426 60c multicolored   1.40   .50
947 A426 100c multicolored   2.25 1.00

Georges Simenon (1903-89), Writer A427

Litho. & Engr.
1994, Oct. 15 *Perf. 13*
948 A427 100c multicolored 2.25 .90
See Belgium No. 1567, France No. 2443.

A428 A429

1994, Oct. 15 Photo. *Perf. 11½*
949 A428 60c multicolored 1.40 .35
Campaign to stop AIDS.

1995, Mar. 7 Photo. *Perf. 11½*
Endangered species.
950 A429 60c European beaver 1.40 .30
951 A429 80c Map butterfly 1.90 .50
952 A429 100c Green tree frog 2.25 .75
953 A429 120c Litte owl 2.75 .90
Nos. 950-953 (4) 8.30 2.45

Swiss Wrestling Assoc., Cent. — A430

Swiss Assoc. of Producers & Distributors of Electricity, Cent. — A431

Swiss News Agency, Cent. — A432

UN, 50th Anniv. A433

1995, Mar. 7
954 A430 60c blue & black 1.40 .55
955 A431 60c multicolored 1.40 .55
956 A432 80c multicolored 1.90 1.50
957 A433 180c multicolored 4.25 1.75
Nos. 954-957 (4) 8.95 4.35

Peace & Freedom A434

Europa: 60c, Dove, faces. 100c, Zeus disguised as bull, abducting Europa, daughter of King of Phoenicia.

Litho., Engr. & Embossed
1995, May 16 *Perf. 13*
958 A434 60c lt blue & dk blue 1.40 .40
959 A434 100c orange & brown 2.25 .85

Switzerland-Liechtenstein Postal Relationship A435

Litho. & Engr.
1995, Sept. 5 *Perf. 13½*
960 A435 60c multicolored 1.40 .50
See Liechtenstein No. 1055.
No. 960 and Liechtenstein No. 1055 are identical. This issue was valid for postage in both countries.

Motion Pictures, Cent. — A436

Scenes from motion pictures: 60c, La Vocation d'Andre Carrel. 80c, Anna Goldin-The Last Witch. 150c, Pipilotti's Mistakes-Absolution.

1995, Sept. 5 Photo. *Perf. 11½*
961 A436 60c multicolored 1.40 .40
962 A436 80c multicolored 1.90 .70
963 A436 150c multicolored 3.50 1.25
Nos. 961-963 (3) 6.80 2.35

Telecom '95, Geneva — A437

1995, Sept. 5
964 A437 180c multicolored 4.25 1.00

Swiss Charities, Solidarity Chain, 50th Anniv. A438

Touring Club, Cent. — A439

Federal Music Festival, Interlaken A440

Swiss Natl. Assoc. Pro Filia, Cent. — A441

Jean Piaget (1896-1980), Psychologist A442

1996, Mar. 12 Photo. *Perf. 11½*
965 A438 70c multicolored 1.60 .50
966 A439 70c multicolored 1.60 .50
967 A440 90c multicolored 2.10 .60
968 A441 90c multicolored 2.10 .60
969 A442 180c multicolored 4.25 2.00
Nos. 965-969 (5) 11.65 4.20

Famous Women — A443

Europa: 70c, S. Corinna Bille (1912-79), author. 110c, Iris von Roten-Meyer (1917-90), writer, painter.

Litho. & Engr.
1996, May 14 *Perf. 13½*
970 A443 70c multicolored 1.60 .50
971 A443 110c multicolored 2.50 1.10

Modern Olympic Games, Cent. — A444

1996, May 14 Litho. *Perf. 13½*
972 A444 180c multicolored 4.25 1.50

Guinness Record Stamp — A445

Design: Aerial view of 11,000 gymnasts arranged as No. 909, making record as world's largest living postage stamp.

1996, June 27 Litho. *Perf. 13½x13*
973 A445 90c multicolored 2.10 .80

Greeting Stamps A446

Various ornate or floral patterns.

Serpentine Die Cut 7 Vert.
1996, Sept. 10 Typo.
Self-Adhesive
Booklet Stamps
974 A446 90c yellow & black 2.10 1.00
975 A446 90c blue & multi 2.10 1.00
976 A446 90c red & multi 2.10 1.00
977 A446 90c green & multi 2.10 1.00
a. Booklet pane of 4, #974-977 8.25
Complete booklet, 2 #977a 16.50

Music Boxes and Automata A447

Designs: 70c, Ring with mechanical figures, musical movement, by Isaac-Daniel Piguet. 90c, Basso-piccolo mandolin cylinder music box, by Eduard Jaccard. 110c, Station automaton, by Paillard and Co. 180c, Kalliope disk music box.

1996, Sept. 10 Photo. *Perf. 11½*
978 A447 70c multicolored 1.60 .40
979 A447 90c multicolored 2.10 .60
980 A447 110c multicolored 2.50 1.00
981 A447 180c multicolored 4.25 1.50
Nos. 978-981 (4) 10.45 3.50

Stamp Design Competition Winners — A448

Designs: 70c, Golden cow. 90c, Smiling creature. 110c, Leaves. 180c, Dove.

1996, Nov. 26 Photo. *Perf. 11½*
982 A448 70c blue & bister 1.60 .55
983 A448 90c multicolored 2.10 .80
984 A448 110c multicolored 2.50 1.00
985 A448 180c multicolored 4.25 1.75
Nos. 982-985 (4) 10.45 4.10

"Globi" as Postman A449

1997, Mar. 11 Litho. *Perf. 13x13½*
986 A449 70c multicolored 1.60 .45

Swiss Railways, 150th Anniv. A450

Designs: 70c, Locomotive 2000, 1990's. 90c, Red Arrow, 1930's. 140c, Pullman coach, 1920's-30's. 170c, Limmat steam locomotive, 1800's.

1997, Mar. 11 Photo. *Perf. 11½*
987 A450 70c multicolored 1.60 .40
988 A450 90c multicolored 2.10 .55
989 A450 140c multicolored 3.25 1.25
990 A450 170c multicolored 4.00 1.75
Nos. 987-990 (4) 10.95 3.95

Gallo-Roman Art — A451

Archaeological finds: 70c, Venus of Octodurus. 90c, Bronze bust of Bacchus. 110c, Ceramic fragment depicting Victoria. 180c, Mosaic theatrical mask.

1997, Mar. 11
991 A451 70c multicolored 1.60 .40
992 A451 90c multicolored 2.10 .50
993 A451 110c multicolored 2.50 .80
994 A451 180c multicolored 4.25 1.25
Nos. 991-994 (4) 10.45 2.95

Swiss Air's North Atlantic Service, 50th Anniv. — A452

1997, Mar. 11 Litho. *Perf. 13½*
995 A452 180c multicolored 4.25 1.10

Swiss Farmers' Union, Cent. — A453

1997, May 13   **Litho.**   **Perf. 13½**
996 A453 70c shown   1.60   .35
997 A453 90c Street map   2.10   .65
Swiss Municipalities' Union, cent. (#997).

Stories and Legends — A454

Europa: Devil and Billy Goat from legend of the "Devil's Bridge."

1997, May 13   **Litho. & Engr.**
998 A454 90c multicolored   2.10 1.10

King of Thailand's Visit to Switzerland, Cent. — A455

King Chulalongkorn (Rama V), Pres. Adolf Deucher.

1997, Sept. 12   **Litho.**   **Perf. 13½**
999 A455 90c multicolored   2.10   .75

Energy 2000 — A456

1997, Sept. 12   **Photo.**   **Perf. 11½**
1000 A456 70c Air (clouds)   1.60   .35
1001 A456 90c Fire   2.10   .65
1002 A456 110c Water   2.50   .95
1003 A456 180c Earth   4.25 1.50
    Nos. 1000-1003 (4)   10.45 3.45

Paul Karrer (1889-1971), Winner of Nobel Prize for Chemistry, 1937 — A457

Design: 110c, Alfred Nobel (1833-96), founder of Nobel Prize.

Litho. & Engr.
1997, Nov. 13   **Perf. 13**
1004 A457 90c gray & blk   2.10   .50
1005 A457 110c lt gray brn & blk   2.50   .75

Nos. 1004-1005 each issued in sheets of 8.
See Sweden Nos. 2254-2255.

Swiss Postal Service A458

Various people from different generations, cultures. Each stamp inscribed in one of Switzerland's four national languages with message to keep in touch.

1997, Nov. 20   **Litho.**   **Perf. 13**
Color of Denomination
1006 A458 70c blue   1.60   .40
1007 A458 70c yellow   1.60   .40
1008 A458 70c green   1.60   .40
1009 A458 70c red   1.60   .40
   a. Strip of 4, #1006-1009   6.50 6.50

Division of Swiss PTT — A459

1998, Jan. 7   **Litho.**   **Perf. 13½**
1010 A459 90c Swisscom   2.10   .40
1011 A459 90c Swiss Post   2.10   .40

Confederation, 150th Anniv. and Helvetic Republic, Bicent. — A460

Stylized design, proclamation in one of four languages, location of denomination: No. 1012, German, LL. No. 1013, Romansch, LR. No. 1014, French, UL. No. 1015, Italian, UR.

1998, Mar. 10   **Photo.**   **Perf. 11½**
1012 A460 90c multicolored   2.10 1.00
1013 A460 90c multicolored   2.10 1.00
1014 A460 90c multicolored   2.10 1.00
1015 A460 90c multicolored   2.10 1.00
   a. Block of 4, #1012-1015   8.50 5.00

Printed in continuous design.

Swiss Old Age and Survivors' Insurance, 50th Anniv. A461

Opening of Natl. Museum, Prangins Castle A462

St. Gallen University, Cent. — A463

1998, Mar. 10
1016 A461 70c multicolored   1.60   .40
1017 A462 70c multicolored   1.60   .40
1018 A463 90c multicolored   2.10   .80
    Nos. 1016-1018 (3)   5.30 1.60

View of Switzerland A464

Designs: 10c, Simplon Pass. 20c, Snow-covered winter scene. 50c, Fence posts along country road. 70c, Hobbyhorses, posts. 90c, Stream, route marker. 110c, Lake, shoreline.

1998, Mar. 10   **Litho.**   **Perf. 13x13½**
1019 A464 10c multicolored   .25   .25
1020 A464 20c multicolored   .45   .25
1021 A464 50c multicolored   1.15   .30
1022 A464 70c multicolored   1.60   .30
1023 A464 90c multicolored   2.10   .30
1024 A464 110c multicolored   2.50   .75
    Nos. 1019-1024 (6)   8.05 2.15

See Nos. 1027-1029.

Sion, Candidate for 2006 Winter Olympic Games — A465

1998, Feb. 12   **Litho.**   **Perf. 13½**
1025 A465 90c multicolored   2.10   .75

National Day — A466

1998, May 12
1026 A466 90c multicolored   2.10 1.10

Europa.

View of Switzerland Type of 1998

140c, City of Zug. 170c, Olive grove, Castagnola. 180c, Road, mountains outside Reutigen.

1998, Sept. 8   **Litho.**   **Perf. 13**
1027 A464 140c multicolored   3.25   .50
1028 A464 170c multicolored   4.00   .60
1029 A464 180c multicolored   4.25   .75
    Nos. 1027-1029 (3)   11.50 1.85

Youth Sports — A467

Die Cut x Serpentine Die Cut
1998, Sept. 8   **Photo.**
Self-Adhesive
Booklet Stamps
1030 A467 70c Roller blading   1.60   .50
1031 A467 70c Snow boarding   1.60   .50
1032 A467 70c Mountain biking   1.60   .50
1033 A467 70c Street basketball   1.60   .50
1034 A467 70c Beach volleyball   1.60   .50
   a. Booklet pane, #1030-1034 + label   8.00
    Complete booklet, 2 #1034a   16.00

Universal Declaration of Human Rights, 50th Anniv. — A468

1998, Nov. 25   **Litho.**   **Perf. 13½**
1035 A468 70c multicolored   1.60   .50

Christmas A469

1998, Nov. 25
1036 A469 90c multicolored   2.10   .75

Bridge 24, Slender West Lake, Yangzhou A470

Chillon Castle, Lake Geneva A470A

Photo. & Engr.
1998, Nov. 25   **Perf. 13½**
1037 A470 20c multicolored   .45   .25
Photo.
1038 A470A 70c multicolored   1.60   .55
   a. Sheet of 4 each, #1038-1039   15.00 15.00
Souvenir Sheet
Perf. 11½
1039 A470A 90c Castle, Bridge 24   2.10 1.50

No. 1039 contains one 53x45mm stamp. See China (PRC) Nos. 2920-2921.
No. 1039 exists with China 1999 World Philatelic Exhibition emblem and a hologram in margin. These were sold for 3.50fr only canceled on cover.

Switzerland Post, 150th Anniv. A471

1999, Jan. 21   **Photo.**   **Perf. 12**
1040 A471 90c multicolored   2.10   .75

Pingu the Penguin as Postman A472

1999, Mar. 9   **Litho.**   **Perf. 13½**
1041 A472 70c Carrying package   1.60   .50
1042 A472 90c In delivery cart   2.10   .65

See Nos. 1064-1065 for redrawn designs.

Comic Book, "Les Amours de Monsieur Vieux Bois," by Rodolphe Töpffer (1799-1846) A473

Vieux Bois: No. 1043, Waving out of window, lady walking away. No. 1044, Down on knees, lady. No. 1045, In air after knocking over furniture. No. 1046, Pulling lady up to lift her over wall. No. 1047, Standing with his lady to be married.

Die Cut x Serpentine Die Cut
1999, Mar. 9
Self-Adhesive
Booklet Stamps
1043 A473 90c multicolored   2.10   .55
1044 A473 90c multicolored   2.10   .55
1045 A473 90c multicolored   2.10   .55
1046 A473 90c multicolored   2.10   .55
1047 A473 90c multicolored   2.10   .55
   a. Booklet pane, #1043-1047 + label   10.50
    Complete booklet, 2 #1047a   21.00

First Non-stop Balloon Flight Around World by Bertrand Piccard and Brian Jones — A473a

1999, Mar. 24   **Litho.**   **Perf. 13½**
1047B A473a 90c multicolored   2.10   .55

UPU, 125th Anniv. — A474

1999, May 5   Photo.   Perf. 12
1048 A474 20c shown   .45   .25
1049 A474 70c UPU emblem   1.60   .65
  a.   Pair, #1048-1049   2.10 1.25

No. 1049 is 56x30mm. Issued in sheets of 8 stamps.

SOS Children's Village, Wabern, 50th Anniv. — A475

1999, May 5   Litho.   Perf. 13½
1050 A475 70c multicolored   1.60   .45

Vintners Festival, Vevey — A476

1999, May 5
1051 A476 90c multicolored   2.10   .55
      Complete booklet, 10 #1051   21.00

Council of Europe, 50th Anniv. — A477

1999, May 5   Photo.   Perf. 11½
1052 A477 90c multicolored   2.10   .55

Swiss National Park — A478

1999, May 5   Litho.   Perf. 13½
1053 A478 90c Horns of an ibex   2.10 1.10
      Europa.

Geneva Convention, 50th Anniv. — A479

1999, May 5
1054 A479 110c multicolored   2.50   .85

Field Marshal Aleksandr Suvorov's Alpine Campaign, 200th Anniv. A481

Designs: 70c, Suvorov and soldiers, monument at Schöllenen Gorge. 110c, Suvorov's vanguard by Lake Klöntal.

1999, Sept. 24   Photo.   Perf. 11¾
1056 A481 70c multicolored   1.60   .50
1057 A481 110c multicolored   2.50   .70

Nos. 1056-1057 each issued in sheets of 8 stamps.
See Russia Nos. 6534-6535.

Rights of the Child — A482

1999, Sept. 24   Litho.   Perf. 13½
1058 A482 70c multicolored   1.60   .45

Carl Lutz (1895-1975), Diplomat, Rescuer of Jews — A483

1999, Sept. 24
1059 A483 90c multicolored   2.10   .55

Christian Friedrich Schönbein (1799-1868), Discoverer of Ozone — A484

1999, Sept. 24
1060 A484 1.10fr multicolored   2.50   .60

Midday in the Alps, by Giovanni Segantini (1858-99) A485

1999, Sept. 24
1061 A485 180c multicolored   4.25 1.25

Christmas — A486

Perf. 13½x13¼
1999, Nov. 23   Litho.
1062 A486 90c multicolored   2.10   .75

Millennium A487

Perf. 11¾x11½
1999, Nov. 23   Photo.
1063 A487 90c multicolored   1.40   .55

No. 1063 was printed in sheets of 8 stamps and 8 se-tenant labels with text or blank. Swiss Post offered to print photos or artwork sent in by customers on the blank labels. Personalized sheets sold for 14fr per sheet.

Pingu The Penguin Type of 1999
Redrawn to Omit Strings on Packages
1999, Dec. 6   Litho.   Perf. 13¼x13½
1064 A472 90c Like #1041   1.60   .55
1065 A472 90c Like #1042   2.10   .70

Intl. Cycling Union, Cent. — A488

2000, Mar. 7   Litho.   Perf. 13¼x13½
1066 A488 70c multicolored   1.60   .40

Swiss Souvenirs — A489

Souvenirs in snow domes: 10c, Alphorn. 20c, Fondue pot. 30c, Wine pitchers. 50c, Figurine of ibex. 60c, Neuchâtel "Pendule" wall clock. 70c, St. Bernard dog.

2000, Mar. 7   Litho.   Perf. 13x13¼
1067 A489 10c multicolored   .25   .25
1068 A489 20c multicolored   .45   .25
1069 A489 30c multicolored   .70   .35
1070 A489 50c multicolored   1.15   .45
1071 A489 60c multicolored   1.40   .50
1072 A489 70c multicolored   1.10   .60
      Nos. 1067-1072 (6)   5.05 2.40
      See No. 1101.

National Council of Women, Cent. A490

2000, May 10   Litho.   Perf. 13¼
1073 A490 70c multi   1.60   .55

Europa, 2000
Common Design Type
2000, May 10
1074 CD17 90c multi   2.10   .75

Embroidery — A491

Embroidered
2000, June 21   Imperf.
Self-Adhesive
1075 A491 5fr multi   16.00 16.00
  a.   Sheet of 4   225.00 225.00

A492

Designs: 120c, Payerne Church, violin. 130c, Church of St. Saphorin, waiter's tray. 180c, Vals hot springs, bather.

2000, June 21   Litho.   Perf. 13x13¼
1076 A492 120c multi   2.75   .75
1077 A492 130c multi   3.00   .80
1078 A492 180c multi   4.25 1.00
      Nos. 1076-1078 (3)   10.00 2.55
      See Nos. 1089-1092, 1103-1105.

2000 Census — A493

2000, Sept. 15   Perf. 13¼x13½
1079 A493 70c multi   1.60   .55

A Perfect World, by Sandra Dobler A494

My Town, by Stephanie Aerschmann A495

Stampin' the Future children's stamp design contest winners: No. 1080, Alien From Outer Space, by Yannik Kehrli. No. 1081, Looks Below the Sun, by Charlotte Bättig.

Serpentine Die Cut 5¾ Vert.
2000, June 15
Booklet Stamps
Self-Adhesive
1080 A494 70c multi   1.60   .60
1081 A494 70c multi   1.60   .60
1082 A494 70c shown   1.60   .60
1083 A495 70c shown   1.60   .60
  a.   Booklet pane, #1080-1083   6.50
        Booklet, 2 #1083a   13.00

The booklet, which was sold unfolded, has rouletting between panes.

2000 Summer Olympics, Sydney A496

2000, Sept. 15   Photo.   Die Cut
Booklet Stamps
Self-Adhesive
1084 A496 90c Swimmer   2.10   .60
1085 A496 90c Cyclist   2.10   .60
1086 A496 90c Runner   2.10   .60
  a.   Booklet pane, #1084-1086   6.50
        Booklet, #1086a   6.50

No. 1086a is separated from booklet cover by rouletting. The booklet was sold folded. See Nos. 1201-1202.

Stamp Day — A497

2000, Nov. 21   Perf. 13¼x13½
**   Litho.**
1087 A497 70c multi   1.60   .40

Christmas — A498

2000, Nov. 21   Photo.   *Perf. 11½*
Granite Paper
1088   A498   90c multi   2.10   .50
See No. 1197c.

Type of 2000
Designs: 200c, Mountain, hiker. 220c, Postbus, children. 300c, Cyclist, bridge and church, Biasca. 400c, Airplane at airport, tourist with suitcase.

2000-01   Litho.   *Perf. 13x13¼*
1089   A492   200c multi   4.50   2.00
1090   A492   220c multi   5.00   2.25
1091   A492   300c multi   7.00   3.00
1092   A492   400c multi   9.25   3.75
Issued: 200c, 300c, 11/21/00. 220c, 400c, 3/13/01.

Alice Rivaz
(1901-98),
Writer — A499

Perf. 13¼x13½
2001, Mar. 13   Litho. & Engr.
1093   A499   70c multi   1.60   .40

Aero Club,
Cent.
A500

2001, Mar. 13   Litho.   *Perf. 13¼*
1094   A500   90c multi   2.10   .55

Congratulations
A501

2001, Mar. 13   *Perf. 13¼x13½*
1095   A501   90c multi   2.10   .60

Caritas,
Cent. — A502

2001, Mar. 13
1096   A502   110c multi   2.50   .75

UN High
Commissioner
for Refugees,
50th
Anniv. — A503

2001, Mar. 13
1097   A503   130c multi   3.00   1.00

Vela Museum,
Ligornetto
A504

2001, May 9
1098   A504   70c multi   1.60   .50

Europa — A505

2001, May 9
1099   A505   90c multi   2.10   .60

Chocosuisse,
Cent. — A506

2001, May 9   Photo.   *Perf. 11½*
Granite Paper
1100   A506   90c multi   2.10   .50
No. 1100 has a scratch-and-sniff coating with a chocolate aroma.

Swiss Souvenirs Type of 2000
Serpentine Die Cut 5¾ Horiz.
2001, May 9   Litho.
Self-Adhesive
1101   A489   70c Like #1072   1.60   .40
   a.   Booklet of 12   19.50
No. 1101 was issued in coil rolls of 100 with backing paper wider than the stamp and the stamps spaced. Also issued in booklets with different backing paper with stamps adjoining. Used examples of each variety are identical.

Type of 1995
Serpentine Die Cut 5¾ Vert.
2001, May 9   Typo.
Self-Adhesive
1102   A404b   90c multi   2.10   .45
   a.   Booklet of 12   25.00

Type of 2000
Designs: 90c, Farm house, Willisau, people feeding horse. 100c, Boat on Lake Geneva, woman at water's edge. 110c, Kleine Matterhorn Glacier, skier.

2001, Sept. 20   Litho.   *Perf. 13x13¼*
1103   A492   90c multi   2.10   .50
1104   A492   100c multi   2.25   .50
1105   A492   110c multi   2.50   .60
   Nos. 1103-1105 (3)   6.85   1.60

The Birth of Venus,
by Arnold Böcklin
(1827-1901)
A507

2001, Sept. 20   *Perf. 13½*
1106   A507   180c multi   4.25   2.00

Souvenir Sheet

Flowers — A508

2001, Sept. 20   *Perf. 13¼x12¾*
1107   A508   Sheet of 4   11.00   11.00
   a.   70c Melastoma
       malabathricum   1.60   .80
   b.   90c Saraca cauliflora   2.10   .90
   c.   110c Leontopodium alpinum   2.00   1.25
   d.   130c Gentiana clusii   3.00   1.50
See Singapore Nos. 984-988.

Illustrations from
Children's Book,
"The Rainbow
Fish," by Marcus
Pfister — A509

2001, Sept. 20   Photo.   *Perf. 12¾x14*
1108   A509   70c Fish, coral   1.60   .40
1109   A509   90c Fish, starfish   2.10   .50

Stamp Day
Stamp Design
Competition
Winner — A510

Perf. 13¼x13½
2001, Nov. 20   Litho.
1110   A510   70c multi   1.60   .45

Christmas — A511

2001, Nov. 20   *Perf. 11½*
Granite Paper
1111   A511   90c multi   2.10   .60
See No. 1197a.

Geneva
Escalade, 400th
Anniv. — A512

Perf. 13¼x13½
2002, Mar. 12   Litho.
1112   A512   70c multi   1.60   .40

Federal
Parliament
Building,
Cent. — A513

2002, Mar. 12
1113   A513   90c multi   2.10   .50

Rega Air
Rescue
Foundation
A514

Litho. with Hologram Affixed
2002, Mar. 12   *Perf. 13x13¾*
1114   A514   180c multi   4.25   2.00

Expo.02, Switzerland — A515

No. 1115: a, "E." b, Backwards "P." c, "0." d, "2."

2002, Mar. 12   Photo.   *Perf. 14x13¼*
Granite Paper
1115   A515   Block of 4   6.50   4.50
   a.-d.   70c Any single   1.60   .80

Swiss Railways,
Cent. — A516

Designs: 70c, RABDe 500 Inter-city tilting train. 90c, Inter-city 2000 double-deck train. 120c, Seetal line railcar. 130c, Re 460 locomotive.

2002, Mar. 12   *Perf. 12¾x14*
1116   A516   70c multi   1.60   .40
1117   A516   90c multi   2.10   .70
1118   A516   120c multi   2.75   .75
1119   A516   130c multi   3.00   1.00
   Nos. 1116-1119 (4)   9.45   2.85

Souvenir Sheet

Arteplage Mobile du Jura — A517

2002, May 15   Photo.   *Perf. 14*
1120   A517   90c multi   2.10   1.25
Expo.02, Switzerland.

Europa
A518

2002, May 15   Litho.   *Perf. 13¼*
1121   A518   70c Clown   1.60   .40
1122   A518   90c Clown, diff.   2.10   .50

Teddy Bears, Cent. — A519

No. 1123 — Teddy bear from: a, France, 1925 (round, with tan frame, 26mm diameter). b, Switzerland, 1950s (square with cut in corners, 25x25mm). c, Germany, 1904 (oval, 23x33mm). d, Switzerland, 2002 (rectangular, 26x23mm). e, England, c. 1920 (round, with blue and red frame, 26mm diameter).

2002, May 15   *Die Cut*
Self-Adhesive
1123   A519   Booklet pane of 5   10.50
   a.-e.   90c Any single   2.10   1.00
   f.   Booklet, 2 #1123   21.00

Cessation of
Production
at Swiss
Post Stamp
Printers
A520

Litho. & Engr.

2002, Sept. 17   **Perf. 13¼**
1124 A520 70c multi   1.60 .40

Ladybug — A521

Serpentine Die Cut 12¼ Vert.
2002, Sept. 17   **Litho.**
Self-Adhesive
1125 A521 90c multi + label   2.10 .55
  a. Booklet pane of 10   21.00

Insects — A522

Designs: 10c, Anax imperator. 20c, Mesoacidalia aglaja. 50c, Rosalia alpina. 100c, Graphosoma lineatum.

Perf. 13¾x14¼
2002, Sept. 17   **Litho.**
1126 A522 10c multi   .25 .25
1127 A522 20c multi   .45 .25
1128 A522 50c multi   1.15 .25
1129 A522 100c multi   2.25 .30
  Nos. 1126-1129 (4)   4.10 1.05

Minerals — A523

Designs: 200c, Quartz crystal. 500c, Titanite.

2002-05   **Litho.**   **Perf. 13¾**
1130 A523 200c multi   4.50 1.50
1131 A523 500c multi   11.50 2.75
  a. Perf. 13¾x14¼   11.50 2.75
  Issued: Nos. 1130-1131, 9/17/02. No. 1131a, 5/10/05.

Switzerland's Entry Into United Nations — A524

Perf. 13¾x14¼
2002, Sept. 10   **Litho.**
1132 A524 90c multi   2.10 .50

Stamp Day — A525

2002, Nov. 19   **Perf. 13¾x14**
1133 A525 70c multi   1.60 .45

World Alpine Skiing Championships, St. Moritz — A526

2002, Nov. 19   **Perf. 14x13¾**
1134 A526 90c multi   2.10 .50

Emblem of Switzerland Tourism — A527

Serpentine Die Cut 13¼ Vert.
2002, Nov. 19
Self-Adhesive
1135 A527 (1.30fr) blue & multi   3.00 .50
  a. Booklet pane of 6   18.00
1136 A527 (1.80fr) red & multi   4.25 .75
  a. Booklet pane of 6   25.00

Nos. 1135-1136 were valid only on post cards sent to European (#1135) or non-European (#1136) addresses, and could not be used in combination with other stamps. No. 1135a sold for 7.20fr, and No. 1136a for 10fr.

Christmas — A528

2002, Nov. 19   Photo.   Perf. 11½
Granite Paper
1137 A528 90c multi   2.10 .50
  See No. 1197b.

Swiss Natl. Association of and for the Blind, Cent. — A529

Litho. & Embossed
2003, Mar. 6   **Perf. 14¾x14½**
1138 A529 70c red & carmine   1.60 .45

100th Natl. Horse Market and Show, Saignelégier A530

2003, Mar. 6   Litho.   Perf. 13¼x13½
1139 A530 90c multi   2.10 .50

2003 World Orienteering Championships, Rapperswil and Jona — A531

2003, Mar. 6
1140 A531 90c multi   2.10 .50

Intl. Year of Water A532

2003, Mar. 6   **Perf. 13x13¼**
1141 A532 90c multi   2.10 .50

Medicinal Plants — A533

Designs: 70c, Hypericum perforatum. 90c, Vinca minor. 110c, Valeriana officinalis. 120c, Arnica montana. 130c, Centaurium minus. 180c, Malva sylvestris. 220c, Matricaria chamomilla.

2003-05   **Perf. 14x13¾**
1142 A533 70c multi   1.60 .50
1143 A533 90c multi   2.10 .50
1144 A533 110c multi   2.50 .65
1145 A533 120c multi   2.75 .75
  a. Perf. 14x14½   2.75 .40
1146 A533 130c multi   3.00 .90
1147 A533 180c multi   4.25 1.10
  a. Perf. 14x14½   4.25 .60
1148 A533 220c multi   5.00 1.50
  a. Perf. 14x14½   5.00 .70
  Nos. 1142-1148 (7)   21.20 5.90
  Issued: Nos. 1142-1148, 3/6/03; Nos. 1145a, 1147a, 1148a, 2005.

Europa — A534

2003, May 8   Litho.   Perf. 13¼x13
1149 A534 90c multi   2.10 .50

Comic Strip Art — A535

No. 1150 — Envelope and: a, Woman, birthday cake. b, Man, heart. c, Man, thunder cloud. d, Woman, musical note. 90c, Envelope, woman, duck.

2003, May 8   **Perf. 14¾**
1150 A535   Block of 4   6.50 4.00
  a.-d. 70c Any single   1.60 .50
Souvenir Sheet
1151 A535 90c multi   2.50 1.25
  20th Intl. Comics Festival, Sierre.

Souvenir Sheet

Trilateral Stamp Exhibition, Ticino — A536

2003, May 8   **Perf. 14¾**
1152 A536   Sheet of 2   2.50 2.50
  a. 20c Eagle   .45 .25
  b. 70c Gentian   1.60 .40

Switzerland's Victory in 2003 America's Cup Yacht Races — A537

2003, Mar 7   Litho.   Perf. 13x13¼
1153 A537 90c multi   2.10 .45
  No. 1153 was not sent to standing order subscribers until September.

Minerals Type of 2002

Designs: 300c, Rutilated quartz. 400c, Green fluorite.

2003, Sept. 9   **Perf. 13¾x14¼**
1154 A523 300c multi   7.00 2.00
1155 A523 400c multi   9.25 3.00

Comic Strip "Diddl," by Thomas Goletz — A538

Designs: 70c, Mice reading love letters. 90c, Mouse chasing flying envelopes.

2003, Sept. 9   **Perf. 13¼x13½**
1156 A538 70c multi   1.60 .45
1157 A538 90c multi   2.10 .55
  See Nos. 1184-1185.

UNESCO World Heritage Sites — A539

Designs: No. 1158, Jungfrau-Aletsch-Bietschhorn. No. 1159, Three Castles, Bellinzona. No. 1160, Old City, Bern. No. 1161, Convent of St. Gall. No. 1162, Benedictine Convent of St. John, Müstair.

2003, Sept. 9   **Perf. 12¾**
1158 A539 90c multi   2.10 .55
1159 A539 90c multi   2.10 .55
1160 A539 90c multi   2.10 .55
1161 A539 90c multi   2.10 .55
1162 A539 90c multi   2.10 .55
  Nos. 1158-1162 (5)   10.50 2.75
  Nos. 1158-1162 each issued in sheets of 6. See NO. 1186.

Stamp Day — A540

Perf. 13¼x13½
2003, Nov. 19   **Litho.**
1163 A540 70c multi   1.60 .45

Four-leaf Clover — A541

Serpentine Die Cut 12¼ Vert.
2003, Nov. 19
Self-Adhesive
1164 A541 130c multi + label   3.00 .65
  a. Booklet of 10   30.00

Christmas — A542

Ornaments: 70c, Horseman. 90c, Santa Claus.

2003, Nov. 19   Photo.   Perf. 11½
1165 A542 70c multi   1.60   .45
1166 A542 90c multi   2.10   .55

See Nos. 1197d-1197e.

Swiss Design — A543

Designs: 15c, Rex potato peeler, 1947, designed by Alfred Neweczeral. 50c, Zipper, 1924, designed by M.O. Winterthaler. 85c, Station clock, 1944, designed by Hanls Hilfiker. No. 1169, Le Fauteuil Grand Confort (black armchair), 1928, designed by Le Corbusier. No. 1170, Landi chair (aluminum chair), 1938, designed by Hans Coray.

Serpentine Die Cut 12
2003-04   Litho.
Self-Adhesive
1167 A543 15c multi   .35   .25
  a.   Booklet pane of 10   3.50
1168 A543 85c multi   2.00 .30
  a.   Booklet pane of 10   19.50
1169 A543 100c multi + etiquette 2.25 .30
  a.   Booklet pane of 10 + 10 etiquettes 25.00
  b.   Nos. 1167-1169 on translucent paper 4.50
1170 A543 100c multi + etiquette 2.25 .30
  a.   Booklet pane of 10 + 10 etiquettes 25.00
Coil Stamp
1171 A543 50c multi   1.15 .25
      Nos. 1167-1171 (5)   8.00 1.40

Issued: 15c, 85c, No. 1169, 12/30; No. 1170, 3/31/04; 50c, 9/7/04.
See No. 1206.

FIFA (Fédération Internationale de Football Association), Cent. — A544

2004, Mar. 9   Perf. 13¼
1172 A544 100c multi   2.25 .55

UEFA (European Football Union), 50th Anniv. — A545

2004, Mar. 9   Perf. 13¼x13½
1173 A545 130c multi   3.00 .65

CERN (European Organization for Nuclear Research), 50th Anniv. — A546

2004, Mar. 9   Perf. 13½x13¼
1174 A546 180c multi   4.25 .90

Comic Strip "Titeuf," by Zep — A547

Titeuf: No. 1175, Giving spring flower to Nadia. No. 1176, Sitting in refrigerator. No. 1177, Running through raked leaves. No. 1178, Pointing at snowman.

2004, Mar. 9   Perf. 14x13½
1175 A547 85c multi   2.00 .45
1176 A547 85c multi   2.00 .45
1177 A547 85c multi   2.00 .45
1178 A547 85c multi   2.00 .45
      Nos. 1175-1178 (4)   8.00 1.80

Souvenir Sheet

Cycling — A548

No. 1179 — Cyclists and marker for: a, Route 5. b, Route 3.

2004, Mar. 9   Perf. 14x13½
1179 A548 Sheet of 2   5.50 5.50
  a.-b.   100c Either single   2.25 .55

Doorbell Button — A549

2004, May 6   Perf. 14½x14¼
1180 A549 85c multi   2.00 .45

Europa A550

2004, May 6   Perf. 14¼x14½
1181 A550 100c multi   2.25 .55

2004 Summer Olympics, Athens A551

2004, May 6   Perf. 13x13¼
1182 A551 100c multi   2.25 .55

See No. 1203.

Zeppelin NT — A552

2004, May 6   Perf. 14x13½
1183 A552 180c multi   4.25 .90

Diddl Type of 2003

Designs: 85c, Diddl with teddy bear, Pimboli, and butterflies. 100c, Diddl with flower.

2004, May 6   Perf. 13¼x13½
1184 A538 85c multi   2.00 .45
1185 A538 100c multi   2.25 .55

UNESCO World Heritage Type of 2003

Design: Monte San Giorgio.

2004, Sept. 7   Perf. 13¾x14¼
1186 A539 100c multi   2.25 .55

Issued in sheets of 6.

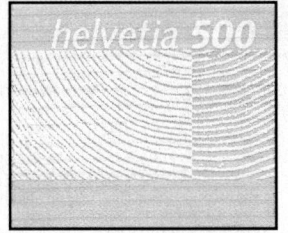

Suisse Balance Health Program A553

2004, Sept. 7   Perf. 13¼x13½
1187 A553 85c multi   2.00 .45

Wood — A554

Silk-screened on Wood
2004, Sept. 7   Imperf.
Self-Adhesive
1188 A554 500c white   11.50 2.75

Cheesemaking A555

Designs: 100c, Cheesemaker inspecting curds and whey. 130c, Cheeses, grapes and nuts.

2004, Sept. 7   Litho.   Perf. 13¼x13½
1189 A555 100c multi   2.25 .55
1190 A555 130c multi   3.00 .70

Animal Protection A556

2004, Sept. 7   Perf. 14x13½
1191 A556 85c Cat   2.00 .45
1192 A556 100c Hedgehog   2.25 .55
1193 A556 130c Pig   3.00 .70
      Nos. 1191-1193 (3)   7.25 1.70

Nos. 1191-1193 each issued in sheets of 6.

Souvenir Sheet

Sitting Helvetia Stamps and Coins, 150th Anniv. — A557

No. 1194: a, Type A17. b, Coin.

Litho. (#1194a), Litho. & Embossed (#1194b)
Perf. 14¼x13¾ on 3 Sides
2004, Sept. 7
1194 A557 Sheet of 2   4.50 4.50
  a.-b.   85c Either single   2.00 .45

Stamp Day — A558

Perf. 13¼x13½
2004, Nov. 23   Litho.
1195 A558 85c multi   2.00 .50

Sports A559

2004, Nov. 23 Litho. Perf. 13x13½
1196 A559 180c multi   4.25 1.10

No. 1196 is identical to United Nations Offices in Geneva No. 433. The stamp, available for use throughout Switzerland, also served as an official stamp for the International Olympic Committee.

Christmas Ornaments Types of 2000-2003
2004, Nov. 23 Photo. Perf. 13x13½
1197   Sheet of 5   12.50 12.50
  a.   A511 85c Snowflake   2.00 .50
  b.   A528 85c Church   2.00 .50
  c.   A498 100c Angel   2.25 .60
  d.   A542 100c Horseman   2.25 .60
  e.   A542 100c Santa Claus   2.25 .60

Photographs by René Burri — A560

No. 1198: a, Children kissing, German inscription. b, Teenagers on bicycle, French inscription. c, Man and woman kissing, Italian inscription. d, Man and woman in bumper car, Romansch inscription.

Serpentine Die Cut 12
2005, Jan. 3   Litho.
Self-Adhesive
1198   Block of 4, #a-d + 4 etiquettes 9.25
  a.-d. A560 100c Any single   2.25 .35
  e.   Booklet pane, 2 each #1198a-1198d + 8 etiquettes 18.50

No. 1198 lacks self-adhesive selvage, and is on a translucent paper that is rouletted on the left and right sides. No. 1198e has a white paper backing, has each stamp and its se-tenant etiquette surrounded by self-adhesive selvage, and is rouletted through the selvage and backing paper.

Swiss Federal Institute of Technology, Zurich, 150th Anniv. A561

2005, Mar. 8   *Perf. 13*
1199 A561 85c multi   2.00   .50

Matterhorn Superimposed Over Inverted Map of Africa — A562

2005, Mar. 8   *Perf. 13x13¼*
1200 A562 85c multi   2.00   .50
Discovery of rocks from Africa making up top of the Matterhorn.

Unspunnen Traditional Costume and Alpine Herdsman's Festival, Bicent. — A563

2005, Mar. 8   *Perf. 13¼x13*
1201 A563 100c multi   2.25   .60

Albert Einstein's Theory of Relativity, Cent. — A564

2005, Mar. 8   *Perf. 13½x13¼*
1202 A564 130c multi   3.00   .75

Cartoon Mouse, by Uli Stein — A565

Mouse with: 85c, Slice of Swiss cheese in typewriter. 100c, Golf club and letter on tee.

2005, Mar. 8   *Perf. 13¼x13½*
1203 A565 85c multi   2.00   .50
1204 A565 100c multi   2.25   .60

Souvenir Sheet

Geneva International Auto Show, Cent. — A566

2005, Mar. 8   *Perf. 13¾x14¼*
1205 A566   Sheet of 2   14.50 14.50
   a.   100c Front of car   2.25   .60
   b.   130c Side of car   3.00   .75

Swiss Design Type of 2003-04
Design: Fixpencil, by Caran d'Ache.
2005, May 10   *Serpentine Die Cut 12*
Self-Adhesive
1206 A543 220c multi + etiquette   5.00   .75
   a.   Serpentine die cut 12¼x12 + etiquette   5.00   .75
   b.   Booklet pane, 6 #1206, 4 #1206a + 10 etiquettes   50.00

Europa A567

2005, May 10   *Perf. 13x13¼*
1207 A567 100c multi   2.25   .60

Soccer for the Visually Impaired A568

2005, May 10   *Perf. 13¾x14¼*
1208 A568 100c multi   2.25   .60
Printed in sheets of 6.

Opening of Paul Klee Center, Bern — A569

2005, May 10   *Perf. 13¼x14*
1209 A569 100c multi   2.25   .60
Printed in sheets of 6.

Stylized Butterflies A570

Serpentine Die Cut 11¾
2005, May 10
Self-Adhesive
1210 A570 100c multi   2.25   .60
   a.   Booklet pane of 10 + 10 labels   25.00

Felix the Bunny, by Annette Langen A571

Felix and: 85c, Lambs, cows. 100c, Swans and Chillon Castle.

2005, May 10   *Perf. 13x13¼*
1211 A571 85c multi   2.00   .50
1212 A571 100c multi   2.25   .60

Subtractive Color Combinations — A572

Additive Color Combinations — A573

Serpentine Die Cut 12½
2005, Sept. 6   Litho.
Self-Adhesive
1213 A572 50c multi   1.15   .30
1214 A573 100c multi   2.25   .55

Swiss Timepieces A574

Designs: 100c, Watchmaker, pocket watch and mechanism. 130c, Woman, wristwatches.

2005, Sept. 6   *Perf. 13¼x13½*
1215 A574 100c multi   2.25   .55
1216 A574 130c multi   3.00   .70

Cell Phone Pictures A575

Images: 85c, On Horseback, by Brigit Rohrbach. 100c, Mountain Hike, by Peter Schumacher. 130c, On Top of the World, by Rémy Sager. 180c, Tracks in the Snow, by Debora Ronchi.

2005, Sept. 6   *Perf. 14¼x14*
1217 A575   85c multi   2.00   .45
1218 A575 100c multi   2.25   .55
1219 A575 130c multi   3.00   .70
1220 A575 180c multi   4.25 1.00
   Nos. 1217-1220 (4)   11.50 2.70

Souvenir Sheet

Friends of Nature Switzerland, Cent. — A576

2005, Sept. 6   *Perf. 13½*
1221 A576   Sheet of 4   11.50 11.50
   a.   85c Skiers   2.00 1.40
   b.   100c Chalet, vert.   2.25 1.60
   c.   110c People fording stream   2.50 1.75
   d.   130c Mountain climber, vert.   3.00 2.10

Stamp Day — A577

2005, Nov. 22   *Perf. 13¼x13½*   Litho.
1222 A577 85c multi   2.00   .45

2006 Winter Olympics, Turin, Italy — A578

2005, Nov. 22   *Perf. 13¾*
1223 A578 100c Curling   2.25   .55
Issued in sheets of 6. See No. 12O4.

Swiss Papal Guards, 500th Anniv. A579

Designs: 85c, Guard and drummers. 100c, Guards and St. Peter's Basilica.

2005, Nov. 22   *Perf. 14x14¼*
1224 A579 85c multi   2.00   .45
1225 A579 100c multi   2.25   .55
Nos. 1224-1225 each issued in sheets of 6. See Vatican City Nos. 1315-1316.

Christmas — A580

Designs: 85c, Crozier and miter. 100c, Gingerbread man.

2005, Nov. 22   *Perf. 13½x13¼*
1226 A580 85c multi   2.00   .45
1227 A580 100c multi   2.25   .55

Reintroduction of Alpine Ibex in Switzerland, Cent. — A581

2006, Mar. 7   Litho.   *Perf. 13¼x13*
1228 A581 85c multi   2.00   .45

Youth Soccer — A582

2006, Mar. 7   *Perf. 13¼x13½*
1229 A582 85c multi   2.00   .45

Cuculus
Canorus
A583

Serpentine Die Cut 12

2006, Mar. 7   **Photo.**

Self-Adhesive

1230 A583 240c multi + eti-
        quette   5.50   .75
a.   Block of 10 + 10 etiquettes   55.00

No. 1230a is on a backing paper with bar
codes on the reverse.
    See Nos. 1273-1276, 1306-1308, 1341-
1342.

Railroad
Anniversaries
A584

Designs: 85c, Simplon Tunnel, cent. 100c,
Bern-Lötschberg-Simplon Railway, cent.

2006, Mar. 7   **Litho.**   **Perf. 14x13¾**
1231 A584 85c multi   2.00   .45
1232 A584 100c multi   2.25   .55

Art Nouveau Exhibition, La Chaux-de-
Fonds — A585

Designs: 100c, "Fir." 180c, "Petal."

2006, Mar. 7
1233 A585 100c multi   2.25   .55
1234 A585 180c multi   4.25   .90

Post Buses,
Cent. — A586

Various post buses and passengers.

Serpentine Die Cut 10¾x11
2006, Mar. 7   **Litho.**

Self-Adhesive

1235 A586 85c blue & multi   2.00   .45
a.   Block of 4 on backing paper   7.75
1236 A586 100c red & multi   2.25   .55
a.   Block of 4 on backing paper   9.25
1237 A586 130c grn & multi   3.00   .65
a.   Block of 4 on backing paper   12.00
b.   Block of 3, #1235-1237 on
     backing paper   7.25
    Nos. 1235-1237 (3)   7.25 1.65

Nos. 1235-1237 each were issued in sheets
of 20. Stamps are adjacent on Nos. 1235a-
1237a and on a shiny, but opaque backing
paper.

Kasperli,
Children's
Theater
Puppet — A587

2006, May 9   **Litho.**   **Perf. 14x13¾**
1238 A587 85c multi   2.00   .45

Europa
A588

2006, May 9   **Perf. 13x13¼**
1239 A588 100c multi   2.25   .60

Mountains — A589

No. 1240: a, Eiger (35x36mm). b, Monch
(30x36mm). c, Jungfrau (39x36mm).

2006, May 9   **Perf. 13¼x13½**
1240 A589 Horiz. strip of 3   6.00 6.00
a.-c.   85c Any single   2.00   .45

Caricatures of
Cows by
Patrice Killoffer
A590

Cow: 85c, On back. 100c, In water. 130c,
Seated. 180c, In snow.

2006, May 9   **Perf. 14x14¼**
1241 A590 85c multi   2.00   .45
1242 A590 100c multi   2.25   .60
1243 A590 130c multi   3.00   .75
1244 A590 180c multi   4.25 1.00
    Nos. 1241-1244 (4)   11.50 2.80

First Session of
United Nations
Human Rights
Council
A591

Perf. 13¾x14¼
2006, June 19   **Litho.**
1245 A591 100c multi   2.25   .60

Dimitri the
Clown — A592

2006, Sept. 7   **Perf. 13¼x13**
1246 A592 100c multi   2.25   .55

Victorinox Swiss
Army
Knives — A593

Designs: 100c, First model, 1897, khaki
pants. 130c, Modern model, blue jeans.

2006, Sept. 7   **Perf. 14x13¾**
1247 A593 100c multi   2.25   .55
1248 A593 130c multi   3.00   .70

Cocolino the
Cooking Cat,
by Oskar
Weiss — A594

Serpentine Die Cut 10¾x11
2006, Sept. 7

Self-Adhesive

1249 A594 85c multi   2.00   .45
a.   Booklet pane of 10   19.50

Fruit — A595

Designs: 200c, Gelterkinder cherries. 300c,
Spätlauber apple. 400c, Hauszwetschge
plums.

2006   **Photo.**   **Serpentine Die Cut 12**
Self-Adhesive
1250 A595 200c multi   4.60 1.10
1251 A595 300c multi   6.90 1.60
a.   Pair, #1250-1251 on backing
     paper   13.80
1252 A595 400c multi   9.20 2.25
    Nos. 1250-1252 (3)   20.70 4.95

Issued: 200c, 300c, 9/7; 400c, 11/21.Nos.
1250-1252 each were printed in sheets of 50.
See also No. 1314.

Town of Olten,
Boy Wearing Train
Conductor's
Hat — A596

Perf. 13½x13¼
2006, Nov. 21   **Litho.**
1253 A596 85c multi   2.00   .50

Stamp Day.

Christmas — A597

Designs: 85c, Star singers. 100c, Advent
wreath.

2006, Nov. 21
1254 A597 85c multi   2.00   .50
1255 A597 100c multi   2.25   .60

Women's
Soccer — A598

2007, Mar. 6   **Litho.**   **Perf. 13¼x13½**
1256 A598 85c multi   2.00   .45

Printed in sheets of 6.

Leonhard Euler
(1707-83),
Mathematician
A599

2007, Mar. 6
1257 A599 130c multi   3.00   .70

Stein am Rhein, 1000th
Anniv. — A600

No. 1258: a, Town Hall (28x36mm). b,
Houses on Town Hall Square (40x36mm). c,
Municipal Fountain (34x36mm).

2007, Mar. 6   **Perf. 13¾x13½**
1258 A600 Horiz. strip of 3   6.00 6.00
a.-c.   85c Any single   2.00   .45

Legends
A601

Designs: 85c, Charlemagne and the Snake.
100c, Fenetta, the Island Maiden. 130c, The
Judge of Bellinzona. 180c, Margaretha.

2007, Mar. 6   **Perf. 13½x14**
1259 A601 85c multi   2.00   .45
1260 A601 100c multi   2.25   .55
1261 A601 130c multi   3.00   .70
1262 A601 180c multi   4.25 1.00
    Nos. 1259-1262 (4)   11.50 2.70

Swiss Club for
Bernese Mountain
Dogs,
Cent. — A602

Serpentine Die Cut 11x10¾
2007, Mar. 6
Self-Adhesive
1263 A602 85c multi   2.00   .45
a.   Block of 4 on backing paper   8.00
No. 1263 was issued in sheets of 20.

Swiss National Bank, Cent. — A603

Designs: 85c, Banknote security devices.
100c, Artwork from 100-franc banknote.

2007, Mar. 6   **Litho.**
Self-Adhesive
1264 A603 85c multi   2.00   .45
a.   Block of 4 on backing paper   8.00
1265 A603 100c multi   2.25   .55
a.   Horiz. pair, #1264-1265   4.25
b.   Block of 4 on backing paper   9.25
Nos. 1264-1265 each were printed in sheets
of 12.

Roger Federer, Tennis Player — A604

2007, Apr. 10   *Perf. 13¾x14¼*
1266 A604 100c multi   2.25 .60

Swiss Assoc. of Day Care Centers, Cent. — A605

2007, Apr. 27   *Perf. 13½x13¾*
1267 A605 85c multi   2.00 .45

Europa — A606

2007, Apr. 27   *Perf. 14*
1268 A606 100c multi   2.25 .60

Scouting, cent. Printed in sheets of 18 + 12 labels.

Art Brut Movement — A607

Designs: 100c, Saint Adolf-Throne-Rock Face-Flower, by Adolf Wölfli. 180c, Untitled work by Carlo Zinelli.

2007, Apr. 27   *Perf. 14¼x14*
1269 A607 100c multi   2.25 .60
1270 A607 180c multi   4.25 1.00

Museum of Communications, Cent. — A608

People with: 85c, Lake in background. 100c, Building in background.

Litho. With Three-Dimensional Plastic Affixed
Serpentine Die Cut 10½
2007, Apr. 27
Self-Adhesive
1271 A608 85c multi   2.00 .45
1272 A608 100c multi   2.25 .60

Bird Type of 2006
Designs: 85c, Fringilla coelebs. 100c, Parus major. 110c, Tichodroma muraria. 180c, Aegolius funereus.

Serpentine Die Cut 12
2007, Sept. 6   Photo.
Self-Adhesive
1273 A583 85c multi   2.00 .30
   a.   Booklet pane of 10   20.00
1274 A583 100c multi + eti-
         quette   2.25 .35
   a.   Booklet pane of 10 + 10 eti-
       quettes   24.00

1275 A583 110c multi   2.50 .40
1276 A583 180c multi   4.25 .65
   a.   Block of 4, #1273-1276, + 2
      etiquettes on backing paper   11.00
      Nos. 1273-1276 (4)   11.00 1.70

No. 1276 was printed with and without an etiquette.

The Dance, by Nina Corti — A609

2007, Sept. 6   Litho.   *Perf. 14¼x14*
1277 A609 85c multi   2.00 .50

Illustration for Children's Book "Schnellen-Ursli," by Alois Carigiet — A610

Serpentine Die Cut 10½x11
2007, Sept. 6
Self-Adhesive
1278 A610 85c multi   2.00 .50
   a.   Booklet pane of 10   20.00

Congratulations — A611

Designs: 85c, Children and hearts. 100c, Boy and stars. 130c, Woman and starbursts.

2007, Sept. 6   Litho.
Self-Adhesive
1279 A611 85c multi   2.00 .30
1280 A611 100c multi   2.25 .35
1281 A611 130c multi   3.00 .45
   a.   Block of 3, #1279-1281, on
      backing paper   7.25
      Nos. 1279-1281 (3)   7.25 1.10

Swiss Settings in British Literature — A612

Designs: 85c, Mönch, from *Frankenstein*, by Mary Shelley. 100c, Staubbach Falls, from "At Staubbach Falls," by William Wordsworth, vert. 130c, Lake Leman, from "The Prisoner of Chillon," by Lord Byron, vert. 180c, Reichenbach Waterfall, from *The Final Problem*, by Sir Arthur Conan Doyle.

Litho. With Foil Application
Perf. 13¼x13½, 13½x13¼
2007, Sept. 6
1282 A612 85c black & silver   2.00 .50
1283 A612 100c black & silver   2.25 .60
1284 A612 130c black & silver   3.00 .75
1285 A612 180c black & silver   4.25 1.10
      Nos. 1282-1285 (4)   11.50 2.95

Skiers and Swiss Post BeeTagg — A613

Serpentine Die Cut 10¾x10½
2007, Oct. 31   Litho.
Self-Adhesive
1286 A613 100c multi   2.25 .60

The BeeTagg design can be read by camera phones to connect the phones to client websites.

Souvenir Sheet

Einsiedeln Abbey — A614

2007, Nov. 20   *Perf. 13¼x14*
1287 A614 85c multi   2.00 1.50

Paper Cuttings — A615

Paper cuttings: 85c, Heart, by Christian Schwizgebel. 100c, Spring, by Pia Arm. 130c, Family Trip, by Christiane and Jacqueline Saugy. 180c, Minuet, by Verena Kühni.

Serpentine Die Cut 10¾
2007, Nov. 20
Self-Adhesive
1288 A615   85c red & black   2.00 .50
   a.   Block of 4 #1288 on backing
      paper   8.00
1289 A615 100c green & black   2.25 .60
   a.   Block of 4 #1289 on backing
      paper   9.25
1290 A615 130c blue & black   3.00 .80
   a.   Block of 4 #1290 on backing
      paper   12.00
1291 A615 180c org & black   4.25 1.10
   a.   Block of 4 #1291 on backing
      paper   17.00
   b.   Block of 4, #1288-1291 on
      backing paper   11.50
      Nos. 1288-1291 (4)   11.50 3.00

Christmas — A616

Designs: 85c, Berne Christmas Fair. 100c, Christmas tree. 130c, Gifts.

2007, Nov. 20   *Perf. 13½x13¼*
1292 A616   85c multi   2.00 .50
1293 A616 100c multi   2.25 .60
1294 A616 130c multi   3.00 .80
      Nos. 1292-1294 (3)   7.25 1.90

Intl. Year of the Potato — A617

2008, Mar. 4   Litho.
1295 A617 85c multi   2.00 .60

Albrecht von Haller (1708-77), Physiologist — A618

2008, Mar. 4   *Perf. 13¼x13½*
1296 A618 85c multi   2.00 .60

The Little Polar Bear, by Hans de Beer — A619

Serpentine Die Cut 10½x11
2008, Mar. 4
Self-Adhesive
1297 A619 85c multi   2.00 .60
   a.   Booklet pane of 10   20.00

Euro 2008 Soccer Championships, Austria and Switzerland — A620

Serpentine Die Cut 12x12¼
2008, Mar. 4   Photo.
Self-Adhesive
1298 A620 100c green & black   2.25 .65
Printed in sheets of 10.

Men's Soccer — A621

2008, Mar. 4   Litho.   *Perf. 13¾x14¼*
1299 A621 100c multi   2.25 .65
Printed in sheets of 6.

Ice Hockey in Switzerland, Cent. — A622

2008, Mar. 4   *Perf. 13x13¼*
1300 A622 100c multi   2.25 .65

Horse Foundation, 50th Anniv. — A623

No. 1301 — Horses and: a, Sun (35x37mm). b, Path and fence (38x37mm). c, Building (31x37mm)

2008, Mar. 4   *Perf. 13½*
1301 A623   Horiz. strip of 3   6.00 6.00
   a.-c.   85c Any single   2.00 .80

Musical Instruments
A624

Designs: 85c, Violin. 100c, Swiss accordion. 130c, Electric guitar. 180c, Saxophone.

2008, Mar. 4		**Litho.**	**Perf. 13x14**	
1302	A624	85c multi	2.00	.60
1303	A624	100c multi	2.25	.65
1304	A624	130c multi	3.00	.85
1305	A624	180c multi	4.25	1.10
		Nos. 1302-1305 (4)	11.50	3.20

Birds Type of 2006

Designs: 120c, Picus canus. 130c, Monticola saxatilis. 220c, Podiceps cristatus.

Serpentine Die Cut 12

2008, May 8			**Photo.**	
		Self-Adhesive		
1306	A583	120c multi	2.75	.50
1307	A583	130c multi	3.00	.50
1308	A583	220c multi + etiquette	5.00	.85
a.		Block of 3, #1306-1308, on backing paper	11.00	
		Nos. 1306-1308 (3)	10.75	1.85

No. 1307 was printed with and without etiquette.

UEFA Euro 2008 Soccer Championships, Austria and Switzerland — A625

Serpentine Die Cut 10½x11

2008, May 8			**Litho.**	
		Self-Adhesive		
1309	A625	85c multi	2.00	.60

No. 1309 was printed in sheets of 10 with a rouletted and slit backing paper. Single stamps also were available on an unslit translucent backing paper.

Swiss Lifesaving Society, 75th Anniv. — A626

2008, May 8			**Perf. 13¼x13½**	
1310	A626	100c multi	2.25	.70

2008 Summer Olympics, Beijing — A627

2008, May 8			**Perf. 14x14¼**	
1311	A627	100c Mountain biking	2.25	.70

See No. 12O5.

Europa
A628

2008, May 8			**Perf. 13x13¼**	
1312	A628	100c multi	2.25	.70

24th Universal Postal Congress, Geneva
A629

2008, July 23			**Perf. 14x13**	
1313	A629	130c multi	3.00	.85

Fruit Type of 2006

Serpentine Die Cut 12

2008, Sept. 4			**Photo.**	
		Self-Adhesive		
1314	A595	500c Catillac pear	11.50	1.75

No. 1314 was printed in sheets of 50. Single stamps also were available on a translucent paper.

Grains — A630

2008, Sept. 4 *Serpentine Die Cut 12*

		Self-Adhesive		
1315	A630	10c Wheat	.25	.25
1316	A630	15c Barley	.35	.25
1317	A630	20c Rye	.45	.25
1318	A630	50c Oats	1.15	.25
a.		Block of 4, #1315-1318 on backing paper	2.25	
		Nos. 1315-1318 (4)	2.20	1.00

Nos. 1315-1318 were each printed in sheets of 50.

Old Rhine Bridge, Bad Sackingen, Germany - Stein, Switzerland — A631

2008, Sept. 4			**Litho.**	**Perf. 14**
1319	A631	100c multi	2.25	.65

Printed in sheets of 10. See Germany No. 2503.

Drawing by Film Maker Fredi M. Murer
A632

2008, Sept. 4			**Perf. 13x13¼**	
1320	A632	100c multi	2.25	.65

Swiss Products
A633

Designs: 85c, Swiss cheese. 100c, Chocolate. 130c, Clock. 180c, Swiss Army knife tools.

2008, Sept. 4			**Perf. 13¾x13**	
1321	A633	85c multi	2.00	.55
1322	A633	100c multi	2.25	.65
1323	A633	130c multi	3.00	.80
1324	A633	180c multi	4.25	1.10
		Nos. 1321-1324 (4)	11.50	3.10

Red Square, by Max Bill (1908-94) — A634

Eggs in a Mirror, Photograph by Hans Finsler (1891-1972)
A635

2008, Nov. 21			**Litho.**	**Perf. 13½**
1325	A634	100c black & red	2.25	.60
1326	A635	130c black & red	3.00	.70

Souvenir Sheet

Stamp Day — A636

2008, Nov. 21			**Perf. 14x13¼**	
1327	A636	85c multi	2.00	.45

Christmas — A637

Silver star and: 85c, Christmas ornament. 100c, Gold star. 130c, Bell.

Litho. With Foil Application

2008, Nov. 21			**Perf. 13½x13¼**	
1328	A637	85c multi	2.00	.45
1329	A637	100c multi	2.25	.60
1330	A637	130c multi	3.00	.70
		Nos. 1328-1330 (3)	7.25	1.75

European Brown Bear — A638

2009, Mar. 5			**Litho.**	
1331	A638	85c multi	2.00	.50

Pro Natura, Cent.

Hans Ulrich Grubenmann (1709-83), Architect, and Rhine Bridge, Schaffhausen
A639

2009, Mar. 5			**Perf. 13¼x13½**	
1332	A639	85c multi	2.00	.50

2009 Intl. Ice Hockey Federation World Championships, Bern and Zurich — A640

2009, Mar. 5			**Perf. 13¾x14¼**	
		Self-Adhesive		
1333	A640	100c multi	2.25	.60

Morteratsch Glacier and Lines Showing Glacier's Retreat
A641

Litho. & Silk-screened				
2009, Mar. 5			**Perf. 14**	
1334	A641	100c multi	2.25	.60

John Calvin (1509-64), Religious Reformer, and St. Peter's Cathedral, Geneva — A642

2009, Mar. 5		**Litho.**	**Perf. 13½x13¼**	
1335	A642	100c multi	2.25	.60

Hans Erni, 100th Birthday — A643

Paintings by Erni: 100c, The Human Mind. 130c, Human Hands.

2009, Mar. 5			**Perf. 14¼x13¾**	
1336	A643	100c multi	2.25	.60
1337	A643	130c multi	3.00	.75

Swiss Museum of Transport, 50th Anniv.
A644

Designs: 85c, Steamship Rigi. 100c, Dufaux race car. 130c, Lockheed Orion 9C Special.

2009, Mar. 5			**Perf. 13x13½**	
1338	A644	85c multi	2.00	.50
1339	A644	100c multi	2.25	.60
1340	A644	130c multi	3.00	.75
		Nos. 1338-1340 (3)	7.25	1.85

Birds Type of 2006

Designs: 140c, Alectoris graeca. 190c, Milvus milvus.

Serpentine Die Cut 12¼x12

2009, May 8				
		Self-Adhesive		
1341	A583	140c multi + etiquette	3.25	.50
1342	A583	190c multi + etiquette	4.50	.70
a.		Pair, #1341-1342 + 2 etiquettes on backing paper	7.75	

European
Wildcat — A645

2009. May 8　　　*Perf. 13¾x14¼*
1343 A645 85c multi　　　2.00　.50

Type Slug and
"@" Symbol on
Printed
Page — A646

2009. May 8　　　*Perf. 14x13*
1344 A646 100c multi　　　2.25　.60

Graphics industry in Switzerland, 550th
anniv.
See Luxembourg No. 1283.

Location of Helvetia Asteroid — A647

2009. May 8　　　*Perf. 12¾x13½*
1345 A647 100c multi　　　2.25　.60
　　　　Europa.

Contemporary
Architecture
A648

Designs: 100c, Stiva da Morts, Vrin, by Gion
A. Caminada. 180c, Pentorama Community
Center, Amriswil, by Müller/Sigrist Architects.

2009. May 8　　　*Perf. 14x13*
1346 A648 100c multi　　　2.25　.60
1347 A648 180c multi　　　4.25　1.10

Trees — A649

2009. May 8　　　*Perf. 13½*
Self-Adhesive
1348 A649　85c Birch　　　2.00　.50
1349 A649 100c Oak　　　2.25　.60
1350 A649 130c Willow　　3.00　.80
　Nos. 1348-1350 (3)　　7.25　1.90

Princess
Lillifee, by
Monika
Finsterbusch
A650

Litho. & Silk-screened
2009. Sept. 3　*Serpentine Die Cut 12*
Self-Adhesive
1351 A650 85c multi　　　2.00　.55
　a.　Booklet pane of 10　　20.00

Swiss Stamp
Dealers
Association,
Cent. — A651

2009, Sept. 3 Litho.　*Perf. 13¼x13½*
1352 A651 100c multi　　　2.25　.65
　Printed in sheets of 12 + 8 labels.

Geneva
Conventions,
60th
Anniv. — A652

2009, Sept. 3　　　*Perf. 14x13*
1353 A652 100c multi　　　2.25　.65

Wedding
A653

Anniversary
A654

Birth — A655

2009, Sept. 3　　　*Perf. 13¾x14¼*
Self-Adhesive
1354 A653 100c multi　　　2.25　.65
1355 A654 100c multi　　　2.25　.65
1356 A655 100c multi　　　2.25　.65
　Nos. 1354-1356 (3)　　6.75　1.95

Red Flowers
With White
Crosses
A656

Various red flowers with white crosses and
German text.

2009, Sept. 3　*Perf. 14x13, 13x14*
1357 A656　85c multi　　　2.00　.55
1358 A656 100c multi　　　2.25　.65
1359 A656 130c multi, vert.　3.00　.85
1360 A656 180c multi, vert.　4.25　1.25
　Nos. 1357-1360 (4)　　11.50　3.30

Movement of Livestock to New
Pastures — A657

No. 1361: a, Sheep and cattle (38x36mm).
b, Cattle (32x36mm). c, Cow and horse
(34x36mm).

2009, Sept. 3　　　*Perf. 13¼x13½*
1361 A657　Horiz. strip of 3　6.00　6.00
　a.-c.　85c Any single　　　2.00　.55

2010
Paralympics,
Vancouver
A658

2009, Nov. 20　　　*Perf. 13½*
1362 A658 130c multi　　　3.00　.85

Souvenir Sheet

Gruyères Castle and Crane — A659

2009, Nov. 20　　　*Perf. 14x13¼*
1363 A659 85c multi　　　2.40　2.40
　　　Stamp Day.

Christmas — A660

Star and: 85c, Cap of Santa Claus. 100c,
Christmas tree. 130c, Gift box.

Litho. With Hologram
2009, Nov. 20　　　*Perf. 13½x13¼*
1364 A660　85c multi　　　2.00　.60
1365 A660 100c multi　　　2.25　.65
1366 A660 130c multi　　　3.00　.85
　Nos. 1364-1366 (3)　　7.25　2.10

Basel Carnival Committee,
Cent. — A661

No. 1367: a, Four marchers, two carrying
parade lantern and sign, Spalentor in background (30x36mm). b, Fifer, drum major,
drummer, wagon, Town Hall in background
(43x36mm). c, Four musicians, Münster
Cathedral in background (30x36mm).

2010, Jan. 12 Litho.　*Perf. 13¾x13½*
1367 A661　Horiz. strip of 3　7.00　7.00
　a.-c.　100c Any single　　　2.25　.65

University of
Basel, 550th
Anniv. — A662

2010, Mar. 4　　　*Perf. 14x13*
1368 A662 85c multi　　　2.00　.55

Intl. Year of
Biodiversity
A663

2010, Mar. 4　　　*Perf. 14¼x13¾*
Self-Adhesive
1369 A663 85c multi　　　2.00　.55

Swiss Cancer
League,
Cent. — A664

2010, Mar. 4　　　*Perf. 14x13*
1370 A664 100c multi　　　2.25　.65

Powered Flight
in Switzerland,
Cent. — A665

Designs: 85c, Ernest Failloubaz, first holder
of pilot's license, and Grandjean monoplane.
100c, Airbus A340 and Zurich Airport. 130c,
Jorge "Géo" Chavez, first man to fly across the
Alps, and Blériot XI monoplane. 180c, Sport
airplane, glider and hot-air balloons.

2010, Mar. 4　　　*Perf. 13¼x13¾*
1371 A665　85c multi　　　2.00　.55
1372 A665 100c multi　　　2.25　.65
1373 A665 130c multi　　　3.00　.85
1374 A665 180c multi　　　4.25　1.25
　Nos. 1371-1374 (4)　　11.50　3.30

2010 Federal
Marksmen's
Festival,
Aarau — A666

2010 Federal
Drumming and
Piping Festival,
Interlaken
A667

Swiss Yodeling
Association,
Cent. — A668

2010 Federal
Costume
Festival,
Schwyz
A669

2010, Mar. 4 Litho.　*Perf. 13¾x14¼*
1375 A666 100c multi　　　2.25　.65
Litho. & Embossed With Foil
Application
1376 A667 100c multi　　　2.25　.65
Litho. & Embossed
1377 A668 100c multi　　　2.25　.65
1378 A669 100c multi　　　2.25　.65
　Nos. 1375-1378 (4)　　9.00　2.60

No. 1375 has a hole drilled into target in
vignette.

Johann Peter
Hebel (1760-
1826),
Poet — A670

2010, May 6 Litho. Perf. 13¼x13½
1379 A670 85c multi 2.00 .55

School Boy with
Slate, by Albert
Anker (1831-
1910)
A671

2010, May 6 Perf. 13½x13
1380 A671 85c multi 2.00 .55

Heidi and
Goats — A672

2010, May 6 Perf. 13¼x13
1381 A672 100c multi 2.25 .65

Europa.

Kunsthaus
Zurich,
Cent.
A673

2010, May 6 Perf. 13¼x13½
Self-Adhesive
1382 A673 100c multi 2.25 .65

Swiss Public
Welfare Society,
Bicent. — A674

2010, May 6 Perf. 13½x13¼
1383 A674 100c multi 2.25 .65

Circus World
Geneva 2010
Circus
Festival — A675

2010, May 6
1384 A675 140c multi 3.25 .85

Railway
Centenaries
A676

Designs: 85c, Niesen Funicular. 100c, Bernina Railway, horiz.

2010, May 6 Perf. 14¼x13¾
1385 A676 85c multi 2.00 .55
Perf. 13¾x14¼
1386 A676 100c multi 2.25 .65

Jimmy Flitz,
Character From
Children's Book
by Roland
Zoss — A677

Serpentine Die Cut 12
2010, Sept. 3 Litho.
Self-Adhesive
1387 A677 85c multi 1.75 .60
a. Booklet pane of 10 17.50

Jeanne Hersch
(1910-2000),
Philosopher
A678

2010, Sept. 3 Perf. 13¼x13½
1388 A678 100c multi 2.00 .65

Words
From "The
Big Dwarf,"
by Franz
Hohler,
Writer
A679

2010, Sept. 3 Perf. 13x13¼
1389 A679 100c green & black 2.00 .65

European Free
Trade
Association,
50th
Anniv. — A680

2010, Sept. 3 Perf. 14x13¾
1390 A680 140c yellow & black 2.75 .90

Gustave
Moynier (1826-
1910) and
Henri Dunant
(1828-1910),
Founders of
Intl. Red
Cross — A681

2010, Sept. 3 Perf. 13¼x13½
1391 A681 190c multi 3.75 1.25

Composers
A682

Designs: 100c, Rolf Liebermann (1910-99).
140c, Heinrich Sutermeister (1910-95).

2010, Sept. 3 Perf. 13x13¼
1392 A682 100c lilac & black 2.00 .65
1393 A682 140c ol brn & blk 2.75 .90

Prehistoric
Animals
A683

Designs: 85c, Theropod. 100c, Ichthyosaur.
140c, Pterosaur.

2010, Sept. 3 Perf. 13¼x13½
1394 A683 85c multi 1.75 .60
1395 A683 100c multi 2.00 .65
1396 A683 140c multi 2.75 .90
Nos. 1394-1396 (3) 6.50 2.15

A684

A685

Optical Art by Youri Messen-
Jaschin — A686

2010, Sept. 3 Perf. 14x13¼
Self-Adhesive
1397 A684 85c multi 1.75 .60
1398 A685 100c multi 2.00 .65
1399 A686 140c black & red 2.75 .90
Nos. 1397-1399 (3) 6.50 2.15

Souvenir Sheet

Tag der Briefmarke
2010 Bern

Zähringer Fountain, Bern — A687

2010, Nov. 4 Perf. 14x13¼
1400 A687 85c multi 1.75 .60

Stamp Day.

Handicrafts
A688

Designs: 200c, Bobbin lacemaking. 300c,
Wood carving.

2010, Nov. 4 Serpentine Die Cut 12
Self-Adhesive
1401 A688 200c multi 4.25 .85
1402 A688 300c multi 6.25 1.25
a. Pair, #1401-1402 10.50
Nos. 1401-1402 also were printed in sheets
of 10. See Nos. 1418-1419.

Christmas — A689

Designs: 85c, Star, candle, conifer sprigs.
100c, Snowflake. 140c, Star, angel.

Litho. With Hologram
2010, Nov. 4 Perf. 13½x13¼
1403 A689 85c multi 1.75 .60
1404 A689 100c multi 2.10 .70
1405 A689 140c multi 3.00 1.00
Nos. 1403-1405 (3) 6.85 2.30

Pettersson and
Findus,
Children's Book
Characters by
Sven Nordqvist
A690

Serpentine Die Cut 12
2011, Mar. 3 Litho.
Self-Adhesive
1406 A690 85c multi 1.90 .65
a. Booklet pane of 10 19.00

Honeybee and
Flower
A691

2011, Mar. 3 Perf. 11¾
1407 A691 85c multi 1.90 .65

Cerebral
Foundation,
50th
Anniv. — A692

2011, Mar. 3 Perf. 13¼x13½
1408 A692 85c multi 1.90 .65

14th World
Gymnaestrada,
Lausanne
A693

2011, Mar. 3
1409 A693 85c multi 1.90 .65

Neuchatel, 1000th Anniv. — A694

2011, Mar. 3
1410 A694 100c multi   2.25   .75

Worldwide Fund for Nature (WWF), 50th Anniv. — A695

2011, Mar. 3
1411 A695 100c multi   2.25   .75

Max Frisch (1911-91), Architect A696

2011, Mar. 3
1412 A696 100c gray & black   2.25   .75

Model of Vitamin C Molecule A697

Litho. & Embossed
2011, Mar. 3   **Perf. 13x13¼**
1413 A697 100c multi   2.25   .75

Intl. Year of Chemistry.

Flowers — A698

Designs: 85c, Cucurbita pepo. 100c, Pisum sativum. 110c, Allium ursinum. 260c, Cynara scolymus.

Serpentine Die Cut 12
2011, Mar. 3   **Litho.**
Self-Adhesive
1414 A698 85c multi   1.90   .65
a.   Booklet pane of 10   19.00
1415 A698 100c multi + eti-   2.25   .75
         quette
a.   Booklet pane of 10 + 10 eti-
         quettes   22.50
1416 A698 110c multi   2.40   .80
1417 A698 260c multi   5.75 1.90
a.   Block of 4, #1414-1417 12.50
      Nos. 1414-1417 (4)   12.30 4.10

Nos. 1414-1415 also were printed in sheets of 50. Nos. 1416-1417 also were printed in sheets of 10. See Nos. 1440-1442.

Handicrafts Type of 2010
Designs: 400c, Potter shaping pot on wheel. 500c, Blacksmith hammering work on anvil.

Serpentine Die Cut 12
2011, May 5   **Litho.**
Self-Adhesive
1418 A688 400c multi   9.25 2.40
1419 A688 500c multi   11.50 3.00
a.   Pair, #1418-1419   21.00

Nos. 1418-1419 also were printed in sheets of 10.

Art Is Resistance, by Thomas Hirschhorn A699

2011, May 5   **Perf. 13¾x14¼**
1420 A699 100c multi   2.40   .80

Venice Art Biennale.

Europa A700

2011, May 5   **Perf. 13½**
1421 A700 100c multi   2.40   .80

Intl. Year of Forests.

Miniature Sheet

Provisional Declaration Naming "Swiss Psalm" as National Anthem, 50th Anniv. — A701

No. 1422: a, Urnerboden (red panels at bottom and right). b, Urnersee bei Flüelen (red panels at left and bottom). c, Urigen (red panels at top and right). d, Schächentaler Windgällen (red panels at left and top).

2011, May 5   **Perf. 13½**
1422 A701 Sheet of 4   2.40 2.40
a.-d. 25c Any single   .80   .25

On each of the four stamps in the sheet, the first verse of the anthem is printed in fluorescent ink in one of Switzerland's four official languages.

Fruit, by Shirana Shahbazi A702

2011, Sept. 2   **Perf. 13¼x13½**
1423 A702 100c multi   2.25   .75

See Liechtenstein No. 1522.

Paul Burkhard (1911-77), Composer A703

2011, Sept. 2   **Perf. 13½**
1424 A703 100c multi   2.25   .75

Works of Handicapped Artists — A704

Designs: 85c, Untitled painting by Bajram Mahmuti. 100c, Emmental, painting by Claudia Aebi-Torre, horiz. 140c, Untitled dot picture, by Christian Oppliger, horiz. 190c, Photograph of dancer and wood sculpture, by Flavia Trachsel.

2011, Sept. 2
1425 A704 85c multi   2.00   .65
1426 A704 100c multi   2.25   .75
1427 A704 140c black   3.25 1.10
1428 A704 190c multi   4.50 1.50
      Nos. 1425-1428 (4)   12.00 4.00

Lavaux Vineyard Terraces UNESCO World Heritage Site — A705

No. 1429: a, Vineyard terraces and steps (26x37mm). b, Village, vineyards, Lake Geneva (41x37mm). c, Open gate and stone wall overlooking Lake Geneva (37x37mm).

2011, Sept. 2   **Litho.**
1429 A705 Horiz. strip of 3 6.75 6.75
a.-c. 100c Any single   2.25   .75

Muggestutz, King of the Dwarves, Book Illustration by Susanna Schmid-Germann A706

2011, Sept. 2 Serpentine Die Cut 12
Self-Adhesive
1430 A706 85c multi   2.00   .65
a.   Booklet pane of 10   20.00

Single examples of No. 1430 on a translucent paper also were made available.

Greetings Stamps A707

Designs: No. 1431, Champagne flutes. No. 1432, Heart. No. 1433, Engagement and wedding rings. No. 1434, Baby's pacifier.

2011, Sept. 2   **Perf. 13¼x13½**
Self-Adhesive
1431 A707 100c multi   2.25   .75
1432 A707 100c multi   2.25   .75
1433 A707 100c multi   2.25   .75
1434 A707 100c multi   2.25   .75
      Nos. 1431-1434 (4)   9.00 3.00

Drawing of Swiss Flag, Machine, Clouds, Rainbow and Musical Notes, by Rap Musician Stress A708

2011, Nov. 17   **Perf. 13½**
1435 A708 100c multi   2.25   .75

Souvenir Sheet

Château de Villa, Sierre — A709

2011, Nov. 17
1436 A709 85c multi   1.90   .65

Stamp Day.

Christmas A710

Christmas trees and: 85c, Chapel. 100c, Gifts on sleigh, village. 140c, Wreath, chalet.

2011, Nov. 17   **Perf. 13¼x13½**
Self-Adhesive
1437 A710 85c multi   1.90   .65
1438 A710 100c multi   2.25   .75
1439 A710 140c multi   3.25 1.10
      Nos. 1437-1439 (3)   7.40 2.50

Flowers Type of 2011
Designs: 140c, Lycopersicon lucopersicum. 180c, Phaeolus coccineus. 190c, Allium cepa.

2012, Mar. 1 Serpentine Die Cut 12
Self-Adhesive
1440 A698 140c multi   3.25   .65
1441 A698 180c multi   4.00   .80
1442 A698 190c multi   4.25   .85
a.   Nos. 1440-1442 on translu-
      cent paper   11.50
      Nos. 1440-1442 (3)   11.50 2.30

Nos. 1440-1442 each were printed in sheets of 10 stamps.

Swiss Brass Band Association, 150th Anniv. — A711

Litho. With Foil Application
2012, Mar. 1   **Perf. 14¼x13¾**
1443 A711 100c multi   2.25   .75

Swiss Civil Code, Cent. A712

2012, Mar. 1 Litho.   **Perf. 13½**
1444 A712 100c multi   2.25   .75

Building of Hermitage in the Steinach Valley by St. Gall (c. 550- c. 645), 1400th Anniv. — A713

2012, Mar. 1   *Perf. 13¼x13½*
1445   A713   100c multi   2.25   .75

Jungfrau Railway, Cent. — A714

2012, Mar. 1
1446   A714   100c multi   2.25   .75

Swiss Tectonic Arena Sardona UNESCO World Heritage Site — A715

No. 1447: a, Buildings in Elm (30x47mm). b, Sun shining through Martinsloch (hole in mountain) (44x47mm). c, Sunshine on Elm Church Tower clock face (30x47mm).

2012, Mar. 1   *Perf. 13½*
1447   A715   Horiz. strip of 3   6.75   6.75
a.-c.   100c Any single   2.25   .75

Beaver — A716

2012, Mar. 1   *Perf. 13½x13¼*
    Self-Adhesive
1448   A716   100c multi   2.25   .75

Children's Book Illustration by Janosch (Horst Eckert) — A717

Serpentine Die Cut 12
2012, Mar. 12
    Self-Adhesive
1449   A717   100c multi   2.25   .75
a.   Serpentine die cut 12¼x12   2.25   .75
b.   Booklet pane of 10 #1449   22.50

Single examples of No. 1449 were made available on a translucent paper. No.1449a is available only on translucent paper.

Cadastral Surveying in Switzerland, Cent. — A718

2012, May 9   *Perf. 13¾x14¼*
1450   A718   100c multi   2.25   .75

Inauguration of Stanserhorn Cabrio Cable Car — A719

2012, May 9   *Perf. 13¼x13½*
1451   A719   100c multi   2.25   .75

Tidying Up Art, by Ursus Wehrli — A720

2012, May 9   Litho.   *Perf. 13½*
1452   A720   100c multi   2.25   .75

Blood Donation — A721

2012, May 9   *Perf. 13½x13¼*
1453   A721   100c multi   2.25   .75

Europa — A722

2012, May 9   *Perf. 13½*
1454   A722   100c multi   2.25   .75

Tell Theaters A723

Actors at: No. 1455, Tell Theater in Altdorf. No. 1456, Open-air Tell Theater in Interlaken.

2012, May 9   *Perf. 13*
    Self-Adhesive
1455   A723   100c multi   2.25   .75
1456   A723   100c multi   2.25   .75
Tell Theaters in Altdorf, 500th anniv.; in Interlaken, cent.

SEMI-POSTAL STAMPS

Nos. B1-B76, B81-B84 were sold at premiums of 2c for 3c stamps, 5c for 5c-20c stamps and 10c for 30c-40c stamps.

Helvetia and Matterhorn — SP2

Perf. 11½, 12
1913, Dec. 1   Typo.   **Wmk. 183**
    Granite Paper
B1   SP2   5c green   2.75   8.25
   Never hinged   7.75

Boy (Appenzell) SP3   Girl (Lucerne) SP4

1915, Dec. 1   *Perf. 11½*
B2   SP3   5c green, *buff*   3.25   8.25
a.   Tête bêche pair   82.50   875.00
   Never hinged   160.00
B3   SP4   10c red, *buff*   100.00   87.50
   Set, never hinged   225.00

Girl (Fribourg) SP5   Dairy Boy (Bern) SP6

Girl (Vaud) — SP7

1916, Dec. 1
B4   SP5   3c vio, *buff*   5.00   37.50
B5   SP6   5c grn, *buff*   11.00   9.25
B6   SP7   10c brn red, *buff*   47.50   77.50
   Nos. B4-B6 (3)   63.50   124.25
   Set, never hinged   175.00

Girl (Valais) SP8   Girl (Unterwalden) SP9

Girl (Ticino) — SP10

1917, Dec. 1
B7   SP8   3c vio, *buff*   3.25   50.00
B8   SP9   5c green, *buff*   7.75   5.50
B9   SP10   10c red, *buff*   19.00   22.50
   Nos. B7-B9 (3)   30.00   78.00
   Set, never hinged   87.50

Uri SP11   Geneva SP12

1918, Dec. 1
    Straw-Surfaced Paper
B10   SP11   10c red, org & blk   7.75   25.00
B11   SP12   15c vio, red, org & blk   9.25   11.00
   Set, never hinged   52.50

Nidwalden SP13   Vaud SP14

Obwalden — SP15

1919, Dec. 1
    Cream-Surfaced Paper
B12   SP13   7½c gray, red & blk   2.50   14.00
B13   SP14   10c lake, grn & blk   2.50   14.00
B14   SP15   15c pur, red & blk   5.00   7.25
   Nos. B12-B14 (3)   10.00   35.25
   Set, never hinged   22.50

Schwyz SP16   Zürich SP17

Ticino — SP18

1920, Dec. 1
    Cream-Surfaced Paper
B15   SP16   7½c gray & red   3.75   11.50
B16   SP17   10c red & lt bl   5.00   12.50
B17   SP18   15c violet, red & bl   2.75   6.00
   Nos. B15-B17 (3)   11.50   30.00
   Set, never hinged   25.00

Valais SP19   Bern SP20

Switzerland — SP21

1921, Dec. 1
    Cream-Surfaced Paper
B18   SP19   10c grn, red & blk   .65   3.00
B19   SP20   20c vio, red, org & blk   1.90   3.50
B20   SP21   40c blue & red   7.25   47.50
   Nos. B18-B20 (3)   9.80   54.00
   Set, never hinged   25.00

Zug SP22   Fribourg SP23

Lucerne SP24   Switzerland SP25

1922, Dec. 1
Cream-Surfaced Paper

B21	SP22	5c org, pale bl & blk	.50	5.50
B22	SP23	10c ol grn & blk	.60	2.50
B23	SP24	20c vio, pale bl & blk	1.00	2.50
B24	SP25	40c bl & red	8.75	47.50
		Nos. B21-B24 (4)	10.85	58.00
		Set, never hinged	26.00	

Basel
SP26

Glarus (St. Fridolin)
SP27

Neuchâtel
SP28

Switzerland
SP29

1923, Dec. 1
Cream-Surfaced Paper

B25	SP26	5c org & blk	.40	3.50
B26	SP27	10c multi	.40	1.90
B27	SP28	20c multi	.45	1.90
B28	SP29	40c dk bl & red	7.75	37.50
		Nos. B25-B28 (4)	9.00	44.80
		Set, never hinged	21.00	

Appenzell
SP30

Solothurn
SP31

Schaffhausen
SP32

Switzerland
SP33

1924, Dec. 1
Cream-Surfaced Paper

B29	SP30	5c dk vio & blk	.25	1.60
B30	SP31	10c grn, red & blk	.40	1.00
B31	SP32	20c car, yel & blk	.65	1.00
B32	SP33	30c bl, red & blk	1.40	11.00
		Nos. B29-B32 (4)	2.70	14.60
		Set, never hinged	6.50	

St. Gallen (Canton)
SP34

Appenzell-Ausser-Rhoden
SP35

Grisons
SP36

Switzerland
SP37

1925, Dec. 1
Cream-Surfaced Paper

B33	SP34	5c vio, grn & blk	.25	1.10
B34	SP35	10c grn & blk	.25	.85
B35	SP36	20c multi	.25	.85
B36	SP37	30c dk bl, red & blk	1.10	8.25
		Nos. B33-B36 (4)	1.85	11.05
		Set, never hinged	4.50	

Thurgau
SP38

Basel
SP39

Aargau
SP40

Switzerland
SP41

1926, Dec. 1
Cream-Surfaced Paper

B37	SP38	5c vio, bis & grn	.25	1.40
B38	SP39	10c gray grn, red & blk	.25	1.40
B39	SP40	20c red, blk & bl	.25	1.40
B40	SP41	30c dk bl & red	1.10	12.50
		Nos. B37-B40 (4)	1.85	16.70
		Set, never hinged	4.50	

Orphan
SP42

Orphan at Pestalozzi School
SP43

SP44

J. H. Pestalozzi
SP45

1927, Dec. 1   Typo.   Wmk. 183
Granite Paper

B41	SP42	5c red vio & yel, *grysh*	.25	1.60
B42	SP43	10c grn & fawn, *grnsh*	.25	.60

Engr.

B43	SP44	20c red	.25	.60

Unwmk.
Photo.

B44	SP45	30c gray bl & blk	1.10	6.50
		Nos. B41-B44 (4)	1.85	9.30
		Set, never hinged	3.25	

Nos. B43-B44 for the centenary of the death of Johann Heinrich Pestalozzi, the Swiss educational reformer.

Lausanne
SP46

Winterthur
SP47

St. Gallen (City) — SP48

J. H. Dunant
SP49

1928, Dec. 1   Typo.   Wmk. 183
Cream-Surfaced Paper.

B45	SP46	5c dk vio, red & blk	.25	1.60
B46	SP47	10c brn, org red & blk	.25	.90
B47	SP48	20c brn red, blk & yel	.25	.90

Unwmk.
Photo.
Thick White Paper

B48	SP49	30c dl bl & red	1.10	7.00
		Nos. B45-B48 (4)	1.85	10.40
		Set, never hinged	3.50	

No. B48 for the centenary of the birth of Jean Henri Dunant, Swiss author, philanthropist and founder of the Red Cross Society.

Lake Lugano and Mt. Salvatore
SP50

Lake Engstlen and Mt. Titlis
SP51

Mt. Lyskamm
SP52

Nicholas von der Flüe
SP53

1929, Dec. 1   Perf. 11x11½

B49	SP50	5c dk vio & red org	.25	1.40
B50	SP51	10c ol brn & gray bl	.25	1.10
B51	SP52	20c brn garnet & bl	.25	1.10
B52	SP53	30c dk blue	1.25	12.50
		Nos. B49-B52 (4)	2.00	16.10
		Set, never hinged	4.00	

No. B52 for Nicholas von der Flüe, the Swiss patriot. By his advice the Swiss Confederation was continued and Swiss independence was saved.

Fribourg
SP54

Altdorf
SP55

Schaffhausen
SP56

Jeremias Gotthelf
SP57

Wmk. 183
1930, Dec. 1   Typo.   Perf. 11½
Cream-Surfaced Paper

B53	SP54	5c dp grn, dl bl & blk	.25	1.40
B54	SP55	10c multicolored	.25	.90
B55	SP56	20c multicolored	.30	.90

Engr.
White Paper

B56	SP57	30c slate blue	1.25	6.00
		Nos. B53-B56 (4)	2.05	9.20
		Set, never hinged	4.00	

No. B56 for Jeremias Gotthelf, pen name of Albrecht Bitzius, pastor and author.

Lakes Silvaplana and Sils
SP58

Wetterhorn
SP59

Lake Geneva
SP60

Alexandre Vinet
SP61

1931, Dec. 1   Photo.   Unwmk.
Granite Paper

B57	SP58	5c dp grn	.45	1.60
B58	SP59	10c dk vio	.40	.85
B59	SP60	20c brn red	.55	1.10

Wmk. 183
Engr.

B60	SP61	30c ultra	4.50	19.00
		Nos. B57-B60 (4)	5.90	22.55
		Set, never hinged	14.00	

No. B60 for Alexandre Rudolph Vinet, critic and theologian.

Flag Swinger
SP62

Putting the Stone
SP63

Wrestling
SP64

Eugen Huber
SP65

1932, Dec. 1   Typo.   Unwmk.
Granite Paper

B61	SP62	5c dk grn & red	.30	1.90
B62	SP63	10c orange	.45	2.25
B63	SP64	20c scarlet	.55	1.90

Wmk. 183
Engr.

B64	SP65	30c ultra	2.25	8.75
		Nos. B61-B64 (4)	3.55	14.80
		Set, never hinged	9.50	

No. B64 for Eugen Huber, jurist and author of the Swiss Civil Law Book.

Girl of Vaud — SP66

Girl of Bern — SP67

Girl of Ticino
SP68

Jean Baptiste
Girard (Le Père
Grégoire)
SP69

1933, Dec. 1   Photo.   Unwmk.
Granite Paper

B65	SP66	5c grn & buff	.30	1.50
B66	SP67	10c vio & buff	.30	1.10
B67	SP68	20c red & buff	.45	2.10

Wmk. 183
Engr.

B68	SP69	30c ultra	2.50	8.50
	Nos. B65-B68 (4)		3.55	13.20
	Set, never hinged		8.25	

Girl of
Appenzell
SP70

Girl of Valais
SP71

Girl of Grisons
SP72

Albrecht von
Haller
SP73

1934, Dec. 1   Photo.   Unwmk.

B69	SP70	5c grn & buff	.30	1.60
B70	SP71	10c vio & buff	.45	1.10
B71	SP72	20c red & buff	.45	1.60

Wmk. 183
Engr.

B72	SP73	30c ultra	2.50	8.75
	Nos. B69-B72 (4)		3.70	13.05
	Set, never hinged		8.25	

Girl of Basel
SP74

Girl of Lucerne
SP75

Girl of Geneva
SP76

Stefano
Franscini
SP77

1935, Dec. 1   Photo.   Unwmk.
Granite Paper

B73	SP74	5c grn & buff	.25	1.75
B74	SP75	10c vio & buff	.45	1.10
B75	SP76	20c red & buff	.45	2.75

Wmk. 183
Engr.

B76	SP77	30c ultra	2.50	8.75
	Nos. B73-B76 (4)		3.65	14.35
	Set, never hinged		8.25	

No. B76 honors Stefano Franscini (1796-1857), political economist and educator.

Alpine
Herdsman — SP78

Perf. 11½
1936, Oct. 1   Photo.   Unwmk.
Granite Paper

B77	SP78	10c + 5c vio	.55	1.00
B78	SP78	20c + 10c dk red	.85	4.25
B79	SP78	30c + 10c ultra	3.75	20.00
	Nos. B77-B79 (3)		5.15	25.25
	Set, never hinged		11.00	

Souvenir Sheet

B80	SP78	Sheet of 3	35.00	125.00
	Never hinged		70.00	
a.	Block of 4 sheets		190.00	875.00
	Never hinged		300.00	

Swiss National Defense Fund Drive.
No. B80 contains stamps similar to Nos. B77-B79, but on grilled granite paper with blue and red fibers instead of black and red. Sold for 2fr. Size: 120x130mm.

Johann Georg
Nägeli
SP79

Girl of
Neuchâtel
SP80

Girl of Schwyz
SP81

Girl of Zurich
SP82

Wmk. 183
1936, Dec. 1   Engr.   Perf. 11½
Granite Paper

B81	SP79	5c grn	.55	.70

Unwmk.
Photo.

B82	SP80	10c vio & buff	.55	.70
B83	SP81	20c red & buff	.25	1.90
B84	SP82	30c ultra & buff	3.50	30.00
	Nos. B81-B84 (4)		4.85	33.30
	Set, never hinged		11.00	

Gen. Henri
Dufour — SP83

Nicholas von
der
Flüe — SP84

Boy
SP85

Girl
SP86

Perf. 11½
1937, Dec. 1   Unwmk.   Engr.

B85	SP83	5c + 5c bl grn	.25	.55
B86	SP84	10c + 5c red vio	.25	.55

Photo.
Granite Paper

B87	SP85	20c + 5c red & silver	.30	.55
B88	SP86	30c + 10c ultra & sil	1.25	5.50
	Set, never hinged		2.05	7.15
			3.50	

25th anniv. of the Pro Juventute (child welfare) stamps.

Souvenir Sheet

1937, Dec. 20   Imperf.

B89	Sheet of 2		6.50	57.50
a.	SP85 20c + 5c red & silver		1.60	17.00
b.	SP86 30c + 10c ultra & silver		1.60	17.00
	Never hinged		7.50	

Simulated perforation in silver. Sheet sold for 1fr.

Tell
Chapel,
Lake
Lucerne
SP87

1938, June 15   Perf. 11½
Granite Paper

B90	SP87	10c + 10c brt vio & yel	.45	1.10
	Never hinged		1.10	
a.	Grilled gum		22.50	77.50
	Never hinged		32.50	

National Fête Day.

Salomon
Gessner
SP88

Girl of St.
Gallen
SP89

Girl of
Uri — SP90

Girl of
Aargau — SP91

1938, Dec. 1   Engr.   Perf. 11½

B91	SP88	5c + 5c dp bl grn	.25	.50

Photo.
Granite Paper

B92	SP89	10c + 5c pur & buff	.25	.55
B93	SP90	20c + 5c red & buff	.25	.55
B94	SP91	30c + 10c ultra	1.60	6.50
	Nos. B91-B94 (4)		2.35	8.10
	Set, never hinged		4.50	

Castle at
Laupen
SP92

1939, June 15

B95	SP92	10c + 10c brn, gray & red	.30	1.10
	Never hinged		1.10	

600th anniversary of the Battle of Laupen. The surtax was used to aid needy mothers.

Hans Herzog
SP93

Girl of Fribourg
SP94

Girl of
Nidwalden
SP95

Girl of Basel
SP96

Perf. 11½
1939, Dec. 1   Unwmk.   Engr.

B96	SP93	5c + 5c dk grn	.25	.45

Photo.
Granite Paper

B97	SP94	10c + 5c rose vio & buff	.25	.45
B98	SP95	20c + 5c org red	.30	1.40
B99	SP96	30c + 10c red & buff	1.60	11.50
	Nos. B96-B99 (4)		2.40	13.80
	Set, never hinged		5.00	

Sempach,
1386 — SP97

Giornico,
1478 — SP98

Calven, 1499
SP99

WWI Ranger
SP100

1940, Mar. 20   Photo.
Granite Paper

B100	SP97	5c + 5c emer, blk & red	.30	1.25
B101	SP98	10c + 5c brn org, blk & car	.30	.55
B102	SP99	20c + 5c brn red, blk & car	2.25	.95
B103	SP100	30c + 10c brt bl, brn blk & red	1.60	8.25

National Fête Day. The surtax was for the National Fund and the Red Cross.

Redrawn

B104	SP99	20c + 5c brn red, blk & car	9.75	6.50
	Nos. B100-B104 (5)		14.20	17.50
	Set, never hinged		26.00	

The base of statue has been heavily shaded. "Calven 1499" moved nearer to bottom line of base. Top line of base removed.

Souvenir Sheet
Unwmk.
1940, July 16   Photo.   Imperf.
Granite Paper

B105	Sheet of 4		250.00	575.00
	Never hinged		425.00	
a.	SP97 5c+5c yel grn, blk & red		11.00	26.00
b.	SP98 10c+5c org yel, blk & red		47.50	210.00
c.	SP99 20c+5c brn red, blk & red (redrawn)		47.50	210.00
d.	SP100 30c+10c chlky bl, blk & red		11.00	26.00

National Fête Day. Sheets measure 125x65mm and sold for 5fr.

Gottfried Keller
SP102

Girl of Thurgau
SP103

Girl of
Solothurn
SP104

Girl of Zug
SP105

1940, Dec. 1   **Engr.**   *Perf. 11½*
B106	SP102	5c + 5c dk bl grn	.25	.40

Photo.
B107	SP103	10c + 5c brn & buff	.25	.30
B108	SP104	20c + 5c org red & buff	.25	.40
B109	SP105	30c + 10c dp ultra & buff	1.40	9.50
	Nos. B106-B109 (4)		2.15	10.60
	Set, never hinged		4.00	

Lake
Lucerne,
Arms of
Cantons
SP106

Tell
Chapel at
Chemin
Creux
SP107

1941, June 15
B110	SP106	10c + 10c multi	.30	.75
B111	SP107	20c + 10c org, red & lt buff	.30	1.25
	Set, never hinged		2.00	

Natl. Fête Day and 650th anniv. of Swiss
Independence.

Johann Lavater
SP108

Girl of
Schaffhausen
SP109

Girl of
Obwalden
SP110

Daniel Jean
Richard
SP111

1941, Dec. 1   **Engr.**
B112	SP108	5c + 5c dk grn	.25	.30
B113	SP111	30c + 10c dp ultra	.80	5.00

Photo.
B114	SP109	10c + 5c chnt & buff	.25	.40
B115	SP110	20c + 5c ver & buff	.25	.40
	Nos. B112-B115 (4)		1.55	6.10
	Set, never hinged		3.50	

Souvenir Sheet
Imperf
B116		Sheet of 2	60.00	*350.00*
a.		SP109 10c +5c chnt & buff	17.00	*125.00*
b.		SP110 20c +5c ver & buff	17.00	*125.00*
		Never hinged	100.00	

Issued in sheets measuring 75x70mm and
sold for 2fr. The surtax was used for charity.

Ancient
Geneva
SP113

Soldiers'
Monument,
Forch
SP114

1942, June 15   *Perf. 11½*
B117	SP113	10c + 10c gray blk, red & yel		.50
B118	SP114	20c + 10c cop red, red & buff		.85
	Set, never hinged		1.25	

National Fête Day, 1942. No. B117 for the
2000th anniv. of the City of Geneva.

Souvenir Sheet
Imperf
B119		Sheet of 2	50.00	*225.00*
a.		SP113 10c +10c gray black, red & yellow	14.00	*80.00*
b.		SP113 20c +10c copper red, red & buff	14.00	*80.00*
		Never hinged	82.50	

Issued in sheets measuring 105x63mm in
commemoration of National Fete and the
2000th anniv. of the City of Geneva. Sold for
2fr. The surtax was divided between the Swiss
Alliance of Samaritans and the National Community Chest.

Niklaus
Riggenbach
SP116

Girl of
Appenzell
SP117

Girl of Glarus
SP118

Konrad Escher
von der Linth
SP119

1942, Dec. 1   **Engr.**   *Perf. 11½*
B120	SP116	5c + 5c deep grn	.25	.50
B121	SP119	30c + 10c royal bl	1.10	4.50

Photo.
B122	SP117	10c + 5c dp brn & buff	.25	.50
B123	SP118	20c + 5c org red	.25	.50
	Nos. B120-B123 (4)		1.85	6.00
	Set, never hinged		3.75	

Intragna
SP120

Parliament
Buildings,
Bern
SP121

1943, June 15   **Photo.**   *Perf. 11½*
B124	SP120	10c + 10c blk brn, buff & dk red	.25	.75
B125	SP121	20c + 10c cop red, buff & dk red	.30	1.50
	Set, never hinged		1.25	

National Fête Day, 1943.

Emanuel von
Fellenberg
SP122

Silver Thistle
SP123

20c+5c, Lady slipper. 30c+10c, Gentian.

1943, Dec. 1   **Engr.**
B126	SP122	5c + 5c green	.25	.50

Photo.
B127	SP123	10c + 5c sl grn & ocher	.25	.50
B128	SP123	20c + 5c copper red & yel	.25	.50
B129	SP123	30c + 10c royal bl & lt bl	1.10	8.50
	Nos. B126-B129 (4)		1.85	10.00
	Set, never hinged		3.25	

Souvenir Sheets

SP126

1943   **Engr.**   *Imperf.*
B130	SP126	Sheet of 12	37.50	*60.00*
a.		10c black, single stamp	1.10	*3.75*
		Never hinged	77.50	

Sold for 5fr. Size: 165x140mm.

SP127

Red Horizontal Lines
B131	SP127	Sheet of 2	42.50	*52.50*
a.		4c black & red	13.00	*20.00*
b.		6c black & red	13.00	*20.00*
		Never hinged	75.00	

Sold for 3fr. Size: 70x75mm.

Arms of Geneva — SP128

B132	SP128	Sheet of 2	40.00	*40.00*
a.		5c green & black	11.50	*15.00*
		Never hinged	65.00	

Sold for 3fr. Size: 72x72mm. Centenary of
Swiss postage stamps. The surtax aided the
Swiss Red Cross.

Heiden
SP129

St. Jacob
SP130

Mesocco
SP131

Basel
SP132

Perf. 11½

1944, June 15   **Photo.**   *Unwmk.*
B133	SP129	5c + 5c dk bl grn, red & buff	.25	2.25
B134	SP130	10c + 10c gray blk, red & buff	.25	.50
B135	SP131	20c + 10c hn, red & buff	.25	1.00
B136	SP132	30c + 10c brt ultra & red	2.10	17.50
	Nos. B133-B136 (4)		2.85	21.25
	Set, never hinged		6.00	

National Fete Day.

Numa Droz
SP133

Edelweiss
SP134

Designs: 20c+5c, Lilium martagon.
30c+10c, Aquilegia alpina.

1944, Dec. 1   **Engr.**
B137	SP133	5c + 5c green	.25	.35

Photo.
B138	SP134	10c + 5c dk sl grn, yel & gray	.25	.40
B139	SP134	20c + 5c red, yel & gray	.35	.40
B140	SP134	30c + 10c bl, gray & lt bl	1.10	8.50
	Nos. B137-B140 (4)		1.95	9.65
	Set, never hinged		4.00	

Symbol of Faith, Hope and Love — SP137

1945

SCHWEIZER SPENDE AN DIE KRIEGSGESCHÄDIGTEN
SPENDE DER MARKENFREUNDE

DON SUISSE POUR LES VICTIMES DE LA GUERRE
DON DES AMIS DU TIMBRE

DONO SVIZZERO PER LE VITTIME DELLA GUERRA
DONO DEGLI AMICI DEL FRANCOBOLLO

Lifeboat Making a Rescue — SP138

1945, Feb. 20   **Perf. 11½**
B141 SP137 10c + 10c multi   .30   .50
B142 SP137 20c + 60c multi   .90   5.75
   Set, never hinged   2.50

Imperf
Souvenir Sheet
B143 SP138 3fr + 7fr bl gray 110.00 225.00
   Never hinged   200.00

Issued in sheets measuring 70x110mm.
Surtax for the benefit of war victims.

Souvenir Sheet

Dove of Basel — SP139

1945, Apr. 14   **Typo.**
B144 SP139 Sheet of 2   70.00 95.00
  a. 10c gray, maroon &   16.00 26.00
    black
   Never hinged   150.00

Cent. of the Basel Cantonal Stamp. The
sheets measure 71x63mm and sold for 3fr.
The surtax was for the Pro Juventute
Foundation.

Numeral of Value and Red Cross — SP140

1945   **Photo.**   **Perf. 12**
B145 SP140 5c + 10c grn & red   .30 .75
   Never hinged   .65

Weaver SP141

Farm of Jura SP142

Farm of Emmental SP143

Frame House, Eastern Switzerland — SP144

1945, June 15   **Engr.**   **Perf. 11½**
B146 SP141 5c + 5c bl grn &   .35 2.00
    red

Photo.
B147 SP142 10c + 10c brn,   .35 .75
    gray bl & red
B148 SP143 20c + 10c hn brn,   .55 .75
    buff & red
B149 SP144 30c + 10c saph &   5.50 35.00
    red
   Nos. B146-B149 (4)   6.75 38.50
   Set, never hinged   14.50

The surtax was for needy mothers.

Ludwig Forrer — SP145

Alpine Dog-Rose SP147

Susanna Orelli — SP146

Crocus SP148

1945, Dec. 1   **Engr.**
B150 SP145 5c + 5c dk grn   .25 .50
B151 SP146 10c + 10c dk red   .25 .50
    brn

Photo.
B152 SP147 20c + 10c rose brn,   .30 .50
    rose & yel org
B153 SP148 30c + 10c dk bl,   1.50 7.50
    gray & lil
   Nos. B150-B153 (4)   2.30 9.00
   Set, never hinged   4.50

Cheese Making SP149

Farm Buildings and Vineyards SP150

House in Appenzell SP151

House in Engadine SP152

1946, June 15   **Engr.**
B154 SP149 5c + 5c bl grn &   .35 2.00
    red

Photo.
B155 SP150 10c + 10c brn,   .25 .75
    buff & red
B156 SP151 20c + 10c henna,   .35 .75
    buff & red
B157 SP152 30c + 10c saph &   3.00 9.50
    red
   Nos. B154-B157 (4)   3.95 13.00
   Set, never hinged   9.50

Rodolphe Toepffer SP153

Narcissus SP154

20c+10c, Mountain sengreen. 30c+10c, Blue thistle.

1946, Nov. 30   **Engr.**
B158 SP153 5c + 5c green   .25 .50

Photo.
B159 SP154 10c + 10c dk sl grn,   .25 .50
    gray & red org
B160 SP154 20c + 10c brn car,   .30 .75
    gray & yel
B161 SP154 30c + 10c dk bl,   1.40 6.00
    gray & pink
   Nos. B158-B161 (4)   2.20 7.75
   Set, never hinged   3.75

Railroad Laborers SP157

Railroad Station, Rorschach SP158

Lüen-Castiel Station — SP159

Flüelen Station SP160

Perf. 11½
1947, June 14   **Engr.**   **Unwmk.**
B162 SP157 5c + 5c dk grn   .25 2.10
    & red

Photo.
B163 SP158 10c + 10c gray   .30 .75
    blk, cream & red

B164 SP159 20c + 10c rose lil,   .30 1.00
    cream & red
B165 SP160 30c + 10c bl, gray   3.50 9.00
    & red
   Nos. B162-B165 (4)   4.35 12.85
   Set, never hinged   10.00

The surtax was for professional education of invalids and for the fight against cancer.

Jakob Burckhardt SP161

Alpine Primrose SP162

20c+10c, Red lily. 30c+10c, Cyclamen.

1947, Dec. 1   **Engr.**
B166 SP161 5c + 5c dk grn   .25 .45

Photo.
B167 SP162 10c + 10c sl blk,   .25 .45
    gray & yel
B168 SP162 20c + 10c red brn,   .30 .40
    gray & cop red
B169 SP162 30c + 10c dk bl,   1.25 5.75
    gray & pink
   Nos. B166-B169 (4)   2.05 7.05
   Set, never hinged   3.50

Sun and Olympic Emblem SP165

Icehockey Player SP167

10c+10c, Snowflake and Olympic Emblem. 30c+10c, Ski-runner.

1948, Jan. 15
B170 SP165 5c + 5c dk bl grn &   .25 1.50
    yel
B171 SP165 10c + 10c choc & bl   .30 1.00
B172 SP167 20c + 10c dp mag,   .40 1.50
    gray & org yel
B173 SP167 30c + 10c dk bl, bl   1.25 5.50
    & gray blk
   Nos. B170-B173 (4)   2.20 9.50
   Set, never hinged   5.50

Issued to publicize the 5th Olympic Winter Games, St. Moritz, Jan. 30-Feb. 8, 1948.

Frontier Guard SP169

House of Fribourg SP170

House of Valais SP171

House of Ticino SP172

1948, June 15   Engr.

B174	SP169	5c + 5c dk grn & red	.25 1.25

Photo.

B175	SP170	10c + 10c sl & gray	.25 .75
B176	SP171	20c + 10c brn red & pink	.30 1.00
B177	SP172	30c + 10c bl & gray	2.25 7.50
		Nos. B174-B177 (4)	3.05 10.50
		Set, never hinged	6.00

Johann R. Wettstein — SP173

1948, Aug. 21   Perf. 11x12½

B178	SP173	Sheet of 2	50.00 65.00
a.		10c rose lilac	14.00 25.00
b.		20c chalky blue	14.00 25.00
		Never hinged	77.50

Intl. Phil. Expo., Basel, Aug. 21-29, 1948. Sheet, size 110x60mm, sold for 3fr, of which the surtax was used for the exhibition and charitable purposes.

Gen. Ulrich Wille SP174	Foxglove SP175

20c+10c, Alpine rose. 40c+10c, Lily of paradise.

1948, Dec. 1   Engr.   Perf. 11½

B179	SP174	5c + 5c dk vio brn	.25 .45

Photo.

B180	SP175	10c + 10c dk grn, yel grn & yel	.25 .45
B181	SP175	20c + 10c brn, crim & buff	.30 .45
B182	SP175	40c + 10c bl, gray & org	1.25 5.50
		Nos. B179-B182 (4)	2.05 6.85
		Set, never hinged	4.50

Postman SP176

Mountain Farmhouse SP177

House of Lucerne SP178

House of Prattigau SP179

Engraved and Photogravure
1949, June 15
Shield in Carmine

B183	SP176	5c + 5c rose vio	.30 1.50

Photo.

B184	SP177	10c + 10c bl grn & car	.30 .75
B185	SP178	20c + 10c dk brn & cr	.30 .75
B186	SP179	40c + 10c bl & pale bl	2.50 10.00
		Nos. B183-B186 (4)	3.40 13.00
		Set, never hinged	7.25

The surtax was for professional education of Swiss youth.

Niklaus Wengi SP180	Anemone Sulphureous SP181

20c+10c, Alpine clematis. 40c+10c, Superb pink.

1949, Dec. 1   Engr.   Perf. 11½

B187	SP180	5c + 5c vio brn	.25 .45

Photo.

B188	SP181	10c + 10c grn, gray & yel	.25 .45
B189	SP181	20c + 10c brn, bl & yel	.25 .45
B190	SP181	40c + 10c bl, lav & yel	1.40 5.50
		Nos. B187-B190 (4)	2.15 6.85
		Set, never hinged	4.00

Adaptation of 1850 Design SP182

Putting the Stone SP183

Designs: 20c+10c, Wrestlers. 30c+10c, Runners. 40c+10c, Target shooting.

1950, June 1   Engr. & Photo.
Shield in Red

B191	SP182	5c + 5c black	.25 .75

Photo.
Inscribed: "I. VIII. 1950"

B192	SP183	10c + 10c green	.50 .80
B193	SP183	20c + 10c brown ol	.50 1.25
B194	SP183	30c + 10c rose lil	3.75 17.00
B195	SP183	40c + 10c dull bl	4.75 11.00
		Nos. B191-B195 (5)	9.75 30.80
		Set, never hinged	20.00

The surtax was for the Red Cross and the Society of Swiss History of Art.

Theophil Sprecher von Bernegg SP184	Admiral Butterfly SP185

Designs: 20c+10c, Blue Underwing Butterfly. 30c+10c, Bee. 40c+10c, Sulphur Butterfly.

1950, Dec. 1   Engr.

B196	SP184	5c + 5c sepia	.25 .30

Photo.

B197	SP185	10c + 10c multi	.25 .40
B198	SP185	20c + 10c multi	.30 .50
B199	SP185	30c + 10c rose lil, gray & dk brn	3.00 13.50

B200	SP185	40c + 10c bl, dk brn & yel	3.00 9.25
		Nos. B196-B200 (5)	6.80 23.95
		Set, never hinged	13.50

Arms of Switzerland and Zurich — SP186

Valaisan Polka SP187	

20c+10c, Flag-swinging. 30c+10c, Hornussen (natl. game). 40c+10c, Blowing alphorn.

1951, June 1   Engr.
Shield in Red

B201	SP186	5c + 5c gray	.25 .50

Photo.
Inscribed: "1. VIII. 1951"
Shield in Red, Figure Shaded in Gray

B202	SP187	10c + 10c green	.40 .50
B203	SP187	20c + 10c ol bis	.60 .85
B204	SP187	30c + 10c red vio	4.50 11.50
B205	SP187	40c + 10c brt blue	4.50 13.50
		Nos. B201-B205 (5)	10.25 26.85
		Set, never hinged	20.00

The surtax was used primarily for needy mothers.

Souvenir Sheet
1951, Sept. 29   Imperf.

B206	SP187	40c brt bl, sheet	175.00 190.00
		Never hinged	275.00

No. B206 sold for 3fr, size: 74x56mm. Natl. Phil. Exhib., LUNABA, Sept. 29-Oct. 7, 1951, Lucerne. The net proceeds were used for Swiss schools abroad.

Johanna Spyri SP189	Dragonfly SP190

Butterflies: 20c+10c, Black-Veined. 30c+10c, Orange-Tip. 40c+10c, Saturnia pyri.

1951, Dec. 1   Engr.   Perf. 11½

B207	SP189	5c + 5c red brn	.25 .30

Photo.

B208	SP190	10c + 10c grn & dk bl	.25 .30
B209	SP190	20c + 10c rose lil, cr & blk	.30 .50
B210	SP190	30c + 10c ol grn, gray & org	2.00 8.50
B211	SP190	40c + 10c bl, dk brn & car	2.50 8.50
		Nos. B207-B211 (5)	5.30 18.10
		Set, never hinged	10.00

Arms of Switzerland, Glarus and Zug — SP191

Doubs River — SP192

Designs: 20c+10c, Lake of St. Gotthard. 30c+10c, Moesa River. 40c+10c, Lake of Marjelen.

1952, May 31   Engr. & Typo.

B212	SP191	5c + 5c gray & red	.25 1.00

Photo.

B213	SP192	10c + 10c blue green	.25 .50
B214	SP192	20c + 10c brown car	.30 .50
B215	SP192	30c + 10c brown	2.50 6.50
B216	SP192	40c + 10c blue	3.00 8.75
		Nos. B212-B216 (5)	6.30 17.25
		Set, never hinged	12.50

The surtax was used primarily for historical research and popular culture.

See Nos. B222-B226, B233-B236, B243-B246, B253-B256.

Portrait of a Boy, by Albert Anker SP193	Ladybug SP194

20c+10c, Barred-wing butterfly. 30c+10c, Argus butterfly. 40c+10c, Silkworm moth.

Perf. 11½
1952, Dec. 1   Unwmk.   Engr.

B217	SP193	5c + 5c brown car	.25 .35

Photo.

B218	SP194	10c + 10c bluish grn, blk & org red	.25 .35
B219	SP194	20c + 10c rose lil, cr & blk	.30 .50
B220	SP194	30c + 10c brn, blk & gray bl	2.00 8.25
B221	SP194	40c + 10c pale vio, brn & buff	1.90 8.75
		Nos. B217-B221 (5)	4.70 18.20
		Set, never hinged	10.00

See Nos. B227-B231, B238-B241.

Types Similar to 1952

Designs: 5c+5c, Arms of Switzerland and Bern. 10c+10c, Reuss River. 20c+10c, Sihl Lake. 30c+10c, Bisse River. 40c+10c, Lake of Geneva.

Engraved and Photogravure
1953, June 1

B222	SP191	5c + 5c gray & red	.25 .75

Photo.

B223	SP192	10c + 10c blue green	.25 .50
B224	SP192	20c + 10c brown car	.30 .75
B225	SP192	30c + 10c brown	2.50 7.00
B226	SP192	40c + 10c brown	2.50 6.50
		Nos. B222-B226 (5)	5.80 15.50
		Set, never hinged	12.50

The surtax was used for Swiss nationals abroad and for disabled persons.

Booklet Panes

Panes consisting of blocks, strips or pairs removed from large sheets of regular issue and fastened or enclosed within a cover or folder, often by stapling or sewing in the sheet margin, are no longer being listed. Such panes contain no straight edges and can easily be made privately.

Types Similar to 1952, Dated "1953"

5c+5c, Portrait of a girl, by Albert Anker. 10c+10c, Nun moth. 20c+10c, Camberwell beauty butterfly. 30c+10c, Purple longicorn beetle. 40c+10c, Self-portrait, Ferdinand Hodler, facing left.

1953, Dec. 1   Engr.   Perf. 11½

B227	SP193	5c + 5c rose brown	.25 .35

Photo.

B228	SP194	10c + 10c multi	.25 .30
B229	SP194	20c + 10c multi	.30 .50
a.		Sheet of 24	200.00
		Never hinged	375.00

b. Bkt. pane, 4 #B229, 2
#B230 32.50
B230 SP194 30c + 10c ol, blk
& red 1.90 8.25

Engr.

B231 SP193 40c + 10c blue 2.75 7.00
Nos. B227-B231 (5) 5.45 16.40
Set, never hinged 12.00

No. B229a consists of 16 No. B229 and 8
No. B230, arranged to include four se-tenant
pairs and four pairs which are both se-tenant
and tête bêche.

Opening Bars of
"Swiss Hymn"
SP195

Jeremias
Gotthelf
SP196

Types Similar to 1952, Dated "1954"

Views: 10c+10c, Neuchatel lake. 20c+10c,
Maggia river. 30c+10c, Cascade, Taubenloch
gorge. 40c+10c, Sils lake.

1954, June 1 Engr. Perf. 11½
B232 SP195 5c + 5c dk bl
grn .25 .75

Photo.

B233 SP192 10c + 10c blue
grn .25 .50
B234 SP192 20c + 10c deep
plum .35 .50
B235 SP192 30c + 10c dk
brown 2.00 6.75
B236 SP192 40c + 10c dp
blue 2.25 7.25
Nos. B232-B236 (5) 5.10 15.75
Set, never hinged 12.00

The surtax was used to aid vocational training and home nursing.
No. B232 commemorates the centenary of
the death of Alberik Zwyssig, composer of the
"Swiss Hymn."

Types Similar to 1952, Dated "1954"

Insects: 10c+10c, Garden tiger. 20c+10c,
Bumble bee. 30c+10c, Ascalaphus. 40c+10c,
Swallow-tail.

1954, Dec. 1 Engr.
B237 SP196 5c + 5c dk red
brn .25 .30

Photo.

B238 SP194 10c + 10c multi .25 .30
B239 SP194 20c + 10c multi .35 .50
B240 SP194 30c + 10c rose
vio, brn &
yel 2.00 6.75
B241 SP194 40c + 10c multi 2.25 7.25
Nos. B237-B241 (5) 5.10 15.10
Set, never hinged 11.00

Type Similar to 1952, Dated "1955," and

Federal Institute of
Technology,
Zurich — SP197

Views: 10c+10c, Saane river. 20c+10c,
Lake of Aegeri. 30c+10c, Grappelen Lake.
40c+10c, Lake of Bienne.

1955, June 1 Engr. Perf. 11½
B242 SP197 5c + 5c gray .25 .75

Photo.

B243 SP192 10c + 10c dp
green .25 .50
B244 SP192 20c + 10c rose
brn .35 .50
B245 SP192 30c + 10c brown 2.00 6.00
B246 SP192 40c + 10c dp
blue 2.25 7.50
Nos. B242-B246 (5) 5.10 15.25
Set, never hinged 11.50

The surtax aided mountain dwellers.
No. B242 for the centenary of the Federal
Institute of Technology in Zurich.

Charles Pictet
de Rochemont
SP198

Peacock
Butterfly
SP199

Insects: 20c+10c, Great Horntail. 30c+10c,
Yellow Bear moth. 40c+10c, Apollo butterfly.

1955, Dec. 1 Unwmk.
B247 SP198 5c + 5c brn car .25 .30

Photo.

Insects in Natural Colors

B248 SP199 10c + 10c yel grn .25 .30
B249 SP199 20c + 10c red .30 .50
B250 SP199 30c + 10c dk
ocher 2.50 4.75
B251 SP199 40c + 10c ultra 2.25 5.75
Nos. B247-B251 (5) 5.55 11.60
Set, never hinged 11.50

Types Similar to 1952, Dated "1956", and

"Woman's
Work" — SP200

Designs: 10c+10c, Rhone at St. Maurice.
20c+10c, Katzensee. 30c+10c, Rhine at Trin.
40c+10c, Lake Wallen.

1956, June 1 Engr. Perf. 11½
B252 SP200 5c + 5c turq bl .25 1.00

Photo.

B253 SP192 10c + 10c green .25 .50
B254 SP192 20c + 10c brn car .30 .75
B255 SP192 30c + 10c brown 2.00 4.75
B256 SP192 40c + 10c ultra 1.75 5.75
Nos. B252-B256 (5) 4.55 12.75
Set, never hinged 10.00

The surtax was for the National Day Collection, the National Library and Academy of Arts
and Letters. No. B252 was issued in honor of
Swiss women.

Carlo Maderno
SP201

Burnet Moth
SP202

Insects: 20c+10c, Purple Emperor.
30c+10c, Blue ground beetle. 40c+10c, Cabbage butterfly.

1956, Dec. 1 Engr. Perf. 11½
B257 SP201 5c + 5c brn car .25 .30

Photo.

Granite Paper

B258 SP202 10c + 10c grn, dk
grn & car
rose .25 .30
B259 SP202 20c + 10c multi .30 .30
B260 SP202 30c + 10c yel & dp
bl 1.40 4.50
B261 SP202 40c + 10c lt ultra,
pale yel &
sep 1.40 5.00
Nos. B257-B261 (5) 3.60 10.40
Set, never hinged 7.50

Red Cross and
Swiss Emblems
SP203

"Charity" — SP204

Engraved and Photogravure

1957, June 1 Unwmk. Perf. 11½
B262 SP203 5c + 5c gray &
red .25 .55

Photo.

Granite Paper

Cross in Deep Carmine

B263 SP204 10c + 10c brt grn
& gray .25 .30
B264 SP204 20c + 10c red &
bl gray .30 .30
B265 SP204 30c + 10c brn &
vio gray 1.75 4.50
B266 SP204 40c + 10c brt bl
& bis 1.90 5.75
Nos. B262-B266 (5) 4.45 11.40
Set, never hinged 10.00

The surtax went to the Red Cross for the
needs of the sick and to combat cancer.

Leonhard
Euler — SP205

Clouded
Yellow — SP206

Insects: 20c+10c, Magpie moth. 30c+10c,
Rose Chafer. 40c+10c, Red Underwing.

1957, Nov. 30 Engr. Perf. 11½
B267 SP205 5c + 5c brn car .25 .30

Photo.

Granite Paper

B268 SP206 10c + 10c multi .25 .30
B269 SP206 20c + 10c lil rose,
blk & yel .30 .50
B270 SP206 30c + 10c rose
brn, ind & brt
grn 1.40 4.50
B271 SP206 40c + 10c multi 1.40 3.50
Nos. B267-B271 (5) 3.60 9.10
Set, never hinged 7.50

> Catalogue values for unused
> stamps in this section, from this
> point to the end of the section, are
> for Never Hinged items.

Mother and
Child — SP207

Fluorite — SP208

Designs: 20c+10c, Ammonite. 30c+10c,
Garnet. 40c+10c, Rock Crystal.

Perf. 11½
1958, May 31 Unwmk. Engr.
B272 SP207 5c + 5c brn car .40 .40

Photo.

Granite Paper

B273 SP208 10c + 10c multi .55 .55
B274 SP208 20c + 10c blk, red
& ol bis .75 .75
B275 SP208 30c + 10c lil rose, dl
yel & mag 3.25 5.25
B276 SP208 40c + 10c blk,
chlky bl & sl
bl 3.25 5.00
Nos. B272-B276 (5) 8.20 11.95
Set, never hinged

The surtax was for needy mothers.
See #B283-B286, B292-B295, B304-B307.

Albrecht von
Haller — SP209

Pansy — SP210

Flowers: 20c+10c, China aster. 30c+10c,
Morning glory. 40c+10c, Christmas rose.

1958, Dec. 1 Engr. Perf. 11½
B277 SP209 5c + 5c brn car .25 .30

Photo.

Granite Paper

B278 SP210 10c + 10c grn, yel &
brn .25 .30
B279 SP210 20c + 10c multi .55 .30
B280 SP210 30c + 10c multi 2.00 3.50
B281 SP210 40c + 10c dk bl, yel
& grn 2.00 3.50
Nos. B277-B281 (5) 5.05 7.90
See Nos. B287-B291.

Mineral Type of 1958 and

Globe and Swiss
Flags — SP211

Designs: 10c+10c, Agate. 20c+10c, Tourmaline. 30c+10c, Amethyst. 40c+10c, Fossil
salamander (andrias).

1959, June 1 Engr. Perf. 11½
B282 SP211 5c + 5c dl grn &
red .40 .50

Photo.

Granite Paper

B283 SP208 10c + 10c gray, yel
grn & ver .50 .50
B284 SP208 20c + 10c blk, lil
rose & bl grn .65 .50
B285 SP208 30c + 10c blk, lt brn
& vio 2.25 3.00
B286 SP208 40c + 10c blk, bl &
gray 2.50 3.00
Nos. B282-B286 (5) 6.30 7.50

Types of 1958

Designs: 5c+5c, Karl Hilty. 10c+10c, Marigold. 20c+10c, Poppy. 30c+10c, Nasturtium.
50c+10c, Sweet pea.

1959, Dec. 1 Engr. Perf. 11½
B287 SP209 5c +5c brn car .25 .25

Photo.

Granite Paper

B288 SP210 10c + 10c dk grn,
grn & yel .30 .25
B289 SP210 20c + 10c mag, red
& grn .50 .25
B290 SP210 30c + 10c multi 2.25 3.00
B291 SP210 50c + 10c multi 2.25 3.00
Nos. B287-B291 (5) 5.55 6.75

Mineral Type of 1958 and

Owl, T-Square
and
Hammer — SP212

Designs: 5c+5c, Smoky quartz. 10c+10c,
Feldspar. 20c+10c, Gryphaea, fossil.
30c+10c, Azurite.

1960, June 1 Photo. Perf. 11½
Granite Paper

B292 SP208 5c + 5c blk, bl &
ocher .55 .75
B293 SP208 10c + 10c blk, yel
grn & pink .60 .50
B294 SP208 20c + 10c blk, lil
rose & yel .85 .50
B295 SP208 30c + 10c multi 4.00 3.75

Engr.

B296 SP212 50c + 10c bl &
gold 4.75 3.50
Nos. B292-B296 (5) 10.75 9.00

Souvenir Sheet
Imperf
Typo.

B297 Sheet of 4 .... 40.00 20.00
#B297 contains 4 50c+10c stamps of design SP212 in gold & blue. Size: 84x75mm. Sold for 3fr.

Alexandre Calame SP213 — Dandelion SP214

Flowers: 20c+10c, Phlox. 30c+10c, Larkspur. 50c+10c, Thorn apple.

1960, Dec. 1   Engr.   Unwmk.
B298	SP213	5c + 5c grnsh bl	.25 .25

Photo.
Granite Paper
B299	SP214	10c + 10c grn, yel & gray		.30 .25
B300	SP214	20c + 10c mag, grn & gray		.45 .25
B301	SP214	30c + 10c org brn, grn & bl		3.50 3.50
B302	SP214	50c + 10c ultra & grn		3.50 3.50
		Nos. B298-B302 (5)		8.00 7.75

See Nos. B308-B312, B329-B333, B339-B343.

Mineral Type of 1958 and

Book of History with Symbols of Time and Eternity — SP215

Designs: 10c+10c, Fluorite. 20c+10c, Petrified fish. 30c+10c, Lazulite. 50c+10c, Petrified fern.

1961, June 1   Engr.   Perf. 11½
B303	SP215	5c + 5c lt blue	.35 .50

Photo.
Granite Paper
B304	SP208	10c + 10c gray, grn & pink	.50 .35
B305	SP208	20c + 10c gray & car rose	.60 .35
B306	SP208	30c + 10c gray, org & grnsh bl	1.60 2.50
B307	SP208	50c + 10c gray, bl & bis	2.25 3.50
		Nos. B303-B307 (5)	5.30 7.20

Types of 1960
Designs: 5c+5c, Jonas Furrer. 10c+10c, Sunflower. 20c+10c, Lily of the valley. 30c+10c, Iris. 50c+10c, Silverweed.

1961, Dec. 1   Engr.   Perf. 11½
B308	SP213	5c + 5c dk blue	.25 .25

Photo.
Granite Paper
B309	SP214	10c + 10c grn, yel & org	.25 .25
B310	SP214	20c + 10c dk red, grn & gray	.30 .25
B311	SP214	30c + 10c multi	1.75 2.00
B312	SP214	50c + 10c dk bl, yel & grn	2.00 2.50
		Nos. B308-B312 (5)	4.55 5.25

Jean Jacques Rousseau SP216 — Half-Thaler, Obwalden, 1732 SP217

Coins: 20c+10c, Ducat, Schwyz, ca. 1653. 30c+10c, "Steer Head" Batzen, Uri, 1659. 50c+10c, Nidwalden Batzen.

Perf. 11½
1962, June 1   Unwmk.   Engr.
B313	SP216	5c + 5c dk blue	.25 .25

Photo.
Granite Paper
B314	SP217	10c + 10c grn & stl bl	.25 .25
B315	SP217	20c + 10c car rose & yel	.50 .50
B316	SP217	30c + 10c org & sl bl	1.25 1.65
B317	SP217	50c + 10c ultra & vio bl	1.25 1.65
		Nos. B313-B317 (5)	3.50 4.30

Apple Blossoms SP218 — Mother and Child SP219

Designs: 10c+10c, Boy chasing duck. 30c+10c, Girl and sunflowers. 50c+10c, Forsythia. 1fr+20c, Mother and child, facing right.

1962, Dec. 1   Perf. 11½
Granite Paper
B318	SP218	5c + 5c bl gray, pink, grn & yel	.25 .25
B319	SP218	10c + 10c grn, pink & dk grn	.25 .25
B320	SP219	20c + 10c org red, brn, grn & pink	.60 .50
B321	SP218	30c + 10c org, red & yel	1.10 2.00
B322	SP218	50c + 10c dp bl, yel & brn	1.50 2.50
		Nos. B318-B322 (5)	3.70 5.50

Souvenir Sheet
Imperf
B323	SP219	1fr + 20c Sheet of 2	5.25 5.25

50th anniv. of the Pro Juventute (Youth Aid) Foundation. No. B323 sold for 3fr.

Anna Heer, M.D. — SP220 — Bandage Roll — SP221

Designs: 20c+10c, Gift parcel. 30c+10c, Plasma bottles. 50c+10c, Red Cross armband.

1963, June 1   Engr.   Perf. 11½
B324	SP220	5c + 5c dk blue	.25 .25

Photo.
Granite Paper
Cross in Red
B325	SP221	10c + 10c lt & dk grn & gray	.25 .25
B326	SP221	20c + 10c rose, gray & blk	.50 .25
B327	SP221	30c + 10c multicolored	1.10 1.50
B328	SP221	50c + 10c bl, gray & blk	1.25 1.50
		Nos. B324-B328 (5)	3.35 3.75

Types of 1960
Designs: 5c+5c, Portrait of a Boy by Albert Anker. 10c+10c, Daisy. 20c+10c, Geranium. 30c+10c, Cornflower. 50c+10c, Carnation.

1963, Nov. 30   Engr.   Perf. 11½
B329	SP213	5c + 5c blue	.25 .30
a.		Booklet pane of 4	3.00

Photo.
B330	SP214	10c + 10c grn, gray & yel	.30 1.25
a.		Booklet pane of 4	4.00
B331	SP214	20c + 10c multi	1.40 2.50
a.		Booklet pane of 4	5.75

B332	SP214	30c + 10c multi	1.40 1.50
B333	SP214	50c + 10c ultra, lil rose & grn	1.75 1.50
		Nos. B329-B333 (5)	5.10 7.05

Nos. B329-B331 were printed on two kinds of paper: I. Fluorescent, with violet fibers. II. Non-fluorescent, the 10c+10c and 20c+10c with mixed red and blue fibers. Nos. B332-B333 exist only on violet-fibered, fluorescent paper. The booklet panes, Nos. B329a, B330a and B331a, exist only on non-fluorescent paper.

Johann Georg Bodmer SP222 — Copper Coin, Zurich SP223

Coins: 20c+10c, Doppeldicken, Basel. 30c+10c, Silver taler, Geneva. 50c+10c, Gold half florin, Bern.

Violet Fibers, Fluorescent Paper
1964, June 1   Engr.   Perf. 11½
B334	SP222	5c + 5c blue	.25 .25

Photo.
B335	SP223	10c + 10c grn, bis & blk	.25 .25
B336	SP223	20c + 10c rose car, gray & blk	.45 .25
B337	SP223	30c + 10c org, gray & blk	.70 .50

Granite Paper, Red and Blue Fibers
B338	SP223	50c + 10c ultra, yel & brn	1.15 .65
		Nos. B334-B338 (5)	2.80 1.90

Fluorescent Paper
Paper of Nos. B334-B425, B427 and B429 is fluorescent and has violet fibers.
Nos. B426, B428 and all semipostals from No. B430 onward are fluorescent but lack violet fibers, unless otherwise noted.

Types of 1960
Designs: 5c+5c, Portrait of a Girl by Albert Anker. 10c+10c, Daffodil. 20c+10c, Rose. 30c+10c, Clover. 50c+10c, Water lily.

1964, Dec. 1   Engr.   Perf. 11½
B339	SP213	5c + 5c grnsh bl	.25 .25

Photo.
B340	SP214	10c + 10c dp grn, yel & org	.25 .25
B341	SP214	20c + 10c dp car, rose & grn	.45 .25
B342	SP214	30c + 10c brn, lil & grn	.70 .55
B343	SP214	50c + 10c multi	1.15 .75
		Nos. B339-B343 (5)	2.80 2.05

Type of Regular Issue, 1965
Souvenir Sheet
10c, 20r Seated Helvetia. 20c, 40r Seated Helvetia.

1965, Mar. 8   Photo.   Imperf.
Granite Paper, Nonfluorescent
B344	A153	Sheet of 2	1.50 1.00
a.		10c grn, pale orange & blk	.75 .50
b.		20c dark red, yel grn & blk	.75 .50

Natl. Postage Stamp Exhib., NABRA, Bern, Aug. 27-Sept. 5, 1965. Sold for 3fr, the net proceeds were used to cover expenses of the exhibition and to promote philately.

Father Theodosius Florentini SP224 — The Temptation of Christ SP225

Ceiling Paintings from Church of St. Martin at Zillis, 12th century: 10c+10c, Symbol of evil (goose with fishtail). 20c+10c, Magi on horseback. 30c+10c, Fishermen on Sea of Galilee.

Perf. 11½
1965, June 1   Engr.
B345	SP224	5c + 5c blue	.25 .25

Photo.
B346	SP225	10c + 10c ol grn, ocher & bl	.25 .25
B347	SP225	20c + 10c dk brn, red & buff	.45 .25
B348	SP225	30c + 10c dk brn, sep & bl	.70 .30
B349	SP225	50c + 10c vio bl, bl & brn	1.15 .30
		Nos. B345-B349 (5)	2.80 1.35

See Nos. B355-B359, B365-B369.

Hedgehogs — SP226

Designs: 10c+10c, Alpine marmots. 20c+10c, Red deer. 30c+10c, European badgers. 50c+10c, Varying hares.

1965, Dec. 1   Photo.   Perf. 11½
B350	SP226	5c + 5c multi	.25 .25
B351	SP226	10c + 10c multi	.25 .25
B352	SP226	20c + 10c multi	.45 .25
B353	SP226	30c + 10c multi	.70 .25
B354	SP226	50c + 10c multi	1.15 .30
		Nos. B350-B354 (5)	2.80 1.30

See Nos. B360-B364.

Types of 1965
5c+5c, Heinrich Federer (1866-1928), writer. 10c+10c, Joseph's dream. 20c+10c, Joseph on his way. 30c+10c, Virgin and Child fleeing to Egypt. 50c+10c, Angel leading the way. Nos. B356-B359 from ceiling paintings, Church of St. Martin at Zillis.

1966, June 1   Engr.   Perf. 11½
B355	SP224	5c + 5c dp blue	.25 .25

Photo.
B356	SP225	10c + 10c multi	.25 .25
B357	SP225	20c + 10c multi	.45 .25
B358	SP225	30c + 10c multi	.70 .25
B359	SP225	50c + 10c multi	1.15 .35
		Nos. B355-B359 (5)	2.80 1.35

Animal Type of 1965
5c+5c, Ermine. 10c+10c, Red squirrel. 20c+10c, Red fox. 30c+10c, Hares. 50c+10c, Two chamois.

1966, Dec. 1   Photo.   Perf. 11½
Animals in Natural Colors
B360	SP226	5c + 5c grnsh bl	.25 .25
B361	SP226	10c + 10c emer	.25 .25
B362	SP226	20c + 10c ver	.45 .25
B363	SP226	30c + 10c brt lemon	.70 .25
B364	SP226	50c + 10c ultra	1.15 .35
		Nos. B360-B364 (5)	2.80 1.35

Types of 1965
Designs: 5c+5c, Dr. Theodor Kocher. 10c+10c, Annunciation to the Shepherds. 20c+10c, Jesus and the Samaritan Woman at the Well. 30c+10c, Adoration of the Magi. 50c+10c St. Joseph. (Ceiling paintings, St. Martin at Zillis.)

Perf. 11½
1967, June 1   Unwmk.   Engr.
B365	SP224	5c + 5c blue	.25 .25

Photo.
B366	SP225	10c + 10c multi	.25 .25
B367	SP225	20c + 10c multi	.45 .25
B368	SP225	30c + 10c multi	.70 .25
B369	SP225	50c + 10c multi	1.15 .35
		Nos. B365-B369 (5)	2.80 1.35

Roe Deer — SP227 — Hunter, Month of May — SP228

Designs: 20c+10c, Pine marten. 30c+10c, Alpine ibex. 50c+20c, Otter.

**1967, Dec. 1   Photo.   *Perf. 11½*
Animals in Natural Colors**

B370	SP227 10c + 10c yel grn	.25	.25
B371	SP227 20c + 10c dp car	.45	.25
B372	SP227 30c + 10c ol bis	.70	.25
B373	SP227 50c + 20c ultra	1.15	.50
	Nos. B370-B373 (4)	2.55	1.25

1968, May 30   Photo.   *Perf. 11½*

Designs from Rose Window, Lausanne Cathedral: 20c+10c, Leo. 30c+10c, Libra. 50c+20c, Pisces.

B374	SP228 10c + 10c multi	.25	.25
B375	SP228 20c + 10c multi	.45	.25
B376	SP228 30c + 10c multi	.70	.30
B377	SP228 50c + 20c multi	1.15	.50
	Nos. B374-B377 (4)	2.55	1.50

Capercaillie — SP229   St. Francis — SP230

Birds: 20c+10c, Bullfinch. 30c+10c, Woodchat shrike. 50c+20c, Firecrest.

**1968, Nov. 28   Photo.   *Perf. 11½*
Birds in Natural Colors**

B378	SP229 10c + 10c dull yel	.25	.25
B379	SP229 20c + 10c olive grn	.45	.25
B380	SP229 30c + 10c lilac rose	.70	.25
B381	SP229 50c + 20c dp violet	1.15	.50
	Nos. B378-B381 (4)	2.55	1.25

See Nos. B386-B389.

1969, May 29   Photo.   *Perf. 11½*

Designs: 10c+10c, St. Francis Preaching to the Birds, Königsfelden Convent Church. 20c+10c, Israelites Drinking from Spring of Moses, Berne Cathedral. 30c+10c, St. Christopher, Laufelfinger Church (now Basel Museum). 50c+20c, Virgin and Child, Chapel at Grapplang (now National Museum).

B382	SP230 10c + 10c multi	.25	.25
B383	SP230 20c + 10c multi	.45	.25
B384	SP230 30c + 10c multi	.70	.25
B385	SP230 50c + 20c multi	1.15	.45
	Nos. B382-B385 (4)	2.55	1.20

Bird Type of 1968

Birds: 10c+10c, European goldfinch. 20c+10c, Golden oriole. 30c+10c, Wall creeper. 50c+20c, Eurasian jay.

**1969, Dec. 1   Photo.   *Perf. 11½*
Birds in Natural Colors**

B386	SP229 10c + 10c gray	.25	.25
B387	SP229 20c + 10c green	.45	.25
B388	SP229 30c + 10c plum	.70	.25
B389	SP229 50c + 20c ultra	1.15	.55
	Nos. B386-B389 (4)	2.55	1.30

Sailor, by Gian Casty, Gellert Schoolhouse, Basel — SP231

Blue Titmice — SP232

Contemporary Stained Glass Windows: 20c+10c, Abstract composition, by Celestino Piatti. 30c+10c, Bull (Assyrian god Marduk), by Hans Stocker. 50c+20c, Man and Woman, by Max Hunziker and Karl Ganz.

1970, May 29   Photo.   *Perf. 11½*

B390	SP231 10c + 10c multi	.25	.25
B391	SP231 20c + 10c multi	.45	.25
B392	SP231 30c + 10c multi	.70	.25
B393	SP231 50c + 20c multi	1.15	.50
	Nos. B390-B393 (4)	2.55	1.25

See Nos. B398-B401.

1970, Dec. 1   Photo.   *Perf. 11½*

Birds: 20c+10c, Hoopoe. 30c+10c, Greater spotted woodpecker. 50c+20c, Crested grebes.

Birds in Natural Colors

B394	SP232 10c + 10c orange	.25	.25
B395	SP232 20c + 10c emerald	.45	.25
B396	SP232 30c + 10c brt rose	.70	.25
B397	SP232 50c + 20c blue	1.15	.75
	Nos. B394-B397 (4)	2.55	1.50

See Nos. B402-B405.

Art Type of 1970

Contemporary Stained Glass Windows: 10c+10c, "Composition," by Jean-François Comment. 20c+10c, Cock, by Jean Prahin. 30c+10c, Fox, by Kurt Volk. 50c+20c, "Composition," by Bernard Schorderet.

1971, May 27   Photo.   *Perf. 11½*

B398	SP231 10c + 10c multi	.25	.25
B399	SP231 20c + 10c multi	.45	.25
B400	SP231 30c + 10c multi	.70	.25
B401	SP231 50c + 20c multi	1.15	.45
	Nos. B398-B401 (4)	2.55	1.20

Bird Type of 1970

Birds: 10c+10c, European redstarts. 20c+10c, White-spotted bluethroats. 30c+10c, Peregrine falcon. 40c+20c, Mallards.

1971, Dec. 1

B402	SP232 10c + 10c multi	.25	.25
B403	SP232 20c + 10c multi	.45	.25
B404	SP232 30c + 10c multi	.70	.25
B405	SP232 40c + 20c multi	.95	.60
	Nos. B402-B405 (4)	2.35	1.35

Harpoon Heads, Late Stone Age — SP233

McGredy's Sunset — SP234

Archaeological Treasures: 20c+10c, Bronze hydria, Hallstadt period. 30c+10c, Gold bust of Emperor Marcus Aurelius, Roman period. 40c+20c, Horseman rider (decorative disk), early Middle Ages.

1972, June 1

B406	SP233 10c + 10c multi	.25	.25
B407	SP233 20c + 10c multi	.45	.25
B408	SP233 30c + 10c multi	.70	.25
B409	SP233 40c + 20c multi	.95	.70
	Nos. B406-B409 (4)	2.35	1.45

1972, Dec. 1   Photo.   *Perf. 11½*

Famous Roses: 20c+10c, Miracle. 30c+10c, Papa Meilland. 40c+20c, Madame Dimitriu.

B410	SP234 10c + 10c multi	.25	.25
B411	SP234 20c + 10c multi	.45	.25
B412	SP234 30c + 10c multi	.70	.25
B413	SP234 40c + 20c multi	.95	1.10
	Nos. B410-B413 (4)	2.35	1.85

Rauraric (Gallic) Jug — SP235

Archeologic Finds: 30c+10c, Bronze head of a Gaul. 40c+20c, Alemannic dress fasteners (fish), 6th century. 60c+20c, Gold bowl, 6th century B.C.

1973, May 29   Photo.   *Perf. 11½*

B414	SP235 15c + 5c multi	.35	.25
B415	SP235 30c + 10c multi	.70	.25
B416	SP235 40c + 20c multi	.95	.60
B417	SP235 60c + 20c multi	1.40	.85
	Nos. B414-B417 (4)	3.40	1.95

See Nos. B422-B425.

Chestnut — SP236

Fruits of the Forest: 30c+10c, Sweet cherries. 40c+20c, Blackberries. 60c+20c, Blueberries.

1973, Nov. 29   Photo.   *Perf. 11½*

B418	SP236 15c + 5c multi	.35	.25
B419	SP236 30c + 10c multi	.70	.25
B420	SP236 40c + 20c multi	.95	.60
B421	SP236 60c + 20c multi	1.40	.70
	Nos. B418-B421 (4)	3.40	1.80

Archaeological Type of 1973

Archaeological Finds: 15c+5c, Polychrome glass bowl. 30c+10c, Bull's head. 40c+20c, Gold fibula. 60c+20c, Ceramic bird.

1974, May 30   Photo.   *Perf. 11½*

B422	SP235 15c + 5c multi	.35	.25
B423	SP235 30c + 10c multi	.70	.30
B424	SP235 40c + 20c multi	.95	.55
B425	SP235 60c + 20c multi	1.40	.70
	Nos. B422-B425 (4)	3.40	1.80

Laurel — SP237

Gold Fibula, 6th Century — SP238

Designs: 30c+20c, Belladonna. 50c+20c, Laburnum. 60c+25c, Mistletoe.

1974, Nov. 29   Photo.   *Perf. 11½*

B426	SP237 15c + 10c multi	.35	.25
B427	SP237 30c + 20c multi	.70	.25
B428	SP237 50c + 20c multi	1.15	.60
B429	SP237 60c + 25c multi	1.40	.80
	Nos. B426-B429 (4)	3.60	1.90

1975, May 30   Photo.   *Perf. 11½*

Archaeological Treasures: 30c+20c, Bronze head of Bacchus, 2nd century. 50c+20c, Bronze daggers, 1800-1600 B.C. 60c+25c, Colored glass bottle, 1st century.

B430	SP238 15c + 10c multi	.35	.25
B431	SP238 30c + 20c multi	.70	.25
B432	SP238 50c + 20c multi	1.15	.70
B433	SP238 60c + 25c multi	1.40	.75
	Nos. B430-B433 (4)	3.60	1.95

Mail Bucket — SP239

Hepatica — SP240

Forest Plants: 30c+20c, Mountain ash berries. 50c+20c, Yellow nettle. 60c+25c, Sycamore maple.

1975, Nov. 27   Photo.   *Perf. 11½*

B434	SP239 10c + 5c multi	.25	.25
B435	SP240 15c + 10c multi	.35	.25
B436	SP240 30c + 20c multi	.70	.30
B437	SP240 50c + 20c multi	1.15	.65
B438	SP240 60c + 25c multi	1.40	.75
	Nos. B434-B438 (5)	3.85	2.20

See Nos. B443-B446.

Castles — SP241

1976, May 28   Photo.   *Perf. 11½*

B439	SP241 20c + 10 Kyburg	.45	.25
B440	SP241 40c + 20 Grandson	.95	.30
B441	SP241 40c + 20 Murten	.95	.30
B442	SP241 80c + 40 Bellinzona	2.25	.85
	Nos. B439-B442 (4)	4.60	1.70

See #B447-B450, B455-B458, B463-B466.

Plant Type of 1975

Medicinal Forest Plants: 20c+10c, Barberry. No. B444, Black elder. 40c+20c, Linden. 80+40c, Pulmonaria.

1976, Nov. 29   Photo.   *Perf. 11½*

B443	SP240 20c + 10c multi	.45	.25
B444	SP240 40c + 20c lil & multi	.95	.25
B445	SP240 40c + 20c terra cotta & multi	.95	.25
B446	SP240 80c + 40c multi	1.90	.80
	Nos. B443-B446 (4)	4.25	1.55

Castle Type of 1976

1977, May 26   Photo.   *Perf. 11½*

B447	SP241 26c + 10c Aigle	.45	.25
B448	SP241 40c + 20c Pratteln	.95	.35
B449	SP241 70c + 30c Sargans	1.60	.90
B450	SP241 80c + 40c Hallwil	1.90	1.00
	Nos. B447-B450 (4)	4.90	2.50

Wild Rose — SP242

Communal Arms — SP243

Designs: Roses.

1977, Nov. 28   Photo.   *Perf. 11½*

B451	SP242 20c + 10c multi	.45	.25
B452	SP242 40c + 20c multi	.95	.25
B453	SP242 70c + 30c multi	1.60	.80
B454	SP242 80c + 40c multi	1.90	1.00
	Nos. B451-B454 (4)	4.90	2.30

See Nos. B492-B496.

Castle Type of 1976

1978, May 26   Photo.   *Perf. 11½*

B455	SP241 20c + 10c Hagenwil	.45	.30
B456	SP241 40c + 20c Burgdorf	.95	.60
B457	SP241 70c + 30c Tarasp	1.60	1.25
B458	SP241 80c + 40c Chillon	1.90	1.50
	Nos. B455-B458 (4)	4.90	3.65

1978, Nov. 28   Photo.   *Perf. 11½*

B459	SP243 20c + 10c Aarburg	.45	.25
B460	SP243 40c + 20c Gruyeres	.95	.25
B461	SP243 70c + 30c Castasegna	1.60	1.00
B462	SP243 80c + 40c Wangen an der Aare	1.90	1.25
	Nos. B459-B462 (4)	4.90	2.75

See #B467-B470, B475-B478, B484-B487.

Castle Type of 1976

1979, May 25   Photo.   *Perf. 11½*

B463	SP241 20c + 10c Oron	.45	.30
B464	SP241 40c + 20c Spiez	.95	.45
B465	SP241 70c + 30c Porrentruy	1.60	1.00
B466	SP241 80c + 40c Rapperswil	1.90	1.50
	Nos. B463-B466 (4)	4.90	3.25

Arms Type of 1978

1979, Nov. 28   Photo.   *Perf. 11*

B467	SP243 20c + 10c Cadro	.45	.25
B468	SP243 40c + 20c Rute	.95	.25
B469	SP243 70c + 30c Schwamendingen	1.60	.85
B470	SP243 80c + 40c Perroy	1.90	1.10
	Nos. B467-B470 (4)	4.90	2.45

Masons' and Carpenters' Sign — SP244

1980, May 29   Photo.   Perf. 11½
B471 SP244 20c + 10c shown   .45   .30
B472 SP244 40c + 20c Barber   .95   .30
B473 SP244 70c + 30c Hat mak-
              er   1.60 1.00
B474 SP244 80c + 40c Baker   1.90 1.25
     Nos. B471-B474 (4)   4.90 2.85

Arms Type of 1978
1980, Nov. 26   Photo.   Perf. 11½
B475 SP243 20c + 10c Cortaillod   .45   .25
B476 SP243 40c + 20c Sierre   .95   .25
B477 SP243 70c + 30c Scuol   1.60   .90
B478 SP243 80c + 40c Wolfen-
              schiessen   1.90   .95
     Nos. B475-B478 (4)   4.90 2.35

Icarus in
Flight
SP245

1981, Mar. 9   Photo.
B479 SP245 2fr + 1fr multi   4.75 3.00

Swissair, 50th Anniversary. Surtax was for
Pro Aero Foundation Issued in sheet of 8.

Post Office Sign,
Aarburg,
1685 — SP246

Post Office Signs (c. 1849).

1981, May 4   Photo.
B480 SP246 20c + 10c shown   .45   .30
B481 SP246 40c + 20c Fribourg   .95   .50
B482 SP246 70c + 30c Gordola   1.60 1.10
B483 SP246 80c + 40c Splugen   1.90 1.25
     Nos. B480-B483 (4)   4.90 3.15

Arms Type of 1978
1981, Nov. 26   Photo.   Perf. 11½
B484 SP243 20c + 10c Uffikon   .45   .25
B485 SP243 40c + 20c Torre   .95   .30
B486 SP243 70c + 30c Benken   1.60   .60
B487 SP243 80c + 40c Prever-
              enges   1.90   .75
     Nos. B484-B487 (4)   4.90 1.90

Sonne Inn
Sign, Willisau
SP247

1982, May 27   Photo.   Perf. 11½
B488 SP247 20c + 10c shown   .45   .25
B489 SP247 40c + 20c A
              L'Onde, St.
              Saphorin   .95   .30
B490 SP247 70c + 30c Three
              Kings,
              Rheinfelden   1.60   .55
B491 SP247 80c + 40c Krone,
              Winterthur   1.90   .70
     Nos. B488-B491 (4)   4.90 1.80
     See Nos. B497-B500.

Rose Type of 1977
Designs: 10c+10c, Letter balance. 20c+10c,
La Belle Portugaise. 40c+20c, Hugh Dickson.
70c+30c, Mermaid. 80c+40c, Madame
Caroline.

1982, Nov. 25   Photo.
B492 SP242 10c + 10c multi   .25   .25
B493 SP242 20c + 10c multi   .45   .25
B494 SP242 40c + 20c multi   .95   .30
B495 SP242 70c + 30c multi   1.60   .80
B496 SP242 80c + 40c multi   1.90 1.10
     Nos. B492-B496 (5)   5.15 1.70

Inn Sign Type of 1982
1983, May 26   Photo.
B497 SP247 20c + 10c Lion Inn,
              Heimiswil,
              1669   .45   .30
B498 SP247 40c + 20c Cross
              Hotel, Sach-
              seln, 1489   .95   .50

B499 SP247 70c + 30c Tankard
              Inn, 1830   1.60   .80
B500 SP247 80c + 40c Au Cava-
              lier Inn, Vaud   1.90   1.00
     Nos. B497-B500 (4)   4.90   2.60

Antique
Toys — SP248

1983, Nov. 24
B501 SP248 20c + 10c Kitchen
              stove, 1850   .45   .25
B502 SP248 40c + 20c Rocking
              horse, 1826   .95   .35
B503 SP248 70c + 30c Doll,
              1870   1.60   .55
B504 SP248 80c + 40c Steam lo-
              comotive, 1900   1.90   .70
     Nos. B501-B504 (4)   4.90 1.85

Ceramic Tiled
Stoves — SP249

1984, May 24   Photo.   Perf. 11½
B505 SP249 35c + 15c 1566   .80   .40
B506 SP249 50c + 20c 1646   1.15   .50
B507 SP249 70c + 30c 1768   1.60   .70
B508 SP249 80c + 40c 18th
              cent.   1.90   .90
     Nos. B505-B508 (4)   5.45 2.50
     See Nos. B660-B663.

Children's
Stories
SP250

1984, Nov. 26   Photo.
B509 SP250 35c + 15c Heidi   .80   .40
B510 SP250 50c + 20c Pinocchio   1.15   .50
B511 SP250 70c + 30c Pippi
              Longstocking   1.60   .70
B512 SP260 80c + 40c Max and
              Moritz   1.90   .90
     Nos. B509-B512 (4)   5.45 2.50

Musical
Museum
Exhibits
SP251

1985, May 28   Photo.   Perf. 11½
B513 SP251 25c + 10c Music
              box, 1895   .60   .25
B514 SP251 35c + 15c Rattle
              box, 18th cent.   .80   .25
B515 SP251 50c + 20c Em-
              menthal neck-
              ed zither, 1828   1.15   .25
B516 SP251 70c + 30c Drum,
              1571   1.60   .30
B517 SP251 80c + 40c Diatonic
              accordion,
              20th cent.   1.90   .35
     Nos. B513-B517 (5)   6.05 1.40

Surtax for Swiss cultural programs.

Hansel and
Gretel
SP252

Fairy tales by Jakob (1785-1863) and Wilhelm (1786-1859) Grimm.

1985, Nov. 26   Photo.
B518 SP252 35c + 15c shown   .80   .25
B519 SP252 50c + 20c Snow
              White   1.15   .25
B520 SP252 80c + 40c Little Red
              Riding Hood   1.90   .35
B521 SP252 90c + 40c Cinderel-
              la   2.10   .40
     Nos. B518-B521 (4)   5.95 1.25

Surtax for Pro Juventute Foundation and
youth welfare orgs.

Man, Vitality
and
Movement
SP253

1986, Feb. 11   Photo.   Perf. 12
B522 SP253 50c + 20c multi   1.15   .25

Surtax for Natl. Sports Federation and cultural programs.

Paintings in
Natl. Museums
SP254

Swiss art: 35c+15c, Bridge in the Sun,
1907, by Giovanni Giacometti (1868-1933).
50c+20c, The Violet Hat, 1907, by Cuno Amiet
(1868-1961). 80c+40c, After the Funeral,
1905, by Max Buri (1868-1915). 90c+40c, Still
Life, 1914, by Felix Valloton (1865-1925).

1986, Apr. 22   Photo.   Perf. 11½
B523 SP254 35c + 15c multi   .80   .25
B524 SP254 50c + 20c multi   1.15   .25
B525 SP254 80c + 40c multi   1.90   .40
B526 SP254 90c + 40c multi   2.10   .45
     Nos. B523-B526 (4)   5.95 1.35

Surtax for Natl. Day Collection &monuments
preservation, social & cultural organizations.

Children's
Toys — SP255

1986, Nov. 25   Photo.
B527 SP255 35c + 15c Teddy
              bear   .80   .25
B528 SP255 50c + 20c Top   1.15   .30
B529 SP255 80c + 40c Steam-
              roller   1.90   .50
B530 SP255 90c + 40c Doll   2.10   .55
     Nos. B527-B530 (4)   5.95 1.60

Surtax was for youth welfare organizations
and the Pro Juventute Foundation.

Antique
Furniture
SP256

Designs: 35c+15c, Saane Valley wall cabi-
net, 1764, Vieux Pays d'Enhaut Museum,
Chateau d'Oex. 50c+20c, Raised chest, 16th
cent., Rhaetian Museum, Chur. 80c+40c,
Ticino canton cradle, 1782, Valmaggia
Museum, Cevio. 90c+40c, Appenzell region
wardrobe, 1698, St. Gallen Historical
Museum.

1987, May 26   Photo.
B531 SP256 35c + 15c multi   .80   .25
B532 SP256 50c + 20c multi   1.15   .35
B533 SP256 80c + 40c multi   1.90   .60
B534 SP256 90c + 40c multi   2.10   .60
     Nos. B531-B534 (4)   5.95 1.80

Surtax for Red Cross and patriotic funds.

**No. 786 Surcharged with Clasped
Hands and "7.9.87" in Red
Photo. & Engr.**
1987, Sept. 7   Perf. 13½x13
B535 A349 50c + 50c multi   1.25   .45

Surtaxed to benefit flood victims.

Christmas   Child
SP257   Development
                   SP258

1987, Nov. 24   Photo.   Perf. 11½
B536 SP257 25c +10c shown   .60   .25
B537 SP258 35c +15c shown   .80   .25
B538 SP258 50c +20c Boy, build-
              ing blocks   1.15   .30
B539 SP258 80c +40c Boy, girl
              in sandbox   1.90   .55
B540 SP258 90c +40c Father,
              child   2.10   .60
     Nos. B536-B540 (5)   6.55 1.95

Surtax for national youth welfare projects
and the Pro Juventute Foundation.
See Nos. B555-B558.

Junkers JU-
52, 1939, and
the
Matterhorn
SP259

1988, Mar. 8   Photo.
B541 SP259 140c +60c multi   3.25 2.50

Pro Aero Foundation, Zurich, 50th Anniv.
Issued in sheets of 8.

SP260   SP261

Minnesingers.

1988, May 24   Photo.
B542 SP260 35c +15c Count Ru-
              dolf of Neu-
              chatel   .80   .25
B543 SP260 50c +20c Rudolf
              von Rotenburg   1.15   .35
B544 SP260 80c +40c Master
              Johannes
              Hadlaub   1.90   .60
B545 SP260 90c +40c The
              Hardegger   2.10   .65
     Nos. B542-B545 (4)   5.95 1.85

700 Years of art and culture.

1988, Nov. 25   Perf. 11½
B546 SP261 35c +15c Reading   .80   .25
B547 SP261 50c +20c Music   1.15   .30
B548 SP261 80c +40c Math   1.90   .55
B549 SP261 90c +40c Art   2.10   .60
     Nos. B546-B549 (4)   5.95 1.70

Child development. Surtax for natl. youth
welfare projects and the Pro Juventute
Foundation.

700 Years of
Art and Culture
SP262

Illuminations in Zurich Central, Bern
Burgher and Lucerne Central libraries: No.
B550, King Friedrich II presenting Bern munic-
ipal charter, 1218, *Bendicht Tschachtlan*

Chronicle, 1470. No. B551, Capt. Adrian von Bubenberg and troops passing through Murten town gate, 1476, *Bern Chronicle*, by Diebold Schilling, 1483. No. B552, Official messenger of Schwyz before the Council of Zurich, c. 1440, *Gerold Edlibach Chronicle*, 1485. No. B553, Schilling presenting manuscript to the mayor and councilmen in the council chamber, Lucerne, c. 1500, *Diebold Schilling's Lucerne Chronicle*, 1513.

1989, May 23

B550	SP262	35c +15c multi	.80	.25
B551	SP262	50c +20c multi	1.15	.30
B552	SP262	80c +40c multi	1.90	.50
B553	SP262	90c +40c multi	2.10	.55
	Nos. B550-B553 (4)		5.95	1.60

Surtax to benefit women's and cultural organizations.

Gymnastics
SP263

1989, Aug. 25   Photo.   Perf. 11½

B554	SP263	50c +20c multi	1.15	.30

Surtax to benefit Swiss Natl. Sports Federation, cultural and social work.

Child Development Type of 1987

1989, Nov. 24

B555	SP258	35c +15c Community work	.80	.25
B556	SP258	50c +20c Friendship	1.15	.25
B557	SP258	80c +40c Vocational training	1.90	.50
B558	SP258	90c +40c Higher education and research	2.10	.55
	Nos. B555-B558 (4)		5.95	1.55

Surtax for natl. youth welfare projects and the Pro Juventute Foundation.

700 Years of Art and Culture — SP264

Street criers: No. B559, Fly swatter and starch-sprinkler vendor. No. B560, Clock vendor. No. B561, Knife grinder. No. B562, Pinewood sellers.

1990, May 22   Photo.

B559	SP264	35c +15c multi	.80	.25
B560	SP264	50c +20c multi	1.15	.30
B561	SP264	80c +40c multi	1.90	.55
B562	SP264	90c +40c multi	2.10	.60
	Nos. B559-B562 (4)		5.95	1.70

Souvenir Sheet

Natl. Philatelic Exhibition, Geneva '90 — SP265

a, Brass badge worn by Geneva Cantonal post drivers before 1849. b, Place du Bourg-de-Four and entrance to Rue Etienne-Dumont. c, Ile Rousseau and Pont des Bergues. d, No. 2L1 on cover.

1990, Sept. 5

B563	SP265	Sheet of 4	5.50	5.50
a.-d.		50c +25c any single	1.15	.35

Child Development
SP266

1990, Nov. 20

B564	SP266	35c +15c Model making	.80	.25
B565	SP266	50c +20c Youth groups	1.15	.30
B566	SP266	80c +40c Sports	1.90	.55
B567	SP266	90c +40c Music	2.10	.60
	Nos. B564-B567 (4)		5.95	1.70

700 Years of Art and Culture SP267

Contemporary paintings by: 50c+20c, Wolf Barth. 70c+30c, Helmut Federle. 80c+40c, Matthias Bosshart. 90c+40c, Werner Otto Leuenberger.

1991, May 14   Photo.   Perf. 11½

B568	SP267	50c +20c multi	1.15	.30
B569	SP267	70c +30c multi	1.60	.45
B570	SP267	80c +40c multi	1.90	.55
B571	SP267	90c +40c multi	2.10	.60
	Nos. B568-B571 (4)		6.75	1.90

Woodland Flowers
SP268

50c+25c, Allium ursinum. 70c+30c, Geranium sylvaticum. 80c+40c, Campanula trachelium. 90c+40c, Hieracium murorum.

1991, Nov. 26

B572	SP268	50c +25c multi	1.15	.40
B573	SP268	70c +30c multi	1.60	.45
B574	SP268	80c +40c multi	1.90	.55
B575	SP268	90c +40c multi	2.10	.60
	Nos. B572-B575 (4)		6.75	2.00

Surtax for youth and family welfare projects and the Pro Juventute Foundation.

Swiss Folk Art — SP269

50c + 20c, Earthenware plate, Heimberg, 18th cent. 70c + 40c, Paper cutout by Johann Jakob Hauswirth (1809-1871). 80c + 40c, Cream spoon, Gruyeres. 90c + 40c, Embroidered silk carnation, Grisons.

1992, May 22   Photo.   Perf. 11½

B576	SP269	50c +20c multi	1.15	.30
B577	SP269	70c +30c multi	1.60	.45
B578	SP269	80c +40c multi	1.90	.50
B579	SP269	90c +40c multi	2.10	.60
	Nos. B576-B579 (4)		6.75	1.85

Surtax for preservation of cultural heritage.

Unfinished Work, by Jean Tinguely
SP270

1992, Aug. 25   Photo.   Perf. 12

B580	SP270	50c +20c blue & black	1.15	.40

Surtax for Natl. Sports Federation and sports-related social and cultural activities.

Wood Puppet of Melchior, 18th Cent. — SP271

Trees — SP272

1992, Nov. 24   Photo.   Perf. 11½

B581	SP271	50c +25c multi	1.15	.35
B582	SP272	50c +25c Copper beech	1.15	.35
B583	SP272	70c +30c Norway maple	1.60	.50
B584	SP272	80c +40c Common oak	1.90	.55
B585	SP272	90c +40c Spruce	2.10	.60
	Nos. B581-B585 (5)		7.90	2.35

Christmas. Surtax for youth and family welfare projects and the Pro Juventute Foundation.

Swiss Folk Art — SP273

Designs: No. B586, Appenzell dairyman's earring. No. B587, Fluhli glassware. 80c + 40c, Painting of cattle drive, by Sylvestre Pidoux. 100c + 40c, Straw hat ornament.

1993, May 5   Photo.   Perf. 11½

B586	SP273	60c +30c multi	1.40	.40
B587	SP273	60c +30c multi	1.40	.40
B588	SP273	80c +40c multi	1.90	.35
B589	SP273	100c +50c multi	2.25	.70
	Nos. B586-B589 (4)		6.95	1.85

Architectural Heritage Type of 1960

Design: 80c+20c, Kapell Bridge and Water Tower, Lucerne.

1993, Sept. 7   Litho.   Perf. 13½x13

B590	A145	80c +20c orange & red	1.90	.45

Surtax for reconstruction of Kapell Bridge with any excess for preservation of architectural heritage.

SP274   SP275

Woodland plants.

1993, Nov. 23   Photo.   Perf. 11½

B591	SP274	60c +30c Christmas wreath	1.40	.40
B592	SP274	60c +30c Male fern	1.40	.40
B593	SP274	80c +40c Guelder rose	1.90	.55
B594	SP274	100c +50c Mnium punctatum	2.25	.65
	Nos. B591-B594 (4)		6.95	2.00

Christmas. Surtax for youth and family welfare projects and the Pro Juventute Foundation.

1994, May 17   Photo.   Perf. 11½

Swiss Folk Art: No. B595, Weight-driven Neuchatel clock. No. B598, Linen-embroidered pomegranate. 80c+40c, Biscuit mold for Krafli. 100c+40c, Paper bird mobile for child's cradle.

B595	SP275	60c +30c multi	1.40	.40
B596	SP275	60c +30c multi	1.40	.40
B597	SP275	80c +40c multi	1.90	.55
B598	SP275	100c +40c multi	2.25	.65
	Nos. B595-B598 (4)		6.95	2.00

Christmas
SP276

Mushrooms
SP277

Designs: No. B600, Wood blewit. 80c+40c, Red boletus. 100c+50c, Shaggy pholiota.

1994, Nov. 28   Litho.   Perf. 11½

B599	SP276	60c +30c multi	1.40	.45
B600	SP277	60c +30c multi	1.40	.45
B601	SP277	80c +40c multi	1.90	.60
B602	SP277	100c +50c multi	2.25	.80
	Nos. B599-B602 (4)		6.95	2.30

Surtax for youth and family welfare projects and the Pro Juventute Foundation.

Swiss Folk Art — SP278

Designs: No. B603, Wooden cream pail. No. B604, Straw hat. 80c+40c, Chest lock, c. 1580. 100c+40c, Langnau pottery sugar bowl.

1995, May 16   Photo.   Perf. 11½

B603	SP278	60c +30c multi	1.40	.50
B604	SP278	60c +30c multi	1.40	.50
B605	SP278	80c +40c multi	1.90	.70
	Complete booklet, 10 #B605		18.50	
B606	SP278	100c +50c multi	2.25	.80
	Nos. B603-B606 (4)		6.95	2.50

Surtax for Swiss Pro Patria Foundation and special cultural, social projects.

Souvenir Sheet

Basler Taube '95 Philatelic Exhibition, Basel — SP279

Designs: a, 80c+30c, like Switzerland #3L1. Engraved panorama of Basel, by Matthaus Merian, 17th cent.: b, 60c+30c, Buildings, twin church steeples. c, 100c+50c, Buildings. d, 100c+50c, Buildings, bridge.

1995, May 16   Photo.   Perf. 13x14

B607	SP279	Sheet of 4	8.00	8.00
a.		80c +30c multi	1.90	.60
b.		60c +30c black & blue	1.40	.55
c.-d.		100c +50c any single	2.25	.90

Nos. B607b-B607d are a continuous design.

Christmas
SP280

Life In and Around Water — SP281

#B608, Angel from "The Annunciation," by Bartolome. #B609, River trout. 80c+40c, Grey wagtail. 100c+50c, Spotted salamander.

1995, Nov. 28   Photo.   Perf. 11½

B608	SP280	60c +30c multi	1.40	.50
		Complete booklet, 10 #B608	14.00	
B609	SP281	60c +30c multi	1.40	.50
B610	SP281	80c +40c multi	1.90	.65
B611	SP281	100c +50c multi	2.25	.80
		Nos. B608-B611 (4)	6.95	2.45

Surtax for Pro Juventute Foundation.

For Sports SP282

1996, Mar. 12   Photo.   Perf. 11½

B612	SP282	70c +30c multi	1.60	.85
		Complete booklet, 10 #B612	16.00	

SP283

Restorations, projects: No. B613, Magdalena Chapel, Wolfenschiessen. No. B614, Underground mills, Col-des-Roches. 90c+40c, Pfäfers Baroque spa complex. 110c+50c, Roman road over Great St. Bernhard.

1996, May 14   Photo.   Perf. 11½

B613	SP283	70c +35c multi	1.60	.60
B614	SP283	70c +35c multi	1.60	.60
B615	SP283	90c +40c multi	2.10	.75
		Complete booklet, 10 #B615	21.00	
B616	SP283	110c +50c multi	2.50	.90
		Nos. B613-B616 (4)	7.80	2.85

Christmas SP284

Life In and Around Water — SP285

1996, Nov. 26   Photo.   Perf. 11½

B617	SP284	70c +35c Star, constellations	1.60	.55
B618	SP285	70c +35c Grayling	1.60	.55
		Complete booklet, 10 #B618	16.00	
B619	SP285	90c +45c Crayfish	2.10	.70
B620	SP285	110c +55c Otter	2.50	.80
		Nos. B617-B620 (4)	7.80	2.60

SP286

Designs: No. B621, St. Valbert Church, Soubey. No. B622, Culture Mill, Lützelflüh. 90c+40c, Ittingen Charterhouse, Thurgau.

110c+50c, Municipal Building, Onsernone Valley.

1997, May 13   Photo.   Perf. 11½

B621	SP286	70c +35c multi	1.60	1.25
B622	SP286	70c +35c multi	1.60	1.25
B623	SP286	90c +40c multi	2.10	1.60
		Complete booklet, 10 #B623	21.00	
B624	SP286	110c +50c multi	2.50	2.00
		Nos. B621-B624 (4)	7.80	6.10

Christmas SP287

Life In and Around Water — SP288

Designs: No. B625, Mistletoe twig. No. B626, Three-spined stickleback. 90c+45c, Yellow-bellied toad. 110c+55c, Ruff.

1997, Nov. 20   Photo.   Perf. 11½

B625	SP287	70c +35c multi	1.60	1.25
B626	SP288	70c +35c multi	1.60	1.25
		Complete booklet, 10 #B626	16.00	
B627	SP288	90c +45c multi	2.10	1.60
B628	SP288	110c +55c multi	2.50	1.90
		Nos. B625-B628 (4)	7.80	6.00

Surtax for Pro Juventute Foundation.

Pro Patria Stamps, 60th Anniv. SP289

Heritage and landscapes: No. B629, St. Gall Rhine Valley. No. B630, Round Church, Saas Balen. No. B631, Natural forest preserves, Bödmeren. No. B632, St. Gotthard Refuge. 110c +50c, Blacksmiths, Corcelles.

1998, May 12   Photo.   Perf. 11½

B629	SP289	70c + 35c multi	1.60	1.25
B630	SP289	70c + 35c multi	1.60	1.25
B631	SP289	90c + 40c multi	2.10	1.50
		Complete booklet, 10 #B631	21.00	
B632	SP289	90c + 40c multi	2.10	1.50
B633	SP289	110c + 50c multi	2.50	1.90
		Nos. B629-B633 (5)	9.90	7.40

Christmas SP290

Life Near Water — SP291

No. B634, Bell, holly on ribbon. No. B635, Ramshorn snail. 90c+45c, Great crested grebe. 110c+55c, Pike.

1998, Nov. 25   Photo.   Perf. 11½

B634	SP290	70c +35c multi	1.60	1.25
B635	SP291	70c +35c multi	1.60	1.25
B636	SP291	90c +45c multi	2.10	1.60
		Complete booklet, 6 #B634, 4 #B636	18.00	
B637	SP291	110c +55c multi	2.50	1.90
		Nos. B634-B637 (4)	7.80	6.00

Pro Patria — SP292

Heritage and landscapes: No. B638, Chestnut groves, Malcantone. No. B639, La Sarraz Castle. 90c+40c, Lake Lucerne steamship. 110c+50c, St. Paul's Chapel, Rhäzüns.

1999, May 5   Litho.   Perf. 13½

B638	SP292	70c +35c multi	1.60	1.40
B639	SP292	70c +35c multi	1.60	1.40
B640	SP292	90c +40c multi	2.10	1.75
		Complete booklet, 10 #B640	21.00	
B641	SP292	110c +50c multi	2.50	2.10
		Nos. B638-B641 (4)	7.80	6.65

Souvenir Sheet

NABA 2000 Philatelic Exhibition, St. Gallen — SP293

a, 70c+30c, St. Laurenzen Church spire. b, 20c+10c, Top of town house. c, 90c+30c, Oriel window.

1999, Sept. 9   Photo.   Perf. 11¾
Sheet of 3

B642	SP293	#a.-c. + label	4.75	4.75
a.		70c+30c multicolored	1.60	1.25
b.		20c+10c multicolored	.45	.40
c.		90c+30c multicolored	2.10	1.60

Christmas SP294

Nicolo the Clown From Children's Book by Verena Pavoni SP295

Designs: No. B643, Children, snowman. No. B644, Nicolo, circus tent. 90c+45c, Nicolo and his father. 110c+55c, Nicolo and donkey.

1999, Nov. 23   Perf. 13½x13¼   Litho.

B643	SP294	70c +35c multi	1.60	1.40
B644	SP295	70c +35c multi	1.60	1.40
B645	SP295	90c +45c multi	2.10	1.75
		Complete booklet, 6 #B644, 4 #B645	18.00	
B646	SP295	110c +55c multi	2.50	2.10
		Nos. B643-B646 (4)	7.80	6.65

Surtax for Pro Juventute Foundation. Se Nos. B660-B663.

Cities With Pro Patria Foundation Renovation Projects SP296

Perf. 13¼x13½
2000, May 10   Litho. & Engr.

B647	SP296	70c +35c Näfles	1.60	1.25
B648	SP296	70c +35c Tengia	1.60	1.25
B649	SP296	90c +40c Brugg	2.10	1.60
B650	SP296	90c +40c Carouge	2.10	1.60
		Booklet, 10 #B650	21.00	
		Nos. B647-B650 (4)	7.40	5.70

Souvenir Sheet

NABA 2000 Philatelic Exhibition, St. Gallen — SP297

Quadrants of stylized No. 5: a, UL. b, UR. c, LL. d, LR.

2000, May 10   Photo.   Perf. 11¾

B651	SP297	Sheet of 4	5.50	5.50
a.		70c+35c multicolored	1.60	1.25
b.-c.		20c+10c any single	.45	.35
d.		90c+45c multicolored	2.10	1.75

Christmas SP298

Illustrations from Little Albert, by Albert Manser SP299

Designs: No. B652, St. Nicholas and Schmutzli in sleigh. No. B653, Children at fence. No. B654, Little Albert with umbrella. No. B655, Children on sleds.

Perf. 13¼x13½

2000, Nov. 21   Litho.

B652	SP298	70c +35c multi	1.60	1.25
B653	SP299	70c +35c multi	1.60	1.25
B654	SP299	90c +45c multi	2.10	1.50
		Booklet, 6 #B653, 4 #B654	18.00	
B655	SP299	90c +45c multi	2.10	1.60
		Nos. B652-B655 (4)	7.40	5.50

Surtax for Pro Juventute Foundation.

Landmarks SP300

Designs: No. B656, Hauterive Abbey. No. B657, La Chaux-de-Fonds Theater. No. B658, Granary, Rorschach. No. B659, Bishop's Castle, Leuk.

2001, May 9   Litho.   Perf. 13¼x13½

B656	SP300	70c +35c multi	1.60	1.25
B657	SP300	70c +35c multi	1.60	1.25
B658	SP300	90c +40c multi	2.10	1.50
B659	SP300	90c +40c multi	2.10	1.50
		Booklet, 10 #B659	21.00	
		Nos. B656-B659 (4)	7.40	5.50

Surtax for Pro Patria Foundation.

Pro Juventute Types of 1999

Art from children's books: No. B660, What's Santa Claus Doing?, by Karin von Oldershausen. No. B661, Leopold the Leopard, from Leopold and the Sun, by Stephan Brülhart. No. B662, Honeybear, from Leopold and the Sun. No. B663, Tom the Monkey, from Leopold and the Sun.

Perf. 13½x13¼

2001, Nov. 20   **Litho.**

B660	SP294	70c +35c multi	1.60 1.25
B661	SP295	70c +35c multi	1.60 1.25
B662	SP295	90c +45c multi	2.10 1.60
	Booklet, 6 #B661, 4 #B662		18.00
B663	SP295	90c +45c multi	2.10 1.60
	Nos. B660-B663 (4)		7.40 5.70

Surtax for Pro Juventute Foundation.

Mills — SP301

Location: No. B664, Bruzella. No. B665, Oberdorf. No. B666, Büren an der Aare. No. B667, Lussery-Villars.

2002, May 15   **Litho.**   **Perf. 13¼x13½**

B664	SP301	70c +35c multi	1.60 1.40
B665	SP301	70c +35c multi	1.60 1.40
B666	SP301	90c +40c multi	2.10 1.60
	Booklet, 10 #B666		21.00
B667	SP301	90c +40c multi	2.10 1.60
	Nos. B664-B667 (4)		7.40 6.00

Surtax for Pro Patria Foundation.

Roses — SP302

Designs: No. B668, Christmas rose (gold background). No. B669, Ingrid Bergman rose (white background). No. B670, Belle Vaudoise rose (orange petals). No. B671, Charmian rose (pink petals). 130c+65c, Frühlingsgold rose.

Perf. 13¾x13¼

2002, Nov. 19   **Litho.**

B668	SP302	70c +35c multi	1.60 1.40
B669	SP302	70c +35c multi	1.60 1.40
B670	SP302	90c +45c multi	2.10 1.90
	Booklet, 6 #B669, 4 #B670		18.00
B671	SP302	90c +45c multi	2.10 1.90
B672	SP302	130c +65c multi	3.00 2.60
	Nos. B668-B672 (5)		10.40 9.20

Surtax for Pro Juventute Foundation. No. B668 is impregnated with a pine needle, cinnamon and clove scent, and Nos. B669-B672 with a rose scent.

Bridges SP303

Designs: No. B673, Wynigen Bridge, Burgdorf, 1776. No. B674, Salginatobel Bridge, Schiers, 1929. No. B675, Pont St. Jean, Saint Ursanne, 15th cent. No. B676, Reuss Bridge, Rottenschwil, 1907.

2003, May 8   **Litho.**   **Perf. 13¼x13½**

B673	SP303	70c +35c multi	1.60 1.60
B674	SP303	70c +35c multi	1.60 1.60
B675	SP303	90c +40c multi	2.10 2.00
	Booklet, 10 #B675		21.00
B676	SP303	90c +40c multi	2.10 2.00
	Nos. B673-B676 (4)		7.40 7.20

Rights of the Child — SP304

Children: 70c+35c, Christmas tree, toy tractor, gift. 85c+35c, Playing as storekeeper and shopper. 90c+45c, Skateboarding with dog. 100c+45c, Playing guitar and drums.

Serpentine Die Cut 10½x11

2003, Nov. 19   **Litho.**

Self-Adhesive

B677	SP304	70c +35c multi	1.75 1.75
a.	Block of 4 on translucent backing paper		7.00
B678	SP304	85c +35c multi	2.00 1.90
a.	Block of 4 on translucent backing paper		8.00
B679	SP304	90c +45c multi	2.10 2.10
a.	Block of 4 on translucent backing paper		8.40
B680	SP304	100c +45c multi	2.25 2.25
a.	Block of 4 on translucent backing paper		9.00
b.	Nos. B677-B680 on translucent backing paper		8.00
c.	Booklet, 6 each #B678, B680		22.50
	Nos. B677-B680 (4)		8.10 8.00

Nos. B677-B680 each were printed in sheets of 20 stamps with a white paper backing.

Small Buildings SP305

Designs: No. B681, Bathing pavilion, Gorgier. No. B682, Granary, Oberramsern. No. B683, Ossuary, Gentilino. No. B684, Dock house, Lucerne.

2004, May 6   **Litho.**   **Perf. 13¾x14¼**

B681	SP305	85c +40c multi	2.00 1.90
B682	SP305	85c +40c multi	2.00 1.90
B683	SP305	100c +50c multi	2.40 2.40
B684	SP305	100c +50c multi	2.40 2.40
	Complete booklet, 6 #B681, 4 #B684		22.50

Complete booklet sold for 14.50fr.

Rights of the Child — SP306

Designs: No. B685, Children playing card game. No. B686, Children, man, giraffe. No. B687, Children, teacher. No. B688, Child, elderly man and woman.

Serpentine Die Cut 10½x11

2004, Nov. 23   **Litho.**

Self-Adhesive

B685	SP306	85c +40c multi	2.25 2.25
a.	Block of 4 on translucent paper		9.00
B686	SP306	85c +40c multi	2.25 2.25
a.	Block of 4 on translucent paper		9.00
B687	SP306	100c +50c multi	2.75 2.75
a.	Block of 4 on translucent paper		11.00
b.	Booklet pane, 6 each #B685, B687		30.00
B688	SP306	100c +50c multi	2.75 2.75
a.	Block of 4 on translucent paper		11.00
b.	Nos. B685-B688 on translucent paper		10.00
	Nos. B685-B688 (4)		10.00 10.00

Nos. B685-B688 were each printed in sheets of 20 stamps. No. B687b sold for 17fr.

Historic Buildings SP307

Designs: No. B689, Rotach Houses, Zurich. No. B690, Monte Carasso Abbey, Monte Carasso. No. B691, St. Katharinental Abbey, Diessenhofen. No. B692, Palais Wilson, Geneva.

2005, May 10   **Litho.**   **Perf. 13¼x13½**

B689	SP307	85c +40c multi	2.10 2.10
B690	SP307	85c +40c multi	2.10 2.10
B691	SP307	100c +50c multi	2.50 2.50
	Complete booklet, 6 #B690, 4 #B691		23.00
B692	SP307	100c +50c multi	2.50 2.50
	Nos. B689-B692 (4)		9.20 9.20

Surtax for Pro Patria Foundation.

Children's Rights SP308

Children and: No. B693, Life preserver. No. B694, Cherries. No. B695, Computer. No. B696 Candle in window.

Serpentine Die Cut 10½x11

2005, Nov. 22   **Photo.**

Self-Adhesive

B693	SP308	85c +40c multi	2.00 1.90
a.	Block of 4 on translucent paper		8.00
B694	SP308	85c +40c multi	2.00 1.90
a.	Block of 4 on translucent paper		8.00
B695	SP308	100c +50c multi	2.25 2.25
a.	Block of 4 on translucent paper		9.00
b.	Booklet pane, 2 each #B693, B695		8.50
	Complete booklet, 3 #B695b		26.00
B696	SP308	100c +50c multi	2.25 2.25
a.	Block of 4 on translucent paper		9.00
b.	Nos. B693-B696 on translucent paper		8.50
	Nos. B693-B696 (4)		8.50 8.30

Nos. B693-B696 were each printed in sheets of 20. Complete booklet sold for €17.

Gardens and Parks — SP309

Designs: No. B697, Prangins Castle, Prangins. No. B698, Heidegg Castle, Gelfingen. No. B699, Birseck Castle, Arlesheim. No. B700, Villa Garbald, Castasegna.

2006, May 9   **Litho.**   **Perf. 14x13¾**

B697	SP309	85c +40c multi	2.10 2.10
B698	SP309	85c +40c multi	2.10 2.10
B699	SP309	100c +50c multi	2.50 2.50
B700	SP309	100c +50c multi	2.50 2.50
	Complete booklet, 6 #B698, 4 #B700		24.00
	Nos. B697-B700 (4)		9.20 9.20

Complete booklet sold for €14.50.

Souvenir Sheet

Wettingen Monastery — SP310

No. B701: a, Building, country name at left. b, Building and bridge, country name at right. c, Main building.

2006, May 9   **Perf. 13¾x14¼**

B701	SP310	Sheet of 3	7.25 7.25
a.-b.	85c+15c Either single		2.00 1.75
c.	100c+50c multi		2.25 2.50
	NABA Baden 2006.		

Souvenir Sheet

NABA Baden 2006 Philatelic Exhibition — SP311

No. B702: a, Baden City Tower. b, Fountain.

Perf. 14¼x13¾ on 3 Sides

2006, Sept. 7   **Litho.**

B702	SP311	Sheet of 2	5.50 5.50
a.-b.	100c +50c Either single		2.25 2.50

Children's Art Competition SP312

Designs: No. B703, Singer, by Veronica Jesus Garcia Pinto. No. B704, Car in garage, by Stephane Arada. No. B705, Bandaged dog, by Lea Mayer. No. B706, Angel, by Ted Scapa, judge of competition.

Serpentine Die Cut 10¾x11

2006, Nov. 21   **Litho.**

Self-Adhesive

B703	SP312	85c +40c multi	2.10 2.10
a.	Block of 4, #B703		8.50
B704	SP312	85c +40c multi	2.10 2.10
a.	Block of 4, #B704		8.50
B705	SP312	100c +50c multi	2.50 2.50
a.	Booklet pane, 6 each #B704-B705		28.00
b.	Block of 4, #B705		10.00
B706	SP312	100c +50c multi	2.50 2.50
a.	Block of 4, #B703-B706		9.25
b.	Block of 4, #B706		10.00
	Nos. B703-B706 (4)		9.20 9.20

Surtax for Pro Juventute Foundation. See also Nos. B711-B714, B719-B722.

Historic Roads SP313

Designs: No. B707, Via Jura, Chateau de Vorbourg. No. B708, Via Jacobi, Chapel of St. Apollonia. No. B709, Via Cook, Grandhotel Giessbach. No. B710, Via Gottardo, Alte Sust.

2007, Apr. 27   **Litho.**   **Perf. 13½x13¼**

B707	SP313	85c +40c multi	2.10 2.10
B708	SP313	85c +40c multi	2.10 2.10
B709	SP313	100c +50c multi	2.50 2.50
	Complete booklet, 6 #B708, 4 #B709		23.00
B710	SP313	100c +50c multi	2.50 2.50
	Nos. B707-B710 (4)		9.20 9.20

Surtax for Pro Patria Foundation. See also Nos. B715-B718, B723-B726.

Children's Art Competition Type of 2006

Designs: No. B711, Camping, by Christine Fischer. No. B712, Mountains, by Jonathan Balest. No. B713, Sunshine, by Morena Rufatti. No. B714, Angels, by Ted Scapa, judge of competition.

Serpentine Die Cut 10½x11

2007, Nov. 20   **Litho.**

Self-Adhesive

B711	SP312	85c +40c multi	2.25 2.25
a.	Block of 4 #B711 on backing paper		9.00
B712	SP312	85c +40c multi	2.25 2.25
a.	Block of 4 #B712 on backing paper		9.00
B713	SP312	100c +50c multi	2.75 2.75
a.	Block of 4 #B713 on backing paper		11.00
b.	Booklet pane, 6 each #B711, B713		30.00
B714	SP312	100c +50c multi	2.75 2.75
a.	Block of 4 #B714 on backing paper		11.00

b.   Block of 4, #B711-B714 on
backing paper   10.00   10.00
Nos. B711-B714 (4)   10.00   10.00

Surtax for Pro Juventute Foundation.

Historic Roads Type of 2007

Designs: No. B715, Via Romana, East Gate, Avenches, and columns, Nyon. No. B716, Via Sbrinz, Schnitzturm Tower. No. B717, Via Stockalper, Old Hospice, Simplon. No. B718, Via Valtellina, Dürrboden Restaurant, Grisons.

2008, May 8   **Litho.**   ***Perf. 13½x13¼***
B715 SP313   85c +40c multi   2.40   2.40
B716 SP313   85c +40c multi   2.40   2.40
B717 SP313   100c +50c multi   3.00   3.00
    Complete booklet, 6
    #B716, 4 #B717   27.00
B718 SP313   100c +50c multi   3.00   3.00
Nos. B715-B718 (4)   10.80   10.80

Surtax for Pro Patria Foundation.

Children's Art Competition Type of 2006

Designs: No. B719, Friendship Unites (Sun and Moon), by Andrea Andreazzi. No. B720, Friendship Provides Support (boy, girl, child in wheelchair), by Manon Peng. No. B721, Friendship is the Source of Happiness (girls and four-leaf clover), by Delia Candolo. No. B722, Friendship is Uplifting (angels), by Ted Scapa, judge of competition.

Serpentine Die Cut 10¾x11
2008, Nov. 21   **Litho.**
Self-Adhesive
B719 SP312   85c +40c multi   2.10   2.10
B720 SP312   85c +40c multi   2.10   2.10
B721 SP312   100c +50c multi   2.50   2.50
   a.   Booklet pane, 6 each
      #B719, B721   28.00
B722 SP312   100c +50c multi   2.50   2.50
   a.   Block of 4, #B719-B722 on
      backing paper   9.25
Nos. B719-B722 (4)   9.20   9.20

No. B721a sold for 17fr. Surtax for Pro Juventute Foundation.

Historic Roads Type of 2003

Designs: No. B723, Via Salina and Bern Gate, Murten. No. B724, Via Francigena and Great St. Bernhard Hospice, Bourg-Saint-Pierre. No. B725, Via Rhenana and salt drilling towers, Rheinfelden. No. B726, Via Spluga and Albertini House, Splügen.

2009, May 8   ***Perf. 13½x13¼***
B723 SP313   85c +40c multi   2.25   2.25
B724 SP313   85c +40c multi   2.25   2.25
B725 SP313   100c +50c multi   2.75   2.75
    Complete booklet, 6
    #B724, 4 #B725   26.00
B726 SP313   100c +50c multi   2.75   2.75
Nos. B723-B726 (4)   10.00   10.00

Complete booklet sold for 14.50fr. Surtax for Pro Patria Foundation.

Souvenir Sheet

Pro Patria Foundation, Cent. — SP314

2009, May 8   **Litho.**   ***Perf. 14x13¼***
B727 SP314   100c +50c multi   2.75   2.75

Surtax for Pro Patria Foundation.

Services of the Pro Juventute Foundation SP315

Designs: No. B728, Letters to Parents (family and arrows). No. B729, Vacation Pass programs (children and tree). No. B730, Advice 147 counseling (boy and girl). No. B731, Semi-postal stamp sales (four children and stylized stamps).

Serpentine Die Cut 12
2009, Nov. 20   **Litho.**
Self-Adhesive
B728 SP315   85c +40c multi   2.50   2.50
   a.   Block of 4 #B728 on backing paper   10.00
B729 SP315   85c +40c multi   2.50   2.50
   a.   Block of 4 #B729 on backing paper   10.00
B730 SP315   100c +50c multi   3.00   3.00
   a.   Booklet pane of 12, 6 each #B728, B730   34.00
   b.   Block of 4 #B730 on backing paper   12.00
B731 SP315   100c +50c multi   3.00   3.00
   a.   Block of 4, #B728-B731, on translucent paper   11.00
   b.   Block of 4 #B731 on backing paper   12.00
Nos. B728-B731 (4)   11.00   11.00

Complete booklet sold for 17fr. Surtax for Pro Juventute Foundation.

Details From Panorama of Battle of Murten, by Louis Braun — SP316

Desings: No. B732, Retreat of Charles the Bold on caparisoned horse. No. B733, Death of Duke of Somerset near tents. No. B734, Confederate troops with flags and halberds. No. B735, Burgundian Cavalry being attacked by Confederate troops.

2010, May 6   **Litho.**   ***Perf. 14***
B732 SP316   85c +40c multi   2.25   2.25
B733 SP316   85c +40c multi   2.25   2.25
B734 SP316   100c +50c multi   2.75   2.75
    Complete booklet, 6
    #B732, 4 #B734   27.00
B735 SP316   100c +50c multi   2.75   2.75
Nos. B732-B735 (4)   10.00   10.00

Surtax for Pro Patria Foundation. Complete booklet sold for 14.50fr.

Boy Saving Money SP317

Designs: No. B736, Boy thinking of teddy bear, piggy bank. No. B737, Boy and piggy bank. No. B738, Boy, teddy bear and piggy bank. No. B739, Piggy bank, boy holding gift.

Serpentine Die Cut 12
2010, Nov. 4   **Litho.**
Self-Adhesive
B736 SP317   85c +40c multi   2.60   2.60
   a.   Block of 4 on translucent backing paper   10.50
B737 SP317   85c +40c multi   2.60   2.60
   a.   Block of 4 on translucent backing paper   10.50
B738 SP317   100c +50c multi   3.25   3.25
   a.   Block of 4 on translucent backing paper   13.00
B739 SP317   100c +50c multi   3.25   3.25
   a.   Block of 4, #B736-B739   12.00
   b.   Booklet pane of 12, 6 each #B736, B739   36.00
   c.   Block of 4 on translucent backing paper   13.00
Nos. B736-B739 (4)   11.70   11.70

Surtax for Pro Juventute Foundation. No. B739b sold for 17fr.

Lake Steamships SP318

Designs: No. B740, PS Gallia. No. B741, PS Piemonte. No. B742, PS Blümlisalp. No. B743, PS La Suisse.

2011, May 5   **Litho.**   ***Perf. 13½***
Color of Denomination
B740 SP318   85c+40c green   3.00   3.00
B741 SP318   85c+40c orange   3.00   3.00
B742 SP318   100c+50c yellow   3.50   3.50
    Complete booklet, 6
    #B741, 4 #B742   35.00
B743 SP318   100c+50c brt pink   3.50   3.50
Nos. B740-B743 (4)   13.00   13.00

Complete booklet sold for 14.50fr. Surtax for Pro Patria Foundation.

Children SP319

Stylized flowers and: No. B744, Young boy, duck, sheep, bear, leaf, crescent moon. No. B745, Two girls, happy face, musical notes, envelope, ice cream cone, heart. No. B746, Two young girls, gift, stars, bell, Christmas tree. No. B747, Boy, sun, fish, ball, paw print.

Serpentine Die Cut 12
2011, Nov. 17
Self-Adhesive
Color of Denomination
B744 SP319   85c +40c blue   2.75   2.75
B745 SP319   85c +40c rose lilac   2.75   2.75
B746 SP319   100c +50c dl org   3.50   3.50
B747 SP319   100c +50c green   3.50   3.50
   a.   Block of 4, #B744-B747, on translucent paper   12.50
   b.   Booklet pane of 12, 3 each #B744-B747   37.50
Nos. B744-B747 (4)   12.50   12.50

Stamps do not touch on No. B747a, but touch in No. B747b. No. B747b sold for 17fr. Surtax for Pro Juventute Foundation.

Girls on Swing SP320

2012, Mar. 1   ***Serpentine Die Cut 12***
Self-Adhesive
B748 SP320   100c +50c multi   3.25   3.25

Pro Juventute Foundation, cent. Surtax for Pro Juventute Foundation.

Architectural Preservation SP321

Designs: No. B749, Eichberg Estate Lion Fountain, Uetendorf. No. B750, Ferme des Troncs storehouse, Mézières. No. B751, Domed stone cellar, Brusio. No. B752, Villa Abendstern summer house, Wädenswil.

2012, May 9   ***Perf. 14¼x13¾***
B749 SP321   85c +40c multi   2.75   2.75
B750 SP321   85c +40c multi   2.75   2.75
B751 SP321   100c +50c multi   3.25   3.25
    Complete booklet, 6
    #B749, 4 #B751   32.50
B752 SP321   100c +50c multi   3.25   3.25
Nos. B749-B752 (4)   12.00   12.00

Complete booklet sold for 14.50fr. Surtax for Pro Patria Foundation.

AIR POST STAMPS

Nos. 134 and 139 Overprinted in Carmine

1919-20   **Wmk. 183**   ***Perf. 11½***
Granite Paper
C1 A25   30c yel brn & pale
        grn ('20)   110.00   *1,250.*
C2 A25   50c dp & pale grn   32.50   110.00
    Set, never hinged   350.00

Counterfeits of overprint and fraudulent cancellations exist.

Airplane AP1

Pilot at Controls of Airplane AP2

Biplane against Sky — AP3

Allegorical Figure of Flight AP4

Perf. 11½, 12 and Compound
1923-25   **Typo.**
C3   AP1   15c brn red & ap
          grn   2.25   8.25
C4   AP1   20c grn & lt grn
          ('25)   .90   *6.00*
C5   AP1   25c dk bl & bl   7.75   22.50
C6   AP2   35c brn & buff   11.00   42.50
C7   AP2   40c vio & gray vio   14.50   45.00
C8   AP3   45c red & ind   1.60   *7.25*
C9   AP3   50c blk & red   12.50   17.00
             Perf. 11½
C10   AP4   65c gray bl & dp bl
          ('24)   3.25   *16.00*
C11   AP4   75c org & brn red
          ('24)   15.00   *55.00*
C12   AP4   1fr vio & dp vio
          ('24)   42.50   32.50
Nos. C3-C12 (10)   111.25   252.00
    Set, never hinged   275.00

For surcharges see Nos. C19, C22, C26.

1933-37   **With Grilled Gum**
C4a   AP1   20c grn & lt grn ('37)   .30   .40
C5a   AP1   25c dk bl & bl ('34)   5.00   *50.00*
C8a   AP3   45c red & indigo ('37)   2.50   *52.50*
C9a   AP3   50c gray grn & scar
          ('35)   1.10   1.60
C10a   AP4   65c gray bl & dp bl
          ('37)   2.75   *8.50*
C11a   AP4   75c org & brn red
          ('36)   27.50   175.00
C12a   AP4   1fr vio & deep vio   2.10   3.25
Nos. C4a-C12a (7)   41.25   291.25
    Set, never hinged   65.00

See Grilled Gum note after No. 145.

Allegory of Air Mail — AP5

Bird Carrying Letter AP6

1929-30   **Granite Paper**
C13   AP5   35c red brn, bis &
          claret   15.00   42.50
C14   AP5   40c dl grn, yel grn
          & bl   57.50   82.50

C15 AP6 2fr blk brn & red brn, gray

C15	AP6 2fr blk brn & red brn, *gray* ('30)	85.00	85.00
	Nos. C13-C15 (3)	157.50	210.00
	Set, never hinged	425.00	

1933-35   With Grilled Gum

C13a	AP5 35c red brn, bis & cl	5.00	50.00
C14a	AP5 40c dk grn, yel grn & bl	37.50	77.50
C15a	AP6 2fr blk brn & red brn ('35)	7.25	12.00
	Nos. C13a-C15a (3)	49.75	139.50
	Set, never hinged	140.00	

Front View of Airplane AP7

1932, Feb. 2   Granite Paper

C16	AP7 15c dp grn & lt grn	.55	1.60
C17	AP7 20c dk red & buff	1.10	2.50
C18	AP7 90c dp bl & gray	7.25	30.00
	Nos. C16-C18 (3)	8.90	34.10
	Set, never hinged	22.50	

Intl. Disarmament Conf., Geneva, Feb. 1932. For surcharges see Nos. C20-C21, C23-C25.

Nos. C3, C10, C16-C18 Surcharged with New Values and Bars in Black or Red

1935-38

C19	AP1 10c on 15c	4.75	37.50
C20	AP7 10c on 15c	.40	.55
a.	Inverted surcharge	6,500.	12,000.
C21	AP7 10c on 20c ('36)	.45	2.25
C22	AP4 10c on 65c ('38)	.25	.40
C23	AP7 30c on 90c ('36)	3.00	14.00
C24	AP7 40c on 20c ('37)	3.75	15.00
C25	AP7 40c on 90c ('36) (R)	3.25	14.50
a.	Vermilion surcharge	92.50	800.00
	Never hinged, #C25a	150.00	
	Nos. C19-C25 (7)	15.85	84.20
	Set, never hinged	40.00	

Stamp similar to No. C22, but from souvenir sheet, is listed as No. 242a.

Type of Air Post Stamp of 1923 Srchd. in Black

1938, May 22   Wmk. 183   Perf. 11½

C26	AP3 75c on 50c gray & scar	6.50	

"Pro Aero" Meeting, May 21-22.
No. C26 was not sold to the public in the ordinary way, but affixed to air mail letters by postal officials. It was not regularly obtainable unused.

Jungfrau — AP8

Designs: 40c, View of Valais. 50c, Lake Geneva. 60c, Alpstein. 70c, View of Ticino. 1fr, Lake Lucerne. 2fr, The Engadine. 5fr, Churfirsten.

Perf. 11½
1941, May 1   Unwmk.   Engr.
Tinted Granite Paper

C27	AP8 30c ultra	.55	.25
C28	AP8 40c gray blk	.55	.25
C29	AP8 50c slate grn	.55	.30
C30	AP8 60c chestnut	.85	.30
C31	AP8 70c plum	.90	.55
C32	AP8 1fr Prus grn	1.75	.60
C33	AP8 2fr car lake	5.75	3.50
C34	AP8 5fr deep blue	19.00	15.00
	Nos. C27-C34 (8)	29.90	20.75
	Set, never hinged	80.00	

See Nos. C43-C44.

Type of 1941 Overprinted in Red

1941, May 12

C35	AP8 1fr blue green	5.50	19.00
	Never hinged		10.00

Issued to commemorate special flights between Payerne and Buochs, May 28, 1941.

Parliament Buildings, Bern AP16

1943, July 13   Photo.

C36	AP16 1fr cop red, buff & blk	1.60	10.00
	Never hinged		3.75

30th anniv. of the 1st Alpine flight, by Oscar Bider, July 13, 1913.

DH-3 Haefeli AP17

Fokker AP18

Lockheed-Orion — AP19

1944, Sept. 1

C37	AP17 10c gray brn & pale grn	.25	.50
C38	AP18 20c rose car & buff	.30	.50
C39	AP19 30c ultra & pale gray	.35	1.25
	Nos. C37-C39 (3)	.90	2.25
	Set, never hinged	1.50	

25th anniv. of the 1st regular air route in Switzerland.

Douglas DC-3 AP20

1944, Sept. 20   Granite Paper

C40	AP20 1.50fr multi	5.50	17.50
	Never hinged		11.00

25th anniv. of the Zurich-Geneva air route.

Zoegling Training Glider AP21

1946, May 1   Granite Paper

C41	AP21 1.50fr henna brn & gray	11.50	27.50
	Never hinged		20.00

Valid for use only on two special flights.

Douglas DC-4 Linking Geneva and New York AP22

1947, Mar. 17   Granite Paper

C42	AP22 2.50fr bl gray, dk bl & red	7.00	20.00
	Never hinged		13.00

Valid only on the Geneva-New York flight of May 2, 1947.
Because of bad weather at NYC the flight ended at Washington.

Types of 1941
1948, Oct. 1   Engr.
Tinted Granite Paper

C43	AP8 30c dk slate bl	4.50	12.50
C44	AP8 40c deep ultra	21.00	2.75
	Set, never hinged	57.50	

Glider in Symbolized Aerodynamic Buoyancy — AP23

1949, Apr. 11   Engr. & Typo.

C45	AP23 1.50fr dk vio & yel	16.00	37.50
	Never hinged		30.00

Valid only on special flights, Apr. 27-29, 1949. Proceeds were for the advancement of national aviation.

> Catalogue values for unused stamps in this section, from this point to the end of the section, are for Never Hinged items.

Glider and Jets AP24

1963, June 1   Photo.   Perf. 11½
Granite Paper

C46	AP24 2fr multicolored	4.00	3.50

50th anniversary of the first Alpine flight by Oscar Bider, July 13, 1913. Valid for postage on July 13, 1963, on flights from Bern to Locarno and Langenbruck to Bern. Proceeds went to the Pro Aero Foundation.

AIR POST SEMI-POSTAL STAMP

> Catalogue values for unused stamps in this section are for Never Hinged items.

Boeing 747 — SPAP1

1972, Feb. 17   Photo.   Perf. 12½
Violet Fibers, Fluorescent Paper

CB1	SPAP1 2fr + 1fr dp bl, red & gray	4.50	2.25

50th anniv. of 1st Swiss Intl. flight, Zurich to Nuremberg, and 25th anniv. of 1st Swissair trans-Atlantic flight, Zurich to NYC. Valid on all mail but obligatory on special flights from Geneva to NYC in May, and from Geneva to Nuremberg in June, 1972.
Surtax was for Pro Aero Foundation and the training of young airmen, and for the Swiss Air Rescue Service.

POSTAGE DUE STAMPS

D1

D2

Wmk. 182
1878-80   Typo.   Perf. 11½

J1	D1 1c ultra	1.90	1.60
J2	D2 2c ultra	1.90	1.60
J3	D2 3c ultra	17.00	16.00
J4	D2 5c ultra	17.00	6.75
J5	D2 10c ultra	180.00	6.00
J6	D2 20c ultra	210.00	6.00
J7	D2 50c ultra	400.00	20.00
J8	D2 100c ultra	525.00	17.00
J9	D2 500c ultra	475.00	27.50
	Nos. J1-J9 (9)	1,827.	102.45

A 5c in design D1 exists.

1882-83   Granite Paper

J10	D2 10c ultra	175.00	40.00
J11	D2 20c ultra	400.00	52.50
J12	D2 50c ultra	2,400.	525.00
J13	D2 100c ultra	800.00	400.00
J14	D2 500c ultra	13,750.	210.00

1883-84   Numerals in Red

J15	D2 5c blue green	42.50	30.00
J16	D2 10c blue green	65.00	25.00
J17	D2 20c blue green	120.00	22.50
J18	D2 50c blue green	140.00	72.50
J19	D2 100c blue green	350.00	350.00
J20	D2 500c blue green	775.00	190.00
	Nos. J15-J20 (6)	1,492.	690.00

1884-97   Numerals in Red

J21	D2 1c olive green	.65	.65
J22	D2 3c olive green	5.75	6.50
J23	D2 5c olive green	1.60	.65
a.	5c yellow green	25.00	12.50
J24	D2 10c olive green	3.75	.85
a.	10c yellow green	110.00	16.00
J25	D2 20c olive green	8.25	1.30
a.	20c yellow green	110.00	16.00
J26	D2 50c olive green	12.00	2.50
a.	50c yellow green	100.00	32.50
J27	D2 100c olive green	14.00	2.75
a.	100c yellow green	100.00	80.00
J28	D2 500c olive green	150.00	160.00
a.	500c yellow green	125.00	60.00

Numerous shades of Nos. J21-J28 exist.

1908-09   Wmk. 183
Numerals in Red

J29	D2 1c olive green	.30	1.10
J30	D2 5c olive green	.60	.90
J31	D2 10c olive green	1.50	2.25
J32	D2 20c olive green	3.00	5.00
J33	D2 50c olive green	15.00	1.10
J34	D2 100c olive green	30.00	2.25
	Nos. J29-J34 (6)	50.40	12.60

D3

1910   Perf. 11½, 12
Numerals in Red

J35	D3 1c blue green	.25	.25
J36	D3 3c blue green	.25	.25
J37	D3 5c blue green	.25	.25
J38	D3 10c blue green	11.00	.25
J39	D3 15c blue green	.65	1.10
J40	D3 20c blue green	17.50	.25
J41	D3 25c blue green	1.25	.65
J42	D3 30c blue green	1.25	.55
J43	D3 50c blue green	1.50	1.10
	Nos. J35-J43 (9)	33.90	4.65

See Nos. S1-S12.

No. J36 Surcharged

1916

J44	D3 5c on 3c bl grn & red	.40	.25

Nos. J35-J36, J43
Surcharged

1924

J45	D3	10c on 1c	.25	8.25
J46	D3	10c on 3c	.25	1.50
J47	D3	20c on 50c	.95	1.50
		Nos. J45-J47 (3)	1.45	11.25

D4

D5

Wmk. 183

1924-26   Typo.   Perf. 11½

Granite Paper

J48	D4	5c ol grn & red	.65	.25
J49	D4	10c ol grn & red	2.75	.25
J50	D4	15c ol grn & red ('26)	2.50	.55
J51	D4	20c ol grn & red	6.00	.25
J52	D4	25c ol grn & red	2.75	.55
J53	D4	30c ol grn & red	2.75	.85
J54	D4	40c ol grn & red ('26)	3.75	.70
J55	D4	50c ol grn & red	3.75	.70
		Nos. J48-J55 (8)	24.90	4.10

1924   With Grilled Gum

J48a	D4	5c olive green & red	.65	.60
J49a	D4	10c olive green & red	2.50	1.10
J51a	D4	20c olive green & red	4.75	1.50
J52a	D4	25c olive green & red	7.25	65.00
		Nos. J48a-J52a (4)	15.15	68.20

See Grilled Gum note after No. 145.

Nos. J50, J53 and J55 Surcharged
with New Value in Black

1937

J56	D4	5c on 15c	.90	4.25
J57	D4	10c on 30c	.90	1.50
J58	D4	20c on 30c	1.50	5.00
J59	D4	40c on 50c	2.50	12.00
		Nos. J56-J59 (4)	5.80	22.75
		Set, never hinged	10.50	

1938   Engr.   Unwmk.

J60	D5	5c scarlet	.40	.25
J61	D5	10c scarlet	.55	.25
J62	D5	15c scarlet	1.25	2.25
J63	D5	20c scarlet	.95	.25
J64	D5	25c scarlet	1.40	1.90
J65	D5	30c scarlet	1.40	1.25
J66	D5	40c scarlet	1.60	.45
J67	D5	50c scarlet	1.90	2.25
		Nos. J60-J67 (8)	9.45	8.85
		Set, never hinged	19.00	

1938   With Grilled Gum

J60a	D5	5c scarlet	.65	1.60
J61a	D5	10c scarlet	.65	1.25
J62a	D5	15c scarlet	1.40	2.50
J63a	D5	20c scarlet	1.25	.55
J64a	D5	25c scarlet	1.40	9.50
J65a	D5	30c scarlet	1.40	2.25
J66a	D5	40c scarlet	2.10	2.10
J67a	D5	50c scarlet	2.50	3.50
		Nos. J60a-J67a (8)	11.35	23.25
		Set, never hinged	29.00	

See Grilled Gum note after No. 145.

OFFICIAL STAMPS

For General Use

With Perforated Cross
In 1935 the government authorized the use of regular postage issues perforated with a nine-hole cross for all government departments. Twenty-seven different stamps were so perforated. These were succeeded in 1938 by the cross overprints.

Values for canceled Official Stamps are for those canceled to order. Postally used stamps sell for considerably more. This note does not apply to Nos. 1O1-1O16, 2O27-2O30, 3O23-3O26.

Counterfeit overprints exist of most official stamps.

Official stamps without unused values were not made available to the public unused.

Regular Issues of 1908-36 Overprinted in Black

1938   Unwmk.   Perf. 11½

O1	A53	3c olive	.25	.25
O2	A54	5c blue green	.25	.25
O3	A55	10c red violet	.95	.45
O4	A56	15c orange	.25	1.60
O5	A58	20c red	.45	.25
O6	A58	25c brown	.45	1.40
O7	A59	30c ultra	.60	1.00
O8	A60	35c yellow green	.60	1.25
O9	A61	40c gray	.60	1.00

Wmk. 183

With Grilled Gum

O10	A25	50c dp grn & pale grn	.60	1.50
O11	A25	60c brn org & buff	1.25	2.50
O12	A25	70c vio & buff	1.25	4.25
O13	A25	80c sl & buff	1.25	3.25
O14	A36	90c grn & red, grn	3.00	3.25
O15	A25	1fr dp cl & pale grn	1.50	3.25
O16	A36	1.20fr brn rose & red, rose	1.50	4.50
O17	A36	1.50fr bl & red, bl	2.50	6.00
O18	A36	2fr gray blk & red, gray	3.00	7.00
		Nos. O1-O18 (18)	20.25	42.95
		Set, never hinged	65.00	

Nos. O14, O16, O17 and O18 are on surface-colored paper.

1938   Unwmk.   With Grilled Gum

O1a	A53	3c olive	4.50	.45
O2a	A54	5c blue green	1.25	.45
O3a	A55	10c red violet	1.50	.55
O4a	A56	15c orange	2.75	1.25
O5a	A68	20c red	1.50	.70
O6a	A58	25c brown	75.00	7.75
O7a	A59	30c ultra	2.50	1.10
O8a	A60	35c yellow green	1.90	1.90
O9a	A61	40c gray	2.50	1.00
		Nos. O1a-O9a (9)	93.40	15.15
		Set, never hinged	190.00	

See Grilled Gum note after No. 145.

Postage Stamps of 1936-42 Overprinted in Black

1942-45   Unwmk.   Perf. 11½

O19	A53	3c olive	.30	2.10
O20	A54	5c blue green	.30	.25
O21	A55	10c dk red brn	.55	.55
O21A	A55	10c orange brn ('45)	.25	.45
O22	A56	15c orange	.60	1.90
O23	A68	20c red	.60	.45
O24	A58	25c lt brown	.60	2.25
O25	A59	30c ultra	.95	.90
O26	A60	35c yellow grn	1.25	2.75
O27	A61	40c gray	1.25	.60
O28	A77	50c dp pur, grnsh	3.75	4.25
O29	A78	60c red brn, buff	4.50	4.25
O30	A79	70c rose vio, pale lil	5.00	8.25

O31	A80	80c blk, pale gray	1.40	1.60
O32	A81	90c dk red, pale rose	1.60	2.25
O33	A82	1fr dk grn, grnsh	1.60	1.60
O34	A83	1.20fr red vio, pale gray	2.25	2.75
O35	A84	1.50fr dk bl, buff	2.25	3.25
O36	A85	2fr mar, pale rose	3.25	4.00
		Nos. O19-O36 (19)	32.25	44.40
		Set, never hinged	60.00	

Same Overprint on Nos. 329-339

1950   Unwmk.   Perf. 12x11½

O37	A118	5c orange	.40	.55
O38	A119	10c yellow grn	.65	.55
O39	A120	15c aqua	5.50	15.00
O40	A121	20c brown car	2.10	.65
O41	A122	25c red	3.25	8.25
O42	A123	30c olive	2.50	3.25
O43	A124	35c red brown	3.50	11.00
O44	A125	40c deep blue	2.75	3.25
O45	A126	50c slate gray	4.50	5.75
O46	A127	60c blue green	5.50	7.75
O47	A128	70c purple	16.00	22.50
		Nos. O37-O47 (11)	46.65	78.50
		Set, never hinged	77.50	

FOR THE WAR BOARD OF TRADE

Regular Issues of 1908-18 Overprinted

1918   Wmk. 183   Perf. 11½, 12

1O1	A26	3c brown org	110.00	225.00
1O2	A26	5c green	10.00	32.50
1O3	A26	7½c gray (I)	300.00	450.00
a.		7½c slate (II)	550.00	950.00
1O4	A28	10c red, buff	15.00	40.00
1O5	A28	15c vio, buff	12.50	45.00
1O6	A28	20c red & yel	125.00	500.00
1O7	A25	25c dp bl	125.00	500.00
1O8	A25	30c yel brn & pale grn	125.00	450.00
		Nos. 1O1-1O8 (8)	822.50	2,242.

Most unused examples of Nos. 1O1-1O8 are reprints made using the original overprint forms. Counterfeits exist.

Overprinted

1918

1O9	A26	3c brown orange	4.25	35.00
1O10	A26	5c green	12.00	52.50
1O11	A26	7½c gray	4.50	22.50
1O12	A28	10c red, buff	45.00	87.50
1O13	A28	15c vio, buff	82.50	
1O14	A25	20c red & yel	8.75	52.50
1O15	A25	25c dp blue	8.75	52.50
1O16	A25	30c yel brn & pale grn	14.50	87.50
		Nos. 1O9-1O16 (8)	180.25	390.00

No. 1O13 was never placed in use. Fraudulent cancellations are found on Nos. 1O1-1O16.

FOR THE LEAGUE OF NATIONS

Regular Issues Overprinted

On 1908-30 Issues

1922-31   Wmk. 183   Perf. 11½, 12

2O1	A26	2½c ol, buff ('28)		.45
2O2	A26	3c ultra, buff ('30)	8.25	
2O3	A26	5c orange, buff	5.50	
2O4	A26	5c gray vio, buff ('26)	2.75	
2O5	A26	5c red vio, buff ('27)	2.25	
2O6	A26	5c dk grn, buff ('31)	25.00	

2O7	A26	7½c dp grn, buff ('28)		.55
2O8	A28	10c green, buff		.55
2O9	A28	10c bl grn, buff ('28)	1.10	
2O10	A28	10c vio, buff ('31)	2.75	
2O11	A28	15c brn red, buff ('28)	1.10	
2O12	A28	20c red vio, buff	8.25	
2O13	A28	20c car, buff ('26)	2.25	
2O14	A28	25c ver, buff	8.25	
2O15	A28	25c car, buff	1.10	
2O16	A28	25c brn, buff ('27)	17.00	
2O17	A28	30c dp bl, buff ('25)	8.25	
2O18	A25	30c yel brn & pale grn	14.00	
2O19	A25	35c yel grn & yel	10.00	
2O20	A25	40c deep blue	1.40	
2O21	A25	40c red vio & grn ('28)	14.00	
2O22	A25	50c dp grn & pale grn	11.00	
2O23	A25	60c brn org & buff	30.00	1.60
2O24	A25	70c vio & buff ('25)	26.00	
2O25	A25	80c slate & buff	2.75	
2O26	A25	1fr dp cl & pale grn	6.75	
2O27	A29	3fr red	32.50	
2O28	A30	5fr ultra	60.00	
2O29	A31	10fr dull violet	140.00	
2O30	A31	10fr gray grn ('30)	140.00	
		Nos. 2O1-2O30 (30)	555.35	

1930-44   With Grilled Gum

2O2a	A26	3c ultra, buff ('33)	10.00
2O6a	A26	5c dk grn, buff ('33)	19.00
2O17a	A28	30c dp bl,buff	425.00
2O22a	A25	50c dp grn & pale grn ('35)	.90 2.25
2O23a	A25	60c brn org & buff ('44)	25.00 225.00
2O24a	A25	70c violet & buff ('32)	1.60 2.25
2O25a	A25	80c slate & buff ('42)	2.75 2.50
2O26a	A25	1fr dp cl & pale grn ('42)	5.25

1935-36

With Grilled Gum

2O31	A36	90c grn & red, grn ('36)	5.00	
2O32	A36	1.20fr brn rose & red, rose ('36)	2.75	4.50
b.		Inverted overprint	4,250.	
2O33	A36	1.50fr bl & red, bl ('36)	2.75	4.50
2O34	A36	2fr gray blk & red, gray ('36)	2.75	5.25

1922-25   Ordinary Gum

2O31a	A36	90c	14.00
2O32a	A36	1.20fr ('25)	14.00
2O33a	A36	1.50fr ('25)	13.00
2O34a	A36	2fr ('25)	12.00

1928

2O35	A39	5fr blue	87.50

On 1932 Issue

1932

2O36	A41	5c peacock bl	19.00
2O37	A41	10c orange	1.60
2O38	A41	20c cerise	1.60
2O39	A41	30c ultra	55.00
2O40	A41	60c olive brn	15.00

Unwmk.

2O41	A42	1fr ol gray & bl	15.00
		Nos. 2O36-2O41 (6)	107.20

On 1934 Issue

1934-35   Wmk. 183

2O42	A46	3c olive	.25
2O43	A47	5c emerald	.65
2O44	A49	15c orange ('35)	1.50
2O45	A51	25c brown	19.00
2O46	A52	30c ultra	1.60
		Nos. 2O42-2O46 (5)	23.00

On 1936 Issue

1937   Unwmk.

2O47	A53	3c olive	.25	.25
2O48	A54	5c blue green	.25	.25
2O49	A55	10c red violet	1.10	
2O50	A56	15c orange	.45	.55
2O51	A57	20c carmine	1.90	
2O52	A58	25c brown	.65	1.10
2O53	A59	30c ultra	.65	1.00
2O54	A60	35c yellow green	.65	1.00
2O55	A61	40c gray	.95	1.25
		Nos. 2O47-2O55 (9)		8.40

1937   With Grilled Gum

2O47a	A53	3c olive	.30
2O48a	A54	5c blue green	.45
2O49a	A55	10c red violet	6.25
2O50a	A56	15c orange	.70
2O51a	A57	20c carmine	2.25
2O52a	A58	25c brown	1.40
2O53a	A59	30c ultra	1.10

2O54a	A60	35c yellow green		4.25
2O55a	A61	40c gray		4.25
	Nos. 2O47a-2O55a (9)			20.95

On 1931 Issue

1937   **Wmk. 183**

2O56	A40	3fr orange brown	190.00

On 1938 Issue

1938   **Unwmk.**   **Perf. 11½**

Granite Paper

2O57	A63	20c red & buff	1.90
2O58	A64	30c blue & lt blue	3.00
2O59	A65	60c brown & buff	5.75
2O60	A66	1fr black & buff	9.25
	Nos. 2O57-2O60 (4)		19.90

Regular Issue of 1938 Overprinted in Black or Red

Granite Paper

2O61	A63	20c red & buff	2.25
2O62	A64	30c blue & lt blue	4.00
2O63	A65	60c brown & buff	7.25
2O64	A66	1fr black & buff (R)	12.50
	Nos. 2O61-2O64 (4)		26.00

Regular Issue of 1938 Overprinted in Black

1939

2O65	A69	3fr brn car, *buff*	3.25	11.00
2O66	A70	5fr slate bl, *buff*	5.50	15.00
2O67	A71	10fr green, *buff*	11.00	32.50
	Nos. 2O65-2O67 (3)		19.75	58.50

Same Overprint in Black on Regular Issues of 1939-42

1942-43

2O68	A55	10c dk red brown		.85
2O68A	A55	10c orange brn ('43)	.40	.85
2O69	A68	20c red	.50	1.00
	Nos. 2O68-2O69 (3)			2.70

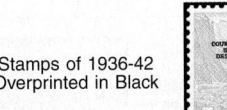

Stamps of 1936-42 Overprinted in Black

1944

2O70	A53	3c olive	.25	.25
2O71	A54	5c blue green	.25	.25
2O72	A55	10c orange brown	.80	.40
2O73	A56	15c orange	.25	.50
2O74	A68	20c red	.40	.75
2O75	A58	25c lt brown	.40	1.00
2O76	A59	30c ultra	.50	1.00
2O77	A60	35c yellow green	.50	1.00
2O78	A61	40c gray	.55	1.25

Nos. 2O73-2O75 and 2O78 exist with grilled gum. Value each $2,000 unused, $2,250 used.

Stamps of 1941 Overprinted in Black

2O79	A77	50c dp pur, *grnsh*	1.00	1.75
2O80	A78	60c red brn, *buff*	1.25	2.50
2O81	A79	70c rose vio, *pale lil*	1.25	2.50
2O82	A80	80c blk, *pale gray*	1.10	2.00
2O83	A81	90c dk red, *pale rose*	1.10	2.00
2O84	A82	1fr dk grn, *grnsh*	1.10	2.25
2O85	A83	1.20fr red vio, *pale gray*	1.75	3.00
2O86	A84	1.50fr dk bl, *buff*	2.00	3.50
2O87	A85	2fr mar, *pale rose*	2.50	4.00

Stamps of 1942 Overprinted in Black

Unwmk.   **Perf. 11½**

2O88	A69	3fr brn car, *cr*	4.50	9.00
2O89	A70	5fr slate bl, *cr*	7.00	12.50
2O90	A71	10fr green, *cr*	12.00	24.00
	Nos. 2O70-2O90 (21)		40.45	75.40
	Set, never hinged		65.00	

FOR THE INTERNATIONAL LABOR BUREAU

Regular Issues Overprinted

On 1908-30 Issues

1923-30   **Wmk. 183**   **Perf. 11½, 12**

3O1	A26	2½c ol grn, *buff* ('28)		.30
3O2	A26	3c ultra, *buff* ('30)		1.10
3O3	A26	5c org, *buff*		.55
3O4	A26	5c red vio, *buff* ('28)		.20
3O5	A26	7½c dp grn, *buff* ('28)		.45
3O6	A28	10c grn, *buff*		.55
3O7	A28	10c bl grn, *buff* ('28)		1.10
3O8	A28	15c brn red, *buff* ('28)		1.10
3O9	A28	20c red vio, *buff*		17.00
3O10	A28	20c car, *buff* ('27)		5.00
3O11	A28	25c car, *buff*		1.25
3O12	A28	25c brn, *buff* ('28)		3.00
3O13	A28	30c dp bl, *buff* ('25)		2.50
3O14	A25	30c yel brn & pale grn		65.00
3O15	A25	35c yel grn & yel		11.00
3O16	A25	40c deep blue		1.25
3O17	A25	40c red vio & grn ('28)		17.00
3O18	A25	50c dp grn & pale grn		5.00
3O19	A25	60c brn org & buff	1.60	1.90
3O20	A25	70c vio & buff ('24)		26.00
3O21	A25	80c slate & buff	14.00	2.25
3O22	A25	1fr dp cl & pale grn		2.75
3O23	A29	3fr red		25.00
3O24	A30	5fr ultra		37.50
3O25	A31	10fr dull violet		150.00
3O26	A31	10fr gray grn ('30)		150.00
	Nos. 3O1-3O26 (26)			528.75

1937-44   **With Grilled Gum**

3O18a	A25	50c dp grn & pale grn ('42)	1.75	2.25
3O20a	A25	70c vio & buff	1.75	2.25
3O21a	A25	80c slate & buff ('44)	25.00	175.00
3O22a	A25	1fr dp cl & pale grn ('42)		3.25

1925-42   **With Grilled Gum**

3O27	A36	90c grn & red, *grn* ('37)		9.75
a.		Ordinary gum		5.00
3O28	A36	1.20fr brn rose & red, *rose* ('42)	14.00	4.00
a.		Ordinary gum		4.50
3O29	A36	1.50fr bl & red, *bl* ('37)	2.75	3.00
a.		Ordinary gum		14.00
3O30	A36	2fr gray blk & red, *gray* ('36)	3.25	6.25
a.		Ordinary gum		32.50
	Nos. 3O27-3O30 (4)			23.00

1928

3O31	A39	5fr blue	82.50

On 1932 Issue

1932

3O32	A41	5c peacock blue	1.10
3O33	A41	10c orange	.90
3O34	A41	20c cerise	1.25
3O35	A41	30c ultra	7.75
3O36	A41	60c olive brown	7.75

Unwmk.

3O37	A42	1fr ol gray & bl	10.00
	Nos. 3O32-3O37 (6)		28.75

On 1936 Issue

1937

3O38	A53	3c olive	.25	.55
3O39	A54	5c blue green	.25	.55
3O40	A55	10c red violet		2.75
3O41	A56	15c orange	.45	1.10
3O42	A57	20c carmine		2.25
3O43	A58	25c brown	.60	1.40
3O44	A59	30c ultra	.60	1.10
3O45	A60	35c yellow green	.60	1.60
3O46	A61	40c gray	.95	1.90
	Nos. 3O38-3O46 (9)		3.70	13.20

1937   **With Grilled Gum**

3O38a	A53	3c olive	1.10
3O39a	A54	5c blue green	1.10
3O40a	A55	10c red violet	1.60
3O41a	A56	15c orange	1.90
3O42a	A57	20c carmine	1.60
3O43a	A58	25c brown	2.25
3O44a	A59	30c ultra	2.25
3O45a	A60	35c yellow green	2.75
3O46a	A61	40c gray	2.25
	Nos. 3O38a-3O46a (9)		16.80

On 1931 Issue

1937   **Wmk. 183**

3O47	A40	3fr orange brown	175.00

On 1934 Issue

3O48	A46	3c olive	5.50

On 1938 Issue

1938   **Unwmk.**   **Perf. 11½**

Granite Paper

3O49	A63	20c red & buff	1.60
3O50	A64	30c blue & lt blue	3.25
3O51	A65	60c brown & buff	6.00
3O52	A66	1fr black & buff	8.75
	Nos. 3O49-3O52 (4)		19.60

Regular Issue of 1938 Overprinted in Black or Red

3O53	A63	20c red & buff (Bk)	3.25
3O54	A64	30c bl & lt bl (Bk)	3.25
3O55	A65	60c brn & buff (Bk)	6.50
3O56	A66	1fr blk & buff (R)	7.00
	Nos. 3O53-3O56 (4)		20.00

Regular Issue of 1938 Overprinted in Black

1939

3O57	A69	3fr brn car, *buff*	4.50	8.25
3O58	A70	5fr slate bl, *buff*	5.50	17.00
3O59	A71	10fr green, *buff*	10.00	30.00
	Nos. 3O57-3O59 (3)		20.00	55.25

Same Overprint in Black on Regular Issues of 1939-42

1942-43

3O60	A55	10c dark red brown		.80
3O60A	A55	10c orange brn ('43)	.50	.80
3O61	A68	20c red	.55	.80
	Nos. 3O60-3O61 (3)			2.40

Stamps of 1936-42 Overprinted in Black

1944

3O62	A53	3c olive	.25	.25
3O63	A54	5c blue green	.25	.25
3O64	A55	10c orange brn	.25	.25
3O65	A56	15c orange	.50	.50
3O66	A68	20c red	.35	.50
3O67	A58	25c lt brown	.55	.70
3O68	A59	30c ultra	.50	1.10
3O69	A60	35c yellow grn	.70	1.25
3O70	A61	40c gray	.75	1.40

Stamps of 1941 Overprinted

3O71	A77	50c dp pur, *grnsh*	1.50	8.00
3O72	A78	60c red brn, *buff*	1.50	8.00
3O73	A79	70c rose vio, *pale lil*	1.75	8.00
3O74	A80	80c blk, *pale gray*	.45	1.40
3O75	A81	90c dk red, *pale rose*	.45	1.40
3O76	A82	1fr dk grn, *grnsh*	.45	1.40
3O77	A83	1.20fr red vio, *pale gray*	.75	1.75
3O78	A84	1.50fr dull bl, *buff*	1.00	2.25
3O79	A85	2fr mar, *pale rose*	1.25	3.00

Stamps of 1942 Overprinted

3O80	A69	3fr brown car, *cr*	3.25	6.00
3O81	A70	5fr slate blue, *cr*	5.00	10.50
3O82	A71	10fr green, *cr*	10.00	20.00
	Nos. 3O62-3O82 (21)		31.45	77.90
	Set, never hinged		60.00	

Nos. 329-339 Overprinted in Black

1950   **Unwmk.**   **Perf. 12x11½**

3O83	A118	5c orange	4.00	4.75
3O84	A119	10c yellow green	4.00	5.25
3O85	A120	15c aqua	5.00	7.50
3O86	A121	20c brown carmine	5.00	7.50
3O87	A122	25c red	6.00	7.75
3O88	A123	30c olive	6.00	7.75
3O89	A124	35c red brown	6.00	7.75
3O90	A125	40c deep blue	6.00	7.75
3O91	A126	50c slate gray	7.50	8.25
3O92	A127	60c blue green	9.00	12.50
3O93	A128	70c purple	10.00	17.50
	Nos. 3O83-3O93 (11)		68.50	94.25
	Set, never hinged		110.00	

Catalogue values for unused stamps in this section, from this point to the end of the section, are for Never Hinged items.

Miners — O1   Globe, Chimney and Wheel — O2

1956-60   **Unwmk.**   **Engr.**   **Perf. 11½**

3O94	O1	5c dark gray	.25	.25
3O95	O1	10c green	.25	.25
3O96	O2	20c vermilion	1.25	2.25
3O97	O2	25c car rose ('60)	.25	.25
3O98	O2	30c orange ver ('60)	.25	.40
3O99	O1	40c blue	1.25	2.75
3O100	O1	50c lt ultra ('60)	.25	.50
3O101	O2	60c reddish brown	.30	.50
3O102	O2	2fr rose violet	1.10	1.50
	Nos. 3O94-3O102 (9)		5.15	8.65

Type of 1960 Overprinted: "Visite du / Pape Paul VI / Genève / 10 juin 1969"

Violet Fibers, Fluorescent Paper

1969, June 10
3O103 O2 30c orange vermilion .30 .30

Visit of Pope Paul VI to the Intl. Labor Bureau to celebrate its 50th anniv., Geneva, June 10.

ILO Headquarters, Geneva — O3

Violet Fibers, Fluorescent Paper

1974, May 30 Photo. Perf. 11½
3O104 O3 80c blue, yellow & gray 1.90 .80

Inauguration of the new International Labor Organization Building.

Young Man at Lathe, Cogwheels O4

Designs: 60c, Woman at drilling machine. 90c, Welder and lab assistant using protective devices and clothing. 100c, Surveyor with theodolite and topographical map. 120c, Professional education for youth.

1975-88 Photo. Perf. 11½
3O105 O4 30c red brn & dk brn .70 .30
3O106 O4 60c ultra & blk 1.40 .60
3O107 O4 100c dk green & blk 2.25 1.00
3O108 O4 120c multicolored 2.75 1.25

Perf. 12x11½
3O109 O4 90c multicolored 2.10 1.50
Nos. 3O105-3O109 (5) 9.20 4.15

Issued: 30c-100c, 2/13; 120c, 8/22/83; 90c, 9/13/88.

ILO, 75th Anniv. — O5

1994, May 17 Litho. Perf. 13
3O110 O5 180c multicolored 2.00 2.00

FOR THE INTERNATIONAL BUREAU OF EDUCATION

Regular Issues of 1936-42, Overprinted in Black

1944 Unwmk. Perf. 11½
4O1 A53 3c olive .40 1.00
4O2 A54 5c blue grn .55 1.25
4O3 A55 10c orange brn .55 1.50
4O4 A56 15c orange .55 1.50
4O5 A58 20c red .55 1.50
4O6 A58 25c lt brown .65 1.75
4O7 A59 30c ultra .85 2.25
4O8 A60 35c yellow grn .85 2.25
4O9 A61 40c gray 1.10 2.50

Regular Issue of 1941, Overprinted in Black

4O10 A77 50c dp pur, grnsh 5.00 13.00
4O11 A78 60c red brn, buff 5.00 13.00
4O12 A79 70c rose vio, pale lil 5.00 13.00
4O13 A80 80c blk, pale gray .60 1.50
4O14 A81 90c dk red, pale rose .70 1.75
4O15 A82 1fr dk grn, grnsh .85 2.25
4O16 A83 1.20fr red vio, pale gray 1.00 2.50
4O17 A84 1.50fr dk bl, buff 1.25 3.00
4O18 A85 2fr mar, pale rose 1.60 4.00

Regular Issue of 1942, Overprinted in Black

4O19 A69 3fr brn car, cr 7.00 17.00
4O20 A70 5fr slate bl, cr 10.00 25.00
4O21 A71 10fr green, cr 15.00 40.00
Nos. 4O1-4O21 (21) 59.05 151.50
Set, never hinged 110.00

No. 306 Overprinted in Carmine

1946
4O22 A104 10c rose violet .25 .50
Never hinged .50

Nos. 316-321 Overprinted in Black

1948 Unwmk. Perf. 11½
4O23 A54 5c chocolate 1.75 3.00
4O24 A55 10c green 1.75 3.00
4O25 A68 20c orange brn 1.75 3.00
4O26 A113 25c carmine 1.75 3.00
4O27 A59 30c grnsh blue 2.00 3.00
4O28 A61 40c ultra 2.00 3.00
Nos. 4O23-4O28 (6) 11.00 18.00
Set, never hinged 20.00

Same Overprint on Nos. 329-339

1950 Perf. 12x11½
Overprint 18mm wide
4O29 A118 5c orange .65 1.75
4O30 A119 10c yellow grn .65 2.10
4O31 A120 15c aqua .65 2.10
4O32 A121 20c brown car 2.00 5.75
4O33 A122 25c red 4.50 10.50
4O34 A123 30c olive 4.50 10.50
4O35 A124 35c red brn 3.50 8.75
4O36 A125 40c deep blue 3.50 8.75
4O37 A126 50c slate gray 4.00 9.75
4O38 A127 60c blue green 4.75 11.50
4O39 A128 70c purple 5.50 13.50
Nos. 4O29-4O39 (11) 34.20 84.95
Set, never hinged 60.00

Catalogue values for unused stamps in this section, from this point to the end of the section, are for Never Hinged items.

Globe and Books — O1

Designs: 20c, 30c, 60c, 2fr, Pestalozzi Monument at Yverdon.

1958-60 Engr. Perf. 11½
4O40 O1 5c dark gray .25 .25
4O41 O1 10c green .25 .25
4O42 O1 20c vermilion 2.25 2.25
4O43 O1 20c car rose ('60) .25 .25
4O44 O1 30c org ver ('60) .25 .35
4O45 O1 40c blue 2.75 2.75
4O46 O1 50c lt ultra ('60) .30 .50
4O47 O1 60c reddish brn .30 .50
4O48 O1 2fr rose violet 1.10 1.50
Nos. 4O40-4O48 (9) 7.70 8.60

FOR THE WORLD HEALTH ORGANIZATION

No. 316-319, 321 Overprinted in Black

1948 Unwmk. Perf. 11½
5O1 A54 5c chocolate 2.25 2.50
5O2 A55 10c green 2.25 3.50
5O3 A68 20c orange brn 2.25 3.50
5O4 A113 25c carmine 2.25 4.50
5O5 A61 40c ultra 2.50 5.00
Nos. 5O1-5O5 (5) 11.50 19.00
Set, never hinged 20.00

Regular Issues of 1941, 1942 and 1949 Overprinted in Black

1948-50
5O6 A118 5c orange .50 1.00
5O7 A119 10c yellow grn .65 1.50
5O8 A120 15c aqua .90 2.00
5O9 A121 20c brown car 2.25 6.00
5O10 A122 25c red 2.25 6.00
5O11 A123 30c olive 1.50 5.00
5O12 A124 35c red brown 2.10 7.00
5O13 A125 40c deep blue 2.10 3.50
5O14 A126 50c slate gray 2.25 6.00
5O15 A127 60c blue green 2.50 7.00
5O16 A128 70c purple 3.00 7.00
5O17 A80 80c blk, pale gray ('48) 2.00 3.75
5O18 A81 90c dk red, pale rose 4.25 8.50
5O19 A82 1fr dk grn, grnsh ('48) 2.50 4.50
5O20 A83 1.20fr red vio, pale gray 5.50 12.00
5O21 A84 1.50fr dk bl, buff 11.00 12.00
5O22 A85 2fr mar, pale rose ('48) 3.50 6.50
5O23 A69 3fr brn car, cr 22.50 37.50
5O24 A70 5fr sl bl, cr ('48) 7.50 11.50
5O25 A71 10fr grn, cr 45.00 65.00
Nos. 5O6-5O25 (20) 123.75 213.25
Set, never hinged 250.00

Catalogue values for unused stamps in this section, from this point to the end of the section, are for Never Hinged items.

WHO Emblem — O2

1957-60 Unwmk. Engr. Perf. 11½
5O26 O2 5c gray .25 .25
5O27 O2 10c lt grn .25 .25
5O28 O2 20c vermilion 2.25 2.25
5O29 O2 20c car rose ('60) .25 .25
5O30 O2 30c org ver ('60) .35 .35
5O31 O2 40c blue 2.75 2.75
5O32 O2 50c lt ultra ('60) .50 .50
5O33 O2 60c red brn .50 .50
5O34 O2 2fr rose lilac 1.50 1.50
Nos. 5O26-5O34 (9) 8.60 8.60

No. 5O32 Overprinted: "ERADICATION DU PALUDISME"

1962, Mar. 19
5O35 O2 50c lt ultra .75 .75

WHO drive to eradicate malaria.

World Health Organization Emblem — O3

1975-95 Typo. Perf. 11½
5O36 O3 30c multi .70 .30
5O37 O3 60c lt bl & multi 1.40 .30
5O38 O3 90c lilac & multi 2.10 .90
5O39 O3 100c orange & multi 2.25 1.00

Litho.
Perf. 12
5O40 O3 140c lt grn, scar & grn 3.25 1.50

Perf. 13½x13
5O41 O3 180c multicolored 4.25 2.10
Nos. 5O36-5O41 (6) 13.95 6.10

Issued: 140c, 5/27/86; 180c, 11/28/95; others, 2/13/75.

FOR THE INTERNATIONAL ORGANIZATION FOR REFUGEES

Stamps of 1941 and 1949 Overprinted in Black

1950 Unwmk. Perf. 12x11½, 11½
6O1 A118 5c orange 11.00 14.00
6O2 A119 10c yellow green 11.00 14.00
6O3 A121 20c brown carmine 11.00 14.00
6O4 A122 25c red 11.00 14.00
6O5 A125 40c deep blue 11.00 14.00
6O6 A80 80c blk, pale gray 11.00 14.00
6O7 A82 1fr dk grn, grnsh 11.00 14.00
6O8 A85 2fr mar, pale rose 11.00 14.00
Nos. 6O1-6O8 (8) 88.00 112.00
Set, never hinged 150.00

FOR THE UNITED NATIONS EUROPEAN OFFICE

See No. 513 for postage issue commemorating the United Nations.

Stamps of 1941-49 Overprinted in Black

1950 Unwmk. Perf. 12x11½, 11½
7O1 A118 5c orange .25 2.25
7O2 A119 10c yellow grn .35 2.25
7O3 A120 15c aqua .55 3.00
7O4 A121 20c brown car .85 4.25
7O5 A122 25c red 1.10 7.50
7O6 A123 30c olive 1.40 7.50
7O7 A124 35c red brown 1.40 7.50
7O8 A125 40c deep blue 2.10 8.75
7O9 A126 50c slate gray 2.50 10.50
7O10 A127 60c blue green 2.75 12.50
7O11 A128 70c purple 3.50 12.50
7O12 A80 80c blk, pale gray 5.50 10.00
7O13 A81 90c dk red, pale rose 5.50 10.00
7O14 A82 1fr dk grn, grnsh 5.50 10.00
7O15 A83 1.20fr red vio, pale gray 6.50 13.00
7O16 A84 1.50fr dk bl, buff 6.50 13.00
7O17 A85 2fr mar, pale rose 6.50 13.00
7O18 A69 3fr brn car, cr 65.00 125.00
7O19 A70 5fr sl bl, cr 67.50 125.00
7O20 A71 10fr grn, cr 90.00 160.00
Nos. 7O1-7O20 (20) 275.25 557.50
Set, never hinged 500.00

UN
Emblem — O1

Statue from UN
Building,
Geneva — O2

1955-59		**Engr.**	**Perf. 11½**	
7O21	O1	5c dk violet brn	.25	.25
7O22	O1	10c green	.25	.25
7O23	O2	20c vermilion	2.00	4.00
7O24	O2	20c car rose ('59)	.25	.25
7O25	O2	30c org ver ('59)	.25	.30
7O26	O1	40c ultra	2.25	4.50
7O27	O1	50c ultra ('59)	.25	.40
7O28	O2	60c red brown	.25	.50
7O29	O2	2fr lilac	.80	1.60
		Nos. 7O21-7O29 (9)	6.55	12.05
		Set, never hinged	12.50	

See Nos. 7O34-7O37. For overprints see
Nos. 7O31-7O32.

United Nations
Emblem — O3

1955, Oct. 24			**Photo.**	
7O30	O3	40c dark blue & bister	1.60	3.75
		Never hinged	3.00	

10th anniv. of the UN, Oct. 24, 1955.

**Catalogue values for unused
stamps in this section, from this
point to the end of the section, are
for Never Hinged items.**

Nos. 7O24 and 7O27 Overprinted in
Black or Red: "ANNÉE MONDIALE
DU RÉFUGIÉ 1959 1960"

1960				
7O31	O2	20c carmine rose	.25	.25
7O32	O1	50c ultra (R)	.50	.50

World Refugee Year, 7/1/59-6/30/60.

Palace of
Nations,
Geneva
O4

1960		**Granite Paper**	**Perf. 11½**	
7O33	O4	5fr blue	3.75	4.00

Types of 1955 Inscribed: "MUSÉE
PHILATÉLIQUE" (O1) or "ONU
MUSÉE PHILATÉLIQUE" (O2)

Engraved; Inscription Typographed

1962, Oct. 24		**Unwmk.**	**Perf. 11½**	
7O34	O1	10c green & red	.25	.25
7O35	O2	30c org ver & ultra	.30	.30
7O36	O1	50c ultra & org	.50	.50
7O37	O2	60c red brn & emer	.60	.60
		Nos. 7O34-7O37 (4)	1.65	1.65

Opening of the Philatelic Museum, UN
European Office, Geneva.

O5   O6
UNCSAT Emblem

1963, Feb. 4		**Engr.**	**Perf. 11½**	
7O38	O5	50c ultra & car rose	.50	.50
7O39	O6	2fr lilac & emer	2.00	2.00

UN Conf. on the Application of Science and
Technology for the Benefit of the Less Developed Areas (UNCSAT), Geneva, Feb. 4-20.

Stamps issued, starting Oct. 4, 1969,
by the UN in Swiss currency for use by
UN staff members or the public are
listed under "United Nations" in Vol. 1 of
this catalogue and in Scott's U.S. Specialized Catalogue. These stamps are
on sale in various UN post offices, but
are valid only in the UN enclave in
Geneva. They are not inscribed
"Helvetia."

FOR THE WORLD
METEOROLOGICAL ORGANIZATION

**Catalogue values for unused
stamps in this section are for
Never Hinged items.**

Sun, Cloud, Rain
and Snow — O1

Design: 20c, 30c, 60c, 2fr, Direction indicator and anemometer.

1956-60		**Unwmk. Engr.**	**Perf. 11½**	
8O1	O1	5c dark gray	.25	.25
8O2	O1	10c green	.25	.25
8O3	O1	20c vermilion	2.25	2.25
8O4	O1	20c car rose ('60)	.25	.25
8O5	O1	30c org ver ('60)	.35	.35
8O6	O1	40c blue	2.75	2.75
8O7	O1	50c lt ultra ('60)	.50	.50
8O8	O1	60c reddish brn	.60	.60
8O9	O1	2fr rose violet	2.00	2.00
		Nos. 8O1-8O9 (9)	9.20	9.20

WMO
Emblem
O2

1973, Aug. 30		**Engr.**	**Perf. 11½**	
		Violet Fibers, Fluorescent Paper		
8O10	O2	30c carmine	.70	.30
8O11	O2	40c blue	.95	.30
8O12	O2	1fr ocher	2.25	1.00
		Nos. 8O10-8O12 (3)	3.90	1.60

**Type O2 Inscribed: "OMI / OMM /
1873 / 1973"**

1973, Aug. 30		**Photo.**	**Perf. 11½**	
		Violet Fibers, Fluorescent Paper		
8O13	O2	80c deep violet & gold	1.90	.80

Intl. meteorological cooperation, cent.

FOR THE INTERNATIONAL BUREAU
OF THE UNIVERSAL POSTAL
UNION

**Catalogue values for unused
stamps in this section are for
Never Hinged items.**

See Nos. 98-103, 204-205, 514, 589-
590 for postage issues commemorating
the UPU.

UPU Monument,
Bern — O1

Design: 10c, 20c, 30c, 60c, Pegasus.

1957-60		**Unwmk. Engr.**	**Perf. 11½**	
9O1	O1	5c gray	.25	.25
9O2	O1	10c lt grn	.25	.25
9O3	O1	20c vermilion	2.25	2.25
9O4	O1	20c car rose ('60)	.25	.25

9O5	O1	30c org ver ('60)	.35	.35
9O6	O1	40c blue	2.75	2.75
9O7	O1	50c lt ultra ('60)	.50	.50
9O8	O1	60c red brn	.60	.60
9O9	O1	2fr rose lilac	2.00	2.00
		Nos. 9O1-9O9 (9)	9.20	9.20

First Class
Mail — O2

Parcel
Post — O3

Money
Orders — O4

Technical
Cooperation
O5

Intl. Reply
and Notication
Service — O6

Express Mail
Service — O7

Post NET
System
O8

1976-95		**Photo.**	**Perf. 11½**	
		Fluorescent Paper		
9O10	O2	40c multi	.95	.40
9O11	O3	80c multi	1.90	.80
9O12	O4	90c multi	2.10	.90
9O13	O5	100c multi	2.25	1.00
9O14	O6	120c multi	2.75	1.25
9O15	O7	140c multi	3.25	1.50
		Perf. 13½x13		
9O16	O8	180c multicolored	4.25	2.10
		Nos. 9O10-9O16 (7)	17.45	7.95

Issued: 120c, 8/22/83; 140c, 3/7/89; 180c,
11/28/95; others, 9/16/76.

UPU, 125th
Anniv.
O9

1999, Mar. 9			**Perf. 13**	
9O17	O9	20c shown	.45	.25
9O18	O9	70c Hand holding rain-		
		bow	1.60	.65

Service Quality
Improvement
O10

2003, Sept. 9	**Litho.**	**Perf. 13¾x14¼**	
9O19	O10	90c multi	2.10	.45

Methods of
Mail Transport
O11

2005, Sept. 6	**Litho.**	**Perf. 13½x14¼**	
9O20	O11	100c multi	2.25	1.60

Postman
O12

2007, Sept. 6	**Litho.**	**Perf. 13¼x13½**	
9O21	O12	180c multi	4.25	3.25

See United Nations No. 944, United Nations
Offices in Geneva No. 475, and United
Nations Offices in Vienna No. 403.

René de Saint-Marceaux (1845-1915),
Sculptor of UPU Monument — O13

	Litho. & Engr.			
2009, Oct. 9			**Perf. 13x13¼**	
9O22	O13	180c multi	4.25	3.50

See France No. 3724.

FOR THE INTERNATIONAL
TELECOMMUNICATION UNION

**Catalogue values for unused
stamps in this section are for
Never Hinged items.**

Transmitter — O1

Designs: 20c, 30c, 60c, 2fr, Antenna.

1958-60		**Unwmk. Engr.**	**Perf. 11½**	
10O1	O1	5c dark gray	.25	.25
10O2	O1	10c green	.25	.25
10O3	O1	20c vermilion	2.25	2.25
10O4	O1	20c car rose ('60)	.25	.25
10O5	O1	30c org ver ('60)	.35	.35
10O6	O1	40c blue	2.75	2.75
10O7	O1	50c lt ultra ('60)	.50	.50
10O8	O1	60c redsh brn	.60	.60
10O9	O1	2fr rose vio	2.00	2.00
		Nos. 10O1-10O9 (9)	9.20	9.20

ITU Headquarters,
Geneva — O2

1973, Aug. 30   Photo.   Perf. 11½
Violet Fibers, Fluorescent Paper
10O10 O2 80c blue & black   .80   .80

Sound
Waves, ITU
Emblem
O3

Airplane,
Ocean
Liner — O4

Radio Waves,
Face on TV,
Microphone
O5

Photogravure and Engraved
1976, Feb. 12   Perf. 11½
Violet Fibers, Fluorescent Paper
10O11 O3 40c dp org & vio bl   .95   .40
10O12 O4 90c bl, vio bl & yel   2.10   .90
10O13 O5 1fr grn & multi   2.25 1.00
        Nos. 10O11-10O13 (3)   5.30 2.30

ITU activities: world telecommunications,
mobile radio and mass media.

Fiber Optic Communication
Links — O6

1988, Sept. 13   Litho.   Perf. 12x11½
10O14 O6 1.40fr multi   3.25 1.40

Radio Waves,
ITU
Emblem — O7

1994, May 17   Litho.   Perf. 13½
10O15 O7 1.80fr multicolored   4.25 2.10

Telecommunications — O8

1999, Mar. 9   Photo.   Perf. 11½
10O16 O8 10c Teleeducation   .25   .25
10O17 O8 100c Telemedicine   2.25 1.10

Stylized
Face — O9

2003, Sept. 9 Litho. Perf. 13¾x14¼
10O18 O9 90c multi   2.10   .45

FOR THE WORLD INTELLECTUAL
PROPERTY ORGANIZATION

> Catalogue values for unused
> stamps in this section are for
> Never Hinged items.

WIPO
Emblem
O1

1982, May 27 Photo.   Perf. 12x11½
11O1 O1 40c shown   .95   .40
11O2 O1 80c Headquarters,
              Geneva   1.90   .80
11O3 O1 100c Industrial symbols 2.25 1.00
11O4 O1 120c Educational and
              artistic symbols   2.75 1.25
1985, Sept. 10 Photo.   Perf. 12x11½
11O5 O1 50c Mind in action   1.15   .95
        Nos. 11O1-11O5 (5)   9.00 4.00

This is an expanding set. Numbers will
change if necessary.

FOR THE INTERNATIONAL
OLYMPIC COMMITTEE

> Catalogue values for unused
> stamps in this section are for
> Never Hinged items.

Olympics Type of Regular Issue

Hand and plant with leaves of Olympic rings
and: 20c, Orange frame. 70c, Green frame.

2000, Sept. 15   Photo.   Die Cut
Booklet Stamps
Self-Adhesive
12O1 A496 20c multi   .45   .25
12O2 A496 70c multi   1.60   .80
   a.   Booklet pane, #12O1-12O2   2.10
        Booklet, #12O2a   2.10

No. 12O2a is separated from booklet cover
by rouletting. The booklet was sold folded.

Olympics Type of Regular Issue,
2004

Design: Runner, "40," Olympic rings, scene
from 1896 Athens Olympics.

2004, May 6   Litho.   Perf. 13x13¼
12O3 A551 100c multi   2.25 1.60

2006 Winter Olympics Type of 2005
2005, Nov. 22 Litho. Perf. 13½x13
12O4 A578 130c Ice hockey   3.00 2.00

        Issued in sheets of 6.

Summer Olympics Type of 2008
2008, May 8   Litho.   Perf. 14x14¼
12O5 A627 180c BMX cycling   4.25 3.50

Bobsled — O1

Perf. 13¼x13½
2009, Nov. 20   Litho.
12O6 O1 100c multi   2.25 2.00

FRANCHISE STAMPS

These stamps were distributed to
many institutions and charitable societies for franking their correspondence.

F1

Control Figures Overprinted in Black
214

Perf. 11½, 12
1911-21   Typo.   Wmk. 183
Blue Granite Paper
S1   F1 2c ol grn & red   .25   .25
S2   F1 3c ol grn & red   2.50   .55
S3   F1 5c ol grn & red   1.10   .25
S4   F1 10c ol grn & red   1.40   .25
S5   F1 15c ol grn & red   21.00 4.00
S6   F1 20c ol grn & red   5.00   .60
        Nos. S1-S6 (6)   31.25 5.90

Without Control Figures
S1a F1 2c olive green & red   .55 19.00
S2a F1 3c olive green & red   .55 25.00
S3a F1 5c olive green & red   4.75 32.50
S4a F1 10c olive green & red   8.25 50.00
S5a F1 15c olive green & red   5.25 125.00
S6a F1 20c olive green & red   9.50 50.00
        Nos. S1a-S6a (6)   28.85 301.50

Control Figures
Overprinted in Black

1926
S7   F1 5c ol grn & red   12.50 4.50
S8   F1 10c ol grn & red   7.75 3.25
S9   F1 20c ol grn & red   10.00 3.75
        Nos. S7-S9 (3)   30.25 11.50

Control Figures
Overprinted in Black

1927   White Granite Paper
S10 F1 5c green & red   5.00   .40
S11 F1 10c green & red   2.50   .25
   b.   Grilled gum   325.00 725.00
S12 F1 20c green & red   3.50   .30
        Nos. S10-S12 (3)   11.00   .95

Without Control Figures
S10a F1 5c green & red   32.50 140.00
S11a F1 10c green & red   32.50 140.00
   c.   Grilled gum   150.00 650.00
S12a F1 20c green & red   32.50 140.00

Nurse — F2

Nun — F3

J. H. Dunant — F4

Control Figures Overprinted in
Black

1935   Perf. 11½
S13 F2 5c turq green   2.25 5.50
   b.   Grilled gum   3.25   .40
S14 F3 10c lt violet   2.25 5.50
   b.   Grilled gum   3.25   .25

S15 F4 20c scarlet   2.25 6.50
   b.   Grilled gum   3.75   .45
        Nos. S13-S15 (3)   6.75 17.50
        Nos. S13b-S15b (3)   10.25 1.10

Without Control Figures
S13a F2 5c turquoise green   1.40 3.75
   c.   Grilled gum   15.00 1.40
S14a F3 10c light violet   1.40 3.75
   c.   Grilled gum   15.00 1.40
S15a F4 20c scarlet   1.40 5.00
   c.   Grilled gum   15.00 1.50
        Nos. S13a-S15a (3)   4.20 12.50
        Nos. S13c-S15c (3)   45.00 4.30

SYRIA

'sir-ē-ə

LOCATION — Asia Minor, bordering on Turkey, Iraq, Lebanon, Israel and the Mediterranean Sea
GOVT. — Republic
AREA — 71,498 sq. mi.
POP. — 14,972,000 (1997 est.)
CAPITAL — Damascus

Syria was originally part of the Turkish province of Sourya conquered by British and Arab forces in late 1918 and later partitioned. The British assumed control of the Palestine and Transjordan regions; the French were permitted to occupy the sanjaks of Lebanon, Alaouites and Alexandretta; and the remaining territory, including the vilayets of Damascus and Aleppo, was established as an independent Arab kingdom, under which the first Syrian stamps were issued.

French forces from Beirut deposed King Faisal in July 1920, and two years of military occupation followed until Syria was mandated to France in July 1922. Syrian autonomy was substituted for the mandate in 1934, but full independence was not again achieved until 1946. In 1958, Syria and Egypt merged to form the United Arab Republic. Syria left this union in 1961, adopting the name Syrian Arab Republic. UAR issues for Syria are listed following Syria's 1919-20 Issues of the Arabian Government.

10 Milliemes = 1 Piaster
40 Paras = 1 Piaster (Arabian Govt.)
100 Centimes = 1 Piaster (1920)
100 Piasters = 1 Syrian Pound

Catalogue values for unused stamps in this country are for Never Hinged items, beginning with Scott 314 in the regular postage section, Scott B13 in the semipostal section, Scott C124 in the airpost section, Scott CB5 in the airpost semipostal section, Scott J40 in the postage due section, and all of the items in the UAR sections.

Watermarks

Wmk. 291 — National Emblem Multiple

Carrier Pigeon — Wmk. 403

Issued under French Occupation

Stamps of France, 1900-07, Surcharged

Perf. 14x13½

1919, Nov. 21   **Unwmk.**

1	A16	1m on 1c gray	225.00	200.00
2	A16	2m on 2c vio brn	575.00	550.00
3	A16	3m on 3c red org	275.00	240.00
4	A20	4m on 15c gray grn	55.00	47.50
5	A22	5m on 5c dp grn	30.00	27.50
6	A22	1p on 10c red	45.00	32.50
7	A22	2p on 25c blue	22.50	15.00
8	A18	5p on 40c red & pale bl	30.00	22.50
9	A18	9p on 50c bis brn & lav	60.00	50.00
10	A18	10p on 1fr cl & ol grn	95.00	80.00
		Nos. 1-10 (10)	1,412.	1,260.

The letters "T.E.O." are the initials of "Territoires Ennemis Occupés." There are two types of the numerals in the surcharges on Nos. 2, 3, 8 and 9.

Stamps of French Offices in Turkey, 1902-03, Surcharged

1919

11	A2	1m on 1c gray	1.25	.80
a.		Inverted surcharge	40.00	
12	A2	2m on 2c violet brn	1.25	.80
a.		Inverted surcharge	40.00	
13	A2	3m on 3c red orange	3.00	1.40
a.		Inverted surcharge	40.00	
14	A3	4m on 15c pale red	1.25	.80
a.		Inverted surcharge	40.00	
15	A2	5m on 5c green	1.25	.80

Overprinted

16	A5	1p on 25c blue	1.25	.75
a.		Inverted overprint	40.00	
17	A6	2p on 50c bis brn & lav	2.25	1.25
18	A6	4p on 1fr claret & ol grn	3.75	2.50
19	A6	8p on 2fr gray vio & yel	11.00	8.00
a.		"T.E.O." double	110.00	110.00
20	A6	20p on 5fr dk bl & buff	325.00	210.00
		Nos. 11-20 (10)	351.25	227.10

On Nos. 17-20 "T.E.O." reads vertically up.
Nos. 1-20 were issued in Beirut and mainly used in Lebanon. Nos. 16-20 were also used in Cilicia.
Inverted surcharges exist on several values of this issue.

Stamps of France, 1900-07, Surcharged

1920

21	A16	1m on 1c gray	5.50	4.50
a.		Inverted surcharge	60.00	
b.		Double surcharge	67.50	
22	A16	2m on 2c vio brn	6.50	4.75
a.		Double surcharge	67.50	
b.		Inverted surcharge	60.00	
23	A22	3m on 5c green	13.00	12.00
a.		Double surcharge	82.50	
b.		Inverted surcharge	100.00	
24	A18	20p on 5fr dk bl & buff	475.00	450.00
		Nos. 21-23 (3)	25.00	21.25

The letters "O.M.F." are the initials of "Occupation Militaire Francaise."

Stamps of France, 1900-07, Surcharged in Black or Red

1920

25	A16	1m on 1c gray	.95	
26	A16	2m on 2c violet brn	1.50	1.00
27	A22	3m on 5c green	2.25	2.00
a.		Double surcharge	67.50	
28	A22	5m on 10c red	2.50	2.25
a.		Inverted surcharge	65.00	65.00
b.		Double surcharge	65.00	65.00

29	A18	20p on 5fr dk bl & buff	72.50	70.00
30	A18	20p on 5fr dk bl & buff (R)	300.00	250.00
		Nos. 25-30 (6)	380.00	326.20

Stamps of France, 1900-21, Surcharged in Black or Red

1920-22

31	A16	25c on 1c gray	2.00	1.00
32	A16	50c on 2c vio	2.00	1.00
33	A16	75c on 3c red org	2.00	1.00
a.		Inverted surcharge	52.50	52.50
b.		Double surcharge	60.00	60.00
34	A22	1p on 5c green (R)	2.25	2.00
a.		Double surcharge	60.00	60.00
35	A22	1p on 5c green	1.25	1.00
a.		Inverted surcharge	35.00	35.00
b.		Double surcharge	45.00	45.00
36	A22	1p on 20c red brn ('21)	.75	.25
a.		Inverted surcharge	35.00	35.00
b.		Double surcharge	35.00	35.00
37	A22	1.25p on 25c bl ('22)	1.50	.95
a.		Inverted surcharge	40.00	40.00
b.		Double surcharge	37.50	37.50
38	A22	1.50p on 30c org ('22)	1.60	.80
a.		Inverted surcharge	27.50	40.00
39	A22	2p on 10c red	1.25	1.00
a.		Inverted surcharge	50.00	50.00
40	A22	2p on 25c bl (R)	1.25	1.00
a.		Inverted surcharge	45.00	45.00
b.		Double surcharge	35.00	35.00
41	A18	2p on 40c red & pale bl ('21)	1.60	.75
42	A20	2.50p on 50c dl bl ('22)	1.40	1.10
a.		Final "S" of "Piastres" omitted	24.00	24.00
b.		Inverted surcharge	30.00	30.00
c.		Double surcharge	35.00	35.00
43	A22	3p on 25c bl (R)	1.40	1.10
a.		Inverted surcharge	45.00	45.00
44	A18	3p on 60c vio & ultra ('21)	1.75	1.10
a.		Inverted surcharge	37.50	37.50
45	A20	5p on 15c gray grn	2.50	2.25
a.		Double surcharge	140.00	150.00
46	A18	5p on 1fr cl & ol grn ('21)	3.00	1.50
47	A18	10p on 40c red & pale bl	3.75	3.25
48	A18	10p on 2fr org & pale bl ('21)	6.00	3.00
49	A18	25p on 50c bis brn & lav	5.50	4.00
a.		Inverted surcharge	100.00	100.00
50	A18	25p on 5fr dk bl & buff ('21)	110.00	95.00
51	A18	50p on 1fr cl & ol grn	25.00	20.00
a.		"PIASRTES"	1,650.	1,650.
b.		Double surcharge	1,700.	1,900.
52	A18	100p on 5fr dk bl & buff (R)	47.50	45.00
53	A18	100p on 5fr dk bl & buff (Bk)	250.00	225.00
a.		"PIASRTES"	1,650.	1,650.
		Nos. 31-53 (23)	475.25	413.05

In first printing, space between "Syrie" and numeral is 2mm, second printing, 1mm.
For overprints see Nos. C1-C9.

Surcharged in Black or Red

1920-23

54	A16	10c on 2c violet ('23)	1.40	.90
a.		Inverted surcharge	35.00	35.00
55	A22	10c on 5c org (R) ('23)	1.00	.65
a.		Inverted surcharge	35.00	35.00
56	A16	25c on 1c dk gray	1.10	.90
a.		Inverted surcharge	40.00	40.00
b.		Double surcharge	52.50	52.50
c.		50c on 1c dk gray (error)	4.50	4.50
57	A22	25c on 5c green ('21)	1.10	.60
a.		Inverted surcharge	35.00	35.00
b.		Double surcharge	35.00	35.00

58	A22	25c on 5c orange ('22)	1.00	.80
a.		"CENTIEMES" omitted	37.50	37.50
b.		Inverted surcharge	35.00	35.00
c.		Double surcharge	37.50	37.50
59	A16	50c on 2c vio brn	1.10	.90
a.		Inverted surcharge	35.00	35.00
b.		Double surcharge	45.00	45.00
60	A22	50c on 10c red ('21)	1.25	.55
a.		Inverted surcharge	35.00	35.00
b.		Double surcharge	35.00	35.00
61	A22	50c on 10c green ('22)	1.50	1.25
a.		Inverted surcharge	35.00	35.00
b.		Double surcharge	37.50	37.50
c.		Double surcharge, one inverted	50.00	50.00
62	A16	75c on 3c red orange	3.00	2.00
a.		Inverted surcharge	35.00	35.00
b.		Double surcharge	45.00	45.00
63	A20	75c on 15c sl grn ('21)	1.40	.90
a.		Double surcharge	35.00	35.00
		Nos. 54-63 (10)	13.85	9.45

Preceding Issues Overprinted

1920

Black Overprint

64	A16	25c on 1c sl gray	12.00	10.00
a.		Double overprint	45.00	
65	A16	50c on 2c vio brn	13.00	11.00
a.		Double overprint	45.00	
66	A22	1p on 5c green	11.00	9.00
a.		Double overprint	45.00	
67	A22	2p. on 25c blue	18.00	14.50
a.		Double overprint	82.50	
68	A20	5p on 15c gray grn	55.00	47.50
a.		Double overprint	140.00	150.00
69	A18	10p on 40c red & pale bl	80.00	75.00
a.		Double overprint	325.00	
70	A18	25p on 50c bis brn & lav	225.00	190.00
a.		Double overprint	600.00	
71	A18	50p on 1fr cl & ol grn	650.00	625.00
a.		Double overprint	2,100.	
72	A18	100p on 5fr dk bl & buff	2,000.	1,900.
a.		Double overprint	3,900.	4,300.
		Nos. 64-72 (9)	3,064.	2,882.

Red Overprint

73	A16	25c on 1c sl gray	12.50	10.00
74	A16	50c on 2c vio brn	11.00	8.50
75	A22	1p on 5c green	11.00	8.50
76	A22	2p on 25c blue	9.00	6.50
77	A20	5p on 15c gray grn	55.00	47.50
a.		Double overprint	190.00	
78	A18	10p on 40c red & pale bl	85.00	75.00
a.		Double overprint	170.00	
79	A18	25p on 50c bis brn & lav	225.00	180.00
a.		Double overprint	450.00	475.00
80	A18	50p on 1fr cl & ol grn	475.00	425.00
a.		Double overprint	1,700.	1,900.
81	A18	100p on 5fr dk bl & buff	1,650.	1,650.
a.		Double overprint	3,500.	3,750.
		Nos. 73-81 (9)	2,533.	2,411.

Nos. 64-81 were used only in the vilayet of Aleppo where Egyptian gold currency was still in use.

A1

Black or Red Surcharge

1921   **Perf. 11½**

82	A1	25c on ¹⁄₁₀p lt brn	1.25	.85
a.		"25 Centiemes" omitted		
83	A1	50c on ²⁄₁₀p grn	1.25	.85
84	A1	1p on ³⁄₁₀p yel	1.75	.85
a.		"⁴⁄₁₀" for "³⁄₁₀"	12.50	12.50
b.		Inverted surcharge	60.00	60.00
85	A1	1p on 5m rose	2.00	1.10
86	A1	2p on 5m rose	2.50	1.25
a.		Tête bêche pair	160.00	160.00
b.		Inverted surcharge	40.00	40.00
c.		Double surcharge	45.00	45.00
87	A1	3p on 1p gray bl	3.00	1.25
a.		Inverted surcharge	40.00	40.00
88	A1	5p on 2p bl grn	5.00	3.50
a.		Inverted surcharge	45.00	45.00

89 A1 10p on 5p vio brn   11.00   5.75
90 A1 25p on 10p gray (R)   13.00   8.00
  a.   Inverted surcharge   45.00   45.00
   Nos. 82-90 (9)   40.75   23.40

Nos. 82-90 are surcharged on stamps of the Arabian Government Nos. 85, 87-93 and have the designs and sizes of those stamps.

Kilis Issue

A2

Sewing Machine Perf. 9
1921   **Handstamped**
      Pelure Paper

91 A2 (1p) violet   50.00   45.00

Issued at Kilis to meet a shortage of the regular issue, caused by the sudden influx of a large number of Armenian refugees from Turkey. The Kilis area was restored to Turkey in Oct. 1923.

Stamps of France, Surcharged

1921-22   *Perf. 14x13½*
92 A18   2p on 40c red & pale bl   1.25   .90
  a.   Inverted surcharge   35.00   35.00
  b.   Double surcharge   35.00   35.00
  c.   Triple surcharge   82.50
93 A18 2.50p on 50c bis brn & lav ('22)   1.40   1.00
  a.   Double surcharge   37.50   37.50
  b.   2p on 50c bister brown & lavender (error)   82.50   67.50
94 A18   3p on 60c vio & ultra   1.25   .90
  a.   Inverted surcharge   35.00   35.00
  b.   Double surcharge   35.00   35.00
95 A18   5p on 1fr cl & ol grn   7.00   6.00
  a.   Inverted surcharge   40.00   40.00
96 A18 10p on 2fr org & pale bl   15.00   11.00
97 A18 25p on 5fr dk bl & buff   13.00   10.00
   Nos. 92-97 (6)   38.90   29.80

On No. 93 the surcharge reads: "2 PIASTRES 50."

For overprints see Nos. C10-C17.

French Mandate

French Stamps of 1900-23 Surcharged

1923
104 A16 10c on 2c vio brn   .40   .25
  a.   Inverted surcharge   27.50   27.50
  b.   Double surcharge   35.00   35.00
105 A22 25c on 5c orange   .75   .75
  a.   Inverted surcharge   27.50   27.50
106 A22 50c on 10c green   .90   .85
  a.   Inverted surcharge   27.50   27.50
  b.   Double surcharge   35.00   35.00
  c.   25c on 10c green (error)   240.00   240.00
107 A20 75c on 15c sl grn   1.60   1.50
  a.   Inverted surcharge   35.00   35.00
  b.   Double surcharge   37.50   37.50
108 A22 1p on 20c red brn   .75   .70
  a.   Inverted surcharge   27.50   27.50
  b.   Double surcharge   35.00   35.00
109 A22 1.25p on 25c blue   1.40   1.25
  a.   Inverted surcharge   40.00   40.00
  b.   Double surcharge   37.50   37.50
110 A22 1.50p on 30c orange   1.10   .90
  a.   Inverted surcharge   27.50   27.50
111 A22 1.50p on 30c red   1.10   .90
112 A20 2.50p on 50c dl bl   .70   .60
  a.   Inverted surcharge   60.00   60.00
  b.   Double surcharge   35.00   35.00

On Pasteur Stamps of 1923
113 A23 50c on 10c green   2.00   1.75
114 A23 1.50p on 30c red   1.75   1.50
115 A23 2.50p on 50c blue   2.00   1.75

Surcharged

116 A18   2p on 40c red & pale bl   .75   .70
  a.   Inverted surcharge   35.00   35.00
  b.   Double surcharge   37.50   37.50
  c.   "Liabn"   450.00   450.00
117 A18   3p on 60c vio & ultra   1.50   1.25
  a.   Inverted surcharge   40.00   40.00
  b.   Double surcharge   75.00   75.00
  c.   "Liabn"   450.00   450.00
118 A18   5p on 1fr cl & ol grn   2.00   1.50
  a.   Inverted surcharge   75.00   75.00
  b.   "Liabn"   450.00   450.00
119 A18 10p on 2fr org & pale bl   7.50   7.00
  a.   "Liabn"   450.00   450.00
120 A18 25p on 5fr dk bl & buff   22.50   20.00
   Nos. 104-120 (17)   48.70   43.15

Stamps of France, 1900-21, Surcharged

1924   *Perf. 14x13½*
121 A16 10c on 2c vio brn   .40   .25
  a.   Inverted surcharge   35.00   35.00
122 A22 25c on 5c orange   .70   .60
  a.   "25" omitted   24.00
123 A22 50c on 10c green   .70   .60
  a.   Inverted surcharge   35.00   35.00
124 A20 75c on 15c sl grn   .70   .60
125 A22 1p on 20c red brn   .60   .50
  a.   "1 PIASTRES"   24.00
126 A22 1.25p on 25c blue   1.10   .90
127 A22 1.50p on 30c orange   1.10   .90
128 A22 1.50p on 30c red   1.00   .85
129 A20 2.50p on 50c dl bl   1.00   .85

Same on Pasteur Stamps of France, 1923
1924
130 A23 50c on 10c grn   .90   .70
  a.   Inverted surcharge   47.50   47.50
131 A23 1.50p on 30c red   1.40   1.10
132 A23 2.50p on 50c blue   .75   .60
  a.   Inverted surcharge   35.00   35.00
   Nos. 121-132 (12)   10.35   8.55

Olympic Games Issue

Stamps of France, 1924, Surcharged

1924
133 A24 50c on 10c gray grn & yel grn   30.00   27.50
134 A25 1.25p on 25c rose & dk rose   30.00   27.50
135 A26 1.50p on 30c brn red & blk   30.00   27.50
136 A27 2.50p on 50c ultra & dk bl   30.00   27.50
   Nos. 133-136 (4)   120.00   110.00

See Nos. 166-169.

Stamps of France 1900-20 Surcharged

137 A18   2p on 40c red & pale bl   .90   .50
138 A18   3p on 60c vio & ultra   .70   .65
139 A18   5p on 1fr claret & ol grn   3.50   3.25
140 A18 10p on 2fr org & pale bl   3.50   3.00
141 A18 25p on 5fr dk bl & buff   5.25   4.50
   Nos. 137-141 (5)   13.85   11.90

For overprints see Nos. C18-C21.

Stamps of France 1900-21, Surcharged

or

1924-25
143 A16 10c on 2c vio brn   .40   .25
  a.   Double surcharge   35.00   35.00
  b.   Inverted surcharge   30.00   30.00
144 A22 25c on 5c orange   .40   .25
  a.   Double surcharge   35.00   35.00
145 A22 50c on 10c green   .75   .50
  a.   Double surcharge   35.00   35.00
  b.   Inverted surcharge   30.00   30.00
146 A20 75c on 15c gray grn   .90   .70
  a.   Double surcharge   35.00   35.00
  b.   Inverted surcharge   30.00   30.00
147 A22 1p on 20c red brn   .60   .40
  a.   Inverted surcharge   26.00   26.00
148 A22 1.25p on 25c blue   .95   .75
  a.   Double surcharge   30.00   30.00
149 A22 1.50p on 30c red   .90   .70
  a.   Double surcharge   35.00   35.00
150 A22 1.50p on 30c orange   26.00   25.00
151 A22   2p on 35c violet ('25)   1.00   .80
152 A18   2p on 40c red & pale bl   .75   .50
  a.   Arabic "Piastre" in singular   1.75   1.75
153 A18   2p on 45c grn & bl ('25)   5.00   4.00
154 A18   3p on 60c vio & ultra   1.10   .75
155 A20   3p on 60c lt vio ('25)   1.25   1.25
156 A20   4p on 85c ver   .45   .25
157 A18   5p on 1fr cl & ol grn   1.25   .75
158 A18 10p on 2fr org & pale bl   2.00   1.50
159 A18 25p on 5fr dk bl & buff   2.75   1.50
   Nos. 143-159 (17)   46.45   39.35

On No. 152a, the surcharge is as illustrated. The correct fourth line ("2 Piastres" -plural), as it appears on Nos. 151, 152 and 153, has four characters, the third resembling "9."

For overprints see Nos. C22-C25.

Same Surcharge on Pasteur Stamps of France
1924-25
160 A23 50c on 10c green   1.25   1.00
161 A23 75c on 15c grn ('25)   1.25   1.00
162 A23 1.50p on 30c red   1.25   1.00
163 A23   2p on 45c red ('25)   1.25   1.00
164 A23 2.50p on 50c blue   1.75   1.25
165 A23   4p on 75c blue   1.75   1.25
   Nos. 160-165 (6)   8.50   6.50

Olympic Games Issue

Stamps of France, 1924, Surcharged in French and Arabic

1924
166 A24 50c on 10c   29.00   29.00
167 A25 1.25p on 25c   29.00   29.00
168 A26 1.50p on 30c   29.00   29.00
169 A27 2.50p on 50c   29.00   29.00
   Nos. 166-169 (4)   116.00   116.00

Same Colors as #133-136

Ronsard Issue
Same Surcharge on France No. 219
1925
170 A28 4p on 75c bl, *bluish*   1.00   .75

Mosque at Hama
A3

Mosque at Damascus
A5

View of Merkab
A4

Designs: 50c, View of Alexandretta. 75c, View of Hama. 1p, Omayyad Mosque, Damascus. 1.25p, Latakia Harbor. 1.50p, View of Damascus. 2p, View of Palmyra. 2.50p, View of Kalat Yamoun. 3p, Bridge of Daphne. 5p, View of Aleppo. 10p, View of Aleppo. 25p, Columns at Palmyra.

Perf. 12½, 13½
1925   Litho.   Unwmk.
173 A3 10c dark violet   .35   .25

     Photo.
174 A4 25c olive black   1.00   .55
175 A4 50c yellow green   .50   .25
176 A4 75c brown orange   .60   .25
177 A5 1p magenta   .60   .25
178 A4 1.25p deep green   2.25   1.10
179 A4 1.50p rose red   .75   .25
180 A4 2p dark brown   2.00   .25
181 A4 2.50p peacock blue   1.50   .50
182 A4 3p orange brn   1.50   .25
183 A4 5p violet   1.25   .25
184 A4 10p violet brown   3.50   .30
185 A4 25p ultra   5.75   4.50
   Nos. 173-185 (13)   21.55   8.95

For surcharges see Nos. 186-206, B1-B12, C26-C45, CB1-CB4.

Surcharged in Black or Red

1926-30
186 A4 1p on 3pi org brn ('30)   2.00   .50
187 A4 2p on 1p25 dp grn (R) ('28)   1.25   .40
  a.   Double surcharge   16.00   16.00
188 A4 3.50p on 75c org brn   1.00   .35
  a.   Double surcharge   16.00   16.00
189 A4 4p on 25c ol blk   1.50   .35
190 A4 4p on 25c ol blk ('27)   1.40   .45
191 A4 4p on 25c ol blk (R) ('28)   1.25   .35
192 A4 4.50p on 75c brn org   1.40   .35
193 A4 6p on 2p50 pck bl   1.10   .35
194 A4 7.50p on 2p50 pck bl
195 A4 7.50p on 2p50 pck bl (R) ('28)   3.50   .90
  a.   Double surcharge   29.00
196 A4 12p on 1p25 dp grn   1.50   .40
  a.   Surcharge on face and back   50.00   42.50
197 A4 15p on 25p ultra   2.75   .90
198 A4 20p on 1p25 dp grn   2.25   .70
   Nos. 186-198 (13)   21.90   6.35

Size of numerals and arrangement of this surcharge varies on the different denominations.
No. 189 has slanting foot on "4."
No. 190, foot straight.

No. 173 Surcharged in Red

1928
199 A3 05c on 10c dk vio   1.00   .25

Stamps of 1925 Ovptd. in Red or Blue

1929 — **Perf. 13½**

200	A4	50c yellow grn (R)	3.50	2.75
201	A5	1p magenta (Bl)	3.50	2.75
202	A4	1.50p rose red (Bl)	3.50	2.75
203	A4	3p orange brn (Bl)	3.50	2.75
204	A4	5p violet (R)	3.50	2.75
205	A4	10p violet brn (Bl)	3.50	2.75
206	A4	25p ultra (R)	3.50	2.75
		Nos. 200-206 (7)	24.50	19.25

Industrial Exhibition, Damascus, Sept. 1929.

View of Hama — A6

View of Alexandretta — A9

Citadel at Aleppo A10

Great Mosque of Damascus A11

Ruins of Bosra A13

Mosque at Homs A15

View of Sednaya A16

Citadel at Aleppo A17

Ancient Bridge at Antioch A18

Mosque at Damascus A22

Designs: 20c, Great Mosque, Aleppo. 25c, Minaret, Hama. 2p, View of Antioch. 4p, Square at Damascus. 15p, Mosque at Hama. 25p, Monastery of St. Simeon the Stylite (ruins). 50p, Sun Temple (ruins), Palmyra.

Perf. 12x12½

1930-36 — **Litho.** — **Unwmk.**

208	A6	10c red violet	.50	.25
209	A6	10c vio brn ('33)	.50	.35
209A	A6	10c vio brn, redrawn ('35)	.50	.25
210	A6	20c dark blue	.50	.25
211	A6	20c brn org ('33)	.50	.25
212	A6	25c gray green	.50	.25
213	A6	25c dk bl gray ('33)	.80	.45

Photo.

Perf. 13

214	A9	50c violet	.50	.25
215	A15	75c org red ('32)	.50	.25
216	A10	1p green	.75	.25
217	A11	1p bis brn ('36)	1.75	.40
218	A11	1.50p bister brown	7.50	3.00
219	A11	1.50p dp grn ('33)	1.00	.50
220	A9	2p dark violet	.75	.25
221	A13	3p yellow green	2.00	.70
222	A10	4p yellow orange	.75	.25
223	A15	4.50p rose carmine	1.75	.55
224	A16	6p grnsh black	2.25	.50
225	A17	7.50p dull blue	2.25	.70
226	A18	10p dark brown	2.00	.50
227	A10	15p deep green	3.50	1.00
228	A18	25p violet brown	3.25	1.10
229	A15	50p olive brown	11.50	4.50
230	A22	100p red orange	22.50	9.75
		Nos. 208-230 (24)	68.30	26.50

On No. 209A Arabic inscriptions, upper right, are entirely redrawn with lighter lines. Hyphen added in "Helio-Vaugirard" imprint. Lines in buildings and background more distinct.

On No. 215 the letters of "VAUGIRARD" in the imprint are reversed as in a mirror.

For overprints and surcharges see Nos. 253-268, 346, M1-M2.

Autonomous Republic

Parliament Building A23

abu-al-Ala al-Maarri — A24

President Ali Bek el Abed — A25

Saladin — A26

1934, Aug. 2 — **Engr.** — **Perf. 12½**

232	A23	10c olive green	1.25	1.50
233	A23	20c black	1.25	1.40
234	A23	25c red orange	1.40	1.50
235	A23	50c ultra	1.50	1.50
236	A23	75c plum	1.50	1.50
237	A24	1p vermilion	3.75	3.00
238	A24	1.50p green	4.50	3.50
239	A24	2p red brown	4.50	3.50
240	A24	3p Prus blue	4.50	3.50
241	A24	4p brt violet	4.75	3.50
242	A24	4.50p carmine	5.00	3.75
243	A24	5p dark blue	5.00	3.75
244	A24	6p dark brown	5.00	3.75
245	A24	7.50p dark ultra	5.25	3.75
246	A25	10p dark brown	7.25	6.00
247	A25	15p dull blue	10.00	8.50
248	A25	25p rose red	15.00	13.00
249	A25	50p dark brown	25.00	20.00
250	A26	100p lake	37.50	32.50
		Nos. 232-250 (19)	143.90	119.40

Proclamation of the Republic. See Nos. C57-C66. For surcharge see No. M3.

Stamps of 1930-36 Overprinted in Red or Black

1936, Apr. 15

253	A9	50c violet (R)	2.75	1.50
254	A10	1p bister brn (Bk)	2.75	1.50
255	A9	2p dk violet (R)	2.75	1.50
256	A13	3p yellow grn (Bk)	3.25	1.50
257	A10	4p yellow org (Bk)	3.25	1.50
258	A15	4.50p rose car (Bk)	3.25	1.50
259	A16	6p grnsh blk (R)	4.00	2.00
260	A17	7.50p dull blue (R)	4.75	2.75
261	A18	10p dk brown (R)	5.75	3.75
		Nos. 253-261 (9)	32.50	17.50

Industrial Exhibition, Damascus, May 1936. See Nos. C67-C71.

Stamps of 1930 Srchd. in Black

1937-38 — **Perf. 13½x13**

262	A10	2.50p on 4p yel org ('38)	.55	.40
263	A22	10p on 100p red orange	1.00	.90

Stamps of 1930-33 Srchd. in Red or Black

1938 — **Perf. 13½**

264	A15	25c on 75c org red (Bk)	.50	.25
265	A11	50c on 1.50p dp grn (R)	.60	.30
266	A17	2p on 7.50p dl bl (R)	1.00	.60
267	A17	5p on 7.50p dl bl (R)	1.75	.90
268	A15	10p on 50p ol brn (Bk)	2.25	.95
		Nos. 264-268 (5)	6.10	3.00

President Hashem Bek el Atassi — A27

1938-43 — **Photo.** — **Unwmk.**

268A	A27	10p dp blue ('43)	1.25	.85
269	A27	12.50p on 10p dp bl (R)	1.50	.90
270	A27	20p dark brown	1.25	.85
		Nos. 268A-270 (3)	4.00	2.60

The 10pi and 20pi exist imperf.

Columns at Palmyra A28

1940 — **Litho.** — **Perf. 11½**

271	A28	5p pale rose	2.00	.65

Exists imperf.

Museum at Damascus — A29

Hotel at Bloudan A30

Kasr-el-Heir A31

1940 — **Typo.** — **Perf. 13x14**

272	A29	10c bright rose	.70	.25
273	A29	20c light blue	.70	.25
274	A29	25c fawn	.75	.25
275	A29	50c ultra	.75	.25

Engr.

Perf. 13

276	A30	1p peacock blue	1.00	.25
277	A30	1.50p chocolate	1.50	.70
278	A30	2.50p dark green	1.00	.30
279	A31	5p violet	1.10	.40
280	A31	7.50p vermilion	2.00	.40
281	A31	50p sepia	3.50	1.25
		Nos. 272-281 (10)	13.00	4.30

For overprints see Nos. 298-299.

President Taj Eddin Hassani A32

1942, Apr. 6 — **Litho.** — **Perf. 11½**

282	A32	50c sage green	4.50	2.50
283	A32	1.50p dull gray brn	4.75	2.50
284	A32	6p fawn	5.00	2.50
285	A32	15p light blue	5.50	2.50
		Nos. 282-285,C96-C97 (6)	28.00	18.25

Proclamation of independence by the Allies, Sept. 27, 1941.

President Taj Eddin Hassani — A33

President Hassani and Map of Syria — A34

1942 — **Photo.** — **Unwmk.**

286	A33	6p rose lake & salm-on rose	4.00	1.25
287	A33	15p dull blue & blue	4.00	1.25
		Nos. 286-287,C98 (3)	12.00	6.50

Nos. 286-287 exist imperf.

1943 — **Litho.**

288	A34	1p light green	4.00	1.50
289	A34	4p buff	4.00	1.50
290	A34	8p pale violet	4.00	1.50
291	A34	10p salmon	4.00	1.50
292	A34	20p dull chalky blue	4.00	1.50
		Nos. 288-292,C99-C102 (9)	32.00	19.50

Proclamation of a United Syria. Exist imperf.

Stamps of 1943 Overprinted with Border in Black

1943

293	A34	1p light green	4.00	1.50
294	A34	4p buff	4.00	1.50
295	A34	8p pale violet	4.00	1.50
296	A34	10p salmon	4.00	1.50
297	A34	20p dl chalky bl	4.25	1.50
		Nos. 293-297,C103-C106 (9)	32.25	19.50

Mourning for President Hassani. Exist imperf.

Nos. 278 and 280 Overprinted in Carmine or Black

1944   **Unwmk.**   *Perf. 13*
298 A30 2.50p dk green (C)   4.50   2.50
299 A31 7.50p vermilion (Bk)   4.75   2.75
Nos. 298-299,C114-C116 (5)   37.75   33.75

1000th anniv. of the Arab poet and philosopher, abu-al-Ala al-Maarri.

President Shukri el
Kouatly — A35

1945, Mar. 15   **Litho.**   *Perf. 11½*
300 A35 4p pale lilac   1.00   .35
301 A35 6p dull blue   1.25   .40
302 A35 10p salmon   1.25   .40
303 A35 15p dark brown   2.00   .50
304 A35 20p slate green   2.00   .50
305 A35 40p orange   3.00   1.00
Nos. 300-305,C117-C123 (13)   26.60   10.35

Resumption of constitutional government.

Fiscal Stamps Overprinted or
Surcharged in Black

A36   A37

A38   A39

1945   **Typo.**   *Perf. 11, 11½x11*
306 A36 12½p on 15p yel grn   4.25   1.25
307 A37 25p buff   8.25   1.75
307A A38 25p on 25s lt vio brn   5.25   1.40
308 A39 50p on 75p brn org   9.50   2.50
309 A39 75p brown org   12.00   3.25
310 A37 100p yellow grn   19.00   4.00
Nos. 306-310 (6)   58.25   14.15

Type of 1945 and Nos. 308 and 310
Overprinted in Black

a   b

1945   **Unwmk.**   *Perf. 11*
311 A37(b) 50p magenta   6.00   1.50
312 A39(a) 50p on 75p brn org   4.50   .90
313 A37(b) 100p yellow green   7.75   1.50
Nos. 311-313 (3)   18.25   3.90

**Catalogue values for unused
stamps in this section, from this
point to the end of the section, are
for Never Hinged items.**

Independent Republic

A40

Fiscal Stamp Overprinted in Carmine
1946
314 A40 200p light blue   35.00   10.00

Sun and Ears   President Shukri
of   el
Wheat — A41   Kouatly — A42

1946   **Litho.**   *Perf. 13x13½*
315 A41 50c brown orange   .60   .25
316 A41 1p violet   1.00   .25
317 A41 2.50p blue gray   1.25   .30
318 A41 5p lt blue green   1.10   .25

Photo.
Perf. 13½x13, 13x13½
319 A42 7.50p dark brown   .60   .25
320 A42 10p Prussian green   .85   .25
321 A42 12.50p deep violet   2.25   .25
Nos. 315-321 (7)   7.65   1.80

For overprints see Nos. 328-329, 335-336.

Arab
Horse
A44

1946-47   **Litho.**
325 A44 50p olive brown   5.75   .90
326 A44 100p dk blue grn ('47)   12.50   2.00
327 A44 200p rose violet ('47)   65.00   5.50
Nos. 325-327 (3)   83.25   8.40

For overprints and surcharges see Nos.
330, 337, 356-357.

Nos. 320, 321 and
325 Overprinted in
Black or Green

1946, Apr. 17
328 A42 10p Prus green   1.25   .45
329 A42 12.50p deep violet   1.75   .65
330 A44 50p olive brown (G)   4.00   1.60
Nos. 328-330,C135 (4)   9.50   3.70

Evacuation of British and French troops
from Syria. For surcharge see No. 347.

President Shukri el
Kouatly — A45

1946   **Unwmk.**   **Litho.**   *Perf. 13½x13*
331 A45 15p red   1.00   .25
332 A45 20p violet   1.50   .25
333 A45 25p ultra   2.25   .30
Nos. 331-333 (3)   4.75   .80

No. 333 Overprinted
in Magenta

1946, Aug. 28
334 A45 25p ultra   3.00   1.10
Nos. 334,C136-C138 (4)   14.50   7.10

8th Arab Medical Cong., Aleppo, 8/28-9/4.

Nos. 328 to 330 With Additional
Overprint in Black

e

f

Perf. 13½x13, 13x13½
1947, June 10
335 A42(e) 10p Prus green   1.50   .25
336 A42(e) 12.50p deep violet   1.60   .25
337 A44(f) 50p olive brown   4.50   .75
Nos. 335-337,C139 (4)   10.10   2.50

Evacuation of British and French troops, 1st
anniv.

Hercules and the
Lion — A46

Mosaics
from
Omayyad
Mosque,
Damascus
A47

1947, Nov. 15   **Litho.**   *Perf. 11½*
338 A46 12.50p slate green   3.00   .40
339 A47 25p gray blue   4.25   .85
Nos. 338-339,C140-C141 (4)   13.75   3.75

1st Arab Archaeological Cong., Damascus,
Nov.
See No. C141a.

Courtyard
of Azem
Palace
A48

Telephone
Building
A49

1947, Nov. 15
340 A48 12.50p deep claret   2.50   .50
341 A49 25p brt blue   3.25   .70
Nos. 340-341,C142-C143 (4)   11.25   3.95

3rd Congress of Arab Engineers, Damascus, Nov.
See No. C143a.

House of
Parliament
A50

Pres. Shukri el
Kouatly — A51

1948, June 23   **Unwmk.**   *Perf. 10½*
342 A50 12.50p black & org   1.00   .25
343 A51 25p deep rose   2.00   .45
Nos. 342-343,C144-C145 (4)   6.15   1.95

Reelection of Pres. Shukri el Kouatly. See
No. C145a.

National   Syrian Flag and
Emblem — A52   Soldier — A53

1948, June 23   **Litho.**
344 A52 12.50p gray & choc   1.50   .25
345 A53 25p multicolored   2.00   .45
Nos. 344-345,C146-C147 (4)   6.25   1.75

Inauguration of compulsory military training.
See No. C147a.

Nos. 215 and 327 Surcharged with
New Value and Bars in Black

1948   *Perf. 13, 13x13½*
346 A15 50c on 75c org red   .50   .25
347 A44 25p on 200p rose vio   2.75   .30

Col. Husni   Palmyra — A56
Zayim — A54

Ain el
Arous
A55

1949, June 20   **Litho.**   *Perf. 11½*
348 A54 25p blue   2.00   .40

Revolution of Mar. 30, 1949. See No. C153.

A souvenir sheet comprises Nos. 348 and C153, imperf. Value $80.

1949, June 20
349 A55 12.50p violet ... 3.75 1.50
350 A56 25p blue ... 6.50 2.75
Nos. 349-350,C154-C155 (4) ... 36.75 22.75

UPU, 75th anniv. See note after #C155.

Pres. Husni Zayim and Map — A57

Wmk. 291
1949, Aug. 6   Litho.   Perf. 11½
351 A57 25p blue & brown ... 6.50 1.25

Election of President Husni Zayim. See Nos. C156, C156a.

Tel-Chehab Waterfall — A58

Damascus Scene A59

1949
352 A58 5p gray ... .75 .25
353 A58 7.50p olive gray ... 1.00 .25
354 A59 12.50p violet brown ... 1.25 .25
355 A59 25p blue ... 2.00 .40
Nos. 352-355 (4) ... 5.00 1.15

See No. 376.

Nos. 327 and 326 Surcharged with New Value and Bars in Black
1950   Unwmk.   Perf. 13x13½
356 A44 2.50p on 200p rose vio ... .40 .25
357 A44 10p on 100p dk bl grn ... .50 .25

National Emblem — A60

Road to Damascus A61

Postal Administration Building, Damascus — A62

1950-51   Litho.   Perf. 11½
358 A60 50c orange brn ... .30 .25
359 A60 2.50p pink ... .40 .25
360 A61 10p purple ('51) ... .50 .25
361 A61 12.50p sage grn ('51) ... .75 .40
362 A62 25p blue ('51) ... 1.75 .25
363 A62 50p black ('51) ... 5.25 .60
Nos. 358-363 (6) ... 8.95 2.00

Nos. 358 to 363 exist imperforate.

Parliament Building, Damascus A63

1951, Apr. 14
364 A63 12.50p gray blk ... .40 .25
365 A63 25p blue ... .75 .35
Nos. 364-365,C162-C163 (4) ... 2.80 1.85

New constitution adopted Sept. 5, 1950. Nos. 364-365 exist imperforate.

Water Wheel, Hama A64

Palace of Justice, Damascus A65

Perf. 11½
1952, Apr. 22   Litho.   Unwmk.
366 A64 50c dark brown ... .30 .25
367 A64 2.50p dark blue ... .35 .25
368 A64 5p blue green ... .40 .25
369 A64 10p red ... .45 .25
370 A65 12.50p gray black ... .75 .25
371 A65 15p lilac rose ... 4.00 .25
372 A65 25p deep blue ... 2.00 .35
373 A65 100p olive brown ... 7.50 2.00
Nos. 366-373 (8) ... 15.75 3.85

Nos. 366-373 exist imperforate.

Type of 1949 and

Crusaders' Fort — A66

Crusaders' Fort — A67

1953   Photo.
374 A67 50c rose red ... .40 .25
375 A66 2.50p dark brown ... .40 .25
376 A58 7.50p green ... .50 .25
377 A67 12.50p deep blue ... 1.75 .25
Nos. 374-377 (4) ... 3.05 1.00

Farm Workers — A68

Family Group A69

Designs: 1pi, 5pi, Farm workers. 10pi, 12½pi, Family group. 20pi, 25pi, 50pi, Factory and construction workers.

1954   Perf. 11½
378 A68 1p olive ... .25 .25
379 A68 2½p brown red ... .30 .25
380 A68 5p deep blue ... .40 .25
381 A69 7½p brown red ... .50 .25
382 A69 10p black ... .60 .25
383 A69 12½p violet ... .70 .25
384 A69 20p deep plum ... .85 .25

385 A69 25p violet ... 1.25 .35
386 A69 50p dark green ... 3.00 .75
Nos. 378-386 (9) ... 7.85 2.85

For overprints see #387-388, UAR 20, 34.

Nos. 382 and 385 Overprinted in Carmine

1954, Oct. 9
387 A69 10p black ... 1.25 .35
388 A69 25p violet ... 1.50 .45
Nos. 387-388,C185-C186 (4) ... 5.85 3.40

Cotton Festival, Aleppo, October 1954.

Globe — A69a   Mother and Child — A70

Arab Postal Union Issue
1955   Photo.   Perf. 13½x13
389 A69a 12½p green ... .50 .25
390 A69a 25p violet ... .95 .35
Nos. 389-390,C191 (3) ... 1.85 .85

Founding of the APU, 7/1/54. Exist imperf. For overprints see #396-399, C203, C207.

1955, May 13   Litho.   Perf. 11½
391 A70 25p red ... .80 .25
Nos. 391,C194-C195 (3) ... 3.30 1.80

Mother's Day.

United Nations Emblem A71

1955   Photo.
392 A71 7½p crimson ... .50 .25
393 A71 12½p Prus green ... 1.00 .50
Nos. 392-393,C200-C201 (4) ... 3.75 1.75

UN, 10th anniv., Oct. 24. For overprints see Nos. 401-402.

Aqueduct at Aleppo A72

1955   Litho.   Unwmk.
394 A72 7.50p lilac ... .55 .25
395 A72 12.50p carmine ... 1.00 .35
Nos. 394-395,C202 (3) ... 3.55 1.70

New aqueduct bringing water from the Euphrates to Northern Syria. Exist imperf.

Nos. 389-390 Overprinted in Ultramarine or Green

1955   Photo.   Perf. 13½x13
396 A69a 12½p green ... .40 .25
397 A69a 25p vio (G) ... 1.25 .40
Nos. 396-397,C203 (3) ... 2.15 .90

APU Congress held at Cairo, Mar. 15.

Nos. 389-390 Overprinted in Black

1956
398 A69a 12½p green ... .50 .25
399 A69a 25p violet ... 1.25 .55
Nos. 398-399,C207 (3) ... 2.25 1.05

Visit of King Hussein of Jordan to Damascus, Apr. 1956.

Cotton — A73

1956   Unwmk.   Litho.   Perf. 11½
400 A73 2½p bluish green ... .50 .25

Issued to publicize a Cotton Festival.

Nos. 392-393 Overprinted in Black

1956   Photo.   Perf. 11½
401 A71 7½p crimson ... .50 .25
402 A71 12½p Prussian green ... .75 .35
Nos. 401-402,C221-C222 (4) ... 4.00 2.45

UN, 11th anniv.

People's Army A74

1957   Litho.   Perf. 11½
403 A74 5p lilac rose ... .30 .25
404 A74 20p gray green ... .50 .25

Formation of the Popular Resistance Movement.
For overprints see Nos. 405-406, 413-414.

Nos. 403-404 Overprinted in Black or Red

1957
405 A74 5p lilac rose ... .30 .25
406 A74 20p gray green (R) ... .65 .30

Evacuation of Port Said by British and French troops, Dec. 22, 1956.

Azem Palace, Damascus A75

1957   Litho.   Perf. 11½
407 A75 12½p lilac   .30   .25
408 A75 15p gray   .50   .25

For overprint see UAR No. 33.

Map of Near East, Scales and Damascus Skyline — A76

Cotton, Bale and Ship — A77

1957   Wmk. 291   Perf. 11½
409 A76 12½p bright green   .40   .25
    Nos. 409,C240-C241 (3)   1.70 1.05

3rd Congress of the Union of Arab Lawyers, Damascus, Sept. 21-25.

1957
410 A77 12½p lt bl grn & blk   .50   .25
    Nos. 410,C242-C243 (3)   2.50 1.15

Cotton Festival, Aleppo, Oct. 3-5.

Children — A78

1957, Oct. 7
411 A78 12½p olive   1.00   .25
    Nos. 411,C244-C245 (3)   3.75 1.25

Intl. Children's Day, Oct. 7.
For overprint see UAR Nos. 13A, C10-C11.

Mailing and Receiving Letter A79

1957   Unwmk.
412 A79 5p magenta   .50   .25

Intl. Letter Writing Week, Oct. 6-12. See No. C246.

Nos. 403-404 Overprinted in Black or Red

1957   Perf. 11½
413 A74 5p lilac rose   .40   .25
414 A74 20p gray green (R)   .50   .25

Digging of fortifications along the Syrian-Israeli frontier.

Scales, Torch and Map A80

1957, Nov. 8   Wmk. 291
415 A80 20p olive gray   .55   .25
    Nos. 415,C247-C248 (3)   1.80 1.10

Congress of Afro-Asian Jurists, Damascus.

Glider A81

1957, Nov. 8   Litho.   Perf. 11½
416 A81 25p red brown   1.10   .30
417 A81 35p green   1.50   .40
418 A81 40p ultra   3.00   .70
    Nos. 416-418 (3)   5.60 1.40

Issued to commemorate a glider festival.

Khaled ibn el Walid Mosque, Homs — A82

1957   Unwmk.   Perf. 12
419 A82 2½p dull brown   .40   .25

Scroll, Communications Building and Telephone — A83

1958   Wmk. 291   Perf. 11½
420 A83 25p ultra   .30   .25
    Nos. 420,C249-C250 (3)   1.05   .75

> **Issues of 1958-61 released by the United Arab Republic are listed following the listings of Syria, Issues of the Arabian Government.**

Syrian Arab Republic

Hall of Parliament, Damascus A83a

1961   Unwmk.   Litho.   Perf. 12
420A A83a 15p magenta   .40   .25
420B A83a 35p olive gray   .75   .25

Establishment of Syrian Arab Republic.

Water Wheel, Hama — A84

Roman Arch of Triumph, Latakia — A85

Qalb Lozah Church, Aleppo A86

7½p, 10p, Khaled ibn el Walid Mosque, Homs.

**   Perf. 11½x11**
1961-62   Unwmk.   Litho.
421 A84 2½p rose red   .30   .25
422 A84 5p blue   .30   .25
423 A84 7½p blue grn ('62)   .30   .25
424 A84 10p orange ('62)   .35   .25
**   Perf. 12x11½**
425 A85 12½p gray brn   .60   .25
426 A86 17½p olive gray ('62)   .50   .25
427 A85 25p dull red brown   .70   .25
428 A86 35p dull green ('62)   .65   .25
    Nos. 421-428 (8)   3.70 2.00

Types of 1961, Regular and Air Post

Designs: 2½p, 5p, 7½p, 10p, Arch, Jupiter Temple. 12½p, 15p, 17½p, 22½p, "The Beauty of Palmyra."

1962   Perf. 11½x11
429 A84 2½p gray blue   .30   .25
430 A84 5p brown orange   .30   .25
431 A84 7½p olive bister   .30   .25
432 A84 10p claret   .30   .25
**   Perf. 12x11½**
**   Size: 26x38mm**
433 AP68 12½p gray olive   .35   .25
434 AP68 15p ultra   .50   .25
435 AP68 17½p brown   .50   .25
436 AP68 22½p grnsh blue   .70   .25
    Nos. 429-436 (8)   3.25 2.00

Martyrs' Memorial — A87

1962, June 11   Litho.
440 A87 12½p tan & sepia   .30   .25
441 A87 35p green & bl grn   .35   .25

1925 Revolution.

Pres. Nazem el-Kodsi — A88

1962, Dec. 14   Perf. 12x11½
442 A88 12½p sepia & lt bl   .30   .25

1st anniv. of the election of Pres. Nazem el-Kodsi. See No. C278.

Queen Zenobia — A89

Central Bank of Syria A90

Designs: 2½p, 5p, "The Beauty of Palmyra." 17½p, Hejaz Railway Station, Damascus. 22½p, Mouassat Hospital, Damascus. 35p, P.T.T. Jalaa Avenue Office, Damascus.

1963   Unwmk.   Perf. 11½x11
443 A89 2½p dk bl gray   .30   .25
444 A89 5p rose lilac   .30   .25
445 A89 7½p dull blue   .35   .25
446 A89 10p olive gray   .70   .25
447 A89 12½p ultra   1.00   .25
448 A89 15p violet brn   1.50   .25

---

449 A90 17½p dull violet   .60   .25
450 A90 22½p brt violet   .30   .25
451 A90 25p bister brown   .30   .25
452 A90 35p bright pink   .35   .25
    Nos. 443-452 (10)   5.70 2.50

Wheat Emblem and Globe — A91

1963, Mar. 21   Litho.   Perf. 12x11½
453 A91 12½p ultra & blk   .30   .25

FAO "Freedom from Hunger" Campaign. See No. C291 and souvenir sheet No. C291a.

Cotton Festival Type of Air Post Issue, 1962, Inscribed "1963"

1963, Sept. 26   Perf. 12x11½
455 AP75 17½p multi   .30   .25
456 AP75 22½p multi   .35   .25

The 1963 Cotton Festival, Aleppo.

Boy Playing Ball and UN Emblem — A92

1963, Oct. 24   Perf. 12x11½
457 A92 12½p emer & sl grn   .30   .25
458 A92 22½p rose red & dk grn   .30   .25

Issued for International Children's Day.

Ugharit Princess — A93

1964   Litho.   Perf. 11½x11
459 A93 2½p gray   .30   .25
460 A93 5p brown   .30   .25
461 A93 7½p rose claret   .30   .25
462 A93 10p emerald   .30   .25
463 A93 12½p light violet   .30   .25
464 A93 17½p ultra   .30   .25
465 A93 20p rose carmine   .45   .25
466 A93 25p orange   .75   .25
    Nos. 459-466 (8)   3.00 2.00

Map of North Africa and Middle East, Flag of Syria, and Crowd A94

1965, Mar. 8   Litho.   Perf. 11½x12
467 A94 12½p multicolored   .30   .25
468 A94 17½p multicolored   .30   .25
469 A94 20p multicolored   .30   .25
    Nos. 467-469 (3)   .90   .75

Mar. 8 Revolution, 2nd anniv.

Weather Map and Anemometer — A95

1965, Mar. 23   Litho.   Unwmk.
470 A95 12½p dl lilac & blk   .30 .25
471 A95 27½p lt blue & blk   .30 .25

Fifth World Meteorological Day.

"Evacuation of Apr. 17, 1946" — A96   Peasants' Union Emblem — A97

1965, Apr. 17   Litho.   Perf. 12x11½
472 A96 12½p bl & brt yel grn   .30 .25
473 A96 27½p rose red & lt lil   .30 .25

19th anniv. of the evacuation of British and French troops from Syria.

1965, Aug.   Unwmk.   Perf. 11½x11
474 A97 2½p blue green   .30 .25
475 A97 12½p purple   .30 .25
476 A97 15p maroon   .30 .25
    Nos. 474-476 (3)   .90 .75

Issued to publicize the Peasants' Union.

Torch, Map of Arab Countries and Farmer, Soldier, Woman, Intellectual and Worker — A98   Workers, Factory and Emblem — A99

1965, Nov. 23   Perf. 12x11½
477 A98 12½p multicolored   .30 .25
478 A98 25p multicolored   .30 .25

National Council of the Revolution, a legislative body working for a socialist and democratic society.

1966, Jan.   Litho.   Perf. 11½x11
479 A99 12½p blue   .30 .25
480 A99 15p carmine   .30 .25
481 A99 20p dull violet   .30 .25
482 A99 25p olive gray   .30 .25
    Nos. 479-482 (4)   1.20 1.00

Establishment of the General Union of Trade Unions.

Roman Lamp A100   Islamic Vessel, 12th Century A101

1966   Litho.   Perf. 11½x11
483 A100 2½p slate green   .30 .25
484 A100 5p magenta   .30 .25
485 A101 7½p brown   .30 .25
486 A101 10p brt rose lilac   .30 .25
    Nos. 483-486 (4)   1.20 1.00

"Evacuation of Troops" — A102   Bust of Core, Terra Cotta Vase — A103

1966, Apr. 17   Litho.   Perf. 12x11½
487 A102 12½p multi   .30 .25
488 A102 27½p multi   .30 .25

20th anniv. of the evacuation of British and French troops from Syria.

1967   Perf. 11½x11

Design: 15p, 20p, 25p, 27½p, Bronze vase in form of seated African woman.

489 A103 2½p brt green   .30 .25
490 A103 5p salmon pink   .30 .25
491 A103 10p grnsh blue   .30 .25
492 A103 12½p dull brown   .30 .25
493 A103 15p brt pink   .30 .25
494 A103 20p brt blue   .30 .25
495 A103 25p green   .30 .25
496 A103 27½p violet blue   .30 .25
    Nos. 489-496 (8)   2.40 2.00

Arab Revolution Monument, Damascus A104

1968, Mar. 8   Litho.   Perf. 12x12½
497 A104 12½p black, yel & brn   .30 .25
498 A104 25p blk, pink & car rose   .30 .25
499 A104 27½p blk, lt grn & grn   .30 .25
    Nos. 497-499 (3)   .90 .75

Mar. 8 Revolution, 5th anniversary.

Map of Syria — A105

1968, Apr. 4   Litho.   Perf. 12x12½
500 A105 12½p pink & multi   .30 .25
501 A105 60p gray & multi   .40 .25

Arab Baath Socialist Party, 21st anniv.

Hands Holding Wrench, Gun and Torch — A106

1968, Apr. 13
502 A106 12½p tan & multi   .30 .25
503 A106 17½p rose & multi   .30 .25
504 A106 60p yellow & multi   .30 .25
    Nos. 502-504 (3)   .90 .75

Issued to publicize the mobilization effort.

Rising Sun, Power Lines and Railroad Tracks A107

1968, Apr. 17   Litho.   Perf. 12½x12
505 A107 12½p multicolored   .30 .25
506 A107 27½p violet & multi   .30 .25

22nd anniv. of the evacuation of British and French troops from Syria.

Oil Wells and Oil Pipe Line on Map — A108

1968, May 1
507 A108 12½p lt & dk grn & ultra   .30 .25
508 A108 17½p pink, brn & ultra   .30 .25

Syrian oil exploitation; completion of the oil pipe line to Tartus.

Map of Palestine and Torch — A109

1968, May   Litho.   Perf. 12x12½
509 A109 12½p ultra, blk & red   .75 .35
510 A109 25p ol bis, blk & red   1.00 .35
511 A109 27½p gray, blk & red   1.50 .50
    Nos. 509-511 (3)   3.25 1.20

Issued for Palestine Day.

Citadel of Aleppo, Wheat and Cogwheel A110

1968, July 18   Litho.   Perf. 12x12½
512 A110 12½p multi   .30 .25
513 A110 27½p multi   .30 .25

Industrial and Agricultural Fair, Aleppo.

Fair Emblem, Globe, Grain, Wheel and Horse — A111

Design: 27½p, Syrian flag, hand with torch, fair emblem, globe, grain and wheel.

Perf. 12x12½, 12½x12
1968, Aug. 25   Litho.
514 A111 12½p dp brn, blk & emer   .30 .25
515 A111 27½p multicolored   .30 .25
516 A111 60p bl gray, blk & dp org   .30 .25
    Nos. 514-516 (3)   .90 .75

15th Intl. Damascus Fair, Aug. 25-Sept. 20.

Woman Carrying Cotton, and Castle of Aleppo — A112

1968, Oct. 3   Litho.   Perf. 12x12½
517 A112 12½p multi   .30 .25
518 A112 27½p multi   .30 .25

13th Cotton Festival, Aleppo.

Al Jahez — A113   Oil Derrick and Pipe Line — A114

1968, Nov. 9   Litho.   Perf. 12x12½
519 A113 12½p black & buff   .30 .25
520 A113 27½p black & gray   .60 .25

9th Science Week; Al Jahez Abu Uthman Amr ben Bahr (776-868).

1968   Perf. 12x11
521 A114 2½p grnsh bl & dk grn   .30 .25
522 A114 5p grn & vio bl   .30 .25
523 A114 7½p lt yel grn & bl   .30 .25
524 A114 10p brt yel & grn   .30 .25
525 A114 12½p yellow & ver   .30 .25
526 A114 15p ol bis & dk brn   .30 .25
527 A114 27½p dl org & dk red brn   .30 .25
    Nos. 521-527 (7)   2.10 1.75

Broken Chains and Sun A115

1969, Mar. 8   Litho.   Perf. 12½x12
Sun in Yellow and Red
528 A115 12½p vio bl & blk   .30 .25
529 A115 25p gray & blk   .30 .25
530 A115 27½p dull grn & blk   .30 .25
    Nos. 528-530 (3)   .90 .75

March 8 Revolution, 6th anniversary.

"Sun of Freedom, Young Man and Woman" — A116

1969, Mar. 29   Perf. 12x12½
531 A116 12½p multi   .30 .25
532 A116 25p multi   .30 .25

Youth Week; 5th Youth Festival, Homs, 4/18-24.

Liberation through
Knowledge and
Construction
A117

1969, Apr. 17   Litho.   Perf. 12x12½
533 A117 12½p yellow & multi   .30 .25
534 A117 27½p gray & multi   .30 .25

23rd anniv. of the evacuation of British and
French troops from Syria.

Mahatma
Gandhi — A118

1969, Oct. 7   Litho.   Perf. 12x12½
535 A118 12½p brown & dull yel   .30 .25
536 A118 27½p green & yellow   .30 .25

Mohandas K. Gandhi (1869-1948), leader in
India's fight for independence.

Cotton — A119

1969, Oct. 10
537 A119 12½p multi   .30 .25
538 A119 17½p multi   .30 .25
539 A119 25p multi   .30 .25
      Nos. 537-539 (3)   .90 .75

14th Cotton Festival, Aleppo.

Map of
Arab
Countries
A120

Designs: 25p, Arab Academy. 27½p,
Damascus University.

1969, Nov. 2   Litho.   Perf. 12½x12
540 A120 12½p ultra & lt grn   .30 .25
541 A120 25p dk pur & dp pink   .30 .25
542 A120 27½p dp bis & yel grn   .30 .25
      Nos. 540-542 (3)   .90 .75

10th Science Week, and 6th Arab Scientific
Conf. No. 541 also for 50th anniv. of the Arab
Academy and No. 542, the 50th anniv. of the
Medical School of the Damascus University.

Symbols
of
Progress
A121

1970, Mar. 8   Litho.   Perf. 12½x12
543 A121 12½p brt bl, blk & bis brn   .30 .25
544 A121 25p red, blk & dp bl   .30 .25
545 A121 27½p lt grn, blk & tan   .30 .25
      Nos. 543-545 (3)   .90 .75

March 8 Revolution, 7th anniversary.

Map of
Arab
League
Countries,
Flag and
Emblem
A122

1970, Mar. 22
546 A122 12½p multi   .30 .25
547 A122 25p gray & multi   .30 .25
548 A122 27½p multi   .35 .25
      Nos. 546-548 (3)   .95 .75

25th anniversary of the Arab League.

Sultan Saladin and Battle of Hattin,
1187, between Saracens and
Crusaders — A123

1970, Apr. 17   Litho.   Perf. 12½x12
549 A123 15p brn & buff   .30 .25
550 A123 35p lilac & buff   .35 .25

24th anniv. of the evacuation of British and
French troops from Syria.

Development of
Agriculture and
Industry — A124

1970-71   Litho.   Perf. 11x11½
551 A124 2½p brn & red ('71)   .30 .25
552 A124 5p orange & bl   .30 .25
553 A124 7½p lil & gray ('71)   .30 .25
554 A124 10p lt & dk brn   .30 .25
555 A124 12½p blue & org ('71)   .30 .25
556 A124 15p grn & red lil   .30 .25
557 A124 20p vio & red brn   .30 .25
558 A124 22½p red brn & blk
            ('71)   .30 .25
559 A124 25p gray & vio bl
            ('71)   .30 .25
560 A124 27½p brt grn & dk brn
            ('71)   .30 .25
561 A124 35p rose red & emer
            ('71)   .35 .25
      Nos. 551-561 (11)   3.35 2.75

Young
Man and
Woman,
Map of
Arab
Countries
A125

1970, May 7   Unwmk.   Perf. 12½x12½
569 A125 15p green & ocher   .30 .25
570 A125 25p brown & ocher   .30 .25

First Youth Week, Latakia, Apr. 23-29.
Inscribed "Youth's First Weak" (sic.).

Refugee
Family
A126

1970, May 15
571 A126 15p multicolored   .30 .25
572 A126 25p gray & multi   .30 .25
573 A126 35p green & multi   .30 .25
      Nos. 571-573 (3)   .90 .75

Issued for Arab Refugee Week.

Cotton — A127

1970, Aug. 18   Litho.   Perf. 12½
574 A127 5p shown   .30 .25
575 A127 10p Tomatoes   .30 .25
576 A127 15p Tobacco   .30 .25
577 A127 20p Beets   .30 .25
578 A127 35p Wheat   .75 .25
  a. Strip of 5, #574-578   2.00 2.00

Industrial and Agricultural Fair, Aleppo.

Boy
Scout,
Tent,
Emblem
and Map
of Arab
Countries
A128

1970, Aug. 25   Perf. 12½x12½
579 A128 15p gray green   .40 .25

9th Pan-Arab Boy Scout Jamboree,
Damascus.

Olive Tree
and
Emblem
A129

1970, Sept. 28   Litho.   Perf. 11½x12
580 A129 15p gray grn, yel & blk   .30 .25
581 A129 25p red brn, yel & blk   .50 .25

Issued to publicize World Olive Year.

Protection of Industry, Agriculture, Arts
and Commerce — A130

1971, Mar. 8   Litho.   Perf. 12½x12½
582 A130 15p olive, yel & bl   .30 .25
583 A130 22½p red brn, yel & ol   .30 .25
584 A130 27½p bl, yel & red brn   .30 .25
      Nos. 582-584 (3)   .90 .75

March 8 Revolution, 8th anniversary.

Workers
Memorial,
Hands
with
Wrench
and Olive
Branch
A131

1971, May 1   Litho.   Perf. 12½x12½
585 A131 15p brn vio, yel & bl   .30 .25
586 A131 25p dk bl, bl & yel   .30 .25

Labor Day.

Child and
Traffic
Lights
A132

World Traffic Day: 25p, Road signs, traffic
lights, children, vert.

1971, May 4   Perf. 11½x12, 12x11½
587 A132 15p black, red & bl   .30 .25
588 A132 25p gray & multi   .30 .25
589 A132 45p black, red & yel   .30 .25
      Nos. 587-589 (3)   .90 .75

Factories,
Cogwheel
and
Cotton
A133

1971, July 15   Litho.   Perf. 12½x12
590 A133 15p lt grn, bl & blk   .30 .25
591 A133 30p red & black   .30 .25

11th Industrial and Agricultural Fair, Aleppo.

Arab Postal Union
Emblem — A134

1971, Sep. 1   Perf. 12x12½
592 A134 15p claret & multi   .30 .25
593 A134 20p vio bl & multi   .30 .25

25th anniv. of the Conference of Sofar, Lebanon, establishing the APU.

Flag, Map of
Syria, Egypt and
Libya — A135

1971, Aug. 13   Perf. 12x11½
594 A135 15p car, dl grn & blk   .30 .25

Confederation of the Arab states of Syria,
Libya and Egypt.

Red Pepper and Chemical Factory
(Fertilizer Industry) — A136

18th Intl. Damascus Fair: 15p, Electronics
industry (TV, telephone, computer). 35p,
Glass industry (old map and glass manufacture). 50p, Carpet industry (carpet and
looms).

1971, Aug. 25   Perf. 12½
595 A136 5p violet & multi   .30 .25
596 A136 15p dull grn & multi   .30 .25
597 A136 35p multicolored   .30 .25
598 A136 50p yel grn & multi   .50 .25
      Nos. 595-598 (4)   1.40 1.00

Pres. Hafez al Assad and Crowd — A137

1971, Nov. Litho. Perf. 12x12½
599 A137 15p vio bl, blk & car .30 .25
600 A137 20p dk & lt grn, car & blk .30 .25
1st anniv. of Correctionist Movement of Nov. 16, 1970.

UNESCO Emblem, Radar, Spacecraft, Telephone A138

1971, Dec. 8
601 A138 15p vio bl & multi .30 .25
602 A138 50p green & multi .30 .25
25th anniv. of UNESCO.

UNICEF Emblem and Playing Children — A139

1971, Dec. 21
603 A139 15p ultra, dk bl & dp car .30 .25
604 A139 25p grnsh bl, ocher & dk bl .30 .25
UNICEF, 25th anniv.

Conference Emblem — A140

1971, Dec. Perf. 12½x12
605 A140 15p blk, grnsh bl & org .30 .25
Scholars' Conference.

Book Year Emblem A141

1972, Jan. 2
606 A141 15p tan, lt bl & vio .30 .25
607 A141 20p brn, lt grn & grn .30 .25
International Book Year.

Wheel, "8" and Scales of Justice — A142

1972, Mar. 8 Litho. Perf. 12x12½
608 A142 15p blue grn & vio .30 .25
609 A142 20p olive bis & car .30 .25
March 8 Revolution, 9th anniversary.

Baath Party Emblem — A143

1972, Mar. 7
610 A143 15p dk blue & multi .30 .25
611 A143 20p violet & multi .30 .25
Arab Baath Socialist Party, 25th anniv.

Eagle, Chimneys, Grain and Oil Rigs — A144

1972, Apr. 17 Perf. 12½x12
612 A144 15p gold, blk & car .30 .25
Federation of Arab Republics, 1st anniv.

Symbolic Flower, Broken Chain — A145

1972, Apr. 17 Perf. 12x11½
613 A145 15p rose red & gray .30 .25
614 A145 50p pale bl grn & gray .30 .25
26th anniv. of the evacuation of British and French troops from Syria.

Hand Holding Wrench and Spade — A146

1972, May 1
615 A146 15p ol grn, bl & blk .30 .25
616 A146 50p vio bl, brn & blk .30 .25
Labor Day.

Environment Emblem, Crystals, Microscope A147

1972, June 5
617 A147 15p multicolored .30 .25
618 A147 50p blue & multi .35 .25
UN Conference on Human Environment, Stockholm, June 5-16.

Dove over Factory — A148

1972, July 17 Litho. Perf. 12x11½
619 A148 15p yellow & multi .30 .25
620 A148 20p yellow & multi .30 .25
Agricultural and Industrial Fair, Aleppo.

Folk Dance — A149

1972, Aug. 25 Litho. Perf. 12x12½
621 A149 15p shown .30 .25
622 A149 20p Women and tambourine player .30 .25
623 A149 50p Men and drummer .50 .25
Nos. 621-623 (3) 1.10 .75
19th International Damascus Fair.

Olympic Rings, Discus, Soccer, Swimming — A150

Warriors on Horseback, Olympic Emblems — A151

Design: 60p, Olympic rings, running, gymnastics, fencing.

1972 Litho. Perf. 12½x12
624 A150 15p ol bis, blk & vio .50 .25
625 A150 20p dull bl, blk & org .60 .25
Souvenir Sheet
Imperf
626 A151 75p lt grn, bl & blk 2.00 2.00
20th Olympic Games, Munich, Aug. 26-Sept. 11, 1972.

Emblem of Revolution and Prancing Horse A152

1973, Mar. 8 Litho. Perf. 11½x12
627 A152 15p brt grn, blk & red .30 .25
628 A152 20p dull org, blk & red .30 .25
629 A152 25p blue, blk & red .30 .25
Nos. 627-629 (3) .90 .75
March 8 Revolution, 10th anniversary.

Heart and WHO Emblem A153

1973, Mar. 21
630 A153 15p gray & multi .30 .25
631 A153 50p lt brown & multi .35 .25
WHO, 25th anniversary.

Cogwheel and Grain Emblem — A154

1973, Apr. 17 Perf. 12x12½
632 A154 15p blue & multi .30 .25
633 A154 20p multicolored .30 .25
27th anniv. of the evacuation of British and French troops from Syria.

Workers and Globe A155

1973, May 1 Perf. 11½x12
634 A155 15p rose & multi .30 .25
635 A155 50p blue & multi .35 .25
Labor Day.

UN, FAO Emblems, People and Symbols — A156

1973, May 7 Perf. 12x11½
636 A156 15p lt grn & red brn .30 .25
637 A156 50p lilac & blue .35 .25
World food program, 10th anniv.

Stock — A157

1973, May 15
638 A157 5p shown .30 .25
639 A157 10p Gardenia .30 .25
640 A157 15p Jasmine .30 .25
641 A157 20p Rose .30 .25
642 A157 25p Narcissus .30 .25
  a. Strip of 5, #638-642 1.50 1.50
   Intl. Flower Show, Damascus.

Children and
Flame — A158

Children's Day: 3 children's heads and flame in different arrangements; 25p, 35p, 70p, vertical.

Perf. 11½x12, 12x11½
1973-74 **Litho.**
643 A158 2½p lt olive grn .30 .25
644 A158 5p orange .30 .25
645 A158 7½p dk brown .30 .25
646 A158 10p crimson .30 .25
647 A158 15p ultra .30 .25
648 A158 25p gray .30 .25
649 A158 35p brt blue .30 .25
650 A158 55p green .30 .25
651 A158 70p rose lilac .35 .25
  Nos. 643-651 (9) 2.75 2.25
  Issued: 15p, 55p, 70p, 5/73; others, 3/74.

Fair
Emblem
A159

1973, June 17 **Perf. 11½x12**
652 A159 15p multicolored .30 .25
  13th Agricultural and Industrial Fair, Aleppo.

Euphrates Dam and Power
Plant — A160

1973, July 5 **Perf. 12½x12**
653 A160 15p green & multi .30 .25
654 A160 50p brown & multi .30 .25
  Euphrates River diversion and dam project.

Woman from Deir
Ezzor — A161

Women's Costumes from: 10p, Hassaké. 20p, As Sahel. 25p, Zakié. 50p, Sarakeb.

1973, July 25 **Litho.** **Perf. 12**
655 A161 5p multicolored .30 .25
656 A161 10p multicolored .30 .25
657 A161 20p multicolored .30 .25
658 A161 25p multicolored .30 .25
659 A161 50p multicolored .30 .25
  a. Strip of 5, #655-659 1.50 1.50
   20th International Damascus Fair.

Map of Palestine,
Barbed Wire,
Human Rights
Emblem — A162

1973, Aug. 20 **Perf. 12x11½**
660 A162 15p lt green & multi .90 .50
661 A162 50p lt blue & multi 1.75 .50
  25th anniversary of the Universal Declaration of Human Rights.

Citadel of
Ja'abar
A163

15p, Minaret of Meskeneh, vert. 25p, Statue of Psyche at Anab al Safinah, vert.

Perf. 11½x12, 12x11½
1973, Sept. 5 **Litho.**
662 A163 10p black, org & blue .30 .25
663 A163 15p black, org & blue .30 .25
664 A163 25p black, org & blue .30 .25
  Nos. 662-664 (3) .90 .75
  Salvage of monuments threatened by Euphrates Dam.

WMO
Emblem
A164

1973, Sept. 12 **Perf. 11½x12**
665 A164 70p yellow & multi .50 .25
  Intl. meteorological cooperation, cent.

Maalula
A165

Design: 50p, Ruins of Afamia.

1973, Oct. 22 **Litho.** **Perf. 11½x12**
666 A165 15p gray blue & blk .30 .25
667 A165 50p brown & blk .30 .25
  Arab Emigrants' Congress, Buenos Aires.

Workers
and
Soldiers
A166

1973, Nov. 16 **Litho.** **Perf. 12½x12**
668 A166 15p ultra & yellow .30 .25
669 A166 25p purple & red brn .30 .25
  3rd anniv. of Correctionist Movement of Nov. 16, 1970.

Nicolaus
Copernicus
A167

Design: 25p, Abu-al-Rayhan al-Biruni.

1973, Dec. 15 **Perf. 12x11½**
670 A167 15p gold & black .30 .25
671 A167 25p gold & black .30 .25
  14th Science Week.

Arms of
Syria and
Emblems
A168

1974, Mar. 8 **Perf. 11x12**
672 A168 20p gray & blue .30 .25
673 A168 25p lt green & vio .30 .25
  11th anniversary of March 8th Revolution.

UPU
Emblem — A169

20p, Air mail letter and UPU emblem, horiz.

1974, Mar. 15 **Perf. 12x11½, 11½x12**
674 A169 15p gray & multi .30 .25
675 A169 20p multicolored .30 .25
676 A169 70p gray & multi .50 .25
  Nos. 674-676 (3) 1.10 .75
  Centenary of Universal Postal Union.

Arab
Postal
Institute
A170

1974, Apr. 10 **Perf. 11½x12**
677 A170 15p multicolored .30 .25
  Inauguration of the Higher Arab Postal Institute, Damascus, Apr. 10.

Sun and
Monument
A171

1974, Apr. 10
678 A171 15p emerald, blk & org .30 .25
679 A171 20p dp org, blk & org .30 .25
  28th anniversary of the evacuation of British and French troops from Syria.

Machine Shop
Worker
A172

Abulfeda
A173

1974, May 1 **Perf. 12x12½**
680 A172 15p black, yel & bl .30 .25
681 A172 50p black, buff & bl .30 .25
  Labor Day.

1974 **Litho.** **Perf. 11½x11**

Design: 200p, al-Farabi.

682 A173 100p pale green .50 .25
683 A173 200p lt brown 1.00 .45

Damascus Fair
Emblem — A174

Design: 25p, Cog wheel and sun.

1974, July 25 **Perf. 11½x11**
684 A174 15p multicolored .30 .25
685 A174 25p blue, blk & yel .30 .25
  21st International Damascus Fair.

Figs — A175

Fruits: 15p, Grapes. 20p, Pomegranates. 25p, Cherries. 35p, Rose hips.

1974, Aug. 21 **Perf. 12x12½**
686 A175 5p gray & multi .30 .25
687 A175 15p gray & multi .30 .25
688 A175 20p gray & multi .30 .25
689 A175 25p gray & multi .30 .25
690 A175 35p gray & multi .30 .25
  a. Strip of 5, #686-690 2.50 2.50
   Agricultural and Industrial Fair, Aleppo.

Burning Fuse and
Flowers — A176

20p, Bomb and star-shaped holes in target.

1974, Oct. 6 **Litho.** **Perf. 12x12½**
691 A176 15p multicolored .75 .25
692 A176 20p multicolored 1.00 .25
  First anniv. of October Liberation War (Yom Kippur War).

Rook and Knight — A177

Design: 50p, Knight and chess board.

1974, Nov. 23
693 A177 15p blue & black ....75 .25
694 A177 50p orange, blk & bl 2.25 .80
Chess Federation, 50th anniversary.

WPY Emblem — A178   Ishtup, Ilum — A179

1974, Dec. 4   Litho.   Perf. 12x12½
695 A178 50p black, slate & red .30 .25
World Population Year.

1975   Perf. 12x11½
Ancient Statuettes: 55p, Woman holding pitcher. 70p, Ur-Nina.
696 A179 20p brt green .30 .25
697 A179 55p brown .30 .25
698 A179 70p gray blue .50 .25
Nos. 696-698 (3) 1.10 .75

"A," People and Sun — A180

1975, Mar. 8   Litho.   Perf. 12x11½
699 A180 15p gray & multi .30 .25
12th anniversary, March 8th Revolution.

Postal Savings Bank Emblem, Family — A181

Design: 20p, Family depositing money, and stamped envelope.

1975, Mar. 17
700 A181 15p brt green & multi .30 .25
701 A181 20p orange & black .30 .25
Publicity for Savings Certificates and Postal Savings Bank.

"Sun" and Dove — A182

1975, Apr. 17   Litho.   Perf. 12x11½
702 A182 15p bister, red & blk .30 .25
703 A182 25p bister, grn & blk .30 .25
29th anniversary of the evacuation of British and French troops from Syria.

"Worker and Industry" — A183

1975, May 1   Litho.   Perf. 12x11½
704 A183 15p blue grn & blk .30 .25
705 A183 25p brown, yel & blk .30 .25
Labor Day.

Camomile A184

Flowers: 10p, Chincherinchi. 15p, Carnation. 20p, Poppy. 25p, Honeysuckle.

1975, May 17
706 A184 5p ultra & multi .30 .25
707 A184 10p lilac & multi .30 .25
708 A184 15p blue & multi .35 .25
709 A184 20p gray grn & multi .40 .25
710 A184 25p vio bl & multi .75 .25
a. Strip of 5, #706-710 2.10 2.10
International Flower Show, Damascus.

Kuneitra Destroyed and Rebuilt — A185

1975, June 5   Perf. 12½
711 A185 50p black & multi .35 .25
Re-occupation of Kuneitra by Syria.

Apples A186

1975, July 7
712 A186 5p shown .30 .25
713 A186 10p Quince .30 .25
714 A186 15p Apricots .35 .25
715 A186 20p Grapes .40 .25
716 A186 25p Figs .50 .25
a. Strip of 5, #712-716 1.90 1.90
Agricultural and Industrial Fair, Aleppo.

22nd Intl. Damascus Fair — A187

1975, July 25   Litho.   Perf. 12x11½
717 A187 15p olive grn & multi .30 .25
718 A187 35p brown & multi .30 .25

Pres. Hafez al Assad A188

1975, Nov. 29   Litho.   Perf. 11½x12
719 A188 15p green & multi .30 .25
720 A188 50p blue & multi .30 .25
5th anniv. of Correctionist Movement of Nov. 16, 1970.

Farm Woman — A189

IWY Emblem and: 15p, Mother. 25p, Student. 50p, Laboratory technician.

1975, Nov. 29   Perf. 12x11½
721 A189 10p buff & multi .30 .25
722 A189 15p rose & black .30 .25
723 A189 25p dull green & blk .35 .25
724 A189 50p orange & blk .50 .25
Nos. 721-724 (4) 1.45 1.00
International Women's Year.

Horse-shaped Bronze Lamp A190   Man's Head Inkstand A191

Designs: 10p, 25p, like 20p. 35p, like 30p. 50p, 60p, Nike. 75p, Hera. 100p, Imdugug-Mari (winged animal). 500p, Palmyrene coin of Vasalathus. 1000p, Abraxas coin.

1976   Perf. 11½x12, 12x11½
725 A190 10p bluish grn .30 .25
726 A190 20p lilac rose .30 .25
727 A190 25p violet blue .30 .25
728 A190 30p brown .30 .25
729 A191 35p olive .30 .25
730 A191 50p brt blue .30 .25
731 A191 60p violet .30 .25
732 A191 75p orange .35 .25
733 A191 100p lilac rose .50 .25
734 A191 500p grnsh gray 2.00 1.75
735 A191 1000p dk green 4.00 2.25
Nos. 725-735 (11) 8.95 6.25
See Nos. 798-803.

National Theater, Damascus and Pres. al Assad A192

1976, Mar. 8   Litho.   Perf. 11½x12
736 A192 25p brt grn, sil & blk .30 .25
737 A192 35p olive, sil & blk .30 .25
13th anniversary of March 8 Revolution.

Syria, Arabian Government #85 — A193

1976, Apr. 12   Perf. 12x12½
738 A193 25p brt green & multi .30 .25
739 A193 35p blue & multi .30 .25
Post's Day.

Nurse and Emblem — A194

1976, Apr. 8   Perf. 12x11½
740 A194 25p blue, blk & red .30 .25
741 A194 100p violet, blk & red .50 .30
Arab Red Cross and Red Crescent Societies, 8th Conference, Damascus.

Eagle and Stars — A195

1976, Apr. 17
742 A195 25p blk, red & brt grn .30 .25
743 A195 35p blk, red & brt grn .30 .25
30th anniversary of the evacuation of British and French troops from Syria.

Hand Holding Wrench — A196

May Day: 60p, Hand holding globe.

1976, May 1
744 A196 25p blue & black .30 .25
745 A196 60p citron & multi .40 .25

654 SYRIA

Cotton and Factory — A197

1976, July 1
746 A197 25p vio & multi .30 .25
747 A197 35p bl & multi .30 .25

Agricultural and Industrial Fair, Aleppo.

Tulips — A198

1976, July 26
748 A198 5p shown .30 .25
749 A198 15p Yellow daisies .30 .25
750 A198 20p Turk's-cap lilies .30 .25
751 A198 25p Irises .50 .25
752 A198 35p Freesia .75 .25
a. Strip of 5, #748-752 2.25 2.25

Intl. Flower Show, Damascus.

People, Globe and Olive Branch A199

60p, Symbolic arrow piercing darkness.

1976, Sept. 2 *Perf. 11½x12*
753 A199 40p yel & multi .30 .25
754 A199 60p multi .35 .25

5th Summit Conference of Non-aligned Countries, Colombo, Sri Lanka, Aug. 9-19.

Soccer, Pan Arab Games Emblem A200

1976, Oct. 6 *Litho.* *Perf. 12½*
755 A200 5p shown .30 .25
756 A200 10p Swimming .30 .25
757 A200 25p Running .30 .25
758 A200 35p Basketball .30 .25
759 A200 50p Javelin .30 .25
a. Strip of 5, #755-759 1.50 1.50

Souvenir Sheet
Imperf
760 A200 100p Steeplechase 2.00 2.00

5th Pan Arab Sports Tournament.
Size of stamp of No. 760: 55x35mm.

"Development" A201

1976, Nov. 16
761 A201 35p multi .30 .25

Correctionist Movement pof Nov. 16, 1970.

The Fox and the Crow — A202

Fairy Tales: 15p, The Hare and the Tortoise, horiz. 20p, Little Red Riding Hood. 25p, The Lamb and the Wolf, horiz. 35p, The Lamb and the Wolf.

1976, Dec. 7 *Perf. 12x12½, 12½x12*
762 A202 10p multi .30 .25
763 A202 15p multi .30 .25
764 A202 20p multi .30 .25
765 A202 25p multi .30 .25
766 A202 35p multi .30 .25
Nos. 762-766 (5) 1.50 1.25

Children's literature.

Syrian Airlines Boeing 747 — A203

1977, Feb. *Litho.* *Perf. 12½x12*
767 A203 35p multi .30 .25

Civil Aviation Day.

Muhammad Kurd-Ali (1876-1953), Philosopher, Birth Cent. — A204

1977, Feb. *Perf. 12x12½*
768 A204 25p lt grn & multi .30 .25

Woman Holding Syrian Flag — A205

1977, Mar. 8 *Litho.* *Perf. 12x12½*
769 A205 35p multi .30 .25

14th anniversary of March 8 Revolution.

Warrior on Horseback — A206

1977, Apr. 10 *Litho.* *Perf. 12½*
770 A206 100p multi .30 .25

31st anniversary of the evacuation of British and French troops from Syria.

APU Emblem — A207

1977, Apr. 12 *Litho.* *Perf. 12x12½*
771 A207 35p silver & multi .30 .25

Arab Postal Union, 25th anniversary.

Tools and Factories A208

1977, May 1 *Perf. 12½x12*
772 A208 60p multi .35 .25

Labor Day.

ICAO Emblem, Plane and Globe A209

1977, May 11
773 A209 100p multi .50 .25

Intl. Civil Aviation Org., 30th anniv.

Pioneers — A210

1977, Aug. 15 *Litho.* *Perf. 12x12½*
774 A210 35p multi .30 .25

Al Baath Pioneer Organization.

Citrus Fruit — A211

1977, Aug. 1
775 A211 10p Lemon .30 .25
776 A211 20p Lime .30 .25
777 A211 25p Grapefruit .30 .25
778 A211 35p Oranges .30 .25
779 A211 60p Tangerines .40 .25
a. Strip of 5, #775-779 1.60 1.60

Agricultural and Industrial Fair, Aleppo.

Flowers A212

1977, Aug. 6 *Litho.* *Perf. 12½x12*
780 A212 10p Mallow .30 .25
781 A212 20p Coxcomb .30 .25
782 A212 25p Morning glories .30 .25
783 A212 35p Almond blossoms .30 .25
784 A212 60p Lilacs .30 .25
a. Strip of 5, #780-784 1.50 1.50

Intl. Flower Show, Damascus.

Coffeepot and Ornament A213

1977, Sept. 10 *Perf. 12x12½*
785 A213 25p blk, bl & red .30 .25
786 A213 60p blk, grn & brn .35 .25

24th Intl. Damascus Fair.

Blind Man, Globe and Eye — A214

1977, Nov. 17 *Litho.* *Perf. 12x12½*
787 A214 55p multi .30 .25
788 A214 70p multi .30 .25

World Blind Week.

Globe and Measures A215

1977, Nov. 5
789 A215 15p grn & multi .30 .25

World Standards Day, Oct. 14.

Microscope, Book, Harp, UNESCO
Emblem — A216

1977, Nov. 5   *Perf. 12½x12*
790 A216 25p multi   .30 .25
30th anniversary of UNESCO.

Archbishop
Capucci, Map of
Palestine,
Bars — A217

1977, Nov. 17   *Perf. 12x12½*
791 A217 60p multi   2.00 .50
Palestinian Archbishop Hilarion Capucci,
jailed by Israel in 1974.

Fight Cancer
Shield, Crab and
Surgeon — A218

1977, Nov. 17
792 A218 100p multi   1.00 .50
Fight Cancer Week.

Dome of the Rock, Jerusalem — A219

1977, Dec. 6   *Perf. 12*
793 A219 5p multi   .50 .25
794 A219 10p multi   .75 .25
Palestinian fighters and their families.

Mural — A220

Designs: 10p, 15p, Murals from Dura-Europos, in National Museum, Damascus.

1978, Jan. 22 Litho.   *Perf. 12x11½*
795 A220 5p gray grn   .30 .25
796 A220 10p vio bl   .30 .25
797 A220 15p brown, horiz.   .30 .25
    Nos. 795-797 (3)   .90 .75

Types of 1976

Designs: 40p, Man's head inkstand. 55p, Nike. 70p, 80p, Hera. 200p, Arab-Islamic astrolabe. 300p, Palmyrene (Herod) coin.

1978 Litho.   *Perf. 12x11½, 11½x12*
798 A191 40p pale org   .30 .25
799 A191 55p brt rose   .30 .25
800 A191 70p vermilion   .35 .25
801 A191 80p green   .35 .25

802 A191 200p lt ultra   1.00 .30
803 A190 300p rose lil   1.50 .50
    Nos. 798-803 (6)   3.80 1.80

Pres. Hafez al
Assad — A221

1978   *Perf. 12x11½*
805 A221 50p multi   .40 .25
Anniversary of "Correction Movement."

Blood Circulation,
WHO
Emblem — A222

1978, Apr. 7 Litho.   *Perf. 12x11½*
806 A222 100p multi   .50 .25
World Health Day, fight against hypertension.

Factory — A223

1978, Apr. 17
807 A223 35p multi   .30 .25
32nd anniversary of the evacuation of British and French troops from Syria.

Rosette — A224

1978, Apr. 21
808 A224 25p blk & grn   .30 .25
14th Arab Engineering Conference, Damascus, Apr. 21-26.

Map of Arab
Countries, Police,
Flag and
Eye — A225

1978, May
809 A225 35p multi   .30 .25
6th Conf. of Arab Police Commanders.

European
Goldfinch
A226

Birds: 20p, Peregrine falcon. 25p, Rock dove. 35p, Eurasian hoopoe. 60p, Old World quail.

1978   *Perf. 11½x12*
810 A226 10p multi   .40 .25
811 A226 20p multi   .40 .25
812 A226 25p multi   .40 .25
813 A226 35p multi   .50 .25
814 A226 60p multi   .60 .25
  a.   Strip of 5, #810-814   2.40 2.40

Trout
A227

Designs: Various fish.

1978, July Litho.   *Perf. 11½x12*
815 A227 10p multi   .40 .25
816 A227 20p multi   .40 .25
817 A227 25p multi   .40 .25
818 A227 35p multi   .50 .25
819 A227 60p multi   .55 .25
  a.   Strip of 5, #815-819   2.25 2.25

Pres. Assad Type of Air Post, 1978
Miniature Sheet

1978, Sept. Litho.   *Imperf.*
820 AP161 100p gold & multi   1.00 1.00
Reelection of President Assad. Size of stamp: 58x80mm.

Flowering
Cactus
A228

Designs: Flowering cacti.

1978   **Litho.**   *Perf. 12½*
821 A228 25p multi   .50 .25
822 A228 30p multi   .50 .25
823 A228 35p multi   .50 .25
824 A228 50p multi   .50 .25
825 A228 60p multi   .50 .25
  a.   Strip of 5, #821-825   2.50 2.50
International Flower Show, Damascus.

Fair
Emblem — A229

1978   **Litho.**   *Perf. 12x12½*
826 A229 25p sil & multi   .30 .25
827 A229 35p sil & multi   .30 .25

Miniature Sheet
Imperf
828 A229 100p sil & multi   1.00 1.00
25th Intl. Damascus Fair. No. 828 shows different ornament, size of stamp: 40x46mm.

Euphrates Dam and Pres.
Assad — A230

1978, Dec. Litho.   *Perf. 12½x12*
829 A230 60p multi   .50 .25
Inauguration of Euphrates Dam.

Pres. Hafez al
Assad — A231

1978, Nov. 16 Litho.   *Perf. 12x12½*
830 A231 60p multi   .40 .25
Nov. 16 Movement.

Racial
Equality
Emblem
A232

1978, Mar. Litho.   *Perf. 12½*
831 A232 35p multi   .40 .25
International Year to Combat Racism.

Averroes — A233

1979, Mar.
832 A233 100p multi   .75 .25
Averroes (1126-1198), Spanish-Arabian philosopher and physician.

Human Rights
Flame and
Globe — A234

1978, Dec.   *Perf. 12x12½*
833 A234 60p multi   .50 .25
30th anniversary of Universal Declaration of Human Rights (in 1978).

Symbolic
Design — A235

Princess, 2nd
Century
Shield — A236

1979, Mar.
834 A235 100p multi .50 .25
16th anniversary of March 8 Revolution.

1979 Litho. Perf. 11½
Designs: 20p, Helmet of Homs. 35p, Ishtar.
836 A236 20p green .30 .25
837 A236 25p rose car .30 .25
838 A236 35p sepia .30 .25
Nos. 836-838 (3) .90 .75

Flame
Emblem — A237

1979 Litho. Perf. 12x11½
846 A237 35p multi .30 .25
Intl. Middle East Dental Congress.

Flame
Emblem — A238

1979
847 A238 35p multi .30 .25
33rd anniversary of evacuation.

Ibn
Assaker,
900th
Anniv.
A239

1979 Perf. 11½x12
848 A239 75p multi .30 .25

Telephone
Lineman — A240

1979, May 1 Litho. Perf. 12x11½
849 A240 50p multi .30 .25
850 A240 75p multi .30 .25
May Day.

Wright
Brothers'
Plane
A241

Designs: 75p, Bleriot's plane crossing
English Channel. 100p, Spirit of St. Louis.

1979 Perf. 11½x12
851 A241 50p multi .30 .25
852 A241 75p multi .30 .25
853 A241 100p multi .50 .25
Nos. 851-853 (3) 1.10 .75
75th anniversary of 1st powered flight.

Girl with IYC
Emblem — A242

Design: 15p, Boy, globe, IYC emblem.

1979 Perf. 12x11½
854 A242 10p multi .30 .25
855 A242 15p multi .35 .25
International Year of the Child.

Power
Plant — A243

1979 Perf. 11x11½
856 A243 5p blue .30 .25
857 A243 10p lil rose .30 .25
858 A243 15p gray grn .30 .25
Nos. 856-858 (3) .90 .75

Flags and
Pavilion — A244

Design: 75p, Lamppost and flags.

1979 Photo. Perf. 12x11½
859 A244 60p multi .30 .25
860 A244 75p multi .35 .25
26th International Damascus Fair.

Correction Movement, 9th
Anniversary — A245

1979 Photo. Perf. 11½x12
861 A245 100p multi .50 .25

Games
Emblem,
Running
A246

1979, Nov.
862 A246 25p shown .30 .25
863 A246 35p Diving .30 .25
864 A246 50p Soccer .30 .25
Nos. 862-864 (3) .90 .75
8th Mediterranean Games, Split, Yugoslavia, Sept. 15-29.

Butterfly — A247

Designs: Various butterflies.

1979, Dec. Litho. Perf. 12x11½
865 A247 20p multi .50 .25
866 A247 25p multi .50 .25
867 A247 30p multi .50 .25
868 A247 35p multi .50 .25
869 A247 50p multi .50 .25
Nos. 865-869 (5) 2.50 1.25

Damascus
Intl. Flower
Show
A248

Design: Roses.

1980, Jan. 9 Litho. Perf. 12½
870 A248 5p multi .50 .25
871 A248 10p multi .50 .25
872 A248 15p multi .50 .25
873 A248 50p multi .50 .25
874 A248 75p multi .50 .25
875 A248 100p multi .80 .25
Nos. 870-875 (6) 3.30 1.50

March 8
Revolution, 17th
Anniv. — A249

1980, Mar. 25 Litho. Perf. 12x11½
876 A249 40p multi .30 .25

Astrolabe
A250

1980, May 2 Perf. 12½
877 A250 50p violet .30 .25
878 A250 100p sepia .50 .25
879 A250 1000p gray grn 4.00 1.25
Nos. 877-879 (3) 4.80 1.75
2nd International History of Arabic Sciences
Symposium, Apr. 5.

Lit Cigarette,
Skull — A251

1980, June 25 Photo. Perf. 12x11½
880 A251 60p Smoker .60 .25
881 A251 100p shown 1.00 .30
World Health Day; anti-smoking campaign.

Evacuation, 34th
Anniversary
A252

1980, June 25 Litho.
882 A252 40p multi .30 .25
883 A252 60p multi .35 .25

Moscow
'80
Emblem
and
Wrestling
A253

1980, July Litho. Perf. 11½x12
884 A253 15p shown .30 .25
885 A253 25p Fencing .30 .25
886 A253 35p Weight lifting .35 .25
887 A253 50p Judo .50 .25
888 A253 75p Boxing 1.00 .25
a. Strip of 5, #884-888 2.50 2.50
Souvenir Sheet
Imperf
888B A253 300p Discus, running 5.00 5.00
22nd Summer Olympic Games, Moscow,
July 19-Aug. 3.

Sinbad
the Sailor
A254

1980 Litho. Perf. 11½x12
889 A254 15p shown .30 .25
890 A254 25p Scheherezade
and Shahrayar .30 .25
891 A254 35p Ali Baba and the
Forty Thieves .35 .25
892 A254 50p Hassan the Clever .50 .25
893 A254 100p Aladdin's Lamp 1.00 .30
a. Strip of 5, #889-893 2.50 2.50
Popular stories.

Savings Certificates — A255

1980
894 A255 25p multi .30 .25

Hegira, 1500th Anniv. — A256

1980 *Perf. 12½x12*
895 A256 35p multi .35 .25

Intl. Flower Show, Damascus A257

1980 *Perf. 12x11½*
896 A257 20p Daffodils .50 .25
897 A257 30p Chrysanthemums .50 .25
898 A257 40p Clematis .55 .25
899 A257 60p Yellow roses .60 .25
900 A257 100p Chrysanthe-
mums, diff. .75 .25
a. Strip of 5, #896-900 3.00 3.00

May Day — A258

1980, May
901 A258 35p multi .40 .25

Children's Day — A259

1980
902 A259 25p multi .40 .25

November 16th Movement, 10th Anniv. — A260

1980 *Perf. 11½x12*
903 A260 100p multi 1.00 .25

Steam-powered Passenger Wagon — A261

1980
904 A261 25p shown .35 .25
905 A261 35p Benz, 1899 .40 .25
906 A261 40p Rolls-Royce, 1903 .60 .25

907 A261 50p Mercedes, 1906 .75 .25
908 A261 60p Austin, 1915 1.00 .30
a. Strip of 5, #904-908 3.25 3.25

Mother's Day — A262

1980 *Perf. 12x11½*
909 A262 40p shown .50 .25
910 A262 100p Mother and child 1.00 .25

27th International Damascus Fair — A263

1981, Jan. 24 *Perf. 11½x12*
911 A263 50p multi .45 .25
912 A263 100p multi .80 .25

Army Day — A264

1981, Jan. 24 *Perf. 12½x12*
913 A264 50p multi .45 .25

A265

1981, Mar. 8 Litho. *Perf. 12x11½*
914 A265 50p multi .35 .25
18th anniv. of March 8th revolution.

A266

1981, Apr. 17 Litho. *Perf. 12x11½*
915 A266 50p multi .35 .25
35th anniversary of evacuation.

World Conference on History of Arab and Islamic Civilization, Damascus — A267

1981, May 30 Photo. *Perf. 12½x12*
916 A267 100p multi .60 .25

Intl. Workers' Solidarity Day — A268

1981, May 30 Litho. *Perf. 12x11½*
917 A268 100p multi .60 .25

Housing and Population Census — A269

1981, June 1
918 A269 50p multi .35 .25

Umayyad Window A270   Abdul Malik Gold Coin A270a

10p, figurine. 15p, Rakkla's cavalier, Abbcid ceramic. 160p, like 5p. 500p, Umar B. Abdul Aziz gold coin.

1981 *Perf. 12x11½, 11½x12*
919 A270 5p crim rose .25 .25
920 A270 10p brt grn .25 .25
921 A270 15p dp rose lil .25 .25
922 A270a 75p blue .35 .25
923 A270 160p dk grn .70 .25
924 A270a 500p dk brn 2.50 1.10
Nos. 919-924 (6) 4.30 2.45

Olives A270b

Harbor A270c

1982 *Perf. 12x11½*
925 A270b 50p ol grn .40 .25
926 A270b 60p bl gray .45 .25
929 A270c 100p lilac .55 .25
930 A270c 180p red 1.10 .55
Nos. 925-930 (4) 2.50 1.30

Saving Certificates Plan — A271

1981, June 22
931 A271 50p gldn brn & blk .35 .25

Avicenna (980-1037), Philosopher and Physician A272

1981, Aug.
932 A272 100p multi .60 .25

Syria-P.L.O. Solidarity, Intl. Conference A273

1981, June 22
933 A273 160p multi 3.50 .90

Grand Mosque, Damascus — A274

1981 *Perf. 12½*
934 A274 50p Glass lamp, 13th
cent. .30 .25
935 A274 180p shown 1.40 .40
936 A274 180p Hunter 1.40 .40
Nos. 934-936 (3) 3.10 1.05

Youth Festival A275

1981 *Perf. 12½*
937 A275 60p multi .40 .25

28th Intl. Damascus Fair — A276

1981 *Perf. 12x11½*
938 A276 50p Ornament .30 .25
939 A276 160p Emblem 1.00 .45

Intl. Palestinian
Solidarity
Day — A277

1981
940 A277 100p multi .75 .25

1300th
Anniv. of
Bulgaria
A278

1981 *Perf. 11½x12*
941 A278 380p multi 2.25 1.00

Intl.
Children's
Day
A279

1981
942 A279 180p multi 1.10 .45

World
Food Day,
Oct. 16
A280

1981
943 A280 180p multi 1.10 .45

9th Intl. Flower
Show, Damascus
A281

Designs: Flowers.

1981 *Perf. 12x11½*
944 A281 25p multi .25 .25
945 A281 40p multi .40 .25
946 A281 50p multi .50 .30
947 A281 60p multi .75 .35
948 A281 100p multi 1.10 .50
a. Strip of 5, #944-948 3.00 2.00

Souvenir Sheet

Koran Competition — A282

1981 **Litho.** *Imperf.*
949 A282 500p multi 5.00 5.00

11th Anniv. of
Correction
Movement
A283

1981, Nov. *Perf. 12x11½*
950 A283 60p multi .45 .30

TB
Bacillus
Centenary
A284

1982 **Litho.** *Perf. 11½x12*
951 A284 180p multi 1.25 .65

Mothers'
Day — A285

Mar. 8th
Revolution, 19th
Anniv. — A286

1982 *Perf. 11½*
952 A285 40p green .25 .25
953 A285 75p brown .50 .25

1982, Mar. *Perf. 12x11½*
954 A286 50p multi .35 .25

Intl. Year of the
Disabled
(1981) — A287

Pres. Hafez al
Assad — A288

1982 *Perf. 12x11½*
955 A287 90p multi .75 .30

1982 *Perf. 11½*
956 A288 150p ultra .90 .50

36th Anniv. of
Evacuation
A289

1982 *Perf. 12x11½*
957 A289 70p multi .50 .25

World Traffic
Day — A290

1982
958 A290 180p multi 1.25 .65

Intl. Workers'
Solidarity
Day — A291

1982
959 A291 180p multi 1.25 .65

World Telecommunication Day,
May 17 — A292

1982
960 A292 180p multi 1.25 .65

Soldier Holding
Rifles — A293

1982 **Photo.** *Perf. 12x11½*
961 A293 50p multi .30 .25

Arab Postal
Union, 30th
Anniv. — A294

1982
962 A294 60p multi .45 .25

1982 World Cup — A295

Various soccer players. 300p, Ball.

1982, July *Perf. 12½*
963 A295 40p multi .25 .25
964 A295 60p multi .40 .25
965 A295 100p multi .65 .40
Nos. 963-965 (3) 1.30 .90

Size: 75x55mm
Imperf
966 A295 300p multi 10.00 10.00

10th Intl. Flower
Show, Damascus
A297

1982 *Perf. 12x11½*
967 A297 50p Honeysuckle .45 .25
968 A297 60p Geraniums .60 .30

Scouting
Year
A298

1982, Nov. 4 *Perf. 11½x12*
969 A298 160p green 1.40 .75

Ladybug
A299

1982 *Perf. 12x12½*
970 Strip of 5 .75 .40
a. A299 5p Dragonfly .25 .25
b. A299 10p Stag Beetle .25 .25
c. A299 20p shown .25 .25
d. A299 40p Grasshopper .25 .25
e. A299 50p Honeybee .30 .25

ITU Plenipotentiaries Conference,
Nairobi, Sept — A300

1982 *Perf. 11½x12*
971 A300 50p Map .30 .25
972 A300 180p Dish antenna 1.40 .75

12th Anniv. of Correction Movement A301

1982, Nov.
973 A301 50p dk bl & sil .35 .25

A302

Factory — A302a

Walled Arch — A302b

Ruins — A302c

1982-83 Litho. Perf. 11½
974 A302 30p brown .25 .25
975 A302a 50p grnish blk .25 .25
976 A302b 70p green .35 .25
977 A302c 200p red 1.00 .55
Nos. 974-977 (4) 1.85 1.30

Issued: 50p, 11/16/83; others, 11/4/82.

Dove and Satellite — A303

1982 Litho. Perf. 12x11½
978 A303 50p multi .50 .30
2nd UN Conference on Peaceful Uses of Outer Space, Vienna, Aug. 9-21.

Intl. Palestinian Solidarity Day — A304

1982
979 A304 50p multi .90 .25

20th Anniv. of March 8th Revolution — A305

1983 Perf. 12½x12
980 A305 60p multi 1.00 .50

World Communications Year — A305a

1983
981 A305a 180p multi 1.25 .65

9th Anniv. of Liberation of Al-Kuneitra — A306

1983, June 26 Litho. Perf. 11½
982 A306 50p View 1.50 .50
983 A306 100p View, diff. 3.00 .65

Arab Pharmacists' Day, Apr. 2 — A307

1983, Apr. 2 Perf. 11½x12
984 A307 100p multi .75 .30

25th Anniv. of Intl. Maritime Org. — A308

1983, June Perf. 12x11½
985 A308 180p multi 1.40 .75

Namibia Day, Aug. 26 A309

1983, Aug. 26 Perf. 11½x12
986 A309 180p multi 1.40 .75

Eibla Sculpture, 3rd Cent. BC A310

1983
987 A310 380p ol & brn 2.50 1.40

World Standards Day — A311

1983, Oct. 14 Photo. Perf. 11½
988 A311 50p Factory, emblem .40 .25
989 A311 100p Measuring equipment .80 .40

11th Intl. Flower Show, Damascus A312

1983, Oct. 14 Litho. Perf. 11½
990 A312 50p multi .40 .25
991 A312 60p multi, diff. .50 .25

World Heritage Day — A313

1983, Oct. 14 Photo. Perf. 11½
992 A313 60p dk brn .50 .25

World Food Day A313a

1983, Oct. 16 Litho. Perf. 11½x12
992A A313a 180p multi 1.50 .75

Waterwheels of Hama — A314

Perf. 11x11½, 11½x11
1982-84 Litho.
993 A314 5p sepia .25 .25
994 A314 10p violet .25 .25
995 A314 20p red .25 .25
997 A314 50p blkish grn .60 .30
Nos. 993-997 (4) 1.35 1.05

Issued: 50p, 11/25/82; others, 1/15/84.
On No. 997 "50" is in outlined numbers.

Statue — A316

1983 Perf. 12
1003 A316 225p brown 2.00 1.00
Intl. Symposium on History and Archaeology of Deir Ez-zor.

View of Aleppo — A317

1983 Perf. 12x12½
1004 A317 245p multi 2.25 1.10
Intl. Symposium on Conservation of Old City of Aleppo, Sept. 26-30.

Mar. 8th Revolution, 21st Anniv. — A318

1984, Mar. 8 Perf. 12½x12
1005 A318 60p Alassad Library .75 .35

Massacre at Sabra and Shatilla A319

1983 Litho. Perf. 11½x12
1006 A319 225p Victims, mother & child 2.00 .50

Mothers' Day — A320

1984, Mar. 21 Perf. 12x11½
1007 A320 245p Mother & child 2.50 1.25

12th Intl. Flower Show, Damascus A321

Various flowers.

1984, May 25
1008 A321 245p multi 2.50 1.25
1009 A321 285p multi 2.75 1.40

1984 Summer Olympics — A322

1984   **Litho.**   **Perf. 12x11½**
1010   Strip of 5   3.00 2.40
  a. A322 30p Swimming   .30   .25
  b. A322 50p Wrestling   .30   .25
  c. A322 60p Running   .60   .30
  d. A322 70p Boxing   .65   .35
  e. A322 90p Soccer   .90   .45
Souvenir Sheet
Imperf
1011 A322 200p Soccer, diff.   3.50 3.50

9th
Regional
Pioneers'
Festival
A323

1984   **Perf. 11½x12**
1012 A323 50p Pioneers   .50   .25
1013 A323 60p Pioneers, diff.   .60   .30

Aleppo
Agricultural &
Industrial
Fair — A324

1984, June 12   Litho.   Perf. 12x12½
1014 A324 150p Peppers, Aleppo
    Castle   1.25 .50

Supreme
Council of
Science,
25th
Anniv.
A325

1985, Feb. 23   **Perf. 12½x12**
1015 A325 65p multi   .40   .25

Aleppo
University,
25th
Anniv.
A326

1985, Feb. 23
1016 A326 45p multi   .25   .25

Syrian
Arab
Army,
39th
Anniv.
A327

1985, Feb. 23
1017 A327 65p brn & gldn brn   .40   .25

Pres.
Assad,
Soldier
Saluting,
Troops
A328

1984, Aug. 1   **Perf. 11½x12**
1018 A328 60p multi   .60   .30
4th General Revolutionary Youth Conference.

ITU Emblem,
Satellite
Dish,
Telephone
A329

1984, Oct. 2   **Perf. 12½**
1019 A329 245p multi   1.75 .90
Intl. Telecommunications Day.

APU Emblem and Administration
Building, Damascus — A330

1984, Oct. 9
1020 A330 60p multi   .60   .30
Arab Postal Union Day.

Gearwheel,
Arabesque
Pattern — A331

Gold
Necklace — A332

1984, Oct. 27   Perf. 12x12½, 12x11½
1021 A331 45p multi   .45   .25
1022 A332 100p multi   1.00 .45
Intl. Fair, Damascus.

Intl. Civil
Aviation
Org., 40th
Anniv.
A333

1984, Oct. 27   **Perf. 11½x12**
1023 A333 45p brt bl & lt bl   .25   .25
1024 A333 245p ultra, brt bl &
    lt bl   1.25 .60

14th
Anniv. of
11-16-70
Movement
A334

1984, Dec. 3   **Perf. 12½x12**
1025 A334 65p red brn, blk & org   .65   .35

Pres. Assad,
Text on Scroll
A335

1984, Nov. 29   **Perf. 12½**
1026 A335 50p grn, brn org & sep   .50   .25
Vow of Dedication taken by Youth of the
Revolution.

Agricultural Exhibition — A336

1984, June 12   **Perf. 12½x12**
1027 A336 65p multi   .65   .35

Al-Kuneitra Memorial, Rose — A337

1984
1028 A337 70p multi   1.25 .35

Roman Arch and Colonnades,
Palmyra — A338

1984, Dec. 3
1029 A338 100p multi   1.00 .50
Intl. Tourism Day.

Woodland Conservation — A339

1984
1030 A339 45p multi   .25   .25

March 8
Revolution, 22nd
Anniv. — A340

1985, Apr. 27
1031 A340 60p multi   .40   .25

UPU Emblem,
Postal
Headquarters,
Damascus
A341

1985, Apr. 27
1032 A341 285p multi   3.00 1.50
World Post Day.

APU Building, Damascus — A342

1985, Apr. 27   **Perf. 12½**
1033 A342 245p multi   2.50 1.25
Arab Parliamentary Union, 10th Anniv.

Natl. Flag,
Map of
Arab
Countries
A343

1985   **Perf. 12½x12**
1034 A343 50p multi   .50   .25
Arab League.

Re-election
of President
Assad
A344

1985, Mar. 12   **Perf. 12½**
1035 A344 200p multi   1.25 .70
1036 A344 300p multi   2.00 1.00
1037 A344 500p multi   3.25 1.75
  a. Souvenir sheet of 3, #1035-
    1037, imperf.   7.00 5.50
    Nos. 1035-1037 (3)   6.50 3.45

Arab Postal
Union, 12th
Congress,
Damascus
A345

1985, Aug. 12   **Perf. 12½x12½**
1038 A345 60p multi   .60   .30

Labor
Day — A346

1985, Aug. 12   *Perf. 12½*
1039 A346 60p Order of Labor   .60 .30

32nd Intl.
Fair,
Damascus
A347

1986, Feb. 1   Litho.   *Perf. 12½*
1040 A347 60p multi   .50 .25

2nd Scientific Symposium — A348

1985, Nov. 16   *Perf. 12½*
1041 A348 60p Locomotives   .60 .30

UN Child
Survival
Campaign
A349

1985, Nov. 16   *Perf. 12½x12*
1042 A349 60p Malnourished child .50 .25

UN, 40th
Anniv. — A350

1985, Nov. 16   *Perf. 12x12½*
1043 A350 245p multi   2.25 1.10

November 16th Movement, 15th
Anniv. — A351

1985, Nov. 16   *Perf. 12½*
1044 A351 60p Pres. Assad, high-
          way   .50 .25

Abdul
Rahman
Dakhei in
Andalusia,
1200th
Anniv.
A352

1986, Feb. 1   *Perf. 12½x12*
1045 A352 60p beige & brn   .60 .30

Tulips — A353

1986, Feb. 1   *Perf. 12½*
1046 A353 30p multi   .30 .25
1047 A353 60p multi, diff.   .60 .30
          Intl. Flower Show, Damascus.

Dental Congress, Damascus — A354

1986   *Perf. 12½x12*
1048 A354 110p yel, grysh grn &
          bl   1.10 .55

World Traffic
Day — A355

1986   *Perf. 12x12½*
1049 A355 330p multi   3.00 1.50

Syrian Investment
Certificates, 15th
Anniv. — A357

1986   Litho.   *Perf. 12x11½*
1055 A357 100p multi   1.00 .50

Liberation of Al-Kuneitra, 12th
Anniv. — A358

1986   Litho.   *Perf. 11½x12*
1056 A358 110p Government Build-
          ing   .75 .40

Day of Internal
Security
Forces — A359

1986   *Perf. 12x11½*
1057 A359 110p multi   .75 .40

Labor
Day — A360

1986, Aug. 12
1058 A360 330p multi   1.25 .60

1986 World Cup
Soccer
Championships,
Mexico — A361

1986, July 7
1059 A361 330p multi   3.25 1.75
1060 A361 370p multi   3.50 1.90
          Booklet Stamp
          Size: 105x80mm
          Imperf
1061 A361 500p Hemispheres,
          ball   5.00 2.50
          Nos. 1059-1061 (3)   11.75 6.15

Pres. Hafez al
Assad — A362

1986-90   Litho.   *Perf. 12x11½*
1068 A362 10p rose   .25 .25
1069 A362 30p dl ultra   .25 .25
1070 A362 50p claret   .40 .25
1071 A362 100p brt lt bl   .65 .30
1072 A362 150p brn vio   1.40 .65
1073 A362 175p violet   1.60 .80
1074 A362 200p pale red brn 1.40 .65
1075 A362 300p brt rose lil 2.00 1.00
1076 A362 500p orange   3.25 1.60
1077 A362 550p pink   5.00 2.50
1078 A362 600p dull grn   5.25 2.75
1079 A362 1000p brt pink   6.50 3.25
1080 A362 2000p pale grn 13.00 6.50
          Nos. 1068-1080 (13) 40.95 20.75
     Issued: 150p, 175p, 550p, 600p, 1988; 50p,
9/30/90.

Intl. Day for
Solidarity with the
Palestinian
People — A363

1986, Aug. 7   Litho.
1081 A363 110p multi   1.10 .55

Mothers'
Day — A364

1986, Aug. 7
1082 A364 100p multi   1.00 .50

March 8 Revolution, 23rd
Anniv. — A365

1986, Aug. 7   *Perf. 11½x12*
1083 A365 110p multi   1.10 .55

Arab Post
Day
A366

1986, Aug. 7
1084 A366 110p multi   1.10 .55

A367

33rd Intl.
Damascus
Fair
A368

1986, Dec. 9   Litho.   *Perf. 11½x12*
1085 A367 110p multi   .90 .45
1086 A368 330p multi   2.50 .60

14th Intl. Flower Show,
Damascus — A369

     Various flowers.

1986, Oct. 11   *Perf. 12½*
1087   Strip of 5   6.50 5.00
  a. A369 10p multi   .25 .25
  b. A369 50p multi   .50 .25
  c. A369 100p multi   1.00 .50
  d. A369 110p multi   1.10 .60
  e. A369 330p multi   3.50 1.75

Syria-Soviet Joint Space Project — A370

World Children's Day — A371

1986, Nov. 16   **Litho.**   **Perf. 12½**
1088 A370 330p multi   3.50 1.75

1986   **Perf. 12x12½, 12½x12**
1089 A371 330p shown   1.75 .90
1090 A371 330p Youth art exhibition, horiz.   1.75 .90

World Post Day A372

1986, Jan. 28   **Perf. 12½x12**
1091 A372 330p multi   1.75 .90

Intl. Tourism Day A373

Women wearing folk costumes, landmarks.

1986
1092 A373 330p multi   1.75 .90
1093 A373 370p multi   2.00 1.00

Pres. Assad, Tishreen Palace — A374

1986, Nov. 16   **Litho.**   **Perf. 12½**
1094 A374 110p multi   1.25 .60

Nov. 16 Corrective Movement.

March 8th Revolution, 24th Anniv. — A375

1987, Mar. 6
1095 A375 100p multi   .60 .30

Intl. Peace Year — A376

1987, Mar. 8   **Perf. 12x11½**
1096 A376 370p multi   2.25 1.25

Arab Baath Socialist Party, 40th Anniv. A377

1987, Apr. 7   **Litho.**   **Perf. 12½**
1097 A377 100p multi   .60 .30

Arab Post Day, 35th Anniv. A378

1987, May 1   **Perf. 11½x12**
1098 A378 110p multi   .70 .35

Evacuation, Day, 41st Anniv. — A379

1987, Apr. 17   **Perf. 12½x12**
1099 A379 100p multi   .60 .30

Labor Day — A380

1987, May 1   **Perf. 12x11½**
1100 A380 330p multi   2.00 1.00

Hitteen's Battle, 800th Anniv. — A381

1987, June 25   **Litho.**   **Perf. 12½**
1101 A381 110p multi   1.00 .45

Al-Kuneitra Monument A382

1987, June 25   **Perf. 12x11½**
1102 A382 100p multi   .65 .30

Child Vaccination Campaign — A383

1987, June 25   **Perf. 11½x12**
1103 A383 100p multi   .50 .30
1104 A383 330p multi   2.00 1.10

A384

A385

Syrian-Soviet Joint Space Flight, July 22-30 — A386

Designs: No. 1105, Launch, July 22. No. 1106, Docking at space station, July 24. No. 1107, Landing, July 30, vert. No. 1108a, Lift-off. No. 1108b, Parachute landing. No. 1108c, Docked at space station. No. 1108d, Cosmonauts.

Perf. 12½, 11½x12, 12x11½
1987   **Litho.**
1105 A384 330p multi   2.00 1.00
1106 A385 330p multi   2.00 1.00
1107 A385 330p multi   2.00 1.00
   Nos. 1105-1107 (3)   6.00 3.00
Souvenir Sheet
Imperf
1108   Sheet of 4   10.00 10.00
a.-d.   A386 300p, any single   2.25 2.25

6th Conference of Arab Ministers of Culture A387

1987, Apr. 21   **Litho.**   **Perf. 12½**
1109 A387 330p dull blue grn & blk   3.00 1.50

President Assad Conversing with Syrian Cosmonaut — A388

1987, Aug. 12
1110 A388 500p multi   3.50 1.75

10th Mediterranean Games, Latakia — A389

Designs: 100p, Gymnastic rings, weight lifting, vert. 330p, Phoenician sailing ship. 370p, Flags spelling "SYRIA." No. 1115a, Emblem, gymnastics. No. 1115b, Emblem, weight lifting. No. 1115c, Emblem, tennis. No. 1115d, Emblem, soccer.

Perf. 12x11½, 11½x12
1987, Sept. 10
1111 A389 100p brt rose lil & blk   .70 .35
1112 A389 110p shown   .75 .40
   Size: 58x28mm
   Perf. 12½
1113 A389 330p multi   2.25 1.10
1114 A389 370p multi   2.50 1.25
   Nos. 1111-1114 (4)   6.20 3.10
   Souvenir Sheet
   Imperf
1115   Sheet of 4   7.75 7.75
a.-d.   A389 300p any single   1.90 1.90

34th Intl. Damascus Fair — A390

1987   **Perf. 12x11½**
1116 A390 330p multi   2.00 1.00

Intl. Flower Show, Damascus A391

1987, Oct. 20   **Perf. 11½x12**
1117 A391 330p Poppies   1.90 1.00
1118 A391 370p Gentian   2.00 1.00

Arbor Day — A392

1987, Oct. 20   **Perf. 12x11½**
1119 A392 330p multi   2.00 1.00

Army
Day — A393

1987, Oct. 20   Litho.   Perf. 12x11½
1120 A393 100p multi   .60   .30

Intl. Palestine
Day — A394

1987, Nov. 16
1121 A394 500p multi   3.50   1.75

Corrective Movement, 17th
Anniv. — A395

1987, Nov. 16   Perf. 12½
1122 A395 150p Assad waving to
            crowd   1.00   .50

World Post Day — A396

1988, Mar. 8   Litho.   Perf. 12½x12
1123 A396 500p multi   3.00   1.50

Intl.
Tourism
Day
A397

Women wearing folk costumes and: No.
1124, Palmyra Ruins. No. 1125, Reconstructed Roman amphitheater, Busra.

1988, Feb. 25   Litho.   Perf. 11½x12
1124 A397 500p multi   3.00   1.50
1125 A397 500p multi   3.00   1.50
      See Nos. 1147-1148, 1178-1179.

Intl. Children's Day — A398

1988, Feb. 27   Perf. 12½
1126 A398 500p multi   3.00   1.50

March 8th
Revolution, 25th
Anniv. — A399

1988, Mar. 15   Litho.   Perf. 12x11½
1127 A399 150p multi   1.00   .50
      Size: 110x81mm
      Imperf
1128 A399 500p multi, diff.   4.75 4.75
      No. 1128 pictures vignette like 150p without
denomination, in diff. colors, and Arab Revolt
flag, text, outline map; denomination at LR in
sheet.

Mothers'
Day — A400

1988, Apr. 12   Litho.   Perf. 12x12½
1129 A400 500p multi   3.00   1.50

Arab Post
Day
A401

1988, Apr. 17   Perf. 12½x12
1130 A401 150p multi   1.00   .50

1946 Evacuation
A402

1988, Apr. 17   Perf. 12½x12
1131 A402 150p multi   1.00   .50

Labor
Day — A403

1988, May 1
1132 A403 550p multi   3.00   1.50

Intl. Flower
Show, Damascus
A404

1988, May 25   Perf. 12x11½
1133 A404 550p Tiger Lily   3.25 1.60
1134 A404 600p Carnations   3.75 1.90

Arab Engineers'
Union — A405

1988, May 25
1135 A405 150p multi   1.00   .50

A406

1988, Aug. 28   Litho.   Perf. 12x11½
1136 A406 600p blk, grn & olive 3.50 1.75
      Intl. Children's Day.

A407

1988, Aug. 28   Perf. 12½
1137 A407 550p multi   3.00 1.50
      Restoration of San'a, Yemen Arab Republic.

Ebla Intl. Symposium on Archaeology
of Idlib — A408

1988, Aug. 28
1138 A408 175p Hieroglyphic
            tablet   1.00   .50
1139 A408 550p Bas-relief (votive
            basin)   3.00 1.50
1140 A408 600p Gold statue,
            3000 B.C.   3.50 1.75
      Nos. 1138-1140 (3)   7.50 3.75

1988
Summer
Olympics,
Seoul
A409

1988, Sept. 17   Perf. 11½x12
1141 A409 550p Cycling   3.50 1.60
1142 A409 600p Soccer   3.75 1.75

Size: 81x61mm
Imperf
1143 A409 1200p Emblem,
            character
            trademark   12.50 12.50
      Nos. 1141-1143 (3)   19.75 15.85

35th Intl. Fair,
Damascus
A410

1988, Aug. 28   Perf. 12x11½
1144 A410 600p multi   3.50 1.75

WHO, 40th
Anniv. — A411

1988, Aug. 28   Litho.   Perf. 12x11½
1145 A411 600p multi   3.25 1.60

Arab Scouting Movement, 50th
Anniv. — A412

1988, Sept. 17   Perf. 12½x12
1146 A412 150p multi   1.50   .75

Tourism Type of 1988

Women wearing folk costumes and: 550p,
Euphrates Bridge, Deir-ez-Zor. 600p, The Tet-
rapylon, Latakia.

1988, Oct. 18
1147 A397 550p multi   3.25 1.60
1148 A397 600p multi   3.50 1.75

World Post
Day — A413

1988, Dec. 7   Litho.   Perf. 12x12½
1149 A413 600p multi   3.50 1.75

Arbor
Day — A414

1988, Nov. 16
1150 A414 600p multi   3.50 1.75

Shelter for the Homeless — A415

1988-89   *Perf. 12½x12*
1151   A415 150p Arab Housing
     Day   .65   .35
1151A A415 175p Intl. Year of
     Shelter for
     the Homeless 1.25   .60
1152   A415 550p World Housing
     Day   2.50 1.25
1153   A415 600p as No. 1151A   2.75 1.50
    Nos. 1151-1153 (4)   7.15 3.70
The IYSH emblem is pictured on the 175p,
550p and 600p.
Issued: 175p, 2/6/89; others, 10/18/88.

Al-Assad University Hospital — A416

1988, Nov. 16   *Litho.*   *Perf. 12½*
1154 A416 150p multi   .90   .45
Corrective Movement, 18th anniv.

World Food
Day — A417

1988, Oct. 18   *Perf. 12x12½*
1155 A417 550p multi   2.75 1.40

Birds
A418

1989, Mar. 21   *Litho.*   *Perf. 11½x12*
1156 A418 600p Goldfinch   1.50   .75
1157 A418 600p Turtledove   1.50   .75
1158 A418 600p Bee eater   1.50   .75
    Nos. 1156-1158 (3)   4.50 2.25

Jawaharlal
Nehru, 1st
Prime
Minister of
Independent
India — A419

1989, Mar. 8   *Perf. 12½*
1159 A419 550p brn & chest   1.10   .55

Mothers'
Day — A420

1989, Mar. 21
1160 A420 550p multi   1.10   .55

Teacher's
Day
A421

1989, Mar. 8   *Litho.*   *Perf. 11½x12*
1161 A421 175p multi   .70   .35

5th General
Congress of
the Union of
Women
A422

1989, Mar. 8   *Perf. 12½*
1162 A422 150p multi   .30   .25

March 8th Revolution, 26th
Anniv. — A423

1989, Mar. 8   *Perf. 11½x12*
1163 A423 150p multi   .30   .25

Arab Board for Medical
Specializations, 10th Anniv. — A424

1989, Feb. 6   *Perf. 12½*
1164 A424 175p multi   .60   .30

1946 Evacuation of British and French
Troops — A425

1989, Apr. 17   *Litho.*   *Perf. 11½x12*
1165 A425 150p multi   .40   .25

Intl. Flower
Show,
Damascus
A426

1989, June 3   *Perf. 12½*
1166   Strip of 5   5.00 4.00
  a. A426 150p Snapdragon   .30   .25
  b. A426 150p Canaria   .30   .25
  c. A426 450p Compositae   .90   .45
  d. A426 850p Clematis sackmani   1.75   .85
  e. A426 900p Gesneriaceae   1.75   .90

A427

1989, May 1   *Perf. 12x11½*
1167 A427 850p blue grn & blk   1.75   .90
Labor Day.

A428

1989, June 6   *Litho.*   *Perf. 12x11½*
1168 A428 175p multi   .30   .25
13th General Congress of the Arab Teachers' Union.

Arab Post
Day — A429

1989, June 6
1169 A429 175p multi   .50   .25

Liberation of Al-
Kuneitra, 15th
Anniv. — A430

1989, June 26
1170 A430 450p multi   1.25   .60

17th
Congress
of the
Arab
Advocates
Union
A431

1989, June 19   *Perf. 11½x12*
1171 A431 175p multi   .50   .25

World
Post Day
A432

1989, June 26
1172 A432 550p multi   1.50   .75

World Telecommunications
Day — A433

1989, June 6
1173 A433 550p multi   1.50   .75

Interparliamentary Union,
Cent. — A434

1989, July 12   *Perf. 12½*
1174 A434 900p multi   2.50 1.25

Butterflies
A435

1989, June 6
1175 A435 550p Small white   1.50   .75
1176 A435 550p Clouded yellow   1.50   .75
1177 A435 550p Painted Lady   1.50   .75
    Nos. 1175-1177 (3)   4.50 2.25

Intl. Tourism Day Type of 1988
Women wearing folk costumes and: 550p,
Jaabar Castle, Rakka. 600p, Temple of the
Bell, Palmyra.

1989, Oct. 16 Litho. Perf. 11½x12
1178 A397 550p multicolored   3.75 1.75
1179 A397 600p multicolored   4.00 2.00

36th Intl. Fair, Damascus A436

1989, Oct. 16 Perf. 12x11½
1180 A436 450p multicolored   3.00 1.50

Fish A437

1989, Oct. 24 Perf. 11½x12
1181 A437 550p Carp   3.75 1.75
1182 A437 600p Trout   4.00 2.00

2nd Anniv. of the Palestinian Uprising — A438

1989, Oct. 24 Perf. 12x11½
1183 A438 550p Child's drawing 3.75 1.75

Corrective Movement, 19th Anniv. — A439

1989, Nov. 16 Litho. Perf. 12½x12
1184 A439 150p multicolored   1.00 .50

A440

1990, Feb. 13 Litho. Perf. 12x11½
1185 A440 850p multicolored   1.00 .50
World Children's Day.

A441

1990
1186 A441 600p multicolored   .70 .35
March 8th Revolution, 27th anniv.

Revolutionary Youth Union A442

1990 Perf. 12½
1187 A442 150p multicolored   .25 .25

World Food Day A443

1990, Feb. 13 Litho. Perf. 11½x12
1188 A443 850p multicolored   1.00 .50
Dated 1989.

Evacuation of British and French Troops, 1946 — A444

1990, Apr. 17 Perf. 12x11½
1189 A444 175p multicolored   .25 .25

Mother's Day — A445

1990, Apr. 17 Perf. 12½
1190 A445 550p multicolored   .65 .30

Labor Day — A446

1990, May 1 Litho. Perf. 12x12½
1191 A446 550p multicolored   .75 .35

World Cup Soccer Championships, Italy — A447

Perf. 11½x12, 12x11½
1192 A447 550p shown   .40 .25
1193 A447 550p Denomination at right   .40 .25
1194 A447 600p Map, soccer ball, vert.   .45 .25
Nos. 1192-1194 (3)   1.25 .75

Miniature Sheet
Imperf
1195 A447 1300p Stadium   3.50 1.75

Intl. Flower Show, Damascus A448

1990, May 27 Perf. 12x11½
1196 A448 600p Lily   1.10 .50
1197 A448 600p Pastelkleurig   1.10 .50
1198 A448 600p Marigold   1.10 .50
1199 A448 600p Viburnum opulus   1.10 .50
1200 A448 600p Swan river daisy 1.10 .50
Nos. 1196-1200 (5)   5.50 2.50

World Health Day — A449

1990, May 1 Litho. Perf. 12½
1201 A449 600p multicolored   2.50 1.25

Liberation of Al-Kuneitra, 16th Anniv. — A450

1990, June 26 Perf. 12x11½
1202 A450 550p multicolored   2.50 1.25

Intl. Literacy Year — A451

1990, June 26
1203 A451 550p multicolored   2.25 1.10

UN Conference on Least Developed Countries — A452

1990, July 10 Perf. 11½x12
1204 A452 600p multicolored   2.40 1.25

37th Damascus Intl. Fair — A453

1990, Aug. 28 Perf. 12x11½
1205 A453 550p multicolored   2.25 1.10

World Meteorology Day — A454

1990, Aug. 28 Perf. 11½x12
1206 A454 450p multicolored   1.90 .95

Arbor Day — A455

1990, Oct. 30 Perf. 12x11½
1207 A455 550p multicolored   2.25 1.10

World Food Day — A456

1990, Oct. 30 Perf. 12½
1208 A456 850p multicolored   3.25 1.75

Al Maqdisi,
Cartographer
A457

1990, Nov. 6 *Perf. 12x11½*
1209 A457 550p multicolored 2.25 1.10

A458 A459

Pres.
Hafez al
Assad
A460

1990, Nov. 16 **Litho.** *Perf. 11½*
1210 A458 50p claret .25 .25
1211 A458 70p gray .25 .25
1212 A458 100p blue .35 .25
1213 A458 150p brown .60 .30

Perf. 12x11½
1214 A459 175p multicolored .70 .35
1215 A459 300p multicolored 1.25 .55
1216 A459 550p multicolored 2.25 1.10
1217 A459 600p multicolored 2.40 1.25

Perf. 11½x12
1219 A460 1000p multicolored 4.00 2.00
1220 A460 1500p multicolored 6.00 3.00
1222 A460 2000p multicolored 8.00 4.00
1224 A460 2500p multicolored 10.00 5.00
Nos. 1210-1224 (12) 36.05 18.30

1992, May 19 **Litho.** *Perf. 11½*
Without Date at Right
1225 A458 150p brown .60 .30
1225A A458 300p violet 1.25 .60
1225B A458 350p gray 1.40 .70
1225C A458 400p red 1.60 .80
Nos. 1225-1225C (4) 4.85 2.40

Souvenir Sheet

Corrective Movement, 20th
Anniv. — A461

a, Pres. Assad with children. b, Assad
addressing crowd. c, Assad, memorial. d,
Assad, dam.

1990, Nov. 16 *Imperf.*
1227 A461 550p Sheet of 4, #a.-
d. 9.00 9.00

UN Development Program, 40th
Anniv. — A462

1990, Dec. 11 *Perf. 11½x12*
1228 A462 550p multicolored 2.25 1.10

Arab Civil
Aviation
Day
A463

1990, Dec. 11
1229 A463 175p multicolored 1.00 .50

World Post
Day — A464

1990, Dec. 11 *Perf. 12x11½*
1230 A464 550p multicolored 2.25 1.10

Intl. Children's
Day — A465

1990, Dec. 11
1231 A465 550p multicolored 2.25 1.10

Arab-Spanish
Cultural
Symposium
A466

1990, Dec. 24
1232 A466 550p multicolored 2.25 1.10

World AIDS
Day — A467

1990, Dec. 24
1233 A467 550p multicolored 2.25 1.10

March 8th Revolution, 28th
Anniv. — A468

1991, Mar. 8 **Litho.** *Perf. 11½x12*
1234 A468 150p multicolored .60 .30

Butterflies
A469

1991, Mar. 17 *Perf. 12½*
1235 A469 550p Small tortoiseshell 2.25 1.10
1236 A469 550p Changeful great
mars 2.25 1.10
1237 A469 550p Papillion
machaon 2.25 1.10
Nos. 1235-1237 (3) 6.75 3.30

Birds — A470

1991, Mar. 17 *Perf. 12x11½*
1238 A470 600p Golden oriole 2.40 1.25
1239 A470 600p European roller 2.40 1.25
1240 A470 600p House sparrow 2.40 1.25
Nos. 1238-1240 (3) 7.20 3.75

Mother's
Day — A471

1991, Mar. 21
1241 A471 550p multicolored 2.25 1.10

1946 Evacuation of British and French
Troops — A472

1991, Apr. 17 *Perf. 11½x12*
1242 A472 150p multicolored .60 .30

Labor Day
A473

1991, May 1
1243 A473 550p multicolored 2.25 1.10

Intl. Flower Show,
Damascus — A474

1991, July 8 *Perf. 12x12½*
1244 A474 550p Narcissus 2.25 1.10
1245 A474 600p Monarda
didyma 2.40 1.25

Liberation
of
Kuneitra,
17th
Anniv.
A475

1991, July 22 *Perf. 11½x12*
1246 A475 550p multicolored 2.25 1.10

11th Mediterranean Games,
Athens — A476

1991, July 22
1247 A476 550p Running 2.25 1.10
1248 A476 550p Soccer 2.25 1.10
1249 A476 600p Equestrian 2.25 1.10

Size: 80x64mm
Imperf.
1250 A476 1300p Dolphins playing water
polo 5.25 5.25
Nos. 1247-1250 (4) 12.00 8.70

38th Damascus
Intl. Fair — A477

1991, Aug. 28 *Perf. 12x12½*
1251 A477 550p multicolored 2.25 1.10

Intl.
Tourism
Day
A478

Designs: 450p, Woman at Khan Asaad
Pasha El Azem. 550p, Woman at Castle of
Arwad Island.

1991, Sept. 27 *Perf. 11½x12*
1252 A478 450p multicolored 1.90 .95
1253 A478 550p multicolored 2.25 1.10

Housing
Day — A479

1991, Oct. 7   *Perf. 12x11½*
1254 A479 175p multicolored   1.00 .50

Intl. Children's
Day — A480

1991, Oct. 16
1255 A480 600p multicolored   2.40 1.25

Physician
Abu Bakr
Al Razi
(Rhazes),
Patient
A481

1991, Nov. 2 *Litho.* *Perf. 12½x12*
1256 A481 550p multicolored   2.25 1.10
   31st Science Week.

World
Post Day
A482

1991, Nov. 12
1257 A482 550p multicolored   2.25 1.10

World
Food Day
A483

1991, Nov. 12
1258 A483 550p multicolored   2.25 1.10

Tomb of
Unknown
Soldier,
Damascus
A484

1991, Nov. 16   *Perf. 12½*
1259 A484 600p multicolored   2.40 1.25
   Size: 65x80mm
   Imperf
1260 A484 1000p multicolored   4.00 2.00

Corrective Movement, 21st
Anniv. — A485

1991, Nov. 16   *Imperf.*
1261 A485 2500p multicolored 10.00 5.00

Protect the Environment — A486

1991, Nov. 20   *Perf. 12½x12*
1262 A486 175p multicolored   .70 .35

World Telecommunications
Fair — A487

1991, Nov. 20   *Perf. 12x12½*
1263 A487 600p multicolored   2.40 1.25

March 8th
Revolution,
29th Anniv.
A488

1992, Mar. 8 *Litho.* *Perf. 12½*
1264 A488 600p multicolored   2.40 1.25

Re-election of Pres. Assad — A489

1992, Mar. 12 *Litho.* *Imperf.*
1265 A489 5000p shown 20.00 10.00
   Size: 100x85mm
1266 A489 5000p inscription at
        right 20.00 10.00
   Nos. 1265-1266 incorporate designs of
#1036, C496 & C506.

Baath
Party,
45th
Anniv.
A490

1992, Apr. 7   *Perf. 12½x12*
1267 A490 850p multicolored   3.50 1.75

Labor
Day — A491

1992, May 1   *Perf. 12x12½*
1268 A491 900p multicolored   3.50 1.75

Mother's
Day — A492

1992, May 19
1269 A492 900p multicolored   3.50 1.75

Evacuation of British and French
Troops, 46th Anniv. — A493

1992, May 19   *Perf. 12½x12*
1270 A493 900p multicolored   3.50 1.75

Traffic Safety
Day — A494

1992, May 19   *Perf. 12x12½*
1271 A494 850p multicolored   3.50 1.75

Intl. Flower Show,
Damascus
A495

Designs: 300p, Linum mucronatum, horiz.
800p, Yucca filamentosa. 900p, Zinnia
elegans.

   Perf. 11½x12, 12x11½
1992, July 5   *Litho.*
1272 A495 300p multicolored   1.25 .65
1273 A495 800p blue & multi   3.25 1.60
1274 A495 900p multicolored   3.50 1.75
   Nos. 1272-1274 (3)   8.00 4.00

1992 Summer
Olympics,
Barcelona
A496

No. 1275: a, 150p, Team handball. b, 150p,
Running. c, 450p, Swimming. d, 750p, Wrestling. 5000p, Incorporates designs of Nos.
1275a-1275d.

1992, July 25 *Litho.* *Perf. 12x11½*
1275 A496 Strip of 4, #a.-d. 6.00 5.00
            Imperf
   Size: 80x124mm
1276 A496 5000p multicolored 20.00 10.00

Anti-Smoking
Campaign
A497

1992, Aug. 28   *Perf. 12x12½*
1277 A497 750p multicolored   3.00 1.50

39th Intl.
Damascus
Fair — A498

1992, Aug. 28
1278 A498 900p multicolored   3.50 1.75

7th Arab Games, Damascus — A499

Designs: a, 750p, Soccer. b, 850p, Pommel horse. c, 900p, Pole vault.

1992, Sept. 4 **Perf. 12½**
1279 A499 Strip of 3, #a.-c. 10.00 5.00

World Post
Day — A500

1992, Oct. 9 **Perf. 12x12½**
1280 A500 600p multicolored 2.40 1.25

World Children's
Day — A501

1992, Nov. 7 **Perf. 12x11½**
1281 A501 850p multicolored 3.50 1.75

Sebtt El Mardini
(826-912)
A502

1992, Nov. 7 **Litho.** **Perf. 12x11½**
1282 A502 850p multicolored 3.50 1.75

1992 Special
Olympics,
Madrid
A503

1992, Nov. 7 **Perf. 12½**
1283 A503 850p multicolored 3.50 1.75

Corrective Movement, 22nd
Anniv. — A504

1992, Nov. 16 **Perf. 11½x12**
1284 A504 450p multicolored 1.75 .90

Arbor
Day — A505

1992, Dec. 31 **Perf. 12x12½**
1285 A505 600p multicolored 2.40 1.25

2nd Intl. Conference of PACO — A506

Design: 1150p, Eye surrounded by scenes of day and night, rainbow.

1993, May 12 **Litho.** **Perf. 12**
1286 A506 1100p multicolored 1.00 .50

Size: 35½x24mm
Perf. 11½x12
1287 A506 1150p multicolored 1.10 .55
Syrian Ophthamological Society, 25th anniv. (#1287).

March 8th Revolution, 30th
Anniv. — A507

1993, Mar. 8 **Litho.** **Perf. 11½x12**
1288 A507 1100p multicolored .80 .40

Butterflies
A508

Designs: a, 1000p, Common blue. b, 1500p, Silver-washed fritillary. c, 2500p, Precis orithya.

1993, Mar. 13
1289 A508 Strip of 3, #a.-c. 4.75 4.75

Mother's
Day — A509

1993, Apr. 17 **Perf. 12x11½**
1290 A509 1100p multicolored .80 .40

Evacuation of British and French
Troops, 47th Anniv. — A510

1993, Apr. 17 **Perf. 11½x12**
1291 A510 1100p multicolored .80 .40

A511

1993, Apr. 17 **Litho.** **Perf. 11½x12**
1292 A511 2500p multicolored 1.75 .85

Agricultural Reform, 25th
Anniv. — A512

1993, Apr. 20 **Litho.** **Perf. 11½x12**
1293 A512 1150p multicolored .90 .45

A513

1993, May 1 **Perf. 12x11½**
1294 A513 1100p multicolored .80 .40
Labor day.

A514

Intl. Flower Show, Damascus: a, 1000p, Alcea setosa. b, 1100p, Primulaceae. c, 1150p, Gesneriaceae.

1993, June 17 **Litho.** **Perf. 12x11½**
1295 A514 Strip of 3, #a.-c. 2.25 2.25

Tourism
A515

1993, Sept. 27 **Perf. 11½x12**
1296 A515 1000p Woman, prism
tomb 1.00 .50

World
Post Day
A516

1993, Oct. 9 **Perf. 12½x12**
1297 A516 1000p multicolored 1.00 .50

World
Child Day
A517

1993, Nov. 6 **Perf. 11½x12**
1298 A517 1150p multicolored 1.10 .55

Ibn El Bittar,
Chemist — A518

1993, Nov. 6 **Perf. 12x11½**
1299 A518 1150p multicolored 1.10 .55

Corrective Movement, 23rd
Anniv. — A519

1993, Nov. 16 **Litho.** **Imperf.**
1300 A519 2500p multicolored 2.50 2.50

Arabian
Horses
A520

1994, Jan.   Litho.   Perf. 12½
1301 A520 1000p shown   .60   .30
1302 A520 1000p White horse   .60   .30
1303 A520 1500p Tan horse   .90   .45
1304 A520 1500p Black horse   .90   .45
 a.   Strip of 4, #1301-1304   3.00   3.00

Arbor Day
A521

1994, Jan.   Litho.   Perf. 12½x12
1305 A521 1100p multicolored   1.75   .85

40th Intl.
Damascus
Fair
A522

1994, Jan.
1306 A522 1100p multicolored   1.75   .85

Basel Al Assad
(1962-94) — A523

1994, Mar. 1   Perf. 12x12½
1307 A523 2500p multicolored   4.00   2.00

March 8th Revolution, 31st
Anniv. — A524

a, Oranges. b, Mandarin oranges. c,
Lemons.

1994, Mar. 8   Perf. 12½x12
1308 A524 1500p Strip of 3, #a.-
    c.   7.50   7.50

Evacuation of British and French
Troops, 48th Anniv. — A525

1994, Apr. 17
1309 A525 1800p multicolored   2.75   1.40

Mother's
Day
A526

1994, May 1   Litho.   Perf. 12½x12
1310 A526 1800p multicolored   2.75   1.40

Labor Day
A527

1994, May 1
1311 A527 1700p multicolored   2.75   1.40

ILO, 75th
Anniv.
A528

1994, June 1
1312 A528 1700p multicolored   2.75   1.40

1994 World Cup Soccer
Championships, U.S. — A529

Various soccer plays.

1994, June 17   Perf. 12½
1313 A529 1700p Pair, #a.-b.   5.75   2.75
Size: 80x80mm
    Imperf
1314 A529 4000p multicolored   6.75   6.75

41st Intl. Fair,
Damascus
A530

1994, Aug. 3   Litho.   Perf. 12x12½
1315 A530 1800p multicolored   1.60   .80

Intl. Flower Show,
Damascus
A531

a, Daisies. b, Red flowers. c. Yellow flowers.

1994, Aug. 3   Perf. 12x11½
1316 A531 1800p Strip of 3, #a.-
    c.   4.50   4.50

Intl. Olympic Committee,
Cent. — A532

1994, Aug. 3   Perf. 11½x12
1317 A532 1700p multicolored   1.50   .75

Butterflies
A533

a, Apollo (shown). b, Purple emperor, value
at right. c, Birdwing, value at left.

1994, Aug. 9   Litho.   Perf. 11½x12
1318 A533 1700p Strip of 3, #a.-
    c.   8.25   8.25

4th Natl.
Census
A534

1994, Aug. 15
1319 A534 1000p multicolored   1.50   .75

Science
Week
A535

Design: £10, Al Kindi, philosopher.

1994, Nov. 5   Perf. 12½
1320 A535 £10 multicolored   1.50   .75

Corrective Movement, 24th
Anniv. — A536

1994, Nov. 16   Imperf.
1321 A536 £25 multicolored   6.50   6.50

ICAO, 50th Anniv. — A537

1994, Dec. 7   Litho.   Perf. 12½
1322 A537 17p multicolored   1.50   .75

Martyr's
Square
A538

1994, Dec. 7   Litho.   Perf. 11½x12
1323 A538 £50 purple   7.25   3.75
    See Nos. 1472-1474, 1518, 1538.

Intl. Children's
Day — A539

1994, Dec. 19   Perf. 12x11½
1324 A539 £10 multicolored   1.50   .75

World Post
Day — A540

1994, Dec. 19
1325 A540 £10 multicolored   1.50   .75

Intl. Tourism
Day — A541

1994, Dec. 19
1326 A541 £17 multicolored   2.50   1.25

March 8 Revolution, 32nd
Anniv. — A542

1995, Mar. 8   Litho.   Perf. 11½x12
1327 A542 £18 multicolored   2.75   1.40

Arab League,
50th Anniv.
A543

1995, Mar. 22   Perf. 12½
1328 A543 £17 multicolored   2.50   1.25

World Water
Day — A544

1995, Apr. 9   Litho.   Perf. 12x12½
1329 A544 £17 multicolored   1.25 .60

Mother's
Day
A545

1995, Apr. 9   Litho.   Perf. 12½x12
1330 A545 £17 multicolored   2.00 1.00

Arbor
Day — A546

1995, Apr. 9   Litho.   Perf. 12x12½
1331 A546 1800p multicolored   1.50 .75

A547

1995, Aug. 13   Litho.   Perf. 12x11½
1332 A547 £18 multicolored   2.75 1.40
UN, 50th anniv.

A548

1995, Aug. 21
1333 A548 £18 multicolored   2.75 1.40
4th World Conference on Women, Beijing.

Desert
Festival,
Tourism
Day
A549

1995, June 25   Perf. 12½x12
1334 A549 £18 multicolored   1.25 .65

A550

1995, June 25   Perf. 12x12½
1335 A550 £10 Labor Day   .75 .40

A551

1995, Apr. 30   Litho.   Perf. 12x11½
1336 A551 £17 multicolored   1.25 .60
Evacuation of British & French Troops, 49th
anniv.

A552   A553

1995, Apr. 30   Litho.   Perf. 12x11½
1337 A542 £17 multicolored   1.40 .70
Intl. Year of the Family.

1995, Apr. 30   Litho.   Perf. 12x12½
1338 A553 £17 multicolored   2.00 1.00
Arab Apiculture Union, 1st anniv.

FAO, 50th
Anniv.
A554

1995, June 25   Perf. 12½x12
1339 A554 £15 multicolored   1.75 .85

42nd Intl.
Fair,
Damascus
A555

1995, Aug. 28   Litho.   Perf. 11½x12
1340 A555 £15 multicolored   1.50 .75

Int'l Flower
Show,
Damascus
A556

1995, July 30   Litho.   Perf. 12½
1341 A556 £10 Astilbe   .50 .25
1342 A556 £10 Evening prim-
                  rose   .50 .25
1343 A556 £10 Blue carpet   .50 .25
  a.   Strip of 3, #1341-1343   1.50 1.50

Second Congress
of Arab Dentists'
Assoc. — A557

1995, Sept. 16   Litho.   Perf. 12x11½
1344 A557 £18 multicolored   1.50 .75

Syrian
Army,
50th
Anniv.
A558

1995, Oct. 2   Litho.   Perf. 11½x12
1345 A558 £18 multicolored   1.40 .70

World
Post Day
A559

1995, Oct. 2   Litho.   Perf. 11½x12
1346 A559 £15 multicolored   1.60 .85

World Children's
Day — A560

1995, Oct. 2   Perf. 12x11½
1347 A560 £18 multicolored   2.00 1.00

Ahmed ben Maged, Cartographer,
500th Death Anniv. — A561

1995, Nov. 4   Litho.   Perf. 11½x12
1348 A561 £18 multicolored   2.00 1.00

Corrective
Movement,
25th Anniv.
A562

Design: £50, like #1349 with Nos. 1044,
720, 1227b, 903.

1995, Nov. 11   Litho.   Perf. 12½
1349 A562 £10 multicolored   1.10 .55
Imperf
Size: 100x64mm
1350 A562 £50 multicolored   5.50 2.75

Songbirds
A563

Designs: a, Group on tree branch. b, One in
snow, flower. c, One on fence rail.

1995, Dec. 5   Litho.   Perf. 12½
1351 A563 £18 Strip of 3, #a.-c.   7.25 7.25

Louis
Pasteur
(1822-95)
A564

1995, Dec. 21   Perf. 12½x12
1352 A564 £18 multicolored   2.00 1.00

March 8 Revolution, 33rd
Anniv. — A565

1996, Mar. 8   Litho.   Perf. 11½x12
1353 A565 £25 Hydro-electric
                  plant   2.00 1.00

Evacuation Day, 50th Anniv. — A566

1996, Apr. 17   Perf. 12½
1354 A566 £10 black & multi   .85 .40
1355 A566 £25 bister & multi   2.00 1.00
Size: 57x46mm
Imperf
1356 A566 £25 bis, blk, & multi   5.25 2.75

Liberation
of
Kuneitra
A567

1996, June 26   Litho.   Perf. 11½x12
1357 A567 £10 multicolored   .60 .30

1996
Summer
Olympic
Games,
Atlanta
A568

1996, July 19   *Perf. 11½x12*
1358 A568 £17 Wrestling   1.10 .55
1359 A568 £17 Swimming   1.10 .55
1360 A568 £17 Running   1.10 .55
  a.   Strip of 3, #1358-1360   3.25 3.25
Size: 55x41mm
Imperf
1361 A568 £25 Soccer   1.60 .80
  Nos. 1358-1361 (4)   4.90 2.45

Intl. Flower Show, Damascus A569

Cactus: No. 1362, Notocactus graessnerii. No. 1363, Mammilaria erythosperma.

1996, July 1   **Litho.**   *Perf. 12½*
1362 A569 £18 multicolored   1.25 .65
1363 A569 £18 multicolored   1.25 .65

Ba'ath Party, 50th Anniv. A570

1996, July 1   *Perf. 11½x12*
1364 A570 £18 multicolored   1.25 .65

Pres. Hafez al-Assad — A571

1995   **Litho.**   *Perf. 11½*
1365 A571 100p bright blue   .25 .25
1366 A571 500p bright orange   .55 .25
1367 A571 £10 bright lilac   1.10 .55
1368 A571 £17 rose lake   1.90 .95
1369 A571 £18 slate green   2.00 1.00
  Nos. 1365-1369 (5)   5.80 3.00

Issued: £10, 5/3; 100p, 500p, £17, £18, 12/31.

Arbor Day — A572

1996, Mar. 8   **Litho.**   *Perf. 12¼x12½*
1370 A572 £17 multicolored   .80 .40

Mother's Day — A573

1996, May 1   *Perf. 12x11½*
1370A A573 £10 multicolored   .50 .25

Labor Day — A574

1996, May 1   *Perf. 12¼x12½*
1371 A574 £15 multicolored   .70 .35

Radio, Cent. — A575

1996, Aug. 18   **Litho.**   *Perf. 12½*
1372 A575 £17 multicolored   1.10 .55

World AIDS Day — A576

1996, Aug. 18   *Perf. 12x11½*
1373 A576 £17 multicolored   1.10 .55

43rd Intl. Fair, Damascus A577

1996, Aug. 28
1374 A577 £17 multicolored   1.10 .55

NICE, 5th Anniv. A578

1996, Sept. 5   *Perf. 11½x12*
1375 A578 £18 multicolored   1.10 .60

World Child Day — A579

1996, Oct. 9   *Perf. 12x11½*
1376 A579 £10 multicolored   .65 .30

World Post Day — A580

1996, Oct. 9
1377 A580 £17 multicolored   1.10 .55

UNICEF, 50th Anniv. — A581

1996, Nov. 20
1378 A581 £17 multicolored   1.10 .55

36th Science Week — A582

Design: Musa Iben Shaker's sons.

1996, Nov. 2   *Perf. 12½x12*
1379 A582 £10 multicolored   .65 .35

Corrective Movement, 26th Anniv. A583

1996, Nov. 16   *Perf. 12½*
1380 A583 £10 multicolored   .65 .35
Size: 65x90mm
Imperf
1381 A583 £50 like No. 1380   3.25 1.60

Natl. Advance Party — A584

1997, Mar. 7   **Litho.**   *Perf. 12x11½*
1382 A584 £3 multicolored   .25 .25

March 8 Revolution, 34th Anniv. — A585

1997, Mar. 8
1383 A585 £15 multicolored   1.00 .50

Arbor Day — A586

1996, Apr. 8   **Litho.**   *Perf. 12x12½*
1384 A586 £10 multicolored   .75 .40

Fish — A587

1996, Apr. 8   *Perf. 12½x12*
1385 A587 £17 Two dorsal fins   1.00 .50
1386 A587 £17 One dorsal fin   1.00 .50
  a.   Pair, #1385-1386   2.00 2.00

Mother's Day — A588

1997, Apr. 8   *Perf. 12x11½*
1387 A588 £15 multicolored   1.00 .50

Baath Party Revolution, 50th Anniv. A589

1997, Apr. 3   *Perf. 12½*
1388 A589 £25 multicolored   1.60 .80
Size: 90x65mm
Imperf
1389 A589 £25 multicolored   1.60 .80

World Tourism
Day — A590

1997, Apr. 8   *Perf. 12x11½*
1390 A590 £17 multicolored   1.10   .60

Evacuation Day, 51st Anniv. — A591

1997, Apr. 17   *Perf. 11½x12*
1391 A591 £15 multicolored   1.00   .50

Labor
Day — A592

1997, May 1   *Perf. 12x11½*
1392 A592 £15 multicolored   1.00   .50

World Book
Day —
A592a

1997, June 16 Litho.   *Perf. 12½*
1392A A592a £10 multicolored   .50   .25

A592b

1997, June 16   *Perf. 12x11½*
1392B A592b £18 multicolored   .70   .35
        No smoking day.

A593

No. 1393, Echino ereus. No. 1394, Iris.

1997, June 21 Litho.   *Perf. 12x11½*
1393 A593 £18 multicolored   1.10   .60
1394 A593 £18 multicolored   1.10   .60
  a.   Pair, #1393-1394   2.25 2.25
        Intl. Flower Show, Damascus.
        See Nos. 1412-1413.

4th Congress of
Arab
Denistry — A594

1997, Sept. 4
1395 A594 £10 multicolored   .65   .35

44th Intl. Fair,
Damascus
A595

1997, Sept. 4
1396 A595 £17 multicolored   1.10   .55

World
Post Day
A596

1997, Sept. 27   *Perf. 11½x12*
1397 A596 £17 multicolored   1.10   .55

World
Children's
Day
A597

1997, Sept. 27
1398 A597 £17 multicolored   1.10   .55

Intl.
Tourism
Day
A598

1997, Sept. 27
1399 A598 £17 multicolored   1.10   .55

37th Science
Week — A599

1997, Nov. 1 Litho.   *Perf. 12x11½*
1400 A599 £17 multicolored   1.10   .55

Corrective
Movement,
27th Anniv.
A600

1997, Nov. 16   *Perf. 12½*
1401 A600 £10 multicolored   .70   .35
        Size: 92x67mm
        Imperf
1402 A600 £50 like #1401   3.25 3.25

Islamic Conference, 30th
Anniv. — A601

1997, Dec. 9 Litho.   *Perf. 11½x12*
1403 A601 £10 multicolored   .70   .35

March 8 Revolution, 35th
Anniv. — A602

1998, Mar. 8 Litho.   *Perf. 12½x12*
1404 A602 £17 multicolored   1.10   .55

Mother's
Day
A603

1998, March 21   *Perf. 11½x12*
1405 A603 £10 multicolored   .70   .35

Evacuation Day,
52nd
Anniv. — A604

1998, Apr. 17 Litho. *Perf. 12x11½*
1406 A604 £10 multicolored   .70   .35

Labor
Day — A605

1998, May 1
1407 A605 £18 multicolored   1.10   .55

World Tourism
Day — A606

1998, July 22 Litho.   *Perf. 12x11½*
1408 A606 £17 Princess of
                Banias   1.10   .55

Mother Teresa
(1910-97)
A607

1998, July 22
1409 A607 £18 multicolored   1.10   .55

1998 World Cup
Soccer
Championships,
France — A608

1998, June 22   *Perf. 12x12½*
1410 A608 £10 shown   .60   .30
        Size: 60x55mm
        Imperf
1411 A608 £25 Soccer players,
                diff.   2.25 1.10

Intl. Flower Show Type of 1997
  Flowers: No. 1412, Plum-colored with yellow
centers. No. 1413, Red hibiscus.

1998, June 22   *Perf. 12x11½*
1412 A593 £17 multicolored   1.10 1.10
1413 A593 £17 multicolored   1.10 1.10
  a.   Pair, #1412-1413   2.25 2.25

45th Intl.
Damascus
Fair
A609

1998, Sept. 26 Litho. *Perf. 11½x12*
1414 A609 £18 multicolored   1.10   .55

World Children's
Day — A610

1998, Sept. 26   *Perf. 12x11½*
1415 A610 £18 multicolored   1.10   .55

World
Post Day
A611

1998, Sept. 26   Litho.   Perf. 11½x12
1416   A611   £18 multicolored   1.10   .55

Day to Stop
Smoking — A612

1998, Sept. 26   Perf. 12x11½
1417   A612   £15 multicolored   .95   .50

Arab Post Day — A613

1998, Sept. 26   Perf. 12½
1418   A613   £10 multicolored   .60   .30

Arab-Israeli October War, 25th
Anniv. — A614

1998, Oct. 6   Imperf.
1419   A614   £25 multicolored   1.60   .80

Science
Week
A615

1998, Nov. 3   Perf. 11½x12
1420   A615   £10 multicolored   .65   .35

Camels
A616

1998, Nov. 25   Perf. 12½
1421   A616   £17 multicolored   1.10   .55

Corrective
Movement,
28th Anniv.
A617

1998, Nov. 16   Litho.   Perf. 12½
1422   A617   £10 multicolored   .65   .30
Size: 99x65mm
Imperf
1423   A617   £25 multicolored   .65   .30

Jerusalem — A618

1998, Nov. 25   Perf. 12½
1424   A618   £10 multicolored   .65   .30

Re-election
of Pres.
Assad
A619

£50, Portrait with designs from Nos. 1036,
C496, C506, & portrait from No. 1265.

1999, Feb. 11   Perf. 12½
1425   A619   £10 red brn & multi   .50   .25
1426   A619   £17 pale yel & multi   .90   .45
1427   A619   £18 pale grn & multi   .95   .45
Size: 140x110mm
Imperf
1428   A619   £50 pale grn & multi   2.50 2.50
   Nos. 1425-1428 (4)   4.85 3.65

Arbor
Day — A620

1999, Apr. 29   Litho.   Perf. 12½
1429   A620   £17 multicolored   1.10   .55

Evacuation Day,
53rd.
Anniv. — A621

1999, Apr. 29   Perf. 12x11½
1430   A621   £18 multicolored   1.10   .55

Mother's
Day — A622

1999, Apr. 29
1431   A622   £17 multicolored   1.10   .55

Intl. Flower Show,
Damascus
A623

Designs: a, Jasminum. b, Acanthaceae.

1999, June 20   Litho.   Perf. 12x11½
1432   A623   £10 Pair, #a.-b.   .85   .45

March 8 Revolution, 36th
Anniv. — A624

1999, Mar. 8   Litho.   Perf. 12¼x12½
1433   A624   £25 shown   1.50   .75
Size: 75x110mm
Imperf
1434   A624   £25 Building, monu-
              ment   1.50   .75

Declaration of Human Rights, 50th
Anniv. — A625

1999, June 5   Perf. 11½x12
1435   A625   £18 multicolored   .95   .45

Labor
Day — A626

1999, June 5   Litho.   Perf. 12x11½
1436   A626   £10 multicolored   .55   .30

10th
Amity
Festival
A627

1999, Aug. 1   Litho.   Perf. 11½x12
1437   A627   £10 multicolored   .65   .30

A628

1999, Oct. 12   Litho.   Perf. 12x11½
1438   A628   £10 multi   .65   .30
Arab Post Day.

A629

1999, Aug. 28   Perf. 11½x12
1439   A629   £15 multi   .95   .45
46th Intl. Fair, Damascus.

A630

1999, Sept. 21   Perf. 12x11½
1440   A630   £17 multi   1.10   .55
Arab Dentists Assoc., 7th Congress.

A631

1999, Nov. 16
1441   A631   £18 multi   1.10   .55
World Children's Day.

A632

1999, Oct. 12
1442   A632   £17 multi   1.10   .55
UPU, 125th anniv.

Corrective Movement, 29th Anniv. — A633

#1443, Building, statue. #1444, Close-up of statue. £25, Building statue, fountain.

1999, Nov. 16   *Perf. 12½*
1443 A633 £17 multi   1.10 .55
1444 A633 £17 multi, vert.   1.10 .55
    Imperf
    Size: 115x76mm
1445 A633 £25 multi   1.60 1.60
   Nos. 1443-1445 (3)   3.80 2.70

Abu Hanifah al-Deilouri, Botanist — A634

1999, Oct. 12   *Perf. 11½x12*
1446 A634 £17 multi   1.10 .55

Christianity, 2000th Anniv. — A635

1999, Nov. 16   *Perf. 12½*
1447 A635 £17 multi   1.10 .55

March 8 Revolution, 37th Anniv. A636

2000, Mar. 8   **Litho.**   *Perf. 12½*
1448 A636 £18 multi   1.10 .55

Mother's Day — A637

2000, Mar. 21
1449 A637 £17 multi   1.00 .50

Evacuation Day, 54th Anniv. — A638

2000, Apr. 17   *Imperf.*
1450 A638 £25 multi   1.50 1.50

Labor Day — A639

2000, May 1   **Litho.**   *Perf. 12x11½*
1451 A639 £10 multi   .40 .25

Installation of Bashar al-Assad as President A640

2000, July 17   *Perf. 12¼*
1452   Strip of 4   1.90 1.90
  a. A640 £3 lt blue & multi   .25 .25
  b. A640 £10 tan & multi   .40 .25
  c. A640 £17 bl gray & multi   .65 .30
  d. A640 £18 gray & multi   .65 .35
    Imperf
    Size: 110x74mm
1453 A640 £50 multi   1.90 1.90

Arab Post Day A641

2000, Aug. 20   **Litho.**   *Perf. 11½x12*
1454 A641 £18 multi   1.10 .55

47th Damascus Fair — A642

2000, Aug. 20
1455 A642 £15 multi   .90 .45

2000 Summer Olympics, Sydney — A643

No. 1456: a, £17, Weight lifting. b, £18, Women's shot put.

2000, Oct. 1   **Litho.**   *Perf. 12x11½*
1456 A643   Pair, #a-b   1.40 .70
    Imperf
    Size: 80x77mm
1457 A643 £25 Javelin   .95 .50

World Tourism Day — A644

2000, Dec. 6   **Litho.**   *Imperf.*
1458 A644 £50 Mosaic   3.00 3.00

World Post Day A645

2000, Aug. 20   *Perf. 11½x12*
1459 A645 £18 multi   1.10 .55

Nasir ad-Din at-Tusi (1201-74), Scientist A646

2000, Nov. 1   **Litho.**   *Perf. 12½x12¼*
1460 A646 £15 multi   .60 .30
  Science week.

Arbor Day — A647

2000, May 15   *Perf. 12x11½*
1461 A647 £18 multi   .65 .35

Butterflies — A648

a, £17, Charaxes jasius. b, £18, Apaturairis.

2000, May 15   *Perf. 12½*
1462 A648   Pair, #a-b   1.40 .70

World Children's Day — A649

2000, Aug. 20   **Litho.**   *Perf. 12x11½*
1463 A649 £10 multi   .60 .30

World Meteorological Organization, 50th Anniv. — A650

2000, Dec. 6
1464 A650 £10 multi   .60 .30

March 8 Revolution, 38th Anniv. — A651

2001   **Litho.**   *Perf. 12x11½*
1465 A651 £25 multi   .95 .50

Mother's Day — A652

2001
1466 A652 £10 multi   .40 .25

Evacuation Day, 55th Anniv. — A653

2001
1467 A653 £25 multi   .95 .50

Book and Author's Rights — A654

2001
1468 A654 £10 multi .40 .25

Intl. Flower Show, Damascus — A655

No. 1469: a, Weigela. b, Mertensia.

2001
1469 A655 £10 Horiz. pair, #a-b .75 .40

Syrian Engineering Syndicate, 50th Anniv. A656

2001, Feb. 1 Litho. Perf. 12½
1470 A656 £17 multi .65 .35

Size: 95x85mm
Imperf
1471 A656 £25 multi .95 .50

Martyr's Square Type of 1994
2001 Perf. 11½x12
1472 A538 100p brt blue grn .25 .25
1473 A538 £10 red .35 .25
1474 A538 £50 blue 1.90 .95
  Nos. 1472-1474 (3) 2.50 1.45

Labor Day — A657

2001 Litho. Perf. 12x11½
1475 A657 £18 multi .75 .40

48th Damascus Fair — A658

2001 Litho. Perf. 12x11½
1476 A658 £10 multi .40 .25

Re-occupation of Kuneitra by Syria, 27th Anniv. — A659

2001 Perf. 11½x12
1477 A659 £17 multi .65 .35

Anti-Smoking Campaign — A660

2001
1478 A660 £18 multi .70 .35

UN High Commissioner for Refugees, 50th Anniv. — A661

2001
1479 A661 £17 multi .65 .35

Tooth Cross-section A662

2001 Perf. 12x11½
1480 A662 £10 multi .40 .25

World Children's Day — A663

2001 Perf. 12x11½
1481 A663 £18 multi .70 .35

A664

2001 Perf. 12x11½
1482 A664 £10 multi .40 .25

Size: 84x111mm
Imperf
1483 A664 £25 multi 1.00 1.00

A665

Aga Khan Award for Architecture — A666

2001 Perf. 11½x12
1484 A665 £10 multi .40 .25
1485 A666 £17 multi .65 .35
1486 A666 £18 multi .70 .35
  Nos. 1484-1486 (3) 1.75 .95

Installation of Bashar al-Assad as President, 1st Anniv. — A667

Assad and: a, £10, Silver frame. b, £17, Gold frame.

2001 Litho. Perf. 12½x12¼
1487 A667 Horiz. pair, #a-b 1.10 .55

Arab Post Day A668

2001 Perf. 11½x12
1488 A668 £18 multi .75 .35

World Post Day A669

2001
1489 A669 £10 multi .40 .25

Arbor Day — A670

2001 Perf. 12x11½
1490 A670 £5 multi .25 .25

World Tourism Day — A671

2001 Perf. 12½
1491 A671 £17 multi .70 .35

Palestinian Intifada — A672

2001 Perf. 12x11½
1492 A672 £17 multi .70 .35

Pres. Hafez al-Assad (1930-2000) — A673

2001 Perf. 12¼x12½
1493 A673 £25 multi 1.00 .50

Correctionist Movement, 31st Anniv. — A674

Text color: £5, Black. £15, Red.

2001 Perf. 11½x12
1494-1495 A674 Set of 2 .80 .40

Evacuation Day, 56th Anniv. — A675

2002, Apr. 7 Litho. Perf. 12x11½
1496 A675 £15 multi .65 .30

Labor Day — A676

2002, May 1   **Perf. 12x12½**
1497 A676 £10 multi   .45 .25

Intl. Flower Show, Damascus — A677

No. 1498: a, £15, Yellow flowers. b, £17, White lilies.

2002, May 1   **Perf. 12x11½**
1498 A677 Horiz. pair, #a-b   1.40 .70

March 8 Revolution, 39th Anniv. A678

2002, Mar. 8   **Litho.**   **Perf. 11½x12**
1499 A678 £15 multi   .65 .30

Mother's Day — A679

2002, Mar. 21   **Perf. 12x11½**
1500 A679 £25 multi   1.10 .55

Gazelle A680

2002, Mar. 8   **Perf. 12½**
1501 A680 £15 multi   .65 .30

Baath Party, 55th Anniv. A681

2002, Apr. 7   **Perf. 11½x12**
1502 A681 £15 multi   .65 .30

2002 World Cup Soccer Championships, Japan and Korea — A682

No. 1503 — Various players: a, £5. b, £10. £25, Goalie making save, horiz.

2002, May 31   **Perf. 12½**
1503 A682 Horiz. pair, #a-b   .65 .30
     Size: 78x65mm
     Imperf
1504 A682 £25 multi   1.10 .55

World Tourism Day — A683

2002, Sep. 27   **Perf. 12½**
1505 A683 £10 multi   .40 .25

First Syrian Railroad, Cent. — A684

2002, Nov. 9
1506 A684 £10 multi   .40 .25

Abd al-Rahman al-Kawakibi (1849-1902), Arab Nationalist — A685

2002, Aug. 13   **Perf. 12x11½**
1507 A685 £10 multi   .40 .25

Intifada — A686

Designs: £10, Flag bearer, four rock throwers, tank. £25, Flag bearer, rock thrower, tank.

2002, Sep. 28   **Perf. 12x11½**
1508 A686 £10 multi   .40 .25
     Size: 66x79mm
     Imperf
1509 A686 £25 multi   1.10 .55

Birds A687

2002, Sep. 27   **Perf. 11½x12**
1510   Vert. strip of 4   1.40 .70
   a. A687 £3 Sand grouse   .25 .25
   b. A687 £5 Francolin   .25 .25
   c. A687 £10 Duck   .40 .25
   d. A687 £15 Goose   .65 .30

Arab Post Day A688

Frame color: £5, Blue. £10, Red violet.

2002, Aug. 3   **Perf. 11½x12**
1511-1512 A688 Set of 2   .65 .30

49th Intl. Damascus Fair — A689

Emblem and: a, £5, "X's." b, £10, Squares and diamonds.

2002, Aug. 28   **Perf. 12x11½**
1513 A689 Horiz. pair, #a-b   .65 .30

World Post Day — A690

No. 1514: a, Dove, envelope, rainbow. b, Envelope, UPU emblem, horiz.

   Perf. 12x11½, 11½x12 (#1514b)
2002, Oct. 9
1514 A690 £10 Horiz. pair, #a-b   .80 .40

Arbor Day — A691

2002, Dec. 26   **Perf. 12x11½**
1515 A691 £10 multi   .40 .25

Intl. Children's Day — A692

2002, Oct. 16   **Perf. 12½**
1516 A692 £10 multi   .40 .25

Corrective Movement, 32nd Anniv. A693

2002, Oct. 16   **Perf. 11½x12**
1517 A693 £10 multi   .40 .25

Martyr's Square Type of 1994
2003, May 5   **Litho.**   **Perf. 11½x12**
1518 A538 300p brown   .25 .25

March 8 Revolution, 40th Anniv. — A694

2003, Mar. 8   **Perf. 12¼x12½**
1519 A694 £15 multi   .65 .30

Teacher's Day — A695

2003, Mar. 8   **Perf. 12x11½**
1520 A695 £17 multi   .75 .40

Mother's Day — A696

2003, Mar. 21
1521 A696 £32 multi   1.40 .70

Evacuation Day, 57th Anniv. — A697

2003, Apr. 17
1522 A697 £15 multi   .65 .30

Labor Day — A698

2003, May 1
1523 A698 £25 multi · 1.10 .55

Intl. Flower Show, Damascus A699

No. 1524: a, Damask roses and violets. b, Anemones. c, Daisies. d, Damask roses and gillyflowers. e, Sunflowers.

2003, June 15 *Perf. 12½x12¼*
1524 Horiz. strip of 5 · 2.25 1.10
a.-e. A699 £10 Any single · .45 .25

50th Intl. Damascus Fair — A700

Designs: £32, Flags, emblems. £50, Open orbs, horiz.

2003, Sep. 3 *Perf. 12x12½*
1525 A700 £32 multi · 1.40 .70
Size: 89x66mm
Imperf
1526 A700 £50 multi · 2.25 2.25

World Tourism Day — A701

2003, Sep. 27 *Perf. 12¼x12½*
1527 A701 £32 multi · 1.40 .70

Election of Pope John Paul II, 25th Anniv. — A702

2003, Oct. 16 *Perf. 12½x12¼*
1528 A702 £32 multi · 1.40 .70

World Post Day A703

2003, Oct. 14 **Litho.** *Perf. 11½x12*
1529 A703 £10 multi · .45 .25

Corrective Movement, 33rd Anniv. — A704

2003, Nov. 16 *Perf. 12x11½*
1530 A704 £15 multi · .65 .30

Intl. Children's Day A705

2003, Dec. 8 *Perf. 11½x12*
1531 A705 £15 multi · .65 .30

Birds A706

2003, Dec. 8 *Perf. 12½x12¼*
1532 Horiz. strip of 5 · 2.75 2.75
a. A706 £5 Woodcock · .25 .25
b. A706 £10 Lapwing · .45 .25
c. A706 £15 European roller · .65 .30
d. A706 £17 Teal · .70 .35
e. A706 £18 Bustard · .75 .40

Pres. Bashar al-Assad — A707

Perf. 11¾x11¼
2003, Dec. 8 **Unwmk.**
1533 A707 £15 brt blue green · .65 .30
1534 A707 £25 blue · 1.10 .55
1535 A707 £50 lilac · 2.10 1.10
Nos. 1533-1535 (3) · 3.85 1.95
See Nos. 1585-1594. Compare with Nos. 1652-1654.

World Summit on the Information Society, Geneva — A708

2003, Dec. 10 *Perf. 12x11½*
1536 A708 £15 multi · .65 .30

Arbor Day — A709

2003, Dec. 25 **Litho.**
1537 A709 £25 multi · 1.10 .55

Martyr's Square Type of 1994
2004 *Perf. 11½x12*
1538 A538 £5 blue · .25 .25

March 8 Revolution, 41st Anniv. — A710

2004, Mar 8 *Perf. 12½x12*
1539 A710 £10 multi · .40 .25

Teacher's Day — A711

2004, Mar. 13 *Perf. 12x11½*
1540 A711 £5 multi · .25 .25

Mother's Day A712

2004, Mar. 21 *Perf. 11½x12*
1541 A712 £15 multi · .65 .30

Evacuation Day, 58th Anniv. — A713

2004, Apr. 17 **Litho.**
1542 A713 £10 multi · .40 .25

Labor Day A714

2004, May 1
1543 A714 £10 multi · .40 .25

A715

A716

A717

A718

FIFA (Fédération Internationale de Football Association), Cent. — A719

2004, May 21 *Perf. 11½x12*
1544 A715 £5 multi · .25 .25
1545 A716 £10 multi · .40 .25
Perf. 12½x12¼
1546 A717 £15 multi · .60 .30
Perf. 12¼x12½
1547 A718 £32 multi · 1.25 .60
Nos. 1544-1547 (4) · 2.50 1.40
Imperf
1548 A719 £25 multi · 1.00 1.00

Intl. Flower
Show, Damascus
A720

No. 1549: a, Gladiola lavender. b, Jasmine.
c, Iris. d, Orange nesrien. e, Tulip.

2004, June 15   **Perf. 12x11½**
1549   Horiz. strip of 5   1.00   1.00
a.-e.   A720 £5 Any single   .25   .25

Children and War Campaign of Intl.
Committee of the Red Cross — A721

2004, June 17   **Perf. 12¼x12½**
1550   A721 £32 red & black   1.25   .60

2004 Summer
Olympics,
Athens — A722

Designs: £5, Track. £10, Boxing, horiz. £25,
Swimming, horiz.

Perf. 12x11½, 11½x12
2004, Aug. 13
1551-1553 A722   Set of 3   1.60   .80

51st Intl.
Damascus
Fair — A723

2004, Sept. 3   **Perf. 12x11½**
1554   A723 £25 multi   1.00   .50

2004
Census
A724

2004, Sept. 14   **Perf. 12½**
1555   A724 £10 multi   .45   .25

World
Tourism
Day
A725

Designs: £5, Locomotive. No. 1557, £10,
Building. No. 1558, £10, Train.

Perf. 11½x12
2004, Sept. 27   **Litho.**   **Unwmk.**
1556-1558 A725   Set of 3   1.00   .50

World Post
Day — A726

2004, Oct. 9   **Litho.**   **Perf. 12x11½**
1559   A726 £17 multi   .70   .35

Intl.
Children's
Day
A727

2004, Oct. 16   **Perf. 11½x12**
1560   A727 £18 multi   .70   .35

Corrective Movement, 34th
Anniv. — A728

2004, Nov. 16   **Perf. 12½x12**
1561   A728 £25 multi   1.00   .50

Arbor
Day — A729

2004, Dec. 30   **Perf. 12x11½**
1562   A729 £10 multi   .40   .25

Northern
Bald
Ibis — A730

Perf. 12½x12¼
2004, Dec. 30   **Litho.**   **Unwmk.**
1563   A730 £10 multi   .40   .25

Farm
Animals
A731

2004, Dec. 30   **Perf. 11½x12**
1564   Vert. strip of 4   2.10   1.10
a.   A731 £5 Shami goat   .25   .25
b.   A731 £15 Awassi ewe   .55   .25
c.   A731 £17 Bull   .65   .30
d.   A731 £18 Shami cow   .70   .35

March 8 Revolution, 42nd
Anniv. — A732

Perf. 12¼x12½
2005, Mar. 8   **Wmk. 403**
1565   A732 £17 multi   .65   .30

Teacher's
Day
A733

2005, Mar. 13   **Perf. 11½x12**
1566   A733 £25 multi   1.00   .50

Mother's
Day — A734

2005, Mar. 21   **Perf. 12x11½**
1567   A734 £18 multi   .70   .35

Arab League,
60th
Anniv. — A735

2005, Mar. 22
1568   A735 £10 multi   .40   .25

National
Day — A736

2005, Apr. 17
1569   A736 £17 multi   .65   .30

Labor
Day — A737

2005, May 1   **Wmk. 403**
1570   A737 £15 multi   .60   .30

Intl. Flower
Show, Damascus
A738

2005, June 15   **Litho.**
1571   Horiz. strip of 5   2.50   1.25
a.   A738 £5 Hyacinth   .25   .25
b.   A738 £10 Sternbergia clusiana   .40   .25
c.   A738 £15 Primula obconica   .55   .30
d.   A738 £17 Primula malacoides   .65   .30
e.   A738 £18 Canaria   .70   .35

Butterflies
A739

No. 1572: a, Papilio ulysses. b, Monarch. c,
Baeotus baeotus. d, Lacewing. e, Tiger
swallowtail.

2005, Aug. 7   **Perf. 12½**
1572   Horiz. strip of 5   2.00   1.00
a.-e.   A739 £10 Any single   .40   .25

52nd Intl.
Damascus
Fair — A740

2005, Sept. 3   **Perf. 12x11½**
1573   A740 £15 multi   .60   .30

Mevlana
Jalal ad-Din
ar-Rumi
(1207-73),
Islamic
Philosopher
A741

2005, Sept. 25   **Perf. 12½x12¼**
1574   A741 £25 multi   1.00   .50

See Afghanistan Nos. 1449-1451, Iran Nos.
2911, and Turkey No. 2971.

World
Tourism
Day
A742

2005, Sept. 27   *Perf. 11½x12*
1575 A742 £17 multi   .65   .30

World Post
Day — A743

2005, Oct. 9   *Perf. 12x11½*
1576 A743 £18 multi   .70   .35

Intl. Children's Day — A744

2005, Oct. 16   *Perf. 12¼x12½*
1577 A744 £17 multi   .65   .30

Corrective Movement, 35th
Anniv. — A745

2005, Nov. 16   *Perf. 11½x12*
1578 A745 £25 multi   1.00   .50

World Summit on the Information
Society, Tunis — A746

2005, Nov. 16   *Perf. 12¼x12½*
1579 A746 £17 multi   .65   .30

Poets
A747

No. 1580: a, Nizar Kabbani (1923-98). b,
Sadalah Wannous (1941-97). c, Omar Abu
Reisheh (1910-90).

2005, Dec. 20   *Perf. 12½x12¼*
1580   Horiz. strip of 3   1.75   .85
   a.   A747 £10 multi   .40   .25
   b.   A747 £17 multi   .65   .30
   c.   A747 £18 multi   .70   .35

Arbor
Day — A748

2005, Dec. 25   **Wmk. 403**
1581 A748 £17 multi   .65   .30

March 8
Revolution, 43rd
Anniv. — A749

Perf. 12x11½
2006, Mar. 8   **Litho.**   **Wmk. 403**
1582 A749 £18 multi   .70   .35

Aleppo,
2006
Capital of
Islamic
Culture
A750

No. 1583: a, £17, Aleppo Castle. b, £18,
Mosque, vert. £25, Emblem and buildings.

2006, Mar. 16   *Perf. 11½x12, 12x11½*
1583 A750   Pair, #a-b   1.40   .70
Imperf
Size: 79x60mm
1584 A750 £25 multi   .95   .50

Pres. Bashir al-Assad Type of 2003
2006   **Wmk. 403**   *Perf. 11¾x11¼*
1585 A707 £1 brt blue   .25   .25
  a.   Dated "2008"   .25   .25
1586 A707 £3 lilac rose   .25   .25
1587 A707 £5 brown   .25   .25
  a.   Dated "2008"   .25   .25
1588 A707 £10 purple   .40   .25
1589 A707 £15 brt blue grn   .60   .30
1590 A707 £17 orange brn   .65   .35
1591 A707 £18 dark blue   .70   .35
1592 A707 £25 blue   .95   .50
1593 A707 £50 lilac   1.90   .95
1594 A707 £100 green   4.00   2.00
  Nos. 1585-1594 (10)   9.95   5.45

Issued: £1, 9/7; £3, 8/24; £5, 8/1; £10, 6/2;
£15, £25, £50, 3/19; £17, 5/11; £18, 6/8; £100,
9/27.

Mother's
Day — A751

Perf. 12x11½
2006, Mar. 21   **Wmk. 403**
1595 A751 £17 multi   .65   .35

National
Day — A752

No. 1596: a, Sultan Pasha al-Atrach (1889-
1982). b, Yousef al-Azmeh (1884-1920). c,
Sheikh Saleh al-Ali (1885-1950). d, Ibrahim
Hanano (1889-1935). e, Ahmad Moraiwed
(1886-1926).

2006, Apr. 17
1596   Horiz. strip of 5   1.90   .95
  a.-e.   A752 £10 Any single   .35   .25

Labor
Day — A753

2006, May 1
1597 A753 £17 multi   .65   .35

Intl. Flower Show, Damascus — A754

No. 1598: a, £5, Hyoscyamus aureus. b,
£10, Cistus salviaefolius.

2006, May 15   *Perf. 11½x12*
1598 A754   Vert. pair, #a-b   .60   .30

2006 World Cup Soccer
Championships, Germany — A755

No. 1599: a, £17, Players, aerial view of
stadium. b, £18, Players under stadium roof.
£50, Players, vert.

2006, June 25   *Perf. 11½x12*
1599 A755   Vert. pair, #a-b   1.40   .70
Imperf
Size: 60x80mm
1600 A755 £50 multi   1.90   .95

Diplomatic Relations Between Syria
and People's Republic of China, 50th
Anniv. — A756

2006, Aug. 1   *Perf. 12½x12¼*
1601 A756 £10 multi   .40   .25

Intl. Year of Deserts and
Desertification — A757

2006, Aug. 13   **Wmk. 403**
1602 A757 £10 multi   .40   .25

53rd Intl.
Damascus
Fair — A758

2006, Sept. 3   *Perf. 12x11½*
1603 A758 £10 multi   .40   .25

A759

World Tourism
Day — A760

2006, Sept. 27   *Perf. 11½x12*
1604 A759 £10 multi   .40 .25
         Perf. 12¼x12½
1605 A760 £10 multi   .40 .25

World Post
Day — A761

2006, Oct. 19   *Perf. 12x11½*
1606 A761 £17 multi   .65 .35

Artists — A762

No. 1607: a, Fateh Almudarres (1922-99). b,
Adham Ismail (1922-63). c, Saeed Makhlouf
(1925-2000). d, Burhan Karkutli (1932-2003).
e, Michael Kirsheh (1900-73).

2006, Nov. 12   Litho.
1607   Horiz. strip of 5   1.90 .95
a.-e. A762 £10 Any single   .35 .25

Corrective Movement, 36th
Anniv. — A763

2006, Nov. 16   *Perf. 12½x12¼*
1608 A763 £15 multi   .60 .30

Arbor Day — A764

2006, Dec. 28   *Perf. 12¼x12½*
1609 A764 £15 multi   .60 .30

Fish
A765

No. 1610: a, Light-colored fish, green and
violet seaweed. b, Dark-colored fish, green
and violet seaweed. c, Light-colored fish,
green seaweed.

2006, Dec. 28   *Perf. 11½x12*
1610 A765 £15 Vert. strip of 3,
         #a-c   1.75 .85

March 8 Revolution, 44th
Anniv. — A766

        Perf. 12¼x12½
2007, Mar. 8   Litho.   Wmk. 403
1611 A766 £17 multi   .65 .35

Mother's
Day — A767

2007, Mar. 21   *Perf. 12½x12¼*
1612 A767 £15 multi   .60 .30

Baath Party,
60th Anniv.
A768

2007, Apr. 7
1613 A768 £25 multi   1.00 .50

National
Day — A769

2007, Apr. 14
1614 A769 £15 multi   .60 .30

Labor
Day — A770

2007, May 1   *Perf. 12½*
1615 A770 £10 multi   .40 .25

Intl. Flower Show, Damascus — A771

No. 1616: a, Freesia. b, Ipomoea purpurea.
o, Plumhago capensis.

2007, June 27   *Perf. 12¼x12½*
1616 A771 £15 Vert. strip of 3,
         #a-c   1.75 .90

Second Term of Pres. Bashar al-
Assad — A772

No. 1617: a, £10, Portrait of Assad. b, £15,
Portrait of Assad, diff.
£25, Assad taking oath, horiz.

        Perf. 12½x12¼
2007, July 17   Litho.   Wmk. 403
1617 A772   Horiz. pair, #a-b   1.00 .50

      Size: 85x70mm
        Imperf
1618 A772 £25 multi   1.00 .50

54th Intl.
Damascus
Fair — A773

      Perf. 12x11½
2007, Aug. 15   Litho.   Wmk. 403
1619 A773 £15 multi   .60 .30

Launch of Sputnik 1, 50th
Anniv. — A774

No. 1620 — Sputnik 1, rocket, "50" and
background color of: a, £15, Green. b, £25,
Brown.

2007, Oct. 4
1620 A774   Horiz. pair, #a-b   1.60 .80

World
Tourism
Day
A775

2007, Nov. 4   *Perf. 11½x12*
1621 A775 £10 multi   .40 .25

World Post
Day — A776

2007, Nov. 4   *Perf. 12½*
1622 A776 £25 multi   1.00 .50

Correctionist Movement, 37th
Anniv. — A777

2007, Nov. 16   *Perf. 12½x12¼*
1623 A777 £15 multi   .60 .30

Arbor Day
A778

2007, Dec. 25   *Perf. 11½x12*
1624 A778 £18 multi   .70 .35

Doctors — A779

No. 1625: a, Dr. Hussny Sabah (1900-86).
b, Dr. Wajieh Al-Barudy (1906-96). c, Dr.
Nadim Shoman (1903-84). d, Dr. Tawfik Izzed-
din (1912-75). e, Dr. Abdussalam Al-Ojaily
(1918-2006).

2007, Dec. 25   **Perf. 12x11½**
1625   Horiz. strip of 5   2.00 1.00
a.-e. A779 £10 Any single   .40 .25

Birds
A780

No. 1626: a, White stork. b, Syrian woodpeckers. c, Shoveler ducks. d, Bee-eater. e,
Turtle dove.

2007, Dec. 30   **Perf. 12½x12¼**
1626   Horiz. strip of 5   2.00 1.00
a.-e. A780 £10 Any single   .40 .25

March 8
Revolution,
45th Anniv.
A781

2008, Mar. 8   **Litho.**
1627 A781 £15 multi   .60 .30

Mother's
Day — A782

2008, Mar. 21   **Perf. 12x11½**
1628 A782 £10 multi   .40 .25

20th Arab
Summit,
Damascus
A783

Emblem, flags and: £10, Map. £25,
Horseman.

2008, Mar. 29   **Perf. 12½x12¼**
1629 A783 £10 multi   .40 .25
          Imperf
          Size: 70x85mm
1630 A783 £25 multi   1.00 .50

Damascus, 2008 Arab Capital of
Culture — A784

Designs: £10, Al-Shamieh School. £15, Al-
Thaheria Library.
£25, Damascus University, vert.

2008, Mar. 30   **Perf. 12¼x12½**
1631-1632 A784   Set of 2   1.00 .50
          Imperf
          Size: 70x84mm
1633 A784 £25 multi   1.00 1.00

National
Day — A785

2008, Apr. 17   **Perf. 12½**
1634 A785 £10 multi   .40 .25

Labor
Day — A786

2008, May 1   **Perf. 12x11½**
1635 A786 £20 multi   .80 .40

Aleppo
University, 50th
Anniv. — A787

2008, May 4   **Wmk. 403**
1636 A787 £15 multi   .60 .30

Intl. Flower
Show,
Damascus
A788

No. 1637: a, Roses. b, Thistles. c, Dahlias.
d, Wallflowers. e, Daisies (margreet).

2008, June 25   **Perf. 12½x12¼**
1637   Horiz. strip of 5   2.00 1.00
a.-e. A788 £10 Any single   .40 .25

Arab Postal Day — A789

No. 1638 — Emblem and: a, Camel caravan. b, Map and pigeon.

2008, Aug. 3   **Perf. 11½**
1638   Horiz. pair   1.40 .70
a.   A789 £15 multi   .60 .30
b.   A789 £20 multi   .80 .40

55th Intl.
Damascus
Fair — A790

2008, Aug. 15   **Perf. 12x11½**
1639 A790 £25 multi   1.00 .50

Hejaz Railway, Cent. — A791

Emblem and: £25, Train on bridge. £50,
Train in tunnel, railway map, vert.

2008, Aug. 19   **Perf. 12½x12¼**
1640 A791 £25 multi   1.00 .50
          Imperf
          Size: 70x85mm
1641 A791 £50 multi   2.00 1.00

2008 Summer Olympics,
Beijing — A792

Designs: £5, Weight lifting. £10, Long jump,
vert.
£25, Swimming.

          Perf. 12¼x12½, 12½x12¼
2008, Aug. 19
1642-1643 A792   Set of 2   .60 .30
          Imperf
          Size: 85x63mm
1644 A792 £25 multi   1.00 .50

Snakes
A793

No. 1645: a, Golan snake. b, Eryx jaculus.
c, Telescopus fallax syriacus.

2008, Sept. 16   **Perf. 12½**
1645   Horiz. strip of 3   2.40 1.25
a.-c. A793 £20 Any single   .80 .40

World Tourism
Day — A794

Designs: £10, Vase. £15, Plate.

2008, Sept. 27   **Perf. 12x11½**
1646 A794 £10 multi   .40 .25
          Size: 32x32mm
          Perf. 12½
1647 A794 £15 multi   .60 .30

World Post
Day — A795

2008, Oct. 19   **Perf. 12x11½**
1648 A795 £18 multi   .80 .40

Corrective Movement, 38th
Anniv. — A796

2008, Nov. 16   **Perf. 12¼x12½**
1649 A796 £10 multi   .45 .25

Arbor
Day
A797

          Perf. 11½x12
2008, Dec. 25   **Litho.   Wmk. 403**
1650 A797 £17 multi   .75 .35

Louis
Braille
(1809-52),
Educator
of the
Blind
A798

2008, Dec. 27
1651 A798 £17 multi   .75 .35

**Pres. Bashir al-Assad Type of 2003
Redrawn**
          Perf. 11¾x11¼
2008-09   **Litho.   Wmk. 403**
With Sans-Serif Numerals
1652 A707 £5 brown   .25 .25
a.   Dated "2010"   .25 .25
1653 A707 £10 purple   .45 .25
a.   Dated "2010"   .45 .25
b.   Dated "2011"   .40 .25

1654 A707 £25 blue — 1.10 .55
a. grn blue, dated "2011" — 1.00 .50
Nos. 1652-1654 (3) — 1.80 1.05

Issued: £25, 2008; £5, £10, 2009. Nos. 1587-1588, 1592 have serifed numerals.

Famous People
A799

No. 1655: a, Mustafa Alaakad (1930-2005), film director and producer. b, Nihad Kalaai (1926-93), artist. c, Maha Al-Saleh (1945-2008), artist. d, Abd Allateef Fathy (1916-86), artist. e, Fahd Kaaekati (1924-82), artist.

2009, Feb. 22 — *Perf. 12½x12¼*
1655 Horiz. strip of 5 — 4.50 2.25
a.-e. A799 £20 Any single — .90 .45

March 8 Revolution, 46th Anniv. — A800

2009, Mar. 8 — *Perf. 12x11½*
1656 A800 £10 multi — .45 .25

Mother's Day — A801

2009, Mar. 21 — *Perf. 12½*
1657 A801 £18 multi — .80 .40

National Day — A802

2009, Apr. 17 — *Perf. 12¼x12½*
1658 A802 £17 multi — .75 .35

Labor Day A803

2009, May 1 — *Perf. 11½x12*
1659 A803 £15 multi — .65 .35

Intl. Flower Fair, Damascus A804

No. 1660: a, Wallflowers. b, Maemozas. c, Irises d, Lilies. e Adalias.

2009, June 15 — **Wmk. 403** — *Perf. 12*
1660 Horiz. strip of 5 — 4.50 2.25
a.-e. A804 £20 Any single — .90 .45

Jerusalem, Capital of Arab Culture A805

2009, Aug. 3 — *Perf. 12½x12¼*
1661 A805 £10 multi — .45 .25

56th Intl. Damascus Fair — A806

2009, Aug. 15 — *Perf. 12x11½*
1662 A806 £15 multi — .65 .35

World Tourism Day — A807

No. 1663 — Sites in Bosra: a, Bab Al-Hawa. b, Mabrak Al-Naqa Mosque. c, Amphitheater.

2009, Sept. 27 — *Perf. 12¼x12½*
1663 A807 £25 Vert. strip of 3, #a-c — 3.25 1.60

Birds — A808

No. 1664: a, Thrasher. b, Redstart. c, Blue-headed yellow wagtail. d, Honeyeater. e, Syrian serin.

2009, Oct. 8 — **Litho.** — *Perf. 12*
1664 Vert. strip of 5 — 4.50 2.25
a.-e. A808 £20 Any single — .90 .45

World Post Day — A809

2009, Oct. 9 — *Perf. 12½*
1665 A809 £50 multi — 2.25 1.10

Corrective Movement, 39th Anniv. — A810

2009, Nov. 16 — *Perf. 12*
1666 A810 £10 multi — .45 .25

Arbor Day — A811

2009, Dec. 31 — **Wmk. 403**
1667 A811 £15 multi — .65 .35

March 8 Revolution, 47th Anniv. A812

2010, Mar. 8 — **Wmk. 403** — *Perf. 12½*
1668 A812 £25 multi — 1.10 .55

Mother's Day — A813

2010, Mar. 21 — *Perf. 12*
1669 A813 £10 multi — .45 .25

National Day — A814

2010, Apr. 17 — *Perf. 12x11½*
1670 A814 £50 multi — 2.25 1.10

Labor Day — A815

2010, May 1 — *Perf. 12½x12¼*
1671 A815 £25 multi — 1.10 .55

Intl. Year of Biodiversity — A816

2010, May 1 — *Perf. 12¼x12½*
1672 A816 £50 multi — 2.25 1.10

2010 World Cup Soccer Championships, South Africa — A817

No. 1673 — Emblem and: a, Players with blue shirts celebrating. b, Players chasing ball. £50, Emblem, World Cup, horiz.

2010, May 1   **Perf. 12¼x12½**
1673 A817 £25 Vert. pair, #a-b   2.25 1.10
Size: 85x67mm
Imperf
1674 A817 £50 multi   2.25 1.10

50th Aleppo Industrial and Agricultural Production Fair — A818

2010, June 24   **Litho.**   **Perf. 12**
1675 A818 £15 multi   .65 .30

Intl. Flower Fair, Damascus A819

No. 1676: a, Calendula. b, Cyclamen. c, Rose. d, Fuchsia. e, Rosa bracteata.

2010, June 25   **Perf. 12½x12¼**
1676   Horiz. strip of 5   5.50 2.75
a.-e. A819 £25 Any single   1.10 .55

Historical and Tourism Sites of Brazil and Syria — A820

2010, June 28   **Perf. 12½x12¼**
1677 A820 £50 multi   2.25 1.10

See Brazil No. 3132.

57th Intl. Damascus Fair — A821

2010, July 14   **Perf. 12x11½**
1678 A821 £50 multi   2.25 1.10

Friendship Between Syria and Chile, 200th Anniv. A822

2010, Sept. 23   **Wmk. 403**   **Perf. 12½**
1679 A822 £25 multi   1.10 .55

Mammals A823

No. 1680: a, Squirrel. b, Hedgehog. c, Ichneumon.

2010, Sept. 23   **Litho.**
1680   Horiz. strip of 3   4.50 2.25
a.-b. A823 £30 Either single   1.25 .65
c. A823 £40 multi   1.75 .85

World Tourism Day — A824

No. 1681: a, Small plaza with flowers. b, Building, dervishes.

2010, Sept. 27   **Perf. 12**
1681 A824 £25 Horiz. pair, #a-b 2.25 1.10

World Post Day — A825

2010, Oct. 9   **Wmk. 403**
1682 A825 £25 multi   1.10 .55

Corrective Movement, 40th Anniv. A826

2010, Nov. 16
1683 A826 £25 multi   1.10 .55

Miniature Sheet

Lawyers — A827

No. 1684: a, Fatihullah al-Sakal (1893-1970). b, Faris al-Khoubi (1877-1962). c, Saeed al-Gazi (1877-1967). d, Abd-el-Salam

al-Tirmanini (1913-2006). e, Mohammad al-Fadel (1919-77). f, Ahmad Fouad al-Koudmani (1905-81)

2010, Dec. 31   **Perf. 12x11½**
1684 A827 £25 Sheet of 6, #a-f   6.50 3.25

March 8 Revolution, 48th Anniv. — A829

Perf. 12x11½
2011, Mar. 8   **Litho.**   **Wmk. 403**
1686 A829 £25 multi   1.10 .55

Mother's Day — A830

2011, Mar. 21
1687 A830 £25 multi   1.10 .55

National Day A831

2011, Apr. 17   **Perf. 11½x12**
1688 A831 £25 multi   1.10 .55

Labor Day A832

2011, May 1   **Wmk. 403**
1689 A832 £50 multi   2.10 1.10

SEMI-POSTAL STAMPS

Nos. 174-185 Srchd. in Red or Black

1926   **Unwmk.**   **Perf. 12½, 13½**
B1 A4 25c + 25c ol blk (R)   2.25 2.00
B2 A4 50c + 25c yel grn   2.25 2.00
B3 A4 75c + 25c brown org   2.25 2.00
B4 A5 1p + 50c magenta   2.25 2.00
B5 A4 1.25p + 50c dp grn (R)   2.25 2.00
B6 A4 1.50p + 50c rose red   2.25 2.00
B7 A4 2p + 75c dk brn (R)   2.25 2.00
B8 A4 2.50p + 75c pck bl (R)   2.25 2.00
B9 A4 3p + 1p org brn (R)   2.25 2.00
B10 A4 5p + 1p violet   2.25 2.00
B11 A4 10p + 2p vio brn   2.25 2.00
B12 A4 25p + 1p ultra (R)   2.25 2.00
Nos. B1-B12 (12)   27.00 24.00
Set, never hinged   36.00

On No. B4 the surcharge is set in six lines to fit the shape of the stamp.

The surcharge was a contribution to the relief of refugees from the Djebel Druze War. See Nos. CB1-CB4.

> Catalogue values for unused stamps in this section, from this point to the end of the section, are for Never Hinged items.

Syrian Arab Republic

Jordanian Flags on Map of Israel, and Arabs — SP1

1965, June 12   **Litho.**   **Perf. 12x11½**
B13 SP1 12½p + 5p multi   .25 .25
B14 SP1 25p + 5p multi   .25 .25

Issued for Palestine Week.

Father with Children and Red Crescent SP2

1968, May   **Litho.**   **Perf. 12½x12**
B15 SP2 12½p + 2½p multi   .25 .25
B16 SP2 27½p + 7½p multi   .25 .25

The surtax was for refugees.

AIR POST STAMPS

    a   b

Nos. 35, 45, 47 Handstamped Type "a" in Violet

1920, Dec.   **Unwmk.**   **Perf. 13½**
C1 A22 1p on 5c   160.00 40.00
C2 A20 5p on 15c   290.00 47.50
C3 A18 10p on 40c   425.00 77.50
Nos. C1-C3 (3)   875.00 165.00

Nos. 36, 46, 48 Overprinted Type "a" in Violet

1921, June 12
C4 A22 1p on 20c   87.50 40.00
C5 A18 5p on 1fr   425.00 150.00
C6 A18 10p on 2fr   425.00 150.00
Nos. C4-C6 (3)   937.50 340.00

Excellent counterfeits exist of Nos. C1-C6.

Nos. 36, 46, 48 Overprinted Type "b"

1921, Oct. 5
C7 A22 1p on 20c   60.00 18.50
C8 A18 5p on 1fr   150.00 37.50
a. Inverted overprint   325.00 240.00
C9 A18 10p on 2fr   200.00 47.50
a. Double overprint   475.00 400.00
Nos. C7-C9 (3)   410.00 103.50

Nos. 92, 94-96 Ovptd.
— c

1922, May 28

C10	A18	2p on 40c	25.00	25.00
a.		Inverted overprint		
C11	A18	3p on 60c	25.00	25.00
C12	A18	5p on 1fr	25.00	25.00
C13	A18	10p on 2fr	25.00	25.00
		Nos. C10-C13 (4)	100.00	100.00

Nos. 116-119 Overprinted Type "c"

1923, Nov. 22

C14	A18	2p on 40c	29.00	29.00
b.		Inverted surcharge		
C15	A18	3p on 60c	29.00	29.00
C16	A18	5p on 1fr	29.00	29.00
C17	A18	10p on 2fr	29.00	29.00
b.		Double overprint		
		Nos. C14-C17 (4)	116.00	116.00

Overprinted "Liabn"

C14a	A18	2p on 40c	400.00	400.00
C15a	A18	3p on 60c	400.00	400.00
C16a	A18	5p on 1fr	400.00	400.00
C17a	A18	10p on 2fr	400.00	400.00

Nos. 137-140 Overprinted Type "c"

1924, Jan. 13

C18	A18	2p on 40c	4.50	4.50
a.		Double overprint	27.50	
C19	A18	3p on 60c	4.50	4.50
a.		Inverted overprint	47.50	
C20	A18	5p on 1fr	4.50	4.50
a.		Double overprint	50.00	30.00
C21	A18	10p on 2fr	4.50	4.50
		Nos. C18-C21 (4)	18.00	18.00

Nos. 152, 154, 157-158 Overprinted

1924, July 17

C22	A18	2p on 40c	7.00	7.00
a.		Inverted overprint	32.50	
C23	A18	3p on 60c	7.00	7.00
a.		Inverted overprint	32.50	
b.		Double overprint	20.00	
C24	A18	5p on 1fr	7.00	7.00
C25	A18	10p on 2fr	7.00	7.00
a.		Inverted overprint	32.50	
		Nos. C22-C25 (4)	28.00	28.00

Regular Issue of 1925 Overprinted in Green

1925, Mar. 1

C26	A4	2p dark brown	2.25	2.25
C27	A4	3p orange brown	2.25	2.25
C28	A4	5p violet	2.25	2.25
C29	A4	10p violet brown	2.25	2.25
		Nos. C26-C29 (4)	9.00	9.00

Nos.180, 182, 183-184 Ovptd. in Red — f

1926

C30	A4	2p dark brown	2.00	2.00
a.		Inverted overprint	40.00	40.00
C31	A4	3p orange brown	2.00	2.00
C32	A4	5p violet	2.50	2.50
a.		Inverted overprint	40.00	40.00
b.		Double overprint	65.00	65.00
C33	A4	10p violet brown	2.50	2.50
a.		Inverted overprint	40.00	40.00
b.		Double overprint	65.00	65.00
		Nos. C30-C33 (4)	9.00	9.00

Nos. C30-C33 received their first airmail use June 16, 1929, at the opening of the Beirut-Marseille line.

For surcharges see Nos. CB1-CB4.

Regular Issue of 1925 Overprinted Type "f" in Red or Black

1929

C34	A4	50c yellow green (R)	1.25	1.25
a.		Inverted overprint	40.00	
b.		Overprint on face and back	22.50	
c.		Double overprint	40.00	
d.		Double overprint, one inverted	60.00	
e.		Pair, one without overprint		
C35	A5	1p magenta (Bk)	1.75	1.75
a.		Reversed overprint		
b.		Red overprint		

C36	A4	25p ultra (R)	5.50	5.50
a.		Inverted overprint	82.50	
b.		Pair, one without overprint		
		Nos. C34-C36 (3)	8.50	8.50

On No. C35, the overprint is vertical, with plane nose down.

No. 197 Overprinted Type "f" in Red

1929, July 9

C37	A4	15p on 25p ultra	4.25	4.25
a.		Inverted overprint		

Air Post Stamps of 1926-29 Ovptd. in Various Colors

1929, Sept. 5

C38	A4	50c yellow grn (R)	3.00	3.00
C39	A5	1p magenta (Bl)	3.00	3.00
C40	A4	2p dk brown (V)	3.00	3.00
C41	A3	3p orange brn (Bl)	3.00	3.00
a.		Inverted overprint	70.00	
C42	A4	5p violet (R)	3.00	3.00
C43	A4	10p violet brn (Bl)	3.00	3.00
C44	A4	25p ultra (R)	3.00	3.00
		Nos. C38-C44 (7)	21.00	21.00

Damascus Industrial Exhibition.

AP1

1930, Jan. 30   Red Surcharge

C45	AP1	2p on 1.25p dp grn	3.00	3.00
a.		Inverted surcharge		
b.		Double surcharge	60.00	

Plane over Homs AP2

Designs: 1pi, City Wall, Damascus. 2pi, Euphrates River. 3pi, Temple Ruins, Palmyra. 5pi, Deir-el-Zor. 10pi, Damascus. 15pi, Aleppo, Citadel. 25pi, Hama. 50pi, Zebdani. 100pi, Telebisse.

1931-33   Photo.   Unwmk.

C46	AP2	50c ocher	1.00	.90
C47	AP2	50c black brn ('33)	1.25	1.00
C48	AP2	1p chestnut brown	1.10	.95
C49	AP2	2p Prus blue	2.75	1.75
C50	AP2	3p blue grn	1.75	1.25
C51	AP2	5p red violet	1.25	1.25
C52	AP2	10p slate grn	1.25	1.25
C53	AP2	15p orange red	2.10	1.50
C54	AP2	25p orange brn	2.75	2.00
C55	AP2	50p black	3.00	2.25
C56	AP2	100p magenta	3.75	2.50
		Nos. C46-C56 (11)	21.95	16.60

Nos. C46 to C56 exist imperforate. Value, $425.

For overprints see Nos. C67-C71, C110-C112, C114-C115, MC1-MC4.

Village of Bloudan AP12

1934, Aug. 2   Engr.   Perf. 12½

C57	AP12	50c yel brown	2.25	2.25
C58	AP12	1p green	2.50	2.50
C59	AP12	2p peacock bl	2.75	2.75
C60	AP12	3p red	3.00	3.00
C61	AP12	5p plum	3.00	3.00
C62	AP12	10p brt violet	27.50	27.50
C63	AP12	15p orange brn	30.00	30.00
C64	AP12	25p dk ultra	35.00	35.00
C65	AP12	50p black	45.00	45.00
C66	AP12	100p red brown	90.00	90.00
		Nos. C57-C66 (10)	241.00	241.00

Proclamation of the Republic. Exist imperf. Value, set $1,200.

Also exists without figures of value. Value, set $900.

Air Post Stamps of 1931-33 Overprinted in Red or Black

1936, Apr. 15   Perf. 13½x13, 13½

C67	AP2	50c black brown	5.25	4.75
C68	AP2	1p chnt brown (Bk)	5.25	4.75
C69	AP2	2p Prus blue	5.25	4.75
C70	AP2	3p blue green	5.25	4.75
C71	AP2	5p red violet (Bk)	5.25	4.75
		Nos. C67-C71 (5)	26.25	23.75

Damascus Fair, May 1936.

Syrian Pavilion at Paris Exposition AP13

1937, July 1   Photo.   Perf. 13½

C72	AP13	½p yellow green	2.75	2.75
C73	AP13	1p green	2.75	2.75
C74	AP13	2p lt brown	2.75	2.75
C75	AP13	3p rose red	2.75	2.75
C76	AP13	5p brown orange	2.75	2.75
C77	AP13	10p grnsh black	4.75	4.75
C78	AP13	15p blue	5.25	5.25
C79	AP13	25p dark violet	6.25	6.25
		Nos. C72-C79 (8)	30.00	30.00

Paris International Exposition. Exist imperf.

Ancient Citadel at Aleppo AP14

Omayyad Mosque and Minaret of Jesus at Damascus AP15

1937   Engr.   Perf. 13

C80	AP14	½p dark violet	.65	.65
C81	AP15	1p black	.65	.65
C82	AP14	2p deep green	.65	.65
C83	AP15	3p deep ultra	.65	.65
C84	AP14	5p rose lake	2.00	2.00
C85	AP15	10p red brown	1.10	1.10
C86	AP15	15p lake brown	4.75	4.75
C87	AP15	25p dark blue	6.00	6.00
		Nos. C80-C87 (8)	16.45	16.45

No. C80 to C87 exist imperforate. Value, set $175.
For overprint see No. C109.

Maurice Noguès and Route of France-Syria Flight — AP16

1938, July   Photo.   Perf. 11

C88	AP16	10p dark green	3.00	3.00
a.		Souv. sheet of 4, perf. 13½	32.50	32.50
b.		Perf. 13½	8.00	8.00

10th anniversary of first Marseille-Beirut flight, by Maurice Noguès.
No. C88a exists imperf.; value $800.

Bridge at Deir-el-Zor AP17

1940   Engr.   Perf. 13

C89	AP17	25c brown black	.25	.25
C90	AP17	50c peacock blue	.25	.25
C91	AP17	1p deep ultra	.30	.30
C92	AP17	2p dk orange brn	.45	.45

C93	AP17	5p green	.95	.95
C94	AP17	10p rose carmine	1.40	1.00
C95	AP17	50p dark violet	3.00	2.25
		Nos. C89-C95 (7)	6.60	5.45

Exist imperf. Value, set $175.

President Taj Eddin Hassani AP18

1942   Litho.   Perf. 11½

C96	AP18	10p blue gray	4.00	4.00
C97	AP18	50p gray lilac	4.25	4.25

Proclamation of Independence by the Allies, Sept. 27, 1941.

President Taj Eddin Hassani AP19   President Hassani and Map of Syria AP20

1942   Photo.

C98	AP19	10p sl grn & yel grn	4.00	4.00

Exists imperforate. Value, $30.

1943   Litho.

C99	AP20	2p dull brown	3.00	3.00
C100	AP20	10p red violet	3.00	3.00
C101	AP20	20p aqua	3.00	3.00
C102	AP20	50p rose pink	3.00	3.00
		Nos. C99-C102 (4)	12.00	12.00

Proclamation of United Syria.

Same, Overprinted with Black Border

1943, May 5

C103	AP20	2p dull brown	3.00	3.00
C104	AP20	10p red violet	3.00	3.00
C105	AP20	20p aqua	3.00	3.00
C106	AP20	50p rose pink	3.00	3.00
		Nos. C103-C106 (4)	12.00	12.00

Mourning for President Hassani. Exist imperf.

President Shukri el Kouatly — AP21

1944

C107	AP21	200p sepia	9.50	7.50
C108	AP21	500p dull blue	14.00	11.00

For overprints see Nos. C113, C116.

Stamps of 1931-44 Overprinted in Black, Blue or Carmine

1944   Perf. 13, 13½, 11½

C109	AP15	10p red brn (Bk)	2.50	2.50
C110	AP2	15p orange red	2.75	2.75
C111	AP2	25p org brown	2.75	2.75
C112	AP2	100p magenta	8.00	6.75
C113	AP21	200p sepia (C)	15.00	12.00
		Nos. C109-C113 (5)	31.00	26.75
		Set, never hinged		50.00

1st congress of Arab lawyers held in Damascus, Sept. 1944.

Nos. C53-C54, C108 Overprinted in Black or Orange

1944

C114	AP2	15p orange red	3.00	3.00
C115	AP2	25p org brown	3.00	3.00
C116	AP21	500p dull blue (O)	22.50	22.50
	Nos. C114-C116 (3)		28.50	28.50
	Set, never hinged		40.00	

See note after No. 299.

President Shukri el Kouatly AP22

1945, Mar. 15   Litho.   Perf. 11½

C117	AP22	5p pale green	.50	.25
C118	AP22	10p dull red	.50	.25
C119	AP22	15p orange	.60	.25
C120	AP22	25p lt blue	1.25	.50
C121	AP22	50p lt violet	1.75	.70
C122	AP22	100p deep brown	3.50	1.25
C123	AP22	200p fawn	8.00	4.00
	Nos. C117-C123 (7)		16.10	7.10
	Set, never hinged		25.00	

Resumption of constitutional government.

> Catalogue values for unused stamps in this section, from this point to the end of the section, are for Never Hinged items.

Plane and Flock of Sheep AP23

Kattineh Dam AP24

Kanawat, Djebel Druze AP25

Sultan Ibrahim Mosque AP26

1946-47   Perf. 13x13½

C124	AP23	3p rose brown	.50	.25
C125	AP23	5p lt bl grn ('47)	.50	.25
C126	AP23	6p dp org ('47)	.50	.25
C127	AP24	10p sl gray ('47)	.35	.25
C128	AP24	15p scarlet ('47)	.35	.25
C129	AP24	25p blue	.45	.25
C130	AP25	50p violet	.75	.25
C131	AP25	100p blue green	1.75	.40
C132	AP25	200p brown ('47)	4.00	1.25
C133	AP26	300p red brn ('47)	16.00	2.50
C134	AP26	500p ol gray ('47)	17.50	3.50
	Nos. C124-C134 (11)		42.65	9.40

For overprints and surcharges see Nos. C135-C139, C148-C152, C157, C172.

No. C129 Overprinted in Red

1946, Apr. 17

C135	AP24	25p blue	2.50	1.00

Evacuation of British and French troops from Syria.

Nos. C129-C131 Overprinted in Magenta

1946, Aug. 28

C136	AP24	25p blue	2.50	1.25
C137	AP24	50p violet	3.00	1.75
C138	AP25	100p blue green	6.00	3.00
	Nos. C136-C138 (3)		11.50	6.00

See note after No. 334.

No. C135 with Additional Overprint in Black

1947, June 10   Perf. 13x13½

C139	AP24	25p blue	2.50	1.25

1st anniv. of the evacuation of British and French troops from Syria.

Window at Kasr El-Heir El-Gharbi AP27

Ram-headed Sphinxes Carved in Ivory, from King Hazael's Bed — AP28

1947, Nov. 15   Litho.   Perf. 11½

C140	AP27	12.50p dark violet	1.50	.50
C141	AP28	50p brown	5.00	2.00
a.	Souv. sheet of 4, #338-339, C140-C141		60.00	60.00

1st Arab Archaeological Cong., Damascus, Nov.

No. C141a sold for 125 piasters.

Kasr El-Heir El-Charqui AP29

Congress Emblem — AP30

1947, Nov. 15

C142	AP29	12.50p olive black	1.00	.50
C143	AP30	50p dull violet	4.50	2.25
a.	Souv. sheet of 4, #340, 341, C142, C143		60.00	60.00

3rd Cong. of Arab Engineers, Damascus, Nov.

No. C143a sold for 125 piasters.

Kouatly Types of Regular Issue

1948, June 22   Litho.   Perf. 10½

C144	A50	12.50p dp bl & vio brn	.65	.25
C145	A51	50p violet brn & grn	2.50	1.00
a.	Souv. sheet, #342, 343, C144, C145, imperf		150.00	150.00

Reelection of Pres. Shukri el Kouatly.

Military Training Types of Regular Issue

1948, June 22

C146	A52	12.50p blue & dk bl	.75	.25
C147	A53	50p green, car & blk	2.00	.80
a.	Souv. sheet of 4, #344, 345, C146, C147, imperf.		140.00	140.00

Inauguration of compulsory military training.

Nos. C124, C126 and C132 to C134 Surcharged with New Value and Bars in Black or Carmine

1948, Oct. 18   Perf. 13x13½

C148	AP23	2.50p on 3p	.30	.25
C149	AP23	2.50p on 6p	.35	.25
C150	AP25	25p on 200p (C)	.80	.25
C151	AP26	50p on 300p	10.00	.75
C152	AP26	50p on 500p	10.00	.75
	Nos. C148-C152 (5)		21.45	2.25

Husni Zayim Type of Regular Issue

1949, June 20   Litho.   Perf. 11½

C153	A54	50p brown	3.75	2.50

Revolution of March 30, 1949.

Pigeons and Globe AP36

Husni Zayim and View of Damascus AP37

1949, June 20   Unwmk.

C154	AP36	12.50p claret	7.50	6.00
C155	AP37	50p gray black	19.00	12.50

UPU, 75th anniv. A souvenir sheet of 4 contains #349, 350, C154, C155. Value $125.

Election Type of Regular Issue

Wmk. 291

1949, Aug. 6   Litho.   Perf. 11½

C156	A57	50p car rose & dk grnsh bl	3.75	2.50
a.	Souv. sheet of 2, #351, C156, imperf.		175.00	175.00

Election of Pres. Husni Zayim.

No. C131 Surcharged with New Value and Bars in Black

1950   Unwmk.   Perf. 13x13½

C157	AP25	2.50p on 100p bl grn	.40	.25

Port of Latakia AP38

1950, Dec. 25   Perf. 11½

C158	AP38	2.50p dull lilac	.50	.25
C159	AP38	10p grnsh blue	1.10	.25
C160	AP38	15p orange brown	2.50	.40
C161	AP38	25p bright blue	5.50	.35
	Nos. C158-C161 (4)		9.60	1.25

Exist imperf. Value, $35. See No. C173. For overprint see No. C169.

Symbolical of Constitution AP39

1951, Apr. 14   Unwmk.

C162	AP39	12.50p crimson rose	.40	.25
C163	AP39	50p brown violet	1.25	1.00

New constitution adopted Sept. 5, 1950. Exist imperf.

Ruins, Palmyra AP40

Citadel at Aleppo AP41

1952, Apr. 22   Litho.   Perf. 11½

C164	AP40	2.50p vermilion	.30	.25
C165	AP40	5p green	.35	.25
C166	AP40	15p violet	.50	.25
C167	AP41	25p deep blue	.75	.35
C168	AP41	100p lilac rose	5.50	1.00
	Nos. C164-C168 (5)		7.40	2.10

Nos. C164-C168 exist imperforate. For overprints see Nos. C170-C171, C186.

Stamps of 1946-52 Overprinted in Black

1953, Feb. 16   Perf. 13x13½, 11½

C169	AP38	10p grnsh blue	2.00	1.00
C170	AP40	15p violet	2.25	1.10
C171	AP41	25p deep blue	3.25	1.60
C172	AP25	50p violet	8.00	2.25
	Nos. C169-C172 (4)		15.50	5.95

UN Social Welfare Seminar, Damascus, Dec. 8-20, 1952.

Type of 1950 and

Post Office, Aleppo AP42

1953, Oct.   Photo.   Perf. 11½

C173	AP38	10p violet blue	.50	.25
C174	AP42	50p red brown	1.60	.30

For overprint see No. C185.

Building at Hama and
PTT Emblem — AP43

University
of Syria,
Damascus
AP44

1954
C175 AP43 5p violet .25 .25
C176 AP43 10p brown .30 .25
C177 AP43 15p dull green .35 .25
C178 AP44 30p dark brown .45 .25
C179 AP44 35p blue .80 .25
C180 AP44 40p orange 1.75 .40
C181 AP44 50p deep plum 1.25 .60
C182 AP44 70p purple 3.25 .70
    Nos. C175-C182 (8) 8.40 2.95

For overprints see UAR Nos. C27-C28.

Monument,
Damascus
Square
AP45

Mosque and Syrian
Flag — AP46

1954, Sept. 2
C183 AP45 40p carmine rose 1.00 .45
C184 AP46 50p green 1.25 .55

Damascus Fair, Sept. 1954.
Nos. C183-C184 exist imperforate.

**Nos. C174 and C168 Overprinted in
Blue or Black**

1954, Oct. 9
C185 AP42 50p red brown (Bl) 1.10 1.00
C186 AP41 100p lilac rose 2.00 1.60

Cotton Festival, Aleppo, October 1954.

Virgin of
Sednaya
Convent
AP47

Omayyad
Mosque
AP48

1955, Mar. 27 Photo. Perf. 11½
C187 AP47 25p deep purple .60 .40
C188 AP47 75p deep blue green 1.75 1.25

50th anniv. of the founding of Rotary Intl.
Exist imperforate.

1955, Mar. 26
C189 AP48 35p cerise .95 .60
C190 AP48 65p deep green 1.75 1.10

1955 Regional Cong. of Rotary Intl.,
Damascus.

**Arab Postal Union Type of Regular
Issue**

1955, Jan. 1 Perf. 13½x13
C191 A69a 5p yellow brown .40 .25

Founding of the APU, July 1, 1954.
For overprints see Nos. C203, C207.

Young
Couple and
View of
Damascus
AP49

60p, Tank and planes leading advancing
troops.

1955, Apr. 16 Litho. Perf. 11½
C192 AP49 40p dark rose lake .60 .30
C193 AP49 60p ultra 2.25 .35

9th anniv. of the evacuation of British and
French troops from Syria.

Mother's Day Type of Regular Issue

1955, May 13 Unwmk.
C194 A70 35p violet 1.00 1.00
C195 A70 40p black 1.50 .95

Issued to publicize Mother's Day.

Emigrants
under Syrian
Flag — AP51

Mother and
Child — AP52

15p, Airplane over globe and fountain.

1955, July 26 Perf. 11½
C196 AP51 5p magenta .55 .25
C197 AP51 15p light blue .75 .40

Emigrants' Congress. Exist imperf.

1955, Oct. 3 Photo.
C198 AP52 25p deep blue .75 .50
C199 AP52 50p plum 1.25 .90

International Children's Day.

Globe,
Scales and
Dove
AP53

1955, Oct. 30
C200 AP53 15p ultra .75 .40
C201 AP53 35p brown black 1.50 .60

10th anniv. of the UN, Oct. 24, 1955.
For overprints see Nos. C221-C222.

Aqueduct Type of Regular Issue

1955, Nov. 21 Litho. Unwmk.
C202 A72 30p dark blue 2.00 1.10

No. C191
Overprinted in
Ultramarine

1955, Dec. 29 Photo. Perf. 13½x13
C203 A69a 5p yellow brown .50 .25

APU Congress, Cairo, Mar. 15, 1955.

Liberation
Monument — AP54

Designs: 65p, Winged figure with shield
and sword. 75p, President Shukri el Kouatly.

1956, Apr. 17 Litho. Perf. 11½
C204 AP54 35p black brown .60 .40
C205 AP54 65p rose red 1.00 .60
C206 AP54 75p dk slate green 1.90 1.00
    Nos. C204-C206 (3) 3.50 2.00

10th anniv. of the evacuation of British and
French troops from Syria.

No. C191
Overprinted in
Black

1956, Apr. 11 Photo. Perf. 13½x13
C207 A69a 5p yellow brown .50 .25

Visit of King Hussein of Jordan to Damascus, Apr. 1956.

President Shukri el
Kouatly — AP55

1956, July 7 Litho. Perf. 11½
C208 AP55 100p black 1.25 1.00
C209 AP55 200p violet 2.50 1.25
C210 AP55 300p dull rose 4.00 2.75
C211 AP55 500p dk bl grn 7.50 5.00
    Nos. C208-C211 (4) 15.25 10.00

**Nos. CB5-CB8 Overprinted with 3
Bars Obliterating Surtax**

1956
C212 SPAP1 25p gray black .60 .25
C213 SPAP2 35p ultra .75 .25
C214 SPAP2 40p rose lilac 1.50 .60
C215 SPAP1 70p Prus green 1.75 .90
    Nos. C212-C215 (4) 4.60 2.00

Gate of Kasr el Heir,
Palmyra — AP56

Designs: 20p, Hand loom and modern mill.
30p, Ox-drawn plow and tractor. 35p, Cogwheels and galley. 50p, Textiles and vase.

1956, Sept. 1 Unwmk.
C216 AP56 15p gray .50 .50
C217 AP56 20p brt ultra .75 .75
C218 AP56 30p blue green 1.00 1.00
C219 AP56 35p blue 1.25 1.25
C220 AP56 50p rose lilac 1.50 1.50
    Nos. C216-C220 (5) 5.00 5.00

3rd International Fair, Damascus.

Nos. C200-
C201
Ovptd. in
Red or
Green

1956, Oct. 30 Photo. Perf. 11½
C221 AP53 15p ultra (R) 1.00 .60
C222 AP53 35p brown blk (G) 1.75 1.25

United Nations, 11th anniversary.

Clay Tablet
with First
Alphabet
AP57

Helmet of Syrian
Legionary and
Ornament — AP58

50p, Lintel from Temple of the Sun, Palmyra.

1956, Oct. 8 Typo.
C223 AP57 20p gray 1.00 .40
C224 AP58 30p magenta 1.25 .50
C225 AP57 50p gray brown 1.90 1.00
    Nos. C223-C225 (3) 4.15 1.90

Intl. Museum Week (UNESCO), Oct. 8-14.

Trees and
Mosque
AP59

1956, Dec. 27 Litho. Perf. 11½
C226 AP59 10p olive bister .40 .25
C227 AP59 50p slate green .90 .45

Day of the Tree, Dec. 27, 1956.
See UAR #36. For overprint see UAR #49.

Mother and
Child
AP60

Sword and
Shields
AP61

SYRIA 687

Design: 60p, Mother holding infant.

1957, Mar. 21   **Unwmk.**
C228 AP60 40p ultra .75 .60
C229 AP60 60p vermilion 1.25 .85

Mother's Day, 1957.

1957, Apr. 20   **Wmk. 291**

Designs: 15p, 35p, Map and "Syria" holding torch. 25p, Pres. Kouatly.

C230 AP61 10p redsh brn .30 .25
C231 AP61 15p bl grn .40 .25
C232 AP61 25p violet .50 .35
C233 AP61 35p cerise .75 .50
C234 AP61 40p gray 1.10 .60
Nos. C230-C234 (5) 3.05 1.95

British-French troop evacuation, 11th anniv.

Ship Loading — AP62

Sugar Production AP63

30p, 40p, Harvesting grain and cotton.

1957, Sept. 1   **Unwmk.**   **Perf. 11½**
C235 AP62 25p magenta .50 .30
C236 AP62 30p light red brown .60 .35
C237 AP63 35p light blue .75 .40
C238 AP62 40p blue green 1.00 .50
C239 AP62 70p olive bister 1.25 .90
Nos. C235-C239 (5) 4.10 2.45

4th International Fair, Damascus.

Arab Lawyers Type of Regular Issue

1957, Sept. 21   **Litho.**   **Wmk. 291**
C240 A76 17½p red .40 .30
C241 A76 40p black .90 .50

Cotton Festival Type of Regular Issue

1957, Oct. 17
C242 A77 17½p org & blk .75 .40
C243 A77 40p lt bl & blk 1.25 .50

Children's Day Type of Regular Issue

1957, Oct. 3
C244 A78 17½p ultra 1.25 .50
C245 A78 20p red brn 1.50 .50

International Children's Day, Oct. 7. For overprints see UAR Nos. C10-C11.

Family Writing and Reading Letters AP64

1957, Oct. 18   **Litho.**   **Unwmk.**
C246 AP64 5p brt grn .40 .25

Intl. Letter Writing Week Oct. 6-12. For overprint see No. C26.

Afro-Asian Jurists Type of Regular Issue

1957, Nov.   **Wmk. 291**   **Perf. 11½**
C247 A80 30p lt bl grn .50 .35
C248 A80 50p lt vio .75 .50

Type of Regular Issue and

Radio, Telegraph and Telephone — AP65

1958, Feb. 12   **Perf. 11½**
C249 A83 10p brt grn .35 .25
C250 AP65 15p brown .40 .25

Syrian Arab Republic
Souvenir Sheet

Syrian Flag — AP67

1961   **Unwmk.**   **Litho.**   **Imperf.**
C253 AP67 50p multi 2.75 2.75

Establishment of Syrian Arab Republic.

"The Beauty of Palmyra" — AP68

Archway, Palmyra — AP69

Design: 200p, 300p, 500p, 1000p, Niche, King Zahir Bibar's tomb.

1961-63   **Litho.**   **Perf. 12x11½**
C255 AP68 45p citron .40 .25
C256 AP68 50p red org .50 .25
C257 AP69 85p sepia 1.00 .30
C258 AP69 100p lilac 1.25 .35
C259 AP69 200p slate grn ('62) 2.25 .65
C260 AP69 300p dk bl ('62) 2.75 .75
C261 AP69 500p lilac ('63) 4.00 1.50
C262 AP69 1000p dk gray ('63) 8.25 2.75
Nos. C255-C262 (8) 20.40 6.80

See Nos. 433-436.

Arab League Building, Cairo, and Emblem — AP70

1962, Apr. 1   **Perf. 12x11½**
C264 AP70 17½p Prus grn & yel grn .30 .25
C265 AP70 22½p dk & lt bl .30 .25
C266 AP70 50p dk brn & dl org .75 .30
Nos. C264-C266 (3) 1.35 .80

Arab League Week, Mar. 22-28.

Malaria Eradication Emblem — AP71

1962, Apr. 7
C267 AP71 12½p ol, lt bl & pur .40 .25
C268 AP71 50p brn, yel & grn .75 .40

WHO drive to eradicate malaria.

Rearing Horse — AP72

Gen. Yusef al-Azmeh AP73

1962, Apr. 17
C269 AP72 45p vio & org .55 .25
C270 AP73 55p vio bl & lt bl .75 .25

Evacuation Day, 1962.

Martyrs' Square Memorial, Globe and Handshake AP74

Design: 40p, 45p, Eastern Gate at Fair.

1962, Aug. 25   **Litho.**   **Perf. 12x11½**
C271 AP74 17½p rose cl & brn .30 .25
C272 AP74 22½p ver & magenta .30 .25
C273 AP74 40p vio brn & lt brn .30 .25
C274 AP74 45p grnsh bl & lt grn .50 .25
Nos. C271-C274 (4) 1.40 1.00

9th International Damascus Fair.

Cotton and Cogwheel AP75

1962, Sept. 20   **Perf. 12x11½**
C275 AP75 12½p multi .35 .25
C276 AP75 50p multi .50 .25

Cotton Festival, Aleppo. See Nos. 455-456.

President Type of Regular Issue

1962, Dec. 14   **Unwmk.**
C278 A88 50p bl gray & tan .75 .25

1st anniv. of the election of Pres. Nazem el-Kodsi.

Queen Zenobia of Palmyra — AP76

1962, Dec. 28   **Perf. 12x11½**
C279 AP76 45p violet 1.00 .25
C280 AP76 50p rose red 1.00 .25
C281 AP76 85p blue green 1.00 .30
C282 AP76 100p rose claret 1.25 .55
Nos. C279-C282 (4) 4.25 1.35

Saad Allah El Jabri — AP77

1962, Dec. 30   **Litho.**
C283 AP77 50p dull blue .50 .25

Saad Allah El Jabri (1894-1947), a leader in Syria's struggle for independence.

Woman from Mohardé — AP78

Regional Costumes: 40p, Marje Sultan. 45p, Kalamoun. 55p, Jabal-Al-Arab. 60p, Afrine. 65p, Hauran.

1963   **Perf. 12**
Costumes in Original Colors
C285 AP78 40p pale lil & blk .55 .25
C286 AP78 45p pink & blk .60 .25
C287 AP78 50p lt grn & blk .60 .25
C288 AP78 55p lt bl & blk .75 .30
C289 AP78 60p tan & blk .80 .30
C290 AP78 65p pale grn & blk 1.00 .30
Nos. C285-C290 (6) 4.30 1.75

Hunger Type of Regular Issue

50p, Wheat emblem & bird feeding nestlings.

Perf. 12x11½
1963, Mar. 21   **Unwmk.**
C291 A91 50p ver & blk .45 .25
a. Souv. sheet of 2, #453, C291, imperf. 1.50 1.50

FAO "Freedom from Hunger" campaign.

Eagle in
Flight — AP79

1963, Apr. 18   **Litho.**
C292 AP79 12½p brt grn   .30 .25
C293 AP79 50p lilac rose   .35 .25
Revolution of Mar. 8, 1963.

Faris el
Khouri — AP80

Arms and
Wreath — AP81

1963, Apr. 27   **Perf. 12x11½**
C294 AP80 17½p gray   .30 .25
C295 AP81 22½p bl grn & blk   .30 .25
Evacuation Day, 1963.

abu-al-Ala al-
Maarri — AP82

1963, Aug. 19   **Perf. 12x11½**
C296 AP82 50p violet blue   .40 .25
abu-al-Ala al-Maarri (973-1057), poet and
philosopher.

Copper Pitcher,
Arch and
Fair — AP83

1963, Aug. 25
C297 AP83 37½p ultra, yel & brn   .45 .25
C298 AP83 50p brt bl, yel & brn   .50 .25
10th International Damascus Fair.

Centenary
Emblem — AP84

50p, Centenary emblem and globe.

1963, Sept. 19   **Litho.**
C299 AP84 15p chlky bl, red & blk   .40 .25
C300 AP84 50p yel grn, blk & red   .50 .25
Centenary of the International Red Cross.

Abou Feras al
Hamadani
AP85

1963, Nov. 13   **Perf. 12x11½**
C301 AP85 50p yel ol & dk brn   .50 .25
Abou Feras (932-968), poet.

Heads of Three
Races and
Flame — AP86

1964, Jan. 6   **Unwmk.**
C302 AP86 17½p multi   .30 .25
C303 AP86 22½p grn, blk & red   .30 .25
C304 AP86 50p vio, blk & red   .40 .25
   a.   Souv. sheet of 3   1.10 1.10
   Nos. C302-C304 (3)   1.00 .75
Universal Declaration of Human Rights,
15th anniv. #C304a contains 3 imperf. stamps
similar to #C302-C304 with simulated
perforations.

Flag,
Torch and
Map of
Arab
Countries
AP87

1964, Mar. 8   **Unwmk.**   **Perf. 11½**
C305 AP87   15p multi   .30 .25
C306 AP87 17½p multi   .30 .25
C307 AP87 22½p multi   .30 .25
   Nos. C305-C307 (3)   .90 .75
Revolution of Mar. 8, 1963, 1st anniv.

Kaaba,
Mecca,
and
Mosque,
Damascus
AP88

1964, Mar. 14   **Litho.**   **Perf. 11½x12**
C308 AP88 12½p bl & blk   .30 .25
C309 AP88 22½p rose lil & blk   .30 .25
C310 AP88 50p lt grn & blk   .35 .25
   Nos. C308-C310 (3)   .95 .75
First Arab Conference of Moslem Wakf Min-
isters, Damascus.

Young
Couple
and View
of
Damascus
AP89

1964, Apr. 17   **Unwmk.**
C311 AP89 20p blue   .30 .25
C312 AP89 25p rose car   .30 .25
C313 AP89 60p emerald   .35 .25
   Nos. C311-C313 (3)   .95 .75
Evacuation Day, Apr. 17, 1964.

Abul Kasim
(Albucasis)
AP90

1964, Apr. 21   **Perf. 12x11½**
C314 AP90 60p brown   .40 .25
4th Arab Congress of Dental and Oral Surgery, Damascus.

Mosaic,
Chahba,
Thalassa
AP91

Perf. 11½x12
1964, June-July   **Litho.**
C315 AP91 27½p car rose   .30 .25
C316 AP91 45p gray   .30 .25
C317 AP91 50p brt grn   .40 .25
C318 AP91 55p slate grn   .40 .25
C319 AP91 60p ultra   .50 .25
   Nos. C315-C319 (5)   1.90 1.25

Hanging Lamp,
Fair
Emblem — AP92

Globe and Fair
Emblem — AP93

1964, Aug. 28   **Perf. 12x11½**
C320 AP92 20p multi   .30 .25
C321 AP93 25p multi   .30 .25
11th International Damascus Fair.

Industrial and
Agricultural
Symbols — AP94

1964, Sept. 22   **Litho.**   **Unwmk.**
C322 AP94 25p multi   .30 .25
**Same Overprinted with two Red
Lines in Arabic**
C323 AP94 25p multi   .30 .25
Cotton Festival, Aleppo. Overprint on No.
C323 translates: "Market for Industrial and
Agricultural Products."

Arms of
Syria and
Aero Club
Emblem
AP95

1964, Oct. 8   **Litho.**   **Perf. 11½x12**
C324 AP95 12½p emer & blk   .30 .25
C325 AP95 17½p crim & blk   .30 .25
C326 AP95 20p brt bl & blk   .40 .25
   Nos. C324-C326 (3)   1.00 .75
10th anniversary of Syrian Aero Club.

Arab Postal Union
Emblem — AP96

1964, Nov. 12   **Litho.**   **Perf. 12x11½**
C327 AP96 12½p org & blk   .30 .25
C328 AP96 20p emer & blk   .30 .25
C329 AP96 25p dp lil rose & blk   .30 .25
   Nos. C327-C329 (3)   .90 .75
10th anniv. of the permanent office of the
APU.

Grain and Hands
Holding
Book — AP97

1964, Nov. 30   **Unwmk.**
C330 AP97 12½p emer & blk   .30 .25
C331 AP97 17½p mar & blk   .30 .25
C332 AP97 20p dp bl & blk   .30 .25
   Nos. C330-C332 (3)   .90 .75
Burning of the library of Algiers, 6/7/62.

Tennis
Player — AP98

17½p, Wrestlers and drummer. 20p, Weight
lifter. 100p, Wrestlers and drummer.

1965, Feb. 7   **Perf. 12x11½**
C333 AP98 12½p multi   .30 .25
C334 AP98 17½p multi   .30 .25
C335 AP98 20p multi, horiz.   .30 .25
   Nos. C333-C335 (3)   .90 .75
Souvenir Sheet
C336 AP98 100p multi   1.25 1.25
18th Olympic Games, Tokyo, 10/10-25/64.
#C336 contains one 45x33mm stamp.

Ramses
Battling
the
Hittites
AP99

Design: 50p, Two statues of Ramses II.

1965, Mar. 21   Litho.   Perf. 11x12
C337 AP99 22½p emer, ultra & blk   .30 .25
C338 AP99 50p ultra, emer & blk   .40 .25
UNESCO world campaign to save historic
monuments in Nubia.

Al-Sharif Al-
Radi — AP100

1965, Apr. 3   Litho.   Perf. 12x11½
C339 AP100 50p gray brn   .50 .25
5th Poetry Festival held in Latakia; Al-Sharif
Al-Radi (970-1015), poet.

Hippocrates and Avicenna — AP101

1965, Apr. 19   Perf. 11½
C340 AP101 60p dl bl grn & blk   .55 .30
"Medical Days of the Near and Middle East,"
a convention held at Damascus Apr. 19-25.

Dagger in Map of
Palestine
AP102

1965, May 15
C341 AP102 12½p multi   .90 .25
C342 AP102 60p multi   1.00 .25
Deir Yassin massacre, Apr. 9, 1948.

ITU Emblem, Old and New
Communication Equipment — AP103

Perf. 11½x12
1965, May 24   Litho.   Unwmk.
C343 AP103 12½p multi   .30 .25
C344 AP103 27½p multi   .30 .25
C345 AP103 60p multi   .50 .25
Nos. C343-C345 (3)   1.10 .75
ITU, centenary.

Syrian
Welcoming
AP104

1965, Aug.   Unwmk.   Perf. 12x11½
C346 AP104 25p pur & multi   .30 .25
C347 AP104 100p blk & multi   .75 .25
Issued to welcome Arab immigrants.

Bridge and
Gate — AP105

27½p, Fair emblem. 60p, Jug & ornaments.

1965, Aug. 28   Litho.
C348 AP105 12½p blk, brt ultra &
brn   .30 .25
C349 AP105 27½p multi   .30 .25
C350 AP105 60p multi   .40 .25
Nos. C348-C350 (3)   1.00 .75
12th International Damascus Fair.

Fair Emblem and
Cotton
Pickers — AP106

1965, Sept. 30   Perf. 12x11½
C351 AP106 25p olive & multi   .30 .25
10th Cotton Festival, Aleppo.

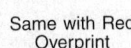

Same with Red
Overprint

1965, Sept. 30
C352 AP106 25p olive & multi   .30 .25
Industrial and Agricultural Fair, Aleppo.

View of
Damascus
and ICY
Emblem
AP107

1965, Oct. 24   Perf. 11½x12
C353 AP107 25p multi   .30 .25
International Cooperation Year.

Radio
Transmitter,
Globe, Syrian
Flag and View of
Damascus
AP108

1966, Feb. 16   Litho.   Perf. 12x11½
C354 AP108 25p multi   .30 .25
C355 AP108 60p multi   .35 .25
3rd Conference of Arab Information Ministers, Damascus, Feb. 14-18.

Hand (shaped
like a dove)
Holding
Flower — AP109

Design: 17½p, Stylized people, horiz.

1966, Mar. 8   Perf. 12x11½, 11½x12
C356 AP109 12½p multi   .30 .25
C357 AP109 17½p multi   .30 .25
C358 AP109 50p multi   .75 .25
Nos. C356-C358 (3)   1.35 .75
March 8 Revolution, 3rd anniversary.

Statues of
Ramses II from
Abu
Simbel — AP110

1966, Mar. 15   Perf. 12x11½
C359 AP110 25p dark blue   .30 .25
C360 AP110 60p dark slate green   .40 .25
Arab "Save the Nubian Monument Week."

UN Headquarters Building and
Emblem — AP111

Design: 100p, UN Flag.

1966, Apr. 11   Litho.   Perf. 11½x12
C361 AP111 25p blk & gray   .30 .25
C362 AP111 50p blk & pale grn   .35 .25
Souvenir Sheet
Imperf
C363 AP111 100p yel, brt bl &
blk   1.25 1.25
20th anniv. (in 1965) of the UN. No. C363
contains one stamp 42x36mm.

Marching
Workers
AP112

1966, May 1   Litho.   Perf. 11½x12
C364 AP112 60p multi   .40 .25
Issued for May Day.

Inauguration of WHO Headquarters,
Geneva — AP113

1966, May 3
C365 AP113 60p blk, bl & yel   .40 .25

Map of Arab
Countries and
Traffic
Signals — AP114

1966, May 4   Perf. 12x11½
C366 AP114 25p gray & multi   .30 .25
Issued to publicize Traffic Day.

Astarte & Tyche,
1st cent.
Basrelief,
Palmyra
AP115

1966, July 26   Litho.   Perf. 12x11½
C367 AP115 50p pale brn   .35 .25
C368 AP115 60p slate   .50 .25

Symbolic Flag,
Wheat, Globe
and Fair Emblem
AP116

1966, Aug. 25   Litho.   Perf. 12x11½
C369 AP116 12½p multi   .30 .25
C370 AP116 60p multi   .35 .25
13th Intl. Damascus Fair, Aug. 25-Sept. 20.

Shuttle and
Symbols of
Agriculture,
Industry and
Cotton — AP117

1966, Sept. 9   Litho.   Perf. 12x11½
C371 AP117 50p sil, blk & plum   .35 .25
11th Cotton Festival, Aleppo.

Symbolic Water Cycle — AP118

1966, Oct. 24   Litho.   Perf. 12x11½
C372 AP118 12½p emer, blk & org .30 .25
C373 AP118 60p ultra, blk & org .35 .25

Hydrological Decade (UNESCO), 1965-74.

Abd-el Kader — AP119

1966, Nov. 7
C374 AP119 12½p brt grn & blk .30 .25
C375 AP119 50p brt grn & red brn .35 .25

Transfer from Damascus to Algiers of the ashes of Abd-el Kader (1807?-1883), Emir of Mascara.

Clasped Hands over Map of South Arabia — AP120

1967, Feb. 8   Litho.   Perf. 12x11½
C376 AP120 20p pink & multi .30 .25
C377 AP120 20p pink & multi .30 .25

3rd Congress of Solidarity with the Workers and People of Aden, Damascus, Jan. 15-18.

Pipelines and Pigeons AP121

1967, Mar. 8   Litho.   Perf. 12x11½
C378 AP121 17½p multi .30 .25
C379 AP121 25p multi .30 .25
C380 AP121 27½p multi .30 .25
　Nos. C378-C380 (3) .90 .75

4th anniversary of March 8 Revolution.

Soldier, Woman and Man Holding Flag — AP122

1967, Apr. 17   Litho.   Perf. 12x11½
C381 AP122 17½p green .30 .25
C382 AP122 25p dp claret .30 .25
C383 AP122 27½p vio blue .30 .25
　Nos. C381-C383 (3) .90 .75

21st anniv. of the evacuation of British and French troops from Syria.

Workers' Monument, Damascus AP123

1967, May 1
C384 AP123 12½p bl grn .30 .25
C385 AP123 50p brt pink .35 .25

Issued for Labor Day, May 1.

Fair Emblem and Gate, Minaret, Omayyad Mosque — AP124

1967, Aug. 25   Litho.   Perf. 12x12½
C386 AP124 12½p multi .30 .25
C387 AP124 60p multi .35 .25

14th Intl. Damascus Fair, Aug. 25-Sept. 20.

Statue of Ur-Nina and ITY Emblem AP125

1967, Sept. 2   Perf. 12½x12
C388 AP125 12½p lt bl, brt rose lil & blk .30 .25
C389 AP125 25p lt bl, ver & blk .30 .25
C390 AP125 27½p lt bl, dk bl & blk .30 .25
　Nos. C388-C390 (3) .90 .75
Souvenir Sheet
Imperf
C391 AP125 60p lt bl & vio bl 1.00 1.00

Intl. Tourist Year.

Cotton Boll and Cogwheel Segment AP126

1967, Sept. 28   Litho.   Perf. 12x12½
C392 AP126 12½p ocher, brn & blk .30 .25
C393 AP126 60p ap grn, brn & blk .40 .25

12th Cotton Festival, Aleppo.

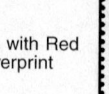

Same with Red Overprint

1967, Sept. 28
C394 AP126 12½p multi .30 .25
C395 AP126 60p multi .35 .25

Industrial and Agricultural Production Fair, Aleppo.

Head of Young Man, Amrith, 4th-5th Century B.C. — AP127

100p, 500p, Bronze bust of a Princess, 2nd cent.

1967, Oct. 7
C396 AP127 45p orange .30 .25
C397 AP127 50p brt pink .40 .25
C398 AP127 60p grnsh bl .50 .25
C399 AP127 100p green .60 .30
C400 AP127 500p brn red 2.25 1.50
　Nos. C396-C400 (5) 4.05 2.55

Ibn el-Naphis AP128

1967, Dec. 28   Litho.   Perf. 12x12½
C401 AP128 12½p grn & org .30 .25
C402 AP128 27½p dk bl & lil rose .30 .25

700th death anniv. of Ibn el-Naphis (1210-1288), Arab physician.

Human Rights Flame and People AP129

Design: 100p, Heads of various races and Human Rights flame.

1968, Feb. 21   Litho.   Perf. 12½x12
C403 AP129 12½p lt grnsh bl, bl & blk .30 .25
C404 AP129 60p pink, blk & dl red .40 .25
Souvenir Sheet
Imperf
C405 AP129 100p multi 1.00 1.00

20th anniv. of the Declaration of Human Rights; Intl. Human Rights Year.

Old Man and Woman Reading AP130

Design: 17½p, 45p, Torch and book.

1968, Mar. 3   Perf. 12x12½
C406 AP130 12½p rose car, blk & org .30 .25
C407 AP130 17½p multi .30 .25
C408 AP130 25p grn, blk & org .30 .25
C409 AP130 45p bl & multi .30 .25
　Nos. C406-C409 (4) 1.20 1.00

Issued to publicize the literacy campaign.

Euphrates Dam Project — AP131

1968, Apr. 11   Litho.   Perf. 12½x12
C410 AP131 12½p multi .30 .25
C411 AP131 17½p multi .30 .25
C412 AP131 25p multi .30 .25
　Nos. C410-C412 (3) .90 .75

Proposed dam across Euphrates River.

WHO Emblem and Avenzoar (1091-1162) — AP132

WHO Emblem and: 25p, Rhazes (Razi, 850-923). 60p, Geber (Jabir 721-776).

1968, June 10   Litho.   Perf. 12½x12
C413 AP132 12½p brn, grn & sal .30 .25
C414 AP132 25p brn, gray & sal .30 .25
C415 AP132 60p brn, gray bl & sal .40 .25
　Nos. C413-C415 (3) 1.00 .75

WHO, 20th anniv.

Monastery of St. Simeon the Stylite AP133

Designs: 17½p, El Tekkieh Mosque, Damascus, vert. 22½p, Columns, Palmyra, vert. 45p, Chapel of St. Paul, Bab Kisan. 50p, Theater of Bosra.

Perf. 12½x12, 12x12½
1968, Oct. 10   Litho.
C416 AP133 15p pale grn & rose brn .30 .25
C417 AP133 17½p redsh brn & dk red brn .30 .25
C418 AP133 22½p grn gray & dk red brn .30 .25
C419 AP133 45p yel & dk red brn .30 .25
C420 AP133 50p lt bl & dk red brn .30 .25
　Nos. C416-C420 (5) 1.50 1.25

Hammer Throw — AP134

Designs: 25p, Discus. 27½p, Running. 60p, Basketball. 50p, Polo, horiz.

1968, Dec. 19   Litho.   Perf. 12x12½
C421 AP134 12½p brt pink, blk & grn .30 .25
C422 AP134 25p red, grn & blk .30 .25

C423 AP134 27½p blk, gray & grn .30 .25
C424 AP134 60p multi .30 .25
Nos. C421-C424 (4) 1.20 1.00

Souvenir Sheet
Imperf

C425 AP134 50p multi 1.00 1.00

19th Olympic Games, Mexico City, Oct. 12-27. #C425 contains one 52x80mm horiz. stamp.

Construction of Damascus Intl. Airport — AP135

1969, Jan. 20 Litho. Perf. 12½x12
C426 AP135 12½p yel, brt bl & grn .30 .25
C427 AP135 17½p org, pur & lt grn .30 .25
C428 AP135 60p car, blk & yel .40 .25
Nos. C426-C428 (3) 1.00 .75

Baal Shamin Temple, Palmyra AP136

Designs: 45p, Interior of Omayyad Mosque, Damascus, vert. 50p, Amphitheater, Palmyra. 60p, Khaled ibn al-Walid Mosque, Homs, vert. 100p, Ruins of St. Simeon, Djebel Samaan.

1969, Jan. 20 Photo. Perf. 12x11½
C429 AP136 25p multi .30 .25
C430 AP136 45p bl & multi .30 .25
C431 AP136 50p multi .30 .25
C432 AP136 60p multi .30 .25
C433 AP136 100p vio & multi .60 .25
Nos. C429-C433 (5) 1.80 1.25

Workers, ILO Emblem, Cogwheel AP137

Design: 60p, ILO emblem.

1969, May 1 Litho. Perf. 12½x12
C434 AP137 12½p multi .30 .25
C435 AP137 27½p multi .30 .25

Miniature Sheet
Imperf

C436 AP137 60p multi .60 .60

ILO, 50th anniv. No. C436 contains one stamp 53½x47mm.

Ballet Dancers AP138

Designs: 12½p, Russian dancers. 45p, Lebanese singer and dancers. 55p, Egyptian dancer and musicians. 60p, Bulgarian dancers.

1969, Aug. 25 Litho. Perf. 12½x12
C437 AP138 12½p multi .30 .25
C438 AP138 27½p bl & multi .30 .25
C439 AP138 45p multi .30 .25

C440 AP138 55p multi .30 .25
C441 AP138 60p multi .40 .25
a. Strip of 5, #C437-C441 1.75 1.75

16th Intl. Fair, Damascus, Aug. 25-Sept. 20.

Children Playing — AP139

1969, Oct. 6 Litho. Perf. 12x12½
C442 AP139 12½p aqua, dk bl & emer .30 .25
C443 AP139 25p brn red, dk bl & lt vio .30 .25
C444 AP139 27½p ultra, dk bl & gray .30 .25
Nos. C442-C444 (3) .90 .75

Issued for Children's Day.

Fortuna — AP140

Designs: 25p, Seated woman from Palmyra. 60p, Motherhood. All sculptures from Greco-Roman period.

1969, Oct. 10
C445 AP140 17½p blk, yel grn & grn .30 .25
C446 AP140 25p dk brn, red brn & lt grn .30 .25
C447 AP140 60p blk, lt gray & bl gray .40 .25
Nos. C445-C447 (3) 1.00 .75

9th Intl. Congress for Classical Archaeology, Oct. 11-20.

Damascus Agricultural Museum — AP141

1969, Dec. 24 Litho. Perf. 12½x12
C448 AP141 12p Cock .30 .25
C449 AP141 17½p Cow .30 .25
C450 AP141 20p Corn .30 .25
C451 AP141 50p Olives .30 .25
a. Strip of 4, #C448-C451 + label 1.25 1.25

Weather Balloon Tracking and UN Emblem AP142

1970, Mar. 23 Litho. Perf. 12½x12
C452 AP142 25p blk, sl grn & yel .30 .25
C453 AP142 60p blk, dk bl & yel .35 .25

10th World Meteorological Day.

Lenin (1870-1924) AP143

1970, Apr. 15 Litho. Perf. 12x12½
C454 AP143 15p red & dk brn .30 .25
C455 AP143 60p red & grn .35 .25

Workers' Syndicate Emblem AP144

1970, May 1 Litho. Perf. 12½x12
C456 AP144 15p dk brn & brt grn .30 .25
C457 AP144 60p dk brn & org .35 .25

Issued for Labor Day.

Radar and Open Book AP145

1970, May 17
C458 AP145 15p brt pink & blk .30 .25
C459 AP145 60p bl & blk .35 .25

International Telecommunications Day.

Opening of UPU Headquarters, Bern — AP146

1970, May 30
C460 AP146 15p multi .30 .25
C461 AP146 60p multi .35 .25

"Zahier Piebers and Maarouf" — AP147

Folk Tales: 10p, Two warriors on horseback. 15p, Two warriors on white horses. 20p, Lady and warrior on horseback. 60p, Warriors, woman and lion.

1970, Aug. 12 Litho. Perf. 12½
C462 AP147 5p lt bl & multi .30 .25
C463 AP147 10p lt bl & multi .30 .25
C464 AP147 15p lt bl & multi .30 .25
C465 AP147 20p lt bl & multi .30 .25
C466 AP147 60p lt bl & multi .50 .25
a. Strip of 5, #C462-C466 1.75 1.75

Al Aqsa Mosque on Fire AP148

1970, Aug. 21 Perf. 12½x12
C467 AP148 15p multi .30 .25
C468 AP148 60p multi .35 .25

1st anniv. of the burning of Al Aqsa Mosque, Jerusalem.

Wood Carving — AP149

Handicrafts: 20p, Jewelry. 25p, Glass making. 30p, Copper engraving. 60p, Shellwork.

1970, Aug. 25 Perf. 12½
C469 AP149 15p vio & multi .30 .25
C470 AP149 20p ol & multi .30 .25
C471 AP149 25p multi .30 .25
C472 AP149 30p multi .30 .25
C473 AP149 60p multi .50 .25
a. Strip of 5, #C469-C473 1.75 1.75

17th Intl. Fair, Damascus.

Education Year Emblem AP150

1970, Nov. 2 Litho. Perf. 12
C474 AP150 15p dl grn & dk brn .30 .25
C475 AP150 60p vio bl & dk brn .35 .25

International Education Year.

UN Emblem, Symbols of Progress, Justice and Peace AP151

1970, Nov. 3
C476 AP151 15p lt ultra, red & blk .30 .25
C477 AP151 60p bl, yel & blk .35 .25

United Nations, 25th anniversary.

Khaled ibn-al-Walid AP152

1970-71 Perf. 12x11½, 12½x12½
C478 AP152 45p brt pink .30 .25
C479 AP152 50p green .35 .25
C480 AP152 60p vio brn .50 .25
C481 AP152 100p dk bl .60 .25
C482 AP152 200p grnsh gray ('71) 1.10 .50
C483 AP152 300p lil ('71) 1.50 .95
C484 AP152 500p gray ('71) 3.00 1.60
Nos. C478-C484 (7) 7.35 4.05

Woman with Garland
AP153

1971, Apr. 17   **Litho.**   **Perf. 12**
C485 AP153 15p dl red, blk & grn   .30 .25
C486 AP153 60p grn, blk & dk red   .35 .25
   25th anniv. of the evacuation of British and French troops from Syria.

People Dancing Around Globe
AP154

1971, Apr. 28   **Litho.**   **Perf. 12½x12**
C487 AP154 15p vio & multi   .30 .25
C488 AP154 60p grn & multi   .30 .25
   Intl. Year against Racial Discrimination.

Pres. Hafez al Assad and Council Chamber — AP155

1971, Sept. 30   **Litho.**   **Perf. 12½x12**
C489 AP155 15p grn & multi   .30 .25
C490 AP155 65p bl & multi   .60 .25
   People's Council and presidential election.

Gamal Abdel Nasser (1918-1970), President of Egypt — AP156

1971, Oct. 17   **Perf. 12x12½**
C491 AP156 15p lt ol grn & brn   .30 .25
C492 AP156 20p gray & brn   .30 .25

Globe and Arrows AP157

1972, May 17   **Litho.**   **Perf. 11½**
C493 AP157 15p bl, vio bl & pink   .30 .25
C494 AP157 50p org, yel & sep   .30 .25
   4th World Telecommunications Day.

Pres. Hafez al Assad — AP158

1972, July   **Litho.**   **Perf. 12x11½**
C495 AP158 100p dk grn   .60 .25
C496 AP158 500p dk brn   3.00 1.10

Airline Emblem, Eastern Hemisphere AP159

1972, Sept. 16   **Litho.**   **Perf. 12x11½**
C497 AP159 15p blk, lt bl & Prus bl   .30 .25
C498 AP159 50p blk, gray & Prus bl   .30 .25
   Syrianair, Syrian airline, 25th anniversary.

Pottery — AP160

   Handicraft Industries: 25p, Rugs. 30p, Metal (weapons). 35p, Straw (baskets, mats). 100p, Wood carving.

1976, July   **Litho.**   **Perf. 12x12½**
C499 AP160 10p multi   .30 .25
C500 AP160 25p multi   .30 .25
C501 AP160 30p multi   .30 .25
C502 AP160 35p multi   .30 .25
C503 AP160 100p multi   .50 .30
 a.   Strip of 5, #C499-C503   1.75 1.75
   23rd Intl. Damascus Fair.

Pres. Hafez al Assad AP161

1978, Sept.   **Litho.**   **Perf. 12½x12**
C504 AP161 25p sil & multi   .50 .25
C505 AP161 35p grn & multi   .50 .25
C506 AP161 60p gold & multi   .50 .25
   Nos. C504-C506 (3)   1.50 .75
   Reelection of Pres. Assad. See No. 820.

AIR POST SEMI-POSTAL STAMPS

   Nos. C30-C33 Surcharged Like Nos. B1-B12 in Black and Red

1926, Apr. 1   **Unwmk.**   **Perf. 13½**
CB1 A4   2p + 1p dk brown   3.00 2.75
CB2 A4   3p + 2p org brn   2.75 2.75
CB3 A4   5p + 3p violet   2.75 2.75
CB4 A4   10p + 5p vio brn   2.75 2.75
   Nos. CB1-CB4 (4)   11.25 11.00
   The new value is in red and rest of the surcharge in black on Nos. CB1-CB3. The entire surcharge is black on No. CB4.
   See note following Nos. B1-B12.

> Catalogue values for unused stamps in this section, from this point to the end of the section, are for Never Hinged items.

Fair Entrance SPAP1

Industry, Handicraft and Farming SPAP2

   Design: 70p+10p, Fairgrounds.

Perf. 11½, Imperf.
1955   **Litho.**   **Unwmk.**
CB5 SPAP1 25p + 5p gray black   .40 .40
CB6 SPAP2 35p + 5p ultra   .40 .40
CB7 SPAP2 40p + 10p rose lilac   .60 .60
CB8 SPAP1 70p + 10p Prus grn   1.10 1.10
   Nos. CB5-CB8 (4)   2.50 2.50
   Intl. Fair, Damascus, Sept. 1955.
   For overprint see Nos. C212-C215.

United Nations Refugee Emblem SPAP3

1966, Dec. 12   **Litho.**   **Perf. 11½x12**
CB9 SPAP3 12½p + 2½p ultra & blk   .25 .25
CB10 SPAP3   50p + 5p grn & blk   .50 .25
   UN Day, 21st anniv.; Refugee Week, Oct. 24-31.

POSTAGE DUE STAMPS

Under French Occupation

French Offices in the Turkish Empire, 1902-03, Surcharged

1920   **Unwmk.**   **Perf. 14x13½**
J1 A3 1p on 10c rose red   160.00 160.00
J2 A3 2p on 20c brn vio   160.00 160.00
J3 A3 3p on 30c lil   160.00 160.00
J4 A4 4p on 40c red & pale bl   160.00 160.00
   Nos. J1-J4 (4)   640.00 640.00

Postage Due Stamps of France, 1893-1920, Surcharged in Black or Red

1920
J5 D2 1p on 10c brown   3.25 3.25
J6 D2 2p on 20c ol grn (R)   3.25 3.25
 a.   "PIASTRE"   900.00 900.00
J7 D2 3p on 30c red   3.25 3.25
 a.   "PIASTRE"
J8 D2 4p on 50c brn vio   4.75 4.75
 a.   3p in setting of 4p   525.00 525.00
   Nos. J5-J8 (4)   14.50 14.50

1921-22
J9 D2 50c on 10c brown   1.40 1.40
 a.   "75" instead of "50"   90.00
 b.   "CENTI MES" instead of "CEN-TIEMES"   7.50
J10 D2 1p on 20c ol grn   1.40 1.40
J11 D2 2p on 30c red   3.25 3.25
J12 D2 3p on 50c brn vio   3.50 3.50
J13 D2 5p on 1fr red brn, straw   5.00 5.00
   Nos. J9-J13 (5)   14.55 14.55

D3

1921   **Perf. 11½**
Red Surcharge
J14 D3 50c on 1p black   3.75 3.75
J15 D3 1p on 1p black   3.75 3.75

D4

1922
J16 D4 2p on 5m rose   10.00 6.50
 a.   "AX" of "TAXE" inverted   175.00 175.00
J17 D4 3p on 1p gray bl   15.00 12.00

French Mandate

Postage Due Stamps of France, 1893-1920, Surcharged

1923
J18 D2 50c on 10c brown   1.50 1.50
J19 D2 1p on 20c ol grn   2.25 2.25
J20 D2 2p on 30c red   1.90 1.90
J21 D2 3p on 50c vio brn   1.90 1.90
J22 D2 5p on 1fr red brn, straw   3.75 3.75
   Nos. J18-J22 (5)   11.30 11.30

Postage Due Stamps of France, 1893-1920, Surcharged

1924
J23 D2 50c on 10c brown   1.00 1.00
J24 D2 1p on 20c ol grn   1.00 1.00
J25 D2 2p on 30c red   1.10 1.10
J26 D2 3p on 50c vio brn   1.50 1.50
J27 D2 5p on 1fr red brn, straw   1.50 1.50
   Nos. J23-J27 (5)   6.10 6.10

Postage Due Stamps of France, 1893-1920, Surcharged

1924
J28 D2 50c on 10c brown   .75 .75
J29 D2 1p on 20c ol grn   .75 .75
J30 D2 2p on 30c red   1.00 1.00
J31 D2 3p on 50c vio brn   1.40 1.40
J32 D2 5p on 1fr red brn, straw   1.75 1.75
   Nos. J28-J32 (5)   5.65 5.65

Water Wheel at Hama D5

Bridge at Antioch — D6

   Designs: 2p, The Tartous. 3p, View of Banias. 5p, Chevaliers' Castle.

1925 Photo. Perf. 13½

J33	D5	50c brown, *yel*	.25	.25
J34	D6	1p violet, *rose*	.25	.25
J35	D5	2p black, *blue*	.55	.55
J36	D5	3p black, *red org*	1.25	1.25
J37	D5	5p black, *bl grn*	1.50	1.50
		Nos. J33-J37 (5)	3.80	3.80

D7

Lion — D8

1931

J38	D7	8p black, *gray blue*	3.50	3.50
J39	D8	15p black, *dull rose*	6.00	6.00

Catalogue values for unused stamps in this section, from this point to the end of the section, are for Never Hinged items.

Syrian Arab Republic

D9

1965 Unwmk. Litho. Perf. 11½x11

J40	D9	2½p violet blue	.25	.25
J41	D9	5p black brown	.25	.25
J42	D9	10p green	.25	.25
J43	D9	17½p carmine rose	.25	.25
J44	D9	25p blue	.25	.25
		Nos. J40-J44 (5)	1.25	1.25

MILITARY STAMPS

Free French Administration

Syria No. 222 Surcharged in Black

1942 Unwmk. Perf. 13

M1	A10	50c on 4p yel org	9.00	8.00

Lebanon Nos. 155 and 142A Surcharged in Carmine

M2	A13	1fr on 5p grnsh bl	9.00	8.00
M3	A25	2.50fr on 12½p dp ultra	9.00	8.00

Camel Corps, Palmyra — M1

Perf. 11½x11¾

1942 Litho.

Bistre Background

M4	M1	1fr deep rose	.75	.55
M5	M1	1.50fr bright violet	.75	.55
M6	M1	2fr orange	.75	.55
M7	M1	2.50fr brown gray	1.00	.85
M8	M1	3fr Prussian blue	1.25	1.10
M9	M1	4fr deep green	2.00	1.60
M10	M1	5fr deep claret	2.25	1.75
		Nos. M4-M10 (7)	8.75	6.95

Nos. M4 to M10 exist imperforate. Value: unused $125; never hinged $200.
For surcharges see Nos. MB1-MB2, MC10.

MILITARY SEMI-POSTAL STAMPS

Free French Administration

RÉSISTANCE

Military Stamps of 1942 Surcharged in Black

+9F

1943 Unwmk. Perf. 11½

MB1	M1	1fr + 9fr deep rose	15.00	17.50
MB2	M1	5fr + 20fr deep claret	15.00	17.50

MILITARY AIR POST STAMPS

Free French Administration

Syria Nos. C55-C56 Srchd. in Black, Carmine or Orange

1942 Unwmk. Perf. 13

MC1	AP2	4fr on 50p blk (C)	8.25	8.25
MC2	AP2	6.50fr on 50p blk (C)	8.25	8.25
MC3	AP2	8fr on 50p blk (O)	8.25	8.25
MC4	AP2	10fr on 100p mag	8.25	8.25
		Nos. MC1-MC4 (4)	33.00	33.00

Winged Shields and Cross of Lorraine MAP1

1942 Litho. Perf. 11½

MC5	MAP1	6.50fr pale pink & rose car	4.00	4.00
MC6	MAP1	10fr lt bl & dl vio	4.50	4.50

Nos. MC5 and MC6 exist imperforate.
See Nos. MC7-MC8. For surcharges see Nos. MC9, MCB1-MCB2.

Souvenir Sheets

1942 Without Gum Perf. 11

MC7		Sheet of 2	37.50	40.00
a.		MAP1 6.50fr pale pink & rose carmine	15.00	15.00
b.		MAP1 10fr lt bl & dl violet	15.00	15.00

Imperf

MC8		Sheet of 2	37.50	40.00
a.		MAP1 6.50fr pale pink & rose carmine	15.00	15.00
b.		MAP1 10fr lt bl & dl violet	15.00	15.00

No. MC5 Surcharged in Rose Carmine With New Value and Bars

1942 Perf. 11½

MC9	MAP1	4fr on 6.50fr	4.00	4.00

Military Stamp of 1942 Srchd. in Black

1943

MC10	M1	4fr on 3fr Prus blue	2.50	2.50

MILITARY AIR POST SEMI-POSTAL STAMPS

Free French Administration

Military Air Post Stamps of 1942 Surcharged in Black

1943 Unwmk. Perf. 11½

MCB1	MAP1	6.50fr + 48.50fr	35.00	37.50
MCB2	MAP1	10fr + 100fr	35.00	37.50

POSTAL TAX STAMPS

Revenue Stamps Overprinted in Red or Black

R1

طابع الجيش السوري
٥ ق. س.
a b

1945 Unwmk. Perf. 10½x11½

RA1	R1(a)	5p dark blue (R)	100.00	22.50

On Stamps Overprinted

RA2	R1(a)	5p dk bl (Bk+Bk)	90.00	27.50
RA3	R1(a)	5p dk bl (Bk+R)	90.00	27.50
RA4	R1(a)	5p dk bl (R+R)	100.00	27.50
RA5	R1(b)	5p dk bl (R+R)	95.00	24.00

On Stamps Overprinted

RA6	R1(a)	5p dk bl (Bk+Bk)	90.00	30.00
RA7	R1(a)	5p dk bl (Bk+R)	90.00	30.00
RA8	R1(a)	5p dk bl (R+R)	90.00	30.00
RA9	R1(b)	5p dk bl (R+R)	110.00	30.00
		Nos. RA1-RA9 (9)	855.00	249.00

The tax was for national defense.

طابع
الجيش السوري
٥ ق. س.

R2

Revenue Stamp Surcharged in Black

1945 Unwmk. Perf. 11

RA10	R2	5p on 25c on 40c rose red	90.00	32.50

The surcharge reads "Tax (postal) for Syrian Army."

Revenue Stamp Surcharged in Black

1945

RA11	R2	5p on 25c on 40c rose red	100.00	32.50

No. RA11 Overprinted in Black

RA12	R2	5p on 25c on 40c	80.00	

The tax on #RA11-RA12 was for the army. This overprint exists on No. RA10.

Revenue stamps without overprints occasionally were used as postage on covers through at least 1948.

ISSUES OF THE ARABIAN GOVERNMENT

The following issues replaced the British Military Occupation (E.E.F.) stamps (Palestine Nos. 2-14) which were used in central and eastern Syria from Nov. 1918 until Jan. 1920.

Turkish Stamps of 1913-18 Handstamped in Various Colors

Also Handstamp Surcharged with New Values as

1 millieme | 1 Egyptian piaster

The Seal reads: "Hakuma al Arabie" (The Arabian Government)

Perf. 11½, 12, 12½, 13½

1919-20 Unwmk.

1	A24	1m on 2pa red lil (254)	.85	.85
2	A25	1m on 4pa dk brn (255)	.85	.85
3	A26	2m on 5pa vio brn (256)	1.40	1.40
4	A15	2m on 5pa on 10pa gray grn (291)	.95	.95
5	A18	2m on 5pa ocher (304)	22.50	22.50
6	A41	2m on 5pa grn (345)	275.00	250.00
7	A18	2m on 5pa ocher (378)	47.50	47.50

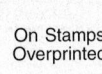
طابع
الجيش السوري
٥ ق. س.

8	A28	4m on 10pa grn (258)	6.50	6.50
9	A28	4m on 10pa grn (271)	.85	.85
10	A22	4m on 10pa bl grn (329)	1.75	1.75
11	A41	4m on 10pa car (346)	37.50	37.50
12	A23	4m on 10pa grn (415)	7.25	7.25
13	A44	4m on 10pa grn (424)	1.25	1.25
14	A11	4m on 10pa on 20pa vio brn (B38)	1.25	1.25
15	A41	4m on 10pa car (B42)	.85	.85
16	SP1	4m on 10pa red vio (B46)	1.40	1.40
17	SP1	4m on 10pa on 20pa car rose (B47)	1.40	1.40
19	A21	5pa ocher (317)		
21	A21	20pa car rose (153)	92.50	110.00
22	A29	20pa red (259)	1.40	1.40
23	A29	20pa red (272)	275.00	275.00
24	A17	20pa car (299)	2.75	2.75
25	A21	20pa car rose (318)	2.75	2.75
26	A22	20pa car rose (330)	11.00	11.00
27	A21	20pa car rose (342)	5.00	5.00
28	A41	20pa ultra (347)	2.75	2.75
29	A16	20pa mag (363)	11.00	11.00
30	A17	20pa car (371)	2.75	2.75
31	A18	20pa car (379)	7.75	7.75
32	A45	20pa dp rose (425)	3.75	3.75
33	A21	20pa car rose (B8)	2.75	2.75
34	A22	20pa car rose (B33)	2.75	2.75
35	A22	20pa car rose (B36)	13.00	13.00
36	A41	20pa ultra (B43)	.55	.55
37	A16	20pa mag (P140)	2.75	2.75
38	A17	20pa car (P144)	250.00	250.00
39	A30	1pi bl (260)	2.75	2.75
40	A31	1pi on 1½pi car & blk (261)	375.00	375.00
41	A30	1pi bl (273)	92.50	92.50
42	A30	1pi on 1pi bl (273)	125.00	125.00
43	A17	1pi blue (300)	4.75	4.75
44	A18	1pi blue (307)	57.50	57.50
45	A22	1pi ultra (331)	5.75	5.75
46	A21	1pi ultra (343)	10.00	10.00
47	A41	1pi vio & blk (348)	1.75	1.75
48	A18	1pi brt bl (389)	5.75	5.75
49	A46	1pi dl vio (426)	1.75	1.75
50	A47	1pi on 50pa ultra (428)	1.10	1.10
51	A21	1pi ultra (B9)	6.00	6.00
52	A22	1pi ultra (B15)	10.00	10.00
53	A18	1pi brt bl (B21)	6.00	6.00
54	A18	1pi blue (B23)	15.00	15.00
55	A22	1pi ultra (B34)	12.50	12.50
56	A41	1pi vio & blk (B44)	2.75	2.75
57	A33	2pi grn & blk (263)	72.50	72.50
58	A13	2pi brn org (289)	2.00	2.00
59	A18	2pi slate (308)	27.50	27.50
60	A18	2pi slate (314)	27.50	27.50
61	A21	2pi bl blk (320)	5.25	5.25
62	A17	2pi org (373)	4.25	4.25
63	A18	5pi brn (310)	12.00	12.00
64	A22	5pi dl vio (333)	23.50	23.50
65	A41	5pi yel brn & blk (349)	4.75	4.75
66	A41	5pi yel brn & blk (418)	4.75	4.75
67	A53	5pi on 2pa Prus bl (547)	7.75	7.75
68	A21	5pi dk vio (B10)	275.00	275.00
69	A17	5pi lil rose (B20)	47.50	47.50
70	A41	5pi yel brn & blk (B45)	4.75	4.75
72	A50	10pi dk grn (431)	130.00	130.00
73	A50	10pi dk vio (432)	110.00	110.00
74	A50	10pi dk brn (433)	375.00	
75	A18	10pi org brn (B2)	350.00	350.00
76	A37	25pi ol grn (267)	350.00	350.00
77	A40	25pi on 200pi brn & blk (287)	500.00	500.00
78	A21	25pi brn (303)	375.00	375.00
79	A51	25pi car, straw (434)	92.50	92.50
81	A52	50pi ind (438)	200.00	200.00

The variety "surcharge omitted" exists on Nos. 1-5, 12-13, 16, 32, 49-50, 67.

A few examples of No. 377 (50pi) and No. 269 (100pi) were overprinted but not regularly issued.

Overprinted

The Inscription reads "Hakum Soria Arabie" (Syrian-Arabian Government)

On Stamp of 1913

83	A26	2m on 5pa vio brn (256)	5.00	5.00

On Stamp of 1916-18

84	A45	20pa dp rose (425)	.55	.55

A1

		Litho.	**Perf. 11½**	
85	A1	5m rose	.55	.55
a.		Tête bêche pair	22.50	10.00
b.		Imperf.		

Independence Issue

Arabic Overprint in Green:
"Souvenir of Syrian Independence March 8, 1920"

86	A1	5m rose	250.00	150.00
a.		Tête bêche pair		
b.		Inverted overprint	375.00	375.00

A2

		Litho.		
		Size: 22x18mm		
87	A2	⅒pi lt brn	.25	.25
		Size: 28x22mm		
88	A2	⅖pi yel grn	.30	.25
a.		⅖pi yellow (error)	10.00	10.00
89	A2	⅗opi yellow	.40	.30
90	A2	1pi gray blue	.35	.25
91	A2	2pi blue grn	2.00	1.00
		Size: 31x25mm		
92	A2	5pi vio brn	2.75	1.50
93	A2	10pi gray	2.75	2.00
		Nos. 86-93 (8)	258.80	155.55

Nos. 86-93 exist imperf.
For overprint see No. J5.

PF1　　　　　PF2

Revenue Stamps Surcharged as on Postage Stamps, for Postal Use

1920		**Unwmk.**	**Perf. 11½**	
94	PF1	5m on 5pa red	.50	.50
95	PF2	1m on 5pa red	.50	.25
96	PF2	2m on 5pa red	.40	.25
97	PF2	1pi on 5pa red	1.00	.65

Surcharged in Syrian Piasters

98	PF2	2pi on 5pa red	.35	.25
99	PF2	3pi on 5pa red	.35	.25
		Nos. 94-99 (6)	3.10	2.00

ISSUES OF THE ARABIAN GOVERNMENT POSTAGE DUE STAMPS

Postage Due Stamps of Turkey, 1914, Handstamped and Surcharged

No. J1　　　　　No. J4

1920		**Unwmk.**	**Perf. 12**	
J1	D1	2m on 5pa claret	6.75	6.75
J2	D2	20pa red	6.75	6.75
J3	D3	1pi dark blue	6.75	6.75
J4	D4	2pi slate	6.75	6.75
		Nos. J1-J4 (4)	27.00	27.00

Type of Regular Issue
Perf. 11½
Litho.

J5	A2	1pi black	1.25	1.25

UNITED ARAB REPUBLIC

> Catalogue values for unused stamps in this section are for Never Hinged items.

See Egypt for stamps of types A1, A4, A7, A8, A14, A17, A19, A20, A24 with denomination in "M" (milliemes).

Issues for Syria

Linked Maps of Egypt and Syria — A1

		Perf. 11½		
1958, Feb. 1		**Unwmk.**	**Litho.**	
1	A1	12½p yellow & green	.25	.25

Establishment of UAR. See No. C1.
See also Egypt No. 436.

Freedom Monument A2

1958, May				
2	A2	5p yel & vio	.40	.25
3	A2	15p yel grn & brn red	.65	.35
		Nos. 2-3,C2-C3 (4)	3.00	1.35

British-French troop evacuation, 12th anniv.

Bronze Rattle — A3　　Hand Holding Torch, Broken Chain and Flag — A4

Antique Art: 15p, Goddess. 20p, Lamgi Mari. 30p, Mithras fighting bull. 40p, Aspasia. 60p, Minerva. 75p, Flask. 100p, Enameled Vase. 150p, Mosaic from Omayyad Mosque, Damascus.

1958, Sept. 14		**Litho.**	**Perf. 12**	
4	A3	10p lt ol grn	.25	.25
5	A3	15p brown org	.25	.25
6	A3	20p rose lilac	.25	.25
7	A3	30p lt brown	.25	.25
8	A3	40p gray	.30	.25
9	A3	60p green	.50	.25
10	A3	75p blue	.80	.30
11	A3	100p brown car	1.20	.40
12	A3	150p dull purple	2.25	.60
		Nos. 4-12 (9)	6.05	2.80

Archaeological collections and museums.

1958, Oct. 14			**Perf. 11½**	
13	A4	12.50p car rose		.25 .25

Establishment of Republic of Iraq.
See Egypt No. 454.

Syria No. 411
Overprinted

1958, Oct. 6		**Wmk. 291**	**Perf. 11½**	
13A	A78	12½p olive	55.00	55.00
		Nos. 13A,C10-C11 (3)	145.00	145.00

Intl. Children's Day, 1958.

View of Damascus — A5

1958, Dec. 10			**Unwmk.**	
14	A5	12½p green		.25 .25

4th Near East Regional Conference, Damascus, Dec. 10-20. See No. C14.

Secondary School, Damascus — A6

1959, Feb. 26		**Litho.**	**Perf. 12**	
15	A6	12½p dull green		.25 .25

See No. 26.

Flags of
UAR and
Yemen
A7

Perf. 13x13½
1959, Mar. 8 **Photo.** **Wmk. 318**
16 A7 12½p grn, red & blk .25 .25
1st anniversary of United Arab States.
See Egypt No. 465.

Arms of
UAR — A8

Mother and
Children — A9

Perf. 12x11½
1959, Feb. 22 **Litho.** **Wmk. 291**
17 A8 12½p grn, blk & red .25 .25
United Arab Republic, 1st anniv.
See Egypt No. 462.

1959, Mar. 21 **Perf. 11½**
18 A9 15p carmine rose .25 .25
19 A9 25p dk slate grn .30 .25
Arab Mother's Day, Mar. 21.
For overprints see Nos. 41-42.

Syria No. 378 Surcharged "U.A.R." in
Arabic and English, and New Value in
Red
1959, Apr. 6 **Photo.** **Unwmk.**
20 A68 2½p on 1p olive .25 .25

Type of 1959 and

A10

Boys' School, Damascus — A11

Designs: 5p, 7½p, 10p, Various
arabesques. 12½p, St. Simeon's Monastery.
17½p, Hittin school. 35p, Normal School for
Girls, Damascus.

1959-61 **Unwmk.** **Litho.** **Perf. 11½**
21 A10 2½p violet .25 .25
22 A10 5p olive bister .25 .25
23 A10 7½p ultra .25 .25
24 A10 10p bl grn .25 .25
25 A11 12½p lt bl ('61) .25 .25
26 A6 17½p brt lilac ('60) .25 .25
27 A11 25p brt grnsh bl .30 .25
28 A11 35p brown ('60) .40 .25
Nos. 21-28 (8) 2.20 2.00

Male Profile and
Fair Emblem — A12

Fair Emblem and Globe — A13

1959, Aug. 30 **Unwmk.** **Perf. 11½**
30 A12 35p gray, grn & vio .40 .25
Souvenir Sheet
Imperf
31 A13 30p dl yel & grn 1.50 1.50
6th International Damascus Fair.

Shield and
Cogwheel — A14

Perf. 13½x13
1959, Oct. 20 **Wmk. 328**
32 A14 50p sepia .60 .35
Issued for Army Day, 1959.
See Egypt No. 491.

Syria Nos.
408 and
386 with
Red
Overprint
Similar to

1959 **Unwmk.** **Litho.** **Perf. 11½**
33 A75 15p gray .25 .25
Photo.
34 A69 50p dk grn .60 .40
The overprints differ in size and lettering:
No. 33 is 28x8½mm; No. 34 is 21x6mm. A
period follows "R" on Nos. 33-34. The Arabic
overprint means "United Arab Republic."
See Nos. C26-C28.

Cogwheel, Wheat
and Cotton — A15

1959, Oct. 30 **Litho.**
35 A15 35p gray, bl & ocher .40 .25
Industrial and Agricultural Production Fair,
Aleppo. For overprint see No. 46.

**Type of Syria Air Post, 1956,
Inscribed "U.A.R."**
1959, Dec. 31 **Unwmk.** **Perf. 13½**
36 AP59 12½p gray ol & bister .25 .25
Day of the Tree. For overprint see No. 49.

A. R.
Kawakbi — A16

1960, Jan. 11 **Perf. 12x11½**
37 A16 15p dark green .25 .25
Kawakbi, Arabic writer, 50th death anniv.

Arms and
Flag — A17

Perf. 13½x13
1960, Feb. 22 **Photo.** **Wmk. 328**
38 A17 12½p red & dk sl grn .25 .25
United Arab Republic, 2nd anniversary.
See Egypt No. 499.

Diesel Train and Old Town — A18

Perf. 11½x11
1960, Mar. 15 **Unwmk.**
39 A18 12½p brn & brt bl .35 .25
Construction of the Latakia-Aleppo railroad.

Arab
League
Center,
Cairo,
and Arms
of UAR
A19

Perf. 13x13½
1960, Mar. 22 **Photo.** **Wmk. 328**
40 A19 12½p dl grn & blk .25 .25
Opening of the Arab League Center and the
Arab Postal Museum in Cairo.
See Egypt No. 502.

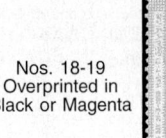

Nos. 18-19
Overprinted in
Black or Magenta

Wmk. 291
1960, Apr. 3 **Litho.** **Perf. 11½**
41 A9 15p car rose .25 .25
42 A9 25p dk slate grn (M) .35 .25
Issued for Arab Mother's Day.

Refugees
Pointing
to Map of
Palestine
A20

Perf. 13x13½
1960, Apr. 7 **Photo.** **Wmk. 328**
43 A20 12½p car rose .40 .25
44 A20 50p green .70 .30
World Refugee Year, 7/1/59-6/30/60.
See Egypt Nos. 503-504.

A21

Perf. 11½
1960, May 12 **Unwmk.** **Litho.**
45 A21 12½p vio, rose & pale grn .25 .25
Evacuation Day, 1960.

No. 35 Overprinted
in Red

1960
46 A15 35p gray, bl & ocher .30 .25
1960 Industrial and Agricultural Production
Fair, Aleppo.

Souvenir Sheet

Flags in Symbolic Design — A22

1960 **Unwmk.** **Imperf.**
47 A22 100p gray, brn & lt bl 1.50 1.50
7th Intl. Damascus Fair.

Child — A23

1960   Litho.   Perf. 11½
48   A23 35p dk grn & fawn   .40 .25
Issued for Children's Day.

No. 36 Overprinted in Carmine

1960   Unwmk.   Perf. 11½
49   AP59 12½p gray ol & bis   .25 .25
Issued to publicize the Day of the Tree.

Coat of Arms   Cogwheel, Retort
and Victory   and Ear of
Wreath — A24   Wheat — A25

Perf. 13½x13
1961, Feb. 22   Photo.   Wmk. 328
50   A24 12½p lt vio   .25 .25
United Arab Republic, 3rd anniversary.
See Egypt No. 517.

Perf. 11½
1961, June 8   Unwmk.   Litho.
51   A25 12½p multi   .25 .25
Industrial and Agricultural Fair, Aleppo.

UAR SEMI-POSTAL STAMP

Catalogue values for unused
stamp in this section is for a Never
Hinged item.

Postal
Emblem — SP1

Perf. 13½x13
1959, Jan. 2   Photo.   Wmk. 318
B1   SP1 20p + 10p bl grn, red &
     blk   .40 .40
Issued for Post Day. The surtax went to the
social fund for postal employees.
See Egypt No. B18 for similar stamp with
denomination in "M" (milliemes).

UAR AIR POST STAMPS

Catalogue values for unused
stamps in this section are for
Never Hinged items.

Map Type of Regular Issue
Perf. 11½
1958, Apr. 3   Unwmk.   Litho.
C1   A1 17½p ultra & brn   .35 .25

Broken
Chain,
Dove and
Olive
Branch
AP1

1958, May 17
C2   AP1 35p rose & blk   .70 .35
C3   AP1 45p bl & brn   1.25 .40
British-French troop evacuation, 12th anniv.

Scout
Putting
up
Tent
AP2

1958, Aug. 31   Perf. 12
C4   AP2 35p dk brn   3.00 1.50
C5   AP2 40p ultra   4.00 2.00
3rd Pan-Arab Boy Scout Jamboree.

View of Damascus Fair — AP3

UAR Flag and Fair Emblem — AP4

Designs: 30p, Minaret, vase and emblem,
vert. 45p, Mosque, chimneys and wheel, vert.

1958, Sept. 1   Litho.   Perf. 11½
C6   AP3 25p vermilion   .70 .60
C7   AP3 30p brt bl grn   1.00 .60
C8   AP3 45p violet   .80 .55
     Nos. C6-C8 (3)   2.50 1.75
Souvenir Sheet
Imperf
C9   AP4 100p brt grn, car &
     blk   50.00 50.00
Fifth Damascus International Fair.

Syria Nos. C244-
C245 Overprinted

1958, Oct. 6   Wmk. 291   Perf. 11½
C10 A78 17½p ultra   45.00 45.00
C11 A78 20p red brn   45.00 45.00
International Children's Day.

Cotton and
Cotton
Material — AP5

1958, Oct. 10   Unwmk.   Perf. 12
C12 AP5 25p brn & yel   .40 .40
C13 AP5 35p brn & brick red   .70 .50
Cotton Festival, Aleppo, Oct. 9-11.

Type of Regular Issue, 1958
1958, Dec. 10
C14 A5 17½p brt vio   .25 .25

Children and
Glider — AP6

1958, Dec. 1   Litho.   Perf. 12
C15 AP6 7½p gray green   .50 .30
C16 AP6 12½p olive   2.00 1.25
1958 glider festival.

UN
Emblem — AP7

1958, Dec. 10
C17 AP7 25p dl pur   .25 .25
C18 AP7 35p light blue   .35 .25
C19 AP7 40p brn red   .45 .30
     Nos. C17-C19 (3)   1.05 .80
10th anniv. of the signing of the Universal
Declaration of Human Rights.

Globe, Radio and Telegraph — AP8

1959, Mar. 1   Perf. 12
C20 AP8 40p grn & blk   .50 .35
Arab Union of Telecommunications.
See Egypt No. 464 for similar stamp with
denomination in "M" (milliemes).

Same Overprinted in Red

1959, Mar. 1
C21 AP8 40p grn & blk   .40 .25
2nd Conference of the Arab Union of Telecommunications, Damascus.

Laurel and Map
of Syria — AP9

Design: 35p, Torch and broken chain.

1959, Apr. 17   Perf. 12x11½
C22 AP9 15p ocher & green   .25 .25
C23 AP9 35p gray & carmine   .40 .25
British-French troop evacuation, 13th anniv.

"Emigration" — AP10

1959, Aug. 4   Unwmk.   Perf. 11½x12
C24 AP10 80p brt grn, blk & red   .70 .40
Convention of the Assoc. of Arab Emigrants
in the US.

Refinery
AP11

1959, Aug. 12   Litho.
C25 AP11 50p bl, blk & car   .90 .40
Opening of first oil refinery in Syria.

Syria Nos. C246 and C181-C182
Overprinted like Nos. 33-34
1959   Perf. 11½
C26 AP64 5p bright green   .25 .25
C27 AP44 50p deep plum   .40 .25
C28 AP44 70p purple   .70 .30
     Nos. C26-C28 (3)   1.35 .80
The overprints differ in size and lettering:
#C26 is 25½x9½mm; #C27-C28 are 27x8mm.
A period follows "R" on #C27-C28.

Cotton Boll and   Boy and Building
Thread — AP12   Blocks — AP13

1959, Oct. 1   Litho.   Perf. 11½
C29 AP12 45p gray blue   .40   .25
C30 AP12 50p claret   .40   .30

Cotton Festival, Aleppo.
For overprints see Nos. C33-C34.

1959, Oct. 5
C31 AP13 25p dl lil, red & dk bl   .25   .25

Issued for Children's Day.

Crane and Compass
AP14

1960   Unwmk.   Perf. 11½
C32 AP14 50p lt brn, crim & blk   .40   .30

7th Damascus International Fair.

Nos. C29-C30
Overprinted in
Claret or Gray Blue

1960   Litho.   Perf. 11½
C33 AP12 45p gray blue (C)   .40   .25
C34 AP12 50p claret (GB)   .45   .30

1960 Cotton Festival, Aleppo.

17th Olympic
Games,
Rome — AP15

1960, Dec. 27   Unwmk.   Perf. 12
C35 AP15 15p Basketball   .25   .25
C36 AP15 20p Swimmer   .35   .25
C37 AP15 25p Fencing   .35   .25
C38 AP15 40p Horsemanship   .60   .30
    Nos. C35-C38 (4)   1.55   1.05

Globe, Laurel and
"UN" — AP16

1960, Dec. 31
C39 AP16 35p multi   .35   .25
C40 AP16 50p bl, red & yel   .40   .25

United Nations, 15th anniversary.

Ibrahim
Hanano — AP17

1961   Litho.   Perf. 12x11½
C41 AP17 50p buff & slate grn   .80   .25

Hanano, leader of liberation movement.

Soldier with
Flag — AP18

1961, Apr. 17   Wmk. 291   Perf. 11½
C42 AP18 40p gray green   1.00   .25

Issued for Evacuation Day, 1961.

Arab and Map of
Palestine — AP19

1961, May 15   Perf. 12
C43 AP19 50p ultra & blk   2.00   .25

Issued for Palestine Day.

Abu-Tammam
AP20

1961, July 20   Unwmk.   Perf. 11½
C44 AP20 50p brown   .50   .25

Abu-Tammam (807-845?), Arabian poet.

Discus
Thrower
and Lyre
AP21

1961, Aug. 23   Litho.   Perf. 11½
C45 AP21 15p crimson & blk   .25   .25
C46 AP21 35p bl grn & vio   .50   .25

5th University Youth Festival.
A souvenir sheet contains one each of Nos.
C45-C46 imperf.

Fair
Emblem — AP22

UAR
Pavilion — AP23

1961, Aug. 25
C47 AP22 17½p vio & grn   .25   .25
C48 AP23 50p brt lil & blk   .35   .25
    a.   Black omitted

8th International Damascus Fair.

St. Simeon's
Monastery
AP24

1961, Oct.   Litho.   Perf. 12
C49 AP24 200p violet blue   1.50   .90

No. C49 was issued by the Syrian Arab
Republic after dissolution of the UAR.

UAR AIR POST SEMI-POSTAL STAMP

Catalogue value for the unused
stamp in this section is for a Never
Hinged item.

Eye, Hand and
UN Emblem
SPAP1

Perf. 12x11½
1961, Apr. 29   Litho.   Wmk. 291
CB1 SPAP1 40p + 10p sl grn &
    blk   .30   .30

UN welfare program for the blind.

TAHITI

tə-'hēt-ē

LOCATION — An island in the South
    Pacific Ocean, one of the Society
    group
GOVT. — A part of the French
    Oceania Colony
AREA — 600 sq. mi.
POP. — 19,029
CAPITAL — Papeete

The stamps of Tahiti were replaced
by those of French Oceania (see
French Polynesia in Vol. 2).

100 Centimes = 1 Franc

Counterfeits exist of surcharges and
overprints on Nos. 1-31.

**Stamps of French Colonies
Surcharged in Black**

a   b

c   d

1882   Unwmk.   Imperf.
1 A8(a) 25c on 35c dk
        vio, org   425.   350.
1A A8(b) 25c on 35c dk
        vio, org   4,500.   4,500.
1B A8(a) 25c on 40c ver,
        straw   6,250.   6,750.

Nos. 1-1B exist with surcharges inverted.
Values for Nos. 1 and 1A are approximately
the same as for normal copies; No. 1B with
surcharge inverted is worth about half the
value of a normal copy.
Surcharge exists reading either up or down
on Nos. 1 and 1A, and double, one inverted on
No. 1B. See Scott Classic Specialized Catalogue of Stamps and Covers for detailed listings of these and later Tahiti issues.

1884   Perf. 14x13½
2 A9(c) 5c on 20c red,
        yel grn   300.   240.
3 A9(d) 10c on 20c red,
        yel grn   350.   300.
Imperf
4 A8(b) 25c on 1fr brnz
        grn, straw   750.   650.

Inverted and vertical surcharges on Nos. 2-
4 are same value as normally placed
surcharges.

Handstamped in Black

1893   Perf. 14x13½
5 A9 1c blk, lil bl   950.00   875.00
6 A9 2c brown, buff   3,200.   2,500.
7 A9 4c claret, lav   1,500.   1,250.
8 A9 5c green, grnsh   55.00   47.50
9 A9 10c black, lav   60.00   52.50
10 A9 15c blue   60.00   47.50
11 A9 20c red, green   72.50   65.00
12 A9 25c yel, straw   8,750.   7,250.
13 A9 25c blk, rose   55.00   47.50
14 A9 35c violet, org   2,600.   2,200.
15 A9 75c carmine, rose   87.50   87.50
16 A9 1fr brnz grn,
        straw   92.50   92.50

Nearly all values of this set are known with
overprint sloping up, sloping down and horizontal. Some occur double. Values the same
as for the listed stamps.
For Nos. 6//16 with inverted overprint, see
the Scott Classic Specialized Catalogue of
Stamps and Covers.
Nos. 6, 12 and 14 are valued in the grade of
Fine.

Overprinted in Black

1893

17	A9	1c blk, *lil bl*	925.00	800.00
18	A9	2c brn, *buff*	3,750.	2,750.
19	A9	4c claret, *lav*	1,850.	1,500.
20	A9	5c grn, *grnsh*	1,100.	950.00
21	A9	10c black, *lav*	350.00	350.00
22	A9	15c blue	55.00	50.00
23	A9	20c red, *grn*	60.00	55.00
24	A9	25c yel, *straw*	50,000.	42,500.
25	A9	25c black, *rose*		50.00
26	A9	35c violet, *org*	2,600.	2,200.
27	A9	75c carmine, *rose*	60.00	55.00
b.		Double overprint	400.00	
28	A9	1fr brnz grn, *straw*	75.00	60.00

Inverted Overprint

17a	A9	1c blk, *lil bl*	1,350.	1,200.
18a	A9	2c brn, *buff*	4,000.	3,900.
19a	A9	4c claret, *lav*	2,000.	1,900.
20a	A9	5c grn, *grnsh*	1,600.	1,500.
21a	A9	10c black, *lav*	950.	900.
22a	A9	15c blue	250.	225.
23a	A9	20c red, *grn*	250.	225.
25a	A9	25c black, *rose*	250.	225.
26a	A9	35c violet, *org*	3,000.	2,800.
27a	A9	75c carmine, *rose*	300.	250.
28a	A9	1fr brnz grn, *straw*	300.	275.

Stamps of French Polynesia Surcharged in Black or Carmine

g   h

1903

29	A1	(g) 10c on 15c bl (Bk)	11.00	11.00
a.		Double surcharge	67.50	67.50
b.		Inverted surcharge	72.50	72.50
30	A1	(h) 10c on 25c blk, *rose* (C)	11.00	11.00
a.		Double surcharge	67.50	67.50
b.		Inverted surcharge	80.00	80.00
31	A1	(h) 10c on 40c red, *straw* (Bk)	13.00	13.00
a.		Double surcharge	80.00	80.00
b.		Inverted surcharge	80.00	80.00
		Nos. 29-31 (3)	35.00	35.00

In the surcharges on Nos. 29-31 there are two varieties of the "1" in "10," i. e. with long and short serif.

SEMI-POSTAL STAMPS

Stamps of French Polynesia Overprinted in Red

1915   Unwmk.   Perf. 14x13½

B1	A1	15c blue	300.00	300.00
a.		Inverted overprint	1,100.	1,000.
B2	A1	15c gray	35.00	35.00
a.		Inverted overprint	425.00	425.00

Counterfeits exist.

POSTAGE DUE STAMPS

Counterfeits exist of overprints on Nos. J1-J26.

Inverted overprints exist on most, and double overprints on many, Tahiti postage due stamps. See the *Scott Classic Specialized Catalogue of Stamps and Covers* for detailed listings.

Postage Due Stamps of French Colonies Handstamped in Black like Nos. 5-16

1893   Unwmk.   Imperf.

J1	D1	1c black	400.	400.
J2	D1	2c black	400.	400.
J3	D1	3c black	450.	450.
J4	D1	4c black	450.	450.
J5	D1	5c black	450.	450.
J6	D1	10c black	450.	450.
J7	D1	15c black	450.	450.
J8	D1	20c black	350.	350.
J9	D1	30c black	450.	450.
J10	D1	40c black	450.	450.
J11	D1	60c black	525.	525.

J12	D1	1fr brown	1,100.	1,100.
J13	D1	2fr brown	1,100.	1,100.
		Nos. J1-J13 (13)	7,025.	7,025.

Overprinted in Black like Nos. 17-28

1893

J14	D1	1c black	2,400.	2,400.
J15	D1	2c black	550.	550.
J16	D1	3c black	550.	550.
J17	D1	4c black	550.	550.
J18	D1	5c black	550.	550.
J19	D1	10c black	550.	550.
J20	D1	15c black	550.	550.
J21	D1	20c black	550.	550.
J22	D1	30c black	550.	550.
J23	D1	40c black	550.	550.
J24	D1	60c black	550.	550.
J25	D1	1fr brown	550.	550.
J26	D1	2fr brown	550.	550.
		Nos. J14-J26 (13)	9,000.	9,000.

TAJIKISTAN

tä-jik-i-'stan

(Tadzhikistan)

LOCATION — Asia, bounded by Uzbekistan, Kyrgyzstan, People's Republic of China and Afghanistan
GOVT. — Republic
AREA — 55,240 sq. mi.
POP. — 6,102,854 (1999 est.)
CAPITAL — Dushanbe

With the breakup of the Soviet Union on Dec. 26, 1991, Tajikistan became independent.

100 Kopecks = 1 Ruble
100 Tanga = 1 Ruble
100 Dinars = 1 Somoni (2000)

Catalogue values for all unused stamps in this country are for Never Hinged items.

Gold Statue of Man on Horse — A1

1992, May 20   Litho.   Perf. 12x12½
1   A1   50k multicolored   .35   .35
For surcharge see No. 12.

Sheik Muslihiddin Mosque A2

1992, May 25   Photo.   Perf. 11½
2   A2   50k multicolored   .30   .30
For surcharges, see Nos. 13-14.

Musical Instruments of Tajikistan — A3

Photo. & Engr.
1992, Aug. 15   Perf. 12x11½
3   A3   35k multicolored   .30   .30
For surcharges see Nos. 5-7.

Ram — A4

1992, Aug. 21   Photo.   Perf. 12x12½
4   A4   30k multicolored   .40   .40

No. 3 Surcharged in Black or Blue

Photo. & Engr.
1992, Nov. 12   Perf. 12x11½
5   A3   15r on 35k   .85   .85
6   A3   15r on 35k (Bl)   2.25   2.25
7   A3   50r on 35k   .85   .85
   Nos. 5-7 (3)   3.95   3.95

Russia No. 5838 Surcharged

1992, Jan. 4   Litho.   Perf. 12x12½
8   A2765   3r on 1k   .35   .35
9   A2765   100r on 1k   2.10   2.10

Russia No. 5984 Surcharged in Violet Blue or Green

No. 1 Surcharged in Black

1992, May 7   Litho.   Perf. 12x12½
10   A2765   10r on 2k (VB)   .95   .95
11   A2765   15r on 2k (Gr)   .95   .95
12   A1   60r on 50k   1.90   1.90
   Nos. 10-12 (3)   3.80   3.80

Location and size of lettering on Nos. 10-11 varies.

No. 2 Surcharged

Methods and Perfs as Before
1992, Sept. 18
13   A2   5r on 50k multi   .45   .45
14   A2   25r on 50k multi   1.10   1.10

Wild Animals A5

Designs: 3r, Ursus arctos. 10r, Cervas elaphus. 15r, Capra falconeri. 25r, Hystrix leucura. 100r, Uncia uncia.

1993, June 8   Litho.   Perf. 13½
15   A5   3r multicolored   .25   .25
16   A5   10r multicolored   .35   .25
17   A5   15r multicolored   .35   .25
18   A5   25r multicolored   .60   .25
19   A5   100r multicolored   2.25   .40
   Nos. 15-19 (5)   3.80   1.40
For surcharge see No. 372.

Fortress, 19th Cent. — A6

Academy — A6a

1r, Statue of Rudaki, poet, vert. 5r, Mountains, river. 10r, Statue with oriental inscription, vert. 15r, Mausoleum of Aini, poet, vert. 20r, Map, flag. 35r, Post office. 50r, Aini Opera House. #29, Theater. #30, Flag, map, diff. #31, Observatory. #32, Academy.

1993-94
20   A6   1r multicolored   .25   .25
22   A6   5r multicolored   .25   .25
23   A6   10r multicolored   .25   .25
24   A6   15r multicolored   .25   .25
25   A6   20r green & multi   .25   .25
26   A6   25r multicolored   .40   .40
27   A6   35r multicolored   .25   .25
28   A6   50r multicolored   .60   .60
29   A6   100r multicolored   .55   .55
30   A6   100r blue & multi   1.10   1.10
31   A6   160r multicolored   .65   .65
32   A6a   160r shown   .65   .65
   Nos. 20-32 (12)   5.45   5.45

Issued: 1r, 5r, 15r, 20r, 25r, 50r, No. 30, 6/8/93, others, 9/8/94.
This is an expanding set. Numbers will change if necessary.
For surcharges, see Nos. 169-171, 231-232, 301, 373.

Souvenir Sheet

1992 Summer Olympics, Barcelona — A7

1993, June 8
33   A7   50r multicolored   8.75   8.75
For surcharge see No. 52A.

Epic Poem "Book of Kings", by Ferdowsi, 1000th Anniv. A8

Designs: 5r, Combat with swords. 20r, Two men on horseback fighting with spears. 30r, Men in combat stopped by guide on giant bird, vert. 50r, Ferdowsi (c. 935-c. 1020), vert.

1993, June 8   Litho.   Perf. 13½
34   A8   5r multicolored   .50   .50
35   A8   20r multicolored   1.40   1.40
36   A8   30r multicolored   1.75   1.75
  a.   Sheet, 2 each # 34-36, + 4 labels   14.00   —
   Nos. 34-36 (3)   3.65   3.65
Souvenir Sheet
37   A8   50r multicolored   3.25   3.25
No. 37 contains one 30x45mm stamp.

Traditional Art Pattern — A8a

1993, July 1   Litho.   Perf. 12x11½
37A   A8a   1.50r multicolored   .70   .70
Dated 1992.
For surcharges see Nos. 62-65.

Ali Hamadani (1314-85), Persian Mystic — A9

1994, Feb. 22   Litho.   Perf. 13½
38   A9   1000r multicolored   3.00   3.00
39   A9   1000r multicolored   3.00   3.00
Name in latin letters on No. 38 and in cyrillic letters on No. 39.

Natl. Arms — A10

1994, Feb. 22
40   A10   10r black brown & multi   .25   .25
41   A10   15r purple & multi   .25   .25
43   A10   35r olive & multi   .25   .25
44   A10   50r red & multi   .25   .25
46   A10   100r green & multi   .30   .30
47   A10   160r blue & multi   .50   .50
   Size: 23x36mm
50   A10   500r blue & multi   .75   .75
52   A10   1000r brown & multi   1.25   1.25
   Nos. 40-52 (8)   3.80   3.80
This is an expanding set. Numbers will change if necessary.

No. 33 Overprinted

1994, Apr. 13   Litho.   Perf. 13½
52A   A7   50r multicolored   7.50   7.50

Prehistoric Animals A11

Designs: No. 53, Diatryma. No. 54, Triceratops. No. 55, Anatosaurus. No. 56, Tyrannosaurus. No. 57, Parasaurolophus. No. 58, Incorrectly inscribed "Tyrannosaurus," with

horns, resembling an Ankalysaurus. No. 59,
Spinosaurus. No. 60, Stegosaurus.

1994, Sept. 8   Litho.   Perf. 13½
53-60 A11 500r Set of 8   7.25 2.50

Issued both in separate sheetlets of nine
and together in a se-tenant sheetlet of nine,
containing Nos. 53-60 and one label. Values:
set of nine sheetlets, $60; se-tenant sheetlet,
$40.

No. 37A
Surcharged
in Green

1995, Mar. 10   Litho.   Perf. 12x11½
62 A8a 100r on 1.50r multi   .25   .25
63 A8a 600r on 1.50r multi   .50   .50
64 A8a 1000r on 1.50r multi   .90   .90
65 A8a 5000r on 1.50r multi   4.25 4.25
a.   Strip, #64-65, 2 ea #62-63   9.00 9.00
      Nos. 62-65 (4)   5.90 5.90

Issued in sheets of 36 stamps. Each vertical
and horizontal strip has stamps in different
order.
For surcharges see Nos. 111-114.

Membership Admissions — A13

Designs: No. 66, Member of UN. No. 67,
Member of UPU, vert. No. 68, Member of
OSCE (Organization of Security & Coopera-
tion in Europe), vert.

1995, May 4   Litho.   Perf. 13½
66 A13 1000r multicolored   1.25 1.00
67 A13 1000r multicolored   1.25 1.00
68 A13 1000r multicolored   1.25 1.00
      Nos. 66-68 (3)   3.75 3.00

Lizards
A14

#69, Alsophylax loricatus. #70, Varanus
griseus. #71, Phrynocephalus mystaceus.
#72, Phrynocephalus helioscopus. #73, Phry-
nocephalus sogdianus. #74, Teratoscincus
scineus.
5000r, Eumeces schneideri.

1995, May 4   Litho.   Perf. 13½
69 A14 500r multicolored   .60   .60
70 A14 500r multicolored   .60   .60
71 A14 500r multicolored   .60   .60
72 A14 500r multicolored   .60   .60
73 A14 500r multicolored   .60   .60
74 A14 500r multicolored   .60   .60
      Nos. 69-74 (6)   3.60 3.60
Souvenir Sheet
75 A14 5000r multicolored   6.25 3.75

For overprints see Nos. 77-78.

Souvenir Sheet

End of World War II, 50th
Anniv. — A15

1995, May 8   Litho.   Perf. 13½
76 A15 5000r multicolored   6.50 6.50
a.   As #76, color diff.   5.50 5.50

On No. 76 emblem in margin is bister, black
& red. No. 76a emblem is yellow, black & red
with missing letter "E" from second line of text.

No. 70
Ovptd.

No. 71
Ovptd.

1995, Dec. 1   Litho.   Perf. 13½
77 A14 500r on #70   4.25 4.25
78 A14 500r on #71   4.25 4.25

Singapore '95 (#77), Beijing '95 (#78).

New Natl. Arms — A16

1995, Dec. 20
79 A16 1r olive & multi   .30   .30
80 A16 2r brown & multi   .30   .30
81 A16 5r green & multi   .30   .30
82 A16 12r red & multi   .50   .50
83 A16 40r green blue & multi   1.00 1.00
      Nos. 79-83 (5)   2.40 2.40

Birds
A17

Designs: No. 84, Syrrhaptes tibetana. No.
85, Perdix daurica turcomana. No. 86, Tetrao-
gallus tibetanus. No. 87, Otis undulata mac-
queeni. No. 88, Larus brunnicephalus. No. 89,
Anser indicus.
600r, Phasianus colchicus.

1996, Feb. 1
84 A17 200r multicolored   1.40 1.40
85 A17 200r multicolored   1.40 1.40
86 A17 200r multicolored   1.40 1.40
87 A17 200r multicolored   1.40 1.40
88 A17 200r multicolored   1.40 1.40
89 A17 200r multicolored   1.40 1.40
      Nos. 84-89 (6)   8.40 8.40
Souvenir Sheet
90 A17 600r multicolored   6.75 6.75

Two each of Nos. 84-89 were issued in
sheet of 12 + label.

UN, 50th
Anniv.
A18

Designs: 100r, UN headquarters, New York.
500r, Headquarters at night.

1996
90A A18 100r multicolored   1.00 1.00
Souvenir Sheet
90B A14 500r multicolored   4.00 4.00

Issued: 100r, 4/10; 500r, 2/1.

Souvenir Sheet

Save the Aral Sea — A19

Designs: a, Felis caracal. b, Salmo trutta
aralensis. c, Hyaena hyaena. d, Pseudoscaphirhynchus kaufmanni. e, Aspiolucius
esocinus.

1996, May 3   Litho.   Perf. 14
91 A19 100r Sheet of 5, #a.-e.   6.00 6.00

See Kazakhstan No. 145, Kyrgyzstan No.
107, Turkmenistan No. 52, Uzbekistan No.
113.

A20

A20a

Designs: Nos. 92-95, 98, Otocolobus manul
(different views). No. 96, Felis chaus oxiana.
No. 97, Felix lynx isabellina.

1996, June 28   Litho.   Perf. 13½
92 A20 100r brown & multi   2.00 2.00
93 A20 100r yellow & multi   2.00 2.00
94 A20 150r blue & multi   2.00 2.00
95 A20 150r lilac & multi   2.00 2.00
96 A20 200r multicolored   2.00 2.00
97 A20 200r multicolored   2.00 2.00
      Nos. 92-97 (6)   12.00 12.00
Souvenir Sheet
98 A20a 500r multicolored   8.00 8.00

World Wildlife Fund (#92-95).

1996
Summer
Olympic
Games,
Atlanta
A21

1996, July 12   Litho.   Perf. 13½
99   A21 200r Judo   1.90 1.90
100 A21 200r Diving   1.90 1.90
101 A21 200r Hammer throw   1.90 1.90
102 A21 200r Soccer   1.90 1.90
103 A21 200r Pierre de
              Coubertin   1.90 1.90
      Nos. 99-103 (5)   9.50 9.50

Kamol Khujandi,
Poet — A22

1996, Sept. 7   Litho.   Perf. 13½
104 A22 500r Cyrillic name
               14mm long   5.00 5.00
a.   Cyrillic name 13mm long   11.00 11.00
105 A22 500r English inscriptions   5.00 5.00

Central
Asian
Postal
Union, 5th
Anniv.
A23

1996, Dec. 25   Perf. 12¾
106 A23 100r multicolored   5.50 5.50

Mountains
A24

1997, July 16   Perf. 13x12¾
107 A24 100r Communism Peak   1.50 1.50
108 A24 100r Peak Korzhenev-
               skoj   1.50 1.50
109 A24 100r Lenin Peak   1.50 1.50
a.   Strip of 3, #107-109   6.50 6.50
Souvenir Sheet
110 A24 500r Mountain climber   6.50 6.50

Nos. 62-65
Srchd.

1997, Oct. 27   Litho.   Perf. 12x11½
111 A8a (A) on 100r #62   1.00 1.00
112 A8a (A) on 600r #63   1.00 1.00
113 A8a (A) on 1000r #64   1.00 1.00
114 A8a (A) on 5000r #65   1.00 1.00
a.   Strip, #113-114, 2 ea #111-112 6.00 6.00
      Nos. 111-114 (4)   4.00 4.00

A25

Traditional Costumes: #115, Woman with
red shawl draped over head, carrying pitcher.
#116, Woman in long formal dress, cape, tiara.
#117, Man wearing long striped coat. #118,
Man wearing long blue coat.

1998, Feb. 20   Litho.   Perf. 12½x13
115 A25 100r multicolored   1.00 1.00
116 A25 100r multicolored   1.00 1.00
117 A25 150r multicolored   1.50 1.50
a.   Pair, #115, 117   2.50 2.50
118 A25 150r multicolored   1.50 1.50
a.   Pair, #116, 118   2.50 2.50
      Nos. 115-118 (4)   5.00 5.00

Handicrafts — A26

1998, Feb. 20   Litho.   Perf. 12¾
119   A26 30r Urn   .50   .50
119A A26 100r Cradles   1.50 1.50

Size: 64x64mm
Imperf

120	A26 300r Ceramic tile	4.00	4.00
	Nos. 119-120 (3)	6.00	6.00

A27

Flowers: 12r, Tulipa greigii. 30r, Crocus korolkowii. 70r, Iris darwasica. 150r, Petilium eduardii. 300r, Juno nicolai.

1998, Apr. 3   Litho.   Perf. 12½x13

121	A27	12r multicolored	.40	.40
122	A27	30r multicolored	.60	.60
123	A27	70r multicolored	1.25	1.25
124	A27	150r multicolored	2.75	2.75
a.		Sheet of 4, #121-124	5.50	5.50
		Nos. 121-124 (4)	5.00	5.00

Souvenir Sheet

125	A27 300r multicolored	5.00	5.00

Stamps in No. 124a have margins continuing the background design of the sheet.

Butterflies
A28

12r, Catocala timur. 30r, Celerio chamyla apocyni. 70r, Colias sieversi. 150r, Papilio alexanor.
300r, Anthocharis tomyris.

1998, Apr. 3   Perf. 13x12½

126	A28	12r multicolored	.75	.75
127	A28	30r multicolored	.90	.90
128	A28	70r multicolored	1.25	1.25
129	A28	150r multicolored	2.50	2.50
a.		Sheet of 4, #126-129	7.00	7.00
		Nos. 126-129 (4)	5.40	5.40

Souvenir Sheet

130	A28 300r multicolored	6.50	6.50

Stamps of No. 129a have margins continuing the background design of the sheet.

Gems
A29

1998, Aug. 21   Litho.   Perf. 13x12¾

131	A29	1r Sapphire	.25	.25
132	A29	1r Ruby	.25	.25
133	A29	12r Lapis lazuli	.35	.35
134	A29	12r Tourmaline	.35	.35
135	A29	150r Spinel	1.90	1.90
136	A29	150r Amethyst	1.90	1.90
a.		Sheet of 6, #131-136, + 2 labels	5.00	5.00
		Nos. 131-136 (6)	5.00	5.00

Souvenir Sheet

137	A29 350r Agate	5.25	5.25

Bobojon Ghafurov, Academician (1908-98) — A30

1998, Aug. 21   Perf. 12¾x13

138	A30 12r blue & multi	.30	.30
139	A30 150r red & multi	2.10	2.10

Each printed in sheets of 10.

Aleksander Pushkin (1799-1837),
Russian Poet — A31

1999, June   Litho.   Perf. 13¼x13½

140	A31 100r Self-portrait drawing	.75	.75
141	A31 270r Painting by Kiprensky	2.25	2.25
a.	Pair, #140-141	3.00	3.00

For surcharges see Nos. 332-335.

"ILLEGAL" STAMPS

Tajikistan postal officials have declared as "illegal" the following items.

Sheets of nine stamps of various denominations depicting:

Elvis Presley, Barry White, Michael Douglas, Robert DeNiro, Grace Kelly, the television show "Ally McBeal," Harry Potter, Batman, Superman (two different sheets), Warner Brothers cartoon characters, U.S. Political Cartoons concerning the 2000 Presidential election, Mushrooms, Mushrooms in Art, Major League Baseball players, Sydney 2002 Olympic Games (two different sheets), Various golfers, U.S. Open Golf Championship, Golfer Eduardo Romero, Tiger Woods (two different sheets), Pope John Paul II, and Masonic emblems.

Sheet of 3 stamps of various denominations depicting Marilyn Monroe.

A32

A32a

A32b

1999, June 5   Litho.   Perf. 13½

142	A32	(40r) multi	.30	.30
143	A32a	(100r) multi	.80	.80
144	A32b	(270r) multi	1.90	1.90
		Nos. 142-144 (3)	3.00	3.00

For surcharge see No. 358.

Samanid
Dynasty — A33

1999, Aug.   Litho.   Perf. 12¾x13

145	A33	30r Lion figurine	.25	.25
146	A33	50r Round emblem	.45	.45
147	A33	100r Handled figurine	.90	.90
148	A33	270r Three figurines	2.50	2.50
		Nos. 145-148 (4)	4.10	4.10

Souvenir Sheet

149	A33 500r King	5.50	5.50
a.	Sheet, #149, 2 ea #145-148	10.00	10.00

Samanid Dynasty, 1100th
Anniv. — A34

No. 150: a, 100r, King. b, 500r, Pres. Emomali Rakhmonov.

1999, Oct.   Litho.   Perf. 13½x13

150	A34 Sheet of 2, #a.-b.	11.00	11.00

Mushrooms
A35

Designs: Nos. 151, 153a, 100r, Pleurotus eryngii. Nos. 152, 153b, 270r, Lepista nuda. 500r, Morchella steppicola.

1999, Nov.   Perf. 13¼x13

151	A35 100r multi	1.25	1.25
152	A35 270r multi	4.00	4.00

Miniature Sheet

153	A35 Sheet, 2 ea #153a-153b	3.75	3.75

Souvenir Sheet

154	A35 500r multi	3.00	3.00

Nos. 151-152 have white borders, while Nos. 153a-153b have borders which continue the sheet's central design.
For surcharge see No. 229.

Fish — A36

Designs: 40r, Ophiocephalus argus. 100r, Barbus brachycephalus. 230r, Schizopygopsis stoliczkai. 270r, Pseudoscaphirhynchus fedtschenkoi.
500r, Pseudoscaphirhynchus kaufmanni.

2000   Litho.   Perf. 13¼x13

155-158	A36 Set of 4	4.25	4.25
158a	Souvenir sheet, #155-158	5.00	5.00

Souvenir Sheet

159	A36 500r multi	5.00	5.00

On Nos. 158-159, Pseudoscaphirhynchus is misspelled "Pseudoscaphihynchus."
For surcharge see No. 218.

UPU, 125th
Anniv. (in
1999) — A37

2000

160	A37 270r multi	1.25	1.25

100 Dinars = 1 Somoni (2000)

Birds of
Prey
A38

Designs: 10d, Pandion haliaetus. 27d, Aquila chrysaetus, vert. 50d, Gyps himalayensis. 70d, Circaetus ferox, vert. 1s, Falco peregrinus, vert.

2001, Jan. 23   Litho.   Perf. 14

161-164	A38 Set of 4	6.75	6.75

Souvenir Sheet

165	A38 1s multi	4.25	4.25

No. 165 contains one 42x56mm stamp. Dated 2000.

Chess — A39

Designs: 15d, Mikhail Botvinnik. 41d, Bobby Fischer.
No. 168: a, 10d, Wilhelm Steinitz. b, 25d, Chess board, five people. c, 50d, José Raul Capablanca. d, 70d, Emanuel Lasker. e, 90d, Chess board, four people. f, 1s, Alexander Alekhine.

2001, May 29   Perf. 14¼x14

166-167	A39 Set of 2	3.00	3.00

Souvenir Sheet

168	A39 Sheet of 6, #a-f	10.00	10.00

No. 26 Surcharged in Green, Red or Black

a

b

c

2001, June 4   Perf. 13½

169	A6(a)	(6d) multi (G)	.65	.65
170	A6(b)	(15d) multi (R)	1.25	1.25
171	A6(c)	(41d) multi (Bk)	3.75	3.75
		Nos. 169-171 (3)	5.65	5.65

Souvenir Sheet

Satellite Communications — A40

2001, July 25   Perf. 13¼x13

172	A40 1.50s multi	3.75	3.75

Souvenir Sheets

Nurec Hydroelectric Station — A41

Pres. Emomali Rakhmonov — A42

Independence, 10th Anniv. — A43

No. 175: a, 41d, Map, flag and arms (29x29mm). b, 54d, Emblem (29x29mm). c, 95d, Ratification of constitution (49x29mm).

2001, Sept. 7   Perf. 13¼x13¾
173 A41 2.50s multi   30.00 30.00
          Perf. 12¾x13¼
174 A42 3s multi   35.00 35.00
          Perf. 14x13¾
175 A43 Sheet of 3, #a-c 25.00 25.00
          Independence, 10th anniv.

Tajikistan postal officials have declared as "illegal" the following items:
Sheets of nine stamps of various denominations depicting Bruce Lee, Michael Jordan, Osama bin Laden, Captain America, Fantastic Four, Queen Mother's 100th Birthday, Formula 1 Racing, Motor Sports and the Netherlands Royal Wedding.
Sheets of six stamps of various denominations depicting Pope John Paul II and Motorcycle racers.
Sheet of three stamps of various denominations depicting Pope John Paul II.

Transportation — A44

Designs: 1s, Tu-154M Airplane.
No. 177: a, 41d, Vehicles on road. b, 90d, Locomotive.

2001, Dec. 12   Litho.   Perf. 14x13¼
176 A44 1s multi   2.75 2.75
          Souvenir Sheet
177 A44 Sheet of 3, #176,
          177a, 177b   6.50 6.50

Commonwealth of Independent States, 10th Anniv. — A45

2001, Dec. 17   Perf. 14¼x14
178 A45 50d multi   2.00 2.00

Souvenir Sheet

Regional Communications Accord — A46

2001, Dec. 17
179 A46 1s multi + 2 labels   3.50 3.50

Avesta, 2700th Anniv. — A47

Zoroastrian: 2d, Goddess Anahita. 3d, Priest.
No. 182: a, 70d, Goddess Haoma. b, 90d, God Farroh. c, 1s, God Surush. d, 2s, Goddess Din.

2002, Jan. 1   Litho.   Perf. 10
180-181 A47 Set of 2   2.00 2.00
          Souvenir Sheet
182 A47 Sheet of 4, #a-d   13.50 13.50
No. 182 contains four 27x44mm stamps. Dated 2001.

Miniature Sheet

UN High Commissioner for Refugees, 50th Anniv. (in 2001) — A48

No. 183: a, Mothers holding children, refugees. b, Military helicopter, sun, refugees. c, Cloud, rainbow, moon, soldier, child.

2002, Jan. 1
183 A48 50d Sheet of 3, #a-c   5.25 5.25
          Dated 2001.

Flora and Fauna of Central Asia — A49

No. 184: a, Bird facing right. b, Bird facing left. c, Mushrooms and snail. d, Rodent. e, Butterfly. f, Butterfly and tulip. g, Cat. h, Cat and tulip.

2002, Apr. 12   Litho.   Perf. 13¾x13½
184   Miniature sheet of 8   9.00 9.00
     a.   A49 6d multi   .50   .50
     b.   A49 15d multi   .50   .50
     c.   A49 41d multi   .50   .50
     d.   A49 50d multi   .60   .60
     e.   A49 95d multi   1.10 1.10
     f.-h. A49 1.50s any single   1.75 1.75

No. 184 exists imperf. Value, $20.

Worldwide Fund for Nature (WWF) — A50

Reed cats: a, 1s, Two cats. b, 1.50s, One cat walking. c, 2s, One cat resting. d, 2s, Three kittens.

2002, Apr. 12   Perf. 14x14¼
185 A50 Block of 4, #a-d   7.00 7.00
     e.   Sheet, 2 #185   16.00 16.00

Dushanbe Zoo, 40th Anniv. — A51

Designs: 2d, Pan troglodytes. 3d, Cervus nippon hortulorum. 10d, Panthera tigris altaice. 41d, Diceros bicornis michaeli. 50d, Giraffa camelopardis reticulata. 1s, Panthera leo.

2002, Aug. 29   Litho.   Perf. 14¼x14
186-191 A51 Set of 6   5.75 5.75

Souvenir Sheet

Navruz — A52

No. 192: a, 1s, Wheat bundle. b, 50d, Dancers in red costumes. c, 1s, Dancer in purple costume.

2002, Aug. 29
192 A52 Sheet of 3, #a-c   5.00 5.00

A53   A54

Istravashan, 2500th Anniv.
A55   A56

2002, Sept. 6
193 A53 50d brown & multi   1.00 1.00
194 A54 50d green & multi   1.00 1.00
195 A55 50d brown & multi   1.00 1.00
196 A56 50d green & multi   1.00 1.00
     Nos. 193-196 (4)   4.00 4.00

No. 168 Overprinted "2002" on Stamps and With Text in Margin
Souvenir Sheet

Designs as before.

2002, Sept. 20   Litho.   Perf. 14¼x14
197 A39 Sheet of 6, #a-f   11.00 11.00

No. 197 is overprinted in bottom sheet margin "Chess Super Championship / between teams of the World and Russia / 08-11.09.2002. Moscow" and in left sheet margin with similar text in Cyrillic characters.
No. 197 exists imperf. Value $300.
No. 197 also exists with violet overprint. Value: perf, $30; imperf $350.

Tajikistan postal officials have declared as "illegal" the following items.
Sheets of nine stamps of various denominations depicting: 20th Century Dreams (6 different sheets), Elephants and Rotary Intl. emblem, Owls, mushrooms and Rotary International emblem, Pandas, Chess, The Beatles, Locomotives, Princess Diana, the movie The Blair Witch Project, Defenders of Peace and Freedom, 2002 Brazilian World Cup Soccer Team, Harry Potter, Cartoon characters from South Park (Christmas), Warner Brothers Cartoon Characters (Christmas).
Sheets of six stamps of various denominations depicting Pokemon characters (eight sheets), Pope John Paul II, Dinosaurs.
Sheet of three stamps of various denominations depicting Elvis Presley.
Souvenir sheets of one stamp with 25.00 denomination depicting Harry Potter (2 different sheets), Penguins,
Souvenir sheet of one stamp with 20.00 denomination depicting Pope John Paul and New York fireman.

New Year 2002 (Year Of the Horse) — A57

No. 198: a, 2d, Thoroughbred racing. b, 3d, Harness racing. c, 95d, Troika. d, 95d, Polo.

No. 199: a, 50d, Dressage. b, 50d, Fox hunting. c, 1s, Steeplechase. d, 1s, Show jumping.

1.50s, Horses in circus act, vert.

2002, Oct. 15   Litho.   Perf. 14x14¼
Blocks of 4, #a-d
198-199 A57   Set of 2   8.00 8.00

Souvenir Sheet
Perf. 14¼x14
200 A57 1.50s multi + 2 labels 4.25 4.25

Oriental Bazaar — A58

No. 201: a, Man in donkey cart. b, Man on donkey. c, Melon vendor. d, Man cooking shashliks.

2002, Dec. 25   Litho.   Perf. 14¼x14
201 A58 65d Block of 4, #a-d   5.50 5.50

Traditional
Sports
A59

Designs: 1d, Archery. 20d, Horse racing. 53d, Polo. 65d, Stone throwing. 1s, Buzkashi. 1.24s, Wrestling.

2002, Dec. 25   Perf. 14x14¼
202-207 A59   Set of 6   6.00 6.00

Lunar
Calendar — A60

Designs: 53d, Sun and zodiac animals. 65d, Zodiac animals and ram. 1s, Ram in circle. 1.50s, Ram.

2003, Mar. 11   Perf. 14¼x14
208-210 A60   Set of 3   5.50 5.50
Souvenir Sheet
211 A60 1.50s multi + 2 labels 4.50 4.50

Monument to Ismail
Somoni — A61

2003, Mar. 11   Perf. 13¼x14
212 A61   1d emerald   .80   .80
213 A61   2d red violet   .80   .80
214 A61   3d blue green   .80   .80
215 A61   4d purple   .80   .80
216 A61   12d brown   .80   .80
217 A61   20d blue   .80   .80
    Nos. 212-217 (6)   4.80 4.80

Souvenir Sheet
No. 158a Surcharged in Purple

No. 218: a, 8d on 40r, Ophiocephalus argus. b, 20d on 100r, Barbus brachycephalus. c, 53d on 230r, Schizopygopsis stoliczkai. d, 66d on 270r, Pseudoscaphihynchus fedtschenkoi.

2003, May 12   Litho.   Perf. 13¼x13
218 A36   Sheet of 4, #a-d   8.00 8.00

2004 Summer Olympics, Athens and 2008 Summer Olympics, Beijing — A62

No. 219: a, 53d, Archery. b, 1s, Track and field. c, 1.23s, Soccer. d, 2s, Gymnastics.

2003, May 20   Perf. 14x13½
219 A62   Sheet of 4, #a-d, +
                    2 labels   10.00 10.00

No. 219 exists imperf. with additional designs in margin. Value $32.50.

Philatelic Exhibitions and Fauna — A63

No. 220: a, 8d, 16th Asian Intl. Stamp Exhibition, China. b, 20d, Panthera tigris. c, 53d, Inachis io. d, 66d, Bangkok 2003 World Philatelic Exhibition. e, 1s, Rupicapra rupicapra. f, 1.50s, Ailuropoda melanoleuca. g, 1.50s, Leontopithecus rosalia. h, 2s, Elephas maximus.

2003, May 20
220 A63   Sheet of 8, #a-h   14.00 14.00
No. 220 exists imperf. Value $35.
For overprint see No. 341.

Intl. Forum on Fresh Water — A64

Designs: No. 221, 1.50s, Peak of Moskvin. No. 222, 1.50s, Iskanderkul.

2003, June 7   Perf. 13½
221-222 A64   Set of 2   6.00 6.00

Nos. 221-222 were printed setenant, both vertically and horizontally, in one sheet.

Famous Men — A65

Designs: No. 223, 1.23s, Nosir Khusrav (1004-88), poet. No. 224, 1.23s, Sadridin Aini (1878-1954), writer.

2003, Sept. 1
223-224 A65   Set of 2   4.75 4.75

Intl. Association of Academies of Science, 10th Anniv. — A66

No. 225: a, Head, satellite dish, airplane, chemicals. b, Association emblem, cosmonaut, robotic hand, computer.

2003, Sept. 1
225 A66 1.23s Horiz. pair, #a-b 5.50 5.50

Intl. Year of Fresh Water — A67

Children's art: a, Fish above lake. b, Sun, river, tree and hills. c, River, hills and trees. d, Waterfalls.

2003, Oct. 20   Perf. 14x14¼
226 A67 66d Block of 4, #a-d   5.00 5.00

Racing Airplanes — A68

No. 227: a, Aero L-29A Delfin Akrobat. b, Yak-55. c, Cessna 172. d, SIAI-Marchetti SF-

---

260. e, Europa XS. f, MBB BO 209 Monsun. g, Mudry Cap 10. h, Soko 2.

2003, Oct. 28   Perf. 14x13½
227 A68 1s Sheet of 8, #a-h   14.00 14.00
No. 227 exists imperf. Value $40.

Fauna of Central Asia — A69

No. 228: a, 8d, Mimas tiliae. 20d, Mustela erminea. 53d, Testudo horsfieldii. 64d, Mantis religiosa. 1.23s, Lanius collurio. 1.27s, Canis aureus. 1.76s, Capra falconeri. 2.29s, Alcedo atthis.

2003, Oct. 28
228 A69   Sheet of 8, #a-h   15.00 15.00
No. 228 exists imperf. Value $40.

No. 153 Surcharged in Red

2004, Jan. 4   Litho.   Perf. 13¼x13
229 A35   Miniature sheet, 2
                   each #a-b   7.00 7.00
  a.   20d on 100r #153a   1.75 1.75
  b.   66d on 270r #153b   3.25 3.25

No. 229 exists surcharged in green. Value, $21.

National Dances — A70

No. 230 — Various dancers and frame color of: a, Brown. b, Purple. c, Green. d, Bright pink.

2004, Jan. 19   Litho.   Perf. 14¼x14
230 A70 53d Block of 4, #a-d   4.75 4.75

Adjacent blocks in sheet are tete-beche. No. 230 exists with visible tagging that reads "Belarus."

**No. 28
Surcharged in
Black and Red**

2004, Apr. 26   Litho.   Perf. 13½
231 A6 A on 50r multi   .90   .90
Sold for 8d on day of issue.

No. 31
Surcharged in
Black

2004, Apr. 26
232 A6 b on 160r multi .90 .90
Sold for 20d on day of issue.

Miniature Sheet

New Year 2004 (Year of the
Monkey) — A71

No. 233: a, 1s, Monkey covering eyes. b,
1.20s, Monkey covering ears. c, 1.50s, Monkey covering mouth.

2004, Aug. 13   Perf. 13¾x13½
233 A71   Sheet of 3, #a-c   6.50 6.50

Dushanbe
Buildings — A72

Designs: 1d, National Circus. 2d, Ferdowsi
National Library. 3d, National Bank. 8d,
Finance Ministry. 20d, Communications Ministry. 50d, City Government Building.

2004, Aug. 13   Perf. 13¾x13¼
234 A72 1d multi   .60 .60
235 A72 2d multi   .60 .60
236 A72 3d multi   .60 .60
237 A72 8d multi   .60 .60
238 A72 20d multi   .60 .60
239 A72 50d multi   1.25 1.25
    Nos. 234-239 (6)   4.25 4.25

FIFA (Fédération Internationale de
Football Association), Cent. — A73

Designs: 50d, Goalie, World Cup. 70d, FIFA
General Secretariat Building, Zurich. 1s,
Player with red shirt, vert. 2s, Player with yellow shirt, vert.

Perf. 13½x13¾, 13¾x13½
2004, Aug. 30
240-243 A73 Set of 4   8.00 8.00
Nos. 240-243 exist imperf. Value, set $35.

Miniature Sheet

2004 Summer Olympics,
Athens — A74

No. 244: a, 30d, Wrestling. b, 45d, Track. c,
55d, Basketball. d, 60d, Shooting. e, 75d,

Equestrian. f, 80d, Women's archery. g, 1.50s,
Soccer. h, 2.50s, Rhythmic gymnastics.

2004, Sept. 6   Perf. 14x13½
244 A74   Sheet of 8, #a-h   13.00 13.00
No. 244 exists imperf. Value $35.

Miniature Sheet

Dushanbe Circus — A75

No. 245: a, 20d, Circus building. b, 50d,
Tightrope walkers. c, 1s, Elephant and trainer.
d, 1.10s, Genie, lamp and cat. e, 1.50s, Man
riding donkey, dog. f, 1.70s, Bareback rider.

2004, Dec. 21   Perf. 14x13½
245 A75   Sheet of 6, #a-f   10.00 10.00
No. 245 exists imperf. Value $25.

Miniature Sheet

Vehicles — A76

No. 246: a, Fire engine. b, Ambulance and
helicopter. c, Police cars. d, Postal van and
train. e, Wrecker and damaged car. f, School
bus.

2004, Dec. 21
246 A76 1s Sheet of 6, #a-f   10.00 10.00
No. 246 exists imperf. Value $25.

Miniature Sheet

Dushanbe as Capital City, 80th
Anniv. — A77

No. 247: a, 20d, New apartment buildings
on Rudaki Ave. b, 46d, Aini State Opera and
Ballet Theater. c, 53d, National Bank. d, 62d,
City Government Building. e, 1.27s, Parliament Building. f, 1.76s, Presidential Palace.

2004, Nov. 16   Litho.   Perf. 11½
247 A77   Sheet of 6, #a-f   14.00 14.00

Musical Instruments — A78

No. 248: a, Gejak and bow. b, Adirna.

2004, Nov. 29   Perf. 11½x11¾
248 A78 2.50s Horiz. pair, #a-b 11.00 11.00
See Kazakhstan No. 470.

Fruit — A79

Designs: Nos. 249, 255, Apples. Nos. 250,
256, Apricots. Nos. 251, 257, Plums. Nos.
252, 258, Pears. Nos. 253, 259, Quince. Nos.
254, 260, Pomegranates.

2005, Mar. 19   Perf. 14x14¼
Panel Color
White Background
249 A79 6d lilac   .25 .25
250 A79 7d blue   .25 .25
251 A79 8d brn orange   .25 .25
252 A79 10d rose   .30 .25
253 A79 11d green   .30 .25
254 A79 12d yel orange   .30 .25
Pale Yellow Background
255 A79 20d purple   .50 .45
256 A79 50d violet   1.00 .90
257 A79 55d red   1.10 1.00
258 A79 75d red violet   1.50 1.25
259 A79 2s dk olive   4.00 3.50
260 A79 3s brown red   6.00 5.50
    Nos. 249-260 (12)   15.75 14.10

Lake Sarez — A80

No. 261: a, Katta Nardjonoi Bay (denomination in white). b, Iriht Bay (denomination in
black).

2005, Apr. 4   Perf. 13½
261 A80 2s Horiz. pair, #a-b   7.00 7.00

Souvenir Sheet

End of World War II, 60th
Anniv. — A81

No. 262: a, 18d. b, 75d.

2005, Apr. 15   Perf. 14¼x14
262 A81   Sheet of 2, #a-b, +
           central label   4.25 4.25

Souvenir Sheet

Hunting — A82

No. 263: a, 1s, Hunter facing left. b, 1.70s,
Hunter facing right. c, 2.30s, Like 1s.

2005, July 27   Perf. 13¾x13½
263 A82   Sheet of 3, #a-c   10.00 10.00
Compare with Type A89.

Airbus A-380 — A83

No. 264 — Inset of airplane and: a, 1.50s,
Left wing. b, 1.50s, Nose. c, 1.80s, Tail. d,
1.80s, Right wing.

2005, July 27   Perf. 13½x14
264 A83   Block of 4, #a-d   12.50 12.50
No. 264 exists imperf. Value $25.

Miniature Sheet

Mammals — A84

No. 265: a, 20d, Hyena on cliff. b, 20d, Turkestan lynx on tree branch. c, 75d, Badger. d,
75d, Fox. e, 80d, Snow leopard. f, 1s, Bear. g,
1.50s, Leopard. h, 1.80s, Tiger.

2005, Aug. 10   Perf. 13½x14
265 A84   Sheet of 8, #a-h   12.50 12.50
No. 265 exists imperf. Value $25.
For overprint, see No. 370.

Worldwide Fund for Nature
(WWF) — A85

No. 266 — Various views of bharals: a, 1s.
b, 1.45s. c, 1.70s. d, 2.25s.

2005, Aug. 26   Perf. 13½x14
266 A85   Block of 4, #a-d   5.00 5.00
No. 266 exists imperf. Value $17.50.

Avicenna (980-1037),
Scientist — A86

2005, Oct. 3   Perf. 13¼x13¾
267 A86 6d Prus bl & blk   .25 .25
268 A86 8d brn & black   .25 .25
269 A86 10d purple & lilac .25 .25
270 A86 12d blue   .45 .45
271 A86 50d blue green   1.40 1.40
272 A86 1s orange   3.00 3.00
    Nos. 267-272 (6)   5.60 5.60

World Post
Day — A87

2005, Oct. 3 — *Perf. 13¼x13¾*

273	A87	5d blue & black	.30	.30
274	A87	7d brown	.30	.30
275	A87	11d green & lt grn	.30	.30
276	A87	20d purple	.50	.50
277	A87	55d gray blue	1.50	1.50
278	A87	75d orange	3.25	3.25
		Nos. 273-278 (6)	6.15	6.15

Mountains — A88

No. 279: a, 1s, Pendjikent. b, 1.50s, Muminabod. c, 2s, Pamir. d, 2.50s, Isfara.

2005, Dec. 6 — *Perf. 13½*

279	A88	Block of 4, #a-d	12.50	12.50

Souvenir Sheet

Hunting — A89

No. 280: a, Hunter holding falcon. b, Hunter killing leopard.

2005, Dec. 31 — *Perf. 13¾x13½*

280	A89	2.50s Sheet of 2, #a-b, + central label	10.00	10.00

Compare with type A82.
No. 280 exists imperf. Value $30.

Fairy Tales — A90

No. 281: a, 55d, The Peasant and the Bear. b, 75d, Three Brothers. c, 2s, Iradj-bogatyr. d, 3s, The Gold Fox.

2006, Mar. 20 — *Perf. 14¼x14*

281	A90	Block of 4, #a-d	10.50	10.50

Stamps in vertical columns are tete-beche.

Traditional Costumes — A91

No. 282: a, 75d, Man from Samarkand wearing red headdress. b, 75d, Man from Sugd wearing blue headdress. c, 1s, Woman from Bukhara with arms together. d, 1s, Woman from Kalayhum with arms apart.

2006, June 20 — *Litho.* *Perf. 14¼x14*

282	A91	Block or horiz. strip of 4, #a-d	6.00	6.00

Printed in sheets of eight containing two of each stamp.

Miniature Sheet

Fauna of Asia — A92

No. 283: a, 8d, Aquila chrysaetos. b, 20d, Panthera tigris longipilis. c, 55d, Hystrix hirsu-tirostris. d, 70d, Alluropoda melanoleuca. e, 75d, Meles meles. f, 1.60s, Ursus arctos. g, 1.92s, Mustela erminea. h, 2s, Bubo coromandus.

2006, June 29 — *Perf. 13¾x13½*

283	A92	Sheet of 8, #a-h	13.00	13.00

No. 283 exists imperf. Value $27.50.

2006 World Cup Soccer Championships, Germany — A93

No. 284: a, 1.50s, Five players. b, 1.50s, Three players and goalie. c, 1.50s, Four players. d, 2s, Three players and goalie, diff.

2006, June 29 — *Perf. 13½x13¾*

284	A93	Block of 4, #a-d	10.00	10.00
	e.	Miniature sheet, 2 each #284a-284d	20.00	20.00

Souvenir Sheet

Kulob, 2700th Anniv. — A94

No. 285: a, Anniversary emblem, flag of Tajikistan. b, Mausoleum of Mir Said Ali Hamadoni.

2006, Aug. 30

285	A94	2s Sheet of 2, #a-b	8.00	8.00

Miniature Sheet

Independence, 15th Anniv. — A95

No. 286: a, 1.50s, Presidential Palace. b, 2.50s, Arms of Tajikistan. c, 3s, Flag of Tajikistan, Pres. Emomali Rakhmonov.

2006, Aug. 30 — *Perf. 14x14¼*

286	A95	Sheet of 3, #a-c, + 3 labels	13.00	13.00

Souvenir Sheet

Commonwealth of Independent States, 15th Anniv. — A96

No. 287: a, Emblem of Commonwealth of Independent States, flags of member nations. b, Emblem of Regional Communications Commonwealth.

2006, Sept. 12 — *Perf. 14¼x14*

287	A96	1.50s Sheet of 2, #a-b, + central label	6.50	6.50

Cotton — A97

2006, Dec. 15 — *Perf. 13½x13¾*

Background Color

288	A97	5d olive green	.35	.35
289	A97	6d rose	.35	.35
290	A97	7d lilac	.35	.35
291	A97	8d light blue	.35	.35
292	A97	20d green	.55	.55
293	A97	75d blue	1.50	1.50
		Nos. 288-293 (6)	3.45	3.45

Headdresses — A98

No. 294 — Various headdresses with gray geometrical design at: a, LR. b, LL. c, UR. d, UL.

2006, Dec. 28 — *Perf. 14x14¼*

294	A98	1.50s Block of 4, #a-d	9.50	9.50

No. 294 exists imperf. Value $25.

Dogs — A99

Designs: 20d, West Siberian laika. 55d, Perdiguero de burgos. 75d, Afghan hound. 1s, Sredneasiatckaia ovtcharka. 2s, Saluki. 3s, Tosa.

2006, Dec. 28 — *Perf. 13¾x13½*

295-300	A99	Set of 6	12.00	12.00

Nos. 295-300 exist imperf. Value, set $25.

No. 32
Surcharged

Methods and Perfs As Before

2007, Mar. 31

301	A6a	75d on 160r #32	2.25	2.25

Souvenir Sheet

Snakes — A100

No. 302: a, Echis carinatus. b, Naja oxiana.

2007, Apr. 30 — *Litho.* *Perf. 14*

302	A100	2s Sheet of 2, #a-b	10.00	10.00

A101   A102

Mevlana (c. 1207-73), Poet — A103

2007, Aug. 30 — *Perf. 13¼x13¾*

303	A101	5d red	.30	.30
304	A101	10d bright blue	.30	.30
305	A101	20d green	.30	.30
306	A101	(25d) dark blue	.45	.45
307	A102	(1.35s) brown violet	2.25	2.25
308	A103	(2.15s) red violet	3.75	3.75
		Nos. 303-308 (6)	7.35	7.35

Jewelry — A104

No. 309: a, 50d, Earring. b, 2s, Necklace. c, 2.50s, Necklace, diff. d, 3s, Earring, diff.

2007, Dec. 18 **Perf. 14¼x14**
309 A104   Block of 4, #a-d   11.00 11.00

Miniature Sheet

Transportation — A105

No. 310: a, 50d, Camels. b, 60d, Steam locomotive. c, 70d, Airplane and helicopter. d, 80d, Pickup truck. e, 90d, Donkey cart. f, 1.50s, Train. g, 1.70s, Bus. h, 2s, Dump truck.

2007, Dec. 27 **Perf. 14x13½**
310 A105   Sheet of 8, #a-h   11.00 11.00

Birds — A106

Designs: Nos. 311, 317a, 1s, Aquila chrysaetos. Nos. 312, 317b, 1.10s, Phasianinae. Nos. 313, 317c, 1.20s, Aix galericulata. Nos. 314, 317d, 1.30s, Otididae. Nos. 315, 317e, 1.40s, Falco cherrug. Nos. 316, 317f, 1.60s Haliaeetus albicilla.

2007, Dec. 27 **Perf. 14x13½**
Stamps With White Frames
311-316 A106   Set of 6   12.50 12.50
Stamps With Colored Frames
317 A106   Sheet of 6, #a-f   12.50 12.50

2008 Summer Olympics, Beijing A107

Designs: 1.50s, Soccer. No. 319, 2s, Hammer throw. No. 320, 2s, Judo. No. 321, 2s, Boxing.

2008, Feb. 28 **Litho.** **Perf. 12½x13**
318-321 A107   Set of 4   7.50 7.50
321a   Miniature sheet, 2 each   15.00 15.00
   #318-321

Cooking Pot — A108

Pitcher — A109

Pot With Lid — A110

Pitcher — A111

2008, Mar. 28 **Perf. 14x14¼**
322 A108   20d brown   .35 .35
323 A108   25d dark blue   .45 .45
324 A109   50d purple   .90 .90
325 A109   1s indigo   1.75 1.75
326 A110   1.35s dark green   2.40 2.40
327 A111   2s brown   3.75 3.75
328 A110   2.15s dark blue   4.00 4.00
329 A111   3s dark red   5.50 5.50
   Nos. 322-329 (8)   19.10 19.10

Souvenir Sheet

Intl. Conference on Water Related Disaster Reduction, Dushanbe — A112

No. 330: a, Avalanche. b, Tornado.

2008, June 19 **Perf. 14¼x14**
330 A112   2.50s Sheet of 2, #a-b,   + label   9.50 9.50

Souvenir Sheet

Buddha Statues, Ajinateppa — A113

No. 331: a, 2.50s, Head of Buddha. b, 3.50s, Buddha reclining.

2008, June 19 **Perf. 14x14¼**
331 A113   Sheet of 2, #a-b, +   4 labels   10.00 10.00

Nos. 140-141 Surcharged in Black or Red

Methods and Perfs. As Before
2008, July 4
Black Surcharge
332   1s on 100r #140   3.25 3.25
333   1s on 100r #141   3.25 3.25
 a.   A31 Pair, #332-333   6.50 6.50
Red Surcharge
334   1s on 100r #140   3.25 3.25
335   1s on 100r #141   3.25 3.25
 a.   A31 Pair, #334-335   6.50 6.50
   Nos. 332-335 (4)   13.00 13.00

Souvenir Sheet

Rudaki (c. 859-940), Poet — A114

No. 336 — Rudaki facing: a, Right. b, Left.

2008, July 9 **Litho.** **Perf. 14¼x14**
336 A114   2.50s Sheet of 2, #a-b,   + label   8.25 8.25

Plants and Insects — A115

No. 337: a, 1.50s, Ribwort and grasshopper. b, 1.50s, Coltfoot and ladybug. c, 2s, Dandelion and beetle. d, 2s, Calendula and bee.

2008, Sept. 29 **Perf. 14x14¼**
337 A115   Block of 4, #a-d   11.00 11.00

Souvenir Sheet

Snakes — A116

No. 338 — Snake facing: a, Right. b, Left.

2008, Sept. 29 **Perf. 13½x14**
338 A116   2.50s Sheet of 2, #a-b   9.50 9.50

Grapes — A117

No. 339 — Color of grapes: a, 1.50s, Purple (Djaus). b, 1.50s, Pink (Black sultana). c, 2s, White (Ladies' fingers). d, 2s, Red (Red Taffi).

2008, Dec. 1 **Perf. 14x14¼**
339 A117   Block of 4, #a-d   10.50 10.50

Musical Instruments — A118

No. 340: a, Gijak of Badahshon. b, Khoirasan local dotaar.

2008, Dec. 1 **Litho.** **Perf. 14x14¼**
340   Horiz. pair + central   label   11.00 11.00
 a.-b.   A118 3s Either single   5.50 5.50
   See Iran No. 2976.

No. 220 Overprinted

Designs as before.

Methods and Perfs As Before
2009, Feb. 1
341 A63   Sheet of 8, #a-h   14.50 14.50
   (#220)

Souvenir Sheet

Paintings — A119

No. 342: a, Flowering Indian Lilac — Luchob, by Zuhur Habibuloev. b, My Mother — My wings, by Sabzali Sharif.

2009, Mar. 31 **Litho.** **Perf. 13½**
342 A119   4s Sheet of 2, #a-b   11.50 11.50

Imam Azam's Celebration Year — A120

2009, July 28
343 A120 4s multi   5.00 5.00

Worldwide Fund for Nature (WWF) A121

Cervus elaphus bactrianus: 1.50s, Head of doe, bucks fighting. 2s, Buck. 2.50s, Buck, two does. 3s, Two does and fawn.

2009, July 28   **Perf. 13½x13¾**
344-347 A121   Set of 4   5.50 5.50
347a   Sheet of 16, 4 each
    #344-347   22.00 22.00
Nos. 344-347, 347a exist imperf.

Animals — A122

Designs: No. 348, 1s, Equus przewalskii. No. 349, 1s, Panthera tigris tigris. No. 350, 1.50s, Camelus bactrianus. No. 351, 1.50s, Caracal caracal. No. 352, 2s, Ailuropoda melanoleuca. No. 353, 2s, Macaca fuscata. No. 354, 2.30s, Elephas maximus. No. 355, 2.30s, Ovis vignei.

2009, July 28   **Perf. 13¾x13½**
348-355 A122   Set of 8   11.00 11.00
355a   Sheet of 8, #348-355   11.00 11.00
Nos. 348-355 were each printed in sheets of 9 + label.

Souvenir Sheet

Animal Circus Performers — A123

No. 356: a, Cat on ball. b, Dog balancing ball on nose.

2009, Sept. 14   **Perf. 14x14¼**
356 A123 3.50s Sheet of 2,
   #a-b   10.50 10.50

Souvenir Sheet

Tajikistan Glaciers — A124

No. 357 — Glaciers on mountain peaks: a, Abu ali ibn Sino. b, Ismoili Somoni.

2009, Sept. 14   **Perf. 13½**
357 A124 4s Sheet of 2, #a-b   11.00 11.00

No. 144 Surcharged

Method and Perf. As Before
2009, Dec. 1
358 A32b 15d on (270r) #144   .40 .40

Melons — A125

No. 359: a, 1.50s, Green melon (whole melon and quarter melon), and large green leaves. b, 1.50s, Yellow and brown melon (whole melon and ⅛ melon slice) and gray leaves. c, 2s, Yellow and brown melon (whole melon and half melon) and gray leaves. d, 2s, Yellow and brown melon (whole melon and quarter melon) and large green leaves.

2009, Dec. 3 Litho.   **Perf. 14x14¼**
359 A125   Block of 4, #a-d   10.50 10.50
Stamps of same denomination are se-tenant within the block. No. 359 exists imperf. Value, $20.

Victory in World War II, 65th Anniv. — A126

No. 360: a, 1.35s, Soldiers and airplanes. b, 2.15s, Soviet Union soldiers holding Nazi flags near Kremlin in Moscow.

2010, Mar. 15 Litho.   **Perf. 14¼x14**
360 A126   Pair, #a-b   3.75 3.75
Printed in sheets containing 3 #360a, 2 #360b + label.

Peonies — A127

No. 361 — Peony with butterfly at: a, 2s, Right. b, 3.20s, Left.

2010, Mar. 30   **Perf. 12½**
361 A127   Pair, #a-b   5.25 5.25
   c.   Souvenir sheet, #361b   3.25 3.25
Printed in sheets containing 3 each #361a-361b.

Rogun Hydroelectric Project — A128

Designs: 10d, Vakhsh River Dam. 15d, Transmission towers and lines. 20d, Turbines. 10s, Tunnel-boring machine.

2010, May 20   **Perf. 13¼x14**
362-365 A128   Set of 4   9.25 9.25

Khaje Abdullah Ansari (1006-88), Mystic A129

2010, July 25   **Perf. 13½**
366 A129 5s multi   5.75 5.75
See Afghanistan No. and Iran No.

Miniature Sheet

Mammals — A130

No. 367: a, 2.50s, Canis lupus. b, 3s, Lynx lynx. c, 3.50s, Elephas maximus. d, 4.50s, Panthera tigris.

2010, Aug. 2   **Perf. 14¼x14**
367 A130   Sheet of 4, #a-d, +
   2 labels   11.50 11.50
Bangkok 2010 Intl. Stamp Exhibition, Portugal 2010 World Philatelic Exhibition.

Souvenir Sheet

Ancient Coins — A131

No. 368: a, 4s, Silver Sasani coin. b, 5s, Gold Shahanshoh Vasudeva coin.

2010, Nov. 19   **Perf. 13½x14**
368 A131   Sheet of 2, #a-b   11.00 11.00

Souvenir Sheet

Traditional Men's Dances — A132

No. 369: a, Man dancing, old man, boy, birds. b, Three men dancing.

2010, Nov. 19   **Perf. 14¼x14**
369 A132 4s Sheet of 2, #a-b   10.50 10.50

No. 265 Overprinted

Methods and Perfs As Before
2010, Apr. 30
370 A84   Sheet of 8, #265c,
   265e, 265f, 265h,
   370a-370d   15.50 15.50
  a.   20d "2010 -" on #265a   .45 .45
  b.   20d Cyrillic text overprinted on
   #265b   .45 .45
  c.   75d "Year of the tiger" overprinted on #265d   1.75 1.75
  d.   1.50s "- 2010" overprinted on
   #265g   3.50 3.50

Souvenir Sheet

New Year 2011 (Year of the Rabbit) — A133

No. 371: a, Rabbit and carrots. b, Rabbit and cat.

2011, Apr. 1 Litho.   **Perf. 14¼x14**
371 A133 2s Sheet of 2, #a-b   5.75 5.75

Nos. 18 and 27 Surcharged

Methods and Perfs As Before
2011, Apr. 27
372 A5 10d on 25r #18   .75 .75
373 A6 15d on 35r #27   1.10 1.10

Locomotives — A134

No. 374: a, 1-5-0, 1947. b, 1-4-0, 1912. c, 1-3-1, 1925. d, 2-3-1, 1925.

2011, June 3 Litho. Perf. 14x14¼
374 A134 1.50s Block of 4, #a-d 6.25 6.25

Apricot Blossoms — A135

No. 375 — Various blossoms: a, 3.50s. b, 4s.

2011, Aug. 10 Perf. 13
375 A135 Horiz. pair, #a-b 5.50 5.50

Miniature Sheet

Independence, 20th Anniv. — A136

No. 376: a, 2.50s, Norak Hydropower Plant (40x28mm). b, 2.50s, Sangtuda Hydropower Plant (40x28mm). c, 2.50s, Rogun Hydropower Plant (40x28mm). d, 3s, President Emomali Rakhmonov (40x84mm).

2011, Aug. 26 Perf. 14x14¼
376 A136 Sheet of 4, #a-d 12.00 12.00

Souvenir Sheet

Commonweath of Independent States, 20th Anniv. — A137

2011, Aug. 26 Perf. 14¼x14
377 A137 3.50s multi 9.50 9.50

Souvenir Sheet

Regional Communications Commonwealth, 20th Anniv. — A138

2011, Sept. 8
378 A138 2.50s multi 9.25 9.25

TANGANYIKA
ˌtan-gə-ˈnyē-kə

LOCATION — Southeastern Africa bordering on the Indian Ocean
GOVT. — Republic within British Commonwealth
AREA — 362,688 sq. mi.
POP. — 9,404,000 (est. 1961)

CAPITAL — Dar es Salaam

Before World War I, this area formed part of German East Africa. It was mandated to Britain after World War I and (in 1946) became a trust territory under the United Nations. In 1935, stamps of the mandate were replaced by those used jointly by Kenya, Uganda and Tanganyika (see Kenya, Uganda and Tanzania). On Dec. 9, 1961, Tanganyika became independent. On Dec. 9, 1962, it became a republic. April 26, 1964, it joined Zanzibar to form the United Republic of Tanganyika and Zanzibar (later renamed Tanzania). See Tanzania.

100 Cents = 1 Rupee
100 Cents = 1 Shilling (1922)
20 Shillings = 1 Pound

> Catalogue values for unused stamps in this country are for Never Hinged items, beginning with Scott 45 in the regular postage section and Scott O1 in the officials section.

Stamps of East Africa & Uganda Protectorates Overprinted

G.E.A.

1921 Wmk. 4 Perf. 14
1 A1 12c gray 7.50 110.00
2 A1 15c ultra 4.00 7.00
3 A1 50c dull violet & blk 11.50 97.50

Overprinted
G.E.A.

4 A2 2r black & red, *blue* 37.50 140.00
5 A2 3r gray green & violet 85.00 210.00
7 A2 5r dull violet & ultra 120.00 290.00
Nos. 1-7 (6) 265.50 854.50

Overprinted in Red or Black
G.E.A.

1922
8 A1 1c black (R) 1.25 21.00
9 A1 10c orange (Bk) 1.60 16.00

A3   Giraffe — A4

Perf. 14½x14
1922-25 Engr. Wmk. 4
10 A3 5c dk violet & blk 2.75 .25
11 A3 5c grn & blk ('25) 5.00 1.75
12 A3 10c green & blk 2.75 .95
13 A3 10c yel & blk ('25) 5.50 1.75
14 A3 15c carmine & blk 2.25 .25
15 A3 20c orange & blk 2.00 .25
16 A3 25c black 6.25 7.50
17 A3 25c blue & blk ('25) 4.50 20.00
18 A3 30c blue & blk 5.75 5.75
19 A3 30c dull vio & blk ('25) 4.75 16.00
20 A3 40c brown & black 3.25 5.25
21 A3 50c gray black 2.75 1.75
22 A3 75c bister & black 3.75 21.00
Perf. 14
23 A4 1sh green & black 3.50 12.50
a. Wmk. sideways 5.50 16.00

24 A4 2sh brn vio & blk 5.25 29.00
a. Wmk. sideways 6.25 18.00
25 A4 3sh blk, wmk. sideways 23.00 32.50
26 A4 5sh red & black 21.00 85.00
a. Wmk. sideways 42.50 97.50
27 A4 10sh dp blue & blk 65.00 130.00
a. Wmk. sideways 140.00 275.00
28 A4 £1 orange & black 200.00 375.00
a. Wmk. sideways 250.00 400.00
Nos. 10-28 (19) 369.00 746.45

On No. 28 the words of value are in a curve between the circle and "POSTAGE & REVENUE."

King George V
A5   A6

1927-31 Typo.
29 A5 5c green & black 2.00 .25
30 A5 10c yellow & black 2.25 .25
31 A5 15c red & black 2.00 .25
32 A5 20c orange & black 3.00 .25
33 A5 25c ultra & black 4.25 2.25
34 A5 30c dull violet & blk 3.25 3.00
35 A5 30c ultra & blk ('31) 29.00 .35
36 A5 40c brown & black 2.25 5.25
37 A5 50c gray & black 2.90 1.10
38 A5 75c olive grn & blk 2.25 17.50
39 A6 1sh green & black 4.75 3.25
40 A6 2sh violet brn & blk 24.00 5.25
41 A6 3sh black 29.00 70.00
42 A6 5sh scarlet & blk 22.50 21.00
43 A6 10sh ultra & black 67.50 110.00
44 A6 £1 brown org & blk 190.00 350.00
Nos. 29-44 (16) 390.90 589.95

> Catalogue values for unused stamps in this section, from this point to the end of the section, are for Never Hinged items.

Independent State

Nurse and Infant — A7   Torch above Mt. Kilimanjaro — A8

5c, Teacher instructing villagers, horiz. 15c, Coffee picker. 20c, Harvesting corn. 30c, Flag, horiz. 50c, Serengeti lions. 1sh, Nurse showing mother to infant & hospital. 2sh, Dar es Salaam harbor. 5sh, Tractor & field workers. 10sh, Diamond mine & rose diamond. 1sh, 2sh, 5sh, 10sh, horiz.

Perf. 14x14½, 14½x14
1961, Dec. 9 Photo. Unwmk.
45 A7 5c sepia & yel grn .30 .30
46 A7 10c Prussian green .30 .30
47 A7 15c sepia & blue .30 .30
b. Blue omitted 650.00
48 A7 20c orange brown .30 .30
49 A7 30c dp green, blk & yel .30 .30
50 A7 50c sepia & yellow .30 .30
Perf. 14½
51 A8 1sh cit brn & gray bl .30 .30
52 A8 1sh30c multicolored 3.50 .30
53 A8 2sh multicolored 1.10 .30
54 A8 5sh Prus grn & dp org 1.10 .30
55 A8 10sh blk, bl & rose 17.50 5.25
a. Rose (diamond) omitted 125.00
56 A8 20sh multicolored 4.50 10.00
Nos. 45-56 (12) 29.80 18.25

Tanganyika's independence, Dec. 9, 1961. For overprints see Nos. O21-O28.

Pres. Julius Nyerere with Pickax — A9

Designs: 50c, Flag hoisting on Mt. Kilimanjaro. 1sh30c, Presidential emblem. 2sh50c, Independence monument, Mnazi Moja.

1962, Dec. 9 Perf. 14½x14
57 A9 30c bright green .25 .25
58 A9 50c multicolored .25 .25
59 A9 1sh30c multicolored .25 .25
60 A9 2sh50c dk blue, blk & red .75 .50
Nos. 57-60 (4) 1.50 1.25

Issued to commemorate the establishment of the Republic of Tanganyika, Dec. 9, 1962.

OFFICIAL STAMPS

> Catalogue values for unused stamps in this section are for Never Hinged items.

Issued for use by the Tanganyika Government

Stamps of Kenya, Uganda & Tanganyika, 1954-59, Overprinted

Perf. 12½x13, 13x12½
1959 Engr. Wmk. 4
O1 A18 5c choc & blk .25 1.25
O2 A19 10c carmine .25 1.25
O3 A20 15c lt bl & blk (on #106) .35 1.25
O4 A19 20c org & blk .25 .25
a. Double overprint 1,300.
O5 A18 30c ultra & black .25 .95
O6 A19 50c dp red lilac .75 .25
O7 A19 1sh dp mag & blk .25 .85
O8 A20 1sh30c pur & red org 5.50 2.25
O9 A20 2sh dp grn & gray 1.40 1.10
O10 A20 5sh black & org 4.00 3.50
O11 A20 10sh ultra & blk 2.25 4.00
O12 A21 £1 black & ver 7.50 17.50
Nos. O1-O12 (12) 23.00 34.40

Stamps of Kenya, Uganda & Tanganyika, 1960, Overprinted

Perf. 14½x14
1960, Oct. 1 Photo. Wmk. 314
O13 A23 5c dull blue .25 2.00
O14 A23 10c lt olive green .25 2.00
O15 A23 15c dull purple .25 2.00
O16 A23 20c brt lilac rose .25 .55
O17 A23 30c brt vermilion .25 .25
O18 A23 50c dull violet .35 1.10

Nos. 129 & 133 of Kenya, Uganda & Tanganyika Overprinted

	Engr.		Perf. 14	
O19	A24	1sh violet & lilac red	.45	.30
O20	A24	5sh rose red & lilac	16.00	1.50
	Nos. O13-O20 (8)		18.05	9.70

Nos. 45-51 and 54 Overprinted "OFFICIAL" in Sans-serif Type of Various Sizes

Perf. 14x14½, 14½x14

1961, Dec. 9 Unwmk.

O21	A7	5c sepia & yellow grn	.25	.25
O22	A7	10c Prussian green	.25	.25
O23	A7	15c sepia & blue	.25	.25
O24	A7	20c orange brown	.25	.25
O25	A7	30c dp grn blk & yel	.25	.25
O26	A7	50c sepia & yellow	.25	.25
O27	A8	1sh citron brn & gray bl	.25	.25
O28	A8	5sh Prus grn & dp org	1.00	1.00
	Nos. O21-O28 (8)		2.75	2.75

TANNU TUVA

'tä-nə 'tü-və

(Tuva People's Republic)

LOCATION — Between Siberia and northwestern Mongolia at the sources of the Yenisei, in the basin formed by the Tannu-Ola and Sayan Mountains.
GOVT. — A former republic closely identified with Soviet Russia in Asia
AREA — 64,000 sq. mi. (approx.)
POP. — 95,000 (1941 est.)
CAPITAL — Kyzyl

This region, traditionally called Uriankhai, was ruled by the Mongols until the mid-18th century, when it became part of the Chinese Empire. Russia and China struggled for control of the country 1914-21, until it became independent as the Tannu Tuva People's Republic in 1921. In 1944 it was incorporated into the U.S.S.R. as an autonomous region of the Russian Soviet Federated Socialist Republic.

Russian, later Soviet, stamps were used in Tuva prior to 1926 and after 1944.

100 Mongo=1 Tugrik
100 Kopecks = 1 Ruble
100 Kopecks = 1 Tugrik (1934)
100 Kopecks = 1 Aksha (1936)

Watermarks

Wmk. 204 — Stars and Diamonds

Wmk. 170 — Greek Border and Rosettes

Most used examples of Nos. 1-38, 45-52a, 54-92 and C1-C18 on the market are cancelled to order, and the used values below are for such stamps.

Tuvan stamps, except for Nos. 117-123 and most of the overprints, were printed by the State Security Printers in Moscow.

Wheel of Truth — A1

	1926	Litho.	Wmk. 204	Perf. 13½
		Size: 20x26mm		
1	A1	1k red	1.50	1.50
2	A1	2k light blue	1.50	1.50
3	A1	5k orange	1.50	1.50
4	A1	8k yel green	2.00	1.75
5	A1	10k violet	2.00	1.75
6	A1	30k dark brown	2.00	1.75
7	A1	50k gray black	2.25	1.75

Size: 22½x30mm
Perf. 10½

8	A1	1r blue green	6.00	3.00
9	A1	3r red brown	8.00	5.75
10	A1	5r dark ultra	13.50	8.00
	Nos. 1-10 (10)		40.25	28.25
	Set, never hinged		77.50	

Nos. 1-10 have crackled white gum. Reprints can be distinguished by their smooth gum.
Nos. 1-10 in different colors are proofs.

Nos. 7-10 Surcharged in Red or Black

Surcharged in Kyzyl.

	1927		Perf. 13½	
11	A1	8k on 50k	25.00	12.50
a.	Inverted surcharge		65.00	
b.	Double surcharge		100.00	

Perf. 10½

12	A1	14k on 1r	25.00	12.50
a.	Inverted surcharge		75.00	
b.	Double surcharge		85.00	
13	A1	18k on 3r (Bk)	25.00	12.50
a.	Inverted surcharge		90.00	
b.	Double surcharge		75.00	
14	A1	28k on 5r (Bk)	25.00	12.50
a.	Inverted surcharge		90.00	
b.	Double surcharge		75.00	
	Nos. 11-14 (4)		100.00	50.00
	Set, never hinged		200.00	

Nos. 11-14 were surcharged with a shiny ink. Reprints are overprinted with a dull ink and are often smudged.

Tuvan Woman — A3

Map of Tannu Tuva A8

Sheep Herding — A11

Fording a Stream — A13

Tuvan Riding Reindeer — A16

Designs: 2k, Stag. 3k, Mountain goat. 4k, Tuvan and tent. 5k, Tuvan man. 10k, Archery competition. 14k, Camel caravan. 28k, Landscape. 50k, Weaving. 70k, Tuvan on horseback.
Printed in Moscow.

	1927	Litho.	Perf. 12½	
15	A3	1k black, lt brown & red	1.00	.60
16	A3	2k purple, dp brown & green	1.20	.55
17	A3	3k black, bl grn & yellow	2.00	.60
18	A3	4k vio bl & choc	.90	.60
19	A3	5k org, blk & dk bl	.90	.65

Perf. 12½x12

20	A8	8k ol brn, pale bl & red brn	1.00	.65
21	A8	10k black, green & brn red	5.50	1.00
22	A8	14k vio bl & red org	10.00	3.50

Perf. 10½

23	A11	18k dk bl & red brn	10.00	5.00
24	A11	28k emer & blk brn	7.25	2.75
25	A13	40k rose & bl grn	5.00	2.50
26	A13	50k black, green & red brown	3.50	2.00
27	A13	70k dl red & bis	7.00	4.00
28	A16	1r yel brn & vio	16.00	6.75
	Nos. 15-28 (14)		71.25	31.15
	Set, never hinged		142.50	

Nos. 15-28 were issued with a crackled white gum. Reprints of the 1k-5k values exist and can be distinguished by their smooth gum.
Nos. 15-28 in different colors are proofs.

Nos. 25-27, 20-22 Surcharged "Tuva", "Posta" and New Values in Various Colors

Surcharged in Moscow.

1932

29	A13	1k on 40k (Bk)	9.00	10.00
30	A13	2k on 50k (Br)	10.00	10.00
31	A13	3k on 70k (Bl)	10.00	10.00
a.	Inverted surcharge		300.00	
32	A8	5k on 8k (Bk)	10.00	10.00
33	A8	10k (Bk)	10.00	10.00
34	A8	15k on 14k (Bk)	15.00	15.00
	Nos. 29-34 (6)		64.00	65.00
	Set, never hinged		128.00	

Issued in connection with the Romanization of the alphabet.
No. 31 with black surcharge was prepared but not issued.

#20//24 Surcharged in Black
Surcharged by numbering machine in Kyzyl.

No. 37

No. 38

	1932-33		Wmk. 204	
35	A8	10k on 8k	180.00	100.00
36	A8	15k on 14k	300.00	200.00
37	A11	35k on 18k	150.00	100.00
	(#23)			
b.	Pair, one without surcharge		—	
c.	Inverted surcharge		500.00	
38	A11	35k on 28k	150.00	100.00
a.	Pair, one without surcharge		—	
	Nos. 35-38 (4)		780.00	500.00
	Set, never hinged		1,550.	

A19

Revenue Stamps Surcharged "Posta" and New Values

Three types: type 1, figures of value 6.7mm high; type 2, figures of value 6.7mm high, letter "p" lengthened at bottom; type 3, figures of value 5.1mm high.
Surcharged in Kyzyl.

	1933		Perf. 12x12½	
39	A19	15k on 6k org yel, type 1	300.00	150.00
40	A19	15k on 6k org yel, type 2	300.00	150.00
b.	Inverted surcharge		—	
41	A19	15k on 6k org yel, type 3	500.00	300.00
42	A19	35k on 15k red brn, type 1	—	4,000.
43	A19	35k on 15k red brn, type 2	—	4,000.
44	A19	35k on 15k red brn, type 3	1,500.	800.00

Mounted Hunter — A20

Tuvan Inside of Yurt — A21

Tuvan Milking Yak — A22

Designs: 2k, Hunter stalking game. 4k, Tractor. 10k, Camel caravan. 15k, Herdsman lassoing reindeer. 20k, Hunter shooting fox with arrow.

Two dies on 10k: Die I, Crown at center top is light and matches the shade of the sky below; Die II, Crown at center top is bold, consistent with rest of design and darker than the sky.

Printed by State Security Printers, Moscow.

Wmk. 170

1934, Apr.   Photo.   Perf. 12

45	A20	1k red orange	1.50	1.00
46	A20	2k olive green	1.50	1.00
47	A21	3k rose red	1.50	1.00
48	A21	4k slate purple	3.50	1.75
49	A22	5k ultramarine	3.50	1.75
50	A22	10k brown, die II	3.50	1.75
51	A22	15k dark lilac	3.50	1.75
52	A22	20k gray black	4.75	2.75
		Nos. 45-52 (8)	23.25	12.75
		Set, never hinged	50.00	
		Set, imperf	50.00	
		Set, imperf., never hinged	100.00	

Nos. 45-52 are inscribed "REGISTERED," but were used as regular postage stamps.

Nos. 46, 48 and 50 exist perf 11, and No. 50 also exists perf 11x10. No. 48 exists perf 11½, reportedly as a color trial proof.

#51 Surcharged in Black

Surcharged by numbering machine in Kyzyl.

1935

53	A22	20k on 15k	175.00	325.00
a.		Inverted surcharge	400.00	

Map of Tuva — A23

Rocky Outcropping — A24

Designs: 3k, 5k, 10k, Different scenes of Yenisei River. 25k, Bei-kem rapids. 50k, Mounted hunters.

Printed by State Security Printers, Moscow.

Wmk. 170

1935, Mar.   Photo.   Perf. 14

54	A23	1k yellow orange	2.25	1.75
55	A23	3k deep green	2.25	1.75
56	A23	5k carmine red	3.00	2.00
57	A23	10k violet	3.25	2.00
b.		Pair, imperf between		
58	A24	15k olive green	3.50	2.50
59	A24	25k violet blue	4.00	2.50
60	A24	50k dark brown	5.75	4.25
		Nos. 54-60 (7)	24.00	15.25
		Set, never hinged	45.00	

Nos. 54-60 in different colors, perf and imperf, are proofs.

Badger
A25

Squirrel — A26

Fox — A27

Elk — A28

Yak — A29

Designs: 5k, Ermine. 25k, Otter. 50k, Lynx. 3t, Bactrian camels. 5t, Bear.
Printed by State Security Printers, Moscow.

1935, Mar.

61	A25	1k orange	1.60	1.00
62	A26	3k emerald green	1.60	1.00
a.		Imperf, pair	300.00	
63	A25	5k rose red	1.60	1.10
64	A27	10k crimson red	1.60	1.10
65	A27	25k orange red	2.50	1.20
66	A27	50k deep blue	2.50	1.20
67	A28	1t violet	2.50	1.20
a.		Imperf, pair	—	
68	A29	2t royal blue	3.50	1.20
69	A29	3t red brown	4.00	1.35
70	A28	5t indigo	5.00	1.75
a.		Imperf, pair	300.00	
b.		Pair, imperf between	—	
		Nos. 61-70 (10)	26.40	12.10
		Set, never hinged	50.00	

Nos. 61-70 in different colors are proofs.

Tuvan Arms — A30

Herdsman on Bull — A32

Athletic Competitions — A33

Soldiers
A34

Designs: 2k, Pres. Ch(aumlaut char='u')rmit-Dazhy. 3k, Tuvan with Bactrian camel. 5k, 8k, Archer. 10k, 15k, Spearfishing. 12k, 20k, Bear-hunting. 30k, Camel and train. 40k, 50k, Horse race. 80k, Partisans. 3t, Partisans confiscating cattle. 5t, 1921 battle scene.

Printed by State Security Printers, Moscow.

1936, July   Perf. 14

71	A30	1k bronze green	2.00	.70
72	A30	2k dark brown	2.50	1.50
74a	A31	4k orange red	3.50	.75
75	A31	5k brown purple	5.00	.70
76	A31	6k myrtle green	4.75	.70
77	A31	8k plum	4.75	.70
78	A31	10k rose red	6.00	1.00
79	A31	12k black brown	7.50	1.25
80a	A31	15k bronze green	13.00	1.25
81	A31	20k deep blue	11.00	1.20
82a	A32	25k orange red	13.00	.90
83	A32	30k plum	30.00	1.25
84a	A32	35k rose red	13.00	1.25
85	A32	40k deep brown	9.00	1.50
86a	A32	50k indigo blue	13.00	1.50
87	A33	70k plum	12.00	2.00
88	A33	80k green	11.00	2.00
89	A34	1a orange red	11.00	2.00
a.		1a rose red (error)	—	
90	A34	2a rose red	11.00	3.00
92	A33	5a black brown	15.00	2.50
73	A30	3k indigo blue	3.25	.75
91	A31	3a indigo blue	17.50	2.00
		Nos. 71-92 (15)	142.50	22.00
		Set, never hinged	325.00	

15th anniversary of independence.
Values for Nos. 71-92 are for the most common varieties. For detailed listings, see the *Scott Classic Specialized Catalogue.*
Imperfs are remainders, later sold by the Soviet Postal Museum.

Values for Nos. 93-98 and 104-116 are for genuine examples. Expertization is essential for these issues.

Issues of 1934-36 Handstamped with Large Numerals and Old Values Obliterated with Bars or Blocks

1938, Aug.

93	A34	5k on 2a (#90a)	400.00
94	AP5	5k on 2a (#C17)	375.00
95	AP1	10k on 1t (#C8)	350.00
96	A24	20k on 50k (#60)	350.00
97	AP5	30k on 2a (#C17)	350.00
98	AP5	30k on 3a (#C18)	325.00

Types of 1935-36 with Modified Designs and New Colors

1938, Dec.   Unwmk.   Perf. 12½

99	A25	5k deep green	60.00
100	A31	10k indigo (dates removed)	60.00

101	AP3	15k red brown ("AIR MAIL," dates removed)	60.00	—
102	A31	20k orange red (dates removed)	85.00	—
103	A33	30k maroon (dates removed)	60.00	—
		Nos. 99-103 (5)	325.00	
		Set, never hinged	500.00	

Some experts believe that these stamps were issued in March 1941.

Stamps of 1934-35 Handstamp Surcharged with New Values in Black or Violet at Kyzyl

1939

104	AP1	10k on 1t (#C8)	225.00
105	AP1	10k on 1t (#B8) (V)	225.00
106	A24	20k on 50k (#60) (V)	200.00

Old values obliterated on Nos. 104-106.

Stamps of 1934-36 Handstamp Surcharged with New Values at Kyzyl

1940, Oct.-1941

107	AP1	10k on 1t (#C8)	—	125.00
a.		Double surcharge		
108	A24	20k on 50k (#60)	—	150.00
109	A27	20k on 50k (#66)	—	350.00
110	A32	20k on 50k (#86a)	—	350.00
111	AP4	20k on 50k (#C14)	—	100.00
112	A33	20k on 70k (#87a)	—	500.00
113	AP4	20k on 75k (#C15)	—	110.00
114	A33	20k on 80k (#88)	—	500.00

The old values are not obliterated on Nos. 107 or 108.

Nos. 91, 92 Handstamp Surcharged with New Values at Kyzyl

1942

115	A33	25k on 3a (#91)	1,200.	—
116	A33	25k on 5a (#92)		—

Government House — A35

Exhibition Hall — A36

Tuvan Woman — A37

1942   Typo.   Unwmk.   Imperf.

117	A35	25k steel blue	950.00	100.00
118	A36	25k steel blue	950.00	100.00
119	A37	25k steel blue	950.00	150.00
		Nos. 117-119 (3)	2,850.	350.00

21st anniversary of independence.

Nos. 117-119 were hand-printed together in small sheetlets of five (117+119+118+117+119), so various se-tenant combinations are possible.

Two additional values, a 25k depicting a Tuvan man and a 50k depicting a soldier on a horse, were prepared, but not issued. A collective proof sheetlet of five, containing Nos. 117-119 and these two values, in the same color as the issued stamps, is also known.

Coat of Arms — A38

Government Building — A39

1943   Perf. 11 (1 or 2 Sides)
Buff Paper

120	A38	25k slate blue	100.00	—
		Vertical strip of 5	900.00	
121	A38	25k black	100.00	—
122	A38	25k blue green	90.00	—
123	A39	50k blue green	90.00	—
		Nos. 120-123 (4)	380.00	

White Paper

120a	A38	25k slate blue	90.00	—
b.		Strip of 3, imperf between	250.00	
121a	A38	25k black	125.00	—
		Vertical strip of five	600.00	
122a	A39	25k blue green	95.00	—
123a	A39	50k blue green	95.00	—
		Nos. 120a-123a (4)	405.00	

22nd anniversary of independence.

Nos. 120 and 121 were each printed in vertical strips of five, perforated 11 between stamps and imperf on outside edges, so that these stamps may be perforated on top edge only, bottom edge only, or on both top and bottom edges. To make maximum use of limited wartime paper supplies, they were sometimes printed in strips of four. These smaller strips are rare.

Nos. 122 and 123 were printed together in blocks of four, containing a vertical pair of the 25k and a vertical pair of the 50k, perforated internally both vertically and horizontally and imperf on the outer edges. Setenant pairs, Value $225 (#122+123), $275 (#122a+123a).

Nos. 121 and 123a were issued with gum, No. 123a both with and without gum, and the balance of the set without gum.

Used examples and covers exist but are extremely rare.

AIR POST STAMPS

Airplane and Yaks — AP1

Airplane and Capercaillie — AP2

Designs, airplane over: 5k, 15k, Camels. 25k, Argali (wild sheep). 75k, Ox and cart. 2t, Roe deer.
Printed by State Security Printers, Moscow.

Wmk. 170
1934, Apr. 4   Photo.   Perf. 14

C1	AP1	1k orange red	1.40	1.00
C2	AP1	5k emer green	1.40	1.00
C3	AP2	10k purple brown	4.50	3.00
C4	AP1	15k rose red	2.75	1.00
C5	AP2	25k slate purple	2.75	1.00
C6	AP1	50k dp bl green	2.75	1.00
C7	AP2	75k lake	2.75	1.00
C8	AP1	1t royal blue	3.50	2.00
C9	AP2	2t ultra, 61x31mm	20.00	25.00
a.		54.5x29mm	40.00	
		Nos. C1-C9 (9)	41.80	36.00
		Set, never hinged	55.00	

Nos. C1-C9 imperf or perf 11½ and stamps printed in different colors are proofs.

Tuvan Leading Laden Yak — AP3

Horseman and Zeppelin AP4

Seaplane Above Dragon — AP5

Designs: 10k, Tuvan plowing. 50k, Villagers with biplane overhead.
Printed by State Security Printers, Moscow.

1936   Unwmk.

C10	AP3	5k indigo & beige	3.00	1.50
C11	AP3	10k purple & cinnamon	4.50	1.50
C12	AP3	15k black brown & pale gray	4.50	1.75
C13	AP4	25k plum & cream	6.00	2.50
c.		Horiz. pair, perf 11, imperf between	—	—
C14	AP4	50k rose red & cream	6.50	2.50
C15	AP4	75k emer grn & pale yellow	10.00	4.00
C16	AP5	1a blue green & pale bl grn	12.00	5.00
C17	AP5	2a rose red & cream	9.50	3.75
C18	AP5	3a dark brown & beige	9.50	3.75
		Nos. C10-C18 (9)	65.50	26.25
		Set, never hinged	120.00	

15th anniversary of independence.

Nos. C10-C18 exist imperf.

TANZANIA

ˌtan-zə-ˈnē-ə

(Tanganyika and Zanzibar)

LOCATION — Southeastern Africa bordering on the Indian Ocean, and a group of islands about 20 miles off the coast
GOVT. — United republic in British Commonwealth
AREA — 364,886 sq. mi.

POP. — 31,270,820 (1999 est.)
CAPITAL — Dodoma

Tanganyika joined Zanzibar on April 26, 1964, to form the United Republic of Tanganyika and Zanzibar. In October 1965 the name was changed to United Republic of Tanzania.

Zanzibar stamps include two (Nos. 331, 334) inscribed "Tanzania."

100 Cents = 1 Shilling

> **Catalogue values for all unused stamps in this country are for Never Hinged items.**

Watermark

Wmk. 387 — Squares and Rectangles

Map — A1

Design: 30c, 1sh30c, Emblem (hands holding torch and spear).

Perf. 14x14½
1964, July 7   Photo.   Unwmk.

1	A1	20c blue & emerald	.25	.25
2	A1	30c brn, dk & lt bl	.25	.25
3	A1	1.30sh ultra, blk & org	.30	.30
4	A1	2.50sh ultra & purple	.65	.65
		Nos. 1-4 (4)	1.45	1.45

Union of Tanganyika and Zanzibar. Not sold in Zanzibar, nor valid there.

Flag
A2

Native Handicraft
A3

Designs: 5c, Hale hydroelectric plant. 15c, Army squad. 20c, Road building. 40c, Giraffes. 50c, Zebras. 65c, Mt. Kilimanjaro. 1sh, Dar es Salaam harbor. 1.30sh, Zinjanthropus skull and Olduvai Gorge excavation. 2.50sh, Sailfish, dhow and map of Mafia Island. 5sh, Sisal industry. 10sh, State House, Dar es Salaam. 20sh, Tanzania coat of arms.

Perf. 14x14½, 14½x14
1965, Dec. 9   Photo.   Unwmk.
Size: 21x17½mm, 17½x21mm

5	A2	5c orange & ultra	.40	.60
6	A2	10c ultra, grn, yel & blk	.40	.60
7	A3	15c grn, bl, brn & buff	.40	.60
8	A2	20c blue & brown	.40	.60
9	A3	30c black & red brn	.40	.60
10	A3	40c blue, yel grn & brn	.40	.60
11	A2	50c yellow grn & blue	.40	.60
12	A2	65c ultra, grn & red brn	.50	.75

Perf. 14½
Size: 41½x25, 25x41½mm

13	A2	1sh bl, grn, yel & brn	.60	.60
14	A2	1.30sh multicolored	.90	.60
15	A2	2.50sh blue & red brn	1.35	.95
16	A2	5sh bl, brt grn & red brn	2.75	1.40
17	A2	10sh blue & yellow	5.50	4.00
18	A3	20sh gray & multi	10.50	9.00
		Nos. 5-18 (14)	24.90	21.50

For overprints see Nos. O1-O8.

Turkeyfish — A4

Fish: 5c, Cardinalfish. 10c, Mudskipper. 15c, Toby puffer. 20c, Two sea horses. 30c, Batfish. 40c, Sweetlips. 50c, Birdfish. 65c, Butterflyfish. 70c, Grouper. 1.30sh, Surgeonfish. 1.50sh, Caesio xanthonotus. 2.50sh, Emperor snapper. 5sh, Moorish idol. 10sh, Striped triggerfish. 20sh, Squirrelfish.

1967-71   Photo.   Perf. 14x14½
Size: 21x17½mm
Fish in Natural Colors

19	A4	5c black & citron	.25	.25
20	A4	10c brown & olive	.25	.25
21	A4	15c brown & blue	.25	.25
22	A4	20c brn & dk bl grn	.25	.25
23	A4	30c black & yel grn	.25	.25
24	A4	40c brown & emerald	.25	.25
25	A4	50c blk & dull bl grn	.25	.25
26	A4	65c blk & gray grn	.70	.70
27	A4	70c blk & olive ('69)	.55	.55

Perf. 14½
Size: 41x25mm

28	A4	1sh brown & multi	.45	.25
29	A4	1.30sh black & olive	.70	.25
30	A4	1.50sh black & ol ('69)	.80	.25
31	A4	2.50sh brn yel & grn	1.40	.25
32	A4	5sh black & bl grn	2.25	.25
33	A4	10sh brn & gray grn	4.75	.60
34	A4	20sh blk & gray olive	11.50	1.40
		Nos. 19-34 (16)	24.85	6.25

Issued: #27, 30, 9/15/69; others, 12/9/67.
Values of Nos. 28-34 are for canceled-to-order stamps with printed cancellations. Postally used examples sell for higher prices.
For overprints see Nos. O9-O16.

Papilio Hornimani
A5

Euphaedra Neophron
A6

Butterflies: 10c, Colotis ione. 15c, Amauris makuyuensis. 20c, Libythea laius. 30c, Danaus chrysippus. 40c, Sallya rosa. 50c, Axiocerses styx. 60c, Eurema hecabe. 70c, Acraea insignis. 1.50sh, Precis octavia. 2.50sh, Charaxes eupale. 5sh, Charaxes pollux. 10sh, Salamis parhassus. 20sh, Papilio ophidicephalus.

1973, Dec. 3   Photo.   Perf. 14½x14

35	A5	5c yellow grn & multi	.35	.35
a.		Booklet pane of 4	1.40	
36	A5	10c lt brown & multi	.35	.35
a.		Booklet pane of 4	1.40	
37	A5	15c ultra & multi	.35	.35
38	A5	20c fawn & multi	.35	.35
a.		Booklet pane of 4	1.40	
39	A5	30c yellow & multi	.35	.35
a.		Booklet pane of 4	1.50	
40	A5	40c multicolored	.35	.35
a.		Booklet pane of 4	1.60	
41	A5	50c citron & multi	.35	.35
a.		Booklet pane of 4	1.50	
42	A5	60c multicolored	.35	.35
43	A5	70c brt green & multi	.35	.35
a.		Booklet pane of 4	1.75	

Perf. 14½

44	A6	1sh green & multi	.60	.60
45	A6	1.50sh orange & multi	1.00	1.00
46	A6	2.50sh multicolored	1.75	1.75
47	A6	5sh multicolored	4.00	4.00
48	A6	10sh lt green & multi	7.50	7.50
49	A6	20sh blue & multi	16.50	15.00
		Nos. 35-49 (15)	34.50	33.00

For surcharges and overprints see Nos. 50-53, 135-136, O17-O26.

Nos. 42, 45-46, 49 Surcharged with New Value and 2 Bars

Perf. 14½x14, 14½

1975, Nov. 17   Photo.

50	A5	80c on 60c multi	4.00	3.75
51	A6	2sh on 1.50sh multi	8.00	7.50
52	A6	3sh on 2.50sh multi	24.00	29.00
53	A6	40sh on 20sh multi	12.00	14.00
		Nos. 50-53 (4)	48.00	54.25

A6a

Designs: 50c, Microwave tower. 1sh, Cordless switchboard and operators, horiz. 2sh, Telephones of 1880, 1930 and 1976. 3sh, Message switching center, horiz.

1976, Apr. 15   Litho.   *Perf. 14½*

54	A6a	50c blue & multi	.25	.25
55	A6a	1sh red & multi	.25	.25
56	A6a	2sh yellow & multi	.25	.30
57	A6a	3sh multicolored	.35	.40
a.		Souvenir sheet of 4	2.25	2.25
		Nos. 54-57 (4)	1.10	1.20

Telecommunications development in East Africa. No. 57a contains 4 stamps similar to Nos. 54-57 with simulated perforations.

Exist imperf. from Format International liquidation stock.

A6b

Designs: 50c, Akii Bua, Ugandan hurdler. 1sh, Filbert Bayi, Tanzanian runner. 2sh, Steve Muchoki, Kenyan boxer. 3sh, Olympic torch, flags of Kenya, Tanzania and Uganda.

1976, July 5   Litho.   *Perf. 14½*

58	A6b	50c blue & multi	.25	.25
59	A6b	1sh red & multi	.25	.25
60	A6b	2sh yellow & multi	.25	.25
61	A6b	3sh blue & multi	.30	.35
a.		Souv. sheet of 4, #58-61, perf. 13	4.25	4.25
		Nos. 58-61 (4)	1.05	1.10

21st Olympic Games, Montreal, Canada, July 17-Aug. 1.

Exist imperf. from Format International liquidation stock.

A6c

Rail Transport in East Africa: 50c, Tanzania-Zambia Railway. 1sh, Nile Bridge, Uganda. 2sh, Nakuru Station, Kenya. 3sh, Class A locomotive, 1896.

1976, Oct. 4   Litho.   *Perf. 14½*

62	A6c	50c lilac & multi	.25	.25
63	A6c	1sh emerald & multi	.30	.25
64	A6c	2sh brt rose & multi	.60	.35
65	A6c	3sh yellow & multi	.90	.60
a.		Souv. sheet of 4, #62-65, perf. 13	7.00	7.00
		Nos. 62-65 (4)	2.05	1.45

A6d

1977, Jan. 10   Litho.   *Perf. 14½*

66	A6d	50c Nile perch	.25	.25
67	A6d	1sh Tilapia	.50	.45
68	A6d	3sh Sailfish	1.25	1.00
69	A6d	5sh Black marlin	2.25	2.25
a.		Souvenir sheet of 4, #66-69	4.25	3.50
		Nos. 66-69 (4)	4.25	3.95

A6e

50c, Masai tribesmen bleeding cow. 1sh, Dancers from Uganda. 2sh, Makonde sculpture. 3sh, Tribesmen skinning hippopotamus.

1977, Jan. 15   *Perf. 13½x14*

70	A6e	50c multicolored	.25	.25
71	A6e	1sh multicolored	.25	.25
72	A6e	2sh multicolored	.40	.30
73	A6e	3sh multicolored	.65	.45
a.		Souvenir sheet of 4, #70-73	2.25	2.25
		Nos. 70-73 (4)	1.55	1.25

2nd World Black and African Festival, Lagos, Nigeria, Jan. 15-Feb. 12.

A6f

50c, Automobile passing through village. 1sh, Winner at finish line. 2sh, Car going through washout. 5sh, Car, elephants and Mt. Kenya.

1977, Apr. 5   Litho.   *Perf. 14*

74	A6f	50c multicolored	.25	.25
75	A6f	1sh multicolored	.25	.25
76	A6f	2sh multicolored	.55	.30
77	A6f	5sh multicolored	1.40	.85
a.		Souvenir sheet of 4, #74-77	3.25	3.25
		Nos. 74-77 (4)	2.45	1.65

25th Safari rally, Apr. 7-11.

A6g

Designs: 50c, Rev. Canon Apolo Kivebulaya. 1sh, Uganda Cathedral. 2sh, Early grass-topped Cathedral. 5sh, Early tent congregation, Kigezi.

1977, June 20   Litho.   *Perf. 14*

78	A6g	50c multicolored	.25	.25
79	A6g	1sh multicolored	.25	.25
80	A6g	2sh multicolored	.25	.25
81	A6g	5sh multicolored	.55	.55
a.		Souvenir sheet of 4, #78-81	2.50	2.50
		Nos. 78-81 (4)	1.40	1.30

Church of Uganda, centenary.

A6h

Endangered species: 50c, Pancake tortoise. 1sh, Nile crocodile. 2sh, Hunter's hartebeest. 3sh, Red Colobus monkey. 5sh, Dugong.

1977, Sept. 26   Litho.   *Perf. 14x13½*

82	A6h	50c multicolored	1.00	.35
83	A6h	1sh multicolored	2.40	.60
84	A6h	2sh multicolored	4.75	2.25
85	A6h	3sh multicolored	8.00	3.25
86	A6h	5sh multicolored	10.50	6.00
a.		Souvenir sheet of 4, #83-86	12.00	12.00
		Nos. 82-86 (5)	26.65	12.45

Prince Philip and Julius Nyerere, 1961 — A7

5sh, Queen Elizabeth II, Prince Philip, Prime Minister Nyerere in London, 1975. 10sh, Royal crown, flags of Tanzania and Commonwealth nations. 20sh, Coronation.

1977, Nov. 23   Litho.   *Perf. 14x13½*

87	A7	50c multicolored	.25	.25
88	A7	5sh multicolored	.25	.25
89	A7	10sh multicolored	.25	.25
90	A7	20sh multicolored	.40	.40
a.		Souvenir sheet of 4, #87-90	1.25	1.25
		Nos. 87-90 (4)	1.15	1.15

25th anniv. of reign of Elizabeth II. For overprints see Nos. 99-102, 179-180.

Women Fetching Water from Stream and Tap — A8

1sh, Flag raising. 3sh, Health care, laboratory and hospital. 5sh, Pres. Julius Nyerere.

1978, Feb. 5   Litho.   *Perf. 13½x14*

91	A8	50c multicolored	.25	.25
92	A8	1sh multicolored	.25	.25
93	A8	3sh multicolored	.25	.25
94	A8	5sh multicolored	.35	.35
a.		Souvenir sheet of 4, #91-94	1.25	1.25
		Nos. 91-94 (4)	1.10	1.10

First anniversary of the New Revolutionary Party (Chama cha Mapinduzi).

A8a

50c, Soccer scene and Joe Kadenge. 1sh, Mohammed Chuma receiving trophy, and his portrait. 2sh, Shot on goal and Omari S. Kidevu. 3sh, Backfield defense and Polly Ouma.

1978, Apr. 17   Litho.   *Perf. 14x13½*

95	A8a	50c green & multi	.25	.25
96	A8a	1sh lt brown & multi	.25	.25
97	A8a	2sh lilac & multi	.25	.25
98	A8a	3sh dk blue & multi	.35	.35
a.		Souvenir sheet of 4, #95-98	2.50	2.50
		Nos. 95-98 (4)	1.10	1.10

World Soccer Cup Championships, Argentina '78, June 1-25.

Nos. 87-90a Overprinted in Large Serifed Letters: "25th ANNIVERSARY / CORONATION / 2nd JUNE 1953"

1978, June 2

99	A7	50c multicolored	.25	.25
100	A7	5sh multicolored	.25	.25
101	A7	10sh multicolored	.25	.25
102	A7	20sh multicolored	.30	.30
a.		Souvenir sheet of 4, #99-102	1.00	1.00
		Nos. 99-102 (4)	1.05	1.05

25th anniv. of coronation of Elizabeth II. Nos. 99-102a also exist overprinted with smaller, sans serif letters, perf. 12. Same values or less. The perf. 12 set does not exist without overprint.

"Do not Drink when Driving" — A9

Designs: 1sh, "Courtesy to the young, old and handicapped." 3sh, "Observe highway code." 5sh, "Do not drive faulty vehicle."

1978, July 1   Litho.   *Perf. 13½x13*

103	A9	50c multicolored	.25	.25
104	A9	1sh multicolored	.25	.25
105	A9	3sh multicolored	.40	.40
106	A9	5sh multicolored	1.60	1.60
a.		Souv. sheet #103-106, perf. 14	2.75	2.75
		Nos. 103-106 (4)	2.50	2.50

Road Safety Campaign.

Lake Manyara Hotel — A10

Designs: 1sh, Lobo Wildlife Lodge. 3sh, Ngorongoro Crater Lodge. 5sh, Ngorongoro Wildlife Lodge. 10sh, Mafia Island Lodge. 20sh, Mikumi Wildlife Lodge.

1978, Sept. 11   Litho.   *Perf. 13½*

107	A10	50c multicolored	.25	.25
108	A10	1sh multicolored	.25	.25
109	A10	3sh multicolored	.25	.25
110	A10	5sh multicolored	.40	.40
111	A10	10sh multicolored	.80	.80
112	A10	20sh multicolored	1.75	1.75
a.		Souvenir sheet of 6, #107-112	7.75	7.75
		Nos. 107-112 (6)	3.70	3.70

Game Lodges of Tanzania.

Chained African — A11

1sh, Division of races (black and white heads). 2.50sh, Racial harmony (black and white handshake and heads). 5sh, End of suppression and rise of freedom (hands breaking loose from chains).

1978, Oct. 24   Litho.   *Perf. 14½x14*

113	A11	50c multicolored	.25	.25
114	A11	1sh multicolored	.25	.25
115	A11	2.50sh multicolored	.40	.40
116	A11	5sh multicolored	.80	.80
a.		Souvenir sheet of 4, #113-116	2.25	2.25
		Nos. 113-116 (4)	1.70	1.70

Anti-Apartheid Year.

Fokker Friendship at Dar Es Salaam Airport — A12

Designs: 1sh, Single-engine Dragon, 1930, Zanzibar. 2sh, British Airways Concorde. 5sh, Wright Brothers' Flyer 1, 1903.

1978, Dec. 28   Litho.   *Perf. 13½*

117	A12	50c multicolored	.30	.30
118	A12	1sh multicolored	.45	.45
119	A12	2sh multicolored	.85	.85

120 A12 5sh multicolored   2.10 2.10
a. Souvenir sheet of 4, #117-120   4.25 4.25
    Nos. 117-120 (4)   3.70 3.70

75th anniversary of 1st powered flight.

Emblem
A13

Design: 5sh, Headquarters buildings.

1979, Feb. 3 Litho. Perf. 14½x14
121 A13 50c multicolored   .25 .25
122 A13 5sh multicolored   .65 .65
a. Souvenir sheet of 2, #121-122   1.60 1.60

Tanzania Post and Telecommunications Corporation, 1st anniversary.

Pres. Nyerere and Children — A14

Designs (UNICEF and Tanzanian IYC Emblems and): 1sh, Kindergarten. 2sh, Vaccination of infant. 5sh, Emblems.

1979, June 25 Litho. Perf. 14½
123 A14 50c multicolored   .25 .25
124 A14 1sh multicolored   .25 .25
125 A14 2sh multicolored   .25 .25
126 A14 5sh multicolored   .50 .50
a. Souvenir sheet of 4, #123-126   2.25 2.25
    Nos. 123-126 (4)   1.25 1.25

International Year of the Child.

Tree Planting — A15

Forest Preservation and Expansion: 1sh, Seedling. 2sh, Rainfall. 5sh, Forest fire.

1979, Sept. 29 Litho. Perf. 14½
127 A15 50c multicolored   .25 .25
128 A15 1sh multicolored   .35 .35
129 A15 2sh multicolored   .60 .60
130 A15 5sh multicolored   1.60 1.60
    Nos. 127-130 (4)   2.80 2.80

Mwenge Satellite Earth Station Opening
A16

1979, Dec. 3 Litho. Perf. 13½
131 A16 10c multicolored   .25 .25
132 A16 40c multicolored   .25 .25
133 A16 50c multicolored   .25 .25
134 A16 5sh multicolored   .25 .25
    Nos. 131-134 (4)   1.00 1.00

Nos. 36, 43 Surcharged

1979 Litho. Perf. 14½x14
135 A5 40c (10 + 30) multi   4.00 4.00
136 A5 50c on 70c multi   6.00 6.00

Tabata Dispensary, Dar-es-Salaam, Rotary Emblem — A17

1980, Mar. 1 Litho. Perf. 13x13½
137 A17 50c shown   .25 .25
138 A17 1sh Ngomvu water project   .25 .25
139 A17 5sh Flying doctor service   .45 .45
140 A17 20sh Torch, anniversary emblem   2.00 2.00
a. Souvenir sheet of 4, #137-140   2.75 2.75
    Nos. 137-140 (4)   2.95 2.95

Rotary International, 75th anniversary. For overprints see Nos. 149-152.

Zanzibar Nos. 49 and 309, "Stamp History" Cancel A18

Cancel and: 50c, Tanganyika #58, postal worker, vert. 10sh, Tanganyika #16, 52. 20sh, Penny Black, Rowland Hill, vert.

1980, Apr. Perf. 14
141 A18 40c multicolored   .25 .25
142 A18 50c multicolored   .25 .25
143 A18 10sh multicolored   .50 .50
144 A18 20sh multicolored   1.00 1.00
a. Souvenir sheet of 4, #141-144   2.75 2.75
    Nos. 141-144 (4)   2.00 2.00

Sir Rowland Hill (1795-1879), originator of penny postage; Tanzanian stamp history.

Overprinted: "LONDON 1980" / PHILATELIC EXHIBITION

1980, May 6 Litho. Perf. 14
145 A18 40c multicolored   .25 .25
146 A18 50c multicolored   .25 .25
147 A18 10sh multicolored   .50 .50
148 A18 20sh multicolored   1.00 1.00
a. Souvenir sheet of 4, #145-148   2.75 2.75
    Nos. 145-148 (4)   2.00 2.00

London 80 Intl. Stamp Exhib., May 6-14.

Nos. 137-140a with Additional Inscription on 1 or 2 Lines: "District 920-55th Annual / Conference, Arusha, Tanzania"

1980, June 23 Litho. Perf. 13x13½
149 A17 50c multicolored   .25 .25
150 A17 1sh multicolored   .25 .25
151 A17 5sh multicolored   .65 .65
152 A17 20sh multicolored   2.75 2.75
a. Souvenir sheet of 4, #149-152   4.00 4.00
    Nos. 149-152 (4)   3.90 3.90

District 920 Rotary Club, 55th Annual Conference, Arusha.

Pan African Postal Union and U.P.U. Emblems A19

1980, July 1 Perf. 13x13½
153 A19 50c purple & blk   .25 .25
154 A19 1sh ultra & blk   .25 .25
155 A19 5sh red orange & blk   .50 .50
156 A19 10sh green & blk   1.00 1.00
    Nos. 153-156 (4)   2.00 2.00

Pan African Postal Union Plenipotentiary Conference, Arusha, Jan. 8-18.

Gidamis Shahanga, Marathon — A20

Tanzanian Olympic Team: 1sh, Nzael Kyomo and sprinters. 10sh, Zakayo Malekwa and javelin. 20sh, William Lyimo and boxers.

1980, Aug. 18 Litho. Perf. 13x13½
157 A20 50c multicolored   .25 .25
158 A20 1sh multicolored   .25 .25
159 A20 10sh multicolored   .75 .75
160 A20 20sh multicolored   1.75 1.75
a. Souvenir sheet of 4, #157-160   3.50 3.50
    Nos. 157-160 (4)   3.00 3.00

22nd Summer Olympic Games, Moscow, July 19-Aug. 3.
Issued also in sheets of 20 (5 of each value).

Spring Hare — A21

1980, Oct. 1 Litho. Perf. 14
161 A21 10c shown   .25 .25
162 A21 20c Genet   .25 .25
163 A21 40c Mongoose   .25 .25
164 A21 50c Ratel   .25 .25
165 A21 75c Rock hyrax   .25 .25
166 A21 80c Leopard   .25 .25

Perf. 14½
Size: 40x24mm
167 A21 1sh Impalas   .25 .25
168 A21 1.50sh Giraffes   .25 .25
169 A21 2sh Zebras   .25 .25
170 A21 3sh Buffalo   .25 .25
171 A21 5sh Lions   .30 .40
172 A21 10sh Rhinoceros   .65 .80
173 A21 20sh Elephants   1.30 1.60
174 A21 40sh Cheetahs   2.60 3.25
    Nos. 161-174 (14)   7.35 8.55

For overprints see Nos. O27-O36.

National Parks Emblem A22

1981, Jan. 26 Litho. Perf. 13x13½
175 A22 50c Ngorongoro Park   .25 .25
176 A22 1sh shown   .25 .25
177 A22 5sh Friends of Serengeti   .50 .50
178 A22 20sh Friends of Ngorongoro   2.00 2.00
    Nos. 175-178 (4)   3.00 3.00

Ngorongoro & Serengeti Parks, 60th anniv. For overprints see Nos. 299-302.

Nos. 89-90 Overprinted

1981, July 29 Litho. Perf. 14x13½
179 A7 10sh multicolored   .35 .35
180 A7 20sh multicolored   .65 .65
a. Souvenir sheet of 2, #179-180   5.50 5.50

Mail Runner A23

1981, Oct. 23 Litho. Perf. 12½x12
181 A23 50c shown   .25 .25
182 A23 1sh Letter sorting   .25 .25
183 A23 5sh Post horn, carrier pigeon   .55 .55
184 A23 10sh Commonwealth members' flags   1.20 1.20
a. Souvenir sheet of 4, #181-184   2.75 2.75
    Nos. 181-184 (4)   2.25 2.25

Commonwealth Postal Administrations Conference, Arusha, June 29-July 10.

Intl. Year of the Disabled A24

1981, Nov. 30 Litho. Perf. 14
185 A24 50c Morris Nyunyusa, blind drummer   .30 .30
186 A24 1sh Sewing   .40 .40
187 A24 5sh Prostheses   1.40 1.40
188 A24 10sh Children   2.75 2.75
    Nos. 185-188 (4)   4.85 4.85

20th Anniv. of Independence — A25

1982, Jan. 13 Litho. Perf. 13x13½
189 A25 50c Pres. Nyerere, flag   .25 .25
190 A25 1sh Zanzibar Electricity Plant   .25 .25
191 A25 3sh Sisal plant, weaver   .50 .50
192 A25 10sh Pupils   1.75 1.75
a. Souvenir sheet of 4, #189-192   3.00 3.00
    Nos. 189-192 (4)   2.75 2.75

Ostrich — A26

1982, Jan. 25 Litho. Perf. 13½
193 A26 50c shown   .65 .65
194 A26 1sh Secretary bird   1.00 1.00
195 A26 5sh Kori bustard   4.25 4.25
196 A26 10sh Saddle-bill stork   8.00 8.00
    Nos. 193-196 (4)   13.90 13.90

1982 World Cup A27

1982, June 2 Litho. Perf. 14
197 A27 50c Jella Mtagwa   .35 .35
198 A27 1sh Stadium   .35 .35
199 A27 10sh Diego Armando Maradona   3.00 3.00
200 A27 20sh Globe   6.50 6.50
a. Souvenir sheet of 4, #197-200   10.50 10.50
    Nos. 197-200 (4)   10.20 10.20

Jade of Seronera and her Cubs A28

Animals Appearing in Movies or TV Shows: 1sh, Wild dog and puppies, Havoc. 5sh, Fifi and sons, Gombe. 10sh, Bahati and twins Rashidi and Ramadhani, Lake Manyara.

1982, July 15   Litho.   Perf. 14
201 A28 50c multicolored   .25 .25
202 A28 1sh multicolored   .30 .30
203 A28 5sh multicolored   1.25 1.25
204 A28 10sh multicolored   2.75 2.75
  a. Souv. sheet, #201-204, perf. 14½ 5.50 5.50
      Nos. 201-204 (4)   4.55 4.55

Scouting
Year
A29

1982, Aug. 25
205 A29 50c Brick laying   .25 .25
206 A29 1sh Camping   .25 .25
207 A29 10sh Tracing marks   1.75 1.75
208 A29 20sh Baden-Powell   3.75 3.75
  a. Souvenir sheet of 4, #205-208 6.50 6.50
      Nos. 205-208 (4)   6.00 6.00

For overprint see No. 303.

World
Food
Day — A30

1982, Oct. 16   Litho.   Perf. 14
209 A30 50c Plowing   .25 .25
210 A30 1sh Dairy cows   .25 .25
211 A30 5sh Corn harvest   .90 .90
212 A30 10sh Grain storage   1.75 1.75
  a. Souvenir sheet of 4, #209-212 3.25 3.25
      Nos. 209-212 (4)   3.15 3.15

TB
Bacillus
Centenary
A31

1982, Dec. 5   Perf. 12½x12
213 A31 50c Child immunization   .25 .25
214 A31 1sh Koch   .25 .25
215 A31 5sh TB emblem   .90 .90
216 A31 10sh WHO emblem   1.75 1.75
      Nos. 213-216 (4)   3.15 3.15

A31a

1983, Mar. 14   Litho.   Perf. 14
217 A31a 50c Pres. Nyerere   .25 .25
218 A31a 1sh Running, boxing   .25 .25
219 A31a 5sh Flags   .75 .75
220 A31a 10sh Pres. Nyerere,
              Royal Family   1.50 1.50
  a. Souvenir sheet of 4, #217-220 3.00 3.00
      Nos. 217-220 (4)   2.75 2.75

Commonwealth Day. For overprint see #407.

5th Anniv. of Posts and
Telecommunications Dept. — A32

1983, Feb. 3   Litho.   Perf. 12½x12
221 A32 50c Letter post   .25 .25
222 A32 1sh Training Institute   .25 .25
223 A32 5sh Satellite communi-
             cations   .80 .80
224 A32 10sh Emblems   1.60 1.60
  a. Souvenir sheet of 4, #221-224 3.00 3.00
      Nos. 221-224 (4)   2.90 2.90

25th Anniv. of Economic Commission
for Africa — A33

1983, Sept. 12   Litho.   Perf. 12½x12
225 A33 50c Eastern & South-
             ern African Man-
             agement Institute,
             Arusha   .45 .45
226 A33 1sh Emblems   .60 .60
227 A33 5sh Mineral collections 2.40 2.40
228 A33 10sh Emblems, diff.   4.75 4.75
  a. Souvenir sheet of 4, #225-228 8.25 8.25
      Nos. 225-228 (4)   8.20 8.20

World Communications Year — A34

1983, Oct. 17   Litho.   Perf. 14
229 A34 50c Rural telephone
             service   .25 .25
230 A34 1sh Emblems   .25 .25
231 A34 5sh Post Office   1.00 1.00
232 A34 10sh Microwave tower   2.00 2.00
  a. Souvenir sheet of 4, #229-232 3.50 3.50
      Nos. 229-232 (4)   3.50 3.50

Historical
Buildings
A35

1983, Dec. 12   Litho.   Perf. 12½x12
233 A35 1sh Bagamoyo Boma   .25 .25
234 A35 1.50sh Beit-El-Ajaib   .30 .30
235 A35 5sh Anglican Church   .70 .70
236 A35 10sh State House, old
             and new   1.25 1.25
  a. Souvenir sheet of 4, #233-236 3.00 3.00
      Nos. 233-236 (4)   2.50 2.50

20th Anniv.
of
Revolution
A36

1984, June 18   Litho.   Perf. 14
237 A36 1sh Muasisi Kwanza   .25 .25
238 A36 1.50sh Clove farming   .30 .30
239 A36 5sh Industrial devel-
             opment   .90 .90
240 A36 10sh Housing develop-
             ments   1.75 1.75
      Nos. 237-240 (4)   3.20 3.20

Souvenir Sheet
241 A36 15sh Map, ship   3.25 3.25

1984
Summer
Olympics
A37

1984, Aug. 6   Perf. 12½x12
242 A37 1sh Boxing   .25 .25
243 A37 1.50sh Running   .25 .25
244 A37 5sh Basketball   .70 .70
245 A37 20sh Soccer   2.00 2.00
  a. Souvenir sheet of 4, #242-245 3.50 3.50
      Nos. 242-245 (4)   3.20 3.20

For overprints see Nos. 275-278.

Intl. Civil
Aviation
Org. 40th
Anniv.
A38

1984, Nov. 15   Litho.   Perf. 13
246 A38 1sh Icarus   .25 .25
247 A38 1.50sh Air Tanzania jets,
             traffic controller   .25 .25
248 A38 5sh Aircraft mainte-
             nance   .90 .90
249 A38 10sh ICAO emblem   1.40 1.40
  a. Souvenir sheet of 4, #246-249 3.25 3.25
      Nos. 246-249 (4)   2.80 2.80

Traditional
Houses
A39

1984, Dec. 20   Perf. 12½x12
250 A39 1sh Sochi   .25 .25
251 A39 1.50sh Isyenga   .25 .25
252 A39 5sh Tembe   .60 .60
253 A39 10sh Banda   1.10 1.10
  a. Souvenir sheet of 4, #250-253 2.50 2.50
      Nos. 250-253 (4)   2.20 2.20

Textile
Industry
A40

5th anniversary of the Southern Africa
Development Coordination Conference.

1985, Apr. 1   Perf. 14
254 A40 1.50sh shown   .50 .50
255 A40 4sh Mining   1.25 1.25
256 A40 5sh Transportation
             and commu-
             nications   1.40 1.40
257 A40 20sh Flags of mem-
             ber nations   6.00 6.00
  a. Souvenir sheet of 4, #254-257 10.00 10.00
      Nos. 254-257 (4)   9.15 9.15

Rare
Species
of
Zanzibar
A41

Perf. 13½x13, 13x13½
1985, May 8   Litho.
258 A41 1sh Tortoise   .50 .50
259 A41 4sh Leopard   1.50 1.50
260 A41 10sh Civet cat   3.00 3.00
261 A41 17.50sh Red colobus,
             vert.   4.75 4.75
      Nos. 258-261 (4)   9.75 9.75

Souvenir Sheet
262   Sheet of 2   3.75 3.75
  a. A41 15sh Black rhinoceros 1.50 1.50
  b. A41 20sh Giant ground pangolin 2.25 2.25

For overprints see Nos. 408-409, 411.

Queen Mother, 85th Birthday — A43

1985, Sept. 30
267 A43 20sh Waving   .25 .25
268 A43 20sh Facing left   .25 .25
269 A43 100sh Wearing green
             hat   .25 .25
  a. Souvenir sheet, #267, 269 .75 .75
270 A43 100sh Facing right   .25 .25
  a. Souvenir sheet, #268, 270 .75 .75
      Nos. 267-270 (4)   1.00 1.00

For overprints see Nos. 295-298.

Tanzania Railways Locomotives — A44

1985, Oct. 7   Litho.   Perf. 14½x14
271 A44 5sh No. 3022   .25 .25
272 A44 10sh No. 3107   .25 .25
273 A44 20sh No. 6004   .35 .35
274 A44 30sh No. 3129   .55 .55
  a. Souvenir sheet of 4, #271-274 1.25 1.25
      Nos. 271-274 (4)   1.40 1.40

Nos. 242-245 Ovptd. with Winners and
"GOLD MEDAL" in 2 or 3 Lines
1985, Oct. 22   Perf. 12½x12
275 A37 1sh Henry Tillman, USA .30 .30
276 A37 1.50sh USA   .30 .30
277 A37 5sh USA   .70 .70
278 A37 20sh France   2.10 2.10
  a. Souvenir sheet of 4, #275-278 8.75 8.75
      Nos. 275-278 (4)   3.40 3.40

Pottery
A45

1985, Nov. 4
279 A45 1.50sh Water and cook-
             ing pots   .25 .25
280 A45 2sh Frying pot and cal-
             dron   .25 .25
281 A45 5sh Woman selling pots   .40 .40
282 A45 40sh Beer pot   3.25 3.25
      Nos. 279-282 (4)   4.15 4.15

Souvenir Sheet
283 A45 30sh Water pot   4.25 4.25

Locomotives — A46

1985, Nov. 25
284 A46 1.50sh Class 64   .25 .25
285 A46 2sh Class 36   .25 .25
286 A46 5sh Shunting
             DFH1013   .60 .60
287 A46 10sh Diesel Electric
             DE1001   1.25 1.25
288 A46 30sh Zanzibar, 1906   3.50 3.50
      Nos. 284-288 (5)   5.85 5.85

Souvenir Sheet
289   Sheet of 2   10.00 10.00
  a. A46 15sh Class 30 steam   4.50 4.50
  b. A46 20sh Class 11 steam   5.50 5.50

For overprints see Nos. 381A-381E.

Intl. Youth
Year — A47

1986, Jan. 20   **Perf. 14**
290	A47	1.50sh Young Pioneers	.25	.25
291	A47	4sh Health care	.50	.50
292	A47	10sh Uhuru torch race	1.00	1.00
293	A47	20sh World map	1.75	1.75
		Nos. 290-293 (4)	3.50	3.50

Souvenir Sheet
294	A47	30sh Agriculture	3.50	3.50

Nos. 267-270 Ovptd. "CARIBBEAN/
ROYAL VISIT/ 1985" in Silver or Gold

1986, Feb. 10   **Perf. 14½x14**
295	A43	20sh on #267	9.00	9.00
296	A43	20sh on #268	9.00	9.00
297	A43	100sh on #269	9.00	9.00
a.		Souvenir sheet, #295, 297	20.00	—
298	A43	100sh on #270	9.00	9.00
a.		Souvenir sheet, #296, 298	20.00	—
		Nos. 295-298 (4)	36.00	36.00

See footnote following No. 303.

Nos. 175-178, 208a Ovptd.
"75th ANNIVERSARY GIRL GUIDES/
1910-1985" in Silver or Black

1986, Feb.   **Litho.**   **Perf. 13x13½, 14**
299	A22	50c multicolored (S)	15.00	15.00
300	A22	1sh multicolored	15.00	15.00
301	A22	5sh multicolored	15.00	15.00
302	A22	20sh multicolored	15.00	15.00

Souvenir Sheet
303		Sheet of 4	45.00	45.00
a.		A29 50c multicolored	—	—
b.		A29 1sh multicolored	—	—
c.		A29 10sh multicolored	—	—
d.		A29 20sh multicolored	—	—

The status of this set, the Caribbean Royal
Visit set and at least 12 stamps overprinted
congratulating the Duke and Duchess of York
on their marriage are in question.

Rotary Intl., World Chess
Championships — A48

1986, Mar. 17   **Perf. 14**
304	A48	20sh shown	.25	.25
305	A48	100sh Chess board	1.25	1.25
a.		Souvenir sheet of 2, #304-305	1.75	1.75

Audubon Birth Bicent. — A49

Illustrations of American bird species by
Audubon.

1986, May 22
306	A49	5sh Mallard	.30	.30
307	A49	10sh American eider	.30	.30
308	A49	20sh Scarlet ibis	.55	.55
309	A49	30sh Roseate spoonbill	.85	.85
a.		Souvenir sheet of 4, #306-309	3.00	3.00
		Nos. 306-309 (4)	2.00	2.00

Gemstones
A50

1986, May 22
310	A50	1.50sh Pearls	.65	.65
311	A50	2sh Sapphires	.80	.80
312	A50	5sh Tanzanite	2.25	2.25
313	A50	40sh Diamonds	12.50	12.50
		Nos. 310-313 (4)	16.20	16.20

Souvenir Sheet
314	A50	30sh Rubies	17.00	17.00

Indigenous
Flowers — A51

1986, June 2
315	A51	1.50sh Hibiscus calyphyllus	.25	.25
316	A51	5sh Aloe graminicola	.25	.25
317	A51	10sh Nersium oleander	.25	.25
318	A51	30sh Nymphaea caerulea	.50	.50
a.		Souvenir Sheet of 4, #315-318	1.25	1.25
		Nos. 315-318 (4)	1.25	1.25

Endangered
Wildlife — A52

1986, June 30   **Litho.**   **Perf. 14x14½**
319	A52	5sh Oryx	.25	.25
320	A52	10sh Giraffe	.25	.25
321	A52	20sh Rhinoceros	.30	.30
322	A52	30sh Cheetah	.40	.40
a.		Miniature sheet of 4, #319-322	1.40	1.40
		Nos. 319-322 (4)	1.20	1.20

UN Child
Survival
Campaign
A53

1986, July 29   **Perf. 12½x12**
323	A53	1.50sh Immunization	.35	.35
324	A53	2sh Growth monitoring	.35	.35
325	A53	5sh Oral rehydration therapy	.35	.35
326	A53	40sh Breast feeding	3.00	3.00
		Nos. 323-326 (4)	4.05	4.05

Souvenir Sheet
327	A53	30sh Healthy child	2.00	2.00

For overprints see Nos. 406, 410, 412.

Marine
Life
A54

1986, Aug. 20
328	A54	1.50sh Butterflyfish	.80	.80
329	A54	4sh Parrotfish	1.75	1.75
330	A54	10sh Sea turtle	3.00	3.00
331	A54	20sh Octopus	4.50	4.50
		Nos. 328-331 (4)	10.05	10.05

Souvenir Sheet
332	A54	30sh Coral	3.75	3.75

Queen Elizabeth II, 60th
Birthday — A55

Photographs: 5sh, Royal family, Buckingham Palace balcony. 10sh, With princes in
open carriage. 40sh, Elizabeth II. 60sh, Greeting crowd.

1987, Mar. 24   **Litho.**   **Perf. 14**
333	A55	5sh multicolored		.20
334	A55	10sh multicolored		.20
335	A55	40sh multicolored		.60
336	A55	60sh multicolored		1.00
a.		Souvenir sheet of 4, #333-336		2.00
		Nos. 333-336 (4)		2.00

1986 World Cup Soccer
Championships, Mexico — A57

Designs: 1.50sh, Map, team captains, officials. 2sh, Foul. 10sh, Goal. 20sh, Goalie
save. 30sh, Argentine natl. team.

1986, Oct. 30   **Litho.**   **Perf. 14**
341	A57	1.50sh multicolored	.30	.30
342	A57	2sh multicolored	.30	.30
343	A57	10sh multicolored	.65	.65
344	A57	20sh multicolored	1.25	1.25
		Nos. 341-344 (4)	2.50	2.50

Souvenir Sheet
345	A57	30sh multicolored	1.50	1.50

Hair Styles — A58

1987, Mar. 16   **Perf. 14½**
346	A58	1.50sh Nungu Nungu	.40	.40
347	A58	2sh Upanga wa Jogoo	.60	.60
348	A58	10sh Morani	1.25	1.25
349	A58	20sh Twende Kilioni	1.75	1.75
		Nos. 346-349 (4)	4.00	4.00

Souvenir Sheet
350	A58	30sh Kusuka Nywele	4.00	4.00

Intl. Peace
Year
A59

Designs: 1.50sh, Julius K. Nyerere, Beyond
War Award winner. 2sh, Peace among
nations. 10sh, Peaceful use of outer space.
20sh, Emblem, UN building. 30sh, Emblem,
handshake.

1986, Dec. 22   **Litho.**   **Perf. 14½**
351	A59	1.50sh multicolored	.55	.55
352	A59	2sh multicolored	.85	.85
353	A59	10sh multicolored	2.10	2.10
354	A59	20sh multicolored	3.00	3.00
		Nos. 351-354 (4)	6.50	6.50

Souvenir Sheet
355	A59	30sh multicolored	2.75	2.75

Natl. Bank of Commerce, 20th
Anniv. — A60

1987, Feb. 6   **Litho.**   **Perf. 14**
356	A60	1.50sh Mobile bank	.50	.50
357	A60	2sh Headquarters	.85	.85
358	A60	5sh Pres. Mwinyi laying foundation stone	1.40	1.40
359	A60	20sh Cotton harvest	3.50	3.50
		Nos. 356-359 (4)	6.25	6.25

New Revolutionary Party (CCM), 10th
Anniv. — A61

1987, Apr. 10   **Perf. 14½x14**
360	A61	2sh Soldiers in formation	.25	.25
361	A61	3sh Woman picking coffee beans	.25	.25
362	A61	10sh Speaker at podium	.40	.40
363	A61	30sh Nyerere, Mwinyi	1.10	1.10
		Nos. 360-363 (4)	2.00	2.00

Arush Declaration, 20th anniv.

Insects
A62

1987, Apr. 22   **Perf. 12½x12**
364	A62	1.50sh Bees	.70	.70
365	A62	2sh Greater grain borer	.95	.95
366	A62	10sh Tse-tse fly	2.10	2.10
367	A62	20sh Wasp	3.50	3.50
		Nos. 364-367 (4)	7.25	7.25

Souvenir Sheet
368	A62	30sh Mosquito	6.00	6.00

Reptiles
A63

1987, July 2
369	A63	2sh Crocodiles	.70	.70
370	A63	3sh Black-striped grass snake	.70	.70
371	A63	10sh Adder	1.40	1.40
372	A63	20sh Green mamba	2.75	2.75
		Nos. 369-372 (4)	5.55	5.55

Souvenir Sheet
373	A63	30sh Tortoise	2.00	2.00

Posts and Telecommunications,
Railways Emblems — A64

1987, July 27   **Perf. 14**
374	A64	2sh shown	.60	.60
375	A64	8sh Air Tanzania, Port Authority	1.40	1.40

Souvenir Sheet

376 A64 20sh Modes of commu-
              nication and
              transportation   5.00 5.00

Traditional
Crafts
A65

1987, Dec. 15 Litho. Perf. 12½x12

377 A65   2sh Baskets   .30   .30
378 A65   3sh Gourds   .30   .30
379 A65 10sh Stools   .50   .50
380 A65 20sh Makonde carvings .90   .90
     Nos. 377-380 (4)   2.00 2.00

Souvenir Sheet

381 A65 40sh Makonde carver at
              work   2.00 2.00

Nos. 284-288 Ovptd.

1987, Dec. 30 Litho. Perf. 12½x12

381A A46 1.50sh multicolored   .70   .70
381B A46   2sh multicolored   .70   .70
381C A46   5sh multicolored   .85   .85
381D A46 10sh multicolored   1.75 1.75
381E A46 30sh multicolored   5.25 5.25
      Nos. 381A-381E (5)   9.25 9.25

Plateosaurus — A66

1988, Apr. 22   Perf. 12½

382 A66   2sh shown   .65   .65
383 A66   3sh Pteranodon   .65   .65
384 A66   5sh Brontosaurus   .65   .65
385 A66   7sh Lions   .70   .70
386 A66   8sh Tiger   .70   .70
387 A66 12sh Orangutans   .80   .80
388 A66 20sh Elephants   1.10 1.10
389 A66 100sh Stegosaurus   2.75 2.75
     Nos. 382-389 (8)   8.00 8.00

Traditional
Games
A67

1988, Feb. 15 Litho. Perf. 12½x12

390 A67   2sh Mdako (marbles)   .50   .50
391 A67   3sh Mieleka (wrestling) .50 .50
392 A67   8sh Bull fight   .50   .50
393 A67 20sh Bao (African
              chess)   .80   .80
     Nos. 390-393 (4)   2.30 2.30

Souvenir Sheet

394 A67 30sh Kulenga shabaha
              (archery)   2.00 2.00
            Dated 1987.

Miniature Sheets

Statue of Liberty, Cent. (in
1986) — A68

No. 395: 1sh, Re-opening gala (evening),
1986. 2sh, Musicians performing. 3sh, Cheer-
leaders. 15sh, Statue holding tablet. 30sh,
Tablet inscription. 40sh, Liberty Island. 50sh,
Re-opening gala (afternoon), 1986. 60sh,
Blimps over Liberty Island.
   No. 396: 4sh, Statue, blimp. 5sh, Torch. 6sh,
Torch and crown observatories lit at night,
scaffolding. 7sh, Worker gilding torch. 8sh,
Statue shrouded in scaffolding. 10sh, Two
workers, torch. 12sh, Head, scaffolding. 18sh,
Celebrant at re-opening (evening). 20sh,
Goodyear blimp, skirt of Statue. 25sh, Boys'
choir, statue. 35sh, Torch held aloft, full moon.
45sh, Worker cleaning tablet.

1988, June 15   Litho.   Perf. 14

395   Sheet of 8 + label   9.00 9.00
  a. A68 1sh multicolored   .25   .25
  b. A68 2sh multicolored   .25   .25
  c. A68 3sh multicolored   .25   .25
  d. A68 15sh multicolored   .60   .60
  e. A68 30sh multicolored   1.25 1.25
  f. A68 40sh multicolored   1.60 1.60
  g. A68 50sh multicolored   2.00 2.00
  h. A68 60sh multicolored   2.40 2.40
396   Sheet of 12   9.00 9.00
  a. A68 4sh multicolored   .25   .25
  b. A68 5sh multicolored   .25   .25
  c. A68 6sh multicolored   .25   .25
  d. A68 7sh multicolored   .25   .25
  e. A68 8sh multicolored   .35   .35
  f. A68 10sh multicolored   .40   .40
  g. A68 12sh multicolored   .45   .45
  h. A68 18sh multicolored   .75   .75
  i. A68 20sh multicolored   .80   .80
  j. A68 25sh multicolored   1.00 1.00
  k. A68 35sh multicolored   1.40 1.40
  l. A68 45sh multicolored   1.75 1.75

Natl.
Monuments — A69

1988, June 15   Litho.

397 A69   5sh Independence
              Torch   .25   .25
398 A69 12sh Arusha Declara-
              tion   .25   .25
399 A69 30sh Askari   .30   .30
400 A69 60sh Independence   .50   .50
     Nos. 397-400 (4)   1.30 1.30

Souvenir Sheet

401 A69 100sh Soldier (Askari
              detail)   2.50 2.50

3rd Natl.
Census,
Aug.
28 — A70

1988, Aug. 8

402 A70   2sh shown   .25   .25
403 A70   3sh Enumeration   .25   .25
404 A70 10sh Health care   .30   .30
405 A70 20sh Population
              figures   .45   .45
     Nos. 402-405 (4)   1.25 1.25

Souvenir Sheet

405A A70 40sh Segments of
              economy and
              society   1.25 1.25

Stamps of 1983-86 Overprinted

Nos. 406 & 410, 412 Overprinted

No. 408
Ovptd.

Nos. 407 & 409,
411 Overprinted

1988, Aug. 15   Perfs. as Before

406 A53   5sh on #325   1.10 1.10
407 A31a 10sh on #220   15.00 15.00
  a. Souv. sheet of 4, #218-220,
         407   10.00 10.00
408 A31a 10sh on #260   5.50 5.50
409 A41 17.50sh on #261   10.00 10.00
410 A53 40sh on #326   13.00 13.00
     Nos. 406-410 (5)   44.60 44.60

Souvenir Sheets

411   Sheet of 2   6.75 6.75
  a. A41 15sh on #262a   1.75 1.75
  b. A41 20sh on #262b   3.75 3.75
412 A53 30sh on #327   6.75 6.75

1988 Olympics,
Seoul and
Calgary — A71

1988, Aug. 29   Perf. 14

414 A71   5sh Biathlon   .50   .50
415 A71 10sh Soccer   .25   .25
416 A71 20sh Cycling   .80   .80
417 A71 25sh Pairs figuring
              skating   .90   .90
418 A71 50sh Fencing   .85   .85
419 A71 50sh Downhill skiing 1.60 1.60
420 A71 70sh Volleyball   1.00 1.00
421 A71 75sh Bobsled   1.90 1.90
     Nos. 414-421 (8)   7.80 7.80

Souvenir Sheets

422 A71 100sh Flags, hockey
              sticks   4.00 4.00
423 A71 100sh Gymnastics   4.00 4.00

   For overprint see No. 534A-534J.

1988
Summer
Olympics,
Seoul
A71a

1988, Sept. 5 Litho. Perf. 12½x12

423A A71a 2sh Javelin   .90   .90
423B A71a 3sh Hurdles   .95   .95
423C A71a 7sh Long distance
              running   1.50 1.50
423D A71a 12sh Relay race   2.00 2.00
     Nos. 423A-423D (4)   5.35 5.35

   A souvenir sheet exists.

Disney Characters, Special
Occasions — A72

1988, Sept. 9   Perf. 14

424 A72   4sh Love You, Dad   .30   .30
425 A72   5sh Happy Birthday   .30   .30
426 A72 10sh Trick or Treat   .45   .45
427 A72 12sh Be Kind to Ani-
              mals   .45   .45
428 A72 15sh Love   .55   .55
429 A72 20sh Let's Celebrate .80   .80
430 A72 30sh Keep In Touch   1.75 1.75
431 A72 50sh Love You, Mom   3.50 3.50
     Nos. 424-431 (8)   8.10 8.10

Souvenir Sheets

432 A72 150sh Let's Work To-
              gether   4.50 4.50
433 A72 150sh Have a Super
              Sunday   4.50 4.50

   Mickey Mouse, 60th anniv.

Domestic
Animals
A73

1988, Sept. 9

434 A73   4sh Goat, vert.   .60   .60
435 A73   5sh Rabbit   .60   .60
436 A73   8sh Cows   .85   .85
437 A73 10sh Cat   1.10 1.10
438 A73 12sh Horse, vert.   1.50 1.50
439 A73 20sh Dog, vert.   2.25 2.25
     Nos. 434-439 (6)   6.90 6.90

Souvenir Sheet

440 A73 100sh Chicken   4.50 4.50

Traditional Musical Instruments — A74

1988, Sept. 30 Litho. Perf. 14

441 A74   2sh Drums   .70   .70
442 A74   3sh Xylophones   .70   .70
443 A74 10sh Thumb pianos   1.50 1.50
444 A74 20sh Fiddles   2.10 2.10
     Nos. 441-444 (4)   5.00 5.00

Souvenir Sheet

445 A74 40sh Violins with cala-
              bash resonators 2.00 2.00
            Dated 1987.

Butterflies
A75

1988, Oct. 17   Perf. 14½

446 A75   8sh Charaxes
              varanes   .75   .75
447 A75 30sh Neptis
              melicerta   1.40 1.40
448 A75 40sh Mylothris
              chloris   1.40 1.40
449 A75 50sh Charaxes
              bohemani   1.75 1.75
450 A75 60sh Myrina ficedula 2.10 2.10
451 A75 75sh Papilio phorcas 2.75 2.75
452 A75 90sh Cyrestis camil-
              lus   3.25 3.25
453 A75 100sh Salamis
              temora   3.25 3.25
     Nos. 446-453 (8)   16.65 16.65

Souvenir Sheets
454 A75 200sh Asterope rosa 7.50 7.50
455 A75 250sh Kallima rumia 8.50 8.50

Intl. Lions Club at Dar es Salaam, 25th Anniv. A76

1988, Nov. 30   Litho.   Perf. 14½
456 A76 2sh Eye operation .40 .40
457 A76 3sh Shallow water well .40 .40
458 A76 7sh Map, rhinoceros 1.25 1.25
459 A76 12sh Donating school desks .50 .50
Nos. 456-459 (4) 2.55 2.55

Souvenir Sheet
460 A76 40sh Emblem 2.00 2.00

Community services: Matibabu Ya Macho Eye Camp (2sh); sanitary water supply in Dar es Salaam (3sh); wildlife conservation (7sh); aid to local schools (12sh).

Intl. Red Cross and Red Crescent Organizations, 125th Annivs. — A77

Design: 2sh, Assisting the wounded and sick. 3sh, Postnatal care clinic. 7sh, Red Cross flag. 12sh, Jean-Henry Dunant, founder. 40sh, Dunant, Thomas Maunier, Louis Appia, Gustave Moynier and Gen. Guillaume Henri Dufour, members of intl. committee that sponsored the conference in 1863 where the Red Cross was founded.

1988, Dec. 30   Litho.   Perf. 12½x12
461 A77 2sh multicolored .50 .50
462 A77 3sh multicolored .50 .50
463 A77 7sh multicolored .55 .55
464 A77 12sh multicolored .80 .80
Nos. 461-464 (4) 2.35 2.35

Souvenir Sheet
465 A77 40sh multicolored 2.00 2.00

Miniature Sheet

Paradise Whydah — A78

Birds: a, Paradise whydah. b, Black-collared barbet. c, Bateleur eagle. d, Openbill storks, lilac-breasted roller. e, Scarlet-tufted malachite sunbird. f, Dark chanting goshawk. g, White-fronted bee-eater, little bee-eater, carmine bee-eater. h, Marabou stork, Narina's trocon. i, African gray parrot. j, Hoopoe. k, Yellow-collared lovebird. l, Yellow-billed hornbill. m, Hammerkop. n, Flamingos, violet-crested turaco. o, Malachite kingfisher. p, Greater flamingo. q, Yellow-billed stork. r, Shoebill stork. s, Saddle-billed stork, blacksmith plover. t, Crowned crane.

1989, Jan. 10   Perf. 14
466 Sheet of 20 30.00 30.00
a.-t. A78 20sh any single .75 .75

Souvenir Sheets
467 A78 350sh Helmeted guineafowl 8.00 8.00
467A A78 350sh Ostrich 8.00 8.00

No. 466 has a continuous design.

Endangered Species
A79   A80

World Wildlife Fund: Various bushbabies, Galago zanzibaricus. 350sh, African palm civet.

1989, Jan. 24   Perf. 14
468 A79 5sh shown .85 .85
469 A79 10sh multi, horiz. 1.00 1.00
470 A79 20sh multi, diff. 1.40 1.40
471 A79 45sh multi, diff., horiz. 2.75 2.75
Nos. 468-471 (4) 6.00 6.00

Souvenir Sheet
472 A79 350sh multi, horiz. 10.00 10.00

1989, Jan. 24
30sh, Black cobra, umbrella acacia. 70sh, Red-tailed tropic bird, tree fern. 100sh, African tree frog, cocoa tree. 150sh, African black-necked heron, Egyptian papyrus. 350sh, Pink-backed pelicans, baobab tree.

473 A80 30sh shown 1.00 1.00
474 A80 70sh multicolored 4.50 4.50
475 A80 100sh multicolored 5.25 5.25
476 A80 150sh multicolored 8.00 8.00
Nos. 473-476 (4) 18.75 18.75

Souvenir Sheet
477 A80 350sh multicolored 9.25 9.25

Steam Locomotives — A81

1989, Jan. 31
478 A81 10sh Class P36, USSR .85 .85
479 A81 25sh Class 12, Belgium .90 .90
480 A81 60sh Class C62, Japan 1.35 1.35
481 A81 75sh Class T1, Pennsylvania R.R. 1.60 1.60
482 A81 80sh Class WP, India 1.75 1.75
483 A81 90sh Class 59, East African Railways 2.00 2.00
484 A81 150sh People Class 4-6-2, China 3.25 3.25
485 A81 200sh Southern Pacific Daylight Express, US 3.25 3.25
Nos. 478-485 (8) 14.95 14.95

Souvenir Sheets
486 A81 350sh Stephenson's Planet, Britain 6.75 6.75
487 A81 350sh Coronation Scot, Britain 6.75 6.75

Nos. 486-487 vert.

World-Class Athletes — A82

Designs: 4sh, Juma Ikangaa, Tanzania, marathon. 8.50sh, Steffi Graf, West Germany, tennis. 12sh, Yannick Noah, France, tennis. 40sh, Pele, Brazil, soccer. 100sh, Erhard Keller, West Germany, speed skater. 125sh, Sadanoyama, Japan, Sumo wrestler. 200sh, Taino, Japan, Sumo wrestler. 250sh, I. Aoki, Japan, golfer. No. 496, Joe Louis, US, world heavyweight boxing champion, 1937-1949. No. 497, T. Nakajima, Japan, golfer.

1989, Feb. 7
488 A82 4sh multicolored .40 .40
489 A82 8.50sh multicolored .40 .40
490 A82 12sh multicolored .40 .40
491 A82 40sh multicolored 1.25 1.25
492 A82 100sh multicolored 3.00 3.00
493 A82 125sh multicolored 3.50 3.50
494 A82 200sh multicolored 5.25 5.25
495 A82 250sh multicolored 6.75 6.75
Nos. 488-495 (8) 20.95 20.95

Souvenir Sheets
496 A82 350sh multicolored 8.50 8.50
497 A82 350sh multicolored 8.50 8.50

History of Space Exploration and 20th Anniv. of the 1st Moon Landing — A83

1989, July 20
498 A83 20sh Luna 3 .50 .50
499 A83 30sh Rendezvous of Gemini 6&7 .60 .60
500 A83 40sh 1st US space walk .65 .65
501 A83 60sh First man on Moon .90 .90
502 A83 70sh Experiments on Moon 1.00 1.00
503 A83 100sh Apollo 15 lunar rover 1.35 1.35
504 A83 150sh Apollo-Soyuz 1.75 1.75
505 A83 200sh Spacelab 2.25 2.25
Nos. 498-505 (8) 9.00 9.00

Souvenir Sheets
506 A83 250sh Futuristic space station 3.75 3.75
507 A83 250sh Eagle lunar module 3.75 3.75

History of space exploration (Nos. 498-500, 503-506); others 20th anniv. of 1st Moon Landing.

St. Mary Magdalene in Penitence A84

Details from paintings by Titian: 10sh, Averoldi Polyptych. 15sh, St. Margaret. 50sh, Venus and Adonis. 75sh, Venus and the Lutenist. 100sh, Tarquin and Lucretia. 125sh, St. Jerome. 150sh, Madonna and Child with Saints. No. 516, St. Catherine of Alexandria at Prayer. No. 517, Adoration of the Holy Trinity. No. 517A, The Supper at Emmaus.

1989, Nov. 15   Litho.   Perf. 13½x14
508 A84 5sh multicolored .35 .35
509 A84 10sh multicolored .35 .35
510 A84 15sh multicolored .35 .35
511 A84 50sh multicolored .80 .80
512 A84 75sh multicolored 1.30 1.30
513 A84 100sh multicolored 1.50 1.50
514 A84 125sh multicolored 1.90 1.90
515 A84 150sh multicolored 2.25 2.25
Nos. 508-515 (8) 8.80 8.80

Souvenir Sheets
516 A84 300sh multicolored 4.00 4.00
517 A84 300sh multicolored 4.00 4.00
517A A84 300sh multicolored 4.00 4.00

500th birth anniv. of Titian.
#517A was not available until Jan. 8, 1991.

World Cup Soccer Championships, Italy — A85

1989, Nov. 15   Perf. 14
Uniform colors
518 A85 25sh green, red & yel 1.00 1.00
519 A85 60sh green, yel & blue 2.10 2.10
520 A85 75sh orange & blue 2.75 2.75
521 A85 200sh blue & white 7.00 7.00
Nos. 518-521 (4) 12.85 12.85

Souvenir Sheets
522 A85 350sh orange & bl, diff. 5.75 5.75
523 A85 350sh grn, yel & bl, diff. 5.75 5.75

Souvenir Sheet

Union Station, Washington, DC — A86

1989, Nov. 17
524 A86 500sh multicolored 9.50 9.50
World Stamp Expo '89.

Fish A87

1989, Dec. 14
525 A87 9sh Tiger tilapia .40 .40
526 A87 13sh Picasso fish .40 .40
527 A87 20sh Powder-blue surgeonfish .55 .55
528 A87 40sh Butterflyfish 1.00 1.00
529 A87 70sh Guenther's notho 1.75 1.75
530 A87 100sh Ansorge's noelebias 2.60 2.60
531 A87 150sh Lyretail panchax 4.00 4.00
532 A87 200sh Regal angelfish 5.50 5.50
Nos. 525-532 (8) 16.20 16.20

Souvenir Sheets
533 A87 350sh Batfish 7.50 7.50
534 A87 350sh Jewel cichlid 7.50 7.50

Nos. 533-534 each contain one 38x51mm stamp.

Nos. 414-423 Ovptd. and Similarly

Perfs. as Before
1989, Dec. 19   Litho.
534A A71 5sh shown .55 .55
534B A71 10sh "Gold - USSR / Silver - Brazil / Bronze - W. Germany" .75 .75
534C A71 20sh "Men's Match Sprint / Lutz Hesslich, DDR" 3.00 3.00
534D A71 25sh "Pairs, Gordeeva & Grinkov, USSR" 1.50 1.50
534E A71 50sh "Epee, Schmitt, W. Germany" 2.40 2.40
534F A71 50sh "Zurbriggen, Switzerland" 2.40 2.40
534G A71 70sh "Men's Team, USA" 3.75 3.75
534H A71 75sh "Gold-USSR / Silver-DDR / Bronze-DDR" 3.00 3.00
Nos. 534A-534H (8) 17.35 17.35

Souvenir Sheets

534I A71 100sh "Ice Hockey: /
Gold-USSR" 11.00 11.00
534J A71 100sh "Women's
Team, /
Gold-USSR" 4.00 4.00

Silver and Bronze medalists overprinted on margins of souvenir sheets.

Inter-Parliamentary Union,
Cent. — A88

Designs: 9sh, Secret ballot. 13sh, Parliament, Dar Es Salaam. 40sh, Sir William Randal Cremer, Frederic Passy. 80sh, Parliament in session. 100sh, IPU emblem.

1989, Dec. 22   *Perf. 12½x12*
535 A88 9sh multicolored .25 .25
536 A88 13sh multicolored .25 .25
537 A88 80sh multicolored .70 .70
538 A88 100sh lt bl, dp bl & blk .80 .80
Nos. 535-538 (4) 2.00 2.00

Souvenir Sheet
539 A88 40sh multicolored 1.40 1.40

Pan-African Postal Union, 10th Anniv. A89

1990, Jan. 17   *Perf. 13½*
540 A89 9sh PAPU emblem .35 .35
541 A89 13sh Post offices boxes .35 .35
542 A89 70sh Mail early, prompt delivery 1.40 1.40
543 A89 100sh Modes of mail delivery 2.40 2.40
Nos. 540-543 (4) 4.50 4.50

Souvenir Sheet
544 A89 40sh Tanzania Post, PAPU, UPU emblems 1.60 1.60

Extinct Animals A90

1990, Feb. 4   *Perf. 14*
545 A90 25sh Tecopa pupfish .75 .75
546 A90 40sh Thylacine 1.10 1.10
547 A90 50sh Quagga 1.50 1.50
548 A90 60sh Passenger pigeon 1.75 1.75
549 A90 75sh Rodriguez saddleback tortoise 2.25 2.25
550 A90 100sh Toolache wallaby 2.75 2.75
551 A90 150sh Texas red wolf 4.25 4.25
552 A90 200sh Utah lake sculpin 5.50 5.50
Nos. 545-552 (8) 19.85 19.85

Souvenir Sheets
553 A90 350sh Hawaiian O-O, vert. 8.00 8.00
554 A90 350sh South island whekau 8.00 8.00

Nina, Admiral's Flag A91

1990, Feb. 20
555 A91 50sh shown 2.10 2.10
556 A91 60sh Pinta, flag 2.50 2.50
557 A91 75sh Santa Maria, flag 3.00 3.00
558 A91 200sh Map of Columbus' first voyage 8.25 8.25
Nos. 555-558 (4) 15.85 15.85

Souvenir Sheet
559 A91 350sh Ships, bird's head 9.50 9.50

Discovery of America, 500th anniv. (in 1992).

Modern Discoveries — A92

Designs: 9sh, Bell X-1 breaking the sound barrier. 13sh, Bathyscaph Trieste reaches the deepest ocean bottom. 150sh, Transistor and computer chips. 250sh, Discovery of DNA structure. 350sh, Voyager 2 visits Neptune.

1990, Feb. 20
560 A92 9sh multicolored .65 .65
561 A92 13sh multicolored .65 .65
562 A92 150sh multicolored 1.50 1.50
563 A92 250sh multicolored 2.50 2.50
Nos. 560-563 (4) 5.30 5.30

Souvenir Sheet
564 A92 350sh multicolored 5.75 5.75

Girl Guides, 60th Anniv. A93

1990, Feb. 22   *Perf. 12½x12*
565 A93 9sh Hiking .25 .25
566 A93 13sh Planting trees .25 .25
567 A93 50sh Teaching writing .70 .70
568 A93 100sh Teaching health care 1.40 1.40
Nos. 565-568 (4) 2.60 2.60

Souvenir Sheet
Perf. 12x12½
569 A93 40sh Nursing school, vert. 1.60 1.60

Disney Characters, Automobiles — A94

1990, Mar. 20   *Perf. 14x13½*
570 A94 20sh Herbie, The Love Bug .45 .45
571 A94 30sh The Absent-Minded Professor's car .50 .50
572 A94 45sh Chitty-Chitty Bang-Bang .65 .65
573 A94 60sh Mr. Toad's wild ride .90 .90
574 A94 75sh Scrooge's limousine 1.10 1.10
575 A94 100sh Shaggy dog's car 1.50 1.50
576 A94 150sh Donald Duck's car 2.40 2.40
577 A94 200sh Firetruck in "Dumbo" 2.50 2.50
Nos. 570-577 (8) 10.00 10.00

Souvenir Sheets
578 A94 350sh Cruella de Vil 6.00 6.00
579 A94 350sh Mickeymobile 6.00 6.00

Black Entertainers A95

1990, Mar. 30   Litho.   *Perf. 14*
580 A95 9sh Miriam Makeba .25 .25
581 A95 13sh Manu Dibango .25 .25
582 A95 25sh Fela .25 .25
583 A95 70sh Smokey Robinson 1.00 1.00
584 A95 100sh Gladys Knight 1.25 1.25
585 A95 150sh Eddie Murphy 2.25 2.25
586 A95 200sh Sammy Davis, Jr. 3.00 3.00
587 A95 250sh Stevie Wonder 3.00 3.00
Nos. 580-587 (8) 11.25 11.25

Souvenir Sheets
Perf. 14½
588 A95 350sh Bill Cosby 3.75 3.75
589 A95 350sh Michael Jackson 3.75 3.75

Union of Tanganyika and Zanzibar, 25th Anniv. (in 1989) — A95a

Designs: 9sh, Fishing. 13sh, Grapes. 50sh, Cloves. 100sh, Presidents Nyerere and Karume exchanging Union instruments, vert. 40sh, Natl. arms, vert.

Perf. 12½x12, 12x12½
1990, Apr. 25   Litho.
589A A95a 9sh multicolored .55 .55
589B A95a 13sh multicolored .55 .55
589C A95a 50sh multicolored 1.75 1.75
589D A95a 100sh multicolored 3.50 3.50
Nos. 589A-589D (4) 6.35 6.35

Souvenir Sheet
589E A95a 40sh multicolored 2.75 2.75

Southern Africa Development Coordinating Conf. (SADCC), 10th Anniv. — A96

1990, Aug. 8   *Perf. 13½*
590 A96 8sh Railway transport .50 .50
591 A96 11.50sh Paper industry .50 .50
592 A96 25sh Tractor production .90 .90
593 A96 100sh Flags, map 2.75 2.75
Nos. 590-593 (4) 4.65 4.65

Souvenir Sheet
Perf. 12½
594 A96 50sh Map 2.50 2.50

A97   A98

Pope John Paul II's Visit to Tanzania: 15sh, Wearing red vestments. 20sh, Wearing miter. 100sh, Papal arms. No. 599: a, Pope with arms outstretched. b, St. Joseph's Cathedral,

Dar Es Salaam. c, Christ the King Cathedral, Moshi. d, Saint Theresa's Cathedral, Tabora. e, Cathedral of the Epiphany, Bugando Mwanza. f, St. Mathias Mulumba Kalemba Cathedral, Songea.

1990, Sept. 1   Litho.   *Perf. 14*
595 A97 10sh shown .30 .30
596 A97 15sh multicolored .45 .45
597 A97 20sh multicolored .50 .50
598 A97 100sh multicolored 1.25 1.25
Nos. 595-598 (4) 2.50 2.50

Souvenir Sheet
599   Sheet of 6 7.00 7.00
   a.-f.   A97 50sh any single .60 .60

1990, Sept. 28

Players from participating countries.
600 A98 10sh West Germany 1.00 1.00
601 A98 60sh Italy 1.75 1.75
602 A98 100sh Scotland 3.00 3.00
603 A98 300sh Yugoslavia 5.25 5.25
Nos. 600-603 (4) 11.00 11.00

Souvenir Sheets
604 A98 400sh Costa Rica 6.00 6.00
605 A98 400sh Belgium 6.00 6.00

World Cup Soccer Championships, Italy.

Birds — A99

1990-91   Litho.   *Perf. 14*
606 A99 5sh Masked weaver .45 .45
607 A99 9sh Emerald cuckoo .45 .45
608 A99 13sh Little bee-eater .80 .80
609 A99 15sh Red bishop .80 .80
610 A99 20sh Bateleur 1.00 1.00
611 A99 25sh Scarlet-chested sunbird 1.00 1.00
   a.   Bklt. pane, 2 ea #606-611 9.00 9.00
611B A99 30sh Pigeons 1.00 1.00
Size: 42x28mm
612 A99 40sh Lesser flamingo 1.00 1.00
613 A99 70sh Helmeted guineafowl 1.10 1.10
614 A99 100sh White pelican 1.25 1.25
615 A99 170sh Saddle-billed stork 1.75 1.75
616 A99 200sh Crowned crane 2.00 2.00
616A A99 300sh Pied crow 2.25 2.25
616B A99 400sh White-headed vulture 2.50 2.50
617 A99 500sh Ostrich 2.50 2.50
Nos. 606-617 (15) 19.85 19.85

Souvenir Sheet
Stamp size: 42x28mm
617A   Sheet of 2 6.25 6.25
   b.   A99 40sh Superb starling 1.10 1.10
   c.   A99 60sh Lilac-breasted roller 1.60 1.60

Issued: 30sh, 300sh, 400sh, 1991; others, 10/1/90.
For surcharges, see Nos. 1723A, 1723B, 2157-2159C, 2267.

Boats A100

1990, Oct. 10   Litho.   *Perf. 12½x12*
618 A100 9sh Canoe .45 .45
619 A100 13sh Outrigger canoe .45 .45
620 A100 25sh Dhow .75 .75
621 A100 100sh Freighter 3.00 3.00
Nos. 618-621 (4) 4.65 4.65

Souvenir Sheet
622 A100 40sh Boat 3.50 3.50

Commonwealth Games, New Zealand — A101

1990, Oct. 22   **Perf. 14**
623	A101	9sh Sprinting	.45	.45
624	A101	13sh Netball, vert.	.75	.75
625	A101	25sh Pole vault	1.05	1.05
626	A101	100sh Long jump, vert.	3.50	3.50
		Nos. 623-626 (4)	5.75	5.75

Souvenir Sheet
627	A101	40sh Boxing	2.50	2.50

Orchids — A102

1990, Nov. 12
628	A102	10sh Phalaenopsis	.40	.40
629	A102	25sh Lycaste	.40	.40
630	A102	30sh Vuylstekeara, Cambria "Plush"	.45	.45
631	A102	50sh Vuylstekeara, Monica "Burnham"	.70	.70
632	A102	90sh Odontocidium	1.25	1.25
633	A102	100sh Oncidioda	1.60	1.60
634	A102	250sh Sophrolaelio- cattleya	4.00	4.00
635	A102	300sh Laeliocattleya	4.50	4.50
		Nos. 628-635 (8)	13.30	13.30

Souvenir Sheets
636	A102	400sh Cymbidium, Baldoyle "Melbury"	6.25	6.25
637	A102	400sh Cymbidium, Tapestry "Long Beach"	6.25	6.25

Expo '90, the Intl. Garden and Greenery Exposition, Osaka, Japan.

1990 World Cup Soccer Championships, Italy — A102a

1990, Nov. 17   **Litho.**   **Perf. 14**
637A	A102a	9sh Long throw-in	.75	.75
637B	A102a	13sh Penalty kick	.75	.75
637C	A102a	25sh Dribbling	1.25	1.25
637D	A102a	100sh Corner kick	4.25	4.25
		Nos. 637A-637D (4)	7.00	7.00

Souvenir Sheet
637E	A102a	50sh Trophy, map	4.50	4.50

Racing A103

5sh, Olympic Soling Class Yacht racing. 20sh, Olympic downhill ski racing. 30sh, Tour de France bicycle race. 40sh, Le Mans 24 hour endurance auto race. 75sh, Olympic 2-man bobsled. 100sh, Belgian Grand Prix motorcycle race. 250sh, Indianapolis 500 auto race. 300sh, Power boat gold cup racing. #646, Colorado 500 enduro motorcycle race. #647, Schneider Trophy air races.

1990, Nov. 19
638	A103	5sh multicolored	.45	.45
639	A103	20sh multicolored	.85	.85
640	A103	30sh multicolored	1.40	1.40
641	A103	40sh multicolored	1.40	1.40
642	A103	75sh multicolored	1.60	1.60
643	A103	100sh multicolored	2.40	2.40
644	A103	250sh multicolored	3.00	3.00
645	A103	300sh multicolored	3.25	3.25
		Nos. 638-645 (8)	14.35	14.35

Souvenir Sheets
646	A103	400sh multicolored	7.00	7.00
647	A103	400sh multicolored	7.00	7.00

1992 Summer Olympics, Barcelona — A104

1990, Nov. 30
648	A104	5sh Archery	.30	.30
649	A104	10sh Women's gymnastics	.30	.30
650	A104	25sh Boxing	.30	.30
651	A104	50sh Two-man kay- ak race	.55	.55
652	A104	100sh Men's volley- ball	1.10	1.10
653	A104	150sh Mens' gym- nastics	1.75	1.75
654	A104	200sh 4x100 meter relay	2.25	2.25
655	A104	300sh Judo	3.50	3.50
		Nos. 648-655 (8)	10.05	10.05

Souvenir Sheets
656	A104	400sh Men's 400 meter hur- dles	5.50	5.50
657	A104	400sh Men's cycling	5.50	5.50

Cog Railroads A105

Cog locomotives: 8sh, Petersberg Cog Rail-way, West Germany. 25sh, Engine *Waumbek* on Mt. Washington Cog Railway, US. 50sh, Doubleheaded cog engines on Dubrovnik-Sarajevo line, Yugoslavia. 100sh, Cog Rail-way, Budapest, Hungary 1874. 150sh, Vordenberg-Eisenerz line, Austria. 200sh, Rimutaka Incline, New Zealand, 1955. 250sh, John Stevens' cog engine, Hoboken, NJ, 1825. 300sh, Pilatusbahn Cog Railway, Swit-zerland, 1889. No. 666, Schneebergbahn of the OBB, Austria. No. 667, Sylvester Marsh, Mt. Washington Cog Railway, 1869.

1990, Dec. 8
658	A105	8sh multicolored	.30	.30
659	A105	25sh multicolored	.30	.30
660	A105	50sh multicolored	.60	.60
661	A105	100sh multicolored	1.10	1.10
662	A105	150sh multicolored	1.75	1.75
663	A105	200sh multicolored	2.25	2.25
664	A105	250sh multicolored	3.25	3.25
665	A105	300sh multicolored	3.75	3.75
		Nos. 658-665 (8)	13.30	13.30

Souvenir Sheets
666	A105	400sh multicolored	6.50	6.50
667	A105	400sh multicolored	6.50	6.50

First Postage Stamps, 150th Anniv. A106

Designs: No. 668, German Post Office at Dar Es Salaam, German East Africa No. 16. No. 669, Mailboat S.S. Reichstag, 1890, Ger-many No. 40 cancelled in Zanzibar. No. 670, Dhows used as mailboats, Zanzibar No. 1. No. 671, Mailplane Singapore I on Lake Victoria, 1928, Tanganyika No. 22. No. 672, Mailplane, Livingston's House, Zanzibar No. 316. No. 673, Passenger-mail train at Moshi Station, Tanganyika No. 52. No. 674, Royal mail coach, 1840. 150sh, Stephenson's *Rocket*, mail car, 1838. 200sh, Handley Page HP-42 mailplane. No. 677, Hand delivery of mail, Thurn & Taxis No. 44 on cover. No. 678, Sir Rowland Hill.

1990, Dec. 12
668	A106	50sh multicolored	1.10	1.10
669	A106	50sh multicolored	1.10	1.10
a.		Pair, #668-669	1.10	1.10
670	A106	75sh multicolored	1.40	1.40
671	A106	75sh multicolored	1.40	1.40
a.		Pair, #670-671	1.50	1.50
672	A106	100sh multicolored	2.10	2.10
673	A106	100sh multicolored	2.10	2.10
a.		Pair, #672-673	2.25	2.25
674	A106	125sh multicolored	2.10	2.10
675	A106	150sh multicolored	3.00	3.00
676	A106	200sh multicolored	3.00	3.00
		Nos. 668-676 (9)	17.30	17.30

Souvenir Sheets
677	A106	350sh multicolored	6.75	6.75
678	A106	350sh multicolored	6.75	6.75

500th anniv. of Thurn and Taxis Post (No. 677).
For overprints see Nos. 928-934.

Intl. Literacy Year — A107

Nos. 679a-681i depict various Walt Disney characters and a letter of the alphabet. No. 682, Mickey's train hauls Russian alphabet. No. 683, Children learning Hebrew.

1990, Dec. 27   **Perf. 13½x14**
Miniature Sheets
679		Sheet of 9	7.50	7.50
a.	A107	1sh "ABC"	.25	.25
b.	A107	2sh "A"	.25	.25
c.	A107	3sh "B"	.25	.25
d.	A107	15sh "C"	.25	.25
e.	A107	55sh "D"	.45	.45
f.	A107	80sh "E"	.65	.65
g.	A107	120sh "F"	.95	.95
h.	A107	145sh "G"	1.10	1.10
i.	A107	200sh "H"	1.60	1.60
680		Sheet of 9	7.25	7.25
a.	A107	10sh "I"	.25	.25
b.	A107	20sh "J"	.25	.25
c.	A107	30sh "K"	.25	.25
d.	A107	40sh "L"	.30	.30
e.	A107	50sh "M"	.40	.40
f.	A107	60sh "N"	.50	.50
g.	A107	100sh "O"	.80	.80
h.	A107	125sh "P"	1.00	1.00
i.	A107	150sh "Q"	1.25	1.25
681		Sheet of 9	7.50	7.50
a.	A107	5sh "R"	.25	.25
b.	A107	18sh "S"	.25	.25
c.	A107	25sh "T"	.25	.25
d.	A107	35sh "U"	.30	.30
e.	A107	45sh "V"	.35	.35
f.	A107	75sh "W"	.60	.60
g.	A107	90sh "X"	.70	.70
h.	A107	160sh "Y"	1.25	1.25
i.	A107	175sh "Z"	1.40	1.40

Souvenir Sheets
682	A107	600sh multicolored	8.50	8.50
683	A107	600sh multicolored	8.50	8.50

Intl. Literacy Year A108

1991, Mar. 15   **Litho.**   **Perf. 14**
684	A108	9sh Learning to read	.30	.30
685	A108	13sh Learning to write	.40	.40
686	A108	25sh Blackboard, books	.55	.55
687	A108	100sh Reading news-papers	.275	2.75
		Nos. 684-687 (4)	1.53	4.00

Souvenir Sheet
688	A108	50sh Adult education	2.50	2.50

For surcharge see No. 1431A.

Mickey Mouse — A109

Character roles: 5sh, Western cowboy. 10sh, Boxer. 15sh, Astronaut. 20sh, Romantic lead with Minnie. 100sh, Swashbuckling hero. 200sh, Detective with Donald Duck and Pistol Pete. 350sh, King with Donald as court jester. 450sh, Sailor with Donald and Goofy. No. 697, Minnie, Mickey as archaeologists in Egypt, Donald as a mummy. No. 698, Mickey as Canadian Mountie.

1991, Feb. 11   **Litho.**   **Perf. 14x13½**
689	A109	5sh multicolored	.45	.45
690	A109	10sh multicolored	.50	.50
691	A109	15sh multicolored	.50	.50
692	A109	20sh multicolored	.50	.50
693	A109	100sh multicolored	2.00	2.00
694	A109	200sh multicolored	4.00	4.00
695	A109	350sh multicolored	4.50	4.50
696	A109	450sh multicolored	4.50	4.50
		Nos. 689-696 (8)	16.95	16.95

Souvenir Sheets
697	A109	600sh multicolored	8.50	8.50
698	A109	600sh multicolored	8.50	8.50

Craters and Caves — A109a

Designs: 3sh, Ngorongoro Crater. 5sh, Kondoa Caves, prehistoric rock paintings. 9sh, Mount Kilimanjaro's inner crater. 12sh, Olduvai Gorge.
Amboni Caves: No. 698f, Open area of cave. g, People viewing cave, large stalactite. h, Woman seated beside welcome sign. i, Man climbing up to view cave.

1991, Mar. 28   **Litho.**   **Perf. 14½**
698A	A109a	3sh multi	3.25	3.25
698B	A109a	5sh multi	3.25	3.25
698C	A109a	9sh multi	4.25	4.25
698D	A109a	12sh multi	6.25	6.25
		Nos. 698A-698D (4)	17.00	17.00

Souvenir Sheet
698E	A109a	10sh Sheet of 4, #f.-i.	8.00	8.00

Nos. 698A-698E were not available to the philatelic community until Mar. 1994.

Miniature Sheet

Peter Paul Rubens, 350th Death Anniv. — A110

Cycle of Decius Mus: No. 699a, Proclama-tion of the Vision. b, Divining of the Entrails. c, Dispatch of the Lictors. d, Dedication to Death. e, Victory and Death of Decius Mus. f, Funeral Rites. No. 700, Trophy of War, vert.

1991, Apr. 10   **Litho.**   **Perf. 14x13½**
699	A110	85sh Sheet of 6, #a.-f.	14.00	14.00

Souvenir Sheet
Perf. 13½x14

700 A110 500sh multicolored   12.00 12.00

Tanzania Investment Bank, 20th Anniv. — A111

Designs: 10sh, Dairy farming. 13sh, Industrial development. 25sh, Engineering. 100sh, Tea harvesting.

1991, June 7   *Perf. 14*
701 A111 10sh multicolored   .40 .40
702 A111 13sh multicolored   .40 .40
703 A111 25sh multicolored   .40 .40
704 A111 100sh multicolored   2.25 2.25
   a.   Souvenir sheet of 4, #701-704   3.25 3.25
      Nos. 701-704 (4)   3.45 3.45

Phila Nippon '91 A112

Japanese locomotives: 10sh, First Japanese steam. 25sh, Series 4500 steam. 35sh, C 62 steam. 50sh, Mikado steam. 75sh, Series 6250 steam. 100sh, C 11 steam. 200sh, E 10 steam. 300sh, Series 8550 steam. No. 713, EF 58 electric. No. 714, DD 51 diesel. No. 715, Series 400 electric. No. 716, EH 10 electric.

1991, Aug. 15   *Litho.*   *Perf. 14*
705 A112 10sh multicolored   1.00 1.00
706 A112 15sh multicolored   1.50 1.50
707 A112 35sh multicolored   1.75 1.75
708 A112 75sh multicolored   2.00 2.00
709 A112 100sh multicolored   2.50 2.50
710 A112 100sh multicolored   3.00 3.00
711 A112 200sh multicolored   3.50 3.50
712 A112 300sh multicolored   4.75 4.75
      Nos. 705-712 (8)   20.00 20.00

Souvenir Sheets
713 A112 400sh multicolored   4.75 4.75
714 A112 400sh multicolored   4.75 4.75
715 A112 400sh multicolored   4.75 4.75
716 A112 400sh multicolored   4.75 4.75

Fauna in Natl. Game Parks A113

Species and park: 10sh, Common zebra, golden-winged sunbird, Ngorongoro Crater Conservation Area. 25sh, Greater kudu, African elephant, Ruaha. 30sh, Sable antelope, red and yellow barbet, Mikumi. 50sh, Wildebeest, leopard, Serengeti. 90sh, Giraffe, white-starred bush robin, Ngurdoto Crater. 100sh, Eland, Abbot's duiker, Kilimanjaro. 250sh, Lion, impala, Lake Manyara. 300sh, Black rhinoceros, ostrich, Tarangire. No. 725, Paradise whydah, oryx, Mkomazi Game Reserve. No. 726, Blue-breasted kingfisher, defassa waterbuck, Selous Game Reserve.

1991, Aug. 22   *Litho.*   *Perf. 14*
717 A113 10sh multicolored   .30 .30
718 A113 25sh multicolored   .65 .65
719 A113 30sh multicolored   .80 .80
720 A113 50sh multicolored   1.25 1.25
721 A113 90sh multicolored   2.10 2.10
722 A113 100sh multicolored   2.50 2.50
723 A113 250sh multicolored   6.00 6.00
724 A113 300sh multicolored   7.50 7.50
      Nos. 717-724 (8)   21.10 21.10

Souvenir Sheets
725 A113 400sh multicolored   9.75 9.75
726 A113 400sh multicolored   9.75 9.75

Butterflies — A114

Designs: 10sh, Vine leaf vagrant. 15sh, Blue spot commodore. 35sh, Orange admiral. 75sh, Wanderer. 100sh, Jackson's leaf. 150sh, Painted empress. 200sh, Double-banded orange. 300sh, Crawshay's sapphire blue. No. 735, Noble swallowtail. No. 736, Club-tailed charaxes. No. 737, Satyr charaxes. No. 738, Green patch swallowtail.

1991, Aug. 28   *Litho.*   *Perf. 14*
727 A114 10sh multicolored   .45 .45
728 A114 15sh multicolored   .45 .45
729 A114 35sh multicolored   .95 .95
730 A114 75sh multicolored   1.90 1.90
731 A114 100sh multicolored   2.50 2.50
732 A114 150sh multicolored   4.00 4.00
733 A114 200sh multicolored   5.00 5.00
734 A114 300sh multicolored   7.50 7.50
      Nos. 727-734 (8)   22.75 22.75

Souvenir Sheets
735 A114 400sh multicolored   5.50 5.50
736 A114 400sh multicolored   5.50 5.50
737 A114 400sh multicolored   5.50 5.50
738 A114 400sh multicolored   5.50 5.50

While Nos. 727-736 have the same issue date as Nos. 737-738, the dollar value of Nos. 737-738 was lower when they were released.

Intelsat, 25th Anniv. A115

Designs: 10sh, Microwave link. 25sh, Earth. 100sh, Mwenge standard "B" Earth station. 500sh, Mwenge standard "A" Earth station. 50sh, World map.

1991, Sept. 5   *Litho.*   *Perf. 14*
739 A115 10sh multicolored   .40 .40
740 A115 25sh multicolored   .55 .55
741 A115 100sh multicolored   2.00 2.00
742 A115 500sh multicolored   8.00 8.00
      Nos. 739-742 (4)   10.95 10.95

Souvenir Sheet
743 A115 50sh multicolored   4.00 4.00

UN Development Program, 40th Anniv. — A116

Designs: 10sh, Irrigated rice farming. 15sh, Vocational training. 100sh, Terrace farming. 500sh, Architectural renovations, vert. 40sh, Helping people to help themselves, vert.

1991, Sept. 16   *Perf. 13½*
744 A116 10sh multicolored   .30 .30
745 A116 15sh multicolored   .30 .30
746 A116 100sh multicolored   1.50 1.50
747 A116 500sh multicolored   7.00 7.00
      Nos. 744-747 (4)   9.10 9.10

Souvenir Sheet
Perf. 13x12½
748 A116 40sh black & blue   2.00 2.00

All Africa Games, Cairo — A117

Perf. 12x12½, 12½x12
1991, Sept. 20
749 A117 10sh Netball   .50 .50
750 A117 15sh Soccer, horiz.   .50 .50
751 A117 100sh Tennis   2.50 2.50
752 A117 200sh Running   3.25 3.25
753 A117 500sh Baseball, horiz.   7.25 7.25
      Nos. 749-753 (5)   14.00 14.00

Souvenir Sheet
754 A117 500sh Basketball   10.50 10.50

Telecom '91 — A118

1991, Oct. 1   *Perf. 13½x14, 14x13½*
755 A118 10sh shown   .30 .30
756 A118 15sh Telecom '91, horiz.   .30 .30
757 A118 35sh arrows   .40 .40
758 A118 100sh like #757, horiz.   1.10 1.10
      Nos. 755-758 (4)   2.10 2.10

World Telecommunications Day (Nos. 757-758).

Dinosaurs A119

1991, Oct. 28   *Perf. 12x12½*
759 A119 10sh Stegosaurus   .30 .30
760 A119 15sh Triceratops   .30 .30
761 A119 25sh Edmontosaurus   .45 .45
762 A119 30sh Plateosaurus   .60 .60
763 A119 35sh Diplodocus   .70 .70
764 A119 100sh Iguanodon   1.90 1.90
765 A119 200sh Silviasaurus   3.75 3.75
      Nos. 759-765 (7)   8.00 8.00

Souvenir Sheet
766 A119 150sh Rhamphorhynchus   4.75 4.75

Animals and Fish A120

No. 767 — Horses: a, Shire. b, Thoroughbred. c, Kladruber. d, Appaloosa. e, Hanoverian. f, Arab. g, Breton. h, Exmoor. i, Connemara. j, Lipizzaner. k, Shetland. l, Percheron. m, Pinto. n, Orlov. o, Palomino. p, Welsh cob.
No. 768 — Cats: a, Japanese bobtail. b, Cornish rex. c, Malayan. d, Tonkinese. e, Abyssinian. f, Russian blue. g, Cymric. h, Somali. i, Siamese. j, Himalayan. k, Singapura. l, Manx. m, Oriental shorthair. n, Maine coon. o, Persian. p, Birman.
No. 769, vert. — African elephants: a, One walking left. b, Two with tusks entangled. c, One facing forward. d, One under tree. e, Adult and calf in water, zebra. f, Adult and calf walking into water. g, Two adults and calf in water. h, Adult and calf standing in water. i, One walking right. j, Two, one raising trunk in air. k,

One raising trunk in air. l, One facing forward, trunk down, zebra. m, Adult, calf at edge of water, antelope. n, Adult and calf, two more in background. o, One walking toward water. p, Adult with trunk on calf.
No. 770 — Aquarium fish: a, Jewel tetra. b, Five-banded barb. c, Simpson platy. d, Guppy, e, Zebra danio. f, Neon tetra. g, Siamese fighting fish. h, Tiger barb. i, Red lyretail. j, Goldfish. k, Pearl gourami. l, Angelfish. m, Clown loach. n, Red swordtail. o, Brown discus. p, Rosy barb.
No. 771 — Birds: a, Budgerigar. b, Rainbow bunting. c, Golden-fronted leafbird. d, Black-headed caique. e, Java sparrow. f, Diamond sparrow. g, Peach-faced lovebird. h, Golden conure. i, Military macaw. j, Celestial parrotlet. k, Sulphur-crested cockatoo. l, Spectacled Amazon parrot. m, Paradise tanager. n, Gouldian finch. o, Masked lovebird. p, Hill mynah.

1991, Oct. 28   *Litho.*   *Perf. 14*
767 A120 50sh Sheet of 16,   19.00 19.00
      #a.-p.   19.00 19.00
768 A120 50sh Sheet of 16,   19.00 19.00
      #a.-p.   19.00 19.00
769 A120 75sh Sheet of 16,   19.00 19.00
      #a.-p.   19.00 19.00
770 A120 75sh Sheet of 16,   19.00 19.00
      #a.-p.   19.00 19.00
771 A120 75sh Sheet of 16,   19.00 19.00
      #a.-p.   19.00 19.00
      Nos. 767-771 (5)   95.00 95.00

For overprints see Nos. 1529-1530.

Paintings by Vincent Van Gogh A121

Designs: 10sh, Peasant Woman Sewing. 15sh, Head of a Peasant Woman with Greenish Lace Cap. 35sh, Flowering Orchard. 75sh, Portrait of a Girl. 100sh, Portrait of a Woman with a Red Ribbon. 150sh, Vase with Flowers. 200sh, Houses in Antwerp. 400sh, Seated Peasant Woman with White Cap. No. 780, The Parsonage Garden at Nuenen in the Snow, horiz. No. 781, Bulb Fields, horiz.

1991, Nov. 20   *Litho.*   *Perf. 13½x14*
772 A121 10sh multicolored   .30 .30
773 A121 15sh multicolored   .30 .30
774 A121 35sh multicolored   .80 .80
775 A121 75sh multicolored   1.60 1.60
776 A121 100sh multicolored   2.00 2.00
777 A121 150sh multicolored   3.00 3.00
778 A121 200sh multicolored   4.00 4.00
779 A121 400sh multicolored   8.00 8.00
      Nos. 772-779 (8)   20.00 20.00

Size: 127x102mm
Imperf
780 A121 400sh multicolored   8.50 8.50
781 A121 400sh multicolored   8.50 8.50

Walt Disney Christmas Cards — A122

Design and date of card: 10sh, "Joy," 1968. 25sh, Mickey, Pluto and Goofy at fireplace, 1981. 35sh, Robin Hood and merry men celebrating, 1973. 75sh, Tree of greetings, Mickey, 1967. 100sh, Goofy, Mickey and Donald trying to catch Santa coming down chimney, 1969, vert. 150sh, Mickey on top of Christmas ornament, 1976, vert. 200sh, Clarabelle Cow with bells, 1935, vert. 300sh, Orphan mice reading book of tricks, 1935, vert. No. 790, Mickey wearing Santa hat and surrounded by Disney characters, 1968, vert. No. 791, Mickey with present for Donald, 1935, vert.

Perf. 13½x14, 14x13½

1991, Dec.   Litho.
782	A122	10sh multicolored	.30	.30
783	A122	25sh multicolored	.55	.55
784	A122	35sh multicolored	.70	.70
785	A122	75sh multicolored	1.40	1.40
786	A122	100sh multicolored	2.00	2.00
787	A122	150sh multicolored	2.50	2.50
788	A122	200sh multicolored	3.00	3.00
789	A122	300sh multicolored	4.00	4.00
		Nos. 782-789 (8)	14.45	14.45

Souvenir Sheets
790	A122	500sh multicolored	8.50	8.50
791	A122	500sh multicolored	8.50	8.50

Elephants
A123

Designs: 10sh, 15sh, 25sh, 100sh, Various pictures of elephas maximus. 30sh, 35sh, 200sh, Various pictures of loxodonta africana. 400sh, Mammut mammuthus.

Perf. 12x12½,12½x12

1991, Nov. 28   Litho.
792	A123	10sh multi, vert.	.60	.60
793	A123	15sh multi, vert.	.60	.60
794	A123	25sh multi, vert.	.90	.90
795	A123	30sh multi, vert.	1.25	1.25
796	A123	35sh multicolored	1.50	1.50
797	A123	100sh multicolored	4.00	4.00
798	A123	200sh multicolored	7.50	7.50
		Nos. 792-798 (7)	16.35	16.35

Souvenir Sheet
799	A123	400sh multicolored	7.25	7.25

Locomotives — A124

1991, Dec. 10   Perf. 12½x12, 12x12½
800	A124	10sh USSR 1930	.25	.25
801	A124	15sh Japan 1964	.25	.25
802	A124	25sh Russia 1834, vert.	.40	.40
803	A124	35sh France 1979	.65	.65
804	A124	60sh France 1972	1.10	1.10
805	A124	100sh United Kingdom 1972	1.60	1.60
806	A124	300sh Russia 1837, vert.	5.25	5.25
		Nos. 800-806 (7)	9.50	9.50

Souvenir Sheet
807	A124	100sh France, 1952, vert.	2.50	2.50

Entertainers — A125

Nos. 808a-808i, 812, Various portraits of Elvis Presley.
Nos. 809a-809i, 813, Various portraits of Marilyn Monroe.
Nos. 810a-810i, 814, Various portraits of Bruce Lee.
Black entertainers: No. 811: a, Scott Joplin. b, Sammy Davis, Jr. c, Joan Armatrading. d, Louis Armstrong. e, Miriam Makeba. f, Lionel Ritchie. g, Whitney Houston, h, Bob Marley. i, Tina Turner. No. 815, Kouyate family.

1992, Feb. 15   Perf. 14
808	A125	75sh Sheet of 9, #a.-i.	9.75	9.75
809	A125	75sh Sheet of 9, #a.-i.	9.75	9.75

810	A125	75sh Sheet of 9, #a.-i.	9.75	9.75
811	A125	75sh Sheet of 9, #a.-i.	9.75	9.75
		Nos. 808-811 (4)	39.00	39.00

Souvenir Sheets
812	A125	500sh multicolored	8.75	8.75
813	A125	500sh multicolored	8.75	8.75
814	A125	500sh multicolored	8.75	8.75
815	A125	500sh multicolored	8.75	8.75
		Nos. 812-815 (4)	35.00	35.00

Nos. 812-815 each contain one 29x43mm stamp.
See #949 for #808 inscribed "15th Anniversary."

Fish of Tanzania
A126

Designs: 10sh, Malacanthus latovittatus. 15sh, Lamprologus tretocephalus. 25sh, Lamprologus calvus. 35sh, Hemichromis bimaculatusl. 60sh, Aphyosemion bivittatum. No. 821, Synanceia verrucosa. 300sh, Aphyosemion ahli. No. 823, Regalecus glesne.

1992, Mar. 8   Perf. 12½x12
816	A126	10sh multicolored	.55	.55
817	A126	15sh multicolored	.70	.70
818	A126	25sh multicolored	.90	.90
819	A126	35sh multicolored	1.10	1.10
820	A126	60sh multicolored	1.50	1.50
821	A126	100sh multicolored	2.00	2.00
822	A126	300sh multicolored	5.25	5.25
		Nos. 816-822 (7)	12.00	12.00

Souvenir Sheet
823	A126	100sh multicolored	3.00	3.00

World War II in the Pacific
A127

Designs: No. 824a, British-designed radar at Pearl Harbor. b, Churchill declares war on Japan. c, Repulse destroyed. d, Prince of Wales sunk. e, Singapore falls to Japanese. f, Hermes is sunk off Ceylon. g, Airfields in Malaya attacked. h, Hong Kong falls to Japanese. i, Japanese Daihatsu landing craft. j, Japanese cruiser Haguro in Java Sea.

1992, Apr. 27   Perf. 14½x15
824	A127	75sh Sheet of 10, #a.-j.	22.50	22.50

Visits of Pope John Paul II — A128

No. 825, 100sh: a, Dominican Republic, 1979. b, Mexico, 1979. c, Poland, 1979. d, Ireland, 1979. e, UN, New York, 1979. f, US, 1979. g, Turkey, 1979. h, Zaire, 1980. i, Congo, 1980. j, Kenya, 1980. k, Ghana, 1980. l, Upper Volta, 1980.
No. 826, 100sh: a, Ivory Coast, 1980. b, France, 1980. c, Brazil, 1980. d, West Germany, 1980. e, Pakistan, 1981. f, Philippines, 1981. g, Guam, 1981. h, Japan, 1981. h, Alaska, 1981. i, Nigeria, 1982. j, Benin, 1982. l, Gabon, 1982.
No. 827, 100sh: a, Equatorial Guinea, 1982. b, Portugal, 1982. c, Great Britain, 1982. d, Argentina, 1982. e, UN, Geneva, 1982. f, San Marino, 1982. g, Spain, 1982. h, Costa Rica, 1983. i, Panama, 1983. j, El Salvador, 1983. k, Nicaragua, 1983. l, Guatemala, 1983.
No. 828, 100sh: a, Honduras, 1983. b, Belize, 1983. c, Haiti, 1983. d, Poland, 1983. e, France, 1983. f, Austria, 1983. g, Alaska, 1984. h, South Korea, 1984. i, Papua New Guinea, 1984. j, Solomon Islands, 1984. k, Thailand, 1984. l, Switzerland, 1984.
No. 829, 100sh: a, Canada, 1984. b, Dominican Republic, 1984. c, Puerto Rico, 1984. d, Venezuela, 1985. e, Ecuador, 1985. f, Peru,

1985. g, Trinidad & Tobago, 1985. h, Netherlands, 1985. i, Luxembourg, 1985. j, Belgium, 1985. k, Togo, 1985. l, Ivory Coast, 1985.
No. 830, 100sh: a, Cameroun, 1985. b, Central African Republic, 1985. c, Zaire, 1985. d, Kenya, 1985. e, Morocco, 1985. f, Liechtenstein, 1985. g, India, 1986. h, Colombia, 1986. i, St. Lucia, 1986. j, France, 1986. k, Bangladesh, 1986. l, Singapore, 1986.
No. 831, 100sh: a, Fiji, 1986. b, New Zealand, 1986. c, Australia, 1986. d, Seychelles, 1986. e, Uruguay, 1987. f, Chile, 1987. g, Argentina, 1987. h, West Germany, 1987. i, Poland, 1987. j, US, 1987. k, Canada, 1987. l, Uruguay, 1988.
No. 832, 100sh: a, Bolivia, 1988. b, Peru, 1988. c, Paraguay, 1988. d, Austria, 1988. e, Zimbabwe, 1988. f, Botswana, 1988. g, Lesotho, 1988. h, Swaziland, 1988. i, Mozambique, 1988. j, France, 1988. k, Madagascar, 1988. l, Reunion, 1989.
No. 833, 100sh: a, Zambia, 1989. b, Malawi, 1989. c, Norway, 1989. d, Iceland, 1989. e, Finland, 1989. f, Denmark, 1989. g, Sweden, 1989. h, Spain, 1989. i, South Korea, 1989. j, Indonesia, 1989. k, Mauritius, 1989. l, Cape Verde, 1990.
No. 834, 100sh: a, Mali, 1990. b, Guinea-Bissau, 1990. c, Burkina Faso, 1990. d, Chad, 1990. e, Czechoslovakia, 1990. f, Mexico, 1990. g, Curacao, 1990. h, Malta, 1990. i, Tanzania, 1990. j, Burundi, 1990. k, Rwanda, 1990. l, Ivory Coast, 1990.

1992, Apr. 13   Perf. 14
Sheets of 12 + 4 Labels
825-834	A128	Set of 10	200.00	200.00

Zanzibar Stone Town
A129

Designs: No. 839a, 150sh, Old fort. b, 300sh, Maruhubi ruins.

1992, Apr. 15   Perf. 12x12½, 12½x12
835	A129	10sh Balcony	.60	.60
836	A129	20sh Bahlnara mosque	1.40	1.40
837	A129	30sh High Court bldg.	2.00	2.00
838	A129	200sh Natl. museum	8.00	8.00
		Nos. 835-838 (4)	12.00	12.00

Souvenir Sheet
839	A129	Sheet of 2, #a.-b.	10.00	10.00

Nos. 835-837 are vert.

Wolfgang Amadeus Mozart, Death Bicent.
A130

Designs: 10sh, Marcella Sembrich as Zerlina in Don Giovanni. 50sh, Symphony Number 41, Jupiter. 300sh, Luciano Pavarotti as Idamente in Idomeneo. 500sh, Wolfgang Amadeus Mozart, vert.

1992, Aug. 1   Perf. 14
840	A130	10sh violet & blk	1.50	1.50
841	A130	50sh multicolored	3.50	3.50
842	A130	300sh violet & blk	8.00	8.00
		Nos. 840-842 (3)	13.00	13.00

Souvenir Sheet
843	A130	500sh olive brn & blk	11.50	11.50

While No. 843 has the same issue date as Nos. 840-842, the dollar value was lower when it were released.
No. 843 contains one 38x50mm stamp.

1992, Aug. 1

Designs: 10sh, Insignia, giraffe and elephant. 15sh, Scouts in canoe. 400sh, John Glenn's Gemini space capsule orbiting Earth. 500sh, Boy scout, vert.

844	A130	10sh multicolored	.45	.45
845	A130	15sh multicolored	.45	.45
846	A130	400sh multicolored	10.50	10.50
		Nos. 844-846 (3)	11.40	11.40

Souvenir Sheet
847	A130	500sh multicolored	8.50	8.50

Lord Robert Baden-Powell, Founder of Boy Scouts, 50th Death Anniv. (in 1991).

While No. 847 has the same issue date as Nos. 844-846, the dollar value was lower when it were released.
No. 847 contains one 38x50mm stamp.

1992, Aug. 1

Charles de Gaulle (1890-1970): 25sh, French Resistance Monument and medal. 30sh, First Free French tank at Omaha beach, Normandy. 150sh, Concorde at de Gaulle Airport. 500sh, France #439 with Cross of Lorraine overprint and Free French stamp, vert.

848	A130	25sh multicolored	.90	.90
849	A130	30sh multicolored	1.00	1.00
850	A130	150sh multicolored	10.00	10.00
		Nos. 848-850 (3)	11.90	11.90

Souvenir Sheet
851	A130	500sh multicolored	13.00	13.00

While No. 851 has the same issue date as Nos. 848-850, the dollar value was lower when it was released.
No. 851 contains one 38x50mm stamp.

Common Chimpanzee
A131

Various chimpanzees in natural habitat.

1992
852	A131	10sh multicolored	.35	.35
853	A131	15sh multicolored	.35	.35
854	A131	35sh multicolored	.85	.85
855	A131	75sh multicolored	1.90	1.90
856	A131	100sh multicolored	2.25	2.25
857	A131	150sh multicolored	3.50	3.50
858	A131	200sh multicolored	4.50	4.50
859	A131	300sh multicolored	7.00	7.00
		Nos. 852-859 (8)	20.70	20.70

Souvenir Sheets
860	A131	400sh Swinging from tree	6.50	6.50
861	A131	400sh Eating termites	6.50	6.50

Spanish Art — A132

Drawings by Goya: 25sh, A Picador mounted on the shoulders of a Chulo, spears a Bull. 100sh, The Dream of Reason brings forth Monsters, vert. 150sh, Another Madness (of Martincho) in the Plaza de Zaragoza. 200sh, Recklessness of Martincho in the Plaza de Zaragoza.
No. 866, Seascape, by Mariano Salvador Maella.

1992   Perf. 13
862	A132	25sh blk & red brn	.50	.50
863	A132	100sh black & brn	1.75	1.75
864	A132	150sh blk & red brn	2.75	2.75
865	A132	200sh blk & red brn	3.00	3.00

Size: 120x95mm
Imperf
866	A132	400sh multicolored	5.00	5.00
		Nos. 862-866 (5)	13.00	13.00

Granada '92.

1992   Perf. 13

Drawings by Diego da Silva Velazquez: 35sh, Philip IV at Fraga. 50sh, The Head of the Stag. 75sh, The Cardinal Infante Don Fernando as a Hunter. 300sh, Pablo de Valladolid. No. 871, Two Men at Table.
867	A132	35sh multicolored	.75	.75
868	A132	50sh multicolored	.90	.90
869	A132	75sh multicolored	1.40	1.40
870	A132	300sh multicolored	3.75	3.75

Size: 120x95mm
Imperf

871	A132	400sh multicolored	5.00	5.00
	Nos. 867-871 (5)		11.80	11.80

Granada '92.

A133

Chimpanzees of Gombe — A134

Designs: No. 872, Melisa and Mike. No. 873, Leakey and David Greybeard. No. 874, Fifi eating termites. No. 875 Galahad.

No. 876a, 10sh, Leakey. b, 15sh, Fifi. c, 20sh, Faben. d, 30sh, David Greybeard. e, 35sh, Mike. f, 50sh, Galahad. g, 100sh, Melisa. h, 200sh, Flo.

No. 877, Fifi, Flo, and Faben.

1992, May 29   Litho.   Perf. 14

872	A133	10sh multicolored	1.00	1.00
873	A133	15sh multicolored	1.25	1.25
874	A133	30sh multicolored	1.75	1.75
875	A133	35sh multicolored	2.00	2.00
	Nos. 872-875 (4)		6.00	6.00

Miniature Sheet

876	A134	Sheet of 8, #a.-h.	12.00	12.00

Souvenir Sheet

877	A133	100sh multicolored	4.50	4.50

Natl. Bank of Commerce, 25th Anniv. — A135

Designs: 10sh, Sorghum plants. 15sh, Samora Avenue branch, computer operator, vert. 30sh, Head office. 35sh, Bankers Training Center. 40sh, Batik tie dyeing.

1992, June 22

878	A135	10sh multicolored	.70	.70
879	A135	15sh multicolored	.80	.80
880	A135	35sh multicolored	1.25	1.25
881	A135	40sh multicolored	1.25	1.25
	Nos. 878-881 (4)		4.00	4.00

Souvenir Sheet

882	A135	30sh multicolored	2.50	2.50

Traditional Dress — A136

Designs: 3sh, Gogo, central area. 5sh, Swahili, coastal area. 9sh, Hehe, southern highlands and Makonde, southern area. 12sh, Maasai, northern area. 40sh, Mwarusha.

1992, Apr. 30   Litho.   Perf. 14½

883	A136	3sh multicolored	.70	.70
884	A136	5sh multicolored	.80	.80
885	A136	9sh multicolored	.90	.90
886	A136	12sh multicolored	1.20	1.20
	Nos. 883-886 (4)		3.60	3.60

Souvenir Sheet

887	A136	40sh multicolored	4.50	4.50

Dated 1989.

1992 Summer Olympics, Barcelona A137

1992, July 23   Perf. 12x12½

888	A137	40sh Basketball	.80	.80
889	A137	100sh Billiards	1.25	1.25
890	A137	200sh Table tennis	2.00	2.00
891	A137	400sh Darts	4.25	4.25
	Nos. 888-891 (4)		8.30	8.30

Souvenir Sheet

892	A137	500sh Weight lifting	6.00	6.00

Fish A138

No. 893: a, Tilapia mariae. b, Capoeta hulstaerti. c, Tropheus moorii. d, Synodontis angelicus. e, Julidochromis dickfeldi. f, Tilapia nilotica. g, Nothobranchius rachovii. h, Pseudotropheus crabro. i, Lamprologus leleupi. j, Pseudotropheus zebra. k, Julidochromis marlieri. l, Chalinochromis brichardi.

Designs: No. 894, Haplochromis "electric blue." No. 895, Lamprologus brevis. No. 896, Nothobranchius palmqvisti.

1992, Oct.   Litho.   Perf. 13½

893	A138	100sh Sheet of 12, #a.-l.	19.00	19.00

Souvenir Sheets

894	A138	500sh multicolored	6.50	6.50
895	A138	500sh multicolored	6.50	6.50
896	A138	500sh multicolored	6.50	6.50

Discovery of America, 500th Anniv. A139

1992, Oct.   Litho.   Perf. 14

897	A139	70sh Sailing ship	1.75	1.75
898	A139	300sh Columbus	6.00	6.00

Souvenir Sheet

899	A139	500sh Columbus, diff.	5.00	5.00

Miniature Sheet

Flowers in Rio de Janeiro Botanical Garden — A140

No. 900: a, Couroupita guianensis. b, Jacaranda acutifolia. c, Psychopsis papilio. d,

Nelumbo nucifera. e, Brownea grandiceps. f, Coffea arabica. g, Monodora myristica. h, Calaranthus rosea. i, Hibiscus schizopetalus. j, Carpobrotus edulis. k, Adenium obesum. l, Delonix regia. m, Agapanthus praecox. n, Zantedeschia aethiopica. o, Protea cynaroides. p, Cassia fistula. q, Aganisia cyanea. r, Heliconia rostrata. s, Cattelya luteola. t, Lagerstroemia speciosa.

500sh, Avenue of Royal Palms, Rio.

1992, Nov. 5   Litho.   Perf. 14½

900	A140	70sh Sheet of 20, #a.-t.	24.00	24.00

Souvenir Sheet

901	A140	500sh multicolored	7.50	7.50

Dinosaurs A141

No. 902: a, Iguanodon. b, Saltasaurus. c, Cetiosaurus. d, Camarasaurus. e, Spinosaurus. f, Stegosaurus. g, Allosaurus. h, Ceratosaurus. i, Lesothosaurus. j, Anchisaurus. k, Ornithomimus. l, Baronyx. m, Pachycephalosaurus. n, Heterodontosaurus. o, Dryosaurus. p, Coelophysis.

1992, Nov. 5   Litho.   Perf. 14

902	A141	100sh Sheet of 16, #a.-p.	22.00	22.00

1992 Olympics, Albertville and Barcelona A142

Designs: 20sh, 4000-meter pursuit cycling, vert. 40sh, Double sculls. 50sh, Water polo. 70sh, Women's single loge. 100sh, Marathon. 150sh, Uneven parallel bars. 200sh, Ice hockey, vert. 400sh, Rings, vert.

No. 911, Tennis, vert. No. 912, Soccer, vert.

1992, Nov. 16   Litho.   Perf. 14

903	A142	20sh multicolored	.35	.35
904	A142	40sh multicolored	.55	.55
905	A142	50sh multicolored	.60	.60
906	A142	70sh multicolored	.85	.85
907	A142	100sh multicolored	1.25	1.25
908	A142	150sh multicolored	1.75	1.75
909	A142	200sh multicolored	2.40	2.40
910	A142	400sh multicolored	4.75	4.75
	Nos. 903-910 (8)		12.50	12.50

Souvenir Sheets

911	A142	500sh multicolored	6.00	6.00
912	A142	500sh multicolored	6.00	6.00

Mickey's Portrait Gallery A142a

Donald Duck in scenes from Disney movies: No. 915, Sea Scouts, 1939. 35sh, Fire Chief, 1940. 50sh, Truant Officer Donald, 1941. 500sh, With Daisy in Mr. Duck Steps Out, 1940.

No. 925, Daisy in Don Donald, 1937.

Disney characters in scenes from Disney movies: No. 913, Hawaiian Holiday, 1937. No. 914, Society Dog Show, 1939. 75sh, Clock Cleaners, 1937. No. 919, Magician Mickey, 1937. No. 920, Goofy and Wilbur, 1939. 200sh, The Nifty Nineties, 1941. 300sh, Society Dog Show, 1939. 400sh, Pluto's Quin-Puplets, 1937. No. 926, Brave Little Tailor, 1938, horiz. No. 927, Forever Goofy.

1992, Nov. 30   Litho.   Perf. 13½x14

913	A142a	25sh multicolored	.50	.50
914	A142a	25sh multicolored	.50	.50
915	A142a	25sh multicolored	.50	.50
916	A142a	35sh multicolored	.65	.65
917	A142a	50sh multicolored	.90	.90
918	A142a	75sh multicolored	1.10	1.10

919	A142a	100sh multicolored	1.25	1.25
920	A142a	100sh multicolored	1.25	1.25
921	A142a	200sh multicolored	2.00	2.00
922	A142a	300sh multicolored	2.75	2.75
923	A142a	400sh multicolored	3.00	3.00
924	A142a	500sh multicolored	3.00	3.00
	Nos. 913-924 (12)		17.40	17.40

Souvenir Sheets

925	A142a	600sh multicolored	5.00	5.00

Perf. 14x13½

926	A142a	600sh multicolored	5.00	5.00

Perf. 13½x14

927	A142a	600sh multicolored	5.00	5.00

Nos. 668-673 & 678 Ovptd. in Black or Red

40th Anniversary of the Accession HM Queen Elizabeth II 1952-1992

1992   Litho.   Perf. 14

928	A106	50sh on #668	.35	.35
929	A106	50sh on #669	.35	.35
a.	Pair, #928-929		.70	.70
930	A106	75sh on #670	.55	.55
931	A106	75sh on #671	.55	.55
a.	Pair, #930-931		1.10	1.10
932	A106	100sh on #672	.75	.75
933	A106	100sh on #673	.75	.75
a.	Pair, #932-933		1.50	1.50
	Nos. 928-933 (6)		3.30	3.30

Souvenir Sheet

934	A106	350sh on #678 (R)	2.50	2.50

Overprint appears on one line in sheet margin of No. 934.

Traditional Hunting A143

Designs: 20sh, Slingshots used on birds. 40sh, Various weapons. 70sh, Bow and arrow used on gazelles. 100sh, Long knife, wooden club used on gazelles. 150sh, Spear and shield used on lion.

1992   Litho.   Perf. 13½

935	A143	20sh multicolored	1.40	1.40
936	A143	70sh multicolored	1.75	1.75
937	A143	100sh multicolored	2.75	2.75
938	A143	150sh multicolored	4.00	4.00
	Nos. 935-938 (4)		9.90	9.90

Souvenir Sheet

Perf. 12½

939	A143	40sh multicolored	3.25	3.25

Shells — A144

Designs: 10sh, Lambis truncata Humphrey. 15sh, Cypraecassis rufa. 25sh, Vexillum rugosum. 30sh, Conus litteratus. 35sh, Corculum cardissa. 50sh, Murex ramosus. 250sh, Melo melo. 300sh, Tridacha gigas.

1992, June 30   Perf. 12x12½

940	A144	10sh multicolored	.45	.45
941	A144	15sh multicolored	.55	.55
942	A144	25sh multicolored	.75	.75
943	A144	30sh multicolored	.75	.75
944	A144	35sh multicolored	.75	.75
945	A144	50sh multicolored	1.10	1.10
946	A144	250sh multicolored	4.50	4.50
	Nos. 940-946 (7)		8.85	8.85

Souvenir Sheet

947	A144	300sh multicolored	6.00	6.00

No. 808 Inscribed Vertically "15th Anniversary"

1992   Litho.   Perf. 14

949	A125	75sh Sheet of 9, #a.-i.	12.00	12.00

TANZANIA

SEAL/SILI
SEA ANIMAL GIANTS **20/-**

Marine
Life
A145

1992		Litho.	Perf. 14	
950	A145	20sh Seal	1.25	1.25
951	A145	30sh Whale	3.00	3.00
952	A145	70sh Shark	1.75	1.75
953	A145	100sh Walrus	3.00	3.00
		Nos. 950-953 (4)	9.00	9.00

Souvenir Sheet

954	A145	500sh Sea turtle	10.00	10.00

A146

WOLFGANG AMADEUS MOZART
[1756-1791]

400/-
TANZANIA

Anniversaries and
Events — A147

Designs: 30sh, Count Ferdinand von Zeppelin. 70sh, Apollo-Soyuz. No. 957, Child being offered apple. No. 958, African elephant. No. 959, Lions Intl. emblem, man being given glasses. No. 960, Zebra. 300sh, Graf Zeppelin. No. 962, Space shuttle in Earth orbit. No. 963, Wolfgang Amadeus Mozart.
No. 964, Voyager 2. No. 965, Unidentified zeppelin. No. 966, African elephant, diff. No. 967, Scene from "The Magic Flute."

1992		Litho.	Perf. 14	
955	A146	30sh multicolored	3.25	3.25
956	A146	70sh multicolored	4.50	4.50
957	A146	150sh multicolored	2.00	2.00
958	A146	150sh multicolored	3.25	3.25
959	A146	200sh multicolored	2.40	2.40
960	A146	200sh multicolored	3.25	3.25
961	A146	300sh multicolored	3.25	3.25
962	A146	400sh multicolored	4.50	4.50
963	A147	400sh multicolored	3.25	3.25
		Nos. 955-963 (9)	29.65	29.65

Souvenir Sheets

964	A146	500sh multicolored	4.50	4.50
965	A146	500sh multicolored	4.50	4.50
966	A146	500sh multicolored	4.50	4.50
967	A147	800sh multicolored	6.50	6.50

Count Zeppelin, 75th death anniv. (#955, 961, 965). Intl. Space Year (#956, 962, 964). Intl. Conference on Nutrition (#957). Earth Summit, Rio de Janeiro (#958, 960, 966). Lions Intl., 75th anniv. (#959). Wolfgang Amadeus Mozart, bicent. of death (in 1991) (#963, 967).
Issued: Nos. 955-956, 961-962, 964-965, Nov.; Nos. 957-960, 966, Dec.

TANZANIA

Abyssinian cat **20/-**

Cats — A147a

1992, Dec. 3		Litho.	Perf. 12x12½	
967A	A147a	20sh Abyssinian	.75	.75
967B	A147a	30sh Havana	.75	.75
967C	A147a	50sh Persian black	.90	.90
967D	A147a	70sh Persian blue	1.10	1.10
967E	A147a	100sh European silver tabby	1.30	1.30

967F	A147a	150sh Persian silver tabby	1.60	1.60
967G	A147a	200sh Maine	2.00	2.00
		Nos. 967A-967G (7)	8.40	8.40

Souvenir Sheet

967H	A147a	300sh European	5.00	5.00

Tanzania

10/-

Model
Trains
A148

Lionel models: 10sh, B & O Tunnel locomotive #5, 2⅞-inch gauge, 1904. 20sh, Liberty Bell #385E, standard gauge, 1930. 30sh, Armored motor car #203, standard gauge, 1917. 50sh, Open trolley #202, standard gauge, 1910-14. 70sh, Macy special #450, standrad gauge. 100sh, Milwaukee Road bipolar electric #381E, standard gauge, 1929. 200sh, New York Central "S" type, standard gauge, 1912. 300sh, 4-4-0 American #7 (thick rim), standard gauge, 1914.
No. 976, Wind-up hand car with Mickey and Minnie Mouse, O-27 gauge, 1936. No. 977, Clear plastic F-3 display model, O gauge, 1947.

1992, Dec. 10		Litho.	Perf. 14	
968	A148	10sh multicolored	.65	.65
969	A148	20sh multicolored	.75	.75
970	A148	30sh multicolored	.80	.80
971	A148	50sh multicolored	1.25	1.25
972	A148	70sh multicolored	1.50	1.50
973	A148	100sh multicolored	1.60	1.60
974	A148	200sh multicolored	2.25	2.25
975	A148	300sh multicolored	3.00	3.00
		Nos. 968-975 (8)	11.80	11.80

Souvenir Sheets

976	A148	500sh multicolored	5.00	5.00
977	A148	500sh multicolored	5.00	5.00

Genoa '92.

TANZANIA

5/-

Birds — A149

1992, Dec. 10		Litho.	Perf. 12x12½	
978	A149	5sh Superb starling	.90	.90
979	A149	10sh Canary	1.10	1.10
980	A149	15sh Four-colored bush shrike	1.10	1.10
981	A149	25sh Grey-headed kingfisher	1.25	1.25
982	A149	30sh Common kingfisher	1.25	1.25
983	A149	35sh Yellow-billed oxpecker	1.25	1.25
984	A149	150sh Black throated honeyquide	3.00	3.00
		Nos. 978-984 (7)	9.85	9.85

Souvenir Sheet
Perf. 12½x12

985	A149	300sh European cuckoo, horiz.	6.00	6.00

TANZANIA

Makonde Art **20/-**

Makonde
Art — A149a

Various carved faces.

1992, Dec. 24		Litho.	Perf. 12x12½	
985A	A149a	20sh multicolored	.30	.30
985B	A149a	30sh multicolored	.30	.30
985C	A149a	50sh multicolored	.50	.50
985D	A149a	70sh multicolored	.70	.70
985E	A149a	100sh multicolored	1.00	1.00

985F	A149a	150sh multicolored	1.50	1.50
985G	A149a	200sh multicolored	2.00	2.00
		Nos. 985A-985G (7)	6.30	6.30

Souvenir Sheet

985H	A149a	350sh multicolored	5.00	5.00

TANZANIA 1992

20/.

RUSSIA 1813

Bicycles
A149b

1992, Dec. 30		Litho.	Perf. 12½x12	
985I	A149b	20sh Russia, 1813	.45	.45
985J	A149b	30sh Germany, 1840	.45	.45
985K	A149b	50sh Germany, 1818	.65	.65
985L	A149b	70sh Germany, 1850	.65	.65
985M	A149b	100sh Italy, 1988	.70	.70
985N	A149b	150sh Sweden, 1982	1.50	1.50
985O	A149b	300sh Italy, 1989	1.75	1.75
		Nos. 985I-985O (7)	6.15	6.15

Souvenir Sheet

985P	A149b	350sh Great Britain, 1887	5.00	5.00

TANZANIA

1992

10/.

Discovery of
America, 500th
Anniv. — A150

Designs: 10sh, Symbols of luck. 15sh, "Is this course right?," compass, chart. 25sh, "Earth!," first sight of land. 30sh, First meetings, horiz. 35sh, Nina, horiz. 75sh, Santa Maria, horiz. 250sh, Ship running aground, vert. 200sh, Columbus.

Perf. 12x12½, 12½x12

1992, Sept. 30		Litho.		
986	A150	10sh multicolored	.35	.35
987	A150	15sh multicolored	.40	.40
988	A150	25sh multicolored	.55	.55
989	A150	30sh multicolored	.60	.60
990	A150	35sh multicolored	.70	.70
991	A150	75sh multicolored	1.25	1.25
992	A150	250sh multicolored	2.25	2.25
		Nos. 986-992 (7)	6.10	6.10

Souvenir Sheet

993	A150	200sh multicolored	6.00	6.00

JEUNE DESSINATEUR
CHARDIN

TANZANIA **100/-**

Louvre
Museum,
Bicent.
A151

No. 994 — Paintings by Jean-Baptiste-Simeon Chardin (1699-1779): a, Young Artist. b, The Buffet. c, The Provider. d, A Mother Working. e, Grace. f, The Copper Fountain. g, House of Cards. h, Child with Teetotum. 500sh, The Ray, horiz.

1993, Mar. 8		Litho.	Perf. 12	
994	A151	100sh Sheet of 8, #a.-h. + label	12.00	12.00

Souvenir Sheet
Perf. 14½

995	A151	500sh multicolored	6.00	6.00

No. 995 contains one 88x55mm stamp.

TANZANIA **100/-**

Coronation Anniversary
1953-1993

Coronation
of Queen
Elizabeth II,
40th Anniv.
A152

No. 996: a, 100sh, Official coronation photograph. b, 150sh, Exeter salt. c, 200sh, Photograph of ceremony, 1953. d, 300sh, Queen, Prince Andrew.
500sh, Princess Elizabeth Opening the New Broadgate Coventry, by Dame Laura Knight, 1948.

1993, June 2		Litho.	Perf. 13½x14	
996	A152	Sheet, 2 ea #a.-d.	14.00	14.00

Souvenir Sheet
Perf. 14

997	A152	500sh multicolored	6.00	6.00

No. 997 contains one 28x43mm stamp.

TANZANIA **20/-**

VALENTINA TERESHKOVA
FIRST WOMAN IN SPACE

Famous
Women — A153

Designs: a, 20sh, Valentina Tereshkova. b, 40sh, Marie Curie. c, 50sh, Indira Gandhi. d, 70sh, Wilma Rudolph. e, 100sh, Margaret Mead. f, 150sh, Golda Meir. g, 200sh, Dr. Elizabeth Blackwell. h, 400sh, Margaret Thatcher.
No. 999, Mother Teresa.

1993, July 15			Perf. 14	
998	A153	Sheet of 8, #a.-h.	15.00	15.00

Souvenir Sheet

999	A153	500sh multicolored	7.00	7.00

TANZANIA **100/-**

ELEPHANT
(Loxodonta africana)

Wildlife — A154

No. 1000 — Wildlife at watering hole: No. 1000: a, Elephant. b, Gazelles. c, Hartebeest. d, Duiker. e, Genet. f, Civet. g, Pelicans. h, Waterbuck. i, Blacksmith plovers. j, Pied kingfisher. k, Black-winged stilts. l, Bush pig.
No. 1000M: n, Brown-hooded kingfisher. o, Sable antelope (n). p, Impala (q). q, Buffalo. r, Leopard. s, Aardvark (t). t, Hippopotamus. u, Spotted hyena. v, Crowned crane (w). w, Crocodile. x, Flamingo. y, Baboon.
No. 1001 — Wildlife on the plains: No. 1001: a, Potto. b, Flamingos. c, Grey-headed kingfisher. d, Red colobus monkey. e, Dik-dik. f, Aardwolf. g, Black-backed jackal. h, Tree pangolin. i, Serval. j, Yellow-billed hornbill. k, Pygmy mongoose. l, Bat-eared fox.
No. 1001M: n, Bushbaby. o, Egyptian vulture. p, Ostrich. q, Greater kudu. r, Diana monkey. s, Giraffe (w). t, Cheetah (s). u, Wildebeeest (t). v, Chimpanzee. w, Warthog. x, Zebra. y, Rhinoceros.
No. 1002, Lions, horiz. No. 1003, African elephants, horiz.

1993, June 30				
1000	A154	100sh Sheet of 12, #a.-l.	12.00	12.00
1000M	A154	100sh Sheet of 12, #n.-y.	12.00	12.00
1001	A154	100sh Sheet of 12, #a.-l.	12.00	12.00
1001M	A154	100sh Sheet of 12, #n.-y.	12.00	12.00
		Nos. 1000-1001M (4)	48.00	48.00

Souvenir Sheets

1002	A154	500sh multi		6.50	6.50
1003	A154	500sh multi		6.50	6.50

For overprints see Nos. 1531, 1534.

Pancake Tortoise A155

1993, June 30

1004	A155	20sh On rock	.60	.50
1005	A155	30sh Drinking	.90	.75
1006	A155	50sh Crawling from under rocks	1.05	.90
1007	A155	70sh Hatchling	1.35	1.20
		Nos. 1004-1007 (4)	3.90	3.35

World Wildlife Federation.

Mushrooms A156

Designs: 20sh, Macrolepiota rhacodes. 40sh, Mycena pura. 50sh, Chlorophyllum molybdites. 70sh, Agaricus campestris. 100sh, Volvariella volvacea. 150sh, Leucoagaricus naucinus. 200sh, Oudemansiella radicata. 300sh, Clitocybe nebularis.

No. 1016, Omphalotus olearius. No. 1017, Lepista nuda.

1993, June 18   Litho.   Perf. 14

1008	A156	20sh multicolored	.35	.35
1009	A156	40sh multicolored	.55	.55
1010	A156	50sh multicolored	.60	.60
1011	A156	70sh multicolored	.85	.85
1012	A156	100sh multicolored	1.40	1.40
1013	A156	150sh multicolored	1.75	1.75
1014	A156	200sh multicolored	2.40	2.40
1015	A156	300sh multicolored	4.00	4.00
		Nos. 1008-1015 (8)	11.90	11.90

Souvenir Sheets

1016	A156	500sh multicolored	5.00	5.00
1017	A156	500sh multicolored	5.00	5.00

Sports — A157

1992, May 28   Litho.   Perf. 12x12½

1018	A157	20sh Boxing	.35	.35
1019	A157	50sh Field hockey	.80	.80
1020	A157	70sh Horse racing	.65	.65
1021	A157	100sh Marathon	.75	.75
1022	A157	150sh Soccer	.95	.95
1023	A157	200sh Diving	1.25	1.25
1024	A157	400sh Basketball	2.40	2.40
		Nos. 1018-1024 (7)	7.15	7.15

Souvenir Sheet
Perf. 12½x12

1025	A157	300sh High jump, horiz.	4.00	4.00

Animals A158

No. 1026: a, Female Grant's zebra, running. b, Male Grant's zebra, standing. c, Female Grant's gazelle. d, Male Grant's gazelle. e, Thompson's gazelle. f, White-bearded gnu, calf.

No. 1027: a, Female cheetah, cubs. b, Young cheetah. c, Lioness carrying her cub. d, Two hunting dogs. e, Three hunting dogs. f, Hunting dogs before an attack.

No. 1028, African rhinoceros. No. 1029, African elephant.

1993, June 30   Litho.   Perf. 14

1026	A158	100sh Sheet of 6, #a.-f.	9.00	9.00
1027	A158	100sh Sheet of 6, #a.-f.	9.00	9.00

Souvenir Sheets

1028	A158	500sh multicolored	10.00	10.00
1029	A158	500sh multicolored	10.00	10.00

For overprints see Nos. 1532-1533, 1535.

A159   A160

1994 Winter Olympics, Lillehammer, Norway: 300sh, Matti Nykanen, ski jumping, 1988. 400sh, Stefan Krause, Jan Behrendt, double luge, 1992. 500sh, Downhill skiing, 1972.

1993, June 10   Litho.   Perf. 14

1030	A159	300sh multicolored	2.25	2.25
1031	A159	400sh multicolored	2.75	2.75

Souvenir Sheet

1032	A159	500sh multicolored	3.50	3.50

1993, June 10

1033	A160	100sh Telescope	.70	.70
1034	A160	300sh Radio telescope	2.25	2.25

Souvenir Sheet

1035	A160	500sh Copernicus	3.50	3.50

Copernicus, 450th anniv. of death.

Picasso (1881-1973) A160a

Various details of painting, Guernica, 1937.

1993, June 10   Litho.   Perf. 14

1035A	A160a	30sh multi	.25	.25
1035B	A160a	200sh multi	1.40	1.40
1035C	A160a	300sh multi	2.00	2.00
		Nos. 1035A-1035C (3)	3.65	3.65

Souvenir Sheet

1035D	A160a	500sh multi	3.50	3.50

Flowers — A161   Polska '93 — A162

Designs: 20sh, Leopard orchid. 30sh, African violet. 40sh, Stapelia semota lutea. 50sh, Busy Lizzie. 60sh, Senecio petraeus. 70sh, Kalanchoe velutina. 100sh, Dwarf ginger lily. 150sh, Nymphaea colorata. 200sh, Thunbergia battiscombei. 250sh, Crossandra nilotica. 300sh, African tulip tree. 350sh, Ruttya fruticosa.

No. 1048, False African violet. No. 1049, Glory lily.

1993, Nov. 8   Litho.   Perf. 13½

1036	A161	20sh multicolored	.50	.50
1037	A161	30sh multicolored	.55	.55
1038	A161	40sh multicolored	.55	.55
1039	A161	50sh multicolored	.55	.55
1040	A161	60sh multicolored	.80	.80
1041	A161	70sh multicolored	.90	.90
1042	A161	100sh multicolored	1.00	1.00
1043	A161	150sh multicolored	1.60	1.60
1044	A161	200sh multicolored	1.90	1.90
1045	A161	250sh multicolored	1.90	1.90
1046	A161	300sh multicolored	2.25	2.25
1047	A161	350sh multicolored	2.25	2.25
		Nos. 1036-1047 (12)	14.75	14.75

Souvenir Sheets
Perf. 13

1048	A161	500sh multicolored	4.25	4.25
1049	A161	500sh multicolored	4.25	4.25

1993   Litho.   Perf. 14

Paintings: 200sh, Stone Masons, by Aleksander Kobzdej, 1952. 300sh, Child Wearing Plumed Helmut, by Z. Waliszewski, 1932.

500sh, In the Marketplace, by Stanislaw Osostowicz, 1939.

1050	A162	200sh multicolored	1.75	1.75
1051	A162	300sh multicolored	2.50	2.50

Souvenir Sheet

1052	A162	500sh multicolored	3.75	3.75

Butterflies A163

No. 1053: a, Gold-banded forester. b, Twin dotted border. c, Aphnaeus flavescens. d, Orange-and-lemon. e, Club-tailed charaxes. f, Broad blue-banded swallowtail. g, African map. h, Buxton's hairstreak. i, Bush charaxes. j, Lilac nymph. k, Large striped swordtail. l, Charaxes acuminatus. m, African leaf. n, African wood white. o, Trimen's false acraea. p, Red line sapphire. q, Mother-of-pearl. r, Flame-bordered charaxes. s, Large blue charaxes. t, Emperor swallowtail.

No. 1054: a, Angled grass yellow. b, Figtree blue. c, Iolaus ismenias. d, Green-veined charaxes. e, Commodore. f, African monarch. g, Bush scarlet. h, Eyed pansy. i, Zebra white. j, Azure hairstreak. k, Yellow pansy. l, Regal purple tip.

No. 1054M: n, Iolaus aphnaeoides. o, Green charaxes. p, Beautiful monarch. q, Short-tailed admiral. r, Dusky dotted border. s, Charaxes anticlea. t, Blue salamis. u, Nepheronia argia. v, Acraea pseudolycia. w, Blue-banded diadem. x, Golden tip. y, Acraea bonasia.

No. 1055, Blood-red cymothoe. No. 1056, Precis octavia. No. 1056A, Noble swallowtail. No. 1056B, Violet-spotted charaxes.

1993, Nov. 8   Litho.   Perf. 13

1053	A163	100sh Sheet of 20, #a.-t.	30.00	30.00
1054	A163	100sh Sheet of 12, #a.-l.	20.00	20.00
1054M	A163	100sh Sheet of 12, #n.-y.	20.00	20.00

Souvenir Sheets

1055	A163	500sh multi	7.00	7.00
1056	A163	500sh multi	7.00	7.00
1056A	A163	500sh multi	7.00	7.00
1056B	A163	500sh multi	7.00	7.00

A164   A165

Players, country: 20sh, Gullit, Holland. 30sh, Sheehy, Ireland. 50sh, Giannini, Italy. 70sh, Cesar, Brazil. 250sh, Barnes, England; Grun, Belgium. 300sh, Chendo, Spain. 350sh, Rijkaard, Holland. 400sh, Matthaeus, Germany.

No. 1065, 500sh, Berti, Italy; Caligiuri, US. No. 1066, 500sh, Walker, England; Gilhaus, Holland.

1993, Nov. 8   Litho.   Perf. 13½

1057-1064	A164	Set of 8	9.50	9.50

Souvenir Sheets

1065-1066	A164	Set of 2	9.50	9.50

1994 World Cup Soccer Championships, US.

1994, Feb. 10

Hummel Figurines: 20sh, Boy with accordian. 40sh, Girl with guitar, boy with banjo. 50sh, Boy with tuba. 70sh, Boy with harmonica, bird. 100sh, Bird in tree, boy seated on fence. 150sh, Boy playing horn. 200sh, Boy with horn, bird. 300sh, Girl playing banjo. 350sh, Boy with cello on back. 400sh, Girls with banjo and sheet music.

No. 1077, 500sh, Four carolers. No. 1078, 500sh, Two figures in tower blowing horns at angel below.

1067-1076	A165	Set of 10	12.50	12.50

Souvenir Sheets

1077-1078	A165	Set of 2	11.00	11.00

Black Athletes — A166

No. 1079: a, 20sh, Arthur Ashe. b, 40sh, Michael Jordan. c, 50sh, Daley Thompson. d, 70sh, Jackie Robinson. e, 100sh, Kareem Abdul-Jabbar. f, 150sh, Florence Joyner. g, 200sh, Jesse Owens. h, 400sh, Jack Johnson. 500sh, Muhammad Ali, horiz.

1993, July 15

1079	A166	Sheet of 8, #a.-h.	9.00	9.00

Souvenir Sheet

1080	A166	500sh multicolored	5.50	5.50

First US Gas Balloon Flight, Bicent. A167

Designs: 200sh, Balloons filling with hot air. 400sh, Jean-Pierre Blanchard (1753-1809), balloon. 500sh, Hot air balloons in flight, vert.

1994, Apr. 25   Litho.   Perf. 14

1081	A167	200sh multicolored	2.25	2.25
1082	A167	400sh multicolored	4.25	4.25

Souvenir Sheet

1083	A167	500sh multicolored	6.50	6.50

Royal Air Force, 75th Anniv. A168

Designs: 200sh, Sopwith Camel. 400sh, BAE Harrier. 500sh, Supermarine Spitfire.

1993, Dec.

1084	A168	200sh multicolored	2.50	2.50
1085	A168	400sh multicolored	4.50	4.50

Souvenir Sheet

1086	A168	500sh multicolored	7.00	7.00

Automotive Anniversaries — A171

Designs: No. 1099, 200sh, 1893 Benz, 1993 500 SEL. No. 1100, 200sh, Henry Ford, 1922 Model T. No. 1101, 400sh, Karl Benz, emblem. No. 1102, 400sh, 1893 Ford, Mustang Cobra.

No. 1103, 500sh, Emblem, 1937 540 K. No. 1104, 500sh, Henry Ford, first Ford factory.

1994, Apr. 25   Litho.   Perf. 14
1099-1102 A171 Set of 4   11.00 11.00
Souvenir Sheets
1103-1104 A171 Set of 2   10.00 10.00

First Benz 4-wheel motor car, cent. (#1099, 1101, 1103). First Ford motor, cent. (#1100, 1102, 1104).

Birds
A172

No. 1105, vert.: a, 20sh, African hawk eagle. b, 30sh, Shoe-bill stork. c, 50sh, Harrier eagle. d, 70sh, Casqued hornbill. e, 100sh, Crowned crane. f, 150sh, Greater flamingo.

No. 1106: a, 200sh, Pelican. b, 250sh, Jacana, black crake. c, 300sh, Ostrich. d, 350sh, Helmeted guinea fowl. e, 400sh, Malachite kingfisher. f, 500sh, Saddle-billed stork.

1994, May 11
1105 A172 Sheet of 6, #a.-f.   10.50 10.50
1106 A172 Sheet of 6, #a.-f.   12.50 12.50

Hong Kong '94
A173

Red-cap white pearl-scale goldfish and: No. 1107, Scarus ghobban. No. 1108, Regal angelfish.

1994, Feb. 18
1107 A173 350sh multicolored   2.25 2.25
1108 A173 350sh multicolored   2.25 2.25
  a.   Pair, #1107-1108   4.50 4.50

Nos. 1107-1108 issued in sheets of 5 pairs. No. 1108a is a continuous design.

Mickey Mouse, 65th Anniv. — A176

Disney characters on tour: 10sh, Boarding plane. 20sh, Dancing, Tonga. 30sh, Lawn bowling, Australia. 40sh, Building igloo, Arctic region. 50sh, Royal Palace Guard, London. 60sh, Esna bazaar, Egypt. 70sh, Zsambox cowboys, Hungary, vert. 100sh, Grand Canal, Venice, vert. 150sh, Dancing, Bali, Indonesia, vert. 200sh, Monks studying text, Bangkok, Thailand, vert. 300sh, Water skiing, Taj Mahal, India, vert. 400sh, Himalayas, Nepal.

No. 1125, Kilimanjaro Uhuru Peak, Kibo, Tanzania, vert. No. 1126, Kigoma railway station, Dar es Salaam, Tanzania, vert. No. 1127, Memorial to Dr. Livingstone, shores of Lake Tanganyika, Tanzania.

1994, Apr. 6   Perf. 14x13½, 13½x14
1113 A176 10sh multicolored   .30 .30
1114 A176 20sh multicolored   .30 .30
1115 A176 30sh multicolored   .30 .30
1116 A176 40sh multicolored   .45 .45
1117 A177 40sh multicolored   .50 .50
1118 A176 60sh multicolored   .55 .55
1119 A176 70sh multicolored   .75 .75
1120 A176 100sh multicolored   1.05 1.05
1121 A176 150sh multicolored   1.50 1.50
1122 A176 200sh multicolored   2.10 2.10
1123 A176 300sh multicolored   3.00 3.00
1124 A176 400sh multicolored   4.00 4.00
  Nos. 1113-1124 (12)   14.80 14.80
Souvenir Sheets
1125 A176 500sh multicolored   4.75 4.75
1126 A176 500sh multicolored   4.75 4.75
1127 A176 500sh multicolored   4.75 4.75

Reptiles
A177

Designs: 20sh, Geochelone elephantopus, vert. 50sh, Iguana iguana, vert. 70sh, Varanus salvator. 100sh, Naja oxiana, vert. 150sh, Chamaeleo jacksonii. 200sh, Eunectes murinus. 250sh, Alligator mississippensis. 500sh, Vipera berus, vert.

Perf. 12x12½, 12½x12
1993, June 28   Litho.
1128-1134 A177 Set of 7   6.75 6.75
Souvenir Sheet
1135 A177 500sh multicolored   5.25 5.25

Nos. 1128-1135 were were not available until July 1994.

Sharks
A178

Designs: 20sh, Isurus oxyrinchus. 30sh, Etmopterus hillianus. 50sh, Galeocerdo cuvier. 70sh, Squatina africana. 100sh, Pristiophorus cirratus. 150sh, Triaenodon obesus. 200sh, Sphyrna lewini.
350sh, Hexanchus griseus, vert.

1993, July 27   Perf. 12½x12
1136-1142 A178 Set of 7   5.25 5.25
Souvenir Sheet
Perf. 12x12½
1143 A178 350sh multicolored   3.25 3.25

Nos. 1136-1143 were not available until July 1994.

Dogs — A179

Designs: 20sh, Gordon setter. 30sh, Zwergschnauzer. 50sh, Labrador retriever. 70sh, Wire fox terrier. 100sh, English springer spaniel. 150sh, Newfoundlander. 200sh, Moscow toy terrier.
350sh, Doberman pinscher.

1993, Sept. 27   Perf. 12x12½
1144-1150 A179 Set of 7   5.75 5.75
Souvenir Sheet
1151 A179 350sh multicolored   2.75 2.75

Nos. 1144-1151 were not available until July 1994.

Horses
A180

Designs: 20sh, Norman-Arab. 40sh, Nonius. 50sh, Boulonnais. 70sh, Arab. 100sh, Anglo-Arab. 150sh, Tarpan. 200sh, Thoroughbred.
No. 1159, Anglo-Norman.

1993, Nov. 30   Perf. 12½x12
1152-1158 A180 Set of 7   6.00 6.00
Souvenir Sheet
Perf. 12x12½
1159 A180 400sh multicolored   3.00 3.00

Nos. 1152-1159 were not available until July 1994.

Military Aircraft
A181

Designs: 20sh, ALFA jet. 30sh, Northrup F-5E. 50sh, Mirage 3NG. 70sh, MB-339C. 100sh, MIG-31. 150sh, C-101 AVIOJET. 200sh, F-16B.
500sh, EAP fighter, vert.

1994, Apr. 25   Litho.   Perf. 12½x12
1160-1166 A181 Set of 7   6.00 6.00
Souvenir Sheet
Perf. 12x12½
1167 A181 500sh multicolored   3.50 3.50

A182

Customs Co-operation Council Meeting, Arusha — A183

Designs: 20sh, Trans-border trade. 50sh, Customs-international trade by ship. 100sh, Customs-air transportation. 150sh, Postal service-customs co-operation, Customs and UPU emblems.
500sh, Emblem.

1994, Aug. 23   Litho.   Perf. 13½
1168-1171 A182 Set of 4   5.00 5.00
Souvenir Sheet
Perf. 12½
1172 A183 500sh multicolored   6.00 6.00

1994 World Cup Soccer Championships, US — A184

No. 1173: a, Giuseppe Signori. b, Ruud Gullit. c, Roberto Mancini. d, Marco Van Basten. e, Dennis Bergkamp. f, Oscar Ruggeri. g, Frank Rijkaard. h, Peter Schmeichel.
1000sh, World Cup trophy.

1994, Sept. 26   Perf. 14
1173 A184 300sh Sheet of 8,
              #a.-h.   10.00 10.00
Souvenir Sheet
1174 A184 1000sh multi   5.50 5.50

1994 World Cup Soccer Championships, US — A184a

Letter in soccer ball: 40sh, B. 50sh, C. 70sh, D. 100sh, E. 170sh, A. 200sh, none. 250sh, F. 500sh, Two players and goalie.

1994, Sept. 30   Litho.   Perf. 12½x12
1174A-1174G A184a Set of 7   10.00 10.00
  i. Souv. sheet of 6, #1174A-
         1174E, 1174G + 3 labels 8.00 8.00
Souvenir Sheet
1174H A184a 500sh multi   5.50 5.50

Dogs — A185

No. 1175, 120sh: a, Alsatian (German Shepherd). b, Japanese chin. c, Shetland sheepdog. d, Italian spinone. e, Great dane. f, English setter. g, Pembroke (welsh corgi). h, St. Bernard. i, Irish wolfhound.

No. 1176, 120sh: a, Afghan hound. b, Basenji (Congo dog). c, Siberian husky. d, Irish setter. e, Norwegian elkhound. f, Bracco Italiano (Italian hound). g, Australian cattle dog. h, German short haired pointer. i, Rhodesian ridgeback.

No. 1177, 120sh: a, Alaskan malamute. b, Scottish cairn terrier. c, American foxhound. d, British bulldog. e, Boston terrier. f, Borzoi (Russian wolfhound). g, Shar pei (Chinese fighting dog). h, Saluki (Persian greyhound). i, Bernese mountain dog.

No. 1178, 120sh: a, Doberman pinscher. b, Chihuahua. c, Bloodhound. d, Keeshond (Dutch barge dog). e, Tibetan spaniel. f, Japanese akita. g, Tervueren (Belgian shepherd dog). h, Chow chow (Chinese Spitz). i, Pharaoh hound.

No. 1179, 1000sh, Like #1175e. No. 1180, 1000sh, Like #1176b.

1994, Sept. 30
Sheets of 9, #a-i
1175-1178 A185 Set of 4   22.00 22.00
Souvenir Sheets
1179-1180 A185 Set of 2   13.50 13.50

Miniature Sheets of 8

Orchids — A186

No. 1181, 200sh: a, Rangaeris amaniensis. b, Eulophia macowanii. c, Cyrtorchis arcuata. d, Centrostigma occultans. e, Cirrhopetalum umbellatum. f, Ansellia gigantea. g, Angraecum ramosum. h, Disa englerana.

No. 1182, 200sh: a, Nervilia stolziana. b, Satyrium orbiculare. c, Schzochilus sulphureus. d, Disa stolzii. e, Platycoryne mediocris. f, Satyrium breve. g, Eulophia nuttii. h, Disa ornithantha.

No. 1183, 1000sh, Eulophia thomsonii, horiz. No. 1184, 1000sh, Phaius P. tankervilliae, horiz.

1994, Oct. 7
Sheets of 8, #a-h
1181-1182 A186 Set of 2   35.00 35.00
Souvenir Sheets
1183-1184 A186 Set of 2   20.00 20.00

Natl. Parks
A187

Designs: 20sh, Ngorongoro Crater. 50sh, Ngurdoto Crater. 70sh, Kilimanjaro Natl. Park. 100sh, Gombe Natl. Park. 150sh, Selous Natl. Park. 200sh, Mikumi Natl. Park. 250sh, Serengeti Natl. Park.
500sh, Lake Manyara Natl. Park, vert.

1993, Oct. 29   Litho.   Perf. 12
1185-1191 A187 Set of 7   4.50 4.50
Souvenir Sheet
1192 A187 500sh multicolored   2.75 2.75
Nos. 1185-1192 are dated 1993 but were not available until Oct. 1994.

Historical African Costumes A188

Designs: 20sh, Berts style. 40sh, Galla style. 50sh, Guinean warrior. 70sh, Goloff style. 100sh, Peul style. 150sh, Abyssinian warrior. 200sh, Pahuin style.
350sh, Zulu style.

1993, Dec. 30
1193-1199 A188 Set of 7   3.25 3.25
Souvenir Sheet
1200 A189 350sh multicolored   2.00 2.00
Nos. 1193-1200 are dated 1993 but were not available until Oct. 1994.

1994 Winter Olympics, Lillehammer A189

Designs: 40sh, Downhill skiing. 50sh, Ice hockey. 70sh, Speed skating. 100sh, Bobsled. 120sh, Figure skating. 170sh, Free style skiing. 250sh, Biathlon.
500sh, Slalom skiing.

1994, Feb. 12
1201-1207 A189 Set of 7   4.50 4.50
Souvenir Sheet
1208 A189 500sh multicolored   2.50 2.50

Sailing Ships — A190

Designs: 40sh, Jahazi. 50sh, Caravel. 70sh, Carrack. 100sh, Galeas. 170sh, Line of battle ship. 200sh, Frigate. 250sh, Brig.
No. 1210, Bark.

1994, Apr. 20
1209-1215 A190 Set of 7   4.00 4.00
Souvenir Sheet
1216 A190 500sh multicolored   2.50 2.50

Prehistoric Animals — A191

Designs: 40sh, Diatruma. 50sh, Tyranosaurus. 100sh, Uintaterius. 120sh, Stiracosaurus. 170sh, Diplodocus. 250sh, Archaeopteryx. 300sh, Sordes.
500sh, Dimetrodon, vert.

1994, June 30
1217-1223 A191 Set of 7   8.00 8.00
Souvenir Sheet
1224 A191 500sh multicolored   3.50 3.50

Intl. Year of the Family — A192

Designs: 40sh, Family. 120sh, Father playing ball with children. 170sh, People at clinic, horiz. 250sh, Woman harvesting in field.
300sh, Emblem.

Perf. 12x12½, 12½x12
1994, Aug. 30   Litho.
1225-1228 A192 Set of 4   4.00 4.00
Souvenir Sheet
1229 A192 300sh multicolored   4.00 4.00

Zanzibar Revolution, 30th Anniv. — A193

Designs: 40sh, Pres. Salmin Amour. 70sh, Abeid Amani Karume, first president. 120sh, Processing cloves, horiz. 250sh, Zanzibar door.
500sh, Hands clasped over map.

1994, Aug. 1
1230-1233 A193 Set of 4   4.00 4.00
Souvenir Sheet
1234 A193 500sh multicolored   3.50 3.50

Arachnids A194

Designs: 40sh, Trombidium. 50sh, Eurypelma. 100sh, Salticus. 120sh, Micrommata rosea, vert. 170sh, Araneus, vert. 250sh, Micrathena, vert. 300sh, Araneus diadematus, vert.
500sh, Hadogenes, vert.

Perf. 12½x12, 12x12½
1994, Aug. 31
1235-1241 A194 Set of 7   5.50 5.50
Souvenir Sheet
1242 A194 500sh multicolored   2.50 2.50

Butterflies and Flowers A195

No. 1243, 120sh: a, Lunaria biennis, papilio glaucus. b, Phlox paniculata, danaus plexippus. c, Rudbeckia gloriosa, papilio troilus. d, Tithonia rotundifolia, hypolimnas antevorta. e, Osteospermum, cirrochroa imperatrix. f, Ursinia anethoides, vanessa atalanta. g, Wahlenbergia gloriosa, limenitis archippus. h, Mentzelia lindleyi, hypolimnas pandarus. i, Paeonia suffruticosa, anthocharis belia.
No. 1244, 120sh: a, Coreopsis laneolata, limenitis sydyi. b, Lantana camara, agraulis vanillae. c, Asclepias tuberosa, danaus chrysippus. d, Verbena canadensis, eurytides marcellus. e, Lonicera japonica, artopoetes pryeri. f, Pentas bussei, heliconius charitonius. g, Echinacea purpurea, limenitis

weidemeyerii. h, Myosotis alpestris, phoebis sennae. i, Aster amellus, timelaea albescens.
No. 1245, 1000sh, Buddleia davidii, papilio polyxenes. No. 1246, 1000sh, Helianthus annuus, vanessa cardui.

1994, Nov. 19   Perf. 14
Sheets of 9, #a-i
1243-1244 A195 Set of 2   18.00 18.00
Souvenir Sheets
1245-1246 A195 Set of 2   13.50 13.50

First Manned Moon Landing, 25th Anniv. A196

No. 1247, 150sh: a, Map of landing site. b, Location of Sea of Tranquility shown on Moon. c, Craters. d, Launch. e, Second stage separation. f, Separation of lunar modules. g, Command module, "Columbia," landing module, "Eagle." h, "Eagle" descending. i, Inside module.
No. 1248, 150sh: a, Michael Collins, Neil Armstrong, Edwin "Buzz" Aldrin. b, "Eagle" on lunar surface. c, Stepping foot on moon. d, Erecting solar wind devices. e, Gathering soil samples. f, Reflection in helmet. g, Astronaut, US flag. h, Carrying equipment. i, "Eagle" ascending from lunar surface.
No. 1249, 150sh: a, "Columbia" above lunar surface, Earth on horizon. b, "Eagle" above lunar surface. c, Release of S-4B rocket. d, Heading toward Earth. e, Re-entering atmosphere. f, Splashdown. g, Pickup at sea. h, Helicopter lifting men on board. i, Astronauts in quarantine.

1994, Nov. 30
Sheets of 9, #a-i
1247-1249 A196 Set of 3   30.00 30.00

Mickey Mouse, Safari Club — A199

Designs: No. 1253, 70sh, Donald, Mickey, lion cubs. No. 1254, 70sh, Goofy leaning on Donald. No, 1255, 100sh, Donald wearing tree disguise. No. 1256, 100sh, Donald under elephant. No. 1257, 120sh, Donald, hippopotamus. No. 1258, 120sh, Mickey writing in diary. No. 1259, 150sh, Goofy carrying gear, Donald, Mickey. No. 1260, 150sh, Mickey, elephant, Donald, Goofy in rain. No. 1261, 200sh, Donald, Goofy, Mickey reading book, lion. No. 1262, 200sh, Goofy, zebras. No. 1263, 250sh, Mickey, giraffe. No. 1264, 250sh, Donald filming picture.
No. 1265, 1000sh, Goofy hanging from tree, vert. No. 1266, 1000sh, Goofy holding camera, Donald, vert. No. 1267, 1000sh, Mickey holding camera, vert.

1994, Dec. 26   Perf. 14x13½
1253-1264 A199 Set of 12   13.00 13.00
Souvenir Sheets
Perf. 13½x14
1265-1267 A199 Set of 3   16.00 16.00

A200

A197

Dinosaurs — A198

No. 1250: a, Brontosaurus (e). b, Albertosaurus. c, Parasaurolophus. d, Pteranodon. e, Stegosaurus. f, Tyrannosaurus. g, Triceratops. h, Ornitholestes. i, Camarasaurus. j, Ankylosaurus. k, Trachodon. l, Allosaurus. m, Corythosaurus. n, Struthiomimus. o, Camptosaurus. p, Heterodontosaurus.
No. 1251: a, Deinonychus. b, Styracosaurus. c, Anatosaurus. d, Plateosaurus. e, Iguanodon. f, Oviraptor. g, Dimorphodon. h, Ornithomimus. i, Lambeosaurus. j, Megalosaurus. k, Cetiosaurus. l, Hypsilophodon. m, Rhamphorhynchus. n, Scelidosaurus. o, Antrodemus. p, Dimetrodon.
1000sh, Brachiosaurus, vert.

1994, Dec. 26
1250 A197 120sh Sheet of
            16, #a.-p.   15.00 15.00
1251 A198 120sh Sheet of
            16, #a.-p.   15.00 15.00
Souvenir Sheet
1252 A197 1000sh multi   8.25 8.25
No. 1250 is a continuous design.

Olympic Gold Medalists — A201

Designs: 350sh, Kristin Otto, Germany, 50m free-style swimming, 1988. 500sh, Carl Lewis, US, track & field, 1984, 1988.
1000sh, Oksana Baiul, Ukraine, women's figure skating, 1994.

1994, Dec. 12   Litho.   Perf. 14
1268 A200 350sh multicolored   1.75 1.75
1269 A200 500sh multicolored   2.50 2.50
Souvenir Sheet
1270 A201 1000sh multicolored   5.00 5.00
Intl. Olympic Committee, cent. (#1270).

D-Day, 50th Anniv. A202

350sh, Combined forces attack Atlantic wall. 600sh, Waterproofed tanks support Marines at Omaha Beach.

No. 1273, 200sh: a, Gen. Eisenhower, US forces, Omaha Beach. b, P-51 Mustang, D-Day armada. c, US Coast Guard cutter, landing craft. d, US troops approaching Omaha Beach. e, US troops landing on Omaha Beach. f, US forces on Omaha Beach.

No. 1274, 200sh: a, Gen. Montgomery, White Ensign flies over Normandy beach. b, British forces with Churchill Avre tank, Gold Beach. c, USS Thompson refueled en route to Omaha Beach. d, HMS Warspite fires on German positions, Sword Beach. e, Royal Marine commandoes landing, Juno Beach. f, Sherman Crab flail tank landing on Normandy beach.

No. 1275, 200sh: a, Supermarine Spitfire over Normandy beaches. b, Bren gun carriers, Gold Beach. c, Le Regiment de la Chaudiere, Juno Beach. d, Canadian forces land on Juno Beach. e, Sherman tank on Normandy beach. f, German artillery fires on D-Day Armada.

No. 1276, 1000sh: US forces prepare to embark from England to Normandy beaches. No. 1277, 1000sh, US forces on Utah Beach. No. 1278, 1000sh, Beach obstacles.

1994, Dec. 12   Litho.   Perf. 14
1271 A202 350sh multicolored   1.75 1.75
1272 A202 600sh multicolored   3.25 3.25
Sheets of 6, #a-f
1273-1275 A202   Set of 3   20.00 20.00
Souvenir Sheets
1276-1278 A202   Set of 3   16.00 16.00

Raptors
A203

Designs: 40sh, Terathopius ecaudatus, vert. 50sh, Spizaetus ornatus, vert. 100sh, Pandion haliaetus, vert. 120sh, Vultur gryphus, vert. 170sh, Haliaetus vocifer. 250sh, Sarcoramphus papa, vert. 400sh, Falco peregrinus.
500sh, Pseudogyps africanus, vert.

Perf. 12x12½, 12½x12
1994, Sept. 30
1279-1285 A203   Set of 7   9.00 9.00
Souvenir Sheet
1286 A203 500sh multicolored   3.50 3.50

Endangered Species — A204

Designs: 40sh, Phascolasctos cinereus. 70sh, Ailurus fulgens. 100sh, Aguila. 120sh, Loxodonta africana. 250sh, Monachus tropicalis. 400sh, Eschrichtius gibbosus. 500sh, Cetacea.
500sh, Panthera tigris, vert.

1994, July 29   Perf. 12½x12
1287-1293 A204   Set of 7   8.50 8.50
Souvenir Sheet
Perf. 12x12½
1294 A204 500sh multicolored   3.75 3.75
No. 1288 shows a Giant Panda, and is incorrectly inscribed with the scientific name of the Lesser Panda.

Crabs — A205

Designs: 40sh, Astacus leptodactytus, horiz. 100sh, Eriocheir sinensis. 120sh, Caneer opillo. 170sh, Cardisoma quanhumi, horiz. 250sh, Birgus latro. 300sh, Menippe mercenaria, horiz. 400sh, Dromia vulgaris.
No. 1302, Callinectes sapidus, horiz.

Perf. 12½x12, 12x12½
1994, Nov. 30   Litho.
1295-1301 A205   Set of 7   6.75 6.75
Souvenir Sheet
1302 A205 500sh multicolored   2.00 2.00

Flowers — A206

Designs: 40sh, Dicentra spectabilis. 100sh, Thunbergia alata. 120sh, Cyrtanthus minimiflorus. 170sh, Nepenthes hybrida. 250sh, Allamanda cathartica. 300sh, Encyclia pentotis. 400sh, Protea lacticolor.
500sh, Tradescantia.

1995, Oct. 31   Perf. 12x12½
1303-1309 A206   Set of 7   6.50 6.50
Souvenir Sheet
1310 A206 500sh multicolored   2.50 2.50
Dated 1994.

Woodstock Music Festival, 25th Anniv. — A207

1995   Litho.   Imperf.
Size: 124x84mm
1311 A207 2000sh Jimi Hendrix   10.00 10.00
Souvenir Sheet
Self-Adhesive
1312 A207 2000sh Carlos Santana   10.00 10.00
Size: 115x122mm
Imperf
Self-Adhesive
1313 A207 2000sh John Lee Hooker   11.00 11.00
Issued: #1311, 2/27; #1312, 5/15; #1313, 8/22.

Space Probes and Satellites A208

Designs: 40sh, Hubble telescope. 100sh, Mariner. 120sh, Voyager 2. 170sh, Work Package 03. 250sh, Orbiting solar observatory (OSO). 300sh, Magellan. 400sh, Galileo.
500sh, FOBOS.

1994, Dec. 30   Litho.   Perf. 12½x12
1319-1325 A208   Set of 7   6.75 6.75
Souvenir Sheet
1326 A208 500sh multicolored   3.50 3.50

Sierra Club, Cent. A209

No. 1327, 150sh, vert: a, Black rhinoceros. b, Aye-aye. c, Aye-aye, holding claw at mouth. d, Giraffes, Masai Mara Reserve. e, Red lechwe, group. f, Red lechwe running. g,

White-handed gibbon, white coat. h, White-handed gibbon, dark coat. i, White-handed gibbon, ready to climb tree.
No. 1328, 150sh: a, Aye-aye. b, Black rhinoceros. c, Aye-aye facing each other. c, Black rhinoceros. d, Red lechwe. e, Lions fighting, Masai Mara Reserve. f, Hyena, Masai Mara Reserve. g, Nile crocodile in water. h, Nile crocodile, mouth open. i, Nile crocodile in grass.

1995, July 6   Litho.   Perf. 14
Sheets of 9, #a-i
1327-1328 A209   Set of 2   18.00 18.00

Fruit A210

Designs: 70sh, Coconuts. 100sh, Pineapple. 150sh, Pawpaw. 200sh, Tomato.
500sh, Coconuts.

1995, June 30
1329-1332 A210   Set of 4   6.00 6.00
Souvenir Sheet
1333 A210 500sh multicolored   5.25 5.25

Miniature Sheets of 9

The Beatles — A211

No. 1334, 100sh: a, George Harrison. b, d, e, f, h, Various group portraits. c, Ringo Starr. g, Paul McCartney. i, John Lennon.
No. 1335, 100sh, vert.: a-i, Various portraits of John Lennon.
No. 1336, 500sh, John Lennon, vert. No. 1337, 500sh, Paul McCartney.

1995   Perf. 12½
Sheets of 9, #a-i
1334-1335 A211   Set of 2   13.00 13.00
Souvenir Sheets
1336-1337 A211   Set of 2   13.00 13.00
No. 1336 contains one 51x76mm stamp. No. 1337 contains one 57x51mm stamp.

Trains A212

No. 1338, 200sh: a, 0-6-0 Italy. b, 0-4-4-OT Mallet, Germany. c, 4-8-0 Tender Engine, Ghana. d, Mallet Tanks, Germany. e, 0-6-2T on the Zillertalbahn, Switzerland. f, Rack Lines, Austria. g, Sweden Jodemans Railway, Norway. h, 4-6-0 Portugal. i, 60CM gauge, Mine Railway, Spain.
No. 1339, 200sh: a, 640 Class 2-6-0s, Italy. b, Norway electric. c, Gordon Highlander 4-40s. d, High Line 9600 class 2-8-0 Japan. e, 4-6-0 Henschel, Portugal. f, Federal German State Railway 220 hydraulic. g, Caledonian 4-2-2, Scotland. h, M2 Locomotive, Denmark. i, Denver & Rio Grande, Western US.
No. 1340, 1000sh, Karl Golsdorf 2-6-0 tank engine, "Germany." No. 1341, 1000sh, High speed ET 403, Germany. No. 1342, 1000sh, AKO 1920, US. No. 1343 1000sh, Porter 2-4-OS, Hawaii.

1995, July 5   Litho.   Perf. 14
Sheets of 9, #a-i
1338-1339 A212   Set of 2   25.00 25.00
Souvenir Sheets
1340-1343 A212   Set of 4   27.50 27.50
Singapore '95.

FAO, 50th Anniv: — A213

No. 1344: a, Boy eating. b, Baby, mother eating. c, Two young people eating.
1000sh, Woman picking fruit, horiz.

1995, Aug. 14
1344 A213 250sh Strip of 3, #a.-c.   4.50 4.50
Souvenir Sheet
1345 A213 1000sh multicolored   5.25 5.25
No. 1344 is a continuous design.

Rotary International, 90th Anniv. — A214

Designs: 600sh, Paul Harris, Rotary emblem. 1000sh, Natl. flag, Rotary emblem.

1995, Aug. 14
1346 A214 600sh multicolored   3.25 3.25
Souvenir Sheet
1347 A214 1000sh multicolored   5.25 5.25

Queen Mother, 95th Birthday A215

No. 1348: a, Drawing. b, With Queen Elizabeth II. c, Formal portrait. d, In black outfit. 1000sh, Blue dress with pearls.

1995, Aug. 14   Perf. 13½x14
1348 A215 250sh Block or strip of 4, #a.-d.   5.00 5.00
Souvenir Sheet
1349 A215 1000sh multicolored   5.25 5.25
No. 1348 was issued in sheets of 8 stamps. Sheets of Nos. 1348-1349 exist with black borders overprinted in sheet margins and text "In Memoriam 1900-2002."

End of World War II, 50th Anniv. A216

No. 1350 — Flags of countries shaped as "VJ:" a, Singapore. b, Fiji. c, Malaysia. d, Marshall Islands. e, Philippines. f, Solomon Islands.
No. 1351: a, Pearl Harbor. b, North Africa. c, Battle of Atlantic. d, War in Soviet Union. e, "D" Day, June 6, 1944. f, Holocaust. g, War in Pacific. h, Hiroshima, Enola Gay, mushroom cloud.
No. 1352, 1000sh, Battle of Britain. No. 1353, 1000sh, British soldier, donkey with backpack.

1995, Aug. 14   Litho.   Perf. 14
1350 A216 250sh Sheet of 6, #a.-f. + label   8.50 8.50

1351 A216 250sh Sheet of 8,
#a.-h. + la-
bel 8.50 8.50

Souvenir Sheets

1352-1353 A216 Set of 2 17.50 17.50

Reptiles
A217

No. 1354: a, African rock python. b, Bell's hinged tortoise. c, Gaboon viper. d, Royal python. e, Savannah monitor. f, Nile monitor. g, Three-horned chameleon. h, Nile crocodile. i, Rough-scaled bush viper. j, Puff adder. k, Rhinocerous viper. l, Leopard tortoise.

No. 1355, 1000sh, Bush viper. No. 1356, 1000sh, Spitting cobra.

1995, Sept. 5

1354 A217 200sh Sheet of 12,
#a.-l. 13.00 13.00

Souvenir Sheets

1355-1356 A217 Set of 2 12.00 12.00

UN, 50th Anniv. — A218

No. 1357 — Various races of people, within group: a, Woman holding baby on shoulders. b, Man holding child in arms. c, One child standing.

1000sh, UN soldier using binoculars.

1995, Aug. 14 Litho. Perf. 14

1357 A218 250sh Strip of 3,
#a.-c. 5.25 5.25

Souvenir Sheet

1358 A218 1000sh multicolored 5.25 5.25

No. 1357 is a continuous design.

Summer Olympics
Gold Medal
Winners — A219

No. 1359 — 200sh, a, Tommie Smith, US, 1968. b, Jack Lovelock, New Zealand, 1936. c, Al Oerter, US, 1956-68. d, Daley Thompson, Great Britain, 1980. e, Greg Louganis, US, 1984-88. f, Sammy Lee, US, 1948. g, Dan Gable, US, 1972. h, Helen Meany, US, 1928. i, Sugar Ray Leonard, US, 1976.

No. 1360, 200sh: a, Robert Mathias, US, 1948-52. b, Larissa Latynina, USSR, 1956. c, Martin Sheridan, US, 1904-08. d, Vera Caslavska, Czechoslovakia, 1968. e, Edwin Moses, US, 1984. f, Jesse Owens, US, 1936. g, Mary Lou Retton, US, 1984. h, Bobby Morrow, US, 1956. i, Joan Benoit, US, 1984.

No. 1361, 1000sh, Florence Griffith Joyner, Jackie Joyner-Kersee, US, 1988. No. 1362, 1000sh, Vasily Alexeyev USSR, 1972-76.

1995, Sept. 18

Sheets of 9, #a-i

1359-1360 A219 Set of 2 16.00 16.00

Souvenir Sheets

1361-1362 A219 Set of 2 10.00 10.00

Wild
Animals
A220

No. 1363: a, Snake, vulture. b, Vulture. c, Giraffe (d, g, h, k, l). d, African bateleur. e, Elephants (f). f, Kob, rhino (b, e, i, j, n). g, Rhinos. h, Baboon. i, Kob (m, n). j, Saddle billed stork, warthog (n). k, Cheetahs (g, j, n). l, African lion (h, k, o, p). m, Vulture. n, Dik-diks. o, Lion cubs. p, Lions (o).

No. 1364: a, Elands. b, Zebras. c, Lions. d, Baboons.

No. 1365, 1000sh, Rhinoceros. No. 1366, 1000sh, Leopard.

1995, Sept. 15

1363 A220 100sh Sheet of 16,
#a.-p. 8.50 8.50

1364 A220 250sh Sheet of 4,
#a.-d. 5.50 5.50

Souvenir Sheets

1365-1366 A220 Set of 2 10.00 10.00

UN, 50th
Anniv.
A221

Designs: 70sh, Corn farming, vert. 100sh, Cultivating land. 150sh, Women spinning cotton in factory. 200sh, Boy drawing at desk, vert.

500sh, UN emblem, "50."

Wmk. 387

1995, Oct. 24 Litho. Perf. 14

1367-1371 A221 Set of 4 4.75 4.75

Souvenir Sheet

1372 A221 500sh multicolored 5.25 5.25

East
African
Treaty,
2nd
Anniv.
A222

Designs: 100sh, Heads of State. 150sh, Map, flags, vert. 180sh, Map, address. 200sh, Fishing on Lake Victoria.

500sh, Heads of State.

1995, Oct. 24

1373-1376 A222 Set of 4 5.50 5.50

Souvenir Sheet

1377 A222 500sh multicolored 5.50 5.50

Hoofed
Animals — A224

Designs: 70sh, Hippopotamus amphibius, horiz. 100sh, Litocranius walleri. 150sh, Sincerus caffer, horiz. 180sh, Antilocapridae, horiz. 200sh, Alcelphus buselaphus. 260sh, Taurotragus oryx. 380sh, Strepsiceros. 500sh, Giraffa camelopardalis.

Perf. 12½x12, 12x12½

1995, May 31 Litho.

1380-1386 A224 Set of 7 7.25 7.25

Souvenir Sheet

1387 A224 500sh multicolored 6.75 6.75

Cactus
Flowers — A225

Designs: 70sh, Weingartia fidaiana. 100sh, Rebutia spegazziniana. 150sh, Caralluma

lugarii. 180sh, Cerochlamys pachyphylla. 200sh, Schlumbergera orssighiana. 260sh, Epiphyllum darrahii. 380sh, Ceropegia nilotica. 500sh, Neoporteria nigrihorrida.

1995, Aug. 31 Perf. 12x12½

1388-1394 A225 Set of 7 7.25 7.25

Souvenir Sheet

1395 A225 500sh multicolored 6.75 6.75

Bats
A226

Designs: 70sh, Cheiromeles torquatus, vert. 100sh, Hypsignatus monstrosus, vert. 150sh, Rhinolophus, ferrum-equinum, vert. 180sh, Plecotus auritus. 200sh, Syconycteris australis, vert. 260sh, Plecotus auritus. vert. 380sh, Otomops martiensseni.

500sh, Pteropus.

1995, July 31 Perf. 12x12½, 12½x12

1396-1402 A226 Set of 7 7.25 7.25

Souvenir Sheet

1403 A226 500sh multicolored 6.50 6.50

Marine
Life of
Coral
Reefs
A227

Designs: 70sh, Medusa. 100sh, Surgeonfish. 150sh, Angelfish. 180sh, Octopus. 200sh, Zebra fish. 260sh, Shark. 380sh, Ray. 500sh, Turtle.

1995, June 15 Perf. 12½x12

1404-1410 A227 Set of 7 7.25 7.25

Souvenir Sheet

1411 A227 500sh multicolored 6.75 6.75

Jerry Garcia
(d. 1995),
Musician
A228

Scenes of Grateful Dead performing on stage and: No. 1413A, Bears. No. 1413B, Skeletons.

1995 Litho. Perf. 12½

1412 A228 200sh multi 10.00 10.00

Souvenir Sheet

1413 A228 1000sh multi 9.50 9.50

Size: 140x92mm

Imperf

Self-Adhesive

1413A A228 2000sh multi 8.25 8.25

1413B A228 2000sh multi 8.25 8.25

No. 1412 was issued in sheets of 9. No. 1413 contains one 51x57mm stamp.
Issued: #1412-1413, 11/15/95; #1413A-1413B, 12/21/95.

Rock and
Roll Stars
A229

No. 1414: a, Chuck Berry. b, Bob Dylan. c, Aretha Franklin. d, The Supremes. e, Buddy Holly. f, Bruce Springsteen. g, Elton John. h, The Rolling Stones. i, Michael Jackson.

1000sh, The Beach Boys (Al Jardin, Mike Love, Brian Wilson, Carl Wilson, Dennis Wilson), horiz.

1995, Dec. 1 Perf. 13½x14

1414 A229 250sh Sheet of 9,
#a.-i. 15.00 15.00

Souvenir Sheet

Perf. 14x13½

1415 A229 1000sh multi 8.50 8.50

Motion
Pictures,
Cent.
A230

No. 1416: a, Noah's Ark, Dolores Costello. b, Ben-Hur, 1926, Ramon Novarro. c, Ben-Hur, 1926, Francis X. Bushman. d, Ben-Hur, 1959, Charlton Heston. e, Ben-Hur, 1959, Haya Harareet. f, Ben-Hur, 1959, Sam Jaffe. g, The Ten Commandments, 1923, Theodore Roberts. h, Samson and Delilah, Victor Mature. i, Samson and Delilah, Hedy Lamarr.

No. 1417, The Ten Commandments, Theodore Roberts.

1995, Dec. 1 Perf. 13½x14

1416 A230 250sh Sheet of 9,
#a.-i. 19.00 19.00

Souvenir Sheet

1417 A230 1000sh multi 8.50 8.50

World Tourism Organization, 20th
Anniv. — A231

Designs: 100sh, Olduvai Gorge, "Cradle of Mankind." 300sh, First State House, Bagamoyo. 400sh, Mount Kilimanjaro.

500sh, Rhinoceroses, Ngorongoro Crater.

1995, Dec. 18 Perf. 14

1418-1420 A231 Set of 3 6.50 6.50

Souvenir Sheet

1421 A231 500sh multicolored 6.25 6.25

Predatory
Animals
A232

Designs: 70sh, Acinonyx jubatus. 100sh, Felus serval. 150sh, Huaena buana. 200sh, Otocyon megalotis. 250sh, Lucaon pictus. 280sh, Pantera pardus. 300sh, Pantera leo. 500sh, Alligator.

1995, Sept. 30   Litho.   Perf. 12½x12
1422-1428 A232   Set of 7   10.50 10.50

Souvenir Sheet
1429 A232   500sh multicolored   5.50 5.50

Horses — A233

No. 1430: a, True black Freisian. b, Appaloosa. c, Arab. d, Paint. e, Chestnut saddlebred. f, Standard thoroughbred. g, Belgian. h, Liver chestnut quarter. i, Hackney. 1000sh, Clydesdale.

1995   Perf. 14
1430 A233   250sh Sheet of 9,
            #a.-i.   19.00 19.00

Souvenir Sheet
1431 A233   1000sh multi   10.50 10.50

No. 685 Surcharged

1995, May 30   Litho.   Perf. 14
1431A A108   70sh on 13sh #685

Paintings from the Metropolitan Museum of Art — A234

No. 1432, 200sh: a, La Orana Maria, by Gauguin. b, Young Herdsman with Cows, by Cuyp. c, Moses and the Burning Bush by, Domenichino. d, Path in the Ile Saint-Martin, Vétheuil, by Monet. e, Dances, Pink and Green, by Degas. f, Terrace at Sainte-Adresse, by Monet. g, The Rehearsal Onstage, by Degas. h, Study for "A Sunday on La Grande Jatte," by Seurat.
No. 1433, 200sh: a, Madame Marsollier and Daughter, by Nattier. b, Christ and the Woman of Samaria, by Rembrandt. c, Rubens and His Wife and Son, by Rubens. d, Portrait of a Young Woman, by Vermeer. e, Portrait of a Man, by Van Dyck. f, Young Woman with a Water Jug, by Vermeer. g, Self Portrait, by Rembrandt. h, Young Man and Woman in an Inn, by Hals.
No. 1434, 1000sh: a, On the Beach at Trouville, by Boudin. No. 1435, 1000sh, A Dance in the Country, by G.D. Tiepolo.

1996, Mar. 7   Perf. 13½x14
Sheets of 8, #a-h, + Label
1432-1433 A234   Set of 2   32.50 32.50

Souvenir Sheets
Perf. 14
1434-1435 A234   Set of 2   20.00 20.00
Nos. 1434-1435 each contain one 81x53mm stamp.

Miniature Sheet

Cats and Dogs — A235

No. 1436 — Cats: a, Siberian. b, Classic silver tabby Persian. c, Brown Burmese. d, Norwegian forest. e, Tabby. f, Blue & white maine coon. g, Brown California spangled cat. h, Black & white bicolor Persian. i, Shaded silver American shorthair.
No. 1437 — Dogs: a, Red labrador. b, St. Bernard. c, Cocker spaniel. d, Black labrador. e, Bernese mountain dog. f, Beagle. g, Miniature pincher. h, Basset hound. i, German shepherd.
No. 1438, Silver tabby British shorthair. No. 1439, Alaskan malamute.

1996, Mar. 4   Litho.   Perf. 14
1436 A235   250sh Sheet of 9,
            #a.-i.   15.00 15.00
1437 A235   250sh Sheet of 9,
            #a.-i.   15.00 15.00

Souvenir Sheets
1438 A235   1000sh multi   8.50 8.50
1439 A235   1000sh multi   8.50 8.50

Souvenir Sheets

Janis Joplin (1943-70), Rock Musician — A235a

Design: No. 1439B, Joplin seated atop a psychedelically-painted Porsche, horiz.

1996, Apr. 10   Litho.   Imperf.
Self-Adhesive
1439A A235a 2000sh shown   22.50 22.50
1439B A235a 2000sh multi   22.50 22.50

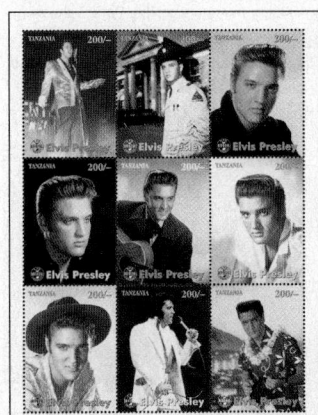

Elvis Presley (1935-77) — A235b

Various photographs with EPE (Elvis Presley Enterprises) official product emblem.

1996, Mar. 13   Litho.   Perf. 12½
1439C A235b 200sh Sheet of
             9, #d.-l.   13.00 13.00

New Year 1996 (Year of the Rat) A236

No. 1440: a, Arvicola oryzivora. b, Meriones hudsonicus. c, Mus missouriensis. d, Mus aureolus.
500sh, Fiber zibethicus.

1996, Apr. 12
1440 A236   200sh Block of 4, #a.-
            d.   4.25 4.25
 e. Souvenir sheet of 1 #1440 4.25 4.25

Souvenir Sheet
1442 A236   500sh multicolored 4.25 4.25
No. 1440 was issued in sheets of 16 stamps.

Deng Xiaoping, Chinese Communist Leader A237

Various portraits.

1996, May 6   Litho.   Perf. 13
1443 A237   250sh Sheet of 6,
            #a.-f.   13.00 13.00

Souvenir Sheet
1444 A237   500sh multicolored 5.50 5.50
CHINA '96, 9th Asian Intl. Philatelic Exhibition (#1443).

Butterflies A238

Designs: 70sh, Dirphia multicolor. 100sh, Inachis io, vert. 150sh, Automerisio. 200sh, Saturnia pyri. 250sh, Arctia villica. 260sh, Arctia caja. 300sh, Celerio euforbiae, vert. 500sh, Zygaena laeta.

Perf. 12½x12, 12x12½
1996, Jan.   Litho.
1445-1451 A238   Set of 7   12.00 12.00

Souvenir Sheet
1452 A238   500sh multicolored 6.00 6.00

China 1996 Intl. Philatelic Exhibition — A239a

1996, June 5   Litho.   Perf. 12½
1460A A239a 300sh multi   5.50 5.50

Souvenir Sheet

Shanghai Intl. Tea Culture Festival — A239b

1996   Litho.   Perf. 12½
1460B A239b 300sh multi   5.00 5.00

Queen Elizabeth II, 70th Birthday — A240

No. 1461: a, Portrait. b, As young woman in evening dress. c, Wearing tiara, jewels. 1000sh, Portrait as young woman.

1996, July 3   Litho.   Perf. 13½x14
1461 A240   300sh Strip of 3,
            #a.-c.   7.00 7.00

Souvenir Sheet
1462 A240   1000sh multicolored 8.00 8.00
No. 1461 was issued in sheets of 9 stamps.

Souvenir Sheet

Frogs A239

Designs: 100sh, Bufo bufo laur. 140sh, Pyxicephalus adspersus. 180sh, Megalixalus laevis. 200sh, Xenopus laevis. 210sh, Hemisus marmoratus. 260sh, Rana beccarii. 300sh, Hyperolius cinctiventrus. 500sh, Rana goliaph.

1996, Jan. 31   Perf. 12½x12
1453-1459 A239   Set of 7   8.50 8.50

Souvenir Sheet
1460 A239   500sh multicolored 7.00 7.00

Crocodiles, Alligators — A241

Designs: 100sh, Melanosuchus niger. 150sh, Caiman latirostris. 200sh, Alligator mississpiensis. 250sh, Gavialis gangeticus. 260sh, Crocodylus niloticus. 300sh, Crocodylus cataphractus. 380sh, Crocodylus rhombifer.
500sh, Crocodile.

1996		Perf. 12½x12	
1463-1469	A241	Set of 7	9.50 9.50

Souvenir Sheet

| 1470 | A241 | 500sh multicolored | 7.50 7.50 |

Snakes
A242

Designs: 100sh, Naja pallida. 140sh, Agkistrodon contortrix. 180sh, Bungarus fasciatus. 200sh, Micrurus frontalis, vert. 260sh, Bitis gabonica, vert. 300sh, Elaphe moellendorffi, vert. 400sh, Vipera ursini, vert.
700sh, Corallus caninus, vert.

1996		Perf. 12½x12, 12x12½	
1471-1477	A242	Set of 7	9.50 9.50

Souvenir Sheet

| 1478 | A242 | 700sh multicolored | 7.50 7.50 |

Famous People, Events — A243

No. 1479, 250sh: a, Gandhi. b, Mao Tsetung. c, Jonas Salk. d, John F. Kennedy. e, Neil Armstrong. f, Mikhail Gorbachev. g, Nelson Mandela. h, Gen. Colin Powell.
No. 1480, 250sh: a, Orville, Wilbur Wright. b, Battle of Verdun, 1916. c, Charles Lindbergh. d, Al Jolson. e, Alexander Fleming. f, Amelia Earhart. g, Franklin Roosevelt, Joseph Stalin, Winston Churchill, Yalta Conference, 1945. h, Atomic bomb blast, 1945, Enrico Fermi.
No. 1481, 1000sh, Deng Xiaoping.

1996, July 15		Litho.	Perf. 14
		Sheets of 8, #a-h	
1479-1480	A243	Set of 2	17.00 17.00

Souvenir Sheet

| 1481 | A243 | multicolored | 8.50 8.50 |

A244

Fruits of East Africa: 140sh, Pineapple. 180sh, Orange, lime. 200sh, Pear, apple. 300sh, Bananas.

1996, Sept. 4		Litho.	Perf. 13
1482-1485	A244	Set of 4	7.50 7.50
1485a		Souv. sheet of 1 #1485	4.25 4.25

Birds — A245

No. 1486, 300sh: a, Vidua macroura. b, Tockus erythrorynchus. c, Trachyphonus erythrocephalus. d, Bubo capensis. e, Gyps ruppellii. f, Sarkidiornis melanotus. g, Dendrocygna bicolor. h, Struthio camelus.
No. 1487, 300sh: a, Gypohierax angolensis. b, Aquila chrysaetos. c, Spilornis rufipectus. d, Eutriorchis astur. e, Haliaeetus albicilla. f, Ichthyophaga ichthyaetus. g, Spilornis holospilus. h, Dryotriorchis spectabilis.
No. 1488, 1000sh: African paradise flycatcher. No. 1489, 1000sh: Haliaeetus leucocephala, horiz.

1996, Sept. 16			Perf. 14
		Sheets of 8, #a-h	
1486-1487	A245	Set of 2	30.00 30.00

Souvenir Sheets

| 1488 | A245 | multicolored | 9.00 9.00 |
| 1489 | A245 | multicolored | 9.00 9.00 |

Reef Fish
A246

Designs: 100sh, Yellowtail wrasse. 150sh, Jewel grouper. 250sh, Barred thick-lipped wrasse. 500sh, Bullethead parrotfish.
No. 1494: a, Golden cardinal fish. b, Yellowhead butterfly fish. c, Common banner fish (diver). d, Zanzibar butterfly fish. e, Lemon damsel. f, Blue and gold fusilier. g, Red firegoby. h, Threadfin fairy basslet. i, Rein rock basslet.
No. 1495, 1000sh, African pygmy angelfish. No. 1496, 1000sh, Blue green chromis.

1996, Sept. 23			
1490-1493	A246	Set of 4	8.50 8.50
1494	A246	200sh Sheet of 9, #a.-i.	13.00 13.00

Souvenir Sheets

| 1495-1496 | A246 | Set of 2 | 8.50 8.50 |

Ferrari Cars A247

No. 1497: a, 1964 250LM. b, 1992 456 GT. c, 1995 F50. d, 1995 F512 M "Testarossa." e, 1984 BB 512. f, 1955 410 S coupe.
1000sh, 1964 250 GTO.

1996, Sept. 27		Litho.	Perf. 14
1497	A247	250sh Sheet of 6, #a.-f.	12.50 12.50

Souvenir Sheet

| 1498 | A247 | 1000sh multi | 8.50 8.50 |

No. 1498 contains one 85x28mm stamp.

Radio, Cent.
A248

Designs: 70sh, Franklin D. Roosevelt, 1st fireside chat, 1933. 100sh, Harry S. Truman

announces US use of atomic bomb, 1945. 150sh, Orson Welles, "Alien Invasion" broadcast, 1938. 200sh, Fiorello La Guardia reads newspaper comics via radio.
1000sh, Robin Williams as Adrian Cronauer, "Good Morning Viet Nam."

1996, July 15		Litho.	Perf. 13½x14
1499-1502	A248	Set of 4	4.25 4.25

Souvenir Sheet

| 1503 | A248 | 1000sh multicolored | 8.50 8.50 |

Mercedes-Benz Automobiles — A249

No. 1504: a, 1952 300SL Coupè 1. b, 1932 680S. c, 1934 500K. d, 1934 Type 150. e, 1934 Type 150 Sport Roadster "Heck." f, 1937 W125.
1000sh, 1936 540K Roadster Class A.

1996, Sept. 27			Perf. 14
1504	A249	250sh Sheet of 6, #a.-f.	12.00 12.00

Souvenir Sheet

| 1505 | A249 | 1000sh multi | 8.50 8.50 |

UNICEF, 50th Anniv. — A250

Designs: 200sh, Child holding bowl. 250sh, Mother breastfeeding infant. 500sh, Tetsuko Kuroyanaga holding child.
1000sh, Girl.

1996, Oct. 4			
1506-1508	A250	Set of 3	7.50 7.50

Souvenir Sheet

| 1509 | A250 | 1000sh multicolored | 7.75 7.75 |

UNESCO, 50th Anniv. — A251

Designs: 200sh, Ngorongoro Conservation Area, Tanzania. 250sh, Los Katios Natl. Park, Colombia. 600sh, Kilwa Kisiwani Makutani Complex, Tanzania.
1000sh, Kilimanjaro Natl. Park, Tanzania.

1996, Oct. 4			
1510-1512	A251	Set of 3	11.00 11.00

Souvenir Sheet

| 1513 | A251 | 1000sh multi | 11.00 11.00 |

Flowers — A252

No. 1514, 300sh: a, Lily of the valley. b, Spanish iris. c, Spiderwort. d, Morning glory. e, Gazania. f, Pansy. g, Begonia. h, Madonna lily.
No. 1515, 300sh: a, Snowdrop. b, Treesia. c, Cosmos. d, Daffodil. e, Blue himalayan

poppy. f, Blue daisy. g, Zinnia flore-pleno. h, Oriental poppy.
No. 1516, 1000sh, Fuchsia. No. 1517, 1000sh, Hanson's lily.

1996, Oct. 25
Sheets of 8, #1-h + Label

1514-1515	A252	Set of 2	35.00 35.00

Souvenir Sheets

| 1516-1517 | A252 | Set of 2 | 20.00 20.00 |

Domestic Cats A253

Designs: 100sh, Lilac point Siamese. 150sh, Somali. 200sh, British blue shorthair.
No. 1521: a, American shorthair silver tabby. b, Scottish fold. c, Persian blue. d, Ocicat.
1000sh, Ragdoll.

1996, Dec. 10		Litho.	Perf. 14
1518-1520	A253	Set of 3	3.50 3.50
1521	A253	300sh Sheet of 4, #a.-d.	8.00 8.00

Souvenir Sheet

| 1522 | A253 | 1000sh multicolored | 8.50 8.50 |

Dogs
A254

Designs: 70sh, Shar-pei. 250sh, Beagle. 600sh, Keeshond.
No. 1527: a, St. Bernard. b, Shetland sheepdog. c, Samoyed. d, Australian cattle dog.
1000sh, Collie.

1996, Dec. 10		Litho.	Perf. 14
1524-1526	A254	Set of 3	6.50 6.50
1527	A254	300sh Sheet of 4, #a.-d.	9.50 9.50

Souvenir Sheet

| 1528 | A254 | 1000sh multicolored | 8.50 8.50 |

Nos. 767-768, 1001-1002, 1026-1028 Ovptd.

a

b

c

1996, Dec. 16

1529	A120(a-b)	50sh Sheet of 16, #a.-p. (#767)	9.75 9.75
1530	A120(c)	50sh Sheet of 16, #a.-p. (#768)	9.75 9.75
1531	A154(a-b)	100sh Sheet of 12, #a.-l. (#1001)	14.50 14.50

1532 A158(c) 100sh Sheet of 6, #a.-f. (#1026) 7.25 7.25
1533 A158(c) 100sh Sheet of 6, #a.-f. (#1027) 7.25 7.25

Souvenir Sheets
1534 A154(c) 500sh on #1002 6.00 6.00
1535 A158(a) 500sh on #1028 6.00 6.00

Size and location of overprint varies. Overprints types a-b appear on alternating stamps of Nos. 1529, 1531.
Nos. 1529-1533 have additional overprints in sheet margin.

Mushrooms A255

No. 1536, 300sh: a, Amanita phalloides. b, Amanita muscaria. c, Morchella vulgaris. d, Tricholoma aurantium. e, Amanita caesarea. f, Psalliota haemorrhoidaria. g, Russula virescens. h, Boletus crocipodius.
No. 1537, 300sh: a, Coprinus comatus. b, Amanitopsis vaginata. c, Clitocybe geotropa. d, Cortinarius violaceus. e, Russula sardonia. f, Cortinarius collinitus. g, Boletus aereus. h, Lepiota procera.
No. 1538, 1000sh, Ganoderma lucidum. No. 1539, 1000sh, Collybia distorta.

1996, Dec. 17
Sheets of 8, #a-h
1536-1537 A255 Set of 2 32.50 32.50
Souvenir Sheets
1538-1539 A255 Set of 2 18.00 18.00

Souvenir Sheet

Watercolor Painting — A256

1996, May 6 Litho. Perf. 13
1540 A256 500sh multicolored 4.75 4.75

China '96. No. 1540 was not available until March 1997.

Sun Yat-Sen (1866-1925) A257

Various portraits.

1997 Perf. 14
1541 A257 300sh Sheet of 6, #a.-f. 13.00 13.00
Souvenir Sheet
1542 A257 1000sh multi 8.50 8.50

Hong Kong '97.

Horses A258

No. 1543: a, Blue Arabian horse. b, English thoroughbred. c, Tennessee walking horse. d, Anglo-Arab horse.
No. 1544: a, Trakehner. b, American saddlebred. c, Morgan. d, Frederiksborg. e, Mirror of #d. f, Mirror of #c. g, Mirror of #b. h, Mirror of #a.
No. 1545, 1000sh, Wielkopolski. No. 1546, 1000sh, Thiawari, vert.

1997, Mar. 20 Litho. Perf. 14
1543 A258 250sh Strip of 4, #a.-d. 8.50 8.50
1544 A258 250sh Sheet of 8, #a.-h. 15.00 15.00
Souvenir Sheets
1545-1546 A258 Set of 2 15.00 15.00

No. 1543 was issued in sheets of 8 stamps with second strip in reverse order.

COMESA A259

Designs140sh, Tourism. 180sh, Fishing. 200sh, Dar es Salaam Port. 300sh, TAZARA Railway.

1997 Perf. 13
1547-1550 A259 Set of 4 7.00 7.00
Souvenir Sheet
1551 A259 500sh Cotton 4.75 4.75

UN Volunteers, 25th Anniv. A260

Designs: 140sh, Health of mother and child. 200sh, Food distribution. 260sh, Clean water distribution. 300sh, Public education. 500sh, Refugee camp.

1997
1552-1555 A260 Set of 4 7.50 7.50
Souvenir Sheet
1556 A260 500sh multicolored 5.50 5.50

Birds A261

Designs: 150sh, Mockingbird. 200sh, House finch. 410sh, Bridled titmouse. 500sh, Cactus wren.
No. 1561: a, Sooty tern. b, Nunbird. c, Mottled wood owl. d, Turquoise-browed mot mot. e, Emerald toucanet. f, Dusky-headed conure.
No. 1562: a, Maguari stork. b, Spoonbills. c, Flamingo. d, Hammerkop. e, Limpkin. f, Pink-backed pelican.
No. 1563, 1000sh, Masked booby. No. 1564, 1000sh, Brown pelican.

1997, May 5 Litho. Perf. 14
1557-1560 A261 Set of 4 8.50 8.50
1561 A261 140sh Sheet of 6, #a.-f. 6.00 6.00
1562 A261 370sh Sheet of 6, #a.-f. 13.00 13.00
Souvenir Sheets
1563-1564 A261 Set of 2 16.00 16.00

Flowers
A262   A263

Designs: 100sh, Plumeria rubra acutifolia. 140sh, 150sh, Liliaceae. 180sh, Alamanda. 200sh, Lilaceae, diff. 210sh, Zinnia. 260sh, Malvaviscus penduliflorus. 300sh, Carna. 380sh, Nerium oleander carneum. 400sh, Hibiscus rosa sinensis. 500sh, Catharanthus roseus. 600sh, Cartharanthus roseus. 700sh, Bougainvillea formosa. 750sh, Acalypha.
No. 1577: a, like #1571. b, like #1569. c, like #1572. d, like #1575.

1997-2004(?) Perf. 14½x15
1565 A262 100sh multi .40 .40
1566 A262 140sh multi .60 .60
1566A A262 150sh multi
1567 A262 180sh multi .75 .75
1568 A262 200sh multi .80 .80
1569 A262 210sh multi .85 .85
1570 A262 260sh multi 1.00 1.00
1571 A262 300sh multi 1.25 1.25
1572 A262 380sh multi 1.50 1.50
1573 A262 400sh multi 1.60 1.60
1573A A262 500sh multi 1.00 1.00
1574 A262 600sh multi 2.50 2.50
1575 A262 700sh multi 3.00 3.00
1576 A262 750sh multi 3.50 3.50
Nos. 1565-1566,1567-1576 (13) 18.75 18.75

Souvenir Sheet
Perf. 14½x14
1577 A263 125sh Sheet of 4, #a.-d. 2.50 2.50

Issued: #1566A, 1997; #1573A, 2004(?); others, 5/19.
For overprint see No. O49. For surcharges see Nos. 2268, 2335, 2337.

Modern Olympic Games, Cent., 1996 Summer Olympic Games, Atlanta, — A264

1996 Litho. Perf. 11½
1578 A264 100sh Tennis .90 .90
1579 A264 150sh Baseball 1.40 1.40
1580 A264 200sh Soccer 1.60 1.60
1581 A264 300sh Boxing 2.75 2.75
Nos. 1578-1581 (4) 6.65 6.65

Chernobyl Disaster, 10th Anniv. A265

Designs: No. 1582, Chabad's Children of Chernobyl. No. 1583, UNESCO.

1997, Apr. 25 Litho. Perf. 13½x14
1582 A265 700sh multicolored 5.50 5.50
1583 A265 700sh multicolored 5.50 5.50

Flowers A266

No. 1583A: b, Prunus dulcis. c, Spassky Clock tower. d, Crataegus monogyna. e, Amica montana. f, Campanula patula. g, Papaver orientalis.
No. 1584: a, Malus niedzwetzkayana. b, Golden domes of the Cathedral of the Annunciation, Moscow. c, Polygonatum multiflorum. d, Leucanthemum vulgare, e, Hypencum perforatum. f, Pulsatilla vulgaris.
No. 1585: a, Laburnum anagyroides, St. Basil's Cathedral, vert. No. 1585A, 1000sh, Rosa canina, Church of Christ Resurrection, Moscow.

1997 Perf. 14x14½
1583A A266 200sh Sheet of 6, #b.-g. 9.50 9.50
1584 A266 300sh Sheet of 6, #a.-f. 14.50 14.50
Souvenir Sheets
1585-1585A A266 Set of 2 20.00 20.00

No. 1585 contains one 30x38mm stamp.

World AIDS Day A267

Designs: 140sh, Condom protects against AIDS, vert. 310sh, Caution, you may contract AIDS. 370sh, Control of AIDS is our responsibility. 410sh, Care and support AIDS orphans. 500sh, Like #1586.

1997 Litho. Perf. 13
1586-1589 A267 Set of 4 9.50 9.50
Souvenir Sheet
1590 A267 500sh multicolored 5.00 5.00

Paintings by Hiroshige (1797-1858) A268

No. 1591: a, Aoi Slope, Outside Toranomon Gate. b, Bikuni Bridge in Snow. c, Mount Atago, Shiba. d, Akasaka Kiribatake. e, Zojoji Pagoda & Akabane. f, Hibiya & Soto-Sakurada from Yamashita-cho.
No. 1592, 1000sh, Shiba Shinmei Shrine. No. 1593, 1000sh, Kanasugibashi Shibaura.

1997, July 21 Litho. Perf. 13½x14
1591 A268 250sh Sheet of 6, #a.-f. 10.50 10.50
Souvenir Sheets
1592-1593 A268 Set of 2 7.00 7.00

Queen Elizabeth II and Prince Philip, 50th Anniv. A269

No. 1594: a, Engagement picture of Queen. b, Royal arms. c, Queen, Prince in casual attire. d, Prince, Queen. e, Balmoral Castle. f, Prince Philip.
1500sh, Formal portrait.

1997, July 21 Litho. Perf. 14
1594 A269 370sh Sheet of 6, #a.-f. 10.50 10.50
Souvenir Sheet
1595 A269 1500sh multi 10.50 10.50

Return of Hong Kong to
China — A270

No. 1596 — Split design comparing modern
and early photographs of: a, Clock Tower,
Tsim Sha Tsu, former terminal of Kowloon-
Canton Railways. b, Legislative Council Build-
ing, previously Supreme Court.
No. 1597: a, Signing of Sino-British Joint
Declaration on Question of Hong Kong, 1984.
b, Deng Xiaoping, Chinese leaders; c, C.F.
Tung, first Chinese chief executive of Hong
Kong, 1996.

1997, July 21   **Perf. 14½**
1596 A270 1000sh Sheet of 2,
     #a.-b.   11.00 11.00
1597 A270 1000sh Sheet of 3,
     #a.-c.   16.00 16.00

No. 1597 contains 3 59x28mm stamps.

Grimm's
Fairy Tales
A271

Mother Goose — A272

No. 1598 — Rumpelstiltskin: a, Woman at
spinning wheel, Prince. b, Woman, Rumpelstiltskin at spinning wheel. c, Prince, woman
playing mandolin.
No. 1599, Girl whistling. No. 1600,
Rumpelstiltskin.

1997   **Perf. 13½x14**
1598 A271 400sh Sheet of 3,
     #a.-c.   7.25 7.25
Souvenir Sheets
Perf. 14
1599 A272 1000sh multicolored   7.25 7.25
Perf. 13½x14
1600 A271 1500sh multicolored   7.25 7.25

1998 Winter
Olympic Games,
Nagano — A273

Designs: 100sh, Torvill & Dean, ice dancing.
200sh, Katarina Witt, figure skating. 500sh,
First Olympic winter games, 1924; curling
introduced. 600sh, Pirmin Zurbriggen, downhill skiing.
No. 1605: a, Dan Jansen, 1000m speed
skating. b, Alberto Tomba, slalom & giant slalom skiing. c, Herma Plank-Szabo, figure skating. d, Donna Weinbrecht, mogul skiing.
No. 1606, 1000sh, Yukio Kasaya, ski jump.
No. 1607, 1000sh, Barbara Ann Scott, figure
skating.

1997, Oct. 6   **Litho.**   **Perf. 14**
1601-1604 A273 Set of 4   9.00 9.00
1605 A273 250sh Block or
   strip of 4,
   #a.-d.   6.50 6.50
Souvenir Sheets
1606-1607 A273 Set of 2   12.50 12.50

Sinking of
MV Bukoba
A274

Designs: 140sh, Ship sinking. 350sh,
Removing bodies. 370sh, Identification of the
dead. 410sh, Mass funeral.
500sh, MV Bukoba.

1997, May 21   **Litho.**   **Perf. 14**
1608-1611 A274 Set of 4   8.50 8.50
Souvenir Sheet
Perf. 14½
1612 A274 500sh multicolored   4.25 4.25

Tourist Attractions of East
Africa — A275

Designs: 140sh, Mount Kilimanjaro. 310sh,
Masai. 370sh, Zanzibar old stonetown. 410sh,
Buffalo, plains of Ruaha.
500sh, Mount Kilimanjaro Kibo Peak.

1997, Oct. 9   **Perf. 13½**
1613-1616 A275 Set of 4   8.50 8.50
Souvenir Sheet
1617 A275 500sh multicolored   4.25 4.25

Endangered
Species
A277

Fauna
A278

1998 World Cup Soccer
Championships, France — A276

Teams: 100sh, Italy, 1938. 150sh, Brazil,
1970. 200sh, Uruguay, 1930. 250sh, W. Germany, 1954. 500sh, Argentina, 1978. 600sh,
England, 1966.
No. 1624, 250sh, vert. — Players: a, Muller,
W. Germany. b, Kocsis, Hungary. c, Pele, Brazil. d, Schillaci, Italy. e, Fontaine, France. f,
Nejedly, Czechoslovakia. g, Rahn, W. Germany. h, Lineker, England.
No. 1625, 250sh — Stadiums: a, The Rose
Bowl, US, 1994. b, Torino Stadium, Italy, 1934.
c, Olympia Stadium, Germany, 1974. d,
Azteca Satdium, Mexico, 1970, 1986. e, Wembley, England, 1966. f, Maracana, Brazil,
1950. g, Centenary Stadium, Uruguay, 1930.
h, Bernabeu Stadium, Spain, 1982.
No. 1626, 1000sh, Pele, Brazil. No. 1627,
1000sh, Eusebio, Portugal.

1997, Oct. 20 **Perf. 14x13½, 13½x14**
1618-1623 A276 Set of 6   6.50 6.50
Sheets of 8, #a-h, + Label
1624-1625 A276 Set of 2   14.50 14.50
Souvenir Sheet
1626-1627 A276 Set of 2   8.50 8.50

No. 1628, 250sh — Animals of Asia: a,
Tiger. b, Japanese macaque. c, Slender loris.
d, Musk deer. e, Przewalski's horse. f, Red
panda.
No. 1629, 250sh — Animals of Latin
America: a, Night monkey. b, Woolly opossum. c, Jaguar. d, Red uakaris. e, Ringtailed
coati. f, Cotton-top tamarin.
No. 1630, 250sh — Animals of North
America: a, Bobcat. b, Moose. c, American
bison. d, Mountain goat. e, Walrus. f, Common
racoon.
No. 1630G — Animals of Africa: h, Cheetah.
i, Zebra. j, Gorilla. k, Brown lesser mouse
lemur. l, Rhinoceros. m. Chimpanzee.
No. 1631, 250sh — Northern wilderness
animals: a, Great horned owl. b, Bald eagle.
c, Coyotes. d, Grizzly bear. e, Caribou (d). f,
Walrus. g, Hooded seal. h, Humpback whale
(g). i, Harp seal.
No. 1632, 250sh — African safari animals a,
Barbary macaque. b, Turaco. c, Giraffe (f). d,
Mountain gorilla, African elephant (a, b, e, g,
h). e, Zebra. f, Grant's gazelle. g, Monarch
butterfly, meerkat. h, African lion. i, Rhinoceros (f).
No. 1633, 1500sh, Maned wolf. No. 1634,
1500sh, Giant panda. No. 1635, 1500sh, Gray
wolf. No. 1636, 1500sh, African elephant, diff.

1997, Oct. 30   **Perf. 14**
Sheets of 6, #a-f
1628-1630 A277   Set of
   3   55.00 55.00
1630G A277 250sh Sheet of
   6, #h.-m.   18.00 18.00
Sheets of 9, #a-i
1631-1632 A278 250sh Set of
   2   50.00 50.00
Souvenir Sheets
1633-1636 A277 1500sh Set of
   4   60.00 60.00

A279   A280

No. 1637 — Modern architecture: a, Sydney
Opera House, Australia. b, Brasilia Cathedral,
Brazil. c, Metropolitan Cathedral of Christ the
King, Liverpool, England. d, Einstein Tower,
Potsdam, Berlin, Germany. e, Solomon Gug-
genheim Museum, New York City, US. f, Pal-
ace of the Natl. Congress, Brasilia.
No. 1638 — Ancient wonders of the world,
vert.: a, Temple of Artemis at Ephesus. b,
Great Pyramid of Cheops. c, Mausoleum at
Halicarnassus. d, Statue of Zeus at Olympia.
e, Hanging Gardens of Babylon. f, Colossus of
Rhodes.
No. 1639, 1000sh, Notre Dame Du Haut
Chapel, Ronchamp, France. No. 1640,
1000sh, Lighthouse of Alexandria.

1997, Nov. 5   **Perf. 14**
1637 A279 140sh Sheet of 6,
   #a.-f.   6.80 6.80

1638 A279 370sh Sheet of 6,
   #a.-f.   17.00 17.00
Souvenir Sheets
1639-1640 A279 Set of 2   17.50 17.50
Nos. 1639-1640 contain one 42x57mm or
57x42mm stamp, respectively.

1997, Nov. 28   **Wmk. 233**
Coastal Birds: 140sh, Red hornbill. 350sh,
Sacred ibis, horiz. 370sh, Sea gulls, horiz.
410sh, Ring-necked dove, horiz.
500sh, Hornbill, ibis, gulls, doves, horiz.
1641-1644 A280 Set of 4   9.00 9.00
Souvenir Sheet
1645 A280 500sh multicolored   3.75 3.75

Aircraft
A281

Fighter Planes: 100sh, P-51D. 200sh, Lockheed P-38J Lightning. 300sh, B-29 Superfortress. 410sh, Lockheed P-80 Shooting Star P-
80 A1. 500sh, Curtiss P-36A.
No. 1651, 150sh — Spitfires: a, MK IX providing altitude cover for bomber formations. b,
MK Vc dog fighting. c, PRMK XIX, Photographic Reconnaissance Development Unit,
RAF. d, MK Vb over North Africa. e, FR XIVE
firing rockets. f, MK VIII (ZPZ), Japanese
bomber. g, Supermarine Seafire being cat-
apulted from HMS Indomitable. h, MK IX during D-Day landings. i, MK XII attacking V1 Flying Bomb.
No. 1652, 150sh — Spitfires: a, MK IXc,
excorting crippled Lancaster Bomber. b, MK
1a dog fighting. c, PR MK XI, 14th Photo
Sqdn., US 8th Air Force. d, MK Vb, North
Africa. e, MK VIII with lightning bolt on nose. f,
MK Vc with RAF, Yugoslav, American markings. g, Supermarine Seafire landing on British carrier. h, MK IXc D-Day. i, MK XII destroying V-1 Flying Bomb.
No. 1653: a, MKII in desert. b, Hurribomber
dog fighting. c, MK 24, photo reconnaissance.
d, Canadian MK 1 foreign squadron. e, Mark
IXC convoy protection. f, Spitfire with clipped
wings flanked by MK 22. g, Hurricanes MKII in
desert. h, Hurribomber.
No. 1654, 1000sh, Boeing P-26. No. 1655,
1000sh, SR-71A. No. 1656, 1000sh, MK Vb.
No. 1657, 1000sh,MK V Float plane. No.
1658, 1000sh, MK 1.

1997, Dec. 23   **Litho.**   **Perf. 14**
1646-1650 A281 Set of 5   11.00 11.00
Sheets of 9, #a-i
1651-1652 A281 Set of 2   15.00 15.00
1653 A281 250sh Sheet of 8,
   #a.-h.   25.00 25.00
Souvenir Sheets
1654-1658 A281 Set of 5   40.00 40.00
No. 1656 contains one 85x28mm stamp.
Nos. 1657-1658 each contain one 57x42mm
stamp.

Jackie
Chan,
Movie
Star
A282

Various portraits.

1997, Dec. 30
1659 A282 370sh Sheet of 6,
   #a.-f.   15.00 15.00

PAPU
(Pan
African
Postal
Union),
18th
Anniv.
A283

Designs: 150sh, Natl. flag of Tanzania, flag
of PAPU. 250sh, PAPU emblem. 400sh, Delivery by EMS motorcycles. 500sh, Giraffes.

1998, Jan. 18   **Perf. 13½**
1660-1663 A283 Set of 4   9.50 9.50

A284   A285

1998   **Litho.**   *Perf. 14*
1664 A284 410sh Mt. Kilimanjaro 3.00 3.00

1998, Jan. 23

Diana, Princess of Wales (1961-97): 150sh, In red jacket. 250sh, In lilac dress. 1000sh, In teal suit with Prince Harry (in sheet margin).

1665 A285 150sh multicolored 1.10 1.10
1666 A285 250sh multicolored 1.90 1.90

Souvenir Sheet

1667 A285 1000sh multicolored 7.00 7.00

Nos. 1665-1666 were each issued in sheets of 9.

Marine Life and Sea Birds A286

No. 1668: a, Black-browed albatross. b, Unidentified bird. c, Xantusi murrelet. d, Empress angelfish. e, Bottle nosed dolphins. f, Queen angelfish. g, Red sponge. h, Unidentified red and tan fish. i, Reef shark. j, Sea star. k, Unidentified white and black fish. l, Stingray.
No. 1669, 250sh: a, Black-saddled pufferfish. b, Harlequin tuskfish. c, Emperor angelfish. d, Foxface. e, Yellow tang. f, Catalina goby. g, Fifteen-spined stickleback. h, Banded pipefish. i, Weather loach.
No. 1670, 250sh, vert.: a, Octopus. b, Pantherfish. c, Hawksbill turtle. d, Skate. e, Jellyfish. f, White tip shark. g, Blue starfish. h, Brain coral. i, Anemone.
No. 1671, 1000sh, Clown fish. No. 1672, 1000sh, Shark. No. 1673, 1000sh, Yellow seahorse, vert.

1998, Jan. 30
1668 A286 200sh Sheet of 12,
    #a.-l.   18.00 18.00

Sheets of 9, #a-i
1669-1670 A286 Set of 2 40.00 40.00

Souvenir Sheets
1671-1673 A286 Set of 3 25.00 25.00

For overprints see #1697-1702.

Traditional Weapons — A287

Designs: 150sh, Slingshot. 250sh, Cutlass and club. 400sh, Gun. 500sh, Bow, arrows.

1998, Mar. 16   **Litho.**   *Perf. 14*
1674-1677 A287 Set of 4 9.00 9.00

New Year 1998 (Year of the Tiger) — A288

No. 1678 — Stylized tiger: a, Walking right. b, Walking left. c, Lying down. d, Seated. 1500sh, Tiger standing.

1998, Mar. 30   **Litho.**   *Perf. 13½*
1678 A288 370sh Sheet of 4,
    #a.-d.   10.00 10.00

Souvenir Sheet
1679 A288 1500sh multi 10.00 10.00

John Denver (1943-97), Rock Musician — A288a

No. 1679A: c, Wearing green sweater. d, Wearing brown sweater (shoulders in middle of stamp). e, Wearing brown sweater (shoulder near corner of stamp). f, Wearing green sweater, hand at face.
1500sh, Wearing blue shirt.

1998, Apr. 30   **Litho.**   *Perf. 14*
1679A A288a 370sh Sheet of
    4, #c-f   5.00 5.00

Souvenir Sheet
1679B A288a 1500sh multi 5.00 5.00

Most examples of Nos. 1679A-1679B were not available in the philatelic marketplace until Dec. 2002.

Antique Automobiles — A289

No. 1680, 370sh: a, 1901 Mercedes 35hp. b, 1903 Ford Model A. c, 1908 Legnano Type A. d, 1908-09 Rolls Royce 40-50hp Silver Ghost. e, 1910 Renault Petit Duc. f, 1913 Fischer Torpedo.
No. 1681, 370sh: a, 1923-24 Peugeot 18cv. b, 1926 Daimler 25-85hp. c, 1932 Bugatti Type 50T. d, 1933 Pierce-Arrow V12 "Silver Arrow." e, 1934 Tatra V8. f, 1937 Grosser Mercedes Benz.
No. 1682, 1000sh, 1900 Benz. No. 1683, 1000sh, 1893 Duryea.

1998, Aug. 4   **Litho.**   *Perf. 14*

Sheets of 6, #a-f
1680-1681 A289 Set of 2 35.00 35.00

Souvenir Sheets
1682-1683 A289 Set of 2 17.50 17.50

Nos. 1682-1683 each contain one 64x48mm stamp.

Flowers and Insects A290

No. 1684, vert: a, Euanthe sanderiana, teirataenia surinama. b, "Clown Mixed." c, Pansies, caterpiller of papilio polyxenes. d, "Prelude." e, Dendrobium primulinum, wasp beetle. f, Carrion beetle, clematis "Lasurstern." g, Sunflowers, "Autumn Beauty" & "Italian White," elder borer, painted daisy. h, Grape hyacinth.
No. 1685, 250sh: a, Platinum sun. b, Vespid wasp, oriental poppy. c, Anemone. d, Ipomoea alba, king's bee hawkmoth. e, Aussie delight, potter wasp. f, Colorado potato beetle, Japanese iris. g, Bomarea caldasii, azure damselfly. h, Hybrid macranthe, queen bumblebee. i, Love with lace iris, click beetle.
No. 1686, 250sh: a, Golden ray lily, South African longhorn beetle. b, Oncidium

maclanthum. c, Agelia petali, dendrobium. c, Cobaea scandens. d, Goldsmith beetle, paphiopedilum gilda. e, Iceland poppies, potter wasp. f, Pink beauty. g, Annual chrysanthemums. h, Little mal. m. femurrubrum.
No. 1687, 1500sh, Carolina Queen. No. 1688, 1500sh, Robert E. Lee daffodils. No. 1689, 1500sh, Orange scarlet hybrid "Tempo." No. 1690, 1500sh, Pansies.

1998, Aug. 18   **Litho.**   *Perf. 14*
1684 A290 250sh Sheet of 8,
    #a.-h.   25.00 25.00

Sheets of 9, #a-i
1685-1686 A290 Set of 2 27.50 27.50

Souvenir Sheets
1687-1690 A290 Set of 2 42.50 42.50

A291

Endangered Species — A292

No. 1691: a, Hyacinth macaw. b, Gibbon. c, Bosman's potto. d, Scarlet crowned barbets. e, Giant anteater. f, Cacomistle. g, Tiger. h, Mara. i, Mandrill. j, Crocodile. k, Wood turtle. l, Baribusa.
No. 1692: a, Giant sable antelope. b, Cheetah. c, Giraffe. d, Black bear. e, African elephant. f, Giant panda.
No. 1693: a, Tiger. b, Bald eagle (a, c). c, Mountain gorilla. d, Sea lion. e, Green sea turtle. f, Hippopotamus.
No. 1694, Emerald tanager.
No. 1695, 1500sh, Florida manatee. No. 1696, 1500sh, Orangutan.

1998, Aug. 31   **Litho.**   *Perf. 14*
1691 A291 200sh Sheet of 12,
    #a.-l.   17.00 17.00
1692 A292 370sh Sheet of 6,
    #a.-f.   15.00 15.00
1693 A292 370sh Sheet of 6,
    #a.-f.   15.00 15.00

Souvenir Sheets
1694 A291 1500sh multi 13.00 13.00
1695-1696 A292 Set of 2 26.00 26.00

Nos. 1692, 1695 each contain 51x38mm stamps. No. 1696 contains 43x28mm stamps.

Nos. 1668-1673 Ovptd.

1998, Sept. 2   **Litho.**   *Perf. 14*
1697 A286 200sh Sheet of 12,
    #a.-l.
    (#1668)   22.50 22.50
1698 A286 250sh Sheet of 9
    #a.-i.
    (#1669)   13.00 13.00
1699 A286 250sh Sheet of 9
    #a.-i.
    (#1670)   13.00 13.00

Souvenir Sheets
1700 A286 1000sh multi
    (#1671)   10.00 10.00
1701 A286 1000sh multi
    (#1672)   10.00 10.00
1702 A286 1000sh multi
    (#1673)   10.00 10.00

The stamps of Nos. 1697-1699, 1701-1702 were ovptd. with Intl. Year of the Ocean emblem and the sheet margins contain one or two emblems with words "INTERNATIONAL YEAR OF THE OCEAN." No. 1700 has overprint only on sheet margin.

Aircraft A293

No. 1703, 300sh: a, Antoinette IV, 1908. b, Deperdussin Racer, 1912. c, Demoiselle,

1909. d, Bleriot XI, 1909. e, Avro FAV Roe, 1912. f, Breguet IV, 1910.
No. 1704, 300sh: a, Deperdussin. b, Ultralight, 1979-86. c, Amphibian, 1929-30. d, Pitts Special, 1930. e, BAC-221, 1960. f, Avro Tutor, 1931.
No. 1705, 300sh: a, KI-44 Tojo. b, Hawker Fury. c, Mustang. d, Zero. e, Travel Air Mystery Ship. f, F8F Bearcat.
No. 1706, 1000sh, USAAF Curtiss P-40M. No. 1707, 1000sh, Biplane. No. 1708, 1000sh, Balloon.

1998, Aug. 4   **Litho.**   *Perf. 14*

Sheets of 6, #a-f
1703-1705 A293 Set of 3 40.00 40.00

Souvenir Sheets
1706-1708 A293 Set of 3 27.50 27.50

No. 1704a incorrectly inscribed 1900.

Eagles A294

No. 1709: a, Pallas's fish. b, Bateleur. c, Martial. d, Golden. e, Wedge-tailed. f, Java hawk.
1500sh, Wedge-tailed, diff.

1998, Aug. 31
1709 A294 370sh Sheet of 6,
    #a.-f.   15.00 15.00

Souvenir Sheet
1710 A294 1500sh multi 11.00 11.00

Fauna and Flora A295

Designs: 250sh, Takahe. 410sh, Lear's macaw. 500sh, Ring-tailed lemur. 600sh, Arabian oryx.
No. 1715, 370sh, : a, Japanese crested ibis. b, Kuai O'o. c, Bourke's hairstreak. d, Quokka. e, Tahitian lorikeet. f, Black-faced tamarin.
No. 1716, 370sh: a, Loggerhead turtle. b, Snow leopard. c, Gurney's pitta. d, Lowland gorilla. e, Echo parakeet. f, Orangutan.
No. 1717, 1500sh, Giant panda. No. 1718, 1500sh, Bengal tiger.

1998, Aug. 31   *Perf. 14x14½*
1711-1714 A295 Set of 4 14.00 14.00

Sheets of 6, #a-f
1715-1716 A295 Set of 2 24.00 24.00

Souvenir Sheets
1717-1718 A295 Set of 2 16.00 16.00

Children's Rights A296

Designs: 150sh, Equal rights for boys and girls. 250sh, Right to education. 400sh, Right not to be beaten, vert. No. 1722, 500sh, Right to be loved, vert.
No. 1723, Right to education.

1998   *Perf. 13*
1719-1722 A296 Set of 4 8.00 8.00

Souvenir Sheet
1723 A296 500sh multicolored 3.25 3.25

Nos. 608, 610 Surcharged

1998   **Method and Perf. as Before**
1723A A99 150sh on 13sh #608
1723B A99 150sh on 20sh #610   — —

Issued: No. 723A, 1/26; No. 1723B, 3/16.

World Stamp Day — A297

Designs: 150sh, UPU Emblem. 250sh, Letter facing and date stamping. 400sh, Trusted messenger. 500sh, Letter posting.
No. 1728, Trusted messenger, letter posting, UPU emblem.

1998, Oct. 9   Wmk. 387   Perf. 14
1724-1727 A297 Set of 4   8.00 8.00
Souvenir Sheet
1728 A297 500sh multicolored   3.25 3.25

A298

Marine Life, Sea Birds A299

Designs: 150sh, Equal sea star. 250sh, Mountain crab. 400sh, Wolffish. 500sh, Purple sea urchin.
No. 1733: a, Barred antshrike. b, Yellow-nosed albatross, common tern. c, Common tern, killer whale. d, Crimson-rumped toucanet. e, French angelfish. f, Grey shark (e). g, Manta ray (f, h). h, Yellow-backed damselfish. i, Green parrot wrasse. j, Silver badgerfish, pyjama wrasse. k, Skate, red-knobbed starfish (h). l, Striped snapper.
No. 1734: a, Common dolphin. b, Blue marlin. c, Arctic tern. d, Blackedge moray. e, Loggerhead turtle. f, Blacktip shark. g, Two-spotted octopus. h, Manta ray. i, Sailfin tang.
No. 1735, 1000sh, Aequipecten opercularis. No. 1736, 1000sh, Chrysaora quinquecirrha. 1500sh, Skate.

1998, Oct. 12
1729-1732 A298 Set of 4   9.00 9.00
1733 A299 200sh Sheet of 12,
            #a.-l.   18.00 18.00
1734 A298 300sh Sheet of 9,
            #a.-i.   22.00 22.00
Souvenir Sheets
1735-1736 A298 Set of 2   12.00 12.00
1737 A299 1500sh multi   9.00 9.00
Intl. Year of the Ocean (#1733-1737).

Mushrooms and Insects — A300

Designs: 140sh, Cardinal beetle, tricholoma batschii. 150sh, Tricholoma catigatum, painted lady. 200sh, Lyophylum decastes, speckled wood butterfly. 250sh, Tricholoma flavovfrens, speckled bush cricket. 370sh, Boletus chrysenteron, shieldbug. 410sh, Boletus zelleri, darter dragonfly. 500sh, Gyroporus castaneus, tortoise beetle. 600sh, Hissing cockroach, boletus satanas.
No. 1746, 250sh: a, Hygrocybe miniata, shieldbug. b, Peacock butterfly, cystolepiata adulterina. c, Collybia dryophila, bush cricket. d, Omphalotus olearius, halloween pennant butterfly. e, Macrolepiota rhacodes, helicon butterfly. f, Macrole piota puellaris, hornet. g, Carpenter bee. h, Mycena epipteryia, South African longhorn beetle. i, Amanita muscaria, skipper butterfly.
No. 1747, 250sh, vert.: a, Leaf hopper cicadia, pleurotus ostreatus. b, Amanita muscaria, froghopper beetle. c, Wasp, amanita umbrinolutea. d, Butterfly, onnia tomentosa. e, Monarch butterfly, ganoderma lucidum. f, Broad-bodied libellua, macrolepiota procera. g, Butterfly anthocharis, suillus granulatus. h, Egyptian grasshopper, cortinarius praestans. i, Flying bush cricket, marasmius rameralis.

No. 1748, 1500sh, Coprinus silvaticus, thornbug. No. 1749, 1500sh, Black swallowtail, chroogomphus rutilus.

1998, Nov. 27
1738-1745 A300 Set of 8   17.00 17.00
Sheets of 9, #a-i
1746-1747 A300 Set of 2   35.00 35.00
Souvenir Sheets
1748-1749 A300 Set of 2   22.50 22.50

Rudolph the Red-Nosed Reindeer A301

No. 1752, 200sh: a, Milo. b, Rudolph (face). c, Leonard. d, Stormella. e, Ridley. f. Boone.
No. 1753, 200sh: a, Santa. b, Rudolph. c, Doggle. d, Edgar. e, Baby Rudolph. f, Toys.
No. 1754, 1000sh, Leonard, horiz. No. 1755, 1000sh, Rudolph. No. 1756, 1000sh, Baby Rudolph with ball on nose, diff. No. 1757, 1000sh, Santa with Rudolph.

Perf. 13½x14, 14x13½
1998, Dec. 15   Litho.
Sheets of 6, #a-f
1752-1753 A301 Set of 2   12.00 12.00
Souvenir Sheets
1754-1757 A301 Set of 4   22.50 22.50

Ferrari Automobiles — A301a

No. 1757A: c, GTO. d, F40. e, 512S. 100sh, Breadvan.

1998, Dec. 16   Litho.   Perf. 14
1757A A301a 500sh Sheet of
              3, #c-e   12.00 12.00
Souvenir Sheet
Perf. 13¾x14¼
1757B A301a 1000sh multi   8.00 8.00
No. 1757A contains three 39x25mm stamps.

Diana, Princess of Wales (1961-97) A302

1998, Dec. 16   Perf. 14
1758 A302 600sh multicolored   3.50 3.50
No. 1758 was issued in sheets of 6.

Picasso — A303

Paintings: No. 1759, 400sh, Jacquelin with Crossedhand, 1954. No. 1760, 400sh, Straw Hat with Blue Foilage, 1936. 500sh, Reading the Letter, 1921.
1500sh, Woman Writing, 1934.

1998, Dec. 16   Perf. 14½
1759-1761 A303 Set of 3   7.50 7.50
Souvenir Sheet
1762 A303 1500sh multicolored   8.50 8.50

Mohandas Gandhi — A304

1998, Dec. 16   Perf. 14
1763 A304 370sh Portrait   3.25 3.25
Souvenir Sheet
1764 A304 1500sh Jawaharlal
            Nehru   11.00 11.00
No. 1763 was issued in sheets of 4.

1998 World Scout Jamboree, Chile A305

No. 1765: a, US Pres. William Howard Taft greets scouts during early years, 1908. b, Early Cub Scout pack enjoys musical camp break, 1930's. c, Dan Beard demonstrates tomahawk throw at Silver Bay, 1912.
1500sh, Ernest Thompson Seton (1860-1946), first Chief Scout.

1998, Dec. 16   Litho.   Perf. 14
1765 A305 600sh Sheet of 3,
            #a.-c.   10.50 10.50
Souvenir Sheet
1766 A305 1500sh multi   9.50 9.50

Royal Air Force, 80th Anniv. A306

No. 1767: a, Panavia Tornado F3. b, Sepecat Jaguar GR1A. c, Jaguar GR1A. d, Jaguar GR1A, diff.
No. 1768, 1000sh, Harrier, Eurofighter. No. 1769, 1000sh, Biplane, hawk.

1998, Dec. 16   Perf. 14
1767 A306 500sh Sheet of 4,
            #a.-d.   13.00 13.00
Souvenir Sheets
1768-1769 A306 Set of 2   14.00 14.00

New Year 1999 (Year of the Rabbit) A307

No. 1770 - Color of rabbit : a, Red brown. b, Spotted. c, Yellow. d, Brown.
1500sh, White.

1999, Jan. 18   Perf. 14
1770 A307 250sh Sheet of 4,
            #a.-d.   7.00 7.00
Souvenir Sheet
1771 A307 1500sh multicolored   9.50 9.50

Tourism in Zanzibar A308

Designs: 100sh, Dhow Harbor, vert. 150sh, Girl on giant tortoise, vert. 250sh, Children with giant tortoise. 300sh, Street in Stone Town, vert. 400sh, Old fort. 500sh, Red colobus monkeys.
600sh, Girl on tortoise, street in Stone Town.

1998, Nov. 10   Litho.   Perf. 14
1772-1777 A308 Set of 6   11.50 11.50
Souvenir Sheet
1778 A308 600sh multicolored   5.00 5.00

Tanzanian Posts Corp., 5th Anniv. A309

Designs: 150sh, Rural post office. 250sh, Overnight mail service. 350sh, Money fax service. 400sh, Post shop business.
500sh, Exterior view of high rise building, vert.

1999, Jan. 1
1779-1782 A309 Set of 4   7.00 7.00
Souvenir Sheet
1783 A309 500sh multicolored   3.50 3.50

Butterflies A310

200sh, Calycopis cecrops. 250sh, Heliconis melpomena, vert. 370sh, Citherias menander, vert. 410sh, Heliconis antiochus, vert.
No. 1788, 200sh: a, Acraea cerasa. b, Acraea semivitrea. c, Euchrysops scintilla. d, Papilio phorcas. e, Euphaedra eusemoides. f, Acraea masamba. g, Phyciodes emerantia. h, Hypothiris tricolor. i, Orimba jansoni.
No. 1789, 200sh: a, Papilio zagreus. b, Chlosyne narva. c, Phyciodes alsina. d, Pyronia bathseba. e, Eurema daira. f, Eurytides xanticles. g, Clossiana titania. h, Euphydryas cynthia. i, Polygonia c-album.
No. 1790, 1500sh, Ornithoptera priamus, vert. No. 1791, 1500sh, Phyciodes, vert.

1999, Feb. 18
1784-1787 A310 Set of 4   7.50 7.50
Sheets of 9, #a-i
1788-1789 A310 Set of 2   15.00 15.00
Souvenir Sheets
1790-1791 A310 Set of 2   19.00 19.00

Birds A311

No. 1792, 370sh: a, Yellow billed stork. b, Black egret. c, Crowned lapwing. d, Snowy plover. e, Crowned crane. f, Saddlebilled stork.
No. 1793, 370sh: a, Great blue heron. b, Chinese egret. c, Horned puffins. d, White faced ibis. e, Greater flamingo. f, Blue footed boobie.
No. 1794, 370sh: a, Blacksmith plover. b, Brolga crane. c, Green-backed heron. d, Straw-necked ibis. e, Little bittern. f, Marabou stork.
No. 1795, 370sh, vert.: a, Sandhill crane. b, Great egret. c, Spoonbill. d, Yellow-crowned night heron. e, Glossy ibis. f, Willet.
No. 1796, 1500sh, Purple heron. No. 1797, 1500sh, Kittliz's sandplover, vert. No. 1798, 1500sh, Black-crowned night heron. No. 1799, 1500sh, Black-headed heron.

1999, Feb. 18
Sheets of 6, #a-f
1792-1795 A311 Set of 4 40.00 40.00
Souvenir sheets
1796-1799 A311 Set of 4 35.00 35.00

A312   A313

Cats
A314

Designs: No. 1800, 200sh, Bengal, horiz. No. 1801, 250sh, Seal lynx point birman. No. 1802, 370sh, Calico British shorthair, horiz. No. 1803, 420sh, Blue & white cornish rex.

Nos. 1804, 100sh, Burmese. No. 1805, 140sh, Burmilla. No. 1806, 150sh, Turkish van. No. 1807, 200sh, Snowshoe. No. 1808, 250sh, Bombay. No. 1809, 370sh, Seychellois longhair.

No. 1810: a, Silver classic tabby. b, Auburn Turkish van. c, Seal bicolor ragdoll. d, European shorthair. e, Black & white British shorthair. f, Gold California spangled. g, Chocolate tipped Burmilla. h, Red classic tabby manx.

No. 1811, 370sh: a, Pekeface Persian. b, American curl shorthair. c, Korat. d, Himalayan Persian. e, Exotic shorthair. f, Scottish fold.

No. 1812, 370sh: a, European shorthair. b, Chartreux. c, British shorthair. d, Maine coon. e, Japanese bobtail. f, Birman.

No. 1813 - Kittens chasing butterflies: a, Black & white kitten, butterfly UL. b, Black & white kitten, butterfly UR. c, Black & yellow kitten, butterfly UR. d, Yellow kitten, butterfly UL.

No. 1814, 1500sh, Black & white Persian, horiz. No. 1815, 1500sh, Cream tabby European shorthair.

No. 1816, 1500sh, American shorthair. No. 1817, 1500sh, American wirehair. No. 1818, Kitten, butterfly, vert.

1999, Feb. 23
1800-1803 A312 Set of 4 9.00 9.00
1804-1809 A313 Set of 6 9.00 9.00
1810 A312 250sh Sheet of 8, #a.-h. 11.00 11.00
Sheets of 6, #a-f
1811-1812 A313 Set of 2 24.00 24.00
1813 A314 500sh Sheet of 4, #a.-d. 11.00 11.00
Souvenir Sheets
1814-1815 A312 Set of 2 20.00 20.00
1816-1817 A313 Set of 2 20.00 20.00
1818 A314 1500sh multi 10.00 10.00

19th Century Ships A315

No. 1819, 370sh: a, Prince Consort (1). b, USS Kearsage (2). c, HMS Victoria (3). d, USS Brooklyn (4). e, Mount Stewart (5). f, Hougomont (6).

No. 1820, 370sh: a, Charles W. Morgan (1). b, RMS Britannia (2). c, Great Britain (3). d, Flying Cloud (4). e, HMS Warrior (5). f, Lightning (6).

No. 1821, 1500sh, Cutty Sark. No. 1822, 1500sh, Great Eastern.

1999, Feb. 9   **Litho.**   **Perf. 14**
Sheets of 6, #a-f
1819-1820 A315 Set of 2 29.00 29.00
Souvenir Sheets
1821-1822 A315 Set of 2 19.00 19.00
Nos. 1821-1822 each contain one 57x43mm stamp.

Military Helicopters — A316

No. 1823: a, Germany DF 4. b, Germany. c, France. d, US, with rocket pods. e, US, with suspended lift sling. f, France, red on tail boom & stabilizers.

1999
1823 A316 370sh Sheet of 6, #a.-f. 15.00 15.00

Unidentified Flying Objects (UFOs) — A317

No. 1824, 370sh: a, US, 1968. b, Trinidad, 1958. c, Belgium, 1990. d, Finland, 1970. e, New Zealand, 1951. f, Australia, 1954.

No. 1825, 370sh: a, McMinnville, 1950. b, Albuquerque, 1963. c, Gulf Breeze, 1988. d, Madre de Dios, 1952. e, Merlin, 1964. f, Mexico City, 1991.

No. 1826, 1500sh, The Arnold Sighting, 1947. No. 1827, 1500sh, The Mantell case, 1948.

1999
Sheets of 6, #a-f
1824-1825 A317 Set of 2 17.00 17.00
Souvenir Sheets
1826-1827 A317 Set of 2 20.00 20.00

Dogs
A318

No. 1828: a, Boston terrier. b, Tyrolean hound. c, Rottweiler. d, Golden retriever. e, English bulldog. f, Spanish greyhound. g, Long-haired dachshund. h, Scottish terrier. i, Pekingese.

1500sh, English cocker spaniel.

1999
1828 A318 200sh Sheet of 9, #a.-i. 10.00 10.00
Souvenir Sheet
1829 A318 1500sh multi 9.50 9.50

Dinosaurs — A319

Designs: 200sh, Stegosaurus (inscribed Edmontonia). 250sh, Archaeopteryx. 370sh, Stegosaurus. 410sh, Lagosuchus.

No. 1834, 370sh: a, Dromiceiomimus. b, Saurolophus. c, Camarosaurus. d, Protoceratops. e, Psittacosaurus. f, Stegoceras.

No. 1835, 370sh: a, Gallimimus. b, Peteinosaurus. c, Lambeosaurus. d, Coelophysis. e, Parasaurolophus. f, Tyrannosaurus rex.

No. 1836, 1500sh, Quetzalcoatlus. No. 1837, 1500sh, Rhomaleosaurus.

1999, Apr. 30   **Litho.**   **Perf. 14**
1830-1833 A319 Set of 4 7.50 7.50
Sheets of 6, #a-f
1834-1835 A319 Set of 2 29.00 29.00
Souvenir Sheets
1836-1837 A319 Set of 2 19.00 19.00

Tourism A320

No. 1838: a, Hoofed animals. b, Mount Kilimanjaro, crater. c, Animal life. d, Sacred ibis. e, Ngorongoro crater. f, Giraffe. g, Lions. h, Dik diks. i, Vulture. j, Lion cubs. k, Elephants. l, African lion. m, Stone Town, Zanzibar. n, National Museum. o, Carved door, Zanzibar. p, Map showing Zanzibar, Pemba, Indian Ocean. q, Herding animals. r, Fishing. s, Lion cub. t, Buildings, boats along shore. u, Masai. v, Birds wading in water. w, Buffalo stampede. x, Like #1838b, closer view.

1999   **Perf. 14½x14**
Booklet Stamps
1838 A320 Souvenir Booklet 11.00
  a.-x.   150sh any single .45 .45
  y.   Booklet pane, #1838a-1838f 2.75
  z.   Booklet pane, #1838g-1838l 2.75
  aa.   Bklt. pane, #1838m-1838r 2.75
  ab.   Bklt. pane, #1838s-1838x 2.75

Space Exploration — A321

Designs: 70sh, Edward White. 100sh, Gemini 7. 150sh, Mir, Russian space station, vert. 200sh, Laika, Russian space dog. 250sh, Apollo Command & Service Modules. 370sh, Apollo Lunar Module.

1500sh, Saturn V Moon Rocket, vert.

1999
1839-1844 A321 Set of 6 8.50 8.50
Souvenir Sheet
1845 A321 1500sh multi 10.00 10.00

Airships, Balloons — A322

No. 1846: a, Graf Zeppelin, 1935 (b). b, Knabenshue Airship, 1905. c, British R-100, 1931. d, Hindenburg, 1937 (c). e, French Balloon, 1783. f, French Balloon, 1912.

1500sh, Sport ballooning.

1999
1846 A322 370sh Sheet of 6, #a.-f. 13.00 13.00
Souvenir Sheet
1847 A322 1500sh multi 8.50 8.50

Marine Life A323

Designs: 200sh, Powder blue surgeon. 250sh, Frilled anemone. 310sh, Red-finned batfish. 410sh, Red beard sponge.

No. 1852, 250sh: a, Right whale. b, Fin whale. c, Humpback whale. d, Tucuxi. e, Gray's beaked whale. f, Sperm whale. g, Bottlenose dolphin. h, Hector's dolphin. i, Hourglass dolphin.

No. 1853, 250sh: a, Horn shark. b, Nurse shark. c, Bonnethead. d, Tiger shark. e, Bull shark. f, Leopard shark. g, Blue shark. h, Zebra shark. i, Oceanic whitetip.

No. 1854, 1500sh, Pacific Electric ray, vert. No. 1855, 1500sh, Loggerhead turtle, vert.

1999, Feb. 9   **Litho.**   **Perf. 14**
1848-1851 A323 Set of 4 5.50 5.50

Sheets of 9, #a.-i.
1852-1853 A323 Set of 2 29.00 29.00
Souvenir Sheets
1854-1855 A323 Set of 2 17.00 17.00

Airplanes A324

Designs: 20sh, Oiseau Bleu, 1929. 100sh, Beechcraft Model 17, 1934. No. 1858, 140sh, US Army Air Corps Beechcraft YC-43. No. 1859, 140sh, Deperdussin, 1913. 150sh, Beechcraft E17B, 1937. 200sh, Beechcraft B17L, 1936. 250sh, Beechcraft Model-G175, 1946. 370sh, Beechcraft Staggerwing Model-C17L.

No. 1864: a, Bird of Passage, Voisin Brothers, 1909. b, BS1, Geoffrey de Havilland, 1913. c, Taube-IGO Etrich, 1910. d, Curtiss Rheims Flyer, Glenn Curtiss, 1909. e, Wright Flyer III, Wright Brothers, 1905. f, Russky Vitvas, Igor Sikorsky, 1913.

No. 1865: a, Sikorsky S-38. b, EFA Eurofighter. c, F-16. d, Hawker Hurricane. e, Artiplast. f, Islander.

No. 1866, 1500sh, Piper Cherokee. No. 1867, 1500sh, MiG.

1999, Feb. 14
1856-1863 A324 Set of 8 8.50 8.50
Sheets of 6
1864 A324 370sh Sheet of 6, #a.-f. 10.50 10.50
1865 A324 370sh Sheet of 6, #a.-f. 10.50 10.50
Souvenir Sheets
1866-1867 A324 Set of 2 19.00 19.00
Nos. 1866-1867 contain one 56x42mm stamp.
Stamp inscriptions are incorrect on Nos. 1865b, 1865c, and perhaps others.

African Wildlife A325

Designs: 100sh, Black rhinoceros. 140sh, Zebra, vert. 150sh, Hippopotamus. 200sh, Nile crocodile. 250sh, African elephant, vert. 370sh, Cape buffalo.

No. 1874, 1500sh, Royal python. No. 1875, 1500sh, Giraffe.

1999, Feb. 18
1868-1873 A325 Set of 6 8.00 8.00
Souvenir Sheets
1874-1875 A325 Set of 2 18.00 18.00

Millennium — A326

Designs: 350sh, High quality health care. 400sh, Good upbringing. 700sh, An abundance of food. 750sh, Clean water for all. 1500sh, Ostrich, "Enhancement of tourism promotion," vert.

1999, Mar. 29
1876-1879 A326 Set of 4 13.00 13.00
Souvenir Sheet
1880 A326 1500sh multi 9.50 9.50

Sharks A327

Designs: 200sh, Sand tiger. 250sh, Mako. 370sh, Great white. 410sh, Bull.
No. 1885: a, Basking. b, Whale. c, Tiger. d, Thresher. e, Caribbean reef. f, Nurse.
No. 1886, 1500sh, Scalloped hammerhead.
No. 1887, 1500sh, Blue.

1999 Litho. Perf. 14
1881-1884 A327 Set of 4 — 7.00 7.00
1885 A327 370sh Sheet of 6,
  #a.-f. — 14.00 14.00
Souvenir Sheets
1886-1887 A327 Set of 2 — 18.50 18.50

Rotary Club of Dar Es Salaam, 50th Anniv. A328

Designs: 150sh, Emblem. 250sh, Polio plus immunization, vert. 350sh, Paul P. Harris, founder of Rotary, Intl., vert. 400sh, Water supply.
500sh, Emblem, vert.

1999, June 30
1888-1891 A328 Set of 4 — 6.50 6.50
Souvenir Sheet
1892 A328 500sh multicolored — 3.25 3.25

Endangered or Extinct Species — A330

No. 1898: a, Atitlan grebe. b, Cabot's tragopan. c, Spider monkey. d, Dibatag. e, Right whale. f, Imperial parrot. g, Cheetah. h, Brown-eared pheasant. i, Leatherback turtle. j, Imperial woodpecker. k, Andean condor. l, Barbary deer. m, Gray gentle lemur. n, Cuban parrot. o, Numbat. p, Short-tailed albatross. q, Green turtle. r, White rhinoceros. s, Diademed sifaka. t, Galapagos penguin.
No. 1899 — Tigers, horiz.: a, Caspian. b, Bengal. c, Javan. d, Indochinese. e, In white phase. f, Sumatran. g, Chinese. h, Bali. i, Siberian.
No. 1900, 1500sh, Rabbit-eared bandicoot.
No. 1901, 1500sh, Grenada dove.

1999, Feb. 18
1898 A330 100sh Sheet of 20,
  #a.-t. — 10.00 10.00
1899 A330 250sh Sheet of 9,
  #a.-i. — 11.00 11.00
Souvenir Sheets
1900-1901 A330 Set of 2 — 15.00 15.00

Queen Mother (b. 1900) — A331

No. 1902: a, In Kenya, 1959. b, In 1980. c, With Prince Charles, 1950. d, İin 1990.
1500sh, In Kenya, 1959, diff.

1999, Aug. 4 Litho. Perf. 14
1902 A331 600sh Sheet of 4,
  #a.-d. + label — 10.00 10.00
Souvenir Sheet Perf. 13¾
1903 A331 1500sh black — 7.00 7.00
No. 1903 contains one 38x51mm stamp.

UPU, 125th Anniv. A332

Designs: 150sh, Mail conveyance. 300sh, Letter writing competition. 350sh, UPU committee meeting. 400sh, EMS Post net track and trace.
500sh, UPU emblem.

Wmk. 387
1999, Aug. 10 Litho. Perf. 14
1904-1907 A332 Set of 4 — 5.50 5.50
Souvenir Sheet
1908 A332 500sh multicolored — 2.50 2.50

Souvenir Sheets

Philex France 99 — A333

Trains: No. 1909, 1500sh, 4-8-2 compound express locomotive. No. 1910, 1500sh, TGV.

1999, Aug. 20 Litho. Perf. 13¾
1909-1910 A333 Set of 2 — 14.00 14.00
Inscriptions are misspelled on Nos. 1909-1910.

Birds of Japan A334

No. 1911, 250sh: a, Steller's sea eagle. b, Japanese blue flycatcher. c, Great gray shrike. d, Kingfisher. e, Hen harrier. f, Siberian meadow bunting. g, Mandarin duck. h, Red-necked grebe. i, Fairy pitta.
No. 1912, 250sh: a, Black paradise flycatcher. b, Laysan albatross. c, Collared Scops owl. d, Ryukyu robin. e, Japanese green woodpecker. f, Lidth's jay. g, White-naped crane. h, Copper pheasant. i, Okinawa rail.
No. 1913, 1500sh, Gyrfalcon. No. 1914, 1500sh, Japanese yellow bunting.

1999, Aug. 20
Sheets of 9, #a.-i.
1911-1912 A334 Set of 2 — 22.50 22.50
Souvenir Sheets
1913-1914 A334 Set of 2 — 15.00 15.00
Inscription on No. 1912b, and perhaps others, is misspelled.
APS StampShow '99 (#1911-1912).

Hokusai Paintings — A335

No. 1915: a, A Ferry Boat at Onmayagashi. b, A Drum Bridge at Kameido. c, Sea Life (fish). d, Sea Life (Octopus). e, Measuring a Pine Tree at Mishima Pass. f, Mount Fuji Seen From the Banks of Minobu River.

1500sh, Mount Fuji and Edo Castle Seen From Nihonbashi, vert.

1999, Aug. 20
1915 A335 400sh Sheet of 6,
  #a.-f. — 13.00 13.00
Souvenir Sheet
1916 A335 1500sh multi — 7.50 7.50

Masks — A336   Military Scenes — A337

Various masks: 150sh, 250sh, 300sh, 350sh.

1999, Aug. 20 Perf. 14
1917-1920 A336 Set of 4 — 5.00 5.00
Souvenir Sheet
1921 A336 1500sh multicolored — 7.00 7.00

1999, Sept. 30
150sh, British defeat Spanish Armada, 1588, horiz. No. 1923, 250sh, Battle of Waterloo. No. 1924, 250sh, Rorke's Drift, 24th Regiment, South Wales Borderers. No. 1925, 250sh, Special Air Services, Desert Storm. No. 1926, 300sh, Soldier on horseback. No. 1927, 300sh, World War I, horiz. No. 1928, 300sh, Bland's Dragoons, Battle of Dettingen. No. 1929, 350sh, Battle of Trafalgar, horiz. No. 1930, 350sh, Light Brigade. No. 1931, 350sh, Squadron 617, the "Dam Busters." No. 1932, 400sh, World War I tank, horiz. No. 1933, 400sh, Battle of Inkerman. No. 1934, 400sh, Battle of Salamanca, horiz. No. 1935, 500sh, Gen. James Wolfe, Battle of Quebec. No. 1936, 500sh, Parachute Regiment, Battle of Arnhem. No. 1937, 500sh, Battle of the Bulge.
No. 1938, 1500sh, Battle of the Nile. No. 1939, 1500sh, Battle of Albuhera.

1922-1937 A337 Set of 16 — 28.00 28.00
Souvenir Sheets
1938-1939 A337 Set of 2 — 14.00 14.00

Ships A338

No. 1940, 400sh: a, Bayan. b, Flying Cloud. c, Mayflower. d, Santa Maria. e, Morning Star. f, Ben Venue.
No. 1941, 400sh: a, Georg Stag. b, E. Starr Jones. c, Indiana. d, Brazilian coasting vessel. e, Nova Queen. f, Rainbow.
No. 1942, 1500sh, Dutch East Indiaman. No. 1943, 1500sh, Junk.

1999, Sept. 30
Sheets of 6, #a.-f.
1940-1941 A338 Set of 2 — 22.50 22.50
Souvenir Sheets
1942-1943 A338 Set of 2 — 15.00 15.00

Trains A339

No. 1944, 400sh: a, Adler 2-2-2, 1835. b, Beuth 2-2-2, 1843. c, Class 500 4-6-0, 1900. d, Northumbrian 0-2-2, 1830. e, Class 4-6-2, 1901. f, Claud Hamilton class 4-4-0.
No. 1945, 400sh: a, Firefly class 2-2-2, 1840. b, Single, 1854. c, 4-4-0, 1891. d, Medoc class 2-4-0, 1857. e, 4-4-0, 1893. f, Numar, 1846.
No. 1946, 1500sh, Planet class 2-2-0, 1830. No. 1947, 1500sh, Vauxhall 2-2-0, 1834. No. 1948, 1500sh, Class PB 4-6-0, 1906. No. 1949, 1500sh, 4-4-0, 1855.

1999, Sept. 30
Sheets of 6, #a.-f.
1944-1945 A339 Set of 2 — 22.50 22.50
Souvenir Sheets
1946-1949 A339 Set of 4 — 15.00 15.00

Airplanes A340

Designs: 200sh, Amref. No. 1951, 250sh, Westwind 2. 300sh, Morning Star. 400sh, Piper Warrior III.
No. 1954: a, Glasair Super II. b, Glastar. c, Cessna 120. d, Europa XS. e, Beechcraft Bonanza. f, Comache GTO. g, Lancir IV. h, Comanche 400.
No. 1955, 1500sh, Glastar, diff. No. 1956, 1500sh, Piper Archer III.

1999, Sept. 30 Litho. Perf. 14
1950-1953 A340 Set of 4 — 6.25 6.25
1954 A340 250sh Sheet of 8,
  #a.-h. — 9.00 9.00
Souvenir Sheets
1955-1956 A340 Set of 2 — 15.00 15.00

Automobiles — A341

No. 1957, 400sh: a, Audi TT Coupe. b, Mitsubishi SST Spyder. c, Honda Dream. d, Renault 20. e, Renault Spider. f, Hyundai Euro I.
No. 1958, 400sh: a, Pininfarina Ethos. b, Jaguar XK120. c, Pininfarina Ethos II. d, Rinspeed E-GO Rocket. e, Volkswagen W12 Roadster. f, Chrysler Pronto Cruiser.
No. 1959, 1500sh, Ferrari Mythos. No. 1960, 1500sh, Hyundai Euro I, diff.

1999, Sept. 30
Sheets of 6, #a.-f.
1957-1958 A341 Set of 2 — 22.50 22.50
Souvenir Sheets
1959-1960 A341 Set of 2 — 14.00 14.00

Flowers A342

Designs; 150sh, Lilium longiflorum. 250sh, Strelitzia reginae. 400sh, Zantedeschia anim lily. 500sh, Iris.
600sh, Like 400sh.

1999, Oct. 6 Litho. Perf. 14
1961-1964 A342 Set of 4 — 6.25 6.25
Souvenir Sheet
1965 A342 600sh multicolored — 3.00 3.00

Butterflies — A343

No. 1966: a, Basilarchia archippus. b, Eueides isabella. c, Colobura dirce. d, Papilio cresphontes. e, Agrias claudia. f, Callicore maimuna.
No. 1967, 1500sh, Anteos clorinade, horiz. No. 1968, 1500sh, Tithorea harmonia, horiz.

TANZANIA

737

1999, Nov. 15
1966 A343 400sh Sheet of 6,
#a.-f. 12.00 12.00
Souvenir Sheets
1967-1968 A343 Set of 2 16.00 16.00

Sea Birds
A344

Designs: 150sh, Rockhopper penguin, vert. No. 1970, 250sh, Jackass penguin, vert. 300sh, Adelie penguin, vert. 350sh, White tern. 400sh, Great frigatebird. 500sh, Brown pelican.
No. 1975, 250sh: a, Manx shearwater. b, Ring-billed gull. c, Herring gull. d, Red-tailed tropic bird. e, Laysan albatross. f, Black-headed gull. g, Blue-footed booby. h, Parakeet auklet. i, Red-legged cormorant.
No. 1976, 250sh: a, Razorbill. b, Southern giant petrel. c, Atlantic puffin. d, Great cormorant. e, Northern gannet. f, Masked booby. g, Tufted puffin. h, Galapagos penguin. i, Macaroni penguin.
No. 1977, 1500sh, King penguin, vert. No. 1978, 1500sh, Emperor penguin, vert.

1999, Nov. 15
1969-1974 A344 Set of 6 10.00 10.00
Sheets of 9, #a.-i.
1975-1976 A344 Set of 2 22.50 22.50
Souvenir Sheets
1977-1978 A344 Set of 2 14.00 14.00

Dogs
A345

No. 1979: a, Boxer. b, Mixed breed. c, Afghan hound. d, Chihuahua. e, Basset hound. f, Cavalier King Charles.
1500sh, Cocker spaniel.

1999, Nov. 15
1979 A345 400sh Sheet of 6,
#a.-f. 10.00 10.00
Souvenir Sheet
1980 A345 1500sh multi 8.00 8.00

Paintings by Xu Beihong (1895-1953)
A346

No. 1981: a, Chang K'uei. b, Fisherman. c, Orchid. d, Cock and Sunflower. e, Eagle. f, Sprite of the Mountain. g, Horse. h, Geese. i, Pigeon and Bamboo. j, Cat and Bamboo.
No. 1982: a, Spring Rain of Li River, horiz. b, The Himalayas, horiz.

1999 *Perf. 12½*
1981 A346 150sh Sheet of 10,
#a.-j. 7.50 7.50
Perf. 13
1982 A346 600sh Sheet of 2,
#a.-b. 6.00 6.00

China 1999 World Philatelic Exhibition.

Return of Macao to People's Republic of China — A347

No. 1983 — Nam Van: a, In 1850s. b, In 1930s. c, At present. d, View of lakes project.

1999 Litho. *Perf. 13¾*
1983 A347 300sh Sheet of 4,
#a.-d. 6.50 6.50

China 1999 World Philatelic Exhibition.

Animals of the Central American Rain Forest — A348

No. 1984: a, Red howler monkey. b, Scarlet macaw. c, Rainbow boa, tree sloth. d, Iguana. e, Fruit bat. f, Rainbow boa. g, Crocodile. h, Manatee. i, Jaguar.
1500sh, Jaguar, diff.

1999, Nov. 15 Litho. *Perf. 14*
1984 A348 350sh Sheet of 9,
#a.-i. 9.50 9.50
Souvenir Sheet
1985 A348 1500sh multi 4.50 4.50

Dinosaurs — A349

No. 1986: a, Tyrannosaurus. b, Coelurus. c, Stegosaurus. d, Corythosaurus. e, Thadeosaurus. f, Brachiosaurus.
1500sh, Ceratosaurus.

1999, Nov. 15
1986 A349 400sh Sheet of 6,
#a.-f. 6.50 6.50
Souvenir Sheet
1987 A349 1500sh multi 4.25 4.25

Nos. 1986-1987 dated 1998. Inscription on No. 1986f is misspelled.

Cats
A350

No. 1988: a, Si-Rex. b, Spotted Mist. c, Angora. d, Persian. e, Sphynx. f, Alaskan Snow.
1500sh, Ragdoll.

1999, Nov. 15
1988 A350 400sh Sheet of 6,
#a.-f. 7.00 7.00
Souvenir Sheet
1989 A350 1500sh multi 4.75 4.75

Mushrooms
A351

150sh, Tricholoma portentosum. 250sh, Tricholomopsis rutilans. 300sh, Russula foetens. 350sh, Russula aeruginea. #1994, 400sh, Cortinarius varius. 500sh, Hygrocybe coccineocrenata.
No. 1996, 400sh: a, Agaricus abruptibulbus. b, Anellaria semiovata. c, Cystoderma carcharias. d, Amanita rubescens. e, Amanita fulva. f, Tricholoma sulphureum.
No. 1997, 400sh: a, Xerocomus rubellus. b, Geastrum rufescens. c, Lactarius salmonicolor. d, Gomphus clavatus. e, Russula rhodopoda. f, Russula paludosa.
No. 1998, 1500sh, Owl. No. 1999, 1500sh, Chipmunk and Strophalia hornemanii, horiz.

1999, Nov. 15
1990-1995 A351 Set of 6 5.50 5.50
Sheets of 6, #a.-f.
1996-1997 A351 Set of 2 13.00 13.00
Souvenir Sheets
1998-1999 A351 Set of 2 7.75 7.75

Flora and Fauna
A352

Designs: No. 2000, 150sh, Lion, vert. No. 2001, 150sh, Mountain gorilla, vert. No. 2002, 250sh, Pygmy hippopotamus, vert. No. 2003, 250sh, Japanese macaque, vert. No. 2004, 300sh, Cheetah. No. 2005, 300sh, Desert hare, vert. No. 2006, 350sh, Horned puffin. No. 2007, 350sh, Salvin's Amazon parrot. No. 2008, 400sh, Blueberries. No. 2009, 400sh, Bird's foot violet. No. 2010, 500sh, Orange groundsel. No. 2011, 500sh, Iguana.
No. 2012, 400sh: a, Polar bear. b, Woodland caribou. c, Snowy owl. d, Arctic fox. e, Willow ptarmigan. f, Arctic hare.
No. 2013, 400sh: a, White-tailed deer. b, Monarch butterfly. c, Yellow trumpet pitcher plants. d, Great blue heron. e, Yellow mud turtle. f, American alligator.
No. 2014, 400sh: a, Three-toed sloth. b, Emerald toucan. c, Praying mantis. d, Mouse opossum. e, Green palm viper. f, Phyllomedusa lemur.
No. 2015, 400sh: a, Ficus stupenda. b, Slow loris. c, Sambar deer. d, Thick-billed green pigeon. e, Bush cricket. f, Monitor lizard.
No. 2016, 1500sh, Three-toed jacamar. No. 2017, 1500sh, Chuckwallas. No. 2018, 1500sh, Swallowtail butterfly. No. 2019, 1500sh, Otter, vert.

1999, Nov. 15
2000-2011 A352 Set of 12 11.00 11.00
Sheets of 6, #a.-f.
2012-2015 A352 Set of 4 14.00 14.00
Souvenir Sheets
2016-2019 A352 Set of 4 15.00 15.00

Flowers — A353

Designs: 150sh, Foxglove. 250sh, Chrysanthemum. 400sh, Amaryllis. 500sh, Hidden lilies.
No. 2024, 350sh, horiz.: a, Gerbara daisies. b, Begonias. c, Clematis. d, Violas. e, Southern magnolia. f, Dwarf balloon flowers. g, Camellias. h, Day lilies. i, Roses.
No. 2025, 350sh, horiz.: a, Daffodils. b, Columbines. c, Nasturtiums. d, Gazanias. e, Rose. f, Crocuses. g, Trumpet vine. h, Dahlia. i, Oriental poppies.

No. 2026, 1500sh, Siberian iris. No. 2027, 1500sh, Water lily, horiz.

1999, Nov. 15 Litho. *Perf. 14*
2020-2023 A353 Set of 4 3.25 3.25
Sheets of 9, #a.-i.
2024-2025 A353 Set of 2 16.00 16.00
Souvenir Sheets
2026-2027 A353 Set of 2 7.50 7.50

Military Vehicles — A354

No. 2028, 400sh: a, French Hotchkiss H35 tank. b, German Panzer IV tank. c, US M4 tank. d, German Tiger tank. e, US Half track. f, British Cromwell tank.
No. 2029, 400sh: a, British MK IV tank. b, Japanese Type 95 tank. c, German Hunting Panther tank. d, French AMX30 tank. e, Israeli Merkava tank. f, US M1 tank.
No. 2030, 1500sh, AH-64A Apache helicopter. No. 2031, 1500sh, Austin armored car, vert.

1999, Sept. 30 Litho. *Perf. 14*
Sheets of 6, #a.-f.
2028-2029 A354 Set of 2 12.00 12.00
Souvenir Sheets
2030-2031 A354 Set of 2 8.00 8.00

African Flowers — A355

Designs: 150sh, Canarina abyssinica. 250sh, Diaphananthe kamerunensis. 350sh, Protea barbigera. 500sh, Angraecum scottianum.
No. 2036, 400sh: a, Bolusanthus speciosus. b, Cassia abbreviata. c, Erythrina lysistemon. d, Leucodendron discolor. e, Romulea fischeri. f, Lupinus princei.
No. 2037, 400sh: a, Ansellia africana. b, Kigelia africana. c, Aerangis brachycarpa. d, Brachycorythis kalbreyeri. e, Begonia meyeriijohannis. f, Saintpaulia ionantha.
No. 2038, 1500sh, Nymphaea caerulea. No. 2039, 1500sh, Aloe petricola.

1999, Nov. 15
2032-2035 A355 Set of 4 3.25 3.25
Sheets of 6, #a.-f.
2036-2037 A355 Set of 2 12.00 12.00
Souvenir Sheets
2038-2039 A355 Set of 2 7.50 7.50

African Wildlife — A356

No. 2040, horiz.: a, Mountain gorilla. b, Zebras. c, East African elephant. d, Crowned cranes. e, Cheetah. f, Tiger. g, Pygmy chimpanzee. h, Hippopotamus.
No. 2041, 1500sh, Giraffes. No. 2042, 1500sh, Rhinoceros.

1999, Nov. 15
2040 A356 300sh Sheet of 8,
         #a.-h.   11.00 11.00
Souvenir Sheets
2041-2042 A356 Set of 2   10.00 10.00

Marine Life A357

Designs: 350sh, Beluga whale. 400sh, Ghost crab. 500sh, Emperor penguin, vert.
No. 2046: a, Herring gulls. b, Dusky dolphin. c, Sandwich tern. d, Humpback whale. e, Right whale. f, Dusky dolphin, sergeant major. g, White-tipped shark. h, Manta ray, trunkfish. i, Purple moon angel. j, Scalloped hammerhead shark. k, Manatee. l, Striped fingerfish.
No. 2047, 1500sh, Humpback whales. No. 2048, 1500sh, Tiger shark.

1999, Nov. 15
2043-2045 A357 Set of 3   5.00 5.00
2046 A357 250sh Sheet of 12,
         #a.-l.   11.00 11.00
Souvenir Sheets
2047-2048 A357 Set of 2   10.00 10.00

Ballet A358

Designs: 300sh, Romeo and Juliet. 350sh, The Dying Swan. 400sh, Giselle, vert. 500sh, Spartacus, vert.
No. 2053, 1500sh, The Firebird, vert. No. 2054, 1500sh, Swan Lake, vert.

1999, Aug. 20   Litho.   Perf. 14
2049-2052 A358 Set of 4   5.00 5.00
Souvenir Sheets
2053-2054 A358 Set of 2   9.00 9.00

17th and 18th Century Indian Art — A359

No. 2055, 500sh: a, Krishna and the Gopis (large tree). c, Krishna Painting the Feet of Radha. c, Krishna Yearning for the Moon (woman with fan). d, Games of Krishna and Radha (boat).
No. 2056, 500sh: a, Balwant Singh Having His Beard Cut. b, Festival of Hou (women at right). c, Ragini Bialvali (woman with fan, woman on seat). d, Krishna Holding a Ball of Butter.
No. 2057, 1500sh, Portrait of Emperor Jahanoir (man with necklace), vert. No. 2058, 1500sh, Krishna and the Gopis, diff., vert. Illustration reduced.

1999, Aug. 20   Perf. 13¾
Sheets of 4, #a-d
2055-2056 A359 Set of 2   10.00 10.00
Souvenir Sheets
2057-2058 A359 Set of 2   8.00 8.00

Fashion Designers — A360

No. 2059: a, Christian Dior. b, Model wearing Dior fashions. c, Bottle of Chanel No. 5, model wearing Chanel Fashions. d, Gabrielle "Coco" Chanel. e, Gianni Versace. f, Model wearing Versace fashions. g, Model wearing Yves Saint Laurent fashions. h, Yves Saint Laurent.
1500sh, Valentino Garavani.

1999, Aug. 20   Perf. 14
2059 A360 300sh Sheet of 8,
         #a-h   6.00 6.00
Souvenir Sheet
2060 A360 1500sh multi   4.00 4.00
Nos. 2059b-2059c, 2059f-2059g are 53x39mm.

Locomotives — A361

No. 2061: a, Class EF 81 Bo-Bo, Japan. b, Class 120 Bo-Bo, West Germany. c, Shao Shan I Co-Co, China. d, TGV, France. e, F40 PH Bo-Bo, US. f, LRC Bo-Bo, Canada.
1500sh, Class 401 Intercity Express, Germany.

1999, Sept. 30
2061 A361 400sh Sheet of 6,
         #a-f   6.00 6.00
Souvenir Sheet
2062 A361 1500sh multi   3.75 3.75

Marine Life A362

Designs: 150sh, Great barracuda. 250sh, Common squid. No. 2065, 300sh, Atlantic salmon. 350sh, Ocean sunfish. 400sh, Lobster. 500sh, Yellowfin tuna.
No. 2069, 300sh: a, Flying fish. b, Sailfish. c, Common dolphin. d, Sperm whale. e, Spinner dolphin. f, Manta ray. g, Green turtle. h, Hammerhead shark. i, Marlin.
No. 2070, 300sh: a, Walrus. b, Killer whale. c, Arctic tern. d, White shark. e, Narwhal. f, Blue whale. g, Giant clam. h, Octopus. i, Conger eel.
No. 2071, 1500sh, Whale shark. No. 2072, 1500sh, Beluga, vert.

1999, Nov. 15
2063-2068 A362 Set of 6   6.00 6.00
Sheets of 9, #a-i
2069-2070 A362 Set of 2   14.00 14.00
Souvenir Sheets
2071-2072 A362 Set of 2   7.50 7.50

Pres. Julius K. Nyerere (1922-99) A363

Nyerere: 200sh, As young man and old man. 500sh, With Edward Moringe Sokoine. 600sh, The Compassionate leader, vert. 800sh, During the early days of independence, vert.
1000sh, Mausoleum.

2000, Apr. 13   Perf. 13
2073-2076 A363 Set of 4   5.00 5.00
Souvenir Sheet
Perf. 13x13½
2077 A363 1000sh multi   2.50 2.50
No. 2077 contains one 35x28mm stamp.

Tourism A364

Designs: 400sh, Lion, Seronera Wildlife Lodge. No. 2079, 800sh, Hippopotami and hyenas, Selous Game Reserve. No. 2080, 800sh, Fish, Mafia Island. No. 2081, 800sh, Giraffes, Lobo Wildlife Lodge. No. 2082, 800sh, Rhinoceros, Ngorongoro Crater Wildlife Lodge. No. 2083, 800sh, Elephant, Mikumi Natl. Park. No. 2084, 800sh, Elephant, Lake Manyara Natl. Park. No. 2085, 800sh, Elephants, rhinoceros, Kibo Peak, Mt. Kilimanjaro.
1000sh, Lion, giraffes, elephant, rhinoceros, Lake Manyara Natl. Park, vert.

Perf. 13x13½, 13½x13
2000, June 10   Litho.
2078-2085 A364 Set of 8   20.00 20.00
Souvenir Sheet
2086 A364 1000sh multi   4.25 4.25
See Nos. 2102-2125.

Activities of World Vision A365

Designs: 200sh, Children with water pots on heads. 600sh, Family preparing food. 800sh, Nurse, family. 1000sh, Education of children.

2000, July 20   Litho.   Perf. 13x13¼
2087-2090 A365 Set of 4   6.00 6.00
Souvenir Sheet
2091 A365 500sh Two children   1.25 1.25

2000 Summer Olympics, Sydney A366

Designs: 150sh, Soccer. 350sh, Basketball, vert. 400sh, Women's 1500-meter race, vert. 800sh, Boxing.
500sh, Medal ceremony, vert.

2000, Sept. 15   Perf. 13¾
2092-2095 A366 Set of 4   4.50 4.50
Souvenir Sheet
2096 A366 500sh multi   1.25 1.25

Universities of East Africa A367

Designs: 150sh, Medical students, Muhimbili University College of Health Sciences. 200sh, Zanzibar University. 600sh, Makerere University, Uganda, vert. 800sh, Egerton University, Kenya.
500sh, Emblem of Inter-university Council for East Africa.

2000   Perf. 13x13¼, 13¼x13
2097-2100 A367 Set of 4   4.25 4.25
Perf. 14½
Size: 84x83mm
2101 A367 500sh multi   1.25 1.25

Tourism Type of 2000
No. 2102, 400sh, No. 2110, 500sh, No. 2118, 600sh, Like #2079. No. 2103, 400sh, No. 2111, 500sh, No. 2119, 600sh, Like #2080. No. 2104, 400sh, No. 2112, 500sh, No. 2120, 600sh, Like #2081. No. 2105, 400sh, No. 2113, 500sh, No. 2121, 600sh, Like #2082. No. 2106, 400sh, No. 2114, 500sh, No. 2122, 600sh, Like #2083. No. 2107, 400sh, No. 2115, 500sh, No. 2123, 600sh, Like #2084. No. 2108, 400sh, No. 2116, 500sh, No. 2124, 600sh, Like #2085. No. 2109, 500sh, No. 2117, 600sh, No. 2125, 800sh, Like #2078.

2000, June 1   Litho.   Perf. 13x13½
2102-2125 A364 Set of 24   50.00 50.00

Flowers A368

150sh, Bacciflava. 250sh, Hybridus pendulus. #2128, 300sh, Rhaphiolepis umbellata. 350sh, Magnoliaeflora. 400sh, Magnolia, vert. 500sh, Margot Koster, vert.
No. 2132, 300sh: a, Viola pedata. b, Magnolia. c, Felicia amelloides. d, Lythrum. e, Hemerocallis. f, Tithonia rotundifolia. g, Lilium. h, Iris. i, Stokesia laevis.

No. 2133, 300sh, vert.: a, Prunus subhirtella. b, Sanguinaria canadensis. c, Rosa palustris. d, Gordonia lasianthius. e, Aquilegia caerulea. f, Fremontodendron. g, Hypericum calycinum. h, Anemone vitifolia. i, Clematis.
No. 2134, Iris cristata, vert. No. 2134A, Aster prikartil.

2000			Perf. 14	
2126-2131	A368	Set of 6	5.00	5.00
Sheets of 9, #a-i				
2132-2133	A368	Set of 2	13.00	13.00
Souvenir Sheet				
2134-2134A	A368	Set of 2	7.50	7.50

Social Security Fund A369

Designs: 200sh, Retirement. 350sh, Employment injury. 600sh, Invalidity. 800sh, Health insurance.

2000	Wmk. 387		Perf. 13¾	
2135-2138	A369	Set of 4	5.00	5.00
Souvenir Sheet				
2139	A369	500sh Maternity	1.25	1.25

Environmental Care — A370

Designs: 200sh, Tree planting campaign. 400sh, Water sources protection. 600sh, Cleaning sewage. 800sh, Protecting forests.

2000	Wmk. 387		Perf. 13x13¼	
2140-2143	A370	Set of 4	5.00	5.00
Souvenir Sheet				
2144	A370	1000sh Mountain	2.50	2.50

Zanzibar Millennium A371

Designs: 150sh, Fishing industry. 200sh, Trade and tourism. 400sh, Child and emblem, vert. 800sh, Right to higher learning, vert. 500sh, Peace and tranquility, vert.

2000	Wmk. 387		Perf. 13¾	
2145-2148	A371	Set of 4	4.50	4.50
Souvenir Sheet				
2149	A371	500sh multi	1.25	1.25

Orchids A372

Designs: 200sh, Vanilla planifolia. 250sh, Pleurothallus tuerckheimii. No. 2152, 370sh, Trichopilia fragrans.
No. 2153, 370sh: a, Cyrtopodium andersonii. b, Cochleanthes discolor. c, Catasetum barbatum. d, Caularthron bicornutum. e, Broughtonia sanguinea. f, Brassavola nodosa.
No. 2154, 370sh: a, Oeceoclades maculata. b, Isochilus linearis. c, Eulophia alta. d, Ionopsis utricularioides. e, Epidendrum ciliare. f, Dimerandra emarginata.
No. 2155, 1500sh, Brassavola cucullata. No. 2156, 1500sh, Epidendrum nocturnum.

2000	Litho.		Perf. 14	
2150-2152	A372	Set of 3	3.50	3.50
Sheets of 6, #a-f				
2153-2154	A372	Set of 2	14.00	14.00
Souvenir Sheets				
2155-2156	A372	Set of 2	8.00	8.00

Nos. 607, 610, 612, 615, 617 Surcharged

Methods and perfs as before

1998-2001				
2157	A99	100sh on 40sh multi		
2158	A99	150sh on 9sh multi		
2159	A99	200sh on 170sh multi		
2159A	A99	230sh on 20sh multi	—	—
2159B	A99	230sh on 170sh multi		
2159C	A99	800sh on 500sh multi	2.00	2.00

Issued: No. 2158, 1/26/98; No. 2157, 8/6/98; No. 2159, 6/4/00; No. 2159C, 4/6/00; No. 2159B, 11/20/00; No. 2159A, 11/20/01.

Rare Birds A373

Designs: 150sh, Taita falcon. 300sh, Banded green. 400sh, Spotted ground thrush. 500sh, Fischer's turaco. 600sh, Blue swallow.

2000	Litho.		Perf. 14	
2160	A373	150sh multi	.75	.75
2161	A373	300sh multi	1.25	1.25
2162	A373	400sh multi	1.75	1.75
2163	A373	500sh multi	2.00	2.00
Souvenir Sheet				
2164	A373	600sh multi	3.00	3.00

Architecture — A374

Designs: 150sh, Ruins of Great Mosque, Kilwa Kisiwani. 200sh, German Boma, Mikindani. 250sh, German Boma, Bagamoyo. 300sh, Butiama Museum, Mara. 350sh, Chief Government Chemist Office. 400sh, Old Post Office, Dar es Salaam. 500sh, Dr. David Livingstone Lodge, Kwihara Tabora. 600sh, Original and present State Houses, vert. 700sh, Ngoni-Nyamwezi traditional houses. 800sh, The People's Palace Beit Elajaib, Zanzibar. 900sh, Tongoni Ruins, Tanga. 1000sh, Karimjee Hall, Dar es Salaam.
1500sh, Old Boma, Mikindani.

2000 (?)	Litho.		Perf. 13	
2165	A374	150sh multi		
2166	A374	200sh multi		
2166A	A374	250sh multi		
2167	A374	300sh multi		
2167A	A374	350sh multi		
2168	A374	400sh multi		
2168A	A374	500sh multi		
2169	A374	600sh multi		
2169A	A374	700sh multi		
2170	A374	800sh multi		
2170A	A374	900sh multi		
2171	A374	1000sh multi		
Souvenir Sheet				
2172	A374	1500sh multi		

For surcharge see No. 2336.

Flora and Fauna — A375

Designs: 100sh, Common babbler. 140sh, Eastern blue darner. 150sh, Cavalier mushroom. 200sh, Orange-barred sulphur. 250sh, Harlequin bug. No. 2179, 370sh, Brassolae liocattleya.
No. 2180, 370sh: a, Common yellowthroat. b, Great orange tip. c, Tiger lily. d, Shaggy mane. e, Sri Lanka grasshopper. f, Woodhouse's toad.
No. 2181, 370sh: a, Golden-crowned warbler. b, Fuchsia. c, Alfalfa butterfly. d, Lycaste aquila. e, Snail. f, Ground beetle.
No. 2182, 1500sh, Rufous-collared sparrow, horiz. No. 2183, 1500sh, Monarch butterfly, horiz.

2000	Litho.		Perf. 14	
2174-2179	A375	Set of 6	3.00	3.00
Sheets of 6, #a-f				
2180-2181	A375	Set of 2	11.00	11.00
Souvenir Sheets				
2182-2183	A375	Set of 2	8.00	8.00

Activities of World Vision — A375a

Design: 200sh, Children have a right to education, horiz. 600sh, Children have a right to happiness, horiz. 800sh, Children have a right not to be exploited. 1000sh, Children have a right to be heard.

2001, Apr. 30	Litho.		Perf. 13	
2183A	A375a	200sh multi	—	—
2183B	A375a	600sh multi	—	—
2183C	A375a	800sh multi	—	—
2183D	A375a	1000sh multi	—	—
Souvenir Sheet				
2183E	A375a	500sh multi	—	—

Endangered Animals A376

Designs: 200sh, Leopard. 400sh, Rhinoceros. No. 2186, 600sh, Crocodile. 800sh, Hunting wild dogs.

No. 2188, 600sh, Cheetah.

2001, June 15	Litho.		Perf. 13	
2184-2187	A376	Set of 4	5.00	5.00
Souvenir Sheet				
2188	A376	600sh multi	1.75	1.75

UN High Commissioner for Refugees, 50th Anniv. — A377

Designs: 200sh, Refugee child being vaccinated. 400sh, Refugees crossing Lake Tanganyika. 600sh, Refugee woman, vert. 800sh, Fleeing refugees, vert.

2001, July 31				
2189-2192	A377	Set of 4	5.00	5.00
2191a		Souvenir sheet of 1	1.75	1.75

Landscapes A378

Designs: 200sh, Rufiji River, Selous Game Reserve. 400sh, Mangapwani Beach, Zanzibar. 600sh, Mountains, Mikumi Natl. Park. 800sh, Balancing Stones, Shore of Lake Victoria, Mwanza, vert.
700sh, Ruaha Natl. Park, vert.

2001, Nov. 30	Litho.		Perf. 13	
2193-2196	A378	Set of 4	5.00	5.00
Souvenir Sheet				
2197	A378	700sh multi	1.75	1.75

Year of Dialogue Among Civilizations A379

Designs: 200sh, Talking with children. 400sh, Formal dress. 600sh, Exchanging ideas. 800sh, Letter writing.
700sh, Communication linkages, vert.

2001, Oct. 9				Litho.
2198-2201	A379	Set of 4	4.50	4.50
Souvenir Sheet				
2202	A379	700sh multi	1.50	1.50

Conservation of Zanzibar Rare Species — A380

Designs: 250sh, Dolphins. 300sh, Coral reefs. 450sh, Coral reefs, diff. 800sh, Zanzibar red colobus, vert.
700sh, Zanzibar red colobus, diff.

2002, Aug. 30	Litho.		Perf. 13	
2203-2206	A380	Set of 4	4.50	4.50
Souvenir Sheet				
2207	A380	700sh multi	1.75	1.75

Historic Sites of East Africa A381

Designs: 250sh, Fort Kilwa. 300sh, Maruhubi Palace ruins, Zanzibar. 400sh, Old Provincial Office, Nairobi, 1913. 800sh, Mparu Tombs, Hoima, Uganda.
700sh, Map of East Africa, ship.

2001, Oct. 19
2208-2211 A381 Set of 4   3.75 3.75
Souvenir Sheet
2212 A381 700sh multi   1.50 1.50

Independence, 40th Anniv. — A382

Designs: 180sh, Tea estates. 230sh, Regional integration with Uganda and Kenya, vert. 350sh, University graduates, vert. 450sh, 1000sh, Lion, elephant, buffalo, cheetah, rhinoceros, Mt. Kilimanjaro. 650sh, Referral hospitals. 950sh, Mining industry.

2001, Dec. 30   Litho.   Perf. 14
2213-2218 A382 Set of 6   6.00 6.00
Souvenir Sheet
2219 A382 1000sh multi   2.10 2.10

Ceremonial Costumes — A383

Designs: 250sh, Makonde mask dance. 350sh, Zanzibar Mwaka koga festival. 400sh, Lizombe dancer. 450sh, Zaramo bride's celebration.
500sh, Like 400sh.

Wmk. 387
2002, Mar. 30   Litho.   Perf. 13¾
2220-2223 A383 Set of 4   4.00 4.00
Souvenir Sheet
2224 A383 500sh multi   1.50 1.50

Mountains A384

Designs: 250sh, Mt. Kilimanjaro. 350sh, Usambara Mountains. 400sh, Uluguru Mountains. 450sh, Mwanihana Peak, Udzungwa Mountains.
500sh, Like 250sh.

2002, June 30   Wmk. 387
2225-2228 A384 Set of 4   4.00 4.00
Souvenir Sheet
2229 A384 500sh multi   1.50 1.50

National Census A385

Census emblem and: 200sh, School children, vert. 250sh, Group of people. 350sh, Family. 600sh, Boy, census figures.
800sh, Group of people, vert.

Perf. 13x13¼ Sync., 13¼x13 Sync.
2002, Aug. 13   Unwmk.
2230-2233 A385 Set of 4   4.00 4.00
Souvenir Sheet
Perf. 13x13¼
2234 A385 800sh multi   1.75 1.75

Arts of Zanzibar A386

Designs: 200sh, Mat making. 250sh, Hand-sewn hats. 350sh, Chair making. 600sh, Hina painting.
800sh, Zanzibar door.

2002, Sept. 13   Unwmk.   Perf. 13¼
2235-2238 A386 Set of 4   3.75 3.75
Souvenir Sheet
Perf. 13
2239 A386 800sh multi   1.75 1.75

Souvenir Sheet

Wildlife — A387

No. 2240: a, Leopard. b, Elephant. c, Rhinoceros. d, Lion. e, Buffalo.

Perf. 13x14
2002, Apr. 30   Wmk. 387
2240 A387 250sh Sheet of 5,
                  #a-e   3.75 3.75
Compare No. 2240 with No. 2251.

Archaeology A388

Designs: 250sh, Ancient city of Kisimkazi, Zanzibar, vert. 400sh, Ruins of Kaole town, Bagamoyo. 450sh, Kondoa Irangi rock paintings, vert. 600sh, Great Mosque, Kilwa Kisiwani.
1000sh, Like 450sh.

Perf. 13¼
2002, Sept. 30   Unwmk.   Litho.
2241-2244 A388 Set of 4   3.50 3.50
Souvenir Sheet
Perf. 13
2245 A388 1000sh multi   2.25 2.25

Wildlife A389

Designs: 400sh, Rhinoceroses. 500sh, Elephant. 600sh, Lion. 800sh, Leopard, vert. 1000sh, Buffalo.
1500sh, Rhinoceros, elephant, lion, leopard, buffalo, vert.

Perf. 13¼x12¾, 12¾x13¼
2003, Apr. 22   Litho.   Wmk. 387
2246-2250 A389 Set of 5   8.00 8.00
Size: 85x115mm
Imperf
2251 A389 1500sh multi   4.00 4.00
Compare No. 2251 with No. 2240.

Cash Crops — A390

Designs: 250sh, Cotton. 300sh, Cashews. 600sh, Sisal. 800sh, Cloves.
1000sh, Tea, horiz.

Perf. 13x13¼ Syncopated
2003, June 10   Unwmk.
2252-2255 A390 Set of 4   3.75 3.75
Souvenir Sheet
Perf. 13¼x13 Syncopated
2256 A390 1000sh multi   2.25 2.25

Activities of World Vision A391

Designs: 300sh, Better nutrition with vitamin A. 600sh, Education opportunity for all children. 800sh, Clean and safe water for all, vert. 1000sh, Malaria prevention with treated mosquito nets.
500sh, Children have a right to be heard.

2003, July 3   Perf. 13
2257-2260 A391 Set of 4   5.25 5.25
Souvenir Sheet
2261 A391 500sh multi   1.25 1.25

Traditional Dances A392

Dances: 300sh, Nyamwezi. 500sh, Luo. 600sh, Pemba. 800sh, Baganda.
1000sh, Masai.

Perf. 13¼x13 Syncopated
2003, July 25
2262-2265 A392 Set of 4   4.25 4.25
Souvenir Sheet
2266 A392 1000sh multi   2.00 2.00

Nos. 612 and 1567 Surcharged

Methods and Perfs As Before
2002
2267 A99   250sh on 40sh #612   .75 .75
2268 A262 250sh on 180sh
                  #1567   .90 .90
Issued: No. 2267, 7/23/02; No. 2268, 8/30/02.

Northern Circuit Tourist Attractions A393

Designs: 300sh, Lion, lioness, Mt. Kilimanjaro. 350sh, Kibo Peak, Mt. Kilimanjaro. 400sh, Zebras, Serengeti Natl. Park. 500sh, Elephants, Kilimanjaro Natl. Park. 600sh, Leopards, Serengeti Natl. Park. 800sh, Rhinoceros, Ngorongoro Crater.
1000sh, Buffalo, Arusha Natl. Park.

2003, Apr. 30   Litho.   Perf. 13¼x13
2269-2274 A393 Set of 6   5.75 5.75
Souvenir Sheet
2275 A393 1000sh multi   2.00 2.00

Landscapes A394

Designs: 300sh, Rufiji Delta. 400sh, Zanzibar shore. 500sh, Lake Manyara, Rift Valley. 800sh, Kalambo Falls, vert.
1000sh, Coastal mangroves.

2003, July 22   Litho.   Perf. 13¼x13
2276-2279 A394 Set of 4   4.00 4.00
Souvenir Sheet
2280 A394 1000sh multi   1.90 1.90

Zanzibar Tourist Attractions A395

Designs: 300sh, Old Fort. 500sh, Door, Beit al Ajaib, vert. 600sh, Coconut palm tree, Michamvi Beach, vert. 800sh, Dhow, Beit al Ajaib.

Perf. 13¼x13, 13x13¼
2003, Sept. 30   Litho.
2281-2284 A395 Set of 4   4.25 4.25
2284a   Souvenir sheet, #2281,
                  2283, 2284   3.25 3.25

Marine Mammals A396

Designs: 300sh, Common dolphin. 350sh, Sperm whale. 400sh, Southern right whale. 600sh, Dugong.
500sh, Bottlenose dolphin.

2003, Oct. 11   Litho.   Perf. 13¼x13
2285-2288 A396 Set of 4   4.25 4.25
Souvenir Sheet
2289 A396 500sh multi   1.75 1.75

Religious Festivals — A396a

Designs: 300sh, Muslims on pilgrimage to Mecca. 500sh, Choir at Christmas. 600sh, Prophet Mohammed's Birthday. 800sh, Church at Christmas.
1000sh, Crucifixion of Jesus.

Wmk. 387
2003, Nov. 4   Litho.   Perf. 14
2289A-2289D A396a Set of 4   4.25 4.25
Souvenir Sheet
2289E A396a 1000sh multi   1.90 1.90

Tanzania Posts Corporation, 10th Anniv. — A397

Designs: 350sh, Counter automation. 400sh, Overnight mail delivery services. 600sh, Workers' participation. 800sh, Expedited mail services.
1000sh, Post Cargo.

Unwmk.

			Perf. 13	
2004, Jan. 19		**Litho.**		
2290-2293	A397	Set of 4	4.00	4.00
2293a		Souvenir sheet, #2290-2293	4.00	4.00

Souvenir Sheet

2294	A397	1000sh multi	1.90	1.90

Western Union Money Transfer A398

Designs: 300sh, Exchange of American and Tanzanian currency. 400sh, Busalanga Primary School. 500sh, Woman, child, Tanzanian currency, vert. 600sh, World map.
800sh, Like 300sh, without Western Union emblem.

Perf. 13¼x13, 13x13¼

			Litho.	
2004, Feb. 3				
2295-2298	A398	Set of 4	3.25	3.25

Souvenir Sheet

2299	A398	800sh multi	1.50	1.50

Girl Guides in Tanzania, 75th Anniv. A399

Designs: 300sh, Guides demonstrating solar cookers. 400sh, Camp training. 600sh, Bravery training. 800sh, Guides assisting at a mother and child clinic session.
1000sh, Like 800sh.

			Perf. 13¼x13	
2004, May 15				
2300-2303	A399	Set of 4	3.75	3.75

Souvenir Sheet

2304	A399	1000sh multi	1.90	1.90

Tanganyika Christian Refugee Service, 40th Anniv. A400

Designs: 350sh, Truck carrying refugees and bicycles. 600sh, Public water source. 800sh, Students in classroom. 1000sh, Afforestation campaign.
1200sh, Four vignettes combined.

Unwmk.

			Perf. 14	
2004, May 24		**Litho.**		
2305-2308	A400	Set of 4	5.00	5.00

Souvenir Sheet
Perf. 14¼

2309	A400	1200sh multi	2.25	2.25

No. 2309 contains one 44x34mm stamp.

Zanzibar Watercraft Races A401

Designs: 350sh, Crowd cheering race winners. 400sh, Punt race. 600sh, Dhow race. 800sh, Sailboat race.
1000sh, Dhow, vert.

			Perf. 13	
2004, June 25				
2310-2313	A401	Set of 4	4.00	4.00
2313a		Souvenir sheet, #2310-2313	4.00	4.00

Souvenir Sheet

2314	A401	1000sh multi	1.90	1.90

Flora, Fauna and Mushrooms — A402

No. 2315, 550sh, horiz. — Animals: a, Red colobus monkey. b, Leopard. c, Giraffe. d, Eland. e, Zebra. f, African elephant.
No. 2316, 550sh, horiz. — Birds: a, European roller. b, Little swift. c, African gray parrot. d, Bateleur. e, European bee-eater. f, Hoopoe.
No. 2317, 550sh, horiz. — Butterflies: a, Gold-banded forester. b, Two-tailed pasha. c, Plain tiger. d, Common dotted border. e, African migrant. f, Forest queen.
No. 2318, 550sh, horiz. — Orchids: a, Cynorkis kassnerana. b, Habenaria rhodocheila. c, Vanilla planifolia. d, Ansellia africana. e, Disa uniflora. f, Calathe rosea.
No. 2319, 550sh, horiz. — Mushrooms: a, Fly mushroom. b, Rosy-gill fairy helmet. c, Purple coincap. d, Velvet shank. e, Thick-footed morel. f, King bolete.
No. 2320, 2000sh, Olive baboon. No. 2321, 2000sh, Gray crowned crane. No. 2322, 2000sh, Blue diadem butterfly. No. 2323, 2000sh, Disa uniflora, diff. No. 2324, 2000sh, Sharp-scaled parasol mushroom.

			Perf. 14	
2004, July 19				
		Sheets of 6, #a-f		
2315-2319	A402	Set of 5	30.00	30.00

Souvenir Sheets

2320-2324	A402	Set of 5	18.50	18.50

Mining A403

Designs: 350sh, Diamond mining at Williamson Diamond Mwadui. 500sh, Semi-processed jewels. No. 2327, 600sh, Drillers in deep mine. 800sh, Gold miners.
No. 2329, Unprocessed gemstones.

			Perf. 13¼x12¾	
2004, July 30				
2325-2328	A403	Set of 4	4.25	4.25
2328a		Souvenir sheet, #2325-2328	4.25	4.25

Souvenir Sheet

2329	A403	600sh multi	1.40	1.40

Southern African Development Community, 24th Anniv. A404

Designs: 350sh, Removal of water hyacinths from beach. 500sh, Irrigation ditch in corn field. 600sh, irrigation ditch at rice paddy. 800sh, Workers installing pipe in borehole, vert.
1000sh, Farm workers hoeing corn field irrigation ditches.

			Perf. 14x13, 13x14	
2004, Aug. 17				
2330-2333	A404	Set of 4	4.25	4.25
2333a		Souvenir sheet, #2330-2333, perf. 13½x13, 13x13½	4.25	4.25

Souvenir Sheet

2334	A404	1000sh multi	1.90	1.90

Nos. 1565, 1569 and 2166
Surcharged

#2335   #2336

Methods and Perfs As Before

2004, Nov. 13				
2335	A262	350sh on 100sh #1565	—	—
2336	A374	350sh on 200sh #2166	—	—
2337	A262	350sh on 210sh #1569	—	—

Children's Rights A405

Inscriptions: No. 2338, 350sh, Involve children in school development. No. 2339, 350sh, Let's equip children with life skills. 400sh, Children need education before employment. 500sh, 1000sh, Disabled children need to be educated.

2004, Nov. 4		**Litho.**	**Perf. 13¼x12¾**	
2338-2341	A405	Set of 4	3.00	3.00

Souvenir Sheet

2342	A405	1000sh multi	1.90	1.90

Law and Peace in the Great Lakes Zone — A405a

Designs: 350sh, Julius K. Nyerere acting as facilitator in Burundi peace negotiations. 500sh, Burundi refugees at border. No. 2342C, 600sh, Nelson Mandela and Tanzania Pres. Banjamin W. Mkapa at Arusha peace talks. 800sh, Pres. Mkapa with Uganda Pres. Yoweri Musaveni and Burundi Pres. Domitien Ndayizeye at Dar es Salaam peace talks.
No. 2342E, 600sh, Arusha Intl. Conference Center.

2004, Oct. 15		**Litho.**	**Perf. 14x13**	
2342A-2342D	A405a	Set of 4	4.25	4.25
2342Df		Souvenir sheet, #2342A-2342D	4.25	4.25

Souvenir Sheet

2342E	A405a	600sh multi	1.10	1.10

Rotary International, Cent. — A406

Designs: 350sh, Rotary officials honor Tanzania Pres. Julius Nyerere. 500sh, Emblem of Dar es Salaam North Tanzania Club, vert. No. 2345 600sh, Eradication of polio. 800sh, Map and flags of District 9200 countries, Eritrea, Ethiopia, Uganda, Kenya and Tanzania, vert.
No. 2347: a, Environmental project. b, Self-reliance to the handicapped. c, Basic health care project, vert. d, Jaipur foot project. e, Malaria project. f, Eradication of river blindness project.
1000sh, Centenary emblem, vert.

2005, Feb. 23		**Litho.**	**Perf. 13**	
2343-2346	A406	Set of 4	4.25	4.25
2347	A406	600sh Sheet of 6, #a-f	6.50	6.50

Souvenir Sheet

2348	A406	1000sh multi	1.90	1.90

Safari Circuit Animals — A407

Designs: 350sh, Lionesses. 500sh, Cheetahs, horiz. No. 2351, 600sh, Red colobus monkey. 800sh, Zebras, horiz.
No. 2353, horiz.: a, Elephants. b, Rhinoceroses. c, Giraffes. d, Crocodile. e, Chimpanzees. f, Buffaloes.
No. 2354, horiz.: a, Leopard. b, Wild hunting dogs.

Perf. 12¾x13¼, 13¼x12¾

2005, Apr. 30				
2349-2352	A407	Set of 4	4.25	4.25
2353	A407	600sh Sheet of 6, #a-f	6.50	6.50
2354	A407	1000sh Sheet of 2, #a-b	3.75	3.75

Zanzibar Heritage and Culture A408

Designs: 350sh, Bull fighting. 400sh, Narrow street in Stone Town, vert. No. 2357, 600sh, Women's traditional dress, vert. 800sh, Clove harvesting, vert.
No. 2359, 600sh: a, House of Wonders. b, Local Taarabu musicians. c, Man holding fish. d, Coconut palm. e, Women's indoor traditional dress. f, Old museum building.
500sh, Pemba-Zanzibar ferry boat.

Perf. 13½x13, 13x13½

			Litho.	
2005, June 30				
2355-2358	A408	Set of 4	4.00	4.00
2359	A408	600sh Sheet of 6, #a-f	6.50	6.50

Souvenir Sheet

2360	A408	500sh multi	1.25	1.25

2004 Summer Olympics, Athens — A409

Designs: No. 2361, 350sh, Greco-Roman wrestlers. No. 2362, 350sh, Baron Godefroy de Blonay, vert. 500sh, Commemorative medal for 1928 Amsterdam Summer Olympics, vert. 1000sh, Greek javelin thrower sculpture, vert.

2005, May 2		**Litho.**	**Perf. 13¼**	
2361-2364	A409	Set of 4	4.00	4.00

Souvenir Sheet

Reign of Pope John Paul, 25th Anniv.
(in 2003) — A410

No. 2365: a, Pope as boy, with mother, 1921. b, Visit to Poland, 1979. c, Meeting with Pres. George W. Bush, 2001. d, In Armenia, 2001.

2005, May 2   *Perf. 13½*
2365 A410 1000sh Sheet of 4,
    #a-d   8.00 8.00

Locomotives, Bicent. — A411

No. 2366: a, West Side Lumber 3-truck shay, Georgetown Loop Railroad. b, LK&P 0-4-0 Saddletanker. c, Double-headed C&T steam locomotive. d, Baldwin 4-6-0, Huckleberry Railroad.
2500sh, Heber Valley Railroad 2-8-0.

2005, May 2
2366 A411 1000sh Sheet of 4,
    #a-d   7.25 7.25
Souvenir Sheet
2367 A411 2500sh multi   4.50 4.50

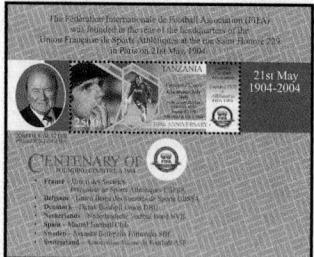

FIFA (Fédération Internationale de
Football Association) Cent. (in
2004) — A412

No. 2368: a, Franco Baresi. b, Daniel Passarella. c, Miroslav Klose. d, Michel Platini.
2500sh, Gianfranco Zola.

2005, May 2   **Litho.**   *Perf. 13½*
2368 A412 1000sh Sheet of 4,
    #a-d   7.25 7.25
Souvenir Sheet
2369 A412 2500sh multi   4.50 4.50

D-Day, 60th Anniv. (in 2004) — A413

No. 2370, vert.: a, Map of invasion. b, Gen. Dwight D. Eisenhower. c, American troops landing at Omaha Beach. d, British Mosquitos. e, Fleet Admiral Ernest J. King. f, Gen. George C. Marshall.
2500sh, Battle for Fox Green Beach.

2006, May 2
2370 A413 600sh Sheet of 6,
    #a-f   6.50 6.50
Souvenir Sheet
2371 A413 2500sh multi   4.50 4.50

Jules Verne (1828-1905),
Writer — A414

No. 2372, 800sh: a, Voyages Extraordinaires. b, Twenty Thousand Leagues Under the Sea. c, A Floating City (book cover). d, Adventures of Three Englishmen and Three Russians in South Africa.
No. 2373, 800sh: a, Mathias Sandorf. b, The Steam House, The Demon of Cawnpore. c, Hector Servadec on the Career of a Comet. d, An Antarctic Mystery.
No. 2374, 800sh: a, Around the World in Eighty Days. b, Dr. Ox's Experiment. c, The Purchase of the North Pole. d, Adrift in the Pacific.
No. 2375, 800sh: a, The Archipelago on Fire. b, The Vanished Diamond. c, Mistress Branican. d, The Castle of the Carpathians.
No. 2376, 800sh: a, The Invasion of the Sea. b, The Floating Island. c, A Floating City (men near ship railing). d, Dick Sands, Boy Captain.
No. 2377, 2000sh, Around the World in Eighty Days, diff. No. 2378, 2000sh, Five Weeks in a Balloon. No. 2379, 2000sh, The Mysterious Island. No. 2380, 2000sh, The Adventures of a Chinaman. No. 2381, 2000sh, The Invasion of the Sea, diff.

2005, May 16   *Perf. 13½*
Sheets of 4, #a-d
2372-2376 A414   Set of 5   29.00 29.00
Souvenir Sheets
2377-2381 A414   Set of 5   18.00 18.00

Fish of
Lake
Victoria
A415

Designs: No. 2382, 350sh, Labeo victorianus. 400sh, Lates niloticus. 600sh, Pundamilia nyererei. 800sh, Brycinus sadleri.
No. 2386, 350sh: a, Haplochromis sharpsnout. b, Haplochromis chilotes. c, Mormyrus kannume. d, Clarias gariepinus. e, Synodontis afrofischeri. f, Protopterus aethiopicus.
500sh, Oreochromis niloticus.

2005, Aug. 30   *Perf. 13¼x13¾*
2382-2385 A415   Set of 4   3.75 3.75
2386 A415 350sh Sheet of 6, #a-
    f   3.75 3.75
Souvenir Sheet
2387 A415 500sh multi   1.25 1.25

Pope John Paul II
(1920-2005), and
Pres. Bill
Clinton — A416

2005, Sept. 22   *Perf. 12¾*
2388 A416 1500sh multi   2.75 2.75
Printed in sheets of 4, with each stamp having a slightly different background.

Rotary International, Cent. — A417

No. 2389: a, Child receiving polio vaccine. b, Dr. Jonas E. Salk, polio researcher. c, Hands, test tube.
2500sh, Salk and Rotary International centenary emblem.

2005, Sept. 22
2389 A417 1200sh Sheet of 3,
    #a-c   6.50 6.50
Souvenir Sheet
2390 A417 2500sh multi   4.50 4.50

Albert Einstein (1879-1955),
Physicist — A418

No. 2391 — Sketch of Einstein and: a, 1979 Swiss 5-franc coin. b, Time Magazine cover. c, Israel #117.
2500sh, Portrait of Einstein.

2005, Sept. 22
2391 A418 1300sh Sheet of 3,
    #a-c   7.00 7.00
Souvenir Sheet
2392 A418 2500sh multi   4.50 4.50

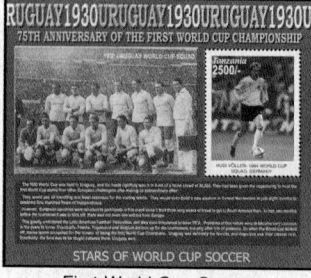

First World Cup Soccer
Championships, 75th Anniv. — A419

No. 2393: a, Christian Ziege. b, Marko Rehmer. c, Jens Nowotny.
2500sh, Rudi Völler.

2005, Sept. 22   *Perf. 13¼*
2393 A419 1200sh Sheet of 3,
    #a-c   6.50 6.50
Souvenir Sheet
2394 A419 2500sh multi   4.50 4.50

Butterflies
A420

Designs: 350sh, Papilio ufipa. No. 2396, 500sh, Mylothris sagala mahale. No. 2397, 600sh, Amauris tartarea tukuyuensis. 800sh, Charaxes lucyae gabriellae.
No. 2399, 600sh: a, Like 350sh. b, Euphaedra neophron kiellandi. c, Like 800sh. d, Abisara zanzibarica. e, Acrae utengulensis.
No. 2400, 500sh, Charaxes usambarae maridadi.

2005, Oct. 27   *Perf. 13¾x13½*
2395-2398 A420   Set of 4   4.00 4.00
2399 A420 600sh Sheet of 6,
    #2397,
    2399a-2399e   6.50 6.50
Souvenir Sheet
2400 A420 500sh multi   .90 .90

Anniversaries
and Events
A421

Designs: 350sh, Person with amputated leg. No. 2402, 500sh, Line of people at polling station. No. 2403, 600sh, Pope John Paul II, kneeling at airport. 800sh, Laurean Cardinal Rugambwa, Pope John Paul II and Pres. Alis Hassan Mwinyi.
No. 2405, 600sh: a, Pres. Julius Nyerere and Abeid Aman Karume signing Union Treaty. b, Woman holding child, casting ballot. c, Pope John Paul II, Pres. Mwinyi and Julius and Maria Nyerere. d, Pope John Paul II and Cardinal Rugambwa and car roof. e, Majimaji Museum, Songea. f, President B. W. Mkapa at fire.
No. 2406, 500sh, Majimaji Monument, vert.

2005, Dec. 9   *Perf. 13¼x12¾*
2401-2404 A421   Set of 4   4.00 4.00
2405 A421 600sh Sheet of 6, #a-
    f   6.25 6.25
Souvenir Sheet
Perf. 12¾x13¼
2406 A421 500sh multi   1.25 1.25
World Diabetes Day (350sh); 2005 general elections (#2402, 2405b), Visit of Pope John Paul II, 15th anniv. (800sh, #2405c, 2405d).

Birds
A422

Designs: 350sh, Rufous-winged sunbird. No. 2408, 500sh, Pemba white-eye. No. 2409, 600sh, Kilombero weaver. 800sh, Usambara eagle owl.
No. 2411, 600sh: a, Pemba scops owl. b, Spike-heeled lark. c, Pemba green pigeon. d, Uluguru bush shrike. e, Yellow-collared love birds. f, Usambara nightjar.
No. 2412, 500sh, Moreau's sunbird, vert.

2006, Mar. 25   *Perf. 13*
2407-2410 A422   Set of 4   4.00 4.00
2411 A422 600sh Sheet of 6, #a-
    f   6.50 6.50
Souvenir Sheet
2412 A422 500sh multi   1.10 1.10
No. 2412 contains one 39x49mm stamp.

2006 World Cup Soccer Championships, Germany — A423

Designs: 350sh, New National Stadium, Dar es Salaam. 500sh, Map of Africa and flags of participating countries, vert. No. 2415, 600sh, Pres. Jakaya Kikwete holding World Cup trophy. 800sh, Mascot for 2006 World Cup, vert. No. 2417, 600sh, World Cup Trophy and 2006 World Cup emblem.

Perf. 13¼x12¾, 12¾x13¼

2006, Mar. 25				
2413-2416	A423	Set of 4	3.75	3.75
2416a		Miniature sheet, #2413-2416	3.75	3.75

Souvenir Sheet

2417	A423	600sh multi	1.50	1.50

Miniature Sheet

Wolfgang Amadeus Mozart (1756-91), Composer — A424

No. 2418: a, Portrait of Mozart (blue panel). b, Mozart's birthplace, Salzburg. c, Poster for Don Giovanni. d, Portrait of Mozart (purple panel).

2006, June 13			Perf. 12¾	
2418	A424	1200sh Sheet of 4, #a-d	8.00	8.00

Release of Elvis Presley Movie, *Jailhouse Rock*, 50th Anniv. — A425

No. 2419 — Presley with: a, Both arms at side. b, Arm raised above head. c, Arms outstretched and jacket pulled up behind head. d, Hand in front of chest.

2006, June 13			Perf. 13½	
2419	A425	1200sh Sheet of 4, #a-d	9.00	9.00

Queen Elizabeth II, 80th Birthday — A426

No. 2420 — Queen: a, Wearing blue robe. b, On reviewing stand. c, On horse. d, Wearing feathered hat.
2500sh, Wearing tiara.

2006, June 13			Perf. 14¼	
2420	A426	1200sh Sheet of 4, #a-d	9.50	9.50

Souvenir Sheet

2421	A426	2500sh multi	5.25	5.25

Rembrandt (1606-69), Painter — A427

No. 2422 — Painting details: a, Jan Pellicorne and His Son Caspar (Jan Pellicorne). b, Jan Pellicorne and His Son Caspar (Caspar). c, Susanna Van Collen, Wife of Jan Pellicorne, and Her Daughter, Eva Susanna (Susanna). d, Susanna Van Collen, Wife of Jan Pellicorne, and Her Daughter, Eva Susanna (Eva Susanna).
3000sh, A Turk.

2006, June 13			Perf. 13¼	
2422	A427	1000sh Sheet of 4, #a-d	6.75	6.75

Imperf
Size: 70x100mm

2423	A427	3000sh multi	5.00	5.00

Beauty of Zanzibar A428

Designs: 350sh, Man and woman in traditional Zanzibar dress. No. 2425, 500sh, Zanzibar Museum. No. 2426, 600sh, Maruhubi Palace ruins. 800sh, Man climbing coconut tree.
No. 2428, 600sh: a, Green turtle at Mnemba Island. b, Red colobus monkey. c, Giant tortoise at Changuu Island. d, Dhow, Zanzibar sunset. e, Dhow sailing near Matemwe. f, Coconut crab, Chumbe Island.
No. 2429, 500sh, vert.: a, Clove foliage and enlargement of flower buds. b, Light Signal Tower.

2006, June 30			Perf. 13½x13	
2424-2427	A428	Set of 4	4.00	4.00
2428	A428	600sh Sheet of 6, #a-f	6.00	6.00

Souvenir Sheet
Perf. 13x13½

2429	A428	500sh Sheet of 2, #a-b	1.75	1.75

Mountains — A429

Designs: 350sh, Mt. Kenya. 400sh, Udzungwa Mountain Range. 600sh, Sanje Falls, vert. 800sh, Ruwenzori Range.
No. 2434, 1000sh: a, Kiko Summit and Mawenzi, Mt. Kilimanjaro. b, Giraffe and Mt. Kilimanjaro.
No. 2435, 1000sh: a, Cattle, herder and Ol Doinyo Lengai. b, Ol Doinyo Lengai summit and crater, vert.

Perf. 13½x13¾, 13¾x13½

2006, Aug. 24				
2430-2433	A429	Set of 4	3.50	3.50

Sheets of 2, #a-b

2434-2435	A429	Set of 2	6.50	6.50

Miniature Sheet

Tazara Railway, 30th Anniv. — A430

No. 2436: a, 350sh, Map of Tanzania and Zambia, waterfall, mountain, people waving, and men signing agreement. b, 350sh, Men and train, elephant and antelope. c, 600sh, Dar es Salaam Station, sign and wreaths with Chinese inscriptions. d, 600sh, New Kapiri Mposhi Station, people near train. e, 800sh, Train, bridge and tunnel, zebra and giraffe. f, 800sh, Train on bridge, lion and lioness.

2006, Oct. 25			Perf. 12	
2436	A430	Sheet of 6, #a-f	6.00	6.00

Worldwide Fund for Nature (WWF) — A431

No. 2437 — Damaliscus lunatus jimela: a, Males butting heads. b, Close-up view of head. c, Adult and juvenile. d, Adult on mound.

2006, Nov. 24			Perf. 13¼	
2437		Horiz. or vert. strip	7.00	7.00
a.-d.		A431 600sh Any single	1.25	1.25
e.		Miniature sheet, 2 each #2437a-2437d	8.00	8.00

Zanzibar Flora and Fauna — A432

No. 2438, 1000sh: a, Coconut crab. b, Frangipane. c, Sykes monkey. d, Green sea turtle.
No. 2439, 1000sh: a, African civet. b, Four-toed elephant shrew. c, Lesser bushbaby. d, Pemba sunbird.
No. 2440, 3000sh, Protoreaster lincki. No. 2441, 3000sh, Tauraco fischeri.

2006, Nov. 24			Perf. 13¼	

Sheets of 4, #a-d

2438-2439	A432	Set of 2	13.50	13.50

Souvenir Sheets

2440-2441	A432	Set of 2	10.00	10.00

Space Achievements — A433

No. 2442 — Intl. Space Station: a, Two rows of solar panels at top, part of Space Station at bottom. b, Connection point for arms holding solar panels. c, Main junction of Space Station. d, Space Station, denomination at UR. e, Space Shuttle with cargo door open. f, Space Station, "International Space Station" just above country name.
No. 2443 — Mars Reconnaissance Orbiter: a, Mars, launch of rocket. b, Orbiter, country name in white at UR. c, Orbiter, country name in red and black at LL. d, Orbiter, country name in white at UL.
No. 2444, 2500sh, Calipso and Cloudsat satellites. No. 2445, 2500sh, Muses-C probe.

2006, June 13		Litho.	Perf. 14	
2442	A433	800sh Sheet of 6, #a-f	7.75	7.75
2443	A433	1150sh Sheet of 4, #a-d	7.50	7.50

Souvenir Sheets

2444-2445	A433	Set of 2	8.00	8.00

Phila Africa 06 Stamp Exhibition, Dar es Salaam A434

2006, Aug. 24			Perf. 13¾	
2446	A434	(700sh) multi	1.10	1.10

Souvenir Sheet

2447	A434	600sh multi	.90	.90

No. 2447 contains one 47x32mm stamp.

Independence, 45th Anniv. — A435

Designs: 350sh, Pres. Julius K. Nyerere with torch. No. 2449, 400sh, University of Dar es Salaam, horiz. No. 2450, 600sh, Vice-president Abeid A. Karume, country name in green. 800sh, Nyerere.
No. 2452, 600sh: a, Prime Minister Rashidi Mfaume Kawawa. b, Nyerere, diff. c, Karume, country name in blue. d, Pres. Ali Hassan Mwinyi. e, Pres. Benjamin W. Mkapa. f, Pres. Jakaya Mrisho Kikwete.
No. 2453, National Uhuru Monument.

2006, Dec. 9			Perf. 13½	
2448-2451	A435	Set of 4	3.50	3.50
2452	A435	600sh Sheet of 6, #a-f	5.75	5.75

Souvenir Sheet

2453	A435	400sh multi	.65	.65

Safari Hunt Animals A436

Designs: 400sh, Wild dog. 600sh, Warthog. No. 2456, 700sh, Zebras. 800sh, Female monkeys and young.

No. 2458, 700sh: a, Elephant. b, Leopard in grass. c, Buffaloes. d, Lion and lioness. e, Leopard in foliage (66x46mm).

2007, Feb. 23   *Perf. 13¾*
2454-2457 A436 Set of 4   4.00 4.00
2458 A436 700sh Sheet of 5,
            #a-e   5.75 5.75

Souvenir Sheet

2459 A436 1000sh multi   1.60 1.60

No. 2459 contains one 47x32mm stamp.

Historical
Zanzibar — A437

Designs: 400sh, Ruins. 600sh, Coral reef and fish west of Pemba, horiz. No. 2462, 700sh, Bet El Ajaib, cloves. 800sh, Coral reef and fish, diff.
No. 2464, 700sh, horiz.: a, Beach. b, Kizimbani Persian Bath. c, Maruhubi Ruins. d, Livingstone House. e, Old Dispensary. f, Cave.
No. 2465, 700sh, Colobus monkey, horiz.

2007, Apr. 26
2460-2463 A437 Set of 4   4.00 4.00
2464 A437 700sh Sheet of 6, #a-
            f   6.75 6.75

Souvenir Sheet

2465 A437 700sh multi   1.10 1.10

Activities of
World Vision
A438

Designs: No. 2466, 400sh, Food security. 600sh, Income generation and nutrition. No. 2468, 700sh, Advocating for children and rights. 800sh, Children's immunization. 1000sh, Education for development.
No. 2471, 700sh: a, Children's immunization. b, Education for development.
No. 2472, 400sh, Income generation and nutrition.

2007, May 31 Litho. Perf. 13¾x13½
2466-2470 A438 Set of 5   5.50 5.50
2471 A438 700sh Sheet of 3,
            #2468, 2471a,
            2471b   3.50 3.50

Souvenir Sheet

2472 A438 400sh multi   .65   .65

Environmental Care — A439

Designs: No. 2473, 400sh, Prof. Mark Mwandosya planting tree at Kiroka Secondary School, Morogoro. No. 2474, 500sh, Shinyanga. 700sh, Kihansi Waterfall, Nectophrynoides asperginis. 800sh, Natural regeneration of the land.
No. 2477, 400sh: a, Illegal mining. b, Tree planting, Morogoro. c, Planted trees in degraded areas. d, Traditional soil and moisture conservation method. e, Tree seedlings for rehabilitating degraded areas. f, Agriculture on steep mountains.
No. 2478, 500sh, Nguru Mountains catchment area.

2007, June 5 Litho. Perf. 14
2473-2476 A439 Set of 4   4.00 4.00
2477 A439 400sh Sheet of 6, #a-
            f   4.00 4.00

Souvenir Sheet

2478 A439 500sh multi   .80   .80

Campaign
Against
AIDS — A440

Inscriptions: No. 2479, 400sh, Let us talk with our children about AIDS. 700sh, Be faithful in your marriage. 800sh, Fight against AIDS is our duty. 1000sh, Examine your health to be free.
No. 2483, 400sh: a, Let us get education about AIDS. b, Prevent yourself from new infection. c, Let us sing to stop AIDS. d, Let us not segregate the people with AIDS.
No. 2484, 400sh, Stop AIDS, keep the promise.

2007, July 14 Litho. Perf. 13¾x13½
2479-2482 A440 Set of 4   4.50 4.50
2483 A440 400sh Sheet of 4, #a-
            d   2.50 2.50

Souvenir Sheet

2484 A440 400sh multi   .65   .65

Reign of
Aga
Khan,
50th
Anniv.
A441

Designs: 400sh, Zanzibar Madrasa Resource Center. No. 2486, 600sh, Aga Khan Hospital, Dar es Salaam, gold frame. 700sh, Lake Manyara Serena Safari Lodge. 800sh, Zanzibar Serena Inn.
No. 2489, 600sh: a, Exterior of Stone Town Cultural Center, Zanzibar. b, View from balcony of Stone Town Cultural Center. c, Medical personnel treating patient at Aga Khan Hospital. d, Aga Khan Hospital, white frame.
1000sh, Women at Zanzibar Madrasa Resource Center, vert.

2007, Aug. 18 Litho. Perf. 14½
2485-2488 A441 Set of 4   4.00 4.00
2489 A441 600sh Sheet of 4,
            #a-d   3.75 3.75

Souvenir Sheet

2490 A441 1000sh multi   1.60 1.60

Campaign
Against
Corruption
A442

Emblem of Prevention of Corruption Bureau: No. 2491, 400sh, Group of people in map of Tanzania. 500sh, Police officer escorting arrested man. 700sh, Man with briefcase as marionette, vert. 800sh, Man initiating bribe.
No. 2495: a, 400sh, Emblem with bright yellow background. b, 600sh, Man, police officer, bus.
No. 2496, 400sh, Emblem with olive green background.

2007, Oct. 9 Litho. Perf. 13¼
2491-2494 A442 Set of 4   4.25 4.25
2495 A442 Sheet of 5, #2492-
            2494, 2495a,
            2495b   5.25 5.25

Souvenir Sheet

2496 A442 400sh multi   .70   .70

Ceremonial
Costumes — A443

Designs: No. 2497, 400sh, Iringa Hehe tribesman in traditional outfit. 600sh, Haya girls in bark cloth outfit. No. 2499, 700sh, Msewe dancers in Pemba, horiz. 800sh, Wabena tribesmen in traditional ceremony, horiz.

No. 2501, 700sh: a, Maasai girls. b, Maasai dancing. c, Singida Nyaturu girl. d, Sambaa tribesman in traditional outfit. e, Wabena woman grinding corn. f, Wairaq man and wife in leather outfit.
No. 2502, 400sh, Wanyaturu girls, horiz.

2007, Oct. 9   *Perf. 14*
2497-2500 A443 Set of 4   4.50 4.50
2501 A443 700sh Sheet of 6, #a-
            f   7.50 7.50

Souvenir Sheet

2502 A443 400sh multi   .70   .70

Pope Benedict
XVI — A444

2007, Oct. 24 Litho. Perf. 13½
2503 A444 600sh multi   1.10 1.10

Printed in sheets of 8.

Wedding of Queen Elizabeth II and
Prince Philip, 60th Anniv. — A445

No. 2504: a, Queen and flowers. b, Couple.

2007, Oct. 24
2504 A445 750sh Pair, #a-b   2.60 2.60

Printed in sheets containing three of each stamp.

Princess Diana (1961-97) — A446

No. 2505 — Diana wearing: a, Purple and red hat, close-up. b, Blue and beige hat, close-up. c, Black and white hat. d, Blue and beige hat. e, Purple and red hat. f, Black and white hat, close-up.
3500sh, Blue and white hat.

2007, Oct. 24
2505 A446 750sh Sheet of 6,
            #a-f   7.75 7.75

Souvenir Sheet

2506 A446 3500sh multi   6.00 6.00

First Helicopter Flight, Cent. — A447

No. 2507: a, Hiller UH-12 Raven. b, Kamov Ka-25 Hormone. c, Cierva autogyro. d, Eurocopter Tiger.
3000sh, Bristol Sycamore.

2007, Oct. 24
2507 A447 1200sh Sheet of 4,
            #a-d   8.25 8.25

Souvenir Sheet

2508 A447 3000sh multi   5.25 5.25

Paintings by Qi Baishi (1864-1957) — A448

No. 2509: a, Wisteria and Bees. b, Pine and Cicada. c, Narcissus, Rock and Quail. d, Pumpkins.
3000sh, Begonias and Butterfly.

2007, Oct. 24   *Perf. 12½*
2509 A448 1000sh Sheet of 4,
            #a-d   7.00 7.00

Souvenir Sheet
                                    Perf. 13½
2510 A448 3000sh multi   5.25 5.25

No. 2509 contains four 32x80mm stamps.

Animals
A449

Designs: 400sh, Wildebeests and zebras grazing. No. 2512, 600sh, Lion and lioness, vert. 700sh, Lioness descending tree, vert. 800sh, Giraffes, vert.
No. 2515, 600sh: a, Leopard on tree, vert. b, Young chimpanzee, vert. c, Lioness resting on tree, vert. d, Adult male chimpanzee, vert. e, Cheetah with a kill. f, Baboons.
No. 2616, 600sh: a, Leopard and cubs. b, Impala.

Perf. 13¾x13½, 13½x13¼
2008, Jan. 30   *Litho.*
2511-2514 A449 Set of 4   4.25 4.25
2515 A449 600sh Sheet of 6, #a-
            f   6.25 6.25

Souvenir Sheet

2516 A449 600sh Sheet of 2, #a-
            b   2.10 2.10

Miniature Sheet

2008 Summer Olympics,
Beijing — A450

No. 2517: a, Basketball. b, Marathon. c, Swimming. d, Javelin.

2008, Apr. 8 Litho. Perf. 12¾
2517 A450 700sh Sheet of 4, #a-
            d   4.50 4.50

Spices of
Zanzibar
A451

Designs: 400sh, Nutmeg. No. 2519, 600sh, Man picking cloves. 700sh, Drying cloves, vert. 1000sh, Cardamom (iliki) seeds.
No. 2522, 600sh: a, Cardamom plants. b, Vanilla beans. c, Ginger. d, Cinnamon (mdalasini). e, Black pepper. f, Paprika peppers.

No. 2523, 600sh, Turmeric (binzari).

2008, Apr. 26   Litho.   *Perf. 13¼*
2518-2521 A451 Set of 4   4.50 4.50
2522 A451 600sh Sheet of 6, #a-
f   6.00 6.00

Souvenir Sheet
2523 A451 600sh multi   1.00 1.00

Marine Life — A452

Designs: 400sh, Sea turtle. No. 2525, 600sh, Dugongs. 700sh, Octopus. 1000sh, Whale shark.
No. 2528, 600sh: a, Lizard fish. b, Eel. c, Sea turtle, diff. d, Lionfish. e, Anemone fish. f, Coelacanths.
No. 2529, 600sh, Seahorses, vert.

2008, Aug. 15   *Perf. 13¾x13½*
2524-2527 A452 Set of 4   4.75 4.75
     Perf. 13¾
2528 A452 600sh Sheet of 6, #a-
f   6.25 6.25

Souvenir Sheet
2529 A452 600sh multi   1.10 1.10

No. 2528 contains six 42x32mm stamps. No. 2529 contains one 35x50mm stamp.

Visit to United States of Pope Benedict XVI — A453

2008, Sept. 3   Litho.   *Perf. 13¼*
2530 A453 1000sh multi   1.75 1.75
Printed in sheets of 4.

Miniature Sheet

Elvis Presley (1935-77) — A454

No. 2531 — Movies: a, Jailhouse Rock. b, Wild in the Country. c, Flaming Star. d, Roustabout.

2008, Sept. 3
2531 A454 1200sh Sheet of 4, #a-d   8.50 8.50

Botanical Gardens — A454a

Designs: 400sh, Flowers, Kitulo Natl. Park. No. 2531F, 600sh, Chameleon and butterfly, Amani Forest. 700sh, Monkey and waterfall, Udzungwa Mountains Forest. 1000sh, Trees, Saadani Natl. Park.
No. 2531I, 600sh: k, Flowers, Kitulo Natl. Park. l, Gazrden House, Vuga-Lushoto. m, Flowers, Udzingwa Mountains. n, Bird at Lake Rushwa, Kagera. o, Rufiji River, Selous Game Reserve. p, Rhinoceros, Ngorongoro Crater.
No. 2531J, 600sh, Bird, Kitulo Natl. Park.

     Perf. 13¾x13½
2008, Nov. 15   Litho.
2531E-2531H A454a Set of 4   4.25 4.25

2531I A454a 600sh Sheet of 6, #k-p   5.75 5.75

Souvenir Sheet
Perf. 13¾
2531J A454a 600sh multi   .95 .95
No. 2531J contains one 50x35mm stamp.

Tanzania Posts Corporation, 15th Anniv. — A455

Designs: 400sh, Window clerk. 600sh, Headquarters, vert.

Perf. 13¾x13½, 13½x13¾
2009, Jan. 20
2532-2533 A455 Set of 2   1.50 1.50

Miniature Sheet

Inauguration of US Pres. Barack Obama — A456

No. 2534 — Pres. Obama and: a, White background. b, Flag. c, Window. d, Wife, Michelle.

2009, Jan. 20   Litho.   *Perf. 11½x12*
2534 A456 1500sh Sheet of 4, #a-d   8.75 8.75

Souvenir Sheet

Signing of Millennium Challenge Compact Aid Package, 1st Anniv. — A457

No. 2535 — a, US Pres. George W. Bush. b, Tanzania Pres. Jakaya Kikwete.

2009, Jan. 27   *Perf. 13½*
2535 A457 1500sh Sheet of 2, #a-b   4.75 4.75

Space Exploration, 50th Anniv. (In 2007) — A458

No. 2536: a, 1200sh, Sputnik III. b, 1500sh, Sputnik III and clouds.
No. 2537: a, Huygens probe and technician. b, Cassini orbiter and Huygens probe in manufacturing facility. c, Titan IV-B/ Centaur launch vehicle. d, Cassini-Huygens in space. e, Saturn, Titan, Huygens probe. f, Huygens probe on Titan.
No. 2538, 1200sh: a, Sputnik II. b, Laika on Monument to the Conquerors of Space, Moscow. c, Statue of Laika. d, Laika the dog.
No. 2539, 1200sh: a, Vostok I. b, Yuri Gagarin. c, Vostok 8K72K. d, Statue of Gagarin.

No. 2540, 1200sh: a, Explorer I and technicians. b, Dr. James Van Allen, Explorer I. c, Explorer I atop Juno I. d, Explorer I in space.
No. 2541, 1200sh — Spitzer Space telescope: a, In space. b, In manufacturing facility, name in black at left. c, In manufacturing facility, name in white at right. d, In space, above Earth.
No. 2542, 3500sh, Sputnik III, horiz. No. 2543, 3500sh, Hubble Space Telescope, vert.

2009, Mar. 13   Litho.   *Perf. 14*
2536 A458 Pair, #a-b   4.25 4.25
2537 A458 750sh Sheet of 6, #a-f   6.75 6.75
Sheets of 4, #a-d
2538-2541 A458 Set of 4   29.00 29.00
Souvenir Sheets
2542-2543 A458 Set of 2   10.50 10.50
No. 2536 was printed in sheets containing 2 pairs.

Peonies A459

2009, Apr. 10   *Perf. 13¼*
2544 A459 570sh multi   .85 .85
Printed in sheets of 8.

Butterflies and Moths — A459a

Designs: 400sh, Mkuranga moth. No. 2544B, 600sh, Udzungwa butterfly, vert. 700sh, Acraea petraea. 800sh, Acraea petraea, diff.
No. 2544E, 600sh, Vanessa cardui. No. 2544F, 600sh, Axiocerses tjoane, vert.

Perf. 13¼x13½, 13½x13¼
2009, June 30
Granite Paper
2544A-2544D A459a Set of 4   3.75 3.75
Souvenir Sheets
2544E-2544F A459a Set of 2   1.90 1.90

Zanzibar Attractions — A459b

Designs: 400sh, Red colobus monkey. No. 2544H, 600sh, House of Wonders, horiz. 700sh, Carved door. 1000sh, Coffee seller.
No. 2544K, 600sh: m, Man dragging outrigger canoe. n, Zanzibar seafront, horiz. o, Giant tortoise, horiz. p, Face of red colobus monkey. q, Chake Chake's Courthouse, horiz. r, Zumari, horiz.
No. 2544L, 600sh, Zanzibar seafront and dhow, horiz.

2009, July 30   *Perf. 14*
2544G-2544J A459b Set of 4   4.25 4.25
2544K A459b 600sh Sheet of 6, #m-r   5.50 5.50
Souvenir Sheet
2544L A459b 600sh multi   .95 .95

Miniature Sheets

A460

Michael Jackson (1958-2009), Singer — A461

No. 2545: a, Dull blue background, no frame. b, Yellow background, with gray frame. c, Orange background, with gray frame. d, Blue background, with gray frame.
No. 2546 — Various photographs with: a, Black background, purple denomination. b, Blue background, purple denomination. c, Blue background, white denomination. d, Black background, white denomination.

2009, Sept. 3   *Perf. 11½x12*
2545 A460 1500sh Sheet of 4, #a-d   9.25 9.25
     Perf. 12x11½
2546 A461 1500sh Sheet of 4, #a-d   9.25 9.25

Chinese Aviation, Cent. — A462

No. 2547 — Helicopters: a, Z-5. b, Z-6. c, Z-8. d, Z-11.
2700sh, Z-9 helicopter.

2009, Nov. 12   *Perf. 14*
2547 A462 950sh Sheet of 4, #a-d   5.75 5.75
Souvenir Sheet
Perf. 14¼
2548 A462 2700sh multi   4.25 4.25
Aeropex 2009, Beijing. No. 2547 contains four 42x28mm stamps.

Youths at Play — A462a
2548A

Designs: 400sh, Girls playing Mdako game. No. 2548B, 600sh, Girls playing tennis. 700sh, Youths dancing. 1000sh, Boy on swing.

No. 2548E, 600sh: g, Boys playing Bao game. h, Boys playing basketball. i, Girls playing handball. j, Boys playing baseball. k, Boys running. l, Girls skipping rope.
No. 2548F, 600sh, Boys playing soccer.

2009, Dec. 30   **Perf. 14**
2548A-2548D A462a   Set of 4   4.00 4.00
2548E   A462a 600sh Sheet of 6,
        #g-l   5.50 5.50

Souvenir Sheet

2548F   A462a 600sh multi   .90   .90

Miniature Sheet

Chinese Zodiac Animals — A463

No. 2549: a, Tiger. b, Ox. c, Rat. d, Horse. e, Rabbit. f, Dragon. g, Snake. h, Pig. i, Dog. j, Cock. k, Monkey. l, Goat.

2010, Jan. 4   Litho.   Perf. 12¼
2549   A463 300sh Sheet of 12,
        #a-l   5.50 5.50

Souvenir Sheet

New Year 2010 (Year of the Tiger) — A464

No. 2550 — Tiger facing: a, Right. b, Left.

2010, Jan. 4   Perf. 12
2550   A464 2700sh Sheet of 2,
        #a-b   8.25 8.25

Miniature Sheets

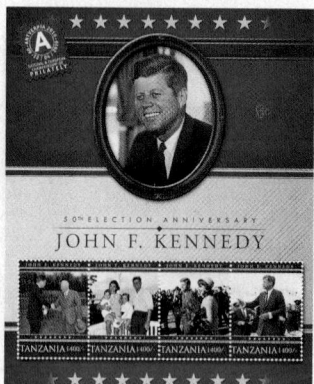

Election of Pres. John F. Kennedy, 50th Anniv. — A465

No. 2551, 1400sh — Pres. Kennedy (brown red panels) with: a, Pres. Dwight D. Eisenhower. b, Wife, Jacqueline, and children. c, Wife and crowd. d, Crowd.
No. 2552, 1400sh — Pres. Kennedy (violet blue panels): a, Shaking woman's hand. b, Leaving Air Force One with wife. c, With wife. d, Looking into space capsule.

2010, June 4   Perf. 11½
            Sheets of 4, #a-d
2551-2552 A465   Set of 2   15.50 15.50

Antverpia 2010 National and European Championship of Philately, Antwerp, Belgium (#2551).

Souvenir Sheet

Boy Scouts of America, Cent. — A466

No. 2553: a, Emblem of Charles L. Sommers National High Adventure Base, Scouts in canoe. b, Emblem of Northern Tier-Bissett National High Adventure Base, Scout skiing. c, Wmblem of Northern Tier-Rogert's Atikokan National High Adventure Base, Scout fishing.

2010, July 15   Perf. 13¼
2553   A466 1900sh Sheet of 3,
        #a-c   7.50 7.50

Miniature Sheets

A467

Princess Diana (1961-97) — A468

No. 2554 — Diana wearing: a, Pink hat with brim with red edge. b, White gown and tiara, looking left. c, Hat with flower. d, Tiara, pink dress and necklace.
No. 2555 — Diana wearing: a, Black and white hat and dress. b, Pink hat. c, White gown and tiara, looking right. d, Tiara, red dress, touching face.

2010, Oct. 14   Perf. 13¼x13
2554   A467 1400sh Sheet of 4,
        #a-d   7.50 7.50
2555   A468 1400sh Sheet of 4,
        #a-d   7.50 7.50

Miniature Sheets

Characters From Star Trek Television Shows — A469

No. 2556, 1400sh — Characters from Star Trek Voyager: a, Capt. Kathryn Janeway. b, Tuvok. c, B'Elanna Torres. d, Chakotay.

No. 2557, 1400sh, vert. — Characters from Star Trek Deep Space Nine: a, Kira Nerys. b, Capt. Benjamin Sisko. c, Quark. d, Jadzia Dax.

2010, Oct. 14   Perf. 11½x12, 12x11½
            Sheets of 4, #a-d
2556-2557 A469   Set of 2   15.00 15.00

A470

National Aeronautics and Space Administration, 50th Anniv. — A471

No. 2558: a, Earth, nose of Space Shuttle. b, Mars, fuselage of Space Shuttle. c, Jupiter. d, Neptune, astronaut.
No. 2559: a, Launch of Apollo 11, July 16, 1969. b, Launch of Space Shuttle Atlantis, May 14, 2010.

2010, Oct. 14
2558   A470 1400sh Sheet of 4,
        #a-d   7.50 7.50
            Souvenir Sheet
            Perf. 13¼x13
2559   A471 1400sh Sheet of 2,
        #a-b   3.75 3.75

Reign of Pope Benedict XVI, 5th Anniv. A472

Pope Benedict XVI: No. 2560, 1400sh, Holding censer. No. 2561, 1400sh, And St. Peter's Basilica.

2010, Dec. 23   Perf. 12
2560-2561 A472   Set of 2   3.75 3.75

Nos. 2560-2561 each were printed in sheets of 4.

Miniature Sheets

A473

Hu Jintao, President of People's Republic of China — A474

No. 2562 — Pres. Hu and: a, Chinese characters at left, English name in white, pale yellow area above first "0" in denomination. b, Chinese characters at right, English name in white, country name and denomination over pink area. c, Chinese characters at right, English name in black, denomination over pale yellow area. d, As "c," denomination over pink area. e, As "a," without pale yellow area above first "0" in denomination. f, As "b," hyphen at right over pale yellow area.
No. 2563 — Pres. Hu: a, Waving. b, Wearing red tie, with black door and knocker in background. c, Wearing blue tie, red and black background. d, Wearing red striped tie, gray background.

2010, Dec. 23
2562   A473 900sh Sheet of 6,
        #a-f   7.25 7.25
2563   A474 1100sh Sheet of 4,
        #a-d   6.00 6.00

Beijing 2010 Intl. Philatelic Exhibition.

Miniature Sheets

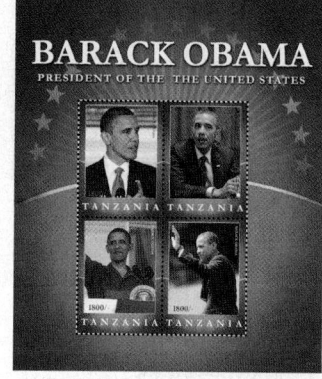

Pres. Barack Obama — A475

No. 2564, 1800sh — Pres. Obama (red and blue frames): a, With finger pointed up. b, Sitting, with arms on desk. c, Behind lectern, with arm raised. d, Waving.
No. 2565, 1800sh — Pres. Obama (purple panels at bottom): a, Writing. b, Standing, with shirt sleeves rolled up. c, Standing, wearing suit and red tie. d, Saluting.

2010, Dec. 23   Litho.
            Sheets of 4, #a-d
2564-2565 A475   Set of 2   19.50 19.50

Start of Chimpanzee Research at Gombe by Jane Goodall, 50th Anniv. — A476

No. 2566, 2500sh: a, Black-and-white photograph of Goodall with chimpanzee. b, Goodall writing. c, Chimpanzees embracing.

No. 2567, 2500sh: a, Goodall shoveling dirt. b, Local people embracing. c, Goodall holding chimpanzee.

No. 2568, 4000sh, Goodall following chimpanzee in forest. No. 2569, 4000sh, Goodall holding camera, looking at chimpanzee. No. 2570, 4000sh, Goodall extending hand to three chimpanzees. No. 2571, 4000sh, Goodall in forest. No. 2572, 4000sh, Chimpanzee looking at ant-covered stick. No. 2573, 4000sh, Goodall holding binoculars, vert. No. 2574, 4000sh, Two chimpanzees, vert.

2010, Dec. 23   **Perf. 12**
Sheets of 3, #a-c
2566-2567 A476 Set of 2   20.50 20.50
Souvenir Sheets
2568-2574 A476 Set of 7   38.00 38.00

Souvenir Sheet

New Year 2011 (Year of the Rabbit) — A477

No. 2575: a, Rabbit standing on hind legs, word "Rabbit" hyphenated. b, Rabbit on all four legs, word "Rabbit" not hyphenated.

2010, Dec. 23
2575 A477 2250sh Sheet of 2,
    #a-b   6.25 6.25

Pan African Postal Union, 30th Anniv. A478

Emblem and: 400sh, Electronic money transfer. 500sh, Integrating physical mail into the digital world. 700sh, Track and trace of postal items.

600sh, Post office internet café service.

2010, Jan. 18   **Perf. 14½**
2576-2578 A478 Set of 3   2.40 2.40
Souvenir Sheet
2579 A478 600sh multi   .90 .90

Wild Animals — A479

Designs: 400sh, Chimpanzees. 500sh, Lion and lioness, horiz. No. 2582, 600sh, Grant's red colobus monkeys, horiz. 700sh, Elephants. 800sh, Gnus, horiz. 1000sh, Waterbuck. 1800sh, Elephant looking for foliage. 2000sh, Zebras, horiz. 2500sh, Hunting dogs, horiz. 3000sh, Buffalo, horiz. 5000sh, Zebras and gazelles grazing, horiz.

No. 2591, 600sh, horiz.: a, Kirk's red colobus monkey. b, Lioness guarding her cubs. c, Udzungwa monkey. d, Female kongoni and juvenile. e, Female hippopotamus with juvenile. f, Leopard with cub.

No. 2592, 600sh, Male giraffe, horiz.

2010, Oct. 28   **Perf. 14**
2580-2590 A479 Set of 11   25.00 25.00
2591 A479 600sh Sheet of 6,
    #a-f   5.00 5.00
Souvenir Sheet
2592 A479 600sh multi   .80 .80

SEMI-POSTAL STAMPS

Natl. Solidarity Walk — SP1

1988, July 1   **Litho.**   **Perf. 14½**
B1 SP1 2sh +1sh Flag, crowd   .70 .70
B2 SP1 3sh +1sh Map, Pres.
    Mwinyi   .70 .70
Souvenir Sheet
B3 SP1 50sh +1sh Flag, Pres.
    Mwinyi   1.75 1.75
Surtax for Chama Cha Mapinduzi party activities.

Natl. Solidarity Walk — SP2

1989, July 1   **Litho.**   **Perf. 14½**
B4 SP2 5sh +1sh Party flag   .45 .45
B5 SP2 10sh +1sh Pres. Mwinyi,
    walk   .45 .45
Souvenir Sheet
B6 SP2 50sh +1sh Pres. Mwinyi   1.40 1.40

Natl. Solidarity Walk SP3

Designs: 4sh + 1sh, Pres. Mwinyi marching with crowd. 9sh + 1sh, Crowd around party flag. 13sh + 1sh, Pres. Mwinyi. 30sh + 1sh, Pres. Mwinyi planting tree. No. B11, Pres. Mwinyi sorting cloves. No. B12, Handshake across map, vert.

1991-92   **Litho.**   **Perf. 13½**
B7 SP3 4sh +1sh multicolored
    ('92)   .75 .75
B8 SP3 9sh +1sh multicolored   1.00 1.00
B9 SP3 13sh +1sh multicolored   1.00 1.00
B10 SP3 30sh +1sh multicolored
    ('92)   1.75 1.75
    Nos. B7-B10 (4)   4.50 4.50

Souvenir Sheets
Perf. 12½
B11 SP3 50sh +1sh multicolored   3.00 3.00
B12 SP3 50sh +1sh multicolored   2.40 2.40
Issued: Nos. B8-B9, 7/6/90. Nos. B7, B10, 7/5/91.

POSTAGE DUE STAMPS

D1   D2

Perf. 13¾x14
1978, July 31   **Litho.**   **Unwmk.**
J1 D1 5c red   .75 1.00
J2 D1 10c green   .75 1.00
J3 D1 20c dark blue   .75 1.00
J4 D1 30c reddish brown   .75 1.00
J5 D1 40c bright rose lilac   .75 1.00
J6 D1 1sh orange   1.25 2.25
    Nos. J1-J6 (6)   5.00 7.25

1967, Jan. 3   **Perf. 14x13½**
J1a D1 5c red   .35 3.00
J2a D1 10c green   .35 3.00
J3a D1 20c dark blue   .55 5.25
J4a D1 30c reddish brown   .90 7.50
J5a D1 40c bright rose lilac   1.25 10.50
J6a D1 1sh orange ('71)   3.25 12.50
    Nos. J1a-J6a (6)   6.65 51.75

1969-71   **Perf. 14x15**
J1b D1 5c red   .70 3.00
J2b D1 10c green   .70 3.00
J3b D1 20c dark blue   1.50 5.25
J4b D1 30c reddish brown   2.10 7.50
J5b D1 40c bright rose lilac   2.75 10.50
J6b D1 1sh orange ('71)   7.25 22.50
    Nos. J1b-J6b (6)   15.00 51.75

1973, Dec. 12   **Perf. 15**
J1c D1 5c red   .40 3.25
J2c D1 10c green   .40 3.25
J3c D1 20c dark blue   .60 6.25
J4c D1 30c reddish brown   .90 9.50
J5c D1 40c bright rose lilac   1.25 13.00
J6c D1 1sh orange   3.00 32.50
    Nos. J1c-J6c (6)   6.55 67.75

1984?   **Perf. 14¾x14**
J1d D1 5c red brown   —   —
J2d D1 10c green   —   —
J4d D1 30c reddish brown   —   —

Additional stamps of this type with this perforation have been reported. The editors would like to examine any examples.

1990   **Litho.**   **Perf. 15x14**
J7 D2 50c dark green   .35 .35
J8 D2 80c bright blue   .35 .35
J9 D2 1sh orange brown   .35 .35
J10 D2 2sh light olive green   .35 .35
J11 D2 3sh purple   .35 .35
J12 D2 5sh gray   .35 .35
J13 D2 10sh brown   .35 .35
J14 D2 20sh bister   .35 .35
    Nos. J7-J14 (8)   2.80 2.80

OFFICIAL STAMPS

Nos. 5-9, 11, 13 and 16 Overprinted: "OFFICIAL"
Perf. 14x14½, 14½x14
1965, Dec. 9   **Photo.**   **Unwmk.**
Size: 21x17½mm, 17½x21mm
O1 A2 5c orange & ultra   .25 .25
O2 A2 10c multicolored   .25 .25
O3 A3 15c grn bl, brn & buff   .25 .25
O4 A2 20c blue & brown   .25 .25
O5 A2 30c black & red brn   .25 .25
O6 A2 50c yellow grn & blk   .25 .25
Perf. 14½
Size: 41½x25
O7 A2 1sh multicolored   .30 .25
O8 A2 5sh bl, brt grn & red
    brn   1.50 1.00
    Nos. O1-O8 (8)   3.30 2.75

Overprint size: 17mm on 5c, 10c, 20c, 50c. 14mm on 15c, 30c. 29x3½mm on 1sh, 5sh.
The overprint was also applied in 1967 in Dar es Salaam to 50c, 1sh and 5sh. Size: 29x3mm.

Nos. 19-23, 25, 27 and 30 Overprinted

Fish in Natural Colors
Size: 21x17½mm
Overprint Litho., 17mm Wide
1967, Dec. 9   **Photo.**   **Perf. 14x14½**
O9 A4 5c black & citron   .50 1.25
O10 A4 10c brown & olive   .50 .60
O11 A4 15c brown & blue   .50 .40
O12 A4 20c brown & dk blue
    grn   .50 .40
O13 A4 30c black & yel grn   .50 .40
O14 A4 50c black & dull bl grn   .50 1.00
Perf. 14½
Size: 41x25mm
Overprint 29mm Wide
O15 A4 1sh brown & multi   1.00 2.00
O16 A4 5sh brown & blue grn   4.00 8.00
    Nos. O9-O16 (8)   8.00 14.05

Overprint Typo., 17½mm Wide
1970-73
O9a A4 5c black & citron   .55 .55
O10a A4 10c brown & olive   .55 .55
O12a A4 20c brn & dk bl grn   .55 .55
O13a A4 30c blk & yel grn   .80 .55
O13B A4 40c multicolored ('73)
    Nos. O9a-O13a (4)   2.45 2.20

The overprint was also applied in 1973 to 15c, 50c, 1sh (28mm wide), and 5sh.

Nos. 35-36, 38, 40-41, 43-47 Overprinted

a   b

1973, Dec. 10   **Photo.**   **Perf. 14½x14**
O17 A5(a) 5c multicolored   1.10 4.00
O18 A5(a) 10c multicolored   1.40 .70
O19 A5(a) 20c multicolored   1.50 .70
O20 A5(a) 40c multicolored   2.25 .70
O21 A5(a) 50c multicolored   2.25 .70
O22 A5(a) 70c multicolored   2.25 .70
Perf. 14½
O23 A6(b) 1sh multicolored   3.25 .80
O24 A6(b) 1.50sh multicolored   3.75 4.00
O25 A6(b) 2.50sh multicolored   5.50 6.00
O26 A6(b) 5sh multicolored   7.50 10.00
    Nos. O17-O26 (10)   30.75 28.30

A larger overprint (17½mm wide instead of 14½mm) was applied locally to 10c, 20c, 40c, and 50c.
Provisional use of some values for regular postage is known.

Nos. 161-171 Overprinted

1980, Oct. 1   **Perf. 14**
O27 A21 10c multicolored   .70 .70
O28 A21 20c multicolored   .70 .70
O29 A21 40c multicolored   .70 .70
O30 A21 50c multicolored   .70 .70
O31 A21 75c multicolored   .70 .70
O32 A21 80c multicolored   .70 .70
Perf. 14½
O33 A21 1sh multicolored   .70 .70
O33A A21 1.50sh multicolored
O34 A21 2sh multicolored   1.40 1.40
O35 A21 3sh multicolored   1.90 1.90
O36 A21 5sh multicolored   3.25 3.25
    Nos. O27-O33,O34-O36 (10) 11.45 11.45

Overprint measures 13mm on Nos. O33-O36; reads up or down.

Nos. 606-614 Inscribed "OFFICIAL"
1990-91   **Litho.**   **Perf. 14**
O37 A99 5sh multi   .60 .60
O38 A99 9sh multi   .60 .60
O39 A99 13sh multi   .60 .60

O40	A99	15sh multi	.60	.60
O41	A99	20sh multi	.90	.90
O42	A99	25sh multi	1.00	1.00
O42A	A99	30sh multi ('91)	1.40	1.40
O43	A99	40sh multi	1.75	1.75
O44	A99	70sh multi	3.00	3.00
O45	A99	100sh multi	4.50	4.50
		Nos. O37-O45 (10)	14.95	14.95

Inscription on Nos. O37-O42A is 15½mm long. Insription on Nos. O43-O45 is 19mm long.

Nos. 1565, 1566, 1568, 1570, 1571, and 1572 Overprinted

1997 (?)		Litho.	Perf. 14½x15
O47	A262	100sh multi	— —
O48	A262	140sh multi	— —
O49	A262	200sh multi	— —
O50	A262	260sh multi	— —
O51	A262	300sh multi	— —
O52	A262	380sh multi	— —

The editors suspect there are additional stamps in this set, and would like to examine any examples.

TETE

'tāt-ə

LOCATION — In southeastern Africa between Nyasaland and Southern Rhodesia
GOVT. — A district of the Portuguese East Africa Colony
AREA — 46,600 sq. mi. (approx.)
POP. — 367,000 (approx.)
CAPITAL — Tete

This district was formerly a part of Zambezia. Stamps of Mozambique replaced those of Tete. See Mozambique.

100 Centavos = 1 Escudo

Vasco da Gama Issue of Various Portuguese Colonies Surcharged

1913		Unwmk.	Perf. 12½, 16
On Stamps of Macao			
1	CD20	¼c on ½a bl grn	5.00	5.00
2	CD21	½c on 1a red	1.75	2.10
3	CD22	1c on 2a red vio	1.75	2.10
4	CD23	2½c on 4a yel grn	1.75	2.10
5	CD24	5c on 8a dk blue	1.75	2.10
6	CD25	7½c on 12a vio brn	2.40	3.00
7	CD26	10c on 16a bis brn	1.75	2.10
8	CD27	15c on 24a bister	1.75	2.10
		Nos. 1-8 (8)	17.90	20.60
On Stamps of Portuguese Africa			
9	CD20	¼c on 2½r bl grn	1.75	2.10
10	CD21	½c on 5r red	1.75	2.10
11	CD22	1c on 10r red vio	1.75	2.10
12	CD23	2½c on 25r yel grn	1.75	2.10
13	CD24	5c on 50r dk blue	1.75	2.10
14	CD25	7½c on 75r vio brn	2.40	3.00
15	CD26	10c on 100r bis brn	1.75	2.10
16	CD27	15c on 150r bister	1.75	2.10
		Nos. 9-16 (8)	14.65	17.70
On Stamps of Timor			
17	CD20	¼c on ½a bl grn	1.75	2.10
18	CD21	½c on 1a red	1.75	2.10
19	CD22	1c on 2a red vio	1.75	2.10
a.		Inverted overprint	30.00	30.00
20	CD23	2½c on 4a yel grn	1.75	2.10
21	CD24	5c on 8a dk blue	1.75	2.10
22	CD25	7½c on 12a vio brn	2.40	3.00
23	CD26	10c on 16a bis brn	1.75	2.10
24	CD27	15c on 24a bister	1.75	2.10
		Nos. 17-24 (8)	14.65	17.70
		Nos. 1-24 (24)	47.20	56.00

Common Design Types pictured following the introduction.

Ceres — A1

1914		Typo.	Perf. 15x14
Name and Value in Black			
25	A1	¼c olive brn	1.40	2.25
26	A1	½c black	1.40	2.25
27	A1	1c blue grn	1.40	2.25
28	A1	1½c lilac brn	1.40	2.25
29	A1	2c carmine	1.40	2.25
30	A1	2½c light vio	1.40	2.25
31	A1	5c deep blue	1.40	2.25
32	A1	7½c yel brn	3.00	3.25
33	A1	8c slate	3.00	3.25
34	A1	10c org brn	3.00	4.00
35	A1	15c plum	4.00	4.50
36	A1	20c yel green	4.00	4.50
37	A1	30c brn, *green*	4.00	4.50
38	A1	40c brn, *pink*	5.00	7.00
39	A1	50c org, *salmon*	8.00	9.00
40	A1	1e grn, *blue*	10.00	10.00
		Nos. 25-40 (16)	53.80	65.75

THAILAND

'tī-,land

(Siam)

LOCATION — Western part of the Malay peninsula in southeastern Asia
GOVT. — Republic
AREA — 198,250 sq. mi.
POP. — 60,609,046 (1999 est.)
CAPITAL — Bangkok

32 Solot = 16 Atts = 8 Sio =
4 Sik = 2 Fuang = 1 Salung
4 Salungs = 1 Tical
100 Satangs (1909) = 1 Tical
= 1 Baht (1912)

Catalogue values for unused stamps in this country are for Never Hinged items, beginning with Scott 264 in the regular postage section, Scott B34 in the semipostal section, Scott C20 in the airpost section, and Scott O1 in the official section.

Watermarks

Wmk. 176 — Chakra

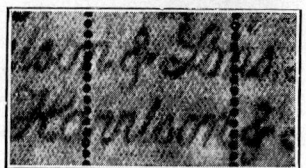

Wmk. 233 — Harrison & Sons, London in Script Letters

Wmk. 299 — Thai Characters and Wavy Lines

Wmk. 329 — Zigzag Lines

Wmk. 334 — Rectangles

Wmk. 340 — Alternating Interlaced Wavy Lines

Wmk. 356 — POSTAGE

Wmk. 368 — JEZ Multiple

Wmk. 371 — Wavy Lines

Wmk. 374 — Circles and Crosses

Wmk. 375 — Letters

Wmk. 377 — Interlocking Circles

Wmk. 385 — CARTOR

Wmk. 387 — Squares and Rectangles

King Chulalongkorn
A1   A2

A4

Perf. 14½, 15

1883, Aug. 4	Unwmk.	Engr.
1 A1 1sol blue	14.00	14.00
b. Imperf., pair		4,500.
2 A1 1att carmine	16.00	16.00
3 A1 1sio vermilion	24.00	24.00
4 A2 1sik yellow	15.00	19.00
5 A4 1sa orange	62.50	62.50
a. 1sa ocher	70.00	70.00
Nos. 1-5 (5)	131.50	135.50

There are three types of No. 1, differing mainly in the background of the small oval at the top.

A 1 fuang red, of similar design to the foregoing, was prepared but not placed in use. Value, $1,500.

For surcharges see Nos. 6-8, 19.

No. 1 Handstamp Surcharged in Red

 a

 b

 c

1 Tical *d*   **1 Tical** *e*

1885, July 1		
6 A1 (a) 1t on 1sol blue	475.	475.
7 A1 (b) 1t on 1sol blue	375.	375.
c. "1" inverted	1,100.	1,100.
8 A1 (c) 1t on 1sol blue	500.	500.

Surcharges of Nos. 6-8 have been counterfeited.

Types "d" and "e" are typeset *official reprints.*

As is usual with handstamps, double impressions, etc., exist.

King Chulalongkorn — A7

1887-91 Typo. Wmk. 176	Perf. 14	
11 A7 1a green ('91)	6.50	2.00
12 A7 2a green & car	6.50	2.00
13 A7 3a grn & blue	12.00	4.00
14 A7 4a grn & org brn	12.00	4.75
15 A7 8a green & yel	12.00	7.00
16 A7 12a lilac & car	17.50	3.50
17 A7 24a lilac & blue	24.00	4.00
18 A7 64a lil & org brn	87.50	29.00
Nos. 11-18 (8)	178.00	56.25

The design of No. 11 has been redrawn and differs in many minor details from Nos. 12-18.

Issue dates: Nos. 12-18, Apr. 1; No. 11, Feb.

For surcharges see Nos. 20-69, 109, 111, 126.

No. 3 Handstamp Surcharged

1889, Aug. Unwmk.	Perf. 15	
19 A1 1a on 1sio	19.00	19.00

Three different handstamps were used. Doubles, etc. exist.

Nos. 12 and 13 Handstamp Surcharged

1889-90 Wmk. 176	Perf. 14	
20 A7 1a on 2a	4.00	3.00
a. "1" omitted	275.00	275.00
c. 1st Siamese character invtd.		
d. First Siamese character omitted	300.00	300.00
21 A7 1a on 3a ('90)	9.00	9.00
a. Inverted "1"	150.00	150.00

For surcharge see No. 29.

22 A7 1a on 2a grn & car	475.00	475.00

24 A7 1a on 2a grn & car	225.00	225.00

25 A7 1a on 2a grn & car	1,000.	1,000.

26 A7 1a on 3a grn & bl		

Some authorities consider No. 26 a forgery. Doubles, etc., exist in this issue.
Issue dates: Nov. 1889. Sept. 1890.

No. 13 Handstamp Surcharged

1891

27 A7 2a on 3a grn & bl	65.00	65.00

28 A7 2a on 3a grn & bl	55.00	55.00
a. Double surcharge	250.00	250.00
b. "2" omitted	250.00	

No. 21 with Additional 2 Att Surcharge

29 A7 2a on 1a on 3a grn & bl	1,500.	1,500.

On No. 29 the 2a surcharge consists of Siamese numeral like No. 27 and English numeral like No. 28.

Most examples of No. 29 show attempts to remove the "1" of the first surcharge.

Typeset Surcharge

30 A7 2a on 3a grn & bl	45.00	45.00

There are 7 types of this surcharge in the setting.
Issued: #27-28, Jan.; #29, Feb.; #30, Mar.

No. 17 Handstamp Surcharged

 f   g

1892, Oct.

33 A7 (f) 4a on 24a lil & bl	50.00	50.00
34 A7 (g) 4a on 24a lil & bl	35.00	35.00

Surcharges exist double on Nos. 33-34 and inverted on No. 33.

Nos. 33-34 Handstamp Surcharged in English

1892, Nov.

35 A7 4a on 24a lil & bl	9.00	9.00
c. Inverted "s"	45.00	45.00

36 A7 4a on 24a lil & bl	14.00	10.00
a. Inverted "s"	40.00	40.00

37 A7 4a on 24a lil & bl	12.50	12.50

38 A7 4a on 24a lil & bl	15.00	15.00

Numerous inverts., doubles, etc., exist.
Nos. 35 and 37 are surcharged examples of No. 33. Nos. 36 and 38 are surcharged examples of No. 34. The "4 atts" surcharge is small on Nos. 35 and 36, and large on Nos. 37 and 38.

Nos. 18 and 17 Typeset Srchd. in English (Shown) and Siamese

1894

39 A7 1a on 64a lil & org brn	3.50	3.50
a. Inverted "s"	45.00	45.00
b. Inverted surcharge	900.00	900.00
d. Italic "s"	60.00	60.00
e. Italic "1"	60.00	60.00

40 A7 1a on 64a lil & org brn	2.00	2.00
a. Inverted capital "S" added to the surcharge	200.00	200.00

 h   j

 k   l

 m

2 Atts. *i*

41 A7 (h) 2a on 64a	26.00	26.00
a. Inverted "s"	42.50	42.50
b. Double surcharge	100.00	100.00
42 A7 (i) 2a on 64a	3,000.	3,000.
43 A7 (j) 2a on 64a	62.50	62.50
44 A7 (k) 2a on 64a	37.50	37.50
45 A7 (l) 2a on 64a	57.50	57.50
46 A7 (m) 2a on 64a	3.00	3.00
a. "Att.s".	45.00	45.00

Nos. 41-46 were in one plate of 120 subjects. The quantities were: h, 38; i, 1; j, 8; k, 18; l, 11 and m, 44.

1894, Oct. 12

47 A7 1a on 64a	3.00	3.00
a. Surcharged on face and back	150.00	
b. As "a," surcharge on back inverted	200.00	
c. Double surcharge	475.00	
d. Inverted surcharge	500.00	
e. Siamese surcharge omitted	400.00	

See No. 67.

48 A7 2a on 64a	3.00	3.00
a. "Att"	35.00	35.00
b. Inverted surcharge	300.00	300.00
c. Surch. on face and back	400.00	400.00
d. Surcharge on back inverted	400.00	400.00
e. Double surcharge	300.00	300.00
f. Double surch., one inverted	1,100.	1,100.
g. Inverted "s"	42.50	42.50

1895, July 23
49	A7	10a on 24a lil & bl		7.00	2.00
a.		Inverted "s"		45.00	45.00
b.		Surch. on face and back		175.00	175.00
c.		Surcharge on back inverted		175.00	175.00

No. 16 Surcharged in English (Shown) and Siamese

1896
50	A7	4a on 12a lil & car		15.00	8.00
a.		Inverted "s"		50.00	50.00
b.		Surcharged on face and back		175.00	175.00
c.		Double surcharge on back		175.00	175.00

Two types of surcharge.

Nos. 16-18 Surcharged in English (Shown) and Siamese Antique Surcharges

1 Atts.
a

b

c

d

e

f

Atts.
Antique Letters

Atts.
Roman Letters

1898-99
51	A7	(a) 1a on 12a		360.00	360.00
52	A7	(b) 1a on 12a		18.00	7.00
53	A7	(c) 2a on 64a ('99)		30.00	9.00
54	A7	(d) 3a on 12a		12.00	4.00
a.		Double surcharge		350.00	350.00
55	A7	(e) 4a on 12a		12.00	5.00
a.		Double surcharge		350.00	350.00
56	A7	(e) 4a on 24a ('99)		40.00	14.00
57	A7	(f) 10a on 24a ('99)		825.00	825.00
		Nos. 51-57 (7)		*1,297.*	*1,224.*

Roman Surcharges

h   i

---

j

k

l

1 Atts.
g

58	A7	(g) 1a on 12a		450.00	450.00
59	A7	(h) 1a on 12a		45.00	20.00
60	A7	(i) 2a on 64a ('99)		35.00	10.00
61	A7	(j) 3a on 12a		85.00	19.00
62	A7	(k) 4a on 12a		40.00	17.00
a.		Double surcharge		175.00	175.00
b.		No period after "Atts."		35.00	35.00
63	A7	(k) 4a on 24a ('99)		60.00	29.00
64	A7	(l) 10a on 24a ('99)		750.00	750.00
		Nos. 58-64 (7)		*1,465.*	*1,292.*

In making the settings to surcharge Nos. 51 to 64 two fonts were mixed.

Antique and Roman letters are frequently found on the same stamp. Such stamps sell for more.

Issue dates: Nos. 54-55, 61-62, Feb. 22. Nos. 51-52, 58-59, June 4. Nos. 56-57, 63-64, Oct. 3.

Nos. 16 and 18 Surcharged in English (Shown) and Siamese Surcharged

m   n

o   p

r

2 Atts.
r

1894-99
65	A7	(m) 1a on 12a		20.00	6.00
66	A7	(n) 1a on 12a		20.00	6.00
a.		Inverted "1"		150.00	150.00
b.		Inverted 1st "t"		150.00	150.00
67	A7	(o) 1a on 64a		5.00	5.00
68	A7	(p) 2a on 64a		24.00	8.00
a.		"1 Atts."		500.00	500.00
69	A7	(r) 2a on 64a		24.00	8.00
		Nos. 65-69 (5)		*93.00*	*33.00*

Issued: No. 67, 10/12/94; others, 2/14/99. See No. 47.

A13   A14

1899, Oct.   Typo.   Unwmk.
70	A13	1a dull green		200.	85.
71	A13	2a dl grn & rose		350.	85.
72	A13	3a carmine & blue		600.	125.
73	A13	4a black & grn		2,200.	325.
74	A13	10a carmine & grn		2,500.	500.
		Nos. 70-74 (5)		*5,850.*	*1,120.*

The King rejected Nos. 70-74 in 1897, but some were released by mistake to three post

---

offices in Oct. 1899. Used values are for stamps canceled to order at Korat in Dec. 1899. Values for postally used stamps are listed in the Scott Classic Specialized catalog.

1899-1904
75	A14	1a gray green		2.00	1.00
76	A14	2a yellow green		2.25	1.25
77	A14	2a scarlet & bl		4.00	2.00
78	A14	3a red & blue		7.00	2.00
79	A14	3a green		20.00	12.00
80	A14	4a dark rose		4.00	1.50
81	A14	4a vio brn & rose		8.00	2.00
82	A14	6a dk rose		35.00	14.00
83	A14	8a dk grn & org		9.00	2.00
84	A14	10a ultra		9.00	3.00
85	A14	12a brn vio & rose		40.00	2.00
86	A14	14a ultra		23.00	18.00
87	A14	24a brn vio & bl		375.00	29.00
88	A14	28a vio brn & bl		25.00	25.00
89	A14	64a brn vio & org brn		70.00	11.00
		Nos. 75-89 (15)		*633.25*	*125.75*

Two types of 1a differ in size and shape of Thai "1" are in drawing of spandrel ornaments. Issue dates: 6a, 14a, 28a, Nos. 77, 79, 81, Jan. 1, 1904; others, Sept. 1899.

For surcharges see Nos. 90-91, 112, 125, 127.

Nos. 78 and 85 With Typewritten Srch. of 6 or 7 Siamese Characters (1 line) in Violet

1902
78a	A14	2a on 3a		*5,000.*	*5,250.*
85a	A14	10a on 12a		*5,000.*	*5,250.*

Nos. 78a and 85a were authorized provisionals, surcharged and issued by the Battambang postmaster.

Nos. 86 and 88 Surcharged in Black

1905, Feb.
90	A14	1a on 14a		10.00	10.00
a.		No period after "Att"		45.00	45.00
b.		Double surcharge		125.00	125.00
91	A14	2a on 28a		12.00	12.00
a.		Double surcharge		125.00	125.00
b.		No period after "Att"		45.00	45.00

King Chulangkorn A15

King Chulalongkorn A16

1905-08   Engr.
92	A15	1a orange & green		2.50	1.00
93	A15	2a violet & slate		3.00	1.00
94	A15	2a green ('08)		11.00	4.00
95	A15	3a green		4.00	2.00
96	A15	3a vio & sl ('08)		12.00	6.25
97	A15	4a gray & red		6.00	1.50
98	A15	4a car & rose ('08)		9.50	2.00
99	A15	5a carmine & rose		8.00	3.00
100	A15	8a blk & ol bis		8.75	1.50
101	A15	9a blue ('08)		23.50	9.00
102	A15	12a blue		18.00	4.00
103	A15	18a red brn ('08)		60.00	22.50
104	A15	24a red brown		34.00	8.00
105	A15	1t dp bl & brn org		45.00	10.00
		Nos. 92-105 (14)		*245.25*	*75.75*

Issue dates: Dec. 1905, Apr. 1, 1908. For surcharges and overprints see Nos. 110, 113-117, 128-138, 161-162, B15, B21.

1907, Apr. 24   Black Surcharge
106	A16	10t gray green		600.00	100.00
107	A16	20t gray green		4,750.	350.00
108	A16	40t gray green		3,400.	475.00
		Nos. 106-108 (3)		*8,750.*	*925.00*

Counterfeits of Nos. 106-108 exist. In the genuine, the surcharged figures correspond to the Siamese value inscriptions on the basic revenue stamps.

No. 17 Surcharged

1907, Dec. 16
109	A7	1a on 24a lil & bl		4.50	1.50
a.		Double surcharge		400.00	

No. 99 Surcharged

1908, Sept.
110	A15	4a on 5a car & rose		11.00	4.00

The No. 110 surcharge is found in two spacings of the numerals: normally 15mm apart, and a narrow, scarcer spacing of 13½mm.

Nos. 17 and 84 Surcharged in Black

| | | | | | |
|---|---|---|---|---|---|
| 111 | A7 | 2a on 24a lil & bl | | 4.50 | 1.20 |
| a. | | Inverted surcharge | | 325.00 | 325.00 |
| 112 | A14 | 9a on 10a ultra | | 13.50 | 5.00 |
| a. | | Inverted surcharge | | 325.00 | 325.00 |

Jubilee Issue

Nos. 92, 95, 110, 100 and 103 Overprinted in Black or Red

1908, Nov. 11
113	A15	1a		3.25	1.60
a.		Siamese date "137" instead of "127"		950.00	950.00
b.		Pair, one without ovpt.			
114	A15	3a		5.50	3.25
115	A15	4a on 5a		5.50	3.25
a.		Horiz. pair, imperf. btwn.		500.00	
116	A15	8a (R)		21.00	21.00
117	A15	18a		32.50	24.00
		Nos. 113-117 (5)		*67.75*	*53.10*

40th year of the reign of King Chulalongkorn.
Nos. 113 to 117 exist with a small "i" in "Jubilee."

Statue of King Chulalongkorn A19

1908, Nov. 11   Engr.   Perf. 13½
118	A19	1t green & vio		52.50	8.00
119	A19	2t red vio & org		72.50	20.00
120	A19	3t pale ol & bl		105.00	16.00
121	A19	5t dl vio & dk grn		160.00	27.50
122	A19	10t bister & car		*1,250.*	87.50

123	A19	20t gray & red brn	525.00	87.50
124	A19	40t sl bl & blk brn	525.00	300.00
		Nos. 118-124 (7)	2,690.	546.50

The inscription at the foot of the stamps reads: "Coronation Commemoration-Forty-first year of the reign-1908."

Stamps of 1887-1904 Surcharged

1909   **Perf. 14**

125	A14	6s on 6a dk rose	2.50	2.00
126	A7	14s on 12a lil & car	110.00	100.00
127	A14	14s on 14a ultra	20.00	18.00
		Nos. 125-127 (3)	132.50	120.00

Nos. 92-102 Surcharged with Bar and

1909, Aug. 15

128	A15	2s on 1a #92	2.50	1.20
129	A15	2s on 2a #93	60.00	60.00
130	A15	2s on 2a #94	2.75	1.20
a.		"2" omitted	85.00	
131	A15	3s on 3a #95	12.00	7.50
132	A15	3s on 3a #96	4.50	1.00
133	A15	6s on 4a #97	64.00	64.00
134	A15	6s on 4a #98	8.00	2.00
135	A15	6s on 5a #99	12.00	8.75
136	A15	12s on 8a #100	7.00	1.40
137	A15	14s on 9a #101	11.00	3.00
138	A15	14s on 12a #102	22.50	21.00
		Nos. 128-138 (11)	206.25	171.05

King Chulalongkorn — A20

1910   **Engr.**   **Perf. 14x14½**

139	A20	2s org & green	2.50	1.50
140	A20	3s green	2.50	1.50
141	A20	6s carmine	6.50	2.50
142	A20	12s blk & ol brn	12.00	2.50
143	A20	14s blue	20.00	2.50
144	A20	28s red brown	47.50	10.00
		Nos. 139-144 (6)	91.00	20.50

Issue dates: 12s, June 5. Others, May 5.
For surcharges see Nos. 163, 223-224.

A21   King Vajiravudh — A22

Printed at the Imperial Printing Works, Vienna

1912   **Perf. 14½**

145	A21	2s brown orange	3.25	1.20
a.		Vert. pair, imperf. btwn.	500.00	500.00
b.		Horiz. pair, imperf. btwn.	500.00	500.00
146	A21	3s yellow green	3.25	1.20
a.		Horiz. pair, imperf. btwn.	500.00	500.00
b.		Vert. pair, imperf. btwn.	500.00	500.00
147	A21	6s carmine rose	4.00	1.50
148	A21	12s gray blk & brn	5.50	2.00
149	A21	14s ultramarine	7.00	2.50
150	A21	28s chocolate	20.00	12.00
151	A21	1b blue & blk	30.00	2.00
a.		Vert. pair, imperf. btwn.	1,250.	1,250.
b.		Horiz. pair, imperf. btwn.	1,250.	1,250.
152	A22	2b car rose & ol brn	35.00	4.00
153	A22	3b yel grn & bl blk	40.00	6.50
154	A22	5h vio & blk	50.00	12.00

155	A22	10b ol grn & vio brn	300.00	95.00
156	A22	20b sl bl & red brn	475.00	95.00
		Nos. 145-156 (12)	973.00	234.90

See Nos. 164-175.
For surcharges and overprints see Nos. 157-160, 176-186, 206, B1-B14, B16-B20, B22, B31-B33.

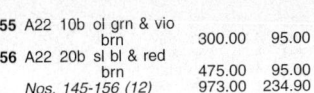

Nos. 147-150 Surcharged in Red or Blue

1914-15

157	A21	2s on 14s (R) ('15)	2.75	.70
a.		Vert. pair, imperf. btwn.	900.00	900.00
b.		Double surcharge	62.50	40.00
158	A21	5s on 6s (Bl)	5.00	.50
a.		Horiz. pair, imperf. btwn.	900.00	900.00
b.		Double surcharge	67.50	67.50
159	A21	10s on 12s (R)	5.00	.50
a.		Double surcharge	67.50	67.50
160	A21	15s on 28s (Bl)	8.50	2.50
		Nos. 157-160 (4)	21.25	4.20

The several settings of the surcharges on Nos. 157-160 show variations in the figures and letters.

Nos. 92-93 Surcharged

1915, Apr. 3

161	A15	2s on 1a org & grn	7.00	5.00
a.		Pair, one without surcharge	350.00	350.00
162	A15	2s on 2a vio & slate	7.00	4.50

No. 143 Surcharged in Red

1916, Oct.

163	A20	2s on 14s blue	4.50	2.00

Printed by Waterlow & Sons, London Types of 1912 Re-engraved

1917, Jan. 1   **Perf. 14**

164	A21	2s orange brown	2.50	1.20
165	A21	3s emerald	2.50	2.50
166	A21	5s rose red	4.00	1.20
167	A21	10s black & olive	3.50	1.20
168	A21	15s blue	4.00	1.40
170	A22	1b bl & gray blk	25.00	4.50
171	A22	2b car rose & brn	70.00	35.00
172	A22	3b yellow grn & blk	525.00	275.00
173	A22	5b dp violet & blk	275.00	190.00
174	A22	10b ol gray & vio	425.00	32.50
a.		Perf. 12½	500.00	47.50
175	A22	20b sea green & brn	600.00	70.00
a.		Perf. 12½	625.00	85.00
		Nos. 164-175 (11)	1,936.	614.50

The re-engraved design of the satang stamps varies in numerous minute details from the 1912 issue. Four lines of the background appear between the vertical strokes of the "M" of "SIAM" in the 1912 issue and only three lines in the 1917 stamps.

The 1912 stamps with value in bahts are 37½mm high; those of 1917 are 39mm. In the latter the king's features, especially the eyes and mouth, are more distinct and the uniform and decorations are more sharply defined.

The 1912 stamps have seven pearls between the earpieces of the crown. On the 1917 stamps there are nine pearls in the same place. Nos. 174 and 175 exist imperforate.

Nos. 164-173 Overprinted in Red

1918, Dec. 2

176	A21	2s orange brown	3.25	3.25
a.		Double overprint	110.00	110.00
177	A21	3s emerald	3.25	3.25
178	A21	5s rose red	4.50	4.50
a.		Double overprint	150.00	150.00
179	A21	10s black & olive	6.75	6.75
180	A21	15s blue	6.75	6.75
181	A22	1b bl & gray blk	27.50	24.00
182	A22	2b car rose & brn	65.00	47.50
183	A22	3b yellow grn & blk	190.00	120.00
184	A22	5b dp vio & blk	400.00	325.00
		Nos. 176-184 (9)	707.00	541.00

Counterfeits of this overprint exist.

Nos. 147-148 Surcharged in Green or Red

1919-20

185	A21	5s on 6s (G)	2.75	1.90
186	A21	10s on 12s (R) ('20)	6.00	1.50

Issue dates: 5s, Nov. 11. 10s, Jan. 1.

King Vajiravudh   Throne Room
A23   A24

1920-26   **Engr.**   **Perf. 14-15, 12½**

187	A23	2s brn, *yel* ('21)	3.50	.70
188	A23	3s grn, *grn* ('21)	3.50	.95
189	A23	3s chocolate ('24)	3.25	.70
190	A23	5s rose, *pale rose*	4.50	.70
191	A23	5s green ('22)	34.00	6.00
192	A23	5s dk vio, *lil* ('26)	7.50	.95
193	A23	10s black & org ('21)	7.00	.70
194	A23	15s bl, *bluish* ('21)	8.50	.70
195	A23	15s carmine ('22)	44.00	6.00
196	A23	25s chocolate ('21)	24.00	2.75
197	A23	25s dk blue ('22)	32.50	1.40
198	A23	50s ocher & blk ('21)	32.50	2.00
		Nos. 187-198 (11)	201.50	22.85

For overprints see Nos. 205, B23-B30.

1926, Mar. 5   **Perf. 12½**

199	A24	1t gray vio & grn	16.00	3.50
200	A24	2t car & org red	35.00	6.00
201	A24	3t ol grn & bl	67.50	25.00
202	A24	5t dl vio & ol grn	95.00	45.00
203	A24	10t red & ol bis	325.00	32.50
204	A24	20t gray bl & brn	375.00	110.00
		Nos. 199-204 (6)	913.50	222.00

This issue was intended to commemorate the fifteenth year of the reign of King Vajiravudh. Because of the King's death the stamps were issued as ordinary postage stamps.

Nos. 195 and 150 with Surcharge similar to 1914-15 Issue in Black or Red

1928, Jan.

205	A23	5s on 15s car	7.00	3.50
206	A21	10s on 28s choc (R)	12.00	2.00

King Prajadhipok
A25   A26

1928   **Engr.**   **Perf. 12½**

207	A25	2s deep red brown	.65	.65
208	A25	3s deep green	.65	.65
209	A25	5s dark violet	.65	.30
210	A25	10s deep rose	.75	.30
211	A25	15s dark blue	.90	.40
212	A25	25s black & org	4.00	1.00
213	A25	50s brn org & blk	2.00	1.25
214	A25	80s blue & black	4.00	2.50
216	A26	1b dk blue & blk	6.00	2.50
217	A26	2b car rose & blk brn	12.00	5.00
218	A26	3b yellow grn & blk	12.00	6.00
219	A26	5b dp vio & gray blk	20.00	6.75
220	A26	10b ol grn & red vio	40.00	10.00
221	A26	20b Prus grn & brn	80.00	18.50
222	A26	40b dk grn & ol brn	160.00	80.00
		Nos. 207-222 (15)	343.60	135.80
		Set, never hinged	500.00	

On the single colored stamps, type A25, the lines in the background are uniform; those of the bicolored values are shaded and do not extend to the frame.

Issue dates: 5s, 10s, 2b-40b, Apr. 15; 2s, 3s, 15s, 25s, 50s, May 1; 1b, June 1; 80s, Nov. 15.

For overprints & surcharge see Nos. 300-301, B34.

Nos. 142, 144 Surcharged in Red or Blue

1930   **Perf. 14**

223	A20	10s on 12s blk & ol brn	8.75	2.75
224	A20	25s on 28s red brn (Bl)	30.00	2.25
		Set, never hinged	50.00	

King Prajadhipok and Chao P'ya Chakri
A27   A28

Statue of Chao P'ya Chakri — A29

1932, Apr. 1   **Engr.**   **Perf. 12½**

225	A27	2s dark brown	2.00	.40
226	A27	3s deep green	3.25	.85
227	A27	5s dull violet	2.00	.40
228	A28	10s red brn & blk	2.00	.25
229	A28	15s dull blue & blk	9.50	1.50
230	A28	25s violet & black	12.50	2.00
231	A28	50s claret & black	55.00	6.00
232	A29	1b blue black	77.50	15.00
		Nos. 225-232 (8)	163.75	26.40
		Set, never hinged	225.00	

150th anniv. of the Chakri dynasty, the founding of Bangkok in 1782, and the opening of the memorial bridge across the Chao Phraya River.

Assembly Hall, Bangkok
A30

1939, June 24   Litho.   Perf. 11, 12
233	A30	2s dull red brown	4.50	2.00
234	A30	3s green	9.50	4.00
235	A30	5s dark violet	6.50	.80
236	A30	10s carmine	14.00	.80
237	A30	15s dark blue	35.00	2.00
		Nos. 233-237 (5)	69.50	9.60
		Set, never hinged	90.00	

7th anniv. of the Siamese Constitution.

King Ananda Mahidol — A32

Chakri Palace, Bangkok — A31

1940   Typo.   Perf. 12½
238	A31	2s dull brown	4.50	1.00
239	A31	3s dp yellow grn	8.00	2.50
a.		Cliché of 5s in plate of 3s	900.00	725.00
240	A31	5s dark violet	5.50	.50
241	A31	10s carmine	20.00	.50
242	A31	15s dark blue	40.00	1.00
		Nos. 238-242 (5)	78.00	5.50
		Set, never hinged	125.00	

Issued: 2s, 3s, 5/13; 5s, 5/24; 15s, 5/28; 10s, 5/30.

King Ananda Mahidol — A32   Plowing Rice Field — A33

Royal Pavilion at Bang-pa-in A34   King Ananda Mahidol A35

1941, Apr. 17   Engr.
243	A32	2s brown	2.00	.45
244	A32	3s deep green	2.75	.85
245	A32	5s violet	1.60	.45
246	A32	10s dark red	1.60	.45
247	A33	15s dp bl & gray blk	2.75	.95
248	A33	25s slate & org	3.50	1.10
249	A33	50s red org & gray	3.25	1.20
250	A34	1b brt ultra & gray	15.00	3.50
251	A34	2b dk car rose & gray	14.00	2.00
252	A34	3b dp grn & gray	35.00	4.25
253	A34	5b blk & rose red	60.00	2.00
a.		Horiz. pair, imperf. btwn.		
254	A34	10b ol blk & yel	95.00	50.00
		Nos. 243-254 (12)	236.45	85.20
		Set, never hinged	375.00	

1943, May 1   Unwmk.   Perf. 11
255	A35	1b dark blue	21.00	2.75
a.		Horiz. pair, imperf. btwn.	100.00	100.00
b.		Vert. pair, imperf. btwn.	100.00	100.00

See No. 274.

Indo-China War Monument A36   Bangkhaen Monument A37

1943   Engr.   Perf. 11, 12½
256	A36	3s dark green	20.00	17.50

Litho.
Perf. 12½x11
257	A36	3s dull green	4.00	2.50

Issue dates: #256, June 1. #257, Nov. 2.

1943, Nov. 25   Perf. 12½, 12½x11

Two types of 10s:
I — Size 19½x24mm.
II — Size 20¾x25¼mm.
258	A37	2s brown orange	2.50	3.25
259	A37	10s car rose (I)	4.00	.80
a.		Type II	8.00	5.00

10th anniv. of the quelling of a counter-revolution led by a member of the royal family on Oct. 11, 1933.

Stamps of similar design, but with values in "cents," are listed under Malaya, Occupation Stamps. See Nos. 2N1-2N6.

King Bhumibol Adulyadej
A38   A39

1947, Dec. 5   Pin-perf. 12½x11
260	A38	5s orange	2.75	3.00
261	A38	10s olive ('48)	2.75	3.00
a.		10s light brown	80.00	80.00
262	A38	20s blue	7.00	2.40
263	A38	50s blue green	14.00	4.75
		Nos. 260-263 (4)	26.50	13.15

Coming of age of King Bhumibol Adulyadej. Issued with and without gum.

> **Catalogue values for unused stamps in this section, from this point to the end of the section, are for Never Hinged items.**

1947-49   Unwmk.   Engr.   Perf. 12½
Size: 20x25mm
264	A39	5s violet	2.00	.30
265	A39	10s red	4.50	.50
266	A39	20s chocolate	2.00	.50
267	A39	50s olive	4.50	.30

Size: 22x27mm
268	A39	1b vio & dp bl	16.00	.45
269	A39	2b ultra & green	55.00	1.60
270	A39	3b brn red & blk	70.00	3.00
271	A39	5b bl grn & brn red	87.50	6.00
272	A39	10b dk brn & pur	325.00	3.00
273	A39	20b blk & rose brn	400.00	9.00
		Nos. 264-273 (10)	966.50	24.45

Issued: 5s, 20s, 11/15/47; 10s, 50s, 1/3/49; 1b-20b, 11/1/48.
For surcharges see Nos. 302-303.

Type of 1943
Perf. 11½, 12½x11½
1948, Jan.   Litho.
274	A35	1b chalky blue	50.00	8.00
a.		Horiz. pair, imperf. btwn.	150.00	150.00
b.		Vert. pair, imperf. btwn.	150.00	150.00

King Bhumibol Adulyadej and Palace
A40   A41

Perf. 12½
1950, May 5   Unwmk.   Engr.
275	A40	5s red violet	2.00	.40
276	A40	10s red	2.50	.40
277	A40	15s purple	13.00	5.00
278	A40	20s chocolate	2.25	.40
279	A40	80s green	25.00	5.00
280	A40	1b deep blue	6.00	.40
281	A40	2b orange yellow	27.50	2.00
282	A40	3b gray	100.00	12.00
		Nos. 275-282 (8)	178.50	25.60

Coronation of Bhumibol Adulyadej as Rama IX, May 5, 1950.

1951-60   Perf. 12½, 13x12½
283	A41	5s rose lilac	2.50	.25
284	A41	10s deep green	2.00	.25
285	A41	15s red brown	2.50	.40
285A	A41	20s chocolate	3.00	.40
286	A41	25s carmine	1.20	.25
287	A41	50s gray olive	3.00	.40
288	A41	1b deep blue	6.50	.40
289	A41	1.15b deep blue	2.00	.50
290	A41	1.25b orange brn	10.00	.50

291	A41	2b dull blue grn	15.00	.50
292	A41	3b gray	20.00	.80
293	A41	5b aqua & red	65.00	2.00
294	A41	10b black brn & vio	325.00	6.00
295	A41	20b gray & olive	325.00	21.00
		Nos. 283-295 (14)	782.70	33.65

Issued: 25s, 2/15; 5s, 10s, 1b, 6/4; 2b, 3b, 12/1; 15s, 2/15/52; 1.15b, 9/1/53; 1.25b, 10/1/54; 5b, 10b, 20b, 2/1/55; 50s, 10/15/56; 20s, 1960.

United Nations Day — A42

1951, Oct. 24
296	A42	25s ultramarine	5.00	4.75

Overprinted in Carmine

1952, Oct.
297	A42	25s ultramarine	3.50	2.75

Overprinted in Carmine

1953, Oct.
298	A42	25s ultramarine	2.75	2.00

Overprinted in Carmine

1954, Oct. 24
299	A42	25s ultramarine	6.00	4.00
		Nos. 296-299 (4)	17.25	13.50

For more overprints see Nos. 315, 320.

Nos. 209 and 210 Overprinted in Black

1955, Jan. 4   Perf. 12½
300	A25	5s dark violet	9.50	20.00
301	A25	10s deep rose	9.50	20.00

No. 266 Surcharged with New Value in Black or Carmine
302	A39	5s on 20s choc	3.50	.75
303	A39	10s on 20s choc (C)	5.00	.75
		Nos. 300-303 (4)	27.50	41.50

King Naresuan (1555-1605), on War Elephant — A43

Tao Suranari — A44

Perf. 13½
1955, Feb. 15   Unwmk.   Engr.
304	A43	25s brt carmine	2.75	.45
305	A43	80s rose violet	25.00	5.00
306	A43	1.25b dark olive grn	70.00	3.00
307	A43	2b deep blue	15.00	3.00
308	A43	3b henna brown	60.00	3.00
		Nos. 304-308 (5)	172.75	13.45

1955, Apr. 15   Perf. 12x13½
309	A44	10s purple	2.50	.40
310	A44	25s emerald	1.90	.40
311	A44	1b brown	40.00	3.00
		Nos. 309-311 (3)	44.40	3.80

Lady Mo, called Tao Suranari (Brave Woman) for her role in stopping an 1826 rebellion.

King Taksin Statue at Thonburi — A45

1955, May 1   Perf. 12½x12
312	A45	5s violet blue	1.90	.30
313	A45	25s Prus green	11.00	.30
314	A45	1.25b red	45.00	3.00
		Nos. 312-314 (3)	57.90	3.60

King Somdech P'ya Chao Taksin (1734-1782).

No. 296 Overprinted in Red

1955, Oct. 24   Perf. 12½
315	A42	25s ultramarine	5.00	4.00

United Nations Day, Oct. 24, 1955.

Don Jedi Monument — A46

1956, Feb. 1   Perf. 13½x13
316	A46	10s emerald	4.75	3.00
317	A46	50s reddish brown	27.50	2.00
318	A46	75s violet	8.00	1.50
319	A46	1.50b brown orange	25.00	1.50
		Nos. 316-319 (4)	65.25	8.00

No. 296 Overprinted in Red Violet

1956, Oct. 24
320	A42	25s ultramarine	6.00	4.50

United Nations Day, Oct. 24, 1956.

Dharmachakra and Deer — A47

20s, 25s, 50s, Hand of peace and Dharmachakra. 1b, 1.25b, 2b, Pagoda of Nakon Phatom.

Wmk. 329

1957, May 13   *Photo.*   *Perf. 13½*

321	A47	5s dark brown	1.50	.65
322	A47	10s rose lake	1.50	.65
323	A47	15s brt green	3.25	1.75
324	A47	20s orange	3.25	2.00
325	A47	25s reddish brown	1.10	.65
326	A47	50s magenta	2.50	.70
327	A47	1b olive brown	2.90	.85
328	A47	1.25b slate blue	35.00	6.00
329	A47	2b deep claret	8.00	1.25
		Nos. 321-329 (9)	59.00	14.50

2500th anniversary of birth of Buddha.

UN Day — A48   Thai Archway — A49

1957, Oct. 24   *Perf. 13½*

330	A48	25s olive	1.60	.80
331	A48	25s bright ocher ('58)	1.60	.80
332	A48	25s indigo ('59)	2.40	.80
		Nos. 330-332 (3)	5.60	2.40

Issued: Oct. 24.

1959, Oct. 15   *Photo.*   *Perf. 13½*

Designs (inscribed "SEAP Games 1959"): 25s, Royal tiered umbrellas. 1.25b, Thai archer, ancient costume. 2b, Wat Arun pagoda and prow of royal barge.

333	A49	10s orange	1.10	.25
334	A49	25s dk carmine rose	1.40	.25
335	A49	1.25b bright green	5.50	1.50
336	A49	2b light blue	4.75	.85
		Nos. 333-336 (4)	12.75	2.85

Issued to publicize the South-East Asia Peninsula Games, Bangkok, Dec. 12-17.

Wat Arun, WRY Emblem — A50   Wat Arun, Bangkok — A51

1960, Apr. 7

337	A50	50s chocolate	1.60	.40
338	A50	2b yellow green	2.40	1.20

WRY, July 1, 1959-June 30, 1960.

1960, Aug.   Wmk. 329   *Perf. 13½*

339	A51	50s carmine rose	.75	.25
340	A51	2b ultramarine	4.75	1.00

Anti-leprosy campaign.

Elephants in Teak Forest — A52   Globe and SEATO Emblem — A53

1960, Aug. 29   *Photo.*   *Perf. 13½*

341	A52	25s emerald	1.60	.40

5th World Forestry Cong., Seattle, WA, Aug. 29-Sept. 10.

1960, Sept. 8

342	A53	50s chocolate	1.60	.40

SEATO Day, Sept. 8.

Siamese Child — A54   Hand with Pen and Globe — A55

1960, Oct. 3   Wmk. 329

343	A54	50s magenta	1.75	.25
344	A54	1b orange	5.00	.75

Children's Day, 1960.

1960, Oct. 3

345	A55	50s carmine rose	1.50	.50
346	A55	2b blue	5.50	1.60

Intl. Letter Writing Week, Oct. 3-9.

UN Emblem and Globe A56   King Bhumibol Adulyadej A57

1960, Oct. 24   *Perf. 13½*

347	A56	50s purple	1.75	.40

15th anniversary of the United Nations. See Nos. 369, 390.

Perf. 13½x13

1961-68   Engr.   Wmk. 334

348	A57	5s rose cl ('62)	.80	.40
349	A57	10s green ('62)	.80	.40
350	A57	15s red brn ('62)	.80	.40
351	A57	20s brown ('62)	.80	.40
352	A57	25s carmine ('63)	.80	.40
353	A57	50s olive ('62)	.80	.40
354	A57	80s orange ('62)	5.00	2.00
355	A57	1b vio bl & brn	5.00	.80
355A	A57	1.25b red & citron ('65)	8.50	2.00
356	A57	1.50b dk vio & yel green	2.50	.80
357	A57	2b red & violet	2.50	2.00
358	A57	3b brn & bl	13.00	.65
358A	A57	4b olive bis & blk ('68)	15.00	3.00
359	A57	5b blue & green	32.50	2.00
360	A57	10b red org & blk	90.00	3.00
361	A57	20b emer & ultra	100.00	6.00
362	A57	25b green & blue	45.00	5.00
362A	A57	40b yellow & blk ('65)	110.00	9.00
		Nos. 348-362A (18)	433.80	38.65

For overprint see No. 588.

Children in Garden — A58   Pen and Envelope with Map — A59

1961, Oct. 2   *Photo.*   Wmk. 329   *Perf. 13½*

363	A58	20s indigo	1.75	.70
364	A58	2b purple	4.50	1.50

Issued for Children's Day.

1961, Oct. 9

1b, 2b, Pen and letters circling globe.

365	A59	25s gray green	.70	.25
366	A59	50s rose lilac	.35	.25
367	A59	1b bright rose	2.00	.40
368	A59	2b ultramarine	2.50	.70
		Nos. 365-368 (4)	5.55	1.60

Intl. Letter Writing Week, Oct. 2-8.

UN Type of 1960

1961, Oct. 24   Wmk. 329   *Perf. 13½*

369	A56	50s maroon	1.60	.70

Issued for United Nations Day, Oct. 24.

Scout Emblem — A60   Scouts Saluting and Tents — A61

Design: 2b, King Vajiravudh and Scouts.

1961, Nov. 1   *Photo.*

370	A60	50s carmine rose	.70	.30
371	A61	1b bright green	1.75	.50
372	A61	2b bright blue	2.75	1.20
		Nos. 370-372 (3)	5.20	2.00

Thai Boy Scouts, 50th anniversary.

Malaria Eradication Emblem and Siamese Designs
A62   A63

1962, Apr. 7   Wmk. 329   *Perf. 13*

373	A62	5s orange brown	.30	.25
374	A62	10s sepia	.30	.25
375	A62	20s blue	1.10	.25
376	A62	50s carmine rose	.30	.25
377	A63	1b green	1.50	.25
378	A63	1.50b dk car rose	3.50	.65
379	A63	2d dark blue	2.00	.35
380	A63	3b violet	5.50	2.50
		Nos. 373-380 (8)	14.50	4.75

WHO drive to eradicate malaria.

View of Bangkok and Seattle Fair Emblem A64

1962, Apr. 21   Wmk. 329   *Perf. 13*

381	A64	50s red lilac	1.50	.30
382	A64	2b deep blue	7.00	.75

"Century 21" Intl. Expo., Seattle, WA, Apr. 21-Oct. 12.

Mother and Child A65   Globe, Letters, Carrier Pigeons A66

1962, Oct. 1   Wmk. 329   *Photo.*   *Perf. 13*

383	A65	25s lt blue green	1.25	.30
384	A65	50s bister brown	1.50	.25
385	A65	1b bright pink	6.75	.75
		Nos. 383-385 (3)	9.50	1.30

Issued for Children's Day.

1962, Oct. 8

Design: 1b, 2b, Quill pen and scroll.

386	A66	25s violet	.70	.30
387	A66	50s red	.50	.25
388	A66	1b lemon	3.50	.60
389	A66	2b lt bluish green	7.00	.70
		Nos. 386-389 (4)	11.70	1.85

Intl. Letter Writing Week, Oct. 7-13.

UN Type of 1960

1962, Oct. 24   *Perf. 13½*

390	A56	50s carmine rose	1.00	.80

United Nations Day, Oct. 24.

Exhibition Emblem — A67

1962, Nov. 1   Unwmk.

391	A67	50s olive bister	1.90	.25

Students' Exhibition, Bangkok.

Woman Harvesting Rice — A68

Wmk. 334

1963, Mar. 21   Engr.   *Perf. 14*

392	A68	20s green	2.00	.65
393	A68	50s ocher	1.50	.25

FAO "Freedom from Hunger" campaign.

Temple Lion — A69

1963, Apr. 1   Wmk. 329   *Perf. 13½*

394	A69	50s green & bister	2.00	.25

1st anniv. of the formation of the Asian-Oceanic Postal Union, AOPU.

New and Old Post and Telegraph Buildings — A70

Wmk. 334

1963, Aug. 4   Engr.   *Perf. 14*

395	A70	50s org, bluish blk & grn	2.40	.80
396	A70	3b grn, dk red & brn	6.50	1.50

80th anniv. of the Post and Telegraph Dept.

King Bhumibol Adulyadej A71   Child with Dolls A72

Perf. 13x13½

1963-71   Wmk. 329   Photo.

397	A71	5s dk car rose	.80	.40
398	A71	10s dark green	.80	.40
399	A71	15s red brown	.80	.40
400	A71	20s black brown	.80	.40
401	A71	25s carmine	.80	.40
402	A71	50s olive gray	1.60	.40
402A	A71	75s brt vio ('71)	1.50	.25
403	A71	80s dull orange	6.50	1.60
404	A71	1b dk bl & dk brn	4.00	.40
404A	A71	1.25b org brn & ol ('65)	16.00	4.50
405	A71	1.50b vio bl & grn	4.50	.80
406	A71	2b dk red & vio	4.50	.40

407	A71	3b brn & dk bl	4.50	.80
407A	A71	4b dp bis & blk ('68)	7.00	2.40
408	A71	5b blue & green	3.25	.80
409	A71	10b orange & blk	27.50	1.50
410	A71	20b brt grn & ind	180.00	8.00
411	A71	25b dk grn & bl	12.00	1.50
411A	A71	40b yel & blk ('65)	225.00	9.50
		Nos. 397-411A (19)	501.85	34.85

Nos. 397-403 were issued in 1963; Nos. 404, 405-407, 408-411 in 1964.
For overprint see No. 589.

1963, Oct. 7   Litho.   Perf. 13½

412	A72	50s rose red	2.00	.25
413	A72	2b dull blue	8.50	.75

Issued for Children's Day.

Garuda Carrying Letter — A73

Design: 2b, 3b, Thai women writing letters.

1963, Oct. 7   Wmk. 329

414	A73	50s lt blue & claret	2.75	.45
415	A73	1b lt grn & vio brn	4.75	.80
416	A73	2b yel brn & turq bl	34.00	3.00
417	A73	3b org brn & yel grn	18.00	3.50
		Nos. 414-417 (4)	59.50	7.75

Intl. Letter Writing Week, Oct. 6-12.

UN Emblem — A74

1963, Oct. 24   Wmk. 329   Perf. 13½

418	A74	50s bright blue	1.50	.40

United Nations Day, Oct. 24.

King Bhumibol Adulyadej — A75

1963, Dec. 5   Photo.   Perf. 13½

419	A75	1.50b blue, org & ind	5.00	1.50
420	A75	5b brt lil rose, org & blk	24.00	4.50

King Bhumibol's 36th birthday.

UNICEF Emblem — A76

1964, Jan. 13   Litho.

421	A76	50s blue	1.00	.40
422	A76	2b olive green	4.50	.80

17th anniv. of UNICEF.

Hand (flags), Pigeon and Globe — A77

Designs: 1b, Girls and world map. 2b, Pen, pencil and unfolded world map. 3b, Globe and hand holding quill.

1964, Oct. 5   Wmk. 329   Perf. 13½

423	A77	50s lilac & lt grn	2.40	.40
424	A77	1b red brown & grn	6.00	1.50
425	A77	2b yellow & vio bl	14.50	1.50
426	A77	3b blue & dk brown	9.50	3.25
		Nos. 423-426 (4)	32.40	6.65

Intl. Letter Writing Week, Oct. 5-11.

UN Emblem and Globe — A78   King and Queen — A79

1964, Oct. 24   Photo.   Perf. 13½

427	A78	50s gray	1.50	.40

United Nations Day, Oct. 24.

1965, Apr. 28   Wmk. 329   Perf. 13½

428	A79	2b brown & multi	16.00	.80
429	A79	5b violet & multi	25.00	4.00

15th wedding anniversary of King Bhumibol Adulyadej and Queen Sirikit.

ITU Emblem, Old and New Communications Equipment — A80

1965, May 17   Photo.

430	A80	1b bright green	7.00	1.50

Cent. of the ITU.

World Map, Letters and Goddess — A81

2b, 3b, World map, letters and handshake.

1965, Oct. 3   Wmk. 329   Perf. 13½

431	A81	50s dp plum, gray & sal	1.75	.60
432	A81	1b dk vio bl, lt vio & yel	5.00	.80
433	A81	2b dk gray, bis & dp org	14.00	1.20
434	A81	3b multicolored	17.50	4.00
		Nos. 431-434 (4)	38.25	6.60

Intl. Letter Writing Week, Oct. 3-9.

A82   A83

Gates of Royal Chapel of Emerald Buddha.

Engr. & Litho.
Perf. 13½x14

1965, Oct. 24   Wmk. 356

435	A82	50s slate grn, bl & ocher	2.00	.40

International Cooperation Year, 1965.

Wmk. 329

1965, Nov. 1   Litho.   Perf. 13½

Map of Thailand and UPU monument, Bern.

436	A83	20s dk blue & lilac	1.00	.40
437	A83	50s gray & blue	2.25	.40
438	A83	1b orange brn & vio bl	7.00	.45
439	A83	3b green & bister	14.00	2.50
		Nos. 436-439 (4)	24.25	3.75

80th anniv. of Thailand's admission to the UPU.

Lotus Blossom and Child — A84

Design: 1b, Boy with book walking up steps.

1966, Jan. 8   Wmk. 334   Perf. 13½

440	A84	50s henna brn & blk	1.50	.40
441	A84	1b green & black	4.00	1.60

Issued for Children's Day, 1966.

Bicycling — A85

1966, Aug. 4   Photo.   Wmk. 329

442	A85	20s shown	1.00	.45
443	A85	25s Tennis	1.40	.45
444	A85	50s Running	1.00	.25
445	A85	1b Weight lifting	4.50	1.50
446	A85	1.25b Boxing	6.50	4.00
447	A85	2b Swimming	9.50	1.20
448	A85	3b Netball	19.00	4.00
449	A85	5b Soccer	52.50	14.00
		Nos. 442-449 (8)	95.40	25.85

5th Asian Games, Bangkok.

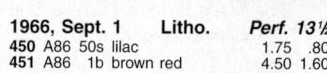

Trade Fair Emblem and Temple of Dawn — A86

1966, Sept. 1   Litho.   Perf. 13½

450	A86	50s lilac	1.75	.80
451	A86	1b brown red	4.50	1.60

1st Intl. Asian Trade Fair, Bangkok.

Letter Writer A87

Design: 50s, 1b, Letters, maps and pen.

1966, Oct. 3   Photo.   Wmk. 329

452	A87	50s scarlet	1.60	.40
453	A87	1b orange brown	3.25	.80
454	A87	2b brt violet	12.00	.80
455	A87	3b brt blue grn	7.00	2.40
		Nos. 452-455 (4)	23.85	4.40

Intl. Letter Writing Week, Oct. 6-12.

UN Emblem — A88

Wmk. 334

1966, Oct. 24   Litho.   Perf. 13½

456	A88	50s ultramarine	1.60	.40

United Nations Day, Oct. 24.

Rice Field A89

1966, Nov. 1   Engr.   Wmk. 329

457	A89	50s dp bl & grnsh bl	4.00	.80
458	A89	3b plum & pink	16.00	4.50

Intl. Rice Year under sponsorship of the FAO.

Pra Buddha Bata Monastery, UNESCO Emblem — A90

1966, Nov. 4   Photo.   Wmk. 329

459	A90	50s black & yel grn	1.25	.25

20th anniv. of UNESCO.

Thai Boxing A91

Designs: 1b, Takraw (three men playing ball). 2b, Kite fighting. 3b, Cudgel play.

1966, Dec. 9   Wmk. 329   Perf. 13½

460	A91	50s black, brn & red	2.00	.80
461	A91	1b black, brn & red	6.50	2.00
462	A91	2b black, brn & red	29.00	4.50
463	A91	3b black, brn & red	27.50	14.00
		Nos. 460-463 (4)	65.00	21.30

5th Asian Games.

Snakehead — A92

Pigmy Mackerel — A93

Fish: 3b, Barb. 5b, Siamese fighting fish.

1967, Jan. 1   Photo.

464	A92	1b brt blue & multi	7.00	1.50
465	A93	2b multicolored	27.50	3.00
466	A93	3b yel grn & multi	15.00	7.00
467	A92	5b pale grn & multi	20.00	8.00
		Nos. 464-467 (4)	69.50	19.50

Dharmachakra, Globe and Temples — A94

Wmk. 329

1967, Jan. 15 Litho. *Perf. 13½*

468	A94	2b black & yellow	6.50	1.20

Establishment of the headquarters of the World Fellowship of Buddhists in Thailand.

Great Hornbill A95

Ascocentrum Curvifolium A96

Birds: 25s, Hill myna. 50s, White-rumped shama. 1b, Diard's fireback pheasant. 1.50b, Spotted dove. 2b, Sarus crane. 3b, White-breasted kingfisher. 5b, Asiatic open-bill (stork).

1967, Feb. 1 Photo.

469	A95	20s tan & multi	1.40	.80
470	A95	25s lt gray & multi	2.00	1.60
471	A95	50s yel grn & multi	3.50	.80
472	A95	1b olive & multi	5.00	1.50
473	A95	1.50b dull yel & multi	5.00	2.40
474	A95	2b pale sal & multi	29.00	3.25
475	A95	3b gray & multi	18.50	7.75
476	A95	5b multicolored	29.00	8.00
		Nos. 469-476 (8)	93.40	26.10

1967, Apr. 1 Wmk. 329 *Perf. 13½*

Orchids: 20s, Vandopsis parishii. 80s, Rhynchostylis retusa. 1b, Rhynchostylus gigantea. 1.50b, Dendrobium falconerii. 2b, Paphiopedilum callosum. 3b, Dendrobium formosum. 5b, Dendrobium primulinum.

477	A96	20s black & multi	1.40	.80
478	A96	50s brt blue & multi	2.00	.40
479	A96	80s black & multi	3.50	1.60
480	A96	1b blue & multi	5.25	1.25
481	A96	1.50b black & multi	5.25	1.25
482	A96	2b ver & multi	24.00	3.25
483	A96	3b brown & multi	18.50	7.75
484	A96	5b multicolored	29.00	6.25
		Nos. 477-484 (8)	88.90	22.55

Thai Architecture — A97

1967, Apr. 6 Engr.

485	A97	50s Mansion	2.00	.80
486	A97	1.50b Pagodas	5.50	3.25
487	A97	2b Bell tower	24.00	3.00
488	A97	3b Temple	16.00	5.50
		Nos. 485-488 (4)	47.50	12.55

Grand Palace and Royal Barge on Chao Phraya River — A98

1967, Sept. 15 Wmk. 329 *Perf. 13½*

489	A98	2b ultra & sepia	9.50	2.00

International Tourist Year, 1967.

Globe, Dove, People and Letters A99

2b, 3b, Clasped hands, globe and doves.

1967, Oct. 8 Photo.

490	A99	50s dk blue & multi	.85	.40
491	A99	1b multicolored	3.25	.80
492	A99	2b brt yel grn & blk	7.00	.80
493	A99	3b brown & blk	12.50	3.00
		Nos. 490-493 (4)	23.60	5.00

Intl. Letter Writing Week, Oct. 6-12.

UN Emblem — A100

1967, Oct. 24 Wmk. 329 *Perf. 13½*

494	A100	50s multicolored	1.40	.25

Issued for United Nations Day, Oct. 24.

Flag and Map of Thailand — A101

1967, Dec. 5 Photo. *Perf. 13½*

495	A101	50s greenish blue, red & vio bl	1.60	.80
496	A101	2b ol gray, red & vio bl	7.00	1.60

50th anniversary of the flag.

Elephant Carrying Teakwood — A102

1968, Mar. 1 Engr. Wmk. 329

497	A102	2b rose claret & gray ol	7.00	.75

See Nos. 537, 566.

Syncom Satellite over Thai Tracking Station — A103

1968, Apr. 1 Photo. *Perf. 13*

498	A103	50s multicolored	.70	.25
499	A103	3b multicolored	3.50	1.25

Earth Goddess — A104

1968, May 1 Wmk. 329 *Perf. 13*

500	A104	50s blk, gold, red & bl grn	2.40	.40

Hydrological Decade (UNESCO), 1965-74.

Snake-skinned Gourami — A105

Fish: 20s, Red-tailed black "shark." 25s, Tor tambroides. 50s, Pangasius sanitwongsei. 80s, Bagrid catfish. 1.25b, Vaimosa rambaiae. 1.50b, Catlocarpio siamensis. 4b, Featherback.

1968, June 1 Photo. *Perf. 13*

501	A105	10s multicolored	1.00	.40
502	A105	20s multicolored	1.75	.40
503	A105	25s multicolored	1.75	.40
504	A105	50s multicolored	4.50	.40
505	A105	80s multicolored	6.00	3.25
506	A105	1.25b multicolored	6.50	4.75
507	A105	1.50b multicolored	24.00	4.00
508	A105	4b multicolored	50.00	17.50
		Nos. 501-508 (8)	95.50	31.10

Arcturus Butterfly — A106

Various butterflies.

1968, July 1 Wmk. 329 *Perf. 13*

509	A106	50s lt blue & multi	5.00	.30
510	A106	1b multicolored	8.00	1.50
511	A106	3b multicolored	22.50	7.00
512	A106	4b buff & multi	32.50	12.00
		Nos. 509-512 (4)	68.00	20.80

Queen Sirikit — A107

Designs: Various portraits of Queen Sirikit.

Photogravure and Engraved
Perf. 13½x14

1968, Aug. 12 Wmk. 334

513	A107	50s gold & multi	.80	.45
514	A107	2b gold & multi	4.50	1.60
515	A107	3b gold & multi	10.00	3.00
516	A107	5b gold & multi	16.00	5.50
		Nos. 513-516 (4)	31.30	10.55

Queen Sirikit's 36th birthday, or third 12-year "cycle."

WHO Emblem and Medical Apparatus — A108

1968, Sept. 1 Photo. *Perf. 12½*

517	A108	50s olive, blk & gray	1.60	.25

20th anniv. of the WHO.

Globe, Pen and Envelope — A109

1b, 3b, Pen nib, envelope and globe.

1968, Oct. 6 Wmk. 329 *Perf. 13½*

518	A109	50s brown & multi	.30	.30
519	A109	1b pale brown & multi	1.40	.55
520	A109	2b multicolored	2.75	.70
521	A109	3b violet & multi	9.50	2.00
		Nos. 518-521 (4)	13.95	3.55

Intl. Letter Writing Week, Oct. 7-13.

UN Emblem and Flags — A110

1968, Oct. 24

522	A110	50s multicolored	1.20	.25

Issued for United Nations Day.

Human Rights Flame and Bas-relief — A111

1968, Dec. 10 Photo. *Perf. 13½*

523	A111	50s sl grn, red & vio	1.60	.25

International Human Rights Year.

King Rama II — A112

1968, Dec. 30 Engr. Wmk. 329

524	A112	50s sepia & bister	1.60	.40

Rama II (1768-1824), who reigned 1809-24.

National Assembly Building — A113

Photogravure and Engraved

1969, Feb. 10 Wmk. 329 *Perf. 13½*

525	A113	50s multicolored	1.00	.25
526	A113	2b multicolored	5.25	1.20

First constitutional election day.

ILO Emblem and Cogwheels — A114

1969, May 1   Photo.   Perf. 13½
527 A114 50s rose vio & dk bl   .85   .25
50th anniv. of the ILO.

Ramwong Dance — A115

Designs: 1b, Candle dance. 2b, Krathop Mai dance. 3b, Nohra dance.

1969, July 15   Wmk. 329   Perf. 13
528 A115 50s multicolored   .65   .30
529 A115 1b multicolored   1.60   .65
530 A115 2b multicolored   2.75   .65
531 A115 3b multicolored   3.25 1.50
    Nos. 528-531 (4)   8.25 3.10

Posting and Receiving Letters — A116

Design: 2b, 3b, Writing and posting letters.

1969, Oct. 5   Photo.   Wmk. 334
532 A116 50s multicolored   .65   .40
533 A116 1b multicolored   1.25   .45
534 A116 2b multicolored   2.40   .65
535 A116 3b multicolored   3.25 1.40
    Nos. 532-535 (4)   7.55 2.90
International Letter Writing Week.

Hand Holding Globe — A117

1969, Oct. 24   Wmk. 329   Perf. 13
536 A117 50s multicolored   1.40   .40
Issued for United Nations Day.

Teakwood Type of 1968
1969, Nov. 18   Engr.   Perf. 13½
537 A102 2b Tin mine   5.00   .65
Issued to publicize tin export, and the 2nd Technical Conf. of the Intl. Tin Council, Bangkok.

Loy Krathong Festival — A118

Designs: 1b, Marriage ceremony. 2b, Khwan ceremony. 5b, Songkran festival.

1969, Nov. 23   Photo.   Wmk. 329
538 A118 50s gray & multi   1.00   .25
539 A118 1b multicolored   1.75   .65
540 A118 2b multicolored   2.75   .55
541 A118 5b multicolored   5.50 1.75
    Nos. 538-541 (4)   11.00 3.20

Biplane, Mailmen and Map of First Thai Airmail Flight, 1919 — A119

1969, Dec. 10   Engr.   Perf. 13½
542 A119 1b multicolored   1.75   .45
50th anniversary of Thai airmail service.

Shadow Play — A120

Photogravure and Engraved
1969, Dec. 18   Wmk. 329
543 A120 50s Phra Rama   .65   .30
544 A120 2b Ramasura   3.50   .40
545 A120 3b Mekhala   3.25 1.20
546 A120 5b Ongkhot   6.00 1.40
    Nos. 543-546 (4)   13.40 3.30

Symbols of Agriculture, Industry and Shipping — A121

1970, Jan. 1   Photo.
547 A121 50s multicolored   .60   .25
Productivity Year 1970.

World Map, Thai Temples and Emblem — A122

1970, Jan. 31   Litho.
548 A122 50s brt blue & blk   1.25   .30
19th triennial meeting of the Intl. Council of Women, Bangkok.

Earth Station Radar and Satellite — A123

Perf. 14½x15
1970, Apr. 1   Litho.   Wmk. 356
549 A123 50s multicolored   .65   .25
Communication by satellite.

Household and Population Statistics — A124

Perf. 13x13½
1970, Apr. 1   Photo.   Wmk. 329
550 A124 1b multicolored   .95   .40
Issued to publicize the 1970 census.

Inauguration of New UPU Headquarters, Bern — A125

Lithographed and Engraved
1970, June 15 Wmk. 334 Perf. 13½
551 A125 50s lt bl, lt grn & grn   .95   .30

Khun Ram Kamhang Teaching (Mural) — A126

1970, July 1   Litho.
552 A126 50s black & multi   1.40   .30
Issued for International Education Year.

Swimming Stadium — A127

1.50b, Velodrome. 3b, Subhajalasaya Stadium. 5b, Kittikachorn Indoor Stadium.

Lithographed and Engraved
1970, Sept. 1   Wmk. 329   Perf. 13½
553 A127 50s yellow, red &
           pur   .85   .30
554 A127 1.50b ultra, grn & dk
           red   2.00   .65
555 A127 3b gold, black &
           dk red   2.50 1.10
556 A127 5b brt grn, ultra &
           dk red   4.00 1.20
    Nos. 553-556 (4)   9.35 3.25
6th Asian Games, Bangkok.

Children Writing Letters — A128

Designs: 1b, Woman writing letter. 2b, Two women reading letters. 3b, Man reading letter.

1970, Oct. 4   Perf. 13½
557 A128 50s black & multi   .65   .25
558 A128 1b black & multi   1.50   .45
559 A128 2b black & multi   3.50   .65
560 A128 3b black & multi   3.50 1.60
    Nos. 557-560 (4)   9.15 2.95
Intl. Letter Writing Week, Oct. 6-12.

Royal Palace, Bangkok, and UN Emblem — A129

1970, Oct. 24   Photo.   Perf. 13½
561 A129 50s multicolored   1.40   .40
25th anniversary of the United Nations.

Heroes of Bangrachan — A130

1b, Monument to Thao Thepkrasattri & Thao Sri Sunthon. 2b, Queen Suriyothai riding elephant. 3b, Phraya Phichaidaphak and battle scene.

1970, Oct. 25   Engr.   Perf. 13½
562 A130 50s pink & violet   .65   .45
563 A130 1b violet & maroon 1.40   .65
564 A130 2b rose & brown   3.50   .65
565 A130 3b blue & green   5.00 1.60
    Nos. 562-565 (4)   10.55 3.35
Heroes from Thai history.

Teakwood Type of 1968
1970, Nov. 1   Engr.
566 A102 2b Rubber plantation 3.25   .70
Issued to publicize rubber export.

King Bhumibol Lighting Flame — A131

1970, Dec. 9   Photo.   Wmk. 329
567 A131 1b multicolored   2.00   .65
Opening of 6th Asian Games, Bangkok.

Woman Playing So Sam Sai — A132

Women Playing Classical Thai Musical Instruments: 2b, Khlui Phiang-O. 3b, Krachappi. 5b, Thon Rammana.

1970, Dec. 20
568 A132 50s multicolored   .65   .40
569 A132 2b multicolored   2.00   .65
570 A132 3b multicolored   2.75   .95
571 A132 5b multicolored   5.25 1.25
    Nos. 568-571 (4)   10.65 3.25

Chocolate Point Siamese Cats — A133

Siamese Cats: 1b, Blue point. 2b, Seal point. 3b, Pure white cat and kittens.

Perf. 13½x14
1971, Mar. 15   Litho.   Wmk. 356
572 A133 50s multicolored   .65   .45
573 A133 1b multicolored   4.50   1.00
574 A133 2b multicolored   6.00   1.10
575 A133 3b multicolored   8.50   2.75
Nos. 572-575 (4)   19.65   5.30

Muang Nakhon Temple — A134

Temples: 1b, Phanom. 3b, Pathom Chedi. 4b, Doi Suthep.

Lithographed and Engraved
1971, Mar. 30   Wmk. 329   Perf. 13½
576 A134 50s rose, black & brn   .70   .30
577 A134 1b emerald, bis & pur   1.40   .40
578 A134 3b org, brn & dk brn   3.00   .65
579 A134 4b ultra, ocher & brn   5.25   2.75
Nos. 576-579 (4)   10.35   4.10

Corn and Tractor in Field A135

1971, Apr. 20   Engr.   Wmk. 329
580 A135 2b multicolored   2.00   .65
Export promotion.

Buddha's Birthplace, Lumbini, Nepal — A136

Buddha's: 1b, Place of Enlightenment, Bihar. 2b, Place of first sermon, Benares. 3b, Place of death, Kusinara.

1971, May 9   Engr.   Perf. 13½
581 A136 50s violet blue & blk   1.00   .30
582 A136 1b green & black   1.25   .55
583 A136 2b dull yellow & blk   3.25   .70
584 A136 3b red & black   2.75   1.50
Nos. 581-584 (4)   8.25   3.05

20th anniv. of World Fellowship of Buddhists.

King Bhumibol and Subjects — A137

Perf. 13½
1971, June 9   Unwmk.   Litho.
585 A137 50s silver & multi   1.40   .30
King Bhumibol's Silver Jubilee.

Floating Market — A138

1971, June 20   Photo.   Wmk. 329
586 A138 4b gold & multi   2.75   .65
Visit Asia Year.

Boy Scouts Saluting — A139

1971, July 1   Litho.
587 A139 50s orange & multi   1.25   .40
60th anniversary of Thai Boy Scouts.

Blocks of four of Nos. 354 and 403 Overprinted in Dark Blue

a

b

Perf. 13½x13
1971, Aug.   Wmk. 334   Engr.
588 A57 (a) Block of 4   8.00   8.00
a.   80s orange, single stamp   2.00   2.00

Perf. 13x13½
Photo.   Wmk. 329
589 A71 (b) Block of 4   8.00   8.00
a.   80s dull orange, single stamp   2.00   2.00

THAILANDPEX '71, Philatelic Exhib., Aug. 4-8.

Woman Writing Letter — A140

Designs: 1b, Women reading mail. 2b, Woman sitting on porch. 3b, Man handing letter to woman.

Wmk. 334
1971, Oct. 3   Litho.   Perf. 13½
590 A140 50s gray & multi   .70   .25
591 A140 1b red brown & multi   1.00   .25
592 A140 2b ultra & multi   1.75   .50
593 A140 3b lt gray & multi   2.75   1.25
Nos. 590-593 (4)   6.20   2.25

Intl. Letter Writing Week, Oct. 6-12.

Wat Benchamabopit (Marble Temple), Bangkok — A141

Perf. 13½x14
1971, Oct. 24   Litho.   Unwmk.
594 A141 50s multicolored   1.50   .45
United Nations Day, Oct. 24.

Duck Raising — A142

Rural occupations: 1b, Raising tobacco. 2b, Fishermen. 3b, Rice winnowing.

Wmk. 329
1971, Nov. 15   Photo.   Perf. 12½
595 A142 50s lt blue & multi   .65   .25
596 A142 1b multicolored   1.00   .40
597 A142 2b blue & multi   1.60   .40
598 A142 3b buff & multi   3.25   1.60
Nos. 595-598 (4)   6.50   2.65

UNICEF Emblem, Mother and Child — A143

1971, Dec. 11   Wmk. 334   Perf. 13½
599 A143 50s blue & multi   .65   .25
25th anniv. of UNICEF.

Thai Costumes, 17th Century — A144

Thai Costumes: 1b, 13th-14th cent. 1.50b, 14th-17th cent. 2b, 18th-19th cent.

Perf. 13½x14
1972, Jan. 12   Litho.   Unwmk.
600 A144 50s multicolored   .80   .40
601 A144 1b multicolored   1.25   .70
602 A144 1.50b multicolored   3.25   .80
603 A144 2b blue & multi   6.00   1.60
Nos. 600-603 (4)   11.30   3.50

Globe A145

Perf. 13x13½
1972, Apr. 1   Photo.   Wmk. 334
604 A145 75s violet blue   1.10   .25
Asian-Oceanic Postal Union, 10th anniv.

King Bhumibol Adulyadej — A146

Perf. 13½x13
1972-77   Litho.   Wmk. 329
Size: 21x26mm
605 A146 10s yellow green   .45   .25
606 A146 20s blue   .70   .25
607 A146 25s rose red   .70   .25
608 A146 75s lilac   1.50   .25
Engr.
609 A146 1.25b yel grn & pink   3.00   .40
610 A146 2.75b red brn & blue grn   2.50   .65
611 A146 3b brn & dk blue ('74)   5.50   .65
612 A146 4b blue & org red ('73)   3.25   .65
613 A146 5b dk vio & red brown   3.50   .70
614 A146 6b green & vio   7.50   .70
615 A146 10b ver & black   6.00   .65
616 A146 20b org & yel grn   6.00   1.10
617 A146 40b dp bis & lilac ('74)   32.50   10.00
618 A146 50b pur & brt grn ('77)   45.00   3.50
619 A146 100b dp org & bl ('77)   65.00   5.50
Nos. 605-619 (15)   183.10   25.50

See Nos. 835-838, 907-908.
For surcharges, see Nos. 2248, 2281-2282.

Iko Women — A147

Hill Tribes: 2b, Musoe musician. 4b, Yao weaver. 5b, Maeo farm woman.

Wmk. 334
1972, May 11   Photo.   Perf. 13½
620 A147 50s multicolored   .30   .25
621 A147 2b dark gray & multi   1.60   .40
622 A147 4b multicolored   8.00   3.50
623 A147 5b multicolored   11.00   1.00
Nos. 620-623 (4)   20.90   5.15

Ruby A148

Precious Stones: 2b, Yellow sapphire. 4b, Zircon. 6b, Star sapphire.

1972, June 7   Litho.

624	A148	75s gray & multi	1.75	.25
625	A148	2b multicolored	8.75	1.00
626	A148	4b multicolored	12.00	4.50
627	A148	6b crimson & multi	15.00	5.00
		Nos. 624-627 (4)	37.50	10.75

Prince Vajiralongkorn A149

Perf. 13½x13

1972, July 28   Photo.   Wmk. 329

628 A149 75s tan & multi   2.00   .40

20th birthday of Prince Vajiralongkorn, heir apparent.

Thai Costume A150

Designs: Costumes of Thai women.

Perf. 14x13½

1972, Aug. 12   Litho.   Wmk. 356

629	A150	75s tan & multi	1.00	.25
630	A150	2b multicolored	2.00	.70
631	A150	4b yellow & multi	5.50	3.25
632	A150	5b gray & multi	6.00	2.50
a.		Souvenir sheet of 4, #629-632	47.50	40.00
		Nos. 629-632 (4)	14.50	6.70

Rambutan — A151

Fruits: 1b, Mangosteen. 3b, Durian. 5b, Mango.

1972, Sept. 7   Wmk. 334   Perf. 13½

633	A151	75s multicolored	1.00	.25
634	A151	1b multicolored	2.40	.55
635	A151	3b pink & multi	6.00	1.40
636	A151	5b lt ultra & multi	12.00	2.50
		Nos. 633-636 (4)	21.40	4.70

Lod Cave, Phangnga — A152

1.25b, Kang Krachan Reservoir. 2.75b, Erawan Waterfalls, Kanchanaburi. 3b, Nok-Kaw Cliff, Loei.

1972, Nov. 15   Litho.   Wmk. 334

637	A152	75s multicolored	.80	.25
638	A152	1.25b multicolored	1.60	1.00
639	A152	2.75b multicolored	5.50	.65
640	A152	3b multicolored	4.50	1.75
		Nos. 637-640 (4)	12.40	3.65

Intl. Letter Writing Week, Oct. 9-15.

Princess Mother Visiting Old People — A153

1972, Oct. 21   Photo.   Wmk. 329

641 A153 75s dk green & ocher   5.00   1.00

Princess Mother Sisangwan, 72nd birthday.

UN Emblem and Globe — A154

Wmk. 334

1972, Nov. 15   Litho.   Perf. 14

642 A154 75s blue & multi   .80   .65

25th anniversary of the Economic Commission for Asia and the Far East (ECAFE).

Educational Center and Book Year Emblem — A155

1972, Dec. 8   Perf. 13½

643 A155 75s multicolored   .65   .25

International Book Year 1972.

Crown Prince Vajiralongkorn A156

1972, Dec. 28   Photo.   Wmk. 329

644 A156 2b brt blue & multi   1.90   .40

Investiture of Prince Vajiralongkorn Salayacheevin as Crown Prince.

Flag, Soldiers and Civilians — A157

1973, Feb. 3   Wmk. 334   Perf. 13½

645 A157 75s multicolored   1.20   .25

25th anniversary of Veterans Day.

Savings Bank, Emblem and Coin — A158

1973, Apr. 1   Wmk. 329

646 A158 75s emerald & multi   .85   .25

60th anniv. of Government Savings Bank.

WHO Emblem and Deity — A159

1973, Apr. 1   Wmk. 329

647 A159 75s brt green & multi   .80   .25

25th World Health Organization Day.

Water Lily A160

Designs: Various water lilies (Thai lotus).

Perf. 11x13

1973, May 15   Litho.   Wmk. 356

648	A160	75s violet & multi	1.00	.25
649	A160	1.50b brown & multi	2.00	.35
650	A160	2b dull grn & multi	3.50	.75
651	A160	4b black & multi	9.00	3.50
		Nos. 648-651 (4)	15.50	4.85

King Bhumibol Adulyadej — A161

Perf. 14x13½

1973-81   Photo.   Wmk. 334

652	A161	5s purple	1.75	.55
653	A161	20s blue	1.75	.55
a.		Perf. 14½, wmk. 233	.30	.25
654	A161	25s rose carmine	2.25	.45

Wmk. 233   Perf. 14½

655	A161	25s brown red ('81)	.30	.25
656	A161	50s dk olive grn ('79)	1.50	.25
657	A161	75s violet	1.25	.25
a.		Perf. 14x13½, wmk. 334	2.25	.45

Wmk. 334   Engr.   Perf. 13

658	A161	5b violet & brown	12.50	1.50
659	A161	6b green & violet	7.50	1.60
660	A161	10b red & black	14.00	2.00
661	A161	20b org & yel grn	175.00	8.00
		Nos. 652-661 (10)	217.80	15.40

For surcharges see Nos. 1168A, 1548, 2249.

Silversmiths — A162

1973, June 15   Litho.   Perf. 13½

662	A162	75s shown	.65	.25
663	A162	2.75b Lacquerware	2.25	.55
664	A162	4b Pottery	5.50	3.00

665	A162	5b Paper umbrellas	5.75	1.00
		Nos. 662-665 (4)	14.15	4.80

Thai handicrafts.

Fresco from Temple of the Emerald Buddha — A163

Designs: Frescoes illustrating Ramayana in Temple of the Emerald Buddha.

1973, July 17   Photo.   Wmk. 329

666	A163	25s multicolored	1.00	.40
667	A163	75s multicolored	1.00	.40
668	A163	1.50b multicolored	3.25	1.25
669	A163	2b multicolored	5.50	1.60
670	A163	2.75b multicolored	2.75	.65
671	A163	3b multicolored	10.00	2.00
672	A163	5b multicolored	13.50	6.75
673	A163	6b multicolored	6.00	2.50
		Nos. 666-673 (8)	43.00	15.55

Development of Postal Service — A164

2b, Telecommunications development.

1973, Aug. 4   Perf. 13½

674	A164	75s multicolored	.70	.40
675	A164	2b multicolored	2.00	.95

90th anniv. of Post and Telegraph Dept.

No. 1 and Other Stamps — A165

Various Stamps and: 1.25b, No. 147. 1.50b, No. 209. 2b, No. 244.

1973, Aug. 4   Photo. & Engr.

676	A165	75s dp rose & dk bl	.65	.25
677	A165	1.25b blue & dp rose	1.75	.50
678	A165	1.50b olive & vio blk	5.50	1.60
679	A165	2b orange & sl grn	4.00	.65
a.		Souvenir sheet of 4	21.00	17.50
		Nos. 676-679 (4)	11.90	3.00

2nd Natl. Phil. Exhib., THAIPEX '73, Aug. 4-8. No. 679a contains 4 stamps with simulated perforations similar to Nos. 676-679.

INTERPOL Emblem — A166

1973, Sept. 3   Photo.

680 A166 75s gray & multi   1.00   .25

Intl. Criminal Police Organization, 50th anniv.

"Lilid Pralaw" — A167

Designs: Scenes from Thai literature.

Perf. 11x13
1973, Oct. 7   Litho.   Wmk. 368
681 A167 75s green & multi   .40   .25
682 A167 1.50b blue & multi   1.60   .60
683 A167 2b multicolored   3.50   1.40
684 A167 5b blue & multi   9.50   2.00
a. Souvenir sheet of 4, #681-
    684, perf. 13x14   40.00 27.50
    Nos. 681-684 (4)   15.00   4.25
Intl. Letter Writing Week, Oct. 7-13.

Wat Suan Dok,
Chiangmai; UN
Emblem — A168

1973, Oct. 24   Perf. 13x11
685 A168 75s blue & multi   1.20   .35
United Nations Day.

Schomburgk's Deer — A169

Wmk. 329
1973, Nov. 14   Photo.   Perf. 13½
686 A169 20s shown   .80   .30
687 A169 25s Kouprey   .80   .30
688 A169 75s Gorals   1.40   .30
689 A169 1.25b Water buffalos 1.90   .95
690 A169 1.50b Javan rhi-
          noceros   8.00   3.25
691 A169 2b Eld's deer   10.00   3.25
692 A169 2.75b Asiatic 2-
          horned rhi-
          noceros   8.00   1.00
693 A169 4b Serows   12.00   8.00
    Nos. 686-693 (8)   42.90 17.35
Protected animals.

Human Rights Flame — A170

Wmk. 371
1973, Dec. 10   Litho.   Perf. 12½
694 A170 75s multicolored   1.40   .45
25th anniversary of the Universal Declaration of Human Rights.

Children and
Flowers — A171

1974, Jan. 12   Litho.   Perf. 13
695 A171 75s multicolored   1.50   .30
Children's Day.

Siriraj Hospital and Statue of Prince
Nakarin — A172

Perf. 13x13½
1974, Mar. 17   Photo.   Wmk. 368
696 A172 75s multicolored   1.25   .40
84th anniversary of Siriraj Hospital, oldest medical school in Thailand.

Phala Piang
Lai — A173

Classical Thai Dances: 2.75b, Phra Lux Phlaeng Rit. 4b, Chin Sao Sai. 5b, Charot Phra Sumen.

Wmk. 334
1974, June 25   Litho.   Perf. 14
697 A173 75s pink & multi   1.20   .40
698 A173 2.75b gray bl & multi 3.00   .65
699 A173 4b gray & multi   6.75   4.00
700 A173 5b yellow & multi   6.75   3.25
    Nos. 697-700 (4)   17.70   8.30

Large Teak Tree in Uttaradit
Province — A174

1974, July 5   Wmk. 329   Perf. 12½
701 A174 75s multicolored   1.00   .40
15th Arbor Day.

People and WPY Emblem — A175

Perf. 10½x13
1974, Aug. 19   Litho.   Wmk. 368
702 A175 75s multicolored   .95   .30
World Population Year, 1974.

Ban Chiang Painted Vase — A176

75s, Royal chariot. 2.75b, Avalokitesavara Bodhisattva. 3b, King Mongkut, Rama IV.

1974, Sept. 19   Wmk. 262   Perf. 12½
703 A176 75s blue & multi   .85   .40
704 A176 2b black, brn & bis 2.25   .85
705 A176 2.75b black, brn & tan 3.00   .70
706 A176 3b black & multi   4.00   2.25
    Nos. 703-706 (4)   10.10   4.20
Centenary of National Museum. Inscribed "BATH" in error.

Purging Cassia — A177

1974, Oct. 6   Wmk. 368   Perf. 11x13
707 A177 75s shown   .75   .25
708 A177 2.75b Butea   2.75   .65
709 A177 3b Jasmine   5.50   1.00
710 A177 4b Lagerstroemia   4.75   2.00
a. Souvenir sheet of 4, #707-
    710, perf. 13½x14   45.00 45.00
    Nos. 707-710 (4)   13.75   3.90
Intl. Letter Writing Week, Oct. 6-12.

"UPU" and UPU Emblem — A178

1974, Oct. 9   Wmk. 371   Perf. 12½
711 A178 75s dk green & multi 1.10   .45
Centenary of Universal Postal Union.

Wat Suthat Thepvararam — A179

Wmk. 329
1974, Oct. 24   Photo.   Perf. 13
712 A179 75s multicolored   1.50   .45
United Nations Day.

Elephant Roundup — A180

Wmk. 371
1974, Nov. 16   Engr.   Perf. 12½
713 A180 4b multicolored   4.75   2.00
Tourist publicity.

Vanda Coerulea — A181

Orchids: 2.75b, Dendrobium aggregatum. 3b, Dendrobium scabrilingue. 4b, Aerides falcata.

Perf. 11x13
1974, Dec. 5   Photo.   Wmk. 368
714 A181 75s red & multi   .95   .30
715 A181 2.75b multicolored 2.25   .70
716 A181 3b olive & multi   4.50   2.00
717 A181 4b green & multi   4.50   2.25
a. Souvenir sheet of 4, #714-
    717, perf. 13½x14   45.00 45.00
    Nos. 714-717 (4)   12.20   5.25
See Nos. 745-748.

Boy — A182

Perf. 14x13½
1975, Jan. 11   Litho.   Wmk. 374
718 A182 75s vermilion & multi 2.40   .55
Children's Day.

Democracy Monument — A183

Designs: 2b, Mother with children and animals, bas-relief from Democracy Monument. 2.75b, Workers, bas-relief from Democracy Monument. 5b, Top of Democracy Monument and quotation from speech of King Rama VII.

Perf. 14x14½
1975, Jan. 26   Wmk. 233
719 A183 75s dull grn & multi .95   .30
720 A183 2b multicolored   2.50   .65
721 A183 2.75b blue & multi 4.50   .70
722 A183 5b multicolored   4.75   1.90
    Nos. 719-722 (4)   12.70   3.55
Movement of Oct. 14, 1973, to re-establish democratic institutions.

Marbled Tiger Cat — A184

1975, Mar. 5   Wmk. 334   Perf. 13½
723 A184 20s shown   1.00   .65
724 A184 75s Gaurs   2.40   .65
725 A184 2.75b Asiatic elephant 8.00 1.25
726 A184 3b Clouded leop-
          ard   7.00   3.25
    Nos. 723-726 (4)   18.40   5.80
Protected animals.

White-eyed River
Martin — A185

Birds: 2b, Paradise flycatchers. 2.75b, Long-tailed broadbills. 5b, Sultan tit.

Wmk. 371

1975, Apr. 2		**Litho.**		***Perf. 12½***	
727	A185	75s	ocher & multi	1.60	.95
728	A185	2b	lt blue & multi	3.75	1.60
729	A185	2.75b	lt violet & multi	4.00	1.60
730	A185	5b	rose & multi	8.00	2.75
		Nos. 727-730 (4)		17.35	6.90

King Bhumibol Adulyadej and Queen
Sirikit — A186

3b, King, Queen, different background design.

Perf. 10½x13

1975, Apr. 28		**Photo.**		**Wmk. 368**	
731	A186	75s	violet bl & multi	2.40	.65
732	A186	3b	multicolored	4.50	1.50

25th wedding anniversary of King Bhumibol Adulyadej and Queen Sirikit.

Round-house Kick — A187

Thai Boxing: 2.75b, Reverse elbow. 3b, Flying knee. 5b, Ritual homage.

Wmk. 371

1975, May 20		**Litho.**		***Perf. 12½***	
733	A187	75s	green & multi	1.60	.45
734	A187	2.75b	blue & multi	4.00	1.20
735	A187	3b	orange & multi	4.75	2.40
736	A187	5b	orange & multi	14.00	4.00
		Nos. 733-736 (4)		24.35	8.05

Tosakanth
Mask — A188

Masks: 2b, Kumbhakarn. 3b, Rama. 4b, Hanuman.

1975, June 10		**Litho.**		**Wmk. 371**	
737	A188	75s	dark gray & multi	1.75	.30
738	A188	2b	dull vio & multi	4.75	.65
739	A188	3b	purple & multi	5.50	1.75
740	A188	4b	multicolored	13.00	6.00
		Nos. 737-740 (4)		25.00	8.70

Thai art and literature.

THAIPEX 75 Emblem — A189

THAIPEX 75 Emblem and: 2.75b, Stamp designer. 4b, Stamp printing plant. 5b, Stamp collector.

1975, Aug. 4		**Wmk. 371**		***Perf. 12½***	
741	A189	75s	yellow & multi	.65	.30
742	A189	2.75b	orange & multi	1.75	.65
743	A189	4b	lt blue & multi	2.75	1.75
744	A189	5b	carmine & multi	3.25	.65
		Nos. 741-744 (4)		8.40	3.35

THAIPEX 75, Third National Philatelic Exhibition, Aug. 4-10.

Orchid Type of 1974

Orchids: 75s, Dendrobium cruentum. 2b, Dendrobium parishii. 2.75b, Vanda teres. 5b, Vanda denisoniana.

Perf. 11x13

1975, Aug. 12		**Photo.**		**Wmk. 368**	
745	A181	75s	olive & multi	.85	.55
746	A181	2b	multicolored	2.25	1.40
747	A181	2.75b	scarlet & multi	4.00	1.40
748	A181	5b	ultra & multi	6.75	2.25
a.		Souv. sheet, #745-748, perf 13½		52.50	52.50
		Nos. 745-748 (4)		13.85	5.60

Mytilus Smaragdinus — A190

Sea Shells: 1b, Turbo marmoratus. 2.75b, Oliva mustelina. 5b, Cypraea moneta.

Perf. 14x14½

1975, Sept. 5		**Litho.**		**Wmk. 375**	
749	A190	75s	yellow & multi	2.00	.85
750	A190	1b	ver & multi	1.75	.25
751	A190	2.75b	blue & multi	5.50	.40
752	A190	5b	green & multi	11.00	3.75
		Nos. 749-752 (4)		20.25	5.25

Yachting and Games Emblem — A191

Designs: 1.25b, Badminton. 1.50b, Volleyball. 2b, Target shooting.

Perf. 11x13

1975, Sept. 20		**Litho.**		**Wmk. 368**	
753	A191	75s	ultra & black	1.00	.30
754	A191	1.25b	brt rose & blk	1.40	.95
755	A191	1.50b	red & black	2.50	1.75
756	A191	2b	apple grn & blk	3.50	1.90
a.		Souv. sheet, #753-756, perf 13½		40.00	40.00
		Nos. 753-756 (4)		8.40	4.90

8th SEAP Games, Bangkok, Sept. 1975.

Pataya
Beach
A192

Views: 2b, Samila Beach. 3b, Prachuap Bay. 5b, Laem Singha Bay.

1975, Oct. 5		**Wmk. 371**		***Perf. 12½***	
757	A192	75s	orange & multi	1.10	.65
758	A192	2b	orange & multi	2.40	1.50
759	A192	3b	orange & multi	6.00	.85
760	A192	5b	orange & multi	7.00	2.00
		Nos. 757-760 (4)		16.50	5.00

Intl. Letter Writing Week, Oct. 6-12.

"u n," UN Emblem, Food and
Education for Children — A193

1975, Oct. 24		**Litho.**		**Wmk. 371**	
761	A193	75s	ultra & multi	1.40	.45

United Nations Day.

Morse Telegraph — A194

Design: 2.75b, Teleprinter and radar.

Perf. 14x14½

1975, Nov. 4		**Litho.**		**Wmk. 334**	
762	A194	75s	multicolored	1.50	.70
763	A194	2.75b	blue & multi	2.25	.80

Centenary of telegraph system.

Sukhrip Khrong Mueang
Barge — A195

Thai ceremonial barges: 1b, Royal escort barge Anekchat Phuchong. 2b, Royal barge Anantanakarat. 2.75b, Krabi Ran Ron Rap barge. 3b, Asura Wayuphak barge. 4b, Asura paksi barge. 5b, Royal barge Sri Suphanahong, 6b, Phali Rang Thawip barge.

Wmk. 371

1975, Nov. 18		**Litho.**		***Perf. 12½***	
764	A195	75s	multicolored	2.40	.45
765	A195	1b	multicolored	4.00	1.90
766	A195	2b	lilac & multi	6.00	2.00
767	A195	2.75b	multicolored	6.75	2.25
768	A195	3b	yellow & multi	8.00	2.75
769	A195	4b	multicolored	8.00	6.00
770	A195	5b	gray & multi	15.00	6.50
771	A195	6b	blue & multi	12.00	6.00
		Nos. 764-771 (8)		62.15	27.85

Thai Flag, Arms
of Chakri Royal
Family — A196

King Bhumibol
Adulyadej — A197

Perf. 15x14

1975, Dec. 5		**Litho.**		**Wmk. 375**	
772	A196	75s	multicolored	2.75	.85
773	A197	5b	multicolored	5.00	1.50

King Bhumibol's 48th birthday.

Shot Put and SEAP Emblem — A198

2b, Table tennis. 3b, Bicycling. 4b, Relay race.

1975, Dec. 9		**Wmk. 368**		***Perf. 11x13***	
774	A198	1b	orange & black	.80	.25
775	A198	2b	brt green & blk	2.75	1.60
776	A198	3b	ocher & blk	3.25	1.75
777	A198	4b	violet & blk	3.50	2.40
a.		Souvenir sheet of 4, #774-777, perf. 13½		37.50	37.50
		Nos. 774-777 (4)		10.30	6.00

8th SEAP Games, Bangkok, Dec. 9-20.

IWY Emblem and Globe — A199

Perf. 14x14½

1975, Dec. 20				**Wmk. 375**	
778	A199	75s	blk, org & vio bl	1.10	.30

International Women's Year.

Children Writing on
Slate — A200

Perf. 13x14

1976, Jan. 10		**Litho.**		**Wmk. 368**	
779	A200	75s	lt green & multi	1.60	.70

Children's Day.

Macrobrachium Rosenbergii — A201

Designs: 2b, Penaeus merguiensis. 2.75b, Panulirus ornatus. 5b, Penaeus monodon.

1976, Feb. 18				***Perf. 11x13***	
780	A201	75s	multicolored	2.50	.30
781	A201	2b	multicolored	4.00	2.00
782	A201	2.75b	multicolored	4.00	.65
783	A201	5b	multicolored	9.50	4.50
		Nos. 780-783 (4)		20.00	7.45

Shrimp and lobster exports.

Golden-backed
Three-toed
Woodpecker
A202

Birds: 1.50b, Greater green-billed malcoha.
3b, Pomatorhinus hypoleucos. 4b, Green
magpie.

Wmk. 371

1976, Apr. 2   Litho.   Perf. 12½
784	A202	1b multicolored	.80	.45
785	A202	1.50b multicolored	.80	.65
786	A202	3b yellow & multi	4.00	1.20
787	A202	4b rose & multi	3.00	.95
		Nos. 784-787 (4)	8.60	3.25

Ban Chiang
Vase — A203

Designs: Ban Chiang painted pottery, various vessels, Bronze Age.

Perf. 14½x14

1976, May 5   Litho.   Wmk. 375
788	A203	1b olive & multi	1.25	.25
789	A203	2b dp blue & multi	5.25	.65
790	A203	3b green & multi	3.75	.55
791	A203	4b org red & multi	6.00	3.50
		Nos. 788-791 (4)	16.25	4.95

Mailman,
1883 — A204

Designs: 3b, Mailman, 1935. 4b, Mailman,
1950. 5b, Mailman, 1974.

Wmk. 377

1976, Aug. 4   Litho.   Perf. 12½
792	A204	1b multicolored	.95	.30
793	A204	3b multicolored	2.75	1.60
794	A204	4b multicolored	4.25	2.40
795	A204	5b multicolored	6.00	1.60
		Nos. 792-795 (4)	13.95	5.90

Development of mailmen's uniforms.

Kinnari — A205

Thai Mythology: 2b, Suphan-mat-cha. 4b,
Garuda. 5b, Naga.

1976, Oct. 3   Wmk. 368   Perf. 11x13
796	A205	1b green & multi	6.00	1.75
797	A205	2b ultra & multi	1.60	.30
798	A205	4b green & multi	2.40	.40
799	A205	5b slate & multi	3.50	.80
		Nos. 796-799 (4)	13.50	3.25

International Letter Writing Week.

UN Emblem,
Drug Addicts,
Alcohol,
Cigarettes,
Drugs — A206

Wmk. 329

1976, Oct. 24   Photo.   Perf. 13½
800	A206	1b ultra & multi	1.20	.40

United Nations Day.

Old and New Telephones — A207

Perf. 14x14½

1976, Nov. 10   Litho.   Wmk. 375
801	A207	1b multicolored	1.20	.40

Centenary of first telephone call by Alexander Graham Bell, Mar. 10, 1876.

Sivalaya-Mahaprasad Hall — A208

Royal Houses: 2b, Cakri-Mahaprasad. 4b,
Mahisra-Prasad. 5b, Dusit-Mahaprasad.

Perf. 14x15

1976, Dec. 5   Wmk. 375   Litho.
802	A208	1b multicolored	.95	.25
803	A208	2b multicolored	6.75	.75
804	A208	4b multicolored	4.00	2.40
805	A208	5b multicolored	5.00	1.60
		Nos. 802-805 (4)	16.70	5.00

Banteng — A209

Protected animals: 2b, Tapir and young. 4b,
Sambar deer and fawn. 5b, Hog deer family.

Wmk. 334

1976, Dec. 26   Litho.   Perf. 11
806	A209	1b multicolored	5.50	2.40
807	A209	2b multicolored	6.50	2.75

Wmk. 368
808	A209	4b multicolored	3.00	.95
809	A209	5b multicolored	3.25	1.00
		Nos. 806-809 (4)	18.25	7.10

Child Casting
Shadow of
Man — A210

Wmk. 329

1977, Jan. 8   Photo.   Perf. 13½
810	A210	1b multicolored	1.40	.30

National Children's Day.

Alsthom's Electric Engine — A211

Locomotives: 2b, Davenport's electric
engine. 4b, Pacific's steam engine. 5b,
George Egestoff's steam engine.

Perf. 11x13

1977, Mar. 26   Litho.   Wmk. 368
811	A211	1b multicolored	1.50	.95
812	A211	2b multicolored	6.00	2.50
813	A211	4b multicolored	13.50	8.00
814	A211	5b multicolored	20.00	6.00
		Nos. 811-814 (4)	41.00	17.45

80th anniv. of State Railroad of Thailand.

Chulalongkorn University
Auditorium — A212

1977, Mar. 26   Photo.
815	A212	1b multicolored	1.50	.40

Chulalongkorn University, 60th anniversary.

Flags of AOPU Members — A213

Wmk. 371

1977, Apr. 1   Litho.   Perf. 12½
816	A213	1b multicolored	1.50	.40

Asian-Oceanic Postal Union (AOPU), 15th
anniv.

Invalid in Wheelchair and
Soldiers — A214

Wmk. 329

1977, Apr. 2   Photo.   Perf. 13½
817	A214	5b multicolored	1.75	.45

Sai-Jai-Thai Day, to publicize Sai-Jai-Thai
Foundation which helps wounded soldiers.

Phra
Aphai
Mani
and
Phisua
Samut
A215

Puppets: 3b, Rusi and Sutsakhon. 4b, Nang
Vali and Usren. 5b, Phra Aphai Mani and Nang
Laweng's portrait.

Perf. 11x13

1977, June 16   Wmk. 368
818	A215	2b multicolored	.80	.25
819	A215	3b multicolored	2.00	.40
820	A215	4b multicolored	1.60	.40
821	A215	5b multicolored	2.40	.65
		Nos. 818-821 (4)	6.80	1.70

Thai plays and literature.

Drum
Dance — A216

Designs: 3b, Dance of dip nets. 4b, Harvest
dance. 5b, Kan dance.

1977, July 14   Photo.   Perf. 13x11
822	A216	2b rose & multi	.30	.25
823	A216	3b lt green & multi	1.60	.45
824	A216	4b yellow & multi	1.40	.40
825	A216	5b lt violet & multi	1.60	.45
		Nos. 822-825 (4)	4.90	1.55

Thailand No. 609, Various Stamps and
Thaipex Emblem — A217

Wmk. 377

1977, Aug. 4   Litho.   Perf. 12½
826	A217	75s multicolored	1.40	.40

THAIPEX 77, 4th National Philatelic Exhibition, Aug. 4-12.

Scenes from Thai Literature — A218

Perf. 11x13

1977, Oct. 5   Photo.   Wmk. 368
827	A218	75s multicolored	2.40	.30
828	A218	2b multi, diff.	2.40	.40
829	A218	5b multi, diff.	3.00	.50
830	A218	6b multi, diff.	4.00	.95
		Nos. 827-830 (4)	11.80	2.55

Intl. Letter Writing Week, Oct. 6-12.

Old and New Buildings, UN
Emblem — A219

1977, Oct. 5   Litho.   Perf. 11x13
831	A219	75s multicolored	1.90	.30

United Nations Day.

King Bhumibol as Scout Leader,
Camp and Emblem — A220

1977, Nov. 21   Photo.   Wmk. 368
832	A220	75s multicolored	2.50	.30

9th National Jamboree, Nov. 21-27.

Diseased Hand and Elbow — A221

1977, Dec. 20   *Perf. 11x13*
833 A221 75s multicolored   1.25 .30

World Rheumatism Year.

Map of South East Asia and ASEAN
Emblem — A222

Wmk. 377
1977, Dec. 1   **Litho.**   *Perf. 12½*
834 A222 5b multicolored   2.25 .45

ASEAN, 10th anniv.

King Type of 1972-74 Redrawn
1976   *Perf. 12½x13*
Size: 21x27mm
835 A146 20s blue   6.00 .65
836 A146 75s lilac   6.00 .65

Engr.
837 A146 10b vermilion & blk   55.00 3.50
838 A146 40b bister & lilac   12.00 2.25
   Nos. 835-838 (4)   79.00 7.05

Numerals are taller and thinner and leaves
in background have been redrawn.

Children Carrying Flag of
Thailand — A223

Wmk. 329
1978, Jan. 9   **Photo.**   *Perf. 13½*
839 A223 75s multicolored   1.75 .45

Children's Day.

Dendrobium Heterocarpum — A224

Orchids: 1b, Dendrobium pulchellum. 1.50b,
Doritis pulcherrima. 2b, Dendrobium
hercoglossum. 2.75b, Aerides odorata. 3b,
Trichoglottis fasciata. 5b, Dendrobium wardi-
anum. 6b, Dendrobium senile.

Perf. 11x14
1978, Jan. 18   **Wmk. 368**
840 A224   75s multicolored   1.60 .55
841 A224   1b multicolored   2.50 1.00
842 A224   1.50b multicolored   3.25 2.00
843 A224   2b multicolored   .65 .25
844 A224   2.75b multicolored   5.50 .25
845 A224   3b multicolored   .65 .25
846 A224   5b multicolored   1.00 .25
847 A224   6b multicolored   1.40 1.25
   Nos. 840-847 (8)   16.55 5.80

9th World Orchid Conference.

Census Chart, Symbols of
Agriculture — A225

Wmk. 377
1978, Mar. 1   **Litho.**   *Perf. 12½*
848 A225 75s multicolored   .65 .25

Agricultural census, Apr. 1978.

Anabas Testudineus — A226

Fish: 2b, Datnioides microlepis. 3b,
Kryptopterus apogon. 4b, Probarbus Jullieni.

Perf. 11x13
1978, Apr. 13   **Photo.**   **Wmk. 368**
849 A226 1b multicolored   2.40 1.60
850 A226 2b multicolored   1.50 .40
851 A226 3b multicolored   1.50 .40
852 A226 4b multicolored   2.25 .50
   Nos. 849-852 (4)   7.65 2.90

Birth of Prince Siddhartha — A227

Murals: 3b, Prince Siddhartha cuts his hair.
5b, Buddha descending from Tavatimsa
Heaven. 6b, Buddha entering Nirvana.

Wmk. 329
1978, June 15   **Photo.**   *Perf. 13½*
853 A227 2b multicolored   2.40 .70
854 A227 3b multicolored   4.75 1.10
855 A227 5b multicolored   9.50 3.75
856 A227 6b multicolored   5.50 2.40
   Nos. 853-856 (4)   22.15 7.95

Story of Gautama Buddha, murals in Puthi
Savan Hall, National Museum, Bangkok.

Bhumibol Dam — A228

Dams and Reservoirs: 2b, Sirikit dam.
2.75b, Vajiralongkorn dam. 6b, Ubol Ratana
dam.

Perf. 14x14½
1978, July 28   **Litho.**   **Wmk. 233**
857 A228   75s multicolored   1.10 .25
858 A228   2b multicolored   1.40 .25
859 A228   2.75b multicolored   2.75 .25
860 A228   6b multicolored   4.25 2.00
   Nos. 857-860 (4)   9.50 2.75

Idea Lynceus — A229

Butterflies: 3b, Sephisa chandra. 5b,
Charaxes durnfordi. 6b, Cethosia penthesilea
methypsia.

Perf. 11x13
1978, Aug. 25   **Litho.**   **Wmk. 368**
861 A229 2b lilac, blk & red   2.00 .70
862 A229 3b multicolored   3.25 .70
863 A229 5b multicolored   3.75 1.75
864 A229 6b multicolored   5.00 2.75
   Nos. 861-864 (4)   14.00 5.90

Chedi Chai
Mongkhon
Temple — A230

Temples: 2b, That Hariphunchai. 2.75b,
Borom That Chaiya. 5b, That Choeng Chum.

1978, Oct. 8   *Perf. 13x11*
865 A230   75s multicolored   1.40 .30
866 A230   2b multicolored   2.00 .30
867 A230   2.75b multicolored   3.25 .30
868 A230   5b multicolored   3.25 1.40
   Nos. 865-868 (4)   9.90 2.30

Intl. Letter Writing Week, Oct. 6-12.

Mother and
Children, UN
Emblem — A231

Perf. 14½x14
1978, Oct. 24   **Litho.**   **Wmk. 375**
869 A231 75s multicolored   .95 .25

United Nations Day.

Boxing, Soccer, Pole Vault — A232

Designs: 2b, Javelin, weight lifting, running.
3b, Ball games and sailing. 5b, Basketball,
hockey stick and boxing gloves.

Perf. 14x14½
1978, Oct.   **Wmk. 233**   **Litho.**
870 A232 75s multicolored   .80 .25
871 A232 2b multicolored   1.10 .55
872 A232 3b multicolored   2.10 .80
873 A232 5b multicolored   4.50 2.40
   Nos. 870-873 (4)   8.50 4.00

8th Asian Games, Bangkok.

Five
Races
and
World
Map
A233

1978, Nov.
874 A233 75s multicolored   .95 .25

Anti-Apartheid Year.

Children Painting Thai Flag — A234

Children and
Children's SOS
Village, Tambol
Bangpu — A235

1979, Jan. 17   *Perf. 14x14½*
875 A234 75s multicolored   .65 .25
876 A235 75s multicolored   1.40 .45

International Year of the Child.

Matuta Lunaris — A236

Crabs: 2.75b, Matuta planipes fabricius. 3b,
Portunus pelagicus. 5b, Scylla serrata.

Wmk. 377
1979, Mar. 22   **Litho.**   *Perf. 12½*
877 A236 2b multicolored   1.60 .65
878 A236 2.75b multicolored   4.75 .80
879 A236 3b multicolored   3.25 .65
880 A236 5b multicolored   5.00 2.75
   Nos. 877-880 (4)   14.60 4.85

A237

1979, June 25
881 A237 1b Sweetsop   1.75 .30
882 A237 2b Pineapple   1.75 .95
883 A237 5b Bananas   4.00 1.00
884 A237 6b Longans (litchi)   2.75 2.00
   Nos. 881-884 (4)   10.25 4.25

See Nos. 1145-1148.

A238

Young man and woman planting tree.

Perf. 13x11
1979, July 10   **Litho.**   **Wmk. 368**
885 A238 75s multicolored   .80 .25

20th Arbor Day.

Pencil, Pen, Thaipex '79
Emblem — A239

Thaipex '79 Emblem and: 2b, Envelopes.
2.75b, Stamp album. 5b, Magnifying glass and
tongs.

1979, Aug. 4		Perf. 11x13	
886	A239	75s multicolored	.65	.25
887	A239	2b multicolored	1.10	.25
888	A239	2.75b multicolored	1.25	.25
889	A239	5b multicolored	3.50	1.40
	Nos. 886-889 (4)		6.50	2.15

Thaipex '79, 5th National Philatelic Exhibition, Bangkok, Aug. 4-12.

Floral
Arrangement
A240

Designs: Decorative arrangements.

1979, Oct. 7	Litho.	Perf. 14½x14 Wmk. 233	
890	A240	75s multicolored	.65	.25
891	A240	2b multicolored	1.10	.25
892	A240	2.75b multicolored	1.75	.25
893	A240	5b multicolored	2.90	1.25
	Nos. 890-893 (4)		6.40	2.00

Intl. Letter Writing Week, Oct. 8-14.

UN Day — A241

1979, Oct. 24	Litho.	Perf. 14½x14
894	A241	75s multicolored	.85	.25

Frigate Makut Rajakumarn — A242

Thai Naval Ships: 3b, Frigate Tapi. 5b, Fast
strike craft, Prabparapak. 6b, Patrol boat T-91.

		Wmk. 329		
1979, Nov. 20	Photo.	Perf. 13½	
895	A242	2b multicolored	2.10	.40
896	A242	3b multicolored	2.10	.85
897	A242	5b multicolored	5.00	2.00
898	A242	6b multicolored	7.50	2.75
	Nos. 895-898 (4)		16.70	6.00

Thai Royal Orders (Medallions and
Ribbons) — A243

Designs: #900a, Rajamitrabhorn Order.
#902a, House of Chakri. #904a, The nine
gems. #906a, Chula Chom Klao. Pairs have
continuous design.

1979, Dec. 5	Litho.	Perf. 13x11 Wmk. 368	
899	1b multicolored	1.40	.40
900	1b multicolored	1.40	.40
a.	A243 Pair, #899-900	3.00	3.00
901	2b multicolored	1.50	.30
902	2b multicolored	1.50	.30
a.	A243 Pair, #901-902	3.25	3.25
903	5b multicolored	3.00	.70
904	5b multicolored	3.00	.70
a.	A243 Pair, #903-904	6.50	6.50
905	6b multicolored	3.75	1.40
906	6b multicolored	3.75	1.40
a.	A243 Pair, #905-906	8.00	8.00
	Nos. 899-906 (8)	19.30	5.60

See Nos. 1278-1285.

King Type of 1972-77

1979, Dec. 23	Litho.	Perf. 13½x13 Wmk. 329 Size: 21x26mm	
907	A146	50s olive green	.60	.25
		Engr.	
908	A146	2b org red & lilac	1.25	.25

Rice
Planting — A245

Children's Day: No. 910, Family in rice field.

1980, Jan. 12	Litho.	Perf. 13x11 Wmk. 368	
909	A245	75s multicolored	.85	.25
910	A245	75s multicolored	.85	.25

Family, House,
Map of
Thailand — A246

1980, Feb. 1	Litho.	Perf. 15x14 Wmk. 233	
911	A246	75s multicolored	.70	.30

Natl. Population & Housing Census, Apr.

Gold-fronted
Leafbird — A247

1980, Feb. 26		Perf. 13x11 Wmk. 368	
912	A247	75s shown	.70	.25
913	A247	2b Yellow-cheeked tit	1.00	.30
914	A247	3b Chestnut-tailed si-		
		va	2.50	.40
915	A247	5b Scarlet minivet	4.50	1.25
	Nos. 912-915 (4)		8.70	2.20

Intl. Commission for Bird Preservation, 9th
Conf. of Asian Section, Chieng-mai, 2/26-29.

Smokers and Lungs, WHO
Emblem — A248

1980, Apr. 7	Wmk. 329	Perf. 13½
916	A248	75s multicolored	.70	.25

World Health Day; fight against cigarette
smoking.

Garuda and
Rotary
Emblem — A249

1980, May 6	Wmk. 368	Perf. 13x11
917	A249	5b multicolored	1.90	.45

Rotary International, 75th anniversary.

Sai Yok Falls, Kanchanaburi — A250

1980, July 1	Litho.	Perf. 14x15 Wmk. 233	
918	A250	1b shown	.65	.25
919	A250	2b Punyaban Falls, Ra-		
		nong	.80	.25
920	A250	5b Heo Suwat Falls,		
		Nakhon Ratch-		
		asima	2.40	1.00
921	A250	6b Siriphum Falls, Chi-		
		ang Mai	2.10	1.40
	Nos. 918-921 (4)		5.95	2.90

Queen
Sirikit — A251

Family with Cattle, Ceres Medal
(Reverse) — A252

No. 524, Ceres medal (obverse), potters.

1980, Aug. 12	Litho.	Perf. 13½, 11x13 (5b) Wmk. 329, 368 (5b)	
922	A251	75s multicolored	.65	.25
923	A252	5b multicolored	1.75	.80
924	A252	5b multicolored	1.75	.80
	Nos. 922-924 (3)		4.15	1.85

Queen Sirikit's 48th birthday.

Khao Phanomrung Temple, Buri
Ram — A253

Intl. Letter Writing Week, Oct. 6-12 (Tem-
ples): 2b, Prang Ku, Chailyaphum. 2.75b,
Phimai, Nakhon Ratchasima. 5b,
Sikhoraphum, Surin.

1980, Oct. 5	Litho.	Perf. 11x13 Wmk. 368	
925	A253	75s multicolored	.80	.30
926	A253	2b multicolored	.80	.30
927	A253	2.75b multicolored	1.20	.45
928	A253	5b multicolored	2.00	1.00
	Nos. 925-928 (4)		4.80	2.05

Princess
Mother — A254

1980, Oct. 21	Litho.	Perf. 15x14 Wmk. 233	
929	A254	75s multicolored	2.75	.55
	Complete booklet, 10 #929		65.00	

Princess Mother, 80th birthday.

Golden Mount,
Bangkok — A255

1980, Oct. 24
930 A255 75s multicolored .... .65 .30
Complete booklet, 10 #930 ...... 16.00

United Nations Day.

King Bhumibol
Adulyadej — A256

Type I   Type II Redrawn

Two types of Nos. 936-938: Type I, asymmetrical shape to mouth and small eye pupils. Type II, symmetrical mouth and large eye pupils.

Perf. 11x13

1980-84(?)		Litho.	Wmk. 368	
932	A256	25s salmon	2.00	.25
933	A256	50s olive green	4.50	.25
b.		Wmk. 233, perf. 14x15	7.50	.40
c.		Wmk. 387, perf. 11x13	1.50	.25
934	A256	75s lilac	.70	.25
935	A256	1.25b yellow green	.70	.25
a.		Wmk. 387, perf. 11x13	2.25	.25
b.		Wmk. 233, perf. 14x15	6.00	.25

Perf. 13½x13

		Engr.	Wmk. 329	
936	A256	3b brn & dk bl (II)	.70	.25
a.	Type I		20.00	1.20
937	A256	5b pur & brn (II)	1.40	.30
a.	Type I		20.00	1.20
938	A256	6b dk grn & pur (II)	1.40	.25
a.	Type I		20.00	1.20
939	A256	8.50b grn & brn org	2.00	.50
940	A256	9.50b olive & dk grn	2.50	.55
		Nos. 932-940 (9)	15.90	2.85

Issued: 25s, 75s, 12/5/80; #935, 9/7/81; #933b, 12/5/81; #933, #935b, 6/8/83; 3b-9.50b, 1983.
See Nos. 1080-1093. For surcharges see Nos. 1226-1226A, 2250.

King Rama VII
Monument
Inauguration
A257

Perf. 15x14

1980, Dec. 10   **Wmk. 233**
946 A257 75s multicolored ...... .75 .30

Bencharongware Bowl — A258

Perf. 11x13

1980, Dec. 15			Wmk. 368	
947	A258	2b shown	1.20	.40
948	A258	2.75b Covered bowls	1.20	.40
949	A258	3b Covered jar	1.75	.60
950	A258	5b Stem plates	1.75	1.00
		Nos. 947-950 (4)	5.90	2.40

King Vajiravudh
Birth Centenary
A259

1981, Jan. 1   Wmk. 233   Perf. 15x14
951 A259 75s multicolored ...... 1.40 .25
Complete booklet, 10 #951 ...... 32.50

Children's
Day — A260

Perf. 13x11

1981, Jan. 16   **Wmk. 368**
952 A260 75s multicolored ...... 1.10 .25
Complete booklet, 10 #952 ...... 16.00

Hegira, 1500th Anniv. — A261

Wmk. 377

1981, Jan. 18   Litho.   Perf. 12½
953 A261 5b multicolored .... 3.25 .75

Dolls in Native Costumes — A262

Wmk. 368

1981, Feb. 6		Litho.	Perf. 13½	
954	A262	75s Palm-leaf fish mobile	.45	.25
		Complete booklet, 10 #954	12.50	
955	A262	75s Teak elephants	.45	.25
		Complete booklet, 10 #955	12.50	
956	A262	2.75b shown	1.25	.60
957	A262	2.75b Baskets	1.25	.60
		Nos. 954-957 (4)	3.40	1.70

CONEX '81 International Crafts Exhibition.

Scout Leader and
Boy on
Crutches — A263

1981, Feb. 28   **Perf. 13x11**
958 A263 75s shown .... .45 .25
Complete booklet, 10 #958 ...... 10.00
959 A263 5b Diamond cutter in wheelchair ...... 1.60 .60

International Year of the Disabled.

Dindaeng-Tarua Expressway
Opening — A264

1981, Oct. 29   **Perf. 13½**
960 A264 1b Klongtoey .... .65 .25
961 A264 5b Vipavadee Rangsit Highway ...... 2.25 .65

Ongkhot, Khon
Mask — A265

Designs: Various Khon masks.

1981, July 1		Litho.	Perf. 13x11	
962	A265	75s shown	.45	.25
963	A265	2b Maiyarab	1.00	.25
964	A265	3b Sukrip	1.60	.50
965	A265	5b Indrajit	2.00	1.25
		Nos. 962-965 (4)	5.05	2.25

Exhibition Emblem, No. 83 — A266

Wmk. 370

1981, Aug. 4		Litho.	Perf. 12	
966	A266	75s shown	.45	.25
967	A266	75s No. 144	.45	.25
968	A266	2.75b No. 198	1.25	.60
969	A266	2.75b No. 226	1.25	.60
		Nos. 966-969 (4)	3.40	1.70

A267

Perf. 15x14

1981, Aug. 26   **Wmk. 233**
970 A267 1.25b multicolored ...... .85 .25
Complete booklet, 10 #970 ...... 16.00

Luang Praditphairo, court Musician, birth centenary. THAIPEX '81 Intl. Stamp Exhibition.

A268

Designs: Dwarfed trees.

1981, Oct. 4			Wmk. 329	
971	A268	75s Mai hok-hian	.65	.25
972	A268	2b Mai kam-ma-lo	1.00	.40
973	A268	2.75b Mai khen	1.40	.30
974	A268	5b Mai khabuan	2.75	1.25
		Nos. 971-974 (4)	5.80	2.20

25th Intl. Letter Writing Week, Oct. 6-12.

World
Food
Day
A269

Wmk. 370

1981, Oct. 16   Litho.   Perf. 12
975 A269 75s multicolored ...... .65 .25

United Nations Day — A270

1981, Oct. 24   Wmk. 368   Perf. 13½
976 A270 1.25b Samran Mukhamat Pavilion ...... .85 .25

King
Cobra
A271

1981, Dec. 1		Wmk. 329	Perf. 13½	
977	A271	75s shown	.65	.25
978	A271	2b Banded krait	1.40	.65
979	A271	2.75b Thai cobra	1.60	.25
980	A271	5b Malayan pit viper	2.00	1.00
		Nos. 977-980 (4)	5.65	2.15

Children's
Day — A272

1982, Jan. 9   Wmk. 370   Perf. 12
981 A272 1.25b multicolored ...... .75 .25
Complete booklet, strip of 4 #981 ...... 10.00

Scouting
Year — A273

1982, Feb. 22
982 A273 1.25b multicolored ...... .70 .25
Complete booklet, strip of 4 #982 ...... 10.00

Bicentenary of Bangkok (Thai Capital) A274

Chakri Dynasty kings. (Rama I-Rama IX).

1982, Apr. 4   Litho.   Perf. 12

983	A274	1b Buddha Yod-Fa (1736-1809)	1.20	.45
984	A274	1.25b shown	1.20	.45
		Complete booklet, strip of 4 #984	6.50	
985	A274	2b Buddha Lert La Naphalai (1767-1824)	1.40	.45
986	A274	3b Nang Klao (1787-1851)	2.25	.65
987	A274	4b Mongkut (1804-1868)	1.60	.80
988	A274	5b Chulalongkorn (1853-1910)	2.75	.85
989	A274	6b Vajiravudh (1880-1925)	2.75	.85
990	A274	7b Prachathipok (1893-1941)	5.25	4.00
991	A274	8b Ananda Mahidol (1925-1946)	2.75	1.50
992	A274	9b Bhumibol Adulyadej (b. 1927)	3.25	1.75
a.		Souv. sheet of 10, 205x142mm	52.50	52.50
b.		Souv. sheet of 10, 195x180mm	52.50	52.50
		Nos. 983-992 (10)	24.40	11.75

Nos. 992a-992b each contain Nos. 983-992. No. 992a sold for 60b, No. 992b for 70b. Values for #992a-992b include folder.

TB Bacillus Centenary — A275

Wmk. 368
1982, Apr. 7   Litho.   Perf. 13½

993	A275	1.25b multicolored	.95 .25
		Complete booklet, strip of 4 #993	6.50

Local Flowers — A276

Perf. 14x14½
1982, June 30   Wmk. 233

994	A276	1.25b Quisqualis indica	.35	.25
		Complete booklet, strip of 4 #994	4.00	
995	A276	1.50b Murraya aniculata	.55	.30
996	A276	6.50b Mesua ferrea	2.00	1.00
997	A276	7b Desmos chinensis	1.60	.50
		Nos. 994-997 (4)	4.50	2.05

Buddhist Temples in Bangkok — A277

1982, Aug. 4   Wmk. 368   Perf. 13½

998	A277	1.25b shown	.45	.25
		Complete booklet, strip of 4 #998	4.00	
999	A277	4.25b Wat Pho	1.10	.40
1000	A277	6.50b Mahathat Yuwarat Rangsarit	1.60	.95
1001	A277	7b Phra Sri Rattana Satsadaram	2.25	.65
a.		Souv. sheet of 4, #998-1001, perf. 12½	90.00	90.00
		Nos. 998-1001 (4)	5.40	2.25

BANGKOK '83 Intl. Stamp Exhibition, Aug. 4-13, 1983. No. 1001a sold for 30b. See Nos. 1025-1026.

A278

1982, Aug. 9   Wmk. 370   Perf. 12

1002	A278	1.25b LANDSAT Satellite	.95 .30
		Complete booklet, strip of 4 #1002	6.50

2nd UN Conference on Peaceful Uses of Outer Space, Vienna, Aug. 9-21.

A279

Prince Purachatra of Kambaengbejra (1882-1936).

1982, Sept. 14   Wmk. 233   Perf. 14

1003	A279	1.25b multicolored	1.25 .30
		Complete booklet, strip of 4 #1003	8.00

26th Intl. Letter Writing Week, Oct. 6-12 — A280

Sangalok Pottery.

1982, Oct. 3   Wmk. 329   Perf. 13½

1004	A280	1.25b Covered glazed jar	.50	.25
		Complete booklet, strip of 4 #1004	6.50	
1005	A280	3b Painted jar	1.75	.50
1006	A280	4.25b Glazed plate	1.00	.65
1007	A280	7b Painted plate	2.25	1.00
		Nos. 1004-1007 (4)	5.50	2.40

UN Day — A281

1982, Oct. 24

1008	A281	1.25b Loha Prasat Tower	.85 .25
		Complete booklet, strip of 4 #1008	8.00

Musical Instruments — A282

1982, Nov. 30   Wmk. 370   Perf. 12

1009	A282	50s Chap, ching	.25	.25
1010	A282	1b Pi nai, pi nok	.70	.25
1011	A282	1.25b Klong that, taphon	.40	.25
		Complete booklet, strip of 4 #1011	6.50	
1012	A282	1.50b Khong mong, krap	.40	.30
1013	A282	6b Khong wong yai	5.00	1.75
1014	A282	7b Khong wong lek	2.00	.65
1015	A282	8b Ranat ek	1.75	.90
1016	A282	9b Ranat thum	1.75	.90
		Nos. 1009-1016 (8)	12.25	5.25

Pileated Gibbon — A283

1982, Dec. 26

1017	A283	1.25b shown	.65	.25
		Complete booklet, strip of 4 #1017	4.00	
1018	A283	3b Pig-tailed macaque	2.00	.45
1019	A283	5b Slow loris	1.50	.55
1020	A283	7b Silvered leaf monkey	1.60	.80
		Nos. 1017-1020 (4)	5.75	2.05

ASEAN Members' Flags — A284

1982, Dec. 26   Wmk. 233

1021	A284	6.50b multicolored	1.75 .65

15th Anniv. of Assoc. of Southeast Asian Nations.

Children's Day — A285

Perf. 14½x14
1983, Jan. 8   Litho.   Wmk. 233

1022	A285	1.25b multicolored	.70 .25
		Complete booklet, strip of 4 #1022	8.50

First Anniv. of Postal Code A286

1983, Feb. 25   Wmk. 329   Perf. 13½

1023	A286	1.25b Codes	.60 .25
		Complete booklet, strip of 4 #1023	7.50
1024	A286	1.25b Code on envelope	.60 .25
		Complete booklet, strip of 4 #1024	7.50

BANGKOK '83 Type of 1982

Design: Old General Post Office.

1983, Feb. 25   Wmk. 368   Photo.

1025	A277	7b multicolored	1.75	.30
1026	A277	10b multicolored	2.75	.65
a.		Souv. sheet of 2, #1025-1026, perf. 12½	32.50	32.50

25th Anniv. of Intl. Maritime Org. — A287

Perf. 14x14½
1983, Mar. 17   Litho.   Wmk. 233

1029	A287	1.25b Chinese junks	.70 .25
		Complete booklet, strip of 4 #1029	6.50

Civil Servants' Day — A288

1983, Apr. 1   Wmk. 370   Perf. 12

1030	A288	1.25b multicolored	.65 .25
		Complete booklet, strip of 4 #1030	6.50

Prince Sithiporn Kridakara (1883-1971) A289

Perf. 14½x14
1983, Apr. 11   Wmk. 233

1031	A289	1.25b multicolored	.70 .25
		Complete booklet, strip of 4 #1031	6.50

Domestic Satellite Communications System Inauguration — A290

Wmk. 368
1983, Aug. 4   Litho.   Perf. 13½

1032	A290	2b Map, dish antenna, satellite	.95 .25

BANGKOK '83 Intl. Stamp Show, Aug. 4-13 — A291

1983, Aug. 4		**Wmk. 370**	**Perf. 12**	
1033	A291	1.25b Mail collection	.25	.25
		Complete booklet, strip of 4 #1033	2.40	
1034	A291	7.50b Posting letters	1.00	.60
1035	A291	8.50b Mail transport	1.25	.75
1036	A291	9.50b Mail delivery	1.75	.75
a.		Souv. sheet of 4, #1033-1036	32.50	32.50
		Nos. 1033-1036 (4)	4.25	2.35

No. 1036a exist imperf, sold for 50b. Value, $200.

A292

Prince Bhanurangsi memorial statue.

Perf. 15x14			
1983, Aug. 4	**Litho.**	**Wmk. 233**	
1037	A292	1.25b multicolored	.80	.25
		Complete booklet, strip of 4 #1037	8.00	

A293

Wmk. 370			
1983, Sept. 27	**Litho.**	**Perf. 12**	
1038	A293	1.25b multicolored	.25	.25
		Complete booklet, strip of 4 #1038	3.50	
1039	A293	7b multicolored	1.50	.75

Malaysia/ Thailand/ Singapore submarine cable inauguration.

Intl. Letter Writing Week — A294

1983, Oct. 6	**Wmk. 329**	**Perf. 13½**	
1040	A294	2b Acropora asper	.70	.25
1041	A294	3b Platygyra lamellina	1.60	.25
1042	A294	4b Fungia	1.00	.70
1043	A294	7b Pectinia lactuca	2.00	1.10
		Nos. 1040-1043 (4)	5.30	2.30

Prince Mahidol of Songkhla — A295

Wmk. 370			
1983, Oct. 10	**Litho.**	**Perf. 12**	
1044	A295	9.50b multicolored	2.00	.75

Siriraj Hospital Faculty of Medicine and Rockefeller Foundation, 60th Anniv. of cooperation.

World Communications Year — A296

3b, Telecommunications equipment, diff.

Perf. 14x14½			
1983, Oct. 24	**Litho.**	**Wmk. 233**	
1045	A296	2b multicolored	.70	.25
1046	A296	3b multicolored	.85	.30

United Nations Day — A297

1983, Oct. 24			
1047	A297	1.25b multicolored	.65	.25
		Complete booklet, strip of 4 #1047	4.50	

Thai Alphabet, 700th Anniv. — A298

Designs: 3b, Painted pottery, Sukothai period. 7b, Thai characters, reign of King Ramkamhaeng. 8b, Buddha, Sukothai period. 9b, Mahathat Temple, Sukothai province.

1983, Nov. 17	**Wmk. 370**	**Perf. 12**	
1048	A298	3b multicolored	1.00	.25
1049	A298	7b multicolored	1.90	.45
1050	A298	8b multi, vert.	1.60	.50
1051	A298	9b multi, vert.	1.75	.65
		Nos. 1048-1051 (4)	6.25	1.85

National Development Program — A299

#1052, King and Queen initiating Royal Projects. #1053, Technical aid. #1054, Terrace farming, Irrigation dam. #1055, Gathering grain. #1056, Receiving the peoples' gratitude.

1984, May 5			
1052	A299	1.25b multicolored	.65	.25
1053	A299	1.25b multicolored	.65	.25
1054	A299	1.25b multicolored	.65	.25
1055	A299	1.25b multicolored	.65	.25
1056	A299	1.25b multicolored	.65	.25
a.		Strip of 5, #1052-1056	3.25	3.25

Children's Day — A300

1984, Jan. 14	**Wmk. 329**	**Perf. 13½**	
1057	A300	1.25b multicolored	.80	.25
		Complete booklet, strip of 4 #1057	8.00	

17th Natl. Games, Jan. 22-28 — A301

1984, Jan. 22			
1058	A301	1.25b Running	.65	.25
		Complete booklet, strip of 4 #1058	6.50	
1059	A301	3b Soccer	.65	.25

5th Rheumatology Congress, Jan. 22-27 — A302

Perf. 14x15			
1984, Jan. 22		**Wmk. 233**	
1060	A302	1.25b Rheumatic joints	.75	.25
		Complete booklet, strip of 4 #1060	6.50	

Armed Forces Day — A303

1984, Jan. 25		**Perf. 15x14**	
1061	A303	1.25b King Naresuan, tanks, jet, ship	.85	.25
		Complete booklet, strip of 4 #1061	8.00	

50th Anniv. of Royal Institute — A304

1984, Mar. 31			
1062	A304	1.25b multicolored	.70	.25
		Complete booklet, strip of 4 #1062	6.50	

Thammasat University, 50th Anniv. — A305

1984, June 27		**Perf. 14x15**	
1063	A305	1.25b Dome Building	.70	.25
		Complete booklet, strip of 4 #1063	6.50	

Asia-Pacific Broadcasting Union, 20th Anniv. — A306

1984, July 1	**Wmk. 387**	**Perf. 12**	
1064	A306	4b Map, emblem	1.25	.40

Seated Buddha, Chiang Saen Style — A307

Seated Buddhas in various styles.

Perf. 14½x14			
1984, July 12		**Wmk. 233**	
1065	A307	1.25b shown	.35	.25
1066	A307	7b Sukothai	1.60	.70
1067	A307	8.50b U-Thong	1.75	1.00
1068	A307	9.50b Ayutthaya	2.40	1.00
		Nos. 1065-1068 (4)	6.10	2.95

Intl. Letter Writing Week — A308

Medicinal Succulents: 1.50b, Alocasia indica. 2b, Aloe barbadensis. 4b, Gynura pseudochina DC. 10b, Rhoeo spathacea.

Wmk. 385			
1984, Oct. 7	**Litho.**	**Perf. 13½**	
1069	A308	1.50b multicolored	.40	.25
1070	A308	2b multicolored	.65	.25
1071	A308	4b multicolored	1.10	.45
1072	A308	10b multicolored	3.00	1.75
		Nos. 1069-1072 (4)	5.15	2.70

Princess Mother (b. 1900) — A309

Perf. 15x14

1984, Oct. 21   **Wmk. 233**
1073 A309 1.50b Portrait   .70 .25

UN Day — A310

1984, Oct. 24   **Wmk. 233**
1074 A310 1.50b Woman thresh-
           ing rice   .65 .25

Local Butterflies — A311

Wmk. 329
1984, Nov. 27   **Photo.**   **Perf. 13½**
1075 A311 2b Bhutanitis lid-
         derdalei   .65 .30
1076 A311 3b Stichophthalma
         louisa   .80 .30
1077 A311 5b Parthenos sylvia   1.40 .90
1078 A311 7b Stichophthalma
         godfreyi   2.40 .90
     Nos. 1075-1078 (4)   5.25 2.40

King Type of 1980
Perf. 13½x13, 14x15 (1.50b, 2b)
Wmk. 329, 233 (1.50b, 2b)
1984-87   **Litho.**
1080 A256   1b Prus blue   .70 .30
1081 A256 1.50b brt yel org
          ('85)   4.50 1.75
1082 A256   2b dk car ('85)   2.25 .25
  a.   Wmk. 387, perf. 11x13½
        ('86?)   4.75 .30
  b.   Wmk. 387, perf. 14½x14
        ('87)   2.40 .30

Engr.
1083 A256   2b hn brn &
          gray vio   13.00 .40
1084 A256   4b turq bl & hn
          brn   1.20 .25
1085 A256 6.50b dk yel grn &
          ol brn   1.50 .70
1086 A256   7b dl red brn &
          sep   1.90 .40
1087 A256 7.50b dk org &
          saph ('85)   1.50 .65
1088 A256   8b brn vio & ol
          grn ('85)   1.75 .55
1089 A256   9b int bl & dk ol
          bis ('85)   2.25 .70
1090 A256 10b hn brn & sl
          grn   2.25 .70
1091 A256 20b dk org & grn   5.25 .65
1092 A256 50b dp vit & grn   10.00 1.75
1093 A256 100b dp org & dk
          bl   18.00 3.25
     Nos. 1080-1093 (14)   66.05 12.30

For surcharges see Nos. 1212, 2251.
Issued: 1b, 1/25/84; No. 1083, 4b, 6.50b,
7b, 10b, 50b, 100b, 12/5/84; 7.50b, 8b, 9b,
1/25/85; 1.50b, 4/6/85; No. 1082, 8/4/85; No.
1082a, 3/3/86; No. 1082b, 6/19/87.

Children's Day — A313

Children's drawings.

Wmk. 385
1985, Jan. 12   **Litho.**   **Perf. 13½**
1101 A313 1.50b Pedestrians,
          overpass   .40 .25
1102 A313 1.50b Climbing over-
          pass, vert.   .40 .25

Bangkok Mail Center Opening — A314

1985, Feb. 25
1103 A314 1.50b multicolored   .70 .25

Phuket Province
Heroes
Bicent. — A315

Perf. 15x14
1985, Mar. 13   **Litho.**   **Wmk. 233**
1104 A315 2b multicolored   .70 .25
Tao-Thep-Krasattri,   Tao-Sri-Sundhorn
Monument.

Government Savings Bank, 72nd
Anniv. — A316

1985, Apr. 1   **Perf. 14x15**
1105 A316 1.50b King Rama VI,
          headquarters   .65 .25

Intl. Telecommunications Satellite Org.,
20th Anniv. — A317

1985, Apr. 6   **Wmk. 387**   **Perf. 12**
1106 A317 2b multicolored   .70 .25

Thai Airways Intl., 25th Anniv. — A318

Wmk. 385
1985, May 1   **Litho.**   **Perf. 13**
1107 A318   2b DC-6   .40 .25
1108 A318 7.50b DC-10   1.60 .80
1109 A318 8.50b Airbus A-300   2.00 .90
1110 A318 9.50b Boeing 747   2.40 1.00
     Nos. 1107-1110 (4)   6.40 2.95

Natl. Flag and
UPU
Emblem — A319

1985, July 1   **Wmk. 387**   **Perf. 12**
1111 A319 2b shown   .55 .25
         Perf. 13½
         Wmk. 385
1112 A319 10b Flag and ITU em-
          blem   1.60 .90
Thai membership to UPU and Intl. Telecommunications Union, cent.

Natl. Communications Day, Aug.
5 — A320

1985, Aug. 4   **Wmk. 329**   **Perf. 13½**
1113 A320 2b multicolored   .70 .25

THAIPEX '85, Aug. 4-13 — A321

1985, Aug. 4   **Wmk. 385**
1114 A321   2b Aisvarya Pavil-
          ion, vert.   .50 .25
1115 A321   3b Varopas Piman
          Pavilion   .80 .25
1116 A321   7b Vehas Camrun
          Pavilion   1.75 .65
1117 A321 10b Vitoon Tassana
          Tower, vert.   2.60 .95
  a.   Souv. sheet of 4, #1114-
        1117   65.00 65.00
     Nos. 1114-1117 (4)   5.65 2.10

No. 1117a exists imperf, sold for 40b. Value,
$700.

Natl. Science Day, Aug. 18 — A322

1985, Aug. 18   **Wmk. 387**   **Perf. 12**
1118 A322 2b King Rama IV, so-
          lar eclipse   1.20 .25

1885 Seal, Modern Map and
Crest — A323

         Perf. 14½x15
1985, Sept. 3   **Wmk. 233**
1119 A323 2b multicolored   .70 .25
Royal Thai Survey Department, Cent.

13th SEA Games, Bangkok, Dec. 8-
17 — A324

Designs: a, Boxing. b, Shot put. c, Badminton. d, Javelin. e, Weight lifting.

1985, Oct. 1   **Wmk. 387**   **Perf. 12**
1120   Strip of 5   8.50 2.50
  a.-e.   A324 2b, any single   .85 .25
  f.   Souv. sheet of 5, #a.-e. + label   35.00 35.00
     No. 1120f sold for 20b.

Climbing
Plants — A325

1985, Oct. 6   **Wmk. 385**   **Perf. 13½**
1121 A325   2b Allemanda
          cathartica   .65 .25
1122 A325   3b Jasminum auricu-
          latum   .90 .25
1123 A325   7b Passiflora
          laurifolia   1.60 .70
1124 A325 10b Antigonon
          leptopus   2.00 .85
     Nos. 1121-1124 (4)   5.15 2.05

International Letter Writing Week.

UN Child Survival
Campaign
A326

1985, Oct. 24
1125 A326 2b multicolored   .70 .25
         UN Day.

Prince
Kromamun
Bidyalabh
Bridhyakorn
(1885-1974),
Govt.
Minister — A327

1985, Nov. 7
1126   A327 2b multi   7.00 .25
1126A A327 2b multi, diff.   1.00 .25
  b.   Pair, #1126-1126A   37.50 37.50
No. 1126A has flower design framing portrait reversed.

Rangsit (1885-1951), Prince of Jainad — A328

Perf. 15x14½
1985, Nov. 12   **Wmk. 233**
1127 A328 1.50b multicolored   .85   .25

Asian-Pacific Postal Union, 5th Congress, Nov. 25-Dec. 4 — A329

1985, Nov. 25   Wmk. 385   Perf. 13½
1128 A329   2b multicolored   .40   .25
1129 A329   10b multicolored   2.00   .85

Intl. Youth Year A330

Perf. 14x15
1985, Nov. 26   **Wmk. 233**
1130 A330 2b multicolored   1.00   .30

12th Asian-Pacific Dental Congress, Bangkok, Dec. 5-10 — A331

1985, Dec. 5
1131 A331 2b multicolored   .85   .25

13th SEA Games — A332

1985, Dec. 8   Wmk. 387   Perf. 12
1132 A332 1b Volleyball   .25   .25
1133 A332 2b Sepak-takraw   .50   .25
1134 A332 3b Women's gym-
          nastics   .80   .30
1135 A332 4b Bowling   1.00   .50
   a.   Souv. sheet, #1132-1135 +
      label   32.50   32.50
    Nos. 1132-1135 (4)   2.55   1.30

No. 1135a sold for 20b.

French Envoys — A333

1985, Dec. 12   Wmk. 385   Perf. 13½
1136 A333   2b shown   .55   .25
1137 A333   8.50b Thai envoys   1.60   .70

Diplomatic relations with France, 300th anniv.

Domestic Express Mail Service Inauguration — A334

1986, Jan. 1
1138 A334 2b multicolored   .85   .25
    Complete booklet, strip of 5
    #1138   8.00

Intl. Express Mail Service, EMS, 3rd anniv.

Wildlife Conservation — A335

Marine turtles.

1986, Jan. 8   **Wmk. 329**
1139 A335   1.50b Chelonia mydas   .70   .30
1140 A335   3b Eretmochelys
          imbricata   1.50   .30
1141 A335   5b Dermochelys
          coriacea   3.00   .70
1142 A335   10b Lepidochelys
          olivacea   2.40   1.00
    Nos. 1139-1142 (4)   7.60   2.30

Natl. Children's Day — A336

Design: Children picking lotus, by Areeya Makarabhundhu, age 12.

1986, Jan. 11   **Wmk. 385**
1143 A336 2b multicolored   .75   .25
    Complete booklet, strip of 5
    #1143   8.00

Statue of Sunthon Phu, Poet — A337

1986, June 26
1144 A337 2b multicolored   .75   .25
    Complete booklet, strip of 5
    #1144   8.00

Fruit Type of 1979
1986, June 26   **Wmk. 385**
1145 A237 2b Watermelon   1.50   .25
    Complete booklet, strip of 5
    #1145   12.50
1146 A237 2b Malay apple   1.50   .25
    Complete booklet, strip of 5
    #1146   12.50
1147 A237 6b Pomelo   1.50   .65
1148 A237 6b Papaya   1.50   .65
    Nos. 1145-1148 (4)   6.00   1.80

Nos. 1145-1148 horiz.

Natl. Year of the Trees A338

1986, July 21
1149 A338 2b multicolored   .70   .25
    Complete booklet, strip of 5
    #1149   5.25

Communications Day — A339

1986, Aug. 4
1150 A339 2b multicolored   .70   .25
    Complete booklet, strip of 5
    #1150   5.25

Bamboo Baskets — A340

1986, Oct. 5
1151 A340 2b Chalom   .50   .25
    Complete booklet, strip of 5
    #1151   5.25
1152 A340 2b Krabung   .50   .25
    Complete booklet, strip of 5
    #1152   5.25
1153 A340 6b Kratib   1.00   .45
1154 A340 6b Kaleb   1.00   .45
    Nos. 1151-1154 (4)   3.00   1.40

Intl. Letter Writing Week.

Intl. Peace Year A341

1986, Oct. 24
1155 A341 2b multicolored   .70   .25
    Complete booklet, strip of 5
    #1155   6.50

Productivity Year — A342

1986, Oct. 24   **Wmk. 329**
1156 A342 2b multicolored   .65   .25
    Complete booklet, strip of 5
    #1156   5.25

6th ASEAN Orchid Congress — A343

1986, Nov. 7   **Wmk. 385**
1157 A343 2b Vanda
          varavuth,
          vert.   .70   .25
    Complete booklet, strip of
    5 #1157   5.25
1158 A343 3b Ascocenda
          emma, vert.   .80   .50
1159 A343 4b Dendrobium
          sri-siam   1.40   1.10
1160 A343 5b Dendrobium
          ekapol pan-
          da   1.40   .95
   a.   Souv. sheet of 4, #1157-
      1160   110.00   110.00
    Nos. 1157-1160 (4)   4.30   2.80

No. 1160a sold for 25b.

Fungi A344

Perf. 13x13½
1986, Nov. 26   Wmk. 329   Photo.
1161 A344 2b Volvariella
          volvacea   .90   .25
    Complete booklet, strip of 5
    #1161   6.50
1162 A344 2b Pleurotus os-
          treatus   .90   .25
    Complete booklet, strip of 5
    #1162   6.50
1163 A344 6b Auricularia poly-
          tricha   2.50   .65
1164 A344 6b Pleurotus cystidi-
          osus   2.50   .65
    Nos. 1161-1164 (4)   6.80   1.80

Fisheries Dept., 60th Anniv. — A345

Wmk. 385
1986, Dec. 16   Litho.   Perf. 13½
1165 A345 2b Morulius
          chrysophekadion   .60   .25
    Complete booklet, strip of 5
    #1165   5.25
1166 A345 2b Notopterus blanci   .60   .25
    Complete booklet, strip of 5
    #1166   5.25
1167 A345 7b Scleropages
          formosus   1.40   .65
1168 A345 7b Pangasianodon gi-
          gas   1.40   .65
    Nos. 1165-1168 (4)   4.00   1.80

No. 653 Surcharged in Dark Olive Green

Perf. 14x13½
1986, Dec.   Photo.   Wmk. 233
1168A A161 1b on 20s blue   .70   .25

Children's Day — A346

Child's drawing.

Perf. 14½x15
1987, Jan. 10   Litho.   Wmk. 387
1169 2b School, playground   .70   .25
1170 2b Pool   .70   .25
  a. A346 Pair, #1169-1170   1.90   1.60

No. 1170a has continuous design.

F-16 & F-5 Fighter Planes,
Pilot — A347

1987, Mar. 27   Wmk. 385   Perf. 13½
1171 A347 2b multicolored   1.10   .25
  Complete booklet, strip of 5
  #1171   10.50

Royal Thai Air Force, 72nd anniv.

King Rama III (Nang Klao, 1787-1851) — A348

Perf. 15x14½
1987, Mar. 31   Wmk. 387
1172 A348 2b multicolored   1.00   .40
  Complete booklet, strip of 5
  #1172   10.50

Ministry of Communications, 75th
Anniv. — A349

1987, Apr. 1
1173 A349 2b multicolored   .70   .25
  Complete booklet, strip of 5
  #1173   5.25

Forestry Year — A350

1987, July 11   Wmk. 385   Perf. 13½
1174 A350 2b multicolored   .70   .25
  Complete booklet, strip of 5
  #1174   5.25

THAIPEX '87 — A351

Gold artifacts.

1987, Aug. 4   Wmk. 385
1175 A351 2b Peacock, vert.   .40   .25
  Complete booklet, strip of 5
  #1175   3.75
1176 A351 2b Hand mirrors, vert.   .40   .25
  Complete booklet, strip of 5
  #1176   3.75
1177 A351 6b Water urn, finger bowls   1.10   .55
1178 A351 6b Dragon vase   1.10   .55
  a. Souv. sheet of 4, #1175-1178   55.00   55.00
  Nos. 1175-1178 (4)   3.00   1.60

No. 1178a exists imperf. Value, $450.

ASEAN, 20th Anniv. — A352

1987, Aug. 20
1179 A352 2b multicolored   .40   .25
  Complete booklet, strip of 5
  #1179   2.75
1180 A352 3b multicolored   .60   .30
1181 A352 4b multicolored   .70   .40
1182 A352 5b multicolored   .95   .45
  Nos. 1179-1182 (4)   2.65   1.40

Natl. Communications Day — A353

1987, Aug. 4
1183 A353 2b multicolored   .80   .25
  Complete booklet, strip of 5
  #1183   6.50

Chulachamklao Royal Military
Academy, Cent. — A354

Design: School crest, King Rama V, and
King Rama IX conferring sword on graduating
officer.

1987, Aug. 5
1184 A354 2b multicolored   1.75   .30
  Complete booklet, strip of 5
  #1184   21.00

Intl. Literacy
Day — A355

1987, Sept. 8
1185 A355 2b multicolored   .70   .25
  Complete booklet, strip of 5
  #1185   6.50

Tourism
Year — A356

2b, Flower-offering ceremony, Saraburi
province. 3b, Duan Sib Festival, Nakhon Si
Thammarat province. 5b, Bang Fai Festival,
Yasothon province. 7b, Loi Krathong Festival,
Sukhothai province.

1987, Sept. 18
1186 A356 2b multicolored   .30   .25
  Complete booklet, strip of 5
  #1186   4.00
1187 A356 3b multicolored   .60   .30
1188 A356 5b multicolored   .90   .40
1189 A356 7b multicolored   1.25   .60
  Nos. 1186-1189 (4)   3.05   1.55

Auditor General's Office, 72nd
Anniv. — A357

1987, Sept. 18
1190 A357 2b multicolored   .70   .25
  Complete booklet, strip of 5
  #1190   6.50

Diplomatic Relations Between
Thailand and Japan, Cent. — A358

1987, Sept. 26   Wmk. 329
1191 A358 2b multicolored   .85   .30
  Complete booklet, strip of 5
  #1191   8.00

Intl. Letter Writing
Week — A359

Floral garlands.

1987, Oct. 4   Wmk. 385
1192 A359 2b Floral tassel   .35   .25
  Complete booklet, strip of 5
  #1192   2.75
1193 A359 3b Tasselled garland   .65   .30
1194 A359 5b Wrist garland   .75   .40
1195 A359 7b Double-ended garland   1.25   .65
  Nos. 1192-1195 (4)   3.00   1.60

Thai Pavilion — A360

1987, Oct. 9   Wmk. 387   Perf. 15
1196 A360 2b multicolored   .95   .25
  Complete booklet, strip of 5
  #1196   6.50

Social Education and Cultural Center
inauguration.

A361

A362

King Bhumibol Adulyadej, 60th
Birthday — A363

Royal ciphers and: #1197, Adulyadej as a
child. #1198, King and Queen, wedding portrait, 1950. #1199, King taking the Oath of
Accession, 1950. #1200, King dressed as a
monk, collecting alms. #1201, Greeting 100
year-old woman. #1202, In military uniform
holding pen and with hill tribes. #1203, Royal
couple visiting wounded servicemen. #1204,
Visiting farm. #1205, Royal family. #1206,
King, Queen Sirikit. #1207, Princess Mother
Somdej Phra Sri Nakarindra Boromrajjonnani,
emblem of Medical Volunteer Assoc. #1208,
Crown Prince Maha Vajiralongkorn, crown
prince's royal standard. #1209, Princess Maha
Chakri Sirindhorn, emblem of Sai Jai Thai
Foundation. #1210, Princess Chulabhorn,
Albert Einstein gold medal awarded by
UNESCO.

Wmk. 329
1987, Dec. 5   Photo.   Perf. 13½
1197 A361 2b shown   .70   .30
1198 A361 2b multicolored   .70   .30
1199 A361 2b multicolored   .70   .30
1200 A361 2b multicolored   .70   .30
1201 A361 2b multicolored   .70   .30
1202 A361 2b multicolored   .70   .30
1203 A361 2b multicolored   .70   .30
1204 A361 2b multicolored   .70   .30
  a. Souv. sheet of #1197-1204   37.50   37.50

Litho.
Wmk. 385
1205 A362 2b multicolored   1.20   .40
1206 A362 2b multicolored   1.20   .40
1207 A362 2b multicolored   1.20   .40
1208 A362 2b multicolored   1.20   .40
1209 A362 2b multicolored   1.20   .40
1210 A362 2b multicolored   1.20   .40

Litho. & Embossed
1211 A363 100b vio blue & gold   65.00   65.00
  Nos. 1197-1211 (15)   77.80   69.80

Size of Nos. 1206-1210: 45x27mm. No.
1211 printed in sheets of 10. Value, $750. No.
1204a sold for 40b.

No. 1081 Surcharged

1987   Litho.   Wmk. 233   Perf. 14x15
1212 A256 2b on 1.50b brt yel org   .85   .25

Children's Day — A364

Perf. 14x14½

1988, Jan. 9	**Litho.**		**Wmk. 387**
1213 A364	2b multicolored	.70	.25
	Complete booklet, strip of 5 #1213	5.25	

Thai Agricultural Cooperatives, 72nd Anniv. — A365

1988, Feb. 26			**Wmk. 387**
1214 A365	2b Prince Bridhyalongkorn, founder	.70	.25
	Complete booklet, strip of 5 #1214	5.25	

Royal Siam Soc., 84th Anniv. A366

1988, Mar. 10			**Perf. 14½x14**
1215 A366	2b multicolored	.65	.25
	Complete booklet, strip of 5 #1215	5.25	

Cultural Heritage Preservation — A367

Ruins in Sukhothai Historic Park.

1988, Apr. 2			**Perf. 14½x14**
1216 A367	2b Wat Phra Phai Luang	.30	.25
	Complete booklet, strip of 5 #1216	4.50	
1217 A367	3b Wat Traphang Thonglang	.60	.30
1218 A367	4b Wat Maha That	.90	.60
1219 A367	6b Thewalai Maha Kaset	1.25	.70
	Nos. 1216-1219 (4)	3.05	1.85

Red Cross Fair A368

1988, Apr.	**Wmk. 387**		**Perf. 14**
1220 A368	2b Prevention of rabies	.70	.25
	Complete booklet, strip of 5 #1220	5.25	

King Rama V, Founder — A369

Perf. 14x14½

1988, Apr. 26			**Wmk. 387**
1221 A369	5b multicolored	2.75	.70

Siriraj Hospital, cent.

Pheasants — A370

Wmk. 329

1988, June 15	**Photo.**		**Perf. 13½**
1222 A370	2b Crested fireback	.30	.25
	Complete booklet, strip of 5 #1222	2.75	
1223 A370	3b Kalij	.60	.25
1224 A370	6b Silver pheasant	1.25	.60
1225 A370	7b Hume's pheasant	1.50	.75
	Nos. 1222-1225 (4)	3.65	1.85

Nos. 935a, 935 Surcharged

a b

Perf. 11x13

1988-92	**Litho.**		**Wmk. 387**
1226 A256(a)	1b on 1.25b	.80	.25
1226A A256(b)	1b on 1.25b	.85	.25
b.	Wmk. 368	1.75	.30

Issued: #1226, 1988; #1226A, Dec. 5, 1992.

Intl. Council of Women, Cent. — A371

1988, June 26	**Wmk. 385**		**Perf. 13½**
1227 A371	2b multicolored	.70	.25
	Complete booklet, strip of 5 #1227	5.25	

King Bhumibol Adulyadej
A372 A372a

Perf. 13½x13

1988-95	**Litho.**		**Wmk. 387**
1228 A372	25s brown	.40	.25

Perf. 14x14½

1229 A372	50s olive	.55	.25
a.	Wmk. 329, perf. 13½x13	.65	.25
1230 A372	1b brt blue	.55	.25
	Complete booklet, 5 #1230	6.00	
a.	Photo, wmk. 233	.80	.25

b.	Photo., wmk. 340, perf. 13½x13¾	.55	.25
1233 A372	2b scarlet	.70	.25
	Complete booklet, 5 #1233	7.50	
a.	Wmk. 329	.55	.25
b.	Photo., wmk. 340, perf. 13½x13¾	.70	.25
	Complete booklet, 5 #1233b	6.00	

Photo.
Wmk. 233
Perf. 14½

1236 A372	1b bright blue	.80	.25
	Nos. 1228-1236 (5)	3.00	1.25

No. 1236 has blue background without halo effect around head. See #1230.

Issued: 25s, 8/12/92; 1b-2b, 7/2/88; 50s, 7/28/93; #1230a, 1236, 1990; #1233a, 1992; #1230b, 1233b, 12/5/94; #1229a, 1995.

Perf. 13½x13

1988-90	**Engr.**		**Wmk. 329**
1241 A372a	3b brn & bluish gray	.80	.25
1242 A372a	4b brt bl & red brn	.95	.25
1243 A372a	5b violet & brn	1.10	.30
1244 A372a	6b green & vio	1.10	.35
1245 A372a	7b red brn & dk brn	.80	.25
1246 A372a	8b red brn & gray ol	1.10	.40
1247 A372a	9b dk blue & brn	1.75	.40
1248 A372a	10b henna brn & blk	1.60	.25
1249 A372a	20b brn org & sage grn	2.40	1.75
1250 A372a	25b olive grn & dark blue	4.50	.90
1251 A372a	50b violet & grn	8.00	1.00
1252 A372a	100b brn org & bluish blk	13.00	2.25
	Nos. 1241-1252 (12)	37.10	8.40

Issued: 3b, 10b, 50b, 100b, 12/5; 5b, 6b, 8b, 9b, 7/1/89; 4b, 7b, 20b, 12/5/89; 25b, 1/9/90.

A373

A374

King Bhumibol's Reign (since 1950) — A375

Designs: No. 1253, King Bhumibol.
Regalia: No. 1254, Great Crown of Victory. No. 1255, Sword of Victory and matching scabbard. No. 1256, Scepter. No. 1257, Fan and feather fly swatter. No. 1258, Royal slippers.
Canopied thrones in the Grand Palace: No. 1259, Queen's round ottoman on 1-tier dais in front of decorative screen. No. 1260, King's throne on 1-tier dais in front of decorative screen. No. 1261, 3-Tier throne with 3 gilded trees. No. 1262, 3-Canopy throne on high gold dais. No. 1263, 3-Tier throne with 4 gilded trees, altar in background. No. 1264, 3-Canopy throne on 5-stair dais, in front of arch flanked by columns.

Wmk. 385

1988, July 2	**Litho.**		**Perf. 13½**
1253 A373	2b shown	2.50	.40

Photo.
Wmk. 329

1254 A374	2b multi, vert.	.65	.30
1255 A374	2b multicolored	.65	.30
1256 A374	2b multicolored	.65	.30
1257 A374	2b multicolored	.65	.30
1258 A374	2b multicolored	.65	.30

Litho.
Perf. 14x14½
Wmk. 387

1259 A375	2b multicolored	.80	.30
1260 A375	2b multicolored	.80	.30
1261 A375	2b multicolored	.80	.30
1262 A375	2b multicolored	.80	.30
1263 A375	2b multicolored	.80	.30
1264 A375	2b multicolored	.80	.30
a.	Souv. sheet of 6, #1259-1264	60.00	60.00
	Nos. 1253-1264 (12)	10.55	3.70

No. 1264a sold for 25b.

Arbor Year A376

Perf. 14½x14

1988, July 29	**Litho.**		**Wmk. 387**
1265 A376	2b multicolored	.65	.25
	Complete booklet, strip of 5 #1265	5.25	

Natl. Communications Day — A377

Wmk. Alternating Interlaced Wavy Lines (340)

1988, Aug. 4			**Perf. 13½**
1266 A377	2b multicolored	.85	.25
	Complete booklet, strip of 5 #1266	6.50	

Intl. Letter Writing Week — A378

Designs: Coconut leaf sculptures.

Perf. 14½x14

1988, Oct. 9			**Wmk. 387**
1267 A378	2b Grasshopper	.40	.25
	Complete booklet, strip of 5 #1267	2.75	
1268 A378	2b Fish	.40	.25
	Complete booklet, strip of 5 #1268	2.75	
1269 A378	6b Bird	1.10	.50
1270 A378	6b Takro (box)	1.10	.50
	Nos. 1267-1270 (4)	3.00	1.50

Housing Development — A379

Wmk. 233

1988, Oct. 24	**Litho.**		**Perf. 14**
1271 A379	2b multicolored	.65	.25
	Complete booklet, strip of 5 #1271	5.25	

Traffic Safety — A380

1988, Nov. 11   Wmk. 329   Perf. 13½
1272 A380 2b multicolored .65 .25
Complete booklet, strip of 5
#1272   6.50

King's Bodyguard, 120th Anniv. — A381

1988, Nov. 11   Wmk. 385
1273 A381 2b Chulalongkorn   4.00 .70
Complete booklet, strip of 5
#1273   50.00

New Year — A382

Flowers.

1988, Dec. 1   Wmk. 387
1274 A382 1b Crotalaria ses-
              siliflora   .65 .30
1275 A382 1b Uvaria grandiflora .65 .30
1276 A382 1b Reinwardtia tri-
              gyna   .65 .30
1277 A382 1b Impatiens griffithii .65 .30
     Nos. 1274-1277 (4)   2.60 1.20

Thai Royal Orders Type of 1979

Floral background: Nos. 1278-1279, Knight Grand Commander, Order of Rama, 1918. Nos. 1280-1281, Knight Grand Cordon, Order of the White Elephant, 1861. Nos. 1282-1283, Knight Grand Cordon, Order of the Crown of Thailand, 1869. Nos. 1284-1285, Ratana Varabhorn Order of Merit, 1911. Pairs have continuous designs.

1988, Dec. 5   Wmk. 385
1278 A243 2b multicolored   .30 .25
1279 A244 2b multicolored   .30 .25
  a.   Pair, #1278-1279   .80 .40
1280 A243 3b multicolored   .65 .25
1281 A244 3b multicolored   .65 .25
  a.   Pair, #1280-1281   1.75 .90
1282 A243 5b multicolored   1.00 .40
1283 A244 5b multicolored   1.00 .40
  a.   Pair, #1282-1283   2.75 1.40
1284 A243 7b multicolored   1.20 .55
1285 A244 7b multicolored   1.20 .55
  a.   Pair, #1284-1285   4.00 2.00
     Nos. 1278-1285 (8)   6.30 2.90

A383

Buddha Monthon Celebrations, Tambol Salaya — A384

Perf. 14x15, 15x14
1988, Dec. 5   Wmk. 233
1286 A383 2b Birthplace   .35 .25
Complete booklet, strip of 5
#1286   2.75
1287 A383 3b Enlightenment
              place   .45 .25
1288 A383 4b Location of 1st
              sermon   .65 .45
1289 A383 5b Place Buddha
              achieved nirva-
              na   .85 .40
1290 A384 6b Statue   1.00 .50
     Nos. 1286-1290 (5)   3.30 1.85
Souvenir Sheet
Perf. 14½x14
1291 A384 6b like No. 1290 27.50 27.50
     No. 1291 sold for 15b.

Children's Day — A385

"Touch" paintings by blind youth: No. 1292, Floating Market, by Thongbai Siyam. No. 1293, Flying Bird, by Kwanchai Kerd-Daeng. No. 1294, Little Mermaid, by Chalermpol Jiengmai. No. 1295, Golden Fish, by Natetip Korsantirak.

Wmk. 387
1989, Jan. 14   Litho.   Perf. 13½
1292 A385 2b multicolored   .45 .25
Complete booklet, strip of 5
#1292   4.00
1293 A385 2b multicolored   .45 .25
Complete booklet, strip of 5
#1293   4.00
1294 A385 2b multicolored   .45 .25
Complete booklet, strip of 5
#1294   4.00
1295 A385 2b multicolored   .45 .25
Complete booklet, strip of 5
#1295   4.00
     Nos. 1292-1295 (4)   1.80 1.00

Communications Authority of Thailand, 12th Anniv. — A386

1989, Feb. 25   Perf. 14½x14
1296 A386 2b multicolored   .70 .25
Complete booklet, strip of 5
#1296   5.25

Chulalongkorn University, 72nd Anniv. — A387

Design: 2b, Statue of Chulalongkorn and King Vajiravudh in front of university auditorium.

1989, Mar. 26
1297 A387 2b multicolored   .80 .25
Complete booklet, strip of 5
#1297   8.00

A388

Perf. 15x14
1989, Mar. 31   Litho.   Wmk. 233
1298 A388 2b shown   .70 .30
Complete booklet, strip of 5
#1298   5.25
Wmk. 387
Perf. 13½
1299 A388 10b Emblem   1.50 .60

Thai Red Cross Society, 96th anniv. (2b); Intl. Red Cross and Red Crescent organizations, 125th annivs. (10b).

A389

Phra Nakhon Khiri Historical Park: 2b, Wat Phra Kaeo. 3b, Chatchawan Wiangchai Observatory. 5b, Phra That Chom Phet Stupa. 6b, Wetchayan Wichian Phrasat Throne Hall.

Perf. 14x14½
1989, Apr. 2   Wmk. 387
1300 A389 2b multicolored   .55 .25
Complete booklet, strip of 5
#1300   4.00
1301 A389 3b multicolored   .90 .45
1302 A389 5b multicolored   1.40 .95
1303 A389 6b multicolored   1.60 1.10
     Nos. 1300-1303 (4)   4.45 2.75

Natl. Lottery Office, 50th Anniv. — A390

1989, Apr. 5   Perf. 13½
1304 A390 2b multicolored   .65 .25
Complete booklet, strip of 5
#1304   5.25

Seashells — A391

1989, June 28   Wmk. 329   Perf. 13½
1305 A391 2b Conus thailandis .30 .25
Complete booklet, strip of 5
#1305   2.75
1306 A391 3b Spondylus
              princeps   .70 .30
1307 A391 6b Cyprea guttata 1.00 .75
1308 A391 10b Nautilus pompili-
              us   3.00 1.60
     Nos. 1305-1308 (4)   5.00 2.90

Arts and Crafts Year A392

Wmk. 387
1989, June 28   Litho.   Perf. 13½
1309 A392 2b Ceramic figurines .40 .25
Complete booklet, strip of 5
#1309   2.75
1310 A392 2b Gold niello ginger
              jar, chicken   .40 .25
Complete booklet, strip of 5
#1310   2.75
1311 A392 6b Textiles   1.10 .50
1312 A392 6b Gemstone flower
              ornament   1.10 .50
     Nos. 1309-1312 (4)   3.00 1.50

Asia-Pacific Telecommunications Organization, 10th Anniv. — A393

APT emblem, map of submarine cable network and satellites of member nations.

1989, July 1   Wmk. 329   Perf. 13½
1313 A393 9b multicolored   1.25 .75

Phya Anuman Rajadhon (1888-1969), Ethnologist A394

1989, July 1   Wmk. 387   Perf. 13½
1314 A394 2b multicolored   .65 .25
Complete booklet, strip of 5
#1314   5.25

9th Natl. Phil. Exhib., Aug. 4-13 — A395

Various mailboxes.

1989, Aug. 4   Wmk. 233   Perf. 15x14
1315 A395 2b multicolored   .40 .25
Complete booklet, strip of 5
#1315   2.75
1316 A395 3b multi, diff.   .45 .25
1317 A395 4b multi, diff.   .65 .35
1318 A395 5b multi, diff.   .80 .40
1319 A395 6b multi, diff.   .95 .50
  a.   Souv. sheet, #1315-1319,
       perf 14   35.00 35.00
     Nos. 1315-1319 (5)   3.25 1.75

No. 1319a sold for 30b. No. 1319a exists imperf. Value, $125.

Wmk. 387

1989, June 26   Litho.   *Perf. 13½*
1320 A396 2b multicolored   .55   .25
  Complete booklet, strip of 5
  #1320   5.25

Intl. Anti-drug Day.

A397

1989, Aug. 4   Wmk. 233   *Perf. 14x15*
1321 A397 2b multicolored   .70   .25
  Complete booklet, strip of 5
  #1321   5.25

Post and Telecommunications School, cent.

A398

1989, Aug. 4   Wmk. 387   *Perf. 13½*
1322 A398 2b multicolored   .55   .25
  Complete booklet, strip of 5
  #1322   5.25

Natl. Communications Day.

Dragonflies — A399

Wmk. 329
1989, Oct. 8   Photo.   *Perf. 13½*
1323 A399 2b shown   .65   .25
  Complete booklet, strip of 5
  #1323   .95
1324 A399 5b multi, diff.   .75   .50
1325 A399 6b multi, diff.   1.25   .60
1326 A399 10b Damselfly   1.60 1.00
  a. Souv. sheet of 4, #1323-
      1326   30.00 30.00
  Nos. 1323-1326 (4)   4.25 2.35

Intl. Letter Writing Week. #1326a sold for 40b.

Transport and Communications
Decade for Asia and the
Pacific — A400

Perf. 14½x14
1989, Oct. 24   Litho.   Wmk. 387
1327 A400 2b multicolored   .55   .25
  Complete booklet, strip of 5
  #1327   5.25

Mental Health   New Year
Care,   1990 — A402
Cent. — A401

1989, Nov. 1   Wmk. 233   *Perf. 15x14*
1328 A401 2b multicolored   .55   .25
  Complete booklet, strip of 5
  #1328   5.25

Perf. 14x14½
1989, Nov. 15   Wmk. 387
Flowering plants.
1329 A402 1b Hypericum uralum   .30   .30
1330 A402 1b Uraria rufescens   .30   .30
1331 A402 1b Manglietia garrettii .30 .30
1332 A402 1b Aeschynanthus
            macranthus   .30   .30
  a. Souv. sheet of 4, #1329-1332 6.50 6.50
  Nos. 1329-1332 (4)   1.20 1.20

No. 1332a sold for 14b.

Insects — A403

Wmk. 329
1989, Nov. 15   Photo.   *Perf. 13½*
1333 A403 2b Catacanthus in-
            carnatus   .40   .25
  Complete booklet, strip of 5
  #1333   2.75
1334 A403 3b Aristobia approxi-
            mator   .60   .30
1335 A403 6b Chrysochroa
            chinensis   .90   .50
1336 A403 10b Enoplotrupes
            sharpi   1.60 1.25
  Nos. 1333-1336 (4)   3.50 2.30

Population and Housing Census of
1990 — A404

Wmk. 387
1990, Jan. 1   Litho.   *Perf. 13½*
1337 A404 2b multicolored   .80   .25
  Complete booklet, strip of 5
  #1337   5.75

Children's Day   Emblems
A405   A406

Perf. 15x14
1990, Jan. 13   Wmk. 233
1338 A405 2b Jumping rope,
            horiz.   .60   .25
  Complete booklet, strip of 5
  #1338   4.00
1339 A405 2b Sports   .60   .25
  Complete booklet, strip of 5
  #1339   4.00

1990, Mar. 29   Wmk. 387   *Perf. 13½*
1340 A406 2b multicolored   .70   .25
  Complete booklet, strip of 5
  #1340   5.75

WHO Fight AIDS Worldwide campaign and
the Natl. Red Cross Soc.

Thai Heritage Conservation
Day — A407

Prize-winning inlaid mother-of-pearl containers: No. 1341, Tiap (footed bowl with lid), vert.
No. 1342, Phan waenfa (two-tiered vessel),
vert. No. 1343, Lung (lidded bowl). No. 1344,
Chiat klom (spade-shaped lidded container
signifying noble rank).

1990, Apr. 2   Photo.   Wmk. 329
1341 A407 2b multicolored   .25   .25
1342 A407 2b multicolored   .25   .25
1343 A407 8b multicolored   1.10   .90
1344 A407 8b multicolored   1.10   .90
  Nos. 1341-1344 (4)   2.70 2.30

A408

Minerals.

Perf. 14x14½
1990, June 29   Litho.   Wmk. 387
1345 A408 2b Tin   .45   .25
1346 A408 3b Zinc   .70   .40
1347 A408 5b Lead   .85   .60
1348 A408 6b Fluorite   1.60 1.25
  a. Souv. sheet of 4, #1345-1348 6.25 6.25
  Nos. 1345-1348 (4)   3.00 2.05

No. 1348a sold for 30b. Exists imperf, value
same as perf.

A409

1990, May 16
1349 A409 2b multicolored   .50   .25

Faculty of Dentistry, Chulalongkorn Univ.,
50th anniv.

Communications Day — A410

1990, Aug. 4   *Perf. 14½x14*
1350 A410 2b multicolored   .65   .25
  Complete booklet, strip of 5
  #1350   5.75

Asian-Pacific Postal Training Center,
20th Anniv. — A411

1990, Sept. 10
1351 A411 2b multicolored   .45   .25
  Complete booklet, strip of 5
  #1351   5.00
1352 A411 8b multicolored   1.40   .70

Rotary Intl. in Thailand, 60th
Anniv. — A412

1990, Sept. 16   *Perf. 13½*
1353 A412 2b Health care   .45   .25
  Complete booklet, strip of 5
  #1353   3.00
1354 A412 3b Immunizations   .60   .30
1355 A412 6b Literacy project   .60   .55
1356 A412 8b Thai museum pro-
            ject   1.20 1.00
  Nos. 1353-1356 (4)   2.85 2.10

Intl. Letter Writing Week, 1990 — A413

1990, Oct. 7   *Perf. 14*
1357 A413 2b multicolored   .45   .25
1358 A413 3b multi, diff.   .70   .40
1359 A413 5b multi, diff.   .85   .60
1360 A413 6b multi, diff.   1.00   .80
  a. Souv. sheet of 4, #1357-1360 6.25 6.25
  Nos. 1357-1360 (4)   3.00 2.05

No. 1360a sold for 30b. Exists imperf, value
same as perf.

Dept. of Comptroller-General,
Cent. — A414

1990, Oct. 7   *Perf. 14½x14*
1361 A414 2b multicolored   1.00   .25
  Complete booklet, strip of 5
  #1361   5.75

A415   A416

1990, Oct. 21   Perf. 14x14½
1362 A415 2b multicolored   4.00   .60
    Complete booklet, strip of 5
    #1362   32.50

Princess Mother, 90th birthday.

1990, Nov. 15 Wmk. 233 Perf. 14½
Flowers: No. 1363, Cyrtandromoea
grandiflora. No. 1364, Rhododendron
arboreum. No. 1365, Merremia vitifolia. No.
1366, Afgekia mahidolae.

1363 A416 1b multicolored   .45   .25
1364 A416 1b multicolored   .45   .25
1365 A416 1b multicolored   .45   .25
1366 A416 1b multicolored   .45   .25
  a.   Sheet of 4, #1363-1366   4.50 4.50
      Nos. 1363-1366 (4)   1.80 1.00

New Year 1991. No. 1366a sold for 10b.
Exists imperf, value same as perf.
  See Nos. 1417-1420.

Wiman Mek Royal Hall — A417

Royal Throne Rooms in the Dusit Palace:
3b, Ratcharit Rungrot Royal House. 4b,
Aphisek Dusit Royal Hall. 5b, Amphon Sathan
Palace. 6b, Udon Phak Royal Hall. 8b,
Anantasamakhom Throne Hall.

Wmk. 329
1990, Dec. 5   Photo.   Perf. 13½
1367 A417 2b multicolored   .45   .25
    Complete booklet, strip of 5
    #1367   3.25
1368 A417 3b multicolored   .65   .25
1369 A417 4b multicolored   .65   .40
1370 A417 5b multicolored   .75   .50
1371 A417 6b multicolored   1.00 .60
1372 A417 8b multicolored   1.60 .90
      Nos. 1367-1372 (6)   5.10 2.90

Somdet Phra Maha Samanachao
Kromphra Paramanuchitchinorot
(1790-1853), Supreme
Patriarch — A418

1990, Dec. 11 Wmk. 387 Perf. 13½
1373 A418 2b multicolored   .60   .25
    Complete booklet, strip of 5
    #1373   6.25

Petroleum Authority, 12th
Anniv. — A419

Perf. 14½x14
1990, Dec. 29   Litho.   Wmk. 387
1374 A419 2b multicolored   .55   .25
    Complete booklet, strip of 5
    #1374   5.25

Locomotives — A420

Designs: 2b, No. 6, Krauss & Co., Germany,
1908. 3b, No. 32, Kyosan Kogyo, Japan, 1949.
5b, No. 715, C56, Japan, 1946. 6b, No. 953,
Mikado, Japan, 1949-1951.

Perf. 14½x14
1990, Dec. 29   Litho.   Wmk. 387
1375 A420 2b multicolored   .70   .25
1376 A420 3b multicolored   1.10 .35
1377 A420 5b multicolored   1.40 1.40
1378 A420 6b multicolored   1.75 1.40
  a.   Souv. sheet of 4, #1375-1378 7.50 7.50
      Nos. 1375-1378 (4)   4.95 3.40

No. 1378a sold for 25b. Exists imperf, value
same as perf.

Children's Day — A421

Children's games: 2b, Tops. 5b, Race. 6b,
Blind-man's buff.

1991, Jan. 12
1379 A421 2b multicolored   .45   .25
    Complete booklet, strip of 5
    #1379   3.50
1380 A421 3b shown   .60   .30
1381 A421 5b multicolored   .80   .40
1382 A421 6b multicolored   1.10 .50
      Nos. 1379-1382 (4)   2.95 1.45

A422

1991, Feb. 17   Perf. 14x14½
1383 A422 2b multicolored   .55   .25
    Complete booklet, strip of 5
    #1383   5.50

Land titling project.

A423

Perf. 14x14½
1991, Mar. 30   Litho.   Wmk. 387
1384 A423 2b Princess Maha   2.50 .25
    Complete booklet, strip of 5
    #1384   20.00
  a.   Souvenir sheet of 1   5.00 5.00

Red Cross. No. 1384a sold for 8b. Exists
imperf, value same as perf.

Cultural
Heritage
A424

Floral decorations: 2b, Indra's heavenly
abode. 3b, Celestial couch. 4b, Crystal ladder.
5b, Crocodile.

Wmk. 329
1991, Apr. 2   Photo.   Perf. 13½
1385 A424 2b multicolored   .40   .25
1386 A424 3b multicolored   .50   .30
1387 A424 4b multicolored   .75   .50
1388 A424 5b multicolored   .85   .60
  a.   Souv. sheet of 4, #1385-1388 8.00 8.00
      Nos. 1385-1388 (4)   2.50 1.65

No. 1388a sold for 30b. Exists imperf, value
same as perf.

Songkran
Day — A425

Perf. 14x14½
1991, Apr. 13 Wmk. 387   Litho.
1389 A425 2b Demon on
            sheep   2.50 1.00
    Complete booklet, strip of 5
    #1389   22.50
  a.   Souvenir sheet of 1   17.00 17.00

No. 1389a sold for 8b. Exists imperf, value
same as perf.
  See #1467, 1530, 1566, 1606, 1662, 1724,
1801, 1869, 1940, 1970, 2017.

Prince Narisranuvattivongs (1863-
1947) — A426

1991, Apr. 28   Perf. 14½x14
1390 A426 2b brown & yellow   .50   .25
    Complete booklet, strip of 5
    #1390   5.00

Mosaics — A427

Various lotus flowers.

1991, May 28   Perf. 13½
1391 A427 2b multi, vert.   .35   .25
    Complete booklet, strip of 5
    #1391   4.00
1392 A427 3b multi, vert.   .55   .25
1393 A427 5b multi   .80   .45
1394 A427 6b multi   1.00 .55
      Nos. 1391-1394 (4)   2.70 1.50

Natl. Communications Day — A428

Wmk. 387
1991, Aug. 4   Litho.   Perf. 13½
1395 A428 2b multicolored   .70   .25
    Complete booklet, strip of 5
    #1395   7.25

Thaipex '91, Natl.
Philatelic
Exhibition
A429

Various fabric designs.

1991, Aug. 4   Perf. 14x14½
1396 A429 2b multicolored   .25   .25
1397 A429 4b multicolored   .40   .35
1398 A429 6b multicolored   .70   .40
1399 A429 8b multicolored   .90   .60
  a.   Souv. sheet of 4, #1396-1399 6.00 6.00
      Nos. 1396-1399 (4)   2.25 1.60

No. 1399a sold for 30b. Exists imperf, value
$32.50. No. 1399a overprinted with Philanip-
pon emblem in lower left corner of margin sold
for 200b. Value, $190.

Intl. Productivity Congress — A430

Perf. 14½x14
1991, Sept. 3   Litho.   Wmk. 387
1400 A430 2b multicolored   .55   .25
    Complete booklet, strip of 5
    #1400   5.00

26th Intl. Council
of Women
Triennial — A431

Wmk. 387
1991, Sept. 23   Litho.   Perf. 13½
1401 A431 2b multicolored   .55   .25
    Complete booklet, strip of 5
    #1401   5.00

Bantam Chickens — A432

Wmk. 329
1991, Oct. 6   Photo.   Perf. 13½
1402 A432 2b Black bantams   .45   .25
1403 A432 3b Black-tailed buff
            bantams   .80   .25
1404 A432 6b Fancy bantams   1.25 .30
1405 A432 8b White bantams   1.75 .80
  a.   Souv. sheet of 4, #1402-1405 7.50 7.50
      Nos. 1402-1405 (4)   4.25 1.60

No. 1405a sold for 35b. Exists imperf, value
same as perf.
  Intl. Letter Writing Week.

World Bank/Intl. Monetary Fund Annual Meetings — A433

Temples, meeting emblem and: 2b, Silver coin of King Rama IV. 4b, Pod Duang money. 8b, Chieng and Hoi money. 10b, Funan, Dvaravati and Srivijaya money.

Perf. 14½x14

1991, Oct. 15   Litho.   Wmk. 387
1406	A433	2b multicolored	.25	.25
		Complete booklet, strip of 5 #1406	3.25	
1407	A433	4b multicolored	.45	.30
1408	A433	8b multicolored	.90	.60
1409	A433	10b multicolored	1.10	.75
a.		Souv. sheet of 4, #1406-1409	6.25	6.25
		Nos. 1406-1409 (4)	2.70	1.90

No. 1409a sold for 35b. Exists imperf, value same as perf.

1993 World Philatelic Exhibition, Bangkok — A434

1991, Oct. 23   Perf. 14x14½
1410	A434	2b No. 118	.25	.25
1411	A434	3b No. 119	.30	.25
1412	A434	4b No. 120	.40	.30
1413	A434	5b No. 121	.55	.40
1414	A434	6b No. 122	.65	.45
1415	A434	7b No. 123	.75	.50
1416	A434	8b No. 124	.85	.60
a.		Souvenir sheet of 1	5.00	5.00
		Nos. 1410-1416 (7)	3.75	2.75

No. 1416a sold for 15b. Exists imperf, value same as perf.

Flower Type of 1990

1991, Nov. 5   Perf. 13½
1417	A416	1b Dillenia obovata	.25	.25
1418	A416	1b Melastoma sanguineum	.25	.25
1419	A416	1b Commelina diffusa	.25	.25
1420	A416	1b Plumbago indica	.25	.25
a.		Souv. sheet of 4, #1417-1420	5.00	5.00
		Nos. 1417-1420 (4)	1.00	1.00

No. 1420a sold for 10b. Exists imperf, value same as perf.

Asian Elephants — A435

Wmk. 329

1991, Nov. 5   Photo.   Perf. 13½
1421	A435	2b shown	.45	.25
1422	A435	4b Pulling logs	.90	.30
1423	A435	6b Lying down	1.00	.45
1424	A435	8b In river	2.00	.90
a.		Souvenir sheet of 1, litho.	7.50	7.50
		Nos. 1421-1424 (4)	4.35	1.90

No. 1424a sold for 22b and stamp does not have border. No. 1424a exists imperf, value same as perf.

Wild Animals — A436

Perf. 14½x14

1991, Dec. 26   Wmk. 387   Litho.
1425	A436	2b Viverra zibetha	.55	.25
		Complete booklet, strip of 5 #1425	3.00	
1426	A436	3b Prionodon linsang	.70	.25
1427	A436	6b Felis temmincki	1.00	.50
1428	A436	8b Ratufa bicolor	1.50	.65
a.		Sheet of 4, #1425-1428	8.50	8.50
		Nos. 1425-1428 (4)	3.75	1.65

No. 1428a sold for 30b. Exists imperf, value same as perf.

Prince Mahidol of Songkla (1891-1929), Medical Pioneer — A437

1992, Jan. 1   Perf. 14x14½
1429	A437	2b multicolored	1.00	.25
		Complete booklet, strip of 5 #1429	7.25	

Department of Mineral Resources, Cent. — A438

No. 1430, Locating fossils. No. 1431, Mining excavation. No. 1432, Drilling for natural gas and petroleum. No. 1433, Digging artesian wells.

Perf. 14½x14

1992, Jan. 1   Litho.   Wmk. 387
1430	A438	2b multicolored	.90	.25
		Complete booklet, strip of 5 #1430	4.50	
1431	A438	2b multicolored	.90	.25
		Complete booklet, strip of 5 #1431	4.50	
1432	A438	2b multicolored	.90	.25
		Complete booklet, strip of 5 #1432	4.50	
1433	A438	2b multicolored	.90	.25
		Complete booklet, strip of 5 #1433	4.50	
		Nos. 1430-1433 (4)	3.60	1.00

Children's Day — A439

Children's drawings on "World Under the Sea": 2b, Divers, fish. 3b, Fish, sea grass. 5b, Mermaid.

1992, Jan. 11   Wmk. 329   Perf. 13½
1434	A439	2b multicolored	.45	.25
		Complete booklet, strip of 5 #1434	3.00	
1435	A439	3b multicolored	.45	.30
1436	A439	5b multicolored, vert.	.90	.50
		Nos. 1434-1436 (3)	1.80	1.05

Duel on Elephants, 400th Anniv. — A440

Perf. 14½x14

1992, Jan. 18   Litho.   Wmk. 387
1437	A440	2b multicolored	.80	.25
		Complete booklet, strip of 5 #1437	7.25	

Orchids (Paphiopedilum) — A441

1992, Jan. 20
1438	A441	2b Bellatulum	.25	.25
1439	A441	2b Exul	.25	.25
1440	A441	3b Concolor	.35	.30
1441	A441	3b Godefroyae	.35	.30
1442	A441	6b Niveum	.70	.55
1443	A441	6b Villosum	.70	.55
1444	A441	10b Parishii	1.25	.90
a.		Souv. sheet of 4, #1438, 1440, 1442, 1444	5.00	5.00
1445	A441	10b Sukhakulii	1.25	.90
a.		Souv. sheet of 4, #1439, 1441, 1443, 1445	5.00	5.00
		Nos. 1438-1445 (8)	5.10	4.00

Fourth Asia Pacific Orchid Conference. Nos. 1444a-1445a each sold for 30b. Each exists imperf, value same as perf.

21st Intl. Society of Sugar Cane Technologists Conf. — A442

1992, Mar. 5   Perf. 14x14½
1446	A442	2b multicolored	1.60	.25
		Complete booklet, strip of 5 #1446	6.00	

Intl. Red Cross A443

Perf. 14½x14

1992, Mar.   Litho.   Wmk. 387
1447	A443	2b multicolored	.50	.25
		Complete booklet, strip of 5 #1447	4.00	

Ministry of Justice, Cent. — A444

Designs: 3b, Prince Rabi Badhanasakdi of Ratchaburi, founder of Thailand's School of Law. 5b, King Rama V, reformer of court system.

1992, Mar. 25   Perf. 13½
1448	A444	3b multicolored	.80	.30
1449	A444	5b multicolored	1.25	.40

Ministry of Agriculture and Cooperatives, Cent. — A445

1992, Apr. 1   Perf. 14½x14
1450	A445	2b gray & multi	.45	.25
		Complete booklet, strip of 5 #1450	3.25	
1451	A445	3b lil & multi	.60	.30
1452	A445	4b pink & multi	.80	.35
1453	A445	5b gray bl & multi	1.00	.40
		Nos. 1450-1453 (4)	2.85	1.30

A446

Ministry of Interior, Cent.: No. 1454, Prince Damrong Rajanubharb, first Minister of the Interior. No. 1455, People voting. No. 1456, Police and fire protection. No. 1457, Water and electricity provided to remote areas.

1992, Apr. 1   Perf. 14x14½
1454	A446	2b multicolored	.35	.25
		Complete booklet, strip of 5 #1454	4.00	
1455	A446	2b multicolored	.35	.35
		Complete booklet, strip of 5 #1455	4.00	
1456	A446	2b multicolored	.35	.35
		Complete booklet, strip of 5 #1456	4.00	
1457	A446	2b multicolored	.35	.35
		Complete booklet, strip of 5 #1457	4.00	
		Nos. 1454-1457 (4)	1.40	1.00

A447

1992, Apr. 1
1458	A447	2b Ships, truck	.25	.25
		Complete booklet, strip of 5 #1458	3.25	
1459	A447	3b Truck, bus, train	.40	.30
1460	A447	5b Airplanes	.60	.40
1461	A447	6b Truck, satellites	.75	.50
		Nos. 1458-1461 (4)	2.00	1.45

Ministry of Transport and Communications, 80th anniv.

Ministry of Education, Cent. — A448

Perf. 14x14½

1992, Apr. 1   Litho.   Wmk. 387
1462	A448	2b multicolored	.45	.25
		Complete booklet, strip of 5 #1462	4.00	

Carts A449

1992, Apr. 2   Perf. 14½x14
1463	A449	2b West	.25	.25
		Complete booklet, strip of 5 #1463	3.25	

1464 A449 3b North .35 .25
1465 A449 5b Northeast .55 .40
1466 A449 10b East 1.10 .90
   a. Souv. sheet of 4, #1463-1466 4.50
   Nos. 1463-1466 (4) 2.25 1.80

Heritage Conservation Day. No. 1466a sold for 30b. Exists imperf without sheet price in margin, value same as perf.

Songkran Day Type of 1991
1992, Apr. 13   *Perf. 14x14½*
1467 A425 2b Demon on monkey, zodiac 1.40 .25
    Complete booklet, strip of 5 #1467 7.00
   a. Souvenir sheet of 1 4.00 4.00

No. 1467a sold for 8b. Exists imperf with sale price in different colors, value same as perf.

Department of Livestock Development, 50th Anniv. — A451

Perf. 14½x14
1992, May 5   Litho.   Wmk. 387
1468 A451 2b multicolored .65 .25
    Complete booklet, strip of 5 #1468 4.00

Wisakhabucha Day — A452

Scenes from Buddha's life: 2b, Birth. 3b, Enlightenment. 5b, Death.

Wmk. 387
1992, May 16   Litho.   *Perf. 14½*
1469 A452 2b multicolored .35 .25
1470 A452 3b multicolored .70 .30
1471 A452 5b multicolored 1.00 .65
   Nos. 1469-1471 (3) 2.05 1.20

Meteorological Department, 50th Anniv. — A453

1992, June 23   *Perf. 14x14½*
1472 A453 2b multicolored .65 .25
    Complete booklet, strip of 5 #1472 4.00

1993 World Philatelic Exhibition, Bangkok — A454

Perf. 14x14½
1992, July 1   Litho.   Wmk. 387
1473 A454 2b No. 18 .25 .25
    Complete booklet, strip of 5 #1473 3.25
1474 A454 3b No. 156 .35 .25
1475 A454 5b No. 222 .55 .40
1476 A454 7b No. 255 .85 .50
1477 A454 8b No. 273 1.00 .65
   a. Souv. sheet of 5, #1473-1477 + label 6.00 6.00
   Nos. 1473-1477 (5) 3.00 2.05

No. 1477a sold for 35b. Exists imperf. with sheet price in blue, value same as #1477a.

Visit ASEAN Year — A455

Designs: 2b, Bua Tong field, Mae Hong Son Province. 3b, Klong Larn Waterfall, Kamphaeng Phet Province. 4b, Coral, Chumphon Province. 5b, Khao Ta-Poo, Phangnga Province.

1992, July 1
1478 A455 2b multicolored .30 .25
    Complete booklet, strip of 5 #1478 3.25
1479 A455 3b multicolored .40 .25
1480 A455 4b multicolored .50 .35
1481 A455 5b multicolored .60 .40
   Nos. 1478-1481 (4) 1.80 1.25

Prince Chudadhuj Dharadilok of Bejraburna (1892-1923) A456

Wmk. 368
1992, July 5   Litho.   *Perf. 13½*
1482 A456 2b multicolored .60 .25
    Complete booklet, strip of 5 #1482 5.00

Natl. Communications Day — A457

Perf. 14½x14
1992, Aug. 4   Litho.   Wmk. 387
1483 A457 2b multicolored .55 .25
    Complete booklet, strip of 5 #1483 4.00

ASEAN, 25th Anniv. — A458

Flags and: 2b, Cultures and sports. 3b, Tourist attractions. 5b, Transportation, communications. 7b, Agriculture.

1992, Aug. 8   Wmk. 368   *Perf. 13½*
1484 A458 2b multicolored .25 .25
    Complete booklet, strip of 5 #1484 3.25
1485 A458 3b multicolored .35 .25
1486 A458 5b multicolored .55 .40
1487 A458 7b multicolored .85 .55
   Nos. 1484-1487 (4) 2.00 1.45

Queen Sirikit, 60th Birthday — A459

#1488, Wedding, with King, Queen being anointed. #1489, Coronation, King and Queen on throne. #1490, Being crowned, Queen with crown, being anointed. #1491, Formal portrait, Queen seated. #1492, Visiting wounded. #1493, Visiting public.

Wmk. 329
1992, Aug. 12   Photo.   *Perf. 13½*
1488 A459 2b multicolored .70 .25
    Complete booklet, strip of 5 #1488 6.00
1489 A459 2b multicolored .70 .25
    Complete booklet, strip of 5 #1489 6.00
1490 A459 2b multicolored .70 .25
    Complete booklet, strip of 5 #1490 6.00
1491 A459 2b multicolored .70 .25
    Complete booklet, strip of 5 #1491 6.00
1492 A459 2b multicolored .70 .25
    Complete booklet, strip of 5 #1492 6.00
1493 A459 2b multicolored .70 .25
    Complete booklet, strip of 5 #1493 6.00
   a. Souv. sheet of 6, #1488-1493 5.00 5.00
   Nos. 1488-1493 (6) 4.20 1.50

No. 1493a sold for 30b. Exists imperf with sale price in different colors, value same as perf.

Royal Regalia of Queen Sirikit — A460

No. 1494, Tray. No. 1495, Kettle. No. 1496, Bowl. No. 1497, Box. No. 1498, Covered dish.

1992, Aug. 12   **Background Colors**
1494 A460 2b dark blue .45 .25
1495 A460 2b violet .45 .25
1496 A460 2b yellow green .45 .25
1497 A460 2b Prussian blue .45 .25
1498 A460 2b dark green .45 .25
   Nos. 1494-1498 (5) 2.25 1.25

Opening of Sirikit Medical Center — A461

Perf. 14½x14
1992, Aug. 12   Litho.   Wmk. 387
1499 A461 2b multicolored .45 .25
    Complete booklet, strip of 5 #1499 4.00

Queen Sirikit, 60th Birthday — A462

Litho. & Embossed
1992, Aug. 12   *Perf. 13½*
1500 A462 100b blue & gold 17.50 17.50

No. 1500 was printed in sheets of 10. Value, $190.

A463

Wmk. 387
1992, Aug. 25   Litho.   *Perf. 13½*
1501 A463 2b multicolored .60 .25
    Complete booklet, strip of 5 #1501 5.00

Prince Wan Waithayakon Krommun Naradhip Bongsprabandh (1891-1976).

A464

1992, Sept. 15   *Perf. 14x14½*
1502 A464 2b multicolored .60 .25
    Complete booklet, strip of 5 #1502 5.00

Professor Silpa Bhirasri, Sculptor, cent. of birth.

Coral A465

Perf. 14½x14
1992, Oct. 4   Litho.   Wmk. 387
1503 A465 2b Catalaphyllia jardinei .55 .25
    Complete booklet, strip of 5 #1503 3.25
1504 A465 3b Porites lutea .80 .25
1505 A465 6b Tubastraea coccinea 1.10 .50
1506 A465 8b Favia pallida 1.60 .70
   a. Souv. sheet of 4, #1503-1506 5.25
   Nos. 1503-1506 (4) 4.05 1.70

Intl. Letter Writing Week. No. 1506a sold for for 30b.

New Year 1993 — A466

Flowers: No. 1507, Rhododendron simsii. No. 1508, Cynoglossum lanceolatum. No.

1509, Tithonia diversifolia. No. 1510, Agapetes parishii.

Perf. 14x13½
1992, Nov. 15   Wmk. 368   Litho.
1507 A466 1b multicolored   .35   .25
1508 A466 1b multicolored   .35   .25
1509 A466 1b multicolored   .35   .25
1510 A466 1b multicolored   .35   .25
a.   Souv. sheet of 4, #1507-1510   3.00 2.00
    Nos. 1507-1510 (4)   1.40 1.00

Nos. 1510a sold for 10b. Exists imperf with sheet price in green, value same as perf.

1st Asian Congress of Allergies and Immunology A467

1992, Nov. 22   Perf. 13½
1511 A467 2b black, red & yellow .45   .25
    Complete booklet, strip of 5
    #1511   5.00

Natl. Assembly, 60th Anniv. — A468

Wmk. 387
1992, Dec. 10   Litho.   Perf. 13½
1512 A468 2b multicolored   .60   .25
    Complete booklet, strip of 5
    #1512   6.00

Bank of Thailand, 50th Anniv. — A469

1992, Dec. 10   Perf. 14½x14
1513 A469 2b multicolored   .60   .25
    Complete booklet, strip of 5
    #1513   5.50

Children's Day — A470

Children's drawings: No. 1514, River scene. No. 1515, Wild animals, forest. No. 1516, Trains, planes, monorail.

1993, Jan. 9   Wmk. 368   Perf. 13½
1514 A470 2b multicolored   .35   .25
    Complete booklet, strip of 5
    #1514   4.00
1515 A470 2b multicolored   .35   .25
    Complete booklet, strip of 5
    #1515   4.00
1516 A470 2b multicolored   .35   .25
    Complete booklet, strip of 5
    #1516   4.00
    Nos. 1514-1516 (3)   1.05   .75

Pottery — A471

Designs: 3b, Jug with bird's neck spout, two bottles. 6b, Pear-shaped vase, two jars. 7b, Three bowls. 8b, Three jars.

1993, Jan. 9   Photo.   Wmk. 329
1517 A471 3b multicolored   .35   .25
1518 A471 6b multicolored   .70   .50
1519 A471 7b multicolored   .80   .55
1520 A471 8b multicolored   .95   .70
a.   Souv. sheet of 4, #1517-1520   5.50 4.00
    Nos. 1517-1520 (4)   2.80 2.00

1993 World Philatelic Exhibition, Bangkok. No. 1520a sold for 35b.

Thai Teachers' Training Institute, Cent. — A472

Perf. 13½x14
1993, Jan. 16   Litho.   Wmk. 368
1521 A472 2b multicolored   .45   .25
    Complete booklet, strip of 5
    #1521   6.00

Kasetsart University, 50th Anniv. — A473

1993, Feb. 2   Wmk. 329   Perf. 13½
1522 A473 2b multicolored   .60   .25
    Complete booklet, strip of 5
    #1522   6.00

Maghapuja Day — A474

Wmk. 387
1993, Mar. 7   Litho.   Perf. 14½
1523 A474 2b multicolored   .70   .25

Queen Sri Bajarindra A475

1993, Mar. 27   Perf. 14x14½
1524 A475 2b multicolored   .80   .25
    Complete booklet, strip of 5
    #1524   7.25

Thai Red Cross, cent.

Office of Attorney General, Cent. — A476

1993, Apr. 1   Wmk. 368   Perf. 12½
1525 A476 2b multicolored   .60   .25
    Complete booklet, strip of 5
    #1525   6.00

Heritage Conservation Day — A477

Historical landmarks, Si Satchanalai Park: 3b, Wat Chedi Chet Thaeo. 4b, Wat Chang Lom. 6b, Wat Phra Si Rattanamahathat (Chaliang). 7b, Wat Suan Kaeo Utthayan Noi.

Wmk. 368
1993, Apr. 2   Litho.   Perf. 13½
1526 A477 3b multicolored   .35   .25
1527 A477 4b multicolored   .45   .30
1528 A477 6b multicolored   .70   .50
1529 A477 7b multicolored   .80   .55
a.   Souv. sheet of 4, #1526-1529   4.50 3.50
    Nos. 1526-1529 (4)   2.30 1.60

No. 1529a sold for 25b.
See Nos. 1561-1564, 1650-1653, 1797-1800.

Songkran Day Type of 1991
Perf. 14x14½
1993   Litho.   Wmk. 387
1530 A425 2b Demon on
             rooster's back,
             zodiac   .40   .25
    Complete booklet, strip of 5
    #1530   2.50
a.   Souvenir sheet of 1   2.50 1.00
b.   As "a," ovptd. in gold   15.00 15.00

No. 1530b overprinted on sheet margin in both Thai and Chinese for Chinpex '93.
Nos. 1530a-1530b sold for 8b and exist imperf. with sale price in different colors. Values same as for perf.
Issued: Nos. 1530, 1530a, 4/13.

Mushrooms — A478

Wmk. 368
1993, July 1   Litho.   Perf. 13½
1531 A478 2b Marasmius   .25   .25
    Complete booklet, strip of 5
    #1531   3.50
1532 A478 4b Coprinus   .50   .30
1533 A478 6b Mycena   .70   .45
1534 A478 8b Cyathus   1.00   .60
a.   Souv. sheet of 4, #1531-1534   4.25 4.25
    Nos. 1531-1534 (4)   2.45 1.60

No. 1534a sold for 30b.

Natl. Communications Day — A479

1993, Aug. 4   Wmk. 387   Perf. 13½
1535 A479 2b multicolored   .45   .25
    Complete booklet, strip of 5
    #1535   5.00

Post and Telegraph Department, 110th Anniv. — A480

Wmk. 387
1993, Aug. 4   Litho.   Perf. 13½
1536 A480 2b multicolored   1.00   .25
    Complete booklet, strip of 5
    #1536   10.50

Queen Suriyothai's Monument — A481

1993, Aug. 12
1537 A481 2b multicolored   .60   .25
    Complete booklet, strip of 5
    #1537   6.00

Fruit — A482

Wmk. 368
1993, Oct. 1   Photo.   Perf. 13½
1538 A482 2b Citrus reticulata .25   .25
    Complete booklet, strip of 5
    #1538   2.50
1539 A482 3b Musa sp.   .40   .25
1540 A482 6b Phyllanthus dis-
             tichus   .75   .45
1541 A482 8b Bouea burmanica   1.00   .60
    Nos. 1538-1541 (4)   2.40 1.55

Thai Ridgeback Dogs — A483

Various dogs.

1993, Oct. 1
1542 A483 2b multicolored   .55   .25
    Complete booklet, strip of 5
    #1542   2.75
1543 A483 3b multicolored   .55   .25
1544 A483 5b multicolored   .80   .40
1545 A483 10b multicolored   2.10   .75
a.   Souv. sheet of 4, #1542-1545   4.50 4.00
    Nos. 1542-1545 (4)   4.00 1.65

Intl. Letter Writing Week. No. 1545a sold for 30b.

5th Conference & Exhibition of ASEAN Council on Petroleum (ASCOPE) — A484

Wmk. 387
1993, Nov. 2   Litho.   Perf. 13½
1546 A484 2b multicolored   .60   .25
    Complete booklet, strip of 5
    #1546   6.00

King Rama VII
(1893-1941)
A485

1993, Nov. 8   **Perf. 14x14½**
1547 A485 2b multicolored   1.00   .25
   Complete booklet, strip of 5
    #1547   9.00

No. 655 Surcharged

1993   Photo.   Wmk. 233   Perf. 14½
1548 A161 1b on 25s brown red   .70   .25

Bencharong and
Lai Nam Thong
Wares — A486

Designs: 3b, Bencharong cosmetic jar,
divinity design. 5b, Bencharong cosmetic jar,
gold knob. 6b, Lai Nam Thong cosmetic jar,
floral design. 7b, Lai Nam Thong cosmetic jar,
floral design, diff.

Wmk. 368
1993, Oct. 1   Photo.   Perf. 13½
1549 A486 3b multicolored   .35   .25
1550 A486 5b multicolored   .55   .40
1551 A486 6b multicolored   .65   .45
1552 A486 7b multicolored   .80   .55
  a.   Souv. sheet of 4, #1549-1552   4.00   4.00
     Nos. 1549-1552 (4)   2.35   1.65

Bangkok '93. No. 1552a sold for 30b.
No. 1552a exists imperf. Value, $22.50.

New Year
1994 — A487

Perf. 14½x14
1993, Nov. 15   Litho.   Wmk. 387
1553 A487 1b Ipomoea cairica   .25   .25
1554 A487 1b Decaschistia
          parviflora   .25   .25
1555 A487 1b Hibiscus tiliaceus   .25   .25
1556 A487 1b Passiflora foetida   .25   .25
  a.   Souv. sheet of 4, #1553-1556   2.00   1.75
     Nos. 1553-1556 (4)   1.00   1.00

No. 1556a sold for 10b.

THAICOM, Natl.
Satellite
Project — A488

1993, Dec. 1   **Perf. 14x14½**
1557 A488 2b multicolored   .50   .25
   Complete booklet, strip of 5
    #1557   5.00

Children's Day — A489

1994, Jan. 8   **Perf. 14½x14**
1558 A489 2b Play land   .45   .25
   Complete booklet, strip of 5
    #1558   4.00

Administrative Building, Chulalongkorn
Hospital, 80th Anniv. — A490

Perf. 14½x14
1994, Mar. 30   Litho.   Wmk. 387
1559 A490 2b multicolored   .45   .25
   Complete booklet, strip of 5
    #1559   4.00

Thai Red Cross.

Royal Institute,
60th
Anniv. — A491

1994, Mar. 31   **Perf. 14x14½**
1560 A491 2b multicolored   .40   .25
   Complete booklet, strip of 5
    #1560   4.00

**Heritage Conservation Day Type of
1993**

Historical landmarks, Phra Nakhon Si
Ayutthaya Park: 2b, Wat Ratchaburana. 3b,
Wat Maha That. 6b, Wat Maheyong. 9b, Wat
Phra Si Samphet.

1994, Apr. 2   **Perf. 14½x14**
1561 A477 2b multicolored   .30   .25
   Complete booklet, strip of 5
    #1561   2.50
1562 A477 3b multicolored   .40   .25
1563 A477 6b multicolored   .80   .50
1564 A477 9b multicolored   1.25   .95
  a.   Souv. sheet of 4, #1561-1564   3.25   3.25
     Nos. 1561-1564 (4)   2.75   1.95

No. 1564a sold for 25b.

Opening of Friendship Bridge,
Thailand-Laos — A492

1994, Apr. 8
1565 A492 9b multicolored   1.75   .75

Songkran Day Type of 1991
1994, Apr. 13   **Litho.**
1566 A425 2b Demon on dog's
          back, zodiac   .35   .25
   Complete booklet, strip of 5
    #1566   3.25
  a.   Souvenir sheet of 1   2.00   1.75
  b.   As "a," inscribed in margin   4.50   4.50

No. 1566a sold for 8b and exists imperf with
frame around stamp and sale price in different
color. Value same as perf.
Sheet margin of No. 1566b has no value
inscription and is overprinted in violet with Thai
and Chinese inscriptions for Beijing Stamp

Exhibition. Issued: May 1994. No. 1566b also
exists imperf. Value same as perf.

Intl. Olympic Committee,
Cent. — A493

Wmk. 387
1994, June 23   Litho.   Perf. 14
1567 A493 2b Soccer   .25   .25
   Complete booklet, strip of 5
    #1567   1.75
1568 A493 3b Running   .35   .25
1569 A493 5b Swimming   .60   .45
1570 A493 6b Weight lifting   .80   .55
1571 A493 9b Boxing   1.10   .80
     Nos. 1567-1571 (5)   3.10   2.30

Thammasat University, 60th
Anniv. — A494

Wmk. 387
1994, June 27   Litho.   Perf. 14
1572 A494 2b multicolored   1.60   .45
   Complete booklet, strip of 5
    #1572   8.00

Asalhapuja
Day — A495

1994, July 22   Wmk. 329   Perf. 13½
1573 A495 2b multicolored   .45   .25

Natl. Communications Day — A496

1994, Aug. 4   **Wmk. 368**
1574 A496 2b multicolored   .45   .25
   Complete booklet, strip of 5
    #1574   4.00

Crabs
A497

3b, Phricotelphusa limula. 5b, Thaipotamon
chulabhorn. 6b, Phricotelphusa sirindhorn.
10b, Thaiphusa sirikit.

Wmk. 340 (340)
1994, Aug. 12   Photo.   Perf. 13½x13
1575 A497 3b multicolored   .55   .25
1576 A497 5b multicolored   .80   .45
1577 A497 6b multicolored   .80   .55

1578 A497 10b multicolored   1.60   .90
  a.   Souv. sheet of 4, #1575-1578   4.50   4.50
  b.   As "a," inscribed in margin   7.25   5.50
     Nos. 1575-1578 (4)   3.75   2.15

No. 1578b has PHILAKOREA '94 Exhibition
emblem added to sheet margin.

Intl. Letter Writing Week — A498

Winning paintings in design contest: 2b,
Gold niello bowls, octagonal footed tray. 6b,
Pumpkin shaped bowls. 8b, Silver niello betel-
nut set. 9b, Covered square bowl with gold
finial, small lotus-shaped footed tray.

Wmk. 368
1994, Oct. 9   Photo.   Perf. 13½
1579 A498 2b multicolored   .25   .25
   Complete booklet, 5 #1579   2.50
1580 A498 6b multicolored   .80   .55
1581 A498 8b multicolored   1.00   .70
1582 A498 9b multicolored   1.10   .80
  a.   Souv. sheet of 4, #1579-1582   4.00   4.00
     Nos. 1579-1582 (4)   3.15   2.30

No. 1582a sold for 30b.

ILO,
75th
Anniv.
A499

Perf. 15x14
1994, Oct. 29   Litho.   Wmk. 387
1583 A499 2b multicolored   .30   .25
   Complete booklet, 5 #1583   4.00

New Year
1995 — A500

Herbs: No. 1584, Utricularia delphinioides.
No. 1585, Utricularia minutissima. No. 1586,
Eriocaulon odoratum. No. 1587, Utricularia
bifida.

1994, Nov. 15   **Perf. 14x14½**
1584 A500 1b multicolored   .25   .25
1585 A500 1b multicolored   .25   .25
1586 A500 1b multicolored   .25   .25
1587 A500 1b multicolored   .25   .25
  a.   Souv. sheet of 4, #1584-1587   2.00   1.75
     Nos. 1584-1587 (4)   1.00   1.00

No. 1587a sold for 10b.

Suan Dusit Teachers College, 60th
Anniv. — A501

Perf. 14½x14
1994, Dec. 4   Litho.   Wmk. 387
1588 A501 2b multicolored   .60   .25
   Complete booklet, 5 #1588   5.50

Council of State, 120th Anniv. — A502

1994, Dec. 5   Wmk. 368   Perf. 13½
1589 A502 2b multicolored   1.40   .25
   Complete booklet, 5 #1589   12.50

ICAO, 50th Anniv. A503

1994, Dec. 7   Perf. 14½x14   Wmk. 387
1590 A503 2b multicolored   .35   .25
   Complete booklet, 5 #1590   5.50

Pharmacy in Thailand, 80th Anniv. — A504

Grinding stones: 2b, Dvaravati, 7th-11th cent. 6b, Lopburi Period, 11th-13th cent. 9b, Bangkok Period, 18th-20th cent.

1994, Dec. 13
1591 A504 2b multicolored   .30   .25
   Complete booklet, 5 #1591   3.00
1592 A504 6b multicolored   .80   .50
1593 A504 9b multicolored   1.10   .80
   Nos. 1591-1593 (3)   2.20   1.55

Bar Assoc., 80th Anniv. — A505

Design: 2b, First Bar Assoc. headquarters, King Vajiravudh, King Bhumibol.

1995, Jan. 1   Wmk. 368   Perf. 13½
1594 A505 2b multicolored   .60   .25
   Complete booklet, 5 #1594   6.25

A506

Children's drawings: No. 1595, Kites Decorate the Summer Sky. No. 1596, Trees and Streams, horiz. No. 1597, Youths and Religion, horiz.

1995, Jan. 14   Wmk. 387   Perf. 14
1595 A506 2b multicolored   .55   .25
   Complete booklet, 5 #1595   3.00
1596 A506 2b multicolored   .55   .25
   Complete booklet, 5 #1596   3.00
1597 A506 2b multicolored   .55   .25
   Complete booklet, 5 #1597   3.00
   Nos. 1595-1597 (3)   1.65   .75

Children's Day.

A507

1995, Mar. 4
1598 A507 2b multicolored   .35   .25
   Complete booklet, 5 #1598   5.00

First Thai newspaper, Bangkok Recorder, 150th anniv.

Royal Thai Air Force, 80th Anniv. A508

1995, Mar. 27   Wmk. 368   Perf. 13½
1599 A508 2b multicolored   .25   .25
   Complete booklet, 5 #1599   4.00

Red Cross Floating Clinic, Wetchapha — A509

1995, Mar. 30
1600 A509 2b multicolored   .25   .25
   Complete booklet, 5 #1600   4.00

Phimai Historical Park — A510

Paintings: 3b, Naga Bridge. 5b, Brahmin Hall. 6b, Gateway of the Inner Wall. 9b, Main Pagoda.

Perf. 14½x14
1995, Apr. 2   Wmk. 387
1601 A510 3b multicolored   .35   .25
1602 A510 5b multicolored   .60   .35
1603 A510 6b multicolored   .80   .50
1604 A510 9b multicolored   1.10   .80
   a.   Souv. sheet of 4, #1601-1604   4.00   4.00
   Nos. 1601-1604 (4)   2.85   1.90

Heritage Conservation Day.
No. 1604a sold for 30b.

Ministry of Defense, 108th Anniv. — A511

Design: 2b, Admin. building, King Rama V.

1995, Apr. 8   Wmk. 387   Perf. 14
1605 A511 2b multicolored   .70   .25
   Complete booklet, 5 #1605   7.50

Songkran Day Type of 1991
1995, Apr. 13   Perf. 11x13
1606 A425 2b Demon on boar's back, zodiac   .30   .25
   a.   Souvenir sheet of 1   1.75   1.00
   Complete booklet, 5 #1606   3.25

No. 1606a sold for 8b and exists imperf with sale price in different color. Value same as perf. No. 1606a and the similar imperf sheet exist with a red marginal inscription in Thai and Chinese (without sale price). Value, each $5.50.

Ministry of Foreign Affairs, 120th Anniv. — A512

2b, Saranrom Palace, King Rama V.

1995, Apr. 14   Perf. 14
1607 A512 2b multicolored   .80   .25
   Complete booklet, 5 #1607   7.50

Visakhapuja Day — A513

Sculptures of Buddha: 2b, Emerald Buddha, temple of Wat Phra Si Rattana Satsadaram, Bangkok. 6b, Phra Phuttha Chinnarat, Wat Phra Si Rattana Maha That, Phitsanulok Province. 8b, Phra Phuttha Sihing, Wat Phra Sing, Chiang Mai Province. 9b, Phra Sukhothai Traimit, Wat Traimit Witthayaram, Bangkok.

Wmk. 340
1995, May 13   Photo.   Perf. 13½
1608 A513 2b multicolored   .25   .25
1609 A513 6b multicolored   .80   .50
1610 A513 8b multicolored   1.00   .70
1611 A513 9b multicolored   1.10   .80
   a.   Souv. sheet of 4, #1608-1611   4.50   4.50
   Nos. 1608-1611 (4)   3.15   2.25

No. 1611a sold for 35b.

ASEAN Environment Year — A514

1995, June 5   Litho.   Wmk. 368
1612 A514 2b multicolored   .25   .25
   Complete booklet, 5 #1612   4.00

Information Technology Year — A515

1995, June 9   Wmk. 340
1613 A515 2b multicolored   .25   .25
   Complete booklet, 5 #1613   4.00

Thailand-People's Republic of China Diplomatic Relations, 20th Anniv. — A516

#1614, Elephants walking right into water. #1615, Elephants walking left into water.

Wmk. 340
1995, July 1   Photo.   Perf. 13½
1614 A516 2b multicolored   .50   .25
1615 A516 2b multicolored   .50   .25
   a.   Pair, Nos. 1614-1615   1.75   1.75
   b.   Souv. sheet, #1614-1615   3.50
   c.   As "b," diff. inscriptions in sheet margin   18.00

No. 1615c contains Jakarta '95 exhibition emblem and does not have sheet value in margin.
#1615b sold for 8b. #1615c sold for 28b.
No. 1615b exists with serial number in sheet margin, The same number is on China (PRC) No. 2462a. These two souvenir sheets were sold as a set. Value, set $26.50.
See People's Republic of China Nos. 2579-2580.

Natl. Communications Day — A517

1995, Aug. 4   Litho.   Perf. 14½x14
1616 A517 2b multicolored   .30   .25
   Complete booklet, 5 #1616   4.50

A518

Domestic cats: 3b, Khoa Manee. 6b, Korat or Si-Sawat. 7b, Seal point Siamese. 9b, Burmese.

1995, Aug. 4   Photo.   Perf. 13½
1617 A518 3b multicolored   .55   .25
1618 A518 6b multicolored   .80   .50
1619 A518 7b multicolored   1.00   .60
1620 A518 9b multicolored   1.60   .80
   a.   Souv. sheet, Nos. 1617-1620   5.50   5.50
   b.   As "a," diff. inscriptions in margin   35.00   35.00
   Nos. 1617-1620 (4)   3.95   2.15

Thaipex '95.
No. 1620b contains Singapore '95 exhibition emblem added to sheet margin and does not have value inscription.
No. 1620a sold for 35b. No. 1620b sold for 46b.
No. 1620a exists imperf. Value $21.00.

A519

1995, Sept. 2   Litho.   Perf. 14x14½
1621 A519 2b multicolored .25 .25
   Complete booklet, 5 #1621 4.50

Revenue Department, 80th anniv.

Natl. Auditing & Office of Auditor
General, 120th Anniv. — A520

1995, Sept. 18   Perf. 14½x14
1622 A520 2b multicolored .25 .25
   Complete booklet, 5 #1622 4.00

Intl. Letter Writing
Week — A521

Wicker: No. 1623, Vase with handles, legs.
No. 1624, Oval-shaped container. No. 1625,
Lamp shade. No. 1626, Vase.

Wmk. 340
1995, Oct. 8   Photo.   Perf. 13½
1623 A521 2b multicolored .25 .25
   Complete booklet, 5 #1623 2.75
1624 A521 2b multicolored .25 .25
   Complete booklet, 5 #1624 2.75
1625 A521 9b multicolored 1.10 .80
1626 A521 9b multicolored 1.10 .80
   a. Souv. sheet, #1623-1626 4.50 4.50
   Nos. 1623-1626 (4) 2.70 2.10

FAO,
50th
Anniv.
A522

1995, Oct. 16   Litho.   Perf. 14½x14
1627 A522 2b multicolored .25 .25
   Complete booklet, 5 #1627 3.50

Total Solar Eclipse in Thailand — A523

1995, Oct. 24   Perf. 13½
1628 A523 2b multicolored .45 .25
   Complete booklet, 5 #1628 2.50

UN,
50th
Anniv.
A524

Perf. 13½x14
1995, Oct. 24   Wmk. 387
1629 A524 2b multicolored .25 .25
   Complete booklet, 5 #1629 2.50

World Agricultural and Industrial
Exhibition, Nkhon Ratchasima
Province — A525

2b, Worldtech '95 Thailand Symbol Tower,
vert. 5b, Farming equipment, food products,
vert. 6b, Computers, equipment. 9b, Factory,
beach.

Perf. 14x14½, 14½x14
1995, Nov. 4   Wmk. 340
1630 A525 2b multicolored .25 .25
   Complete booklet, 5 #1630 2.50
1631 A525 5b multicolored .60 .40
1632 A525 6b multicolored .80 .50
1633 A525 9b multicolored 1.10 .80
   Nos. 1630-1633 (4) 2.75 1.95

New Year
1996 — A526

#1634, Adenium obesum. #1635, Bauhinia
acuminata. #1636, Cananga odorata. #1637,
Thumbergia erecta.

1995, Dec. 9   Perf. 13½
1634 A526 2b multicolored .25 .25
1635 A526 2b multicolored .25 .25
   a. Souvenir sheet, #1634-1635 4.50
1636 A526 2b multicolored .25 .25
1637 A526 2b multicolored .25 .25
   a. Souvenir sheet, #1634-1637 2.75 2.25
   b. As "a," inscribed in margin 13.50 10.00
   c. Souvenir sheet, #1636-1637 8.00 7.00
   Nos. 1634-1637 (4) 1.00 1.00

No. 1637a sold for 15b.
Nos. 1635a, 1637c have "CHINA '96"
emblem inscribed in sheet margin and sold for
22b each. No. 1637b is inscribed in sheet margin with "Indonesia '96" emblem and has the
gold 15b value removed. No. 1637b sold for
14b.
Issued: #1635a, 1637b-1637c, 5/18/96.

Veterinary Science in Thailand, 60th
Anniv. — A527

1995, Dec. 9   Perf. 14½x14
1638 A527 2b multicolored .50 .25
   Complete booklet, 5 #1638 4.00

A528

Perf. 14x14½
1996, Jan. 12   Litho.   Wmk. 340
1639 A528 2b multicolored .50 .25
   Complete booklet, 5 #1639 5.00

Siriraj School of Nursing and Midwifery, cent.

A529

Paintings of Buddha instructing people with:
No. 1640, Bright light, deer. No. 1641, Chil-
dren, animal, person reclined, horiz. No. 1642,
Followers, large tree, river.

1996, Jan. 13   Wmk. 387   Perf. 13½
1640 A529 2b multicolored .50 .25
   Complete booklet, 5 #1640 2.75
1641 A529 2b multicolored .50 .25
   Complete booklet, 5 #1641 2.75
1642 A529 2b multicolored .50 .25
   Complete booklet, 5 #1642 2.75
   Nos. 1640-1642 (3) 1.50 .75

Natl. Children's Day.

Natl. Aviation Day — A530

Perf. 14½x14
1996, Jan. 13   Wmk. 340
1643 A530 2b multicolored .30 .25
   Complete booklet, 5 #1643 4.00

Asia-Europe
Economic
Meeting — A531

Perf. 14x14½
1996, Mar. 1   Litho.   Wmk. 340
1644 A531 2b multicolored .25 .25
   Complete booklet, 5 #1644 4.00

Maghapuja Day — A532

Scenes from the Ten Jataka stories: 2b,
Man on knee, another holding chariot. 6b, Two
people flying over sea. 8b, Archer approaching
man with arrow in side. 9b, Charioteer
pointing.

Wmk. 340
1996, Mar. 3   Photo.   Perf. 13½
1645 A532 2b multicolored .25 .25
1646 A532 6b multicolored .80 .50
1647 A532 8b multicolored 1.00 .70
1648 A532 9b multicolored 1.10 .80
   a. Souvenir Sheet, #1645-1548 6.25 5.50
   Nos. 1645-1648 (4) 3.15 2.25

No. 1648a sold for 36b.

Cremation of Princess Mother Somdej
Phra Sri Nakharindra
Barommarajjonnani — A533

Litho. & Embossed
Perf. 14½x14
1996, Mar. 10   Wmk. 340
1649 A533 2b gold & multi .80 .25
   Complete booklet, 5 #1649 6.25

**Heritage Conservation Day Type of
1993**

Historical landmarks, Kamphaeng Phet
Park: 2b, Wat Phra Kaeo. 3b, Wat Phra Non.
6b, Wat Chang Rop. 9b, Wat Phra Si Iriyabot.

Wmk. 387
1996, Apr. 2   Litho.   Perf. 13½
1650 A477 2b multicolored .25 .25
   Complete booklet, 5 #1650 2.75
1651 A477 3b multicolored .45 .25
1652 A477 6b multicolored .80 .50
1653 A477 9b multicolored 1.10 .80
   a. Souvenir sheet, #1650-1653 3.75 3.75
   Nos. 1650-1653 (4) 2.60 1.80

No. 1653a sold for 28b.

Chiang Mai, 700th Anniv. — A534

Anniv. logo of Chiang Mai and: 2b, Buddhist
Pagoda of Wat Chiang Man. 6b, Sculpted
angel on wall, Wat Chet Yot's Pagoda. 8b,
Insignia of Wat Phan Tao's Vihara. 9b,
Sattaphanta.

Wmk. 340
1996, Apr. 12   Photo.   Perf. 13½
1654 A534 2b multicolored .25 .25
   Complete booklet, 5 #1654 2.75
1655 A534 6b multicolored .80 .50
1656 A534 8b multicolored 1.00 .70
1657 A534 9b multicolored 1.10 .80
   a. Souvenir sheet, #1654-1657 3.25 3.25
   Nos. 1654-1657 (4) 3.15 2.25

No. 1657a sold for 37b.

Second Intl.
Asian Hornbill
Workshop
A535

#1658, White-crowned. #1659, Rufous-
necked. #1660, Plain-pouched. #1661,
Rhinoceros.

1996, Apr. 12
1658 A535 3b multicolored .35 .25
1659 A535 3b multicolored .35 .25
1660 A535 9b multicolored 1.10 .80
1661 A535 9b multicolored 1.10 .80
   a. Souvenir sheet, #1658-1661 5.50 5.50
   b. As "a," inscribed in margin 10.00 8.00
   Nos. 1658-1661 (4) 2.90 2.10

No. 1661a sold for 35b. No. 1661b was
issued 6/8/96, contains CAPEX '96 exhibition
emblem in sheet margin, no value inscription,
and sold for 47b.

Songkran Day Type of 1991
Perf. 13½x14
1996, Apr. 13   Litho.   Wmk. 387
1662 A425 2b Demon on rat's
        back, zodiac .25 .25
   Complete booklet, 5 #1662 3.50
   a. Souvenir sheet of 1 2.75 2.75

b.	Souv. sheet, #1389, 1467, 1530, 1566, 1606, 1662	4.00	4.00
c,	As "a," inscribed in margin	6.00	6.00
d.	As "b," inscribed in margin	17.50	15.00

No. 1662c contains CHINA '96 exhibition emblem and "CHINA '96-9th Asian International Philatelic Exhibition" in Chinese and English and no value inscription in sheet margin. No. 1662d contains CHINA '96 and Hong Kong '96 exhibition emblems in margin and no value inscription.

#1662a sold for 8b. #1662b sold for 20b. #1662c, issued 5/15/96, sold for 14b. #1662d, issued 5/10/96, sold for 25b. #1662a-1662d exist imperf.

King Bhumibol Adulyadej, 50th Anniv. of Assession to the Throne A536

King Bhumibol Adulyadej, 50th Anniv. of Assession to the Throne A537

Designs: No. 1663, Royal Ablutions Ceremony. No. 1664, Pouring of the Libation. No. 1665, Grand Audience. No. 1666, Royal Progress by Land. No. 1667, Audience from Balcony.

1996, June 9   Photo.   Perf. 11½
Granite Paper

1663	A536	3b multicolored	.45	.25
a.		Souvenir sheet	1.50	
1664	A536	3b multicolored	.45	.25
a.		Souvenir sheet	1.50	
1665	A536	3b multicolored	.45	.25
a.		Souvenir sheet	1.50	
1666	A536	3b multicolored	.45	.25
a.		Souvenir sheet	1.50	
1667	A536	3b multicolored	.45	.25
a.		Souvenir sheet	1.50	

Litho. & Typo.
Wmk. 387
Perf. 13½

1668	A537	100b gold & multi	13.50	9.00
		Nos. 1663-1668 (6)	15.75	10.25

Nos. 1663a 1664a, 1665a, 1666a, 1667a have a continuous design and each sold for 8b.

No. 1668 was issued in panes of 10. Value, $150.

Development Programs of King Bhumibol Adulyadej — A538

#1669, Using Vetiver grass to prevent soil erosion. #1670, Chai pattana aerator to improve water quality. #1671, Rain making project to counter droughts. #1672, Dam, natural water resource development. #1673, Reforestation.

Wmk. 340
1996, June 9   Litho.   Perf. 13½

1669	A538	3b multicolored	.35	.25
1670	A538	3b multicolored	.35	.25
1671	A538	3b multicolored	.35	.25
1672	A538	3b multicolored	.35	.25

1673	A538	3b multicolored	.35	.25
a.		Souv. sheet, #1669-1673+label	4.00	3.50
		Nos. 1669-1673 (5)	1.75	1.25

No. 1671 has a holographic image. Soaking in water may affect the hologram. No. 1673a sold for 25b.

Royal Utensils — A539

#1674, Gold-enameled cuspidor, golden spittoon. #1675, Royal betel, areca-nut set, vert. #1676, Royal water urn, vert.

Wmk. 329
1996, June 9   Photo.   Perf. 13½

1674	A539	3b green & multi	.35	.25
1675	A539	3b blue & multi	.35	.25
1676	A539	3b purple & multi	.35	.25
a.		Souvenir sheet, #1674-1676	3.00	2.25
		Nos. 1674-1676 (3)	1.05	.75

No. 1676a sold for 17b.

Modern Olympic Games, Cent. — A540

2b, Pierre de Coubertin, grave site. 3b, 1st lighting of Olympic torch, Olympia, Greece. 5b, Olympic Stadium, Athens, Olympic flag. 9b, Discus thrower, medal from 1896 games.

Perf. 14x14½
1996, June 23   Litho.   Wmk. 340

1677	A540	2b multicolored	.25	.25
		Complete booklet, 5 #1677	2.50	
1678	A540	3b multicolored	.35	.25
1679	A540	5b multicolored	.60	.45
1680	A540	9b multicolored	1.10	.80
		Nos. 1677-1680 (4)	2.30	1.75

Nat. Communications Day — A541

1996, Aug. 4   Wmk. 340

1681	A541	2b King using radio	.55	.25
		Complete booklet, 5 #1681	4.00	

Royal Forest Department, Cent. — A542

Perf. 14½x14
1996, Sept. 18   Litho.   Wmk. 340
Type of Forest

1682	A542	3b Tropical rain	.30	.25
1683	A542	6b Hill evergreen	.80	.50
1684	A542	7b Swamp	.90	.60

1685	A542	9b Mangrove	1.10	.80
a.		Souvenir sheet, #1682-1685	5.00	5.00
		Nos. 1682-1685 (4)	3.10	2.15

No. 1685a sold for 35b.

Intl. Letter Writing Week — A543

Classical Thai novels, characters: No. 1686, "Ramayana," King Rama following deer. No. 1687, "Inao," Inao kidnapping Budsaba, taking her to cave. No. 1688, "Ngao Pa," Lumhap touring forest. No. 1689, "Mathanapatha," Nang Mathana being cursed.

Wmk. 340
1996, Oct. 6   Photo.   Perf. 13½

1686	A543	3b multicolored	.35	.25
1687	A543	3b multicolored	.35	.25
1688	A543	9b multicolored	1.10	.80
1689	A543	9b multicolored	1.10	.80
a.		Souvenir sheet, #1686-1689	5.00	5.00
		Nos. 1686-1689 (4)	2.90	2.10

No. 1689a sold for 36b. For surcharges, see Nos. 2530-2531.

Rotary Intl. 1996 Asia Regional Conference A544

Perf. 14x14½
1996, Oct. 25   Litho.   Wmk. 340

1690	A544	2b multicolored	.25	.25
		Complete booklet, 5 #1609	2.50	

UNESCO, 50th Anniv. — A545

1996, Nov. 4   Perf. 14½x14

1691	A545	2b multicolored	.25	.25
		Complete booklet, 5 #1691	2.50	

Royal Barge — A546

1996, Nov. 7   Unwmk.   Perf. 11½
Granite Paper

1692	A546	9b multicolored	1.75	1.25
a.		Souvenir sheet of 1	3.25	2.75

No. 1692a sold for 16b.

New Year 1997 — A547

Designs: No. 1693, Limnocharis flava. No. 1694, Crinum thaianum, vert. No. 1695, Monochoria hastata, vert. No. 1696, Nymphoides indicum.

Perf. 14x14½, 14½x14
1996, Nov. 15   Litho.   Wmk. 387

1693	A547	2b multicolored	.25	.25
1694	A547	2b multicolored	.25	.25
1695	A547	2b multicolored	.25	.25

1696	A547	2b multicolored	.25	.25
a.		Souvenir sheet, #1693-1696	2.75	2.75
b.		*Nos. 1693-1696 (4)*	7.50	7.50
			1.00	1.00

No. 1696a sold for 15b. No. 1696b inscribed in sheet margin with Hong Kong '97 emblem and vertical Chinese inscription. No. 1696b issued 2/12/97.

Ducks A548

#1697, Sarkidiornis melanotos. #1698, Dendrocygna javanica, vert. #1699, Cairina scutulata, vert. #1700, Nettapus coromandelianus.

Wmk. 340
1996, Dec. 1   Photo.   Perf. 13½

1697	A548	3b multicolored	.35	.25
1698	A548	3b multicolored	.35	.25
1699	A548	7b multicolored	.90	.60
1700	A548	7b multicolored	.90	.60
a.		Souvenir sheet, #1697-1700	5.50	5.50
		Nos. 1697-1700 (4)	2.50	1.70

No. 1700a sold for 33b.

UNICEF, 50th Anniv. — A549

Perf. 14½x14
1996, Dec. 11   Litho.   Wmk. 340

1701	A549	2b multicolored	.25	.25
		Complete booklet, 5 #1701	2.50	

King Bhumibol Adulyadej — A550

Perf. 14x14½
1996, Dec. 5   Litho.   Wmk. 340

1702	A550	2b carmine	.35	.25
		Complete booklet, 5 #1702	4.50	
a.		Unwmkd., granite paper	.50	.25

No. 1702a issued 9/1/98.
See Nos. 1725-1729, 1743-1745, 1756-1757, 1794-1795, 1819-1820, 1876-1879, 2067, 2212-2213, 2435, 2465A.

Thailand's 1st Olympic Gold Medal, 1996 — A552

Litho. & Embossed
Perf. 14½x14
1996, Dec. 16   Wmk. 340

1704	A552	6b multicolored	.80	.50

Mahavajiravudh School, Songkhla, Cent. — A553

Perf. 14x14½
1997, Jan. 1 — Wmk. 387

1705	A553	2b multicolored	.25	.25
		Complete booklet, 5 #1705	2.50	

Children's Day — A554

Children' paintings: No. 1706, Children processing fish. No. 1707, Monument, children in praise.

1997, Jan. 11 — Wmk. 340

1706	A554	2b multicolored	.25	.25
		Complete booklet, 5 #1706	1.75	
1707	A554	2b multicolored	.25	.25
		Complete booklet, 5 #1707	1.75	

Communications Authority of Thailand, 20th Anniv. — A555

Perf. 14½x14
1997, Feb. 25 — Litho. — Wmk. 340

1708	A555	2b multicolored	.25	.25
		Complete booklet, 5 #1708	2.50	

Statue of Prince Bhanurangsi A556

1997, Feb. 25 — Perf. 14x14½

1709	A556	2b multicolored	.25	.25
		Complete booklet, 5 #1709	2.50	

Laksi Mail Center A557

#1710, Outside view of building. #1711, Computerized mail sorting machine.

1997, Feb. 25 — Perf. 14½x14

1710	A557	2b multicolored	.45	.25
1711	A557	2b multicolored	.45	.25
a.		Pair, #1710-1711	1.00	.50

State Railway, Cent. — A558

3b, 0-6-0 Type. 4b, Garratt. 6b, Sulzer diesel. 7b, Hitachi diesel leaving tunnel.

Wmk. 387
1997, Mar. 26 — Litho. — Perf. 13

1712	A558	3b multicolored	.35	.25
a.		Souvenir sheet of 1	2.75	2.75

1713	A558	4b multicolored	.50	.35
1714	A558	6b multicolored	.80	.50
1715	A558	7b multicolored	1.00	.60
a.		Souv. sheet of 4, #1712-1715	4.00	4.00
		Nos. 1712-1715 (4)	2.65	1.70

No. 1712a sold for 20b, No. 1715a sold for 30b.

Chulalongkorn University, 80th Anniv. — A559

Designs: No. 1716, Palace of Prince Maha Vajirunhis. No. 1717, Faculty of Arts building.

Perf. 14½x14
1997, Mar. 26 — Wmk. 340

1716	A559	2b yellow & multi	.45	.25
		Complete booklet, 5 #1716	2.00	
1717	A559	2b rose & multi	.45	.25
		Complete booklet, 5 #1717	2.00	

Thai Red Cross A560

1997, Mar. 28

1718	A560	3b Rajakarun building	.35	.25

Govt. Savings Bank, 84th Anniv. — A561

1997, Apr. 1

1719	A561	2b multicolored	.25	.25
		Complete booklet, 5 #1719	2.00	

Heritage Conservation Day — A562

Phanomrung historical Park: No. 1720, Outer stairway. No. 1721, Pavilion. No. 1722, Passage, stairway to sanctuary. No. 1723, Naga balustrade, Central Gate of Eastern Gallery.

1997, Apr. 2

1720	A562	3b multicolored	.35	.25
1721	A562	3b multicolored	.35	.25
1722	A562	7b multicolored	.90	.60
1723	A562	7b multicolored	.90	.60
a.		Souvenir sheet, #1720-1723	4.00	4.00
		Nos. 1720-1723 (4)	2.50	1.70

No. 1723a sold for 30b.

Songkran Day Type of 1991
1997-2002 — Wmk. 340 — Perf. 14x14½

1724	A425	2b Demon on ox's back, zodiac	.30	.25
		Complete booklet, 5 #1724	1.60	
a.		Souvenir sheet of 1	2.25	1.60
b.		Unwmk., granite paper	.25	.25

Issued: Nos. 1724, 1724a, 4/13/97; No. 1724b, 4/13/02. No. 1724b issued only in No. 2017b.

No. 1724a sold for 8b and exists imperf. Values same.

King Bhumibol Adulyadej Type of 1996
Litho, Litho & Engraved (#1728-1729)
Perf. 14x14½
1997, May 5 — Wmk. 340

1725	A550	4b blue & red brown	1.25	.25
a.		Perf. 13¼, unwmkd.	1.00	.25
b.		Unwmkd., granite paper	1.00	.25
1726	A550	5b pur & org brn	1.25	.30
a.		Perf. 13½, unwmk., granite paper	1.75	.30
b.		Unwmkd., granite paper	1.25	.25
1727	A550	7b pink & green	1.40	1.40

Wmk. 329
Perf. 13½x13

1728	A550	10b orange & dk brown	2.25	.90
1729	A550	20b violet & maroon	3.75	1.75
		Nos. 1725-1729 (5)	9.90	4.60

Issued: No. 1726a, 12/28/98; No. 1725a, 10/8/99. 1725b, 1726b, 12/1/00.

Waterfowl — A563

Designs: No. 1730, Pheasant-tailed jacana. No. 1731, Bronze-winged jacana. No. 1732, Painted stork. No. 1733, Black-winged stilt.

Perf. 11½x12
1997, May 15 — Photo. — Unwmk.
Granite Paper

1730	A563	3b multicolored	.55	.55
1731	A563	3b multicolored	.55	.55
1732	A563	7b multicolored	1.25	1.25
1733	A563	7b multicolored	1.25	1.25
a.		Souvenir sheet, #1730-1733	6.00	6.00
b.		As "a," with added inscription	10.00	10.00
		Nos. 1730-1733 (4)	3.60	3.60

No. 1733a sold for 30b. No. 1733b has PACIFIC 97 emblem in sheet margin, while sales price has been removed from sheet margin. No. 1728b sold for 42b.

King Bhumibol Adulyadej, National Telecommunications — A564

2b, King using hand-held radio, "Suthee" aerial. 3b, King using hand-held radio for communication in local areas. 6b, King using computer. 9b, King, classroom using satellite information.

Perf. 14½x14
1997, June 9 — Litho. — Wmk. 340

1734	A564	2b multicolored	.35	.35
		Complete booklet, 5 #1734	2.00	
1735	A564	3b multicolored	.55	.55
1736	A564	6b multicolored	1.10	1.10
1737	A564	9b multicolored	1.75	1.75
a.		Souvenir sheet, #1734-1737	6.00	6.00
		Nos. 1734-1737 (4)	3.75	3.75

No. 1737a sold for 30b. For surcharges, see Nos. 2407-2408, 2532, 2586.

Motion Pictures in Thailand, Cent. — A565

Designs: No. 1738, King Rama VII filming movie, film showing King Chulalongkorn's state visit to Europe. No. 1739, Early motion picture equipment, advertisement, Prince Sanbassatra, founder of Thai motion picures. No. 1740, Poster from "Double Luck," band playing in front of movie theater. No. 1741, Open air theater, poster from "Going Astray."

1997, June 10

1738	A565	3b multicolored	.55	.55
1739	A565	3b multicolored	.55	.55
1740	A565	7b multicolored	1.25	1.25
1741	A565	7b multicolored	1.25	1.25
		Nos. 1738-1741 (4)	3.60	3.60

Faculty of Medicine, Chulalongkorn University, 50th Anniv. — A566

King Rama VIII, building, operating room.

1997, June 11

1742	A566	2b multicolored	.45	.25
		Complete booklet, 5 #1742	2.25	

King Bhumibol Adulyadej Type of 1996
Perf. 14x14½
1997, July 19 — Litho. — Wmk. 340

1743	A550	6b grn & gray vio	.40	.30
1744	A550	9b dk bl & brn org	.60	.45

Litho. & Engr.
Wmk. 329
Perf. 13½x13

1745	A550	100b lem & dk bl grn	6.25	4.75
		Nos. 1743-1745 (3)	7.25	5.50

Thai-Russian Diplomatic Relations, Cent. — A567

Design: Peterhof Palace, King Chulalongkorn (King Rama V).

1997, July 3 — Litho. — Perf. 14½x14

1746	A567	2b multicolored	.35	.25
		Complete booklet, 5 #1746	3.25	

Asalhapuja Day — A568

3b, Mahosathajataka (scene with man on elephant). 4b, Bhuridattajataka (scene with two men, large snake). 6b, Candakumarajataka (scene with pot of fire, three men on knees, man in sky, Buddha). 7b, Naradajataka (scene with people praising human figure with four arms hovering above roof).

Perf. 11½ Syncopated
1997, July 19 — Photo. — Unwmk.
Granite Paper

1747	A568	3b multicolored	.55	.55
a.		Souvenir sheet of 1	1.75	.90
b.		As "a," inscribed in margin	3.25	3.25
1748	A568	4b multicolored	.70	.70
a.		Souvenir sheet of 1	1.75	.90
b.		As "a," inscribed in margin	3.25	3.25
1749	A568	6b multicolored	1.10	1.10
a.		Souvenir sheet of 1	1.75	.90
b.		As "a," inscribed in margin	3.25	3.25
1750	A568	7b multicolored	1.25	1.25
a.		Souvenir sheet of 1	2.75	1.75
b.		Souvenir sheet, #1747-1750	6.00	4.50
c.		As "a," inscribed in margin	27.50	27.50
		Nos. 1747-1750 (4)	3.60	3.60

#1747a sold for 6b; #1748a for 8b; #1749a for 10b; #1750a for 12b; #1750b for 30b.

Sheet margins of lack value inscriptions, but contain Shanghai '97 exhibition emblem (#1747b, 1748b), Chinese insription; Bangkok '97 exhibition emblem (#1749b, 1750c).

No. 1750b exists imperf. It was issued for sale only at overseas stamp exhibitions.

For surcharges see Nos. 2380, 2382.

1997 Thailand Philatelic Exhibition — A569

Houses from: 2b, Northern region. 5b, Central region. 6b, Northeastern region. 9b, Southern region.

Wmk. 329

1997, Aug. 2   Litho.   Perf. 13½
1751	A569	2b multicolored	.25	.25
	Complete booklet, 5 #1751	1.60	
1752	A569	5b multicolored	.70	.70
1753	A569	6b multicolored	.80	.80
1754	A569	9b multicolored	1.25	1.25
a.	Souvenir sheet, #1751-1754	17.50	17.50
	Nos. 1751-1754 (4)	3.00	3.00

No. 1754a sold for 32b.
No. 1754a exists imperf, sold with an exhibition book. Value, $15.

Natl. Communications Day — A570

Perf. 14x14½

1997, Aug. 4   Wmk. 340
1755	A570	2b multicolored	.25	.25
	Complete booklet, 5 #1755	2.00	

Greeting Stamps — A570a

Lotus flowers: No. 1755A, Nymphaea capensis. No. 1755B, Nymphaea stellata.

Perf. 14x14½

1997, Aug. 4   Litho.   Wmk. 387
Booklet Stamps
1755A	A570a	(2b) multicolored	1.50	1.50
1755B	A570a	(2b) multicolored	1.50	1.50
c.	Bklt. pane, 5 ea #1755A-1755B + 4 labels	30.00	
	Complete bklt., #1755Bc	35.00	

Nos. 1755A-1755B were sold only at 7-11 stores, not at post offices or philatelic agencies.

King Bhumibol Adulyadej Type of 1996
Litho. & Engr.
Perf. 13½x13

1997, Aug. 8   Wmk. 329
1756	A550	25b bl grn & ol blk	8.00	3.25
1757	A550	200b lil rose & vio blk	17.50	9.00

ASEAN, 30th Anniv. — A571

Designs: No. 1758, Thi Lo Su Falls, Tak. No. 1759, Luang Chiang Dao Mountain, Chiang Mai. No. 1760, Phromthep Cape, Phuket. No. 1761, Thalu Island, Chumphon.

Perf. 14½x14

1997, Aug. 8   Wmk. 340
1758	A571	2b multicolored	.25	.25
	Complete booklet, 5 #1758	1.25	
1759	A571	2b multicolored	.25	.25
	Complete booklet, 5 #1759	1.25	
1760	A571	9b multicolored	1.25	1.25
1761	A571	9b multicolored	1.25	1.25
	Nos. 1758-1761 (4)	3.00	3.00

Dinosaurs — A572

Designs: 2b, Phuwiangosaurus sirindhornae. 3b, Siamotyrannus isanensis. 6b, Siamosaurus suteethorni. 9b, Psittacosaurus sattayaraki.

Perf. 13½x13 Syncopated

1997, Aug. 28   Photo.   Unwmk.
1762	A572	2b multicolored	.25	.25
	Complete booklet, 5 #1762	1.25	
1763	A572	3b multicolored	.35	.35
1764	A572	6b multicolored	.50	.35
1765	A572	9b multicolored	1.00	.60
a.	Souvenir sheet, #1762-1765	3.25	2.00
	Nos. 1762-1765 (4)	2.10	1.45

No. 1765a sold for 30b.
For surcharge see No. 2355.

King Chulalongkorn's Visit to Switzerland, Cent. — A573

Perf. 14x14½

1997, Sept. 12   Litho.   Wmk. 340
1766	A573	2b multicolored	.45	.25
	Complete booklet, 5 #1766	6.75	

Intl. Letter Writing Week — A574

Winning drawings: No. 1767, Tricycle, combining rickshaw and tricycle. No. 1768, Tricycle with side seat. No. 1769, Motor tricycle. No. 1770. Motor tricycle with light on roof.

Perf. 11½x12

1997, Oct. 5   Photo.   Unwmk.
Granite Paper
1767	A574	3b multicolored	.25	.25
1768	A574	3b multicolored	.25	.25
1769	A574	9b multicolored	.90	.50
1770	A574	9b multicolored	.90	.50
a.	Souvenir sheet, #1767-1770	2.75	2.00
	Nos. 1767-1770 (4)	2.30	1.50

No. 1770a sold for 30b.

Shells of Thailand and Singapore A575

Designs: No. 1771, Drupa morum. No. 1772, Nerita chamaelon. No. 1773, Littoraria melanostoma. No. 1774, Cryptospira elgans.

1997, Oct. 9   Litho.   Perf. 11½
Granite Paper
1771	A575	2b multicolored	.25	.25
	Complete booklet, 5 #1771	1.75	
1772	A575	2b multicolored	.25	.25
	Complete booklet, 5 #1772	1.75	
1773	A575	9b multicolored	.90	.45
1774	A575	9b multicolored	.90	.45
a.	Souvenir sheet, #1771-7774	2.75	2.75
	Nos. 1771-1774 (4)	2.30	1.40

No. 1774a sold for 30b. See Singapore Nos. 825-828A.

Chalerm Prakiat Energy Conserving Building — A576

Perf. 14½x14

1997, Nov. 10   Litho.   Wmk. 340
1775	A576	2b multicolored	.25	.25
	Complete booklet, 5 #1775	2.00	

Christening of Suphannahong Royal Barge, 86th Anniv. — A577

Perf. 11½

1997, Nov. 13   Photo.   Unwmk.
Granite Paper
1776	A577	9b multicolored	.80	.50
a.	Souvenir sheet of 1	2.25	1.75
b.	As "a," ovptd. in margin	4.00	2.75
c.	As "a," ovptd. in margin	7.25	7.25

#1776a, 1776b, 1776c sold for 20b.
The sheet margin of #1776b is ovptd in gold with Thai and Chinese inscriptions for Bangkok/China 98. Issued 10/16/98.
No. 1776c overprinted in margin with World Stamp Expo 2000 emblem in gold. Issued 7/7/00.
For surcharge, see No. 2512.

New Year 1998 — A578

Flowers: No. 1777, Cassia alata. No. 1778, Strophanthus caudatus. No. 1779, Clinacanthus nutans. No. 1780, Acanthus ilicifolius.

1997, Nov. 15   Litho.   Perf. 13½x13
Granite Paper
1777	A578	2b multicolored	.25	.25
1778	A578	2b multicolored	.25	.25
1779	A578	2b multicolored	.25	.25
1780	A578	2b multicolored	.25	.25
a.	Souvenir sheet, #1777-1780	1.75	.90
b.	As "a," with added inscription	3.50	2.75
	Nos. 1777-1780 (4)	1.00	1.00

No. 1780a sold for 15b. No. 1780b contains Indepex '97 exhibition emblem, but no value inscription in sheet margin.

King Bhumibol Adulyadej's 70th Birthday — A579

#1781, Playing saxophone. #1782, Painting picture. #1783, Building sailboat. #1784, Wearing gold medal, sailboats. 6b, Taking photograph. 7b, Writing book. 9b, Working at computer.

1997, Dec. 5   Photo.   Perf. 11½
Granite Paper
1781	A579	2b multicolored	.25	.25
1782	A579	2b multicolored	.25	.25
1783	A579	2b multicolored	.25	.25
1784	A579	2b multicolored	.25	.25
1785	A579	6b multicolored	.50	.35
1786	A579	7b multicolored	.70	.45
1787	A579	9b multicolored	.90	.50
	Nos. 1781-1787 (7)	3.10	2.30

For surcharge see No. 2381.

A580

Winners in Yuvabadhana Foundation, "Sports Develop Mind and Body" drawing competition: No. 1788, Children in wheelchair race. No. 1789, Flying kites. No. 1790, Gymnastics. No. 1791, Windsurfing.

Perf. 14x14½

1998, Jan. 10   Litho.   Wmk. 340
1788	A580	2b multicolored	.25	.25
	Complete booklet, 5 #1788	3.25	
1789	A580	2b multicolored	.25	.25
	Complete booklet, 5 #1789	3.25	
1790	A580	2b multicolored	.25	.25
	Complete booklet, 5 #1790	3.25	
1791	A580	2b multicolored	.25	.25
a.	Complete booklet, 5 #1791	3.25	
	Nos. 1788-1791 (4)	1.00	1.00

Natl. Childrens' Day.

A581

1998, Jan. 17   Unwmk.
Granite Paper
1792	A581	2b multicolored	.25	.25
	Complete booklet, 5 #1792	3.50	

20th Asia Pacific Dental Congress.

A582

1998, Feb. 3   Wmk. 340
1793	A582	2b multicolored	.25	.25
	Complete booklet, 5 #1793	3.25	

Veteran's Day, 50th anniv.

King Bhumibol Adulyadej Type of 1996

1998, Feb. 25   Photo.   Perf. 11½x12
Granite Paper
1794	A550	50s dk ol & lt ol	.35	.25

Litho. & Engr.
Perf. 13½x13
Wmk. 329
1795	A550	50b dp vio & dk grn	7.25	2.25

A583

Perf. 14x14½
1998, Mar. 27   Litho.   Wmk. 340
1796 A583 2b Queen Sirikit   .35   .25
  Complete booklet, 5 #1796   5.00

1998 Thai Red Cross Fair.

Heritage Conservation Day Type of 1993

Paintings of Phanomrung Historical Park: 3b, Main Tower. 4b, Minor Tower. 6b, Scripture Repository. 7b, Lintel depicting Vishnu sleeping in ocean, doorway of Main Tower.

Perf. 14½x14
1998, Apr. 2   Litho.   Wmk. 340
1797 A477 3b multicolored   .25   .25
1798 A477 4b multicolored   .25   .25
1799 A477 6b multicolored   .45   .45
1800 A477 7b multicolored   .50   .50
  a. Souvenir sheet, #1797-1800   2.75   2.75

No. 1800a sold for 27b.

Songkran Day Type of 1991
1998-2002   Perf. 14x14½
1801 A425 2b Demon on tiger's
             back, zodiac   .25   .25
  Complete booklet, 5 #1801   3.25
  a. Souvenir sheet of 1   1.75   1.00
  b. As "a," inscribed in margin   3.50   2.25
  c. Unwmkd., granite paper   .25   .25

Issued: Nos. 1801-1801b, 4/13/98. No. 1801c, 4/13/02. No. 1801c issued only in No. 2017b.
No. 1801a sold for 8b and exists imperf. Values same.
Sheet margin of No. 1801b contains flags of Thailand and China (PRC), Thai and Chinese inscriptions, no value inscription, and exists imperf.
No. 1801b sold for 8b and was issued 10/16/98.

Wild Cats A584

Paintings: 2b, Felis viverrina. 4b, Panthera tigris. 6b, Panthera pardus. 8b, Felis chaus.

1998, Apr. 13   Perf. 14½x14
1802 A584 2b multicolored   .35   .25
  Complete booklet, 5 #1802   4.00
1803 A584 4b multicolored   .50   .25
1804 A584 6b multicolored   .50   .45
1805 A584 8b multicolored   .70   .50
  a. Souvenir sheet, #1802-1805   3.50   2.75
  Nos. 1802-1805 (4)   2.05   1.45

No. 1805a sold for 30b.

AEROTHAI (Aeronautical Radio of Thailand, Ltd.), 50th Anniv. — A585

1998, Apr. 15
1806 A585 2b multicolored   .25   .25
  Complete booklet, 5 #1806   3.25

Visakhapuja Day — A586

Paintings of the "Ten Jataka Stories:" 3b, Riding horse above buildings, Vidhurajataka. 4b, In chariot, Vessantarajataka. 6b, Two figures seated before larger figure, Vessantarajataka. 7b, Figures in front of building, Vessantarajataka.

1998, May 10   Perf. 13½
1807 A586 3b multicolored   .35   .25
1808 A586 4b multicolored   .50   .25
1809 A586 6b multicolored   .70   .45
1810 A586 7b multicolored   .90   .50
  a. Souvenir sheet, #1807-1810   2.75   2.00
  Nos. 1807-1810 (4)   2.45   1.45

No. 1810a sold for 30b.

Adm. Abhakara Kiartiwongse (1880-1923), Father of Royal Thai Navy — A587

1998, May 19   Perf. 14½x14
1811 A587 2b multicolored   .35   .25
  Complete booklet, 5 #1811   5.00

Educational Development — A588

Perf. 14½x14
1998, June 15   Litho.   Wmk. 340
1812 A588 2b multicolored   .25   .25
  Complete booklet, 5 #1812   4.00

King Chulalongkorn's 1st State Visit to Europe, Cent. — A589

Unwmk.
1998, July 1   Litho.   Perf. 13
Granite Paper
1813 A589 6b multicolored   .70   .45

Litho. & Embossed
1814 A589 20b multicolored   1.75   1.25

Intl. Year of the Ocean A590

2b, Orchaella brevirostris. 3b, Tursiops truncatus. 6b, Physeter catodon. 9b, Dugong dugon.

1998, July 19   Litho.   Perf. 14½x14
Granite Paper
1815 A590 2b multicolored   .35   .25
  Complete booklet, 5 #1815   2.75

1816 A590 3b multicolored   .35   .25
1817 A590 6b multicolored   .55   .45
1818 A590 9b multicolored   .90   .50
  a. Souvenir sheet, #1815-1818   4.50   4.50
  Nos. 1815-1818 (4)   2.15   1.45

No. 1818a sold for 30b.
For surcharges see Nos. 2356-2357.

King Bhumibol Adulyadej Type of 1996
1998   Photo.   Unwmk.   Perf. 11½x12
Granite Paper
1819 A550 2b carmine   .50   .25
1820 A550 9b violet & brn org   1.25   .45

For surcharges, see Nos. 2335, 2585.

Irrigation Engineering in Thailand, 60th Anniv. — A591

Perf. 14½x14
1998, Aug. 1   Litho.   Unwmk.
Granite Paper
1821 A591 2b multicolored   .25   .25
  Complete booklet, 5 #1821   3.25

Natl. Communications Day — A592

1998, Aug. 4
Granite Paper
1822 A592 2b multicolored   .25   .25
  Complete booklet, 5 #1822   3.25

School of Political Science, Chulalongkorn University, 50th Anniv. — A593

1998, Aug. 19
Granite Paper
1823 A593 2b multicolored   .25   .25
  Complete booklet, 5 #1823   3.25

Sukhothai Thammathirat Open University, Award for Excellence — A594

1998, Sept. 5   Litho.   Perf. 14½x14
Granite Paper
1824 A594 2b multicolored   .25   .25
  Complete booklet, 5 #1824   3.25

Amazing Thailand, 1998-99, Thai Arts and Culture A595

1998, Sept. 15   Perf. 13½
Granite Paper
1825 A595 3b With bow & arrow   .25   .25
1826 A595 3b Combat   .25   .25
1827 A595 7b Seizing opponent   .70   .50
1828 A595 7b Sky hovering   .70   .50
  Nos. 1825-1828 (4)   1.90   1.50

Chinese Stone Statues — A596

Warriors holding: No. 1829, Staff with loop. No. 1830, Spear with slightly curved blade. No. 1831, Mace. No. 1832, Spear with jagged blade.

1998, Sept. 15   Perf. 14x14½
Granite Paper
1829 A596 2b multicolored   .25   .25
  Complete booklet, 5 #1829   2.50
1830 A596 2b multicolored   .25   .25
  Complete booklet, 5 #1830   3.25
1831 A596 10b multicolored   .90   .60
1832 A596 10b multicolored   .90   .60
  a. Souvenir sheet, #1829-
      1832, perf 13¼   3.25   2.25
  b. As "a," with added marginal
      inscription   20.00   16.00
  Nos. 1829-1832 (4)   2.30   1.70

China 1999 World Philatelic Exhibition (#1832b). #1832a-1832b sold for 35b.
#1832 is perf 13¼ and was issued 8/21/99.

Intl. Letter Writing Week — A597

Himavanta mythical animals created by ancient Thai artists: #1836, Kraisara Rajasiha, 3 king lions, white body, golden collars. #1837, Gajasiha, 2 tusked lions. #1838, Kesara Singha, 2 hoofed lions. #1839, Singha, 3 gray lions.

Perf. 11½
1998, Oct. 3   Photo.   Unwmk.
Granite Paper
1836 A597 2b multicolored   .25   .25
  Complete booklet, 5 #1836   3.25
1837 A597 2b multicolored   .25   .25
  Complete booklet, 5 #1837   3.25
1838 A597 12b multicolored   .70   .70
1839 A597 12b multicolored   .70   .70
  a. Souvenir sheet, #1836-1839   3.50   2.75
  Nos. 1836-1839 (4)   1.90   1.90

No. 1839a sold for 40b.

Thai Presidency of the Intl. Assoc. of Lions Clubs — A598

1998, Oct. 8　Litho.　Perf. 14½x14
Granite Paper

1840 A598 2b multicolored　　.25　.25
　　Complete booklet, 5 #1840　4.00

New Year
1999 — A599

Flowers: No. 1841, Barleria lupulina. No. 1842, Gloriosa superba. No. 1843, Asclepias curassavica. No. 1844, Sesamum indicum.

Perf. 14½x14
1998, Nov. 15　Photo.　Unwmk.
Granite Paper

1841 A599 2b multicolored　　.25　.25
1842 A599 2b multicolored　　.25　.25
1843 A599 2b multicolored　　.25　.25
1844 A599 2b multicolored　　.25　.25
　a.　Souvenir sheet, #1841-1844　2.00 1.75
　　Nos. 1841-1844 (4)　　1.00 1.00

No. 1844a sold for 15b.

Knight Grand Cross, Most Admirable
Order of the Direkgunabhorn — A600

Perf. 14x14½
1998, Dec. 5　Litho.　Unwmk.
Granite Paper

1845 15b shown　　　　　1.25　.70
1846 15b Decoration　　　1.25　.70
　a.　A600 Pair, #1845-1846　3.25 1.60

Children's Day — A601

Paintings from competition, "Sports develop body and mind:" No. 1847, Sepak Takraw (game of kicking ball over net). No. 1848, Swimming. No. 1849, Volleyball. No. 1850, Equestrian sports.

Perf. 14½x14
1999, Jan. 9　Litho.　Unwmk.
Granite Paper

1847 A601 2b multicolored　　.35　.25
　　Complete booklet, 5 #1847　3.25
1848 A601 2b multicolored　　.35　.25
　　Complete booklet, 5 #1848　3.25
1849 A601 2b multicolored　　.35　.25
　　Complete booklet, 5 #1849　3.25
1850 A601 2b multicolored　　.35　.25
　　Complete booklet, 5 #1850　3.25
　　Nos. 1847-1850 (4)　　1.40 1.00

Asian and Pacific Decade of Disabled
Persons — A602

1999, Jan. 10　　　　　Granite Paper

1851 A602 2b multicolored　　.45　.25
　a.　Complete booklet, 5 #1851　3.25

Thai Rice Production — A603

#1852, Planting rice. #1853, Harvesting rice by hand. #1854, Harvesting rice with machinery. #1855, Rice in field, bowl of rice.

1999, Feb. 25　Litho.　Perf. 14½x14
Granite Paper

1852 A603 6b multicolored　　.45　.45
1853 A603 6b multicolored　　.45　.45
1854 A603 12b multicolored　　.90　.90
1855 A603 12b multicolored　　.90　.90
　a.　Souvenir sheet, #1852-1855　3.25 3.25
　　Nos. 1852-1855 (4)　　2.70 2.70

No. 1855a sold for 45b.

Maghapuja Day (Buddhist
Holiday) — A604

Designs: 3b, Birth of Mahajanaka. 6b, Mani Mekkhala carrying Mahajanaka to Mithila City. 9b, Two mango trees. 15b, Mahajanaka founding an educational institution.

1999, Mar. 1　Litho.　Perf. 13½
Granite Paper

1856 A604 3b multicolored　　.30　.25
1857 A604 6b multicolored　　.60　.45
1858 A604 9b multicolored　　.80　.60
1859 A604 15b multicolored　　1.25 1.00
　a.　Souvenir sheet, #1856-1859　4.50 3.50
　　Nos. 1856-1859 (4)　　2.95 2.30

No. 1859a sold for 45b.

Somdetch Phra
Sri Savarindira
Baromma Raja
Devi Phra Phan
Vassa Ayika
Chao, Queen
Grandmother
A605

Perf. 14x14½
1999, Mar. 30　Litho.　Wmk. 340

1860 A605 2b multicolored　　.35　.25
　　Complete booklet, 5 #1860　5.00

1999 Red Cross Fair.

Bangkok 2000 World Youth Stamp
Expo, 13th Asian Intl. Stamp
Expo — A606

Thai children's games: No. 1861, Kite flying. No. 1862, Wheel rolling. No. 1863, Catching last one in line (children going under arms). No. 1864, Snatching baby from mother snake.

Perf. 14½x14
1999, Mar. 30　　　　　Unwmk.
Granite Paper

1861 A606 2b multicolored　　.35　.25
1862 A606 2b multicolored　　.35　.25
1863 A606 15b multicolored　　1.10 1.00

1864 A606 15b multicolored　　1.10 1.00
　a.　Souvenir sheet, #1861-1864,
　　　perf. 13½　　　　4.50
　　Nos. 1861-1864 (4)　　2.90 2.50

No. 1864a sold for 45b.

Heritage
Conservation
Day — A607

Various Thai silk designs for "Mudmee" textiles.

1999, Apr. 2　　　　Perf. 14x14½
Granite Paper

1865 A607 2b bl grn & multi　　.25　.25
　　Complete booklet, 5 #1865　3.25
1866 A607 4b red & multi　　.45　.25
1867 A607 12b vermilion & multi　1.00　.90
1868 A607 15b black & multi　　1.40 1.10
　a.　Souvenir sheet, #1865-1868　4.50 3.50
　　Nos. 1865-1868 (4)　　3.10 2.50

No. 1868a sold for 45b.

Songkran Day Type of 1991
1999, Apr. 13
Granite Paper

1869 A425 2b Woman on rabbit's
　　　back, zodiac　　　.25　.25
　　Complete booklet, 5 #1869　3.25
　a.　Souvenir sheet of 1　　1.40 1.40
　b.　As "a," with added marginal inscription　　　　　5.00 5.00

China 1999 World Philatelic Exhibition (#1869b). #1869a-1869b sold for 8b and exist imperf. Values same.
Issued: #1869b, 8/21.

Consumer Protection Years, 1998-
99 — A608

1999, Apr. 30　　　　Perf. 14½x14
Granite Paper

1870 A608 2b multicolored　　.35　.25
　　Complete booklet, 5 #1870　3.50

King Bhumibol Adulyadej's 72nd
Birthday — A609

Royal palaces: No. 1871, Chitralada Villa, Dusit Palace, Bangkok, tree branch at UL. No. 1872, Phu Ping Ratchaniwet Palace, circular drive, white fence. No. 1873, Phu Phan Ratchaniwet Palace, adjoining buildings, light posts. No. 1874, Thaksin Ratchaniwet Palace, four trees reaching to second story windows.

1999, May 5　Photo.　Perf. 11½
Granite Paper

1871 A609 6b multicolored　　.65　.45
1872 A609 6b multicolored　　.65　.45
1873 A609 6b multicolored　　.65　.45
1874 A609 6b multicolored　　.65　.45
　a.　Souvenir sheet, #1871-1874　4.50 3.50
　　Nos. 1871-1874 (4)　　2.60 1.80

No. 1874a sold for 40b.

Political Science
Dept.,
Thammasat
University, 50th
Anniv. — A610

1999, June 14　Litho.　Perf. 14x14½

1875 A610 3b multicolored　　.25　.25

King Bhumibol Adulyadej Type of
1996
Litho. & Engr.

1999　　Wmk. 329　　Perf. 13

1876 A550 12b bl grn & bl　　1.25　.80
1877 A550 15b yel brn & grn　　2.00　.45
1878 A550 30b pink & brown　　2.90 2.00

Size: 25x30mm
Perf. 12¾x13¼

1879 A550 500b org & claret　35.00 19.00
　　Nos. 1876-1879 (4)　　41.15 22.25

Issued: 12b, 15b, 30b, 7/1; 500b, 9/10.

UPU,
125th
Anniv.
A611

Designs: 2b, Floating Vessel of Light Festival. 15b, Buddhist Candle Festival, Ubon Ratchathani.

1999, July 1　Litho.　Perf. 14½x14
Granite Paper

1880 A611 2b multicolored　　.35　.25
　　Complete booklet, 5 #1880　2.90
1881 A611 15b multicolored　　1.10 1.00

Customs Dept., 125th Anniv. — A612

1999, July 3

1882 A612 6b multicolored　　.60　.45

Natl. Communications Day — A613

1999, Aug. 4　Litho.　Perf. 14½x14
Granite Paper

1883 A613 4b multicolored　　.25　.25

Thaipex '99 — A614

1999, Aug. 4　　　　Granite Paper
Color of Rabbits

1884 A614 6b black & white　　.60　.45
1885 A614 6b golden brown,
　　　brown　　　　　.60　.45
1886 A614 12b white　　　1.00　.80

1887 A614 12b gray   1.00   .80
a. Souvenir sheet, #1884-1887,
    perf. 13½   4.00   4.00
Nos. 1884-1887 (4)   3.20   2.50

No. 1887a sold for 50b and exists imperf.
Value, $15.

Bangkok 2000 Stamp
Exhibition — A615

Scenes from Thai folk tales and literature:
No. 1888, Boy on dragon-like horse. No. 1889,
Rishi transforming tiger cub and calf into
humans. No. 1890, Boy exiting conch shell.
No. 1891, Children playing with kitchenware.

1999, Aug. 4   *Perf. 14½x14*
Granite Paper
1888 A615 2b multicolored   .35   .25
1889 A615 2b multicolored   .35   .25
1890 A615 15b multicolored   1.10   1.00
1891 A615 15b multicolored   1.10   1.00
a. Souvenir sheet, #1888-1891,
    perf. 13½   4.50   3.50
Nos. 1888-1891 (4)   2.90   2.50

No. 1891a sold for 45b.

King
Bhumibol
Adulyadej's
72nd Birthday
A616

King: No. 1892, On father's knee. No. 1893,
With mother, sister and brother. No. 1894,
With brother, in suits. No. 1895, With brother,
in military uniforms. No. 1896, With wife on
wedding day. No. 1897, At coronation ceremony. No. 1898, As Buddhist monk. No. 1899,
With Queen, Prince and Princesses. No.
1900, Wearing royal robe.

1999, Sept. 10   Photo.   *Perf. 11¾*
Granite Paper
1892 A616 3b multicolored   .35   .25
1893 A616 3b multicolored   .35   .25
1894 A616 3b multicolored   .35   .25
1895 A616 6b multicolored   .60   .35
1896 A616 6b multicolored   .60   .35
1897 A616 6b multicolored   .60   .35
1898 A616 12b multicolored   1.25   .80
1899 A616 12b multicolored   1.25   .80
1900 A616 12b multicolored   1.25   .80
a. Souvenir sheet, #1892-1900   10.50   9.00
Nos. 1892-1900 (9)   6.60   4.20

No. 1900a sold for 90b.

Intl. Year of Older Persons — A617

1999, Oct. 1   Litho.   *Perf. 14½x14*
Granite Paper
1901 A617 2b multi   .35   .25
   Complete booklet, 5 #1901   3.50

Bauhinia
Variegata — A618

Intl. Letter Writing Week: No. 1903, Bombax
ceiba. No. 1904, Radermachera ignea (orange
flowers). No. 1905, Bretschneidera sinensis
(pink flowers).

1999, Oct. 2   *Perf. 14x14½*
Granite Paper
1902 A618 2b shown   .35   .25
   Complete booklet, 5 #1902   2.40
1903 A618 2b multi   .35   .25
   Complete booklet, 5 #1903   3.25
1904 A618 12b multi   1.10   .80
1905 A618 12b multi   1.10   .80
a. Souvenir sheet, #1902-1905,
    perf. 13¼   3.50   2.75
Nos. 1902-1905 (4)   2.90   2.10

No. 1905a sold for 35b.

King Bhumibol Adulyadej's 72nd
Birthday — A619

King: #1906, And vehicle. #1907, And Buddhist monks. #1908, And Queen. #1909, And
soldiers. #1910, And crowd. #1911, And disabled boy. #1912, Wearing green army uniform. #1913, In white suit with camera. #1914,
With crowd waving flags.

1999, Oct. 21   Photo.   *Perf. 14½*
Granite Paper
1906 A619 3b multi   .25   .25
1907 A619 3b multi   .25   .25
1908 A619 3b multi   .25   .25
1909 A619 6b multi   .50   .35
1910 A619 6b multi   .50   .35
1911 A619 6b multi   .50   .35
1912 A619 12b multi   1.10   .80
1913 A619 12b multi   1.10   .80
1914 A619 12b multi   1.10   .80
a. Souvenir sheet, #1906-1914   7.25   6.25
Nos. 1906-1914 (9)   5.55   4.20

No. 1914a sold for 90b. Numbers have been
reserved for additional stamps in this set.

Design
A39 — A620

**Litho. & Embossed with Foil
Application**
1999, Dec. 5   Wmk. 387   *Perf. 13¼*
1915 A620 100b blue & bronze   7.00   7.00
1916 A620 100b blue & silver   7.00   7.00
1917 A620 100b blue & gold   7.00   7.00
a. Souvenir sheet, #1915-1917   25.00   20.00
Nos. 1915-1917 (3)   21.00   21.00

King Bhumibol Adulyadej's 72nd birthday.
No. 1917a sold for 350b.

New Year
2000 — A621

Medicinal plants: No. 1918, Thunbergia
laurifolia. No. 1919, Gmelina arborea. No.
1920, Prunus cerasoides. No. 1921, Fagraea
fragrans.

       Perf. 14½x14¼
1999, Nov. 15   Litho.
Granite Paper
1918 A621 2b multi   .25   .25
1919 A621 2b multi   .25   .25
1920 A621 2b multi   .25   .25
a. Souv. sheet, 5 ea #1918-
    1920 + 10 labels   30.00
1921 A621 2b multi   .35   .25
a. Souvenir sheet, #1918-1921   2.25   1.75
Nos. 1918-1921 (4)   1.10   1.00

No. 1921a sold for 15b.
No. 1920a was issued 3/25/00 and sold for
60b. For an additional fee the blank labels
could be personalized with photos taken at a
booth not operated by the Thailand postal
authorities at the Bangkok 2000 Stamp
Exhibition.

Investiture of
Crown Prince
Vajiralongkorn,
27th
Anniv. — A622

1999, Dec. 28   *Perf. 14x14½*
Granite Paper
1922 A622 3b multi   .60   .25

Lake of Lilies, Thale Noi — A623

Kulap Khao Flowers, Doi Chang
Dao — A624

Krachieo Flowers, Pa Hin
Ngam — A625

Bua Tong Flowers, Doi Mae
Ukor — A626

      Perf. 14½x14¼
2000   Litho.   Unwmk.
Granite Paper
1923 A623   Sheet of 12,   8.00   5.50
a.-l.   3b Any single   .55   .35
1924 A624   Sheet of 12,   8.00   5.50
a.-l.   3b Any single   .55   .35
1925 A625   Sheet of 12,   8.00   5.50
a.-l.   3b Any single   .55   .35
1926 A626   Sheet of 12,   8.00   5.50
a.-l.   3b Any single   .55   .35
Nos. 1923-1926 (4)   32.00   22.00

Issued: #1923, 1/1; #1924, 2/25; #1925,
7/16. #1926, 11/15.

Bees — A627

#1927, Apis andreniformis. #1928, Apis
florea. #1929, Apis cerana. #1930, Apis
dorsata.

2000, Mar. 19   Photo.   *Perf. 11¾*
Granite Paper
1927-1930   A627 3b Set of 4   1.75   1.40
Souvenir Sheets of 1
1927a-1930a   Set of 4   4.50   3.00

Nos. 1927a-1930a do not have white margin
on stamps and sold for 8b each.

Bangkok 2000 Stamp
Exhibition — A628

Ceremonies: #1931, 2b, 1st month blessing
(family & baby). #1932, 2b, Tonsure. #1933,
15b, Teacher respect (teacher, 3 children).
#1934, 15b, Novice ordination.

2000, Mar. 25   Litho.   *Perf. 14½x14*
Granite Paper
1931-1934   A628   Set of 4   4.00   3.25
1934a   Souvenir sheet, #1931-1934,
    perf. 13½x14   5.50   4.50

No. 1934a sold for 45b. No 1934a exists
imperf. Value, $20.

Thai
Red
Cross
Fair
A629

2000, Mar. 30   *Perf. 14½x14*
Granite Paper
1935 A629 3b multi   .35   .35

Thai Heritage Conservation — A630

Chok cloths from: 3b, Hat Seio. 6b, Mae Chaem. 8b, Ban Rai. 12b, Khu Bua.

2000, Apr. 2   Wmk. 387   Perf. 13¼
1936-1939 A630 Set of 4   4.75 3.75
1939a   Souvenir sheet, #1936-1939   5.50 4.50
    No. 1939a sold for 40b.

Songkran Day Type of 1991
Perf. 14x14½
2000, Apr. 13   Litho.   Unwmk.
Granite Paper
1940 A425 2b Angel on serpent   .35 .25
          Booklet, 5 #1940   3.75
a.   Souvenir sheet of 1   1.60 .75
    No. 1940a sold for 8b and exists imperf.

50th Wedding Anniv. of King and Queen — A631

No. 1941 — King Bhumibol Adulyadej and Queen Sirikit: a, Sitting on grass. b, Standing. c, Sitting on thrones. d, With family. e, Standing, wearing regalia.

2000, Apr. 28   Photo.   Perf. 11¾
Granite Paper
1941   Vert. strip of 5   6.50 5.00
a.-e. A631 10b Any single   1.25 1.00

Asalhapuja Day — A632

2000, July 16   Litho.   Perf. 14x14½
Granite Paper
1942 A632 3b multi   .65 .35

Crown Prince Maha Vajiralongkorn, 48th Birthday — A633

2000, July 28   Perf. 14½x14
Granite Paper
1943 A633 2b multi   .45 .25
          Booklet, 5 #1943   5.00
a.   Souvenir sheet of 1, perf. 13¼ 1.60 .80
    No. 1943a sold for 8b.

Natl. Communications Day — A634

2000, Aug. 4
Granite Paper
1944 A634 3b multi   .35 .25

A635

Intl. Letter Writing Week — A636

Various tea sets.

Perf. 14½x14
2000, Oct. 7   Litho.   Unwmk.
Granite Paper
1945 A635   6b shown   .65 .55
1946 A635   6b multi, diff.   .65 .55
1947 A636 12b shown   1.25 1.10
1948 A636 12b multi, diff.   1.25 1.10
a.   Souvenir sheet, #1945-1948,
           perf. 13¼   5.00 4.50
    Nos. 1945-1948 (4)   3.80 3.30
    No. 1948a sold for 45b.

Princess Srinagarindra, Birth Cent. — A637

2000, Oct. 21   Granite Paper
1949 A637 2b multi   .45 .25
          Booklet, 5 #1949   3.75
a.   Souvenir sheet of 1, perf. 13¼ 1.60 .80
    No. 1949a sold for 8b.

Royal Barge Anantanakkharat — A638

Perf. 13¼x14
2000, Nov. 15   Photo.   Wmk. 340
1950 A638 9b multi   1.00 .75
a.   Souvenir sheet of 1   2.25 1.60
    No. 1950a sold for 15b.

New Year 2001 — A639

Flowers: No. 1951, 2b, Clerodendrum philippinum. No. 1952, 2b, Capparis micracantha. No. 1953, 2b, Belamcanda chinensis. No. 1954, 2b, Memecylon caeruleum.

Perf. 14½x14¼
2000, Nov. 15   Litho.   Unwmk.
Granite Paper
1951-1954 A639 Set of 4   1.25 .85
1954a   Souvenir sheet, #1951-1954 2.25 1.60
    No. 1954a sold for 15b.

Parrots — A640

Designs: 2b, Psittacula alexandri. 5b, Psittacula eupatria. 8b, Psittinus cyanurus. 10b, Psittacula roseata.

2001, Jan. 13   Perf. 14x14½
Granite Paper
1955-1958 A640 Set of 4   3.50 2.25
          Booklet, 5 #1955   3.75
a.   Souvenir sheet,
          #1955-1958, perf. 13¼   4.50 3.25
b.   As "a," without price
          and with show emblem in margin 20.00 15.00
    No. 1955a sold for 35b. No. 1955b, Hong Kong 2001 Stamp Exhibition, sold for 50b.

King Chulalongkorn and Land Deed — A641

2001, Feb. 17   Granite Paper
1959 A641 5b multi   .55 .45
    Dept. of Lands, cent.

Marine Life — A642

Designs: a, Ray. b, Turtle. c, Jellyfish, fish. d, Lionfish. e, Black, yellow fish, coral. f, Eel. g, School of striped fish, angelfish, coral, vert. h, Pufferfish, blue fish, vert. i, Shark, fish.
    Stamp sizes: Nos. 1960a-1960f, 29x24mm, Nos. 1960g-1960h, 29x48mm. No. 1960i, 58x42mm.

Perf. 13¾x14¼
2001, Mar. 15   Photo.
Granite Paper
1960 A642   Sheet of 9   6.50 5.50
a.-f.   3b Any single   .55 .35
g.-i.   6b Any single   .75 .55
    For surcharge, see No. 2511.

Gems A643

Designs: 3b, Diamond. 4b, Green sapphire. 6b, Pearl. 12b, Blue sapphire.

2001   Litho.   Perf. 14½x14
Granite Paper
1961-1964 A643 Set of 4   2.25 2.25
a.   Souvenir sheet, #1961-1964,
          perf. 13½x14   4.50 3.25
b.   As "a," ovptd. in margin in gold 13.00 11.00
    Issued, Nos. 1961-1964a, 3/30; No. 1964b, 6/9.

No. 1964a sold for 35b.
No. 1964b has Belgica 2001 emblem overprint.

Red Cross A644

Perf. 14½x14
2001, Apr. 1   Litho.   Unwmk.
Granite Paper
1965 A644 4b multi   .60 .25

Ancient Brocades From Nakhon Si Thammarat National Museum — A645

Colors of brocade: 2b, Orange red, lilac, and gold. 3b, Green and gold. No. 1968, 10b, Orange and gold. No. 1969, 10b, Bright pink and gold.

2001, Apr. 2   Perf. 14x14½
Granite Paper
1966-1969 A645 Set of 4   3.00 2.25
          Booklet, 5 #1966   3.00
a.   Souvenir sheet of #1966-1969, perf. 13¼ 4.50 3.25
    Heritage Conservation Day.
    No. 1969a sold for 35b.

Songkran Day Type of 1991
Perf. 13½x13¾
2001-2002   Wmk. 387
1970 A425 2b Man on snake, zodiac .60 .25
          Booklet, 5 #1970   3.75
a.   Souvenir sheet of 1   1.60 1.10
b.   Unwmkd., granite paper, perf. 14x14½ 3.00 3.00
    Issued: Nos. 1970-1970a, 4/13/01. No. 1970b, 4/13/02. No. 1970b issued only in No. 2017b.
    No. 1970a sold for 8b and exists imperf.

Visakhapuja Day — A646

2001, May 7   Unwmk.   Perf. 14x14½
Granite Paper
1971 A646 3b multi   .55 .35

Demon Statues — A647

Designs: 2b, Maiyarap.   5b, Wirunchambang. 10b, Thotsakan. 12b, Sahatsadecha.

Perf. 14x14½
2001, June 13 Litho. Unwmk.
Granite Paper
1972-1975 A647 Set of 4 3.50 2.60
Booklet, 5 #1972 4.00
1975a Souvenir sheet, #1972-
1975, perf. 13½ 4.50 3.25
No. 1975a sold for 33b.

Prince Purachartra Jayakara and Rotary Intl. Emblem — A648

2001, July 1 Granite Paper
1976 A648 3b multi .50 .25
Rotary Intl. in Thailand, 66th anniv.

Mushrooms — A649

Designs: 2b, Schizophyllum commune. 3b, Lentinus giganteus. 5b, Pleurotus citrinopileatus. 10b, Pleurotus flabellatus.

2001, July 4 Photo. Perf. 13¾x14
Granite Paper
1977-1980 A649 Set of 4 2.75 2.00
Booklet, 5 # 1977 3.75
1980a Souvenir sheet, #1977-
1980, perf. 13½ 4.50 3.25
No. 1980 sold for 26b.

Insects A650

Designs: 2b, Cheirotonus parryi. 5b, Mouhotia batesi. 6b, Cladognathus giraffa. 12b, Mormolyce phyllodes.

2001, July 4 Wmk. 329 Perf. 13½
1981-1984 A650 Set of 4 2.90 2.25
Booklet, 5 #1981 3.75
a. Souvenir sheet,
#1981-1984 5.50 4.50
b. As "a," with Phila
Nippon '01 emblem
in margin 13.00 12.00
No. 1984a sold for 34b.
No. 1984b sold for 34b, and was issued 8/1.

Natl. Communications Day — A651

Perf. 14½x14
2001, Aug. 4 Litho. Unwmk.
Granite Paper
1985 A651 4b multi .50 .45

Thaipex '01 — A652

Various domesticated fowl: 3b, 4b, 6b, 12b.

2001, Aug. 4 Photo. Perf. 13¼
Granite Paper
1986-1989 A652 Set of 4 3.00 2.25
1989a Souvenir sheet, #1986-
1989 4.50 3.25
No. 1989a sold for 33b. No. 1989a also exists imperf. Value, $17.50.

Queen Suriyothai, Heroine of Thailand — A653

2001, Aug. 12 Litho. Perf. 14x14¾
Granite Paper
1990 A653 3b multi .55 .45
a. Souvenir sheet of 1, perf. 13¼ 2.75 1.25
No. 1990a sold for 10b.

Queen Sirikit's Visit to the People's Republic of China — A654

2001, Aug. 12 Perf. 14¾x14
Granite Paper
1991 A654 5b multi .75 .45

Butterflies — A655

Designs: 2b, Pachliopta aristolochiae goniopeltis. 4b, Rhinopalpa polynice. 10b, Poritia erycinoides. 12b, Spindasis lohita.

Perf. 13½ Syncopated
2001, Sept. 10 Photo.
1992-1995 A655 Set of 4 4.00 2.75
Booklet, 5 #1992 3.00
1995a Souvenir sheet, #1992-
1995 5.50 4.50
1995b As "a," with Hafnia '01
emblem in margin 16.00 16.00
No. 1995a sold for 40b.
No. 1995b issued 11/16. No. 1995b sold for 43b.

Intl. Letter Writing Week — A656

Medicinal herbs: 2b, Piper nigrum. 3b, Solanum trilobatum. 5b, Boesenbergia rotunda. 10b, Ocimum tenuiflorum.

Perf. 14x14½
2001, Oct. 6 Litho. Unwmk.
Granite Paper
1996-1999 A656 Set of 4 2.75 1.90
Booklet, 5 #1996 3.75
1999a Souvenir sheet, #1996-
1999, perf. 13½x13¼ 3.75 3.25
No. 1999a sold for 25b.

Police Cadet Academy, Cent. — A657

2001, Oct. 13 Litho. Perf. 14½x14
Granite Paper
2000 A657 5b multi .75 .55

Royal Barge Anekkachat Puchong — A658

2001, Nov. 15 Photo. Perf. 14¼
Granite Paper
2001 A658 9b multi 1.00 .90
a. Souvenir sheet of 1 3.25 2.25
No. 2001a sold for 17b.

New Year 2002 — A659

Flowers: No. 2002, 2b, Pedicularis siamensis. No. 2003, 2b, Schouten glomerata. No. 2004, 2b, Gentiana crassa. No. 2005, 2b, Colquhounia coccinea.

2001, Nov. 15 Litho. Perf. 14x14½
Granite Paper
2002-2005 A659 Set of 4 1.10 1.00
2005a Souvenir sheet, #2002-
2005 2.25 1.75
No. 2005a sold for 11b.

Laying of Foundation Stone for Suvarnabhumi Airport Passenger Terminal — A660

2002, Jan. 19 Litho. Perf. 14½x14
Granite Paper
2006 A660 3b multi .50 .35

Rose — A661

2002, Feb. 1 Perf. 13¾
Granite Paper
2007 A661 4b multi 3.75 1.50

12th World Congress of Gastroenterology A662

2002, Feb. 24 Perf. 14x14½
Granite Paper
2008 A662 3b multi .50 .30

Communications Authority of Thailand, 25th Anniv. — A663

No. 2009: a, Satellite dish, CAT Telecom Co. emblem. b, Envelope, mailbox, Thailand Post emblem.

2002, Feb. 25 Perf. 14½x14
Granite Paper
2009 A663 3b Horiz. pair, #a-b 1.10 .75
c. Souvenir sheet, #2009, perf.
13¼x13½ 1.60 1.10
No. 2009c sold for 10b.

Maghapuja Day — A664

2002, Feb. 26 Perf. 14½x14
Granite Paper
2010 A664 3b multi 1.60 1.10

2002 Red Cross Fair A665

2002, Mar. 30 Granite Paper
2011 A665 4b multi .50 .40

Ministry of Transport and Communications, 90th Anniv. — A666

2002, Apr. 1 Litho. Perf. 14½x14
Granite Paper
2012 A666 3b multi .50 .30

Heritage Conservation Day — A667

String puppets: No. 2013, 3b, Man. No. 2014, 3b, Woman. 4d, Demon. 15b, Monkey.

2002, Apr. 2   *Perf. 14x14½*
Granite Paper
2013-2016	A667	Set of 4	2.50	2.50
2016a		Souvenir sheet, #2013-2016, perf. 13¼	4.50	3.50

No. 2016a sold for 30b.

Songkran Day Type of 1991
2002, Apr. 13   *Perf. 14x14½*
Granite Paper
2017	A425	2b Angel on horse, zodiac	.60	.25
a.		Souvenir sheet of 1	2.00	2.00
b.		Souvenir sheet, #1724b, 1801c, 1869, 1940, 1970b, 2017	3.00	3.00
c.		As "b," with Beijing 2002 emblem in margin and selling price removed	17.50	17.50

Nos. 2017a and 2017b sold for 8b and 14b respectively. Both exist imperf.
Issued: No. 2017c, 9/29. No. 2017c sold for 30b.

Fighting Fish A668

Designs: No. 2018, 3b, Betta imbellis. No. 2019, 3b, Betta splendens. 4b, Betta splendens, diff. 15b, Betta splendens, diff.

2002, May 15   Litho.   *Perf. 14½x14*
Granite Paper
2018-2021	A668	Set of 4	3.00	2.50
2021a		Souvenir sheet, #2018-2021, perf. 13½	4.50	4.00
2021b		As "a," with Amphilex 2002 emblem and selling price removed	15.00	15.00

Issued: No. 2021a, 8/30. No. 2021a sold for 30b; No. 2021b sold for 31b.

Temples — A669

Designs: No. 2022, 3b, Wat Phra Si Rattanasatsadaram. No. 2023, 3b, Wat Phra Chetuphon Wimon Mangkhalaram. 4b, Wat Arun Ratchawararam. 12b, Wat Benchamabophit Dusit Wanaram.

2002, June 17   *Perf. 14½x14*
Granite Paper
2022-2025	A669	Set of 4	3.00	2.25
2025a		Souvenir sheet, #2022-2025, perf. 13½	3.25	2.75
2025b		As "a," with Philakorea 2002 emblem and selling price removed	15.00	15.00

Issued: No. 2025b, 8/2. Nos. 2025a and 2025b each sold for 27b.

Crown Prince Maha Vajiralongkorn, 50th Birthday — A670

2002, July 28   *Perf. 14x14½*
Granite Paper
2026	A670	3b multi	.55	.30

Natl. Communications Day — A671

2002, Aug. 4   Granite Paper
2027	A671	4b multi	.50	.40

Thailand — Australia Diplomatic Relations, 50th Anniv. — A672

Designs: No. 2028, 3b, Nelumbo nucifera (pink flower). No. 2029, 3b, Nymphaea immutabilis (purple flower).

2002, Aug. 6   *Perf. 14½x14*
Granite Paper
2028-2029	A672	Set of 2	1.10	.75
2029a		Souvenir sheet, #2028-2029, perf. 13½	1.60	1.50

See Australia Nos. 2072-2073. No. 2029a sold for 9b.

Queen Sirikit, 70th Birthday — A673

Designs: No. 2030, 3b, Queen and roses. No. 2031, 3b, Queen Sirikit rose. 4b, Queen Sirikit orchid. 15b, Queen Sirikit dona shrub.

2002, Aug. 12   *Perf. 14½x14*
Granite Paper
2030-2033	A673	Set of 4	2.25	2.25
2033a		Souvenir sheet, #2030-2033, perf. 13½	3.75	3.50

No. 2033a sold for 31b.

National Archives, 50th Anniv. — A674

2002, Aug. 18   *Perf. 14½x14*
2034	A674	3b multi	.50	.30

Thai Bank Notes, Cent. A675

2002, Sept. 7   Engr.   *Perf. 13½*
Granite Paper
2035	A675	5b org & brown	.75	.50
a.		Souvenir sheet of 1	3.75	3.25

No. 2035a sold for 11b.

Vimanmek Mansion Art Objects — A676

Designs: No. 2036, 3b, Round, lidded betel nut box. No. 2037, 3b, Bowl. 4b, Bowl, diff. 12b, Rectangular betel nut box.

2002, Sept. 7   Litho.   *Perf. 14½x14*
Granite Paper
2036-2039	A676	Set of 4	2.75	2.00
2039a		Souvenir sheet, #2036-2039, perf. 13½	3.25	3.25

No. 2039a sold for 26b.

Royal Palaces A677

Designs: No. 2040, 4b, Thailand. No. 2041, 4b, Sweden.

Perf. 12½x13½ Syncopated
2002, Oct. 5   Litho. & Engr.
2040-2041	A677	Set of 2	1.10	.75

See Sweden No. 2445.

Intl. Letter Writing Day A678

Designs: No. 2042, 3b, Animal-shaped coconut grater. No. 2043, 3b, Strainer. 4b, Coconut shell ladle. 15b, Earthenware stove and pot.

2002, Oct. 5   Litho.   *Perf. 14½x14*
Granite Paper
2042-2045	A678	Set of 4	2.25	2.00
2045a		Souvenir sheet, #2042-2045, perf. 13½	4.50	3.25

No. 2045a sold for 31b.

Bangkok 2003 World Philatelic Exhibition — A679

Foods from: No. 2046, 3b, Central Thailand (red tablecloth). No. 2047, 3b, Southern Thailand (brown and yellow tablecloth). 4b, Northeastern Thailand. 15b, Northern Thailand.

2002, Oct. 5   *Perf. 14½x14*
2046-2049	A679	Set of 4	2.90	2.25
2049a		Souvenir sheet, #2046-2049, perf. 13½	4.50	3.50

No. 2049a sold for 30b.

New Year 2003 — A680

Flowers: No. 2050, 3b, Guaiacum officinale. No. 2051, 3b, Nyctanthes arbor-tristis. No. 2052, 3b, Barleria cristata. No. 2053, 3b, Thevetia peruviana.

2002, Nov. 15   Litho.
Granite Paper
2050-2053	A680	Set of 4	1.50	1.10
2053a		Souvenir sheet, #2050-2053	2.75	2.25

No. 2053a sold for 16b.

20th World Scout Jamboree — A681

Designs: 3b, Scouts. 12b, Jamboree site.

2002, Dec. 28   *Perf. 14½x14*
Granite Paper
2054-2055	A681	Set of 2	1.90	1.25

New Year 2003 (Year of the Goat) — A682

2003, Jan. 1   *Perf. 13*
Granite Paper
2056	A682	3b multi	.50	.25

See Nos. 2108, 2161, 2341a.

National Children's Day — A683

Pangpond and his: a, Dog, Big (blue background). b, Friend, Hanuman (orange background). c, Girlfriend, Namo (green background). d, Teacher (red background).

2003, Jan. 11   *Perf. 14½x14*
Granite Paper
2057	A683	3b Block of 4, #a-d	1.25	1.00

Rose — A684

2003, Feb. 1   *Perf. 13*
Granite Paper
2058	A684	4b multi	.75	.30

No. 2058 is impregnated with rose scent. Compare with Type A716.

Blue Green, by Fua Haribhitak A685

Portrait of Chira Chongkon, by Chamras Kietkong A686

Moonlight, by Prasong Padmanuja A687

Lotus Flowers, by Thawee Nandakwang — A688

2003, Feb. 24   *Perf. 13¼*
Granite Paper

2059	A685	3b multi	.35	.25
2060	A686	3b multi	.35	.25
2061	A687	3b multi	.35	.25
2062	A688	15b multi	1.40	1.25
	Nos. 2059-2062 (4)		2.45	2.00

Bangkok 2003 World Philatelic Exhibition — A689

Tourist attractions: No. 2063, 3b, Doi Inthanon Temple, Chiang Mai. No. 2064, 3b, River Kwai Bridge, Kanchanaburi. No. 2065, 3b, Phu Kradung (cliff), Loei. 15b, Maya Bay, Krabi.

2003, Mar. 3   *Perf. 14½x14*
Granite Paper

2063-2066	A689	Set of 4	2.60	2.10
2066a		Souvenir sheet, #2063-2066, perf. 13¼	4.50	3.25

No. 2066a sold for 29b.

King Bhumibol Adulyadej Type of 1996
Perf. 14x14½

2003, Mar. 14   Litho.   Unwmk.
Granite Paper

2067	A550	1b blue	.45	.25

2003 Red Cross Fair — A690

2003, Mar. 28   *Perf. 14x14½*
Granite Paper

2068	A690	3b multi	.50	.30

Kick Boxing — A691

Designs: No. 2069, 3b, Boxers punching. No. 2070, 3b, Boxer in black trunks with knee raised. No. 2071, 3b, Boxer in red trunks kicking. 15b, Boxer in red trunks kicking, diff.

2003, Apr. 2   Litho.   *Perf. 13¼*
Granite Paper

2069-2072	A691	Set of 4	3.00	2.10
2072a		Souvenir sheet, #2069-2072	4.50	3.50
2072b		As "a," with China 2003 Philatelic Exhibition emblem in margin	13.00	11.00

No. 2072a sold for 29b.
Issued: No. 2072b, 11/20. No. 2072b sold for 29b.

Princess Maha Chakri Sirindhorn, 48th Birthday — A692

2003, Apr. 2   *Perf. 14x14½*
Granite Paper

2073	A692	3b multi	.50	.25

Princess Galyani Vadhana, 80th Birthday — A693

2003, May 6   **Granite Paper**

2074	A693	3b multi	1.00	.50

Kings Chulalongkorn and Vajiravudh A694

2003, May 6   **Granite Paper**

2075	A694	3b multi	.55	.30

Inspector General Dept., cent.

King Prajadhipok Day — A695

2003, May 30   *Perf. 14½x14*
Granite Paper

2076	A695	3b multi	.55	.30

Bantam Chickens — A696

Designs: No. 2077, 3b, White ears jungle fowl. No. 2078, 3b, Sugarcane husk colored. No. 2079, 3b, Black-tailed white. 15b, Dark gray.

2003   Litho.   *Perf. 13*
Granite Paper

2077-2080	A696	Set of 4	3.00	2.10
2080a		Souvenir sheet, #2077-2080	4.50	3.25
2080b		As "a," with Lanka Philex 2003 emblem in margin	20.00	16.00

Issued: Nos. 2077-2080, 2080a, 6/10; No. 2080b, 7/31. Nos. 2080a and 2080b each sold for 29b.

Asalhapuja Day — A697

2003, July 13   *Perf. 14x14½*
Granite Paper

2081	A697	3b multi	1.40	.40

National Communications Day — A698

2003, Aug. 4   *Perf. 14½x14*
Granite Paper

2082	A698	3b multi	.50	.25

Communications Organization Emblems — A699

No. 2083: a, Thailand Post Company Limited. b, Communications Authority of Thailand (23x27mm). c, CAT Telecom Public Company Limited.

Perf. 14¼x14½
2003, Aug. 14   Litho.   Wmk. 340

2083	A699	3b Horiz. strip of 3, #a-c	1.25	.90

King Chulalongkorn (1853-1910) A700

Litho. & Embossed
2003, Sept. 20   Unwmk.   *Perf. 13¼*

2084	A700	100b gold & multi	8.25	6.50
a.		Souvenir sheet of 4	35.00	35.00

No. 2084a issued 9/30.
No. 2084a exists imperf. with Bangkok 2003 emblem at lower left. Value, $50.

Government Housing Bank, 50th Anniv. — A701

2003, Sept. 24   Litho.   *Perf. 14½x14*
Granite Paper

2085	A701	3b multi	.50	.25

Bangkok 2003 World Philatelic Exhibition — A702

Handicrafts: No. 2086, 3b, Basketry. No. 2087, 3b, Pottery. No. 2088, 3b, Leatherwork. 15b, Wood carving.

2003, Oct. 4
Granite Paper

2086-2089	A702	Set of 4	2.60	2.10
2089a		Souvenir sheet, #2086-2089, perf. 13¼	3.75	3.25

A varnish with a rough surface was applied to portions of the designs.
No. 2089a sold for 29b. No 2089a exists imperf. Value, $16.

Trees of Thailand and Canada — A703

No. 2090: a, Cassia fistula (Thailand). b, Maple leaves (Canada).

2003, Oct. 4   *Perf. 14x14½*
Granite Paper

2090	A703	3b Horiz. pair, #a-b	1.25	1.10
c.		Souvenir sheet, #2090, perf. 13¼	2.50	2.50

No. 2090c sold for 9b.

Lychees — A704

Rose
Apples — A705

Fruit: No. 2093, Coconuts. 15b, Jackfruit.

2003, Oct. 4
Granite Paper

2091	A704	3b shown	.45	.25
2092	A705	3b shown	.45	.25
2093	A704	3b multi	.45	.25
2094	A704	15b multi	1.60	1.25
a.		Souvenir sheet, #2091-2094, perf. 13¼	4.50	3.25
		Nos. 2091-2094 (4)	2.95	2.00

International Letter Writing Week. No. 2094a sold for 29b.

Oct. 14, 1973 Student Uprisings, 30th Anniv. — A706

2003, Oct. 14   *Perf. 14½x14*
Granite Paper

2095	A706	3b multi	.50	.25

Asia-Pacific Economic Cooperation Meeting — A707

2003, Oct. 20   **Granite Paper**

2096	A707	3b multi	.50	.25

New Year
2004 — A708

Flowers: No. 2097, 3b, Bougainvillea spectabilis. No. 2098, 3b, Eucrosia bicolor. No. 2099, 3b, Canna x generalis. No. 2100, 3b, Zinnia violacea.

2003, Nov. 15   *Perf. 14½x14¼*
Granite Paper

2097-2100	A708	Set of 4	1.25	1.10
2100a		Souvenir sheet, #2097-2100	2.25	1.75
2100b		As "a," with 2004 Hong Kong Stamp Expo emblem in margin	7.00	6.50

No. 2100a sold for 16b.
Issued: No. 2100b, 1/30/04. No. 2100b sold for 16b.

Thailand Flag   Thai Pavilion
A709   A710

Elephants   Cassia Fistula
A711   A712

2003, Dec. 1   *Perf. 14¼x14½*
Granite Paper

2101	A709	3b multi	.45	.25
2102	A710	3b multi	.45	.25
2103	A711	3b multi	.45	.25
2104	A712	3b multi	.45	.25
		Nos. 2101-2104 (4)	1.80	1.00

Compare with types A865a-A865d.

Elephants — A713

No. 2105: a, Asian elephant. b, African elephants.

2003, Dec. 9   *Perf. 14½x14*
Granite Paper

2105	A713	3b Horiz. pair, #a-b	1.00	.75
c.		Souvenir sheet, #2105a, perf. 13¼	2.75	2.25

No. 2105c sold for 9b.
Thailand-South Africa diplomatic relations, 10th anniv. See South Africa No. 1330.

King Bhumibol Adulyadej Type of 1996

2003, Dec. 3   **Litho.**   *Perf. 14x14½*
Granite Paper

2106	A550	50s olive brown	.75	.25
2107	A550	1b blue	.75	.25

Issued: 50s, 12/3; 1b, 1/22/04

Zodiac Animal Type of 2003

2004, Jan. 1   **Litho.**   *Perf. 13*
Granite Paper

2108	A682	3b Monkey	.50	.25

See No. 2341b.

Children's Day — A714

2004, Jan. 10   *Perf. 14½x14*
Granite Paper

2109	A714	3b multi	.50	.25

Paintings of
Hem Vejakorn
A715

Designs: No. 2110, 3b, A Scene in Thai History (dancers). No. 2111, 3b, Maha Bharatayudh (charioteer). No. 2112, 3b, Khun Chang — Khun Phaen (women with horse). No. 2113, 3b, Phra Lor (woman and rooster).

2004, Jan. 17   *Perf. 13¼*
Granite Paper

2110-2113	A715	Set of 4	1.40	1.10
2113a		Souvenir sheet, #2110-2113	3.25	2.25

No. 2113a sold for 16b.

Rose — A716

2004, Feb. 1   *Perf. 13*
Granite Paper

2114	A716	4b multi	.65	.30

Compare with type A684. No. 2114 is impregnated with rose scent.

Turtles — A717

Designs: No. 2115, 3b, Cuora amboinensis. No. 2116, 3b, Platysternon megacephalum. No. 2117, 3b, Indotestudo elongata. No. 2118, 3b, Heosemys spinosa.

2004, Mar. 1   *Perf. 14½x14*
Granite Paper

2115-2118	A717	Set of 4	1.75	1.25
2118a		Souvenir sheet, #2115-2118, perf. 13¼	3.25	3.00
2118b		Similar to "a," with 2004 Singapore World Stamp Championship emblem in margin	8.75	7.50

Issued: No. 2118b, 8/28.
Nos. 2118a and 2118b sold for 16b.

Siam Society, Cent. — A718

2004, Mar. 10   *Perf. 14½x14*

2119	A718	3b multi	.50	.25

2004 Red Cross
Fair — A719

2004, Mar. 29   *Perf. 14x14½*
Granite Paper

2120	A719	3b multi	.50	.25

Heritage
Conservation
Day — A720

Fringe colors of hand woven clothes: No. 2121, 3b, Rose red. No. 2122, 3b, Blue. No. 2123, 3b, Green. No. 2124, 3b, Orange red. Denomination is at LL on Nos. 2122, 2124.

2004, Apr. 2   **Litho.**   *Perf. 14x14½*
Granite Paper

2121-2124	A720	Set of 4	1.60	1.25
2124a		Souvenir sheet, #2121-2124, perf. 13¼	3.25	2.75
2124b		As "a," with España 2004 emblem in margin, perf. 13¼	10.00	9.00

Issued: No. 2124b, 5/22. No. 2124a sold for 16b; No. 2124b for 18b.

Architecture in Thailand and
Italy — A721

No. 2125: a, Golden Mountain Temple, Bangkok. b, Colosseum, Rome.

2004, Apr. 21   *Perf. 14½x14*
Granite Paper

2125	A721	3b Horiz. pair, #a-b	2.75	2.50
2125c		Souvenir sheet, #2125, perf. 13¼	24.00	20.00

No. 2125c sold for 10b.
See Italy No. 2602.

Sculpture
A722

Designs: No. 2126, 3b, One-sided Drum, by Chit Rienpracha (yellow green background). No. 2127, 3b, Dance Drama, by Sitthidet Saenghiran (rose red background). No. 2128, 3b, Heavenly Flute, by Khien Yimsiri (Prussian blue background). No. 2129, 3b, The Calf, by Paitun Muangsomboom, horiz.

2004, May 3   *Perf. 13¼*

2126-2129	A722	Set of 4	1.40	.95

Unseen Tourist Attractions — A723

No. 2130: a, Non Ngai Buddha, Suphan Buri. b, Khao Laem Dam, Kanchanaburi. c, Mural, Temple fo the Emerald Buddha, Bangkok. d, Ko Li-Pe, Satun. e, Buddha, Wat Phra Thong, Phuket. f, Khao Luang National Park, Nakhon Si Thammarat. g, Miracle Beach, Ko Damikhwan, Krabi. h, Hornbill, Hala-Bala Forest, Narathiwat. i, Long Ru Waterfall, Ubon Ratchathani. j, Prasat Hin Phanom Rung, Buri Ram. k, Red maple leaves, Phu Kradueng National Park, Loei. l, Phukhao Ya, Ranong. m, Ko Kradat, Trat. n, Op Luang National Park, Chiang Mai. o, Dusky leaf monkey, Phetchaburi. p, Lalu, Sra Kaeo. q, Pu Kai, Mu Ko Similan, Phang-Nga. r, Tha Le Noi Waterfowl Park. Phatthalung. s, Phu Pha Thoep, Mukdahan National Park. t, Phi Maen Cave, Mae Hong Son.

2004, May 31   *Perf. 13*
Granite Paper

2130	A723	3b Sheet of 20, #a-t	10.00	8.00

See Nos. 2137, 2147, 2158.

Buddha
Sculptures
A724

No. 2131: a, Phra Nangpaya. b, Phra
Kampaeng Soumkhor. c, Phra Somdej Wat
Rakangkhositaram. d, Phar Rod. e, Phra
Phongsuphan.

Litho. & Embossed
2004, June 1 *Perf. 13¼*
Granite Paper
2131 Horiz. strip of 5 12.00 9.50
a.-e. A724 9b Any single 2.40 1.75
f. Souvenir sheet, #2131a-
2131e 20.00 20.00

No. 2131f sold for 53b.

Visakhapuja
Day — A725

2004, June 2 Litho. *Perf. 14x14½*
Granite Paper
2132 A725 3b multi .50 .25

Bridges — A726

Designs: No. 2133, 5b, Phra Buddha Yodfa
Bridge. No. 2134, 5b, Rama VI Bridge. No.
2135, 5b, Rama VIII Bridge. No. 2136, 5b,
Rama IX Bridge.

2004, July 1 Litho. *Perf. 14¼x14½*
Granite Paper
2133-2136 A726 Set of 4 2.25 1.25

On Nos. 2135 and 2136 portions of the
design were produced by a thermographic
process which produces a shiny, raised effect.

Unseen Tourist Attractions Type of
2004

No. 2137: a, Wat Pho Prathap Chang,
Phichit. b, Phra Prathan Chaturathit, Wat
Phumin, Nan. c, Thalenai, Angthong Archipel-
ago, Surat Thani. d, Wat Na Phra Men, Phra
Nakhon Si Ayutthaya. e, Sanam Chan Palace,
Nakhon Pathom. f, Piyamitr Tunnel, Yala. g,
Ban Khamchanot, Udon Thani. h, Rail line
along Pasak Cholasit Dam, Lop Buri. i, Khlong
Lan Waterfall, Khlong Lan National Park,
Kamphaeng Phet. j, Mo-I-Daeng Cliff, Khao
Phra Wihan National Park, Si Sa Ket. k,
Changkra Wild Orchid Park, Khon Kaen. l,
Canoeists at Ti Lo Re, Tak. m, Khao Ta Mong
Lai, Prachuap Khiri Khan. n, Suriya Patithin
solar calendar, Prasat Phu Phek, Sakon
Nakhon. o, Traditional boat racing, Chumphon.
p, Mokochu Range Mae Wong National Park,
Nakhon Sawan. q, Ordination by elephant in
the sixth month, Surin. r, Rock climbing, Tan
Rattana Waterfall, Khao Yai National Park,
Prachin Buri. s, Monks collecting alms on
horseback, Chiang Rai. t, Cycling in Thung
Salaeng Luang, Phitsanulok.

2004, July 28 *Perf. 13*
Granite Paper
2137 A723 3b Sheet of 20, #a-t 10.00 8.00

Jasmine
Flower — A727

Litho. & Embossed
2004, Aug. 2 *Perf. 13*
Granite Paper
2138 A727 5b multi .55 .30

No. 2138 is impregnated with a jasmine
scent.

Princess Maha
Chakri Sirindhorn
Information
Technology
Program — A728

2004, Aug. 4 Litho. *Perf. 14x14½*
Granite Paper
2139 A728 3b multi .50 .25

National Communications Day — A729

2004, Aug. 4 *Perf. 14½x14*
Granite Paper
2140 A729 3b multi .50 .25

Opening of First Subway Line — A730

2004, Aug. 12 Litho. *Perf. 14½x14*
Granite Paper
2141 A730 3b multi .50 .25

Queen Sirikit,
72nd
Birthday
A731

Litho. & Embossed
2004, Aug. 12 *Perf. 13¼*
2142 A731 100b multi 7.00 4.50

Boats
A732

Designs: No. 2143, 3b, Thai junk. No. 2144,
3b, Sampan boat. No. 2145, 3b, Krachaeng
boat. 15b, Packet boat.

2004-05 Litho. *Perf. 14½x14*
Granite Paper
2143-2146 A732 Set of 4 2.00 1.40
2146a Souvenir sheet, #2143-
2146, perf. 13¼ 3.25 3.00
b. As "a," with Pacific Explorer
2005 emblem in margin 9.00 8.00

No. 2146a sold for 29b. No. 2146b sold for
30b.
Issued: Nos. 2143-2146a, 9/1/04; No.
2146b, 4/21/05.

Unseen Tourist Attractions Type of
2004

No. 2147: a, Phra Nang Din, Phayad. b,
Phra That Kong Khao Noi, Yasothon. c, Phra
Atchana, Wat Sri Chum, Sukothai. d, Wat
Bang Kung, Samut Songkhram. e, Ku Kut, Wat
Phrathat Chamthewi, Lamphun. f, Dolphin
watching, Chachoengsao. g, Tak Bat Dok Mai
tradition, Saraburi. h, Hat Chao Lao,
Chanthaburi. i, Phu Kum Khao dinosaur fos-
sils, Kalasin. j, Reversed stupa, Wat Phra That
Lampang Luang, Lampang. k, Khu Khut
Waterfowl Park, Songkhla. l, Plant Market
Khlong 15, Nakhon Nayok. m, Huppatad,
Uthai Thani. n, Thai Muang Beach, Nakhon
Phanom. o, Wild gaur, Khao Yai National Park,
Nakhon Ratchasima. p, Canoeing, Le Khao
Kop Cave, Trang. q, Sea of flowers, Pru Soi
Dao, Uttaradit. r, Kolae boat, Ban Paseyawo,
Pattani. s, Sea of Mist, Thap Boek, Phu Hin
Rongkla National Park, Phetchabun. t, Bats,
Khao Chung Phran, Ratchaburi.

2004, Sept. 28 *Perf. 13*
Granite Paper
2147 A723 3b Sheet of 20, #a-t 10.00 8.00

Intl. Letter
Writing
Week — A733

Kites: No. 2148, 3b, Snake. No. 2149, 3b,
Star-shaped. No. 2150, 3b, Diamond-shaped
with tail. 15b, Buffalo.

2004, Oct. 9 Litho. *Perf. 14x14½*
Granite Paper
2148-2151 A733 Set of 4 2.00 1.40
2151a Souvenir sheet, #2148-
2151, perf. 13¼ 3.25 3.00
2151b Similar to "a," with Beijing
2004 emblem in margin 9.00 8.00

Issued: No. 2151b, 10/28. No. 2151a sold
for 29b; No. 2151b for 30b.

King Mongkut
(1804-68)
A734

2004, Oct. 18 *Perf. 14x14½*
Granite Paper
2152 A734 4b multi .50 .25

E-customs System — A735

2004, Nov. 15 *Perf. 14½x14*
Granite Paper
2153 A735 3b multi .50 .25

New Year
2005 — A736

Flowers: No. 2154, 3b, Wrightia sirikitiae.
No. 2155, 3b, Eria amica. No. 2156, 3b,
Burmannia coelestris. No. 2157, 3b, Utricu-
laria bifida.

2004, Nov. 15 *Perf. 14¼x14½*
Granite Paper
2154-2157 A736 Set of 4 3.00 2.00
2157a Souvenir sheet, #2154-
2157, perf. 14¼x14½ 5.00 5.00

No. 2157a sold for 16b.

Unseen Tourist Attractions Type of
2004

No. 2158: a, Phra That Cho Hae, Phrae. b,
Wat Karuna, Chai Nat. c, Wat Nang Sao,
Samut Sakhon. d, Phra Mutao Pagoda,
Nonthaburi. e, Phu Kao Phu Phan Kham
National Park, Nong Bua Lam Phu. f, Airvata
(three-headed elephant), Erawan Museum,
Samut Prakan. g, Wat Chedi Hoi, Pathum
Thani. h, White krajiaw field, Chaiyaphum. i,
Chet Si Waterfall, Nong Khai. j, Summer Pal-
ace, Ko Si Chang, Choi Buri. k, Traditional
Drum-making village (Ban Bang Phae), Ang
Thong. l, Ko Thalu, Rayong. m, Kosamphi For-
est Park, Maha Sarakham. n, Cannonball tree,
Wat Phra Non Chaksi, Sing Buri. o, Tung Kula
Rong Hai, Roi Et. p, Phu Sra Dok Bua, Amnat
Charoen.

2004, Nov. 26 *Perf. 13*
Granite Paper
2158 A723 3b Sheet of 16, #a-p,
+ 4 labels 9.00 8.00

Bangkok Fashion City
Initiative — A737

No. 2159: a, 3b, Man and woman. b, 3b,
Woman in pink dress. c, 3b, Woman with
green shirt. d, 15b, Woman with brown
eyeshade.

2004, Dec. 5 *Perf. 14x14½*
Granite Paper
2159 A737 Horiz. strip of 4, #a-
d 2.25 2.25
e. Souvenir sheet, #2159a-2159d,
perf. 13½ 3.25 2.75

No. 2159e sold for 30b.

Queen Rambhai
Bharni (1904-84)
A738

2004, Dec. 20 *Perf. 14x14½*
Granite Paper
2160 A738 3b multi .50 .25

Zodiac Animal Type of 2003
2005, Jan. 1 *Perf. 13*
Granite Paper
2161 A682 3b Cock .50 .30

See No. 2341c.

Children's Day — A739

2005, Jan. 8   Perf. 14½x14
Granite Paper
2162 A739 3b multi   .50 .25

Thailand - Argentina Diplomatic Relations, 50th Anniv. — A740

No. 2163: a, Tango dancers, Argentina. b, Tom-tom dancers, Thailand.

2005, Feb. 2   Perf. 13¼
Granite Paper
2163 A740 3b Horiz. pair, #a-b   1.10 1.00
    See Argentina Nos. 2312-2313.

Rose — A741

2005, Feb. 10   Perf. 12½
Flocked Paper
2164 A741 10b multi   1.10 .80
No. 2164 is impregnated with rose scent.

Maghapuja Day — A742

2005, Feb. 23   Perf. 14x14½
Granite Paper
2165 A742 3b multi   .50 .25

Rotary International, Cent. — A743

2005, Feb. 23   Perf. 14½x14
Granite Paper
2166 A743 3b multi   .50 .25

Red Cross A744

2005, Mar. 30   Litho.
Granite Paper
2167 A744 3b multi   .50 .25

Princess Maha Chakri Sirindhorn, 50th Birthday — A774a

2005, Apr. 2   Litho.   Perf. 13¼
Granite Paper
2167A A774a 3b multi   .50 .25

A745

Hanging Art — A746

2005, Apr. 2   Litho.   Perf. 13¼
Granite Paper
2168 A745 3b shown   .35 .25
2169 A746 3b shown   .35 .25
2170 A746 3b multi, diff.   .35 .25
2171 A745 15b multi, diff.   1.40 .55
    a.   Souvenir sheet, #2168-2171   3.25 2.75
    Nos. 2168-2171 (4)   2.45 1.30
Heritage Conservation Day. No. 2171 sold for 30b.

Authors Born in 1905 — A747

Designs: No. 2172, 3b, Dokmaisod (olive green background). No. 2173, 3b, Sri Burapha (Prussian blue background). No. 2174, 3b, Maimuangderm (dark blue background). No. 2175, 3b, Arkatdumkeung Rabibhadana (rose pink background).

2005, May 5   Perf. 14½x14
Granite Paper
2172-2175 A747 Set of 4   2.25 2.10
    2175a   Souvenir sheet, #2172-
            2175, perf. 13¼   5.00 4.50
    No. 2175a sold for 17b.

Insects — A748

No. 2176: a, Coccinella transversalis. b, Chrysochroa buqueti rugicollis (47x28mm). c, Sagra femorata. d, Chrysochroa maruyamai (47x28mm).

Litho. & Embossed
2005, May 31   Perf. 14¼x14½
Granite Paper
2176   Horiz. strip or block of
          4   2.25 1.60
    a.-d. A748 5b Any single   .55 .40
    e.   Sheet, 2 each #2176a-2176d 3.00 3.00
Embossed portions of stamps are covered with a glossy varnish.
No. 2176e issued May 2006, Washington 2006 World Philatelic Exhibition. No. 2176e sold for 54b.

Heart Balloons and Mail Truck — A749

Balloons — A749a

2005   Litho.   Perf. 13
Granite Paper
2177   A749   3b multi   .75 .50
2177A A749a 3b multi   .75 .50
Issued: No. 2177, June; No. 2177A, 7/15. Nos. 2177 and 2177A were issued in sheets of 12 + 12 personalizable labels the same size as the stamp.

Buddha Amulets A750

No. 2178: a, Phra Ruang Lang Rang Puen. b, Phra Hu Yan. c, Phra Chinnarat Bai Sema. d, Phra Mahesuan. e, Phra Tha Kradan.

Litho. & Embossed
2005, June 19   Perf. 13¼
Granite Paper
2178   Horiz. strip of 5   4.50 4.50
    a.-e. A750 9b Any single   .90 .90
    f.   Souvenir sheet, #2178a-
          2178e   12.00 12.00
    g.   As "f," with Taipei 2005 em-
          blem in margin   12.00 12.00
    No. 2178f sold for 55b.
No. 2178g issued 8/19/05. No. 2178g sold for 85b.

Thailand - People's Republic of China Diplomatic Relations, 30th Anniv. — A751

Panda: a, Showing tongue. b, Feeding on bamboo.

2005, July 1   Litho.   Perf.
Granite Paper
2179 A751 Horiz. pair   1.10 .90
    a.-b.   3b Either single   .45 .30
    c.   Souvenir sheet, #2179a-2179b 3.25 2.75
No. 2179 has perf. 13¼ line of perforations between the two stamps, and the surrounding selvage is rouletted 11¾. No. 2179c, which sold for 15b, lacks the perforations between the stamps and has no rouletting.

Thaipex 2005 — A752

Dancers in play "Chuck Nark": No. 2180, 3b, Pra Rama and Princess Srida. No. 2181, 3b, Hanuman (white mask). No. 2182, 3b, Thotsakan (green mask). 15b, Pra Rama and Thotsakan.

Litho. with Foil Application
2005, Aug. 3   Perf. 13¼
Granite Paper
2180-2183 A752 Set of 4   2.60 2.00
    2183a   Souvenir sheet, #2180-
            2183   4.50 3.25
No. 2183a sold for 30b. No. 2183a exists imperf. Value $25.

Natl. Communications Day — A753

2005, Aug. 4   Litho.   Perf. 14½x14
Granite Paper
2184 A753 3b multi   .50 .25

Building Gables — A754

No. 2185: a, Prasat Phanom Rung. b, Phra Prang at Wat Phra Phai Luang. c, Uposatha Hall at Wat Khao Bandai It. d, Scripture Library at Wat Phra Sing Woramahawihan.

Perf. 13¼x13½
2005, Aug. 4   Photo.   Wmk. 340
2185   Horiz. strip of 4 + cen-
          tral label   2.75 2.25
    a.-d. A754 5b Any single   .55 .40

Orchids — A755

Designs: No. 2189, 3b, Rhynchostylis gigantea Alba (white flowers). No. 2190, 3b, Rhynchostylis gigantea (pink and red flowers). No. 2191, 3b, Dendrobium gratiosissimum. 15b, Dendrobium thyrsiflorum.

Perf. 14½

2005, Sept. 1	**Litho.**		**Unwmk.**
	Granite Paper		
2189-2192 A755	Set of 4	2.50	2.50
2192a	Souvenir sheet, #2189-2192, perf. 13¼	3.50	3.50

No. 2192a sold for 30b.

Intl. Day of Peace — A756

2005, Sept. 21		**Perf. 13**
	Granite Paper	
2193 A756 3b multi		.50 .25

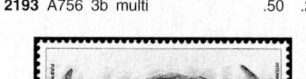

Intl. Letter Writing Week — A757

Water buffalo: No. 2194, 3b, Head. No. 2195, 3b, Standing in field. No. 2196, 3b, In mud. 15b, Attached to plow.

Perf. 14½x14

2005, Oct. 8	**Litho.**		**Unwmk.**
	Granite Paper		
2194-2197 A757	Set of 4	2.50	2.50
2197a	Souvenir sheet, #2194-2197, perf. 13¼	4.50	3.25

National Library, Cent. — A758

2005, Oct. 12		**Perf. 14½x14**
	Granite Paper	
2198 A758 3b multi		.50 .25

Abolition of Slavery, Cent. — A759

2005, Oct. 23		**Litho.**
	Granite Paper	
2199 A759 3b multi		.50 .30

New Year 2006 — A760

Flowers: No. 2200, 3b, Beaumontia murtonii. No. 2201, 3b, Hibiscus mutabilis. No. 2202, 3b, Hibiscus rosa-sinensis. No. 2203, 3b, Cochlospermum religiosum.

2005, Nov. 15			**Perf. 14x14½**
	Granite Paper		
2200-2203 A760	Set of 4	1.25	1.25
2203a	Souvenir sheet, #2200-2203	2.25	2.00

No. 2203a sold for 17b.

Princess Bejaratana, 80th Birthday — A761

2005, Nov. 24		**Perf. 14x14½**
	Granite Paper	
2204 A761 3b multi		.50 .30

Siamese Roosters — A762

Designs: No. 2205, 3b, Golden Rooster, by Pichai Nirand (olive green panel). No. 2206, 3b, Rooster at Dawn, by Prayat Pongdam (black panel). No. 2207, 3b, Legendary Rooster, by Chakrabhand Posayakrit (dancing woman, brown panel). No. 2208, 3b, Divine Rooster, by Chalermchai Kositpipat (blue panel), horiz.

Perf. 14x14½, 14½x14

2005, Nov. 24			
2205-2208 A762	Set of 4	1.25	1.25

King Bhumibol Adulyadej's "New Theory" Agriculture — A763

No. 2209: a, King, easel, farmers, animals. b, King and farmers.

2005, Dec. 5			**Perf. 14¼x14½**
	Granite Paper		
2209	Horiz. pair, #a-b, + central label	.85	.85
a.-b.	A763 3b Either single	.35	.30

Buddhist Monks A764

No. 2210: a, Somdet Phra Phutthachan (1788-1872). b, Phra Ratchamuni Samiram Khunupamachan (1582-1682). c, Phra Achan Man Bhuridatto (1870-1949). d, Khruba Si wichai (1877-1938).

Litho. & Engr.			
2005, Dec. 5			**Perf. 13½**
	Granite Paper		
2210	Horiz. strip of 4	2.25	2.25
a.-d.	A764 5b Any single	.55	.50
e.	Souvenir sheet, #2210a-2210d	3.50	3.50

No. 2210e sold for 30b.

Dec. 26, 2004 Tsunami, 1st Anniv. — A765

No. 2211: a, Wave. b, Undivided Kindness of Thai People, by Chanipa Temprom.

2005, Dec. 26	**Litho.**		**Perf. 14½x14**
	Granite Paper		
2211 A765 3b Horiz. pair, #a-b		2.50	1.75

King Bhumibol Adulyadej Type of 1996

2006	**Litho.**			**Perf. 14x14½**
	Granite Paper			
2212 A550	10b orange & brown		2.00	1.00
2213 A550	15b yel brn & green		3.00	1.50

New Year 2006 (Year of the Dog) — A766

2006, Jan. 1	**Litho.**	**Perf. 13**
	Granite Paper	
2214 A766 3b multi		.50 .30

Prince Chaturantarasmi Krom Phra Chakrabardibongse (1856-1900), Finance Minister — A767

2006, Jan. 13		**Perf. 14x14½**
	Granite Paper	
2215 A767 3b multi		.50 .30

Natl. Children's Day — A768

Winning designs in children's stamp design competition with panel colors of: No. 2216, 3b, Orange brown. No. 2217, 3b, Blue. No. 2218, 3b, Red violet. No. 2219, 3b, Green.

2006, Jan. 14			**Perf. 14½x14**
	Granite Paper		
2216-2219 A768	Set of 4	1.25	1.25

Rose — A769

Litho. & Embossed		
2006, Feb. 7		**Perf. 13**
	Granite Paper	
2220 A769 5b multi		.75 .50

Diplomatic Relations Between Thailand and Iran, 50th Anniv. — A770

2006, Feb. 11	**Litho.**	**Perf. 14½x14**
	Granite Paper	
2221 A770 3b multi		.50 .30

Queen Sirikit Center for Breast Cancer — A771

2006, Mar. 29		**Perf. 14½x14**
	Granite Paper	
2222 A771 3b multi		.50 .25

Heritage Conservation Day — A772

Sites in Phu Phrabat Historical Park: No. 2223, 3b, Buddha's Footprint (monument). No. 2224, 3b, Upright rocks and trees, horiz. No. 2225, 3b, Thao Barot horse stable (rock overhang), horiz. 15b, Nang Usa rock pillar.

2006, Apr. 2   *Perf. 14x14½, 14½x14*
Granite Paper
2223-2226	A772	Set of 4	2.50	2.50
2226a		Souvenir sheet, #2223-2226, perf. 13¼	4.50	3.25

No. 2226a sold for 36b.

Thon Buri Palace — A773

No. 2227: a, Throne Hall. b, King Taksin's Shrine. c, Two Chinese-style residences. d, King Pinklao's residence.

2006, Apr. 2   *Perf. 14½x14*
Granite Paper
2227	A773	3b Block of 4, #a-d	1.40	1.40
e.		Souvenir sheet, #2227, perf. 13¼	2.75	2.25

No. 2227e sold for 17b.

A774

King Bhumibol Adulyadej, 60th Anniv. of Accession — A775

King Bhumibol Adulyadej: No. 2228, 3b, Wearing tie, red brown background (shown). No. 2229, 3b, Wearing tie, blue background. No. 2230, 3b, Wearing tie, olive brown background. No. 2231, 3b, Without tie, blue violet background. No. 2232, Without tie, green background. No. 2233, 3b, Without tie, brown background.

2006   Photo.   *Perf. 13¼*
Granite Paper
2228-2233	A774	Set of 6	8.00	7.00
2233a		Miniature sheet, #2228-2233	16.00	16.00

Litho. & Embossed With Foil Application
2234	A775	100b gold & multi	9.00	9.00

Issued: Nos. 2228-2233, 2233a, 5/5; No. 2234, 6/9. No. 2233a sold for 30b.

Visakhapuja Day — A776

2006, May 12   Litho.   *Perf. 14x14½*
Granite Paper
2235	A776	3b multi	.50	.30

Buddhadasa Bhikkhu (1906-93), Buddhist Philosopher A777

No. 2236: a, Buddhadasa seated between trees. b, Profile of Buddhadasa. c, Gathering of monks. d, Stone fence.

2006, May 27   *Perf. 13*
Granite Paper
2236		Horiz. strip of 4	1.60	1.60
a.-d.	A777	3b Any single	.30	.30
e.		Miniature sheet, #2236a-2236d	2.00	2.00

No. 2236e sold for 17b.

Anemonefish — A778

Designs: No. 2237, 3b, Amphiprion clarkii. No. 2238, 3b, Amphiprion perideraion. No. 2239, 3b, Amphiprion ocellaris. No. 2240, 3b, Amphiprion polymnus.

2006, June 24   *Perf. 14½x14*
Granite Paper
2237-2240	A778	Set of 4	1.40	1.40
2240a		Miniature sheet, #2237-2240, perf. 13½	2.75	2.25
2240b		As "a," with Belgica '06 emblem in margin	11.00	11.00

Issued: Nos. 2237-2240, 2240a, 6/24; No. 2240b, Dec. No. 2240a sold for 20b; No. 2240b, for 30b.

Natl. Communications Day — A779

2006, Aug. 4   Litho.
Granite Paper
2241	A779	3b multi	.50	.30

Mitrephora Sirikitiae — A780

Litho. & Embossed
2006, Aug. 12   *Perf. 13*
Granite Paper
2242	A780	5b multi	.55	.40

Royal Dog Tongdaeng A781

Dog: No. 2243, 3b, Sitting. No. 2244, 3b, Standing. No. 2245, 3b, Laying down. No. 2246, 3b, With puppies.

2006   Litho.   *Perf. 13½*
Granite Paper
2243-2246	A781	Set of 4	1.40	1.10
2246a		Miniature sheet, #2243-2246	2.25	2.25
2246b		As "a," with MonacoPhil 2006 emblem in margin	10.00	10.00

Issued: Nos. 2243-2246, 2246a, 9/1; No. 2246b, Dec. No. 2246a sold for 17b; No. 2246b, for 26b.

Suvarnabhumi Airport — A782

2006, Sept. 28   *Perf. 14½x14*
Granite Paper
2247	A782	3b multi	.50	.30

Nos. 606, 653a, 934 and 1081 Surcharged

Methods, Perfs and Watermarks As Before
2006, Sept. 15
2248	A146	2b on 20s #606	16.00	16.00
2249	A161	2b on 20s #653a	1.10	.35
a.		2b on 20s #653	75.00	75.00
2250	A256	2b on 75s #934	2.75	2.75
2251	A256	2b on 1.50b #1081	2.75	2.75
		Nos. 2248-2251 (4)	22.60	21.85

Location and size of surcharges differs.

Fireworks — A783

2006, Apr. 20   Litho.   *Perf. 13*
Granite Paper
2252	A783	3b multi + label	2.75	2.75

Printed in sheets of 10 stamps + 10 labels that could be personalized. Sheets sold for 100b. Value, $32.50.

Intl. Letter Writing Week — A784

Carnivorous plants: No. 2253, 3b, Nepenthes mirabilis. No. 2254, 3b, Rafflesia kerrii. No. 2255, 3b, Sapria poilanei. 15b, Drosera burmannii.

2006   Litho.   Unwmk.   *Perf. 14½x14*
Granite Paper
2253-2256	A784	Set of 4	2.50	1.60
2256a		Miniature sheet, #2253-2256, perf. 13½	3.25	2.75
2256b		As "a," with Beijing 2006 emblem in margin	10.00	10.00

Issued: Nos. 2253-2256, 2256a, 10/9; No. 2256b, Dec. No. 2256a sold for 29b; No. 2256b, for 44b.

New Year 2007 — A785

Flowers: No. 2257, 3b, Hypoxis aurea. No. 2258, 3b, Murdannia gigantea. No. 2259, 3b, Impatiens phuluangensis. No. 2260, 3b, Caulokaempferia alba.

2006, Nov. 15   *Perf. 14½x14*
Granite Paper
2257-2260	A785	Set of 4	1.25	.90
2260a		Miniature sheet, #2257-2260	2.50	2.25

No. 2260a sold for 16b.

Royal Thai Naval Academy, Cent. — A786

2006, Nov. 20
Granite Paper
2261	A786	3b multi	.50	.30

King Bhumibol Adulyadej, 60th Anniv. of Accession A787

King Bhumibol Adulyadej: No. 2262, 5b, Standing in forest. No. 2263, 5b, Seated on walkway, taking notes. No. 2264, 5b, Standing on wooden plank over water. No. 2265, 5b, Pointing to ground. No. 2266, 5b, Riding cow. No. 2267, 5b, Walking up hill.

2006, Dec. 5   Photo.   *Perf. 13½*
Granite Paper
2262-2267	A787	Set of 6	3.75	2.50
2267a		Miniature sheet, #2262-2267	5.50	5.50

No. 2267a sold for 44b. No. 2267a exists imperf. Value, $275.

Opening of Second Thai-Lao Friendship Bridge — A788

No. 2268 — Bridge and flag of: a, Thailand (denomination at LL). b, Laos (denomination at LR).

2006, Dec. 20   Litho.   *Perf. 14½x14*
Granite Paper
2268	A788	3b Horiz. pair, #a-b	1.10	1.10

New Year 2007 (Year of the Pig) — A789

2007, Jan. 1 **Perf. 13**
Granite Paper
2269 A789 3b multi .50 .30
See No. 2341d.

Natl. Children's Day — A790

No. 2270 — Children's drawings: a, Rainbow, birds and butterflies. b, Cat with green face and butterflies. c, Spotted animals. d, Birds, cloud, sun and girl riding horse.

2007, Jan. 13 **Perf. 14½x14**
Granite Paper
2270 A790 3b Block of 4, #a-d 2.25 1.25

Siam Commercial Bank Public Company, Cent. — A791

2007, Jan. 30 **Perf. 14x14½**
Granite Paper
2271 A791 3b multi .50 .30

Bangkok 2007 Intl. Stamp Exhibition — A792

Various carved wooden dolls depicting Thai children with background colors of: No. 2272, 5b, Blue. No. 2273, 5b, Olive green. No. 2274, 5b, Brown olive. No. 2275, 5b, Rose.

Litho. With Foil Application
2007, Feb. 1 **Perf. 13**
Granite Paper
2272-2275 A792 Set of 4 2.25 1.75
2275a Miniature sheet, #2272-2275 3.75 3.25
No. 2275a sold for 33b.

Yellow Rose — A793

2007, Feb. 7 **Litho.** **Perf. 13**
Granite Paper
2276 A793 5b multi .55 .40
No. 2276 is impregnated with a rose scent.

A794

A795

A796

Carved Fruits and Vegetables — A797

2007, Mar. 1 **Litho.** **Perf. 14½x14**
Granite Paper
2277 A794 5b multi .55 .40
2278 A795 5b multi .55 .40
2279 A796 5b multi .55 .40
2280 A797 5b multi .55 .40
a. Souvenir sheet, #2277-2280, perf. 13¼ 3.50 3.25
Nos. 2277-2280 (4) 2.20 1.60
No. 2280a sold for 26b.

No. 617 Surcharged in Bronze and Black

Methods, Perfs and Watermarks As Before
2007, Mar. 29
2281 A146 50b on 40b #617 6.50 6.50
2282 A146 100b on 40b #617 10.00 10.00

Postman on Scooter — A798

Unwmk.
2007, Mar. 29 **Litho.** **Perf. 13**
Granite Paper
2283 A798 3b multi .35 .30
No. 2283 was printed in sheets of 10 and in sheets of 10 + 10 labels that could be personalized.

Thailand Red Cross Tuberculosis Laboratory — A799

2007, Mar. 29 **Litho.** **Perf. 14½x14**
2285 A799 3b multi .35 .30

A800

A801

A802

Buddhist Ecclesiastical Ceremonial Fans of King Chulalongkorn Era — A803

Litho. With Foil Application
2007, Apr. 2 **Perf. 13¼**
Granite Paper
2286 A800 5b multi .55 .40
2287 A801 5b multi .55 .40
2288 A802 5b multi .55 .40
2289 A803 5b multi .55 .40
a. Souvenir sheet, #2286-2289 3.75 3.25
Nos. 2286-2289 (4) 2.20 1.60
No. 2289a sold for 27b.

Flowers — A804

No. 2290: a, Lotus flower at UR, sunflowers in center and LR. b, Sunflower at UR, two lotus flowers. c, Rose, sunflower and lotus flowers. d, Three roses.

2007, Apr. 23 **Litho.** **Perf. 13**
Granite Paper
2290 Vert. strip of 4 1.60 1.60
a.-d. A804 3b Any single .35 .30

King Bhumibol Adulyadej, 80th Birthday — A805

Litho. & Embossed With Foil Application
2007, May 5 **Perf. 13¼**
Granite Paper
2291 A805 9b multi 1.40 1.40

Princess Galyani Vadhana, 84th Birthday — A806

2007, May 6 **Litho.** **Perf. 14x14½**
2292 A806 3b multi .65 .50

Visakhapuja Day — A807

2007, May 31 **Perf. 14¼x14½**
Granite Paper
2293 A807 3b multi .45 .40

Seaside Tourist Areas — A808

No. 2294: a, Mu Ko Similan National Park. b, Ko Khai. c, Ko Chang. d, Khao Tapu. e, Hat Cha-am. f, Ao Maya. g, Ko Panyi. h, Hat Chao Mai. i, Thale Waek. j, Hat Pattaya.

2007, June 1 **Perf. 14½x14**
Granite Paper
2294 Sheet of 10 11.00 11.00
a.-j. A808 15b Any single 1.10 1.10

Waterfalls — A809

Waterfall at: No. 2295, 3b, Doi Inthanon National Park. No. 2296, 3b, Thung Salaeng Luang National Park. No. 2297, 3b, Khuean Srinagarindra National Park. No. 2298, 3b, Phu Hin Rong Kla National Park.

2007, June 1   *Perf. 14½x14*
Granite Paper
2295-2298 A809   Set of 4   1.40 1.40
2298a   Souvenir sheet, #2295-
   2298, perf. 13½   2.90 2.25
No. 2298a sold for 16b.

Phi Takhon Masks — A810

No. 2299 — Masks with rice steamer hat in: a, White, black background. b, Black, white background. c, Red, black background. d, White, white background.
10b, Two people wearing masks.

2007, June 23   *Perf. 13¼*
Granite Paper
2299 A810   3b Horiz. strip of 4,
   #a-d   1.60 1.60
Souvenir Sheet
Perf. 14x14½
2300 A810 10b multi   2.00 2.00
No. 2300 contains one 60x48mm stamp.

A811

A812

A813

Rock Formations in Pa Hin Ngam National Park — A814

2007, July 2   Litho.   *Perf. 13¼x12¾*
2301 A811 5b multi   .55 .40
2302 A812 5b multi   .55 .40
2303 A813 5b multi   .55 .40
2304 A814 5b multi   .55 .40
   a.   Souvenir sheet, #2301-2304   4.75 3.75
   Nos. 2301-2304 (4)   2.20 1.60
No. 2304a sold for 39b. Portions of the designs of Nos. 2301-2304 and 2304a were printed with a thermographic process producing a shiny, raised effect. A gritty substance was added to these areas to produce a rough texture.

Temples — A815

Designs: No. 2305, 5b, Wat Rajaorasaram. No. 2306, 5b, Wat Rajapradit Sathitmahasimaram. No. 2307, 5b, Wat Rajabopit Sathitmahasimaram. No. 2308, 5b, Wat Suthatthepwararam.

2007, July 2   Litho.   *Perf. 14½x14*
Granite Paper
2305-2308 A815   Set of 4   2.25 1.75
2308a   Souvenir sheet, #2305-
   2308, perf. 13¼   3.50 3.25
No. 2308a sold for 27b.

Bird Figurines A816

Bird figurines covered with beetle wing: No. 2309, 5b, Duck with wings spread. No. 2310, 5b, Bird on rock. No. 2311, 5b, Bird with long tail feathers. No. 2312, 5b, Rooster.

Litho. With Foil Application
2007, Aug. 3   *Perf. 14x14½*
Granite Paper
2309-2312 A816   Set of 4   2.60 1.75
2312a   Souvenir sheet, #2309-
   2312   3.75 3.25
No. 2312a sold for 33b. Bangkok 2007 Intl. Stamp Exhibition.

Natl. Communications Day — A817

2007, Aug. 4   Litho.   *Perf. 14½x14*
Granite Paper
2313 A817 3b multi   .30 .30

24th Summer Universiade, Bangkok — A818

2007, Aug. 8   *Perf. 13¼*
Granite Paper
2314 A818 3b multi   .30 .30

Miniature Sheet

Association of South East Asian Nations (ASEAN), 40th Anniv. — A819

No. 2315: a, Secretariat Building, Bandar Seri Begawan, Brunei. b, National Museum of Cambodia. c, Fatahillah Museum, Jakarta, Indonesia. d, Typical house, Laos. e, Malayan Railway Headquarters Building, Kuala Lumpur, Malaysia. f, Yangon Post Office, Myanmar (Burma). g, Malacañang Palace, Philippines. h, National Museum of Singapore. i, Vimanmek Mansion, Bangkok. j, Presidential Palace, Hanoi, Viet Nam.

2007, Aug. 8   *Perf. 13¼*
Granite Paper
2315 A819 3b Sheet of 10, #a-j   5.50 4.50
See Brunei No. 607, Burma No. 370, Cambodia No. 2339, Indonesia Nos. 2120-2121, Laos Nos. 1717-1718, Malaysia No. 1170, Philippines Nos. 3103-3105, Singapore No. 1265, and Viet Nam Nos. 3302-3311.

Miniature Sheet

Diplomatic Relations Between Thailand and Japan, 120th Anniv. — A820

No. 2316: a, Buddhist statue. b, Pagoda. c, Elephant. d, Dragon. e, Pink and white orchids. f, White flowers. g, Thai dancer. h, Japanese dancer.

2007, Sept. 26   Litho.   *Perf. 13¼*
Granite Paper
2316 A820   3b Sheet of 8, #a-h   4.50 3.25
See Japan No. 2998.

Intl. Letter Writing Week — A821

Utensils: No. 2317, 3b, Betel nut scissors. No. 2318, 3b, Betel nut masher. No. 2319, 3b, Cylinder-and-piston igniter. No. 2320, 3b, Earthenware oil lamp or incense dish.

2007, Oct. 8   Litho.   *Perf. 14½x14*
Granite Paper
2317-2320 A821   Set of 4   1.75 1.10
2320a   Miniature sheet, #2317-2320,
   perf. 13¼   3.00 2.75
No. 2320a sold for 18b.

Miniature Sheets

Provincial Seals — A822

No. 2321, 3b — Seals of: a, Bangkok. b, Krabi. c, Kanchanaburi. d, Kalasin. e, Kamphaeng Phet. f, Khon Kaen. g, Chanthaburi. h, Chachoengsao. i, Chon Buri. j, Chai Nat.
No. 2322, 3b — Seals of: a, Chaiyaphum. b, Chumphon. c, Chiang Rai. d, Chiang Mai. e, Trang. f, Trat. g, Tak. h, Nakhon Nayok. i, Nakhon Pathom. j, Nakhon Phanom.

Litho. & Embossed With Foil Application
2007, Oct. 11   *Perf. 13½*
Granite Paper
Sheets of 10, #a-j
2321-2322 A822   Set of 2   5.50 5.50

Miniature Sheet

People at Work — A823

No. 2323: a, People in palm tree. b, Cook feeding people on wooden walkway. c, People near elephant carving. d, Buddhist monk in canoe. e, People under lanterns. f, Artisan with hammer. g, Woman with flowers. h, Man weaving fishing basket. i, People in boats filled with fruits and vegetables. j, People logging with elephants.

2007, Oct. 26   Litho.   *Perf. 13*
Granite Paper
2323 A823 3b Sheet of 10, #a-j   5.50 5.50

Ministry of Defense, 120th Anniv. — A824

2007, Nov. 11   *Perf. 14x14½*
Granite Paper
2324 A824 3b multi   .35 .30

New Year 2008 — A825

Designs: No. 2325, 3b, Pink Plumeria rubra, denomination in red. No. 2326, 3b, Plumeria obtusa. No. 2327, 3b, White and yellow Plumeria rubra, denomination in pink. No. 2328, 3b, Red Plumeria rubra, denomination in red.

2007, Nov. 15   Perf. 14x14½
Granite Paper
2325-2328 A825 Set of 4   1.25 1.25
2328a   Souvenir sheet, #2325-
                2328   2.90 2.90
No. 2328a sold for 18b.

Patrol
Boat — A826

Perf. 14½x14¼
2007, Nov. 20   Litho.
Granite Paper
2329 A826 3b multi   .55   .30

White Elephant of King Bhumibol
Adulyadej — A827

Designs: No. 2330, 5b, King touching elephant's trunk. No. 2331, 5b, Elephant on lawn. No. 2332, 5b, Elephant on lawn with handlers, vert. No. 2333, 5b, King touching elephant's head, vert.

Perf. 14¾x14, 14x14¾
2007, Dec. 5   Litho.
Granite Paper
2330-2333 A827 Set of 4   1.75 1.75
2333a   Souvenir sheet, #2333,
                perf. 13½   2.75 2.25
No. 2333a sold for 10b.

Miniature Sheet

King Bhumibol Adulyadej, 80th
Birthday — A828

No. 2334 — King: a, 5b, As small boy. b, 5b, As boy, sitting in wagon. c, 5b, As student, reading book. d, 5b, Wearing suit, sepia photograph. e, 5b, Wearing cap. f, 5b, Wearing red uniform. g, 5b, Wearing suit and red tie. h, 5b, Wearing gold robe. i, 80b, Wearing Buddhist robe.

Litho., Litho. & Embossed With
Hologram Affixed (80b)
2007, Dec. 5   Perf. 13¼x13½
2334 A828 Sheet of 9, #a-i   16.00 12.00

No. 1820
Surcharged in Gold

Methods and Perfs As Before
2007, Dec. 18
Granite Paper
2335 A550 15b on 9b #1820   2.00   .75

Busabok
Mala
A829

Queen's Collection — A830

No. 2337: a, Miniature model of royal barge Anantanakharai. b, Miniature model of royal barge Suphannahongse. c, Sappagab Phragajatarn. d, Sappagab Khram. e, Water jars. f, Miniature vanity set. g, Yan Lipao basketry. h, Evening bag.

Litho. & Embossed With Foil
Application
2007, Dec. 18   Perf. 13¼x13½
2336 A829 20b multi   3.00 3.00
  a.   Souvenir sheet of 1   6.00 6.00
Granite Paper
Perf. 13
2337 A830 5b Sheet of 8, #a-h   4.50 3.75
No. 2336a sold for 40b.

Nos. B78-B79
Surcharged in
Black

Methods, Perfs and Watermarks As
Before
2007, Jan. 16
2338   Horiz. strip of 4 (#B78) —   —
  a.-d. SP13 5b on 2b+1b #B78a-B78d,
                Any single   —   —
2339   Horiz. strip of 4 (#B79) —   —
  a.-d. SP13 5b on 2b+1b #B79a-B79d,
                Any single   —   —

New Year Types of 2003-2007 and

New Year 2008
(Year of the
Rat) — A831

Unwmk.
2008, Jan. 1   Litho.   Perf. 13
Granite Paper
2340 A831 3b multi   .35   .30
2341   Sheet of 6, #2214,
                2340, 2341a-2341d   3.50 3.25
  a.   A682 3b As #2056, with gold
                rings with colored centers   .30   .30
  b.   A682 3b As #2108, with gold
                rings with colored centers   —   —
  c.   A682 3b As #2161, with gold
                rings with colored centers   .30   .30
  d.   A789 3b As #2269, with gold
                rings and dots   .30   .30
  e.   As #2341, with Taipei 2008
                emblem in margin   10.00 10.00
No. 2341 sold for 30b. On Nos. 2056, 2108 and 2161, gold rings have white centers. No. 2269 has gold dots only.

A832

A833

A834

A835

Children's Art — A836

No. 2342: a, Stilt walkers, by Kemtis Kumsrijan. b, Flying kites, by Natapol Saelim. c, Puppet show, by Sirada Chokeyangkul. d, Thien Phansa, by Salinthip Narongpun. e, People thanking rice plants, by Amornthep Jitnak.

2008, Jan. 12   Litho.   Perf. 14½x14
Granite Paper
2342   Horiz. strip of 5   2.00 2.00
  a.   A832 3b multi   .35   .30
  b.   A833 3b multi   .35   .30
  c.   A834 3b multi   .35   .30
  d.   A835 3b multi   .35   .30
  e.   A836 3b multi   .35   .30
Children's Day.

Chinese New Year — A837

No. 2343: a, Mask, black denomination at UR (29x48mm). b, Mask, black denomination at LL (29x48mm). c, Masks, green denomination at UL (29x24mm). d, People celebrating, green denomination at LL (29x24mm).

2008, Feb. 1   Litho.   Perf. 14½x14¼
Granite Paper
2343 A837 5b Block of 4, #a-d   2.25 2.25
  e.   Souvenir sheet, #2343a-2343b 2.50 2.50
No. 2343e sold for 20b. For surcharges, see No. 2358.

Pink
Rose — A838

2008, Feb. 7   Litho.   Perf. 13
Granite Paper
2344 A838 5b multi   .45   .40
No. 2344 is impregnated with a rose scent.

Postman in
Boat — A839

2008, Mar. 3   Perf. 14¼
Granite Paper
2345 A839 3b multi   .25   .25

Stylized People
Holding
Heart — A840

2008, Mar. 17
Granite Paper
2346 A840 3b multi   .35   .30
Printed in sheets of 10 and in sheets of 10 + 10 labels that could be personalized.

Nos. B78-B79
Surcharged in
Gold and Black

Methods, Perfs and Watermarks As Before
2008, Mar. 26
2347	Horiz. strip of 4 (#B78)	4.00	3.00
a.-d.	SP13 15b on 2b+1b #B78a-		
	B78d, Any single	1.00	.75
2348	Horiz. strip of 4 (#B79)	4.00	3.00
a.-d.	SP13 15b on 2b+1b #B79a-		
	B79d, Any single	1.00	.75

Miniature Sheet

Chatukham Rammathep — A841

No. 2349: a, Statue, maroon panels, "Chatukham" above denomination. b, Gold amulet, light gray background. c, Statue, maroon panels, "Rammathep" above denomination. d, Statue, yellow panels, "Chatukham" above denomination. e, Gold amulet with inner ring, dark gray background. f, Statue, yellow panels, "Rammathep" above denomination. g, Silver and brown amulet, bister background. h, Silver amulet, blue background. i, Silver and red amulet, orange brown background. j, Silver and red amulet, olive green background. k, Black amulet, pale blue green background. l, Red brown amulet, pink background.

Litho. & Embossed
Perf. 13½x13¼
2008, Mar. 29   Unwmk.
2349	A841 9b Sheet of 12, #a-l	10.00	10.00

No. 2349 was printed in sheets of 12 with and without a row of perforations through the center of the sheet. For surcharges, see No. 2588.

A842

A843

A844

Angels and Demons — A845

2008, Apr. 2   Litho.   Perf. 14x14½
Granite Paper
2350	A842 3b multi	.35	.30
2351	A843 3b multi	.35	.30
2352	A844 3b multi	.35	.30
2353	A845 3b multi	.35	.30
a.	Miniature sheet, #2350-2353, perf. 13¼	3.00	3.00
	Nos. 2350-2353 (4)	1.40	1.20

No. 2353a sold for 20b.

Miniature Sheet

Provincial Seals — A846

No. 2354 — Seals of: a, Nakhon Ratchasima. b, Nakhon Si Thammarat. c, Nakhon Sawan. d, Nonthaburi. e, Narathiwat. f, Nan. g, Buri Ram. h, Pathum Thani. i, Prachuap Khiri Khan. j, Prachin Buri.

Litho. & Embossed With Foil Application
2008, Apr. 2   Perf. 13
Granite Paper
2354	A846 3b Sheet of 10, #a-j	5.50	5.50

Nos. 1764, 1817-1818 Surcharged in Gold and Black

c

Methods and Perfs As Before
2008
2355	A572(c) 15b on 6b #1764	.95	.95
	Granite Paper		
2356	A590(c) 15b on 6b #1817	.95	.95
2357	A590(c) 15b on 9b #1818	.95	.95
	Nos. 2355-2357 (3)	2.85	2.85

Nos. 2343a, 2343c, 2343d, and Items Similar to Nos. 2343b and 2343e Surcharged in Gold and Black — d

Methods and Perfs As Before
2008, Apr. 25
Granite Paper
2358	Block of 4 (#2343)	4.50	4.50
a.	A837(d) 15b on 5b #2343a	1.10	1.10
b.	A837(d) 15b on 5b stamp similar to #2343a	1.10	1.10
c.-d.	A837(c) 15b on 5b Either single, #2343c-2343d	1.10	1.10
e.	A837(d) 15b on 5b sheet similar to #2343e	4.50	3.75

No. 2358b is a surcharge on an unissued stamp similar to No. 2343b that was printed with the incorrectly-spelled inscription "Chinese Neww Year." The extra "w" is obliterated

by a gold circle in the surcharge on No. 2358b found in in the block of four or in the souvenir sheet, No. 2358e.

Diplomatic Relations Between Thailand and Turkey, 50th Anniv. — A847

No. 2359: a, Flag of Thailand, Wat Rajannada, Bangkok. b, Flag of Turkey, Blue Mosque, Istanbul.

2008, May 12   Litho.   Perf. 13¼
Granite Paper
2359	A847 3b Horiz. pair, #a-b	.55	.55

See Turkey Nos. 3108-3109.

Sunflowers A848

2008, May 16   Perf. 13
Granite Paper
2360	A848 3b multi	.25	.25

Visakhapuja Day — A849

2008, May 19   Perf. 14¼x14½
Granite Paper
2361	A849 3b multi	.35	.30

A850

A851

A852

World Environment Day — A853

2008, June 5   Perf. 13½
Granite Paper
2362	A850 3b multi	.25	.25
2363	A851 3b multi	.25	.25
2364	A852 3b multi	.25	.25
2365	A853 3b multi	.25	.25
	Nos. 2362-2365 (4)	1.00	1.00

Miniature Sheet

Orchids — A854

No. 2366: a, Brassocattleya Ploenpit Star. b, Aerides falcata. c, Arachnis Hookeriana x Vanda Doctor Anek. d, Phalaenopsis Little Mary. e, Dendrobium sutiknoi. f, Paphiopedilum callosum. g, Grammatophyllum speciosum. h, Vascostylis Prapawan. i, Vanda Robert's Delight.

2008, June 13   Litho.   Perf. 14x14½
Granite Paper
2366	A854 3b Sheet of 9, #a-i	3.25	3.25

A855

A856

A857

A858

A859

A860

A861

A862

A863

A864

Bangkok
Attractions
A864

2008, July 11   **Perf. 13¼x13½**
Granite Paper

2367		Sheet of 10	4.50	4.50
a.	A855	3b multi	.35	.25
b.	A856	3b multi	.35	.25
c.	A857	3b multi	.35	.25
d.	A858	3b multi	.35	.25
e.	A859	3b multi	.35	.25
f.	A860	3b multi	.35	.25
g.	A861	3b multi	.35	.25
h.	A862	3b multi	.35	.25
i.	A863	3b multi	.35	.25
j.	A864	3b multi	.35	.25

Miniature Sheet

Mountain Region Attractions — A865

No. 2368: a, Phu Chi Fa. b, Phu Pha Thoep. c, Heo Narok Waterfall. d, Phang-Ung. e, Sun Crack. f, Phu Khao Hin Pakarang. g, Phae Mueang Phi Earth Pillar. h, Phu Kradueng. i, Phu Soi Dao. j, Khun Mae Ya.

2008, July 11   **Litho.**
Granite Paper

2368	A865	15b Sheet of 10, #a-j	11.00	11.00

Thailand Flag
— A865a

Elephants —
A865c

Thai Pavilion —
A865b

Cassia Fistula
— A865d

2008, July 25 Litho.   **Perf. 14¼x14½**

2368K	A865a	3b multi	.45	.25
2368L	A865b	3b multi	.45	.25
2368M	A865c	3b multi	.45	.25
2368N	A865d	3b multi	.45	.25
		Nos. 2368K-2368N (4)	1.80	1.00

Nos. 2368K-2368N were printed by a different printer than Nos. 2101-2104.

No. 2368K has a taller, rounder "3" than No. 2101.

No. 2368L has a black line under the building railing at bottom. On No. 2102, the railing touches the white frame of the stamp.

On No. 2368M, the country name, having small dots of color in the lettering, appears pale gray, and the entire vignette has a fuzzy appearance. On No. 2103, the country name is all white and the vignette is sharper.

On No. 2368N, the area without flowers has a blue appearance, and the flowers have a greener appearance. On No. 2104, the area without flowers has a purple appearance, and the flowers appear browner. The screens used on these stamps differ, with No. 2368N having coarser dots than No. 2104. Under magnification the bottom edge of the vignette has more of a saw-tooth appearance on No. 2368N than on No. 2104.

Postman, Tree
and
Dove — A866

2008, Aug. 1   **Perf. 14¼**
Granite Paper

2369	A866	3b multi	.35	.30
a.		Perf. 13	4.50	4.50

A867

Thailand Postal Service, 125th
Anniv. — A868

Designs: No. 2370, 3b, Unissued 1-fuang stamp of 1883 and various modern Thailand stamps. No. 2371, 3b, Old and modern post offices. No. 2372, 3b, Old and modern post office counters. No. 2373, 3b, Old and modern postal delivery men. No. 2374, 3b, Old and modern postal trucks.

No. 2375: a, 5b, Thailand #2 in black and Post Office. b, 5b, Thailand #3. c, 5b, Thailand #4. d, 10b, Thailand #5a. e, 25b, Hologram of Thailand #1 with added Thai words.

Litho., Litho. With Hologram Affixed (#2375e)

2008   **Perf. 14½x14**
Granite Paper

2370-2374	A867	Set of 5	1.60	1.10
		Perf. 13¼x13½		
2375	A868	Sheet of 5 #a-e	4.50	4.50

Communications
Day — A869

2008, Aug. 4   **Litho.**   **Perf. 14x14½**
Granite Paper

2376	A869	3b multi	.35	.30

End of telegraph message service in Thailand.

Painting of
Flowers by
Princess Maha
Chakri Sirindhorn
A870

2008, Aug. 4   **Perf. 13½x13¼**
Granite Paper

2377	A870	5b multi	.45	.40

Peacocks
A871

Designs: No. 2378, 10b, Peacock on branch. No. 2379, 10b, Peacock with tail feathers raised.

Litho. & Embossed With Hologram Affixed

2008, Aug. 9   **Perf. 13¼**
Granite Paper

2378-2379	A871	Set of 2	2.00	1.60
2379a		Souvenir sheet, #2378-2379	3.75	3.25

No. 2379a sold for 30b.

Nos. 1749-1750, 1785 Surcharged in
Black

Methods and Perfs As Before
2008, Oct. 1
Granite Paper

2380	A568	10b on 6b #1749	3.25	3.25
2381	A579	10b on 6b #1785	3.25	3.25
2382	A568	50b on 7b #1750	7.50	7.50
		Nos. 2380-2382 (3)	14.00	14.00

Diplomatic Relations Between
Thailand and Republic of Korea, 50th
Anniv. — A872

No. 2383: a, Chakri Maha Prasat Throne Hall, Thailand (denomination at L). b, Juhamnu Mansion, Changdeok Palace, Korea (denomination at R).

2008, Oct. 1   **Litho.**   **Perf. 14½x14**
Granite Paper

2383	A872	3b Horiz. pair, #a-b	.55	.55

See South Korea No. 2295.

Intl. Letter Writing
Week — A873

Shadow puppets: No. 2384, 3b, Rishi. No. 2385, 3b, Shiva. No. 2386, 3b, Shadow play preluder. No. 2387, 3b, Theng the Jester.

2008, Oct. 4   **Perf. 14x14½**
Granite Paper

2384-2387	A873	Set of 4	.90	.90
2387a		Souvenir sheet, #2384-2387, perf. 13½	2.40	2.40

No. 2387a sold for 18b.

Miniature Sheet

Provincial Seals — A874

No. 2388 — Seal of: a, Pattani. b, Phra Nakhon Si Ayutthaya. c, Phang-Nga. d, Phatthalung. e, Phayao. f, Phichit. g, Phitsanulok. h, Phetchaburi. i, Phetchabun. j, Phrae.

Litho. & Embossed With Foil Application
2008, Oct. 10   **Perf. 13¾**
Granite Paper

2388	A874	3b Sheet of 10, #a-j	4.50	4.50

Thailand No.
119 — A875

2008, Oct. 23 Litho. *Perf. 13½x13¼*
Granite Paper

2389 A875 5b multi   .45   .40

Equestrian statue of King Chulalongkorn, cent.

New Year
2009 — A876

Water lilies: No. 2390, 3b, Nymphaea "Suwanna." No. 2391, 3b, Nymphaea "Tan-khwan." No. 2392, 3b, Nymphaea "Tanpong." No. 2393, 3b, Nymphaea "Mangala-Ubol."

2008, Nov. 15 Litho. *Perf. 14x14½*
Granite Paper

2390-2393 A876 Set of 4   .70   .55
2393a   Souvenir sheet of 4,
             #2390-2393   .95   .75

No. 2393a sold for 17b. A sheet similar to No. 2393a, with the China 2009 World Stamp Exhibition emblem in the sheet margin, sold for 30b.

Miniature Sheet

Cremation of Princess Galyani
Vadhana (1933-2008) — A877

No. 2394 — Princess: a, As child. b, Wearing sash. c, Wearing cap. d, Wearing red dress.

2008, Nov. 11   *Perf. 14x14¾*
Granite Paper

2394 A877 5b Sheet of 4, #a-d   3.00   1.75

No. 2394 exists imperf. Value, $160.

King
Bhumibol
Adulyadej,
81st Birthday
A878

2008, Dec. 3   *Perf. 13¼*
Granite Paper

2395 A878 3b multi   .25   .25

Somdet Chao
Phraya Borom
Maha
Sisuriyawong
(1808-83),
Regent of King
Chulalongkorn
A879

2008, Dec. 23   *Perf. 14x14¾*
Granite Paper

2396 A879 3b multi   .35   .30

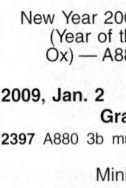

New Year 2009
(Year of the
Ox) — A880

2009, Jan. 2   *Perf. 14¼*
Granite Paper

2397 A880 3b multi   .35   .30

Miniature Sheet

Children's Day — A881

No. 2398 — Characters from "Phra Abhai Manee," poem by Phra Sunthorn Voharn: a, Sri Suvan with pole. b, Phra Abhai Manee with flute. c, Mermaid and fish. d, Giant woman in water. e, Sud Sakhon falling. f, Old man with tiger skin clothes. g, Naked man with stick. h, King's daughter.

2009   *Perf. 14¾x14*
Granite Paper

2398 A881 3b Sheet of 8, #a-h   6.50   6.50
 i.   Souvenir sheet, #2398a-2398d,
        perf. 13¼   9.00   9.00

Issued: No. 2398, 1/10, No. 2398i, May. Honk Kong 2009 Intl. Philatelic Exhibition (No. 2398i).

A882

A883

A884

Prince
Bhanurangsi
(1860-1928),
Founder of Thai
Postal
Service — A885

2009, Jan. 11   *Perf. 14x14¾*
Granite Paper

2399 A882 3b multi   .35   .30
2400 A883 3b multi   .35   .30
2401 A884 3b multi   .35   .30
2402 A885 3b multi   .35   .30
 a.   Souvenir sheet of 4, #2399-
      2402, perf. 13½   2.25   2.25
      Nos. 2399-2402 (4)   1.40   1.20

No. 2402a sold for 20b. No. 2402a exists imperf. Value, $27.50.

White
Rose — A886

Litho. & Embossed
2009, Feb. 6   *Perf. 13*
Granite Paper

2403 A886 5b multi   .45   .40

School of Postal Services — A887

2009, Feb. 22 Litho. *Perf. 14¾x14*
Granite Paper

2404 A887 3b multi   .35   .30

Red
Cross
A888

2009, Mar. 30
Granite Paper

2405 A888 3b multi   .35   .30

Prince Krom
Luang Wongsa
Dhiraj Snid (1808-
71),
Physician — A889

2009, Mar. 30   *Perf. 14x14¾*
Granite Paper

2406 A889 3b multi   .35   .30

Nos. 1736-1737 Surcharged in Gold

Methods, Perfs and Watermarks As
Before
2009, Apr. 1
2407 A564 30b on 6b #1736   *22.50 11.00*
2408 A564 46b on 9b #1737   *37.50 16.00*

Prasat Ta Muean, Surin
Province — A890

Prasat Ta Muean Thom, Surin
Province — A891

Prasat Ta Muean Tot, Surin
Province — A892

Prasat Sadok Kok Thom, Sa Kaeo
Province — A893

Perf. 14¾x14
2009, Apr. 2 Litho. Unwmk.
Granite Paper

2409 A890 3b multi   .35   .30
2410 A891 3b multi   .35   .30
2411 A892 3b multi   .35   .30
2412 A893 3b multi   .35   .30
 a.   Souvenir sheet of 4, #2409-
      2412, perf. 13½   2.00   2.00
      Nos. 2409-2412 (4)   1.40   1.20

Royal Headgear
A894

Designs: No. 2413, 5b, Gold brocade hat.
No. 2414, 5b, Felt hat. No. 2415, 5b, Battle
helmet. No. 2416, 5b, Grand diamond hat.

2009, Apr. 6   *Perf. 13*
Granite Paper

| 2413-2416 | A894 | Set of 4 | 1.75 | 1.75 |
| 2416a | | Souvenir sheet of 4, #2413-2416 | 2.40 | 2.40 |

No. 2416a sold for 25b.

Visakhapuja Day — A895

2009, May 8   *Perf. 14¼x14½*
Granite Paper

| 2417 | A895 | 3b multi | .35 | .30 |

Statues of Hindu
Gods — A896

Designs: No. 2418, 5b, Ganesa. No. 2419,
5b, Brahma. No. 2420, 5b, Narayana. No.
2421, 5b, Siva.

Litho. & Embossed
2009, June 2   *Perf. 13¼*
Granite Paper

| 2418-2421 | A896 | Set of 4 | 1.75 | 1.75 |
| 2421a | | Souvenir sheet of 4, #2418-2421 | 2.40 | 2.40 |

No. 2421a sold for 25b. No. 2421a exists
imperf. Value, $125.

Orchids — A897

Designs: No. 2422, 3b, Cattleya Queen
Sirikhit. No. 2423, 3b, Paphiopedilum Princess
Sangwan. No. 2424, 3b, Sirindhornia
pulchella. No. 2425, 3b, Phalaenopsis Prin-
cess Chulabhorn. No. 2426, 3b, Dendrobium
"Pink Nagarindra." No. 2427, 3b, Ascocenda
Sukontharat. No. 2428, 3b, Dendrobium
"Soamsawali."

2009, June 5   **Litho.**   *Perf. 14½x14*
Granite Paper

| 2422-2428 | A897 | Set of 7 | 1.25 | .95 |
| 2428a | | Sheet of 7, #2422-2428, perf. 13¼ | 1.75 | 1.40 |

No. 2428a sold for 30b.

Diplomatic Relations Between
Thailand and the Philippines, 60th
Anniv. — A898

No. 2429 — Stick dancers with denomination in: a, Pale yellow. b, Light blue.

2009, June 14
Granite Paper

| 2429 | A898 | 3b Horiz. pair, #a-b | .35 | .30 |

Thammasat
University, 75th
Anniv. — A899

2009, June 27   *Perf. 14x14½*

| 2430 | A899 | 3b multi | .35 | .30 |

A900

A901

A902

Candle
Procession
Festival — A903

2009, July 6   *Perf. 14x14½*

2431	A900	3b multi	.55	.50
2432	A901	3b multi	.55	.50
2433	A902	3b multi	.55	.50
2434	A903	3b multi	.55	.50
a.		Souvenir sheet of 4, #2431-2434, perf. 13¼	3.00	3.00
		Nos. 2431-2434 (4)	2.20	2.00

No. 2434a sold for 20b.

**King Bhumibol Adulyadej Type of
1996**
Die Cut Perf. 13¼x13¾

2009, Aug. 4   **Litho.**
Self-Adhesive

| 2435 | A550 | 3b bister brn & bl | .35 | .30 |

Natl. Communications Day — A904

2009, Aug. 4   *Perf. 14½x14*
Granite Paper

| 2436 | A904 | 3b multi | .35 | .30 |

Hun Lakorn Lek Puppetry — A905

Puppets and puppeteers with: No. 2437,
25b, Orange panel at right. No. 2438, 25b,
Orange panel at left.
No. 2439, 25b, No orange panel.

**Litho. With Three-Dimensional
Plastic Affixed**
2009, Aug. 4   *Perf. 17*
Self-Adhesive

| 2437-2438 | A905 | Set of 2 | 5.50 | 5.50 |

Souvenir Sheet
Perf. 12¼x12

| 2439 | A905 | 25b multi | 5.50 | 5.50 |

Miniature Sheet

Provincial Seals — A906

No. 2440 — Seals of: a, Phuket. b, Maha
Sarakham. c, Mukdahan. d, Mae Hong Son. e,
Yasothon. f, Yala. g, Roi Et. h, Ranong. i,
Rayong. j, Ratchaburi.

**Litho. & Embossed With Foil
Application**
2009, Sept. 7   *Perf. 13*
Granite Paper

| 2440 | A906 | 3b Sheet of 10, #a-j | 3.25 | 3.25 |

Guan Yin
Bodhisat
A907

2009, Sept. 9   **Litho.**   *Perf. 14½x14¼*
Granite Paper

| 2441 | A907 | 9b multi | 1.00 | 1.00 |
| a. | | Souvenir sheet of 1 | 1.60 | 1.60 |

No. 2441a sold for 15b. No. 2441a exists
imperf. without gum. Value, $160.

Natl. Telecommunications
Commission — A908

2009, Oct. 1   *Perf. 14x14½*
Granite Paper

| 2442 | A908 | 3b multi | .35 | .30 |

Royal
Carriages
A909

Designs: No. 2443, 3b, Four-wheeled dog
cart. No. 2444, 3b, Postillion landau. No. 2445,
3b, C-spring phaeton. No. 2446, 3b, Glass
state coach.

2009, Oct. 7   *Perf. 13¼x13½*
Granite Paper

| 2443-2446 | A909 | Set of 4 | 1.25 | 1.25 |
| 2446a | | Souvenir sheet of 4, #2443-2446 | 2.25 | 2.25 |

No. 2446a sold for 20b.

A910

A911

A912

Intl. Letter Writing Week — A913

2009, Oct. 9   *Perf. 14x14½*
Granite Paper

2447	A910	3b multi	.35	.30
2448	A911	3b multi	.35	.30
2449	A912	3b multi	.35	.30
2450	A913	3b multi	.35	.30
a.		Souvenir sheet of 4, #2447-2450, perf. 13½	2.25	2.25
		Nos. 2447-2450 (4)	1.40	1.20

No. 2450a sold for 20b.

New Year 2010 — A914

Flowers: No. 2451, 3b, Drosera peltata. No. 2452, 3b, Sonerila griffithii. No. 2453, 3b, Cyanotis arachnoidea. No. 2454, 3b, Caulokaempferia saxicola.

2009, Nov. 15   *Perf. 14½x14*
Granite Paper

2451-2454	A914	Set of 4	1.25	1.25
2454a		Souvenir sheet of 4, #2451-2454	1.60	1.60

No. 2454a sold for 15b.

Princess Bejaratana Ratsuda, 84th Birthday — A915

2009, Nov. 24   *Perf. 13¼*
Granite Paper

2455	A915	3b multi	.45	.40

Royal Thai Army Medical Department, 110th Anniv. — A916

Designs: No. 2456, 3b, Building, medic treating soldier. No. 2457, 3b, Soldier with rifle, knapsack and medical bag, soldiers carrying litter to medical helicopter. No. 2458, 3b, Medic treating soldier, doctors in surgery. No. 2459, 3b, Hospital, soldier saluting.

2009, Nov. 25   *Perf. 14½x14*
Granite Paper

2456-2459	A916	Set of 4	1.25	1.25
2459a		Souvenir sheet of 4, #2456-2459	16.00	—

King Bhumibol Adulyadej, 82nd Birthday — A917

2009, Dec. 5   *Perf. 14½x14*
Granite Paper

2460	A917	9b multi	1.00	1.00

Thailand Earth Observation Satellite — A918

2009, Dec. 5   *Litho.*
Granite Paper

2461	A918	3b multi	.35	.30

A gritty substance has been applied to portions of the design.

Education for the Blind — A919

2009, Dec. 12   **Litho. & Embossed**
Granite Paper

2462	A919	3b multi	.35	.30

New Year 2010 (Year of the Tiger) — A920

2010, Jan. 1   **Litho.**   *Perf. 13*
Granite Paper

2463	A920	3b multi	.25	.25

2010 Population and Housing Census — A921

2010, Jan. 5   **Litho.**   *Perf. 13½*
Granite Paper

2465	A921	3b multi	.25	.25

King Bhumibol Adulyadej Type of 1996

2010, Jan. 8   *Perf. 14x14½*
Granite Paper

2465A	A550	3b bister brn & bl	.25	.25

Young Phra Sang A922

Chao Ngo and Nang Rotchana — A923

Phra Sang A924

Phra Sang Playing Polo — A925

2010, Jan. 9   *Perf. 14½x14*
Granite Paper

2466	A922	3b multi	.25	.25
2467	A923	3b multi	.25	.25
2468	A924	3b multi	.25	.25
2469	A925	3b multi	.25	.25
		Nos. 2466-2469 (4)	1.00	1.00

Characters from Sang Thong. National Children's Day.

Euah Suntornsanan (1910-81), Composer and Musician — A926

2010, Jan. 21   *Perf. 14x14½*
Granite Paper

2470	A926	3b multi	.25	.25

Child Praying A927

Birthday Cake A928

Flowers A929

Heart A930

Moon and Stars A931

Balloons A932

2010, Jan. 28   **Litho.**   *Perf. 14x14½*
Granite Paper (#2471-2476)

2471	A927	3b multi	.25	.25
2472	A928	3b multi	.25	.25
2473	A929	3b multi	.25	.25
2474	A930	3b multi	.25	.25
2475	A931	3b multi	.25	.25
2476	A932	3b multi	.25	.25
		Nos. 2471-2476 (6)	1.50	1.50

Litho. With Holographic Film
Self-Adhesive
Die Cut Perf. 13½x13¾

2477	A927	3b multi	.25	.25
2478	A928	3b multi	.25	.25
2479	A929	3b multi	.25	.25
2480	A930	3b multi	.25	.25
2481	A931	3b multi	.25	.25
2482	A932	3b multi	.25	.25
a.		Sheet of 6, #2477-2482	1.50	
		Nos. 2477-2482 (6)	1.50	1.50

No. 2482a sold for 25b.

Red Rose — A933

Litho. & Embossed
2010, Feb. 5   *Perf. 13*
Granite Paper

2483	A933	5b multi	.30	.25

A rose-scented scratch-and-sniff panel was applied over a rose leaf. A souvenir sheet containing one No. 2483 sold for 14b.

A934

A935

Chinese Deities — A936

2010, Feb. 8   **Litho.**   *Perf. 14x14½*
Granite Paper

2484	A934	5b multi	.30	.25
2485	A935	5b multi	.30	.25
2486	A936	5b multi	.30	.25
a.		Souvenir sheet of 3, #2484-2486, perf. 13½x13¼	1.50	1.10
		Nos. 2484-2486 (3)	.90	.75

No. 2486a sold for 24b.

A937

A938

A939

Fantasy World Painting
Competition — A940

2010, Feb. 25   Litho.   Perf. 13½
Granite Paper

2487	A937	5b multi	.30	.25
2488	A938	5b multi	.30	.25
2489	A939	5b multi	.30	.25
2490	A940	5b multi	.30	.25
a.		Souvenir sheet of 4, #2487-2490	1.75	1.40
		Nos. 2487-2490 (4)	1.20	1.00

Bangkok 2010 Intl. Stamp Exhibition. No. 2490a sold for 28b.

Red
Cross — A941

2010, Mar. 30   Perf. 13½
Granite Paper

2491	A941	3b multi	.25	.25

Postman
Carrying
Parcel — A942

2010, Mar. 30   Perf. 13
Granite Paper

2492	A942	3b multi	.25	.25

Heritage Conservation Day — A943

Designs: No. 2493, 3b, Jalimangalasana Residence, Sanam Chandra Palace. No. 2494, 3b, Phiman Chakri Hall, Phyathai Palace. No. 2495, 3b, Phra Ram Ratchaniwet Palace. No. 2496, 3b, Main Building, Srapathum Palace.

2010, Apr. 2   Perf. 14½x14
Granite Paper

2493-2496	A943	Set of 4	.75	.55
2496a		Souvenir sheet of 4, #2493-2496, perf. 13½	1.25	.95

No. 2496a sold for 19b.

King Chao
Phraya
Chakkri
(Rama I)
(1736-1809)
A944

2010, Apr. 6   Perf. 13¼
Granite Paper

2497	A944	3b multi	.25	.25

Wedding of King Bhumibol Adulyadej
and Queen Sirikit, 60th Anniv. — A945

King and Queen: No. 2498, 15b, As young couple. No. 2499, 15b, As older couple.

**Litho. & Embossed With Foil
Application**
2010, Apr. 28   Perf. 13¼

2498-2499	A945	Set of 2	1.90	1.40
2499a		Souvenir sheet of 2, #2498-2499	3.75	3.00

Values for Nos. 2498-2499 are for stamps with surrounding selvage. No. 2499a sold for 60b.

Thai Airways International, 50th
Anniv. — A946

Airplanes: No. 2500, 3b, DC-6. No. 2501, 3b, DC-10. No. 2502, 3b, Boeing 747-400. No. 2503, 3b, Airbus A340-600.

Litho. & Embossed
2010, May 1   Perf. 14¼x14½
Granite Paper

2500-2503	A946	Set of 4	.75	.55
2503a		Souvenir sheet of 4, #2500-2503	1.40	1.10

No. 2503a sold for 22b.

Coronation of
King
Bhumibol
Adulyadej,
60th Anniv.
A947

2010, May 5   Litho.   Perf. 13¼
Granite Paper

2504	A947	9b multi	.55	.40

Visakhapuja Day — A948

2010, May 28   Perf. 14¼x14½
Granite Paper

2505	A948	3b multi	.25	.25
a.		Souvenir sheet of 4, #2293, 2361, 2417, 2505	1.25	.95

No. 2505a sold for 20b.

Tourism Authority of Thailand, 50th
Anniv. — A949

Designs: No. 2506, 3b, Wat Arun, Bangkok. No. 2507, 3b, Royal barge. No. 2508, 3b, Canoeists near shore. No. 2509, 3b, Tourists on elephants fording river.

2010, June 1   Litho.
Granite Paper

2506-2509	A949	Set of 4	.75	.55

Election
Commission, 12th
Anniv. — A950

2010, June 9   Perf. 13½
Granite Paper

2510	A950	3b multi	.25	.25

Miniature Sheet
No. 1960 Surcharged in Silver

Designs as before.

Method and Perf. As Before
2010, June 16
Granite Paper

2511	A642	Sheet of 9	55.00	42.50
a.-f.		100b on 3b Any single	6.00	4.50
g.-i.		100b on 6b Any single	6.00	4.50

No. 1776 Surcharged in Gold

Method and Perf. As Before
2010, June 16
Granite Paper

2512	A577	200b on 9b #1776	12.50	9.50

Bangkok General
Post Office
Building, 70th
Anniv. — A951

Designs: No. 2513, 3b, Sculptures of Type A15 stamp, Garuda. No. 2514, 3b, Sculptures of Type A29 stamp, man at table. 5b, General Post Office Building, horiz. (57x23mm).

Perf. 14x14½, 14½x14
2010, June 24   Litho.
Granite Paper

2513-2515	A951	Set of 3	.70	.55

King Nang
Khlao Chao
Youhua
(Rama III)
(1787-1851)
A952

2010, July 21   Perf. 13¼
Granite Paper

2516	A952	3b multi	.25	.25

Miniature Sheet

Provincial Seals — A953

No. 2517 — Seals of: a, Lop Buri. b, Lampang. c, Lamphun. d, Loei. e, Si Sa Ket. f, Sakon Nakhon. g, Songkhla. h, Satun. i, Samut Prakan. j, Samut Songkhram.

Litho. With Foil Application
2010, July 23   Perf. 13
Granite Paper

2517	A953	3b Sheet of 10, #a-j	1.90	1.40

National Communications Day — A954

2010, Aug. 4   Litho.   Perf. 14½x14
Granite Paper

2518	A954	3b multi	.25	.25

Peacock
A955

Inscriptions: No. 2519, 15b, Thai Silk. No. 2520, 15b, Thai Silk Blend. No. 2521, 25b, Classic Thai Silk. No. 2522, 25b, Royal Thai Silk.

Litho. With Foil Application on Affixed Silk Oval

2010, Aug. 4   **Perf. 13¼**
2519-2522 A955 Set of 4   5.00 3.75

Bangkok 2010 Intl. Stamp Exhibition. A souvenir sheet containing one No. 2522 sold for 60b.

Orchids — A956

Rhynchostylis gigantea varieties: No. 2523, 3b, Speckle. No. 2524, 3b, Kultana strain. No. 2525, 3b, Alba. No. 2526, 3b, Rubrum.

2010, Aug. 5   Litho.   Perf. 14x14½
Granite Paper
2523-2526 A956   Set of 4   .75 .55
2526a   Souvenir sheet of 4,
              #2523-2526, perf. 13½   1.25 .95

No. 2526a sold for 20b. A sheet similar to No. 2526a with the emblem of the 4th Siam Paragon Bangkok Royal Orchid Paradise sold for 80b.

Thai Literature Heritage — A957

2010, Aug. 7   Perf. 14½x14
Granite Paper
2527 A957 3b multi   .25 .25

Flag of   Cassia
Thailand — A958   Flowers — A959

2010, Aug. 12   Perf. 14¼x14½
Granite Paper
2528 A958 3b multi   .25 .25
2529 A959 3b multi   .25 .25

Nos. 1687 and 1689 Surcharged

Methods, Perfs. and Watermarks As Before

2010, Aug. 27
2530 A543 10b on 3b #1687   .65 .50
2531 A543 10b on 9b #1689   .65 .50

No. 1736 Surcharged in Gold

Method, Perf. and Watermark As Before

2010, Sept. 1
2532 A564 10b on 6b #1736   .65 .50

Miniature Sheet

Queen Savang Vadhana (1862-1955) — A960

No. 2533: a, Queen Savang Vadhana. b, Prince Mahidol and his wife, Princess Srinagarindra. c, King Bhumibol Adulyadej and women (denomination in yellow), horiz. d, King Bhumibol Adulyadej and Queen Sirikit (denomination in dark blue), horiz.

**Perf. 13¼ (#2533a),
13¼x13¼x14½x13¼ (#2533b),
14½x14**

2010, Sept. 10   Litho.   Unwmk.
Granite Paper
2533 A960 3b Sheet of 4, #a-d   .80 .60

Royal Thai Mint, 150th Anniv. — A961

No. 2534: a, Coin, old Mint building, denomination at LR. b, Coin, new Mint building, denomination at LL.

Litho. & Embossed
2010, Sept. 17   Perf. 13¼
Granite Paper
2534   Horiz. pair   .70 .55
 a.-b.   A961 5b Either single .35 .25
 c.   Souvenir sheet of 2, #2534a-
           2534b   1.40 1.10

No. 2534c sold for 20b.

National Youth Day — A962

2010, Sept. 20 Litho. Perf. 14½x14
Granite Paper
2535 A962 3b multi   .25 .25

Tin Toys — A963

Designs: No. 2536, 3b, Wind-up rabbit and chicken. No. 2537, 3b, Chinese rattle drums. No. 2538, 3b, Pop gun. No. 2539, 3b, Boats. No. 2540, 3b, Boy on tricycle. No. 2541, 3b, Tops.

2010, Oct. 5   Perf. 13
Granite Paper
2536-2541 A963 Set of 6   1.25 .95

A souvenir sheet containing Nos. 2536-2538 and a souvenir sheet containing Nos. 2539-2541 exist. Each sold for 20b.

Curves — A964

2010, Oct. 5   Perf. 13¼
Granite Paper
2542 A964 3b green   .25 .25
2543 A964 3b lemon   .25 .25
2544 A964 3b blue   .25 .25
      Nos. 2542-2544 (3)   .75 .75

Department of Comptroller General, 120th Anniv. — A965

2010, Oct. 7   Perf. 14½x14
Granite Paper
2545 A965 3b multi   .25 .25

Goddess Guan Yin — A966

2010, Oct. 10   Perf. 14½x14¼
Granite Paper
2546 A966 9b multi   .60 .45
 a.   Souvenir sheet of 1   1.10 .85

No. 2546a sold for 15b.

King Bhumibol Adulyadej — A967

2010   Litho.   Perf. 13½x13¼
Granite Paper
2547 A967   1b blue   .25 .25
2548 A967   2b lake   .25 .25
2549 A967   3b green   .25 .25
2550 A967   5b fawn   .35 .30
2551 A967   6b violet   .40 .30
2552 A967   7b lilac rose   .50 .35
2553 A967   9b yel bister   .60 .45
2554 A967 10b brown & blk   .70 .55
2555 A967 12b bl grn & gray
            bl   .80 .60
2556 A967 15b bis & dk grn   1.00 .75
 a.   Souvenir sheet of 10,
           #2547-2556   5.25 4.25

Litho. & Engr.
2557 A967 50b pur & bl grn   3.50 2.60
2558 A967 100b apple grn &
            grn   6.75 5.25
2559 A967 200b rose & brn   13.50 10.00

Size:24x29mm
2560 A967 500b org brn & brn   34.00 26.00
 a.   Souvenir sheet of 4, #2557-
           2560   60.00 45.00
      Nos. 2547-2560 (14)   62.85 47.90

Issued: Nos. 2547-2556, 2556a, 10/10; Nos. 2557-2560, 2560a, 11/11.

King Chulalongkorn (Rama V) (1853-1910) A968

2010, Oct. 15   Litho.   Perf. 13¼
Granite Paper
2561 A968 9b multi   .60 .45

Vajiravudh College, Cent. — A969

2010, Nov. 11   Perf. 13½
Granite Paper
2562 A969 3b multi   .25 .25

A970

A971

A972

Fireworks
A973

2010, Nov. 15   *Perf. 13½*
Granite Paper

2563	A970	3b multi	.25	.25
2564	A971	3b multi	.25	.25
2565	A972	3b multi	.25	.25
2566	A973	3b multi	.25	.25
a.	Souvenir sheet of 4, #2563-2566		1.40	1.10
	Nos. 2563-2566 (4)		1.00	1.00

No. 2566a sold for 20b.

King
Bhumibol
Adulyadej,
83rd Birthday
A974

Litho. With Rice Grain Affixed
2010, Dec. 5   *Perf. 13¼*
Granite Paper

2567	A974	9b multi	.60	.45

New Year 2011
(Year of the
Rabbit) — A975

2011, Jan. 1   **Litho.**   *Perf. 13*
Granite Paper

2568	A975	3b multi	.25	.25

Khun Chang — A976

Khun Phaen — A977

Kumanthong — A978

Pimpiralai — A979

2011, Jan. 8   *Perf. 13¼*
Granite Paper

2569	A976	3b multi	.25	.25
2570	A977	3b multi	.25	.25
2571	A978	3b multi	.25	.25
2572	A979	3b multi	.25	.25
	Nos. 2569-2572 (4)		1.00	1.00

Khun Chang Khun Phaen, epic poem.

Fruits and
Vegetables
A980

Designs: No. 2573, 3b, Bottle gourd. No. 2574, 3b, Lime. No. 2575, 3b, Tomato. No. 2576, 3b, Pumpkin.

2011, Jan. 15   *Perf. 13½*
Granite Paper

2573-2576	A980	Set of 4	.80	.60

Li Tie
Guai — A981

Han Zhong
Li — A982

Lu Dong
Bin — A983

Zhang Guo
Lao — A984

Lan Cai
He — A985

He Xian
Gu — A986

Han Xiang
Zi — A987

Cao Guo
Jiu — A988

2011, Feb. 1   **Litho. & Embossed**
Granite Paper

2577	A981	3b multi	.25	.25
2578	A982	3b multi	.25	.25
2579	A983	3b multi	.25	.25
2580	A984	3b multi	.25	.25
2581	A985	3b multi	.25	.25
2582	A986	3b multi	.25	.25
2583	A987	3b multi	.25	.25
2584	A988	3b multi	.25	.25
a.	Souvenir sheet of 8, #2577-2584		2.60	2.00
	Nos. 2577-2584 (8)		2.00	2.00

Eight Chinese Immortals.

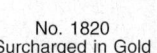

No. 1820
Surcharged in Gold

No. 1737 Surcharged in Gold

No. 2349
Surcharged

Methods, Perfs and Papers As
Before
2011

2585	A550	12b on 9b #1820	.80	.60
2586	A564	50b on 9b #1737	3.25	2.50
2588	A841	Sheet of 12	39.00	39.00
a.-l.	50b on 9b Any single, #2349a-2349l		3.25	2.50

Issued: Nos. 2585, 2586, 2588, 2/2.

Charoen Krung
Road, 150th
Anniv. — A989

2011, Feb. 5   **Litho.**   *Perf. 14½x14¼*
Granite Paper

2589	A989	3b multi	.25	.25

Love — A990

No. 2590 — Heart of: a, Roses. b, Concentric lines.

2011, Feb. 7   *Perf. 13*
Granite Paper

2590	A990	5b Horiz. pair, #a-b	.65	.50

Suankularb Long Building, Bangkok,
Cent. — A991

2011, Mar. 8   *Perf. 14½x14*
Granite Paper

2591	A991	3b multi	.25	.25

Fine Arts
Department,
Cent. — A992

2011, Mar. 27   **Perf. 14x14½**
Granite Paper
2592 A992 3b multi   .25   .25

Princess Maha
Chakri Sirindhorn
Wearing Red
Cross
Uniform — A993

2011, Mar. 30   **Perf. 13¼**
Granite Paper
2593 A993 3b multi   .25   .25

A994

A995

A996

Muang Tam Religious Sanctuary,
Prakhon Chai — A997

2011, Apr. 2   **Perf. 14½x14**
Granite Paper
2594 A994 3b multi   .25   .25
2595 A995 3b multi   .25   .25
2596 A996 3b multi   .25   .25
2597 A997 3b multi   .25   .25
  a.   Souvenir sheet of 4, #2594-
       2597   1.40 1.10
     Nos. 2594-2597 (4)   1.00 1.00
Thai Heritage Conservation Day. No. 2597a
sold for 20b.

Momrajawongse
Kukrit Pramoj
(1911-95), Prime
Minister — A998

Kukrit Pramoj: No. 2598, 3b, Wearing uniform with sash, yellow orange panel at right.
No. 2599, 3b, Wearing traditional costume,
olive green panel at right. No. 2600, 3b, With
dogs, brown panel at right, horiz. No. 2601,
3b, With Mao Zedong, gray panel at right,
horiz.

2011, Apr. 20   **Perf. 13¼**
Granite Paper
2598-2601 A998 Set of 4   .80   .60

Diplomatic Relations Between
Thailand and Laos, 60th
Anniv. — A999

No. 2602: a, Woman, denomination at LR.
b, Woman, denomination at LL. c, Cassia fistula flowers, denomination at LR. d, Plumeria
flowers, denomination at LL.

2011, Apr. 22   **Perf. 14x14½**
Granite Paper
2602 A999 3b Block of 4, #a-d   .80   .60

Postman With
Fork, Spoon and
Foods — A1000

2011, May 10   Litho.   **Perf. 13**
Granite Paper
2603 A1000 3b multi   .25   .25

Pridi Banomyong (1900-83), Prime
Minister — A1001

No. 2605 — Banomyong: a, In suit and tie.
b, Wearing uniform and sash.

2011, May 11   Litho.   **Perf. 13¼**
Granite Paper
2605 A1001 3b Horiz. pair, #a-b   .40   .30

Panyananda Bhikkhu (1911-2007),
Buddhist Monk — A1002

Bhikkhu and: No. 2606, 3b, Thai text. No.
2607, 3b, Buddhist temple. No. 2608, 3b,
Sculpture. No. 2609, 3b, Shell-shaped award.

2011, May 11   **Perf. 13¼**
Granite Paper
2606-2609 A1002 Set of 4   .80   .60

Visakhapuja
Day — A1003

2011, May 17   **Perf. 14½x14¼**
Granite Paper
2610 A1003 3b multi   .25   .25
A souvenir sheet containing one example of
No. 2610 sold for 10b.

Orchid Varieties
A1004

Designs: No. 2611, 3b, Dendrobium
"Cherluk Red." No. 2612, 3b, Dendrobium "Lai
Sirin." No. 2613, 3b, Dendrobium "Suree
Peach." No. 2614, 3b, Dendrobium "Cheetah."

2011, June 2   **Perf. 14x14½**
Granite Paper
2611-2614 A1004 Set of 4   .80   .60
2614a   Souvenir sheet of 4,
            #2611-2614, perf. 13½   1.40 1.10
No. 2614a sold for 20b. A sheet similar to
No. 2614a, but with the emblem of the 5th
Siam Paragon Bangkok Royal Orchid Paradise
and the date of the show, sold for 100b.

Department of Science Service, 120th
Anniv. — A1005

2011, June 23   **Perf. 14½x14**
Granite Paper
2615 A1005 3b multi   .25   .25
No. 2615 was printed in sheets of 20 with
stamps from the right column having purple
engine turning lines in the background.

Scouting in Thailand, Cent. — A1006

2011, July 1   **Perf. 13¼**
Granite Paper
2616 A1006 3b multi   .25   .25

A1007

Diplomatic Relations Between
Thailand and Portugal, 500th
Anniv. — A1008

No. 2617: a, Portuguese caravel, rowboats,
Thai buildings and temples. b, Elephant and
riders at dockside.
No. 2618: a, Portuguese caravel, Thai buildings. b, Thai boats and buildings.

2011, July 20   **Perf. 13½**
Granite Paper
2617 A1007 3b Horiz. pair, #a-b   .40   .30
2618 A1008 3b Horiz. pair, #a-b   .40   .30

See Portugal Nos. 3334-3335.

Miniature Sheet

Provincial Seals — A1009

No. 2619 — Seals of: a, Samut Sakhon. b,
Sa Kaeo. c, Saraburi. d, Sing Buri. e,
Sukhothai. f, Suphan Buri. g, Surat Thani. h,
Surin. i, Nong Khai. j, Nong Bua Lam Phu.

**Litho. & Embossed With Foil
Application**
2011, July 20   **Perf. 13½**
Granite Paper
2619 A1009 3b Sheet of 10, #a-j   2.00 1.50
Sheets of ten identical stamps were available, but these appear to have been sold locally
and not through the philatelic bureau.

Thai Alphabet
A1010

No. 2620 — Various characters of Thai
alphabet that are the first consonants of the
word for: a, Chicken. b, Eggs. c, Bottles. d,
Water buffalo. e, Person wearing red shirt. f,
Bell. g, Snake. h, Plates. i, Cymbals on string.
j, Elephant. k, Chain on stump. l, Trees. m,
Woman weaing pink blouse. n, Headdress. o,
Javelin. p, Pedestal. q, Mandodari (girl wearing headdress). r, Old man. s, Child wearing
Buddhist monk's robe. t, Child in overalls. u,
Turtle. v, Bags. w, Soldier. x, Flag.
No. 2621 — Various characters of Thai
alphabet that are the first consonants of the
word for: a, Mouse. b, Leaves. c, Fish. d, Bee
on flowers. e, Lids of pots. f, Bowl. g, Teeth. h,
Sailboat. i, Horse. j, Yaksha (Buddhist giant).
k, Boat. l, Monkey. m, Ring. n, Pavilion. o,

Hermit in cave. p, Tiger. q, Chest. r, Kite. s, Basin with flower. t, Owl.

2011, July 29   Litho.   Perf. 14¼
Granite Paper

2620	Sheet of 24	6.00	6.00
a.-x.	A1010 1b Any single	.25	.25
2621	Sheet of 20 + 4 labels	5.00	5.00
a.-t.	A1010 1b Any single	.25	.25

Communications
Day — A1011

2011, Aug. 4   Perf. 14x14½
Granite Paper

| 2622 | A1011 3b multi | | .25 | .25 |

A1012

A1013

A1014

Likay Performers
A1015

Litho. With Glitter Affixed
2011, Aug. 4   Perf. 14x14½
Granite Paper

2623	A1012 5b multi	.35	.30
2624	A1013 5b multi	.35	.30
2625	A1014 5b multi	.35	.30
2626	A1015 5b multi	.35	.30
a.	Souvenir sheet of 4, #2623-2626, perf. 13½	2.00	1.50
	Nos. 2623-2626 (4)	1.40	1.20

Thaipex 2011 Intl. Philatelic Exhibition, Bangkok. No. 2626a sold for 30b.

Philatelists Association of
Thailand — A1016

2011, Aug. 9   Litho.   Perf. 13¼
Granite Paper

| 2627 | A1016 3b multi | .25 | .25 |

Miniature Sheet

Queen Savang Vadhana (1862-
1955) — A1017

No. 2628 — Queen Savang Vadhana: a, As child, with King Chulalongkorn (pink background). b, With Crown Prince Maha Vajirunhis (olive green background. c, With Prince Mahitala Dhibesra Adulyadej Vikrom and Princess Valaya Alongkorn (blue violet background), horiz. d, With King Ananda Mahidol, King Bhumibol Adulyadej, Princess Galyani Vadhana, and Prince Rangsit Prayurasakdi (blue green background), horiz.

2011, Sept. 10   Perf. 13¼
Granite Paper

| 2628 | A1017 3b Sheet of 4, #a-d | .80 | .60 |

Worldwide Fund for Nature
(WWF) — A1018

Cats: No. 2629, 3b, Marbled cat. No. 2630, 3b, Asiatic golden cat. No. 2631, 3b, Leopard cat. No. 2632, 3b, Flat-headed cat.

2011, Sept. 26   Perf. 13
Granite Paper

| 2629-2632 | A1018   Set of 4 | .80 | .60 |
| 2632a | Souvenir sheet of 4, #2629-2632, + label | 1.40 | 1.10 |

No. 2632a sold for 20b.

SEMI-POSTAL STAMPS

Nos. 164-175
Overprinted in Red

1918, Jan. 11   Unwmk.   Perf. 14

B1	A21	2s orange brown	2.40	2.40
B2	A21	3s emerald	2.40	2.40
B3	A21	5s rose red	4.75	4.75
B4	A21	10s black & olive	8.00	8.00
B5	A21	15s blue	8.75	6.00
B6	A22	1b blue & gray blk	45.00	32.50
B7	A22	2b car rose & brn	65.00	27.50
B8	A22	3b yel grn & blk	100.00	55.00
B9	A22	5b dp vio & blk	250.00	80.00
a.		Double overprint	775.00	400.00
B10	A22	10b ol grn & vio brn	625.00	240.00
B11	A22	20b sea grn & brn	2,250.	1,400.
		Nos. B1-B11 (11)	3,361.	1,856.

Excellent counterfeit overprints are known. These stamps were sold at an advance over face value, the excess being given to the Siamese Red Cross Society.

Stamps of 1905-19
Handstamp
Overprinted

1920, Feb.
On Nos. 164, 146, 168

B12	A21	2s (+ 3s) org brn	42.50	42.50
B13	A21	3s (+ 2s) green	45.00	45.00
B14	A21	15s (+ 5s) blue	140.00	120.00

On No. 105

| B15 | A15 | 1t (+ 25s) | 375.00 | 350.00 |

On Nos. 185-186

B16	A21	5s on 6s (+ 5s)	62.50	62.50
a.		Overprint inverted		
B17	A21	10s on 12s (+ 5s)	70.00	70.00
		Nos. B12-B17 (6)	735.00	690.00
		Set, never hinged	1,125.	

Sold at an advance over face value, the excess being for the benefit of the Wild Tiger Corps. Counterfeits exist.

Stamps of 1905-20
Handstamp
Overprinted

On Nos. 164, 146, 168

B18	A21	2s (+ 3s) org brn	40.00	40.00
B19	A21	3s (+ 2s) green	40.00	40.00
a.		Pair, one without ovpt.		
B20	A21	15s (+ 5s) blue	65.00	65.00

On No. 105

| B21 | A15 | 1t (+ 25s) | 290.00 | 290.00 |

On No. 186

| B22 | A21 | 10s on 12s (+ 5s) | 65.00 | 65.00 |

On No. 190

B23	A23	5s (+ 5s)	100.00	100.00
		Nos. B18-B23 (6)	600.00	600.00
		Set, never hinged	925.00	

Sold at an advance over face value, the excess being for the benefit of the Wild Tiger Corps. Counterfeits exist.

Nos. 187-188, 190,
193-194, 196, 198
Overprinted in Blue or
Red

1920, Dec. 21

B24	A23	2s brown, *yel*	15.00	15.00
B25	A23	3s grn, *grn* (R)	15.00	15.00
B26	A23	5s rose, *pale rose*	15.00	15.00
B27	A23	10s blk & org (R)	15.00	15.00
B28	A23	15s bl, *bluish* (R)	30.00	30.00
B29	A23	25s chocolate	100.00	100.00
B30	A23	50s ocher & blk (R)	225.00	225.00
		Nos. B24-B30 (7)	415.00	415.00
		Set, never hinged	625.00	

Nos. B12-B30 were sold at an advance over face value, the excess being for the benefit of the Wild Tiger Corps. Counterfeits exist.

Nos. 170-172
Surcharged in Red

1939, Apr. 6   Unwmk.   Perf. 14

B31	A22	5s + 5s on 1b	22.50	22.50
B32	A22	10s + 5s on 2b	27.50	27.50
B33	A22	15s + 5s on 3b	27.50	27.50
		Nos. B31-B33 (3)	77.50	77.50
		Set, never hinged	130.00	

Founding of the Intl. Red Cross Soc., 75th anniv.
Bottom line of overprint is different on Nos. B32-B33.

> **Catalogue values for unused stamps in this section, from this point to the end of the section, are for Never Hinged items.**

No. 214 Surcharged
in Carmine

1952   Unwmk.   Perf. 12½

| B34 | A25 | 80s + 20s blue & blk | 22.50 | 15.00 |

New constitution.

Red Cross and
Dancer — SP1

Lithographed, Cross Typographed
1953, Apr. 6   Wmk. 299   Perf. 11
Cross in Red, Dancer Dark Blue

B35	SP1	25s + 25s yellow grn	12.50	5.00
B36	SP1	50s + 50s brt rose	25.00	8.00
B37	SP1	1b + 1b lt blue	32.50	9.00
		Nos. B35-B37 (3)	70.00	22.00

60th anniv. of the founding of the Siamese Red Cross Society.

Nos. B35-B37
Overprinted in
Black

1955, Apr. 3
Cross in Red, Dancer Dark Blue

B38	SP1	25s + 25s yel grn	24.00	16.00
B39	SP1	50s + 50s brt rose	160.00	110.00
B40	SP1	1b + 1b lt blue	210.00	160.00
		Nos. B38-B40 (3)	394.00	286.00

Counterfeits exist.

Red Cross Cent. Emblem — SP2

1963 Wmk. 334 Litho. Perf. 13½
B41 50s + 10s cross at right .80 .40
B42 50s + 10s cross at left .80 .40
　　a. SP2 Pair, #B41-B42 2.40 1.60
　　　Cent. of the Intl. Red Cross.

Nos. B41-B42
Surcharged

1973, Feb. 15
B43 SP2 75s + 25s on 50s + 10s 1.40 1.20
B44 SP3 75s + 25s on 50s + 10s 1.40 1.20
　　a. Pair, #B43-B44 3.00 2.40
　　　Red Cross Fair, Feb. 15-19.

Nos. B41-B42
Surcharged

1974, Feb. 2
B45 SP2 75s + 25s on 50s + 10s 1.40 1.40
B46 SP3 75s + 25s on 50s + 10s 1.40 1.40
　　a. Pair, #B45-B46 2.90 2.90
　　　Red Cross Fair, Feb. 1974. Position of
surcharge reversed on No. B46.

Nos. B41-B42
Surcharged

1975, Feb 11 52
B47 SP2 75s + 25s on 50s + 10s 1.40 1.40
B48 SP3 75s + 25s on 50s + 10s 1.40 1.40
　　a. Pair, #B47-B48 2.90 2.90
　　　Red Cross Fair, Feb. 1975. Position of
surcharge reversed on No. B48.

Nos. B41-B42
Surcharged

1976, Feb. 26
B49 SP2 75s + 25s on 50s + 10s 1.40 1.40
B50 SP3 75s + 25s on 50s + 10s 1.40 1.40
　　a. Pair, #B49-B50 2.90 2.90
　　　Red Cross Fair, Feb. 16-Mar. 1. Position of
surcharge reversed on #B50.

Nos. B41-B42
Surcharged

1977, Apr. 6 Wmk. 334 Perf. 13½
B51 SP2 75s + 25s on 50s + 10s 1.40 .65
B52 SP3 75s + 25s on 50s + 10s 1.40 .65
　　a. Pair, #B51-B52 2.90 2.90
　　　Red Cross Fair 1977.

Red Cross　　　Eye and Blind
Blood　　　　　People
Collection　　　SP5
SP4

Wmk. 329
1978, Apr. 6 Photo. Perf. 13
B53 SP4 2.75b + 25s multi 2.25 2.00
　　　"Give blood, save life."
　　　For surcharge see No. B58.

Perf. 14x13½
1979, Apr. 6 Litho. Wmk. 368
B54 SP5 75s + 25s multi .85 .50
　　　"Give an eye, save new life." Red Cross Fair.
Surtax was for Thai Red Cross.
For surcharge see No. B59.

Extracting Snake Venom, Red
Cross — SP6

1980, Apr. Perf. 11x13
B55 SP6 75s + 25s multi 1.10 .95
　　　Complete booklet, 10 #B55 24.00
　　　Red Cross Fair. Surtax was for Thai Red
Cross.
For surcharge see No. B60.

Nurse Helping Victim — SP7

1981, Apr. 6 Wmk. 377 Perf. 12½
B56 SP7 75 + 25s red & gray grn 1.50 1.40
　　　Red Cross Fair (canceled). Surtax was for
Thai Red Cross.
For surcharge see No. B65.

Red
Cross
Fair
SP8

Perf. 13x13½
1983, Apr. 6 Litho. Wmk. 329
B57 SP8 1.25b + 25s multi 1.20 1.00
　　　Surtax was for Thai Red Cross.

No. B53 Surcharged

1984, Apr. 6 Photo. Perf. 13
B58 SP4 3.25b + 25s on 2.75b + 25s 2.25 4.50
　　　Red Cross Fair. Surtax was for Thai Red
Cross. Overprint translates: Red Cross
Donation.

No. B54
Surcharged

Wmk. 368
1985, Mar. 30 Litho. Perf. 13
B59 SP5 2b + 25c on 75s + 25s 1.90 1.90
　　　Surtax for the Thai Red Cross.

No. B55 Overprinted and Surcharged

1986, Apr. 6 Wmk. 368 Perf. 11x13
B60 SP6 2b + 25s on 75s + 25s 2.25 2.25
　　　Natl. Children's Day. Surtax for Natl. Red
Cross Society. Overprint translates "Red
Cross Donation."

Natl. Scouting Movement, 75th Anniv.,
15th Asia-Pacific Conference,
Thailand — SP9

　　#B61, Scouts, saluting, community service.
#B62, Scout activities. #B63, King & queen at
ceremony. #B64, 15th Asia-Pacific conf.

1986, Nov. 7 Wmk. 385 Perf. 13½
B61 SP9 2b + 50s multi .50 .35
B62 SP9 2b + 50s multi .50 .35
B63 SP9 2b + 50s multi .50 .35
B64 SP9 2b + 50s multi .50 .35
　　　Nos. B61-B64 (4) 2.00 1.40
　　　Surtax for the Natl. Scouting Fund.

No. B56 Surcharged

1987, Apr. Wmk. 377 Perf. 12½
B65 SP7 2b + 50s on 75s + 25s 2.00 1.60

Sports
SP10　　　　　SP11

　　Designs: No. B66, Hurdles, medal winners.
No. B67, Race, nurse treating injured cyclist.
No. B68, Boxers training. No. B69, Soccer.

1989, Dec. 16 Wmk. 387 Perf. 13½
B66 SP10 2b +1b multi .40 .30
B67 SP10 2b +1b multi .40 .30
B68 SP10 2b +1b multi .40 .30
B69 SP10 2b +1b multi .40 .30
　　　Nos. B66-B69 (4) 1.60 1.20
　　　Surtax for sports welfare organizations.

1990, Dec. 16
B70 SP11 2b +1b Judo .60 .35
B71 SP11 2b +1b Archery .60 .35
B72 SP11 2b +1b High jump .60 .35
B73 SP11 2b +1b Windsurfing .60 .35
　　　Nos. B70-B73 (4) 2.40 1.40
　　　Surtax for sports welfare organization.

Sports — SP12

Wmk. 387
1991, Dec. 16 Litho. Perf. 13½
B74 SP12 2b +1b Jogging .35 .35
B75 SP12 2b +1b Cycling .35 .35
B76 SP12 2b +1b Soccer, jump-
　　　ing rope .35 .35
B77 SP12 2b +1b Swimming .35 .35
　　　Nos. B74-B77 (4) 1.40 1.40
　　　Surtax for sports welfare organizations.

18th South East
Asian Games,
Chiang
Mai — SP13

　　No. B78: a, Water polo. b, Tennis. c, Hur-
dles. d, Gymnastics.
　　No. B79: a, Fencing. b, Pool. c, Diving. d,
Pole vault.

1994, Dec. 16 Wmk. 340
B78 SP13 2b +1b Strip of 4,
　　　#a.-d. 2.25 1.75
　　e. Souvenir sheet, #B78 2.00 2.00
Wmk. 387
B79 SP13 2b +1b Strip of 4,
　　　#a.-d. 2.25 1.75
　　e. Souvenir sheet, #B79 2.00 2.00
　　　Nos. B78e, B79e sold for 15b.
Issued: #B78, 12/16/94; #B79, 12/9/95.
For surcharges see Nos. 2338-2339, 2347-
2348.

SP14

13th Asian Games, Bangkok — SP15

1998, Mar. 27 Perf. 14½x14
B80 SP14 2b +1b Shooting .25 .25
B81 SP14 3b +1b Rhythmic
　　　gymnastics .35 .25
B82 SP14 4b +1b Swimming .45 .35
B83 SP14 7b +1b Wind-surfing .70 .55
　　　Nos. B80-B83 (4) 1.75 1.40

Perf. 14½x14
1998, Dec. 6 Litho. Unwmk.
Granite Paper
B84 SP15 2b +1b Field hockey .35 .25
B85 SP15 3b +1b Wrestling .45 .25
B86 SP15 4b +1b Rowing .55 .35
B87 SP15 7b +1b Equestrian .90 .55
　　　Nos. B84-B87 (4) 2.25 1.40

AIR POST STAMPS

Garuda — AP1

1925 Unwmk. Engr. Perf. 14, 14½
C1 AP1 2s brown, yel 8.00 .50
C2 AP1 3s dark brown 8.00 .50
C3 AP1 5s green 20.00 .55
C4 AP1 10s black & org 32.50 1.00
C5 AP1 15s carmine 8.00 1.50
C6 AP1 25s dark blue 16.00 1.50

THAILAND (continued)

C7	AP1	50s brown org & blk		60.00	9.00
C8	AP1	1b blue & brown		40.00	11.00
		Nos. C1-C8 (8)		192.50	25.55
		Set, never hinged		290.00	

Issue dates: 2s, 50s, Apr. 21; others, Jan. 3.

Nos. C1-C8 received this overprint ("Government Museum 2468") in 1925, but were never issued. The death of King Vajiravudh caused cancellation of the fair at which this set was to have been released.

They were used during 1928 only in the interdepartmental service for accounting purposes of the money-order sections of various Bangkok post offices, and were never sold to the public. Values for set: unused, $1,200; used, $45.

1930-37   *Perf. 12½*

C9	AP1	2s brown, *yel*		9.50	1.00
C10	AP1	5s green		2.40	.40
C11	AP1	10s black & org		8.00	.40
C12	AP1	15s carmine		32.50	8.00
C13	AP1	25s dark blue ('37)		4.00	1.20
a.		Vert. pair, imperf. btwn.		450.00	
C14	AP1	50s brn org & blk ('37)		4.00	2.40
		Nos. C9-C14 (6)		60.40	13.40
		Set, never hinged		90.00	

Monument of Democracy, Bangkok — AP2

1942-43   Engr.   *Perf. 11*

C15	AP2	2s dk org brn ('43)		3.25	2.40
C16	AP2	3s dk grn ('43)		32.50	24.00
a.		Vert. pair, imperf. btwn.		100.00	100.00
C17	AP2	5s deep claret		3.25	1.20
a.		Horiz. pair, imperf. btwn.		75.00	75.00
b.		Vert. pair, imperf. btwn.		75.00	75.00
C18	AP2	10s carmine ('43)		15.00	100.00
a.		Vert. pair, imperf. btwn.		100.00	100.00
C19	AP2	15s dark blue		5.25	2.00
a.		Vert. pair, imperf. btwn.		100.00	100.00
		Nos. C15-C19 (5)		59.25	30.80
		Set, never hinged		90.00	

> **Catalogue values for unused stamps in this section, from this point to the end of the section, are for Never Hinged items.**

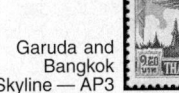

Garuda and Bangkok Skyline — AP3

1952-53   *Perf. 13x12½*

C20	AP3	1.50b red violet ('53)		5.50	1.20
C21	AP3	2b dark blue		16.00	2.50
C22	AP3	3b gray ('53)		20.00	1.40
		Nos. C20-C22 (3)		41.50	5.10

Issue dates: June 15, 1952. Sept. 15, 1953.

OFFICIAL STAMPS

> **Catalogue values for unused stamps in this section are for Never Hinged items.**

O1   O2

Perf. 10½ Rough

1963, Oct. 1   Typo.   Unwmk.
Without Gum

O1	O1	10s pink & dp car	.25	.25
O2	O1	20s brt grn & car rose	.25	.25
O3	O1	25s blue & dp car	.30	.35
O4	O1	50s deep carmine	1.10	2.00
O5	O2	1b silver & car rose	1.25	3.00
O6	O2	2b bronze & car rose	2.25	2.25
		Nos. O1-O6 (6)	5.40	8.10

Issued as an official test from Oct. 1, 1963, to Jan. 31, 1964, to determine the amount of mail sent out by various government departments.

Nos. O5, O9, O10 exist with oval frame of type O1.

1964   **Without Gum**

O7	O1	20s green	.50	.50
O8	O1	25s blue	.50	.50
O9	O2	1b silver	1.00	1.00
O10	O2	2b bister	2.50	2.50
		Nos. O7-O10 (4)	4.50	4.50

Others values exist printed in one color.

THRACE

'thrās

LOCATION — In southeastern Europe between the Black and Aegean Seas
GOVT. — Former Turkish Province
AREA — 89,361 sq. mi. (approx.)

Thrace underwent many political changes during the Balkan Wars and World War I. It was finally divided among Turkey, Greece and Bulgaria.

100 Lepta = 1 Drachma
40 Paras = 1 Piaster
100 Stotinki = 1 Leva (1919)

> A large number of minor overprint errors exist on most issues of Thrace. See the *Scott Classic Specialized Catalogue of Stamps and Covers 1840-1940* for much more specialized listings.

Giumulzina District Issue

Turkish Stamps of 1909 Surcharged in Blue or Red

1913   Unwmk.   *Perf. 12, 13½*

1	A21	10 l on 20pa rose (Bl)		45.00	45.00
a.		Inverted overprint		160.00	
b.		Double overprint		160.00	
2	A21	25 l on 10pa bl grn		67.50	67.50
a.		Inverted overprint		175.00	
b.		Double overprint		175.00	
3	A21	25 l on 20pa rose (Bl)		67.50	67.50
a.		Inverted overprint		190.00	
b.		Double overprint		190.00	
c.		Béhié ovpt. (#162)		190.00	
4	A21	25 l on 1pi ultra		100.00	100.00
a.		Inverted overprint		200.00	
b.		Double overprint		200.00	
		Nos. 1-4 (4)		280.00	280.00

Counterfeits exist of Nos. 1-4.
Eight other values exist, bearing surcharges differing in color or denomination from Nos. 1-4. These stamps were not issued. Values, each: unused $165; never hinged $350.

Turkish Inscriptions
A1   A2

Type 1

Type 2

1913   Litho.   *Imperf.*
Laid Paper
Control Mark in Rose
Without Gum

5	A1	1pi blue, type 1		17.00	17.00
a.		Double print		250.00	
b.		Type 2		80.00	75.00
6	A1	2pi violet		20.00	20.00
a.		Double print		500.00	190.00
b.		Type 2			190.00

Wove Paper

7	A2	10pa vermilion		35.00	32.50
8	A2	20pa blue		35.00	32.50
9	A2	1pi violet		37.50	32.50
		Nos. 5-9 (5)		144.50	134.50

Turkish Stamps of 1908-13
Surcharged in Red or Black

١ بز عروشن .P

1913   *Perf. 12*

10	A22	1pi on 2pa ol grn		25.00	25.00
10A	A22	1pi on 2pa ol grn (R)		25.00	25.00
11	A22	1pi on 5pa ocher		25.00	25.00
11A	A22	1pi on 5pa ocher (R)		25.00	25.00
12	A22	1pi on 20pa rose		30.00	30.00
13	A21	1pi on 5pi dk vio			
13A	A21	1pi on 5pi dk vio (R)		62.50	62.50
				62.50	62.50
14	A21	1pi on 10pi dl red		100.00	100.00
15	A19	1pi on 25pi dk grn		400.00	450.00
		Nos. 10-15 (9)		805.00	805.00

On Nos. 13-15 the surcharge is vertical, reading up. No. 15 exists with double surcharge, one black, one red.
Nos. 10-15 exist with forged surcharges.

Bulgarian Stamps of 1911 Handstamped Surcharged in Red or Blue

غزلى ترکيا
حکومت مقل
انرهش ١

1913

16	A20	10pa on 1s myr grn (R)		20.00	20.00
17	A21	20pa on 2s car & blk		20.00	20.00
a.		Inverted overprint		60.00	
18	A23	1pi on 5s grn & blk (R)		20.00	20.00
a.		Inverted overprint		125.00	125.00
19	A22	2pi on 3s lake & blk		26.00	26.00
a.		Inverted overprint		80.00	
20	A24	2½pi on 10s dp red & blk		40.00	40.00
a.		2½pi on 2s			250.00
21	A25	5pi on 15s brn bis		67.50	67.50
a.		Inverted overprint			250.00
		Nos. 16-21 (6)		193.50	193.50

Same Surcharges on Greek Stamps
On Issue of 1911

1913   *Serrate Roulette 13½*

22	A24	10pa on 1 l grn			
23	A24	10pa on 1 l grn (R)		21.00	21.00
24	A26	10pa on 5 l grn		22.50	22.50
25	A25	10pa on 25 l ultra		110.00	110.00
26	A25	20pa on 2 l car rose (R)		32.50	32.50
27	A24	1pi on 3 l ver		20.00	20.00
a.		Value omitted		65.00	65.00
b.		Red overprint		20.00	20.00
28	A26	2pi on 5 l grn		57.50	57.50
29	A24	2½pi on 10 l car			
				57.50	57.50
30	A25	5pi on 40 l dp bl (R)		110.00	110.00
		Nos. 22-30 (9)		451.00	451.00

On Occupation Stamps of 1912

31	O1	10pa on 1 l brn		14.00	14.00
a.		Value omitted		100.00	
32	O1	20pa on 1 l brn		14.00	14.00
33	O1	1pi on 1 l brn		14.00	14.00
		Nos. 31-33 (3)		42.00	42.00

These surcharges were made with handstamps, two of which were required for each surcharge. The upper handstamp, reads "Administration of Autonomous Western Thrace" in old Turkish. The lower handstamp expresses the new value. On horizontal designs, the text appears on the right, and the value appears on the left. On inverted overprints on horizontal stamps, this is reversed. One or both parts may be found inverted or omitted.
Nos. 16-33 exist with forged surcharges.

OCCUPATION STAMPS

Issued under Allied Occupation

Bulgarian Stamps of 1915-19 Handstamped in Violet Blue

Perf. 11½, 11½x12, 14

1919   Unwmk.

N1b	A43	1s black		2.50	2.00
N2	A43	2s olive green		2.50	2.00
N3	A44	5s green		.85	.85
N4	A44	10s rose		.85	.85
N5	A44	15s violet		.85	.85
N6	A26	25s indigo & black		.85	.85
		Nos. N1b-N6 (6)		8.40	7.40

The overprint on Nos. N1-N6 exists applied both ascending and descending, as well as inverted in both positions. On the 1s value, the usual position of the overprint is upright; on the rest of the set, the overprint is usually inverted, reading from lower right to upper left. See the *Scott Classic Specialized Catalogue of Stamps and Covers* for detailed listings.

Bulgarian Stamps of 1911-19 Overprinted in Red or Black

1919

N7	A43	1s black (R)		.25	.25
N8	A43	2s olive green		.25	.25
N9	A44	5s green		.25	.25
N10	A44	10s rose		.25	.25
N11	A44	15s violet		.25	.25
N12	A26	25s indigo & black		.25	.25
N13	A29	1 l chocolate		4.00	4.00
N14	A37a	2 l brown orange		6.00	6.00
N15	A38	3 l claret		10.00	10.00
		Nos. N7-N15 (9)		21.50	21.50

Overprint is vertical, reading up, on Nos. N9-N13.
The following varieties are found in the setting of "INTERALLIEE": Inverted "V" for "A", second "L" inverted, "F" instead of final "E."

Bulgarian Stamps of 1919 Overprinted

1920

N16	A44	5s green	.25	.25
d.		Imperf, pair	67.50	
N17	A44	10s rose	.25	.25
N18	A44	15s violet	.25	.25
N19	A44	50s yellow brown, ovpt. reading up	1.25	1.25
d.		Ovpt. reading down	21.00	25.00
h.		As "d," imperf, pair	140.00	
		Nos. N16-N19 (4)	2.00	2.00

Various typographical errors in the overprint are found on all values.

Bulgarian Stamps of 1919 Overprinted

1920   **Perf. 12x11½**

N20	A44	5s green	.25	.25
a.		Inverted overprint	32.50	50.00
b.		Pair, one without ovpt.	42.50	65.00
c.		Imperf, pair	42.50	65.00
d.		As "c," inverted overprint	50.00	75.00
N21	A44	10s rose	.25	.25
a.		Inverted overprint	25.00	37.50
b.		Double ovpt., one on gum side	42.50	65.00
c.		Imperf, pair	42.50	65.00
d.		As "c," inverted overprint	50.00	75.00
N22	A44	15s violet	.25	.25
a.		Inverted overprint	25.00	37.50
b.		Imperf, pair	42.50	65.00
c.		As "c," inverted overprint	50.00	75.00
N23	A44	25s deep blue	.25	.25
a.		Inverted overprint	25.00	37.50
b.		Imperf, pair	42.50	65.00
c.		As "c," inverted overprint	50.00	75.00
N24	A44	50s ocher	.25	.25
a.		Inverted overprint	32.50	50.00

Imperf

N25	A44	30s chocolate	1.25	1.25
a.		Inverted overprint	32.50	50.00
		Nos. N20-N25 (6)	2.50	2.50

No. N25 is not known without overprint.

ISSUED UNDER GREEK OCCUPATION

Counterfeits exist of Nos. N26-N84.

For Use in Western Thrace

Greek Stamps of 1911-19 Overprinted "Administration Western Thrace" in Greek

Serrate Roulette 13½

1920   **Litho.**   **Unwmk.**

N26	A24	1 l green	.25	.65
a.		Inverted overprint	15.00	
b.		Double overprint	15.00	
c.		Double overprint, one inverted	75.00	
N27	A25	2 l rose	.25	.40
N28	A24	3 l vermilion	.25	.40
a.		Inverted overprint	17.50	
N29	A26	5 l green	.25	.40
a.		Inverted overprint	25.00	
b.		Double overprint	25.00	
N30	A24	10 l rose	.40	.85
N31	A25	15 l dull blue	.35	.65
a.		Inverted overprint	20.00	
b.		Double overprint	20.00	
c.		Dbl. ovpt., one inverted	24.00	
N32	A25	25 l blue	.40	.85
N34	A25	40 l indigo	1.90	4.00
N35	A26	50 l violet brn	1.90	5.00
N36	A27	1d ultra	6.50	14.00
N37	A27	2d vermilion	25.00	32.50
a.		Double overprint	75.00	
		Nos. N26-N37 (11)	37.45	59.70

The 20 l value with this overprint was not issued. Values: unused $25; never hinged $60.

Engr.

N38	A25	2 l car rose	.85	.85
N39	A24	3 l vermilion	.95	.95
N39A	A25	20 l slate	25.00	
N39B	A25	25 l blue	30.00	
N39C	A25	30 l rose	35.00	
N40	A27	1d ultra	25.00	20.00
N41	A27	2d vermilion	35.00	30.00
N42	A27	3d car rose	50.00	70.00
N43	A27	5d ultra	20.00	30.00
N44	A27	10d deep blue	20.00	30.00
		Nos. N38-N44 (10)	241.80	

Nos. N38-N44 were not issued. Values for used examples of Nos. N38-N39 and N40-N44 are for cancelled-to-order stamps.

Nos. N42-N44 are overprinted on the reissues of Greece Nos. 210-212. See footnote below Greece No. 213.

Overprinted   **ΔΙΟΙΚΗΣΙΣ ΔΥΤΙΚΗΣ ΘΡΑΚΗΣ**

N45	A28	25d deep blue	50.00	30.00

This overprint reads: "Administration Western Thrace."

With Additional Overprint

Litho.

N46	A24	1 l green	4.25	3.00
N47	A25	2 l rose	.25	.40
a.		Inverted overprint	77.50	
N47B	A26	5 l green	21.00	
N48	A24	10 l rose	.55	.65
a.		Inverted overprint	17.50	
N49	A25	20 l slate	.55	.65
a.		Inverted overprint	17.50	
N49B	A25	25 l blue	30.00	
N50	A26	30 l rose (#240)	.65	1.00

Engr.

N50A	A26	30 l rose (#244)	65.00	
N51	A27	2d vermilion	30.00	27.50
N52	A27	3d car rose	40.00	25.00
N53	A27	5d ultra	35.00	30.00
N54	A27	10d deep blue	35.00	20.00
		Nos. N46-N54 (12)	252.25	108.20

Nos. N46, N47B, N49B, N50A, N51, N53 and N54 were not issued. Used values for Nos. N46, N51, N53 and N54 are for canceled-to-order stamps.

For Use in Eastern and Western Thrace

Greek Stamps of 1911-19 Overprinted "Administration Thrace" in Greek

1920   **Litho.**

N55	A24	1 l green	.25	.85
a.		Inverted overprint	17.50	
b.		Double overprint	17.50	
N56	A25	2 l rose	.25	.40
a.		Inverted overprint	12.50	
b.		Double overprint	15.00	
c.		Triple overprint	25.00	
N57	A24	3 l vermilion	.25	.40
a.		Inverted overprint	17.50	
b.		Double overprint	15.00	
c.		Double overprint, one inverted	17.50	
N58	A26	5 l green	.25	.45
a.		Inverted overprint	17.50	
b.		Double overprint	30.00	
N59	A24	10 l rose	.40	.70
a.		Inverted overprint	82.50	
N59B	A25	15 l dull blue	50.00	
a.		Inverted overprint	50.00	
N60	A25	20 l slate	.65	1.25
a.		Inverted overprint	15.00	
b.		Double overprint	15.00	
N61	A25	25 l blue	1.25	2.00
N62	A25	40 l indigo	2.40	6.50
N63	A26	50 l violet brn	3.00	8.50
N64	A27	1d ultra	12.50	20.00
N65	A27	2d vermilion	25.00	35.00

Engr.

N65A	A25	2 l rose	1.75	3.00
N66	A24	3 l vermilion	2.00	3.00
N67	A25	20 l gray lilac	8.00	22.50
N68	A28	25d deep blue	60.00	90.00
		Nos. N55-N68 (16)	167.95	194.55

Nos. N59B and N65A-N68 were not issued. Used values for Nos. N65A-N68 are for canceled-to-order stamps.

With Additional Overprint as Nos. N46-N54

Litho.

N68A	A24	1 l green	4.00	6.00
N69	A25	2 l car rose	.25	.50
a.		Inverted overprint	30.00	
b.		Double overprint	30.00	
N70	A26	5 l green	4.00	8.00
N71	A25	20 l slate	.25	.50
b.		Double overprint	350.00	275.00
N72	A26	30 l rose	.25	.50

Engr.

N73	A27	3d car rose	11.00	17.50
N74	A27	5d ultra	21.00	45.00
N75	A27	10d deep blue	35.00	60.00
		Nos. N68A-N75 (8)	75.75	138.00

Nos. N68A, N70 and N74-N75 were not issued. Used values are for canceled-to-order stamps.

Turkish Stamps of 1916-20 Srchd. in Blue, Black or Red

1920   **Perf. 11½, 12½**

N76	A43	1 l on 5pa org (Bl)	.40	.50
a.		Inverted overprint	35.00	
b.		Double overprint	25.00	25.00
c.		Double overprint, one inverted	45.00	45.00
d.		Double overprint, one on gummed side	35.00	
N77	A32	5 l on 3pi blue	.40	.50
a.		Inverted overprint	85.00	85.00
b.		Double overprint	60.00	60.00
N78	A30	20 l on 1pi bl grn	.50	.70
a.		Inverted overprint	25.00	25.00
b.		Double overprint	25.00	25.00
c.		Double overprint, one inverted	35.00	35.00
d.		Double overprint, one on gummed side	35.00	
N79	A53	25 l on 5pi on 2pa Prus bl (R)	.60	.75
a.		Inverted overprint	42.50	42.50
b.		Double overprint	42.50	42.50
N80	A49	50 l on 5pi bl & blk (R)	4.75	4.75
N81	A45	1d on 20pa dp rose (Bl)	1.60	1.40
a.		Double overprint	35.00	35.00
N82	A22	2d on 10pa on 2pa ol grn (R)	2.50	2.50
a.		Double overprint	30.00	30.00
N83	A57	3d on 1pi dp bl (R)	9.50	9.50
a.		Inverted overprint	50.00	50.00
b.		Double overprint	60.00	60.00
N84	A23	5d on 20pa rose	9.00	9.00
a.		Inverted overprint	67.50	67.50
b.		Double overprint, one inverted	67.50	67.50
		Nos. N76-N84 (9)	29.25	29.60

On Nos. N83 and N84, the normal overprint is reading down. On the inverted overprints, it is reading up.

Nos. N77, N78 and N84 are on the 1920 issue with designs modified. Nos. N81, N82 and N83 are on stamps with the 1919 overprints.

POSTAGE DUE STAMPS

Issued under Allied Occupation

Bulgarian Postage Due Stamps of 1919 Overprinted like Nos. N7-N15 Reading Vertically Up

1919   **Unwmk.**   **Perf. 12x11½**

NJ1	D6	5s emerald	.40	.40
NJ2	D6	10s purple	.85	.85
NJ3	D6	50s blue	2.50	2.50
		Nos. NJ1-NJ3 (3)	3.75	3.75

Type of Bulgarian Postage Due Stamps of 1919-22 Overprinted

1920   **Imperf.**

NJ4	D6	5s emerald	.40	.40
a.		Inverted overprint	37.50	
NJ5	D6	10s deep violet	1.65	1.65
a.		Inverted overprint	37.50	
NJ6	D6	20s salmon	1.40	.50
NJ7	D6	50s blue	1.25	1.25

Perf. 12x11½

NJ8	D6	10s deep violet	1.00	.80
		Nos. NJ4-NJ8 (5)	5.70	4.60

No. NJ6 issued without gum.

TIBET

təˈbet

LOCATION — A high tableland in Central Asia

GOVT. — A semi-independent state, nominally under control of China (under Communist China since 1950-51). In 1965 Tibet became a nominally autonomous region of the People's Republic of China.

AREA — 463,200 sq. mi.

POP. — 1,500,000 (approx.)

CAPITAL — Lhasa

Tibet's postage stamps were valid only within its borders.

6 ⅔ Trangka = 1 Sang

"Stamps" produced by the "Tibetan Government in Exile" have no postal value. These include four-value sets for Himalayan animals and the UPU that were put on sale in the early 1970s.

Excellent counterfeits of Nos. 1-18 exist. Numerous shades of all values. All stamps issued without gum.

Small bits of foreign matter (inclusions) are to be expected in Native Paper. These do not reduce the value of the stamp unless they have caused serious damage to the design or paper.

A1   Lion — A2

1912-50   Unwmk.   Typo.   *Imperf.*
Native Paper

1	A1	⅛t green	40.00	45.00
2	A1	⅛t blue	40.00	55.00
a.		⅛t ultramarine	50.00	60.00
3	A1	⅛t violet	40.00	55.00
4	A1	⅔t carmine	50.00	60.00
a.		"POTSAGE"	150.00	175.00
5	A1	1t vermilion	55.00	75.00
6	A1	1s sage green ('50)	100.00	110.00
		Nos. 1-6 (6)	325.00	400.00

The "POTSAGE" error is found on all shades of the ⅔t (positions 6 and 7).
Pin-perf. examples of Nos. 1 and 3 exist.
Issued in sheets of 12.

Beware of private reproductions of #1-5 that were printed in the US around 1986. Sheets of 12 bear "J. Crow Co." imprint. The set of 5 sheets was sold for $5.

Printed Using Shiny Enamel Paint
1920

1a	A1	⅛t green	60.00	40.00
2b	A1	⅛t blue	500.00	500.00
3d	A1	⅛t purple	100.00	110.00
4h	A1	⅔t carmine	100.00	110.00
i.		"POTSAGE"	225.00	250.00
5c	A1	1t carmine	350.00	400.00

In some 1920-30 printings, European enamel paint was used instead of ink. It has a glossy surface.

1914

7	A2	4t milky blue	750.	850.
a.		4t dark blue	1,100.	1,100.
8	A2	8t carmine rose	165.	175.
a.		8t carmine	1,100.	1,100.

Issued in sheets of 6.

Printed Using Shiny Enamel Paint
1920

7b	A2	4t blue	1,350.	1,500.
8b	A2	8t carmine	1,350.	1,500.

See note following No. 5c.

A3

Thin White Native Paper
1933   *Pin-perf.*

9	A3	½t orange	95.00	100.00
10	A3	⅔t dark blue	95.00	120.00
11	A3	1t rose carmine	95.00	120.00
12	A3	2t scarlet	95.00	120.00
13	A3	4t emerald	95.00	120.00
		Nos. 9-13 (5)	475.00	580.00

Issued in sheets of 12.
Exist imperf.

Heavy Toned Native Paper
1934   *Imperf.*

14	A3	½t yellow	16.00	18.00
15	A3	⅔t blue	14.00	15.00
16	A3	1t orange ver	14.00	15.00
a.		1t carmine	16.00	18.00
17	A3	2t red	14.00	15.00
a.		2t orange vermilion	14.00	15.00
18	A3	4t green	14.00	15.00
a.		25x25mm instead of 24x24mm	55.00	65.00
		Nos. 14-18 (5)	72.00	78.00

Nos. 14-18 are also known with a private pin-perf.
The ½t and 1t exist printed on both sides.
Issued in sheets of 12.

OFFICIAL STAMPS

O1

O2

Various Designs and Sizes Inscribed "STAMP"

Sizes: No. O1, 32½x32½mm. No. O2, 38x28½mm. No. O3, 34x33mm. No. O4, 44x44mm. No. O5, 66x66mm.

1945   Unwmk.   Typo.   *Imperf.*
Native Paper

O1	O1	½t bronze green	
O2	O2	⅛t slate black	
O3	O1	⅔t reddish brown	
O4	O1	1⅛t olive green	
O5	O1	1s dark gray blue	

The status of Nos. O1-O5 is in question. Other values exist.

TIMOR

ˈtē-ˌmor

LOCATION — The eastern part of Timor island, Malay archipelago

GOVT. — Former Portuguese Overseas Territory

AREA — 7,330 sq. mi.

POP. — 660,000 (est. 1974)

CAPITAL — Dili

The Portuguese territory of Timor was annexed by Indonesia May 3, 1976. Timor-Leste achieved independent statehood status on May 20, 2002.

1000 Reis = 1 Milreis
78 Avos = 1 Rupee (1895)
100 Avos = 1 Pataca
100 Centavos = 1 Escudo (1960)
100 Cents = 1 Dollar (2000)

Catalogue values for unused stamps in this country are for Never Hinged items, beginning with Scott 256 in the regular postage section, Scott J31 in the postage due section, and Scott RA11 in the postal tax section.

Watermark

Wmk. 232 —
Maltese Cross

Stamps of Macao
Overprinted in Black
or Carmine

1885   Unwmk.   *Perf. 12½, 13½*

1	A1	5r black (C)	5.50	1.60
a.		Double overprint	50.00	50.00
b.		Triple overprint	115.00	
2	A1	10r green	8.00	3.50
a.		Overprint on Mozambique stamp	22.50	14.00
b.		Overprinted on Portuguese India stamp	210.00	150.00
3	A1	20r rose, perf. 13½	9.00	4.50
a.		Double overprint	27.50	
b.		Perf. 12½	9.50	5.00
4	A1	25r violet	2.25	1.10
a.		Perf. 13½	30.00	17.50
5	A1	40r yellow	5.50	3.00
a.		Double overprint	17.50	
b.		Inverted overprint	21.00	21.00
c.		Perf. 13½	14.00	11.00
6	A1	50r blue	5.75	2.00
a.		Perf. 13½	15.00	12.00
7	A1	80r slate	12.50	4.00
8	A1	100r lilac	6.00	1.75
a.		Double overprint	25.00	
b.		Perf. 13½	9.00	3.50
9	A1	200r org, perf. 13½	11.00	4.00
a.		Perf. 12½	12.50	4.75
10	A1	300r brown	10.00	3.50
		Nos. 1-10 (10)	75.50	28.95

The 20r bister, 25r rose and 50r green were prepared for use but not issued.

The reprints are printed on a smooth white chalky paper, ungummed, with rough perforation 13½, and on thin white paper with shiny white gum and clean-cut perforation 13½.

King Luiz — A2   King Carlos — A3

1887   Embossed   *Perf. 12½*

11	A2	5r black	2.50	1.90
12	A2	10r green	4.00	3.00
13	A2	20r bright rose	4.25	3.00
14	A2	25r violet	8.00	3.50
15	A2	40r chocolate	14.00	5.25
16	A2	50r blue	15.00	6.00
17	A2	80r gray	16.50	8.00
18	A2	100r yellow brown	25.00	10.50
19	A2	200r gray lilac	32.50	17.50
20	A2	300r orange	35.00	18.50
		Nos. 11-20 (10)	156.75	77.15

Reprints of Nos. 11, 16, 18 and 19 have clean-cut perforation 13½.

For surcharges see Nos. 34-43, 83-91.

Macao No. 44
Surcharged in Black

1892   Without Gum   *Perf. 12½, 13*

21	A7	30r on 300r orange	10.00	6.75

For surcharge see No. 44.

1894   Typo.   *Perf. 11½*

22	A3	5r yellow	1.25	.65
23	A3	10r red violet	1.75	.65
24	A3	15r chocolate	3.00	.95
25	A3	20r lavender	3.75	1.10
26	A3	25r green	4.50	.80
27	A3	50r light blue	5.75	3.50
a.		Perf. 13½	160.00	125.00
28	A3	75r rose	7.25	2.75
29	A3	80r light green	7.75	4.25
30	A3	100r brown, *buff*	5.75	2.75
31	A3	150r car, *rose*	13.00	8.00
32	A3	200r dk bl, *lt bl*	13.50	10.50
33	A3	300r dk bl, *salmon*	15.00	12.00
		Nos. 22-33 (12)	82.25	47.90

For surcharges and overprints see Nos. 92-102, 120-122, 124-128, 131-133, 183-193, 199.

Stamps of 1887
Surcharged in Red,
Green or Black

1895   Without Gum   *Perf. 12½*

34	A2	1a on 5r black (R)	1.00	.85
35	A2	2a on 10r green	1.25	.85
a.		Double surcharge	17.50	

36	A2	3a on 20r brt rose (G)	2.75	1.75
37	A2	4a on 25r violet	2.75	1.10
38	A2	6a on 40r choc	6.00	3.00
39	A2	8a on 50r blue (R)	4.00	2.25
40	A2	13a on 80r gray	15.50	10.00
41	A2	16a on 100r yellow brn	17.50	7.75
42	A2	31a on 200r gray lilac	32.50	20.00
43	A2	47a on 300r org (G)	35.00	22.50
		Nos. 34-43 (10)	118.25	70.05

No. 21 Surcharged

1895   Without Gum   Perf. 12½, 13

44	A7	5a on 30r on 300r org	16.00	5.75

Common Design Types pictured following the introduction.

Vasco da Gama Issue
Common Design Types

1898	Engr.		Perf. 14 to 15	
45	CD20	½a blue green	1.50	.85
46	CD21	1a red	1.50	.85
47	CD22	2a red violet	1.50	.85
48	CD23	4a yellow green	1.50	.85
49	CD24	8a dark blue	3.00	1.25
50	CD25	12a violet brown	3.50	1.40
51	CD26	16a bister brown	4.00	1.90
52	CD27	24a bister	5.00	2.50
		Nos. 45-52 (8)	21.50	10.45

400th anniversary of Vasco da Gama's discovery of the route to India.
For overprints and surcharge see Nos. 148-155.

King Carlos
A5   A6

1898-1903   Typo.   Perf. 11½
Name & Value in Black Except #79

53	A5	½a gray	.35	.25
a.		Perf. 12½	2.50	1.75
54	A5	1a orange	.35	.30
a.		Perf. 12½	2.50	1.75
55	A5	2a light green	.35	.30
56	A5	2½a brown	1.25	1.10
57	A5	3a gray violet	1.25	1.10
58	A5	3a gray green ('03)	1.50	1.00
59	A5	4a sea green	1.60	1.00
60	A5	5a rose ('03)	1.50	1.00
61	A5	6a pale yel brn ('03)	1.50	1.00
62	A5	8a blue	2.00	1.10
63	A5	9a red brown ('03)	1.50	1.25
64	A5	10a slate blue ('00)	2.00	1.10
65	A5	10a gray brown ('03)	1.50	1.00
66	A5	12a rose	4.25	3.00
67	A5	12a dull blue ('03)	18.00	10.00
68	A5	13a violet	4.50	3.75
69	A5	13a red lilac ('03)	3.50	1.75
70	A5	15a gray lilac ('03)	5.50	3.75
71	A5	16a dark bl, bl	4.50	3.75
72	A5	20a brn, yelsh ('00)	5.25	3.75
73	A5	22a brn org, pink ('03)	5.25	3.50
74	A5	24a brown, buff	5.50	3.75
75	A5	31a red lil, pinkish	5.50	3.75
76	A5	31a brn, straw ('03)	5.75	3.50
77	A5	47a dk blue, rose	9.00	4.25
78	A5	47a red vio, pink ('03)	6.50	3.50
79	A5	78a blk & red, bl ('00)	12.50	6.75
80	A5	78a dl bl, straw ('03)	17.50	10.00
		Nos. 53-80 (28)	129.65	80.25

Most of Nos. 53-80 were issued without gum. For surcharges & overprints see #81-82, 104-119, 129-130, 134-147, 195-196.

1899   Black Surcharge

81	A6	10a on 16a dk bl, bl	3.75	2.50
82	A6	20a on 31a red lil, pnksh	3.75	2.50

Surcharged in Black

1902   On Issue of 1887

83	A2	5a on 25r violet	2.50	1.75
84	A2	5a on 200r gray lil	4.00	2.00
85	A2	6a on 10r blue grn	100.00	50.00
86	A2	6a on 300r orange	3.75	3.50
87	A2	9a on 40r choc	4.50	3.50
88	A2	9a on 100r yel brn	4.50	3.50
89	A2	15a on 20r rose	4.50	3.50
90	A2	15a on 50r blue	100.00	50.00
91	A2	22a on 80r gray	8.75	6.50
		Nos. 83-91 (9)	232.50	124.75

Reprints of Nos. 83-88, 90-91, 104A have clean-cut perf. 13½.

On Issue of 1894

92	A3	5a on 5r yellow	1.90	1.10
a.		Inverted surcharge	40.00	30.00
93	A3	5a on 25r green	2.25	1.10
94	A3	5a on 50r lt blue	2.25	1.40
95	A3	6a on 20r lavender	2.25	1.40
96	A3	9a on 15r choc	2.25	1.40
97	A3	9a on 75r rose	2.25	1.40
98	A3	15a on 10r red vio	4.00	2.25
99	A3	15a on 100r brn, buff	4.00	2.25
100	A3	15a on 300r bl, sal	4.00	2.25
101	A3	22a on 80r lt green	6.00	4.00
102	A3	22a on 200r bl, blue	8.00	4.00

On Newspaper Stamp of 1893

103	N2	6a on 2½r brn	1.00	.85
a.		Inverted surcharge	27.50	27.50
		Nos. 92-103 (12)	40.15	23.40

Nos. 93-97, 99-102 issued without gum.

Stamps of 1898 Overprinted in Black

104	A5	3a gray violet	4.00	1.90
104A	A5	12a rose	6.00	3.75

Reprint noted after No. 91.

No. 67 Surcharged in Black

1905

105	A5	10a on 12a dull blue	8.25	4.25

Stamps of 1898-1903 Overprinted in Carmine or Green

1911

106	A5	½a gray	.30	.30
a.		Inverted overprint	20.00	20.00
107	A5	1a orange	.30	.30
a.		Perf. 12½	16.00	16.00
108	A5	2a light green	.40	.35
109	A5	3a gray green	.50	.35
110	A5	5a rose (G)	.50	.35
111	A5	6a yel brown	.50	.35
112	A5	9a red brown	.75	.45
113	A5	10a gray brown	.75	.45
114	A5	13a red lilac	.80	.50
115	A5	15a gray lilac	1.60	1.25
116	A5	22a brn org, pink	1.60	1.25
117	A5	31a brown, straw	1.60	1.25
118	A5	47a red vio, pink	3.00	2.50
119	A5	78a dl bl, straw	4.75	3.50
		Nos. 106-119 (14)	17.35	13.15

Preceding Issues Overprinted in Red

1913   Without Gum
On Provisional Issue of 1902

120	A3	5a on 5r yellow	5.00	4.00
121	A3	5a on 25r green	5.00	4.00
122	A3	5a on 50r lt bl	6.00	7.00
123	N2	6a on 2½r brn	6.00	7.00
124	A3	6a on 20r lavender	5.00	4.00
125	A3	9a on 15r choc	5.00	4.00
126	A3	15a on 100r brn, buff	6.00	5.50
127	A3	22a on 80r lt grn	9.00	8.00
128	A3	22a on 200r bl, bl	8.00	7.50

On Issue of 1903

129	A5	3a gray green	6.00	7.50

On Issue of 1905

130	A5	10a on 12a dull bl	6.00	4.00
		Nos. 120-130 (11)	67.00	62.50

Overprinted in Green or Red

1913
On Provisional Issue of 1902

131	A3	9a on 75r rose (G)	6.00	6.00
132	A3	15a on 10r red vio (G)	5.00	5.00
a.		Inverted overprint	35.00	35.00
133	A3	15a on 300r bl, sal (R)	8.00	8.00
a.		"REUBPLICA"	19.00	19.00
b.		"REPBLICAU"	19.00	19.00

On Issue of 1903

134	A5	5a rose (G)	4.00	4.00
		Nos. 131-134 (4)	23.00	23.00

Stamps of 1898-1903 Overprinted in Red

1913

135	A5	6a yellow brown	4.00	1.75
136	A5	9a red brown	4.00	1.75
137	A5	10a gray brown	4.00	1.75
138	A5	13a violet	6.00	2.50
a.		Inverted overprint	40.00	40.00
139	A5	13a red lilac	5.00	2.50
140	A5	15a gray lilac	6.00	3.25
141	A5	22a brn org, pnksh	7.00	3.50
142	A5	31a red lil, pnksh	7.00	3.50
143	A5	31a brown, straw	9.00	5.50
144	A5	47a blue, pink	10.00	5.50
145	A5	47a red vio, pink	12.00	8.00
146	A5	78a dl bl, straw	12.00	6.50

No. 79 Overprinted in Red

147	A5	78a blk & red, bl	12.00	8.00
		Nos. 135-147 (13)	98.00	54.00

Vasco da Gama Issue of 1898 Overprinted or Surcharged in Black

1913

148	CD20	½a blue green	.65	.60
149	CD21	1a red	.65	.60
150	CD22	2a red violet	.65	.60
151	CD23	4a yellow green	.65	.60
152	CD24	8a dark blue	1.40	1.10
153	CD25	10a on 12a vio brn	2.50	2.00

154	CD26	16a bister brown	2.00	1.75
155	CD27	24a bister	2.75	2.25
		Nos. 148-155 (8)	11.25	9.50

Ceres — A7

1914-23   Typo.   Perf. 15x14, 12x11½
Name and Value in Black

156	A7	½a olive brown	.25	.25
157	A7	1a black	.25	.25
158	A7	1½a yel grn ('23)	.60	1.10
159	A7	2a blue green	.25	.25
160	A7	3a lilac brown	1.00	.75
161	A7	4a carmine	1.00	.75
162	A7	6a light violet	1.00	.75
163	A7	7a lt green ('23)	1.75	1.75
164	A7	7½a ultra ('23)	3.25	3.50
165	A7	9a blue ('23)	4.00	6.75
166	A7	10a deep blue	1.25	.75
167	A7	11a gray ('23)	4.00	6.75
168	A7	12a yellow brown	1.50	1.25
169	A7	15a lilac ('23)	9.00	8.00
170	A7	16a slate	2.25	4.25
171	A7	18a dp blue ('23)	11.00	7.00
172	A7	19a gray grn ('23)	11.00	6.00
173	A7	20a org brown	16.50	6.75
174	A7	36a turq blue ('23)	10.00	4.75
175	A7	40a plum	10.00	5.00
176	A7	54a choc ('23)	11.00	8.00
177	A7	58a brown, grn	11.00	7.25
178	A7	72a brt rose ('23)	17.50	17.50
179	A7	76a brown, rose	13.00	7.25
180	A7	1p org, salmon	24.50	12.50
181	A7	3p green, blue	40.00	27.50
182	A7	5p car rose ('23)	92.00	60.00
		Nos. 156-182 (27)	298.85	206.60

For surcharges see Nos. 200-201, MR1.

Preceding Issues Overprinted in Carmine

1915   Perf. 11½
On Provisional Issue of 1902

183	A3	5a on 5r yellow	1.00	.55
184	A3	5a on 25r green	1.00	.55
185	A3	5a on 50r lt blue	1.00	.55
186	A3	6a on 20r lavender	1.00	.55
187	A3	9a on 15r chocolate	1.00	.55
188	A3	9a on 75r rose	1.50	.55
189	A3	15a on 10r red vio	1.50	1.50
190	A3	15a on 100r brn, buff	2.00	1.50
191	A3	15a on 300r bl, sal	2.00	3.00
192	A3	22a on 80r lt grn	3.25	2.75
193	A3	22a on 200r bl, bl	5.00	5.00

On No. 103

194	N2	6a on 2½r, perf. 13½	1.00	.55
a.		Perf. 12½	2.00	1.25
b.		Perf. 11½	4.00	1.75

On No. 104

195	A5	3a gray violet	1.00	.60

On No. 105

196	A5	10a on 12a dull bl	1.10	.60
		Nos. 183-196 (14)	23.35	18.80

Type of 1915 with Additional Surcharge in Black

Perf. 11½

199	A3	½a on 5a on 50r lt bl	15.50	8.50
a.		Perf. 13½	35.00	12.50

Nos. 178 and 169 Surcharged

1932   Perf. 12x11½

200	A7	6a on 72a brt rose	1.50	1.25
201	A7	12a on 15a lilac	1.50	1.25

"Portugal" and Vasco
da Gama's Flagship
"San Gabriel" — A8

Perf. 11½x12

1935		Typo.	**Wmk. 232**	
202	A8	½a bister	.25	.25
203	A8	1a olive brown	.25	.25
204	A8	2a blue green	.25	.25
205	A8	3a red violet	.60	.60
206	A8	4a black	.60	.30
207	A8	5a gray	.70	.65
208	A8	6a brown	.85	.60
209	A8	7a bright rose	1.00	1.00
210	A8	8a bright blue	1.10	1.10
211	A8	10a red orange	1.60	1.20
212	A8	12a dark blue	2.75	2.10
213	A8	14a olive green	3.25	2.10
214	A8	15a maroon	3.00	2.75
215	A8	20a apple green	3.50	2.75
216	A8	30a apple green	5.00	3.00
217	A8	40a violet	9.00	5.00
218	A8	50a olive bister	10.00	5.00
219	A8	1p light blue	24.50	14.00
220	A8	2p brn orange	50.00	25.00
221	A8	3p emerald	67.50	40.00
222	A8	5p dark violet	100.00	52.50
		Nos. 202-222 (21)	285.70	160.40

Common Design Types

1938		Unwmk. Engr.	**Perf. 13½x13**	

Name and Value in Black

223	CD34	1a gray green	.25	.25
224	CD34	2a orange brown	.25	.30
225	CD34	3a dk violet brn	.25	.30
226	CD34	4a brt green	.25	.65
227	CD35	5a dk carmine	.25	2.50
228	CD35	6a slate	.45	.25
229	CD35	8a rose violet	.65	1.10
230	CD37	10a brt red violet	.65	1.75
231	CD37	12a red	1.10	2.50
232	CD37	15a orange	1.75	2.50
233	CD36	20a blue	1.75	.80
234	CD36	40a gray black	3.75	1.25
235	CD36	50a brown	3.75	1.25
236	CD38	1p brown carmine	7.50	5.00
237	CD38	2p olive green	17.50	4.00
238	CD38	3p blue violet	22.50	9.50
239	CD38	5p red brown	45.00	14.00
		Nos. 223-239 (17)	107.60	47.90

For overprints see Nos. 245A-245K.

Mozambique Nos.
273, 276, 278, 280,
282 and 283
Surcharged in Black

1946			**Perf. 13½x13**	
240	CD34	1a on 15c dk vio brn	9.00	5.50
241	CD35	4a on 35c brt grn	9.00	5.50
242	CD35	8a on 50c brt red vio	9.00	5.50
243	CD36	10a on 70c brn vio	9.00	5.50
244	CD36	12a on 1e red	9.00	5.50
245	CD37	20a on 1.75e blue	9.00	5.50
		Nos. 240-245 (6)	54.00	33.00

Nos. 223-227 and 229-234
Overprinted "Libertacao"

1947				
245A	CD34	1a gray green	22.00	15.00
245B	CD34	2a org brown	37.50	17.50
245C	CD34	3a dk vio brn	15.00	8.50
245D	CD34	4a brt green	15.00	10.00
245E	CD35	5a dark car	7.50	3.50
245F	CD35	8a rose violet	3.00	2.00
245G	CD37	10a brt red vio	10.00	5.00
245H	CD37	12a red	12.50	6.00
245I	CD37	15a orange	6.00	3.50
245J	CD36	20a blue	77.50	60.00
m.		Inverted overprint	125.00	100.00
245K	CD36	40a gray black	25.00	14.00
		Nos. 245A-245K (11)	231.00	145.00

Timor Woman — A9

Designs: 3a, Gong ringer. 4a, Girl with basket. 8a, Aleixo de Ainaro. 10a, 1p, 3p, Heads
of various chieftains. 20a, Warrior and horse.

1948		Litho.	**Perf. 14**	
246	A9	1a aqua & dk brn	.50	.50
247	A9	3a gray & dk brn	1.10	.60
248	A9	4a pink & dk grn	1.40	.60
249	A9	8a red & blue blk	1.10	.50
250	A9	10a blue grn & org	1.10	.60
251	A9	20a ultra, aqua & bl	1.40	.50
252	A9	1p org, bl & ultra	19.00	4.00
253	A9	3p vio & dk brn	21.50	6.50
a.		Sheet of 8, #246-253	75.00	75.00
		Nos. 246-253 (8)	47.10	13.80

No. 253a sold for 5p.

Lady of Fatima Issue
Common Design Type

1948, Oct.

254	CD40	8a slate gray	3.00	3.00

UPU Issue

UPU
Symbols — A10

1949		Unwmk.	**Perf. 14.**	
255	A10	16a brown & buff	9.50	10.50

UPU, 75th anniversary.

> Catalogue values for unused
> stamps in this section, from this
> point to the end of the section, are
> for Never Hinged items.

Craftsman
A11

Timor Woman
A12

1950			**Perf. 14½**	
256	A11	20a dull vio blue	1.10	.70
257	A12	50a dull brown	5.50	1.90

Holy Year Issue
Common Design Types

1950, May			**Perf. 13x13½**	
258	CD41	40a green	1.50	1.25
259	CD42	70a black brown	2.25	2.00

Blackberry
Lily — A13

Designs: Various flowers.

1950		Unwmk. Litho.	**Perf. 14½**	
260	A13	1a multicolored	.35	.30
261	A13	3a multicolored	1.40	1.00
262	A13	10a multicolored	1.75	1.00
263	A13	16a multicolored	3.50	1.25
264	A13	20a multicolored	1.40	1.00
265	A13	30a multicolored	1.75	1.10
266	A13	70a multicolored	2.25	1.25
267	A13	1p multicolored	4.00	3.50
268	A13	3p multicolored	7.50	6.00
269	A13	5p multicolored	12.75	8.00
		Nos. 260-269 (10)	36.65	24.40

Holy Year Extension Issue
Common Design Type

1951			**Perf. 14**	
270	CD43	86a bl & pale bl + label	2.00	1.75

Stamp without label attached sells for much
less.

Medical Congress Issue
Common Design Type

Design: Weighing baby.

1952		Litho.	**Perf. 13½**	
271	CD44	10a ol blk & brn	1.00	1.00

St. Francis Xavier Issue

Statue of St. Francis
Xavier — A14

Designs: 16a, Miraculous Arm of St. Francis. 1p, Tomb of St. Francis.

1952, Oct. 25			**Perf. 14**	
272	A14	1a black	.25	.25
273	A14	16a blk brn & brn	1.00	.80
274	A14	1p dk car & gray	5.00	2.00
		Nos. 272-274 (3)	6.25	3.05

400th death anniv. of St. Francis Xavier.

Madonna and
Child — A15

Stamp of Portugal
and Arms of
Colonies — A16

1953			**Perf. 13x13½**	
275	A15	3a dk brn & dull gray	.25	.25
276	A15	16a dk brown & cream	1.00	.80
277	A15	50a dk bl & dull gray	3.00	1.40
		Nos. 275-277 (3)	4.25	2.25

Exhibition of Sacred Missionary Art, Lisbon,
1951.

Stamp Centenary Issue

1953		Photo.	**Perf. 13**	
278	A16	10a multicolored	1.10	1.00

Sao Paulo Issue
Common Design Type

1954		Litho.	**Perf. 13½**	
279	CD46	16a dk brn red, bl & blk	.85	.70

Map of
Timor — A17

1956		Unwmk.	**Perf. 14x12½**	

**Inscription and design in brown,
red, green, ultramarine & yellow**

280	A17	1a pale salmon	.25	.25
281	A17	3a pale gray blue	.25	.25
282	A17	8a buff	.30	.25
283	A17	24a pale green	.40	.25
284	A17	32a lemon	.50	.25
285	A17	40a pale gray	.75	.30
286	A17	1p yellow	1.75	1.10
287	A17	3p pale blue	4.25	1.50
		Nos. 280-287 (8)	8.45	4.15

For surcharges see Nos. 291-300.

Brussels Fair Issue

Exhibition Emblems
and View — A18

1958			**Perf. 14½**	
288	A18	40a multicolored	.50	.40

Tropical Medicine Congress Issue
Common Design Type

Design: Calophyllum inophyllum.

1958			**Perf. 13½**	
289	CD47	32a multicolored	3.00	2.75

Symbolical
Globe — A19

1960		Unwmk. Litho.	**Perf. 13½**	
290	A19	4.50e multicolored	.50	.35

500th death anniv. of Prince Henry the
Navigator.

Nos. 280-287 Surcharged with New
Value and Bars
**Inscription and design in brown,
red, green, ultramarine & yellow**

1960		Unwmk.	**Perf. 14x12½**	
291	A17	5c on 1a pale salmon	.25	.25
292	A17	10c on 3a pale gray bl	.25	.25
293	A17	20c on 8a buff	.25	.25
294	A17	30c on 24a pale grn	.30	.25
295	A17	50c on 32a lemon	.40	.25
296	A17	1e on 40a pale gray	.50	.25
297	A17	2e on 40a pale gray	.60	.25
298	A17	5e on 1p yellow	.75	1.00
299	A17	10e on 3p pale blue	1.75	2.50
300	A17	15e on 3p pale blue	2.50	2.00
		Nos. 291-300 (10)	7.55	7.25

Carved Elephant
Jar — A20

Native Art: 10c, House on stilts. 20c,
Madonna and Child. 30c, Silver rosary. 50c,
Two men in boat, horiz. 1e, Silver box in shape
of temple. 2.50e, Archer. 4.50e, Elephant. 5e,
Man climbing tree. 10e, Woman carrying pot
on head. 20e, Cockfight. 50e, House on stilts
and animals.

Multicolored Designs

1961		Litho.	**Perf. 11½x12**	
301	A20	5c pale violet	.25	.25
302	A20	10c pale green	.25	.30
a.		Value & legend inverted	72.50	72.50
303	A20	20c pale blue	.25	.30
304	A20	30c rose	.25	.25
305	A20	50c pale grnsh bl	.25	.25
306	A20	1e bister	.70	.25
307	A20	2.50e pale ol bis	.50	.25
308	A20	4.50e lt salmon	.50	.25
309	A20	5e lt gray	.60	.25
310	A20	10e gray	1.40	.30
311	A20	20e yellow	2.75	1.00
312	A20	50e lt bluish gray	9.25	2.50
		Nos. 301-312 (12)	16.95	6.20

Sports Issue
Common Design Type

Sports: 50c, Duck hunting. 1e, Horseback
riding. 1.50e, Swimming. 2e, Gymnastics.
2.50e, Soccer. 15e, Big game hunting.

1962, Mar. 22		Unwmk.	**Perf. 13½**	

Multicolored Designs

313	CD48	50c gray & bis	.25	.25
314	CD48	1e olive bister	.60	.30
315	CD48	1.50e gray & bl grn	.70	.40
316	CD48	2e buff	.85	.35
317	CD48	2.50e gray	1.00	.50
318	CD48	15e salmon	3.00	1.90
		Nos. 313-318 (6)	6.40	3.70

Anti-Malaria Issue
Common Design Type

Design: Anopheles sundaicus.

1962		Litho.	**Perf. 13½**	
319	CD49	2.50e multicolored	.75	.60

National Overseas Bank Issue
Common Design Type

Design: 2.50e, Manuel Pinheiro Chagas.

1964, May 16   Unwmk.   *Perf. 13½*
320 CD51 2.50e grn, gray, yel, lt bl
                 & blk   .75 .60

ITU Issue
Common Design Type
1965, May 17   Litho.   *Perf. 14½*
321 CD52 1.50e multicolored   1.50 .90

National Revolution Issue
Common Design Type
Design: 4.50e, Dr. Vieira Machado Academy and Dili Health Center.

1966, May 28   Litho.   *Perf. 11½*
322 CD53 4.50e multicolored   1.50 .90

Navy Club Issue
Common Design Type
10c, Capt. Gago Coutinho and gunboat Patria. 4.50e, Capt. Sacadura Cabral and seaplane Lusitania.

1967, Jan. 31   Litho.   *Perf. 13*
323 CD54 10c multicolored   2.00 1.00
324 CD54 4.50e multicolored   2.00 1.00

| Sepoy Officer, | Our Lady of |
| 1792 — A21 | Fatima — A22 |

Designs: 1e, Officer, 1815. 1.50e, Infantry soldier, 1879. 2e, Infantry soldier, 1890. 2.50e, Infantry officer, 1903. 3e, Sapper, 1918. 4.50e, Special forces soldier, 1964. 10e, Paratrooper, 1964.

1967, Feb. 12   Photo.   *Perf. 13½*
325 A21 35c multicolored   .25 .30
326 A21   1e multicolored   1.50 1.00
327 A21 1.50e multicolored   .60 .30
328 A21   2e multicolored   .60 .25
329 A21 2.50e multicolored   .60 .25
330 A21   3e multicolored   .75 .35
331 A21 4.50e multicolored   1.10 .45
332 A21 10e multicolored   2.25 .65
        Nos. 325-332 (8)   7.65 3.55

1967, May 13   Litho.   *Perf. 12½x13*
333 A22 3e multicolored   .60 .30
Apparition of the Virgin Mary to three shepherd children at Fatima, Portugal, 50th anniv.

Cabral Issue

| Map of Brazil, by Lopo Homem- |
| Reinéis, 1519 — A23 |

1968, Apr. 22   Litho.   *Perf. 14*
334 A23 4.50e multicolored   .80 .50
See note after Macao No. 416.

Admiral Coutinho Issue
Common Design Type
Design: 4.50e, Adm. Coutinho and frigate Adm. Gago Coutinho.

1969, Feb. 17   Litho.   *Perf. 14*
335 CD55 4.50e multicolored   1.10 .85

| View of Dili, |
| 1834 — A24 |

1969, July 25   Litho.   *Perf. 14*
336 A24 1e multicolored   .30 .25
Bicentenary of Dili as capital of Timor.

---

da Gama Medal	Emblem of King
in St. Jerome's	Manuel, St.
Convent — A25	Jerome's
	Convent — A26

Vasco da Gama Issue
1969, Aug. 29   Litho.   *Perf. 14*
337 A25 5e multicolored   .40 .30
Vasco da Gama (1469-1524), navigator.

Administration Reform Issue
Common Design Type
1969, Sept. 25   Litho.   *Perf. 14*
338 CD56 5e multicolored   .40 .25

King Manuel I Issue
1969, Dec. 1   Litho.   *Perf. 14*
339 A26 4e multicolored   .40 .25
King Manuel I, 500th birth anniv.

| Capt. Ross Smith, Arms of Great |
| Britain, Portugal and Australia, and |
| Map of Timor |
| A27 |

1969, Dec. 9
340 A27 2e multicolored   .50 .40
50th anniv. of the first England to Australia flight of Capt. Ross Smith and Lt. Keith Smith.

Marshal Carmona Issue
Common Design Type
Antonio Oscar Carmona in civilian clothes.

1970, Nov. 15   Litho.   *Perf. 14*
341 CD57 1.50e multicolored   .25 .25

Lusiads Issue

	Sailing Ship and
	Monks Preaching
	to
	Islanders — A28

1972, May 25   Litho.   *Perf. 13*
342 A28 1e brown & multi   .25 *.35*
4th centenary of publication of The Lusiads by Luiz Camoens.

Olympic Games Issue
Common Design Type
Design: 4.50e, Soccer, Olympic emblem.

1972, June 20   *Perf. 14x13½*
343 CD59 4.50e multicolored   .50 .50

Lisbon-Rio de Janeiro Flight Issue
Common Design Type
Design: 1e, Sacadura Cabral and Gago Coutinho in cockpit of "Lusitania."

1972, Sept. 20   Litho.   *Perf. 13½*
344 CD60 1e multicolored   .25 .40

WMO Centenary Issue
Common Design Type
1973, Dec. 15   Litho.   *Perf. 13*
345 CD61 20e multicolored   1.75 *2.00*

United Nations Transitional Authority in East Timor

A30

2000, Apr. 29   Litho.   *Perf. 12x11¾*
350 A30 Dom. red & multi   35.00 50.00
351 A30 Int. blue & multi   50.00 75.00
No. 350 sold for 10c and No. 351 sold for 50c on day of issue.

INDEPENDENT STATE OF TIMOR-LESTE

Independence — A31

Designs: 25c, Crocodile. 50c, Palm fronds. $1, Coffee beans and picker. $2, Flag.

2002, May 20   Litho.   *Perf. 14½x14*
352-355 A31 Set of 4   20.00 35.00

A32

Flag and: 10c, Pres. Xanana Gusmao. 50c, Map of country.

2002   Litho.   *Perf. 13x13¼*
356-357 A32 Set of 2   12.50 15.00

A33

Independence From Portugal, 30th Anniv. — A34

Designs: 15c, Timorese flag, old man. 25c, Timorese flag, child. 50c, Timorese coin, rooster. 75c, Timorese flag, Pres. Nicolau Lobato.

2005, Nov. 28   Litho.   *Perf. 12x12½*
358 A33 15c multi   .75 .75
359 A33 25c multi   1.00 1.00
360 A33 50c multi   2.00 2.00
361 A34 75c multi   3.00 3.00
       Nos. 358-361 (4)   6.75 6.75

AIR POST STAMPS

Common Design Type
1938   Unwmk.   Engr.   *Perf. 13½x13*
Name and Value in Black

C1 CD39 1a scarlet   .85 .45
C2 CD39 2a purple   .90 .55
C3 CD39 3a orange   .90 .60
C4 CD39 5a ultra   1.00 .65
C5 CD39 10a lilac brown   2.00 1.00
C6 CD39 20a dark green   3.50 1.75
C7 CD39 50a red brown   6.00 4.00

C8 CD39 70a rose carmine   9.00 7.50
C9 CD39 1p magenta   17.50 8.25
       Nos. C1-C9 (9)   25.25 25.25
No. C7 exists with overprint "Exposicao Internacional de Nova York, 1939-1940" and Trylon and Perisphere. Counterfeits exist. For overprints see Nos. C15-C23.

Mozambique Nos. C3, C4, C6, C7 and C9 Surcharged in Black

1946   Unwmk.   *Perf. 13½x13*
C10 CD39 8a on 50c orange   9.00 5.00
C11 CD39 12a on 1e ultra   9.00 5.00
C12 CD39 40a on 3e dk green   9.00 5.00
C13 CD39 50a on 5e red brn   9.00 5.00
C14 CD39 1p on 10e mag   9.00 5.00
       Nos. C10-C14 (5)   45.00 25.00

Nos. C1-C9 Overprinted "Libertacao"
1947
C15 CD39 1a scarlet   25.00 19.00
C16 CD39 2a purple   25.00 19.00
C17 CD39 3a orange   26.50 20.00
C18 CD39 5a ultra   25.00 19.00
C19 CD39 10a lilac brown   8.00 4.75
C20 CD39 20a dark green   8.75 5.50
C21 CD39 50a red brown   8.00 4.50
C22 CD39 70a rose carmine   35.00 14.00
C23 CD39 1p magenta   15.00 7.50
       Nos. C15-C23 (9)   176.25 113.25

POSTAGE DUE STAMPS

D1

1904   Unwmk.   Typo.   *Perf. 12*
Without Gum
Name and Value in Black

J1 D1 1a yellow green   .75 .50
J2 D1 2a slate   .75 .50
J3 D1 5a yellow brown   2.50 1.50
J4 D1 6a red orange   2.75 2.25
J5 D1 10a gray brown   3.00 2.00
J6 D1 15a red brown   4.75 3.25
J7 D1 24a dull blue   7.50 6.00
J8 D1 40a carmine   9.00 6.75
J9 D1 50a orange   14.00 8.00
J10 D1 1p dull violet   22.50 15.00
       Nos. J1-J10 (10)   67.50 45.75

Overprinted in Carmine or Green

1911   **Without Gum**
J11 D1 1a yellow green   .25 .25
J12 D1 2a slate   .30 .25
  a. Inverted overprint
J13 D1 5a yellow brown   .60 .40
J14 D1 6a deep orange   .80 .50
J15 D1 10a gray brown   1.50 .70
J16 D1 15a brown   1.75 1.10
J17 D1 24a dull blue   2.50 2.00
J18 D1 40a carmine (G)   3.25 2.50
J19 D1 50a orange   3.75 2.50
J20 D1 1p dull violet   7.50 7.00
       Nos. J11-J20 (10)   22.20 17.20

Nos. J1-J10 Overprinted in Red or Green

1913 — Without Gum
J21	D1	1a yellow green	8.00	9.00
J22	D1	2a slate	8.00	9.00
J23	D1	5a yellow brown	6.00	6.00
J24	D1	6a deep orange	6.00	6.00
a.		Inverted surcharge	30.00	
J25	D1	10a gray brown	6.00	6.00
J26	D1	15a red brown	6.00	6.00
J27	D1	24a dull blue	7.00	7.00
J28	D1	40a carmine (G)	7.00	7.00
J29	D1	50a orange	10.00	12.00
J30	D1	1p gray violet	10.00	12.00
		Nos. J21-J30 (10)	74.00	80.00

Catalogue values for unused stamps in this section, from this point to the end of the section, are for Never Hinged items.

Common Design Type
1952 Photo. & Typo. Perf. 14
Numeral in Red, Frame Multicolored
J31	CD45	1a chocolate	.40	.40
J32	CD45	3a brown	.40	.40
J33	CD45	5a dark green	.40	.40
J34	CD45	10a green	.40	.40
J35	CD45	30a purple	.65	.65
J36	CD45	1p brown carmine	1.25	1.25
		Nos. J31-J36 (6)	3.50	3.50

WAR TAX STAMP

Regular Issue of 1914 Surcharged in Red

1919 Unwmk. Perf. 15x14
Without Gum
MR1	A7	2a on ½a ol brn	30.00	22.50

See note after Macao No. MR2.

NEWSPAPER STAMPS

King Luiz — N1

Stamps of Macao Surcharged in Black
1892 Unwmk. Perf. 12½
Without Gum
P1	N1	2½r on 20r brt rose	2.00	.75
a.		"TIMOR" inverted		
P2	N1	2½r on 40r chocolate	2.00	.75
a.		"TIMOR" inverted		
b.		Perf. 13½	4.50	3.00
c.		As "a," perf. 13½		
P3	N1	2½r on 80r gray	2.00	.75
a.		"TIMOR" inverted	18.00	11.50
b.		Perf. 13½		
		Nos. P1-P3 (3)	6.00	2.25

N2   N3

1893-95 Typo. Perf. 11½, 13½
P4	N2	2½r brown	.40	.35
a.		Perf. 12½	2.00	1.50
P5	N3	½a on 2½r brn ('95)	.45	.30

For surcharges see Nos. 103, 123, 194.

POSTAL TAX STAMPS
Pombal Issue
Common Design Types
1925 Unwmk. Perf. 12½
RA1	CD28	2a lake & black	.30	.30
RA2	CD29	2a lake & black	.30	.30
RA3	CD30	2a lake & black	.30	.30
		Nos. RA1-RA3 (3)	.90	.90

Type of War Tax Stamp of Portuguese India Overprinted in Red

1934-35 Perf. 12
RA4	WT1	2a green & blk	6.50	8.00
RA5	WT1	5a green & blk	8.00	8.00
Surcharged in Black
RA6	WT1	7a on ½a rose & blk ('35)	10.00	9.00
		Nos. RA4-RA6 (3)	24.50	25.00

The tax was for local education.

Type of War Tax Stamp of Portuguese India Overprinted in Black

1936 Perf. 12x11½
RA7	WT1	10a rose & black	7.00	9.00
1937 Perf. 11½
RA8	WT1	10a green & blk	5.50	8.25

PT1

1948 Unwmk. Typo. Perf. 11½
Without Gum
RA9	PT1	10a dark blue	3.00	2.00
RA10	PT1	20a green	3.50	3.00

The 20a bears a different emblem.

Catalogue values for unused stamps in this section, from this point to the end of the section, are for Never Hinged items.

PT2

1960 Without Gum Perf. 11½
RA11	PT2	70c dark blue	1.50	1.25
RA12	PT2	1.30e green	2.25	2.25

See Nos. RA13-RA16. For surcharges see Nos. RA20-RA25.

Type of 1960 Redrawn
1967 Typo. Perf. 10½
Without Gum
RA13	PT2	70c deep blue	12.00	12.00
RA14	PT2	1.30e emerald	16.00	12.50

The denominations of Nos. RA13-RA14 are 2mm high. They are 2½mm high on Nos. RA11-RA12. Other differences exist. The printed area of No. RA13 measures 18x31mm; "Republica" 16mm.

Type of 1960
Serif Type Face
1967
RA14A	PT2	70c deep blue	12.00	10.00

Type of 1960, 2nd Redrawing
1967-68 Typo. Perf. 10½
Without Gum
RA15	PT2	70c violet blue	.60	.60
RA16	PT2	1.30e bluish grn ('68)	1.25	1.25

The printed area measures 13x30mm on Nos. RA15-RA16; "Republica" measures 10½mm.

Woman and Star — PT3

1969-70 Litho. Perf. 13½
RA17	PT3	30c vio bl & lt bl ('70)	.25	.25
RA18	PT3	50c dl org & maroon	.25	.25
RA19	PT3	1e yellow & brown	.25	.25
		Nos. RA17-RA19 (3)	.75	.75

The 2.50e and 10e in design PT3 were revenue stamps. Value $1.50 each.

Nos. RA15-RA16 Surcharged in Red or Carmine

1970 Typo. Perf. 10½
Without Gum
RA20	PT2	30c on 70c	7.00	6.00
RA21	PT2	30c on 1.30e	6.00	6.00
RA22	PT2	50c on 70c	275.00	200.00
RA23	PT2	50c on 1.30e	7.25	7.25
RA24	PT2	1e on 70c (C)	325.00	225.00
RA25	PT2	1e on 1.30e	10.00	10.00
		Nos. RA20-RA25 (6)	630.25	454.25

POSTAL TAX DUE STAMPS
Pombal Issue
Common Design Types
1925 Unwmk. Perf. 12½
RAJ1	CD28	4a lake & black	.40	1.00
RAJ2	CD29	4a lake & black	.40	1.00
RAJ3	CD30	4a lake & black	.40	1.00
		Nos. RAJ1-RAJ3 (3)	1.20	3.00

TOBAGO
tə-ˈbā-ˌgō

LOCATION — An island in the West Indies lying off the Venezuelan coast north of Trinidad
GOVT. — British Colony
AREA — 116 sq. mi.
POP. — 25,358
CAPITAL — Scarborough (Port Louis)

In 1889 Tobago, then an independent colony, was united with Trinidad under the name of Colony of Trinidad and Tobago. It became a ward of that colony January 1, 1899.

12 Pence = 1 Shilling
20 Shillings = 1 Pound

Queen Victoria
A1   A2

Wmk. Crown and C C (1)
1879 Typo. Perf. 14
1	A1	1p rose	130.00	90.00
2	A1	3p blue	130.00	75.00
3	A1	6p orange	60.00	80.00
4	A1	1sh green	425.00	80.00
a.		Half used as 6p on cover		
5	A1	5sh slate	800.00	800.00
6	A1	£1 violet	4,500.	

Stamps of the above set with revenue cancellations sell for a small fraction of the price of postally used examples.
Stamps of Type A1, watermarked Crown and C A, are revenue stamps.

1880 Manuscript Surcharge
7	A1	1p on half of 6p org	5,500.	875.

1880
8	A2	½p brown violet	60.00	90.00
9	A2	1p red brown	140.00	70.00
a.		Half used as ½p on cover		2,250.
10	A2	4p yellow green	325.00	32.50
a.		Half used as 2p on cover		2,250.
11	A2	6p bister brown	400.00	125.00
12	A2	1sh bister	90.00	100.00
a.		Imperf.		
		Nos. 8-12 (5)	1,015.	417.50

No. 11 Surcharged in Black

1883
13	A2	2½p on 6p bister brn	90.00	90.00
a.		Double surcharge	4,000.	2,000.

1882-96 Wmk. Crown and C A (2)
14	A2	½p brown vio ('82)	2.25	16.00
15	A2	½p dull green ('86)	2.75	1.40
16	A2	1p red brown ('82)	9.00	2.75
a.		Diagonal half used as ½p on cover		—
17	A2	1p rose ('89)	5.00	1.75
18	A2	2½p ultra ('83)	11.00	1.10
a.		2½p dull blue ('83)	55.00	3.00
b.		2½p bright blue	12.00	1.10
19	A2	4p yel grn ('82)	210.00	100.00
20	A2	4p gray ('85)	5.50	3.75
a.		Imperf., pair	2,250.	
21	A2	6p bis brn ('84)	625.00	550.00
a.		Imperf.		
22	A2	6p brn org ('86)	2.75	6.50
23	A1	1sh olive bis ('94)	3.25	22.50
24	A2	1sh brn org ('96)	17.50	85.00

Stamps of 1882-96 Surcharged in Black

Nos. 25-29   No. 30

1886-92
25	A2	½p on 2½p ultra	8.50	21.00
a.		Inverted surcharge		
b.		Pair, one without surcharge	15,000.	
c.		Space between "½" and "PENNY" 3mm	35.00	75.00
d.		Double surcharge	2,500.	2,000.
26	A2	½p on 4p gray	27.50	80.00
a.		Space between "½" and "PENNY" 3mm		
b.		Double surcharge	3,500.	
27	A2	½p on 6p bis brn	3.75	22.50
a.		Inverted surcharge	3,250.	
b.		Space between "½" and "PENNY" 3mm	30.00	125.00
c.		Double surcharge	3,750.	
28	A2	½p on 6p brn org	140.00	180.00
a.		Space between "½" and "PENNY" 3mm	375.00	425.00
b.		Double surcharge		2,750.

29	A2	1p on 2½ ultra	100.00	20.00
a.		Space between "1" and		
		"PENNY" 4mm	300.00	*90.00*
b.		Half used as ½p on cover		*1,650.*
30	A2	2½p on 4p gray	19.00	9.00
a.		Double surcharge	3,500.	3,500.
		Nos. 25-30 (6)	298.75	*332.50*

Revenue Stamp Type
A1 Surcharged in Black

½d
POSTAGE

1896

31	A1	½p on 4p lilac & rose	90.00	50.00
a.		Space between "½" and "d"		
		1½ to 2½mm	150.00	*82.50*

Tobago stamps were replaced by those of
Trinidad or Trinidad and Tobago.

TOGO
'tō-ˌgō

LOCATION — Western Africa, bordering on the Gulf of Guinea
GOVT. — Republic
AREA — 20,400 sq. mi.
POP. — 4,320,000 (1997 est.)
CAPITAL — Lome

The German Protectorate of Togo was occupied by Great Britain and France in World War I, and later mandated to them. The British area became part of Ghana. The French area was granted internal autonomy in 1956 and achieved independence in 1958.

100 Pfennig = 1 Mark
12 Pence = 1 Shilling
100 Centimes = 1 Franc

Catalogue values for unused stamps in this country are for Never Hinged items, beginning with Scott 309 in the regular postage section, Scott B11 in the semipostal section, Scott C14 in the airpost section, Scott J32 in the postage due section, and Scott O1 in the official section.

Watermark

Wmk. 125 — Lozenges

German Protectorate

AREA — 34,934 sq. mi.
POP. — 1,000,368 (1913)

Stamps of Germany Overprinted in Black

1897		Unwmk.	Perf. 13½x14½	
1	A9	3pf dark brown	5.50	7.25
a.		3pf yellow brown	9.25	25.00
b.		3pf reddish brown	47.50	140.00
c.		3pf pale gray brown	1,600.	1,200.
2	A9	5pf green	5.00	2.90
3	A10	10pf carmine	6.00	3.25
4	A10	20pf ultra	6.00	13.50
5	A10	25pf orange	35.00	60.00
6	A10	50pf red brown	35.00	60.00
		Nos. 1-6 (6)	92.50	146.90

A3

Kaiser's Yacht, the "Hohenzollern" — A4

1900		Typo.	Perf. 14	
7	A3	3pf brown	1.00	1.25
8	A3	5pf green	12.00	2.00
9	A3	10pf carmine	22.00	1.75
10	A3	20pf ultra	1.00	1.50
11	A3	25pf org & blk, yel	1.00	10.00
12	A3	30pf org & blk, sal	1.40	10.00
13	A3	40pf lake & blk	1.00	10.00
14	A3	50pf pur & blk, sal	1.40	7.50
15	A3	80pf lake & blk, rose	2.50	17.00

		Engr.		
		Perf. 14½x14		
16	A4	1m carmine	3.50	55.00
17	A4	2m blue	5.50	85.00
18	A4	3m black vio	7.25	150.00
19	A4	5m slate & car	120.00	500.00
		Nos. 7-19 (13)	179.55	851.00

Counterfeit cancellations are found on Nos. 10-19 and 22.

1909-19		Wmk. 125	Typo.	Perf. 14	
20	A3	3pf brown ('19)	.85	
21	A3	5pf green	1.25	2.25
22	A3	10pf carmine ('14)	1.75	110.00

		Engr.		
		Perf. 14½x14		
23	A4	5m slate & carmine ('19)	24.00	
		Nos. 20-23 (4)	27.85	

Nos. 20 and 23 were never placed in use.

British Protectorate

Nos. 7, 10-19, 21-22 Overprinted or Surcharged

First (Wide) Setting
3mm between Lines
2mm between "Anglo" & "French"
Wmk. 125 (5pf, 10pf); Unwmkd.

1914, Oct. 1			Perf. 14, 14½	
33	A3	½p on 3pf brown	225.00	175.00
a.		Thin "y" in "penny"	500.00	450.00
34	A3	1p on 5pf green	225.00	175.00
a.		Thin "y" in "penny"	500.00	500.00
35	A3	3pf brown	130.00	100.00
36	A3	5pf green	125.00	100.00
37	A3	10pf carmine	150.00	110.00
a.		Inverted overprint	9,000.	4,000.
b.		Unwmk.		6,250.
38	A3	20pf ultra	37.50	50.00
39	A3	25pf org & blk, yel	37.50	42.50
40	A3	30pf org & blk, sal	42.50	60.00
41	A3	40pf lake & blk	275.00	275.00
42	A3	50pf pur & blk, sal	11,000.	9,000.
43	A3	80pf lake & blk, rose	275.00	300.00
44	A4	1m carmine	5,750.	2,800.
45	A4	2m blue	9,500.	11,000.
a.		Inverted overprint	12,000.	
b.		"Occupation" double	18,000.	13,000.

On Nos. 33-34, the surcharge line ("Half penny" or "One penny") was printed separately and its position varies in relation to the 3-line overprint. On Nos. 46-47, the surcharge and overprint lines were printed simultaneously.

Second (Narrow) Setting
2mm between Lines
2mm between "Anglo" & "French"

1914, Oct.				
46	A3	½p on 3pf brown	45.00	30.00
a.		Thin "y" in "penny"	70.00	70.00
b.		"TOG"	475.00	350.00
47	A3	1p on 5pf green	5.00	5.00
a.		Thin "y" in "penny"	15.00	17.50
b.		"TOG"	150.00	125.00
48	A3	3pf brown	5,500.	1,000.
a.		"Occupation" omitted		
49	A3	5pf green	1,400.	800.00
50	A3	10pf carmine		3,100.
51	A3	20pf ultra	26.00	14.00
a.		"TOG"	3,500.	3,000.
b.		Vert. pair, #51 & #38	13,750.	
52	A3	25pf org & blk, yel	32.50	35.00
a.		"TOG"	13,750.	
53	A3	30pf org & blk, sal	22.50	32.50
54	A3	40pf lake & blk	5,500.	1,750.
55	A3	50pf pur & blk, sal		7,500.
56	A3	80pf lake & blk, rose	2,750.	2,100.
57	A4	1m carmine	8,500.	4,500.
58	A4	2m blue		10,000.
59	A4	3m black violet		55,000.
60	A4	5m slate & car		55,000.

Third Setting
1¼mm btwn. "Anglo" & "French"
2mm between Lines
"Anglo-French" 15mm Wide

1915, Jan. 7				
61	A3	3pf brown	9,000.	3,250.
62	A3	5pf green	225.	150.
63	A3	10pf carmine	225.	150.
64	A3	20pf ultra	1,600.	600.
64A	A3	40pf lake & blk		8,500.
65	A3	50pf pur & blk, sal	15,000.	10,000.

Stamps of Gold Coast Overprinted Locally

1915, May		Wmk. 3	Perf. 14	
66	A7	½p green	.35	2.75
a.		Double overprint	525.00	550.00
67	A8	1p scarlet	.35	.60
a.		Double ovpt.	375.00	500.00
b.		Inverted ovpt.	200.00	275.00
c.		As "b," "Togo" omitted	8,000.	
68	A7	2p gray	.35	1.40
69	A7	2 ½p ultra	3.00	5.50

Chalky Paper
70	A7	3p violet, yel	3.00	3.75
71	A7	6p dl vio & red vio	2.50	2.00
72	A7	1sh black, grn	2.50	9.00
a.		Double overprint	1,300.	
73	A7	2sh vio & bl, bl	15.00	17.50
74	A7	2sh6p blk & red, bl	5.25	26.00
75	A7	10sh grn & red, grn	50.00	70.00
76	A7	20sh vio & blk, red	150.00	175.00

Surfaced-Colored Paper
77	A7	3p violet, yel	4.50	22.50
78	A7	5sh grn & red, yel	9.25	17.50
		Nos. 66-78 (13)	246.05	353.50

Nos. 66-78 exist with small "F" in "French" and thin "G" in "Togo." Several values are known without the hyphen between "Anglo-French" and all but No. 77 without the first "O" in "Occupation."

Stamps of Gold Coast Overprinted in London

1916, Apr.		Ordinary Paper		
80	A7	½p green	.35	3.00
81	A8	1p scarlet	.35	1.00
a.		Inverted overprint		
82	A7	2p gray	.60	1.75
83	A7	2 ½p ultra	.70	1.75

Chalky Paper
84	A7	3p violet, yel	4.50	1.50
85	A7	6p dl vio & red vio	2.50	1.25
86	A7	1sh black, grn	5.00	10.00
a.		1sh black, emerald	350.00	750.00
b.		1sh black, bl grn, on back	9.50	17.50
87	A7	2sh vio & ultra, bl	5.25	9.75
88	A7	2sh6p blk & red, bl	5.25	8.00
89	A7	10sh grn & red, yel	25.00	30.00
90	A7	10sh grn & red, bl grn, ol back	20.00	80.00
a.		10sh green & red, grn	27.50	75.00
91	A7	20sh vio & blk, red	160.00	190.00
		Nos. 80-91 (12)	229.50	338.00

The overprint on Nos. 80-91 is in heavier letters than on Nos. 66-78 and the 2nd and 3rd lines are each ½mm longer. The letter "O" on Nos. 80-91 is narrower and more oval.

Issued under French Occupation
Stamps of German Togo Surcharged

c

---

d   e

f   g

h   i

Wmk. Lozenges (5pf and 10pf) (125), Unwmk. (other values)

1914			Perf. 14, 14½	
151	A3(c+d)	5c on 3pf brn	80.00	80.00
152	A3(c+e)	5c on 3pf brn	75.00	75.00
153	A3(c+f)	5c on 3pf brn	87.50	87.50
154	A3(c+g)	10c on 5pf grn	28.00	28.00
a.		Double surcharge	1,350.	1,350.
155	A3(c+h)	10c on 5pf grn	28.00	28.00
156	A3(c+i)	10c on 5pf grn	55.00	55.00
158	A3(c)	20pf ultra	65.00	65.00
a.		3 ½mm between "TOGO" and "Occupation"	1,000.	1,000.
159	A3(c)	25pf org & blk, yel	92.50	92.50
160	A3(c)	30pf org & blk, sal	100.00	100.00
161	A3(c)	40pf lake & black	700.00	725.00
162	A3(c)	80pf lake & blk, rose	700.00	725.00
		Nos. 151-162 (11)	2,011.	2,061.

Surcharged or Overprinted in Sans-Serif Type

1915				
164	A3	5c on 3pf brown	24,000.	5,250.
165	A3	5pf green	1,200.	525.
166	A3	10pf carmine	1,300.	500.
a.		Inverted overprint	31,000.	19,000.
167	A3	20pf ultra	1,600.	1,200.
168	A3	25pf org & blk, yel	17,250.	8,000.
169	A3	30pf org & blk, sal	17,250.	8,000.
170	A3	40pf lake & blk	17,250.	8,000.
171	A3	50pf pur & blk, sal	24,000.	14,000.
171A	A3	80pf red & blk, rose		65,000.
172	A4	1m carmine		75,000.
173	A4	2m blue	32,000.	26,000.
174	A4	3m black vio		47,500.
175	A4	5m slate & car	47,500.	55,000.

Stamps of Dahomey, 1913-17, Overprinted

1916-17		Unwmk.	Perf. 13½x14	
176	A5	1c violet & blk	.30	.55
177	A5	2c choc & rose	.30	.55
178	A5	4c black & brn	.55	.90
a.		Double overprint	550.00	550.00
179	A5	5c yel grn & bl grn	.80	.80
180	A5	10c org red & rose	.80	.80

181	A5	15c brn org & dk vio ('17)	2.00	2.00
182	A5	20c gray & choc	.80	1.20
183	A5	25c ultra & dp bl	1.20	1.20
184	A5	30c choc & vio	1.20	1.60
185	A5	35c brown & blk	2.00	2.40
186	A5	40c blk & red org	1.60	2.00
187	A5	45c gray & ultra	2.00	2.40
188	A5	50c choc & brn	2.00	2.40
189	A5	75c blue & vio	7.25	8.75
190	A5	1fr bl grn & blk	9.50	12.00
191	A5	2fr buff & choc	13.50	16.00
192	A5	5fr vio & do bl	16.00	18.50
		Nos. 176-192 (17)	61.80	74.05

All values of the 1916-17 issue exist on chalky paper and all but the 15c, 25c and 35c on ordinary paper. See the *Scott Classic Specialized Catalogue of Stamps & Covers* for detailed listings.

French Mandate

AREA — 21,893 sq. mi.
POP. — 780,497 (1938)

Type of Dahomey,
1913-39, Overprinted

1921

193	A5	1c gray & yel grn	.30	.50
a.		Overprint omitted	140.00	140.00
194	A5	2c blue & org	.30	.50
195	A5	4c ol grn & org	.30	.50
196	A5	5c dull red & blk	.30	.50
a.		Overprint omitted	475.00	475.00
197	A5	10c bl grn & yel grn	.70	.80
198	A5	15c brown & car	.80	.90
199	A5	20c bl grn & org	1.20	1.20
200	A5	25c slate & org	1.20	1.20
201	A5	30c dp rose & ver	1.60	2.00
202	A5	35c red brn & yel grn	1.20	1.60
203	A5	40c red brn & ol	2.00	2.00
204	A5	45c red brn & ol	1.60	2.00
205	A5	50c deep blue	1.60	1.60
206	A5	75c dl red & ultra	2.00	2.40
207	A5	1fr gray & ultra	2.00	2.40
208	A5	2fr ol grn & rose	6.75	7.25
209	A5	5fr orange & blk	12.00	13.00
		Nos. 193-209 (17)	35.85	40.35

Stamps and Type of 1921 Surcharged

No. 210   No. 213

1922-25

210	A5	25c on 15c ol brn & rose red	.55	.65
211	A5	25c on 2fr ol grn & rose	.70	.90
212	A5	25c on 5fr org & blk	.70	.90
a.		"TOGO" omitted	300.00	325.00
213	A5	60c on 75c vio, *pnksh*	1.20	1.60
a.		"60" omitted	225.00	240.00
214	A5	65c on 45c red brn & ol	1.60	2.00
a.		"TOGO" omitted	225.00	225.00
215	A5	85c on 75c dull red & ultra	2.40	2.75
		Nos. 210-215 (6)	7.15	8.80

Issue years: #213, 1922; #211-212, 1924; others, 1925.

Coconut
Grove
A6

Cacao
Trees — A7

Oil Palms
A8

1924-38   **Typo.**

216	A6	1c yellow & blk	.25	.40
217	A6	2c dp rose & blk	.25	.40
218	A6	4c dk blue & blk	.25	.40
219	A6	5c dp org & blk	.25	.40
220	A6	10c red vio & blk	.25	.40
221	A6	15c green & blk	.25	.40
222	A7	20c gray & blk	.30	.50
223	A7	25c grn & blk, *yel*	.70	.80
224	A7	30c gray grn & blk	.30	.40
225	A7	30c dl grn & lt grn ('27)	.80	.80
226	A7	35c lt brown & blk ('38)	.80	.95
227	A7	35c dp bl grn & grn	.80	.80
228	A7	40c red org & blk	.30	.40
229	A7	45c carmine & blk	.30	.40
230	A7	50c ocher & blk, *bluish*	.55	.65
231	A7	55c vio bl & car rose ('38)	1.05	1.05
232	A7	60c vio brn & blk, *pnksh*	.30	.40
233	A7	60c dp red ('26)	.50	.70
234	A7	65c gray lil & brn	.70	.80
235	A7	75c blue & black	.70	.80
236	A7	80c ind & dl vio ('38)	2.00	2.00
237	A7	85c brn org & brn	1.25	1.30
238	A7	90c brn red & cer ('27)	.95	1.20
239	A8	1fr red brn & blk, *bluish*	.90	.95
240	A8	1fr blue ('26)	.70	.90
241	A8	1fr gray lil & grn ('28)	3.25	3.25
242	A8	1fr dk red & red org ('38)	1.05	1.05
243	A8	1.10fr vio & dk brn ('28)	4.75	6.50
244	A8	1.25fr mag & rose ('33)	1.60	2.00
245	A8	1.50fr bl & lt bl ('27)	.80	.95
246	A8	1.75fr bis & pink ('33)	9.50	6.00
247	A8	1.75fr vio bl & ultra ('38)	1.50	1.50
248	A8	2fr bl blk & blk, *bluish*	1.25	1.30
249	A8	3fr bl grn & red org ('27)	1.40	1.60
250	A8	5fr red org & blk, *bluish*	2.10	2.40
251	A8	10fr ol brn & rose ('26)	2.75	3.25
252	A8	20fr brn red & blk, *yel* ('26)	3.25	4.00
		Nos. 216-252 (37)	46.60	52.00

For surcharges see Nos. 253, 301-302, B8-B9.

No. 240 Surcharged with New Value and Bars in Red

1926

253	A8	1.25fr on 1fr lt bl	.70	.70

Common Design Types
pictured following the introduction.

Colonial Exposition Issue
Common Design Types
Engr., "TOGO" Typo. in Black

1931, Apr. 13   **Perf. 12½**

254	CD70	40c deep green	6.50	6.50
255	CD71	50c violet	6.50	6.50
256	CD72	90c red orange	6.50	6.50
257	CD73	1.50fr dull blue	6.50	6.50
		Nos. 254-257 (4)	26.00	26.00
		Set, never hinged	42.00	

Paris International Exposition Issue
Common Design Types

1937   **Perf. 13**

258	CD74	20c deep violet	1.90	1.90
259	CD75	30c dark green	1.90	1.90
260	CD76	40c carmine rose	1.90	1.90
261	CD77	50c dark brown	1.90	1.90
262	CD78	90c red	1.90	1.90
263	CD79	1.50fr dark green	1.90	1.90
		Nos. 258-263 (6)	11.40	11.40
		Set, never hinged	17.50	

Colonial Arts Exhibition Issue
Souvenir Sheet
Common Design Type

1937   **Imperf.**

264	CD77	3fr Prus bl & blk	8.00	9.50
		Never hinged	12.00	

Caillié Issue
Common Design Type

1939, Apr. 5   **Perf. 12½x12**

265	CD81	90c org brn & org	.95	.95
266	CD81	2fr brt violet	1.10	1.10
267	CD81	2.25fr ultra & dk bl	1.10	1.10
		Nos. 265-267 (3)	3.15	3.15
		Set, never hinged	4.50	

New York World's Fair Issue
Common Design Type

1939, May 10

268	CD82	1.25fr carmine lake	1.25	1.25
		Never hinged	1.60	
269	CD82	2.25fr ultra	1.25	1.25
		Never hinged	1.60	

Togolese Women
A9   A12

Mono River
Bank
A10

Hunters
A11

1941   **Engr.**   **Perf. 12½**

270	A9	2c brown vio	.25	.30
271	A9	3c yellow grn	.25	.30
272	A9	4c brown blk	.25	.30
273	A9	5c lilac rose	.25	.30
274	A9	10c light blue	.25	.30
275	A9	15c chestnut	.25	.25
276	A10	20c plum	.25	.25
277	A10	25c violet blue	.25	.25
278	A10	30c brown blk	.25	.25
279	A10	40c dk carmine	.30	.40
280	A10	45c dk green	.30	.40
281	A10	50c chestnut	.30	.30
282	A10	60c red violet	.65	.70
283	A11	70c black	.95	1.05
284	A11	90c lt violet	1.35	1.60
285	A11	1fr yellow grn	.55	.65
286	A11	1.25fr cerise	1.20	2.40
287	A11	1.40fr orange brn	.80	.90
288	A11	1.60fr orange	.80	.95
289	A11	2fr lt ultra	.90	.95
290	A12	2.25fr ultra	1.45	2.40
291	A12	2.50fr lilac rose	.95	1.05
292	A12	3fr brown vio	1.10	1.20
293	A12	5fr vermilion	1.10	1.20
294	A12	10fr rose violet	1.75	1.90
295	A12	20fr brown blk	2.50	2.60
		Nos. 270-295 (26)	19.20	23.15
		Set, never hinged	29.00	

For surcharges see Nos. 303-308, B7, B10.

Mono River
Bank and
Marshal
Pétain
A12a

1941   **Engr.**   **Perf. 12½x12**

296	A12a	1fr green	.80	
297	A12a	2.50fr blue	.80	

Nos. 296-297 were issued by the Vichy government in France, but were not placed on sale in Togo.

For surcharges, see Nos. B10D-B10E.

Types of 1941 Without "RF"

1942-44   **Perf. 12½**

298	A9	10c blue green	.30	
299	A9	15c yel brn & black	.70	
300	A10	20c lilac brn & black	.90	
300A	A11	1fr yellow grn	.95	
300B	A11	1.50fr lilac & green	.70	
300C	A12	3fr brown violet	.95	
300D	A12	5fr red brown	.95	
300E	A12	10fr rose violet	1.50	
300F	A12	20fr brown blk	1.75	
		Nos. 298-300F (9)	8.70	
		Set, never hinged	13.00	

Nos. 298-300F were issued by the Vichy government in France, but were not placed on sale in Togo.

Nos. 231, 238, 284 Surcharged in Various Colors

a

b

Perf. 14x13½, 12½

1943-44   **Unwmk.**

301	A7(a)	1.50fr on 55c (Bk)	1.20	.85
302	A7(a)	1.50fr on 90c (Bk)	1.20	.85
303	A11(b)	3.50fr on 90c (Bk)	.80	.70
304	A11(b)	4fr on 90c (R)	1.20	.85
305	A11(b)	5fr on 90c (Bl)	2.00	1.50
306	A11(b)	5.50fr on 90c (Br)	2.00	1.50
307	A11(b)	10fr on 90c (G) ('44)	2.00	1.50
308	A11(b)	20fr on 90c (R)	3.25	2.00
		Nos. 301-308 (8)	13.65	9.75
		Set, never hinged	18.00	

Catalogue values for unused stamps in this section, from this point to the end of the section, are for Never Hinged items.

Extracting Palm
Oil — A13

Hunter — A14

Cotton
Spinners — A15

Village of
Atakpamé
A16

Red-fronted Gazelles — A17

Houses of the Cabrais
A18

1947, Oct. 6   Engr.   Perf. 12½
309	A13	10c dark red	.50	.30
310	A13	30c brt ultra	.50	.30
311	A13	50c bluish green	.50	.30
312	A14	60c lilac rose	.50	.30
313	A14	1fr chocolate	.70	.50
314	A14	1.20fr yellow grn	.90	.55
315	A15	1.50fr brown org	.90	.65
316	A15	2fr olive	.90	.65
317	A15	2.50fr gray blk	2.10	1.20
318	A16	3fr slate	1.00	.65
319	A16	3.60fr rose car	1.50	.95
320	A16	4fr Prus green	1.10	.50
321	A17	5fr black brn	2.50	.50
322	A17	6fr ultra	2.50	1.45
323	A17	10fr orange red	3.50	.50
324	A18	15fr dp yel grn	3.25	.70
325	A18	20fr grnsh black	3.25	.95
326	A18	25fr lilac rose	3.50	1.00
		Nos. 309-326 (18)	29.60	11.95

Military Medal Issue
Common Design Type
Engr. & Typo.

1952, Dec. 1   Perf. 13
327	CD101	15fr multicolored	6.50	4.75

Gathering Palm Nuts
A19

1954, Nov. 29   Engr.
328	A19	8fr vio & vio brn	1.60	.80
329	A19	15fr indigo & dk brn	2.00	.80

Goliath Beetle — A20

1955, May 2
330	A20	8fr black & green	3.50	1.75

Intl. Exhibition for Wildlife Protection, Paris, May 1955.

FIDES Issue
Common Design Type

Design: 15fr, Teacher and children planting tree.

1956   Unwmk.   Perf. 13x12½
331	CD103	15fr dk vio brn & org brn	4.75	2.40

Republic

Woman Holding Flag — A21

1957, June 8   Engr.   Perf. 13
332	A21	15fr dk bl grn, sepia & red	.70	.25

Konkomba Helmet — A22

Teak Forest A23

Design: 4fr, 5fr, 6fr, 8fr, 10fr, Buffon's kob.

1957, Oct.   Unwmk.
333	A22	30c violet & claret	.30	.25
334	A22	50c indigo & blue	.30	.25
335	A22	1fr pur & lil rose	.30	.25
336	A22	2fr dk brn & olive	.30	.25
337	A22	3fr black & green	.30	.25
338	A22	4fr blue & gray	.60	.25
339	A22	5fr bluish gray & mag	.60	.25
340	A22	6fr crim rose & bl gray	.65	.25
341	A22	8fr bluish gray & vio	.65	.25
342	A22	10fr grn & red brn	.65	.25
343	A23	15fr multicolored	.45	.25
344	A23	20fr violet, mar & org	.50	.25
345	A23	25fr indigo & bis brn	.65	.25
346	A23	40fr dk brn, ol & dk grn	1.10	.35
		Nos. 333-346 (14)	7.35	3.60

See Nos. 350-363.

Flags, Dove and UN Emblem — A24

1958, Dec. 10   Engr.   Perf. 13
347	A24	20fr dk grn & rose red	.65	.25

Universal Declaration of Human Rights, 10th anniversary.

Flower Issue
Common Design Type

Designs: 5fr, Flower of Bombax tree (kapok). 20fr, Tectona grandis (teakwood) flower, horiz.

Perf. 12x12½, 12½x12

1959, Jan. 15   Photo.   Unwmk.
348	CD104	5fr dp bl, rose & grn	.50	.25
349	CD104	20fr black, yel & grn	.50	.25

Types of 1957
Inscribed:"Republique du Togo"

1959, Jan. 15   Engr.   Perf. 13
Designs as Before
350	A22	30c ultra & gray	.45	.25
351	A22	50c org & brt grn	.45	.25
352	A22	1fr red lil & lt ol grn	.45	.25
353	A22	2fr olive & bl grn	.45	.25
354	A22	3fr vio & rose car	.45	.25
355	A22	4fr lil rose & pale pur	.45	.25
356	A22	5fr green & brown	.45	.25
357	A22	6fr ultra & gray bl	.45	.25
358	A22	8fr sl grn & bis	.45	.25
359	A22	10fr vio & lt brn	.45	.25
360	A23	15fr dk brn, bis & cl	.45	.25
361	A23	20fr blk, bl grn & brn	.45	.25
362	A23	25fr sep, red brn, ol & vio	.60	.25
363	A23	40fr dk grn, org brn & bl	.60	.25
		Nos. 350-363 (14)	6.60	3.50

"Five Continents," Ceiling Painting, Palais des Nations, Geneva — A25

1959, Oct. 24   Engr.   Perf. 12½
Centers in Dark Ultramarine
364	A25	15fr brown	.35	.25
365	A25	20fr purple	.35	.25
366	A25	25fr dark orange	.35	.25
367	A25	40fr dark green	.55	.25
368	A25	60fr carmine rose	.60	.30
		Nos. 364-368 (5)	2.20	1.30

Issued for United Nations Day, Oct. 24.

Skier A26

Bicyclist A27

Sports: 50c, Ice Hockey. 1fr, Tobogganing. 15fr, Discus thrower, vert. 20fr, Boxing, vert. 25fr, Runner.

1960   Unwmk.   Perf. 13
369	A26	30c sl grn, car & bl grn	.45	.25
370	A26	50c red & black	.45	.25
371	A26	1fr red, blk & emer	.45	.25
372	A27	10fr brown, ultra & sl	.45	.25
373	A27	15fr dk red brn & grn	.45	.25
374	A27	20fr dk grn, gldn brn & brn	.55	.25
375	A27	25fr orange, mag & brn	.65	.25
		Nos. 369-375 (7)	3.45	1.75

8th Winter Olympic Games, Squaw Valley, Calif. (Nos. 369-371); 17th Olympic Games, Rome (Nos. 372-375).

Prime Minister Sylvanus Olympio and Togo Flag — A28

1960, Apr. 27   Litho.
Center in Green, Red, Yellow & Brown
376	A28	30c black & buff	.25	.25
377	A28	50c brown & buff	.25	.25
378	A28	1fr lilac & buff	.25	.25
379	A28	10fr blue & buff	.25	.25
380	A28	20fr red & buff	.25	.25
381	A28	25fr green & buff	.25	.25
		Nos. 376-381 (6)	1.50	1.50

Proclamation of Togo's full independence, Apr. 27, 1960.
See Nos. C31-C33.

Flags of "Big Four," and British Flag — A29

1960, May 21   Perf. 14x14½
382	A29	50c shown	.35	.25
383	A29	1fr USSR	.35	.25
384	A29	20fr France	.35	.25
385	A29	25fr US	.35	.25
		Nos. 382-385 (4)	1.40	1.00

Summit Conference of France, Great Britain, United States and USSR, Paris, May 16.

Flag of Togo and UN Emblem A30

1961, Jan. 6   Perf. 14½x15
Flag in red, olive green & yellow
386	A30	30c red	.30	.25
387	A30	50c brown	.30	.25
388	A30	1fr ultramarine	.30	.25
389	A30	10fr maroon	.30	.25
390	A30	25fr black	.30	.25
391	A30	30fr violet	.30	.25
		Nos. 386-391 (6)	1.80	1.50

Togo's admission to United Nations.

Crowned Cranes over Map — A31

Augustino de Souza — A32

1961, Apr. 1   Perf. 14½x15
392	A31	1fr multicolored	.40	.25
393	A31	10fr multicolored	.40	.25
394	A31	15fr multicolored	.50	.25
395	A31	30fr multicolored	.70	.25
		Nos. 392-395 (4)	2.00	1.00

1961, Apr. 27   Litho.   Perf. 15
396	A32	50c yellow, red & blk	.35	.25
397	A32	1fr emerald, brn & blk	.35	.25
398	A32	10fr grnsh bl, vio & blk	.35	.25
399	A32	25fr salmon, grn & blk	.35	.25
400	A32	30fr rose lil, bl & blk	.35	.25
		Nos. 396-400 (5)	1.75	1.25

1st anniv. of independence; "Papa" Augustino de Souza, leader of the independence movement.

Daniel C. Beard A33

Designs: 1fr, Lord Baden-Powell. 10fr, Togolese Scout and emblems. 25fr, Togolese Scout and flag, vert. 30fr, Symbolic tents and fire, vert. 100fr, Three hands of different races giving Scout sign.

1961, Oct. 7   Photo.   Perf. 13
401	A33	50c brt rose & grn	.45	.25
402	A33	1fr dp violet & car	.45	.25
403	A33	10fr dk gray & brn	.45	.25
404	A33	25fr multicolored	.45	.25
405	A33	30fr grn, red & org brn	.55	.25
406	A33	100fr rose car & bl	1.25	.25
		Nos. 401-406 (6)	3.60	1.50

Togolese Boy Scouts; 20th anniv. of the deaths of Daniel C. Beard and Lord Baden-Powell.

Four imperf. souvenir sheets each contain the six stamps, Nos. 401-406. Two sheets have a solid background of bright yellow, two a background of pale grayish brown. One yellow and one brown sheet have simulated perforations around the stamps. Size: 120x145mm. "REPUBLIQUE DU TOGO" is inscribed in white on bottom sheet margin. Value, each $4.

Plane, Ship and Part of Map of Africa — A34

Part of Map of Africa and: 25fr, Electric train and power mast. 30fr, Tractor and oil derricks. 85fr, Microscope and atomic symbol.

1961, Oct. 24   Litho.
Black Inscriptions; Map in Ocher
407	A34	20fr vio bl, org & yel	.50	.25
408	A34	25fr gray, org & yel	.50	.25
409	A34	30fr dk red, yel & org	.60	.25
410	A34	85fr blue, yel & org	1.10	.25
a.		Souvenir sheet of 4	4.00	2.75
		Nos. 407-410 (4)	2.70	1.00

UN Economic Commission for Africa. No. 410a contains one each of Nos. 407-410, imperf., printed without separating margin between the individual stamps to show a complete map of Africa.

Children Dancing
around
Globe — A35

Cmdr. Alan B.
Shepard — A36

UNICEF Emblem, children and globe.

1961, Dec. 9   Unwmk.   Perf. 13½
Black Inscription; Multicolored
Design
411 A35 1fr ultra   .40 .25
412 A35 10fr red brown   .40 .25
413 A35 20fr lilac   .40 .25
414 A35 25fr gray   .40 .25
415 A35 30fr bright blue   .45 .25
416 A35 85fr deep lilac   .85 .25
    Nos. 411-416 (6)   2.90 1.50
    UNICEF, 15th anniv.
Nos. 411-416 assembled in two rows show
the globe and children of various races dancing around it.

1962, Feb. 24   Perf. 15x14
Design: 1fr, 30fr, Yuri A. Gagarin.
417 A36 50c green   .40 .25
418 A36 1fr carmine rose   .40 .25
419 A36 25fr blue   .40 .25
420 A36 30fr purple   .40 .25
    Nos. 417-420 (4)   1.60 1.00
    Astronauts of 1961.
Issued in sheets of 50 and in miniature
sheets of 12 stamps plus four central labels
showing photographs of Alan B. Shepard
(US), Virgil I. Grissom (US), Yuri A. Gagarin
(USSR), Gherman S. Titov (USSR).

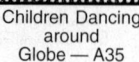

No. 417 Surcharged
in Black

1962, Apr. 7
421 A36 100fr on 50c green   2.40 .50
  a. Carmine surcharge   2.40 .50
Orbital flight of Lt. Col. John H. Glenn, Jr.,
US, Feb. 20, 1962.

Independence
Monument,
Lomé — A37

Woman
Carrying Fruit
Basket — A38

1962, Apr. 27   Litho.   Perf. 13½x14
422 A37 50c multicolored   .35 .25
423 A38 1fr green & pink   .35 .25
424 A37 5fr multicolored   .35 .25
425 A38 20fr purple & yel   .35 .25
426 A37 25fr multicolored   .35 .25
427 A38 30fr red & yellow   .35 .25
  a. Souv. sheet of 3, #424-425, 427,
    imperf.   2.40 1.75
    Nos. 422-427 (6)   2.10 1.50
2nd anniversary of Togo's independence.

Malaria
Eradication
Emblem
A39

1962, June 2   Perf. 13½x13
Multicolored Design
428 A39 10fr yellow green   .55 .25
429 A39 25fr pale lilac   .55 .25
430 A39 30fr ocher   .55 .25
431 A39 85fr light blue   1.10 .25
    Nos. 428-431 (4)   2.75 1.00
WHO drive to eradicate malaria.

Capitol, Pres. John F. Kennedy and
Pres. Sylvanus Olympio — A40

1962, July 4   Unwmk.   Perf. 13
Inscription and Portraits
in Slate Green
432 A40 50c yellow   .25 .25
433 A40 1fr blue   .25 .25
434 A40 2fr vermilion   .25 .25
435 A40 5fr lilac   .25 .25
436 A40 25fr pale violet   .45 .25
437 A40 100fr brt green   1.75 .80
  a. Souvenir sheet, imperf.   6.00 5.75
    Nos. 432-437 (6)   3.20 2.05
Visit of Pres. Sylvanus Olympio of Togo to
the US, Mar. 1962.

Mail Coach and Stamps of
1897 — A41

50c, Mail ship, stamps of 1900. 1fr, Mail
train, stamps of 1915. 10fr, Motorcycle truck,
stamp of 1924. 25fr, Mail truck, stamp of 1941.
30fr, DC-3, stamp of 1947.

1963, Jan. 12   Photo.   Perf. 13
438 A41 30c multicolored   .50 .25
439 A41 50c multicolored   .50 .25
440 A41 1fr multicolored   .50 .25
441 A41 10fr vio, dp org & blk   .50 .25
442 A41 25fr dk red brn, blk &
    yel grn   .50 .25
443 A41 30fr ol brn & lil rose   .50 .25
    Nos. 438-443,C34 (7)   5.00 1.95
65th anniv. of Togolese mail service.
For souvenir sheet see No. C34a.

Hands
Reaching
for FAO
Emblem
A42

1963, Mar. 21   Perf. 14
444 A42 50c bl, org & dk brn   .60 .25
445 A42 1fr ol grn, org & dk brn   .60 .25
446 A42 25fr brn, dk brn & org   .60 .25
447 A42 30fr vio, blk & org   .80 .25
    Nos. 444-447 (4)   2.60 1.00
FAO "Freedom from Hunger" campaign.

Togolese Flag and Lomé
Harbor — A43

1963, Apr. 27   Litho.   Perf. 13x12½
Flag in Red, Green and Yellow
448 A43 50c red brn & blk   .30 .25
449 A43 1fr dk car rose & blk   .30 .25
450 A43 25fr dull bl & blk   .30 .25
451 A43 50fr bister & blk   .40 .25
    Nos. 448-451 (4)   1.30 1.00
3rd anniversary of independence.

Centenary
Emblem — A44

1963, June 1   Photo.   Perf. 14
Flag in Red, Olive Green, Yellow
452 A44 25fr blue, blk & red   1.10 .25
453 A44 30fr dull grn, blk & red   1.50 .25
International Red Cross centenary.

Lincoln,
Broken
Fetters,
Maps of
Africa and
US. — A45

1963, Oct.   Unwmk.   Perf. 13x14
454 A45 50c multicolored   .35 .25
455 A45 1fr multicolored   .35 .25
456 A45 25fr multicolored   .35 .25
    Nos. 454-456,C35 (4)   2.80 1.20
Centenary of the emancipation of the American slaves. See souvenir sheet No. C35a.
For overprints see Nos. 473-475, C41.

UN Emblem and
"15" — A46

Hibiscus — A47

1963, Dec. 10   Photo.   Perf. 14x13
457 A46 50c ultra, dk bl & rose
    red   .35 .25
458 A46 1fr yel grn, dk bl &
    rose red   .35 .25
459 A46 25fr lil, dk bl & rose red   .95 .25
460 A46 85fr gold, dk bl & rose
    red   1.25 .30
    Nos. 457-460 (4)   2.90 1.05
15th anniv. of the Universal Declaration of
Human Rights.

1964   Perf. 14
Designs: 50c, Orchid. 2fr, Butterfly. 5fr,
Hinged tortoise. 8fr, Ball python. 10fr, Bunea
alcinoe (moth). 20fr, Octopus. 25fr, John Dory
(fish). 30fr, French angelfish. 40fr, Hippopotamus. 60fr, Bohor reedbuck. 85fr, Anubius
baboon.
    Size: 22½x31mm
461 A47 50c multicolored   1.25 .25
462 A47 1fr yellow, car & grn   1.25 .25
463 A47 2fr lilac, yel & blk   1.25 .25
464 A47 5fr gray & multi   1.25 .25
465 A47 8fr cit, red brn & blk   1.25 .25
466 A47 10fr multicolored   1.25 .25
467 A47 20fr dl bl, yel & brn   1.25 .25
468 A47 25fr dl bl, grn & yel   1.25 .25
469 A47 30fr multicolored   1.55 .25
470 A47 40fr grn, red brn & blk   1.90 .25
471 A47 60fr grnsh bl & red brn   2.75 .25
472 A47 85fr lt grn, brn & org   4.00 .25
    Nos. 461-472 (12)   20.20 3.00
See Nos. 511-515, C36-C40, J56-J63.

Nos. 454-456 Overprinted Diagonally:
"En Mémoire de / JOHN F. KENNEDY
/ 1917-1963"

1964, Mar. 7   Perf. 13x14
473 A45 50c multicolored   .35 .25
474 A45 1fr multicolored   .35 .25
475 A45 25fr multicolored   .35 .25
    Nos. 473-475 (3)   1.05 .75
Issued in memory of John F. Kennedy.
See No. C41 and note on souvenir sheets
following it.

Isis of
Kalabsha
A48

Designs: 25fr, Head of Ramses II. 30fr, Colonnade of Birth House at Philae.

1964, Mar. 8   Litho.   Perf. 14
476 A48 20fr blk, pale grn & red   .60 .25
477 A48 25fr black & lil rose   .60 .25
478 A48 30fr black & citron   .70 .25
  a. Souvenir sheet of 3   3.25 2.50
    Nos. 476-478 (3)   1.90 .75
UNESCO world campaign to save historic
monuments in Nubia. No. 478a contains three
imperf. stamps similar to Nos. 476-478 with
simulated perforations.

Phosphate
Mine,
Kpeme
A49

25fr, Phosphate plant, Kpeme. 60fr,
Phosphate train. 85fr, Loading ship with
phosphate.

1964, Apr. 27   Unwmk.   Perf. 14
479 A49 5fr brown & bis brn   .30 .25
480 A49 25fr dk pur & brn car   .30 .25
481 A49 60fr dk green & olive   .70 .25
482 A49 85fr vio blk & Prus bl   1.00 .25
    Nos. 479-482 (4)   2.30 1.00
Fourth anniversary of independence.

African Breaking
Slavery Chain, and
Map — A50

1964, May 25   Photo.   Perf. 14x13
483 A50 5fr dp orange & brn   .40 .25
484 A50 25fr olive grn & brn   .40 .25
485 A50 85fr rose car & brn   1.00 .25
    Nos. 483-485,C42 (4)   3.30 1.05
1st anniv. of the meeting of African heads of
state at Addis Ababa.

Pres.
Nicolas
Grunitzky
and
Butterfly
A51

1964, Aug. 18   Litho.   Perf. 14
486 A51 1fr shown   .55 .25
487 A51 5fr Dove   .55 .25
488 A51 25fr Flower   .55 .25
489 A51 45fr as 1fr   .90 .25
490 A51 85fr Flower   1.75 .25
    Nos. 486-490 (5)   4.30 1.25
National Union and Reconciliation.

Soccer
A52

1964, Oct.   Photo.   *Perf. 14*
491	A52	1fr shown	.50	.25
492	A52	5fr Runner	.50	.25
493	A52	25fr Discus	.50	.25
494	A52	45fr as 1fr	.65	.25
		Nos. 491-494,C43 (5)	4.05	1.30

18th Olympic Games, Tokyo, Oct. 10-25. For souvenir sheet see No. C43a.

Cooperation Issue
Common Design Type

1964, Nov. 7   Engr.   *Perf. 13*
495	CD119	25fr mag, dk brn & ol bis	.80	.25

Dirigible and Balloons — A53

25fr, 45fr, Otto Lilienthal's glider, 1894; Wright Brothers' plane, 1903; Boeing 707.

1964, Dec. 5   Photo.   *Perf. 14x13*
496	A53	5fr org lil & grn	.90	.25
497	A53	10fr brt grn, dl bl & dk red	.90	.25
498	A53	25fr bl, vio bl & org	.90	.25
499	A53	85fr brt pink, vio bl & grn	1.10	.25
a.		Souv. sheet of 4	8.75	7.25
		Nos. 496-499,C44 (5)	5.05	1.50

Inauguration of the national airline, Air Togo. #499a contains 4 imperf. stamps similar to #497-499 and #C44 with simulated perfs.

Orbiting Geophysical Observatory and Mariner — A54

Space Satellites: 15fr, 25fr, Tiros, Telstar and Orbiting Solar Observatory. 20fr, 50fr, Nimbus, Syncom and Relay.

1964, Dec. 12   Litho.   *Perf. 14*
500	A54	10fr dp rose, bl & yel	.40	.25
501	A54	15fr multi	.40	.25
502	A54	20fr yel, grn & vio	.40	.25
503	A54	25fr multi	.40	.25
504	A54	45fr brt grn, dk bl & yel	.55	.25
505	A54	50fr yel, grn & org	.75	.25
a.		Souv. sheet, #502-505, imperf.	3.00	2.50
		Nos. 500-505 (6)	2.90	1.50

Intl. Quiet Sun Year.

Togo Olympic Stamps Printed in Israel — A55

Arms of Israel and Togo — A56

Pres. Nicolas Grunitzky of Togo and: 20fr, Church of the Mount of Beatitudes. 45fr, Ruins of Synagogue at Capernaum.

Perf. 13½x14½, 14x13½

1964, Dec. 26   Photo.
506	A55	5fr rose violet	.40	.25
507	A56	20fr grnsh bl, grn & dl pur	.40	.25
508	A56	25fr red & bluish grn	.40	.25
509	A56	45fr dl yel, ol & dl pur	.85	.25
510	A56	85fr mag & bluish grn	.65	.25
a.		Souv. sheet of 4, imperf.	4.50	3.50
		Nos. 506-510 (5)	2.70	1.25

Israel-Togo friendship.

Type of Regular Issue, 1964

1965, June   Unwmk.   *Perf. 14*

Designs: 3fr, Morpho aega butterfly. 4fr, Scorpion. 6fr, Bird-of-paradise flower. 15fr, Flap-necked chameleon. 45fr, Ring-tailed palm civet.

Size: 23x31mm
511	A47	3fr bister & multi	1.40	.25
512	A47	4fr org & bluish blk	1.40	.25
513	A47	6fr multi	1.40	.25
514	A47	15fr brt pink, yel & brn	1.40	.25
515	A47	45fr dl grn, org & brn	2.00	.25
		Nos. 511-515 (5)	7.60	1.25

Syncom Satellite, Radar Station and ITU Emblem — A57

1965, June   *Perf. 13x14*
516	A57	10fr Prus blue	.45	.25
517	A57	20fr olive bister	.45	.25
518	A57	25fr bright blue	.45	.25
519	A57	45fr crimson	.65	.25
520	A57	50fr green	.75	.25
		Nos. 516-520 (5)	2.75	1.25

ITU, centenary.

Abraham Lincoln — A58

Discus Thrower, Flags of Togo and Congo — A59

1965, June 26   Photo.   *Perf. 13x14*
521	A58	1fr magenta	.40	.25
522	A58	5fr dull green	.40	.25
523	A58	20fr brown	.40	.25
524	A58	25fr slate	.40	.25
		Nos. 521-524,C45 (5)	3.85	1.35

Death cent. of Abraham Lincoln. For souvenir sheet see No. C45a.

1965, July   Unwmk.   *Perf. 14x13*

Flags and: 10fr, Javelin thrower. 15fr, Handball player. 25fr, Runner.

Flags in Red, Yellow and Green
525	A59	5fr deep magenta	.40	.25
526	A59	10fr dark blue	.40	.25
527	A59	15fr brown	.40	.25
528	A59	25fr dark purple	.40	.25
		Nos. 525-528,C46 (5)	3.35	1.35

1st African Games, Brazzaville, July 18-25.

Winston Churchill and "V" — A60

Stalin, Roosevelt and Churchill at Yalta — A61

Perf. 13½x14, 14x13½

1965, Aug. 7   Photo.
529	A60	5fr dull green	.45	.25
530	A61	10fr brt vio & gray	.45	.25
531	A60	20fr brown	.45	.25
532	A61	45fr Prus bl & gray	.80	.25
		Nos. 529-532,C47 (5)	4.15	1.40

Sir Winston Spencer Churchill (1874-1965), British statesman and World War II leader.

Unisphere and New York Skyline — A62

10fr, Togolese dancers & drummer, Unisphere. 50fr, Michelangelo's Pieta & Unisphere.

1965, Aug. 28   Photo.   *Perf. 14*
533	A62	5fr grnsh bl & vio blk	.35	.25
534	A62	10fr yel grn & dk brn	.35	.25
535	A62	25fr brn org & dk grn	.35	.25
536	A62	50fr vio & sl grn	.50	.25
537	A62	85fr rose red & brn	1.10	.30
a.		Souvenir sheet of 2	2.75	1.75
		Nos. 533-537 (5)	2.65	1.30

New York World's Fair, 1964-65. No. 537a contains two imperf. stamps similar to Nos. 536-537 with simulated perforations.

"Constructive Cooperation" and Olive Branch — A63

Designs: 25fr, 40fr, Hands of various races holding globe and olive branch. 85fr, Handclasp, olive branch and globe.

1965, Sept. 25   Unwmk.   *Perf. 14*
538	A63	5fr violet, lt bl & org	.35	.25
539	A63	15fr brn, org & gray	.35	.25
540	A63	25fr blue & orange	.35	.25
541	A63	40fr dp car, gray & org	.55	.25
542	A63	85fr green & org	1.00	.30
		Nos. 538-542 (5)	2.60	1.30

International Cooperation Year.

Major White and Gemini 4 — A64

25fr, Lt. Col. Alexei Leonov and Voskhod 2.

1965, Nov. 25   Photo.   *Perf. 13½x14*
543	A64	25fr dp bl & brt car rose	.60	.25
544	A64	50fr green & brown	1.00	.25

"Walks in Space" of Lt. Col. Alexei Leonov (USSR) and Major Edward H. White (US). Printed in sheets of 12 with ornamental borders.

For overprints and surcharges see Nos. 563-566.

Adlai E. Stevenson and UN Headquarters — A65

5fr, "ONU" and doves. 10fr, UN emblem and headquarters. 20fr, "ONU" and orchids.

1965, Dec. 15   *Perf. 14x13½*
545	A65	5fr dk brn, yel & lt bl	.40	.25
546	A65	10fr org, dk bl & grn	.40	.25
547	A65	20fr dk grn, yel grn & org brn	.40	.25
548	A65	25fr brt vio, dk bl & bluish grn	.40	.25
		Nos. 545-548,C48 (5)	3.35	1.40

UN, 20th anniv.; Adlai E. Stevenson (1900-1965), US ambassador to the UN.

Pope Paul VI, Plane and UN Emblem — A66

15fr, 30fr, Pope addressing UN General Assembly & UN emblem, vert. 20fr, Pope, NYC skyline with UN Headquarters.

1966, Mar. 5   Litho.   *Perf. 12*
549	A66	5fr blue & multi	.40	.25
550	A66	15fr lt violet & multi	.40	.25
551	A66	20fr bister & multi	.40	.25
552	A66	30fr lt ultra & multi	.40	.25
		Nos. 549-552,C49-C50 (6)	4.60	1.50

Visit of Pope Paul VI to the UN, New York City, Oct. 4, 1965.

Surgical Operation and Togolese Flag — A67

Togolese Flag and: 10fr, 30fr, Blood transfusion. 45fr, Profiles of African man and woman.

1966, May 7   Litho.   *Perf. 12*
553	A67	5fr multicolored	.40 .25
554	A67	10fr multicolored	.40 .25
555	A67	15fr multicolored	.40 .25
556	A67	20fr multicolored	.40 .25
557	A67	45fr multicolored	.60 .25
	Nos. 553-557,C51 (6)		4.45 1.60

Togolese Red Cross, 7th anniversary.

Talisman Roses and WHO
Headquarters, Geneva — A68

Various flowers & WHO Headquarters.

1966, May   Litho.   *Perf. 12*
558	A68	5fr lt yel grn & multi	.45 .25
559	A68	10fr pale pink & multi	.45 .25
560	A68	15fr dull yel & multi	.45 .25
561	A68	20fr pale gray & multi	.45 .25
562	A68	30fr tan & multi	.45 .25
	Nos. 558-562,C52-C53 (7)		4.65 1.75

Inauguration of WHO Headquarters, Geneva.

Nos. 543-544 Overprinted or
Surcharged in Red

1966, July 11   Photo.   *Perf. 13½x14*
563	A64	50fr Envolée Surveyor 1	.70 .25
564	A64	50fr Envolée Gemini 9	.70 .25
a.	Pair, #563-564		1.50 .60
565	A64	100fr on 25fr Envolée Luna 9	1.60 .25
566	A64	100fr on 25fr Envolée Venus 3	1.60 .25
a.	Pair, #565-566		3.50 .90
	Nos. 563-566 (4)		4.60 1.00

US and USSR achievements in Space.

Wood
Carver — A69

Arts and Crafts: 10fr, Basket maker. 15fr,
Woman weaver. 30fr, Woman potter.

1966, Sept.   Photo.   *Perf. 13x14*
567	A69	5fr blue, yel & dk brn	.40 .25
568	A69	10fr emer, org & dk brn	.40 .25
569	A69	15fr ver, yel & dk brn	.40 .25
570	A69	30fr lilac, dk brn & yel	.40 .25
	Nos. 567-570,C55-C56 (6)		4.85 1.50

Togolese
Dancer — A70

Designs: 5fr, Togolese man. 20fr, Woman
dancer from North Togo holding branches.
25fr, Male dancer. 30fr, Male dancer from
North Togo with horned helmet. 45fr,
Drummer.

1966, Nov.   Photo.   *Perf. 13x14*
571	A70	5fr emerald & multi	.55 .25
572	A70	10fr dl yel & multi	.55 .25
573	A70	20fr lt ultra & multi	.55 .25
574	A70	25fr dp orange & multi	.55 .25
575	A70	30fr red violet & multi	.55 .25
576	A70	45fr blue & multi	.65 .25
	Nos. 571-576,C57-C58 (8)		5.75 2.00

Soccer Players and Jules Rimet
Cup — A71

Various Soccer Scenes.

1966, Dec. 14   Photo.   *Perf. 14x13*
577	A71	5fr blue, brn & red	.50 .25
578	A71	10fr brick red & multi	.50 .25
579	A71	20fr ol, brn & dk grn	.50 .25
580	A71	25fr vio, brn & org	.50 .25
581	A71	30fr ocher & multi	.50 .25
582	A71	45fr emerald, brn & mag	.60 .25
	Nos. 577-582,C59-C60 (8)		5.60 2.00

England's victory in the World Soccer Cup
Championship, Wembley, July 30. For souvenir sheet see No. C60a.

African Mouthbreeder and
Sailboat — A72

Designs: 10fr, Yellow jack and trawler. 15fr,
Banded distichodus and seiner. 25fr,
Jewelfish and galley. 30fr, like 5fr.

1967, Jan. 14   Photo.   *Perf. 14*
Fish in Natural Colors
583	A72	5fr lt ultra & blk	.45 .25
584	A72	10fr brn org & brn	.45 .25
585	A72	15fr brt rose & dk bl	.45 .25
586	A72	25fr olive & blk	.45 .25
587	A72	30fr grnsh bl & blk	.60 .25
	Nos. 583-587,C61-C62 (7)		5.90 1.85

African Boy and Greyhound — A73

UNICEF Emblem and: 10fr, Boy and Irish
setter. 20fr, Girl and doberman.

1967, Feb. 11   Photo.   *Perf. 14x13½*
588	A73	5fr orange, plum & blk	.65 .25
589	A73	10fr yel grn, red brn & dk grn	.65 .25
590	A73	15fr brt rose, brn & blk	.65 .25
591	A73	20fr bl, vio bl & blk	.65 .25
592	A73	30fr ol, sl grn & blk	.65 .25
	Nos. 588-592,C63-C64 (7)		6.75 1.85

UNICEF, 20th anniv. (in 1966).

French A-1 Satellite — A74

5fr, Diamant rocket, vert. 15fr, Fr-1 satellite,
vert. 20fr, 40fr, D-1 satellite. 25fr, A-1 satellite.

Perf. 14x13½, 13½x14
1967, Mar. 18   Photo.
593	A74	5fr multi	.40 .25
594	A74	10fr multi	.40 .25
595	A74	15fr multi	.40 .25
596	A74	20fr multi	.40 .25
597	A74	25fr multi	.40 .25
598	A74	40fr multi	.50 .25
	Nos. 593-598,C65-C66 (8)		5.50 2.05

French achievements in space.

Johann Sebastian Bach and
Organ — A75

UNESCO Emblem and: 10fr, Ludwig van
Beethoven, violin and oboe. 15f, Duke Elling-
ton, saxophone, trumpet, drums. 20fr, Claude
A. Debussy, piano and harp. 30fr, like 15fr.

1967, Apr. 15   Photo.   *Perf. 14x13½*
599	A75	5fr org & multi	.60 .25
600	A75	10fr multi	.60 .25
601	A75	15fr multi	.60 .25
602	A75	20fr lt bl & multi	.60 .25
603	A75	30fr lil & multi	.60 .25
	Nos. 599-603,C67-C68 (7)		7.00 1.75

20th anniv. (in 1966) of UNESCO.

EXPO Emblem, British Pavilion and
Day Lilies — A76

10fr, French pavilion, roses. 30fr, African village, bird-of-paradise flower.

1967, May 30   Photo.   *Perf. 14***
604	A76	5fr brt pink & multi	.45 .25
605	A76	10fr dull org & multi	.45 .25
606	A76	30fr blue & multi	.45 .25
	Nos. 604-606,C69-C72 (7)		6.45 1.90

EXPO '67 Intl. Exhibition, Montreal, Apr. 28-
Oct. 27.
For overprints see Nos. 628-630, C86-C89.

Lions
Emblem — A77

20fr, 45fr, Lions emblem and flowers.

1967, July 29   Photo.   *Perf. 13x14*
607	A77	10fr yellow & multi	.45 .25
608	A77	20fr multicolored	.45 .25
609	A77	30fr green & multi	.55 .25
610	A77	45fr blue & multi	.80 .25
	Nos. 607-610 (4)		2.25 1.00

50th anniversary of Lions International.

Montagu's Harriers — A78

5fr, Bohor reedbucks. 15fr, Zebras. 20fr,
30fr, Marsh harriers. 25fr, Leopard.

1967, Aug. 19   Photo.   *Perf. 14x13½*
611	A78	5fr lilac & org brn	.55 .25
612	A78	10fr dk red, yel & dl bl	.55 .25
613	A78	15fr grn, blk & lil	.55 .25
614	A78	20fr dk brn, yel & dl bl	.55 .25
615	A78	25fr brn, ol & yel	.55 .25
616	A78	30fr vio, yel & dl bl	.65 .25
	Nos. 611-616,C79-C80 (8)		6.10 2.00

Stamp Auction and Togo Nos. 16 and
C42 — A79

10fr, 45fr, Exhibition, #67 (British) & 520.
15fr, 30fr, Stamp store, #230. 20fr, Stamp
packet vending machine, #545.

1967, Oct. 14   Photo.   *Perf. 14x13*
**Stamps on Stamps in Original
Colors**
617	A79	5fr purple	.30 .25
618	A79	10fr dk brown	.30 .25
619	A79	15fr deep blue	.30 .25
620	A79	20fr slate green	.35 .25
621	A79	30fr red brown	.50 .25
622	A79	45fr Prus blue	.80 .25
	Nos. 617-622,C82-C83 (8)		5.80 2.15

70th anniv. of the 1st Togolese stamps. For
souvenir sheet see No. C82a.
See Nos. 853-855, C205.

Monetary Union Issue
Common Design Type
1967, Nov. 4   Engr.   *Perf. 13*
623	CD125	30fr dk bl, vio bl & brt grn	.60 .25

Broad Jump, Summer Olympics
Emblem and View of Mexico
City — A80

15fr, Ski jump, Winter Olympics emblem, ski
lift. 30fr, Runners, Summer Olympics emblem,
view of Mexico City. 45fr, Bobsledding, Winter
Olympics emblem, ski lift.

1967, Dec. 2   Photo.   *Perf. 13x14*
624	A80	5fr orange & multi	.50 .25
625	A80	15fr multicolored	.50 .25
626	A80	30fr multicolored	.50 .25
627	A80	45fr multicolored	.80 .25
	Nos. 624-627,C84-C85 (6)		5.15 1.95

1968 Olympic Games. For souvenir sheet
see No. C85a.

Nos. 604-606 Overprinted: "JOURNÉE
NATIONALE / DU TOGO / 29
SEPTEMBRE 1967"

1967, Dec.   *Perf. 14*
628	A76	5fr multicolored	.30 .25
629	A76	15fr multicolored	.30 .25
630	A76	30fr blue & multi	.40 .25
	Nos. 628-630,C86-C89 (7)		5.40 1.85

National Day, Sept. 29, 1967.

The Gleaners, by François Millet and Phosphate Works, Benin — A81

Industrialization of Togo: 20fr, 45fr, 90fr, The Weaver at the Loom, by Vincent van Gogh, and textile plant, Dadia.

1968, Jan.		Photo.	Perf. 14	
631	A81	10fr olive & multi	.45	.25
632	A81	20fr multicolored	.45	.25
633	A81	30fr brown & multi	.55	.25
634	A81	45fr multicolored	.65	.25
635	A81	60fr dk blue & multi	.95	.25
636	A81	90fr multicolored	1.60	.25
		Nos. 631-636 (6)	4.65	1.50

Togolese Women Brewing Beer — A82

The Beer Drinkers, by Edouard Manet — A83

Design: 45fr, Modern beer bottling plant.

1968, Mar. 26		Litho.	Perf. 14	
637	A82	20fr emerald & multi	.55	.25
638	A83	30fr dk car & multi	.70	.25
639	A82	45fr orange & multi	.85	.25
		Nos. 637-639 (3)	2.10	.75

Publicity for local beer industry.

Symbolic Water Cycle, Flower and Cogwheels A84

1968, Apr. 6
640	A84	30fr multicolored	.65	.25

Hydrological Decade (UNESCO), 1965-74. See No. C90.

Viking Ship and Portuguese Brigantine — A85

10fr, Fulton's steamship and modern steamship. 20fr, Harbor activities and map of Africa.

1968, Apr. 26		Photo.	Perf. 14x13½	
641	A85	5fr brt green & multi	.55	.25
642	A85	10fr dp orange & multi	.55	.25
643	A85	20fr green & multi	.55	.25
644	A85	30fr yel grn & multi	.55	.25
		Nos. 641-644,C91-C92 (6)	5.55	1.50

Inauguration of Lomé Harbor.

Adenauer and 1968 Europa Emblem — A86

1968, May 25		Photo.	Perf. 14	
645	A86	90fr olive grn & brn org	1.90	.25

Konrad Adenauer (1876-1967), chancellor of West Germany (1949-63).

Adam and Eve Expelled from Paradise, by Michelangelo — A87

Paintings: 20fr, The Anatomy Lesson of Dr. Tulp, by Rembrandt. 30fr, The Anatomy Lesson, by Rembrandt (detail). 45fr, Jesus Healing the Sick, by Raphael.

1968, June 22		Photo.	Perf. 14	
646	A87	15fr crimson & multi	.50	.25
647	A87	20fr multicolored	.50	.25
648	A87	30fr green & multi	.50	.25
649	A87	45fr multicolored	.60	.25
		Nos. 646-649,C93-C94 (6)	5.10	1.50

WHO, 20th anniv.

Olympic Monument, San Salvador Island, Bahamas — A88

1968, July 27			Perf. 14x13½	
650	A88	15fr Wrestling	.40	.25
651	A88	20fr Boxing	.40	.25
652	A88	30fr Judo	.40	.25
653	A88	45fr Running	.50	.25
		Nos. 650-653,C95-C96 (6)	4.55	1.50

19th Olympic Games, Mexico City, 10/12-27.

Chick Holding Lottery Ticket — A89

Scout Before Tent — A90

45fr, Lottery ticket, horseshoe & 4-leaf clover.

1968, Oct. 5		Litho.	Perf. 14	
654	A89	30fr dk green & multi	.65	.25
655	A89	45fr multicolored	.75	.25

2nd anniversary of National Lottery.

1968, Nov. 23
10fr, 45fr, Scout leader training cub scouts, horiz. 20fr, First aid practice, horiz. 30fr, Scout game.

656	A90	5fr dp org & multi	.35	.25
657	A90	10fr emerald & multi	.35	.25
658	A90	20fr multicolored	.35	.25
659	A90	30fr multicolored	.45	.25
660	A90	45fr blue & multi	.55	.25
		Nos. 656-660,C97-C98 (7)	4.75	1.85

Issued to honor the Togolese Boy Scouts.

Adoration of the Shepherds, by Giorgione — A91

Paintings: 20f, Adoration of the Magi, by Pieter Brueghel. 30fr, Adoration of the Magi, by Botticelli. 45fr, Adoration of the Magi, by Durer.

1968, Dec. 28		Litho.	Perf. 14	
661	A91	15fr green & multi	.45	.25
662	A91	20fr multicolored	.45	.25
663	A91	30fr multicolored	.55	.25
664	A91	45fr multicolored	.65	.25
		Nos. 661-664,C100-C101 (6)	5.60	1.60

Christmas.

Martin Luther King, Jr. — A92

Portraits and Human Rights Flame: 20fr, Professor René Cassin (author of Declaration of Human Rights). 45fr, Pope John XXIII.

1969, Feb. 1		Photo.	Perf. 13½x14	
665	A92	15fr brn org & sl grn	.60	.25
666	A92	20fr grnsh bl & vio	.60	.25
667	A92	30fr ver & slate bl	.60	.25
668	A92	45fr olive & car rose	.80	.25
		Nos. 665-668,C102-C103 (6)	5.45	1.65

International Human Rights Year.
For overprints see Nos. 683-686, C110-C111.

Omnisport Stadium and Soccer — A93

Stadium and: 15fr, Handball. 20fr, Volleyball. 30fr, Basketball. 45fr, Tennis.

1969, Apr. 26		Photo.	Perf. 14x13½	
669	A93	10fr emer, dp car & dk brn	.50	.25
670	A93	15fr org, ultra & dk brn	.50	.25
671	A93	20fr yel, ol & dk brn	.50	.25
672	A93	30fr dl grn, bl & dk brn	.50	.25
673	A93	45fr org, lil & dk brn	.60	.25
		Nos. 669-673,C105-C106 (7)	5.15	1.80

Opening of Omnisport Stadium, Lomé.

Astronaut and Eagle on Moon, Earth and Stars in Sky — A94

Designs: 1f, 30f, Lunar Module Eagle Landing on Moon. 45fr, Astronaut and Eagle on moon, earth and stars in sky.

1969, July 21		Litho.	Perf. 14	
674	A94	1fr green & multi	.40	.25
675	A94	20fr brown & multi	.40	.25
676	A94	30fr scarlet & multi	.40	.25
677	A94	45fr ultra & multi	.70	.25
		Nos. 674-677,C107-C108 (6)	4.65	1.75

Man's 1st landing on the moon, 7/20/69. US astronauts Neil A. Armstrong & Col. Edwin E. Aldrin, Jr., with Lieut. Col. Michael Collins piloting Apollo 11.
For overprints see #710-712, C120-C121.

Christ at Emmaus, by Velazquez A95

Paintings: 5fr, The Last Supper, by Tintoretto. 20fr, Pentecost, by El Greco. 30fr, The Annunciation, by Botticelli. 45fr, Like 10fr.

1969, Aug. 16		Litho.	Perf. 14	
678	A95	5fr red, gold & multi	.50	.25
679	A95	10fr multicolored	.50	.25
680	A95	20fr grn, gold & multi	.50	.25
681	A95	30fr multicolored	.50	.25
682	A95	45fr pur, gold & multi	.70	.25
		Nos. 678-682,C109 (6)	5.70	1.75

Nos. 665-668 Overprinted

1969, Sept. 1		Photo.	Perf. 13½x14	
683	A92	15fr brn org & sl grn	.55	.25
684	A92	20fr grnsh bl & vio	.55	.25
685	A92	30fr ver & slate bl	.55	.25
686	A92	45fr olive & car rose	.65	.25
		Nos. 683-686,C110-C111 (6)	5.15	1.55

Gen. Dwight D. Eisenhower (1890-1969), 34th President of the US.

African Development Bank and Emblem — A96

Designs: 45fr, Bank emblem and hand holding railroad bridge and engine.

1969, Sept. 10   Photo.   *Perf. 13x14*
687 A96 30fr ultra, blk gold & grn 1.25 .25
688 A96 45fr grn, dk bl, gold & dk red 1.75 .25

5th anniv. of the African Development Bank. See No. C112.

Louis Pasteur and Help for 1968 Flood Victims — A97

Designs: 15fr, Henri Dunant and Red Cross workers meeting Biafra refugees at airport. 30fr, Alexander Fleming and help for flood victims. 45fr, Wilhelm C. Roentgen and Red Cross workers with children in front of Headquarters.

1969, Sept. 27   Litho.   *Perf. 14*
689 A97 15fr red & multi .50 .25
690 A97 20fr emerald & multi .50 .25
691 A97 30fr purple & multi .50 .25
692 A97 45fr brt blue & multi .70 .25
   Nos. 689-692,C113-C114 (6) 5.20 1.70

League of Red Cross Societies, 50th anniv.

Glidji Agricultural Center A98

Designs (Emblem of Young Pioneer and Agricultural Organization and): 1fr, Corn harvest. 3fr, Founding meeting of Agricultural Pioneer Youths, Mar. 7, 1967. 4fr, Class at Glidji Agricultural School. 5fr, Boys forming human pyramid. 7fr, Farm students threshing. 8fr, Instruction in gardening. 10fr, 50fr, Cooperative village. 15fr, Gardening School. 20fr, Cattle breeding. 25fr, Chicken farm. 30fr, Independence parade. 40fr, Boys riding high wire. 45fr, Tractor and trailer. 60fr, Instruction in tractor driving.

1969-70   Litho.   *Perf. 14*
693 A98 1fr multi ('70) .45 .25
694 A98 2fr multi .45 .25
695 A98 3fr multi ('70) .45 .25
696 A98 4fr multi ('70) .45 .25
697 A98 5fr ultra & multi .45 .25
698 A98 7fr multi ('70) .45 .25
699 A98 8fr red & multi .45 .25
700 A98 10fr bl & multi ('70) .45 .25
701 A98 15fr red & multi ('70) .45 .25
702 A98 20fr lilac & multi .45 .25
703 A98 25fr multi ('70) .45 .25
704 A98 30fr brt bl & multi .45 .25
705 A98 40fr brt yel & multi .45 .25
706 A98 45fr rose lil & multi .60 .25
707 A98 50fr blue & multi .60 .25
708 A98 60fr orange & multi .60 .25
   Nos. 693-708,C115-C119 (21) 27.65 6.55

Books and Map of Africa A99

1969, Nov. 27   Litho.   *Perf. 14*
709 A99 30fr lt blue & multi .60 .25

12th anniv. of the Intl. Assoc. for the Development of Libraries in Africa.

Christmas Issue
Nos. 674-675, 677 Overprinted "JOYEUX NOEL"

1969, Dec.   Litho.   *Perf. 14*
710 A94 1fr green & multi .55 .25
711 A94 20fr brown & multi 1.90 .35
712 A94 45fr ultra & multi 3.50 .65
   Nos. 710-712,C120-C121 (5) 15.45 2.35

George Washington — A100

Portraits: 20fr, Albert Luthuli. 30fr, Mahatma Gandhi. 45fr, Simon Bolivar.

1969, Dec. 27   Photo.   *Perf. 14x13½*
713 A100 15fr dk brn, emer & buff .55 .25
714 A100 20fr dk brn, org & buff .55 .25
715 A100 30fr dk brn, grnsh bl & ocher .55 .25
716 A100 45fr dk brn, sl grn & dl yel .55 .25
   Nos. 713-716,C122-C123 (6) 5.05 1.60

Issued to honor leaders for world peace. For overprint & surcharges see #764-766, C143.

Plower, by M.K. Klodt and ILO Emblem A101

Paintings and ILO Emblem: 10fr, Gardening, by Camille Pissarro. 20fr, Fruit Harvest, by Diego Rivera. 30fr, Spring Sowing, by Vincent van Gogh. 45fr, Workers, by Rivera.

1970, Jan. 24   Litho.   *Perf. 12½x13*
717 A101 5fr gold & multi .80 .25
718 A101 10fr gold & multi .80 .25
719 A101 20fr gold & multi .80 .25
720 A101 30fr gold & multi 1.00 .25
721 A101 45fr gold & multi 1.40 .25
   Nos. 717-721,C124-C125 (7) 9.80 1.75

ILO, 50th anniversary.

Togolese Hair Styles — A102

Various hair styles. 20fr, 30fr, vertical.

1970, Feb. 21   *Perf. 13x12½, 12½x13*
722 A102 5fr multicolored .60 .25
723 A102 10fr ver & multi .60 .25
724 A102 20fr purple & multi .60 .25
725 A102 30fr yellow grn & multi .80 .25
   Nos. 722-725,C126-C127 (6) 5.60 1.65

Togo No. C127 and Independence Monument, Lomé — A103

30fr, Pres. Etienne G. Eyadéma, Presidential Palace and Independence Monument. 50fr, Map of Togo, dove and Independence Monument, vert.

Perf. 13x12½, 12½x13
1970, Apr. 27   Litho.
726 A103 20fr multicolored .70 .25
727 A103 30fr multicolored .70 .25
728 A103 50fr multicolored 1.10 .25
   Nos. 726-728,C128 (4) 3.60 1.00

10th anniv. of independence.

Inauguration of UPU Headquarters, Bern — A104

1970, May 30   Photo.   *Perf. 14x13½*
729 A104 30fr orange & pur 1.25 .25
   See No. C129.

Soccer, Jules Rimet Cup and Flags of Italy and Uruguay — A105

Designs (Various Scenes from Soccer, Rimet Cup and Flags of): 10fr, Great Britain and Brazil. 15fr, USSR and Mexico. 20fr, Germany and Morocco. 30fr, Romania and Czechoslovakia.

1970, June 27   Litho.   *Perf. 13x14*
730 A105 5fr olive & multi .60 .25
731 A105 10fr pink & multi .60 .25
732 A105 15fr yellow & multi .60 .25
733 A105 20fr multicolored .60 .25
734 A105 30fr emerald .90 .25
   Nos. 730-734,C130-C132 (8) 7.05 2.10

Soccer Championships for the Jules Rimet Cup, Mexico City, May 30-June 21, 1970.

Lenin and UNESCO Emblem A106

1970, July 25   Litho.   *Perf. 12½*
735 A106 30fr fawn & multi 1.90 .25

Lenin (1870-1924), Russian communist leader. See No. C133.
For surcharge see No. C179.

EXPO '70 Emblem and View of US Pavilion — A107

Designs: 2fr, Paper carp flying over Sanyo pavilion. 30fr, Russian pavilion. 50fr, Tower of the Sun pavilion. 60fr, French and Japanese pavilions.

1970, Aug. 8   Litho.   *Perf. 13*
Size: 56½x35mm
736 A107 2fr gray & multi .65 .25
Size: 50x33mm
737 A107 30fr blue & multi .65 .25
738 A107 30fr blue & multi .65 .25
739 A107 50fr blue & multi .80 .25
740 A107 60fr blue & multi .95 .25
   a. Strip of 4, #737-740 3.50 1.90
   Nos. 736-740 (5) 3.70 1.25

EXPO '70 Intl. Exhibition, Osaka, Japan, Mar. 15-Sept. 13. No. 740a has continuous view of EXPO. See No. C134.

Neil A. Armstrong, Michael Collins and Edwin E. Aldrin, Jr. — A108

Designs: 2fr, US flag, moon rocks and Apollo 11 emblem. 20fr, Astronaut checking Surveyor 3 on moon, and Apollo 12 emblem. 30fr, Charles Conrad, Jr., Richard F. Gordon, Jr., Alan L. Bean and Apollo 12 emblem. 50fr, US flag, moon rocks and Apollo 12 emblem.

1970, Sept. 26
741 A108 1fr multi .50 .25
742 A108 2fr multi .50 .25
743 A108 20fr multi .50 .25
744 A108 30fr multi .65 .25
745 A108 50fr multi 1.25 .25
   Nos. 741-745,C135 (6) 6.90 2.00

Moon landings of Apollo 11 and 12.
For overprints see Nos. 746-750, C136.

Nos. 741-745 Inscribed:
"FELICITATIONS / BON RETOUR APOLLO XIII"

1970, Sept. 26
746 A108 1fr multi .55 .25
747 A108 2fr multi .55 .25
748 A108 20fr multi .55 .25
749 A108 30fr multi .70 .25
750 A108 50fr multi 1.25 .25
   Nos. 746-750,C136 (6) 6.35 1.85

Safe return of the crew of Apollo 13.

Forge of Vulcan, by Velazquez, and ILO Emblem — A109

Paintings and Emblems of UN Agencies: 15fr, Still Life, by Delacroix, and FAO emblem. 20fr, Portrait of Nicholas Kratzer, by Holbein, and UNESCO emblem. 30fr, UN Headquarters, New York, and UN emblem. 50fr, Portrait of a Little Girl, by Renoir, and UNICEF emblem.

1970, Oct. 24   Litho.   *Perf. 13x12½*
751 A109 1fr car, gold & dk brn .65 .25
752 A109 15fr ultra, gold & blk .65 .25
753 A109 20fr grnsh bl, gold & dk grn .65 .25
754 A109 30fr lil & multi .80 .25
755 A109 50fr org brn, gold & sepia 1.25 .25
   Nos. 751-755,C137-C138 (7) 6.85 1.80

United Nations, 25th anniversary.

Euchloron Megaera — A110

Butterflies and Moths: 2fr, Cymothoe chrysippus. 30fr, Danaus chrysippus. 50fr, Morpho.

1970, Nov. 21   Litho.   *Perf. 13x14*
756 A110 1fr yellow & multi 2.00 .25
757 A110 2fr lt vio & multi 2.00 .25
758 A110 30fr multicolored 2.00 .25
759 A110 50fr orange & multi 3.75 .25
   Nos. 756-759,C139-C140 (6) 20.25 1.50

For surcharge see No. 859.

Nativity, by Botticelli — A111

Paintings: 20fr, Adoration of the Shepherds, by Veronese. 30fr, Adoration of the Shepherds, by El Greco. 50fr, Adoration of the Kings, by Fra Angelico.

1970, Dec. 26   Litho.   Perf. 12½x13
760	A111	15fr gold & multi	.65	.25
761	A111	20fr gold & multi	.65	.25
762	A111	30fr gold & multi	.65	.25
763	A111	50fr gold & multi	1.10	.25
	Nos. 760-763,C141-C142 (6)		6.80	1.55

Christmas.

Nos. 715, C123, 714 Surcharged and Overprinted: "EN MEMOIRE / Charles De Gaulle / 1890-1970"

1971, Jan. 9   Photo.   Perf. 14x13½
764	A100	30fr multicolored	2.00	.25
765	A100	30fr on 90fr multi	2.00	.25
766	A100	150fr on 20fr multi	8.50	.35
	Nos. 764-766,C143 (4)		24.00	1.45

"Aerienne" obliterated with heavy bar on No. 765.

De Gaulle and Churchill — A112

De Gaulle and: 30fr, Dwight D. Eisenhower. 40fr, John F. Kennedy. 50fr, Konrad Adenauer.

1971, Feb. 20   Photo.   Perf. 13x14
767	A112	20fr blk & brt blue	.90	.25
768	A112	30fr blk & crimson	.90	.25
769	A112	40fr blk & dp green	1.40	.25
770	A112	50fr blk & brown	1.60	.25
	Nos. 767-770,C144-C145 (6)		10.00	1.50

Nos. 764-770 issued in memory of Charles de Gaulle (1890-1970), President of France.

Resurrection, by Raphael — A113

Easter: 30fr, Resurrection, by Master of Trebon. 40fr, like 1fr.

1971, Apr. 10   Litho.   Perf. 10½x11½
771	A113	1fr gold & multi	.50	.25
772	A113	30fr gold & multi	.50	.25
773	A113	40fr gold & multi	.50	.25
	Nos. 771-773,C146-C148 (6)		5.20	1.55

Cmdr. Alan B. Shepard, Jr. — A114

Designs: 10fr, Edgar D. Mitchell and astronaut on moon. 30fr, Stuart A. Roosa, module on moon. 40fr, Take-off from moon, and spaceship.

1971, May   Litho.   Perf. 12½
774	A114	1fr blue & multi	.40	.25
775	A114	10fr green & multi	.40	.25
776	A114	30fr dull red & multi	.40	.25
777	A114	40fr dk green & multi	.45	.25
	Nos. 774-777,C149-C151 (7)		5.90	2.55

Apollo 14 moon landing, Jan. 31-Feb. 9.
For overprints see Nos. 788, C162-C164.

Cacao Tree and Pods — A115

Designs: 40fr, Sorting and separating beans and pods. 50fr, Drying cacao beans.

1971, June 6   Litho.   Perf. 14
778	A115	30fr multicolored	.80	.25
779	A115	40fr ultra & multi	.85	.25
780	A115	50fr multicolored	1.60	.25
	Nos. 778-780,C152-C154 (6)		6.60	1.85

International Cacao Day, June 6.

Napoleon, Death Sesquicentennial — A115a

Die Cut Perf. 12
1971, June 11   Embossed
780A	A115a	1000fr gold	47.50	47.50
b.	Sheet of 1, imperf.		32.50	32.50

No. 780Ab contains one 48x69mm stamp.

Control Tower and Plane — A116

1971, June 26   Litho.   Perf. 14
781	A116	30fr multicolored	1.00	.25

10th anniv. of the Agency for the Security of Aerial Navigation in Africa and Madagascar (ASECNA). See No. C155.

Great Market, Lomé — A117

Tourist publicity: 30fr, Bird-of-paradise flower and sculpture of a man. 40fr, Aledjo Gorge and anubius baboon.

1971, July 17
782	A117	20fr multicolored	.55	.25
783	A117	30fr multicolored	.55	.25
784	A117	40fr multicolored	.65	.25
	Nos. 782-784,C156-C158 (6)		5.35	1.65

For surcharge and overprint see Nos. 804, C172.

Great Fetish of Gbatchoume — A118

Religions of Togo: 30fr, Chief Priest in front of Atta Sakuma Temple. 40fr, Annual ceremony of the sacred stone.

1971, July 31   Litho.   Perf. 14½
785	A118	20fr multicolored	.40	.25
786	A118	30fr multicolored	.40	.25
787	A118	40fr multicolored	.50	.25
	Nos. 785-787,C159-C161 (6)		3.65	1.50

No. 777 Overprinted in Silver: "EN MEMOIRE / DOBROVOLSKY — VOLKOV — PATSAYEV / SOYUZ 11"

1971, Aug.   Perf. 12½
788	A114	40fr multicolored	.50	.25
	Nos. 788,C162-C164 (4)		6.15	1.65

Russian astronauts Lt. Col. Georgi T. Dobrovolsky, Vladislav N. Volkov and Victor I. Patsayev, who died during the Soyuz 11 space mission, June 6-30, 1971.

Sapporo '72 Emblem and Speed Skating — A119

Sapporo '72 Emblem and: 10fr, Slalom skiing. 20fr, Figure skating, pairs. 30fr, Bobsledding. 50fr, Ice hockey.

1971, Oct. 30   Perf. 14
789	A119	1fr multicolored	.30	.25
790	A119	10fr multicolored	.30	.25
791	A119	20fr multicolored	.30	.25
792	A119	30fr multicolored	.30	.25
793	A119	50fr multicolored	.55	.25
	Nos. 789-793,C165 (6)		4.00	1.75

11th Winter Olympic Games, Sapporo, Japan, Feb. 3-13, 1972.

Toy Crocodile and UNICEF Emblem — A120

Toys and UNICEF Emblem: 30fr, Fawn and butterfly. 40fr, Monkey. 50fr, Elephants.

1971, Nov. 27
794	A120	20fr multicolored	.35	.25
795	A120	30fr violet & multi	.35	.25
796	A120	40fr green & multi	.45	.25
797	A120	50fr bister & multi	.65	.25
	Nos. 794-797,C167-C168 (6)		3.60	1.50

UNICEF, 25th anniv.
For overprints see Nos. 918, C263-C264.

Virgin and Child, by Botticelli — A121

Virgin and Child by: 30fr, Master of the Life of Mary. 40fr, Dürer. 50fr, Veronese.

1971, Dec. 24   Perf. 14x13
798	A121	10fr purple & multi	.60	.25
799	A121	30fr green & multi	.60	.25
800	A121	40fr brown & multi	.90	.25
801	A121	50fr dk blue & multi	1.25	.25
	Nos. 798-801,C169-C170 (6)		6.70	1.80

Christmas.

St. Mark's Basilica — A122

Design: 40fr, Rialto Bridge.

1972, Feb. 26   Litho.   Perf. 14
802	A122	30fr multicolored	.70	.25
803	A122	40fr multicolored	.90	.25
	Nos. 802-803,C171 (3)		4.35	1.05

UNESCO campaign to save Venice.

No. 784 Surcharged with New Value, Two Bars and "VISITE DU PRESIDENT / NIXON EN CHINE / FEVRIER 1972"

1972, Mar.   Litho.   Perf. 14
804	A117	300fr on 40fr multi	4.50	1.60

Visit of Pres. Richard M. Nixon to the People's Republic of China, Feb. 20-27.
See No. C172.

Crucifixion, by Master MS — A123

Easter (Paintings): 30fr, Pietà, by Botticelli.

1972, Mar. 31
805	A123	25fr gold & multi	.80	.25
806	A123	30fr gold & multi	.80	.25
807	A123	40fr gold & multi	1.00	.25
	Nos. 805-807,C173-C174 (5)		7.25	1.25

Heart, Smith, WHO
Emblem — A124

Heart, WHO Emblem and: 40fr, Typist. 60fr,
Athlete with javelin.

1972, Apr. 4
808	A124	30fr multicolored	.45	.25
809	A124	40fr multicolored	.60	.25
810	A124	60fr multicolored	.95	.25
	Nos. 808-810,C175 (4)		3.60	1.20

"Your heart is your health," World Health
Day.

Org. of African and Malagasy Union
Conf. — A124a

Die Cut Perf. 12x12½
**1972, Apr. 24　　Litho. & Embossed
Self-adhesive**
810A	A124a 1000fr gold, red & grn	10.00	10.00

On No. 810A embossing may cut through
stamp and embossed backing paper may not
adhere well to the unused stamps.
For overprint see No. 893A.

Video
Telephone — A125

1972, June 24　　Litho.　　*Perf. 14*
811	A125	40fr violet & multi	1.00	.25

4th World Telecommunications Day. See
No. C176.
For overprints see Nos. 880, C229.

Grating Cassava　　　　Basketball
A126　　　　　　　　　　A127

25fr, Cassava collection by truck, horiz.

1972, June 30
812	A126	25fr yellow & multi	.45	.25
813	A126	40fr multicolored	.60	.25
	Nos. 812-813,C177-C178 (4)		3.40	1.00

Cassava production.
For overprint & surcharge see #866-867.

1972, Aug. 26　　Litho.　　*Perf. 14*
814	A127	30fr shown	.40	.25
815	A127	40fr Running	.45	.25
816	A127	50fr Discus	.60	.25
	Nos. 814-816,C180-C181 (5)		5.30	1.85

20th Olympic Games, Munich, 8/26-9/11.
For overprints see Nos. C234-C235.

Pin-tailed
Whydah — A128

Birds: 30fr, Broad-tailed widowbird. 40fr,
Yellow-shouldered widowbird. 60fr, Yellow-
tailed widowbird.

1972, Sept. 9
817	A128	25fr citron & multi	1.00	.25
818	A128	30fr lt blue & multi	1.40	.25
819	A128	40fr multicolored	1.40	.25
820	A128	60fr lt green & multi	2.10	.25
	Nos. 817-820,C182 (5)		9.15	1.45

Paul P. Harris,
Rotary
Emblem — A129

50fr, Flags of Togo and Rotary Club.

1972, Oct. 7　　Litho.　　*Perf. 14*
821	A129	40fr green & multi	.45	.25
822	A129	50fr multicolored	.80	.25
a.		Souvenir sheet of 2	2.50	1.50
	Nos. 821-822,C183-C185 (5)		4.50	1.90

Rotary International, Lomé. No. 822a contains 2 stamps with simulated perforations
similar to Nos. 821-822.
For overprints see Nos. 862, 898, C212-
C213, C244-C235.

Mona Lisa,
by
Leonardo
da Vinci
A130

40fr, Virgin and Child, by Giovanni Bellini.

1972, Oct. 21
823	A130	25fr gold & multi	1.00	.25
824	A130	40fr gold & multi	1.25	.25
	Nos. 823-824,C186-C188 (5)		10.40	1.50

West African Monetary Union Issue
Common Design Type
Design: 40fr, African couple, city, village
and commemorative coin.

1972, Nov. 2　　Engr.　　*Perf. 13*
825	CD136 40fr red brn, rose red & gray	.60	.25

Presidents Pompidou and Eyadema,
Party Headquarters — A131

1972, Nov. 23　　Litho.　　*Perf. 14*
826	A131	40fr purple & multi	1.90	.25

Visit of Pres. Georges Pompidou of France
to Togo, Nov. 1972. See No. C189.

Christmas
A132

Paintings: 25fr, Anunciation, Painter
Unknown. 30fr, Nativity, Master of
Vyshchibrod. 40fr, Like 25fr.

1972, Dec. 23
827	A132	25fr gold & multi	.55	.25
828	A132	30fr gold & multi	.55	.25
829	A132	40fr gold & multi	.65	.25
	Nos. 827-829,C191-C193 (6)		6.70	1.80

Raoul Follereau and Lepers — A133

1973, Jan. 23　　Photo.　　*Perf. 14x13½*
830	A133	40fr violet & green	2.25	.25

World Leprosy Day and 20th anniv. of the
Raoul Follereau Foundation. See No. C194.

WHO　　　　　　　Christ on the
Emblem — A134　　　Cross — A135

1973, Apr. 7　　Photo.　　*Perf. 14x13*
831	A134	30fr blue & multi	.50	.25
832	A134	40fr dp yellow & multi	.65	.25

WHO, 25th anniv.

1973, Apr. 21　　Litho.　　*Perf. 14*
833	A135	25fr shown	.50	.25
834	A135	30fr Pietá	.50	.25
835	A135	40fr Ascension	.60	.25
	Nos. 833-835,C195 (4)		3.00	1.15

Easter.

Eugene Cernan, Ronald Evans,
Harrison Schmitt, Apollo 17
Badge — A136

Design: 40fr, Lunar rover on moon.

1973, June 2　　Litho.　　*Perf. 14*
836	A136	30fr multicolored	.50	.25
837	A136	40fr multicolored	.60	.25
	Nos. 836-837,C196-C197 (4)		5.95	1.60

Apollo 17 moon mission, Dec. 7-19, 1972.

Scouts Pitching
Tent — A137

20fr, Campfire, horiz. 30fr, Rope climbing.

1973, June 30
838	A137	10fr multicolored	.45	.25
839	A137	20fr multicolored	.45	.25
840	A137	30fr violet & multi	.45	.25
841	A137	40fr ocher & multi	.60	.25
	Nos. 838-841,C198-C199 (6)		7.05	2.15

24th Boy Scout World Conference (1st in
Africa), Nairobi, Kenya, July 16-21.
For overprints see Nos. C265-C266.

Nicolaus
Copernicus, 500th
Anniv.
Birth — A138

Designs: 10fr, Heliocentric system. 20fr,
Nicolaus Copernicus. 30fr, Seated figure of
Astronomy and spacecrafts around earth and
moon. 40fr, Astrolabe.

1973, July 18
842	A138	10fr multicolored	.65	.25
843	A138	20fr multicolored	.65	.25
844	A138	30fr multicolored	.65	.25
845	A138	40fr lilac & multi	.85	.25
	Nos. 842-845,C200-C201 (6)		7.10	1.80

Red Cross
Ambulance
Crew
A139

1973, Aug. 4
846	A139	40fr multicolored	1.60	.25

Togolese Red Cross. See No. C202.
For overprints see Nos. 846, C294.

Teacher and Students — A140

40fr, Hut and man reading under tree, vert.

1973, Aug. 18   Litho.   Perf. 14
847 A140 30fr multicolored   .50 .25
848 A140 40fr multicolored   .65 .25
　　Nos. 847-848,C203 (3)   2.65 .85
Literacy campaign.

African Postal Union Issue
Common Design Type

1973, Sept. 12   Engr.   Perf. 13
849 CD137 100fr yel, red & claret 1.25 .35

INTERPOL
Emblem and
Headquarters
A141

Weather Vane
and WMO
Emblem
A142

1973, Sept. 29   Photo.   Perf. 13½x14
850 A141 30fr yel, brn & gray grn .55 .25
851 A141 40fr yel grn, bl & mag   .65 .25
50th anniv. of Intl. Criminal Police Org.

1973, Oct. 4   Perf. 14x13
852 A142 40fr yel, dp brn & grn 1.00 .25
Intl. meteorological cooperation, cent. See No. C204.

Type of 1967
Designs: 25fr, Old and new locomotives, No. 795. 30fr, Mail coach and bus, No. 613. 90fr, Mail boat and ship, Nos. C61 and 469.

1973, Oct. 20   Photo.   Perf. 14x13
853 A79 25fr multicolored   .60 .25
854 A79 30fr purple & green   .80 .25
855 A79 90fr dk blue & multi 2.10 .35
　　Nos. 853-855,C205 (4)   6.00 1.20
Togolese postal service, 75th anniv.

John F. Kennedy
and Adolf
Schaerf — A143

Virgin and Child,
Italy, 15th
Century — A144

Designs: 30fr, Kennedy and Harold MacMillan. 40fr, Kennedy and Konrad Adenaeur.

1973, Nov. 22   Litho.   Perf. 14
856 A143 20fr blk, gray & vio .55 .25
857 A143 30fr blk, rose & brn .55 .25
858 A143 40fr blk, lt grn & grn .65 .25
　　Nos. 856-858,C206-C208 (6) 9.10 2.55
John F. Kennedy (1917-1963).

No. 758 Surcharged with New Value, 2 Bars and Overprinted in Ultramarine: "SECHERESSE SOLIDARITE AFRICAINE"

1973, Dec.   Photo.   Perf. 13x14
859 A110 100fr on 30fr multi 1.40 .50
African solidarity in drought emergency.

1973, Dec. 22   Litho.   Perf. 14
30fr, Adoration of the Kings, Italy, 15th cent.
860 A144 25fr gold & multi .50 .25
861 A144 30fr gold & multi .65 .25
　　Nos. 860-861,C210-C211 (3) 4.45 1.30
Christmas.

No. 821 Overprinted: "PREMIERE CONVENTION / 210eme DISTRICT / FEVRIER 1974 / LOME"

1974, Feb. 21   Litho.   Perf. 14
862 A129 40fr green & multi .40 .25
　　Nos. 862,C212-C213 (3) 2.05 .85
First convention of Rotary Intl., District 210, Lomé, Feb. 22-24.

Soccer and
Games'
Cup
A145

Various soccer scenes and games' cup.

1974, Mar. 2   Litho.   Perf. 14
863 A145 20fr lt blue & multi .25 .25
864 A145 30fr yellow & multi   .40 .25
865 A145 40fr lilac & multi   .45 .25
　　Nos. 863-865,C214-C216 (6) 6.10 2.65
World Soccer Championships, Munich, Germany, June 13-July 7.

Nos. 812-813 Overprinted and Surcharged: "10e ANNIVERSAIRE DU P.A.M."

1974, Mar. 25   Litho.   Perf. 14
866 A126 40fr multicolored .65 .25
867 A126 100fr on 25fr multi 1.40 .50
10th anniv. of World Food Program. Overprint on No. 866 is in one line; 2 lines on No. 867 and 2 bars through old denomination.

Girl Before Mirror,
by
Picasso — A146

Paintings by Picasso: 30fr, The Turkish Shawl. 40fr, Mandolin and Guitar.

1974, Apr. 6
868 A146 20fr vio blue & multi .40 .25
869 A146 30fr maroon & multi   .65 .25
870 A146 40fr multicolored   .85 .25
　　Nos. 868-870,C217-C219 (6) 9.50 2.45
Pablo Picasso (1881-1973), Spanish painter.

Kpeme
Village and
Wharf
A147

Design: 40fr, Tropicana tourist village.

1974, Apr. 20
871 A147 30fr multicolored .45 .25
872 A147 40fr multicolored .45 .25
　　Nos. 871-872,C220-C221 (4) 3.25 1.10

Mailman, UPU
Emblem — A148

Design: 40fr, Mailman, different uniform.

1974, May 10   Litho.   Perf. 14
873 A148 30fr salmon & multi .45 .25
874 A148 40fr multicolored   .50 .25
　　Nos. 873-874,C222-C223 (4) 2.90 1.10
UPU, centenary.

Map and
Flags of
Members
— A148a

1974, May 29   Litho.   Perf. 13x12½
875 A148a 40fr blue & multi .60 .25
15th anniversary of the Council of Accord.

Fisherman
with Net
A149

40fr, Fisherman casting net from canoe.

1974, June 22   Litho.   Perf. 14
876 A149 30fr multicolored .55 .25
877 A149 40fr multicolored .65 .25
　　Nos. 876-877,C224-C226 (5) 5.70 1.65
Lagoon fishing.

Pioneer Communicating with
Earth — A150

30fr, Radar station and satellite, vert.

1974, July 6   Perf. 14
878 A150 30fr multicolored .35 .25
879 A150 40fr multicolored .40 .25
　　Nos. 878-879,C227-C228 (4) 3.65 1.50
US Jupiter space probe.

No. 811 Overprinted with INTERNABA Emblem in Silver Similar to No. C229

1974, July
880 A125 40fr multicolored 3.00 .55
INTERNABA 1974 Intl. Philatelic Exhibition, Basel, June 7-16. See No. C229.
No. 880 exists overprint in black. Value, unused $10.

Tympanotomus
Radula — A151

Designs: Seashells.

1974, July 13   Litho.   Perf. 14
881 A151 10fr shown   .85 .25
882 A151 20fr Tonna galea .85 .25
883 A151 30fr Conus mercator 1.00 .25
884 A151 40fr Cardium costatum 1.40 .25
　　Nos. 881-884,C230-C231 (6) 8.10 1.70

Groom with
Horses
A152

Design: 40fr, Trotting horses.

1974, Aug. 3   Litho.   Perf. 14
885 A152 30fr multicolored .90 .25
886 A152 40fr multicolored 1.10 .25
　　Nos. 885-886,C232-C233 (4) 6.50 1.20
Horse racing.

Leopard
A153

1974, Sept. 7   Litho.   Perf. 14
887 A153 20fr shown   .70 .25
888 A153 30fr Giraffes   .70 .25
889 A153 40fr Elephants .95 .25
　　Nos. 887-889,C236-C237 (5) 6.70 1.50
Wild animals of West Africa.

1974, Oct. 14
890 A153 30fr Herding cattle .40 .25
891 A153 40fr Milking cow   .55 .25
　　Nos. 890-891,C238-C239 (4) 3.30 1.10
Domestic animals.

Churchill
and Frigate
F390
A154

Design: 40fr, Churchill and fighter planes.

1974, Nov. 1   Photo.   Perf. 13x13½
892 A154 30fr multicolored .55 .25
893 A154 40fr multicolored .70 .25
　　Nos. 892-893,C240-C241 (4) 5.25 1.55
Winston Churchill (1874-1965).

No. 810A Ovptd. "Inauguration de l'hotel de la Paix 9-1-75"

Litho. & Embossed
1975, Jan. 9   Perf. 12½
Self-adhesive
893A A124a 1000fr gold, red & grn 10.00 10.00
On No. 893A embossing may cut through stamp and embossed backing paper may not adhere well to the unused stamps.

Chlamydocarya Macrocarpa — A155

Flowers of Togo: 25fr, Strelitzia reginae, vert. 30fr, Storphanthus sarmentosus, vert. 60fr, Clerodendrum scandens.

1975, Feb. 15   Litho.   Perf. 14
894 A155 25fr multicolored .60 .25
895 A155 30fr multicolored .60 .25
896 A155 40fr multicolored .80 .25
897 A155 60fr multicolored 1.10 .25
　　Nos. 894-897,C242-C243 (6) 8.35 1.80

No. 821 Overprinted: "70e ANNIVERSAIRE / 23 FEVRIER 1975"

1975, Feb. 23   Litho.   Perf. 14
898 A129 40fr green & multi .55 .25
　　Nos. 898,C244-C245 (3) 2.45 .85
Rotary Intl., 70th anniv.

Radio
Station,
Kamina
A156

30fr, Benedictine Monastery, Zogbegan. 40fr, Causeway, Atchinedji. 60fr, Ayome Waterfalls.

1975, Mar. 1   Photo.   Perf. 13x14
899	A156 25fr multicolored	.35	.25
900	A156 30fr multicolored	.35	.25
901	A156 40fr multicolored	.45	.25
902	A156 60fr multicolored	.65	.25
	Nos. 899-902 (4)	1.80	1.00

Jesus Mocked, by El Greco — A157

Paintings: 30fr, Crucifixion, by Master Janoslet. 40fr, Descent from the Cross, by Bellini. 90fr, Pietà, painter unknown.

1975, Apr. 19   Litho.   Perf. 14
903	A157 25fr black & multi	.35	.25
904	A157 30fr black & multi	.45	.25
905	A157 40fr black & multi	.55	.25
906	A157 90fr black & multi	1.10	.30
	Nos. 903-906,C246-C247 (6)	5.45	1.85

Easter.

Stilt Walking, Togolese Flag A158

Design: 30fr, Flag and dancers.

1975, Apr. 26   Litho.   Perf. 14
907	A158 25fr multicolored	.40	.25
908	A158 30fr multicolored	.40	.25
	Nos. 907-908,C248-C249 (4)	2.00	1.00

15th anniv. of independence.

Rabbit Hunter with Club A159

40fr, Beaver hunter with bow and arrow.

1975, May 24   Photo.   Perf. 13x13½
909	A159 30fr multicolored	.75	.25
910	A159 40fr multicolored	.95	.25
	Nos. 909-910,C250-C251 (4)	5.55	1.10

Pounding Palm Nuts A160

Design: 40fr, Man extracting palm oil, vert.

1975, June 28   Litho.   Perf. 14
911	A160 30fr multicolored	.95	.25
912	A160 40fr multicolored	.95	.25
	Nos. 911-912,C252-C253 (4)	5.65	1.50

Palm oil production.

Apollo-Soyuz Link-up — A161

1975, July 15
913	A161 30fr multicolored	.40	.25
	Nos. 913,C254-C258 (6)	5.80	1.85

Apollo Soyuz space test project (Russo-American cooperation), launching July 15; link-up July 17.

Women's Heads, IWY Emblem — A162

1975, July 26   Litho.   Perf. 12½
914	A162 30fr blue & multi	.50	.25
915	A162 40fr multicolored	.60	.25

International Women's Year.

Dr. Schweitzer and Children — A163

1975, Aug. 23   Litho.   Perf. 14x13½
916	A163 40fr multicolored	.75	.25
	Nos. 916,C259-C261 (4)	4.50	1.30

Dr. Albert Schweitzer (1875-1965), medical missionary and musician.

Merchant Writing Letter, by Vittore Carpaccio A164

1975, Oct. 9   Litho.   Perf. 14
917	A164 40fr multicolored	.60	.25

Intl. Letter Writing Week. See No. C262.

No. 797 Overprinted: "30ème Anniversaire / des Nations-Unies"

1975, Oct. 24   Litho.   Perf. 14
918	A120 50fr multi	.50	.25
	Nos. 918,C263-C264 (3)	1.85	.75

UN, 30th anniv.

Virgin and Child, by Mantegna A165

Paintings of the Virgin and Child: 30fr, El Greco. 40fr, Barend van Orley.

1975, Dec. 20   Litho.   Perf. 14
919	A165 20fr red & multi	.35	.25
920	A165 30fr bl & multi	.40	.25
921	A165 40fr red & multi	.50	.25
	Nos. 919-921,C267-C269 (6)	4.70	1.75

Christmas.

Crashed Plane and Pres. Eyadema A166

1976, Jan. 24   Photo.   Perf. 13
922	A166 50fr multi	11.00	.45
923	A166 60fr multi	26.00	.50

Airplane crash at Sara-kawa, Jan. 24, 1974, in which Pres. Eyadema escaped injury.

1976 Summer Olympics, Montreal — A166a

Litho. & Embossed
1976, Feb. 24   Perf. 11
923A	A166a 1000fr Diving	15.00	—
923B	A166a 1000fr Track	15.00	—
923C	A166a 1000fr Pole vault	15.00	—
923D	A166a 1000fr Equestrian	15.00	—
923E	A166a 1000fr Cycling	15.00	—
	Nos. 923A-923E (5)	75.00	

Exist imperf.

Frigates on the Hudson — A167

American Bicentennial: 50fr, George Washington, by Gilbert Stuart, and Bicentennial emblem, vert.

1976, Mar. 3   Litho.   Perf. 14
924	A167 35fr multicolored	.45	.25
925	A167 50fr multicolored	.65	.25
	Nos. 924-925,C270-C273 (6)	5.50	1.80

For overprints see Nos. C280-C283.

ACP and CEE Emblems A168

50fr, Map of Africa, Europe and Asia.

1976, Apr. 24   Photo.   Perf. 13x14
926	A168 10fr orange & multi	.30	.25
927	A168 50fr pink & multi	.50	.30
	Nos. 926-927,C274-C275 (4)	2.00	1.05

First anniv. of signing of treaty between Togo and European Common Market, Lomé, Feb. 28, 1975.

Cable-laying Ship — A169

30fr, Telephone, tape recorder, speaker.

1976, Mar. 10   Photo.   Perf. 13x14
928	A169 25fr ultra & multi	.35	.25
929	A169 30fr pink & multi	.35	.25
	Nos. 928-929,C276-C277 (4)	2.45	1.15

Centenary of first telephone call by Alexander Graham Bell, Mar. 10, 1876.

Blind Man and Insect — A170

Marine Exhibition Hall — A171

1976, Apr. 8   Perf. 14x13
930	A170 50fr brt grn & multi	.90	.25

World Health Day: "Foresight prevents blindness." See No. C278.

Air Post Type, 1976, and Type A171

10fr, Pylon, flags of Ghana, Togo and Dahomey.

1976   Litho.   Perf. 14
931	A171 5fr multicolored	.55	.25
932	AP19 10fr multicolored	.55	.25
933	A171 50fr multicolored	.80	.45
	Nos. 931-933,C279 (4)	2.90	1.20

Marine Exhibition, 10th anniv. (5fr, 50fr). Ghana-Togo-Dahomey electric power grid, 1st anniversary (10fr).
Issue dates: 50fr, May 8; 5fr, 10fr, August.

Running — A172

Montreal Olympic Emblem and: 30fr, Kayak. 50fr, High jump.

1976, June 15   Photo.   Perf. 14x13
934	A172 25fr multicolored	.30	.25
935	A172 30fr multicolored	.30	.25
936	A172 50fr multicolored	.45	.25
	Nos. 934-936,C284-C286 (6)	4.10	2.05

21st Olympic Games, Montreal, Canada, July 17-Aug. 1.
For overprints see Nos. 947, C298-C299.

Titan 3 and Viking Emblem — A173

50fr, Viking trajectory, Earth to Mars.

1976, July 15   Litho.   Perf. 14
937	A173 30fr blue & multi	.35	.25
938	A173 50fr rose & multi	.50	.25
	Nos. 937-938,C287-C290 (6)	4.70	2.00

US Viking Mars missions.

Young Routy at Celeyran, by Toulouse-Lautrec A174

Paintings by Toulouse-Lautrec: 20fr, Model in Studio. 35fr, Louis Pascal, portrait.

1976, Aug. 7 — Litho. — Perf. 14

939	A174	10fr black & multi	.50 .25
940	A174	20fr black & multi	.50 .25
941	A174	35fr black & multi	.65 .25

Nos. 939-941,C291-C293 (6) 6.30 1.80

Henri Toulouse-Lautrec (1864-1901), French painter, 75th death anniversary.

No. 846 Overprinted: "Journée / Internationale / de l'Enfance"

1976, Nov. 27 — Litho. — Perf. 14

942	A139	40fr multi	.40 .25

Intl. Children's Day. See No. C294.

Adoration of the Shepherds, by Pontormo — A175

Paintings: 30fr, Nativity, by Carlo Crivelli. 50fr, Virgin and Child, by Jacopo da Pontormo.

1976, Dec. 18

943	A175	25fr multi	.45 .25
944	A175	30fr multi	.45 .25
945	A175	50fr multi	.65 .25

Nos. 943-945,C295-C297 (6) 5.85 2.35

Christmas.

Mohammed Ali Jinnah, Flags of Togo and Pakistan — A176

1976, Dec. 24 — Litho. — Perf. 13

946	A176	50fr multi	.60 .25

Jinnah (1876-1948), first Governor General of Pakistan.

No. 936 Overprinted: "CHAMPIONS OLYMPIQUES / SAUT EN HAUTEUR / POLOGNE"

1976, Dec. — Photo. — Perf. 14x13

947	A172	50fr multi	.55 .25

Nos. 947,C298-C299 (3) 2.95 1.15

Olympic winners.

Queen Elizabeth II, Silver Jubilee — A176a

Designs: No. 947A, Portrait. No. 947B, Wearing coronation regalia.

Litho. & Embossed

1977, Jan. 10 — Perf. 11

947A	A176a	1000fr silver & multi	8.00

Souvenir Sheet

947B	A176a	1000fr silver & multi	9.00

Exist imperf.

Kpeme Phosphate Mine, Sara-kawa Crash A177

1977, Jan. 13 — Photo. — Perf. 13x14

948	A177	50fr multi	.55 .25

Nos. 948,C300-C301 (3) 2.30 .85

Presidency of Etienne Eyadema, 10th anniv.

Musical Instruments A178

1977, Feb. 7 — Litho. — Perf. 14

949	A178	5fr Gongophone	.50 .25
950	A178	10fr Tamtam, vert.	.50 .25
951	A178	25fr Dondon	.50 .25

Nos. 949-951,C302-C304 (6) 4.80 1.55

Victor Hugo and his Home A179

1977, Feb. 26 — Perf. 13x14

952	A179	50fr multi	.65 .25

Victor Hugo (1802-1885), French writer, 175th birth anniversary. See No. 959, C316. For overprints see Nos. 959, C316.

Beethoven and Birthplace, Bonn A180

50fr, Bronze bust, 1812, & Heiligenstadt home.

1977, Mar. 7 — Perf. 14

953	A180	30fr multi	.50 .25
954	A180	75fr multi	.75 .25

Nos. 953-954,C306-C307 (4) 5.15 3.85

Benz, 1894, Germany — A181

Early Automobiles: 50fr, De Dion Bouton, 1903, France.

1977, Apr. 11 — Litho. — Perf. 14

955	A181	35fr multi	.55 .25
956	A181	80fr multi	.80 .25

Nos. 955-956,C308-C311 (6) 6.70 2.10

Lindbergh, Ground Crew and Spirit of St. Louis — A182

50fr, Lindbergh and Spirit of St. Louis.

1977, May 9

957	A182	25fr multi	.35 .25
958	A182	50fr multi	.60 .25

Nos. 957-958,C312-C315 (6) 4.65 1.55

Charles A. Lindbergh's solo transatlantic flight from New York to Paris, 50th anniv.

No. 952 Overprinted: "10ème ANNIVERSAIRE DU / CONSEIL INTERNATIONAL / DE LA LANGUE FRANCAISE"

1977, May 17 — Litho. — Perf. 14

959	A179	50fr multi	.60 .25

Intl. French Language Council, 10th anniv. See No. C316.

African Slender-snouted Crocodile — A183

Endangered wildlife: 15fr, Nile crocodile.

1977, June 13

960	A183	5fr multi	.35 .25
961	A183	15fr multi	.35 .25

Nos. 960-961,C317-C320 (6) 5.90 1.60

Agriculture School, Tove A184

1977, July 11 — Litho. — Perf. 14

962	A184	50fr multi	.50 .25

Nos. 962,C321-C323 (4) 3.60 1.20

Agricultural development.

Landscape with Cart, by Peter Paul Rubens (1577-1640) — A185

Rubens Painting: 35fr, Exchange of the Princesses at Hendaye, 1623.

1977, Aug. 8

963	A185	15fr multi	.45 .25
964	A185	35fr multi	.60 .25

Nos. 963-964,C324-C325 (4) 3.35 1.00

Orbiter 101 on Ground — A186

Designs: 30fr, Launching of Orbiter, vert. 50fr, Ejection of propellant tanks at take-off.

1977, Oct. 4 — Litho. — Perf. 14

965	A186	20fr multi	.30 .25
966	A186	30fr multi	.40 .25
967	A186	50fr multi	.50 .25

Nos. 965-967,C326-C328 (6) 4.50 1.60

Space shuttle trials in the US.

Lafayette Arriving in Montpelier, Vt. — A187

Design: 25fr, Lafayette, age 19, vert.

1977, Nov. 7 — Perf. 14x13, 13x14

968	A187	25fr multi	.35 .25
969	A187	50fr multi	.60 .25

Nos. 968-969,C329-C330 (4) 2.70 1.00

Arrival of the Marquis de Lafayette in North America, 200th anniv.

Lenin, Cruiser Aurora, Red Flag A188

1977, Nov. 7 — Litho. — Perf. 12

970	A188	50fr multi	1.20 .25

Russian October Revolution, 60th anniv.

Virgin and Child, by Lorenzo Lotto — A189

Edward Jenner — A190

Virgin and Child by: 30fr, Carlo Crivelli. 50fr, Cosimo Tura.

1977, Dec. 19 — Perf. 14

971	A189	20fr multi	.30 .25
972	A189	30fr multi	.35 .25
973	A189	50fr multi	.50 .25

Nos. 971-973,C331-C333 (6) 4.80 1.65

Christmas.

Perf. 14x13, 13x14

1978, Jan. 9 — Litho.

Design: 20fr, Vaccination clinic, horiz.

974	A190	5fr multi	.25 .25
975	A190	20fr multi	.25 .25

Nos. 974-975,C334-C335 (4) 1.25 1.00

Worldwide eradication of smallpox.

Orville and Wilbur Wright — A191

Design: 50fr, Wilbur Wright flying at Kill Devil Hill, 1902.

1978, Feb. 6 — Litho. — Perf. 14

976	A191	35fr multi	.35 .25
977	A191	50fr multi	.50 .25

Nos. 976-977,C336-C339 (6) 7.10 1.95

75th anniversary of first motorized flight.

Anniversaries and Events — A192

Designs: No. 978, High jump. No. 979, Westminster Abbey. No. 980, Soccer players, World Cup. No. 981, Apollo 8. No. 982, Duke of Wellington, by Goya. No. 983, Hurdles. No. 984, Coronation coach. No. 985, Soccer players. No. 986, Apollo launch. No. 987, Dona Isabel Cobos de Porcel, by Goya.

1978, Mar. 13 — Litho. — Perf. 11

978	A192	1000fr gold & multi	9.00
979	A192	1000fr gold & multi	9.00
980	A192	1000fr gold & multi	9.00

981 A192 1000fr gold & multi	9.00	
982 A192 1000fr gold & multi	9.00	

Souvenir Sheets

983 A192 1000fr gold & multi	12.00	
984 A192 1000fr gold & multi	12.00	
985 A192 1000fr gold & multi	12.00	
986 A192 1000fr gold & multi	12.00	
987 A192 1000fr gold & multi	12.00	

Nos. 978, 983, 1980 Summer Olympics, Moscow. Nos. 979, 984, Coronation of Queen Elizabeth II, 25th anniv. Nos. 980, 985, 1978 World Cup Soccer Championships, Argentina. Nos. 981, 986, 1st manned lunar orbit, 10th anniv. Nos. 982, 987, Death sesquicent. of Francisco Goya.

For overprints see Nos. 1056A-1056B, 1094A-1094B.

Exist imperf.

John, the Evangelist and Eagle — A197

Evangelists: 10fr, Luke and ox. 25fr, Mark and lion. 30fr, Matthew and angel.

1978, Mar. 20 Litho. Perf. 13½x14

988 A197 5fr multi		.25	.25
989 A197 10fr multi		.25	.25
990 A197 25fr multi		.25	.25
991 A197 30fr multi		.25	.25
a. Souvenir sheet of 4		.90	.60
Nos. 988-991 (4)		1.00	1.00

No. 991a contains one each of Nos. 988-991 with simulated perforations.

Anchor, Fishing Harbor, Lomé A199

1978, Apr. 26 Photo. Perf. 13

997 A199 25fr multi		.25	.25
Nos. 997,C340-C342 (4)		3.05	1.15

Venera I, USSR — A200

Designs: 30fr, Pioneer, US, horiz. 50fr, Venera, fuel base and antenna.

1978, May 8 Litho. Perf. 14

998 A200 20fr multi		.25	.25
999 A200 30fr multi		.30	.25
1000 A200 50fr multi		.40	.25
Nos. 998-1000,C343-C345 (6)		3.90	1.60

US Pioneer and USSR Venera space missions.

Soccer — A201

50fr, Soccer players and Argentina '78 emblem.

1978, June 5 Perf. 14

1001 A201 30fr multi		.35	.25
1002 A201 50fr multi		.50	.25
Nos. 1001-1002,C346-C349 (6)		6.15	1.95

11th World Cup Soccer Championship, Argentina, June 1-25.

Celerifère, 1818 A202

History of the Bicycle: 50fr, First bicycle sidecar, c. 1870, vert.

Perf. 13x14, 14x13

1978, July 10 Photo.

1003 A202 25fr multi		.35	.25
1004 A202 50fr multi		.70	.25
Nos. 1003-1004,C350-C353 (6)		5.20	1.70

Thomas A. Edison, Sound Waves — A203   Dunant's Birthplace, Geneva — A204

Design: 50fr, Victor's His Master's Voice phonograph, 1905, and dancing couple.

1978, July 8 Photo. Perf. 14x13

1005 A203 30fr multicolored		.30	.25
1006 A203 50fr multicolored		.40	.25
Nos. 1005-1006,C354-C357 (6)		5.35	1.85

Centenary of the phonograph, invented by Thomas Alva Edison.

1978, Sept. 4 Photo. Perf. 14x13

Designs: 10fr, Henri Dunant and red cross. 25fr, Help on battlefield, 1864, and red cross.

1007 A204 5fr Prus bl & red		.25	.25
1008 A204 10fr red brn & red		.25	.25
1009 A204 25fr grn & red		.25	.25
Nos. 1007-1009,C358 (4)		1.20	1.00

Dunant (1828-1910), founder of Red Cross.

Threshing, by Raoul Dufy — A205

50fr, Horsemen on Seashore, by Paul Gauguin.

1978, Nov. 6 Litho. Perf. 14

1010 A205 25fr multi		.30	.25
1011 A205 50fr multi		.50	.25
Nos. 1010-1011,C359-C362 (6)		4.70	2.15

Eiffel Tower, Paris — A206

Virgin and Child, by Antonello da Messina — A207

1978, Nov. 27 Photo. Perf. 14x13

1012 A206 50fr multi		.50	.25
Nos. 1012,C365-C367 (4)		3.90	1.70

Centenary of the Congress of Paris.

1978, Dec. 18 Litho. Perf. 14

Paintings (Virgin and Child): 30fr, by Cario Crivelli. 50fr, by Francesco del Cossa.

1013 A207 20fr multi		.30	.25
1014 A207 40fr multi		.40	.25
1015 A207 50fr multi		.50	.25
Nos. 1013-1015,C368-C370 (6)		4.65	2.20

Christmas.

Capt. Cook's Ship off New Zealand — A208

Design: 50fr, Endeavour in drydock, N.E. Coast of Australia, horiz.

1979, Feb. 12 Litho. Perf. 14

1016 A208 25fr multi		.25	.25
1017 A208 50fr multi		.45	.25
Nos. 1016-1017,C371-C374 (6)		4.25	2.55

200th death anniv. of Capt. James Cook.

Entry into Jerusalem A209

Easter: 40fr, The Last Supper, horiz. 50fr, Descent from the Cross, horiz.

1979, Apr. 9

1018 A209 30fr multi		.30	.25
1019 A209 40fr multi		.35	.25
1020 A209 50fr multi		.40	.25
Nos. 1018-1020,C375-C377 (6)		3.70	2.10

Einstein Observatory, Potsdam — A210

Design: 50fr, Einstein and James Ramsay MacDonald, Berlin, 1931.

1979, July 2 Photo. Perf. 14x13

1021 A210 35fr multi		.35	.25
1022 A210 50fr multi		.45	.25
Nos. 1021-1022,C380-C383 (6)		4.85	2.45

Albert Einstein (1879-1955), theoretical physicist.

Children and Children's Village Emblem — A211   Man Planting Tree — A212

IYC: 10fr, Mother and children. 15fr, Map of Africa, Children's Village emblem, horiz. 20fr, Woman and children walking to Children's Village, horiz. 25fr, Children sitting under African fan palm. 30fr, Map of Togo with location of Children's Villages.

1979, July 30 Photo. Perf. 14x13

1023 A211 5fr multi		.25	.25
1024 A211 10fr multi		.25	.25
1025 A211 15fr multi		.25	.25
1026 A211 20fr multi		.25	.25
1027 A211 25fr multi		.25	.25
1028 A211 30fr multi		.25	.25
a. Souv. sheet of 2, #1027-1028		.75	.45
Nos. 1023-1028 (6)		1.50	1.50

1979, Aug. 13 Perf. 14x13

1029 A212 50fr lilac & green		.60	.25

Second Arbor Day. See No. C384.

Sir Rowland Hill (1795-1879), Originator of Penny Postage — A213

30fr, French mail-sorting office, 18th cent., horiz. 50fr, Mailbox, Paris, 1850.

1979, Aug. 27

1030 A213 20fr multi		.25	.25
1031 A213 30fr multi		.30	.25
1032 A213 50fr multi		.40	.25
Nos. 1030-1032,C385-C387 (6)		3.80	2.05

Norris Locomotive, 1843 — A214

35fr, Stephenson's "Rocket," 1829, vert.

1979, Oct. 1 Litho. Perf. 14

1033 A214 35fr multi		.50	.25
1034 A214 50fr multi		.70	.25
Nos. 1033-1034,C388-C391 (6)		5.70	2.60

Olympic Flame, Lake Placid 80 Emblem, Slalom — A215

1980 Olympic Emblems, Olympic Flame and: 30fr, Yachting 50fr, Discus.

1979, Oct. 18   Litho.   Perf. 13½
1035	A215	20fr multi	.25 .25
1036	A215	30fr multi	.30 .25
1037	A215	50fr multi	.40 .25
	Nos. 1035-1037,C392-C394 (6)		*3.90 2.05*

13th Winter Olympic Games, Lake Placid, NY, 2/12-24/80 (90fr); 22nd Summer Olympic Games, Moscow, 7/19-8/3/80.

Catholic Priests
A216

Design: 30fr, Native praying, vert.

1979, Oct. 29   Perf. 13x14
1038	A216	30fr multi	.35 .25
1039	A216	50fr multi	.50 .25
	Nos. 1038-1039,C396-C397 (4)		*2.00 1.05*

Religions in Togo.

Astronaut Walking on Moon — A217

Design: 50fr, Space capsule orbiting moon.

1979, Nov. 5
1040	A217	35fr multi	.30 .25
1041	A217	50fr multi	.40 .25
	Nos. 1040-1041,C398-C401 (6)		*5.25 2.65*

Apollo 11 moon landing, 10th anniversary.

Telecom 79 — A218

1979, Nov. 26   Photo.   Perf. 13x14
1042	A218	50fr multi	.40 .25

3rd World Telecommunications Exhibition, Geneva, Sept. 20-26. See No. C402.

Holy Family — A219

Christmas: 30fr, Virgin and Child. 50fr, Adoration of the Kings.

1979, Dec. 17   Litho.   Perf. 14
1043	A219	20fr multi	.30 .25
1044	A219	30fr multi	.35 .25
1045	A219	50fr multi	.50 .25
	Nos. 1043-1045,C403-C405 (6)		*4.50 2.20*

Rotary Emblem — A220

Rotary Emblem and: 30fr, Anniversary emblem. 40fr, Paul P. Harris, Rotary founder.

1980, Jan. 14
1046	A220	25fr multi	.25 .25
1047	A220	30fr multi	.35 .25
1048	A220	40fr multi	.40 .25
	Nos. 1046-1048,C406-C408 (6)		*4.25 2.45*

Rotary International, 75th anniversary.

Biathlon, Lake Placid '80 Emblem — A221

1980, Jan. 31   Litho.   Perf. 13½
1049	A221	50fr multi	.40 .25
	Nos. 1049,C409-C411 (4)		*3.00 1.50*

13th Winter Olympic Games, Lake Placid, NY, Feb. 12-24. See No. C412.

1980 Winter Olympics, Lake Placid — A221a

Gold medalist: No. 1049F, Hanni Wenzel, Liechtenstein, women's slalom. No. 1049G, Eric Heiden, US, men's speed skating. No. 1049H, Jouko Tormanen, Finland, 90-meter ski jumping. No. 1049I, Erich Schaerer, Josef Benz, Switzerland, 2-man bobsled. No. 1049J, US, ice hockey.

1980   Litho.   Perf. 11
1049A	A221a	1000fr multi	20.00 4.50
1049B	A221a	1000fr multi	20.00 4.50
1049C	A221a	1000fr multi	20.00 4.50
1049D	A221a	1000fr multi	20.00 4.50
1049E	A221a	1000fr multi	20.00 4.50
	Nos. 1049A-1049E (5)		*100.00 22.50*

Souvenir Sheets
1049F	A221a	1000fr gold & multi	—
1049G	A221a	1000fr gold & multi	—
1049H	A221a	1000fr gold & multi	—
1049I	A221a	1000fr gold & multi	—
1049J	A221a	1000fr gold & multi	—

Exist imperf.

Swimming, Moscow '80 Emblem — A222

1980, Feb. 29   Litho.   Perf. 13½
1050	A222	20fr shown	.25 .25
1051	A222	30fr Gymnastics	.25 .25
1052	A222	50fr Running	.45 .25
	Nos. 1050-1052,C413-C415 (6)		*5.95 3.25*

22nd Summer Olympic Games, Moscow, July 19-Aug. 3.

Christ and the Angels, by Andrea Mantegna A223

Easter 1980 (Paintings by): 40fr, Carlo Crivelli. 50fr, Jacopo Pontormo.

1980, Mar. 31   Perf. 14
1053	A223	30fr multi	.35 .25
1054	A223	40fr multi	.40 .25
1055	A223	50fr multi	.45 .25
	Nos. 1053-1055,C416-C418 (6)		*3.90 2.00*

Jet over Map of Africa A224

1980, Mar. 24   Litho.   Perf. 12½
1056	A224	50fr multi	.60 .25

ASECNA (Air Safety Board), 20th anniv. See No. C419.

Nos. 979, 984 Ovptd. "Londres / 1980"

Litho. & Embossed
1980, May 6   Perf. 11
1056A	A192	1000fr gold & multi	6.50 —

Souvenir Sheet
1056B	A192	1000fr gold & multi	7.25 —

12th World Telecommunications Day — A225

1980, May 17   Photo.   Perf. 14x13½
1057	A225	50fr multi	.50 .25

See No. C420.

Red Cross over Globe Showing Lomé, Togo — A226

1980, June 16   Photo.   Perf. 14x13
1058	A226	50fr multi	.60 .25

Togolese Red Cross. See No. C421.

Jules Verne (1828-1905), French Science Fiction Writer — A227

50fr, Shark (20,000 Leagues Under the Sea).

1980, July 14   Litho.   Perf. 14
1059	A227	30fr multi	.30 .25
1060	A227	50fr multi	.45 .25
	Nos. 1059-1060,C422-C425 (6)		*4.20 2.00*

Baroness James de Rothschild, by Ingres — A228

Paintings by Jean Auguste Dominique Ingres (1780-1867): 30fr, Napoleon I on Imperial Throne. 40fr, Don Pedro of Toledo and Henri IV.

1980, Aug. 29   Litho.   Perf. 14
1061	A228	25fr multi	.25 .25
1062	A228	35fr multi	.35 .25
1063	A228	40fr multi	.40 .25
	Nos. 1061-1063,C426-C428 (6)		*4.25 2.05*

Minnie Holding Mirror for Leopard A229

Disney Characters and Animals from Fazao Reserve: 2fr, Goofy (Dingo) cleaning teeth of hippopotamus. 3fr, Donald holding snout of crocodile. 4fr, Donald dangling over cliff from horn of rhinoceros. 5fr, Goofy riding water buffalo. 10fr, Monkey taking picture of Mickey. 100fr, Mickey as doctor examining giraffe with sore throat. 200fr, Pluto in party hat. No. 1071, Elephant giving shower to Goofy. No. 1072, Lion carrying Goofy by seat of his pants. No. 1072A, Pluto.

1980, Sept. 15   Perf. 11
1064	A229	1fr multi	.25 .25
1065	A229	2fr multi	.25 .25
1066	A229	3fr multi	.25 .25
1067	A229	4fr multi	.25 .25
1068	A229	5fr multi	.25 .25
1069	A229	10fr multi	.25 .25
1070	A229	100fr multi	.75 .35

1070A	A229	200fr multi	1.50	.75
1071	A229	300fr multi	2.25	1.10
		Nos. 1064-1071 (9)	6.00	3.70

Souvenir Sheets

| 1072 | A229 | 300fr multi | 8.00 | 3.00 |
| 1072A | A229 | 300fr multi | 4.00 | 1.50 |

50th anniv. of the Disney character Pluto.

Market
Activities,
Women
Preparing
Meat
A230

1980-81   **Perf. 14**

1073	A230	1fr Grinding savo	.25	.25
1074	A230	2fr shown	.25	.25
1075	A230	3fr Truck going to market	.25	.25
1076	A230	4fr Unloading produce	.25	.25
1077	A230	5fr Sugar cane vendor	.25	.25
1078	A230	6fr Barber curling child's hair, vert.	.25	.25
1079	A230	7fr Vegetable vendor	.25	.25
1080	A230	8fr Sampling mangos, vert.	.25	.25
1081	A230	9fr Grain vendor	.25	.25
1082	A230	10fr Spiced fish vendor	.25	.25
1083	A230	15fr Clay pot vendor	.25	.25
1084	A230	20fr Straw baskets	.25	.25
1085	A230	25fr Selling lemons and onions, vert.	.25	.25
1086	A230	30fr Straw baskets, diff.	.25	.25
1087	A230	40fr Shore market	.30	.25
1087A	A230	45fr Vegatable stall	.30	.25
1088	A230	50fr Women carrying produce, vert.	.40	.25
1088A	A230	60fr Rice wine	.40	.25
		Nos. 1073-1088A (18)	4.90	4.50

Issued: 45fr, 60fr, 3/8/81; others, 3/17/80. Nos. 1087A, 1088A dated 1980.
See Nos. C440-C445, J68-J71. For overprints see Nos. C486-C487.

Commemorative Wreath — A231

Famous Men of the Decade: 40fr, Mao Tse-tung, vert.

1980, Feb. 11   **Perf. 14x13**

1089	A231	25fr multi	.40	.25
1090	A231	40fr emer grn & dk grn	.60	.25
		Nos. 1089-1090,C429-C431 (5)	5.10	1.80

World Tourism Conference, Manila, Sept. 27 — A232

1980, Sept. 15   **Litho.**   **Perf. 14**

| 1091 | A232 | 50fr Hotel tourism emblem, vert. | .50 | .25 |
| 1092 | A232 | 150fr shown | 1.50 | .75 |

Map of
Australia
and Human
Rights
Flame
A233

1980, Oct. 13   **Photo.**   **Perf. 13x14**

1093	A233	30fr shown	.30	.25
1094	A233	50fr Europe and Asia map	.50	.25
		Nos. 1093-1094,C432-C433 (4)	2.20	1.25

Declaration of Human Rights, 30th anniv.

Nos. 980,
985 Ovptd.
in Gold &
Black

Litho. & Embossed

1980, Nov. 24   **Perf. 11**

| 1094A | A192 | 1000fr gold & multi | 9.00 | — |

Souvenir Sheet

| 1094B | A192 | 1000fr gold & multi | 8.00 | — |

No. 1094B ovptd. with additional text and black bars in sheet margin.

Melk
Monastery,
Austria, 18th
Century
A234

Perf. 14½x13½

1980, Dec. 22   **Litho.**

1095	A234	20fr shown	.25	.25
1096	A234	30fr Tarragon Cathedral, Spain, 12th cent.	.35	.25
1097	A234	55fr St. John the Baptist, Florence, 1964	.55	.25
		Nos. 1095-1097,C435-C437 (6)	4.35	2.25

Christmas.

African Postal
Union, 5th
Anniversary
A235

1980, Dec. 24   **Photo.**   **Perf. 13½**

| 1098 | A235 | 100fr multi | .75 | .35 |

February
2nd Hotel
Opening
A236

1981, Feb. 2   **Litho.**   **Perf. 12½x13**

| 1099 | A236 | 50fr multi | .60 | .25 |

See No. C437B.

A236a

1981, Dec. 21   **Litho.**   **Perf. 12½**

| 1100 | A236a | 70fr lt grn & multi | .70 | .35 |

West African Rice Development Assoc.
See No. C461.

A237

Easter (Rembrandt Paintings): 30fr, Rembrandt's Father. 40fr, Self-portrait. 50fr, Artist's father as an old man. 60fr, Rider on Horseback.

1981, Apr. 13   **Perf. 14½x13½**

1101	A237	30fr multi	.35	.25
1102	A237	40fr multi	.40	.25
1103	A237	50fr multi	.50	.25
1104	A237	60fr multi	.60	.30
		Nos. 1101-1104,C438-C439 (6)	4.50	2.15

Wedding of Prince Charles and Lady Diana Spencer — A237a — 1105

1981, July 29   **Litho.**   **Perf. 11**

| 1105 | A237a | 1000fr gold & multi | 7.25 | 5.75 |

Souvenir Sheet

Litho. & Embossed

| 1106 | A237a | 1000fr Charles & Diana, diff. | 8.00 | 4.00 |

No. 1105 printed with embossed se-tenant label.
For overprints see Nos. 1143A-1143B.

Red-headed Rock Fowl — A238

1981, Aug. 10   **Perf. 13½x14½**

1107	A238	30fr shown	.45	.25
1108	A238	40fr Splendid sunbird	.55	.25
1109	A238	60fr Violet-backed starling	.90	.25
1110	A238	90fr Red-collared widowbird	1.40	.30
		Nos. 1107-1110,C446-C447 (6)	5.60	1.65

1982 World Soccer Championships, Spain — A238a

Flags (Nos. 1110A-1110E) or Players (Nos. 1110F-1110J) and stadiums: Nos. 1110A, 1110F, Athletico de Madrid. Nos. 1110B, 1110G, Real Madrid C.F. Nos. 1110C, 1110H, R.C.D. Espanol. Nos. 1110D, 1110I, Real Zaragoza. Nos. 1110E, 1110J, Valencia.

Set of 5

Litho. & Embossed

1981, Aug. 17   **Perf. 11**

| 1110A-1110E | A238a | 1000fr | 45.00 | 11.00 |

Souvenir Sheets

| 1110F-1110J | A238a | 1000fr | 40.00 | 12.00 |

African
Postal
Union
Ministers,
6th Council
Meeting,
July 28-20
A239

1981, Aug. 31   **Litho.**   **Perf. 12½**

1111	A239	70fr Dish antenna	.50	.25
1112	A239	90fr Computer operator, vert.	.70	.35
1113	A239	105fr Map	.80	.40
		Nos. 1111-1113 (3)	2.00	1.00

Intl. Year of
the
Disabled
A240

1981, Aug. 31   **Perf. 14**

| 1114 | A240 | 70fr Blind man | .95 | .45 |
| | | Nos. 1114,C448-C449 (3) | 3.55 | 1.70 |

See No. C449A.

Woman with
Hat, by
Picasso,
1961 — A241

Picasso Birth Centenary: Sculptures.

1981, Sept. 14   **Perf. 14½x13½**

1116	A241	25fr shown	.35	.25
1117	A241	50fr She-goat	.65	.25
1118	A241	60fr Violin, 1915	.70	.25
		Nos. 1116-1118,C450-C452 (6)	6.40	2.55

Aix-la-Chapelle Cathedral,
Germany — A242

World Heritage Year: 40fr, Geyser, Yellowstone Natl. Park. 50fr, Nahanni Natl. Park, Canada. 60fr, Stone churches, Ethiopia.

1981, Sept. 28   **Perf. 13½x14½**
1119	A242	30fr multi	.30	.25
1120	A242	40fr multi	.35	.25
1121	A242	50fr multi	.40	.25
1122	A242	60fr multi	.50	.35
	Nos. 1119-1122,C453-C454 (6)		4.15	2.35

Yuri Gagarin's Vostok I, 20th. — A243

Space Anniversaries: 50fr, 20th Anniv. of Alan Shepard's Flight. 60fr, Lunar Orbiter I, 15th.

1981, Nov.   **Perf. 14**
1123	A243	25fr multi	.25	.25
1124	A243	50fr multi	.45	.25
1125	A243	60fr multi	.55	.30
	Nos. 1123-1125,C455-C456 (5)		3.00	1.75

Christmas
A244

Rubens Paintings: 20fr, Adoration of the Kings. 30fr, Adoration of the Shepherds. 50fr, St. Catherine.

Perf. 14½x13½
1981, Dec. 10   **Litho.**
1126	A244	20fr multi	.25	.25
1127	A244	30fr multi	.25	.25
1128	A244	50fr multi	.40	.25
	Nos. 1126-1128,C457-C459 (6)		5.20	2.75

15th Anniv. of Natl. Liberation — A245

1982, Jan. 13   **Litho.**   **Perf. 12½**
1129	A245	70fr Dove, flag	.70	.35
1130	A245	90fr Citizens, Pres. Eyadema, vert.	.90	.45
	Nos. 1129-1130,C462-C463 (4)		3.20	1.55

Scouting
Year
A246

1982, Feb. 25   **Litho.**   **Perf. 14**
1131	A246	70fr Pitching tent	.55	.25
	Nos. 1131,C464-C467 (5)		4.50	1.80

Easter — A247

Designs: The Ten Commandments.

1982, Mar. 15   **Perf. 14x14½**
1132	A247	10fr multi	.25	.25
1133	A247	25fr multi	.25	.25
1134	A247	30fr multi	.25	.25
1135	A247	45fr multi	.30	.25
1136	A247	50fr multi	.35	.25
1137	A247	70fr multi	.45	.25
1138	A247	90fr multi	.60	.30
	Nos. 1132-1138,C469-C470 (9)		3.95	2.55

Papilio
Dardanus
A248

1982, July 15   **Litho.**   **Perf. 14½x14**
1139	A248	15fr shown	.60	.25
1140	A248	20fr Belenois calypso	.60	.25
1141	A248	25fr Palla decius	.60	.25
	Nos. 1139-1141,C474-C475 (5)		5.80	1.60

1982 World
Cup — A249

Designs: Various soccer players.

1982, July 26   **Perf. 14x14½**
1142	A249	25fr multi	.25	.25
1143	A249	45fr multi	.35	.25
	Nos. 1142-1143,C477-C479 (5)		4.90	2.50

For overprints see Nos. 1150-1155.

Nos. 1105-1106 Ovptd. on one or two
lines

1982, Oct. 28   **Litho.**   **Perf. 11**
1143A	A237a	1000fr gold & multi	8.00	4.00

Souvenir Sheet
Litho. & Embossed
1143B	A237a	1000fr gold & multi	9.25	3.50

Christmas
A250

Madonna of Baldacchino, by Raphael. #1144-1148 show details; #1149 entire painting.

1982, Dec. 24   **Litho.**   **Perf. 14½x14**
1144	A250	45fr multi	.45	.25
1145	A250	70fr multi	.65	.30
1146	A250	105fr multi	1.00	.40
1147	A250	130fr multi	1.40	.45
1148	A250	150fr multi	1.50	.55
	Nos. 1144-1148 (5)		5.00	1.95

Souvenir Sheet
Perf. 14x14½
1149	A250	500fr multi, vert.	4.50	1.75

Nos. 1142-1143, C477-C480
Overprinted: VAINQUER / COUPE DU
MONDE / FOOTBALL 82 / "ITALIE"

1983, Jan. 31   **Litho.**   **Perf. 14x14½**
1150	A249	25fr multi	.25	.25
1151	A249	45fr multi	.35	.25
1152	A249	105fr multi	.75	.40
1153	A249	200fr multi	1.60	.70
1154	A249	300fr multi	2.25	1.10
	Nos. 1150-1154 (5)		5.20	2.70

Souvenir Sheet
1155	A249	500fr multi	4.50	2.75

Italy's victory in 1982 World Cup. Nos. 1152-1155 airmail.

20th Anniv. of West
African Monetary
Union
(1982) — A251

1983, May   **Litho.**   **Perf. 12½x12**
1156	A251	70fr Map	.60	.25
1157	A251	90fr Emblem	.80	.30

Visit of Pres. Mitterand of France, Jan.
13-15 — A252

1983, Jan. 13   **Litho.**   **Perf. 13**
1158	A252	35fr Sokode Regional Hospital	.35	.25
a.		Souvenir sheet, imperf.	1.00	.55
1159	A252	45fr Citizens joining hands	.40	.25
a.		Souvenir sheet, imperf.	1.00	.55
1160	A252	70fr Soldiers, vert.	.60	.30
a.		Souvenir sheet, imperf.	1.00	.55
1161	A252	90fr Pres. Mitterand, vert.	.85	.35
a.		Souvenir sheet, imperf.	1.00	.55
1162	A252	105fr Pres. Eyadema, Mitterand, vert.	.95	.40
a.		Souvenir sheet, imperf.	1.00	.55
1163	A252	130fr Greeting crowd	1.25	.50
a.		Souvenir sheet, imperf.	1.00	.55
	Nos. 1158-1163 (6)		4.40	2.05

Nos. 1161-1163 airmail.

Easter — A253

Paintings: 35fr, Mourners at the Death of Christ, by Bellini. 70fr, Crucifixion, by Raphael. 90fr, Descent from the Cross, by Carracci. 500fr Christ, by Reni.

1983   **Litho.**   **Perf. 13½x14½**
1164	A253	35fr multi	.35	.25
1165	A253	70fr multi, vert.	.65	.25
1166	A253	90fr multi	1.00	.25
	Nos. 1164-1166 (3)		2.00	.75

Souvenir Sheet
Perf. 14½x13½
1167	A253	500fr multi	4.50	1.75

90fr, 500fr airmail.

Folkdances — A254

1983, Dec. 1   **Perf. 14½x14**
1168	A254	70fr Kondona	.65	.25
1169	A254	90fr Kondona, diff.	.80	.25
1170	A254	105fr Touboule	.95	.25
1171	A254	130fr Adjogbo	1.00	.25
	Nos. 1168-1171 (4)		3.40	1.00

90fr, 105fr, 130fr airmail.

World
Communications
Year — A255

1983, June 20   **Litho.**   **Perf. 14x14½**
1172	A255	70fr Drummer	.60	.25
1173	A255	90fr Modern communication	.70	.25

90fr airmail.

Christmas — A256

1983, Dec.   **Perf. 13½x14½**
1174	A256	70fr Catholic Church, Kante	.55	.25
1175	A256	90fr Altar, Dapaong Cathedral	.65	.25
1176	A256	105fr Protestant Church, Dapaong	.80	.25
	Nos. 1174-1176 (3)		2.00	.75

Souvenir Sheet
1177	A256	500fr Ecumenical Church, Pya	4.50	1.75

90fr, 105fr, 500fr airmail.

Sarakawa Presidential Assassination
Attempt, 10th Anniv. — A257

1984, Jan. 24   Litho.   Perf. 13
1178	A257	70fr Wrecked plane	.60	.25
1179	A257	90fr Plane, diff.	.70	.25
1180	A257	120fr Memorial Hall	1.00	.25
1181	A257	270fr Pres. Eyadema statue, vert.	2.25	.45
		Nos. 1178-1181 (4)	4.55	1.20

120fr, 270fr airmail.

20th Anniv.
of World
Food
Program
(1983)
A258

1984, May 2   Litho.   Perf. 13
1182	A258	35fr Orchard	.25	.25
1183	A258	70fr Fruit tree	.55	.25
1184	A258	90fr Rice paddy	.65	.25
		Nos. 1182-1184 (3)	1.45	.75

Souvenir Sheet
1185	A258	300fr Village, horiz.	3.25	2.10

25th Anniv. of
Council of
Unity — A259

1984, May 29   Perf. 12
1186	A259	70fr multi	.65	.25
1187	A259	90fr multi	.85	.25

Easter
1984 — A260

Various stained-glass windows.

1984   Litho.   Perf. 14x14½
1188	A260	70fr multi	.55	.25
1189	A260	90fr multi	.65	.25
1190	A260	120fr multi	.85	.25
1191	A260	270fr multi	1.90	.50
1192	A260	300fr multi	2.10	.55
		Nos. 1188-1192 (5)	6.05	1.80

Souvenir Sheet
1193	A260	500fr multi	4.50	3.50

Nos. 1189-1193 airmail.

Centenary of German-Togolese
Friendship — A261

#1194, Degbenou Catholic Mission, 1893.
#1195, Kara Bridge, 1911. #1196, Treaty Site,
Baguida, 1884. #1197, Degbenou Students,
1893. #1198, Sansane Administrative Post,
1908. #1199, Adjido Official School.
#1200, Sokode Cotton Market, 1910.
#1201, William Fountain, Atakpame, 1906.
#1202, Lome Main Street, 1895, No. 19.
#1203, Police, 1905. #1204, Lome Railroad
Construction. #1205, Governor's Palace,
Lome, 1905. #1206, No. 9, Commerce Street,
Lome.
#1207, Nos. 10, 17. #1208, Lome Wharf,
1903. #1209, G. Nachtigal. #1210, Wilhelm II.
#1211, O.F. de Bismark. #1212, J. de
Puttkamer. #1213, A. Koehler. #1214, W.
Horn. #1215, J.G. de Zech. #1216, E. Bruck-
ner. #1217, A.F. de Mecklenburg. #1218, H.G.
de Doering. #1219, Land Development, 1908.
#1220, Postal Courier, No. 8. #1221, Treaty
Signers, 1885. 150fr, German & Togolese
Children, Flags. #1223, Aneho Line Locomo-
tive, 1905. #1224, Mallet Locomotive, 1907.
#1225, German Ship "Mowe," 1884. #1226,
"La Sophie," 1884. 300fr, Pres. Eyadema,
Helmut Kohl.

1984, July 5   Litho.   Perf. 13
1194	A261	35fr multi	.50	.25
1195	A261	35fr multi	.50	.25
1196	A261	35fr multi	.50	.25
1197	A261	35fr multi	.50	.25
1198	A261	35fr multi	.50	.25
1199	A261	35fr multi	.50	.25
1200	A261	35fr multi	.50	.25
1201	A261	45fr multi, vert.	.50	.25
1202	A261	45fr multi	.50	.25
1203	A261	45fr multi	.50	.25
1204	A261	45fr multi	.50	.25
1205	A261	45fr multi	.50	.25
1206	A261	45fr multi	.50	.25
1207	A261	70fr multi	.60	.25
1208	A261	70fr multi	.60	.25
1209	A261	90fr multi, vert.	.75	.25
1210	A261	90fr multi, vert.	.75	.25
1211	A261	90fr multi, vert.	.75	.25
1212	A261	90fr multi, vert.	.75	.25
1213	A261	90fr multi, vert.	.75	.25
1214	A261	90fr multi, vert.	.75	.25
1215	A261	90fr multi, vert.	.75	.25
1216	A261	90fr multi, vert.	.75	.25
1217	A261	90fr multi, vert.	.75	.25
1218	A261	90fr multi, vert.	.75	.25
1219	A261	90fr multi, vert.	.75	.25
1220	A261	120fr multi, vert.	1.00	.25
1221	A261	120fr multi	1.00	.25
1222	A261	150fr multi	1.25	.25
1223	A261	270fr multi	2.25	.45
1224	A261	270fr multi	2.25	.45
1225	A261	270fr multi	2.25	.45
1226	A261	270fr multi	2.25	.45
1227	A261	300fr multi	2.40	.50
		Nos. 1194-1227 (34)	30.60	9.55

Souvenir sheets of one exist for each
design. Stamp size: 65x80mm. Value, set of
34, $35.

Donald
Duck, 50th
Anniv.
A262

1984, Sept. 21   Litho.   Perf. 11
1230	A262	1fr Donald, Chip	.55	.25
1231	A262	2fr Donald, Chip and Dale	.55	.25
1232	A262	3fr Louie, Chip and Dale	.55	.25
1233	A262	5fr Donald, Chip	.55	.25
1234	A262	10fr Daisy Duck, Donald	.55	.25

1235	A262	15fr Goofy, Donald	.55	.25
1236	A262	105fr Huey, Dewey and Louie	.80	.25
1237	A262	500fr Nephews, Donald	3.75	.70
1238	A262	1000fr Nephews, Donald	8.25	1.40
		Nos. 1230-1238 (9)	16.10	3.85

Souvenir Sheets
Perf. 14
1239	A262	1000fr Surprised Donald	10.00	10.00
1240	A262	1000fr Perplexed Donald	10.00	10.00

Nos. 1236-1240 airmail.
For overprints see Nos. C551-C554.

Endangered Mammals — A263

1984, Oct. 1   Litho.   Perf. 15x14½
1241	A263	45fr Manatee swimming	1.25	.50
1242	A263	70fr Manatee eating	2.00	.50
1243	A263	90fr Manatees floating	3.00	1.00
1244	A263	105fr Young manatee, mother	5.00	1.00
		Nos. 1241-1244 (4)	11.25	3.00

Souvenir Sheets
Perf. 14x15, 15x14
1245	A263	1000fr Olive Colobus monkey, vert.	12.00	7.25
1246	A263	1000fr Galago (Bushbaby)	12.00	7.25

Nos. 1243-1246 airmail. See #1444-1447.

Birth
Centenary
of Eleanor
Roosevelt
A264

1984, Oct. 10   Litho.   Perf. 13½
1247	A264	70fr shown	.55	.25
1248	A264	90fr Mrs. Roosevelt, Statue of Liberty	.70	.25

No. 1248 airmail.

Classic Automobiles — A265

1984, Nov. 15   Litho.   Perf. 15
1249	A265	1fr 1947 Bristol	.85	.25
1250	A265	2fr 1925 Frazer Nash	.85	.25
1251	A265	3fr 1950 Healey	.85	.25
1252	A265	4fr 1925 Kissell	.85	.25
1253	A265	50fr 1927 La Salle	.85	.25
1254	A265	90fr 1921 Minerva	1.00	.25
1255	A265	500fr 1950 Morgan	5.75	.70
1256	A265	1000fr 1921 Napier	12.00	1.40
		Nos. 1249-1256 (8)	23.00	3.60

Souvenir Sheets
1257	A265	1000fr 1941 Nash	9.00	2.00
1258	A265	1000fr 1903 Peugeot	9.00	2.00

Nos. 1254-1258 airmail.
For overprints see Nos. 1328-1331, C542-
C544, C564-C565.

Christmas
A266

Perf. 14½x13½
1984, Nov. 23   Litho.
1259	A266	70fr Connestable Madonna	.60	.25
1260	A266	290fr Cowper Madonna	2.25	.50
1261	A266	300fr Alba Madonna	2.25	.55
1262	A266	500fr Madonna of the Curtain	4.00	.85
		Nos. 1259-1262 (4)	9.10	2.15

Souvenir Sheet
1263	A266	1000fr Madonna with Child	8.00	6.75

Nos. 1260-1263 airmail.

African Locomotives — A267

1984, Nov. 30   Litho.   Perf. 15
1264	A267	1fr Decapod, Madeira	.55	.25
1265	A267	2fr 2-6-0, Egypt	.55	.25
1266	A267	3fr 4-8-2+2-8-4, Algeria	.55	.25
1267	A267	4fr Congo-Ocean diesel	.55	.25
1268	A267	50fr 0-4-0+0-4-0, Libya	.55	.25
1269	A267	90fr #49, Malawi	.65	.25
1270	A267	105fr 1907 Mallet, Togo	.80	.25
1271	A267	500fr 4-8-2, Rhodesia	3.50	.80
1272	A267	1000fr Beyer-Garratt, East Africa	7.00	1.60
		Nos. 1264-1272 (9)	14.70	4.15

Souvenir Sheets
1273	A267	1000fr 2-8-2, Ghana	9.00	6.00
1274	A267	1000fr Locomotive, Senegal	9.00	6.00

Nos. 1269-1274 airmail.
For overprints see Nos. 1343-1346, 1356-
1360, C541, C566.

Economic Convention, Lome — A268

1984, Dec. 8   Litho.   Perf. 12½
1275		100fr Map of the Americas	.80	.25
1276		130fr Map of Eurasia, Africa	1.10	.25
1277		270fr Map of Asia, Australia	1.90	.50
a.	A268	Strip of 3, #1275-1277	4.50	4.50

Souvenir Sheet
1278	A268	500fr President Eyadema	4.50	4.00

No. 1277a has continuous design.

Intl. Civil
Aviation
Org., 40th
Anniv.
A269

Map of Togo, ICAO emblem and: 70fr, Lockheed Constellation, 1944. 105fr, Boeing 707, 1954. 200fr, Doublas DC-8-61, 1966. 500fr, Bac/Sud Concorde, 1966. 1000fr, Icarus, by Hans Erni.

1984, Oct. 15	Litho.	Perf. 15x14		
1279 A269	70fr multi		.80	.25
1280 A269	105fr multi		1.00	.25
1281 A269	200fr multi		1.60	.25
1282 A269	500fr multi		4.00	.75
Nos. 1279-1282 (4)			7.40	1.50

Souvenir Sheet

1283 A269	1000fr multi	7.25	7.00

Nos. 1280-1283 airmail.

Mosaic of the 12 Apostles, Baptistry of the Aryans, Ravenna, Italy, — A270

Designs: 1fr, St. Paul. 2fr, St. Thomas. 3fr, St. Matthew. 4fr, St. James the Younger. 5fr, St. Simon. 70fr, St. Thaddeaus Judas. 90fr, St. Bartholomew. 105fr, St. Philip. 200fr, St. John. 270fr, St. James the Greater. 400fr, St. Andrew. 500fr, St. Peter. No. 1296, The Last Supper, by Andrea del Castagno, c. 1421-1457, horiz. No, 1297, Coronation of the Virgin, by Raphael, 1483-1520, horiz.

1984, Dec. 14		Perf. 15		
1284 A270	1fr multi		1.10	.25
1285 A270	2fr multi		1.10	.25
1286 A270	3fr multi		1.10	.25
1287 A270	4fr multi		1.10	.25
1288 A270	5fr multi		1.10	.25
1289 A270	70fr multi		1.10	.25
1290 A270	90fr multi		1.10	.25
1291 A270	105fr multi		1.10	.25
1292 A270	200fr multi		2.50	.25
1293 A270	270fr multi		3.50	.35
1294 A270	400fr multi		4.75	.45
1295 A270	500fr multi		5.75	.55
Nos. 1284-1295 (12)			25.30	3.60

Souvenir Sheets

1296-1297 A270	1000fr each	15.00	4.50

Nos. 1290-1297 airmail.

For overprints see Nos. C545-C547.

Race Horses A271

1985, Jan. 10				
1298 A271	1fr	Allez France	.85	.25
1299 A271	2fr	Arkle, vert.	.85	.25
1300 A271	3fr	Tingle Creek, vert.	.85	.25
1301 A271	4fr	Interco	.85	.25
1302 A271	50fr	Dawn Run	.85	.25
1303 A271	90fr	Seattle Slew, vert.	.85	.25
1304 A271	500fr	Nijinsky	4.00	.60
1305 A271	1000fr	Politician	8.00	1.25
Nos. 1298-1305 (8)			17.10	3.35

Souvenir Sheets

1306 A271	1000fr Shergar	9.00	6.50
1307 A271	1000fr Red Rum	9.00	6.50

Nos. 1303-1307 airmail.

For overprints see Nos. 1353-1355A.

Easter — A272

Paintings by Raphael (1483-1520).

Perf. 13½x14½, 14½x13½				
1985, Mar. 7				
1308 A272	70fr	Christ and His Flock	.90	.25
1309 A272	90fr	Christ and the Fishermen	.90	.25
1310 A272	135fr	The Blessed Christ, vert.	1.10	.25
1311 A272	150fr	The Entombment, vert.	1.40	.25
1312 A272	250fr	The Resurrection, vert.	2.25	.35
Nos. 1308-1312 (5)			6.55	1.35

Souvenir Sheet

1313 A272	1000fr The Transfiguration	9.50	7.50

Nos. 1309-1313 airmail.

Technical & Cultural Cooperation Agency, 15th Anniv. — A273

1985, Mar. 20		Perf. 12½		
1314 A273	70fr multi		.60	.25
1315 A273	90fr multi		.60	.25

Philexafrica '85, Lome — A274

1985, May 9		Perf. 13		
1316 A274	200fr	Woman carrying fruit basket	2.40	.25
1317 A274	200fr	Man plowing field	2.40	.25
a.		Pair, #1316-1317 + label	5.00	4.50

Scarification Ritual — A275

1985, May 14		Perf. 14x15		
1318 A275	25fr	Kabye (Pya)	.60	.25
1319 A275	70fr	Mollah (Kotokoli)	.60	.25
1320 A275	90fr	Maba (Dapaong)	.60	.25
1321 A275	105fr	Kabye (Pagouda)	.75	.25
1322 A275	270fr	Peda	1.75	.30
Nos. 1318-1322 (5)			4.30	1.30

Nos. 1320-1322 airmail.

Seashells A276

70fr, Clavatula muricata. 90fr, Marginella desjardini. 120fr, Clavatula nifat. 135fr, Cypraea stercoraria. 270fr, Conus genuanus. 1000fr, Dancers wearing traditional shell decorations.

1985, June 1		Perf. 15x14		
1323 A276	70fr multi		1.10	.25
1324 A276	90fr multi		1.10	.25
1325 A276	120fr multi		1.40	.25

1326 A276	135fr multi		1.40	.25
1327 A276	270fr multi		3.00	.35
Nos. 1323-1327 (5)			8.00	1.35

Souvenir Sheet

1327A A276	1000fr multi	9.50	7.50

Nos. 1324-1327A airmail.

Nos. 1253, 1256-1258 Overprinted "Exposition Mondiale 1985 / Tsukuba, Japon"

1985, June		Perf. 15		
1328 A265	50fr #1253		1.50	.25
1329 A265	1000fr #1256		11.50	3.50

Souvenir Sheets

1330 A265	1000fr #1257	9.75	3.75
1331 A265	1000fr #1258	9.75	3.75

EXPO '85.

Audubon Birth Bicent. — A277

Illustrations by artist-naturalist J.J. Audubon (1785-1851).

1985, Aug. 13		Perf. 13		
1332 A277	90fr	Larus bonapartii	.95	.25
1333 A277	120fr	Pelecanus occidentalis	1.25	.25
1334 A277	135fr	Cassidix mexicanus	1.25	.25
1335 A277	270fr	Aquila chrysaetos	2.50	.35
1336 A277	500fr	Picus erythrocephalus	4.50	.60
Nos. 1332-1336 (5)			10.45	1.70

Souvenir Sheet

1337 A277	1000fr	Dendroica petechia	9.50	7.50

Nos. 1332, 1334 and 1336-1337 airmail.

Dove, UN Emblem — A278

Kara Port Construction — A279

Designs: 115fr, Hands, UN emblem. 250fr, Millet crop, Atalote Research Facility. 500fr, UN, Togo flags, statesmen.

1985, Oct. 24	Litho.	Perf. 13		
1338 A278	90fr multi		.80	.25
1339 A278	115fr multi		.95	.25
1340 A279	150fr multi		1.25	.25
1341 A279	250fr multi		2.00	.35
1342 A279	500fr multi		4.00	.65
Nos. 1338-1342 (5)			9.00	1.75

UN, 40th anniv. Nos. 1340-1342 are airmail.

Nos. 1267, 1270, 1272, 1273 Ovptd. with Rotary Emblem and "80e ANNIVERSAIRE DU / ROTARY INTERNATIONAL"

1985	Litho.	Perf. 15		
1343 A267	4fr multi		.65	.40
1344 A267	105fr multi		1.25	1.10
1345 A267	1000fr multi		12.50	6.50
Nos. 1343-1345 (3)			14.40	8.00

Souvenir Sheet

1346 A267	1000fr multi	12.50	6.50

Nos. 1344-1346 are airmail.

Christmas A280

Religious paintings and statuary: 90fr, The Garden of Roses Madonna. 115fr, Madonna and Child, Byzantine, 11th cent. 150fr, Rest During the Flight to Egypt, by Gerard David (1450-1523). 160fr, African Madonna, 16th cent. 250fr, African Madonna, c. 1900. 500fr, Mystic Madonna, by Sandro Botticelli (1444-1510).

Perf. 14½x13½				
1985, Dec. 10		Litho.		
1347 A280	90fr multi		.80	.25
1348 A280	115fr multi		1.00	.25
1349 A280	150fr multi		1.40	.25
1350 A280	160fr multi		1.40	.25
1351 A280	250fr multi		2.00	.40
Nos. 1347-1351 (5)			6.60	1.40

Souvenir Sheet

1352 A280	500fr multi	4.50	3.50

Nos. 1348-1352 air airmail. No. 1352 contains one stamp 36x51mm.

Nos. 1302, 1305-1307 Ovptd. "75e Anniversaire / du Scoutisme Feminin"

1986, Jan.		Perf. 15		
1353 A271	50fr multi		1.60	.30
1354 A271	1000fr multi		15.00	3.50

Souvenir Sheet

1355 A271	1000fr multi	9.50	7.50
1355A A271	1000fr multi	9.50	7.50

Nos. 1354-1355A airmail.

Nos. 1268-1269, 1271, 1273-1274 Ovptd. "150e ANNIVERSAIRE / DE CHEMIN FER 'LUDWIG'"

1985, Dec. 27	Litho.	Perf. 15		
1356 A267	50fr multi		1.25	.35
1357 A267	90fr multi		1.25	.60
1358 A267	500fr multi		8.00	3.50
Nos. 1356-1358 (3)			10.50	4.45

Souvenir Sheets

1359 A267	1000fr No. 1273	9.00	6.50
1360 A267	1000fr No. 1274	9.00	6.50

Halley's Comet A281

Designs: 70fr, Suisei space probe, comets. 90fr, Vega-1 probe. 150fr, Space telescope. 200fr, Giotto probe, comet over Togo. 1000fr, Edmond Halley, Sir Isaac Newton.

1986, Mar. 27		Perf. 13		
1361 A281	70fr multi		.65	.25
1362 A281	90fr multi		.80	.30
1363 A281	150fr multi		1.40	.45
1364 A281	200fr multi		1.90	.60
Nos. 1361-1364 (4)			4.75	1.60

Souvenir Sheet

1365 A281	1000fr multi	8.25	6.50

Nos. 1362-1365 are airmail.

For overprints see Nos. 1405-1409.

Flowering and Fruit-bearing Plants A282

1986, June   *Perf. 14*
1366	A282	70fr Anacardium occidentale	.65	.25
1367	A282	90fr Ananas comosus	.85	.30
1368	A282	120fr Persea americana	1.10	.40
1369	A282	135fr Carica papaya	1.25	.45
1370	A282	290fr Mangifera indica, vert.	2.75	.90
		Nos. 1366-1370 (5)	6.60	2.30

Nos. 1368-1370 airmail.

1986 World Cup Soccer Championships, Mexico — A283

Various soccer plays.

1986, May 5   **Litho.**   *Perf. 15x14*
1371	A283	70fr multi	.60	.25
1372	A283	90fr multi	.65	.30
1373	A283	130fr multi	1.00	.40
1374	A283	300fr multi	2.25	.90
		Nos. 1371-1374 (4)	4.50	1.85

Souvenir Sheet
1375	A283	1000fr multi	8.25	6.50

Nos. 1372-1375 are airmail.
For overprints see Nos. 1394-1397.

Mushrooms — A284

1986, June 9   *Perf. 13x12½*
1376	A284	70fr Ramaria moelleriana	1.10	.25
1377	A284	90fr Hygrocybe firma	1.40	.30
1378	A284	150fr Kalchbrennera corallocephala	2.25	.45
1379	A284	200fr Cookeina tricholoma	3.00	.60
		Nos. 1376-1379 (4)	7.75	1.60

Intl. Youth Year — A285

1986, June   *Perf. 13½x14½*
1380	A285	25fr shown	.80	.25
1381	A285	90fr Youths, doves	2.10	.30

Dated 1985.

Wrestling — A286

1986, July 16   *Perf. 14x15, 15x14*
1382	A286	15fr Single-leg take-down move	.40	.25
1383	A286	20fr Completing take-down	.40	.25
1384	A286	70fr Pinning combination	.65	.25
1385	A286	90fr Riding	.95	.35
		Nos. 1382-1385 (4)	2.40	1.10

Nos. 1384-1385 horiz. No. 1385 is airmail.

Wedding of Prince Andrew and Sarah Ferguson — A287

1986, July 23   *Perf. 14*
1386	A287	10fr Sarah Ferguson	.45	.25
1387	A287	1000fr Prince Andrew	11.50	2.75

Souvenir Sheet
1388	A287	1000fr Couple	7.50	6.00

Nos. 1387-1388 are airmail.

Easter A288

Paintings (details): 25fr, 1000fr, The Resurrection, by Andrea Mantegna (1431-1506), vert. 70fr, The Calvary, by Paolo Veronese (1528-1588), vert. 90fr, The Last Supper, by Jacopo Tintoretto (1518-1594). 200fr, Christ at the Tomb, by Alonso Berruguette (1486-1561).

      Perf. 14x15, 15x14
1986, Mar. 24   **Litho.**
1389	A288	25fr multi	.45	.25
1390	A288	70fr multi	.60	.25
1391	A288	90fr multi	.75	.30
1392	A288	200fr multi	1.75	.60
		Nos. 1389-1392 (4)	3.55	1.40

Souvenir Sheet
1393	A288	1000fr multi	7.50	5.00

Nos. 1391-1393 are airmail.

Nos. 1371-1374 Ovptd. or Inscribed
"DEMI-FINALE / ARGENTINE 2 / BELGIQUE 0,"
"DEMI-FINALE / ALLEMAGNE / DE L'OUEST 2 / FRANCE 0,"
"3 eme et 4 eme PLACE / FRANCE 4 / BELGIQUE 2,"
& "FINALE / ARGENTINE 3 / ALLEMAGNE / DE L'OUEST 2"

1986, Aug. 4   **Litho.**   *Perf. 15x14*
1394	A283	70fr multi	.60	.25
1395	A283	90fr multi	.75	.30
1396	A283	130fr multi	1.00	.40
1397	A283	300fr multi	2.40	.90
		Nos. 1394-1397 (4)	4.75	1.85

Nos. 1395-1397 are airmail.

Hotels — A289

1986, Aug. 18   *Perf. 12½*
1398	A289	70fr Fazao	.60	.25
1399	A289	90fr Sarakawa	.80	.35
1400	A289	120fr Le Lac	1.00	.40
		Nos. 1398-1400 (3)	2.40	1.00

Nos. 1399-1400 are airmail.

Keran Natl. Park A290

1986, Sept. 15   **Litho.**   *Perf. 14½*
1401	A290	70fr Wild ducks	.95	.25
1402	A290	90fr Antelope	1.10	.25
1403	A290	100fr Elephant	1.25	.30
1404	A290	130fr Waterbuck	1.75	.35
		Nos. 1401-1404 (4)	5.05	1.15

Nos. 1402-1404 are airmail.

Nos. 1361-1365 Ovptd. with Halley's Comet Emblem in Silver

1986, Oct. 9   *Perf. 13*
1405	A281	70fr multi	1.60	.25
1406	A281	90fr multi	1.90	.30
1407	A281	150fr multi	3.25	.50
1408	A281	200fr multi	4.25	.65
		Nos. 1405-1408 (4)	11.00	1.70

Souvenir Sheet
1409	A281	1000fr multi	21.00	7.25

Nos. 1406-1409 are airmail.

Frescoes from Togoville Church — A291

Togoville Church — A292

1986, Dec. 22   **Litho.**   *Perf. 14½x15*
1410	A291	45fr Annunciation	.40	.25
1411	A291	120fr Nativity	1.00	.30
1412	A291	130fr Adoration of the Magi	1.10	.35
1413	A291	200fr Flight into Egypt	1.75	.55
		Nos. 1410-1413 (4)	4.25	1.45

Souvenir Sheet
1414	A292	1000fr multi	7.50	6.00

Christmas. Nos. 1411-1414 are airmail.

Phosphate Mining — A293

Natl. Liberation, 20th Anniv. — A294

1987, Jan. 13   **Litho.**   *Perf. 12½*
1415	A293	35fr shown	.30	.25
1416	A293	50fr Sugar refinery, Anie	.40	.25
1417	A293	70fr Nangbeto Dam	.50	.25
1418	A293	90fr Hotel, post office in Lome	.70	.40
1419	A293	100fr Post office, Kara	.80	.40
1420	A293	120fr Peace monument	.90	.45
1421	A293	130fr Youth vaccination campaign	1.00	.60
		Nos. 1415-1421 (7)	4.60	2.60

Souvenir Sheet
      Perf. 13
1422	A294	500fr shown	3.50	3.25

Nos. 1419-1422 are airmail.

Easter — A295

Paintings in Nadoba Church, Keran: 90fr, The Last Supper. 130fr, Christ on the Cross. 300fr, The Resurrection. 500fr, Evangelization in Tamberma, fresco, horiz.

1987, Apr. 13   **Litho.**   *Perf. 14½x15*
1423	A295	90fr multi	.65	.35
1424	A295	130fr multi	.95	.45
1425	A295	300fr multi	2.10	1.00
		Nos. 1423-1425 (3)	3.70	1.80

Souvenir Sheet
      Perf. 15x14½
1426	A295	500fr multi	4.00	3.75

Nos. 1424-1426 are airmail.

World Rugby Cup A296

1987, May 11   *Perf. 15x14½*
1427	A296	70fr Dive	.75	.25
1428	A296	130fr Running with the ball	1.50	.45
1429	A296	300fr Scrimmage	3.00	1.10
		Nos. 1427-1429 (3)	5.25	1.80

Souvenir Sheet
      Perf. 14½x15
1430	A296	1000fr Stands, goal, vert.	9.50	9.50

Nos. 1427-1429 are horiz. Nos. 1428-1430 are airmail.

Indigenous Flowers A297

1987, June 22   **Litho.**   *Perf. 13*
1431	A297	70fr Adenium obesum	.70	.25
1432	A297	90fr Amorphophallus abyssinicus, vert.	.85	.25
1433	A297	100fr Ipomoea mauritana	.95	.30

1434 A297 120fr Salacia togoica,
vert. 1.25 .35
Nos. 1431-1434 (4) 3.75 1.15

Nos. 1432-1434 are airmail.

Fish
A298

1987, Sept. 8 **Litho.** *Perf. 13*
1435 A298 70fr Chaetodon
hoefleri .75 .30
1436 A298 90fr Tetraodon
lineatus .85 .35
1437 A298 120fr Chaetodipterus
goreensis 1.10 .50
1438 A298 130fr Labeo parvus 1.25 .55
Nos. 1435-1438 (4) 3.95 1.70

1988 Summer Olympics,
Seoul — A299

Buddha and athletes

1987, Sept. 14 *Perf. 12½*
1439 A299 70fr Long jump .60 .30
1440 A299 90fr Relay .75 .35
1441 A299 200fr Cycling 1.75 .80
1442 A299 250fr Javelin 2.25 .85
Nos. 1439-1442 (4) 5.35 2.30

Souvenir Sheet
1443 A299 1000fr Tennis 7.50 5.50

Nos. 1440-1443 are airmail.

World Wildlife Fund Type of 1984
1987, Dec. 15 **Litho.** *Perf. 14*
Size: 32x24mm
1444 A263 60fr like 45fr 3.25 .50
1445 A263 75fr like 70fr 3.75 .75
1446 A263 80fr like 90fr 3.75 1.00
1447 A263 100fr like 105fr 5.00 1.50
Nos. 1444-1447 (4) 15.75 3.75

No. 1447 is airmail.

Christmas
A300

Paintings: 40fr, Springtime in Paradise,
horiz.. 45fr, Creation of Man, Sistine Chapel,
by Michelangelo, horiz.. 105fr, Presentation in
the Temple. 270fr, Original Sin. 500fr, Nativity,
horiz.

Perf. 15x14, 14x15
1987, Dec. 15 **Litho.**
1448 A300 40fr multi .40 .25
1449 A300 45fr multi .45 .25
1450 A300 105fr multi 1.10 .45
1451 A300 270fr multi 2.75 1.00
Nos. 1448-1451 (4) 4.70 1.95

Souvenir Sheet
1452 A300 500fr multi 4.50 4.00

Nos. 1450-1452 are airmail.

Eradication of
Tuberculosis
A301

1987, Dec. 28 *Perf. 12½x13, 13x12½*
1453 A301 80fr Inoculation,
horiz. .55 .30
1454 A301 90fr Family under
umbrella .65 .30
1455 A301 115fr Hospital, horiz. .80 .40
Nos. 1453-1455 (3) 2.00 1.00

Health for all by the year 2000. Nos. 1454-
1455 are airmail.

Intl. Fund for Agricultural Development
(IFAD), 10th Anniv. — A302

1988, Feb. 25 **Litho.** *Perf. 13½*
1456 A302 90fr multi .75 .30

Easter
1988 — A303

Stained-glass windows: 70fr, Jesus and the
Disciples at Emmaus. 90fr, Mary at the Foot of
the Cross. 120fr, The Crucifixion. 200fr, St.
Thomas Touching the Resurrected Christ.
500fr, The Agony of Jesus on the Mount of
Olives.

1988, June 6 **Litho.** *Perf. 14x15*
1457 A303 70fr multi .55 .25
1458 A303 90fr multi .85 .35
1459 A303 120fr multi 1.10 .50
1460 A303 200fr multi 1.90 .85
Nos. 1457-1460 (4) 4.40 1.95

Souvenir Sheet
1461 A303 500fr multi 4.50 3.50

Nos. 1459-1461 are airmail.

Paintings by Picasso (1881-
1973) — A304

Designs: 45fr, The Dance. 160fr, Portrait of
a Young Girl. No. 1464, Gueridon. No. 1465,
Mandolin and Guitar.

1988, Apr. 25 **Litho.** *Perf. 12½x13*
1462 A304 45fr multi .50 .25
1463 A304 160fr multi 1.60 .75
1464 A304 300fr multi 3.50 1.50
Nos. 1462-1464 (3) 5.60 2.50

Souvenir Sheet
1465 A304 300fr multi 3.25 2.75

Nos. 1464-1465 are airmail.

A305

1988, Aug. 30 *Perf. 14x15*
1466 A305 70fr Basketball .60 .30
1467 A305 90fr Tennis .80 .35
1468 A305 120fr Archery 1.10 .50
1469 A305 200fr Discus 1.75 .80
Nos. 1466-1469 (4) 4.25 1.95

Souvenir Sheet
1470 A305 500fr Marathon 4.00 3.00

1988 Summer Olympics, Seoul. Nos. 1468-
1470 are airmail.

A306

1988, Oct. 28 **Litho.** *Perf. 13*
1471 A306 80fr shown .65 .35
1472 A306 125fr Emblems .95 .45

WHO, 40th anniv.

Traditional
Costumes
A307

1988, July 25 **Litho.** *Perf. 13½*
1473 A307 80fr Watchi chief .95 .25
1474 A307 125fr Watchi woman 1.40 .70
1475 A307 165fr Kotokoli 1.90 .85
1476 A307 175fr Ewe 4.00 1.90
Nos. 1473-1476 (4) 8.25 3.70

Souvenir Sheet
1477 A307 500fr Moba 4.00 3.00

PHILTOGO 3,
Aug. 11-
12 — A308

Children's drawings by: 10fr, B. Gossner.
35fr, K. Ekoue-Kouvahey. 70fr, A. Abbey. 90fr,
T.D. Lawson. 120fr, A. Tazzar.

1988, Dec. 3
1478 A308 10fr multi .30 .25
1479 A308 35fr multi .40 .25
1480 A308 70fr multi .75 .30
1481 A308 90fr multi .80 .35
1482 A308 120fr multi 1.10 .50
Nos. 1478-1482 (5) 3.35 1.65

Christmas — A309

Paintings: 80fr, Adoration of the Magi, by
Brueghel. 150fr, The Virgin, Infant Jesus, Sts.
Jerome and Dominic, by Lippi. 175fr,
Madonna, Infant Jesus, St. Joseph and Infant
John the Baptist, by Barocci. 195fr, Virgin and
Child, by Bellini. 750fr, The Holy Family and a
Shepherd, by Titian.

1988, Dec. 15 *Perf. 14½x15*
1483 A309 80fr multi .70 .35
1484 A309 150fr multi 1.40 .60
1485 A309 175fr multi 1.60 .70
1486 A309 195fr multi 1.90 .80
Nos. 1483-1486 (4) 5.60 2.45

Souvenir Sheet
1487 A309 750fr multi 6.00 4.50

Nos. 1484-1487 are airmail.

Natl.
Industries
A310

1988, May 28 **Litho.** *Perf. 13*
1488 A310 125fr Cement factory .80 .40
1489 A310 165fr Bottling plant 1.40 .60
1490 A310 195fr Phosphate mine 1.40 .70
1491 A310 200fr Plastics factory 1.75 .80
1492 A310 300fr Manufacturing
plant 2.25 1.10
Nos. 1488-1492 (5) 7.60 3.60

John F.
Kennedy
A311

Designs: 125fr, Arrival in Paris, 1961. 155fr,
At Hotel de Ville, vert. 165fr, With De Gaulle at
Elysee Palace, vert. 180fr, Boarding Air Force
One with Jackie at Orly, France. 750fr, Ken-
nedy and De Gaulle, natl. colors, vert.

1988, July 30 **Litho.** *Perf. 14*
1493 A311 125fr multi .95 .40
1494 A311 155fr multi 1.25 .55
1495 A311 165fr multi 1.40 .60
1496 A311 180fr multi 1.75 .65
Nos. 1493-1496 (4) 5.35 2.20

Souvenir Sheet
Perf. 13½x13
1497 A311 750fr multi 6.00 4.75

Hairstyles
A312

1988, Nov. 20 *Perf. 13*
1498 A312 80fr shown .55 .25
1499 A312 125fr multi, diff. .85 .40
1500 A312 170fr multi, diff. 1.25 .55
1501 A312 180fr multi, diff., vert. 1.50 .60
Nos. 1498-1501 (4) 4.15 1.80

Souvenir Sheet
Perf. 14
1502 A312 500fr multi, diff. 4.00 3.25

Sarakawa
Plane Crash,
15th Anniv.
A313

Portrait and various views of the wreckage.

1989, Jan. 24 *Perf. 13½*
1503 A313 10fr multi .25 .25
1504 A313 80fr multi, vert. .70 .35
1505 A313 125fr multi 1.10 .55
Nos. 1503-1505 (3) 2.05 1.15

1990 World Cup Soccer
Championships, Italy — A314

ITALIA '90 emblem, flag of Togo, athletes
and architecture: 80fr, Cathedral of St.
Januarius, Naples. 125fr, Milan Cathedral.
165fr, Bevilacqua Palace, Verona. 175fr, Bap-
tistery of San Giovanni, Florence. 380fr,
Madama Palace, Turin. 425fr, Cathedral of
San Lorenzo, Genoa. 650fr, The Colosseum,
Rome.

1989, Jan. 10   Litho.   Perf. 13½
1506	A314	80fr multi	.65	.30
1507	A314	125fr multi	1.00	.45
1508	A314	165fr multi	1.40	.60
1509	A314	175fr multi	1.50	.65
1510	A314	380fr multi	3.00	1.50
1511	A314	425fr multi	3.50	1.50
		Nos. 1506-1511 (6)	11.05	5.00

Souvenir Sheet
1512	A314	650fr multi	5.25	5.25

Nos. 1510-1512 are airmail.

A316

Prince Emanuel of Liechtenstein
Foundation — A316a

1988 Summer Olympics, Seoul: Flags of
Liechtenstein, Togo, athletes, Pres. Eyadema.
No. 1522A, Olympic rings. No. 1522B, Ten-
nis players Miroslav Mecir, Steffi Graf, vert.

1989, May 25   Litho.   Perf. 13½
1520	A316	80fr Boxing	1.25	.30
1521	A316	125fr Long jump	1.50	.45
1522	A316	165fr Running	2.50	.55
		Nos. 1520-1522 (3)	4.75	1.30

Litho. & Embossed
1522A	A316a	1500fr gold & multi	10.00
1522B	A316a	1500fr gold & multi	10.00

Nos. 1522A-1522B are airmail and exist
imperf. and in souvenir sheets of 1 both perf.
and imperf.

Federal
Republic
of
Germany,
40th
Anniv.
A317

1989, June 1
1523	A317	90fr Palace	.90	.40
1524	A317	125fr Statesmen, vert.	1.25	.60
1525	A317	180fr Natl. flag, crest	1.50	.75
		Nos. 1523-1525 (3)	3.65	1.75

Council for Rural Development, 30th
Anniv. — A318

1989, June 19   Perf. 15x14
1526	A318	75fr Flags, well, trac-tor, field	.80	.40

See Ivory Coast No. 874.

Intl. Red
Cross,
125th
Anniv.
A319

1989, June 30   Perf. 13½
1527	A319	90fr shown	.70	.35
1528	A319	125fr Geneva Con-vention, 1864	.90	.50

French
Revolution,
Bicent.
A320

Designs: 90fr, Storming of the Bastille, vert.
125fr, Tennis Court Oath. 180fr, Abolition of
privileges. 1000fr, Declaration of Human
Rights and Citizenship, vert.

1989, July 15
1529	A320	90fr multi	.85	.40
1530	A320	125fr multi	1.10	.50
1531	A320	180fr multi	1.60	.70
		Nos. 1529-1531 (3)	3.55	1.60

Souvenir Sheet
1532	A320	1000fr multi	9.50	3.25

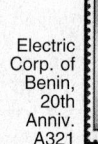

Electric
Corp. of
Benin,
20th
Anniv.
A321

1989, July 15
1533	A321	80fr multi	.65	.30
1534	A321	125fr multi	1.10	.45

A322

PHILEXFRANCE '89, French
Revolution, Bicent. — A322a

Figures and scenes from the revolution:
90fr, Jacques Necker (1732-1804), financier,
statesman, and The Three Estates. 190fr, Guy
Le Chapelier (1754-1794), politician, and abolition of feudalism (seigniorial privileges), Aug.
4, 1789. 425fr, Talleyrand-Perigord (1754-
1838), statesman, and Lafayette's Oath at the
Festival of Federation, July 14, 1790. 480fr,
Paul Barras (1755-1829), revolutionary, and
overthrowing of Robespierre during the
Revolution of 9th Thermidor, July 27, 1794.
750fr, Georges Jacques Danton (1759-1794),
revolutionary leader, and arrest of Louis XVI at
Varennes, June 21, 1791, horiz. Nos. 1537-
1539 are airmail.
No. 1539A, Assassination of Jean-Paul
Marat (1743-93). No. 1539B, Fabré
d'Eglantine (1750-94), making of the calendar
of the republic.

1989   Litho.   Perf. 13½
1535	A322	90fr multi	.70	.65
1536	A322	190fr multi	1.40	.70
1537	A322	425fr multi	3.25	1.75
1538	A322	480fr multi	3.75	1.90
		Nos. 1535-1538 (4)	9.10	5.00

Souvenir Sheet
1539	A322	750fr multi	8.00	2.00

Litho. & Embossed
1539A	A322a	1500fr gold & multi	15.00

Souvenir Sheet
1539B	A322a	1500fr gold & multi	8.00

#1539A-1539B are airmail and exist imperf.
Nos. 1535-1538 exist in souvenir sheets of
1, No. 1539A in souvenir sheets of 1, perf. and
imperf.
Issued: 90fr-750fr, 6/12; 1500fr, 7/15.

Gen.
Kpalime's
Role in Natl.
Unity and
Peace
Struggle, 20th
Anniv.
A323

1989, Aug. 21
1540	A323	90fr shown	.80	.35
1541	A323	125fr Giving speech	1.10	.55

A324

Butterflies.

1990, Apr. 30   Litho.   Perf. 13½
1542	A324	5fr Danaus chrysippus	.60	.25
1543	A324	10fr Morpho aega	.60	.25
1544	A324	15fr Papilio demodocus	.60	.25
1545	A324	90fr Papilio darda-nus	2.10	.60
		Nos. 1542-1545 (4)	3.90	1.35

Souvenir Sheet
1545A	A324	500fr Papilio zalmox-is	5.50	2.75

No. 1545A is airmail.

A325

1989, Dec. 1   Litho.   Perf. 13½
1546	A325	40fr Apollo 11 liftoff	.50	.25
1547	A325	90fr Module transpo-sition	1.00	.35
1548	A325	150fr Eagle	1.50	.55
1549	A325	250fr Splashdown	2.75	1.00
		Nos. 1546-1549 (4)	5.75	2.15

Souvenir Sheet
1550	A325	500fr Astronaut on Moon	4.00	2.75

1st Moon Landing, 20th anniv.

Lome IV Conference, Dec.
1989 — A326

1989, Dec. 15   Litho.   Perf. 13
1551	A326	100fr "Dec. 89"	.80	.40
1552	A326	100fr "15 Dec. 89"	.80	.40

A327

Boy Scouts,
Flora and
Fauna
A327a

#1559A, Kalchbrennera corallocephala.
#1559B, Spindasis mozambica.

1990, Jan. 8   Litho.   Perf. 13½
1553	A327	80fr Myrina silenus	.75	.35
1554	A327	90fr Phlebobus silvaticus	.80	.40
1555	A327	125fr Volvariella es-culenta	1.10	.55
1556	A327	165fr Hypolicaena antifaunus	1.40	.80
1557	A327	380fr Termitomyces striatus	3.25	1.50
1558	A327	425fr Axiocerces harpax	3.50	1.75
		Nos. 1553-1558 (6)	10.80	5.35

Souvenir Sheet
1559	A327	750fr Cupidopsis jo-bates	7.50	1.40

Litho. & Embossed
1559A	A327a	1500fr gold & multi	12.00

Souvenir Sheet
1559B	A327a	1500fr gold & multi	12.00

Nos. 1557-1559B are airmail. Nos. 1559A-
1559B exist imperf. No. 1559A exists in souvenir sheet of 1 both perf. and imperf.

People's Republic of Togo, 20th Anniv. — A328

1990, Jan. 8
1560 A328 45fr Government House, Kara .45 .25
1561 A328 90fr Pres. Eyadema, House .80 .40

Pan-African Postal Union, 10th Anniv. — A329

1990, Jan. 1 *Perf. 13½*
1562 A329 125fr bronze, blk & bl 1.25 .55

Ninth Convention of Lions Club International Multidistrict 403, Lome — A329a

Frame color: 90fr, Blue. 125fr, Rose. 165fr, Yellow.

1990, May 5 *Litho.* *Perf. 13½*
1562A-1562C A329a Set of 3 3.50 3.50

US-Togo Relations A330

180fr, Pres. Bush, Pres. Eyadema, horiz.

1990, July 20 *Litho.* *Perf. 13½*
1563 A330 125fr multicolored .95 .50
1564 A330 180fr multicolored 1.40 .70
Size: 90 x 75mm
1565 A330 125fr multicolored 1.00 .50
1566 A330 180fr multicolored 1.40 .70
Nos. 1563-1566 (4) 4.75 2.40

Nos. 1565-1566 printed in sheets of 1.

Reptiles A331

1990, May 22
1567 A331 1fr Varanus niloticus .25 .25
1568 A331 25fr Vipere bitis arietans .25 .25
1569 A331 60fr Naja melaneuloca .75 .40
1570 A331 90fr Python de sebae 1.10 .50
Nos. 1567-1570 (4) 2.35 1.40

Cowrie Shell Ornaments A332

1990, July, 20 *Litho.* *Perf. 13½*
1571 A332 90fr shown .90 .45
1572 A332 125fr Shell necklace 1.40 .65
1573 A332 180fr Shells on horned helmet 1.75 .90
Nos. 1571-1573 (3) 4.05 2.00

Stamp Day A333

1990, Aug. 23
1574 A333 90fr multicolored .90 .40

Traditional Homes A334

1990, Sept. 9
1575 A334 90fr shown .80 .40
1576 A334 125fr multi, diff. 1.10 .55
1577 A334 190fr multi, diff. 1.75 .85
Nos. 1575-1577 (3) 3.65 1.80

Charles de Gaulle (1890-1970), Speech at Brazzaville, 1944 — A335

1990, Aug. 30 *Litho.* *Perf. 14*
1578 A335 125fr multicolored 1.25 .65

New Lome Airport A336

1990, Sept. 17 *Perf. 13½*
1579 A336 90fr multicolored .90 .40

Children's Art — A337

1990, Sept. 28 *Litho.* *Perf. 13½*
1580 A337 90fr multicolored .90 .40

Forest Wildlife — A342

1991, June 5 *Litho.* *Perf. 13½x14*
1593 A342 90fr Chimpanzee .90 .35
1594 A342 170fr Green parrot 1.60 .75
1595 A342 185fr White parrot 1.60 .80
Nos. 1593-1595 (3) 4.10 1.90

Python Regius A343

Various snakes emerging from eggs.

1992, Aug. 24 *Litho.* *Perf. 13½*
1596 A343 90fr multicolored .70 .35
1597 A343 125fr multicolored 1.10 .55
1598 A343 175fr multicolored 1.75 .85
1599 A343 300fr multicolored 2.50 1.25
Nos. 1596-1599 (4) 6.05 3.00

Dated 1991.

Voodoo Dances A344

Various women dancing.

1992, Aug. 24
1600 A344 90fr multicolored .80 .40
1601 A344 125fr multicolored 1.25 .60
1602 A344 190fr multicolored 1.75 .85
Nos. 1600-1602 (3) 3.80 1.85

Dated 1991.

A345

1994 World Cup Soccer Championships, US — A346

Various soccer players in action: 5fr, 10fr, 25fr, 60fr, 90fr, 100fr, 200fr, 1000fr.
1500fr, Player in white & green uniform. 3000fr, Two players in air, horiz.

1994, Nov. 15 *Litho.* *Perf. 14*
1603-1610 A345 Set of 8 6.75 3.50
Souvenir Sheets
1611 A346 1500fr multicolored 7.50 3.50
1612 A346 3000fr multicolored 12.50 6.25

UPU, 120th Anniv. — A347

1994, July 29 *Perf. 13½*
1613 A347 180fr multicolored .70 .35

A miniature sheet may exist.

Stamp Day — A348

1994, Oct. 9
1614 A348 90fr pale bl & multi .60 .25
1615 A348 125fr pale yel & multi .75 .40

Intl. Olympic Committee, Cent. — A348a

Designs, each 300fr: b, Pierre de Coubertin, Olympic Hymn. c, Original members of IOC. d, Olympic flame.
900fr, Pierre de Coubertin holding document.

1994, Oct. *Litho.* *Perf. 13½*
1615A A348a Strip of 3, #b.-d. 4.25 4.25
Souvenir Sheet
1615E A348a 900fr multicolored 4.25 2.10

Nos. 1615A, 1615E exist imperf. No. 1615c is 60x51mm. No. 1615E is airmail and contains one 36x51mm stamp.

Birds A349

Designs: #1616, 5fr, Secretary bird, vert. #1617, 10fr, Paradise flycather, vert. #1618, 25fr, African spoonbill. #1619, 60fr, Cordon bleu waxbill, vert. #1620, 90fr, Orange-breasted sunbird, vert. #1621, 100fr, Yellow-billed hornbill, vert. #1621A, 180fr, Barn owl. #1622, 200fr, African hoopoe. #1622A, 300fr, Firecrowned bishop, vert. #1623, 1000fr, Redthroated bee eater, vert.

1995 *Litho.* *Perf. 14*
1616-1623 A349 Set of 10 7.75 3.75
Souvenir Sheet
1624 A349 1500fr Vulture 7.50 3.50

Issued: 180fr, 300fr, 8/7; others, 1/23.

A350

Motion Picture, Alien: a, Alien creature. b, Humans in combat with creature. c, Sigourney Weaver.

1994   Litho.   Perf. 13½
1625   A350 600fr Strip of 3, #a.-c. 7.50 3.75
   No. 1625b is 60x48mm. No. 1625 is a continuous design and exists in souvenir sheets of 1.

A351

No. 1626, each 600fr: a, Edwin "Buzz" Aldrin. b, Eagle, olive branch, Neil Armstrong. c, Michael Collins.
   No. 1627, each 600fr: a, Apollo emblem, footprint. b, Crew of Apollo 11. c, Moon rock, NASA emblem.

1994   Strips of 3, #a.-c.
1626-1627 A351 Set of 2   15.00 7.50
   First manned Moon landing, 25th anniv.
   Nos. 1626b, 1627b are each 60x47mm. Nos. 1626-1627 are continuous designs and exist in souvenir sheets of 1.

Dinosaurs — A352

   125fr, Polacanthus. 180fr, Pachycephalosaurus. 425fr, Coelophysis. 480fr, Brachiosaurus. 500fr, Dilophosaurus. 1500fr, Scutellosaurus.
   No. 1634, Velociraptor, vert.

1994
1628-1633 A352 Set of 6   13.00 6.50
Souvenir Sheet
1634   A352 1500fr multicolored   6.25 3.00
   No. 1634 is airmail.

Flowers — A353

   Designs: 15fr, Belvache de Madagascar. 90fr, Oeuillets. 125fr, Agave, horiz.

1995, May 12
1635-1637 A353 Set of 3   1.10 .55

Easter — A354

   Details or entire paintings: 90fr, The Resurrection, by A. Mantegna. 180fr, Calvary, by

Veronese. 190fr, The Last Supper, by Tintoretto, horiz.

1995, May 12
1638-1640 A354 Set of 3   2.10 1.10

Fish
A355

   10fr, Pike. 90fr, Capitaine. 180fr, Carp.

1995, May 12
1641-1643 A355 Set of 3   2.10 1.10

Miniature Sheets of 6 and 8

VJ Day, 50th Anniv. A356

   Japanese leaders: No. 1644a, Adm. Isoroko Yamamoto. b, Gen. Hideki Tojo. c, Vice Adm. Shigeru Fukudome. d, Adm. Shigetaro Shimada. e, Contre-Adm. Chuichi Nagumo. f, Gen. Shizu Ichi Tanaka.
   No. 1646, Japanese signing peace agreement.
   VE Day: No. 1645a, 200fr, German fighter planes making final attacks. b. 200fr, Allies win Battle of the Atlantic. c, 200fr, Ludendorf Bridge at Remagen is taken intact. d, 200fr, Russian rockets fired at Berlin. e, 45fr, Hostilities suspended in Italy. f, 90fr, Russians capture devastated Warsaw. g, 125fr, Russian tanks enter Berlin. h, 500fr, UN flag.
   No. 1647, German U-236 surrenders.

1995, July 20   Litho.   Perf. 14
1644   A356 200fr #a.-f.   4.75 2.50
1645   A356 #a.-h.   6.25 3.25
Souvenir Sheets
1646   A356 1500fr multicolored   6.00 3.00
1647   A356 1500fr multicolored 10.00 5.00

UN, 50th Anniv. — A357

   No. 1648: a, 25fr, Doves, earth from space. b, 90fr, Doves, UN headquarters. c, 400fr, Doves, earth from space.
   1000fr, Earth, dove.

1995, June 26
1648   A357 Strip of 3, #a.-c.   2.40 1.25
Souvenir Sheet
1649   A357 1000fr multicolored   6.25 3.00

1995 Boy Scout Jamboree, Holland — A358

   Designs: 90fr, Nat. flag. 190fr, Scout oath. 300fr, Lord Baden-Powell.
   1500fr, Scout salute.

1995, July 20
1650-1652 A358 Set of 3   2.75 1.40
Souvenir Sheet
1653   A358 1500fr multicolored   6.00 3.00

Queen Mother, 95th Birthday A359

   No. 1654: a, Formal portrait. b, Cutting cake. c, As younger woman wearing jewels, waving. d, Drawing.
   No. 1654E, Holding umbrella. No. 1654F, Formal portrait as young woman.
   No. 1655, Royal attire, pearls.
   No. 1655A, Early picture of King George VI, Queen Mother.

1995, July 20   Perf. 13½x14
1654   A359 250fr Strip of 4,
            #a.-d.   5.00 2.50
1654E A359 250fr multicolored 1.25 .65
1654F A359 250fr multicolored 1.25 .65
   g.   Block or strip of 4, #1654a,
        1654d, 1654E, 1654F   5.00 2.50
   Nos. 1654-1654F (3)   7.50 3.80
Souvenir Sheets
1655   A359 1000fr multicolored 4.00 2.00
1655A A359 1000fr multicolored 4.00 2.00
   Nos. 1654, 1654Fg were issued in sheets of 8 stamps.
   Issued: #1654, 1655, 7/20; # 1654E, 1654F, 1655A, 11/22.

FAO, 50th Anniv. — A360

   No. 1656: a, 45fr, Cattle. b, 125fr, Water buffalo. c, 200fr, Boy, man with water buffaloes.
   1000fr, Woman milking cow.

1995, Mar. 3   Litho.   Perf. 14
1656   A360 Strip of 3, #a.-c.   2.25 1.10
Souvenir Sheet
1657   A360 1000fr multicolored   4.50 2.10
   No. 1656 is a continuous design.

A361

   No. 1658, each 200fr: a, Elihu Root, peace, 1912. b, Alfred Fried, peace, 1911. c, Henri Moisson, chemistry, 1906. d, Charles Barkla, physics, 1917. e, Rudolf Eucken, literature, 1908. f, Carl von Ossietzky, peace, 1935. g, Sir Edward Appleton, physics. 1947. h, Camillo Golgi, physiology, 1906. i, Wilhelm Roentgen, physics, 1901.
   No. 1659, each 200fr: a, Manfred Eigen, chemistry, 1967. b, Donald J. Cram, chemistry, 1987. c, Paul J. Flory, chemistry, 1974. d, Johann Deisenhofer, chemistry, 1988. e, P.W. Bridgman, physics, 1946. f, Otto Stern, physics, 1943. g, Arne Tiselius, chemistry, 1948. h, J. Georg Bednorz, physics, 1987. i, Albert Claude, medicine, 1974.
   Each 1500fr: No. 1660, Albert Einstein, physics, 1921. No. 1661, Woodrow Wilson, peace, 1919.

1995, Aug. 21
   Miniature Sheets of 9, a-i
1658-1659 A361 Set of 2   25.00 12.00
Souvenir Sheets
1660-1661 A361 Set of 2   12.50 6.50
   Nobel Prize winners.

A362

1995, July 20
1662   A362 1000fr shown   4.25 2.00
Souvenir Sheet
1663   A362 1000fr Natl. flag, Rotary emblem   4.25 2.00
   Rotary Intl., 90th anniv.

Miniature Sheets

Fauna
A363

   Primates, each 200fr, vert: No. 1664a, Black-faced monkey in tree. b, Brown monkey in tree. c, Black monkey. d, Baboon.
   Wild animals, each 200fr: No. 1665a, Hyena. b, Hyrax. c, Mongoose. d, Elephant. e, Mandrill. f, Okapi. g, Hippopotamus. h, Flamingo. i, Wild boar.
   1500fr, Potto.

1995, Oct. 2   Litho.   Perf. 14
1664   A363 Sheet of 4, #a.-d.   3.25 1.60
1665   A363 Sheet of 9, #a.-i.   7.25 3.50
Souvenir Sheet
1666   A363 1500fr multicolored   6.00 3.00

FAO, 50th Anniv. A364

1995, Mar. 3   Litho.   Perf. 14
1667   A364 125fr shown   .50 .25
Souvenir Sheet
1668   A364 300fr like No. 1667 1.50 .75

Sir Rowland Hill (1795-1879) A365

1995, June 3   Perf. 13½
1669   A365 125fr multicolored   .75 .40

UN, 50th Anniv. — A366

1995, June 26
1670   A366 180fr multicolored   .90 .50

Miniature Sheets of 8

Mushrooms
A367

No. 1671: a, Cortinarius violaceus. b, Hygrocybe flavescens. c, Mycena haematopus. d, Coprinus micaceus. e, Helvella lacunosa. f, Flammulina velutipes. g, Aleuria aurantia. h, Geastrum triplex.

No. 1672: a, Russula laurocerasi. b, Phyllotopsis nidulans. c, Xeromphalina campanella. d, Psathyrella hydrophila. e, Entoloma murraii. f, Hygrophorus speciosus. g, Mycena leaiana. h, Cystoderma amianthinum.

No. 1673, each 200fr: a, Amanita muscaria. b, Amanita virosa. c, Galerina autumnalis. d, Omphalotus illudens. e, Naematoloma fasciculare. f, Paxillus involutus. g, Russula emetica. h, Scleroderma citrinum.

No. 1674, each 200fr: a, Armillaria ponderosa. b, Agaricus augustus. c, Gomphidius subroseus. d, Morchella esculenta. e, Stropharia rugoso. f, Boletus edulis. g, Clitocybe nuda. h, Lactarius deliciosus.

Each 1500fr: No. 1675, Trametes versicolor. No. 1676, Collybia iocephala.

1995, Nov. 1		Perf. 14	
1671	A367	180fr #a.-h.	9.00 4.50
1672	A367	195fr #a.-h.	10.00 4.75
1673-1674	A367	Set of 2, #a.-h.	21.00 10.50

Souvenir Sheets

1675-1676	A367	Set of 2	20.00 10.00

Miniature Sheets

History of Transportation — A368

Steam locomotives: No. 1677, each 200fr: a, SNCF Class 231 D Le Havre-Paris Express. b, Princess Royal Class Pacific, England. c, Class 52 2-10-0, German Railroad. d, Class "15A" 4-6-4+4-6-4 Beyer-Garratt, Rhodesia. e, Japanese 2-8-0. f, Class 940, 2-8-2 engine, Italy.

Various vehicles: No. 1678, each 200fr: a, Semi truck. b, Roman chariot. c, Motorcycle. d, Hummer 4-wheel drive. e, Bicycle. f, London autobus. g, Lunar rover. h, 1954 Jaguar XK 140. i, Ski-doo.

No. 1679, First land vehicle to break sound barrier.

1995, Dec. 1		Litho.	Perf. 14	
1677	A368	Sheet of 6, #a.-f.	5.50 2.75
1678	A368	Sheet of 9, #a.-i.	8.00 3.75

Souvenir Sheet

1679	A368	1500fr multicolored	6.50 3.50

No. 1679 contains one 85x28mm stamp.

World Post
Day
A369

Designs: 220fr, Selling stamps. 315fr, Sorting stamps. 335fr, Post office workers handling large sacks of mail.

1995		Litho.	Perf. 13½	
1680-1682	A369	Set of 3	4.50 2.25

Christmas
A370

Paintings: 90fr, Nativity scene, vert. 325fr, Adoration of the Magi, vert. 340fr, 500fr, Adoration of the shepherds.

1995, Sept. 13		Litho.	Perf. 13½	
1683-1685	A370	Set of 3	4.00 2.00

Souvenir Sheet

Perf. 12½

1686	A370	500fr multi, vert.	3.75 1.90

Sheets of 6

Wildlife of
Africa
A371

No. 1687: a, Gorilla. b, Uroota suraka. c, Pan troglodytes. d, Panthera pardus. e, Crocodylus niloticus. f, Leptailurus serval.

No. 1688a, Papilio tynderaeus. b, Bongo taurotragus. c, Epiphora aldiba. d, Cephalophus zebra. e, Cercopithecus cephus. f, Arctocebus calabarensis.

1996, May 10		Litho.	Perf. 14	
1687	A371	150fr #a.-f.	3.75 1.90
1688	A371	180fr #a.-f.	4.75 2.50

China '96, 9th Asian Intl. Philatelic Exhibition.

A372

Designs: 50fr, Olympic Stadium, Mexico, 1968, horiz. 90fr, Yevgeny Petrov, skeet shooter, Mexico, 1968, horiz. 220fr, Lia Manoliu, women's discus, Mexico, 1968, horiz. 325fr, Dumb-bell lifting, discontinued sport.

Medal winners from past games: No. 1693, each 200fr: a, China, Women's Volleyball, 1984. b, Wayne Wells, wrestling, 1972. c, Bob Beaman, long jump, 1968. d, Victor Kurentsov, weight lifting, 1968. e, Shirley Strong, 100m hurdles, 1984. f, Nadia Comaneci, balance beam, 1976. g, Giovanni Parisi, boxing, 1988. h, Emil Zatopek, 10,000m, 1948. i, USSR, Brazil, Germany, soccer, 1988.

1000fr, Helen Mayer, fencing, 1936.

1996, July 8		Litho.	Perf. 14	
1689-1692	A372	Set of 4	2.75 1.40
1693	A372	Sheet of 9, #a.-i.	7.25 3.50

Souvenir Sheet

1694	A372	1000fr multicolored	4.00 2.00

1996 Summer
Olympics,
Atlanta — A373

100fr, Women's gymnastics. 150fr, Women's tennis. 200fr, Javelin. 300fr, Men's field hockey. 400fr, Weight lifting. 500fr, Men's soccer.

1000fr, Synchronized swimming.

1996, Mar. 25			Perf. 12½	
1695-1700	A373	Set of 6	7.50 3.75

Souvenir Sheet

1701	A373	1000fr multicolored	5.50 2.75

Butterflies
A374

Designs: 40fr, Euphaedra eleus, vert. 90fr, Papilio dardanus, vert. 220fr, Iolaus timon. 315fr, Charaxes cynthia.

1996, June 17		Litho.	Perf. 13	
1702-1705	A374	Set of 4	2.75 1.50

Beetles — A375

Designs: 100fr, Purpuricenus kaehleri. 150fr, Carabus auronitens. 200fr, Semanotus rassicus. 300fr, Rosalia alpina. 400fr, Mylabris variabilis. 500fr, Odontolabis cuvera. 1000fr, Psalidognathus atys.

1996, May 5				
1706-1711	A375	Set of 6	7.75 3.75

Souvenir Sheet

Perf. 12½

1712	A375	1000fr multicolored	5.50 2.75

No. 1712 contains one 40x32mm stamp.

1998 World Cup
Soccer
Championships,
France — A376

French flag, various action scenes: 100fr, 150fr, 200fr, 300fr, 400fr, 500fr.

1996, Apr. 10			Perf. 12½	
1713-1718	A376	Set of 6	7.75 3.75

Souvenir Sheet

1719	A376	1000fr multicolored	5.50 2.75

World Wildlife Fund — A377

Designs: a, 325fr, Cephalophus drosalis. b, 220fr, Cephalophus maxwelli. c, 180fr, Cephalophus rufilatus. d, 370fr, Cephalophus syvicultor.

1500fr, Cephalophus dorsalis, diff.

1996, July 30			Perf. 14	
1720	A377	Block of 4, #a.-d.	7.00 3.00

Souvenir Sheet

1721	A377	1500fr multicolored	8.25 4.00

No. 1720 was issued in sheets of 16 stamps.

Endangered Species — A378

Designs, vert: 220fr, Zebra. 315fr, Cheetah. 325fr, Antelope. 335fr, Madoqua Kirki.

No. 1726, each 200fr: a, African elephants. b, Toucan (c, d, e, f.) c, Mamba (f). d, Lionesses. e, Impala. f, Nyala. g, Hippoppotamus. h, Crocodile. i, Kingfisher.

Each 1500 fr: No. 1727, Buphagus erythrorhynchus, vert. No. 1728, Leopard, vert.

1996, July 30				
1722-1725	A378	Set of 4	8.50	4.00
1726	A378	Sheet of 9, #a.-i.	9.50	4.75

Souvenir Sheets

1727-1728	A378	Set of 2	17.00	9.25

Endangered
Species
A379

75fr, Elephant. 90fr, Crocodile. 315fr, Deer.

1996, July 30		Litho.	Perf. 13	
1729-1731	A379	Set of 3	5.50 3.00

Traditional
Musical
Instruments
A380

90fr, Gongs. 220fr, Cymbals (balafon). 325fr, String instrument. 500fr, Drums.

1996, July 15				
1732-1735	A380	Set of 4	5.00 2.50

Traditional
Dances
A381

Designs: 10fr, Kamou dance, Kabyes. 90fr, Kondona dance, Kabyes. 220fr, Bassar. 315fr, Kloto. 335fr, Voudoussis.

1996, June 30				
1736-1740	A381	Set of 5	8.00 4.00

New Year 1997
(Year of the
Ox) — A382

Paintings, by Ren Bonian (1840-95): No. 1741: a, Herdboy on Buffalo. b, Return from the Pasture. c, Grazing by the Pond. 500fr, Reading Beside an Ox.

1997, Jan. 2			Perf. 14	
1741	A382	180fr Strip of 3, #a.-c.	2.50 2.50
d.		Souvenir sheet of 6, 2x #a-c	5.00 5.00

Souvenir Sheet

Perf. 13½x14

1742	A382	500fr multicolored	2.75 2.75

No. 1741 was issued in sheets of 6 stamps. No. 1742 contains one 34x46mm stamp.

Fruits
A383

100fr, Mango. 150fr, Bananas. 200fr, Peaches. 300fr, Papaya. 400fr, Lemon. 500fr, Coconuts.
1000fr, Various fruits.

1996, June 2   Litho.   Perf. 12½
1743-1748 A383 Set of 6   7.25 7.25

Souvenir Sheet
Perf. 13
1749 A383 1000fr multicolored   5.25 5.25

No. 1749 contains one 40x32mm stamp.

Souvenir Sheet

Chinese Stone Carving — A384

1996, May 10   Litho.   Perf. 12
1750 A384 370fr multicolored   1.50 1.50

China '96. No. 1750 was not available until March 1997.

Jaffar Ballogou, Boxer — A384a

1996   Litho.   Perf. 13
1750A A384a 90fr red & multi   —
1750B A384a 220fr blk & multi   —
1750C A384a 315fr red & multi   —

World Telecommunications Day.

UNESCO, 50th Anniv. A385

World Heritage Sites: No. 1751, each 235fr: a, Axum archaeological site, Ethiopia. b, Victoria Falls, Zambia. c, Archaeological site, Zimbabwe. d, Nature reserve, Niger. e, Arguin Natl. Park, Mauritania. f, Goree Island, Senegal. g, Timgad Ruins, Algeria. h, Ait Ben-Haddou, Morocco.
No. 1752, each 235fr: a, Kyoto, Japan. b, Waterfalls, Colombia. c, Necropolis, Egypt. d, Old Rama Church, Finland. e, Palladian villa, Vicenza, Italy. f, Rock paintings, China. g, Church, Ouro Preto, Brazil. h, Rhodes, Greece.
No. 1753, each 235fr: a, Exterior of Cistercian Abbey, Fontenay, France. b, Dubrovnik, Croatia. c, Interior of Cistercian Abbey, Fontenay. d, e, Quedlinberg, Germany. f, Ironbridge Gorge, England. g, Grand Canyon, U.S. h, Village, Ironbridge Gorge, England.
Each 1000fr: No. 1754, Kyoto, Japan, horiz. No. 1755, Mt. Huangshan, China, horiz. No. 1756, Village, Ironbridge, England, horiz.

1997, Mar. 24   Litho.   Perf. 14
Sheets of 8, a-h, + Label
1751-1753 A385 Set of 3   25.00 25.00

Souvenir Sheets
1754-1756 A385 Set of 3   12.50 12.50

Cats A386

150fr, American shorthair. 200fr, Siamese, vert. 300fr, Java. 400fr, "Ocicat," vert. 500fr, Scottish fold. No. 1762, 1000fr, Persian, vert. No. 1763, Colorpoint shorthair, vert.

1997   Litho.   Perf. 12½
1757-1762 A386 Set of 6   12.00 12.00

Souvenir Sheet
1763 A386 1000fr multicolored   4.50 4.50

No. 1763 contains one 32x40mm stamp.

Military Uniforms — A387

Designs: 150fr, Officer of cuirassiers. 200fr, Norman regiment officer. 300fr, Volunteer battalion foot soldier. 400fr, Berlin Campaign Militiaman. 500fr, Foot soldier. No. 1769, 1000fr, Musketeer.
No. 1770, Belling Regiment Hussar.

1997   Perf. 13x12½
1764-1769 A387 Set of 6   12.00 12.00

Souvenir Sheet
1770 A387 1000fr multicolored   4.50 4.50

No. 1770 contains one 40x32mm stamp.

Return of Hong Kong to China — A388

Deng Xiaoping (1904-97) — A388a

Views of city: 220fr, Chinese flag as inscription, skyscraper. 315fr, Chinese flag as inscription, night scene. 325fr, Circular stair railing, skyscraper at night. 340fr, Chinese flag, view of city through inscription. 370fr, Deng Xiaoping (1904-97), fireworks over city.
#1775A: a, shown. b, Looking left.

1997, June 2   Perf. 14
1771-1775 A388 Set of 5   7.50 7.50
Sheet of 2
Perf. 13½
1775A A388a 500fr #a.-b.   4.50 4.50

Nos. 1771-1773 are 28x44mm and were each issued in sheets of 4. Nos. 1774-1775 were each issued in sheets of 3.

Queen Elizabeth II and Prince Philip, 50th Wedding Anniv. A389

No. 1776: a, Queen. b, Royal arms. c, Queen in yellow hat, Prince in military uniform. d, Queen in white hat, Prince. e, Windsor Castle. f, Prince.
1000fr, Portrait of Queen, Prince.

1997, June 25
1776 A389 315fr Sheet of 6, #a.-f.   7.50 7.50

Souvenir Sheet
1777 A389 1000fr multicolored   4.50 4.50

Locomotives — A390

150fr, Light locomotive, Adams Bridges. 200fr, Norris Type, England 1866. 300fr, Jones and Ports locomotive with long boiler, 1848. 400fr, Cargo and passenger locomotive, Ansaldo, 1850. 500fr, Birkenhead, Italy, 1863. #1783, 1000fr, Quarter locomotive, New York, 1890.
#1783A, Six-wheeled locomotive, Robert Stephenson, 1830, vert.

1996, Dec. 5   Litho.   Perf. 12½x12
1778-1783 A390 Set of 6   12.00 12.00

Souvenir Sheet
Perf. 12½
1783A A390 1000fr multi   4.50 4.50

Birds — A391

150fr, Poephila guttata. 200fr, Lonchura malacca. 300fr, Acanthis cannabina. 400fr, Fringilla coelebs. 500fr, Emblema guttata. #1789, 1000fr, Passerina amoena.
#1789A, Chloebia gouldiae.

1996, Nov. 27   Perf. 13
1784-1789 A391 Set of 6   11.00 11.00

Souvenir Sheet
1789A A391 1000fr multi   4.50 4.50

Nos. 1784-1789 are dated 1996.
No. 1789A contains one 32x40mm stamp.

Turtles A392

Designs: 150fr, Asterochelys yniphora. 200fr, Staurotypus triporcatus. 300fr, Puxidea mouhoti. 400fr, Geomyda spengleri. 500fr, Cuora galbinifrons. #1795, 1000fr, Malaclemys terrapin.
#1795A, Asterochelys radiata.

1996, Nov. 30
1790-1795 A392 Set of 6   11.00 11.00

Souvenir Sheet
1795A A392 1000fr multi   4.50 4.50

Nos. 1790-1795 are dated 1996.
No. 1795A contains one 40x32mm stamp.

Natl. Liberation, 30th Anniv. — A393

1997   Litho.   Perf. 13½
1796 A393 90fr yellow & multi   .30 .30
1797 A393 220fr green & multi   .75 .75

Diana, Princess of Wales (1961-97) A394

Nos. 1798a-1798i: Various portraits of Princess Diana in designer gowns, each 180fr.
Views up close, each 180fr: No. 1799, like #1798a. No. 1799A, Like #1798b. No. 1800, like #1798c. No. 1801, like #1798d. No. 1802, like #1798e. No. 1802A, Like #1798f. No. 1802B, Like #1798g. No. 1803, like #1798h. No. 1804, like #1798i.

1997
1798 A394 Sheet of 9, #a.-i.   7.50 7.50

Souvenir Sheets
1799-1804 A394 Set of 9   50.00 50.00

Diana, Princess of Wales (1961-97) — A395

Nos. 1805-1807, Various pictures of Diana during her lifetime as Princess of Wales.
Each 1000fr: Pictures of Diana with (in margin): No. 1808, French Pres. Giscard d'Estaing. No. 1809, Mother Teresa. No. 1810, US First Lady Hillary Clinton.

1998, Jan. 2   Perf. 14
Sheets of 6
1805 A395 240fr #a.-f.   5.00 5.00
1806 A395 315fr #a.-f.   6.50 6.50
1807 A395 340fr #a.-f.   7.25 7.25

Souvenir Sheets
1808-1810 A395 Set of 3   10.50 10.50

Souvenir Sheet

Marilyn Monroe (1926-62) — A396

1997   Litho.   Perf. 13½
1811 A396 2000fr multicolored   8.50 8.50

New Year 1998
(Year of the
Tiger) — A397

Various paintings of tigers, by Liu Jiyou
(1918-83): No. 1812: a, 180fr. b, 200fr. No.
1813: a, 90fr. b, 100fr, c, 180fr. d, 200fr.

1998, Jan. 5   Litho.   Perf. 14
1812 A397 Sheet of 2, #a.-b.   1.25 1.25
1813 A397 Sheet of 4, #a.-d.   2.00 2.00
No. 1812 contains two 26x65mm stamps.

Hiroshige (1797-1858),
Painter — A398

Paintings: No. 1814: a, Sixty-Nine Stations
of the Kisokaido Road: Mochizuki. b, Eight
Views of Lake Biwa Evening Snow at Mt. Hira.
c, Kinkizan Temple on Enoshima Island,
Sagami Provence. d, Cherry Blossoms. e,
Evening Snow at Asakusa. f, Miyanokoshi.
No. 1815: a, Two Terrapins (Fan print). b,
Swimming Carp. c, Takanawa by Moonlight. d,
Night Rain at Karasaki. e, Chiryu: The Sum-
mer Horse Fair. f, Shower over the
Nihonbashi.
No. 1816, vert: a, Takata Riding Grounds. b,
Sugatami & Omokage Bridges & Jariba at
Takata. c, Dam on the Otonashi River at Oji. d,
Basho's Hermitage and Camellia Hill. e, Fudo
Falls, Oji. f, Takinogawa Oji.
Each 1000fr: No. 1817, Bird in a Tree. No.
1818, Title Page for Hiroshige's One Hundred
Views of Edo, by Baisotei. No. 1819, Memorial
Portrait of Hiroshige, by Utagawa. No. 1820,
Street Stalls and Tradesmen in Jouricho. No.
1821, Cherry Blossom, Morning Glory, Cranes
and Rabbits. No. 1822, Three Wild Geese Fly-
ing Across the Moon. No. 1823, Suwa Bluff,
Nippori. Nos. 1817-1823 are vert.

Perf. 14x13½, 13½x14
1998, Mar. 2   Litho.
Sheets of 6
1814 A398 220fr #a.-f.   5.50 5.50
1815 A398 315fr #a.-f.   7.50 7.50
1816 A398 370fr #a.-f.   8.50 8.50

Souvenir Sheets
Perf. 13½x14
1817-1823 A398 Set of 7   30.00 30.00
Nos. 1817-1823 each contain one
26x72mm stamp.

Fauna, Flora, Minerals — A399

Dolphins and whales: No. 1824: a, Souffleur
nesarnack. b, Lagenorhynque. c, Sotalie du
cameroun. d, Petit rorqual. e, Rorqual commun. f, Faux orque.
Insects and spiders: No. 1825: a, Lasius
niger. b, Sceliphron spirifex. c, Peucetia. d,
Mygale. e, Theraphoside. f, Dynaste hercule.
Precious stones, minerals: No. 1826: a,
Ruby. b, Diamond in kimberlite. c, Cut diamond. d, Rock salt. e, Tiger's eye. f, Uraninite.
Moths and butterflies: No. 1827: a, Pirate. b,
Euchromie des liserons. c, Asterope. d, Psalis
de kiriakoff. e, Sphinx de fabricius. f, Pensee
bleue.

Mushrooms: No. 1828: a, Lepiote. b,
Hypholome. c, Lactaire. d, Russule fetide. e,
Russule doree. f, Strophaire.
Each 2000fr: No. 1829, Tricholome a odeur
de savon. No. 1830, Potto.

1998(?)   Litho.   Perf. 13½
Sheets of 6
1824 A399 180fr #a.-f.   4.00 4.00
1825 A399 250fr #a.-f.   5.75 5.75
1826 A399 300fr #a.-f.   6.75 6.75
1827 A399 400fr #a.-f.   9.00 9.00
1828 A399 450fr #a.-f.   10.25 10.25

Souvenir Sheets
1829-1830 A399 Set of 2   15.50 15.50
Intl. Scouting, 90th Anniv. (#1825, 1827-
1830). Nos. 1829-1830 each contain one
41x60mm stamp.

Jerry Garcia (1942-95) — A400

Various portraits.

1998   Litho.   Perf. 13½
1831 A400 250fr Sheet of 9,
#a.-i.   7.75 7.75

Souvenir Sheet
1832 A400 2000fr multicolored   7.00 7.00
No. 1832 contains one 42x51mm stamp.

Dinosaurs — A401

Various unidentified dinosaurs.

1998
1833 A401 290fr Sheet of 9,
#a.-i.   10.00 10.00

Souvenir Sheet
1834 A401 2000fr multicolored   7.50 7.50
No. 1834 contains one 42x51mm stamp.

1998 Winter Olympic Games,
Nagano — A402

No. 1835: a, Hockey. b, Speed skating. c,
Pairs figure skating. d, Luge. e, Curling. f,
Bobsledding.
No. 1836: a, Downhill skiing. b, Freestyle ski
jumping (blue skis). c, Ski jumping. d, Downhill
skiier in tuck. e, Snow boarding. f, Freestyle
skiing (red skis).

1998
Sheets of 6
1835 A402 250fr #a.-f.   5.75 5.75
1836 A402 300fr #a.-f.   6.75 6.75
Nos. 1835-1836 each have 3 labels.

1998 World Cup Soccer
Championships, France — A403

Player, country, vert: No. 1837, Kluivert,
Netherlands. No. 1838, Asprilla, Colombia.
No. 1839, Bergkamp, Netherlands. No. 1840,
Gascoigne, England. No. 1841, Ravanelli,
Italy. No. 1842, Sheringham, England.
No. 1843: a, Paul Gascoigne, England, diff.
b, Ryan Giggs, Wales. c, Roy Keane, Ireland.
d, Stuart Pearce, England. e, Tony Adams,
England. f, Teddy Sheringham, England, diff.
g, Paul Ince, England. h, Steve McManaman,
England.
No. 1844: a, Rossi, Italy. b, Lineker,
England. c, Lato, Poland. d, Futre, Poland. e,
Klinsmann, Germany. f, Hurst, England. g,
Kempes, Argentina. h, McCoist, Scotland.
World Cup Champions, year, vert: — #1845:
a, Argentina, 1978. b, Italy, 1982. c, England,
1966. d, Uruguay, 1930. e, Germany, 1954. f,
Argentina, 1986. g, Brazil, 1994.
Each 1500fr: No. 1846, Ronaldo, Brazil,
vert. No. 1847, Gary Lineker, England, vert.
No. 1848, Shearer, England, vert.

Perf. 13½x14, 14x13½
1998, July 10   Litho.
1837-1842 A403 370fr Set of 6 10.00 10.00
Sheets of 8 + Label
1843 A403 220fr #a.-h.   6.50 7.75
1844 A403 315fr #a.-h.   11.00 11.00
Sheet of 7 + 2 Labels
1845 A403 325fr #a.-g.   10.00 10.00
Souvenir Sheets
1846-1848 A403 Set of 3   18.00 18.00

Bella Bellow (d. 1973),
Singer — A403a

1998-2002   Litho.   Perf. 13½
1848A A403a 5fr yel orange
1848B A403a 10fr olive green
1848C A403a 25fr emerald
1848D A403a 40fr violet
1848E A403a 50fr greenish
black
  s. gray green, dated "2002"   —
1848F A403a 75fr yel orange
1848G A403a 100fr orange
1848H A403a 125fr blue
1848I A403a 200fr brt purple
1848J A403a 240fr red violet
1848K A403a 280fr green
1848L A403a 300fr Prus blue
1848M A403a 320fr red orange
1848N A403a 340fr car lake
1848O A403a 390fr car rose

1848P A403a 450fr brt blue
('02)   —
1848R A403a 500fr gray olive
('02)   —
1848T A403a 1000frgray   —
No. 1848E is dated "1998." At least three
additional values were issued in this set. The
editors would like to examine any examples.

Star Wars Movies — A404

Return of the Jedi — #1849: a, Princess
Leia. b, Darth Vader. c, Han Solo. d, R2-D2,
C-3PO. e, Emperor Palpatine. f, Chewbacca.
g, Leia on speeder. h, Luke Skywalker. i,
Storm trooper on speeder.
Empire Strikes Back — #1850: a, Lando
Calrissian. b, Yoda. c, Chewbacca. d, C-3PO,
R2-D2. e, Luke Skywalker. f, Darth Vader. g,
Battle on snow planet. h, Leia. i, Rider on
snow planet.
2000fr, Han Solo, Luke Skywalker, Princess
Leia, R2-D2.

1997   Litho.   Perf. 13½
Sheets of 9
1849 A404 190fr #a.-i.   6.50 6.50
1850 A404 350fr #a.-i.   11.50 11.50
Souvenir Sheet
1851 A404 2000fr multicolored   8.00 8.00
No. 1851 contains one 42x60mm.

Jacqueline Kennedy Onassis (1929-
94) — A405

No. 1852: Various portraits.
No. 1853: Various portraits of John F. Kennedy (1917-63).

1997
Sheets of 9
1852 A405 250fr #a.-i.   10.00 10.00
1853 A405 400fr #a.-i.   12.00 12.00

Diana, Princess of Wales (1961-97) — A406

No. 1854: Various portraits.
2000fr, Diana in black (Mother Teresa in sheet margin).

1997
Sheet of 8 + Label
1854 A406 500fr #a.-h.   16.00 16.00
Souvenir Sheet
1854I A406 2000fr multicolored   10.00 10.00

Marilyn Monroe (1926-62) — A407

Various portraits, each 300fr.

1997   **Litho.**   **Perf. 13½**
1855 A407 Sheet of 9, #a.-i.   11.00 11.00

Minerals
A408

Designs: 100fr, Calcite. 150fr, Turquoise, vert. 200fr, Pyrite, vert. 300fr, Tourmaline, vert. 400fr, Pyrargirite, vert. 500fr, Malachite. 1000fr, Beryl, vert.

1999   **Litho.**   **Perf. 12¾**
1856-1861 A408 Set of 6   6.00 6.00
Souvenir Sheet
Perf. 13
1861A A408 1000fr multicolored 4.00 4.00
No. 1861A contains one 32x40mm stamp.

Butterflies — A408a

Designs: 100fr, Quercusia quercus. 150fr, Pseudacraea boisduvali. 200fr, Argynnis paphia. 300fr, Erebia pandrose. 400fr, Euphydryas maturna. 500fr, Pyronia tithonus. 1000fr, Charaxes pollux.

1999, June 7   Litho.   Perf. 12¾
1861B-1861G A408a Set of 6   5.75 5.75
Souvenir Sheet
Perf. 13
1861H A408a 1000fr multi   3.75 3.75
No. 1861H contains one 40x32mm stamp.

Flowers — A409

Designs: No. 1862, Caralluma burchardii. No. 1863, Dimorphotheca barberiae. No. 1864, Hoya carnosa. No. 1865, Amaryllis belladonna. No. 1866, Watsonia beatricis. No. 1867, Anthurium schezerianum. No. 1868, Thumbergia alata. No. 1869, Arctotis breviscapa. No. 1870, Glauciun flavum. No. 1871, Impatiens petersiana. No. 1872, Chrysanthemum segetum. No. 1873, Zantedeschia aethiopica, horiz.

1999   **Perf. 12¼**
1862 A409 100fr brown   .30   .30
1863 A409 100fr violet   .30   .30
1864 A409 100fr pale red   .30   .30
1865 A409 150fr dark grn bl   .55   .55
1866 A409 150fr red brown   .55   .55
1867 A409 150fr violet blue   .55   .55
1868 A409 200fr orange   .75   .75
1869 A409 200fr bright grn bl .75   .75
1870 A409 300fr olive   1.10 1.10
1871 A409 300fr blue   1.10 1.10
1872 A409 500fr brown   1.75 1.75
1873 A409 1000fr bright pink   3.75 3.75
      Nos. 1862-1873 (12)   11.75 11.75

1998 World Cup Soccer Championship, France — A410

Predominant colors of player's shirts. No. 1874: a, Yellow. b, White. c, Blue. d, Red.
No. 1875: a, White. b, Blue. c, Red. d, Green.
No. 1876: a, White, with black shorts. b, Yellow, with blue shorts. c, Yellow, with yellow shorts. d, White, with white shorts.
No. 1877: a, Red. b, Green. c, White. d, Red & white striped.
No. 1878: a, Blue. b, Yellow. c, Red. d, White.
No. 1879: a, Orange. b, White. c, Red. d, Multicolored diamonds.
No. 1880: a, White, with black shorts. b, White, with blue and red chest stripes. c, White, with green trim. d, White, with red and blue arm stripes.
No. 1881: a, Blue & white stripes. b, Red & white checks. c, Yellow & green. d, Blue.
2000fr, Player, map of France.

1998   **Litho.**   **Perf. 13¼**
Sheets of 4
1874 A410 180fr #a.-d.   3.25 3.25
1875 A410 200fr #a.-d.   3.50 3.50
1876 A410 250fr #a.-d.   4.25 4.25
1877 A410 290fr #a.-d.   5.00 5.00
1878 A410 300fr #a.-d.   5.25 5.25
1879 A410 350fr #a.-d.   6.25 6.25
1880 A410 400fr #a.-d.   6.75 6.75
1881 A410 425fr #a.-d.   7.25 7.25
      Nos. 1874-1881 (8)   41.50 41.50
Souvenir Sheet
1882 A410 2000fr multicolored 7.50 7.50

Birds
1882A

Designs: 100fr, Luscinia svecica. 150fr, Oriolus oriolus. 200fr, Carduelis carduelis. 300fr, Parus caeruleus. 400fr, Fringilla coelebs. 500fr, Parus montanus.
1000fr, Regulus ignicapillus.

1999   **Litho.**   **Perf. 12¾**
1882A-1882F A410a Set of 6   6.00 6.00
Souvenir Sheet
Perf. 13x13¼
1882G A410a 1000fr multi   4.00 4.00
No. 1882G contains one 40x32mm stamp.

Antique Automobiles — A410b

Designs: 100fr, 1913 Peugeot Bebe. 150fr, 1950 Rolls-Royce. 200fr, 1921 Stutz Bearcat. 300fr, 1923 Ford Model T. 400fr, 1907 Packard. 500fr, 1950 Citroen II Legere sedan.
1000fr, 1929 Ford Model A Tudor sedan.

1999   **Perf. 12¾**
1882H-1882M A410b Set of 6   6.00 6.00
Souvenir Sheet
Perf. 13
1882N A410b 1000fr multi   4.00 4.00
No. 1882N contains one 40x32mm stamp.

Mushrooms — A410c

Designs: 100fr, Ganoderma lucidum. 150fr, Cantharellus lutescens. 200fr, Lactarius deliciosus. 300fr, Amanita caesarea. 400fr, Cortinarius violaceus. 500fr, Amanita rubescens. 1000fr, Clitopilus prunulus.

1999, Feb. 23   Litho.   Perf. 12¾
1882O-1882T A410c Set of 6   —   —
Souvenir Sheet
Perf. 13¼
1882U A410c 1000fr multi   —   —

Cats — A411

No. 1883: a, 100fr, Colorpoint. b, 150fr, British shorthair.
No. 1884: a, 200fr, Ocicat. b, 300fr, Ragdoll.
No. 1885: a, 400fr, Balinese. b, 500fr, California Spangled.
1000fr, Somali.

1999   **Litho.**   **Perf. 12½**
1883 A411 Pair, #a.-b.   .85   .85
1884 A411 Pair, #a.-b.   1.90 1.90
1885 A411 Pair, #a.-b.   3.50 3.50
      Nos. 1883-1885 (3)   6.25 6.25
Souvenir Sheet
1886 A411 1000fr multicolored 4.00 4.00

Millennium
A412

No. 1886A, Invention of Paper by Chinese (with millennium emblem).
No. 1887 — Chinese Science & Technology: a, Lacquerware. b, Counting rods. c, Sericulture. d, Acupuncture. e, "Tuned chime bell." f, Piston bellows. g, Compass. h, Manufacture of steel. i. Crossbow. j, Spinning wheel. k, Water conservancy. l, Pulse taking. m, Multi-tube seed drill. n, Rotary winnowing fan. o, Like #1886A (no millennium emblem). p, Silk loom (60x40mm). q, Wheelbarrow.
No. 1888 — Highlights of the 11th Century: a, Chinese invent gunpowder. b, Islamic bronze griffin. c, Battle of Clontarf. d, William becomes Duke of Normandy. e, Norman knight. f, Spinning wheels in use in China. g, Yaroslav becomes Grand Prince of Kiev. h, Polyphonic singing introduced. i, Macbeth becomes King of Scotland. j, Edward the Confessor becomes King of England. k, Astrolabe. l, Harp introduced in Europe. m, Trier Cathedral. n, Mandingo Empire founded in Africa. o, Toltecs invade Yucatan. p, Vikings reach North Americam (60x40mm). q, Movable type used in China.
No. 1889 — Western Paintings of the 20th century by: a, Henri Matisse. b, Pablo Picasso. c, Marc Chagall. d, Wassily Kandinsky. e, Fernand Léger. f, Piet Mondrian. g, George Bellows. h, Georgia O'Keeffe. i, Salvador Dali. j, Francis Bacon. k, Edward Hopper. l, Andy Warhol. m, Helen Frankenthaler. n, Richard Anuszkiewicz. o, Audrey Flack. p, Jackson Pollack, Lee Krasner (60x40mm). q, Jean-Michel Basquiat.

1999   **Litho.**   **Perf. 13¼x13**
1886A A412 120fr multi   .70   .70
Sheets of 17
Perf. 12½
1887 A412 120fr #a.-q. + label 9.00 9.00
1888 A412 130fr #a.-q. + label 9.00 9.00
1889 A412 140fr #a.-q. + label 11.00 11.00

Inscriptions on Nos. 1887b, 1887e, 1888i, and perhaps others, are incorrect or misspelled.
Issued: 130fr, 7/20.

US Civil War Photographs A413

Various Civil War photographs making up a photomosaic of Abraham Lincoln, each 300fr.

1999, July 20   Litho.   Perf. 13½
1890 A413 Sheet of 8, #a.-h.   10.00 10.00
See Nos. 1939-1940.

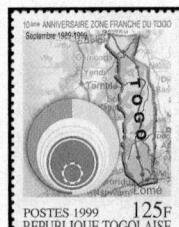

Free Trade Zone, 10th Anniv. — A414

Symbol and: 125fr, Map. 240fr, Clouds. 340fr, Wall.

1999   Litho.   Perf. 12¾
1891 A414 125fr multi   .45 .45
1892 A414 240fr multi   .85 .85
1893 A414 340fr multi   1.25 1.25
    Nos. 1891-1893 (3)   2.55 2.55

Rural Development Council, 40th Anniv. — A414a

1999   Litho.   Perf. 13x13¼
1893A A414a 100fr green & mul-ti   —
1893B A414a 125fr blue & multi   —
1893C A414a 240fr red & multi
1893D A414a 380fr vio & multi
1893E A414a 390fr blk & multi

Other stamps for this subject may exist. The editors would like to examine any examples. Numbers may change.

Goldfish A415

Various depictions of Carassius auratus: 100fr, 150fr, 200fr, 300fr, 400fr, 500fr.

1999
1894-1899 A415 Set of 6   6.00 6.00
Souvenir Sheet
Perf. 13
1899A A415 1000fr multi   4.00 4.00
No. 1899A contains one 40x31mm stamp.

SOS Children's Villages, 50th Anniv. — A416

1999   Litho.   Perf. 13¼x13
1900 A416 125fr multi ('01)   .70 .70
1901 A416 240fr multi
1902 A416 340fr multi

Additional stamps may have been issued in this set. The editors would like to examine any examples.

Sailing Vessels — A417

Designs: 100fr, Phoenician boat. 150fr, Roman cargo boat. 200fr, New Guinea fishing boat. 300fr, Caravel, vert. 400fr, 16th cent. English ship, vert. 500fr, 17th cent. English ship, vert.
1000fr, Steamship with sails.

1999   Litho.   Perf. 12½
1905-1910 A417 Set of 6   6.00 6.00
Souvenir Sheet
Perf. 12¼x12
1911 A417 1000fr multi   4.00 4.00
No. 1911 contains one 42x30mm stamp.

Dogs — A417a

Designs: 100fr, St. Bernard. 150fr, Teckel. 200fr, German shepherd. 300fr, Italian hound. 400fr, Yorkshire terrier. 500fr, Schnauzer.

1999   Litho.   Perf. 12¾
1911A-1911F A417a Set of 6   6.00 6.00
Souvenir Sheet
Perf. 12½
1911G A417a 1000fr Afghan hound   4.00 4.00
No. 1911G contains one 40x31mm stamp.

Trains A417b

Designs: 100fr, Baldwin 0-4-0. 150fr, Baldwin 2-6-2. 200fr, Baldwin gasoline locomotive. 300fr, H.K. Porter 0-4-0. 400fr, H.K. Porter 2-6-2. 500fr, Vulcan 0-4-0.

1999   Litho.   Perf. 12¾
1911H-1911M A417b Set of 6   6.00 6.00
Souvenir Sheet
1911N A417b 1000fr Jordanian locomotive   4.00 4.00
No. 1911N contains one 40x31mm stamp.

Orchids A417c

Designs: 100fr, Gramangis ellisii. 150fr, Habenaria columbae. 200fr, Epidendrum atroporpureum. 300fr, Odontoglossum majale. 400fr, Oncidium splendidum. 500fr, Zygopetalum mackai.

1000fr, Paphiopedilum pairieanum.

1999, Nov. 8   Litho.   Perf. 12x12¼
1911O-1911T A417c Set of 6   7.25 7.25
Souvenir Sheet
Perf. 12½
1911U A417c 1000fr multi   4.00 4.00
No. 1911U contains one 31x39mm stamp.

New Year 2000 (Year of the Dragon) — A418

Various views of dragon: 100fr, 150fr, 200fr, 300fr, 400fr, 500fr.
1000fr, Head of dragon, horiz.

2000   Perf. 12¾x12
1912-1917 A418 Set of 6   6.25 6.25
Souvenir Sheet
Perf. 13¼
1918 A418 1000fr multi   3.50 3.50
No. 1918 contains one 40x32mm stamp.

Wild Cats A419

Designs: 100fr, Panthera tigris. 150fr, Acinonyx jubatus. 200fr, Felis concolor. 300fr, Panthera leo, female. 400fr, Felis pardalis. 500fr, Panthera leo, male.
1000fr, Panthera tigris, diff.

2000   Perf. 13
1919-1924 A419 Set of 6   6.25 6.25
Souvenir Sheet
1925 A419 1000fr multi   3.50 3.50
No. 1925 contains one 40x32mm stamp.

Flowers — A420

No. 1926, 290fr: a, Cyrtanthus contractus. b, Sandersonia aurantíaca. c, Anomateca grandiflora. d, Helichrysum ecklonis. e, Striga elegans. f, Nymphaea odorata.
No. 1927, 290fr: a, Leomotis leonii. b, Strelitzia reginae. c, Freesia refracta. d, Garzania nivea. e, Dimophotheca sinuata. f, Pelargonium domesticum.
No. 1928, 290fr: a, Gloriosa rothchiliana. b, Clematis vitalba. c, Rochea falcato. d, Plumbago capensis. e, Thunbergia alata. f, Lampranthus coccineus.
No. 1929, 1500fr, Epiphyllum hybrid. No. 1930, 1500fr, Agapanthus africanus.
Illustration reduced.

Wildlife A421

Designs: 200fr, Thompson's gazelle. 300fr, Felis margarita. 400fr, Blesbok. 500fr, Kob.
No. 1935, 290fr, vert.: a, Hoopoe. b, Harpactira spider. c, Marabou. d, Bee-eater. e, Oryx. f, Okapi. g, Wart hog. h, Baboon.
No. 1936, 290fr, vert.: a, Hornbill. b, Pygmy kingfisher. c, Vulture. d, Bateleur eagle. e, Kudu. f, Hyena. g, Gorilla. h, Lizard.
No. 1937, 1500fr, Eland, vert. No. 1938, 1500fr, Mongoose, vert.

2000, July 28   Litho.   Perf. 14
Sheets of 6, #a-f
1926-1928 A420 Set of 3   24.00 24.00
Souvenir Sheets
1929-1930 A420 Set of 2   13.50 13.50

2000, July 28
1931-1934 A421 Set of 4   6.75 6.75
Sheets of 8, #a-h
1935-1936 A421 Set of 2   22.50 22.50
Souvenir Sheets
1937-1938 A421 Set of 2   13.50 13.50

Mushrooms A421a

Designs: 100fr, Hebeloma crustuliniforme. 150fr, Polyporellus squamosus, horiz. 200fr, Morchella deliciosa. 300fr, Disciotis venosa, horiz. 400fr, Cantharellus tubiformis. 500fr, Otidea onotica, horiz.
1000fr, Ixocomus granulatus, horiz.

2000, July 30   Litho.   Perf. 12¾
1938A-1938F A421a Set of 6   6.25 6.25
Souvenir Sheet
Perf. 13
1938G A421a 1000fr multi   3.50 3.50
No. 1938G contains one 39x31mm stamp.

Civil War Photographs Type of 1999

No. 1939, 290fr: Various photographs with a science theme making up a photomosaic of Albert Einstein.
No. 1940, 290fr: Various photographs with an Oriental theme making up a photomosaic of Mao Zedong.

2000, Sept. 5   Perf. 13¾
Sheets of 8, #a-h
1939-1940 A413 Set of 2   24.00 24.00

Queen Mother, 100th Birthday — A422

No. 1941: a, With Princesses Elizabeth and Margaret, 1931. b, With daughter, 1940. c, Black and white photo. d, In 1990.
1500fr, With Princess Margaret, 1939.

2000, Sept. 5   **Perf. 14**
1941 A422 650fr Sheet of 4,
    #a-d, + label   12.50 12.50

Souvenir Sheet
Perf. 13¾
1942 A422 1500fr With Princess Margaret, 1939   7.25 7.25

No. 1942 contains one 38x51mm stamp.

Popes — A423

No. 1943, 400fr: a, Anastasius I, 399-401. b, Boniface I, 418-22. c, Gaius, 283-96. d, Hilarius, 461-68. e, Hyginus, 136-40. f, Innocent I, 402-17.
No. 1944, 400fr: a, Martin I, 649-55. b, Nicholas I, 858-67. c, Paschal I, 817-24. d, Paul I, 757-67. e, Pelagius, 556-61. f, Pelagius II, 579-90.
No. 1945, 400fr: a, Sergius, 687-701. b, Sergius II, 844-47. c, Severinus, 640. d, Sisinnius, 708. e, Stephen II, 752-57. f, Stephen IV, 816-17.
No. 1946, 1500fr, Pontian, 230-35. No. 1947, 1500fr, Pelagius II, diff. No. 1948, 1500fr, Stephen V, 885-91.
Illustration reduced.

2000, Sept. 5   **Perf. 12x12¼**
Sheets of 6, #a-f
1943-1945 A423 Set of 3   32.50 32.50
Souvenir Sheets
1946-1948 A423 Set of 3   20.00 20.00

British Monarchs — A424

No. 1949, 400fr: a, Charles II, 1660-85. b, Anne, 1702-14. c, George I, 1714-27. d, George IV, 1820-30. e, James II, 1685-88. f, George II, 1727-60.
No. 1950, 400fr: a, Elizabeth II, 1952-present. b, Edward VIII, 1936. c, George VI, 1936-52. d, George V, 1910-36. e, Edward VII, 1901-10. f, William IV, 1830-37.
No. 1951, 1500fr, William III and Mary, 1689-1702. No. 1952, 1500fr, Victoria, 1837-1901.

2000, Sept. 5
Sheets of 6, #a-f
1949-1950 A424 Set of 2   22.50 22.50
Souvenir Sheets
1951-1952 A424 Set of 2   13.50 13.50

Millennium Type of 1999

Highlights of 1950-59: a, US sends troops to defend South Korea. b, Rock and roll hits the air waves. c, Death of Eva Peron. d, Structure of DNA revealed by Watson and Crick. e, Sir Edmund Hillary and Tenzing Norgay reach peak of Mt. Everest. f, John F. Kennedy marries Jacqueline Bouvier. g, Coronation of Queen Elizabeth II. h, Millionth Volkswagen produced. i, German soccer team wins World Cup. j, Roger Bannister runs 1st 4-minute mile. k, Dr. Jonas Salk develops polio vaccine. l, 1st McDonald's franchise. m, New phone lines cross Atlantic. n, Soviet Union launches Sputnik. o, Jack Kerouac writes "On the Road." p, China begins "Great Leap Forward." q, Communist revolution in Cuba. r, Computer chip patented.

2000   **Perf. 12¾x12½**
1953 A412 200fr Sheet of 18,
    #a-r, + label   17.50 17.50

36th Organization of African Unity Summit, Lomé — A425

OAU emblem, map of Africa, doves and panel color of: 10fr, Bright yellow. 25fr, Green. 100fr, Dull yellow. 125fr, Blue violet. 250fr, Red violet. 375fr, Red. 400fr, Brown. 425fr, Orange.
No. 1954: a, Peace dove statue. b, Hotel du 2 Février. c, Congress building, Lomé. d, Alédjo Fault. e, Temberma hut. f, Cacao plantation.
No. 1955: a, Pres. Gnassingbé Eyadema, map of Europe and Africa, handshakes. b, Algerian Pres. Abdelazir Bouteflika, Pres. Eyadema, and map of Africa. c, Pres. Eyadema and OAU emblem. d, Map of Africa, doves, OAU emblem.
Illustration reduced.

2000   **Litho.**   **Perf. 14x13¾**
1953S-1953Z A425 Set of 8   7.25 7.25
Sheets of 6 and 4
1954 A425 350fr #a-f   7.50 7.50
1955 A425 550fr #a-d   7.75 7.75

Trains — A426

No. 1956, 425fr: a, Richard Trevethick's engine. b, Stephenson's Adler. c, Crampton Continent. d, Atlantic Coastlines 4-4-2. e, Great Northern Railway Ivatt Atlantic. f, Great Western Railway City of Truro 4-4-0.
No. 1957, 425fr: a, Paris-Lyon-Mediterranean Railway, compound 4-8-2. b, Canadian Pacific Railway Royal Hudson 4-6-4. c, London-Midland Railway Duchess. d, New York Central Twentieth Century Limited. e, New Zealand Government Railway J class 4-8-4. f, British Railways Evening Star 5-10-0.
No. 1958, 1800fr, Eurostar. No. 1959, 1800fr, TGV Atlantique.

2000, Sept. 8   **Litho.**   **Perf. 14**
Sheets of 6, #a-f
1956-1957 A426 Set of 2   22.50 22.50
Souvenir Sheets
1958-1959 A426 Set of 2   16.00 16.00

Ships — A427

No. 1960, 425fr: a, Norse knaar. b, Hanseatic cog. c, Iberian caravel. d, Henri Grace à Dieu. e, Ark Royal. f, Dutch Hooker.
No. 1961, 425fr: a, HMS Victory. b, HMS Warrior. c, Cutty Sark. d, USS Olympia. e, Empress of Canada. f, James Clark Ross.
No. 1962, 1800fr, Discovery. No. 1963, 1800fr, Sea Cat ferry.

2000, Sept. 8   **Litho.**   **Perf. 14**
Sheets of 6, #a-f
1960-1961 A427 Set of 2   22.50 22.50
Souvenir Sheets
1962-1963 A427 Set of 2   16.00 16.00

Dogs and Cats — A428

Designs: 275fr, Bloodhound. 300fr, Sphinx cat. 325fr, Basset hound. 350fr, Cocker spaniel. No. 1968, 375fr, American curl cat. 400fr, Scottish fold cat.
No. 1970, 375fr, horiz. — Dogs: a, Bearded collie. b, Chow chow. c, Boxer. d, Irish setter. e, Bracco Italiano. f, Pointer.
No. 1971, 375fr, horiz. — Cats: a, Devon Rex. b, Cornish Rex. c, Siamese. d, Balinese. e, Birman. f, Korat.
No. 1972, 1500fr, Yorkshire terrier. No. 1973, 1500fr, Chinchilla cat.

Perf. 13½x13¼, 13¼x13½
2001, Dec. 17   **Litho.**
1964-1969 A428 Set of 6   10.00 10.00
Sheets of 6, #a-f
1970-1971 A428 Set of 2   22.50 22.50
Souvenir Sheets
1972-1973 A428 Set of 2   15.00 15.00

Marine Life — A429

No. 1974, 200fr (31x31mm): a, Priacanthus arenatus. b, Diplodus annularis. c, Lithognathus mormyrus. d, Selene vomer. e, Penaeus duorarum. f, Arbacia lixula. g, Serranus scriba. h, Trachurus trachurus. i, Lepas anatifera. j, Octopus vulgaris. k, Scorpaena scrofa. l, Dardanus arrosor.
No. 1975, 250fr (31x31mm): a, Porcupine fish. b, Blue shark. c, Sting ray. d, Physalia physalis. e, Turtles. f, Coryphaena hippurus. g, Caranx hippos. h, Sawfish. i, Todaropsis eblanae. j, Pompano. k, Diplodus cervinus. l, Barracuda.
No. 1976, 1500fr, Octopus vulgaris, diff. No. 1977, 1500fr, Blue shark, diff.

2001, Dec. 17   **Perf. 12½**
Sheets of 12, #a-l
1974-1975 A429 Set of 2   26.00 26.00
Souvenir Sheets
Perf. 13¼x13½
1976-1977 A429 Set of 2   15.00 15.00

African Wildlife A430

Designs: 150fr, Okapia johnstoni, vert. 200fr, Sagittarius serpentarius. 250fr, Lemur catta, vert. 300fr, Gorilla gorilla. 350fr, Genetta genetta, vert. 400fr, Fennecus zerda.
No. 1984, 380fr: a, Papio hamadryas. b, Felis serval. c, Suricata suricatta. d, Orycteropus afer. e, Connochataetes taurinus. f, Tragelaphus strepsiceros.
No. 1985, 380fr: a, Panthera pardus. b, Loxodonta africana. c, Cercopithecus hamlyni. d, Ephippiorhynchuus senegalensis. e, Hippopotamus amphibius. f, Hippotragus niger.
No. 1986, 415fr: a, Equus burchelli boehmi. b, Ceratotherium simum. c, Achionyx jubatus. d, Gazella dama. e, Crocuta crocuta. f, Lyacon pictus.
No. 1987, 1500fr, Crocodylus niloticus. No. 1988, 1500fr, Panthera leo, vert. No. 1989, 1500fr, Giraffa camelopardalis.

Perf. 13½x13¼, 13¼x13½
2001, Dec. 17
1978-1983 A430 Set of 6   8.00 8.00
Sheets of 6, #a-f
1984-1986 A430 Set of 3   35.00 35.00
Souvenir Sheets
1987-1989 A430 Set of 3   22.50 22.50

United We Stand A431

2002, Mar. 18   **Litho.**   **Perf. 14**
1990 A431 400fr multi   2.00 2.00

Bella Bellow Type of 1998-2002
2002-04   **Litho.**   **Perf. 13½**
1990A A403a 20fr yel green   — —
1990B A403a 30fr brown   — —
1990C A403a 110fr blue green   — —
1990D A403a 150fr aquamarine   — —
1990E A403a 250fr red   — —
1990F A403a 400fr yellow green   — —
1990G A403a 550fr pale orange   — —
1990H A403a 650fr black   — —
1990I A403a 1000fr rose   — —
1990J A403a 3000fr light blue   — —

The editors suspect that additional stamps were issued in this set and would like to examine any examples.
Numbers may change.

2004 Summer Olympics, Athens — A432

Designs: 150fr, Chariot rider and horses. 300fr, Pin from 1960 Rome Olympics. 450fr, Emblem of 1960 Squaw Valley Winter Olympics, vert. 500fr, Diver, vert.

2004, Aug. 25   **Litho.**   **Perf. 13¼**
1991-1994 A432 Set of 4   6.50 6.50

Pres. Gnassingbé Eyadema (1935-2005) A433

2004   **Perf. 13½x13¼**
Panel Color

1995	A433	25fr dark blue	.25	.25
1996	A433	50fr yel green	.25	.25
1997	A433	150fr olive green	.60	.60
1998	A433	400fr dull brown	1.60	1.60
1999	A433	550fr green	2.25	2.25
2000	A433	650fr brt blue	2.75	2.75
2001	A433	1000fr lilac	4.25	4.25
2002	A433	2000fr salmon pink	8.25	8.25
2003	A433	3000fr blue green	12.50	12.50
		Nos. 1995-2003 (9)	32.70	32.70

Pope John Paul II
(1920-2005)
A435

2006, Jan. 24   Litho.   Perf. 13½
2007 A435 550fr multi   2.50 2.50
Printed in sheets of 4.

Jules Verne (1828-1905),
Writer — A436

No. 2008:, a, Home of Verne from 1882-1900. b, Monument to Verne, Amiens, France. c, Sculpture of Verne, Amiens. d, Mysterious Island.

2006, Jan. 24   Litho.   Perf. 13½
2008 A436 550fr Sheet of 4,
              #a-d   10.00 10.00

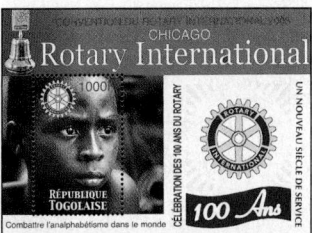

Rotary International, Cent. (in 2005) — A437

No. 2009 — Children and denomination in: a, Yellow in upper right. b, Red. c, Yellow in upper left.
1000fr, Child.

2006, Jan. 24
2009 A437 700fr Sheet of 3,
              #a-c   10.00 10.00
Souvenir Sheet
2010 A437 1000fr multi   4.50 4.50

Friedrich von Schiller (1759-1805),
Writer — A438

No. 2011, vert. — Schiller: a, Monument. b, Bust. c, Portrait.
1000fr, Birthplace of Schiller.

2006, Jan. 24
2011 A438 700fr Sheet of 3,
              #a-c   10.00 10.00
Souvenir Sheet
2012 A438 1000fr multi   4.50 4.50

World Cup Soccer Championships,
75th Anniv. (in 2005) — A439

No. 2013: a, David Beckham. b, Ronaldo Nazario. c, Fernando Hierro.
1000fr, Eusebio.

2006, Jan. 24
2013 A439 700fr Sheet of 3,
              #a-c   10.00 10.00
Souvenir Sheet
2014 A439 1000fr multi   4.50 4.50

V-E Day, 50th Anniv. (in 2005) — A440

No. 2015, vert.: a, Monument to victory. b, New York Times front page with war reports. c, Soldiers at Battle of the Bulge, 1944. d, Airplanes. e, Sculpture of Holocaust victim.
1000fr, DUKW.

2006, Jan. 24   Litho.   Perf. 13¼
2015 A440 400fr Sheet of 5, #a-
              e   7.50 7.50
Souvenir Sheet
2016 A440 1000fr multi   3.75 3.75

V-J Day, 50th Anniv. (in 2005) — A441

No. 2017: a, USS Charles Carroll. b, BB-35. c, LCT-515. d, LST-388. e, Destroyer Thompson DD-627. f, USS Thomas Jefferson.
1000fr, Battle of Iwo Jima.

2006, Jan. 24
2017 A441 350fr Sheet of 6, #a-
              f   7.75 7.75
Souvenir Sheet
2018 A441 1000fr multi   3.75 3.75

Railroads, Bicent. — A442

No. 2019: a, DX5287. b, W192. c, Central Pacific Jupiter. d, LWDHAM.
No. 2020, 1000fr, Rovos Ralf Class 25NC. No. 2021, 1000fr, Class 242 streamlined tank locomotive.

2006, Jan. 24
2019 A442 550fr Sheet of 4, #a-
              d   8.25 8.25
Souvenir Sheets
2020-2021 A442 Set of 2   7.50 7.50

Léopold Sédar Senghor
Year — A443

2006, July 28
2022	A443	150fr multi	.60	.60
2023	A443	550fr multi	2.25	2.25
2024	A443	650fr multi	2.60	2.60
2025	A443	1000fr multi	4.00	4.00
2026	A443	2000fr multi, horiz.	8.00	8.00
2027	A443	3000fr multi, horiz.	12.00	12.00
2028	A443	5000fr multi, horiz.	20.00	20.00
2029	A443	10,000fr multi, horiz.	40.00	40.00
		Nos. 2022-2029 (8)	89.45	89.45

Souvenir Sheet

Wolfgang Amadeus Mozart (1756-91),
Composer — A444

2006, Dec. 21   Perf. 14
2030 A444 1500fr multi   6.00 6.00

Space Achievements — A445

Designs: 150fr, Luna 9. 300fr, Hayabusa probe. 450fr, Venus Express. 500fr, Space Shuttle Discovery, vert.
No. 2035: a, Intl. Space Station. b, Deep Impact probe. c, Muse Asteroid. d, Artist's view of L1 spacecraft. e, Odyssey. f, Calipso.
No. 2036: a, Viking 1 in oribit around Mars. b, Viking 1. c, Phobos. d, Viking Lander 1.
No. 2037, 1500fr, Mars Reconnaissance Orbiter. No. 2038, 1500fr, Apollo 11, vert.

2006, Dec. 21   Perf. 13¼
2031-2034 A445 Set of 4   5.75 5.75
2035 A445 400fr Sheet of 6,
              #a-f   9.50 9.50
2036 A445 550fr Sheet of 4,
              #a-d   8.75 8.75
Souvenir Sheets
2037-2038 A445 Set of 2   12.00 12.00

Worldwide Fund for Nature
(WWF) — A446

No. 2039 — Cyclanorbis senegalensis: a, On sand, facing left. b, With foliage, facing left. c, Head. d, With foliage, facing right.

2006, Dec. 28
2039 A446 350fr Block or strip
              of 4, #a-d   5.75 5.75
   e.   Minature sheet, 2 each #a-d 11.50 11.50

Birds — A447

No. 2040: a, Platnea alba. b, Ceryle rudis. c, Ardea alba. d, Ephipphorhynchus senegalensis.
1500fr, Ephipphorhynchus senegalensis, diff.

2006, Dec. 28   *Perf. 14*
2040 A447 450fr Sheet of 4, #a-d   7.25 7.25

Souvenir Sheet
2041 A447 1500fr multi   6.00 6.00

Mushrooms — A448

No. 2042: a, Coprinus micaceus. b, Cookeina sulcipes. c, Hygrocybe firma. d, Chlorophyllum molybdites.
1500fr, Volvariella esculenta.

2006, Dec. 28
2042 A448 450fr Sheet of 4, #a-d   7.25 7.25

Souvenir Sheet
2043 A448 1500fr multi   6.00 6.00

Butterflies — A449

No. 2044, horiz.: a, Papilio nobilis. b, Colotis celimene. c, Salamis anacardii. d, Eronia cleodora.
1500fr, Colotis regina.

2006, Dec. 28   *Perf. 14*
2044 A449 450fr Sheet of 4, #a-d   7.25 7.25

Souvenir Sheet
2045 A449 1500fr multi   6.00 6.00

Orchids — A450

No. 2046, vert.: a, Triphora trianthophora. b, Amerorchis rotundifolia. c, Cypripedium x andrewsii. d, Pogonia ophioglossoides.
1500fr, Platanthera x keenanii.

2006, Dec. 28   *Perf. 14*
2046 A450 450fr Sheet of 4, #a-d   7.25 7.25

Souvenir Sheet
2047 A450 1500fr multi   6.00 6.00

Rembrandt (1606-69), Painter A451

Designs: 50fr, Three Oriental Figures (Jacob and Laban). 100fr, The Pancake Woman. 150fr, The Goldsmith. 250fr, The Golf Player. 325fr, The Persian. 350fr, Jacob and Rachel Listening to an Account of Joseph's Dreams.
1250fr, The Conspiracy of Julius Civilis, horiz.

2006   *Perf. 14¼*
2048-2053 A451 Set of 6   5.00 5.00
Imperf
Size: 106x76mm
2054 A451 1250fr multi   5.00 5.00

Souvenir Sheets

A452

Elvis Presley (1935-77) — A453

No. 2055 — Country name in: a, Pale blue. b, Pale yellow. c, Pink. d, Pale green.
No. 2056 — Country name in: a, Pale blue. b, Pale yellow. c, Pink. d, Pale green.

2006, Dec. 21   *Litho.*   *Perf. 14*
2055 A452 550fr Sheet of 4, #a-d 8.75 8.75
2056 A453 550fr Sheet of 4, #a-d 8.75 8.75

New Year 2007 (Year of the Pig) A454

2008, Jan. 21   *Litho.*   *Perf. 13½*
2057 A454 275fr multi   1.25 1.25
Printed in sheets of 4.

Pope Benedict XVI — A455

2008, Jan. 21   *Perf. 12½x12¾*
2058 A455 300fr multi   1.40 1.40
Printed in sheets of 8.

Miniature Sheet

Inauguration of Pres. John F. Kennedy, 47th Anniv. — A456

No. 2059: a, Band passing reviewing stand. b, Kennedy taking oath of office. c, Capitol. d, Kennedy giving inaugural address.

2008, Jan. 21   *Perf. 13¼*
2059 A456 450fr Sheet of 4, #a-d 8.00 8.00

Wedding of Queen Elizabeth II and Prince Philip, 60th Anniv. — A457

No. 2060: a, Couple, white frame. b, Queen, pink frame. c, Couple, light blue frame. d, Queen, light blue frame. e, Couple, pink frame. f, Queen, white frame.
1250fr, Couple, diff., green frame.

2008, Jan. 21   *Perf. 12¾*
2060 A457 400fr Sheet of 6, #a-f   11.00 11.00

Souvenir Sheet
2061 A457 1250fr multi   5.75 5.75

Princess Diana (1961-97) — A458

No. 2062, vert.: a, Wearing double-stranded pearl necklace, large photo. b, Wearing white hat, cropped photo. c, Wearing black and white houndstooth dress, large photo. d,

Wearing double-stranded pearl necklace, cropped photo. e, Wearing white hat, large photo. f, Wearing black and white houndstooth dress, cropped photo.
1500fr, Wearing black jacket.

2008, Jan. 21
2062 A458 400fr Sheet of 6, #a-f   11.00 11.00

Souvenir Sheet
2063 A458 1500fr multi   6.75 6.75

Campaign to Prevent AIDS — A459

Red AIDS ribbon and: 200fr, Colored squares. 350fr, Hand, horiz. 650fr, Man and woman carrying Togo flags, horiz.

2008, Feb. 8   *Perf. 11½*
2064-2066 A459 Set of 3   5.75 5.75
Dated 2007.

Miniature Sheet

2008 Summer Olympics, Beijing — A460

No. 2067: a, Swimming. b, Running. c, Soccer. d, Sailing.

2008, Aug. 18   *Litho.*   *Perf. 12*
2067 A460 240fr Sheet of 4, #a-d 4.50 4.50

Peony A461

2009, Apr. 10   *Litho.*   *Perf. 13¼*
2068 A461 200fr multi   .80 .80
Printed in sheets of 8.

Miniature Sheet

Pope Benedict XVI — A462

No. 2069 — Pope Benedict XVI: a, Seated, with hands in prayer. b, With covered chalices. c, Wearing miter. d, Wearing red vestments and red and gold stole. e, Wearing white vestments, hand raised. f, Seated with hands crossed.

2010, Feb. 11   *Perf. 11½*
2069 A462 350fr Sheet of 6, #a-f 8.75 8.75

Miniature Sheet

U.S. Pres. Barack Obama — A463

No. 2070 — Pres. Obama: a, With people in background. b, With blue sky in background. c, On telehone. d, Wearing suit, with hand raised.

2010, Feb. 11			**Perf. 12x11½**	
2070	A463	450fr Sheet of 4, #a-d	7.50	7.50

A464

A465

Michael Jackson (1958-2009), Singer — A466

No. 2071 — Jackson with microphone: a, Near mouth, gray area at top. b, Near eyes, black area behind head. c, Near eyes, tan area behind head. d, Near mouth, black area behind head.

No. 2072 — Jackson wearing a: a, White costume with pearls. b, Black costume with sequins. c, Sunglasses, with hands together. d, Sunglasses, hands not visible.

2010, Feb. 11			**Perf. 11½x12**	
2071	A464	450fr Sheet of 4, #a-d	7.50	7.50
		Perf. 11½		
2072	A465	450fr Sheet of 4, #a-d	7.50	7.50
		Souvenir Sheet		
2073	A466	1000fr black & gray	4.25	4.25

A467

A468

A469

Phataginus Tricuspis
A470

2010, Mar. 6		**Perf. 13x13¼**	
2074	Horiz. strip of 4	9.00	9.00
a.	A467 550fr multi	2.25	2.25
b.	A468 550fr multi	2.25	2.25
c.	A469 550fr multi	2.25	2.25
d.	A470 550fr multi	2.25	2.25
e.	Sheet of 8, 2 each #2074a-2074d, + 2 labels	18.00	18.00

SEMI-POSTAL STAMPS

Curie Issue
Common Design Type

1938	**Unwmk.**	**Engr.**	**Perf. 13**	
B1	CD80	1.75fr + 50c brt ultra	20.00	20.00
		Never hinged	32.50	

French Revolution Issue
Common Design Type
Photo., Name and Value Typo. in Black

1939				
B2	CD83	45c + 25c green	9.50	9.50
B3	CD83	70c + 30c brown	9.50	9.50
B4	CD83	90c + 35c red org	9.50	9.50
B5	CD83	1.25fr + 1fr rose pink	9.50	9.50
B6	CD83	2.25fr + 2fr blue	9.50	9.50
		Nos. B2-B6 (5)	47.50	47.50
		Set, never hinged	80.00	

French Revolution, 150th anniv. Surtax for defense of the colonies.

Nos. 281, 236, 245, 289 Surcharged in Red or Black

SECOURS + 1 fr. NATIONAL

1941			**Perf. 14 x 13½, 12½**	
B7	A10	50c + 1fr	3.25	3.25
B8	A7	80c + 2fr	6.50	6.50
B9	A8	1.50fr + 2fr	6.50	6.50
B10	A11	2fr + 3fr (R)	6.50	6.50
		Nos. B7-B10 (4)	22.75	22.75

Catalogue values for unused stamps in this section, from this point to the end of the section, are for Never Hinged items.

Common Design Type and

Togolese Militiaman SP1

Military Infirmary SP2

1941		**Photo.**	**Perf. 13½**	
B10A	SP1	1fr + 1fr red	1.25	
B10B	CD86	1.50fr + 3fr maroon	1.25	
B10C	SP2	2.50fr + 1fr blue	1.25	
		Nos. B10A-B10C (3)	3.75	

Nos. B10A-B10C were issued by the Vichy government in France, but were not placed on sale in Togo.

Nos. 296-297 Surcharged in Black or Red

1944		**Engr.**	**Perf. 12x12½**	
B10D		50c + 1.50fr on 2.50fr deep blue (R)	.95	
B10E		+ 2.50fr on 1fr green	1.10	

Colonial Development Fund.
Nos. B10D-B10E were issued by the Vichy government in France, but were not placed on sale in Togo.

Tropical Medicine Issue
Common Design Type

1950		**Engr.**	**Perf. 13**	
B11	CD100	10fr + 2fr indigo & dk bl	5.50	4.00

The surtax was for charitable work.

Republic

Patient on Stretcher — SP3

Uprooted Oak Emblem — SP4

Designs: 30fr+5fr, Feeding infant. 50fr+10fr, Blood transfusion.

1959		**Engr.**	**Perf. 13**	
B12	SP3	20fr + 5fr multicolored	.75	.75
a.		Souvenir sheet of 4	5.00	5.00
B13	SP3	30fr + 5fr bl, car & brn	.75	.75
a.		Souvenir sheet of 4	5.00	5.00
B14	SP3	50fr + 10fr emer, brn & car	.75	.75
a.		Souvenir sheet of 4	5.00	5.00
		Nos. B12-B14 (3)	2.25	2.25

Issued for the Red Cross.
Nos. B12a, B13a, B14a exist imperf.; same values.

1960		**Unwmk.**	**Perf. 13**	

#B16 similar to #B15, with emblem on top.

B15	SP4	25fr + 5fr dk bl, brn & yel grn	.45	.45
B16	SP4	45fr + 5fr dk bl, brn & ol	.80	.80

World Refugee Year, July 1, 1959-June 30, 1960. The surtax was for aid to refugees.

AIR POST STAMPS

Common Design Type

1940	**Unwmk.**	**Engr.**	**Perf. 12½x12**	
C1	CD85	1.90fr ultra	.40	.40
C2	CD85	2.90fr dark red	.65	.65
C3	CD85	4.50fr dk gray grn	.80	.80
C4	CD85	4.90fr yellow bister	.90	.90
C5	CD85	6.90fr deep orange	1.30	1.30
		Nos. C1-C5 (5)	4.05	4.05
		Set, never hinged	6.00	

Common Design Type
Inscribed "Togo" across top

1942			
C6	CD88	50c car & bl	.25
C7	CD88	1fr brn & blk	.40
C8	CD88	2fr grn & red brn	.50
C9	CD88	3fr dk bl & scar	.65
C10	CD88	5fr vio & brn red	.80

Frame Engraved, Center Typographed

C11	CD89	10fr ultra, ind & org	1.10	
C12	CD89	20fr rose car, mag & gray blk	1.10	
C13	CD89	50fr yel grn, dl grn & lt vio	1.75	2.25
		Nos. C6-C13 (8)	6.55	
		Set, never hinged	8.75	

There is doubt whether Nos. C6-C12 were officially placed in use.

Catalogue values for unused stamps in this section, from this point to the end of the section, are for Never Hinged items.

Elephants — AP1

Plane — AP2

Plane — AP3

Post Runner and Plane — AP4

1947, Oct. 6		**Engr.**	**Perf. 12½**	
C14	AP1	40fr blue	8.75	4.00
C15	AP2	50fr lt ultra, & red vio	4.75	1.60
C16	AP3	100fr emer & dk brn	8.00	2.50
C17	AP4	200fr lilac rose	13.00	4.00
		Nos. C14-C17 (4)	34.50	12.10

UPU Issue
Common Design Type

1949, July 4			**Perf. 13**	
C18	CD99	25fr multi	8.75	7.25

Liberation Issue
Common Design Type

1954, June 6				
C19	CD102	15fr indigo & pur	8.00	6.50

Freight Highway — AP5

1954, Nov. 29				
C20	AP5	500fr indigo & dk grn	60.00	45.00

Republic

Independence Allegory — AP6

Unwmk.

1957, Oct. 29　　Engr.　　Perf. 13

C21　AP6　25fr bl, olive bister & ver　.60　.30

1st anniv. of Togo's autonomy.

Flag and Torch — AP7

Great White Egret — AP8

1957, Oct. 29

C22	AP7	50fr multi	.65	.35
C23	AP7	100fr multi	1.10	.60
C24	AP7	200fr multi	2.25	1.00
C25	AP8	500fr ind, lt bl & grn	18.00	6.75
		Nos. C22-C25 (4)	22.00	8.70

Types of 1957 inscribed: "Republique du Togo" and

Flag, Plane and Map — AP9

1959, Jan. 15　　Engr.　　Perf. 13

C26	AP9	25fr ultra, emer & vio brn	.40	.25
C27	AP7	50fr dk bl, dl grn & red	.60	.35
C28	AP7	100fr multi	1.40	.60
C29	AP7	200fr dk grn, red & ultra	3.50	1.25
C30	AP8	500fr blk brn, rose lil & grn	14.00	3.50
		Nos. C26-C30 (5)	19.90	5.95

Hotel Le Benin AP10

Eagle and Map of Togo — AP11

Perf. 14½x15, 15x14½

1960, Apr. 27　　Litho.　　Unwmk.

C31	AP10	100fr crim, emer & yel	1.75	.25
C32	AP10	200fr multi	4.00	.40
C33	AP11	500fr grn & gldn brn	8.50	1.00
		Nos. C31-C33 (3)	14.25	1.65

Proclamation of Togo's full independence, Apr. 27, 1960.

Mail Service Type

100fr, Boeing 707 and stamps of 1960.

1963, Jan. 12　　Photo.　　Perf. 13

C34	A41	100fr multi	2.00	.45
a.		Souvenir sheet of 4	6.00	5.00

No. C34a contains 4 stamps similar to Nos. 441-443 and C34, with simulated perforations.

Emancipation Type

1963, Oct.　　Unwmk.　　Perf. 13x14

C35	A45	100fr multi	1.75	.45
a.		Souv. sheet of 4, #454-456, C35, imperf.	3.50	3.00

For overprint see No. C41.

Type of 1964 Regular Issue

50fr, Black-bellied seed-cracker. 100fr, Blue-billed mannikin. 200fr, Redheaded lovebird. 250fr, African gray parrot. 500fr, Yellow-breasted barbet.

1964-65　　Photo.　　Perf. 14
Size: 22½x31mm
Birds in Natural Colors

C36	A47	50fr yel grn	3.00	.30
C37	A47	100fr ocher	6.00	.35
C38	A47	200fr dl bl grn	11.50	.90
C39	A47	250fr dl rose ('65)	15.50	1.10
C40	A47	500fr violet	30.00	1.60
		Nos. C36-C40 (5)	66.00	4.25

No. C35 Overprinted Diagonally: "En Mémoire de / JOHN F. KENNEDY / 1917-1963"

1964, Feb.　　　　　Perf. 13x14

C41	A45	100fr multi	2.25	.30

Issued in memory of John F. Kennedy.

Same overprint was applied to stamps of No. C35a, with black border and commemorative inscription added. Two sheets exist: with and without gray silhouetted head of Kennedy covering all four stamps. Value: without silhouette, $17.50; with silhouette, $25.

Liberation Type

1964, May 25　　　　Perf. 14x13

C42	A50	100fr dl bl grn & dk brn	1.50	.30

Olympic Games Type

1964, Oct.　　Photo.　　Perf. 14

C43	A52	100fr Tennis	1.90	.30
a.		Souv. sheet of 3, #493-494, C43, imperf.	3.25	2.50

Flag of Togo and Jet — AP12

1964, Dec. 5　　Unwmk.　　Perf. 14x13

C44	AP12	100fr multi	1.25	.50

Inauguration of the national airline "Air Togo." For souvenir sheet see No. 499a.

Lincoln Type

1965, June　　Photo.　　Perf. 13½x14

C45	A58	100fr ol gray	2.25	.35
a.		Souv. sheet of #545, C45, imperf	3.00	2.25

Sports Type

100fr, Soccer player, flags of Togo and Congo.

1965, July　　Unwmk.　　Perf. 14x13

C46	A59	100fr multi	1.75	.35

Churchill Type

1965, Aug. 7　　Photo.　　Perf. 13½x14

C47	A60	85fr car rose	2.00	.40
a.		Souv. sheet of #532, C47, imperf	3.25	2.50

UN Type

100fr, Apple, grapes, wheat and "ONU."

1965, Dec. 15　　　　Perf. 14x13½

C48	A65	100fr dk bl & bis	1.75	.40
a.		Souvenir sheet of 2	2.40	1.75

No. C48a contains two imperf. stamps similar to Nos. 548 and C48 with simulated perforations.

Pope Type

Designs: 45fr, Pope speaking at UN rostrum, world map and UN emblem. 90fr, Pope, plane and UN emblem.

1966, Mar. 5　　Litho.　　Perf. 12

C49	A66	45fr emer & multi	.90	.25
C50	A66	90fr gray & multi	2.10	.25
a.		Souvenir sheet of 2, #C49-C50	3.75	2.50

Red Cross Type

Jean Henri Dunant and Togolese Flag.

1966, May 7　　Litho.　　Perf. 12

C51	A67	100fr multi	2.25	.35

WHO Type

Flowers: 50fr, Daisies and WHO Headquarters. 90fr, Talisman roses and WHO Headquarters.

1966, May　　Litho.　　Perf. 12

C52	A68	50fr lt bl & multi	.90	.25
C53	A68	90fr gray & multi	1.50	.25
a.		Souvenir sheet of 2, #C52-C53	3.00	2.00

Air Afrique Issue
Common Design Type

1966, Aug. 31　　Photo.　　Perf. 13

C54	CD123	30fr brt grn, blk & lem	.80	.25

Arts and Crafts Type

60fr, Basket maker. 90fr, Wood carver.

1966, Sept.　　　　Perf. 13x14

C55	A69	60fr ultra, org & blk	1.25	.25
C56	A69	90fr brt rose, yel & blk	2.00	.25

Dancer Type

50fr, Woman from North Togo holding branches. 60fr, Man from North Togo with horned helmet.

1966, Nov.　　Photo.　　Perf. 13x14

C57	A70	50fr multi	1.10	.25
C58	A70	60fr olive & multi	1.25	.25

Soccer Type

Designs: Different Soccer Scenes.

1966, Dec. 14　　Photo.　　Perf. 14x13

C59	A71	50fr org, brn & pur	1.10	.25
C60	A71	60fr ultra, brn & org	1.40	.25
a.		Souvenir sheet of 3, #582, C59-C60, imperf.	3.25	2.40

Fish Type

Designs: 45fr, Yellow jack and trawler. 90fr, Banded distichodus and seiner.

1967, Jan. 14　　　　Perf. 14
Fish in Natural Colors

C61	A72	45fr org & brn	1.00	.25
C62	A72	90fr emer & dk bl	2.50	.35

UNICEF Type

UNICEF Emblem and: 45fr, Girl and miniature poodle. 90fr, African boy and greyhound.

1967, Feb. 11　　Photo.　　Perf. 14x13½

C63	A73	45fr yel, red brn & blk	1.40	.25
C64	A73	90fr ultra, dk grn & blk	2.10	.35
a.		Souvenir sheet of 2	4.00	2.25

No. C64a contains 2 imperf., lithographed stamps with simulated perforations similar to Nos. C63-C64.

Satellite Type

50fr, Diamant rocket. 90fr, Fr-1 satellite.

1967, Mar. 18　　Photo.　　Perf. 13½x14

C65	A74	50fr multi, vert.	1.10	.25
C66	A74	90fr multi, vert.	1.90	.30
a.		Souvenir sheet of 2	3.00	2.10

No. C66a contains 2 imperf. stamps similar to Nos. C65-C66 with simulated perforations.

Musician Type

UNESCO Emblem and: 45fr, Johann Sebastian Bach and organ. 90fr, Ludwig van Beethoven, violin and oboe.

1967, Apr. 15　　Photo.　　Perf. 14x13½

C67	A75	45fr multi	1.25	.25
C68	A75	90fr pink & multi	2.75	.25
a.		Souvenir sheet of 2	4.00	2.25

No. C68a contains 2 imperf. stamps similar to Nos. C67-C68 with simulated perforations.

EXPO '67 Type

EXPO '67 Emblem and: 45fr, French pavilion, roses. 60fr, British pavilion, day lilies. 90fr, African village, bird-of-paradise flower. 105fr, US pavilion, daisies.

1967, May 30　　Photo.　　Perf. 14

C69	A76	45fr multi	.70	.25
C70	A76	60fr multi	1.10	.25
C71	A76	90fr yel & multi	1.40	.30
C72	A76	105fr multi	1.90	.35
		Nos. C69-C72 (4)	5.10	1.05

For overprints see Nos. C86-C89.

Mural by José Vela Zanetti — AP13

The designs are from a mural in the lobby of the UN Conf. Building, NYC. The mural depicting mankind's struggle for a lasting peace is shown across 3 stamps twice in the set: on the 5fr, 15fr, 30fr and 45fr, 60fr, 90fr.

1967, July 15　　Litho.　　Perf. 14

C73	AP13	5fr multi	.40	.25
C74	AP13	15fr org & multi	.40	.25
C75	AP13	30fr multi	.45	.25
C76	AP13	45fr multi	.70	.25
C77	AP13	60fr car & multi	1.10	.25
C78	AP13	90fr ind & multi	1.75	.30
a.		Souvenir sheet of 3, #C76-C78	4.00	2.75
		Nos. C73-C78 (6)	4.80	1.55

Issued to publicize general disarmament.

Animal Type

1967, Aug. 19　　Photo.　　Perf. 14x13½

C79	A78	45fr Lion	1.10	.25
C80	A78	60fr Elephant	1.60	.25

African Postal Union Issue, 1967
Common Design Type

1967, Sept. 9　　Engr.　　Perf. 13

C81	CD124	100fr bl, brt grn & ol brn	1.90	.30

Stamp Anniversary Type

Designs: 90fr, Stamp auction and Togo Nos. 16 and C42. 105fr, Father and son with stamp album and No. 474.

1967, Oct. 14　　Photo.　　Perf. 14x13
Stamps on Stamps in Original Colors

C82	A79	90fr olive	1.25	.25
a.		Souvenir sheet of 3	3.00	2.50
C83	A79	105fr dk car rose	2.00	.40

No. C82a contains 3 imperf. stamps similar to Nos. 621-622 and C82 with simulated perforations.

Pre-Olympics Type

View of Mexico City, Summer Olympics emblem and: 60fr, Runners. 90fr, Broad jump.

1967, Dec. 2　　　　Perf. 13x14

C84	A80	60fr pink & multi	1.50	.45
C85	A80	90fr multi	1.50	.50
a.		Souv. sheet of 3, #627, C84-C85, imperf.	5.00	3.00

Nos. C69-C72 Overprinted: "JOURNÉE NATIONALE / DU TOGO / 29 SEPTEMBRE 1967"

1967, Dec.　　Photo.　　Perf. 14

C86	A76	45fr multi	.60	.25
C87	A76	60fr multi	.90	.25
C88	A76	90fr yel & multi	1.40	.25
C89	A76	105fr multi	1.75	.25
		Nos. C86-C89 (4)	4.40	1.00

Issued for National Day, Sept. 29, 1967.

Hydrological Decade Type

1968, Apr. 6　　Litho.　　Perf. 14

C90	A84	60fr multi	1.75	.25

Ship Type

Designs: 45fr, Fulton's and modern steamships. 90fr, US atomic ship Savannah and atom symbol.

1968, Apr. 26   Photo.   Perf. 14x14½
C91 A85 45fr yel & multi   1.10   .25
C92 A85 90fr bl & multi   2.25   .25
  a.   Souvenir sheet of 2   4.50 2.25

No. C92a contains 2 imperf. stamps similar to Nos. C91-C92 with simulated perforations.

WHO Type

Paintings: 60fr, The Anatomy Lesson, by Rembrandt (detail). 90fr, Jesus Healing the Sick, by Raphael.

1968, June 22   Photo.   Perf. 14
C93 A87 60fr multi   1.25   .25
C94 A87 90fr pur & multi   1.75   .25
  a.   Souvenir sheet of 2   4.00 3.25

No. C94a contains 2 imperf. stamps similar to Nos. C93-C94 with simulated perforations.

Olympic Games Type

1968, July 27   Perf. 14x13½
C95 A88 60fr Wrestling   1.10   .25
C96 A88 90fr Running   1.75   .25
  a.   Souvenir sheet of 2   3.00 2.40

No. C96a contains 2 imperf. stamps similar to Nos. C95-C96 with simulated perforations.

Boy Scout Type

60fr, First aid practice, horiz. 90fr, Scout game.

1968, Nov. 23   Litho.   Perf. 14
C97 A90 60fr ol & multi   1.10   .25
C98 A90 90fr org & multi   1.60   .35
  a.   Souvenir sheet of 2   3.25 1.90

No. C98a contains 2 imperf. stamps with simulated perforations similar to Nos. C97-C98.

PHILEXAFRIQUE Issue

The Letter, by Jean Auguste Franquelin
AP14

1968, Nov. 9   Photo.   Perf. 12½x12
C99 AP14 100fr multi   2.75 1.75

PHILEXAFRIQUE Philatelic Exhibition in Abidjan, Feb. 14-23. Printed with alternating light ultramarine label.

Christmas Type

Paintings: 60fr, Adoration of the Magi, by Pieter Brueghel. 90fr, Adoration of the Magi, by Dürer.

1968, Dec. 28   Litho.   Perf. 14
C100 A91 60fr red & multi   1.40   .25
C101 A91 90fr multi   2.10   .35
  a.   Souvenir sheet   4.50 2.25

No. C101a contains 2 imperf. stamps similar to Nos. C100-C101 with simulated perforations.

Human Rights Type

Human Rights Flame and: 60fr, Robert F. Kennedy. 90fr, Martin Luther King, Jr.

1969, Feb. 1   Photo.   Perf. 13½x14
C102 A92 60fr brt rose lil & vio bl 1.25 .25
C103 A92 90fr emer & brn   1.60   .40
  a.   Souvenir sheet   3.00 2.10

No. C103a contains 2 imperf. stamps similar to Nos. C102-C103 with simulated perforations.

For overprints see Nos. C110-C111.

2nd PHILEXAFRIQUE Issue
Common Design Type

Design: 50fr, Togo #16 and Aledjo Fault.

1969, Feb. 14   Engr.   Perf. 13
C104 CD128 50fr red brn, grn &
             car rose   2.25   .45

Sports Type

Stadium and: 60fr, Boxing. 90fr, Bicycling.

1969, Apr. 26   Photo.   Perf. 14x13½
C105 A93 60fr bl, red & dk brn   .95   .25
C106 A93 90fr ultra, brt pink & dk
           brn   1.60   .30
  a.   Souvenir sheet   3.00 2.10

No. C106a contains 2 imperf. stamps similar to Nos. C105-C106 with simulated perforations.

Lunar Type

Designs: 60fr, Astronaut exploring moon surface. 100fr, Astronaut gathering rocks.

1969, July 21   Litho.   Perf. 14
C107 A94 60fr dk bl & multi   1.00   .25
C108 A94 100fr multi   1.75   .50
  a.   Souvenir sheet   16.00 8.00

No. C108a contains 4 imperf. stamps with simulated perforations similar to Nos. 676-677 and C107-C108, magenta margin. No. C108a also exists with colors of 30fr and 100fr stamps changed, and margin in orange. Value, unused $6, used $2.

For overprints see Nos. C120-C121.

Painting Type

Painting: 90fr, Pentecost, by El Greco.

1969, Aug. 16   Litho.   Perf. 14
C109 A95 90fr multi   3.00   .50
  a.   Souvenir sheet   3.25 1.75

No. C109a contains two imperf. stamps with simulated perforations similar to Nos. 682 and C109.

Nos. C102-C103 Overprinted Like Nos. 683-686

1969, Sept. 1   Photo.   Perf. 13½x14
C110 A92 60fr brt rose lil & vio bl 1.10 .25
C111 A92 90fr emer & brn   1.75   .30
  a.   Souv. sheet of 2   3.00 2.00

#C111a is #C103a with Eisenhower overprint.

Bank Type

Design: 100fr, Bank emblem and hand holding cattle and farmer.

1969, Sept. 10   Photo.   Perf. 13x14
C112 A96 100fr multi   1.25   .40

Red Cross Type

60fr, Wilhelm C. Roentgen & Red Cross workers with children in front of Togo Headquarters. 90fr, Henri Dunant & Red Cross workers meeting Biafra refugees at airport.

1969, Sept. 27   Litho.   Perf. 14
C113 A97 60fr brn & multi   1.25   .30
C114 A97 90fr ol & multi   1.75   .40
  a.   Souv. sheet of 2   3.25 2.25

No. C114a contains 2 imperf. stamps with simulated perforations similar to Nos. C113-C114.

Agricultural Center Type

Emblem of Young Pioneer and Agricultural Organization and: 90fr, Manioc harvest. 100fr, Instruction in gardening. 200fr, Corn harvest. 250fr, Marching drum corps. 500fr, Parade of Young Pioneers.

1969-70   Litho.   Perf. 14
C115 A98 90fr multi   1.50   .25
C116 A98 100fr org & multi   1.75   .30
C117 A98 200fr multi ('70)   3.50   .40
C118 A98 250fr ol & multi   4.25   .70
C119 A98 500fr multi ('70)   9.00   .90
  Nos. C115-C119 (5)   20.00 2.50

Christmas Issue

Nos. C107-C108, C108a Overprinted: "JOYEUX NOEL"

1969, Dec.   Litho.   Perf. 14
C120 A94 60fr multi   3.75   .45
C121 A94 100fr multi   5.75   .65
  a.   Souvenir sheet of 4   67.50 67.50

Peace Leaders Type

60fr, Friedrich Ebert. 90fr, Mahatma Gandhi.

1969, Dec. 27   Litho.   Perf. 14x13½
C122 A100 60fr dk brn, dk red &
            yel   1.10   .25
C123 A100 90fr dk brn, vio bl &
            ocher   1.75   .35

For surcharges see Nos. 765, C143.

ILO Type

Paintings and ILO Emblem: 60fr, Spring Sowing, by Vincent van Gogh. 90fr, Workers, by Diego de Rivera.

1970, Jan. 24   Litho.   Perf. 12½x13
C124 A101 60fr gold & multi   2.00   .25
C125 A101 90fr gold & multi   3.00   .25
  a.   Souvenir sheet of 2   4.00 1.60

No. C125a contains two stamps similar to Nos. C124-C125, with simulated perforations.

Hair Styles Type

Various hair styles. 45fr, vert. 90fr, horiz.

1970, Feb. 21   Perf. 12½x13, 13x12½
C126 A102 45fr car & multi   1.00   .25
C127 A102 90fr multi   2.00   .40

Independence Type

Design: 60fr, Togo No. C33 and Independence Monument, Lomé.

1970, Apr. 27   Litho.   Perf. 13x12½
C128 A103 60fr yel & multi   1.10   .25

UPU Type

1970, May 30   Photo.   Perf. 14x13½
C129 A104 50fr grnsh bl & dk car   .90   .25

Soccer Type

Various Scenes from Soccer, Rimet Cup and Flags of: 50fr, Sweden and Israel. 60fr, Bulgaria and Peru. 90fr, Belgium and Salvador.

1970, June 27   Litho.   Perf. 13x14
C130 A105 50fr multi   .90   .25
C131 A105 60fr lil & multi   1.25   .25
C132 A105 90fr multi   1.60   .35
  a.   Souvenir sheet of 4   4.00 4.00
  Nos. C130-C132 (3)   3.75   .75

No. C132a contains 4 stamps similar to Nos. 734, C130-C132, but imperf. with simulated perforations.

Lenin Type

Design: 50fr, Lenin Meeting Peasant Delegation, by V. A. Serov, and UNESCO emblem.

1970, July 25   Litho.   Perf. 12½
C133 A106 50fr multi   2.25   .25

For overprint see No. C179.

EXPO '70 Type
Souvenir Sheet

150fr, Mitsubishi pavilion, EXPO '70 emblem.

1970, Aug. 8   Litho.   Perf. 13
C134 A107 150fr yel & multi   5.50 3.50
  Inscribed "AERINNE"

No. C134 contains one stamp 86x33mm.

Astronaut Type

Design: 200fr, James A. Lovell, Fred W. Haise, Jr. and Tom Mattingly (replaced by John L. Swigert, Jr.) and Apollo 13 emblem.

1970, Sept. 26
C135 A108 200fr multi   3.50   .75
  a.   Souv. sheet of 3   4.50 3.25

Space flight of Apollo 13. No. C135a contains 3 stamps similar to Nos. 741, 744 and C135, with simulated perforations.
For overprint see No. C136.

Nos. C135, C135a Inscribed: "FELICITATIONS / BON RETOUR APOLLO XIII"

1970, Sept. 26
C136 A108 200fr multi   2.75   .60
  a.   Souvenir sheet of 3   3.75 2.75

Safe return of the crew of Apollo 13.

UN Type

Paintings and Emblems of UN Agencies: 60fr, The Mailman Roulin, by van Gogh, and UPU emblem. 90fr, The Birth of the Virgin, by Vittore Carpaccio, and WHO emblem.

1970, Oct. 24   Litho.   Perf. 13x12½
C137 A109 60fr grn, gold & blk   1.10   .25
C138 A109 90fr red org, gold &
            brn   1.75   .30
  a.   Souvenir sheet of 4   3.50 2.50

No. C138a contains one each of Nos. 754-755 and C137-C138 with simulated perforations.

Moth Type

Moths: 60fr, Euchloron megaera. 90fr, Pseudacraea boisduvali.

1970, Nov. 21   Photo.   Perf. 13x14
C139 A110 60fr multi   5.25   .25
C140 A110 90fr multi   5.25   .25

Christmas Type

Paintings: 60fr, Adoration of the Magi, by Botticelli. 90fr, Adoration of the Kings, by Tiepolo.

1970, Dec. 26   Litho.   Perf. 12½x13
C141 A111 60fr gold & multi   1.50   .25
C142 A111 90fr gold & multi   2.25   .30
  a.   Souv. sheet of 2, #C141-C142 3.50 1.75

No. C122 Surcharged and Overprinted: "EN MEMOIRE / Charles De Gaulle / 1890-1970"

1971, Jan. 9   Photo.   Perf. 14x13½
C143 A100 200fr on 60fr   11.50   .60

De Gaulle Type

Designs: 60fr, De Gaulle and Pope Paul VI. 90fr, De Gaulle and satellite.

1971, Feb. 20   Photo.   Perf. 13x14
C144 A112 60fr blk & dp vio   2.20   .25
C145 A112 90fr blk & bl grn   3.00   .25
  a.   Souvenir sheet of 4   8.50 3.00

Nos. C143-C145 issued in memory of Charles De Gaulle (1890-1970), President of France. No. C145a contains 4 imperf. stamps similar to Nos. 769-770, C144-C145.

Easter Type

Paintings: 50fr, Resurrection, by Matthias Grunewald. 60fr, Resurrection, by Master of Trebon. 90fr, Resurrection, by El Greco.

1971, Apr. 10   Litho.   Perf. 10½x11½
C146 A113 50fr gold & multi   .85   .25
C147 A113 60fr gold & multi   1.25   .25
C148 A113 90fr gold & multi   1.60   .30
  a.   Souvenir sheet of 4, #773,
          C146-C148   4.50 2.50
  Nos. C146-C148 (3)   3.70   .70

Apollo 14 Type

Designs: 50fr, 200f, Apollo 14 badge 100fr, Take-off from moon, and spaceship.

1971, May   Litho.   Perf. 12½
C149 A114 50fr grn & multi   .65   .25
C150 A114 100fr multi   1.10   .45
C151 A114 200fr org & multi   2.50   .85
  a.   Souv. sheet of 4   5.75 5.50
  Nos. C149-C151 (3)   4.25 1.50

No. C151a contains 4 stamps similar to Nos. 777 and C149-C151 with simulated perforations.
For surcharge and overprints see Nos. C162-C164.

Cacao Type

60fr, Ministry of Agriculture. 90fr, Cacao tree and & pods. 100fr, Sorting & separating beans from pods.

1971, June 6   Litho.   Perf. 14
C152 A115 60fr multi   .95   .25
C153 A115 90fr multi   1.40   .40
C154 A115 100fr multi   1.75   .45
  Nos. C152-C154 (3)   4.10 1.05

ASECNA Type

1971, June 26
C155 A116 100fr multi   1.60   .35

Tourist Type

Designs: 50fr, Château Viale and antelope. 60fr, Lake Togo and crocodile. 100fr, Old lime furnace, Tokpli, and hippopotamus.

1971, July 17
C156 A117 50fr multi   .90   .25
C157 A117 60fr multi   1.10   .25
C158 A117 100fr multi   1.60   .40
  Nos. C156-C158 (3)   3.60   .80

For overprint see No. C172.

Religions Type

Designs: 50fr, Mohammedans praying in front of Lomé Mosque. 60fr, Protestant service. 90fr, Catholic bishop and priests.

1971, July 31   Litho.   Perf. 14½
C159 A118 50fr multi   .60   .25
C160 A118 60fr multi   .65   .25
C161 A118 90fr multi   1.10   .25
  a.   Souvenir sheet of 4, #787,
          C159-C161   4.25 2.50
  Nos. C159-C161 (3)   2.35   .65

Nos. C149-C151 Overprinted and
Surcharged in Black or Silver: "EN
MEMOIRE / DOBROVOLSKY —
VOLKOV — PATSAYEV / SOYUZ 11"

C162	A114	90fr on 50fr multi	1.25 .35
C163	A114	100fr multi (S)	1.40 .40
C164	A114	200fr multi	3.00 .65
a.		Souvenir sheet of 4, #788,	
		C162-C164	7.00 7.00
		Nos. C162-C164 (3)	5.65 1.40

See note after No. 788.

Olympic Type

200fr, Sapporo '72 emblem and Ski jump.

1971, Oct. 30   Litho.   Perf. 14

C165	A119	200fr multi	2.25 .50
a.		Souvenir sheet of 4	4.25 3.50

No. C165 contains 4 stamps with simulated
perforations similar to Nos. 791-793 and C165
printed on glazed paper.

African Postal Union Issue, 1971
Common Design Type

Design: 100fr, Adjogbo dancers and
UAMPT Building, Brazzaville, Congo.

1971, Nov. 13   Photo.   Perf. 13x13½

C166	CD135	100fr bl & multi	1.25 .40

Intl. Organization for the Protection of
Children (U.I.P.E.) — AP14a

Die Cut Perf. 10½

			Embossed
C166A	AP14a	1500fr gold	20.00

UNICEF Type

Toys: 60fr, Turtle. 90fr, Parrot.

1971, Nov. 27   Litho.   Perf. 14

C167	A120	60fr lt bl & multi	.70 .25
C168	A120	90fr multi	1.10 .25
a.		Souvenir sheet of 4	2.75 2.50

No. C168a contains 4 stamps with simu-
lated perforations similar to Nos. 796-797 and
C167-C168.
For overprints see Nos. C263-C264.

Christmas Type

Virgin and Child by: 60fr, Giorgione. 100fr,
Raphael.

1971, Dec. 24   Perf. 14x13

C169	A121	60fr olive & multi	1.25 .30
C170	A121	100fr multi	2.10 .50
a.		Souvenir sheet of 4	6.25 6.25

No. C170a contains 4 stamps with simulated perforations similar to Nos. 800-801,
C169-C170.

Venice Type

Design: 100fr, Ca' d'Oro, Venice.

1972, Feb. 26   Litho.   Perf. 14

C171	A122	100fr multi	2.75 .55
a.		Souvenir sheet of 3	6.75 4.25

No. C171a contains 3 stamps similar to
Nos. 802-803, C171 with simulated
perforations.

No. C156 Overprinted "VISITE DU
PRESIDENT / NIXON EN CHINE /
FEVRIER 1972"

1972, Mar.   Litho.   Perf. 14

C172	A117	50fr multi	.80 .25

Visit of Pres. Richard M. Nixon to the People's Republic of China, Feb. 20-27.

Easter Type

Paintings: 50fr, Resurrection, by Thomas
de Coloswa. 100fr, Ascension by Andrea
Mantegna.

1972, Mar. 31

C173	A123	50fr gold & multi	1.90 .25
C174	A123	100fr gold & multi	2.75 .25
a.		Souvenir sheet of 4	3.50 1.90

No. C174a contains 4 stamps similar to
Nos. 806-807, C173-C174 with simulated
perforations.

Heart Type

100fr, Heart, WHO emblem and smith.

1972, Apr. 4

C175	A124	100fr multi	1.60 .45
a.		Souvenir sheet of 2	3.25 1.40

No. C175a contains 2 stamps similar to
Nos. 810 and C175 with simulated
perforations.

Telecommunications Type

Design: 100fr, Intelsat 4 over Africa.

1972, June 24   Perf. 14

C176	A125	100fr multi	1.60 .30

For overprint see No. C229.

Cassava Type

60fr, Truck and cassava processing factory,
horiz. 80fr, Children, mother holding tapioca
cake.

1972, June 30

C177	A126	60fr multi	1.10 .25
C178	A126	80fr multi	1.25 .25

No. C133 Surcharged in Deep
Carmine:
"VISITE DU PRESIDENT / NIXON EN
RUSSIE / MAI 1972"

1972, July 15   Litho.   Perf. 12½

C179	A106	300fr on 50fr multi	4.75 1.40

President Nixon's visit to the USSR, May
1972. Old denomination obliterated with
6x5mm rectangle.

Olympic Type

1972, Aug. 26   Litho.   Perf. 14

C180	A127	90fr Gymnastics	1.10 .40
a.		Souv. sheet of 2	4.00 1.90
C181	A127	200fr Basketball	2.75 .70

No. C180a contains 2 stamps with simu-
lated perforations similar to Nos. 816 and
C180.
For overprints see Nos. C234-C235.

Bird Type

Bird: 90fr, Rose-ringed parakeet.

1972, Sept. 9

C182	A128	90fr multi	3.25 .45
a.		Souvenir sheet of 4	15.00 3.00

No. C182a contains 4 stamps similar to
Nos. 818-820, C182 with simulated
perforations.

Rotary Type

Rotary Emblem and: 60fr, Map of Togo,
olive branch. 90fr, Flags of Togo and Rotary
Club. 100fr, Paul P. Harris.

1972, Oct. 7   Litho.   Perf. 14

C183	A129	60fr brn & multi	.75 .25
C184	A129	90fr multi	1.10 .50
C185	A129	100fr multi	1.40 .65
		Nos. C183-C185 (3)	3.25 1.35

For overprints see Nos. C212-C213, C244-
C245.

Painting Type, 1972

Designs: 60fr, Mystical Marriage of St.
Catherine, by Assistant to the P. M. Master.
80fr, Self-portrait, by Leonardo da Vinci. 100fr,
Sts. Mary and Agnes by Botticelli.

1972, Oct. 21

C186	A130	60fr gold & multi	1.90 .25
C187	A130	80fr gold & multi	2.25 .30
C188	A130	100fr gold & multi	4.00 .45
a.		Souvenir sheet of 4	5.00 2.25
		Nos. C186-C188 (3)	8.15 .95

No. C188a contains 4 stamps with simulated perforations similar to Nos. 824, C186-
188.

Presidential Visit Type

Design: 100fr, Pres. Pompidou and Col. Etienne Eyadema, front view of party
headquarters.

1972, Nov. 23   Litho.   Perf. 14

C189	A131	100fr multi	2.40 .40

Johann Wolfgang
von Goethe
(1749-1832),
German Poet and
Dramatist
AP15

1972, Dec. 2   Photo.   Perf. 13x14

C190	AP15	100fr grn & multi	1.60 .40

Christmas Type

Paintings: 60fr, Nativity, by Master
Vyshchibrod. 80fr, Adoration of the Kings,
anonymous. 100fr, Flight into Egypt, by
Giotto.

1972, Dec. 23   Litho.   Perf. 14

C191	A132	60fr gold & multi	1.25 .25
C192	A132	80fr gold & multi	1.60 .35
C193	A132	100fr gold & multi	2.10 .45
a.		Souvenir sheet of 4	5.00 2.75
		Nos. C191-C193 (3)	4.95 1.00

No. C193a contains 4 stamps with simulated perforations similar to Nos. 829, C191-
C193.

Leprosy Day Type

Design: 100fr, Dr. Armauer G. Hansen,
apparatus, microscope and Petri dish.

1973, Jan. 23   Photo.   Perf. 14x13½

C194	A133	100fr rose car & bl	3.00 .40

World Leprosy Day and centenary of the
discovery of the Hansen bacillus, the cause of
leprosy.

Miniature Sheets

1972 Summer Olympics,
Munich — AP15a

Medalists, each 1500fr.: #C194A, Mark
Spitz, US, swimming. #C194B, L. Linsenhoff,
West Germany, equestrian. #C194C, D.
Morelon, France, cycling.

Litho. & Embossed

1973, Jan.   Perf. 13½

C194A-C194C	AP15a	Set of 3	375.00

Exist imperf.

Miniature Sheet

Apollo 17 Moon Landing — AP15b

1973, Jan.

C194D	AP15b	1500fr gold & multi	55.00

Exists imperf.

Easter Type

1973, Apr. 21   Litho.

C195	A135	90fr Christ in Glory	1.40 .40
a.		Souvenir sheet of 2	2.75 1.75

No. C195a contains one each of Nos. 835
and C195 with simulated perforations.

Apollo 17 Type

Designs: 100fr, Astronauts on moon and
orange rock. 200fr, Rocket lift-off at Cape
Kennedy and John F. Kennedy.

1973, June 2   Litho.   Perf. 14

C196	A136	100fr multi	1.60 .45
C197	A136	200fr multi	3.25 .65
a.		Souvenir sheet of 2	4.25 3.00

No. C197a contains 2 stamps similar to
Nos. C196-C197 with simulated perforations.

Boy Scout Type

100fr, Canoeing, horiz. 200fr, Campfire,
horiz.

1973, June 30   Litho.   Perf. 14

C198	A137	100fr bl & multi	1.60 .45
C199	A137	200fr bl & multi	3.50 .70
a.		Souvenir sheet of 2	4.50 2.50

No. C199a contains 2 stamps similar to
Nos. C198-C199 with simulated perforations.
For overprints see Nos. C265-C266.

Copernicus Type

Designs: 90fr, Heliocentric system. 100fr,
Nicolaus Copernicus.

1973, July 18

C200	A138	90fr multi	1.90 .35
C201	A138	100fr bis & multi	2.40 .45
a.		Souv. sheet of 2, #C200-C201	4.00 1.90

Red Cross Type

Design: 100fr, Dove carrying Red Cross
letter, sun, map of Togo.

1973, Aug. 4

C202	A139	100fr multi	3.25 .35

For overprint see No. C294.

Literacy Type

Design: 90fr, Woman teacher in classroom.

1973, Aug. 18   Litho.   Perf. 14

C203	A140	90fr multi	1.50 .35

WMO Type

1973, Oct. 4   Photo.   Perf. 14x13

C204	A142	200fr dl bl, pur & brn	2.00 .60

Type 1967

Early & contemporary planes, #758, C36.

1973, Oct. 20   Photo.   Perf. 14x13

C205	A79	100fr multi	2.50 .35
a.		Souvenir sheet of 2	3.00 1.75

75th anniversary of Togolese postal service.
No. C205a contains 2 stamps similar to Nos.
855 and C205 with simulated perforations.

Kennedy Type

Designs: 90fr, Kennedy and Charles De
Gaulle. 100fr, Kennedy and Nikita Krushchev.
200fr, Kennedy and model of Apollo
spacecraft.

1973, Nov. 22   Litho.   Perf. 14

C206	A143	90fr blk & pink	1.60 .45
C207	A143	100fr blk, lt bl & bl	1.75 .60
C208	A143	200fr blk, buff & brn	4.00 .75
a.		Souvenir sheet of 3	4.00 2.00
		Nos. C206-C208 (3)	7.35 1.80

No. C208a contains 2 stamps similar to
Nos. C207-208 with simulated perforations.

Human Rights
Flame and
People — AP16

1973, Dec. 8   Photo.   Perf. 13x14
C209 AP16 250fr lt bl & multi   2.40 .80

25th anniversary of the Universal Declaration of Human Rights.

Christmas Type

Paintings: 90fr, Virgin and Child. 100fr, Adoration of the Kings. Both after 15th century Italian paintings.

1973, Dec. 22   Litho.   Perf. 14
C210 A144 90fr gold & multi   1.40 .35
C211 A144 100fr gold & multi   1.90 .65
  a.   Souvenir sheet of 2   2.75 1.50

No. C211a contains 2 stamps with simulated perforations similar to Nos. C210-C211.

Nos. C183 and C185 Overprinted:
"PREMIERE CONVENTION / 210eme
DISTRICT / FEVRIER 1974 / LOME"

1974, Feb. 21   Litho.   Perf. 14
C212 A129 60fr brn & multi   .65 .25
C213 A129 100fr multi   1.00 .35

First convention of Rotary International, District 210, Lomé, Feb. 22-24.

Soccer Type

Various soccer scenes and games' cup.

1974, Mar. 2   Litho.   Perf. 14
C214 A145 90fr multi   1.10 .45
C215 A145 100fr multi   1.40 .50
C216 A145 200fr multi   2.50 .95
  a.   Souvenir sheet of 2   5.25 3.25
        Nos. C214-C216 (3)   5.00 1.90

No. C216a contains 2 stamps with simulated perforations similar to Nos. C215-C216.

Picasso Type

Paintings: 90fr, The Muse. 100fr, Les Demoiselles d'Avignon. 200fr, Sitting Nude.

1974, Apr. 6   Litho.   Perf. 14
C217 A146 90fr brn & multi   1.60 .40
C218 A146 100fr pur & multi   2.00 .45
C219 A146 200fr multi   4.00 .85
  a.   Souvenir sheet of 2   7.00 4.00
        Nos. C217-C219 (3)   7.60 1.70

No. C219a contains 3 stamps similar to Nos. C217-C219 with simulated perforations.

Coastal Views Type

Designs: 90fr, Fishermen on Lake Togo. 100fr, Mouth of Anecho River.

1974, Apr. 20
C220 A147 90fr multi   1.10 .25
C221 A147 100fr multi   1.25 .35
  a.   Souvenir sheet of 2   2.50 1.25

No. C221a contains 2 stamps with simulated perforations similar to Nos. C220-C221.

UPU Type

Designs: Old mailmen's uniforms.

1974, May 10   Litho.   Perf. 14
C222 A148 50fr multi   .70 .25
C223 A148 100fr multi   1.25 .35
  a.   Souvenir sheet of 2   40.00 17.00

No. C223a contains 2 stamps similar to Nos. C222-C223, rouletted.

Fishing Type

Designs: 90fr, Fishermen bringing in net with catch. 100fr, Fishing with rod and line. 200fr, Fishing with basket, vert.

1974, June 22   Litho.   Perf. 14
C224 A149 90fr multi   1.00 .25
C225 A149 100fr multi   1.10 .25
C226 A149 200fr multi   2.40 .65
  a.   Souvenir sheet of 3   5.25 2.50
        Nos. C224-C226 (3)   4.50 1.15

No. C226a contains 3 stamps with simulated perforations similar to Nos. C224-C226.

Jupiter Probe Type

Designs: 100fr, Rocket take-off, vert. 200fr, Satellite in space.

1974, July 6   Perf. 14
C227 A150 100fr multi   .90 .35
C228 A150 200fr multi   2.00 .65
  a.   Souvenir sheet of 2   5.50 4.00

No. C228a contains 2 stamps similar to Nos. C227-C228 with simulated perforations; imperf. or rouletted.

No. C176
Overprinted in Black

1974, July   Perf. 14
C229 A125 100fr multi   3.50 1.20

INTERNABA 1974 Intl. Philatelic Exhibition, Basel, June 7-16.
No. C229 exists overprinted in silver. Value, unused $11.

Seashell Type

1974, July 13   Litho.   Perf. 14
C230 A151 90fr Alcithoe ponsonbyi   1.75 .30
C231 A151 100fr Casmaria iredalei   2.25 .40
  a.   Souvenir sheet of 2   4.50 1.40

No. C231a contains 2 stamps similar to Nos. C230-C231 with simulated perforations.

Horse Racing Type

90fr, Steeplechase. 100fr, Galloping horses.

1974, Aug. 3   Litho.   Perf. 14
C232 A152 90fr multi   2.10 .30
C233 A152 100fr multi   2.40 .40
  a.   Souvenir sheet of 2   6.50 2.25

No. C233a contains one each of Nos. C232-C233 with simulated perforations.

Nos. C180, C180a and C181
Overprinted: "COUPE DU MONDE /
DE FOOTBALL / VAINQUEURS /
REPUBLIQUE FEDERALE /
d'ALLEMAGNE"

1974, Aug. 19
C234 A127 90fr multi   .75 .25
  a.   Souvenir sheet of 2   18.00
C235 A127 200fr multi   1.50 .65

World Cup Soccer Championship, Munich, 1974, victory of German Federal Republic. For description of No. C234a see note after No. C181.

Animal Type

1974, Sept. 7   Litho.   Perf. 14
C236 A153 90fr Lions   2.10 .45
C237 A153 100fr Rhinoceroses   2.25 .40
  a.   Souvenir sheet of 3   3.75 1.90

Wild animals of West Africa. No. C237a contains 3 stamps similar to Nos. 889, C236-C237 with simulated perforations.

1974, Oct. 14
C238 A153 90fr Herd at waterhole   1.10 .25
C239 A153 100fr Village and cows   1.25 .35
  a.   Souvenir sheet of 2   2.50 1.25

Domestic animals. No. C239a contains 2 stamps with simulated perforations similar to Nos. C238-C239.

Churchill Type

Designs: 100fr, Churchill and frigate. 200fr, Churchill and fighter planes.

1974, Nov. 1   Photo.   Perf. 13x13½
C240 A154 100fr multi   1.25 .35
C241 A154 200fr org & multi   2.75 .70
  a.   Souvenir sheet of 2   4.50 2.10

No. C241a contains 2 stamps similar to Nos. C240-C241; perf. or imperf.

Flower Type

Flowers of Togo: 100fr, Clerodendrum thosonae. 200fr, Gloriosa superba.

1975, Feb. 15   Litho.   Perf. 14
C242 A155 100fr multi   1.75 .30
C243 A155 200fr multi   3.50 .50
  a.   Souvenir sheet of 2   8.25 2.75

No. C243a contains one each of Nos. C242-C243, perf. 13x14 or imperf.

Nos. C184-C185 Overprinted: "70e
ANNIVERSAIRE / 23 FEVRIER 1975"

1975, Feb. 23   Litho.   Perf. 14
C244 A129 90fr multi   .90 .25
C245 A129 100fr multi   1.00 .35

Rotary International, 70th anniversary.

Easter Type

Paintings: 100fr, Christ Rising from the Tomb, by Master MS. 200fr, Holy Trinity (detail), by Dürer.

1975, Apr. 19   Litho.   Perf. 14
C246 A157 100fr multi   1.00 .25
C247 A157 200fr multi   2.00 .55
  a.   Souvenir sheet of 2   3.50 2.00

No. C247a contains 2 stamps similar to Nos. C246-C247 with simulated perforations.

Independence Type

50fr, National Day parade, flag and map of Togo. 60fr, Warriors' dance and flag of Togo.

1975, Apr. 26   Litho.   Perf. 14
C248 A158 50fr multi, vert.   .50 .25
C249 A158 60fr multi   .70 .25
  a.   Souvenir sheet of 2   1.50 .75

No. C249a contains 2 stamps similar to Nos. C248-C249 with simulated perforations.

Hunt Type

Designs: 90fr, Running deer. 100fr, Wild boar hunter with shotgun.

1975, May 24   Photo.   Perf. 13x13½
C250 A159 90fr multi   1.75 .30
C251 A159 100fr multi   2.10 .30

Palm Oil Type

Designs: 85fr, Selling palm oil in market, vert. 100fr, Oil processing plant, Alokoegbe.

1975, June 28   Litho.   Perf. 14
C252 A160 85fr multi   1.75 .50
C253 A160 100fr multi   2.00 .50

Apollo-Soyuz Type and

Soyuz Spacecraft
AP17

Designs: 60fr, Donald K. Slayton, Vance D. Brand and Thomas P. Stafford. 90fr, Aleksei A. Leonov and Valery N. Kubasov. 100fr, Apollo-Soyuz link-up, American and Russian flags. 200fr, Apollo-Soyuz emblem and globe.

1975, July 15
C254 AP17 50fr yel & multi   .50 .25
C255 A161 60fr lil & multi   .70 .25
C256 A161 90fr bl & multi   .85 .25
C257 A161 100fr grn & multi   1.25 .40
C258 A161 200fr yel & multi   2.10 .45
  a.   Souv. sheet of 4, #C255-C258   6.00 3.50
        Nos. C254-C258 (5)   5.40 1.50

See note after No. 913.

Schweitzer Type

Dr. Schweitzer: 80fr, playing organ, vert. 90fr, with pelican, vert. 100fr, and Lambarene Hospital.

1975, Aug. 23   Litho.   Perf. 14x13½
C259 A163 80fr multi   1.10 .30
C260 A163 90fr multi   1.25 .35
C261 A163 100fr multi   1.40 .40
        Nos. C259-C261 (3)   3.75 1.05

Letter Writing Type

80fr, Erasmus Writing Letter, by Hans Holbein.

1975, Oct. 9   Litho.   Perf. 14
C262 A164 80fr multi   1.00 .25

Nos. C167-C168a Overprinted:
"30ème Anniversaire / des Nations-
Unies"

1975, Oct. 24   Litho.   Perf. 14
C263 A120 60fr multi   .60 .25
C264 A120 90fr multi   .75 .25
  a.   Souvenir sheet of 4   3.00 1.90

UN, 30th anniv. #C264a contains Nos. 796 (with overprint), 918, C263-C264.

Nos. C198-C199 Overprinted: "14ème
JAMBORÉE / MONDIAL / DES
ÉCLAIREURS"

1975, Nov. 7
C265 A137 100fr multi   .55 .25
C266 A137 200fr multi   1.10 .50
  a.   Souvenir sheet of 2   3.25 2.00

14th World Boy Scout Jamboree, Lillehammer, Norway, July 29-Aug. 7. No. C266a contains one each of Nos. C265-C266 with simulated perforations.

Christmas Type

Paintings of the Virgin and Child: 90fr, Nativity, by Federico Barocci. 100fr, Bellini. 200fr, Correggio.

1975, Dec. 20   Litho.   Perf. 14
C267 A165 90fr bl & multi   .80 .25
C268 A165 100fr red & multi   .90 .25
C269 A165 200fr bl & multi   1.75 .50
  a.   Souv. sheet of 2, #C268-C269   3.50 2.00
        Nos. C267-C269 (3)   3.45 1.00

Bicentennial Type

Paintings (and Bicentennial Emblem): 60fr, Surrender of Gen. Burgoyne, by John Trumbull. 70fr, Surrender at Trenton, by Trumbull, vert. 100fr, Signing of Declaration of Independence, by Trumbull. 200fr, Washington Crossing the Delaware, by Emanuel Leutze.

1976, Mar. 3   Litho.   Perf. 14
C270 A167 60fr multi   .65 .25
C271 A167 70fr multi   .75 .25
C272 A167 100fr multi   1.00 .25
C273 A167 200fr multi   2.00 .55
  a.   Souv. sheet of 2, #C272-C273   4.00 2.00
        Nos. C270-C273 (4)   4.40 1.20

No. C273a also exists imperf. Value $22.50. For overprints see Nos. C280-C283.

Common Market Type

Designs: 60fr, ACP and CEE emblems. 70fr, Map of Africa, Europe and Asia.

1976, Apr. 24   Photo.   Perf. 13x14
C274 A168 60fr lt bl & multi   .55 .25
C275 A168 70fr yel & multi   .65 .25

Telephone Type

Designs: 70fr, Thomas A. Edison, old and new communications equipment. 105fr, Alexander Graham Bell, old and new telephones.

1976, Mar. 10   Photo.   Perf. 13x14
C276 A169 70fr multi   .75 .25
C277 A169 105fr multi   1.00 .40
  a.   Souv. sheet of 2, #C276-C277   2.25 1.40

No. C277a exists imperf. Value $10.00.

Eye Examination
AP18

Pylon, Flags of
Ghana, Togo,
Dahomey
AP19

1976, Apr. 8   Perf. 14x13
C278 AP18 60fr dk red & multi   .60 .25

World Health Day: "Foresight prevents blindness."

1976, May 8   Litho.   Perf. 14
C279 AP19 60fr multi   1.00 .25

Ghana-Togo-Dahomey electric power grid, 1st anniv. See No. 932.

Nos. C270-C273, C273a, Overprinted: "INTERPHIL / MAI 29-JUIN 6, 1976"

1976, May 29

C280	A167	60fr multi	.50	.25
C281	A167	70fr multi	.55	.25
C282	A167	100fr multi	.80	.25
C283	A167	200fr multi	1.60	.55
a.		Souvenir sheet of 2	3.00	3.00
		Nos. C280-C283 (4)	3.45	1.30

Interphil 76 Intl. Philatelic Exhibition, Philadelphia, Pa., May 29-June 6. Overprint on No. C281 in 3 lines; overprint on No. C283a applied to each stamp.

Olympic Games Type

Montreal Olympic Emblem and: 70fr, Yachting. 105fr, Motorcycling. 200fr, Fencing.

1976, June 15   Photo.   Perf. 14x13

C284	A172	70fr multi	.60	.25
C285	A172	105fr multi	.85	.40
C286	A172	200fr multi	1.60	.65
a.		Souvenir sheet of 2, #C285-C286, perf. 14	3.00	2.25
		Nos. C284-C286 (3)	3.05	1.30

For overprints see Nos. C298-C299.

Viking Type

60fr, Viking landing on Mars. 70fr, Nodus Gordii (view on Mars). 105fr, Lander over Mare Tyrrhenum. 200fr, Landing on Mars.

1976, July 15   Litho.   Perf. 14

C287	A173	60fr bis & multi	.55	.25
C288	A173	70fr multi	.65	.25
C289	A173	105fr bl & multi	.90	.40
C290	A173	200fr multi	1.75	.60
a.		Souv. sheet of 2, #C289-C290, perf. 14x13½	3.50	2.25
		Nos. C287-C290 (4)	3.85	1.40

Toulouse-Lautrec Type, 1976

Paintings: 60fr, Carmen, portrait. 70fr, Maurice at the Somme. 200fr, "Messalina."

1976, Aug. 7   Litho.   Perf. 14

C291	A174	60fr blk & multi	.90	.25
C292	A174	70fr blk & multi	1.00	.25
C293	A174	200fr blk & multi	2.75	.55
a.		Souv. sheet of 2, #C292-C293, perf. 13½x14	5.00	2.25
		Nos. C291-C293 (3)	4.65	1.00

No. C202 Overprinted: "Journeé / Internationale / de l'Enfance"

1976, Nov. 27   Perf. 14

C294	A139	100fr multi	.55	.35

International Children's Day.

Christmas Type

Paintings: 70fr, Holy Family, by Lorenzo Lotto. 105fr, Virgin and Child with Saints, by Jacopo da Pontormo. 200fr, Virgin and Child with Saints, by Lotto.

1976, Dec. 18

C295	A175	70fr multi	.80	.25
C296	A175	105fr multi	1.25	.45
C297	A175	200fr multi	2.25	.90
a.		Souv. sheet of 2, #C296-C297	3.50	2.00
		Nos. C295-C297 (3)	4.30	1.55

No. C284 Overprinted: "CHAMPIONS OLYMPIQUES / YACHTING — FLYING DUTCHMAN / REPUBLIQUE FEDERALE ALLEMAGNE"
No. C286 Overprinted: "CHAMPIONS OLYMPIQUES / ESCRIME FLEURET PAR EQUIPES / REPUBLIQUE FEDERALE ALLEMAGNE"

1976, Dec.   Photo.   Perf. 14x13

C298	A172	70fr multi	.65	.25
C299	A172	200fr multi	1.75	.65
a.		Souvenir sheet of 2	3.50	2.50

Olympic winners. No. C299a (on No. C286a) contains Nos. C285 and C299.

Eyadema Anniversary Type

60fr, National Assembly Building. 100fr, Pres. Eyadema greeting people at Aug. 30th meeting.

1977, Jan. 13   Photo.   Perf. 13x14

C300	A177	60fr multi	.65	.25
C301	A177	100fr multi	1.10	.35
a.		Souv. sheet of 2, #C300-C301	2.00	1.25

Musical Instrument Type

Musical Instruments: 60fr, Atopani. 80fr, African violin, vert. 105fr, African flutes, vert.

1977, Feb. 7   Litho.   Perf. 14

C302	A178	60fr multi	.90	.25
C303	A178	80fr multi	1.00	.25
C304	A178	105fr multi	1.40	.30
a.		Souv. sheet of 2, #C303-C304	2.75	1.50
		Nos. C302-C304 (3)	3.30	.70

Victor Hugo Type

Victor Hugo in exile on Guernsey Island.

1977, Feb. 26   Perf. 13x14

C305	A179	60fr multi	.80	.25
a.		Souvenir sheet of 2, #952, C305	1.25	.75

For overprint see No. C316.

Beethoven Type

Designs: 100fr, Beethoven's piano and 1818 portrait. 200fr, Beethoven on his deathbed and Holy Trinity Church, Vienna.

1977, Mar. 7   Perf. 14

C306	A180	100fr multi	1.40	.35
C307	A180	200fr multi	2.50	3.00
a.		Souv. sheet of 2, #C306-C307	3.25	1.75

Automobile Type

Early Automobiles: 60fr, Cannstatt-Daimler, 1899, Germany. 70fr, Sunbeam, 1904, England. 100fr, Renault, 1908, France. 200fr, Rolls Royce, 1909, England.

1977, Apr. 11   Litho.   Perf. 14

C308	A181	60fr multi	.80	.25
C309	A181	70fr multi	.90	.25
C310	A181	100fr multi	1.25	.35
C311	A181	200fr multi	2.40	.75
a.		Souv. sheet of 2, #C310-C311	5.00	1.90
		Nos. C308-C311 (4)	5.35	1.50

Lindbergh Type

Designs: 60fr, Lindbergh and son Jon, birds in flight. 85fr, Lindbergh home in Kent, England. 90fr, Spirit of St. Louis over Atlantic Ocean. 100fr, Concorde over NYC.

1977, May 9

C312	A182	60fr multi	.65	.25
C313	A182	85fr multi	.95	.25
C314	A182	90fr multi	1.00	.25
C315	A182	100fr multi	1.10	.30
a.		Souv. sheet of 2, #C314-C315	2.40	1.40
		Nos. C312-C315 (4)	3.70	.90

No. C305 Overprinted: "10ème ANNIVERSAIRE DU / CONSEIL INTERNATIONAL / DE LA LANGUE FRANCAISE"

1977, May 17   Litho.   Perf. 14

C316	A179	60fr multi	.70	.25

10th anniv. of the French Language Council.

Wildlife Type

60fr, Colobus monkeys. 90fr, Chimpanzee, vert. 100fr, Leopard. 200fr, West African manatee.

1977, June 13

C317	A183	60fr multi	.70	.25
C318	A183	90fr multi	1.00	.25
C319	A183	100fr multi	1.10	.25
C320	A183	200fr multi	2.40	.35
a.		Souv. sheet of 2, #C319-C320	4.00	1.75
		Nos. C317-C320 (4)	5.20	.95

Agriculture Type

Designs: 60fr, Corn silo. 100fr, Hoeing and planting by hand. 200fr, Tractor on field.

1977, July 11   Litho.   Perf. 14

C321	A184	60fr multi	.50	.25
C322	A184	100fr multi	.85	.25
C323	A184	200fr multi	1.75	.45
a.		Souv. sheet of 2, #C322-C323, perf. 13x14	3.40	1.60
		Nos. C321-C323 (3)	3.10	.85

Rubens Type

Paintings: 60fr, Heads of Black Men, 1620. 100fr, Anne of Austria, 1624.

1977, Aug. 8

C324	A185	60fr multi	.90	.25
C325	A185	100fr multi	1.40	.25
a.		Souv. sheet of 2, #C324-C325, perf. 14x13	2.10	1.25

Orbiter Type

90fr, Retrieval of unmanned satellite in space. 100fr, Satellite's return to space after repairs. 200fr, Manned landing of Orbiter.

1977, Oct. 4   Litho.   Perf. 14

C326	A186	90fr multi, vert.	.75	.25
C327	A186	100fr multi	.80	.25
C328	A186	200fr multi	1.75	.35
a.		Souv. sheet of 2, #C327-C328	3.00	1.50
		Nos. C326-C328 (3)	3.30	.75

Lafayette Type

60fr, Lafayette landing in New York, 1824. 105fr, Lafayette and Washington at Valley Forge.

1977, Nov. 7   Perf. 13x14

C329	A187	60fr multi	.65	.25
C330	A187	105fr multi	1.10	.25
a.		Souv. sheet of 2, #C329-C330	1.75	1.00

Christmas Type

Virgin & Child by: 90fr, 200fr, Carlo Crivelli, diff. 100fr, Bellini.

1977, Dec. 19   Perf. 14

C331	A189	90fr multi	.85	.25
C332	A189	100fr multi	.90	.25
C333	A189	200fr multi	1.90	.40
a.		Souv. sheet of 2, #C332-C333	3.50	1.75
		Nos. C331-C333 (3)	3.65	.80

Jenner Type

Designs: 50fr, Edward Jenner. 60fr, Smallpox vaccination clinic, horiz.

1978, Jan. 9   Perf. 14x13, 13x14

C334	A190	50fr multi	.35	.25
C335	A190	60fr multi	.40	.25
a.		Souvenir sheet of 2	1.40	.65

No. C335a contains 2 stamps with simulated perforations similar to Nos. C334-C335.

Wright Brothers Type

Designs: 60fr, Orville Wright's 7½-minute flight. 70fr, Orville Wright injured in first aircraft accident, 1908. 200fr, Wrights' bicycle shop, Dearborn, Mich. 300fr, First flight, 1903.

1978, Feb. 6   Litho.   Perf. 14

C336	A191	60fr multi	.60	.25
C337	A191	70fr multi	.65	.25
C338	A191	200fr multi	2.00	.35
C339	A191	300fr multi	3.00	.60
a.		Souvenir sheet of 2	9.25	5.25
		Nos. C336-C339 (4)	6.25	1.35

No. C339a contains one each of Nos. C338-C339 with simulated perforations.

Port of Lomé Type, 1978

Anchor and: 60fr, Industrial harbor. 100fr, Merchant marine harbor. 200fr, Bird's-eye view of entire harbor.

1978, Apr. 26   Photo.   Perf. 13

C340	A199	60fr multi	.45	.25
C341	A199	100fr multi	.75	.25
C342	A199	200fr multi	1.60	.40
a.		Souv. sheet of 2, #C341-C342	3.00	1.50
		Nos. C340-C342 (3)	2.80	.80

Space Type

Designs: 90fr, Module camera, horiz. 100fr, Module antenna. 200fr, Pioneer, US, in orbit.

1978, May 8   Litho.   Perf. 14

C343	A200	90fr multi	.70	.25
C344	A200	100fr multi	.75	.25
C345	A200	200fr multi	1.50	.35
a.		Souv. sheet of 2, #C344-C345, perf. 13½x14	2.50	1.50
		Nos. C343-C345 (3)	2.95	.75

Soccer Type

Various soccer scenes & Argentina '78 emblem.

1978, June 5   Perf. 14

C346	A201	60fr multi	.50	.25
C347	A201	80fr multi	.65	.25
C348	A201	100fr multi	1.75	.40
C349	A201	300fr multi	2.40	.55
a.		Souvenir sheet of 2, #C348-C349, perf. 13½x14	3.75	2.25
		Nos. C346-C349 (4)	5.30	1.35

Bicycle Type

History of Bicycle: 60fr, Bantam, 1896, vert. 85fr, Fold-up bicycle for military use, 1897. 90fr, Draisienne, 1816, vert. 100fr, Penny-farthing, 1884, vert.

Perf. 14x13, 13x14

1978, July 10   Photo.

C350	A202	60fr multi	.80	.25
C351	A202	85fr multi	1.00	.25
C352	A202	90fr multi	1.10	.35
C353	A202	100fr multi	1.25	.35
a.		Souv. sheet of 2, #C352-C353	3.00	1.60
		Nos. C350-C353 (4)	4.15	1.10

Phonograph Type

60fr, Edison's original phonograph, horiz. 80fr, Emile Berliner's phonograph, 1888. 200fr, Berliner's improved phonograph, 1894, horiz. 300fr, His Master's Voice phonograph, 1900, horiz.

Perf. 13x14, 14x13

1978, July 8   Photo.

C354	A203	60fr multi	.45	.25
C355	A203	80fr multi	.60	.25
C356	A203	200fr multi	1.40	.35
C357	A203	300fr multi	2.20	.50
a.		Souv. sheet of 2, #C356-C357	3.50	2.00
		Nos. C354-C357 (4)	4.65	1.25

Red Cross Type

Design: 60fr, Red Cross and other pavilions at Paris Exhibition, 1867.

1978, Sept. 4   Photo.   Perf. 14x13

C358	A204	60fr pur & red	.45	.25
a.		Souv. sheet of 2, #1009, C358	1.10	.55

Paintings Type

60fr, Langlois Bridge, by Vincent van Gogh. 70fr, Witches' Sabbath, by Francisco Goya. 90fr, Jesus among the Doctors, by Albrecht Dürer. 200fr, View of Arco, by Dürer.

1978, Nov. 6   Litho.   Perf. 14

C359	A205	60fr multi	.60	.25
C360	A205	70fr multi	.65	.30
C361	A205	90fr multi	.90	.40
C362	A205	200fr multi	1.75	.70
a.		Souv. sheet of 2, #C361-C362	3.25	1.40
		Nos. C359-C362 (4)	3.90	1.60

Birth and death anniversaries of famous painters.

Philexafrique II — Essen Issue
Common Design Types

#C363, Warthog and Togo No. C36. #C364, Firecrest and Thurn and Taxis No. 1.

1978, Nov. 1   Litho.   Perf. 13x12½

C363	CD138	100fr multi	2.50	2.00
C364	CD139	100fr multi	2.50	2.00
a.		Pair, #C363-C364 + label	5.00	5.00

Congress of Paris Type

60fr, Mail ship "Slieve Roe" 1877, post horn. 105fr, Congress of Paris medal. 200fr, Locomotive, 1870. All horizontal.

1978, Nov. 27   Photo.   Perf. 14x13

C365	A206	60fr multi	.55	.25
C366	A206	105fr multi	.95	.45
C367	A206	200fr multi	1.90	.75
a.		Souv. sheet of 2, #C366-C367	3.00	1.50
		Nos. C365-C367 (3)	3.40	1.40

Christmas Type

Paintings (Virgin and Child): 90fr, 200fr, by Carlo Crivelli, diff. 100fr, by Cosimo Tura.

1978, Dec. 17

C368	A207	60fr multi	.75	.35
C369	A207	100fr multi	.95	.40
C370	A207	200fr multi	1.75	.70
a.		Souv. sheet of 2, #C369-C370	3.25	1.40
		Nos. C368-C370 (3)	3.45	1.45

Capt. Cook Type

Designs: 60fr, "Freelove," Whitby Harbor, horiz. 70fr, Trip to Antarctica, 1773, horiz. 90fr, Capt. Cook. 200fr, Sails of Endeavour.

1979, Feb. 12   Litho.   Perf. 14

C371	A208	60fr multi	.50	.25
C372	A208	70fr multi	.55	.25
C373	A208	90fr multi	.75	.30
C374	A208	200fr multi	1.75	1.25
a.		Souv. sheet of 2, #C373-C374	3.00	1.75
		Nos. C371-C374 (4)	3.55	2.00

Easter Type

60fr, Resurrection. 100fr, Ascension. 200fr, Jesus appearing to Mary Magdalene.

1979, Apr. 9

C375	A209	60fr multi	.45	.25
C376	A209	100fr multi	.70	.40
C377	A209	200fr multi	1.50	.70
a.		Souv. sheet of 2, #C376-C377	2.75	1.40
		Nos. C375-C377 (3)	2.65	1.30

UPU Emblem, Drummer — AP20

Design: 100fr, UPU emblem, hands passing letter, satellites.

1979, June 8   Engr.   Perf. 13
C378 AP20 60fr multi   1.40 .50
C379 AP20 100fr multi   1.20 1.00

Philexafrique II, Libreville, Gabon, June 8-17.

Einstein Type

Designs: 60fr, Sights and actuality diagram. 85fr, Einstein playing violin, vert. 100fr, Atom symbol and formula of relativity, vert. 200fr, Einstein portrait, vert.

Perf. 14x13, 13x14

1979, July 2   Photo.
C380 A210 60fr multi   .50 .25
C381 A210 85fr multi   .80 .40
C382 A210 100fr multi   .85 .45
C383 A210 200fr multi   1.90 .85
  a. Souv. sheet of 2, #C382-C383   3.00 1.50
    Nos. C380-C383 (4)   4.05 1.90

Tree Type

Design: 60fr, Man watering tree.

1979, Aug. 13   Perf. 14x13
C384 A212 60fr blk & brn   .40 .25

Rowland Hill Type

Designs: 90fr, Bellman, England, 1820. 100fr, "Centercycles" used for parcel delivery, 1883, horiz. 200fr, French P.O. railroad car, 1848, horiz.

1979, Aug. 27   Photo.
C385 A213 90fr multi   .65 .30
C386 A213 100fr multi   .70 .35
C387 A213 200fr multi   1.50 .65
  a. Souv. sheet of 2, #C386-C387   2.50 1.25
    Nos. C385-C387 (3)   2.85 1.30

Train Type

Historic Locomotives: 60fr, "Le General," 1862. 85fr, Stephenson's, 1843. 100fr, "De Witt Clinton," 1831. 200fr, Joy's "Jenny Lind," 1847.

1979, Oct. 1   Litho.   Perf. 14
C388 A214 60fr multi   .75 .25
C389 A214 85fr multi   1.10 .45
C390 A214 100fr multi   1.25 .50
C391 A214 200fr multi   1.40 .90
  a. Souv. sheet of 2, #C390-C391   6.00 3.00
    Nos. C388-C391 (4)   4.50 2.05

Olympic Type

1980 Olympic Emblems and: 90fr, Ski jump. No. C393, Doubles canoeing, Olympic flame. No. C394, Rings. No. C395a, Bobsledding, horiz. No. C395b, Gymnast, horiz.

1979, Oct. 18   Litho.   Perf. 13½
C392 A215 90fr multi   .65 .30
C393 A215 100fr multi   .70 .35
C394 A215 200fr multi   1.60 .65
    Nos. C392-C394 (3)   2.95 1.30

Souvenir Sheet

C395   Sheet of 2   2.50 1.25
  a. A215 100fr multi   .65 .35
  b. A215 200fr multi   1.40 .65

Religion Type

Designs: 60fr, Moslems praying. 70fr, Protestant ministers.

1979, Oct. 29   Perf. 13x14
C396 A216 60fr multi   .55 .25
C397 A216 70fr multi   .60 .30
  a. Souv. sheet, #C396-C397   1.75 .65

Apollo 11 Type

60fr, Astronaut leaving Apollo 11. 70fr, US flag. 200fr, Sun shield. 300fr, Lunar take-off.

1979, Nov. 5
C398 A217 60fr multi   .45 .25
C399 A217 70fr multi   .50 .25
C400 A217 200fr multi   1.50 .65
C401 A217 300fr multi   2.10 1.00
  a. Souv. sheet of 2, #C400-C401   4.00 1.75
    Nos. C398-C401 (4)   4.55 2.10

Telecom Type

Design: 60fr, Telecom 79, dish antenna.

1979, Nov. 26   Photo.   Perf. 14x13
C402 A218 60fr multi   .70 .25

Miniature Sheets

President Eyadema, 10th Anniv. of the People's Republic — AP21

Litho. & Embossed

1979, Nov. 30   Perf. 13½
C402A AP21 1000fr In uniform   6.00   —

Imperf

C402B AP21 1000fr In suit, vert.   6.00   —
    Exist imperf.

Christmas Type

90fr, Adoration of the Kings. 100fr, Presentation of Infant Jesus. 200fr, Flight into Egypt.

1979, Dec. 17   Litho.   Perf. 14
C403 A219 90fr multi   .85 .35
C404 A219 100fr multi   .90 .40
C405 A219 200fr multi   1.60 .70
  a. Souv. sheet of 2, #C404-C405   3.50 1.50
    Nos. C403-C405 (3)   3.35 1.45

Rotary Type

3-H Emblem and: 90fr, Man reaching to sun. 100fr, Fish, grain. 200fr, Family, globe.

1980, Jan. 14
C406 A220 90fr multi   .80 .40
C407 A220 100fr multi   .85 .45
C408 A220 200fr multi   1.60 .85
  a. Souv. sheet of 2, C407-C408   3.25 1.60
    Nos. C406-C408 (3)   3.25 1.70

Rotary Intl., 75th anniv.; 3-H program (health, hunger, humanity).

Winter Olympic Type, 1980

1980, Jan. 31   Litho.   Perf. 13½
C409 A221 60fr Downhill skiing   .45 .25
C410 A221 100fr Speed skating   .75 .35
C411 A221 200fr Cross-country
            skiing   1.40 .65
    Nos. C409-C411 (3)   2.60 1.20

Souvenir Sheet

C412   Sheet of 2   2.50 1.25
  a. A221 100fr Ski jump, horiz.   .65 .35
  b. A221 200fr Hockey, horiz.   1.25 .65

Olympic Type

1980, Feb. 29   Litho.   Perf. 13½
C413 A222 100fr Fencing   .90 .45
C414 A222 200fr Pole vault   1.60 .80
C415 A222 300fr Hurdles   2.10 1.00
  a. Souv. sheet of 2, #C414-C415   4.75 2.50
    Nos. C413-C415 (3)   5.00 2.50

Easter Type

Easter 1980 (Paintings by): 60fr, Lorenzo Lotto. 100fr, El Greco. 200fr, Carlo Crivelli.

1980, Mar. 31   Perf. 14
C416 A223 60fr multi   .50 .25
C417 A223 100fr multi   .70 .35
C418 A223 200fr multi   1.50 .65
  a. Souv. sheet of 2, #C417-C418   2.50 1.25
    Nos. C416-C418 (3)   2.70 1.20

ASECNA Type

1980, Mar. 24   Litho.   Perf. 12½
C419 A224 60fr multi   .60 .25

Telecommunications Type

1980, May 17   Photo.   Perf. 13½x14
C420 A225 60fr "17 MAI", vert.   .60 .25

Red Cross Type

1980, June 16   Photo.   Perf. 14x13
C421 A226 60fr Nurses, patient   .60 .25

Jules Verne Type

Designs: 60fr, Rocket (From Earth to Moon). 80fr, Around the World in 80 Days. 100fr,

---

Rocket and moon (From Earth to Moon). 200fr, Octopus (20,000 Leagues Under the Sea).

1980, July 14   Litho.   Perf. 14
C422 A227 60fr multi   .50 .25
C423 A227 80fr multi   .65 .25
C424 A227 100fr multi   .80 .35
C425 A227 200fr multi   1.50 .65
  a. Souv. sheet of 2, #C424-C425,
      perf. 13½x14   2.50 1.25
    Nos. C422-C425 (4)   3.45 1.45

Ingres Type

Ingres Paintings: 90fr, Jupiter and Thetis. 100fr, Countess d'Haussonville. 200fr, "Tu Marcellus Eris."

1980, Aug. 29   Litho.   Perf. 14
C426 A228 90fr multi   .80 .30
C427 A228 100fr multi   .85 .35
C428 A228 200fr multi   1.60 .65
  a. Souv. sheet of 2, #C427-C428   3.00 1.25
    Nos. C426-C428 (3)   3.25 1.30

Famous Men Type

90fr, Salvador Allende, vert. 100fr, Pope Paul VI, vert. 200fr, Jomo Kenyatta, vert.

1980, Feb. 11   Litho.   Perf. 14x13
C429 A231 90fr ultra & lt bl grn   1.00 .30
C430 A231 100fr pur & pink   1.10 .35
C431 A231 200fr brn & yel bis   2.00 .65
  a. Souv. sheet of 2, #C430-C431   3.25 1.25
    Nos. C429-C431 (3)   4.10 1.30

Human Rights Type

1980, Oct. 13   Perf. 13x14
C432 A233 60fr Map of Ameri-
            cas   .40 .25
C433 A233 150fr Map of Africa   1.00 .50
  a. Souv. sheet of 2, #C432-C433   1.75 1.25

American Order of Rosicrucians Emblem — AP22

1980, Nov. 17   Litho.   Perf. 13
C434 AP22 60fr multi   .60 .25

General Conclave of the American Order of Rosicrucians, meeting of French-speaking countries, Lome, Aug.

Christmas Type

Designs: 100fr, Cologne Cathedral, Germany, 13th cent. 150fr, Notre Dame, Paris, 12th cent. 200fr, Canterbury Cathedral, England, 11th cent.

1980, Dec. 22   Perf. 14½x13½
C435 A234 100fr multi   .70 .35
C436 A234 150fr multi   1.10 .50
C437 A234 200fr multi   1.40 .65
  a. Souv. sheet of 2, #C436-C437   3.00 1.40
    Nos. C435-C437 (3)   3.20 1.50

Hotel Type of 1981

1981, Feb. 2   Litho.   Perf. 12½x13
C437B A236 60fr multi   .60 .25

Easter Type of 1981

Rembrandt Paintings: 100fr, Artist's Mother. 200fr, Man in a Ruff.

1981, Apr. 13   Litho.   Perf. 14½x13½
C438 A237 100fr multi   .90 .40
C439 A237 200fr multi   1.75 .70
  a. Souv. sheet of 2, #C438-C439   3.50 1.50

Market Type

1981, Mar. 8   Litho.   Perf. 14
C440 A230 90fr Fabric dealer   .60 .30
C441 A230 100fr Bananas   .65 .35
C442 A230 200fr Clay pottery   1.40 .65
C443 A230 250fr Setting up   1.60 .90
C444 A230 500fr Selling   3.50 1.60
C445 A230 1000fr Measuring
            grain   6.50 3.50
    Nos. C440-C445 (6)   14.25 7.20

For overprints see Nos. C486-C487.

Bird Type

Perf. 13½x14½

1981, Aug. 10   Litho.
C446 A238 50fr Violet-backed
           sunbird   .80 .25
C447 A238 100fr Red bishop   1.50 .35
  a. Souv. sheet, #C446-C447   5.50 2.50

IYD Type

1981, Aug. 31   Perf. 14
C448 A240 90fr Carpenter   .85 .40
C449 A240 200fr Basketball
            players   1.75 .85

Souvenir Sheet

C449A A240 300fr Weaver   2.75 1.60

Picasso Type

1981, Sept. 14   Perf. 14½x13½
C450 A241 90fr Violin and Bot-
          tle on Table,
          1916   1.10 .40
C451 A241 100fr Baboon and
          Young   1.10 .50
C452 A241 200fr Mandolin and
          Clarinet, 1914 2.50 .90
  a. Souv. sheet of 2, #C451-C452   4.25 1.75
    Nos. C450-C452 (3)   4.70 1.80

World Heritage Year Type

1981, Sept. 28   Perf. 13½x14½
C453 A242 100fr Cracow Muse-
          um, Poland   .85 .40
C454 A242 200fr Goree Isld., Se-
          negal   1.75 .85
  a. Souv. sheet of 2, #C453-C454   2.75 1.50

Space Type

1981, Nov.   Perf. 14
C455 A243 90fr multi   .85 .45
C456 A243 100fr multi   .90 .50

Souvenir Sheet

Perf. 13x14

C456A A243 300fr multi, vert.   2.25 1.25

10th anniv. of Soyuz 10 (90fr) and Apollo 14 (100fr).

Christmas Type

Rubens Paintings: 100fr, Adoration of the Kings. 200fr, Virgin and Child. 300fr, Virgin giving Chasuble to St. Idefonse.

Perf. 14½x13½

1981, Dec. 10   Litho.
C457 A244 100fr multi   .70 .35
C458 A244 200fr multi   1.50 .65
C459 A244 300fr multi   2.10 1.00
  a. Souv. sheet of 2, #C458-C459   4.00 1.90
    Nos. C457-C459 (3)   4.30 2.00

West African Rice Development Assoc. Type

1981, Dec. 21   Litho.   Perf. 12½
C461 A236a 105fr yel & multi   .70 .35

Liberation Type

Designs: 105fr, Citizens holding hands, Pres. Eyadema, vert. 130fr, Hotel.

1982, Jan. 13   Litho.   Perf. 12½
C462 A245 105fr multi   .70 .35
C463 A245 130fr multi   .90 .40

Scouting Year Type

1982, Feb. 25   Litho.   Perf. 14
C464 A246 90fr Semaphore   .75 .30
C465 A246 120fr Tower   1.00 .40
C466 A246 130fr Scouts, canoe   1.10 .40
C467 A246 135fr Scouts, tent   1.10 .45
    Nos. C464-C467 (4)   3.95 1.55

Souvenir Sheet

Perf. 13x14

C468 A246 500fr Baden-Powell   4.25 1.60

Easter Type

1982, Apr.   Perf. 14x14½
C469 A247 105fr multi   .70 .35
C470 A247 120fr multi   .80 .40

Souvenir Sheet

C471 A247 500fr multi   4.00 1.60

PHILEXFRANCE '82 Intl. Stamp Exhibition, Paris, June 11-21 — AP23

1982   **Litho.**   *Perf. 13*
C472 AP23 90fr shown .70 .30
C473 AP23 105fr ROMOLYMPHIL
'82, vert. .90 .35

Issue dates: 90fr, June 11; 105fr, May 19.

Butterfly Type
1982, July 15   *Perf. 14½x14*
C474 A248 90fr Euxanthe eurio-
nome 1.90 .40
C475 A248 105fr Mylothris rhodo-
pe 2.10 .45

Souvenir Sheet
C476 A248 500fr Papilio zalmoxis 4.25 1.60

World Cup Type
1982, July 26   *Perf. 14x14½*
C477 A249 105fr multi .80 .35
C478 A249 200fr multi 1.40 .65
C479 A249 300fr multi 2.10 1.00
Nos. C477-C479 (3) 4.30 2.00

Souvenir Sheet
C480 A249 500fr multi 4.00 1.65

For overprints see Nos. 1152-1155.

Pre-Olympics,
1984 Los
Angeles — AP24

1983, Oct. 3   **Photo.**   *Perf. 12½*
C481 AP24 70fr Boxing .55 .25
C482 AP24 90fr Hurdles .70 .25
C483 AP24 105fr Pole vault .80 .25
C484 AP24 130fr Runner .90 .25
Nos. C481-C484 (4) 2.95 1.00

Souvenir Sheet
C485 AP24 500fr Runner, diff. 4.00 1.50

Nos. C443-C444 Overprinted: "19E
CONGRES UPU HAMBOURG 1984"

1984, June   **Litho.**   *Perf. 14*
C486 A230 250fr multi 1.75 1.00
C487 A230 500fr multi 3.75 2.00

1984 Summer Olympics — AP25

1984, July 27   *Perf. 13*
C488 AP25 70fr Pole vault .45 .25
C489 AP25 90fr Bicycling .45 .25
C490 AP25 120fr Soccer .75 .25
C491 AP25 250fr Boxing 1.50 .40
C492 AP25 400fr Running 2.25 .65
Nos. C488-C492 (5) 5.40 1.80

Souvenir Sheet
C493 AP25 1000fr like 120fr,
without flag 7.50 6.50

Nos. C488-C490, C493 vert.

Olympic
Champions
AP26

1984, Nov. 15   **Litho.**   *Perf. 15*
C494 AP26 500fr Jim Thorpe,
US 7.25 3.25
C495 AP26 500fr Jesse
Owens, US 7.25 3.25
C496 AP26 500fr Muhammad
Ali, US 40.00 3.25
C497 AP26 500fr Bob Bea-
mon, US 7.25 3.25
Nos. C494-C497 (4) 61.75 13.00

Souvenir Sheets
C498 AP26 500fr Bill Stein-
kraus, US 7.25 3.25
C499 AP26 500fr New Zealand
rowing team 7.25 3.25
C500 AP26 500fr Pakistani
hockey
team 7.25 3.25
C501 AP26 500fr Yukio Endo,
Japan 7.25 3.25

West German Olympians
1984, Nov. 15
C502 AP26 500fr Dietmar
Mogenburg 7.25 3.25
C503 AP26 500fr Fredy
Schmidtke 7.25 3.25
C504 AP26 500fr Matthias
Behr 7.25 3.25
C505 AP26 500fr Sabine
Everts 7.25 3.25
Nos. C502-C505 (4) 29.00 13.00

Souvenir Sheets
C506 AP26 500fr Karl-Heinz
Radschin-
sky 7.25 3.25
C507 AP26 500fr Pasquale
Passarelli 7.25 3.25
C508 AP26 500fr Michale
Gross 7.25 3.25
C509 AP26 500fr Jurgen Hing-
sen 7.25 3.25

For overprints see Nos. C521-C536, C563.

Peace and
Human
Rights — AP28

230fr, Map of Togo, globe, doves. 270fr,
Palm tree, emblem. 500fr, Opencast mining
operation. 1000fr, Human Rights Monument,
UN, NYC.

1985, Jan. 14   **Litho.**   *Perf. 13½x14*
C510 AP28 230fr multi 1.50 .25
C511 AP28 270fr multi 1.90 .30
C512 AP28 500fr multi 3.50 .50
C513 AP28 1000fr multi 7.00 1.00
Nos. C510-C513 (4) 13.90 2.05

Tribal
Dances
AP29

1985, July   *Perf. 15x14*
C514 AP29 120fr Adifo, Adangbe .85 .25
C515 AP29 135fr Fouet (whip),
Kente .85 .25
C516 AP29 290fr Idjombi,
Pagouda 2.00 .30
C517 AP29 500fr Moba,
Dapaong 3.50 .50
Nos. C514-C517 (4) 7.20 1.30

Visit of Pope John Paul II — AP30

90fr, The Pope outside Lome Cathedral.
130fr, Blessing crowd in St. Peter's Square.
500fr, Greeting Pres. Eyadema.

1985, Aug. 9   *Perf. 13*
C518 AP30 90fr multi .75 .25
C519 AP30 130fr multi, vert. 1.25 .25
C520 AP30 500fr multi 3.50 .50
Nos. C518-C520 (3) 5.50 1.00

Nos. C495, C497, C499, C502, C505-
508 Overprinted with Winners Names,
Country and Type of Olympic Medal

1985, Aug.   *Perf. 15*
C521 AP26 500fr Kirk Baptiste,
US 6.50 1.50
C522 AP26 500fr Carl Lewis,
US 6.50 1.50
C523 AP26 500fr Patrik
Sjoberg,
Sweden 6.50 1.50
C524 AP26 500fr Glynis Nunn,
Australia 6.50 1.50
Nos. C521-C524 (4) 26.00 6.00

Souvenir Sheets
C525 AP26 500fr Rowing
eights, Ca-
nada 3.50 3.00
C526 AP26 500fr Rolf Milser,
W. Germa-
ny 3.50 3.00
C527 AP26 500fr Takashi Irie,
Japan 3.50 3.00
C528 AP26 500fr Frederic
Delcourt,
France 3.50 3.00

Nos. C494, C496, C503-C504, C498,
C500, C501, C509 Ovptd. with
Winners Names, Country and Type of
Olympic Medal

1985, Sept. 19   **Litho.**   *Perf. 15*
C529 AP26 500fr Italy 6.50 1.50
C530 AP26 500fr Kevin Barry 6.50 1.50
C531 AP26 500fr Rolf Golz 6.50 1.50
C532 AP26 500fr Philippe
Boisse 6.50 1.50
Nos. C529-C532 (4) 26.00 6.00

Souvenir Sheets
C533 AP26 500fr Karen Stives 3.50 3.00
C534 AP26 500fr R.F.A. (West
Germany) 3.50 3.00
C535 AP26 500fr Koji
Gushiken 3.50 3.00
C536 AP26 500fr Daley
Thompson 3.50 3.00

Traditional Instruments — AP31

Youth and Development — AP32

Designs: No. C537, Xylophone, Kante horn,
tambour. No. C538, Bongo drums, castanets,
bassar horn. No. C539, Communications. No.
C540, Agriculture and industry.

1985   **Litho.**   *Perf. 13*
C537 AP31 100fr multi .90 .60
C538 AP31 100fr multi .90 .60
    a. Pair, #C537-C538 3.00 3.00
C539 AP32 200fr multi 1.75 1.25
C540 AP32 200fr multi 1.75 1.25
    a. Pair, #C539-C540 7.50 7.50
Nos. C537-C540 (4) 5.30 3.70

PHILEXAFRICA '85, Lome, Togo, 11/16-24.
Issued: 100fr, Nov. 4; 200fr, Nov. 16.

No. 1274 Ovptd. with Organization
Emblem and "80e Anniversaire du
Rotary International."

1985, Nov. 15   **Litho.**   *Perf. 15*
Souvenir Sheet
C541 A267 1000fr multi 20.00 6.50

Nos. 1254-1255, 1258 Ovptd. "10e
ANNIVERSAIRE DE APOLLO-
SOYUZ" in 1 or 2 lines

1985, Dec. 27   **Litho.**   *Perf. 15*
C542 A265 90fr multi 1.25 .40
C543 A265 500fr multi 6.75 2.00

Souvenir Sheet
C544 A265 1000fr multi 8.50 2.90

Nos. 1294-1295, 1297 Ovptd. "75e
ANNIVERSAIRE DE LA MORT DE
HENRI DUNANT FONDATEUR DE LA
CROIX ROUGE" in 2 or 4 lines

1985, Dec. 27
C545 A270 400fr multi 4.75 1.50
C546 A270 500fr multi 6.25 2.00

Souvenir Sheet
C547 A270 1000fr multi 7.50 6.00

Statue of Liberty,
Cent. — AP33

1986, Apr. 10   *Perf. 13*
C548 AP33 70fr Eiffel Tower .55 .25
C549 AP33 90fr Statue of Liber-
ty .65 .25
C550 AP33 500fr Empire State
Building 3.75 1.40
Nos. C548-C550 (3) 4.95 1.90

Nos. 1237-1240 Ovptd. with
AMERIPEX '86 Emblem

1986, May 22   *Perf. 11*
C551 A262 500fr multi 6.50 1.40
C552 A262 1000fr multi 12.50 2.75

Souvenir Sheets
Perf. 14
C553 A262 1000fr No. 1239 8.50 3.50
C554 A262 1000fr No. 1240 8.50 3.50

Air Africa,
25th Anniv.
AP34

1986, Dec. 29   **Litho.**   *Perf. 12½x13*
C555 AP34 90fr multi .75 .25

Konrad Adenauer (1876-1967) West
German Chancellor — AP35

1987, July 15   **Litho.**   *Perf. 12½x13*
C556 AP35 120fr At podium .90 .60
C557 AP35 500fr With Pres. Ken-
nedy, 1962 3.50 3.00

Souvenir Sheet
Perf. 13x12½
C558 AP35 500fr Portrait, vert. 3.50 3.00

Berlin,
750th
Anniv.
AP36

Designs: 90fr, Wilhelm I (1781-1864) coin,
Victory statue. 150fr, Frederick III (1831-1888)
coin, Brandenburg Gate. 300fr, Wilhelm II
(1882-1951) coin, Reichstag building. 750fr,
Otto Leopold von Bismarck (1815-1898), first
chancellor of the German empire, and Charlot-
tenburg Palace.

TOGO

1987, Aug. 31 **Litho.** *Perf. 13½*
C559 AP36 90fr multi .60 .30
C560 AP36 150fr multi 1.00 .50
C561 AP36 300fr multi 2.00 1.00
Nos. C559-C561 (3) 3.60 1.80

Souvenir Sheet
C562 AP36 750fr multi 5.50 4.25

Nos. C506, 1258, 1273 and 1274
Overprinted in Black for Philatelic
Exhibitions

a

b

c

d

Additional overprints appear on souvenir
sheets away from stamps.

1988, Apr. 25 **Litho.** *Perf. 15*
Souvenir Sheets
C563 AP26 (a) 500fr #C506 9.50 3.00
C564 A265 (b) 1000fr #1258 10.00 5.50
C565 A265 (c) 1000fr #1273 10.00 5.50
C566 A267 (d) 1000fr #1274 10.00 5.50
Nos. C563-C566 (4) 39.50 19.50

AIR POST SEMI-POSTAL STAMPS

Nursery — SPAP1

Perf. 13½x12½
1942, June 22 **Unwmk.** **Photo.**
CB1 SPAP1 1.50fr + 3.50fr green .65
CB2 SPAP1 2fr + 6fr brown .65

Native children's welfare fund.
Nos. CB1-CB2 were issued by the Vichy
government in France, but were not placed on
sale in Togo.

Colonial Education Fund
Common Design Type
1942, June 22 **Engr.**
CB3 CD86a 1.20fr + 1.80fr blue
& red .70

No. CB3 was issued by the Vichy government in France, but was not placed on sale in
Togo.

POSTAGE DUE STAMPS

Postage Due Stamps of
Dahomey, 1914
Overprinted

1921 **Unwmk.** *Perf. 14x13½*
J1 D2 5c green .70 .95
J2 D2 10c rose .70 1.00
J3 D2 15c gray 1.45 2.00
J4 D2 20c brown 2.60 2.75
J5 D2 30c blue 3.00 3.25
J6 D2 50c black 2.40 2.75
J7 D2 60c orange 2.40 2.75
J8 D2 1fr violet 4.50 5.25
Nos. J1-J8 (8) 17.75 20.70

Cotton
Field — D3

1925 **Typo.** **Unwmk.**
J9 D3 2c blue & blk .25 .40
J10 D3 4c dl red & blk .25 .40
J11 D3 5c ol grn & blk .25 .40
J12 D3 10c cerise & blk .30 .50
J13 D3 15c orange & blk .80 .95
J14 D3 20c red vio & blk .50 .65
J15 D3 25c gray & blk 1.05 1.20
J16 D3 30c ocher & blk .50 .65
J17 D3 50c brown & blk 1.10 1.20
J18 D3 60c green & blk 1.10 1.20
J19 D3 1fr dk vio & blk 1.10 1.30
Nos. J9-J19 (11) 7.20 8.85

Type of
1925 Issue
Surcharged

1927
J20 D3 2fr on 1fr rose red &
vio 6.50 7.25
J21 D3 3fr on 1fr org brn, blk
& ultra 6.50 7.25

Mask — D4

1941 **Engr.** *Perf. 13*
J22 D4 5c brown black .25 .30
J23 D4 10c yellow green .25 .30
J24 D4 15c carmine .25 .30
J25 D4 20c ultra .30 .40
J26 D4 30c chestnut .65 .70
J27 D4 50c olive green 1.60 1.75
J28 D4 60c violet .80 .95
J29 D4 1fr light blue 1.10 1.25
J30 D4 2fr orange vermilion 1.00 1.10
J31 D4 3fr rose violet 1.25 1.40
Nos. J22-J31 (10) 7.45 8.45

For type D4 without "RF," see Nos. J31A-
J31F.

Type of 1941 Without "RF"
1942-44
J31A D4 5c brown black .25
J31B D4 10c green & violet .30
J31C D4 15c car rose & brn .40
J31D D4 30c brown & black .65
J31E D4 2fr brn org & brn vio .80
J31F D4 3fr violet & green .80
Nos. J31A-J31F (6) 3.20

Nos. J31A-J31F were issued by the Vichy
government in France, but were not placed on
sale in Togo.

Catalogue values for unused
stamps in this section, from this
point to the end of the section, are
for Never Hinged items.

Carved Figures — D5

1947
J32 D5 10c brt ultra .30 .30
J33 D5 30c red .30 .30
J34 D5 50c dp yellow grn .30 .30
J35 D5 1fr chocolate .55 .55
J36 D5 2fr carmine .55 .55
J37 D5 3fr gray blk .55 .55
J38 D5 4fr ultra 1.05 .95
J39 D5 5fr sepia 1.25 1.10
J40 D5 10fr dp orange 1.30 1.25
J41 D5 20fr dk blue vio 1.90 1.50
Nos. J32-J41 (10) 8.05 7.35

Republic

Konkomba Helmet
D6 D7

1957 **Engr.** *Perf. 14x13*
J42 D6 1fr brt violet .25 .25
J43 D6 2fr brt orange .25 .25
J44 D6 3fr dk gray .25 .25
J45 D6 4fr brt red .25 .25
J46 D6 5fr ultra .25 .25
J47 D6 10fr dp green .35 .35
J48 D6 20fr dp claret .50 .50
Nos. J42-J48 (7) 2.10 2.10

1959 *Perf. 14x13*
J49 D7 1fr orange brn .25 .35
J50 D7 2fr lt blue grn .25 .35
J51 D7 3fr orange .25 .35
J52 D7 4fr blue .25 .45
J53 D7 5fr lilac rose .25 .45
J54 D7 10fr violet blue .45 .65
J55 D7 20fr black .80 .85
Nos. J49-J55 (7) 2.50 3.45

Type of Regular Issue
Shells: 1fr, Conus papilionaceus. 2fr,
Marginella faba. 3fr, Cypraea stercoraria. 4fr,
Strombus latus. 5fr, Costate cockle (sea shell).
10fr, Cancellaria cancellata. 15fr, Cymbium
pepo. 20fr, Tympanotomus radula.

1964-65 **Unwmk.** **Photo.** *Perf. 14*
Size: 20x25½mm
J56 A47 1fr gray grn & red brn
('65) .40 .25
J57 A47 2fr tan & ol grn ('65) .40 .25
J58 A47 3fr gray, brn & yel ('65) .40 .25
J59 A47 4fr tan & multi ('65) .40 .25
J60 A47 5fr sep, org & grn .60 .30
J61 A47 10fr sl bl, brn & bis .80 .40
J62 A47 15fr grn & brn 1.90 1.00
J63 A47 20fr sl, dk brn & yel 2.40 1.25
Nos. J56-J63 (8) 7.30 3.95

Tomatoes — D8

1969-70 **Litho.** *Perf. 14*
J64 D8 5fr yellow & multi .45 .25
J65 D8 10fr blue & multi .45 .25
J66 D8 15fr multi ('70) .65 .30
J67 D8 20fr multi ('70) .90 .40
Nos. J64-J67 (4) 2.45 1.20

Market Type
1981, Mar. 8 **Litho.** *Perf. 14*
Size: 23x32mm, 32x23mm
J68 A230 5fr Millet, vert. .25 .25
J69 A230 10fr Packaged goods .25 .25
J70 A230 25fr Chickens .25 .25
J71 A230 50fr Ivory vendor .30 .25
Nos. J68-J71 (4) 1.05 1.00

OFFICIAL STAMPS

Catalogue values for unused
stamps in this section are for
never hinged items.

O1

1991? **Litho.** *Perf. 13½*
O1 O1 15fr multicolored .20 —
O2 O1 100fr multicolored .35 —
O3 O1 125fr multicolored .40 —
O4 O1 500fr multicolored 1.40 —

1991?
O5 O1 10fr multicolored — —
O6 O1 90fr yellow & multi .30

1991?
O7 O1 180fr ap grn & multi .50

1991
O8 O1 50fr yellow & multi .25 .25
O9 O1 300fr grn & multi 1.00 1.00

The editors would like information on dates
of issue and stamps of other denominations.
The catalogue numbers will change.

TOKELAU
'tō-kə-ˌlau

(Union Islands)

LOCATION — Pacific Ocean 300 miles
north of Apia, Western Samoa
GOVT. — A dependency of New
Zealand
AREA — 4 sq. mi.
POP. — 1,487 (1996)

The Tokelau islands consist of three
atolls: Atafu, Nukunono and Fakaofo,
which span 100 miles of ocean.

12 Pence = 1 Shilling
100 Cents = 1 Dollar (1967)

Catalogue values for all unused
stamps in this country are for
Never Hinged items.

Map and
Scene on
Atafu — A1

Nukunono
Dwelling
and
Map — A2

Fakaofo
Shore Line
and
Map — A3

Perf. 13½x13
1948, June 22 **Wmk. 253** **Engr.**
1 A1 ½p red brown & rose lilac .25 .45
2 A2 1p dp green & orange brn .25 .35
3 A3 2p deep ultra & green .30 .35
Nos. 1-3 (3) .80 1.15

For surcharges see Nos. 5, 9-11.

Coronation Issue

Queen Elizabeth II — A3a

1953, May 25   Photo.   Perf. 14x14½
4   A3a 3p brown   4.00 2.75

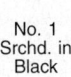

No. 1 Srchd. in Black

Perf. 13½x13
1956, Mar. 27   Engr.   Wmk. 253
5   A1 1sh on ½p   4.25 4.25

Postal-Fiscal Type of New Zealand, 1950, Surcharged

Wmk. 253
1966, Nov.   Typo.   Perf. 14
6   A109 6p light blue   2.00 1.25
7   A109 8p light green   2.50 1.50
8   A109 2sh pink   3.00 2.00
     Nos. 6-8 (3)   7.50 4.75

Nos. 1-3 Surcharged with New Value and Dots Obliterating Old Denomination

1967, July 10   Engr.   Perf. 13½x13
9   A2 1c on 1p   .60   .60
10   A3 2c on 2p   1.40 1.40
11   A1 10c on ½p   4.75 4.75
     Nos. 9-11 (3)   6.75 6.75

The 1c and 2c surcharges include two dots, the 10c surcharge has only one.

Postal Fiscal Type of New Zealand, 1950, Surcharged

1967, July 10   Typo.   Perf. 14
12   A109 3c light lilac   .35   .35
13   A109 5c light blue   .70   .70
14   A109 7c light green   1.10 1.10
15   A109 20c pink   2.50 2.50
     Nos. 12-15 (4)   4.65 4.65

1877, British Protectorate — A4

History of Tokelau: 10c, 1916, part of Gilbert and Ellice Islands Colony. 15c, 1925, administration transferred to New Zealand. 20c, 1948, New Zealand Territory.

Perf. 13x12½
1969, Aug. 8   Litho.   Wmk. 253
16   A4 5c ultra, yellow & blk   1.10   .45
17   A4 10c rose red, yel & blk   1.25   .85
18   A4 15c dull grn, yel & blk   1.40 1.40
19   A4 20c brown, yel & blk   1.75 1.75
     Nos. 16-19 (4)   5.50 4.45

Nativity, by Federico Fiori — A4a

Adoration, by Correggio — A4b

1969, Oct. 1   Photo.   Perf. 13½x14
20   A4a 2c multicolored   .40   .40
     Christmas.

Perf. 12½
1970, Oct. 1   Unwmk.   Litho.
21   A4b 2c multicolored   .40   .40
     Christmas.

"Dolphin," 1765, Map of Atafu — A5   Fan — A6

Designs: 10c, "Pandora," 1791, and map of Nukunono. 25c, "General Jackson," 1835, and map of Fakaofo, horiz.

1970, Dec. 9   Unwmk.   Perf. 13½
22   A5 5c yellow & multi   1.25   .90
23   A5 10c multicolored   2.75 1.60
24   A5 25c pink & multi   6.00 4.75
     Nos. 22-24 (3)   10.00 7.25

Discovery of Tokelau Islands.

1971, Oct. 20   Litho.   Perf. 14
Native Handicrafts: 2c, Round vessel. 3c, Hexagonal box. 5c, Shoulder bag. 10c, Handbag. 15c, Jewelry box with beads. 20c, Outrigger canoe model. 25c, Fish hooks.
25   A6 1c olive & multi   .25   .25
26   A6 2c red & multi   .30   .25
27   A6 3c dk violet & multi .45   .25
28   A6 5c dull blue & multi .50   .25
29   A6 10c dp orange & multi .60   .30
30   A6 15c emerald & multi   .85   .55
31   A6 20c multicolored   1.10   .70
32   A6 25c violet blue & multi 1.25 .90
     Nos. 25-32 (8)   5.30 3.45

Windmill Pump, Map of Atafu — A7   Horny Coral — A8

South Pacific Commission Emblem and: 10c, Community well, map of Fakaofo. 15c, Eradication of rhinoceros beetle, map of Nukunono. 20c, members.

1972, Sept. 6   Litho.   Perf. 14x13½
33   A7 5c lt blue grn & multi   .75   .25
34   A7 10c grnsh blue & multi   .95   .45
35   A7 15c lilac & multi   1.10   .60
36   A7 20c violet bl & multi   1.50   .95
     Nos. 33-36 (4)   4.30 2.25

South Pacific Commission, 25th anniversary. On 15c, "PACIFIC" reads "PACFIC."

1973, Sept. 12   Litho.   Perf. 13x13½
37   A8 3c shown   1.40 1.10
38   A8 5c Soft coral   1.40 1.25
39   A8 15c Mushroom coral 2.25 2.10
40   A8 25c Staghorn coral 2.75 2.50
     Nos. 37-40 (4)   7.80 6.95

Cowrie (Cypraea Mauritiana) A9

Cowrie shells: 5c, Cypraea tigris. 15c, Cypraea talpa. 25c, Cypraea argus.

1974, Nov. 13   Litho.   Perf. 14
41   A9 3c apple grn & multi   1.50 1.10
42   A9 5c dk blue & multi   1.75 1.10
43   A9 15c blue & multi   2.50 2.25
44   A9 25c green & multi   2.75 2.50
     Nos. 41-44 (4)   8.50 6.95

Moorish Idol — A10

Fish: 10c, Long-nosed butterflyfish. 15c, Lined butterflyfish. 25c, Red firefish.

1975, Nov. 19   Litho.   Perf. 14
45   A10 5c blue & multi   .70   .30
46   A10 10c brown & multi   1.25   .65
47   A10 15c lilac & multi   1.90 1.10
48   A10 25c multicolored   3.25 2.10
     Nos. 45-48 (4)   7.10 4.15

Canoe Making A11

Designs: 2c, Reef fishing. 3c, Woman preparing pandanus leaves for weaving. 5c, Communal kitchen (umu). 9c, Wood carving. 20c, Husking coconuts. 50c, Wash day. $1, Meal time. 9c, 20c, 50c, $1, vertical.

1976, Oct. 27   Litho.   Perf. 14
49   A11 1c pink & multi   .55 1.10
50   A11 2c multicolored   .40 1.40
51   A11 3c lt blue & multi   .35   .70
52   A11 5c yellow & multi   .40   .70
53   A11 9c bister & multi   .25   .85
54   A11 20c multicolored   .25   .70
55   A11 50c tan & multi   .35   .85
56   A11 $1 multicolored   .70 2.10
     Nos. 49-56 (8)   3.25 8.40

1981, July 17   Perf. 15
49a A11 1c   .50   .65
51a A11 3c   .50   .65
52a A11 5c   .50   .65
53a A11 9c   .90 1.00
54a A11 20c   .90 1.00
55a A11 50c   1.75 2.00
56a A11 $1   5.00 5.00
     Nos. 49a-56a (7)   10.05 10.95

White Tern — A12

Birds of Tokelau: 10c, Turnstone. 15c, White-capped noddy. 30c, Brown noddy.

1977, Nov. 16   Litho.   Perf. 14½x15
57   A12 8c multicolored   .50   .35
58   A12 10c multicolored   .65   .40
59   A12 15c multicolored   .80   .65
60   A12 30c multicolored   1.75 1.40
     Nos. 57-60 (4)   3.70 2.80

Westminster Abbey — A13

10c, King Edward's Chair. 15c, Scepter, Crown, Orb, Bible and Staff of State. 30c, Elizabeth II.

1978, June 28   Litho.   Perf. 14
61   A13 8c multicolored   .25   .25
62   A13 10c multicolored   .35   .35
63   A13 15c multicolored   .55   .55
64   A13 30c multicolored   1.00 1.00
     Nos. 61-64 (4)   2.15 2.15

25th anniv. of coronation of Elizabeth II.

Canoe Racing A14

Designs: Various canoe races.

1978, Nov. 8   Litho.   Perf. 13½x14
65   A14 8c multicolored   .40   .40
66   A14 12c multicolored   .55   .55
67   A14 15c multicolored   .65   .65
68   A14 30c multicolored   1.10 1.10
     Nos. 65-68 (4)   2.70 2.70

1979, Nov. 7   Photo.   Perf. 14
69   A14 10c Rugby   .35   .35
70   A14 15c Cricket   .70   .70
71   A14 20c Rugby, diff.   .70   .70
72   A14 30c Cricket, diff. .85   .85
     Nos. 69-72 (4)   2.60 2.60

1980, Nov. 5   Litho.   Perf. 13½
73   A14 10c Surfing   .25   .25
74   A14 20c Surfing, diff. .30   .25
75   A14 30c Swimming   .45   .45
76   A14 50c Swimming, diff. .60   .55
     Nos. 73-76 (4)   1.60 1.45

1981, Nov. 4   Photo.   Perf. 14
77   A14 10c Pole vaulting, vert.   .35   .35
78   A14 20c Volleyball, vert.   .40   .35
79   A14 30c Running, vert.   .50   .40
80   A14 50c Volleyball, vert., diff. .60   .60
     Nos. 77-80 (4)   1.85 1.70

Wood Carving — A15   Octopus Lure Fishing — A16

1982, May 5   Litho.   Perf. 13½x13
81   A15 10s shown   .35   .35
82   A15 22s Bow-drilling sea shells   .35   .35
83   A15 34s Bowl finishing .50   .50
84   A15 60s Basket weaving 1.00 1.00
     Nos. 81-84 (4)   2.20 2.20

1982, Nov. 3   Litho.   Perf. 14
Designs: Fishing Methods.
85   A16 5s shown   .25   .25
86   A16 18s Multiple-hook   .25   .25
87   A16 23s Ruvettus   .25   .25
88   A16 34s Netting flying fish .40   .40
89   A16 63s Noose   .70   .70
90   A16 75s Bonito   .85   .85
     Nos. 85-90 (6)   2.70 2.70

Outrigger Canoe A17

1983, May 4   Litho.
91	A17	5s shown	.25	.25
92	A17	18s Whale boat	.25	.25
93	A17	23s Aluminium whale boat	.25	.25
94	A17	34s Alia fishing boat	.30	.30
95	A17	63s Cargo ship	.65	.65
96	A17	75s Seaplane	.90	.90
		Nos. 91-96 (6)	2.60	2.60

Traditional Games A18

1983, Nov. 2   Litho.   Perf. 14
97	A18	5s Javelin throwing	.25	.25
98	A18	18s Tifaga string game	.25	.25
99	A18	23s Fire making	.25	.25
100	A18	34s Shell throwing	.30	.30
101	A18	63s Handball	.65	.65
102	A18	75s Mass wrestling	.90	.90
		Nos. 97-102 (6)	2.60	2.60

Planting, Harvesting Copra — A19

Copra Industry: b, Husking, splitting. c, Drying, cutting. d, Bagging, weighing. e, Shipping. Continuous design.

1984, May 2   Litho.   Perf. 13½x13
103	Strip of 5	3.00	3.00
a.-e.	A19 48s any single	.45	.45

Local Fish — A20

1984, Dec. 5   Litho.   Perf. 14½x14
104	A20	1c Manini	.30	.30
105	A20	2c Hahave	.30	.30
106	A20	5c Uloulo	.30	.30
107	A20	9c Ume Ihu	.30	.30
108	A20	23c Lifilafi	.40	.40
109	A20	34c Fagamea	.55	.55
110	A20	50c Kakahi	.70	.70
111	A20	75c Palu Po	1.25	1.25
112	A20	$1 Mokoha	1.60	1.60
113	A20	$2 Hakula	2.75	2.75
		Nos. 104-113 (10)	8.45	8.45

Trees, Fruits and Herbs — A21

1985, June 26   Litho.   Perf. 13½
114	A21	5c Mati	.25	.25
115	A21	18c Nonu	.25	.25
116	A21	32c Ulu	.45	.45
117	A21	48c Fala	.65	.65
118	A21	60c Kanava	.85	.85
119	A21	75c Niu	1.00	1.00
		Nos. 114-119 (6)	3.45	3.45

Public Buildings and Churches A22

Designs: 5c, Administration Center, Atafu. 18c, Administration Center, Nukunonu. 32c, Administration Center, Fakaofo. 48c, Congregational Church, Atafu. 60c, Catholic Church, Nukunonu. 75c, Congregational Church, Fakaofo.

1985, Dec. 4
120	A22	5c multicolored	.25	.25
121	A22	18c multicolored	.25	.25
122	A22	32c multicolored	.45	.45
123	A22	48c multicolored	.65	.65
124	A22	60c multicolored	.85	.85
125	A22	75c multicolored	1.00	1.00
		Nos. 120-125 (6)	3.45	3.45

Hospitals and Schools A23

Designs: 5c, Atafu Hospital. 18c, St. Joseph's Hospital, Fakaofo. 32c, Fenuafala Hospital, Fakaofo. 48c, Matauala School, Atafu. 60c, Matiti School, Nukunonu. 75c, Fenuafala School, Fakaofo.

1986, May 7   Perf. 13½
126	A23	5c multicolored	.25	.25
127	A23	18c multicolored	.25	.25
128	A23	32c multicolored	.45	.45
129	A23	48c multicolored	.65	.65
130	A23	60c multicolored	.85	.85
131	A23	75c multicolored	1.00	1.00
		Nos. 126-131 (6)	3.45	3.45

Fauna A24

1986, Dec. 3   Litho.   Perf. 14
132	A24	5c Coconut crab	.25	.25
133	A24	18c Pigs	.25	.25
134	A24	32c Chickens	.50	.50
135	A24	48c Turtles	.75	.75
136	A24	60c Goats	.90	.90
137	A24	75c Ducks	1.10	1.10
		Nos. 132-137 (6)	3.75	3.75

Flora A25

1987, May 6
138	A25	5c Gahu	.60	.60
139	A25	18c Puka	.85	.85
140	A25	32c Higano	1.10	1.10
141	A25	48c Tialetiale	1.50	1.50
142	A25	60c Gagie	1.75	1.75
143	A25	75c Puapua	1.90	1.90
		Nos. 138-143 (6)	7.70	7.70

Olympic Sports A26

1987, Dec. 2   Litho.   Perf. 14x14½
144	A26	5c Javelin	.40	.40
145	A26	18c Shot put	.70	.70
146	A26	32c Long jump	.90	.90
147	A26	48c Hurdles	1.00	1.00
148	A26	60c Running	1.25	1.25
149	A26	75c Wrestling	1.75	1.75
		Nos. 144-149 (6)	6.00	6.00

Australia Bicentennial, SYDPEX '88 — A27

Re-enactment of the arrival of the First Fleet in Sydney Harbor, Jan. 26, 1988 (in a continuous design): a, Ships in harbor, building (LL). b, Ships in harbor, tall ship (LR). c, Ships in harbor, Sydney Opera House. d, Bridge. e, North Sydney.

1988, July 30   Litho.   Perf. 13½x13
150	Strip of 5	14.00	14.00
a.-e.	A27 50c any single	2.40	2.40

Political Development A28

Designs: 5c, Transfer of administration from the New Zealand Department of Maori and Island Affairs to the Ministry of Foreign Affairs, 1975. 18c, The General Fono empowered as the decision-making body of Tokelau, 1977. 32c, 1st Visit of New Zealand's prime minister, 1985. 48c, 1st Visit of UN representatives, 1976. 60c, 1st Tokelau delegation to go to the UN, 1987. 75c, 1st Tokelau appointed to the office of Official Secretary, 1987.

1988, Aug. 10   Perf. 14½
151	A28	5c multicolored	.25	.25
152	A28	18c multicolored	.40	.40
153	A28	32c multicolored	.85	.85
154	A28	48c multicolored	1.25	1.25
155	A28	60c multicolored	1.50	1.50
156	A28	75c multicolored	2.00	2.00
		Nos. 151-156 (6)	6.25	6.25

Island Christmas A29

Designs: 5c, Three Wise Men *(Na Makoi)*. 20c, Holy family *(He Tala)*. 40c, Escape into Egypt *(Fakagagalo ki Aikupito)*. 60c, Christmas presents *(Meaalofa Kilihimahi)*. 70c, Christ child *(Pepe ko Iesu)*. $1, Christmas parade *(Holo Tamilo)*.

1988, Dec. 7   Litho.   Perf. 13½
157	A29	5c multicolored	.30	.30
158	A29	20c multicolored	.30	.30
159	A29	40c multicolored	.70	.70
160	A29	60c multicolored	1.10	1.10
161	A29	70c multicolored	1.25	1.25
162	A29	$1 multicolored	1.75	1.75
		Nos. 157-162 (6)	5.40	5.40

Food Gathering A30

Fishing and gathering coconuts. Printed setenant in continuous designs.
No. 163: a, Launching outrigger canoe. b, Outrigger canoe and sailboat starboard side. c, Outrigger canoe and sailboat stern.
No. 164: a, Outrigger and sailboat port side. b, Islander carrying baskets of coconuts. c, Gathering coconuts from palm trees.

1989, June 28   Litho.   Perf. 14x14½
163	Strip of 3	5.25	5.25
a.-c.	A30 50c any single	1.60	1.60
164	Strip of 3	5.25	5.25
a.-c.	A30 50c any single	1.60	1.60

Women's Work and Leisure — A31

1990, May 2   Litho.   Perf. 14½
165	A31	5c Weavers	.85	.65
166	A31	20c Washing clothes	1.25	1.25
167	A31	40c Resting among palm trees	2.10	1.75
168	A31	60c Weaving mat	2.50	2.75
169	A31	80c Weaving, diff.	3.50	3.75
170	A31	$1 Basket weaver	3.75	4.00
		Nos. 165-170 (6)	13.95	14.15

Souvenir Sheet

Penny Black, 150th Anniv. — A32

1990, May 3   Litho.   Perf. 11½
171	A32	$3 multicolored	20.00	20.00

Men's Handicrafts — A33

1990, Aug. 1   Photo.   Perf. 13
172	A33	50c shown	1.75	1.50
173	A33	50c Carving pots	1.75	1.50
174	A33	50c Tying rope on pot	1.75	1.50
a.		Strip of 3, #172-174	6.75	6.75
175	A33	50c Finishing pots	1.75	1.50
176	A33	50c Shaping a canoe	1.75	1.50
177	A33	50c Three men working	1.75	1.50
a.		Strip of 3, #175-177	6.75	6.75

1992 Summer Olympics, Barcelona — A34

1992, July 8   Litho.   Perf. 13½
178	A34	40c Swimming	1.00	1.00
179	A34	60c Long jump	1.50	1.50
180	A34	$1 Volleyball	3.25	3.25
181	A34	$1.80 Running	4.25	4.25
		Nos. 178-181 (4)	10.00	10.00

Discovery of America, 500th Anniv. A35

1992, Dec. 18
182	A35	40c Santa Maria	1.25	1.25
183	A35	60c Columbus	1.50	1.50
184	A35	$1.20 Columbus' fleet	3.50	3.50
185	A35	$1.80 Landfall	4.75	4.75
		Nos. 182-185 (4)	11.00	11.00

Coronation
of Queen
Elizabeth II,
40th Anniv.
A36

1993, July 8   Litho.   Perf. 13½
186 A36 25c Queen, early por-
           trait   .85   .85
187 A36 40c Prince Philip   1.40 1.40
188 A36 $1 Queen, recent por-
           trait   2.50 2.50
189 A36 $2 Queen & Prince
           Philip   4.25 4.25
      Nos. 186-189 (4)   9.00 9.00

Birds
A37

25c, Numenius tahitiensis. 40c, Phaethon
rubricauda. $1, Egretta sacra. $2, Pluvialis
fulva.

1993-94   Litho.   Perf. 13½
190 A37 25c multicolored   1.10 1.10
191 A37 40c multicolored   1.60 1.60
192 A37 $1 multicolored   2.75 2.75
193 A37 $2 multicolored   3.50 3.50
  a.   Souvenir sheet of 4, #190-193,
       perf. 14x14½   10.00 10.00
      Nos. 190-193 (4)   8.95 8.95

No. 193a contains Hong Kong '94 emblem,
inscription in Chinese and English in sheet
margin and sold for $20 HK at the show.
Issued: #190-193, 12/15/93; #193a, 2/1/94.

PHILAKOREA '94 — A38

1994, Aug. 16   Litho.   Perf. 12
194 A38 $2 White heron   4.50 4.50
  a.   Souvenir sheet of 1   7.00 7.00

No. 194a has a continuous design.

Handicrafts
A39

1995   Litho.   Perf. 13½
195 A39 5c Outrigger canoe   .30   .30
196 A39 25c Plaited fan   .40   .40
197 A39 40c Plaited baskets   .65   .65
198 A39 50c Fishing box   .85   .85
199 A39 80c Water bottle   1.25 1.25
200 A39 $1 Fishing hook   1.75 1.75
201 A39 $2 Coconut gourds   3.25 3.25
202 A39 $5 Shell necklace   8.50 8.50
      Nos. 195-202 (8)   16.95 16.95

Souvenir Sheet

New Year 1995 (Year of the
Boar) — A40

1995, Feb. 3   Litho.   Perf. 14
203 A40 $5 multicolored   10.00 10.00
  a.   Ovptd. in sheet margin   16.00 16.00
  b.   Ovptd. in sheet margin   9.50 9.50

No. 203a ovptd. in red in sheet margin
"POST'X 95 / 3-6 February / 1995 / AUCK-
LAND" surrounded by simulated perforations.
No. 203b ovptd. in red in sheet margin with
Singapore '95 exhibition emblem.

Pacific
Imperial
Pigeon
A41

1995, Apr. 27   Litho.   Perf. 13½
204 A41 25c shown   .85   .85
205 A41 40c Full view   1.40 1.40
206 A41 $1 In tree, red ber-
           ries   2.25 2.25
207 A41 $2 Nesting   4.00 4.00
      Nos. 204-207 (4)   8.50 8.50

World Wildlife Fund.

Reef
Fish — A42

Designs: 25c, Long nosed butterfly fish. 40c,
Emperor angelfish. $1, Moorish idol. $2, Lined
butterfly fish.
$3, Red fire fish.

1995, Sept. 1   Litho.   Perf. 12
208 A42 25c multicolored   .55   .55
209 A42 40c multicolored   .85   .85
210 A42 $1 multicolored   2.10 2.10
211 A42 $2 multicolored   4.50 4.50
      Nos. 208-211 (4)   8.00 8.00

Souvenir Sheet
212 A42 $3 multicolored   6.00 6.00

No. 212 contains one 40x35mm stamp and
is inscribed in sheet margin for Singapore '95.

Butterflies — A43

Designs: 25c, Danaus plexippus. 40c, Precis villida samoensis. $1, Hypolimnas bolina.
$2, Euploea lewenii.

1995, Oct. 16   Litho.   Perf. 12
213 A43 25c multicolored   .75   .75
214 A43 40c multicolored   1.25 1.25
215 A43 $1 multicolored   3.00 3.00
216 A43 $2 multicolored   4.50 4.50
      Nos. 213-216 (4)   9.50 9.50

Sea Turtles
A44

1995, Nov. 27   Litho.   Perf. 12
217 A44 25c Hawksbill   .85   .85
218 A44 40c Leatherback   1.25 1.25
219 A44 $1 Green   3.00 3.00
220 A44 $2 Loggerhead   4.50 4.50
      Nos. 217-220 (4)   9.60 9.60

Souvenir Sheet
221 A44 $3 like #220   6.50 6.50

No. 221 contains one 50x40mm stamp and
is a continuous design.

Souvenir Sheet

New Year 1996 (Year of the
Rat) — A45

1996, Feb. 19   Litho.   Perf. 12
222 A45 $3 Pacific rat   6.00 6.00
  a.   Ovptd. in sheet margin   6.00 6.00
  b.   Ovptd. in sheet margin   6.00 6.00

Overprinted in sheet margin with red exhibition emblem: No. 222a, CHINA '96; No. 222b,
TAIPEI '96.

Common Design Types
pictured following the introduction.

Queen Elizabeth II, 70th Birthday
Common Design Type

Various portraits of Queen, scenes of Tokelau: 40c, Nukunonu. $1, Atafu, silhouette of
island, boat. $1.25, Atafu, building on island,
boat. $2, Atafu, huts.
$3, Queen wearing tiara, formal dress.

1996, Apr. 22   Litho.   Perf. 13½
223 CD354 40c multicolored   .65   .65
224 CD354 $1 multicolored   2.10 2.10
225 CD354 $1.25 multicolored   2.40 2.40
226 CD354 $2 multicolored   3.25 3.25
      Nos. 223-226 (4)   8.40 8.40

Souvenir Sheet
227 CD354 $3 multicolored   6.00 6.00

Dolphins — A46

1996, July 15   Litho.   Perf. 14
228 A46 40c Fraser's   1.50 1.50
229 A46 $1 Common   3.25 3.25
230 A46 $1.25 Striped   3.25 3.25
231 A46 $2 Spotted   4.75 4.75
      Nos. 228-231 (4)   12.75 12.75

Shells
A47

Designs: 40c, Cypraea talpa. $1, Cypraea
mauritiana. $1.25, Cypraea argus. $2,
Cypraea tigris.
$3, Cypraea mauritana, diff.

1996, Oct. 16   Litho.   Perf. 12
232 A47 40c multicolored   .85   .85
233 A47 $1 multicolored   1.90 1.90
234 A47 $1.25 multicolored   2.50 2.50
235 A47 $2 multicolored   3.75 3.75
      Nos. 232-235 (4)   9.00 9.00

Souvenir Sheet
236 A47 $3 multicolored   6.00 6.00

No. 236 contains one 50x40mm stamp with
a continuous design.

Souvenir Sheet

New Year 1997 (Year of the
Ox) — A48

1997, Feb. 12   Litho.   Perf. 15x14
237 A48 $2 multicolored   4.25 4.25
  a.   Overprinted in gold   4.50 4.50
  b.   Overprinted in red   4.75 4.75

No. 237a ovptd. in sheet margin HONG
KONG '97 / STAMP EXHIBITION" in English
and Chinese.
No. 237b overprinted in sheet margin with
Pacific 97 emblem. Issued 5/29.

Humpback
Whale
A49

Designs: 40c, With school of fish. $1, Calf,
adult, young adult. $1.25, With mouth open,
school of fish. $2, Adult, calf.
$3, Mouth, head of whale.

1997, May 29   Litho.   Perf. 12
238 A49 40c multicolored   .75   .75
239 A49 $1 multicolored   1.75 1.75
240 A49 $1.25 multicolored   2.50 2.50
241 A49 $2 multicolored   3.50 3.50
      Nos. 238-241 (4)   8.50 8.50

Souvenir Sheet
242 A49 $3 multicolored   4.75 4.75
  a.   Ovptd. in sheet margin   5.00 5.00

No. 242a ovptd. in sheet margin, "AUPEX
'97 / 13-16 NOVEMBER / NZ NATIONAL /
STAMP EXHIBITION." Issued: 11/13.

South Pacific Commission, 50th
Anniv. — A50

1997, Sept. 17   Litho.   Perf. 14
243 A50 40c Church, waterfront   .70   .70
244 A50 $1 Beach, child   1.75 1.75
245 A50 $1.25 Island   2.25 2.25
246 A50 $2 Atoll   3.50 3.50
      Nos. 243-246 (4)   8.20 8.20

Year of the
Coral
Reef — A51

Designs: No. 247, Gorgonian coral, emperor
angelfish. No. 248, Soft coral. No. 249, Mushroom coral. No. 250, Staghorn coral. No. 251,
Staghorn coral, Moorish idol.

1997, Oct. 20   Litho.   Perf. 13½
247 A51 $1 multicolored   1.40 1.40
248 A51 $1 multicolored   1.40 1.40
249 A51 $1 multicolored   1.40 1.40
250 A51 $1 multicolored   1.40 1.40
251 A51 $1 multicolored   1.40 1.40
  a.   Strip of 5, #247-251   7.00 7.00

Souvenir Sheet

New Year 1998 (Year of the Tiger) — A52

1998, Jan. 28   Litho.   Perf. 14x14½
252 A52 $2 multicolored   2.75 2.75
  a.   Ovptd. in sheet margin   3.50 3.50

No. 252a overprinted in sheet margin with emblem of Singpex '98 Stamp Exhibition, Singapore.

Diana, Princess of Wales (1961-97)
Common Design Type

Designs: No. 252B, Holding yellow flowers. No. 253: a, Wearing high-collared ruffled blouse. b, Wearing red beret. c, Wearing pink and yellow jacket.

1998, May 15   Litho.   Perf. 14½x14
252B CD355 $1 multi   1.50 1.50
Souvenir Sheet
253   CD355 $1 Sheet of 4,
        #252B, 253a-
        253c   7.00 7.00

No. 253 sold for $4 + 50c, with surtax from international sales being donated to the Princess Diana Memorial Fund and surtax from national sales being donated to designated local charity.

Souvenir Sheet

First Stamps of Tokelau, 50th Anniv. — A53

Designs: a, #3. b. #1. c, #2.

1998, June 22   Litho.   Perf. 14½
254 A53 $1 Sheet of 3, #a.-c.   4.50 4.50

Beetles
A54

Designs: 40c, Oryctes rhinoceros. $1, Tribolium castaneum. $1.25, Coccinella repanda. $2, Amarygmus hyorophiloides. $3, Coccinella repanda, diff.

1998, Aug. 24   Litho.   Perf. 14
255 A54 40c multicolored   .55   .55
256 A54 $1 multicolored   1.50 1.50
257 A54 $1.25 multicolored   1.90 1.90
258 A54 $2 multicolored   2.75 2.75
      Nos. 255-258 (4)   6.70 6.70
Souvenir Sheet
259 A54 $3 multicolored   4.50 4.50

Tropical
Flowers
A55

40c, Ipomoea pes-caprae. $1, Ipomoea littoralis. $1.25, Scaevola taccada. $2, Thespesia populnea.

1998, Nov. 19   Litho.   Perf. 14
260 A55 40c multicolored   .55   .55
261 A55 $1 multicolored   1.40 1.40
262 A55 $1.25 multicolored   1.75 1.75
263 A55 $2 multicolored   2.75 2.75
      Nos. 260-263 (4)   6.45 6.45

Souvenir Sheet

New Year 1999 (Year of the Rabbit) — A56

1999, Feb. 16   Litho.   Perf. 14
264 A56 $3 multicolored   4.50 4.50
  a.   Ovptd. in sheet margin   4.50 4.50

No. 264a overprinted in sheet margin with emblem of IBRA '99 Intl. Stamp Exhibtion, Nuremburg. Issued: 4/27.

Souvenir Sheet

Australia '99, World Stamp Exhibition — A57

1999, Mar. 19
265 A57 $3 HMS Pandora   5.50 5.50

First Manned Moon Landing, 30th Anniv. — A58

Designs: 25c, Lift-off. 50c, Separation of stages. 75c, Aldrin deploying instruments on moon. $1, Planting flag. $1.25, Returning to Earth. $2, Splashdown.
  $3, Apollo 11, Moon, Earth.

Perf. 13½x13¼
1999, Aug. 31   Litho.
266 A58 25c multicolored   .35   .35
267 A58 50c multicolored   .70   .70
268 A58 75c multicolored   1.00 1.00
269 A58 $1 multicolored   1.50 1.50
270 A58 $1.25 multicolored   2.00 2.00
271 A58 $2 multicolored   3.00 3.00
      Nos. 266-271 (6)   8.55 8.55
Souvenir Sheet
272 A58 $3 multicolored   4.50 4.50
  a. Ovptd. in silver "World Stamp
      Expo 2000 7-16 July
      Anaheim - U.S.A." on sheet
      margin   5.00 *5.00*

Crabs
A59

1999   Litho.   Perf. 14¼x14½
273 A59 40c Coconut   .65   .65
274 A59 $1 Ghost   1.60 1.60
275 A59 $1.25 Land hermit   2.10 2.10
276 A59 $2 Purple hermit   3.25 3.25
      Nos. 273-276 (4)   7.60 7.60
Souvenir Sheet
277 A59 $3 Ghost, diff.   4.50 4.50

Black-naped
Tern — A60

Designs: 40c, Chick and egg. $1, On nest. $1.25, Pair near water. $2, Pair in flight.

Perf. 13½x14
1999, Dec. 31   Litho.   Unwmk.
278-281 A60 Set of 4   7.00 7.00

Souvenir Sheet

New Year 2000 (Year of the Dragon) — A61

2000   Litho.   Perf. 14x14¼
282 A61 $3 multi   5.00 5.00
  a.   Overprinted in sheet margin 4.50 4.50

No. 282a overprinted in sheet margin with emblem "Bangkok 2000," "World Youth Stamp Exhibition" and Thai text.

Souvenir Sheet

The Stamp Show 2000, London — A62

Unwmk.
2000, May 22   Litho.   Perf. 14
283 A62 $6 multi   8.00 8.00

Queen Mother, 100th Birthday — A63

Various photos. Denominations 40c, $1.20, $1.80, $3.

Perf. 14½x14¼
2000, Aug. 4   Wmk. 373
284-287 A63 Set of 4   9.00 9.00

Lizards
A64

Designs: 40c, Gehyra oceanica. $1, Lepidodactylus lugubris. $1.25, Gehyra mutilata. $2, Emoia cyanura.

2001, Feb. 1   Litho.   Perf. 14
288-291 A64 Set of 4   7.00 7.00

Souvenir Sheet

New Year 2001 (Year of the Snake) — A65

2001, Feb. 1
292 A65 $3 multi   5.50 5.50
  a.   With gold ovpt. in margin   5.50 5.50

Overprint in margin on No. 292a is for Hong Kong 2001 Stamp Exhibition.

Hippocampus
Histrix — A66

Various views of seahorses. Denominations: 40c, $1, $1.25, $2.

2001, Aug. 23   Litho.   Perf. 14
293-296 A66 Set of 4   7.00 7.00
Souvenir Sheet
297 A66 $3 multi   4.50 4.50

Island
Scenery
A67

Designs: 40c, Sky over Atafu. $1, Waters of Fakaofo. $2, Sunrise over Nukunonu village. $2.50, Ocean, Nukunonu.

Unwmk.
2001, Dec. 17   Litho.   Perf. 14
298-301 A67 Set of 4   9.00 9.00
  a.   Souvenir sheet, #298-301   9.00 9.00

Issued: No. 301a issued 5/27/06 for Washington 2006 World Philatelic Exhibition.

Reign Of Queen Elizabeth II, 50th Anniv. Issue
Common Design Type

Designs: Nos. 302, 306a, 40c, Princess Elizabeth, Prince Philip on honeymoon, 1947. Nos. 303, 306b, $1, Wearing purple hat. Nos. 304, 306c, $1.25, Holding Prince Charles, 1948. Nos. 305, 306d, $2, In 1996. No. 306e, $3, 1955 portrait by Annigoni (38x50mm).

Perf. 14¼x14½, 13¾ (#306e)
2002, Feb. 6   Litho.   Wmk. 373
With Gold Frames
302-305 CD360 Set of 4   7.00 7.00
Souvenir Sheet
Without Gold Frames
306 CD360 Sheet of 5, #a-e   11.00 11.00

Souvenir Sheet

New Year 2002 (Year of the Horse) — A68

2002, Feb. 12   Litho.   Perf. 14
307   A68 $4 multi   6.00   6.00
a.   As #307, with gold ovpt. in mar-
      gin   6.00   6.00

No. 307a was issued 2/22 and has overprint reading "STAMPEX 2002 / HONG KONG / 22-24 FEBRUARY 2002."

Worldwide Fund for Nature (WWF) — A69

Various views of Pelagic thresher shark: 40c, $1, $2, $2.50.

2002, July 2   Litho.   Perf. 14¼
308-311   A69   Set of 4   9.50   9.50

Queen Mother Elizabeth (1900-2002)
Common Design Type

Designs: 40c, Wearing broad-brimmed hat (black and white photograph). $2, Wearing blue hat.
No. 314: a, $2.50, Wearing hat (black and white photograph). b, $4, Wearing purple hat.

Wmk. 373
2002, Aug. 5   Litho.   Perf. 14¼
With Purple Frames
312-313   CD361   Set of 2   4.75   4.75
Souvenir Sheet
Without Purple Frames
Perf. 14½x14¼
314   CD361   Sheet of 2, #a-b   10.50   10.50

New Zealand Navy Ships That Have Stopped at Tokelau A70

Designs: 40c, HMNZS Kaniere. $1, HMNZS Endeavour. $2, HMNZS Wellington. $2.50, HMNZS Monowai.

2002, Dec. Litho. Unwmk. Perf. 14
315-318   A70   Set of 4   9.00   9.00

Souvenir Sheet

New Year 2003 (Year of the Ram) — A71

2003, Feb. 3
319   A71 $4 multi   6.00   6.00
a.   With Bangkok 2003 overprint in
      gold in margin   6.00   6.00
      Issued: No. 319a, 10/13.

Coronation of Queen Elizabeth II, 50th Anniv.
Common Design Type

Designs: Nos. 320, 322a, $2.50, Queen with maids of honor. Nos. 321, 322b, $4, Queen with Prince Philip.

Perf. 14¼x14½
2003, June 2   Litho.   Wmk. 373
Vignettes Framed, Red Background
320-321   CD363   Set of 2   10.00   10.00
Souvenir Sheet
Vignettes Without Frame, Purple Panel
322   CD363   Sheet of 2, #a-b   10.00   10.00

Prince William, 21st Birthday
Common Design Type

No. 323: a, Color photograph at right. b, Color photograph at left.

Wmk. 373
2003, June 21   Litho.   Perf. 14¼
323   Horiz. pair   6.25   6.25
a.   CD364 $1.50 multi   2.00   2.00
b.   CD364 $3 multi   4.25   4.25

Souvenir Sheet

Welpex 2003 Stamp Show, Wellington, New Zealand — A72

Unwmk.
2003, Nov. 7   Litho.   Perf. 14
324   A72 $4 multi   6.00   6.00

Souvenir Sheet

New Year 2004 (Year of the Monkey) — A73

2004   Litho. with Foil Application
325   A73 $4 multi   6.00   6.00
a.   With 2004 Hong Kong Stamp Ex-
      po emblem in gold in margin   6.00   6.00
      Issued: No. 325, 1/22; No. 325a, 1/28.

Island Scenes A74

Designs: 40c, Atafu dawn. $1, Return of the fishermen, Nukunonu. $2, A Fakaofo calm evening glow. $2.50, Solitude in Atafu.

2004, June 30   Litho.   Perf. 14¼x14
326-329   A74   Set of 4   7.00   7.00

No. 324 Overprinted in Silver

2004, Aug. 8   Litho.   Perf. 14
330   A72 $4 multi   6.25   6.25

Fregata Ariel A75

Designs: 40c, Bird on nest. $1, Birds in flight. $2, Birds on nest and in flight. $2.50, Bird on nest, diff.

2004, Dec. 20   Litho.   Perf. 14
331-334   A75   Set of 4   9.00   9.00

Souvenir Sheet

New Year 2005 (Year of the Rooster) — A76

2005, Feb. 9
335   A76 $4 multi   6.00   6.00
a.   Ovptd. in gold in margin with Pa-
      cific Explorer 2005 emblem   6.00   6.00
      No. 335a issued 4/21/05.

Pope John Paul II (1920-2005) A77

2005, Aug. 18   Litho.   Perf. 14
336   A77 $1 multi   1.50   1.50

Visit of HMNZS Te Kaha A78

Various views of ship: 40c, $1, $2, $2.50.

2005, Dec. 15   Litho.   Perf. 14
337-340   A78   Set of 4   9.00   9.00

Souvenir Sheet

New Year 2006 (Year of the Dog) — A79

2006, Jan. 29
341   A79 $4 multi   6.00   6.00

Queen Elizabeth II, 80th Birthday A80

Queen: 40c, With head on hands. $1, In wedding gown. No. 344, $2, Wearing tiara. No. 345, $2.50, Wearing blue hat.
No. 346: a, $2, Like $1. b, $2.50, Like #344.
No. 347: a, #346a overprinted "KIWIPEX." b, #346b overprinted "2006"

2006   Litho.   Perf. 14
With White Frames
342-345   A80   Set of 4   9.00   9.00
Souvenir Sheets
Without White Frames
346   A80   Sheet of 2, #a-b   6.00   6.00
Overprinted in Metallic Blue
347   A80   Sheet of 2, #a-b   6.00   6.00

Issued: Nos. 342-346, 4/21; No. 347, 11/2. No. 347 is also overprinted in sheet margin "National Stamp Exhibition, Christchurch, New Zealand."

Souvenir Sheet

New Year 2007 (Year of the Pig) — A81

2007, Feb. 18   Litho.   Perf. 14
348   A81 $4 multi   6.00   6.00

Worldwide Fund for Nature (WWF) A82

Pacific golden plover: 40c, Flock of birds. $1, Head. $2, Bird standing on one leg. $2.50, Birds and driftwood.

2007, Oct. 19   Litho.   Perf. 14
349-352   A82   Set of 4   9.00   9.00
352a   Miniature sheet of 16, 4
              each #349-352   36.00 36.00

Marine Life — A83

Designs: 10c, Bicolor angelfish. 20c, Staghorn coral. 40c, Black-tipped reef sharks. 50c, Sea star. $1, Porcupine fish. $1.50, Thorny seahorses. $2, Spotted eagle rays. $2.50, Small giant clams. $5, Green turtles. $10, Slate pencil urchin.

2007, Dec. 19 — Perf. 14½x14¼

353	A83	10c multi	.25	.25
354	A83	20c multi	.30	.30
355	A83	40c multi	.65	.65
356	A83	50c multi	.80	.80
357	A83	$1 multi	1.60	1.60
358	A83	$1.50 multi	2.40	2.40
359	A83	$2 multi	3.25	3.25
360	A83	$2.50 multi	4.00	4.00
361	A83	$5 multi	7.75	7.75
362	A83	$10 multi	15.50	15.50
a.		Miniature sheet, #353-362	37.50	37.50
		Nos. 353-362 (10)	36.50	36.50

Souvenir Sheet

New Year 2008 (Year of the Rat) — A84

2008, Feb. 7 — Perf. 14
363	A84	$4 multi	6.50 6.50

Sir Edmund Hillary (1919-2008), Mountaineer A85

2008, Nov. 5 — Litho. — Perf. 14¼
364-367	A85	Set of 4	7.25 7.25

Souvenir Sheet
Perf. 13¾x13¼
368	A85	$5 multi	6.00 6.00

Hillary: 50c, As young man. $1, Wearing plaid shirt. $2, Wearing hat and glasses. $2.50, Wearing blue jacket. $5, On mountain, horiz.

Local Scenes A86

Designs: 50c, Buildings near seashore. $1, Boats on beach. $2, Trees. $2.50, Boat anchored near buildings. $5, Islets.

2008, Nov. 7 — Perf. 14¼
369-372	A86	Set of 4	7.25 7.25

Souvenir Sheet
Perf. 13¾x13¼
373	A86	$5 multi	6.00 6.00

Tarapex National Exhibition, New Plymouth, New Zealand (#373).

Souvenir Sheet

New Year 2009 (Year of the Ox) — A87

2009, Jan. 26 — Litho. — Perf. 14
374	A87	$4 multi	6.00 6.00

Coins of the Pacific Area — A88

Obverse and reverse of: 50c, Chile 1875 one-peso. $1, Great Britain 1911 one-sovereign. $2, New Zealand 1950 half-crown. $2.50, Tokelau 1997 ten-dollar.

2009, Dec. 22 — Litho. — Perf. 14x14¼
375-378	A88	Set of 4	8.50 8.50
378a		Souvenir sheet of 4, #375-378	8.50 8.50

For overprint, see No. 380.

Souvenir Sheet

New Year 2010 (Year of the Tiger) — A89

2010, Feb. 12 — Perf. 13¼x13½
379	A89	$4 multi	5.75 5.75

No. 378a Overprinted in Gold

Designs as before.

Method and Perf. As Before
2010, May 8
380	A88	Sheet of 4, #a-d	8.25 8.25

London 2010 Festival of Stamps.

2009 Tokelauan Bible Translation A90

Open Bible and: 50c, Atafu Church. $1, Fakaofo Church. $2, Nukunonu Church. $2.50, Closed Tokelauan Bibles.

Perf. 13½x13¼
2010, Sept. 21 — Litho.
381-384	A90	Set of 4	9.00 9.00

Souvenir Sheet

New Year 2011 (Year of the Rabbit) — A91

Perf. 13¼x13¾
2011, Feb. 3 — Unwmk.
385	A91	$5 multi	7.75 7.75

Worldwide Fund for Nature (WWF) A92

Yellow-bellied sea snake: 50c, On rocks. $1, On beach. $2, In sea. $2.50, Three in sea.

2011, Mar. 25 — Unwmk. — Perf. 13½
386-389	A92	Set of 4	9.50 9.50
389a		Miniature sheet of 16, 4 each #386-389	38.00 38.00

Souvenir Sheet

Wedding of Prince William and Catherine Middleton — A93

Perf. 14¾x14¼
2011, Apr. 29 — Wmk. 406
390	A93	$6 multi	9.50 9.50

Christmas — A94

Designs: 40c, Christmas tree. 45c, Ornament. $1.40, Stocking. $2, Angel.

2011, Nov. 16 — Unwmk. — Perf. 13½
391-394	A94	Set of 4	6.75 6.75

TONGA

ˈtäŋ-gə

LOCATION — A group of islands in the south Pacific Ocean, south of Samoa
GOVT. — Kingdom in British Commonwealth
AREA — 289 sq. mi.
POP. — 109,082 (1999 est.)
CAPITAL — Nuku'alofa

This group, also known as the Friendly Islands, became a British Protectorate in 1900 under the Anglo-German Agreement of 1899. On June 4, 1970, the United Kingdom ceased to have any responsibility for the external relations of Tonga.

12 Pence = 1 Shilling
20 Shillings = 1 Pound
100 Seniti = 1 Pa'anga (1967)

Catalogue values for unused stamps in this country are for Never Hinged items, beginning with Scott 87 in the regular postage section, Scott B1 in the semipostal section, Scott C1 in the air post section Scott CE1 in the air post special delivery section, Scott CO1 in the air post official section, and Scott O11 in the officials section.

Watermarks

Wmk. 62 — NZ and Small Star Wide Apart

Wmk. 79 — Turtles

King George I — A1

Perf. 12x11½
1886-92 — Typo. — Wmk. 62
1	A1	1p car rose ('87)	11.50	4.00
a.		Perf. 12½	450.00	7.00
b.		Perf. 12½x10		
2	A1	2p violet ('87)	42.50	3.50
a.		Perf. 12½	57.50	14.00
3	A1	6p ultra ('88)	57.50	2.75
a.		Perf. 12½		
4	A1	6p org yel ('92)	18.00	30.00
5	A1	1sh blue grn ('88)	62.50	7.25
a.		Perf. 12½	110.00	4.50
b.		Half used as 6p on cover		
		Nos. 1-5 (5)	192.00	47.50

For surcharges and overprints see #6-9, 24.

Nos. 1 and 2 Surcharged or Overprinted in Black

a   b

1891, Nov. 10 — Perf. 12x11½
6	A1(a)	4p on 1p car rose	3.50	12.50
a.		No period after "PENCE"	57.50	125.00
7	A1(a)	8p on 2p violet	40.00	100.00

1891, Nov. 23 — Perf. 12½

Two types of overprint:
I — Solid stars, rays pointed and short.
II — Open-center stars, rays blunt and long.

8	A1(b)	1p car rose (I)	50.00	65.00
a.		Overprinted with 3 stars (I)	400.00	
b.		Overprinted with 4 stars (I)	550.00	
c.		Overprinted with 5 stars (I)	800.00	
d.		Type II	50.00	65.00
e.		Perf. 12x11½ (I or II)	350.00	
9	A1(b)	2p violet (I)	80.00	42.50
a.		Type II	80.00	42.50
b.		Perf. 12x11½ (I or II)	425.00	

Coat of Arms   George I
A4   A5

1892, Nov. 10 — Typo. — Perf. 12x11½
10	A4	1p rose	14.00	25.00
a.		Diagonal half used as ½p on cover		975.00
11	A5	2p olive gray	27.50	18.00
12	A4	4p red brown	55.00	80.00
13	A5	8p violet	62.50	200.00
14	A5	1sh brown	90.00	125.00
		Nos. 10-14 (5)	249.00	448.00

For surcharges and overprints see Nos. 15-23, 25-28, 36-37, O1-O10.

Types A4 and A5 Surcharged in Carmine or Black

c d

e f

1893
15	A4(c)	½p on 1p ultra (C)	26.00	30.00
a.		Surcharge omitted		
16	A4(c)	½p on 1p ultra	50.00	55.00
17	A5(d)	2½p on 2p blue grn (C)	21.00	13.50
18	A5(d)	2½p on 2p blue grn	19.00	19.00
a.		Double surcharge	3,000.	2,000.
19	A4(e)	5p on 4p org yel (C)	4.50	7.50
20	A5(f)	7½p on 8p rose (C)	27.50	85.00
		Nos. 15-20 (6)	148.00	210.00

Stamps of 1886-92 Surcharged in Blue or Black

g h

1894
21	A4	½p on 4p red brn (Bl)	2.25	8.00
a.		"SURCHARGE"	10.00	22.50
b.		Pair, one without surcharge		
c.		"HALF PENNY" omitted		
22	A5	½p on 1sh brn (Bk)	2.75	12.50
a.		Double surcharge	310.00	
b.		"SURCHARGE"	11.50	45.00
c.		As "b," double surcharge	1,000.	
23	A5	2½p on 8p vio (Bk)	8.00	9.25
a.		No period after "SURCHARGE"	37.50	62.50
24	A1	2½p on 1sh blue grn (Bk)	65.00	27.50
a.		No period after "SURCHARGE"	200.00	
b.		Perf. 12x11½	17.50	47.50
		Nos. 21-24 (4)	78.00	57.25

Type A5 with Same Surcharges in Carmine

1895
			Unwmk.	
25	A5(g)	1p on 2p lt blue	50.00	30.00
26	A5(h)	1½p on 2p lt bl, perf. 12x11	55.00	45.00
a.		Perf. 12	70.00	45.00
27	A5(h)	2½p on 2p lt blue	45.00	50.00
b.		Without period	250.00	250.00

28	A5(h)	7½p on 2p lt bl, perf. 12x11	70.00	50.00
a.		Perf. 12	475.00	
		Nos. 25-28 (4)	220.00	175.00

King George II — A13

1895, Aug. 16   Perf. 12
29	A13	1p gray green	27.50	30.00
a.		Diagonal half used as ½p on cover		850.00
b.		Horiz. pair, imperf. btwn.	—	7,500.
30	A13	2½p dull rose	24.00	15.00
31	A13	5p brt blue, perf. 12x11	26.00	57.50
a.		Perf. 12	32.50	57.50
b.		Perf. 11	400.00	
32	A13	7½p yellow	37.50	55.00
		Nos. 29-32 (4)	115.00	157.50

Type A13 Redrawn and Surcharged "g" or "h" in Black
33	A13(g)	½p on 2½p red	47.50	37.50
a.		"SURCHARCE"	85.00	70.00
b.		Period after "Postage"	95.00	75.00
34	A13(g)	1p on 2½p red	95.00	50.00
a.		Period after "Postage"	170.00	110.00
35	A13(h)	7½p on 2½p red	62.50	75.00
a.		Period after "Postage"	110.00	120.00
		Nos. 33-35 (3)	205.00	162.50

Half Penny

Nos. 26 and 28 with Additional Surcharge in Violet and Black

1896, May   Perf. 12x11
36	A5	½p on 1½p on 2p	500.00	
a.		Tongan surch. reading up	475.00	475.00
b.		Perf. 12	475.00	475.00
c.		As "a," perf. 12	500.00	500.00
d.		"Haalf"	3,500.	
37	A5	½p on 7½p on 2p	97.50	125.00
a.		"Half penny" inverted	3,250.	
b.		"Half penny" double		
c.		Tongan surch. reading up	97.50	125.00
d.		Tongan surcharge as "c" and double		
e.		"Hafl Penny"	2,200.	2,500.
f.		"Hafl" only	5,500.	
g.		"Hwlf"		
h.		Periods instead of hyphens after words	1,100.	
j.		Perf. 12	925.00	

Coat of Arms — A17   Ovava Tree — A18

George II — A19

Prehistoric Trilithon, Tongatabu — A20

Breadfruit A21   Coral Formations A22

View of Haabai A23

Red-breasted Musk Parrot — A24

View of Vavau — A25

Type I   Type II

Two types of 2p:
I — Top of sword hilt shows above "2."
II — No hilt shown.

Wmk. 79 Sideways
	1897-1934	Engr.	Perf. 14	
38	A17	½p dark blue	.70	3.00
39	A17	½p green ('34)	1.10	1.40
40	A18	1p dp red & blk	.90	.90
41	A19	2p bis & sep (I)	20.00	7.00
a.		bister & gray, type II	35.00	3.75
42	A19	2½p lt blue & blk	8.00	1.60
a.		"½" without fraction bar	110.00	75.00
43	A20	3p ol grn & blk	4.00	9.75
44	A21	4p dull vio & grn	4.25	4.50
45	A19	5p orange & blk	35.00	16.00
46	A22	6p red	9.00	7.00
47	A19	7½p green & blk	20.00	26.00
a.		Center inverted	6,500.	
48	A19	10p carmine & blk	50.00	55.00
49	A19	1sh red brn & blk	16.00	9.00
50	A23	2sh dk ultra & blk	30.00	32.50
51	A24	2sh6p dk violet	65.00	50.00
52	A25	5sh dull red & blk	26.00	32.50
		Nos. 38-52 (15)	289.95	256.15

See Nos. 73-74, 77-78, 80-81. For surcharges see Nos. 63-69.

Stamp of 1897 Overprinted in Black

1899, June 1
53	A18	1p red & black	40.00	72.50
a.		"1889" instead of "1899"	250.00	400.00
b.		Comma omitted after June		
c.		Double overprint		

Marriage of George II to Lavinia, June 1, 1899. The letters "T L" are the initials of Taufa'ahau, the King's family name, and Lavinia.

Queen Salote — A26

Dies of 2p:
Die I — Ball of "2" smaller.
Die II — Ball of "2" larger. "U" has spur at left.

1920-35   Engr.   Wmk. 79
54	A26	1½p gray blk ('35)	.55	3.50
55	A26	2p violet & sepia	12.00	15.00
56	A26	2p dl vio & blk (I) ('24)	15.00	2.75
a.		Die II	6.00	9.50
57	A26	2½p blue & black	9.00	45.00
58	A26	2½p ultra ('34)	5.00	1.10
59	A26	5p red org & blk	3.75	5.50
60	A26	7½p green & blk	2.00	2.00
61	A26	10p carmine & blk	2.90	5.50
62	A26	1sh red brown & blk	1.40	4.00
		Nos. 54-62 (9)	51.60	83.25

See Nos. 75-76, 79.

Stamps of 1897 Srchd. in Dark Blue or Red

1923
63	A19	2p on 5p org & blk	1.10	1.00
64	A19	2p on 7½p grn & blk	27.50	32.50
65	A19	2p on 10p car & blk	18.00	57.50
66	A19	2p on 1sh red brn & blk	75.00	25.00
67	A23	2p on 2sh ultra & blk (R)	12.00	7.00
68	A24	2p on 2sh6p dk vio (R)	35.00	7.50
69	A25	2p on 5sh dull red & blk (R)	3.50	2.50
		Nos. 63-69 (7)	172.10	133.00

Queen Salote — A27

Inscribed "1918-1938"
1938, Oct. 12   Perf. 14
70	A27	1p carmine & blk	.65	4.00
71	A27	2p violet & blk	8.00	3.00
72	A27	2½p ultra & blk	8.00	3.75
		Nos. 70-72 (3)	16.65	10.75
		Set, never hinged	32.00	

Accession of Queen Salote Tupou, 20th anniv.
See Nos. 82-86.

Types of 1897-1920
1942	Engr.	Wmk. 4

Die III of 2p:

Foot of "2" longer than in Die II, extending beyond curve of loop.

73	A17	½p green	.30	2.75
74	A18	1p scarlet & blk	1.75	2.75
75	A26	2p dull vio & blk (II)	4.50	3.00
a.		Die III	5.50	10.00
76	A26	2½p ultra	1.10	2.00
77	A20	3p green & black	.40	4.25
78	A22	6p orange red	2.00	2.25
79	A26	1sh red brown & gray blk	3.00	3.50
80	A24	2sh6p dk violet	25.00	30.00
81	A25	5sh dull red & brn blk	12.00	60.00
		Nos. 73-81 (9)	50.05	110.50
		Set, never hinged	70.00	

Type of 1938, Inscribed "1918-1943"
1944, Jan. 25

82	A27	1p rose car & blk	.25	1.10
83	A27	2p purple & blk	.25	1.10
84	A27	3p dk yel grn & blk	.25	1.10
85	A27	6p red orange & blk	.40	2.00
86	A27	1sh dk red brn & blk	.25	2.00
		Nos. 82-86 (5)	1.40	7.30
		Set, never hinged	2.00	

25th anniv. of the accession of Queen Salote.

> **Catalogue values for unused stamps in this section, from this point to the end of the section, are for Never Hinged items.**

UPU Issue
Common Design Types
Engr.; Name Typo. on 3p, 6p
Perf. 13½, 11x11½
1949, Oct. 10   **Wmk. 4**

87	CD306	2½p ultra	.40	.90
88	CD307	3p deep olive	1.75	3.25
89	CD308	6p deep carmine	.55	.55
90	CD309	1sh red brown	.55	.55
		Nos. 87-90 (4)	3.25	5.25

Common Design Types
pictured following the introduction.

A28

A29

Queen Salote — A30

1950, Nov. 1   **Photo.**   **Perf. 12½**

91	A28	1p cerise	1.20	1.00
92	A29	5p green	1.20	2.75
93	A30	1sh violet	1.20	3.00
		Nos. 91-93 (3)	3.60	8.75

50th anniv. of the birth of Queen Salote.

Map and Island Scene — A31

Badges and Royal Palace A32

2½p, Queen Salote & coastal scene. 3p, Queen Salote & ship "Bellona." 5p, Flag of Tonga, island view. 1sh, Arms of Tonga & Great Britain.

Perf. 13x13½ (1p), 13½x13, 12½ (3p)
1951, July 2   **Engr.**   **Wmk. 4**

94	A31	½p deep green	.30	3.25
95	A32	1p carmine & black	.30	3.25
96	A32	2½p choc & dp grn	.60	3.25
97	A31	3p ultra & org yel	2.75	3.25
98	A32	5p dp green & car	3.75	1.50
99	A32	1sh purple & orange	3.75	1.50
		Nos. 94-99 (6)	11.45	16.00

50th anniv. of the treaty of friendship between Tonga and Great Britain.

Royal Palace, Nukualofa A33

Map of Tonga Islands — A34

Designs: 1½p, Fisherman. 2p, Canoe and schooners. 3p, Swallows' Cave, Vavau. 3½p, Map of Tongatabu. 4p, Vavau harbor. 5p, Post Office, Nukualofa. 6p, Fuaamotu airport. 8p, Wharf, Nukualofa. 2sh, Beach at Lifuka, Haapai. 5sh, Mutiny on the Bounty. 10sh, Queen Salote. £1, Arms of Tonga.

Perf. 11½x11, 11x11½
1953, July 1   **Wmk. 79**

100	A33	1p chocolate & blk	.30	.25
101	A33	1½p emerald & ultra	.30	.25
102	A33	2p black & aqua	.30	.25
103	A34	3p dk grn & ultra	.30	.25
104	A33	3½p carmine & yel	.30	.25
105	A33	4p rose car & yel	.30	.25
106	A33	5p choc & ultra	.30	.25
107	A33	6p black & dp ultra	.40	.25
108	A33	8p purple & emer	.45	.25
109	A34	1sh black & ultra	.75	.40
110	A33	2sh choc & ol grn	5.00	.90
111	A33	5sh purple & yel	15.00	5.00
112	A34	10sh black & yellow	9.00	6.00
113	A34	£1 ultra, car & yel	11.00	10.50
		Nos. 100-113 (14)	43.70	25.05

For surcharges and overprints see Nos. 119-126, 158-174, 182-202, 210-215, 218-221, 237, 269-273, C34-C39, C47-C54, C87-C91, CO4-CO6, CO11-CO20, CO27-CO43.

Whaling Ship and Longboat A35

1p, Stamp of 1886. 4p, Post Office, Customs & Treasury Building & Queen Salote. 5p, Diesel-driven ship Aoniu. 1sh, Plane over Tongatabu.

1961, Dec. 1   **Photo.**   **Perf. 14½x13½**

114	A35	1p brn org & car rose	.30	.25
115	A35	2p ultra	.90	.30
116	A35	4p bright green	.30	.30
117	A35	5p purple	.90	.30
118	A35	1sh red brown	1.00	.60
		Nos. 114-118 (5)	3.40	1.75

75th anniversary of postal service.
For surcharges & overprints see #146-151, 216-221, C16-C21, C55-C57, CO1-CO3, CO9-CO10.

Stamps of 1953 and 1961 Overprinted in Red: "1862 / TAU'ATAINA / EMANCIPATION / 1962"
Perf. 11½x11, 11x11½, 14½x13
Engr.; Photo. (4p)
1962, Feb. 7   **Wmk. 79**

119	A33	1p choc & blk	.25	.60
120	A35	4p brt green	.25	.65
121	A33	5p choc & ultra	.25	.65
122	A33	6p black & dp ultra	.25	1.10
123	A33	8p purple & emer	.50	1.60
124	A34	1sh black & ultra	.35	.80
125	A34	2sh on 3p dk grn & ultra	.60	3.75
126	A33	5sh purple & yellow	6.25	3.75
		Nos. 119-126 (8)	8.70	12.90

Cent. of emancipation. See Nos. CO1-CO6.

Freedom from Hunger Issue
Common Design Type with Portrait of Queen Salote
Perf. 14x14½
1963, June 4   **Wmk. 79**   **Photo.**

127	CD314	11p ultra	.70	.35

Coat of Arms, ¼ Koula Coin, Reverse A36

Designs: 2p, 9p, 2sh, Queen Salote (head), ¼-koula coin, obverse.

Litho.; Embossed on Gilt Foil
1963, July 15   **Unwmk.**   **Die Cut**
Diameter: 40mm

128	A36	1p dp carmine	.25	.25
129	A36	2p violet blue	.25	.25
130	A36	6p dp green	.30	.30
131	A36	9p magenta	.35	.35
132	A36	1sh6p violet	.70	.70
133	A36	2sh emerald	.75	.75
		Nos. 128-133,C1-C6,CO7 (13)	14.75	14.75

1st gold coinage of Polynesia. Backed with paper inscribed in salmon-colored alternating rows: "TONGA" and "THE FRIENDLY ISLANDS" in multiple.
For surcharges see #140-145, C11-C15, CO8.

Red Cross Centenary Issue
Common Design Type with Portrait of Queen Salote
Wmk. 79
1963, Sept. 2   **Litho.**   **Perf. 13**

134	CD315	2p black & red	.25	.25
135	CD315	11p ultra & red	.75	1.00

Queen Salote on ¼-Koula Coin A37

Litho.; Embossed on Gilt Foil
1964, Oct. 19   **Unwmk.**   **Die Cut**

136	A37	3p pink	.25	.25
137	A37	9p light blue	.25	.25
138	A37	2sh yellow green	.50	.50
139	A37	5sh pale lilac	1.50	1.50
		Nos. 136-139,C7-C10 (8)	5.95	5.95

Pan-Pacific and Southeast Asia Women's Association Conf., Nukualofa, Aug. 1964. See note on paper backing after No. 133.
For surcharges & overprints see #152-157, 263-268.

Nos. 128-133 Surcharged in Red, White or Black

1965, Mar. 18

140	A36	1sh3p on 1sh6p (R)	.25	.25
141	A36	1sh9p on 9p (W)	.25	.25
142	A36	2sh6p on 6p (R)	.25	.25
143	A36	5sh on 1p	22.50	22.50
144	A36	5sh on 2p	4.00	4.00
145	A36	5sh on 2sh	.90	.90
		Nos. 140-145,C11-C15,CO8 (12)	88.90	88.90

Nos. 114-115 Overprinted and Surcharged in Purple or Red

Perf. 14½x13½
1966, June 18   **Photo.**   **Wmk. 79**

146	A35	1p (P)	.25	.25
147	A35	3p on 1p (P)	.25	.25
148	A35	6p on 2p (R)	.25	.25
149	A35	1sh2p on 2p (R)	.25	.25
150	A35	2sh on 2p (R)	.35	.25
151	A35	3sh on 2p (R)	.35	.25
		Nos. 146-151,C16-C21,CO9-CO10 (14)	5.75	4.15

Centenary of Tupou College and of secondary education.

Nos. 136-137 Overprinted and Surcharged in Silver on Black or Ultramarine

Litho.; Embossed on Gilt Foil
1966, Dec. 16   **Unwmk.**   **Die Cut**

152	A37	3p pink (U)	.25	.25
153	A37	5p on 9p lt blue	.25	.25
154	A37	9p lt bl	.25	.25
155	A37	1sh7p on 3p pink (U)	.55	.55
156	A37	3sh6p on 9p lt blue	.95	.95
157	A37	6sh6p on 3p pink (U)	1.75	1.75
		Nos. 152-157,C22-C26 (11)	9.50	9.50

Nos. 100-110, 147 and 151 Srchd. in Black or Red

Perf. 11½x11, 11x11½, 14½x13½
1967, Mar. 25   **Wmk. 79**

158	A33	1s on 1p	.25	.25
159	A33	2s on 4p	.25	.25
160	A33	3s on 5p	.25	.25
161	A33	4s on 5p	.25	.25
162	A33	5s on 3½p	.25	.25
163	A33	6s on 8p	.25	.25
164	A33	7s on 1½p	.25	.25
165	A33	8s on 6p	.25	.25
166	A34	9s on 3p	.25	.25
167	A34	10s on 1sh	.30	.30
168	A35	11s on 3p on 1p	.40	.40
169	A35	21s on 3sh on 2p	.60	.60

170	A33	23s on 1p	.65 .65
171	A33	30s on 2sh (R) (1-line surcharge)	1.40 1.40
172	A33	30s on 2sh (R) (3-line surcharge)	1.50 1.50
173	A33	50s on 6p (R)	1.75 1.75
174	A33	60s on 2p (R)	2.25 2.25
		Nos. 158-174 (17)	11.10 11.10

The size, typeface and arrangement of surcharge vary on the different denominations.

King Taufa'ahau IV — A38

Designs: 1s, 4s, 28s, 1pa, Coat of Arms, reverse of new palladium coins.
Diameter: 1s, 44mm; 2s, 50s, 52mm; 4s, 59mm; 15s, 68mm; 28s, 40mm; 1pa, 74mm

Litho.; Embossed on Palladium Foil

1967, July 4		**Unwmk.**	**Die Cut**
175	A38	1s orange & brt bl	.25 .25
176	A38	2s brt bl & dp mag	.25 .25
177	A38	4s emerald & mag	.25 .25
178	A38	15s blue grn & vio	.35 .35
179	A38	28s blk & brt red lil	.60 .60
180	A38	50s red & vio bl	1.10 1.10
181	A38	1pa ultra & brt rose	2.75 2.75
		Nos. 175-181,C27-C33 (14)	13.20 13.20

Coronation of King Taufa'ahau IV, July 4, 1967. Backed with paper inscribed in yellow alternating rows: "Tonga The Friendly Islands" and "Historically The First Palladium Coinage." For surcharges and overprints see Nos. 203-209, C40-C46, CO21-CO24,

Types of Regular Issue, 1953, Surcharged

Wmk. 79

1967, Dec. 15		**Engr.**	**Die Cut**
182	A33	1s on 1p yellow & blk	.25 .25
183	A33	2s on 2p carmine & ultra	.25 .25
184	A34	3s on 3p brown org & yel	.25 .25
185	A33	4s on 4p purple & yel	.25 .25
186	A33	5s on 5p green & yel	.25 .25
187	A34	10s on 10p rose red & yel	.25 .25
188	A33	20s on 2sh carmine & ultra	.25 .25
189	A33	50s on 5sh sepia & yel	2.00 2.00
190	A34	1pa on 10sh orange yel	.75 .75
		Nos. 182-190,C34-C36,CO12-CO14 (15)	8.10 8.10

Arrival of US Peace Corps.

Nos. 100-111 Srchd. in Red, Black or Ultra

Perf. 11½x11, 11x11½

1968, Apr. 6		**Engr.**	**Wmk. 79**
191	A33	1s on 1p (R)	.25 .25
192	A33	2s on 4p	.25 .25
193	A34	3s on 3p (U)	.25 .25
194	A33	4s on 5p (R)	.25 .25
195	A33	5s on 2p (R)	.25 .25
196	A33	6s on 6p (R)	.25 .25
197	A33	7s on 1½p (R)	.25 .25
198	A33	8s on 8p (R)	.25 .25
199	A33	9s on 3½p	.30 .30
200	A34	10s on 1sh (R)	.30 .30
201	A33	20s on 5sh (R)	1.25 1.25
202	A33	2pa on 2sh (R)	2.75 2.75
		Nos. 191-202,C37-C39,CO15-CO18 (19)	13.75 13.75

Surcharge on 3s and 10s is vertical.

Nos. 175-181 Overprinted: "H.M'S BIRTHDAY / 4 July 1968" in Gold on Red Panel on 1s, 4s, 28s and 1pa. "HIS MAJESTY'S 50th BIRTHDAY" in Silver on Blue Panel on 2s, 15s and 50s

Litho.; Embossed on Palladium Foil

1968, July 4		**Unwmk.**	**Die Cut**
203	A38	1s orange & brt bl	.25 .25
204	A38	2s brt bl & dp mag	.25 .25
205	A38	4s emerald & mag	.25 .25
206	A38	15s blue grn & vio	.55 .55
207	A38	28s blk & brt red lil	1.10 1.10
208	A38	50s red & vio bl	1.90 1.90
209	A38	1pa ultra & brt rose	4.00 4.00
		Nos. 203-209,C40-C46,CO21-CO24 (18)	33.20 29.15

Types of 1953 Surcharged in Red, Black or Green: "Friendly Islands / Field & Track Trials / South Pacific Games / Port Moresby 1969"
Designs as before.

Wmk. 79

1968, Dec. 19		**Engr.**	**Die Cut**
210	A33	5s on 5p green & yel (R)	.25 .25
211	A34	10s on 1sh cer & buff	.25 .25
212	A33	15s on 2sh rose car & bl	.25 .25
213	A33	25s on 2p rose car & bl	.30 .25
214	A33	50s on 1p yel & blk	.50 .30
215	A34	75s on 10sh org (G)	.85 .45
		Nos. 210-215,C47-C54,CO19-CO20 (16)	8.40 5.25

Issued to publicize the field and track trials for the third South Pacific Games, Port Moresby, 1969. The overprint is in 5 lines on the horizontal stamps, in 7 lines on vertical stamps. On the vertical stamps "Trial" is printed on the line ahead of "Field & Track." On #215 the denomination is spelled out.

Nos. 149-150 and Types of 1953 Surcharged

Perf. 14½x13½

1968		**Photo.**	**Wmk. 79**
216	A35	1s on 1sh3p on 2p	1.60 1.60
217	A35	1s on 2sh on 2p	1.60 1.60

		Engr.	**Die Cut**
218	A33	1s on 6p yellow & blk	.90 .90
219	A33	2s on 3½p dk blue	1.00 1.00
220	A33	3s on 1½p lt green	1.00 1.00
221	A33	4s on 8p black & pale grn	1.10 1.10
		Nos. 216-221,C55-C57 (9)	12.00 10.20

Banana — A39

Unwmk.

1969, Apr. 21		**Typo.**	**Die Cut**
		Self-adhesive	
222	A39	1s yellow, black & red	1.00 .85
223	A39	2s yel, black & emer	1.10 1.00
224	A39	3s yellow, black & lil	1.25 1.10
225	A39	4s yellow, black & ultra	1.40 1.10
226	A39	5s yel, blk & ol grn	1.75 1.75
		Nos. 222-226 (5)	6.50 5.80

Packed in boxes of 200. See Nos. 248-252, 297-301, O11-O15, design A75.

Peelable Backing Inscribed
Starting in 1969, self-adhesive stamps are attached to peelable paper backing printed with "TONGA where time begins" in multiple rows and various colors, unless otherwise stated.

Shot-putter — A40

1969, Aug. 13		**Litho.**	**Die Cut**
		Self-adhesive	
227	A40	1s bister, red & blk	.25 .25
228	A40	3s bis, red & emer	.25 .25
229	A40	6s bister, red & bl	.25 .25
230	A40	10s bister, red & pur	.25 .25
231	A40	30s bister, red & bl	.30 .30
		Nos. 227-231,C58-C62,CO25-CO26 (12)	8.15 8.15

3rd Pacific Games, Port Moresby, Papua and New Guinea, Aug. 13-23.

Oil Derrick and Map of Tonga Islands — A41

1969, Dec. 23		**Litho.**	**Die Cut**
		Self-adhesive	
232	A41	3s brown & multi	.25 .25
233	A41	7s brt blue & multi	.25 .25
234	A41	20s multicolored	.70 .70
235	A41	25s orange & multi	1.00 1.00
236	A41	35s henna brn & multi	1.40 1.40

Type of Regular Issue, 1953, Surcharged in Red:
"1969 / OIL / SEARCH / T$1.10" and Oil Derrick Obliterating Old Denomination

		Wmk. 79	**Die Cut**
237	A34	1.10pa on £1 green & multi	4.50 4.50
		Nos. 232-237,C63-C67,CO27 (12)	16.25 16.25

First scientific search for oil in Tonga.

British and Tongan Royal Families — A42

Litho.; Gold Embossed

1970, Mar. 7		**Self-adhesive**	**Die Cut**
238	A42	3s multicolored	.25 .25
239	A42	5s multicolored	.25 .25
240	A42	10s multicolored	.55 .40
241	A42	25s multicolored	1.25 .90
242	A42	50s multicolored	2.75 2.00
		Nos. 238-242,C68-C72,CO28-CO30 (13)	27.55 18.85

Visit of Elizabeth II, Prince Philip and Princess Anne, Mar. 1970.

Open Book, George Tupou I and II, Salote Tupou III, Taufa'ahau Tupou IV and Tonga Flag — A43

Litho.; Gold Embossed

1970, June 4			
		Self-adhesive	
243	A43	3s multicolored	.25 .25
244	A43	7s multicolored	.25 .25
245	A43	15s multicolored	.60 .60

246	A43	25s multicolored	.70 .70
247	A43	50s multicolored	1.25 1.25
		Nos. 243-247,C73-C77,CO31-CO33 (13)	15.10 15.10

Tonga's independence and entry into the British Commonwealth of Nations.
For surcharges see Nos. CO49-CO51, CO71.

Banana Type of 1969 redrawn and

Coconut — A44

1970, June 9			**Typo.**
		Self-adhesive	
248	A39	1s yellow, blk & mag	.40 .40
249	A39	2s yellow, blk & bl	.50 .50
250	A39	3s yellow, blk & brn	.50 .50
251	A39	4s yellow, blk & grn	.50 .50
252	A39	5s yellow, blk & org	.55 .55

Typo.; Embossed on Gilt Foil
Coconut Brown

253	A44	6s blue, grn & mag	.65 .65
254	A44	7s purple & green	.70 .70
255	A44	8s gold, grn & vio bl	.75 .75
256	A44	9s carmine & green	.85 .85
257	A44	10s gold, grn & org	.85 .85
		Nos. 248-257,O11-O20 (20)	16.00 16.00

Nos. 248-252 have no white shading in upper part of the banana, Nos. 222-226 have white shading. Nos. 253-256 have self-adhesive control numbers in lower left corner of paper backing. Paper backing is green on Nos. 253-257.
See Nos. 302-306, O26-O30.

Red Cross and Arms of Tonga A45

1970, Oct. 17		**Litho.**	**Die Cut**
		Self-adhesive	
258	A45	3s red, black & grn	.25 .25
259	A45	7s red, blk & vio bl	.25 .25
260	A45	15s red, blk & red lil	.55 .55
261	A45	25s red, black & brt grn	.90 .90
262	A45	75s red, black & grn	4.50 4.50
		Nos. 258-262,C78-C82,CO34-CO36 (13)	29.35 29.35

Centenary of the British Red Cross.

Nos. 153, 152 Surcharged

Litho.; Embossed on Gilt Foil

1971, Jan. 31			**Die Cut**
263	A37	2s on 9p lt blue	.25 .25
264	A37	3s on 9p lt blue	.25 .25
265	A37	5s on 3p pink	.35 .25
266	A37	15s on 9p lt blue	1.10 .65

267	A37	25s on 3p pink	1.50 1.00
268	A37	50s on 3p pink	3.50 2.10

Nos. 263-268,C83-C86,CO37-
CO40 (14)   35.10 24.55

In memory of Queen Salote (1900-65). The "In Memoriam" inscription is in silver on black panel on the 2s, 3s and 15s; in silver on ultramarine panel on the 5s, 25s and 50s. The dates and denominations are all on black panels in silver and metallic red, green, bronze, magenta or gold respectively.

Type of Regular Issue, 1953, Surcharged in Red and Black

1971 Engr. Wmk. 79 Imperf

269	A33	3s on 8p black & pale grn	.25 .25
270	A33	7s on 4p pur & yel	.25 .25
271	A33	25s on 1p yel & blk	.55 .40
272	A33	75s on 2sh car & ultra	3.25 2.10

Nos. 269-272,C87-C89,CO41-
CO43 (10)   14.05 9.40

Philatokyo 71, Philatelic Exposition, Tokyo, Apr. 19-29.

Type of Regular Issue, 1971, Surcharged

1971

273	A34	15s on 1sh car & buff	.50 .50

Nos. 273,C90-C91 (3)   4.00 4.00

Centenary of Japanese postal service.

Self-adhesive & Imperf.
Starting with Nos. 274-278, all issues are self-adhesive and imperforate, unless otherwise stated.

Pole Vault — A46

1971, July Litho. Unwmk. Die Cut

274	A46	3s green, blk & brn	.25 .25
275	A46	7s red, blk & brn	.25 .25
276	A46	15s green, blk & brn	.35 .35
277	A46	25s rose lil, blk & brn	.45 .45
278	A46	50s dk bl, blk & brn	.95 .95

Nos. 274-278,C92-C96,CO44-
CO46 (13)   9.80 9.80

4th South Pacific Games, Papeete, French Polynesia, Sept. 8-19.
For surcharges see Nos. 332, C140.

Gold Medal of Merit — A47

24s, Silver Medal of Merit. 38s, Bronze Medal of Merit, obverse (King Taufa'ahau IV).

Litho; Embossed
1971, Oct. 30   **Imperf.**

279	A47	3s gold & multi	.25 .25
280	A47	24s silver & multi	.40 .40
281	A47	38s bronze & multi	.80 .80

Nos. 279-281,C99-C101,CO49-
CO51 (9)   9.55 9.55

First investiture of Tongan Medal of Merit. For surcharges see Nos. 333-336.

Juggler, UNICEF Emblem A48

1971, Dec. Litho. Die Cut

282	A48	2s violet & multi	.25 .25
283	A48	4s multicolored	.25 .25
284	A48	8s blue & multi	.25 .25
285	A48	16s emerald & multi	.35 .35
286	A48	30s lil rose & multi	.65 .65

Nos. 282-286,C102-
C106,CO52-CO54 (13)   14.15 14.15

25th anniv. of UNICEF.

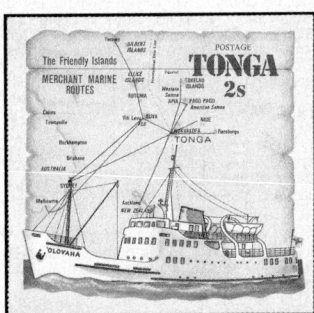

Merchant Marine Routes from Tonga and "Olovaha" — A49

1972, Apr. 14

287	A49	2s blue & multi	.35 .35
288	A49	10s magenta & multi	.85 .35
289	A49	17s brown & multi	1.25 .35
290	A49	21s dk green & multi	1.40 .50
291	A49	60s multicolored	6.50 4.00

Nos. 287-291,C107-
C111,CO55-CO57 (13)   41.95 28.75

Togan Merchant Marine publicity
For surcharges see Nos. C124, CO66-CO69.

King Taufa'ahau IV Coronation Coin, ¼ Hau — A50

Litho.; Embossed on Metallic Foil
1972, July 15

292	A50	5s silver & multi	.25 .25
293	A50	7s silver & multi	.25 .25
294	A50	10s silver & multi	.25 .25
295	A50	17s silver & multi	.40 .40
296	A50	60s silver & multi	1.40 1.40

Nos. 292-296,C112-
C116,CO58-CO60 (13)   15.45 15.45

Coronation of King Taufa'ahau IV, 5th anniv.

Coconut Type of 1970 and

Banana
A51

Watermelon — A52

1972, Sept. 30   **Typo.**

297	A51	1s brt yel, red & blk	.35 .25
298	A51	2s brt yel, bl & blk	.40 .25
299	A51	3s brt yel, emer & blk	.45 .25
300	A51	4s brt yel & blk	.45 .25
301	A51	5s brt yel & brn blk	.45 .25
302	A44	6s brn, org & grn	.50 .25
303	A44	7s brn, ultra & grn	.55 .30
304	A44	8s brn, mag & grn	.55 .30
305	A44	9s brn, red & grn	.55 .30
306	A44	10s brn, bl & grn	.65 .35
307	A52	15s green, org brn & ultra	1.40 .50
308	A52	20s grn, bl & red	1.50 .70
309	A52	25s grn, red & brn	1.75 .80
310	A52	40s grn, bl & org	3.00 1.75
311	A52	50s grn, dk bl & yel	3.00 2.00

Nos. 297-311,O21-O35 (30)   28.85 17.35

Paper backing is brown on Nos. 302-311. Nos. 302-306 have self-adhesive control number in lower left corner of paper backing.

Flag Raising, Minerva Reef — A53

1972, Dec. 9   **Litho.**

312	A53	5s black & multi	.25 .25
313	A53	7s green & multi	.25 .25
314	A53	10s purple & multi	.25 .25
315	A53	15s orange & multi	.35 .35
316	A53	40s ultra & multi	1.40 1.40

Nos. 312-316,C119-
C123,CO63-CO65 (13)   12.75 9.25

Tonga's proclamation of sovereignty over the Minerva Reefs, June 1972.

Tongan Coins and Bank Building — A54

1973, Mar. 30   **Litho.**

317	A54	5s silver & multi	.25 .25
318	A54	7s silver & multi	.25 .25
319	A54	10s silver & multi	.25 .25
320	A54	20s silver & multi	.45 .25
321	A54	30s silver & multi	.60 .35

Nos. 317-321,C125-
C129,CO66-CO68 (13)   17.95 17.10

Establishment of Bank of Tonga.

Handshake, Outrigger Canoe — A55

1973, June 29

322	A55	5s silver & multi	.30 .25
323	A55	7s silver & multi	.45 .25
324	A55	15s silver & multi	1.40 .55
325	A55	21s silver & multi	1.90 .70
326	A55	55s silver & multi	6.75 3.25

Nos. 322-326,C130-
C134,CO69-CO71 (13)   135.00 70.10

Tongan Boy Scout Movement, 25th anniv.

Capt. Cook's Report and Tongan Rulers — A56

Litho.; Embossed on Gilt Foil
1973, Oct. 2

327	A56	6s multicolored	.50 .45
328	A56	8s multicolored	.50 .45
329	A56	11s multicolored	.70 .55
330	A56	35s multicolored	4.75 1.90
331	A56	40s multicolored	4.75 2.25

Nos. 327-331,C135-
C139,CO72-CO74 (13)   60.00 31.45

Bicentenary of Capt. Cook's arrival. Design is from the manuscript in British Museum.

Nos. 278, 281, C100-C101 and 280 Surcharged and Overprinted in Silver or Gold on Red (12s, 14s) or Black Panels (5s, 20s, 50s): "Commonwealth Games Christchurch 1974"

1973, Dec. 19   **Litho.**

332	A46	5s on 50s (G)	.25 .25

Litho.; Embossed

333	A47	12s on 38s (S)	.45 .25
334	A47	14s on 75s (G)	.45 .25
335	A47	20s on 1pa (G)	.80 .35
336	A47	50s on 24s (S)	1.60 1.25

Nos. 332-336,C140-
C144,CO75-CO77 (13)   14.95 11.30

10th British Commonwealth Games, Christchurch, N.Z., Jan. 24-Feb. 2, 1974.

Letter Addressed to Tonga, Names of UPU Members — A57

1974, June 20   **Typo.**

337	A57	5s tan & multi	.25 .25
338	A57	10s tan & multi	.25 .25
339	A57	15s tan & multi	.45 .45
340	A57	20s tan & multi	.50 .50
341	A57	25s tan & multi	1.60 1.60

Nos. 337-341,C154-
C158,CO87-CO89 (13)   14.55 14.55

Centenary of Universal Postal Union.

Girl Guide Badges — A58

1974, Sept. 11   **Litho.**

342	A58	5s multicolored	.45 .30
343	A58	10s multicolored	.85 .50
344	A58	20s multicolored	2.00 1.25

345 A58 40s multicolored 4.00 2.40
346 A58 60s multicolored 5.50 3.25
Nos. 342-346,C159-
C163,CO90-CO92 (13) 49.00 29.20

Girl Guides of Tonga.
For surcharges see Nos. C189, C192.

Sailing
Ship
and
Anchors
A59

1974, Dec. 11
347 A59 5s blue & multi .40 .35
348 A59 10s blue & multi .90 .45
349 A59 25s blue & multi 2.00 .80
350 A59 50s blue & multi 4.00 2.75
351 A59 75s blue & multi 6.00 4.50
Nos. 347-351,C164-
C168,CO93-CO95 (13) 47.00 27.00

Establishment of Royal Marine Institute.

Dateline Hotel, Nukualofa — A60

1975, Mar. 11
352 A60 5s blue & multi .25 .25
353 A60 10s green & multi .25 .25
354 A60 15s scarlet & multi .35 .35
355 A60 30s purple & multi .75 .75
356 A60 1pa orange & multi 2.75 2.75
Nos. 352-356,C169-
C173,CO96-CO98 (13) 15.15 15.15

First meeting of South Pacific area Prime
Ministers. See note after No. 226.

Boxing and Games' Emblem — A61

1975, June 11 Litho.
357 A61 5s black & multi .25 .25
358 A61 10s green & multi .35 .35
359 A61 20s brown & multi .55 .55
360 A61 25s orange & multi .65 .65
361 A61 65s violet & multi 1.40 1.40
Nos. 357-361,C174-
C178,CO99-CO101 (13) 13.35 13.35

5th South Pacific Games, Guam, Aug. 1-10.
See note after No. 226.
For surcharges see Nos. 412, 482.

King
Taufa'ahau IV
Coin — A62

Designs (FAO Coins): 5s, Chicken. 20s, like
1pa, (small coin, 27mm). 50s, School of fish.
2pa, Animals and plants on reverse, King on
obverse (large coin, 42mm).

1975, Sept. 3
362 A62 5s red, sil & blk .25 .25
363 A62 20s ultra, grn, sil &
blk .55 .55
364 A62 50s blue, sil & blk 1.10 1.10
365 A62 1pa silver & black 3.75 3.75
366 A62 2pa silver & black 3.75 3.75
Nos. 362-366,C179-C183 (10) 13.25 13.25

Coinage issued for the benefit of the FAO.
Size of paper backing of 2pa: 82x50mm;
others 45x45mm. See note after No. 226.
For surcharge see Nos. 413.

Coat of Arms, 5pa Coin,
Reverse — A63

George Tupou I Coin, Reverse and
Obverse — A64

Coins: 20s, King Taufa'ahau IV. 50s, King
George Tupou II, 50pa obverse and reverse.
75s, 20pa reverse.

Litho.; Embossed on Gilt Foil
1975, Nov. 4
Pink Background
367 A63 5s black, sil & vio bl .25 .25
368 A64 10s gold, blk & red .35 .25
369 A63 20s black, sil & grn .60 .35
370 A64 50s gold, blk & vio 1.25 1.25
371 A63 75s black, sil & red lil 2.25 2.25
Nos. 367-371,C184-
C188,CO102-CO104 (13) 14.95 13.40

Centenary of Constitution of Tonga. Size of
paper backing of Nos. 367 and 369:
65x60mm; of No. 371, 87x78mm. See note
after No. 226.
For surcharges see Nos. C232, C296.

Montreal Olympic Games
Emblem — A65

1976, Feb. 24 Litho.
372 A65 5s red, ultra & blk .40 .35
373 A65 10s red, green & blk .60 .35
374 A65 25s red, lt brown &
blk 1.40 .80
375 A65 35s red, lilac & blk 1.75 1.10
376 A65 70s red, bister & blk 3.50 2.75
Nos. 372-376,C189-
C193,CO105-CO107 (13) 31.00 20.05

21st Olympic Games, Montreal, Canada,
July 17-Aug. 1. See note after No. 226.
For surcharges see Nos. 414, 478.

William Hooper, William Floyd, John
Penn, Francis Lightfoot Lee — A66

Signers of Declaration of Independence,
Flags of US and Tonga: 10s, Benjamin Frank-
lin, Thomas Nelson, Jr., Benjamin Harrison,
William Ellery. 15s, Oliver Wolcott, Lyman
Hall, William Whipple, Carter Braxton. 25s,
George Taylor, Thomas Stone, Arthur Middle-
ton, Richard Stockton. 75s, Stephen Hopkins,
Elbridge Gerry, James Wilson, Francis
Hopkinson.

1976, May 26 Litho.
377 A66 9s buff & multi .45 .25
378 A66 10s buff & multi .45 .25
379 A66 15s buff & multi .65 .50
380 A66 25s buff & multi 1.00 1.00
381 A66 75s buff & multi 5.75 4.50
Nos. 377-381,C194-
C198,CO108-CO110 (13) 34.50 21.45

American Bicentennial. Printed on peelable
buff paper backing, inscribed in carmine with
facsimile of Declaration of Independence.
For surcharges see #481, C233, C236-
C237, C297.

Nathaniel Turner and John
Thomas — A67

1976, Aug. 25
382 A67 5s yellow & multi .25 .25
383 A67 10s multicolored .40 .25
384 A67 20s multicolored .90 .50
385 A67 25s multicolored 1.00 .55
386 A67 85s multicolored 2.75 2.75
Nos. 382-386,C199-
C203,CO111-CO113 (13) 18.75 16.65

Sesquicentennial of the arrival of Methodist
missionaries and establishment of Christianity
in Tonga. Printed on peelable paper backing
inscribed in manuscript with segments of John
Thomas's Tonga diary.
For surcharges see Nos. 415-416, 479-480.

Wilhelm I and George Tupou I — A68

1976, Nov. 1
387 A68 9s yellow & multi .35 .30
388 A68 15s yellow & multi .55 .50
389 A68 22s yellow & multi .80 .70
390 A68 50s yellow & multi 1.40 1.25
391 A68 73s yellow & multi 1.90 1.75
Nos. 387-391,C204-
C208,CO114-CO116 (13) 16.55 15.65

Tonga-Germany Friendship Treaty, centenary. Printed on peelable paper backing showing reproduction of original treaty.

Queen Salote in Coronation
Procession, 1953 — A69

1977, Feb. 7 Litho.
392 A69 11s blue & multi .40 .40
393 A69 20s green & multi .50 .50
394 A69 30s vio blue & multi .30 .30
395 A69 50s lt green & multi .45 .45
396 A69 75s violet & multi .80 .80
Nos. 392-396,C209-
C213,CO117-CO119 (13) 45.80 23.55

25th anniv. of the reign of Elizabeth II.
Printed on peelable paper backing showing
replica of handwritten Proclamation of
Accession.
For surcharge see No. 417.

Various Coins — A70

1977, July 4
397 A70 10s multicolored .25 .25
398 A70 15s multicolored .30 .30
399 A70 25s multicolored .40 .40
400 A70 50s multicolored .85 .85
401 A70 75s multicolored 1.50 1.50
Nos. 397-401,C214-
C218,CO120-CO122 (13) 13.50 13.50

10th anniversary of coronation of King
Taufa'ahau IV. Printed on peelable paper
backing showing multicolored replicas of Tongan stamps.

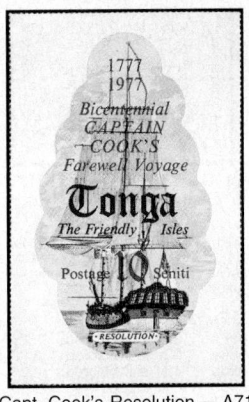

Capt. Cook's Resolution — A71

1977, Sept. 27   Litho.
402 A71 10s multicolored 1.00 .75
403 A71 17s multicolored 2.25 1.25
404 A71 25s multicolored 2.50 2.50
405 A71 30s multicolored 3.50 3.00
406 A71 40s multicolored 3.50 3.00
Nos. 402-406,C219-
C223,CO123-CO125 (13) 81.95 61.90

Bicentenary of Capt. Cook's farewell voyage.

Humpback Whale — A72

1977, Dec. 16
407 A72 15s ultra & black 4.25 .85
408 A72 22s green & black 4.50 1.50
409 A72 31s orange & black 5.25 2.00
410 A72 38s lilac & black 5.50 5.25
411 A72 64s red & black 9.25 5.50
Nos. 407-411,C224-
C228,CO126-CO128 (13) 87.25 38.15

Whale protection.

Stamps of 1975-77 Surcharged in
Black, Green, Brown or Black on Silver
1978, Feb. 17
412 A61 15s on 20s
(#359;B) 2.00 1.75
413 A62 15s on 5s
(#362;B) 2.00 1.75
414 A65 15s on 10s
(#373;G) 2.00 1.75
415 A67 15s on 5s
(#382;Br) 2.00 1.75
416 A67 15s on 10s
(#383;B) 2.00 1.75
417 A69 15s on 11s
(#392;B on
S) 2.00 3.00
418 OA11 15s on 38s
(#CO99;B) 2.00 1.75
Nos. 412-418,C229-C238
(17) 79.75 70.50

The surcharge on No. 413 is only the "1,"
and on No. 418 includes "postage."

Flags of Canada and Tonga A73

1978, May 5   Litho.
419 A73 10s red & multi .25 .25
420 A73 15s red & multi .35 .35
421 A73 20s red & multi .45 .45
422 A73 25s red & multi .60 .60
423 A73 45s red & multi 2.00 2.00
Nos. 419-423,C239-
C243,CO129-CO131 (13) 14.05 14.05

11th Commonwealth Games, Edmonton,
Canada, Aug. 3-12. See note after No. 226.

King Taufa'ahau IV — A74

1978, July 4
424 A74 2s multicolored .25 .25
425 A74 5s multicolored .25 .25
426 A74 10s multicolored .25 .25
427 A74 25s multicolored .65 .65
428 A74 75s multicolored 2.00 2.00
Nos. 424-428,C244-
C248,CO132-CO134 (13) 13.10 13.10

60th birthday of King Taufa'ahau IV. See
note after No. 226.

Two Bananas
A75

Coconut — A76

Designs: 1s to 5s, Bananas. 6s to 10s,
Coconuts. 15s to 1pa, Pineapples.

1978, Sept. 29   Typo.
429 A75 1s yellow & black .30 .30
430 A75 2s yellow & dk blue .30 .30
431 A75 3s multicolored .40 .40
432 A75 4s multicolored .40 .40
433 A75 5s multicolored .40 .40
434 A76 6s multicolored .60 .60
435 A76 7s multicolored .60 .60
436 A76 8s multicolored .60 .60
437 A76 9s multicolored .60 .60
438 A76 10s brown & green .60 .60
439 A76 15s green & lt brown 1.75 1.75
440 A76 20s multicolored 2.00 2.00
441 A76 30s multicolored 2.25 2.25
442 A76 50s multicolored 2.75 2.75
443 A76 1pa multicolored 3.25 3.25
Nos. 429-443,O36-O50 (30) 31.95 31.95

Nos. 429-443 issued in coils; self-adhesive
control numbers on paper backing, except on
1s and 5s. See note after No. 226.
See No. 529.

Whale — A77

1978, Dec. 15   Litho. & Typo.
444 A77 15s shown 4.00 2.00
445 A77 18s Bat 4.00 2.00
446 A77 25s Turtle 4.00 2.00
447 A77 28s Parrot 6.50 3.00
448 A77 60s like 15s 10.50 6.00
Nos. 444-448,C249-
C253,CO150-CO152 (13) 85.75 45.50

Wildlife conservation. See note after No. 226.

Introduction of Metric System — A78

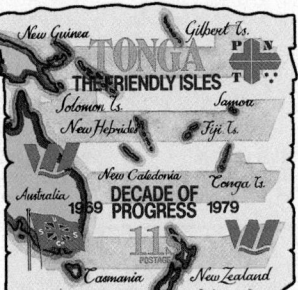

Shipping Routes, South Pacific
Map — A79

Peace
Corps — A80

22s, New church buildings. 50s, Air routes
to Auckland, Suva, Apia & Pago Pago.

1979, Feb. 16   Litho.
449 A78 5s multicolored .25 .25
450 A79 11s multicolored .35 .25
451 A80 18s multicolored .50 .40
452 A79 22s multicolored .60 .50
453 A79 50s multicolored 1.50 .80
Nos. 449-453,C254-
C258,CO153-CO155 (13) 14.30 9.25

Decade of Progress. Paper backing shows
map of Tonga.

Tongan First Day Covers — A81

1979, June 1
454 A81 5s multicolored .25 .25
455 A81 10s multicolored .25 .25
456 A81 25s multicolored .60 .60
457 A81 50s multicolored 1.25 1.25
458 A81 1pa multicolored 1.75 1.75
Nos. 454-458,C259-
C263,CO156-CO158 (13) 12.50 12.50

10th anniversary of introduction of self-
adhesive stamps and for Bernard Mechanick,
inventor of self-adhesive, free-form stamps;
death centenary of Sir Rowland Hill.
Printed on peelable paper backing showing
advertisement.
For surcharges and overprints see Nos.
469-473.

Eua Island through Camera
Lens — A82

1979, Nov. 23   Litho.
459 A82 10s multicolored .25 .25
460 A82 18s multicolored .45 .45
461 A82 31s multicolored .75 .75
462 A82 50s multicolored 1.10 1.10
463 A82 60s multicolored 1.40 1.40
Nos. 459-463,C275-
C279,CO170-CO172 (13) 12.05 12.05

Printed on peelable paper backing showing
film and camera.

King George Tupou I, Admiral du
Bouzet, Map of Tonga — A83

1980, Jan. 9   Litho.
464 A83 7s multicolored .25 .25
465 A83 10s multicolored .35 .35
466 A83 14s multicolored .45 .45
467 A83 50s multicolored 1.40 1.40
468 A83 75s multicolored 1.90 1.90
Nos. 464-468,C280-
C284,CO173-CO175 (13) 13.55 13.55

Tongan-French Friendship Treaty, 125th
anniversary. Printed on peelable paper; multicolored backing shows map of Tonga.

Nos. 454-458 Surcharged and
Overprinted in Black on Silver: "1980
OLYMPIC GAMES," Moscow '80 and
Bear Emblems

1980, Apr. 30   Litho.
469 A81 13s on 5s multi .50 .50
470 A81 20s on 10s multi .75 .75
471 A81 25s multicolored .90 .90
472 A81 33s on 50s multi 1.10 1.10
473 A81 1pa multicolored 3.50 3.50
Nos. 469-473,C285-
C289,CO176-CO178 (13) 18.15 18.15

Boy Scout Cooking over
Campfire — A84

1980, Sept. 30   Litho.
474 A84 9s multicolored .25 .25
475 A84 13s multicolored .40 .40
476 A84 15s multicolored .45 .45
477 A84 30s multicolored .90 .90
Nos. 474-477,C290-
C293,CO179-CO180 (10) 17.00 17.00

Boy Scout Jamboree; Rotary Intl., 75th
anniv. Peelable backing shows map of Tonga.

Nos. 361, 375, 380, 384-385
Surcharged

				Litho.
1980, Dec. 3				**Litho.**
478	A65	9s on 35s multi	.50	.50
479	A67	13s on 20s multi	.75	.75
480	A67	13s on 25s multi	.75	.75
481	A66	19s on 25s multi	1.10	1.10
482	A61	1pa on 65s multi	6.25	6.25
		Nos. 478-482,C294- C299,CO181 (12)	27.85	27.85

Intl. Year of the Disabled — A85

1981, Sept. 9				**Litho.**
483	A85	2pa multicolored	3.25	3.25
484	A85	3pa multicolored	5.00	5.00
		Nos. 483-484,C300-C302 (5)	10.45	10.45

Prince Charles and Lady Diana — A86

Designs: 13s, Charles, King Taufa'ahau. 47s, 1.50pa, Couple, diff.

1981, Oct. 21				**Litho.**
485	A86	13s multicolored	.25	.25
486	A86	47s multicolored	.50	.50
487	A86	1.50pa multicolored	1.75	1.75
488	A86	3pa multicolored	3.50	3.50
		Nos. 485-488 (4)	6.00	6.00

Royal Wedding and Gt. Britain-Tonga Friendship Treaty centenary. Issued in sheets of 20 (2x10) and 5 labels in vert. center row. For surcharge see No. B1.

Bicentenary of Discovery of Vavau by Francisco Maurelle A87

18th century Spanish engravings and maps.

1981, Nov. 25				**Litho.**
489	A87	9s multicolored	.60	.50
490	A87	13s multicolored	.90	.60
491	A87	47s multicolored	2.75	1.40
492	A87	1pa multicolored	6.75	6.75
a.		Souvenir sheet, imperf.	13.00	13.00
		Nos. 489-492 (4)	11.00	9.25

No. 492a contains one No. 492 (32x25mm).

Bible Class, 1830 Print — A88

1981, Nov. 25				
493	A88	9s Open book	.30	.30
494	A88	13s Book, diff.	.50	.40
495	A88	32s Type	1.10	1.10
496	A88	47s shown	1.60	1.60
		Nos. 493-496 (4)	3.50	3.40

Christmas 1981 and sesquicentennial of books printed in Tonga.

175th Anniv. of Capture of The Port-au-Prince — A89

1981, Dec. 16				**Litho.**
497	A89	29s Battle	1.00	.75
498	A89	32s Battle, diff.	1.25	.90
499	A89	47s Map	1.60	1.50
500	A89	47s Sinking ship	1.60	1.50
a.		Pair, #499-500	3.25	
501	A89	1pa Ship	3.50	3.50
		Nos. 497-501 (5)	8.95	8.15

Nos. CO179-CO180 Surcharged

1982, Jan. 4				**Litho.**
502	OA19	5pa on 25s multi	17.50	17.50
503	OA19	5pa on 2pa multi	17.50	17.50

Scouting Year — A90

1982, Feb. 22				**Litho.**
504	A90	29s Brownsea Isld. Camp, 1907	1.00	.60
505	A90	32s Baden-Powell, horse	1.00	.65
506	A90	47s Imperial Jamboree, 1924	1.50	1.00
507	A90	1.50pa "Scouting for Boys"	4.50	3.00
508	A90	2.50pa Mafeking stamp	8.00	5.00
		Nos. 504-508 (5)	16.00	10.25

1982 World Cup — A91

Designs: Various soccer players, map showing match sites.

1982, July 7				**Litho.**
509	A91	32s multicolored	.85	.60
510	A91	47s multicolored	1.25	.85
511	A91	75s multicolored	1.90	1.40
512	A91	1.50pa multicolored	3.50	2.50
		Nos. 509-512 (4)	7.50	5.35

Inter-island Transport A92

9s, 13s, Ferry Olovaha. 47s, 1pa SPIA Twin Otter (Niuatoputapu Airport opening).

1982, Aug. 11				
513	A92	9s multicolored	.50	.25
514	A92	13s multicolored	.60	.30
515	A92	47s multicolored	2.00	1.00
516	A92	1pa multicolored	4.00	2.75
		Nos. 513-516 (4)	7.10	4.30

Tin Can Mail Centenary A93

13s, 32s, 47s, Collecting mail. 2pa, Map. Nos. 517-519 form continuous design.

1982, Sept. 29				**Litho.**
517	A93	13s multicolored	.25	.25
518	A93	32s multicolored	.55	.55
519	A93	47s multicolored	.90	.90
a.		Souv. sheet of 3 (13s, 32s, 47s)	2.00	2.00
520		2pa multicolored	3.50	3.50
a.		Souvenir sheet of 1	3.50	3.50
		Nos. 517-520 (4)	5.20	5.20

No. 520 comes with different labels. For surcharges see Nos. 526-528.

Tonga College Centenary — A94

1982, Oct. 25			Size: 42x30mm (5s)
521	A94	5s Students	.35 .35
522	A94	29s King George Tupou I	2.25 2.25
523	A94	29s Monument	2.25 2.25
a.		Pair, #522-523	5.00
		Nos. 521-523 (3)	4.85 4.85

Nos. 521-523 inscribed in English or Tongan.

12th Commonwealth Games, Brisbane, Australia, Sept. 30-Oct. 9 — A95

1982, Oct. 25				
524	A95	32s Decathlon, vert.	1.60	.75
525	A95	1.50pa Opening ceremony	8.25	8.25

Nos. 517-519 Overprinted in Red or Silver in 1 or 2 Lines: "Christmas / Greetings / 1982"

1982, Nov. 17				
526	A93	13s multicolored	.30	.30
527	A93	32s multicolored	.70	.70
528	A93	47s multicolored	1.00	1.00
		Nos. 526-528 (3)	2.00	2.00

Pineapple Type of 1978 and

Fruit — A96

1982, Nov. 17				
529	A76	13s multicolored	5.50	5.50
530	A96	2pa multicolored	12.00	12.00
531	A96	3pa multicolored	15.00	15.00
		Nos. 529-531 (3)	32.50	32.50

Capt. Cook's Resolution, 1777 and Canberra, 1983 — A96a

32s, like 29s. 47s, 1.50pa, Montgolfier Bros. balloon, 1783, Concorde. 2.50pa, Concorde, Canberra. 29s se-tenant with label showing Resolution.

1983, Feb. 22				**Litho.**
532	A96a	29s multicolored	2.25	1.50
533	A96a	32s multicolored	3.00	1.50
534	A96a	47s multicolored	4.25	2.50
535	A96a	1.50pa multicolored	11.00	11.00
		Nos. 532-535 (4)	20.50	16.50

Souvenir Sheet

536	A96a	2.50pa multicolored	6.50	6.50

Pacific Forum of Sea and Air Transport (29s, 32s, 2.50pa); manned flight bicentenary (47s, 1.50pa).

For overprints see Nos. O68-O70.

A96b

1983, Mar. 14				
537	A96b	29s Map	1.40	1.40
538	A96b	32s Dancers	1.60	1.60
539	A96b	47s Fishermen	2.25	2.25
540	A96b	1.50pa King Taufa'ahau IV, flag	7.00	7.00
		Nos. 537-540 (4)	12.25	12.25

Commonwealth Day.

Niuafo'ou Airport Opening A97

1983, May 11				**Litho.**
541	A97	32s De Havilland Otter	.90	.50
542	A97	47s like 32s	1.25	.50
543	A97	1pa Boeing 707	2.10	1.40
544	A97	1.50pa like 1pa	3.75	2.10
		Nos. 541-544 (4)	8.00	4.50

World Communications Year — A98

1983, June 22				**Litho.**
545	A98	29s Intelsat IV	.50	.50
546	A98	32s Intelsat IV-A	.60	.60
547	A98	75s Intelsat V	1.40	1.40

			Size: 45x32mm
548	A98	2pa Apollo 15 Moon post cover	3.50 3.50
		Nos. 545-548 (4)	6.00 6.00

10th Anniv. of Bank of Tonga A99

Various banknotes.

1983, Aug. 3 — Litho.
549	A99	1pa multicolored		2.25	2.25
550	A99	2pa multicolored		4.25	4.25

Printing Press, 1830 — A100

1983, Sept. 22 — Litho.
551	A100	13s shown		.30	.30
552	A100	32s Woon's arrival,	1831	.75	.75
553	A100	1pa Print		1.75	1.75
554	A100	2pa Tonga Chronicle		3.75	3.75
		Nos. 551-554 (4)		6.55	6.55

Sesquicentennial of printing in Tonga (by missionary William Woon).

Christmas 1983 A101

Designs: Various sailboats off Vava'u.

1983, Nov. 17 — Litho.
555	A101	29s multicolored	.50	.40
556	A101	32s multicolored	.60	.50
557	A101	1.50pa multicolored	2.40	2.40
558	A101	2.50pa multicolored	4.25	4.25
		Nos. 555-558 (4)	7.75	7.55

Abel Tasman, Discoverer of Tonga, and his Zeehan — A102

Navigators and Explorers of the Pacific and their Ships.

1984, Mar. 12 — Litho.
559	A102	32s shown	2.00	2.00
560	A102	47s Samuel Wallis, Dolphin	2.75	2.75
561	A102	90s William Bligh, Bounty	5.00	5.00
562	A102	1.50pa James Cook, Resolution	9.00	9.00
		Nos. 559-562 (4)	18.75	18.75

See Nos. 593-596.

Swainsonia Casta — A103

Shells, fish.

1984-85 — Litho.
563	A103	1s shown	.50	1.90
564	A103	2s Porites (coral)	1.25	1.90
565	A103	3s Holocentrus ruber	1.60	2.25
566	A103	5s Cypraea mappa viridis	.60	1.90
567	A103	6s Dardanus megistos (crab)	1.60	2.25
568	A103	9s Stegostoma fasciatum	1.60	.90
a.		Perf. 14½ ('85)	1.60	.90
569	A103	10s Conus bullatus	1.25	.95
570	A103	13s Pterois volitans	1.90	.95
571	A103	15s Conus textile	1.25	2.25
572	A103	20s Dascyllus aruanus	2.75	2.75
573	A103	29s Conus aulicus	2.25	1.25
574	A103	32s Acanthurus leucosternon	4.00	1.25
575	A103	47s Lambis truncata	4.00	2.00

Size: 39x25mm
576	A103	1pa Millepora dichotama (coral)	12.00	12.00
577	A103	2pa Birgus latro (crab)	17.50	19.00
578	A103	3pa Chicoreus palma-rosae	11.00	19.00
579	A103	5pa Thunnus albacares	13.50	22.50
		Nos. 563-579 (17)	78.55	95.00

See Nos. 682-692, 701-709, 756-759. For surcharges and overprints see Nos. 618-625, 808-810, O52-O67, O71-O77.

Tonga Chronicle, 20th Anniv. — A104

1984, June 26
580	A104	3s multicolored	.25	.25
a.		Sheet of 12	.75	
581	A104	32s multicolored	.50	.50
a.		Sheet of 12	7.00	

Nos. 580-581 issued in sheets of 12; sheet backgrounds show pages of Chronicle, giving each stamp a different background.

1984 Summer Olympics A105

1984, July 23
582	A105	29s Running	.40	.40
583	A105	47s Javelin	.65	.65
584	A105	1.50pa Shot put	2.00	2.00
585	A105	3pa Torch	4.25	4.25
		Nos. 582-585 (4)	7.30	7.30

Intl. Dateline Centenary — A106

1984, Aug. 20
586	A106	47s George Airy, Greenwich Meridian pioneer	2.00	1.50
587	A106	2pa Sandford Fleming, time zone pioneer	9.00	6.00

Ausipex '84 — A107

1984, Sept. 17
588	A107	32s Australia #18	1.25	.85
589	A107	1.50pa Tonga #51	5.50	3.75

Souvenir Sheet
589A		Sheet of 2, #588-589	5.50	5.50

Nos. 588-589 each printed se-tenant with label showing exhibition emblem.

No. 589A contains two imperf. stamps similar to Nos. 588-589, but with denomination replacing logo. No. 589A without denominations was not valid for postage.

Christmas 1984 — A108

Christmas Carols in local settings.

1984, Nov. 12 — Litho.
590	A108	32s Silent Night	.90	.50
591	A108	47s Away in a Manger	1.60	.80
592	A108	1pa I Saw Three Ships	3.25	3.25
		Nos. 590-592 (3)	5.75	4.55

Famous Mariners

Designs: 32s, Willem Schouten (c. 1580-1625), The Eendracht, 1616. 47s, Jakob Le Maire (1585-1616), The Hoorn, 1615. 90s, Lt. Fletcher Christian, The Bounty, 1789. 1.50pa, Francisco Maurelle, La Princessa, 1781.

1985, Feb. 27 — Litho. — Die Cut
593	A102	32s multicolored	1.50	1.50
a.		Perf. 14	50.00	
594	A102	47s multicolored	3.75	1.75
595	A102	90s multicolored	6.75	5.00
596	A102	1.50pa multicolored	12.00	7.75
		Nos. 593-596 (4)	25.00	16.00

Nos. 593-596 each printed se-tenant with self-adhesive label picturing anchor.

Geological Survey of Tonga Trench for Oil — A110

Designs: 29s, Tonga Trench and islands. 32s, Marine exploration, seismic surveying. 47s, Search for oil off Tongatapu, vert. No. 600, Exploration of sea bed, vert. No. 601, Angler fish.

1985, Apr. 10
597	A110	29s multicolered	1.50	1.10
598	A110	32s multicolored	1.60	1.10
599	A110	47s multicolored	2.50	1.60
600	A110	1.50pa multicolored	8.25	8.25
		Nos. 597-600 (4)	13.85	12.05

Souvenir Sheet
601	A110	1.50pa multicolored	13.00	7.75
a.		Perf. 14	13.00	7.75

Nos. 597-600 printed in sheets of 40, 2 panes of 20 separated by labels inscribed "Proof 1," etc.

Adventures of Will Mariner — A111

29s, Readying Port au Prince for sail, Gravesend, 1805. 32s, Captured & set afire, 1806. 47s, Mariner taken prisoner by Chief Finow, Tonga. 1.50pa, Passage to China aboard brig Favourite. 2.50pa, Returning to England aboard East Indiaman Cuffnells, 1810.

1985, June 18 — Die Cut
602	A111	29s multicolored	.60	.50
a.		Perf. 14	.60	.50
603	A111	32s multicolored	.65	.55
a.		Perf. 14	.65	.55
604	A111	47s multicolored	1.00	.80
a.		Perf. 14	1.00	.80
605	A111	1.50pa multicolored	3.75	3.75
a.		Perf. 14	3.75	
606	A111	2.50pa multicolored	6.00	6.00
a.		Perf. 14	6.00	
		Nos. 602-606 (5)	12.00	11.60
		Nos. 602a-606a (5)	12.00	11.60

Mutiny on the Bounty, Film 50th Anniv. A112

Designs: a, Byron Russell (Quintal), Stanley Fields (Muspratt) and Charles Laughton (Capt. Bligh). b, Laughton, Donald Crisp (Burkitt), Eddie Quillon (Ellison) and David Thursby (Maxwell). c, Clark Gable (Fletcher Christian). d, Russell, Alec Craig (McCoy), Laughton and Fields. e, Laughton and Franchot Tone (Roger Byam).

1985, July 16 — Perf. 14
607		Strip of 5	62.50	62.50
a.-e.	A112	47s, any single	10.00	5.00

Sheets consist of four strips of 5 and a central strip of labels showing film credits.

Queen Mother, 85th Birthday A113

Designs: 32s, Age 10. 47s, At Hadfield Girl Guides rally, 1931. 1.50pa, In Guide uniform. 2.50pa, Portrait by Norman Parkinson, 1985.

1985, Aug. 20 — Imperf.
608	A113	32s multicolored	1.25	.90
a.		Perf. 14	2.00	1.50
609	A113	47s multicolored	2.00	1.50
a.		Perf. 14	3.25	2.40
610	A113	1.50pa multicolored	6.00	6.00
a.		Perf. 14	9.25	9.25
611	A113	2.50pa multicolored	9.75	9.75
a.		Perf. 14	15.00	15.00
		Nos. 608-611 (4)	19.00	18.15
		Nos. 608a-611a (4)	29.50	28.15

Girl Guides movement, 75th anniv.

Christmas — A114

1985, Nov. 12
612	A114	32s No room at the inn	.50	.35
613	A114	42s Shepherds follow star	.75	.50
614	A114	1.50pa The three kings	2.75	2.75
615	A114	2.50pa Holy family	4.25	4.25
		Nos. 612-615 (4)	8.25	7.85

Self-adhesive Discontinued

In 1986, imperforate self-adhesive stamps attached to peelable paper backing were no longer issued, unless otherwise stated.

Halley's Comet A115

Designs: Nos. 616a, 617a, Comet. Nos. 616b, 617b, Edmond Halley. Nos. 616c, 617c, Solar system. Nos. 616d, 617d, Telescope. Nos. 616e, 617e, Giotto space probe.

1986, Mar. 26 — Perf. 14
616		Strip of 5	19.00	19.00
a.-e.	A115	42s, any single	3.00	3.00
617		Strip of 5	19.00	19.00
a.-e.	A115	57s, any single	3.00	3.00

Nos. 564, 570, 565, 568, 567, 572, 577 and 579 Surcharged

1986, Apr. 16   Litho.   Imperf.
Self-adhesive

618	A103	4s on 2s, #564	1.10	2.25
619	A103	4s on 13s, #570	1.10	2.25
620	A103	42s on 3s, #565	2.90	1.75
621	A103	42s on 9s, #568	2.90	1.75
622	A103	57s on 6s, #567	3.50	2.50
623	A103	57s on 20s, #572	3.50	2.50
624	A103	2.50pa on 2pa, #577	11.00	11.00
625	A103	2.50pa on 5pa, #579	11.00	11.00
		Nos. 618-625 (8)	37.00	35.00

Royal Links with the United Kingdom A116

1986, May 22   Perf. 14

626	A116	57s Taufa'ahau IV	1.50	1.50
627	A116	57s Elizabeth II	1.50	1.50
a.		Pair, #626-627	3.50	3.50

Size: 40x40mm

628	A116	2.50pa King and queen	6.00	6.00
		Nos. 626-628 (3)	9.00	9.00

Queen Elizabeth II, 60th birthday. No. 628 printed in sheets of 5 plus one label.

AMERIPEX '86, Chicago, May 22- June 1 — A117

Peace Corps activities: No. 629, Health care. No. 630, Education.

1986, May 22

629	A117	57s multicolored	1.10	1.10
630	A117	1.50pa multicolored	3.00	3.00
a.		Souv. sheet, #629, 630, imperf	4.75	4.75
b.		Pair, #629-630	5.75	5.75

Peace Corps in Tonga, 20th anniv.

Intl. Sporting Events — A118

Designs: 42s, 1986 Field Hockey World Cup, London. 57s, Women's basketball, 13th Commonwealth Games, Scotland. 1pa, Boxing, Commonwealth Games. 2.50pa, 1986 World Cup Soccer Championships, Mexico.

1986, July 23   Litho.   Perf. 14

631	A118	42s multicolored	1.25	1.25
632	A118	57s multicolored	2.00	2.00
633	A118	1pa multicolored	3.25	3.25
634	A118	2.50pa multicolored	8.00	8.00
		Nos. 631-634 (4)	14.50	14.50

Postage Stamp Cent. A119

Stamps on stamps: No. 635, #1. No. 636, #47a. No. 637, #91. No. 638, #628. No. 639a, #40, UL portion of #C29. No. 639b, UR portion of #C29, left side #245. No. 639c, Center of #245, Type AP10. No. 639d, Left side #245, #C148. No. 639e, LL portion of #C29, #429, #440. No. 639f, LR portion of #C29, #C135. No. 639g, #507. No. 639h, #514. Nos. 639a-639h, vert.

1986, Aug. 27

635	A119	32s multi	2.50	1.75
636	A119	42s multi	2.75	2.00
637	A119	57s multi	3.50	2.00
638	A119	2.50pa multi	5.75	5.75
		Nos. 635-638 (4)	14.50	11.50

Souvenir Sheet

639		Sheet of 8	15.00	15.00
a.-h.		A119 50s, any single	1.50	1.50

Christmas — A120

Designs: 32s, Girls wearing shell jewelry. 42s, Boy, totem poles, vert. 57s, Folk dancers, vert. 2pa, outrigger canoe.

1986, Nov. 12   Litho.   Perf. 14

640	A120	32s multicolored	2.50	.75
641	A120	42s multicolored	2.75	1.00
642	A120	57s multicolored	3.00	1.50
643	A120	2pa multicolored	6.25	6.25
		Nos. 640-643 (4)	14.50	9.50

Nos. 641-642 Ovptd. with Jamboree Emblem and "BOY SCOUT / JAMBOREE / 5th-10th DEC '86" in Silver

1986, Dec. 2   Litho.   Perf. 14

644	A120	42s multicolored	3.50	3.50
645	A120	57s multicolored	3.75	3.75

Dumont d'Urville's Second Voyage A121

Designs: 32s, D'Urville and ship Astrolabe. 42s, Four Tongan girls, detail fron D'Urville's engraving, Voyage au Pole et dans l'Oceanie. 1pa, Map of voyage. 2.50pa, Wreck of the Astrolabe.

1987, Feb. 24

646	A121	32s multicolored	4.25	2.00
647	A121	42s multicolored	4.25	2.00
648	A121	1pa multicolored	10.00	6.00
649	A121	2.50pa multicolored	16.00	16.00
		Nos. 646-649 (4)	34.50	26.00

Dumont d'Urville (1790-1842), explorer and admiral.

Wildlife Conservation — A122

Fauna: a, Noah's Ark. b, Eagles. c, Giraffes, birds. d, Seagulls. e, Elephants, ostriches. f, Elephant. g, Lions, zebras, antelopes. h, Chimpanzees. i, Antelope, frogs. j, Tigers, lizard. k, Tiger, snake. l, Butterfly.

1987, May 6   Perf. 13½

650		Sheet of 12	67.50	67.50
a.-l.		A122 42s any single	4.25	4.25

1st Inter-island Canoe Race, Tonga to Samoa — A123

1987, July 1   Perf. 14

651	A123	32s Two paddlers	.55	.45
652	A123	42s Five paddlers	.85	.70
653	A123	57s Three paddlers	1.10	.90
654	A123	1.50pa Two, diff.	3.00	3.00
a.		Souvenir sheet of 4, #651-654	10.00	10.00
		Nos. 651-654 (4)	5.50	5.05

Coronation of King Taufa'ahau IV, 20th Anniv. — A124

Booklet Stamps

1987-88   Imperf.
Self-Adhesive

655	A124	1s green & yel grn	.35	.85
655A	A124	2s blk & pale yel org	4.00	4.00
656	A124	5s black & brt pink	.35	.85
a.		Bklt. pane of 12 (6 5s plus 1 1s, 2 10s, 3 15s with gutter between)	5.00	
657	A124	10s black & bluish lil	.45	.95
658	A124	15s brn blk & org ver	.60	.95
a.		Bklt. pane of 12 (1s, 2 2s, 3 10s, plus 2 5s, 10s, 3 15s with gutter between) ('88)	14.00	
659	A124	32s Prus bl & aqua	.70	1.00
a.		Bklt. pane, 4 32s, 2 15s + 4 10s, 2 1s with gutter between)	7.00	
b.		Bklt. pane, 6 32s + 2 2s, 4 1s with gutter btwn. ('88)	14.00	
		Nos. 655-659 (6)	6.45	8.60

Issued: 2s, 7/4/88; others, 7/1/87.

Parliament, 125th Anniv. — A125

1987, Sept. 2   Litho.   Perf. 14½

660	A125	32s multicolored	.50	.50
661	A125	42s multicolored	.75	.75
662	A125	75s multicolored	1.50	1.50
663	A125	2pa multicolored	3.00	3.00
		Nos. 660-663 (4)	5.75	5.75

Christmas 1987 — A126

Cartoons featuring Octopus as Santa Claus and mouse as his helper.

1987, Nov. 18   Litho.   Perf. 14

664	A126	42s Sack of gifts	1.50	.80
665	A126	57s Delivering them by canoe	1.75	1.75
666	A126	1pa By automobile	3.25	3.25
667	A126	3pa Sipping tropical drinks	8.00	8.00
		Nos. 664-667 (4)	14.50	13.80

King Taufa'ahau Tupou IV, 70th Birthday — A127

Portrait and: 32s, M.V. *Olovaha* inter-island ship, athlete pole vaulting and offshore oil derrick. 42s, Banknote and coins, Ha'Amonga Trilithon and traditional craftsman. 57s, Rowing, Red Cross nurse and communications

---

satellite. 2.50pa, Tonga Scouts emblem, No. 506 and Friendly Islands Airways passenger plane.

1988, July 4   Litho.   Perf. 11½

668	A127	32s multicolored	2.25	1.00
669	A127	42s multicolored	1.60	1.10
670	A127	57s multicolored	1.75	1.10
671	A127	2.50pa multicolored	8.00	8.00
		Nos. 668-671 (4)	13.60	11.20

See Nos. 744-747 for stamps inscribed for the silver jubilee.

Souvenir Sheet

Australia Bicentennial — A128

Designs: a, Cook and his journal. b, List of stores shipped aboard the *Lady Juliana*, the ship, Arthur Philip, 1st gov. of New South Wales, 1788, and left half of the list of sentences of all the prisoners tried at Glo'ster Assizes. c, Right half of list of sentences, Australia Type A59 redrawn and aerial view of an early settlement. d, Robert O'Hara Burke (1820-61) and W.J. Wills (1834-61), the 1st explorers to cross Australia from south to north. e, Emu pictured on a Player's cigarette card, U.R. Stuart's (gold) prospecting license and opals. f, Australian Commonwealth Military Forces emblem, WW I recruit on cigarette card, and war poster. g, Souv. card commemorating 1st overland mail delivery by transcontinental railway, and Australia Type A4 on cover. h, Hand-canceled cover commemorating the 1st England-Australia transcontinental airmail flight, Nov. 12-Dec.10, 1919, aviator Capt. Ross Smith (1892-1922) and Great Britain #588. i, Don Bradman and Harold Larwood, cricket champions of the 1930s, on cigarette cards, and era newspaper frontispiece. j, Frontispiece of Hulton's natl. weekly *Picture Post* Victory Special issue, and WW II campaign medals. k, Australia #676 and a sheep station. l, Sydney Harbor Bridge, Opera House and theater tickets to *The Bartered Bride*.

1988, July 11   Litho.   Perf. 13½

672	A128	Sheet of 12	45.00	45.00
a.-l.		42s any single	3.00	3.00

1988 Summer Olympics, Seoul — A129

1988, Aug. 11   Perf. 14

673	A129	57s Running	.90	.90
674	A129	75s Yachting	1.10	1.10
675	A129	2pa Cycling	5.50	5.50
676	A129	3pa Women's tennis	6.50	6.50
		Nos. 673-676 (4)	14.00	14.00

Music of Tonga A130

1988, Sept. 9   Litho.   Perf. 14

677	A130	32s shown	.45	.35
678	A130	42s Choir	.65	.50
679	A130	57s Tonga Police Band	.80	.70
680	A130	2.50pa The Jets	3.50	3.50
		Nos. 677-680 (4)	5.40	5.05

Souvenir Sheet

681		Sheet of 2	3.50	3.50
a.	A130	57s like 2.50pa	1.10	1.10
b.	A130	57s Olympic eternal flame	1.10	1.10

SPORT AID '88.

Marine Type of 1984

Two types of background shading on No. 690:
Type I: Shading at top and sides extends to vert. & horiz. edges of design.
Type II: Shading is oval shaped.

1988   Litho.   Perf. 14½
Size: 27x34mm

682	A103	1s like No. 563	.30	.30
683	A103	2s like No. 564	.40	.40
684	A103	5s like No. 566	.55	.55
685	A103	6s like No. 567	1.10	1.10
686	A103	10s like No. 569	.65	.65
687	A103	15s like No. 571	.65	.65
688	A103	20s like No. 572	.95	.95
689	A103	32s like No. 574	1.10	1.10
690	A103	42s Fregata ariel, type I	4.00	.95
a.		Type II	35.00	
691	A103	57s Sula leuco-gaster	4.75	1.25

Size: 41x27mm
Perf. 14

692	A103	3pa Like No. 578	3.00	9.00
		Nos. 682-692 (11)	17.45	16.90

Issued: 1s, 5s, 10s, 20s, 32s, Oct. 4; 2s, 6s, 15s, 42s, 57s, 3pa, Oct. 18.
Nos. 683-684, 686, 689 exist inscribed "1990."
See #701-709. For surcharge see #808.

Tonga-US Treaty, Cent. A131

1988, Oct. 20   Perf. 14

693	A131	42s *Resolution*	1.00	.75
694	A131	57s *Santa Maria*	1.50	1.10
695	A131	2pa Capt. Cook, Columbus	5.50	5.50
a.		Souvenir sheet of 3, #693-695	7.25	7.25
		Nos. 693-695 (3)	8.00	7.35

Christmas — A132

Designs (a, Intl. Red Cross, b, Natl. Red Cross): 15s, Girl, teddy bear. 32s, Nurse reading to child. 42s, Checking pulse. 57s, Tucking child into bed. 1.50pa, Boy in wheelchair.

1988, Nov. 17   Litho.   Perf. 14½

696	A132	15s Pair, #a.-b.	.50	.50
697	A132	32s Pair, #a.-b.	1.00	1.00
698	A132	42s Pair, #a.-b.	1.10	1.10
699	A132	57s Pair, #a.-b.	1.90	1.90
700	A132	1.50pa Pair, #a.-b.	4.75	4.75
		Nos. 696-700 (5)	9.25	9.25

Intl. Red Cross 125th anniv. and 25th anniv. of the natl. Red Cross.

Marine Type of 1984

1989, Mar. 2   Litho.
Size: 27x34mm

701	A103	4s like No. 570	1.90	1.90
702	A103	7s Diomedea exulans	4.50	3.00
703	A103	35s Hippocampus	4.00	3.25
704	A103	50s like No. 573	4.50	2.40

Size: 41x27mm
Perf. 14

705	A103	1pa Chelonia mydas	7.25	5.50
706	A103	1.50pa Megaptera novaeangliae	14.50	9.00
707	A103	2pa like No. 577	10.50	10.50
709	A103	5pa like No. 579	17.00	20.00
		Nos. 701-709 (8)	64.15	55.55

Mutiny on the *Bounty*, Bicent. — A133

32s, Map of Tofua & Kao Isls., breadfruit. 42s, *Bounty*, chronometer. 57s, William Bligh & castaways in longboat. 2pa, Mutineers on the *Bounty*, vert. 3pa, Castaways.

Perf. 13½x14, 14x13½
1989, Apr. 28   Photo.

710	A133	32s multicolored	4.50	2.50
711	A133	42s multicolored	7.50	3.25
712	A133	57s multicolored	10.00	4.75
		Nos. 710-712 (3)	22.00	10.50

Souvenir Sheet

713		Sheet of 2	17.00	17.00
a.	A133	2pa multicolored	5.00	5.00
b.	A133	3pa multicolored	7.50	7.50

Butterflies A134

1989, May 15   Litho.   Perf. 14½

714	A134	42s *Hypolimnas bolina*	1.25	.85
715	A134	57s *Jamides bochus*	1.60	1.10
716	A134	1.20pa *Melanitis leda solandra*	3.75	2.75
717	A134	2.50pa *Danaus plexippus*	7.25	7.25
		Nos. 714-717 (4)	13.85	11.95

Opening of the Natl. Sports Stadium and the South Pacific Mini Games, Aug. 22 A135

Rugby (No. 718): a, Rugby Public School, 1870. b, Dave Gallaher and the Springboks vs. East Midlands, 1906. c, King George V inspecting Cambridge team of 1922 and Wavell Wakefield, captain of England. d, Ernie Crawford, captain of Ireland, Danie Craven demonstrating the dive pass and cigarette cards from the 1930's. e, Sioni Mafi, captain of Tonga, and match scene.
Tennis (No. 719): a, Royal tennis, 1659. b, Walter Clopton Wingfield and game of lawn tennis, 1873. c, Oxford and Cambridge teams of 1884. d, Bunny Ryan in 1910 and cigarette cards. e, Tennis players, 1980's.
Cricket (No. 720): a, Match in 1743 and bronze memorial to Fuller Pilch. b, W.G. Grace, 19th cent. c, *The Boys Own Paper*, 1909. d, Australian team of 1909 and cigarette cards. e, The Ashes trophy and modern match scene.

1989, Aug. 22   Litho.   Perf. 14

718		Strip of 5	6.25	6.25
a.-e.	A135	32s any single	1.00	1.00
719		Strip of 5	9.50	9.50
a.-e.	A135	42s any single	1.50	1.50
720		Strip of 5	14.50	14.50
a.-e.	A135	57s any single	2.50	2.50
		Nos. 718-720 (3)	30.25	30.25

Printed in sheets of 10 containing descriptions and emblem.

Natl. Aviation History — A136

Designs: 42s, Short S30. 57s, Vought F4U Corsair. 90s, Boeing 737. 3pa, Montgolfier brothers' hot-air balloon, the Wright Flyer, Concorde jet and space shuttle.

1989, Oct. 23   Litho.   Perf. 14½x14

721	A136	42s multicolored	3.25	1.60
722	A136	57s multicolored	3.75	2.00
723	A136	90s multicolored	6.50	6.00

Size: 97x126½mm

724	A136	3pa multicolored	16.00	16.00
		Nos. 721-724 (4)	29.50	25.60

1st Flight to Tonga, 1939 (42s); military base on the island, 1943 (57s); civil aviation, Fua'amotu Airport (90s); aviation through the ages (3pa).

Flying Home for Christmas A137

1989, Nov. 9   Perf. 14x13½

725	A137	32s Aircraft landing	2.40	1.10
726	A137	42s Islanders waving, aircraft	2.75	1.10
727	A137	57s Tongan in outrigger canoe, aircraft	3.00	1.50
728	A137	3pa Islanders waving, aircraft, diff.	8.00	8.00
		Nos. 725-728 (4)	16.15	11.70

World Stamp Expo '89 A138

20th UPU Congress, Washington, DC — A139

Postal history and communications (No. 730): a, Sir Rowland Hill, penny blacks on Mulready envelope. b, Clipper ship, early train. c, Pony Express advertisement, stagecoach, post rider. d, Hot-air balloon and flight cover. e, Samuel Morse, miniature, telegraph key. f, Early Royal Mail truck, mailbox. g, Biplane and early aviators. h, Zeppelin flight cover, HMS *Queen Mary*. i, Helicopter, truck. j, Computer operator, facsimile machine. k, Apollo 11 mission emblem, flight cover, planetary bodies. l, American space shuttle, UPU monument.

1989, Nov. 17   Litho.   Perf. 14

729	A138	57s Pair, #730k-730 l	3.50	3.50

Souvenir Sheet
Perf. 13½

730	A139	Sheet of 12	42.50	42.50
a.-l.	A139	57s any single	2.50	2.50

A140   A141

1990, Feb. 14   Litho.   Perf. 14

731	A140	42s Boxing	1.25	.75
732	A140	57s Archery	2.25	1.50
733	A140	1pa Bowls	3.00	3.00
734	A140	2pa Swimming	5.00	5.00
		Nos. 731-734 (4)	11.50	10.25

1990 Commonwealth Games.

1990, Apr. 11   Litho.   Perf. 14

Protect the Environment: 32s, Wave power, ocean pollution. 57s, Wind power, acid rain. $1.20, Solar power, ozone layer. $2.50, Green earth, rain forests.

735	A141	32s multicolored	2.50	.90
736	A141	57s multicolored	3.50	1.50
737	A141	1.20pa multicolored	7.00	7.00
		Nos. 735-737 (3)	13.00	9.40

Souvenir Sheet

738	A141	2.50pa multicolored	13.00	13.00

First Postage Stamps, 150th Anniv. A142

1990   Litho.   Perf. 14

739	A142	42s G. B. #1	2.10	1.50
740	A142	42s G. B. #2	2.10	1.50
a.		Pair, #739-740	3.75	3.75
741	A142	57s Tonga #1	2.50	1.50
742	A142	1.50pa Tonga #CO180	6.00	6.00
743	A142	2.50pa Tonga #736	9.00	9.00
		Nos. 739-743 (5)	21.70	19.50

King's Birthday Type of 1988 Inscribed "Silver Jubilee of His Majesty King Taufa'ahau Tupou IV 1965-1990"

1990, July 4   Litho.   Perf. 11½

744	A127	32s like No. 668	1.50	1.00
745	A127	42s like No. 669	1.50	1.00
746	A127	57s like No. 670	2.25	1.25
747	A127	2.50pa like No. 671	7.75	7.75
		Nos. 744-747 (4)	13.00	11.00

Native Catamaran — A143

1990, June 6   Perf. 14½

748	A143	32s buff & green	1.60	.75
749	A143	42s buff & bl, diff.	1.60	.85
750	A143	1.20pa buff & brn, diff.	4.25	4.25
751	A143	3pa buff & vio, diff.	8.50	8.50
		Nos. 748-751 (4)	15.95	14.35

Banded Iguana A144

1990, Sept. 12   Litho.   Perf. 14

752	A144	32s multicolored	2.00	1.25
753	A144	42s multi, diff.	2.50	1.75
754	A144	57s multi, diff.	3.25	2.25
755	A144	1.20pa multi, diff.	8.25	4.75
		Nos. 752-755 (4)	16.00	10.00

Marine Type of 1984

1990, July 6   Litho.   Perf. 14
Size: 20x22mm

756	A103	2s like No. 564	1.25	.85
a.		Booklet pane of 10	12.50	12.50
757	A103	5s like No. 566	1.25	.85
a.		Booklet pane of 10	12.50	12.50
758	A103	10s like No. 569	1.25	.85
a.		Booklet pane of 10	12.50	12.50
759	A103	32s like No. 574	2.25	2.25
a.		Booklet pane of 10	22.50	22.50
		Nos. 756-759 (4)	6.00	4.80

Nos. 756-758 exist inscribed "1992."
For surcharges see Nos. 809-810.
Issue date: #756a-759a, Sept. 4.

UN Development Program, 40th Anniv. — A145

1990, Oct. 25   Litho.   Perf. 14

760	A145	57s Tourism	2.00	2.00
761	A145	57s Agriculture, fisheries	2.00	2.00
a.		Pair, #760-761	4.50	4.50
762	A145	3pa Education	10.00	10.00
763	A145	3pa Healthcare	10.00	10.00
a.		Pair, #762-763	22.50	22.50
		Nos. 760-763 (4)	24.00	24.00

Rotary Intl. — A146

1990, Nov. 28

764	A146	32s shown	1.00	.55
765	A146	42s Two boys	1.50	.80
766	A146	2pa Three children	5.00	5.00
767	A146	3pa Two girls	6.50	6.50
		Nos. 764-767 (4)	14.00	12.85

Accident Prevention A147

No. 768: a, d, Care at work; hard hats save lives. b, c, Keep matches and medicines out of children's reach. e, as "d," corrected inscription.
No. 769: a, d, Don't drink and drive. b, c, Crash helmets save lives; mind cyclists and children.
No. 770: a, d, Listen to forecasts; learn to swim. b, c, Swim from safe beaches; beware of broken glass.
"a" and "b" have English inscriptions, denominations at top; "c" and "d" have Tongan inscriptions, denominations at bottom.

Strips of 4 + Label

1991, Apr. 10   Litho.   Perf. 14½

768	A147	32s #a.-d.	5.25	5.25
f.		Strip of 4, #a.-c., e.	35.00	
769	A147	42s #a.-d.	7.50	7.50
770	A147	57s #a.-d.	9.25	9.25
		Nos. 768-770 (3)	22.00	22.00

Center label is a progressive proof.
No. 768d was incorrectly inscribed, "Ngauo tokanga." No. 768e was issued 8/11/91 with correct inscription, "Ngaue tokanga."
For surcharges see Nos. 811, 1124.

A148

1991, July 2   Litho.   Perf. 14½

771	A148	42s Fish	.80	.70
772	A148	57s Island, boat	.95	.85
773	A148	2pa Fruit, island	3.50	3.50
774	A148	3pa Turtle, beach	6.25	6.25
		Nos. 771-774 (4)	11.50	11.30

Heilala week.

A149

Racing yachts: a, Red spinnaker. b, Yellow spinnaker. c, Green striped spinnaker. d, Yacht at sunset. e, Yacht, moon.

Miniature Sheet of 5 + Label

1991, July 2

775	A149	1pa #775a-775e	13.00	13.00

Around the world yacht race.

Church of Jesus Christ of Latter Day Saints in Tonga, Cent. — A150

1991, Aug. 19

776	A150	42s Tonga Temple	1.75	1.75
777	A150	57s Temple at night	2.75	2.75

Rowing Festival A151

1991, Oct. 29   Litho.   Perf. 14

778	A151	42s Women's coxed eight	1.00	1.00
779	A151	57s Men's longboat	1.50	1.50
780	A151	1pa Outrigger	2.75	2.75
781	A151	2pa Bow of large canoe	5.25	5.25
782	A151	2pa Stern of large canoe	5.25	5.25
a.		Pair, #781-782	11.00	11.00
		Nos. 778-782 (5)	15.75	15.75

For surcharges see Nos. 898-899C.

Telecommunications — A152

No. 783: a, Recording television program. b, Communications Satellite. c, Watching television program.
No. 784: a, Man on telephone, woman at computer. b, Communications satellite, diff. c, Man in city on telephone.

No. 785: a, Seaman on sinking ship broadcasting SOS. b, Man on telephone, satellite relay station. c, Rescue missions.
No. 786: a, Weather satelite. b, Men at computers. c, Television weather report, storm.

1991, Oct. 15   Litho.   Perf. 14½

783	A152	15s Strip of 3, #a.-c.	1.50	1.50
784	A152	32s Strip of 3, #a.-c.	3.00	3.00
785	A152	42s Strip of 3, #a.-c.	4.25	4.25
786	A152	57s Strip of 3, #a.-c.	5.75	5.75
		Nos. 783-786 (4)	14.75	14.75

For surcharges, see 1095-1098.

Christmas — A153

Designs: 32s, Turtles pulling Santa's sleigh. 42s, Santa on roof. 57s, Family with presents. 3.50pa, Waving goodbye to Santa.

1991, Nov. 11   Perf. 14

787	A153	32s multicolored	1.00	.70
788	A153	42s multicolored	1.25	.90
789	A153	57s multicolored	1.75	1.75
790	A153	3.50pa multicolored	10.00	10.00
		Nos. 787-790 (4)	14.00	13.35

For surcharges, see 1120-1122.

Armed Forces — A154

1991, Dec. 15

791	A154	42s Royal Tonga Marine	1.00	1.00
792	A154	42s Patrol boat Pangai	1.00	1.00
a.		A154 Pair, #791-792	2.50	2.50
793	A154	57s Patrol boat Neiafu	1.50	1.50
794	A154	57s Tonga Royal Guards	1.50	1.50
a.		A154 Pair, #793-794	3.50	3.50
795		2pa King Tupou IV, military parade	5.25	5.25
796		2pa Patrol boat Savea	5.25	5.25
a.		A154 Pair, #795-796	11.00	11.00
		Nos. 791-796 (6)	15.50	15.50

Miniature Sheet

Discovery of America, 500th Anniv. — A155

Designs: a, Columbus. b, Monastery of Santa Maria de la Chevas. c, Obverse and reverse of coin of Ferdinand and Isabella. d, Spain #C48, #426. e, Compass, astrolabe. f, Santa Maria. g, Map, Columbus' signature. h, Columbus arriving in New World. i, Lucayan artifacts, parrot. j, Pineapple, artifacts. k, Columbus announcing his discovery. l, Medal of Columbus, signature.

1992, Apr. 28   Litho.   Perf. 13½

797	A155	57s Sheet of 12, #a.-l.	42.50	42.50

Marine Type of 1984 and

A155a

Perf. 13x13½, 14 (15s, 20s, 10pa)
1992-93   Litho.

798	A155a	1s Swainsonia casta	.25	.25
799	A155a	3s Holocentrus ruber	.25	.25
800	A155a	5s Cypraea mappa viridis	.25	.25
801	A155a	10s Conus bullatus	.25	.25
802	A103	15s like #567	.30	.30
803	A155a	20s Dascyllus aruanus	.35	.35
804	A155a	45s Lambis truncata	.75	.75
805	A155a	60s Conus aulicus	1.00	1.00
806	A155a	80s Pterois volitans	1.40	1.40

Size: 27x41mm

807	A103	10pa like #568	20.00	20.00
		Nos. 798-807 (10)	24.80	24.80

Issued: 1s, 3s, 5s, 10s, 20s, 45s, 60s, 80s, May 12, 1993. 15s, 10pa, May 5, 1992.
See Nos. 874-884. Area covered by background colors on Nos. 874, 876-879 has been reduced in size. See Nos. 920-924.
For inscribed stamps see Nos. O78-O87.

Surcharges

On #688

On #756 in Blue

On #759

On #769 in Red and Black

1992-93   Litho.   Perf. 14½, 14

808	A103	1s on 20s #688	.25	.25
809	A103	10s on 2s #756	65.00	65.00
810	A103	45s on 32s #759	4.00	4.00
811	A147	60s on 42s Strip of 4, #a.-d. + label	16.00	16.00

Issued: 1s, 5/19; 45s, 60s, 8/11; 10s, 1993.

Miniature Sheet

World War II in Pacific, 50th Anniv. A156

Designs: a, Newspaper headline, Japanese attack on Pearl Harbor. b, Map of Bataan, Corregidor, and Manila, pilot's wings, airplanes. c, Newspaper headline, troops landing in Gilbert Islands, Marine Corps emblem, dogtags. d, Uniform patch, B-29 "Enola Gay," troops landing on Iwo Jima. e, Map of Battle of Midway, Admiral Nimitz. f, Southwest Pacific campaign map, Gen. MacArthur. g, Map of Saipan and Tinian, Lt. Gen. Holland Smith. h, Map outlining bombing of Japan, Maj. Gen. Curtis Lemay. i, Mitsubishi A6M Zero. j, Douglas SBD Dauntless. k, Grumman F4F Wildcat. l, Supermarine Seafire.

1992, May 26   Litho.   Perf. 14

814	A156	42s Sheet of 12, #a.-l.	30.00	30.00

1992 Summer Olympics, Barcelona — A157

1992, June 16

815	A157	42s Boxing	1.25	.85
816	A157	57s Diving	1.75	1.10
817	A157	1.50pa Tennis	4.50	4.50
818	A157	3pa Cycling	9.50	9.50
		Nos. 815-818 (4)	17.00	15.95

For surcharges, see 1123, 1125.

King Taufa'ahau IV, 25th Anniv. of Coronation A158

Designs: 45s, 2pa, King, Queen Halaevalu. No. 820a, King, crown. b. Extract from investiture ceremony. c, King, #C33.

1992, July 4   **Perf. 13½x13**

819	A158	45s multicolored	1.25	.90

Size: 51x38mm

Perf. 12½x12

820	A158	80s Strip of 3, #a.-		
		c.	6.50	6.50
821	A158	2pa multicolored	5.25	5.25
		Nos. 819-821 (3)	13.00	12.65

Sacred Bats of Kolovai — A159

Designs: No. 822a, Bats in flight. b, Close-up of flying bat. c, Flying bats, tree. d, Bats hanging in tree. e, Bat hanging from tree limb. Origin of sacred bats: No. 823a, 45s, Kula leaving for Upolu to be tattooed as Tongan chief. b, 45s, Kula looking through path of fires. c, 2pa, Kula walking down path, Hina. d, 2pa, Hina waving, Kula leaving with pet fruit bats.

Nos. 823a-823d are horiz.

1992, Oct. 20   **Litho.**   **Perf. 14**

822	A159	60s Strip of 5, #a.-e.	13.00	13.00

Souvenir Sheet

Perf. 14½

823	A159	Sheet of 4, #a.-d.	14.00	14.00

Christmas A160

1992, Nov. 10   **Perf. 14**

824	A160	60s Pearls	1.50	1.10
825	A160	80s Reef fish	2.00	1.40
826	A160	2pa Pacific orchids	4.75	4.75
827	A160	3pa Eua parrots	7.25	7.25
		Nos. 824-827 (4)	15.50	14.50

For surcharges, see Nos. 894-897.

Anniversaries and Events — A161

Designs: 60s, Tonga flag, Rotary emblem. 80sh, John F. Kennedy, Peace Corps emblem. 1.50pa, FAO, WHO emblems. 3.50pa, Globe, Rotary Foundation emblem.

1992, Dec. 15   **Perf. 14½**

828	A161	60s multicolored	1.40	1.00
829	A161	80s multicolored	1.90	1.40
830	A161	1.50pa multicolored	3.50	3.50
831	A161	3.50pa multicolored	8.50	8.50
		Nos. 828-831 (4)	15.30	14.40

Rotary Intl. in Tonga, 25th anniv. (#828). Peace Corps in Tonga, 25th anniv. (#829). Intl. Conference of FAO and WHO (#830). Rotary Foundation of Rotary Intl., 75th anniv. (#831). For overprint see No. 869.

Family Planning — A163

Outdoor silhouette scenes: No. 832, Mother, girl, butterflies. No. 833, Child on tricycle pulling kite. No. 834, Girl, kittens. No. 835, Adult, child playing chess.

1993, Jan. 26   **Perf. 14x13½**

832	A163	15s Pair, #a.-b.	2.50	2.50
833	A163	45s Pair, #a.-b.	3.50	3.50
834	A163	60s Pair, #a.-b.	5.00	5.00
835	A163	2pa Pair, #a.-b.	15.00	15.00
		Nos. 832-835 (4)	26.00	26.00

Nos. 832a-835a have Tongan inscriptions. Nos. 832b-835b have English inscriptions and are mirror images of Nos. 832a-835a.

Health and Fitness — A164

Designs: 60s, Fresh fruit, fish, anti-smoking and anti-drug symbols. 80s, Anti-smoking symbol, weight training. 1.50pa, Anti-drug symbol, water sports. 2.50pa, Fresh fruit, fish, cyclist, jogger.

1993, Mar. 16   **Litho.**   **Perf. 14**

836	A164	60s multicolored	2.00	2.00
837	A164	80s multicolored	2.75	2.75
838	A164	1.50pa multicolored	5.25	5.25
839	A164	2.50pa multicolored	8.50	8.50
		Nos. 836-839 (4)	18.50	18.50

Tonga Fire Service, 25th Anniv. A165

1993, May 18   **Litho.**   **Perf. 14**

840	A165	45s Fireman's badge	2.00	2.00
841	A165	45s Police van, badge	2.00	2.00
a.		Pair, #840-841	4.50	3.50
842	A165	60s Police band	2.50	2.50
843	A165	60s Putting out fire	2.50	2.50
a.		Pair, #842-843	5.50	4.50
844	A165	2pa Fire truck at station	9.00	9.00

845	A165	2pa Policeman, police dog	9.00	9.00
a.		Pair, #844-845	20.00	15.00
		Nos. 840-845 (6)	27.00	27.00

Tonga Police Training College, 25th anniv. (#841-842, 845). For surcharges see Nos. 943-948.

A166

Abel Tasman's Voyage to Eua, 350th Anniv.: 30s, Map of islands. 60s, Sailing ships, Heemskirk and Zeehaen. 80s, Sailing ships, natives in canoes. 3.50pa, Landing on Eua.

1993, June 21

846	A166	30s multicolored	.80	.50
847	A166	60s multicolored	1.75	1.10
848	A166	80s multicolored	2.25	2.25
849	A166	3.50pa multicolored	10.00	10.00
		Nos. 846-849 (4)	14.80	13.85

A167

King Taufa'ahau IV, 75th Birthday: 45s, 2pa, Musical instruments. No. 851a, Sporting events. b, Ancient landmarks. c, Royal Palace.

1993, July 1   **Litho.**   **Perf. 13x13½**

850	A167	45s multicolored	.65	.65

Perf. 12x12½

Size: 37x48mm

851	A167	80s Strip of 3, #a.-c.	5.00	5.00
852	A167	2pa multicolored	3.00	3.00
		Nos. 850-852 (3)	8.65	8.65

A168   A168a

Children's Stamp Designs: Nos. 853a, 854a, Beach scene. Nos. 853b, 854b, "Maui-The Fisher of the Islands." Nos. 853c, 854c, Raft on ocean. Nos. 853d, 854d, Woman with hands in mixing bowl. Nos. 853e, 854e, "Maui and his Hook." Nos. 853f, 854f, "Communication in the South Pacific."

1993, Dec. 1   **Litho.**   **Perf. 14**

853	A168	10s Strip of 6, #a.-f.	3.00	3.00
854	A168	80s Strip of 6, #a.-f.	14.00	14.00

1993, Nov. 10   **Litho.**   **Perf. 14**

Christmas traditions: 60s, Festive dinner. 80s, Shooting cannon. 1.50pa, Musicians. 3pa, Going to church.

855	A168a	60s multicolored	1.50	1.25
856	A168a	80s multicolored	2.00	1.50
857	A168a	1.50pa multicolored	3.75	3.75
858	A168a	3pa multicolored	7.75	7.75
		Nos. 855-858 (4)	15.00	14.25

Miniature Sheet

Kindness to Animals — A169

Designs: a, 80s, Boy holding puppy. b, 80s, Girl holding kitten. c, 60s, Boy holding rooster (b). d, 60s, Girl with butterfly. e, 60s, Three dogs. f, 60s, Boy, puppy.

1994, Jan. 14   **Perf. 14½**

859	A169	Sheet of 6, #a.-f.	17.50	17.50

For overprint see No. 868.

Game Fishing — A170

1994, Feb. 28   **Litho.**   **Perf. 12**

860	A170	60s Tiger shark	1.50	1.00
861	A170	80s Dolphin fish	2.00	1.40
862	A170	1.50pa Yellow fin tuna	4.00	4.00
863	A170	2.50pa Pacific blue marlin	6.50	6.50
		Nos. 860-863 (4)	14.00	12.90

1994 World Cup Soccer Championships, US — A171

Designs: No. 864a, Player's legs. No. 864b, World Cup trophy. No. 865a, American player in red, white, & blue. No. 865b, German player in black shorts, white shirt.

1994, June 1   **Perf. 14x14½**

864	A171	80s Pair, #a.-b.	4.00	4.00
865	A171	2pa Pair, #a.-b.	10.00	10.00

Pan Pacific & South East Asia Women's Assoc. Conference — A172

Career women: No. 866a, Lawyer. No. 866b, Policewoman. No. 867a, Doctor. No. 867b, Nurse.

1994, Aug. 18   **Litho.**   **Perf. 14**

866	A172	45s Pair, #a.-b.	3.50	3.50
867	A172	2.50pa Pair, #a.-b.	10.50	10.50

No. 859 Overprinted

1994, Nov. 10   Litho.   Perf. 14½
868   A169   Sheet of 6, #a.-f.   8.50   8.50

No. 831
Ovptd. in
Dark Blue

1994, Nov. 17   Litho.   Perf. 14½
869   A161   60s on 3.50pa multi   4.00   4.00

Types of 1969-85 and

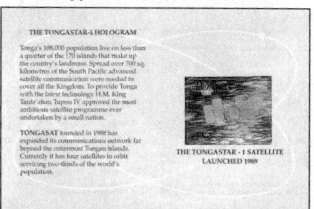

Tongastar 1 Satellite — A173

Design: a, 10s, Type A39 banana, size 22x11mm. b, 25s, Type AP12. c, Booklet pane, 12 #870a, 3 #870b. d, 45s, like #608. e, 45s, like #609. f, 45s, like #610. g, 45s, like #611. h, Booklet pane of 3 each #870d-870e, 2 #870f, 1 #870g. i, 60s, Type A72. j, 60s, Type OA19. k, 80s, Type OA17. l, Booklet pane, #870i-870k. m, 2pa, Tongastar 1. n, Booklet pane of 1 #870m.

Unwmk.
1994, Dec. 14   Litho.   Die Cut
Self-adhesive

870   A173   Souvenir booklet   27.50

First full-scale production of self-adhesive stamps by Tonga, 25th anniv. (#870). Satellite communications network for Tongan Islands (#870m).
No. 870b is airmail. Nos. 870j-870k are air post official stamps.
No. 870m contains a holographic image. Soaking in water may affect the hologram.

Marine Type of 1992-93 Redrawn
1994-95   Litho.   Perf. 14
874   A155a   10s like #801   .25   .25
876   A155a   20s like #803   .35   .35
877   A155a   150 like #804   .80   .80
878   A155a   60s like #805   1.10   1.10
879   A155a   80s like #806   1.40   1.40
Size: 41x27mm, 41x27mm
880   A155a   1pa like #705,
               horiz.   2.25   2.25
881   A155a   2pa like #577,
               horiz.   4.25   4.25
882   A155a   5pa like #578,
               horiz.   6.25   6.25
883   A155a   5pa like #706   10.00   10.00
884   A155a   10pa like #568   21.00   21.00
       Nos. 874-884 (10)   47.65   47.65

Area covered by background colors on Nos. 874, 876-879 has been reduced in size.
Issued: 1pa, 2pa, 3pa, 6/21/94; 5pa, 9/21/94; 4pa, 1/18/95; 10s, 20s, 45s, 60s, 80s, 9/25/95.
This is an expanding set. Numbers may change.

FAO,
50th
Anniv.
A174

1995, May 16   Litho.   Perf. 14
886   A174   5pa multicolored   17.00   17.00

Tonga's Entry into British
Commonwealth, 25th Anniv. — A175

Children with bicycles from parts of Commonwealth.

1995, June 6
887   A175   45s Polynesia   1.10   .90
888   A175   60s Asia   1.50   1.25
889   A175   80s Africa   1.75   1.75
890   A175   2pa India   4.50   4.50
891   A175   2.50pa Europe   6.00   6.00
       Nos. 887-891 (5)   14.85   14.40

1995 Rugby World Cup, South
Africa — A176

Designs: No. 892a, Player running right with ball, two others. b, Two players. No. 893a, Three players. b, Player ready to catch ball.

1995, June 20   Perf. 14½
892   A176   80s Pair, #a.-b.   6.00   6.00
893   A176   2pa Pair, #a.-b.   13.50   13.50

Nos. 892-893 were each issued in sheets of 4 stamps.
For surcharges see Nos. 954A, 956A.

Nos. 824-827 Surcharged

i

j

1995, June 30   Litho.   Perf. 14
894   60s Pair   4.50   4.50
  a.   A160(i) on #824   2.00   2.00
  b.   A160(j) on #824   2.00   2.00
895   60s Pair   4.50   4.50
  a.   A160(i) on 80s #825   2.00   2.00
  b.   A160(j) on 80s #825   2.00   2.00
896   60s Pair   4.50   4.50
  a.   A160(i) on 2pa #826   2.00   2.00
  b.   A160(j) on 2pa #826   2.00   2.00
897   60s Pair   4.50   4.50
  a.   A160(i) on 3pa #827   2.00   2.00
  b.   A160(j) on 3pa #827   2.00   2.00
       Nos. 894-897 (4)   18.00   18.00

Nos. 779-782 Surcharged

1995, June 30   Litho.   Perf. 14
898   A151   60s on 57s #779   1.60   1.60
899   A151   80s on 2pa #781   2.00   2.00
899A   A151   80s on 2pa #782   2.00   2.00
  b.   Pair, #899-899A   4.00   4.00
899C   A151   1pa on #780   2.50   2.50
       Nos. 898-899C (4)   8.10   8.10

Victory in the
Pacific, 50th
Anniv. — A177

Nos. 900, 901: a, Soldier climbing from rope ladder. b, Ship, soldiers. c, Ship, landing craft with troops, soldiers up close. d, Ship, landing craft with troops. e, Map.

1995, Aug. 1   Litho.   Perf. 14x14½
900   A177   60s Strip of 5, #a.-e.   10.00   10.00
901   A177   80s Strip of 5, #a.-e.   12.00   12.00

Nos. 900-901 are continuous designs and were issued together in sheet containing ten stamps.

Singapore '95 — A178

Designs: No. 902a, 45s, #887. b, 60s, #888. 2pa, Boy cycling in Singapore.

1995, Sept. 1   Litho.   Perf. 12
902   A178   Pair, #a.-b.   3.75   3.75
Souvenir Sheet
903   A178   2pa multicolored   5.25   5.25

Souvenir Sheet

Beijing Intl. Coin & Stamp Show
'95 — A179

Design: 1.40pa, Mount Song, Henan Province, China.

1995, Sept. 14   Perf. 14½
904   A179   1.40pa multicolored   5.00   5.00

End of World War II, UN, 50th
Anniv. — A180

No. 905a, Holocaust survivors. b, UN emblem, "50." c, Children of Holocaust survivors in celebration.
No. 906a, Mushroom cloud from atom bomb explosion. b, Like #905b. c, Space shuttle.

1995, Oct. 20   Litho.   Perf. 13
905   A180   60s Strip of 3, #a.-c.   4.00   4.00
906   A180   80s Strip of 3, #a.-c.   7.50   7.50

Nos. 905b, 906b are 23x31mm.

Christmas and
New Year — A181

Orchids: 20s, Calanthe triplicata. Nos. 908, Spathoglottis plicata, inscribed "MERRY CHRISTMAS." No. 909, like #908, inscribed "A HAPPY 1996." No. 910, Dendrobium platygastrium, inscribed "MERRY CHRISTMAS". No. 911, like #910, inscribed "A HAPPY 1996." 80s, Goodyera rubicunda. 2pa, Dendrobium toki. 2.50pa, Phaius tankervilliae.

1995, Nov. 15   Litho.   Perf. 14x14½
907   A181   20s multicolored   .75   .75
908   A181   45s multicolored   1.00   1.00
909   A181   45s multicolored   1.00   1.00
910   A181   60s multicolored   1.25   1.25
911   A181   60s multicolored   1.25   1.25
912   A181   80s multicolored   1.75   1.75
913   A181   2pa multicolored   5.00   5.00
914   A181   2.50pa multicolored   6.00   6.00
       Nos. 907-914 (8)   18.00   18.00

Humpback Whale — A182

1996, Jan. 7   Perf. 14
915   A182   45s In water   2.10   2.10
916   A182   60s With calf   3.25   3.25
917   A182   1.50pa Sounding   6.50   6.50
918   A182   2.50pa Breaching   9.25   9.75
       Nos. 915-918 (4)   21.10   21.60

World Wildlife Fund.

Miniature Sheet

New Year 1996 (Year of the
Rat) — A183

Denomination: a, UR. b, UL. c, LR. d, LL.

1996, Feb. 23
919   A183   60s Sheet of 4,
               #a.-d.   7.50   7.50

No. 919 is a continuous design.
See Nos. 930-932, 932E, 942, 986.

Marine Type of 1992-93 Redrawn
1996, May 31   Litho.   Perf. 14
Size: 40x26mm
920   A155a   1pa like #880   2.25   2.25
921   A155a   2pa like #881   4.75   4.75
922   A155a   3pa like #882   7.50   7.50
923   A155a   5pa like #883   12.00   12.00
924   A155a   10pa like #884   25.00   25.00
       Nos. 920-924 (5)   51.50   51.50

Size of "TONGA" on Nos. 920-923 is smaller than on Nos. 880-883. Name of species appears at top instead of bottom on Nos. 920-924. Background colors vary. Inscribed "1996."

1996 Summer Olympic Games, Atlanta — A184

Statues of classical Greek figures, modern athletes: 45s, Zeus, runner. 80s, The Discus Thrower. 2pa, The Javelin Thrower. 3pa, The Horseman, dressage competitor.

1996, July 2   Litho.   Perf. 14

925	A184	45s multicolored	1.25	.80
926	A184	80s multicolored	2.00	1.90
927	A184	2pa multicolored	5.75	5.75
928	A184	3pa multicolored	9.00	9.00
		Nos. 925-928 (4)	18.00	17.45

For surcharges & overprint see Nos. 949-952.

13th Congress of Intl. Union of Preshistoric and Protohistoric Sciences — A185

a, Prehistoric man using fire, knife, bow & arrow, animals. b, Ancient Egyptians, Greeks, Romans.

1996, Sept. 5   Litho.   Perf. 12

929	A185	1pa Pair, #a.-b.	7.50	7.50

No. 929 was issued in sheets of 6 stamps.

New Year 1996 (Year of the Rat) Type

Denomination: a, UR. b, UL. c, LR. d, LL.

1996, June 27   Litho.   Perf. 14
Sheets of 4

930	A183	10s #a.-d.	1.40	1.40
931	A183	20s #a.-d.	2.75	2.75
932	A183	45s #a.-d.	6.75	6.75
932E	A183	60s #a.-d.	10.00	10.00

The denominations are larger on No. 932E than those on No. 919.

Christmas A186

Paintings: 20s, Virgin and Child, by Sassoferrato. 60s, Adoration of the Shepherds, by Murillo. 80s, Virgin and Child, by Delaroche. 1pa, Adoration of the Shepherds, by Champaigne.

1996, Oct. 29   Litho.   Perf. 14

933	A186	20s multicolored	.75	.50
934	A186	60s multicolored	2.50	1.50
935	A186	80s multicolored	2.75	2.50
936	A186	1pa multicolored	8.50	8.50
		Nos. 933-936 (4)	14.50	13.00

UNICEF, 50th Anniv. — A187

Children in sports activities: a, Running, playing rugby. b, Tennis. c, Cycling.

1996, Oct. 29

937	A187	80s Strip of 3, #a.-c.	9.00	9.00

No. 937 is a continuous design.

Queen Halaevalu Mata'aho, 70th Birthday — A188

Designs: 60s, Queen, natl. flag. No. 939a, Queen, coin with portrait. No. 939b, Coin with natl. arms, Queen.

1996, Nov. 27   Litho.   Perf. 12

938	A188	60s multicolored	3.50	3.50
939	A188	2pa Pair, #a.-b.	10.50	10.50

Towards the Year 2000 — A189

Year "2000" rising out of Pacific, Tonga landmarks: Nos. 940a, 941a, The Ha'amonga stone monument, globe, Kao Island. Nos. 940b, 941b, Mount Talau overlooking Port of Reguge, Royal Palance, Tongatapu, communication satellite.

1996, Dec. 9

940	A189	80s Pair, #a.-b.	4.00	4.00
941	A189	2pa Pair, #a.-b.	9.50	9.50

New Year Type of 1996 Redrawn with Ox

Denomination located: a, 60s, UR. b, 60s, UL. c, 80s, LR. d, 2pa, LL.

1997, Jan. 24   Litho.   Perf. 14

942	A183	Sheet of 4, #a.-d.	11.00	11.00

New Year 1997 (Year of the Ox).

Nos. 840-845 Surcharged

1997, Mar. 3   Litho.   Perf. 14

943	A165	10s on 45s #840	3.50	3.25
944	A165	10s on 45s #841	3.50	3.25
a.		Pair, #943-944	6.00	6.00
945	A165	10s on 60s #842	3.50	3.25
946	A165	10s on 60s #843	3.50	3.25
a.		Pair, #945-946	6.00	6.00
947	A165	20s on 2pa #844	4.00	3.75
948	A165	20s on 2pa #845	4.00	3.75
a.		Pair, #947-948	7.00	7.00
		Nos. 943-948 (6)	22.00	20.50

Nos. 925-928 Surcharged & Overprinted.

1997, Mar. 24   Litho.   Perf. 14

949	A184	10s on 45s #925	.90	.90
950	A184	10s on 80s #926	.90	.90
951	A184	10s on 2pa #927	.90	.90
952	A184	3pa #928	9.25	9.25
		Nos. 949-952 (4)	11.95	11.95

Size and location of surcharge varies.

Nos. 892-893 Surcharged

a   b

1997, Mar. 24   Perf. 14½
Sheets of 4

954A	A176	10s on 80s	2.00	2.00
956A	A176	1pa on 2pa	15.00	15.00

#954A contains #892a (a), #892b (a), #892b (b), #892a (b). #956A contains #893a (a), #893b (a), #893b (b), #893a (b).

Christianity in Tonga, Birth of King George Tupou I, Bicent. — A190

#957, 961a, 962a, Arrival of missionary ship, Duff, Captain James Wilson. #958, King George Tupou I, village. #959, 961b, 962b, People in water, rowboats coming ashore from Duff. #960, 961c, 962c, Natives, missionaries, Duff.

1997, Apr. 28   Perf. 14

957	A190	10s multicolored	.25	.25
958	A190	10s multicolored	.25	.25
959	A190	10s multicolored	.25	.25
960	A190	10s multicolored	.25	.25
a.		Sheet of 6, #957, 959-960, 3 #958	4.00	4.00
961	A190	60s Strip of 3, #a.-c.	5.00	5.00
962	A190	80s Strip of 3, #a.-c.	7.00	7.00

Nos. 961-962 were each issued in sheets of 9 stamps.
See Nos. 972-975.

Souvenir Sheet

Pacific Swallow, Golden Gate Bridge — A191

1997, May 30

963	A191	2pa multicolored	7.50	7.50

Pacific '97.

Tonga High School, 50th Anniv. A192

Designs: 20s, Students in uniforms outside of school. 60s, Dressed for sports. 80s, Brass band. 3.50pa, Running competition.

1997, June 4

964	A192	20s multicolored	.75	.40
965	A192	60s multicolored	1.75	1.10
966	A192	80s multicolored	2.25	1.50
967	A192	3.50pa multicolored	9.25	9.25
		Nos. 964-967 (4)	14.00	12.25

A193

Nos. 968, 970: a, Queen, King with bowed heads, royal escorts. b, Coronation ceremony. c, Queen, King. 45s, 2pa, King's crown.

1997, June 30   Litho.   Perf. 13x13½

968	A193	10s Strip of 3, #a.- c.	1.25	1.25
969	A193	45s multicolored	1.75	1.75

Size: 34x47mm
Perf. 12

970	A193	60s Strip of 3, #a.- c.	7.00	7.00
971	A193	2pa multicolored	8.50	8.50

King Taufa'ahau IV, Queen Halaevalu Mata'aho, 50th wedding anniv., coronation, 30th anniv.

Christianity in Tonga Type of 1997

1997, Aug. 27   Perf. 14
Size: 27x18mm

972	A190	10s like #957	.25	.25
973	A190	10s like #958	.25	.25
974	A190	10s like #959	.25	.25
975	A190	10s like #960	.25	.25
a.		Sheet of 12, 6 #973, 2 each #972, #974-975	6.00	6.00

A194

Mushrooms: Nos. 976a, 977a, Lenzites elegans. Nos. 976b, 977b, Marasmiellus semiustus. No. 976c, 978a, Aseroe rubra. Nos. 976d, 978b, Podoscypha involuta. Nos. 976e, 979a, Microporus xanthopus. Nos. 976f, 979b, Lentinus tuberregium.

1997, Oct. 1   Litho.   Perf. 14

976	A194	10s Strip of 6, #a.- f.	2.25	2.25

Size: 26x40mm

977	A194	20s Pair, #a.-b.	2.00	2.00
978	A194	60s Pair, #a.-b.	6.00	6.00
979	A194	2pa Pair, #a.-b.	19.00	19.00
c.		Sheet of 6, #977-979	32.50	32.50

No. 976 is a continuous design.

Diana, Princess of Wales (1961-97)
Common Design Type

Various portraits: a, 10s. b, 80s. c, 1pa. d, 2.50pa.

Perf. 13½x14

1998, May 29   Litho.   Unwmk.

980	CD355	Strip of 4, #a.-d	5.75	5.75

No. 980 sold for 4.40pa + 50s with surtax from international sales going to the Princess Diana Memorial Fund and surtax from local sales going to designated local charity.

Flying Home for Christmas A195

878   TONGA

Designs: 60s, Airplane on ground, people waving. 80s, People waving, house, plane overhead. 1.50pa, Man in outrigger canoe waving to airplane. 3.50pa, Man, woman, people in boat on lake waving, airplane overhead.

1997, Oct. 20   Litho.   Perf. 14x13½
981	A195	60s bister & red	.90	.90
982	A195	80s bister & red	1.20	1.20
983	A195	1.50pa bister & red	2.20	2.20
984	A195	3.50pa bister & red	5.20	5.20
		Nos. 981-984 (4)	9.50	9.50

King Taufa'ahau
Tupou IV, 80th
Birthday — A196

1998, July 4   Litho.   Perf. 14
985	A196	2.70pa multicolored	7.00	7.00
a.	Souv. sheet, #985, Niuafo'ou #207		10.00	10.00

New Year 1998 (Year of the Tiger)

Tiger: a, 55s, Leaping down. b, 80s, Lying down. c, 1pa, Leaping upward. d, 1pa, Stalking.

1998, July 23
986	A183	Sheet of 4, #a.-d.	6.00	6.00

No. 986 is a continuous design. Singpex '98.
For surcharges, see No. 1098.

Birds
A197

5s, Fairy tern, vert. 10s, Tongan whistler, vert. 15s, Common barn owl, vert. 20s, Purple swamp hen, vert. 30s, Red-footed booby, vert. 40s, Banded rail. 50s, Swamp harrier. 55s, Blue-crowned lorikeet, vert. 60s, Great frigate bird, vert. 70s, Friendly ground dove. 80s, Red-tailed tropic bird, vert. 1pa, Red shining parrot, vert. 2pa, Pacific pigeon, vert. 3pa, Pacific golden plover. 5pa, Tongan megapode.

Perf. 14x14½, 14½x14
1998, Aug. 26   Litho.
992	A197	5s multicolored	.25	.25
993	A197	10s multicolored	.25	.25
994	A197	15s multicolored	.25	.25
995	A197	20s multicolored	.30	.30
996	A197	30s multicolored	.50	.50
997	A197	40s multicolored	.65	.65
998	A197	50s multicolored	.75	.75
999	A197	55s multicolored	.90	.90
1000	A197	60s multicolored	.95	.95
1001	A197	70s multicolored	1.10	1.10
1002	A197	80s multicolored	1.25	1.25
1003	A197	1pa multicolored	1.60	1.60
1004	A197	2pa multicolored	3.00	3.00
1005	A197	3pa multicolored	4.75	4.75
1006	A197	5pa multicolored	8.00	8.00
		Nos. 992-1006 (15)	24.50	24.50

For surcharges, see Nos. 1077A, 1077B, 1099-1114, 1126, 1147.

Fish
A198

Designs: a, 10s, Chaetodon pelewensis. b, 55s, Chaetodon lunula. c, 1pa, Chaetodon ephippium.

1998, Sept. 23   Litho.   Perf. 14
1008	A198	Strip of 3, #a.-c.	4.75	4.75

Intl. Year of the Ocean. No. 1008 was issued in sheets of 9 stamps.

Christmas
A199

Designs: 10s, Angel, "Kilisimasi Fiefia." 80s, Angel, "Merry Christmas." 1pa, Children, candle, "Ta'u Fo'ou Monu'ia." 1.60pa, Children, candle, "Happy New Year."

1998, Nov. 12   Litho.   Perf. 14x14½
1009	A199	10s multicolored	.60	.40
1010	A199	80s multicolored	2.50	1.25
1011	A199	1pa multicolored	2.75	2.25
1012	A199	1.60pa multicolored	3.50	3.50
		Nos. 1009-1012 (4)	9.35	7.40

New Year
1999
(Year of
the
Rabbit)
A200

a, 10s, Three rabbits. b, 55s, Rabbit eating. c, 80s, Rabbit looking upward. d, 1pa, Rabbit hopping.

1999, Feb. 16   Perf. 14
1013	A200	Sheet of 4, #a.-d.	4.50	4.50

Explorers — A201

Explorer, ship: 55s, Tasman, Heemserck, 1643. 80s, La Perouse, Astrolabe, 1788. 1pa, William Bligh, Bounty, 1789. 2.50pa, James Cook, Resolution, 1777.

1999, Mar. 19   Litho.   Perf. 14
1014	A201	55s multicolored	1.10	.60
1015	A201	80s multicolored	1.60	1.10
1016	A201	1pa multicolored	2.25	2.00
1017	A201	2.50pa multicolored	5.00	5.00
a.	Souvenir sheet of 1		5.25	5.25
		Nos. 1014-1017 (4)	9.95	8.75

Australia '99 World Stamp Expo (#1017a).

Scenic
Views,
Vava'u
A202

Designs: 10s, Neiafu. 55s, Boats on water, Port of Refuge. 80s, Aerial view, Port of Refuge. 1pa, Sunset, Neiafu. 2.50pa, Mounu Island.

1999, May 19   Perf. 14½
1018	A202	10s multicolored	.50	.40
1019	A202	55s multicolored	1.00	.60
1020	A202	80s multicolored	1.60	.80
1021	A202	1pa multicolored	1.75	1.40
1022	A202	2.50pa multicolored	3.50	3.50
		Nos. 1018-1022 (5)	8.35	6.70

For surcharge see No. 1148.

Flowers
A203

Designs: 10s, Fagraea berteroana. 80s, Garcinia pseudoguttfera. 1pa, Phlaeria disperma, vert. 2.50pa, Gardenia taitensis, vert.

Perf. 13¼x13, 13x13¼
1999, Sept. 29   Litho.
1023	A203	10s multicolored	.30	.30
1024	A203	80s multicolored	1.40	1.40
1025	A203	1pa multicolored	1.75	1.75
1026	A203	2.50pa multicolored	4.25	4.25
		Nos. 1023-1026 (4)	7.70	7.70

Millennium — A204

Designs: a, 55s, Ha'amonga monument, people, clocks at 11:15 to 11:25. b, 80s, Monument, people, clocks at 11:30 to 11:40. c, 1pa, People, clocks at 11:45 to 11:55. d, 2.50pa, King Taufa'ahau IV, clocks at 12:00, 12:05.

1999, Dec. 1
1027	A204	Strip of 4, #a.-d.	7.00	7.00

Millennium — A205

Clock, dove and: 10s, Flowers. 1pa, Ha'amonga Monument. 2.50pa, Native boat. 2.70pa, Crown.

Litho. & Embossed
2000, Jan. 1   Perf. and Die Cut
1028	A205	10s multi	.25	.25
1029	A205	1pa multi	1.50	1.50
1030	A205	2.50pa multi	3.50	3.50
1031	A205	2.70pa multi	4.00	4.00
a.	Souv. sheet, #1030-1031		8.00	8.00
		Nos. 1028-1031 (4)	9.25	9.25

Values are for stamps with attached selvage.

Souvenir Sheet

New Year 2000 (Year of the Dragon) — A206

Various dragons; a, 10s. b, 55s, c, 80s. d, 1pa.

Litho. with Foil Application
2000, Feb. 4   Perf. 14½
1032	A206	Sheet of 4, #a.-d.	5.00	5.00

Souvenir Sheet

The Stamp Show 2000, London — A207

Litho. with Foil Application
2000, May 22   Perf. 13x13¼
1033	A207	Sheet of 2	5.50	5.50
a.	1pa Queen Mother		1.50	1.50
b.	2.50pa Queen Salote Tupou III		3.50	3.50

Geostationary
Orbital Slot
Program — A208

Designs: 10s, Proton RU500 lauch vehicle, vert. 1pa, LM3 launch vehicle. 2.50pa, Apstar 1. 2.70pa, Gorizont.

Litho. with Foil Application
2000, July 5   Perf. 14½x15, 15x14½
1034-1037	A208	Set of 4	9.00	9.00
1037a		Souvenir sheet, #1036-1037	8.25	8.25

World Stamp Expo 2000, Anaheim.

2000 Summer
Olympics,
Sydney — A209

No. 1038: a, Runner, koalas, sailboats. b, Boxers, kangaroos, Ayers Rock. c, Torchbearers, Ayers Rock, Sydney Opera House (60x45mm). d, Discus thrower, Sydney Harbour Bridge, flower. e, Weight lifter, kookaburra, fish.

2000, Sept. 15   Litho.   Perf. 14
1038		Horiz. strip of 5	5.50	5.50
a.-e.	A209 80s Any single		1.00	1.00

Commonwealth Membership, 30th Anniv. — A210

Designs: 10s, Education. 55s, Arts. 80s, Health. 2.70pa, Agriculture.

2000, Oct. 25
1039-1042	A210	Set of 4	5.50	5.50

For surcharge see No. 1149.

Souvenir Sheet

New Year 2001 (Year of the Snake) — A211

No. 1043 — Various snakes: a, 10s. b, 55s, c, 80s, d, 1pa.

Litho. with Foil Application
2001, Feb. 1   Perf. 14¼
1043	A211	Sheet of 4, #a-d	4.50	4.50

Hong Kong 2001 Stamp Exhibition.

Dance — A212

Designs: 10s, Ma'ulu'ulu. 55s, Me'etupaki. 80s, Tau'olunga. 2.70pa, Faha'iula.

2001, Apr. 4   Litho.   Perf. 13¼
1044-1047 A212   Set of 4   5.50 5.50

For surcharge see No. 1151.

Year of the Mangrove A213

Designs: 10s, Fiddler crab. 55s, Black duck, gray mullet, vert. 80s, Red mangrove, emperor fish, vert. 1pa, Reef heron, mangrove. 2.70pa, Mangrove crab.

2001, May 5   Litho.   Perf. 13¾
1048-1052 A213   Set of 5   6.75 6.75
1052a   Souvenir sheet, #1048-
           1052, perf. 13½   7.25 7.25

For surcharge see No. 1150.

Sport Fishing — A214

2001, July 31   Perf. 14¾x14
1053   Horiz. strip of 4 with
        central label   8.25 8.25
  a. A214 45s Sailfish   .50 .50
  b. A214 80s Blue marlin 1.00 1.00
  c. A214 2.40pa Wahoo   3.00 3.00
  d. A214 2.60pa Dorado   3.25 3.25

Fruit — A215

**2001, Sept. 19   Serpentine Die Cut
Self-Adhesive**
1054   Horiz. strip of 5   6.25 6.25
  a. A215 10s Banana   .25 .25
  b. A215 45s Coconut   .50 .50
  c. A215 60s Pineapple   .75 .75
  d. A215 80s Watermelon   .85 .85
  e. A215 2.40pa Passion fruit 2.40 2.40

Shells A216

Designs: 10s, Haliotis ovina. 80s, Turbo petholatus. 1pa, Trochus niloticus. 2.70pa, Turbo marmoratus.

Perf. 12¾
2001, Dec. 13   Litho.   Unwmk.
1055-1058 A216   Set of 4   7.00 7.00

Values are for stamps with surrounding selvage.

**Reign Of Queen Elizabeth II, 50th
Anniv. Issue**
Common Design Type
Souvenir Sheet

No. 1059: a, 15s, Princess Elizabeth as child. b, 90s, Wearing yellow hat. c, 1.20pa, With Princess Anne and Prince Charles. d, 1.40pa, Wearing crown. e, 2.25pa, 1955 portrait by Annigoni (38x50mm).

Perf. 14¼x14½, 13¾ (2.25pa)
2002, Feb. 6   Litho.   Wmk. 373
1059 CD360   Sheet of 5, #a-e   8.00 8.00

Souvenir Sheet

New Year 2002 (Year of the Horse) — A217

Various horses: a, 65s. b, 80s. c, 1pa. d, 2.50pa.

Litho. With Foil Application
2002, Feb. 12   Unwmk.   Perf. 14
1060 A217   Sheet of 4, #a-d   7.50 7.50

Intl. Year of Ecotourism — A218

Designs: 5s, Whale, surfer. 15s, Woman, shoreline. 70s, Beach, fish. 1.40pa, Arch. man. 2.25pa, Boats, man.

2002, Apr. 9   Litho.   Perf. 13¼x13¾
1061-1065 A218   Set of 5   6.75 6.75

Pearls A219

Pearls and: 90s, Workers preparing oysters for pearl cultivation. 1pa, Diver checking strung oysters. 1.20pa, Woman, pearl on necklace. 2.50pa, Islands.

2002, June 12   Litho.   Perf. 13½
1066-1069 A219   Set of 4   8.00 8.00
1069a   Souvenir sheet, #1068-
           1069   6.00 6.00

Values are for stamps with surrounding selvage.

Participation of Tongan Team in Rugby Sevens Tournament — A220

Designs: 15s, Player leaping for ball. 30s, Players ready for scrum. 90s, Player attempting tackle. 4pa, Players on ground.

2002, July 27
1070-1073 A220   Set of 4   9.00 9.00

Values are for stamps with surrounding selvage.

Weaving — A221

Designs: 30s, Woman and young girl. 90s, Woman with work hanging on line, boy with baskets. 1.40pa, Women weaving baskets. 2.50pa, Woman weaving basket lid.

2002, Sept. 17   Perf. 12¼
1074-1077 A221   Set of 4   7.00 7.00

No. 999 Surcharged

Type 1 — Slash Over First "5"

No. 1003 Surcharged

Methods and Perfs As Before
2002, Sept.
1077A A197 5s on 55s #999,
              Type 1   — —
1077B A197 15(s) on $1 #1003 — —
       See Nos. 1099-1114 for additional surcharges on No. 999.

'Eua National Park, 10th Anniv. — A222

Various depictions of red shining parrots 45s, 1pa, 1.50pa, 2.50pa.

2002, Nov. 27   Litho.   Perf. 12¼
1078-1081 A222   Set of 4   7.50 7.50

New Year 2003 (Year of the Ram) — A223

No. 1082: a, 65s, One ram. 80s, Three sheep. 1pa, Three sheep, diff. 2.50pa, Two sheep.

2003, Apr. 14   Litho.   Perf. 13¼
1082 A223   Sheet of 4, #a-d   7.00 7.00

Coronation of Queen Elizabeth II, 50th Anniv. — A224

Designs: 90s, Queen Elizabeth II in coach. 1.20pa, Queen Salote of Tonga. 1.40pa, Queen Salote in coach. 2.50pa, Queen Elizabeth II.

Litho. With Foil Application
2003, June 2
1083-1086 A224   Set of 4   10.00 10.00

Boats of Abel Tasman — A225

Various boats: 15s, 75s, 90s, 2.50pa.

2003, Aug. 7   Litho.   Perf. 13¼
1087-1090 A225   Set of 4   9.00 9.00
1090a   Souvenir sheet, #1087-1090   9.00 9.00

Beaches — A226

Flower and: 15s, Euakafa Beach. 90s, Pangaimotu Beach. 1.40pa, Fafa Beach. 2.25pa, Nuku Beach.

2003, Sept. 11
1091-1094 A226   Set of 4   8.50 8.50

Nos. 784, 785a, 785b, 785c, 786
Surcharged

Methods and Perfs As Before
2003, Sept.
1095   A152 10s on 32s Horiz.
             strip of 3,
             #784a-784c   — —
1096   A152 10s on 42s #785a — —
1097   A152 10s on 42s #785b — —
1097A A152 10s on 42s #785c — —

1098 A152 10s on 57s Horiz.
strip of 3,
#786a-786c — —

No. 999 Surcharged

Type 2 — Small numerals and cent sign

Type 3 — Small numerals and "s"

Type 4 — Thin numerals and "s"

Type 5 — Large numerals and "s"

Type 6 — Medium-sized numerals and "s"

Type 7 — Very large, bold numerals and "c"

Methods and Perfs As Before
2003-04

1099	A197	05s on 55s, Type 3	—	—
a.	Obliterators 2x1½mm			
1100	A197	05s on 55s, Type 4	—	—
1101	A197	5s on 55s, Type 5	—	—
1102	A197	5c on 55s, Type 7	—	—
1103	A197	10s on 55s, Type 5	—	—
1104	A197	10s on 55s, Type 5	—	—
1105	A197	10c on 55s, Type 7	—	—
1106	A197	15c on 55s, Type 2	—	—
1107	A197	15s on 55s, Type 2	—	—
1108	A197	15s on 55s, Type 5	—	—
1109	A197	15s on 55s, Type 7	—	—
1110	A197	20c on 55s, Type 2	—	—
1111	A197	20s on 55s, Type 4	—	—
1112	A197	20s on 55s, Type 5	—	—
1113	A197	45s on 55s, Type 5	—	—
1114	A197	45s on 55s, Type 6	—	—

Earliest known uses: Nos. 1099, 1106, 1110, 10/03; Nos. 1100, 1103, 1107, 1111, 12/03; Nos. 1101, 1108, 2/04; Nos. 1113, 4/04; Nos. 1104, 1112, 1114, 6/04; Nos. 1105, 1109, 8/04; No. 1102, 9/04;

Churches
A227

Designs: 15s, Catholic Church, Neiafu, Vava'u. 90s, Wesleyan Church, Uiha, Ha'apai. 1.40pa, Cathedral of the Immaculate Conception of Mary. 2.25pa, Free Wesleyan Church, Nuku'alofa.

2003, Nov. 10
1115-1118	A227	Set of 4	8.50	8.50

Christmas.

Year of the Monkey 2004

New Year 2004 (Year of the Monkey) — A228

No. 1119: a, 60s, Spider monkey. b, 80s, Ring-tailed lemur. c, 1pa, Cotton-top tamarin. d, 2.50pa, White-cheeked gibbon.

2004, Feb. 12   Litho.   Perf. 13¼
1119	A228	Sheet of 4, #a-d	6.00	6.00

Nos. 770, 787, 788, 815, 816, 1001, Niuafo'ou Nos. 140, 141 and 145 Surcharged

Type 1 — Small denomination and obliterator

Type 2 — Large denomination and obliterator

Methods and Perfs As Before
2004
1120	A153	10s on 32s #787	—	—
1121	A153	10s on 42s #788, Type 1	—	—
1122	A153	10s on 42s #788, Type 2	—	—
1123	A157	10s on 42s #815	—	—
1124	A147	10s on 57s Horiz. strip of 4, + central label, #770a-770d	—	—
1125	A157	10s on 57s #816	—	—
1126	A197	60s on 70s #1001	—	—

On Stamps of Niuafo'ou
1127	A25	10s on 42s #140	—	—
1128	A26	10s on 42s #145	—	—
1129	A25	10s on 57s #141	—	—

Size and location of obliterators and new denominations varies. Earliest known use: No. 1126, 3/04; Nos. 1120, 1121, 4/04; Nos. 1122, 1123, 1124, 1125, 1127, 1128, 1129, 6/04. The surcharged Niuafo'ou stamps were not necessarily sent only to Niuafo'ou for sale there.

Fruit Plants — A229

Designs: 45s, Mango. 60s, Pineapple. 80s, Coconut. 1.80pa, Banana.

2004, Sept. 21   Litho.   Perf. 14¼x14
1130-1133	A229	Set of 4	4.50	4.50

Christmas
A230

Designs: 65s, Madonna and Child. 80s, Journey to Bethlehem. 1.20pa, Annunciation to the Shepherds. 2.50pa, Magi.

2004, Dec.   Perf. 14
1134-1137	A230	Set of 4	8.25	8.25

Royalty — A231

Designs: 65s, King George Tupou I. 90s, King George Tupou II. 1.40pa, Queen Salote Tupou III. 3.05pa, King Taufa'ahau Tupou IV.

2004, July 7   Litho.   Perf. 14
1138-1141	A231	Set of 4	6.75	6.75

Souvenir Sheet

Year of the Rooster 2005
Sheet Value $4.95

New Year 2005 (Year of the Rooster) — A232

No. 1142 — Various roosters with panel color of: a, 65s, Yellow orange. b, 80s, Light green. c, 1pa, Tan. d, 2.50pa, Gray blue.

2005, Feb. 12
1142	A232	Sheet of 4, #a-d	8.50	8.50

Souvenir Sheet

Whales — A233

No. 1143 — Various whales with denominations in: a, 65s, Purple. b, 80s, Yellow. c, 1pa, Green. d, 2.50pa, Pink.

2005, May 4   Perf. 13¼
1143	A233	Sheet of 4, #a-d	8.25	8.25

Coronation of King Siaosi Tupou V — A234

King Siaosi Tupou V wearing: 30s, Uniform and sash. 1pa, Tuxedo and sash. 5pa, Robe and crown.

Litho. With Foil Application
2008, Aug. 1   Perf. 14
1144-1145	A234	Set of 2	1.50	1.50

Souvenir Sheet
1146	A234	5pa multi	5.50	5.50

No. 1146 contains one 30x60mm stamp.

Tonga Nos. 999, 1019, 1040, 1045, 1049, and Niuafo'ou Nos. 203, 211, 225 and 235 Surcharged

Methods and Perfs As Before
2008-10
On Stamps of Tonga
1147	A197	30s on 55s #999, type 1	—	—
1148	A202	30s on 55s #1019, type 1	—	—
1149	A210	30s on 55s #1040, type 2	—	—
1150	A213	30s on 55s #1049, type 2	—	—
1151	A212	70s on 55s #1045, type 1	—	—

On Stamps of Niuafo'ou
1152	A41	30s on 55s #203, type 2	—	—
1153	A44	30s on 55s #211, type 2	—	—
1154	A52	30s on 55s #225, type 2	—	—
1155	A11	70s on 55s #200, type 2	—	—
1156	A56	70s on 55s #235, type 2	—	—

Size, location and obliterators of surcharges vary. Surcharged Niuafo'ou stamps were used in Tonga.

Issued: No. 1147, Nov. 2009; No. 1148, Nov. 2008; Nos. 1149, 1153, July 2008; No. 1150, Feb. 2010; No. 1151, June 2010; Nos. 1152, 1154, 2008; Nos. 1155, 1156, May 2010.

Type 1 — Serifed Surcharge
Christmas — A235

No. 1157: a, 3pa, Lighthouse ornament on Christmas tree. b, 5pa, Christmas lights and Free Church of Tonga Cathedral.

2011, Dec. 24   Litho.   Perf. 14
1157	A235	Horiz. pair, #a-b	9.25	9.25

Birds
A236

Designs: 60s, Prosopeia tabuensis. 2.25pa,
Anas superciliosa. 2.40pa, Halcyon chloris.
2.50pa, Egretta novaehollandiae. 2.70pa,
Aplonis tabuensis. 3pa, Megapodius pritchardii. 3.40pa, Megapodius pritchardii, diff. 4pa,
Lalage maculosa. 5pa, Tyto alba. 6.60pa, Halcyon chloris, diff. 7.30pa, Prosopeia tabuensis, diff. 10pa, Swamp harrier.

2012, Feb. 6   **Perf. 14**
Stamps With White Frames

1158	A236	60s multi	.75	.75
1159	A236	2.25pa multi	2.75	2.75
1160	A236	2.40pa multi	3.00	3.00
1161	A236	2.50pa multi	3.00	3.00
1162	A236	2.70pa multi	3.25	3.25
1163	A236	3pa multi	3.75	3.75
1164	A236	3.40pa multi	4.00	4.00
1165	A236	4pa multi	4.75	4.75
1166	A236	5pa multi	6.00	6.00
1167	A236	6.60pa multi	8.00	8.00
1168	A236	7.30pa multi	8.75	8.75
1169	A236	10pa multi	12.00	12.00
	Nos. 1158-1169 (12)		60.00	60.00

Stamps Without White Frames

1170		Sheet of 12	60.00	60.00
a.	A236	60s multi	.75	.75
b.	A236	2.25pa multi	2.75	2.75
c.	A236	2.40pa multi	3.00	3.00
d.	A236	2.50pa multi	3.00	3.00
e.	A236	2.70pa multi	3.25	3.25
f.	A236	3pa multi	3.75	3.75
g.	A236	3.40pa multi	4.00	4.00
h.	A236	4pa multi	4.75	4.75
i.	A236	5pa multi	6.00	6.00
j.	A236	6.60pa multi	8.00	8.00
k.	A236	7.30pa multi	8.75	8.75
l.	A236	10pa multi	12.00	12.00

Reign of Queen
Elizabeth II, 60th
Anniv. — A237

2012, Mar. 6   **Perf. 14¾x14**

1171	A237	3.40pa multi	4.00	4.00

Souvenir Sheet

1172	A237	10pa multi	12.00	12.00

Worldwide Fund for Nature
(WWF) — A238

Various depictions of Thorny seahorse: 45s,
2pa, 2.40pa, 3.40pa.

2012, Mar. 12   **Perf. 14¼x14**

1173-1176	A238	Set of 4	9.75	9.75
1176a		Sheet of 16, 4 each		
		#1173-1176	39.00	39.00

SEMI-POSTAL STAMP

Catalogue values for unused
stamps in this section are for
Never Hinged items.

No. 488 Surcharged in Silver for
Cyclone Relief

1982, Apr. 14   **Litho.**

B1	A86	3pa + 50s multi	7.00	7.00

AIR POST STAMPS

Catalogue values for unused
stamps in this section are for
Never Hinged items.

Type of Regular Gold Coin Issue

Designs: 10p, 1sh1p, Queen Salote standing, ½-koula coin, obverse. 11p, Coat of arms,
½-koula coin, reverse. 2sh1p, 2sh9p, Queen
Salote standing, 1-koula coin, obverse. 2sh4p,
Coat of arms, 1-koula coin, reverse.

Litho.; Embossed on Gilt Foil
1963, July 15   **Unwmk.**   *Die Cut*
Diameter: 54mm

C1	A36	10p dp carmine	.50	.50
C2	A36	11p green	.70	.70
C3	A36	1sh1p violet blue	.70	.70

Diameter: 80mm

C4	A36	2sh1p magenta	1.25	1.25
C5	A36	2sh4p emerald	1.25	1.25
C6	A36	2sh9p violet	2.00	2.00
	Nos. C1-C6 (6)		6.40	6.40

See note after No. 133.

Map of Tongatabu and ¼-Koula
Coin — AP1

Litho.; Embossed on Gilt Foil
1964, Oct. 19

C7	AP1	10p deep green	.30	.30
C8	AP1	1sh2p black	.45	.45
C9	AP1	3sh6p carmine	.95	.95
C10	AP1	6sh6p purple	1.75	1.75
	Nos. C7-C10 (4)		3.45	3.45

Pan-Pacific and Southeast Asia Women's
Association Conf., Nukualofa, Aug. 1964. See
note after No. 133.

Nos. C1-C2, C4-C6 Surcharged like
Regular Issue, 1965, in Black, White
or Red

1965, Mar. 18

C11	A36	2sh3p on 10p (B)	.75	.75
C12	A36	2sh9p on 11p (W)	1.50	1.50
C13	A36	4sh6p on 2sh1p	20.00	20.00
C14	A36	4sh6p on 2sh4p	20.00	20.00
C15	A36	4sh6p on 2sh9p	12.00	12.00
	Nos. C11-C15 (5)		54.25	54.25

Nos. 114-115, 117-118 Overprinted or
Surcharged

Perf. 14½x13½

1966, June 18   **Wmk. 79**

C16	A35	5p purple	.25	.25
C17	A35	10p on 1p brn org & car rose	.25	.25
C18	A35	1sh red brown	.30	.25
C19	A35	2sh9p on 2p ultra	.35	.25

C20	A35	3sh6p on 5p purple	.35	.25
C21	A35	4sh6p on 1sh red brn	.75	.25
	Nos. C16-C21 (6)		2.25	1.20

Centenary of Tupou College and secondary
education. The overprint or surcharge is
spaced differently on other values.

Nos. C7-C8 Overprinted and
Surcharged in Silver or Gold on Black,
or in Black on Gold

Litho.; Embossed on Gilt Foil
1966, Dec. 16   **Unwmk.**   *Die Cut*

C22	AP1	10p (S on B)	.25	.25
C23	AP1	1sh2p (B on G)	.25	.25
C24	AP1	4sh on 10p (S on B)	1.00	1.00
C25	AP1	5sh6p on 1sh2p (B on G)	1.50	1.50
C26	AP1	10sh6p on 1sh2p (G on B)	2.50	2.50
	Nos. C22-C26 (5)		5.40	5.40

In memory of Queen Salote (1900-65).

**King Taufa'ahau Type of Regular
Issue, 1967**

Designs: 7s, 11s, 23s, 2pa, Taufa'ahau IV,
obverse of new palladium coins. 9s, 21s, 29s,
Coat of Arms, reverse.

Litho.; Embossed on Palladium Foil
1967, July 4

Diameter: 7s, 44mm; 9s, 29s, 52mm; 11s,
59mm; 21s, 68mm; 23s, 40mm; 2pa, 74mm.

C27	A38	7s red & black	.25	.25
C28	A38	9s maroon & emer	.25	.25
C29	A38	11s brt blue & org	.30	.30
C30	A38	21s black & emer	.55	.55
C31	A38	23s magenta & emer	.60	.60
C32	A38	29s vio blue & emer	.70	.70
C33	A38	2pa magenta & orange	5.00	5.00
	Nos. C27-C33 (7)		7.60	7.60

See note after No. 181.

Regular
Issues of
1953 Srchd.
in Red or
Black

Wmk. 79
1967, Dec. 15   **Engr.**   *Die Cut*

C34	A33	11s on 3½p ultra (R)	.30	.30
C35	A33	21s on 1½p emerald	.35	.35
C36	A33	23s on 3½p ultra (R)	.35	.35
	Nos. C34-C36 (3)		1.00	1.00

Arrival of the United States Peace Corps.

No. 112 Surcharged
in Red

1968, Apr. 6   **Engr.**   **Perf. 11x11½**

C37	A34	11s on 10sh blk & yel	.45	.45
C38	A34	21s on 10sh blk & yel	.60	.60
C39	A34	23s on 10sh blk & yel	.60	.60
	Nos. C37-C39 (3)		1.65	1.65

Nos. C27-C33 Overprinted: "HIS
MAJESTY'S 50th BIRTHDAY" in Silver
on Blue Panel on 7s, 11s, 23s and
2pa. "H.M.'s BIRTHDAY / 4 . JULY .
1968" in Gold on Red Panel on 9s,
21s and 29s

Litho.; Embossed on Palladium Foil
1968, July 4   **Unwmk.**   *Die Cut*

C40	A38	7s red & black	.25	.25
C41	A38	9s maroon & emer	.25	.25
C42	A38	11s brt blue & org	.25	.25
C43	A38	21s black & emerald	.75	.35

C44	A38	23s mag & emerald	.75	.35
C45	A38	29s vio blue & emer	1.00	.40
C46	A38	2pa magenta & org	6.75	6.00
	Nos. C40-C46 (7)		9.90	7.70

50th birthday of King Taufa'ahau IV.

Types of 1953 Surcharged: "Friendly
Islands / Field & Track Trials / South
Pacific Games / Port Moresby 1969 /
AIRMAIL"

Designs as before.

1968, Dec. 19   **Engr.**   **Wmk. 79**

C47	A33	6s on 6p yel& blk	.25	.25
C48	A33	7s on 4p purple & yel	.25	.25
C49	A33	8s on 8p blk & lt grn	.25	.25
C50	A33	9s on 1½p emerald	.25	.25
C51	A34	11s on 3p brn org & yel	.25	.25
C52	A33	21s on 3½p dk blue	.30	.30
C53	A33	38s on 5sh sepia & yel	2.10	.50
C54	A34	1pa on 10sh orange yel	1.00	.60
	Nos. C47-C54 (8)		4.40	2.40

Issued to publicize the field and track trials
for the third South Pacific Games, Port
Moresby, 1969. The overprint is in 5 lines on
the horizontal stamps, in 7 lines on the vertical
stamps. On the vertical stamps "Trial" is
printed on the line ahead of "Field & Track." On
No. C54 the denomination is spelled out.

Nos. C19-C21 Surcharged

Perf. 14½x13½

1968   **Photo.**   **Wmk. 79**

C55	A35	1s on 2sh9p on 2p ultra	1.60	1.00
C56	A35	1s on 3sh6p on 5p pur	1.60	1.00
C57	A35	1s on 4sh6p on 1sh red brown	1.60	1.00
	Nos. C55-C57 (3)		4.80	3.00

**Pacific Games Type of Regular
Issue**

Design: Boxer.

1969, Aug. 13   **Litho.**   *Die Cut*
Self-adhesive

C58	A40	9s orange, blk & pur	.30	.30
C59	A40	11s orange, blk & dk bl	.30	.30
C60	A40	20s org, blk & yel grn	.50	.50
C61	A40	60s orange, blk & scar	1.25	1.25
C62	A40	1pa orange, blk & grn	1.75	1.75
	Nos. C58-C62 (5)		4.10	4.10

See note after No. 231.

Oil Derrick on
Map of
Tongatabu and
King Taufa'ahau
IV — AP2

Litho.; Gold Embossed
1969, Dec. 23   **Self-adhesive**

C63	AP2	9s multicolored	.30	.30
C64	AP2	10s multicolored	.30	.30
C65	AP2	24s multicolored	.90	.90
C66	AP2	29s multicolored	1.00	1.00
C67	AP2	38s multicolored	1.40	1.40
	Nos. C63-C67 (5)		3.90	3.90

1st scientific search for oil in Tonga.

King Taufa'ahau IV and Queen
Elizabeth II — AP3

Litho.; Gold Embossed
1970, Mar. 7   **Self-adhesive**

C68	AP3	7s multicolored	.40	.30
C69	AP3	9s multicolored	.50	.35
C70	AP3	24s multicolored	1.25	.65

C71	AP3	29s multicolored	1.50	.75
C72	AP3	38s multicolored	2.10	1.00
		Nos. C68-C72 (5)	5.75	3.05

See note after No. 242.

King Taufa'ahau Tupou IV
Medal — AP4

Litho.; Gold Embossed

1970, June 4   Self-adhesive

C73	AP4	9s grnsh bl, ver & gold	.30	.30
C74	AP4	10s lilac, bl & gold	.30	.30
C75	AP4	24s yel, grn & gold	.75	.75
C76	AP4	29s ultra, org & gold	1.10	1.10
C77	AP4	38s ocher, emer & gold	1.60	1.60
		Nos. C73-C77 (5)	4.05	4.05

See note after No. 247.

**Red Cross Type of Regular Issue
Without Coat of Arms**

1970, Oct. 17   Litho.   Die Cut
Self-adhesive

C78	A45	9s red & silver	.25	.25
C79	A45	10s red & magenta	.25	.25
C80	A45	18s red & brt green	.75	.75
C81	A45	38s red & brt blue	2.75	2.75
C82	A45	1pa red & green	6.00	6.00
		Nos. C78-C82 (5)	10.00	10.00

Centenary of the British Red Cross.

Nos. C22-C24 Surcharged

**Lithographed; Embossed on Gilt
Foil**

1971, Jan. 31   Die Cut

C83	AP1	9s on #C22 (S on B)	.70	.25
C84	AP1	24s on #C24 (O on B)	1.50	1.00
C85	AP1	29s on #C23 (R on B)	2.10	1.25
C86	AP1	38s on #C23 (G on B)	3.25	1.60
		Nos. C83-C86 (4)	7.55	4.05

In memory of Queen Salote (1900-1965).

Regular
Issues of
1953, Srchd
in Red and
Black

1971   Engr.   Wmk. 79   Imperf

C87	A33	9s on 1½p green	.25	.25
C88	A33	10s on 4p purple & yel	.25	.25
C89	A33	38s on 1p yellow & blk	1.10	.60
		Nos. C87-C89 (3)	1.60	1.00

See note after No. 272.

Types of Regular Issue Surcharged in
Purple or Black: "AIRMAIL," New
Denomination and "HONOURING
JAPANESE POSTAL CENTENARY
1871-1971"

1971

| C90 | A34 | 18s on 1sh car & buff (P) | .50 | .50 |
| C91 | A33 | 1pa on 2sh car & ultra | 3.00 | 3.00 |

Surcharge on #C90 in 6 lines, on #C91 in 4.

Self-adhesive & Imperf.
Starting with Nos. C92-C96, all airmail issues are self-adhesive and
imperforate, unless otherwise stated.

High Jump — AP5

1971, July   Litho.   Unwmk.

C92	AP5	9s brown, mag & blk	.25	.25
C93	AP5	10s brown, blue & blk	.25	.25
C94	AP5	24s brn, dk grn & blk	.45	.45
C95	AP5	29s brown, vio & blk	.75	.75
C96	AP5	38s brown, red & blk	1.00	1.00
		Nos. C92-C96 (5)	2.60	2.60

4th South Pacific Games, Papeete, French
Polynesia, Sept. 8-19.
For surcharges see Nos. C141-C142.

Prehistoric
Trilithon,
King's Watch
and Portrait
AP6

Litho. and Embossed

1971, July 20

| C97 | AP6 | 14s dk brown & multi | .75 | .75 |
| C98 | AP6 | 21s ocher & multi | 1.10 | 1.10 |

2nd anniversary of man's first landing on the
moon and the placement of a Bulova Accutron
there. See Nos. C117-118, CO47-CO48,
CO61-CO62. Advertisement on peelable
paper backing.

Medal Type of Regular Issue

Designs: 10s, Gold Medal of Merit, obverse
(King Taufa'ahau IV). 75s, Silver Medal of
Merit, obverse (King Taufa'ahau IV). 1pa,
Bronze Medal of Merit, reverse.

1971, Oct. 30   Litho. & Embossed

C99	A47	10s gold & multi	.25	.25
C100	A47	75s silver & multi	1.60	1.60
C101	A47	1pa bronze & multi	1.75	1.75
		Nos. C99-C101 (3)	3.60	3.60

Girl with Blocks
and UNICEF
Emblem — AP7

1971, Dec.   Litho.

C102	AP7	10s multicolored	.30	.30
C103	AP7	15s multicolored	.35	.35
C104	AP7	25s multicolored	.60	.60
C105	AP7	50s multicolored	1.40	1.40
C106	AP7	1pa multicolored	2.75	2.75
		Nos. C102-C106 (5)	5.40	5.40

25th anniversary of UNICEF.

Ship Type of Regular Issue

Design: Map of Merchant Marine routes
from Tonga and cargo ship "Niuvakai."

1972, Apr. 14

C107	A49	9s ver & multi	.85	.35
C108	A49	12s multicolored	1.10	.35
C109	A49	14s dk purple & multi	1.25	.35
C110	A49	75s olive & multi	6.75	5.00
C111	A49	90s black & multi	7.00	6.50
		Nos. C107-C111 (5)	16.95	12.55

For surcharge and overprint see No. C124.

Coin Type of Regular Issue

Design: Coins on top; panel at bottom
inscribed "5th anniversary world's first palladium coinage."

Litho.; Embossed on Metallic Foil

1972, July 15

C112	A50	9s silver & multi	.30	.30
C113	A50	12s silver & multi	.35	.35
C114	A50	14s silver & multi	.50	.50
C115	A50	21s silver & multi	.75	.75
C116	A50	75s silver & multi	2.25	2.25
		Nos. C112-C116 (5)	4.15	4.15

**Watch Type of 1971
Litho. and Embossed**

1972, July 20

| C117 | AP6 | 17s multicolored | .85 | .85 |
| C118 | AP6 | 38s multicolored | 1.75 | 1.75 |

Advertisement on peelable paper backing.

Proclamation of Sovereignty — AP8

1972, Dec. 9   Litho.

C119	AP8	9s ultra & multi	.25	.25
C120	AP8	12s red brown & multi	.25	.25
C121	AP8	14s magenta & multi	.35	.35
C122	AP8	38s brn org & multi	1.00	1.00
C123	AP8	1pa olive & multi	2.75	2.75
		Nos. C119-C123 (5)	4.55	4.55

Tonga's proclamation of sovereignty over
the Minerva Reefs, June 1972.

No. C107 Surcharged

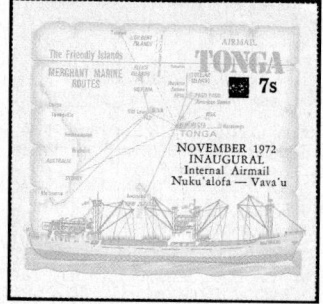

1972, Nov.   Litho.

| C124 | A49 | 7s on 9s multicolored | 3.00 | 3.00 |

Inauguration of internal airmail service
Nukualofa-Vavau, Nov. 1972.

Tongan Bank Notes and Bank
Building — AP9

1973, Mar. 30   Litho.

C125	AP9	9s multicolored	.25	.25
C126	AP9	12s ultra & multi	.25	.25
C127	AP9	17s dp car & multi	.40	.25
C128	AP9	50s lt blue & multi	1.50	1.25
C129	AP9	90s multicolored	2.75	2.75
		Nos. C125-C129 (5)	5.15	4.60

Establishment of Bank of Tonga.

Boy Scout Emblem — AP10

1973, June 29   Litho.

C130	AP10	9s silver & multi	.70	.35
C131	AP10	12s silver & multi	.85	.45
C132	AP10	14s silver & multi	1.25	.70
C133	AP10	17s silver & multi	1.40	.85
C134	AP10	1pa silver & multi	15.00	9.25
		Nos. C130-C134 (5)	19.20	11.60

See note after No. 326.
For surcharges see Nos. C143-C144.

"Resolution" — AP11

1973, Oct. 2   Litho.

C135	AP11	9s multicolored	.80	.40
C136	AP11	14s multicolored	1.50	.60
C137	AP11	29s multicolored	4.50	2.75
C138	AP11	38s multicolored	5.50	3.00
C139	AP11	75s multicolored	10.50	4.25
		Nos. C135-C139 (5)	22.80	11.00

Bicentenary of Capt. Cook's arrival.

Nos. 277, C96, C94, C130 and C132
Surcharged in Silver, Violet or Black:
"Commonwealth Games Christchurch
1974"

1973, Dec. 19

C140	A46	7s on 25s multi (S)	.25	.25
C141	AP5	9s on 38s multi (V)	.25	.25
C142	AP5	24s multicolored (B)	.95	.35
C143	AP10	29s on 9s multi (V)	1.10	.50
C144	AP10	40s on 14s multi (B)	1.60	1.10
		Nos. C140-C144 (5)	4.10	2.35

10th British Commonwealth Games, Christchurch, New Zealand, Jan. 24-Feb. 2, 1974.
No. C140 is overprinted "AIRMAIL" in black;
the silver surcharge and overprint are on black
panels.

Parrot of
Eua — AP12

1974, Mar. 20   **Litho.**

C145	AP12	7s multicolored	.50	.25
C146	AP12	9s multicolored	.60	.30
C147	AP12	12s multicolored	.60	.30
C148	AP12	14s multicolored	.90	.45
C149	AP12	18s multicolored	1.00	.50
C150	AP12	29s multicolored	1.75	.90
C151	AP12	38s multicolored	2.50	1.25
C152	AP12	50s multicolored	3.00	1.50
C153	AP12	75s multicolored	4.50	2.25
		Nos. C145-C153 (9)	15.35	7.70

Printed in rolls of 500. Self-adhesive
red control number in upper left corner.

Carrier Pigeon Scattering Letters over
Tonga — AP13

1974, June 20   **Typo.**

C154	AP13	14s lt blue & multi	.45	.45
C155	AP13	21s lt blue & multi	.55	.55
C156	AP13	60s lt blue & multi	1.75	1.75
C157	AP13	75s lt blue & multi	1.90	1.90
C158	AP13	1pa lt blue & multi	2.50	2.50
		Nos. C154-C158 (5)	7.15	7.15

Centenary of Universal Postal Union.

Girl Guide Leaders — AP14

1974, Sept. 11   **Litho.**

C159	AP14	14s blue & multi	.80	.50
C160	AP14	16s blue & multi	1.40	.80
C161	AP14	29s blue & multi	2.75	1.60
C162	AP14	31s blue & multi	3.50	2.10
C163	AP14	75s blue & multi	7.50	4.50
		Nos. C159-C163 (5)	15.95	9.50

Girl Guides of Tonga.
For surcharges and overprints see Nos.
C190-C191, C193.

Freighter "James Cook" and List of
Tongan Merchantmen — AP15

1974, Dec. 11

C164	AP15	9s blue & multi	.80	.30
C165	AP15	14s blue & multi	1.40	.55
C166	AP15	17s blue & multi	1.50	.60
C167	AP15	60s blue & multi	5.50	3.75
C168	AP15	90s blue & multi	8.75	4.75
		Nos. C164-C168 (5)	17.95	9.95

Establishment of Royal Marine Institute.

Beach
AP16

Designs: 12s, 14s, like 9s. 17s, 38s, Surf.

1975, Mar. 11   **Litho.**

C169	AP16	9s gold & multi	.25	.25
C170	AP16	12s gold & multi	.25	.25
C171	AP16	14s gold & multi	.30	.30
C172	AP16	17s gold & multi	.30	.30
C173	AP16	38s gold & multi	.95	.95
		Nos. C169-C173 (5)	2.00	2.00

First meeting of South Pacific area Prime
Ministers. See note after No. 226.
For surcharges see Nos. C229, C298.

Women's Discus and Games'
Emblem — AP17

1975, June 11

C174	AP17	9s multicolored	.35	.35
C175	AP17	12s multicolored	.45	.45
C176	AP17	14s multicolored	.45	.45
C177	AP17	17s black & multi	.60	.60
C178	AP17	90s olive & multi	2.40	2.40
		Nos. C174-C178 (5)	4.25	4.25

5th South Pacific Games, Guam, Aug. 1-10.
See note after No. 226.
For surcharges see Nos. C230-C231.

FAO Type of 1975

Designs (FAO Coins): 12s, Coins showing
cattle, corn and pig. 14s, Cornucopias; coins
showing king, family planning emblem and
melons. 25s, Bananas and treasure chest.
50s, King Taufa'ahau. 1pa, Palms.

1975, Sept. 3

C179	A62	12s multicolored	.45	.45
C180	A62	14s blue & multi	.45	.45
C181	A62	25s silver, blk & org	.70	.70
C182	A62	50s car, sil & blk	1.25	1.25
C183	A62	1pa silver & black	2.50	2.50
		Nos. C179-C183 (5)	5.35	5.35

Size of paper backing of 14s: 82x50mm;
others 45x45mm. See note after No. 226.

Coin Type of 1975

Coins: 9s, King Taufa'ahau IV, obverse. 12s,
Queen Salote III, 75pa reverse and obverse.
14s, 10pa reverse. 38s, King Taufa'ahau IV,
10pa reverse and observe. 1pa, Heads of four
constitutional monarchs.

1975, Nov. 4   **Lt. Blue Background**

C184	A63	9s black, sil & red	.35	.25
C185	A63	12s gold, blk & grn	.45	.35
C186	A63	14s black, sil & ol	.45	.35
C187	A63	38s gold, blk & org	1.00	.50
C188	A63	1pa black, sil & blue	2.60	2.60
		Nos. C184-C188 (5)	4.85	4.00

Size of paper backing of 1pa: 87x78mm,
others 65x60mm. See note after No. 226.

Nos. 344-345, C160, C163
Surcharged and Overprinted in
Carmine on Silver, Green or Gold

a

Type 2 — Unserifed Surcharge b

1976, Feb. 24   **Litho.**

C189	A58 (a)	12s on 20s (S)	.80	.50
C190	AP14 (b)	14s on 16s (Gr)	.80	.50
C191	AP14 (b)	16s (G)	1.00	.50
C192	A58 (a)	38s on 40s (G)	2.50	.70
C193	AP14 (b)	75s (S)	4.50	2.75
		Nos. C189-C193 (5)	9.60	4.95

21st Olympic Games, Montreal, Canada,
July 17-Aug. 1. See note after No. 226.

Bicentennial Type of 1976

Signers of Declaration of Independence,
Flags of US and Tonga: 12s, Abraham Clark,
George Ross, Thomas Lynch, Jr., Charles
Carroll, Roger Sherman (no flags). 14s, Rob-
ert Treat Paine, Thomas Jefferson, Thomas
McKean, John Adams. 17s, Button Gwinnett,
Lewis Morris, Caesar Rodney, Richard Henry
Lee. 38s, John Hart, Samuel Huntington,
Philip Livingston, John Morton. 1pa, John
Hancock, Joseph Hewes, Josiah Bartlett, John
Witherspoon.

1976, May 26

C194	A66	12s buff & multi	.65	.25
C195	A66	14s buff & multi	.75	.25
C196	A66	17s buff & multi	.80	.45
C197	A66	38s buff & multi	3.50	1.00
C198	A66	1pa buff & multi	6.75	4.25
		Nos. C194-C198 (5)	12.45	6.10

See note after No. 381.

Missionary Ship "Triton" — AP18

1976, Aug. 25   **Litho.**

C199	AP18	9s pink & multi	.35	.30
C200	AP18	12s multicolored	.55	.40
C201	AP18	14s multicolored	.60	.45
C202	AP18	17s buff & multi	.80	.55
C203	AP18	38s multicolored	1.40	.90
		Nos. C199-C203 (5)	3.70	2.60

See note after No. 386.
For surcharges see Nos. C234, C294,
C299.

Treaty Signing Ceremony,
Nukualofa — AP19

1976, Nov. 1

C204	AP19	11s multicolored	.45	.40
C205	AP19	17s multicolored	.60	.55
C206	AP19	18s multicolored	.65	.60
C207	AP19	31s multicolored	1.10	1.00
C208	AP19	39s multicolored	1.40	1.25
		Nos. C204-C208 (5)	4.20	3.80

See note after No. 391.
For surcharges see Nos. C235, C295.

Elizabeth II and Taufa'ahau IV — AP20

1977, Feb. 7

C209	AP20	15s gray & multi	1.60	.55
C210	AP20	17s gray & multi	2.25	.80
C211	AP20	22s gray & multi	22.50	10.00
C212	AP20	31s gray & multi	3.00	1.75
C213	AP20	39s gray & multi	6.00	3.00
		Nos. C209-C213 (5)	35.35	16.10

See note after No. 396.

Coronation Coin — AP21

1977, July 4   **Litho.**
C214 AP21 11s multicolored .40 .40
C215 AP21 15s multicolored .50 .50
C216 AP21 18s multicolored .50 .50
C217 AP21 39s multicolored .80 .80
C218 AP21 1pa multicolored 2.75 2.75
    Nos. C214-C218 (5) 4.95 4.95

See note after No. 401.
See Nos. CO120-CO122.

Capt. Cook Medal and Journal
Quotation — AP22

1977, Sept. 27
C219 AP22 15s multicolored .90 .75
C220 AP22 22s multicolored 1.40 1.25
C221 AP22 31s multicolored 3.50 3.00
C222 AP22 50s multicolored 10.00 5.00
C223 AP22 1pa multicolored 21.00 9.00
    Nos. C219-C223 (5) 36.80 19.00

Bicentenary of Capt. Cook's farewell voyage.
See Nos. CO123-CO125.

Sei and Fin Whales — AP23

1977, Dec. 16
C224 AP23 11s blk, vio & bl 4.25 .80
C225 AP23 17s blk, red & bl 4.75 .90
C226 AP23 18s blk, grn & bl 4.75 1.10
C227 AP23 39s blk, brn & bl 5.75 2.25
C228 AP23 50s blk, mag & bl 7.25 0.50
    Nos. C224-C228 (5) 26.75 8.55

Whale protection.
See Nos. CO126-CO128.

Stamps of 1975-77 Surcharged in
Various Colors

1978
C229 AP16 17s on 38s
    (#C173;Gr) 2.25 1.50
C230 AP17 17s on 9s
    (#C174;B) 2.25 1.50
C231 AP17 17s on 12s
    (#C175;DBl) 2.25 1.50
C232 A63 17s on 38s
    (#C187;B) 2.25 1.50
C233 A66 17s on 12s
    (#C194; R on
    G) 2.25 1.50
C234 AP18 17s on 9s (#C199;
    B) 2.25 1.50
C235 AP19 17s on 18s
    (#C206; G on
    Brn) 2.25 1.50
C236 A66 1pa on 75s (#381;
    Gr on S) 11.75 9.50
C237 A66 1pa on 38s
    (#C197; DBl
    on G) 11.75 9.50

C238 OA15 1pa on 1.10pa
    (#CO119; S
    on DBl) 26.50 27.50

Edmonton Games Type of 1978

Canadian Maple leaf and Tongan coat of
arms.

1978, May 5   **Litho.**
C239 A73 17s red & multi .45 .45
C240 A73 35s red & multi .90 .90
C241 A73 38s red & multi .95 .95
C242 A73 40s red & multi 2.00 2.00
C243 A73 65s red & multi 1.50 1.50
    Nos. C239-C243 (5) 5.80 5.80

See note after No. 423.

King Type of 1978

Design: Head of King Taufa'ahau IV within
6-pointed star.

1978, July 4
C244 A74 11s multicolored .25 .25
C245 A74 15s multicolored .35 .35
C246 A74 17s multicolored .45 .45
C247 A74 39s multicolored 1.00 1.00
C248 A74 1pa multicolored 2.50 2.50
    Nos. C244-C248 (5) 4.55 4.55

See note after No. 226.

Wildlife Type of 1978

1978, Dec. 15   **Litho. & Typo.**
C249 A77 17s Whale 4.00 2.00
C250 A77 22s Bat 4.00 2.00
C251 A77 31s Turtle 4.00 2.00
C252 A77 39s Parrot 8.50 3.50
C253 A77 45s like 17s 8.75 4.00
    Nos. C249-C253 (5) 29.25 13.50

Wildlife conservation. See note after No. 226.

Types of 1979

Designs: 15s, like No. 453. 17s, like No.
450. 31s, Rotary emblem. 39s, Ministry and
tourism buildings, Bank of Tonga, GPO. 1pa,
Dish antenna and map of Tonga.

1979, Feb. 16   **Litho.**
C254 A79 15s multicolored .40 .30
C255 A79 17s multicolored .50 .35
C256 A78 31s vio blue & gold .75 .45
C257 A79 1pa multicolored 1.10 .65
C258 A79 1pa multicolored 2.75 1.60
    Nos. C254-C258 (5) 5.50 3.35

Decade of Progress. Paper backing shows
map of Tonga.

Type of 1979

Tongan self-adhesive, free-form stamps.

1979, June 1
C259 A81 15s multicolored .35 .35
C260 A81 17s multicolored .45 .45
C261 A81 18s multicolored .60 .60
C262 A81 31s multicolored .75 .75
C263 A81 39s multicolored 1.00 1.00
    Nos. C259-C263 (5) 3.15 3.15

See note after No. 458.

Jet — AP24

1979, Aug. 17
C264 AP24 5s multicolored .25 .25
C265 AP24 11s multicolored .35 .25
C266 AP24 14s multicolored .50 .35
C267 AP24 15s multicolored .50 .35
C268 AP24 17s multicolored .65 .45
C269 AP24 18s multicolored .70 .50
C270 AP24 22s multicolored .75 .55
C271 AP24 31s multicolored 1.10 .75
C272 AP24 39s multicolored 1.40 .95
C273 AP24 75s multicolored 2.50 1.75
C274 AP24 1pa multicolored 3.50 2.50
    Nos. C264-C274 (11) 12.20 8.65

Nos. C264-C274 issued in coils; self-adhesive control number in lower left corner of
paper backing except on 14s, 18s, 22s, 75s.
See note after No. 226.
See Nos. C303-C305.

View Type of 1979

Design: Kao Island. See note after No. 463.

1979, Nov. 23
C275 A82 5s multicolored .25 .25
C276 A82 15s multicolored .45 .45
C277 A82 17s multicolored .45 .45

C278 A82 39s multicolored 1.00 1.00
C279 A82 75s multicolored 1.75 1.75
    Nos. C275-C279 (5) 3.85 3.85

Friendship Treaty Type of 1980

George Tupou I, Napoleon III, Adventure.
See notes over #464 & after #468.

1980, Jan. 9   **Litho.**
C280 A83 15s multicolored .45 .45
C281 A83 17s multicolored .55 .55
C282 A83 22s multicolored .60 .60
C283 A83 31s multicolored .85 .85
C284 A83 39s multicolored 1.00 1.00
    Nos. C280-C284 (5) 3.45 3.45

Nos. C259-C263 Surcharged and
Overprinted in Black on Silver: "1980
OLYMPIC GAMES," Moscow '80 and
Bear Emblems

1980, Apr. 30   **Litho.**
C285 A81 9s on 15s multi .30 .30
C286 A81 16s on 15s multi .65 .65
C287 A81 29s on 18s multi 1.00 1.00
C288 A81 32s on 31s multi 1.10 1.10
C289 A81 47s on 39s multi 1.75 1.75
    Nos. C285-C289 (5) 4.80 4.80

22nd Summer Olympic Games, Moscow,
July 19-Aug. 3.

Scouting Activities in Rotary
Emblem — AP25

1980, Sept. 30   **Litho.**
C290 AP25 29s multicolored 1.00 1.00
C291 AP25 32s multicolored 1.00 1.00
C292 AP25 47s multicolored 1.50 1.50
C293 AP25 1pa multicolored 3.00 3.00
    Nos. C290-C293 (4) 6.50 6.50

Boy Scout Jamboree; Rotary International,
75th anniversary. Peelable backing shows
map of Tonga.

Nos. C170, C185, C195, C200-C201,
C208 Surcharged

1980, Dec. 3   **Litho.**
C294 AP18 29s on 14s multi 1.75 1.75
C295 AP19 29s on 39s multi 1.75 1.75
C296 A63 32s on 12s multi 2.00 2.00
C297 A66 32s on 14s multi 2.00 2.00
C298 AP16 47s on 12s multi 2.75 2.75
C299 AP18 47s on 12s multi 2.75 2.75
    Nos. C294-C299 (6) 13.00 13.00

IYD Type of 1981

1981, Sept. 9   **Litho.**
         Size: 25x32mm
C300 A85 29s multicolored .50 .50
C301 A85 32s multicolored .60 .60
C302 A85 47s multicolored 1.10 1.10
    Nos. C300-C302 (3) 2.20 2.20

Jet Type of 1979

1982, Nov. 17   **Litho.**
C303 AP24 29s pink & black 1.50 1.00
C304 AP24 32s pale yel & blk 1.75 1.25
C305 AP24 47s lt brown & blk 2.75 1.75
    Nos. C303-C305 (3) 6.00 4.00

**AIR POST SPECIAL DELIVERY
STAMP**

Catalogue values for unused
stamps in this section are for
Never Hinged items.

Owl — APSD1

1990, Feb. 21   **Litho.**   **Perf. 11½**
CE1 APSD1 10pa multi 17.00 17.00

AIR POST OFFICIAL STAMPS

Catalogue values for unused
stamps in this section are for
Never Hinged items.

Nos. 115, 117-118, 111-113
Overprinted "OFFICIAL AIR MAIL /
1862 / TAU'ATAINA / EMANCIPATION
/ 1962" in Red

Engr.; Photo. (A35)
1962, Feb. 7   **Wmk. 79**
CO1 A35 2p ultra 16.00 7.50
CO2 A35 5p purple 16.00 8.00
CO3 A35 1sh red brown 9.00 4.00
CO4 A33 5sh pur & yel 90.00 55.00
CO5 A34 10sh black & yel 42.50 22.50
CO6 A34 £1 ultra, car &
    yel 75.00 37.50
    Nos. CO1-CO6 (6) 248.50 134.50

Centenary of emancipation.

Type of Regular Gold Coin Issue

Design: 15sh, Queen Salote standing, 1-
koula coin, obverse.

Litho.; Embossed on Gilt Foil
1963, July 15   **Unwmk.**   **Die Cut**
       Diameter: 80mm
CO7 A36 15sh black 5.75 5.75

Note after No. 133 also applies to No. CO7.

No. CO7 Surcharged like Regular
Issue of 1965 in Black

1965, Mar. 18
CO8 A36 30sh on 15sh black 6.50 6.50

No. 116 Surcharged in Italic Letters
Similarly to Nos. C16-C21

Perf. 14½x13½
1966, June 18   **Wmk. 79**
CO9 A35 10sh on 4p brt green .80 .50
CO10 A35 20sh on 4p brt green 1.00 .65

Centenary of Tupou College and secondary
education.

No. 111 Surcharged in Red:
"OFFICIAL / AIRMAIL / ONE
PA'ANGA"

1967, Mar. 25   **Engr.**   **Perf. 11½x11**
CO11 A33 1p on 5sh pur & yel 3.00 3.00

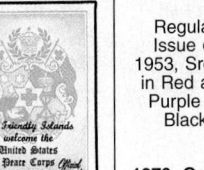

Type of Regular Issue Surcharged

1967, Dec. 15   **Wmk. 79**   *Die Cut*
CO12   A34   30s on £1 multi   .55   .55
CO13   A34   70s on £1 multi   .80   .80
CO14   A34   1.50pa on £1 multi   1.25   1.25
    Nos. CO12-CO14 (3)   2.60   2.60
    Arrival of US Peace Corps.

No. 113 Surcharged with New Value and "OFFICIAL/AIRMAIL"

1968, Apr. 6   **Engr.**   *Perf. 11x11½*
CO15   A34   40s on £1 multi   .75   .75
CO16   A34   60s on £1 multi   1.00   1.00
CO17   A34   1pa on £1 multi   1.50   1.50
CO18   A34   2pa on £1 multi   2.25   2.25
    Nos. CO15-CO18 (4)   5.50   5.50

Type of 1953 Surcharged: "Friendly Islands / Trials / Field & Track / South Pacific / Games / Port Moresby / 1969 / OFFICIAL AIRMAIL"

1968, Dec. 19   **Engr.**   *Die Cut*
         Wmk. 79
CO19   A34   20s on £1 grn & multi   .35   .25
CO20   A34   1pa on £1 grn & multi   1.00   .60

No. 176 Overprinted and Surcharged in Gold on Colored Panels (Green, Emerald, Violet or Lilac) like Nos. 203-209.

Litho.; Embossed on Palladium Foil
1968   **Unwmk.**
CO21   A38   40s on 2s (G)   1.90   .90
CO22   A38   60s on 2s (E)   2.50   1.60
CO23   A38   1pa on 2s (V)   3.75   3.75
CO24   A38   2pa on 2s (L)   6.75   6.75
    Nos. CO21-CO24 (4)   14.90   13.00
    50th birthday of King Taufa'ahau IV.

Pacific Games Type of Regular Issue

Design: Boxer.

1969, Aug. 13   **Litho.**   *Die Cut*
         Self-adhesive
CO25   A40   70s gray, red & grn   1.25   1.25
CO26   A40   80s gray, red & org   1.50   1.50
    See note after No. 231.

Type of Regular Issue, 1953, Surcharged: "OFFICIAL AIRMAIL / 1969 OIL / SEARCH / 90s" and Oil Derrick Obliterating Old Denomination

1969, Dec. 23   *Die Cut Wmk. 79*
CO27   A34   90s on £1 grn & multi   4.25   4.25
    First scientific search for oil in Tonga.

Type of Regular Issue, 1953, Surcharged: "Royal Visit / MARCH / 1970 / OFFICIAL / AIRMAIL" in Black, Violet Blue or Emerald

1970, Mar. 7   **Engr.**   **Wmk. 79**
CO28   A34   75s on 1sh   4.25   3.00
CO29   A34   1pa on 1sh (VBl)   5.50   4.00
CO30   A34   1.25pa on 1sh (E)   7.00   4.00
    Nos. CO28-CO30 (3)   16.75   12.00
    See note after No. 242.

Regular Issue Srchd. in Black, Red or Emerald

1970, June 4   **Wmk. 79**   *Die Cut*
CO31   A33   50s on 5sh (B)   1.50   1.50
CO32   A33   90s on 5sh (R)   2.50   2.50
CO33   A33   1.50pa on 5sh (E)   4.00   4.00
    Nos. CO31-CO33 (3)   8.00   8.00
    See note after No. 247.

Regular Issue of 1953, Srchd. in Red and Purple or Black

1970, Oct. 17   **Engr.**   *Die Cut*
CO34   A33   30s on 1½p (B & R)   1.90   1.90
CO35   A33   80s on 5sh (P & R)   5.00   5.00
CO36   A33   90s on 5sh (P & R)   6.00   6.00
    Nos. CO34-CO36 (3)   12.90   12.90
    Centenary of the British Red Cross.

Type of Regular Issue, 1953, Surcharged in Black, Purple, Blue or Green

1971, Jan. 31   **Engr.**   *Die Cut*
CO37   A34   20s on 10sh (Bk)   1.25   .85
CO38   A34   30s on 10sh (P)   2.10   1.25
CO39   A34   50s on 10sh (Bl)   3.50   2.10
CO40   A34   2pa on 10sh (G)   13.75   11.75
    Nos. CO37-CO40 (4)   20.60   15.95
    In memory of Queen Salote (1900-1965).

Type of Regular Issue, 1953, Surcharged in Red and Blue, Black or Purple

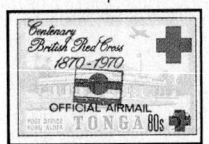

1971   **Engr.**   **Wmk. 79**   *Imperf*
Colors: Green & Yellow
CO41   A33   30s on 5p (R & Bl)   1.40   .80
CO42   A33   80s on 5p (R & Bk)   3.25   2.10
CO43   A33   90s on 5p (R & P)   3.50   2.40
    Nos. CO41-CO43 (3)   8.15   5.30
    See note after No. 272.

Self-adhesive & Imperf. Starting with Nos. CO44-CO46, all airmail official issues are self-adhesive and imperforate, unless otherwise stated.

Soccer Ball — OA1

1971, July   **Litho.**   **Unwmk.**
CO44   OA1   50s multi   1.10   1.10
CO45   OA1   90s multi   1.50   1.50
CO46   OA1   1.50pa multi   2.25   2.25
    Nos. CO44-CO46 (3)   4.85   4.85
    4th South Pacific Games, Papeete, French Polynesia, Sept. 8-19.
    For overprints see Nos. CO75-CO77.

Watch Type of Air Post Issues Litho. and Embossed

1971, July 20
CO47   AP6   14s brown & multi   1.25   1.25
CO48   AP6   21s brn red & multi   1.75   1.75
    Advertisement on peelable paper backing.

Nos. 243-244, 246 Surcharged

Litho.; Gold Embossed
1971, Oct. 30
CO49   A43   60s on 3s multi   1.25   1.25
CO50   A43   80s on 25s multi   1.50   1.50
CO51   A43   1.10pa on 7s multi   1.75   1.75
    Nos. CO49-CO51 (3)   4.50   4.50
    First investiture of Tongan Medal of Honor.

"UNICEF" — OA2

1971, Dec.   **Litho.**
CO52   OA2   70s black & multi   2.00   2.00
CO53   OA2   80s multicolored   2.50   2.50
CO54   OA2   90s multicolored   2.50   2.50
    Nos. CO52-CO54 (3)   7.00   7.00
    25th anniversary of UNICEF.
    For overprint see No. CO70.

Ship Type of Regular Issue

Design: Map of Merchant Marine routes from Tonga and tanker "Aoniu."

1972, Apr. 14
CO55   A49   20s multi   1.90   .90
CO56   A49   50s multi   4.00   2.75
CO57   A49   1.20pa multi   8.75   7.00
    Nos. CO55-CO57 (3)   14.65   10.65

Coin Type of Regular Issue

Design: Coins in center, inscription panel above, date below coins.

Litho.; Embossed on Metallic Foil
1972, July 15
CO58   A50   50s silver & multi   1.75   1.75
CO59   A50   70s silver & multi   2.50   2.50
CO60   A50   1.50pa silver & multi   4.50   4.50
    Nos. CO58-CO60 (3)   8.75   8.75

Watch Type of Air Post Issue

1972, July 20   **Litho.; Embossed**
CO61   AP6   17s multicolored   1.25   1.25
CO62   AP6   38s ocher & multi   2.50   2.50
    Advertisement on peelable paper backing.

Flags and Map of Tonga Islands — OA3

1972, Dec. 9   **Litho.**
CO63   OA3   25s black & multi   .55   .55
CO64   OA3   75s multicolored   1.60   1.60
CO65   OA3   1.50pa multicolored   3.50   3.50
    Nos. CO63-CO65 (3)   5.65   2.15
    Tonga's proclamation of sovereignty over the Minerva Reefs, June 1972.

No. 290 Surcharged in Black, Ultramarine or Green

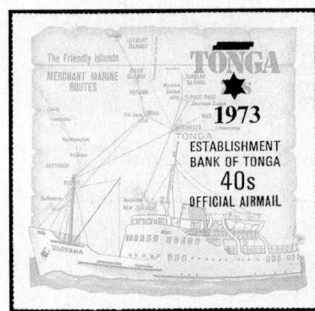

1973, Mar. 30   **Litho.**
CO66   A49   40s on 21s (B)   2.00   2.00
CO67   A49   85s on 21s (U)   4.00   4.00
CO68   A49   1.25pa on 21s (G)   5.00   5.00
    Nos. CO66-CO68 (3)   11.00   11.00
    Establishment of Bank of Tonga.

Nos. CO55, CO53 and 247 Overprinted or Surcharged in Silver:

New value, 4 wavy lines, fleur-de-lis and

No. CO70

Silver surcharge and overprint on dark blue panels

1973, June 29
CO69   A49   30s on 20s   15.00   4.00
CO70   OA2   80s multi   37.50   14.50
CO71   A43   1.40pa on 50s   52.50   35.00
    Nos. CO69-CO71 (3)   105.00   53.50
    25th anniv. of Tongan Boy Scout movement.

Tanker James Cook and Cook Medal — OA4

1973, Oct. 2   **Litho.**
CO72   OA4   25s multi   4.00   1.60
CO73   OA4   80s multi   10.00   5.00
CO74   OA4   1.30pa multi   12.00   8.25
    Nos. CO72-CO74 (3)   26.00   14.85
    Bicentenary of Capt. Cook's arrival.

Nos. CO44-CO46 Overprinted in Dark Blue, Black or Green with Games' Emblems and: "1974 / Commonwealth / Games / Christchurch"

1973, Dec. 19

CO75	OA1	50s multi (DBl)	1.50	1.50
CO76	OA1	90s multi (B)	2.25	2.00
CO77	OA1	1.50pa multi (G)	3.50	3.00
Nos. CO75-CO77 (3)			7.25	6.50

10th British Commonwealth Games, Christchurch, N.Z., Jan. 24-Feb. 2, 1974.

Peace Dove OA5

1974, Mar. 20 Litho.

CO78	OA5	7s multicolored	.50	.25
CO79	OA5	9s multicolored	.65	.35
CO80	OA5	12s multicolored	.65	.35
CO81	OA5	14s multicolored	.90	.50
CO82	OA5	17s multicolored	1.00	.65
CO83	OA5	29s multicolored	1.75	1.10
CO84	OA5	38s multicolored	2.50	1.40
CO85	OA5	50s multicolored	3.00	3.00
CO86	OA5	75s multicolored	4.25	4.25
Nos. CO78-CO86 (9)			15.20	11.85

Printed in rolls of 500. Self-adhesive lilac control number in upper left corner.

"UPU Centenary" — OA6

1974, June 20 Typo.

CO87	OA6	25s red, green & blk	1.00	1.00
CO88	OA6	35s yel, red lil & blk	1.10	1.10
CO89	OA6	70s dp org, bl & blk	2.25	2.25
Nos. CO87-CO89 (3)			4.35	4.35

Centenary of Universal Postal Union.

Lady Baden-Powell — OA7

1974, Sept. 11 Litho.

CO90	OA7	45s emer & multi	4.50	2.75
CO91	OA7	55s emer & multi	6.50	3.75
CO92	OA7	1pa emer & multi	9.25	5.50
Nos. CO90-CO92 (3)			20.25	12.00

Girl Guides of Tonga. *
For overprints see Nos. CO105-CO107.

Handshake and Institute's Emblem — OA8

Institute's Emblem and Banknotes — OA9

1974, Dec. 11

CO93	OA8	30s multicolored	3.25	1.60
CO94	OA8	35s multicolored	3.75	2.10
CO95	OA9	80s red & multi	8.75	4.50
Nos. CO93-CO95 (3)			15.75	8.20

Establishment of Royal Marine Institute.

Arch and Palms — OA10

Designs: 75s, 1.25pa, Dawn over lagoon.

1975, Mar. 11 Litho.

CO96	OA10	50s multi	1.75	1.75
CO97	OA10	75s multi	3.00	3.00
CO98	OA10	1.25pa multi	4.00	4.00
Nos. CO96-CO98 (3)			8.75	8.75

First meeting of South Pacific area Prime Ministers. See note after No. 226.

Track and Games' Emblem — OA11

1975, June 11

CO99	OA11	38s multi	1.00	1.00
CO100	OA11	75s multi	1.90	1.90
CO101	OA11	1.20pa multi	3.00	3.00
Nos. CO99-CO101 (3)			5.90	5.90

5th South Pacific Games, Guam, Aug. 1-10. See note after No. 226.
For surcharge see No. 418.

Four Constitutional Monarchs — OA12

Litho.; Embossed on Gilt Foil
1975, Nov. 4

CO102	OA12	17s multicolored	.80	.65
CO103	OA12	60s multicolored	2.00	1.75
CO104	OA12	90s multicolored	2.60	2.60
Nos. CO102-CO104 (3)			5.40	5.00

No. CO90-CO92 Overprinted in Carmine on Blue, Silver or Gold

1976, Feb. 24 Litho.

CO105	OA7	45s multicolored (B)	3.50	1.40
CO106	OA7	55s multicolored (S)	3.50	1.60
CO107	OA7	1pa multicolored (G)	6.75	6.75
Nos. CO105-CO107 (3)			13.75	9.75

21st Olympic Games, Montreal, Canada, July 17-Aug. 1. See note after No. 226.

Bicentennial Type of 1976

Signers of Declaration of Independence: 20s, William Paca, Francis Lewis, George Read, Edward Rutledge, Thomas Heyward, Jr. 50s, George Walton, Matthew Thornton, Robert Morris, William Williams, James Smith. 1.15pa, Benjamin Rush, Samuel Adams, Samuel Chase, George Wythe, George Clymer.

1976, May 26

CO108	A66	20s buff & multi	1.25	1.00
CO109	A66	50s buff & multi	4.00	2.50
CO110	A66	1.15pa buff & multi	8.50	5.25
Nos. CO108-CO110 (3)			13.75	8.75

See note after No. 381.

Inside View of Lifuka Chapel — OA13

1976, Aug. 25 Litho.

CO111	OA13	65s multicolored	2.75	2.75
CO112	OA13	85s multicolored	3.00	3.00
CO113	OA13	1.15pa multicolored	4.00	4.00
Nos. CO111-CO113 (3)			9.75	9.75

See note after No. 386.
For surcharge see No. CO181.

OA14

1976, Nov. 1

CO114	OA14	30s silver & multi	.85	.85
CO115	OA14	60s silver & multi	2.00	2.00
CO116	OA14	1.25pa silver & multi	4.50	4.50
Nos. CO114-CO116 (3)			7.35	7.35

See note after No. 391.

Flags of Great Britain and Tonga — OA15

1977, Feb. 7 Litho.

CO117	OA15	35s multi	5.00	3.25
CO118	OA15	45s multi	1.00	.50
CO119	OA15	1.10pa multi	2.00	1.25
Nos. CO117-CO119 (3)			8.00	5.00

See note after No. 396.
For surcharge see No. C238.

Coin Type of Air Post Stamps 1977

Design: Coronation coin, inscriptions in round upper panel.

1977, July 4

CO120	AP21	20s multicolored	.75	.75
CO121	AP21	40s multicolored	1.50	1.50
CO122	AP21	80s multicolored	3.00	3.00
Nos. CO120-CO122 (3)			5.25	5.25

See note after No. 401.

Capt. Cook Type of Air Post Stamps 1977

Design: Inscription and flying dove.

1977, Sept. 27

CO123	AP22	20s gold & multi	1.40	1.40
CO124	AP22	55s on 20s multi	10.00	10.00
CO125	AP22	85s on 20s multi	21.00	21.00
Nos. CO123-CO125 (3)			32.40	32.40

Printed on peelable paper backing showing dark brown replica of entry in Capt. Cook's diary.

Whale Type of Air Post Stamps 1977

Design: Blue whale.

1977, Dec. 16

CO126	AP23	45s multicolored	7.75	3.50
CO127	AP23	65s multicolored	11.00	5.00
CO128	AP23	85s multicolored	13.00	6.00
Nos. CO126-CO128 (3)			31.75	14.50

Whale protection.

Games' Emblem and Athletes OA16

1978, May 5 Litho.

CO129	OA16	30s red & multi	.70	.70
CO130	OA16	60s red & multi	1.40	1.40
CO131	OA16	1pa red & multi	2.50	2.50
Nos. CO129-CO131 (3)			4.60	4.60

See note after No. 423.

King Type of 1978

Head of King Taufa'ahau IV on medal.

1978, July 4

CO132	A74	26s multicolored	.65	.65
CO133	A74	85s multicolored	2.00	2.00
CO134	A74	90s multicolored	2.50	2.50
Nos. CO132-CO134 (3)			5.15	5.15

See note after No. 226.

Wildlife Type of 1978

1978, Dec. 15   Litho. & Typo.

CO150	A77	40s Whale	8.25	4.00
CO151	A77	50s Bat	8.25	4.00
CO152	A77	1.10pa Turtle	11.00	9.00
Nos. CO150-CO152 (3)			27.50	17.00

Wildlife conservation. See note after No. 226.

Types of 1979

Designs: 38s, Red Cross and star. 74s, like No. 451. 80s, like No. 450.

1979, Feb. 16   Litho.

CO153	A78	38s multicolored	1.10	.70
CO154	A80	74s multicolored	2.00	1.40
CO155	A79	80s multicolored	2.50	1.60
Nos. CO153-CO155 (3)			5.60	3.70

Decade of Progress. Paper backing shows map of Tonga.

Hands Peeling off No. CO118 — OA17

1979, June 1

CO156	OA17	45s multicolored	1.25	1.25
CO157	OA17	65s multicolored	1.75	1.75
CO158	OA17	80s multicolored	2.25	2.25
Nos. CO156-CO158 (3)			5.25	5.25

See note after No. 458.
For surcharges see Nos. CO176-CO178.

Parrot — OA18

1979, Aug. 1

CO159	OA18	5s multicolored	.25	.25
CO160	OA18	11s multicolored	.25	.25
CO161	OA18	14s multicolored	.35	.35
CO162	OA18	15s multicolored	.35	.35
CO163	OA18	17s multicolored	.45	.45
CO164	OA18	18s multicolored	.50	.50
CO165	OA18	22s multicolored	.55	.55
CO166	OA18	31s multicolored	.75	.75
CO167	OA18	39s multicolored	1.00	1.00
CO168	OA18	75s multicolored	1.90	1.90
CO169	OA18	1pa multicolored	2.40	2.40
Nos. CO159-CO169 (11)			8.75	8.75

Nos. CO159-CO169 issued in coils. See note after No. 226.
The 5s exists with denomination in magenta and the leaves behind the bird missing. This seems to be a special printing that was not available for postal purposes.

View Type of 1979

Design: Niuatoputapu and Tafahi Islands. See note after No. 463.

1979, Nov. 23   Litho.

CO170	A82	35s multicolored	.85	.85
CO171	A82	45s multicolored	1.10	1.10
CO172	A82	1pa multicolored	2.25	2.25
Nos. CO170-CO172 (3)			4.20	4.20

Friendship Treaty Type of 1980

Design: Church. See note after No. 468.

1980, Jan. 9   Litho.

CO173	A83	40s multicolored	1.10	1.10
CO174	A83	55s multicolored	1.40	1.40
CO175	A83	1.25pa multicolored	3.25	3.25
Nos. CO173-CO175 (3)			5.75	5.75

Nos. CO156-CO158 Surcharged and Overprinted in Black on Silver: "1980 OLYMPIC GAMES," Moscow '80 and Bear Emblems

1980, Apr. 30   Litho.

CO176	OA17	26s on 45s	1.00	1.00
CO177	OA17	40s on 65s	1.60	1.60
CO178	OA17	1.10pa on 80s	4.00	4.00
Nos. CO176-CO178 (3)			6.60	6.60

22nd Summer Olympic Games, Moscow, July 19-Aug. 3.

Tents and Rotary Emblem — OA19

1980, Sept. 30   Litho.

CO179	OA19	25s multicolored	1.75	1.75
CO180	OA19	2pa multicolored	6.75	6.75

Boy Scout Jamboree; Rotary Intl., 75th anniv. Peelable backing shows map of Tonga. For surcharges see Nos. 502-503.

No. CO111 Surcharged

1980, Dec. 3   Litho.

CO181	OA13	2pa on 65s multi	5.50	5.50

OFFICIAL STAMPS

Types of Postage Issue of 1892 Overprinted in Carmine

Perf. 12x11½

1893, Feb. 13   Wmk. 62

O1	A4	1p ultra	11.50	55.00
a.	Half used as ½p on cover			
O2	A5	2p ultra	30.00	62.50
O3	A4	4p ultra	55.00	110.00
O4	A5	8p ultra	100.00	200.00
O5	A5	1sh ultra	110.00	210.00
Nos. O1-O5 (5)			306.50	637.50

Values are for stamps of good color. Faded and discolored stamps sell for much less.
The overprinted initials stand for "Gaue Faka Buleaga" (On Government Service).

Nos. O1-O5 with Additional Surcharge Handstamped in Black

1893

O6	A4	½p on 1p ultra	20.00	57.50
O7	A5	2½p on 2p ultra	27.50	50.00
O8	A4	5p on 4p ultra	27.50	50.00
O9	A5	7½p on 8p ultra	27.50	92.50
O10	A5	10p on 1sh ultra	32.50	95.00
Nos. O6-O10 (5)			135.00	345.00

Catalogue values for unused stamps in this section, from this point to the end of the section, are for Never Hinged items.

Redrawn Banana and Coconut Types of Regular Issue, 1970, Inscribed "Official Post"

1970, June 9   Typo.   Die Cut

Self-adhesive

O11	A39	1s yel, blk & dp car	.55	.55
O12	A39	2s yel, blk & blue	.70	.70
O13	A39	3s yel, blk & brn	.70	.70
O14	A39	4s yel, blk & emer	.70	.70
O15	A39	5s yel, blk & org	.80	.80

Litho.; Embossed on Gilt Foil

O16	A44	6s brown & multi	.95	.95
O17	A44	7s brown & multi	1.00	1.00
O18	A44	8s brown & multi	1.10	1.10
O19	A44	9s brown & multi	1.50	1.50
O20	A44	10s brown & multi	1.75	1.75
Nos. O11-O20 (10)			9.75	9.75

Nos. O13, O17-O18 and O20 have self-adhesive control numbers in lower left corner of paper backing.

Types of Regular Issue 1970-72

1972, Sept. 30   Typo.

Self-adhesive

O21	A51	1s yel, red & brn	.25	.25
O22	A51	2s yel, grn & brn	.30	.25
O23	A51	3s yel, emer & brn	.35	.25
O24	A51	4s yel, blk & brn	.35	.25
O25	A51	5s yellow & brn	.35	.25
O26	A44	6s brown & green	.45	.25
O27	A44	7s brown & green	.50	.30
O28	A44	8s brown & green	.50	.30
O29	A44	9s brown & green	.50	.30
O30	A44	10s brown & green	.60	.35
O31	A52	15s green & ultra	1.00	.50
O32	A52	20s green & ver	.55	.70
O33	A52	25s green & dk brn	1.40	.90
O34	A52	40s green & org	2.50	1.75
O35	A52	50s green & vio bl	3.00	2.25
Nos. O21-O35 (15)			13.30	8.70

Paper backing is brown on Nos. O26-O35. Nos. O30-O35 have self-adhesive control number in lower left corner, Nos. O21-O29 lower right corner.

Types of Regular Issue 1978

Designs: 1s-5s, Bananas (similar to type A75). 6s-10s, Coconuts. 15s-1pa, Pineapples.

1978, Sept. 29   Typo.

O36	A75	1s yellow & lilac	.30	.30
O37	A75	2s yellow & brown	.30	.30
O38	A75	3s multicolored	.40	.40
O39	A75	4s multicolored	.40	.40
O40	A75	5s multicolored	.40	.40
O41	A76	6s multicolored	.60	.60
O42	A76	7s multicolored	.60	.60
O43	A76	8s multicolored	.60	.60
O44	A76	9s multicolored	.60	.60
O45	A76	10s multicolored	.60	.60
O46	A76	15s multicolored	1.50	1.50
O47	A76	20s multicolored	1.60	1.60
O48	A76	30s multicolored	1.75	1.75
O49	A76	50s multicolored	2.25	2.25
O50	A76	1pa multicolored	3.25	3.25
Nos. O36-O50 (15)			15.15	15.15

Nos. O36-O50 issued in coils; self-adhesive control numbers on paper backing except on 1s. See note after No. 226.

Type of 1984 Overprinted "OFFICIAL"

1984-85   Litho.   Die Cut

O52	A103	1s multicolored	.50	.50
O53	A103	2s multicolored	.50	.50
O54	A103	3s multicolored	.50	.50
O55	A103	4s multicolored	.50	.50
O56	A103	6s multicolored	.50	.50
O57	A103	9s multicolored	.75	.75
a.	Perf. 14½ ('85)			
O58	A103	10s multicolored	.75	.75
O59	A103	13s multicolored	1.25	1.25
O60	A103	15s multicolored	1.25	1.25
O61	A103	20s multicolored	1.50	1.50
O62	A103	29s multicolored	1.75	1.75
O63	A103	32s multicolored	1.75	1.75
O64	A103	47s multicolored	2.00	2.00
O65	A103	1pa multicolored	4.00	4.00
O66	A103	2pa multicolored	7.00	7.00
O67	A103	5pa multicolored ('85)	12.00	12.00
Nos. O52-O67 (16)			36.50	36.50

Nos. 532-534 Ovptd. "OFFICIAL"

1983, Feb. 22   Litho.   Die Cut

O68	A96a	29s multicolored	4.75	4.75
O69	A96a	32s multicolored	4.75	4.75
O70	A96a	47s multicolored	10.00	10.00
Nos. O68-O70 (3)			19.50	19.50

O68-O70 handstamped.

Nos. 564-565, 567-568, 570, 572 and 577 Surcharged "OFFICIAL"

1986, Apr. 16   Litho.   Die Cut

Self-adhesive

O71	A103	4s on 2s, #564	1.00	1.00
O72	A103	4s on 13s, #570	1.00	1.00
O73	A103	42s on 3s, #565	3.25	3.25
O74	A103	42s on 9s, #568	3.25	3.25
O75	A103	57s on 4s, #567	3.50	3.50
O76	A103	57s on 20s, #572	3.50	3.50
O77	A103	2.50pa on 2pa, #577	12.00	12.00
Nos. O71-O77 (7)			27.50	27.50

Marine Type Inscribed "POSTAGE & REVENUE" and "OFFICIAL"

1995-96   Litho.   Perf. 14

O78	A155a	10s multicolored	.60	.60
O79	A155a	20s multicolored	.90	.40
O80	A155a	45s multicolored	1.10	.70
O81	A155a	60s multicolored	1.40	.95
O82	A155a	80s multicolored	1.75	1.25
O83	A155a	1pa multicolored	2.25	1.75
O84	A155a	2pa multicolored	4.00	4.00
O85	A155a	3pa multicolored	5.00	5.00
O86	A155a	5pa multicolored	9.75	9.75
O87	A155a	10pa multicolored	14.00	14.00
Nos. O78-O87 (10)			40.75	38.40

Issued: 10s-80s, 9/25/95; 1pa-10pa, 5/31/96.

NIUAFO'OU

Tin Can Island

Catalogue values for all unused stamps in this country are for Never Hinged items.

Nos. 1-63 are self-adhesive stamps on peelable inscribed backing paper and imperforate.

Niuafo'ou Airport Type of Tonga

1983, May 11   Litho.   Die Cut

1	A97	29s multicolored	1.75	1.75
2	A97	1pa multicolored	4.75	4.75

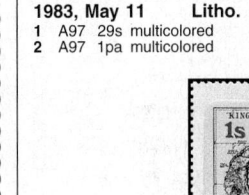

Map of Niuafo'ou — A1

1983, May 11

3	A1	1s buff, blk & red	.45	.45
4	A1	2s buff, blk & brt green	.45	.45
5	A1	3s buff, blk & brt blue	.45	.45
6	A1	4s buff, blk & brn org	.45	.45
7	A1	5s buff, blk & deep rose lil	.45	.45
8	A1	6s buff, blk & grnsh blue	.45	.45
9	A1	9s buff, blk & lt ol grn	.45	.45
10	A1	10s buff, blk & brt bl	.45	.45
11	A1	13s buff, blk & brt grn	.50	.50
12	A1	15s buff, blk & brn org	.60	.60
13	A1	20s buff, blk & grnsh blue	.75	.75
14	A1	29s buff, blk & deep rose lil	1.25	1.25
15	A1	32s buff, blk & lt ol grn	1.40	1.40
16	A1	47s buff, blk & red	1.90	1.90
Nos. 3-16 (14)			10.00	10.00

See Nos. 19-22.

Tonga No. 520 Surcharged or Ovptd. in Purple or Gold "NIUAFO'OU / Kingdom of Tonga"

1983, May 11

17	A93	1pa on 2pa multi (P)	3.25	3.25
18	A93	2pa multicolored (G)	6.75	6.75

Nos. 17-18 each exist se-tenant with label.

Map Type of 1983
Value Typo. in Violet Blue

1983, May 30
19	A1	3s buff & black	.30	.30
20	A1	5s buff & black	.30	.30
21	A1	32s buff & black	1.50	1.50
22	A1	2pa buff & black	8.00	8.00
		Nos. 19-22 (4)	10.10	10.10

The denomination on Nos. 19-22 added like a surcharge and is larger than on Nos. 5-7, 15, covering part of the design.
Nos. 19-22 each exist se-tenant with label.

Eruption of Niuafo'ou, Sept. 9, 1946
A2

1983, Sept. 29
23	A2	5s shown	.50	.35
24	A2	29s Lava flow	1.90	1.25
25	A2	32s Moving to high ground	2.10	1.25
26	A2	1.50pa Evacuation to Eua	6.50	6.50
		Nos. 23-26 (4)	11.00	9.35

Birds — A3

1983, Nov. 15
27	A3	1s Purple swamphen	1.00	1.00
28	A3	2s White-collared king-fisher	1.00	1.00
29	A3	3s Red-headed par-rotfinch	1.00	1.00
30	A3	5s Banded rail	1.25	1.25
31	A3	6s Niuafo'ou megapode	1.60	1.60
32	A3	9s Giant forest honey-eater	2.50	2.50
33	A3	10s Purple swamphen, drinking	2.50	2.50
34	A3	13s Banded rail, diff.	2.75	2.75
35	A3	15s Niuafo'ou megapode, diff.	2.75	2.75

Size: 25x39mm
36	A3	20s like #34	3.25	3.25
37	A3	29s Red-headed par-rotfinch, diff.	3.50	3.50
38	A3	32s White-collared king-fisher, diff.	3.50	3.50
39	A3	47s like #35	4.25	4.25

Size: 32x42mm
40	A3	1pa like #33	8.00	9.75
41	A3	2pa like #35	11.00	14.00
		Nos. 27-41 (15)	49.85	54.60

Nos. 34-36, 39 and 41 horiz.
For surcharges see Nos. 66-73.

Wildlife A4

1984, Mar. 7
42	A4	29s Green turtle	.90	.90
43	A4	32s Flying fox, vert.	.90	.90
44	A4	47s Humpback whale	3.25	2.10
45	A4	1.50pa Niuafo'ou megapode, vert.	6.00	8.25
		Nos. 42-45 (4)	11.05	12.15

Map A5

1984, Aug. 20
46	A5	47s Intl. Date Line, Cent.	1.10	1.10
47	A5	2pa shown	3.75	3.75

AUSIPEX '84 — A6

A7

1984, Sept. 17
48	A6	32s Australia No. 15	.90	.90
49	A6	1.50pa No. 10	4.50	4.50

Souvenir Sheet
50		Sheet of 2	5.00	5.00

No. 50 contains two imperf. stamps similar to Nos. 48-49, but with denomination replacing logo. No. 50 without denominations was not valid for postage.

1985, Feb. 20

Jacob Le Maire, 400th Birth Anniv.: 13s, Dutch band entertaining natives. 32s, Natives preparing kava. 47s, Native outrigger canoes. 1.50pa, Le Maire's ship at anchor.

51	A7	13s multicolored	.50	.50
52	A7	32s multicolored	1.10	1.10
53	A7	47s multicolored	1.50	1.50
54	A7	1.50pa multicolor	4.50	5.50
		Nos. 51-54 (4)	7.60	8.60

Souvenir Sheet
55	A7	1.50pa multicolored	4.00	4.00

Mail Ships A8

1985, May 22   *Die Cut*
56	A8	9s Ysabel, 1902	.60	.60
a.		Perf. 14	.90	.90
57	A8	13s Tofua I, 1908	1.25	1.25
a.		Perf. 14	1.90	1.90
58	A8	47s Mariposa, 1934	1.90	1.90
a.		Perf. 14	2.75	2.75
59	A8	1.50pa Matua, 1936	4.25	6.00
a.		Perf. 14	6.50	9.00
		Nos. 56-59 (4)	8.00	9.75
		Nos. 56a-59a (4)	12.05	14.55

Rocket Mail — A9

Designs: 32s, Preparing to fire rocket. 42s, Rocket airborne. 57s, Captain watching rocket's progress. 1.50pa, Islanders reading mail.

1985, Nov. 5
60	A9	32s multicolored	1.50	.90
61	A9	42s multicolored	2.00	1.10
62	A9	57s multicolored	2.75	1.60
63	A9	1.50pa multicolored	5.75	6.50
		Nos. 60-63 (4)	12.00	10.10

Self-adhesive stamps discontinued.

Halley's Comet — A10

Nos. 64, 65: a, Drawing of Comet in 684. b, Comet shown in Bayeux Tapestry, 1066. c, Edmond Halley. d, Comet, 1910. e, Infrared photography, 1986.

1986, Mar. 26   *Perf. 14*
64	A10	42s Strip of #a.-e.	36.00	32.50
65	A10	57s Strip of #a.-e.	36.00	32.50

Nos. 32-39 Surcharged in Blue

1986, Apr. 16   *Die Cut*
Self-Adhesive
66	A3	4s on 9s #32	1.50	2.75
67	A3	4s on 10s #33	1.50	2.75
68	A3	42s on 13s #34	3.75	2.75
69	A3	42s on 15s #35	3.75	2.75
70	A3	57s on 29s #37	4.75	3.25
71	A3	57s on 32s #38	4.75	3.25
72	A3	2.50pa on 20s #36	13.00	14.00
73	A3	2.50pa on 47s #39	13.00	14.00
		Nos. 66-73 (8)	46.00	45.50

Placement of surcharge varies.

AMERIPEX '86 Type of Tonga
1986, May 22   *Perf. 14*
74	A117	57s Surveying	3.00	3.00
75	A117	1.50pa Agriculture	5.50	5.50
a.		Souv. sheet of 2, #74-75, imperf.	10.00	10.00

Peace Corps in Tonga, 25th anniv.

First Tongan Postage Stamps, Cent. A11

1986, Aug. 27
76	A11	42s Swimmers with mail	1.60	1.60
77	A11	57s Loading tin can mail into canoe	2.10	2.10
78	A11	1pa Rocket mail	3.75	3.75
79	A11	2.50pa Outrigger canoe	6.50	6.50
		Nos. 76-79 (4)	13.95	13.95

Souvenir Sheet
80	A11	2.50pa Outrigger canoe, diff.	14.00	14.00

Red Cross — A12

1987, Mar. 11   *Perf. 14x14½*
81	A12	15s Balanced diet	1.25	1.25
82	A12	42s Post-natal care	3.25	3.25
83	A12	1pa Insects spread disease	4.75	4.75
84	A12	2.50pa Fight against drugs, alcohol, smoking	7.50	7.50
		Nos. 81-84 (4)	16.75	16.75

Sharks A13

1987, Apr. 29   *Perf. 14*
85	A13	29s Hammerhead	3.00	2.75
86	A13	32s Tiger	3.00	2.75
87	A13	47s Gray nurse	3.50	3.00
88	A13	1pa Great white	6.00	8.25
		Nos. 85-88 (4)	15.50	16.75

Souvenir Sheet
89	A13	2pa Shark attack	18.00	18.00

Aviators and Aircraft A14

Designs: 42s, Capt. E. C. Musick and Sikorsky S-42. 57s, Capt. J.W. Burgess and Shorts S-30. 1.50pa, Sir Charles Kingsford Smith and Fokker F.VIIb-3m. 2pa, Amelia Earhart and Lockheed Electra 10A.

1987, Sept. 2
90	A14	42s multicolored	2.50	1.75
91	A14	57s multicolored	3.00	2.00
92	A14	1.50pa multicolored	4.50	4.50
93	A14	2pa multicolored	5.25	5.25
		Nos. 90-93 (4)	15.25	13.50

First Niuafo'ou Postage Stamps, 5th Anniv. A15

Designs: 42s, 57s, Niuafo'ou megapode, No. 15. 1pa, 2pa, Concorde, No. 1.

1988, May 18
94	A15	42s multicolored	1.50	1.00
95	A15	57s multicolored	1.50	1.10
96	A15	1pa multicolored	5.00	3.75
97	A15	2pa multicolored	6.00	4.75
		Nos. 94-97 (4)	14.00	10.60

#96-97, Niuafo'ou Airport Inauguration, 5th anniv.

Settlement of Australia, Bicent. Type of Tonga
Miniature Sheet

Designs: a, Arrival of First Fleet, Sydney Cove, Jan. 1788. b, Aborigines. c, Early settlement. d, Soldier on guard. e, Herd of sheep. f, Horseman. g, Locomotive, kangaroos. h, Train, kangaroos. i, Flying doctor service. j, Cricket players. k, Stadium, batsman guarding wicket. l, Sydney Harbor Bridge, Opera House.

1988, July 11   *Perf. 13½*
98	A128	42s Sheet of 12, #98a-98 l	50.00	50.00

Polynesian Islands — A16

Birds and landmarks: 42s, Audubon's shearwater, blowholes at Houma, Tonga. 57s, Kiwi, Akaroa Harbor, New Zealand. 90s, Red-tailed tropicbird, Rainmaker Mountain, Samoa. 2.50pa, Laysan albatross, Kapoho Volcano, Hawaii.

1988, Aug. 18   *Perf. 14*
99	A16	42s multicolored	1.50	1.00
100	A16	57s multicolored	2.50	1.60
101	A16	90s multicolored	2.75	2.75
102	A16	2.50pa multicolored	5.25	5.25
		Nos. 99-102 (4)	12.00	10.60

Miniature Sheet

Mutiny on the Bounty, Bicent. — A17

Designs: a, Sextant. b, William Bligh. c, Royal Navy lieutenant. d, Midshipman. e, Contemporary newspaper, Tahitian girl. f, Breadfruit. g, *Mutiny on the Bounty* excerpt, pistol grip. h, Pistol barrel, illustration of Bounty castaways. i, Tahitian girl, newsprint. j, Bligh's and Fletcher Christian's signatures. k, Christian, Pitcairn Island. l, Tombstone of John Adams.

1989, Apr. 28   **Perf. 13½**
103   A17   42s Sheet of 12, #a.-l.   30.00   30.00

Marine Conservation — A18

1989, June 2   **Perf. 14**
104	A18	32s Hatchet fish	1.40	1.40
105	A18	42s Snipe eel	1.60	1.60
106	A18	57s Viper fish	2.00	2.00
107	A18	1.50pa Angler fish	5.00	5.00
		Nos. 104-107 (4)	10.00	10.00

Evolution of the Earth — A19

Designs: 1s, Formation of the crust. 2s, Cross-section of crust. 5s, Volcanism. 10s, Surface cools. 13s, Gem stones. 15s, Oceans form. 20s, Mountains develop. 32s, River valley. 42s, Silurian Era plant life. 45s, Early marine life. 50s, Trilobites, Cambrian Era marine life. 57s, Carboniferous Era forest, coal seams. 60s, Dinosaurs feeding. 80s, Dinosaurs fighting. 1pa, Carboniferous Era insect, amphibians. 1.50pa, Stegosaurus, Jurassic Era. 2pa, Birds and mammals, Jurassic Era. 5pa, Hominid family, Pleistocene Era. 10pa, Mammoth, saber tooth tiger.

1989-93   **Perf. 14½**
108	A19	1s multicolored	.70	.70
109	A19	2s multicolored	.70	.70
110	A19	5s multicolored	.90	.90
111	A19	10s multicolored	.90	.90
111A	A19	13s multicolored	1.10	1.10
112	A19	15s multicolored	.90	.90
113	A19	20s multicolored	.90	.90
114	A19	32s multicolored	1.10	1.10
115	A19	42s multicolored	1.50	1.50
115A	A19	45s multicolored	1.50	1.50
116	A19	50s multicolored	1.60	1.60
117	A19	57s multicolored	1.60	1.60
117A	A19	60s multicolored	1.75	1.75
117B	A19	80s multicolored	2.10	2.10

Size: 26x40mm
Perf. 14
118	A19	1pa multicolored	3.00	3.00
119	A19	1.50pa multicolored	4.75	4.75
120	A19	2pa multicolored	4.75	4.75
121	A19	5pa multicolored	9.25	9.25

Perf. 14
121A	A19	10pa multicolored	16.00	16.00
		Nos. 108-121A (19)	55.00	55.00

Issued: 1s-10s, 15s-42s, 50s-57s, 6/6/89; 13s, 45s, 60s, 80s, 5/3/93; 10pa, 9/14/93; others, 8/1/89.

A20

1989, Nov. 17   **Perf. 14**
122   A20   57s multicolored   1.90   1.90

Miniature Sheet

Nos. 108-121 with UPU emblem: Nos. 123a-123e, #108-112, Nos. 123f-123j, #113-117, Nos. 123k-123n, #118-121.
123		Sheet of 15, #a.-n.,		
		122	27.50	27.50
a.-e.	A19 32s any single, perf. 14½		1.00	1.00
f.-j.	A19 42s any single, perf. 14½		1.50	1.50
k.-n.	A19 57s any single, perf. 14		2.00	2.00

Miniature Sheet

Lake Vai Lahi, Niuafo'ou A21

a, d, Left part of lake. b, e, Small islands in center of lake. c, f, Small islet in right side of lake.

1990, Apr. 4   **Perf. 14**
124		Sheet of 6	11.00	11.00
a.-c.	A21 42s any single		1.00	1.00
d.-f.	A21 1pa any single		2.25	2.25

Nos. 124a-124c and 124d-124f printed in continuous designs.

Penny Black, 150th Anniv. A22

Tin Can Mail and: 42s, Penny Black. 57s, US #2. 75s, Western Australia #1. 2.50pa, Cape of Good Hope #178.

1990, May 1
125	A22	42s multicolored	1.75	1.40
126	A22	57s multicolored	1.90	1.60
127	A22	75s multicolored	2.10	2.10
128	A22	2.50pa multicolored	7.25	7.00
		Nos. 125-128 (4)	13.00	12.10

Polynesian Whaling — A23

Designs: 15s, Whale surfacing. 42s, Whale diving beneath outrigger canoe. 57s, Tail flukes. 1pa, 2pa, Old man, two whales.

1990   **Perf. 11½**
129	A23	15s multicolored	2.50	2.50
130	A23	42s multicolored	3.50	3.50
131	A23	57s multicolored	3.75	3.75
132	A23	2pa multicolored	9.75	9.75
		Nos. 129-132 (4)	19.50	19.50

Souvenir Sheet
Perf. 14x14½
133   A23   1pa multicolored   20.00   20.00

Issue dates: #133, Sept. 4, others, June 6.
The entire souvenir sheet, No. 133, shows a modified No. 132. The 37½x30½mm stamp shows the two whales.
For surcharges see Nos. 139, 174-178.

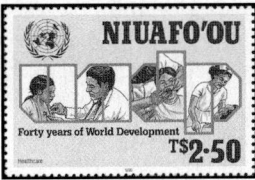

UN Development Program, 40th Anniv. — A24

Designs: No. 134a, Agriculture and fisheries. No. 134b, Education. No. 135a, Health care. No. 135b, Communications.

1990, Oct. 25   **Perf. 14**
134	A24	57s Pair, #a.-b.	3.00	3.00
135	A24	2.50pa Pair, #a.-b.	12.00	12.00

Charting of Niuafo'ou, Bicent. — A24a

Designs: No. 136a, 32s, The Bounty. b, 42s, Chart showing location of Niuafo'ou and Tonga. c, 57s, The Pandora.
No. 137a, 2pa, Capt. Edwards of the Pandora. b, 3pa, Capt. Bligh of the Bounty.

1991, July 25   **Litho.**   **Perf. 14½**
136   A24a   57s Strip of 3, #a.-c.   6.00   6.00

Souvenir Sheet
137   A24a   Sheet of 2, #a.-b.   18.00   18.00

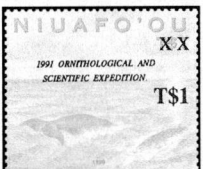

No. 133 Surcharged in Dark Blue Violet

1991, July 31   **Litho.**   **Perf. 14x14½**
139   A23   1pa on 1pa #133   13.00   13.00
"1991 Ornithological and Scientic Expedition" overprint appears on souvenir sheet at top center.

Ceresium Unicolor — A25

1991, Sept. 11   **Perf. 14½x14**
140	A25	42s Larva stage	1.25	1.25
141	A25	57s Mature beetle	1.50	1.50
142	A25	1.50pa Larva stage, diff.	3.75	3.75
143	A25	2.50pa Mature beetle on tree limb	6.50	6.50
		Nos. 140-143 (4)	13.00	13.00

For surcharges, see Tonga Nos. 1127, 1129.

Christmas A26

Legend of the origin of the coconut tree: 15s, No. 146a, Heina bathing in lake being watched by eel. 42s, No. 146b, Heina weeping over plant growing from eel's grave. No. 146c, 1.50pa, Heina's boy climbing coconut tree. No. 146d, 3pa, "Eel's face" on coconut.

1991, Nov. 12   **Litho.**   **Perf. 14½**
144	A26	15s multicolored	.75	.75
145	A26	42s multicolored	2.00	2.00
146	A26	Sheet of 4, #a.-d.	17.50	17.50
		Nos. 144-146 (3)	20.25	20.25

For surcharge, see Tonga No. 1128.

Nos. 144-145 inscribed "Christmas Greetings 1991." No. 146 contains Nos. 144-145, 146a-146d inscribed "A Love Story."

Miniature Sheet

Discovery of America, 500th Anniv. — A27

Designs: a, Columbus. b, Queen Isabella, King Ferdinand. c, Columbus being blessed by Abbot of Palos. d, Men in boat, 15th century compass. e, Wooden traverse, wind rose, Nina. f, Bow of Santa Maria. g, Stern of Santa Maria. h, Pinta. i, Two men raising cross. j, Explorers, natives. k, Columbus kneeling before King and Queen. l, Columbus' second coat of arms.

1992, Apr. 28   **Litho.**   **Perf. 13½**
147   A27   57s Sheet of 12, #a.-l.   35.00   35.00

Miniature Sheet

World War II in Pacific, 50th Anniv. A28

Newspaper headline and: a, Battleship ablaze at Pearl Harbor. b, Destroyed aircraft. c, Japanese A6M Zero fighter. d, Declaration of war, Pres. Franklin D. Roosevelt. e, Japanese T95 tank, Gen. MacArthur, Japanese naval ensign. f, Douglas SBD Dauntless dive bomber, Admiral Nimitz. g, Bren gun, Gen. Sir Thomas Blamey. h, Australian mortar crew, Kokoda Trail. i, US battleship, Maj. Gen. Julian C. Smith. j, Aircraft carrier USS Enterprise. k, American soldier, flag, Maj. Gen. Curtis Lemay. l, B-29 bomber, surrender ceremony on USS Missouri in Tokyo bay.

1992, May 12   **Litho.**   **Perf. 14**
148   A28   42s Sheet of 12, #a.-l.   27.50   27.50

King Taufa'ahau IV, 25th Anniv. of Coronation A29

45s, 2pa, King, Queen Halaevalu during coronation. No. 150a, King, Tongan national anthem. b, Extract from investiture ceremony. c, Tongan national anthem, singers.

1992, July 4   **Perf. 13½x13**
149   A29   45s multicolored   1.10   1.10

Size: 51x38mm
Perf. 12½x12
150	A29	80s Strip of 3, #a.-c.	6.00	6.00
151	A29	2pa multicolored	5.00	5.00
		Nos. 149-151 (3)	12.10	12.10

Megapodius Pritchardii — A30

1992, Sept. 15   Litho.   Perf. 14
152 A30 45s Female & male   2.25   2.25
153 A30 60s Female with egg   2.75   2.75
154 A30 80s Chick   4.00   4.00
155 A30 1.50pa Head of male   7.00   7.00
   Nos. 152-155 (4)   16.00 16.00
           World Wildlife Fund.

First
Niuafo'ou
Postage
Stamps,
10th Anniv.
A31

1993, May 3   Litho.   Perf. 14x14½
156 A31 60s Nos. 4, 117A   1.90   1.90
157 A31 80s Nos. 7, 117B   2.40   2.40

Aviation in
Niuafo'ou,
10th
Anniv. — A32

Airplanes of: 1pa, South Pacific Island Airways. 2.50pa, Friendly Islands Airways.

1993, May 3
158 A32   1pa multicolored   3.50   3.50
159 A32 2.50pa multicolored   7.50   7.50

King's 75th Birthday Type of Tonga

King and: 45s, 2pa, Patrol boat Pangai. No. 161a, Sporting events. b, Aircraft and communications. c, Musical instruments.

1993, July 1   Perf. 13x13½
160 A167 45s multicolored   1.00   1.00
                  Perf. 12x12½
                  Size: 37x48mm
161 A167 80s Strip of 3, #a.-
            c.   5.50   5.50
162 A167 2pa multicolored   4.25   4.25
   Nos. 160-162 (3)   10.75 10.75

Wildlife — A33

Designs: a, Two parrots. b, Bird with fish. c, Butterfly, beetle. d, Birds, dragonfly, butterfly. e, Bird in flight, two on ground.

1993, Aug. 10   Litho.   Perf. 14
163 A33 60s Strip of 5, #a.-e.   8.00   8.00

   No. 163 is a continuous design.

Winners of Children's Painting
Competition — A34

Designs: Nos. 164a, 165a, Ofato Beetle Grubs of Niuafo'ou, by Peni Finau. Nos. 164b, 165b, Crater Lake Megapode, Volcano, by Paea Puletau.

1993, Dec. 1   Litho.   Perf. 14
164 A34 10s Pair, #a.-b.   1.00   1.00
165 A34 1pa Pair, #a.-b.   7.50   7.50

Beetles
A35

1994, Mar. 15   Litho.   Perf. 14
168 A35   60s Scarabaeidea   1.75   1.75
169 A35   80s Coccinellidea   2.10   2.10
170 A35 1.50pa Cerambycidea   3.75   3.75
171 A35 2.50pa Pentatomidae   6.75   6.75
   Nos. 168-171 (4)   14.35 14.35

A36   A37

Sailing Ships: a, Stern of HMS Bounty. b, Bow of HMS Bounty. c, HMS Pandora. d, Whaling ship. e, Trading schooner.

1994, June 21   Litho.   Perf. 14
172 A36 80s Strip of 5, #a.-e. 17.50 17.50

   No. 172 is a continuous design.

1994, Sept. 21   Litho.   Perf. 14½

1946 Volcanic Eruption: a, Blue-crowned lorikeet, lava flow. b, Black Pacific ducks, lava flow. c, Megapodes, palm trees (b). d, White-tailed tropic birds, people evacuating island (c). e, People wading out to sailboats, Pacific reef heron.

173 A37 80s Strip of 5, #a.-e.   9.50   9.50

   No. 173 is a continuous design.

Nos. 129-133 Surcharged in Blue

1995, June 30   Litho.   Perf. 11½
174 A23   60s on 42s #130   3.00   3.00
175 A23   80s on 15s #129   3.75   3.75
176 A23   80s on 57s #131   4.00   4.00
177 A23   2pa on #132   9.25   9.25
   Nos. 174-177 (4)   20.00 20.00

Souvenir Sheet
178 A23 1.50pa on 1pa #133   11.00 11.00

Size and location of surcharge varies. Surcharge on No. 178 includes "COME WHALE WATCHING / IN THE SOUTH PACIFIC."

Victory in the Pacific Type of Tonga

Nos. 179, 180: a, Soldier holding rifle. b, Soldier aiming rifle, tank. c, Front of tank. d, Troops coming off boat, firing weapons. e, Troops on beach.

1995, Aug. 1   Litho.   Perf. 14x14½
179 A177 60s Strip of 5, #a.-e. 13.00 13.00
180 A177 80s Strip of 5, #a.-e. 17.00 17.00

Nos. 179-180 are continuous designs and were issued together in sheets containing 10 stamps.

Singapore '95 Type of Tonga

Designs, vert: No. 181a, 45s, like #117A. b, 60s, like #117B.
   2pa, Plesiosaurus.

1995, Sept. 1   Litho.   Perf. 12
181 A178   Pair, #a.-b.   4.25   4.25
              Souvenir Sheet
182 A178 2pa multicolored   5.75   5.75

**Beijing Intl. Coin & Stamp Show '95
Type of Tonga**
Souvenir Sheet

Design: 1.40pa, The Great Wall of China.

1995, Sept. 14   Perf. 14½
183 A179 1.40pa multicolored   5.50   5.50

**End of World War II, UN, 50th Anniv.
Type of Tonga**

No. 184: a, London blitz. b, UN emblem, "50." c, Concorde.
No. 185: a, Building of Siam-Burma Railway by Allied prisoners of war. b, Like #184b. c, Japanese bullet train.

1995, Oct. 20   Litho.   Perf. 14
184 A180 60s Strip of 3, #a.-
            c.   5.50   5.50
185 A180 80s Strip of 3, #a.-
            c.   7.50   7.50

   Nos. 184b, 185b are 23x31mm.

Mailmen
of
Niuafo'ou
A38

Portrait, illustration of postal history: 45s, Charles Stuart Ramsey, companions, floating with poles. 60s, Ramsey with can of mail encountering shark. 1pa, Walter George Quensell, mail being lowered from ship to canoes. 3pa, Quensell, original "tin can" mail cancels.

1996, Aug. 21   Litho.   Perf. 14
186 A38 45s multicolored   1.25   1.25
187 A38 60s multicolored   1.75   1.75
188 A38 1pa multicolored   3.00   3.00
189 A38 3pa multicolored   9.00   9.00
   Nos. 186-189 (4)   15.00 15.00

**Congress of Preshistoric and
Protohistoric Sciences Type of
Tonga**

a, Prehistoric man making drawings, fire, living in huts, animals. b, Ancient Egyptians, Romans.

1996, Sept. 5   Perf. 12
190 A185 1pa Pair, #a.-b.   7.00   7.00

Evacuation of
Niuafo'ou, 50th
Anniv. — A39

a, Island, two canoes. b, Volcano, four canoes. c, Edge of island, canoe. d, Canoe. e, People boarding MV Matua.

1996, Dec. 2   Perf. 14
191 A39 45s Strip of 5, #a.-e.   6.00   6.00
192 A39 60s Strip of 5, #a.-e.   9.00   9.00

Nos. 191-192 are continuous designs and were issued together in sheet containing 10 stamps.

UNICEF, 50th Anniv. Type of Tonga

Children's toys on checkerboard: a, Dolls, truck, balls on pegs. b, Tricycle, car, balls on pegs, teddy bear, train. c, Car, helicopter, roller skates, books, blocks.

1996, Oct. 29   Litho.   Perf. 14
193 A187 80s Strip of 3, #a.-c.   6.50   6.50

   No. 193 is a continuous design.

Ocean Environment — A40

Various zooplankton and phytoplankton.

1997, May 19   Litho.   Perf. 14
194 A40   60s red & multi   1.50   1.50
195 A40   80s brown & multi   2.00   2.00
196 A40 1.50pa blue & multi   4.00   4.00
197 A40 2.50pa green & multi   7.00   7.00
   Nos. 194-197 (4)   14.50 14.50

Pacific '97 Type of Tonga
Souvenir Sheet

Design: Oakland Bay Bridge, back-naped tern.

1997, May 30
198 A191 2pa multicolored   7.00   7.00

**1997 Wedding Anniv., Coronation
Anniv. Type of Tonga**

No. 199: a, King Taufa'ahau, Queen Halaevalu Mata'aho on wedding day. b, King in coronation regalia.
   5pa, King in coronation procession, horiz.

1997, June 30   Litho.   Perf. 12
                  Size: 34x47mm
199 A193 80s vert. pair, #a.-
                                   5.00   5.00
              Souvenir Sheet
200 A193 5pa multicolored   13.00 13.00

No. 199 was issued in sheets of 6 stamps.

Diana, Princess of Wales (1961-97)
Common Design Type

Various portraits: a, 10s. b, 80s, c, 1pa. d, 2.50pa.

                  Perf. 13½x14
1998, May 29   Litho.   Unwmk.
201 CD355 Sheet of 4, #a.-d.   7.75   7.75

No. 201 sold for 4.40pa + 50s with surtax from international sales going to the Princess Diana Memorial Fund and surtax from local sales going to designated local charity.

Blue Crowned
Lorikeet — A41

World Wildlife Fund: 10s, Young birds in nest. 55s, Adult on branch of flower. 80s, Adult on branch of bush. 3pa, Two adults on tree branch.

1998, May 15   Litho.   Perf. 14½x15
202 A41 10s multicolored   1.25   1.25
203 A41 55s multicolored   2.75   2.75
204 A41 80s multicolored   3.25   3.25
205 A41 3pa multicolored   10.00 10.00
   a. Sheet, 2 each #202-205   37.50 37.50
   Nos. 202-205 (4)   17.25 17.25

For surcharges see Tonga Nos. 1152, 1155.

**King Taufa'ahau Tupou IV Type of
Tonga**

1998, July 4   Litho.   Perf. 14
207 A196 2.70pa multicolored   5.00   5.00

See Tonga #985a for souvenir sheet containing one #207.

Fish
A43

a, 10s, Amphipiron melanopus. b, 55s, Amphipiron perideraion. c, 80s, Amphipiron chrysopterus.

1998, Sept. 23   Litho.   Perf. 14
208 A43   Strip of 3, #a.-c.   2.50   2.50

Intl. Year of the Ocean. No. 208 was issued in sheets of 9 stamps.

Year of the Tiger Type of Tonga

Designs: a, 55s, Head of tiger with mouth open. b, 80s, Two tigers standing. c, 1pa, Two tigers lying down. 1pa, Head of tiger.

1998, July 23   Perf. 14
209 A183   Sheet of 4, #a.-d.   6.00   6.00

No. 209 is a continuous design. Singpex '98.

Christmas
A44

Designs: 20s, Angel playing mandolin. 55s, Angel playing violin. 1pa, Children singing, bells. 1.60pa, Children singing, candles.

1998, Nov. 12   Perf. 14x14½
210 A44   20s multicolored   .40   .40
211 A44   55s multicolored   1.10   1.10
212 A44   1pa multicolored   2.00   2.00
213 A44   1.60pa multicolored 3.00   3.00
   Nos. 210-213 (4)   6.50   6.50

For surcharge see Tonga No. 1153.

New Year 1999 (Year of the Rabbit)
A45

Stylized rabbits: a, 10s. b, 55s. c, 80s. d, 1pa.

1999, Feb. 16   Perf. 14
214 A45   Sheet of 4, #a.-d.   4.25   4.25

Jakob le Maire (1585-1616), Explorer — A46

1999, Mar. 19   Litho.   Perf. 14
215 A46   80s shown   1.40   1.40
216 A46   2.70pa Tongiaki canoe 4.50 4.50
   a.   Souvenir sheet, #215-216 6.00 6.00
Australia '99 World Stamp Expo (#216a).

Flowers
A47

55s, Cananga odorata. 80s, Gardenia tannaensis, vert. 1pa, Coleus amboinicus, vert. 2.50pa, Hernandia moerenhoutiana.

Perf. 13x13¼, 13¼x13
1999, Sept. 29   Litho.
217 A47   55s multicolored   .75   .75
218 A47   80s multicolored   1.25   1.25
219 A47   1pa multicolored   1.50   1.50
220 A47   2.50pa multicolored 4.00   4.00
   Nos. 217-220 (4)   7.50   7.50

Souvenir Sheet

Millennium — A48

a, 1pa, Dove. b, 2.50pa, Native boat.

2000, Jan. 1   Litho.   Perf. 14½x15
221 A48   Sheet of 2, #a.-b.   5.00   5.00

Souvenir Sheet

New Year 2000 (Year of the Dragon) — A49

Various dragons; a, 10s. b, 55s. c, 80s. d, 1pa.

Litho. with Foil Application
2000, Feb. 4   Perf. 14½
222 A49   Sheet of 4, #a.-d.   4.50   4.50

Souvenir Sheet

The Stamp Show 2000, London — A50

Litho. with Foil Application
2000, May 22   Perf. 13x13¼
223 A50   Sheet of 2   6.25   6.25
   a. $1.50 Queen Mother   2.00   2.00
   b. $2.50 Queen Salote Tupou III 3.25 3.25

Souvenir Sheet

World Stamp Expo 2001, Anaheim — A51

No. 224: a, 10s, Man and woman. b, 2.50pa, Satellite dish. c, 2.70pa, Intelsat.

2000, July 7   Litho.   Perf. 13x13¼
224 A51   Sheet of 3, #a-c   8.25   8.25

Butterflies — A52

Designs: 55s, Jamides bochus. 80s, Blue moon. 1pa, Eurema hecabe aprica. 2.70pa, Monarch.

2000, Oct. 25   Perf. 14
225-228 A52   Set of 4   8.00   8.00

For surcharge see Tonga No. 1154.

Souvenir Sheet

New Year 2001 (Year of the Snake) — A53

No. 229 — Various snakes: a, 10s. b, 55s, c, 80s, d, 1pa.

Litho. with Foil Application
2001, Feb. 1   Perf. 14¼
229 A53   Sheet of 4, #a-d   4.25   4.25

Hong Kong 2001 Stamp Exhibition.

Fish — A54

Designs: 80s, Prognichthys sealei. 1pa, Xiphias gladius. 2.50pa, Katsuwonus pelamis.

2001, June 5   Litho.   Perf. 13¾
230-232 A54   Set of 3   7.25   7.25
232a   Souvenir sheet, #230-232 7.25 7.25

Souvenir Sheet

Fruit — A55

No. 233: a, 55s, Papaya. b, 80s, Limes. c, 1pa, Mangos. d, 2.50pa, Bananas.

Perf. 14¼x14
2001, Sept. 19   Litho.   Unwmk.
233 A55   Sheet of 4, #a-d   8.50   8.50

Barn Owl
A56

Designs: Nos. 234, 238a, 10s, Owl in flight. Nos. 235, 238b, 55s, Adult feeding young. Nos. 236, 238c, 2.50pa, Four owls. Nos. 237, 238d, 2.70pa, Owl's head.

2001, Nov. 21   Perf. 12¾x13¼
Without Vertical Bister Line Separating Panels
234-237 A56   Set of 4   10.00 10.00

Souvenir Sheet
With Vertical Bister Line Separating Panels
238 A56   Sheet of 4, #a-d   10.00 10.00

For surcharge see Tonga No. 1156.

Reign Of Queen Elizabeth II, 50th Anniv. Issue
Common Design Type
Souvenir Sheet

No. 239: a, 15s, Princess Elizabeth with Queen Mother. b, 90s, Wearing purple hat. c, 1.20pa, As young woman. d, 1.40pa, Wearing red hat. e, 2.25pa, 1955 portrait by Annigoni (38x50mm).

Perf. 14¼x14½, 13¾ (2.25pa)
2002, Feb. 6   Litho.   Wmk. 373
239 CD360   Sheet of 5, #a-e   7.00   7.00

Souvenir Sheet

New Year 2002 (Year of the Horse) — A517

Various horses: a, 65s. b, 80s. c, 1pa. d, 2.50pa.

Litho. With Foil Application
2002, Feb. 12   Unwmk.   Perf. 14
240 A57   Sheet of 4, #a-d   8.50   8.50

Megapodius Pritchardii
A58

Designs: 15s, Bird, eggs. 70s, Two birds. 90s, Bird, vert. 2.50pa, Two birds, vert.

Perf. 14x13½, 13½x14
2002, Apr. 9   Litho.
241-244 A58   Set of 4   7.00   7.00
244a   Souvenir sheet, #243-244 6.00 6.00

Nos. 243-244 lack white frame around stamp.

Cephalopods
A59

Designs: 80s, Octopus vulgaris. 1pa, Sepioteuthis lessoniana. 2.50pa, Nautilus belauensis.

2002, July 25   Litho.   Perf. 13¾
245-247 A59   Set of 3   7.00   7.00
247a   Souvenir sheet, #245-247 7.00 7.00

Souvenir Sheet

Mail Planes — A60

No. 248: a, 80c, Casa C-212 Aviocar. b, 1.40pa, Britten-Norman Islander. c, 2.50pa, DHC 6-300 Twin Otter.

2002, Nov. 27   Litho.   Perf. 12¾
248 A60   Sheet of 3, #a-c   8.00   8.00

New Year 2003 (Year of the Ram) Type of Tonga

No. 249: a, 65s, One ram. 80s, Three sheep. 1pa, Three sheep, diff. 2.50pa, Two sheep.

2003, Apr. 14   Litho.   Perf. 13¼
249 A223   Sheet of 4, #a-d   6.00   6.00

Coronation of Queen Elizabeth II, 50th Anniv. Type of Tonga

Designs: 90s, Queen Elizabeth II. 1.20pa, Queen Elizabeth II seated. 1.40pa, Queen Salote of Tonga in coach. 2.50pa, Queen Salote.

2003, June 2   Litho.
250-253 A224   Set of 4   10.00   10.00

New Year (Year of the Monkey) Type of Tonga

No. 254: a, 60s, Spider monkey. b, 80s, Ring-tailed lemur. c, 1pa, Cotton-top tamarin. d, 2.50pa, White-cheeked gibbon.

2004, Feb. 12   Litho.   Perf. 13¼
254 A228   Sheet of 4, #a-d   6.00   6.00

Trees Type of Tonga

Designs: 45s, Pawpaw (papaya). 60s, Banana. 80s, Coconut. 1.80pa, Lime.

2004   Litho.   Perf. 14¼x14
255-258 A229   Set of 4   4.50   4.50

Christmas Type of Tonga

Designs: 15s, Madonna and Child. 90s, Journey to Bethlehem. 1.20pa, Annunciation to the Shepherds. 2.60pa, Magi.

2004, Dec.   Perf. 14
259-262 A230   Set of 4   5.75   5.75

Royalty Type of Tonga

Designs: 30s, King George Tupou I. 65s, King George Tupou II. 80s, Queen Salote Tupou III. 3.05pa, King Taufa'ahau Tupou IV.

2004, July 7   Litho.   Perf. 14
263-266 A231   Set of 4   5.75   5.75
266a   Souvenir sheet, #263-266   5.75   5.75

New Year 2005 (Year of the Rooster) Type of Tonga
Souvenir Sheet

No. 267 — Various roosters with panel color of: a, 65s, Gray. b, 80s, Grayish tan. c, 1pa, Gray. d, 2.50pa, Yellow green.

2005, Feb. 12
267 A232   Sheet of 4, #a-d   5.25   5.25

Christmas — A61

No. 268: a, 3.40pa, Palm frond and Christmas lights. b, 5pa, Grass and snowflakes.

2011, Dec. 24
268 A61   Horiz. pair, #a-b   9.75   9.75

Miniature Sheets

Megaptera Novaeangliae — A62

No. 269 — Various depictions of humpback whale: a, 1pa. b, 1.40pa. c, 1.60pa.
No. 270 — Various depictions of humpback whale: a, 2pa. b, 2.25pa. c, 2.40pa.

2012, Jan. 16
269 A62   Sheet of 3, #a-c, + label   4.75   4.75
270 A62   Sheet of 3, #a-c, + label   8.00   8.00

Worldwide Fund for Nature (WWF) — A63

Various depictions of Zebra shark: 45s, 2pa, 2.40pa, 3.40pa.

2012, Mar. 12   Perf. 14¼x14
271-274 A63   Set of 4   9.75   9.75
274a   Sheet of 16, 4 each #271-274   39.00   39.00

Butterflies — A64

Designs: 45s, Australian meadow-argus. 1.95pa, Crow butterfly. 2pa, Monarch butterfly. 2.40pa, Monarch butterfly, diff. 2.50pa, Blue moon butterfly. 3pa, Australian meadow-argus, diff. 3.40pa, Crow butterfly, diff. 4pa, Blue moon butterfly, diff. 5pa, Monarch butterfly, diff. 6pa, Blue moon butterfly, diff. 7.30pa, Crow butterfly, diff. 8pa, Australian meadow-argus, diff.

2012, Apr. 20   Perf. 12¾x12½
Stamps With White Backgrounds
275 A64   45s multi   .55   .55
276 A64   1.95pa multi   2.25   2.25
277 A64   2pa multi   2.40   2.40
278 A64   2.40pa multi   2.75   2.75
279 A64   2.50pa multi   3.00   3.00
280 A64   3pa multi   3.50   3.50
281 A64   3.40pa multi   4.00   4.00
282 A64   4pa multi   4.75   4.75
283 A64   5pa multi   6.00   6.00
284 A64   6pa multi   7.00   7.00
285 A64   7.30pa multi   8.50   8.50
286 A64   8pa multi   9.50   9.50
    Nos. 275-286 (12)   54.20   54.20

Stamps With Light Blue Background
287   Sheet of 12   55.00   55.00
a.   A64 45s multi   .55   .55
b.   A64 1.95pa multi   2.25   2.25
c.   A64 2pa multi   2.40   2.40
d.   A64 2.40pa multi   2.75   2.75
e.   A64 2.50pa multi   3.00   3.00
f.   A64 3pa multi   3.50   3.50
g.   A64 3.40pa multi   4.00   4.00
h.   A64 4pa multi   4.75   4.75
i.   A64 5pa multi   6.00   6.00
j.   A64 6pa multi   7.00   7.00
k.   A64 7.30pa multi   8.50   8.50
l.   A64 8pa multi   9.50   9.50

TRANSCAUCASIAN FEDERATED REPUBLIC

ˌtranˌt s-ko-'kā-zhən 'fe-də-rāted ri-'pə-blik

LOCATION — In southeastern Europe, south of the Caucasus Mountains between the Black and Caspian Seas
GOVT. — Former republic
AREA — 71,255 sq. mi.
POP. — 5,851,000 (approx.)
CAPITAL — Tiflis

The Transcaucasian Federation was made up of the former autonomies of Armenia, Georgia and Azerbaijan. Its stamps were replaced by those of Russia.

100 Kopecks = 1 Ruble

Russian Stamps of 1909-17 Overprinted in Black or Red

1923   Unwmk.   Perf. 14½x15
1   A15   10k dark blue   3.00   5.00
2   A14   10k on 7k lt bl   3.00   5.00
3   A11   25k grn & gray vio   3.00   5.00
4   A11   35k red brn & grn (R)   3.00   5.00
a.   Double overprint   40.00   50.00
5   A8   50k brn red & grn   3.00   5.00
6   A9   1r pale brn, brn & org   10.00   12.00
7   A12   3½r mar & lt grn   35.00

Imperf
8   A9   1r pale brn, brn & red org   5.00   6.00
    Nos. 1-8 (8)   65.00
    Nos. 1-6,8 (7)   43.00

No. 7 was prepared but not issued.

Overprinted on Stamps of Armenia Previously Handstamped:

a   c

Perf. 14½x15
9   A11(c)   25k grn & gray vio   250.00   250.00
10   A8(c)   50k vio & grn   250.00   150.00

Perf. 13½
11   A9(a)   1r pale brn, brn & org   100.00   50.00
12   A9(c)   1r pale, brn, brn & org   150.00   50.00

Imperf
13   A9(c)   1r pale brn, brn & red org   35.00   35.00
    Nos. 9-13 (5)   785.00   535.00

Counterfeit overprints exist.

Oil Fields — A1

Soviet Symbols — A2

1923   Perf. 11½
14   A1   40,000r red violet   3.00   3.50
15   A1   75,000r dark grn   3.00   3.50
16   A1   100,000r blk vio   3.00   3.50
17   A1   150,000r red   3.00   3.50
18   A2   200,000r dull grn   3.00   3.50
19   A2   300,000r blue   3.00   3.50
20   A2   350,000r dark brn   3.00   3.50
21   A2   500,000r rose   3.00   3.50
    Nos. 14-21 (8)   24.00   28.00

Nos. 14-15 Srchd. in Brown

1923
22   A1   700,000r on 40,000r   3.00   5.00
a.   Imperf., pair   40.00
23   A1   700,000r on 75,000r   3.00   5.00
a.   Imperf., pair   40.00

Types of Preceding Issue with Values in Gold Kopecks

1923, Oct. 24
25   A2   1k orange   2.50   2.75
26   A2   2k blue green   2.50   2.75
27   A2   3k rose   3.50   2.75
28   A2   4k gray brown   2.25   2.75
29   A1   5k dark violet   2.25   2.75
30   A1   9k deep blue   2.25   2.75
31   A1   18k slate   2.25   2.75
    Nos. 25-31 (7)   17.50   19.25

Nos. 14-21, 25-31 exist imperf. but are not known to have been issued in that condition. Value, $14 each.

TRANSVAAL

tranˌt s-'väl

(South African Republic)

LOCATION — Southern Africa
GOVT. — A former British Colony
AREA — 110,450 sq. mi.
POP. — 1,261,736 (1904)
CAPITAL — Pretoria

Transvaal was known as the South African Republic until 1877 when it was occupied by the British. The republic was restored in 1884 and continued until 1900 when it was annexed to Great Britain and named "The Transvaal."

12 Pence = 1 Shilling
20 Shillings = 1 Pound

Most unused stamps between Nos. 1-96, 119-122 and 136-137 were issued with gum, but do not expect gum on scarcer stamps as few examples retain their original gum. In many cases removal of the remaining gum may enhance the preservation of the stamps. Otherwise, values for unused stamps are for examples with original gum as defined in the catalogue introduction.

Very fine imperforate stamps will have adequate to large margins. However, rouletted stamps are valued as partly rouletted, with straight edges, and rouletted just into the design, as the rouletting methods were quite inaccurate.

First Republic

Coat of Arms
A1   A2
Mecklenburg Printings
By Adolph Otto, Gustrow
Fine Impressions
Thin Paper

A1 has spread wings on eagle.

1869   Unwmk.   Imperf.
1   A1   1p brown lake   500.00
a.   1p red   675.00   675.00
2   A1   6p ultra   230.00   230.00
3   A1   1sh dark green   800.00   800.00
a.   Tete beche pair   —

Rouletted 15½, 16
4   A1   1p red   125.00
5   A1   6p ultra   115.00   115.00
6   A1   1sh blue green   150.00   150.00
a.   1sh yellow green   200.00   185.00
b.   1sh deep green   260.00   275.00

Nos. 1-6 were printed from 2 sets of plates, differing in the spacing between the stamps.
The only known example of No. 3a is in a museum.
See Nos. 9-24, 26-33, 35-36, 38-39, 41-42, 43-49, 119, 122. For overprints see Nos. 53-61, 63-66, 68-72, 75-78, 81-83, 86-87, 90-91, 94.

1871-74
7   A2   3p lilac   92.50   100.00
a.   3p violet   110.00   115.00
8   A2   6p brt ultra ('74)   70.00   27.50
a.   Half used as 3p on cover   1,650.

Many forgeries exist in colors duller or lighter than the genuine stamps.
In forgeries of type A1, all values, the "D" of "EENDRAGT" is not noticeably larger than the other letters and does not touch the top of the

ribbon. In type A1 genuine stamps, the "D" is large and touches the ribbon top. The eagle's eye is a dot and its face white on the genuine stamps; the eye is a loop or blob attached to the beak, and the beak is strongly hooked, on the forgeries. Many forgeries of the 1sh have the top line of the ribbon broken above "EENDRAGT."

Forgeries of type A2 usually can be detected only by color.

A sharply struck cancellation of a numeral in three rings is found on many of these forgeries. The similar genuine cancellation is always roughly or heavily struck.

See Nos. 25, 34, 437, 40, 42B, 120-121. For overprints see Nos. 50-52, 62, 67, 73-74, 79-80, 84-85, 88-89, 92-93, 95-96.

Local Printings
(A) By M. J. Viljoen, Pretoria
Poor Impressions,
Overinked and Spotted
Thin Soft Paper

1870			Imperf.	
9	A1	1p pink	92.50	
a.		1p rose red	115.00	
b.		1p carmine	80.00	92.50
10	A1	6p dull ultra	375.00	80.00
a.		Tete beche pair	—	

The only known examples of No. 10a are in museums.

Rouletted 15½, 16

11	A1	1p carmine	800.00	300.00
a.		Rouletted 6½	—	1,100.
12	A1	6p dull ultra	230.00	100.00

Hard Paper, Thick to Medium
Imperf

13	A1	1p carmine	85.00	100.00
14	A1	6p ultra		
15	A1	1sh gray green	150.00	140.00
a.		1sh dark green	—	
b.		Tete beche pair	23,000.	
c.		Half used as 6p on cover	—	2,100.

The existence of No. 14 is questionable.

Rouletted 15½, 16

16	A1	1p light carmine	85.00	100.00
a.		1p carmine	62.50	70.00
17	A1	6p ultra	125.00	125.00
a.		Tete beche pair	30,000.	21,000.
18	A1	1sh dark green	185.00	92.50
a.		1sh gray green	750.00	750.00

Examples of Nos. 16-18 are sometimes so heavily inked as to be little more than blots of color.

(B) By J. P. Borrius, Potchefstroom
Clearer Impressions Though Often
Overinked
Thick Porous Paper

1870			Imperf.	
19	A1	1p black	160.00	135.00
20	A1	6p indigo		

Rouletted 15½, 16

21	A1	1p black	25.00	32.50
22	A1	6p gray blue	160.00	70.00
a.		6p indigo	115.00	92.50
b.		6p bright ultra	—	

Thin Transparent Paper

23	A1	1p black	225.00	750.00
24	A1	1p brt carmine	200.00	62.50
a.		1p deep carmine	80.00	47.50
25	A2	3p gray lilac	125.00	75.00
26	A1	6p ultra	80.00	35.00
27	A1	1sh yellow green	100.00	50.00
a.		1sh deep green	100.00	50.00
b.		Half used as 6p on cover	—	2,100.

Thick Soft Paper

28	A1	1p dull rose	450.00	85.00
a.		1p brown rose	575.00	140.00
b.		Printed on both sides	—	
29	A1	6p dull blue	100.00	50.00
a.		6p bright blue	230.00	75.00
b.		6p ultramarine	200.00	75.00
c.		Rouletted 6½	—	
30	A1	1sh yellow green	975.00	750.00

The paper of Nos. 28 to 30 varies considerably in thickness.

(C) By P. Davis & Son, Natal
Thin to Medium Paper

1874			Perf. 12½	
31	A1	1p red	150.00	50.00
a.		1p brownish red	150.00	50.00
32	A1	6p deep blue	200.00	70.00
a.		6p blue	185.00	62.50
b.		Horiz. pair, imperf. between	—	

(D) By the Stamp Commission,
Pretoria
Pelure Paper

1875-76			Imperf.	
33	A1	1p pale red	70.00	65.00
a.		1p orange red	65.00	32.50
b.		1p brown red	80.00	40.00
c.		Pin perf.	775.00	475.00

34	A2	3p gray lilac	80.00	55.00
a.		3p dull violet	90.00	55.00
b.		Pin perf.	—	500.00
35	A1	6p blue	77.50	55.00
a.		6p pale blue	77.50	62.50
b.		6p dark blue	82.50	57.50
c.		Tete beche pair, thin opaque paper	20,000.	
d.		Tete beche pair, pelure, transparent paper	—	
e.		Pin perf.	—	400.00

The only known examples of No. 35c are in museums.

Rouletted 15½, 16

36	A1	1p orange red	450.00	155.00
a.		Rouletted 6½	1,250.	250.00
37	A2	3p dull violet	500.00	165.00
a.		Rouletted 6½	1,100.	320.00
38	A1	6p blue	215.00	130.00
a.		Rouletted 6½	1,275.	140.00

The paper of this group varies slightly in thickness and is sometimes divided into pelure and semipelure. We believe there was only one lot of the paper and that the separation is not warranted.

Thick Hard Paper
Imperf

39	A1	1p orange red ('76)	32.50	25.00
40	A2	3p lilac	425.00	140.00
41	A1	6p deep blue	70.00	22.50
a.		6p blue	115.00	27.50
b.		Tete beche pair	20,000.	

Rouletted 15½, 16

42	A1	1p orange red ('76)	475.00	175.00
a.		Rouletted 6½ ('75)	700.00	175.00
42B	A2	3p lilac	400.00	
43	A1	6p deep blue	700.00	325.00
a.		6p blue	875.00	125.00
b.		Rouletted 6½ ('75)	750.00	300.00

Soft Porous Paper
Imperf

44	A1	1p orange red	150.00	62.50
45	A1	6p deep blue	225.00	650.00
a.		6p dull blue	400.00	110.00
46	A1	1sh yellow green	460.00	140.00
a.		Half used as 6p on cover	—	1,850.

Rouletted 15½, 16

47	A1	1p orange red	—	425.00
a.		Rouletted 6½	—	525.00
48	A1	6p deep blue	—	185.00
a.		Rouletted 6½	—	1,275.
49	A1	1sh yellow grn	800.00	400.00
a.		Rouletted 6½	—	1,400.
b.		Rouletted 15½-16x16½	800.00	400.00

First British Occupation

Stamps and Types of
1875 Overprinted

Red Overprint
Pelure Paper

1877		Unwmk.	Imperf.	
50	A2	3p lilac	1,500.	210.00
a.		Overprinted on back	3,750.	3,750.
b.		Double ovpt., red and black	7,000.	

Rouletted 15½, 16

51	A2	3p lilac	—	1,850.
a.		Rouletted 6½	—	2,600.

Thin Hard Paper
Imperf

52	A2	3p lilac	1,500.	350.00

Soft Porous Paper

53	A1	6p blue	1,850.	210.00
a.		6p deep blue	—	300.00
b.		Inverted overprint	—	6,000.
c.		Double overprint	5,250.	1,150.
54	A1	1sh yellow grn	750.00	210.00
a.		Inverted overprint	—	5,250.
b.		Half used as 6p on cover	—	2,100.

Rouletted 15½, 16

55	A1	6p blue	—	2,000.
a.		Rouletted 6½	—	2,750.
56	A1	1sh yellow grn	2,000.	875.00
a.		Rouletted 6½	4,750.	2,750.
b.		As "a.", overprint inverted	—	7,500.

Black Overprint
Pelure Paper
Imperf

57	A1	1p red	360.00	145.00

Rouletted 15½, 16

58	A1	1p red	—	1,350.

Thick Hard Paper
Imperf

59	A1	1p red	35.00	27.50
a.		Inverted overprint	650.00	575.00

Rouletted 15½, 16

60	A1	1p red	185.00	57.50
a.		Rouletted 6½	750.00	240.00
b.		Inverted overprint	—	
c.		Double overprint	—	1,275.

Soft Porous Paper
Imperf

61	A1	1p red	35.00	27.50
a.		Double overprint	—	1,400.
62	A2	3p lilac	110.00	52.50
a.		3p deep lilac	200.00	97.50
b.		Inverted overprint	—	
63	A1	6p dull blue	200.00	100.00
a.		6p bright blue	185.00	35.00
b.		6p dark blue	185.00	250.00
c.		Inverted overprint	1,650.	
d.		Double overprint	4,000.	2,400.
64	A1	6p blue, rose	115.00	55.00
a.		Tete beche pair	—	
b.		Inverted overprint	140.00	55.00
c.		Overprint omitted	4,000.	2,900.
d.		Half used as 3p on cover	—	
65	A1	1sh yellow grn	150.00	65.00
a.		Tete beche pair	23,500.	24,000.
b.		Inverted overprint	1,400.	500.00
c.		Half used as 6p on cover	—	1,750.

The only known examples of No. 64a are in museums.

Rouletted 15½, 16

66	A1	1p red	100.00	85.00
a.		Rouletted 6½	750.00	175.00
67	A2	3p lilac	240.00	75.00
a.		Rouletted 6½	—	875.00
68	A1	6p dull blue	240.00	75.00
a.		Inverted overprint	—	875.00
b.		Rouletted 6½	—	1,400.
c.		As "a," rouletted 6½	—	4,750.
69	A1	6p blue, rose	300.00	80.00
a.		Inverted overprint	650.00	80.00
b.		Rouletted 6½	—	
c.		Tete beche pair	—	
d.		Overprint omitted	—	
e.		As "a," rouletted 6½	—	750.00
f.		As "d," rouletted 6½	—	
70	A1	1sh yellow grn	325.00	100.00
a.		Inverted overprint	1,400.	575.00
b.		Rouletted 6½	550.00	150.00
c.		As "a," rouletted 6½	1,750.	700.00

In this issue the space between "V. R." and "TRANSVAAL" is normally 8½mm but in position 11 it is 12mm. In this and the following issues there are numerous minor varieties of the overprint, missing periods, etc.
The only known examples of No. 69c are in museums.

Types A1 and A2
Overprinted

1877-79			Imperf.	
71	A1	1p red, blue	70.00	35.00
a.		"Transvral"	6,500.	2,900.
b.		Inverted overprint	925.00	475.00
c.		Double overprint	4,750.	
d.		Overprint omitted	—	
72	A1	1p red, org ('78)	30.00	24.00
a.		Printed on both sides	—	
b.		Pin perf.	—	
73	A2	3p lilac, buff	75.00	32.50
a.		Inverted overprint	—	875.00
b.		Pin perf.	—	
74	A2	3p lilac, grn ('79)	175.00	50.00
a.		Inverted overprint	—	2,350.
b.		Double overprint	—	
c.		Pin perf.	—	
75	A1	6p blue, grn	115.00	45.00
a.		Tete beche pair	—	20,000.
b.		Inverted overprint	—	1,275.
c.		Half used as 3p on cover	—	
d.		Pin perf.	—	
76	A1	6p blue, bl ('78)	80.00	32.50
a.		Tete beche pair	—	
b.		Overprint omitted	—	2,750.
c.		Inverted overprint	—	1,275.
d.		Half used as 3p on cover	—	925.00
e.		Double overprint	—	3,750.
f.		Pin perf.	—	
		Nos. 71-76 (6)	545.00	219.00

The only known examples of No. 76a are in museums.

Rouletted 15½, 16

77	A1	1p red, blue	125.00	45.00
a.		"Transvral"	—	3,500.
b.		Inverted overprint	—	
c.		Double overprint	—	
78	A1	1p red, org ('78)	47.50	32.50
a.		Horiz. pair, imperf. vert.	—	
b.		Rouletted 6½	300.00	115.00
79	A2	3p lilac, buff	125.00	32.50
a.		Inverted overprint	—	3,500.
b.		Vert. pair, imperf. horiz.	875.00	
80	A2	3p lilac, grn ('79)	800.00	175.00
a.		Inverted overprint	—	
b.		Rouletted 6½	750.00	325.00
81	A1	6p blue, green	110.00	32.50
a.		Inverted overprint	—	750.00
b.		Overprint omitted	—	4,750.
c.		Tete beche pair	—	
d.		Half used at 3p on cover	—	800.00
e.		Rouletted 6½	—	1,275.

82	A1	6p blue, bl ('78)	325.00	65.00
a.		Inverted overprint	—	1,050.
b.		Overprint omitted	—	4,000.
c.		Tete beche pair	—	
d.		Horiz. pair, imperf. vert.	—	
e.		Half used as 3p on cover	—	900.00
f.		Double overprint	—	
g.		Rouletted 6½	—	350.00
h.		As "a," rouletted 6½	—	
		Nos. 77-82 (6)	1,532.	382.50

The only known examples of No. 81c are in museums. The existence of No. 82c is questioned.

Types A1 and A2
Overprinted

Imperf

83	A1	1p red, org ('78)	80.00	52.50
84	A2	3p lilac, buff ('78)	92.50	40.00
a.		Pin perf.	875.00	875.00
85	A2	3p lilac, grn ('79)	160.00	40.00
a.		Inverted overprint	—	2,300.
b.		Overprint omitted	—	
c.		Printed on both sides	—	1,150.
86	A1	6p blue, bl ('78)	160.00	35.00
a.		Tete beche pair	18,000.	
b.		Inverted overprint	—	800.00
		Nos. 83-86 (4)	492.50	167.50

Rouletted 15½, 16

87	A1	1p red, org ('78)	200.00	140.00
a.		Rouletted 6½	—	350.00
88	A2	3p lilac, buff ('78)	210.00	125.00
a.		Vert. pair, imperf. horiz.	—	
b.		Rouletted 6½	—	400.00
89	A2	3p lilac, grn ('79)	800.00	175.00
a.		Inverted overprint	—	
b.		Overprint omitted	—	
c.		Rouletted 6½ ('97)	—	350.00
90	A1	6p blue, bl ('78)	500.00	125.00
a.		Tete beche pair	—	
b.		Inverted overprint	—	1,275.
c.		Rouletted 6½	—	400.00
d.		As "b," rouletted 6½	—	

Types A1 and A2
Overprinted

1879			Imperf.	
91	A1	1p red, orange	55.00	35.00
a.		1p red, yellow	57.50	45.00
b.		Small capital "T"	350.00	200.00
92	A2	3p lilac, green	52.50	30.00
a.		Small capital "T"	300.00	115.00
93	A2	3p lilac, blue	57.50	35.00
a.		Small capital "T"	325.00	110.00
		Nos. 91-93 (3)	165.00	100.00

Rouletted 15½, 16

94	A1	1p red, yellow	400.00	240.00
a.		1p red, orange	875.00	450.00
b.		Small capital "T"	1,100.	750.00
c.		Rouletted 6½	750.00	750.00
d.		Pin perf.	—	875.00
95	A2	3p lilac, green	875.00	300.00
a.		Small capital "T"	—	1,000.
b.		Rouletted 6½	1,150.	750.00
96	A2	3p lilac, blue	—	210.00
a.		Small capital "T"	—	800.00
b.		Rouletted 6½	—	950.00
c.		Pin perf.	—	1,000.

Queen Victoria — A3

1878-80		Engr.	Perf. 14, 14½	
97	A3	½p vermilion ('80)	30.00	100.00
98	A3	1p red brown	19.00	5.25
99	A3	3p claret	30.00	9.25
100	A3	4p olive green	32.50	9.25
101	A3	6p slate	19.00	6.50
a.		Half used as 3p on cover	—	
102	A3	1sh green	140.00	55.00
103	A3	2sh blue	225.00	95.00
		Nos. 97-103 (7)	495.50	280.25

For surcharges see Nos. 104-118, 138-139.

No. 101 Surcharged in Red or Black

(a) Surcharged

1879

104	A3	1p on 6p slate (R)	200.00	95.00
105	A3	1p on 6p slate (Bk)	55.00	27.50

(b) Surcharged

106	A3	1p on 6p slate (R)	750.00	400.00
107	A3	1p on 6p slate (Bk)	275.00	95.00

(c) Surcharged

108	A3	1p on 6p slate (R)	750.00	400.00
109	A3	1p on 6p slate (Bk)	275.00	95.00

(d) Surcharged

110	A3	1p on 6p slate (R)	375.00	210.00
111	A3	1p on 6p slate (Bk)	110.00	55.00
a.	Pair, one without surcharge		—	

(e) Surcharged

112	A3	1p on 6p slate (R)	700.00	375.00
113	A3	1p on 6p slate (Bk)	240.00	87.50

(f) Surcharged

114	A3	1p on 6p slate (R)	325.00	185.00
115	A3	1p on 6p slate (Bk)	110.00	50.00

(g) Surcharged

116	A3	1p on 6p slate (R)	7,000.	1,850.
117	A3	1p on 6p slate (Bk)	700.00	185.00

Surcharge distinctions: a, "PENNY" in gothic capitals. b, "1" has heavy serif at base; "P," thin serif at base. c, No serif at base of "1." d, Heavy serifs at base of "1" and "p." e, Italics. f, "1" has long, sloping serif at top, thin serif at base. g, Tail of "y" missing.

Second Republic

No. 100 Surcharged

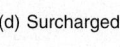

1882   Unwmk.   Perf. 14, 14½

118	A3	1p on 4p olive grn	20.00	7.00
a.	Inverted surcharge		375.00	250.00

1883   Perf. 12

119	A1	1p black	8.00	3.00
a.	Imperf.			
b.	Vert. pair, imperf. horiz.		650.00	400.00
c.	Horiz. pair, imperf. vert.		325.00	
120	A2	3p red	17.50	3.50
a.	Horiz. pair, imperf. vert.			1,000.
b.	Half used as 1p on cover			750.00
121	A2	3p black, rose	32.50	7.50
a.	Half used as 1p on cover			750.00
122	A1	1sh green	80.00	7.00
a.	Tete beche pair		1,150.	185.00
b.	Half used as 6p on cover			550.00
		Nos. 119-122 (4)	138.00	21.00

The so-called reprints of this issue are forgeries. They were made from the counterfeit plates described in the note following No. 8,

plus a new false plate for the 3p. The false 3p plate has many small flaws and defects.

Forgeries of No. 120 are in dull orange red, clearly printed on whitish paper, and those of No. 121 in brownish or grayish black on bright rose. Genuine examples of No. 120 lack the orange tint and the paper is yellowish; genuine examples of No. 121 are in black without gray or brown shade, on dull lilac rose paper.

A 6p in slate on white, apparently of this issue, is a late print from the counterfeit plate.

A4

Perf. 13½, 11½x12, 12½, 12½x12

1885-93   Typo.

123	A4.	½p gray	1.75	.25
a.	Imperf. at top and bottom (used strip of 4)			
124	A4	1p rose	1.20	.25
125	A4	2p brown	3.00	4.00
126	A4	2p olive bis ('87)	2.40	.25
127	A4	2½p purple ('93)	3.50	.65
128	A4	3p violet	3.75	2.50
129	A4	4p bronze green	5.25	1.50
130	A4	6p blue	4.50	3.75
a.	Imperf.			
131	A4	1sh green	3.75	1.50
132	A4	2sh6p yellow	14.00	3.75
133	A4	5sh steel blue	10.00	6.50
134	A4	10sh pale brown	40.00	13.00
135	A4	£5 dark green ('92)	4,000.	225.00
		Nos. 123-134 (12)	93.10	37.90

Reprints of Nos. 123-137, 140-163, 166-174 closely resemble the originals. Paper is whiter; perf. 12½, large holes.

Excellent counterfeits of No. 135 exist.

For overprint and surcharges see Nos. 140-147, 163, 213.

Nos. 120, 122
Surcharged

1885   Perf. 12

136	A2	½p on 3p red	8.75	13.00
a.	Surcharge reading down		8.75	13.00
137	A1	½p on 1sh green	32.50	65.00
a.	Surcharge reading down		32.50	65.00
b.	Tete beche pair			450.00

Almost all examples of No. 137b have telegraph cancellations. Postally used examples are rare.

Nos. 101, 128 Surcharged in Red or Black

Perf. 14

138	A3	½p on 6p slate	85.00	115.00
139	A3	2p on 6p slate	11.00	17.50
a.	Horiz. pair, imperf. vert.			

Perf. 11½x12, 12½x12

140	A4	½p on 3p vio (Bk)	7.50	7.50
a.	"PRNNY"		55.00	75.00
b.	2nd "N" of "PENNY" invtd.		105.00	115.00

No. 128 Surcharged

No. 141   No. 142

1887

141	A4	2p on 3p violet	2.40	5.00
a.	Double surcharge		210.00	210.00
142	A4	2p on 3p violet	11.50	10.50
a.	Double surcharge			400.00

Nos. 126, 130, 131 Surcharged

Nos. 143-144   Nos. 145-146

No. 147

1893   Red Surcharge

143	A4	½p on 2p olive bis	.90	3.00
a.	Inverted surcharge		3.00	3.50
b.	Bars 14mm apart		1.75	3.00
c.	As "b," inverted		5.75	11.50

Black Surcharge

144	A4	½p on 2p olive bis	1.00	3.00
a.	Inverted surcharge		5.25	5.75
b.	Bars 14mm apart		1.75	3.75
c.	As "b," inverted		23.00	18.50
145	A4	1p on 6p blue	2.00	2.00
a.	Inverted surcharge		2.60	3.00
b.	Double surcharge		65.00	52.50
c.	Pair, one without surcharge		260.00	
d.	Bars 14mm apart		3.00	3.00
e.	As "d," inverted		6.50	5.25
f.	As "d," double			95.00
146	A4	2½p on 1sh green	2.60	6.25
a.	Inverted surcharge		8.00	8.50
b.	Fraction line misplaced "⅔½"		50.00	87.50
c.	As "b," inverted		400.00	350.00
d.	Bars 14mm apart		3.75	8.75
e.	As "d," inverted		11.00	21.00
147	A4	2½p on 1sh green	8.00	7.00
a.	Inverted surcharge		10.00	10.00
b.	Bars 14mm apart		13.00	13.00
c.	As "b," inverted		24.00	24.00
d.	Double surcharge		92.50	105.00
		Nos. 143-147 (5)	14.50	21.25

A13

Wagon with Two Shafts

1894   Typo.   Perf. 12½

148	A13	½p gray	1.50	.90
149	A13	1p rose	2.40	.25
150	A13	2p olive bister	2.40	.25
151	A13	6p blue	3.25	.60
152	A13	1sh yellow grn	17.50	22.00
		Nos. 148-152 (5)	27.05	24.00

Counterfeits of #148-152 are plentiful.
See note following No. 135 for reprints.

1895-96   Wagon with Pole

153	A13	½p gray	1.50	.25
154	A13	1p rose	1.50	.25
155	A13	2p olive bister	1.75	.35
156	A13	3p violet	3.00	1.00
157	A13	4p slate	3.50	1.00
158	A13	6p blue	3.50	1.00
159	A13	1sh green	4.00	1.75
160	A13	5sh slate blue ('96)	20.00	35.00
161	A13	10sh red brown ('96)	20.00	8.00
		Nos. 153-161 (9)	58.75	48.60

Most of the unused examples of Nos. 153-161 now on the market are reprints.
See Nos. 166-174. For surcharge and overprints see Nos. 162, 214-220, 232-235.
See note following No. 135 for reprints.

Nos. 159, 127 Surcharged in Red or Green

1895

162	A13	½p on 1sh green (R)	1.75	.25
a.	Inverted surcharge		5.25	5.25
b.	"Pennij" instead of "Penny"		70.00	80.00
c.	Double surcharge		75.00	105.00
163	A4	1p on 2½p pur (G)	.60	.30
a.	Inverted surcharge		20.00	20.00
b.	Surcharge sideways		—	
c.	Surcharge on back			4,000.
d.	Space between "1" and "d"		1.50	1.75

ZEGELREGT
6d
ZES PENCE

A16

1895   Perf. 11½

164	A16	6p rose (G)	2.40	2.60
a.	Vertical pair, imperf. between			

Counterfeits of No. 164 are on the 6p dark red revenue stamp of 1898, and have a shiny green ink for the overprint. The false overprint is also found on other revenue denominations, though only the 6p rose was converted to postal use.

Coat of Arms, Wheat Field and Railroad Train — A17

1895, Sept. 6   Litho.

165	A17	1p red	2.40	2.60
a.	Imperf.			
b.	Vertical pair, imperf. between		150.00	160.00

Penny Postage in Transvaal. Horiz. pair, imperf. between also exists.
For overprint see No. 245.

With Pole

1896   Typo.   Perf. 12½

166	A13	½p green	1.20	.25
167	A13	1p rose & grn	1.20	.25
168	A13	2p brown & grn	1.20	.25
169	A13	2½p ultra & grn	2.40	.25
170	A13	3p red vio & grn	3.00	3.00
171	A13	4p olive & grn	3.00	3.50
172	A13	6p violet & grn	2.00	2.00
173	A13	1sh bister & grn	2.60	.80
174	A13	2sh6p lilac & grn	3.00	3.50
		Nos. 166-174 (9)	19.60	13.80

See note following No. 135 for reprints.
For overprints and surcharges see Nos. 202-212, 214-235, 237-244, 246-251, Cape of Good Hope Nos. N5-N8.

Pietersburg Issue

Date large; "P" in Postzegel large — A18

Date small; "P" in Postzegel large — A19

Date small; "P" in Postzegel small — A20

1901   Typeset   Imperf.

Initials in Red

175	A18	½p black, green	37.50	
a.	Initials omitted		125.00	
b.	Initials in black		45.00	
176	A19	½p black, green	50.00	
a.	Initials omitted		125.00	
b.	Initials in black		52.50	
177	A20	½p black, green	50.00	
a.	Initials omitted		125.00	
b.	Initials in black		52.50	

Initials in Black

178	A18	1p black, rose	5.00	
179	A19	1p black, rose	6.50	
180	A20	1p black, rose	8.00	
181	A18	2p black, orange	7.50	
182	A19	2p black, orange	20.00	
183	A20	2p black, orange	25.00	
184	A18	4p black, dull blue	12.50	
185	A19	4p black, dull blue	15.00	
186	A20	4p black, dull blue	40.00	
187	A18	6p black, green	16.50	

188	A19	6p black, *green*	20.00	
189	A20	6p black, *green*	55.00	
190	A18	1sh black, *yellow*	12.50	
191	A19	1sh black, *yellow*	20.00	
192	A20	1sh black, *yellow*	30.00	

Perf. 11½
Initials in Red

193	A18	½p black, *green*	6.50	
194	A19	½p black, *green*	20.00	
195	A20	½p black, *green*	15.00	

Initials in Black

196	A18	1p black, *rose*	3.00	
a.		Horiz. pair, imperf. vert.	65.00	
197	A19	1p black, *rose*	3.50	
a.		Horiz. pair, imperf. vert.	100.00	
198	A20	1p black, *rose*	6.50	
a.		Horiz. pair, imperf. vert.	100.00	
199	A18	2p black, *orange*	7.50	
200	A19	2p black, *orange*	9.50	
201	A20	2p black, *orange*	17.00	

Nos. 193-201 inclusive are always imperforate on one side.

The setting consisted of 12 stamps of type A18, 6 of type A19, and 6 of type A20. Numerous type-setting varieties exist. The perforated stamps are from the first printing and were put into use first. Used stamps are not valued because all seem to show evidence of having been canceled to order.

Second British Occupation
Issued under Military Authority

Nos. 166-174, 160-161, 135 Overprinted

1900		Unwmk.	Perf. 12½	
202	A13	½p green	.35	.60
a.		"V.I.R."	700.00	
203	A13	1p rose & grn	.35	.50
204	A13	2p brown & grn	4.00	3.00
a.		"V.I.R."	700.00	750.00
205	A13	2½p ultra & grn	1.25	3.00
206	A13	3p red vio & grn	1.25	2.60
207	A13	4p olive & grn	3.75	3.25
a.		"V.I.R."	700.00	
208	A13	6p violet & grn	3.75	2.00
209	A13	1sh bister & grn	3.75	4.50
210	A13	2sh6p hel & grn	4.75	14.00
211	A13	5sh slate blue	9.50	20.00
212	A13	10sh red brown	11.50	22.00
213	A4	£5 dark green	2,500.	925.00
		Nos. 202-212 (11)	44.20	75.45

Nos. 202-213 have been extensively counterfeited. The overprint on the forgeries is clear and clean, with small periods and letters showing completely. In the genuine, letters are worn and lack many or all serifs; the periods are large and oval.

The genuine overprint exists inverted; double; with period missing after "V," after "R," after "I," etc.

Issued in Lydenburg

Overprinted in Black

1900				
214	A13	½p green	160.00	160.00
215	A13	1p rose & grn	150.00	140.00
216	A13	2p brown & grn	1,400.	1,000.
217	A13	2½p ultra & grn	2,600.	1,050.
218	A13	4p olive & grn	3,750.	1,050.
219	A13	6p violet & grn	3,250.	1,000.
220	A13	1sh bister & grn	5,500.	3,250.

Beware of counterfeits.

No. 167 Surcharged

221	A13	3p on 1p rose & grn	130.00	110.00

Issued in Rustenburg

Nos. 166-170, 172-174 Handstamped in Violet

1900			Perf. 12½	
223	A13	½p green	175.00	130.00
224	A13	1p rose & grn	130.00	100.00
225	A13	2p brown & grn	375.00	190.00
226	A13	2½p ultra & grn	210.00	130.00
227	A13	3p red vio & grn	300.00	175.00
229	A13	6p violet & grn	1,400.	500.00
230	A13	1sh bister & grn	2,000.	1,100.
231	A13	2sh6p hel & grn		8,000.

Issued in Schweizer Reneke
Nos. 166-168 and 172 Handstamped "BESIEGED" in Black

1900		Typo.	Perf. 12½	
232	A13	½p green	290.00	
233	A13	1p rose & green	300.00	
234	A13	2p brown & green	450.00	
235	A13	6p violet & green	1,150.	
		Nos. 232-235 (4)	2,190.	

Same Overprint on Cape of Good Hope No. 59 and Type of 1893
Perf. 14

236	A15	½p green	600.00	
236A	A15	1p carmine	600.00	

In 1902 five revenue stamps overprinted "V.R.I." are said to have been used postally in Volksrust. There seems to be some doubt that this issue was properly authorized for postal use.

Issued in Wolmaransstad

Nos. 166-173 Handstamped in Blue or Red

1900				
237	A13	½p green	290.00	450.00
238	A13	1p rose & grn	200.00	325.00
239	A13	2p brown & grn	2,100.	2,100.
240	A13	2½p ultra & grn (R)		2,100.
241	A13	3p red vio & grn	3,500.	3,750.
242	A13	4p olive & grn	4,750.	5,250.
243	A13	6p violet & grn	5,250.	5,750.
244	A13	1sh bister & grn		11,000.

No. 165 Overprinted in Blue

245	A17	1p red	200.00	350.00

Regular Issues
No. 166-168, 170-171, 174 Surcharged or Overprinted

1901-02				
246	A13	½p on 2p brn & grn	.80	1.20
247	A13	½p green	.60	1.75
248	A13	1p rose & grn	.60	.25
a.		Overprint "E" omitted	87.50	
249	A13	3p red vio & grn	2.60	4.25
250	A13	4p olive & grn	2.75	6.25
251	A13	2sh6p hel & grn	10.50	30.00
		Nos. 246-251 (6)	17.85	43.70

Excellent counterfeits of Nos. 246-251 are plentiful. See note after No. 213 for the recognition marks of the counterfeits.

Edward VII — A27

Nos. 260, 262 to 267 and 275 to 280 have "POSTAGE" at each side; the other stamps of type A27 have "REVENUE" at the right.

Wmk. Crown and C A (2)

1902-03		Typo.	Perf. 14	
252	A27	½p gray grn & blk	2.00	.25
253	A27	1p rose & blk	1.50	.25
254	A27	2p violet & blk	5.00	1.20
255	A27	2½p ultra & blk	11.50	1.50
256	A27	3p ol grn & blk	10.50	1.00
257	A27	4p choc & blk	10.50	2.00
258	A27	6p brn org & blk	5.00	1.20
259	A27	1sh ol grn & blk	16.50	20.00
260	A27	1sh red brn & blk	15.00	5.00
261	A27	2sh brown & blk	60.00	70.00
262	A27	2sh yel & blk	17.50	18.50
263	A27	2sh6p black & vio	18.50	17.50
264	A27	5sh vio & blk, *yel*	35.00	45.00
265	A27	10sh vio & blk, *red*	75.00	47.50
266	A27	£1 violet & grn	325.00	190.00
267	A27	£5 violet & org	1,650.	750.00
		Nos. 252-266 (15)	608.50	420.90

Issue dates: 3p, 4p, Nos. 260, 262, £1, £5, 1903. Others, Apr. 1, 1902.

1904-09			Wmk. 3	
268	A27	½p gray grn & blk	10.50	3.50
269	A27	1p rose & blk	8.00	1.20
270	A27	2p violet & blk	15.00	2.40
271	A27	2½p ultra & blk	22.00	10.00
272	A27	3p ol grn & blk	4.00	.60
273	A27	4p choc & blk	5.50	.80
274	A27	6p brn org & blk	13.00	2.40
275	A27	1sh red brn & blk	10.50	.60
276	A27	2sh yellow & blk	27.50	10.50
277	A27	2sh6p blk & red vio	55.00	10.00
278	A27	5sh vio & blk, *yel*	29.00	1.75
279	A27	10sh vio & blk, *red*	80.00	3.50
280	A27	£1 violet & grn	350.00	40.00
		Nos. 268-280 (13)	630.00	87.25

The 2p and 3p are on chalky paper, the 2½p, 4p, 6p and £1 on both chalky and ordinary, and the other values on ordinary paper only.

Issue years: ½p, 1p, 5sh, 1904. 2½p, 6p, 1sh, 1905. 2p, 3p, 4p, 2sh, 1906. 10sh, 1907. £1, 1908. 2sh6p, 1909.

1905-10				
281	A27	½p green	2.75	.25
a.		Booklet pane of 6	—	
282	A27	1p carmine	1.50	.25
a.		Wmk. 16 (anchor) ('07)	—	375.00
b.		Booklet pane of 6	—	
283	A27	2p dull vio ('10)	4.00	.75
284	A27	2½p ultra ('10)	20.00	10.00
		Nos. 281-284 (4)	28.25	11.25

Wmk. 16 is illustrated in the Cape of Good Hope.

Some of the above stamps are found with the overprint "C. S. A. R." for use by the Central South African Railway, the control mark being applied after the stamps had left the post office.

POSTAGE DUE STAMPS

D1

Wmk. Multiple Crown and C A (3)

1907		Typo.	Perf. 14	
J1	D1	½p green & blk	4.00	1.50
J2	D1	1p carmine & blk	4.75	1.00
J3	D1	2p brown org	5.75	1.50
J4	D1	3p blue & blk	8.75	5.00
J5	D1	5p violet & blk	2.75	14.00
J6	D1	6p red brown & blk	5.00	14.00
J7	D1	1sh black & car	14.00	10.00
		Nos. J1-J7 (7)	45.00	47.00

Most canceled stamps of #J1-J7 were used outside the Transvaal under the Union of South Africa administration in 1910-16.

The stamps of Transvaal were replaced by those of South Africa.

TRINIDAD
'tri-nə-ˌdad

LOCATION — West Indies, off the Venezuelan coast
GOVT. — British Colony which became part of the Colony of Trinidad and Tobago in 1889
AREA — 1,864 sq. mi.
POP. — 387,000
CAPITAL — Port of Spain

12 Pence = 1 Shilling
20 Shillings = 1 Pound

In 1847 David Bryce, owner of the "Lady McLeod," issued a blue, lithographed, imperf. stamp to prepay his 5-cent rate for carrying letters on his sail-equipped steamer between Port of Spain and San Fernando, another Trinidad port. The stamp pictures the "Lady McLeod" above the monogram "LMcL," expressing no denomination. Value, unused, $50,000, used (pen canceled), $12,500. Used stamps canceled by having a corner skinned off are worth less.

Values for unused stamps are for examples with original gum as defined in the catalogue introduction. However, Nos. 9-12 are seldom found with gum, and these are valued without gum.

Values for Nos. 18-26 are for stamps with pin perforations on two or three sides. Stamps with pin perforations on all four sides are not often seen and command large premiums.

Very fine examples of Nos. 27-47 will have perforations touching the design on one or more sides due to the narrow spacing of the stamps on the plates and imperfect perforating methods. These stamps with perfs clear of the design on all four sides are scarce and command substantially higher prices.

"Britannia"
A1　　　　A2

1851-56　Unwmk. Engr.　Imperf.
Blued Paper

1	A1	(1p) brick red ('56)	200.00	85.00
a.		(1p) brown red ('53)	360.00	77.50
2	A1	(1p) purple brown	20.00	90.00
3	A1	(1p) blue	21.00	72.50
a.		(1p) deep blue, deeply blued paper	175.00	95.00
4	A1	(1p) gray brn ('53)	57.50	90.00
a.		(1p) gray ('52)	90.00	77.50
		Nos. 1-4 (4)	298.50	337.50

1854-57　White Paper

6	A1	(1p) brown red ('57)	3,250.	77.50
7	A1	(1p) gray	55.00	95.00
8	A1	(1p) black violet	32.50	100.00

See Nos. 14, 18, 22, 27, 33, 39, 43, 45, 48, 58. For surcharges see Nos. 62-64.

1852　Litho.
Fine Impressions
Yellowish Paper

9	A2	(1p) blue	11,500.	1,950.
a.		(1p) deep blue	11,500.	1,950.
b.		White paper		1,950.

1853　Bluish Paper

10	A2	(1p) blue	10,000.	2,400.

Same, Lines of Background More or Less Worn
1855-60　Thin Paper

11	A2	(1p) slate blue	5,500.	800.00
12	A2	(1p) blue	5,000.	500.00
a.		(1p) greenish blue		800.00
13	A2	(1p) rose	17.50	750.00
a.		(1p) dull red	17.50	725.00

A3

1859　Engr.　Imperf.
White Paper

14	A1	(1p) dull rose	—	—
15	A3	4p gray lilac	125.00	400.00
a.		4p dull lilac		
16	A3	6p green	15,000.	525.00
17	A3	1sh slate blue	125.00	425.00

Pin-perf. 12½

18	A1	(1p) dull rose red	2,000.	70.00
a.		(1p) lake	2,250.	70.00
19	A3	4p brown lilac	—	1,250.
a.		4p dull purple	7,500.	1,250.
20	A3	6p deep green	3,500.	250.00
a.		6p yellow green	3,500.	250.00
21	A3	1sh black violet	9,000.	1,750.

Pin-perf. 14

22	A1	(1p) rose red	275.00	35.00
a.		(1p) carmine	325.00	37.50
23	A3	4p brown lilac	250.00	150.00
a.		4p violet	600.00	160.00
b.		4p dull violet	1,650.	125.00
24	A3	6p deep green	800.00	100.00
25	A3	6p yellow green	200.00	160.00
a.		Vert. pair, imperf. between		8,000.
26	A3	1sh black violet	9,000.	1,150.

1860　Clean-cut Perf. 14 to 15½

27	A1	(1p) dull rose	175.00	67.50
a.		(1p) lake	100.00	40.00
b.		Horiz. pair, imperf. vert.	3,000.	
29	A3	4p violet brown	200.00	95.00
a.		4p dull violet		375.00

30	A3	6p deep green	300.00	175.00
31	A3	6p yellow green	475.00	110.00
32	A3	1sh black violet		

1861　Rough Perf. 14 to 16½

33	A1	(1p) dull rose	160.00	32.50
34	A3	4p gray lilac	750.00	100.00
35	A3	4p brown lilac	325.00	85.00
a.		4p dull violet	750.00	115.00
36	A3	6p green	475.00	85.00
a.		6p blue green	325.00	95.00
37	A3	1sh indigo	1,000.	350.00
a.		1sh purplish blue	1,675.	550.00

Thick Paper
1863　Perf. 11½ to 12

39	A1	(1p) carmine	160.00	25.00
a.		Perf. 11½-12x11	2,000.	600.00
40	A3	4p dull violet	225.00	72.50
41	A3	6p dp blue green	1,350.	100.00
a.		Perf. 11½-12x11		8,000.
42	A3	1sh indigo	2,750.	110.00

Perf. 12½

43	A1	(1p) lake	60.00	25.00

Perf. 13

45	A1	(1p) lake	30.00	25.00
46	A3	6p emerald	500.00	60.00
47	A3	1sh brt violet	4,500.	300.00

1864-72　Wmk. 1　Perf. 12½

48	A1	(1p) red	65.00	3.50
a.		(1p) lake	65.00	7.25
b.		(1p) rose	65.00	3.00
c.		(1p) carmine	65.00	3.50
d.		Imperf., pair	800.00	800.00
49	A3	4p brt violet	150.00	18.00
a.		4p pale violet	250.00	21.00
b.		Imperf.		600.00
50	A3	4p lilac	200.00	21.00
a.		4p gray lilac		
51	A3	4p gray ('72)	160.00	7.50
52	A3	6p blue green	175.00	9.00
a.		6p emerald	110.00	17.50
53	A3	6p yellow grn	100.00	6.00
a.		6p dp grn	500.00	9.00
b.		Imperf., pair		800.00
54	A3	1sh purple	200.00	10.00
a.		1sh lilac	150.00	10.00
b.		1sh violet	150.00	10.00
c.		1sh red lilac	160.00	11.00
d.		Imperf.		750.00
55	A3	1sh orange yel ('72)	175.00	2.00
		Nos. 48-55 (8)	1,225.	77.00

See Nos. 59-61A, 65. For surcharge see No. 67.

Queen Victoria — A4

1869-94　Typo.　Perf. 12½

56	A4	5sh dull lake	200.00	90.00
a.		Imperf., pair	1,250.	

Perf. 14

57	A4	5sh claret ('94)	67.50	100.00

For overprint see No. O7.

1876　Engr.　Perf. 14

58	A1	(1p) carmine	42.50	2.75
a.		(1p) red	60.00	2.75
b.		(1p) carmine	42.50	2.75
c.		Half used as ½p on cover		750.00
59	A3	4p gray	140.00	1.50
60	A3	6p yellow green	115.00	4.00
a.		6p deep green	150.00	3.00
61	A3	1sh orange yellow	150.00	4.50
		Nos. 58-61 (4)	447.50	12.75

Perf. 14x12½

61A	A3	6p yellow green		6,750.

Value for No. 61A is for stamp with perfs barely touching the design.

Type A1 Surcharged in Black

HALFPENNY

1879　Wmk. 1　Perf. 14

62	A1	½p lilac	14.50	10.00

Same Surcharge
1882　Wmk. Crown and C A (2)

63	A1	½p lilac	250.00	90.00
64	A1	1p carmine	60.00	2.50
a.		Half used as ½p on cover		675.00

Type of 1859
1882　Wmk. 2

65	A3	4p gray	215.00	12.00

No. 60 Surcharged by pen and ink in Black or Red

1882　Wmk. 1

67	A3	1p on 6p green (R)	13.00	7.50
a.		Half used as ½p on cover		400.00
b.		Black surcharge		1,900.

Counterfeits of No. 67b are plentiful. Various handwriting exists on both 60 and 60a.

A7

1883-84　Typo.　Wmk. 2

68	A7	½p green	8.50	1.50
69	A7	1p rose	16.00	.60
a.		Half used as ½p on cover		950.00
70	A7	2½p ultra	20.00	.70
a.		2½p blue	21.00	.75
71	A7	4p slate	3.50	.70
72	A7	6p olive brn ('84)	6.00	6.50
73	A7	1sh orange brn ('84)	8.50	4.75
		Nos. 68-73 (6)	62.50	14.75

For overprints see Nos. O1-O6.

A8　　　　A9

ONE ONE
Type I　Type II

ONE PENNY:
Type I — Round "O" in "ONE."
Type II — Oval "O" in "ONE."

1896-1904　Perf. 14

74	A8	½p lilac & green	4.00	.35
75	A8	½p gray grn ('02)	.75	2.40
76	A8	1p lil & car, type I	4.25	.25
77	A8	1p lil & car, type II ('00)	400.00	4.75
78	A8	1p blk, red, type II ('01)	2.25	.25
a.		Value omitted	36,000.	
79	A8	2½p lilac & ultra	7.25	.25
80	A8	2½p vio & bl, bl ('02)	20.00	.75
81	A8	4p lilac & orange	7.75	21.00
82	A8	4p grn & ultra, buff ('02)	2.25	20.00
83	A8	5p lilac & violet	9.50	16.00
84	A8	6p lilac & black	9.00	6.50
85	A8	1sh grn & org brn	8.25	7.75
86	A8	1sh blk & bl, yel ('04)	22.50	6.50

Wmk. C A over Crown (46)

87	A9	5sh green & org	55.00	90.00
88	A9	5sh lil & red vio ('02)	60.00	77.50
89	A9	10sh grn & ultra	250.00	425.00
		Revenue cancel		30.00
90	A9	£1 grn & car	180.00	275.00
		Nos. 74-90 (17)	1,042.	954.25

No. 82 also exists on chalky paper. Nos. 88 and 90 exist on both ordinary and chalky paper.
Circular "Registrar General" cancels are revenue usage and of minimal value.
See Nos. 92-104.

Landing of
Columbus — A10

1898   **Engr.**   **Wmk. 1**
91   A10   2p gray vio & yel brn   2.50   1.25
     Overprinted "SPECIMEN"   60.00

400th anniv. of the discovery of the island of Trinidad by Columbus, July 31, 1498.

1904-09   **Wmk. 3**   **Chalky Paper**
92   A8   ½p gray green   9.00   2.25
  a.   Ordinary paper   6.00   1.25
93   A8   1p blk, *red*, type II   10.00   .25
  a.   Ordinary paper   10.00   .25
94   A8   2½p vio & bl, *bl*   27.50   1.10
95   A8   4p blk & car, *yel*
          ('06)   4.50   11.00
96   A8   6p lilac & blk ('05)   21.00   18.00
97   A8   6p vio & dp vio
          ('06)   8.50   14.00
98   A8   1sh blk & bl, *yel*   24.00   9.50
99   A8   1sh blk & bl, *yel*   13.00   22.50
100   A8   1sh blk, *grn* ('06)   2.25   1.50
101   A9   5sh lil & red vio
          ('07)   65.00   110.00
102   A9   £1 grn & car ('07)   200.00   300.00
     Nos. 92-102 (11)   384.75   490.10

For overprints see Nos. O8-O9.

1906-07
103   A8   1p carmine ('07)   2.50   .25
104   A8   2½p ultramarine   7.00   .25

A11   A12

1909   **Ordinary Paper**
105   A11   ½p gray green   8.00   .25
106   A12   1p carmine   8.00   .25
107   A11   2½p ultramarine   22.50   3.75
     Nos. 105-107 (3)   38.50   4.25

For overprint see No. O10.

POSTAGE DUE STAMPS

D1

Wmk. Crown and C A (2)
1885, Jan. 1   **Typo.**   **Perf. 14**
J1   D1   ½p black   22.50   55.00
J2   D1   1p black   9.00   .25
J3   D1   2p black   40.00   .25
J4   D1   3p black   60.00   .50
J5   D1   4p black   47.50   5.50
J6   D1   5p black   27.50   .70
J7   D1   6p black   45.00   9.00
J8   D1   8p black   65.00   4.00
J9   D1   1sh black   80.00   9.00
     Nos. J1-J9 (9)   396.50   84.20

1906-07   **Wmk. 3**
J10   D1   1p black   7.00   .25
J11   D1   2p black   35.00   .25
J12   D1   3p black   15.00   3.25
J13   D1   4p black   15.00   18.00
J14   D1   5p black   17.50   16.00
J15   D1   6p black   7.25   13.00
J16   D1   8p black   14.50   16.00
J17   D1   1sh black   21.00   42.50
     Nos. J10-J17 (8)   132.25   109.25

See Trinidad and Tobago Nos. J1-J16.

OFFICIAL STAMPS

Postage Stamps of
1869-84 Overprinted in
Black

1893-94   **Wmk. 2**   **Perf. 14**
O1   A7   ½p green   42.50   65.00
O2   A7   1p rose   45.00   72.50
O3   A7   2½p ultra   55.00   110.00
O4   A7   4p slate   57.50   115.00
O5   A7   6p olive brown   57.50   115.00
O6   A7   1sh orange brown   77.50   160.00

Wmk. Crown and C C (1)
Perf. 12½
O7   A4   5sh dull lake   190.00   750.00
     Nos. O1-O7 (7)   525.00   1,387.

Nos. 92 and 103
Overprinted

1909-10   **Wmk. 3**   **Perf. 14**
O8   A8   ½p gray green   2.50   9.00
O9   A8   1p carmine   2.25   9.50
  a.   Double overprint   375.00
  b.   Inverted overprint   900.00   275.00
  c.   Vertical overprint   140.00   160.00

Same Overprint on No. 105

1910
O10   A11   ½p gray green   9.00   12.00

Stamps of Trinidad have been superseded by those inscribed "Trinidad and Tobago."

TRINIDAD & TOBAGO

ˈtri-nə-ˌdad and tə-ˈbā-ˌgō

LOCATION — West Indies off the coast of Venezuela
GOVT. — Republic
AREA — 1,980 sq. mi.
POP. — 1,102,096 (1999 est.)
CAPITAL — Port-of-Spain

The two British colonies of Trinidad and Tobago were united from 1889 until 1899, when Tobago became a ward of the united colony. From 1899 until 1913 postage stamps of Trinidad were used. The two islands became a state in August 1962, and the independent Republic of Trinidad and Tobago on August 1, 1976.

12 Pence = 1 Shilling
20 Shillings = 1 Pound
100 Cents = 1 Dollar (1935)

Catalogue values for unused stamps in this country are for Never Hinged items, beginning with Scott 62 in the regular postage section and Scott J9 in the postage due section.

"Britannia"
A1   A2

1913   **Typo.**   **Wmk. 3**   **Perf. 14**
Ordinary Paper
1   A1   ½p green   3.50   .25
2   A1   1p scarlet   1.75   .25
  a.   1p carmine   2.75   .25

4   A1   2½p ultra   8.00   .50
Chalky Paper
5   A1   4p scar & blk, *yel*   .80   7.00
6   A1   6p red vio & dull vio   11.00   8.00
7   A1   1sh black, *emerald*   1.75   3.50
  a.   1sh black, *green*   2.00   5.00
  b.   1sh black, *bl grn, ol back*   11.00   10.00
     Nos. 1-2,4-7 (6)   26.80   19.50

1914   **Surface-colored Paper**
8   A1   4p scar & blk, *yel*   2.00   11.00
9   A1   1sh black, *green*   1.60   12.00
Chalky Paper
10   A2   5sh dull vio & red
          vio   75.00   110.00
11   A2   £1 green & car   190.00   250.00
     Nos. 8-11 (4)   268.60   383.00

1921-22   **Wmk. 4**
Ordinary Paper
12   A1   ½p green   3.50   2.75
13   A1   1p scarlet   .75   .40
14   A1   1p brown ('22)   .75   1.90
15   A1   2p gray ('22)   1.25   1.50
16   A1   2½p ultra   1.00   22.50
17   A1   3p ultra ('22)   6.00   4.00
Chalky Paper
18   A1   6p red vio & dull
          vio   3.50   19.00
19   A2   5sh dull vio & red
          vio   65.00   160.00
20   A2   £1 green & car   150.00   325.00
     Nos. 12-20 (9)   231.75   537.05

For overprints see #B2-B3, MR1-MR13, O1-O5.

"Britannia" and
King
George V — A3

1922-28   **Ordinary Paper**
21   A3   ½p green   .55   .25
22   A3   1p brown   .55   .25
23   A3   1½p rose red   2.50   .25
24   A3   2p gray   .55   1.40
25   A3   3p ultra   .55   1.40
Chalky Paper
26   A3   4p red & blk, *yel*
          ('28)   3.75   3.75
27   A3   6p red vio & dl vio   2.50   29.00
28   A3   6p red & grn, *emer*
          ('24)   1.40   .70
29   A3   1sh blk, *emer* ('25)   6.25   2.00
30   A3   5sh vio & dull vio   25.00   42.50
31   A3   £1 rose & green   150.00   275.00
Wmk. Multiple Crown and C A (3)
Chalky Paper
32   A3   4p red & blk, *yel*   3.75   14.00
33   A3   1sh blk, *emerald*   4.00   11.00
     Nos. 21-33 (13)   201.35   381.50

First Boca — A4

Designs: 2c, Agricultural College. 3c, Mt. Irvine Bay, Tobago. 6c, Discovery of Lake Asphalt. 8c, Queen's Park, Savannah. 12c, Town Hall, San Fernando. 24c, Government House. 48c, Memorial Park. 72c, Blue Basin.

1935-37   **Engr.**   **Wmk. 4**   **Perf. 12**
34   A4   1c emer & bl, perf.
          12½ ('36)   .40   .25
  a.   Perf. 12   .50   1.10
35   A4   2c lt brn & ultra,
          perf. 12   2.00   1.25
  a.   Perf. 12½ ('36)   1.50   .25
36   A4   3c red & black,
          perf. 12½ ('36)   3.25   .40
  a.   Perf. 12   1.75   .40
37   A4   6c bl & brn, perf.
          12   5.00   3.00
  a.   Perf. 12½ ('37)   12.00   7.00
38   A4   8c red org & yel
          grn   4.50   4.25
39   A4   12c dk violet & blk   4.00   2.25
  a.   Perf. 12½ ('37)   12.00   8.50
40   A4   24c ol grn & blk   6.50   2.50
  a.   Perf. 12½ ('37)   18.00   15.00
41   A4   48c slate green   11.00   19.00
42   A4   72c mag & sl grn   35.00   40.00
     Nos. 34-42 (9)   71.65   72.90

Common Design Types
pictured following the introduction.

Silver Jubilee Issue
Common Design Type
1935, May 6   **Perf. 11x12**
43   CD301   2c black & ultra   .40   1.00
44   CD301   3c car & blue   .40   2.00
45   CD301   6c ultra & brn   2.00   3.50
46   CD301   24c brn vio &
              ind   9.00   21.00
     Nos. 43-46 (4)   11.80   27.50
     Set, never hinged   22.00

Coronation Issue
Common Design Type
1937, May 12   **Perf. 13½x14**
47   CD302   1c deep green   .25   .25
48   CD302   2c yellow brown   .25   .25
49   CD302   8c deep orange   .50   .50
     Nos. 47-49 (3)   1.00   1.00
     Set, never hinged   1.50

First
Boca — A13

George VI — A14

Various Frames and: 2c, Agricultural College. 3c, Mt. Irvine Bay, Tobago. 4c, Memorial Park. 5c, General Post Office and Treasury. 6c, Discovery of Lake Asphalt. 8c, Queen's Park, Savannah. 12c, Town Hall, San Fernando. 24c, Government House. 60c, Blue Basin.

Perf. 11½x11
1938-41   **Wmk. 4**   **Engr.**
50   A13   1c emer &
          blue   .50   .25
51   A13   2c lt brn & ul-
          tra   .60   .25
52   A13   3c dk car & blk   7.00   1.00
52A   A13   3c vio brn & bl
          grn ('41)   .25   .25
53   A13   4c brown   17.50   2.50
53A   A13   4c red ('41)   .30   .25
54   A13   5c mag ('41)   .30   .25
55   A13   6c brt bl & sep   1.25   .75
56   A13   8c red org &
          yel grn   1.50   1.00
57   A13   12c dk vio & blk   2.00   .25
58   A13   24c dk ol grn &
          blk   2.75   .25
59   A13   60c mag & sl
          grn   6.50   1.75
Perf. 12
60   A14 $1.20 dk grn ('40)   8.00   1.50
61   A14 $4.80 rose pink
          ('40)   22.50   50.00
     Nos. 50-61 (14)   70.95   60.25
     Set, never hinged   115.00

Watermark sideways on Nos. 50-59.

Catalogue values for unused stamps in this section, from this point to the end of the section, are for Never Hinged items.

Peace Issue
Common Design Type
Perf. 13½x14
1946, Oct. 1   **Engr.**   **Wmk. 4**
62   CD303   3c brown   .25   .25
63   CD303   6c deep blue   .25   .25

Silver Wedding Issue
Common Design Types
1948, Nov. 22 Photo.   **Perf. 14x14½**
64   CD304   3c red brown   .25   .25

           Engr.   **Perf. 11½x11**
65   CD305 $4.80 rose car   32.50   40.00

UPU Issue
Common Design Types
Engr.; Name Typo. on 6c, 12c
Perf. 13½, 11x11½
1949, Oct. 10   **Wmk. 4**
66   CD306   5c red violet   .40   .40
67   CD307   6c indigo   2.00   2.00
68   CD308   12c rose violet   .50   .50
69   CD309   24c olive   .50   .50
     Nos. 66-69 (4)   3.40   3.40

University Issue
Common Design Types
Inscribed: "Trinidad"

1951, Feb. 16   Engr.   Perf. 14x14½

70	CD310	3c chocolate & grn	.25	.25
71	CD311	12c purple & blk	.60	.50

Types of 1938 with Portrait of Queen Elizabeth II

1953, Apr. 20   Perf. 11½x11

72	A13	1c yel grn & dp blue	.25	.25
73	A13	2c org brn & sl blue	.25	.25
74	A13	3c vio brn & blue grn	.25	.25
75	A13	4c red	.25	.25
76	A13	5c magenta	.55	.35
77	A13	6c blue & brown	.55	.35
78	A13	8c red org & dp grn	2.50	.35
79	A13	12c dk violet & blk	.35	.25
80	A13	24c dk ol grn & blk	2.50	.35
81	A13	60c rose car & grnsh blk	25.00	1.25

Perf. 11½

82	A14	$1.20 dark green	1.40	.65
a.		Perf. 12	3.50	2.00
83	A14	$4.80 rose pink	10.00	16.00
a.		Perf. 12	15.00	17.50
		Nos. 72-83 (12)	43.55	20.45

For surcharge see No. 85.

Coronation Issue
Common Design Type

1953, June 3   Perf. 13½x13

84	CD312	3c dark green & blk	.25	.25

No. 73 Surcharged "ONE CENT"
Perf. 11½x11

1956, Dec. 20   Wmk. 4

85	A13	1c on 2c org brn & sl blue	1.75	2.00

West Indies Federation
Common Design Type
Perf. 11½x11

1958, Apr. 22   Engr.   Wmk. 314

86	CD313	5c green	.25	.25
87	CD313	6c blue	.25	.40
88	CD313	12c carmine rose	.30	.25
		Nos. 86-88 (3)	.80	.90

Cipriani
Memorial, Port-
of-Spain
A27

Queen's Hall,
Port-of-Spain
A28

Designs: 5c, Whitehall. 6c, Treasury Building. 8c, Governor General's House. 10c, General Hospital, San Fernando. 12c, Oil refinery. 15c, Crest of colony. 25c, Scarlet ibis. 35c, Lake Asphalt (Pitch). 50c, Jinnah Memorial Mosque. 60c, Anthurium lilies. $1.20, Copper-rumped hummingbird and hibiscus. $4.80, Map.

Perf. 13½x14, 14x13½

1960, Sept. 24   Photo.   Wmk. 314
Size: 22½x25mm, 25x22½mm

89	A27	1c dark gray & buff	.25	.25
a.		Wmkd. sideways ('66)	.50	.50
90	A28	2c ultra	.25	.25
91	A28	5c dark blue	.25	.25
92	A28	6c lt red brown	.25	.25
93	A28	8c yellow green	.25	.35
94	A28	10c light purple	.25	.25
95	A28	12c bright red	.25	.25
96	A28	15c orange	1.10	.55
97	A28	25c dk blue & crim	.90	.25
98	A28	35c green & black	4.00	.25
99	A28	50c blue, yel & olive	.40	.45
100	A27	60c multicolored	.60	.25
a.		Perf. 14 ('65)	160.00	40.00

Size: 48x25mm

101	A28	$1.20 multicolored	16.00	3.00
102	A28	$4.80 lt bl & lt yel grn	25.00	17.50
		Nos. 89-102 (14)	49.75	24.10

See #116. For overprints see #123-124, 126.

Scouts and Map of Trinidad and Tobago — A29

1961, Apr. 4   Perf. 13½x14

103	A29	8c multicolored	.25	.25
104	A29	25c multicolored	.35	.35

2nd Caribbean Scout Jamboree, Valsayn Park, Trinidad, Apr. 4-14.

Independent State

Underwater Scene from Painting by Carlisle Chang — A30

Designs: 8c, Elizabeth II and new Terminal Building, Piarco Airport. 25c, Elizabeth II and Hilton Hotel. 35c, Map and greater bird of paradise. 60c, Map and scarlet ibis.

1962, Aug. 31   Photo.   Perf. 14½

105	A30	5c blue green	.35	.25
106	A30	8c slate	.55	.25
107	A30	25c purple	.35	.25
108	A30	35c emer, yel, brn & blk	3.00	.25
109	A30	60c ultra, black & ver	3.75	4.00
		Nos. 105-109 (5)	8.00	5.00

Issued to mark Trinidad and Tobago's independence, Aug. 31, 1962.

Freedom from Hunger Issue

Protein Food — A31

1963, June 1   Perf. 14x13½

110	A31	5c henna brown	.25	.25
111	A31	8c citron	.25	.25
112	A31	25c violet blue	.60	.60
		Nos. 110-112 (3)	1.10	1.10

See note in Common Design section.

Girl Guide Emblem A32

Perf. 14½x14

1964, Sept. 15   Wmk. 314

113	A32	6c red, dk blue & yel	.25	.25
114	A32	25c brt blue, dk bl & yel	.25	.25
115	A32	35c lt green, dk bl & yel	.30	.30
		Nos. 113-115 (3)	.80	.80

50th anniv. of the Trinidad and Tobago Girl Guide Association.

Arms of Independent State — A33

1964, Sept. 15   Perf. 14x13½

116	A33	15c orange	.40	.40

For overprint see No. 125.

ICY Emblem A34

Unwmk.
1965, Nov. 15   Litho.   Perf. 12
Granite Paper

117	A34	35c dull yel, red brn & grn	.70	.70

International Cooperation Year, 1965.

Eleanor Roosevelt — A35

Perf. 13½x14

1965, Dec. 10   Wmk. 314

118	A35	25c vio blue, red & blk	.40	.40

Issued to honor Eleanor Roosevelt and to publicize the Eleanor Roosevelt Memorial Foundation.

"Redhouse," Parliament Building — A36

8c, Map of Trinidad & Tobago, royal yacht "Britannia," arms of State. 25c, Flag, map. 35c, Flag, Trinity Hills, General Post Office, sugar cane, coconut palms, derricks.

1966, Feb. 8   Photo.   Wmk. 314

119	A36	5c ultra, red, blk & grn	.55	.25
120	A36	8c ultra, sil, blk & yel brn	2.50	.30
121	A36	25c red, blk & emerald	2.50	1.40
122	A36	35c ultra, red, blk & grn	2.50	1.90
		Nos. 119-122 (4)	8.05	3.85

Visit of Elizabeth II and Prince Philip.

Nos. 93, 94, 116 and 100 Overprinted:
"FIFTH YEAR OF / INDEPENDENCE /
31st AUGUST 1967"
Perf. 14x13½, 13½x14

1967, Aug. 31   Photo.   Wmk. 314

123	A28	8c yellow green	.25	.25
124	A28	10c lt purple	.25	.25
125	A33	15c orange	.25	.25
126	A27	60c multicolored	.30	.30
		Nos. 123-126 (4)	1.05	1.05

On 60c, the overprint is arranged in 5 lines.

Carnival Symbols A37

Designs: 10c, Calypso King, vert. 15c, Steel band. 25c, Chinese masks. 35c, Carnival King, vert. 60c, Carnival Queen, vert.

Unwmk.
1968, Feb. 16   Litho.   Perf. 12

127	A37	5c pink & multi	.25	.25
128	A37	10c vio blue & multi	.25	.25
129	A37	15c multicolored	.25	.25
130	A37	25c multicolored	.25	.25
131	A37	35c dk purple & multi	.25	.25
132	A37	60c brown ol & multi	.45	.45
		Nos. 127-132 (6)	1.70	1.70

Issued to publicize the Trinidad Carnival.

WHO Emblem and Eye Examination A38

Dancing Children and Human Rights Flame A39

Wmk. 314

1968, May 7   Photo.   Perf. 14

133	A38	5c rose red, gold & blk	.25	.25
134	A38	25c orange, gold & blk	.30	.30
135	A38	35c brt blue, gold & blk	.40	.40
		Nos. 133-135 (3)	.95	.95

1968, Aug. 5   Perf. 14

136	A39	5c carmine, yel & blk	.25	.25
137	A39	10c brt blue, yel & blk	.25	.25
138	A39	25c yel grn, yel & blk	.25	.25
		Nos. 136-138 (3)	.75	.75

International Human Rights Year.

Bicycling and Map A40

Designs (Olympic Rings, Map of Trinidad and Tobago and): 15c, Weight lifting. 25c, Relay race. 35c, Running. $1.20, Map of Mexico and flags of Mexico and Trinidad and Tobago.

Photo.; Gold Impressed (except $1.20)

1968, Oct. 12   Perf. 14

139	A40	5c vio, gold & multi	.25	.25
140	A40	15c red, gold & multi	.25	.25
141	A40	25c org, gold & multi	.25	.25
142	A40	35c brt grn, gold & multi	.35	.25
143	A40	$1.20 blue, gold & multi	1.25	.80
		Nos. 139-143 (5)	2.35	1.80

19th Olympic Games, Mexico City, 10/12-27.

Cacao A41

Designs: 3c, Sugar refinery. 5c, Redtailed chachalaca. 6c, Oil refinery. 8c, Fertilizer plant. 10c, Green hermit (hummingbird) vert. 12c, Citrus fruit, vert. 15c, Coat of arms, vert. 20c, 25c, Flag and map of islands, vert. 30c, Wild poinsettia, vert. 40c, Scarlet ibis. 50c, Maracas Bay. $1, Blooming tabebuia (tree) vert. $2.50, Fishermen hauling in net. $5, Red House, Port-of-Spain.

Photo.; Silver or Gold Impressed

1969, Apr. 1   Wmk. 314   Perf. 14

144	A41	1c silver & multi	.25	.25
145	A41	3c gold & multi	.25	.25
a.		Wmk. upright ('74)	.60	.60
146	A41	5c gold & multi	.25	.25
a.		Wmk. upright ('73)	8.00	4.50
147	A41	6c gold & multi	.25	.25
a.		Wmk. upright ('74)	.30	.25
148	A41	8c silver & multi	.25	.25
149	A41	10c gold & multi	.25	.25
b.		Wmk. 373 ('76)	.30	.25
150	A41	12c silver & multi	.25	.25
151	A41	15c silver & multi	.25	.25
152	A41	20c gold & multi	.25	.25
153	A41	25c silver & multi	.30	.25
154	A41	30c silver & multi	.35	.25
155	A41	40c gold & multi	.55	.35
156	A41	50c silver & multi	.70	.50
157	A41	$1 gold & multi	1.75	1.25
158	A41	$2.50 gold & multi	4.25	5.00
159	A41	$5 gold & multi	8.75	9.00
		Nos. 144-159 (16)	18.90	18.85

For overprint see No. 187.

Capt. A. A. Cipriani, ILO Emblem and Gate A42

ILO, 50th Anniv.: 15c, Industrial Court's & ILO emblems, & Woodford Square gate.

1969, May 1   Photo.   Perf. 12   Unwmk.
160 A42 6c dp car, gold & blk   .25 .25
161 A42 15c brt blue, gold & blk   .25 .25

Union Jack and Flags of CARIFTA Members A43

Designs: 6c, Cornucopia, vert. 30c, Map of Caribbean, vert. 40c, Jet plane and "Strength through Unity" emblem.

1969, Aug. 1   Perf. 14x13½, 13½x14
162 A43 6c lilac, gold & multi   .25 .25
163 A43 10c multicolored   .25 .25
164 A43 30c red, emer, blk & gold   .25 .25
165 A43 40c blue, blk, grn & gold   .35 .35
    Nos. 162-165 (4)   1.10 1.10

Caribbean Free Trade Area (CARIFTA).

Moon Landing and Earth — A44

40c, Lunar landing module & astronauts on moon. $1, Astronauts Aldrin at control panel, Armstrong collecting rocks.

1969, Sept. 1   Litho.   Perf. 14
166 A44 6c multi   .25 .25
167 A44 40c multi, vert.   .30 .30
168 A44 $1 multi   .75 .75
    Nos. 166-168 (3)   1.30 1.30

See note after US No. C76.

Maces of Senate and House of Representatives — A45

10c, Chamber of Parliament. 15c, View of Kennedy Complex, University of the West Indies at St. Augustine. 40c, Cannon & view of Scarborough from Fort King George.

1969, Oct. 23   Photo.   Wmk. 314   Perf. 14x13½
169 A45 10c multicolored   .25 .25
170 A45 15c multicolored   .25 .25
171 A45 30c lt blue & multi   .25 .25
172 A45 40c multicolored   .25 .25
    Nos. 169-172 (4)   1.00 1.00

15th Conf. of the Commonwealth Parliamentary Assoc., Port-of-Spain, Oct. 4-19.

Congress Emblem and Landscape A46   Carnival King as "Man in the Moon" A47

6c, Congress emblem (steel drum and bird). 30c, Palms, landscape and emblem, horiz.

1969, Nov. 2   Litho.   Unwmk.   Perf. 14x13½, 13½x14
173 A46 6c red, black & gold   .25 .25
174 A46 30c lt blue, plum & gold   .25 .25
175 A46 40c ultra, black & gold   .25 .25
    Nos. 173-175 (3)   .75 .75

24th Cong. of the Intl. Junior Chamber of Commerce.

1970, Feb. 2   Wmk. 314   Perf. 14

Designs: 6c, Carnival Queen as "City Beneath the Sea." 15c, Bambara god (antelope) from the Band of the Year. 30c, Pheasant Queen (Chanticleer) of Malaya. 40c, Steel Band of the Year with 1969 Calypso and Road March Kings, horiz.

176 A47 5c dk brown & multi   .25 .25
177 A47 6c dk blue & multi   .25 .25
178 A47 15c violet bl & multi   .25 .25
179 A47 30c dk green & multi   .25 .25
180 A47 40c green & multi   .25 .25
    Nos. 176-180 (5)   1.25 1.25

Issued to publicize the Trinidad Carnival.

Mahatma Gandhi and Indian Flag — A48

Design: 10c, Gandhi monument, vert.

1970, Mar. 2   Photo.   Unwmk.   Perf. 12
181 A48 10c ultra & multi   .60 .50
182 A48 30c crimson & multi   1.40 1.10

Mohandas K. Gandhi (1869-1948), leader in India's fight for independence.

"Culture, Science, Arts and Technology" A49

UN, 25th Anniv.: 10c, Children of various races, map of Trinidad and Tobago and "UNICEF." 20c, Noah's ark, rainbow, dove and UN emblem.

1970, June 26   Photo.   Perf. 13½
183 A49 5c multicolored   .25 .25
184 A49 10c multicolored   .50 .50
185 A49 20c multicolored   .75 .75
    Nos. 183-185 (3)   1.50 1.50

UPU Headquarters, Bern — A50

1970, June 26   Unwmk.   Perf. 12
186 A50 30c ultra & multi   .50 .50

Opening of new UPU Headquarters in Bern.

No. 146 Overprinted: "NATIONAL / COMMERCIAL / BANK / ESTABLISHED / 1.7.70"
Photo.; Gold Embossed
1970, July 1   Wmk. 314   Perf. 14
187 A41 5c gold & multi   .30 .25

San Fernando Town Hall — A51

Designs: 3c, East Indian Immigrants, 1820, after painting by Cazabon, vert. 40c, Ships in San Fernando Harbor, 1860, after painting by Michel J. Cazabon.

1970, Nov.   Litho.   Wmk. 314   Perf. 14x13½, 13½x14
188 A51 3c bister & multi   .25 .25
189 A51 5c lemon & multi   .25 .25
190 A51 40c lemon & multi   .75 .75
    Nos. 188-190 (3)   1.25 1.25

Municipality of San Fernando, 125th anniv.

Madonna and Child, by Titian — A52

Paintings: 3c, Adoration of the Shepherds, School of Saville. 30c, Adoration of the Shepherds, by Louis Le Nain. 40c, Virgin and Child with St. John and Angel, by Morando. $1, Adoration of the Magi, by Paolo Veronese.

1970, Dec. 8   Unwmk.   Litho.   Perf. 13½
191 A52 3c dull org & multi   .25 .25
  a. Booklet pane of 2   .20
192 A52 5c brt pink & multi   .25 .25
  a. Booklet pane of 2   .25
193 A52 30c lt utra & multi   .25 .25
  a. Booklet pane of 2   .60
194 A52 40c yellow grn & multi   .25 .25
  a. Booklet pane of 2   .75
  b. Souvenir sheet of 4, #191-194   2.75 2.75
195 A52 $1 pale lilac & multi   .60 .60
    Nos. 191-195 (5)   1.60 1.60

Brocket Deer — A53

1971, Aug. 9   Litho.   Perf. 14x13½   Wmk. 314
196 A53 3c shown   .40 .25
197 A53 5c Collared peccary   .50 .25
198 A53 6c Paca   .60 .40
199 A53 30c Agouti   1.75 3.25
200 A53 40c Ocelot   1.75 2.40
    Nos. 196-200 (5)   5.00 6.55

Capt. A. A. Cipriani A54   Virgin and Child with St. John, by Bartolommeo A55

Design: 30c, Chaconia medal (for distinction in social field).

1971, Aug. 31   Perf. 14
201 A54 5c multicolored   .25 .25
202 A54 30c multicolored   .30 .30

9th anniversary of independence. Capt. Arthur Andrew Cipriani (died 1945) was mayor of Port of Spain and member of First Executive Council.

1971, Oct. 25   Litho.   Perf. 14x14½

Christmas: 5c, Local creche. 10c, Virgin and Child with Sts. Jerome and Dominic, by Filippino Lippi. 15c, Virgin and Child with St. Anne, by Gerolamo dai Libri.

203 A55 3c yellow & multi   .25 .25
204 A55 5c dull blue & multi   .25 .25
205 A55 10c red & multi   .25 .25
206 A55 15c orange & multi   .35 .35
    Nos. 203-206 (4)   1.10 1.10

Satellite Earth Station, Matura A56

Dish Antenna A57

Design: 40c, Satellite over earth (Africa).

1971, Nov. 18   Perf. 14
207 A56 10c ultra & multi   .25 .25
208 A57 30c green & multi   .25 .25
209 A57 40c black & multi   .35 .35
  a. Souvenir sheet of 3   2.25 2.25
    Nos. 207-209 (3)   .85 .85

Opening of Satellite Earth Station at Matura. No. 209a contains 3 imperf. stamps with simulated perforations similar to Nos. 207-209.

Morpho Hybrid A58

Butterflies: 5c, Purple mort bleu. 6c, Jaune d'abricot. 10c, Purple king shoemaker. 20c, Southern white pape. 30c, Little jaune.

1972, Feb. 18   Photo.   Wmk. 314
210 A58 3c olive & multi   1.00 .80
211 A58 5c ocher & multi   1.50 .25
212 A58 6c yellow & multi   1.75 .80
213 A58 10c yel grn & multi   2.00 .30
214 A58 20c lilac & multi   3.00 2.40
215 A58 30c dull grn & multi   4.50 3.00
    Nos. 210-215 (6)   13.75 7.55

S.S. Lady McLeod and Stamp A59

10c, Map of Trinidad and Tobago. 30c, Commemorative inscription.

1972, Apr. 12   Litho.   Perf. 14½x14
216	A59	5c blue & multi	.25	.25
217	A59	10c blue & multi	.25	.25
218	A59	30c blue & multi	.65	.65
a.		Souvenir sheet of 3, #216-218	1.50	1.50
		Nos. 216-218 (3)	1.15	1.15

125th anniv. of the Lady McLeod stamp.

Trinity Cross — A60

Medals: 10c, Chaconia medal. 20c, Hummingbird medal. 30c, Medal of Merit.

1972, Aug. 28   Photo.   Perf. 13½x13
219	A60	5c blue & multi	.25	.25
220	A60	10c multicolored	.25	.25
221	A60	20c yellow grn & multi	.25	.30
222	A60	30c brt rose & multi	.25	.40
a.		Souvenir sheet of 4, #219-222	1.25	1.25
		Nos. 219-222 (4)	1.00	1.20

10th anniversary of independence. See Nos. 235-238.

Olympic Rings, Relay Race Medal, 1964 A61

Olympic Rings and: 20c, Bronze medal, 200-meters, 1964. 30c, Bronze medals, weight lifting, 1952. 40c, Silver medal, 400-meters, 1964. 50c, Silver medal, weight lifting, 1948.

1972, Sept. 7   Litho.   Perf. 14
223	A61	10c yellow & multi	.25	.25
224	A61	20c multicolored	.30	.30
225	A61	30c lilac & multi	.40	.40
226	A61	40c lt blue & multi	.50	.50
227	A61	50c orange & multi	.60	.60
a.		Souv. sheet of #223-227 + label	2.50	2.50
		Nos. 223-227 (5)	2.05	2.05

20th Olympic Games, Munich, 8/26-9/11.

Holy Family, by Titian A62

Christmas: 3c, Adoration of the Kings, by Dosso Dossi. 30c, Like 5c.

1972, Nov. 9   Photo.   Wmk. 314
228	A62	3c blue & multi	.25	.25
229	A62	5c rose lilac & multi	.25	.25
230	A62	30c lt green & multi	.50	.50
a.		Souvenir sheet of 3, #228-230	2.25	2.25
		Nos. 228-230 (3)	1.00	1.00

ECLA Headquarters, Santiago, Chile — A63

Designs: 20c, INTERPOL emblem. 30c, WMO emblem. 40c, University of West Indies Administration Building.

1973, Aug. 15   Litho.   Wmk. 314
231	A63	10c orange & multi	.25	.25
232	A63	20c multicolored	.25	.25
233	A63	30c ultra & multi	.35	.35
234	A63	40c lilac & multi	.45	.45
a.		Souvenir sheet of 4, #231-234	1.40	1.40
		Nos. 231-234 (4)	1.30	1.30

Economic Commission for Latin America, 25th anniv. (10c); Intl. Criminal Police Organization, 50th anniv. (20c); Intl. Meteorological cooperation, cent. (30c); Admission of 1st students to the University of West Indies, 25th anniv. (40c).

Medal Type of 1972 Redrawn

Medals: 10c, Trinity Cross. 20c, Medal of Merit. 30c, Chaconia medal. 40c, Hummingbird medal.

1973, Aug. 30   Photo.   Perf. 14½x14
235	A60	10c dark green & multi	.25	.25
236	A60	20c dark brown & multi	.25	.25
237	A60	30c dark blue & multi	.25	.25
238	A60	40c deep violet & multi	.40	.40
a.		Souv. sheet, #235-238, perf. 14	1.50	1.50
		Nos. 235-238 (4)	1.15	1.15

11th anniv. of independence. "Trinidad and Tobago" in one line on #235-238.

General Post Office, Port of Spain A64

40c, Conference Hall & flags, Chagaramas.

1973, Oct. 8   Photo.   Perf. 14
239	A64	30c multicolored	.25	.25
240	A64	40c multicolored	.40	.40
a.		Souvenir sheet of 2, #239-240	1.25	1.25

2nd Commonwealth Conf. of Postal Administrations, Trinidad, Oct. 8-20. On #240a the perforations extend through margin and divide map.

Virgin and Child, by Murillo — A65

1973, Oct. 22   Perf. 14½x14
241	A65	5c pink & multi	.25	.25
242	A65	$1 lt blue & multi	.80	.80
a.		Souv. sheet of 2, #241-242, perf. 14	1.25	1.25

Christmas 1973.

Post Office and UPU Emblem — A66

UPU, Cent.: 50c, Map of Islands, UPU emblem, means of transportation.

1974, Nov. 18   Photo.   Perf. 13½x14
243	A66	40c brt purple & multi	.50	.50
244	A66	50c blue gray & multi	.75	.75
a.		Souvenir sheet of 2, #243-244	27.50	30.00

Humming Bird I, Transatlantic Crossing, 1960 — A67

Design: 50c, Globe, Humming Bird II, Harold and Kwailan La Borde.

1974, Dec. 2   Perf. 14½
245	A67	40c multicolored	.50	.50
246	A67	50c multicolored	.70	.70
a.		Souvenir sheet of 2, #245-246	3.50	3.50

First anniversary of the voyage around the world by Harold and Kwailan La Borde aboard Humming Bird II, 1969-1973.

"Equality" and IWY Emblem A68

1975, June 23   Litho.   Wmk. 314
247	A68	15c multicolored	.25	.25
248	A68	30c multicolored	.50	.50

International Women's Year 1975.

Dr. Pawan and Laboratory Equipment — A69

25c, Vampire bat, microscope, syringe, bat's head.

Perf. 14x14½
1975, Sept. 23   Photo.   Wmk. 373
249	A69	25c yellow & multi	.50	.50
250	A69	30c lt blue & multi	.60	.60

Isolation of rabies virus by Dr. Joseph Lennox Pawan (1887-1957).

Boeing 707, BWIA Emblem, Air Routes A70

Designs: 30c, Boeing 707 on ground. 40c, Boeing 707 in the air.

Wmk. 373
1975, Nov. 27   Litho.   Perf. 14½
251	A70	20c dark blue & multi	.50	.50
252	A70	30c deep ultra & multi	.70	.70
253	A70	40c dull green & multi	.90	.90
a.		Souvenir sheet of 3, #251-253	2.75	2.75
		Nos. 251-253 (3)	2.10	2.10

British West Indian Airways, 35th anniv.

Land of the Hummingbird Costume — A71

Carnival 1976: $1, Carib Prince riding pink ibis. Designs show prize-winning costumes from 1974 carnival.

1976, Jan. 12   Photo.   Perf. 14½
254	A71	30c multicolored	.40	.40
255	A71	$1 multicolored	1.10	1.10
a.		Souvenir sheet of 2, #254-255	1.75	1.75

Angostura Building, Port of Spain A72

Designs (Exposition Medals, obverse and reverse): 35c, New Orleans, 1885-86. 45c, Sydney, 1879. 50c, Brussels, 1897.

1976, July 14   Litho.   Perf. 13
256	A72	5c bister & multi	.25	.25
257	A72	35c yellow grn & multi	.25	.25
258	A72	45c blue & multi	.30	.30
259	A72	50c violet & multi	.30	.30
a.		Souv. sheet, #256-259, perf. 14	1.25	1.25
		Nos. 256-259 (4)	1.10	1.10

Sesquicentennial of the manufacture of Angostura Bitters.

Map of West Indies, Bats, Wicket and Ball A72a

Prudential Cup — A72b

1976, Oct. 4   Unwmk.   Perf. 14
260	A72a	35c lt blue & multi	.55	.55
261	A72b	45c lilac rose & blk	.75	.75
a.		Souvenir sheet of 2, #260-261	2.75	2.75

World Cricket Cup, won by West Indies Team, 1975.

Columbus Sailing through the Bocas, by A. Camps-Campins — A73

Paintings: 10c, View, by Jean Michael Cazabon. 20c, Landscape, by Cazabon. 35c, Los Gallos Point, by Cazabon. 45c, Corbeaux Town, by Cazabon.

1976, Nov. 1   Litho.   Wmk. 373
262	A73	5c ocher & multi	.55	.55
263	A73	10c lilac & multi	.55	.55
264	A73	20c green & multi	.55	.55
265	A73	35c red orange & multi	.55	.55
266	A73	45c blue & multi	.65	.65
a.		Souvenir sheet of 5, #262-266	3.00	3.00
		Nos. 262-266 (5)	2.85	2.85

For overprints see Nos. 325, 327.

Hasely Crawford and Gold Medal A74

1977, Jan. 4   Litho.   Perf. 12½
267	A74	25c multicolored	.50	.45
a.		Souvenir sheet of 1	.70	.60

Hasely Crawford, winner of 100-meter dash at Montreal Olympic Games.

Sikorsky S-38 (Lindbergh's Plane) — A75

Designs: 35c, Charles Lindbergh delivering first airmail to Port of Spain, 1927. 45c, Boeing 707, British West Indies Airways. 50c, Boeing 747, British Airways.

1977, Apr.   Wmk. 373   Perf. 13
268	A75	20c lt blue & multi	.30	.30
269	A75	35c lt blue & multi	.50	.50
270	A75	45c lt blue & multi	.60	.60
271	A75	50c lt blue & multi	1.10	.75
a.		Souv. sheet, #268-271, perf. 14	5.25	5.25
		Nos. 268-271 (4)	2.50	2.15

Airmail to Trinidad & Tobago, 50th anniv.

Trinidad and
Tobago
Flag — A76

35c, Coat of arms. 45c, Government House.

1977, July 26   Litho.   Perf. 13½x13
272	A76	20c yellow & multi	.40	.40
273	A76	35c red & multi	.70	.70
274	A76	45c lt blue & multi	.90	.90
a.		Souv. sheet, #272-274, perf. 14	2.25	2.25
		Nos. 272-274 (3)	2.00	2.00

Inauguration of the Republic, Aug. 1, 1976.

White
Poinsettia — A77

Christmas: 45c, 50c, Red poinsettia.

1977, Oct. 11   Litho.   Perf. 14½
275	A77	10c multicolored	.25	.25
276	A77	35c multicolored	.40	.40
277	A77	45c multicolored	.55	.55
278	A77	50c multicolored	.60	.60
a.		Souvenir sheet of 4, #275-278	1.75	1.75
		Nos. 275-278 (4)	1.80	1.80

Robinson
Crusoe
Hotel,
Tobago
A78

15c, Turtle Beach Hotel, Tobago. 25c,
Mount Irvine Hotel, Tobago. 70c, Mount Irvine
beach, Tobago. $5, Holiday Inn, Trinidad.

Wmk. 373
1978, Jan. 17   Litho.   Perf. 14
279	A78	6c multicolored	.25	.25
280	A78	15c multicolored	.25	.25
281	A78	25c multicolored	.25	.25
282	A78	70c multicolored	.45	.45
283	A78	$5 multicolored	3.25	3.25
a.		Souvenir sheet of 5, #279-283	4.50	4.50
		Nos. 279-283 (5)	4.45	4.45

For overprint see No. 326.

Paphinia
Cristata
A79

Orchids: 30c, Caularthron bicornutum. 40c,
Miltassia. 50c, Oncidium ampiliatum. $2.50,
Oncidium papilio.

1978, June 7   Wmk. 373   Perf. 14
284	A79	12c multicolored	.75	.75
285	A79	30c multicolored	.85	.85
286	A79	40c multicolored	1.10	1.10
287	A79	50c multicolored	1.50	1.50
288	A79	$2.50 multicolored	6.75	6.75
a.		Souvenir sheet of 5, #284-288	11.50	11.50
		Nos. 284-288 (5)	10.95	10.95

Miss Universe and
Trophy — A80

Designs: 35c, Portrait with crown. 45c, Miss
Universe in evening dress.

1978, Aug. 2   Litho.   Perf. 14½
289	A80	10c multicolored	.55	.55
290	A80	35c multicolored	.75	.75
291	A80	45c multicolored	.95	.95
a.		Souvenir sheet of 3, #289-291	2.50	2.50
		Nos. 289-291 (3)	2.25	2.25

Janelle (Penny) Commissiong, Miss Universe, 1977.

Tayra
A81

1978, Nov. 7   Perf. 13½x14
292	A81	15c shown	.25	.25
293	A81	25c Ocelot	.35	.30
294	A81	40c Porcupine	.55	.50
295	A81	70c Yellow anteater	1.10	.75
a.		Souvenir sheet of 4, #292-295	2.75	2.75
		Nos. 292-295 (4)	2.25	1.80

"Burst of
Beauty" — A82

Costumes: 10c, Rain worshipper. 35c,
Zodiac. 45c, Praying mantis. 50c, Eye of the
hurricane. $1, Steel orchestra.

1979, Feb. 1   Litho.   Perf. 13½
296	A82	5c multicolored	.25	.25
297	A82	10c multicolored	.25	.25
298	A82	35c multicolored	.25	.25
299	A82	45c multicolored	.30	.30
300	A82	50c multicolored	.35	.35
301	A82	$1 multicolored	.70	.70
		Nos. 296-301 (6)	2.10	2.10

Day Care
Center — A83

IYC Emblem and: 10c, School lunch program. 35c, Dental care. 45c, Nursery school.
50c, Free school bus. $1, Medical care.

Unwmk.
1979, June 5   Litho.   Perf. 13
302	A83	5c multicolored	.25	.25
303	A83	10c multicolored	.25	.25
304	A83	35c multicolored	.25	.25
305	A83	45c multicolored	.30	.30
306	A83	50c multicolored	.30	.30
307	A83	$1 multicolored	.65	.65
a.		Souvenir sheet of 6, #302-307	1.90	1.90
		Nos. 302-307 (6)	2.00	2.00

International Year of the Child.

Geothermal
Exploration
A84

Designs: 35c, Hydrogeology. 45c, Petroleum exploration. 70c, Preservation of the
environment.

1979, July 3   Wmk. 373
308	A84	10c multicolored	.25	.25
309	A84	35c multicolored	.30	.30
310	A84	45c multicolored	.35	.35
311	A84	70c multicolored	.55	.55
a.		Souvenir sheet of 4, #308-311	2.50	2.50
		Nos. 308-311 (4)	1.45	1.45

4th Latin American Geological Cong., July
7-15.

Map of Tobago and Tobago No.
1 — A85

15c, Tobago #2, 7. 35c, Tobago #28, 11.
45c, Tobago #25, 4. 70c, Great Britain #28
used in Scarborough and Tobago #5. $1, Gen-
eral Post Office, Scarborough and Tobago #6.

Perf. 13½x14
1979, Aug. 1   Litho.   Wmk. 373
312	A85	10c multicolored	.25	.25
313	A85	15c multicolored	.25	.25
314	A85	35c multicolored	.25	.25
315	A85	45c multicolored	.30	.30
316	A85	70c multicolored	.45	.45
317	A85	$1 multicolored	.65	.65
a.		Souvenir sheet of 6, #312-317	2.50	2.50
		Nos. 312-317 (6)	2.15	2.15

Centenary of Tobago's postage stamps.

Rowland Hill, Trinidad and Tobago No.
109 — A86

Hill and: 45c, Trinidad and Tobago #273. $1,
Trinidad #62, Tobago #10.

1979, Oct. 4   Perf. 13
318	A86	25c multicolored	.25	.25
319	A86	45c multicolored	.40	.40
320	A86	$1 multicolored	.80	.80
a.		Souvenir sheet of 3, #318-320	2.25	2.25
		Nos. 318-320 (3)	1.45	1.45

Sir Rowland Hill (1795-1879), originator of
penny postage.

Poui
Tree
A87

Designs: 10c, Court House. 50c, Royal Train
locomotive. $1.50, Bacchante freighter.

Wmk. 373
1980, Jan. 21   Litho.   Perf. 14½
321	A87	5c multicolored	.25	.25
322	A87	10c multicolored	.25	.25
323	A87	50c multicolored	.45	.45
324	A87	$1.50 multicolored	1.40	1.40
a.		Souvenir sheet of 4, #321-324	2.75	2.75
		Nos. 321-324 (4)	2.35	2.35

Princes Town centenary.

Nos. 262, 279, 263 Overprinted in 3 or
5 Lines:
"1844-1980 POPULATION
CENSUS 12th MAY 1980"

1980, Apr. 8   Litho.   Perf. 14
325	A73	5c multicolored	.25	.25
326	A78	6c multicolored	.25	.25
327	A73	10c multicolored	.25	.25
		Nos. 325-327 (3)	.75	.75

Scarlet Ibis Hen
and Nest — A88

Scarlet Ibis: b, Nest and eggs. c, Chick in
nest. d, Male. e, Male and female.

Wmk. 373
1980, May 6   Litho.   Perf. 14½
328		Strip of 5, multi	5.75	5.75
a.-e.		A88 single stamp	.90	.90

Bronze
and Silver
Medals,
1948,
1952
A89

Wmk. 373
1980, July 22   Litho.   Perf. 14
329	A89	10c shown	.25	.25
330	A89	15c Hasely Crawford, 1976 gold medal	.25	.25
331	A89	70c 1964 silver, bronze medals	.65	.65
		Nos. 329-331 (3)	1.15	1.15

Souvenir Sheet
332	A89	$2.50 Moscow '80 em- blem, vert.	2.40	2.40

22nd Summer Olympic Games, Moscow,
July 19-Aug. 3.

Charcoal Production — A90

Wmk. 373
1980, Sept. 8   Litho.   Perf. 14
333	A90	10c shown	.25	.25
334	A90	55c Logging	.30	.30
335	A90	70c Teak plantation	.40	.40
336	A90	$2.50 Watershed man- agement	1.50	1.50
a.		Souvenir sheet of 4, #333-336	3.00	3.00
		Nos. 333-336 (4)	2.45	2.45

11th Commonwealth Forestry Conference.

Elizabeth Bourne, Judiciary and
Isabella Tesbier, Government — A91

Decade for Women: No. 338, Beryl
McBurnie, dance and culture; Audrey Jeffers,
social work. No. 339, Dr. Stella Abidh, public
health; Louise Horne, nutrition.

1980, Sept. 29
337	A91	$1 multicolored	.70	.70
338	A91	$1 multicolored	.70	.70
339	A91	$1 multicolored	.70	.70
		Nos. 337-339 (3)	2.10	2.10

Stadium and Netball League Emblem — A92

1980, Oct. 21
340 A92 70c multicolored .55 .55

1979 World Netball Tournament, Port-of-Spain.

Athlete, Man in Wheelchair, IYD Emblem — A93

Wmk. 373
1981, Apr. 6   Litho.   Perf. 14½
341 A93 10c shown .25 .25
342 A93 70c Amputee with crutch .35 .35
343 A93 $1.50 Blind people .85 .85
344 A93 $2 IYD emblem 1.10 1.10
Nos. 341-344 (4) 2.55 2.55

International Year of the Disabled.

Marine Preservation — A94

1981, July 7   Litho.   Perf. 13x13½
345 A94 10c Land .25 .25
346 A94 55c shown .40 .40
347 A94 $3 Sky 2.50 2.50
a. Souvenir sheet of 3, #345-347 5.00 5.00
Nos. 345-347 (3) 3.15 3.15

World Food Day — A95

1981, Oct. 16   Litho.   Perf. 14½x14
348 A95 10c Produce .25 .25
349 A95 15c Rice threshing, mill .25 .25
350 A95 45c Bigeye .40 .40
351 A95 55c Cow, pig, goats .50 .50
352 A95 $1.50 Poultry 1.25 1.25
353 A95 $2 Smallmouth grunt 1.75 1.75
a. Souvenir sheet of 6, #348-353 5.00 5.00
Nos. 348-353 (6) 4.40 4.40

President Awards — A96

1981, Nov. 30   Perf. 14
354 A96 10c First aid .25 .25
355 A96 70c Motor mechanics .55 .55
356 A96 $1 Hiking .75 .75
357 A96 $2 President giving award 1.50 1.50
Nos. 354-357 (4) 3.05 3.05

Commonwealth Pharmaceutical Conference A97

1982, Feb. 12   Litho.   Perf. 14½x14
358 A97 10c Pharmacist .75 .75
359 A97 $1 Pluchea symphitfolia 3.00 3.00
360 A97 $2 Nopalea cochenilifera 5.25 5.25
Nos. 358-360 (3) 9.00 9.00

Scouting Year — A98

1982, June 28   Litho.   Perf. 14
361 A98 15c Production .60 .60
362 A98 55c Tolerance 1.75 1.75
363 A98 $5 Discipline 7.00 7.00
Nos. 361-363 (3) 9.35 9.35

25th Anniv. of Tourist Board — A99

Perf. 13½x14
1982, Oct. 18   Litho.   Wmk. 373
364 A99 55c Charlotteville .45 .45
365 A99 $1 Boating .85 .85
366 A99 $3 Fort George 2.50 2.50
Nos. 364-366 (3) 3.80 3.80

Pa Pa Bois — A100

Designs: Various folklore characters.

1982, Nov. 8
367 A100 10c multicolored .25 .25
368 A100 15c multicolored .25 .25
369 A100 65c multicolored .55 .55
370 A100 $5 multicolored 4.25 4.25
a. Souvenir sheet of 4, #367-370 7.50 7.50
Nos. 367-370 (4) 5.30 5.30

Canefarmers' Centenary — A101

1982, Dec. 13   Litho.   Perf. 14
371 A101 30c Harvest .40 .40
372 A101 70c Loading bullock cart .95 .95
373 A101 $1.50 Field 2.00 2.00
a. Souvenir sheet of 3, #371-373, perf. 14½ 4.00 4.00
Nos. 371-373 (3) 3.35 3.35

20th Anniv. of Independence — A102

1982, Dec. 28   Perf. 13½x14
374 A102 10c Natl. Stadium .40 .40
375 A102 35c Caroni Arena Water Treatment Plant .75 .75
376 A102 50c Mount Hope Maternity Hospital 1.50 1.50
377 A102 $2 Natl. Insurance Board Mall, Tobago 2.00 2.00
Nos. 374-377 (4) 4.65 4.65

Commonwealth Day — A103

1983, Mar. 14   Perf. 14
378 A103 10c Flags .25 .25
379 A103 55c Satellite view .40 .40
380 A103 $1 Oil industry, vert. .75 .75
381 A103 $2 Maps, vert. 1.50 1.50
Nos. 378-381 (4) 2.90 2.90

10th Anniv. of CARICOM — A104

1983, July 11   Litho.   Perf. 14
382 A104 35c Jet, map 2.00 2.00

World Communications Year — A105

1983, Aug. 5   Perf. 14½
383 A105 15c Operator .25 .25
384 A105 55c Scarborough PO, Tobago .70 .70
385 A105 $1 Textel Building 1.25 1.25
386 A105 $3 Morne Bleu Receiving Station 3.75 3.75
Nos. 383-386 (4) 5.95 5.95

Commonwealth Finance Ministers Conference — A106

Wmk. 373
1983, Sept. 19   Litho.   Perf. 14
387 A106 $2 multicolored 1.50 1.50

World Food Day — A107

1983, Oct. 17   Perf. 14x13½
388 A107 10c Kingfish .55 .55
389 A107 55c Flying fish 1.10 1.10
390 A107 70c Queen conch 1.50 1.50
391 A107 $4 Red shrimp 7.50 7.50
Nos. 388-391 (4) 10.65 10.65

Flowers — A108

1983, Dec. 14   Wmk. 373   Perf. 14
No Year Imprint Below Design
392 A108 5c Bois pois .25 .25
b. Imprint "1989" .25 .25
393 A108 10c Maraval Lily .25 .25
b. Imprint "1985" .25 .25
c. Imprint "1986" .25 .25
d. Imprint "1987" .25 .25
e. Imprint "1989" .25 .25
394 A108 15c Star grass .25 .25
395 A108 20c Bois caco .25 .25
396 A108 25c Strangling fig .25 .25
397 A108 30c Cassia moschata .25 .25
398 A108 50c Chalice flower .60 .65
399 A108 65c Black stick .70 .85
400 A108 80c Columnea scandens .90 1.00
401 A108 95c Cats Claws 1.00 1.25
402 A108 $1 Bois l'agli 1.10 1.25
403 A108 $1.50 Eustoma exeltatum 1.60 2.00

Size: 38½x26mm
404 A108 $2 Chaconia, horiz. 2.25 2.50
405 A108 $2.50 Chysothemis pulchella, horiz. 3.00 3.25
406 A108 $5 Centratherum punctatum, horiz. 6.00 6.75
407 A108 $10 Savanna flower, horiz. 11.50 13.00
Nos. 392-407 (16) 30.15 34.00

1984, Oct.
"1984" Imprint Below Design
392a A108 5c multicolored 4.00 4.00
393a A108 10c multicolored 3.00 3.00
394a A108 15c multicolored 3.00 3.00
396a A108 25c multicolored 5.00 5.00
Nos. 392a-396a (4) 15.00 15.00

1985-89   Wmk. 384
"1985" Imprint Below Design
392f A108 5c multicolored 1.25 1.25
401f A108 95c multicolored .80 .80
402f A108 $1 multicolored .85 .85
406f A108 $5 multicolored 3.25 3.25
407f A108 $10 multicolored 6.50 6.50
Nos. 392f-407f (5) 12.65 12.65

"1986" Imprint Below Design
393g A108 10c multicolored .25 .25

"1987" Imprint Below Design
393h A108 10c multicolored .25 .25
397h A108 30c multicolored .25 .25
399h A108 65c multicolored .60 .60
400h A108 80c multicolored .75 .75
401h A108 95c multicolored .85 .85
402h A108 $1 multicolored 1.00 .60
403h A108 $1.50 multicolored 1.50 1.50
404h A108 $2 multicolored 1.90 1.90
406h A108 $5 multicolored 5.00 5.00
407h A108 $10 multicolored 10.00 10.00
Nos. 393h-407h (10) 22.10 21.70

"1988" Imprint Below Design
393i A108 10c multicolored .85 .85
395i A108 20c multicolored .35 .35
396i A108 25c multicolored .85 .85
397i A108 30c multicolored .35 .35
399i A108 65c multicolored .60 .40
400i A108 80c multicolored .75 .75
401i A108 95c multicolored .95 .95
406i A108 $5 multicolored 5.00 5.00
407i A108 $10 multicolored 10.00 10.00
Nos. 393i-407i (9) 19.70 19.30

"1989" Imprint Below Design
393j A108 10c multicolored .25 .25
395j A108 20c multicolored .35 .25
396j A108 25c multicolored .85 .85
397j A108 30c multicolored .35 .25
399j A108 65c multicolored .60 .40
402j A108 $1 multicolored 1.00 .60
403j A108 $1.50 multicolored 1.50 1.50
404j A108 $2 multicolored 1.90 1.90
405j A108 $2.50 multicolored 2.50 2.50
406j A108 $5 multicolored 5.00 5.00
407j A108 $10 multicolored 10.00 10.00
Nos. 393j-407j (11) 24.30 23.50

Castles on Chess
Board
A109

1984 Summer
Olympics
A110

World Chess Federationn, 60th Anniv.: Various chess pieces.

Wmk. 373

1984, Sept. 12   Litho.   Perf. 14
408	A109	50c multicolored	1.75	1.75
409	A109	70c multicolored	2.50	2.50
410	A109	$1.50 multicolored	5.25	5.25
411	A109	$2 multicolored	7.25	7.25
		Nos. 408-411 (4)	16.75	16.75

1984, Sept. 21   Perf. 14x14½
412	A110	15c Swimming	.25	.25
413	A110	55c Running	.65	.65
414	A110	$1.50 Yachting	1.60	1.60
415	A110	$4 Bicycling	4.25	4.25
a.		Souvenir sheet of 4, #412-415	8.00	8.00
		Nos. 412-415 (4)	6.75	6.75

St. Mary's Children's Home, 125th
Anniv. — A111

1984, Nov. 13   Litho.   Perf. 13½
416	A111	10c Children's band	.25	.25
417	A111	70c St. Mary's Home	.90	.90
418	A111	$3 Group scene	3.50	3.50
		Nos. 416-418 (3)	4.65	4.65

Christmas
1984
A112

1984, Nov.   Litho.   Perf. 14
419	A112	10c Parang Band	.35	.35
420	A112	30c Musical notes, Poinsettia	.40	.40
421	A112	$1 Bandola, Cuatro, Bandolin	1.50	1.50
422	A112	$3 Fiddle, Guitar, Double Bass	4.50	4.50
		Nos. 419-422 (4)	6.75	6.75

Emancipation, 150th
Anniv. — A113

1984, Oct. 22   Litho.   Perf. 13½x13
423	A113	35c Slave ship	.75	.75
424	A113	55c Map, Slave Triangle	1.25	1.25
425	A113	$1 Book by Eric Williams	2.25	2.25
426	A113	$2 Toussaint L'Ouverture	4.75	4.75
a.		Souvenir sheet of 4, #423-426	10.50	10.50
		Nos. 423-426 (4)	9.00	9.00

Labor
Day — A114

Labor leaders: No. 427, A.A. Cipriani and T.U.B. Butler. No. 428, A. Cola Rienzi and C.T.W.E. Worrell. No. 429, C.P. Alexander and Q. O'Connor.

Wmk. 373

1985, June 17   Litho.   Perf. 14
427	A114	55c dull rose & blk	1.75	1.75
428	A114	55c brt green & blk	1.75	1.75
429	A114	55c lt orange & blk	1.75	1.75
		Nos. 427-429 (3)	5.25	5.25

Ships
A115

Wmk. 373

1985, Aug 20   Litho.   Perf. 14½
430	A115	30c Lady Nelson	.60	.60
431	A115	95c Lady Drake	1.75	1.75
432	A115	$1.50 Federal Palm	2.75	2.75
433	A115	$2 Federal Maple	3.50	3.50
		Nos. 430-433 (4)	8.60	8.60

UN
Decade
for
Women
A116

Women in the arts, public service and education: No. 434, Sybil Atteck, Marjorie Padmore. No. 435, May Cherrie, Evelyn Tracey. No. 436, Jessica Smith-Phillips, Irene Omilta McShine.

1985, Oct. 30   Wmk. 384   Perf. 14
434	A116	$1.50 multicolored	2.00	2.00
435	A116	$1.50 multicolored	2.00	2.00
436	A116	$1.50 multicolored	2.00	2.00
		Nos. 434-436 (3)	6.00	6.00

Intl. Youth
Year — A117

Anniversaries and events: 10c, Natl. Cadet Force, 75th anniv. 65c, Girl Guides, 75th anniv.

1985, Nov. 27   Perf. 14x14½
437	A117	10c Cadet emblem	1.00	1.00
438	A117	65c Badges, anniv. emblem	2.40	2.40
439	A117	95c shown	3.25	3.25
		Nos. 437-439 (3)	6.65	6.65

A118   A119

Sisters of St. Joseph de Cluny in Trinidad, 150th Anniv.: 10c, Sister Anne-Marie Javouhey, founder. 65c, St. Joseph's Convent, Port-of-Spain. 95c, Statue of Sr. Anne-Marie.

Perf. 14x14½

1986, Mar. 19   Litho.   Wmk. 384
440	A118	10c multicolored	.25	.25
441	A118	65c multicolored	.60	.60
442	A118	95c multicolored	1.00	1.00
		Nos. 440-442 (3)	1.85	1.85

Wmk. 384

1986, Apr. 21   Litho.   Perf. 14½
443	A119	10c At the Cenotaph	.30	.30
444	A119	15c Aboard HMY Britannia	.30	.30
445	A119	30c With Pres. Clarke	.30	.30
446	A119	$5 Receiving bouquet	4.25	4.25
		Nos. 443-446 (4)	5.15	5.15

Queen Elizabeth II, 60th birthday.

Locomotives, AMERIPEX '86 — A120

Perf. 14½x14

1986, May 26   Wmk. 373
447	A120	65c Arma tank locomotive	.40	.40
448	A120	95c Canadian-built No. 22	.65	.65
449	A120	$1.10 Tender engine	.75	.75
450	A120	$1.50 Saddle tank	1.00	1.00
a.		Souvenir sheet of 4, #447-450	3.00	3.00
		Nos. 447-450 (4)	2.80	2.80

Boy Scouts,
75th Anniv.
A121

1986, July 21   Wmk. 384   Perf. 14
451	A121	$1.70 Campsite	1.50	1.50
452	A121	$2 Uniforms, 1911, 1986	2.00	2.00

Dr. Eric Williams (1911-1981), First
Prime Minister — A122

Wmk. 373

1986, Sept. 25   Litho.   Perf. 14
453	A122	10c Graduating college, 1935	.75	.75
454	A122	30c Wearing red tie	1.00	1.00
a.		Black tie	1.00	1.00
455	A122	95c Pro-Chancellor of UWI	1.75	1.75
456	A122	$5 Williams, prime minister's residence	5.50	5.50
a.		Souvenir sheet of 4, #453-456	8.50	8.50
		Nos. 453-456 (4)	9.00	9.00
		Nos. 453-454 vert.		

Intl. Peace
Year
A123

1986, Oct. 30   Wmk. 384
457	A123	95c shown	.60	.60
458	A123	$3 Dove	2.40	2.40

Giselle LaRonde,
Miss World
1986 — A124

Wmk. 384

1987, July 27   Litho.   Perf. 14
459	A124	10c Wearing folk costume	.85	.85
460	A124	30c Bathing suit	1.75	1.75
461	A124	95c Crown	3.50	3.50
462	A124	$1.65 Crown and sash	5.25	5.25
		Nos. 459-462 (4)	11.35	11.35

Republic
Bank,
150th
Anniv.
A125

Designs: 10c, Colonial Bank, Port of Spain. 65c, Cocoa plantation. 95c, Oil fields. $1.10, Tramcar, Belmont Tramway Co.

Wmk. 373

1987, Dec. 21   Litho.   Perf. 14
463	A125	10c buff, red brn & blk	.60	.60
464	A125	65c buff, red brn & blk	.85	.85
465	A125	95c buff, red brn & blk	2.50	2.50
466	A125	$1.10 buff, red brn & blk	2.75	2.75
		Nos. 463-466 (4)	6.70	6.70

Defense Force,
25th
Anniv. — A126

Various army, coast guard and navy uniforms.

Wmk. 384

1988, Feb. 29   Litho.   Perf. 14
467	A126	10c Army	1.50	.40
468	A126	30c Army (women)	2.75	.50
469	A126	$1.10 Navy, army, coast guard	4.00	3.25
470	A126	$1.50 Navy	5.00	4.75
		Nos. 467-470 (4)	13.25	8.90

Cricket
A127

Bat, wicket posts, ball, 18th cent. belt buckle and batters: 30c, George John. 65c, Learie Constantine. 95c, Sonny Ramadhin. $1.50, Gerry Gomez. $2.50, Jeffrey Stollmeyer.

Wmk. 373

1988, June 6   Litho.   Perf. 14
471	A127	30c multicolored	1.60	.55
472	A127	65c multicolored	3.00	1.40
473	A127	95c multicolored	3.25	2.25
474	A127	$1.50 multicolored	4.00	4.00
475	A127	$2.50 multicolored	5.25	5.75
		Nos. 471-475 (5)	17.10	13.95

Oilfield Workers'
Trade Union, 50th
Anniv. — A128

50, Star, oil well and: 10c, Uriah Buzz Butler, labor leader. 30c, Adrian C. Rienzi, pres. from 1937-42. 65c, John Rojas, pres. from 1943-62. $5, George Weekes, pres. from 1962-87.

Wmk. 384

1988, July 11	Litho.	Perf. 14½
476 A128 10c multicolored	.25	.25
477 A128 30c multicolored	.25	.25
478 A128 65c multicolored	.55	.55
479 A128 $5 multicolored	2.50	2.50
Nos. 476-479 (4)	3.55	3.55

Borough of Arima, Cent. — A129

20c, Mary Werges, Santa Rosa Church. 30c, Gov. W. Robinson, royal charter. $1.10, Mayor C.P. Lopez greeting Gov. Robinson at train station. $1.50, Mayor J.F. Wallen, centennial emblem.

Wmk. 384

1988, Aug. 22	Litho.	Perf. 14½
480 A129 20c multicolored	.30	.30
481 A129 30c multicolored	.30	.30
482 A129 $1.10 multicolored	1.75	1.75
483 A129 $1.50 multicolored	1.75	1.75
Nos. 480-483 (4)	4.10	4.10

Lloyds of London, 300th Anniv.
Common Design Type

Designs: 30c, Queen Mother at the "Topping Out" ceremony of new Lloyds's building, 1984. $1.10, BWIA Tristar 500, horiz. $1.55, ISCOTT iron and steel mill, horiz. $2, *Atlantic Empress* on fire off Tobago.

1988, Nov. 21	Litho.	Perf. 14
484 CD341 30c multicolored	.85	.35
485 CD341 $1.10 multicolored	3.00	1.75
486 CD341 $1.55 multicolored	2.75	2.40
487 CD341 $2 multicolored	5.25	3.50
Nos. 484-487 (4)	11.85	8.00

Unification of the Islands, Cent. — A130

Torch and: 40c, Natl. arms, 1889, and 1p Type A1. $1, Badge from Tobago flag and Tobago No. 31. $1.50, Badge from Trinidad flag and Trinidad No. 71. $2.25, Natl. arms, 1989, and No. 274.

Wmk. 384

1989, Mar. 20	Litho.	Perf. 14½
488 A130 40c multicolored	1.25	.30
489 A130 $1 multicolored	3.00	1.25
490 A130 $1.50 multicolored	3.25	3.25
491 A130 $2.25 multicolored	3.75	3.75
Nos. 488-491 (4)	11.25	8.55

Rare Species A131

Designs: a, *Pipile pipile*. b, *Phyllodytes auratus*. c, *Cebus albifrons trinitatis*. d, *Tamandua tetradactyla*. e, *Lutra longicaudis*. Printed in a continuous design.

Perf. 14x14½

1989, July 31		Wmk. 373
492 Strip of 5	22.50	22.50
a.-e. A131 $1 any single	2.40	2.40

A132

1989, Oct. 2		Perf. 14½
493 A132 10c Men using walking sticks	1.25	.50
494 A132 40c City Hall	.80	.50
495 A132 $1 Guides and leader	3.25	1.25
496 A132 $2.25 Volunteers, anniv. emblem	4.00	3.75
Nos. 493-496 (4)	9.30	6.00

Blind Welfare, 75th anniv. (10c), Port-of-Spain City Hall, 75th anniv. (40c), Girl Guides, 75th anniv. ($1), and Red Cross, 50th anniv. ($2.25).

A133

Drum instruments played in a steel band.

Perf. 14½x14

1989, Nov. 30		Wmk. 384
497 A133 10c Tenor	.40	.40
498 A133 40c Guitar	.40	.40
499 A133 $1 Cello	.70	.80
500 A133 $2.25 Bass	1.75	2.00
Nos. 497-500 (4)	3.25	3.60

Mushrooms A134

1990, May 3		Perf. 14x13½
501 A134 10c *Xeromphalina tenuipes*	.60	.60
502 A134 40c *Dictyophora indusiata*	1.00	1.00
503 A134 $1 *Leucocoprinus birnbaumii*	2.40	2.40
504 A134 $2.25 *Crinipellis perniciosa*	5.00	5.00
Nos. 501-504 (4)	9.00	9.00

Stamp World London '90.

Scarlet Ibis A135

1990, Sept. 7		Perf. 14
505 A135 40c Immature bird	2.50	.50
506 A135 80c Mating display	2.75	2.00
507 A135 $1 Adult male	3.25	2.00
508 A135 $2.25 Adult, egg & young	5.50	5.00
Nos. 505-508 (4)	14.00	9.50

World Wildlife Fund.

Yellow Oriole — A136

1990, Dec. 17	Litho.	Wmk. 384
509 A136 20c shown	.30	.30
510 A136 25c Green rumped parrotlet	.65	.40
511 A136 40c Fork-tailed flycatcher	.30	.30
512 A136 50c Copper rumped hummingbird	.70	.55
513 A136 $1 Bananaquit	.85	.55
514 A136 $2 Semp	1.25	1.25
515 A136 $2.25 Channel-billed toucan	.65	.65

516 A136 $2.50 Bay headed tanager	.70	.70
517 A136 $5 Green honey-creeper	4.50	4.50
a. Souvenir sheet of 1, wmk. 373	4.50	4.50
518 A136 $10 Cattle egret	3.25	3.25
519 A136 $20 Golden olive woodpecker	9.50	9.50
520 A136 $50 Peregrine falcon	24.00	24.00
Nos. 509-520 (12)	46.65	45.95

No. 517a issued 2/3/97 for Hong Kong '97. For overprints & surcharge see #565-568, 597A.

1994-98		Wmk. 373
510a A136 25c	.90	.90
512a A136 50c	.60	.60
513a A136 $1	.90	.90
514a A136 $2	2.00	2.00
516a A136 $2.50	2.40	2.40
517b A136 $5	4.75	4.75
518a A136 $10	9.75	9.75
519a A136 $20	20.00	20.00
Nos. 510a-519a (8)	41.30	41.30

Issued: #510a, 8/94; #512a, 4/95; #510a, 8/94; #513a, 3/3/97; #516a, 518a, 519a, 10/14/98; #517b, 6/1996.
#510a, 513a, 514a, 517b dated 1990; #517a dated 1997.

University of the West Indies A137

Chancellors and Campus Buildings: 40c, HRH Princess Alice, Administration Building. 80c, Sir Hugh Wooding, Main Library. $1, Sir Allen Lewis, Faculty of Engineering. $2.25, Sir Shridath Ramphal, Faculty of Medical Studies.

Perf. 13½x14

1990, Oct. 15	Litho.	Wmk. 373
521 A137 40c multicolored	.60	.60
522 A137 80c multicolored	1.10	1.10
523 A137 $1 multicolored	1.60	1.60
524 A137 $2.25 multicolored	3.50	3.50
Nos. 521-524 (4)	6.80	6.80

British West Indies Airways, 50th Anniv. A138

Airplanes: 40c, Lockheed Lodestar. 80c, Vickers Viking 1A. $1, Vickers Viscount 702. $2.25, Boeing 707. $5, Lockheed TriStar 500.

1990, Nov. 27		Perf. 14
525 A138 40c multicolored	1.90	.65
526 A138 80c multicolored	2.75	1.90
527 A138 $1 multicolored	3.00	1.90
528 A138 $2.25 multicolored	5.50	7.00
Nos. 525-528 (4)	13.15	11.45

Souvenir Sheet

1990, Nov. 27		
529 A138 $5 multicolored	8.75	8.75

Ferns A139

1991, July 1		Perf. 13½
530 A139 40c Lygodium volubile	.65	.65
531 A139 80c Blechnum occidentale	1.25	1.25
532 A139 $1 Gleichenia bifida	1.60	1.60
533 A139 $2.25 Polypodium lycopodioides	3.50	3.50
Nos. 530-533 (4)	7.00	7.00

Trinidad & Tobago in World War II — A140

Designs: 40c, Firing practice by Trinidad & Tobago regiment. 80c, Fairey Barracuda surprises U-boat. $1, Avro Lancaster returns from bombing raid. $2.25, River class frigate on convoy duty. No. 538a, Supermarine Spitfire. b, Vickers Wellington.

Perf. 13½x14

1991, Dec. 7	Litho.	Wmk. 384
534 A140 40c multicolored	1.40	1.40
535 A140 80c multicolored	2.75	2.75
536 A140 $1 multicolored	3.50	3.50
537 A140 $2.25 multicolored	7.50	7.50
Nos. 534-537 (4)	15.15	15.15

Souvenir Sheet of 2

538 A140 $2.50 #a.-b.	22.50	22.50

H. E. Rapsey — A141

Inca Clathrata Quesneli — A142

Holy Name Convent — A143

1992, Mar. 30	Wmk. 373	Perf. 14
539 A141 40c multicolored	.80	.80
540 A142 80c multicolored	1.60	1.60
541 A143 $1 multicolored	2.10	2.10
Nos. 539-541 (3)	4.50	4.50

#539, Building and Loan Assoc., cent. #540, Trinidad & Tobago Field Naturalists' Club. #541, Holy Name Convent, cent.

Religions of Trinidad and Tobago — A145

#544, Baptist, baptism by immersion. #545, Muslim, minaret. #546, Hindu, Brahman..the source of all. #547, Christianity, cross. #548, Baha'i, slogan.

1992, Apr. 21	Litho.	Perf. 14
544 A145 40c multicolored	1.25	1.25
545 A145 40c multicolored	1.25	1.25
546 A145 40c multicolored	1.25	1.25

547 A145 40c multicolored   1.25 1.25
548 A145 40c multicolored   1.25 1.25
   Nos. 544-548 (5)   6.25 6.25

BWIA Aircraft A146

Wmk. 373

1992, Aug. 6   Litho.   Perf. 14
549 A146 $2.25 MD83   4.50 4.50
550 A146 $2.25 L1011   4.50 4.50

Natl. Museum and Art Gallery, Cent. A147

Wmk. 384

1992, Dec. 7   Litho.   Perf. 14½
551 A147 $1 multicolored   .75 .75

Christmas — A148

1992, Dec. 21
552 A148 40c multicolored   .50 .50

Trinidad Guardian, 75th Anniv. — A149

1992, Dec. 23
553 A149 40c multicolored   .50 .50

Philatelic Society of Trinidad & Tobago, 50th Anniv. A150

1992, Dec. 30
554 A150 $2.25 multicolored   1.75 1.75

CARICOM (Caribbean Economic Community), 20th Anniv. — A151

Map of CARICOM nations, portraits of West Indian men: 50c, $1.50, $2.75, $3, Derek Walcott, Sir Shridath Ramphal, William Demas.
$6, Order of the Caribbean Community.

Perf. 13x13½

1994, Jan. 31   Litho.   Wmk. 373
555 A151 50c pink & multi   .30 .30
556 A151 $1.50 green & multi   .90 .90
557 A151 $2.75 gray & multi   1.90 1.90
558 A151 $3 violet & multi   1.90 1.90
   Nos. 555-558 (4)   5.00 5.00

Souvenir Sheet
Perf. 13½x13
559 A151 $6 multicolored   4.50 4.50
No. 559 contains one 34x56mm stamp.

Drum Instruments Played in a Steel Band — A152

1994, Feb. 11   Perf. 14x15
560 A152 50c Quadrophonic pan   .35 .35
561 A152 $1 Tenor base pan   .75 .75
562 A152 $2.25 Six pan   1.60 1.60
563 A152 $2.50 Rocket pan   1.75 1.75
   Nos. 560-563 (4)   4.45 4.45

Aldwyn Roberts Kitchener, Calypso Singer — A153

1994, Feb. 11   Perf. 14
564 A153 50c multicolored   2.50 2.50

Nos. 510-511, 514, 518 Ovptd. with Hong Kong '94 Exhibition Emblem

Wmk. 384

1994, Feb. 18   Litho.   Perf. 14
565 A136 25c multicolored   .40 .40
566 A136 40c multicolored   .40 .40
567 A136 $2 multicolored   1.50 1.50
568 A136 $10 multicolored   7.75 7.75
   Nos. 565-568 (4)   10.05 10.05

Hotels & Lodges A154

#569, Trinidad Hilton. #570, Sandy Point Village, Tobago. #571, Asa Wright Nature Center and Lodge. #572, ML's Bed and Breakfast.

Wmk. 373

1994, Aug. 10   Litho.   Perf. 14
569 A154 $3 multicolored   1.75 1.75
570 A154 $3 multicolored   1.75 1.75
571 A154 $3 multicolored   1.75 1.75
572 A154 $3 multicolored   1.75 1.75
   Nos. 569-572 (4)   7.00 7.00

Snakes A155

50c, Boa constrictor. $1.25, Horse whip or vine snake. $2.50, Bushmaster. $3, Large coral snake.

Wmk. 373

1994, Sept. 19   Litho.   Perf. 14
573 A155 50c multicolored   .40 .40
574 A155 $1.25 multicolored   1.10 1.10
575 A155 $2.50 multicolored   2.10 2.10
576 A155 $3 multicolored   2.40 2.40
   Nos. 573-576 (4)   6.00 6.00

Trinidad Art Society, 50th Anniv. — A156

Artworks: No. 577, Copper sculpture, by Ken Morris. No. 578, Fisherman, by Sybil Atteck. No. 579, Snowballman, by Mahmoud P. Alladin.

1995, Mar. 6   Wmk. 384
577 A156 50c multicolored   1.10 1.10
578 A156 50c multicolored   1.10 1.10
579 A156 50c multicolored   1.10 1.10
   Nos. 577-579 (3)   3.30 3.30

Conservation — A157

Designs: $1.25, Leatherback turtle. $2.50, POS Lighthouse, vert. $3, "Knowsley" Ministry of Foreign Affairs.

1995, Aug. 7
580 A157 $1.25 multicolored   .85 .85
581 A157 $2.50 multicolored   1.75 1.75
582 A157 $3 multicolored   2.10 2.10
   Nos. 580-582 (3)   4.70 4.70

Brian Lara, Cricket Hero — A158

Designs: $1.25, Batting. $2.50, In batting stance. $3, Batting, diff.
No. 587: a, $3.75, With arms raised at crowd. b, $5.01, Down on one knee with bat.

Perf. 13x13½

1996, May 15   Litho.   Wmk. 373
583 A158 50c multicolored   .40 .40
584 A158 $1.25 multicolored   .95 .95
585 A158 $2.50 multicolored   1.75 1.75
586 A158 $3 multicolored   2.10 2.10
   Nos. 583-586 (4)   5.20 5.20

Souvenir Sheet
587 A158 Sheet of 2, #a.-b.   6.00 6.00

Trinidad & Tobago Remembers World War II — A159

50c, Red Cross Economy Label. $1.25, Battleship USS Missouri. $2.50, US servicemen playing baseball, Queen's Park, Savannah, 1942. $3, Fulmar 1, Royal Naval Air Station.
No. 592: a, Grumman Goose seaplane. b, US Navy Airship.

Wmk. 373

1996, June 7   Litho.   Perf. 14
588 A159 50c multicolored   .60 .60
589 A159 $1.25 multicolored   1.40 1.40
590 A159 $2.50 multicolored   2.75 2.75
591 A159 $3 multicolored   3.25 3.25
   Nos. 588-591 (4)   8.00 8.00

Souvenir Sheet of 2
592 A159 $3 #a.-b.   12.00 12.00

A160

Wendy Fitzwilliam, 1998 Miss Universe: $1.25, Lying on beach. $2.50, In traditional costume. $3, Wearing evening gown. $5, After coronation.

1999, May 3   Litho.   Perf. 14
593 A160 50c multicolored   .60 .60
594 A160 $1.25 multicolored   1.25 1.25
595 A160 $2.50 multicolored   2.40 2.40
596 A160 $3 multicolored   2.75 2.75
   Nos. 593-596 (4)   7.00 7.00

Souvenir Sheet
597 A160 $5 multicolored   7.00 7.00

No. 511 Surcharged

1999   Method and Perf. as Before
597A A136 75c on 40c multi   —

A161

Angostura Bitters, 175th Anniv.: 75c, Angostura Bitters bottle. $3, Distillery. $4.50, Bitters bottle, cocktails.

Self-Adhesive
Serpentine Die Cut

2000, Jan. 27   Litho.
598 A161 75c multi   .60 .60
599 A161 $3 multi   2.40 2.40
600 A161 $4.50 multi   3.50 3.50
  a. Souvenir sheet, #598-600   6.50 6.50

Tourism A162

Shoreline scenes: 75c, Maracas Bay. $1, Pirates Bay. $3.75, Pigeon Point. $5, Toco, North Coast.

2000, July 25 Litho. Perf. 14¼x14½
601 A162 75c multi   .40 .40
602 A162 $1 multi   .60 .60
603 A162 $3.75 multi   2.75 2.75
604 A162 $5 multi   3.25 3.25

Christmas A163

Design: 75c, Caroni landscape. $3.75, Pastelles, sorrel and ginger beer. $4.50, Musicians under palm trees. $5.25, Angels with steel drums.

Perf. 14¼x14½

2000, Nov. 14				Litho.
605	A163	75c multi	.40	.40
606	A163	$3.75 multi	2.75	2.75
607	A163	$4.50 multi	3.00	3.00
608	A163	$5.25 multi	3.75	3.75

No. 515
Surcharged

Method and Perf. as Before

2001?			
609	A136	75c on $2.25 multi	—

National
Mail Center
A164

Designs: $3, Building entrance. $10, Side of building.

Perf. 14¼x14½

2000, Nov. 20				Litho.
610-611	A164	Set of 2	7.00	7.00

Endangered
Fauna
A165

Designs: 25c, Paca, 50c, Prehensile-tailed porcupine. 75c, Iguana. $1, Leatherback turtle. $2, Golden tegu. $2, Red howler monkey. $4, Weeping capuchin monkey, vert. $5, River otter. $10, Ocelot. $20, Trinidad piping guan, vert.

Perf. 14¼x14½, 14½x14¼

2001, Feb. 6				Litho.
612	A165	25c multi	.25	.25
613	A165	50c multi	.25	.25
614	A165	75c multi	.35	.35
615	A165	$1 multi	.50	.50
616	A165	$2 multi	1.10	1.10
617	A165	$3 multi	1.50	1.50
618	A165	$4 multi	2.10	2.10
619	A165	$5 multi	2.75	2.75
620	A165	$10 multi	5.75	5.75
621	A165	$20 multi	11.50	11.50
		Nos. 612-621 (10)	26.05	26.05

Salvation Army in
Trinidad & Tobago,
Cent. — A166

Designs: 75c, Emblem. $2, William Booth Memorial Hall.

Perf. 14½x14¼

2001, Aug. 9				
622-623	A166	Set of 2	2.00	2.00
623a		Souvenir sheet, #622-623, perf. 13¾x14¼	2.00	2.00

Natl. Library,
150th Anniv.
A167

Designs: 75c, Port of Spain Public Library, Carnegie Free Library. $3.25, New National Library building.

Perf. 14¼x14½

2001, Aug. 9				
624-625	A167	Set of 2	3.00	3.00
625a		Souvenir sheet, #624-625	3.00	3.00

Under 17 World Soccer
Championships — A168

Designs: $2, Emblem of Soca Warriors. $3.25, National flag. $4.50, Lion holding flag. $5.25, Stadiums.

Perf. 14½x14

2001, Sept. 6				
626-629	A168	Set of 4	9.00	9.00
629a		Souvenir sheet, #626-629	9.00	9.00

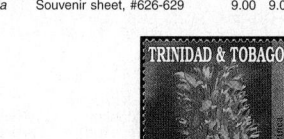

Flowers — A169

Designs: $1, Pachystachys coccinea. $2.50, Heliconia psittacorum. $3.25, Brownea latifolia, horiz. $3.75, Oncidium papilio.

2001			**Perf. 14½x14¼, 14¼x14½**	
630-633	A169	Set of 4	7.25	7.25

Christmas — A170

People and: $1, Boats, church. $3.75, Flowers. $4.50, House, flowers. $5.25, Church, post office.

2001			**Perf. 14½x14¼**	
634-637	A170	Set of 4	8.00	8.00
637a		Souvenir sheet, #634-637	9.00	9.00

Butterflies
A171

Designs: $1, Cracker. $3.75, Tiger. $4.50, Four continent. $5.25, "89."

2002, June 19		Litho.	**Perf. 13¼x13**	
638-641	A171	Set of 4	10.00	10.00

Hummingbirds
A172

Designs: $1, Rufous-breasted hermit. $2.50, Black-throated mango. $3.25, Tufted coquette. $3.75, White-chested emerald.

2002 ?			**Perf. 13x13¼**	
642-645	A172	Set of 4	8.00	8.00

Historic
Forts
A173

Designs: $1, Fort Picton. $3.75, Fort George. $4.50, Fort King George. $5.25, Fort James.

2002 ?			**Perf. 13¼x13**	
646-649	A173	Set of 4	9.00	9.00
649a		Souvenir sheet, #646-649	9.00	9.00

Reign of
Queen
Elizabeth II,
50th Anniv.
A174

Queen: $3.75, At Governor General's House. $4.50, With Mayor E. Taylor of Port of Spain. $5.25, At Red House, addressing Parliament, #119, and former personal flag of the Queen.

$10, In limousine, waving to crowd.

2002		Litho.	**Perf. 13¾**	
650-652	A174	Set of 3	9.00	9.00

Souvenir Sheet

653	A174	$10 multi	6.50	6.50

Independence, 40th Anniv. — A175

2002				
654	A175	$1 multi	1.00	1.00

Christmas
A176

Designs: $1, Child opening gift of steel drum, vert. $2.50, People, musicians, house. $3.75, Houses. $5.25, Santa Claus on horse-drawn cart, vert.

		Perf. 14½x14¼, 14¼x14½		
2002, Nov. 20				**Litho.**
655-658	A176	Set of 4	6.00	6.00

Pan-American
Health
Organization,
Cent. — A177

Designs: $1, Emblem. $2.50, National headquarters, Port of Spain. $3.25, Steel drum with symbols. $4.50, Joseph L. Pawan (1887-1957), discoverer of vampire bat rabies.

2002, Dec. 2			**Perf. 14½x14¼**	
659-662	A177	Set of 4	7.00	7.00

Cricket
Players — A178

Designs: $1, Ian Raphael Bishop. $2.50, Deryck Lance Murray. $4.50, Augustine Lawrence Logie. $5.25, Ann Browne John.

2003, Feb. 7			**Perf. 13**	
663-666	A178	Set of 4	7.50	7.50

Carnival
A179

Various costumed participants: $1, $2.50, $3.75, vert., $4.50, vert., $5.25, vert.

		Perf. 14¼x14½, 14½x14¼		
2003, Feb. 25				**Litho.**
667-671	A179	Set of 5	8.00	8.00
671a		Souvenir sheet of 1	5.00	5.00

Inauguration of Intl. Criminal
Court — A180

Designs: $1, Trinidad & Tobago Pres. Arthur N. R. Robinson and UN Secretary General Kofi Annan. $2.50, Robinson, Prof. Benjamin Ferencz, Prof. Cherif Bassiouni, Philippe Kirsch, UN Undersecretary for Legal Affairs Hans Corell. $3.75, Robinson and Corell. $4.50, Robinson, Emma Bonino, and Italian Pres. Carlo Ciampi.

$6, Robinson, vert.

		Perf. 14¾x14½, 14½x14¾		
2003, Feb. 25				
672-675	A180	Set of 4	7.00	7.00

Souvenir Sheet

676	A180	$6 multi	5.00	5.00

Rainforest Flora &
Fauna — A181

No. 677: a, Mountain immortelle. b, Blue-crowned motmot. c, Red howler monkey. d, Butterfly orchid. e, Channel-billed toucan. f, Ocelot. g, Bromeliads. h, Lineated woodpecker. i, Tamandua. j, Emperor butterfly.

Serpentine Die Cut 12½
2003, Feb. 24 **Litho.**
Self-Adhesive
677 Booklet pane of 10 9.00
a.-j. A181 $1 Any single .85 .85

Lighthouses
A182

Designs: $1, Port-of-Spain. $3.75, Chacachacare. $4.50, Port-of-Spain, diff. $5.25, Chacachacare, diff.
No. 681B, Like No. 679, spelled "Chacacharie." No. 681C, Like No. 681, spelled "Chacacharie."

2002-03 **Perf. 14½x14¼**
678-681 A182 Set of 4 9.50 9.50
681a Souvenir sheet, #678-681 9.50 9.50
681B A182 $3.75 multi — —
681C A182 $5.25 multi — —

Nos. 678, 680, 681B and 681C were issued on 11/6/02 and all were withdrawn from sale later that day when the incorrect spelling of the lighthouse was discovered. Nos. 678 and 680 were put back on sale, along with new stamps with the corrected spelling of the lighthouse, Nos. 679 and 681, and the souvenir sheet with the stamps with the corrected spelling, No. 681a, on 5/26/03. The editors would like to examine any examples of the souvenir sheet with stamps with the incorrect spelling.

Scenes of Village
Life — A183

Designs: $1, Dancing the cocoa. $2.50, Dirt oven. $3.75, River washing. $4.50, Box cart racing. $5.25, Pitching marbles.

2003, Oct. 28
682-686 A183 Set of 5 7.00 7.00

Marine
Life — A184

Designs: $1, Boulder brain coral. $2.50, Hawksbill turtle. $3.75, Green moray eel. $4.50, Creole wrasse. $5.25, Black-spotted sea goddess.
$10, Queen angelfish.

2003, Oct. 28 **Perf. 14¼x14½**
687-691 A184 Set of 5 10.00 10.00
Souvenir Sheet
692 A184 $10 multi 10.00 10.00

Christmas — A185

Paintings by Jean Michel Cazabon (1813-88): $1, View of Port-of-Spain from Laventille Hill. $2.50, View of Diego Martin from Fort George. $3.75, Corbeaux Town, Trinidad. $4.50, Rain Clouds over Cedros. $5.25, Los Galos, Icacos Bay.
No. 698: a, $5, River at St. Ann's. b, $6.50, House in Trinidad.

2003, Nov. 17 **Perf. 13¾**
693-697 A185 Set of 5 8.00 8.00
Souvenir Sheet
698 A185 Sheet of 2, #a-b 8.00 8.00

World
AIDS
Day
A186

Designs: $1, Unite against AIDS. $2.50, Stigma isolates. $3.75, Care stops AIDS, vert. $4.50, Family protects, vert.
$10, People and AIDS ribbon.

2003, Nov. 21
699-702 A186 Set of 4 6.00 6.00
Souvenir Sheet
703 A186 $10 multi 6.00 6.00

2004
Carnival — A187

Calypso musicians: $1, Aldric Farrel, "The Lord Pretender." $2.50, Roy Lewis, "The Mystic Prowler." $3.75, Lord Kitchener, The Mighty Sparrow and The Roaring Lion. $4.50, McArthur Linda Sandy-Rose, "Calypso Rose." $5.25, Nap Hepburne, Lord Brynner and The Mighty Sparrow.
$10, McArthur Linda Sandy-Rose, diff.

2004, Feb. 18
704-708 A187 Set of 5 8.00 8.00
Souvenir Sheet
709 A187 $10 multi 6.00 6.00

2004 Summer
Olympics,
Athens — A188

Designs: $1, Track and field. $2.50, Boxing. $3.75, Taekwondo. $4.50, Swimming.

2004, July 19 **Litho.** **Perf. 13**
710-713 A188 Set of 4 6.00 6.00

Intl. Year
Commemorating
the Struggle
Against Slavery
and Its
Abolition — A189

Designs: $1, Slave ship. $2.50, Rada community, Belmont. $3.75, Daaga, Prince of Popo. $4.50, Slaves singing freedom songs, horiz. $5.25, Providence Estate Aqueduct, Tobago, horiz.
$15, Sandy's escape, horiz.

2004, Sept. 23 **Litho.** **Perf. 13**
714-718 A189 Set of 5 8.00 8.00
Souvenir Sheet
719 A189 $15 multi 8.00 8.00

Christmas
A190

Paintings by Arthur Aldwin "Boscoe" Holder: $1, Lady with Ginger Lilies. $2.50, View from Maracas Lookout. $3.75, Lady in Peacock Chair. $4.50, Caribbean Beauty in White, horiz. $5.25, Teteron Bay, Chaguaramas, horiz.
$10, Creole Ladies in Straw Hats, horiz.

2004, Nov. 22
720-724 A190 Set of 5 7.00 7.00
Souvenir Sheet
725 A190 $10 multi 5.00 5.00

Fruits — A191

Designs: $1, Mango. $2.50, Lime. $3.75, Pineapple. $4.50, Coconut, horiz. $5.25, Orange, horiz.
$10, Guava, horiz.

2004, June 7
726-730 A191 Set of 5 7.00 7.00
Souvenir Sheet
731 A191 $10 multi 6.00 6.00

Carnival — A192

Designs: $1, Dame Lorraine. $2.50, Jab Jab. $3.25, Burrokeet, horiz. $3.75, Midnight Robber. $4.50, Fancy Indian.
$15, Fancy Sailor.

2005, Jan. 18 **Litho.** **Perf. 13**
732-736 A192 Set of 5 7.00 7.00
Souvenir Sheet
737 A192 $15 multi 7.00 7.00

Brian Lara,
Cricket
Player — A193

Various photos of Lara in action: $1, $2.50, $3.75, $4.50, $5.25.
$15, Lara walking under raised cricket bats.

2005, Apr. 12 **Litho.** **Perf. 13**
738-742 A193 Set of 5 7.50 7.50
Souvenir Sheet
743 A193 $15 multi 7.50 7.50

Tobago Heritage
Festival — A194

Designs: $1, Belé. $2.50, Dancing the jig. $3.75, Goat race, horiz. $4.50, Harvest Festival, horiz. $5.25, Drumming Festival, horiz.
$15, Traditional Tobago wedding.

Perf. 13½x13¼, 13¼x13½
2005, Aug. 15
744-748 A194 Set of 5 7.50 7.50
Souvenir Sheet
Perf. 13¼
749 A194 $15 multi 7.50 7.50

Medicinal
Herbs
A195

Designs: 25c, Rachet. 50c, Chandelier. 75c, Worm grass. $1, Black sage. $3, Wonder of the world. $3.25, Vervine. $4, Aloe vera. $5, Senna. $10, Bois bande. $20, Herbal garden.

2005, May 18 **Perf. 13¼x13**
750 A195 25c multi .25 .25
751 A195 50c multi .25 .25
752 A195 75c multi .30 .30
753 A195 $1 multi .35 .35
754 A195 $3 multi 1.00 1.00
755 A195 $3.25 multi 1.10 1.10
756 A195 $4 multi 1.40 1.40
757 A195 $5 multi 1.75 1.75
758 A195 $10 multi 3.50 3.50
759 A195 $20 multi 7.00 7.00
Nos. 750-759 (10) 16.90 16.90

Fish and Marine
Life — A196

No. 760: a, Foureye butterfly fish. b, Caribbean reef squid. c, Hawksbill turtle. d, Southern sting ray. e, Queen angelfish. f, Giant anemone. g, Peppermint shrimp. h, Rough file clam. i, White-speckled hermit crab. j, Christmas tree worm.

Serpentine Die Cut 12½
2005, May 1 **Litho.**
Self-Adhesive
760 Booklet of 10 7.00
a.-j. A196 $1 Any single .65 .65

Sir Solomon Hochoy (1905-83), First
Governor-General — A197

Hochoy and: $1, Prime Minister Dr. Eric E. Williams. $2.50, Haile Selassie. $3.75, His wife, Thelma. $4.50, Queen Elizabeth II. $5.25, Honor Guard.
$15, Hochoy in uniform.

2005, Aug. 22 **Perf. 13½x13**
761-765 A197 Set of 5 7.50 7.50
Souvenir Sheet
Perf. 13½x13¼
766 A197 $15 multi 7.00 7.00

Introduction of Women Police, 50th
Anniv. — A198

2005, Sept. 30   *Perf. 12¾*
767 A198 $15 black   6.50 6.50

Souvenir Sheet

Children Against Cancer — A199

2005, Nov. 7   *Perf. 13½x13¼*
768 A199 $15 multi   9.50 9.50
No. 768 sold for $20.

Anansi and the
Cricket
Match — A200

Anansi: $1, And friends reading cricket bro-
chure. $2.50, And friends hiding in bathroom.
$3.75, And friends under umbrella. $4.50,
Holding bag, talking to woman. $5.25, Laugh-
ing at friends paying woman.
$15, Anansi rubbing stomach.

2005, Dec. 12   *Perf. 13½x13*
769-773 A200 Set of 5   7.00 7.00
Souvenir Sheet
774 A200 $15 multi   6.00 6.00

Pope John Paul
II (1920-2005)
A201

Scenes from Pope's 1985 visit to Trinidad &
Tobago: $1, Leaving airplane. $2.50, Kissing
ground. $3.75, Shaking hands with priest.
$4.50, With bishop, waving. $5.25, Celebrating
mass.
$15, Waving to crowd from police vehicle.

2006, Apr. 10 Litho. *Perf. 13½x13¼*
775-779 A201 Set of 5   7.00 7.00
Souvenir Sheet
780 A201 $15 multi   6.00 6.00

2006 World Cup Soccer
Championships, Germany — A202

Various images of Trinidad & Tobago soccer
players in action: $1, $2.50, $3.75, $4.50.

2006, June 28   *Litho.*
781-784 A202 Set of 4   9.00 9.00
Initial reports said this set was available only
with the purchase of a first day cover for $50,
but the stamps have been made available individually at face value.

CARICOM Single
Market and
Economy
A203

Designs: $1, Cables, palm tree. $2.50,
Lighthouse, check. $3.75, Cell phone, diver.
$4.50, Sprinter's hands, beach, horiz. $5.25,
Hands on computer keyboard, globe, horiz.
$15, Map of Caribbean, horiz.

Perf. 13½x13¼, 13¼x13½
2006, July 3
785-789 A203 Set of 5   6.50 6.50
Souvenir Sheet
790 A203 $15 multi   6.50 6.50

Souvenir Sheet

Orchid Society, 50th Anniv. — A204

2006, Sept. 5   *Perf. 13½x13¼*
791 A204 $15 multi   6.00 6.00

Arrival of
Chinese to
Trinidad and
Tobago,
Bicent.
A205

Art: $1, Guayaguayare Beach, by Ou Hing
Wan. $2.50, Hosay, by Carlisle Chang. $3.75,
Saddle Road, by Amy Leong Pang, vert.
$4.50, Mother & Child, sculpture by Patrick
Chu Foon, vert. $5.25, Still Life, by Sybil
Atteck, vert.
$15, Inherent Nobility of Man, by Chang,
vert.

Perf. 14¼x14½, 14½x14¼
2006, Oct. 11
792-796 A205 Set of 5   7.00 7.00
Souvenir Sheet
Perf. 13x13¼
797 A205 $15 multi   6.50 6.50

Children's
Games — A206

Designs: $1, Rim driving. $2.50, Top spinning. $3.75, Playing 3A. $4.50, Farmer in the
Den.
$15, Tire swing.

2006, Nov. 29   *Perf. 13¼*
798-801 A206 Set of 4   5.00 5.00
Souvenir Sheet
802 A206 $15 multi   6.00 6.00

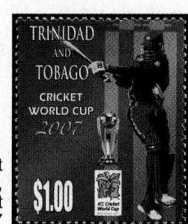

2007 Cricket
World Cup,
West
Indies — A207

2007 Cricket World Cup emblem, Cricket
World Cup and: $1, Batsman. $2, Bowler.
$2.50, Bowler, diff. $3.75, Batsman, diff.
$4.50, Wicketkeeper.
$15, Cricket World Cup.

2007, Mar. 15   Litho.   *Perf. 13*
803-807 A207 Set of 5   4.50 4.50
Souvenir Sheet
Perf. 13½
808 A207 $15 multi   4.75 4.75
No. 808 contains one 27x45mm stamp.

Reopening of
Red House,
Cent. — A208

Designs: $1, Red House, c. 1907. $2.50,
Parliament Chamber. $3.75, Cenotaph and
Eternal Flame. $5.25, Rotunda and fountain.
$15, Dome.

2007, Sept. 14   *Perf. 13½x13¼*
809-812 A208 Set of 4   4.00 4.00
Souvenir Sheet
813 A208 $15 multi   4.75 4.75

St. Mary's
Children's
Home, 150th
Anniv. — A209

Designs: $1, Main entrance, c. 1930. $2.50,
Fountain. $3.75, St. Mary's Anglican Church.
$4.50, St. Mary's Children's Home Cub Scout
pack.

2007, Sept. 21
814-817 A209 Set of 4   3.75 3.75

Historic
Buildings
A210

Designs: $1, Roomor. $2, Killarney. $2.50,
Queen's Royal College. $3.25, Hayes Court.
$3.75, Knowsley. $4.50, Mille Fleurs. $10,
Boissiere House. $20, Archbishop's House.
$50, White Hall.

2007, Dec. 14   Litho.   *Perf. 13*
818 A210 $1 multi   .35   .35
819 A210 $2 multi   .65   .65
820 A210 $2.50 multi   .80   .80
821 A210 $3.25 multi   1.10 1.10
822 A210 $3.75 multi   1.25 1.25
823 A210 $4.50 multi   1.50 1.50
824 A210 $10 multi   3.25 3.25
825 A210 $20 multi   6.50 6.50
826 A210 $50 multi   16.00 16.00
Nos. 818-826 (9)   31.40 31.40

Souvenir Sheet

Ozone Layer Protection — A211

2008, Jan. 24 Litho. *Perf. 13x13¼*
827 A211 $15 multi   4.75 4.75

Miniature Sheet

2008 Summer Olympics,
Beijing — A212

No. 828: a, Running. b, Table tennis. c,
Cycling. d, Swimming.

2008, June 16   *Perf. 12*
828 A212 $3.50 Sheet of 4, #a-d 4.75 4.75

Scouting,
Cent. (in
2007)
A213

Designs: $1, Cub scouts. $2.50, Scouts.
$3.75, Venturers. $4.50, Leaders.
$15, Lord Robert Baden-Powell, vert.

2008, July 29 Litho. *Perf. 13¼x13¼*
829-832 A213 Set of 4   4.00 4.00
Souvenir Sheet
Perf. 13½x13¼
833 A213 $15 multi   5.00 5.00

University of the West Indies, 60th Anniv. — A214

Designs: $1, Sir Arthur Lewis, first West Indian principal. $2.50, Princess Alice, Countess of Athlone, first Chancellor. $3.75, Sir Philip Sherlock, first principal of St. Augustine Campus. $4.50, Administration Building, St. Augustine Campus, horiz. $5.25, Samaan tree, St. Augustine Campus, horiz.
$15, Administration Building, St. Augustine Campus, at night.

Perf. 13½x13¼, 13¼x13½
2008, Oct. 3
834-838 A214 Set of 5   5.50 5.50
Souvenir Sheet
839 A214 $15 multi   5.00 5.00

Worldwide Fund for Nature (WWF) — A215

No. 840 — Brazilian porcupine: a, Adult on branch (shown). b, Head. c, Adult and juvenile. d, Juvenile on branch.

2008, Nov. 3   Perf. 13½x13¼
840   Strip or block of 4   5.00 5.00
a.-d. A215 $3.75 Any single   1.25 1.25
e.   Miniature sheet, 2 each
       #840a-840d   10.00 10.00

Commonwealth Heads of Government Meeting, Port of Spain — A216

Designs: $1, International Finance Center, Waterfront Complex, Port of Spain. $2.50, Steel drums. $3.75, Pigeon Point, Tobago. $4.50, Queen Elizabeth II and Commonwealth Secretaries-General chief Emeka Anyaoku, Kamalesh Sharma, Sir Shridath Ramphal, and Sir Donald McKinnon. $5.25, Scarlet ibis.
$15, Emblem of Commonwealth Heads of Government Meeting.

2009, Nov. 16   Perf. 13¼
841-845 A216 Set of 5   5.50 5.50
Souvenir Sheet
Perf. 14x13¾
846 A216 $15 multi   4.75 4.75
No. 846 contains one 33x45mm stamp.

Souvenir Sheet

Trinidad & Tobago Postal Corporation, 10th Anniv. — A217

No. 847: a, Head office. b, Retail counter.

Litho. & Embossed
2009, Dec. 18   Perf. 13¾x13¼
847 A217 $10 Sheet of 2, #a-b   6.50 6.50

Miniature Sheets

Intl. Year of Biodiversity — A218

No. 848: a, $1, Collared peccary. b, $1, No Man's Land, Bon Accord, Tobago. c, $2.50, Butterfly orchid. d, $2.50, Hot peppers. e, $3.75, Paria Bay, Trinidad. f, $3.75, Ornate hawk eagle. g, $4.50, Trinidad piping-guan. h, $4.50, Royal poinciana tree. i, $5.25, Trinidad select hybrid cocoa pods. j, $5.25, Water buffalos, Aripo Livestock Station.
No. 849: a, $1, Agouti. b, $1, Fishermen at Grafton Beach, Tobago. c, $2.50, Caroni Swamp and Bird Sanctuary, Trinidad. d, $2.50, Red bracket deer. e, $3.75, Turkey vulture. f, $3.75, White-chested emerald hummingbird. g, $4.50, Leatherback turtle. h, $4.50, Nariva Swamp, Trinidad. i, $5.25, Soldado Rock, Gulf of Paria. j, $5.25, Orchid.

2010, May 26 Litho. Perf. 13¼x12½
Sheets of 10, #a-j
848-849 A218 Set of 2   21.50 21.50
London 2010 Festival of Stamps.

Syrians and Lebanese in Trinidad & Tobago, Cent. — A219

Designs: $1, Rahme Sabga, peddler. $2.50, Kashish, peddler. $3.75, Grand Bazaar Shopping Center. $4.50, Nicholas Tower.
$15, Woman wearing traditional Arab head covering.

2010, July 20   Perf. 13¼x13
850-853 A219 Set of 4   3.75 3.75
Souvenir Sheet
854 A219 $15 multi   4.75 4.75

Trinidad & Tobago Cadet Force, Cent. — A220

Various photographs of cadets: $1, $2.50, $3.75, $4.50, $5.25.
$15, Rifles, Sir George Ruthven Le Hunte, Cadet Force founder, and Pres. George Maxwell Richards.

2010, Dec. 1   Perf. 13x13¼
855-859 A220 Set of 5   5.50 5.50
Souvenir Sheet
860 A220 $15 multi   4.75 4.75

Tobago House of Assembly, 30th Anniv. A221

Designs: $1, Tobago House of Assembly. $2.50, Englishman's Bay. $3.75, St. Patrick's Anglican Church. $4.50, Fort King George. $5.25, Buccoo Goat Race.
$15, Pigeon Point Heritage Park.

2010, Dec. 4   Perf. 13x13¼
861-865 A221 Set of 5   5.50 5.50
Souvenir Sheet
Perf. 13¼
866 A221 $15 multi   4.75 4.75

Festivities A222

Designs: $1, Spiritual Baptist Liberation Day. $2.50, Eid ul-Fitr. $3.75, Christmas. $4.50, Diwali.
$15, Parang.

2010, Dec. 10   Perf. 13¼x13
867-870 A222 Set of 4   3.75 3.75
Souvenir Sheet
Perf. 13¼
871 A222 $15 multi   4.75 4.75

Carnival — A223

Designs: $1, Participant in Sky People costume designed by Peter Minshall. $2.50, Children portraying Pierrot Grenade. $3.75, Junior Carnival Queen on Broadway. $4.50, Children's Carnival on Frederick Street. $5.25, Participant in Black Indian Chief costume designed by Larrie Approo.
$15, Participant in Pan Woman costume designed by Wendy Kallicharan.

2011, Mar. 1   Perf. 12
872-876 A223 Set of 5   5.50 5.50
Souvenir Sheet
877 A223 $15 multi   4.75 4.75

Dr. Eric Williams (1911-81), Prime Minister — A224

Designs: $1, Williams with Sir V. S. Naipaul, Michael Anthony, and Andre Deutsch. $1.50, Williams playing cricket with C. L. R. James and Sir Learie Constantine. $2.50, Williams by Georgia M. Cordner. $4.50, Williams with John Lennon and Ringo Starr. $5.25, Williams and Jawaharlal Nehru.
$15, Williams with Sir Winston Churchill.

2011, Apr. 5 Litho. Perf. 13¼x13
878-883 A224 Set of 6   6.00 6.00
Souvenir Sheet
884 A224 $15 multi   4.75 4.75

SEMI-POSTAL STAMPS

Emblem of Red Cross SP1

Perf. 11, 12
1914, Sept. 18 Typo. Unwmk.
B1   SP1 (½p) red (on cover)   250.00
This stamp was allowed to pay ½p postage on one day, Sept. 18, 1914, on circulars distributed by the Red Cross. Value on cover is for proper Red Cross usage. Value unused, $15.

No. 2 Overprinted in Red (Cross) and Black (Date)

a   b

1915, Oct. 21 Wmk. 3 Perf. 14
B2   A1 (a) 1p scarlet   2.25 2.25

1916, Oct. 19
B3   A1 (b) 1p scarlet   .80 3.25
a.   Date omitted

POSTAGE DUE STAMPS

D1

1923-45 Typo. Wmk. 4 Perf. 14
J1   D1 1p black   .95   1.90
J2   D1 2p black   1.90   1.90
J3   D1 3p black ('25)   1.90   2.75
J4   D1 4p black ('29)   3.50 25.00
J5   D1 5p black ('45)   42.50 110.00
J6   D1 6p black ('45)   67.50 42.50
J7   D1 8p black ('45)   52.50 200.00
J8   D1 1sh black ('45)   90.00 140.00
  Nos. J1-J8 (8)   260.75 524.05

> **Catalogue values for unused stamps in this section, from this point to the end of the section, are for Never Hinged items.**

Denominations in Cents

1947, Sept. 1

J9	D1	2c black	2.50	3.25
J10	D1	4c black	1.50	4.50
J11	D1	6c black	1.90	9.00
J12	D1	8c black	1.90	27.50
J13	D1	10c black	1.90	4.00
J14	D1	12c black	1.90	22.50
J15	D1	16c black	3.50	52.50
J16	D1	24c black	12.50	11.00
		Nos. J9-J16 (8)	27.60	134.25

Nos. J9-J16 also exist on chalky paper.

Wmk. 4a (error)

J9a	D1	2c	60.00
J11a	D1	6c	125.00
J14a	D1	12c	150.00

D2

1970 Unwmk. Litho. Perf. 14x13½
Size: 18x23mm

J17	D2	2c green	.25	2.75
J18	D2	4c carmine rose	.25	4.25
J19	D2	6c brown	.55	5.50
J20	D2	8c lt violet	.70	6.25
J21	D2	10c brick red	.70	6.25
J22	D2	12c dull orange	.90	6.25
J23	D2	16c brt yellow grn	.90	4.25
J24	D2	24c gray	.90	4.50
J25	D2	50c blue	.90	5.00
J26	D2	60c olive green	.90	5.00
		Nos. J17-J26 (10)	6.95	50.00

Perf. 13½x14
1976-77 Litho. Unwmk.
Size: 17x21mm

J27	D2	2c green	.25	1.75
J28	D2	4c carmine rose	.25	1.75
J29	D2	6c brown	.25	2.40
J30	D2	8c lt violet	.30	2.40
J31	D2	10c brick red	.30	2.40
J32	D2	12c dull orange	.45	3.25
		Nos. J27-J32 (6)	1.80	13.95

Issued: 4c, 12c, 4/1/76; 2c, 6c, 8c, 10, 1977.

The letters in the top label on Nos. J27-J32 are larger with D's and O's more squarish than the oval letters on Nos. J17-J26. "Postage Due" is 13mm long and is composed of finer letters than on Nos. J17-J26, which have a 14mm inscription.

WAR TAX STAMPS

Nos. 1-2 Overprinted

1917 Wmk. 3 Perf. 14

MR1	A1	1p scarlet	3.50	4.25
a.		Invtd. overprint	200.00	250.00

Overprinted

MR2	A1	½p green	.30	.30
a.		Overprinted on face and back	425.00	
b.		Pair, one without over-print	275.00	
MR3	A1	1p scarlet	.80	2.25
a.		Pair, one without over-print	425.00	800.00
b.		Double overprint	125.00	

Overprinted

MR4	A1	½p green	.30	6.50
MR5	A1	1p scarlet	.30	1.00

Overprinted

MR6	A1	½p green	.30	3.25
MR7	A1	1p scarlet	3.50	1.25

Overprinted

MR8	A1	½p green	.30	3.25
MR9	A1	1p scarlet	35.00	27.50

Overprinted

MR10	A1	1p scarlet	.80	1.40
a.		Inverted overprint	100.00	100.00

Overprinted

MR11	A1	1p scarlet	1.75	.30
a.		Double overprint	200.00	200.00
b.		Inverted overprint	125.00	125.00

Overprinted

1918

MR12	A1	½p green	.30	2.00
MR13	A1	1p scarlet	.90	1.75
a.		Double overprint	125.00	
b.		Horiz. pair, one without overprint		1,000.

The War Tax Stamps show considerable variations in the colors, thickness of the paper, distinctness of the watermark, and the gum. Counterfeits exist of the errors of Nos. MR1-MR13.

OFFICIAL STAMPS

Regular Issue of 1913 Overprinted

1913 Wmk. 3 Perf. 14

O1	A1	½p green	1.25	7.50

Same Overprinted

1914

O2	A1	½p green	2.25	15.00

Same Overprinted

1916

O3	A1	½p green	1.50	3.50
a.		Double overprint	27.50	

Same Overprint without Period

1917

O4	A1	½p green	1.00	7.50

Same Overprinted

1917, Aug. 22

O5	A1	½p green	1.75	20.00

The official stamps are found in several shades of green and on paper of varying thickness.

TRIPOLITANIA

tri-ˌpä-lə-ˈtā-nyə

LOCATION — In northern Africa, bordering on Mediterranean Sea
GOVT. — A former Italian Colony
AREA — 350,000 sq. mi. (approx.)
POP. — 570,716 (1921)
CAPITAL — Tripoli

Formerly a Turkish province, Tripolitania became part of Italian Libya. See Libya.

100 Centesimi = 1 Lira

Used values in italics are for postally used stamps. CTO's or stamps with fake cancels sell for about the same as unused, hinged stamps.

Watermark

Wmk. 140 — Crowns

Propaganda of the Faith Issue
Italian Stamps Overprinted

1923, Oct. 24 Wmk. 140 Perf. 14

1	A68	20c ol grn & brn org	11.00	47.50
2	A68	30c claret & brn org	11.00	47.50
3	A68	50c vio & brn org	5.50	55.00
4	A68	1 l blue & brn org	5.50	75.00
		Nos. 1-4 (4)	33.00	225.00
		Set, never hinged	80.00	

Fascisti Issue

Italian Stamps Overprinted in Red or Black

1923, Oct. 29 Unwmk.

5	A69	10c dk green (R)	13.00	16.00
6	A69	30c dk violet (R)	13.00	16.00
7	A69	50c brown car	13.00	20.00

Wmk. 140

8	A70	1 l blue	13.00	45.00
9	A70	2 l brown	13.00	52.50
10	A71	5 l blk & bl (R)	13.00	75.00
		Nos. 5-10 (6)	78.00	224.50
		Set, never hinged	180.00	

Manzoni Issue
Stamps of Italy, 1923, Overprinted in Red

1924, Apr. 1 Wmk. 140 Perf. 14

11	A72	10c brown red & blk	12.50	65.00
12	A72	15c blue grn & blk	12.50	65.00
13	A72	30c black & slate	12.50	65.00
14	A72	50c org brn & blk	12.50	65.00
15	A72	1 l blue & blk	80.00	375.00
16	A72	5 l violet & blk	525.00	2,800.
		Nos. 11-16 (6)	655.00	3,435.
		Set, never hinged	1,630.	

On Nos. 15 and 16 the overprint is placed vertically at the left side.

Victor Emmanuel Issue

Italy Nos. 175-177 Overprinted

1925-26 Unwmk. Perf. 11

17	A78	60c brown car	.80	9.50
18	A78	1 l dark blue	1.60	9.50
a.		Perf. 13½	7.25	35.00

Perf. 13½

19	A78	1.25 l dk blue ('26)	2.40	32.50
a.		Perf. 11	1,750.	2,200.
		Nos. 17-19 (3)	4.80	51.50
		Set, #17-19, 18a, 19a, never hinged	3,500.	

Saint Francis of Assisi Issue
Italy Nos. 178-180 Overprinted

1926, Apr. 12 Wmk. 140 Perf. 14

20	A79	20c gray green	2.40	13.00
21	A80	40c dark violet	2.40	13.00
22	A81	60c red brown	2.40	26.00

Italy No. 182 and Type of A83 Overprinted in Red

Unwmk.

23	A82	1.25 l dark blue	2.40	32.50
24	A83	5 l + 2.50 l ol grn	6.50	65.00
		Nos. 20-24 (5)	16.10	149.50
		Set, never hinged	40.00	

Volta Issue

Type of Italy Overprinted

1927, Oct. 10   Wmk. 140   *Perf. 14*

25 A84	20c purple	4.75	35.00
26 A84	50c deep orange	8.00	22.50
a.	Double overprint	175.00	
27 A84	1.25 l brt blue	11.00	55.00
	Nos. 25-27 (3)	23.75	112.50
	Set, never hinged	60.00	

Monte Cassino Issue
Types of Italy Overprinted in Red or Blue

1929, Oct. 14

28 A96	20c dk green (R)	5.50	20.00
29 A96	25c red org (Bl)	5.50	20.00
30 A98	50c + 10c crim (Bl)	5.50	22.50
31 A98	75c + 15c ol brn (R)	5.50	22.50
32 A96	1.25 l + 25c dk vio (R)	13.00	40.00
33 A98	5 l + 1 l saph (R)	13.00	45.00

Overprinted in Red

Unwmk.

34 A100	10 l + 2 l gray brn	13.00	65.00
	Nos. 28-34 (7)	61.00	235.00
	Set, never hinged	142.00	

Royal Wedding Issue
Type of Italy Overprinted

1930, Mar. 17   Wmk. 140

35 A101	20c yellow green	1.60	4.75
36 A101	50c + 10c dp org	1.20	8.00
37 A101	1.25 l + 25c rose red	1.20	16.00
	Nos. 35-37 (3)	4.00	28.75
	Set, never hinged	12.00	

Ferrucci Issue
Types of Italy Overprinted in Red or Blue

1930, July 26

38 A102	20c violet (R)	5.50	5.50
39 A103	25c dk green (R)	5.50	5.50
40 A103	50c black (R)	5.50	11.00
41 A103	1.25 l deep blue (R)	5.50	20.00
42 A104	5 l + 2 l dp car (Bl)	11.00	35.00
	Nos. 38-42,C1-C3 (8)	60.00	157.50
	Set, never hinged	140.00	

Virgil Issue
Types of Italy Overprinted in Red or Blue

1930, Dec. 4   Photo.

43 A106	15c violet black	1.20	9.50
44 A106	20c orange brown	1.20	4.00
45 A106	25c dark green	1.20	4.00
46 A106	30c lt brown	1.20	4.00
47 A106	50c dull violet	1.20	4.00
48 A106	75c rose red	1.20	8.00
49 A106	1.25 l gray blue	1.20	9.50

Unwmk.
Engr.

50 A106	5 l + 1.50 l dk vio	3.50	45.00
51 A106	10 l + 2.50 l ol brn	3.50	67.50
	Nos. 43-51,C4-C7 (13)	33.20	287.50
	Set, never hinged	82.50	

Saint Anthony of Padua Issue
Types of Italy Overprinted in Blue or Red

1931, May 7   Photo.   Wmk. 140

52 A116	20c brown (Bl)	1.60	20.00
53 A116	25c green (R)	1.60	6.50
54 A118	30c gray brn (Bl)	1.60	6.50
55 A118	50c dull vio (Bl)	1.60	6.50
56 A120	1.25 l slate bl (R)	1.60	35.00

Overprinted in Red or Black

Unwmk.   Engr.

57 A121	75c black (R)	1.60	20.00
58 A122	5 l + 2.50 l dk brn (Bk)	7.50	72.50
	Nos. 52-58 (7)	17.10	167.00
	Set, never hinged	45.00	

Native Village Scene A14

1934, Oct. 16   Wmk. 140

73 A14	5c ol grn & brn	4.00	20.00
74 A14	10c brown & black	4.00	20.00
75 A14	25c scar & indigo	4.00	16.00
76 A14	50c purple & brown	4.00	16.00
77 A14	60c org brn & ind	4.00	24.00
78 A14	1.25 l dk bl & grn	4.00	40.00
	Nos. 73-78,C43-C48 (12)	48.00	272.00
	Set, never hinged	120.00	

2nd Colonial Arts Exhibition, Naples.

SEMI-POSTAL STAMPS

Many issues of Italy and Italian Colonies include one or more semipostal denominations. To avoid splitting sets, these issues are generally listed as regular postage, airmail, etc., unless all values carry a surtax.

Holy Year Issue
Italian Stamps of 1924 Overprinted in Black or Red

1925   Wmk. 140   *Perf. 12*

B1 SP4	20c+ 10c dk grn & brn	3.25	22.50
B2 SP4	30c+ 15c dk brn & brn	3.25	24.00
B3 SP4	50c+ 25c vio & brn	3.25	22.50
B4 SP4	60c+ 30c dp rose & brn	3.25	27.50
B5 SP8	1 l + 50c dp bl & vio (R)	3.25	35.00

B6 SP8	5 l + 2.50 l org brn & vio (R)	3.25	52.50
	Nos. B1-B6 (6)	19.50	184.00
	Set, never hinged	45.00	

Colonial Institute Issue

Peace Substituting Spade for Sword — SP1

1926, June 1   Typo.   *Perf. 14*

B7 SP1	5c + 5c brown	.95	9.50
B8 SP1	10c + 5c ol brn	.95	9.50
B9 SP1	20c + 5c bl grn	.95	9.50
B10 SP1	40c + 5c brn red	.95	9.50
B11 SP1	60c + 5c orange	.95	9.50
B12 SP1	1 l + 5c blue	.95	20.00
	Nos. B7-B12 (6)	5.70	67.50
	Set, never hinged	14.50	

The surtax was for the Italian Colonial Institute.

> **Fiera Campionaria Tripoli**
> See Libya for stamps with this inscription.

Types of Italian Semi-Postal Stamps of 1926 Overprinted like Nos. 17-19

1927, Apr. 21   Unwmk.   *Perf. 11*

B19 SP10	40c + 20c dk brn & blk	2.40	35.00
B20 SP10	60c + 30c brn red & ol brn	2.40	35.00
B21 SP10	1.25 l + 60c dp bl & blk	2.40	55.00
B22 SP10	5 l + 2.50 l dk grn & blk	4.00	80.00
	Nos. B19-B22 (4)	11.20	205.00
	Set, never hinged	27.50	

The surtax was for the charitable work of the Voluntary Militia for Italian National Defense.

Allegory of Fascism and Victory — SP2

1928, Oct. 15   Wmk. 140

B29 SP2	20c + 5c bl grn	3.25	13.00
B30 SP2	30c + 5c red	3.25	13.00
B31 SP2	50c + 10c pur	3.25	22.50
B32 SP2	1.25 l + 20c dk bl	4.00	27.50
	Nos. B29-B32 (4)	13.75	76.00
	Set, never hinged	32.50	

46th anniv. of the Societa Africana d'Italia. The surtax aided that society.

Types of Italian Semi-Postal Stamps of 1928 Ovptd.

1929, Mar. 4   Unwmk.   *Perf. 11*

B33 SP10	30c + 10c red & blk	4.00	22.50
B34 SP10	50c + 20c vio & blk	4.00	26.00
B35 SP10	1.25 l + 50c brn & bl	4.75	45.00
B36 SP10	5 l + 2 l ol grn & blk	4.75	80.00
	Nos. B33-B36 (4)	17.50	173.50
	Set, never hinged	45.00	

The surtax on these stamps was for the charitable work of the Voluntary Militia for Italian National Defense.

Types of Italian Semi-Postal Stamps of 1926, Overprinted in Black or Red Like Nos. B33-B36

1930, Oct. 20

B50 SP10	30c + 10c dp grn & bl (Bk)	27.50	47.50
B51 SP10	50c + 10c dk grn & vio (R)	27.50	65.00
B52 SP10	1.25 l + 30c blk brn & red (R)	27.50	80.00
B53 SP10	5 l + 1.50 l ind & grn (R)	87.50	225.00
	Nos. B50-B53 (4)	170.00	417.50
	Set, never hinged	400.00	

Ancient Arch — SP3

1930, Nov. 27   Photo.   Wmk. 140

B54 SP3	50c + 20c ol brn	4.00	22.50
B55 SP3	1.25 l + 20c dp bl	4.00	22.50
B56 SP3	1.75 l + 20c green	4.00	25.00
B57 SP3	2.55 l + 50c purple	8.00	40.00
B58 SP3	5 l + 1 l deep car	8.00	60.00
	Nos. B54-B58 (5)	28.00	170.00
	Set, never hinged	64.00	

25th anniv. of the Italian Colonial Agricultural Institute. The surtax was for the benefit of that institution.

AIR POST STAMPS

Ferrucci Issue
Type of Italian Air Post Stamps Overprinted in Blue or Red like #38-42

1930, July 26   Wmk. 140   *Perf. 14*

C1 AP7	50c brown vio (Bl)	4.75	9.50
C2 AP7	1 l dk blue (R)	4.75	16.00
C3 AP7	5 l + 2 l dp car (Bl)	17.50	55.00
	Nos. C1-C3 (3)	25.00	76.50
	Set, never hinged	68.00	

Virgil Issue
Types of Italian Air Post Stamps Overprinted in Red or Blue like #43-51

1930, Dec. 4   Photo.

C4 AP8	50c deep green	2.40	11.00
C5 AP8	1 l rose red	2.40	11.00

Unwmk.
Engr.

C6 AP8	7.70 l + 1.30 l dk brn	6.50	55.00
C7 AP8	9 l + 2 l gray	6.50	55.00
	Nos. C4-C7 (4)	17.80	126.00
	Set, never hinged	44.00	

Airplane over Columns of the Basilica, Leptis — AP1

Arab Horseman Pointing at Airplane AP2

1931-32   Photo.   Wmk. 140

C8 AP1	50c rose car	.80	.25
C9 AP1	60c red org	2.40	9.50
C10 AP1	75c dp bl ('32)	2.40	8.00
C11 AP1	80c dull violet	11.00	16.00
C12 AP2	1 l deep blue	1.60	.25
C13 AP2	1.20 l dk brown	30.00	20.00

C14 AP2 1.50 l org red 13.00 *20.00*
C15 AP2 5 l green 34.00 *32.50*
  Nos. C8-C15 (8) 95.20 *106.50*
  Set, never hinged 213.00

For surcharges and overprint see Nos. C29-C32.

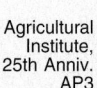

Agricultural
Institute,
25th Anniv.
AP3

1931, Dec. 7
C16 AP3 50c dp blue 3.25 *22.50*
C17 AP3 80c violet 3.25 *22.50*
C18 AP3 1 l gray black 3.25 *32.50*
C19 AP3 2 l deep green 8.00 *45.00*
C20 AP3 5 l + 2 l rose red 11.00 *92.50*
  Nos. C16-C20 (5) 28.75 *215.00*
  Set, never hinged 72.50

Graf Zeppelin Issue

Mercury, by Giovanni da Bologna, and
Zeppelin
AP4

Designs: 3 l, 12 l, Mercury. 10 l, 20 l, Guido
Reni's "Aurora." 5 l, 15 l, Arch of Marcus
Aurelius.

1933, May 5
C21 AP4 3 l dark brown 11.00 *145.00*
C22 AP4 5 l purple 11.00 *145.00*
C23 AP4 10 l deep green 11.00 *240.00*
C24 AP4 12 l deep blue 11.00 *260.00*
C25 AP4 15 l carmine 11.00 *260.00*
C26 AP4 20 l gray black 11.00 *350.00*
  Nos. C21-C26 (6) 66.00 *1,400.*
  Set, never hinged 160.00

For overprints and surcharges see Nos.
C38-C42.

North Atlantic Flight Issue

Airplane,
Lion of St.
Mark
AP7

1933, June 1
C27 AP7 19.75 l blk & ol
  brn 21.00 *650.00*
C28 AP7 44.75 l dk bl & lt
  grn 21.00 *650.00*
  Set, never hinged 100.00

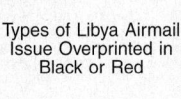

Type of
1931
Ovptd. or
Srchd.

1934, Jan. 20
C29 AP2 2 l on 5 l org brn 4.00 *87.50*
C30 AP2 3 l on 5 l grn 4.00 *87.50*
C31 AP2 5 l on 5 l ocher 4.00 *100.00*
C32 AP2 10 l on 5 l rose 5.50 *100.00*
  Nos. C29-C32 (4) 17.50 *375.00*
  Set, never hinged 40.00

For use on mail to be carried on a special
flight from Rome to Buenos Aires.

Types of Libya Airmail
Issue Overprinted in
Black or Red

1934, May 1 **Wmk. 140**
C38 AP4 50c rose red 12.00 *145.00*
C39 AP4 75c lemon 12.00 *145.00*
C40 AP4 5 l + 1 l brn 12.00 *145.00*
C41 AP4 10 l + 2 l dk bl 240.00 *850.00*
C42 AP5 25 l + 3 l pur 240.00 *850.00*
  Nos. C38-C42,CE1-CE2
  (7) 540.00 *2,425.*
  Set, never hinged 1,350.

"Circuit of the Oases."

Plane
Shadow on
Desert
AP11

Designs: 25c, 50c, 75c, Plane shadow on
desert. 80c, 1 l, 2 l, Camel corps.

1934, Oct. 16 **Photo.**
C43 AP11 25c sl bl & org red 4.00 *20.00*
C44 AP11 50c dk grn & ind 4.00 *16.00*
C45 AP11 75c dk brn & org
  red 4.00 *16.00*
C46 AP11 80c org brn & ol
  grn 4.00 *20.00*
C47 AP11 1 l scar & ol grn 4.00 *24.00*
C48 AP11 2 l dk bl & brn 4.00 *40.00*
  Nos. C43-C48 (6) 24.00 *136.00*
  Set, never hinged 60.00

Second Colonial Arts Exhibition, Naples.

AIR POST SEMI-POSTAL STAMPS

King Victor
Emmanuel
III
SPAP1

1934, Nov. 5 **Wmk. 140** **Perf. 14**
CB1 SPAP1 25c + 10c
  gray grn 6.50 *24.00*
CB2 SPAP1 50c + 10c
  brn 6.50 *24.00*
CB3 SPAP1 75c + 15c
  rose
  red 6.50 *24.00*
CB4 SPAP1 80c + 15c blk
  brn 6.50 *24.00*
CB5 SPAP1 1 l + 20c
  red brn 6.50 *24.00*
CB6 SPAP1 2 l + 20c brt
  bl 6.50 *24.00*
CB7 SPAP1 3 l + 25c
  pur 24.00 *120.00*
CB8 SPAP1 5 l + 25c
  org 24.00 *120.00*
CB9 SPAP1 10 l + 30c
  rose vio 24.00 *120.00*
CB10 SPAP1 25 l + 2 l dp
  grn 24.00 *120.00*
  Nos. CB1-CB10 (10) 135.00 *624.00*
  Set, never hinged 325.00

65th birthday of King Victor Emmanuel III;
non-stop flight from Rome to Mogadiscio.
For overprint see No. CBO1.

AIR POST SEMI-POSTAL OFFICIAL STAMP

Type of Air Post Semi-Postal Stamps
Overprinted Crown and "SERVIZIO DI
STATO" in Black

1934 **Wmk. 140** **Perf. 14**
CBO1 SPAP1 25 l + 2 l cop
  red 2,750. *5,250.*
  Never hinged 5,250.

AIR POST SPECIAL DELIVERY STAMPS

Type of Libya Overprinted in Black
Like Nos. C38-C42

1934, May 1 **Wmk. 140** **Perf. 14**
CE1 APSD1 2.25 l red or-
  ange 12.00 *145.00*
CE2 APSD1 4.50 l + 1 l dp
  rose 12.00 *145.00*
  Set, never hinged 70.00

AUTHORIZED DELIVERY STAMP

Authorized Delivery Stamp of Italy
1930, Overprinted like Nos. 38-42

1931, Mar. **Wmk. 140** **Perf. 14**
EY1 AD2 10c dark brown 16.00 *40.00*
  Never hinged 40.00

TRISTAN DA CUNHA

ˌtris-tən-də-ˈkü-nə

LOCATION — Group of islands in the
south Atlantic Ocean midway
between the Cape of Good Hope and
South America
GOVT. — A dependency of St. Helena
AREA — 40 sq. mi.
POP. — 313 (1988)

  12 Pence = 1 Shilling
100 Cents = 1 Rand (1961)
  12 Pence = 1 Shilling (1963)
  20 Shillings = 1 Pound
100 Pence = 1 Pound (1971)

**Catalogue values for all unused
stamps in this country are for
Never Hinged items.**

Stamps of St.
Helena, 1938-
49,
Overprinted in
Black

1952, Jan. 1 **Wmk. 4** **Perf. 12½**
1 A24 ½p purple .25 *2.75*
2 A24 1p blue grn & blk .85 *1.90*
3 A24 1½p car rose & blk .85 *1.90*
4 A24 2p carmine & blk .85 *1.90*
5 A24 3p gray 1.10 *1.90*
6 A24 4p ultra 5.50 *3.00*
7 A24 6p gray blue 5.50 *3.00*
8 A24 8p olive 5.50 *7.50*
9 A24 1sh sepia 5.00 *2.50*
10 A24 2sh6p deep claret 24.00 *17.50*
11 A24 5sh brown 27.50 *22.50*
12 A24 10sh violet 52.50 *37.50*
  Nos. 1-12 (12) 129.40 *103.85*
  Set, hinged 85.00

Common Design Types
pictured following the introduction.

Coronation Issue
Common Design Type
1953, June 2 **Engr.** **Perf. 13½x13**
13 CD312 3p dk green & black 1.10 1.75

Tristan
Crayfish — A1

Carting
Flax — A2

Designs: 1½p, Rockhopper penguin. 2p,
Factory. 2½p, Mollymauk. 3p, Island boat. 4p,
View of Tristan. 5p, Potato patches. 6p, Inac-
cessible Island. 9p, Nightingale Island. 1sh, St.
Mary's Church. 2sh 6p, Elephant seal. 5sh,
Flightless rail. 10sh, Island spinning wheel.

1954-58 **Perf. 12½**
14 A1 ½p choc & red .25 .25
  a. Bklt. pane of 4 ('58) 2.50
15 A2 1p green & choc .25 *.60*
  a. Bklt. pane of 4 4.00
16 A1 1½p dp plum & blk 2.00 1.40
  a. Bklt. pane of 4 ('58) 7.00
17 A2 2p org & vio blue .35 .25
18 A2 2½p carmine & blk 1.75 .70
19 A1 3p ol grn & ultra .80 1.40
  a. Bklt. pane of 4 ('58) 10.50
20 A2 4p dp bl & aqua .80 .75
  a. Bklt. pane of 4 ('58) 13.00
21 A2 5p gray & bl grn .80 .75
22 A2 6p vio & dk ol grn .80 .75
23 A2 9p henna brn &
  rose lil .80 .55
24 A2 1sh choc & ol grn .80 .55
25 A2 2sh6p blue & choc 20.00 10.00
26 A2 5sh red org & blk 55.00 15.00
27 A2 10sh red vio & org 25.00 16.00
  Nos. 14-27 (14) 109.40 48.95
  Set, hinged 70.00

Starfish — A3

Fish: 1p, Concha. 1½p, Klipfish. 2p, Heron
fish (saury). 2½p, Snipefish ("swordfish"). 3d,
Tristan crawfish. 4p, Soldier fish. 5p, Five finger fish. 6p, Mackeral scad. 9p, Stumpnose.
1sh, Bluefish. 2sh6p, Snoek (snake mackerel).
5sh, Shark. 10sh, Atlantic right whale.

Perf. 12½x13
1960, Feb. 1 **Engr.** **Wmk. 314**
28 A3 ½p orange &
  black .25 .25
  a. Booklet pane of 4 1.50
29 A3 1p rose lilac &
  blk .25 .25
  a. Booklet pane of 4 2.50
30 A3 1½p grnsh bl & blk .35 .25
  a. Booklet pane of 4 2.75
31 A3 2p green & black .45 .35
32 A3 2½p brown & black .50 .35
33 A3 3p rose red & blk 1.40 1.40
  a. Booklet pane of 4 8.00
34 A3 4p gray ol & blk 1.25 .65
  a. Booklet pane of 4 7.00
35 A3 5p org yel & blk 1.60 .70
36 A3 6p blue & black 1.60 .80
37 A3 9p rose car & blk 1.90 .70
38 A3 1sh brn org & blk 2.75 .60
39 A3 2sh6p vio blue & blk 12.50 12.50
40 A3 5sh emerald & blk 15.00 16.00
41 A3 10sh violet & blk 50.00 50.00
  Nos. 28-41 (14) 89.80 84.80

1961, Apr. 15 **Perf. 12½x13**
42 A3 ½c like No. 28 .25 .25
43 A3 1c like No. 29 .25 .25
44 A3 1½c like No. 30 .40 .40
45 A3 2c like No. 31 .75 .75
46 A3 2½c like No. 33 1.10 1.10
47 A3 3c like No. 34 1.10 1.10
48 A3 4c like No. 35 1.40 1.40
49 A3 5c like No. 36 1.40 1.40
50 A3 7½c like No. 37 1.40 1.40
51 A3 10c like No. 38 2.25 1.60
52 A3 25c like No. 39 9.00 9.00
53 A3 50c like No. 40 22.50 17.50
54 A3 1r like No. 41 45.00 40.00
  Nos. 42-54 (13) 86.80 76.15

Nos. 46, 49-51 surcharged for "Tristan
Relief" are listed as St. Helena Nos. B1-B4.

Types of St.
Helena, 1961
Overprinted

Perf. 11½x12, 12x11½

1963, Apr. 12		**Photo.**	**Wmk. 4**	
55	A29	1p rose, ultra, yel & grn	.25	1.00
56	A29	1½p bis, sep, yel & grn	.25	.40
57	A29	2p gray & red	.25	1.00
58	A30	3p dk bl, rose & grnsh bl	.30	1.00
a.		Double overprint		
59	A29	4½p slate, brn & car	.55	.70
60	A29	6p cit, brn & dp car	.80	.40
61	A29	7p vio, blk & red brn	.55	.40
62	A29	10p bl & dp claret	.55	.40
63	A29	1sh red brn, grn & yel	.55	.40
64	A29	1sh6p gray bl & blk	5.50	1.10
65	A29	2sh6p grnsh bl, yel & red	1.75	.75
66	A29	5sh grn, brn & yel	7.00	1.75
67	A29	10sh gray bl, blk & sal	7.00	1.75
		Nos. 55-67 (13)	25.30	11.05

Freedom from Hunger Issue
Common Design Type
Perf. 14x14½

1963, Oct. 2		**Photo.**	**Wmk. 314**	
68	CD314	1sh6p rose carmine	1.00	.40

Red Cross Centenary Issue
Common Design Type

1964, Jan. 2		**Litho.**	**Perf. 13**	
69	CD315	3p black & red	.75	.40
70	CD315	1sh6p ultra & red	1.25	.60

Flagship of Tristáo da Cunha, 1506 — A4

Queen Elizabeth II — A5

½p, Map of South Atlantic Ocean. 1½p, Dutch ship Heemstede, first landing, 1643. 2p, New England whaler. 3p, Confederate ship Shenandoah. 4½p, H.M.S. Galatea, 1867. 6p, H.M.S. Cilicia, 1942. 7p, H.M. Royal Yacht Britannia, 1957. 10p, H.M.S. Leopard, Evacuation, 1961. 1sh, Dutch ship Tjisadane, 1961. 1sh6p, M.V. Tristania. 2sh6p, M.V. Boissevain, returning islanders, 1963. 5sh, M.S. Bornholm, returning islanders, 1963.

Perf. 11x11½

1965, Feb. 17		**Engr.**	**Wmk. 314**	
71	A4	½p black & dk blue	.25	.25
a.		Booklet pane of 4	.25	
72	A4	1p black & emerald	.85	.25
a.		Booklet pane of 4	4.25	
73	A4	1½p black & ultra	.85	.25
a.		Booklet pane of 4	4.25	
74	A4	2p black & lilac	.85	.25
75	A4	3p blk & grnsh bl	.85	.25
a.		Booklet pane of 4	4.25	
76	A4	4½p black & brown	.85	.25
77	A4	6p black & green	.70	.30
a.		Booklet pane of 4	4.25	
78	A4	7p black & ver	.85	.40
79	A4	10p black & dk brn	.85	.40
80	A4	1sh black & lil rose	.85	.50
81	A4	1sh6p black & olive	4.50	2.75
82	A4	2sh6p black & brn org	3.00	3.00
83	A4	5sh black & violet	6.00	4.00

Perf. 11½x11

84	A5	10sh lil rose & dk bl	2.00	1.50
		Nos. 71-84 (14)	23.25	14.35

See Nos. 113-115. For surcharges see Nos. 108, 141-152. For overprints see Nos. 132.

ITU Issue
Common Design Type

1965, May 11		**Litho.**	**Perf. 11x11½**	
85	CD317	3p vermilion & gray	.60	.25
86	CD317	6p purple & orange	.90	.40

Intl. Cooperation Year Issue
Common Design Type

1965, Oct. 25		**Wmk. 314**	**Perf. 14½**	
87	CD318	1p blue grn & claret	.25	.30
88	CD318	6p lt violet & green	1.40	.45

Churchill Memorial Issue
Common Design Type
Wmk. 314

1966, Jan. 24		**Photo.**	**Perf. 14**	

Design in Black, Gold and Carmine Rose

89	CD319	1p bright blue	.25	.25
90	CD319	3p green	.40	.25
91	CD319	6p brown	1.60	.70
92	CD319	1sh6p violet	4.75	1.50
		Nos. 89-92 (4)	7.00	2.70

World Cup Soccer Issue
Common Design Type

1966			**Perf. 14**	
93	CD320	3p multicolored	.25	.25
94	CD321	2sh6p multicolored	1.25	.55

Nos. 93-94 were issued Oct. 1 in Tristan da Cunha, but on July 1 in St. Helena.

Light Dragoon of 19th Century and Sailing Ship — A6

Wmk. 314

1966, Aug. 15		**Litho.**	**Perf. 14½**	
95	A6	3p pale green & multi	.25	.25
96	A6	6p tan & multi	.25	.25
97	A6	1sh6p gray & multi	.50	.30
98	A6	2sh6p multicolored	.85	.45
		Nos. 95-98 (4)	1.85	1.25

150th anniv. of the establishment of a garrison on Tristan da Cunha.

WHO Headquarters Issue
Common Design Type

1966, Oct. 1		**Litho.**	**Perf. 14**	
99	CD322	6p multicolored	.35	.25
100	CD322	5sh multicolored	1.90	1.00

UNESCO Anniversary Issue
Common Design Type

1966, Dec. 1		**Litho.**	**Perf. 14**	
101	CD323	10p "Education"	.35	.25
102	CD323	1sh6p "Science"	.75	.40
103	CD323	2sh6p "Culture"	1.40	.75
		Nos. 101-103 (3)	2.50	1.40

Calshot Harbor A7

Perf. 14x14½

1967, Jan. 2		**Litho.**	**Unwmk.**	
104	A7	10p dull green & multi	.25	.25
105	A7	10p brown & multi	.25	.25
106	A7	1sh6p dull blue & multi	.25	.25
107	A7	2sh6p orange brn & multi	.25	.25
		Nos. 104-107 (4)	1.00	1.05

Opening of the artificial Calshot Harbor.

No. 76 Surcharged with New Value and Three Bars
Perf. 11x11½

1967, May 10		**Engr.**	**Wmk. 314**	
108	A4	4p on 4½p blk & brn	.45	.30

Tristan da Cunha, Prince Alfred, Queen Elizabeth II and Prince Philip — A8

1967, July 10		**Litho.**	**Perf. 14x14½**	
109	A8	3p blue grn, dk grn & blk	.25	.25
110	A8	6p dk carmine & blk	.25	.25
111	A8	1sh6p brt grn, gray grn & blk	.25	.25
112	A8	2sh6p dull ultra, sep & blk	.25	.30
		Nos. 109-112 (4)	1.00	1.05

Cent. of the visit of Prince Alfred, First Duke of Edinburgh, to Tristan da Cunha.

Types of 1965

Designs: 4p, H.M.S. Challenger, 1870. 10sh, South African research vessel, R.S.A. £1, Queen Elizabeth II.

Perf. 11x11½

1967, Sept. 1		**Engr.**	**Wmk. 314**	
113	A4	4p black & orange	5.25	3.75
114	A4	10sh black & dull grn	16.00	14.00

Perf. 11½x11

115	A5	£1 brn org & dk blue	16.00	17.50
		Nos. 113-115 (3)	37.25	35.25

Wandering Albatross Nest — A9

Birds: 1sh, Big-billed buntings. 1sh6p, Tristan thrushes. 2sh6p, Great shearwaters.

Perf. 14x14½

1968, May 15		**Photo.**	**Wmk. 314**	
116	A9	4p multicolored	.25	.25
117	A9	1sh multicolored	.60	.30
118	A9	1sh6p multicolored	1.00	.50
119	A9	2sh6p multicolored	1.40	.85
		Nos. 116-119 (4)	3.25	1.90

Union Jack and St. Helena Flag — A10

Design: 9p, 2sh6p, Map showing locations of St. Helena and Tristan da Cunha.

1968, Nov. 1		**Litho.**	**Wmk. 314**	
120	A10	6p violet & multi	.25	.25
121	A10	9p brn, bl grn & vio bl	.25	.25
122	A10	1sh6p green & multi	.25	.25
123	A10	2sh6p dp car, bl grn & vio bl	.35	.35
		Nos. 120-123 (4)	1.10	1.10

30th anniv. of Tristan da Cunha as a Dependency of St. Helena.

Frigate A11

Designs: 1sh, Cape Horner. 1sh6p, Barque. 2sh6p, Tea Clipper.

Perf. 11x11½

1969, June 1		**Engr.**	**Wmk. 314**	
124	A11	4p brt blue	.25	.25
125	A11	1sh rose carmine	.45	.40
126	A11	1sh6p green	.65	.50
127	A11	2sh6p sepia	1.10	.90
		Nos. 124-127 (4)	2.45	2.05

Islanders Going to First Religious Service, 1851 — A12

Designs: 4p, Tristan da Cunha, birds and ship. 1sh6p, Landing at the beach. 2sh6p, St. Mary's Church, 1969, and procession.

Perf. 14½x14

1969, Nov. 1		**Litho.**	**Wmk. 314**	
128	A12	4p multicolored	.25	.40
129	A12	9p multicolored	.25	.40
130	A12	1sh6p multicolored	.35	.55
131	A12	2sh6p multicolored	.50	.55
		Nos. 128-131 (4)	1.35	1.90

Issued to honor the work of the United Society for the Propagation of the Faith.

No. 77 Overprinted in Deep Orange: "NATIONAL / SAVINGS"
Perf. 11x11½

1970, May 15		**Engr.**	**Wmk. 314**	
132	A4	6p black & green	.45	.25

Issued to promote national savings. No. 132 also used as savings stamp.

In 1971, No. 132 was locally surcharged "2½p" and 3 short bars by means of a rubber handstamp. Value $7.

Globe and Red Cross A13

1sh9p, 2sh6p, British & Red Cross flags, vert.

Perf. 13½x13, 13x13½

1970, June 1			**Litho.**	
133	A13	4p emer, red & grnsh bl	.30	.25
134	A13	9p bister, red & grnsh bl	.45	.25
135	A13	1sh9p gray, vio bl & red	.75	.35
136	A13	2sh6p rose cl, vio bl & red	1.00	.60
		Nos. 133-136 (4)	2.50	1.45

Centenary of the British Red Cross Society.

Rock Lobster and Lobster Men Placing Trap — A14

10p, 2sh6p, Workers in processing plant and side view of rock lobster (jasus tristani).

Perf. 12½x13

1970, Nov. 1		**Litho.**	**Wmk. 314**	
137	A14	4p lilac rose & multi	.25	.30
138	A14	10p dull yel & multi	.25	.35
139	A14	1sh6p brown org & multi	.75	.60
140	A14	2sh6p olive & multi	1.10	.75
		Nos. 137-140 (4)	2.35	2.00

Tristan da Cunha rock lobster (crawfish) industry.

Nos. 72-74, 77-83, 113-114
Surcharged with New Value and Three
Bars

Perf. 11x11½

1971, Feb. 15		Engr.		Wmk. 314	
141	A4	½p on 1p		.25	.25
142	A4	1p on 2p		.25	.25
143	A4	1½p on 4p		.35	.25
144	A4	2½p on 6p		.35	.25
145	A4	3p on 7p		.35	.25
146	A4	4p on 10p		.35	.25
147	A4	5p on 1sh		.35	.25
148	A4	7½p on 1sh6p		2.10	2.10
149	A4	12½p on 2sh6p		3.00	3.00
150	A4	15p on 1½p		3.00	3.50
151	A4	25p on 5sh		3.00	6.25
152	A4	50p on 10sh		4.25	12.50
		Nos. 141-152 (12)		17.60	29.10

"Quest" — A15

4p, Presentation of Scout Troop flag in front of Tristan school. 7½p, Great Britain #167a with Tristan da Cunha cancellation. 12½p, Sir Ernest Henry Shackleton, boat & expedition cancellations.

Perf. 13½x14

1971, June 1		Litho.	Wmk. 314	
153	A15	1½p lt blue & multi	1.10	.25
154	A15	4p buff, yel grn & blk	1.10	.45
155	A15	7½p pale grn, rose lil & blk	1.10	1.00
156	A15	12½p buff & multi	1.90	3.70
		Nos. 153-156 (4)	5.20	3.70

50th anniversary of the Shackleton-Rowett South Atlantic expedition.

"Victory" at Trafalgar and Thomas Swain Catching Nelson — A16

Ships and Island Families: 2½p, "Emily of Stonington" and inscribed P. W. Green, 1836. 4p, "Italia" and inscribed Gaetano Lavarello, 1892, and Andrea Repetto. 7½p, "Falmouth" and Corp. William Glass, 1816. 12½p, American Whaler and inscribed 1836 Joshua Rogers, 1849, Capt. Andrew Hangan.

1971, Nov. 1				
157	A16	1½p bister & multi	.25	.25
158	A16	2½p multicolored	.25	.25
159	A16	4p gray & multi	.50	.55
160	A16	7½p multicolored	.80	.85
161	A16	12½p blue & multi	1.25	1.40
		Nos. 157-161 (5)	3.05	3.30

Cow Pudding — A17　　　Coxswain — A18

Native Flora: 1p, Peak berry and crater lake. 1½p, Sand flower, horiz. 2½p, New Zealand flax, horiz. 3p, Island tree. 4p, Bog fern and snow-capped mountain. 5p, Dog catcher and albatrosses. 7½p, Celery and terns. 12½p, Pepper tree and waterfall. 25p, Foul berry, horiz. 50p, Tussock and penguins. £1, Tussac and islands, horiz.

Perf. 13½x13, 13x13½

1972, Feb. 26			Wmk. 314	
162	A17	½p gray & multi	.25	.25
163	A17	1p salmon & multi	.25	.25
164	A17	1½p green & multi	.25	.25
165	A17	2½p multicolored	.25	.25
166	A17	3p multicolored	.25	.25
167	A17	4p lemon & multi	.35	.30
168	A17	5p yel grn & multi	.50	.30
169	A17	7½p dull yel & multi	2.10	1.75
170	A17	12½p multicolored	1.40	1.00
171	A17	25p gray & multi	2.75	2.40

Litho. and Engr.

172	A17	50p multicolored	6.75	4.50
173	A17	£1 lt blue & multi	12.00	4.50
		Nos. 162-173 (12)	27.10	16.00

1972, June 1　Litho.　Perf. 14

2½p, Launching longboat. 4p, Men rowing longboat. 12½p, Longboat under sail.

174	A18	2½p multi, horiz.	.25	.25
175	A18	4p multi, horiz.	.25	.25
176	A18	7½p multi	.60	.40
177	A18	12½p multi	1.00	.50
		Nos. 174-177 (4)	2.10	1.40

Silver Wedding Issue, 1972
Common Design Type

Design: Queen Elizabeth II, Prince Philip, thrush and wandering albatrosses.

Perf. 14x14½

1972, Nov. 20		Photo.	Wmk. 314	
178	CD324	2½p multicolored	.25	.25
179	CD324	7½p ultra & multi	.50	.45

Altar, St. Mary's Church — A19

1973, July 8　Litho.　Perf. 13½

180	A19	25p dk blue & multi	1.40	1.40

St. Mary's Church, Tristan da Cunha, 50th anniv.

"Challenger" off Tristan, Steil's Sounding Instrument — A20

Designs: 4p, Challenger's laboratory. 7½p, Challenger off Nightingale Island. 12½p, Map of Challenger's voyage. Each stamp shows an instrument for deep sea soundings.

1973, Oct. 15　　　　Wmk. 314
Perf. 13½x14

181	A20	4p multicolored	.25	.25
182	A20	5p multicolored	.30	.30
183	A20	7½p multicolored	.50	.50
184	A20	12½p multicolored	1.00	1.00
a.		Souv. sheet, #181-184, perf. 13½	2.75	2.75
		Nos. 181-184 (4)	2.05	2.05

Centenary of "Challenger's" visit to Tristan da Cunha during oceanographic exploration world trip, 1872-76.

View of English Port from Shipboard — A21

5p, Inspectors at volcano rim. 7½p, Islanders disembarking from "Bornholm." 12½p, Islanders on board ship approaching Tristan da Cunha.

1973, Nov. 10　　　　Perf. 14½

185	A21	4p yellow, blk & gold	.25	.25
186	A21	5p multicolored	.30	.25
187	A21	7½p multicolored	.45	.30
188	A21	12½p multicolored	.60	.40
		Nos. 185-188 (4)	1.60	1.20

10th anniversary of return of islanders to Tristan da Cunha.

Princess Anne's Wedding Issue
Common Design Type

1973, Nov. 14		Wmk. 314	Perf. 14	
189	CD325	7½p multicolored	.25	.25
190	CD325	12½p bl grn & multi	.25	.25

Rockhopper Penguin — A22

Designs: Rockhopper penguins.

1974, May 1		Litho.		
191	A22	2½p shown	3.25	1.25
192	A22	5p Colony	3.50	1.65
193	A22	7½p Penguins fishing	4.00	2.00
194	A22	25p Penguin and fledgling	8.25	5.00
		Nos. 191-194 (4)	19.00	9.90

Souvenir Sheet

Map of Tristan da Cunha, Penguin and Sea Gull — A23

1974, Oct. 1		Wmk. 314	Perf. 13½	
195	A23	35p multicolored	6.00	5.25

Blenheim Palace A24

25p, Churchill and Queen Elizabeth II.

Wmk. 373

1974, Nov. 30		Litho.	Perf. 14	
196	A24	7½p black & yellow	.25	.25
197	A24	25p black & brown	.50	.50
a.		Souvenir sheet of 2, #196-197	1.10	1.10

Sir Winston Churchill (1874-1965).

Plocamium Fuscorubrum — A25

Aquatic Plants: 5p, Ulva lactuca. 10p, Epymenia flabellata. 20p, Macrocystis pyrifera.

Perf. 13x14

1975, Apr. 16			Wmk. 314	
198	A25	4p lilac & multi	.25	.25
199	A25	5p ultra & multi	.25	.25
200	A25	10p yellow & multi	.40	.30
201	A25	20p lt green & multi	.75	.65
		Nos. 198-201 (4)	1.65	1.45

Killer Whales — A26

Wmk. 314

1975, Nov. 1		Litho.	Perf. 13½	
202	A26	2p shown	.35	.25
203	A26	3p Rough-toothed dolphins	.65	.25
204	A26	5p Atlantic right whale	1.75	.85
205	A26	20p Finback whales	4.25	1.90
		Nos. 202-205 (4)	7.00	3.25

Tristan da Cunha No. 1 A27

Designs: 9p, Tristan da Cunha #13, vert. 25p, Freighter Tristania II.

Perf. 13½x14, 14x13½

1976, May 6		Litho.	Wmk. 373	
206	A27	5p lilac, vio & blk	.25	.25
207	A27	9p bluish gray, grn & blk	.25	.25
208	A27	25p multicolored	.85	.85
a.		Souvenir sheet of 3	3.50	3.50
		Nos. 206-208 (3)	1.35	1.35

Festival of Stamps 1976. #208a contains one each of Ascension #214, St. Helena #297 and Tristan da Cunha #208.

The Patches A28

Views, by Roland Svensson: 3p, Tristan house, vert. 10p, Tristan Settlement and Cliffs. 20p, Huts at Nightingale, vert.

1976, Oct. 4		Litho.	Perf. 14	
209	A28	3p multicolored	.25	.25
210	A28	5p multicolored	.25	.25
211	A28	10p multicolored	.30	.30
212	A28	20p multicolored	.50	.50
a.		Souvenir sheet of 4, #209-211	1.75	1.75
		Nos. 209-212 (4)	1.30	1.30

An artist's view of Tristan da Cunha. See Nos. 234-237, 268-271.

Royal Yacht Britannia — A29

15p, Royal standard. 25p, Royal family.

1977, Feb. 7		Wmk. 373	Perf. 13	
213	A29	10p multicolored	.25	.25
214	A29	15p multicolored	.25	.25
215	A29	25p multicolored	.30	.30
		Nos. 213-215 (3)	.80	.80

25th anniv. of the reign of Elizabeth II. For surcharges see Nos. 220-221.

H.M.S. Eskimo, Sept. 1970 A30

Royal Naval Ships and Arms: 10p, Naiad, Nov. 1968. 15p, Jaguar, Mar. 1964. 20p, London, Dec. 1964. Dates of visits to island.

1977, Oct. 1   Litho.   Perf. 14½

216	A30	5p multicolored	.25	.25
217	A30	10p multicolored	.25	.25
218	A30	15p multicolored	.30	.30
219	A30	20p multicolored	.35	.35
a.		Souvenir sheet of 4, #216-219	2.00	2.00
		Nos. 216-219 (4)	1.15	1.15

Nos. 214-215 Surcharged with New Value and Bar

1977, Oct. 13   Wmk. 373   Perf. 13

220	A29	4p on 15p multi	3.25	6.50
221	A29	7½p on 25p multi	3.25	6.50

Giant Fulmars — A31

Perf. 13½x14, 14x13½
1977, Dec. 1   Litho.

222	A31	1p Pterodroma macroptera, horiz.	.25	.45
223	A31	2p Fregetta marina, horiz.	.25	.75
224	A31	3p Macronectes giganteus	.25	.75
225	A31	4p Pterodroma mollis	.25	.85
226	A31	5p Diomedea exulans	.25	.85
227	A31	10p Pterodroma brevirostris	.30	.85
228	A31	15p Sterna vittata	.55	1.25
229	A31	20p Puffinus gravis	.75	1.25
230	A31	25p Pachyptila vittata	.90	1.25
231	A31	50p Catharacta skua	2.00	1.25
232	A31	£1 Pelecanoides urinatrix	2.75	2.25
233	A31	£2 Diomedea chlororynchos	5.75	3.00
		Nos. 222-233 (12)	14.25	14.75

Nos. 224-233 are vertical. For overprints see Nos. 318-319.

Painting Type of 1976

Views by Roland Svensson: 5p, St. Mary's Church. 10p, Longboats. 15p, A Tristan home. 20p, Harbor, 1970.

Wmk. 373
1978, Mar. 1   Litho.   Perf. 14½

234	A28	5p multicolored	.25	.25
235	A28	10p multicolored	.25	.25
236	A28	15p multicolored	.35	.35
237	A28	20p multicolored	.50	.50
a.		Souvenir sheet of 4, #234-237	1.75	1.75
		Nos. 234-237 (4)	1.35	1.35

An artist's view of Tristan da Cunha.

Elizabeth II Coronation Anniversary
Common Design Types
Souvenir Sheet

1978, Apr. 21   Unwmk.   Perf. 15

238		Sheet of 6	1.60	1.60
a.		CD326 25p King's Bull	.30	.30
b.		CD327 25p Elizabeth II	.30	.30
c.		CD328 25p Tristan crawfish	.30	.30

No. 238 contains 2 se-tenant strips of Nos. 238a-238c, separated by horizontal gutter with commemorative and descriptive inscriptions and showing central part of coronation procession with coach.

Sodalite — A32

Local Minerals: 5p, Aragonite. 10p, Sulphur. 20p, Lava containing pyroxene crystal.

Perf. 13½x14
1978, June 9   Litho.   Wmk. 373

239	A32	5p multicolored	.45	.45
240	A32	5p multicolored	.50	.50
241	A32	10p multicolored	.80	.80
242	A32	20p multicolored	1.25	1.25
		Nos. 239-242 (4)	3.00	3.00

Fish A33

1978, Sept. 29   Litho.   Perf. 14

243	A33	5p Klipfish	.30	.30
244	A33	10p Fivefinger	.30	.30
245	A33	15p Concha	.40	.40
246	A33	20p Soldier	.50	.50
		Nos. 243-246 (4)	1.50	1.50

Orangeleaf and Navy Flag — A34

Royal Fleet Auxiliary Vessels: 10p, Tarbatness. 20p, Tidereach. 25p, Reliant.

1978, Nov. 24   Litho.   Perf. 12½

247	A34	5p multicolored	.25	.25
248	A34	10p multicolored	.25	.25
249	A34	20p multicolored	.35	.35
250	A34	25p multicolored	.40	.40
a.		Souvenir sheet of 4, #247-250	1.50	2.75
		Nos. 247-250 (4)	1.25	1.25

Fur Seals — A35

Wildlife conservation: 5p, Elephant seal. 15p, Tristan thrush. 20p, Tristan buntings.

Wmk. 373
1979, Jan. 3   Litho.   Perf. 14

251	A35	5p multicolored	.30	.30
252	A35	10p multicolored	.30	.30
253	A35	15p multicolored	.35	.35
254	A35	20p multicolored	.45	.45
		Nos. 251-254 (4)	1.40	1.40

Tristan Longboat — A36

Ships: 10p, Queen Mary. 15p, Queen Elizabeth. 20p, QE II. 25p, QE II, longboat, view of Tristan.

1979, Feb. 8   Perf. 14½

255	A36	5p multicolored	.25	.25
256	A36	10p multicolored	.25	.25
257	A36	15p multicolored	.25	.25
258	A36	20p multicolored	.35	.35
		Nos. 255-258 (4)	1.10	1.10

Souvenir Sheet

259	A36	25p multicolored	1.00	1.50

Visit of cruise ship QE II, Feb. 8.

Tristan da Cunha No. 12 A37

Tristan da Cunha Stamps: 10p, No. 26. 25p, No. 58. vert. 50p, 1p-local "potatoe" stamp.

Perf. 14½x14, 14x14½
1979, Aug. 27   Litho.   Wmk. 373

260	A37	5p multicolored	.25	.25
261	A37	10p multicolored	.25	.25
262	A37	25p multicolored	.40	.40
		Nos. 260-262 (3)	.90	.90

Souvenir Sheet

263	A37	50p multicolored	.75	.75

Sir Rowland Hill (1795-1879), originator of penny postage.

The Padre's House, IYC Emblem A38

IYC Emblem, Children's Drawings: 10p, "Houses in the Village." 15p, "St. Mary's Church." 20p, "Rockhopper Penguins."

1979, Nov. 26   Litho.   Perf. 14

264	A38	5p multicolored	.25	.25
265	A38	10p multicolored	.25	.25
266	A38	15p multicolored	.25	.25
267	A38	20p multicolored	.25	.25
		Nos. 264-267 (4)	1.00	1.00

International Year of the Child.

Painting Type of 1976

Views (Sketches by Roland Svensson): 5p, Stoltenhoff Island. 10p, Nightingale from the East. 15p, The Administrator's abode, vert. 20p, "Ridge where the goat jumped off," vert.

1980, Feb.   Litho.   Perf. 14

268	A28	5p multicolored	.25	.25
269	A28	10p multicolored	.25	.25
270	A28	15p multicolored	.25	.25
271	A28	20p multicolored	.25	.25
a.		Souvenir sheet of 4, #268-271	1.00	1.00
		Nos. 268-271 (4)	1.00	1.00

Mail Pickup Boat — A40

1980, May 6   Litho.   Perf. 14

272	A40	5p shown	.25	.25
273	A40	10p Unloading mail	.25	.25
274	A40	15p Truck transport	.25	.25
275	A40	20p Delivery bell	.25	.25
276	A40	25p Distribution	.30	.30
		Nos. 272-276 (5)	1.30	1.30

London 80 Intl. Stamp Exhib., May 6-14.

Queen Mother Elizabeth Birthday
Common Design Type

1980, Aug. 11   Litho.   Perf. 14

277	CD330	14p multicolored	.45	.45

Golden Hinde — A41

1980, Sept. 6   Perf. 14½

278	A41	5p shown	.25	.25
279	A41	10p Drake's route	.25	.25
280	A41	20p Sir Francis Drake	.25	.25
281	A41	25p Queen Elizabeth I	.35	.35
		Nos. 278-281 (4)	1.10	1.10

Sir Francis Drake's circumnavigation, 400th anniversary.

Humpty Dumpty A42

Wmk. 373
1980, Oct. 31   Litho.   Perf. 13½

282		Sheet of 9	2.10	2.10
a.	A42	15p shown	.25	.25
b.	A42	15p Mary had a Little Lamb	.25	.25
c.	A42	15p Little Jack Horner	.25	.25
d.	A42	15p Hey Diddle Diddle	.25	.25
e.	A42	15p London Bridge	.25	.25
f.	A42	15p Old King Cole	.25	.25
g.	A42	15p Sing a Song of Sixpence	.25	.25
h.	A42	15p Tom Tom the Piper's Son	.25	.25
i.	A42	25p Owl and the Pussy Cat	.25	.25

Christmas 1980.

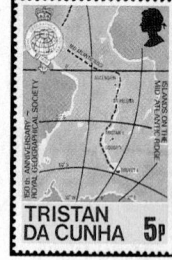

Islands on Mid-Atlantic Ridge, Society Emblem — A43

Royal Geographical Soc., 150th Anniv. (Maps and Expeditions): 10p, Tristan da Cunha, Francis Beaufort, 1806. 15p, Tristan Island, Norwegian expedition, 1937-1938. 20p, Gough Island, scientific survey, 1955-1956.

1980, Dec. 15

283	A43	5p multicolored	.25	.25
284	A43	10p multicolored	.25	.25
285	A43	15p multicolored	.35	.35
286	A43	20p multicolored	.35	.35
		Nos. 283-286 (4)	1.10	1.10

Rev. Edwin Dodgson A44

1981, Mar. 23   Wmk. 373   Perf. 14

287	A44	10p portrait, vert.	.25	.25
288	A44	20p shown	.35	.35
289	A44	30p Dodgson preaching, vert.	.45	.45
a.		Souvenir sheet of 3, #287-289	1.00	1.00
		Nos. 287-289 (3)	1.05	1.05

Centenary of arrival of Rev. Edwin H. Dodgson, who saved population from starvation.

Map of Tristan da Cunha showing L'heure du Berger Route, 1767 (Dalrymple's Map, 1781) — A45

Early Maps and Charts By: 5p, 21p, Capt. Denham, 1853 (diff.). 35p, Ivan Keulen, 1700.

1981, May 22

290	A45	5p multicolored	.25	.25
291	A45	14p multicolored	.40	.30
292	A45	21p multicolored	.50	.50
		Nos. 290-292 (3)	1.15	1.05

Souvenir Sheet

293	A45	35p multicolored	.70	.85

Royal Wedding Issue
Common Design Type
Wmk. 373

1981, July 22 — Litho. — Perf. 14
294 CD331 5p Bouquet .25 .25
295 CD331 20p Charles .25 .25
296 CD331 50p Couple .45 .45
Nos. 294-296 (3) .95 .95

Hiking — A46

1981, Sept. 14
297 A46 5p shown .25 .25
298 A46 10p Camping .25 .25
299 A46 20p Map reading .25 .25
300 A46 25p Prince Philip .35 .25
Nos. 297-300 (4) 1.10 1.00

Duke of Edinburgh's Awards, 25th anniv.

Inaccessible Island Rail — A47

1981, Nov. 1 — Litho. — Perf. 13½x14
301 Strip of 4 1.40 1.40
a. A47 10p Nest .30 .30
b. A47 10p Eggs .30 .30
c. A47 10p Chicks .30 .30
d. A47 10p Adult rail .30 .30

Six-gilled Shark A48

1982, Feb. 8 — Litho. — Perf. 13½x14
302 A48 5p shown .25 .25
303 A48 14p Porbeagle shark .45 .30
304 A48 21p Blue shark .75 .55
305 A48 35p Hammerhead shark 1.10 .85
Nos. 302-305 (4) 2.55 1.95

Marcella — A49

1982, Apr. 5 — Litho. — Perf. 14
306 A49 5p shown .40 .40
307 A49 15p Eliza Adams .40 .40
308 A49 30p Corinthian .55 .55
309 A49 50p Samuel & Thomas .90 .90
Nos. 306-309 (4) 2.25 2.25

See Nos. 324-327.

Princess Diana Issue
Common Design Type
Perf. 14½x14

1982, July 1 — Litho. — Wmk. 373
310 CD333 5p Arms .25 .25
311 CD333 15p Diana .75 .25
312 CD333 30p Wedding 1.50 .35
313 CD333 50p Portrait 2.25 .60
Nos. 310-313 (4) 4.75 1.45

Scouting Year — A50

Perf. 13½x13, 13x13½
1982, Aug. 23 — Litho.
314 A50 5p Baden-Powell, vert. .25 .25
315 A50 20p Brownsea Isld. camp, 1907, vert. .35 .35
316 A50 50p Saluting .95 .95
Nos. 314-316 (3) 1.55 1.55

Souvenir Sheet
Perf. 14
317 A50 50p Tree illustration, vert. 1.50 1.25

Nos. 226, 230 Overprinted: "1st PARTICIPATION / COMMONWEALTH / GAMES 1982"
Perf. 13½x14
1982, Sept. 28 — Litho. — Wmk. 373
318 A31 5p multicolored .25 .25
319 A31 25p multicolored .40 .40

12th Commonwealth Games, Brisbane, Australia, Sept. 30-Oct. 9.

Formation of Volcanic Island A51

1982, Nov. 1 — Perf. 14x14½
320 A51 5p shown .30 .30
321 A51 15p Surface cinder cones .45 .45
322 A51 25p Eruption .55 .55
323 A51 35p 1961 eruption .70 .70
Nos. 320-323 (4) 2.00 2.00

Ship Type of 1982
1983, Feb. 1 — Litho. — Perf. 14
324 A49 5p Islander, vert. .25 .25
325 A49 20p Roscoe .50 .50
326 A49 35p Columbia .90 .75
327 A49 50p Emeline, vert. 1.25 1.10
Nos. 324-327 (4) 2.90 2.60

Tractor Pulling Trailer A52

1983, May 2 — Litho. — Perf. 14
328 A52 5p shown .25 .25
329 A52 15p Pack mules .25 .25
330 A52 30p Oxen pulling cart .50 .40
331 A52 50p Jeep .80 .60
Nos. 328-331 (4) 1.80 1.50

Map of South Atlantic A53

Island History.

Wmk. 373
1983, Aug. 1 — Litho. — Perf. 14
332 A53 1p shown .25 .25
333 A53 3p Tristao d'Acunha's flag-ship .25 .25
334 A53 4p Landing, 1643 .25 .25
335 A53 5p 17th cent. views .25 .25
336 A53 10p Landing party, 1815 .25 .25
337 A53 15p Settlement .35 .45
338 A53 18p Governor Glass's house .45 .50
339 A53 20p Rev. W.F. Taylor, Peter Green .50 .60
340 A53 25p Three-master John and Eliza-beth .75 .90
341 A53 50p Dependency dec-laration of St. Helena, 1938 1.40 1.75
342 A53 £1 Commissioning ceremony 2.75 3.50
343 A53 £2 Evacuation, 1961 5.75 7.25
Nos. 332-343 (12) 13.20 16.20

Raphael, 500th Birth Anniv. — A54

1983, Oct. 27 — Litho. — Perf. 14½
344 A54 20p multicolored .25 .25
345 A54 25p multicolored .65 .50
346 A54 40p multicolored 1.10 .90
Nos. 344-346 (3) 2.00 1.65

Souvenir Sheet
347 A54 50p multi, horiz. 1.50 1.25

Details from Christ's Charge to St. Peter.

St. Helena Colony Sesquicentenary — A55

1984, Jan. 3 — Litho. — Perf. 14
348 A55 10p No. 7 .25 .25
349 A55 15p No. 9 .30 .25
350 A55 25p No. 10 .50 .40
351 A55 60p No. 12 1.25 1.00
Nos. 348-351 (4) 2.30 1.90

Local Fungi A56

1984, Mar. 26
352 A56 10p Agrocybe praecox, vert. .65 .75
353 A56 20p Laccaria tetraspora, vert. 1.10 1.10
354 A56 30p Agrocybe cylin-dracea 1.75 1.75
355 A56 50p Sarcoscypha coc-cinea 2.75 2.75
Nos. 352-355 (4) 6.25 6.35

Constellations A57

Sheep Shearing — A58

1984, July 30 — Perf. 14½
356 A57 10p Orion .25 .25
357 A57 20p Scorpius .55 .45
358 A57 25p Canis Major .65 .55
359 A57 50p Crux 1.40 1.10
Nos. 356-359 (4) 2.85 2.35

1984, Oct. 1
360 A58 9p shown .25 .25
361 A58 17p Carding wool .40 .35
362 A58 29p Spinning .70 .60
363 A58 45p Knitting 1.10 1.00
a. Souvenir sheet of 4, #360-363 2.75 2.25
Nos. 360-363 (4) 2.45 2.20

Stamps from No. 363a do not have white border around the design.

Christmas 1984 A59

1984, Dec. 3 — Perf. 14
364 A59 10p Three angels, Christmas dinner .25 .25
365 A59 20p Two angels, cart .50 .45
366 A59 30p Candles, sailboat .80 .70
367 A59 50p Trees, Nativity 1.25 1.10
Nos. 364-367 (4) 2.80 2.50

Shipwrecks — A60

1985, Feb. 4 — Perf. 14x13½, 13½x14
368 A60 10p HMS Julia, 1817, vert. .90 .45
369 A60 25p Bell from Mabel Clark, 1878, vert. 1.40 1.10
370 A60 35p Barque Glenhuntley, 1898 2.00 1.50
Nos. 368-370 (3) 4.30 3.05

Souvenir Sheet
371 A60 60p Map of shipwreck sites 2.50 2.00

No. 371 contains one 48x32mm stamp. See Nos. 393-396, 412-415.

Queen Mother 85th Birthday
Common Design Type
Perf. 14½x14
1985, June 7 — Litho. — Wmk. 384
372 CD336 10p With Prince Charles, 1954 .30 .30
373 CD336 20p With Margaret at Ascot .55 .55
374 CD336 30p Queen Mother .80 .80
375 CD336 50p Holding Prince Henry 1.00 1.00
Nos. 372-375 (4) 2.65 2.65

Souvenir Sheet
376 CD336 80p With Anne 2.75 2.75

Flags A61

10p, Jonathan Lambert & flag of 1811, Isles of Refreshment. 15p, Cannon & flag of 21st Light Dragoons, 1816-17, Fort Malcolm. 25p, HMS Falmouth, 1816, & flag of HMS Atlantic Isle, HMS JOB 9, 1942-46. 60p, View of Tristan & Union Jack, 1816 to date.

1985, Sept. 30 — Wmk. 373 — Perf. 14
377 A61 10p multicolored .55 .45
378 A61 15p multicolored .70 .60
379 A61 25p multicolored 1.25 1.10
380 A61 60p multicolored 3.25 2.40
Nos. 377-380 (4) 5.75 4.55

Nos. 378-380 vert.

Loss of The Lifeboat, Cent. — A62

1985, Nov. 28
381	A62	10p Lifeboat, barque West Riding	.30	.30
382	A62	30p Map	.90	.90
383	A62	50p Death toll	1.50	1.50
		Nos. 381-383 (3)	2.70	2.70

Halley's Comet A63

1986, Mar. 3   **Wmk. 384**
384	A63	10p Bayeux Tapestry, c. 1092	.60	.60
385	A63	20p Trajectory around Earth	1.00	1.00
386	A63	30p Comet over Inaccessible Is.	1.40	1.40
387	A63	50p Ship Paramour	2.10	2.10
		Nos. 384-387 (4)	5.10	5.10

Queen Elizabeth II 60th Birthday
Common Design Type

Designs: 10p, With Prince Charles, 1950. 15p, Birthday Parade, wearing uniform of Scots Guards, 1976. 25p, At Westminster Abbey, London, 1972, wearing mantle and robes of the Most Noble Order of Bath. 45p, Silver Jubilee Tour, Canada, 1977. 65p, Visiting Crown Agents' offices, 1983.

1986, Apr. 21   **Perf. 14½**
388	CD337	10p scarlet, blk & sil	.25	.25
389	CD337	15p ultra & multi	.35	.35
390	CD337	25p green & multi	.60	.60
391	CD337	45p violet & multi	1.00	1.00
392	CD337	65p rose vio & multi	1.40	1.40
		Nos. 388-392 (5)	3.60	3.60

For overprints see Nos. 429-433.

Shipwrecks Type of 1985
1986, June 2   **Perf. 13½**
393	A60	9p SV Allanshaw, 1893	.50	.50
394	A60	20p Church font from Edward Vittery, 1881	1.00	1.00
395	A60	40p Figurehead, 1940	2.00	2.00
		Nos. 393-395 (3)	3.50	3.50

Souvenir Sheet
    Perf. 13½x13
396	A60	65p Barque Italia, 1892	3.50	3.50
		Nos. 394-395 vert.		

Royal Wedding Issue, 1986
Common Design Type

Designs: 10p, Informal portrait. 40p, Andrew operating helicopter.

1986, July 23   **Perf. 14**
397	CD338	10p multicolored	.25	.25
398	CD338	40p multicolored	1.25	1.25

A64   A65

1986, Sept. 30
399	A64	5p Wandering albatross	.25	.25
400	A64	10p Daisy	.60	.50
401	A64	20p Vanessa butterfly	1.25	1.00

402	A64	25p Wilkins's bunting	1.50	1.25
403	A64	50p Ring-eye	2.75	2.50
		Nos. 399-403 (5)	6.35	5.50

Flora & fauna of Inaccessible Island.

1987, Jan. 23   **Perf. 14½**

Indigenous Flightless Species and Habitats: 10p, Flightless moth, Edinburgh Settlement. 25p, Strap-winged fly, Crater Lake. 35p, Flightless rail, Inaccessible Island. 50p, Gough Island moorhen, Gough Island.
404	A65	10p multicolored	.50	.50
405	A65	25p multicolored	1.25	1.25
406	A65	35p multicolored	1.75	1.75
407	A65	50p multicolored	2.50	2.50
		Nos. 404-407 (4)	6.00	6.00

Rockhopper Penguins A66

1987, June 22
408	A66	10p Swimming	.65	.65
409	A66	20p Nesting	1.40	1.40
410	A66	30p Adult and young	2.10	2.10
411	A66	50p Adult's head	3.75	3.75
		Nos. 408-411 (4)	7.90	7.90

Shipwrecks Type of 1985

Designs: 11p, Castaways attacking sea elephant, vert. 17p, Henry A. Paull, 1879, Sandy Point. 45p, Gustav Stoltenhoff, Stoltenhoff Is., vert. 70p, Map of wrecks off Inaccessible Is.

1987, Apr. 2   **Perf. 14**
412	A60	11p olive gray & blk	.65	.65
413	A60	17p dark violet & blk	1.10	1.10
414	A60	45p myrtle green & blk	3.25	3.25
		Nos. 412-414 (3)	5.00	5.00

Souvenir Sheet
415	A60	70p light blue, royal blue & apple grn	5.00	5.00

Norwegian Scientific Expedition, 50th Anniv. — A67

10p, Microscope and textbooks symbolic of expedition results. 20p, Scientists tagging a mollymawk. 30p, Expedition headquarters on the island. 50p, S.S. Thorshammer.

Wmk. 384
1987, Dec. 7   **Litho.**   **Perf. 14**
416	A67	10p multicolored	1.00	.90
417	A67	20p multicolored	2.10	1.50

Wmk. 373
418	A67	30p multicolored	3.00	2.10
419	A67	50p multicolored	4.50	3.50
		Nos. 416-419 (4)	10.60	8.00

Fauna of Nightingale Island — A68

1988, Mar. 21   **Wmk. 384**   **Perf. 14**
420	A68	5p Tristan bunting	.30	.30
421	A68	10p Tristan thrush	.55	.55
422	A68	20p Yellow-nosed albatross	1.00	1.00
423	A68	25p Great shearwater	1.25	1.25
424	A68	50p Elephant seal	2.75	2.75
		Nos. 420-424 (5)	5.85	5.85

Handicrafts A69

1988, May 30   **Perf. 14½**
425	A69	10p Painted penguin eggs	.40	.40
426	A69	15p Moccasins	.55	.55
427	A69	35p Woolen clothing	1.40	1.40
428	A69	50p Model canvas boats	1.90	1.90
		Nos. 425-428 (4)	4.25	4.25

Nos. 388-392 Ovptd. "40TH WEDDING ANNIVERSARY" in Silver

1988, Mar. 9
429	CD337	10p scar, blk & sil	.25	.25
430	CD337	15p ultra & multi	.40	.40
431	CD337	25p green & multi	.65	.65
432	CD337	45p violet & multi	1.10	1.10
433	CD337	65p rose vio & multi	1.60	1.60
		Nos. 429-433 (5)	4.00	4.00

19th Cent. Whaling A70

1988, Oct. 6   **Perf. 14x14½**
434	A70	10p "Trying out" blubber	.70	.70
435	A70	20p Harpoon guns	1.25	1.25
436	A70	30p Scrimshaw	2.10	2.10
437	A70	50p Ships	3.50	3.50
		Nos. 434-437 (4)	7.55	7.55

Souvenir Sheet
438	A70	£1 Right whale	5.50	5.50

Lloyds of London, 300th Anniv.
Common Design Type

10p, Lloyds's new building, 1988. 25p, Cargo ship *Tristania II*, horiz. 35p, Supply ship *St. Helena*, horiz. 50p, Square-rigger *Kobenhavn*, lost at sea.

1988, Nov. 7   **Perf. 14**
439	CD341	10p multicolored	.50	.50
440	CD341	25p multicolored	1.50	1.50
441	CD341	35p multicolored	2.00	2.00
442	CD341	50p multicolored	2.75	2.75
		Nos. 439-442 (4)	6.75	6.75

Paintings of the Island, 1824, by Augustus Earle (1793-1838) — A71

Designs: 1p, Government House. 3p, Squall off Tristan. 4p, Rafting Blubber. 5p, Tristan. 10p, Man Killing an Albatross. 15p, View on the Summit. 20p, Nightingale Island. 25p, Tristan, diff. 35p, "Solitude," Watching the Horizon. 50p, North Eastern. £1, Tristan, diff. £2, Governor Glass and His Companions.

1988, Dec. 10
443	A71	1p multicolored	.25	.25
444	A71	3p multicolored	.25	.25
445	A71	4p multicolored	.25	.25
446	A71	5p multicolored	.25	.25
447	A71	10p multicolored	.35	.35
448	A71	15p multicolored	.50	.60
449	A71	20p multicolored	.65	1.10
450	A71	25p multicolored	.85	1.25
451	A71	35p multicolored	1.25	2.00
452	A71	50p multicolored	1.60	2.75
453	A71	£1 multicolored	3.25	5.50
454	A71	£2 multicolored	6.50	10.50
		Nos. 443-454 (12)	15.95	25.05

Gough Is. Fauna — A72

1989, Feb. 6   **Litho.**   **Wmk. 384**
455	A72	5p Giant petrel	.45	.45
456	A72	10p Gough moorhen	.80	.80
457	A72	20p Gough bunting	1.50	1.50
458	A72	25p Sooty albatross	1.75	1.75
459	A72	50p Amsterdam fur seal	3.50	3.50
		Nos. 455-459 (5)	8.00	8.00

Ferns — A73

1989, May 22   **Wmk. 373**   **Perf. 14**
460	A73	10p Eriosorus cheilanthoides	.60	.60
461	A73	25p Asplenium alvarezense	1.50	1.50
462	A73	35p Elaphoglossum hybridum	2.25	2.25
463	A73	50p Ophioglossum opacum	3.00	3.00
		Nos. 460-463 (4)	7.35	7.35

A74

1989, Nov. 20   **Wmk. 384**
464	A74	10p Cattle egret	1.40	1.10
465	A74	25p Spotted sandpiper	3.00	2.50
466	A74	35p Purple gallinule	4.50	3.50
467	A74	50p Barn swallow	5.75	4.75
		Nos. 464-467 (4)	14.65	11.85

Artifacts on Exhibit in the Nautical Museum A75

1989, Sept. 25
468	A75	10p Surgeon's mortar	.60	.60
469	A75	20p Parts of a harpoon	1.25	1.25
470	A75	30p Compass with binnacle hood	1.90	1.90
471	A75	60p Rope-twisting device	3.75	3.75
		Nos. 468-471 (4)	7.50	7.50

Moths A76

1990, Feb. 1   **Perf. 14**
472	A76	10p Peridroma saucia	.75	.75
473	A76	15p Ascalapha odorata	1.25	1.25
474	A76	35p Agrius cingulata	3.00	3.00

475 A76 60p Eumorpha
        labruscae   5.50   5.50
    Nos. 472-475 (4)   10.50 10.50

Starfish
(Echinoderms)
A77

1990, June 12   Perf. 14x13½
476 A77 10p shown   .85   .85
477 A77 20p multi, diff.   1.60   1.50
478 A77 30p multi, diff.   2.75   2.25
479 A77 60p multi, diff.   4.75   4.50
    Nos. 476-479 (4)   9.95   9.10

Queen Mother, 90th Birthday
Common Design Types
1990, Aug. 4 Wmk. 384 Perf. 14x15
480 CD343 25p Queen Mother at
           the Coliseum   1.25   1.10

Perf. 14½
481 CD344 £1 Broadcasting to
           women of the
           empire, 1939   5.00   4.50

Dunnottar
Castle,
1942 — A78

Designs: 15p, RMS St. Helena, 1977-1990.
35p, Launching new RMS St. Helena, 1989.
60p, Duke of York launching new RMS St.
Helena. £1, New RMS St. Helena.
1990, Sept. 13 Wmk. 373 Perf. 14½
482 A78 10p multicolored   .95   .95
483 A78 15p multicolored   1.50   1.50
484 A78 35p multicolored   4.00   3.25
485 A78 60p multicolored   6.25   5.50
    Nos. 482-485 (4)   12.70 11.20
Souvenir Sheet
486 A78 £1 multicolored   10.00 10.00
    See Ascension Nos. 493-497, St. Helena
Nos. 535-539.

Royal Navy
Warships
A79

Perf. 14½x14
1990, Nov. 30 Litho. Wmk. 373
487 A79 10p Pyramus, 1829   1.25   1.25
488 A79 25p Penguin, 1815   3.25   3.00
489 A79 35p Thalia, 1886   4.50   4.25
490 A79 50p Sidon, 1858   6.50   6.00
    Nos. 487-490 (4)   15.50 14.50

    See Nos. 547-550.

1991, Feb. 4
491 A79 10p Milford, 1938   2.25   1.60
492 A79 25p Dublin, 1923   3.50   2.75
493 A79 35p Yarmouth, 1919   4.75   4.00
494 A79 50p Carlisle, 1938   5.25   6.00
    Nos. 491-494 (4)   15.75 14.35

Souvenir Sheet

Royal Viking Sun — A80

Wmk. 384
1991, Apr. 1   Litho.   Perf. 14
495 A80 £1 multicolored   11.00 11.00

Prince
Philip,
70th
Birthday
A81

Designs: 10p, HMS Galatea, Prince Alfred.
25p, Royal Visit, 1957. 30p, HMY Britannia,
Prince Philip. 50p, Settlement of Edinburgh,
Prince Philip.
1991, June 10   Wmk. 373
496 A81 10p multicolored   1.50   1.25
497 A81 25p multicolored   3.25   3.00
498 A81 30p multicolored   4.25   3.50
499 A81 50p multicolored   6.50   6.00
    Nos. 496-499 (4)   15.50 13.75

Birds
A82

1991, Oct. 1
500 A82 8p Gough moorhens   2.75   1.60
501 A82 10p Gough bunting   2.75   1.90
502 A82 12p Gough moorhen
            in nest   3.00   1.90
503 A82 15p Gough bunting
            with chicks   3.25   2.25
    Nos. 500-503 (4)   11.75   7.65
    World Wildlife Fund.

Discovery of America, 500th
Anniv. — A83

1992, Jan. 23
504 A83 10p STV Eye of the
            Wind   .95   .75
505 A83 15p STV Soren Lar-
            sen   1.25   1.10
506 A83 35p STV Pinta, Nina,
            Santa Maria   3.00   2.75
507 A83 60p Columbus, Santa
            Maria   5.75   4.75
    Nos. 504-507 (4)   10.95   9.35
    World Columbian Stamp Expo '92, Chicago
and Genoa '92 Intl. Philatelic Exhibitions.

**Queen Elizabeth II's Accession to
the Throne, 40th Anniv.**
Common Design Type
1992, Feb. 6
508 CD349 10p multicolored   .60   .55
509 CD349 20p multicolored   1.25   1.10
510 CD349 25p multicolored   1.50   1.25
511 CD349 35p multicolored   2.10   1.90
512 CD349 65p multicolored   4.00   3.50
    Nos. 508-512 (5)   9.45   8.30

Fish — A84

Designs: 10p, Caesioperca coatsii. 15p,
Mendosoma lineatum. 35p, Physiculus kar-
rerae. 60p, Decapterus longimanus.

1992, June 1
513 A84 10p multicolored   .80   .55
514 A84 15p multicolored   1.50   1.10
515 A84 35p multicolored   3.00   2.40
516 A84 60p multicolored   5.50   4.25
    Nos. 513-516 (4)   10.80   8.30

Wreck of the Italia, Cent. — A85

Designs: 10p, Italia leaving Greenock. 45p,
In mid-Atlantic. 65p, Driving ashore on Stony
Beach. £1, Italia in peaceful waters.
1992, Sept. 18   Perf. 13½x14
517 A85 10p multicolored   .95   .80
518 A85 45p multicolored   3.75   3.50
519 A85 65p multicolored   5.75   5.25
    Nos. 517-519 (3)   10.45   9.55
Souvenir Sheet
520 A85 £1 multicolored   10.50 10.50
    Genoa '92 Intl. Philatelic Exhibition (#520).

Insects — A86

15p, Stenoscelis hylastoides. 45p, Troglos-
captomyza brevilamellata. 60p, Senilites
tristanicola.

Perf. 14x13½
1993, Feb. 2   Litho.   Wmk. 384
521 A86 15p multicolored   1.25   1.25
522 A86 45p multicolored   3.50   3.50
523 A86 60p multicolored   4.50   4.00
    Nos. 521-523 (3)   9.25   8.75

Coronation of
Queen Elizabeth
II, 40th
Anniv. — A87

Designs: 10p, Ampulla, spoon. 15p, Orb.
35p, Imperial State Crown. 60p, St. Edward's
Crown.
1993, June 14   Perf. 14½
524 A87 10p green & black   .85   .70
525 A87 15p red vio & black   1.25   1.10
526 A87 35p purple & black   2.75   2.40
527 A87 60p blue & black   4.50   4.25
    Nos. 524-527 (4)   9.35   8.45

Resettlement to Tristan, 30th
Anniv. — A88

Ships: No. 528, Tristania, Frances Repetto.
No. 529, Boissevain. 50p, Bornholm.
1993, Nov. 10   Perf. 13½x14
528 A88 35p multicolored   2.75   2.50
529 A88 35p multicolored   2.75   2.50
  a.   Pair, #528-529   6.50   6.00
530 A88 50p multicolored   4.50   4.25
    Nos. 528-530 (3)   10.00   9.25

Christmas — A89

Entire paintings or details: 5p, Madonna
with Child, School of Botticelli. 15p, The Holy
Family, by Daniel Gran. 35p, The Holy Virgin
and Child, by Rubens. 65p, The Mystical Marriage of St. Catherine with the Holy Child, by
Jan Van Balen.
1993, Nov. 30 Wmk. 373 Perf. 13
531 A89 5p multicolored   .65   .65
532 A89 15p multicolored   2.00   1.50
533 A89 35p multicolored   4.25   3.25
534 A89 65p multicolored   6.75   6.00
    Nos. 531-534 (4)   13.65 11.40

Ships
A90

Designs: 1p, Duchess of Atholl, 1929. 3p,
Empress of Australia, 1935. 5p, Anatolia,
1937. 8p, Viceroy of India, 1939. 10p,
Rangitata, 1943. 15p, Caronia, 1950. 20p,
Rotterdam, 1960. 25p, Leonardo da Vinci,
1972. 35p, Vistafjord, 1974. £1, World Discoverer, 1984. £2, Astor, 1984. £5, RMS St.
Helena, 1992.
1994, Feb. 3 Wmk. 384 Perf. 14
535 A90 1p multicolored   .30   .35
536 A90 3p multicolored   .30   .35
537 A90 5p multicolored   .30   .35
538 A90 8p multicolored   .30   .35
539 A90 10p multicolored   .40   .50
540 A90 15p multicolored   .60   .70
541 A90 20p multicolored   .80   .90
542 A90 25p multicolored   1.00   1.10
543 A90 35p multicolored   1.50   1.75
544 A90 £1 multicolored   3.75   4.50
545 A90 £2 multicolored   7.75   9.00
546 A90 £5 multicolored   20.00 17.00
    Nos. 535-546 (12)   37.00 36.85

Royal Navy Warships Type of 1990
1994, May 2   Wmk. 373
547 A79 10p HMS Nigeria,
            1948   1.10   1.10
548 A79 25p HMS Phoebe,
            1949   2.75   2.75
549 A79 35p HMS Liverpool,
            1949   3.50   3.50
550 A79 50p HMS Magpie,
            1955   5.50   5.50
    Nos. 547-550 (4)   12.85 12.85

Sharks
A91

1994, Aug.   Wmk. 384
551 A91 10p Blue shark   .95   .95
552 A91 45p Seven-gill shark   4.25   4.25
553 A91 65p Mako shark   5.75   5.75
    Nos. 551-553 (3)   10.95 10.95

Farm Animals — A92

1994, Nov.   Wmk. 373
554 A92 10p Donkeys   .85   .85
555 A92 20p Cattle   1.90   1.90
556 A92 35p Ducks, geese   3.50   3.50
557 A92 60p Girl feeding lamb   6.25   6.25
    Nos. 554-557 (4)   12.50 12.50

    See Nos. 601-604.

Local
Transport
A93

Designs: 15p, Pick-up truck. 20p, Leyland
Daf Sherpa van. 45p, Yamaha motorcycle,
scooter. 60p, Administrator's Landrover.

Wmk. 384
1995, Feb. 27   Litho.   Perf. 14
558 A93 15p multicolored   1.25 1.25
559 A93 20p multicolored   1.50 1.50
560 A93 45p multicolored   3.50 3.50
561 A93 60p multicolored   5.00 5.00
    Nos. 558-561 (4)   11.25 11.25

End of World War II, 50th Anniv.
Common Design Types

Designs: 15p, Lewis gun instruction, 1943.
20p, Tristan defense volunteers, 1943-46. 45p,
Radio, weather stations. 60p, HNS Birmingham, 1942. £1, Reverse of War Medal, 1939-45.

Perf. 13x13½
1995, June 19   Litho.   Wmk. 373
562 CD351 15p multicolored   1.60 1.60
563 CD351 20p multicolored   2.25 2.25
564 CD351 45p multicolored   4.50 4.50
565 CD351 60p multicolored   6.50 6.50
    Nos. 562-565 (4)   14.85 14.85

Souvenir Sheet
Perf. 14
566 CD352 £1 multicolored   8.00 8.00

Souvenir Sheet

Queen Mother, 95th Birthday — A94

1995, Aug. 4   Litho.   Perf. 14½x14
567 A94 £1.50 multicolored   9.00 9.00

UN, 50th Anniv.
Common Design Type

20p, Bedford 4-ton truck. 30p, Saxon
armored personnel carrier. 45p, Mi26 heavy
lift helicopter. 50p, RFA Sir Tristram transporting UN vehicles.

1995, Oct. 24   Perf. 13½x13
568 CD353 20p multicolored   1.90 1.90
569 CD353 30p multicolored   3.25 3.25
570 CD353 45p multicolored   4.50 4.50
571 CD353 50p multicolored   5.25 5.25
    Nos. 568-571 (4)   14.90 14.90

Seals
A95

Sub Antarctic fur seal: 10p, On rock. 35p,
Coming out of water with young.
Southern elephant seal: 45p, On beach with
young. 50p, In water.

1995, Nov. 3   Perf. 13½
572 A95 10p multicolored   .75   .75
573 A95 35p multicolored   3.00 3.00
574 A95 45p multicolored   4.50 4.50
575 A95 50p multicolored   4.75 4.75
    Nos. 572-575 (4)   13.00 13.00

Queen Elizabeth II, 70th Birthday
Common Design Type

Various portraits of Queen, island scenes:
15p, Tristan from sea. 20p, Traditional cottage.
45p, The Residency. 60p, With Prince Philip.

1996, Apr. 22   Litho.   Perf. 13½
576 CD354 15p multicolored   1.00 1.00
577 CD354 20p multicolored   1.40 1.40
578 CD354 45p multicolored   3.00 3.00
579 CD354 60p multicolored   3.75 3.75
    Nos. 576-579 (4)   9.15 9.15

New Harbor — A96

15p, View of Old Harbor. 20p, Earthmoving,
New Harbor construction. 45p, Crane, new
construction. 60p, View of New Harbor. Nos.
581-582 are 45x28mm.

1996, July 5   Wmk. 373   Perf. 13
580 A96 15p multicolored   1.90 1.90
581 A96 20p multicolored   3.00 3.00
582 A96 45p multicolored   4.00 4.00
583 A96 60p multicolored   5.00 5.00
    Nos. 580-583 (4)   13.90 13.90

Nos. 581-582 are 45x28mm.

A97

Gough Island Birds: 15p, Gough moorhen.
20p, Wandering albatross. 45p, Sooty albatross. 60p, Gough bunting.

1996, Oct. 1   Perf. 14
584 A97 15p multicolored   1.00 1.00
585 A97 20p multicolored   1.50 1.50
586 A97 45p multicolored   3.50 3.50
587 A97 60p multicolored   5.00 5.00
  a.   Souvenir sheet of 1   6.00 6.00
    Nos. 584-587 (4)   11.00 11.00

No. 587a for return of Hong Kong to China,
July 1, 1997. Issued 6/20/97.

A98

Presentation of Portrait of Queen Victoria,
Cent.: 20p, 19th cent. map of Trista da Cunha.
30p, HMS Magpie. 45p, Peter Green, former
governor. 50p, Detail of portrait of Queen Victoria, by Heinrich Von Angell.

1996, Dec. 18   Perf. 13½
588 A98 20p multicolored   1.60 1.60
589 A98 30p multicolored   2.50 2.50
590 A98 45p multicolored   3.50 3.50
591 A98 50p multicolored   4.00 4.00
    Nos. 588-591 (4)   11.60 11.60

The South Atlantic had begun to form by the late Cretaceous Period (100 million years ago). Volcanic islands had started to form as the South American and African continents split apart. The warm tropical seas teemed with life. In shallow areas coral life was abundant, belemnites and ammonites swam there with diverse bony fishes such as *Enchodus*. Such animals were prey for the large aquatic reptiles known as *Clidastes* and *Platecarpus* which could grow up to 15m in length. Plesiosaurs such as *Trinacromerum* still thrived and reached up to 10m but Ichthyosaurs and marine crocodiles were rare but other marine reptiles included the turtle *Archelon*.

Atlantic Marine Fauna of the
Cretaceous — A99

Designs: a, Archelon. b, Trinacromerum. c,
Platecarpus. d, Clidastes.

1997, Feb. 10   Wmk. 384   Perf. 14
592 A99 35p Sheet of 4, #a.-d. 12.00 12.00
          See No. 619.

Visual Communications — A100

Designs: No. 593, Smoke signals. No. 594,
HMS Eurydice. No. 595, HMS Challenger. No.
596, Flag hoists. No. 597, Semaphore. No.
598, HMS Carlisle. No. 599, Light signals. No.
600, HMS Cilicia.

1997   Litho.   Wmk. 384   Perf. 14½
593   10p multicolored   .50   .50
594   10p multicolored   .50   .50
  a.   A100 Pair, #593-594 1.25 1.25
595   15p multicolored   .70   .70
596   15p multicolored   .70   .70
  a.   A100 Pair, #595-596 2.00 2.00
597   20p multicolored   .85   .85
598   20p multicolored   .85   .85
  a.   A100 Pair, #597-598 2.50 2.50
599   35p multicolored   1.50 1.50
600   35p multicolored   1.50 1.50
  a.   Pair, #599-600   4.25 4.25
    Nos. 593-600 (8)   7.10 7.10

Farm Animals Type of 1994
1997, Aug. 26   Litho.   Perf. 14
601 A92 20p Chickens   1.40 1.40
602 A92 30p Cattle   2.40 2.40
603 A92 45p Sheep   3.50 3.50
604 A92 50p Dogs   3.75 3.75
    Nos. 601-604 (4)   11.05 11.05

Queen Elizabeth II and Prince Philip,
50th Wedding Anniv. — A101

Designs: No. 605, Queen up close. No. 606,
Prince riding polo pony. No. 607, Queen with
horse. No. 608, Prince up close. No. 609,
Prince in military attire, Queen in green coat.
No. 610, Princess Anne riding horse.
£1.50, Queen, Prince riding in open carriage, horiz.

1997, Nov. 20   Wmk. 373   Perf. 14
605   15p multicolored   .70   .70
606   15p multicolored   .70   .70
  a.   A101 Pair, #605-606 2.00 2.00
607   20p multicolored   1.00 1.00
608   20p multicolored   1.00 1.00
  a.   A101 Pair, #607-608 3.25 3.25
609   45p multicolored   2.10 2.10
610   45p multicolored   2.10 2.10
  a.   A101 Pair, #609-610 6.75 6.75
    Nos. 605-610 (6)   7.60 7.60
Souvenir Sheet
611 A101 £1.50 multicolored 14.00 14.00

First Lobster
Survey, 50th
Anniv. — A102

Ships: 15p, Hilary, Melodie. 20p, Tristania II,
Hekla. 30p, Pequena, Frances Repetto. 45p,
Tristania, Gillian Gaggins. 50p, MFV. Kelso,
MV. Edinburgh.
£1.20, Fr. C.P. Lawrence, lobster.

1998, Feb. 6   Perf. 14½
612 A102 15p multicolored   .85   .85
613 A102 20p multicolored   1.25 1.25
614 A102 30p multicolored   1.90 1.90
615 A102 45p multicolored   3.00 3.00
616 A102 50p multicolored   3.00 3.00
    Nos. 612-616 (5)   10.00 10.00
Souvenir Sheet
617 A102 £1.20 multicolored 12.00 12.00

Diana, Princess of Wales (1961-97)
Common Design Type

a, In beige dress. b, In white top with black
collar. c, In striped top. d, In lilac & white print
dress.

1998, May 15   Perf. 14½x14
618 CD355 35p Strip of 4, #a.-d. 6.00 6.00

No. 618 sold for £1.40 + 20p with surtax
from international sales going to the Princess
Diana Memorial Fund and surtax from local
sales going to a designated local charity.

Atlantic Marine Fauna Type of 1997

Fauna of the Miocene Epoch: a,
Carcharodon. b, Orycterocetus. c, Eurhi-
nodelphis. d, Hexanchus (six gilled shark),
myliobatis.

1998, July 8   Perf. 14
619 A99 45p Sheet of 4, #a.-d. 15.00 15.00

Visiting
Cruise
Ships
A103

1998, Sept. 15   Perf. 14
620 A103 15p Livonia   1.50 1.50
621 A103 20p Professor
            Molchanov   2.00 2.00
622 A103 45p Explorer   4.50 4.50
623 A103 60p Hanseatic 6.00 6.00
    Nos. 620-623 (4)   14.00 14.00

Sailing
Ships
A104

1998, Nov. 23   Wmk. 373   Perf. 14½
624 A104 15p H.G. Johnson,
            1892   1.50 1.50
625 A104 35p Theodore, 1893 3.25 3.25
626 A104 45p Hesperides,
            1893   4.50 4.50
627 A104 50p Bessfield, 1894 4.75 4.75
    Nos. 624-627 (4)   14.00 14.00
1999, Mar. 19
628 A104 20p Derwent, 1895   2.00 2.00
629 A104 30p Strathgryffe,
            1898   2.75 2.75
630 A104 50p Celestial Em-
            pire, 1898 4.50 4.50
631 A104 60p Lamorna, 1902   4.75 4.75
    Nos. 628-631 (4)   14.00 14.00
    Nos. 624-631 (8)   28.00 28.00

Wandering Albatross — A105

World Wildlife Fund: 5p, Two adults. 8p, Adult, juvenile in nest. 12p, Adult spreading wings. 15p, Two in flight.

1999, Apr. 27   Wmk. 373   Perf. 14
632	A105	5p multicolored	.65	.65
633	A105	8p multicolored	.70	.70
634	A105	12p multicolored	.75	.75
635	A105	15p multicolored	.85	.85
a.		Strip of 4, #632-635	3.25	3.25
		Nos. 632-635 (4)	2.95	2.95

Issued in sheets of 16.

Wedding of Prince Edward and Sophie Rhys-Jones
Common Design Type
Perf. 13¾x14

1999, June 18   Litho.   Wmk. 384
636	CD356	45c Separate portraits	2.25	2.25
637	CD356	£1.20 Couple	5.75	5.75

Queen Mother's Century
Common Design Type

Queen Mother: 20p, With Princess Elizabeth on her 18th birthday. 30p, With King George VI at Balmoral. 50p, With Royal Family, 94th birthday. 60p, As colonel-in-chief of Black Watch. £1.50, Age 5 photo, airplanes from Battle of Britain, 1940.

1999, Aug. 18   Wmk. 384   Perf. 13½
638	CD358	20p multi	1.25	1.25
639	CD358	30p multi	2.00	2.00
640	CD358	50p multi	3.00	3.00
641	CD358	60p multi	3.75	3.75
		Nos. 638-641 (4)	10.00	10.00

Souvenir Sheet
642	CD358	£1.50 black	10.00	10.00

Millennium — A106

Various birds.

2000, Jan. 1   Wmk. 373   Perf. 14
Color of Queen's Head
643	A106	20p bister	1.00	1.00
644	A106	30p green	1.75	1.75
645	A106	50p blue	3.25	3.25
646	A106	60p brown	4.00	4.00
		Nos. 643-646 (4)	10.00	10.00

Royalty — A107

British monarchs on 8p-£5: 1p, King Manuel I of Portugal. 3p, Frederick Henry, Prince of Orange. 5p, Empress Maria Theresa of Austria. 8p, King George III. 10p, King George IV. 15p, King Willian IV. 20p, Queen Victoria. 25p, Edward VII. 35p, George V. £1, Edward VIII. £2, George VI. £5, Elizabeth II.

2000, Feb. 1   Wmk. 384   Perf. 14
647	A107	1p multi	.25	.25
648	A107	3p multi	.25	.25
649	A107	5p multi	.25	.25
650	A107	8p multi	.30	.30
651	A107	10p multi	.40	.40
652	A107	15p multi	.60	.80
653	A107	20p multi	.75	1.00
654	A107	25p multi	1.00	1.10
655	A107	35p multi	1.60	1.90
656	A107	£1 multi	3.75	5.25

657	A107	£2 multi	8.25	10.00
658	A107	£5 multi	20.00	24.50
		Nos. 647-658 (12)	37.40	46.00

The Stamp Show 2000, London
A108

Designs: 15p, Longboat under oars. 45p, Longboat under sail. 50p, Cutty Sark, 1876. 60p, Cutty Sark, 2000. £1.50, Cutty Sark visiting Tristan da Cunha, 1876.

Wmk. 373
2000, May 22   Litho.   Perf. 14
659	A108	15p multi	1.25	1.25
660	A108	45p multi	3.00	3.00
661	A108	50p multi	3.25	3.25
662	A108	60p multi	4.00	4.00
		Nos. 659-662 (4)	11.50	11.50

Souvenir Sheet
663	A108	£1.50 multi	11.00	11.00

Prince William, 18th Birthday
Common Design Type

William: Nos. 664, 668a, As toddler, with Princes Charles and Harry, vert. Nos. 665, 668b, Holding paper, vert. Nos. 666, 668c, Wearing scarf. Nos. 667, 668d, Wearing suit and wearing sweater. No. 668e, As child, with Shetland pony.

Perf. 13¾x14¼, 14¼x13¾

2000, June 21   Litho.   Wmk. 373
Stamps With White Border
664	CD359	45p multi	2.25	2.25
665	CD359	45p multi	2.25	2.25
666	CD359	45p multi	2.25	2.25
667	CD359	45p multi	2.25	2.25
		Nos. 664-667 (4)	9.00	9.00

Souvenir Sheet
Stamps Without White Border
Perf. 14¼
668	CD359	45p Sheet of 5, #a-e	12.00	12.00

Ships and Helicopters — A109

No. 669, 10p: a, SA Agulhas. b, SA 330J Puma, 1999.
No. 670, 15p: a, HMS London. b, Westland Wessex HAS 1, 1964.
No. 671, 20p: a, HMS Endurance. b, Westland Lynx HAS 3, 1996.
No. 672, 50p: a, USS Spiegel Grove. b, Sikorsky UH-19F, 1963.

Wmk. 373
2000, Sept. 4   Litho.   Perf. 14
Pairs, #a-b
669-672	A109	Set of 4	15.00	15.00

First Election of Winston Churchill to Parliament, Cent. — A110

Designs: 20p, During siege of Sidney Street, 1911. 30p, With Franklin D. Roosevelt, 1941. 50p, VE Day broadcast, 1945. 60p, Greeting Queen Elizabeth, 1955.

Perf. 13¾x14
2000, Oct. 2   Wmk. 373
673-676	A110	Set of 4	10.00	10.00

New Year 2001 (Year of the Snake) — A111

No. 677: a, 30p, Inaccessible Island rail. b, 45p, Black-faced spoonbill.

Wmk. 373
2001, Feb. 1   Litho.   Perf. 14½
677	A111	Sheet of 2, #a-b	10.00	10.00

Hong Kong 2001 Stamp Exhibition.

Age of Victoria
A112

Designs: 15p, Letter, 1846. 20p, Prince Alfred, Duke of Edinburgh, vert. 30p, HMS Galatea. 35p, Queen Victoria, vert. 50p, Charles Dickens, vert. 60p, Resupplying ships. £1.50, Jubilee celebrations.

Wmk. 373
2001, May 24   Litho.   Perf. 14
678-683	A112	Set of 6	12.00	12.00

Souvenir Sheet
684	A112	£1.50 multi	9.00	9.00

Longboats — A113

No. 685: a, Boat with dark and light blue striped sails, island in distance. b, Boat with red and blue striped and white sails, boat with blue, red and yellow striped and blue and white striped sails. c, Prow and sail of boat, two boats in distance. d, Boat with blue red and yellow striped and blue and white striped sails. e, Boat with dark and light blue sails near shore. f, Boat with red and blue striped and white sails. g, Boat with gray, red and white sails. h, Boat with sails down.

2001, July 12
685	A113	30p Sheet of 8, #a-h	11.00	11.00

Nos. 669-672 Overprinted in Blue Violet

Wmk. 373
2001, Sept. 17   Litho.   Perf. 14
686	A109	10p Pair, #a-b	1.75	1.75
687	A109	15p Pair, #a-b	2.50	2.50
688	A109	20p Pair, #a-b	3.25	3.25
689	A109	50p Pair, #a-b	8.50	8.50
		Nos. 686-689 (4)	16.00	16.00

Souvenir Sheet

Birdlife International World Bird Festival — A114

Spectacled petrel: a, Head. b, Diving (island in background). c, In flight with legs extended. d, Diving (sea in background). e, Chick.

Wmk. 373
2001, Oct. 1   Litho.   Perf. 14½
690	A114	35p Sheet of 5, #a-e	11.00	11.00

Royal Navy Ships A115

Designs: No. 691, 20p, HMS Penguin, 1815. No. 692, 20p, HMS Julia, 1817. No. 693, 35p, HMS Beagle, 1901. No. 694, 35p, HMS Puma, 1962. No. 695, 60p, HMS Monmouth, 1997. No. 696, 60p, HMS Somerset, 1999.

Wmk. 373
2001, Oct. 31   Litho.   Perf. 14
691-696	A115	Set of 6	12.00	12.00

Churches A116

Designs: No. 697, 35p, Exterior, St. Joseph's Catholic Church. No. 698, 35p, Exterior, St. Mary's Anglican Church. No. 699, 60p, Stained glass window, St. Joseph's. No. 700, 60p, Altar, St. Mary's.

Perf. 13¼x13½, 13½x13¼
2001, Nov. 27
697-700	A116	Set of 4	13.00	13.00

Christmas, Arrival of first USPG missionary, 150th anniv.

Tristan da Cunha Postage Stamps, 50th Anniv. A117

Designs: Nos. 701, 45p, 705a, 45p, #5, 6, 9, 10 canceled. Nos. 702, 20p, 705, 45p, #7, 8, 11, 12 canceled. Nos. 703, 50p, 705c, 45p, #1-4 canceled. Nos. 704, 60p, 705d, 45p, Men at post office, 1952.

2002, Jan. 1   Perf. 13½
Without "Tristan da Cunha" in Script
701-704	A117	Set of 4	10.50	10.50

Souvenir Sheet
With "Tristan da Cunha" in Script at Top or Bottom of Stamps
705	A117	45p Sheet of 4, #a-d	11.50	11.50

Reign Of Queen Elizabeth II, 50th Anniv. Issue
Common Design Type

Designs: Nos. 706, 710a, 15p, Princess Elizabeth, 1947. Nos. 707, 710b, 30p, Wearing tiara, 1991. Nos. 708, 710c, 45p, Wearing red coat. Nos. 709, 710d, 50p, Wearing purple hat, 1997. No. 710e, 60p, 1955 portrait by Annigoni (38x50mm).

Perf. 14¼x14½, 13¾ (#710e)
2002, Feb. 6   Litho.   Wmk. 373
With Gold Frames
706-709 CD360   Set of 4   8.00 8.00
Souvenir Sheet
Without Gold Frames
710 CD360   Sheet of 5, #a-e   11.00 11.00

Fishing Industry — A118

Designs: 20p, Pelagic armorhead. 35p, Yellowtail. 50p, Splendid alfonsino. 60p, Ship San Liberatore.

Wmk. 373
2002, May   Litho.   Perf. 14
711-713 A118   Set of 3   6.75 6.75
714   Souvenir sheet, #711-713,
         714a   8.50 8.50
  a.   A118 60p multi   1.75 1.75

Queen Mother Elizabeth (1900-2002)
Common Design Type
Designs: 20p, Wearing hat (black and white photograph). £1.50, Wearing blue green hat. No. 717: a, 75p, Holding baby (black and white photograph). b, 75p, Wearing dark blue hat.

Wmk. 373
2002, Aug. 5   Litho.   Perf. 14¼
With Purple Frames
715-716 CD361   Set of 2   8.00 8.00
Souvenir Sheet
Without Purple Frames
Perf. 14½x14¼
717 CD361   Sheet of 2, #a-b   8.00 8.00

Marine Mammals — A119

No. 718: a, Gray's beaked whale. b, Dusky dolphin. c, False killer whale. d, Long-finned pilot whale. e, Sperm whale. f, Shepherd's beaked whale.
£2, Humpback whale.

Wmk. 373
2002, Sept. 24   Litho.   Perf. 13¼
718 A119 30p Sheet of 6, #a-f 12.00 12.00
Souvenir Sheet
719 A119   £2 multi   11.00 11.00

HMS Herald Survey, 150th Anniv. — A120

Designs: 20p, Captain Denham and officers. 35p, HMS Herald in Bay of Biscay. 50p, Surveying, Oct. 30, 1852. 60p, HMS Herald and Torch at sunset, 1852.

2002, Nov. 11   Perf. 14x14¾
720-723 A120   Set of 4   8.00 8.00

Guinness Book of World Records — A121

No. 724: a, Great Barrier Reef (longest reef). b, Greenland (biggest island). c, Sahara Desert (biggest desert). d, Amazon and Nile Rivers (longest rivers). e, Mt. Everest (biggest mountain). f, Tristan da Cunha (most remote inhabited island).
£2, Like No. 724f.

Wmk. 373
2003, Jan. 10   Litho.   Perf. 13¾
724 A121 30p Sheet of 6, #a-f   9.50 9.50
Souvenir Sheet
725 A121   £2 multi   12.00 12.00

Atlantic Yellow-nosed Albatross — A122

Designs: Nos. 726, 730a, 15p, Heads of two birds. Nos. 727, 730b, 30p, Bird on nest, vert. Nos. 728, 730c, 45p, Bird in flight, vert. Nos. 729, 730d, Two birds in flight. No. 730e, £1, Two birds in flight, diff.

Perf. 14¼x13¾, 13¾x14¼
2003, May 7   Litho.
Stamps With White Frames
726-729 A122   Set of 4   7.00 7.00
Souvenir Sheet
Stamps Without Frames
Perf. 14¼x14½
730 A122   Sheet of 5, #a-e   12.00 12.00
Birdlife International.

Head of Queen Elizabeth II
Common Design Type
Wmk. 373
2003, June 2   Litho.   Perf. 13¾
731 CD362   £2.80 multi   11.00 11.00

Coronation of Queen Elizabeth II, 50th Anniv.
Common Design Type
Designs: Nos. 732, 20p, 734a, Queen and extended family. Nos. 733, £1.50, 734b, Bishops paying homage to Queen at coronation.

Perf. 14¼x14½
2003, June 2   Litho.   Wmk. 373
Vignettes Framed, Red Background
732-733 CD363   Set of 2   8.00 8.00
Souvenir Sheet
Vignettes Without Frame, Purple Panel
734 CD363 75p Sheet of 2, #a-b 8.00 8.00

Prince William, 21st Birthday
Common Design Type
No. 735: a, William in polo uniform at right. b, In sweater at left.

Wmk. 373
2003, June 21   Litho.   Perf. 14¼
735   Horiz. pair   7.00 7.00
  a.-b.   CD364 50p Either single 3.00 3.00

William Glass (1787-1853), Governor — A123

No. 736: a, Arrival of Glass on HMS Falmouth, 1816. b, As corporal, stationed on Tristan da Cunha. c, Glass and family onshore, 1817. d, Glass family with dog. e, Gov. Glass conducting daughter's marriage ceremony, 1833. f, Glass as old man.

Perf. 14¼x14½
2003, Nov. 24   Litho.   Wmk. 373
736 A123 30p Sheet of 6, #a-f, +
         6 labels   7.00 7.00

Royal Navy Ships — A124

No. 737, 20p: a, RFA Tideflow. b, RFA Tidespring.
No. 738, 35p: a, RFA Gold Rover. b, RFA Diligence.
No. 739, 60p: a, RFA Wave Chief. b, HMY Britannia.

Wmk. 373
2003, Dec. 8   Litho.   Perf. 14
Horiz. pairs, #a-b
737-739 A124   Set of 3   9.50 9.50

History of Writing Implements — A125

Designs: 15p, Cave paintings and pigment blocks. 20p, Clay tablet. 35p, Egyptian writing palette. 45p, Goose quill pen. 50p, Fountain pen. 60p, Ballpoint pen.
£1.50, Word processing.

2004, Jan. 8   Perf. 13¾
740-745 A125   Set of 6   8.50 8.50
Souvenir Sheet
Litho. with Margin Embossed
746 A125   £1.50 multi   8.00 8.00

Worldwide Fund for Nature (WWF) — A126

Subantarctic fur seal: No. 747, 35p, Underwater. No. 748, 35p, Pair on rocks. No. 749, 35p, Seal on rock. No. 750, 35p, Head.

Wmk. 373
2004, July 12   Litho.   Perf. 14
747-750 A126   Set of 4   6.50 6.50
  750a   Sheet, 4 each #747-750 27.50 27.50

New Flag — A127

2004, July 27   Unwmk.   Die Cut
Self-Adhesive
Booklet Stamp
751 A127 30p multi   1.50 1.50
  a.   Booklet pane of 6   9.00
         Complete booklet, 2 #751a 18.00

Merchant Ships — A128

Designs: No. 752, 20p, RMS Dunnottar Castle. No. 753, 20p, RMS Caronia. No. 754, 35p, SA Agulhas. No. 755, 35p, MV Edinburgh. No. 756, 60p, MV Explorer. No. 757, 60p, MV Hanseatic.

Wmk. 373
2004, Nov. 9   Litho.   Perf. 13¼
752-757 A128   Set of 6   10.50 10.50

Battle of Trafalgar, Bicent. — A129

Designs: 15p, Admiral Horatio Nelson's quadrant. 20p, HMS Royal Sovereign breaks the line, horiz. 25p, Thomas Swain aids the wounded Nelson, horiz. 35p, HMS Victory breaks the line, horiz. 50p, Nelson. 60p, HMS Victory, horiz.
No. 764: a, Capt. Thomas Masterman Hardy. b, HMS Victory.

Perf. 13¼
2005, Jan. 20   Litho.   Unwmk.
758-763 A129   Set of 6   8.75 8.75
Souvenir Sheet
764 A129 75p Sheet of 2, #a-b 6.75 6.75

No. 763 has particles of wood from the HMS Victory embedded in the areas covered by a thermographic process that produces a shiny, raised effect.

Island Flora, Fauna and Scenes — A130

No. 765 — Tristan da Cunha: a, Rockhopper penguins. b, Southern elephant seals. c, Tristan rock lobster. d, Crowberry. e, Tristan da Cunha island settlement and volcano.
No. 766 — Gough Island: a, Gough moorhen. b, Subantarctic fur seal. c, Bluefish. d, Gough tree fern. e, South African Weather Station.
No. 767 — Inaccessible Island: a, Inaccessible rail. b, Dusky dolphins. c, Sebastes capensis. d, Pepper tree. e, Inaccessible Island Waterfall.
No. 768 — Nightingale Island: a, Tristan thrush. b, Southern right whale. c, Fivefinger fish. d, Tussock grass. e, Nightingale Island.
No. 769 — Middle Island: a, Broad-billed prion. b, False killer whale. c, Wreckfih. d, Fern. e, Middle Island.
No. 770 - Stoltenhoff Island: a, Brown skua. b, Shepherd's beaked whales. c, Snoeks. d, Sea bind weed. e, Stoltenhoff Island.

2005   Wmk. 373   Perf. 13¾
765   Horiz. strip of 5 10.00 10.00
  a.-e.   A130 50p Any single 2.00 2.00

766		Horiz. strip of 5	10.00	10.00
a.-e.	A130	50p Any single	2.00	2.00
767		Horiz. strip of 5	10.00	10.00
a.-e.	A130	50p Any single	2.00	2.00
768		Horiz. strip of 5	10.00	10.00
a.-e.	A130	50p Any single	2.00	2.00
769		Horiz. strip of 5	10.00	10.00
a.-e.	A130	50p Any single	2.00	2.00
770		Horiz. strip of 5	10.00	10.00
a.-e.	A130	50p Any single	2.00	2.00

Issued: No. 765, 2/21; No. 766, 3/28; No. 767, 4/18; No. 768, 2/7/06; No. 769, 3/30/06; No. 770, 9/27/06.
See No. 796.

Birds
A131

Designs: 1p, Kerguelen petrel. 3p, Sooty albatross. 5p, Antarctic tern. 8p, Tristan bunting. 10p, Cape petrel. 15p, Tristan moorhen. 20p, Giant fulmar. 25p, Brown skua. 35p, Great-winged petrel. £1, Broad-billed prion. £2, Soft-plumaged petrel. £5, Rockhopper penguin.

Perf. 14¼x14¾

2005, June 1   Litho.   Wmk. 373

771	A131	1p multi	.25	.25
772	A131	3p multi	.25	.25
773	A131	5p multi	.25	.25
774	A131	8p multi	.30	.30
775	A131	10p multi	.35	.35
776	A131	15p multi	.55	.55
777	A131	20p multi	.75	.75
778	A131	25p multi	.90	.90
779	A131	35p multi	1.25	1.25
780	A131	£1 multi	4.00	4.00
781	A131	£2 multi	8.00	8.75
782	A131	£5 multi	20.00	21.00
	Nos. 771-782 (12)		*36.85*	*38.60*

Pope John Paul II
(1920-2005)
A132

Wmk. 373

2005, Aug. 18   Litho.   Perf. 14

783	A132	50p multi	2.10	2.10

Battle of Trafalgar, Bicent. — A133

Designs: 20p, HMS Victory. 70p, Ships in battle, horiz. £1, Admiral Horatio Nelson.

Perf. 13¼

2005, Oct. 18   Litho.   Unwmk.

784-786	A133	Set of 3	7.00	7.00

Discovery of Tristan da Cunha, 500th Anniv. — A134

No. 787: a, 30p, Discovery by Tristao d'Acunha, 1506. b, 30p, First survey, 1767. c, 30p, Jonathan Lambert of Salem, 1810. d, 50p, William Glass, 1816. e, 50p, Duke of Gloucester (ship), 1824. f, 80p, Wreck of the Emily, 1836.

No. 788: a, 30p, Thomas Swain (1774-1862). b, 30p, HMS Challenger, 1873. c, 30p, Rev. Edwin Dodgson arrives, 1881. d, 50p, Wreck of the Italia, 1892. e, 50p, HMS Milford, 1938. f, 80p, Norwegian Expedition, 1937-38.

No. 789: a, 30p, World War II TDV training. b, 30p, HMS Atlantic Isle, 1944. c, 30p, Hands holding potatoes, 1946 potato stamp. d, 50p, Tristan da Cunha #5. e, 50p, Volcano eruption and evacuation, 1961. f, 80p, Gough Island Scientific Expedition, 1955.

No. 790: a, 30p, Royal Society Expedition, 1962. b, 30p, Resettlement, 1963. c, 30p, Denstone Expedition to Inaccessible Island, 1982. d, 50p, RMS St. Helena, 1992. e, 50p, New coat of arms, 2002. f, 80p, Hurricane disaster, 2001.

Perf. 14¼x14½

2006   Litho.   Wmk. 373

787	A134	Sheet of 6, #a-f	10.00	10.00
788	A134	Sheet of 6, #a-f	10.00	10.00

Perf. 14¼x14¾

789	A134	Sheet of 6, #a-f	11.00	11.00
790	A134	Sheet of 6, #a-f	11.00	11.00

Issued: Nos. 787-788, 2/2; Nos. 789-790, 6/1.

Queen Elizabeth II, 80th Birthday
A135

Queen: No. 791, 60p, As child. No. 792, 60p, Wearing feathered hat. No. 793, 60p, Wearing red hat. No. 794, 60p, Wearing sunglasses.

No. 795: a, 50p, Like No. 792. b, 50p, Like No. 793.

2006, Apr. 21   Perf. 14

791-794	A135	Set of 4	9.50	9.50

Souvenir Sheet

795	A135	50p Sheet of 2, #a-b	4.00	4.00

Island Flora, Fauna and Scenes Type of 2005-06
Miniature Sheet

No. 796: a, Map of Tristan da Cunha, flag. b, Map of Inaccessible Island, wandering albatross. c, Map of Nightingale Island, humpback whale. d, Map of Middle Island, traditional longboats. e, Map of Stoltenhoff Island, mackerel. f, Map of Gough Island, sub-antarctic fur seal.

Wmk. 373

2007, Jan. 22   Litho.   Perf. 13¾

796		Sheet of 6	13.00	13.00
a.-f.	A130	50p Any single	2.10	2.10

Local Vehicles
A136

Designs: 15p, Wave Dancer fishery patrol boat. 20p, Ambulance. 30p, Inshore rescue craft. 45p, Police Land Rover. 50p, Fire engine. 85p, Administrator's Land Rover.

Perf. 12½x13

2007, Apr. 17   Litho.   Unwmk.

797-802	A136	Set of 6	10.00	10.00

Wedding of Queen Elizabeth II and Prince Philip, 60th Anniv. — A137

Designs: No. 803, 50p, Shown. No. 804, 50p, Queen waving. No. 805, 50p, Queen and

---

Prince (black and white photograph). No. 806, 50p, Queen and Prince (color photograph). £2, Queen in wedding gown.

2007, June 1   Wmk. 373   Perf. 13¾

803-806	A137	Set of 4	8.00	8.00

Souvenir Sheet
Perf. 14

807	A137	£2 multi	8.00	8.00

No. 807 contains one 42x57mm stamp.

Miniature Sheet

BirdLife International — A138

No. 808 — Great shearwater: a, In flight, facing right. b, In flight, facing left, showing land and sky. c, On ground, showing land and sky. d, In flight facing left, showing land and water. e, On ground, showing land only. f, Chick.

2007, July 1   Unwmk.   Perf. 13¾

808	A138	50p Sheet of 6, #a-f	13.00	13.00

Scouting, Cent.
A139

Designs: 15p, Scout J. W. S. Marr and his book, *Into the Frozen South*, hands tying knot. 20p, The Quest frozen in, Marr, hands tightening rope. £1.25, Flag raising ceremony, hand with compass. £1.40, Children of Tristan da Cunha, trumpeter.

No. 813, vert.: a, Marr and Questie, the ship's cat. b, Lord Robert Baden-Powell.

2007, July 9   Wmk. 373

809-812	A139	Set of 4	13.00	13.00

Souvenir Sheet

813	A139	£1.50 Sheet of 2, #a-b	13.00	13.00

A140

A141

A142

A143

A144

Princess Diana (1961-97)
A145

Perf. 13x12½

2007, Nov. 30   Litho.   Unwmk.

814	A140	50p multi	2.25	2.25
815	A141	50p multi	2.25	2.25
816	A142	50p multi	2.25	2.25
817	A143	50p multi	2.25	2.25
818	A144	50p multi	2.25	2.25
819	A145	50p multi	2.25	2.25
	Nos. 814-819 (6)		*13.50*	*13.50*

Military Uniforms — A146

Designs: No. 820, 15p, Officer, 21st Light Dragoon. No. 821, 15p, Corporal, Royal Artillery. No. 822, 20p, Privates, Royal Artillery. No. 823, 20p, Lieutenant, Royal Artillery. No. 824, £1, Soldiers from Cape Regiment. No. 825, £1, Soldiers from South Africa Army Engineering Corps.

Unwmk.

2007, Dec. 10   Litho.   Perf. 14

820-825	A146	Set of 6	11.50	11.50

Marine Invertebrates
A147

Designs: 15p, Tristan rock lobster. 20p, Trumpet anemone. 35p, Starfish. No. 829, 60p, Tristan urchin. No. 830, 60p, Sponge. 85p, Strawberry anemone.

2007, Dec. 10   Unwmk.   Perf. 13¼

826-831	A147	Set of 6	11.50	11.50

A148

Royal Air Force, 90th Anniv. — A149

Designs: No. 832, 30p, Royal Aircraft Factory S. E. 5a. No. 833, 30p, Hawker Hart. No. 834, 30p, Hawker Typhoon. No. 835, 30p, Avro Vulcan. No. 836, 30p, SEPECAT Jaguar. £1.50, Sir Hugh Trenchard reviewing troops.

Wmk. 373

2008, Apr. 1	Litho.		Perf. 14
832-836 A148	Set of 5	6.00	6.00

Souvenir Sheet

| 837 A149 | £1.50 black | 6.00 | 6.00 |

Nos. 832-836 each were printed in sheets of 8 + central label.

Tristan Fisheries, 60th Anniv. — A150

Designs: 15p, Fishing boats in harbor. 20p, Fishing boats. 30p, Offloading and loading fish. 70p, Sorting tails. 80p, Wrapping and packaging of rock lobster tails. £1.25, Shipping for export.

Perf. 13¼x13

2008, July 1	Litho.		Unwmk.
838-843 A150	Set of 6	13.50	13.50

Allan B. Crawford (1912-2007), Writer — A151

Designs: 15p, Crawford. 20p, Local Tristan da Cunha stamp. 50p, First map of Tristan da Cunha. 60p, Members of 1937-38 Norwegian Scientific Expedition, Crawford's book, *I Went to Tristan*, horiz. 85p, Men at opening of Marion Island Meteorological Office, Crawford's book, *Tristan da Cunha and the Roaring Forties*, horiz. £1.20, Crawford and his book, *Penguins, Potatoes and Postage Stamps*, horiz.

Perf. 13x13¼, 13¼x13

2008, Aug. 1	Litho.		Unwmk.
844-849 A151	Set of 6	14.00	14.00

End of World War I, 90th Anniv. A152

Paintings: No. 850, 50p, End of Richthofen, by Charles H. Hubbell. No. 851, 50p, Lion Leads in Jutland, by W. L. Wyllie. No. 852, 50p, Oppy Wod, by John Nash. No. 853, 50p, A Battery Shelled, by Percy Wyndham Lewis. No. 854, 50p, Somme Tank, by Louis Dauphin. No. 855, 50p, The Angels of Mons, by R. Crowhurst, vert. £1, Wreath of Remembrance, vert.

Wmk. 406

2008, Sept. 16	Litho.		Perf. 14
850-855 A152	Set of 6	11.00	11.00

Souvenir Sheet

| 856 A152 | £1 multi | 3.75 | 3.75 |

Ships A153

Tristao da Cunha (1460-1540), Explorer — A154

Designs: No. 857, 50p, Mary Rose. No. 858, 50p, Endurance. No. 859, 50p, Cutty Sark. No. 860, 50p, Suomen Joutsen. No. 861, 50p, RFA Lyme Bay. No. 862, MS Explorer.

Wmk. 406

2009, Mar. 9	Litho.		Perf. 14
857-862 A153	Set of 6	9.00	9.00

Souvenir Sheet

| 863 A154 | £1 multi | 3.00 | 3.00 |

Naval Aviation, Cent. A155

Designs: 25p, Felixstowe F.2A. 35p, Short S.27. No. 866, 50p, Blackburn Dart. No. 867, 50p, Sikorsky Hoverfly helicopter. £1.50, Lieutenant Commander C. R. Samson in Short S.27 taking off from HMS Hibernia, 1912.

Wmk. 406

2009, Apr. 17	Litho.		Perf. 14
864-867 A155	Set of 4	4.75	4.75

Souvenir Sheet

| 868 A155 | £1.50 multi | 4.50 | 4.50 |

Nos. 864-867 each were printed in sheets of 8 + central label.

Space Exploration A156

Designs: 25p, Goddard Rocket, 1936. 35p, X-24B Spaceplane, 1972. 60p, Launch of Apollo 11, 1969. 90p, Space Shuttle Discovery ferried by Boeing 747, 2005. £1, X-43C experimental hypersonic aircraft. £1.50, Astronauts on Moon, painting by Capt. Alan Bean, vert.

Wmk. 406

2009, July 20	Litho.		Perf. 13¼
869-873 A156	Set of 5	10.50	10.50

Souvenir Sheet
Perf. 13x13½

| 874 A156 | £1.50 multi | 5.00 | 5.00 |

First man on the Moon, 40th anniv. No. 874 contains one 40x60mm stamp.

Potato Production — A157

No. 875, 25p: a, Preparing seed potatoes. b, Planting.
No. 876, 35p: a, Digging out. b, Harvesting.

No. 877, £1.10: a, Potato blossoms. b, Potato fields.

Unwmk.

2009, Aug. 3	Litho.		Perf. 13
Horiz. Pairs, #a-b			
875-877 A157	Set of 3	11.50	11.50

Island Traditions A158

Designs: 25p, Sheep shearing. 35p, Ratting Day. 70p, Longboats to Nightingale. £1.60, Old Year's Night Okalolies.

2009, Sept. 28			
878-881 A158	Set of 4	9.25	9.25

See Nos. 927-930.

Mail Delivery on Tristan da Cunha A159

Designs: 25p, Mail arriving by ship. 35p, Transporting mail to post office. £1, Hitting the gong. £1.60, Giving out the mail.

Unwmk.

2009, Nov. 23	Litho.		Perf. 13
882-885 A159	Set of 4	10.50	10.50

British History A160

Designs: No. 886, 35p, Battle of Hastings. No. 887, 35p, Peasants' Revolt. No. 888, 35p, King Henry VIII. No. 889, 35p, English Reformation. No. 890, 35p, Elizabethan era. No. 891, 35p, English Civil War. No. 892, 35p, Scientific innovation. No. 893, 35p, Bonnie Prince Charlie.

Wmk. 406

2010, Jan. 15	Litho.		Perf. 13¼
886-893 A160	Set of 8	9.00	9.00

See Nos. 902-909, 944-951.

A161

A162

A163

A164

A165

Battle of Britain, 70th Anniv. A166

Design: £1.50, Sir Douglas Bader, vert.

Wmk. 406

2010, Mar. 18	Litho.		Perf. 13
894 A161	25p black & gray	.80	.80
895 A162	25p black & gray	.80	.80
896 A163	50p black & gray	1.60	1.60
897 A164	50p black & gray	1.60	1.60
898 A165	70p black & gray	2.10	2.10
899 A166	70p black & gray	2.10	2.10
Nos. 894-899 (6)		9.00	9.00

Souvenir Sheet

| 900 A166 | £1.50 black & gray | 4.75 | 4.75 |

Souvenir Sheet

Great Britain No. 159 — A167

2010, May 8			Perf. 14x14¼
901 A167	£1.50 multi	4.50	4.50

London 2010 Festival of Stamps.

British History Type of 2010

Designs: No. 902, 35p, Thomas Becket. No. 903, 35p, Battle of Agincourt. No. 904, 35p, Battle of Trafalgar. No. 905, 35p, Engineering & transportation. No. 906, 35p, Wireless age. No. 907, 35p, Votes for women. No. 908, 35p, The Great Depression. No. 909, 35p, Second World War.

Wmk. 406

2010, July 16	Litho.		Perf. 13¼
902-909 A160	Set of 8	9.00	9.00

Surnames of Island Families A168

Surnames of island families, flags and birds: No. 910, 50p, Hagan and Rogers, US flag, bald eagle. No. 911, 50p, Repetto and Lavaretto, Italian flag, hoopoe. No. 912, 50p, Glass, Scottish flag, golden eagle. No. 913, 50p, Green, Netherlands flag, oystercatcher. No. 914, 50p, Swain, English flag, avocet.

Perf. 12½x13

2010, Sept. 6			Unwmk.
910-914 A168	Set of 5	7.75	7.75

Conservation — A169

Designs: 1p, New Conservation R1 boat. 3p, Eradication of New Zealand flax on Nightingale Island. 5p, Banding Tristan albatross. 8p, Hag's Tooth, Gough Island UNESCO World Heritage Site. 10p, Inaccessible rail. 15p, Inaccessible Island UNESCO World Heritage Site. 25p, Counting seals. 35p, Eradication of Sagina plant on Gough Island. 70p, Eradication of Loganberry plants at Sandy Point. £1, Banding Yellow-nosed albatross. £2, Gough bunting. £5, Counting penguins.

2010, Nov. 1		Litho.	Perf. 13	
915	A169	1p multi	.25	.25
916	A169	3p multi	.25	.25
917	A169	5p multi	.25	.25
918	A169	8p multi	.25	.25
919	A169	10p multi	.35	.35
920	A169	15p multi	.50	.50
921	A169	25p multi	.80	.80
922	A169	35p multi	1.10	1.10
923	A169	70p multi	2.25	2.25
924	A169	£1 multi	3.25	3.25
925	A169	£2 multi	6.50	6.50
926	A169	£5 multi	16.50	16.50
	Nos. 915-926 (12)		32.25	32.25

Island Traditions Type of 2009

Designs: 25p, Thatching a roof. 35p, Bullock cart. 70p, Music. £1.60, Pillow dance.

2010, Nov. 24			
927-930	A158	Set of 4	9.25 9.25

Service of Queen Elizabeth II and Prince Philip — A170

Designs: 25p, Queen Elizabeth II. 35p, Queen and Prince Philip. No. 933, 50p, Queen and Prince Philip, diff. No. 934, 50p, Queen (wearing hat) and Prince Philip. No. 935, 70p, Queen and Prince Philip, diff. No. 936, 70p, Prince Philip.
£1.50, Queen and Prince Philip, diff.

2011, Mar. 14			Perf. 13¼	
931-936	A170	Set of 6	9.75	9.75
936a		Souvenir sheet of 6, #931-936, + 3 labels	9.75	9.75
Souvenir Sheet				
937	A170	£1.50 multi	5.00	5.00

Cruise Ships — A171

Designs: 25p, MV Professor Multanovskiy. 35p, MV Aleksey Maryshev. 70p, MV Professor Molchanov. £1.10, MV Plancius. £1.50, MV Plancius.

2011, Apr. 12				Unwmk.
	Perf. 14x14¾			
938-941	A171	Set of 4		8.00 8.00
Souvenir Sheet				
942	A171	£1.50 multi		5.00 5.00

Souvenir Sheet

Wedding of Prince William and Catherine Middleton — A172

Perf. 14¾x14¼

2011, Apr. 29		Wmk. 406
943	A172 £3 multi	10.00 10.00

British History Type of 2010

Designs: No. 944, 35p, Magna Carta. No. 945, 35p, Wars of the Roses. No. 946, 35p, The Gunpowder Plot. No. 947, 35p, Great Fire of London. No. 948, 35p, Battle of Waterloo. No. 949, 35p, Age of Empire. No. 950, 35p, Industry and Commerce. No. 951, 35p, First World War.

2011, May 24	Wmk. 406	Perf. 13¼
944-951 A160	Set of 8	9.25 9.25

Photographs of Wedding of Prince William and Catherine Middleton — A173

Couple: No. 952, 70p, Standing, holding hands. No. 953, 70p, Kissing. No. 954, 70p, In coach, waving, horiz. No. 955. 70p, In car, waving, horiz.

2011, Sept. 1	Unwmk.	Perf. 12½
952-955 A173	Set of 4	9.00 9.00

Eruption of Queen Mary's Peak, 50th Anniv. A174

Queen Mary's Peak and: No. 956, 25p, Tholoid. No. 957, 35p, October 1961 eruption. No. 958, 95p, Islanders leave aboard the MV Tjisadane. No. 959, £1.10, Islanders arrive in Cape Town.
No. 960, MV Tjisadane.

2011, Oct. 10	Unwmk.	Perf. 14
956-959 A174	Set of 4	8.50 8.50
Souvenir Sheet		
960 A174	£2 multi	6.25 6.25

Volcano Eruption Type of 2011

Queen Mary's Peak and: No. 961, 25p, Returning with the report. No. 962, 35p, Resettlement survey team. No. 963, 95p, HMS Protector Whirlwind helicopter. No. 964, £1.10, Royal Society members.
No. 965, 32p, Landing party.

2012, Jan. 30	Unwmk.	Perf. 14
961-964 A174	Set of 4	8.50 8.50
Souvenir Sheet		
965 A174	£2 multi	6.50 6.50

Reign of Queen Elizabeth II, 60th Anniv. — A175

Queen Elizabeth II: 25p, Color photograph. 35p, Color photograph, diff. No. 968, 50p, Black-and-white photograph. No. 969, 50p, Color photograph, diff. No. 970, 70p, Color photograph, diff. No. 971, 70p, Black-and-white photograph, diff.
£1.50, Queen Elizabeth II wearing crown.

2012, Feb. 6	Unwmk.	Perf. 13¼
966-971 A175	Set of 6	9.50 9.50
971a	Sheet of 6, #966-971, + 3 labels	9.50 9.50
Souvenir Sheet		
972 A175	£1.50 multi	4.75 4.75

Miniature Sheet

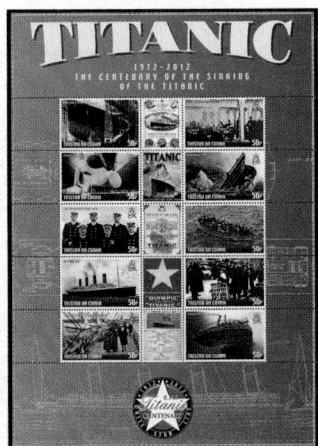

Sinking of the Titanic, Cent. — A176

No. 973: a, Titanic being built in Harland & Wolff Shipyard. b, First class dining room. c, Titanic's propellers. d, Sinking of the ship. e, Captain. E. J. Smith and crew. f, Survivors in lifeboat. g, Titanic setting sail. h, Newspaper reports. i, Passengers strolling on board. j, Discovery of the wreck.

2012, Feb. 27	Unwmk.	Perf. 13¼
973 A176	50p Sheet of 10, #a-j, + 5 labels	16.00 16.00

POSTAGE DUE STAMPS

Type of Barbados 1934-47
Perf. 14

1957, Feb. 1		Wmk. 4	Typo.
Chalky Paper			
J1	D1	1p rose red	3.50 7.00
J2	D1	2p orange yellow	4.25 9.25
J3	D1	3p green	4.50 11.50
J4	D1	4p ultramarine	5.25 13.50
J5	D1	5p deep claret	6.50 16.00
	Nos. J1-J5 (5)		24.00 57.25

Numeral — D2

Perf. 13½x14

1976, Sept. 3		Litho.	Wmk. 373	
J6	D2	1p lilac rose	.25	.70
J7	D2	2p grayish green	.25	1.00
J8	D2	4p violet	.25	1.00
J9	D2	5p light blue	.25	1.00
J10	D2	10p brown	.65	1.50
	Nos. J6-J10 (5)		1.65	5.20

1976, May 31			Wmk. 314	
J6a	D2	1p lilac rose	.35	.70
J7a	D2	2p grayish green	.35	1.00
J8a	D2	4p violet	.35	1.00
J9a	D2	5p light blue	.35	1.00
J10a	D2	10p brown	.75	1.50
	Nos. J6a-J10a (5)		2.15	5.20

Outline Map of Tristan da Cunha — D3

Perf. 15x14

1986, Nov. 20		Litho.	Wmk. 384	
J11	D3	1p pale yel brn & brn	.25	.25
J12	D3	2p orange & brown	.25	.25
J13	D3	5p crimson rose & brn	.25	.25
J14	D3	7p lt lilac & black	.25	.25
J15	D3	10p pale ultra & blk	.30	.30
J16	D3	25p lt green & blk	.75	.90
	Nos. J11-J16 (6)		2.05	2.20

TRUCIAL STATES

'trü-shəl 'stāts

LOCATION — Qatar Peninsula, Persian Gulf
GOVT. — Sheikdoms under British Protection
AREA — 32,300 sq. mi.
POP. — 86,000
CAPITAL — Dubai

The Trucial States are: Abu Dhabi, Ajman, Dubai, Fujeira, Ras al Khaima, Sharjah and Kalba, and Umm al Qiwain.

Stamps inscribed "Trucial States" were issued and used only in Dubai. Beginning Aug. 1972 all Trucial States used the stamps of United Arab Emirates.

100 Naye Paise = 1 Rupee

Catalogue values for all unused stamps in this country are for Never Hinged items.

7 Palm Trees — A1   Dhow — A2

Perf. 14½x14

1961, Jan. 7		Photo.	Unwmk.	
1	A1	5np emerald	1.75	.40
2	A1	15np red brown	.75	.40
3	A1	20np ultra	1.60	.40
4	A1	30np orange	.75	.35
5	A1	40np purple	.75	.40
6	A1	50np brown olive	.75	.40
7	A1	75np gray	.90	.40
	Engr.		**Perf. 13x12½**	
8	A2	1r emerald	8.00	4.00
9	A2	2r black	8.00	24.00
10	A2	5r rose red	9.50	26.50
11	A2	10r violet blue	15.00	27.50
	Nos. 1-11 (11)		47.75	84.75

Stamps inscribed "Trucial States" were withdrawn in June, 1963, when the individual states began issuing their own stamps.

TUNISIA

tü-'nē-zh͟ē͟ə

LOCATION — Northern Africa, bordering on the Mediterranean Sea
GOVT. — Republic
AREA — 63,362 sq. mi.
POP. — 9,513,603 (1999 est.)
CAPITAL — Tunis

The former French protectorate became a sovereign state in 1956 and a republic in 1957.

100 Centimes = 1 Franc
1000 Millimes = 1 Dinar (1959)

Catalogue values for unused stamps in this country are for Never Hinged items, beginning with Scott 163 in the regular postage section, Scott B78 in the semipostal section, Scott C13 in the airpost section, Scott CB1 in the airpost semi-postal section, and Scott J33 in the postage due section.

Coat of Arms — A1

Perf. 14x13½

1888-97   Typo.   Unwmk.

1	A1	1c black, *blue*	5.50	4.75
2	A1	2c pur brn, *buff*	5.50	4.75
3	A1	5c green, *grnsh*	37.50	16.00
4	A1	15c blue, *grysh*	65.00	30.00
5	A1	25c black, *rose*	130.00	80.00
6	A1	40c red, *straw*	130.00	87.50
7	A1	75c car, *rose*	130.00	95.00
8	A1	5fr gray vio, *grysh*	575.00	375.00
		Nos. 1-8 (8)	1,078.	693.00

All values exist imperforate.
Reprints were made in 1893 and some values have been reprinted twice since then. The shades usually differ from those of the originals. Stamps from the 1897 printing are on thicker paper, with white gum instead of grayish, and have a background of horizontal ruled lines.

A2   A3

1888-1902

9	A2	1c blk, *lil bl*	2.00	1.20
10	A2	2c pur brn, *buff*	2.00	1.20
11	A2	5c grn, *grnsh*	8.00	1.20
12	A2	5c yellow grn ('99)	7.25	1.20
13	A2	10c blk, *lav* ('93)	12.00	2.00
14	A2	10c red ('01)	7.25	1.20
15	A2	15c blue, *grysh*	55.00	1.20
16	A2	15c gray ('01)	11.00	2.40
17	A2	20c red, grn ('99)	20.00	2.50
18	A2	25c blk, *rose*	28.00	2.40
19	A2	25c blue ('01)	22.50	3.25
20	A2	35c brown ('02)	55.00	4.00
21	A2	40c red, *straw*	24.00	2.40
22	A2	75c car, *rose*	190.00	92.50
23	A2	75c dp vio, *org* ('93)	35.00	11.00
24	A3	1fr olive, *olive*	40.00	10.50
25	A3	2fr dull violet ('02)	180.00	150.00
26	A3	5fr red lil, *lav*	225.00	87.50
		Bar cancellation		.50

Quadrille Paper

27	A2	15c bl, *grysh* ('93)	52.50	1.20
		Nos. 9-27 (19)	976.50	378.85

For surcharges see Nos. 28, 58-61.

No. 27 Surcharged in Red

1902

28	A2	25c on 15c blue	4.00	4.00

Mosque at Kairouan A4

Plowing A5

Ruins of Hadrian's Aqueduct A6

Carthaginian Galley — A7

1906-26   Typo.

29	A4	1c blk, *yel*	.25	.25
30	A4	2c red brn, *straw*	.25	.25
31	A4	3c lt red ('19)	.25	.25
32	A4	5c grn, *grnsh*	.40	.25
33	A4	5c orange ('21)	.30	.25
34	A5	10c red	.40	.30
35	A5	10c green ('21)	.50	.40
36	A5	15c vio, *pnksh*	1.40	.30
a.		Imperf., pair	175.00	
37	A5	15c brn, *org* ('23)	.30	.30
38	A5	20c brn, *pnksh*	.30	.30
39	A5	25c deep blue	1.90	.75
a.		Imperf., pair		
40	A5	25c violet ('21)	.55	.30
41	A6	30c red brn & vio ('19)	1.20	.80
42	A5	30c pale red ('21)	1.20	1.20
43	A6	35c ol grn & brn	10.50	2.40
44	A6	40c blk brn & red brn	5.25	.80
45	A5	40c blk, *pnksh* ('23)	1.20	.80
46	A5	40c gray grn ('26)	.25	.25
47	A5	50c blue ('21)	.90	.90
48	A6	60c ol grn & vio ('21)	1.10	.95
49	A6	60c ver & rose ('25)	.80	.50
50	A6	75c red brn & red	1.10	.80
51	A6	75c ver & dl red ('26)	.55	.55
52	A7	1fr red & dk brn	1.20	.80
53	A7	1fr ind & ultra ('25)	.55	.50
54	A7	2fr brn & ol grn	6.75	2.00
55	A7	2fr grn & red, *pink* ('25)	1.10	.50
56	A7	5fr violet & blue	12.00	5.25
57	A7	5fr gray vio & grn ('25)	1.10	.65
		Nos. 29-57 (29)	53.55	23.55

For surcharges and overprints see Nos. 62-64, 70-73 115-116, B1-B23, B25-B27, B29-B30, B32-B36, C1-C6.

Stamps and Type of 1888-1902 Surcharged

1908, Sept.

58	A2	10c on 15c gray, *lt gray* (R)	2.00	2.00
59	A3	35c on 1fr ol, *ol* (R)	4.75	4.75
60	A3	40c on 2fr dl vio (Bl)	8.75	8.75
61	A3	75c on 5fr red lil, *lav* (Bl)	6.75	6.75
		Nos. 58-61 (4)	22.25	22.25

No. 36 Surcharged

1911

62	A5	10c on 15c vio, *pinkish*	2.00	.80
a.		Inverted surcharge		2,400.

No. 34 Surcharged

1917, Mar. 16

63	A5	15c on 10c red	1.20	.40
a.		"15c" omitted	40.00	
b.		Double surcharge	87.50	

No. 36 Surcharged

1921

64	A5	20c on 15c vio, *pinkish*	1.20	.40

Arab and Ruins of Dougga — A9

1922-26   Typo.   Perf. 13½x14

65	A9	10c green	.25	.25
66	A9	10c rose ('26)	.30	.30
67	A9	30c rose	1.20	1.20
68	A9	30c lilac ('26)	.50	.50
69	A9	50c blue	.80	.80
		Nos. 65-69 (5)	3.05	3.05

For surcharges see Nos. 117, B24, B28, B31.

Stamps and Type of 1906 Surcharged in Red or Black

a   b

1923-25

70	A4(a)	10c on 5c grn, *grnsh* (R)	.50	.50
a.		Double surcharge	92.50	
b.		Inverted surcharge	130.00	
c.		Double surcharge, one inverted	130.00	
71	A5(b)	20c on 15c violet (Bk)	.95	.30
a.		Double surcharge	130.00	
72	A5(b)	30c on 20c yel brn (Bk) ('25)	.50	.50
73	A5(b)	50c on 25c blue (R)	.95	.40
a.		Double surcharge	130.00	
b.		Inverted surcharge	120.00	
		Nos. 70-73 (4)	2.90	1.70

Arab Woman Carrying Water — A10

Grand Mosque at Tunis — A11

Mosque, Tunis — A12

Roman Amphitheater, El Djem (Thysdrus) — A13

1926-46   Typo.   Perf. 14x13½

74	A10	1c lt red	.25	.25
75	A10	2c olive grn	.25	.25
76	A10	3c slate blue	.25	.25
77	A10	5c yellow grn	.25	.25
78	A10	10c rose	.25	.25
78A	A10	10c brown ('46)	.25	.25
79	A11	15c gray lilac	.25	.25
80	A11	20c deep red	.30	.25
81	A11	25c gray green	.50	.30
82	A11	25c lt violet ('28)	.75	.30
83	A11	30c lt violet	.50	.50
84	A11	30c blue grn ('28)	.50	.30
84A	A12	30c dk ol grn ('46)	.25	.25
85	A11	40c deep brown	.30	.25
85A	A12	40c lil rose ('46)	.30	.30
86	A11	45c emerald ('40)	1.10	1.10
87	A12	50c black	.30	.25
88	A12	50c ultra ('34)	.80	.30
88B	A12	50c emerald ('40)	.25	.25
88C	A12	50c lt blue ('46)	.30	.30
89	A12	60c red org ('40)	.25	.25
89A	A12	60c ultra ('45)	.25	.25
90	A12	65c ultra ('38)	.65	.30
91	A12	70c dark red ('40)	.25	.25
92	A12	75c vermilion	.50	.50
93	A12	75c lilac rose ('28)	1.05	.40
94	A12	80c blue green	1.00	.50
94A	A12	80c blk brn ('40)	.30	.30
94B	A12	80c emerald ('45)	.50	.30
95	A12	90c org red ('28)	.40	.40
96	A12	90c ultra ('39)	10.00	10.00
97	A12	1fr brown violet	.80	.50
97A	A12	1fr rose ('40)	.25	.25
98	A13	1.05fr dl bl & mag	.75	.55
98A	A12	1.20fr blk brn ('45)	.50	.30
99	A13	1.25fr gray bl & dk bl	.75	.50
100	A13	1.25fr car rose ('40)	1.20	1.20
100A	A13	1.30fr bl & vio bl ('42)	.30	.30
101	A13	1.40fr brt red vio ('40)	1.35	1.35
102	A13	1.50fr bl & dp bl ('28)	1.25	.70
102A	A13	1.50fr rose red & red org ('42)	.55	.55
102B	A12	1.50fr rose lil ('46)	.25	.25
103	A13	2fr rose & ol brn	1.50	.50
104	A13	2fr red orange ('39)	.40	.40
104A	A12	2fr Prus grn ('45)	.30	.25
105	A13	2.25fr ultra ('39)	1.05	1.05
105A	A13	2.40fr red ('46)	.75	.55
106	A13	2.50fr green ('40)	.90	.90
107	A13	3fr dl bl & org ('39)	1.90	.75
108	A13	3fr violet ('39)	.40	.40
108A	A13	3fr black brn ('46)	.30	.25
108B	A13	4fr ultra ('45)	1.10	.65
109	A13	5fr red & grn, *grnsh* ('40)	2.75	.90
110	A13	5fr dp red brn ('46)	1.40	1.40
110A	A13	5fr dk green ('46)	.50	.50
110B	A13	6fr dp ultra ('45)	.80	.50
111	A13	10fr brn red & blk, *bluish* ('46)	11.00	3.00
112	A13	10fr rose pink ('46)	.90	.90
112A	A13	10fr ver ('46)	.80	.50
112B	A13	10fr ultra ('46)	.75	.40
112C	A13	15fr rose lil ('45)	.50	.25
113	A13	20fr lil & red, *pnksh* ('28)	2.40	1.20
113A	A13	20fr dk green ('45)	.90	.50
113B	A13	25fr violet ('45)	.90	.75
113C	A13	50fr carmine ('45)	1.75	.95
113D	A13	100fr car rose ('45)	2.00	1.20
		Nos. 74-113D (66)	66.95	44.75

See Nos. 152A-162, 185-189, 199-206.
For surcharges and overprints see Nos. 114, 118-121, 143-152, B74-B77, B87-B88, B91-B95, B98, C7-C12.

No. 99 Surcharged with New Value and Bars in Red

1927, Mar. 24

114	A13	1.50fr on 1.25fr	.80	.30

Stamps of 1921-26 Surcharged

1928, May 1
115	A4	3c on 5c orange	.30	.25
116	A5	10c on 15c brn, *org*	.80	.30
c.		Double surcharge	140.00	
117	A9	25c on 30c lilac	.75	.40
118	A12	40c on 80c bl grn	.80	.50
119	A12	50c on 75c ver	.95	.55
		Nos. 115-119 (5)	3.60	2.00

No. 83 Surcharged

1929
120	A11	10c on 30c lt violet	1.90	1.10

No. 120 exists precanceled only. The value in first column is for a stamp which has not been through the post and has original gum. The value in the second column is for a postally used, gumless stamp. See No. 199a.

No. 85 Surcharged with New Value and Bars

1930
121	A11	50c on 40c dp brn	6.00	.85

A14   A15

A16

A17

Perf. 11, 12½, 12½x13
1931-34   Engr.
122	A14	1c deep blue	.25	.25
123	A14	2c yellow brn	.25	.25
124	A14	3c black	.50	.50
125	A14	5c yellow grn	.25	.25
126	A14	10c red	.25	.25
127	A15	15c dull violet	.75	.65
128	A15	20c dull brown	.25	.25
129	A15	25c rose red	.30	.25
130	A15	30c deep green	.65	.55
131	A15	40c red orange	.30	.30
132	A16	50c ultra	.30	.30
133	A16	75c yellow	2.40	2.10
134	A16	90c red	.80	.80
135	A16	1fr olive black	.55	.50
136	A16	1fr dk brown ('34)	.55	.50
137	A17	1.50fr brt ultra	.95	.75
138	A17	2fr deep brown	.90	.90
139	A17	3fr blue green	10.50	10.50
140	A17	5fr car rose	28.00	22.50
a.		Perf. 12½	45.00	40.00
141	A17	10fr black	52.50	37.50
142	A17	20fr dark brown	65.00	52.50
		Nos. 122-142 (21)	166.20	132.35

For surcharges see Nos. B54-B73.

Nos. 88, 102 Surcharged in Red or Black

1937   *Perf. 14x13½*
143	A12	65c on 50c (R)	.65	.25
b.		Double surcharge	120.00	100.00
144	A13	1.75fr on 1.50fr (R)	6.50	1.60
a.		Double surcharge	110.00	110.00
b.		In pair with unsurcharged stamp	275.00	

1938
145	A12	65c on 50c (Bk)	.90	.30
a.		Double surcharge, one inverted	200.00	200.00
146	A13	1.75fr on 1.50fr (R)	9.50	8.00

Stamps of 1938-39 Surcharged in Red or Carmine

1940
147	A12	25c on 65c ultra (C)	.25	.25
148	A12	1fr on 90c ultra (R)	.55	.55
a.		Double surcharge	130.00	

Stamps of 1938-40 Surcharged in Red or Black

1941
149	A12	25c on 65c ultra (R)	.30	.30
150	A13	1fr on 1.25fr car rose	.65	.65
151	A13	1fr on 1.40fr brt red vio	.75	.75
152	A13	1fr on 2.25fr ultra (R)	.75	.75
		Nos. 149-152 (4)	2.45	2.45

Types of 1926 Without RF
1941-45   Typo.   *Perf. 14x13½*
152A	A11	30c carmine ('45)	.25	.25
152B	A12	1.20fr int blue ('45)	.25	.25
153	A12	1.50fr brn red ('42)	.50	.50
154	A13	2.40fr & brt pink ('42)	.50	.50
155	A13	2.50fr dk bl & lt bl	.50	.50
156	A13	3fr lt violet ('42)	.30	.30
157	A13	4fr blk & bl vio ('42)	.50	.50
158	A13	4.50fr ol grn & brn ('42)	.70	.70
159	A13	5fr brown blk ('42)	.65	.65
160	A13	10fr lil & dull vio	.65	.55

161	A13	15fr henna brn ('42)	5.25	4.50
162	A13	20fr lt vio & car	3.00	1.75
		Nos. 152A-162 (12)	13.05	10.95

> Catalogue values for unused stamps in this section, from this point to the end of the section, are for Never Hinged items.

One Aim Alone - Victory A18

Mosque and Olive Tree A19

1943   Litho.   *Perf. 12*
163	A18	1.50fr rose	.40	.25

1944-45   Unwmk.   *Perf. 11½*
Size: 15½x19mm
165	A19	30c yellow ('45)	.30	.25
166	A19	40c org brn ('45)	.30	.25
168	A19	60c red org ('45)	.65	.50
169	A19	70c rose pink ('45)	.30	.25
170	A19	80c Prus grn ('45)	.40	.30
171	A19	90c violet ('45)	.40	.30
172	A19	1fr red ('45)	.40	.30
173	A19	1.50fr dp bl ('45)	.40	.30

Size: 21¼x26½mm
175	A19	2.40fr red	.65	.50
176	A19	2.50fr red brn	.65	.50
177	A19	3fr lt vio	.90	.70
178	A19	4fr brt bl vio	.65	.50
179	A19	4.50fr apple grn	.65	.50
180	A19	5fr gray	.90	.70
181	A19	6fr choc ('45)	.65	.50
182	A19	10fr brn lake ('45)	.95	.80
183	A19	15fr copper brn	.95	.80
184	A19	20fr lilac	1.10	.90
		Nos. 165-184 (18)	11.20	8.85

For surcharge see No. B79.

Types of 1926
1946-47   Typo.   *Perf. 14x13½*
185	A12	2fr emerald ('47)	.65	.50
186	A12	3fr rose pink	.40	.25
187	A12	4fr violet ('47)	.95	.50
188	A13	4fr violet ('47)	1.10	.50
189	A12	6fr carmine ('47)	.30	.25
		Nos. 185-189 (5)	3.40	2.00

Neptune, Bardo Museum A20

1947-49   Engr.   *Perf. 13*
190	A20	5fr dk grn & bluish blk	1.25	.95
191	A20	10fr blk brn & bluish blk	.65	.30
192	A20	18fr dk bl gray & Prus bl ('48)	1.90	1.10
193	A20	25fr dk bl & bl grn ('49)	2.40	1.20
		Nos. 190-193 (4)	6.20	3.55

For surcharge see No. B108.

Detail from Great Mosque at Kairouan A21

1948-49
194	A21	3fr dk bl grn & bl grn	1.10	.65
195	A21	4fr dk red vio & red vio	.80	.50
196	A21	6fr red brn & red	.30	.25
197	A21	10fr purple ('49)	.65	.30
198	A21	12fr henna brn	1.10	.75
198A	A21	12fr dk brn & org brn ('49)	1.00	.65
198B	A21	15fr dk red ('49)	.90	.65
		Nos. 194-198B (7)	5.85	3.75

See No. 225. For surcharge see No. B103.

Types of 1926
1947-49   Typo.   *Perf. 14x13½*
199	A12	2.50fr brown orange	.80	.50
a.		2.50fr brown	1.50	.80
200	A12	4fr brown org ('49)	1.40	.50
201	A12	4.50fr lt ultra	.95	.50
202	A12	5fr blue ('48)	.80	.65
203	A12	5fr lt bl grn ('49)	1.40	.50
204	A13	6fr rose red	.30	.25
205	A13	15fr rose red	1.40	.75
206	A13	25fr red orange	2.00	1.00
		Nos. 199-206 (8)	9.05	4.40

No. 199a is known only precanceled. See note after No. 120.

Dam on the Oued Mellegue A22

1949, Sept. 1   Engr.   *Perf. 13*
207	A22	15fr grnsh black	3.50	.80

UPU Symbols and Tunisian Post Rider — A23

Berber Hermes at Carthage — A24

1949, Oct. 28   Bluish Paper
208	A23	5fr dark green	2.00	1.60
209	A23	15fr red brown	1.60	1.60
		Nos. 208-209,C13 (3)	6.75	5.20

UPU, 75th anniversary.
Nos. 208-209 exist imperf.

1950-51
210	A24	15fr red brown	1.25	.80
211	A24	25fr indigo ('51)	1.25	.80
212	A24	50fr dark green ('51)	2.75	.80
		Nos. 210-212 (3)	5.25	2.40

Horse, Carthage Museum — A25

1950, Dec. 26   Typo.   *Perf. 13½x14*
Size: 21½x17½mm
213	A25	10c aquamarine	.30	.25
214	A25	50c brown	.30	.25
215	A25	1fr rose lilac	.30	.25
216	A25	2fr gray	.40	.30
217	A25	4fr vermilion	.65	.50
218	A25	5fr blue green	.40	.25
219	A25	8fr deep blue	.65	.40
220	A25	12fr red	1.60	.60
221	A25	15fr carmine rose ('50)	.65	.50
		Nos. 213-221 (9)	5.25	3.45

See Nos. 222-224, 226-228.

1951-53   Engr.   *Perf. 13x14*
Size: 22x18mm
222	A25	15fr carmine rose	1.40	.75
223	A25	15fr ultra ('53)	1.60	.65
224	A25	30fr deep ultra	2.75	.80
		Nos. 222-224 (3)	5.75	2.20

Type of 1948-49
1951, Aug. 1   *Perf. 13*
225	A21	30fr dark blue	1.60	1.25

Horse Type of 1950
1952   Typo.   *Perf. 13½x14*
226	A25	3fr brown orange	.80	.50
227	A25	12fr carmine rose	1.40	.55
228	A25	15fr ultra	.80	.25
		Nos. 226-228 (3)	3.00	1.30

Charles Nicolle — A26

Flags, Pennants and Minaret — A27

1952, Aug. 4   Engr.   Perf. 13
229 A26 15fr black brown   2.00 1.00
230 A26 30fr deep blue   2.00 1.00

Founding of the Society of Medical Sciences of Tunisia, 50th anniv.

1953, Oct. 18
231 A27 8fr black brn & choc   1.60 1.20
232 A27 12fr dk green & emer   1.60 1.20
233 A27 15fr indigo & ultra   1.60 1.20
234 A27 18fr dk pur & pur   1.60 1.20
235 A27 30fr dk car & car   1.60 1.20
        Nos. 231-235 (5)   8.00 6.00

First International Fair of Tunis.

Courtyard at Sousse — A28

Sidi Bou Maklouf Mosque A29

Designs: 1fr, Courtyard at Sousse. 2fr, 4fr, Citadel, Takrouna. 5fr, 8fr, View of Tatahouine. 10fr, 12fr, Oasis of Matmata. 15fr, Street Corner, Sidi Bou Said. 20fr, 25fr, Genoese fort, Tabarka. 30fr, 40fr, Bab-El-Khadra gate. 50fr, 75fr, Four-story building, Medenine.

Perf. 13½x13 (A28), 13
1954, May 29
236 A28 50c emerald   .30 .25
237 A28 1fr carmine rose   .30 .25
238 A28 2fr violet brown   .40 .30
239 A28 4fr turq blue   .55 .30
240 A28 5fr violet   .55 .30
241 A28 8fr black brown   .55 .30
242 A28 10fr dk blue grn   .55 .30
243 A28 12fr rose brown   .55 .30
244 A28 15fr dp ultra   2.60 .40
245 A29 18fr chocolate   2.25 .75
246 A29 20fr dp ultra   1.40 .30
247 A29 25fr indigo   1.40 .30
248 A29 30fr dp claret   1.50 .30
249 A29 40fr dk Prus grn   1.75 .65
250 A29 50fr dk violet   2.75 .30
251 A29 75fr carmine rose   6.50 2.40

Typo.
Perf. 14x13½
252 A28 15fr ultra   .90 .25
        Nos. 236-252 (17)   24.80 7.85

Imperforates exist. Value $50. See Nos. 271-287. For surcharge see No. B125.

Mohammed al-Amin, Bey of Tunis — A30

1954, Oct.   Perf. 13
253 A30 8fr bl & dk bl   1.20 1.00
254 A30 12fr lil gray & indigo 1.30 1.00
255 A30 15fr dp car & brn lake   1.40 1.00
256 A30 18fr red brn & blk brn   1.40 1.00
257 A30 30fr bl grn & dk bl grn 2.00 1.60
        Nos. 253-257 (5)   7.30 5.60

Theater Drapes, Dove and Sun — A31

1955
258 A31 15fr dk red brn, bl & org 1.25 1.00

Essor, Tunisian amateur theatrical society.

Rotary Emblem, Map and Symbols of Punic, Roman, Arab and French Civilizations A32

1955, May 14   Unwmk.
259 A32 12fr vio brn & blk brn   1.20 .95
260 A32 15fr vio gray & dk brn   1.30 .95
261 A32 18fr rose vio & dk pur   1.40 1.00
262 A32 25fr blue & dp ultra   1.40 1.00
263 A32 30fr dk Prus grn & ind   2.00 1.60
        Nos. 259-263 (5)   7.30 5.50

Rotary International, 50th anniv.

Bey of Tunis A33

Embroiderers A34

1955   Engr.   Perf. 13½x13
264 A33 15fr dark blue   .85 .25

1955, July 25   Perf. 13
15fr, 18fr, Potters. 20fr, 30fr, Florists.
265 A34 5fr rose brown   1.20 .95
266 A34 12fr ultra   1.20 .95
267 A34 15fr Prussian green 1.30 1.00
268 A34 18fr red   1.30 1.00
269 A34 20fr dark violet   1.50 1.20
270 A34 30fr violet brown   1.50 1.20
        Nos. 265-270 (6)   8.00 6.30

For surcharge see No. B126.

Independent Kingdom
Types of 1954 Redrawn with "RF" Omitted

1956, Mar. 1   Perf. 13½x13, 13 (A29)
271 A28 50c emerald   .25 .25
272 A28 1fr carmine rose   .25 .25
273 A28 2fr violet brown   .25 .25
274 A28 4fr turquoise blue .25 .25
275 A28 5fr violet   .25 .25
276 A28 8fr black brown   .25 .25
277 A28 10fr dk blue grn   .25 .25
278 A28 12fr rose brown   .25 .25
279 A29 15fr deep ultra   1.25 .25
280 A29 18fr chocolate   .35 .25
281 A29 20fr deep ultra   .25 .25
282 A29 25fr indigo   .25 .25
283 A29 30fr deep claret   1.10 .25
284 A29 40fr dk Prus grn   1.10 .25
285 A29 50fr dark violet   .85 .25
286 A29 75fr carmine rose   1.60 1.10

Perf. 14x13
Typo.
287 A28 15fr ultra   .25 .25
        Nos. 271-287 (17)   9.00 5.10

Mohammed al-Amin Bey of Tunis — A35

Farhat Hached — A36

Designs: 12fr, 18fr, 30fr, Woman and Dove. 5fr, 20fr, Bey of Tunis.

1956   Unwmk.   Engr.   Perf. 13
288 A35 5fr deep blue   .25 .25
289 A35 12fr brown violet   .35 .35
290 A35 15fr red   .35 .35
291 A35 18fr dk blue gray   .50 .40
292 A35 20fr dark green   .50 .40
293 A35 30fr copper brown   1.00 .50
        Nos. 288-293 (6)   2.95 2.25

Issued to commemorate Tunisian autonomy.

1956, May 1
294 A36 15fr rose brown   .35 .35
295 A36 30fr indigo   .40 .40

Farhat Hached (1914-1952), nationalist leader.

Grapes — A37

Fruit Market A38

Designs: 15fr, Hand holding olive branch. 18fr, Wheat harvest. 20fr, Man carrying food basket ("Gifts for the wedding").

1956-57   Unwmk.   Engr.   Perf. 13
296 A37 12fr lil, vio & vio brn   .65 .25
297 A37 15fr ind, dk ol grn & red brn .75 .25
298 A37 18fr brt violet blue   1.10 .40
299 A37 20fr brown orange   1.10 .40
300 A38 25fr chocolate   1.50 1.00
301 A38 30fr deep ultra   1.60 .65
        Nos. 296-301 (6)   6.70 2.95

Habib Bourguiba — A39

Farmers and Workers A40

Perf. 14 (A39), 11½x11 (A40)
1957, Mar. 20
302 A39 5fr dark blue   .25 .25
303 A39 12fr magenta   .25 .25
304 A39 20fr ultra   .35 .35
305 A40 25fr green   .40 .25
306 A39 30fr chocolate   .50 .40
307 A40 50fr crimson rose   .90 .60
        Nos. 302-307 (6)   2.65 2.10

First anniversary of independence.

Dove and Handclasp A41

Labor Bourse, Tunis — A42

1957, July 5   Engr.   Perf. 13
308 A41 18fr dk red violet .35 .35
309 A42 20fr crimson   .40 .40
310 A41 25fr green   .40 .40
311 A42 30fr dark blue   .50 .50
        Nos. 308-311 (4)   1.65 1.65

5th World Congress of the Intl. Federation of Trade Unions, Tunis, July 5-13.

Republic

Officer and Soldier — A43

1957, Aug. 8   Typo.   Perf. 11
312 A43 20fr rose pink   14.00 19.00
313 A43 25fr light violet   14.00 15.00
314 A43 30fr brown orange   14.00 15.00
        Nos. 312-314 (3)   42.00 49.00

Proclamation of the Republic.

Bourguiba in Exile, Ile de la Galité A44

1958, Jan. 18   Engr.   Perf. 13
315 A44 20fr blue & dk brn .50 .40
316 A44 25fr lt blue & vio .50 .40

6th anniv. of Bourguiba's deportation.

Map of Tunisia — A45

25fr, Woman & child. 30fr, Hand holding flag.

1958, Mar. 20   Perf. 13
317 A45 20fr dk brown & emer .35 .25
318 A45 25fr blue & sepia   .35 .25
319 A45 30fr red brown & red   .50 .25
        Nos. 317-319 (3)   1.20 .75

2nd anniv. of independence. See No. 321.

Andreas Vesalius and Abderrahman ibn Khaldoun — A46

1958, Apr. 17   Unwmk.
320 A46 30fr bister & slate grn .50 .25

World's Fair, Brussels, Apr. 17-Oct. 19.

Redrawn Type of 1958

1958, June 1   Engr.   Perf. 13
321 A45 20fr brt bl & ocher   .50 .50

Date has been changed to "1 Juin 1955-1958."

3rd anniv. of the return of Pres. Habib Bourguiba.

Gardener — A47   A48

1958, May 1
322 A47 20fr multicolored   .50 .30

Labor Day, May 1.

1958, July 25   Unwmk.   Perf. 13
Blue Paper
323 A48 5fr dk vio brn & ol   .50 .25
324 A48 10fr dk grn & yel grn   .50 .25
325 A48 15fr org red & brn lake   .50 .25
326 A48 20fr vio, ol grn & yel   .50 .25
327 A48 25fr red lilac   .50 .25
    Nos. 323-327 (5)   2.50 1.25

First anniversary of the Republic.

Pres. Habib   Fishermen
Bourguiba — A49   Casting
                Net — A50

1958, Aug. 3   Unwmk.   Perf. 13
328 A49 20fr vio & brn lake   .35 .25

Pres. Bourguiba's 55th birthday.

1958, Oct. 18   Engr.   Perf. 13
329 A50 25fr dk brn, grn & red   .65 .35

6th International Fair, Tunis.

UNESCO
Building,
Paris
A51

1958, Nov. 3
330 A51 25fr grnsh black   .60 .35

Opening of UNESCO Headquarters, Nov. 3.

Woman   Hand Planting
Opening   Symbolic
Veil — A52   Tree — A53

Habib
Bourguiba
at Borj le
Boeuf
A54

1959, Jan. 1   Engr.   Perf. 13
331 A52 20m greenish blue   .40 .25

Emancipation of Tunisian women.

1959, Mar. 2   Unwmk.   Perf. 13

10m, Shield with flag and people holding torch. 20m, Habib Bourguiba at Borj le Boeuf, Sahara.

332 A53 5m vio brn, car & sal   .25 .25
333 A53 10m multicolored   .35 .25
334 A53 20m blue   .40 .25
335 A54 30m grnsh bl, ind & org brn   .75 .50
    Nos. 332-335 (4)   1.75 1.25

25th anniv. of the founding of the Neo-Destour Party at Kasr Helal, Mar. 2, 1934.

"Independence" — A55

1959, Mar. 20
336 A55 50m olive, blk & red   .80 .40

3rd anniversary of independence.

Map of Africa and
Drawings — A56

1959, Apr. 15   Litho.   Perf. 13
337 A56 40m lt bl & red brn   .65 .40

Africa Freedom Day, Apr. 15.

Camel
Camp and
Mosque,
Kairouan
A57

Horseback   Olive
Rider — A58   Picker — A59

Open
Window
A58a

Designs: ½m, Woodcock in Ain-Draham forest. 2m, Camel rider. 3m, Saddler's shop. 4m, Old houses of Medenine, gazelle and youth. 6m, Weavers. 8m, Woman of Gafsa. 10m, Unveiled woman holding fruit. 12m, Ivory craftsman. 15m, Skanes Beach, Monastir, and mermaid. 16m, Minaret of Ez-Zitouna University, Tunis. 20m, Oasis of Gabès. 25m, Oil, flowers and fish of Sfax. 30m, Modern and Roman aqueducts. 40m, Festival at Kairouan

---

(drummer and camel). 45m, Octagonal minaret, Bizerte (boatman). 50m, Three women of Djerba island. 60m, Date palms, Djerid. 70m, Tapestry weaver. 75m, Pottery of Nabeul. 90m, Le Kef (man on horse). 100m, Road to Sidi-bou-Said. 200m, Old port of Sfax. ½d, Roman temple, Sbeitla. 1d, Farmer plowing with oxen, Beja.

1959-61   Unwmk.   Engr.   Perf. 13
338 A58 ½m emer, brn & bl grn ('60)   .25 .25
339 A57 1m lt bl & ocher   .25 .25
340 A58 2m multicolored   .25 .25
341 A58 3m slate green   .25 .25
342 A57 4m red brn ('60)   .25 .25
343 A58 5m gray green   .25 .25
344 A58 6m rose violet   .25 .25
345 A58 8m vio brn ('60)   .85 .35
346 A58 10m ol, dk grn & car   .25 .25
347 A58 12m vio bl & ol bis ('61)   .65 .25
348 A57 15m brt blue ('60)   .35 .25
349 A57 16m grnsh blk ('60)   .35 .25
350 A58a 20m grnsh blue   1.25 .35
351 A58 20m grnsh blk, ol & mar ('60)   2.10 .25
352 A57 25m multi ('60)   .35 .25
353 A58a 30m brn, grnsh bl & ol   .50 .25
354 A59 40m dp grn ('60)   1.90 .25
355 A58a 45m brt grn ('60)   .75 .35
356 A58a 50m Prus grn, dk bl & rose ('60)   1.10 .25
357 A58a 60m grn & red brn ('60)   1.10 .40
358 A59 70m multi ('60)   1.60 .60
359 A59 75m ol gray ('60)   1.50 .65
360 A58a 90m brt grn, ultra & choc ('60)   1.50 .65
361 A59 95m multicolored   2.10 1.25
362 A58a 100m dk bl, ol & brn   2.10 1.10
363 A58a 200m brt bl, bis & car   5.50 2.75
363A A59 ½d lt brn ('60)   13.50 7.50
363B A58a 1d sl grn & bis ('60)   25.00 15.00
    Nos. 338-363B (28)   66.05 34.95

  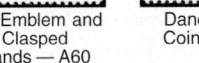

UN Emblem and   Dancer and
Clasped   Coin — A61
Hands — A60

1959, Oct. 24
364 A60 80m org brn, brn & ultra   .85 .60

UN Day, Oct. 24.

1959, Nov. 4
365 A61 50m grnsh bl & blk   .65 .65

Central Bank of Tunisia, first anniversary.

Uprooted Oak
Emblem — A62

Doves and
WRY
Emblem
A63

1960, Apr. 7   Engr.   Perf. 13
366 A62 20m blue black   .50 .35
367 A63 40m red lil & dk grn   .65 .50

World Refugee Year, 7/1/59-6/30/60.

Girl, Boy and   Cyclist — A65
Scout
Badge — A64

Designs: 25m, Hand giving Scout sign. 30m, Bugler and tent. 40m, Peacock and Scout emblem. 60m, Scout and campfire.

1960, Aug. 9
368 A64 10m lt blue green   .30 .30
369 A64 25m green, red & brn   .45 .35
370 A64 30m vio bl, grn & mar   .55 .35
371 A64 40m black, car & bl   .60 .45
372 A64 60m dk brn, vio blk & lake   1.25 .60
    Nos. 368-372 (5)   3.15 2.05

4th Arab Boy Scout Jamboree, Tunis, Aug.

1960, Aug. 25

Designs: 10m, Olympic rings forming flower. 15m, Girl tennis player and minaret. 25m, Runner and minaret. 50m, Handball player and minaret.

373 A65 5m dk brown & olive   .30 .30
374 A65 10m sl, red vio & emer   .30 .30
375 A65 15m rose red & rose car   .30 .30
376 A65 25m grnsh bl & gray bl   .45 .45
377 A65 50m brt green & ultra   .85 .85
    Nos. 373-377 (5)   2.20 2.20

17th Olympic Games, Rome, 8/25-9/11.

Symbolic Forest   National Fair
Design — A66   Emblems — A67

Designs: 15m, Man working in forest. 25m, Tree superimposed on leaf. 50m, Symbolic tree and bird.

1960, Aug. 29
378 A66 8m multicolored   .30 .25
379 A66 15m dark green   .45 .25
380 A66 25m dk pur, crim & brt grn   .60 .30
381 A66 50m Prus grn, yel grn & rose lake   1.00 .55
    Nos. 378-381 (4)   2.35 1.35

5th World Forestry Congress, Seattle, Wash., Aug. 29-Sept. 10.

1960, June 1
382 A67 100m black & green   .85 .60

5th Natl. Fair, Sousse, May 27-June 12.

Pres. Bourguiba   Pres. Bourguiba
Signing   A69
Constitution
A68

1960, June 1
383 A68 20m choc, red & emer   .50 .40
384 A69 20m grayish blk   .25 .25
385 A69 30m blue, dl red & blk   .35 .25
386 A69 40m grn, dl red & blk   .50 .25
    Nos. 383-386 (4)   1.60 1.15

Promulgation of the Constitution (No. 383).

UN Emblem and Arms — A70

Dove and "Liberated Tunisia" — A71

1960, Oct. 24   Engr.   Perf. 13
387 A70 40m mag, ultra & gray grn .65 .60

15th anniversary of the United Nations.

1961, Mar. 20   Perf. 13

Design: 75m, Globe and arms.

388 A71 20m maroon, bis & bl .25 .25
389 A71 30m blue, vio & brn .30 .25
390 A71 40m yel grn & ultra .60 .45
391 A71 75m bis, red lil & Prus bl .75 .55
    Nos. 388-391 (4) 1.90 1.50

5th anniversary of independence.

Map of Africa, Woman and Animals — A72

Mother and Child with Flags — A73

Map of Africa: 60m, Negro woman and Arab. 100m, Arabic inscription and Guinea masque. 200m, Hands of Negro and Arab.

1961, Apr. 15   Engr.   Unwmk.
392 A72 40m bis brn, red brn & dk grn .30 .25
393 A72 60m sl grn, blk & org brn .35 .30
394 A72 100m sl grn, emer & vio .75 .45
395 A72 200m dk brn & org brn 1.40 1.10
    Nos. 392-395 (4) 2.80 2.10

Africa Freedom Day, Apr. 15.

1961, June 1   Unwmk.   Perf. 13

Designs: 50m, Tunisians. 95m, Girl with wings and half-moon.

396 A73 25m pale vio, red & brn .35 .25
397 A73 50m bl grn, sep & brn .25 .25
398 A73 95m pale vio, rose lil & ocher .75 .40
    Nos. 396-398 (3) 1.60 .90

National Feast Day, June 1.

Dag Hammarskjold A74

Arms of Tunisia A75

1961, Oct. 24   Photo.   Perf. 14
399 A74 40m ultramarine .65 .35

UN Day; Dag Hammarskjold (1905-1961), Secretary General of the UN, 1953-61.

1962, Jan. 18   Perf. 11½
Arms in Original Colors
400 A75 1m black & yellow .25 .25
401 A75 2m black & pink .25 .25
402 A75 3m black & lt blue .25 .25
403 A75 6m black & gray .25 .25
    Nos. 400-403 (4) 1.00 1.00

Tunisia's campaign for independence, 10th anniv.

Mosquito in Spider Web and WHO Emblem — A76

Designs: 30m, Symbolic horseback rider spearing mosquito. 40m, Hands crushing mosquito, horiz.

1962, Apr. 7   Engr.   Perf. 13
404 A76 20m chocolate .50 .35
405 A76 30m red brn & slate grn .40 .35
406 A76 40m dk brn, mar & grn .90 .40
    Nos. 404-406 (3) 1.80 1.10

WHO drive to eradicate malaria.

Boy and Map of Africa — A77

African Holding "Africa" — A78

1962, Apr. 15   Photo.   Perf. 14
407 A77 50m brown & orange .60 .40
408 A78 100m blue, blk & org .85 .60

Africa Freedom Day, Apr. 15.

Farm Worker — A79

Industrial Worker — A80

1962, May 1   Unwmk.
409 A79 40m multicolored .50 .25
410 A80 60m dark red brown .60 .35

Labor Day.

"Liberated Tunisia" — A81

Woman of Gabès — A82

1962, June 1   Typo.   Perf. 13½x14
411 A81 20m salmon & blk .60 .35

National Feast Day, June 1.

1962-63   Photo.   Perf. 11½

Women in costume of various localities: 10m, 30m, Mahdia. 15m, Kairouan. 20m, 40m,

Hammamet. 25m, Djerba. 55m, Ksar Hellal. 60m, Tunis.

412 A82 5m multi .65 .25
413 A82 10m multi .85 .40
414 A82 15m multi ('63) 1.25 .60
415 A82 20m multi 1.25 .65
416 A82 25m multi ('63) 1.25 .65
417 A82 30m multi 1.50 .85
418 A82 40m multi 1.60 .85
419 A82 50m multi 1.60 1.00
420 A82 55m multi ('63) 2.50 1.25
421 A82 60m multi ('63) 3.25 1.60
    Nos. 412-421 (10) 15.70 8.10

6 stamps issued July 25, 1962 (July 25) for the 6th anniv. of Tunisia's independence. 4 issued June 1, 1963 for Natl. Feast Day. See Nos. 470-471.

UN Emblem, Flag and Dove — A83

Aboul-Qasim Chabbi — A84

30m, Leaves, globe, horiz. 40m, Dove, globe.

1962, Oct. 24   Unwmk.
422 A83 20m gray, blk & scar .35 .25
423 A83 30m multicolored .50 .25
424 A83 40m claret brn, blk & bl .75 .40
    Nos. 422-424 (3) 1.60 .90

Issued for United Nations Day, Oct. 24.

1962, Nov. 20   Engr.   Perf. 13
425 A84 15m purple .40 .25

Aboul-Qasim Chabbi (1904-34), Arab poet.

Pres. Habib Bourguiba A85

Hached Telephone Exchange A86

1962, Dec. 7   Photo.   Perf. 12½x13½
426 A85 20m bright blue .25 .25
427 A85 30m rose claret .25 .25
428 A85 40m green .25 .25
    Nos. 426-428 (3) .75 .75

1962, Dec. 7   Litho.

Designs: 10m, Carthage Exchange. 15m, Sfax telecommunications center. 50m, Telephone operators. 100m, Symbol of automatization. 200m, Belvedere Central Exchange.

429 A86 5m multicolored .30 .25
430 A86 10m multicolored .35 .25
431 A86 15m multicolored .55 .35
432 A86 50m multicolored .85 .55
433 A86 100m multicolored 1.90 1.00
434 A86 200m multicolored 2.75 1.60
    Nos. 429-434 (6) 6.70 4.00

1st Afro-Asian Philatelic Exhibition; automation of the telephone system.

Dove over Globe — A87

"Hunger" — A88

1963, Mar. 21   Engr.   Perf. 13
435 A87 20m brt bl & brn .35 .25
436 A88 40m bis brn & dk brn .50 .25

FAO "Freedom from Hunger" campaign.

Runner and Walker — A89

Centenary Emblem — A90

1963, Feb. 17   Litho.   Perf. 13
437 A89 30m brn, blk & grn .65 .50

Army Sports Day; 13th C.I.S.M. cross country championships.

1963, May 8   Engr.   Perf. 13
438 A90 20m brn, gray & red .60 .35

Centenary of International Red Cross.

"Human Rights" — A91

Hand Raising Gateway of Great Temple of Philae — A92

1963, Dec. 10   Unwmk.   Perf. 13
439 A91 30m grn & dk brn .50 .35

15th anniv. of the Universal Declaration of Human Rights.

1964, Mar. 8   Engr.
440 A92 50m red brn, bis & bluish blk .50 .35

UNESCO world campaign to save historic monuments in Nubia.

Sunshine, Rain and Barometer — A93

1964, Mar. 8   Unwmk.   Perf. 13
441 A93 40m brn, red lil & slate .50 .25

4th World Meteorological Day, Mar. 23.

Mohammed Ali — A94

1964, May 15   Engr.
442 A94 50m sepia .50 .40

Mohammed Ali (1894-1928), labor leader.

Map of Africa and
Symbolic
Flower — A95

Pres. Habib
Bourguiba — A96

1964, May 25   Photo.   Perf. 13x14
443 A95 60m multicolored   .60 .35
Addis Ababa charter on African Unity, 1st
anniv.

1964, June 1   Engr.   Perf. 12½x13½
444 A96 20m vio bl   .25 .25
445 A96 30m black   .25 .25

"Ship and
Torch" — A97

1964, Oct. 19   Photo.   Perf. 11½x11
446 A97 50m blk & grn   .50 .35
Neo-Destour Congress, Bizerte. "Bizerte" in
Arabic forms the ship and "Neo-Destour Congress 1964" the torch of the design.

Communication Equipment and ITU
Emblem — A98

1965, May 17   Engr.   Perf. 13
447 A98 55m gray & blue   .60 .35
ITU, centenary.

Carthaginian
Coin — A99

Girl with
Book — A100

Perf. 12½x14
1965, July 9   Photo.   Unwmk.
448 A99   5m grn & blk brn   .25 .25
449 A99 10m bis & blk brn   .35 .25
450 A99 75m bl & blk brn   .85 .25
    Nos. 448-450 (3)   1.45 .75
Festival of Popular Arts, Carthage.

1965, Oct. 1   Engr.   Perf. 13
451 A100 25m brt bl, blk & red   .35 .25
452 A100 40m blk, bl & red   .40 .25
453 A100 50m red, bl & blk   .50 .25
   a. Souvenir sheet of 3, #451-453   5.50 5.50
    Nos. 451-453 (3)   1.25 .85
Girl Students' Center; education for women.
No. 453a sold for 200m. Issued perf. and
imperf.; same value.

Links and ICY
Emblem — A101

Man Pouring
Water — A102

1965, Oct. 24
454 A101 40m blk, brt bl & rose lil   .50 .25
International Cooperation Year.

1966, Jan. 18   Photo.   Perf. 13x14
Symbolic Designs: 10m, Woman and pool.
30m, Woman pouring water. 100m, Mountain
and branches.

Inscribed "Eaux Minerales"
455 A102 10m gray, ocher & dk
                red   .35 .25
456 A102 20m multicolored   .50 .40
457 A102 30m yel, bl & red   .50 .40
458 A102 100m ol, bl & yel   1.40 .75
    Nos. 455-458 (4)   2.75 1.80
Mineral waters of Tunisia.

President
Bourguiba
and Hands
A103

"Promotion of
Culture" — A104

25m, "Independence" (arms raised), flag
and doves. 40m, "Development."

1966, June 1   Engr.   Perf. 13
459 A103   5m dl pur & vio   .25 .25
460 A103 10m gray grn & sl grn   .25 .25

Perf. 11½
Photo.
461 A104 25m multi   .25 .25
462 A104 40m multi, horiz.   .65 .25
463 A104 60m multi   1.00 .40
    Nos. 459-463 (5)   2.40 1.40
10th anniversary of independence.

Map of Africa
through View
Finder, Plane and
UN
Emblem — A105

1966, Sept. 12   Engr.   Perf. 13
464 A105 15m lilac & mul-
                ticolored   .35 .25
465 A105 35m blue & multi   .40 .25
466 A105 40m multicolored   .60 .40
   a. Souvenir sheet, #464-466   11.00 11.00
    Nos. 464-466 (3)   1.35 .90
2nd UN Regional Cartographic Conference
for Africa, held in Tunisia, Sept. 12-24.
No. 466a sold for 150m. Issued perf. and
imperf.; same value.

UNESCO
Emblem
and Nine
Muses
A106

1966, Nov. 4   Perf. 13
467 A106 100m blk & brn   1.10 .40
UNESCO, 20th anniv.

Runners and
Mediterranean
Map — A107

1967, Mar. 20   Engr.   Perf. 13
468 A107 20m dk red, brn ol & bl   .25 .25
469 A107 30m brt bl & blk   .50 .35
Mediterranean Games, Sept. 8-17.

Types of 1962-63 and 1965-66 with
EXPO '67 Emblem and Inscription and

Symbols of Various
Activities — A108

Designs: 50m, Woman of Djerba. 75m,
Woman of Gabes. 155m, Pink flamingoes.

Photo.; Engr. (A108)
1967, Apr. 28   Perf. 11½, 13 (A108)
470 A82   50m multicolored   .50 .25
471 A82   75m multicolored   .75 .35
472 A108 100m dk grn, sl bl &
                blk   1.25 .50
473 A108 110m dk brn, ultra &
                red   1.60 .65
474 AP6   155m multicolored   2.40 .85
    Nos. 470-474 (5)   6.50 2.45
EXPO '67, Intl. Exhibition, Montreal, Apr.
28-Oct. 27.

Tunisian Pavilion, Pres. Bourguiba and
Map of Tunisia — A109

Designs: 105m, 200m, Tunisian Pavilion
and bust of Pres. Bourguiba.

1967, June 13   Engr.   Perf. 13
475 A109   65m red lil & dp org   .50 .40
476 A109 105m multicolored   .60 .40
477 A109 120m brt bl   .75 .40
478 A109 200m red, lil & blk   1.25 .60
    Nos. 475-478 (4)   3.10 1.80
Tunisia Day at EXPO '67.

"Tunisia"
Holding 4-
leaf Clovers
A110

Woman Freeing
Doves — A111

1967, July 25   Litho.   Perf. 13½
479 A110 25m multicolored   .25 .25
480 A111 40m multicolored   .40 .25
10th anniversary of the Republic.

Tennis Courts, Players and Games'
Emblem — A112

10m, Games' emblem & sports emblems,
vert. 15m, Swimming pool & swimmers. 35m,
Sports Palace & athletes. 75m, Stadium &
athletes.

1967, Sept. 8   Engr.   Perf. 13
481 A112   5m sl grn & hn brn   .25 .25
482 A112 10m brn red & multi   .25 .25
483 A112 15m black   .25 .25
484 A112 35m dk brn & Prus bl   .50 .25
485 A112 75m dk car rose, vio &
                bl grn   .95 .50
    Nos. 481-485 (5)   2.30 1.50
Mediterranean Games, Tunis, Sept. 8-17.

Bird, Punic
Period — A113

History of Tunisia: 20m, Sea horse, medallion from Kerkouane. 25m, Hannibal, bronze
bust, Volubilis. 30m, Stele, Carthage. 40m,
Hamilcar, coin. 60m, Mask, funereal pendant.

1967, Dec. 1   Litho.   Perf. 13½
486 A113 15m gray grn, pink &
                blk   .35 .25
487 A113 20m dp bl, red & blk   .35 .25
488 A113 25m dk grn & org brn   .50 .25
489 A113 30m grnsh gray, pink &
                blk   .50 .25
490 A113 40m red brn, yel & blk   .65 .25
491 A113 60m multicolored   .75 .35
    Nos. 486-491 (6)   3.10 1.60

"Mankind" and
Human Rights
Flame — A114

1968, Jan. 18   Engr.   Perf. 13
492 A114 25m brick red   .50 .40
493 A114 60m deep blue   .50 .25
International Human Rights Year.

Computer
Fantasy
A115

1968, Mar. 20   Engr.   Perf. 13
494 A115 25m mag, bl vio & ol   .40   .35
495 A115 40m ol grn, red brn &
           brn   .40   .35
496 A115 60m ultra, slate & brn   .50   .40
    Nos. 494-496 (3)   1.30   1.10

Introduction of electronic equipment for postal service.

Physician and
Patient — A116

Arabian
Jasmine — A117

1968, Apr. 7   Engr.   Perf. 13
497 A116 25m dp grn & brt grn   .50   .40
498 A116 60m magenta & carmine   .50   .40

WHO, 20th anniversary.

1968-69   Photo.   Perf. 11½
Flowers: 5m, Flax. 6m, Canna indica. 10m, Pomegranate. 15m, Rhaponticum acaule. 20m, Geranium. 25m, Madonna lily. 40m, Peach blossoms. 50m, Caper. 60m, Ariana rose. 100m, Jasmine.

Granite Paper
499 A117 5m multicolored   .25   .25
500 A117 6m multicolored   .25   .25
501 A117 10m multicolored   .35   .25
502 A117 12m multicolored   .35   .25
503 A117 15m multicolored   .40   .25
504 A117 20m multicolored   .50   .25
505 A117 25m multicolored   .65   .30
506 A117 40m multicolored   .75   .40
507 A117 50m multicolored   1.00   .40
508 A117 60m multicolored   1.40   .65
509 A117 100m multicolored   1.90   .90
    Nos. 499-509 (11)   7.80   4.15

Issued: 12, 50, 60, 100m, 4/9/68; others, 3/20/69.

Flower with Red
Crescent and
Globe — A118

Flutist — A119

25m, Dove with Red Crescent and globe.

1968, May 8   Engr.   Perf. 13
510 A118 15m Prus bl, grn & red   .40   .35
511 A118 25m brt rose lil & red   .50   .35

Red Crescent Society.

1968, June 1   Litho.   Perf. 13
512 A119 20m vio & multi   .40   .25
513 A119 50m multicolored   .50   .40

Stamp Day.

Jackal
A120

Animals: 8m, Porcupine. 10m, Dromedary. 15m, Dorcas gazelle. 20m, Desert fox (fennec). 25m, Desert hedgehog. 40m, Arabian horse. 60m, Boar.

1968-69   Photo.   Perf. 11½
514 A120 5m dk brn, lt bl & blue   .35   .25
515 A120 8m dk vio brn & yel
          grn   .50   .25
516 A120 10m dk brn, lt bl &
          ocher   .65   .25
517 A120 15m dk brn, ocher &
          yel grn   .75   .25

518 A120 20m dl yel & dk brn   1.25   .50
519 A120 25m blk, tan & brt grn   1.60   .65
520 A120 40m blk, lil & pale grn   2.00   1.00
521 A120 60m dk brn, buff & yel
          grn   3.00   1.40
    Nos. 514-521 (8)   10.10   4.55

Issued: 5, 8, 20, 60m, 9/15/68; others, 1/18/69.

Worker and ILO
Emblem — A121

60m, Young man & woman holding banner.

1969, May 1   Engr.   Perf. 13
522 A121 25m Prus bl, blk & bis   .40   .35
523 A121 60m rose car, bl & yel   .60   .40

ILO, 50th anniversary.

Veiled
Women
and
Musicians
with Flute
and Drum
A122

1969, June 20   Litho.   Perf. 14x13½
524 A122 100m dp yel grn & multi   .95   .40

Stamp Day.

Tunisian Coat
of
Arms — A123

Symbols of
Industry — A124

1969, July 25   Photo.   Perf. 11½
525 A123 15m yel & multi   .25   .25
526 A123 25m pink & multi   .35   .25
527 A123 40m gray & multi   .40   .25
528 A123 60m lt bl & multi   .50   .25
    Nos. 525-528 (4)   1.50   1.00

1969, Sept. 10   Perf. 13x12
529 A124 60m blk, red & yel   .50   .30

African Development Bank, 5th anniv.

Lute — A125

Nurse and
Maghrib
Flags — A126

Musical Instruments: 50m, Zither, horiz. 70m, Rebab (2-strings). 90m, Drums and flute, horiz.

1970, Mar. 20   Photo.   Perf. 11½
Granite Paper
530 A125 25m multicolored   .50   .40
531 A125 50m multicolored   .65   .40
532 A125 70m multicolored   .95   .40
533 A125 90m multicolored   1.25   .40
    Nos. 530-533 (4)   3.35   1.60

1970, May 4   Photo.   Perf. 11½
534 A126 25m lilac & multi   .35   .25

6th Medical Seminar of Maghrib Countries (Morocco, Algeria, Tunisia and Libya), Tunis, May 4-10.

Common Design Types
pictured following the introduction.

UPU Headquarters Issue
Common Design Type
1970, May 20   Engr.   Perf. 13
535 CD133 25m dl red & dk ol bis   .50   .25

Mail
Service
Symbol
A127

35m, Mailmen of yesterday and today, vert.

1970, Oct. 15   Litho.   Perf. 12½x13
Size: 37x31½mm
536 A127 25m pink & multi   .30   .25
Size: 22x37½mm
Perf. 13x12½
537 A127 35m blk & multi   .40   .25

Stamp Day.

Dove,
Laurel and
UN
Emblem
A128

1970, Oct. 24   Photo.   Perf. 13x12½
538 A128 40m multicolored   .50   .25

United Nations, 25th anniversary.

Jasmine Vendor
and Veiled
Woman — A129

Lenin, after N.N.
Joukov — A130

Scenes from Tunisian Life: 25m, "The 3rd Day of the Wedding." 35m, Perfume vendor. 40m, Fish vendor. 85m, Waiter in coffeehouse.

1970, Nov. 9   Photo.   Perf. 14
539 A129 20m dk grn & multi   .25   .25
540 A129 25m multicolored   .30   .25
541 A129 35m multicolored   .50   .40
542 A129 40m dp car & multi   .60   .40
543 A129 85m brt bl & multi   .95   .40
  a. Souvenir sheet of 5, #539-543   7.50   7.50
    Nos. 539-543 (5)   2.60   1.70

No. 543a sold for 500m. Issued perf. and imperf.; same value.

1970, Dec. 28   Engr.   Perf. 13
544 A130 60m dk car rose   1.25   .30

Lenin (1870-1924), Russian communist leader.

Radar, Flags and
Carrier
Pigeon — A131

1971, May 17   Litho.   Perf. 13x12½
545 A131 25m lt bl & multi   .50   .40

Coordinating Committee for Post and Telecommunications Administrations of Maghrib Countries.

UN Headquarters,
Symbolic
Flower — A132

1971, May 10   Photo.   Perf. 12½x13
546 A132 80m brt rose lil, blk & yel   .50   .30

Intl. year against racial discrimination.

"Telecommunications" — A133

1971, May 17   Perf. 13x12½
547 A133 70m sil, blk & lt grn   .50   .25

3rd World Telecommunications Day.

Earth,
Moon,
Satellites
A134

Design: 90m, Abstract composition.

1971, June 21   Photo.   Perf. 13x12½
548 A134 15m brt bl & blk   .40   .25
549 A134 90m scar & blk   .75   .30

Conquest of space.

"Pottery
Merchant"
A135

Life in Tunisia (stylized drawings): 30m, Esparto weaver selling hats and mats. 40m, Poultry man. 50m, Dyer.

1971, July 24   Photo.   Perf. 14x13½
550 A135 25m gold & multi   .40   .25
551 A135 30m gold & multi   .40   .25
552 A135 40m gold & multi   .50   .25
553 A135 50m gold & multi   .65   .25
  a. Sheet of 4, #550-553, perf. 13½ 7.50   7.50
    Nos. 550-553 (4)   1.95   1.00

No. 553a sold for 500m. Issued perf. and imperf.; same value.

Pres. Bourguiba Sick in 1938 A136

Designs: 25m, Bourguiba and "8," vert. 50m, Bourguiba carried in triumph, vert. 80m, Bourguiba and irrigation dam.

1971, Oct. 11   Perf. 13½x13, 13x13½
554 A136 25m multicolored   .25   .25
555 A136 30m multicolored   .25   .25
556 A136 50m multicolored   .40   .35
557 A136 80m blk, ultra & grn   .60   .35
    Nos. 554-557 (4)   1.50 1.20

8th Congress of the Neo-Destour Party.

Shah Mohammed Riza Pahlavi and Stone Head 6th Century B.C. — A137

50m, King Bahram-Gur hunting, 4th cent. 100m, Coronation, from Persian miniature, 1614.

1971, Oct. 17   Perf. 11½
Granite Paper
558 A137 25m multicolored   .35   .35
559 A137 50m multicolored   .40   .25
560 A137 100m multicolored   .75   .30
    a. Souvenir sheet of 3, #558-560 4.50 4.50
    Nos. 558-560 (3)   1.50   .90

2500th anniv. of the founding of the Persian empire by Cyrus the Great. No. 560a sold for 500m. Issued perf. and imperf.; same value.

Pimento and Warrior A138

2m, Mint & farmer. 5m, Pear & 2 men under pear tree. 25m, Oleander & girl. 60m, Pear & sheep. 100m, Grapefruit & fruit vendor.

1971, Nov. 15   Litho.   Perf. 13
561 A138 1m lt bl & multi   .25   .25
562 A138 2m gray & multi   .30   .30
563 A138 5m citron & multi   .40   .30
564 A138 25m lilac & multi   .65   .40
565 A138 60m multicolored   1.25   .30
566 A138 100m buff & multi   1.90   .50
    a. Souvenir sheet of 6, #561-566 8.50 8.50
    Nos. 561-566 (6)   4.75 2.05

Fruit, flowers and folklore. No. 566a sold for 500m. Exists imperf.; same value.

Dancer and Musician — A139

1971, Nov. 22   Photo.   Perf. 11½
567 A139 50m blue & multi   .50   .25

Stamp Day.

Map of Africa, Communication Symbols A139a

UNICEF Emblem, Mother and Child A140

Perf. 13½x12½
1971, Nov. 30   Litho.
568 A139a 95m multicolored   .60   .50

Pan-African telecommunications system.

1971, Dec. 6   Photo.   Perf. 11½
569 A140 110m multicolored   .60   .40

UNICEF, 25th anniv.

Symbolic Olive Tree and Oil Vat — A141

Gondolier in Flood Waters — A142

1972, Jan. 9   Litho.   Perf. 13½
570 A141 60m multicolored   .50   .25

International Olive Year.

1972, Feb. 7   Photo.   Perf. 11½
Designs: 30m, Young man and Doge's Palace. 50m, Gondola's prow and flood. 80m, Rialto Bridge and hand holding gondolier's hat, horiz.

571 A142 25m lt bl & multi   .30   .25
572 A142 30m blk & multi   .50   .25
573 A142 50m yel grn, gray & blk   .50   .40
574 A142 80m bl & multi   .95   .40
    Nos. 571-574 (4)   2.25 1.30

UNESCO campaign to save Venice.

Man Reading and Book Year Emblem — A143

"Your Heart is Your Health" — A144

1972, Mar. 27   Photo.   Perf. 11½
Granite Paper
575 A143 90m brn & multi   .60   .50

International Book Year.

1972, Apr. 7   Perf. 13x13½
World Health Day: 60m, Smiling man pointing to heart.

576 A144 25m grn & multi   .40   .25
577 A144 60m red & multi   .65   .40

"Only one Earth" Environment Emblem — A145

1972, June 5   Engr.   Perf. 13
578 A145 60m lemon & slate green   .60   .25

UN Conference on Human Environment, Stockholm, June 5-16.

Hurdler, Olympic Emblems A146

1972, Aug. 26   Photo.   Perf. 11½
579 A146 5m Volleyball   .25   .25
580 A146 15m shown   .30   .25
581 A146 20m Athletes   .30   .25
582 A146 25m Soccer   .30   .25
583 A146 60m Swimming, women's   .50   .25
584 A146 80m Running   .65   .30
    a. Souv. sheet of 6   4.50 4.50
    Nos. 579-584 (6)   2.30 1.55

20th Olympic Games, Munich, Aug. 26-Sept. 11. No. 584a contains 6 imperf. stamps similar to Nos. 579-584. Sold for 500m.

Chessboard and Pieces — A147

1972, Sept. 25   Photo.   Perf. 11½
585 A147 60m grn & multi   3.00 1.00

20th Men's Chess Olympiad, Skopje, Yugoslavia, Sept.-Oct.

Fisherman A148

1972, Oct. 23   Litho.   Perf. 13½
586 A148 5m shown   .25   .25
587 A148 10m Basket maker   .25   .25
588 A148 25m Musician   .35   .25
589 A148 50m Married Berber woman   .85   .25
590 A148 60m Flower merchant   1.10   .35
591 A148 80m Festival   1.40   .50
    a. Souvenir sheet of 6, #586-591 5.00 5.00
    Nos. 586-591 (6)   4.20 1.85

Life in Tunisia. No. 591a sold for 500m; exists imperf.

Post Office, Tunis A149

Litho. & Engr.
1972, Dec. 8   Perf. 13
592 A149 25m ver, org & blk   .30   .25

Stamp Day.

Dome of the Rock, Jerusalem A150

1973, Jan. 22   Photo.   Perf. 13½
593 A150 25m multicolored   .50   .35

Globe, Pen and Quill — A151

Family — A152

Design: 60m, Lyre and minaret.

1973, Mar. 19   Photo.   Perf. 14x13½
594 A151 25m gold, brt mag & brn   .25   .25
595 A151 60m bl & multi   .40   .25

9th Congress of Arab Writers.

1973, Apr. 2   Perf. 11½
Family Planning: 25m, profiles and dove.
596 A152 20m grn & multi   .25   .25
597 A152 25m lil & multi   .40   .35

"10" and Bird Feeding Young A153

Design: 60m, "10" made of grain and bread, and hand holding spoon.

1973, Apr. 26   Photo.   Perf. 11½
598 A153 25m multicolored   .65   .25
599 A153 60m multicolored   .65   .25

World Food Program, 10th anniversary.

Roman Head and Ship A154

Drawings of Tools and: 25m, Mosaic with ostriches and camel. 30m, Mosaic with 4 heads and 4 emblems. 40m, Punic stele to the sun, vert. 60m, Outstretched hand & arm of Christian preacher; symbols of 4 Evangelists. 75m, 17th cent. potsherd with Arabic inscription, vert.

1973, May 6
600 A154 5m multicolored   .35   .25
601 A154 25m multicolored   .50   .40
602 A154 30m multicolored   .50   .40
603 A154 40m multicolored   .75   .40
604 A154 60m multicolored   .95   .40
605 A154 75m multicolored   1.00   .50
    a. Souvenir sheet of 6   9.25 9.25
    Nos. 600-605 (6)   4.05 2.35

UNESCO campaign to save Carthage. No. 605a contains 6 imperf. stamps similar to Nos. 600-605. Sold for 500m.

Overlapping
Circles — A155

Map of Africa as
Festival
Emblem — A156

Design: 75m, Printed circuit board.

1973, May 17 Photo. Perf. 14x13½
606 A155 60m yel & multi   .40 .25
607 A155 75m vio & multi   .50 .25
5th Intl. Telecommunications Day.

1973, July 15 Photo. Perf. 13½x13
40m, African heads, festival emblem in eye.
608 A156 25m multicolored   .40 .35
609 A156 40m multicolored   .50 .35
Pan-African Youth Festival, Tunis.

Scout Emblem and
Pennants — A157

1973, July 23 Litho. Perf. 13½x13
610 A157 25m multicolored   .40 .35
International Boy Scout Organization.

Crescent-shaped Racing Cars — A158

1973, July 30 Perf. 13x13½
611 A158 60m multicolored   .50 .40
2nd Pan-Arab auto race.

Highway
Cloverleaf
A159

Traffic Lights and
Signs — A160

Stylized
Camel — A161

Perf. 12½x13, 13x12½
1973, Sept. 28   Litho.
612 A159 25m lt bl & multi   .65 .40
613 A160 30m multicolored   .75 .35
Highway safety campaign.

1973, Oct. 8 Photo. Perf. 13½
Stamp Day: 10m, Stylized bird and philatelic symbols, horiz.
614 A161 10m multicolored   .40 .25
615 A161 65m multicolored   .50 .40

Copernicus
A162

African Unity
A163

Lithographed and Engraved
1973, Oct. 16   Perf. 13x12½
616 A162 60m blk & multi   1.25 .30

1973, Nov. 4 Photo. Perf. 14x13½
617 A163 25m blk & multi   .50 .25
10th anniv. of the OAU.

Handshake and
Emblems
A164

Globe, Hand
Holding
Carnation
A165

1973, Nov. 15 Litho. Perf. 14½x14
618 A164 65m yel & multi   .50 .40
25th anniv. of Intl. Criminal Police Org.

1973, Dec. 10 Photo. Perf. 11½
619 A165 60m blk & multi   .65 .35
25th anniv. of Universal Declaration of Human Rights.

WMO Headquarters and
Emblem — A166

Design: 60m, Globe and emblem.

1973, Dec. 24 Litho. Perf. 14x14½
620 A166 25m multicolored   .50 .25
621 A166 60m multicolored   .65 .30
Intl. meteorological cooperation, cent.

Bourguiba in the
Desert,
1945 — A167

Portraits of Pres. Habib Bourguiba: 25m, Exile transfer from Galite Island to Ile de la Groix, France, 1954. 60m, Addressing crowd, 1974. 75m, In Victory Parade, 1955. 100m, In 1934.

1974, Mar. 2 Photo. Perf. 11½
622 A167 15m plum & multi   .30 .25
623 A167 25m multicolored   .30 .25
624 A167 60m multicolored   .30 .25
625 A167 75m multicolored   .40 .25

626 A167 100m multicolored   .50 .40
a. Souvenir sheet of 5, #622-626 2.75 2.75
Nos. 622-626 (5)   1.80 1.40
40th anniv. of the Neo-Destour Party. No. 626a sold for 500m. Issued perf. and imperf.; same value.

Scientist with
Microscope
A168

1974, Mar. 21   Perf. 14
627 A168 60m multicolored   1.00 .50
6th African Congress of Micropaleontology, Mar. 21-Apr. 3.

Woman with
Telephones and
Globe — A169

60m, Telephone dial, telephones, wires.

1974, July 1 Photo. Perf. 11½
628 A169 15m multicolored   .40 .40
629 A169 60m multicolored   .50 .50
Introduction of international automatic telephone dialing system.

WPY
Emblem
and
Symbolic
Design
A170

1974, Aug. 19 Photo. Perf. 11½
630 A170 110m multicolored   .65 .40
World Population Year.

Pres. Bourguiba
and Sun Flower
Emblem — A171

60m, Bourguiba and cactus flower, horiz. 200m, Bourguiba and verbena, horiz.

1974, Sept. 12 Photo. Perf. 11½
631 A171 25m blk, ultra & grnsh
  bl   .25 .25
632 A171 60m red, car & yel   .30 .25
633 A171 200m blk, brt lil & grn 1.10 .60
a. Souv. sheet, #631-633, imperf. 3.75 3.75
Nos. 631-633 (3)   1.65 1.10
Congress of the Socialist Destour Party.

Jets
Flying
over
Old
World
Map
A172

1974, Sept. 23 Litho. Perf. 12½
634 A172 60m brn & multi   .60 .40
25th anniversary of Tunisian aviation.

Symbolic Carrier
Pigeons — A173

Handshake,
Letter, UPU
Emblem — A174

1974, Oct. 9 Photo. Perf. 13
635 A173 25m multicolored   .40 .25
636 A174 60m multicolored   .50 .35
Centenary of Universal Postal Union.

Le Bardo, National
Assembly — A175

Pres. Bourguiba
Ballot — A176

1974, Nov. 3 Photo. Perf. 11½
637 A175 25m grn, bl & blk   .40 .30
638 A176 100m org & blk   .60 .40
Legislative (25m) and presidential elections (100m), Nov. 1974.

Mailman with
Letters and
Bird — A177

Water
Carrier — A178

1974, Dec. 5 Litho. Perf. 14½x14
639 A177 75m lt vio & multi   .50 .25
Stamp Day.

1975, Feb. 17 Photo. Perf. 13½
640 A178 5m shown   .25 .25
641 A178 15m Perfume vendor   .25 .25
642 A178 25m Laundresses   .25 .25
643 A178 60m Potter   .50 .25
644 A178 110m Fruit vendor   1.00 .65
a. Souvenir sheet of 5, #640-644 5.00 5.00
Nos. 640-644 (5)   2.25 1.65
Life in Tunisia. No. 644a sold for 500m. Issued perf. and imperf.; same value.

Steel Tower,
Skyscraper — A179

Geometric
Designs
and Arrow
A180

Perf. 14x13½, 13½x14

1975, Mar. 17 **Photo.**
645 A179 25m yel, org & blk .25 .25
646 A180 65m ultra & multi .75 .35

Union of Arab Engineers, 13th Conference,
Tunis, Mar. 17-21.

Brass Coffeepot and Plate — A181

15m, Horse and rider. 25m, Still life. 30m,
Bird cage. 40m, Woman with earrings. 60m,
Design patterns.

1975, Apr. 14 **Perf. 13x14, 14x13**
647 A181 10m blk & multi .25 .25
648 A181 15m blk & multi .25 .25
649 A181 25m blk & multi .35 .25
650 A181 30m blk & multi, vert. .40 .25
651 A181 40m blk & multi, vert. .40 .25
652 A181 60m blk & multi .65 .30
  Nos. 647-652 (6) 2.30 1.55

Artisans and their works.

Communications and Weather
Symbols — A182

1975, May 17 **Photo.** **Perf. 11½**
653 A182 50m lt bl & multi .30 .25

World Telecommunications Day (communications serving meteorology).

Youth and
Hope — A183

Tunisian Woman,
IWY
Emblem — A184

65m, Bourguiba arriving at La Goulette,
Tunis.

1975, June 1 **Photo.** **Perf. 11½**
654 A183 25m multi .25 .25
655 A183 65m multi, horiz. .40 .25

Victory (independence), 20th anniversary.

1975, June 19 **Litho.** **Perf. 14x13½**
656 A184 110m multicolored .75 .35

International Women's Year.

Children
Crossing
Street
A185

1975, July 5 **Photo.** **Perf. 13½x14**
657 A185 25m multicolored .30 .25

Highway safety campaign, July 1-Sept. 30.

Djerbian
Minaret,
Hotel
and
Marina,
Jerba
A186

Old & new Tunisia: 15m, 17th cent. minaret
& modern hotel, Tunis. 20m, Fortress, earring
& hotel, Monastir. 65m, View of Sousse, hotel
& pendant. 500m, Town wall, mosque &
palms, Tozeur. 1d, Mosques & Arab ornaments, Kairouan.

1975, July 12 **Litho.** **Perf. 14x14½**
658 A186 10m multicolored .25 .25
659 A186 15m multicolored .25 .25
660 A186 20m multicolored .25 .25
661 A186 65m multicolored .60 .40
662 A186 500m multicolored 4.00 1.75
663 A186 1d multicolored 6.50 2.50
  Nos. 658-663 (6) 11.85 5.40

Victors — A187

Symbolic
Ship
A188

1975, Aug. 23 **Photo.** **Perf. 13½**
664 A187 25m olive & multi .25 .25
665 A188 50m blue & multi .40 .25

7th Mediterranean Games, Algiers, 8/23-9/6.

Flowers in Vase,
Birds Holding
Letters — A189

1975, Sept. 29 **Litho.** **Perf. 13½x13**
666 A189 100m blue & multi .50 .25

Stamp Day.

Sadiki College, Young
Bourguiba — A190

Engr. & Litho.
1975, Nov. 17 **Perf. 13**
667 A190 25m sepia, orange & olive .30 .25

Sadiki College, centenary.

Duck — A191

Vergil — A192

Mosaics: 10m, Fish. 25m, Lioness, horiz.
60m, Head of Medusa, horiz. 75m, Circus
spectators.

1976, Feb. 16 **Photo.** **Perf. 13**
668 A191 5m multicolored .30 .25
669 A191 10m multicolored .30 .25
670 A192 25m multicolored .75 .50
671 A192 60m multicolored .75 .50
672 A192 75m multicolored .90 .50
673 A192 100m multicolored 1.40 .50
  a. Souvenir sheet of 6, #668-673 7.00 7.00
  Nos. 668-673 (6) 4.40 2.50

Tunisian mosaics, 2nd-5th centuries.
No. 673a sold for 500m. Issued perf. and
imperf.; same value.

Telephone
A193

1976, Mar. 10 **Litho.** **Perf. 14x13½**
674 A193 150m blue & multi .65 .35

Centenary of first telephone call by Alexander Graham Bell, Mar. 10, 1876.

Pres.
Bourguiba
and
"20" — A194

Pres. Bourguiba and: 100m, "20" and symbolic Tunisian flag. 150m, "Tunisia" rising from
darkness, and 20 flowers.

1976, Mar. 20 **Photo.** **Perf. 11½**
675 A194 40m multicolored .25 .25
676 A194 100m multicolored .50 .25
677 A194 150m multicolored .75 .35
  Nos. 675-677 (3) 1.50 .85

Souvenir Sheets
Perf. 11½, Imperf.
678 Sheet of 3 3.50 3.50
  a. A194 50m like 40m .50 .50
  b. A194 200m like 100m 1.00 1.00
  c. A194 250m like 150m 1.50 1.50

20th anniversary of independence.

Blind Man with
Cane
A195

Procession and
Buildings
A196

1976, Apr. 7 **Engr.** **Perf. 13**
679 A195 100m black & red .50 .25

World Health Day: "Foresight prevents
blindness."

1976, May 31 **Photo.** **Perf. 12x11½**
680 A196 40m multicolored .40 .25

Habitat, UN Conf. on Human Settlements,
Vancouver, Canada, May 31-June 11.

Face and Hands
Decorated with
Henna — A197

Old and new Tunisia: 50m, Sponge fishing
at Jerba. 65m, Textile industry. 110m, Pottery
of Guellala.

1976, June 15 **Photo.** **Perf. 13x13½**
681 A197 40m multicolored .25 .25
682 A197 50m multicolored .50 .25
683 A197 65m multicolored .50 .25
684 A197 110m multicolored .65 .50
  Nos. 681-684 (4) 1.90 1.25

The
Spirit of
'76, by
Archibald
M.
Willard
A198

1976, July 4 **Perf. 13x14**
685 A198 200m multicolored 1.75 .85

Souvenir Sheets
Perf. 13x14, Imperf.
686 A198 500m multicolored 5.00 5.00

American Bicentennial.

Running
A199

Montreal Olympic Games Emblem and:
75m, Bicycling. 120m, Peace dove.

1976, July 17 **Photo.** **Perf. 11½**
687 A199 50m gray, red & blk .25 .25
688 A199 75m red, yel & blk .40 .25
689 A199 120m orange & multi .65 .35
  Nos. 687-689 (3) 1.30 .85

21st Olympic Games, Montreal, Canada,
July 17-Aug. 1.

Child
Reading — A200

Heads and
Bird — A201

1976, Aug. 23   Litho.   Perf. 13
690 A200 100m brown & multi   .50   .25
Books for children.

1976, Sept. 30   Litho.   Perf. 13
691 A201 150m orange & multi   .75   .25
Non-aligned Countries, 15th anniv. of 1st
Conference.

Mouradite
Mausoleum, 17th
Century — A202

Cultural Heritage: 100m, Minaret, Kairouan
Great Mosque and psalmodist. 150m, Monastir Ribat monastery and Alboracq (sphinx).
200m, Barber's Mosque, Kairouan and man's
bust.

1976, Oct. 25   Photo.   Perf. 14
692 A202 85m multicolored   .40   .25
693 A202 100m multicolored   .50   .25
694 A202 150m multicolored   .75   .25
695 A202 200m multicolored   1.10   .40
  Nos. 692-695 (4)   2.75   1.15

Globe
and
Emblem
A203

1976, Dec. 24   Photo.   Perf. 13x14
696 A203 150m multicolored   .85   .35
25th anniv. of UN Postal Administration.

Electronic Tree
and ITU
Emblem — A204

1977, May 17   Photo.   Perf. 14x13½
697 A204 150m multicolored   .85   .50
9th World Telecommunications Day.

"Communication," Sassenage Castle,
Grenoble — A205

1977, May 19   Litho.   Perf. 13½x13
698 A205 100m multicolored   .90   .40
10th anniv. of Intl. French Language Council.

Soccer
A206

1977, June 27   Photo.   Perf. 13½
699 A206 150m multicolored   1.00   .50
Junior World Soccer Tournament, Tunisia,
June 27-July 10.

Gold Coin, 10th
Century — A207

Cultural Heritage: 15m, Stele, Gorjani Cemetery, Tunis, 13th century. 20m, Floral design,
17th century illumination. 30m, Bird and flowers, glass painting, 1922. 40m, Antelope, from
11th century clay pot. 50m, Gate, Sidi Bou
Said, 20th century.

1977, July 9   Photo.   Perf. 13
700 A207 10m multicolored   .25   .25
701 A207 15m multicolored   .25   .25
702 A207 20m multicolored   .25   .25
703 A207 30m multicolored   .40   .25
704 A207 40m multicolored   .50   .25
705 A207 50m multicolored   .50   .25
  a. Miniature sheet of 6, #700-705   3.75   3.75
  Nos. 700-705 (6)   2.15   1.50

"The Young
Republic" and
Bourguiba
A208

Habib Bourguiba and: 100m, "The Confi-
dent Republic" and 20 doves. 150m, "The
Determined Republic" and 20 roses.

1977, July 25   Photo.   Perf. 13x13½
706 A208 40m multicolored   .40   .25
707 A208 100m multicolored   .50   .25
708 A208 150m multicolored   .85   .35
  a. Souvenir sheet of 3, #706-708   2.75   2.75
  Nos. 706-708 (3)   1.75   .85
20th anniv. of the Republic. No. 708a sold
for 500m. Exists imperf., same value.

Symbolic Cancellation, APU
Emblem — A209

1977, Aug. 16   Litho.   Perf. 13x12½
709 A209 40m multicolored   .25   .25
Arab Postal Union, 25th anniversary.

Diseased Knee,
Gears and
Globe — A210

1977, Sept. 26   Photo.   Perf. 14x13½
710 A210 120m multicolored   .75   .35
World Rheumatism Year.

Farmer, Road, Water and
Electricity — A211

1977, Dec. 15   Photo.   Perf. 13½
711 A211 40m multicolored   .35   .25
Rural development.

Factory
Workers — A212

Pres. Bourguiba,
Torch and
"9" — A213

Designs: 20m, Bus driver and trains, horiz.
40m, Farmer driving tractor, horiz.

1978, Mar. 6   Perf. 13x14, 14x13
712 A212 20m rose red & multi   .25   .25
713 A212 40m black & green   .25   .25
714 A212 100m multicolored   .50   .35
  Nos. 712-714 (3)   1.00   .85
5th development plan, creation of new jobs.

1978, Apr. 9   Engr.   Perf. 13
715 A213 40m shown   .25   .25
716 A213 60m Bourguiba and "9"   .25   .25
40th anniv. of 1st fight for independence,
4/9/38.

A214

1978, May 2   Photo.   Perf. 13x13½
717 A214 150m Policeman   .90   .35
6th Regional African Interpol Conference,
Tunis, May 2-5.

A215

Designs: 40m, Tunisian Goalkeeper.
150m., Soccer player, maps of South America
and Africa, flags.

1978, June 1   Photo.   Perf. 13x14
718 A215 40m multicolored   .35   .25
719 A215 150m multicolored   1.00   .40
11th World Cup Soccer Championship,
Argentina, June 1-25.

Destruction of Apartheid, Map of
South Africa — A216

Fight Against Apartheid: 100m, White and
black doves flying in unison.

1978, Aug. 30   Litho.   Perf. 13½x14
720 A216 50m multicolored   .25   .25
721 A216 100m multicolored   .50   .35

"Pollution is a
Plague"
A217

"Eradication of
Smallpox"
A218

Designs: 50m, "The Sea, mankind's patri-
mony." 120m, "Greening of the desert."

1978, Sept. 11   Photo.   Perf. 14x13
722 A217 10m multicolored   .25   .25
723 A217 50m multicolored   .50   .25
724 A217 120m multicolored   1.20   .35
  Nos. 722-724 (3)   1.95   .85
Protection of the environment.

1978, Oct. 16   Litho.   Perf. 12½
725 A218 150m multicolored   .75   .40
Global eradication of smallpox.

Jerba
Wedding
A219

5m, Horseman from Zlass. 75m, Women
potters from the Mogods. 100m, Dove over
Marabout Sidi Mahrez cupolas, Tunis. 500m,
Plowing in Jenduba. 1d, Spring Festival in
Tozeur (man on swing).

1978, Nov. 1   Photo.   Perf. 13
726 A219 5m multi, vert.   .25   .25
727 A219 60m multi   .35   .25
728 A219 75m multi   .50   .25
729 A219 100m multi   .50   .25
730 A219 500m multi   3.75   1.25
731 A219 1d multi   6.00   2.50
  Nos. 726-731 (6)   11.35   4.75
Traditional Arab calligraphy.

Lenin and Red
Banner over
Kremlin — A220

1978, Nov. 7   Perf. 13½
732 A220 150m multicolored   1.20   .50
Russian October Revolution, 60th anniv.

Farhat Hached, Union Emblem — A221

1978, Dec. 5   Photo.   Perf. 14
733 A221 50m multicolored   .40 .25
Farhat Hached (1914-1952), founder of General Union of Tunisian Workers.

Family — A222   Sun with Man's Face — A223

1978, Dec. 15   Photo.   Perf. 13½
734 A222 50m multicolored   .50 .25
Tunisian Family Planning Assoc., 10th anniv.

1978, Dec. 25   Perf. 14
735 A223 100m multicolored   .75 .25
Sun as a source of light and energy.

Plane, Weather Map and Instruments — A224

1978, Dec. 29
736 A224 50m multicolored   .40 .25
Tunisian civil aviation and meteorology, 20th anniv.

Habib Bourguiba and Constitution — A225

1979, May 31   Photo.   Perf. 14x13½
737 A225 50m multicolored   .40 .25
20th anniversary of Constitution.

El Kantaoui Port A226

1979, June 3   Perf. 13½x14
738 A226 150m multicolored   .75 .35
Development of El Kantaoui as a resort area.

Landscapes — A227

1979, July 14   Perf. 12½x13½
739 A227 50m Korbous   .25 .25
740 A227 100m Mides   .40 .25

Bow Net Weaving — A228   Pres. Bourguiba, "10" and Hands — A229

1979, Aug. 15   Photo.   Perf. 11½
741 A228 10m shown   .35 .25
742 A228 50m Beekeeping   .85 .25

1979, Sept. 5
743 A229 50m multicolored   .35 .25
Socialist Destour Party, 10th Congress.

Modes of Communication, ITU Emblem — A230

1979, Sept. 20   Litho.   Perf. 11½
744 A230 150m multicolored   .90 .50
3rd World Telecommunications Exhibition, Geneva, Sept. 20-26.

Arab Achievements — A231

1979, Oct. 1   Perf. 14½
745 A231 50m multicolored   .25 .25

Children Crossing Street, IYC Emblem — A232

1979, Oct. 16   Perf. 14x13½
746 A232 50m shown   .25 .25
747 A232 100m Child and birds   .60 .25
International Year of the Child.

Dove, Olive Tree, Map of Tunisia — A233   Woman Wearing Crown — A234

1979, Nov. 1   Litho.   Perf. 12
748 A233 150m multicolored   .90 .40
2nd International Olive Oil Year.

1979, Nov. 3   Perf. 14½
749 A234 50m multicolored   .25 .25
Central Bank of Tunisia, 20th anniversary.

Children and Jujube Tree — A235

1979, Dec. 25   Litho.   Perf. 15x14½
750 A235 20m shown   .30 .25
751 A235 30m Peacocks   .60 .25
752 A235 70m Goats   1.10 .35
753 A235 85m Girl, date palm   1.10 .40
    Nos. 750-753 (4)   3.10 1.25

Postal Code Introduction — A236

1980, Mar. 20   Photo.   Perf. 14
754 A236 50m multicolored   .40 .25

Fight Against Cigarette Smoking A237

1980, Apr. 7
755 A237 150m multicolored   .75 .25

Pres. Bourguiba in Flower, Open Book — A238

1980, June 1   Photo.   Perf. 11½
756 A238 50m shown   .25 .25
757 A238 100m Dove, Bourguiba, mosque   .90 .40
Victory (independence), 25th anniversary.

Butterfly and Gymnast A239

1980, June 3   Photo.   Perf. 12x11½
Granite Paper
758 A239 100m multicolored   .50 .25
Turin Gymnastic Games, June 1-7.

Artisans
A240   A241

1980, July 21   Photo.   Perf. 13½
759 A240 30m multicolored   .30 .25
760 A241 75m multicolored   .50 .25

ibn-Khaldun (1332-1406), Historian — A242

1980, July 28   Perf. 14
761 A242 50m multicolored   .25 .25

Avicenna (Arab Physician), Birth Millenium — A243

1980, Aug. 18   Engr.   Perf. 12½x13
762 A243 100m redsh brn & sepia   .90 .35

Arab Achievements — A244

1980, Aug. 25   Photo.   Perf. 13½x14
763 A244 50m multicolored   .40 .25

Port Sidi bou Said A245

1980, Sept. 4   Perf. 14
764 A245 100m multicolored   .75 .35

World Tourism Conference, Manila, Sept. 27 — A246

1980, Sept. 27   Photo.   Perf. 14
765 A246 150m multicolored   .65 .25

Wedding in Jerba, by Yahia (1903-
1969) — A247

1980, Oct. 1   *Perf. 12*
766 A247 50m multicolored   .60 .40

Tozeur-Nefta
International Airport
Opening — A248

1980, Oct. 13   Photo.   *Perf. 13x13½*
767 A248 85m multicolored   .40 .25

Eye and
Text
A249

1980, Oct. 26   Litho.   *Perf. 13½x14*
768 A249 100m multicolored   1.10 .50

7th Afro-Asian Ophthalmologic Congress.

Hegira,
1500th
Anniv.
A250

1980, Nov. 9
769 A250 50m Spiderweb   .25 .25
770 A250 80m City skyline   .40 .25

Film Strip and
Woman's
Head — A251

1980, Nov. 15   Photo.   *Perf. 14x13½*
771 A251 100m multicolored   .50 .35

Carthage Film Festival.

Orchid
A252

1980, Nov. 17   *Perf. 13½x14*
772 A252 20m shown   .65 .35
773 A252 25m Wild cyclamen   .85 .35
Size: 39x27mm
Perf. 14
774 A252 50m Mouflon   1.60 .35
775 A252 100m Golden eagle   3.50 .40
Nos. 772-775 (4)   6.60 1.45

Campaign
to Save
Kairouan
Mosque
A253

1980, Dec. 29   Photo.   *Perf. 12*
Granite Paper
776 A253 85m multicolored   .40 .25

Heinrich von
Stephan (1831-
1897), Founder of
UPU — A254

Blood Donors'
Assoc., 20th
Anniv. — A255

1981, Jan. 7
777 A254 150m multicolored   .75 .40

1981, Mar. 5   Litho.   *Perf. 14x13½*
778 A255 75m multicolored   .75 .50

Pres. Bourguiba
and Flag — A256

1981, Mar. 20   Photo.   *Perf. 12x11½*
Granite Paper
779 A256 50m shown   .25 .25
780 A256 60m Stork, "25"   .40 .25
781 A256 85m Doves   .65 .40
782 A256 120m Victory on
   winged horse   .65 .40
a.   Souvenir sheet of 4, #779-782   3.25 3.25
Nos. 779-782 (4)   1.95 1.30

25th anniversary of independence. No. 782
sold for 500m. Exists imperf., same value.

Pres.
Bourguiba
and
Flower
A257

1981, Apr. 10   Photo.   *Perf. 12x11½*
783 A257 50m shown   .25 .25
784 A257 75m Bourguiba, flower,
   diff.   .40 .25

Destourien Socialist Party Congress.

Mosque
Entrance,
Mahdia
A258

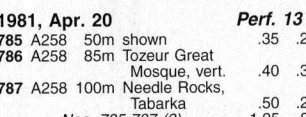

1981, Apr. 20   *Perf. 13½*
785 A258 50m shown   .35 .25
786 A258 85m Tozeur Great
   Mosque, vert.   .40 .35
787 A258 100m Needle Rocks,
   Tabarka   .50 .25
Nos. 785-787 (3)   1.25 .85

A259

Youth
Festival — A260

1981, May 17   Litho.   *Perf. 14x15*
788 A259 150m multicolored   .70 .35

13th World Telecommunications Day.

1981, June 2   Photo.   *Perf. 11½*
Granite Paper
789 A260 100m multicolored   .50 .25

A261   A262

1981, June 15   Photo.   *Perf. 14*
790 A261 150m multicolored   .75 .35

Kemal Ataturk (1881-1938), 1st president of
Turkey.

1981, July 15   Photo.   *Perf. 11½x12*
791 A262 150m Skifa, Mahdia   .85 .40

Mohammed Tahar Ben Achour (1879-
1973), Scholar — A263

1981, Aug. 6   *Perf. 13*
792 A263 200m multicolored   1.10 .50

25th Anniv. of Personal Status Code
(Women's Liberation) — A264

1981, Aug. 13
793 A264 50m Woman   .25 .25
794 A264 100m shown   .50 .35

Intl. Year of the
Disabled — A265

1981, Sept. 21   Photo.   *Perf. 13½*
795 A265 250m multicolored   1.25 .65

Pilgrimage to
Mecca — A266

World Food
Day — A267

1981, Oct. 7   Photo.   *Perf. 13½*
796 A266 50m multicolored   .40 .25

1981, Oct. 16   Litho.   *Perf. 12*
Granite Paper
797 A267 200m multicolored   1.10 .65

Traditional
Jewelry
A268

150m, Mneguech silver earrings. 180m
Mahfdha (silver medallion worn by married
women). 200m, Essalta gold headdress.

1981, Dec. 7   Photo.   *Perf. 14*
798 A268 150m multi, vert.   .75 .35
799 A268 180m multi   .90 .40
800 A268 200m multi, vert.   1.10 .50
Nos. 798-800 (3)   2.75 1.25

Bizerta
Bridge
A269

1981, Dec. 14   Litho.   *Perf. 12x11½*
Granite Paper
801 A269 230m multicolored   1.00 .50

A270

Chemist compounding honey mixture, manuscript miniature, 1224.

1982, Apr. 3   Photo.   *Perf. 13*
802 A270 80m multicolored   .65 .35

Arab Chemists' Union, 16th anniv.

A271

1982, May 12   Photo.   *Perf. 13½*
803 A271 150m multicolored   1.00 .60

Oceanic Enterprise Symposium, Tunis,
5/12-14.

A272

A273

1982, June 26　　　　　**Perf. 12½**
Granite Paper
804　A272　80m multicolored　　　.40　.25
The Productive Family Employment campaign.

1982, July 25　Litho.　Perf. 14x13½
25th Anniv. of Republic: Pres. Bourguiba and Various Women.

805　A273　80m multicolored　　　.35　.25
806　A273　100m multicolored　　　.50　.35
807　A273　200m multicolored　　　.85　.40
　　　Nos. 805-807 (3)　　　　1.70　1.00

Scouting Year — A274

Perf. 14½x14, 14x14½
1982, Aug. 23
808　A274　80m multicolored　　　.40　.25
809　A274　200m multicolored　　　.85　.25
75th anniv. of scouting and 50th anniv. of scouting in Tunisia (80m, horiz.).

Tunisian Fossils — A274a

Designs: 80m, Pseudophillipsia azzouzi, vert. 200m, Mediterraneotrigonia cherahilensis, vert. 280m, Numidiopleura enigmatica. 300m, Micreschara tunisiensis, vert. 500m, Mantelliceras pervinquieri, vert. 1000m, Elephas africanavus.

1982, Sept. 20　Photo.　Perf. 11½x12
809A　A274a　80m multi　　　1.00　.40
809B　A274a　200m multi　　　2.00　.60
809C　A274a　280m multi　　　2.40　.75
809D　A274a　300m multi　　　3.00　1.00
809E　A274a　500m multi　　　6.00　1.60
809F　A274a　1000m multi　　12.00　3.00
　　　Nos. 809A-809F (6)　　26.40　7.35

A275

A276

1982, Sept. 29　　　　**Perf. 14x13½**
810　A275　80m shown　　　.50　.25
Size: 23x40mm
811　A275　200m Woman, buildings　.85　.50
30th Anniv. of Arab Postal Union.

1982, Oct. 1　Photo.　Perf. 12
Granite Paper
812　A276　200m multicolored　　　.85　.25
ITU Plenipotentiaries Conf., Nairobi

World Food Day A277

Tahar Haddad (1899-1935), Social Reformer A278

1982, Oct. 16　Litho.　Perf. 13
813　A277　200m multicolored　　　.90　.35

1982, Oct. 25　　　　　　**Engr.**
814　A278　200m dark brown　　　.80　.25

TB Bacillus Centenary A279

1982, Nov. 16　Litho.　Perf. 13½
815　A279　100m multicolored　　　.90　.25

Folk Songs and Stories — A280

1982, Nov. 22　Photo.　Perf. 14
816　A280　20m Dancing in the Rain　　　　　　　　.25　.25
817　A280　30m Woman Sweeping　　　　　　　　.25　.25
818　A280　70m Fisherman and the Child　　　　　　.25　.25
819　A280　80m Rooster and the Oranges, horiz.　.30　.25
820　A280　100m Woman and the Mirror, horiz.　.50　.25
821　A280　120m The Two Girls, horiz.　　　　　.65　.30
　　　Nos. 816-821 (6)　　　2.20　1.55

Intl. Palestinian Solidarity Day — A281

1982, Nov. 30　Litho.　Perf. 13x12
822　A281　80m multicolored　　　.40　.25

Farhat Hached (1914-1952) A282

Bourguiba Dam Opening A283

1982, Dec. 6　Engr.　Perf. 13
823　A282　80m brown red　　　.40　.25

1982, Dec. 20　Litho.　Perf. 13½
824　A283　80m multicolored　　　.50　.25

Environmental Training College Opening — A284

1982, Dec. 29　Photo.　Perf. 11½
Granite Paper
825　A284　80m multicolored　　　.40　.25

World Communications Year — A285

1983, May 17　Litho.　Perf. 13½x14
826　A285　200m multicolored　　　.60　.35

20th Anniv. of Org. of African Unity — A286

1983, May 25　Photo.　Perf. 12
Granite Paper
827　A286　230m ultra & grnsh bl　.85　.50

30th Anniv. of Customs Cooperation Council — A287

1983, May 30　Litho.　Perf. 13½
828　A287　100m multicolored　　　.40　.25

Aly Ben Ayed (1930-1972), Actor — A288

1983, Aug. 15　Engr.　Perf. 13
829　A288　80m dk car, dl red & gray　.35　.35

Stone-carved Face, El-Mekta — A289

Pre-historic artifacts: 20m, Neolithic necklace, Kel el-Agab. 30m, Mill and grindstone, Redeyef. 40m, Orynx head rock carving, Gafsa. 80m, Dolmen Mactar. 100m, Acheulian Bi-face flint, El-Mekta.

1983, Aug. 20　Photo.　Perf. 11½x12
830　A289　15m multicolored　　　.25　.25
831　A289　20m multicolored　　　.40　.25
832　A289　30m multicolored　　　.40　.25
833　A289　40m multicolored　　　.40　.25
834　A289　80m multicolored　　　.50　.40
835　A289　100m multicolored　　.65　.40
　　　Nos. 830-835 (6)　　　2.60　1.80

Sports for All A290

1983, Sept. 27　Litho.　Perf. 12½
836　A290　40m multicolored　　　.25　.25

World Fishing Day A291

1983, Oct. 17　　　　　　**Perf. 14½**
837　A291　200m multicolored　　1.00　.25

Evacuation of French Troops, 20th Anniv. — A292

1983, Oct. 17　Litho.　Perf. 14x13½
838　A292　80m multicolored　　　.40　.25

Tapestry Weaver, by Hedi Khayachi (1882-1948) — A293

1983, Nov. 22　Photo.　Perf. 11½
Granite Paper
839　A293　80m multicolored　　　.65　.40

Natl. Allegiance A294

Jet, Woman's Head, Emblem A295

1983, Nov. 30   Litho.   Perf. 14½
840 A294 100m Children, flag   .40 .25

1983, Dec. 21   Perf. 13½
841 A295 150m multicolored   .65 .25

Pres. Bourguiba A296

Destourien Socialist Party, 50th Anniv.: Portraits of Bourguiba. 200m, 230m horiz.

Perf. 12½x12, 12x12½
1984, Mar. 2   Photo.
Granite Paper
842 A296 40m multicolored   .25 .25
843 A296 70m multicolored   .25 .25
844 A296 80m multicolored   .40 .25
a. Pair, #843-844   .75 .75
845 A296 150m multicolored   .65 .40
a. Pair, #842, 845   1.00 1.00
846 A296 200m multicolored   .85 .40
847 A296 230m multicolored   .90 .60
a. Pair, #846-847   2.00 2.00
    Nos. 842-847 (6)   3.30 2.15

Nos. 844a, 845a and 847a were printed checkerwise in sheets of ten.

4th Molecular Biology Symposium A297

1984, Apr. 3   Perf. 13½x13
848 A297 100m Map, diagram   .60 .35

Ibn El Jazzar, Physician — A298

Economic Development Program, 20th Anniv. — A299

1984, May 15   Photo.   Perf. 14x13
849 A298 80m multicolored   .50 .40

1984, June 15   Perf. 11½
Granite Paper
850 A299 230m Merchant, worker   .90 .40

Coquette, The Sorceress and the Fairy Carabosse A300

Perf. 13½x14, 14x13½
1984, Aug. 27   Photo.
851 A300 20m shown   .25 .25
852 A300 80m Counting with fingers   .40 .25
853 A300 100m Boy riding horse, vert.   .50 .25
    Nos. 851-853 (3)   1.15 .75

Legends and folk tales.

Family and Education Org., 20th Anniv. — A301

1984, Sept. 4   Perf. 13x14
854 A301 80m Family looking into future   .40 .25

Natl. Heritage Protection A302

Aboul-Qasim Chabbi, Poet (1909-1934) A303

1984, Sept. 13   Perf. 14
855 A302 100m Medina Mosque Minaret, hand   .50 .35

1984, Oct. 9   Engr.   Perf. 12½x13
856 A303 100m multicolored   .40 .25

40th Anniv., ICAO A304

1984, Oct. 25   Photo.   Perf. 13
857 A304 200m Aircraft tail, bird   .90 .60

Sahara Festival A305

1984, Dec. 3   Litho.   Perf. 14½
858 A305 20m Musicians   .65 .25

20th Anniv., Intelsat A306

Perf. 13½x14½
1984, Dec. 25   Photo.
859 A306 100m Tunisian Earth Station   .40 .25

Mediterranean Landscape, by Jilani Abdelwaheb (Abdul) — A307

1984, Dec. 31   Photo.   Perf. 14½
860 A307 100m multicolored   .65 .40

EXPO '85, Tsukuba, Japan A308

1985, Mar. 20   Photo.   Perf. 12
861 A308 200m multicolored   .85 .50

Civil Protection Week — A309

1985, May 13   Litho.   Perf. 14
862 A309 100m Hands, water and fire   .50 .40

Pres. Habib Bourguiba, Crowded Pier — A310

Pres. Bourguiba: 75m, On horseback, vert. 200m, Wearing hat, vert. 230m, Waving to crowd.

1985, June 1   Perf. 12½
863 A310 75m multicolored   .60 .60
864 A310 100m multicolored   1.00 1.00
865 A310 200m multicolored   1.40 1.40
866 A310 230m multicolored   1.60 1.60
    Nos. 863-866 (4)   4.60 4.60

Natl. independence, 30th anniv.

Head of a Statue, Carthage and Pres. Bourguiba A311

1985, June 4   Perf. 14
867 A311 250m multicolored   1.00 .65

EXPO '85.

Intl. Amateur Film Festival, Kelibia — A312

Natl. Folk Tales — A313

1985, July 20   Perf. 14½x13
868 A312 250m multicolored   1.20 .65

1985, July 29   Perf. 14
869 A313 25m Sun, Sun Shine Again, horiz.   .25 .25
870 A313 50m I Met a Man With Seven Wives   .25 .25
871 A313 100m Uncle Shisbene   .40 .25
    Nos. 869-871 (3)   .90 .75

Intl. Youth Year — A314

1985, Sept. 30   Perf. 14½x13½
872 A314 250m multicolored   .90 .60

The Perfumers' Courtyard, 1912, by Hedi Larnaout — A315

1985, Oct. 4   Perf. 14
873 A315 100m multicolored   .50 .25

Regional Bridal Costumes A316

UN, 40th Anniv. A317

1985, Oct. 22   Perf. 12
874 A316 20m Matmata   .25 .25
875 A316 50m Moknine   .25 .25
876 A316 100m Tunis   .40 .25
    Nos. 874-876 (3)   .90 .75

1985, Oct. 24   Perf. 14x13½
877 A317 250m multicolored   .90 .60

Self-Sufficiency in Food Production — A318

Perf. 13½x14½
1985, Nov. 26   **Photo.**
878 A318 100m Makhtar stele of feast   .40 .25

League of Arab States, 40th Anniv. A319

1985, Nov. 29   **Litho.**   *Perf. 13½x14*
879 A319 100m multicolored   .50 .25

Aziza Othmana (d. 1669) — A320   Land Law, Cent. — A321

1985, Dec. 16   **Engr.**   *Perf. 12½x13*
880 A320 100m dk grn, hn brn & brn   .50 .25

1985, Dec. 25   **Litho.**   *Perf. 13½*
881 A321 100m multicolored   .40 .25

Natl. Independence, 30th Anniv. — A322

Perf. 13x13½, 13½x13
1986, Mar. 20   **Photo.**
882 A322 100m Dove, vert.   .35 .25
883 A322 120m Rocket   .40 .25
884 A322 280m Horse and rider   1.10 .65
885 A322 300m Balloons, vert.   1.20 .75
   a. Souvenir sheet of 4, #882-885   3.50 3.50
     Nos. 882-885 (4)   3.05 1.90

No. 885a exists imperf. Same value.

A323   A324

1986, Apr. 30   **Litho.**   *Perf. 14x13½*
886 A323 300m multicolored   1.50 .40
887 A324 380m multicolored   1.90 .50

Prof. Hulusi Behcet (1889-1948), discovered virus causing Behcet's Disease affecting eyes and joints. 3rd Mediterranean Rheumatology Day (#886). Intl. Geographical Ophtalmological Soc. Cong. (#887).

12th Destourian Socialist Party Congress A325

1986, June 19   **Photo.**   *Perf. 12*
888 A325 120m shown   .40 .25
889 A325 300m Torchbearer   1.10 .75

A326

Regional bridal costumes.

1986, Aug. 25   **Litho.**   *Perf. 14*
890 A326 40m Homi-Souk   .25 .25
891 A326 280m Mahdia   .90 .60
892 A326 300m Nabeul   1.20 .65
     Nos. 890-892 (3)   2.35 1.50

A327

1986, Sept. 20   **Engr.**   *Perf. 13*
893 A327 160m dark red   .65 .25

Hassen Husni Abdul-Wahab (1883-1968), historian, archaeologist

Founding of Carthage, 2800th Anniv. — A328

1986, Oct. 18   **Engr.**   *Perf. 13*
894 A328 2d dark violet   8.00 3.00

Protohistoric Artifacts — A329

Design: 10m, Flint arrowhead, El Borma, c. 3000 B.C. 20m, Rock cut-out dwelling, Sejnane, c. 1000 B.C. 50m, Lintel bas-relief from a cult site in Tunis, c. 1000 B.C., horiz. 120m, Base of a Neolithic vase, Kesra. 160m, Phoenician trireme, petroglyph, c. 800 B.C., horiz. 250m, Ceramic pot, c. 700 B.C., found at Sejnane, vert.

1986, Oct. 30   **Litho.**   *Perf. 13½*
895 A329 10m multicolored   .25 .25
896 A329 20m multicolored   .25 .25
897 A329 50m multicolored   .40 .25
898 A329 120m multicolored   .65 .25
899 A329 160m multicolored   .85 .40
900 A329 250m multicolored   1.60 .60
     Nos. 895-900 (6)   4.00 2.00

Bedouins, by Ammar Farhat — A330

1986, Nov. 20   **Photo.**   *Perf. 13½*
901 A330 250m multicolored   1.40 .40

Intl. Peace Year A331

1986, Nov. 24   *Perf. 13½x13*
902 A331 300m multicolored   1.10 .40

FAO, 40th Anniv. — A332

1986, Nov. 27   *Perf. 13x13½*
903 A332 280m multicolored   .90 .60

Computer Education Inauguration A333

1986, Dec. 8   *Perf. 13½*
904 A333 2d multicolored   7.50 2.75

Breast-feeding for Child Survival — A334   Wildlife, Natl. Parks — A335

1986, Dec. 22   **Photo.**   *Perf. 14*
905 A334 120m multicolored   .50 .25

1986, Dec. 29   *Perf. 12*

Designs: 60m, Mountain gazelle, Chambi Natl. Park. 120m, Addax, Bou. Hedma. 350m, Seal, Zembretta. 380m, Greylag goose, Ichkeul.

Granite Paper
906 A335 60m multicolored   .25 .25
907 A335 120m multicolored   .50 .35
908 A335 350m multicolored   1.40 1.00
909 A335 380m multicolored   1.75 1.10
     Nos. 906-909 (4)   3.90 2.70

City of Monastir, Cent. — A336

1987, Jan. 24   **Litho.**   *Perf. 12x11½*
Granite Paper
910 A336 120m Pres. Bourguiba, city arms   .40 .25

Invention of the Telegraph by Samuel F.B. Morse, 150th Anniv. A337

1987, June 15   **Litho.**   *Perf. 13½x14*
911 A337 500m multicolored   1.75 1.00

30th Anniv. of the Republic A338

Pres. Bourguiba and women of various sects.

1987, July 25   **Photo.**   *Perf. 13½*
912 A338 150m multi   .35 .25
913 A338 250m multi   .60 .35
914 A338 350m multi, diff.   .85 .55
915 A338 500m multi, diff.   1.25 .75
   a. Souvenir sheet of 4, #912-915   4.00 4.00
     Nos. 912-915 (4)   3.05 1.90

No. 915a sold for 1.50d. Exists imperf.

UN Universal Vaccination by 1990 Campaign — A339

1987, Sept. 14   *Perf. 12*
Granite Paper
916 A339 250m multicolored   .85 .50

The Street, by Azouz ben Raiz (1902-1962) A340

1987, Sept. 22   **Granite Paper**
917 A340 250m multicolored   1.00 .50

Arab Day for Shelter of the Homeless A341

1987, Oct. 5   **Photo.**   *Perf. 12x11½*
Granite Paper
918 A341 150m multicolored   .50 .25

Advisory Council for Postal Research, 30th Anniv. A342

1987, Oct. 9 *Perf. 14*
919 A342 150m Express mail .50 .25
920 A342 350m Use postal code 1.10 .60

The Arabs, by Ibn-Mandhour (1233-1312), Lexicographer A343

1987, Oct. 26 *Engr.* *Perf. 13*
921 A343 250m plum 1.00 .50

Pasteur Institute, Tunis A344

1987, Nov. 21 *Perf. 13x12½*
922 A344 250m blk, grn & rose lake 1.00 .50

Pasteur Institute, Paris, cent.

Intl. Year of the Vine (Wine) — A345

1987, Nov. 27 *Photo.* *Perf. 14*
923 A345 250m multicolored 1.00 .50

6th Volleyball Championships of African Nations — A346

1987, Dec. 2 *Litho.* *Perf. 14x13½*
924 A346 350m multicolored 1.40 .70

African Basketball Championships A347

Folk Costumes A348

1987, Dec. 15
925 A347 350m multicolored 1.50 .70

1987, Dec. 25 *Photo.*
926 A348 20m Midoun .25 .25
927 A348 30m Tozeur .25 .25
928 A348 150m Sfax .85 .40
 Nos. 926-928 (3) 1.35 .90

Flowering Plants — A349

1987, Dec. 29 *Perf. 14½*
929 A349 30m Narcissus tazetta .25 .25
930 A349 150m Gladiolus communis .60 .30
931 A349 400m Iris xiphium 1.50 .80
932 A349 500m Tulipa sylvestris 1.90 1.00
 Nos. 929-932 (4) 4.25 2.35

Declaration of Nov. 7, 1987 A350

Cameo portrait of Pres. Zine el Abidine Ben Ali and: 150m, Scales of Justice. 200m, Girl with flowers (party badges) in her hair, vert. 350m, Mermaid, doves, natl. coat of arms. 370m, "CMA," emblem of the Maghreb states (Tunisia, Mauritania, Morocco, Algeria and Libya), vert.

1988, Mar. 21 *Photo.* *Perf. 12*
Granite Paper
933 A350 150m multicolored .50 .25
934 A350 200m multicolored .60 .30
935 A350 350m multicolored 1.10 .55
936 A350 370m multicolored 1.10 .60
 Nos. 933-936 (4) 3.30 1.70

Youth and Change A351

1988, Mar. 22 *Litho.* *Perf. 14x14½*
937 A351 75m shown .25 .25
938 A351 150m Happy family .50 .25

Martyr's Day, 50th Anniv. A352

Perf. 13x13½, 13½x13
1988, Apr. 9 *Photo.*
939 A352 150m shown .45 .25
940 A352 500m Monument, vert. 1.50 .75

Opening Conference of the Constitutional Democratic Assembly — A353

1988, July 30 *Perf. 12x11½*
Granite Paper
941 A353 150m Flag, Pres. Ben Ali .50 .25

1988 Summer Olympics, Seoul A354

1988, Sept. 20 *Photo.* *Perf. 13½*
942 A354 150m shown .50 .25
943 A354 430m Running, boxing, weight lifting, wrestling 1.40 1.00

A355

1988, Sept. 21
944 A355 200m multicolored .60 .35
Restoration of the City of San'a, Yemen.

A356

1988, Nov. 7 *Photo.* *Perf. 14*
945 A356 150m multicolored .40 .30
Appointment of Pres. Zine El Abidine Ben Ali, 1st anniv.

Amilcar Beach, 1942, by A. Debbeche — A357

1988, Nov. 21 *Photo.* *Perf. 13½x13*
946 A357 100m multicolored .50 .25

Tunis Air, 40th Anniv. A358

1988, Nov. 28 *Photo.* *Perf. 12x11½*
Granite Paper
947 A358 500m multicolored 1.60 .80

UN Declaration of Human Rights, 40th Anniv. — A359

1988, Dec. 10 *Perf. 12*
Granite Paper
948 A359 370m black 1.10 .60

Tunisian Postage Stamp Cent. — A360

1988, Dec. 16 *Perf. 12½*
Granite Paper
949 A360 150m multicolored .65 .40

A361

A362

Decorative doorways.

1988, Dec. 26 *Perf. 14x13½*
950 A361 50m multi .25 .25
951 A361 70m multi, diff. .25 .25
952 A361 100m multi, diff. .25 .25
953 A361 150m multi, diff. .40 .25
954 A361 370m multi, diff. .90 .40
955 A361 400m multi, diff. 1.10 .40
 Nos. 950-955 (6) 3.15 1.80

1989, Mar. 7 *Engr.* *Perf. 13½x13*
956 A362 1000m dark blue 2.75 1.60

Ali Douagi (1909-49).

Natl. Day for the Handicapped A363

1989, May 30 *Photo.* *Perf. 13½*
957 A363 150m multicolored .50 .25

Education A364

1989, July 10 *Perf. 14*
958 A364 180m multicolored .50 .25

Family Planning Assoc., 20th Anniv. — A365

1989, Aug. 14 *Litho.* *Perf. 14*
959 A365 150m multicolored .40 .25

Family
Care
A366

1989, Aug. 14   Litho.   Perf. 14
960 A366 150m multicolored   .40 .25

Fauna
A367

1989, Aug. 28   Photo.   Perf. 13½x14
961 A367 250m Tortoise   1.00 .50
962 A367 350m Oryx   1.40 .65

Intl. Fair, Tunis
A368

Mohamed
Beyram V (1840-
1889)
A369

1989, Oct. 16   Photo.   Perf. 14
963 A368 150m shown   .40 .25
964 A368 370m Pavilion, horiz.   .90 .60

1989, Oct. 28   Engr.   Perf. 13
965 A369 150m blk & dp rose lil   .40 .25

Theater, Carthage
A370

Monument
A371

1989, Nov. 3   Photo.   Perf. 14
966 A370 300m multicolored   .85 .40

1989, Nov. 7   Perf. 11½x12
Granite Paper
967 A371 150m multicolored   .40 .25

Appointment of Pres. Zine El Abidine Ben
Ali, 2nd Anniv.

Nehru — A372

Flags — A373

1989, Nov. 29   Engr.   Perf. 13
968 A372 300m dark brown   .90 .35

Jawaharlal Nehru, 1st prime minister of
independent India.

1990, Jan. 15   Photo.   Perf. 12x11½
Granite Paper
969 A373 200m multicolored   .60 .35

Maghreb Union summit, Tunis.

Museum
of Bardo,
Cent.
A374

1990, Feb. 20   Litho.   Perf. 13½
970 A374 300m multicolored   .90 .50

Pottery
A375

1990, Mar. 22   Perf. 14
971 A375   75m multicolored   .35 .25
972 A375 100m multi, diff.   .50 .35

Sheep Museum — A376

1990, Apr. 13   Litho.   Perf. 13½
973 A376 400m Sheep   1.25 .75
974 A376 450m Ram's head   1.60 .85
  a.   Souvenir sheet of 2, #973-974   3.75 3.75

No. 974a sold for 1000m, exists imperf. Nos.
973-974 inscribed 1989.

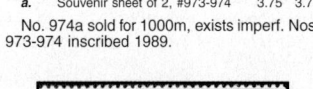

Tunisian Olympic Movement — A377

1990, May 27
975 A377 150m multicolored   .40 .25

Child's
Drawing
A378

1990, June 5   Perf. 14
976 A378 150m multicolored   .40 .25

Traditional costumes.
A379

1990, July 13   Photo.   Perf. 14x14½
977 A379 150m Sbiba   .50 .35
978 A379 500m Bou Omrane   1.60 .85

A380

Relic from Punic city of Dougga.

1990, Aug. 1   Litho.   Perf. 14
979 A380 300m multicolored   .85 .50

Intl.
Literacy
Year
A381

1990, Sept. 8   Photo.   Perf. 12x11½
Granite Paper
980 A381 120m multicolored   .40 .25

A382   A383

1990, Oct. 15   Perf. 11½x12
Granite Paper
981 A382 150m multicolored   .50 .25

Importance of water.

1990, Nov. 7   Granite Paper
982 A383 150m shown   .40 .25
983 A383 150m Clock tower   .40 .25

Appointment of Pres. Zine El Abidine Ben
Ali, 3rd anniv.

A384   A385

1990, Nov. 16   Engr.   Perf. 13½x13
984 A384 150m green   .50 .25

Kheireddine Et-Tounsi (1822-1889), politician.

1990, Dec. 17   Photo.   Perf. 13½
Fauna and flora.

985 A385 150m Cervus elaphus
                 barbarus   .40 .25
986 A385 200m Cynara
                 cardenculus   .65 .35
987 A385 300m Bubalus bubalis   1.00 .40
988 A385 600m Ophris lutea   2.10 .85
  Nos. 985-988 (4)   4.15 1.85

Maghreb Arab
Union, 2nd
Anniv. — A386

1991, Jan. 21   Photo.   Perf. 13½
989 A386 180m multicolored   .50 .25

Harbor of
Tabarka — A387

1991, Mar. 17
990 A387 450m multicolored   1.25 .50

Fish — A388

1991, Sept. 10   Photo.   Perf. 14x13
991 A388 180m Pagre   .60 .25
992 A388 250m Rouget de roche   1.25 .40
993 A388 450m Maquereau   1.25 .60
994 A388 550m Pageot commun   2.10 .90
  Nos. 991-994 (4)   5.20 2.15

Child
Welfare — A389

1991, Sept. 29   Perf. 14
995 A389 450m multicolored   1.60 .85

  A390

1991, Oct. 9   Perf. 13½x14
996 A390 400m multicolored   1.25 .50

A391   A392

Jewelry.

Perf. 14x13, 13x14
1991, Oct. 22   Litho.
997 A391 120m Ring, bracelets,
                 horiz.   .40 .25
998 A391 180m Necklace   .50 .25

999 A391 220m Earrings .65 .35
1000 A391 730m shown 2.50 1.10
Nos. 997-1000 (4) 4.05 1.95

1991, Nov. 7 **Perf. 11½**
1001 A392 180m multicolored .50 .25

Appointment of Pres. Zine El Abidine Ben Ali, 4th anniv.

Tunis-Carthage Center — A393

1991, Nov. 22 **Engr.** **Perf. 13**
1002 A393 80m red, blue & green .70 .40

A394

1991, Dec. 12 **Photo.** **Perf. 14**
1003 A394 450m bright blue 1.40 .55

World Day of the Rights of Man.

A395

1991, Dec. 26 **Engr.** **Perf. 12½x13**
1004 A395 200m blue .50 .35

Mahmoud Bayram Et Tounsi (1893-1960), poet.

Expo '92, Seville — A396

1992, Apr. 20 **Photo.** **Perf. 13½**
1005 A396 180m multicolored .50 .25

General Post Office, Tunis, Cent. — A397

Perf. 13x12½, 12½x13
1992, June 15 **Engr.**
1006 A397 180m red brn, horiz. .50 .25
1007 A397 450m dark brown 1.40 .45

"When the Subconscious Awakes," by Moncef ben Amor — A398

1992, July 21 **Litho.** **Perf. 13½**
1008 A398 500m multicolored 1.50 .50

1992 Summer Olympics, Barcelona A399

1992, Aug. 4
1009 A399 180m Running .85 .40
1010 A399 450m Judo, vert. 1.90 .65

Birds — A400   A401

1992, Sept. 22 **Photo.** **Perf. 11½**
Granite Paper
1011 A400 100m Merops apiaster .60 .25
1012 A400 180m Carduelis carduelis 1.10 .40
1013 A400 200m Serinus serinus 1.25 .50
1014 A400 500m Carduelis chloris 2.50 1.00
Nos. 1011-1014 (4) 5.45 2.15

1992, Oct. 21 **Perf. 11½x12**
Granite Paper
1015 A401 180m multicolored .65 .40

UN Conference on Rights of the Child.

African Human Rights Conference, Tunis — A402

1992, Nov. 2 **Photo.** **Perf. 11½**
Granite Paper
1016 A402 480m multicolored 1.60 .85

A403   A404

1992, Nov. 7 **Granite Paper**
1017 A403 180m multicolored .65 .40
1018 A404 730m multicolored 2.10 1.10

Appointment of Pres. Zine El Abidine Ben Ali, 5th anniv.

Arbor Day A405

1992, Nov. 8 **Perf. 11½x12**
Granite Paper
1019 A405 180m Acacia tortilis .75 .50

Intl. Conference on Nutrition, Rome — A406

1992, Dec. 15 **Litho.** **Perf. 13½**
1020 A406 450m multicolored 1.60 .65

Traditional Costumes — A407

1992, Dec. 23
1021 A407 100m Chemesse .40 .25
1022 A407 350m Hanifites 1.10 .50

Mosaics A408

1992, Dec. 29
1023 A408 100m Goat .40 .25
1024 A408 180m Duck .85 .35
1025 A408 350m Horse 1.40 .50
1026 A408 450m Gazelle 1.50 .90
Nos. 1023-1026 (4) 4.15 2.00

World Conference on Human Rights, Vienna — A409

1993, June 8 **Litho.** **Perf. 13½**
1027 A409 450m multi — —

Arab-African Fair of Tunisia — A410

1993, July 10 **Litho.** **Perf. 13½x14**
1028 A410 450m multicolored 1.40 .50

Relaxation in the Patio, by Ali Guermassi A411   Reassembly of the Democratic Congress A412

1993, July 20 **Litho.** **Perf. 13½**
1029 A411 450m multicolored 1.40 .50

1993, July 29 **Perf. 13½**
1030 A412 180m multicolored .50 .25

A413

A414

1993 **Perf. 13**
1031 A413 20m Wolf .90 .25
1032 A414 60m Hoya carnosa .60 .25

Appointment of Pres. Zine El Abidine, 6th Anniv.
A414A   A415

1993, Nov. 7 **Perf. 13½**
1033 A414A 180m multicolored .50 .25
1034 A415 450m multicolored 1.40 .50

Kairouan Tapestries — A416

Designs: Various ornate patterns.

1993, Dec. 13 **Perf. 13½**
1035 A416 100m multicolored .25 .25
1036 A416 120m multicolored .35 .25
1037 A416 180m multicolored .60 .35
1038 A416 350m multicolored 1.40 .75
Nos. 1035-1038 (4) 2.60 1.60

Pasteur Institute of Tunis, Cent. A417

Design: 450m, Charles Nicolle (1866-1936), bacteriologist, 1928 Nobel medal.

1993, Oct. 12   **Litho.**   **Perf. 13½**
1039   A417   450m multicolored   1.40   .65

A418

School Activities A419

1993, Dec. 30   **Litho.**   **Perf. 13½**
1040   A418   180m Music   .50   .25
1041   A419   180m Art, reading   .50   .25

19th African Cup of Nations Soccer Tournament — A420

1994, Mar. 26
1042   A420   180m shown   .50   .25
1043   A420   350m Two players, diff.   1.00   .35
1044   A420   450m Map, player   1.40   .65
   Nos. 1042-1044 (3)   2.90   1.25

Presidential and Legislative Elections — A421

1994, Mar. 20
1045   A421   180m multicolored   .50   .25

Election of Pres. Zine El Abidine ben Ali — A422

1994, May 15   **Photo.**   **Perf. 11½**
   Granite Paper
1046   A422   180m multicolored   .50   .35
1047   A422   350m multicolored   1.00   .75
  a.   Souvenir sheet, #1046-1047   2.50   2.50

No. 1047a exists imperf.

ILO, 75th Anniv. — A423

1994, May 12   **Perf. 13½x14**
1048   A423   350m multicolored   1.20   .35

Intl. Year of the Family — A424   Plants — A425

1994, May 15   **Litho.**   **Perf. 14x13½**
1049   A424   180m multicolored   .85   .50

1994, June 2
1050   A425   50m Prunus spinosa   .25   .25
1051   A425   100m Xeranthemum inapertum   .25   .25
1052   A425   200m Orchis simia   .65   .30
1053   A425   1d Scilla peruviana   3.00   1.50
   Nos. 1050-1053 (4)   4.15   2.30

Organization of African Unity Summit Meeting, Tunis — A426

1994, June 3   **Perf. 13½**
1054   A426   480m multicolored   1.50   .75

Intl. Olympic Committee, Cent. A427

1994, July 7   **Litho.**   **Perf. 13½**
1055   A427   450m multicolored   1.50   .65

Philakorea '94 — A428

1994, Aug 18   **Litho.**   **Perf. 13¼x13½**
1056   A428   450m multi   1.50   .65

A429   A430

Butterflies: 100m, Colias croceus, horiz. 180m, Vanessa atalanta, horiz. 300m, Papilio podalirius. 350m, Danaus chrysippus, horiz. 450m, Vanessa cardui. 500m, Papilio machaon.

Perf. 13½x14, 14x13½
1994, Oct. 13   **Litho.**
1057   A429   100m multicolored   .40   .25
1058   A429   180m multicolored   .65   .35
1059   A429   300m multicolored   .90   .50
1060   A429   350m multicolored   1.25   .65
1061   A429   450m multicolored   1.60   .85
1062   A429   500m multicolored   1.90   .90
   Nos. 1057-1062 (6)   6.70   3.50

1994, Nov. 16   **Perf. 13½**
1063   A430   350m Pres. Ali, "7," horiz.   1.00   .50
1064   A430   730m "7," Emblem   2.00   1.00

Pres. Zine El Abdine, 7th anniv. of taking office.

41st Military Boxing World Championships A431

1994, Nov. 18   **Litho.**   **Perf. 13½x14**
1065   A431   450m multicolored   1.40   .70

Intl. Civil Aviation Organization, 50th Anniv. — A432

1994, Dec. 7   **Litho.**   **Perf. 13¾x14**
1066   A432   450m multi   1.00   .50

Wildlife — A433

1994, Dec. 27   **Litho.**   **Perf. 13½**
1067   A433   180m Anser anser   .65   .40
1068   A433   350m Aythya ferina, Aythya fuligula   1.10   .85
1069   A433   500m Bubalus bubalis   1.60   1.25
1070   A433   1d Lutra lutra, horiz.   3.00   2.75
   Nos. 1067-1070 (4)   6.35   5.25

"Composition," by Ridha Bettaieb — A434

1994, Dec. 29   **Litho.**   **Perf. 13**
1071   A434   500m multicolored   1.40   .85

Arab League, 50th Anniv. — A435   Art of Glass Blowing — A436

1995, May 29   **Litho.**   **Perf. 13½**
1072   A435   180m multicolored   .55   .40

1995, June 29
1073   A436   450m Water bottle   1.25   .90
1074   A436   730m Incense burner   2.00   1.50

Aboulkacem Chebbi (1909-34), Poet — A437

1995, Aug. 12   **Litho.**   **Perf. 13½**
1075   A437   180m multicolored   .40   .40

4th World Conference on Women, Beijing A438

1995, Sept. 6   **Litho.**   **Perf. 13½**
1076   A438   180m multicolored   .55   .40

FAO, 50th Anniv. A439

1995, Oct. 2   **Litho.**   **Perf. 13½x13**
1077   A439   350m multicolored   .80   .65

Hannibal (247-183BC), Carthaginian General — A440

1995, Nov. 14   **Engr.**   **Perf. 14x13½**
1078   A440   180m maroon   .65   .40
  a.   Souvenir sheet of 1   2.50   2.50

No. 1078a sold for 1d and exists imperf.

United Nations, 50th Anniv. A441

1995, Oct. 24   **Litho.**   **Perf. 14x13½**
1079   A441   350m multicolored   .80   .65

A442   A443

1995, Nov. 7   Litho.   Perf. 13x13½
1080 A442 180m multicolored   .50 .35
1081 A443 350m multicolored   .95 .65
Appointment of Pres. Zine El Abidine ben Ali, 8th anniv.

Campaign Against Desertification — A444

1995, Oct. 31   Litho.   Perf. 13¼
1082 A444 180m multi   .35 .35

Human Rights Day — A445

1995, Dec. 10   Litho.   Perf. 13x13½
1083 A445 350m multicolored   .95 .65

Pedestrian Security A446

1995, Dec. 19   Perf. 13½x13
1084 A446 350m multicolored   .80 .65

Flora and Fauna A447   Traditional Costumes A448

Designs: 50m, Ophrys lapethica. 180m, Gazella dorcas. 300m, Scupellaria cypria. 350m, Chlamydotis undulata.

1995, Dec. 28   Perf. 13½
1085 A447 50m multicolored   .25 .25
1086 A447 180m multicolored   .50 .25
1087 A447 300m multicolored   .80 .55
1088 A447 350m multicolored   .95 .75
    Nos. 1085-1088 (4)   2.50 1.80

1996, Mar.16   Perf. 14x13½
1089 A448 170m Jebra, Khamri   .50 .40
1090 A448 200m Kaftan brode, Hammamet   .50 .40

A449   A450

Independence, 40th Anniv.: 390m, Dove, rainbow, "20, 40."

1996, Mar. 20   Perf. 13x13½
1091 A449 200m multicolored   .55 .30
1092 A449 390m multicolored   1.00 .75

1996, Jan. 20   Litho.   Perf. 13x13½
1093 A450 440m multicolored   1.25 .85
Natl. Trade Union, 50th anniv.

Painting, "Hannana," by Noureddine Khayachi (1917-87) — A451

1996, Apr. 25   Litho.   Perf. 13½
1094 A451 810m multicolored   1.90 1.60

A451a   A452

1996, June 5   Litho.   Perf. 13x13½
1094A A451a 390m multicolored   .90 .75
Environment Day.

1996, June 8   Litho.   Perf. 13x13½
1095 A452 200m multicolored   .55 .35
CAPEX '96.

Insects A453

1996, May 23   Litho.   Perf. 14x13½
1096 A453 200m Coccinella septempunctata   .60 .40
1097 A453 810m Apis mellifica   2.75 2.00

1996 Summer Olympic Games, Atlanta A455

Olympic emblem, and: 20m, Flags, Olympic rings, athletic field. 200m, Torch bearer, fireworks, "100," globe, vert. 390m, Early Olympic wrestlers.

1996, July 19   Litho.   Perf. 13
1099 A455 20m multicolored   .25 .25
1100 A455 200m multicolored   .50 .35
1101 A455 390m multicolored   1.00 .85
    Nos. 1099-1101 (3)   1.75 1.45

Code of Personal Status (Women's Liberation), 40th Anniv. — A456

1996, Aug. 13   Perf. 14
1102 A456 200m multicolored   .50 .35

Landmarks A457   Intl. Year to Fight Poverty A458

Designs: 20m, Ramparts of Sousse, horiz. 200m, Numidian Mausoleum, Dougga. 390m, Arch of Trajan, Makthar, horiz.

1996, Sept. 16   Photo.   Perf. 11½
Granite Paper
1103 A457 20m multicolored   .25 .25
1104 A457 200m multicolored   .45 .35
1105 A457 390m multicolored   1.00 .85
    Nos. 1103-1105 (3)   1.70 1.45

1996, Oct. 17   Litho.   Perf. 13x13½
1106 A458 390m multicolored   .85 .65

Appointment of Pres. Zine El Abidine, 9th Anniv.
A459   A460

1996, Nov. 7
1107 A459 200m multicolored   .45 .35
1108 A460 390m multicolored   .75 .75

National Day of Saharan Tourism — A461

Designs: No. 1109, Camels, oasis, balloon. No. 1110, Decorative designs.

1996, Nov. 12   Litho.   Perf. 13¼x13
1109 200m multi   .40 .35
1110 200m multi   .40 .35
  a. A461 Horiz. pair, #1109-1110   1.00 1.00

Ezzitouna Mosque, 1300th Anniv. — A462

1996, Nov. 25   Litho.   Perf. 14x13½
1111 A462 250m multicolored   .55 .40

Natl. Solidarity Day
A463   A464

1996, Dec. 8   Perf. 13x13½
1112 A463 500m multicolored   .95 .95
1113 A464 500m multicolored   .95 .95

World Human Rights Day — A465   UNICEF, 50th Anniv. — A466

1996, Dec. 10
1114 A465 500m multicolored   1.10 .90

1996, Dec. 11
1115 A466 810m multicolored   1.75 1.50

Musical Instruments — A467

1996, Dec. 26   Litho.   Perf. 13½
1116 A467 250m Mezoued   .60 .50
1117 A467 300m Gombri   .75 .60
1118 A467 350m Tabla   .85 .65
1119 A467 500m Tar Tounsi (Riq)   1.25 .90
    Nos. 1116-1119 (4)   3.45 2.65

Perf. 13½x13¼
1119A   Vert. strip of 4   — —
  b. A467 20m Tabla, 38x25mm   — —
  c. A467 30m Mezoued, 38x25mm   — —
  d. A467 50m Gombri, 38x25mm   — —
  e. A467 100m Tar Tounsi, 38x25mm   — —

World Book and Copyright Day A468

1997, Apr. 23   Litho.   Perf. 13½
1120 A468 1d multicolored   2.40 1.75

Marine Life A469

Designs: 50m, Mytilus galloprovincialis. 70m, Tapes decussatus. 350m, Octopus vulgaris. 500m, Sepia officinalis.

1997, May 13
1121 A469 50m multicolored   .25 .25
1122 A469 70m multicolored   .25 .25
1123 A469 350m multicolored   .85 .65
1124 A469 500m multicolored   1.40 1.25
    Nos. 1121-1124 (4)   2.75 2.40

PACIFIC 97, Intl. Stamp Exhibition, San Francisco — A470

1997, May 29 Photo. Perf. 11½x12
Granite Paper
1125 A470 250m multicolored .60 .40

A471   A472

1997, June 16 Litho. Perf. 13½
1126 A471 350m multicolored .90 .65
Mediterranean Games, Bari.

1997, July 15
1127 A472 250m multicolored .60 .40
Tunis, 1997 Cultural Capital.

Republic, 40th Anniv. A473

A474

1997, July 25
1128 A473 130m multicolored .35 .25
1129 A474 500m multicolored 1.25 1.00

Reptiles A475

100m, Uromastix acanthinurus. 350m, Chamaeleo chamaeleon, vert. 500m, Varanus griseus.

1997, Sept. 9 Litho. Perf. 13½
1130 A475 100m multicolored .25 .25
1131 A475 350m multicolored 1.00 .65
1132 A475 500m multicolored 1.25 1.10
Nos. 1130-1132 (3) 2.50 2.00

Rosa Gallica Flore Pleno — A476

1997, Sept. 23 Litho. Perf. 13½
1134 A476 350m multicolored .90 .85

Intl. Day for Protection of the Elderly A477

1997, Oct. 1 Litho. Perf. 13½
1135 A477 250m multicolored .60 .40

Tunisian Works of Art — A478

#1136, "L'Automne," by Ammar Farhat. #1137, Sculpture, "Pecheur D'Hommes," by Hedi Selmi. #1138, "Au Cafe-Maure," by Farhat. #1139, "Le Viellard au Kanoun," by Farhat. #1140, "Cafe Des Nattes-Sidi Bou Said," by Hedi Khayachi. #1141, "Le Kouttab," by Yahia Turki. 1000d, "La Fileuse," by Farhat.

1997, Nov. 5
1136 A478 250m multi, vert. .55 .55
1137 A478 250m multi, vert. .55 .55
1138 A478 250m multi, vert. .55 .55
1139 A478 250m multi, vert. .55 .55
1140 A478 500m multi 1.10 1.10
1141 A478 500m multi 1.10 1.10
1142 A478 1000m multi, vert. 2.25 2.25
  a. Sheet of 7, #1136-1142, + 3 labels 7.25 7.25
Nos. 1136-1142 (7) 6.65 6.65

No. 1142a issued 11/7.

A479

A480

1997, Nov. 7
1143 A479 250m multicolored .60 .40
1144 A480 500m multicolored 1.10 1.10
Pres. Zine El Abidine, 10th anniv. of taking office.

Desert Rose — A481

1997, Nov. 29
1145 A481 250m multicolored .60 .40

Intl. Human Rights Day — A482

1997, Dec. 10 Litho. Perf. 13½
1146 A482 500m multicolored .90 .90

Horses A483

Designs: 50m, Arabian. 70m, Barb. 250m, Arabian barb, vert. 500m, Arabian, vert.

1997, Dec. 18 Perf. 12½x13
1147 A483 50m multicolored .25 .25
1148 A483 70m multicolored .25 .25
1149 A483 250m multicolored .75 .40
1150 A483 500m multicolored 1.50 .75
Nos. 1147-1150 (4) 2.75 1.65

Bombing of Sakiet Sidi Yoncef, 40th Anniv. A484

1998, Feb. 8
1151 A484 250m multicolored .60 .30

School Health Week A485

1998, Feb. 16 Litho. Perf. 12½x13
1152 A485 250m multicolored .60 .30

Bar Assoc. of Tunisia, Cent. — A486

1998, Mar. 27 Perf. 13x12½
1153 A486 250m multicolored .60 .30

Martyr's Day, 60th Anniv.
A487   A488

1998, Apr. 9
1154 A487 250m multicolored .50 .30
1155 A488 520m multicolored 1.10 .55

Okba Ibn Nafaa Mosque, Kairouan — A489

1998, May 28 Litho. Perf. 13
1156 A489 500m multicolored 1.25 .60

1998 World Cup Soccer Championships, France — A490

250m, Tunisian team. 500m Player, trophy.

1998, June 10 Litho. Perf. 13
1157 A490 250m multi .60 .30
1158 A490 500m multi, vert. 1.25 .60

Crustaceans — A491

1998, July 8 Perf. 12½x13
1159 A491 110m Crab .25 .25
1160 A491 250m Shrimp .60 .30
1161 A491 1000m Lobster 2.25 1.10
Nos. 1159-1161 (3) 3.10 1.65

21st Reassembly of the Democratic Congress (RCD) — A492

#1162, Pres. Zine El Abidine ben Ali, flag, emblems. #1163, People holding torches, flag, dove.

1998, July 30 Perf. 13
1162 A492 250m multi .60 .30
1163 A492 250m multi, vert. .60 .30

36th Intl. Congress on the History of
Medicine — A493

1998, Sept. 6   Litho.   *Perf. 13*
1164 A493 500m multicolored   1.25   .60

Paintings — A494

#1165, "The Weaver," by Ali Guermassi
(1923-92). #1166, "Woman Musician," by
Noureddine Khayachi (1917-87). 500m, Still
life by Ali Khouja (1947-91).

1998, Oct. 8
1165 A494 250m multi   .60   .30
1166 A494 250m multi, vert.   .60   .30
1167 A494 500m multi, vert.   1.25   .60
    Nos. 1165-1167 (3)   2.45 1.20

Central
Bank of
Tunisia,
40th Anniv.
A495

1998, Nov. 10   Litho.   *Perf. 13*
1168 A495 250m multicolored   .60   .30

A496

1998, Nov. 7
1169 A496 250m multicolored   .60   .30

Appointment of Pres. Zine El Abidine ben
Ali, 11th anniv.

Universal
Declaration
of Human
Rights,
50th Anniv.
A497

1998, Dec. 10   Litho.   *Perf. 12½x13*
1170 A497 250m multicolored   .65   .35

Averroes (Ibn Rushd) (1126-1198),
Philosopher — A498

1998, Dec. 12
1171 A498 500m multicolored   1.25   .60

Musicians
A499

1998, Dec. 21   *Perf. 12½x13, 13x12½*
1172 A499 250m Kaddour Srarfi   .60   .30
1173 A499 250m Saliha, vert.   .60   .30
1174 A499 500m Ali Riahi, vert.   1.25   .60
    Nos. 1172-1174 (3)   2.45 1.20

Boukornine Natl. Park — A500

1998, Dec. 29   Litho.   *Perf. 13*
1175 A500 70m Gazelles   .25   .25
1176 A500 110m Rabbit   .25   .25
1177 A500 250m Eagles   .60   .30
1178 A500 500m Cyclamens   1.25   .60
    Nos. 1175-1178 (4)   2.35 1.40

Fruit Trees
A501

1999, Feb. 27   Litho.   *Perf. 13*
1179 A501 250m Orange   .65   .30
1180 A501 250m Date, vert.   .65   .30
1181 A501 500m Olive   1.25   .60
    Nos. 1179-1181 (3)   2.55 1.20

Archaeological Sites — A502

50m, Gate, Thuburbo Majus. 250m, Thermal baths, Bulla Regia. 500m, Zaghouan
Aqueduct.

1999, Mar. 31   Litho.   *Perf. 13*
1182 A502 50m multi, vert.   .25   .25
1183 A502 250m multi   .55   .30
1184 A502 500m multi   1.25   .60
    Nos. 1182-1184 (3)   2.05 1.15

Paintings by
Tunisian
Artists
A503

Designs: No. 1185, "L'Intemporel," by
Moncef Ben Amor. No. 1186, "Fiancailles," by
Ali Guermassi. No. 1187, "La Poterie," by
Ammar Farhat. No. 1188, "Vendeur
d'ombrelles et d'eventails," by Yahia Turki.

1999, May 6   Litho.
1185 A503 250m multicolored   .55   .30
1186 A503 250m multicolored   .55   .30
1187 A503 500m multicolored   1.10   .55
1188 A503 500m multicolored   1.10   .55
    Nos. 1185-1188 (4)   3.30 1.70

Constitution, 40th Anniv. — A504

1999, June 1   Litho.   *Perf. 13*
1189 A504 250m multicolored   .85   .40

Flowers — A505

70m, Acacia cyanophilla. #1191, Bouganvil-
lea spectabilis. #1192, Papaver rhoeas. 500m,
Dianthus caryophylius.

1999, June 25   Litho.   *Perf. 12¾*
1190 A505 70m multicolored   .25   .25
1191 A505 250m multicolored   .65   .30
1192 A505 250m multicolored   .65   .30
1193 A505 500m multicolored   1.40   .70
   a.   Souvenir sheet, #1190-1193,
      imperf.   5.50 5.50
    Nos. 1190-1193 (4)   2.95 1.55

    No. 1193a sold for 1.50d.

Philex France 99 — A506

1999, July 2   *Perf. 13x12¾*
1194 A506 500m multicolored   1.75   .85

Tahar Haddad (b. 1899), Women's
Rights Advocate — A507

1999, Aug. 13   Litho.
1195 A507 500m multicolored   1.75   .85

Marine Life
A508

1999, Sept. 22   *Perf. 12¾*
1196 A508 250m Caretta caretta   .90   .45
1197 A508 500m Epinephelus
         marginatus   1.75   .85

National Organ Donation Day — A509

1999, Oct. 2   *Perf. 13x12¾*
1198 A509 250m multicolored   .90   .45

UPU, 125th   Elections — A511
Anniv. — A510

1999, Oct. 9   *Perf. 12¾*
1199 A510 500m multicolored   1.50   .75

1999, Oct. 10   Litho.
1200 A511 500m multicolored   1.75   .85

Tamarisk
A512

1999, Oct. 28   Litho.   *Perf. 12¾x13*
1201 A512 250m shown   .75   .35
1202 A512 500m Dromedary   1.50   .75

Appointment of
Pres. Zine El
Abidine Ben Ali,
12th
Anniv. — A513

1999, Nov. 7   *Perf. 13x12¾*
1203 A513 250m multi   .90   .45

Human Rights   Famous
Day — A514   Tunisians — A515

1999, Dec. 10   Litho.   *Perf. 13x12¾*
1204 A514 250m multi   .90   .45

1999, Dec. 28   *Perf. 13x12¾, 12¾x13*
#1205, Ahmed Ibn Abi Dhiaf (1802-74), his-
torian. #1206, Abdelaziz Thaalbi (1876-1944),
anti-colonial leader. 500m, Khemaies Tarnane
(1894-1964), musician.

1205 A515 250m multi   .75   .35
1206 A515 250m multi   .75   .35
1207 A515 500m multi, horiz.   1.50   .75
    Nos. 1205-1207 (3)   3.00 1.45

Millennium — A516

1999, Dec. 31 **Perf. 13**
1208 A516 250m multi .90 .45

A517

A518

Archaeology
A519

Design: 100m, Methred cup. 110m, Aghlabide plate. 250m, Zaghouan water temple. 500m, Ulysses and the Sirens mosaic.

2000, Apr. 22 **Litho.** **Perf. 13x13¼**
1209 A517 100m multi .35 .35
1210 A517 110m multi .45 .45
Perf. 13¼
1211 A518 250m multi 1.00 1.00
1212 A519 500m multi 2.00 2.00
Nos. 1209-1212 (4) 3.80 3.80

Ferry Carthage — A520

2000, Apr. 29 **Perf. 13¼x13**
1213 A520 500m multi 1.60 .80
a. Souvenir sheet, imperf. 7.50 3.75
No. 1213a sold for 2d.

Expo 2000, Hanover — A521

2000, June 1 **Perf. 13¼x13**
1214 A521 1d multi 3.50 1.75

Trees
A522

Designs: 50m, Carob. 100m, Apricot. 250m, Avocado, vert. 400m, Apple.

2000, July 5 **Litho.** **Perf. 12¾**
1215-1218 A522 Set of 4 3.00 1.50

2001 Mediterranean Games, Tunis — A523

2000, Sept. 2 **Litho.** **Perf. 13**
1219 A523 500m multi 1.60 .80
a. Souvenir sheet of 1, imperf. 3.75 1.90
No. 1219a sold for 1500m.

2000 Summer Olympics, Sydney — A524

2000, Sept. 22 **Perf. 12¾**
1220 A524 500m multi 1.60 .80
Souvenir Sheet
Imperf
1221 A524 1500m multi 3.75 1.90

Flowers — A525

Designs: 110m, Freesias. 200m, Chrysanthemums. No. 1224, 250m, "Golden Times" roses. No. 1225, 250m, Vase with flowers (33x49mm). 500m, "Calibra" roses.

2000, Oct. 21 **Perf. 12¾, 13 (#1225)**
1222-1226 A525 Set of 5 4.75 2.40

Appointment of Pres. Zine El Abidine Ben Ali, 13th Anniv.
A526

2000, Nov. 7 **Perf. 13**
1227 A526 250m multi 1.00 .50

Art — A527

Designs: 100m, Still Life, by Hédi Khayachi. No. 1229, 250m, Landscape, by Abdelaziz Berraies. No. 1230, 250m, The Knife Sharpener, by Ali Guermassi. 400m, Date and Milk Seller, by Yahia Turki, vert.

2000, Nov. 18
1228-1231 A527 Set of 4 3.00 1.50

Intl. Human Rights Day — A528

2000, Dec. 10
1232 A528 500m multi 1.75 .85

Shells — A529

Designs: 50m, Neverita josephinia. No. 1234, 250m, Phyllonotus trunculus. No. 1235, 250m, Columbella rustica. 1d, Arca noe.

2000, Dec. 29 **Perf. 13x13¼**
1233-1236 A529 Set of 4 5.25 2.50

A530

Famous Tunisians
A531

Designs: No. 1237, 250m, Imam Sahnoun. No. 1238, 250m, Imam Ibn Arafa. No. 1239, 250m, Ali Belhaouane (1909-58), vert. 1d, Mohamed Jamoussi (1910-82), musician.

2000, Dec. 30 **Perf. 12¾**
1237 A530 250m shown .75 .35
1238 A530 250m multi .75 .35
1239 A531 250m multi .75 .35
1240 A531 1d shown 3.00 1.50
Nos. 1237-1240 (4) 5.25 2.55

Tunisian Presidency of UN Security Council — A532

2001, Feb. 19 **Litho.** **Perf. 13**
1241 A532 250m multi 1.10 .55

World Fund of Solidarity
A533

2001, Mar. 29
1242 A533 500m multi 1.60 .80

Year of Digital Culture — A534

2001, May 17 **Perf. 12¾**
1243 A534 250m multi 1.10 .55

Mohamed Dorra, Child Killed in Israeli-Palestinian Violence — A535

2001, May 30
1244 A535 600m multi 2.25 1.10

A536 A537

Designs: No. 1245, 19th cent. ceramic tile, Qallaline. No. 1246, Gigthis, horiz. No. 1247, Tunis City Hall, horiz. 500m, Needles of Tabarka.

2001, Aug. 24
1245 A536 250m multi .55 .25
1246 A537 250m multi .55 .25
1247 A537 250m multi .55 .25
1248 A537 500m multi 1.00 .50
Nos. 1245-1248 (4) 2.65 1.25

2001
Mediterranean
Games,
Tunis — A538

Designs: No. 1249, 250m, No. 1251b, Track, stadium. No. 1250, 500m, No. 1251a, Runners, medal.

2001, Sept. 2   **Perf. 12¾**
1249-1250 A538   Set of 2   1.50 .75
Souvenir Sheet
Imperf
1251 A538 750m Sheet of 2,
       #a-b   3.00 1.50

Paintings — A539

Designs: No. 1252, 250m, Sidi Bou Said, by Pierre Boucherle. No. 1253, 250m, Still Life, by Boucherle. No. 1254, 250m, Dream in Traditional Space, by Aly Ben Salem, vert. 500m, Traditional Open-air Marriage, by Ben Salem.

2001, Sept. 29   Litho.   Perf. 13
1252-1255 A539   Set of 4   2.75 1.40

Year of
Dialogue
Among
Civilizations
A540

2001, Oct. 9   **Perf. 12¾x13**
1256 A540 500m multi   1.10 .55

National Employment Fund — A541

2001, Oct. 10
1257 A541 250m multi   .60 .30

Appointment of
Pres. Zine El
Abidine Ben Ali,
14th Anniv. — A542

2001, Nov. 7   **Perf. 13x12¾**
1258 A542 250m multi   .60 .30

Butterflies — A543

Designs: Nos. 1259, 1263a, 250m, Ariane. No. 1260, 250m, No. 1263c, 500m, Pacha à

deux queues. Nos. 1261, 1263b, 250m, Demi-deuil. Nos. 1262, 1263d, 500m, Grand paon de nuit.

2001, Nov. 15   **Perf. 13x13¼**
1259-1262 A543   Set of 4   3.00 1.50
Souvenir Sheet
Imperf
1263 A543   Sheet of 4, #a-d   3.50 1.75

Birds — A544

Designs: No. 1264, 250m, No. 1268a, 300m, Bec-croise des sapins. 500m, Mesange charbonnière. No. 1266, 600m, Cigogne blanche. No. 1267, 600m, Geai des chenes.

2001, Nov. 22   **Perf. 13**
1264-1267 A544   Set of 4   4.50 2.25
Souvenir Sheet
1268 A544   Sheet, #1265-1267,
             1268a   5.00 2.50

Intl. Human Rights
Day — A545

2001, Dec. 10   **Perf. 13x12¾**
1269 A545 250m multi   .60 .30

Famous
Men
A546

Designs: No. 1270, 250m, Ibrahim ibn al-Aghlab (757-812), founder of Aghlabid dynasty. No. 1271, 250m, Ibn Rachiq al Kairaouani (1000-71). 350m, Abdelaziz Laroui (1898-1971). 650m, Assad ibn al-Fourat (759-828).

2001, Dec. 29   **Perf. 12¾x13**
1270-1273 A546   Set of 4   3.25 1.60

Arabic
Calligraphy
A547

Designs: No. 1274, 350m, Shown. No. 1275, 350m, Calligraphy, vert.

2001, Dec. 31 Perf. 12¾x13, 13x12¾
1274-1275 A547   Set of 2   2.25 1.10

Archaeology
A548   A549

Designs: 250m, Kef casbah. 390m, Amphitheater, Oudhna, horiz. No. 1278, Baron of Erlanger Palace. No. 1279, Mosaic of Virgil.

Perf. 13x12¾, 12¾x13
2002, Mar. 26   **Litho.**
1276 A548 250m multi   .55 .25
1277 A548 390m multi   .85 .40
1278 A549 600m multi   1.25 .60
1279 A549 600m multi   1.25 .60
    Nos. 1276-1279 (4)   3.90 1.85

Animals of Zembra
and Zembretta Natl.
Park — A550

Designs: No. 1280, 250m, No. 1284a, 400m, Ovis musimon. No. 1281, 250m, No. 1284b, 400m, Oryctolagus cuniculus. No. 1282, 600m, Falco peregrinus brookei. No. 1283, 600m, Larus audouinii.

2002, Apr. 10   **Perf. 13**
1280-1283 A550   Set of 4   3.50 1.75
Souvenir Sheet
1284 A550   Sheet, #1282-1283,
             1284a-1284b   3.75 1.90

Sahara Desert
Tourism
A551

Designs: No. 1285, 250m, No. 1289a, 400m, Gazella leptoceros. No. 1286, 390m, No. 1289b, 400m, Sahara village. No. 1287, 600m, Horseman. No. 1288, 600m, Tamaghza.

2002, May 22   **Perf. 13¼**
1285-1288 A551   Set of 4   3.75 1.90
Souvenir Sheet
1289 A551   Sheet, #1287-1288,
             1289a-1289b, im-
             perf.   4.00 2.00

2002 World Cup Soccer
Championships, Japan and
Korea — A552

World Cup, Emblem of Tunisia and World Cup tournament and: No. 1290, 390m, No. 1292a, 500m, Player, map of Japan and Korea. No. 1291, 600m, 1292b, 1000m, Ball in goal net.

2002, May 29   **Perf. 13**
1290-1291 A552   Set of 2   2.00 1.00
Souvenir Sheet
1292 A552   Sheet of 2, #a-b   3.00 1.50

Famous
Men — A553

Designs: 100m, Sheikh Mohamed Senoussi (1851-1900). No. 1294, 250m, Mosbah Jarbou (1914-58). No. 1295, 250m, Mohamed Daghbaji (1885-1924). 1.10d, Abou al-Hassen al-Housri (1029-95).

2002, July 18   **Perf. 12¾**
1293-1296 A553   Set of 4   3.50 1.75

World Handicapped Games — A554

Tunisian flag and: 100m, Wheelchair racer. 700m, Discus thrower, vert.

2002, July 20
1297-1298 A554   Set of 2   1.75 .85

27th World
Veterinary
Congress,
Tunis
A555

2002, Sept. 25   Litho.   Perf. 12¾
1299 A555 600m multi   1.25 .60

Travel International Club, 20th
Anniv. — A556

2002, Oct. 25   Litho.   Perf. 13x13¼
1300 A556 600m multi   1.25 .60

Appointment of
Pres. Zine El
Abidine Ben Ali,
15th Anniv. — A557

2002, Nov. 7   **Perf. 13x12¾**
1301 A557 390m multi   .85 .40

Assassination of
Farhat Hached
(1914-52) — A558

2002, Dec. 3   Litho.   Perf. 13x12¾
1302 A558 390m multi   .85 .40

Intl. Human Rights
Day — A559

2002, Dec. 10
1303 A559 700m multi   1.50 .75

Art Type of 2001

Designs: No. 1304, 250m, Space for Gazelles, by Aly Ben Salem. No. 1305, 250m, Popular Arts, by Ammar Farhat, vert. No. 1306, 250m, Marriage, by Habib Bouabana, vert. 900m, Still Life, by Pierre Boucherle, vert.

2002, Dec. 28   **Perf. 13**
1304-1307 A539   Set of 4   3.50 1.75

Mosaics
A560

Designs: 390m, Spinner. 600m, Africa.

2003, Feb. 28
1308-1309 A560 Set of 2   2.10 1.00

Scouting in Tunisia, 70th
Anniv. — A561

"70" and scouts: 250m, Reading map, at computer, planting tree. 600m, Saluting flag, at computer, vert.

2003, Mar. 29   Litho.   Perf. 13
1310-1311 A561 Set of 2   1.75 .85

National Book
Year — A562

2003, Apr. 23
1312 A562 390m multi   .85 .40

The Washerwoman, by Yahia
Turki — A563

2003, June 13
1313 A563 1d multi   2.10 1.00

National
Tourism
Day — A564

2003, June 28   Perf. 13¼
1314 A564 600m multi   1.25 .60

Parks — A565

Designs: 200m, Farhat Hached Park, Rades. 250m, Friguia Animal Park. 390m, La Marsa Park. 1d, Ennahli Park.

2003, June 28   Perf. 13
1315-1318 A565 Set of 4   4.00 2.00

A566   A567

2003, July 28   Litho.   Perf. 13x12¾
1319 A566 250m multi   .70 .35

Congress of Ambition.

2003, Aug. 3
1320 A567 390m multi   .90 .45

Pres. Habib Bourguiba (1903-2000).

A568

Flora and Fauna — A569

Designs: Nos. 1321a, 50m, 1326, 600m, Oryx dammah. Nos. 1321b, 50m, 1324, 250m, Nyctanthes sambac. Nos. 1321c, 100m, 1323, 250m, Aries. Nos. 1321d, 100m, 1327, 1d, Myrtus communis. Nos. 1321e, 200m, 1325, 390m, Struthio camelus. Nos. 1321f, 200m, 1322, 100m, Rosa canina.

2003, Sept. 25   Perf. 12¾
1321   Strip of 6   1.60 .80
  a.-b. A568 50m Either single   .25 .25
  c.-d. A568 100m Either single   .25 .25
  e.-f. A568 200m Either single   .45 .25
1322-1327 A569 Set of 6   5.75 2.75

No. 1321 was issued in a sheet of 6 strips that sold for 4500m.

Appointment of
Pres. Zine El
Abidine Ben Ali,
16th Anniv. — A570

2003, Nov. 7   Litho.   Perf. 13x12¾
1328 A570 250m multi   .60 .30

First 5+5
Dialogue
Summit,
Tunis — A571

2003, Dec. 5   Perf. 13¼
1329 A571 600m multi   1.25 .60

Universal
Declaration of
Human
Rights — A572

2003, Dec. 10   Perf. 13x12¾
1330 A572 350m multi   .75 .35

Silver Items
A573

Designs: No. 1331, 600m, Machmoum. No. 1332, 600m, Jewelry.

2003, Dec. 18   Perf. 12¾x13
1331-1332 A573 Set of 2   2.50 1.25
1332a   Souvenir sheet, #1331-1332   2.50 2.50

No. 1332a sold for 1.50d.

African Soccer
Championships — A574

Designs: 250m, Stylized soccer players, African cup, map. 600m, Map of Africa as soccer player.

2004, Jan. 24   Perf. 13
1333-1334 A574 Set of 2   1.90 .95
Values are for stamps with surrounding selvage.

Ksar Helal
Congress, 70th
Anniv. — A575

2004, Mar. 2   Litho.   Perf. 13x12¾
1335 A575 250m multi   .60 .30

Arab League
Conference,
Tunis
A576

2004, May 22   Perf. 13
1336 A576 600m multi   1.25 .60

Copper Handicrafts — A577

Designs: 100m, Water jar, 18th cent. 200m, Ewer, 18th cent. 250m, Bucket, 19th cent. 600m, Brazier, 18th cent. 700m, Amphora, 18th cent. 1000m, Ewer, 19th cent.

2004, June 5   Perf. 13x13¼
1337-1342 A577 Set of 6   6.25 3.00
1343   Sheet, 3 each #1337, 1338, 1343a-1343d   7.50 3.75
  a. A577 50m Like #1340   .25 .25
  b. A577 150m Like #1342   .30 .25
  c. A577 250m Like #1341   .60 .30
  d. A577 300m Like #1339   .70 .35

No. 1343 sold for 3500m.

Coins and
Banknotes
A578

Designs: No. 1344, 250m, Gold coin, 706. No. 1345, 250m, Gold coin, 1767. No. 1346, 600m, Punic silver coin, 300 B.C. No. 1347, 600m, Punic gold coin, 310-290 B.C. 1000m, Banknote, 1847 (65x30mm).

2004, July 23   Perf. 13¼
1344-1348 A578 Set of 5   5.75 2.75
1348a   Souvenir sheet, #1344-1348 + label   5.75 2.75

No. 1348a sold for 3000m.

African
Development
Bank, 40th
Anniv.
A579

2004, Sept. 10   Litho.   Perf. 13
1349 A579 700m multi   1.50 .75

Children's Art — A580

2004, Oct. 20
1350 A580 250m multi .60 .30

Presidential and Legislative Elections A581

2004, Oct. 24
1351 A581 250m multi .60 .30

Appointment of Pres. Zine El Abidine Ben Ali, 17th Anniv. A582

2004, Nov. 7
1352 A582 250m multi .60 .30

El Abidine Mosque, Carthage — A583

2004, Nov. 11
1353 A583 250m multi .60 .30

Birds — A584

Designs: 100m, Oxyura leucocephala. No. 1355, 600m, Phoenicurus moussieri. No. 1356, 600m, Aythya nyroca. 1000m, Marmaronetta angustirostris.

2004, Nov. 20 *Perf. 13¼*
1354-1357 A584 Set of 4 5.00 2.50

Universal Declaration of Human Rights — A585

2004, Dec. 10 *Perf. 13x12¾*
1358 A585 350m multi .75 .35

Famous People A586

Designs: 250m, Ibn Chabbat (1221-85), writer. 500m, Ibn Charaf (1000-67), writer. No. 1361, 600m, Princess Elyssa. No. 1362, 600m, Hatem El Mekki (1918-2003), stamp designer, and #580, 619. No. 1363, 600m, Dr. Mongi Ben Hmida (1928-2002), neurologist.

2004, Dec. 18 *Perf. 12¾x13*
1359-1363 A586 Set of 5 5.50 2.75

World Handball Championships — A587

2005, Jan. 23 *Perf. 13*
1364 A587 600m multi 1.25 .60

Native Costumes — A588

Designs: 250m, Takhlila, Hammam Sousse. No. 1366, 390m, Tarf-Ras ceremonial costume, Kerkennah. No. 1367, 390m, Karmassoud jebba. 600m, Traditional bridal costume, Matmata.

2005, Mar. 16 *Perf. 13x12¾*
1365-1368 A588 Set of 4 3.50 1.75

World Summit on the Information Society, Tunis A589

2005, Apr. 7 *Litho. Perf. 13*
1369 A589 600m multi 1.25 .60

Sculptures of the Punic and Roman Eras — A590

Designs: No. 1370, 250m, Victory, 2nd cent. No. 1371, 250m, Aesculapius, 2nd-3rd cent. 600m, Pottery mask of a woman's face, 4th-5th cent. B.C. 1000m, Baal Ammon, 1st cent.

2005, May 18 *Perf. 13¼*
1370-1373 A590 Set of 4 4.50 2.25

World No Tobacco Day — A591

2005, May 31 *Perf. 13¼x13*
1374 A591 250m multi .60 .30

Rotary International, Cent. — A592

2005, June 22 *Perf. 13x12¾*
1375 A592 600m multi 1.25 .60

Intl. Year of Sport and Physical Education — A593

2005, July 1
1376 A593 600m multi 1.25 .60

World Scout Conference A594

2005, Sept. 5
1377 A594 600m multi 1.25 .60

Intl. Year of Physics A595

2005, Oct. 15 *Litho. Perf. 13*
1378 A595 2d multi 4.00 2.00

Appointment of Pres. Zine El Abidine Ben Ali, 18th Anniv. A596

2005, Nov. 8
1379 A596 250m multi .55 .25

World Summit on the Information Society, Tunis — A597

2005, Nov. 12 *Litho. Perf. 13¼x13*
1380 A597 600m multi .90 .45

Universal Declaration of the Rights of Man, 57th Anniv. A598

2005, Dec. 10 *Litho. Perf. 13*
1381 A598 350m multi 1.10 .55

Medicinal Plants — A599

Designs: 250m, Foeniculum. No. 1383, 600m, Mentha aquatica. No. 1384, 600m, Lavandula angustifloia. 1000m, Origanum majorana.

2005, Dec. 22
1382-1385 A599 Set of 4 5.25 2.50
1386 Booklet pane, 2 each #1383-1384, 1386a, 1386b 9.75 —
a. A599 600m Like #1382 1.25 .60
b. A599 600m Like #1385 1.25 .60
Complete booklet, #1386 9.75

Ibn Khaldun (1332-1406), Philosopher
A600

2006, Mar. 15   **Litho.**   **Perf. 13x12¾**
1387 A600 390m multi   .90 .45

A601

Independence, 50th Anniv. — A602

Designs: No. 1390, Stylized map and flag, doctor examining child. No. 1391, Bridge and ship. No. 1392, Stylized woman holding torch. No. 1393, Woman and book. No. 1394, Computer, man, woman, "@," and stylized dove.

2006, Mar. 18   **Perf. 13x12¾, 12¾x13**
1388 A601 250m shown   .60 .30
1389 A602 250m shown   .60 .30
1390 A601 250m multi   .60 .30
1391 A601 250m multi   .60 .30
1392 A601 390m multi   .85 .40
1393 A601 390m multi   .85 .40
1394 A601 390m multi   .85 .40
   a.   Souvenir sheet, #1388-1394, + 2 labels   5.00 5.00
   Nos. 1388-1394 (7)   4.95 2.40

    No. 1394a sold for 2.50d.

Dialogue Among Civilizations and Religions
A603

2006, Apr. 26   **Litho.**   **Perf. 13½**
1395 A603 1.35d multi   2.75 1.40

Punic and Roman Era Jewelry
A604

Designs: No. 1396, 250m, Gold and garnet vestment clasps. No. 1397, 250m, Gold-plated bronze earrings. No. 1398, 600m, Ring depicting god Baal Hammon. No. 1399, 600m, Gold and amethyst pendants.

2006, May 18   **Litho.**   **Perf. 13¼**
1396-1399 A604   Set of 4   3.75 1.90

Special Handicapped Employment Program — A605

2006, May 29   **Perf. 13**
1400 A605 2.35d multi   4.50 2.25

National Cleanliness and Environmental Protection Program — A606

2006, June 11
1401 A606 250m multi   .60 .30

2006 World Cup Soccer Championships, Germany — A607

Map, flags of Germany and Tunisia and: 250m, Feet of soccer players. 600m, Soccer player.

2006, June 14
1402-1403 A607   Set of 2   1.90 .95

Tunisian Army, 50th Anniv.
A608

2006, June 24
1404 A608 250m multi   .60 .30

Diplomatic Relations Between Tunisia and Japan, 50th Anniv.
A609

2006, July 7
1405 A609 700m multi   1.40 .70

Vacation Safety Program — A610

2006, July 31
1406 A610 250m multi   .60 .30

Personal Status Code, 50th Anniv.
A611

2006, Aug. 8
1407 A611 2.35d multi   4.50 2.25

Appointment of Pres. Zine El Abidine Ben Ali, 19th Anniv.
A612

2006, Nov. 7
1408 A612 250m multi   .60 .30

Universal Declaration of Human Rights — A613

2006, Dec. 10
1409 A613 700m multi   1.40 .70

Traditional Clothing and Textiles
A614

Designs: No. 1410, 250m, Jelwa (wedding dress). No. 1411, 250m, Silk jebba. 1.10d, Klim. 1.35d, Woolen blanket from Gafsa.

2007, Mar. 16   **Litho.**   **Perf. 13**
1410-1413 A614   Set of 4   6.75 3.25

Independence, 51st Anniv. — A615

2007, Mar. 20
1414 A615 250m multi   .60 .30

Youth and Digital Culture
A616

2007, Mar. 21
1415 A616 250m multi   .60 .30

Natl. Energy Conservation Program
A617

2007, Apr. 7
1416 A617 1d multi   2.10 1.00

Dialogue Between Cultures, Civilizations and Religions
A618

2007, May 7   **Litho.**   **Perf. 13**
1417 A618 600m multi   1.25 .60

Archaeological Sites — A619

Designs: No. 1418, 250m, Baths of Caracalla, Dougga. No. 1419, 250m, Punic city of Kerkouane. No. 1420, 600m, Baths, Makthar. No. 1421, 600m, Capitol, Sbeitla.

2007, May 18   **Perf. 13½**
1418-1421 A619   Set of 4   3.75 1.90

Carthage Investment Forum — A620

2007, June 21   *Perf. 13*
1422 A620 600m multi   1.25   .60

National Tourism Day — A621

Designs: No. 1423, 250m, Sahara tourism. No. 1424, 250m, Beach tourism. No. 1425, 600m, Tabarka Jazz Festival. No. 1426, 600m, Golf tourism.

2007, June 28
1423-1426 A621   Set of 4   3.75 1.90

A622

Republic of Tunisia, 50th Anniv. A623

2007, July 25   Litho.   *Perf. 13*
1427 A622 250m multi   .60   .30
1428 A623 250m multi   .60   .30

Appointment of Pres. Zine El Abidine Ben Ali, 20th Anniv. A624

2007, Nov. 7   Litho.   *Perf. 13*
1429 A624 250m multi   .60   .30

Friendship Between Germany and Tunisia, 50th Anniv. A625

2007, Dec. 17
1430 A625 600m multi   1.25   .60

Intl. Human Solidarity Day — A626

2007, Dec. 20
1431 A626 1.35d multi   3.00 1.50

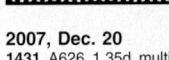

French Air Raid on Sakiet Sidi Youssef, 50th Anniv. A627

2008, Feb. 8   Litho.   *Perf. 13*
1432 A627 250m multi   .60   .30

Government Accounting Board, 40th Anniv. — A628

2008, Mar. 8   Litho.   *Perf. 13*
1433 A628 250m multi   .45   .25

Universal Declaration of Human Rights, 60th Anniv. — A629

2008, Mar. 10
1434 A629 600m multi   1.10   .55

World Meteorological Day — A630

2008, Mar. 23
1435 A630 250m multi   .45   .25

Terra Cotta Objects — A631

Designs: 250m, Water jug, 19th cent. No. 1437, 600m, Goblet, 3rd cent. B.C. No. 1438, 600m, Plate, 10th cent. B.C. 1.10d, Lamp, 1st cent. B.C.

2008, May 18   *Perf. 13x12¾*
1436-1439 A631   Set of 4   4.50 2.25

National Day of the Disabled A632

2008, May 29   *Perf. 13*
1440 A632 250m multi   .45   .25

Fish — A633

Designs: No. 1441, 250m, Mugil cephalus. No. 1442, 250m, Thunnus thynnus. No. 1443, 600m, Sparus aurata. No. 1444, 600m, Dicentrarchus labrax.

2008, June 5   Litho.   *Perf. 13x13¼*
1441-1444 A633   Set of 4   3.00 1.50
1444a   As #1444, with incomplete frame lines   1.10   .55
1444b   Souvenir sheet, #1441-1443, 1444a   3.25 1.60

No. 1444b sold for 1.800d.

Democratic Constitutional Rally — A634

2008, July 30   *Perf. 13*
1445 A634 250m multi   .45   .25

Souvenir Sheet

Arab Post Day — A635

No. 1446 — Emblem and: a, World map, pigeon. b, Camel caravan.

2008, Aug. 3   *Perf. 12¾*
1446 A635 600m Sheet of 2, #a-b   2.00 1.00

2008 Summer Olympics, Beijing A636

Olympic rings, star and crescent, emblem of 2008 Summer Olympics, symbols of athletic events and: No. 1447, 250m, Colored dots and ribbons. No. 1448, 600m, Starbursts.

2008, Aug. 8   *Perf. 13½*
1447-1448 A636   Set of 2   1.40   .70
1448a   Souvenir sheet of 2 #1447-1448   1.50   .75

No. 1448a sold for 900m.

Dialogue With Youth A637

2008, Sept. 20   Litho.   *Perf. 13¼*
1449 A637 250m multi   .40   .25

Appointment of Pres. Zine El Abidine Ben Ali, 21st Anniv. A638

2008, Nov. 7   *Perf. 13x13¼*
1450 A638 250m multi   .40   .25

University of Tunisia, 50th Anniv. — A639

2008, Nov. 11   *Perf. 13¼x13*
1451 A639 250m multi   .40 .25

Famous Men A640

Designs: No. 1452, 250m, Ridha El Kalai (1931-2004), musician. No. 1453, 250m, Ammar Farhat (1911-87), painter. No. 1454, 600m, Mahmoud Messadi (1911-2004), writer. No. 1455, 600m, Hedi Jouini (1909-90), musician.

2008, Dec. 20   *Perf. 12¾x13, 13x12¾*
1452-1455 A640 Set of 4   2.60 1.25

Arab Maghreb Union, 20th Anniv. — A641

2009, Feb. 17   Litho.   *Perf. 13*
1456 A641 250m multi   .35 .25

Aboul Qasem Chebbi (1909-34), Poet — A642

2009, Feb. 24   *Perf. 12¾*
1457 A642 250m multi   .35 .25

Kairouan, 2009 Islamic Cultural Capital — A643

Designs: No. 1458, 250m, Mausoleum of Abi Zamaa al-Balawi. No. 1459, 250m, Okba Ibn Nafaa Mosque. 1000m, Emblem.

2009, Mar. 8
1458-1460 A643 Set of 3   2.25 1.10
1460a   Souvenir sheet, #1458-1460   2.25 1.10

Woven Fiber Crafts A644

Designs: No. 1461, 250m, Esparto basket and jug holder. No. 1462, 250m, Rattan mat. No. 1463, 600m, Palm fiber fan. No. 1464, 600m, Rattan basket.

2009, Mar. 16   *Perf. 13¼*
1461-1464 A644 Set of 4   2.50 1.25

Intl. Society for Military Law and the Law of War, 18th Congress A645

2009, May 5   Litho.   *Perf. 13*
1465 A645 700m multi   1.10 .55

Constitution, 50th Anniv. — A646

2009, June 1
1466 A646 250m multi   .40 .25

Fruit — A647

Designs: 250m, Eryobotrica japonica. No. 1468, 600m, Cerasus spp. No. 1469, 600m, Ficus carica. No. 1470, 600m, Prunus persica.

2009, June 5   *Perf. 13¼*
1467-1470 A647 Set of 4   3.00 1.50
1470a   Sheet of 4, #1467-1470   3.25 1.60

No. 1470a sold for 2.10d.

16th Mediterranean Games, Pescara, Italy — A648

2009, June 26   Litho.   *Perf. 13*
1471 A648 600m multi   .90 .45

Presidential and Legislative Elections A649

2009, Oct. 25   Litho.   *Perf. 13x13¼*
1472 A649 250m multi   .40 .25

Appointment of Pres. Zine El Abidine Ben Ali, 22nd Anniv. A650

2009, Nov. 7
1473 A650 390m multi   .65 .30

Universal Declaration of Human Rights, 61st Anniv. A651

2009, Dec. 10
1474 A651 1.35d multi   2.10 1.10

Tunisian Cuisine A652

Designs: 250m, Tajine à la viande (meat tagine). 700m, Salade mechouia (grilled vegetable salad). 1000m, Poisson grillé (grilled fish). 1100m, Couscous à la viande (couscous with meat).

2009, Dec. 26   *Perf. 13¼*
1475-1478 A652 Set of 4   4.75 2.40
1478a   Souvenir sheet of 4, #1475-1478   4.75 2.40

Arab Women's Day — A653

2010, Feb. 1   *Perf. 13¼x13*
1479 A653 1350m multi   2.00 1.00

Intl. Year of Rapprochement of Cultures — A654

2010, Feb. 6   *Perf. 13x13¼*
1480 A654 2350m multi   3.50 1.75

Intl. Youth Year — A655

2010, Mar. 21   *Perf. 13¼x13*
1481 A655 390m multi   .60 .30

Expo 2010, Shanghai A656

2010, May 1   *Perf. 13¼*
1482 A656 390m multi   .55 .30

Organic Foods and Food Products A657

Designs: No. 1483, 250m, Cynara scolymus. No. 1484, 250m, Prunus dulcis. No. 1485, 250m, Punica granatum. No. 1486, 600m, Capsicum annuum. No. 1487, 600m, Opuntia ficus-indica. No. 1488, 600m, Solanum lycopersicum. No. 1489, 600m, Olea europaea and picher of olive oil. No. 1490, 600m, Phoenix dactylifera.

2010, May 12
1483-1490 A657 Set of 8   5.00 2.50
1490a   Souvenir sheet, #1483-1490   5.00 2.50

Tunisia, a Technological Pole — A658

2010, May 17   *Perf. 13*
1491 A658 390m multi   .55 .25

Year of Peace and Security in Africa
A659

2010, June 25
1492 A659 250m multi .35 .25

Landmarks in Medina of Tunis — A660

Designs: No. 1493, 250m, Bab El Khadra. No. 1494, 250m, Bab Jedid. No. 1495, 250m, Dar Hsine. No. 1496, 250m, Dar Ben Abdallah. 600m, Bab Bhar. 1000m, Bab Saâdoun.

2010, July 2 Perf. 12¾
1493-1498 A660 Set of 6 3.50 1.75

2010 Youth Olympics, Singapore
A661

2010, Aug. 4 Perf. 13
1499 A661 700m multi .95 .45

Famous Men — A662

Designs: 250m, Zoubeir Turki (1924-2009), painter. 600m, Jaâfar Majed (1940-2009), poet. 1000m, Ali Ben Salem (1910-2001), painter. 1100m, Mustapha Khraief (1910-67), poet.

2010, Oct. 10 Perf. 12¾
1500-1503 A662 Set of 4 4.25 2.10

Third Congress of Organization of Arab Women, Tunis — A663

2010, Oct. 28 Perf. 13
1504 A663 1350m multi 2.00 1.00

Appointment of Pres. Zine El Abidine Ben Ali, 23rd Anniv.
A664

2010, Nov. 7
1505 A664 390m multi .55 .30

National Year of Tunisian Cinema
A665

2010, Nov. 27 Litho.
1506 A665 390m multi .55 .25

Universal Declaration of Human Rights, 62nd Anniv.
A666

2010, Dec. 10
1507 A666 390m multi .55 .25

A667

A668

A669

Revolution of 2010-11
A670

2011, Mar. 25 Litho. Perf. 13
1508 A667 250m multi .40 .25
1509 A668 390m multi .60 .30
1510 A669 600m multi .90 .45
1511 A670 1350m multi 2.00 1.00
Nos. 1508-1511 (4) 3.90 2.00

World Book and Copyright Day — A671

2011, Apr. 23
1512 A671 2350m multi 3.50 1.75

World Press Freedom Day — A672

2011, May 3
1513 A672 250m multi .40 .25

Children's Art — A673

Designs: 700m, I Love My Country, by Syrine Zouari. 1350m, Spring, by Mustapha Gader, vert.

2011, May 20 Perf. 13
1514-1515 A673 Set of 2 3.00 1.50

Medicinal Plants
A674

Designs: No. 1516, 250m, Allium sativum. No. 1517, 250m, Pimpinella anisum. 600m, Lippia tryphilla. 1000m, Rosemarinus officinalis.

2011, June 28 Perf. 13¼
1516-1519 A674 Set of 4 3.00 1.50

Phila Nippon 2011 Intl. Philatelic Exhibition, Yokahama, Japan
A675

2011, July 28
1520 A675 250m multi .40 .25

Human Rights Day — A676

2011, Dec. 10 Perf. 13
1521 A676 390m multi .55 .25

January 14 Revolution, 1st Anniv.
A679

2012, Jan. 14
1522 A677 390m multi .55 .25

Pottery
A678

Designs: Nos. 1523, 1527a, 250m, Maajina plate. Nos. 1524, 1527b, 600m, Borniya jar. Nos. 1525, 1527c, 900m, Charbiya jug. Nos. 1526, 1527d, 1000m, Quallaline receptacle.

2012, Mar. 23 Perf. 13¼
Stamps With White Backgrounds
1523-1526 A678 Set of 4 3.75 1.90
Souvenir Sheet
Stamps With Buff Backgrounds
1527 A678 Sheet of 4, #a-d 3.75 1.90

SEMI-POSTAL STAMPS

No. 36 Overprinted in Red

1915, Feb.   Unwmk.   Perf. 14x13½
B1   A5   15c vio, *pnksh*   1.60 1.60

No. 32 Overprinted in Red

1916, Feb. 15
B2   A4   5c grn, *grnsh*   2.40 2.40

Types of Regular Issue of 1906 in New Colors and Surcharged

1916, Aug.
B3   A5   10c on 15c brn vio,
           bl   1.30 1.30
B4   A5   10c on 20c brn, *org*   1.50 1.50
B5   A5   10c on 25c bl, *grn*   4.00 4.00
B6   A6   10c on 35c ol grn &
           vio   8.00 8.00
B7   A6   10c on 40c bis & blk   5.25 5.25
B8   A6   10c on 75c vio brn
           & grn   12.00 12.00
B9   A7   10c on 1fr red & grn   8.00 8.00
B10 A7   10c on 2fr bis & bl   110.00 110.00
B11 A7   10c on 5fr vio & red   140.00 140.00
     Nos. B3-B11 (9)   290.05 290.05

Nos. B3-B11 were sold at their face value but had a postal value of 10c only. The excess was applied to the relief of prisoners of war in Germany.

Types of Regular Issue of 1906 in New Colors and Surcharged in Carmine

1918
B12 A5   15c on 20c blk, *grn*   2.40 2.40
B13 A5   15c on 25c dk bl,
           buff   2.40 2.40
B14 A6   15c on 35c gray grn
           & red   3.25 3.25
B15 A6   15c on 40c brn & lt
           bl   5.50 5.50
B16 A6   15c on 75c red brn
           & blk   13.00 13.00
B17 A7   15c on 1fr red & vio   35.00 35.00
B18 A7   15c on 2fr bis brn &
           red   110.00 110.00
B19 A7   15c on 5fr vio & blk   190.00 190.00
     Nos. B12-B19 (8)   361.55 361.55

The different parts of the surcharge are more widely spaced on the stamps of types A6 and A7. These stamps were sold at their face value but had a postal value of 15c only. The excess was intended for the relief of prisoners of war in Germany.

Types of 1906-22 Surcharged

1923
B20 A4   0c on 1c blue   1.20 1.20
B21 A4   0c on 2c ol brn   1.20 1.20
B22 A4   1c on 3c green   1.20 1.20
B23 A4   2c on 5c red vio   1.20 1.20
B24 A9   3c on 10c vio, *blu-
           ish*   1.20 1.20
B25 A5   5c on 15c ol grn   1.20 1.20
B26 A5   5c on 20c bl, *pink*   2.40 2.40
B27 A5   5c on 25c vio, *blu-
           ish*   2.40 2.40
B28 A9   5c on 30c orange   2.40 2.40
B29 A6   5c on 35c bl & vio   4.75 4.75
B30 A6   5c on 40c bl & brn   4.75 4.75
B31 A9   10c on 50c blk, *blu-
           ish*   6.50 6.50
B32 A6   10c on 60c ol brn &
           bl   8.75 8.75

B33 A6   10c on 75c vio & lt
           grn   9.50 9.50
B34 A7   25c on 1fr mar & vio   9.50 9.50
B35 A7   25c on 2fr bl & rose   30.00 30.00
B36 A7   25c on 5fr grn & ol
           brn   80.00 80.00
     Nos. B20-B36 (17)   168.15 168.15

These stamps were sold at their original values but had postal franking values only to the amounts surcharged on them. The difference was intended to be used for the benefit of wounded soldiers.

This issue was entirely speculative. Before the announced date of sale most of the stamps were taken by postal employees and practically none of them were offered to the public.

Mail Delivery — SP1

Type of Parcel Post Stamps, 1906, with Surcharge in Black

1925, June 7   Perf. 13½x14
B37 SP1   1c on 5c brn &
            red, *pink*   .80   .80
  a.   Surcharge omitted   160.00 160.00
B38 SP1   2c on 10c brn &
            bl, *yel*   .80   .80
B39 SP1   3c on 20c red vio
            & rose, *lav*   1.60 1.60
B40 SP1   5c on 25c sl grn
            & rose, *bluish*   1.60 1.60
B41 SP1   5c on 40c rose &
            grn, *yel*   1.60 1.60
B42 SP1   10c on 50c vio &
            bl, *lav*   3.25 3.25
B43 SP1   10c on 75c grn &
            ol, *grnsh*   3.25 3.25
B44 SP1   25c on 1fr bl &
            grn, *bluish*   3.25 3.25
B45 SP1   25c on 2fr rose &
            vio, *pnksh*   14.50 14.50
B46 SP1   25c on 5fr red &
            brn, *lem*   52.50 52.50
     Nos. B37-B46 (10)   83.15 83.15

These stamps were sold at their original values but paid postage only to the amount of the surcharged values. The difference was given to Child Welfare societies.

Tunis-Chad Motor Caravan SP2

1928, Feb.   Engr.   Perf. 13½
B47 SP2   40c + 40c org brn   1.60 1.60
B48 SP2   50c + 50c dp vio   2.00 2.00
B49 SP2   75c + 75c dk bl   2.00 2.00
B50 SP2   1fr + 1fr carmine   2.00 2.00
B51 SP2   1.50fr + 1.50fr brt bl   2.00 2.00
B52 SP2   2fr + 2fr dk grn   2.40 2.40
B53 SP2   5fr + 5fr red brn   2.40 2.40
     Nos. B47-B53 (7)   14.40 14.40

The surtax on these stamps was for the benefit of Child Welfare societies.

Nos. 122-135, 137-142 Surcharged in Black

a

b

1938   Perf. 11, 12½, 12½x13
B54 A14(a)   1c + 1c   3.25 3.25
B55 A14(a)   2c + 2c   3.25 3.25
B56 A14(a)   3c + 3c   3.25 3.25
B57 A14(a)   5c + 5c   3.25 3.25

B58 A14(a)   10c + 10c   3.25 3.25
B59 A15(a)   15c + 15c   3.25 3.25
B60 A15(a)   20c + 20c   3.25 3.25
B61 A15(a)   25c + 25c   3.25 3.25
B62 A15(a)   30c + 30c   3.25 3.25
B63 A15(a)   40c + 40c   3.25 3.25
B64 A16(a)   50c + 50c   3.25 3.25
B65 A16(a)   75c + 75c   3.25 3.25
B66 A16(a)   90c + 90c   3.25 3.25
B67 A16(a)   1fr + 1fr   3.25 3.25
B68 A17(b)   1.50fr + 1fr   3.25 3.25
B69 A17(b)   2fr + 1.50fr   5.50 5.50
B70 A17(b)   3fr + 2fr   6.50 6.50
B71 A17(b)   5fr + 3fr   24.00 24.00
  a.   Perf. 12½   120.00 120.00
B72 A17(b)   10fr + 5fr   52.50 52.50
B73 A17(b)   20fr + 10fr   80.00 80.00
     Nos. B54-B73 (20)   217.25 217.25

50th anniversary of the post office.

Nos. 86, 100-101, 105 Surcharged in Black, Blue or Red

1941   Perf. 14x13½
B74 A11   1fr on 45c (Bk)   .65   .65
B75 A13   1.30fr on 1.25fr (Bl)   .65   .65
B76 A13   1.50fr on 1.40fr (Bk)   .65   .65
B77 A13   2fr on 2.25fr (R)   .90   .90
     Nos. B74-B77 (4)   2.85 2.85

The surcharge measures 11x14mm on #B74.

Catalogue values for unused stamps in this section, from this point to the end of the section, are for Never Hinged items.

British, French and American Soldiers SP3

1943   Litho.   Perf. 12
B78 SP3   1.50fr + 8.50fr crimson   .65   .25
Liberation of Tunisia.

Children — SP3a

1944   Engr.   Perf. 13½
B78A SP3a   1.20fr + 1.30fr brown   1.25
B78B SP3a   1.50fr + 2fr black
             brown   1.25
B78C SP3a   2fr + 3fr dark
             green   1.25
B78D SP3a   3fr + 4fr red or-
             ange   1.25
     Nos. B78A-B78D (4)   5.00

National welfare fund.
Nos. B78A-B78D were issued by the Vichy government in France, but were not issued in Tunisia.

Native Scene — SP4

Surcharged in Black

1944   Perf. 11½
B79 SP4   2fr + 48fr red   1.60 1.60
The surtax was for soldiers.

Sidi Mahrez Mosque — SP5

Ramparts of Sfax — SP6

Fort Saint — SP7

Sidi-bou-Said — SP8

1945   Unwmk.   Litho.   Perf. 11½
B80 SP5   1.50fr + 8.50fr choc &
            red   1.60 1.25
B81 SP6   3fr + 12fr dk bl grn &
            red   1.60 1.25
B82 SP7   4fr + 21fr brn org &
            red   1.60 1.25
B83 SP8   10fr + 40fr red & blk   1.60 1.25
     Nos. B80-B83 (4)   6.40 5.00

The surtax was for soldiers.

France No. B193 Overprinted in Black — c

1945   Perf. 14x13½
B84 SP147   2fr + 1fr red org   .80   .55

The surtax was for the aid of tuberculosis victims.

Same Overprint on Type of France, 1945

1945   Engr.   Perf. 13
B85 SP150   2fr + 3fr dk grn   1.25   .65
Stamp Day.

Same Overprint on France No. B192
1945
B86 SP146   4fr + 6fr dk vio brn   .80   .55

The surtax was for war victims of the P.T.T.

Types of 1926
Surcharged in Carmine

1945   Typo.   Perf. 14x13½
B87 A10   4fr + 6fr on 10c ultra   .70   .55
B88 A12   10fr + 30fr on 80c dk grn   .70   .55

The design of type A12 is redrawn, omitting "RF." The surtax was for war veterans.

Tunisian Soldier — SP9

1946   Unwmk.   Engr.   Perf. 13
B89 SP9   20fr + 30fr grn, red & blk   2.00   1.60

The surtax aided Tunisian soldiers in Indo-China.

Type of France Overprinted Type "c" in Carmine

1946
B90 SP160   3fr + 2fr dk bl   1.60   1.25
Stamp Day.

Stamps and Types of 1926-46 Surcharged in Carmine and Black

1946   Perf. 14x13½
B91 A12   80c + 50c emerald   1.60   1.25
B92 A12   1.50fr + 1.50fr rose lil   1.60   1.25
B93 A12   2fr + 2fr Prus grn   1.60   1.25
B94 A13   2.40fr + 2fr sal pink   1.60   1.25
B95 A13   4fr + 4fr ultra   2.40   1.60
Nos. B91-B95 (5)   8.80   6.60

The two parts of the surcharge are more widely spaced on stamps of type A13.

Type of France Overprinted Type "c" in Carmine

1947   Perf. 13
B96 SP172   4.50fr + 5.50fr sepia   1.60   1.25

On Type of France Surcharged in Carmine with New Value and Bars
B97 SP158   10fr + 15fr on 2fr + 3fr brt ultra   1.60   1.25

Type of 1926 Surcharged in Carmine

1947   Typo.   Perf. 14x13½
B98 A13   10fr + 40fr black   1.60   1.25

Feeding Young Bird — SP10

1947   Engr.   Perf. 13
B99 SP10   4.50fr + 5.50fr dk bl grn   2.00   1.60
B100 SP10   6fr + 9fr brt ultra   2.00   1.60

B101 SP10   8fr + 17fr dp car   2.00   1.60
B102 SP10   10fr + 40fr dk pur   2.00   1.60
Nos. B99-B102 (4)   8.00   6.40

The surtax was for child welfare.

Type of Regular Issue of 1948 Surcharged in Blue

1948
B103 A21   4fr + 10fr ol grn & org   1.60   1.25

The surtax was for anti-tuberculosis work.

Arch of Triumph, Sbeitla SP11

1948
B104 SP11   10fr + 40fr ol grn & olive   2.00   1.60
B105 SP11   18fr + 42fr dk bl & indigo   2.00   1.60

Surtax for charitable works of the army.

Arago Type of France Overprinted in Carmine

1948
B106 SP176   6fr + 4fr brt car   1.60   1.25
Stamp Day, Mar. 6-7.

Sleeping Child SP12

1949, June 1
B107 SP12   25fr + 50fr dk grn   3.25   2.40

The surtax was for child welfare.

Neptune Type of 1947 Surcharged in Black with Lorraine Cross and "FFL+15F"

1949, Dec. 8
B108 A20   10fr + 15fr dp ultra & car   2.00   1.60

The surtax was for the Tunisian section of the Association of Free French.

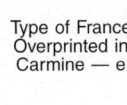

Type of France Overprinted in Carmine — e

1949, Mar. 26
B109 SP180   15fr + 5fr indigo   2.00   1.60
Stamp Days, Mar. 26-27.

Type of France, 1950, Ovptd. Like No. B106 in Ultramarine

1950, Mar. 11   Unwmk.   Perf. 13
B110 SP183   12fr + 3fr greenish black   2.75   2.40

Stamp Days, Mar. 11-12.

Tunisian and French Woman Shaking Hands SP13

1950, June 5
B111 SP13   15fr + 35fr red   2.00   1.60
B112 SP13   25fr + 45fr dp ultra   2.00   1.60

The surtax was for Franco-Tunisian Mutual Assistance.

Arab Soldier — SP14

1950, Aug. 21   Engr.
B113 SP14   25fr + 25fr dp bl   3.25   2.40

The surtax was for old soldiers.

Type of France Overprinted Type "c" in Black

1951, Mar. 10
B114 SP186   12fr + 3fr brnsh gray   2.40   1.60
Stamp Days, Mar. 10-11.

Mother Carrying Child SP15

1951, June 19   Engr.   Perf. 13
B115 SP15   30fr + 15fr dp ultra   3.50   2.75

The surtax was for child welfare.

National Cemetery of Gammarth SP16

1952, June 15
B116 SP16   30fr + 10fr blue   3.25   2.40

Surtax aided orphans of the military services.

Type of France Overprinted Type "e" in Lilac

1952, Mar. 8   Unwmk.
B117 SP190   12fr + 3fr purple   2.00   1.60
Stamp Day, Mar. 8.

Stucco Work, Bardo SP17   Boy Campers SP18

1952, May 5   Engr.   Perf. 13
B118 SP17   15fr + 1fr ultra & indigo   1.60   1.25

Surtax for charitable works of the army.

1952, June 15
B119 SP18   30fr + 10fr dk grn   3.25   2.40

The surtax was for the Educational League vacation camps.

Type of France Surcharged Type "c" and Surtax

1952, Oct. 15
B120 A226   15fr + 5fr bl grn   3.25   2.40

Creation of the French Military Medal, cent.

Type of France Overprinted Type "c"

1953, Mar. 14
B121 SP193   12fr + 3fr vermilion   2.40   2.00
"Day of the Stamp."

Type of France Overprinted Type "c"

1954, Mar. 20
B122 SP196   12fr + 3fr indigo   2.40   2.00
Stamp Day.

Balloon Post, 1870 SP19

1955, Mar. 19
B123 SP19   12fr + 3fr red brown   2.40   2.00
Stamp Days, Mar. 19-20.

Independent Kingdom

Franz von Taxis SP20

1956, Mar. 17
B124 SP20   12fr + 3fr dark green   1.25   1.25
Stamp Days, Mar. 17-18

Republic

No. 246 Surcharged in Red

1957, Aug. 8   Engr.
B125 A29   20fr + 10fr dp ultra   .75   .75
15th anniversary of the army.

Florist Type of 1955 with Added Inscriptions, Surcharged in Red

1957, Oct. 19   Perf. 13
B126 A34   20fr + 10fr dk vio   .60   .60

No. B126 is inscribed "5e. Foire Internationale" at bottom and lines of Arabic at either side.

Mailman
Delivering
Mail — SP21

Ornamental
Cock — SP22

1959, May 1   Engr.   Perf. 13
B127 SP21 20fr + 5fr dk brn &
                 org brn   .50   .50
Day of the Stamp. The surtax was for the
Post Office Mutual Fund.

1959, Oct. 24   Litho.   Perf. 13
B128 SP22 10m + 5m yel, lt bl &
                 red   .35   .35
Surtax for the Red Crescent Society.

Mailman on
Camel
Phoning — SP23

Dancer of
Kerkennah
Holding
Stamp — SP24

1960, Apr. 16   Engr.   Perf. 13
B129 SP23 60m + 5m ol, org & ul-
                 tra   .75   .75
Day of the Stamp.

1961, May 6   Unwmk.   Perf. 13
Stamp Day: 15m+5m, Mail truck, horiz.
20m+6m, Hand holding magnifying glass and
stamps. 50m+5m, Running boy, symbols of
mail.

B130 SP24 12m + 4m multi   .60   .60
B131 SP24 15m + 5m multi   .75   .75
B132 SP24 20m + 6m multi   .85   .85
B133 SP24 50m + 5m multi   .95   .95
    Nos. B130-B133 (4)   3.15 3.15

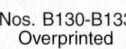

Nos. B130-B133
Overprinted

1963, Oct. 24
B134 SP24 12m + 4m cl, vio & ol .35   .35
B135 SP24 15m + 5m ol, cl & vio
                 bl   .40   .40
B136 SP24 20m + 6m multi   .50   .50
B137 SP24 50m + 5m multi   .85   .85
    Nos. B134-B137 (4)   2.10 2.10
United Nations Day.

Old Man, Red
Crescent
SP25

Nurse Holding
Bottle of Blood
SP26

Tunisian Red Crescent: 75m+10m, Mother,
child and Red Crescent.

1972, May 8   Engr.   Perf. 13
B138 SP25 10m + 10m pur & dk
                 red   .40   .35
B139 SP25 75m + 10m bis brn &
                 dl red   .60   .40

1973, May 10   Engr.   Perf. 13
Design: 60m+10m, Red Crescent and
blood donors' arms, horiz.
B140 SP26 25m + 10m multi   .50   .40
B141 SP26 60m + 10m gray &
                 car   .85   .40
Red Crescent appeal for blood donors.

Blood
Donors — SP27

Red Crescent Society: 75m+10m, Blood
transfusion, symbolic design.

1974, May 8   Photo.   Perf. 14x13
B142 SP27 25m + 10m multi   .40   .40
B143 SP27 75m + 10m multi   .50   .50

Man Holding
Scales with
Balanced
Diet — SP28

1975, May 8   Photo.   Perf. 11½
B144 SP28 50m + 10m multi   .50   .40
Tunisian Red Crescent fighting malnutrition.

Blood Donation,
Woman and
Man — SP29

1976, May 8   Photo.   Perf. 11½
B145 SP29 40m + 10m multi   .50   .35
Tunisian Red Crescent Society.

Litter
Bearers
and Red
Crescent
SP30

1977, May 8   Photo.   Perf. 13½x14
B146 SP30 50m + 10m multi   .50   .40
Tunisian Red Crescent Society.

Blood Donors
SP31

Hand and Red
Crescent
SP32

1978, May 8   Photo.   Perf. 13x14
B147 SP31 50m + 10m multi   .50   .40
Blood drive of Tunisian Red Crescent
Society.

1979, May 8   Photo.   Perf. 13½
B148 SP32 50m + 10m multi   .50   .40
Tunisian Red Crescent Society.

Red Crescent Society
SP33   SP34

1980, May 8   Photo.   Perf. 13½
B149 SP33 50m + 10m multi   .50   .40

1981, May 8   Perf. 14½x13½
B150 SP34 50m + 10m multi   .40   .35

Dome of
the Rock,
Jerusalem
SP35

1981, Nov. 29   Photo.   Perf. 13½
B151 SP35 50m + 5m multi   .55   .35
B152 SP35 150m + 5m multi   1.00   .60
B153 SP35 200m + 5m multi   1.60   .70
    Nos. B151-B153 (3)   3.15 1.65
Intl. Palestinian Solidarity Day.

Red
Crescent
Society
SP36

1982, May 8   Photo.   Perf. 13½
B154 SP36 80m + 10m multi   .50   .40

Red Crescent
Society — SP37

1983, May 8   Litho.   Perf. 14x13½
B155 SP37 80m + 10m multi   .60   .35

Sabra and Chatilla Massacre — SP38

1983, Sept. 20   Photo.   Perf. 13
B156 SP38 80m + 5m multi   .50   .50

Red Crescent Society — SP39

1984, May 8   Litho.   Perf. 12½
B157 SP39 80m + 10m First aid   .50   .40

Red Crescent Society
SP40   SP41

1985, May 8   Litho.   Perf. 14
B158 SP40 100m + 10m multi   .40   .25

1986, May 9   Litho.   Perf. 14½x13½
B159 SP41 120m + 10m Map of
                 Tunisia   .50   .40

Red Crescent
Society — SP42

1987, May 8   Litho.   Perf. 13x13½
B160 SP42 150m + 10m multi   .60   .45

Intl. Red Cross and Red Crescent
Organizations, 125th Annivs. — SP43

1988, May 9   Photo.   Perf. 14
B161 SP43 150m + 10m multi   .60   .40

Red Crescent
Society
SP44

1989, May 8   Photo.   Perf. 11½
                    Granite Paper
B162 SP44 150m +10m multi   .45   .30

Red Crescent Society
SP45   SP46

1990, May 8   Litho.   Perf. 14x13½
B163 SP45 150m +10m multi   .45   .25

1991, May 8   Litho.   Perf. 13½
B164 SP46 180m +10m multi   .60   .45

Red Crescent
Society — SP47

1993, Aug. 17   Litho.   Perf. 14x13½
B165 SP47 120m +30m multi   .60   .30

AIR POST STAMPS

No. 43
Surcharged
in Red

1919, Apr.   Unwmk.   Perf. 14x13½
C1   A6 30c on 35c ol grn &
         brn   1.60 1.60
  a. Inverted surcharge   180.00
  b. Double surcharge   180.00
  c. Double inverted surcharge   210.00
  d. Double surcharge, one invert-
      ed   180.00

Type A6,
Overprinted
in Rose

1920, Apr.
C2   A6 30c ol grn, bl & rose   1.25 1.25

Nos. 53
and 55
Overprinted
in Red

1927, Mar. 24
C3   A7 1fr indigo & ultra   1.25   .80
C4   A7 2fr grn & red, pink   3.50 2.40

Nos. 51
and 57
Srchd. in
Black or
Red

C5   A6 1.75fr on 75c (Bk)   1.25   .80
C6   A7 1.75fr on 5fr (R)   3.50 2.40

Type A13 Ovptd. like #C3-C4 in Blue
1928, Feb.
C7   A13 1.30fr org & lt vio   4.00 1.60
C8   A13 1.80fr gray grn & red   4.75 1.25
C9   A13 2.55fr lil & ol brn   2.40 1.25
     Nos. C7-C9 (3)   11.15 4.10

Type A13 Surcharged like #C5-C6 in
Blue
1930, Aug.
C10 A13 1.50fr on 1.30fr org &
          lt vio   2.75   .95
C11 A13 1.50fr on 1.80fr gray
          grn & red   4.75   .80
C12 A13 1.50fr on 2.55fr lil & ol
          brn   9.50 2.40
     Nos. C10-C12 (3)   17.00 4.15

> **Catalogue values for unused stamps in this section, from this point to the end of the section, are for Never Hinged items.**

UPU Type of Regular Issue
1949, Oct. 28   Engr.   Perf. 13
C13 A23 25fr dk bl, bluish   2.75 2.00
UPU, 75th anniv. Exists imperf.; value $40.

Bird from
Antique
Mosaic,
Museum of
Sousse
AP2

1949   Unwmk.
C14 AP2 200fr dk bl & indigo   8.75 2.40

(Arabic on
one
line) — AP3

1950-51
C15 AP3 100fr bl grn & brn   5.50 1.60
C16 AP3 200fr dk bl & ind ('51)   9.50 4.00

Monastir
AP4

Coast at
Korbous
AP5

Design: 1000fr, Air view of Tozeur mosque.
1953-54
C17 AP4 100fr dk bl, ind &
          dk grn ('54)   5.25 1.25
C18 AP4 200fr cl, blk brn &
          red brn
          ('54)   7.25 2.00
C19 AP5 500fr dk brn & ul-
          tra   40.00 14.50
C20 AP5 1000fr dk green   67.50 30.00
     Nos. C17-C20 (4)   120.00 47.75
     Imperforates exist.

Independent Kingdom
Types of 1953-54 Redrawn with "RF"
Omitted

1956, Mar. 1
C21 AP4 100fr slate bl, indigo
          & dk grn   1.75   .75
C22 AP4 200fr multi   3.25 1.50
C23 AP5 500fr dk brn & ultra   6.75 6.00
C24 AP5 1000fr dk green   13.50 11.00
     Nos. C21-C24 (4)   25.25 19.25

Republic

Desert
Swallows — AP6

Birds: #C26, Butcherbird. #C27, Cream-colored courser. 100m, European chaffinch. 150m, Pink flamingoes. 200m, Barbary partridges. 300m, European roller. 500m, Bustard.

1965-66   Photo.   Perf. 12½
Size: 23x31mm
C25 AP6 25m multi   .85   .35
C26 AP6 55m blk & lt bl   1.25   .85
C27 AP6 55m multi ('66)   1.25   .65
Size: 22½x33mm
Perf. 11½
C28 AP6 100m multi   1.75 1.00
C29 AP6 150m multi ('66)   5.75 2.50
C30 AP6 200m multi ('66)   6.25 2.75
C31 AP6 300m multi ('66)   9.00 5.50
C32 AP6 500m multi   13.00 6.75
     Nos. C25-C32 (8)   39.10 20.35
     See No. 474.

AIR POST SEMI-POSTAL STAMP

> **Catalogue value for the unused stamp in this section is for a Never Hinged item.**

Window, Great
Mosque of
Kairouan — SPAP1

1952, May 5   Engr.   Perf. 13
CB1 SPAP1 50fr + 10fr blk &
            gray grn   4.75 3.50
Surtax for charitable works of the army.

POSTAGE DUE STAMPS

Regular postage stamps perforated with holes in the form of a "T," the holes varying in size and number, were used as postage due stamps from 1888 to 1901.

For listings, see the *Scott Classic Specialized Catalogue of Stamps and Covers.*

D1

Perf. 14x13½
1901-03   Unwmk.   Typo.
J1   D1 1c black   .55   .50
J2   D1 2c orange   1.05   .65
J3   D1 5c blue   .80   .50
J4   D1 10c brown   .80   .65
J5   D1 20c blue green   4.50   .95
J6   D1 30c carmine   3.50   .90
J7   D1 50c brown violet   2.00   .95
J8   D1 1fr olive green   1.60   .95
J9   D1 2fr carmine, grn   4.50 2.50
J10 D1 5fr blk, yellow   57.50 40.00
     Nos. J1-J10 (10)   76.80 48.55

No. J10 Surcharged in
Blue

1914, Nov.
J11 D1 2fr on 5fr blk, yellow   1.60 1.60

In Jan. 1917 regular 5c postage stamps were overprinted "T" in an inverted triangle and used as postage due stamps.

D2

1922-49
J12 D2 1c black   .30   .30
J13 D2 2c black, yellow   .30   .30
J14 D2 5c violet brown   .70   .30
J15 D2 10c blue   .55   .50
J16 D2 10c yel green ('45)   .25   .25
J17 D2 20c orange, yel   .55   .50
J18 D2 30c brown ('23)   .55   .30
J19 D2 50c rose red   1.05   .50
J20 D2 50c blue vio ('45)   .25   .25
J21 D2 60c violet ('28)   1.05   .50
J22 D2 80c bister ('28)   .90   .40
J23 D2 90c orange red ('28)   1.10   .65
J24 D2 1fr green   .65   .30
J25 D2 2fr olive grn, straw   1.30   .55
J26 D2 2fr car rose ('45)   .30   .30
J27 D2 3fr vio, pink ('29)   .50   .30
J28 D2 4fr grnsh bl ('45)   .50   .50
J29 D2 5fr violet   .90   .65
J30 D2 10fr cerise ('49)   .50   .50
J31 D2 20fr olive gray ('49)   1.40 1.10
     Nos. J12-J31 (20)   13.60 8.95

Inscribed: "Timbre Taxe"
1950   Unwmk.   Perf. 14x13½
J32 D2 30fr blue   1.75 1.50

> **Catalogue values for unused stamps in this section, from this point to the end of the section, are for Never Hinged items.**

Independent Kingdom

Grain and Fruit — D3

1957, Apr. 1   Engr.   Perf. 14x13
J33 D3 1fr bright green   .25   .25
J34 D3 2fr orange brown   .25   .25
J35 D3 3fr bluish green   .50   .50
J36 D3 4fr indigo   .50   .50
J37 D3 5fr lilac   .50   .50
J38 D3 10fr carmine   .50   .50
J39 D3 20fr chocolate   1.60 1.60
J40 D3 30fr blue   2.10 2.10
     Nos. J33-J40 (8)   6.20 6.20

Republic
Inscribed "Republique Tunisienne"
1960-77
J41 D3 1m emerald   .25   .25
J42 D3 2m red brown   .25   .25
J43 D3 3m bluish green   .25   .25
J44 D3 4m indigo   .25   .25
J45 D3 5m lilac   .25   .25
J46 D3 10m carmine rose   .50   .50
J47 D3 20m violet brown   .75   .75
J48 D3 30m blue   .90   .90
J49 D3 40m lake ('77)   .25   .25
J50 D3 100m blue green ('77)   .50   .50
     Nos. J41-J50 (10)   4.15 4.15

PARCEL POST STAMPS

Mail
Delivery — PP1   Gathering
                        Dates — PP2

1906   Unwmk.   Typo.   Perf. 13½x14
Q1   PP1 5c grn & vio brn   .80   .65
Q2   PP1 10c org & red   1.20   .80
Q3   PP1 20c dk brn & org   2.00   .80
  a. Center double   525.00 5,500.
Q4   PP1 25c blue & brn   2.75   .80
Q5   PP1 40c gray & rose   3.25   .80
Q6   PP1 50c vio brn & vio   2.75   .80
Q7   PP1 75c bis brn & bl   4.00   .80
Q8   PP1 1fr red brn & red   3.25   .55

Q9	PP1	2fr carmine & bl	9.50	1.20
Q10	PP1	5fr vio & vio brn	27.50	1.60
	Nos. Q1-Q10 (10)		57.00	8.80

1926

Q11	PP2	5c pale brn & dk bl	.50	.50
Q12	PP2	10c rose & vio	.65	.50
Q13	PP2	20c yel grn & blk	.65	.65
Q14	PP2	25c org brn & blk	.65	.65
Q15	PP2	40c dp rose & dp grn	2.75	.65
Q16	PP2	50c lt vio & blk	2.00	.90
Q17	PP2	60c ol & brn red	2.00	.80
Q18	PP2	75c gray vio & bl grn	2.00	.80
Q19	PP2	80c ver & ol brn	2.00	.80
Q20	PP2	1fr Prus bl & dp rose	2.40	.80
Q21	PP2	2fr vio & mag	4.75	.80
Q22	PP2	4fr red & blk	5.25	.80
Q23	PP2	5fr red brn & dp vio	8.00	1.20
Q24	PP2	10fr dl red & grn, *grnsh*	16.00	1.20
Q25	PP2	20fr yel grn & dp vio, *lav*	30.00	2.00
	Nos. Q11-Q25 (15)		79.60	13.05

Parcel post stamps were discontinued July 1, 1940.

TURKEY

'tər-kē

LOCATION — Southeastern Europe and Asia Minor, between the Mediterranean and Black Seas
GOVT. — Republic
AREA — 300,947 sq. mi.
POP. — 65,599,206 (1999 est.)
CAPITAL — Ankara

The Ottoman Empire ceased to exist in 1922, and the Republic of Turkey was inaugurated in 1923.

40 Paras = 1 Piaster
40 Paras = 1 Ghurush (1926)
40 Paras = 1 Kurush (1926)
100 Kurush = 1 Lira

Catalogue values for unused stamps in this country are for Never Hinged items, beginning with Scott 817 in the regular postage section, Scott B69 in the semipostal section, Scott C1 in the airpost section, Scott J97 in the postage due section, Scott O1 in the official section, Scott P175 in the newspaper section, and Scott RA139 in the postal tax section.

Watermarks

Wmk. 394 — "PTT," Crescent and Star

Wmk. 405

Turkish Numerals

١ ٢ ٣ ٤ ٥
1 2 3 4 5

٦ ٧ ٨ ٩ ٠
6 7 8 9 0

"Tughra," Monogram of Sultan Abdul-Aziz
A1   A2

A3   A4

1863   Unwmk.   Litho.   *Imperf.*
Red Band: 20pa, 1pi, 2pi
Blue Band: 5pi
Thin Paper

1	A1	20pa blk, *yellow*	75.00	20.00
a.		Tête bêche pair	250.00	200.00
b.		Without band	100.00	
c.		Green band		
2	A2	1pi blk, *dl vio*	125.00	20.00
a.		1pi black, *gray*	125.00	21.50
b.		Tête bêche pair	400.00	300.00
c.		Without band	140.00	
d.		Design reversed		175.00
e.		1pi blk, *yel* (error)	250.00	150.00
4	A3	2pi blk, *grnsh bl*	115.00	20.00
a.		2pi black, *ind*	115.00	21.50
b.		Tête bêche pair	400.00	300.00
c.		Without band	140.00	
5	A4	5pi blk, *rose*	225.00	45.00
a.		Tête bêche pair	500.00	400.00
b.		Without band	250.00	
c.		Green band	275.00	
d.		Red band	275.00	

Thick, Surface Colored Paper

6	A1	20pa blk, *yellow*	250.00	37.50
a.		Tête bêche pair	450.00	450.00
b.		Design reversed	325.00	325.00
c.		Without band	225.00	225.00
d.		Paper colored through	225.00	225.00
7	A2	1pi blk, *gray*	300.00	35.00
a.		Tête bêche pair	900.00	900.00
b.		Design reversed		
c.		Without band		
d.		Paper colored through	350.00	225.00
		Nos. 1-7 (6)	1,090.	177.50

The 2pi and 5pi had two printings. In the common printing, the stamps are more widely spaced and alternate horizontal rows of 12 are inverted. In the first and rare printing, the stamps are more closely spaced and no rows are tête bêche.
See Nos. J1-J4.

Crescent and Star, Symbols of Turkish Caliphate — A5

Surcharged

The bottom characters of this and the following surcharges denote the denomination. The characters at top and sides translate, "Ottoman Empire Posts."

1865   Typo.   *Perf. 12½*

8	A5	10pa deep green	11.00	35.00
c.		"1" instead of "10" in each corner	300.00	300.00
9	A5	20pa yellow	6.00	3.00
a.		Star without rays	7.00	4.00
10	A5	1pi lilac	12.50	4.00
a.		Star without rays	17.50	3.00
11	A5	2pi blue	6.50	4.00
12	A5	5pi carmine	5.50	4.50
d.		Inverted surcharge		
13	A5	25pi red orange	325.00	250.00

Imperf., Pairs

8b	A5	10pa	125.00	125.00
9b	A5	20pa	125.00	125.00
10b	A5	1pi	100.00	90.00
11a	A5	2pi	100.00	90.00
12b	A5	5pi	110.00	110.00
13a	A5	25pi	750.00	750.00

See Nos. J6-J35. For overprints and surcharges see Nos. 14-52, 64-65, 446-461, 467-468, J71-J77, Eastern Rumelia 1.

Surcharged

1867

14	A5	10pa gray green	9.50	
a.		Imperf., pair	55.00	
15	A5	20pa yellow	15.00	
a.		Imperf., pair	75.00	
16	A5	1pi lilac	20.00	
a.		Imperf., pair	110.00	
b.		Imperf., with surcharge of 5pi	25.00	
17	A5	2pi blue	5.50	45.00
a.		Imperf.		
18	A5	5pi rose	4.50	45.00
b.		Imperf.		
19	A5	25pi orange	3,600.	
		Nos. 14-18 (5)	54.50	

Nos. 14, 15, 16 and 19 were never placed in use.

Surcharged

1869   *Perf. 13½*

20	A5	10pa dull violet	100.00	12.00
a.		Printed on both sides		
b.		Imperf., pair	90.00	80.00
c.		Inverted surcharge		90.00
d.		Double surcharge		
e.		10pa yellow (error)		300.00
21	A5	20pa pale green	400.00	14.00
a.		Printed on both sides	450.00	275.00
22	A5	1pi yellow	10.00	2.50
c.		Inverted surcharge	100.00	
d.		Double surcharge		
e.		Surcharged on both sides		
f.		Printed on both sides		
23	A5	2pi orange red	200.00	10.00
b.		Imperf., pair	125.00	125.00
c.		Printed on both sides		125.00
d.		Inverted surcharge	70.00	70.00
e.		Surcharged on both sides		140.00
24	A5	5pi blue	4.25	10.00
25	A5	5pi gray	30.00	37.50
26	A5	25pi dull rose	37.50	125.00
		Nos. 20-26 (7)	781.75	211.00

Pin-perf., Perf. 5 to 11 and Compound

1870-71

27	A5	10pa lilac	550.00	25.00
28	A5	10pa brown	500.00	15.00
29	A5	20pa gray green	75.00	8.00
a.		Printed on both sides		
30	A5	1pi yellow	550.00	10.00
a.		Inverted surcharge	500.00	80.00
b.		Without surcharge		
31	A5	2pi red	8.00	5.00
a.		Imperf.	20.00	20.00
b.		Printed on both sides		40.00
c.		Surcharged on both sides		
32	A5	5pi blue	5.00	12.50
a.		5pi greenish blue	6.00	8.00
33	A5	5pi slate	40.00	50.00
a.		Printed on both sides		
b.		Surcharged on both sides		40.00
34	A5	25pi dull rose	40.00	75.00
		Nos. 27-34 (8)	1,768.	200.50

1873   *Perf. 12, 12½*

35	A5	10pa dark lilac	475.00	25.00
a.		Inverted surcharge		90.00
36	A5	10pa olive brown	110.00	17.50
a.		10pa bister	110.00	11.00
37	A5	2pi vermilion	3.50	4.50
a.		Surcharged on both sides	22.50	22.50
		Nos. 35-37 (3)	588.50	47.00

Surcharged

1874-75   *Perf. 13½*

38	A5	10pa red violet	52.50	7.50
a.		Imperf., pair	210.00	50.00
39	A5	20pa yellow green	15.00	5.00
b.		Imperf., pair	30.00	13.00
c.		Double surcharge		
40	A5	1pi yellow	210.00	30.00
a.		Imperf., pair	100.00	80.00

Perf. 12, 12½

41	A5	10pa red violet	25.00	10.00
a.		Inverted surcharge	45.00	60.00
		Nos. 38-41 (4)	302.50	52.50

Surcharged

1876, Apr.   *Perf. 13½*

42	A5	10pa red lilac	2.00	.50
a.		Inverted surcharge	70.00	
b.		Imperf., pair	15.00	15.00
43	A5	20pa pale green	2.00	.50
b.		Inverted surcharge	70.00	
c.		Imperf., pair	15.00	15.00
44	A5	1pi yellow	2.00	.50
a.		Imperf., pair	27.50	27.50
46	A5	5pi gray blue	1,700.	
47	A5	25pi dull rose	1,700.	
		Nos. 42-44 (3)	6.00	

Nos. 46 and 47 were never placed in use.
See Nos. 64-65.

Surcharged

Surcharged

1876, Jan.

48	A5	¼pi on 10pa violet	3.00	2.50
49	A5	½pi on 20pa yel grn	6.25	2.50
50	A5	1¼pi on 50pa rose	2.25	2.50
a.		Imperf., pair	60.00	
51	A5	2pi on 2pi redsh brn	40.00	7.50
52	A5	5pi on 5pi gray blue	10.00	85.00
		Nos. 48-52 (5)	61.50	100.00

The surcharge on Nos. 48-52 restates in French the value originally expressed in Turkish characters.
The vast majority of No. 51 unused are without gum.

A7

1876, Sept.   Typo.   *Perf. 13½*

53	A7	10pa black & rose lil	2.00	6.25
54	A7	20pa red vio & grn	62.50	5.00
55	A7	50pa blue & yellow	1.25	10.00
56	A7	2pi black & redsh brn	1.60	5.00
57	A7	5pi red & blue	3.00	12.50
b.		Cliché of 25pi in plate of 5pi	400.00	375.00
58	A7	25pi claret & rose	15.00	85.00
a.		Imperf.	160.00	
		Nos. 53-58 (6)	85.35	123.75

Nos. 56-58 exist perf. 11½, but were not regularly issued.
See Nos. 59-63, 66-91, J36-J38. For overprints see Nos. 462-466, 469-476, J78-J79, P10-P14, Eastern Rumelia 2-40.

1880-84   *Perf. 13½*

59	A7	5pa black & ol ('81)	3.00	6.50
a.		Imperf.	30.00	
60	A7	10pa black & grn ('84)	3.00	3.50
61	A7	20pa black & rose	55.00	2.00
62	A7	1pi blk & bl *(piastres)*	75.00	3.00
a.		1pi black & gray blue	85.00	
b.		Imperf.	40.00	
63	A7	1pi blk & bl *(piastre)* ('81)	110.00	5.00
		Nos. 59-63 (5)	246.00	20.00

A cliché of No. 63 was inserted in a plate of the Eastern Rumelia 1pi (No. 13). This was found in the remainder stock.
Nos. 60-61 and 63 exist perf. 11½, but were not regularly issued.

1881-82
Surcharged like Apr., 1876 Issue

64	A5	20pa gray	4.25	6.25
a.		Inverted surcharge	13.50	
b.		Imperf., pair	25.00	
65	A5	2pi pale salmon	3.00	1.00
a.		Inverted surcharge	22.50	

1884-86   *Perf. 11½, 13½*

66	A7	5pa lil & pale lil ('86)	200.00	150.00
67	A7	10pa grn & pale grn	1.60	1.25
68	A7	20pa rose & pale rose	1.60	1.25
69	A7	1pi blue & lt blue	1.60	1.25

Perf. 11½

70	A7	2pi ocher & pale ocher	2.25	1.25
71	A7	5pi red brn & pale brn	20.00	25.00
c.		5pi ocher & pale ocher (error)	12.00	12.00

Perf. 11½, 13½

73	A7	25pi blk & pale gray ('86)	300.00	425.00
		Nos. 66-73 (7)	527.05	605.00

Imperf

66a	A7	5pa		60.00
67a	A7	10pa		20.00
68b	A7	20pa		20.00
69b	A7	1pi		20.00
73a	A7	25pi		150.00

1886   *Perf. 13½*

74	A7	5pa black & pale gray	2.00	2.50
75	A7	2pi orange & lt bl	2.00	2.00
76	A7	5pi grn & pale grn	3.00	25.00
77	A7	25pi bis & pale bis	45.00	150.00
		Nos. 74-77 (4)	52.00	179.50

Imperf

74a	A7	5pa		20.00
75b	A7	2pi		20.00
76b	A7	5pi		20.00
77a	A7	25pi		35.00

Stamps of 1884-86, bisected and surcharged as above, 10pa, 20pa, 1pi and 2pi or surcharged "2" in red are stated to have been made privately and without authority. With the aid of employees of the post office, stamps were passed through the mails.

1888   Perf. 13½

83	A7	5pa green & yellow	2.50	5.00
84	A7	2pi red lilac & bl	1.50	1.50
85	A7	5pi dk brown & gray	5.00	20.00
86	A7	25pi red & yellow	30.00	150.00
		Nos. 83-86 (4)	39.00	176.50

Imperf

83a	A7	5pa		20.00
84a	A7	2pi		20.00
85a	A7	5pi		20.00
86a	A7	25pi		25.00

Nos. 74-86 exist perf. 11½, but were not regularly issued.

1890   Perf. 11½, 13½

87	A7	10pa green & gray	8.00	1.00
88	A7	20pa rose & gray	1.60	1.00
89	A7	1pi blue & gray	125.00	1.00
90	A7	2pi yellow & gray	2.25	7.50
91	A7	5pi buff & gray	5.00	22.50
		Nos. 87-91 (5)	141.85	33.00

Imperf

87a	A7	10pa		20.00
88a	A7	20pa		20.00
89a	A7	1pi		100.00
90b	A7	2pi		100.00
91a	A7	5pi		25.00

Arms and Tughra of "El Gazi" (The Conqueror) Sultan Abdul Hamid
A10   A11

A12   A13

A14

1892-98   Typo.   Perf. 13½

95	A10	10pa gray green	2.25	.50
96	A11	20pa violet brn ('98)	1.25	.50
a.		20pa dark pink	7.50	.45
b.		20pa pink	35.00	.45
97	A12	1pi pale blue	110.00	4.00
98	A13	2pi brown org	3.00	1.00
a.		Tête bêche pair	30.00	30.00
99	A14	5pi dull violet	9.00	15.00
a.		Turkish numeral in upper right corner reads "50" instead of "5"	30.00	15.00
		Nos. 95-99 (5)	125.50	21.00

See Nos. J39-J42. For surcharges and overprints see Nos. 100, 288-291, 350, 355-359, 477-478, B38, B41, J80-J82, P25-P34, P36, P121-P122, P134-P137, P153-P154.

No. 95 Surcharged in Red

1897

100	A10	5pa on 10pa gray grn	3.00	1.25
a.		"Cniq" instead of "Cinq"	10.00	10.00

Turkish stamps of types A11, A17-A18, A21-A24, A26, A28-A39, A41 with or without Turkish overprints and English surcharges with "Baghdad" or "Iraq" are listed under Mesopotamia in Vol. 4.

Turkish stamps of types A19 and A21 with Double-headed Eagle and "Shqipenia" handstamp are listed under Albania in Vol. 1.

A16

1901   Typo.   Perf. 13¼
For Foreign Postage

102	A16	5pa bister	1.25	.60
103	A16	10pa yellow green	1.25	.60
104	A16	20pa magenta	1.25	.60
a.		Perf. 12	2.50	1.00
105	A16	1pi violet blue	1.50	1.00
106	A16	2pi gray blue	2.50	1.00
107	A16	5pi ocher	8.50	3.50
108	A16	25pi dark green	100.00	30.00
109	A16	50pi yellow	250.00	100.00
		Nos. 102-109 (8)	366.25	137.30

A17

Perf. 12, 13¼
For Domestic Postage

110	A17	5pa purple	1.25	.50
111	A17	10pa green	1.25	.50
112	A17	20pa carmine	1.25	.50
113	A17	1pi blue	1.25	.50
a.		Imperf.	20.00	
114	A17	2pi orange	2.00	.50
115	A17	5pi lilac rose	5.75	1.00

Perf. 13½

116	A17	25pi brown	10.00	2.00
a.		Perf. 12	25.00	8.50
117	A17	50pi yellow brown	37.50	5.00
a.		Perf. 12	55.00	17.00
		Nos. 110-117 (8)	60.25	10.50

Nos. 110-113 exist perf. 12x13½.
See Nos. J43-J46.
For overprints and surcharges see Nos. 165-180, 292-303, 340-341, 361-377, 479-493, B19-B20, B37, P37-P48, P69-P80, P123-P126, P138-P146, P155-P164.

A18

1905   Perf. 12, 13½ and Compound

118	A18	5pa ocher	1.00	.50
119	A18	10pa dull green	1.00	.50
a.		Imperf.	4.00	3.50
120	A18	20pa carmine	1.00	.50
a.		Imperf.	4.00	3.50
121	A18	1pi blue	1.00	.50
122	A18	2pi slate	1.50	.50
123	A18	2½pi red violet	1.50	.50
a.		Imperf.	11.00	9.00

124	A18	5pi brown	2.00	.50
125	A18	10pi orange brn	3.75	.50
126	A18	25pi olive green	12.50	15.00
127	A18	50pi deep violet	50.00	30.00

See Nos. J47-J48. For overprints and surcharges see Nos. 128-131, 181-182, 304-314, 351-354, 378-389, 494-508, B1-B3, B21-B23, B39-B40, P49-P54, P127-P129, P147-P150, P165-P171.

Overprinted in Carmine or Blue

1906

128	A18	10pa dull green (C)	3.00	1.00
129	A18	20pa carmine (Bl)	3.00	1.00
130	A18	1pi blue (C)	3.00	1.00
131	A18	2pi slate (C)	17.50	5.00
		Nos. 118-131 (14)	101.75	57.00

Stamps bearing this overprint were sold to merchants at a discount from face value to encourage the use of Turkish stamps on foreign correspondence, instead of those of the various European powers which maintained post offices in Turkey. The overprint is the Arab "B," for "Béhié," meaning "discount."

A19

1908

132	A19	5pa ocher	1.25	.50
133	A19	10pa blue green	1.75	.30
134	A19	20pa carmine	40.00	.50
135	A19	1pi bright blue	15.00	.50
a.		1pi ultramarine	50.00	10.00
136	A19	2pi blue black	10.00	.50
137	A19	2½pi violet brown	6.00	.50
138	A19	5pi dark violet	80.00	.50
139	A19	10pi red	70.00	2.50
140	A19	25pi dark green	12.00	5.00
141	A19	50pi red brown	50.00	35.00

See Nos. J49-J50. For overprints and surcharges see Nos. 142-145, 314B-316B, 390-396, 509-516A, B4-B6, B17, B24-B27, P55-P60, P130-P131, P151, P172, Thrace 15.

Overprinted in Carmine or Blue

142	A19	10pa blue green (C)	7.50	2.50
143	A19	20pa carmine (Bl)	7.50	2.50
144	A19	1pi brt blue (C)	15.00	2.50
145	A19	2pi blue black (C)	25.00	12.50
		Nos. 132-145 (14)	341.00	65.80

A20

Perf. 12, 13½ & Compound
1908, Dec. 17

146	A20	5pa ocher	1.00	.50
147	A20	10pa blue green	1.50	.50
148	A20	20pa carmine	2.00	1.00
149	A20	1pi ultra	3.00	1.00
150	A20	2pi gray black	12.50	15.00
		Nos. 146-150 (5)	20.00	18.00

Imperf

146a	A20	5pa	3.00	3.00
147a	A20	10pa	4.00	4.00
148a	A20	20pa	5.50	5.50
149a	A20	1pi	3.00	3.00

Granting of a Constitution, the date of which is inscribed on the banderol: "324 Temuz 10" (July 24, 1908).
For overprints see Nos. 397, 517.

Tughra and "Reshad" of Sultan Mohammed V — A21

1909, Dec.

151	A21	5pa ocher	1.00	.50
152	A21	10pa blue green	1.00	.50
a.		Imperf.	3.00	3.00
153	A21	20pa carmine rose	1.00	.50
154	A21	1pi ultra	3.00	.50
a.		1pi bright blue	12.50	.50
155	A21	2pi blue black	3.00	.50
156	A21	2½pi dark brown	90.00	20.00
157	A21	5pi dark violet	12.00	1.00
158	A21	10pi dull red	37.50	1.00
159	A21	25pi dark green	350.00	100.00
160	A21	50pi red brown	150.00	80.00

The 2pa olive green, type A21, is a newspaper stamp, No. P68.
Two types exist for the 10pa, 20pa and 1pi. In the second type, the damaged crescent is restored.
See Nos. J51-J52. For overprints and surcharges see Nos. 161-164, 317-327, 342-343, 398-406, 518-528, 567, B7-B14, B18, B28-B32, P61-P68, P81, P132-P133, P152, P173, Turkey in Asia 67, 72, Thrace 1-4, 13, 13A, 14.

Overprinted in Carmine or Blue

161	A21	10pa blue grn (C)	1.75	.75
a.		Imperf.		
162	A21	20pa car rose (Bl)	1.75	.75
163	A21	1pi ultra (C)	3.50	2.00
a.		Imperf.	4.00	
b.		1pi bright blue	6.50	3.00
164	A21	2pi blue black (C)	75.00	30.00
a.		Imperf.		
		Nos. 151-164 (14)	730.50	238.00

Stamps of 1901-05 Overprinted in Carmine or Blue

The overprint was applied to 18 denominations in four settings with change of city name, producing individual sets for each city: "MONASTIR," "PRISTINA," "SALONIQUE" and "USKUB."

1911, June 26   Perf. 12, 13½

165	A16	5pa bister	4.50	4.50
166	A16	10pa yel grn	4.50	4.50
167	A16	20pa magenta	9.00	9.00
168	A16	1pi violet blue	9.00	9.00
169	A16	2pi gray blue	9.00	9.00
170	A16	5pi ocher	40.00	60.00
171	A16	25pi dark green	60.00	75.00
172	A16	50pi yellow	100.00	125.00
173	A17	5pa purple	4.50	4.50
174	A17	10pa green	4.50	4.50
175	A17	20pa carmine	9.00	9.00
176	A17	1pi blue	9.00	9.00
177	A17	2pi orange	9.00	9.00
178	A17	5pi lilac rose	40.00	60.00
179	A17	25pi chocolate	85.00	125.00
180	A17	50pi yel brn	100.00	125.00
181	A18	2½pi red violet	65.00	100.00
182	A18	10pi org brn	60.00	125.00
		Nos. 165-182 (18)	622.00	802.00

Sultan's visit to Macedonia. The Arabic overprint reads: "Souvenir of the Sultan's Journey, 1329." Values same for all cities. See Nos. P69-P81.

General Post Office, Constantinople
A22

1913, Mar. 14   Perf. 12

237	A22	2pa olive green	1.00	.50
238	A22	5pa ocher	1.00	.50
239	A22	10pa blue green	1.00	.50
240	A22	20pa carmine rose	1.00	.50
241	A22	1pi ultra	1.00	.50
242	A22	2pi indigo	2.00	.50

243	A22	5pi dull violet	3.50	1.00
244	A22	10pi dull red	6.00	3.00
245	A22	25pi gray green	22.50	22.50
246	A22	50pi orange brown	85.00	125.00

See Nos. J53-J58. For overprints and surcharges see Nos. 247-250, 328-339, 344, 407-414, 529-538, 568, B15-B16, B33-B36, Turkey in Asia 68, Thrace 10, 10A, 11, 11A, 12, N82.

Overprinted in Carmine or Blue

247	A22	10pa blue green (C)	1.00	.50
248	A22	20pa car rose (Bl)	1.00	.50
249	A22	1pi ultra (C)	1.00	.50
250	A22	2pi indigo (C)	17.50	7.50
		Nos. 237-250 (14)	144.50	163.50

Mosque of Selim, Adrianople — A23

1913, Oct. 23   Engr.

251	A23	10pa green	1.50	1.00
252	A23	20pa red	2.50	2.00
253	A23	40pa blue	6.00	3.00
		Nos. 251-253 (3)	10.00	6.00

Recapture of Adrianople (Edirne) by the Turks.

See Nos. 592, J59-J62. For overprints and surcharge see Nos. 415-417, 539-540, J59-J62, J67-J70, J83-J86, Thrace N84.

Obelisk of Theodosius in the Hippodrome A24

Column of Constantine A25

Leander's Tower — A26

One of the Seven Towers — A27

Fener Bahçe (Garden Lighthouse) A28

The Castle of Europe on the Bosporus A29

Mosque of Sultan Ahmed — A30

Monument to the Martyrs of Liberty A31

Fountains of Suleiman A32

Cruiser "Hamidie" A33

View of Kandili on the Bosporus A34

War Ministry (Later Istanbul University) — A35

Sweet Waters of Europe Park A36

Mosque of Suleiman A37

The Bosporus A38

Sultan Ahmed's Fountain A39

Sultan Mohammed V — A40

Designs A24-A39: Views of Constantinople.

1914, Jan. 14   Litho.

254	A24	2pa red lilac	.75	.40
255	A25	4pa dark brown	.75	.40
256	A26	5pa violet brown	.75	.40
257	A27	6pa dark blue	.75	.40

Engr.

258	A28	10pa green	2.00	.40
259	A29	20pa red	2.00	.40
260	A30	1pi blue	.75	.50
	b.	Booklet pane of 2+2 labels		
261	A31	1½pi car & blk	1.25	.75
262	A32	1¾pi sl & red brn	1.50	1.00
263	A33	2pi green & blk	2.00	.40
264	A34	2½pi org & ol grn	2.00	.50
265	A35	5pi dull violet	4.00	1.00
266	A36	10pi red brown	8.00	1.00
267	A37	25pi olive green	125.00	5.50
268	A38	50pi carmine	8.00	3.00
269	A39	100pi deep blue	75.00	27.50
		Cut cancellation		12.00
270	A40	200pi green & blk	550.00	400.00
		Cut cancellation		25.00
		Nos. 254-270 (17)	784.25	443.55

See Nos. 590-591, 593-598.

For overprints and surcharges see Nos. 271-287, 419, 541, 552-553, 574A, 601, 603-604, P174, Turkey in Asia 1-3, 5-9, 73-74, Thrace N77, N78.

Nos. 258-260, 262-263 Ovptd. in Red or Blue

271	A28	10pa green (R)	3.00	.75
272	A29	20pa red (Bl)	10.00	.75
273	A30	1pi blue (R)	3.00	.75
275	A32	1¾pi sl & red brn (Bl)	4.00	1.25
276	A33	2pi green & blk (R)	50.00	5.00
		Nos. 271-276 (5)	70.00	8.50

No. 261 Surcharged

1914, July 23

277	A31	1pi on 1½pi car & blk	3.25	2.50
	a.	"1330" omitted	2.50	1.50
	b.	Double surcharge		
	c.	Triple surcharge	5.00	5.00

7th anniv. of the Constitution. The surcharge reads "10 July, 1330, National fête" and has also the numeral "1" at each side, over the original value of the stamp.

Stamps of 1914 Overprinted in Black or Red

278	A26	5pa violet brn (Bk)	1.75	.50
279	A28	10pa green (R)	3.25	.50
280	A29	20pa red (Bk)	4.00	.50
281	A30	1pi blue (R)	10.00	1.50
282	A33	2pi grn & blk (R)	15.00	1.50
283	A35	5pi dull violet (R)	50.00	4.25
284	A36	10pi red brown (R)	190.00	65.00
		Nos. 278-284 (7)	274.00	73.75

This overprint reads "Abolition of the Capitulations, 1330".

No. 269 Surcharged

1915

286	A39	10pi on 100pi	62.50	22.50
	a.	Inverted surcharge	—	—

No. 270 Surcharged

287	A40	25pi on 200pi	25.00	8.00

Preceding Issues Overprinted in Carmine or Black

1915

On Stamps of 1892

288	A10	10pa gray green	1.00	.50
	a.	Inverted overprint	7.50	7.50
289	A13	2pi brown orange	1.50	.50
	a.	Inverted overprint	7.50	7.50
290	A14	5pi dull violet	4.00	.50
	a.	On No. 99a	17.00	17.00

On Stamp of 1897

291	A15	5pa on 10pa gray grn	1.00	.50
	a.	Inverted overprint	5.00	5.00
	b.	On No. 100a	10.00	10.00

On Stamps of 1901

292	A16	5pa bister	1.00	.50
293	A16	1pi violet blue	3.00	.50
294	A16	2pi gray blue	2.50	.50
295	A16	5pi ocher	20.00	.50
296	A16	25pi dark green	50.00	20.00
297	A17	5pa purple	1.00	.50
298	A17	10pa green	1.50	.50
299	A17	20pa carmine	1.50	.50
	a.	Inverted overprint	7.50	7.50
300	A17	1pi blue	1.50	.50
	a.	Inverted overprint	5.00	5.00
301	A17	2pi orange	2.00	.50
	a.	Inverted overprint	7.50	7.50
	b.	Double ovpt. (R and Bk)	5.00	5.00
302	A17	5pi lilac rose	2.50	.50
303	A17	25pi brown	12.50	2.00

On Stamps of 1905

304	A18	5pa ocher	1.00	.50
305	A18	10pa dull green	1.00	.50
	a.	Inverted overprint	5.00	5.00
306	A18	20pa carmine	1.00	.50
	a.	Inverted overprint	5.00	5.00
307	A18	1pi brt blue	1.50	.50
	a.	Inverted overprint	5.00	5.00
308	A18	2pi slate	2.50	.50
	a.	Inverted overprint	10.00	10.00
309	A18	2½pi red violet	1.50	.50
310	A18	5pi brown	2.00	.50
	a.	Inverted overprint	10.00	10.00
311	A18	10pi orange brown	12.50	.50
312	A18	25pi olive green	50.00	8.00

On Stamps of 1906

313	A18	10pa dull green	2.00	.50
314	A18	2pi slate	5.00	.50
	a.	Inverted overprint	5.00	5.00

On Stamps of 1908

314B	A19	2pi blue black	225.00	50.00
315	A19	2½pi violet brown	5.00	1.50
315A	A19	5pi dark violet	100.00	35.00
315B	A19	10pi red	15.00	7.50
316	A19	25pi dark green	30.00	10.00
	a.	Inverted overprint	17.00	17.00

With Additional Overprint

316B	A19	2pi blue black	15.00	5.00

On Stamps of 1909

317	A21	5pa ocher	1.00	.50
	a.	Inverted overprint	10.00	10.00
	b.	Double overprint	10.00	5.00
318	A21	20pa car rose	1.00	.50
	a.	Inverted overprint	5.00	5.00
319	A21	1pi ultra	2.00	.50
	a.	Inverted overprint	5.00	5.00
320	A21	2pi blue blk	2.50	.75
	a.	Inverted overprint	5.00	5.00
321	A21	2½pi dark brn	67.50	25.00
322	A21	5pi dark violet	.75	.50
	a.	Inverted overprint	6.50	6.50

323	A21	10pi dull red	10.00	.50
324	A21	25pi dark green	1,750.	1,200.

With Additional Overprint

325	A21	20pa carmine rose	2.00	.50
a.		Inverted overprint	5.00	5.00
326	A21	1pi ultra	2.00	.50
327	A21	2pi blue black	3.50	.50

On Stamps of 1913

328	A22	5pa ocher	1.00	.50
a.		Inverted overprint	7.50	7.50
329	A22	10pa blue green	1.00	.50
a.		Inverted overprint	10.00	10.00
330	A22	20pa carmine rose	1.00	.50
a.		Inverted overprint	7.50	7.50
331	A22	1pi ultra	1.50	.50
a.		Inverted overprint	5.00	5.00
332	A22	2pi indigo	2.00	.50
a.		Inverted overprint	5.00	5.00
333	A22	5pi dull violet	3.00	.50
334	A22	10pi dull red	10.00	.50
a.		Inverted overprint	10.00	10.00
335	A22	25pi gray green	30.00	20.00

With Additional Overprint

336	A22	10pa blue green	1.00	.50
337	A22	20pa carmine rose	1.00	.50
338	A22	1pi ultra	2.00	.50
339	A22	2pi indigo	7.50	3.00
a.		Inverted overprint	10.00	10.00

See Nos. P121-P133.

Stamps of 1901-13 Overprinted

1916

340	A17	5pa purple	1.00	.50
a.		5pa purple, #P43	80.00	80.00
341	A17	10pa green	1.00	.50
a.		Double overprint	6.50	6.50
b.		10pa yellow green, #103	80.00	80.00
342	A21	20pa car rose, #153	2.00	.75
a.		20pa carmine rose, #162	110.00	110.00
343	A21	1pi ultra	5.50	1.00
344	A22	5pi dull violet	10.00	3.00
		Nos. 340-344 (5)	20.00	5.75

Occupation of the Sinai Peninsula.

Old General Post Office of Constantinople A41

1916, May 29 Litho. Perf. 12½, 13½

345	A41	5pa green	.75	.50
346	A41	10pa carmine	.75	.50
347	A41	20pa ultra	1.00	.50
348	A41	1pi violet & blk	1.50	.50
349	A41	5pi yel brn & blk	20.00	2.50
		Nos. 345-349 (5)	24.00	4.75

Introduction of postage in Turkey, 50th anniv. For overprints see Nos. 418, B42-B45.

Stamps of 1892-1905 Overprinted

a

b

1916

On Stamps of 1892-98

355	A10(a)	10pa gray green	1.00	.50
355A	A11(a)	20pa violet brown	1.00	.50
b.		Inverted overprint	10.00	10.00
356	A12(a)	1pi gray blue	50.00	50.00
357	A13(a)	2pi brown org	5.00	1.50
358	A14(a)	5pi dull violet	50.00	50.00

On Stamp of 1897

359	A15(b)	5pa on 10pa gray grn	.75	.50

On Stamps of 1901

361	A16(a)	5pa bister	.75	.50
a.		Double overprint	7.50	7.50
362	A16(a)	10pa yel grn	1.00	.50
363	A16(a)	20pa magenta	.75	.50
364	A16(a)	1pi violet blue	1.00	.50
a.		Inverted overprint	7.50	7.50
365	A16(a)	2pi gray blue	5.00	1.00
366	A16(b)	5pi on 25pi dk grn	55.00	55.00
367	A16(b)	10pi on 25pi dk grn	55.00	55.00
368	A16(a)	25pi dark green	55.00	55.00
369	A17(a)	5pa purple	75.00	50.00
370	A17(a)	10pa green	2.00	1.50
371	A17(a)	20pa carmine	.75	.50
a.		Inverted overprint	7.50	7.50
372	A17(a)	1pi blue	1.00	.50
a.		Inverted overprint	7.50	7.50
373	A17(a)	2pi orange	1.50	.50
374	A17(b)	10pi on 25pi brown	5.00	1.50
375	A17(b)	10pi on 50pi yel brn	7.50	1.50
376	A17(a)	25pi brown	7.50	1.50
377	A17(a)	50pi yel brn	10.00	2.50

On Stamps of 1905

378	A18(a)	5pa ocher	.75	.50
379	A18(a)	20pa carmine	1.00	.50
a.		Inverted overprint	10.00	5.00
380	A18(a)	1pi brt blue	2.00	.50
a.		Inverted overprint	10.00	5.00
381	A18(a)	2pi slate	1.50	1.00
382	A18(a)	2½pi red violet	7.50	1.50
383	A18(b)	10pi on 25pi ol grn	10.00	3.00
384	A18(b)	10pi on 50pi dp vio	10.00	4.00
385	A18(a)	25pi olive green	10.00	5.00
386	A18(a)	50pi deep violet	7.50	5.00

On Stamps of 1906

387	A18(a)	10pa dull green	1.50	.60
388	A18(a)	20pa carmine	1.50	1.00
389	A18(a)	1pi brt blue	1.50	1.00

On Stamps of 1908

390	A19(a)	2½pi violet brown	67.50	67.50
391	A19(b)	10pi on 25pi dk grn	20.00	12.50
392	A19(b)	10pi on 50pi red brn	67.50	67.50
393	A19(b)	25pi on 50pi red brn	67.50	67.50
394	A19(a)	25pi dark green	15.00	5.00
395	A19(a)	50pi red brown	50.00	50.00

With Additional Overprint

396	A19(a)	2pi blue black	67.50	67.50

On Stamps of 1908-09

397	A20(a)	5pa ocher	67.50	67.50
398	A21(a)	5pa ocher	50.00	50.00
399	A21(a)	10pa blue green	50.00	50.00
400	A21(a)	20pa carmine rose	50.00	50.00

1916

350	A10	10pa gray grn (R)	2.00	2.00
351	A18	20pa carmine (Bl)	3.75	2.50
352	A18	1pi blue (R)	10.00	5.00
353	A18	2pi slate (Bk)	12.50	5.00
354	A18	2½pi red violet (Bk)	20.00	2.25
		Nos. 350-354 (5)	48.25	13.75

National Fête Day. Overprint reads "10 Temuz 1332" (July 23, 1916).

Preceding Issues Overprinted or Surcharged in Red or Black

401	A21(a)	1pi ultra	2.00	1.00
402	A21(a)	2pi blue black	4.00	2.00
403	A21(a)	2½pi dark brown	50.00	50.00
404	A21(a)	5pi dark violet	50.00	50.00

With Additional Overprint

405	A21(a)	1pi ultra	67.50	67.50
406	A21(a)	2pi blue black	50.00	50.00

On Stamps of 1913

407	A22(a)	5pa ocher	1.00	.75
408	A22(a)	20pa carmine rose	1.50	.50
409	A22(a)	1pi ultra	1.50	.50
410	A22(a)	2pi indigo	3.00	1.00
411	A22(b)	10pi on 50pi org brn	12.50	10.00
412	A22(a)	25pi gray green	7.50	5.00
413	A22(a)	50pi orange brown	15.00	12.50

With Additional Overprint

414	A22(a)	1pi ultra	2.00	1.00

On Commemorative Stamps of 1913

415	A23(a)	10pa green	1.25	.50
416	A23(a)	20pa red	2.00	.75
417	A23(a)	40pa blue	6.00	2.50

On Commemorative Stamp of 1916

418	A41(a)	5pi yel brn & blk	1.00	.50

No. 277 Surcharged in Blue

419	A31	60pa on 1pi on 1½pi	3.00	3.50
a.		"1330" omitted	40.00	40.00

See Nos. P134-P152, J67-J70.

Turkish Artillery A42

Mosque at Orta Köy, Constantinople — A43

Lighthouse on Bosporus — A44

Monument to Martyrs of Liberty — A45

Map of the Dardanelles; Sultan Mohammed V — A46

Map of the Dardanelles A47

Istanbul Across the Golden Horn A48

Pyramids of Egypt A49

Dolma Bahçe Palace and Mohammed V — A50

Sentry and Shell — A51

Sultan Mohammed V — A52

1916-18 Typo. Perf. 11½, 12½

420	A42	2pa violet	1.50	.75
421	A43	5pa orange	1.00	.75
424	A44	10pa green	1.00	1.00

Engr.

425	A45	20pa deep rose	1.00	.75
426	A46	1pi dull violet	3.00	.50

Typo.

428	A47	50pa ultra	1.50	.50
429	A48	2pi org brn & ind	3.00	.50
430	A49	5pi pale blue & blk	17.50	2.00

Engr.

431	A50	10pi dark green	8.75	5.00
432	A50	10pi dark violet	32.50	2.50
433	A50	10pi dark brown	14.00	2.50
434	A51	25pi carmine, straw	2.25	1.50
437	A52	50pi carmine	5.00	5.00
438	A52	50pi indigo	2.00	2.50
439	A52	50pi green, straw	2.50	10.00
		Nos. 420-439 (15)	96.50	35.75

For overprints and surcharges see Nos. 541B-541E, 554-560, 565-566, 569-574, 575, 577-578, 579A-580, Turkey in Asia 4, 10, 64-66, Thrace N76, N80, N81. Compare designs A42-A43 with A53-A54.

Forgeries of Nos. 446-545 abound.

Preceding Issues Overprinted or Surcharged in Red, Black or Blue

d

e

f   g

1917

On Stamps of 1865

446	A5(d)	20pa yellow (R)	45.00	67.50
a.		Star without rays (R)	50.00	57.50
447	A5(d)	1pi pearl gray (R)	45.00	67.50
a.		Star without rays (R)	50.00	57.50
448	A5(d)	2pi blue (R)	45.00	67.50
449	A5(d)	5pi carmine (Bk)	45.00	67.50

On Stamp of 1867

450	A5(d)	5pi rose (Bk)	45.00	67.50

On Stamps of 1870-71

451	A5(d)	2pi red (Bl)	45.00	67.50
452	A5(d)	5pi blue (Bl)	45.00	67.50
453	A5(d)	25pi dull rose (Bl)	45.00	67.50

On Stamp of 1874-75

454	A5(d)	10pa red violet (Bl)	45.00	67.50

On Stamps of April, 1876

455	A5(d)	10pa red lilac (Bl)	45.00	67.50
a.		10pa red violet (Bl)	50.00	67.50
457	A5(d)	20pa pale green (R)	45.00	67.50
458	A5(d)	1pi yellow (Bl)	45.00	67.50

On Stamps of January, 1876

459	A5(d)	¼pi on 10pa rose lil (Bl)	45.00	67.50
460	A5(d)	½pi on 20pa yel grn (R)	45.00	67.50
461	A5(d)	1¼pi on 50pa rose (Bl)	45.00	67.50

On Stamps of September, 1876

462	A7(d)	50pa blue & yel (R)	45.00	67.50
463	A7(d)	2pi blk & redsh brn (R)	45.00	67.50
464	A7(d)	25pi claret & rose (Bk)	45.00	67.50

On Stamps of 1880-84

465	A7(d)	5pa black & ol (R)	45.00	67.50
466	A7(d)	10pa black & grn (R)	45.00	67.50

On Stamps of 1881-82

467	A5(d)	20pa gray (Bl)	45.00	67.50
468	A5(d)	2pi pale sal (Bl)	45.00	67.50

On Stamps of 1884-86

469	A7(d)	10pa grn & pale grn (Bk)	45.00	67.50
470	A7(d)	2pi ocher & pale ocher (Bk)	45.00	67.50
471	A7(d)	5pi red brn & pale brn (Bk)	45.00	67.50

On Stamps of 1886

472	A7(d)	5pa blk & pale gray (R)	3.00	1.75
a.		Inverted overprint	30.00	30.00
473	A7(d)	2pi org & bl (Bk)	4.50	2.50
a.		Inverted overprint	35.00	35.00
474	A7(d)	5pi grn & pale grn (R)	45.00	67.50
475	A7(d)	25pi bis & pale bis (Bk)	45.00	67.50

On Stamp of 1888

476	A7(d)	5pi dk brn & gray (Bk)	45.00	67.50

On Stamps of 1892-98

477	A11(d)	20pa vio brn (R)	4.00	3.00
478	A13(d)	2pi brn org (R)	4.00	3.50
a.		Tête bêche pair	13.50	13.50

On Stamps of 1901

479	A16(d)	5pa bister (R)	3.00	3.00
a.		Inverted overprint	20.00	20.00
480	A16(d)	20pa mag (Bk)	2.00	1.50
a.		Inverted overprint	25.00	25.00
481	A16(d)	1pi vio bl (R)	3.00	3.00
a.		Inverted overprint	20.00	20.00
482	A16(d)	2pi gray bl (R)	5.00	5.00
483	A16(d)	5pi ocher (R)	32.50	50.00
484	A16(e)	10pi on 50pi yel (R)	32.50	50.00
485	A16(d)	25pi dk grn (R)	100.00	50.00
486	A17(d)	5pa purple (Bk)	32.50	50.00

487	A17(d)	10pa green (R)	5.00	5.00
488	A17(d)	20pa car (Bk)	2.00	1.50
a.		Inverted overprint	20.00	20.00
489	A17(d)	1pi blue (R)	1.00	.90
490	A17(d)	2pi org (Bk)	3.00	3.00
a.		Inverted overprint	20.00	20.00
491	A17(d)	5pi lil rose (R)	32.50	50.00
492	A17(e)	10pi on 50pi yel brn (R)	32.50	50.00
493	A17(d)	25pi brown (R)	5.00	5.00

On Stamps of 1905

494	A18(d)	5pa ocher (R)	2.00	1.00
a.		Inverted overprint	20.00	20.00
495	A18(d)	10pa dl grn (R)	32.50	50.00
496	A18(d)	20pa car (Bk)	1.00	1.00
a.		Double ovpt., one invtd.	35.00	35.00
b.		Inverted overprint	35.00	35.00
497	A18(d)	1pi blue (R)	1.50	1.00
a.		Inverted overprint	35.00	35.00
498	A18(d)	2pi slate (R)	5.00	5.00
499	A18(d)	2½pi red vio (Bk)	5.00	5.00
a.		Inverted overprint	20.00	20.00
500	A18(d)	5pi brown (R)	35.00	45.00
501	A18(d)	10pi orange brn (R)	35.00	50.00
502	A18(e)	10pi on 50pi dp vio (R)	35.00	50.00
503	A18(d)	25pi ol grn (R)	35.00	50.00

On Nos. 128-131

504	A18(d)	10pa dl grn (R)	1.50	1.00
a.		Inverted overprint	20.00	20.00
505	A18(d)	20pa car (Bk)	1.00	.75
a.		Double ovpt., one invtd.	20.00	20.00
b.		Inverted overprint	20.00	20.00
506	A18(d)	1pi brt bl (Bk)	1.00	.75
a.		Inverted overprint	20.00	20.00
507	A18(d)	1pi brt bl (R)	1.50	1.25
a.		Inverted overprint	20.00	20.00
508	A18(d)	2pi slate (Bk)	35.00	50.00
		Nos. 494-508 (15)	227.00	311.75

On Stamps of 1908

509	A19(d)	5pa ocher (R)	1.50	1.25
510	A19(d)	10pa bl grn (R)	20.00	20.00
510A	A19(d)	1pi brt blue (R)	125.00	140.00
511	A19(d)	2pi bl blk (R)	35.00	50.00
512	A19(d)	2½pi violet brn (Bk)	35.00	35.00
512A	A19(d)	10pi red (R)	150.00	225.00
513	A19(e)	10pi on 50pi red brn (R)	35.00	50.00
514	A19(d)	25pi dark green (R)	35.00	50.00

With Additional Overprint

514A	A19(d)	10pa bl grn (Bk)	150.00	225.00
515	A19(d)	1pi brt bl (Bk)	35.00	50.00
516	A19(d)	2pi bl blk (R)	5.00	5.00
516A	A19(d)	2pi bl blk (Bk)	35.00	67.50

On Stamps of 1908-09

517	A20(d)	5pa ocher (R)	3.00	3.00
518	A21(d)	5pa ocher (R)	2.00	1.00
a.		Double overprint	20.00	20.00
b.		Dbl. ovpt., one inverted	20.00	20.00
519	A21(d)	10pa bl grn (R)	2.00	1.50
520	A21(d)	20pa carmine rose (Bk)	2.00	1.50
a.		Double overprint	35.00	35.00
521	A21(d)	1pi ultra (R)	1.50	1.00
a.		1p bright blue (R)	30.00	30.00
522	A21(d)	2pi bl blk (R)	5.00	5.00
523	A21(d)	2½pi dk brn (Bk)	35.00	50.00
524	A21(d)	5pi dk vio (R)	35.00	50.00
525	A21(d)	10pi dull red (R)	35.00	50.00

With Additional Overprint

525A	A21(d)	10pa bl grn (Bk)	175.00	225.00
526	A21(d)	1pi ultra (Bk)	125.00	190.00

527	A21(d)	1pi ultra (R)	5.00	4.00
a.		1pi bright blue (R)	125.00	140.00
528	A21(d)	2pi bl blk (R)	35.00	50.00

On Stamps of 1913

529	A22(d)	5pa ocher (R)	2.50	2.00
530	A22(d)	10pa bl grn (R)	35.00	50.00
531	A22(d)	20pa car rose (Bk)	2.50	2.50
532	A22(d)	1pi ultra (R)	2.50	3.50
533	A22(d)	2pi indigo (R)	3.50	3.50
534	A22(d)	5pi dl vio (R)	35.00	50.00
535	A22(d)	10pi dl red (Bk)	45.00	50.00

With Additional Overprint

536	A22(d)	10pa bl grn (Bk)	1.50	1.50
a.		Inverted overprint	20.00	20.00
537	A22(d)	1pi ultra (Bk)	3.00	3.00
a.		Inverted overprint	20.00	20.00
538	A22(d)	2pi indigo (Bk)	35.00	100.00

On Commemorative Stamps of 1913

539	A23(d)	10pa green (R)	5.00	5.00
a.		Inverted overprint	20.00	20.00
540	A23(d)	40pa blue (R)	7.00	7.00
a.		Inverted overprint	20.00	20.00

On No. 277, with Addition of New Value

541	A31	60pa on 1pi on 1½pi (Bk)	5.00	3.00
a.		"1330" omitted	45.00	45.00

On Stamps of 1916-18

541B	A51(f)	25pi car, straw	5.00	5.00
541C	A52(g)	50pi carmine	17.50	17.50
541D	A52(g)	50pi indigo	35.00	50.00
541E	A52(g)	50pi green, straw	15.00	27.50

Ovptd. on Eastern Rumelia No. 12

542	A4(d)	20pa blk & rose (R)	35.00	35.00

Ovptd. in Black on Eastern Rumelia #15-17

543	A4(d)	5pa lilac & pale lilac	45.00	45.00
544	A4(d)	10pa green & pale green	45.00	45.00
545	A4(d)	20pa carmine & pale rose	45.00	45.00

Some experts question the status of Nos. 510A, 512A and 525A.
See Nos. J71-J86, P153-P172.

Soldiers in Trench — A52a

1917

545A	A52a	5pa on 1pi red	1.25	.75

It is stated that No. 545A was never issued without surcharge.
See Nos. 548f, 545A, 602.

Turkish Artillery A53

1917   Typo.   Perf. 11½, 12½

546	A53	2pa Prussian blue		150.00

In type A42 the Turkish inscription at the top is in one group, in type A53 it is in two groups. It is stated that No. 546 was never placed in use. Examples were distributed through the Universal Postal Union at Bern.
For surcharges see Nos. 547-548, Turkey in Asia 69-70.

Surcharged

547	A53	5pi on 2pa Prus bl	15.00	1.75
a.		Inverted surcharge	20.00	9.00
b.		Turkish "5" omitted at lower left		

Surcharged

1918

548	A53	5pi on 2pa Prus blue	15.00	2.00
g.		Inverted surcharge	20.00	10.00

Top line of surcharge on Nos. 547-548 reads "Ottoman Posts."
For surcharge see Thrace No. N79.

No. 545A Surcharged

1918

548A	A52a	2pa on 5pa on 1pi red	2.50	1.75
b.		Double surcharge	10.00	10.00
c.		Inverted surcharge	10.00	10.00
d.		Double surcharge inverted	10.00	10.00
e.		Dbl. surch., one inverted	10.00	10.00
f.		In pair with No. 545A	17.50	17.50

Enver Pasha and Kaiser Wilhelm II on Battlefield A54

St. Sophia and Obelisk of the Hippodrome A55

1918   Typo.   Perf. 12, 12½

549	A54	5pa brown red	100.00	
550	A55	10pa gray green	100.00	

The stamps, of which very few saw postal use, were converted into paper money by pasting on thick yellow paper and reperforating.
Values are for stamps with original gum. Examples removed from the yellow paper are worth $8 each.

Armistice Issue

Overprinted in Black or Red

1919, Nov. 30

On Stamps of 1913

552	A34	2½pi org & ol grn	125.00	300.00
553	A38	50pi carmine	125.00	300.00

On Stamps of 1916-18

554	A46	1pi dull violet (R)	7.50	10.00
555	A47	50pa ultra (R), perf 11½	1.00	1.50
556	A48	2pi org brn & ind	1.75	2.00
557	A49	5pi pale bl & blk (R), perf 11½	1.75	2.00
558	A50	10pi dark green (R)	6.25	10.00
559	A51	25pi carmine, straw	6.25	10.00

560 A52 50pi grn, *straw* 6.25 10.00
(R)

Fountain in Desert near Sinai — A56

Sentry at Beersheba — A57

Turkish Troops at Sinai A58

Typo.

562 A56 20pa claret 1.25 *2.00*
563 A57 1pi blue (R) 125.00 150.00
564 A58 25pi slate blue (R) 125.00 150.00
Nos. 552-564 (12) 532.00 947.50

The overprint reads: "Souvenir of the Armistice, 30th October 1334." Nos. 562-564 are not known to have been regularly issued without overprint.

See No. J87. For overprints and surcharges see Nos. 576, 579, 582, 583-584, 586, Turkey in Asia 71, Thrace N83.

Stamps of 1911-19 Overprinted in Turkish

"Accession to the Throne of His Majesty, 3rd July 1334-1918," the Tughra of Sultan Mohammed VI and sometimes Ornaments and New Values

Dome of the Rock, Jerusalem — A59

1919
565 A42 2pa violet 1.00 *2.50*
566 A43 5pa orange .75 .50
567 A21 5pa on 2pa ol grn .75 .50
a. Inverted surcharge 10.00 10.00
568 A22 10pa on 2pa ol grn 1.00 .50
569 A44 10pa green 1.25 1.50
a. Inverted overprint 25.00 25.00
570 A45 20pa deep rose 1.25 .50
a. Inverted overprint 12.00 12.00
571 A46 1pi dull violet 1.25 1.00
572 A47 60pa on 50pi ultra 1.25 1.00
573 A48 60pa on 2pi org brn & ind 1.00 .50
574 A48 2pi orange brn & ind 1.00 1.00
574A A34 2½pi orange & ol grn 25.00 37.50
575 A49 5pi pale blue & blk 1.00 1.00
576 A56 10pi on 20pa cl 1.00 1.00
577 A50 10pi dark brown 2.50 2.50
578 A51 25pi carmine, straw 2.00 2.00
579 A57 35pi on 1pi blue 1.50 2.00
579A A52 50pi carmine 25.00 *37.50*
580 A52 50pi green, straw 6.00 5.00
581 A59 100pi on 10pa green 6.00 5.00
582 A58 250pi on 25pi sl bl 6.00 5.00
Nos. 565-582 (20) 86.50 108.50

See note after #586. See #J88-J91.
For overprint and surcharge see Nos. 585, Thrace N82.

Surcharged with Ornaments, New Values and

Perf. 11½, 12½

583 A56 20pa claret 1.75 10.00
584 A57 1pi deep blue 2.50 17.50
585 A59 60pa on 10pa green 1.50 7.50
586 A58 25pi slate blue 7.50 50.00
a. Inverted overprint 100.00
Nos. 583-586 (4) 13.25 85.00

#576, 579, 581, 582, 583-586 were prepared in anticipation of the invasion and conquest of Egypt by the Turks. They were not issued at that time but subsequently received various overprints in commemoration of Sultan Mehmet Sadi's accession to the throne (#565-582) and of the 1st anniv. of this event (#583-586).

For surcharge see Thrace No. N83.

Designs of 1913 Modified

1920 **Litho.** **Perf. 11, 12**
590 A26 5pa brown orange 1.00 .50
Engr.
591 A28 10pa green 1.00 .50
592 A23 20pa rose 1.00 .50
593 A30 1pi blue green 3.75 .50
594 A32 3pi blue 1.00 .50
595 A34 5pi gray 50.00 .50
596 A36 10pi gray violet 12.50 .50
597 A37 25pi dull violet 5.00 2.50
598 A38 50pi brown 5.00 10.00
Nos. 590-598 (9) 80.25 16.00

On most stamps of this issue the designs have been modified by removing the small Turkish word at right of the tughra of the Sultan. In the 3pi and 5pi the values have been altered, while for the 25pi the color has been changed.

For surcharges see Thrace Nos. N77, N78, N84.

1921-22 **Black Surcharge**
600 SP1 30pa on 10pa red vio 1.50 .50
a. Double surcharge 37.50 37.50
b. Imperf.
601 A28 60pa on 10pa green 1.50 .50
a. Double surcharge 22.50 22.50
602 A52a 4½pi on 1pi red 8.00 3.25
a. Inverted surcharge 20.00 20.00
603 A32 7½pi on 3pi blue 15.00 1.00
604 A32 7½pi on 3pi bl (R) 25.00 2.50
('22)
a. Double surcharge 35.00 30.00
Nos. 600-604 (5) 51.00 7.75

Turkish Stamps of 1916-21 with Greek surcharge as above in blue or black are of private origin.

Issues of the Republic

Crescent and Star — A64

TWO PIASTERS:
Type I — "2" measures 3¼x1¾mm
Type II — "2" measures 2¾x1½mm

FIVE PIASTERS:
Type I — "5" measures 3½x2¼mm
Type II — "5" measures 3x1¾mm

Perf. 11, 12, 13½, 13½x12
1923-25 **Litho.**
605 A64 10pa gray black .25 .25
606 A64 20pa citron .25 .25
607 A64 1pi deep violet .25 .25
a. Slanting numeral in lower left corner .50 .25
608 A64 1½pi emerald .25 1.50
609 A64 2pi bluish grn (I) 2.00 .50
a. 2pi deep green (II) .75 .25
610 A64 3pi yel brn 1.00 .50
611 A64 3¾pi lilac brown 2.50 2.50
612 A64 4½pi carmine .75 1.00
613 A64 5pi purple (I) 3.50 1.50
a. 5pi violet (II) 12.50 1.00
614 A64 7½pi blue 2.50 .50
615 A64 10pi slate 7.50 1.00
a. 10pi blue 7.50 1.00
616 A64 11¼pi dull rose 2.50 2.00
617 A64 15pi brown 10.00 1.00
618 A64 18¾pi myrtle green 4.50 3.00
619 A64 22½pi orange 6.00 2.00
620 A64 25pi black brown 30.00 2.50
621 A64 50pi gray 75.00 4.00
622 A64 100pi dark violet 150.00 8.50
624 A64 500pi deep green 500.00 160.00
Cut cancellation 1.60
Nos. 605-624 (19) 798.75 192.75
Set, never hinged 3,000.

#605-610, 612-617 exist imperf. & part perf.

Bridge of Sakarya and Mustafa Kemal — A65

1924, Jan. 1 **Perf. 12**
625 A65 1½pi emerald .75 .30
626 A65 3pi purple .90 .50
627 A65 4½pi pale rose 5.00 2.00
628 A65 5pi yellow brown 4.00 2.00
629 A65 7½pi deep blue 5.00 2.00
630 A65 50pi orange 22.50 10.00
631 A65 100pi brown violet 52.50 20.00
632 A65 200pi olive brown 72.50 35.00
Nos. 625-632 (8) 163.15 71.80
Set, never hinged 750.00

Signing of Treaty of Peace at Lausanne.

The Legendary Blacksmith and his Gray Wolf — A66

Sakarya Gorge — A67

Fortress of Ankara — A68

Mustafa Kemal Pasha — A69

1926 **Engr.**
634 A66 10pa slate .50 .25
635 A66 20pa orange .50 .25
636 A66 1g brt rose 1.50 .25
637 A67 2g green 1.50 .25
638 A67 2½g gray black 2.00 .25
639 A67 3g copper red 2.50 .25
640 A68 5g lilac gray 4.00 .75
641 A68 6g red 1.00 .25
642 A68 10g deep blue 7.50 .50
643 A68 15g deep orange 10.00 .50
644 A69 25g dk green & blk 15.00 1.25
645 A69 50g carmine & blk 20.00 1.50
646 A69 100g olive grn & blk 35.00 2.00
647 A69 200g brown & blk 90.00 5.50
Nos. 634-647 (14) 190.00 13.75
Set, never hinged 800.00

Stamps of 1926 Overprinted in Black, Silver or Gold

1927, Sept. 9
648 A66 1g brt rose .50 .50
649 A67 2g green .50 1.00
650 A67 2½g gray black 1.50 2.00
651 A67 3g copper red 2.00 2.50
652 A68 5g lilac gray 2.50 4.00
653 A68 6g red 1.50 1.50
654 A68 10g deep blue 3.50 3.50
655 A68 15g deep orange 5.00 5.00
656 A69 25g dk green & blk (S) 15.00 20.00
657 A69 50g car & blk (S) 27.50 37.50
658 A69 100g ol grn & blk (G) 60.00 75.00
Nos. 648-658 (11) 119.50 152.50
Set, never hinged 425.00

Agricultural and industrial exhibition at Izmir, Sept. 9-20, 1927.
The overprint reads: "1927" and the initials of "Izmir Dokuz Eylul Sergisi" (Izmir Exhibition, September 9).

Second Izmir Exhibition Issue
Nos. 634-647 Overprinted in Red or Black

On A66-A68

On A69

1928, Sept. 9
659 A66 10pa slate (R) .50 .40
660 A66 20pa orange .50 .40
661 A66 1g brt rose 1.00 1.00
662 A67 2g green (R) 1.50 1.50
663 A67 2½g gray blk (R) 1.50 1.50
664 A67 3g copper red 1.50 1.50
665 A68 5g lilac gray (R) 2.00 2.00

666	A68	6g red	.50	.50
667	A68	10g deep blue	3.50	3.00
668	A68	15g deep orange	5.00	2.00
669	A69	25g dk grn & blk		
		(R)	15.00	6.25
670	A69	50g car & blk	17.50	20.00
671	A69	100g ol grn & blk		
		(R)	40.00	50.00
672	A69	200g brn & blk (R)	62.50	62.50
		Nos. 659-672 (14)	152.50	153.05
		Set, never hinged	650.00	

The overprint reads "Izmir, September 9, 1928."

Nos. 636, 652, 654
Surcharged in Black
(#673) or Red (#674-
675)

1929

673	A66	20pa on 1g brt rose	.50	.25
a.		Inverted surcharge	3.50	3.50
674	A68	2½k on 5g lilac gray	1.00	.50
a.		Inverted surcharge	7.50	7.50
675	A68	6k on 10g deep blue	6.00	.75
		Nos. 673-675 (3)	7.50	1.50
		Set, never hinged	40.00	

Railroad Bridge
over Kizil
Irmak — A70

A71

A72   A73

Latin Inscriptions
Without umlaut over first "U" of
"CUMHURIYETI"

1929   **Engr.**

676	A70	2k gray black	5.00	1.00
677	A70	2½k green	3.00	1.00
678	A70	3k violet brown	4.00	1.50
679	A71	6k dark violet	25.00	1.00
680	A72	12½k deep blue	35.00	3.75
681	A73	50k carmine & blk	60.00	8.75
		Nos. 676-681 (6)	132.00	17.00
		Set, never hinged	400.00	

See Nos. 682-691, 694-695, 697, 699. For surcharges & overprints see #705-714, 716-717, 719, 721, 727, 765-766, 770-771, 777, C2, C7.

Sakarya
Gorge — A74

Mustafa Kemal
Pasha — A75

With umlaut over first "U" of
"CUMHURIYETI"

1930

682	A71	10pa green	.25	.25
683	A70	20pa gray violet	.25	.25
684	A70	1k olive green	.50	.50
685	A71	1½k olive black	.50	.40
686	A70	2k dull violet	3.00	.50
687	A70	2½k deep green	2.00	.50
688	A70	3k brown orange	20.00	1.50
689	A71	4k deep rose	7.50	.50
690	A72	5k rose lake	11.50	.50
691	A71	6k indigo	7.50	.50
692	A74	7½k red brown	.25	.25
694	A72	12½k deep ultra	.75	.25
695	A72	15k deep orange	.75	.50
696	A74	17½k dark gray	.75	.50
697	A72	20k black brown	50.00	2.00

698	A74	25k olive brown	1.00	1.00
699	A72	30k yellow brown	1.75	1.00
700	A74	40k red violet	1.50	1.00
701	A75	50k red & black	3.50	1.25
702	A75	100k olive grn & blk	3.50	1.25
703	A75	200k dk green & blk	3.75	1.50
704	A75	500k chocolate & blk	17.50	22.50
		Nos. 682-704 (22)	138.00	38.40
		Set, never hinged	500.00	

For surcharges and overprints see Nos. 715, 718, 720, 722-726, 767-769, 772-773, 775-776, 778-780, 823-828, 848-850, C1, C3-C6, C8-C11.

Nos. 682-704 Surcharged in Red or
Black

a   b

c

1930, Aug. 30

705	A71(a)	10pa on 10pa (R)	.50	1.25
706	A70(b)	10pa on 20pa	.50	1.50
707	A70(b)	20pa on 1ku	1.00	1.50
708	A71(a)	1k on 1½k (R)	.50	1.25
709	A70(b)	1½k on 2k	1.00	1.50
710	A70(b)	2k on 2½k (R)	2.50	2.00
711	A70(b)	2½k on 3k	2.00	1.50
712	A71(a)	3k on 4k	2.00	2.00
713	A72(a)	4k on 5k	2.50	1.00
714	A71(a)	5k on 6k (R)	3.50	4.00
715	A74(a)	6k on 7½k	.75	.50
716	A72(a)	7½k on 12½k (R)	1.25	1.00
717	A72(a)	12½k on 15k	1.25	1.00
718	A74(b)	15k on 17½k (R)	5.00	4.00
719	A72(b)	17½k on 20k (R)	5.00	2.50
720	A74(b)	20k on 25k (R)	7.50	2.00
721	A72(b)	25k on 30k	5.00	2.50
722	A74(b)	30k on 40k	7.50	2.50
723	A75(c)	40k on 50k	15.00	7.50
724	A75(c)	50k on 100k (R)	70.00	16.00
725	A75(c)	100k on 200k (R)	85.00	27.50
726	A75(c)	250k on 500k (R)	75.00	35.00
		Nos. 705-726 (22)	294.25	118.00
		Set, never hinged	800.00	

Inauguration of the railroad between Ankara and Sivas.

There are numerous varieties in these settings as: "309," "390," "930" inverted, no period after "D," no period after "Y" and raised period before "Y."

No. 685 Surcharged
in Red

1931, Apr. 1

727	A71	1k on 1½k olive blk	1.00	.25

Olive Tree with Roots
Extending to All
Balkan
Capitals — A76

1931, Oct. 20   **Engr.**   **Perf. 12**

728	A76	2½k dark green	.40	.25
729	A76	4k carmine	.50	.25
730	A76	6k steel blue	.50	.25

731	A76	7½k dull red	.50	.25
732	A76	12k deep orange	1.00	.25
733	A76	12½k dark blue	1.00	.25
734	A76	30k dark violet	1.75	1.50
735	A76	50k dark brown	3.00	.75
736	A76	100k brown violet	6.25	1.50
		Nos. 728-736 (9)	14.90	5.25
		Set, never hinged	30.00	

Second Balkan Conference.

A77   A78

Mustafa Kemal Pasha
(Kemal Atatürk) — A79

1931-42   **Typo.**   **Perf. 11½, 12**

737	A77	10pa blue green	.25	.25
738	A77	20pa deep orange	.25	.25
739	A77	30pa brt violet ('38)	.25	.25
740	A78	1k dk slate green	.25	.25
740A	A77	1½k magenta ('42)	.55	.25
741	A78	2k dark violet	.50	.25
741A	A78	2k yel grn ('40)	.50	.25
742	A77	2½k green	.50	.25
743	A78	3k brn org ('38)	1.50	.25
744	A78	4k slate	2.50	.25
745	A78	5k rose red	.25	.25
745A	A78	5k brown blk ('40)	2.00	.50
746	A78	6k deep blue	3.00	.25
746A	A78	6k rose ('40)	.80	.30
747	A77	7½k deep rose ('32)	.50	.25
747A	A78	8k brt blue ('38)	3.50	.25
b.		8k dark blue ('36)	3.50	.25
748	A77	10k black brn ('32)	1.00	.25
748A	A77	10k deep blue ('40)	7.00	.60
749	A77	12k bister ('32)	1.00	.25
750	A79	12½k indigo ('32)	1.00	.25
751	A77	15k org yel ('32)	1.00	.25
752	A77	20k olive grn ('32)	1.00	.25
753	A77	25k Prus blue ('32)	2.50	1.00
754	A77	30k magenta ('32)	7.50	.50
755	A79	100k maroon ('32)	200.00	5.50
756	A79	200k purple ('32)	3.75	2.00
757	A79	250k chocolate ('32)	100.00	11.50
		Nos. 737-757 (27)	342.60	26.65
		Set, never hinged	750.00	

See Nos. 1015-1033, 1117B-1126. For overprints see Nos. 811-816.

Symbolizing 10th
Anniversary of
Republic — A80

President Atatürk — A81

1933, Oct. 29   **Perf. 10**

758	A80	1½k blue green	1.25	1.00
759	A80	2k olive brown	1.25	1.00
760	A81	3k dull red	1.25	1.00
761	A81	6k deep blue	1.25	1.00
762	A80	12½k dark blue	3.25	2.50

763	A80	25k dark brown	8.00	5.00
764	A81	50k orange brown	20.00	15.00
		Nos. 758-764 (7)	36.25	26.50
		Set, never hinged	75.00	

10th year of the Turkish Republic. The stamps were in use for three days only.

Nos. 682, 685, 692, 694, 696-698, 702
Overprinted or Surcharged in Red

1934, Aug. 26   **Perf. 12**

765	A71	10pa green	.50	1.00
766	A71	1k on 1½k	1.00	.75
767	A74	2k on 25k	1.50	1.25
768	A74	5k on 7½k	5.00	5.00
769	A74	6k on 17½k	2.50	2.00
770	A72	12½k deep ultra	7.50	5.00
771	A72	15k on 20k	50.00	45.00
772	A74	20k on 25k	35.00	37.50
773	A75	50k on 100k	40.00	37.50
		Nos. 765-773 (9)	143.00	135.00
		Set, never hinged	600.00	

Izmir Fair, 1934.

Nos. 696, 698, 701-
704 Surcharged in
Black

1936, Oct. 26

775	A74	4k on 17½k	1.00	.50
776	A74	5k on 25k	1.00	.50
777	A73	6k on 50k	1.00	.50
778	A75	10k on 100k	1.75	1.00
779	A75	20k on 200k	5.50	2.00
780	A75	50k on 500k	10.00	3.25
		Nos. 775-780 (6)	20.25	7.75
		Set, never hinged	75.00	

"1926" in Overprint

775a	A74	4k on 17½k	6.50	3.75
776a	A74	5k on 25k	7.00	3.75
777a	A73	6k on 50k	7.00	3.75
778a	A75	10k on 100k	9.00	4.50
779a	A75	20k on 200k	20.00	10.00
780a	A75	50k on 500k	55.00	27.50
		Nos. 775a-780a (6)	104.50	53.25
		Set, never hinged	250.00	

Re-militarization of the Dardanelles.

Hittite Bronze
Stag — A82

Thorak's Bust
of Kemal
Atatürk — A83

1937, Sept. 20   **Litho.**   **Perf. 12**

781	A82	3k light violet	1.75	1.25
782	A83	6k blue	3.00	2.00
783	A82	7½k bright pink	4.75	3.75
784	A83	12½k indigo	10.00	7.50
		Nos. 781-784 (4)	19.50	14.50
		Set, never hinged	40.00	

2nd Turkish Historical Congress, Istanbul, Sept. 20-30.

Arms of Turkey,
Greece, Romania
and
Yugoslavia — A84

1937, Oct. 29   **Perf. 11½**

785	A84	8k carmine	6.75	3.50
786	A84	12½k dark blue	15.00	4.75
		Set, never hinged	40.00	

The Balkan Entente.

Street in Izmir A85

Fig Tree — A87

30pa, View of Fair Buildings. 3k, Tower, Government Square. 5k, Olive branch. 6k, Woman with grapes. 7½k, Woman picking grapes. 8k, Izmir Harbor through arch. 12k, Statue of Pres. Ataturk. 12½k, Pres. Ataturk.

1938, Aug. 20　Photo.　Perf. 11½
Inscribed: "Izmir Enternasyonal Fuari 1938"

789	A85	10pa dark brown	.50	.60
790	A85	30pa purple	.75	.50
791	A87	2½k brt green	1.25	1.00
792	A87	3k brown orange	1.25	.50
793	A87	5k olive green	2.25	.75
794	A85	6k brown	5.00	.40
795	A87	7½k scarlet	5.00	2.50
796	A87	8k brown lake	3.50	1.50
797	A87	12k rose violet	6.25	3.50
798	A87	12½k deep blue	10.00	8.50
		Nos. 789-798 (10)	35.75	19.75
		Set, never hinged	70.00	

Izmir International Fair.

President Ataturk Teaching Reformed Turkish Alphabet A95

1938, Nov. 2

799	A95	2½k brt green	1.00	.55
800	A95	3k orange	1.25	.55
801	A95	6k rose violet	1.50	.65
802	A95	7½k deep rose	1.75	1.00
803	A95	8k red brown	2.00	1.10
804	A95	12½k brt ultra	2.50	1.25
		Nos. 799-804 (6)	10.00	5.10
		Set, never hinged	20.00	

Reform of the Turkish alphabet, 10th anniv.

Army and Air Force A96

Ataturk Driving Tractor — A98

3k, View of Kayseri. 7½k, Railway bridge. 8k, Scout buglers. 12½k, President Ataturk.

1938, Oct. 29
Inscribed: "Cumhuriyetin 15 inc yil donumu hatirasi"

805	A96	2½k dark green	.45	.35
806	A96	3k red brown	.45	.35
807	A98	6k bister	.75	.35
808	A96	7½k red	1.25	.90
809	A96	8k rose violet	4.00	2.50
810	A98	12½k deep blue	2.25	1.75
		Nos. 805-810 (6)	9.15	6.20
		Set, never hinged	20.00	

15th anniversary of the Republic.

Stamps of 1931-38 Overprinted in Black

1938, Nov. 21　Perf. 11½x12

811	A78	3k brown orange	.50	.35
812	A78	5k rose red	.50	.35
813	A78	6k deep blue	.75	.50
814	A77	7½k deep rose	.80	.55
815	A78	8k dark blue	2.00	.75
a.		8k bright blue	225.00	150.00
816	A79	12½k indigo	3.75	1.75
		Nos. 811-816 (6)	8.30	4.25
		Set, never hinged	15.00	

President Kemal Atatürk (1881-1938). The date is that of his funeral.

> **Catalogue values for unused stamps in this section, from this point to the end of the section, are for Never Hinged items.**

Turkish and American Flags — A102

Presidents Inönü and F. D. Roosevelt and Map of North America A103

Designs: 3k, 8k, Inonu and Roosevelt. 7½k, 12½k, Kemal Ataturk and Washington.

1939, July 15　Photo.　Perf. 14

817	A102	2½k ol grn, red & bl	.25	.25
818	A103	3k dk brn & bl grn	.50	.25
819	A102	6k purple, red & bl	.50	.25
820	A103	7½k org ver & bl grn	1.00	.40
821	A103	8k dp cl & bl grn	.75	.40
822	A103	12½k brt bl & bl grn	2.00	.85
		Nos. 817-822 (6)	5.00	2.40

US constitution, 150th anniversary.

Nos. 698, 702-704 Surcharged in Black

1939, July 23　Unwmk.　Perf. 13

823	A74	3k on 25k	.40	.25
824	A75	6k on 200k	.65	.50
825	A74	7½k on 25k	.75	.50
826	A75	12k on 100k	1.00	.50
827	A75	12½k on 200k	2.00	.50
828	A75	17½k on 500k	3.00	1.00
		Nos. 823-828 (6)	7.80	3.25

Annexation of Hatay.

Railroad Bridge A105

Locomotive A106

Track Through Mountain Pass A107

Design: 12½k, Railroad tunnel, Atma Pass.

1939, Oct. 20　Typo.　Perf. 11½

829	A105	3k lt orange red	3.25	3.25
830	A106	6k chestnut	3.75	3.75
831	A107	7½k rose pink	5.25	5.25
832	A107	12½k dark blue	8.75	8.75
		Nos. 829-832 (4)	21.00	21.00

Completion of the Sivas to Erzerum link of the Ankara-Erzerum Railroad.

Atatürk Residence in Ankara — A109

Kemal Atatürk — A110

A111

Designs: 5k, 6k, 7½k, 8k, 12½k, 17½k, Various portraits of Ataturk, "1880-1938."

1939-40　　　　　　Photo.

833	A109	2½k brt green	1.00	.50
834	A110	3k dk blue gray	1.00	.50
835	A110	5k chocolate	1.25	.75
836	A110	6k chestnut	1.25	.75
837	A110	7½k rose red	3.75	1.00
838	A110	8k gray green	1.75	1.00
839	A110	12½k brt blue	2.00	1.50
840	A110	17½k brt rose	6.50	2.00
		Nos. 833-840 (8)	18.50	8.00

Souvenir Sheet

841	A111	100k blue black	70.00	100.00

Death of Kemal Ataturk, first anniversary. Size of No. 841: 90x120mm. Issued: 2½k, 6k, 12½k, 11/11/39; others, 1/3/40.

Namik Kemal A118

Arms of Turkey, Greece, Romania and Yugoslavia A119

1940, Jan. 3

842	A118	6k chestnut	1.25	.60
843	A118	8k dk olive grn	3.00	1.50
844	A118	12k brt rose red	3.50	2.00
845	A118	12½k brt blue	7.50	3.00
		Nos. 842-845 (4)	15.25	7.10

Birth cent. of Namik Kemal, poet and patriot.

Perf. 11½
1940, Jan. 1　Typo.　Unwmk.

846	A119	8k light blue	3.50	1.00
847	A119	10k deep blue	7.00	2.25

The Balkan Entente.

Nos. 703-704 Surcharged in Red or Black

1940, Aug. 20　　Perf. 12

848	A75	6k on 200k dk grn & blk (R)	.75	1.00
849	A75	10k on 200k dk grn & blk	1.25	1.50
850	A75	12k on 500k choc & blk	2.00	2.50
		Nos. 848-850 (3)	4.00	5.00

13th International Izmir Fair.

Map of Turkey and Census Figures A120

1940, Oct. 1　Typo.　Perf. 11½

851	A120	10pa dark blue green	.25	.25
852	A120	3k orange	1.25	1.25
853	A120	6k carmine rose	1.50	1.50
854	A120	10k dark blue	2.50	2.50
		Nos. 851-854 (4)	5.50	5.50

Census of Oct. 20, 1940.

Runner — A121

Pole Vaulter — A122

Hurdler A123

Discus Thrower — A124

1940, Oct. 5

855	A121	3k olive green	2.50	2.50
856	A122	6k rose	7.50	3.50
857	A123	8k chestnut brown	3.50	4.00
858	A124	10k dark blue	5.50	10.00
		Nos. 855-858 (4)	19.00	20.00

11th Balkan Olympics.

Mail Carriers on Horseback A125

Postman of 1840 and 1940 — A126

Old Sailing Vessel and Modern Mailboat — A127

Design: 12k, Post Office, Istanbul.

1940, Dec. 31   Typo.   Perf. 10
859 A125   3k gray green   .50   .50
860 A126   6k rose   .75   .75
861 A127 10k dark blue   1.00   1.00
862 A127 12k olive brown   1.50   1.50
    Nos. 859-862 (4)   3.75   3.75

Centenary of the Turkish post.

Harbor Scene A129

Statue of Atatürk — A132

Designs: 3k, 6k, 17½k, Various Izmir Fair buildings. 12k, Girl picking grapes.

1941, Aug. 20   Litho.   Perf. 11½
Inscribed: "Izmir Enternasyonal Fuari 1941"
863 A129 30pa dull green   .35   .25
864 A129   3k olive gray   .50   .25
865 A129   6k salmon rose   .75   .25
866 A132 10k blue   .95   .30
867 A129 12k dull brown vio   1.10   .45
868 A129 17½k dull brown   1.75   1.25
    Nos. 863-868 (6)   5.40   2.75

Izmir International Fair, 1941.

Tomb of Barbarossa II — A135

Barbarossa's Fleet in Battle — A136

Barbarossa II (Khair ed-Din) — A137

1941
869 A135 20pa dark violet   .25   .25
870 A136   3k light blue   .75   .75
871 A136   6k rose red   1.25   1.25
872 A136 10k deep ultra   1.50   1.50
873 A136 12k dull brn & bis   1.75   1.75
874 A137 17½k multicolored   2.25   2.25
    Nos. 869-874 (6)   7.75   7.75

400th death anniv. of Barbarossa II.

President Inönü
A138   A138a

1942-45   Perf. 11½x11, 11
875   A138 0.25k yellow bis   .25   .25
876   A138 0.50k lt yellow grn   .25   .25
877   A138   1k gray green   .25   .25
877A A138   1½k brt vio ('45)   .25   .25
878   A138   2k bluish green   .30   .25
879   A138   4k fawn   .30   .30
880   A138   4½k slate   .30   .30
881   A138   5k light blue   .35   .25
882   A138   6k salmon
                   rose   .30   .25
883   A138   6¾k ultra   .25   .25
884   A138   9k blue violet   .80   .25
885   A138   10k dark blue   .30   .25
886   A138 13½k brt pink   .30   .25
887   A138   16k Prus green   .50   .25
888   A138 17½k rose lake   .50   .25
889   A138   20k brown violet   .50   .50
890   A138 27½k orange   .50   .50
891   A138   37k buff   .50   .50
892   A138   50k purple   1.60   .25
893   A138 100k olive bister   .25   3.00
894   A138a 200k brown   17.50   2.50
    Nos. 875-894 (21)   30.60 11.10

Ankara — A139   Antioch — A141

0.50k, Mohair goats. 1½k, Ankara Dam. 2k, Oranges. 4k, Merino sheep. 4½k, Train. 5k, Tile decorating. 6k, Atatürk statue, Ankara. 6¾k, 10k, Pres. Ismet Inonu. 13½k, Grand National Assembly. 16k, Arnavutkoy, Istanbul. 17½k, Republic monument, Istanbul. 20k, Safety monument, Ankara. 27½k, Post Office, Istanbul. 37k, Monument at Afyon. 50k, "People's House," Ankara. 100k, Atatürk & Inonu. 200k, Pres. Inonu.

1943, Apr. 1   Perf. 11
896 A139 0.25k citron   .25   .25
897 A139 0.50k brt green   .40   .25
898 A141   1k yellow olive   .25   .25
899 A141   1½k deep violet   .25   .25
900 A139   2k brt blue green   .40   .25
901 A139   4k copper red   2.00   .50
902 A139   4½k black   2.00   .25
903 A141   5k sapphire   1.25   .50
904 A139   6k carmine rose   .25   .25
905 A139   6¾k brt ultra   .25   .25
906 A139   10k dark blue   .25   .25
907 A141 13½k brt red violet   .30   .25
908 A141   16k myrtle green   3.50   .25
909 A139 17½k brown orange   1.00   .25
910 A139   20k sepia   1.25   .25
911 A139 27½k dk orange   1.50   1.00
912 A139   37k lt yellow brn   1.25   .40
913 A141   50k purple   10.00   .25
914 A139 100k dk olive grn   12.50   2.50

915 A139 200k dark brown   9.00   2.00
  a.   Souvenir sheet   70.00 100.00
    Nos. 896-915 (20)   47.85 10.40

No. 915a contains one stamp similar to No. 915, perf. 13½ and printed in sepia. Issued Apr. 20.

For surcharge see No. 928.

Girl with Grapes — A158

Entrance to Izmir Fair A159

Fair Building A160

1943, Aug. 20   Litho.   Perf. 11½
916 A158   4½k dull olive   .25   .25
917 A159   6k carmine rose   .25   .25
918 A160   6¾k blue   .25   .25
919 A159   10k dark blue   .50   .25
920 A158 13½k sepia   1.00   1.00
921 A160 27½k dull gray   1.50   1.75
    Nos. 916-921 (6)   3.75   3.75

Izmir International Fair.

Soccer Team on Parade A161

Turkish Flag and Soldier — A162

Designs: 6¾k, Bridge. 10k, Hospital. 13½k, View of Ankara. 27½k, President Inonu.

1943, Oct. 29   Perf. 11x11½, 11½x11
Inscribed: "Cumhuriyetin 20 nci Yildonomu Hatirasi"
922 A161   4½k lt olive grn   1.50   1.75
923 A162   6k rose red   .50   .25
924 A161   6¾k ultra   .50   .25
925 A161   10k violet blue   .50   .25
926 A161 13½k olive   .75   .25
927 A162 27½k lt brown   .95   .75
    Nos. 922-927 (6)   4.70   3.50

Republic, 20th anniv. Nos. 922-927 exist imperf.

No. 905 Surcharged with New Value in Red

1945   Perf. 11
928 A139 4½k on 6¾k brt ultra 1.00   .45

Recording Census Data — A167

President Ismet Inönü — A169

1945, Oct. 21   Litho.   Perf. 11½
929 A167   4½k olive black   .65   .25
930 A167   9k violet   .75   .25
931 A167   10k violet blue   .75   .25
932 A167   18k dark red   1.50   .60
    Nos. 929-932 (4)   3.65   1.35

Souvenir Sheet
Imperf
933 A167   1 l chocolate   75.00 100.00

Census of 1945.

Perf. 11½ to 12½
1946, Apr. 1   Unwmk.
934 A169 0.25k brown red   .25   .25
935 A169   1k dk slate grn   .25   .25
936 A169   1½k plum   .50   .25
937 A169   9k purple   1.00   .25
938 A169   10k deep blue   1.50   .25
939 A169   50k chocolate   5.00   .25
    Nos. 934-939 (6)   8.50   1.50

U.S.S. Missouri A170

1946, Apr. 5   Perf. 11½
940 A170   9k dark purple   .75   .30
941 A170   10k dk chalky blue   1.25   .60
942 A170 27½k olive green   3.00   3.50
  a.   Imperf., pair   50.00
    Nos. 940-942 (3)   5.00   4.40

Visit of the USS Missouri to Istanbul, 4/5.

Sower A171

Dove and Flag-Decorated Banderol A172

1946, June 16   Perf. 11½ to 12½
943 A171   9k violet   .25   .25
944 A171   10k dark blue   .40   .25
945 A171   18k olive green   .65   1.00
946 A171 27½k red orange   1.25   2.50
    Nos. 943-946 (4)   2.55   4.00

Passing of legislation to distribute state lands to poor farmers.

1947, Aug. 20   Photo.   Perf. 12
947 A172   15k violet & dk bl   .40   .25
948 A172   20k blue & dk blue   1.00   .50
949 A172   30k brown & gray blk .40   .25
950 A172   1 l ol grn & dk grn .50   .50
    Nos. 947-950 (4)   2.30   1.50

Izmir International Fair.

Victory Monument, Afyon Karahisar A173

Ismet Inönü as General A174

Kemal Atatürk as
General — A175

1947, Aug. 30
951 A173 10k dk brn & pale brn   .50   .30
952 A174 15k brt violet & gray   .35   .25
953 A175 20k dp blue & gray   .55   .25
954 A173 30k grnsh blk & gray   1.00   .30
955 A174 60k ol gray & pale brn 1.50   .65
956 A175 1 l dk green & gray   2.50 1.25
   Nos. 951-956 (6)   6.40 3.00

25th anniv. of the Battle of Dumlupinar, Aug.
30, 1922.

Grapes
and
Istanbul
Skyline
A176

1947, Sept. 22
957 A176 15k rose violet   .40   .25
958 A176 20k deep blue   .75   .50
959 A176 60k dark brown   1.25   .75
   Nos. 957-959 (3)   2.40 1.50

International Vintners' Congress, Istanbul.

Approaching Train,
Istanbul Skyline and
Sirkeci
Terminus — A177

1947, Oct. 9
960 A177 15k rose violet   .60   .30
961 A177 20k brt blue   1.00   .75
962 A177 60k olive green   2.40 1.90
   Nos. 960-962 (3)   4.00 2.95

International Railroad Congress, Istanbul.

President Ismet Inönü
A178   A179

1948   Unwmk.   Engr.   Perf. 12, 14
963 A178 0.25k dark red   .30   .25
964 A178   1k olive black   .30   .25
965 A178   2k brt rose lilac .30   .25
966 A178   3k red orange   .30   .25
967 A178   4k dark green   .30   .25
968 A178   5k blue   .30   .25
969 A178 10k chocolate   .75   .25
970 A178 12k deep red   1.25   .30
971 A178 15k violet   .75   .25
972 A178 20k deep blue   1.00   .50
973 A178 30k brown   1.50   .30
974 A178 60k black   4.00   .10
975 A179   1 l olive green 8.00   .50
976 A179   2 l dark brown 30.00 5.00
977 A179   5 l deep plum   17.50 27.50
   Nos. 963-977 (15)   66.55 36.60

For overprints see Nos. O13-O42.

President Ismet Inönü and Lausanne
Conference — A180

Conference
Building
A180a

1948, July 23   Photo.   Perf. 11½
978 A180 15k rose lilac   .70   .70
979 A180a 20k blue   .90   .90
980 A180a 40k gray green   1.10 1.10
981 A180   1 l brown   1.75 1.75
   Nos. 978-981 (4)   4.45 4.45

25th anniversary of Lausanne Treaty.

Statue of Kemal
Atatürk,
Ankara — A181

1948, Oct. 29
982 A181 15k violet   .50   .40
983 A181 20k blue   .60   .50
984 A181 40k gray green   1.25 1.10
985 A181 1 l brown   2.75 2.25
   Nos. 982-985 (4)   5.10 4.25

25th anniv. of the proclamation of the
republic.

A182   A183

A184

Wrestlers
A185

1949, June 3
986 A182 15k rose lilac   2.40   .60
987 A183 20k blue   2.75 1.25
988 A184 30k brown   2.75   .60
989 A185 60k green   4.00 3.50
   Nos. 986-989 (4)   11.90 5.95

5th European Wrestling Championships,
Istanbul, June 3-5, 1949.

Ancient
Galley
A186

Galleon   Monument to
Mahmudiye   Khizr
A187   Barbarossa
                 A188

Designs: 15k, Cruiser Hamidiye. 20k, Submarine Sakarya. 30k, Cruiser Yavuz.

1949, July 1
990 A186 5k violet   .75   .50
991 A187 10k brown   .75   .50
992 A186 15k lilac rose   .75   .50
993 A186 20k gray blue   1.75   .90
994 A186 30k gray   1.00   .50
995 A188 40k olive gray   3.50 1.75
   Nos. 990-995 (6)   8.50 4.65

Fleet Day, July 1, 1949.

A189

UPU
Monument,
Bern
A190

Perf. 11½
1949, Oct. 9   Unwmk.   Photo.
996 A189 15k violet   .55   .30
997 A189 20k blue   .55   .30
998 A190 30k dull rose   .55   .30
999 A190 40k green   1.10   .55
   Nos. 996-999 (4)   2.75 1.45

UPU, 75th anniversary.

Istanbul
Fair
Building
A191

1949, Oct. 1   Litho.   Perf. 10
1000 A191 15k brown   .60   .30
1001 A191 20k blue   .60   .30
1002 A191 30k olive   .80   .60
   Nos. 1000-1002 (3)   2.00 1.20

Istanbul Fair, Oct. 1-31.

Boy and Girl and   Aged Woman
Globe — A192   Casting
                    Ballot — A193

Kemal
Atatürk
and Map
A194

1950, Aug. 13   Perf. 11½
1003 A192 15k purple   .25   .25
1004 A192 20k deep blue   .60   .60

2nd World Youth Council Meeting, 1950. No.
1004 exists imperf. Value $12.

1950, Aug. 30
1005 A193 15k dark brown   .60   .25
1006 A193 20k dark blue   .60   .25
1007 A194 30k dk blue & gray 1.00 .50
   Nos. 1005-1007 (3)   2.20 1.00

Election of May 14, 1950.

Hazel   Symbolical of
Nuts — A195   1950
                     Census — A196

Designs: 12k, Acorns. 15k, Cotton. 20k,
Symbolical of the fair. 30k, Tobacco.

1950, Sept. 9
1008 A195 8k gray grn & buff   .60   .60
1009 A195 12k magenta   1.25 1.25
1010 A195 15k brn blk & lt brn   .60   .60
1011 A195 20k dk blue & aqua   1.75 1.75
1012 A195 30k brn blk & dull org 1.75 1.75
   Nos. 1008-1012 (5)   5.95 5.95

Izmir International Fair, Aug. 20-Sept. 20.

1950, Oct. 9   Litho.   Perf. 11½
1013 A196 15k dark brown   .35   .25
1014 A196 20k violet blue .95   .25

General census of 1950.

Atatürk Types of 1931-42
Perf. 10x11½, 11½x12
1950-51   Typo.
1015 A77 10p dull red brn   .25   .25
1016 A77 10p vermilion ('51)   .35   .50
1017 A77 20p blue green   1.50   .35
1018 A78   1k olive green   .25   .25
1019 A78   2k plum   .25   .25
1020 A78   2k dp yellow
             ('51)   .75   .30
1021 A78   3k yellow orange   1.25   .45
1022 A78   3k gray ('51)   .75   .25
1023 A78   4k green ('51)   .75   .25
1024 A78   5k blue   1.25   .45
1025 A78   5k plum ('51)   5.25   .45
1026 A77 10k brown orange   2.25   .25
1027 A77 15k purple   2.75   .45
1028 A77 15k brown car-
             mine   18.00   .35
1029 A77 20k dark blue   30.00   .35
1030 A77 30k pink ('51)   25.50   .75
1031 A79 100k red brown
             ('51)   7.50 1.10
1032 A79 200k dark brown   15.00 1.50
1033 A79 200k rose violet
             ('51)   15.00 2.25
   Nos. 1015-1033 (19)   128.60 10.75

16th Century Flight
of Hezarfen Ahmet
Celebi — A197

Plane over
Istanbul
A198

40k, Biplane over Taurus Mountains.

1950, Oct. 17   Litho.   Perf. 11
1034 A197 20k dk green & blue   .50   .35
1035 A197 40k dk brown & blue   .75   .75
1036 A198 60k purple & blue   1.25   .90
      Nos. 1034-1036 (3)   2.50   2.00

Regional meeting of the ICAO, Istanbul, Oct. 17.

Farabi
A199

1950, Dec. 1   Unwmk.   Perf. 11½
Multicolored Center
1037 A199 15k blue   .75   .75
1038 A199 20k blue violet   .75   .75
1039 A199 60k red brown   4.25   2.75
1040 A199 1 l gold & bl vio   4.75   4.25
      Nos. 1037-1040 (4)   10.50   8.50

Death millenary of Farabi, Arab philosopher.

Mithat Pasha and Security Bank
Building — A200

Design: 20k, Agricultural Bank.

1950, Dec. 21   Photo.
1041 A200 15k rose violet   1.00   1.00
1042 A200 20k blue   1.00   1.00

3rd Congress of Turkish Cooperatives, Istanbul, Dec. 25, 1950.

Floating a
Ship
A201

Lighthouse — A202

1951, July 1
1043 A201 15k shown   .75   .75
1044 A201 20k Steamship   .75   .75
1045 A201 30k Diver rising   1.50   1.50
1046 A202 1 l shown   2.75   2.75
      Nos. 1043-1046 (4)   5.75   5.75

25th anniv. of the recognition of coastal rights in Turkish waters to ships under the Turkish flag.

Mosque of
Sultan
Ahmed
A203

Henry Carton de
Wiart — A204

Designs: 20k, Dolma Bahce Palace. 60k, Rumeli Hisari Fortress.

1951, Aug. 31   Photo.   Perf. 13½
1047 A203 15k dark green   .40   .25
1048 A203 20k deep ultra   .60   .30
1049 A204 30k brown   .90   .35
1050 A203 60k purple brown   1.75   1.75
      Nos. 1047-1050 (4)   3.65   2.65

40th Interparliamentary Conf., Istanbul.

Allegory of
Food and
Agriculture
A205

Designs: 20k, Dam. 30k, United Nations Building. 60k, University, Ankara.

1952, Jan. 3   Unwmk.   Perf. 14
Inscribed: "Akdeniz Yetistirme Merkezi. Ankara 1951."
1051 A205 15k green   1.00   .65
1052 A205 20k blue violet   1.10   .75
1053 A205 30k blue   2.50   2.00
1054 A205 60k red   3.75   3.25
   a.   Souvenir sheet of 4   95.00   95.00
      Nos. 1051-1054 (4)   8.35   6.65

UN Mediterranean Economic Instruction Center.
No. 1054a contains one each of Nos. 1051-1054, imperf., with inscriptions in dark blue gray.

Abdulhak Hamid
Tarhan, Poet,
Birth
Cent. — A206

1952, Feb. 5   Photo.   Perf. 13½
1055 A206 15k dark purple   .50   .50
1056 A206 20k dark blue   .50   .50
1057 A206 30k brown   .50   .50
1058 A206 60k dark olive grn   1.75   1.75
      Nos. 1055-1058 (4)   3.25   3.25

Ruins, Bergama
A207

Pavilion, Istanbul
A208

Designs: 1k, Ruins, Bergama. 2k, Ruins, Milas. 3k, Karatay Gate, Konya. 4k, Kozak plateau. 5k, Urgup. 10k, 12k, 15k, 20k, Kemal Ataturk. 30k, Mosque, Bursa. 40k, Mosque, Istanbul. 50, Tarsus Cataract. 75k, Rocks, Urgup. 1 l, Palace, Istanbul. 5 l, Museum interior, Istanbul.

1952, Mar. 15   Perf. 13½
1059 A207 1k brown orange   .25   .25
1060 A207 2k olive green   .25   .25
1061 A207 3k rose brown   .25   .25
1062 A207 4k blue green   .70   .70
1063 A207 5k brown   .25   .25
1064 A207 10k dark brown   .25   .25
1065 A207 12k brt rose car   .70   .70
1066 A207 15k purple   .30
1067 A207 20k chalky blue   1.10   .25
1068 A207 30k grnsh gray   .70   .25
1069 A207 40k slate blue   5.00   .25
1070 A208 50k olive   .70
1071 A208 75k slate   .70   .30
1072 A208 1 l deep purple   .70   .25
1073 A208 2 l brt ultra   2.75   .40
1074 A208 5 l sepia   42.50   10.50
      Nos. 1059-1074 (16)   57.10   15.35

Imperfs, value, set $75.
For surcharge & overprint see #1075, 1255.

No. 1059 Surcharged with New Value
in Black

1952, June 1
1075 A207 0.50k on 1k brn org   .25   .25

Technical
Faculty
Building
A209

1952, Aug. 20   Perf. 12x12½
1076 A209 15k violet   .65   .65
1077 A209 20k blue   .95   .95
1078 A209 60k brown   1.60   1.60
      Nos. 1076-1078 (3)   3.20   3.20

8th Intl. Congress of Theoretic and Applied Mechanics.

Turkish
Soldier — A210

Pigeons
Bandaging
Wounded
Hand — A212

20k, Soldier with Turkish flag. 30k, Soldier & child with comic book. 60k, Raising Turkish flag.

1952, Sept. 25   Perf. 14
1079 A210 15k Prus blue   .40   .40
1080 A210 20k deep blue   .60   .60
1081 A210 30k brown   .85   .85
1082 A210 60k olive blk & car   1.75   1.75
      Nos. 1079-1082 (4)   3.60   3.60

Turkey's participation in the Korean war.

1952, Oct. 29   Perf. 12½x12
20k, Flag, rainbow and ruined homes.

Dated "1877-1952"
1085 A212 15k dk green & red   .80   .40
1086 A212 20k blue & red   2.00   .70

Turkish Red Crescent Society, 75th anniv.

Relief From Panel
of Aziziye
Monument — A213

Aziziye
Monument
A214

Design: 40k, View of Erzerum.

1952, Nov. 9   Perf. 11
1087 A213 15k purple   .60   .30
1088 A214 20k blue   .65   .50
1089 A214 40k olive gray   1.00   .70
      Nos. 1087-1089 (3)   2.25   1.50

75th anniv. of the Battle of Aziziye at Erzerum.

Rumeli
Hisari
Fortress
A215

Troops Entering
Constan-
tinople — A216

Sultan Mohammed
II — A217

Designs: 8k, Soldiers moving cannon. 10k, Mohammed II riding into sea, and Turkish armada. 12k, Landing of Turkish army. 15k, Ancient wall, Constantinople. 30k, Mosque of Faith. 40k, Presenting mace to Patriarch Yenadios. 60k, Map of Constantinople, c. 1574. 1 l, Tomb of Mohammed II. 2.50 l, Portrait of Mohammed II.

1953, May 29   Photo.   Perf. 11½
Inscribed: "Istanbulun Fethi 1453-1953"
1090 A215 5k brt blue   1.25   .60
1091 A215 8k gray   1.90   .60
1092 A215 10k blue   .60   .60
1093 A215 12k rose lilac   1.25   .60
1094 A215 15k brown   .90   .30
1095 A216 20k vermilion   .25   .30
1096 A216 30k dull green   2.40   1.25
1097 A215 40k violet blue   4.25   1.50
1098 A215 60k chocolate   3.00   1.50
1099 A215 1 l blue green   7.25   2.10

Perf. 12
1100 A217 2 l multi   15.00   6.00
1101 A217 2.50 l multi   9.00   9.00
   a.   Souvenir sheet   175.00   90.00
      Nos. 1090-1101 (12)   48.05   24.35

Conquest of Constantinople by Sultan Mohammed II, 500th anniv.

Ruins of
the
Odeon,
Ephesus
A218

15k, Church of St. John the Apostle. 20k, Shrine of Virgin Mary, Panaya Kapulu. 40k, Ruins of the Double Church. 60k, Shrine of the Seven Sleepers. 1 l, Restored house of the Virgin Mary.

1953, Aug. 16   Litho.   Perf. 13½
Multicolored Center
1102 A218 12k sage green   .30   .30
1103 A218 15k lilac   .25   .25
1104 A218 20k dk slate blue   .30   .30
1105 A218 40k light green   .65   .65
1106 A218 60k violet blue   .85   .85
1107 A218 1 l brown red   2.50   2.50
      Nos. 1102-1107 (6)   4.85   4.85

Pres. Celal Bayar, Mithat Pasha. Herman Schulze-Delitzsch and People's Bank — A219

Design: 20k, Pres. Bayar, Mithat Pasha and University of Ankara.

1953, Sept. 2   Photo.   Perf. 10½
1108 A219 15k orange brown   1.00   .50
1109 A219 20k Prus green   1.00   .50

5th Intl. People's Credit Congress, Istanbul, Sept.

Combined Harvester A220

Kemal Atatürk — A221

Designs: 15k, Berdan dam. 20k, Military parade. 30k, Diesel train. 35k, Yesilkoy airport.

1953, Oct. 29   Perf. 14
1110 A220 10k olive bister   .30   .25
1111 A220 15k dark gray   .30   .25
1112 A220 20k rose red   .75   .75
1113 A220 30k olive green   1.25 1.25
1114 A220 35k dull blue   .75   .75
1115 A221 55k dull purple   1.75 1.75
Nos. 1110-1115 (6)   5.10 5.00

Turkish Republic, 30th anniv.

Kemal Atatürk and Mausoleum at Ankara — A222

1953, Nov. 10
1116 A222 15k gray black   .75   .35
1117 A222 20k violet brown   1.10   .55

15th death anniv. of Kemal Ataturk.

Type of 1931-42
Without umlaut over first "U" of "CUMHURIYETI"
Perf. 11½x12, 10x11½
1953-56   Typo.   Unwmk.
1117B A77 20p yellow   .30   .25
1118 A78 1k brown orange   .30   .25
1119 A78 2k rose pink ('53)   .50   .25
1120 A78 3k yellow brn ('53)   .50   .25
1120A A78 4k slate ('56)   1.50   .40
1121 A78 5k blue   2.00   .25
1121A A78 8k violet ('56)   .50   .25
1122 A77 10k dark olive ('53)   .50   .25
1123 A77 12k brt car rose ('53)   .50   .25
1124 A77 15k fawn   .60   .25
1125 A77 20k rose lilac   3.50   .40
1126 A77 30k lt blue grn ('54)   1.25   .25
Nos. 1117B-1126 (12)   11.95 3.30

Compass and Map A223

Designs: 20k, Globe, crescent and stars. 40k, Tree symbolical of 14 NATO members.

1954, Apr. 4   Photo.   Perf. 14
1127 A223 15k brown   1.75 1.25
1128 A223 20k violet blue   2.25 1.75
1129 A223 40k dark green   15.50 13.00
Nos. 1127-1129 (3)   19.50 16.00

NATO, 5th anniv.

Industry, Engineering and Agriculture — A224

Justice and Council of Europe Flag — A225

1954, Aug. 8   Litho.   Perf. 10½
1130 A224 10k brown   3.25 2.40
1131 A225 15k dark green   3.00 1.25
1132 A225 20k blue   3.25 1.25
1133 A224 30k brt violet   14.50 10.00
Nos. 1130-1133 (4)   24.00 14.90

Council of Europe, 5th anniv.

Flag Signals to Plane — A226

Amaury de La Grange and Plane A227

Design: 45k, Kemal Ataturk and air fleet.

1954, Sept. 20   Perf. 12½
1134 A226 20k black brown   .40   .25
1135 A227 35k dull violet   .60   .25
1136 A227 45k deep blue   1.00   .30
Nos. 1134-1136 (3)   2.00   .80

47th Congress of the Intl. Aeronautical Federation, Istanbul, 1954.

Souvenir Sheet

A228

1954, Oct. 18   Imperf.
1137 A228   Sheet of 3   16.00 7.00
a.   20k aquamarine   1.25   .85
b.   30k violet blue   1.50   .85
c.   1 l red violet   3.00 1.90

First anniv. of Law of Oct. 17, 1953, reorganizing the Department of Post, Telephone and Telegraph.

Ziya Gokalp A229

Kemal Atatürk A230

1954, Oct. 25   Perf. 11
1138 A229 15k rose lilac   .25   .25
1139 A229 20k dark green   .35   .25
1140 A229 30k crimson   .60   .35
Nos. 1138-1140 (3)   1.20   .85

30th death anniv. of Ziya Gokalp, author and historian.

1955, Mar. 1   Perf. 12½
1141 A230 15k carmine rose   .25   .25
1142 A230 20k blue   .25   .25
1143 A230 40k dark gray   .30   .25
1144 A230 50k blue green   .55   .25
1145 A230 75k orange brown   .65   .25
Nos. 1141-1145 (5)   2.00 1.25

Relief Map of Dardanelles — A231

Artillery Loaders — A232

30k, Minelayer Nusrat. 60k, Col. Kemal Ataturk.

1955, Mar. 18   Perf. 10½
1146 A231 15k green   .25   .25
1147 A232 20k orange brown   .25   .25
1148 A231 30k ultra   .30   .25
1149 A232 60k olive gray   .90   .45
Nos. 1146-1149 (4)   1.70 1.20

Battle of Gallipoli, 40th anniversary.

Aerial Map A233

1955, Apr. 14   Perf. 11
1150 A233 15k gray   .35   .25
1151 A233 20k aquamarine   .35   .25
1152 A233 50k brown   .60   .25
1153 A233 1 l green   1.10   .50
Nos. 1150-1153 (4)   2.40 1.25

City Planning Congress, Ankara, 1955.

Carnation — A234

1955, May 19   Litho.   Perf. 10
1154 A234 10k shown   .55   .55
1155 A234 15k Tulip   .55   .55
1156 A234 20k Rose   .85   .55
1157 A234 50k Lily   2.00 1.10
Nos. 1154-1157 (4)   3.95 2.75

National Flower Show, Istanbul, May 20-Aug. 20.

Battle First Aid Station A235

30k, Gulhane Military Hospital, Ankara.

1955, Aug. 28   Unwmk.   Perf. 12
1158 A235 20k red, lake & gray   .60   .25
1159 A235 30k dp grn & yel grn   .95   .30

XVIII Intl. Congress of Military Medicine, Aug. 8-Sept. 1, Istanbul.

Soccer Game A236

Emblem and Soccer Ball — A237

1 l, Emblem with oak & olive branches.

1955, Aug. 30   Perf. 10
1160 A236 15k light ultra   .70   .25
1161 A237 20k crimson rose   .85   .25
1162 A236 1 l light green   1.75 1.10
Nos. 1160-1162 (3)   3.30 1.60

Intl. Military Soccer Championship games, Istanbul, Aug. 30.

Sureté Monument, Ankara A238

20k, Dolma Bahce Palace. 30k, Police College, Ankara. 45k, Police Martyrs' Monument, Istanbul.

1955, Sept. 5   Perf. 10
Inscribed: "Enterpol Istanbul 1955"
1163 A238 15k blue green   .30   .30
1164 A238 20k brt violet   .45   .45
1165 A238 30k gray black   .55   .40
1166 A238 45k lt brown   1.10   .65
Nos. 1163-1166 (4)   2.40 1.80

24th general assembly of the Intl. Criminal Police, Istanbul, Sept. 5-9.

Early
Telegraph
Transmitter
A239

Modern
Transmitter
A240

Perf. 13½x14, 14x13½

1955, Sept. 10   **Photo.**
1167 A239 15k olive .25 .25
1168 A240 20k crimson rose .25 .25
1169 A239 45k fawn .60 .25
1170 A240 60k ultra .60 .60
  Nos. 1167-1170 (4) 1.70 1.35
Centenary of telecommunication.

Academy of
Science,
Istanbul
A241

Designs: 20k, University. 60k, Hilton Hotel.
1 l, Kiz Kulesi (Leander's Tower).

1955, Sept. 12   **Perf. 13½x14**
1171 A241 15k yellow orange .35 .35
1172 A241 20k crimson rose .35 .35
1173 A241 60k purple .45 .35
1174 A241 1 l deep blue .85 .60
  Nos. 1171-1174 (4) 2.00 1.65

10th meeting of the governors of the Intl.
Bank of Reconstruction and Development and
the Intl. Monetary Fund, Istanbul, Sept. 12-16.

Surlari,
Istanbul
A242

Mosque of
Sultan
Ahmed — A243

Congress
Emblem — A244

Designs: 30k, Haghia Sophia. 75k, Map of
Constantinople, by Christoforo Buondel-
monti, 1422.

1955, Sept. 15   **Litho.**   **Perf. 11½**
1175 A242 15k grnsh blk & Prus
    grn .50 .25
1176 A243 20k vermilion & org .40 .25
1177 A242 30k sepia & vio brn .40 .25
1178 A243 75k ultramarine 1.10 .75
  Nos. 1175-1178 (4) 2.40 1.50

10th Intl. Congress of Byzantine Research,
Istanbul, Sept. 15-21, 1955.

1955, Sept. 26   **Perf. 10½x11**

30k, Chalet in Istanbul. 55k, Bridges.

Inscribed: "Beynelmiel X. Vol
Kongresi Istanbul 1955"
1179 A244 20k red violet .25 .25
1180 A244 30k dk grn & yel grn .25 .25
1181 A244 55k dp bl & brt bl 1.10 .55
  Nos. 1179-1181 (3) 1.60 1.05
10th International Transportation Congress.

Map of
Turkey,
Showing
Population
Increase
A245

1955, Oct. 22   **Unwmk.**   **Perf. 10**
Map in Rose
1182 A245 15k lt & dk gray & red .35 .25
1183 A245 20k lt & dk vio & red .25 .25
1184 A245 30k lt & dk ultra & red .30 .25
1185 A245 60k lt & dk bl grn &
    red .70 .30
  Nos. 1182-1185 (4) 1.60 1.05
Census of 1955.

Waterfall,
Antalya — A246

Alanya and
Seljukide
Dockyards
A247

Designs: 30k, Theater at Aspendos. 45k,
Ruins at Side. 50k, View of Antalya. 65k, St.
Nicholas Church at Myra (Demre) and St.
Nicholas.

Perf. 14x13½, 13½x14
1955, Dec. 10   **Photo.**   **Unwmk.**
1186 A246 18k bl, ol grn & ultra .25 .25
1187 A247 20k blue, ultra & brn .25 .25
1188 A247 30k dl grn, ol bis &
    grn .25 .25
1189 A246 45k yel grn & brn 2.25 1.00
1190 A247 50k Prus grn & ol bis .40 .30
1191 A247 65k orange ver & blk .50 .40
  Nos. 1186-1191 (6) 3.90 2.45

Kemal Atatürk — A248

1955-56   **Litho.**   **Perf. 12½**
1192 A248 0.50k carmine .25 .25
1193 A248 1k yellow orange .25 .25
1194 A248 2k brt blue .25 .25
1195 A248 3k scarlet .25 .25
1196 A248 5k lt brown .30 .25
1197 A248 6k lt blue grn .30 .25
1198 A248 10k blue green .30 .25
1199 A248 18k rose violet .30 .25
1200 A248 20k lt violet bl .40 .25
1201 A248 25k olive green .50 .25
1202 A248 30k violet .50 .25
1203 A248 40k fawn .60 .30
1204 A248 75k slate blue 1.75 .50
  Nos. 1192-1204 (13) 5.95 3.55
Issue dates: 3k, 1955. Others, 1956.

Tomb at
Nigde — A249

Zubeyde
Hanum — A250

1956, Apr. 12   **Perf. 10½**
1205 A249 40k violet bl & bl .25 .25
25th anniv. of the Turkish History Society.
The tomb of Hüdavent Hatun, a sultan's
daughter, exemplifies Seljukian architecture of
the 14th century.

1956, May 13   **Perf. 11**
1206 A250 20k pale brn & dk brn .35 .30
Imperf
1207 A250 20k lt grn & dk grn 1.10 1.75
Mother's Day; Zubeyde Hanum, mother of
Kemal Ataturk.

Shah
and
Queen
of Iran
A251

1956, May 15   **Unwmk.**   **Perf. 11**
1208 A251 100k grn & pale
    grn 1.25 1.25
Imperf
1209 A251 100k red & pale
    grn 12.00 8.50
Visit of the Shah and Queen of Iran to Turkey, May 15.

Erenkoy
Sanitarium
A252

1956, July 31   **Perf. 11**
1210 A252 50k dk bl grn & pink .95 .25
Anti-Tuberculosis work among PTT
employees.

Symbol of Izmir
Fair — A253

A254

1956, Aug. 20   **Perf. 11**
1211 A253 45k brt green .35 .25
Souvenir Sheet
Imperf
1212 A254 Sheet of 2 6.00 5.00
 a. 50k rose red 2.50 .65
 b. 50k bright ultramarine 2.50 .65
25th Intl. Fair, Izmir, 8/20-9/20. See #C28.

Hands Holding
Bottled
Serpent — A255

1956, Sept. 10   **Litho.**   **Perf. 10½**
1213 A255 25k multicolored .30 .30
 a. Tete beche pair 1.25
25th Intl. Anti-Alcoholism Congress, Istanbul
Sept. 10-15.
Printed both in regular sheets and in sheets
with alternate vertical rows inverted.

Medical Center
at
Kayseri — A256

Sariyar
Dam — A257

1956, Nov. 1   **Perf. 12½x12**
1214 A256 60k violet & yel .30 .30
750th anniv. of the first medical school and
clinic in Anatolia.

1956, Dec. 2   **Litho.**   **Perf. 10½**
1215 A257 20k vermilion .30 .30
1216 A257 20k bright blue .30 .30
Inauguration of Sariyar Dam.

Freestyle
Wrestling
A258

Design: 65k, Greco-Roman wrestling.

1956, Dec. 8   **Unwmk.**   **Perf. 10½**
1217 A258 40k brt yel grn & brn .60 .40
1218 A258 65k lt bluish gray &
    dp car .60 .40
16th Olympic Games, Melbourne, Nov. 22-
Dec. 8, 1956.

Mehmet Akif
Ersoy — A259

1956, Dec. 26
1219 A259 20k brn & brt yel grn .25 .25
1220 A259 20k rose car & lt gray .25 .25
1221 A259 20k vio bl & brt pink .25 .25
  Nos. 1219-1221 (3) .75 .75
20th death anniv. of Mehmet Akif Ersoy,
author of the Turkish National Anthem.
Each value bears a different verse of the
anthem.

Theater in
Troy — A260

Trojan
Vase — A261

Design: 30k, Trojan Horse.

Perf. 13½x14, 14x13½
1956, Dec. 31   Photo.   Unwmk.
1222 A260 15k green   1.40 .85
1223 A261 20k red violet   1.40 .85
1224 A260 30k chestnut   2.00 .85
  Nos. 1222-1224 (3)   4.80 2.55

Excavations at Troy.

Mobile
Chest X-
Ray Unit
A262

1957, Jan. 1   Litho.   Perf. 12
1225 A262 25k ol brn & red   .25 .25

Fight against tuberculsois.

Kemal Atatürk — A263

1956-57   Perf. 12½
1226 A263 ½k blue green   .25 .25
1227 A263 1k yellow orange   .25 .25
1228 A263 3k gray olive   .25 .25
1229 A263 5k violet   .25 .25
1230 A263 6k rose car ('57)   .35 .25
1231 A263 10k rose violet   .30 .25
1232 A263 12k fawn ('57)   .40 .25
1233 A263 15k lt violet bl   .30 .25
1234 A263 18k carmine ('57)   .40 .25
1235 A263 20k lt brown   .30 .25
1236 A263 25k lt blue green   .30 .25
1237 A263 30k slate blue   .30 .25
1238 A263 40k olive ('57)   .50 .25
1239 A263 50k orange   .40 .25
1240 A263 60k brt blue ('57)   .60 .35
1241 A263 70k Prus green ('57) 2.00 .35
1242 A263 75k brown   1.50 .35
  Nos. 1226-1242 (17)   8.65 4.55

Pres. Heuss of
Germany — A264

1957, May 5   Unwmk.   Perf. 10½
1243 A264 40k yellow & brown   .25 .25

Visit of Pres. Theodor Heuss of Germany to
Turkey, May 5. See No. C29.

View of
Bergama
and Ruin
A265

40k, Dancers in kermis at Bergama.

1957, May 24
1244 A265 30k brown   .25 .25
1245 A265 40k green   .25 .25

20th anniv. of the kermis at Bergama
(Pergamus).

Symbols of
Industry and
Flags
A266

1957, July 1   Photo.   Perf. 13½x14
1246 A266 25k violet   .40 .40
1247 A266 40k gray blue   .40 .40

Turkish-American collaboration, 10th anniv.

Osman
Hamdi Bey
A267

Hittite Sun Course from Alaça
Höyük — A268

1957, July 6   Perf. 10½
1248 A267 20k beige, pale brn &
             blk   .35 .25
1249 A268 30k Prussian green   .40 .25

75th anniv. of the Academy of Art. The 20k
exists with "cancellation" omitted.

King of
Afghanistan — A269

1957, Sept. 1   Litho.   Perf. 10½
1250 A269 45k car lake & pink .25 .25

Visit of Mohammed Zahir Shah, King of
Afghanistan, to Turkey. See No. C30.

Medical
Center,
Amasya
A270

Design: 65k, Suleiman Medical Center.

1957, Sept. 29   Unwmk.   Perf. 10½
1251 A270 25k vermilion & yellow .25 .25
1252 A270 65k brt grnsh bl & cit-
             ron   .30 .25

11th general meeting of the World Medical
Assoc.

Mosque of
Suleiman
A271

Architect Mimar
Koca Sinan (1489-
1587)
A272

1957, Oct. 18   Perf. 11
1253 A271 20k gray green   .25 .25
1254 A272 100k brown   .60 .40

400th anniv. of the opening of the Mosque
of Suleiman, Istanbul.

No. 1073 Surcharged with New Value
and "ISTANBUL Filatelik n. Sergisi
1957"

1957, Nov. 11   Photo.   Perf. 13½
1255 A208 50k on 2 l brt ultra   .30 .25

1957 Istanbul Philatelic Exhibition.

Forestation Map of Turkey — A273

25k, Forest & hand planting tree, vert.

1957, Nov. 18   Litho.   Perf. 10½
1256 A273 20k green & brown   .25 .25
1257 A273 25k emerald & bl grn .25 .25

Centenary of forestry in Turkey.
Nos. 1256-1257 each come with two different tabs attached (four tabs in all) bearing various quotations.

A274

1957, Nov. 23
1258 A274 50k pink, vio, red &
             yel   .50 .25

400th death anniv. of Fuzuli (Mehmet Suleiman Ogiou), poet.

A275

1957, Nov. 28   Photo.   Perf. 14x13½
1259 A275 65k dk Prus blue   .30 .30
1260 A275 65k rose violet   .30 .30

Benjamin Franklin (1706-1790).

Green Dome,
Tomb of
Mevlana, at
Konya — A276

Mevlana — A278

Konya
Museum
A277

Perf. 11x10½, 10½x11
1957, Dec. 17   Litho.   Unwmk.
1261 A276 50k green, bl & vio .25 .25
1262 A277 100k dark blue   .75 .25

Miniature Sheet
Imperf

1263 A278 100k multicolored   1.75 1.40

Jalal-udin Mevlana (1207-1273), Persian
poet and founder of the Mevlevie dervish
order. No. 1263 contains one stamp
32x42mm.

Kemal Atatürk (Double
Frame; Serifs) — A279

1957   Unwmk.   Perf. 11½
        Size: 18x22mm
1264 A279 ½k lt brown   .25 .25
1265 A279 1k lt violet bl   .25 .25
1266 A279 2k black violet   .25 .25
1267 A279 3k orange   .25 .25
1268 A279 5k blue green   .25 .25
1269 A279 6k dk slate grn   .25 .25
1270 A279 10k violet   .25 .25
1271 A279 12k brt green   .25 .25
1272 A279 15k dk blue grn   .25 .25
1273 A279 18k rose carmine   .25 .25
1274 A279 20k brown   .25 .25
1275 A279 25k brown red   .25 .25
1276 A279 30k brt blue   .25 .25
1277 A279 40k slate blue   .30 .25
1278 A279 50k yellow orange   .30 .25
1279 A279 60k black   .40 .25
1280 A279 70k rose violet   .40 .25
1281 A279 75k gray olive   .50 .25
        Size: 21x29mm
1282 A279 100k carmine   .85 .25
1283 A279 250k olive   2.25 .25
  Nos. 1264-1283 (20)   8.25 5.05

College
Emblem — A280

View of
Adana — A281

1958, Jan. 16   Litho.   Perf. 10½x11
1288 A280 20k bister, ind & org .25 .25
1289 A280 25k dk blue, bis & org .25 .25

"Turkiye" on top of 25k. 75th anniv. of the
College of Economics and Commerce,
Istanbul.

1958   Photo.   Perf. 11½
        Size: 26x20½mm
1290 A281 5k Adana   .25 .25
1291 A281 5k Adapazari   .25 .25
1292 A281 5k Adiyaman   .25 .25
1293 A281 5k Afyon   .25 .25
1294 A281 5k Amasya   .25 .25
1295 A281 5k Ankara   .25 .25

1296	A281	5k Antakya	.25	.25
1297	A281	5k Antalya	.25	.25
1298	A281	5k Artvin	.25	.25
1299	A281	5k Aydin	.25	.25
1300	A281	5k Balikesir	.25	.25
1301	A281	5k Bilecik	.25	.25
1302	A281	5k Bingol	.25	.25
1303	A281	5k Bitlis	.25	.25
1304	A281	5k Bolu	.25	.25
1305	A281	5k Burdur	.25	.25
1306	A281	5k Bursa	.25	.25
1307	A281	5k Canakkale	.25	.25
1308	A281	5k Cankiri	.25	.25
1309	A281	5k Corum	.25	.25
1310	A281	5k Denizli	.25	.25
1311	A281	5k Diyarbakir	.25	.25

Size: 32½x22mm

1312	A281	20k Adana	.25	.25
1313	A281	20k Adapazari	.25	.25
1314	A281	20k Adiyaman	.25	.25
1315	A281	20k Afyon	.25	.25
1316	A281	20k Amasya	.25	.25
1317	A281	20k Ankara	.25	.25
1318	A281	20k Antakya	.25	.25
1319	A281	20k Antalya	.25	.25
1320	A281	20k Artvin	.25	.25
1321	A281	20k Aydin	.25	.25
1322	A281	20k Balikesir	.25	.25
1323	A281	20k Bilecik	.25	.25
1324	A281	20k Bingol	.25	.25
1325	A281	20k Bitlis	.25	.25
1326	A281	20k Bolu	.25	.25
1327	A281	20k Burdur	.25	.25
1328	A281	20k Bursa	.25	.25
1329	A281	20k Canakkale	.25	.25
1330	A281	20k Cankiri	.25	.25
1331	A281	20k Corum	.25	.25
1332	A281	20k Denizli	.25	.25
1333	A281	20k Diyarbakir	.25	.25
		Nos. 1290-1333 (44)	11.00	11.00

1959

Size: 26x20½mm

1334	A281	5k Edirne	.25	.25
1335	A281	5k Elazig	.25	.25
1336	A281	5k Erzincan	.25	.25
1337	A281	5k Erzurum	.25	.25
1338	A281	5k Eskisehir	.25	.25
1339	A281	5k Gaziantep	.25	.25
1340	A281	5k Giresun	.25	.25
1341	A281	5k Gumusane	.25	.25
1342	A281	5k Hakkari	.25	.25
1343	A281	5k Isparta	.25	.25
1344	A281	5k Istanbul	.25	.25
1345	A281	5k Izmir	.25	.25
1346	A281	5k Izmit	.25	.25
1347	A281	5k Karakose	.25	.25
1348	A281	5k Kars	.25	.25
1349	A281	5k Kastamonu	.25	.25
1350	A281	5k Kayseri	.25	.25
1351	A281	5k Kirklareli	.25	.25
1352	A281	5k Kirsehir	.25	.25
1353	A281	5k Konya	.25	.25
1354	A281	5k Kutahya	.25	.25
1355	A281	5k Malatya	.25	.25

Size: 32½x22mm

1356	A281	20k Edirne	.25	.25
1357	A281	20k Elazig	.25	.25
1358	A281	20k Erzincan	.25	.25
1359	A281	20k Erzurum	.25	.25
1360	A281	20k Eskisehir	.25	.25
1361	A281	20k Gaziantep	.25	.25
1362	A281	20k Giresun	.25	.25
1363	A281	20k Gumusane	.25	.25
1364	A281	20k Hakkari	.25	.25
1365	A281	20k Isparta	.25	.25
1366	A281	20k Istanbul	.25	.25
1367	A281	20k Izmir	.25	.25
1368	A281	20k Izmit	.25	.25
1369	A281	20k Karakose	.25	.25
1370	A281	20k Kars	.25	.25
1371	A281	20k Kastamonu	.25	.25
1372	A281	20k Kayseri	.25	.25
1373	A281	20k Kirklareli	.25	.25
1374	A281	20k Kirsehir	.25	.25
1375	A281	20k Konya	.25	.25
1376	A281	20k Kutahya	.25	.25
1377	A281	20k Malatya	.25	.25
		Nos. 1334-1377 (44)	11.00	11.00

1960

Size: 26x20½mm

1378	A281	5k Manisa	.25	.25
1379	A281	5k Maras	.25	.25
1380	A281	5k Mardin	.25	.25
1381	A281	5k Mersin	.25	.25
1382	A281	5k Mugla	.25	.25
1383	A281	5k Mus	.25	.25
1384	A281	5k Nevsehir	.25	.25
1385	A281	5k Nigde	.25	.25
1386	A281	5k Ordu	.25	.25
1387	A281	5k Rize	.25	.25
1388	A281	5k Samsun	.25	.25
1389	A281	5k Siirt	.25	.25
1390	A281	5k Sinop	.25	.25
1391	A281	5k Sivas	.25	.25
1392	A281	5k Tekirdag	.25	.25
1393	A281	5k Tokat	.25	.25
1394	A281	5k Trabzon	.25	.25
1395	A281	5k Tunceli	.25	.25
1396	A281	5k Urfa	.25	.25
1397	A281	5k Usak	.25	.25
1398	A281	5k Van	.25	.25
1399	A281	5k Yozgat	.25	.25
1400	A281	5k Zonguldak	.25	.25

Size: 32½x22mm

1401	A281	20k Manisa	.25	.25
1402	A281	20k Maras	.25	.25
1403	A281	20k Mardin	.25	.25
1404	A281	20k Mersin	.25	.25
1405	A281	20k Mugla	.25	.25
1406	A281	20k Mus	.25	.25
1407	A281	20k Nevsehir	.25	.25
1408	A281	20k Nigde	.25	.25
1409	A281	20k Ordu	.25	.25
1410	A281	20k Rize	.25	.25
1411	A281	20k Samsun	.25	.25
1412	A281	20k Siirt	.25	.25
1413	A281	20k Sinop	.25	.25
1414	A281	20k Sivas	.25	.25
1415	A281	20k Tekirdag	.25	.25
1416	A281	20k Tokat	.25	.25
1417	A281	20k Trabzon	.25	.25
1418	A281	20k Tunceli	.25	.25
1419	A281	20k Urfa	.25	.25
1420	A281	20k Usak	.25	.25
1421	A281	20k Van	.25	.25
1422	A281	20k Yozgat	.25	.25
1423	A281	20k Zonguldak	.25	.25
		Nos. 1378-1423 (46)	11.50	11.50
		Nos. 1290-1423 (134)	26.80	26.80

Ruins at Pamukkale A282

Designs: 25k, Travertines at Pamukkale.

1958, May 18   Litho.   Perf. 12

1424	A282	20k brown	.25	.25
1425	A282	25k blue	.25	.25

"Industry" A283

Symbolizing New Europe A284

1958, Oct. 10   Unwmk.   Perf. 10½

1426	A283	40k slate blue	.25	.25

National Industry Exhibition.

Europa Issue

1958, Oct. 10

1427	A284	25k vio & dull pink	.50	.25
1428	A284	40k brt ultra	.50	.25

Letters A285

1958, Oct. 5

1429	A285	20k orange & blk	.25	.25

Intl. Letter Writing Week, Oct. 5-11.

Atatürk 20th Anniv. Death — A286

1958, Nov. 10   Perf. 12

1430		25k Flame and mausoleum	.25	.25
1431		75k Atatürk	.25	.25
a.	A286	Pair, #1430-1431	.45	.25

20th death anniv. of Kemal Atatürk.

Emblem — A288

1959, Jan. 10   Litho.   Perf. 10

1432	A288	25k dk violet & yel	.25	.25

25th anniv. of the Agricultural Faculty of Ankara University.

Blackboard and School Emblem — A289

1959, Jan. 15   Perf. 10½

1433	A289	75k black & yellow	.30	.30

75th anniv. of the establishment of a secondary boys' school in Istanbul.

State Theater, Ankara A290

Design: 25k, Portrait of Sinasi.

1959, Mar. 30   Unwmk.   Perf. 10½

1434	A290	20k red brn & emer	.25	.25
1435	A290	25k Prus grn & org	.25	.25

Centenary of the Turkish theater; Sinasi, writer of the first Turkish play in 1859.

Globe and Stars A291

1959, Apr. 4   Perf. 10

1436	A291	105k red	.25	.25
1437	A291	195k green	1.00	.50

10th anniversary of NATO.

Aspendos Theater A292

1959, May 1   Litho.   Perf. 10½

1438	A292	20k bis brn & vio	.25	.25
1439	A292	20k grn & ol bis	.25	.25

Aspendos (Belkins) Festival.

No. B70 Surcharged in Ultramarine

1959, May 5

1440	SP25	105k on 15k + 5k org	.55	.25

Council of Europe, 10th anniversary.

Basketball — A293

1959, May 21   Perf. 10

1441	A293	25k red org & dk bl	.25	.25

11th European and Mediterranean Basketball Championship.

"Karadeniz" A294

Telegraph Mast — A295

Kemal Atatürk — A296

Designs: 1k, Turkish Airlines' SES plane. 10k, Grain elevator, Ankara. 15k, Iron and Steel Works, Karabück. 20k, Euphrates Bridge, Birecik. 25k, Zonguldak Harbor. 30k, Gasoline refinery, Batman. 40k, Rumeli Hisari Fortress. 45k, Sugar factory, Konya. 55k, Coal mine, Zonguldak. 75k, Railway. 90k, Crane loading ships. 100k, Cement factory, Ankara. 120k, Highway. 150k, Harvester. 200k, Electric transformer.

Perf. 10½, 11, 11½, 12½, 13½

1959-60   Litho.   Unwmk.

1442	A294	1k indigo	.25	.25
1443	A294	5k brt blue ('59)	.25	.25
1444	A294	10k blue	.25	.25
1445	A294	15k brown	.70	.25
1446	A294	20k slate green	.25	.25
1447	A294	25k violet	.25	.25
1448	A294	30k lilac	.45	.35
1449	A294	40k blue	.70	.25
1450	A294	45k dull violet	.70	.25
1451	A294	55k olive brown	.70	.25
1452	A295	60k green	.95	.25
1453	A295	75k gray olive	3.50	.50
1454	A295	90k dark blue	7.75	.25
1455	A295	100k gray	10.50	.25
1456	A295	120k magenta	3.50	.35
1457	A294	150k orange	3.50	.45
1458	A295	200k yellow green	4.25	.45
1459	A295	250k black brown	4.25	.55
1460	A296	500k dark blue	7.00	.85
		Nos. 1442-1460 (19)	49.70	6.25

Postage Due Stamps of 1936 Surcharged

1959, June 1   Perf. 11½

1461	D6	20k on 20pa brown	.85	.25
1462	D6	20k on 2k lt blue	.25	.25
1463	D6	20k on 3k brt vio	.25	.25
1464	D6	20k on 5k Prus bl	.25	.25
1465	D6	20k on 12k brt rose	.25	.25
		Nos. 1461-1465 (5)	1.85	1.25

Anchor Emblem — A297

Design: 40k, Sea Horse emblem.

1959, July 4 — **Perf. 11**
1466 A297 30k multicolored .25 .25
1467 A297 40k multicolored .25 .25

50th anniv. of the Merchant Marine College.

11th Century Warrior A298

1959, Aug. 26 — **Litho.** — **Perf. 11**
1468 A298 2½ l rose lil & lt bl 1.00 .70

Battle of Malazkirt, 888th anniversary.

A299

Ornament — A300

Design: 40k, Mosque.

1959, Oct. 19 — **Unwmk.** — **Perf. 12½**
1469 A299 30k black & red .25 .25
1470 A299 40k lt blue, blk & ocher .25 .25
1471 A300 75k dp blue, yel & red .50 .25
  Nos. 1469-1471 (3) 1.00 .75

Turkish Artists Congress, Ankara.

Kemal Ataturk — A301

Litho.; Center Embossed
1959, Nov. 10 — **Perf. 14**
1472 A301 500k dark blue 3.00 1.00
  a. Min. sheet of 1, red, imperf. 3.75 2.00

School of Political Science, Ankara A302

Emblem — A303
Crossed Swords Emblem — A304

1959, Dec. 4 — **Photo.** — **Perf. 13½**
1473 A302 40k green & brown .25 .25
1474 A302 40k red brown & bl .25 .25
1475 A303 1 l lt & dk vio & buff .70 .25
  Nos. 1473-1475 (3) 1.20 .75

Political Science School, Ankara, cent.

Inscribed: "Kara Harbokulunum 125 Yili"

Design: 40k, Bayonet and flame.

1960, Feb. 28 — **Litho.** — **Perf. 10½**
1476 A304 30k vermilion & org .25 .25
1477 A304 40k brown, car & yel .25 .25

125th anniv. of the Territorial War College.

Window on World and WRY Emblem A305

150k, Symbolic shanties & uprooted oak emblem.

1960, Apr. 7
1478 A305 90k brt grnsh bl & blk .25 .25
1479 A305 105k yellow & blk .30 .25

World Refugee Year, 7/1/59-6/30/60.

Spring Flower Festival — A306

1960, June 4 — **Photo.** — **Perf. 11½**
Granite Paper
1480 A306 30k Carnations .50 .25
1481 A306 40k Jasmine .70 .25
1482 A306 75k Rose 1.00 .25
1483 A306 105k Tulip 1.40 .50
  Nos. 1480-1483 (4) 3.60 1.25

Atatürk Square, Nicosia A307

Design: 105k, Map of Cyprus.

1960, Aug. 16 — **Litho.** — **Perf. 10½**
1484 A307 40k blue & pink .25 .25
1485 A307 105k blue & yellow .35 .25

Independence of the Republic of Cyprus.

Women and Nest A308

Design: 30k, Globe and emblem.

1960, Aug. 22 — **Photo.** — **Perf. 11½**
1486 A308 30k lt vio & yel .25 .25
1487 A308 75k grnsh bl & gray .35 .25

16th meeting of the Women's Intl. Council.

Soccer A309

#1489, Basketball. #1490, Wrestling. #1491, Hurdling. #1492, Steeplechase.

1960, Aug. 25
1488 A309 30k yellow green .55 .45
1489 A309 30k black .55 .45
1490 A309 30k slate blue .55 .45
1491 A309 30k purple .55 .45
1492 A309 30k brown .55 .45
  a. Sheet of 25, #1488-1492 20.00 11.50
  Nos. 1488-1492 (5) 2.75 2.25

17th Olympic Games, Rome, 8/25-9/11. Printed in sheets of 25 (5x5) with every horizontal and every vertical row containing one of each design. Also printed in normal sheets of 100.

Common Design Types pictured following the introduction.

Europa Issue, 1960
Common Design Type
1960, Sept. 19
Size: 33x22mm
1493 CD3 75k green & bl grn .85 .50
1494 CD3 105k dp bl & lt bl 1.25 .85

Agah Efendi and Front Page of Turcamani Ahval — A310

1960, Oct. 21 — **Photo.** — **Perf. 11½**
1495 A310 40k brown blk & sl .25 .25
1496 A310 60k brn blk & bis brn .25 .25

Centenary of Turkish journalism.

UN Emblem and Torch — A311

Design: 105k, UN headquarters building and UN emblem forming "15," horiz.

1960, Oct. 24 — **Unwmk.**
1497 A311 90k brt bl & dk bl .30 .30
1498 A311 105k lt bl grn & brn .30 .30

15th anniversary of the United Nations.

Army Emblem A312
Tribunal A313

Design: 195k, "Justice," vert.

1960, Oct. 14 — **Litho.** — **Perf. 13**
1499 A312 40k violet & bister .25 .25
1500 A313 105k red, gray & brn .25 .25
1501 A313 195k grn, rose red & brn .45 .25
  Nos. 1499-1501 (3) .95 .75

Trial of ex-President Celal Bayar and ex-Premier Adnan Menderes.

Revolutionaries and Statue — A314

Prancing Horse, Broken Chain — A315

Designs: 30k, Ataturk and hand holding torch. 105k, Youth, soldier and broken chain.

1960, Dec. 1 — **Photo.** — **Perf. 14½**
1502 A314 10k gray & blk .25 .25
1503 A314 30k purple .25 .25
1504 A314 40k brt red & blk .25 .25
1505 A314 105k blue blk & red .40 .25
  Nos. 1502-1505 (4) 1.15 1.00

Revolution of May 27, 1960.

Faculty Building A316

Sculptured Head of Ataturk — A317

Designs: 40k, Map of Turkey and sun disk.

1961, Jan. 9 — **Litho.** — **Perf. 13**
1506 A316 30k slate grn & gray .30 .25
1507 A316 40k brn blk & bis brn .40 .25
1508 A317 60k dk green & buff .50 .25
  Nos. 1506-1508 (3) 1.20 .75

25th anniv. of the Faculty of Languages, History and Geography, University of Ankara.

Communication and Transportation — A318

40k, Highway construction, telephone & telegraph. 75k, New parliament building, Ankara.

1961, Apr. 27 — **Unwmk.** — **Perf. 13**
1509 A318 30k dull vio & blk .25 .25
1510 A318 40k green & black .35 .25
1511 A318 75k dull blue & blk .45 .25
  Nos. 1509-1511 (3) 1.05 .75

9th conference of ministers of the Central Treaty Org. (CENTO), Ankara.

Flag and People — A319

Legendary Wolf and Osman Warriors A320

Design: 60k, "Progress" (Ataturk showing youth the way).

1961, May 27 — **Litho.**
1512 A319 30k multicolored .25 .25
1513 A320 40k sl grn & yel .25 .25
1514 A319 60k grn, pink & dk red .55 .25
  Nos. 1512-1514 (3) 1.05 .75

First anniversary of May 27 revolution.

Rockets A321

Designs: 40k, Crescent and star emblem, "50" and Jet. 75k, Atatürk, eagle and jets, vert.

1961, June 1
1515	A321	30k brn, org yel & blk	.25	.25
1516	A321	40k violet & red	.25	.25
1517	A321	75k slate blk & bis	.55	.25
		Nos. 1515-1517 (3)	1.05	.75

50th anniversary of Turkey's air force.

Europa Issue, 1961
Common Design Type

1961, Sept. 18   *Perf. 13*
Size: 32x22mm
1518	CD4	30k dk violet bl	.55	.35
1519	CD4	40k gray	.65	.35
1520	CD4	75k vermilion	1.25	.60
		Nos. 1518-1520 (3)	2.45	1.30

Tulip and Cogwheel
A322

Open Book and Olive Branch
A324

Torch, Hand and Cogwheel
A323

1961, Oct. 21   *Unwmk.*   *Litho.*
1521	A322	30k slate, pink & sil	.25	.25
1522	A323	75k ultra, org & blk	.35	.25

Technical and professional schools, cent.

1961, Oct. 29
1523	A324	30k red, blk & olive	.25	.25
1524	A324	75k brt blue, blk & grn	.30	.25

Inauguration of the new Parliament.

Kemal Atatürk
A325   A326

1961-62   *Litho.*   *Perf. 10x10½*
Size: 20x25mm
1525	A325	1k brown org ('62)	.90	.25
1526	A325	5k blue	1.50	.25
1527	A325	10k sepia	2.40	.25
1528	A326	10k car rose	2.40	.25
1529	A325	30k dull grn ('62)	7.00	.30
		Size: 21½x31mm		
1530	A325	10 l violet ('62)	14.50	1.90
		Nos. 1525-1530 (6)	28.70	3.20

NATO Emblem and Dove — A327

Design: 105k, NATO emblem, horiz.

1962, Feb. 18   *Unwmk.*   *Perf. 13*
1545	A327	75k dl bl, blk & sil	.25	.25
1546	A327	105k crimson, blk & sil	.60	.25

10th anniv. of Turkey's admission to NATO.

Scouts at Campfire
A328

60k, Scouts with flag. 105k, Scouts saluting.

1962, July 22   *Litho.*
1547	A328	30k lt grn, blk & red	.25	.25
1548	A328	60k gray, blk & red	.60	.25
1549	A328	105k tan, blk & red	.80	.25
		Nos. 1547-1549 (3)	1.65	.75

Turkish Boy Scouts, 50th anniversary.

Soldier Statue — A329

Oxcart from Victory Monument, Ankara
A330

Design: 75k, Atatürk.

1962, Aug. 30   *Unwmk.*   *Perf. 13*
1550	A329	30k slate green	.25	.25
1551	A330	40k gray & sepia	.25	.25
1552	A329	75k gray blk & lt gray	.80	.25
		Nos. 1550-1552 (3)	1.30	.25

40th anniv. of Battle of Dumlupinar.

Europa Issue, 1962
Common Design Type

1962, Sept. 17
Size: 37x23mm
1553	CD5	75k emerald & blk	.65	.40
1554	CD5	105k red & blk	.85	.50
1555	CD5	195k blue & blk	1.50	.65
		Nos. 1553-1555 (3)	3.00	1.55

Brown imprint.

Virgin Mary's House, Ephesus
A331

20pa Stamp of 1863
A332

40k, Inside view after restoration, horiz. 75k, Outside view, horiz. 105k, Statue of Virgin Mary.

1962, Dec. 8   *Photo.*   *Perf. 13½*
1556	A331	30k multicolored	.25	.25
1557	A331	40k multicolored	.25	.25
1558	A331	75k multicolored	.35	.25
1559	A331	105k multicolored	.45	.25
		Nos. 1556-1559 (4)	1.30	1.00

1963, Jan. 13   *Perf. 13x13½*
Issue of 1863: 30k, 1pi. 40k, 2pi. 75k, 5pi.
1560	A332	10k yellow, brn & blk	.25	.25
1561	A332	30k rose, lil & blk	.25	.25
1562	A332	40k lt bl, bluish grn & blk	.25	.25
1563	A332	75k red brn, rose & blk	.45	.25
		Nos. 1560-1563 (4)	1.20	1.00

Centenary of Turkish postage stamps. See No. 1601, souvenir sheet.

Starving People
A333

Designs: 40k, Sowers. 75k, Hands protecting Wheat Emblem, and globe.

1963, Mar. 21   *Unwmk.*   *Perf. 13*
1564	A333	30k dp bl & dk bl	.25	.25
1565	A333	40k brn org & brn	.25	.25
1566	A333	75k grn & dk grn	.55	.25
		Nos. 1564-1566 (3)	1.05	.75

FAO "Freedom from Hunger" campaign.

Julian's Column, Ankara — A334

Ethnographic Museum
A335

10k, Ankara Citadel. 30k, Gazi Institute of Education. 50k, Atatürk's mausoleum. 60k, President's residence. 100k, Ataturk's home, Cankaya. 150k, Parliament building.

1963   *Litho.*   *Perf. 13*
1568	A334	1k sl grn & yel grn	.65	.65
1569	A334	1k purple	.25	.25
1570	A335	5k sepia & buff	.65	.65
1571	A335	10k lil rose & pale bl	.65	.25
1573	A335	30k black & violet	.65	.25
1574	A335	50k blue & yellow	.65	.65
1575	A335	60k dk blue gray	4.00	.65
1576	A335	100k olive brown	2.40	.15
1577	A335	150k dull green	12.00	1.60
		Nos. 1568-1577 (9)	21.90	5.10

Map of Turkey and Atom Symbol
A336

Designs: 60k, Symbols of medicine, agriculture, industry and atom. 100k, Emblem of Turkish Atomic Energy Commission.

1963, May 27   *Unwmk.*   *Perf. 13*
1584	A336	50k red brn & blk	.25	.25
1585	A336	60k grn, dk grn, yel & red	.25	.25
1586	A336	100k violet bl & bl	.55	.30
		Nos. 1584-1586 (3)	1.05	.80

Turkish nuclear research center, 1st anniv.

Meric Bridge
A337

Sultan Murad I — A338

Designs: 10k, Üçserefeli Mosque. 60k, Summerhouse, Edirne Palace.

1963, June 17
1587	A338	10k dp bl & yel grn	.25	.25
1588	A337	30k red org & ultra	.25	.25
1589	A337	60k dk bl, red & brn	.25	.25
1590	A338	100k multicolored	1.10	.35
		Nos. 1587-1590 (4)	1.85	1.10

600th anniv. of the conquest of Edirne (Adrianople).

Soldier and Rising Sun
A339

1963, June 28
1591	A339	50k red, blk & gray	.25	.25
1592	A339	100k red, blk & ol	.45	.25

600th anniversary of the Turkish army.

Plowing
A340

Mithat Pasha — A341

Design: 50k, Agriculture Bank, Ankara.

Perf. 13x13½, 13½x13
1963, Aug. 27   *Photo.*   *Unwmk.*
1593	A340	30k brt yel grn, red brn & grn	.25	.25
1594	A340	50k pale vio & Prus bl	.25	.25
1595	A341	60k gray & green	.30	.25
		Nos. 1593-1595 (3)	.80	.75

Centenary of Agriculture Bank, Ankara.

Sports and Exhibition Palace, Istanbul and #5 — A342

Designs: 50k, Sultan Ahmed Mosque & Turkey in Asia #22. 60k, View of Istanbul & Turkey in Asia #83. 100k, Rumeli Hisari Fortress & #679. 130k, Ankara Fortress & #C2.

1963, Sept. 7   *Litho.*   *Perf. 13*
1596	A342	10k blk, yel & rose	.25	.25
a.		Rose omitted	37.50	37.50
1597	A342	50k blk, grn & rose lil	.30	.25
1598	A342	60k dk brn, dk bl & blk	.35	.25
1599	A342	100k dk vio & lil rose	.50	.25
1600	A342	130k brn, tan & dp org	.75	.25
		Nos. 1596-1600 (5)	2.15	1.25

"Istanbul 63" Intl. Stamp Exhibition.

Type of 1963 Inscribed: "F.I.P. GÜNÜ"
Souvenir Sheet

Issues of 1863: 10k, 20pa. 50k, 1pi. 60k, 2pi. 130k, 5pi.

Unwmk.
1963, Sept. 13   *Litho.*   *Imperf.*
1601		Sheet of 4	2.00	1.50
a.	A332	10k yel, brown & blk	.25	.25
b.	A332	50k lilac, pink & blk	.25	.25
c.	A332	60k bluish grn, lt bl & blk	.40	.25
d.	A332	130k red brn, pink & blk	.50	.25

Intl. Philatelic Federation.

Europa Issue, 1963
Common Design Type
1963, Sept. 16
Size: 32x24mm
1602	CD6	50k red & black	.60	.25
1603	CD6	130k bl grn, blk & bl	.80	.35

Atatürk and First Parliament Building A343

Atatürk and: 50k, Turkish flag. 60k, New Parliament building.

1963, Oct. 29   Photo.   Perf. 13½
1604	A343	30k blk, gold, yel & mar	.25	.25
1605	A343	50k dk grn, gold, yol & red	.30	.25
1606	A343	60k dk brn, gold & yel	.40	.25
		Nos. 1604-1606 (3)	.95	.75

40th anniversary of Turkish Republic.

Atatürk, 25th Death Anniv. — A344

1963, Nov. 10
1607	A344	50k red, gold, grn & brn	.40	.25
1608	A344	60k red, gold, bl & brn	.55	.25

NATO, 15th Anniv. A346

130k, NATO emblem and olive branch.

1964, Apr. 4   Litho.   Perf. 13
1610	A346	50k grnsh bl, vio bl & red	.45	.25
1611	A346	130k red & black	.75	.70

12 Stars and Europa with Torch A347

Design: 130k, Torch and stars.

1964, May 5   Litho.   Perf. 12
1612	A347	50k red brn, yel & vio bl	.40	.25
1613	A347	130k vio bl, lt bl & org	.80	.50

15th anniversary of Council of Europe.

Hüseyin Rahmi Gürpinar, novelist — A348

Portraits: 1k, Hüseyin Rahmi Gürpinar, novelist. 5k, Ismail Hakki Izmirli, scientist. 10k, Sevket Dag, painter. 50k, Recaizade Mahmut Ekrem, Writer. 60k, Gazi Ahmet Muhtar Pasha, commander. 100k, Ahmet Rasim, writer. 130k, Salih Zeki, mathematician.

1964   Litho.   Perf. 13½x13
1614	A348	1k red & blk	.25	.25
1615	A348	5k dull grn & blk	.25	.25
1616	A348	10k tan & blk	.25	.25
1617	A348	50k ultra & dk bl	1.25	.25

1618	A348	60k gray & blk	1.40	.25
1619	A348	100k grnsh bl & dk bl	1.50	.25
1620	A348	130k brt grn & dk grn	6.50	.65
		Nos. 1614-1620 (7)	11.40	2.15

Mosque of Sultan Ahmed A349

Kiz Kulesi, Mersin — A350

Designs: No. 1622, Zeus Temple, Silifke. No. 1623, View of Amasra. No. 1625, Augustus' Gate and minaret, Ankara.

1964, June 11   Unwmk.   Perf. 13
1621	A349	50k gray ol & yel grn	.25	.25
1622	A349	50k claret & car	.25	.25
1623	A349	50k dk bl & vio bl	.25	.25
1624	A350	60k sl grn & dk gray	.40	.25
1625	A350	60k dk brn & org brn	.40	.25
		Nos. 1621-1625 (5)	1.55	1.25

Kars Castle — A351

Alp Arslan, Conqueror of Kars, 1064 — A352

1964, Aug. 16   Unwmk.   Perf. 13
1626	A351	50k blk & pale vio	.40	.40
1627	A352	130k blk, gold, sal & pale vio	1.25	.60

900th anniversary of conquest of Kars.

Europa Issue, 1964
Common Design Type
1964, Sept. 14   Litho.   Perf. 13
Size: 22x33mm
1628	CD7	50k org, ind & sil	.90	.50
1629	CD7	130k lt bl, mag & cit	1.75	.85

Fuat, Resit and Ali Pashas — A353

Design: 60k, Mustafa Resit Pasha, vert.

1964, Nov. 3   Perf. 13
Sizes: 48x33mm (50k, 100k); 22x33mm (60k)
1630	A353	50k multicolored	.55	.25
1631	A353	60k multicolored	.75	.25
1632	A353	100k multicolored	1.10	.25
		Nos. 1630-1632 (3)	2.40	1.05

125th anniversary of reform decrees.

Parachutist — A354

Designs: 90k, Glider, horiz. 130k, Ataturk watching squadron in flight.

1965, Feb. 16   Litho.   Perf. 13
1633	A354	60k lt bl, blk, red & yel	.25	.25
1634	A354	90k bister & multi	.50	.25
1635	A354	130k lt blue & multi	.80	.25
		Nos. 1633-1635 (3)	1.55	.75

Turkish Aviation League, 40th anniv.

Emblem A355

Designs: 50k, Radio mast and waves, vert. 75k, Hand pressing button.

1965, Feb. 24   Unwmk.   Perf. 13
1636	A355	30k multicolored	.25	.25
1637	A355	50k multicolored	.25	.25
1638	A355	75k multicolored	.55	.25
		Nos. 1636-1638 (3)	1.05	.75

Telecommunications meeting of the Central Treaty Org., CENTO.

Coast of Ordu — A356

50k, Manavgat Waterfall, Antalya. 60k, Sultan Ahmed Mosque, Istanbul. 100k, Hali Rahman Mosque, Urfa. 130k, Red Tower, Alanya.

1965, Apr. 5   Litho.
1639	A356	30k multicolored	.25	.25
1640	A356	50k multicolored	.35	.25
1641	A356	60k multicolored	.35	.25
1642	A356	100k multicolored	.65	.25
1643	A356	130k multicolored	.95	.25
		Nos. 1639-1643 (5)	2.55	1.25

ITU Emblem, Old and New Communication Equipment — A357

1965, May 17   Perf. 13
1644	A357	50k multicolored	.35	.25
1645	A357	130k multicolored	.65	.25

ITU, centenary.

ICY Emblem A358

1965, June 26   Litho.   Unwmk.
1646	A358	100k red org, red brn & brt grn	.40	.25
1647	A358	130k gray, lil & ol grn	.65	.35

International Cooperation Year.

Hands Holding Book A358a

Map and Flags of Turkey, Iran and Pakistan A358b

1965, July 21   Unwmk.   Perf. 13
1648	A358a	50k org brn, yel & dk brn	.30	.25
1649	A358b	75k dl bl, red, grn blk & org	.45	.25

1st anniv. of the signing of the Regional Cooperation Development Pact by Turkey, Iran and Pakistan.
See Iran 1327-1328, Pakistan 217-218.

Kemal Ataturk — A359

1965   Litho.   Perf. 12½
1650	A359	1k brt green	.40	.25
1651	A359	5k violet blue	.80	.25
1652	A359	10k blue	1.25	.25
1653	A359	25k gray	2.75	.25
1654	A359	30k magenta	2.00	.25
1655	A359	50k brown	3.25	.30
1656	A359	150k orange	11.50	.75
		Nos. 1650-1656 (7)	21.95	2.30

Europa Issue, 1965
Common Design Type
1965, Sept. 27   Perf. 13
Size: 32x23mm
1665	CD8	50k gray, ultra & grn	1.25	.70
1666	CD8	130k tan, blk & grn	2.25	1.40

Map of Turkey and People A360

Designs: 50k, "1965." 100k, "1965," symbolic eye and man, vert.

Unwmk.
1965, Oct. 24   Litho.   Perf. 13
1667	A360	10k multicolored	.30	.25
1668	A360	50k grn, blk & lt yel grn	.40	.25
1669	A360	100k orange, sl & blk	.75	.25
		Nos. 1667-1669 (3)	1.45	.75

Issued to publicize the 1965 census.

Plane over Ankara Castle A361

Designs: 30k, Archer and Ankara castle. 50k, Horsemen with spears (ancient game). 100k, Three stamps and medal. 150k, Hands holding book, vert.

1965, Oct. 25
1670	A361	10k brt vio, yel & red	.25	.25
1671	A361	30k multicolored	.25	.25
1672	A361	50k lt gray ol, ind & red	.25	.25
1673	A361	100k gray & multi	.60	.30
		Nos. 1670-1673 (4)	1.35	1.05

Souvenir Sheet
Imperf
1674	A361	150k multicolored	2.75	2.50

1st Natl. Postage Stamp Exhibition "Ankara 65."

Resat Nuri Guntekin, Novelist — A362

Portraits: 5k, Besim Omer Akalin, M.D. 10k, Tevfik Fikret, poet. 25k, Tanburi Cemil, composer. 30k, Ahmet Vefik Pasha, playwright. 50k, Omer Seyfettin, novelist. 60k, Kemalettin Mimaroglu, architect. 150k, Halit Ziya Usakligil, novelist. 220k, Yahya Kemal Beyatli, poet.

1965		Litho.	Perf. 13½x13
Black Portrait and Inscriptions			
1675	A362	1k rose	.25 .25
1676	A362	5k blue	.45 .25
1677	A362	10k buff	.45 .25
1678	A362	25k dull red brn	.75 .25
1679	A362	30k gray	.75 .25
1680	A362	50k orange	1.10 .25
1681	A362	60k red lilac	1.25 .25
1682	A362	150k lt green	1.75 .25
1683	A362	220k tan	3.00 .45
		Nos. 1675-1683 (9)	9.75 2.45

Training Ship Savarona A363

Designs: 60k, Submarine "Piri Reis." 100k, Cruiser "Alpaslan." 130k, Destroyer "Gelibolu." 220k, Destroyer "Gemlik."

1965, Dec. 6		Photo.	Perf. 11½
1684	A363	50k blue & brown	.35 .25
1685	A363	60k blue & black	.50 .25
1686	A363	100k blue & black	.80 .25
1687	A363	130k blue & vio blk	1.25 .40
1688	A363	220k blue & indigo	1.75 .65
		Nos. 1684-1688 (5)	4.65 1.80

First Congress of Turkish Naval Society.

Kemal Ataturk — A364

Halide Edip Adivar, Writer — A365

1965		Litho.	Perf. 13½
Imprint: "Apa Ofset Basimevi"			
Black Portrait and Inscriptions			
1689	A364	1k rose lilac	.50 .25
1690	A364	5k lt green	.70 .25
1691	A364	10k blue gray	.90 .25
1692	A364	50k olive bister	1.10 .30
1693	A364	150k silver	1.75 .70
		Nos. 1689-1693 (5)	4.95 1.75

See Nos. 1724-1728.

1966		Litho.	Perf. 13½

Portraits: 25k, Huseyin Sadettin Arel, writer and composer. 30k, Kamil Akdik, graphic artist. 60k, Abdurrahman Seref, historian. 130k, Naima, historian.

1694	A365	25k gray & brn blk	.90 .25
1695	A365	30k rose vio & blk brn	1.10 .25
1696	A365	50k blue & black	1.25 .25
1697	A365	60k lt grn & blk brn	1.40 .25
1698	A365	130k lt vio bl & blk	1.90 .25
		Nos. 1694-1698 (5)	6.55 1.25

Tiles, Green Mausoleum, Bursa — A366

Tiles: 60k, Spring flowers, Hurrem Sultan Mausoleum, Istanbul. 130k, Stylized flowers, 16th century.

1966, May 15		Litho.	Perf. 13½x13
1699	A366	50k multicolored	.85 .25
1700	A366	60k multicolored	1.40 .50
1701	A366	130k multicolored	2.10 .60
		Nos. 1699-1701 (3)	4.35 1.35

On No. 1700 the black ink was applied by a thermographic process and varnished, producing a shiny, raised effect to imitate the embossed tiles of the design source.

Volleyball A367

View of Bodrum A368

1966, May 20			Perf. 13x13½
1702	A367	50k tan & multi	.40 .25

4th Intl. Military Volleyball Championship.

1966, May 25		Perf. 13x13½, 13½x13

Views: 30k, Kusadasi. 50k, Anadolu Hisari, Istanbul. 90k, Marmaris. 100k, Izmir.

1703	A368	10k multi	.25 .25
1704	A368	30k multi	.65 .25
1705	A368	50k multi, horiz.	.35 .25
1706	A368	90k multi	.35 .25
1707	A368	100k multi, horiz.	.45 .25
		Nos. 1703-1707 (5)	2.05 1.25

Inauguration of Keban Dam — A369

Design: 60k, View of Keban Dam area.

1966, June 10			Perf. 13½
1708	A369	50k multicolored	.30 .25
1709	A369	60k multicolored	.50 .25

Visit of King Faisal of Saudi Arabia A370

1966, Aug. 29		Litho.	Perf. 13½x13
1710	A370	100k car rose & dk car	.75 .30

Symbolic Postmark and Stamp A371

Designs: 60k, Flower made of stamps. 75k, Stamps forming display frames. 100k, Map of Balkan states, magnifying glass and stamp.

1966, Sept. 3			Perf. 13½x13
1711	A371	50k multicolored	.25 .25
1712	A371	60k multicolored	.25 .25
1713	A371	75k multicolored	.55 .25
		Nos. 1711-1713 (3)	1.05 .75

Souvenir Sheet
Imperf

1714	A371	100k multicolored	2.50 2.10

2nd "Balkanfila" stamp exhibition, Istanbul.

Sultan Suleiman on Horseback A372

90k, Mausoleum, Istanbul. 130k, Suleiman.

1966, Sept. 6			Perf. 13½x13
1715	A372	60k multicolored	.65 .25
1716	A372	90k multicolored	1.10 .40
1717	A372	130k multicolored	2.25 .65
		Nos. 1715-1717 (3)	4.00 1.30

Sultan Suleiman the Magnificent (1496?-1566). On No. 1717 a gold frame was applied by raised thermographic process.

Europa Issue, 1966
Common Design Type

1966, Sept. 26		Litho.	Perf. 13x13½
Size: 22x33mm			
1718	CD9	50k lt bl, vio bl & blk	1.10 .65
a.		Black (inscriptions & imprint) omitted	65.00
1719	CD9	130k lil, dk red lil & blk	2.25 1.10

Symbols of Education, Science and Culture A373

1966, Nov. 4		Litho.	Perf. 13
1720	A373	130k brn, bis brn & yel	.50 .25

UNESCO, 20th anniversary.

Middle East University of Technology A374

Designs: 100k, Atom symbol. 130k, design symbolizing sciences.

1966, Nov. 15			
1721	A374	50k multicolored	.25 .25
1722	A374	55k multicolored	.55 .25
1723	A374	130k multicolored	.85 .55
		Nos. 1721-1723 (3)	1.65 1.05

10th anniv. of the Middle East University of Technology.

Ataturk Type of 1965
Imprint: "Kiral Matbaasi — Ist"

1966		Litho.	Perf. 12½
Black Portrait and Inscriptions			
1724	A364	25k yellow	.35 .25
1725	A364	30k pink	.50 .25
1726	A364	50k rose lilac	1.50 .25
1727	A364	90k pale brown	1.25 .25
1728	A364	100k gray	1.50 .25
		Nos. 1724-1728 (5)	5.10 1.25

Statue of Ataturk, Ankara — A375

Equestrian Statues of Ataturk: No. 1729A, Statue in Izmir. No. 1729B, Statue in Samsun.

Without Imprint

1967		Litho.	Perf. 13x12½
Size: 23x16mm			
1729	A375	10k black & yellow	.30 .25
Inscribed "1967"			
Imprint: Kiral Matbaasi			
Size: 22x15mm			
1729A	A375	10k black & salmon	.30 .25
1729B	A375	10k black & lt grn	.30 .25
		Nos. 1729-1729B (3)	.90 .75

Issued for use on greeting cards. See Nos. 1790-1791A, 1911.

Puppets Karagöz and Hacivat — A376

Intl. Tourist Year Emblem and: 60k, Sword and shield game. 90k, Traditional military band. 100k, raised effect.

Perf. 13x13½, 13½x13			
1967, Mar. 30			Litho.
1730	A376	50k multicolored	.90 .25
1731	A376	60k multicolored	1.25 .25
1732	A376	90k multicolored	1.60 .45
1733	A376	100k multicolored	2.50 .65
		Nos. 1730-1733 (4)	6.25 1.60

Intl. Tourist Year. On No. 1733 the black ink was applied by a thermographic process and varnished, producing a shiny, raised effect.

Woman Vaccinating Child, Knife and Lancet — A377

Fallow Deer — A378

1967, Apr. 1			Perf. 13x13½
1734	A377	100k multicolored	.60 .25

250th anniv. of smallpox vaccination (variolation) in Turkey. The gold was applied by a thermographic process and varnished, producing a shiny, raised effect.

1967, Apr. 23		Litho.	Perf. 13x13½
1735	A378	50k shown	.50 .25
1736	A378	60k Wild goat	.65 .25
1737	A378	100k Brown bear	.90 .25
1738	A378	130k Wild boar	1.25 .40
		Nos. 1735-1738 (4)	3.30 1.15

Soccer Players and Emblem with Map of Europe A379

130k, Players at left, smaller emblem.

1967, May 1   *Perf. 13*
1739 A379 50k multicolored   1.00   .25
1740 A379 130k yellow & multi   1.40   .50
20th Intl. Youth Soccer Championships.

Sivas Hospital A380

1967, July 1   Litho.   *Perf. 13*
1741 A380 50k multicolored   .40   .25
750th anniversary of Sivas Hospital.

Selim Sirri Tarcan A381

60k, Olympic Rings, Baron Pierre de Coubertin.

1967, July 20
1742 A381 50k lt blue & multi   .35   .25
1743 A381 60k lilac & multi   .35   .25
   a.   Pair, #1742-1743   .80   .65
1st Turkish Olympic competitions.

Ahmed Mithat, Writer — A382

Portraits: 5k, Admiral Turgut Reis. 50k, Sokullu Mehmet, statesman. 100k, Nedim, poet. 150k, Osman Hamdi, painter.

1967   Litho.   *Perf. 12½*
1744 A382 1k green & blk   .65   .25
1745 A382 5k dp bister & blk   1.00   .25
1746 A382 50k brt violet & blk   1.40   .25
1747 A382 100k citron & blk   2.50   .40
1748 A382 150k yellow & blk   4.00   .40
   Nos. 1744-1748 (5)   9.55   1.55

Ruins of St. John's Church, Ephesus A383

Design: 130k, Inside view of Virgin Mary's House, Ephesus.

1967, July 26   *Perf. 13*
1749 A383 130k multicolored   .40   .25
1750 A383 220k multicolored   .95   .50
Visit of Pope Paul VI to the House of the Virgin Mary in Ephesus, July 26.

Plate on Firing Grid and Ornaments A384

1967, Sept. 1
1751 A384 50k pale lil, blk, ind & bl   .50   .25
5th International Ceramics Exhibition.

View of Istanbul and Emblem A385

1967, Sept. 4   Litho.   *Perf. 13*
1752 A385 130k dk blue & gray   .80   .25
9th Congress of the Intl. Commission of Large Dams.

Stamps, Ornament and Map of Turkey A386   Kemal Ataturk A387

Design: 60k, Grapes and stamps.

1967
1753 A386 50k multicolored   .35   .25
1754 A386 60k multicolored   .45   .25
   a.   Souvenir sheet, #1753-1754   2.50   2.50
   Intl. Trade Fair, Izmir.

1967   Litho.   *Perf. 11½x12*
     Booklet Stamps
1755 A387 10k black & lt ol grn   3.25   .80
   a.   Booklet pane of 10   100.00
   b.   Booklet pane of 25   250.00
1756 A387 50k black & pale rose   3.25   .80
   a.   Booklet pane of 2   40.00
   b.   Bklt. pane, 5 #1755, 4 #1756 + label   35.00

Symbolic Water Cycle — A388

1967, Dec. 1   Litho.   *Perf. 13*
1757 A388 90k lt grn, blk & org   .60   .25
1758 A388 130k lilac, blk & org   .70   .60
Hydrological Decade (UNESCO), 1965-74.

Child and Angora Cat, Man with Microscope — A389

60k, Horse and man with microscope.

1967, Dec. 23   *Perf. 13*
1759 A389 50k multicolored   .50   .25
1760 A389 60k multicolored   .70   .40
125th anniv. of Turkish veterinary medicine.

Human Rights Flame — A390

1968, Jan. 1   *Perf. 13x13½*
1761 A390 50k rose lil, dk bl & org   .25   .25
1762 A390 130k lt bl, dk bl & red org   .75   .25
International Human Rights Year.

Archer on Horseback — A391

Miniatures, 16th Century: 50k, Investiture. 60k, Sultan Suleiman the Magnificent receiving an ambassador, vert. 100k, Musicians.

    Perf. 13x13½, 13½x13
1968, Mar. 1   Litho.
1763 A391 50k multicolored   .70   .70
1764 A391 60k multicolored   1.40   1.40
1765 A391 90k multicolored   1.75   1.75
1766 A391 100k multicolored   2.10   2.10
   Nos. 1763-1766 (4)   5.95   5.95

Kemal Ataturk — A392

1968   Litho.   *Perf. 12½*
1767 A392 1k dk & lt blue   .35   .25
1768 A392 5k dk & lt green   .55   .25
1769 A392 50k org brn & yel   2.10   .25
1770 A392 200k dk brown & pink   6.50   .30
   Nos. 1767-1770 (4)   9.50   1.05

Law Book and Oak Branch A393

1968, Apr. 1   *Perf. 13*
1771 A393 50k multicolored   .35   .35
1772 A394 60k multicolored   .40   .40
Centenary of the Court of Appeal.

Mithat Pasha and Scroll A394

Designs: 50k, Scales of Justice. 60k, Ahmet Cevdet Pasha and scroll.

1968, Apr. 1
1773 A393 50k multicolored   .30   .25
1774 A394 60k multicolored   .50   .25
Centenary of the Supreme Court.

    Europa Issue, 1968
   Common Design Type
1968, May 6   Litho.   *Perf. 13*
    Size: 31½x23mm
1775 CD11 100k pck bl, yel & red   *1.75*   .75
1776 CD11 130k green, yel & red   *3.25*   1.25

Yacht Kismet — A395

1968, June 15   Litho.   *Perf. 13*
1777 A395 50k lt ultra & multi   .80   .80
Round-the-world trip of the yacht Kismet, Aug. 22, 1965-June 14, 1968.

"Fight Usury" A396

1968, June 19
1778 A396 50k multicolored   .50   .50
Centenary of the Pawn Office, Istanbul.

Sakarya Battle and Independence Medal — A397

130k, Natl. anthem & reverse of medal.

1968, Aug. 30   *Perf. 13x13½*
1779 A397 50k gold & multi   .50   .40
1780 A397 130k gold & multi   .75   .60
Turkish Independence medal. The gold on Nos. 1779-1780 was applied by a thermographic process and varnished, producing a shiny, raised effect.

Ataturk and Galatasaray High School — A398

50k, "100" and old and new school emblems. 60k, Portraits of Beyazit II and Gulbaba.

1968, Sept. 1   Litho.
1781 A398 50k gray & multi   .25   .25
1782 A398 60k tan & multi   .50   .50
1783 A398 100k lt blue & multi   .75   .75
   Nos. 1781-1783 (3)   1.50   1.50
Centenary of Galatasaray High School.

Charles de Gaulle — A399

1968, Oct. 25   Litho.   *Perf. 13*
1784 A399 130k multicolored   1.25   .70
Visit of President Charles de Gaulle of France to Turkey.

Kemal Ataturk — A400

Ataturk and his Speech to Youth — A401

50k, Ataturk's tomb and Citadel of Ankara. 60k, Ataturk looking out a train window. 250k, Framed portrait of Ataturk in military uniform.

1968, Nov. 10
1785	A400	30k orange & blk	.30 .25
1786	A400	50k brt grn & sl grn	.30 .25
1787	A400	60k bl grn & blk	.35 .25
1788	A401	100k blk, gray & brt grn	.70 .25
1789	A401	250k multicolored	1.25 .40
		Nos. 1785-1789 (5)	2.90 1.40

30th death anniv. of Kemal Ataturk.

Ataturk Statue Type of 1967
Equestrian Statues of Ataturk: No. 1790, Statue in Zonguldak. No. 1791, Statue in Antakya. No. 1791A, Statue in Bursa.

Imprint: Kiral Matbaasi 1968
1968-69   Litho.   Perf. 13x12½
Size: 22x15mm
1790	A375	10k black & lt blue	.25 .25
1791	A375	10k blk & brt rose lil	.25 .25

Perf. 13½
Imprint: Tifdruk Matbaacilik Sanayii A. S. 1969
Size: 21x16½mm
1791A	A375	10k dk grn & tan ('69)	.30 .25
		Nos. 1790-1791A (3)	.80 .75

Ince Minare Mosque, Konya — A402

Historic Buildings: 10k, Doner Kumbet (tomb), Kayseri. 50k, Karatay Medresse (University Gate), Konya. 100k, Ortakoy Mosque, Istanbul. 200k, Ulu Mosque, Divriki.

1968-69   Photo.   Perf. 13x13½
1792	A402	1k dk brn & buff ('69)	.25 .25
1793	A402	10k plum & dl rose ('69)	.50 .25
1794	A402	50k dk ol grn & gray	.65 .25
1795	A402	100k dk & lt grn ('69)	1.75 .40
1796	A402	200k dp bl & lt bl ('69)	2.75 .55
		Nos. 1792-1796 (5)	5.90 1.70

ILO Emblem A403

1969, Apr. 15   Litho.   Perf. 13
1797	A403	130k dk red & black	.80 .25
		ILO, 50th anniv.	

Sultana Hafsa, Medical Pioneer A404

1969, Apr. 26   Litho.   Perf. 13½x13
1798	A404	60k multicolored	1.25 1.00

Europa Issue, 1969
Common Design Type
1969, Apr. 28   Perf. 13
Size: 32x23mm
1799	CD12	100k dull vio & multi	1.60 .65
1800	CD12	130k gray grn & multi	2.25 1.60

Kemal Ataturk — A405   Map of Istanbul — A407

Ataturk and S.S. Bandirma A406

1969, May 19   Litho.   Perf. 13
1801	A405	50k multicolored	.40 .25
1802	A406	60k multicolored	.60 .35

50th anniv. of the landing of Kemal Ataturk at Samsun.

1969, May 31
1803	A407	130k vio bl, lt bl, gold & red	.55 .25

22nd Congress of the Intl. Chamber of Commerce, Istanbul.

Educational Progress A408

Agricultural Progress A409

Designs: 90k, Pouring ladle and industrial symbols. 100k, Road sign (highway construction). 180k, Oil industry chart and symbols.

1969   Litho.   Perf. 13½x13
1804	A408	1k black & gray	.25 .25
1805	A408	1k black & bis brn	.25 .25
1806	A408	1k black & lt grn	.25 .25
1807	A408	1k black & lt vio	.25 .25
1808	A408	1k black & org red	.25 .25
1809	A409	50k brown & ocher	.65 .25
1810	A409	90k blk & grnsh gray	1.10 .25
1811	A408	100k black & org red	1.50 .25
1812	A408	180k violet & orange	2.50 .25
		Nos. 1804-1812 (9)	7.00 2.25

Issued: 1, 100k, 4/8; 50k, 6/11; 90, 180k, 8/15.

Sultan Suleiman Receiving Sheik Abdul Latif — A410

Designs: 80k, Lady Serving Wine, Safavi miniature, Iran. 130k, Lady on Balcony, Mogul miniature, Pakistan.

1969, July 21   Litho.   Perf. 13
1813	A410	50k yellow & multi	.45 .25
1814	A410	80k yellow & multi	.75 .25
1815	A410	130k yellow & multi	1.25 .50
		Nos. 1813-1815 (3)	2.45 1.00

5th anniv. of the signing of the Regional Cooperation for Development Pact by Turkey, Iran and Pakistan.
See Iran 1513-1515, Pakistan 274-276.

Kemal Ataturk — A411

Design: 60k, Ataturk monument and bas-relief showing congress.

1969, July 23
1816	A411	50k black & gray	.40 .25
1817	A411	60k black & grnsh gray	.60 .35

50th anniversary, Congress of Erzerum.

Sivas Congress Delegates A412

Design: 50k, Congress Hall.

1969, Sept. 4   Litho.   Perf. 13
1818	A412	50k dk brn & dp rose	.35 .35
1819	A412	60k olive blk & yel	.45 .45

50th anniv. of the Congress of Sivas (preparation for the Turkish war of independence).

Bar Dance — A413

Folk Dances: 50k, Candle dance (çaydaçira). 60k, Scarf dance (halay). 100k, Sword dance (kiliç-kalkan). 130k, Two male dancers (zeybek), vert.

1969, Sept. 9
1820	A413	30k brown & multi	.45 .25
1821	A413	50k multicolored	.55 .25
1822	A413	60k multicolored	.90 .25
1823	A413	100k yellow & multi	1.00 1.00
1824	A413	130k multicolored	1.60 .55
		Nos. 1820-1824 (5)	4.50 2.30

1914 Airplane "Prince Celaleddin" A414

75k, First Turkish letter carried by air.

1969, Oct. 18   Litho.   Perf. 13
1825	A414	60k dk blue & blue	.35 .25
1826	A414	75k black & bister	.45 .25

55th anniv. of the first Turkish mail transported by air.

"Kutadgu Bilig" A415

1969, Nov. 20   Litho.   Perf. 13
1827	A415	130k ol bis, brn & gold	.55 .25

900th anniv. of "Kutadgu Bilig," a book about the function of the state, compiled by Jusuf of Balasagun in Tashkent, 1069.

Ataturk's Arrival in Ankara, after a Painting — A416

Design: 60k, Ataturk and his coworkers in automobiles arriving in Ankara, after a photograph.

1969, Dec. 27   Litho.   Perf. 13
1828	A416	50k multicolored	.75 .25
1829	A416	60k multicolored	1.25 .30

50th anniv. of Kemal Ataturk's arrival in Ankara, Dec. 27, 1919.

Bosporus Bridge, Map of Europe and Asia — A417

Design: 60k, View of proposed Bosporus Bridge and shore lines.

1970, Feb. 20   Litho.   Perf. 13
1830	A417	60k gold & multi	.75 .30
1831	A417	130k gold & multi	1.50 .65

Foundation ceremonies for the bridge across the Bosporus linking Europe and Asia.

Kemal Ataturk and Signature A418   Kemal Ataturk A419

1970   Litho.   Perf. 13
1832	A418	1k dp orange & brn	.25 .25
1833	A419	5k silver & blk	.25 .25
1834	A419	30k citron & blk	.35 .25
1835	A419	50k lt olive & blk	.45 .25
1836	A419	50k pink & blk	.75 .25
1837	A419	75k lilac & blk	1.50 .25
1838	A419	100k blue & blk	1.00 .25
		Nos. 1832-1838 (7)	4.55 1.75

For surcharge see No. 2078.

Education Year
Emblem — A420

Turkish EXPO
'70
Emblem — A421

1970, Mar. 16
1839 A420 130k ultra, pink & rose
lil   .80 .25
International Education Year.

1970, Mar. 27
100k, EXPO '70 emblem & Turkish pavilion.

1840 A421 50k gold & multi   .25 .25
1841 A421 100k gold & multi   .60 .25
EXPO '70 International Exhibition, Osaka,
Japan, Mar. 15-Sept. 13.

Opening of
Grand
National
Assembly
A422

Design: 60k, Session of First Grand
National Assembly, 1920.

1970, Apr. 23
1842 A422 50k multicolored   .35 .25
1843 A422 60k multicolored   .45 .25
Turkish Grand National Assembly, 50th
anniv.

Emblem of
Cartographic
Service
A423

Map of Turkey and Gen. Mehmet
Sevki Pasha — A424

Designs: 60k, Plane and aerial mapping
survey diagram. 100k, Triangulation point in
mountainous landscape.

Perf. 13½x13 (A423), 13x13½ (A424)
1970, May 2   **Litho.**
1844 A423 50k blue & multi   .40 .25
1845 A424 60k blk, gray grn &
brick red   .40 .25
1846 A423 100k multicolored   .60 .35
1847 A424 130k multicolored   1.00 .50
    Nos. 1844-1847 (4)   2.40 1.35
Turkish Cartographic Service, 75th anniv.

Europa Issue, 1970
Common Design Type
1970, May 4   ***Perf. 13***
Size: 37x23mm
1848 CD13 100k ver, blk & org   1.50 .75
1849 CD13 130k dk bl grn, blk &
org   3.50 1.50

Inauguration of UPU Headquarters,
Bern — A425

1970, May 20
1850 A425 60k blk & dull blue   .30 .25
1851 A425 130k blk & dl ol grn   .65 .25

Lady with
Mimosa, by
Osman Hamdi
(1842-1910)
A426

Paintings: No. 1853, Deer, by Seker Ahmet
(1841-1907). No. 1854, Portrait of Fevzi
Cakmak, by Avni Lifij (d. 1927). No. 1855, Sailboats, by Nazmi Ziya (1881-1937); horiz.

1970   **Litho.**   ***Perf. 13***
Size: 29x49mm
1852 A426 250k multicolored   1.25 .35
1853 A426 250k multicolored   1.25 .35
Size: 32x49mm
1854 A426 250k multicolored   1.25 .35
Size: 73½x33mm
1855 A426 250k multicolored   1.25 .35
    Nos. 1852-1855 (4)   5.00 1.40
Issued: #1852-1853, 6/15; #1854-1855,
12/15.

Turkish Folk
Art — A427

1970, June 15
1856 A427 50k multicolored   .40 .25
3rd National Stamp Exhibition, ANKARA 70,
Oct. 28-Nov. 4. Pane of 50, each stamp se-
tenant with label. This 50k, in pane of 50 without labels, was re-issued Oct. 28 with Nos.
1867-1869.

View of
Fethiye
A428

80k, Seeyo-Se-Pol Bridge, Esfahan, Iran.
130k, Saiful Malook Lake, Pakistan.

1970, July 21   **Litho.**   ***Perf. 13***
1857 A428 60k multicolored   .35 .25
1858 A428 80k multicolored   .50 .25
1859 A428 130k multicolored   .75 .35
    Nos. 1857-1859 (3)   1.60 .85
6th anniv. of the signing of the Regional
Cooperation for Development Pact by Turkey,
Iran and Pakistan.
See Iran 1558-1560, Pakistan 290-292.

Sultan Balim's
Tomb — A429

Haci Bektas
Veli — A430

30k, Tomb of Haci Bektas Veli, horiz.

1970, Aug. 16   **Litho.**   ***Perf. 13***
1860 A429 30k multicolored   .25 .25
1861 A429 100k multicolored   .70 .25
1862 A430 180k multicolored 1.40 .25
    Nos. 1860-1862 (3)   2.35 .75
700th death anniv. of Haci Bektas Veli,
mystic.

Hittite Sun
Disk and
"ISO"
A431

1970, Sept. 15
1863 A431 110k car rose, gold &
blk   .45 .45
1864 A431 150k ultra, gold & blk   .75 .45
8th General Council Meeting of the Intl.
Standardization Org., Ankara.

UN Emblem,
People and
Globe — A432

Stamp "Flower"
and
Book — A433

100k, UN emblem and propeller, horiz.

1970, Oct. 24   **Litho.**   ***Perf. 13***
1865 A432 100k gray & multi   .45 .25
1866 A432 220k multicolored   .75 .35
25th anniversary of the United Nations.

1970, Oct. 28
Designs: 60k, Ataturk monument and
stamps, horiz. 130k, Abstract flower.
1867 A433 10k multicolored   .25 .25
1868 A433 60k blue & multi   .40 .25
Souvenir Sheet
1869 A433 250k dk green & org 2.50 1.90
3rd National Stamp Exhibition, ANKARA 70,
Oct. 28-Nov. 4. See note below No. 1856.

InönüBattle Scene — A434

Design: No. 1871, Second Battle of Inönü.

1971   **Litho.**   ***Perf. 13***
1870 A434 100k multicolored   .80 .25
1871 A434 100k multicolored   .80 .25
1st and 2nd Battles of Inönü, 50th anniv.
Issue dates: #1870, Jan. 10; #1871, Apr. 1.

Village on River Bank, by Ahmet
Sekür — A435

Painting: No. 1872, Landscape, Yildiz Palace Garden, by Ahmet Ragip Bicakcilar.

1971, Mar. 15   **Litho.**   ***Perf. 13***
1872 A435 250k multicolored 1.25 .40
1873 A435 250k multicolored 1.25 .40
See #1901-1902, 1909-1910, 1937-1938.

Campaign
Against
Discrimination
A436

1971, Mar. 21   **Litho.**   ***Perf. 13***
1874 A436 100k multicolored   .45 .25
1875 A436 250k gray & multi   .85 .35
Intl. Year against Racial Discrimination.

Europa Issue, 1971
Common Design Type
1971, May 3   **Litho.**   ***Perf. 13***
Size: 31½x22½mm
1876 CD14 100k lt bl, cl & mag 2.10 1.00
1877 CD14 150k dp org, grn &
red   3.50 1.50

Kemal Ataturk
A437   A438

1971
1878 A437   5k gray & ultra   .60 .25
1879 A437 25k gray & dk red   .90 .25
1880 A438 25k brown & pink   .60 .25
1881 A437 100k gray & violet 1.25 .25
1882 A438 100k green & salm-
on   1.25 .35
1883 A438 250k blue & gray 3.00 .60
1884 A437 400k tan & olive
grn   5.00 .70
    Nos. 1878-1884 (7) 12.60 2.65

Pres. Kemal
Gürsel — A439

Mosque of
Selim,
Edirne — A440

1971, May 27   **Litho.**   ***Perf. 13***
1885 A439 100k multicolored   .50 .25
Revolution of May 27, 1960; Kemal Gürsel
(1895-1966), president.

1971, July 21   **Litho.**   ***Perf. 13***
150k, Religious School, Chaharbagh, Iran.
200k, Badshahi Mosque, Pakistan.
1886 A440 100k multi   .40 .25
1887 A440 150k multi   .55 .25
1888 A440 200k multi, horiz.   .80 .25
    Nos. 1886-1888 (3)   1.75 .75
Regional Cooperation by Turkey, Iran and
Pakistan, 7th anniversary.
See Iran 1599-1601, Pakistan 305-307.

Alp Arslan and Battle of
Malazkirt — A441

Design: 250k, Archers on horseback.

1971, Aug. 26   Litho.   Perf. 13x13½
1889 A441 100k multicolored   .75   .25
1890 A441 250k red, org & blk   1.20   .40
900th anniversary of the Battle of Malazkirt,
which established the Seljuk Dynasty in Asia
Minor.

Battle of Sakarya — A442

1971, Sept. 13
1891 A442 100k violet & multi   1.00   .45
50th anniversary of the victory of Sakarya.

Turkey-Bulgaria Railroad — A443

Designs: 110k, Ferry and map of Lake Van.
250k, Turkey-Iran railroad.

1971
1892 A443 100k multicolored   .75   .25
1893 A443 110k multicolored   .75   .25
1894 A443 250k yellow & multi   1.75   .60
      Nos. 1892-1894 (3)   3.25 1.10
Turkish railroad connections with Bulgaria
&Iran. Issued: 110, 250k, 9/27; 100k, 10/4.

Soccer and
Map of
Mediterranean
A444

200k, Runner and stadium, vert. 250k, Shot
put and map of Mediterranean, vert.

1971, Oct. 6
1895 A444 100k dull vio & blk   .45   .25
1896 A444 200k brn, blk & emer   .80   .35

Souvenir Sheet
Imperf
1897 A444 250k ol bis & slate
                  grn   2.00 1.75
Mediterranean Games, Izmir.

Tomb of Cyrus the Great — A445

Designs: 100k, Harpist, Persian mosaic,
vert. 150k, Ataturk and Riza Shah Pahlavi.

1971, Oct. 13
1898 A445   25k lt blue & multi   .35   .25
1899 A445 100k multicolored   .80   .25
1900 A445 150k dk brown & buff   1.25   .35
      Nos. 1898-1900 (3)   2.40   .85
2500th anniversary of the founding of the
Persian empire by Cyrus the Great.

Painting Type of 1971
No. 1901, Sultan Mohammed I and his Staff.
No. 1902, Palace with tiled walls.

1971, Nov. 15   Litho.   Perf. 13
1901 A435 250k multicolored   1.25   .40
1902 A435 250k multicolored   1.25   .40

Yunus
Emre — A446

1971, Dec. 27   Litho.   Perf. 13
1903 A446 100k brown & multi   .65   .25
650th death anniv. of Yunus Emre, Turkish
folk poet.

First Turkish World Map and Book
Year Emblem — A447

1972, Jan. 3   Perf. 13
1904 A447 100k buff & multi   .50   .25
International Book Year.

Doves and NATO
Emblem — A448

1972, Feb. 18   Litho.   Perf. 13
1905 A448 100k dull grn, blk &
                  gray   1.40   .40
1906 A448 250k dull bl, blk &
                  gray   1.75 1.00
Turkey's membership in NATO, 20th anniv.

Europa Issue 1972
Common Design Type
1972, May 2   Litho.   Perf. 13
Size: 22x33mm
1907 CD15 110k blue & multi   3.00 1.00
1908 CD15 250k brown & multi   4.50 2.00

Painting Type of 1971
No. 1909, Forest, Seker Ahmet. No. 1910,
View of Gebze, Anatolia, by Osman Hamdi.

1972, May 15   Litho.
1909 A435 250k multicolored   1.25   .35
1910 A435 250k multicolored   1.25   .35

Ataturk Statue Type of 1967
Imprint: Ajans - Turk/Ankara 1972
Design: 25k, Ataturk Statue in front of Eth-
nographic Museum, Ankara.

Perf. 12½x11½
1972, June 12   Litho.
Size: 22x15½mm
1911 A375   25k black & buff   .25   .25

Fisherman, by
Cevat
Dereli — A449

Paintings: 125k, Young Man, by Abdur
Rehman Chughtai (Pakistan). 150k, Persian
Woman, by Behzad.

1972, July 21   Litho.   Perf. 13
1912 A449 100k gold & multi   .90   .25
1913 A449 125k gold & multi   1.50   .40
1914 A449 150k gold & multi   1.60   .55
      Nos. 1912-1914 (3)   4.00 1.20
Regional Cooperation for Development Pact
among Turkey, Iran and Pakistan, 8th anniv.
See Iran 1647-1649, Pakistan 322-324.

Ataturk and Commanders at Mt.
Koca — A450

Designs: No. 1916, Battle of the Com-
mander-in-chief. No. 1917, Turkish army
entering Izmir. 110k, Artillery and cavalry.

1972   Litho.   Perf. 13x13½
1915 A450 100k lt ultra & blk   1.00   .25
1916 A450 100k pink & multi   1.00   .25
1917 A450 100k yellow & multi   1.00   .25
1918 A450 110k orange & multi   1.00   .25
      Nos. 1915-1918 (4)   4.00 1.00
50th anniv. of fight for establishment of independent Turkish republic. Issued: #1915,
1918, 8/26; #1916, 8/30; #1917, 9/9.

"Cancer is
Curable"
A451

1972, Oct. 10   Litho.   Perf. 12½x13
1919 A451 100k blk, brt bl & red   .40   .25
Fight against cancer.

International
Railroad Union
Emblem — A452

1972, Dec. 31   Litho.   Perf. 13
1920 A452 100k sl grn, ocher & red .50 .25
Intl. Railroad Union, 50th anniv.

Kemal
Ataturk — A453

1972-76   Litho.   Perf. 13½x13
Size: 21x26mm
1921 A453   5k gray & blue   .25   .25
1922 A453   25k orange ('75)   .35   .25
1923 A453 100k buff & red brn
                  ('73)   1.25   .25
1924 A453 100k lt gray & gray
                  ('75)   .45   .25
1925 A453 110k lt bl & vio bl   1.00   .35
1926 A453 125k dull grn ('73)   1.60   .25
1927 A453 150k tan & brown   1.25   .25
1928 A453 150k lt grn & grn
                  ('75)   .35   .25
1929 A453 175k yel & lil ('73)   2.25   .35
1930 A453 200k buff & red   1.60   .25
1931 A453 250k pink & pur
                                     .40   .25
1931A A453 400k gray & Prus
                  bl ('76)   .45   .25
1932 A453 500k pink & violet   2.75   .65
1933 A453 500k gray & ultra
                                    1.00   .30
Size: 22x33mm
Perf. 13
1934 A453   10 l pink & car
                  rose ('75)   2.25   .30
      Nos. 1921-1934 (15)   17.20 4.45
See Nos. 2060-2061. For surcharges see
Nos. 2180-2181.

Europa Issue 1973
Common Design Type
1973, Apr. 4   Litho.   Perf. 13
Size: 32x23mm
1935 CD16 110k gray & multi   3.25 1.75
1936 CD16 250k multicolored   6.75 2.75

Painting Type of 1971
Paintings: No. 1937, Beyazit Almshouse,
Istanbul, by Ahmet Ziya Akbulut. No. 1938,
Flowers, by Suleyman Seyyit, vert.

1973, June 15   Litho.   Perf. 13
1937 A435 250k multicolored   1.25   .50
1938 A435 250k multicolored   1.25   .50

Helmet, Sword   Mausoleum of
and Oak   Antiochus
Leaves — A454   I — A455

Design: 100k, Helmet, sword and laurel.

1973, June 28   Perf. 13x12½
1939 A454   90k brown, gray &
                  grn   .65   .25
1940 A454 100k brown, lem &
                  grn   .65   .25
Army Day.

1973, July 21   Litho.   Perf. 13
Designs: 100k, Colossal heads, mausoleum
of Antiochus I (69-34 B.C.), Commagene, Turkey. 150k, Statue, Shahdad Kerman, Persia,
3000 B.C. 200k, Street, Mohenjo-daro,
Pakistan.
1941 A455 100k lt blue & multi   .35   .25
1942 A455 150k olive & multi   .50   .25
1943 A455 200k brown & multi   .75   .95
      Nos. 1941-1943 (3)   1.60 1.45
Regional Cooperation for Development Pact
among Turkey, Iran and Pakistan, 9th anniv.
See Iran 1714-1716, Pakistan 343-345.

Minelayer
Nusret
A456

Designs: 25k, Destroyer Istanbul. 100k,
Speedboat Simsek and Naval College. 250k,
Two-masted training ship Nuvid-i Futuh.

1973, Aug. 1
Size: 31½x22mm
1944 A456   5k Prus bl & multi   .25   .25
1945 A456   25k Prus bl & multi   .25   .25

1946 A456 100k Prus bl & multi   1.10   .25
Size: 48x32mm
1947 A456 250k blue & multi   2.50   .40
   Nos. 1944-1947 (4)   4.10 1.15

abu-al-Rayhan al-Biruni   Emblem of Darussafaka Foundation
A457   A458

1973, Sept. 4   **Litho.**   *Perf. 13x12½*
1948 A457 250k multicolored   .80   .80

abu-al-Rayhan al-Biruni (973-1048), philosopher and mathematician.

1973, Sept. 15   *Perf. 13*
1949 A458 100k silver & multi   .30   .25

Centenary of the educational and philanthropic Darussafaka Foundation.

BALKANFILA IV Emblem — A459

Designs: 110k, Symbolic view and stamps. 250k, "Balkanfila 4."

1973   **Litho.**   *Perf. 13*
1950 A459 100k gray & multi   .35   .25
1951 A459 110k multicolored   .25   .25
1952 A459 250k multicolored   .45   .25
   Nos. 1950-1952 (3)   1.05   .75

BALKANFILA IV, Philatelic Exhibition of Balkan Countries, Izmir, Oct. 26-Nov. 5. Issued: 100k, Sept. 26; 110k, 250k, Oct. 26.

Sivas Shepherd Dog — A460

1973, Oct. 4
1953 A460   25k shown   .25   .25
1954 A460 100k Angora cat   1.00   .25

Kemal Ataturk — A461

1973, Oct. 10   **Litho.**   *Perf. 13*
1955 A461 100k gold & blk brn   .40   .25

35th death anniv. of Kemal Ataturk.

Flower and "50" — A462

Ataturk — A463

250k, Torch & "50." 475k, Grain & cogwheel.

1973, Oct. 29
1956 A462 100k purple, red & bl   .25   .25
1957 A462 250k multicolored   .70   .25
1958 A462 475k brt blue & org   1.10   .50
   Nos. 1956-1958 (3)   2.05 1.00

Souvenir Sheet
Imperf
1959 A463 500k multicolored   3.50 2.00

50th anniv. of the Turkish Republic. #1959 contains one stamp with simulated perforations.

Bosporus Bridge A464

150k, Istanbul & Bosporus Bridge. 200k, Bosporus Bridge, children & UNICEF emblem, vert.

1973, Oct. 30   *Perf. 13*
1960 A464 100k multicolored   .35   .25
1961 A464 150k multicolored   .55   .35
1962 A464 200k multicolored   .60   .35
   Nos. 1960-1962 (3)   1.50   .95

Inauguration of the Bosporus Bridge from Istanbul to Üsküdar, Oct. 30, 1973; UNICEF; children from East and West brought closer through Bosporus Bridge (No. 1962).

Mevlana's Tomb and Dancers — A465   Jalal-udin Mevlana — A466

1973, Dec. 1   *Perf. 13x12½*
1963 A465 100k blk, lt ultra & grn   .50   .25
1964 A466 250k blue & multi   .80   .35

Jalal-udin Mevlana (1207-1273), poet and founder of the Mevlevie dervish order.

Cotton and Ship — A467

Export Products: 90k, Grapes. 100k, Figs. 250k, Citrus fruits. 325k, Tobacco. 475k, Hazelnuts.

1973, Dec. 10   **Litho.**   *Perf. 13*
1965 A467   75k black, gray & bl   .25   .25
1966 A467   90k black, olive & bl   .40   .25
1967 A467 100k black, emer & bl   .55   .25
1968 A467 250k blk, brt yel & bl   1.40   .35

1969 A467 325k blk, yel & bl   1.40   .35
1970 A467 475k blk, org brn & bl   2.10   .55
   Nos. 1965-1970 (6)   6.10 2.00

Pres. Inönü — A468   Hittite King, 8th Century B.C. — A469

1973, Dec. 25   **Litho.**   *Perf. 13*
1971 A468 100k sepia & buff   .50   .25

Ismet Inönü, (1884-1973), first Prime Minister and second President of Turkey.

1974, Apr. 29   **Litho.**   *Perf. 13*

Europa: 250k, Statuette of a Boy, (2nd millenium B.C.).
1972 A469 110k multicolored   5.50 1.50
1973 A469 250k lt blue & multi   9.50 3.50

Silver and Gold Figure, 3000 B.C. — A470   Child Care — A471

Archaeological Finds: 175k, Painted jar, 5000 B.C., horiz. 200k, Vessels in bull form, 1700-1600 B.C., horiz. 250k, Pitcher, 700 B.C.

1974, May 24   **Litho.**   *Perf. 13*
1974 A470 125k multicolored   .35   .25
1975 A470 175k multicolored   .60   .25
1976 A470 200k multicolored   .75   .25
1977 A470 250k multicolored   1.10   .40
   Nos. 1974-1977 (4)   2.80 1.15

1974, May 24
1978 A471 110k gray blue & blk   .40   .25

Sisli Children's Hospital, Istanbul, 75th anniv.

Anatolian Rug, 15th Century A472

Designs: 150k, Persian rug, late 16th century. 200k, Kashan rug, Lahore.

1974, July 21   **Litho.**   *Perf. 12½x13*
1979 A472 100k blue & multi   1.00   .25
1980 A472 150k brown & multi   1.50   .25
1981 A472 200k red & multi   3.00   .25
   Nos. 1979-1981 (3)   5.50   .75

10th anniversary of the Regional Cooperation for Development Pact among Turkey, Iran and Pakistan.
See Iran 1806-1808, Pakistan 365-367.

Dove with Turkish Flag over Cyprus A473

1974, Aug. 26   **Litho.**   *Perf. 13*
1982 A473 250k multicolored   .95   .45

Cyprus Peace Operation.

Wrestling A474   Arrows Circling Globe A475

90k, 250k, various wrestling holds, horiz.

1974, Aug. 29
1983 A474   90k multicolored   .25   .25
1984 A474 100k multicolored   .40   .25
1985 A474 250k multicolored   .70   .25
   Nos. 1983-1985 (3)   1.35   .75

World Freestyle Wrestling Championships.

1974, Oct. 9   **Litho.**   *Perf. 13*

UPU Emblem and: 110k, "UPU" in form of dove. 200k, Dove.
1986 A475 110k bl, gold & dk bl   .25   .25
1987 A475 200k green & brown   .30   .25
1988 A475 250k multicolored   .55   .30
   Nos. 1986-1988 (3)   1.10   .80

Centenary of Universal Postal Union.

"Law Reforms" A476

"National Economy" A477   "Education" A478

1974, Oct. 29
1989 A476   50k blue & black   .25   .25
1990 A477 150k red & multi   .35   .25
1991 A478 400k multicolored   .80   .40
   Nos. 1989-1991 (3)   1.40   .90

Works and reforms of Kemal Ataturk.

Arrows Pointing Up — A479

Cogwheel and Map of Turkey A480

1974, Nov. 29   Litho.   Perf. 13
1992 A479 25k brown & black .25 .25
1993 A480 100k brown & gray .45 .25
3rd 5-year Development Program (#1992), and industrialization progress (#1993).

Volleyball — A481

1974, Dec. 30
1994 A481 125k shown .25 .25
1995 A481 175k Basketball .45 .25
1996 A481 250k Soccer .80 .25
   Nos. 1994-1996 (3) 1.50 .75

Automatic Telex Network A482

Postal Check A483

Radio Transmitter and Waves A484

1975, Feb. 5   Litho.   Perf. 13
1997 A482 5k black & yellow .25 .25
1998 A483 50k ol grn & org .25 .25
1999 A484 100k blue & black .30 .25
   Nos. 1997-1999 (3) .80 .75
Post and telecommunications.

Child Entering Classroom A485

Children's paintings: 50k, View of village. 100k, Dancing children.

1975, Apr. 23   Litho.   Perf. 13
2000 A485 25k multicolored .25 .25
2001 A485 50k multicolored .25 .25
2002 A485 100k multicolored .30 .25
   Nos. 2000-2002 (3) .80 .75

Karacaoglan Monument in Mut, by Huseyin Gezer — A486

1975, Apr. 25
2003 A486 110k dk grn, bis & red .50 .30
Karacaoglan (1606-1697), musician.

Orange Harvest in Hatay, by Cemal Tollu — A487

Europa: 250k, Yoruk Family on Plateau, by Turgut Zaim.

1975, Apr. 28
2004 A487 110k bister & multi 2.75 1.10
2005 A487 250k bister & multi 4.25 2.00

Porcelain Vase, Turkey A488

Designs: 200k, Ceramic plate, Iran, horiz. 250k, Camel leather vase, Pakistan.

Perf. 13½x13, 13x13½
2006 A488 110k multicolored 1.25 .35
2007 A488 200k multicolored 1.75 .60
2008 A488 250k ultra & multi 1.75 .95
   Nos. 2006-2008 (3) 4.75 1.90
Regional Cooperation for Development Pact among Turkey, Iran and Pakistan.
See Iran 1871-1873, Pakistan 383-385.

Horon Folk Dance — A489

Regional Folk Dances: 125k, Kasik. 175k, Bengi. 250k, Kasap. 325k, Kafkas, vert.

1975, Aug. 30   Litho.   Perf. 13
2009 A489 100k blue & multi .55 .25
2010 A489 125k green & multi .75 .25
2011 A489 175k rose & multi .90 .25
2012 A489 250k multicolored 1.10 .25
2013 A489 325k orange & multi 1.75 .40
   Nos. 2009-2013 (5) 5.05 1.40

Knight Slaying Dragon — A490   The Plunder of Salur Kazan's House — A491

Design: 175k, Two Wanderers, horiz.

1975, Oct. 15   Litho.   Perf. 13
2014 A490 90k multicolored .25 .25
2015 A490 175k multicolored .40 .30
2016 A491 200k multicolored .60 .40
   Nos. 2014-2016 (3) 1.25 .95
Illustrations for tales by Dede Korkut.

Common Carp A492

1975, Nov. 27   Litho.   Perf. 12½x13
2017 A492 75k Turbot 1.25 .80
2018 A492 90k shown 1.60 .95
2019 A492 175k Trout 2.40 1.25
2020 A492 250k Red mullet 4.75 1.40
2021 A492 475k Red bream 6.00 2.00
   Nos. 2017-2021 (5) 16.00 6.40

Women's Participation A493

Insurance Nationalization — A494

Fine Arts — A495

1975, Dec. 5   Perf. 12½x13, 13x12½
2022 A493 100k bis, blk & red .25 .25
2023 A494 110k violet & multi .30 .25
2024 A495 250k multicolored .40 .25
   Nos. 2022-2024 (3) .95 .75
Works and reforms of Ataturk.

Ceramic Plate — A496

Europa: 400k, Decorated pitcher.

1976, May 3   Litho.   Perf. 13
2025 A496 200k purple & multi 5.00 2.00
2026 A496 400k multicolored 10.00 3.00

Sultan Ahmed Mosque A497

1976, May 10
2027 A497 500k gray & multi .95 .45
7th Islamic Conference, Istanbul.

Lunch in the Field A498

Children's Drawings: 200k, Boats on the Bosporus, vert. 400k, Winter landscape.

1976, May 19   Litho.   Perf. 13
2028 A498 50k multicolored .25 .25
2029 A498 200k multicolored .25 .25
2030 A498 400k multicolored .45 .25
   Nos. 2028-2030 (3) .95 .75
Samsun 76, First National Junior Philatelic Exhibition, Samsun.

Storks, Sultan Marsh A499

Conservation Emblem and: 200k, Horses, Manyas Lake. 250k, Borabay Lake. 400k, Manavgat Waterfall.

1976, June 5
2031 A499 150k multicolored 2.50 .80
2032 A499 200k multicolored .85 .25
2033 A499 250k multicolored 1.40 .25
2034 A499 400k multicolored 1.60 .35
   Nos. 2031-2034 (4) 6.35 1.65
European Wetland Conservation Year.

Nasreddin Hodja Carrying Liver — A500   Montreal Olympic Emblem and Flame — A501

Turkish Folklore: 250k, Friend giving recipe for cooking liver. 600k, Hawk carrying off liver and Hodja telling hawk he cannot enjoy liver without recipe.

1976, July 5   Litho.   Perf. 13
2035 A500 150k multicolored .40 .25
2036 A500 250k multicolored .60 .25
2037 A500 600k multicolored 1.40 .50
   Nos. 2035-2037 (3) 2.40 1.00

1976, July 17
Designs: 400k, "76," Montreal Olympic emblem, horiz. 600k, Montreal Olympic emblem and ribbons.
2038 A501 100k red & multi .25 .25
2039 A501 400k red & multi .75 .40
2040 A501 600k red & multi 1.40 .60
   Nos. 2038-2040 (3) 2.40 1.25
21st Olympic Games, Montreal, Canada, 7/17-8/1.

Kemal Ataturk A502

Designs: 200k, Riza Shah Pahlavi. 250k, Mohammed Ali Jinnah.

1976, July 21   Litho.   Perf. 13½
2041 A502 100k multicolored .30 .25
2042 A502 200k multicolored .40 .25
2043 A502 250k multicolored .60 .30
   Nos. 2041-2043 (3) 1.30 .80
Regional Cooperation for Development Pact among Turkey, Pakistan and Iran, 12th anniversary.
See Iran 1903-1905, Pakistan 412-414.

"Ataturk's Army" A503

Ataturk's Speeches A504

"Peace at Home and in the World" A505

1976, Oct. 29   Litho.   Perf. 13
2044	A503	100k black & red	.25	.25
2045	A504	200k gray grn & multi	.30	.25
2046	A505	400k blue & multi	.70	.30
		Nos. 2044-2046 (3)	1.25	.80

Works and reforms of Ataturk.

Hora A506

1977, Jan. 19   Litho.   Perf. 13
2047	A506	400k multicolored	.95	.30

MTA Sismik 1 "Hora" geophysical exploration ship.

Keyboard and Violin Sound Hole — A507

1977, Feb. 24   Litho.   Perf. 13x13½
2048	A507	200k multicolored	.50	.25

Turkish State Symphony Orchestra, sesquicentennial.

Ataturk and "100" — A508

Design: 400k, Hand holding ballot.

1977, Mar. 21   Litho.   Perf. 13
2049	A508	200k black & red	.50	.25
2050	A508	400k black & brown	.95	.50

Centenary of Turkish Parliament.

Hierapolis (Pamukkale) A509

Europa: 400k, Zelve (mountains and poppies).

1977, May 2   Litho.   Perf. 13½x13
2051	A509	200k multicolored	6.00	2.00
2052	A509	400k multicolored	10.00	3.00

Terra Cotta Pot, Turkey A510

Designs: 225k, Terra cotta jug, Iran. 675k, Terra cotta bullock cart, Pakistan.

1977, July 21   Litho.   Perf. 13
2053	A510	100k multicolored	.35	.25
2054	A510	225k multicolored	1.10	.35
2055	A510	675k multicolored	2.10	.75
a.		Souv. sheet, #2053-2055	9.50	9.50
		Nos. 2053-2055 (3)	3.55	1.35

Regional Cooperation for Development Pact among Turkey, Iran and Pakistan, 13th anniv. See Iran 1946-1948, Pakistan 431-433.

Finn-class Yacht — A511

200k, Three yachts. 250k, Symbolic yacht.

1977, July 28
2056	A511	150k lt bl, bl & blk	.30	.25
2057	A511	200k ultra & blue	.55	.25
2058	A511	250k ultra & black	.75	.25
		Nos. 2056-2058 (3)	1.60	.75

European Finn Class Sailing Championships, Istanbul, July 28.

Ataturk Type of 1972

1977, June 13   Litho.   Perf. 13½x13
2060	A453	100k olive	.75	.25
2061	A453	200k brown	1.00	.25

Kemal Ataturk — A512

Imprint: "GUZEL SANATLAR MATBAASI A.S. 1977"

1977, Sept. 23   Litho.   Perf. 13
Size: 20½x22mm
2062	A512	200k blue	.75	.25
2063	A512	200k Prussian blue	1.00	.25

Imprint: "TIFDRUK-ISTANBUL 1978"

1978, June 28   Photo.   Perf. 13
Size: 20x25mm
2065	A512	10k brown	.50	.25
2066	A512	50k grnsh gray	.75	.25
2067	A512	1 l fawn	.75	.25
2068	A512	2½ l purple	1.00	.25
2069	A512	5 l blue	1.25	.25
2072	A512	25 l dl grn & lt bl	3.00	.30
2073	A512	50 l dp org & tan	4.00	.70
		Nos. 2065-2073 (7)	11.25	2.25

No. 1832 Surcharged with New Value and Wavy Lines

1977, Aug. 17
2078	A418	10k on 1k dp org & brn	.30	.25

"Rationalism" A513   "National Sovereignty" A514

"Liberation of Nations" — A515

1977, Oct. 29   Litho.   Perf. 13
2079	A513	100k multicolored	.25	.25
2080	A514	200k multicolored	.25	.25
2081	A515	400k multicolored	.80	.25
		Nos. 2079-2081 (3)	1.30	.75

Works and reforms of Ataturk.

Mohammad Allama Iqbal — A516   Trees and Burning Match — A517

1977, Nov. 9   Perf. 13x12½
2082	A516	400k multicolored	.80	.25

Mohammad Allama Iqbal (1877-1938), Pakistani poet and philosopher.

1977, Dec. 15   Litho.   Perf. 13

Design: 250k, Sign showing growing tree.
2083	A517	50k green, blk & red	.25	.25
2084	A517	250k gray, grn & blk	.60	.25

Forest conservation. See type A542.

Wrecked Car — A518

Passing on Wrong Side — A519   Traffic Sign, "Slow!" — A520

Two types of 50k:
I — Number on license plate.
II — No number on plate.

Traffic Safety: 250k, Tractor drawing overloaded farm cart. 800k, Accident caused by incorrect passing. 10 l, "Use striped crossings."

1977-78   Perf. 13½x13, 13x13½
2085	A518	50k ultra, blk & red, II	.60	.55
a.		Type I	.70	.55
2086	A519	150k red, gray & blk	.25	.25
2087	A518	250k ocher, blk & red	.50	.25
2088	A520	500k gray, red & blk	.50	.25

2089	A520	800k multicolored	1.10	.25
2090	A520	10 l dl grn, blk & brn	1.75	.35
		Nos. 2085-2090 (6)	4.70	1.90

Issued: 500k, 1977; others, 1978.
For No. 2089 surcharged, see No. 2182.

Ishak Palace, Dogubeyazit — A521

Europa: 5 l, Anamur Castle.

1978, May 2   Litho.   Perf. 13
2091	A521	2½ l multicolored	7.00	2.50
2092	A521	5 l multicolored	12.00	3.50

Riza Shah Pahlavi — A522

1978, June 16   Litho.   Perf. 13x13½
2093	A522	5 l multicolored	.50	.50

Riza Shah Pahlavi (1877-1944) of Iran, birth centenary.

Yellow Rose, Turkey A523

3½ l, Pink roses, Iran. 8 l, Red roses, Pakistan.

1978, July 21   Litho.   Perf. 13
2094	A523	2½ l multi	.30	.25
2095	A523	3½ l multi	.60	.25
2096	A523	8 l multi	1.50	.45
		Nos. 2094-2096 (3)	2.40	.95

Regional Cooperation for Development Pact among Turkey, Iran and Pakistan. See Iran 1984-1986, Pakistan 449-451.

Anti-Apartheid Emblem — A524

1978, Aug. 14   Litho.   Perf. 13½x13
2097	A524	10 l multicolored	.85	.25

Anti-Apartheid Year.

View of Ankara — A525

Design: 5 l, View of Tripoli, horiz.

Perf. 13x12½, 12½x13
1978, Aug. 17
2098	A525	2½ l multi	.30	.25
2099	A525	5 l multi	.75	.25

Turkish-Libyan friendship.

Souvenir Sheet

Bridge and Mosque — A526

1978, Oct. 25   *Imperf.*
2100 A526 15 l multicolored   1.50 1.00
Edirne '78, 2nd Natl. Phil. Youth Exhib.

Independence Medal A527   Latin Alphabet A529

Speech Reform A528

1978, Oct. 29   *Perf. 13x13½, 13½x13*
2101 A527 2½ l multi   .25 .25
2102 A528 3½ l multi   .30 .25
2103 A529 5 l multi   .45 .25
   Nos. 2101-2103 (3)   1.00 .75
Ataturk's works and reforms.

House on Bosporus, 1699 — A530

Turkish Houses: 2½ l, Izmit, 1774, vert. 3½ l, Kula, 17th cent., vert. 5 l, Milas, 18th-19th cent., vert. 8 l, Safranbolu, 18th-19th cent.

Perf. 13x12½, 12½x13
1978, Nov. 22
2104 A530 1 l multi   .40 .25
2105 A530 2½ l multi   .60 .25
2106 A530 3½ l multi   .60 .40
2107 A530 5 l multi   .90 .40
2108 A530 8 l multi   1.50 .45
   Nos. 2104-2108 (5)   4.00 1.75

Carrier Pigeon, Plane, Horseback Rider, Train A531

Europa: 5 l, Morse key, telegraph and Telex machine. 7½ l, Telephone dial and satellite.

1979, Apr. 30   *Litho.*   *Perf. 13*
2109 A531 2½ l multicolored   3.00 1.00
2110 A531 5 l org brn & blk   5.00 1.00
2111 A531 7½ l brt blue & blk   5.75 1.50
   Nos. 2109-2111 (3)   13.75 3.50

Plowing, by Namik Ismail A532

Paintings: 7½ l, Potters, by Kamalel Molk, Iran. 10 l, At the Well, by Allah Baksh, Pakistan.

1979, Sept. 5   *Litho.*   *Perf. 13½x13*
2112 A532 5 l multi   .25 .25
2113 A532 7½ l multi   .50 .25
2114 A532 10 l multi   .75 .35
   Nos. 2112-2114 (3)   1.50 .85
Regional Cooperation for Development Pact among Turkey, Pakistan and Iran, 15th anniversary.
See Iran 2020-2022, Pakistan 486-488.

A533   A534

1979, Sept. 17   *Perf. 13*
2115 A533 5 l Colemanite   .35 .25
2116 A533 7½ l Chromite   .50 .25
2117 A533 10 l Antimonite   .80 .25
2118 A533 15 l Sulphur   1.00 .30
   Nos. 2115-2118 (4)   2.65 1.05
10th World Mining Congress.

1979, Sept. 24

8-shaped road, train tunnel, plane and emblem.

2119 A534 5 l multicolored   .40 .25
European Ministers of Communications, 8th Symposium.

Youth — A535

Secularization A536

Design: 5 l, National oath.

1979, Oct. 29   *Perf. 13x12½, 12½x13*
2120 A535 2½ l multi   .25 .25
2121 A536 3½ l multi   .25 .25
2122 A535 5 l black & orange   .30 .25
   Nos. 2120-2122 (3)   .80 .75
Ataturk's works and reforms.

Poppies — A537

1979, Nov. 26   *Litho.*   *Perf. 13x13½*
2123 A537 5 l shown   .25 .25
2124 A537 7½ l Oleander   .45 .25
2125 A537 10 l Late spider orchid   .70 .25
2126 A537 15 l Mandrake   1.10 .25
   Nos. 2123-2126 (4)   2.50 1.00
See Nos. 2154-2157.

Kemal Ataturk
A538   A538a

Perf. 12½x11½, 13x12½(No. 2131)
1979-81   *Litho.*
2127 A538 50k olive ('80)   .25 .25
2128 A538 1 l grn & lt grn   .40 .25
2129 A538 2½ l purple   .60 .25
2130 A538 2½ l bl grn & lt bl ('80)   .40 .25
2131 A538 2½ l orange ('81)   .50 .25
2132 A538 5 l ultra & gray   .90 .25
   a.   Sheet of 8   7.25 6.00
2133 A538 7½ l brown   .90 .30
2134 A538 7½ l red ('80)   1.25 .30
2135 A538 10 l rose carmine   1.50 .40
2136 A538 20 l gray ('80)   2.25 .50
   Nos. 2127-2136 (10)   8.95 3.00
No. 2132a for Ankara '79 Philatelic Exhibition, Oct. 14-20.
For surcharge see No. 2261.

1980-82   *Photo.*   *Perf. 13½*
2137 A538a 7½ l red brown   .50 .25
   c.   Sheet of 4   4.00 2.50
2137A A538a 10 l brown   1.00 .25
2138 A538a 20 l lilac   1.00 .25
2138A A538a 30 l gray   1.25 .30
2139 A538a 50 l orange red   2.25 .30
2140 A538a 75 l brt green   3.00 .75
2141 A538a 100 l blue   4.00 1.00
   Nos. 2137-2141 (7)   13.00 3.10
No. 2137c for ANTALYA '82 4th Natl. Junior Stamp Show. Exists both per perf 13½ and imperf. Same value.
Issued: #2137, 7/15/81; #2137c, 10/3/82; 30 l, 9/23/81; others, 12/10/80.
See Nos. 2164-2169.

Turkish Printing, 250th Anniversary — A539

1979, Nov. 30   *Litho.*   *Perf. 13*
2142 A539 10 l multicolored   .60 .45

2nd International Olive Oil Year — A540

Perf. 12½x13, 13x12½
1979, Dec. 20   *Litho.*
2143 A540 5 l shown   .25 .25
2144 A540 10 l Globe, oil drop, vert.   .45 .25

Uskudarli Hoca Ali Riza Bey (1857-1930), Painter — A541

Europa: 15 l, Ali Sami Boyar (1880-1967), painter. 20 l, Dr. Hulusi Behcet (1889-1948), physician, discovered Behcet skin disease.

1980, Apr. 28   *Perf. 13*
2145 A541 7½ l multi   1.75 1.00
2146 A541 15 l multi   2.50 1.25
2147 A541 20 l multi   3.25 1.25
   Nos. 2145-2147 (3)   7.50 3.50

Forest Conservation A542   Earthquake Destruction A543

1980, July 3   *Perf. 13½x13*
2148 A542 50k ol grn & red org   .30 .25
See type A517. For surcharge see No. 2262.

1980, Sept. 8   *Perf. 13*
2149 A543 7½ l shown   .30 .25
2150 A543 20 l Seismograph   .70 .50
7th World Conference on Earthquake Engineering, Istanbul.

Games' Emblem, Sports — A544   Hegira — A545

1980, Sept. 26   *Perf. 13x13½*
2151 A544 7½ l shown   .25 .25
2152 A544 20 l Emblem, sports, diff.   .70 .25
First Islamic Games, Izmir.

1980, Nov. 9
2153 A545 20 l multicolored   .80 .40

Plant Type of 1979
1980, Nov. 26   *Perf. 13*
2154 A537 2½ l Manisa tulip   .25 .25
2155 A537 7½ l Ephesian bell-flower   .50 .25
2156 A537 15 l Angora crocus   .75 .25
2157 A537 20 l Anatolian orchid   1.25 .25
   Nos. 2154-2157 (4)   2.75 1.00

Avicenna Treating Patient A546

Avicenna (Arab Physician), Birth Millenium: 20 l, Portrait, vert.

1980, Dec. 15
2158 A546 7½ l multi   .40 .25
2159 A546 20 l multi   .70 .30

Balkanfila VIII Stamp Exhibition, Ankara A547

1981, Jan. 1   *Litho.*   *Perf. 13*
2160 A547 10 l red & black   .75 .25

Kemal
Ataturk — A548

1981, Feb. 4   *Perf. 13*
2163 A548 10 l lilac rose   .50 .25

Ataturk Type of 1980
1983-84   *Perf. 13x13½*
2164 A538a 15 l grnsh blue   .25 .25
2165 A538a 20 l orange ('84)   .30 .25
2167 A538a 65 l bluish grn   .95 .25
2169 A538a 90 l lilac rose   1.25 .25
  Nos. 2164-2169 (4)   2.75 1.00

  Issued: #2164, 2167, 2169, 11/30; #2165, 7/25.

Sultan Mehmet the
Conqueror (1432-
1481) — A549

1981, May 3   *Litho.*   *Perf. 13x12½*
2173 A549 10 l multicolored   .45 .35
2174 A549 20 l multicolored   .90 .70

Gaziantep
(Folk
Dance)
A550

Antalya
A551

1981, May 4   *Litho.*   *Perf. 13*
2175 A550 7½ l shown   .25 .25
2176 A550 10 l Balikesir   .35 .25
2177 A550 15 l Kahramanmaras   1.75 .75
2178 A551 35 l shown   4.00 1.10
2179 A551 70 l Burdur   5.00 2.25
  Nos. 2175-2179 (5)   11.35 4.60

  Nos. 2178-2179 show CEPT (Europa) emblem.

  Nos. C40, 1925, 1931A, 2089
  Surcharged in Black with New Value
  and Wavy Lines
1981, June 3   *Perf. 13½x13*
2179A AP7 10 l on 60k   .90 .25
2180 A453 10 l on 110k   .90 .25
2181 A453 10 l on 400k   .90 .25
2182 A520 10 l on 800k   .90 .25
  Nos. 2179A-2182 (4)   3.60 1.00

A552

1981, June 22   *Perf. 13x12½*
2183 A552 7½ l Rug, Bilecik   .25 .25
2184 A552 10 l Embroidery   .35 .25
2185 A552 15 l Drum, zurna
          players   .55 .25
2186 A552 20 l Embroidered
          napkin   .55 .25
2187 A552 30 l Rug, diff.   1.10 .25
  Nos. 2183-2187 (5)   2.80 1.25

  22nd Intl. Turkish Folklore Congress.

Kemal Ataturk
A553

1981, May 19   *Litho.*   *Perf. 14x15*
2188 A553 2½ l No. 1801   .30 .25
2189 A553 7½ l No. 1816   .30 .25
2190 A553 10 l No. 1604   .40 .25
2191 A553 20 l No. 804   .75 .25
2192 A553 25 l No. 777   .90 .30
2193 A553 35 l No. 1959   1.25 .50
  Nos. 2188-2193 (6)   3.90 1.80

  Souvenir Sheet
2194   Sheet of 6   20.00 10.00
  a. A553 2½ l like 2½ l   .25 .25
  b. A553 37½ l like 7½ l   .50 .25
  c. A553 50 l like 10 l   .75 .25
  d. A553 100 l like 20 l   1.50 .40
  e. A553 125 l like 25 l   2.00 .75
  f. A553 175 l like 35 l   3.00 1.00

  Souvenir Sheet

Balkanfila VIII Stamp Exhibition,
Ankara — A554

1981, Aug. 8   *Litho.*   *Perf. 13*
2195 A554   Sheet of 2   6.00 5.00
  a.   50 l No. B68   2.75 2.75
  b.   50 l No. 733   2.75 2.50

5th General Congress of European
Physics Society
A555

1981, Sept. 7   *Perf. 12½x13*
2196 A555 10 l red & multi   .70 .25
2197 A555 30 l blue & multi   1.10 .40

World
Food Day
A556

1981, Oct. 16
2198 A556 10 l multicolored   .40 .25
2199 A556 30 l multicolored   .95 .25

Constituent Assembly
Inauguration — A557

1981, Oct. 23   *Perf. 13*
2200 A557 10 l multicolored   .55 .25
2201 A557 30 l multicolored   1.25 .25

Ataturk — A558

Portraits of Ataturk.
1981-82   *Perf. 11½x12½, 13 (#2204)*
2202 A558 1 l green   .25 .25
2203 A558 2½ l purple   .25 .25
2204 A558 2½ l gray & org   .50 .25
2205 A558 5 l blue   .25 .25
2206 A558 10 l orange   .25 .25
2207 A558 35 l brown   .70 .25
  Nos. 2202-2207 (6)   2.20 1.50

  Issued: #2204, 12/10/81; others, 1/27/82.

Literacy
Campaign
A559

Energy
Conservation
A560

1981, Dec. 24   *Perf. 13½*
2217 A559 2½ l Procession   .45 .25

1982, Jan. 11   *Perf. 13*
2218 A560 10 l multicolored   .45 .25

Magnolias, by
Ibrahim Calli
(b. 1882)
A561

Sultanhan
Caravanserai
A562

1982, Mar. 17   *Perf. 13x13½, 13½x13*
2219 A561 10 l shown   .50 .25
2220 A561 20 l Fishermen, horiz.   .95 .25
2221 A561 30 l Sewing Woman   1.25 .25
  Nos. 2219-2221 (3)   2.70 .75

Europa Issue
1982, Apr. 26   *Perf. 13x12½*
2222 A562 30 l shown   .75 .25
2223 A562 70 l Silk Route   1.60 .50
  a. Min. sheet, 2 each #2222-2223   7.00 7.00
  b. Pair, #2222-2223   2.50 1.00

1250th Anniv. of
Kul-Tigin
Monument, Kosu
Saydam,
Mongolia — A563

1982, June 9   *Perf. 13*
2224 A563 10 l Monument   .25 .25
2225 A563 30 l Kul-Tigin (685-
          732), Gok-Turk-
          ish commander   .70 .25

Pendik
Shipyard
Opening
A564

1982, July 1   *Perf. 12½x13*
2226 A564 30 l Ship, emblem   .65 .25

Mountains
of Anatolia
A565

1982, July 17   *Perf. 13*
2227 A565 7½ l Agri Dagi, vert.   .30 .25
2228 A565 10 l Buzul Dagi   .55 .25
2229 A565 15 l Demirkazik, vert.   .85 .25
2230 A565 20 l Erciyes   1.10 .25
2231 A565 30 l Kackar Dagi,
          vert.   1.75 .25
2232 A565 35 l Uludag   2.25 .25
  Nos. 2227-2232 (6)   6.80 1.50

Beyazit
State
Library
Centenary
A566

1982, Sept. 27
2233 A566 30 l multicolored   .70 .35

Musical Instruments of
Anatolia — A567

1982, Oct. 13
2234 A567 7½ l Davul   .60 .25
2235 A567 10 l Baglama   .60 .25
2236 A567 15 l shown   .90 .25
2237 A567 20 l Kemence   1.10 .25
2238 A567 30 l Ney   1.50 .25
  Nos. 2234-2238 (5)   4.70 1.25

Roman
Temple
Columns,
Sardis
A568

1982, Nov. 3
2239 A568 30 l multi   1.25 .40

Family Planning and Mother-Child
Health — A569

1983, Jan. 12   *Litho.*   *Perf. 13*
2240 A569 10 l Family on map   .25 .25
2241 A569 35 l Mother and child   .75 .25

30th Anniv. of Customs Cooperation
Council — A570

1983, Jan. 26
2242 A570 45 l multi   1.10 .25

1982 Constitution — A571

1983, Jan. 27
2243 A571 10 l Ballot box   .50 .25
2244 A571 30 l Open book, scale   .75 .30

Manastirli Bey
A572

1983, Mar. 16   **Litho.**
2245 A572 35 l multi   .90 .25

Manastirli Hamdi Bey (1890-1945), telegrapher of news of Istanbul's occupation to Ataturk, 1920.

Europa Issue

Piri Reis,
Geographer
A573

1983, May 5   **Litho.**   **Perf. 12½x13**
2246 A573   50 l   shown   15.00   2.50
2247 A573 100 l   Ulugh Beg
          (1394-1449),
          astronomer   35.00   7.50

Youth
Week
A574

1983, May 16
2248 A574 15 l multi   .50 .25

World Communications Year — A575

1983, May 16   **Perf. 13**
2249 A575 15 l   Carrier pigeon,
          vert.   .40 .25
2250 A575 50 l   Phone lines   .80 .25
2251 A575 70 l   Emblem, vert.   1.50 .25
     Nos. 2249-2251 (3)   2.70 .75

50th
Anniv. of
State Civil
Aviation
A576

1983, May 20   **Litho.**   **Perf. 13**
2252 A576 50 l   Plane, jet   1.10 .25
2253 A576 70 l   Airport   1.50 .45

18th
Council of
Europe Art
Exhibition
A577

15 l, Eros, 2nd cent. BC, vert. 35 l, Two-headed duck, Hittite, 14th cent BC. 50 l, Zinc jugs, plate, 16th cent., vert. 70 l, Marcus Aurelius and his wife Faustina the Young, 2nd cent.

1983, May 22   **Perf. 13**
2254 A577 15 l   multi   .60 .25
2255 A577 35 l   multi   1.50 .25
2256 A577 50 l   multi   1.60 .25
2257 A577 70 l   multi   1.75 .25
     Nos. 2254-2257 (4)   5.45 1.00

Council of Europe's
"The Water's Edge"
Campaign — A578

Coastal Views.

1983, June 1   **Litho.**   **Perf. 13x12½**
2258 A578 10 l   Olodeniz   .65 .40
2259 A578 25 l   Olympus   .65 .40
2260 A578 35 l   Kekova   1.40 .80
     Nos. 2258-2260 (3)   2.70 1.60

Nos. 2127, 2148 Surcharged
Perf. 12½x11½, 13½x13

1983, June 8
2261 A538 5 l   on 50k olive   .25 .25
2262 A542 5 l   on 50k ol grn &
          red org   .25 .25

Kemal   Aga Khan
Ataturk   Architecture Award
A579   A580

1983, June 22   **Perf. 13**
2263 A579   15 l   bl grn & bl   .40 .25
  a.   Sheet of 5 + label   3.50 2.50
2264 A579   50 l   green & blue   1.60 .25
2265 A579 100 l   orange & blue   3.50 .55
     Nos. 2263-2265 (3)   5.50 1.05

For surcharge see No. 2432.

1983, Sept. 4   **Photo.**   **Perf. 11½**
2266 A580 50 l   View of Istanbul   1.10 .25

60th Anniv. of
the Republic
A582

1983, Oct. 29   **Perf. 13½x13**
2268 A582 15 l   multi   .30 .25
2269 A582 50 l   multi   .95 .25

Columns, Aphrodisias — A583

1983, Nov. 2   **Perf. 13**
2270 A583 50 l   multi   1.10 .85

UNESCO Campaign
for Istanbul and
Goreme — A584

1984, Feb. 15   **Litho.**   **Perf. 13**
2271 A584 25 l   St. Sophia Basili-
          ca   .50 .25
2272 A584 35 l   Goreme   .75 .25
2273 A584 50 l   Istanbul   1.00 .25
     Nos. 2271-2273 (3)   2.25 .75

Natl. Police
Org. Emblem
A585

1984, Apr. 10   **Litho.**   **Perf. 13**
2274 A585 15 l multi   .50 .30

Europa (1959-
84)
A586

1984, Apr. 30   **Perf. 13½x13**
2275 A586   50 l   blue & multi   15.00 2.50
2276 A586 100 l   gray & multi   26.00 5.00

Mete
Khan, Hun
Ruler, 204
BC, Flag
A587

Sixteen States (Hun Rulers and Flags): 20 l, Panu, Western Hun empire (48-216). 50 l, Attila, 375-454. 70 l, Aksunvar, Ak Hun empire, 420-562.

1984, June 20   **Litho.**   **Perf. 13**
2277 A587 10 l   multi   .75 .25
2278 A587 20 l   multi   1.00 .40
2279 A587 50 l   multi   2.00 .50
2280 A587 70 l   multi   3.50 .50
     Nos. 2277-2280 (4)   7.25 1.65

See Nos. 2315-2318, 2349-2352, 2382-2385.

Occupation of
Cyprus, 10th
Anniv.
A588

1984, July 20   **Litho.**   **Perf. 13**
2281 A588 70 l   Dove, olive
          branch   1.60 .75

Wild Flowers   Armed Forces Day
A589   A590

1984, Aug. 1   **Perf. 11½x12½**
2282 A589   10 l   Marshmallow
          flower   .25 .25
2283 A589   20 l   Red poppy   .30 .25
2284 A589   70 l   Sowbread   1.00 .25
2285 A589 200 l   Snowdrop   2.75 .35
2286 A589 300 l   Tulip   4.50 .45
     Nos. 2282-2286 (5)   8.80 1.55

See Nos. 2301-2308. For surcharges see Nos. 2467, 2479-2480.

1984, Aug. 26   **Perf. 13½x13**
2287 A590 20 l   Soldier, dove,
          flag   .45 .25
2288 A590 50 l   Sword   .90 .25
2289 A590 70 l   Arms, soldier,
          flag   1.40 .25
2290 A590 90 l   Map, soldier   1.75 .25
     Nos. 2287-2290 (4)   4.50 1.00

Trees and Wood   Pres. Ismet
Products   Inonu (1884-
A591   1973),
               A592

Seed, Tree and Product: 10 l, Liquidambar, liquidambar grease. 20 l, Oriental spruce, stringed instrument. 70 l, Oriental beech, chair. 90 l, Cedar of Lebanon, ship.

1984, Sept. 19   **Perf. 13x12½**
2291 A591 10 l   multi   .55 .25
2292 A591 20 l   multi   .55 .25
2293 A591 70 l   multi   1.40 .25
2294 A591 90 l   multi   2.00 .25
     Nos. 2291-2294 (4)   4.50 1.00

1984, Sept. 24   **Perf. 13**
2295 A592 20 l   Portrait   1.10 .25

First Intl. Turkish
Carpet
Congress — A593

1984, Oct. 7   **Perf. 13x13½**
2296 A593 70 l   Seljukian carpet,
          13th cent.   1.10 .75

Ruins of
Ancient
City of
Harran
A594

1984, Nov. 7   **Perf. 13½x13**
2297 A594 70 l   Columns, arch   1.75 1.25

Turkish
Women's
Suffrage, 50th
Anniv.
A595

1984, Dec. 5   **Litho.**   **Perf. 13**
2298 A595 20 l   Women voting   .45 .25

40th Anniv.,
ICAO — A596

1984, Dec. 7   **Litho.**   **Perf. 13**
2299 A596 100 l   Icarus, ICAO
          emblem   1.75 1.40

Souvenir Sheet

No. 1047 — A597

1985, Jan. 13   Litho.   Imperf.
2300 A597   Sheet of 4, 2 each   4.50 3.50
a.-b.   70 l, any single   .55   .55
Istanbul '87. No. 2300b has denomination in lower right.

Flower Type of 1984
1985   Perf. 11½x12½
2301 A589   5 l Narcissus   .75   .30
Perf. 12½x13
2308 A589   100 l Daisy   1.40   .25
Issue dates: #2301, Feb. 6; #2308, July 31.
For surcharge see No. 2465.

Turkish Aviation League, 60th Anniv. A598

1985, Feb. 16   Perf. 13
2310 A598   10 l Parachutist, glider   .30   .25
2311 A598   20 l Hot air balloon, vert.   .75   .55

INTELSAT, 20th Anniv. — A599

1985, Apr. 3
2312 A599   100 l multi   1.75   .90

Europa Issue

Ulvi Cemal Erkin (1906-1972) and Kosekce — A600

Composers and music: 200 l, Mithat Fenmen (1916-1982) and Concertina.

1985, Apr. 29   Perf. 13½x13
2313 A600   100 l multi   25.00   3.50
2314 A600   200 l multi   35.00   5.00

States Type of 1984
Sixteen States (Kagan rulers and flags): 10 l, Bilge, Gokturk Empire (552-743) and Orhon-Turkish alphabet. 20 l, Bayan, Avar Empire (565-803). 70 l, Hazar, Hazar Empire (651-983). 100 l, Kutlug Kul Bilge, Uygur State (774-1335).

1985, June 20
2315 A587   10 l multi   .60   .25
2316 A587   20 l multi   1.25   .25
2317 A587   70 l multi   2.40   .25
2318 A587   100 l multi   4.75   .25
Nos. 2315-2318 (4)   9.00 1.00

Intl. Youth Year A601

1985, Aug. 8
2319 A601   100 l multi   1.25   .95
2320 A601   120 l multi   2.00 1.60

Postal Code Inauguration A602

1985, Sept. 4   Perf. 13
Background Color
2321 A602   10 l pale yel brn   .40   .25
2322 A602   20 l fawn   .60   .25
2323 A602   20 l gray green   .60   .25
2324 A602   20 l brt blue   .60   .25
2325 A602   70 l rose lilac   1.40   .25
2326 A602   100 l gray   1.90   .45
Nos. 2321-2326 (6)   5.50 1.70

Symposium of Natl. Palaces — A603

1985, Sept. 25   Perf. 13½x13
2327 A603   20 l Aynalikavak, c. 1703   .50   .25
2328 A603   100 l Beylerbeyi, 1865   1.75   .25

UN, 40th Anniv. A604

1985, Oct. 24
2329 A604   100 l multi   1.25 1.00

Alanya Fortress and City A605

1985, Nov. 7
2330 A605   100 l multi   1.75   .90

A606

A607

1985, Nov. 12   Perf. 13x13½
2331 A606   100 l multi   1.75 1.00
Turkish Meteorological Service, 60th anniv.

1985, Dec. 14
2332 A607   20 l multi   .50   .25
Isik Lyceum, Istanbul, cent.

Ataturk — A608

Perf. 11½x12½
1985, Dec. 18   Litho.
2334 A608   10 l pale bl & ultra   .30   .25
2335 A608   20 l beige & brn   .40   .25
2336 A608   100 l lt pink & claret   1.50   .25
Nos. 2334-2336 (3)   2.20   .75
For surcharges see Nos. 2433-2434, 2449.

7th Intl. Children's Festival, Ankara A609

Various children's drawings.

1986, Apr. 23   Litho.   Perf. 12½x13
2342 A609   20 l multi   .50   .45
2343 A609   100 l multi   1.60   .45
2344 A609   120 l multi   1.90 1.90
Nos. 2342-2344 (3)   4.00 2.80

Europa Issue

Pollution A610

1986, Apr. 28   Perf. 13
2345 A610   100 l shown   12.00 2.50
2346 A610   200 l Bandaged leaf   17.50 5.00

1st Ataturk Intl. Peace Prize — A611

1986, May 19   Litho.   Perf. 13
2347 A611   20 l gold & multi   .65   .65
2348 A611   100 l silver & multi   1.60   .95

States Type of 1984
Sixteen States (Devleti rulers and flags): 10 l, Bilge Kul Kadir Khan, Kara Khanids State (840-1212). 20 l, Alp-Tekin, Ghaznavids State (963-1183). 100 l, Seldjuk Bey, Seldjuks State (1040-1157). 120 l, Muhammed Harezmsah, Khwarizm-Shahs State (1157-1231).

1986, June 20
2349 A587   10 l multi   .50   .25
2350 A587   20 l multi   1.40   .40
2351 A587   100 l multi   2.10   .70
2352 A587   120 l multi   5.00 1.40
Nos. 2349-2352 (4)   9.00 2.75

1st Turkish Submarine, Cent. — A612

1986, June 16   Litho.   Perf. 13
2353 A612   20 l Torpedo sub Abdulhamid   1.00   .50

Kirkpinar Wrestling Matches, Edirne — A613

1986, June 30
2354 A613   10 l Oiling bodies   .75   .75
2355 A613   20 l Five wrestlers   .75   .75
2356 A613   100 l Two wrestlers   2.10 1.40
Nos. 2354-2356 (3)   3.60 2.90

Organization for Economic Cooperation and Development, 25th Anniv. — A614

1986, Sept. 30   Litho.   Perf. 13½x13
2357 A614   100 l multi   1.40   .45

Automobile, Cent. — A615

1986, Oct. 15
2358 A615   10 l Benz Veloci-pede, 1886   .90   .60
2359 A615   20 l Rolls-Royce Sil-ver Ghost, 1906   1.25   .60
2360 A615   100 l Mercedes Tour-ing Car, 1928   2.40 1.25
2361 A615   200 l Abstract speed-ing car   3.50 1.75
Nos. 2358-2361 (4)   8.05 4.20

Paintings A616

Designs: 100 l, Bouquet with Tulip, by Feyhaman Duran (1886-1970). 120 l, Landscape with Fountain, by H. Avni Lifij (1886-1927), horiz.

1986, Oct. 22   Perf. 13½x13, 13x13½
2362 A616   100 l multi   1.00   .60
2363 A616   120 l multi   3.00   .85

Celal Bayar (1883-1986), 3rd President — A617

1986, Oct. 27   Perf. 13
2364 A617   20 l shown   .70   .25
2365 A617   100 l Profile   1.10   .25

Kubad-Abad Ruins, Beysehir Lake — A618

1986, Nov. 7   Perf. 13½x13
2366 A618   100 l multi   1.75   .65

Mehmet Akif Ersoy (1873-1936), Composer of the Turkish National Anthem — A619

1986, Dec. 27 Litho. ***Perf. 13½x13***
2367 A619 20 l multi .50 .25

Road Safety — A620

1987, Feb. 4 Litho. ***Perf. 13x13½***
2368 A620 10 l Use seatbelts .25 .25
2369 A620 20 l Don't drink alcohol and drive .45 .25
2370 A620 150 l Observe speed limit 1.60 .25
Nos. 2368-2370 (3) 2.30 .75

For surcharges see Nos. 2466, 2477-2478.

Butterflies A621

1987, Feb. 25 ***Perf. 13½x13***
2371 A621 10 l Celerio euphorbiae 1.00 .25
2372 A621 20 l Vanessa atalanta 1.50 .50
2373 A621 100 l Euplagia quadripunctaria 5.00 1.75
2374 A621 120 l Colias crocea 6.00 2.50
Nos. 2371-2374 (4) 13.50 5.00

Intl. Year of Shelter for the Homeless — A622

1987, Mar. 18 Litho. ***Perf. 13x13½***
2375 A622 200 l multi 1.25 .75

Karabuk Iron and Steel Works, 50th Anniv. A623

1987, Apr. 3 Litho. ***Perf. 13½x13***
2376 A623 50 l Interior .65 .25
2377 A623 200 l Exterior 1.60 .25

Natl. Sovereignty — A624

1987, Apr. 23 ***Perf. 13½x13***
2378 A624 50 l multi .55 .25

Founding of the Turkish state, 67th anniv.

Architecture — A625

Europa: 50 l, Turkish History Institute, 1951-67, designed by Turgut Cansever with Ertur Yener. 200 l, Social Insurance Institute, 1963, designed by Sedad Hakki Eldem.

1987, Apr. 28 ***Perf. 13***
2379 A625 50 l multi *10.00 2.00*
2380 A625 200 l multi *25.00 4.00*

92nd Session, Intl. Olympic Committee, Istanbul, May 9-12 — A626

1987, May 9 Litho. ***Perf. 13x13½***
2381 A626 200 l multi 1.75 1.00

States Type of 1984

Sixteen states (Devleti and Imparatorlugu rulers and flags): 10 l, Batu Khan, Golden Horde State (1227-1502). 20 l, Kutlug Timur Khan, Great Timur Empire (1368-1507). 50 l, Babur Shah, Babur Empire (1526-1858). 200 l, Osman Bey Gasi, Ottoman Empire (1299-1923).

1987, June 20 ***Perf. 12½x13***
2382 A587 10 l multi .60 .30
2383 A587 20 l multi 1.25 .35
2384 A587 50 l multi 1.90 .35
2385 A587 200 l multi 4.00 1.25
Nos. 2382-2385 (4) 7.75 2.25

Album of the Conqueror, Mehmet II, 15th Cent., Topkapi Palace Museum — A627

Untitled paintings by Mehmet Siyah Kalem: 10 l, Two warriors, vert. 20 l, Three men, donkey. 50 l, Blackamoor whipping horse. 200 l, Demon, vert.

Perf. 13½x13, 13x13½
1987, July 1 Litho.
2386 A627 10 l multi .75 .40
2387 A627 20 l multi 1.00 .40
2388 A627 50 l multi 1.25 .40
2389 A627 200 l multi 2.00 1.00
Nos. 2386-2389 (4) 5.00 2.20

Natl. Palaces A628

1987, Sept. 25 ***Perf. 13½x13***
2390 A628 50 l Ihlamur, c. 1850 1.00 .60
2391 A628 200 l Kucuksu Pavilion, 1857 2.00 .75

See Nos. 2425-2426.

"Tughra," Suleiman's Calligraphic Signature — A629

Designs: 30 l, Portrait, vert. 200 l, Suleiman Receiving a Foreign Minister, contemporary miniature, vert. 270 l, Bust, detail of bas-relief, The Twenty-Three Law-Givers, entrance to the gallery of the US House of Representatives.

Litho., Litho. & Engr. (270 l)
1987, Oct. 1 ***Perf. 13½x13, 13x13½***
2392 A629 30 l multi .50 .35
2393 A629 50 l shown .75 .45
2394 A629 200 l multi 2.25 .90
2395 A629 270 l multi 2.75 1.25
Nos. 2392-2395 (4) 6.25 2.95

Suleiman the Magnificent (1494-1566), sultan of the Turkish Empire (1520-1566). On No. 2395, the gold ink was applied by a thermographic process producing a shiny, raised effect.

A630

Presidents: a, Cemal Gursel (1961-1966). b, Cevdet Sunay (1966-1973). c, Fahri S. Koruturk (1973-1980). d, Kenan Evren (1982-). e, Ismet Inonu (1938-1950). f, Celal Bayar (1950-1960). g, Mustafa Kemal Ataturk (1923-1938).

1987, Oct. 29 Litho. ***Imperf.***
Souvenir Sheet
2396 A630 Sheet of 7 6.75 6.75
a.-f. 50 l any single .65 .65
g. 100 l multi, 26x37mm .85 .85

A631

1988, Apr. 9 Litho. ***Perf. 13***
2397 A631 50 l shown *.75 .50*
2398 A631 200 l Mosque, architectural elements *2.25 1.00*

Joseph (Mimar) Sinan (1489-1588), architect.

Health — A632

1988, May 4
2399 A632 50 l Immunization, horiz. .25 .25
2400 A632 200 l Fight drug abuse .65 .25
2401 A632 300 l Safe work conditions, horiz. .95 .25
2402 A632 600 l Organ donation 2.10 .55
Nos. 2399-2402 (4) 3.95 1.30

Europa Issue

Telecommunications — A633

Transport and communication: 200 l, Modes of transportation, vert.

1988, May 2 Litho. ***Perf. 13, 12½***
2403 A633 200 l multi *5.00 2.00*
2404 A633 600 l multi *15.00 3.00*

Steam, Electric and Diesel Locomotives A634

50 l, American Standard steam engine, c. 1850. 100 l, Steam engine produced in Esslingen for Turkish railways, 1913. 200 l, Henschel Krupp steam engine, 1926. 300 l, E 43001 Toshiba electric engine produced in Japan, 1987. 600 l, MTE-Tulomsas #24361 diesel-electric high-speed engine, 1984.

1988, May 24 ***Perf. 13***
2405 A634 50 l buff, brn & blk 1.40 .55
2406 A634 100 l buff, brn & blk 2.75 1.10
2407 A634 200 l buff, brn & blk 4.50 1.90
2408 A634 300 l buff, brn & blk 5.50 2.25
2409 A634 600 l buff, brn & blk 7.75 3.50
Nos. 2405-2409 (5) 21.90 9.30

Court of Cassation (Supreme Court), 120th Anniv. A635

1988, July 1 Litho. ***Perf. 13½x13***
2410 A635 50 l multi .75 .45

Bridge Openings — A636

Designs: 200 l, Fatih Sultan Mehmet Bridge, Kavacik-Hisarustu. 300 l, Seto Ohashi (Friendship) Bridges, the Minami and Kita.

1988, July 3 Litho. ***Perf. 13x13½***
2411 A636 200 l multi 1.90 1.10
2412 A636 300 l multi 3.00 1.50

Telephone System A637

1988, Aug. 24 Litho. ***Perf. 13½x13***
2413 A637 100 l multi .45 .25

1988 Summer Olympics, Seoul
A638

Perf. 12½x13, 13x12½

1988, Sept. 17 Litho.
2414 A638 100 l Running .60 .25
2415 A638 200 l Archery 1.00 .25
2416 A638 400 l Weight lifting 1.40 .35
2417 A638 600 l Gymnastics, vert. 2.00 .45
Nos. 2414-2417 (4) 5.00 1.30

Naim Suleymanoglu, 1988 Olympic Gold Medalist, Weight Lifting — A639

1988, Oct. 5 Litho. **Perf. 13x12½**
2418 A639 1000 l multi 8.00 4.00

Aerospace Industries A640

1988, Oct. 28 Perf. 13½x13, 13x13½
2419 A640 50 l Gear, aircraft, vert. .25 .25
2420 A640 200 l shown .90 .25

Butterflies A641

1988, Oct. 28 **Perf. 13½x13**
2421 A641 100 l Gonepteryx rhamni 1.60 .85
2422 A641 200 l Chazara briseis 4.00 1.40
2423 A641 400 l Allancastria cerisyi godart 6.50 2.50
2424 A641 600 l Nymphalis antiopa 8.25 4.00
a. Souvenir sheet of 4, #2421-2424 35.00 35.00
Nos. 2421-2424 (4) 20.35 8.75
ANTALYA '88.

Natl. Palaces Type of 1987
1988, Nov. 3 Litho. **Perf. 13**
2425 A628 100 l Maslak Royal Lodge, c. 1890 .55 .55
2426 A628 400 l Yildiz Sale Pavilion, 1889 1.25 1.25

Souvenir Sheet

Kemal Ataturk — A642

1988, Nov. 10 **Perf. 13x13½**
2427 A642 400 l multi 1.75 1.75

Medicinal Plants of Anatolia A643

1988, Dec. 14 Litho. **Perf. 13**
2428 A643 150 l Tilia rubra .55 .25
2429 A643 300 l Malva silvestris .70 .25
2430 A643 600 l Hyoscyamus niger 1.40 .25
2431 A643 900 l Atropa belladonna 2.75 .45
Nos. 2428-2431 (4) 5.40 1.20

Stamps of 1983-85 Surcharged

Perf. 13, 11½x12½
1989, Feb. 8 Litho.
2432 A579 50 l on 15 l No. 2263 .25 .25
2433 A608 75 l on 10 l No. 2334 .45 .25
2434 A608 150 l on 20 l No. 2336 1.10 .25
Nos. 2432-2434 (3) 1.80 .75
Surcharge on No. 2432 is slightly different.

Artifacts in the Museum of Anatolian Civilizations, Ankara — A644

Designs: 150 l, Seated Goddess with Child, neolithic bisque figurine, Hacilar, 6th millennium B.C. 300 l, Lead figurine, Alisar Huyuk, Assyrian Trading Colonies Era, c. 19th cent. B.C. 600 l, Human-shaped vase, Kultepe, Assyrian Trading Colonies Era, 18th cent. B.C. 1000 l, Ivory mountain god, Bogazkoy, Hittite Empire, 14th cent. B.C.

1989, Feb. 8 Litho. **Perf. 13½x13**
2435 A644 150 l multi .80 .25
2436 A644 300 l multi 1.25 .80
2437 A644 600 l multi 2.00 1.60
2438 A644 1000 l multi 4.00 2.40
Nos. 2435-2438 (4) 8.05 5.05
See Nos. 2458-2461, 2495-2498, 2520-2523, 2617-2620.

NATO, 40th Anniv. A645

Wmk. 394
1989, Apr. 4 Litho. **Perf. 13½**
2439 A645 600 l multi 1.75 .25

Europa Issue

Children's Games — A646

Perf. 13x12½
1989, Apr. 23 **Wmk. 394**
2440 A646 600 l Leapfrog 20.00 3.50
2441 A646 1000 l Open the door, Headbezirgan 30.00 5.00

Steamships — A647

Perf. 13½x13
1989, July 1 Litho. **Wmk. 394**
2442 A647 150 l Sahilbent 3.00 1.75
2443 A647 300 l Ragbet 4.50 2.40
2444 A647 600 l Tari 6.00 3.00
2445 A647 1000 l Guzelhisar 9.00 4.50
Nos. 2442-2445 (4) 22.50 11.65

French Revolution, Bicent. — A648   Kemal Ataturk — A649

Wmk. 394
1989, July 14 Litho. **Perf. 14**
2446 A648 600 l multi 1.75 .25

1989, Aug. 16 **Perf. 13x13½**
2447 A649 2000 l gray & bluish gray 3.00 .50
2448 A649 5000 l gray & deep red brn 7.00 2.00
See Nos. 2485-2486, 2538-2541. For surcharge see No. 2656.

No. 2336 Surcharged in Bright Blue
Perf. 11½x12½
1989, Aug. 31 Litho. **Unwmk.**
2449 A608 500 l on 20 l .70 .25

Photography, 150th Anniv. — A650

1989, Oct. 17 **Perf. 13½x13**
2450 A650 175 l Camera .40 .25
2451 A650 700 l Shutter 1.40 .25

State Exhibition of Paintings and Sculpture A651

Designs: 200 l, *Manzara*, by Hikmet Onat. 700 l, *Sari Saz*, by Bedri Rahmi Eyuboglu. 1000 l, *Kadin*, by Zuhtu Muridoglu.

Perf. 13½x13
1989, Oct. 30 Litho. **Wmk. 394**
2452 A651 200 l multicolored .30 .25
2453 A651 700 l multicolored 1.25 .25
2454 A651 1000 l multicolored 1.60 .35
Nos. 2452-2454 (3) 3.15 .85

Jawaharlal Nehru, 1st Prime Minister of Independent India — A652

1989, Nov. 14 **Perf. 13½x12½**
2455 A652 700 l multicolored 1.10 .25

Sea Turtles A653

1989, Nov. 16 **Perf. 13½x13**
2456 A653 700 l Caretta caretta 4.00 1.25
2457 A653 1000 l Chelonia mydas 8.00 2.50
a. Souv. sheet of 2, #2456-2457 24.00 20.00

Artifacts Type of 1989
Perf. 13x12½, 12½x13
1990, Feb. 8 Litho. **Wmk. 394**
2458 A644 100 l Ivory female deity .30 .30
2459 A644 200 l Ceremonial vessel .50 .50
2460 A644 500 l Seated goddess pendant 1.00 .75
2461 A644 700 l Carved lion 1.75 1.25
Nos. 2458-2461 (4) 3.55 2.80
Nos. 2458 and 2460 vert.

Wars of Dardanelles, 1915 — A654

1990, Mar. 18 **Perf. 13**
2462 A654 1000 l multicolored 1.10 .25

EXPO '90 Intl. Garden and Greenery Exposition, Osaka — A655

Perf. 12½x13
1990, Apr. 1 **Wmk. 394**
2463 1000 l Bridge at left 1.50 .35
2464 1000 l Pavilion at left 1.50 .35
a. A655 Pair, #2463-2464 3.25 1.25

Nos. 2301, 2368 and 2284 Surcharged
Perfs. as Before
1990, Apr. 4 Litho.
2465 A589 50 l on 5 l #2301 .75 .25
2466 A620 100 l on 10 l #2368 2.00 .25
2467 A589 200 l on 70 l #2284 4.50 .30
Nos. 2465-2467 (3) 7.25 .80

Grand Natl. Assembly, 70th Anniv. — A657   Europa 1990 — A658

1990, Apr. 23 **Perf. 13**
2468 A657 300 l multicolored .50 .50

1990, May 2
Post offices.
2469 A658 700 l Ulus, Ankara 7.50 2.75
2470 A658 1000 l Sirkeci, Istanbul, horiz. 10.00 3.00

8th European Supreme Courts Conf. A659

1990, May 7 Litho. Perf. 12½x13
2471 A659 1000 l multicolored 2.25 1.10

Salamandra Salamandra — A660

World Environment Day: No. 2473, Triturus vittatus. No. 2474, Bombina bombina. No. 2475, Hyla arborea, vert.

1990, June 5 Perf. 13½x13
2472 A660 300 l multicolored .70 .70
2473 A660 500 l multicolored .70 .70
2474 A660 1000 l multicolored 1.50 1.50
2475 A660 1500 l multicolored 2.50 2.50
Nos. 2472-2475 (4) 5.40 5.40

Turkey-Japan Relations, Cent. — A661

1990, June 13 Perf. 12½x13
2476 A661 1000 l multicolored 1.75 1.10

Traffic Types of 1987 and Nos. 2283-2284 Surcharged

1990, June 20 Perf. 14
2477 A620 150 l on 10 l 7.00 1.75
2478 A620 300 l on 20 l 11.00 1.75

Perf. 11½x12½
2479 A589 300 l on 70 l #2284 3.00 .75
2480 A589 1500 l on 20 l #2283 8.75 .75
Nos. 2477-2480 (4) 29.75 5.00

Boats in Saintes Marines — A662

Paintings by Vincent Van Gogh (1853-1890): 300 l, Self-portrait, vert. 1000 l, Vase with Sunflowers, vert. 1500 l, Road of Cypress and Stars.

Wmk. 394
1990, July 29 Litho. Perf. 13
2481 A662 300 l multicolored 2.25 1.50
2482 A662 700 l multicolored 4.00 2.25
2483 A662 1000 l multicolored 4.75 3.25
2484 A662 1500 l multicolored 5.25 4.50
Nos. 2481-2484 (4) 16.25 11.50

Ataturk Type of 1989
1990, Aug. 1 Unwmk. Perf. 14
2485 A649 500 l gray & olive
grn 1.40 .25
2486 A649 1000 l gray & rose vio 1.75 .70

A664

A665

Perf. 13x13½
1990, Aug. 22 Wmk. 394
2487 A664 300 l multicolored .50 .50
Intl. Literacy Year.

1990, Oct. 17 Litho. Perf. 13x13½
State exhibition of paintings and sculpture by: 300 l, Nurullah Berk. 700 l, Cevat Dereli. 1000 l, Nijad Sirel.
2488 A665 300 l multicolored .45 .25
2489 A665 700 l multicolored .90 .35
2490 A665 1000 l multicolored 1.40 .50
Nos. 2488-2490 (3) 2.75 1.10

PTT, 150th Anniv. A666

Past and present communication methods: 200 l, Post rider, truck, train, airplane, ship. 250 l, Telegraph key, computer terminal. 400 l, Telephone switchboard, computerized telephone exchange. 1500 l, Power lines, satellite.

1990, Oct. 23 Perf. 14
2491 A666 200 l multicolored .25 .25
2492 A666 250 l multicolored .25 .25
2493 A666 400 l multicolored .80 .25
2494 A666 1500 l multicolored 3.00 5.75
a. Souv. sheet of 4, #2491-2494 5.00 3.75
Nos. 2491-2494 (4) 4.30 6.50

For surcharges see Nos. 2657-2659.

Artifacts Type of 1989
300 l, Figurine of a woman, c. 5000-4500 BC. 500 l, Sistrum, c. 2100-2000 BC. 1000 l, Spouted vessel with 3-footed pedestal, c. 2000-1750 BC. 1500 l, Ceremonial vessel, 1900-1700 BC.

1991, Feb. 8 Litho. Perf. 13x12½
2495 A644 300 l multi .40 .25
2496 A644 500 l multi .75 .45
2497 A644 1000 l multi 1.10 .75
2498 A644 1500 l multi 2.25 1.10
Nos. 2495-2498 (4) 4.50 2.55

Nos. 2495-2498 are vert.

Lakes of Turkey A667

Wmk. 394
1991, Apr. 24 Litho. Perf. 13
2499 A667 250 l Abant .25 .25
2500 A667 500 l Egridir .75 .25
2501 A667 1500 l Van 2.10 1.10
Nos. 2499-2501 (3) 3.10 1.60

Europa — A668

Unwmk.
1991, May 6 Litho. Perf. 13
2502 A668 1000 l multicolored 15.00 3.50
2503 A668 1500 l multi, diff. 22.50 4.00

Natl. Statistics Day — A669

1991, May 9 Perf. 13½x13
2504 A669 500 l multicolored .45 .25

Eastern Mediterranean Fiber Optic Cable System — A670

1991, May 13
2505 A670 500 l multicolored .45 .25

European Conf. of Transportation Ministers — A671

1991, May 22 Perf. 13
2506 A671 500 l multicolored .90 .60

Caricature Art A672

500 l, "Amcabey" by Cemal Nadir Guler. 1000 l, "Abdulcanbaz" by Turhan Selcuk, vert.

Wmk. 394
1991, Sept. 11 Litho. Perf. 13
2507 A672 500 l multicolored .70 .25
2508 A672 1000 l multicolored 1.10 .60

Ceramics A673

Wall facings: 500 l, 13th cent. Seljuk bird. 1500 l, 16th cent. Ottoman floral pattern.

1991, Sept. 23 Perf. 13½x13
2509 A673 500 l multicolored .40 .25
2510 A673 1500 l multicolored 1.40 .65

Symposium on Intl. Protection of Human Rights, Antalya — A674

1991, Oct. 4 Perf. 13x12½
2511 A674 500 l multicolored .45 .25

Southeastern Anatolia Irrigation and Power Project A675

1991, Oct. 6 Unwmk. Perf. 13½x13
2512 A675 500 l multicolored .45 .25

Turkish Fairy Tales — A676

Baldboy: 500 l, With genie. 1000 l, At party. 1500 l, Plowing field.

1991, Oct. 9 Perf. 13x13½
2513 A676 500 l multicolored .40 .25
2514 A676 1000 l multicolored .90 .45
2515 A676 1500 l multicolored 1.40 .65
Nos. 2513-2515 (3) 2.70 1.35

Snakes A677

Perf. 12½x13
1991, Oct. 23 Wmk. 394
2516 A677 250 l Eryx jaculus 2.40 .60
2517 A677 500 l Elaphe
quatuor-
lineata 3.50 1.25
2518 A677 1000 l Vipera
xanthina 7.25 2.40
2519 A677 1500 l Vipera
kaznakovi 9.50 4.25
Nos. 2516-2519 (4) 22.65 8.50

World Environment Day.

Antiquities Type of 1989
300 l, Statuette of Mother Goddess, Neolithic, 6000 B.C., vert. 500 l, Hasanoglan statuette, Early Bronze Age, 3000 B.C., vert. 1000 l, Inandik vase, Old Hittite, 18th cent. B.C., vert. 1500 l, Lion statuette, Urartian, 8th cent. B.C., vert.

Wmk. 394
1992, Feb. 12 Litho. Perf. 13
2520 A644 300 l multicolored .30 .25
2521 A644 500 l multicolored .45 .25
2522 A644 1000 l multicolored .90 .45
2523 A644 1500 l multicolored 1.50 .65
Nos. 2520-2523 (4) 3.15 1.60

Discovery of America, 500th Anniv. A678

Wmk. 394
1992, May 4 Litho. Perf. 13
2524 A678 1500 l shown 7.00 2.00
2525 A678 2000 l Balloons,
vert. 12.50 3.00

Europa.

Settlement of Jews in Turkey, 500th Anniv. A679

1992, May 15 Perf. 12½x13
2526 A679 1500 l multicolored 1.00 1.00

A681

A682

Wmk. 394
1992, June 1   **Litho.**   *Perf. 13*
2529 A681 500 l multicolored   .45   .45

Turkish Court of Accounts, 130th anniv.

1992, June 4
2530 A682 1500 l multicolored   .90   .90

Economics Congress, Izmir.

World Environment Day — A683

1992, June 5   **Litho.**   *Perf. 13*
2531	A683	500 l	Vanellus vanellus	.60	.60
2532	A683	1000 l	Oriolus oriolus	.90	.60
2533	A683	1500 l	Tadorna tadorna	1.25	.60
2534	A683	2000 l	Halcyon smyrnensis, vert.	1.75	1.25

Nos. 2531-2534 (4)   4.50   3.05

Ataturk Type of 1989 and

Kemal Ataturk — A683a   A683b

10,000 l, Full face. 100,000 l, Facing left.

Perf. 13, 14 (#2539, 2541, 2543-2544A)

1992-96   **Litho.**   **Unwmk.**
2538	A649	250 l	gold, brn & org	1.50	.25
2539	A649	5000 l	gold & vio	2.00	.40
2540	A649	10,000 l	gold & blue	4.50	1.90
2541	A649	20,000 l	gold & lil rose	8.00	1.60
2542	A683a	50,000 l	multi	4.50	1.75
2543	A683b	50,000 l	lake & pink	3.50	.90
2544	A683b	100,000 l	grn bl & yel org	4.50	1.75

Nos. 2538-2544 (7)   28.50   8.55

Issued: 250 l, 10,000 l, 5/28/92; 5000 l, 20,000 l, 9/29/93; #2542, 11/10/94; #2543, 100,000 l, 6/1/96.
For surcharges see Nos. 2655, 2732.

Black Sea Economic Cooperation Summit — A684

Wmk. 394
1992, June 25   **Litho.**   *Perf. 13*
2545 A684 1500 l multicolored   .90   .45

1992 Summer Olympics, Barcelona A685

1992, July 25   **Wmk. 394**
2546	A685	500 l	Doves	.45	.25
2547	A685	1000 l	Boxing	.60	.35
2548	A685	1500 l	Weight lifting	1.10	.45
2549	A685	2000 l	Wrestling	2.25	.65

Nos. 2546-2549 (4)   4.40   1.70

Anatolian Folktales — A686

Scenes: 500 l, Woman carrying milk to soldiers. 1000 l, Pouring milk into trough. 1500 l, Soldiers dipping into trough.

Perf. 13x12½
1992, Sept. 23   **Litho.**   **Wmk. 394**
2550	A686	500 l	multicolored	.25	.25
2551	A686	1000 l	multicolored	.60	.25
2552	A686	1500 l	multicolored	1.00	.45

Nos. 2550-2552 (3)   1.85   .95

Turkish Handicrafts — A687

500 l, Embroidered flowers. 1000 l, Dolls in traditional costumes, vert. 3000 l, Saddlebags.

1992, Oct. 21   *Perf. 13½x13, 13x13½*
2553	A687	500 l	multicolored	.25	.25
2554	A687	1000 l	multicolored	.55	.25
2555	A687	3000 l	multicolored	1.50	.80

Nos. 2553-2555 (3)   2.30   1.30
See Nos. 2585-2588, 2611-2612.

Fruits — A688

Wmk. 394
1992, Nov. 25   **Litho.**   *Perf. 13*
2556	A688	500 l	Cherries	.35	.25
2557	A688	1000 l	Peaches	.70	.25
2558	A688	3000 l	Grapes	1.40	.60
2559	A688	5000 l	Apples	3.00	1.00

Nos. 2556-2559 (4)   5.45   2.10
See Nos. 2565-2568.

Famous Men — A689

Designs: No. 2560, Sait Faik Abasiyanik (1906-54), writer. No. 2561, Fikret Mualla Saygi (1904-67), artist. No. 2562, Cevat Sakir Kabaagacli (1886-1973), author. No. 2563, Muhsin Ertugrul (1892-1979), actor and producer. No. 2564, Asik Veysel Satiroglu (1894-1973), composer.

Perf. 14, 13½x13 (#2561, 2564)
1992, Dec. 30   **Litho.**
2560	A689	T	multicolored	1.10	.25
2561	A689	T	multicolored	1.10	.25
2562	A689	M	multicolored	1.50	.25
2563	A689	M	multicolored	1.50	.25
2564	A689	M	multicolored	1.50	.25

Nos. 2560-2564 (5)   6.70   1.25

Value on day of issue: Nos. 2560-2561, 500 l. Nos. 2562-2564, 1000 l.
See Nos. 2577-2581.

Fruit Type of 1992
Wmk. 394
1993, Apr. 28   **Litho.**   *Perf. 13*
2565	A688	500 l	Bananas	.60	.35
2566	A688	1000 l	Oranges	.60	.60
2567	A688	3000 l	Pears	1.25	.95
2568	A688	5000 l	Pomegranates	2.50	1.75

Nos. 2565-2568 (4)   4.95   3.65

Europa — A690

Sculptures by: 1000 l, Hadi Bara. 3000 l, Zuhtu Muridoglu.

1993, May 3
2569 A690 1000 l multicolored   1.25   .60
2570 A690 3000 l multicolored   2.25   1.00

A691

Wmk. 394
1993, July 6   **Litho.**   *Perf. 13*
2571 A691 2500 l lt bl, dk bl & gold   .90   .60

Economic Cooperation Organization Meeting, Istanbul.

Houses — A692

Various houses from Black Sea region.

1993, July 7
2572	A692	1000 l	multicolored	.75	.25
2573	A692	2500 l	multi, horiz.	.75	.60
2574	A692	3000 l	multicolored	1.50	.90
2575	A692	5000 l	multi, horiz.	1.50	1.25

Nos. 2572-2575 (4)   4.50   3.00

See Nos. 2604-2607, 2631-2634, 2647-2650, 2676-2679.

Hodja Ahmet Yesevi (1093-1166), Poet — A693

1993, July 28
2576 A693 3000 l lt bl, dk bl & gold   1.00   .40

Famous Men Type of 1992
Designs: No. 2577, Haci Arif Bey (1831-84), composer. No. 2578, Neyzen Tevfik Kolayli (1878-1953), poet. No. 2579, Munir Nurettin Selcuk (1900-81), composer, musician. No. 2580, Cahit Sitki Taranci (1910-56), poet. No. 2581, Orhan Veli Kanik (1914-50), writer.

Perf. 14, 13½x13 (2578-2580)
1993, Aug. 4   **Litho.**   **Unwmk.**
2577	A689	T	brown & red brown	1.10	.25
2578	A689	T	brown & red brown	1.10	.25
2579	A689	M	brown & red brown	1.50	.25

2580	A689	M	brown & red brown	1.50	.25
2581	A689	M	brown & red brown	1.50	.25

Nos. 2577-2581 (5)   6.70   1.25

Value on day of issue: Nos. 2577-2578, 500 l. Nos. 2579-2581, 1000 l.

Istanbul, Proposed Site for 2000 Olympics A694

1993, Aug. 11   *Perf. 12½x13*
2582 A694 2500 l multicolored   .90   .45

Protection of Mediterranean Sea Against Pollution — A695

Unwmk.
1993, Oct. 12   **Litho.**   *Perf. 13*
2583 A695 1000 l Amphora on sea floor   .25   .25
2584 A695 3000 l Dolphin jumping   1.60   .65

Handicrafts Type of 1992
Perf. 12½x13, 13x12½
1993, Oct. 21   **Wmk. 394**
2585	A687	1000 l	Painted rug	.25	.25
2586	A687	3000 l	Earrings	.95	.25
2587	A687	5000 l	Money purse, vert.	2.00	.95

Nos. 2585-2587 (3)   3.20   1.45

Republic, 70th Anniv. — A696

1993, Oct. 29   **Wmk. 394**   *Perf. 13*
2588 A696 1000 l multicolored   .45   .45

Civil Defence Organization — A697

Perf. 12½x13
1993, Nov. 25   **Unwmk.**
2589 A697 1000 l multicolored   .45   .45

Turksat Satellite — A698   Natl. Water Project — A699

Designs: 1500 l, Satellite, globe, map of Turkey. 5000 l, Satellite transmissions to areas in Europe and Asia.

Perf. 13x13½
1994, Jan. 21   Litho.   Wmk. 394
2590 A698 1500 l multicolored   .25   .25
2591 A698 5000 l multicolored   1.10   .25

1994, Feb. 28   Perf. 13x12½
2592 A699 1500 l multicolored   .45   .35

Native
Cuisine
A700

Perf. 12½x13
1994, Mar. 23   Litho.   Wmk. 394
2593 A700 1000 l Ezogel in
                    corbasi   .65   .65
2594 A700 1500 l Mixed dolma   .65   .65
2595 A700 3500 l Shish kebabs   .65   .65
2596 A700 5000 l Baklava   1.25   .65
    Nos. 2593-2596 (4)   3.20 2.60

Europa
A701

1500 l, Marie Curie (1867-1934), chemist,
vert. 5000 l, Albert Einstein (1879-1955),
physicist.

Unwmk.
1994, May 2   Litho.   Perf. 13
2597 A701 1500 l multicolored   .50   .50
2598 A701 5000 l multicolored   1.50 1.50

World Environment Day — A703

Views of: 6000 l, Antalya. 8500 l, Mugla,
vert.

Wmk. 394
1994, June 5   Litho.   Perf. 13
2602 A703 6000 l multicolored   1.25   .90
2603 A703 8500 l multicolored   1.90 1.25

Houses Type of 1993
2500 l, 2-story housing complex. 3500 l, 3-
story home with balconies. 6000 l, Tri-level
country home. 8500 l, 2-story home.

1994, July 7
2604 A692 2500 l multi, horiz.   .60   .60
2605 A692 3500 l multi, horiz.   .60   .60
2606 A692 6000 l multi, horiz.   .60   .60
2607 A692 8500 l multi, horiz.   1.75   .60
    Nos. 2604-2607 (4)   3.55 2.40

Tourism
A704

1994, Aug. 3
2608 A704 5000 l Hiking   .75   .45
2609 A704 10,000 l Rafting   1.50   .75

Project of
the Year
2001
A705

1994, Aug. 27
2610 A705 2500 l multicolored   .50   .50

Handicrafts Type of 1992
Designs: 7500 l, Kusak pattern used on 18th
cent. clothing, vert. 12,000 l, Pacalik pattern
used on 19th cent. clothing.

1994, Oct. 21
2611 A687 7500 l multicolored   1.00   .50
2612 A687 12,500 l multicolored   1.75 1.75

Mushrooms — A706

1994, Nov. 16
2613 A706 2500 l Morchella
                    conica   .50   .50
2614 A706 5000 l Agaricus
                    bernardii   .90   .90
2615 A706 7500 l Lactarius
                    deliciosus   1.60 1.60
2616 A706 12,500 l Macrolepiota
                    procera   3.25 3.25
    Nos. 2613-2616 (4)   6.25 6.25
    See Nos. 2637-2640.

Antiquities Type of 1989
Lydian Treasures, 6th cent. B.C.: 2500 l, Silver pitcher, vert. 5000 l, Silver incense burner,
vert. 7500 l, Gold, glass necklace. 12,500 l,
Gold brooch.

1994, Dec. 7
2617 A644 2500 l multicolored   .60   .45
2618 A644 5000 l multicolored   .90   .50
2619 A644 7500 l multicolored   1.40   .75
2620 A644 12,500 l multicolored   2.50 1.00
    Nos. 2617-2620 (4)   5.40 2.70

Nevruz,
New Day
A707

1995, Mar. 21
2621 A707 3500 l multicolored   .45   .45

Europa — A708

1995, May 5
2622 A708 3500 l Flowers   1.00 1.00
2623 A708 15,000 l Olive branch   2.00 2.00

Istanbul '96 World Stamp
Exhibition — A709

a, 7000 l, Buildings. b, 25,000 l, Tower,
buildings. c, 7000 l, Mosque, city along harbor.
c, 25,000 l, Residential area, mosque, harbor.

1995, May 24
2624 A709 Block of 4, #a.-d.   7.25 3.50
    Nos. 2624a-2624b and 2624c-2624d are
each continuous designs.

European Nature Conservation
Year — A710

1995, June 5
2625 A710 5000 l Field of pop-
                    pies   .50   .25
2626 A710 15,000 l Trees   1.50   .70
2627 A710 25,000 l Mountain val-
                    ley   2.50 1.25
    Nos. 2625-2627 (3)   4.50 2.20

A711   A712

1995, Feb. 1
2628 A711 15,000 l red & blue   1.75 1.75
    Motion Pictures, cent.

1995, Apr. 23
2629 A712 5000 l multicolored   .45   .45
1sh Conference of the Moslem Women Par-
liamentaries, Pakistan.

Houses Type of 1993
5000 l, 2-story block house. 10,000 l, Tower
of part-stone house. 15,000 l, Interior view of
2-story house, horiz. 20,000 l, Three unit-con-
necting apartment, horiz.

1995, July 7
2631 A692 5000 l multicolored   .75   .35
2632 A692 10,000 l multicolored   1.10   .40
2633 A692 15,000 l multicolored   1.25   .55
2634 A692 20,000 l multicolored   1.40 1.10
    Nos. 2631-2634 (4)   4.50 2.40

UN, 50th
Anniv. — A713

1995, Oct. 24
2635 A713 15,000 l shown   .80   .40
2636 A713 30,000 l UN emblem,
                    "50"   1.60   .80

Mushroom Type of 1994
Designs: 5000 l, Amanita phalloides.
10,000 l, Lepiota helveola. 20,000 l, Gyromitra
esculenta. 30,000 l, Amanita gemmata.

1995, Nov. 16
2637 A706 5000 l multicolored   .65   .65
2638 A706 10,000 l multicolored   1.10 1.10
2639 A706 20,000 l multicolored   2.25 2.25
2640 A706 30,000 l multicolored   2.50 2.50
    Nos. 2637-2640 (4)   6.50 6.50

Children's
Rights
A714

6,000 l, Rainbow, hearts, flower, sun in sky.
10,000 l, Child's hand drawing letter "A."

1996, Mar. 13
2641 A714 6,000 l multicolored   .40   .40
2642 A714 10,000 l multicolored   1.10 1.00

Fauna — A715

Designs: a, 5,000 l, Bee. b, 10,000 l, Dog. c,
15,000 l, Rooster. d, 30,000 l, Fish.

1996, Apr. 10   Unwmk.
2643 A715 Sheet of 4, #a.-d.   5.00 5.00
    ISTANBUL '96.

Famous
Women
A716

Perf. 12½x13
1996, May 5   Litho.   Unwmk.
2644 A716 10,000 l Nene Hatun   1.50 1.50
2645 A716 40,000 l Halide Edip
                    Adivar   3.00 3.00
    Europa.

World Environment Day — A717

Unwmk.
1996, June 3   Litho.   Perf. 13
2646 A717 50,000 l multicolored   1.75   .90

Houses Type of 1993
Designs: 10,000 l, Tri-level block house,
horiz. 15,000 l, Two story with bay window,
gate at entrance to side courtyard, horiz.
25,000 l, Two story townhouse, double
wooden doors at bottom. 50,000 l, Flat-roofed,
two-story townhouse.

1996, July 7   Perf. 13
2647 A692 10,000 l multicolored   .45   .25
2648 A692 15,000 l multicolored   .75   .50
2649 A692 25,000 l multicolored   1.00   .55
2650 A692 50,000 l multicolored   2.10 1.10
    Nos. 2647-2650 (4)   4.30 2.25

1996 Summer Olympic Games,
Atlanta — A718

a, 10,000 l, Archery. b, 15,000 l, Wrestling.
c, 25,000 l, Weight lifting. d, 50,000 l, Hurdles.

1996, July 19
2651 A718 Sheet of 4, #a.-d.   6.50 6.50
    ISTANBUL '96.

Turkish
Press,
50th
Anniv.
A719

1996, July 24   Perf. 12½x13
2652 A719 15,000 l multicolored   .60   .30

Euro '96, European Soccer
Championships, Great Britain — A720

1996, June 8 *Perf. 13*
2653 A720 15,000 l Player, vert. 1.10 .45
2654 A720 50,000 l Soccer ball,
flags 2.50 1.25

Nos. 2447, 2491, 2493-2494, 2538
Surcharged in Orange or Deep Violet
Blue

or

Perfs., Printing Methods as Before
1996, July 22
2655 A649 T on 250 l #2538
(O) 1.10 .25
2656 A649 T on 2000 l #2447 1.10 .25
2657 A666 M on 200 l #2491 1.75 .25
2658 A666 M on 400 l #2493 1.75 .25
2659 A666 M on 1500 l #2494 1.75 .25
Nos. 2655-2659 (5) 7.45 1.25

Nos. 2655-2656 and 2657-2659 had face
values of 10,000 l and 15,000 l on day of
issue.
See No. 2732.

Methods of Transportation — A721

a, 25,000 l, Airplane (b). b, 50,000 l, Helicopter, ship (d). c, 75,000 l, Train. d, 100,000 l,
Bus (c).

Unwmk.
1996, Sept. 27 *Litho.* *Perf. 13*
2660 A721 Sheet of 4, #a.-d. 14.00 10.00
ISTANBUL '96. Exists imperf. Value, $85.

New Year
A722

Unwmk.
1996, Oct. 23 *Litho.* *Perf. 13*
2661 A722 15,000 l multicolored .55 .30

Social and
Cultural
Heritage
A723

10,000 l, Public Library, Bayezit, Amasya.
15,000 l, Mosque and hospital, Divrigi.

1996, Dec. 17 *Litho.* *Perf. 13*
2662 A723 10,000 l multicolored .35 .35
2663 A723 15,000 l multicolored .55 .55

Stories and Legends — A724

Europa: 25,000 l, Little children dressed in
flowers and leaves riding a giant peacock.
70,000 l, Genie, man riding a giant bird.

1997, May 5 *Litho.* *Perf. 13*
2664 A724 25,000 l multicolored 1.25 1.25
2665 A724 70,000 l multicolored 2.50 2.50

White Cat — A725

Designs: a, 25,000 l, Tail, hindquarters. b,
50,000 l, Back legs. c, 75,000 l, Front legs. d,
150,000 l, Face.

1997, Apr. 23
2666 A725 Sheet of 4, #a.-d. 10.00 8.25

Language
Day — A726

1997, May 13 *Litho.* *Perf. 13*
2667 A726 25,000 l multicolored .50 .50

World Environment Day — A727

1997, June 5
2668 A727 35,000 l multicolored .90 .90

Orchids — A728

Designs: 25,000 l, Ophrys tenthredinifera.
70,000 l, Ophrys apifera.

1997, May 28
2669 A728 25,000 l multicolored .80 .25
2670 A728 70,000 l multicolored 1.90 .55

25th Intl.
Istanbul
Festival
A729

1997, June 13 *Perf. 13½*
Background Color
2671 A729 15,000 l blue .25 .25
2672 A729 25,000 l pink .65 .65
2673 A729 70,000 l blue green 1.60 1.60
2674 A729 75,000 l purple 2.00 2.00
2675 A729 100,000 l green blue 2.75 2.75
Nos. 2671-2675 (5) 7.25 7.25

House Type of 1993
Inscribed: 25,000 l, Bir Urfa Evi, vert.
40,000 l, Bir Mardin Evi. 80,000 l, Bir
Diyarbakir Evi. 100,000 l, Kemaliye'de Bir Ev,
vert.

1997, July 7 *Litho.* *Perf. 13*
2676 A692 25,000 l multicolored .50 .50
2677 A692 40,000 l multicolored .90 .90
2678 A692 80,000 l multicolored 1.75 1.75
2679 A692 100,000 l multicolored 2.25 2.25
Nos. 2676-2679 (4) 5.40 5.40

A730 A731

Flowers: 40,000 l, Lilium candidum.
100,000 l, Euphorbia pulcherima.

1997, Sept. 8 *Litho.* *Perf. 13*
2680 A730 40,000 l multicolored 1.10 .25
2681 A730 100,000 l multicolored 2.50 .65

1997, Sept. 13
World Air Games: No. 2682, Hang gliding.
No. 2683, Sailplane. No. 2684, Man pointing
up at biplanes. No. 2685, Hot air balloon.
2682 A731 40,000 l multi 1.10 1.10
2683 A731 40,000 l multi 1.10 1.10
2684 A731 100,000 l multi 3.25 3.25
2685 A731 100,000 l multi 4.25 4.25
Nos. 2682-2685 (4) 9.70 9.70

Forestry
Congress
A732

1997, Oct. 13 *Litho.* *Perf. 13*
2686 A732 50,000 l multicolored 1.40 1.40

15th European
Gymnastics
Congress — A733

1997, Oct. 13
2687 A733 100,000 l multicolored 2.75 2.75

Traditional
Women's
Headcovers
A734

1997, Nov. 19 *Litho.* *Perf. 13*
2688 A734 50,000 l Gaziantep 1.50 .75
2689 A734 50,000 l Canakkale 1.50 .75
2690 A734 100,000 l Isparta 2.50 1.50
2691 A734 100,000 l Bursa 2.50 1.50
Nos. 2688-2691 (4) 8.00 4.50

See Nos. 2711-2714, 2748-2751, 2765-
2768, 2790-2793.

1998 Winter Olympic Games,
Nagano — A735

Slalom skiers: No. 2692, #1 on bib. No.
2693, #119 on bib.

1998, Feb. 7 *Litho.* *Perf. 13*
2692 125,000 l multicolored 2.00 2.00
2693 125,000 l multicolored 2.00 2.00
a. A735 Pair, #2692-2693 4.25 4.25

Intl. Year of the Ocean — A736

Designs: a, 50,000 l, Turtle, jellyfish. b,
75,000 l, Fish, octopus. c, 125,000 l, Coral,
crab. d, 125,000 l, Fish, coral, starfish.

1998, Apr. 18 *Litho.* *Perf. 13*
2694 A736 Sheet of 4, #a.-d. 8.00 8.00

Dardenelles
Campaign — A737

Memorial Statues: #2695, "Mother with Children," Natl. War Memorial, Wellington. #2696,
"With Great Respect to the Mehmetcik, Gallipoli" (Turkish soldier carrying wounded
ANZAC).

1998, Mar. 18 *Litho.* *Perf. 13*
2695 A737 125,000 l multicolored 1.75 1.75
2696 A737 125,000 l multicolored 1.75 1.75

See New Zealand Nos. 1490-1491.

A738

Europa (National Festivals and Holidays):
100,000 l, Kemal Ataturk, natl. flag, people
celebrating. 150,000 l, Ataturk, natl. flag, children of different races celebrating together.

1998, May 5
2697 A738 100,000 l multicolored 1.25 1.25
2698 A738 150,000 l multicolored 2.25 2.25

A739

Tulips: 50,000 l, Sylvestris. 75,000 l, Armena (pink). 100,000 l, Armena (violet). 125,000 l, Saxatilis.

1998, May 1   Litho.   Perf. 13
2699 A739 50,000 l multicolored .75 .75
2700 A739 75,000 l multicolored 1.60 1.60
2701 A739 100,000 l multicolored 1.90 1.90
2702 A739 125,000 l multicolored 3.00 3.00
    Nos. 2699-2702 (4) 7.25 7.25

Souvenir Sheet

World Environment Day — A740

Owls: a, Two on branches. b, One flying, one standing.

1998, June 5   Litho.   Perf. 13½
2703 A740 150,000 l Sheet of 2, #a.-b. 6.25 6.25

Contemporary Arts — A741

75,000 l, Couple dancing. 100,000 l, Man playing cello. 150,000 l, Ballerina.

1998, Aug. 14   Litho.   Perf. 13
2704 A741 75,000 l multi 1.10 .50
2705 A741 100,000 l multi, vert. 1.40 .70
2706 A741 150,000 l multi, vert. 2.10 1.10
    Nos. 2704-2706 (3) 4.60 2.30

Kemal Ataturk — A742

1998, Aug. 20   Litho.   Perf. 13
2707 A742 150,000 l cl & brn 1.60 .65
2708 A742 175,000 l bl & rose brn 2.25 .85
2709 A742 250,000 l brn & cl 3.00 1.25
2710 A742 500,000 l brn & dk bl 6.50 2.50
    Nos. 2707-2710 (4) 13.35 5.25

Women's Headcovers Type of 1997
1998, Nov. 24   Litho.   Perf. 13
2711 A734 75,000 l Afyon .85 .40
2712 A734 75,000 l Ankara .85 .40
2713 A734 175,000 l Mus 1.90 .95
2714 A734 175,000 l Mugla 1.90 .95
    Nos. 2711-2714 (4) 5.50 2.70

Turkish Republic, 75th Anniv. — A743

275,000 l, Flag, silhouette of Ataturk.

1998, Oct. 29   Litho.   Perf. 13
2715 A743 175,000 l shown 1.75 .90
 a. Souvenir sheet of 1, imperf. 1.75 1.25
2716 A743 275,000 l red & blk 2.75 1.40
 a. Souvenir sheet of 1, imperf. 2.75 2.00
    Nos. 2715a, 2716a have simulated perforations.

Famous People A744

#2717, Ihap Hulusi Görey (1898-1986). #2718, Bedia Muvahhit (1897-1993). No. 2719, Feza Gürsey (1921-92). #2720, Haldun Taner (1915-86). #2721, Vasfi Riza Zobu (1902-92).

1998, Dec. 31   Photo.   Perf. 13
2717 A744 M gray bl, bl & plum 1.50 .30
2718 A744 M lil, dp lil & plum 1.50 .30
2719 A744 T org, brn & plum 2.00 .50
2720 A744 T gray vio, vio & plum 2.00 .50
2721 A744 T grn, blk & plum 2.00 .50
    Nos. 2717-2721 (5) 9.00 2.10
    On day of issue, Nos. 2717-2718 were valued at 50,000 l each, and Nos. 2719-2721 were valued at 75,000 l each.

NATO, 50th Anniv. A745

1999, Apr. 4   Litho.   Perf. 13
2722 A745 200,000 l multicolored 2.75 2.10

Ottoman Empire, 700th Anniv. A746

Designs: No. 2723, Man on horse surrounded by people in buildings. No. 2724, Man on horse, three men in foreground. No. 2725, Men seated.
No. 2726, Man on white horse, castle. No. 2727, Group of women, horiz.

1999, Apr. 12
2723 A746 175,000 l multicolored 1.75 1.25
2724 A746 175,000 l multicolored 1.75 1.25
2725 A746 175,000 l multicolored 1.75 1.25
    Nos. 2723-2725 (3) 5.25 3.75
Size: 79x119mm, 119x79mm
Imperf
2726 A746 200,000 l multicolored 2.25 2.25
2727 A746 200,000 l multicolored 2.25 2.25

Europa A747

Natl. Parks: 175,000 l, Köprülü Canyon, vert. 200,000 l, Kackarlar.

Perf. 13¼x13, 13x13¼
1999, May 5   Litho.
2728 A747 175,000 l multicolored 2.00 2.00
2729 A747 200,000 l multicolored 2.00 2.00

World Environment Day — A748

No. 2730: a, 100,000 l, Tetrax tetrax. 200,000 l, Hoplopterus spinosus.
No. 2731: a, 100,000 l, Marbled duck. b, 200,000 l, Sitta kruperi.

1999, June 3   Litho.   Perf. 13¼
2730 A748 Sheet of 2, #a.-b. 3.50 3.50
2731 A748 Sheet of 2, #a.-b. 3.50 3.50
    See Nos. 2763-2764, 2800-2801.

No. 2538 Surcharged in Violet Blue

1999   Litho.   Perf. 13
2732 A649 T on 250 l #2537 .75 .40
    No. 2732 sold for 50,000 l on day of issue.

Souvenir Sheet

National Congress During the War for Independence — A749

Designs: a, 100,000 l, Ataturk, two other men, building. b, 100,000 l, Ataturk, two other men seated. c, 200,000 l, Two men standing in front of building. d, 200,000 l, Ataturk standing in front of building.

Perf. 13¼x13
1999, June 22   Litho.   Unwmk.
2733 A749 Sheet of 4, #a.-d. 6.25 6.25

Art — A750

1999, July 8   Litho.   Perf. 13x13¼
2734 A750 250,000 l shown 2.25 1.10
2735 A750 250,000 l multi, diff. 2.25 1.10

Tourism — A751

Perf. 13x13¼, 13¼x13
1999, Sept. 19   Litho.
No. 2736, Temple to Zeus. No. 2737, Antakya Archaelogical Museum, horiz. No. 2738, Golf course, Antalya. No. 2739, Sailboat off Bodrum.
2736 A751 125,000 l multi 1.40 1.40
2737 A751 125,000 l multi 1.40 1.40
2738 A751 225,000 l multi 2.10 2.10
2739 A751 225,000 l multi 2.10 2.10
    Nos. 2736-2739 (4) 7.00 7.00

Dams A752

225,000 l, Cubuk 1. 250,000 l, Atatürk.

1999, Sept. 19   Litho.   Perf. 13¼x13
2740 A752 225,000 l multi 2.25 2.25
2741 A752 250,000 l multi 2.25 2.25

Kemal Atatürk — A753

1999, Sept. 27   Litho.   Perf. 13¾
2742 A753 225,000 l grn & brn 2.50 .55
2743 A753 250,000 l brn & lil 2.50 .65
2744 A753 500,000 l pink & grn 3.75 1.40
2745 A753 1,000,000 l bl & red 9.00 4.00
    Nos. 2742-2745 (4) 17.75 6.60

Thanks for Earthquake Rescue Efforts — A754

Designs: 225,000 l, Hands holding wreckage, flowers, vert. 250,000 l, Rescuers, handclasp.

Perf. 13¼x13, 13x13¼
1999, Oct. 15   Litho.
2746 A754 225,000 l multi 1.40 .65
2747 A754 250,000 l multi 1.75 .75

Women's Headcovers Type of 1997
1999, Nov. 24   Litho.   Perf. 13¼
2748 A734 150,000 l Manisa 1.10 .55
2749 A734 150,000 l Nigde 1.10 .55
2750 A734 250,000 l Antalya 2.00 .90
2751 A734 250,000 l Amasya 2.00 .90
    Nos. 2748-2751 (4) 6.20 2.90

Caravansaries — A755

1999, Dec. 24   Litho.   Perf. 13¼x13
2752 A755 150,000 l Sarapsa .65 .25
2753 A755 250,000 l Obruk 1.00 .45

Millennium A756

Designs: 275,000 l, Earth, brain, satellite. 300,000 l, Monachus monachus.

2000, Feb. 1	Litho.	Perf. 13¼	
2754	A756	275,000 l multi	2.00 2.00
2755	A756	300,000 l multi	2.00 2.00

Merchant Ships A757

125,000 l, Bug. 150,000 l, Gülcemal. 275,000 l, Nusret. 300,000 l, Bandirma.

2000, Mar. 16			
2756	A757	125,000 l multi	.65 .65
2757	A757	150,000 l multi	.90 .90
2758	A757	275,000 l multi	2.40 2.40
2759	A757	300,000 l multi	2.75 2.75
	Nos. 2756-2759 (4)		6.70 6.70

See Nos. 2813-2816, 2840-2843.

Grand National Assembly, 80th Anniv. — A758

Perf. 13x13¼, 13¼x13

2000, Apr. 23			Litho.
2760	A758	275,000 l shown	1.00 1.00
2761	A758	300,000 l Sprouts, horiz.	1.10 1.10

Europa, 2000
Common Design Type

2000, May 9			Perf. 13x13¼
2762	CD17	300,000 l multi	2.00 2.00

World Environment Day Type of 1999
Souvenir Sheets

No. 2763, 275,000 l: a, Aquila heliaca. b, Picus viridis.
No. 2764, 275,000 l: a, Oxyura leucocephala. b, Recurvirostra avosetta.

2000, June 5	Litho.	Perf. 13¼
	Sheets of 2, #a-b	
2763-2764 A748	Set of 2	8.00 8.00

Women's Headcover Type of 1997

Designs: No. 2765, 275,000 l, Trabzon. No. 2766, 275,000 l, Tunceli. No. 2767, 275,000 l, Corum. No. 2768, 275,000 l, Izmir.

2000, July 15		
2765-2768 A734	Set of 4	7.25 7.25

Souvenir Sheet

Nomadic Life A759

a, Woman at loom, woman seated. b, Women & containers. c, Women, 2 goats, carpet on tent rope. d, Woman, children, 6 goats, carpet on rope.

2000			
2769		Sheet of 4	9.00 9.00
a.-d.	A759	300,000 l Any single	1.60 1.60

Military Leaders — A760

Designs: 100,000 l, Gen. Yakup Sevki Subasi. 200,000 l, Lt. Gen. Musa Kazim Karabekir (c. 1882-1948). 275,000 l, Marshal Mustafa Fevzi Cakmak (1876-1950). 300,000 l, Gen. Cevat Cobanli (1871-1938).

2000		
2770-2773 A760	Set of 4	5.50 5.50

2000 Summer Olympics, Sydney A761

Designs: 125,000 l, Rhythmic gymnastics. 150,000 l, Swimming. 275,000 l, High jump. 300,000 l, Archery.

2000		
2774-2777 A761	Set of 4	5.50 5.50

Crocuses — A762

Designs: 250,000 l, Crocus chrysanthus. 275,000 l, Crocus olivieri. 300,000 l, Crocus biflorus. 1,250,000 l, Crocus sativus.

2000, Oct. 9	Litho.	Perf. 13¾x14
2778-2781 A762	Set of 4	12.00 5.50

Architecture — A763

Designs: 200,000 l, Arslan Baba. 275,000 l, Karasaç Ana. 300,000 l, Hoca Ahmet Yesevi.

2000, Oct. 19	Litho.	Perf. 13¼x13
2782-2784 A763	Set of 3	8.00 8.00

Turksat 2A — A764   Women's Clothing — A765

2001, Jan. 25	Litho.	Perf. 13x13¾
2785 A764	200,000 l multi	1.25 1.25

2001, Mar. 19

Designs: No. 2786, 200,000 l, Afyon. No. 2787, 200,000 l, Balikesir. No. 2788, 325,000 l, Kars. No. 2789, 325,000 l, Tokat.

2786-2789 A765	Set of 4	6.25 6.25

See Nos. 2822-2825, 2757-2760, 2880-2883.

Women's Headcovers Type of 1997

Designs: 200,000 l, Mersin-Silifke. 250,000 l, Sivas. 425,000 l, Aydin. 450,000 l, Hakkari.

2001, Apr. 16	Litho.	Perf. 13¼
2790-2793 A734	Set of 4	7.25 7.25

Europa — A766

Waterfalls: 450,000 l, Düdenbasi. 500,000 l, Yerköprü.

2001, May 5		Perf. 13
2794-2795 A766	Set of 2	3.00 3.00

Aviators A767

Designs: 250,000 l, Capt. Ismail Hakki Bey. 300,000 l, Lieut. Nuri Bey. 450,000 l, Lieut. Sadik Bey. 500,000 l, Capt. Fethi Bey.

2001, May 15		
2796-2799 A767	Set of 4	5.00 5.00

World Environment Day Type of 1999

No. 2800, 300,000 l: a, Turdus pilaris. b, Carduelis carduelis.
No. 2801, 450,000 l: a, Merops apiaster. b, Upupa epops.

2001, June 5		Perf. 13¼
	Sheets of 2, #a-b	
2800-2801 A748	Set of 2	7.00 7.00

Kemal Ataturk — A768   Medicinal Plants — A769

Ataturk (1881-1938) and: 300,000 l, Turkish flag. 450,000 l, Birthplace

2001, May 19		Perf. 13
2802-2803 A768	Set of 2	3.25 3.25

2001, June 27		Perf. 13¾

Designs: 250,000 l, Myrtus communis. 300,000 l, Achillea millefolium. 450,000 l, Hypericum perforatum. 500,000 l, Rosa moyesii. 1,750,000 l, Crataegus oxyacantha.

2804-2808 A769	Set of 5	11.00 2.50

Horses A770

Designs: 300,000 l, Horse and foal. No. 2810, 450,000 l, Three horses. No. 2811, 450,000 l, Two horses galloping. 500,000 l, Horse, vert.

2001, July 16		Perf. 13
2809-2812 A770	Set of 4	5.50 5.50

Merchant Ships Type of 2000

Designs: 250,000 l, Resitpasa. No. 2814, 300,000 l, Mithatpasa. No. 2815, 300,000 l, Gülnihal, 500,000 l, Aydin.

2001, Sept. 3		Perf. 13¼
2813-2816 A757	Set of 4	5.00 5.00

Architecture A771

Designs: No. 2817, 300,000 l, Sirvansahlar Palace, Baku, Azerbaijan. No. 2818, 300,000 l, Sultan Tekes Mausoleum, Urgench, Uzbekistan. 450,000 l, Timur Mausoleum, Samarkand, Uzbekistan. 500,000 l, While Tlightning Mausoleum, Bursa.

2001, Oct. 15		
2817-2820 A771	Set of 4	6.25 6.25

Sultan Nevruz A772

2002, Mar. 21	Litho.	Perf. 13¼
2821 A772	400,000 l multi	2.25 2.25

Women's Clothing Type of 2001

Designs: 350,000 l, Kastamonu. 400,000 l, Canakkale. 500,000 l, Amasya-Ilisu. 600,000 l, Elazig.

2002, Apr. 16		Perf. 13x13¼
2822-2825 A765	Set of 4	7.25 7.25

Europa — A773

2002, May 5	Litho.	Perf. 13x13¼
2826 A773	500,000 l multi	1.50 1.50

2002 World Cup Soccer Championships, Japan and Korea — A774

Designs: 400,000 l, Players, referee. 600,000 l, Crowd, player making scissors kick.

2002, May 31	Litho.	Perf. 13¼x13
2827-2828 A774	Set of 2	4.50 4.50

Famous Men — A775

Designs: 100,000 l, Muzaffer Sarisözen (1898-1963), musician. 400,000 l, Arif Nihat Asya (1904-75), writer. 500,000 l, Vedat Tek (1873-1942), architect. 600,000 l, Hilmi Ziya Ulken (1901-74), philosopher. 2,500,000 l, Ibrahim Calli (1882-1960), painter.

2002, June 3		Perf. 13¾x14
2829-2833 A775	Set of 5	16.00 5.50

Souvenir Sheet

Wild Cats — A776

No. 2834: a, Panthera pardus tulliana. b, Lynx lynx. c, Panthera tigris. d, Caracal caracal.

2002, June 20   *Perf. 13¼x13*
2834 A776 400,000 l Sheet of 4,
     #a-d   9.00 9.00

Souvenir Sheet

Shells — A777

Various shells: a, 400,000 l. b, 500,000 l. c, 600,000 l. d, 750,000 l.

2002, June 25
2835 A777   Sheet of 4, #a-d   9.00 9.00

Third Place Finish of Turkish Team in World Cup Soccer Championships — A778

Designs: 400,000 l, Players in action. 700,000 l, Team photo.

2002, July 29   *Perf. 13x13¼*
2836-2837 A778   Set of 2   4.50 4.50

String Instruments A779

Designs: 450,000 l, Violin. 700,000 l, Bass.

2002, Oct. 10   *Perf. 13¼x13*
2838-2839 A779   Set of 2   4.50 4.50

Merchant Ships Type of 2000

Designs: 450,000 l, Ege. 500,000 l, Ayvalik. No. 2842, 700,000 l, Karadeniz. No. 2843, 700,000 l, Marakaz.

2002, Nov. 4   Litho.   *Perf. 13*
2840-2843 A757   Set of 4   8.00 8.00

Souvenir Sheet

Turkish and Hungarian Buildings — A780

No. 2844: a, 450,000 l, Gazi Kassim Pasha Mosque, Pécs, Hungary. b, 700,000 l, Rakoczi House, Tekirdag, Turkey.

2002, Dec. 2   Litho.   *Perf. 13¼*
2844 A780   Sheet of 2, #a-b   4.50 4.50
   See Hungary Nos. 3819-3820.

BJK Soccer Team, Cent. — A781

Team emblem and: 500,000 l, Eagle, Turkish and team flags. 700,000 l, Eagle, stadium. 750,000 l, Soccer players. 1,000,000 l, Eagle's head.

2003, Mar. 3   *Perf. 13x13¼*
2845-2848 A781   Set of 4   8.00 8.00

A782   A783

Europa: 500,000 l, Travel poster. 700,000 l, Ankara State Theater poster.

2003, May 9   Litho.   *Perf. 13*
2849-2850 A782   Set of 2   3.00 3.00

2003, May 29
Conquest of Constantinople, 550th Anniv.: No. 2851, 500,000 l, Leaders at table. No. 2852, 500,000 l, Sultan Mehmet II seated. 700,000 l, Robe. 1,500,000 l, Sultan Mehmet II and cartouche.

2851-2854 A783   Set of 4   7.25 7.25

Souvenir Sheet

World Environment Day — A784

No. 2855: a, Gazella subgutturosa. b, Cervus elaphus. c, Capreolus capreolus. d, Cervus dama.

2003, June 5
2855 A784 500,000 l Sheet of 4,
     #a-d   6.25 6.25

Zodiac A785

2003, June 19   *Perf. 13¼*
2856 A785 500,000 l multi   1.40 1.40

Women's Clothing Type of 2001

Designs: No. 2857, 500,000 l, Sivas. No. 2858, 500,000 l, Gaziantep. No. 2859, 700,000 l, Erzincan. No. 2860, 700,000 l, Ankara-Beypazari.

2003, July 8   *Perf. 13*
2857-2860 A765   Set of 4   7.25 7.25

Fruit Blossoms — A786

Blossoms: 500,000 l, Ayva cicegi (quince). 700,000 l, Erik cicegi (plum). 750,000 l, Kiraz cicegi (cherry). 1,000,000 l, Nar cicegi (pomegranate). 3,000,000 l, Portakal cicegi (orange).

2003, July 25   *Perf. 13¾x14*
2861-2865 A786   Set of 5   13.50 7.25

Brass Instruments A787

Designs: 600,000 l, French horn. 800,000 l, Trumpet.

2003, Sept. 23   Litho.   *Perf. 13¼x13*
2866-2867 A787   Set of 2   4.50 4.50

Republic of Turkey, 80th Anniv. A788

Kemal Ataturk, flag and: No. 2868, 600,000 l, Cavalry. No. 2869, 600,000 l, Buildings.

2003, Oct. 29   Litho.   *Perf. 13¼x13*
2868-2869 A788   Set of 2   3.50 3.50

Navy Ships A789

Designs: No. 2870, 600,000 l, Karadeniz. No. 2871, 600,000 l, Gediz. No. 2872, 700,000 l, Salihreis. No. 2873, 700,000 l, Kocatepe.

2003, Nov. 14
2870-2873 A789   Set of 4   9.00 9.00

Agriculture Bank, 140th Anniv. — A790

2003, Nov. 20   *Perf. 13x13¼*
2874 A790 600,000 l multi   1.75 1.75

Buildings Associated with Kemal Ataturk — A791

Designs: 600,000 l, House, Trabzon. 700,000 l, Museum, Sakarya. 800,000 l, House, Selanik. 1,000,000 l, Museum, Ankara.

2003, Dec. 12
2875-2878 A791   Set of 4   7.25 7.25

PTT Bank — A792

2004, Mar. 3   *Perf. 14*
2879 A792 600,000 l multi   1.75 .80

Women's Clothing Type of 2001

Designs: 600,000 l, Edirne. No. 2881, 700,000 l, Tunceli. No. 2882, 700,000 l, Burdur. 800,000 l, Trabzon.

2004, Apr. 30   *Perf. 13x13¼*
2880-2883 A765   Set of 4   7.25 7.25

Europa — A793

Designs: 700,000 l, Skier, windsurfer. 800,000 l, Tourist at archaeological ruins, ships.

2004, May 9
2884-2885 A793   Set of 2   3.00 3.00

Souvenir Sheet

World Environment Day — A794

No. 2886: a, Falco tinnunculus. b, Buteo buteo. c, Aquila chrysaetos. d, Milvus migrans.

2004, June 5   *Perf. 13¼x13*
2886 A794 700,000 l Sheet of 4,
     #a-d   6.25 6.25

Caravansaries — A795

Designs: 600,000 l, Mamahatun Caravansary, Erzincan. 700,000 l, Cardak Caravasary, Denizli.

2004, June 7
2887-2888 A795 Set of 2 3.50 3.50

Gendarmerie, 165th Anniv. — A796

2004, June 14 *Perf. 13x13¼*
2889 A796 600,000 l multi 1.40 .70

Birds — A797

Designs: 100,000 l, Regulus regulus. 250,000 l, Sylvia rueppelli. 600,000 l, Hippolais polyglotta. 700,000 l, Passer domesticus. 800,000 l, Emberiza bruniceps. 1,000,000 l, Fringilla coelebs. 1,500,000 l, Phoenicurus phoenicurus. 3,500,000 l, Erithacus rubecula.

2004, July 23 *Perf. 14*
2890	A797	100,000 l multi	.25 .25
2891	A797	250,000 l multi	.35 .25
2892	A797	600,000 l multi	.80 .40
2893	A797	700,000 l multi	1.40 .70
2894	A797	800,000 l multi	1.50 .75
2895	A797	1,000,000 l multi	2.00 1.00
2896	A797	1,500,000 l multi	3.00 1.40
2897	A797	3,500,000 l multi	6.75 3.25
	Nos. 2890-2897 (8)		16.05 8.00

2004 Summer Olympics, Athens A798

Designs: 600,000 l, Wrestling. No. 2899, 700,000 l, Weight lifting. No. 2900, 700,000 l, Women's track and field, vert. 800,000 l, Wrestling.

Perf. 13¼x13, 13x13¼
2004, Aug. 13
2898-2901 A798 Set of 4 6.25 6.25

Souvenir Sheet

Navy Submarines — A799

No. 2902: a, 600,000 l, 18 Mart. b, 700,000 l, Preveze. c, 700,000 l, Anafartalar. d, 800,000 l, Atilay.

2004, Sept. 14 *Perf. 13x13¼*
2902 A799 Sheet of 4, #a-d 6.25 6.25

Piri Reis (1465-1554), Admiral and Map Compiler — A800

2004, Sept. 20
2903 A800 600,000 l multi 1.40 1.40

Waterfalls A801

Designs: 600,000 l, Kapuzbasi Waterfall. 700,000 l, Sudüsen Waterfall, vert.

2004, Oct. 19 *Perf. 13x13¼, 13¼x13*
2904-2905 A801 Set of 2 3.50 3.50

Buildings Associated With Kemal Ataturk — A802

Designs: 600,000 l, Ataturk Summer House, Bursa. No. 2907, 700,000 l, Ataturk House Museum, Erzurum. No. 2908, 700,000 l, Ataturk House, Havza. 800,000 l, State Railways Director's Building, Ankara.

2004, Nov. 8 *Litho.* *Perf. 13¼x13*
2906-2909 A802 Set of 4 6.25 6.25

Souvenir Sheet

Turkish Stars Aerobatics Team — A803

No. 2910: a, 600,000 l, Two airplanes. b, 700,000 l, Five airplanes. c, 800,000 l, Seven airplanes flying upwards. d, 900,000 l, Seven airplanes flying left.

2004, Dec. 7 *Litho.* *Perf. 13¼x13*
2910 A803 Sheet of 4, #a-d 9.00 9.00

Provinces A804

2005, Jan. 1 *Litho.* *Perf. 14*
2914	A804	1k Adana	.25 .25
2915	A804	5k Adiyaman	.25 .25
2916	A804	10k Afyon	.25 .25
2917	A804	25k Agri	.35 .25
2918	A804	50k Amasya	.70 .35
2919	A804	60k Ankara	.85 .40
2920	A804	60k Bitlis	.85 .40
2921	A804	70k Antalya	1.00 .50
2922	A804	70k Bolu	1.00 .50
2923	A804	80k Artvin	1.10 .55
2924	A804	80k Burdur	1.10 .55
2925	A804	90k Aydin	1.25 .60
2926	A804	1 l Balikesir	1.50 .75
2927	A804	1.50 l Bilecik	2.25 1.10
2928	A804	3.50 l Bingol	5.00 2.50
2929	A804	3.50 l Bursa	5.00 2.50
	Nos. 2914-2929 (16)		22.70 11.70

A805 A806

Designs: 60k, Batiburnu Lighthouse, Canakkale. 70k, Zonguldak Lighthouse, Zonguldak.

2005, Mar. 18 *Litho.* *Perf. 13x13¼*
2930-2931 A805 Set of 2 2.75 1.40

2005, Apr. 1
Marmaris Intl. Maritime Festival: 70k, Sailboat. 80k, Sailboat, sun on horizon.
2932-2933 A806 Set of 2 2.75 1.40

A807

2005, Apr. 10
2934 A807 70k multi 1.40 .70
Turkish Police, 160th anniv.

A808

Grand National Assembly, 85th anniv.: 60k, Torch, star and crescent. 70k, Crescent and fireworks over Grand National Assembly.

2005, Apr. 23
2935-2936 A808 Set of 2 2.25 1.10

Europa — A809

2005, May 9
2937 A809 70k multi 1.10 .55

Caftans of Sultans — A810

Caftan of Sultan: No. 2938, 70k, Ahmed I (shown). No. 2939, 70k, Ahmed I, diff. No. 2940, 70k, Murad III. No. 2941, 70k, Selim.

2005, May 20
2938-2941 A810 Set of 4 5.00 2.50

Souvenir Sheet

World Environment Day — A811

No. 2942: a, 60k, Pagellus bogaraveo. b, 70k, Epinephelus guaza. c, 70k, Merlanyus euxinus. d, 80k, Maena smaris.

2005, June 5 *Litho.* *Perf. 13¼x13*
2942 A811 Sheet of 4, #a-d 5.50 2.75

Tapestries & Carpets — A812

Designs: 60k, Carpet from Hereke region, Turkey. 70k, L'humanité Assaillie par les Sept Pechés Capitaux tapestry, Belgium.

2005, June 22 *Litho.* *Perf. 13x13¼*
2943-2944 A812 Set of 2 2.25 1.10
See Belgium Nos. 2098-2099.

World Architecture Congress, Istanbul — A813

2005, July 3
2945 A813 70k multi 1.40 .70

Mosaics A814

Designs: 60k, Akelos. No. 2947, 70k, Oceanos and Tethys. No. 2948, 70k, Achilles. 80k, Menad.

2005, July 5 *Perf. 13¼x13*
2946-2949 A814 Set of 4 5.50 2.75

Clocks — A815

Designs: 60k, Musical clock, 1770. 70k, Clock, 1867.

2005, July 20 *Perf. 13x13¼*
2950-2951 A815 Set of 2 2.25 1.25

Turkish Grand Prix, Istanbul — A816

2005, Aug. 19   Litho.   Perf. 13x13¼
2952 A816 70k multi   1.40 .65

Philanthropic Businessmen — A817

Designs: 60k, Sakip Sabanci (1933-2004). 70k, Vehbi Koç (1901-96).

2005, Sept. 21   Litho.   Perf. 13¼x13
2953-2954 A817 Set of 2   2.25 1.25

Provinces
A818

2005, Sept. 28   Perf. 13¾
2955 A818 50k Canakkale   .75   .35
2956 A818 60k Cankiri   1.00   .50
2957 A818 60k Corum   1.00   .50
2958 A818 60k Denizli   1.00   .50
2959 A818 60k Diyarbakir   1.00   .50
2960 A818 60k Edirne   1.00   .50
2961 A818 60k Elazig   1.00   .50
2962 A818 70k Erzincan   1.25   .60
2963 A818 70k Erzurum   1.25   .60
2964 A818 70k Eskisehir   1.25   .60
2965 A818 70k Gaziantep   1.25   .60
2966 A818 70k Giresun   1.25   .60
2967 A818 70k Gumushane   1.25   .60
2968 A818 1 l Hakkari   1.75   .80
2969 A818 1.50 l Hatay   2.50 1.25
2970 A818 2.50 l Isparta   4.25 2.10
Nos. 2955-2970 (16)   22.75 11.10

Mevlana Jalal ad-Din ar-Rumi (1207-73), Islamic Philosopher A819

2005, Sept. 30   Perf. 13x13¼
2971 A819 70k multi   1.40 .65

See Afghanistan Nos. 1449-1451, Iran No. 2911 and Syria No. 1574.

Galatasaray Sports Club, Cent. — A820

Club emblem and: No. 2972, 60k, Soccer stadium crowd, lion and "100." No. 2973, 70k, Soccer stadium, trophy.
No. 2974: a, 60k, Man, lion and "100." b, 70k, Club emblem, building. c, 80k, Soccer players. d, 1 l, Soccer players with trophy.

2005, Oct. 11   Perf. 13x13¼
2972-2973 A820 Set of 2   2.25 1.10
Souvenir Sheet
Perf. 13¼x13
2974 A820 Sheet of 4, #a-d   5.00 2.50
No. 2974 contains four 41x26mm stamps.

Start of Negotiations for Turkish Admission to European Union — A821

2005, Nov. 3   Perf. 13¼x13
2975 A821 70k multi   1.40 .65

Vegetables — A824

Designs, 60k, Allium porrum (leeks). 70k, Allium sativum (garlic). 80k, Allium cepa (onions).

2005, Nov. 21   Litho.   Perf. 13x13¼
2978-2980 A824 Set of 3   3.50 1.75

Europa Stamps, 50th Anniv. (in 2006) — A825

Designs: No. 2981, 60k, Vignette of #1907. No. 2982, 70k, Vignette of #1628. 80k, Vignette of #B120. 1 l, Vignette of #1719.
No. 2985, horiz.: a, 10k, #1520. b, 25k, #1800. c, 60k, #1553. d, 70k, #1775.
No. 2986, horiz.: a, 10k, #1493. b, 25k, #1936. c, 60k, #1602. d, 70k, #1876.

2005, Dec. 15   Litho.   Perf. 13x13¼
2981-2984 A825 Set of 4   8.00 4.00
Souvenir Sheets
Perf. 13¼x13
2985 A825 Sheet of 4, #a-d   9.00 4.50
Imperf
2986 A825 Sheet of 4, #a-d   13.50 6.75

2006 Winter Olympics, Turin A826

Designs: 60k, Speed skating. 70k, Skiing.

2006, Feb. 10   Perf. 13¼x13
2987-2988 A826 Set of 2   2.00 1.00

March 29 Total Solar Eclipse A827

2006, Mar. 29   Litho.   Perf. 13¼x13
2989 A827 70k multi   1.10 .55

Support for Education A828

2006, Apr. 10
2990 A828 60k multi   .95 .45

Karaoglan, Cartoon Hero — A829

Karaoglan: 60k, With bow and arrow. No. 2992, 70k, Attacking swordsman. No. 2993, 70k, On horseback. 80k, On horseback, diff.

2006, Apr. 20   Perf. 13x13¼
2991-2994 A829 Set of 4   4.25 2.10

Izzet Baysal (1907-2000), Architect — A830

2006, May 11   Litho.   Perf. 13¼x13
2995 A830 60k multi   .85 .45

A831

A832

A833

A834

A835

A836

A837

A838

A839

Kemal Ataturk (1881-1938) — A840

2006, May 19
2996   Block of 10   7.50 3.75
  a. A831 60k multi   .75   .35
  b. A832 60k multi   .75   .35
  c. A833 60k multi   .75   .35
  d. A834 60k multi   .75   .35
  e. A835 60k multi   .75   .35
  f. A836 60k multi   .75   .35
  g. A837 60k multi   .75   .35
  h. A838 60k multi   .75   .35
  i. A839 60k multi   .75   .35
  j. A840 60k multi   .75   .35

Europa — A841

2006, May 30   Perf. 13x13¼
2997 A841 70k multi   .90 .45

Miniature Sheet

World Environment Day — A842

No. 2998: a, 25k, Parched earth. b, 50k, Tree. c, 60k, Tree, diff. d, 70k, Forest.

2006, June 5
2998　A842　Sheet of 4, #a-d　　2.75　1.40
Intl. Year of Deserts and Desertification.

2006 World Cup Soccer Championships, Germany — A843

Designs: No. 2999, 70k, Player dribbling ball. No. 3000, 70k, Player kicking ball, horiz.

2006, June 9　Perf. 13x13¼, 13¼x13
2999-3000　A843　Set of 2　　1.90　.95

Airplanes A844

Designs: 60k, Deperdussin monoplane. No. 3002, 70k, Bleriot monoplane. No. 3003, 70k, R. E. P. monoplane.

2006, June 22　Perf. 13¼x13
3001-3003　A844　Set of 3　　2.60　1.40
See Nos. 3034-3036.

Treasures of Karun — A845

Designs: No. 3004, 70k, Bracelet and coins. No. 3005, 70k, Winged sun disc pectoral and bracelet. 80k, Lion's head bracelets.

2006, July 10　Perf. 13x13¼
3004-3006　A845　Set of 3　　2.75　1.40

Provinces A846

2006, Sept. 11　Perf. 13¼x13
3007	A846	10k Kahramanmaras	.25	.25
3008	A846	10k Manisa	.25	.25
3009	A846	50k Kirsehir	.70	.35
3010	A846	50k Kocaeli	.70	.35
3011	A846	60k Izmir	.80	.40
3012	A846	60k Konya	.80	.40
3013	A846	60k Mardin	.80	.40
3014	A846	60k Mugla	.80	.40
3015	A846	70k Istanbul	.95	.50
3016	A846	70k Mersin	.95	.50
3017	A846	1 l Kastamonu	1.40	.70
3018	A846	1 l Kirklareli	1.40	.70
3019	A846	1.60 l Kayseri	2.25	1.10
3020	A846	2 l Malatya	2.75	1.40
3021	A846	4 l Kars	5.50	2.75
3022	A846	4 l Kutahya	5.50	2.75

Nos. 3007-3022 (16)　25.80　13.20
See nos. 3055-3062.

Scenes From Movie, "Selvi Boylum Al Yazmalim" — A847

Various scenes: 60k, 70k.

2006, Sept. 16　Perf. 13x13¼
3023-3024　A847　Set of 2　　1.75　.85

Turkish Railroads, 150th Anniv. A848

Designs: 60k, Steam locomotive. 70k, Electric train.

2006, Sept. 23　Perf. 13¼x13
3025-3026　A848　Set of 2　　1.75　.85

Central Bank, 75th Anniv. A849

2006, Oct. 3
3027　A849　60k multi　　.80　.40

Intl. Telecommunications Union Conference, Antalya — A850

Conference emblem and: 60k, Globe with spotlight on Turkey. 70k, Map with lines drawn to Turkey.

2006, Nov. 6　Perf. 13x13¼
3028-3029　A850　Set of 2　　1.90　.95

Middle East Technical University, Ankara, 50th Anniv. — A851

2006, Nov. 15　Litho.　Perf. 13x13¼
3030　A851　60k multi　　.85　.40

Turkish Atomic Energy Authority, 50th Anniv. A852

2006, Nov. 22　Litho.　Perf. 13¼x13
3031　A852　60k multi　　.85　.40

Geothermal Resources — A853

Designs: 60k, Four steam clouds. 70k, Steam leaving smokestack.

2006, Dec. 11
3032-3033　A853　Set of 2　　1.90　.95

Airplanes Type of 2006

Designs: 60k, Breguet XIV B-2. No. 3035, 70k, Albatros C-XV. No. 3036, 70k, Fiat R2.

2007, Mar. 15　Litho.　Perf. 13¼x13
3034-3036　A844　Set of 3　　3.00　1.50

A854

A855

A856

Hittite Artifacts A857

2007, Mar. 30
3037	A854	60k multi	.90	.45
3038	A855	60k multi	.90	.45
3039	A856	60k multi	.90	.45
3040	A857	60k multi	.90	.45

Nos. 3037-3040 (4)　3.60　1.80

Third Meeting of Economic Cooperation Organization Postal Authorities, Tehran — A858

2007, Apr. 5　Perf. 13x13¼
3041　A858　60k multi　　.90　.45
See Iran No. 2917, Kazakhstan No. 526 and Pakistan No. 1101.

Tekirdag as Part of Turkey, 650th Anniv. A859

2007, Apr. 14　Perf. 13¼x13
3042　A859　60k multi　　.90　.45

Fenerbahce Sports Club, Cent. — A860

Club emblem and: No. 3043, 60k, Men witnessing signing ceremony. No. 3044, 70k, Quotation and Arabic text.
No. 3045 — Club emblem and: a, 60k, Lighthouse. b, 70k, Three men seated at table. c, 80k, Building, stadium interior. d, 90k, Stadium exterior.

2007, May 3 — Perf. 13x13¼
3043-3044 A860 Set of 2   2.00 1.00

Souvenir Sheet
Perf. 13¼x13

3045 A860 Sheet of 4, #a-d   4.50 4.50

No. 3045 contains four 38x23mm stamps. No. 3045 exists affixed to a booklet cover which was only sold in a set with an imperforate sheet of eight 41x31mm stamps depicting various athletes, two first day covers, and a folder, for 25 l. Value $15.

Souvenir Sheet

Mevlana Jalal ad-Din ar-Rumi (1207-73), Islamic Philosopher — A861

No. 3046: a, 25k, Portrait. b, 50k, Arabic calligraphy. c, 60k, Dervishes. d, 70k, Mausoleum.

2007, May 8 — Perf. 13x13¼
3046 A861 Sheet of 4, #a-d   3.25 1.60

Europa
A862

Designs: 60k, Turkish Scouting emblem, Scout at campfire. 70k, Scouts saluting.

2007, May 9 — Perf. 13¼
3047-3048 A862 Set of 2   2.00 1.00

Scouting, cent.

Mehmetcik Foundation, 25th Anniv. — A863

2007, May 17 — Litho. Perf. 13¼x13
3049 A863 60k multi   .95 .45

Souvenir Sheet

World Environment Day — A864

No. 3050: a, 25k, Goats. b, 50k, Cattle. c, 60k, Sheep. d, 70k, Chickens.

2007, June 5 — Litho. Perf. 13¼x13
3050 A864 Sheet of 4, #a-d   3.00 1.50

Turkish Cuisine — A865

Designs: No. 3051, 1 l, Nohutlu Bulgur Pilavi (chick pea and bulgur pilaf). No. 3052, 1 l, Yüksük Corbasi (soup). 2 l, Asure (vegetables).

2007, June 20 — Litho. Perf. 13¼
3051-3053 A865 Set of 3   6.25 3.25

Black Sea Economic Cooperation Organization, 15th Anniversary Summit
A866

2007, June 25 — Perf. 13¼
3054 A866 60k multi   .95 .95

Provinces Type of 2006
2007, July 10 — Perf. 13¼x13

3055	A846	10k	Siirt	.25 .25
3056	A846	50k	Ordu	.80 .40
3057	A846	60k	Rize	.95 .45
3058	A846	1 l	Nigde	1.60 .80
3059	A846	2 l	Nevsehir	3.25 1.60
3060	A846	2 l	Samsun	3.25 1.60
3061	A846	4 l	Mus	6.25 3.25
3062	A846	4 l	Sakarya	6.25 3.25

Nos. 3055-3062 (8)   22.60 11.60

Turkish Language Association, 75th Anniv. — A867

2007, July 12 — Perf. 13x13¼
3063 A867 70k multi   1.10 .55

Roses
A869

Color of rose: No. 3065, 60k, White. No. 3066, 60k, Red. No. 3067, 60k, Yellow.

2007, Aug. 16 — Litho. Perf. 13¼
3065-3067 A869 Set of 3   2.75 1.40

Shadow Play Characters
A870

Designs: 60k, Tuzsuz Deli Bekir and Efe. 70k, Hacivat and Karagöz. 80k, Tiryaki and Celebi.

2007, Sept. 13 — Litho. Perf. 13¼x13
3068-3070 A870 Set of 3   3.75 1.90

Miniature Sheet

Balkanfila XIV Intl. Philatelic Exhibition, Istanbul — A871

No. 3071: a, 60k, Blue Mosque, Galata Tower. b, 70k, Hagia Sophia. c, 80k, City walls and painting. d, 1 l, Bosporus Bridge.

2007, Oct. 28
3071 A871 Sheet of 4, #a-d   5.25 2.60

An imperforate sheet containing a 60k dove and flags stamp, a 70k bridge stamp, 80k flags stamp and a 1 l flags and map of Turkey stamp exists. It sold for considerably above face value.

Mimar Sinan (1489-1588), Architect A873

Sinan and: 60k, Büyükcekmece Bridge. No. 3074, 70k, Bath of Roxelana (Haseki Hürrem Sultan Hamami Ayasofya). No. 3075, 70k, Selimye Mosque, Edirne. 80k, Suleiman Mosque, Istanbul.

2007, Nov. 14 — Perf. 13¼
3073-3076 A873 Set of 4   4.75 2.40

World Philosophy Day — A874

2007, Nov. 22 — Perf. 13x13¼
3077 A874 60k multi   1.00 .50

Cartoon Character "Keloglan" — A875

Designs: 60k, Keloglan in giant's hand. No. 3079, 70k, Keloglan leaving house. No. 3080, 70k, Keloglan on horse. 80k, Keloglan with carpet and birds.

2007, Nov. 28
3078-3081 A875 Set of 4   4.75 2.40

Provinces Type of 2006
2007, Dec. 4 — Perf. 13¼x13

3082	A846	5k	Tunceli	.25 .25
3083	A846	10k	Tokat	.25 .25
3084	A846	65k	Sanliurfa	1.10 .55
3085	A846	65k	Trabzon	1.10 .55
3086	A846	80k	Sivas	1.40 .70
3087	A846	85k	Usak	1.50 .75
3088	A846	1 l	Tekirdag	1.75 .90
3089	A846	4.50 l	Sinop	7.75 4.00

Nos. 3082-3089 (8)   15.10 7.95

TRT Television, 40th Anniv. A876

Designs: 65k, Emblem. 80k, Emblem and headquarters.

2008, Jan. 31 — Litho. Perf. 12¾x13
3090-3091 A876 Set of 2   2.50 1.25

Nasreddin Hoca Fables, 800th Anniv. — A877

Hoca: 25k, And two men at table. 65k, Sitting backward on horse. 80k, Showing two pots to man. 85k, Spooning water into lake.

2008, Feb. 7 — Perf. 13x13¼
3092-3095 A877 Set of 4   4.25 2.10

A878

St. Valentine's Day — A879

2008, Feb. 14 — Perf. 13
3096 A878 65k multi   1.10 .55
3097 A879 80k multi   1.40 .70

Miniature Sheet

Amasya Medical Center, 700th Anniv. — A880

No. 3098: a, 50k, Building. b, 65k, Six musicians. c, 80k, Seven people. d, 85k, Four people.

2008, Mar. 13 — Perf. 13x13¼
3098 A880 Sheet of 4, #a-d   4.50 2.25

Urartian Cultural Artifacts A881

Designs: No. 3099, 65k, Carved ivory spirit figure (Fildisi Kanati Cin). No. 3100, 65k, Gold earring, bronze pin and necklace (Altin küpe, Tunc igne, Boncuk kolye). No. 3101, 80k, Bronze cauldron (Uc ayak uzerinde tunc kazan). No. 3102, 80k, Harput Castle (Harput Kalesi).

2008, Mar. 27   **Perf. 13¼x13**
3099-3102 A881   Set of 4   4.50 2.25

Military Aircraft A882

Designs: 65k, Consolidated B24 D. 80k, Curtiss Hawk. 85k, PZL XXIV.

2008, Apr. 25
3103-3105 A882   Set of 3   3.75 1.90
See Nos. 3148-3150.

Europa A883

Designs: 65k, Letter, fingers making heart. 80k, Pen, inkwell.

2008, May 9   **Litho.**   **Perf. 13¼**
3106-3107 A883   Set of 2   2.40 1.25

Diplomatic Relations Between Turkey and Thailand, 50th Anniv. A884

Designs: 65k, Loha Prasat, Bangkok, Thailand. 80k, Sultan Ahmed Mosque, Istanbul.

2008, May 12   **Litho.**   **Perf. 13¼x13**
3108-3109 A884   Set of 2   2.40 1.25
See Thailand No. 2359.

National Olympic Committee, Cent. — A885

Olympic Committee emblem and: 65k, Dove and Olympic flag. 80k, Parading athletes. 85k, Stadium. 1 l, Athlete and Olympic flag.

2008, May 26   **Perf. 13x13¼**
3110-3113 A885   Set of 4   5.25 2.60

Provinces A886

2008, May 28   **Perf. 13¼x13**
3114 A886   5k Zonguldak   .25 .25
3115 A886   50k Yozgat   .80 .40
3116 A886   65k Aksaray   1.10 .55
3117 A886   65k Kirikkale   1.10 .55
3118 A886   80k Karaman   1.40 .70
3119 A886   85k Van   1.40 .70

3120 A886   1 l Bayburt   1.60 .80
3121 A886   4.50 l Batman   7.25 3.75
   Nos. 3114-3121 (8)   14.90 7.70
   See Nos. 3129-3137.

Miniature Sheet

World Environment Day — A887

No. 3122: a, 25k, Boy and polar bears. b, 65k, Sea ice. c, 80k, Mountains and stream. d, 85k, Girl, flower, parched earth.

2008, June 5   **Perf. 13x12¾**
3122 A887   Sheet of 4, #a-d   4.25 2.10

Turkish Diplomats Who Saved Jews During World War II — A888

Birds and: 65k, Selehattin Ulkümen (1914-2003). 80k, Necdet Kent (1911-2002).

2008, July 17   **Perf. 12¾x13**
3123-3124 A888   Set of 2   2.50 1.25

2008 Summer Olympics, Beijing — A889

Designs: 25k, Archery. 65k, Taekwondo, vert. No. 3127, 80k, Weight lifting. No. 3128, 80k, Wrestling.

     Perf. 13x13¼, 13¼x13
2008, Aug. 8   **Litho.**
3125-3128 A889   Set of 4   4.25 2.10

Provinces Type of 2008
    Perf. 13¼x13, 13x13¼
2008, Aug. 29
3129 A886   50k Kilis   .85 .40
3130 A886   65k Bartin, vert.   1.10 .55
3131 A886   1 l Ardahan   1.75 .85
3132 A886   1 l Igdir   1.75 .85
3133 A886   1.50 l Yalova   2.60 1.25
3134 A886   2 l Karabuk   3.50 1.75
3135 A886   2 l Osmaniye   3.50 1.75
3136 A886   4.50 l Düzce   7.75 3.75
3137 A886   4.50 l Sirnak   7.75 3.75
   Nos. 3129-3137 (9)   30.55 14.90

Glassware — A890

Designs: 65k, Bowl. 80k, Vase.

2008, Sept. 11   **Perf. 13x12¾**
3138-3139 A890   Set of 2   2.25 1.10

Battle of Preveza, 470th Anniv. — A891

Designs: 65k, Khair ed-Din (Barbarossa), battle, map. 80k, Kemal Ataturk, ships.

2008, Sept. 27   **Perf. 13x13¼**
3140-3141 A891   Set of 2   2.25 1.10

Miniature Sheet

Friendship Between Turkey and Indonesia — A892

No. 3142: a, 80k Blue Mosque, Turkey. b, 65k Istiqlal Mosque, Indonesia. c, 80k Bosporus Bridge, Turkey. d, 65k Barelang Bridge, Indonesia. e, 80k Whirling dervishes. f, 65k Saman dance. g, 80k Turkish tulip (ters lale). h, 65k Flame of Irian (Mucuna bennettii). i, 80k Turkish Van cat. j, 65k Flat-headed cat (Yassibas kedi).

2008, Oct. 24   **Perf. 13x13¼**
3142 A892   Sheet of 10, #a-j   9.50 4.75
   See Indonesia No. 2167.

Republic of Turkey, 85th Anniv. A893

Kemal Ataturk, Turkish flag and: No. 3143, 80k, Airplane, ship, truck and train. No. 3144, 80k, Computer keyboard, satellite, dish antenna.

2008, Oct. 29   **Litho.**   **Perf. 12¾x13**
3143-3144 A893   Set of 2   2.10 1.10

Turkish Maritime Enterprises, 160th Anniv. A894

Designs: 65k, Docked ship. No. 3146, 80k, Emblem. No. 3147, 80k, Ship at sea, horiz.

   Perf. 13½x13¼, 13¼x13½
2008, Nov. 29   **Litho.**
3145-3147 A894   Set of 3   3.00 1.50

Military Aircraft Type of 2008
Designs: 65k, C-47 Dakota. 80k, F-100 D Super Sabre. 1 l, F-86 E Sabre.

2009, Mar. 12   **Litho.**   **Perf. 13¼x13**
3148-3150 A882   Set of 3   3.25 1.60

Miniature Sheet

Fifth World Water Forum, Istanbul — A895

No. 3151 — Emblem and: a, 25k, Head, Earth, water. b, 65k, Bosporus Bridge, water drop. c, 80k, Bosporus Bridge, waterfall. d, 80k, Waterfall, parched land, clay jug pouring water.

2009, Mar. 16   **Perf. 13x13¼**
3151 A895   Sheet of 4, #a-d   3.25 1.60

Sultan's Boats — A896

Boats from Istanbul Sea Museum: No. 3152, 80k, Boat with yellow hull and short bowsprit, gray green sky. No. 3153, 80k, Boat with brown hull, long bowsprit, blue gray sky.

2009, Apr. 2
3152-3153 A896   Set of 2   2.10 1.10

Council of Europe, 60th Anniv. A897

European Court for Human Rights, 50th Anniv. A898

2009, May 5   **Perf. 13¼x13**
3154 A897 80k multi   1.10 .55
3155 A898 80k multi   1.10 .55

Mother's Day — A899

Designs: 65k, Bird, hatchlings in nest shaped like heart. 80k, Mother's hands holding infant, hearts. No. 3158, 1 l, Mother and child. No. 3159, 1 l, Hands of mother and baby, flower.

2009, May 10   **Perf. 13¾**
3156-3159 A899   Set of 4   4.50 2.25
Nos. 3156-3159 each have perforations in a heart shape in the vignette.

Ceramics — A900

Designs: 80k, Ceramic pot, Portugal. 85k, Faience mosque lamp, Turkey.

2009, May 12   *Perf. 13x13¼*
3160-3161 A900   Set of 2   2.25 1.10
See Portugal Nos. 3111-3112.

Miniature Sheet

Arrival of Kemal Ataturk at Samsun, 90th Anniv. — A901

No. 3162: a, 25k, Congress Building, Sivas. b, 65k, Congress Building, Erzurum. c, 65k, Government building, Amasya. d, 80k, Statue of Ataturk, Samsun.

2009, May 19   *Litho.*
3162 A901   Sheet of 4, #a-d   3.25 1.60

Ministry of Transport and Communication, 70th Anniv. — A902

Designs: 50k, Ship, map. 65k, Bridge, highway interchange, bus. 80k, Earth, satellite, dish antenna, envelopes, computer, cellular phone. No. 3166, 1 l, Map, train. No. 3167, 1 l, Postal worker delivering parcel, envelope, airplane, globe.

2009, May 27   *Perf. 13¼x13*
3163-3167 A902   Set of 5   5.25 2.60

Miniature Sheet

World Environment Day — A903

No. 3168 — Butterflies: a, 25k, Aporia crataegi. b, 65k, Lasiommate megera. c, 80k, Plebeius agestis. d, 80k, Gonepteryx rhamni.

2009, June 5   *Perf. 13x13¼*
3168 A903   Sheet of 4, #a-d   3.25 1.60

Kemal Ataturk — A904

Various photographs of Ataturk.

2009, June 5   *Perf. 13½ Syncopated*
3169 A904   5k multi   .25 .25
3170 A904   10k multi   .25 .25
3171 A904   25k multi   .35 .25
3172 A904   50k multi   .65 .35
3173 A904   65k multi   .85 .40
3174 A904   80k multi   1.10 .55
3175 A904   85k multi   1.10 .55
3176 A904   1 l multi   1.40 .70
3177 A904   2 l multi   2.60 1.40
3178 A904   4.50 l multi   6.00 3.00
    Nos. 3169-3178 (10)   14.55 7.70

Europa
A905

Designs: 80k, Cacabey Astronomy Madrassa, Kirsehir. 1 l, Ali Kuscu (1403-74), astronomer.

2009, June 16   *Perf. 13¼x13*
3179-3180 A905   Set of 2   2.40 1.25

Items of the Phrygians — A906

Designs: 65k, Pitcher. 80k, Clay ceremonial cup with birds. No. 3183, 1 l, Goose-shaped clay ceremonial cup. No. 3184, 1 l, Cauldron.

2009, June 25   *Perf. 13x13¼*
3181-3184 A906   Set of 4   4.50 2.25

Embroidery — A907

Various embroidered pieces with background color of: 75k, Blue. 90k, Pink.

2009, July 2   *Perf. 13¼x13*
3185-3186 A907   Set of 2   2.25 1.10

Kemal Ataturk — A908

Various photographs of Ataturk.

2009, July 16   *Perf. 13½ Syncopated*
3187 A908   75k multi   1.10 .55
3188 A908   90k multi   1.25 .60
3189 A908   5 l multi   7.00 3.50
    Nos. 3187-3189 (3)   9.35 4.65

Miniature Sheet

Haci Bektas Veli (1209-71), Mystic — A909

No. 3190: a, 75k, Haci Bektas Veli, birds. b, 75k, Birds over town. c, 90k, Dancers. d, 90k, Haci Bektas Veli, deer, lion, birds.

2009, Aug. 12   *Perf. 13x13¼*
3190 A909   Sheet of 4, #a-d   4.50 2.25

Postal Cooperation Between Turkey and Bosnia and Herzegovina — A910

2009, Oct. 9   *Litho.*
3191 A910   90k multi   1.25 .60
See Bosnia and Herzegovina No. 656.

Namik Kemal Yolga (1914-2001), Diplomat Who Rescued Jews in World War II — A911

2009, Oct. 20   *Perf. 13¼x13*
3192 A911   75k multi   1.00 .50

Castles A912

Designs: 25k, Kolan Castle, Adana. 75k, Afyon Castle. 90k, Amasya Castle. 1 l, Ankara Castle.

2009, Nov. 5
3193-3196 A912   Set of 4   4.00 2.00

Mekteb-i Mülkiye Political Science Faculty, 150th Anniv. A913

Designs: 75k, Political Science Faculty Building, anniversary emblem. 90k, Anniversary emblem.

2009, Dec. 4   *Perf. 13¼x13*
3197-3198 A913   Set of 2   2.25 1.10

Süleyman Celebi (1351-1422), Writer — A914

Cengiz Aytmatov (1928-2008), Writer — A915

2009, Dec. 17
3199 A914   75k multi   1.00 .50
3200 A915   90k multi   1.25 .60

Miniature Sheets

A916

Istanbul, 2010 Capital of European Culture — A917

No. 3201: a, Silhouette of Hagia Sophia, red sky. b, Sculpture. c, Artwork of main dome of Blue Mosque. d, Blue Mosque, blue sky. e, Tower on coastline, blue sky. f, Bread. g, Tram. h, Haydarpasa Station, cloudy sky.
No. 3202: a, Silhouettes of buildings, pink sky. b, Religious painting. c, Fishermen. d, Man in boat, Bosporus Bridge. e, Ship. f, Birds over Bosporus. g, Topkapi Palace. h, Silhouettes of Hagia Sophia and Blue Mosque, orange red sky.

2010, Jan. 7   *Perf. 13x13x¼*
3201 A916   75k Sheet of 8, #a-h   8.00 4.00
    Perf. 13¼x13
3202 A917   75k Sheet of 8, #a-h   8.00 4.00

2010 Winter Olympics, Vancouver A918

Designs: 25k, Slalom skier. 75k, Snowboarder. No. 3205, 90k, Cross-country skier. No. 3206, 90k, Speed skater.

2010, Feb. 12   *Perf. 13¼*
3203-3206 A918   Set of 4   3.75 1.90

Military Aircraft A919

Designs: 75k, F-4. 90k, F-16. 1 l, CN-235.

2010, Mar. 18   *Perf. 13x13¼*
3207-3209 A919   Set of 3   3.50 1.75

Early Bronse Age Items — A920

Designs: 75k, Twinned figures. 90k, Ceremonial symbol. No. 3212, 1 l, Necklace. No. 3213, 1 l, Sculpture of nursing woman, vert.

    Perf. 13¼x13½, 13½x13¼
2010, Mar. 31
3210-3213 A920   Set of 4   5.00 2.50

Anatolian News Agency, 90th Anniv, A921

2010, Apr. 6   *Perf. 13¼x13*
3214 A921   75k multi   1.00 .50

A922

National Assembly, 90th
Anniv. — A923

2010, Apr. 23   *Perf. 13x13¼*
3215 A922 75k multi   1.00 .50
3216 A923 90k multi   1.25 .60

Sile Lighthouse,
150th
Anniv. — A924

2010, May 1
3217 A924 75k multi   1.00 .50

Labor Day — A925

Designs: No. 3218, 80k, Dove with olive
branch. No. 3219, 80k, Hands holding globe.
No. 3220, 110k, Dove with banner. No. 3221,
110k, Worker.

2010, May 1   *Perf. 13x12¾*
3218-3221 A925   Set of 4   5.00 2.50

Yunus
Emre (c.
1240-c.
1321),
Poet
A926

Emre and: 75k, Tomb, Eskisehir. 90k, Poem,
vert.

2010, May 3   *Perf. 13¼x13, 13x13¼*
3222-3223 A926   Set of 2   2.10 1.10

Europe
Day
A927

2010, May 9   *Perf. 12¾x13*
3224 A927 75k multi   .95 .45

Europa
A928

Children's stories: 80k, Balik Cobani (The
Fish and the Shepherd). 110k, Book of Dede
Korkut.

2010, May 9   *Perf. 13¼x13*
3225-3226 A928   Set of 2   2.40 1.25

RASAT
Observational
Satellite — A929

2010, May 17   *Perf. 13x13¼*
3227 A929 75k multi   .95 .45

Miniature Sheet

World Environment Day — A930

No. 3228 — Flowers: a, Crocus stevenii. b,
Crocus mathewii. c, Astragalus lineatus. d,
Erica bocquetii.

2010, June 5
3228 A930 110k Sheet of 4, #a-d 5.75 3.00

Sultan's Boats — A931

Boats from Istanbul Sea Museum: 80k, Boat
with red orange and white hull. 110k, Boat with
white and gold hull with bird figurehead.

2010, June 14   *Perf. 13x13¼*
3229-3230 A931   Set of 2   2.50 1.25

Kemal
Atatürk — A932

Various portraits.

Perf. 13½ Syncopated
2010, June 24
3231 A932   25k multi   .35 .25
3232 A932   80k multi   1.10 .55
3233 A932   110k multi   1.40 .70
3234 A932   355k multi   4.50 2.25
   Nos. 3231-3234 (4)   7.35 3.75

2010 World Men's Basketball
Championships, Turkey
A933   A934

2010, Aug. 28   *Perf. 13x12¾*
Background Color
3235 A933   80k blue   1.10 .55
3236 A934   80k brown   1.10 .55
3237 A933   110k yellow brown 1.50 .75
3238 A934   110k red   1.50 .75
   Nos. 3235-3238 (4)   5.20 2.60

Miniature Sheet

Japan Year in Turkey — A935

No. 3239: a, 80k, Bridge in Ritsurin Garden,
Takamatsu, Japan. b, 80k, Traditional Japanese dancer. c, 80k, Japanese dancers with
drums. d, 80k, Tokyo skyline. e, 80k, Noh theater. f, 110k, Samurai headgear. g, 110k, Mt.
Fuji. h, 110k, Kokeshi dolls. i, 110k, Turkish
frigate Ertugrul. j, 110k, Sushi.

2010, Sept. 2   *Perf. 13x13¼*
3239 A935   Sheet of 10, #a-j   13.00 6.50
   See Japan No.

Souvenir Sheet

Religious Buildings in Spain and
Turkey — A936

No. 3240: a, 80k, Santa María de la Mayor
Collegiate Church, Toro, Spain. b, 110k,
Ortaköy Mosque, Istanbul.

2010, Oct. 18   *Perf. 12¾x13*
3240 A936   Sheet of 2, #a-b   2.75 1.40
   See Spain No. 3240.

Miniature Sheet

11th Economic Cooperation
Orgaization Summit, Istanbul — A937

No. 3241 — Emblem with background color
of: a, 90k, Blue. b, 100k, Lilac. c, 130k, Rose.
d, 150k, Green

2010, Dec. 20   *Perf. 13x12¾*
3241 A937   Sheet of 4, #a-d   6.25 3.00

Miniature Sheet

2011 Winter Universiade,
Erzurum — A938

No. 3242 — Emblems and: a, 90k, Twin
Minaret Madrasa, Erzurum. b, 90k, Ice hockey
player. c, 1.30 l, Mascot. d, 1.30 l, Ski jumper.

2011, Jan. 27   *Perf. 13¼x13*
3242 A938   Sheet of 4, #a-d   5.75 2.75

Lilies
A939

Various lilies.

2011, Feb. 4   *Perf. 13¾*
3243 A939   25k multi   .35 .25
3244 A939   1 l multi   1.25 .65
3245 A939   3.65 l multi   4.75 2.40
3246 A939   6 l multi   7.75 3.75
   Nos. 3243-3246 (4)   14.10 7.05

Values are for stamps with surrounding
selvage.

Souvenir Sheet

Treaty of Moscow, 90th Anniv. — A940

No. 3247: a, Turkish flag, building. b, Treaty
negtiators.

2011, Feb. 4   *Perf. 13¼x13*
3247 A940 90k Sheet of 2, #a-b 2.40 1.25

Evliya Celebi (1611-82), Travel
Writer — A941

Map and: 90k, Celebi writing, silhouette of
Celebi on horse. 1.30 l, Celebi on horse.

2011, Mar. 25   *Perf. 13x13¼*
3248-3249 A941   Set of 2   3.00 1.50

Fish
A942

Designs: No. 3250, 1.30 l, Trigla lucerna. No. 3251, 1.30 l, Diplodus vulgaris. No. 3252, 1.30 l, Xiphias gladius.

2011, Apr. 28   **Perf. 13¼x13**
3250-3252 A942   Set of 3   5.25 2.60

Organization for Economic Cooperation and Development, 50th Anniv. — A943

2011, May 5   **Perf. 13x13¼**
3253 A943 1.30 l multi   1.75 .85

Europa A944

Forest and: 90k, Woodpecker. 1.30 l, Deer.

2011, May 9   **Perf. 13¼x13**
3254-3255 A944 Set of 2   2.75 1.40

Intl. Year of Forests.

Week of the Disabled A945

Week of the Disabled emblem, stylized person in wheelchair, Turkish text, and: 90k, Stylized person walking. 1.30 l, Hand with blackboard eraser.

2011, May 10   **Litho.**
3256-3257 A945 Set of 2   2.75 1.40

Souvenir Sheet

Kemal Atatürk (1881-1938) — A946

2011, May 19   **Perf. 13x13¼**
3258 A946 90k multi   1.25 .60

Miniature Sheet

Turkish Air Force, Cent. — A947

No. 3259: a, Jet on ground, blue skies. b, Jets over bridge. c, Jet in flight. d, Jet on runway, gray skies.

2011, June 1   **Perf. 13¼x13**
3259 A947 1.30 l Sheet of 4 #a-d 6.75 3.50
A sheet of four imperforate 1.30 l vertical stamps depicting jets in flight sold for 30 l.

Miniature Sheet

World Environment Day — A948

No. 3260: a, 25k, Anas acuta. b, 90k, Streptopelia turtur. c, 1.30 l, Phasianus colchicus. d, 1.30 l, Alectoris chukar.

2011, June 5   **Perf. 13¾**
3260 A948 Sheet of 4, #a-d   4.75 2.40

Korean War, 60th Anniv. A949

2011, June 25   **Perf. 13¼x13**
3261 A949 1.30 l multi   1.60 .80

Social Services and Child Protection Agency, 90th Anniv. — A950

2011, June 30   **Perf. 13x13¼**
3262 A950 90k multi   1.10 .55

Miniature Sheet

Kirkpinar Oil Wrestling Festival, 650th Anniv. — A951

No. 3263: a, 90k, Two wrestlers, both heads visible. b, 90k, Two wrestlers, heads not visible. c, 1.30 l, Two wrestlers. d, 1.30 l, Two wrestlers and referee.

2011, July 8   **Perf. 13¼x13**
3263 A951 Sheet of 4, #a-d   5.50 2.75

Miniature Sheet

Tourist Attractions of Van — A952

No. 3264: a, 25k, Van Castle. b, 90k, Hüsrev Pasha Mosque. c, 1.30 l, Bridge and fish. d, 1.30 l, Akdamar Church, Van cat.

2011, July 12   **Perf. 13x13¼**
3264 A952 Sheet of 4, #a-d   4.25 2.10

2011 European Youth Summer Olympic Festival, Trabzon A953

Festival mascot and: 25k, Festival emblem. 90k, Festival emblem, diff. No. 3267, 1.30 l, Festival flag and balloons. No. 3268, 1.30 l, Festival emblem, vert.

2011, July 23   **Perf. 13¼x13, 13x13¼**
3265-3268 A953 Set of 4   4.25 2.10

Yildiz Technical University, Cent. A954

Centenary emblem and: 90k, University building. 1.30 l, Star, University building.

2011, Aug. 22   **Perf. 13¼x13**
3269-3270 A954 Set of 2   2.50 1.25

Fruit — A955

Designs: 10k, Pyracantha coccinea. 1 l, Prunus persica. 1.30 l, Prunus avium. 3.65 l, Rubus fruticosus.

Perf. 13½ Syncopated
2011, Aug. 26
3271 A955 10k multi   .25 .25
3272 A955 1 l multi   1.10 .55
3273 A955 1.30 l multi   1.50 .75
3274 A955 3.65 l multi   4.25 2.10
Nos. 3271-3274 (4)   7.10 3.65

39th Mechanized Infantry Brigade — A956

Designs: 50k, Turkish flag and soldiers carrying flag. 90k, Turkish flag and soldiers. 1.30 l, Soldiers on ship, horiz.

2011, Oct. 6   **Litho.**
3275-3277 A956 Set of 3   3.00 1.50

Sultan's Boats — A957

Designs: 90k, Boat with pointed tip. 1.30 l, Boat with white hull and eagle figurehead.

2011, Nov. 28   **Perf. 13x13¼**
3278-3279 A957 Set of 2   2.40 1.25

Photographs of Turkish People and Agriculture — A958

Designs: No. 3280, 50k, Woman and string of pepers. No. 3281, 50k, Workers in field of protected plants. No. 3282, 1 l, Boy swimming in water with livestock, horiz. No. 3283, 1 l, Farm worker in field of plants under protective tents, horiz.

2011, Dec. 28   **Perf. 13x13¼, 13¼x13¼**
3280-3283 A958 Set of 4   3.25 1.60

SEMI-POSTAL STAMPS

Regular Issues Overprinted in Carmine or Black

Overprint reads: "For War Orphans"
Perf. 12, 13½ and Compound
1915   **Unwmk.**
On Stamps of 1905
B1 A18 10pa dull grn (#119)   1.00 .75
B2 A18 10pi orange brown   12.50 .80
On Stamp of 1906
B3 A18 10pa dull grn (#128)   40.00 25.00
On Stamp of 1908
B4 A19 10pa blue green   1.50 .75
B5 A19 5pi dark violet   75.00 12.50
Nos. B1-B5 (5)   130.00 39.80

With Additional Overprint

B6 A19 10pa blue green   240.00 175.00
On Stamps of 1909
B7 A21 10pa blue green   1.00 .75
  a. Inverted overprint   22.50 22.50
  b. Double overprint, one invtd.   30.00 30.00
B8 A21 20pa carmine rose   1.00 .75
  a. Inverted overprint   27.50 27.50
B9 A21 1pi ultra   1.00 .75
B10 A21 5pi dark violet   8.75 1.50
  Nos. B7-B10 (4)   11.75 3.75

With Additional Overprint

B11 A21 10pa blue green   1.00 .75
  b. Double overprint, one inverted   5.00 5.00
B12 A21 20pa carmine rose   1.50 .75
B13 A21 1pi ultra   2.00 .75
On Stamps of 1913
B14 A22 10pa blue green   1.00 .75
  a. Inverted overprint   22.50 22.50
B15 A22 1pi ultra   1.00 .75
  a. Double overprint   5.00 5.00
  Nos. B11-B15 (5)   6.50 3.75

With Additional Overprint

B16	A22	10pa blue green	1.75	.75
a.		Inverted overprint	27.50	27.50

On Newspaper Stamp of 1908

B17	A19	10pa blue green	360.00	175.00

On Newspaper Stamp of 1909

B18	A21	10pa blue green	1.75	1.00

Regular Issues Overprinted in Carmine or Black

1916

On Stamps of 1901

B19	A17	1pi blue	1.00	.50
B20	A17	5pi lilac rose	10.00	1.50

On Stamps of 1905

B21	A18	1pi brt blue	7.50	2.00
B22	A18	5pi brown	7.50	5.00

On Stamp of 1906

B23	A18	1pi brt blue	1.00	.75

On Stamps of 1908

B24	A19	20pa carmine (Bk)		*300.00*
B25	A19	10pi red	500.00	200.00

With Additional Overprint

B26	A19	20pa carmine	8.00	8.00
B27	A19	1pi brt blue (C)	20.00	5.00

On Stamps of 1909

B28	A21	20pa carmine rose	2.00	1.25
B29	A21	1pi ultra	1.50	1.00
B30	A21	10pi dull red	175.00	100.00

With Additional Overprint

B31	A21	20pa carmine rose	1.50	.75
B32	A21	1pi ultra	2.00	1.00

On Stamps of 1913

B33	A22	20pa carmine rose	2.00	1.50
B34	A22	1pi ultra	2.00	1.00
a.		Inverted overprint	5.00	5.00
B35	A22	10pi dull red	22.50	15.00

With Additional Overprint

B36	A22	20pa carmine rose	2.00	1.25

On Newspaper Stamps of 1901

B37	A16	5pi ocher	11.50	6.00
a.		5pa bister, No. P37	150.00	150.00

Regular Issues Surcharged in Black

On Stamp of 1898

B38	A11	10pa on 20pa vio brn	2.00	1.50

On Stamp of 1905

B39	A18	10pa on 20pa carmine	2.00	1.50

On Stamp of 1906

B40	A18	10pa on 20pa carmine	1.50	1.25

On Newspaper Stamp of 1893-99

B41	A11	10pa on 20pa violet brn	2.00	1.50
		Nos. B38-B41 (4)	*7.50*	*5.75*

Nos. 346-349 Overprinted

B42	A41	10pa carmine	1.00	.75
a.		Inverted overprint	6.75	6.75
B43	A41	20pa ultra	1.00	.75
a.		Inverted overprint	6.75	6.75
B44	A41	1pi violet & blk	1.00	.90
a.		Inverted overprint	6.75	6.75
B45	A41	5pi yel brn & blk	1.00	.75
a.		Inverted overprint	11.00	11.00
		Nos. B42-B45 (4)	*4.00*	*3.15*

Nos. B42-B45 formed part of the Postage Commemoration issue of 1916.

A Soldier's Farewell — SP1

1917, Feb. 20   Engr.   Perf. 12½

B46	SP1	10pa red violet	1.25	.50

For surcharges see Nos. 600, B47.

Stamp of Same Design Surcharged

B47	SP1	10pa on 20pa car rose	2.00	.50

Badge of the Society — SP9

School Teacher — SP10

Marie Sklodowska Curie — SP16

Kemal Atatürk — SP23

Designs: 2k+2k, Woman farmer. 2½k+2½k, Typist. 4k+4k, Aviatrix and policewoman. 5k+5k, Women voters. 7½k+7½k, Yildiz Palace, Istanbul. 10k+10k, Carrie Chapman Catt. 12½k+12½k, Jane Addams. 15k+15k, Grazia Deledda. 20k+20k, Selma Lagerlof. 25k+25k, Bertha von Suttner. 30k+30k, Sigrid Undset.

1935, Apr. 17   Photo.   Perf. 11½
Inscribed: "XII Congres Suffragiste International"

B54	SP9	20pa + 20pa brn	.50	.50
B55	SP10	1k + 1k rose car	.75	.50
B56	SP10	2k + 2k sl bl	1.00	.75
B57	SP10	2½k + 2½k yel grn	1.00	.75
B58	SP10	4k + 4k blue	1.50	1.00
B59	SP10	5k + 5k dl vio	2.50	2.00
B60	SP10	7½k + 7½k org red	2.50	2.00
B61	SP16	10k + 10k org	2.50	2.50
B62	SP16	12½k + 12½k dk bl	2.50	2.00
B63	SP16	15k + 15k violet	5.00	5.00
B64	SP16	20k + 20k red org	7.50	6.25
B65	SP16	25k + 25k grn	15.00	14.00
B66	SP16	30k + 30k ultra	90.00	100.00
B67	SP16	50k + 50k dk sl grn	175.00	150.00
B68	SP23	100k + 100k brn car	125.00	140.00
		Nos. B54-B68 (15)	*432.25*	*427.75*
		Set, never hinged	750.00	

12th Congress of the Women's Intl. Alliance.

> **Catalogue values for unused stamps in this section, from this point to the end of the section, are for Never Hinged items.**

Katip Chelebi — SP24

Perf. 10½
1958, Sept. 24   Litho.   Unwmk.

B69	SP24	50k + 10k gray	.35	.25

Mustafa ibn 'Abdallah Katip Chelebi Hajji Khalifa (1608-1657), Turkish author.

Road Building Machine SP25

Kemal Atatürk — SP26

Design: 25k+5k, Tanks and planes.

1958, Oct. 29

B70	SP25	15k + 5k orange	.25	.25
B71	SP26	20k + 5k lt red brn	.25	.25
B72	SP25	25k + 5k brt grn	.25	.25
		Nos. B70-B72 (3)	*.75*	*.75*

The surtax went to the Red Crescent Society and to the Society for the Protection of Children.
For surcharge see No. 1440.

Ruins, Göreme SP27

1959, July 8   Litho.   Perf. 10

B73	SP27	105k + 10k pur & buff	.50	.25

Issued for tourist publicity.

Istanbul SP28

1959, Sept. 11

B74	SP28	105k + 10k lt bl & red	.50	.25

15th International Tuberculosis Congress.

Manisa Asylum SP29

Merkez Muslihiddin SP30

Kermis at Manisa: 90k+5k, Sultan Camil Mosque, Manisa, vert.

1960, Apr. 17   Unwmk.   Perf. 13

B75	SP29	40k + 5k grn & lt bl	.25	.25
B76	SP29	40k + 5k vio & rose lil	.25	.25
B77	SP29	90k + 5k dp cl & car rose	.60	.25
B78	SP30	105k + 10k multi	.80	.25
		Nos. B75-B78 (4)	*1.90*	*1.00*

Census Chart SP31

Census Symbol — SP32

1960, Sept. 23   Photo.   Perf. 11½
Granite Paper

B79	SP31	30k + 5k bl & rose pink	.25	.25
B80	SP32	50k + 5k grn, dk bl & ultra	.35	.25

Issued for the 1960 Census.

Old Observatory SP33

Fatin Gökmen — SP34

Designs: 30k+5k, Observatory emblem. 75k+5k, Building housing telescope.

1961, July 1   Litho.   Perf. 13
B81	SP33 10k + 5k grnsh bl & grn	.25	.25
B82	SP33 30k + 5k vio & blk	.75	.75
B83	SP34 40k + 5k brown	.25	.25
B84	SP33 75k + 5k olive grn	.75	.75
	Nos. B81-B84 (4)	2.00	2.00

Kandili Observatory, 50th anniversary.

Anti-Malaria Work — SP35

UNICEF, 10th anniv.: 30k+5k, Mother and infant, horiz. 75k+5k, Woman distributing pasteurized milk.

1961, Dec. 11   Unwmk.   Perf. 13
B85	SP35 10k + 5k Prus green	.25	.25
B86	SP35 30k + 5k dull violet	.30	.25
B87	SP35 75k + 5k dk olive bis	.60	.25
	Nos. B85-B87 (3)	1.15	.75

Malaria Eradication Emblem, Map and Mosquito SP36

1962, Apr. 7   Litho.
B88	SP36 30k + 5k dk & lt brn	.30	.25
B89	SP36 75k + 5k blk & lil	.35	.25

WHO drive to eradicate malaria.

Poinsettia SP37   Wheat and Census Chart SP38

Flowers: 40k+10k, Bird of paradise flower. 75k+10k, Water lily.

1962, May 19   Perf. 12½x13½
Flowers in Natural Colors
B90	SP37 30k + 10k lt bl & blk	.25	.25
B91	SP37 40k + 10k lt bl & blk	.45	.25
B92	SP37 75k + 10k lt bl & blk	.95	.40
	Nos. B90-B92 (3)	1.65	.90

Inscribed: "Umumi Ziraat Sayimi"
1963, Apr. 14   Photo.   Perf. 11½

Design: 60k+5k, Wheat and chart, horiz.

B93	SP38 40k + 5k gray grn & yel	.25	.25
B94	SP38 60k + 5k org yel & blk	.25	.25

1961 agricultural census. Two black bars obliterate "Kasim 1960" inscription.

Red Lion and Sun, Red Crescent, Red Cross and Globe SP39

Designs: 60k+10k, Emblems in flowers, vert. 100k+10k, Emblems on flags.

1963, Aug. 1   Perf. 13
B95	SP39 50k + 10k multi	.25	.25
B96	SP39 60k + 10k multi	.40	.25
B97	SP39 100k + 10k multi	.60	.45
	Nos. B95-B97 (3)	1.25	.95

Centenary of International Red Cross.

Angora Goat — SP40   Olympic Torch Bearer — SP41

Animals: 10k+5k, Steppe cattle, horiz. 50k+5k, Arabian horses, horiz. 60k+5k, Three Angora goats. 100k+5k, Montofon cattle, horiz.

1964, Oct. 4   Litho.   Perf. 13
B98	SP40 10k + 5k multi	.35	.25
B99	SP40 30k + 5k multi	.35	.25
B100	SP40 50k + 5k multi	.60	.25
B101	SP40 60k + 5k multi	.85	.25
B102	SP40 100k + 5k multi	1.10	.25
	Nos. B98-B102 (5)	3.25	1.25

Issued for Animal Protection Day.

1964, Oct. 10   Unwmk.

Designs: 10k+5k, Running, horiz. 60k+5k, Wrestling. 100k+5k, Discus.

B103	SP41 10k + 5k org brn, blk & red	.40	.25
B104	SP41 50k + 5k ol, blk & red	.40	.25
B105	SP41 60k + 5k bl, blk & red	1.00	.25
B106	SP41 100k + 5k vio, blk, red & sil	1.40	.40
	Nos. B103-B106 (4)	3.20	1.15

18th Olympic Games, Tokyo, Oct. 10-25.

Map of Dardanelles and Laurel SP42

Designs: 90k+10k, Soldiers and war memorial, Canakkale. 130k+10k, Turkish flag and arch, vert.

1965, Mar. 18   Litho.   Perf. 13
B107	SP42 50k + 10k vio, yel & gold	.25	.25
B108	SP42 90k + 10k vio bl, bl, yel & grn	.60	.25
B109	SP42 130k + 10k dk brn, red & yel	1.10	.90
	Nos. B107-B109 (3)	1.95	1.40

50th anniversary of Battle of Gallipoli.

Tobacco Plant — SP43   Goddess, Basalt Carving — SP44

50k+5k, Tobacco leaves and Leander's tower, horiz. 100k+5k, Tobacco leaf.

1965, Sept. 16   Unwmk.   Perf. 13
B110	SP43 30k + 5k brn, lt brn & grn	.25	.25
B111	SP43 50k + 5k vio bl, ocher & pur	.60	.25
B112	SP43 100k + 5k blk, ol grn & ocher	1.00	.50
	Nos. B110-B112 (3)	1.85	1.00

Second International Tobacco Congress.

Perf. 13½x13, 13x13½
1966, June 6   Litho.

Archaeological Museum, Ankara: 30k+5k, Eagle and rabbit, ivory carving, horiz. 60k+5k, Bronze bull. 90k+5k, Gold pitcher.

B113	SP44 30k + 5k multi	.25	.25
B114	SP44 50k + 5k multi	.55	.25
B115	SP44 60k + 5k multi	.85	.45
B116	SP44 90k + 5k multi	1.10	.60
	Nos. B113-B116 (4)	2.75	1.55

Grand Hotel Ephesus SP45

Designs: 60k+5k, Konak Square, Izmir, vert. 130k+5k, Izmir Fair Grounds.

1966, Oct. 18   Litho.   Perf. 12
B117	SP45 50k + 5k multi	.25	.25
B118	SP45 60k + 5k multi	.45	.25
B119	SP45 130k + 5k multi	.95	.55
	Nos. B117-B119 (3)	1.65	1.05

33rd Congress of the Intl. Fair Assoc.

Europa Issue, 1967
Common Design Type
1967, May 2   Litho.   Perf. 13x13½
Size: 22x33mm
B120	CD10 100k + 10k multi	1.00	1.00
a.	Dark blue ("Europa") omitted		
B121	CD10 130k + 10k multi	2.50	1.75

Cloverleaf Crossing, Map of Turkey SP46

130k+5k, Highway E5 & map of Turkey.

1967, June 30   Litho.   Perf. 13
B122	SP46 60k + 5k multi	.60	.25
B123	SP46 130k + 5k multi, vert.	1.00	.60

Inter-European Express Highway, E5.

WHO Emblem SP47

1968, Apr. 7   Litho.   Perf. 13
B124	SP47 130k + 10k lt ultra, blk & yel	.80	.25

WHO, 20th anniversary.

Efem Pasha, Dr. Marko Pasha and View of Istanbul — SP48

60k+10k, Omer Pasha, Dr. Abdullah Bey & wounded soldiers. 100k+10k, Ataturk & Dr. Refik Saydam in front of Red Crescent headquarters, vert.

1968, June 11   Litho.   Perf. 13
B125	SP48 50k + 10k multi	.45	.25
B126	SP48 60k + 10k multi	.60	.30
B127	SP48 100k + 10k multi	.95	.45
	Nos. B125-B127 (3)	2.00	1.00

Centenary of Turkish Red Crescent Society.

NATO Emblem and Dove SP49

NATO, 20th anniv.: 130k+10k, NATO emblem and globe surrounded by 15 stars, symbols of the 15 NATO members.

1969, Apr. 4   Litho.   Perf. 13
B128	SP49 50k + 10k brt grn, blk & lt bl	.45	.25
B129	SP49 130k + 10k bluish blk, bl & gold	.75	.35

Red Cross, Crescent, Lion and Sun Emblems SP50

Design: 130k+10k, Conference emblem and Istanbul skyline.

1969, Aug. 29   Litho.   Perf. 13
B130	SP50 100k + 10k dk & lt bl & red	.50	.30
B131	SP50 130k + 10k red, lt bl & blk	.80	.45

21st Intl. Red Cross Conf., Istanbul.

Erosion Control SP51

60k+10k, Protection of flora (dead tree). 130k+10k, Protection of wildlife (bird of prey).

1970, Feb. 9   Litho.   Perf. 13
B132	SP51 50k + 10k multi	.40	.40
B133	SP51 60k + 10k multi	.60	.60
B134	SP51 130k + 10k multi	1.40	1.40
	Nos. B132-B134 (3)	2.40	2.40

1970 European Nature Conservation Year.

Globe and Fencer SP52

Design: 130k+10k, Globe, fencer and folk dancer with sword and shield.

1970, Sept. 13   Litho.   Perf. 13
B135	SP52 90k + 10k bl & blk	.50	.25
B136	SP52 130k + 10k ultra, lt bl, blk & org	.70	.25

International Fencing Championships.

"Children's Protection" SP53

Designs: 100k+15k, Hand supporting child, vert. 110k+15k, Mother and child.

1971, June 30   Litho.   Perf. 13
Star and Crescent Emblem in Red
B137	SP53 50k + 10k lil rose & blk	.25	.25
B138	SP53 100k + 15k brn, rose & blk	.45	.25
B139	SP53 110k + 15k org brn, bis & blk	.55	.25
	Nos. B137-B139 (3)	1.25	.75

50th anniv. of the Child Protection Assoc.

UNICEF, 25th Anniv. — SP54   "Your Heart is your Health" — SP55

1971, Dec. 11
B140	SP54 100k + 10k multi	.50	.25
B141	SP54 250k + 15k multi	1.10	.70

1972, Apr. 7 Litho. *Perf. 13*
B142 SP55 250k + 25k gray, blk & red .80 .60
World Health Day.

Olympic Emblems, Runners SP56

100k+15k, Olympic rings & motion emblem. 250k+25k, Olympic rings & symbolic track ('72).

1972, Aug. 26
B143 SP56 100k + 15k multi .40 .25
B144 SP56 110k + 25k multi .50 .25
B145 SP56 250k + 25k multi .70 .45
Nos. B143-B145 (3) 1.60 .95
20th Olympic Games, Munich, 8/26-9/11.

Emblem of Istanbul Technical University SP57

1973, Apr. 21 Litho. *Perf. 13*
B146 SP57 100k + 25k multi .50 .25
Istanbul Technical University, 200th anniv.

Dove and "50" SP58

1973, July 24 Litho. *Perf. 12½x13*
B147 SP58 100k + 25k multi .50 .25
Peace Treaty of Lausanne, 50th anniversary.

World Population Year — SP59

1974, June 15 Litho. *Perf. 13*
B148 SP59 250k + 25k multi .75 .35

Guglielmo Marconi (1874-1937), Italian Electrical Engineer and Inventor SP60

1974, Nov. 15 Litho. *Perf. 13½*
B149 SP60 250k + 25k multi .75 .35

Dr. Albert Schweitzer SP61 / Africa with South-West Africa SP62

1975, Jan 14 Litho. *Perf. 13*
B150 SP61 250k + 50k multi .90 .45
Dr. Albert Schweitzer (1875-1965), medical missionary and music scholar.

1975, Aug. 26 Litho. *Perf. 13x12½*
B151 SP62 250k + 50k multi .70 .35
Namibia Day (independence for South-West Africa).

Ziya Gökalp SP63 / Spoonbill SP64

1976, Mar. 23 Litho. *Perf. 13*
B152 SP63 200k + 25k multi .55 .25
Ziya Gökalp (1876-1924), philosopher.

1976, Nov. 19 Litho. *Perf. 13*
Birds: 150k+25k, European roller. 200k+25k, Flamingo. 400k+25k, Hermit ibis, horiz.
B153 SP64 100k + 25k multi .65 .25
B154 SP64 150k + 25k multi .80 .25
B155 SP64 200k + 25k multi 1.25 .35
B156 SP64 400k + 25k multi 2.25 .45
Nos. B153-B156 (4) 4.95 1.30

Decree by Mehmet Bey, and Ongun Holy Bird — SP65

1977, May 13 Litho. *Perf. 13*
B157 SP65 200k + 25k grn & blk .50 .25
700th anniv. of Turkish as official language.

10th World Energy Conference SP66

Design: 600k+50k, Conference emblem and globe with circles.

1977, Sept. 19 Litho. *Perf. 12½*
B158 SP66 100k + 25k multi .40 .25
B159 SP66 600k + 50k multi 1.25 .50

Running SP67

Designs: 2½ l+50k, Gymnastics. 5 l+ 50k, Table tennis. 8 l+50k, Swimming.

1978, July 18 Litho. *Perf. 13*
B160 SP67 1 l + 50k multi .30 .25
B161 SP67 2½ l + 50k multi .40 .30
B162 SP67 5 l + 50k multi .80 .30
B163 SP67 8 l + 50k multi 1.50 .35
Nos. B160-B163 (4) 3.00 1.20
GYMNASIADE '78, World School Games, Izmir.

Ribbon and Chain SP68

Design: 5 l+50k, Ribbon and flower, vert.

Perf. 12½x13, 13x12½
1978, Sept. 3 Litho.
B164 SP68 2½ l + 50k multi .75 .25
B165 SP68 5 l + 50k multi 1.00 .25
European Declaration of Human Rights, 25th anniversary.

Children, Head of Ataturk SP69 / Black Francolin SP70

IYC Emblem and: 5 l+50k, Children with globe as balloon. 8 l+50k, Kneeling person and child, globe.

1979, Apr. 23 Litho. *Perf. 13x13½*
B166 SP69 2½ l + 50k multi .35 .25
B167 SP69 5 l + 50k multi .55 .25
B168 SP69 8 l + 50k multi .85 .35
Nos. B166-B168 (3) 1.75 .85
International Year of the Child.

1979, Dec. 3 Litho. *Perf. 13x13½*
#B170, Great bustard. #B171, Crane. #B172, Gazelle. #B173, Mouflon muffelwild.
B169 SP70 5 l + 1 l multi .90 .25
B170 SP70 5 l + 1 l multi .90 .25
B171 SP70 5 l + 1 l multi .90 .25
B172 SP70 5 l + 1 l multi .90 .25
B173 SP70 5 l + 1 l multi .90 .25
a. Strip of 5, #B169-B173 6.00 6.00
European Wildlife Conservation Year. No. B173a has continuous design.

Flowers, Trees and Sun SP71 / Rodolia Cardinalis SP72

Environment Protection: 7½ l+ 1 l Sun, water. 15 l+1 l, Industrial pollution, globe. 20 l+1 l, Flower in oil puddle.

1980, June 4 Litho. *Perf. 13*
B174 SP71 2½ l + 1 l multi .25 .25
B175 SP71 7½ l + 1 l multi .25 .25
B176 SP71 15 l + 1 l multi .45 .25
B177 SP71 20 l + 1 l multi .50 .35
Nos. B174-B177 (4) 1.45 1.10

1980, Dec. 3 Litho. *Perf. 13*
Useful Insects: 7½ l+1 l, Bracon hebetor; 15 l+1 l, Calosoma sycophanta; 20 l+1 l, Deraeocoris rutilus.
B178 SP72 2½ l + 1 l multi .25 .25
B179 SP72 7½ l + 1 l multi .45 .25
B180 SP72 15 l + 1 l multi .80 .25
B181 SP72 20 l + 1 l multi 1.00 .25
Nos. B178-B181 (4) 2.50 1.00

Intl. Year of the Disabled SP73 / TB Bacillus Centenary SP75

Insects SP74

1981, Mar. 25 Litho. *Perf. 13*
B182 SP73 10 l + 2½ l multi .30 .25
B183 SP73 20 l + 2½ l multi .45 .25

1981, Dec. 16 Litho. *Perf. 13*
Useful Insects: No. B184, Cicindela campestris. No. B185, Syrphus vitripennis. No. B186, Ascalaphus macaronius. No. B187, Empusa fasciata.
B184 SP74 10 l + 2½ l multi .50 .25
B185 SP74 20 l + 2½ l multi .85 .25
B186 SP74 30 l + 2½ l multi 1.40 .45
B187 SP74 40 l + 2½ l multi 1.75 .60
Nos. B184-B187 (4) 4.50 1.55
See Nos. B190-B194, B196-B200.

1982, Mar. 24 *Perf. 13x12½*
Portraits: #B188, Dr. Tevfik Saglam (1882-1963). #B189, Robert Koch.
B188 SP75 10 l + 2½ l multi .50 .25
B189 SP75 30 l + 2½ l multi 1.25 .25

Insect Type of 1981
Useful Insects: 10 l+2½ l, Eurydema spectabile. 15 l+2½ l, Dacus oleae. 20 l+2½ l, Klapperichicen viridissima. 30 l+2½ l, Leptinotarsa decemlineata. 35 l+2½ l, Rhynchites auratus.

1982, Aug. 18 Litho. *Perf. 13*
B190 SP74 10 l + 2½ l multi .60 .25
B191 SP74 15 l + 2½ l multi .90 .25
B192 SP74 20 l + 2½ l multi .90 .25
B193 SP74 30 l + 2½ l multi 1.00 .25
B194 SP74 35 l + 2½ l multi 1.10 .25
Nos. B190-B194 (5) 4.50 1.25

Richard Wagner (1813-1883), Composer — SP76

1983, Feb. 13
B195 SP76 30 l + 5 l multi 1.10 1.00

Insect Type of 1981
Harmful Insects: 15 l+5 l, Eurygaster Intergriceps Put. 25 l+5 l, Phyllobius nigrofasciatus Pes. 35 l+5 l, Cercopis intermedia Kbm. 50 l+10 l, Graphosoma lineatum (L). 75 l+10 l, Capnodis miliaris (King).

1983, Sept. 14 Litho. *Perf. 13*
B196 SP74 15 l + 5 l multi .50 .25
B197 SP74 25 l + 5 l multi .65 .25
B198 SP74 35 l + 5 l multi .85 .25
B199 SP74 50 l + 10 l multi 1.25 .25
B200 SP74 75 l + 10 l multi 1.75 .40
Nos. B196-B200 (5) 5.00 1.40

Topkapi Museum Artifacts SP77

1984 Summer Olympics SP78

1984, May 30   Litho.   Perf. 13
B201 SP77 20 l + 5 l Kaftan,
             16th cent.   .60 .25
B202 SP77 70 l + 15 l Ewer   1.90 .75
B203 SP77 90 l + 20 l Swords   3.00 .85
B204 SP77 100 l + 25 l Lock, key 3.50 1.00
     Nos. B201-B204 (4)   9.00 2.85

Surtax was for museum. See Nos. B208-B211, B213-B216, B218-B221.

1984, July 28

Designs: 20 l+5 l, Banners, horiz. 70 l+15 l, Medalist. 100 l+20 l, Running, horiz.
B205 SP78 20 l + 5 l multi   1.10 .70
B206 SP78 70 l + 15 l multi   1.25 1.10
B207 SP78 100 l + 20 l multi   2.10 1.40
     Nos. B205-B207 (3)   4.45 3.20

Artifacts Type of 1984

Ceramicware: 10 l+5 l, Iznik plate. 20 l+10 l, Iznik boza pitcher and mug, 16th cent. 100 l+15 l, Du Paquier ewer and basin, 1730. 120 l+20 l, Ching dynasty plate, 1522-1566.

1985, May 30   Litho.   Perf. 13
B208 SP77 10 l + 5 l multi   .65 .25
B209 SP77 20 l + 10 l multi   1.10 .50
B210 SP77 100 l + 15 l multi 2.25 1.40
B211 SP77 120 l + 20 l multi 3.25 1.75
     Nos. B208-B211 (4)   7.25 3.90

Rabies Vaccine, Cent. — SP79

1985, July 16   Perf. 13x13½
B212 SP79 100 l + 15 l Pasteur 1.75 1.10

Artifacts Type of 1984

20 l+5 l, Metal and ceramic incense burner, c. 17th cent. 100 l+10 l, Jade lidded mug decorated with precious gems, 16th cent. 120 l+15 l, Dagger designed by Mahmut I, 1714. 200 l+30 l, Willow buckler, defensive shield, undated.

1986, May 30   Litho.   Perf. 13x12½
B213 SP77 20 l + 5 l multi   .90 .45
B214 SP77 100 l + 10 l multi 1.75 .70
B215 SP77 120 l + 15 l multi 2.00 .90
B216 SP77 200 l + 30 l multi 4.00 1.40
     Nos. B213-B216 (4)   8.65 3.45

General Assembly of NATO SP80

1986, Nov. 13   Litho.   Perf. 13½x13
B217 SP80 100 l + 20 l multi 2.75 .85

Artifacts Type of 1984

Designs: 20 l+5 l, Crystal and gold ewer, 16th cent., vert. 50 l+10 l, Emerald and gold pendant, 17th cent. 200 l+15 l, Sherbet jug, 19th cent., vert. 250 l+30 l, Crystal and gold pen box, 16th cent.

1987, May 30   Litho.   Perf. 13
B218 SP77 20 l + 5 l multi   .75 .25
B219 SP77 50 l + 10 l multi   1.10 .45
B220 SP77 200 l + 15 l multi 1.40 1.10
B221 SP77 250 l + 30 l multi 2.25 1.40
     Nos. B218-B221 (4)   5.50 3.20

15th Intl. Chemotherapy Congress, Istanbul — SP81

1987, July 19   Litho.   Perf. 13
B222 SP81 200 l + 25 l multi 1.75 .25

Intl. Road Transport Union (IRU) 21st World Congress SP82

1988, June 13   Litho.   Perf. 12½x13
B223 SP82 200 l + 25 l multi .90 .25

European Environmental Campaign Balancing Nature and Development — SP83

Designs: 100 l+25 l, Hands, desert reclamation. 400 l+50 l, Eye, road, planted field.

1988, Oct. 19   Litho.   Perf. 12½x13
B224 SP83 100 l + 25 l multi .50 .25
B225 SP83 400 l + 50 l multi 1.75 .40

Silkworm Industry SP84

Perf. 13½x13
1989, Apr. 15   Litho.   Wmk. 394
B226 SP84 150 l + 50 l Silkworm .50 .25
B227 SP84 600 l + 100 l Cocoon,
             strands   1.75 .40

Council of Europe, 40th Anniv. SP85

1989, May 5   Litho.   Perf. 13
B228 SP85 600 l + 100 l multi 1.75 .45

European Tourism Year SP86

1990, Apr. 26   Wmk. 394
B229 SP86 300 l + 50 l Antalya .50 .25
B230 SP86 1000 l + 100 l Istanbul 1.25 .40

Fight Against Addictions — SP87

Fight Against: No. B231, Smoking. No. B232, Drugs, horiz.

1990, June 26   Litho.   Perf. 13
B231 SP87 300 l + 50 l multi .60 .25
B232 SP87 1000 l + 100 l multi 1.60 .75

Yunus Emre (died c.1321), Poet SP88   SP89

1991, June 26   Litho.   Perf. 13
B233 SP88 500 l + 100 l multi .65 .35
B234 SP89 1500 l + 100 l multi 1.60 .75

Wolfgang Amadeus Mozart (1756-1791), Composer — SP90

1991, July 24
B235 SP90 1500 l + 100 l multi 1.75 .90

Turkish Supreme Court, 30th Anniv. SP91

1992, Apr. 25
B236 SP91 500 l + 100 l multi .50 .25

Scouts Planting Tree SP92

#B238 Mountain climber on rope, vert.

1992, Dec. 18
B237 SP92 1000 l + 200 l multi 1.00 .60
B238 SP92 3000 l + 200 l multi 1.75 1.00

Travertine, Pamukkale — SP93

Different views of rock formations.

1993, June 6
B239 SP93 1000 l + 200 l multi .75 .25
B240 SP93 3000 l + 500 l multi 1.50 .55

Intl. Day for Natural Disaster Reduction SP94

1993, Oct. 13   Perf. 12½x13
B241 SP94 3000 l + 500 l multi 1.40 .75

Intl. Olympic Committee, Cent. — SP95

1994, Aug. 17   Perf. 13
B242 SP95 12,500 l + 500 l multi 1.75 1.10

Trees SP96

Designs: No. B243, Platanus orientalis. No. B244, Cupressus sempervirens, vert.

1994, Nov. 30
B243 SP96 7500 l + 500 l multi 1.25 .95
B244 SP96 12,500 l + 500 l multi 2.40 1.75

TBMM (Great Natl. Assembly), 75th Anniv. SP97

1995, Apr. 23
B245 SP97 3500 l + 500 l multi .45 .25

The Epic of Manas SP98

Designs: No. B246, Lancers charging. No. B247, Abay Kunanbay (1845-1904), poet, vert.

1995, June 28
B246 SP98 3500 l + 500 l multi .45 .25
B247 SP98 3500 l + 500 l multi .45 .25

For the People of Bosnia-Herzegovina — SP99

1996, Feb. 28
B248 SP99 10,000 l + 2500 l multi .75 .75

Ankara University, 50th Anniv. SP100

Unwmk.
1996, Nov. 20   Litho.   Perf. 13
B249 15,000 l + 2500 l multi .65 .30

Fight Against Cancer, 50th Anniv. SP101

1997, Feb. 18   Litho.   Perf. 12½x13
B250 SP101 25,000 l + 5000 l
             multi   .65 .30

Pakistan Independence, 50th Anniv. — SP102

Mohammed Ali Jinnah (1876-1948).

1997, Mar. 23　Litho.　Perf. 13
B251　SP102　25,000 l　+5000 l
　　　　multi　　　　　.60　.30

Universal Declaration of Human Rights SP103

Stylized designs: 75,000 l, Puzzle piece with outlines of people's faces. 175,000 l, Heart-shaped kite with people as tail.

1998, Dec. 10　Litho.　Perf. 13½
B252　SP103　75,000 l　+25,000 l　1.00　.50
B253　SP103　175,000 l　+25,000 l　2.00　1.00

GATA (Gulhane Military Medical Academy), Cent. SP104

1998, Dec. 30　Litho.　Perf. 13
B254　SP104　75,000 l　+10,000 l
　　　　multi　　　　1.40　.70

Kemal Ataturk's Entry Into War College, Cent. — SP105

1999, Mar. 13　Litho.　Perf. 13
B255　SP105　75,000 l　+5,000 l
　　　　multi　　　　.90　.25

Council of Europe, 50th Anniv. SP106

1999, Apr. 30　Litho.　Perf. 13¼
B256　SP106　175,000 l　+10,000 l　2.75　1.40

Church, Mosque and Synagogue — SP107

Dancers SP108

2000, May 25　Litho.　Perf. 13¼
B257　SP107　275,000 l　+10,000 l　2.00　2.00
B258　SP108　300,000 l　+10,000 l　2.00　2.00

Tombs and Mausoleums — SP109

150,000 l+25,000 l, Usta Sagirt Kumbeti Ahlat, vert. 200,000 l+25,000 l, Kocbasli Mezar Tasi Tunceli. 275,000 l+25,000 l, Isabey Turbesi, Uskup, vert. 300,000 l+25,000 l, Yusuf bin Kuseyr Turbesi, Nahcivan, vert.

2000
B259-B262　SP109　Set of 4　7.25　7.25

Coins SP110

Various coins with background colors of: No. B263, 300,000 l + 25,000 l, Red. No. B264, 300,000 l + 25,000 l, Blue green. 450,000 l + 25,000 l, Dark carmine. 500,000 l + 25,000 l, Blue violet.

2001, Oct. 1　Litho.　Perf. 13
B263-B266　SP110　Set of 4　6.25　6.25

Caravansaries — SP111

Designs: 300,000 l + 25,000 l, Ashab i Kehf Han, Afsin. 500,000 l + 25,000 l, Horozlu Han, Konya.

2001, Nov. 19　Litho.　Perf. 13
B267-B268　SP111　Set of 2　4.00　4.00

Turkey's Admission to NATO, 50th Anniv. SP112

2002, Feb. 18
B269　SP112　400,000 l + 25,000 l　2.25　2.25

Trains SP113

Designs: 500,000 l + 25,000 l, Steam locomotive. 700,000 l + 25,000 l, Electric locomotive.

2002, Sept. 16　Litho.　Perf. 13¼x13
B270-B271　SP113　Set of 2　5.50　5.50

Trains SP114

Designs: 600,000 l+50,000 l, Trolley. 800,000 l+50,000 l, Subway.

2003, Sept. 9　Litho.　Perf. 13¼x13
B272-B273　SP114　Set of 2　3.50　3.50

Ibrahim Hakki Erzurumlu (1703-72), Writer — SP115

2003, Dec. 24　Litho.　Perf. 13x13¼
B274　SP115　600,000 l　+50,000 l
　　　　multi　　　　1.40　1.40

Lighthouses SP116

Designs: 600,000 l + 50,000 l, Kerempe Lighthouse, Kastamonu. 700,000 l + 50,000 l, Taslikburnu Lighthouse, Antalya.

2004, Apr. 5
B275-B276　SP116　Set of 2　4.50　4.50

Scouting — SP117

Designs: 600,000 l + 50,000 l, Girl Scout in foreground. 700,000 l + 50,000 l, Boy Scout in foreground.

2004, Sept. 30
B277-B278　SP117　Set of 2　3.50　3.50

Rotary International, Cent. — SP118

2005, Feb. 23　Litho.　Perf. 13x13¼
B279　SP118　80k　+10k multi　　1.50　1.50

Intl. Year of Physics SP119

2005, Sept. 13　Litho.　Perf. 13¼x13
B280　SP119　70k　+10k multi　　1.25　1.25

World Forests Day SP120

2006, Mar. 21　Litho.　Perf. 13¼x13
B281　SP120　60k　+10k multi　　1.10　1.10

Mehmet Akif Ersoy (1873-1936), Poet — SP121

Ersoy at: 60k+10k, Left. 70k+10k, Right.

2006, Oct. 13　Litho.　Perf. 13¼x13
B282-B283　SP121　Set of 2　2.10　2.10

Coast Guard Command, 25th Anniv. — SP122

2007, July 13　Litho.　Perf. 13x13¼
B284　SP122　60k + 10k multi　　1.10　1.10

Marbled Art — SP123

Designs: 60k+10k, White flowers. 70k+10k, Red tulips.

2007, Dec. 6　　　　Perf. 13¼x13
B285-B286　SP123　Set of 2　2.60　2.60

Kasgarli Mahmut (1008-1105), Lexicographer — SP124

Kasgarli: 65k+10k, On horseback. 80k+10k, Holding book.

2008, Apr. 10　Litho.　Perf. 13¼x13
B287-B288　SP124　Set of 2　2.60　2.60

Railway Terminals in Istanbul — SP125

Designs: 65k+10k, Haydarpasa Terminal. 80k+10k, Sirkeci Terminal.

2008, Oct. 15　Litho.　Perf. 13x13¼
B289-B290　SP125　Set of 2　2.25　2.25

Ethics Day
SP126

2009, May 25   *Perf. 13¼x13*
B291 SP126 65k +10k multi   1.00 1.00

Katip Celebi
(1609-57),
Historian
SP127

Celebi, book and: 75k+10k, Quill pen.
90k+10k, Ships.

2009, July 16
B292-B293 SP127 Set of 2   2.60 2.60

Locomotives — SP128

Various locomotives: 80k+10k, 110k+10k.

2010, Aug. 4   *Perf. 12¾x13*
B294-B295 SP128 Set of 2   3.00 3.00

Rugs
SP129

Various rugs: 80k+10k, 110k+10k.

2010, Nov. 17
B296-B297 SP129 Set of 2   3.00 3.00

Hasankeyf — SP130

2011, Sept. 21   *Perf. 13x13¼*
B298 SP130 130k +10k multi   1.60 1.60

State
Personnel
Department,
50th Anniv.
SP131

2011, Dec. 17   *Perf. 13¼x13*
B299 SP131 100k +10k multi   1.25 1.25

AIR POST STAMPS

> Catalogue values for unused stamps in this section are for **Never Hinged** items.

Nos. 692, 695, 698, 700 Overprinted or Surcharged in Brown or Blue

1934, July 15   **Unwmk.**   *Perf. 12*
C1   A74   7½k (Br)   .75   .25
C2   A72   12½k on 15k (Br)   .75   .25
C3   A74   20k on 25k (Br)   .75   .25
C4   A74   25k (Bl)   1.00   .40
C5   A74   40k (Br)   2.25 1.25
     Nos. C1-C5 (5)   5.50 2.40

Regular Stamps of
1930 Surcharged in
Brown

1937
C6   A74   4½k on 7½k red brn   5.00   1.00
C7   A72   9k on 15k dp org   40.00 20.00
C8   A74   35k on 40k red vio   10.00   4.25
     Nos. C6-C8 (3)   55.00 25.25

Nos. 698, 703-704
Surcharged in Black

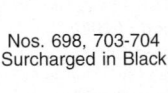

1941, Dec. 18
C9   A74   4½k on 25k   2.00   1.50
C10   A75   9k on 200k   9.75   8.25
C11   A75   35k on 500k   6.25   5.25
     Nos. C9-C11 (3)   18.00 15.00

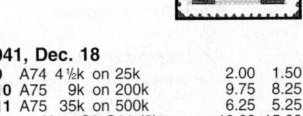

Plane over
Izmir
AP1

Planes over: 5k, 40k, Izmir. 20k, 50k,
Ankara. 30k, 1 l, Istanbul.

1949, Jan. 1   **Photo.**   *Perf. 11½*
C12   AP1   5k gray & vio   .25   .25
C13   AP1   20k bl gray & brn   .25   .25
C14   AP1   30k bl gray & ol brn   1.00   .25
C15   AP1   40k bl & dp ultra   1.00 1.00
C16   AP1   50k gray vio & red brn   1.00   .25
C17   AP1   1 l gray bl & dk grn   3.00   .65
     Nos. C12-C17 (6)   6.50 2.65

For overprints see Nos. C19-C21.

Plane Over
Rumeli
Hisari
Fortress
AP2

1950, May 19   **Unwmk.**
C18 AP2 2½ l gray bl & dk grn 22.50 14.00

Nos. C12, C14 and C16 Overprinted
in Red

1951, Apr. 9   *Perf. 11½*
C19 AP1   5k gray & vio   1.50   .50
C20 AP1   30k bl gray & ol brn   2.00   .60
C21 AP1   50k gray vio & red brn   2.50   .70
     Nos. C19-C21 (3)   6.00 1.80

Industrial Congress, Ankara, Apr. 9.

Yesilkoy
Airport and
Plane
AP3

Designs: 20k, 45k, Yesilkoy Airport and
plane in flight. 35k, 55k, Ankara Airport and
plane. 40k, as No. C22.

1954, Nov. 1   *Perf. 14*
C22 AP3   5k red brn & bl   1.00   .25
C23 AP3   20k brn org & bl   .65   .25
C24 AP3   35k dk grn & bl   .65   .25
C25 AP3   40k dp car & bl   .65   .25
C26 AP3   45k violet & bl   1.50   .25
C27 AP3   55k black & bl   4.00   .50
     Nos. C22-C27 (6)   8.45 1.75

Symbol of Izmir
Fair — AP4

1956, Aug. 20   **Litho.**   *Perf. 10½*
C28 AP4 25k reddish brown   .35   .30

25th Intl. Fair at Izmir, Aug. 20-Sept. 20.

Heuss Type of Regular Issue, 1957
1957, May 5
C29 A264 40k sal pink & magenta   .35   .30

**Zahir Shah Type of Regular Issue,
1957**
1957, Sept. 1
C30 A269 25k grn & lt grn   .25   .25

Hawk — AP5

Crane — AP6

Birds: 40k, 125k, Swallows. 65k, Cranes.
85k, 195k, Gulls. 245k, Hawk.

1959, Aug. 13   **Litho.**   *Perf. 10½*
C31 AP5   40k bright lilac   .50   .25
C32 AP5   65k blue green   3.00   .40
C33 AP5   85k bright blue   1.00   .40
C34 AP5   105k yel & sepia   .75   .40
C35 AP6   125k brt violet   1.00   .40
C36 AP6   155k yel green   1.25   .40
C37 AP6   195k violet blue   1.50   .40
C38 AP6   245k brn & brn org   3.50 1.00
     Nos. C31-C38 (8)   12.50 3.65

De Havilland
Rapide
Biplane
AP7

Designs: 60k, Fokker Friendship transport
plane. 130k, DC9-30. 220k, DC-3. 270k, Viscount 794.

1967, July 13   **Litho.**   *Perf. 13½x13*
C39 AP7   10k pink & blk   .40   .25
C40 AP7   60k lt grn, red & blk   .65   .25
C41 AP7   130k bl, blk & red   .90   .25
C42 AP7   220k lt brn, blk & red   1.40   .35
C43 AP7   270k org, blk & red   2.25   .45
     Nos. C39-C43 (5)   5.60 1.55

For surcharge see No. 2179A.

Kestrel — AP8

Birds: 60k, Golden eagle. 130k, Falcon.
220k, Sparrow hawk. 270k, Buzzard.

1967, Oct. 10   **Litho.**   *Perf. 13*
C44 AP8   10k brown & salmon   1.10   .25
C45 AP8   60k brown & yellow   .85   .25
C46 AP8   130k brown & lt bl   2.10   .25
C47 AP8   220k brown & lt grn   3.25   .45
C48 AP8   270k org brn & gray   4.75   .65
     Nos. C44-C48 (5)   12.05 1.85

F-104 Jet
Plane — AP9

Turkish Air
Force
Emblem
and Jets
AP10

Designs: 200k, Victory monument, Afyon,
and Jets. 325k, F-104 jets and pilot. 400k, Bleriot XI plane with Turkish flag. 475k, Flight of
Hezarfen Ahmet Celebi from Galata Tower to
Uskudar.

1971, June 1   **Litho.**   *Perf. 13*
C49 AP9   110k multi   .90   .25
C50 AP9   200k multi   2.00   .25
C51 AP10   250k multi   2.00   .45
C52 AP9   325k multi   3.10   .45

C53	AP10 400k multi	3.50	.55
C54	AP10 475k multi	4.50	.65
	Nos. C49-C54 (6)	16.00	2.60

The gold ink on No. C51 is applied by a thermographic process which gives a raised and shiny effect.

F-28
Plane — AP11

1973, Dec. 11   Litho.   Perf. 13

C55	AP11 110k shown	.65	.25
C56	AP11 250k DC-10	1.10	.30

POSTAGE DUE STAMPS

Same Types as Regular Issues of Corresponding Dates

1863   Unwmk.   Imperf.
Blue Band

J1	A1 20pa blk, *red brn*	100.00	32.50
a.	Tête bêche pair	225.00	225.00
b.	Without band	50.00	
c.	Red band	90.00	45.00
J2	A2 1pi blk, *red brn*	150.00	22.50
a.	Tête bêche pair	225.00	225.00
b.	Without band	50.00	
J3	A3 2pi blk, *red brn*	500.00	70.00
a.	Tête bêche pair	650.00	450.00
b.	Without band	100.00	
J4	A4 5pi blk, *red brn*	300.00	80.00
a.	Tête bêche pair	425.00	425.00
b.	Without band	100.00	
c.	Red band	150.00	
	Nos. J1-J4 (4)	1,050.	205.00

1865   Perf. 12½

J6	A5 20pa brown	4.00	5.00
J7	A5 1pi brown	4.00	5.00
b.	Half used as 20pa on cover		
c.	Printed on both sides	25.00	
J8	A5 2pi brown	12.50	25.00
a.	Half used as 1pi on cover		
J9	A5 5pi brown	5.00	30.00
a.	Half used as 2½pi on cover		
J10	A5 25pi brown	45.00	100.00
	Nos. J6-J10 (5)	70.50	165.00

Exist imperf. Values, $60 to $100 each. The 10pa brown is an essay. Value about $2,750.

1867

J11	A5 20pa bister brn	9.00	100.00
J12	A5 1pi bister brn	9.00	
a.	With surcharge of 5pi	13.50	
b.	Imperf., pair	65.00	
J13	A5 2pi fawn	75.00	
J14	A5 5pi fawn	17.50	
J15	A5 25pi bister brn	21,250.	
	Nos. J11-J14 (4)	110.50	

Nos. J12-J15 were not placed in use.

1869   Perf. 13½
With Yellow-Brown Border

J16	A5 20pa bister brn	10.00	10.00
a.	Without surcharge		
J17	A5 1pi bister brn	550.00	20.00
a.	Without surcharge		
J18	A5 2pi bister brn	800.00	20.00
J19	A5 5pi bister brn	2.25	12.50
b.	Without border		
c.	Printed on both sides	15.00	—
J20	A5 25pi bister brn		
	Nos. J16-J19 (4)	1,362.	62.50

With Brown Border

Color of border ranges from brown to reddish brown and black brown.

J21	A5 20pa bister brn	125.00	20.00
a.	Inverted surcharge		
b.	Without surcharge		
J22	A5 1pi bister brn	550.00	12.50
a.	Without surcharge		
J23	A5 2pi bister brn	450.00	12.50
b.	Inverted surcharge		
J24	A5 5pi bister brn	2.50	15.00
b.	Without surcharge		
J25	A5 25pi bister brn	37.50	100.00
	Nos. J21-J25 (5)	1,165.	160.00

Pin-perf., Perf. 5 to 11½ and Compound

1871
With Brick Red Border

J26	A5 20pa bister brn	1,250.	50.00
J27	A5 1pi bister brn		5,000.
J28	A5 2pi bister brn	110.00	140.00
J29	A5 5pi bister brn	7.50	25.00

With Black Brown Border

J31	A5 20pa bister brn	150.00	3.50
a.	Half used as 10pa on cover		

b.	Imperf., pair		16.50
c.	Printed on both sides	40.00	40.00
J32	A5 1pi bister brn	225.00	2.50
a.	Half used as 20pa on cover		
c.	Inverted surcharge	50.00	35.00
J33	A5 2pi bister brn	6.00	9.00
a.	Half used as 1pi on cover		
c.	Imperf., pair		16.50
J34	A5 5pi bister brn	2.50	20.00
a.	Half used as 2½pi on cover		
c.	Printed on both sides		
J35	A5 25pi bister brn	40.00	125.00
a.	Inverted surcharge		
	Nos. J31-J35 (5)	423.50	160.00

1888   Perf. 11½ and 13½

J36	A7 20pa black	4.00	12.50
J37	A7 1pi black	4.00	12.50
J38	A7 2pi black	4.00	15.00
b.	Diagonal half used as 1pi		
	Nos. J36-J38 (3)	12.00	40.00

Imperf

J36a	A7 20pa		11.00
J37a	A7 1pi		11.00
J38a	A7 2pi		11.00

Perf.   13½ 1892

J39	A11 20pa black	7.00	12.50
J40	A12 1pi black		

1901

J42	A11 20pa black, *deep rose*	2.50	20.00

1901

J43	A17 10pa black, *deep rose*	4.00	6.00
J44	A17 20pa black, *deep rose*	3.75	8.75
J45	A17 1pi black, *deep rose*	3.00	10.00
J46	A17 2pi black, *deep rose*	2.50	15.00
	Nos. J43-J46 (4)	13.25	39.75

1905   Perf. 12

J47	A18 1pi black, *deep rose*	3.00	10.00
J48	A18 2pi black, *deep rose*	4.50	20.00

1908, Perf. 12, 13½ and Compound

J49	A19 1pi black, *deep rose*	80.00	7.50
J50	A19 2pi black, *deep rose*	12.50	45.00

1909

J51	A21 1pi black, *deep rose*	15.00	50.00
J52	A21 10pa black, *deep rose*	150.00	175.00
a.	Imperf.	65.00	

1913   Perf. 12

J53	A22 2pa black, *deep rose*	1.00	.50
J54	A22 5pa black, *deep rose*	1.00	.50
J55	A22 10pa black, *deep rose*	1.00	.50
J56	A22 20pa black, *deep rose*	1.00	.50
J57	A22 1pi black, *deep rose*	4.50	10.00
J58	A22 2pi black, *deep rose*	8.00	17.50
	Nos. J53-J58 (6)	16.50	29.50

Adrianople Issue
Nos. 251-253 Surcharged in Black, Blue or Red

1913

J59	A23 2pa on 10pa green (Bk)	3.25	.35
J60	A23 5pa on 20pa red (Bl)	3.25	.35
J61	A23 10pa on 40pa blue (R)	10.00	.80
J62	A23 20pa on 40pa blue (Bk)	32.50	11.00
	Nos. J59-J62 (4)	49.00	12.50

For surcharges see Nos. J67-J70, J83-J86.

D1

D2

D3

D4

1914   Engr.

J63	D1 5pa claret	1.25	10.00
J64	D2 20pa red	1.25	10.00
J65	D3 1pi dark blue	1.25	10.00
J66	D4 2pi slate	1.25	10.00
	Nos. J63-J66 (4)	5.00	40.00

For surcharges and overprints see Nos. J87-J91.

Nos. J59 to J62 Surcharged in Red or Black

1916

J67	A23 10pa on 2pa on 10pa (R)	55.00	55.00
J68	A23 20pa on 5pa on 20pa	55.00	55.00
J69	A23 40pa on 10pa on 40pa	55.00	55.00
J70	A23 40pa on 20pa on 40pa (R)	55.00	55.00
	Nos. J67-J70 (4)	220.00	220.00

Preceding Issues Overprinted in Red, Black or Blue

1917

On Stamps of 1865

J71	A5 20pa red brn (Bl)	45.00	67.50
J72	A5 1pi red brn (Bl)	45.00	67.50
J73	A5 2pi bis brn (Bl)	45.00	67.50
J74	A5 5pi bis brn (Bl)	45.00	67.50
J75	A5 25pi dk brn (Bl)	45.00	67.50
	Nos. J71-J75 (5)	225.00	337.50

On Stamp of 1869
Red Brown Border

J76	A5 5pi bis brn (R)	45.00	67.50

On Stamp of 1871
Black Brown Border

J77	A5 5pi bis brn (R)	75.00	50.00

On Stamps of 1888

J78	A7 1pi black (R)	45.00	67.50
J79	A7 2pi black (R)	45.00	67.50

On Stamps of 1892

J80	A11 20pa black (R)	2.50	2.50
J81	A12 1pi black (R)	2.50	2.50
J82	A13 2pi black (R)	2.50	2.50
	Nos. J80-J82 (3)	7.50	7.50

Adrianople Issue
On Nos. J59 to J62 with Addition of New Value

J83	A23 10pa on 2pa on 10pa (R)	1.25	1.00
J84	A23 20pa on 5pa on 20pa (Bk)	1.50	1.00
J85	A23 40pa on 10pa on 40pa (Bk)	2.00	1.50
a.	"40pa" double		
J86	A23 40pa on 20pa on 40pa (R)	3.75	3.50
	Nos. J83-J86 (4)	8.50	7.00

Nos. J71-J86 were used as regular postage stamps.

Armistice Issue

No. J65 Overprinted

1919, Nov. 30

J87	D3 1pi dark blue	125.00	150.00

Accession to the Throne Issue
Postage Due Stamps of 1914 Overprinted in Turkish "Accession to the Throne of His Majesty. 3rd July, 1334-1918"

1919

J88	D1 10pa on 5pa claret	25.00	37.50
J89	D2 20pa red	25.00	37.50
J90	D3 1pi dark blue	25.00	37.50
J91	D4 2pi slate	25.00	37.50
	Nos. J88-J91 (4)	100.00	150.00

Railroad Bridge over Kizil Irmak — D5

Kemal Atatürk — D6

1926   Engr.

J92	D5 20pa ocher	1.25	2.50
J93	D5 1g red	2.00	5.00
J94	D5 2g blue green	3.00	5.00
J95	D5 3g lilac brown	3.50	12.50
J96	D5 5g lilac	6.00	20.00
	Nos. J92-J96 (5)	15.75	45.00
	Set, never hinged	30.00	

Catalogue values for unused stamps in this section, from this point to the end of the section, are for Never Hinged items.

1936   Litho.   Perf. 11½

J97	D6 20pa brown	.25	.25
J98	D6 2k light blue	.25	.25
J99	D6 3k bright violet	.25	.25
J100	D6 5k Prussian blue	.25	.25
J101	D6 12k bright rose	.35	.25
	Nos. J97-J101 (5)	1.35	1.25

For surcharges see Nos. 1461-1465.

LOCAL ISSUES

Type I

Type III

Type V

Type II

Type IV

Type VI

During 1873//1882 Turkish stamps with the above overprints were used for local postage in Constantinople (types 1-5) and Mount Athos (type 6).

MILITARY STAMPS

For the Army in Thessaly

Tughra and
Bridge at
Larissa — M1

1898, Apr. 21   Unwmk.   Perf. 13

M1	M1	10pa yellow green	10.00	7.50
M2	M1	20pa rose	10.00	7.50
M3	M1	1pi dark blue	10.00	7.50
M4	M1	2pi orange	10.00	7.50
M5	M1	5pi violet	10.00	7.50
		Nos. M1-M5 (5)	50.00	37.50

Issued for Turkish occupation forces to use in Thessaly during the Greco-Turkish War of 1897-98.
Forgeries of Nos. M1-M5 are perf. 11½.

OFFICIAL STAMPS

Catalogue values for unused stamps in this section are for Never Hinged items.

O1

Perf. 10 to 12 and Compound

1948		Typo.	Unwmk.	
O1	O1	10pa rose brown	.50	.25
O2	O1	1k gray green	.50	.25
O3	O1	2k rose violet	.50	.25
O4	O1	3k orange	.50	.25
O5	O1	5k blue	25.00	.90
O6	O1	10k brown org	7.50	.25
O7	O1	15k violet	2.50	.25
O8	O1	20k dk blue	3.00	.25
O9	O1	30k olive bister	5.00	.80
O10	O1	50k black	5.00	.80
O11	O1	1 l bluish grn	5.00	.80
O12	O1	2 l lilac rose	10.00	1.00
		Nos. O1-O12 (12)	65.00	6.05

Regular Issue of 1948
Overprinted Type "a" in
Black

1951

O13	A178	5k blue	.25	.25
O14	A178	10k chocolate	.30	.25
O15	A178	20k deep blue	.60	.25
O16	A178	30k brown	.90	.25
		Nos. O13-O16 (4)	2.05	1.00

Overprint "a" is 15½mm wide. Points of crescent do not touch star. The 0.25k (No. 963) exists with overprint "a" but its status is questionable.

b	c

Overprinted Type "b" in Dark Brown

1953

O17	A178	0.25k dk red	.25	.25
O18	A178	5k blue	.30	.25
O19	A178	10k chocolate	.40	.25
O20	A178	15k violet	1.00	.25
O21	A178	20k deep blue	6.00	1.00
O22	A178	30k brown	1.25	.30
O23	A178	60k black	1.25	.25
		Nos. O17-O23 (7)	10.60	2.55

Overprint "b" is 14mm wide. Lettering thin with sharp, clean corners.

Overprinted Type "c" in Black or Green Black

1953-54

O23A	A178	0.25k dk red (G Bk)		
		('53)	.25	.25
f.		Black overprint	4.00	4.00
g.		Violet overprint ('53)	4.00	4.00
O23B	A178	10k chocolate	12.50	.65
O23C	A178	15k violet	15.00	1.00
O23D	A178	30k brown	6.50	.65
O23E	A178	60k black	8.00	1.00
		Nos. O23A-O23E (5)	42.25	3.55

Lettering of type "c" heavy with rounded corners.

Small Star — d	Large Star — e

Overprinted or Surcharged Type "d" in Black

1955

O24	A178	0.25k dark red	.30	.25
O25	A178	1k olive black	.30	.25
O26	A178	2k brt rose lil	.30	.25
O27	A178	3k red orange	.40	.25
O28	A178	4k dk green	.50	.25
O29	A178	5k on 15k vio	.50	.25
O31	A178	10k on 15k vio	.60	.25
O32	A178	15k violet	.60	.25
O33	A178	20k deep blue	.70	.25
O35	A178	40k on 1 l ol grn	.80	.35
O36	A179	75k on 2 l dk brn	1.10	.80
O37	A179	75k on 5 l dp plum	8.00	8.00
		Nos. O24-O37 (12)	14.10	11.40

Type "d" measures 15x16mm. Overprint on Nos. O35-O37 measures 19x22mm. Nos. O29, O31, O35-O37 have two bars and new value added.

Overprinted or Surcharged Type "e" in Black

1955

O25a	A178	1k olive black	.40	.25
O29a	A178	5k on 15k violet	1.10	.25
O30	A178	5k blue	1.50	.25
O31a	A178	10k on 15k violet	2.50	1.00
c.		"10" without serif	.50	.30
O33a	A178	20k deep blue	.80	.30
O34	A178	30k brown	.50	.25

Heavy crescent — f	Thin crescent — g

Overprinted or Surcharged Type "f" in Black

1957

O24b	A178	0.25k dark red	.50	.25
O25b	A178	1k olive black	.40	.30
O31b	A178	10k on 15k violet	.80	.30
O35b	A179	75k on 1 l olive grn	1.50	.50
O38b	A178	½k on 1k ol blk	.40	.25
		Nos. O24b-O38b (5)	3.60	1.60

Type "f" crescent is larger and does not touch wavy line. The surcharged "10" on No. O31b exists only without serifs. The overprint on O35b measures 17x22½mm.

Overprinted or Surcharged Type "g" in Black

1957

O38	A178	½k on 1k ol blk	.40	.30
O39	A178	1k ol blk	.40	.30
O40	A178	2k on 4k dk grn	.40	.30
O41	A178	3k on 4k dk grn	.40	.30
O42	A178	10k on 12k dp red	.40	.30
		Nos. O38-O42 (5)	2.00	1.50

The shape of crescent and star on type "g" varies on each value. Overprint measures 14x18mm. The surcharged stamps have two bars and new value added.

O2	O3

1957		Litho.	Perf. 10½	
O43	O2	5k blue	.25	.25
O44	O2	10k orange brn	.25	.25
O45	O2	15k lt violet	.25	.25
O46	O2	20k red	.25	.25
O47	O2	30k gray olive	.25	.25
O48	O2	40k brown vio	.25	.25
O49	O2	50k grnsh blk	.25	.25
O50	O2	60k lt yel grn	.30	.25
O51	O2	75k yellow org	.50	.25
O52	O2	100k green	.75	.25
O53	O2	200k deep rose	1.25	.50
		Nos. O43-O53 (11)	4.55	3.00

1959		Unwmk.	Perf. 10	
O54	O2	5k rose	.25	.25
O55	O2	10k ol grn	.25	.25
O56	O2	15k car rose	.25	.25
O57	O2	20k lilac	.25	.25
O58	O2	40k blue	.25	.25
O59	O2	60k orange	.25	.25
O60	O2	75k gray	.50	.25
O61	O2	100k violet	.65	.25
O62	O2	200k red brn	1.10	.65
		Nos. O54-O62 (9)	3.75	2.65

1960		Litho.	Perf. 10½	
O63	O3	1k orange	.25	.25
O64	O3	5k vermilion	.25	.25
O65	O3	10k gray grn	.35	.25
O67	O3	30k red brn	.25	.25
O70	O3	60k green	.25	.25
O71	O3	1 l rose lilac	.30	.25
O72	O3	1 ½ l brt ultra	.95	.25
O74	O3	2 ½ l violet	1.50	.35
O75	O3	5 l blue	3.50	.85
		Nos. O63-O75 (9)	7.60	2.95

For surcharge see No. O83.

O4

1962		Typo.	Perf. 13	
O76	O4	1k olive bister	.30	.25
O77	O4	5k brt green	.30	.25
O78	O4	10k red brown	.30	.25
O79	O4	15k dk blue	.30	.25
O80	O4	25k carmine	.30	.25
O81	O4	30k ultra	.30	.25
		Nos. O76-O81 (6)	1.80	1.50

For surcharge see No. O82.

Nos. O81 and O70 Surcharged

1963

O82	O4	50k on 30k ultra	.35	.25

Perf. 10½
Litho.

O83	O3	100k on 60k green	.50	.25

O5	O6

1963		Litho.	Perf. 12½	
O84	O5	1k gray	.50	.25
O85	O5	5k salmon	.50	.25
O86	O5	10k green	.50	.25
O87	O5	50k car rose	.50	.25
O88	O5	100k ultra	1.00	.50
		Nos. O84-O88 (5)	3.00	1.50

For surcharge see No. O139.

1964		Unwmk.	Perf. 12½	
O89	O6	1k gray	.25	.25
O90	O6	5k blue	.25	.25
O91	O6	10k yellow	.25	.25
O92	O6	30k red	.40	.25
O93	O6	50k lt green	.50	.25
O94	O6	60k brown	1.50	.25
O95	O6	80k pale grnsh bl	3.50	.40

O96	O6	130k indigo	3.00	.60
O97	O6	200k lilac	7.50	.80
		Nos. O89-O97 (9)	17.15	3.30

For surcharge see No. O140.

O7

1965		Litho.	Perf. 13	
O98	O7	1k emerald	.25	.25
O99	O7	10k ultra	.25	.25
O100	O7	50k orange	.35	.25
		Nos. O98-O100 (3)	.85	.75

For surcharge see No. O141.

Carpet Designs O8	Seljuk Tile, 13th Century O9

1k, Usak. 50k, Bergama. 100k, Ladik. 150k, Seljuk. 200k, Nomad. 500k, Anatolia.

1966		Litho.	Perf. 13	
O101	O8	1k orange	.25	.25
O102	O8	50k green	.25	.25
O103	O8	100k brt pink	.30	.25
O104	O8	150k violet blue	.65	.25
O105	O8	200k olive bister	.80	.25
O106	O8	500k lilac	3.00	.40
		Nos. O101-O106 (6)	5.25	1.65

For surcharge see No. O142.

1967		Litho.	Perf. 11½x12	
O107	O9	1k dk bl & lt bl	.30	.25
O108	O9	50k org & dk bl	.30	.25
O109	O9	100k lil & dk bl	.30	.25
		Nos. O107-O109 (3)	.90	.75

For surcharge see No. O143.

Leaf Design — O10

1968		Litho.	Perf. 13	
O110	O10	50k brn & lt grn	.25	.25
O111	O10	150k blk & dl yel	.50	.25
O112	O10	500k red brn & lt bl	1.60	.25
		Nos. O110-O112 (3)	2.35	.75

O11	O12

1969, Aug. 25		Litho.	Perf. 13	
O113	O11	1k lt grn & red	.25	.25
O114	O11	10k lt grn & bl	.25	.25
O115	O11	50k lt grn & brn	.25	.25
O116	O11	100k lt grn & red vio	.40	.25
		Nos. O113-O116 (4)	1.15	1.00

1971, Mar. 1		Litho.	Perf. 11½x12	
O117	O12	5k brown & blue	.25	.25
O118	O12	10k vio bl & ver	.25	.25
O119	O12	30k org & vio bl	.25	.25
O120	O12	50k Prus bl & sepia	.35	.25
O121	O12	75k yellow & green	.60	.25
		Nos. O117-O121 (5)	1.70	1.25

O13

1971, Nov. 15   Litho.   *Perf. 11½x12*

O122	O13	5k lt bl & gray	.25	.25
O123	O13	25k cit & lt brn	.25	.25
O124	O13	100k org & olive	.25	.25
O125	O13	200k dk brn & bis	.40	.25
O126	O13	250k rose lil & vio	.60	.25
O127	O13	500k dk bl & brt bl	.95	.45
		Nos. O122-O127 (6)	2.70	1.70

O14   O15

1972, Apr. 7   Litho.   *Perf. 13*

O128	O14	5k buff & blue	.25	.25
O129	O14	100k buff & olive	.25	.25
O130	O14	200k buff & carmine	.55	.25
		Nos. O128-O130 (3)	1.05	.75

1973, Sept. 20   Litho.   *Perf. 13*

O131	O15	100k violet & buff	.65	.25

O16

1974, June 17   Litho.   *Perf. 13½x13*

O132	O16	10k sal pink & brn	.25	.25
O133	O16	25k blue & dk brn	.25	.25
O134	O16	50k brt pink & brn	.25	.25
O135	O16	150k lt grn & brn	.40	.25
O136	O16	250k rose & brn	.65	.25
O137	O16	500k yellow & brn	1.25	.25
		Nos. O132-O137 (6)	3.05	1.50

O17

1975, Nov. 5   Litho.   *Perf. 12½x13*

O138	O17	100k lt blue & maroon	.25	.25

Nos. O84, O89, O98, O101, O107
Surcharged in Red or Black
Perf. 12½, 13, 11½x12

1977, Aug. 17   Litho.

O139	O5	5k on 1k gray	.25	.25
O140	O6	5k on 1k gray	.25	.25
O141	O7	5k on 1k emer	.25	.25
O142	O8	5k on 1k org (B)	.25	.25
O143	O9	5k on 1k dk & lt bl	.25	.25
		Nos. O139-O143 (5)	1.25	1.25

O18   O19

1977, Dec. 29   Litho.   *Perf. 13½x13*

O144	O18	250k lt bl & grn	.35	.25

1978   Photo.   *Perf. 13½*

O145	O19	50k pink & rose	.25	.25
O146	O19	2½ l buff & grnsh blk	.25	.25
O147	O19	4½ l lil rose & sl grn	.40	.25
O148	O19	5 l lt blue & pur	.40	.25
O149	O19	10 l lt grn & grn	.85	.25
O150	O19	25 l yellow & red	2.25	.25
		Nos. O145-O150 (6)	4.40	1.50

O20   O21

1979   Litho.   *Perf. 13½*

O151	O20	50k dp org & brn	.25	.25
O152	O20	2½ l bl & dk bl	.25	.25

1979, Dec. 20   Litho.   *Perf. 13½*

O153	O21	50k sal & dk bl	.25	.25
O154	O21	1 l lt grn & red	.25	.25
O155	O21	2½ l lil rose & red	.30	.25
O156	O21	5 l lt bl & mag	.30	.25
O157	O21	7½ l lt lil & dk bl	.30	.25
O158	O21	10 l yel & dk bl	.40	.25
O159	O21	35 l gray & rose ('81)	1.25	.25
O160	O21	50 l pnksh & dk bl ('81)	1.50	.25
		Nos. O153-O160 (8)	4.55	2.00

O22

1981, Oct. 23   Litho.   *Perf. 13½*

O161	O22	5 l yel & red	2.00	.25
O162	O22	10 l salmon & red	2.50	.25
O163	O22	35 l gray & rose	3.00	.25
O164	O22	50 l pink & dk bl	3.50	.25
O165	O22	75 l pale grn & grn	6.00	.25
O166	O22	100 l lt bl & dk bl	8.00	.45
		Nos. O161-O166 (6)	25.00	1.70

O23   O24

1983-84   Litho.   *Perf. 12½x13*
Background Color

O167	O23	5 l yellow	1.00	.25
O168	O23	15 l yellow bister	1.25	.25
O169	O23	20 l gray ('84)	.50	.25
O170	O23	50 l sky blue	3.00	.25
O171	O23	65 l pink	3.75	.25
O172	O23	70 l pale rose ('84)	.75	.25
O173	O23	90 l bister brn	5.50	.25
O174	O23	90 l bl gray ('84)	1.10	.25
O175	O23	100 l lt green ('84)	1.75	.25
O176	O23	125 l lt green	6.00	.50
O177	O23	230 l pale salmon ('84)	3.00	.40
		Nos. O167-O177 (11)	27.60	3.15

For surcharges see Nos. O184, O186-O190.

1986-87

O178	O24	5 l yel & vio	.40	.25
O179	O24	10 l org & vio	.40	.25
O180	O24	20 l gray & vio	.40	.25
O180A	O24	50 l pale blue & dp ultra ('87)		
O181	O24	100 l lt yel grn & vio	2.00	.25
O182	O24	300 l pale vio & vio blue ('87)	2.50	.25
		Nos. O178-O182 (6)	6.20	1.50

For surcharges see Nos. O183, O185.

Nos. O179, O168, O180, O172, O173,
O177 Surcharged in Dark Orange

1989

O183	O24	500 l on 10 l	2.00	.25
O184	O23	500 l on 15 l	2.00	.25
O185	O24	500 l on 20 l	2.00	.25
O186	O23	1000 l on 70 l	3.00	.25
O187	O23	1000 l on 90 l	3.00	.25
O188	O23	1250 l on 230 l	4.00	.50
		Nos. O183-O188 (6)	16.00	1.75

Issued: #O183, O185-O188, 8/9; #O184, 6/7.

Nos. O171, O173 &
O174 Surcharged in
Black

1991, Mar. 27

O189	O23	100 l on 65 l	.40	.25
O189A	O23	250 l on 90l (#O173)	—	
O190	O23	250 l on 90 l(#O174)	.80	.25

O25   O26

Perf. 11½x12½

1992, Mar. 24   Litho.

O191	O25	3000 l lt brn & dk brn	2.00	.30
O192	O25	5000 l lt grn & dk grn	6.00	.50

1992, Dec. 2   Litho.   *Perf. 12½x13*

O193	O26	1000 l bl grn & vio	.50	.25
O194	O26	10,000 l vio bl & bl grn	4.50	.50

O27

1993, Sept. 27   Litho.   *Perf. 12½x13*

O195	O27	1000 l brown & green	1.00	.25
O196	O27	1500 l brown & green	1.50	.25
O197	O27	5000 l green & claret	4.00	.40
		Nos. O195-O197 (3)	6.50	.90

O28   O29

1994, May 9   Litho.   *Perf. 11½x12*

O198	O28	2500 l pink & violet	1.00	.25
O199	O28	25,000 l yel & brn	2.75	.50

1995, Jan. 25

O200	O29	3500 l violet & lt vio	1.00	.25
O201	O29	17,500 l bl grn & lt grn	4.00	.45

O30   O31

1995, May 17

O202	O30	50,000 l ol & apple grn	3.25	1.60

1995, Nov. 8   Litho.   *Perf. 12½x13*

O203	O31	5000 l salmon & org	.75	.25

O32   O32a

O32b   O32c

1996, July 10   Litho.   *Perf. 11½x12¼*

O204	O32	15,000 l bl & red	1.00	.25
O205	O32a	20,000 l grn & pur	1.50	.25
O206	O32b	50,000 l pur & grn	2.00	.40
O207	O32c	100,000 l red & bl	3.00	.75
		Nos. O204-O207 (4)	7.50	1.65

O33

1997, Feb. 5   Litho.   *Perf. 12½x13*

O208	O33	25,000 l red & blue	.55	.30

O34   O35

1997, Aug. 4   Litho.   *Perf. 12½x13*

O209	O34	40,000 l multicolored	.55	.30
O210	O35	250,000 l multicolored	3.50	1.75

O36   O37

O38   O39

1998, June 10   Litho.   *Perf. 12½x13*

O211	O36	40,000 l dk bl & lt bl	.40	.25
O212	O37	100,000 l purple	1.00	.50
O213	O38	200,000 l brn & pale bl grn	1.90	1.00
O214	O39	500,000 l brn & pale bl grn	4.75	2.50
		Nos. O211-O214 (4)	8.05	4.25

O40

1998, July 29   Litho.   *Perf. 12½x13*

O215	O40	75,000 l multicolored	.75	.30

O41   O42

1999   Litho.   *Perf. 11½x12¼*

O216	O41	(R) vio & blue grn	2.50	.45
O217	O42	(RT) black & pink	4.50	.45

O43   O44

O45   O46

2000, Apr. 3   Litho.   Perf. 11½x12¼

O218	O43	50,000 l blue & pink	.40	.25
O219	O44	75,000 l brn & gray	.50	.25
O220	O45	500,000 l red brn & lt bl	3.00	.40
O221	O46	1,250,000 l dk bl & buff	6.00	1.00
		Nos. O218-O221 (4)	9.90	1.90

O46a

O46b

Perf. 11½x12¼
2000, Nov. 20   Litho.

O221A	O46b	R blue & yel grn	—	—
O221B	O46a	RT dk bl & lt bl	—	—

No. O221B sold for 500,000 l on day of issue. No. O221A sold for 300,000 l on day of issue.

O47

Perf. 11½x12¼
2001, Dec. 13   Litho.

O222	O47	R blue & yel org	1.00	.25

Sold for 300,000 l on day of issue.

O48   O49

O50   O51

O52

Perf. 11½x12¼
2002, Dec. 10   Litho.

O223	O48	50,000 l multi	.25	.25
O224	O49	100,000 l multi	.25	.25
O225	O50	250,000 l multi	.50	.30
O226	O51	500,000 l multi	1.00	.60
O227	O52	1,500,000 l multi	3.75	1.75
		Nos. O223-O227 (5)	5.75	3.15

O53   O54

O55   O56

Perf. 11½x12¼
2003, Aug. 18   Litho.

O228	O53	500,000 l bl & red	1.00	.70
O229	O54	750,000 l bl & yel	1.50	.80
O230	O55	1,000,000 l bl & grn	1.50	1.00
O231	O56	3,000,000 l bl & yel	5.00	2.10
		Nos. O228-O231 (4)	9.00	4.60

O57

2003, Oct. 13   Litho.   Perf. 11½x12¼

O232	O57	R pink & purple	1.25	.85

Sold for 600,000 l on day of issue.

Buildings
O58

Designs: 100,000 l, Hamidiye Etfal Children's Sanitorium. 500,000 l, Heating Plant, Silahtaraga. 600,000 l, PTT Headquarters, Ankara, vert. 1,000,000 l, Finance Ministry building, Ankara, vert. 3,500,000 l, Old Post and Telegraph Ministry building, Istanbul.

2004, Oct. 15   Perf. 13¼x13, 13x13¼

O233	O58	100,000 l multi	.25	.25
O234	O58	500,000 l multi	.75	.50
O235	O58	600,000 l multi	.80	.60
O236	O58	1,000,000 l multi	1.50	1.00
O237	O58	3,500,000 l multi	5.50	2.00
		Nos. O233-O237 (5)	8.80	4.35

Building Type of 2004

Design: 60k, Prime Minister's Building, Ankara.

2005, Jan. 1   Litho.   Perf. 14

O238	O58	60k multi	.90	.90

Buildings
O59

Designs: 10k, Museum of the Republic, Ankara. 25k, Culture and Tourism Ministry, Ankara. 50k, State Guest House, Ankara. 60k, Sculpture Museum, Ankara. 1 l, Ethnographic Museum, Ankara. 3.50 l, National Library, Ankara.

2005, July 4   Litho.   Perf. 13¼x13
Frame Color

O239	O59	10k orange	.25	.25
O240	O59	25k orange	.35	.35
O241	O59	50k yel green	.75	.75
O242	O59	60k blue	.90	.90
O243	O59	1 l yellow	1.50	1.50
O244	O59	3.50 l dull org	5.25	5.25
		Nos. O239-O244 (6)	9.00	9.00

Kemal
Ataturk — O60

Various portraits.

2006, Apr. 21   Litho.   Perf. 13x13¼
Background Color

O245	O60	10k blue	.25	.25
O246	O60	50k brown	.75	.75
O247	O60	60k dark red	.95	.95
O248	O60	1 l blue green	1.50	1.50
O249	O60	3.50 l red	5.50	5.50
		Nos. O245-O249 (5)	8.95	8.95

Kemal
Ataturk — O61

Various portraits.

Perf. 13x13½
2007, Feb. 26   Wmk. 405

O250	O61	10k multi	.25	.25
O251	O61	50k multi	.70	.70
O252	O61	60k multi	.85	.85
O253	O61	1 l multi	1.40	1.40
O254	O61	4 l multi	5.75	5.75
		Nos. O250-O254 (5)	8.95	8.95

Kemal
Ataturk — O62

2007, Dec. 4   Wmk. 405

O255	O62	65k multi	1.10	1.10

Kemal Ataturk
O63   O64

Perf. 13x13¼
2008, Feb. 29   Wmk. 405

O256	O63	5k multi	.25	.25
O257	O64	65k multi	1.10	1.10
O258	O64	85k multi	1.40	1.40
O259	O64	1 l multi	1.75	1.75
O260	O64	3.35 l multi	5.50	5.50
O261	O64	4.50 l multi	7.50	7.50
		Nos. O256-O261 (6)	17.50	17.50

O65

O66

Kemal Ataturk
O67   O68

Perf. 13x13¼, 13¼x13
2008, Dec. 4   Wmk. 405

O262	O65	5k multi	.25	.25
O263	O66	50k multi	.65	.65
O264	O67	65k multi	.85	.85
O265	O68	1 l multi	1.25	1.25
		Nos. O262-O265 (4)	3.00	3.00

Flowers
O69

Designs: 5k, Nergis (daffodils). 10k, Nilüfer (water lily). 25k, Papatya (daisies). 50k, Cigdem (crocuses). 65k, Zambak (lilies). 75k, Yildiz (dahlia). 1 l, Kardelen (snowdrops). 3.35 l, Menekse (violet). 4.50 l, Ortanca (hydrangea). 5 l, Sardunya (geraniums).

2009   Wmk. 405   Perf. 13¾

O266	O69	5k multi	.25	.25
O267	O69	10k multi	.25	.25
O268	O69	25k multi	.35	.35
O269	O69	50k multi	.65	.65
O270	O69	65k multi	.85	.85
O271	O69	75k multi	1.10	1.10
O272	O69	1 l multi	1.25	1.25
O273	O69	3.35 l multi	4.25	4.25
O274	O69	4.50 l multi	5.75	5.75
O275	O69	5 l multi	7.00	7.00
		Nos. O266-O275 (10)	21.70	21.70

Issued: 75k, 5 l, 7/16; others, 3/26.

Flowers — O70

Designs: 5k, Ayçiçegi (sunflowers). 10k, Gelincik (poppies). 25k, Carkifelek (passion flower). 80k, Zinya (zinnia). 1 l Gül (rose).

Perf. 13x13¼
2010, Aug. 26   Wmk. 405

O276	O70	5k multi	.25	.25
O277	O70	10k multi	.25	.25
O278	O70	25k multi	.35	.35
O279	O70	80k multi	1.10	1.10
O280	O70	1 l multi	1.40	1.40
		Nos. O276-O280 (5)	3.35	3.35

Stylized
Flowers — O71

Various stylized flowers.

2010, Dec. 10   Wmk. 405

O281	O71	5k multi	.25	.25
O282	O71	50k multi	.70	.70
O283	O71	80k multi	1.10	1.10
O284	O71	90k multi	1.25	1.25
O285	O71	1 l multi	1.40	1.40
		Nos. O281-O285 (5)	4.70	4.70

Stylized Flowers Type of 2010

Various stylized flowers.

Perf. 13½ Syncopated
2011, Apr. 18   Wmk. 405
Inscribed "2011"

O286	O71	10k multi	.25	.25
O287	O71	1 l multi	1.40	1.40
O288	O71	2.80 l multi	3.75	3.75
O289	O71	6 l multi	7.75	7.75
		Nos. O286-O289 (4)	13.15	13.15

Abstract Art — O72

Various abstract designs.

Perf. 13x13¼

2011, Dec. 19 **Wmk. 405**
O290 O72 10k multi .25 .25
O291 O72 1 l multi 1.10 1.10
O292 O72 2 l multi 2.25 2.25
O293 O72 7 l multi 7.50 7.50
Nos. O290-O293 (4) 11.10 11.10

NEWSPAPER STAMPS

N1

Black Overprint
1879 Unwmk. Perf. 11½ and 13½
P1 N1 10pa blk & rose
lilac 225.00 225.00

Other stamps found with this "IMPRIMES" overprint were prepared on private order and have no official status as newspaper stamps. Counterfeits exist of No. P1.

The 10pa surcharge, on half of 20pa rose and pale rose was made privately. See note after No. 77.

Regular Issue of 1890 Handstamped in Black

Nos. P10-P29 were overprinted with a single wooden handstamp. Variations in size are due to inking and pressure.

The handstamps on Nos. P10-P29 are found double, inverted and sideways. Counterfeit overprints comprise most of the examples offered for sale in the marketplace.

1891 **Perf. 13½, 11½**
P10 A7 10pa grn & gray 40.00 12.50
a. Imperf. 22.50 12.50
P11 A7 20pa rose & gray 75.00 15.00
P12 A7 1pi blue & gray 210.00 150.00
P13 A7 2pi yel & gray 525.00 400.00
P14 A7 5pi buff & gray 1,050. 750.00
Nos. P10-P14 (5) 1,900. 1,327.

Blue Handstamp
P10b A7 10pa green & gray 210.00 125.00
P11a A7 20pa rose & gray 340.00 250.00
P12a A7 1pi blue & gray 425.00 375.00
Nos. P10b-P12a (3) 975.00 750.00

This overprint in red and on 2pi and 5pi in blue is considered bogus.

Same Handstamp on Regular Issue of 1892

1892 **Perf. 13½**
P25 A10 10pa gray green 500.00 100.00
P26 A11 20pa rose 1,250. 375.00
P27 A12 1pi pale blue 110.00 150.00
P28 A13 2pi brown org 200.00 175.00
P29 A14 5pi pale violet 1,800. 1,250.
a. On No. 99a 500.00
Nos. P25-P29 (5) 3,860. 2,050.

Regular Issues of 1892-98 Overprinted in Black

1893-98
P30 A10 10pa gray grn 3.75 2.50
P31 A11 20pa vio brn ('98) 3.00 1.50
a. 20pa dark pink 2.50 1.25
b. 20pa pink 325.00 22.50
P32 A12 1pi pale blue 3.00 1.50
P33 A13 2pi brown org 27.50 12.50
a. Tete beche pair 22.50
P34 A14 5pi pale violet 85.00 75.00
a. On No. 99a 140.00 65.00
Nos. P30-P34 (5) 122.25 93.00

For surcharge and overprints see Nos. B41, P134-P136, P153-P154.

No. 95 Surcharged

1897
P36 A10 5pa on 10pa gray grn 5.00 3.00
a. "Cniq" instead of "Cinq" 15.00 15.00

For overprint see No. P137.

Nos. 102-107 Overprinted in Black

1901 **Perf. 12, 13½ and Compound**
P37 A16 5pa bister 1.75 1.00
a. Inverted overprint
P38 A16 10pa yellow grn 6.25 6.25
P39 A16 20pa magenta 32.50 7.50
P40 A16 1pi violet blue 60.00 22.50
P41 A16 2pi gray blue 125.00 37.50
P42 A16 5pi ocher 300.00 90.00
Nos. P37-P42 (6) 525.50 164.75

For overprints see Nos. B37, P69-P74, P123, P138-P141, P155-P158.

Same Overprint on Nos. 110-115

1901
P43 A17 5pa purple 8.75 2.00
P44 A17 10pa green 32.50 2.50
P45 A17 20pa magenta 8.75 1.50
a. Overprinted on back
P46 A17 1pi blue 25.00 2.00
P47 A17 2pi orange 87.50 4.00
a. Inverted overprint
P48 A17 5pi lilac rose 160.00 27.50
Nos. P43-P48 (6) 322.50 39.50

For overprints see Nos. P75-P80, P124-P126, P142-P146, P159-P164.

Same Overprint on Regular Issue of 1905

1905
P49 A18 5pa ocher 2.50 1.00
P50 A18 10pa dull green 30.00 1.50
P51 A18 20pa carmine 2.50 1.25
P52 A18 1pi pale blue 2.50 1.25
P53 A18 2pi slate 70.00 10.00
P54 A18 5pi brown 175.00 20.00
Nos. P49-P54 (6) 282.50 35.00

For overprints see Nos. P127-P129, P147-P150, P165-P171.

Regular Issue of 1908 Overprinted in Carmine or Blue

1908
P55 A19 5pa ocher (Bl) 10.00 .50
P56 A19 10pa blue grn (C) 17.50 .50
P57 A19 20pa carmine (Bl) 22.50 1.00
P58 A19 1pi brt blue (C) 100.00 2.50
P59 A19 2pi blue blk (C) 150.00 7.50
P60 A19 5pi dk violet (C) 200.00 17.50
Nos. P55-P60 (6) 500.00 29.50

For overprints see Nos. B17, P130-P131, P151, P172.

Same Overprint on Regular Issue of 1909

1909
P61 A21 5pa ocher (Bl) 3.50 1.25
a. Imperf.
P62 A21 10pa blue grn (C) 8.75 1.50
P63 A21 20pa car rose (Bl) 60.00 1.75
a. Imperf.
P64 A21 1pi brt blue (C) 100.00 5.00
P65 A21 2pi blue blk (C) 250.00 30.00
P66 A21 5pi dk violet (C) 500.00 65.00
Nos. P61-P66 (6) 922.25 104.50

For surcharge and overprints see Nos. B18, P67-P68, P81, P132-P133, P152.

No. 151 Surcharged in Blue

1910 **Perf. 12, 13½ and Compound**
P67 A21 2pa on 5pa ocher .75 .75

1911 **Perf. 12**
P68 A21 2pa olive green 1.00 .50

Newspaper Stamps of 1901-11 Overprinted in Carmine or Blue

The overprint was applied to 13 denominations in four settings with change of city name, producing individual sets for each city: "MONASTIR," "PRISTINA," "SALONIQUE" and "USKUB."

1911, June 26 **Perf. 12, 13½**
P69 A16 5pa bister 20.00 22.50
P70 A16 10pa yellow grn 20.00 22.50
P71 A16 20pa magenta 20.00 22.50
P72 A16 1pi violet blue 20.00 22.50
P73 A16 2pi gray blue 25.00 30.00
P74 A16 5pi ocher 50.00 60.00
P75 A17 5pa purple 10.00 12.50
P76 A17 10pa green 10.00 12.50
P77 A17 20pa carmine 10.00 12.50
P78 A17 1pi blue 10.00 12.50
P79 A17 2pi orange 12.00 15.00
P80 A17 5pi lilac rose 30.00 30.00
P81 A21 2pa olive green 3.00 3.75
Nos. P69-P81 (13) 240.00 278.75

Values for each of the 4 city sets of 13 are the same.
The note after No. 182 will also apply to Nos. P69-P81.

Newspaper Stamps of 1901-11 Overprinted in Carmine or Black

1915
On Stamps of 1893-98
P121 A10 10pa gray green 6.00 .50
a. Inverted overprint 10.00 10.00
P122 A13 2pi yellow brn 1.50 1.00
a. Inverted overprint 10.00 10.00
On Stamps of 1901
P123 A16 10pa yellow grn 1.00 .50
P124 A17 5pa purple 1.00 1.00
P125 A17 20pa carmine 2.00 1.00
P126 A17 5pi lilac rose 20.00 5.00
On Stamps of 1905
P127 A18 5pa ocher 2.00 1.00
a. Inverted overprint 7.50 7.50
P128 A18 2pi slate 17.50 5.00
P129 A18 5pi brown 1.00 .60
On Stamps of 1908
P130 A19 2pi blue blk 1,375. 550.00
P131 A19 5pi dk violet 10.00 1.25

On Stamps of 1909
P132 A21 5pa ocher 1.00 .50
P133 A21 5pi dk violet 100.00 35.00
Nos. P121-P129,P131-P133 (12) 172.00 52.35

Preceding Newspaper Issues with additional Overprint in Red or Black

1916
On Stamps of 1893-98
P134 A10 10pa gray green 2.00 .75
P135 A11 20pa violet brn 1.00 .75
P136 A14 5pi dull violet 50.00 50.00
On Stamp of 1897
P137 A10 5pa on 10pa gray grn .60 .50
On Stamps of 1901
P138 A16 5pa bister .50 .30
P139 A16 10pa yellow grn .90 .90
P140 A16 20pa magenta 1.00 .90
a. Inverted overprint 10.00 10.00
P141 A16 1pi violet blue 1.00 1.00
P142 A17 5pa purple 50.00 50.00
P143 A17 10pa green 50.00 50.00
P144 A17 20pa carmine 1.50 .90
P145 A17 1pi blue 1.50 .90
P146 A17 2pi orange 1.50 .90
On Stamps of 1905
P147 A18 5pa ocher 1.00 .75
P148 A18 10pa dull green 50.00 50.00
P149 A18 20pa carmine 50.00 50.00
P150 A18 1pi pale blue 1.75 1.00
On Stamp of 1908
P151 A19 5pa ocher 62.50 62.50
On Stamp of 1909
P152 A21 5pa ocher 62.50 62.50
Nos. P134-P152 (19) 389.25 384.55

Preceding Newspaper Issues with additional Overprint in Red or Black

1917
On Stamps of 1893-98
P153 A12 1pi gray (R) 2.50 2.00
P154 A11 20pa vio brn (R) 3.75 3.75
On Stamps of 1901
P155 A16 5pa bister (Bk) 1.50 1.25
a. Inverted overprint 20.00 20.00
P156 A16 10pa yellow grn (R) 1.50 1.25
P157 A16 20pa magenta (Bk) 1.50 1.25
P158 A16 2pi gray blue (R) 40.00 30.00
P159 A17 5pa purple (Bk) 2.25 2.25
a. Inverted overprint 20.00 20.00
b. Double overprint 20.00 20.00
c. Double ovpt., one inverted 25.00 25.00
P160 A17 10pa green (R) 22.50 35.00
P161 A17 20pa carmine (Bk) 1.50 1.25
P162 A17 1pi blue (R) 3.00 3.00
P163 A17 2pi orange (Bk) 2.50 2.50
P164 A17 5pi lilac rose (R) 32.50 50.00
On Stamps of 1905
P165 A18 5pa ocher (R) 2.50 2.00
a. Inverted overprint 10.00 10.00
P166 A18 5pa ocher (Bk) 3.00 2.50
a. Inverted overprint 10.00 10.00
P167 A18 10pa dull green (R) 2.50 2.00
P168 A18 20pa carmine (Bk) 2.50 2.00
a. Double overprint 15.00 15.00
P169 A18 1pi blue (R) 2.50 2.00
a. Inverted overprint 25.00 25.00
P170 A18 2pi slate (R) 32.50 50.00
P171 A18 5pi brown (R) 32.50 50.00
On Stamp of 1908
P172 A19 5pa ocher (R) 32.50 50.00
Nos. P153-P172 (20) 225.50 294.00

Nos. P153-P172 were used as regular postage stamps.

#P173

#P174

1919
Blue Surcharge and Red Overprint

P173	A21	5pa on 2pa ol grn	1.25	1.00
a.		Red overprint double	12.50	5.00
b.		Blue surcharge double	12.50	5.00

1920
Red Surcharge

P174	A25	5pa on 4pa brn	1.25	.50

Catalogue values for unused stamps in this section, from this point to the end of the section, are for Never Hinged items.

Dove and Citadel of Ankara — N6

1952-55		Litho.	Perf. 12½
P175	N6	0.50k grnsh gray	.25	.25
P176	N6	0.50k violet ('53)	.25	.25
		Perf. 10½, 10		
P177	N6	0.50k red org ('54)	.25	.25
P178	N6	0.50k brown ('55)	.25	.25
		Nos. P175-P178 (4)	1.00	1.00

POSTAL TAX STAMPS

Map of Turkey and Red Crescent PT1

1928		Unwmk.	Typo.	Perf. 14
		Crescent in Red		
RA1	PT1	½pi lt brown	.30	.25
RA2	PT1	1pi red violet	.30	.25
RA3	PT1	2½pi orange	.30	.25
		Engr.		
		Various Frames		
RA4	PT1	5pi dk brown	.60	.45
RA5	PT1	10pi yellow green	.75	.55
RA6	PT1	20pi slate	1.25	.60
RA7	PT1	50pi dark violet	3.75	1.40
		Nos. RA1-RA7 (7)	7.25	3.75
		Set, never hinged	13.00	

The use of these stamps on letters, parcels, etc. in addition to the regular postage, was obligatory on certain days in each year.

For surcharges see Nos. RA16, RA21-RA22.

Cherubs Upholding Star — PT2

1932

RA8	PT2	1k ol bis & red	1.00	.30
RA9	PT2	2½k dk brn & red	1.25	.30
RA10	PT2	5k green & red	1.50	.30
RA11	PT2	25k black & red	3.00	1.00
		Nos. RA8-RA11 (4)	6.75	1.90
		Set, never hinged	9.00	

For surcharges and overprints see Nos. RA12-RA15, RA28-RA29, RA36-RA38.

No. RA8 Surcharged

20 para

RA12	PT2	20pa on 1k	1.00	.50
RA13	PT2	3k on 1k	1.75	.70
a.		3 "kruus"	2.50	2.50

By a law of Parliament the use of these stamps on letters and telegraph forms, in addition to the regular fees, was obligatory from Apr. 20-30 of each year. The inscription in the tablet at the bottom of the design states that the money derived from the sale of the stamps is devoted to child welfare work.

No. RA8 Surcharged

20 para

1933

RA14	PT2	20pa on 1k ol bis & red	1.00	.50
RA15	PT2	3k on 1k ol bis & red	1.75	1.00

No. RA5 Surcharged

5 Beş Kuruş

RA16	PT1	5k on 10pi yel grn & red	1.50	.75
		Nos. RA14-RA16 (3)	4.25	2.25

PT3

PT4

1933			Perf. 11, 11½
RA17	PT3	20pa gray vio & red	1.00	.50
RA18	PT4	1k violet & red	1.00	.50
RA19	PT4	5k dk brown & red	2.50	.50
RA20	PT3	15k green & red	3.50	.50
		Nos. RA17-RA20 (4)	8.00	2.00
		Set, never hinged	12.00	

Nos. RA17 and RA20 were issued in Ankara; Nos. RA18 and RA19 in Izmir. For overprint see No. RA27.

Nos. RA3, RA1 Surcharged in Black

5 Beş kuruş

1933-34				
RA21	PT1	1k on 2½pi orange	.50	.30
RA22	PT1	5k on ½pi lt brown	1.50	.50

Map of Turkey PT5

1934-35		Crescent in Red	Perf. 12
RA23	PT5	½k blue ('35)	.25	.25
RA24	PT5	1k red brown	.25	.25
RA25	PT5	2½k brown ('35)	.50	.25
RA26	PT5	5k blue green ('35)	1.25	.25
		Nos. RA23-RA26 (4)	2.25	1.00
		Set, never hinged	5.00	

Frame differs on No. RA26.
See Nos. RA30-RA35B. For surcharge see No. RA63.

Nos. RA17, RA8-RA9 Overprinted "P.Y.S." in Roman Capitals

1936			Perf. 11, 14
RA27	PT3	20pa gray vio & red	.40	.25
RA28	PT2	1k ol bis & red	.40	.25
RA29	PT2	3k on 2½k dk brn & red	.75	.30
		Nos. RA27-RA29 (3)	1.55	
		Set, never hinged	12.00	

Type of 1934-35, Inscribed "Türkiye Kizilay Cemiyeti"

1938-46			Perf. 8½-11½

Type I — Imprint, "Devlet Basimevi". Crescent red.
Type II — Imprint, "Alaeddin Kiral Basimevi". Crescent carmine.
Type III — Imprint, "Damga Matbaasi". Crescent red.

Crescent in Red or Carmine

RA30	PT5	½k blue (I)	.50	.25
a.		Type II	4.00	1.00
b.		Type III	.50	.25
RA31	PT5	1k red vio (I)	.40	.25
a.		Type II	6.50	2.00
b.		Type III	.50	.25
RA32	PT5	2½k orange (I)	.30	.25
a.		Type III	2.00	1.00
RA33	PT5	5k blue grn (I)	.50	.25
RA33A	PT5	5k choc (III) ('42)	1.00	.25
RA34	PT5	10k pale grn (I)	1.50	.30
a.		Type III	2.00	1.00
RA35	PT5	20k black (I)	1.00	.25
RA35A	PT5	50k pur (III) ('46)	7.50	1.00
RA35B	PT5	1 l blue (III) ('44)	30.00	2.50
		Nos. RA30-RA35B (9)	44.20	6.05
		Set, never hinged	75.00	

No. RA9 Surcharged in Black

20 Para P.Y.S.

1938			Perf. 14
RA36	PT2	20pa on 2½k	1.00	.50
RA37	PT2	1k on 2½k	1.00	.50

No. RA9 Surcharged in Black

P.Y.S 20 Para

1938		Unwmk.	Perf. 14
RA37A	PT2	20pa on 2½k	1.25	.60
RA37B	PT2	1k on 2½k	1.50	.75

No. RA9 Surcharged "1 Kurus" in Black

1939			Perf. 14
RA38	PT2	1k on 2½k dk brn & red	.50	.50

Child — PT6

Nurse with Child — PT7

1940		Typo.	Perf. 12
		Star in Carmine		
RA39	PT6	20pa bluish grn	.30	.25
RA40	PT6	1k violet	.30	.25
RA41	PT7	1k lt blue	.30	.25
RA42	PT6	2½k pale red lil	.30	.25
RA43	PT6	3k black	.35	.25
RA44	PT7	5k pale violet	.30	.25
RA45	PT7	10k blue green	1.00	.40
RA46	PT7	15k dark blue	.75	.30
RA47	PT7	25k olive bister	2.50	1.25
RA48	PT7	50k olive gray	6.00	2.50
		Nos. RA39-RA48 (10)	12.10	5.95
		Set, never hinged	30.00	

Soldier and Map of Turkey — PT8

1941-44			Perf. 11½
RA49	PT8	1k purple	.40	.25
RA50	PT8	2k light blue	2.50	.25
RA51	PT8	3k chestnut	2.75	.50
RA51A	PT8	4k mag ('44)	9.50	.35
RA52	PT8	5k brt rose	7.75	2.50
RA53	PT8	10k dk blue	11.00	4.00
		Nos. RA49-RA53 (6)	33.90	7.85
		Set, never hinged	75.00	

The tax was used for national defense.

Baby — PT9

Nurse and Baby — PT13

Nurse and Children PT10

Nurse Feeding Child PT11

Nurse and Child PT12

Nurse and Child — PT14

President Inonu Holding Child — PT15

Children PT16

1942 Unwmk. Typo. *Perf. 11½*
Star in Red

RA54	PT9	20pa brt violet	.40	.25
RA55	PT9	20pa chocolate	.40	.25
RA56	PT10	1k dk slate grn	.40	.25
RA57	PT11	2½k yellow grn	.40	.30
RA58	PT12	3k dark blue	.40	.30
RA59	PT13	5k brt pink	.40	.30
RA60	PT14	10k lt blue	.70	.40
RA61	PT15	15k dk red brn	1.10	.70
RA62	PT16	25k brown	1.75	1.00
		Nos. RA54-RA62 (9)	5.95	3.75

See Nos. RA175, RA179-RA180.

No. RA32 Surcharged with New Value in Brown

1942 *Perf. 10*

RA63	PT5	1k on 2½k org & red (I)	.25	.25

Child Eating — PT17

Nurse and Child — PT18

Nurse and Child PT19

Child and Red Star — PT20

President Inönü and Child — PT21

Inscribed: "Sefcat Pullari 23 Nisan 1943 Cocuk Esirgeme Kurumu."

1943 Star in Red *Perf. 11*

RA64	PT17	50pa lilac	.25	.25
RA65	PT17	50pa gray green	.25	.25
RA66	PT18	1k lt ultra	.25	.25
RA67	PT19	3k dark red	.30	.25
RA68	PT20	15k cream & blk	1.50	.40
RA69	PT21	100k brt violet blue	2.50	1.60
a.		Souvenir sheet, #RA64-RA69, imperf.	5.50	5.50
		Nos. RA64-RA69 (6)	5.05	3.00

Star and Crescent PT23

Hospital PT24

Nurse and Children PT25

Baby PT26

Nurse Bathing Baby — PT27

Nurse Feeding Child — PT28

Baby with Bottle — PT29

Child — PT30

Hospital — PT31

Perf. 10 to 12 and Compound
1943-44
Star in Red

RA71	PT23	20pa deep blue	.40	.30
RA72	PT24	1k gray green	.40	.25
RA73	PT25	3k pale gray brn	.40	.25
RA74	PT26	5k yellow orange	.70	.30
RA75	PT26	5k violet brn	.30	.25
RA76	PT27	10k red	.40	.25
RA77	PT28	15k red violet	.60	.40
RA78	PT29	25k pale violet	.90	.50
RA79	PT30	50k lt blue	2.00	1.00
RA80	PT31	100k lt green	5.00	4.00
		Nos. RA71-RA80 (10)	11.10	7.55
		Set, never hinged	22.00	

For surcharge see No. RA156.

Nurse Holding Baby — PT32

Nurse Feeding Child — PT33

Child — PT34

Star and Crescent PT35

1945-47 Unwmk. Litho. *Perf. 11½*
Star in Red

RA81	PT32	1k lilac brn	.40	.25
a.		1k rose violet	.50	.25

RA82	PT33	5k yellow grn	.70	.25
a.		5k green	.70	.25
RA83	PT34	10k red brown	.50	.25
RA84	PT35	250k gray black	9.50	3.50
RA84A	PT35	500k dull vio ('47)	37.50	12.50
		Nos. RA81-RA84A (5)	48.60	16.75
		Set, never hinged	90.00	

Imprint on No. RA82: "Kagit ve Basim isleri A.S. ist." On No. RA82a: "Guzel Sanatlar Matbaasi — Ankara."

Nurse and Wounded Soldier PT36

President Inönü and Victim of Earthquake PT37

Removing Wounded from Hospital Ship — PT38

Nurse and Soldier — PT39

Feeding the Poor — PT40

Wounded Soldiers on Landing Raft — PT41

Symbolical of Red Crescent Relief — PT42

1945 *Perf. 12x10, 10x12*
Crescent in Red

RA85	PT36	20pa dp bl & brn org	.50	.25
RA86	PT37	1k dp bl & ol bis	.50	.25
RA87	PT38	2½k dp bl & red	1.00	.50
RA88	PT39	5k dp bl & red	2.00	1.00
RA89	PT40	10k dp bl & lt grn	2.00	1.00
RA90	PT41	50k blk & gray grn	4.50	2.00
RA91	PT42	1 l black & yel	15.00	7.50
		Nos. RA85-RA91 (7)	25.50	12.50
		Set, never hinged	45.00	

See Nos. RA181-RA182.

Ankara Sanatorium PT43

1946 *Perf. 12*

RA92	PT43	20k red & lt bl	.65	.30

See No. RA210. For surcharge see No. RA186.

Covering Sleeping Child — PT44

Designs: 1k, Mother and child. 2½k, Nurse at playground. 5k, Doctor examining infant. 15k, Feeding child. 25k, Bathing child. 50k, Weighing baby. 150k, Feeding baby.

1946 Litho. *Perf. 12½*
Inscribed: "25ci Yil Hatirasi 1946"
Star in Carmine

RA93	PT44	20pa brown	.35	.25
RA94	PT44	1k blue	.35	.25
RA95	PT44	2½k carmine	.35	.25
RA96	PT44	5k vio brn	.60	.25
RA97	PT44	15k violet	.90	.50
RA98	PT44	25k gray grn	1.25	.60
RA99	PT44	50k bl grn	1.75	1.50
RA100	PT44	150k gray brn	3.25	1.75
		Nos. RA93-RA100 (8)	8.80	5.35
		Set, never hinged	15.00	

For surcharge see No. RA155.

Hospital Ship — PT52

Ambulance Plane — PT53

Hospital Train — PT54

Ambulance PT55

Boy Scout and Red Crescent Flag — PT56

Stretcher Bearers and Wounded Soldier PT57

Nurse and Hospital — PT58

Sanatorium
PT59

1946 *Perf. 11½*

RA101	PT52	1k multi	1.25	1.25
RA102	PT53	4k multi	1.25	1.25
RA103	PT54	10k multi	3.50	3.50
RA104	PT55	25k multi	4.50	4.50
RA105	PT56	40k multi	8.50	8.50
RA106	PT57	70k multi	6.00	6.00
RA107	PT58	1 l multi	5.50	5.50
RA108	PT59	2½ l multi	12.50	12.50
		Nos. RA101-RA108 (8)	43.00	43.00

For overprints see Nos. RA139-RA146.

Souvenir Sheet

Pres. Inönü and Child — PT60

1946 **Unwmk.** **Typo.** *Imperf.*
Without Gum

RA109	PT60	250k slate blk,		
		pink & red	20.00	17.50

Turkish Society for the Prevention of Cruelty to Children, 25th anniv.

Nurse and
Wounded Soldier
PT61

Pres. Inönü and
Victim of
Earthquake
PT62

Nurse and
Soldier — PT64

Symbolical of
Red Crescent
Relief — PT67

1946-47 **Litho.** *Perf. 11½*
Crescent in Red

RA113	PT61	20pa dk bl vio & ol		
		('47)	.25	.25
RA114	PT62	1k dk brn & yel	.45	.25
RA115	PT64	5k dp bl & red	.45	.25
RA116	PT67	1 l brn blk & yel	1.90	1.25
		Nos. RA113-RA116 (4)	3.05	2.00

PT68

Nurse and
Wounded
Soldier — PT69

Victory and
Soldier — PT70

1947 **Crescent in Red**

RA117	PT68	250k brn blk &		
		grn	5.25	2.00
RA118	PT69	5 l sl gray &		
		org	8.75	3.50

Booklet Pane of One
Perf. 11½ (top) x Imperf.

RA119	PT70	10 l deep blue	22.50	—

Black numerals above No. RA119 indicate position in booklet.

President Inönü
and Victim of
Earthquake
PT71

Nurse and Child
PT72

1947 *Perf. 11½*

RA120	PT71	1k dk brn, pale bl &		
		red	.25	.25
RA121	PT72	2½k bl vio & car	.25	.25

See Nos. RA221-RA223. For surcharge see No. RA154.

Nurse Offering
Encouragement
PT73

Plant with Broken
Stem
PT74

Perf. 8½, 11½x10, 11x10½

1948-49 **Typo.** **Unwmk.**
Crescent in Red

RA122	PT73	½k ultra ('49)	.55	.25
RA123	PT73	1k indigo	.25	.25
RA124	PT73	2k lilac rose	.25	.25
RA125	PT73	2½k org ('49)	.25	.25
RA126	PT73	3k bl grn	.25	.25
RA127	PT73	4k gray ('49)	.35	.25
RA128	PT73	5k blue	.70	.25
RA129	PT73	10k pink	1.25	.25
RA130	PT73	25k chocolate	1.60	.25

Perf. 10

RA130A	PT74	50k ultra & bl		
		gray ('49)	2.25	.75
RA130B	PT74	100k grn & pale		
		grn ('49)	5.25	1.00
		Nos. RA122-RA130B (11)	12.95	4.00
		Set, never hinged	30.00	

For surcharges see Nos. RA151-RA153, RA187.

Nurse and
Children — PT75

Various Scenes with Children.

Inscribed: "1948 Cocuk Yili Hatirasi"

1948 **Litho.** *Perf. 11*
Star in Red

RA131	PT75	20pa dp ultra	.30	.25
RA132	PT75	20pa rose lilac	.30	.25
RA133	PT75	1k dp Prus bl	.50	.30
RA134	PT75	3k dk brn vio	.75	.50
RA135	PT75	15k slate black	1.50	1.25
RA136	PT75	30k orange	3.50	3.50
RA137	PT75	150k yellow grn	4.50	4.00
RA138	PT75	300k brown red	7.00	6.50
		Nos. RA131-RA138 (8)	18.35	16.05
		Set, never hinged	30.00	

No. RA136 is arranged horizontally. For overprints and surcharges see Nos. RA199-RA206.

> **Catalogue values for unused stamps in this section, from this point to the end of the section, are for Never Hinged items.**

Nos. RA101
to RA108
Overprinted in
Carmine

1949 *Perf. 11½*

RA139	PT52	1k multi	10.00	10.00
RA140	PT53	4k multi	10.00	10.00
RA141	PT54	10k multi	10.00	10.00
RA142	PT55	25k multi	10.00	10.00
RA143	PT56	40k multi	20.00	20.00
RA144	PT57	70k multi	10.00	10.00
RA145	PT58	1 l multi	10.00	10.00
RA146	PT59	2½ l multi	10.00	10.00
		Nos. RA139-RA146 (8)	90.00	90.00

Ruins and
Tent — PT76

Booklet Panes of One
1949 *Perf. 10 (top) x Imperf.*

RA149	PT76	5k gray, vio gray &		
		red	3.00	2.00
RA150	PT76	10k red vio, sal &		
		red	3.00	2.00

Black numerals above each stamp indicate its position in the booklet.

No. RA124 Surcharged in Black

1950 **Unwmk.** *Perf. 8½*

RA151	PT73	20pa on 2k	1.25	1.00

Postal Tax Stamps of 1944-48
Surcharged with New Value in Black
or Carmine
Perf. 8½ to 12½ and Compound

1952

RA152	PT73	20pa on 3k bl grn	.50	.25
RA153	PT73	20pa on 4k gray	.75	.25
RA154	PT72	1k on 2½k bl vio		
		& car (C)	1.00	1.50
RA155	PT44	1k on 2½k car	2.00	1.00
RA156	PT25	1k on 3k pale		
		gray brn	2.00	1.00
		Nos. RA152-RA156 (5)	6.25	4.00

"Protection"
PT77

Various Symbolical Designs Inscribed
"75 iNCi" etc.

1952 **Typo.** *Perf. 10*
Crescent in Carmine

RA157	PT77	5k bl grn & bl	2.00	1.50
RA158	PT77	15k yel grn, bl &		
		cr	2.00	1.50
RA159	PT77	30k bl, grn & brn	2.00	1.50
RA160	PT77	1 l blk, bl & cr	2.00	1.50
a.		Souvenir sheet, #RA157-RA160, imperf.	30.00	30.00
		Nos. RA157-RA160 (4)	8.00	6.00

Printed in sheets of 20 containing one horizontal row of each value.

Nurse and
Children
PT78

Design: 1k, Nurse and baby.

1954 **Litho.** *Perf. 10½*
Star in Red

RA161	PT78	20pa aqua	.60	.35
RA162	PT78	20pa yellow	.90	.35
RA163	PT12	1k deep blue	1.50	.80
		Nos. RA161-RA163 (3)	3.00	1.50

Globe and
Flag — PT79

Designs: 5k, Winged nurse in clouds. 10k, Protecting arm of Red Crescent.

1954

RA164	PT79	1k multi	.25	.25
RA165	PT79	5k multi	.50	.25
RA166	PT79	10k car, grn & gray	1.00	.25
		Nos. RA164-RA166 (3)	1.75	.75

See Nos. RA208, RA211-RA213. For surcharges see Nos. RA187A-RA187B.

Florence
Nightingale — PT80

Selimiye
Barracks
PT81

30k, Florence Nightingale, full-face.

1954, Nov. 4
Crescent in Carmine

RA167	PT80	20k gray grn & dk		
		brn	.50	.50
RA168	PT80	30k dl brn & blk	.75	.50
RA169	PT81	50k buff & blk	1.25	.50
		Nos. RA167-RA169 (3)	2.50	1.50

Arrival of Florence Nightingale at Scutari, cent.

Type of 1942 and

Children Kissing — PT82

Nurse Holding Baby — PT83

1955, Apr. 23   **Star in Red**

RA170	PT82	20pa chalky bl	.25	.25
RA171	PT82	20pa org brn	.25	.25
RA172	PT82	1k lilac	.25	.25
RA173	PT82	3k gray bis	.25	.25
RA174	PT82	5k orange	.25	.25
RA175	PT12	10k green	2.50	.75
RA176	PT83	15k dk blue	.25	.25
RA177	PT83	25k brn car	1.50	1.40
RA178	PT83	50k dk gray grn	2.00	1.50
RA179	PT12	2½ l dull brn	375.00	125.00
RA180	PT12	10 l rose lil	875.00	250.00
Nos. RA170-RA180 (11)			1,257.	380.15

Types of 1945
Inscribed: "Turkiye Kizilay Dernegi"

1955   Litho.   Perf. 10½x11½, 10½
Crescent in Red

RA181	PT36	20pa vio brn & lem	.25	.25
RA182	PT41	1k blk & gray grn	.25	.25

Nurse — PT85

Nurses on Parade PT86

Design: 100k, Two nurses under Red Cross and Red Crescent flags and UN emblem.

Perf. 10½

1955, Sept. 5   Unwmk.   Litho.
Crescent and Cross in Red

RA183	PT85	10k blk & pale brn	.75	.35
RA184	PT86	15k dk grn & pale yel grn	.75	.45
RA185	PT85	100k lt ultra	3.50	1.75
Nos. RA183-RA185 (3)			5.00	2.55

Meeting of the board of directors of the Intl. Council of Nurses, Istanbul, Aug. 29-Sept. 5, 1955.

Nos. RA92 and RA130B Surcharged "20 Para"

1955

RA186	PT43	20p on 20k	.50	.40

Typo.

RA187	PT74	20p on 100k (surch. 11½x2mm)	.60	.40
c.		Surcharge 13½x2½mm	1.00	.75

No. RA164 Surcharged with New Value and Two Bars

1956   Litho.   Perf. 10½

RA187A	PT79	20p on 1k multi	.25	.25
RA187B	PT79	2.50k on 1k multi	.25	.25

Woman and Children — PT87

Designs: 10k, 25k, 50k, Flag and building. 250k, 5 l, 10 l, Mother nursing baby.

1956   Litho.   Perf. 10½
Star in Red

RA188	PT87	20pa red org	.50	.50
RA189	PT87	20pa gray grn	.50	.50
RA190	PT87	1k purple	.50	.50
RA191	PT87	1k grnsh bl	.50	.50
RA192	PT87	3k lt red brn	1.00	.50
RA193	PT87	10k rose car	2.00	2.00
RA194	PT87	25k brt grn	4.00	2.00
RA195	PT87	50k brt ultra	6.00	2.50
RA196	PT87	250k red lilac	15.00	5.00
RA197	PT87	5 l sepia	35.00	18.00
RA198	PT87	10 l dk sl grn	57.50	30.00
Nos. RA188-RA198 (11)			122.50	59.00

Nos. RA131-RA138 Overprinted and Surcharged in Black or Red: "IV. DUNYA Cocuk Gunu 1 Ekim 1956"

1956, Oct. 1   Unwmk.   Perf. 11

RA199	PT75	20pa (R)	12.00	12.00
RA200	PT75	20pa	12.00	12.00
RA201	PT75	1k (R)	12.00	12.00
RA202	PT75	3k (R)	12.00	12.00
RA203	PT75	15k (R)	12.00	12.00
RA204	PT75	25k on 30k	12.00	12.00
RA205	PT75	100k on 150k (R)	12.00	12.00
RA206	PT75	250k on 300k	18.00	18.00
Nos. RA199-RA206 (8)			102.00	102.00

The tax was for child welfare.

Type of 1954, Redrawn Type of 1946, and

Flower — PT88

Crescent in Red

1957   Unwmk.   Perf. 10½

RA207	PT88	½k lt ol gray & brn	.50	.25
RA208	PT79	1k ol bis, blk & grn	.50	.25
RA209	PT88	2½k yel grn & bl grn	.50	.25
RA210	PT43	20k red & lt bl	2.75	1.25
RA211	PT79	25k lt gray, blk & grn	2.75	1.25
RA212	PT79	50k bl, dk grn & grn	8.00	1.50
RA213	PT79	100k vio, blk & grn	8.75	3.00
Nos. RA207-RA210 (7)			25.75	7.75

No. RA210 inscribed "Turkiye Kizilay Cemiyeti." No. RA92 inscribed ". . . . Dernegi."

Children — PT89

1957   Unwmk.   Perf. 10½

RA214	PT89	20pa car & red	.25	.25
RA215	PT89	20pa grn & red	.25	.25
RA216	PT89	1k ultra & car	.25	.25
RA217	PT89	3k red org & car	1.50	1.50
Nos. RA214-RA217 (4)			2.25	2.25

"Blood Donor and Recipient" — PT90

Designs: 75k, Figure showing blood circulation. 150k, Blood transfusion symbolism.

1957, May 22
Size: 24x40mm

RA218	PT90	25k gray, blk & red	.25	.25

Size: 22½x37½mm

RA219	PT90	75k grn, blk & red	.50	.30
RA220	PT90	150k yel grn & red	1.25	.60
Nos. RA218-RA220 (3)			2.00	1.15

Redrawn Type of 1947
Inscribed: "V Dunya Cocuk Gunu"

1957   Star in Red   Perf. 10½

RA221	PT72	100k blk & bis brn	1.25	.75
RA222	PT72	150k blk & yel grn	1.25	.75
RA223	PT72	250k blk & vio	2.50	1.00
Nos. RA221-RA223 (3)			5.00	2.50

The tax was for child welfare.

Child and Butterfly — PT91

Various Butterflies. 50k, 75k horiz.

1958   Litho.   Unwmk.

RA224	PT91	20k gray & red	.75	.75
RA225	PT91	25k multi	.75	.75
RA226	PT91	50k multi	1.50	1.50
RA227	PT91	75k grn, yel & blk	2.00	2.00
RA228	PT91	150k multi	2.50	2.50
Nos. RA224-RA228 (5)			7.50	7.50

Florence Nightingale — PT92

1958   Crescent in Red

RA229	PT92	1 l bluish green	.40	.25
RA230	PT92	1½ l gray	.60	.50
RA231	PT92	2½ l blue	.80	.60
Nos. RA229-RA231 (3)			1.80	1.35

Turkey stopped issuing postal tax stamps in June, 1958. Similar stamps of later date are private charity stamps issued by the Red Crescent Society and the Society for the Protection of Children.

POSTAL TAX AIR POST STAMPS

Air Fund Issues

These stamps were obligatory on all air mail for 21 days a year. Tax for the Turkish Aviation Society: 20pa for a postcard, 1k for a regular letter, 2 1/2k for a registered letter, 3k for a telegram, 5k-50k for a package, higher values for air freight. Postal tax air post stamps were withdrawn Aug. 21, 1934 and remainders destroyed later that year.

Biplane PTAP1

Type PTAP1

Perf. 11, Pin Perf.

1926   Unwmk.   Litho.
Size: 35x25mm

RAC1		20pa brn & pale grn	3.00	.30
RAC2		1g blue grn & buff	2.00	.30

Size: 40x29mm

RAC3		5g vio & pale grn	8.00	1.00
RAC4		5g car lake & pale grn	35.00	15.00
Nos. RAC1-RAC4 (4)			48.00	16.60
Set, never hinged			275.00	

PTAP2

PTAP3

1927-29   Type PTAP2

RAC5		20pa dl red & pale grn	1.50	.50
RAC6		1k green & yel	1.25	.50

Type PTAP3
Perf. 11½

RAC7		2k dp cl & yel grn	1.50	.50
RAC8		2½k red & yel grn	8.00	1.60
RAC9		5k dk bl gray & org	1.25	.50
RAC10		10k dk grn & rose	5.00	1.25
RAC11		15k green & yel	5.00	1.00
RAC12		20k ol brn & yel	7.00	2.00
RAC13		50k dk bl & cob bl	10.00	4.50
RAC14		100k car & lt bl	110.00	80.00
Nos. RAC5-RAC14 (10)			150.50	92.35
Set, never hinged			825.00	

#RAC1, RAC5, RAC7 and RAC11 Surcharged in Black (RAC15-RAC16, RAC18-RAC19) or Red (Others)

1930-31

RAC15		1k ("Bir kurus") on RAC1	200.00	75.00
RAC16		1k ("Bir Kurus") on RAC5	1.50	.50
RAC17		100pa ("Yuz Para") on RAC7	2.00	.75
RAC18		5k ("Bes Kurus") on RAC5	8.00	1.50
RAC19		5k ("5 Kurus") on RAC5	3.00	.75
RAC20		10k ("On kurus") on RAC7	4.00	1.25
RAC21		50k ("Elli kurus") on RAC7	12.00	4.00
RAC22		1 l ("Bir lira") on RAC7	37.50	9.00
RAC23		5 l ("Bes lira") on RAC11	2,000.	400.00
Nos. RAC15-RAC23 (9)			2,268.	492.75
Set, never hinged			5,000.	

PTAP4

PTAP5

1931-32   Litho.   Perf. 11½

RAC24	PTAP4	20pa black	5.00	1.75

Typo.

RAC25	PTAP5	1k brown car ('32)	2.00	.50
RAC26	PTAP5	5k red ('32)	4.00	.75
RAC27	PTAP5	10k green ('32)	6.00	1.50
		Nos. RAC24-RAC27 (4)	17.00	4.50

PTAP6

1933   **Type PTAP6**

RAC28	10pa ("On Para") grn	3.50	2.00
RAC29	1k ("Bir Kurus") red	8.00	2.75
RAC30	5k ("Bes Kurus") lil	12.00	3.00
	Nos. RAC28-RAC30 (3)	23.50	7.75

TURKEY IN ASIA

'tər-kē in 'ā-zhə

(Anatolia)

40 Paras = 1 Piaster

This designation, which includes all of Turkey in Asia Minor, came into existence during the uprising of 1919, led by Mustafa Kemal Pasha. Actually there was no separation of territory, the Sultan's sovereignty being almost immediately reduced to a small area surrounding Constantinople. The formation of the Turkish Republic and the expulsion of the Sultan followed in 1923. Subsequent issues of postage stamps are listed under Turkey (Republic).

Issues of the Nationalist Government

Turkish Stamps of 1913-18 Surcharged in Black or Red

(The Surcharge reads "Angora 3 Piastres")

1920   **Unwmk.**   **Perf. 12**

On Stamps of 1913

1	A24	3pi on 2pa red lilac	4.75	5.25
2	A25	3pi on 4pa dk brn	37.50	37.50
3	A27	3pi on 6pa dk bl	250.00	150.00

On Stamp of 1916-18

4	A42	3pi on 2pa vio (Bk)	35.00	20.00
		Nos. 1-4 (4)	327.25	212.75

Turkish Stamps of 1913-18 Hstmpd. in Black or Red

(The Srch. reads "Post, Piastre 3")

1921   **Perf. 12**

On Stamps of 1913

5	A24	3pi on 2pa red lilac	35.00	25.00
a.		On No. 1	47.50	72.50
6	A25	3pi on 4pa dk brown	30.00	30.00
a.		On No. 2	160.00	175.00
7	A25	3pi on 4pa dk brn (R)	150.00	175.00
a.		On No. 2	160.00	175.00
8	A27	3pi on 6pa dk blue	125.00	150.00
a.		On No. 3	300.00	325.00
9	A27	3pi on 6pa bl (R)	62.50	75.00
a.		On No. 3	110.00	140.00

On Stamps of 1916-18

10	A42	3pi on 2pa vio (R)	62.50	75.00
a.		On No. 4	97.50	125.00
		Nos. 5-10 (6)	465.00	530.00

Turkish Revenue Stamps Handstamped in Turkish "Osmanli Postalari, 1336" (Ottoman Post, 1920).

عثمانلى پوسته كرى
١٣٣٦

Type a

Dash at upper left is set high. Bottom (date) line is 8½mm long.

عثمانلى پوسته لرى
١٣٣٦

Type b

Dash at upper left is set lower. Bottom (date) line is 10mm long.

عثمانلى پوسته لرى
١٣٣٦

Type c

Dash at upper left is set lower. Bottom (date) line is 9mm long.

Religious Tribunals Revenue R1

12	R1	1pi grn (a, b, c)	750.00	300.00
13	R1	5pi ultra (a, b)	16,000.	15,500.
14	R1	50pi gray grn (a, b, c)	25.00	35.00
		Cut cancellation		3.00
15	R1	100pi buff (a)	140.00	97.50
a.		100pi yellow (a)	95.00	72.50
		Cut cancellation		7.50
16	R1	500pi org (a)	225.00	150.00
		Cut cancellation		20.00
17	R1	1000pi brn (a)	3,000.	1,750.
		Cut cancellation		175.00

See Nos. 29-32.

Court Costs Revenue R2

Black Overprint

18	R2	10pa grn (b, c)	110.00	100.00
19	R2	1pi ultra (a, c)	—	19,000.
20	R2	5pi rose (c)	17,500.	—
21	R2	50pi ocher (a, b, c)	50.00	50.00
a.		50pi yellow (a, b, c)	12.00	17.00
		Cut cancellation, #21, 21a		2.00
22	R2	100pi brown (a)	150.00	100.00
		Cut cancellation		20.00
23	R2	500pi slate (a)	325.00	325.00
		Cut cancellation		20.00

See Nos. 24, 33-39.

Notary Public Revenue — R3

Design R2 Overprinted "Katibi Adliye Masus dur" in Red

24	R3	50pi ocher (a)	1,250.	150.00
		Cut cancellation		20.00

Laborer's Passport Tax Stamp — R4

Notary Public Revenue — R5

Black Overprint

25	R4	2pi emerald (a, c)	—	22,000.
26	R5	100pi yellow brn (a)	1,250.	150.00
		Cut cancellation		30.00

See Nos. 46-48.

Theater Tax Stamp — R6

Land Registry Revenue — R7

27	R6	20pa black	5,000.	5,000.
28	R7	2pi blue black	6,250.	6,250.

See Nos. 40, 45.

Hejaz Railway Tax Stamp — R8

Perf. 11½

28A	R8	2pi dk red & bl (b)	1,750.	1,750.

Turkish Revenue Stamps Overprinted in Turkish "Osmanli Postalari, 1337" (Ottoman Post, 1921)

On #29-63

عثمانلى پوسته لرى
١٣٣٧

Perf. 12

29	R1	10pa slate	17.00	14.50
a.		Handstamped overprint	100.00	50.00
b.		Double overprint		
30	R1	1pi green	32.50	20.00
a.		Inverted overprint	35.00	22.50
b.		Handstamped overprint	3,500.	3,250.
31	R1	5pi ultra	29.00	14.50
a.		"1337" inverted	100.00	90.00
b.		Half used as 2½pi on cover		
c.		Handstamped overprint	875.00	875.00
		Nos. 29-31 (3)	78.50	49.00

Handstamped Overprint

32	R1	50pi green	7,250.	7,250.

Design R2 Overprinted

33	R2	10pa green	24.50	24.50
a.		Handstamped overprint	3,500.	3,500.
34	R2	1pi ultra	50.00	25.00
a.		Handstamped overprint	875.00	875.00
35	R2	5pi red	24.50	25.00
a.		Inverted overprint		
b.		"1337" inverted	100.00	100.00
c.		Half used as 2½pi on cover		
d.		Handstamped overprint	7,500	7,500.
36	R2	50pi ocher, handstamped ovpt.	500.00	100.00
		Cut cancellation		20.00
		Nos. 33-36 (4)	599.00	174.50

Design R3 Overprinted Additional Turkish Overprint in Red or Black

37	R3	10pa green (R)	100.00	60.00
38	R3	1pi ultra (R)	72.50	50.00
39	R3	5pi rose (Bk)	72.50	50.00
a.		"1337" inverted	200.00	200.00
b.		Handstamped overprint	7,000.	7,000.
		Nos. 37-39 (3)	245.00	160.00

Design R7 Overprinted

40	R7	2pi blue black	125.00	110.00
a.		Handstamped overprint	5,500.	5,500.

R12

Overprinted in Black

1921   **Perf. 12**

41	R12	5pi green	150.00	125.00
		Cut cancellation		17.50
a.		Handstamped overprint	5,500.	5,000.

Museum Tax Stamp R13

Overprinted in Black

42	R13	1pi ultra	425.00	400.00
a.		Handstamped overprint	5,500.	5,500.
43	R13	5pi deep green	475.00	450.00
a.		Handstamped overprint	5,500.	5,500.

Handstamped Overprint

44 R13 5pi dark vio   7,000. 7,000.
The overprint variety "337" for "1337" exists on Nos. 42-43.

Design R6
Overprinted

Perf. 12, 12½

45 R6 20pa black   12.50   5.00
a.   Date 4½mm high   15.00
b.   "337" for "1337"   25.00

Design R5
Overprinted

46 R5 10pa green   25.00   25.00
a.   Overprint 21mm long
b.   "131" for "1337"
47 R5 1pi ultra   37.50   25.00
a.   "13" for "1337"   50.00   50.00
b.   "131" for "1337"   50.00   50.00
c.   Inverted overprint   90.00   90.00
d.   Handstamped overprint   4,500.   4,500.
48 R5 5pi red   62.50   25.00
a.   Inverted overprint   90.00   90.00
b.   "131" for "1337"   85.00   85.00
c.   Handstamped overprint   4,500.   4,400.
      Nos. 46-48 (3)   125.00   75.00

R16

Perf. 11½, 11½x11
Overprinted in Black

49 R16 10pa pink   4.00   1.50
a.   Imperf.
b.   Date "1237"   5.00   2.00
d.   Inverted overprint
e.   Handstamped overprint   1,950.   1,950.
50 R16 1pi yellow   10.00   5.00
a.   Overprint 18mm long   10.00   5.00
b.   Date "1332"   12.00
c.   Date "1317"
d.   Inverted overprint
e.   Handstamped overprint   1,950.   1,950.
51 R16 2pi yellow grn   12.50   5.00
a.   Date "1237"   15.00
b.   Date "1317"
c.   Imperf.
d.   Inverted overprint   40.00   9.00
e.   Handstamped overprint   —   —
52 R16 5pi red   20.00   1.00
a.   Horiz. pair, imperf. vert.
b.   Inverted overprint   25.00   7.50
c.   Double overprint   30.00   12.50
d.   Date "1332"   45.00
e.   Half used as 2½pi on cover
f.   Overprint 18mm long   20.00   7.50
g.   Handstamped overprint   1,950.   1,950.
      Nos. 49-52 (4)   46.50   12.50

Design R8 Overprinted
TURKISH INSCRIPTIONS

20 Paras   1 Piaster

2 Piasters   5 Piasters

Dark Red & Blue

1921   *Perf. 11½*
53 R8 20pa on 1pi   75.00   75.00
54 R8 1pi on 1pi   7.50   4.00
55 R8 2pi on 1pi   7.50   4.00
a.   Inverted surcharge
56 R8 5pi on 1pi   12.00   6.00
      Nos. 53-56 (4)   102.00   89.00
      See No. 57.

No. 54 Overprinted

57 R8 1pi on 1pi dk red & bl   50.00   50.00

Hejaz Railway Tax
Stamp — R19

Overprinted in Black

58 R19 1pi grn & brn red   6.00   4.00
a.   Double overprint
b.   Handstamped overprint

The errors "1307," "1331" and "2337" occur once in each sheet of Nos. 53-58.

Naval League
Labels — R20

Overprinted in Black

1921   *Perf. 12x11½*
59 R20 1pa orange   10.00   15.00
a.   Date "1327"   15.00   3.50
60 R20 2pa indigo   10.00   15.00
61 R20 5pa green   12.50   17.50
62 R20 10pa brown   25.00   30.00
63 R20 40pa red brown   175.00   190.00
      Nos. 59-63 (5)   232.50   267.50

The error "2337" occurs on all values of this issue.
The Naval League stamps have pictures of three Turkish warships. They were sold for the benefit of sailors of the fleet but did not pay postage until they were overprinted in 1921.

Turkish Stamps of 1915-20
Overprinted

a

b

The overprints on Nos. 64-77 read "Adana December 1st, 1921." This issue commemorated the withdrawal of the French from Cilicia. On No. 71 the lines of the overprint are further apart than on Nos. 68-70 and 73-74.

1921   *Perf. 12*
64 A44 (a) 10pa grn (424)   10.00   7.00
65 A45 (a) 20pa deep rose
              (425)   10.00   7.00
a.   Inverted overprint   20.00
66 A51 (a) 25pi car, *straw*
              (434)   20.00   25.00
a.   Double overprint
b.   Inverted overprint   37.50   37.50
      Nos. 64-66 (3)   40.00   39.00
On Newspaper Stamp of 1915
67 A21 (a) 5pa och (P132)   90.00   150.00
On Stamp of 1915
68 A22 (b) 5pa och (328)   350.00   400.00
On Stamps of 1917-18
69 A53 (b) 5pi on 2pa
              (547)   15.00   17.50
70 A53 (b) 5pi on 2pa
              (548)   15.00   17.50
On Stamp of 1919
71 A57 (b) 35pi on 1pi bl
              (Bk; 579)   42.50   50.00
a.   Inverted surcharge
On Newspaper Stamp of 1915
72 A21 (b) 5pa och (P132)   200.00   200.00
On No. 72 the overprint is vertical, half reading up and half reading down.
On Stamps of 1920
73 A32 (b) 3pi blue (594)   15.00   12.50
74 A36 (b) 10pi gray vio
              (596)   20.00   20.00
On Postage Due Stamps of 1914
75 D1 (a) 5pa claret
              (J63)   350.00   350.00
76 D2 (a) 20pa red (J64)   350.00   400.00
a.   Inverted overprint
77 D3 (b) 1pi dk bl
              (J65)   350.00   400.00
a.   Inverted overprint   750.00   750.00
      Nos. 75-77 (3)   1,050.   1,150.

Withdrawal of the French from Cilicia. Forged overprints exist.

Pact of Revenge,
Burning Village at
Top — A21

Izmir
Harbor — A22

Mosque of
Selim,
Adrianople
A23

Mosque of   Soldier — A25
Selim,
Konya — A24

Legendary
Gray
Wolf — A26

Snake Castle
and Seyhan
River,
Adana — A27

Parliament
Building at
Sivas — A28

A29

Mosque at
Urfa — A30

Map of
Anatolia
A31

Declaration of Faith
from the
Koran — A32

1922   **Litho.**   *Perf. 11½*
78 A21 10pa violet brn   1.00   .25
79 A22 20pa blue grn   1.00   .25
80 A23 1pi dp blue   1.50   .35
81 A24 2pi red brown   3.00   .50
82 A25 5pi dk blue   3.00   .50
83 A26 10pi dk brown   12.50   .75
a.   Vert. pair, imperf between   100.00
b.   Vert. strip of 3, imperf between   300.00
84 A27 25pi rose   15.00   2.00
85 A28 50pi indigo   1.00   15.00
86 A29 50pi dk gray   1.00   1.25
87 A30 100pi violet   75.00   8.00
      Cut cancellation   1.25
88 A31 200pi slate   200.00   62.50
      Cut cancellation   5.00
89 A32 500pi green   125.00   27.50
      Cut cancellation   10.00
      Nos. 78-89 (12)   439.00   118.85
      Set, never hinged   2,075.

Imperf

79a A22 20pa   25.00   30.00
80a A23 1pi   15.00   20.00
82a A25 5pi   15.00   20.00
84a A27 25pi   35.00   30.00
85a A28 50pi   27.50   30.00

Stamps of
Type A23
Overprinted

1922

90	A23	1pi deep blue	7.25	15.00
91	A23	5pi deep blue	7.25	20.00
92	A23	10pi brown	7.25	20.00
93	A23	25pi rose	10.00	25.00
94	A23	50pi slate	12.50	25.00
95	A23	100pi violet	17.50	37.50
96	A23	200pi black vio	17.50	50.00
97	A23	500pi blue green	25.00	75.00
		Nos. 90-97 (8)	104.25	267.50
		Set, never hinged	200.00	

Withdrawal of the French from Cilicia and the return of the Kemalist Natl. army. The overprint reads: "Adana, Jan. 5, 1922."

No. 90-97 without overprint were presented to some high government officials.

First
Parliament
House,
Ankara — A33

1922   **Litho.**

98	A33	5pa violet	.75	2.50
99	A33	10pa green	1.75	2.50
100	A33	20pa pale red	2.50	2.00
101	A33	1pi brown org	12.00	1.50
102	A33	2pi red brown	20.00	4.25
103	A33	3pi rose	5.00	.60
a.		Arabic "13" in right corner	10.00	7.50
b.		Thin grayish paper	55.00	7.50
		Nos. 98-103 (6)	42.00	13.35
		Set, never hinged	140.00	

Nos. 98-103, 103b exist imperf. In 1923 several stamps of Turkey and Turkey in Asia were overprinted in Turkish for advertising purposes. The overprint reads: "Izmir Economic Congress, 17 Feb., 1339."

POSTAGE DUE STAMPS

D1

1922   **Litho.**   **Perf. 11½**

J1	D1	20pa dull green	1.00	5.00
a.		Imperf.		
J2	D1	1pi gray green	1.00	5.00
J3	D1	2pi red brown	2.50	17.50
J4	D1	3pi rose	4.50	25.00
J5	D1	5pi dark blue	6.00	55.00
		Nos. J1-J5 (5)	15.00	
		Set, never hinged	55.00	

TURKISH REPUBLIC OF NORTHERN CYPRUS

'tər-kish ri-'pə-blik of 'nor-thərn 'sī-prəs

LOCATION — Northern 40% of the Island of Cyprus in the Mediterranean Sea off the coast of Turkey.

Established following Turkish invasion of Cyprus in 1974. On Nov. 15, 1983 Turkey declared the Turkish Republic of Northern Cyprus to be independent. No other country has recognized this country.

1000 Milliemes = 1 Pound
100 Kurus = 1 Turkish Lira (1978)

> **Catalogue values for all unused stamps in this country are for Never Hinged items.**

> Letters bearing these stamps enter international mail via the Turkish Post Office.

Watermark

Wmk. 390

Republic of Turkey, 50th Anniv.
A1   A2

Designs: 3m, Woman sentry. 5m, Military parade. 10m, Flag bearers. 15m, Anniversary emblem. 20m, Ataturk statue. 50m, Painting, "The Fallen." 70m, Turkish flag, map of Cyprus.

Perf. 12x11½, 11½x12

1974, July 27   Litho.   Unwmk.

1	A1	3m multicolored	45.00	37.50
2	A2	5m multicolored	.75	.50
3	A1	10m multicolored	.90	.50
4	A2	15m multicolored	1.50	.90
5	A1	20m multicolored	1.25	.70
6	A1	50m multicolored	4.00	2.75
7	A2	70m multicolored	35.00	15.00
		Nos. 1-7 (7)	88.40	57.85

First day covers are dated 1/29/73.

Nos. 5, 3 Surcharged

1975, Mar. 3   Perf. 12x11½

8	A1	30m on 20m, #5	1.25	1.00
9	A1	100m on 10m, #3	3.00	2.25

Surcharge appears in different positions.

Historical
Sites and
Landmarks
A3

Designs: 3m, Namik Kemal's bust, Famagusta. 5m, 30m, Kyrenia Harbor. 10m, Ataturk Statue, Nicosia. 15m, St. Hilarion Castle. 20m, Ataturk Square, Nicosia. 25m, Coastline, Famagusta. 50m, Lala Mustafa Pasha Mosque, Famagusta vert. 100m, Kyrenia Castle. 250m, Kyrenia Castle, exterior walls. 500m, Othello Tower, Famagusta vert.

1975-76   Perf. 13

10	A3	3m pink & multi	.40	.30
11	A3	5m bl & multi	.40	.30
12	A3	10m pink & multi	.45	.40
13	A3	15m pink & multi	.50	.40
14	A3	15m bl & multi	.50	.40
15	A3	20m pink & multi	3.00	.40
16	A3	20m bl & multi	.50	.40
17	A3	25m pink & multi	.70	.50
18	A3	30m pink & multi	1.00	.75
19	A3	50m pink & multi	1.50	1.00
20	A3	100m pink & multi	1.75	1.25
21	A3	250m pink & multi	2.50	1.75
22	A3	500m pink & multi	3.50	3.00
		Nos. 10-22 (13)	16.70	10.85

Issued: #10, 12-13, 15, 17-22, 4/21; #11, 14, 16, 8/2/76. #1, 14, 16 have different inscriptions and "1976."
For surcharges see Nos. 28-29.

Peace in
Cyprus — A4

Designs: 50m, Map, olive branch, severed chain. 150m, Map, globe, olive branch, vert.

1975, July 20   Perf. 13½x13, 13x13½

23	A4	30m multicolored	.40	.25
24	A4	50m multicolored	.50	.35
25	A4	150m multicolored	1.10	1.00
		Nos. 23-25 (3)	2.00	1.60

Europa — A5

Paintings: 90m, Pomegranates by I.V. Guney. 100m, Harvest Time by F. Direkoglu.

1975, Dec. 29   Perf. 13

26	A5	90m multicolored	2.00	1.00
27	A5	100m multicolored	3.00	1.50

Nos. 19, 20
Surcharged

1976, Apr. 28   Perf. 13

28	A3	10m on 50m, #19	.50	.50
29	A3	30m on 100m, #20	1.25	1.25

Europa — A6

1976, May 3

30	A6	60m Expectation	.75	.30
31	A6	120m Man in Meditation	1.50	.65

Fruits — A7

1976, June 28

32	A7	10m Ceratonia siliqua	.25	.25
33	A7	25m Citrus nobilis	.30	.25
34	A7	40m Fragaria vesca	.40	.25
35	A7	60m Citrus sinensis	.50	.30
36	A7	80m Citrus limon	.75	.45
		Nos. 32-36 (5)	2.20	1.50

For surcharges see Nos. 66-69.

Olympic Games,
Montreal — A8

Design: 100m, Olympic rings, doves, horiz.

1976, July 17

37	A8	60m multicolored	.75	.25
38	A8	100m multicolored	1.00	.35

Liberation
Monument — A9

1976, Nov. 1   Perf. 13x13½

39	A9	30m multi	.50	.25
40	A9	150m multi, diff.	.90	.45

Europa — A10

1977, May 2   Perf. 13

41	A10	80m Salamis Bay	2.00	.75
42	A10	100m Kyrenia Port	3.00	1.25

Handicrafts
A11

1977, June 27

43	A11	15m Pottery	.35	.25
44	A11	30m Gourds, vert.	.55	.25
45	A11	125m Baskets	.95	.30
		Nos. 43-45 (3)	1.85	.80

Landmarks
A12

Designs: 20m, Arap Ahmet Pasha Mosque, Nicosia, vert. 40m, Paphos Castle. 70m, Bekir Pasha aqueduct, Larnaca. 80m, Sultan Mahmut library, Nicosia.

1977, Dec. 2   Perf. 13x13½, 13½x13

46	A12	20m multicolored	.25	.25
47	A12	40m multicolored	.30	.25
48	A12	70m multicolored	.40	.25
49	A12	80m multicolored	.60	.40
		Nos. 46-49 (4)	1.55	1.15

Namik Kemal
(1840-1888),
Writer — A13

1977, Dec. 21   Perf. 13

50	A13	30m Bust, home	.30	.25
51	A13	140m Portrait, vert.	.90	.50

Social Security — A14　　　Europa — A15

Designs: 275k, Man with sling, crutch. 375k, Woman with children.

1978, Apr. 17　　　　　　Perf. 13x13½
52　A14　150k blk, bl & yel　　　.30　.25
53　A14　275k blk, grn & red org　.40　.25
54　A14　375k blk, red org & bl　.70　.25
　　　Nos. 52-54 (3)　　　　　1.40　.75

1978, May 2　Perf. 13x13½, 13½x13
225k, Oratory in Buyuk Han, Nicosia. 450k, Reservoir, Selimiye Mosque, Nicosia.

55　A15　225k multi　　　　3.25　1.00
56　A15　450k multi, horiz.　　6.50　1.50

Transportation A16

1978, July 10　　　　　Perf. 13½x13
57　A16　75k Roadway　　　　.30　.25
58　A16　100k Hydrofoil　　　.40　.25
59　A16　650k Airplane　　　.70　.70
　　　Nos. 57-59 (3)　　　　1.40　1.20

National Oath — A17

1978, Sept. 13
60　A17　150k Dove, olive branch　.35　.25
61　A17　225k Stylized pen, vert.　.50　.25
62　A17　725k Stylized dove　　.90　.65
　　　Nos. 60-62 (3)　　　　1.75　1.15

Kemal Ataturk — A18

1978, Nov. 10
63　A18　75k bl grn & lt grn　　.25　.25
64　A18　450k brn & buff　　　.25　.25
65　A18　650k Prus bl & lt bl　.30　.30
　　　Nos. 63-65 (3)　　　　.80　.80

Nos. 33-36 Surcharged

1979, June 4
66　A7　50k on 25m　　　　.40　.25
67　A7　1 l on 40m　　　　.50　.25
68　A7　3 l on 60m　　　　.75　.25
69　A7　5 l on 80m　　　　.90　.25
　　　Nos. 66-69 (4)　　　　2.55　1.00

Souvenir Sheet

Turkish Invasion of Cyprus, 5th Anniv. — A19

1979, July 2　　　　　　　　Imperf.
70　A19　15 l multicolored　　3.75　3.25

Europa A20

Communications: 3 l, Stamps, building, map. 8 l, Early and modern telephones, globe, satellite.

1979, Aug. 20　Litho.　　Perf. 13
71　A20　2 l multicolored　　1.50　.40
72　A20　3 l multicolored　　2.00　.65
73　A20　8 l multicolored　　4.25　1.00
　　　Nos. 71-73 (3)　　　　7.75　2.05

Intl. Consultative Radio Committee, 50th Anniv. — A21

1979, Sept. 24
74　A21　2 l blue & multi　　.25　.25
75　A21　5 l gray & multi　　.25　.25
76　A21　6 l green & multi　　.35　.30
　　　Nos. 74-76 (3)　　　　.85　.80

Intl. Year of the Child A22

Childrens' drawings of children.

1979, Oct. 29
77　A22　1½ l multi, vert.　　.25　.25
78　A22　4½ l multicolored　　.35　.30
79　A22　6 l multi, vert.　　.45　.40
　　　Nos. 77-79 (3)　　　　1.05　.95

Press reports in Jan. 1980 state that the 1979 UPU Congress declared Turkish Cyprus stamps invalid for international mail.

A23　　　　　Europa — A24

Anniv. and events: 2½ l, Lala Mustafa Pasha Mosque, Famagusta. 10 l, Arap Ahmet Pasha Mosque, Lefkosa. 20 l, Holy Kaaba, Mosque.

1980, Mar. 23
80　A23　2½ l multicolored　　.25　.25
81　A23　10 l multicolored　　.45　.25
82　A23　20 l multicolored　　.70　.70
　　　Nos. 80-82 (3)　　　　1.40　1.20

1st Islamic Conference in Turkish Cyprus (2½ l). General Assembly of World Islam Congress (10 l). Moslem year 1400 AH (20 l).

1980, May 23
83　A24　5 l Ebu-Suud Efendi　.75　.40
84　A24　30 l Sultan Selim II　2.50　.80

Historic Landmarks A25

Designs: 2½ l, Omer's Shrine, Kyrenia. 3½ l, Entrance gate, Famagusta. 5 l, Funerary monuments, Famagusta. 10 l, Bella Paise Abbey, Kyrenia. 20 l, Selimiye Mosque, Nicosia.

1980, June 25
Blue Paper
85　A25　2½ l buff & Prus bl　.25　.25
86　A25　3½ l pale pink & dk grn　.25　.25
87　A25　5 l pale bl grn & dk car　.25　.25
88　A25　10 l lt grn & red lil　.25　.25
89　A25　20 l buff & dk bl　　.40　.35
　　　Nos. 85-89 (5)　　　　1.40　1.35

For overprints and surcharges see Nos. 198-200.

Cyprus Postage Stamps, Cent. A26

1980, Aug. 16
90　A26　7½ l No. 5, vert.　　.25　.25
91　A26　15 l No. 199　　　　.35　.25
92　A26　50 l Social welfare, vert.　.90　.80
　　　Nos. 90-92 (3)　　　　1.50　1.30

Palestinian Solidarity A27

15 l, Dome of the Rock, entrance, vert.

1980, Mar. 24
93　A27　15 l multicolored　　.30　.25
94　A27　35 l multicolored　　.75　.60

World Muslim Congress Statement — A28

1981, Mar. 24
95　A28　1 l In Turkish　　　.35　.25
96　A28　35 l In English　　.90　.65

Ataturk by Feyhamam Duran — A29

1981, May 19
97　A29　20 l multicolored　　1.00　.65

Printed with se-tenant label promoting Ataturk Stamp Exhibition.

Europa A30

Folk dances.

1981, June 29
98　A30　10 l multicolored　　.90　.40
99　A30　30 l multi, diff.　　2.25　1.00

Souvenir Sheet

Ataturk, Birth Cent. — A31

1981, July 23　　　　　　Imperf.
100　A31　150 l multicolored　2.25　1.75

No. 100 has simulated perfs.

Flowers A32

Designs: 1 l, Convolvulus althaeoides, vert. 5 l, Cyclamen persicum. 10 l, Mandragara officinarum. 25 l, Papaver rhoeas, vert. 30 l, Arum dioscoridis, vert. 50 l, Chrysanthemum segetum. 100 l, Cistus salyiaefolius, vert. 150 l, Ferula communis.

1981-82　　　　　　　　Perf. 13
101　A32　1 l multicolored　　.25　.25
102　A32　5 l multicolored　　.25　.25
103　A32　10 l multicolored　　.25　.25
104　A32　25 l multicolored　　.40　.40
105　A32　30 l multicolored　　.45　.45
106　A32　50 l multicolored　　.75　.75
107　A32　100 l multicolored　1.50　1.50
108　A32　150 l multicolored　2.25　2.25
　　　Nos. 101-108 (8)　　　6.10　6.10

Issue dates: 1 l, 10 l, 25 l, 150 l, Sept. 28; 5 l, 30 l, 50 l, 100 l, Jan. 22, 1982.
For surcharge & overprints see #138-141, 201.

Intl. Year for Disabled Persons A33

Fight Against Apartheid — A34

World Food Day — A35

1981, Oct. 16
109	A33	7½ l multicolored	.25	.25
110	A34	10 l multicolored	.35	.30
111	A35	20 l multicolored	.65	.50
	Nos. 109-111 (3)		1.25	1.05

Palestinian Solidarity A36

1981, Nov. 29
112	A36	10 l multicolored	.25	.25

Royal Wedding of Prince Charles and Lady Diana Spencer — A37

1981, Nov. 30
113	A37	50 l multicolored	1.00	.70

Charter of Cyprus, 1865 — A38

Turkish Forces Landing in Tuzla — A39

1982, July 30
114		Sheet of 4	5.00	5.00
a.	A38	30 l multicolored	1.00	1.00
b.	A39	70 l multicolored	1.00	1.00

Europa. #114 contains 2 each #114a, 114b.

Buffavento Castle — A40

Windsurfing — A41

Kantara Castle A42

Tourism: 30 l, Shipwreck museum.

Perf. 12½x12, 12x12½
1982, Aug. 20
116	A40	5 l multicolored	.25	.25
117	A41	10 l multicolored	.30	.25
118	A42	15 l multicolored	.35	.30
119	A42	30 l multicolored	.60	.40
	Nos. 116-119 (4)		1.50	1.20

Art Treasures — A43

Designs: 30 l, The Wedding by Aylin Orek. 50 l, Carob Pickers by Ozden Nazim, vert.

1982, Dec. 3   *Perf. 13x13½, 13½x13*
120	A43	30 l multicolored	.50	.30
121	A43	50 l multicolored	.75	.50

Robert Koch, TB Bacillus A44

World Cup Soccer Championships, Spain — A45

Scouting, 75th Anniv. — A46

1982, Dec. 15   *Perf. 12½*
122	A44	10 l multicolored	.25	.25
123	A45	30 l multicolored	.75	.60
124	A46	70 l multicolored	2.00	1.50
	Nos. 122-124 (3)		3.00	2.35

Paintings A47

30 l, Calloused Hands by Salih Oral. 35 l, Malya-Limassol Bus by Emin Cizenel.

1983, May 16   *Perf. 13½x13*
125	A47	30 l multicolored	.90	.75
126	A47	35 l multicolored	1.25	1.00

Miniature Sheet

Europa — A48

a, Map by Piri Reis. b, Cyprus seen from Skylab.

1983, June 30   *Perf. 13*
127	A48	Sheet of 2	60.00	30.00
a.-b.		100 l any single	15.00	15.00

25th Anniv. of Turkish Resistance A49

Designs: 15 l, No. 3. 20 l, Exploitation, Suppression & Resurrection by Aziz Hasan. 25 l, Resistance by Guner Pir.

1983, Aug. 1   *Perf. 13*
129	A49	15 l multi, vert.	.30	.30
130	A49	20 l multi	.45	.45
131	A49	25 l multi, vert.	.50	.50
	Nos. 129-131 (3)		1.25	1.25

World Communications Year — A50

1983, Aug. 1
132	A50	30 l shown	.60	.60
133	A50	50 l Letters	1.00	1.00

Birds A51

1983, Oct. 10
134	A51	10 l Merops apiaster	.25	.25
135	A51	15 l Carduelis carduelis	.35	.25
136	A51	50 l Erithacus rubecula	1.00	.70
137	A51	65 l Oriolus oriolus	1.40	1.00
a.		Block of 4, #134-137	3.50	3.00
	Nos. 134-137 (4)		3.00	2.20

Nos. 103, 108 Ovptd.

Nos. 101, 104 Ovptd. or Srchd.

1983, Dec. 7
138	A32	10 l multicolored	.25	.25
139	A32	15 l on 1 l multi	.25	.25
140	A32	25 l multicolored	.35	.35
141	A32	150 l multicolored	2.00	2.00
	Nos. 138-141 (4)		2.85	2.85

Europa, 25th Anniv. A52

1984, May 30   *Perf. 12x12½*
142	A52	50 l blk, yel & brn	1.00	.50
143	A52	100 l blk, bl & ultra	2.00	1.00
a.		Pair, #142-143	3.25	2.75

Olympics, Los Angeles A53

Perf. 12½x12, 12x12½
1984, June 19
144	A53	10 l Olympic flame, vert.	.30	.25
145	A53	20 l Olympic rings	.40	.25
146	A53	70 l Judo	.80	.60
	Nos. 144-146 (3)		1.50	1.10

Ataturk Cultural Center A54

Perf. 12x12½
1984, July 20   Wmk. 390
147	A54	120 l blk, yel & brn	.90	.90

Turkish Invasion of Cyprus, 10th Anniv. A55

1984, July 20
148	A55	20 l shown	.40	.40
149	A55	70 l Map, flag, olive branch	.70	.70

Forest Conservation — A56

1984, Aug. 20
150	A56	90 l multicolored	1.25	.75

Paintings — A57

20 l, Old Turkish Houses in Nicosia by Cevdet Cagdas. 70 l, Scenery by Olga Rauf.

1984, Sept. 21   *Perf. 13*
151 A57 20 l multicolored   .40   .40
152 A57 70 l multicolored   1.10 1.10

Proclamation of Turkish Republic of Northern Cyprus — A58

Unanimous Vote by Legislative Assembly — A59

Perf. 12½x12, 12x12½
1984, Nov. 15
153 A58 20 l multicolored   .50   .30
154 A59 70 l multicolored   .95   .70

Independence, 1st Anniv.

European Taekwondo Championship, Kyrenia — A60

1984, Dec. 10
155 A60 10 l Competitors   .30   .25
156 A60 70 l Flags   .60   .55

Balance of the Spirit — A61

Paintings by Saulo Mercader: 20 l, The Look, vert.

1984, Dec. 10 *Perf. 12½x13, 13x12½*
157 A61 20 l multicolored   .25   .25
158 A61 70 l multicolored   .50   .50

Visit by Nuremburg Chamber Orchestra A62

1984, Dec. 10   *Perf. 12½*
159 A62 70 l multicolored   1.00   .50

Dr. Fazil Kucuk (1906-1984), Politician — A63

70 l, Kucuk reading newspaper, c. 1970.

1985, Jan.
160 A63 20 l multicolored   .50   .25
161 A63 70 l multicolored   .70   .50

Domestic Animals A64

1985, May 29   *Perf. 12x12½*
162 A64 100 l Capra   .55   .55
163 A64 200 l Bos taurus   1.10 1.10
164 A64 300 l Ovis aries   1.60 1.60
165 A64 500 l Equus asinus   2.75 2.75
     Nos. 162-165 (4)   6.00 6.00

Europa — A65

Composers: No. 166, George Frideric Handel (1685-1759). No. 167, Domenico Scarlatti (1685-1757). No. 168, Johann Sebastian Bach (1685-1750). No. 169, Buhurizade Mustafa Itri (1640-1712).

1985, June 26   *Perf. 12½x12*
166 A65 20 l grn & multi   .30   .25
167 A65 20 l brn lake & multi   .30   .25
168 A65 100 l bl & multi   1.25   .80
169 A65 100 l brn & multi   1.25   .80
  a. Block of 4, #166-169   3.75 3.75

Printed in sheets of 16, containing 4 No. 169a.

Paintings — A66

Paintings: 20 l, Pastoral Life by Ali Atakan. 50 l, Woman Carrying Water by Ismet V. Guney.

1985, Aug.   *Perf. 12½x13*
170 A66 20 l multicolored   .35   .35
171 A66 50 l multicolored   .55   .55

Intl. Youth Year A67

Wmk. 390
1985, Oct. 29 Litho.   *Perf. 12½*
172 A67 20 l shown   .40   .25
173 A67 100 l Globe, dove   .90   .60

Northern Cyprus Air League — A68

Development of Rabies Vaccine, Cent. — A69

Ismet Inonu (1884-1973), Turkish Pres. — A70

UN, 40th Anniv. A71

Blood Donor Services A72

1985, Nov. 29
174 A68 20 l multicolored   .25   .25
175 A69 50 l Pasteur   .30   .30
176 A70 100 l brown   .60   .60
177 A71 100 l multicolored   .60   .60
178 A72 100 l multicolored   .60   .60
     Nos. 174-178 (5)   2.35 2.35

Paintings — A73

20 l, House with Arches by Gonen Atakol. 100 l, Ataturk Square by Yalkin Muhtaroglu.

1986, June 20   *Perf. 13*
179 A73 20 l multicolored   .25   .25
180 A73 100 l multicolored   .40   .40

Miniature Sheet

Europa — A74

1986, June 20   *Perf. 12x12½*
181 A74   Sheet of 2   16.00 16.00
  a. 100 l Gyps fulvus   4.00 2.00
  b. 200 l Roadside litter   8.00 4.00

Karagoz Puppets — A75

1986, July 25   *Perf. 12½x13*
182 A75 100 l multicolored   .90   .40

Anatolian Artifacts A76

Designs: 10 l, Ring-shaped composite pottery, Kernos, Old Bronze Age (2300-1050 B.C.). 20 l, Bird-shaped lidded pot, Skuru Hill tomb, Morphou, late Bronze Age (1600-1500 B.C.), vert. 50 l, Earthenware jug, Vryse, Kyrenia, Neolithic Age (4000 B.C.). 100 l, Terra sigillata statue of Artemis, Sea of Salamis, Roman Period (200 B.C.), vert.

1986, Sept. 15   *Perf. 12½*
183 A76 10 l multicolored   .25   .25
184 A76 20 l multicolored   .25   .25
185 A76 50 l multicolored   .25   .25
186 A76 100 l multicolored   .50   .50
     Nos. 183-186 (4)   1.25 1.25

For surcharge see No. 295A.

Defense Forces, 10th Anniv. — A77

World Food Day — A78

World Cup Soccer Championships, Mexico — A79

Halley's Comet A80

1986, Oct. 13
187 A77 20 l multicolored   .25   .25
188 A78 50 l multicolored   .30   .30
189 A79 100 l multicolored   .35   .35
190 A80 100 l multicolored   .40   .40
     Nos. 187-190 (4)   1.30 1.30

Development Projects — A81

1986, Nov. 17
191 A81 20 l Water resources   .25   .25
192 A81 50 l Housing   .25   .25
193 A81 100 l Airport   .45   .45
     Nos. 191-193 (3)   .95   .95

Royal Wedding of Prince Andrew and Sarah Ferguson — A82

Anniv. and events: No. 195, Queen Elizabeth II, 60th birthday.

Perf. 12½x13

1986, Nov. 20   Wmk. 390
194 A82 100 l multicolored   .50 .35
195 A82 100 l multicolored   .50 .35
  a. Pair, #194-195   1.00 .70

Trakhoni Station, 1904 A83

1986, Dec. 31
196 A83 50 l shown   .35 .25
197 A83 100 l Locomotive #1,
   1904   .90 .60

Rail transport, 1904-1951.

Nos. 86, 88-89, 105 Overprinted or Surcharged

a

b

1987, May 18   Unwmk.   Perf. 13
198 A25(a) 10 l on #89   .40 .25
199 A25(a) 15 l on 3½ l, #86   .40 .25
200 A25(a) 20 l on #88   .50 .25
201 A32(b) 30 l on #105   .80 .35
  Nos. 198-201 (4)   2.10 1.10

Paintings — A84

Designs: 50 l, Shepherd by Feridun Isiman. 125 l, Pear Woman by Mehmet Uluhan.

Perf. 12½x13

1987, May 27   Wmk. 390
202 A84 50 l multicolored   .35 .25
203 A84 125 l multicolored   .85 .40

Europa A85

Modern architecture: 50 l, Bauhaus-style house, designed by A. Vural Behaeddin, 1973. 200 l, House, designed by Necdet Turgay, 1979.

1987, June 30   Perf. 12½
204 A85 50 l multicolored   2.00 .40
205 A85 200 l multicolored   5.00 1.75
  a. Bklt. pane, 2 each #204-205   16.00

No. 205a contains two copies each of Nos. 204-205, printed alternately, with unprinted selvage at each end of the pane, perf between stamps and selvage and imperf on outside edges. Thus, singles from the pane gauge 12½ by imperf.

Folk Dancers — A86

1987, Aug. 20
206 A86 20 l multicolored   .25 .25
207 A86 50 l multi, diff.   .25 .25
208 A86 200 l multi, diff.   .50 .50
209 A86 1000 l multi, diff.   2.50 2.50
  Nos. 206-209 (4)   3.50 3.50

For surcharge see No. 295B.

Infantry Regiment, 1st Anniv. — A87

5th Islamic Summit Conf., Kuwait — A88

Pharmaceutical Federation — A89

1987, Sept. 30
210 A87 50 l multicolored   .25 .25
211 A88 200 l multicolored   .50 .50
212 A89 200 l multicolored   .50 .50
  Nos. 210-212 (3)   1.25 1.25

Ahmet Belig Pasha (1851-1924), Egyptian Judge — A90

Mehmet Emin Pasha (1813-1871), Turkish Grand Vizier — A91

Famous men: 125 l, Mehmet Kamil Pasha (1832-1913), grand vizier.

1987, Oct. 22
213 A90 50 l brn & yel   .25 .25
214 A91 50 l multicolored   .25 .25
215 A91 125 l multicolored   .35 .30
  Nos. 213-215 (3)   .85 .80

Pres. Rauf Denktash, Turkish Prime Minister Turgut Ozal A92

1987, Nov. 2
216 A92 50 l multi   .25 .25

New Kyrenia Harbor A93

Wmk. 390
1987, Nov. 20   Litho.   Perf. 12½
217 A93 150 l shown   .40 .40
218 A93 200 l Eastern Mediterranean University   .55 .55

Chair Weaver, by Osman Guvenir — A94

Paintings: 20 l, Woman Making Pastry, by Ayhan Mentes, vert. 150 l, Woman Weaving a Rug, by Zekai Yesiladali, vert.

Wmk. 390
1988, May 2   Litho.   Perf. 13
219 A94 20 l multi   .25 .25
220 A94 50 l multi   .45 .25
221 A94 150 l multi   .85 .35
  Nos. 219-221 (3)   1.55 .85

Europa A95

1988, May 31   Perf. 12½
222 A95 200 l Tugboat Piyale Pasha   2.75 1.00
223 A95 500 l Satellite dish,
   broadcast tower,
   vert.   4.00 1.25

Bayrak Radio and Television Corporation, 25th anniv. (500 l).

Tourism A96

Photographs: 150 l, Nicosia, by Aysel Erduran. 200 l, Famagusta, by Sonia Halliday and Laura Lushington. 300 l, Kyrenia, by Halliday and Lushington.

1988, June 17
224 A96 150 l multi   .25 .25
225 A96 200 l multi   .35 .35
226 A96 300 l multi   .50 .50
  Nos. 224-226 (3)   1.10 1.10

Turkish Prime Ministers — A97

No. 227, Bulent Ecevit, 1970's. No. 228, Bulent Ulusu, Sept. 21, 1980-Dec. 13, 1983. No. 229, Turgut Ozal, from Dec. 13, 1983.

1988, July 20
227 A97 50 l shown   .25 .25
228 A97 50 l multi   .25 .25
229 A97 50 l multi   .25 .25
  Nos. 227-229 (3)   .75 .75

Civil Defense A98

1988, Aug. 8   Perf. 12x12½
230 A98 150 l multicolored   .35 .35

Summer Olympics, Seoul A99

1988, Sept. 17   Perf. 12½
231 A99 200 l shown   .30 .30
232 A99 250 l Women's running   .40 .40
233 A99 400 l Seoul   .65 .65
  Nos. 231-233 (3)   1.35 1.35

Sedat Simavi (1896-1953), Turkish Journalist — A100

Intl. Conferences, Kyrenia — A101

North Cyprus Intl. Industrial Fair — A102

Intl. Red. Cross and Red Crescent Organizations, 125th Anniv. — A103

US-USSR Summit Meeting on Nuclear Arms Reduction A104

WHO, 40th
Anniv. — A105

1988, Oct. 17   Perf. 12½x12, 12x12½
234 A100   50 l olive grn   .25   .25
235 A101 100 l multi   .25   .25
236 A102 300 l multi   .55   .55
237 A103 400 l multi   .85   .85
238 A104 400 l Gorbachev and
                  Reagan   .85   .85
239 A105 600 l multi   1.10   1.10
      Nos. 234-239 (6)   3.85   3.85

Miniature Sheet

Portraits and Photographs of Kemal
Ataturk — A106

b, Holding canteen. c, In uniform. d, Facing
left.

1988, Nov. 10   Perf. 12½
240 A106   Sheet of 4   3.00   2.00
a.-d.   250 l any single   .45   .30

Souvenir Sheet

Turkish Republic of Northern Cyprus,
5th Anniv. — A107

1988, Nov. 15   Imperf.
241 A107 500 l multicolored   3.25   1.75

Dervis Pasha Mansion, 19th Cent.,
Nicosia — A108

Designs: 400 l, Gamblers' Inn, 17th cent.,
Asmaalti Meydani. 600 l, Camii Cedit Mosque,
1902, Paphos, vert.

1989, Apr. 28   Perf. 13
242 A108 150 l shown   .30   .30
243 A108 400 l multi   .80   .80
244 A108 600 l multi   1.25   1.25
      Nos. 242-244 (3)   2.35   2.35

Europa — A109

1989, May 31   Perf. 12½x12
245 A109   600 l Girl, doll   3.00   1.00
246 A109 1000 l Flying kite   4.00   1.25
a.   Bklt. pane, 2 each #245-246,
        perf. 12½   14.00

Geneva
Peace
Summit,
Aug. 24,
1988
A110

1989, June 30   Perf. 12½
247 A110 500 l blk & dark red   1.00   1.00

Wildlife
A111

1989, July 31
248 A111   100 l Alectoris chukar .25   .25
249 A111   200 l Lepus cyprius   .40   .40
250 A111   700 l Francolinus
                   francolinus   1.40   1.40
251 A111 2000 l Vulpes vulpes   4.00   4.00
      Nos. 248-251 (4)   6.05   6.05

Natl. Development Projects — A112

Perf. 12½x12, 12x12½
1989, Sept. 29
252 A112 100 l Road construc-
                  tion   .25   .25
253 A112 150 l Sanitary water
                  supply   .30   .30
254 A112 200 l Afforestation   .40   .40
255 A112 450 l Telecommunica-
                  tions   .90   .90
256 A112 650 l Power station   1.25   1.25
257 A112 700 l Irrigation ponds 1.40   1.40
      Nos. 252-257 (6)   4.50   4.50

Nos. 253-256 vert.

Free Port, Famagusta, 15th
Anniv. — A113

Turkish Cypriot
Post, 25th
Anniv. — A114

Saded Newspaper, Cent. — A115

Intl. Marine Organization, 30th
Anniv. — A116

Erenkoy
Uprising,
25th
Anniv.
A117

Perf. 12x12½, 12½x13 (450 l)
1989, Nov. 17
258 A113   100 l multicolored   .25   .25
259 A114   450 l multicolored   .90   .90
260 A115   500 l multicolored   1.00   1.00
261 A116   600 l multicolored   1.25   1.25
262 A117 1000 l multicolored   2.00   2.00
      Nos. 258-262 (5)   5.40   5.40

Erdal Inonu   Agriculture
A118   A119

1989, Dec. 15   Perf. 12½x12
263 A118 700 l multicolored   1.40   1.40
Visit of Inonu, Turkish politician, to northern
Cyprus.

1989, Dec. 25   Perf. 12x12½, 12½x12
264 A119 150 l Mule drawn   .30   .30
265 A119 450 l Ox drawn   .90   .90
266 A119 550 l Millstone, olive
                  press   1.10   1.10
      Nos. 264-266 (3)   2.30   2.30

Nos. 264-265 horiz.

World
Health
Day
A120

Perf. 12x12½
1990, Apr. 19   Litho.   Wmk. 390
267 A120 200 l shown   .40   .25
268 A120 700 l Cigarette, heart 1.50   .40

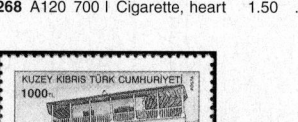

Europa
A121

Post offices.

Perf. 12x12½
1990, May 31   Litho.   Wmk. 390
269 A121 1000 l Yenierenkoy   3.00   1.50
270 A121 1500 l Ataturk
                   Meydani   4.50   2.00
a.   Souv. sheet, 2 #269, 2 #270 18.00 16.00

World Cup Soccer Championships,
Italy — A122

1990, June 8
271 A122   300 l Turkish Cypriot
                   team   .65   .65
272 A122 1000 l Ball, emblem,
                   globe   2.00   2.00

A123

World Environment Day: Birds.

1990, June 5   Perf. 12
273 A123   150 l Turdus
                   philomelos   4.00   .75
274 A123   300 l Sylvia atri-
                   capilla   5.75   1.25
275 A123   900 l Phoenicurus
                   ochruros   12.00   2.75
276 A123 1000 l Phyllosopus
                   collybita   15.00   5.00
      Nos. 273-276 (4)   36.75   9.75

For surcharge see No. 386.

A125

Designs: 300 l, Painting by Filiz Ankac. 1000
l, Sculpture by Sinasi Tekman, vert.

1990, July 31   Perf. 13x12½, 12½x13
279 A125   300 l multicolored   .65   .65
280 A125 1000 l multicolored   2.00   2.00

A126

Wmk. 390
1990, Aug. 24   Litho.   Perf. 12½
281 A126   150 l Amphitheater,
                   Soli   .35   .35
282 A126 1000 l Mosaic, Soli   2.00   2.00
European Tourism Year.

Visit by
Turkish
President
Kenan
Evren
A127

1990, Sept. 19
283 A127 500 l multicolored   1.00   1.00

Traffic
Safety
A128

1990, Sept. 21
284 A128 150 l Wear seat belts .35 .35
285 A128 300 l Obey the speed
limit .65 .65
286 A128 1000 l Obey traffic signals 2.00 2.00
Nos. 284-286 (3) 3.00 3.00

A129   Flowers — A130

1990, Oct. 1
287 A129 1000 l multicolored 2.00 2.00
Visit by Turkish Prime Minister Yildirim
Akbulut.

Perf. 12½x12
1990, Oct. 31   Litho.   Wmk. 390
288 A130 150 l Rosularia cypria .35 .25
289 A130 200 l Silene fraudra-
trix .40 .25
290 A130 300 l Scutellaria
sibthorpii .65 .25
291 A130 600 l Sedum
lampusae 1.25 .30
292 A130 1000 l Onosma caes-
pitosum 2.00 .50
293 A130 1500 l Arabis cypria 3.25 .80
Nos. 288-293 (6) 7.90 2.35

For surcharges see Nos. 295C, 387.

Intl.
Literacy
Year
A131

1990, Nov. 24   Perf. 12x12½
294 A131 300 l Ataturk as teacher .65 .25
295 A131 750 l A, b, c, books,
map 1.60 .40

Nos. 183, 206, 288
Surcharged

1991, June 3
Perfs. & Printing Methods as Before
295A A76 250 l on 10 l #183 .25 .25
295B A86 250 l on 20 l #206 .25 .25
295C A130 500 l on 150 l #288 .35 .25
Nos. 295A-295C (3) .85 .75

Shape of obliterator varies.

Orchids — A132

1991, July 8   Litho.   Perf. 14
296 A132 250 l Ophrys lapethica .55 .55
297 A132 500 l Ophrys kotschyi 1.60 1.60
See Nos. 303-306.

A133

Europa: a, Hermes space shuttle. b,
Ulysses probe.

Perf. 12½x12
1991, July 29   Litho.   Wmk. 390
Miniature Sheet
298 A133 2000 l Sheet of 2,
#a.-b. 10.00 8.00

Public
Fountains
A134

Wmk. 390
1991, Sept. 9   Litho.   Perf. 12
299 A134 250 l Kuchuk
Medrese .25 .25
300 A134 500 l Djafer Pasha .35 .35
301 A134 1500 l Sarayonu
Square 1.10 1.10
302 A134 5000 l Arabahmet
Mosque 3.50 3.50
Nos. 299-302 (4) 5.20 5.20

Orchid Type of 1991
1991, Oct. 10   Perf. 14
303 A132 100 l Serapias levan-
tina .25 .25
304 A132 500 l Dactylorhiza
romana .40 .40
305 A132 2000 l Orchis simia 1.40 1.40
306 A132 3000 l Orchis sancta 2.00 2.00
Nos. 303-306 (4) 4.05 4.05

Hindiler by Salih M. Cizel — A135

Painting: 500 l, Dusme by Asik Mene.

Wmk. 390
1991, Nov. 5   Litho.   Perf. 13
307 A135 250 l multicolored .25 .25
308 A135 500 l multicolored .25 .25
See type A143. For surcharge see No. 381.

World Food Day
A136

Basbakan
Mustafa Cagatay
(1937-1989)
A137

Eastern
Mediterranean
University — A138

Wolfgang
Amadeus
Mozart,
Death
Bicent.
A139

1991, Nov. 20   Perf. 12
309 A136 250 l multicolored .25 .25
310 A137 500 l multicolored .30 .30
311 A138 500 l multicolored .30 .30
312 A139 1500 l multicolored .85 .85
Nos. 309-312 (4) 1.70 1.70

For surcharge see No. 380.

World
AIDS Day
A140

1991, Dec. 13   Perf. 12
313 A140 1000 l multicolored .55 .55

Lighthouses — A141

1991, Dec. 16   Perf. 12x12½
314 A141 250 l Canbulat Burcu,
Famagusta .25 .25
315 A141 500 l Yat Limani,
Kyrenia .30 .30
316 A141 1500 l Turizm Limani,
Kyrenia .85 .85
Nos. 314-316 (3) 1.40 1.40

Tourism
A142

Designs: 250 l, Elephant and hippopotamus
fossils, Kyrenia. 500 l, Roman fish ponds,
Lambusa (58 BC-398 AD). 1500 l, Roman
tomb and church, Lambusa (58 BC-1192 AD).

1991, Dec. 27
317 A142 250 l multicolored .25 .25
318 A142 500 l multicolored .30 .30
319 A142 1500 l multicolored .85 .85
Nos. 317-319 (3) 1.40 1.40

Paintings
A143

Designs: 500 l, Ebru, by Arife Kandulu.
3500 l, Nicosia, by Ismet Tartar.

Wmk. 390
1992, Mar. 31   Litho.   Perf. 14
320 A143 500 l multicolored .25 .25
321 A143 3500 l multicolored 1.75 1.75
See type A135.

Tourism
A144

No. 322, Ancient building, Famagusta. No.
323, Trap shooting range, Nicosia. 1000 l,
Salamis Bay resort, Famagusta. 1500 l,
Casino, Kyrenia.

1992, Apr. 21   Perf. 13½x14, 14x13½
322 A144 500 l multi .25 .25
323 A144 500 l multi .25 .25
324 A144 1000 l multi .50 .50
325 A144 1500 l multi, vert. .75 .75
Nos. 322-325 (4) 1.75 1.75

Souvenir Sheet

Discovery of America, 500th
Anniv. — A145

Europa: a, 1500 l, Santa Maria, Nina and
Pinta. b, 3500 l, Columbus.

1992, May 29   Perf. 13½x14
326 A145 Sheet of 2, #a.-b. 10.00 10.00

Sea
Turtles
A146

Perf. 13½x14
1992, June 30   Litho.   Wmk. 390
327 A146 1000 l Green turtle 3.00 3.00
328 A146 1500 l Loggerhead
turtle 3.50 3.50
a.   Souv. sheet, 2 ea #327-328 14.00 14.00
World Wildlife Fund.

1992
Summer
Olympics,
Barcelona
A147

#329: a, Women's gymnastics, vert. b, Ten-
nis, vert. 1000 l, High jump. 1500 l, Cycling.

1992, July 25   Perf. 14x13½
329 A147 500 l Pair, #a-b. .75 .75

Perf. 13½x14
330 A147 1000 l multicolored .50 .50
331 A147 1500 l multicolored .75 .75
Nos. 329-331 (3) 2.00 2.00

Electric
Power
Plant,
Kyrenia
A148

Social
Insurance,
15th Anniv.
A149

Intl.
Federation
of Women
Artists
A150

Veterinary
Services
A151

Perf. 13½x14

1992, Sept. 30   Litho.   Wmk. 390

332	A148	500 l multicolored	.25	.25
333	A149	500 l multicolored	.25	.25
334	A150	1500 l multicolored	.75	.75
335	A151	1500 l multicolored	.75	.75
		Nos. 332-335 (4)	2.00	2.00

Civil
Aviation
Office,
17th Anniv.
A152

Meteorology Office, 18th
Anniv. — A153

Mapping,
14th
Anniv.
A154

Perf. 13½x14

1992, Nov. 20   Litho.   Wmk. 390

336	A152	1000 l multicolored	.50	.50
337	A153	1000 l multicolored	.50	.50
338	A154	1200 l multicolored	.60	.60
		Nos. 336-338 (3)	1.60	1.60

Native
Cuisine
A155

Food: 2000 l, Zulbiye (pastry). 2500 l, Cicek
Dolmasi (stuffed squash flowers). 3000 l, Tatar
Boregi (flaky pastry dish). 4000 l, Seftali kebab
(meat dish).

1992, Dec. 14

339	A155	2000 l multicolored	1.00	1.00
340	A155	2500 l multicolored	1.25	1.25
341	A155	3000 l multicolored	1.50	1.50
342	A155	4000 l multicolored	2.00	2.00
		Nos. 339-342 (4)	5.75	5.75

Intl. Conference on Nutrition, Rome.
See Nos. 388-390.

Tourism
A156

Designs: 500 l, Church and Monastery of St.
Barnabas. 10,000 l, Bowl.

Perf. 13½x14

1993, Apr. 1   Litho.   Wmk. 390

343	A156	500 l multi	.25	.25
344	A156	10,000 l multi	5.00	5.00

Souvenir Sheet

Europa — A157

Contemporary paintings by: a, 2000 l, Turk-
sal Ince. b, 3000 l, Ilkay Onsoy.

Perf. 14x13½

1993, May 5   Litho.   Wmk. 390

345	A157	Sheet of 2, #a.-b.	2.00	2.00

Trees — A158

1993, June 11   Perf. 14x13½

346	A158	500 l Olea europea	.25	.25
347	A158	1000 l Eucalyptus camaldulensis	.50	.50
348	A158	3000 l Platanus orientalis	1.50	1.50
349	A158	4000 l Pinus brutia te- nore	2.00	2.00
		Nos. 346-349 (4)	4.25	4.25

Arabahmet Rehabilitation
Project — A159

Perf. 13½x14

1993, Sept. 20   Litho.   Wmk. 390

350	A159	1000 l shown	.25	.25
351	A159	3000 l Homes, diff.	.50	.50

Creation of Turkish Republic of
Northern Cyprus, 10th Anniv.
A160

Designs: No. 353, Flags changing to dove,
vert. 1000 l, Dove flying from flag. 5000 l,
Flowers forming "10," map.

Perf. 13½x14, 14x13½

1993, Nov. 15   Litho.   Wmk. 390

352	A160	500 l multicolored	.25	.25
353	A160	500 l multicolored	.25	.25
354	A160	1000 l multicolored	.25	.25
355	A160	5000 l multicolored	.80	.80
		Nos. 352-355 (4)	1.55	1.55

Ataturk, 55th Death
Anniv. — A161

State
Theaters,
30th Anniv.
A162

Turkish Resistance Organization, 35th
Anniv. — A163

Turkish
News
Agency,
20th
Anniv.
A164

Tchaikovsky, Death Cent. — A165

Perf. 14x13½, 13½x14

1993, Dec. 27   Litho.   Wmk. 390

356	A161	500 l multicolored	.25	.25
357	A162	500 l multicolored	.25	.25
358	A163	1500 l multicolored	.30	.30
359	A164	2000 l multicolored	.40	.40
360	A165	5000 l multicolored	1.10	1.10
		Nos. 356-360 (5)	2.30	2.30

Soyle Falci,
by Goral
Ozkan
A166

Design: 6500 l, Sculpture, IV Hareket, by
Senol Ozdevrim.

1994, Mar. 31   Perf. 14

361	A166	1000 l multicolored	.25	.25
362	A166	6500 l multicolored	1.40	1.40

Fazil Kucuk (1906-84), Physician and
Political Leader — A167

1994, Apr. 1

363	A167	1500 l multicolored	.30	.30

Souvenir Sheet

Archaeological Discoveries — A168

Europa: a, Neolithic village, Ayios Epectitos
Vrysi. b, Neolithic man, early tools found in
excavation.

1994, May 16   Perf. 13½

364	A168	8500 l Sheet of 2, #a.-		
		b.	3.00	3.00

1994 World Cup Soccer
Championships, US — A169

1994, June 30

365	A169	2500 l Trophy, vert.	.25	.25
366	A169	10,000 l US map	.80	.80

Turkish
Postal
Service in
Northern
Cyprus,
30th Anniv.
A170

1994, June 30

367	A170	50,000 l multicolored	4.00	4.00

A171

A172

Turkish
Peace
Operation,
20th
Anniv.
A173

1994, July 20   Perf. 14

368	A171	2500 l shown	.25	.25
369	A172	5000 l Monument	.40	.40
370	A172	7000 l Monument, diff.	.50	.50
371	A173	8500 l shown	.65	.65
		Nos. 368-371 (4)	1.80	1.80

First Rural Postal Cancellations, Cent. — A174

Postmarks, stamps: 1500 l, Karpas, Cyprus #131. 2500 l, Gazi Magusa (Famagusta), #71. 5000 l, Bey Keuy, Cyprus #150. 7000 l, Aloa, Cyprus, #179. 8500 l, Pyla, Cyprus #152.

1994, Aug. 15   **Perf. 13½**
372 A174 1500 l multicolored   .25 .25
373 A174 2500 l multicolored   .25 .25
374 A174 5000 l multicolored   .35 .35
375 A174 7000 l multicolored   .55 .55
376 A174 8500 l multicolored   .70 .70
    Nos. 372-376 (5)   2.10 2.10

Sea Shells — A175

1994, Nov. 15   **Perf. 14**
377 A175 2500 l Charonia
              tritonis   .25 .25
378 A175 12,500 l Tonna galea   .70 .35
379 A175 12,500 l Cypraea talpa   .70 .35
    Nos. 377-379 (3)   1.65 .95

Nos. 307, 309 Surcharged

1994, Dec. 12 Perfs., etc. as Before
380 A136 1500 l on 250 l multi   .25 .25
381 A135 2500 l on 250 l multi   .25 .25
    Size and location of surcharge varies.

European Nature Conservation Year — A176

Designs: 2000 l, Donkeys on mountain top. 3500 l, Shoreline. 15,000 l, Donkeys in field.

1995, Feb. 10   Wmk. 390   Perf. 14
382 A176 2000 l multicolored   .25 .25
383 A176 3500 l multicolored   .25 .25
384 A176 15,000 l multicolored   1.00 1.00
    Nos. 382-384 (3)   1.50 1.50

Souvenir Sheet

Peace and Freedom — A177

Europa: a, Globe, dove. b, Doves over Europe.

1995, Apr. 20   **Perf. 13½x14**
385 A177 15,000 l Sheet of 2,
    #a.-b.   2.50 2.50

Nos. 275 & 290 Surcharged

1995, Apr. 21   Perfs., etc. as Before
386 A123 2000 l on 900 l #275   1.75 1.50
387 A130 3500 l on 300 l #290   3.50 3.50
    Size and location of surcharge varies.

Native Cusine Type of 1992

Food: 3500 l, Sini katmeri. 10,000 l, Kolokas musakka, Bullez kizartma. 14,000 l, Enginar dolmasi.

Perf. 13½x14
1995, May 29   Litho.   Wmk. 390
388 A155 3500 l multicolored   .25 .25
389 A155 10,000 l multicolored   .55 .55
390 A155 14,000 l multicolored   .80 .80
    Nos. 388-390 (3)   1.60 1.60

Butterflies A178

1995, June 30
391 A178 3500 l Papilio
              machaon   .25 .25
392 A178 4500 l Charaxes jasi-
              us   .25 .25
393 A178 15,000 l Cynthia cardui .70 .70
394 A178 30,000 l Vanessa ata-
              lanta   1.40 1.40
    Nos. 391-394 (4)   2.60 2.60

Visit by Turkish Pres. Suleyman Demirel A179

1995, Aug. 21   **Perf. 13½**
395 A179 5000 l multicolored   .25 .25

Tourism A180

Designs: 3500 l, Beach scene, Kyrenia. 7500 l, Sailboats. 15,000 l, Ruins, Famagusta,

---

vert. 20,000 l, St. George Cathedral, Famagusta, vert.

1995, Aug. 21
396 A180 3500 l multicolored   .25 .25
397 A180 7500 l multicolored   .40 .40
398 A180 15,000 l multicolored   .80 .80
399 A180 20,000 l multicolored   1.00 1.00
    Nos. 396-399 (4)   2.45 2.45

State Printing Office, 20th Anniv. A181

Turkish Natl. Assembly, 75th Anniv. A182

Louis Pasteur (1822-95) A183

UN, 50th Anniv. A184

G. Marconi (1874-1937), Radio, Cent. — A185

Motion Pictures, Cent. — A186

Perf. 13½x14, 14x13½
1995, Nov. 7   Litho.   Wmk. 390
400 A181 3000 l multicolored   .25 .25
401 A182 3000 l multicolored   .25 .25
402 A183 5000 l multicolored   .25 .25
403 A184 22,000 l multicolored   1.25 1.25
404 A185 30,000 l multicolored   1.60 1.60
405 A186 30,000 l multicolored   1.60 1.60
    Nos. 400-405 (6)   5.20 5.20

A187   A188

Tombstone inscriptions, Orhon and Yenisey river region: 5000 l, Kültigin Heykelinin Basi. 10,000 l, Kültigin Yaziti.

1995, Dec. 28   **Perf. 14x13½**
406 A187 5000 l multicolored   .25 .25
407 A187 10,000 l multicolored   .55 .55
    Reading of Orhon Epitaphs, cent.

1996, Jan. 31
408 A188 10,000 l multicolored   .55 .55
    Bosnia-Herzegovina.

Fish A189

Designs: 60,000 l, Mullus surmuletus. 10,000 l, Thalassoma pavo. 28,000 l, Diplodus vulgaris. 40,000 l, Epinephelus guaza.

1996, Mar. 29   **Perf. 14**
409 A189 6,000 l multicolored   .25 .25
410 A189 10,000 l multicolored   .30 .30
411 A189 28,000 l multicolored   .80 .80
412 A189 40,000 l multicolored   1.10 1.10
    Nos. 409-412 (4)   2.45 2.45
    For surcharge see no. 506.

Tourism A190

Designs: 100,000 l, Pomegranate tree, vert. 150,000 l, Pomegranate fruit, vert. 250,000 l, Bellapais Monastery. 500,000 l, Folk dancing.

Perf. 14x13½, 13½x14
1996, Apr. 26   Litho.   Wmk. 390
413 A190 100,000 l multi   3.00 3.00
414 A190 150,000 l multi   5.00 5.00
415 A190 250,000 l multi   7.00 7.00
416 A190 500,000 l multi   15.00 15.00
    Nos. 413-416 (4)   30.00 30.00

Famous Women A191

Europa: 15,000 l, Beria Remzi Ozoran. 50,000 l, Kadriye Hulusi Hacibulgur.

1996, May 31   **Perf. 13½x14**
417 A191 15,000 l multicolored   .50 .50
418 A191 50,000 l multicolored   2.00 2.00

World Environment Day — A192

Designs: a, Older, dying trees in mountainous area. b, Newly-planted trees.

1996, June 28   **Perf. 13½**
419 A192 50,000 l Sheet of 2,
    #a.-b.   1.10 1.10

1996 Summer Olympic Games,
Atlanta — A193

a, 15,000 l, Basketball. b, 50,000 l, Javelin.
c, 15,000 l, Discus. d, 50,000 l, Volleyball.

1996, July 31
420 A193 Sheet of 4, #a.-d.   3.00 3.00

Euro '96, European Soccer
Championship, Great Britain — A194

1996, Oct. 31   *Perf. 13½x14*
421 A194 15,000 l shown   .40 .40
422 A194 35,000 l Flags, soccer
       ball   1.40 1.40
   a.   Pair, #421-422   2.00 2.00

Civil
Defense
A195

Security
Forces — A196

Nasreddin
Hodja
A197

Children's
Rights
A198

    Perf. 13½x14, 14x13½
1996, Dec. 23   **Litho.**   **Wmk. 390**
423 A195 10,000 l multicolored   .25 .25
424 A196 20,000 l multicolored   .50 .50
425 A197 50,000 l multicolored   1.25 1.25
426 A198 75,000 l multicolored   1.90 1.90
    Nos. 423-426 (4)   3.90 3.90

Paintings — A199

Designs: 25,000 l, Buildings, people, by
Lebibe Sonuc. 70,000 l, Woman seated
beside plant, by Ruzen Atakan.

1997, Jan. 31   *Perf. 14*
427 A199 25,000 l multicolored   .65 .65
428 A199 70,000 l multicolored   1.75 1.75

Mushrooms   Natl. Flag on
A200   Mountainside
            A201

Designs: 15,000 l, Amanita phallioides. No.
430, Morchella esculenta. No. 431, Pleurotus
eryngii. 70,0000 l, Amanita muscaria.

1997, Mar. 31
429 A200 15,000 l multicolored   .45 .45
430 A200 25,000 l multicolored   .65 .65
431 A200 25,000 l multicolored   .65 .65
432 A200 70,000 l multicolored   1.75 1.75
    Nos. 429-432 (4)   3.50 3.50

1997, Apr. 23
433 A201 60,000 l multicolored   1.50 1.50

Stories
and
Legends
A202

Europa: 25,000 l, Woman with broom, children playing, man with donkey. 70,000 l, Well,
apple tree, man behind bushes.

1997, May 30   *Perf. 13½x14*
434 A202 25,000 l multicolored   .75 .75
435 A202 70,000 l multicolored   1.75 1.75

Visit by
Turkish
Leaders
A203

Designs: 15,000 l, Prime Minister Necmed-
din Erbakan, vert. 80,000 l, Pres. Süleyman
Demirel.

    Perf. 14x13½, 13½x14
1997, June 20
436 A203 15,000 l multicolored   .30 .30
437 A203 80,000 l multicolored   1.50 1.50

A204   A205

Raptors: No. 438, Aquila chrysaetos. No.
439, Falco eleanorae. 75,000 l, Falco tinnunculus. 100,000 l, Pernis apivorus.

1997, July 31   *Perf. 14x13½*
438 A204 40,000 l multicolored   .55 .55
439 A204 40,000 l multicolored   .55 .55
440 A204 75,000 l multicolored   1.00 1.00
441 A204 100,000 l multicolored   1.40 1.40
    Nos. 438-441 (4)   3.50 3.50

1997, Oct. 28
   Old Coins Used in Cyprus: 25,000 l, 1861
Abdül Aziz gold lira. 40,000 l, 1808 Mahmud II

---

gold rumi. 75,000 l, 1566 Selim II gold lira.
100,000 l, 1909 Mehmed V gold besibirlik.
442 A205 25,000 l multicolored   .35 .35
443 A205 40,000 l multicolored   .55 .55
444 A205 75,000 l multicolored   1.00 1.00
445 A205 100,000 l multicolored   1.40 1.40
    Nos. 442-445 (4)   3.30 3.30

Turk
Lisesi,
Cent.
A206

Scouting,
90th
Anniv.
A207

Fight Against
AIDS — A208

Diesel
Engine,
Cent.
A209

    Perf. 13½x14, 14x13½
1997, Dec. 22   **Litho.**   **Wmk. 390**
446 A206   25,000 l multicolored   .30 .30
447 A207   40,000 l multicolored   .50 .50
448 A208 100,000 l multicolored   1.25 1.25
449 A209 150,000 l multicolored   1.75 1.75
    Nos. 446-449 (4)   3.80 3.80

Ismet Sevki (1884-1957) and Ahmet
Sevki (1874-1959),
Photographers — A210

1998, Jan. 28   *Perf. 13½x14*
450 A210 40,000 l shown   .50 .50
451 A210 105,000 l Ahmet Sevki,
       vert.   1.25 1.25

Insects
A211

Designs: 40,000 l, Agrion splendens.
65,000 l, Ascalaphus macaronius. 125,000 l,
Podalonia hirsuta. 150,000 l, Rhyssa
persuasoria.

1998, Mar. 30
452 A211 40,000 l multicolored   .40 .40
453 A211 65,000 l multicolored   .65 .65
454 A211 125,000 l multicolored   1.25 1.25
455 A211 150,000 l multicolored   1.50 1.50
    Nos. 452-455 (4)   3.80 3.80

Doors — A212

1998, Apr. 30   *Perf. 14x13½*
456 A212 115,000 l shown   1.10 1.10
457 A212 140,000 l Door, steps   1.40 1.40

Natl.
Festival
A213

Europa: 150,000 l, Globe, map of Cyprus,
flags, vert.

1998, May 30   *Perf. 13½x14, 14x13½*
458 A213   40,000 l multicolored   .65 .65
459 A213 150,000 l multicolored   2.10 2.10

Intl. Year
of the
Ocean
A214

Various marine life.

1998, June 30   *Perf. 13½x14*
460 A214 40,000 l multicolored   .30 .30
461 A214 90,000 l multicolored   .65 .65

Visit by
Turkish
Prime
Minister
Mesut
Yilmaz
A215

1998, July 20
462 A215 75,000 l multicolored   .55 .55

Turkish Pres.   1998 World Cup
Süleyman   Soccer
Demirel — A216   Championships,
            France — A217

Design: 175,000 l, Pres. Demirel, Pres.
Rauf R. Denktash, view of ocean, horiz.

1998, July 25   *Perf. 13½x14, 14x13½*
463 A216 75,000 l multicolored   .55 .55
464 A216 175,000 l multicolored   1.25 1.25

Establishment of Yaylacik water program.

1998, July 31   *Perf. 13½x14, 13x13½*

75,000 l, Team coming across field, fans in
stadium. 175,000 l, Holding up World Cup
trophy.

465 A217 75,000 l multi, horiz.   .55 .55
466 A217 175,000 l multi   1.25 1.25

Visit of Turkish Deputy Prime Minister Bülent Ecevit — A218

Traditional Crafts — A219

1998, Sept. 5   *Perf. 14*
467 A218 200,000 l multicolored   1.50 1.50

1998, Oct. 26   *Perf. 13½x14, 14x13½*
468 A219   50,000 l Kalayci, horiz.   .40 .40
469 A219   75,000 l Sepetci   .60 .60
470 A219 130,000 l Bileyici   1.00 1.00
471 A219 400,000 l Oymaci, horiz.   3.00 3.00
    Nos. 468-471 (4)   5.00 5.00

Bayrak Radio & Television, 35th Anniv. A220

Turkish Cyprus, 15th Anniv. A221

Turkish Republic, 75th Anniv. A222

Universal Declaration of Human Rights, 50th Anniv. — A223

No. 476a, 75,000 l, Natl. flag, map of Turkish Cyprus.

1998, Nov. 15
472 A220   50,000 l multicolored   .40 .40
473 A221   75,000 l multicolored   .55 .55
474 A222   75,000 l multicolored   .55 .55
475 A223 175,000 l multicolored   1.25 .65
    Nos. 472-475 (4)   2.75 2.15
Souvenir Sheet
476   Sheet of 2, #473, #476a   1.10 1.10

A224

1999, Jan. 15   *Perf. 14*
477 A224 75,000 l multicolored   .55 .55
    Dr. Fazil Kücük (1906-84), politician.

A225

Scene from "Othello," by Verdi: a, Singers standing. b, Singer on floor.

1999, Jan. 30
478 A225 200,000 l Sheet of 2, #a.-b.   2.00 2.00

Snakes A226

Designs: 50,000 l, Malpolon monspessulanus insignitus. 75,000 l, Hierophis jugularis. 195,000 l, Vipera lebetina. 220,000 l, Natrix natrix.

1999, Mar. 26   *Perf. 13½x14*
479 A226   50,000 l multicolored   .40 .40
480 A226   75,000 l multicolored   .60 .60
481 A226 195,000 l multicolored   1.60 1.60
482 A226 220,000 l multicolored   1.75 1.75
    Nos. 479-482 (4)   4.35 4.35

Europa A227

1999, May 17   *Perf. 14*
483 A227   75,000 l Sütunlu Cave   .75 .75
484 A227 200,000 l Incirli Cave, vert.   1.75 1.75

Turkish Peace Operation, 25th Anniv. A228

Wmk. 390
1999, July 20   **Litho.**   *Perf. 13¾*
485 A228 150,000 l shown   1.25 1.25
486 A228 250,000 l Dove, map, sun   2.00 2.00

Turkish Postal Administration in Cyprus, 35th Anniv. — A229

1999, Nov. 12   **Litho.**   *Perf. 13¾*
487 A229 75,000 l multicolored   .25 .25

UPU, 125th Anniv. A230

1999, Nov. 12
488 A230 225,000 l multicolored   .80 .80

Total Solar Eclipse, Aug. 11 — A231

1999, Nov. 12
489 A231 250,000 l multicolored   .90 .90

Destruction of Turkish Heritage in Southern Cyprus — A232

Photos of: 75,000 l, Building, Limassol. 150,000 l, Mosque, Evdim. 210,000 l, Bayraktar Mosque, Nicosia (Lefkosa). 1,000,000 l, Cami-i Kebir Mosque, Paphos (Baf), vert.

1999, Dec. 3
490 A232   75,000 l multi   .25 .25
491 A232 150,000 l multi   .55 .55
492 A232 210,000 l multi   .75 .75
493 A232 1,000,000 l multi   3.75 3.75
    Nos. 490-493 (4)   5.30 5.30

Millennium A233

Designs: 75,000 l, Cellular phone. 150,000 l, "Welcome 2000." 275,000 l, Computer. 300,000 l, Satellite.

2000, Mar. 3   **Litho.**   *Perf. 13¾*
494 A233   75,000 l multi   .25 .25
495 A233 150,000 l multi   .50 .50
496 A233 275,000 l multi   .95 .95
497 A233 300,000 l multi   1.00 1.00
    Nos. 494-497 (4)   2.70 2.70

Beach Scenes A234

Designs: 300,000 l, Umbrella, pail, shovel, beach ball, sailboats. 340,000 l, Beach chair.

2000, Apr. 29   **Litho.**   *Perf. 13¾*
498 A234 300,000 l multi   1.00 1.00
499 A234 340,000 l multi   1.10 1.10

Europa, 2000
Common Design Type and

A235

2000, May 31   **Wmk. 390**   *Perf. 14*
500   Sheet of 2   1.90 1.90
  a.   CD17 300,000 l multi   .95 .95
  b.   A235 300,000 l multi   .95 .95

4th Intl. Music Festival, Bellapais Abbey A236

Designs: 150,000 l, Bellapais Abbey. 350,000 l, Blended colors, vert.

Visit of Turkish Pres. Ahmet N. Sezer — A237

2000, June 21   *Perf. 13¾*
501 A236 150,000 l multi   .45 .45
502 A236 350,000 l multi   1.10 1.10

2000, June 22
503 A237 150,000 l multi   .45 .45

2000 Summer Olympics, Sydney A238

125,000 l, Torch and Olympic rings, vert. 200,000 l, Runner.

2000, July 25
504-505 A238 Set of 2   .90 .90

No. 409 Surcharged

Method & Perf. as Before
2000, Sept. 28   **Wmk. 390**
506 A189 50,000 l on 6000 l   .25 .25

Flora and Fauna — A239

Designs: 125,000 l, Praying mantis on flower. 200,000 l, Butterfly on flower. 275,000 l, Bee on flower. 600,000 l, Snail on flower stem.

Wmk. 390
2000, Oct. 16   **Litho.**   *Perf. 13¾*
507-510 A239 Set of 4   3.75 3.75

Kerchief Borders A240

Background colors: 125,000 l, Yellow. 200,000 l, Lilac. 265,000 l, Green. 350,000 l, Brown.

2000, Nov. 28
511-514 A240 Set of 4   3.00 3.00

Restored Buildings, Nicosia (Lefkosa) A241

Designs: 125,000 l, Lusignan House. 200,000 l, Eaved House.

Wmk. 390
2001, Mar. 28   **Litho.**   *Perf. 13¾*
515-516   A241   Set of 2   .75   .75

Art — A242

Works by: 125,000 l, Inci Kansu. 200,000 l, Emel Samioglu. 350,000 l, Ozden Selenge, vert. 400,000 l, Ayhatun Atesin.

2001, Mar. 30
517-520   A242   Set of 4   2.50   2.50

Europa — A243   World Environment Day — A244

Designs: 200,000 l, Degirmenlik Reservoir. 500,000 l, Waterfall, Sinar.

2001, May 31
521-522   A243   Set of 2   1.60   1.60

2001, June 22
Designs: 125,000 l, Atomic model, x-ray images. 450,000 l, X-ray images, radiation symbol.
523-524   A244   Set of 2   1.10   1.10

Police Uniforms — A245

Uniforms from: 125,000 l, 1885. 200,000 l, 1933. 500,000 l, 1934. 750,000 l, 1983.

2001, Aug. 24
525-528   A245   Set of 4   2.75   2.75

Automobiles — A246

Designs: 175,000 l, 1954 MG TF. 300,000 l, 1948 Vauxhall 14. 475,000 l, 1922 Bentley. 600,000 l, 1955 Jaguar XK 120.

Wmk. 390
2001, Nov. 2   **Litho.**   *Perf. 13¾*
529-532   A246   Set of 4   1.90   1.90

Publication of The Genocide Files, by Harry Scott Gibbons — A247

2001, Dec. 24
533   A247   200,000 l multi   .30   .30

July 20th Technical School, Cent. A248

2001, Dec. 24
534   A248   200,000 l multi   .30   .30

Cartoon Art — A249

Designs: 250,000 l, Chef with grinder and book, by Utku Karsu, vert. 300,000 l, People singing "We Are the World," malnourished Africans, by Musa Kayra. 475,000 l, Can of diet cola airdropped for a malnourished African, by Serhan Gazi, vert. 850,000 l, Child viewing city and painting a country scene, by Mustafa Tozaki, vert.

Wmk. 390
2002, Feb. 28   **Litho.**   *Perf. 13¾*
535-538   A249   Set of 4   2.60   2.60

Tourism A250

Underwater photographs: 250,000 l, Turtle swimming. 300,000 l, Starfish on coral. 500,000 l, Fish. 750,000 l, Shipwreck.

2002, Mar. 27
539-542   A250   Set of 4   2.50   2.50

Souvenir Sheet

Europa — A251

No. 543: a, Man on stilts. b, Tightrope walker.

Wmk. 390
2002, May 27   **Litho.**   *Perf. 13¾*
543   A251   600,000 l Sheet of 2,
       #a-b   1.50   1.50

2002 World Cup Soccer Championships, Japan and Korea — A252

Designs: 300,000 l, Soccer team. 1,000,000 l, "Lift Embargo on Sports."

2002, June 24
544-545   A252   Set of 2   1.60   1.60

Native Costumes — A253

Designs: 250,000 l, Woman. 300,000 l, Man. 425,000 l, Man, diff. 700,000 l, Woman, diff.

2002, Aug. 8
546-549   A253   Set of 4   2.00   2.00

Children's Art — A254

Art by: 300,000 l, M. A. Alpdogan. 600,000 l, S. Avci, vert.

Wmk. 390
2002, Sept. 30   **Litho.**   *Perf. 13¾*
550-551   A254   Set of 2   .90   .90

Sports Personalities — A255

Designs: 300,000 l, Sureyya Ayhan, winner of women's 1500m race at 2002 European Track and Field Championships. 1,000,000 l, Park Jung-tae (1944-2002), father of modern taekwondo.

2002, Oct. 28
552-553   A255   Set of 2   1.60   1.60

Famous Men — A256

Designs: 100,000 l, Oguz Karayel (1933-96), soccer player. 175,000 l, Mete Adanir (1961-89), soccer player. 300,000 l, M. Necati Ozkan (1899-1970). 575,000 l, Osman Turkay (1927-2001), poet, horiz.

2002, Dec. 3
554-557   A256   Set of 4   1.40   1.40

Art — A257

Paintings by: 250,000 l, S. Bayraktar. 1,000,000 l, F. Sükan.

Wmk. 390
2003, Feb. 21   **Litho.**   *Perf. 13¾*
558-559   A257   Set of 2   1.50   1.50

Souvenir Sheet

Europa — A258

Poster art: a, Tree. b, Question mark.

2003, May 8
560   A258   600,000 l Sheet of 2,
       #a-b   1.60   1.60

Birds A259

Designs: 100,000 l, Oenanthe cypriaca. 300,000 l, Sylvia melanothorax. 500,000 l, Phalacrocorax pygmeus, vert. 600,000 l, Phoenicopterus ruber, vert.

2003, June 3
561-564   A259   Set of 4   2.10   2.10

Chests A260

Chest from: 250,000 l, Seher. 300,000 l, Lapta. 525,000 l, Baf. 1,000,000 l, Karpaz ve Akatu.

Perf. 13¾x14
2003, July 25   **Litho.**   **Wmk. 390**
565-568   A260   Set of 4   3.00   3.00

Flowers — A261

Designs: 150,000 l, Gladiolus triphyllus. 175,000 l, Tulipa cypria. 500,000 l, Ranunculus asiaticus. 525,000 l, Narcissus tazetta.

2003, Oct. 21   *Perf. 14x13¾*
569-572   A261   Set of 4   1.75   1.75

National Anniversaries — A262

No. 573 — Kemal Ataturk and flag of: a, Turkey. b, Turkish Republic of Northern Cyprus.

2003, Nov. 14   *Perf. 13¾x14*
573   A262   3,000,000 l Horiz. pair,
       #a-b   8.50   8.50

Republic of Turkey, 80th anniv. (#573a), Turkish Republic of Northern Cyprus, 20th anniv. (#573b).

Federation of Agricultural Producers, 60th Anniv. A263

2003, Dec. 12
574 A263 300,000 l multi   .45 .45

Lions International in Turkish Republic of Northern Cyprus, 40th Anniv. — A263a

2003, Dec. 12
575 A264 500,000 l multi   .70 .70

Turkish Postal Service in Northern Cyprus, 40th Anniv. A264

Emblem and: 250,000 l, Mailbox and Nicosia Post Office. 1,500,000 l, Globe, winged envelopes.

Perf. 13¾x14
2004, Apr. 30   Litho.   Wmk. 390
576-577 A264   Set of 2   2.40 2.40

Souvenir Sheet

Europa — A265

No. 578: a, Beach, sailboat. b, Woman holding drink, beach.

2004, May 25
578 A265 600,000 l Sheet of 2,
             #a-b   1.60 1.60
             Exists imperf.

Eurasia Postal Union A266

2004, June 7
579 A266 300,000 l multi   .40 .40

Flowers — A267

Designs: 250,000 l, Salvia veneris. 300,000 l, Phlomis cypria. 500,000 l, Pimpinella cypria. 600,000 l, Rosularia cypria.

2004, July 9   Perf. 14x13¾
580-583 A267   Set of 4   2.40 2.40

Soccer Stadiums A268

Stadium and: 300,000 l, European Soccer Championships emblem. 1,000,000 l, UEFA (European Football Union) 50th anniv. emblem.

2004, Aug. 20   Perf. 13¾x14
584-585 A268   Set of 2   1.75 1.75

2004 Summer Olympics, Athens — A269

No. 586, 300,000 l: a, Sailing, handball. b, Boxing, equestrian.
No. 587, 500,000 l: a, Weight lifting, gymnastics. b, Canoeing, tennis.

2004, Sept. 24   Perf. 14x13¾
Horiz. pairs, #a-b
586-587 A269   Set of 2   2.25 2.25

Eastern Mediterranean University, 25th Anniv. (in 2004) — A270

2005, Feb. 15   Litho.   Perf. 13¾x14
588 A270 15k multi   .25 .25

Cyprus Turkish Philatelic Association, 25th Anniv. (in 2004) — A271

2005, Feb. 15
589 A271 30k multi   .50 .50

Website for Universities in Turkish Republic of Northern Cyprus — A272

2005, Feb. 15
590 A272 50k multi   .80 .80

A273

Tourism A274

2005, Mar. 9
591 A273 10k multi   .25 .25
592 A274 1 l multi   1.60 1.60

Children's Drawings — A275

Drawings of men and women by: 25k, E. Demirci. 50k, E. Oztemiz.

2005, Apr. 22   Perf. 14x13¾
593-594 A275   Set of 2   1.10 1.10

Europa — A276

No. 595: a, Woman at left, round table. b, Oven, square table, woman at right.

2005, May 30   Perf. 13¾x14
595 A276 60k Pair, #a-b   1.75 1.75
 c.   Souvenir sheet, 2 #595   3.50 3.50

Flowers — A277

Designs: 15k, Fianthus cyprius. 25k, Delphinium caseyi. 30k, Brassica hilarionis. 50k, Limonium albidum.

2005, July 8   Perf. 14x13¾
596-599 A277   Set of 4   1.90 1.90
          See Nos. 608-613.

Arts in Towns A278

Designs, 10k, Beach, umbrellas, musical symbols, artist's palette, olive branches, Kyrenia (Girne). 25k, Musical symbols, mosque, Famagusta (Gazimagusa). 50k, Dancers, building, Nicosia (Lefkosa). 1 l, Theater and masks, Kyrenia, Famagusta and Nicosia.

Perf. 13½x13¾
2005, Sept. 9   Litho.   Wmk. 390
600-603 A278   Set of 4   2.75 2.75

Ercan Airport — A279

2005, Nov. 23   Perf. 13¾x13½
604 A279 50k multi   .75 .75

University of Northern Cyprus A280

2005, Nov. 23   Perf. 13½x13¾
605 A280 1 l multi   1.50 1.50

Europa Stamps, 50th Anniv. A281

Designs: No. 606, 1.40 l, Map of Cyprus. No. 607, 1.40 l, Photo of Cyprus from space, satellite.

2006, Jan. 6
606-607 A281   Set of 2   4.25 4.25
607a   Souvenir sheet, #606-607 4.25 4.25
          No. 607a exists imperf.

Flowers Type of 2005

Designs: 15k, Helianthemum obtusifolium. 25k, Iris sisyrhinchium, horiz. 40k, Ranunculus asiaticus, horiz. 50k, Crocus veneris, horiz. 60k, Anemone coronaria, horiz. 70k, Cyclamen persicum.

Perf. 14x13¾, 13¾x14
2006   Litho.   Wmk. 390
608-613 A277   Set of 6   3.75 3.75

Art — A282

Design: 55k, Sculpture by S. Oztan. 60k, Painting by M. Hastürk.

Perf. 13¾x13½
2006, Apr. 7   Litho.   Wmk. 390
614-615 A282   Set of 2   1.75 1.75

Dr. Fazil Kucuk (1906-84), Politician — A283

2006, May 18
616 A283 40k multi   .50 .50

1038 TURKISH REPUBLIC OF NORTHERN CYPRUS

Kemal Ataturk
(1881-1938)
A284

2006, May 18
617 A284 1 l multi   1.25 1.25

Europa — A286

Designs: No. 618, 70k, Birds and stars. No.
619, 70k, Pregnant woman, fetus, flags of
European countries.

2006, May 18
618-619 A286   Set of 2   1.75 1.75
619a   Souvenir sheet, #618-619   1.75 1.75

No. 619a exists imperf.

2006 World Cup Soccer
Championships, Germany — A287

No. 620: a, 50k, World Cup trophy, map of
Germany, mascots, soccer ball and field. b,
1 l, Soccer ball, player, Brandenburg Gate.

2006, July 7   Perf. 13¾x13½
620 A287   Pair, #a-b   2.00 2.00

Birds   Forest Fire
A288   Prevention
               A289

Designs: 40k, Vanellus vanellus. 50k, Anas
platyrhynchos. 60k, Alcedo atthis. 1 l,
Himantopus himantopus.

2006, Sept. 22
621-624 A288   Set of 4   3.50 3.50

2006, Oct. 10   Perf. 14x13¾
625 A289 50k multi   .70 .70

Naci Talat
(1945-91),
Politician
A290

2006, Oct. 10   Perf. 14
626 A290 70k multi   .95 .95

Eastern
Mediterranean Intl.
Regatta — A291

2006, Oct. 10   Perf. 14x13¾
627 A291 1.50 l multi   2.10 2.10

Environmental
Conference — A292

Designs: 50k, Leaf. 80k, Globe, plant and
drought-stricken ground.

Wmk. 390
2007, Feb. 19 Litho.   Perf. 14
628-629 A292   Set of 2   1.90 1.90

Antique
Household
Items
A293

Designs: 70k, Pitcher. 80k, Iron. 1.50 l, Oil
lamp, vert. 2 l, Gas burner and pot, vert.

2007, Apr. 6   Perf. 13¾x14, 14x13¾
630-633 A293   Set of 4   7.50 7.50

Europa — A294

Emblems, tent, campfire, hand giving Scout
sign, dove and: No. 634, 80k, One Scout. No.
635, 80k, Three Scouts playing musical
instruments.

2007, May 4   Perf. 14x13¾
634-635 A294   Set of 2   2.40 2.40
635a   Souvenir sheet, #634-635,
       imperf.   2.40 2.40

Scouting, cent.

Painting by O.
Keten — A295

Painting
by S.
Cavusoglu
A296

2007, July 12 Perf. 14x13¾, 13¾x14
636 A295 50k multi   .80 .80
637 A296 70k multi   1.10 1.10

Occupations of the Past — A297

Designs: 40k, Rattan weaver. 65k, Fruit
peddler. 70k, Shoemaker. 1 l, Shoeshiner.

2007, Sept. 14   Perf. 13¾x14
638-641 A297   Set of 4   4.75 4.75

Methods of Postal
Transport — A298

Designs: 50k, Carrier pigeons. 60k,
Mounted postman, coach, automobile. 1 l,
Postman on bicycle, horiz. 1.25 l, Postman on
motor scooter, horiz.

Perf. 14x13¾, 13¾x14
2007, Nov. 16
642-645 A298   Set of 4   5.75 5.75

Flowers — A299   Europa — A300

Designs: 25k, Asphodelus aestivus. 50k,
Ophrys fusca. 60k, Bellis perennis. 70k,
Ophrys sphegodes. 80k, Dianthus strictus.
1.60 l, Ophrys argolica. 2.20 l, Crocus cyprius.
3 l, Limodorum abortivum. 5 l, Carlina
pygmaea. 10 l, Ophrys kotschyi.

Wmk. 390
2008, Mar. 20 Litho.   Perf. 14
646 A299 25k multi   .40   .40
647 A299 50k multi   .80   .80
648 A299 60k multi   .95   .95
649 A299 70k multi   1.10 1.10
650 A299 80k multi   1.25 1.25
651 A299 1.60 l multi 2.50 2.50
652 A299 2.20 l multi 3.50 3.50
653 A299 3 l multi   4.75 4.75
654 A299 5 l multi   7.75 7.75
655 A299 10 l multi   15.50 15.50
       Nos. 646-655 (10) 38.50 38.50

2008, May 8   Perf. 14x13¾
Designs: No. 656, 80k, Woman writing letter. No. 657, 80k, Quill pen, world map.
656-657 A300   Set of 2   2.60 2.60

Souvenir Sheet

2008 Summer Olympics,
Beijing — A301

No. 658: a, Diving. b, Gymnastics.

2008, July 24
658 A301 65k Sheet of 2, #a-b   2.25 2.25
Exists imperf.

Souvenir Sheet

Turkish Resistance Organization, 50th
Anniv. — A302

No. 659: a, Emblem and "50." b, Monument,
Lefkosa.

2008, Aug. 1   Imperf.
659 A302 1 l Sheet of 2, #a-b   3.50 3.50

Nicosia   Inner Wheel
(Lefkosa)   International
Municipal   A304
Government,
50th Anniv.
A303

Cyprus
Turkish
Airlines Jet
A305

Civil Defense
Organization
A306

Perf. 14x13¾, 13¾x14

2008, Sept. 18
660	A303	55k multi	.85	.85
661	A304	80k multi	1.25	1.25
662	A305	1 l multi	1.60	1.60
663	A306	1.50 l multi	2.40	2.40
		Nos. 660-663 (4)	6.10	6.10

Turkish Declaration of Independence of Northern Cyprus, 25th Anniv. — A307

2008, Nov. 15   *Perf. 14*
664	A307	1 l multi	1.25	1.25

Tradesmen — A308

Designs: 60k, Upholsterer. 70k, Miller. 80k, Bicycle mechanic. 2 l, Circumcisor.

2008, Nov. 20   *Perf. 13¾x14*
665-668	A308	Set of 4	5.25	5.25

Archaeology — A309

Items from Soli archaeological site: 60k, Gold ring. 2 l, Gold crown.

Perf. 13¾x14
2009, Mar. 23   Litho.   Wmk. 390
669-670	A309	Set of 2	3.25	3.25

Europa — A310

No. 671: a, Solar system. b, Galaxy and comet.

2009, May 5
671	A310	80k Pair, #a-b	2.10	2.10

Intl. Year of Astronomy.

Medicinal Plants — A311

Designs: 50k, Cistus creticus. 60k, Capparis spinosa. 70k, Pancratium maritimum. 1 l, Passiflora caerulea.

2009, July 9   *Perf. 14x13¾*
672-675	A311	Set of 4	3.75	3.75

Reptiles and Amphibians — A312

Designs: 80k, Agama stellio. 1.50 l, Bufo viridis.

2009, Sept. 14   *Perf. 13¼*
676-677	A312	Set of 2	3.25	3.25

Turkish Cypriot Air Traffic Controllers Association — A313

Turkish Cypriot Chamber of Commerce — A314   Ziya Rizki (1919-94), Politician A315

2009, Nov. 12   *Perf. 13¾x14*
678	A313	65k multi	.90	.90

Perf. 14x13¾
679	A314	1 l multi	1.40	1.40
680	A315	1.50 l multi	2.00	2.00
		Nos. 678-680 (3)	4.30	4.30

Turkish Cypriot Representation at Organization of the Islamic Conference, 34th Anniv. — A316

Emblem and: 70k, Map of Islamic Conference countries, flag, mosque, arch. 1 l, Mosque, flag, arch.

2010, Mar. 17   *Perf. 14x13¾*
681-682	A316	Set of 2	2.25	2.25

Europa A317

2010, May 28   *Perf. 13¾x14*
683	A317	Pair	2.00	2.00
a.		80k Two faces	1.00	1.00
b.		80k Girl reading book	1.00	1.00
c.		As "a," perf. 13¾ horiz.	1.00	1.00
d.		As "b," perf. 13¾ horiz.	1.00	1.00
e.		Vert. pair, #683c-683d	2.00	2.00
f.		Booklet pane, 2 #683e	4.00	
		Complete booklet, #683f	4.00	

Worldwide Fund for Nature (WWF) A318

Designs: No. 684, 25k, Larus melanocephalus. No. 685, 25k, Larus audouinii. No. 686, 30k, Larus ridibundus. No. 687, 30k, Larus genei.

2010, June 4   *Perf. 14*
684-687	A318	Set of 4	1.40	1.40

2010 World Cup Soccer Championships, South Africa — A319

2010 World Cup Soccer Championships emblem and: 50k, World Cup trophy, crowd. 2 l, Flag of South Africa, elephants, soccer player, mascot.

2010, July 8   *Perf. 14x13¾*
688-689	A319	Set of 2	3.25	3.25

Foreign Press Association — A320

Journalists: 60k, Kemal Asik (1925-89). 70k, Abdi Ipekçi (1929-79). 80k, Adem Yavuz (1943-74). 1 l, Sedat Simavi (1896-1953).

2010, Sept. 1   *Perf. 14*
690-693	A320	Set of 4	4.25	4.25

Cruise Ships and Tourist Attractions A321

Various ships and attractions: 1.50 l, 2 l.

2010, Oct. 20   *Perf. 13¾x14*
694-695	A321	Set of 2	5.00	5.00

Workers for Turkish Cypriot Society — A322

Designs: 50k, Ozdemir Sennaroglu (1931-85). 60k, Osman Orek (1925-99). 70k, Salih Miroglu (1953-2005). 80k, Ozker Ozgür (1940-2005).

2010, Dec. 24   *Perf. 14x13¾*
696-699	A322	Set of 4	3.50	3.50

American University, Girne (Kyrenia), 25th Anniv. A323

2010, Dec. 24   *Perf. 13¾x14*
700	A323	1 l multi	1.40	1.40

Politicians — A324

Designs: 80k, Dr. Niyazi Manyera (1911-99), Republic of Cyprus Minister of Health. 1.10 l, Mustafa Fazil Plümer (1914-2001), Republic of Cyprus Agriculture Minister. 2 l, Osman Orek (1925-99), Prime Minister of Turkish Republic of Northern Cyprus. 2.20 l, Dr. Fazil Küçük (1906-84), Vice-president of Republic of Cyprus.

2011, Mar. 9   *Perf. 14x13¾*
701-704	A324	Set of 4	7.75	7.75

Tourism A325

Designs: 50k, Ayios Philon Church. 80k, Ayios Trias Basilica, vert. 1.10 l, Aphendrika. 2 l, Apostolos Andreas Monastery, vert.

2011, Apr. 18   *Perf. 13¾x14, 14x13¾*
705-708	A325	Set of 4	5.75	5.75

Europa — A326

Designs: No. 709, 1.50 l, Ladybug, forest on hillside. No. 710, 1.50 l, Pinecone, forest.

Perf. 14x13¾
2011, May 16   Wmk. 390
709-710	A326	Set of 2	4.00	4.00
710a		Souvenir sheet of 2, #a709-710	4.00	4.00

Intl. Year of Forests.

Wedding of Prince William and Catherine Middleton — A327

2011, May 27
711	A327	1 l multi	1.25	1.25

Trees — A328

Designs: 1 l, Quercus infectoria. 2.50 l, Olea europaea.

2011, July 18
712-713   A328   Set of 2   4.00 4.00

Art — A329

Design: 60k, Drawing by Birol Ruhi. 70k, Painting by Kemal Ankaç. 80k, Sculpture by Baki Bogaç. 1 l, Painting by Salih Bayraktar, horiz.

Perf. 14x13¾, 13¾x14
2011, Sept. 14
714-717   A329   Set of 4   3.50 3.50

Flora — A330

Designs: 25k, Ziziphus lotus. 50k, Cynara cardunculus. 60k, Oxalis pes-caprae. 70k, Malva sylvestris. 80k, Rubus sanctus. 1.50 l, Crataegus monogyna.

2011, Nov. 25   **Perf. 13¾**
718-723   A330   Set of 6   4.75 4.75

Miniature Sheet

Rauf Denktash (1924-2012), First President of Turkish Republic of Northern Cyprus — A331

No. 724 — Denktash: a, 60k, With dove on arm, flag in background. b, 60k, With flag in background. c, 1 l, At microphone. d, 1 l, Wearing striped tie.

2012, Mar. 16   **Perf. 14**
724   A331   Sheet of 4, #a-d   3.75 3.75

POSTAL TAX STAMP

Trees — PT1

1995, July 24   **Litho.**   **Perf. 14**
RA1   PT1 1000 l black & green   2.00 1.25

TURKMENISTAN

.tərk-ˌme-nə-'stan

LOCATION — Southern Asia, bounded by Kazakhstan, Uzbekistan, Iran and Afghanistan
GOVT. — Independent republic, member of the Commonwealth of Independent States
AREA — 188,417 sq. mi.
POP. — 4,366,383 (1999 est.)
CAPITAL — Ashgabat

With the breakup of the Soviet Union on Dec. 26, 1991, Turkmenistan and ten former Soviet republics established the Commonwealth of Independent States.

100 Kopecks = 1 Ruble

Manat (1994)

Catalogue values for all unused stamps in this country are for Never Hinged items.

Dagdan Necklace, 19th Century — A1

Designs: No. 3, Girl in traditional costume, horiz. No. 4, Akhaltekin horse and rider in native riding dress. No. 5, Mollanepes Theater, horiz. 15r, National arms. No. 7, Pres. Saparmurad Niyazov at left, national flag, horiz. No. 8, Niyazov at right, flag, horiz. No. 9, Map of Turkmenistan.

1992   **Litho.**   **Perf. 12x12½**
1   A1   50k multicolored   .30 .30
Perf. 12½
2   A1   10r multicolored   .35 .35
3   A1   10r multicolored   .40 .40
4   A1   10r multicolored   .40 .40
5   A1   10r multicolored   .40 .40
6   A1   15r multicolored   .70 .70
7   A1   25r multicolored   1.10 1.10
8   A1   25r multicolored   2.50 2.50
     Nos. 1-8 (8)   6.15 6.15

Size: 112x79mm
Imperf
9   A1   10r multicolored   8.25 8.25

Issued: 50k, 1992; #8, 12/8; others, 8/27. Nos. 2-8 exist imperf. Value, set $100.

Nos. 4, 6 Overprinted

1992, Dec. 12   **Color of Overprint**
10   A1   10r black   4.50 4.50
11   A1   10r brown   4.50 4.50
12   A1   10r red   4.50 4.50
13   A1   10r vermilion   — —
14   A1   10r carmine   4.50 4.50
15   A1   10r green   4.50 4.50
16   A1   15r black   4.50 4.50
17   A1   15r brown   4.50 4.50
18   A1   15r red   4.50 4.50
19   A1   15r pink   — —
20   A1   15r blue   4.50 4.50
21   A1   15r yellow   — —
     Nos. 10-21 (12)   40.50 40.50

1992 Summer Olympics, Barcelona A2

Designs: a, 1r, Weight lifting. b, 3r, Equestrian. c, 5r, Wrestling. d, 10r, Rowing. e, 15r, Emblem of Turkmenistan Olympic Committee. No. 23, Flags, symbols for modern pentathalon, weight lifting, rowing, gymnastics.

1992, Dec. 15   Photo.   Perf. 10½x10
22   A2   Strip of 5, #a.-e.   9.25 9.25
Imperf
23   A2   15r multicolored   11.00 11.00
For surcharge see No. 33.

Musical Instruments — A3

Photo. & Engr.
1992, Sept. 13   **Perf. 12x11½**
28   A3   35k buff, red brn, gold & black   .30 .30

Horse A4

1992, Aug. 9   **Photo.**   **Perf. 12**
29   A4   20k shown   .25 .25
30   A4   40k Snake, vert.   .25 .25

A5

1992, Nov. 29   **Litho.**   **Perf. 12x11½**
31   A5   1r multicolored   .30 .30

US Pres. Bill Clinton, Pres. Saparmurad Niyazov — A6

Designs dated: a. 21.30.93. b. 22.03.93. c, 23.03.93. d, 24.03.93. e, 25.03.93.

1993, Mar. 21   **Litho.**   **Perf. 10½**
32   A6   100r Strip of 5, #a.-e.   12.00 12.00
Pres. Niyazov's visit to New York City & Washington DC.
Exists imperf. Value, $25.

No. 22 Surcharged

1993, Apr. 1   **Photo.**   **Perf. 10½x10**
33   A2   Strip of 5   7.00 7.00
   a.   25r on 1r   1.40 1.40
   b.   10r on 3r   .65 .65
   c.   15r on 5r   .75 .75
   d.   15r on 10r   .75 .75
   e.   50r on 15r   2.40 2.40
     Size of surcharge varies.

Phoca Caspica — A7

World Wildlife Fund A8

Phoca caspica: #34a, 25r, Facing right. #34b, 500r, Facing left. 15r, Lying in snow. 50r, On rocks. 100r, Mother and young. 150r, Swimming.

1993, Oct. 11   **Litho.**   **Perf. 13½**
34   A7   Pair #a.-b.   3.75 3.75
35   A8   15r multicolored   .60 .60
36   A8   50r multicolored   .95 .95
37   A8   100r multicolored   1.60 1.60
38   A8   150r multicolored   3.25 3.25
   a.   Bklt. pane, 2 ea #34-38   28.00 28.00
     Booklet, #38a   32.50
     Nos. 34-38 (5)   10.15 10.15

Formation of Tovarishch Society for Exploitation of Turkmen Oil Fields, 115th Anniv. — A9

Designs: 1m, Two men viewing oil field. 1.5m, Early tanker Turkmen. 2m, Oil well. 3m, Alfred Nobel, Ludwig Nobel, Robert Nobel, Petr Bilderling, vert. 5m, Early oil field.

1994, June 26   **Litho.**   **Perf. 13**
39   A9   1m multicolored   .60 .60
40   A9   1.5m multicolored   .90 .90
41   A9   2m multicolored   1.25 1.25
42   A9   3m multicolored   1.90 1.90
   a.   Miniature sheet of 8 + label   17.50 17.50
     Nos. 39-42 (4)   4.65 4.65

Souvenir Sheet
43   A9   5m multicolored   4.50 4.50

See Azerbaijan Nos. 416-418a.

Repetek Natl. Park A10

Designs: 3m, Repetek Institute. No. 45, Desert, camels. No. 46, Echus carinatus. No. 47, Varanus griseus. 20m, Testudo horsfieldi. No. 49, Haloxylon ammodendron.

1994, Dec. 11 Litho. *Perf. 13*

44	A10	3m multicolored	.50	.50
45	A10	5m multicolored	.55	.55
46	A10	5m multicolored	.55	.55
a.		Miniature sheet of 8 + label	10.00	10.00
47	A10	10m multicolored	1.10	1.10
48	A10	20m multicolored	2.00	2.00
		Nos. 44-48 (5)	4.70	4.70

Souvenir Sheet

49	A10	10m multicolored	2.50	2.50

Intl. Olympic Committee, Cent. — A11

1994, Dec. 30 Litho. *Perf. 14*

50	A11	11.25m multicolored	2.75	2.75

Souvenir Sheet

51	A11	20m multicolored	5.00	5.00

Miniature Sheet

Save the Aral Sea — A12

Designs: a, Feis caracal. b, Salmo trutta aralensis. c, Hyaena hyaena. d, Pseudoscaphirhynchus kaufmanni. e, Aspiolucius esocinus.

1996, Apr. 29 Litho. *Perf. 14*

52	A12	100m Sheet of 5, #a.-e.	8.00	8.00

Independence, 5th Anniv. — A13

#53, Map of Turkmenistan on globe, vert. #54, Train pulling into station. #55, Natl. Airport, vert. #56, Iranian Pres. Rafsanjani, Turkmenistan Pres. Saparmurad Niyazov, Turkish Pres. Demirel. 500m, UN Secretary-General Boutros Boutros-Gali, Pres. Niyazov, vert. 1000m, Natl. flag, arms.

1996, Oct. 27 Litho. *Perf. 14*

53	A13	100m multicolored	.50	.50
54	A13	100m multicolored	.55	.55
55	A13	300m multicolored	1.40	1.40
56	A13	300m multicolored	1.60	1.60
57	A13	500m multicolored	2.10	2.10
58	A13	1000m multicolored	4.25	4.25
		Nos. 53-58 (6)	10.40	10.40

1996 Summer Olympic Games, Atlanta A14

1997, May 5 Litho. *Perf. 14x14½*

59	A14	100m Judo	.70	.70
60	A14	300m Boxing	1.60	1.60
61	A14	300m Track & field	1.60	1.60
62	A14	300m Wrestling	1.60	1.60
63	A14	500m Shooting	3.25	3.25
		Nos. 59-63 (5)	8.75	8.75

Souvenir Sheet

64	A14	1000m Olympic torch	6.25	6.25

Items inscribed "Turkmenistan" that were not authorized by Turkmenistan postal officials but which have appeared on the market include:

Single stamps of 100m depicting Princess Diana (3 different stamps), Mother Teresa, Pope John Paul II and Mother Teresa, 50th Anniv. of India, and 50th Anniv. of Pakistan.

Sheets of 4 stamps with denominations of 100m depicting JAPEX 98 / Cats.

Sheets of 9 stamps with denominations of 100m depicting the Titanic, Trains, Golfers, Japanese Armor, Japanese Paper Dolls, and Japanese Art.

Sheets of 6 stamps with denominations of 120m depicting Millennium (8 different sheets).

Sheets of 6 stamps with denominations of 120m depicting Pokémon, and Brad Pitt.

Sheets of 4 stamps with denominations of 195m depicting Greenpeace, Elvis Presley, Birds, Orchids, and Japanese Fashion.

Sheets of 6 stamps with denominations of 195m depicting Marilyn Monroe.

Sheets of 9 stamps with denominations of 195m depicting Cacti, and Minerals.

Sheets of 4 stamps with denominations of 250m depicting Akira Kurosawa.

Sheets of 2 stamps with denominations of 390m depicting Brazilian soccer players from 1998 World Cup.

Sheets of 9 stamps with denominations of 1000m depicting IBRA / Mushrooms (2 different sheets).

Souvenir sheets of 1 stamp with various denominations depicting Hokusai Artwork (2 different sheets), Pope John Paul II (2 different sheets), the Titanic (2 different sheets), 1998 Winter Olympics (2 sheets), Year of the Tiger (2 sheets), 50th Anniv. of Israel, Princess Diana, Queen Mother, Che Guevara, Frank Sinatra, Marilyn Monroe, Elvis Presley, International Year of Older Persons / Bob Hope, 1998 World Cup Soccer Championships, Severiano Ballasteros, Jacques Villeneuve, Leaders of the World / Automobiles, and Maria de Medici / Millennium.

Women's Traditional Clothing — A15

Various costumes.

1999, July 5 Litho. *Perf. 14*

65	A15	500m multi	.90	.90
66	A15	1000m multi	1.50	1.50
67	A15	1200m multi	2.10	2.10
68	A15	2500m multi	2.75	2.75
69	A15	3000m multi	3.50	3.50
		Nos. 65-69 (5)	10.75	10.75

Falcons — A16

a, 1000m, Falco tinnunculus. b, 1000m, Falco peregrinus, looking left. c, 1000m, Falco peregrinus, looking right. d, 2500m, Falco tinnunculus, diff. e, 3000m, Falco peregrinus, diff.

2000, Mar. 30 Litho. *Perf. 14*

70	A16	Sheet of 5, #a-e	15.00	15.00

Horn — A17

2000, Oct. Litho. *Imperf.*

Self-Adhesive

71	A17	A multi	1.75	1.75

Sold for 5000m on day of issue.

UN Resolution on the Permanent Neutrality of Turkmenistan, 5th Anniv. — A18

UN emblem, "5," and flags of Turkmenistan and resolution co-sponsors: a, Afghanistan. b, Armenia. c, Azerbaijan. d, Bangladesh. e, Belarus. f, Colombia. g, Czech Republic. h, Egypt. i, France. j, Georgia. k, India. l, Indonesia. m, Iran. n, Kenya. o, Kyrgyzstan. p, Malaysia. q, Mauritius. r, Pakistan. s, Moldova. t, Russia. u, Senegal. v, Tajikistan. w, Turkey. x, Ukraine.

2000, Dec. Litho. *Perf. 14*

72		Sheet of 24 + label	70.00	70.00
a.-x.	A18	3000m Any single	2.75	2.75

Trade Center Building A19

Flag and Arms A20

2001, Apr. 24 Litho. *Imperf.*

Self-Adhesive

73	A19	B multi	1.00	1.00
74	A20	U multi	2.00	2.00

No. 73 sold for 1,200m, No. 74 sold for 3,000m on day of issue.

Horses — A21

No. 75, horiz.: a, Perenli. b, Garader. c, Pyyada. d, Tyllanur. e, Arkadas. f, Yanardag. No. 76, 5000m, Yanardag, diff., horiz. (denomination at LR). No. 77, 5000m, Yanardag, diff., horiz. (denomination at UR). No. 78: a, Bitarap. b, Yanardag, diff.

2001, Aug. 20 Litho. *Perf. 14½x14*

75	A21	3000m Sheet of 6, #a-f	9.00	9.00

Size: 116x90mm

Imperf

76-77	A21	Set of 2	10.00	10.00

Souvenir Sheet

Perf. 14x14½

78	A21	5000m Sheet of 2, #a-b	8.00	8.00

Items inscribed "Turkmenistan" that were not authorized by Turkmenistan postal officials but which have appeared on the market include:

Sheets of 9 stamps with denominations of 50m depicting Kim Basinger, Matt Damon, and Pope John Paul II.

Sheets of 9 stamps with denominations of 100m depicting Leading Personalities of the 20th Century.

Sheets of 6 stamps with denominations of 120m depicting Leonardo DiCaprio, and Princess Diana.

Sheets of 8 stamps with denominations of 120m and one label depicting scenes and people from the 20th Century (3 different sheets).

Sheets of 9 stamps with denominations of 120m depicting Princess Diana, Musical group V.I.P., Television show "Xena, Warrior Princess," Elizabeth Taylor, Bruce Lee, Jackie Chan, Tiger Woods, Muhammad Ali, Monaco Grand Prix race cars, Auto racer David Coulthard, Soccer player David Beckham, Euro 2000 European Football Championships, Rugby players, Tennis Stars of the Millennium, Sportsmen of the Millennium, Elephants, Cats, Butterflies, and Pokémon.

Sheets of 2 stamps with denominations of 390m depicting Soccer players from the 1998 World Cup (2 different sheets depicting French and Japanese players).

Souvenir sheets of 1 with denominations of 975m depicting the Mona Lisa, Marilyn Monroe, and Lucille Ball.

A22

Independence, 10th Anniv. — A23

No. 79 — 500m coins with reverses showing: a, Building with domed roof, coin denomination at right. b, Building with domed roof and tower, coin denomination at left. c, Building with pointed, conical roof. d, Building with archway. e, Building with domed roof on cubic base. f, Statue.

No. 80 — Archaeological sites: a, Soltan Sanjar. b, Nusay. c, Gyz Gala. d, Urgenç. e, Anew. f, Köne Urgenç.

No. 81 — Items in National museum: a, Horn. b, 19th cent. carpet. c, Musical instrument. d, Statue of nude woman. e, Vase. f, 20th cent. decoration.

No. 82, horiz. — Hotels: a, Ahal. b, Gara Altyn. c, Demiryolçy. d, Altyn Suw. e, Köpetdag. f, Aziya.

No. 83 — Buildings: a, Altyn Asyryn Yasayys Jaylary. b, Bitaraplyk Binasy (Arch of Neutrality). c, Türkmendöwletätiyaçlandyrys. d, Random Tower. e, Türkmenbasy Bank. f, Altyn Asyr Söwda Merkezi (Trade Center Building).

No. 84 — Monuments to: a, Oguz Han. b, Seljuk Bay. c, Bayram Han. d, Soltan Sanjar. e, Gorkut Ata. f, Görogly Beg.

No. 85 — Monuments to: a, Sahyrlary Bayram Han. b, Sahyrlary Kemine. c, Sahyrlary Zelili. d, Sahyrlary Seydi. e, Sahyrlary Mollanepes. f, Sahyrlary Mätäji.

2001   Litho.   Imperf.

79	A22	500m Sheet of 6, #a-f	3.00	3.00
80	A23	1000m Sheet of 6, #a-f	5.00	5.00
81	A23	1200m Sheet of 6, #a-f	7.00	7.00
82	A23	1250m Sheet of 6, #a-f	8.00	8.00
83	A23	1250m Sheet of 6, #a-f	8.00	8.00
84	A23	3000m Sheet of 6, #a-f	15.00	15.00
85	A23	3000m Sheet of 6, #a-f	15.00	15.00
		Nos. 79-85 (7)	61.00	61.00

Issued: Nos. 79-80, 10/17; No. 81, 10/19; Nos. 82-83, 10/23; Nos. 84-85, 10/21.

Mohammed Ali Jinnah (1876-1948), First Governor General of Pakistan — A24

2001, Dec. 25   Litho.   Perf. 13

86	A24	500m multi	1.10	1.10

Birds — A25

No. 87, 3000m: a, Motacilla flava. b, Lanius isabellinus. c, Oenanthe oenanthe. d, Corvus monedula. e, Corvus cornix. f, Upupa pyrrhocorax.

No. 88, 3000m: a, Sylvia communis. b, Cuculus canorus. c, Sylvia curruca. d, Corvus pica. e, Corvus frugilegus. f, Corvus corax.

No. 89, 5000m, Anas crecca. No. 90, 5000m, Riparia riparia.

2002, Dec. 1   Litho.   Perf. 14

Sheets of 6, #a-f

87-88	A25	Set of 2	21.00	21.00

Souvenir Sheets

89-90	A25	Set of 2	6.50	6.50

Butterflies — A26

No. 91, 3000m, vert.: a, Vanessa indica. b, Cynthia cardui. c, Pararge aegeria. d, Pieris rapae. e, Lysandra bellargus. f, Anthocharis cardamines.

No. 92, 3000m, vert.: a, Pandoriana pandora. b, Chazara briseis. c, Aphantopus hyperantus. d, Iolana iolas. e, Pararge schakra. f, Maniola jurtina.

No. 93, 5000m, Hamearis lucina. No. 94, 5000m, Quercusia quercus.

Sheets of 6, #a-f

2002, Dec. 1

91-92	A26	Set of 2	21.00	21.00

Souvenir Sheets

93-94	A26	Set of 2	6.50	6.50

Mosque — A27

2003, Feb.   Litho.   Imperf.

Self-Adhesive

95	A27	B multi	1.00	.80

Independence and Peace Monument, Ashkhabad — A28

2003, July 25   Self-Adhesive

96	A28	G multi	1.50	1.50

Building and Flags — A29

2004, Feb. 25   Self-Adhesive

97	A29	B multi	1.00	1.00

Dog — A30

2004, Aug. 13   Self-Adhesive

98	A30	A multi	1.00	1.00

Building — A31

2005   Self-Adhesive   Perf. 11¼

99	A31	M multi	1.25	1.25

Souvenir Sheet

Permanent Neutrality of Turkmenistan, 10th Anniv. — A32

No. 100: a, UN Secretary General Kofi Annan and Turkmenistan Pres. Saparmurad Niyazov. b, Sculpture on building, UN emblem.

2005, Dec. 1   Litho.   Perf. 11½

100	A32	5000m Sheet of 2, #a-b	17.50	17.50

Souvenir Sheets

A33

A34

A35

Akhal-Teke Horses — A36

No. 101: a, Horse's head. b, Horse rearing up.

No. 102: a, Pony nursing. b, Horse walking left.

No. 103: a, Horse facing right. b, Horse facing left.

No. 104: a, Gray horse and mountain. b, Brown horse and mountain.

2005, Dec. 1

101	A33	2500m Sheet of 2, #a-b	6.75	6.75
102	A34	2500m Sheet of 2, #a-b	6.75	6.75
103	A35	2500m Sheet of 2, #a-b	6.75	6.75
104	A36	2500m Sheet of 2, #a-b	6.75	6.75
		Nos. 101-104 (4)	27.00	27.00

Miniature Sheet

Ashgabat Architecture — A37

No. 105: a, 3000m, Building with dome, fountain at left. b, 3000m, Rukhiyet Palace (building with three green domes, automobiles). c, 3000m, Building with three golden domes and fountain. d, 3000m, Goktepe Mosque (green domes). e, 3000m, Mosque with golden domes. f, 3000m, Statue of Akhal-Teke horses. g, 3000m, Domed building with fence. h, 3000m, Central Bank and flags. i, 5000m, Neutrality Arch at night, vert. j, 5000m, Oil and Gas Ministry Building with flagpoles at right, vert. k, 5000m, President Hotel with flagpoles at left, vert. l, Independence Monument with statues at left and right, vert. Sizes: Nos. 105a-105h, 40x30mm; Nos. 105i-105l, 40x60mm.

2006   Litho.   Perf. 13x12¾

105	A37	Sheet of 12, #a-l, + label	25.00	25.00

Independence, 15th Anniv. — A38

2006   Litho.   Imperf.

Self-Adhesive

106	A38	multi	1.00	1.00

Miniature Sheets

Pres. Saparmurat Niyazov (1940-2006) — A39

Nos. 108 and 109 — Pres. Niyazov: a, On reviewing stand, tank in background (34x47mm). b, At airplane's door, waving (34x47mm). c, Walking past women in red costumes (34x24mm). d, Wearing suit, seated in chair (34x24mm). e, Lifting girl, helicopter in background (34x24mm). f, Standing with children in front of helicopter (34x24mm). g, Turning key on box on table (34x24mm). h, Waving at crowd (34x24mm). i, Walking from under canopy (34x47mm). j, Seated in front of microphones (34x24mm). k, Standing in farm field (50x24mm). l, Cutting ribbon (34x24mm). m, Standing on red carpet, holding bowl (34x47mm).

Litho. with Foil Application

2007			Perf.	11½

Stamps With Light Blue Panels

107	A39	A Sheet of 13, #a-m	32.50	32.50

Stamps With Green Panels

108	A39	A Sheet of 13, #a-m	32.50	32.50

Leopard — A40

2007		Litho.	Rouletted 8

Self-Adhesive

109	A40	A multi		1.50	1.50

TURKS & CAICOS ISLANDS

'tərks ənd͜ ' kā-kəs 'ī-lənds

LOCATION — A group of islands in the West Indies, at the southern extremity of the Bahamas
GOVT. — British colony; a dependency of Jamaica until 1959
AREA — 192 sq. mi.
POP. — 16,863 (1999 est.)
CAPITAL — Grand Turk

12 Pence = 1 Shilling
20 Shillings = 1 Pound
100 Cents = 1 US Dollar (1969)

> **Catalogue values for unused stamps in this country are for Never Hinged items, beginning with Scott 90.**

Dependency's Badge
A6   A7

1900-04		Engr.	Wmk. 2	Perf. 14
1	A6	½p green	3.00	4.50
2	A6	1p rose	4.00	.85
3	A6	2p black brown	1.10	1.40
4	A6	2½p gray blue ('04)	2.00	1.10
a.	2½p blue ('00)		9.00	17.50

5	A6	4p orange	4.25	8.00
6	A6	6p violet	2.75	7.50
7	A6	1sh purple brn	3.75	20.00

			Wmk. 1	
8	A7	2sh violet	47.50	75.00
9	A7	3sh brown lake	70.00	95.00
		Nos. 1-9 (9)	138.35	213.35

1905-08			**Wmk. 3**	
10	A6	½p green	5.75	.25
11	A6	1p carmine	18.00	.55
12	A6	3p violet, yel ('08)	2.50	7.00
		Nos. 10-12 (3)	26.25	7.80

King Edward VII — A8

1909, Sept. 2			**Perf. 14**	
13	A8	½p yellow green	.85	.45
14	A8	1p carmine	1.40	.45
15	A8	2p gray	4.50	1.60
16	A8	2½p ultra	6.50	4.25
17	A8	3p violet, yel	2.75	2.75
18	A8	4p red, yel	3.75	8.00
19	A8	6p violet	8.00	7.00
20	A8	1sh black, green	8.00	9.50
21	A8	2sh red, grn	40.00	55.00
22	A8	3sh black, red	42.50	45.00
		Nos. 13-22 (10)	118.25	134.00

Turk's-Head Cactus   George V
A9   A10

1910-11			**Wmk. 3**	
23	A9	¼p claret	2.00	1.10
24	A9	¼p red ('11)	.70	.50
		See Nos. 36, 44.		

1913-16				
25	A10	½p yellow green	.55	2.00
26	A10	1p carmine	1.10	2.50
27	A10	2p gray	2.50	4.00
28	A10	2½p ultra	2.50	3.50
29	A10	3p violet, yel	2.50	12.50
30	A10	4p scarlet, yel	1.10	11.00
31	A10	5p olive grn ('16)	7.50	25.00
32	A10	6p dull violet	2.75	4.00
33	A10	1sh orange	1.75	5.75
34	A10	2sh red, bl grn	14.00	35.00
a.		2sh red, grnsh white ('19)	30.00	80.00
b.		2sh red, emerald ('21)	55.00	80.00
35	A10	3sh black, red	17.50	30.00
		Nos. 25-35 (11)	53.75	135.25

Issued: 5p, 5/18/16; others, 4/1/13.
For overprints see Nos. MR1-MR13.

1921, Apr. 23			**Wmk. 4**	
36	A9	¼p red	4.75	22.00
37	A10	½p green	3.00	6.25
38	A10	1p scarlet	1.10	6.25
39	A10	2p gray	1.10	21.00
40	A10	2½p ultra	2.00	8.50
41	A10	5p olive green	9.00	60.00
42	A10	6p dull violet	7.50	60.00
43	A10	1sh brown orange	11.00	37.50
		Nos. 36-43 (8)	39.45	221.50

A11   A12

Inscribed "Postage"

1922-26				
44	A9	¼p gray black ('26)	1.10	1.25
45	A11	½p green	4.00	4.50
46	A11	1p brown	.65	3.75
47	A11	1½p rose red ('25)	9.00	21.00
48	A11	2p gray	.65	7.00
49	A11	2½p violet, yel	.65	2.40
50	A11	3p ultra	.65	7.00
51	A11	4p red, yel	1.60	21.00
52	A11	5p yellow grn	1.25	30.00
53	A11	6p dull violet	.95	10.00
54	A11	1sh orange	1.10	25.00
55	A11	2sh red, green	2.75	12.50

			Wmk. 3	
56	A11	2sh red, green ('25)	35.00	95.00
57	A11	3sh black, red ('25)	7.00	37.50
		Nos. 44-57 (14)	66.35	277.90

Issued: #47, 56-57, 11/24; #44, 10/11; others, 11/20.

Inscribed "Postage and Revenue"

1928, Mar. 1			**Wmk. 4**	
60	A12	½p green	.95	.60
61	A12	1p brown	.95	.90
62	A12	1½p red	.95	4.00
63	A12	2p dk gray	.95	.60
64	A12	2½p vio, yel	.95	6.25
65	A12	3p ultra	.95	8.75
66	A12	6p brown vio	.95	9.25
67	A12	1sh brown org	4.50	9.25
68	A12	2sh red, grn	7.75	45.00
69	A12	5sh green, yel	13.50	45.00
70	A12	10sh violet, bl	62.50	125.00
		Nos. 60-70 (11)	94.90	254.60

Common Design Types pictured following the introduction.

Silver Jubilee Issue
Common Design Type

1935, May 6			**Perf. 11x12**	
71	CD301	½p green & blk	.40	1.00
72	CD301	3p ultra & brn	2.10	5.25
73	CD301	6p ol grn & lt bl	2.10	6.00
74	CD301	1sh brn vio & ind	4.00	4.00
		Nos. 71-74 (4)	8.60	16.25
		Set, never hinged	16.00	

Coronation Issue
Common Design Type

1937, May 12			**Perf. 13½x14**	
75	CD302	½p deep green	.25	.25
76	CD302	2p gray	.45	.65
77	CD302	3p brt ultra	.60	.65
		Nos. 75-77 (3)	1.30	1.55
		Set, never hinged	1.75	

Raking Salt — A13

Salt Industry — A14

1938-45			**Wmk. 4**	**Perf. 12½**
78	A13	¼p black	.25	.25
79	A13	½p green	2.40	.25
80	A13	1p brown	.45	.25
81	A13	1½p carmine	.45	.25
82	A13	2p gray	.70	.30
83	A13	2½p orange	2.50	1.10
84	A13	3p ultra	.30	.30
85	A13	6p rose violet	6.00	3.25
85A	A13	6p blk brn ('45)	.25	.25
86	A13	1sh bister	2.40	11.00
86A	A13	1sh dk ol grn ('45)	.25	.25
87	A14	2sh rose car	25.00	17.00
88	A14	5sh green	30.00	25.00
89	A14	10sh dp violet	7.50	8.50
		Nos. 78-89 (14)	78.45	67.95
		Set, never hinged	125.00	

> **Catalogue values for unused stamps in this section, from this point to the end of the section, are for Never Hinged items.**

Peace Issue
Common Design Type

1946, Nov. 4		Engr.	**Perf. 13½x14**	
90	CD303	2p gray black	.25	.25
91	CD303	3p deep blue	.25	.25

Silver Wedding Issue
Common Design Types

1948, Sept. 13		Photo.	**Perf. 14x14½**	
92	CD304	1p red brown	.25	.30
		Perf. 11½x11		
		Engr.; Name Typo.		
93	CD305	10sh purple	14.00	19.00

Dependency's Badge — A17

Flag and Merchant Ship — A18

Map of the Islands A19

Victoria and George VI A20

1948, Dec. 14		Engr.	**Perf. 12½**	
94	A17	½p green	.25	.25
95	A17	2p carmine	.45	.25
96	A18	3p deep blue	.70	.25
97	A19	6p violet	.90	.40
98	A20	2sh ultra & blk	1.40	2.25
99	A20	5sh blue grn & blk	4.00	7.00
100	A20	10sh chocolate & blk	6.25	7.00
		Nos. 94-100 (7)	13.95	17.40

Cent. of political separation from the Bahamas.

UPU Issue
Common Design Types
Engr.; Name Typo. on 3p, 6p
Perf. 13½, 11x11½

1949, Oct. 10			**Wmk. 4**	
101	CD306	2½p red orange	.25	1.50
102	CD307	3p indigo	1.90	1.25
103	CD308	6p chocolate	.75	.75
104	CD309	1sh olive	.75	.50
		Nos. 101-104 (4)	3.65	4.00

Loading Bulk Salt — A21

Dependency's Badge — A22

Designs: 1p, Salt Cay. 1½p, Caicos mail. 2p, Grand Turk. 2½p, Sponge diving. 3p, South Creek. 4p, Map. 6p, Grand Turk Light. 1sh, Government House. 1sh6p, Cockburn Harbor. 2sh, Government offices. 5sh, Salt Loading.

1950, Aug. 2		Engr.	**Perf. 12½**	
105	A21	½p deep green	.95	.60
106	A21	1p chocolate	.80	1.25
107	A21	1½p carmine	1.40	.90
108	A21	2p red orange	.70	.60
109	A21	2½p olive green	1.25	.80
110	A21	3p ultra	.35	.60
111	A21	4p rose car & blk	4.00	1.25
112	A21	6p ultra & blk	3.00	.80
113	A21	1sh bl gray & blk	1.40	.60
114	A21	1sh6p red & blk	12.50	5.25
115	A21	2sh ultra & emer	4.50	5.75
116	A21	5sh black & ultra	27.00	11.50
117	A22	10sh purple & blk	27.00	27.50
		Nos. 105-117 (13)	84.85	57.40

Coronation Issue
Common Design Type

1953, June 2			**Perf. 13½x13**	
118	CD312	2p red orange & blk	.40	1.10

M. S.
Kirksons
A23

Design: 8p, Flamingos in flight.

1955, Feb. 1   Wmk. 4   Perf. 12½
119 A23 5p emerald & blk   .80   .80
120 A23 8p yellow brn & blk   3.25   .80

Queen
Elizabeth II — A24

Bonefish
A25

Pelican and
Salinas
A26

Designs: 2p, Red grouper. 2½p, Spiny lobster. 3p, Albacore. 4p, Muttonfish snapper. 5p, Permit. 6p, Conch. 8p, Flamingos. 1sh, Spanish mackerel. 1sh6p, Salt Cay. 2sh, Caicos sloop. 5sh, Cable office. 10sh, Dependency's badge.

Perf. 13½x14 (1p), 13½x13
1957-60   Engr.   Wmk. 314
121 A24 1p lil rose & dk
          bl   .25   .25
122 A25 1½p orange &
          slate   .25   .25
123 A25 2p ol & brn red   .25   .25
124 A25 2½p brt grn & car   .25   .25
125 A25 3p purple & blue   .25   .25
126 A25 4p blk & dp rose   1.25   .25
127 A25 5p brown & grn   1.25   .75
128 A25 6p ultra & car   1.90   .85
129 A25 8p black & ver   3.25   .25
130 A25 1sh blk & dk blue   1.25   .25
131 A25 1sh6p vio bl & dk
          brn   13.00   2.10
132 A25 2sh lt brn & vio bl   13.00   4.00
133 A25 5sh brt car & blk   1.90   3.00

Perf. 14
134 A26 10sh purple & blk   12.50 13.00

Perf. 14x14½
Photo.
135 A26 £1 dk red & brn   55.00 26.00
     Nos. 121-135 (15)   105.55 51.70
     Issued: £1, 11/1/60; others, 11/25/57.

Map of
Islands
A27

Perf. 13½x14
1959, July 4   Wmk. 4   Photo.
136 A27 6p ol grn & salmon   .70   .70
137 A27 8p violet & salmon   .80   .80
     Granting of a new constitution.

Freedom from Hunger Issue
Common Design Type
Perf. 14x14½
1963, June 4   Wmk. 314
138 CD314 8p carmine rose   .50   .50

Red Cross Centenary Issue
Common Design Type
1963, Sept. 2   Litho.   Perf. 13
139 CD315 2p black & red   .25   .40
140 CD315 8p ultra & red   .70   .70

Shakespeare Issue
Common Design Type
1964, Apr. 23   Photo.   Perf. 14x14½
141 CD316 8p green   .40   .40

ITU Issue
Common Design Type
Perf. 11x11½
1965, May 17   Litho.   Wmk. 314
142 CD317 1p ver & brown   .25   .25
143 CD317 2sh emer & lt blue   .65   .65

Intl. Cooperation Year Issue
Common Design Type
1965, Oct. 25   Wmk. 314   Perf. 14½
144 CD318 1p blue grn & claret .25   .25
145 CD318 8p lt violet & green .60   .60

Churchill Memorial Issue
Common Design Type
1966, Jan. 24   Photo.   Perf. 14
**Design in Black, Gold and Carmine
Rose**
146 CD319   1p bright blue   .25   .25
147 CD319   2p green   .25   .25
148 CD319   8p brown   .35   .25
     a.   Gold impression double 200.00
149 CD319 1sh6p violet   .75   1.00
     Nos. 146-149 (4)   1.60   1.75

Royal Visit Issue
Common Design Type
1966, Feb. 4   Litho.   Perf. 11x12
Portraits in Black
150 CD320   8p violet blue   .40   .30
151 CD320 1sh6p dk car rose   .80   .40

Andrew Symmers Landing with Union
Jack — A28

Designs: 8p, Andrew Symmers, his signature, Royal Warrant and Union Jack. 1sh6p, New coat of arms, Royal Cypher and St. Edward's crown.

Perf. 13½
1966, Oct. 1   Unwmk.   Photo.
152 A28   1p dk blue & dp org   .25   .25
153 A28   8p dk blue, dl yel &
           car   .25   .25
154 A28 1sh6p multicolored   .25   .25
     Nos. 152-154 (3)   .75   .75

200th anniv. of the landing of Andrew Symmers, British agent, establishing the ties with Great Britain.

UNESCO Anniversary Issue
Common Design Type
Wmk. 314
1966, Dec. 1   Litho.   Perf. 14
155 CD323 1p "Education"   .25   .25
156 CD323 8p "Science"   .30   .30
157 CD323 1sh6p "Culture"   .50   .50
     Nos. 155-157 (3)   1.05   1.05

Turk's-head
Cactus — A29

Boat
Building
A30

Designs: 2p, Donkey cart. 3p, Sisal industry. 4p, Conch industry. 6p, Salt industry. 8p, Skin diving. 1sh, Fishing. 1sh6p, Water skiing. 2sh, Crawfish industry. 3sh, Map of Islands. 5sh,

Fishing industry. 10sh, Coat of arms. £1, Queen Elizabeth II.

Perf. 14½x14, 14x14½
1967, Feb. 1   Photo.   Wmk. 314
158 A29   1p vio, red & yel   .25   .35
159 A30 1½p choc & org yel   1.10   .35
160 A29   2p gray, yel & sl   .25   .35
161 A30   3p green & dk brn   .25   .35
162 A30   4p grnsh bl, blk &
           pink   2.50   .35
163 A29   6p blue & dk brn   1.75   .35
164 A29   8p aqua, dk bl &
           yel   .55   .35
165 A30 1sh grnsh bl & red
           brn   .25   .35
166 A29 1sh6p brt grnsh bl,
           yel & brn   .40   .60
167 A30 2sh multicolored   1.10   1.75
168 A30 3sh grnsh bl & mar   1.10   .75
169 A30 5sh sky bl, dk bl &
           yel   1.50   2.50
170 A30 10sh multicolored   2.75   4.00
171 A29   £1 dk car rose, sil
           & dk bl   4.00   8.50
     Nos. 158-171 (14)   17.75 20.90

     See #181, 217-230. For surcharges see #182-195.

Turks
Islands
No. 1
A31

Designs: 6p, Turks Islands No. 2 and portrait of Queen Elizabeth on simulated stamp. 1sh, Turks Islands No. 3 (like 1p).

1967, May 1   Photo.   Perf. 14½
172 A31   1p lilac rose & blk   .25   .25
173 A31   6p gray & black   .25   .25
174 A31 1sh Prus blue & blk   .40   .40
     Nos. 172-174 (3)   .90   .90

Centenary of Turks Islands stamps.

Human
Rights
Flame
A32

1968, Apr. 1   Perf. 14x14½
175 A32   1p lt green & multi   .25   .25
176 A32   8p lt blue & multi   .25   .25
177 A32 1sh6p multicolored   .25   .25
     Nos. 175-177 (3)   .75   .75

International Human Rights Year.

Martin
Luther
King, Jr.
and
Protest
March of
1968
A33

1968, Oct. 1   Photo.   Wmk. 314
178 A33   2p dk blue, dk & lt brn .25 .25
179 A33   8p dk car rose, dk & lt
           brn   .25   .25
180 A33 1sh6p dp vio, dk & lt brn .25 .25
     Nos. 178-180 (3)   .75   .75

Martin Luther King, Jr. (1929-68), American civil rights leader.

Nos. 158-171 Surcharged

Designs as before and: ¼c, Coat of arms like 10sh.

Perf. 14x14½, 14½x14
1969, Sept. 8   Photo.   Wmk. 314
181 A30   ¼c lt gray & multi   .25   .25
182 A29   1c on 1p multi   .25   .25
183 A29   2c on 2p multi   .25   .25
184 A29   3c on 3p multi   .25   .25
185 A30   4c on 4p multi   .25   .25
186 A29   5c on 6p multi   .25   .25
187 A29   7c on 8p multi   .25   .25
188 A30   8c on 1½p multi   .25   .25
189 A30 10c on 1sh multi   .25   .25
190 A29 15c on 1sh6p multi   .25   .25
191 A30 20c on 2sh multi   .30   .50
192 A30 30c on 3sh multi   .40   .65
193 A30 50c on 5sh multi   .60   .95
194 A30 $1 on 10sh multi   1.40   2.25
195 A29 $2 on £1 multi   6.00   9.50
     Nos. 181-195 (15)   11.20 16.35

     The surcharge is differently arranged on each denomination to fit the design; the old denomination is obliterated with a rectangle on the 8c and 15c.
     See Nos. 217-230.

1969   Wmk. 314 Sideways
182a A29   1c on 1p   .25   .30
183a A29   2c on 2p   .25   .30
184a A29   3c on 3p   .25   .30
186a A29   5c on 6p   .25   .30
187a A29   7c on 8p   .25   .40
190a A29 15c on 1sh6p   .30   .50
195a A29 $2 on £1   3.00   5.00
     Nos. 182a-195a (7)   4.55   7.10

Nativity with
John the
Baptist — A34

Designs from the Book of Hours of Eleanora, Duchess of Tuscany: 3c, 30c, Flight into Egypt.

Perf. 13x12½
1969, Oct. 20   Litho.   Wmk. 314
196 A34   1c plum & multi   .25   .25
197 A34   3c dk blue & multi   .25   .25
198 A34 15c olive & multi   .25   .25
199 A34 30c yellow brn & multi .25   .25
     Nos. 196-199 (4)   1.00   1.00

Christmas.

Coat of
Arms — A35

1970, Feb. 2   Litho.   Perf. 13x12½
200 A35   7c brown & multi   .25   .25
201 A35 35c violet blue & multi .75   .75

     New Constitution, inaugurated 6/16/69.
     See No. 769.

Christ Bearing
the Cross, by
Dürer — A36

Albrecht Dürer Engravings: 7c, Christ on the Cross. 50c, The Lamentation for Christ.

TURKS & CAICOS ISLANDS

Perf. 13½x14

1970, Mar. 17   Engr.   Wmk. 314

202	A36	5c dp blue & blk	.25	.25
203	A36	7c vermilion & blk	.25	.25
204	A36	50c dk brown & multi	.40	1.00
		Nos. 202-204 (3)	.90	1.50

Easter.

Dickens and "Oliver Twist" Scene A37

Charles Dickens and Scene from: 3c, "A Christmas Carol." 15c, "Pickwick Papers." 30c, "The Old Curiosity Shop."

Litho. & Engr.

1970, June 17   Perf. 13½x13

205	A37	1c yel, red brn & blk	.25	.25
206	A37	3c sal pink, sl & blk	.25	.25
207	A37	15c salmon, bl & blk	.30	.30
208	A37	30c lt blue, ol & blk	.60	.60
		Nos. 205-208 (4)	1.40	1.40

Charles Dickens (1812-70), English novelist.

Red Cross Ambulance, 1870 — A38

5c, 30c, Red Cross ambulance, 1970.

1970, Aug. 4   Litho.   Perf. 13½x14

209	A38	1c orange & multi	.25	.25
210	A38	5c ocher & multi	.25	.25
211	A38	15c brt pink & multi	.25	.25
212	A38	30c multicolored	.50	.50
		Nos. 209-212 (4)	1.25	1.25

Centenary of British Red Cross Society.

Gen. George Monck, Duke of Albemarle, and his Coat of Arms — A39

Designs: 8c, 35c, Coats of arms of Charles II and Queen Elizabeth II.

1970, Dec. 1   Litho.   Perf. 12½x13½

213	A39	1c multicolored	.25	.25
214	A39	8c multicolored	.25	.25
215	A39	10c multicolored	.30	.30
216	A39	35c multicolored	1.00	.95
		Nos. 213-216 (4)	1.80	1.75

Tercentenary of the issue of Letters Patent to the Six Lords Proprietors.

Types of 1967

Values in Cents and Dollars

Designs: 1c, Turk's-head cactus. 2c, Donkey cart. 3c, Sisal industry. 4c, Conch industry. 5c, Salt industry. 7c, Skin diving. 8c, Boat building. 10c, Fishing. 15c, Water skiing. 20c, Crawfish industry. 30c, Map of Islands. 50c, Fishing industry. $1, Arms of Colony. $2, Queen Elizabeth II.

Perf. 14x14½, 14½x14

1971, Feb. 2   Photo.   Wmk. 314

217	A29	1c violet, red & yel	.25	.30
218	A29	2c gray, yel & slate	.25	.30
219	A29	3c green & dk brn	.25	.30
220	A30	4c grnsh bl, blk & pink	.25	.30
221	A29	5c blue & dk brown	.25	.30
222	A29	7c aqua, dk bl & yel	.25	.30
223	A30	8c choc & org yel	.25	.30
224	A30	10c grnsh bl & red brn	.35	.40
225	A29	15c brt grnsh bl, yel & brn	.65	.70

226	A30	20c multicolored	.95	1.10
227	A30	30c grnsh bl & mar	1.40	1.60
228	A30	50c sky bl, dk bl & yel	2.25	2.50
229	A30	$1 blue & multi	4.50	4.75
230	A29	$2 dk car rose, sil & dk blue	8.25	9.50
		Nos. 217-230 (14)	20.10	22.65

The ¼c, released with this set is a shade of No. 181, the background being a greenish, slightly darker gray.

Queen Conch and Emblem A40

Tourist publicity (Sun, Sea and Sand Emblem and): 1c, Seahorse, vert. 15c, American oyster catcher. 30c, Blue Marlin.

Perf. 14½x14, 14x14½

1971, May 2   Litho.   Wmk. 314

232	A40	1c multicolored	.35	.35
233	A40	3c multicolored	.35	.35
234	A40	15c multicolored	.55	.55
235	A40	30c multicolored	1.10	1.10
		Nos. 232-235 (4)	2.35	2.35

Pirate Sloop A41

Designs: 3c, Pirates burying treasure. 15c, Marooned pirate. 30c, Buccaneers.

1971, July 17   Perf. 14½x14

236	A41	2c multicolored	.25	.25
237	A41	3c multicolored	.25	.25
238	A41	15c multicolored	.70	.70
239	A41	30c multicolored	1.40	1.40
		Nos. 236-239 (4)	2.60	2.60

A42

Adoration of the Virgin and Child, from Wilton Diptych, French School, c. 1395 — A43

1971, Oct. 12   Litho.   Perf. 14x13½

240	A42	2c dull brn & multi	.25	.25
241	A43	2c dull brn & multi	.25	.25
242	A42	8c green & multi	.25	.25
243	A43	8c green & multi	.25	.25
244	A42	15c dk blue gray & multi	.25	.25
245	A43	15c dk blue gray & multi	.25	.25
		Nos. 240-245 (6)	1.50	1.50

Christmas.

Rocket Launch, Cape Canaveral — A44

10c, Space capsule in orbit around earth. 15c, Map of Turks & Caicos Islands & splashdown. 20c, Distinguished Service Medal, vert.

1972, Feb. 21   Perf. 13½

246	A44	5c lt blue & blk	.25	.25
247	A44	10c multicolored	.25	.25
248	A44	15c lt green & multi	.25	.25
249	A44	20c blue & multi	.25	.25
		Nos. 246-249 (4)	1.00	1.00

First orbital flight by US astronaut Lt. Col. John H. Glenn, Jr., and splashdown off Turks and Caicos Islands, 10th anniversary.

The Three Crosses, by Rembrandt — A45

Details from Etchings by Rembrandt: 2c, Christ Before Pilate, vert. 30c, Descent from the Cross, vert.

1972, Mar. 17   Perf. 14x13½, 13½x14

250	A45	2c lilac & black	.25	.25
251	A45	15c pink & black	.25	.25
252	A45	30c yellow & black	.40	.40
		Nos. 250-252 (3)	.90	.90

Easter.

Richard Grenville and "Revenge" — A46

Discoverers and explorers of the Americas: ¼c, Christopher Columbus, Niña, Pinta and Santa Maria, vert. 10c, Capt. John Smith and three-master, vert. 30c, Juan Ponce de León and three-master.

1972, July 4

253	A46	¼c multicolored	.25	.25
254	A46	8c multicolored	1.40	.25
255	A46	10c multicolored	1.40	.35
256	A46	30c multicolored	3.00	1.00
		Nos. 253-256 (4)	6.05	1.85

Silver Wedding Issue, 1972

Common Design Type

Design: Queen Elizabeth II, Prince Philip, turk's-head cactus and spiny lobster.

Perf. 14x14½

1972, Nov. 20   Photo.   Wmk. 314

257	CD324	10c ultra & multi	.25	.25
258	CD324	20c multicolored	.25	.25

Treasure Hunting, c. 1700 — A47

Designs: 5c, Replica of silver bank medallion, 1687, obverse. 10c, Same, reverse. 30c, Scuba diver, 1973.

Perf. 14x14½

1973, Jan. 18   Litho.   Wmk. 314

259	A47	3c Prus blue & multi	.25	.25
260	A47	5c plum, silver & blk	.25	.25
261	A47	10c brt rose, silver & blk	.25	.25
262	A47	30c violet blue & multi	.90	.90
a.		Souvenir sheet of 4, #259-262	2.25	2.25
		Nos. 259-262 (4)	1.65	1.65

Treasure hunting.

Arms of Jamaica, Turks and Caicos Islands — A48

1973, Apr. 16   Litho.   Perf. 13½x14

263	A48	15c buff & multi	.35	.35
264	A48	35c lt green & multi	.75	.75

Centenary of annexation to Jamaica.

Sooty Tern — A49

Birds: 1c, Magnificent frigate bird. 2c, Noddy tern. 3c, Blue gray gnatcatcher. 4c, Little blue heron. 5c, Catbird. 7c, Black-whiskered vireo. 8c, Osprey. 10c, Flamingo. 15c, Brown pelican. 20c, Parula warbler. 30c, Northern mockingbird. 50c, Ruby-throated hummingbird. $1, Bahama bananaquit. $2, Cedar waxwing. $5, Painted bunting.

Wmk. 314 Sideways

1973, Aug. 1   Litho.   Perf. 14

265	A49	¼c yellow & multi	.25	.25
266	A49	1c pink & multi	.25	.25
267	A49	2c orange & multi	.25	.25
268	A49	3c lilac rose & multi	.55	.50
269	A49	4c lt blue & multi	.25	.25
270	A49	5c lt green & multi	.40	.25
271	A49	7c salmon & multi	.45	.30
272	A49	8c blue & multi	.55	.50
273	A49	10c brt blue & multi	.65	.65
274	A49	15c tan & multi	1.00	.90
275	A49	20c brt yel & multi	2.75	2.50
276	A49	30c yellow & multi	2.25	2.10
277	A49	50c yellow & multi	3.50	3.25
278	A49	$1 blue & multi	6.75	6.75
279	A49	$2 gray & multi	15.00	13.50
		Nos. 265-279 (15)	34.85	32.20

1974-75   Wmk. 314 Upright

266a	A49	1c pink & multi ('75)	.60	.80
267a	A49	2c orange & multi	1.25	1.60
268a	A49	3c lil rose & multi ('75)	2.00	2.50
275a	A49	20c brt yel & multi ('75)	6.25	8.00
		Nos. 266a-275a (4)	10.10	12.90

1976-77   Wmk. 373

265a	A49	¼c yellow & multi ('77)	.25	.25
266b	A49	1c pink & multi ('77)	.25	.25
267b	A49	2c orange & multi ('77)	.25	.25
268b	A49	3c lilac rose & multi ('77)	.25	.25
269a	A49	4c lt bl & multi ('77)	.25	.25
270a	A49	5c lt grn & multi ('77)	.25	.25
273a	A49	10c brt bl & multi ('77)	.25	.25
274a	A49	15c tan & multi ('77)	.40	.65
275b	A49	20c brt yel & multi	.50	.80
276a	A49	30c yel & multi ('77)	.75	1.25
277a	A49	50c yel & multi ('77)	1.25	2.00
278a	A49	$1 blue & multi ('77)	2.50	4.00
279b	A49	$2 gray & multi ('77)	5.25	8.00
279A	A49	$5 lt grn & multi	13.50	21.00
		Nos. 265a-279A (14)	25.90	39.45

Bermuda Sloop — A50

Old Sailing Ships: 5c, HMS Blanche. 8c, US privateer Grand Turk and packet Hinchinbrooke. 10c, HMS Endymion. 15c, RMS Medina. 20c, HMS Daring.

1973, July 19   Litho.   Perf. 13½

280	A50	2c multicolored	.25	.25
281	A50	5c multicolored	.25	.25
282	A50	8c multicolored	.25	.25
283	A50	10c multicolored	.25	.25
284	A50	15c multicolored	.35	.35
285	A50	20c multicolored	.50	.50
a.		Souvenir sheet of 6, #280-285	2.50	2.50
		Nos. 280-285 (6)	1.85	1.85

Princess Anne's Wedding Issue
Common Design Type

1973, Nov. 14　　Wmk. 314　　*Perf. 14*
286 CD325 12c blue grn & multi　.25　.25
287 CD325 18c slate & multi　.25　.25

Lucayan
Stool
A51

Designs: Lucayan artifacts.

1974, July 17　　Litho.　　*Perf. 14½*
288 A51 6c shown　.25　.25
289 A51 10c Broken wood bowl　.25　.25
290 A51 12c Greenstone axe　.25　.25
291 A51 18c Wood bowl　.25　.25
292 A51 35c Animal head, frag-
　　　　　ment of stool　.25　.25
　a.　Souvenir sheet of 5, #288-292　2.50　2.50
　　　　Nos. 288-292 (5)　1.25　1.25

Carvings made by Lucayan Indians, first
inhabitants of the islands.

Grand
Turk
G.P.O.
A52

UPU Emblem and: 12c, Map of Turks and
Caicos Islands and local mail sloop. 18c,
"United Service" (globe and "UPU"). 55c,
Design symbolic of the Islands joining the
UPU in 1881.

1974, Oct. 9　　Wmk. 314　　*Perf. 14*
293 A52 4c yellow & multi　.25　.25
294 A52 12c blue & multi　.25　.25
295 A52 18c violet & multi　.25　.25
296 A52 55c lt blue & multi　.55　.55
　　　　Nos. 293-296 (4)　1.30　1.30

Centenary of Universal Postal Union.

"His
Finest
Hour"
A53

12c, Churchill and Franklin D. Roosevelt.

1974, Nov. 30　　Wmk. 373
297 A53 12c multicolored　.25　.25
298 A53 18c multicolored　.25　.25
　a.　Souvenir sheet of 2, #297-298　.70　.70

Sir Winston Churchill (1874-1965).

Spanish Captain,　　Old Windmill, Salt
c. 1492 — A54　　　　Cay — A55

Uniforms: 20c, Officer, Royal Artillery, 1783.
25c, Officer, 67th Foot, 1798. 35c, Private,
First West India Regiment, 1833.

1975, Mar. 26　　Wmk. 314　　*Perf. 14½*
299 A54 5c blue & multi　.25　.25
300 A54 20c blue & multi　.30　.30
301 A54 25c blue & multi　.35　.35
302 A54 35c blue & multi　.50　.50
　a.　Souvenir sheet of 4, #299-302　1.60　1.60
　　　　Nos. 299-302 (4)　1.40　1.40

1975, Oct. 16　　Litho.　　Wmk. 373
Salt industry: 10c, Pink salt pans, horiz. 20c,
Salt raking at Salt Cay, horiz. 25c,
Unprocessed salt ready for shipment.
303 A55 6c violet & multi　.25　.25
304 A55 10c lt brown & multi　.25　.25
305 A55 20c red & multi　.35　.35
306 A55 25c magenta & multi　.45　.45
　　　　Nos. 303-306 (4)　1.30　1.30

Star
Coral
A56

1975, Dec. 4　　Litho.　　Wmk. 373
307 A56 6c shown　.30　.30
308 A56 10c Elkhorn coral　.35　.30
309 A56 20c Brain coral　.70　.60
310 A56 25c Staghorn coral　.85　.70
　　　　Nos. 307-310 (4)　2.20　1.90

Schooner
A57

American Bicentennial: 20c, Ship of the line.
25c, Frigate Grand Turk. 55c, Ketch.

1976, May 28　　*Perf. 14x13½*
311 A57 6c orange & multi　.25　.25
312 A57 20c violet blue & multi　.40　.30
313 A57 25c brown & multi　.50　.35
314 A57 55c multicolored　.90　.80
　a.　Souvenir sheet of 4, #311-314　2.25　2.25
　　　　Nos. 311-314 (4)　2.05　1.70

Turks
and
Caicos
Islands
No. 151
A58

25c, Turks and Caicos Islands No. 150.

1976, July 14　　Wmk. 373　　*Perf. 14½*
315 A58 20c carmine & multi　.50　.45
316 A58 25c violet blue & multi　.60　.55

Visit of Queen Elizabeth II and Prince Philip
to the Caribbean, 10th anniversary.

Virgin and Child,
by Carlo
Dolci — A59

Christmas: 10c, Virgin and Child with St.
John, by Botticelli. 20c, Adoration of the Kings,
from Retable by the Master of Paradise. 25c,
Adoration of the Kings, illuminated page,
French, 15th century.

1976, Nov. 10　　Litho.　　*Perf. 14x13½*
317 A59 6c multicolored　.25　.25
318 A59 10c orange & multi　.25　.25
319 A59 20c red lilac & multi　.25　.25
320 A59 25c multicolored　.25　.25
　　　　Nos. 317-320 (4)　1.00　1.00

Queen with
Regalia — A60

Designs: 6c, Queen presenting Order of
British Empire to E. T. Wood, Grand Turk,
1966. 55c, Royal family on balcony of Buckingham Palace. $5, Portrait of Queen from photo-
graph taken during her 1966 visit to Grand
Turk.

1977　　Litho.　　*Perf. 14x13½*
321 A60 6c multicolored　.25　.25
322 A60 25c multicolored　.25　.25
323 A60 55c multicolored　.50　.50
　　　　Nos. 321-323 (3)　1.00　1.00

Souvenir Sheet
Perf. 14

324 A60 $5 multicolored　3.00　3.00

25th anniv. of the reign of Elizabeth II.
Nos. 322 and 323 were also issued in book-
let panes of 2.
Issued: #321-323, Feb. 7; #324, Dec. 6.

Friendship 7 Capsule — A61

Designs: 3c, Lunar rover, vert. 6c, Tracking
Station on Grand Turk. 20c, Moon landing
craft, vert. 25c, Col. Glenn's rocket leaving
launching pad, vert. 50c, Telstar 1 satellite.

Wmk. 373
1977, June 20　　Litho.　　*Perf. 13½*
325 A61 1c multicolored　.25　.25
326 A61 3c multicolored　.25　.25
327 A61 6c multicolored　.25　.25
328 A61 20c multicolored　.25　.25
329 A61 25c multicolored　.25　.25
330 A61 50c multicolored　.50　.50
　　　　Nos. 325-330 (6)　1.75　1.75

US Tracking Station on Grand Turk, 25th
anniversary.

Adoration of the
Kings, 1634 by
Rubens — A63

Rubens Paintings: ¼c, Flight into Egypt. 1c,
Adoration of the Kings, 1624. 6c, Madonna
with Garland. 20c, $1, Virgin and Child Adored
by Angels. $2, Adoration of the Kings, 1618.

1977, Dec. 23
331 A63 ¼c multicolored　.25　.25
332 A63 ½c multicolored　.25　.25
333 A63 1c multicolored　.25　.25
334 A63 6c multicolored　.25　.25
335 A63 20c multicolored　.25　.25
336 A63 $2 multicolored　1.50　1.50
　　　　Nos. 331-336 (6)　2.75　2.75

Souvenir Sheet

337 A63 $1 multicolored　1.90　1.90

Christmas and 400th birth anniversary of
Peter Paul Rubens (1577-1640).

Map of
Turks
Island
Passage
A64

Designs: 20c, Grand Turk lighthouse and
sailboat (LUG cargo vessel). 25c, Deepsea
fishing yacht. 55c, S.S. Jamaica Planter.

Wmk. 373, Unwmkd.
1978, Feb. 2　　Litho.　　*Perf. 13½*
338 A64 6c multicolored　.30　.30
339 A64 20c multicolored　.50　.40
340 A64 25c multicolored　.60　.50
341 A64 55c multicolored　1.25　1.25
　a.　Souv. sheet of 4, #338-341,
　　　unwmkd.　2.75　2.75
　　　　Nos. 338-341 (4)　2.65　2.45

Turks Island Passage, a major Caribbean
shipping route.
No. 341a exists watermarked. Value $50.

Queen Victoria in
Coronation
Regalia — A65

British Monarchs in Coronation Regalia:
10c, Edward VII. 25c, George V. $2,
George VI. $2.50, Elizabeth II.

1978, June 2　　Litho.　　*Perf. 14*
342 A65 6c multicolored　.25　.25
343 A65 10c multicolored　.25　.25
344 A65 25c multicolored　.25　.25
345 A65 $2 multicolored　1.00　1.00
　　　　Nos. 342-345 (4)　1.75　1.75

Souvenir Sheet

346 A65 $2.50 multicolored　1.75　1.75

25th anniversary of coronation of Queen
Elizabeth II. Nos. 342-345 also issued in
sheets of 3 plus label, perf. 12.

Wilbur
Wright
and
Flyer 3
A66

Aviation Progress: 6c, Cessna 337 and
Wright brothers. 10c, Southeast Airlines' Elec-
tra and Orville Wright. 15c, C47 cargo plane
on South Caicos runway. 35c, Norman-Britten
Islander at Grand Turk airport. $1, Orville
Wright and Flyer, 1902. $2, Wilbur Wright and
Flyer.

1978, June 29　　Litho.　　*Perf. 14½*
347 A66 1c multicolored　.25　.25
348 A66 6c multicolored　.25　.25
349 A66 10c multicolored　.25　.25
350 A66 15c multicolored　.25　.25
351 A66 35c multicolored　.60　.60
352 A66 $2 multicolored　1.90　1.90
　　　　Nos. 347-352 (6)　3.50　3.50

Souvenir Sheet

353 A66 $1 multicolored　1.00　1.00

Coronation of Queen Elizabeth II, 25th
Anniv. — A67

Designs: 15c, Ampulla and anointing spoon.
25c, St. Edward's crown. $2 Queen Elizabeth
II

Imperf. x Roulette 5

1978, July 24   Litho.
Self-adhesive
354		Souvenir booklet	3.75
a.		A67 Bklt. pane of 3, 15c, 25c, $2	2.40
b.		15c value from #354a	.25
c.		25c value from #354a	.25
d.		$2 value from #354a	1.90
e.		A67 Bklt. pane, 3 each, 15c, 25c	1.35

No. 354 contains #354a-354b printed on peelable paper backing with music and text of hymns.

11th Commonwealth Games, Edmonton, Canada, Aug. 3-12 — A68

1978, Aug. 3   Litho.   *Perf. 15*
355	A68	6c shown	.25	.25
356	A68	20c Weight lifting	.25	.25
357	A68	55c Boxing	.45	.45
358	A68	$2 Bicycling	1.05	1.05
		Nos. 355-358 (4)	2.00	2.00

Souvenir Sheet
359	A68	$1 Sprinting	1.40	1.40

Fish A69

1978-79   Litho.   *Perf. 14¼*
No Year Imprint Below Design
360	A69	1c Indigo hamlet	.25	.25
361	A69	2c Tobacco fish	.25	.25
362	A69	3c Passing Jack	.25	.25
363	A69	4c Porkfish	.25	.25
364	A69	5c Spanish grunt	.25	.25
365	A69	7c Yellowtail snapper	.25	.25
366	A69	8c Foureye butter-flyfish	.25	.25
367	A69	10c Yellow fin grouper	.25	.25
368	A69	15c Beau Gregory	.30	.30
369	A69	20c Queen angelfish	.40	.40
370	A69	30c Hogfish	.60	.60
371	A69	50c Fairy Basslet	1.00	1.00
372	A69	$1 Clown wrasse	1.90	1.90
373	A69	$2 Stoplight par-rotfish	4.25	4.25
374	A69	$5 Queen triggerfish	10.00	10.00
		Nos. 360-374 (15)	20.45	20.45

Issue dates: 1c, 3c, 5c, 10c, 15c, 20c, Nov. 17, 1978; others Feb. 6, 1979.

1981, Dec. 15   *Perf. 12½x12*
"1981" Imprint Below Design
360a	A69	1c multicolored	.25	.25
364a	A69	5c multicolored	.25	.25
367a	A69	10c multicolored	.25	.25
369a	A69	20c multicolored	.55	.55
371a	A69	50c multicolored	1.25	1.25
372a	A69	$1 multicolored	2.50	2.50
373a	A69	$2 multicolored	5.50	5.50
374a	A69	$5 multicolored	13.00	13.00
		Nos. 360a-374a (8)	23.55	23.55

1983, Jan. 25   *Perf. 14¼x12*
"1983" Imprint Below Design
368b	A69	15c multicolored	1.90	1.00
369b	A69	20c multicolored	1.25	1.25
372b	A69	$1 multicolored	3.00	3.00
373b	A69	$2 multicolored	4.25	4.25
374b	A69	$5 multicolored	10.00	10.00
		Nos. 368b-374b (5)	20.40	19.50

Virgin with the Goldfinch, by Dürer — A70

Dürer Paintings: 20c, Virgin and Child with St. Anne. 35c, Nativity, horiz. $1, Adoration of the Kings, horiz. $2, Praying Hands.

1978, Dec. 11   Litho.   *Perf. 14*
375	A70	6c multicolored	.25	.25
376	A70	20c multicolored	.25	.25
377	A70	35c multicolored	.45	.45
378	A70	$2 multicolored	1.75	1.75
		Nos. 375-378 (4)	2.70	2.70

Souvenir Sheet
379	A70	$1 multicolored	2.50	2.50

Christmas and 450th death anniversary of Albrecht Dürer (1471-1528), German painter.

Ospreys A71

Endangered Species: 20c, Green turtle. 25c, Queen conch. 55c, Rough-toothed dolphin. $1, Humpback whale. $2, Iguana.

1979, May 17   Litho.   *Perf. 14*
380	A71	6c multicolored	.30	.30
381	A71	20c multicolored	.90	.40
382	A71	25c multicolored	1.20	.50
383	A71	55c multicolored	2.50	1.20
384	A71	$1 multicolored	4.50	2.25
		Nos. 380-384 (5)	9.40	4.65

Souvenir Sheet
385	A71	$2 multicolored	6.00	5.50

The Beloved, by Dante Gabriel Rossetti A72

Paintings and IYC Emblem: 25c, Tahitian Girl, by Paul Gauguin. 55c, Calmady Children, by Sir Thomas Lawrence. $1, Mother and Daughter (detail), by Gauguin. $2, Marchesa Elena Grimaldi, by Van Dyck.

1979, July 2   Litho.   *Perf. 14*
386	A72	6c multicolored	.25	.25
387	A72	25c multicolored	.25	.25
388	A72	55c multicolored	.35	.35
389	A72	$1 multicolored	.65	.65
		Nos. 386-389 (4)	1.50	1.50

Souvenir Sheet
390	A72	$2 multicolored	1.00	1.00

International Year of the Child.

Stampless Cover and "Medina" — A73

Designs: 20c, Map of Islands and Rowland Hill. 45c, Stamped envelope and "Orinoco." 75c, Paddlewheeler "Shannon" and letter. $1, Royal Packet "Trent," map of Islands. $2, New and old seals.

1979, Sep. 10   Litho.   *Perf. 14*
391	A73	6c multicolored	.25	.25
392	A73	20c multicolored	.25	.25
393	A73	45c multicolored	.50	.50
394	A73	75c multicolored	.90	.90
395	A73	$1 multicolored	1.10	1.10

Perf. 12
396	A73	$2 multicolored ('80)	3.25	3.25
a.		Souv. sheet of 1, perf. 14 ('79)	1.75	1.75
		Nos. 391-396 (6)	6.25	6.25

Nos. 391-395 were issued in sheets of 40, and in sheets of 5 stamps plus label, in changed colors, perf. 12.

No. 396 issued May 6, 1980 in sheet of 5 plus label picturing signal flags and map.

Souvenir Sheet
No. 396a Overprinted

1979, Sept. 10   Litho.   *Perf. 14*
397	A73	$2 multicolored	1.25	1.25

Brasiliana 79 Intl. Philatelic Exhibition, Rio de Janeiro, Sept. 15-23.

Cuneiform Script — A74

Designs: 5c, Egyptian papyrus; Chinese writing. 15c, Greek runner; Roman post horse; Roman ship. 25c, Pigeon post; railway post; steamship postal packet. 40c, Balloon post; first airmail plane; supersonic airmail jet. $1, Original stamp press (3 designs each of 5c, 15c, 25c, 40).

Imperf. x Roulette 5, Imperf. ($1)
1979, Sept. 27   Litho.
Self-adhesive
398		Souvenir booklet	6.00
a.		A74 Bklt. pane of 1 ($1)	
b.		A74 Bklt. pane, 3 each 5c, 15c	
c.		A74 Bklt. pane, 3 each 25c, 40c	

Sir Rowland Hill (1795-1879), originator of penny postage. No. 398 contains 3 booklet panes on peelable paper backing with descriptions of stamp designs.

International Year of the Child A74a

Designs: Aquatic scenes.

1979, Nov. 2   Litho.   *Perf. 11*
399	A74a	¼c Pluto and starfish	.25	.25
400	A74a	½c Minnie Mouse	.25	.25
401	A74a	1c Mickey Mouse skin-diving	.25	.25
402	A74a	2c Goofy riding turtle	.25	.25
403	A74a	3c Donald and dolphin	.25	.25
404	A74a	4c Mickey Mouse and fish	.25	.25
405	A74a	5c Goofy surfing	.25	.25
406	A74a	25c Pluto and lobster	.60	.25
407	A74a	$1 Daisy Duck water-skiing	2.40	1.00
		Nos. 399-407 (9)	4.75	3.00

Souvenir Sheet
Perf. 13½x14
408	A74a	$1.50 Goofy	2.10	1.50

St. Nicholas, Icon, 17th Century — A75

Icons or Illuminations: 3c, Emperor Otto II, 10th century. 6c, St. John, Book of Lindisfarne. 15c, Christ and angels. 20c, Christ attended by angels, Book of Kells, 9th century. 25c, St. John the Evangelist. 65c, Christ enthroned, 17th century. $1, St. John, 8th century. $2, St. Matthew, Book of Lindisfarne.

1979, Nov. 26
409	A75	1c multicolored	.25	.25
410	A75	3c multicolored	.25	.25
411	A75	6c multicolored	.25	.25
412	A75	15c multicolored	.25	.25
413	A75	20c multicolored	.25	.25
414	A75	25c multicolored	.25	.25
415	A75	65c multicolored	.25	.25
416	A75	$1 multicolored	.25	.25
		Nos. 409-416 (8)	2.00	2.00

Souvenir Sheet
417	A75	$2 multicolored	1.25	1.25

Christina's World, by Andrew Wyeth — A76

Art Treasures: 10c, Ivory leopards, Benin, 19th century. 20c, The Kiss, by Gustav Klimt, vert. 25c, Portrait of a Lady, by Rogier van der Weyden, vert. 80c, Sumerian bull's head harp, 2600 B.C., vert. $1, The Wave, by Hokusai. $2, Holy Family, by Rembrandt, vert.

1979, Dec. 19   Litho.   *Perf. 13½*
418	A76	6c multicolored	.25	.25
419	A76	10c multicolored	.25	.25
420	A76	20c multicolored	.25	.25
421	A76	25c multicolored	.25	.25
422	A76	80c multicolored	.30	.30
423	A76	$1 multicolored	.45	.45
		Nos. 418-423 (6)	1.75	1.75

Souvenir Sheet
424	A76	$2 multicolored	1.75	1.75

Pied-billed Grebe — A77

1980, Feb. 20   Litho.   *Perf. 14*
425	A77	20c shown	.75	.40
426	A77	25c Ovenbirds	.90	.45
427	A77	35c Marsh hawks	1.25	.65
428	A77	55c Yellow-bellied sap-sucker	2.00	.90
429	A77	$1 Blue-winged teals	3.50	1.75
		Nos. 425-429 (5)	8.40	4.15

Souvenir Sheet
430	A77	$2 Glossy ibis	4.25	4.25

Stamp Under Magnifier, Perforation Gauge, London 1980 Emblem A78

1980, May 6   Litho.   *Perf. 14x14½*
431	A78	25c shown	.25	.25

432 A78 40c Stamp in tongs,
gauge .35 .35
Souvenir Sheet
433 A78 $2 Exhibition Hall 1.10 1.10
London 1980 International Stamp Exhibition, May 6-14.

Trumpet
Triton
A79

1980, June 26 Litho. Perf. 14
434 A79 15c shown .25 .25
435 A79 20c Measled cowry .30 .30
436 A79 30c True tulip .40 .40
437 A79 45c Lion's paw .60 .60
438 A79 55c Sunrise tellin .75 .75
439 A79 70c Grown cone 1.00 1.00
Nos. 434-439 (6) 3.30 3.30

Queen Mother
Elizabeth, 80th
Birthday — A80

1980, Aug. 4 Litho. Perf. 14
440 A80 80c multicolored .70 .70
Souvenir Sheet
Perf. 12
441 A80 $1.50 multicolored 1.50 1.50

Pinocchio — A81

Christmas: Scenes from Walt Disney's Pinocchio.

1980, Sept. 25 Perf. 11
442 A81 ¼c multicolored .25 .25
443 A81 ½c multicolored .25 .25
444 A81 1c multicolored .25 .25
445 A81 2c multicolored .25 .25
446 A81 3c multicolored .25 .25
447 A81 4c multicolored .25 .25
448 A81 5c multicolored .25 .25
449 A81 75c multicolored 1.10 1.10
450 A81 $1 multicolored 1.50 1.50
Nos. 442-450 (9) 4.35 4.35
Souvenir Sheet
451 A81 $2 multi, vert. 4.50 4.50

Medical Examination, Lions — A82

1980, Oct. 8 Litho. Perf. 14
452 A82 10c shown .25 .25
453 A82 15c Scholarships,
Kiwanis .25 .25
454 A82 45c Education, Soroptimists .60 .60
455 A82 $1 Lobster boat, Rotary .90 .90
Nos. 452-455 (4) 2.00 2.00
Souvenir Sheet
456 A82 $2 Funds for schools,
Rotary 2.25 2.25
Lions, Rotary, Kiwanis and Soroptimists service organizations; 75th anniv. of Rotary Intl.

Martin Luther King, Jr. (1929-68) — A83

Human Rights Leaders: 30c, John F. Kennedy. 45c, Roberto Clemente (1934-72), baseball player. 70c, Frank Worrel (1927-67), cricket player. $1, Harriet Tubman (1823-1913), born slave, helped others escape to freedom. $2, Marcus Garvey (1887-1940), Jamaican black nationalist leader.

1980, Dec. 22 Litho. Perf. 14
457 A83 20c multicolored .25 .25
458 A83 30c multicolored .35 .35
459 A83 45c multicolored .60 .60
460 A83 70c multicolored .95 .95
461 A83 $1 multicolored 1.35 1.35
Nos. 457-461 (5) 3.50 3.50
Souvenir Sheet
462 A83 $2 multicolored 2.00 2.00

Racing
Yachts
A84

Designs: Racing yachts.

1981, Jan. 29 Litho. Perf. 14
463 A84 6c multicolored .25 .25
464 A84 15c multicolored .25 .25
465 A84 35c multicolored .40 .40
466 A84 $1 multicolored .85 .85
Nos. 463-466 (4) 1.75 1.75
Souvenir Sheet
467 A84 $2 multicolored 1.75 1.75
South Caicos Regatta. No. 467 contains one 28x42mm stamp.

Pluto
Listening to
Sea
Shell — A85

1981, Feb. 16 Perf. 13½x14
468 A85 10c shown .50 .50
469 A85 75c Pluto on raft,
dolphin 2.00 2.00
Souvenir Sheet
470 A85 $1.50 Pluto 4.25 4.25
50th anniversary of Walt Disney's Pluto.

Night Queen
Cactus — A86

1981, Feb. 10 Perf. 14
471 A86 25c shown .30 .30
472 A86 35c Ripsaw cactus .40 .40
473 A86 55c Royal strawberry
cactus .70 .70
474 A86 80c Caicos cactus 1.10 1.10
Nos. 471-474 (4) 2.50 2.50
Souvenir Sheet
475 A86 $2 Turks head cactus 2.25 2.25

Donald Duck
and Louie
with Easter
Egg — A87

Easter: Various Disney characters with Easter eggs.

1981, Mar. 20 Litho. Perf. 11
476 A87 10c multicolored .30 .30
477 A87 25c multicolored .60 .60
478 A87 60c multicolored 1.60 1.60
479 A87 80c multicolored 2.00 2.00
Nos. 476-479 (4) 4.50 4.50
Souvenir Sheet
480 A87 $4 multicolored 7.50 7.50

Woman with Fan,
1909 — A88

1981, May 28 Litho. Perf. 14
481 A88 20c shown .25 .25
482 A88 45c Woman with Pears,
1909 .65 .65
483 A88 80c The Accordionist,
1911 1.10 1.10
484 A88 $1 The Aficionado,
1912 1.40 1.40
Nos. 481-484 (4) 3.40 3.40
Souvenir Sheet
485 A88 $2 Girl with a Mandolin, 1910 3.00 3.00
Pablo Picasso (1881-1973).

Royal Wedding Issue
Common Design Type and

A88a

1981, June 23 Litho. Perf. 14
486 CD331a 35c Couple .25 .25
487 CD331a 65c Kensington
Palace .30 .30
488 CD331a 90c Charles .40 .40
Nos. 486-488 (3) .95 .95
Souvenir Sheet
489 CD331 $2 Glass coach 1.25 1.25

Self-adhesive
Imperf. x Roulette 5 (20c, $1),
Imperf. ($2)
1981, July 7
490 Booklet 4.00
a. A88a Pane of 6 (3x20c, Lady Diana, 3x$1, Charles) 2.25
b. A88a Pane of 1 ($2, Couple 1.75
Nos. 486-488 also printed in sheets of 5 plus label, perf. 12, in changed colors.

Underwater Marine Biology
Observation — A89

1981, Aug. 21 Litho. Perf. 14
491 A89 15c shown .30 .30
492 A89 40c Underwater photography .65 .65
493 A89 75c Diving for wreckage 1.10 1.10
494 A89 $1 Diver, dolphins 1.50 1.50
Nos. 491-494 (4) 3.55 3.55
Souvenir Sheet
495 A89 $2 Diving flag 3.75 3.75

Br'er Rabbit Barricading his
Door — A90

Christmas: Scenes from Walt Disney's Uncle Remus.

1981, Nov. 2 Litho. Perf. 14x13½
496 A90 ¼c multicolored .30 .30
497 A90 ½c multicolored .30 .30
498 A90 1c multicolored .30 .30
499 A90 2c multicolored .30 .30
500 A90 3c multicolored .30 .30
501 A90 4c multicolored .30 .30
502 A90 5c multicolored .30 .30
503 A90 75c multicolored 1.40 1.40
504 A90 $1 multicolored 1.90 1.90
Nos. 496-504 (9) 5.40 5.40
Souvenir Sheet
505 A90 $2 multicolored 4.50 4.50

Flags of
Turks and
Caicos
Islands
A91

Maps of Various Islands: a, Grand Turk. b, Salt Cay. c, South Caicos. d, East Caicos. e, Middle Caicos. f, North Caicos. g, Caicos Cays. h, Providenciales. i, West Caicos.

1981, Dec. 1 Perf. 14
506 Strip of 10 5.50 5.50
a.-j. A91 20c any single .55 .55

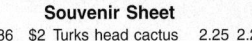
Caribbean
Buckeyes — A92

1982, Jan. 21 Litho. Perf. 14
507 A92 20c shown .40 .40
508 A92 35c Clench's hairstreaks .75 .75
509 A92 65c Gulf fritillarys 1.25 1.25
510 A92 $1 Bush sulphurs 2.10 2.10
Nos. 507-510 (4) 4.50 4.50
Souvenir Sheet
511 A92 $2 Turk Isld. leaf butterfly 5.00 5.00

Scouting
Year — A93

1982, Feb. 17   Litho.   Perf. 14
512 A93 40c Flag ceremony .90 .90
513 A93 50c Building raft 1.10 1.10
514 A93 75c Cricket match 1.50 1.50
515 A93 $1 Nature study 2.00 2.00
　　Nos. 512-515 (4) 5.50 5.50
Souvenir Sheet
516 A93 $2 Baden-Powell, sa-
　　lute 4.50 4.50

1982 World Cup
Soccer — A94

Designs: Various soccer players.

1982, Apr. 30   Litho.   Perf. 14
517 A94 10c multicolored .25 .25
518 A94 25c multicolored .35 .35
519 A94 45c multicolored .60 .60
520 A94 $1 multicolored 1.25 1.25
　　Nos. 517-520 (4) 2.45 2.45
Souvenir Sheet
521 A94 $2 multi, horiz. 2.25 2.25

#517-520 issued in sheets of 5 + label.

Phillis Wheatley (1753-1784), Poet,
and Washington Crossing
Delaware — A95

Washington's 250th Birth Anniv. and F.D.
Roosevelt's Birth Centenary: 35c, Washing-
ton, Benjamin Banneker (1731-1806), astrono-
mer and mathematician, map. 65c, FDR,
George Washington Carver (1864-1943). 80c,
FDR with stamp collection. $2, FDR examining
Washington stamp.

1982, May 3   Litho.   Perf. 14
522 A95 20c multicolored .35 .35
523 A95 35c multicolored .70 .70
524 A95 65c multicolored 1.25 1.25
525 A95 80c multicolored 1.75 1.75
　　Nos. 522-525 (4) 4.05 4.05
Souvenir Sheet
526 A95 $2 multicolored 3.50 3.50

Second
Thoughts, by
Norman
Rockwell — A96

1982, June 23   Litho.   Perf. 14x13½
527 A96 8c shown .30 .30
528 A96 15c The Proper Gratuity .30 .30
529 A96 20c Before the Shot .35 .35
530 A96 25c The Three Umpires .45 .45
　　Nos. 527-530 (4) 1.40 1.40

Princess Diana Issue
Common Design Type
1982   Litho.   Perf. 14½x14
530A CD332 8c Sandringham .30 .25
530B CD332 35c Wedding 1.40 .55
530C CD332 $1.10 Diana 4.50 1.75
　　Nos. 530A-530C (3) 6.20 2.55

1982, July 1   Perf. 14½x14
531 CD332 55c Sandringham 1.50 1.00
532 CD332 70c Wedding 1.50 1.00
533 CD332 $1 Diana 2.75 1.75
　　Nos. 531-533 (3) 5.75 3.75

Also issued in sheetlets of 5 + label.

Souvenir Sheet
534 CD332 $2 Diana, diff. 5.00 4.00

Skymaster over Caicos Cays — A97

1982, Aug. 26   Litho.   Perf. 14
535 A97 8c shown .25 .25
536 A97 15c Jetstar, Grand
　　Turk .35 .35
537 A97 65c Helicopter, South
　　Caicos 1.00 1.00
538 A97 $1.10 Seaplane, Pro-
　　videnciales 1.90 1.90
　　Nos. 535-538 (4) 3.50 3.50
Souvenir Sheet
539 A97 $2 Boeing 727 3.25 3.25

Christmas — A98

Christmas: Scenes from Walt Disney's
Mickey's Christmas Carol.

1982, Dec. 1   Litho.   Perf. 13½
540 A98 1c multicolored .25 .25
541 A98 1c multicolored .25 .25
542 A98 2c multicolored .25 .25
543 A98 2c multicolored .25 .25
544 A98 3c multicolored .25 .25
545 A98 3c multicolored .25 .25
546 A98 4c multicolored .25 .25
547 A98 65c multicolored 1.10 1.10
548 A98 $1.10 multicolored 2.50 1.50
　　Nos. 540-548 (9) 5.35 4.35
Souvenir Sheet
549 A98 $2 multicolored 5.25 5.25

Trams and Locomotives — A99

1983, Jan. 18   Litho.   Perf. 14
550 A99 15c West Caicos trol-
　　ley tram .30 .30
551 A99 55c West Caicos
　　steam locomotive 1.10 1.10
552 A99 90c Mule-drawn tram,
　　East Caicos 1.60 1.60
553 A99 $1.60 Sisal locomotive,
　　East Caicos 3.00 3.00
　　Nos. 550-553 (4) 6.00 6.00
Souvenir Sheet
554 A99 $2.50 Steam engine 4.50 4.50

A99a

1983, Mar. 14
555 A99a 1c Woman crossing
　　guard .35 .35
556 A99a 8c Wind and solar en-
　　ergy sources .35 .35
557 A99a 65c Sailing 1.60 1.60
558 A99a $1 Cricket game 2.50 2.50
　a. Block or strip of 4, #555-558 5.75 5.75

Commonwealth Day.

Easter — A100

Crucifixion, by Raphael. $2.50 shows entire
painting.

1983, Apr. 7   Litho.   Perf. 14
559 A100 35c Mary Magda-
　　lene, St. John .50 .50
560 A100 50c Mary .70 .70
561 A100 95c Angel looking to
　　heaven 1.10 1.10
562 A100 $1.10 Angel looking to
　　earth 1.25 1.25
　　Nos. 559-562 (4) 3.55 3.55
Souvenir Sheet
563 A100 $2.50 multicolored 5.00 5.00

Piked
Whale
A101

1983   Litho.   Perf. 14
564 A101 50c shown 1.60 1.60
565 A101 65c Right whale 2.25 2.25
566 A101 70c Killer whale 2.50 2.50
567 A101 95c Sperm whale 3.50 3.50
568 A101 $1.10 Gooseback
　　whale 4.00 4.00
569 A101 $2 Blue whale 7.00 7.00
570 A101 $2.20 Humpback
　　whale 8.00 8.00
571 A101 $3 Longfin pilot
　　whale 10.50 10.50
　　Nos. 564-571 (8) 39.35 39.35
Souvenir Sheet
572 A101 $3 Fin whale 15.00 15.00

Issued: 50c, $2.20, #571, 5/16; 70c, 95c,
$2, 6/13; others 7/11. Issued in sheets of 4.
For overprints see Nos. 637-639.

Manned Flight
Bicentenary
A102

1983, Aug. 30   Litho.   Perf. 14
573 A102 25c 1st hydrogen bal-
　　loon, 1783 .35 .35
574 A102 35c Friendship 7, 1962 .50 .50
575 A102 70c Montgolfiere, 1783 .90 .90
576 A102 95c Columbia space
　　shuttle 1.25 1.25
　　Nos. 573-576 (4) 3.00 3.00
Souvenir Sheet
577 A102 $2 Montgolfiere, Co-
　　lumbia 3.00 3.00

Ships
A103

1985   Litho.   Perf. 12½x12
578 A103 4c Dug-out canoe .25 .25
579 A103 5c Santa Maria .25 .25
580 A103 8c Spanish trea-
　　sure galleons .25 .25
581 A103 10c Bermuda
　　sloop .35 .25
582 A103 20c Privateer
　　Grand Turk .90 1.10
583 A103 25c Nelson's Frig-
　　ate Boreas 1.00 1.40
584 A103 30c Warship En-
　　dymion 1.50 2.00
585 A103 35c Bark Caesar 1.75 2.40
586 A103 50c Schooner
　　Grapeshot 2.50 3.00
587 A103 65c Invincible 3.25 4.25
588 A103 95c Magicienne 4.50 6.00
589 A103 $1.10 Durban 5.50 7.00
590 A103 $2 Sentinel 9.00 12.00
591 A103 $3 Minerva 14.00 19.00
592 A103 $5 Caicos sloop 22.50 29.00
　　Nos. 578-592 (15) 67.50 88.15

Issued: 4c, 8c, 10c, 30c, 65c, $1.10, $5,
Mar.; 5c, 20c, 25c, 35c, 50c, 95c, $2, Aug. 12;
$3, Dec.

1983-84   Perf. 14
578a A103 4c .25 .25
579a A103 5c .25 .25
580a A103 8c .25 .25
581a A103 10c .30 .25
582a A103 20c .90 .95
583a A103 25c 1.10 1.25
584a A103 30c 1.00 1.25
585a A103 35c 1.75 1.60
586a A103 50c 2.25 2.25
587a A103 65c 3.25 3.00
588a A103 95c 4.50 4.00
589a A103 $1.10 5.25 4.75
590a A103 $2 14.50 13.50
591a A103 $3 21.00 22.50
592a A103 $5 66.55 64.80
　　Nos. 578a-592a (15) 66.55 64.80

Issued: 10c, 30c, 65c, $1.10-$3, 10/5/83;
8c, 25c, 50c, 95c, 12/16/83; 4c, 5c, 20c, 35c,
$5, 1/9/84.

For overprints see Nos. 744-746.

Christmas
A104

Designs: Scenes from Walt Disney's Oh
Christmas Tree.

1983, Nov.   Perf. 11
593 A104 1c Fifer Pig .25 .25
594 A104 1c Fiddler Pig .25 .25
595 A104 2c Practical Pig .25 .25
596 A104 2c Pluto .25 .25
597 A104 3c Goofy .25 .25
598 A104 3c Mickey Mouse .25 .25
599 A104 35c Gyro Gearloose .60 .60
600 A104 50c Ludwig Von
　　Drake .80 .80
601 A104 $1.10 Huey, Dewey
　　and Louie 1.90 1.90
　　Nos. 593-601 (9) 4.80 4.80
Souvenir Sheet
Perf. 13½
602 A104 $2.50 Around the tree 6.50 6.50

John F. Kennedy (1917-1963), 20th
Death Anniv. — A105

1983, Dec. 22   Litho.   Perf. 14
603 A105 20c multicolored   .35   .35
604 A105 $1 multicolored   1.75 1.75

Classic
Cars
A106

1984, Mar. 15   Litho.   Perf. 14
605 A106 4c Cadillac V-16,
                 1933 + label   .25   .25
606 A106 8c Rolls Royce
                 Phantom III,
                 1937 + label   .25   .25
607 A106 10c Saab 99, 1969
                 + label   .25   .25
608 A106 25c Maserati Bora,
                 1973 + label   .75   .75
609 A106 40c Datsun 260Z,
                 1970 + label   1.25 1.25
610 A106 55c Porsche 917,
                 1971 + label   1.75 1.75
611 A106 80c Lincoln Conti-
                 nental, 1939 +
                 label   2.50 2.50
612 A106 $1 Triumph TR3A,
                 1957 + label   3.00 3.00
       Nos. 605-612 (8)   10.00 10.00

Souvenir Sheet
613 A106 $2 Daimler, 1886   3.75 3.75

125th anniv. of first commercially productive
oil well, Drake's Rig, Titusville, Pa. Nos. 605-
612 se-tenant with labels showing flags and
auto museum names. No. 613 for 150th birth
anniv. of Gotlieb Daimler, inventor of high-
speed internal combustion engine.

Easter — A107

450th death anniv. of Antonio Allegri Correggio (Various cameo portraits of Correggio,
paintings): 15c, Rest on the Flight to Egypt
with St. Francis. 40c, St. Luke and St.
Ambrose. 60c, Diana and her Chariot. 95c,
Deposition of Christ. $2, Nativity with St. Eliza-
beth and the Infant St. John.

1984, Apr. 9
614 A107 15c multicolored   .30   .30
615 A107 40c multicolored   .95   .95
616 A107 60c multicolored   1.25 1.25
617 A107 95c multicolored   1.75 1.75
       Nos. 614-617 (4)   4.25 4.25

Souvenir Sheet
618 A107 $2 multi, horiz.   3.25 3.25

1984 Los Angeles Olympics — A108

Various Disney characters participating in
Olympic sports.

1984, Feb. 21   Litho.   Perf. 14
619 A108 1c 500-meter   .30   .30
620 A108 1c Diving   .30   .30
621 A108 2c Single kayak   .30   .30
622 A108 2c 1000-meter kayak   .30   .30
623 A108 3c Highboard diving   .30   .30
624 A108 3c Kayak slalom   .30   .30

625 A108 25c Freestyle swim-
                 ming   .80   .80
626 A108 75c Water polo   2.25 2.25
627 A108 $1 Yachting   3.00 3.00
       Nos. 619-627 (9)   7.85 7.85

Souvenir Sheet
628 A108 $2 Platform diving   6.25 6.25

1984, Apr.   Perf. 12½x12
Same Designs
619a A108 1c   .30   .30
620a A108 1c   .30   .30
621a A108 2c   .30   .30
622a A108 2c   .30   .30
623a A108 3c   .30   .30
624a A108 3c   .30   .30
625a A108 25c   .75   .75
626a A108 75c   2.10 2.10
627a A108 $1   2.75 2.75
       Nos. 619a-627a (9)   7.40 7.40

Souvenir Sheet
628a A108 $2   6.50 6.50

Nos. 619a-628a inscribed with Olympic
rings emblem. Printed in sheets of 5.

Sir Arthur Conan Doyle (1859-
1930) — A109

Scenes from the Adventures of Sherlock
Holmes.

1984, July 16   Litho.   Perf. 14
629 A109 25c Second Stain   3.50 2.10
630 A109 45c Final Problem   4.75 3.50
631 A109 70c Empty House   6.75 5.25
632 A109 85c Greek Interpret-
                 er   8.25 6.75
       Nos. 629-632 (4)   23.25 17.60

Souvenir Sheet
633 A109 $2 Doyle, vert.   19.00 22.50

Nos. 567-568, 572 Overprinted with
UPU Emblem and: "19TH UPU
CONGRESS / HAMBURG, WEST
GERMANY./ 1874-1984"

1984   Litho.   Perf. 14
637 A101 95c multicolored   4.50 3.00
638 A101 $1.10 multicolored   4.50 3.50

Souvenir Sheet
639 A101 $3 multicolored   8.00 8.00

AUSIPEX '84
A110

Darwin, Ship, Map of Australia, Fauna.

1984, Aug. 22   Perf. 14x13½
640 A110 5c Clown fish   1.05   .85
641 A110 35c Monitor lizard   3.25 3.25
642 A110 50c Rainbow lori-
                 keets   4.50 3.75
643 A110 $1.10 Koalas   6.00 5.00
       Nos. 640-643 (4)   14.80 12.85

Souvenir Sheet
644 A110 $2 Grey kangaroo   5.75 5.75

Christmas — A111

Scenes from Walt Disney's The Toy Tinkers.

1984   Litho.   Perf. 14
645 A111 20c multicolored   1.00   .50
646 A111 35c multicolored   1.40   .70
647 A111 50c multicolored   2.00 1.00
648 A111 75c multicolored   2.75 1.75
649 A111 $1.10 multicolored   3.25 2.50
       Nos. 645-649 (5)   10.40 6.45

Souvenir Sheet
650 A111 $2 multicolored   5.00 5.00

No. 648 issued in sheets of 8. Issue dates:
75c, Nov. 26, others, Oct. 8.

Audubon Birth
Bicentenary
A112

Cameo portrait of Audubon, signature and
illustrations from Birds of North America.

1985, Jan. 28   Litho.   Perf. 14
651 A112 25c Dendroica
                 magnoliae   2.25 1.10
652 A112 45c Asio flammeus   3.50 2.25
653 A112 70c Zenaida
                 macroura   4.25 4.25
654 A112 85c Progne subis   4.25 4.75
       Nos. 651-654 (4)   14.25 12.35

Souvenir Sheet
655 A112 $2 Haematopus os-
                 tralegus   6.75 6.00

Intl. Civil
Aviation
Org.,
40th
Anniv.
A113

Pioneers & inventions: 8c, Leonardo da
Vinci, 15th century glider wing. 25c, Sir Alliott
Verdon Roe, 1949 C. 102 Jet. 65c, Robert H.
Goddard, first liquid fuel rocket launch, 1926.
$1, Igor Sikorsky, 1939 Sikorsky VS300. $2,
Aviator Amelia Earhart, 1937 Lockheed 10E
Electra.

1985, Feb. 21
656 A113 8c multicolored   .85   .45
657 A113 25c multicolored   2.50   .60
658 A113 65c multicolored   4.25 2.25
659 A113 $1 multicolored   6.50 5.25
       Nos. 656-659 (4)   14.10 8.55

Souvenir Sheet
660 A113 $2 multicolored   4.75 4.75

Arrival of
the
Statue of
Liberty in
New
York,
Cent.
A114

Designs: 20c, Flags of US, France, Franklin,
Lafayette. 30c, Designer Frederic A. Bartholdi,
engineer Gustave Eiffel, Statue, Eiffel Tower.
65c, Isere, arriving in New York with Statue,
1885. $1.10, Fund raisers Louis Agassiz, H.
W. Longfellow, Charles Sumner, Joseph Pulit-
zer. $2, Dedication day, Oct. 28, 1886.

1985, Mar. 28
661 A114 20c multicolored   1.10   .80
662 A114 30c multicolored   1.60   .95
663 A114 65c multicolored   3.50 2.10
664 A114 $1.10 multicolored   3.75 2.50
       Nos. 661-664 (4)   9.95 6.35

Souvenir Sheet
665 A114 $2 multicolored   6.00 6.00

Royal
Navy
A115

Designs: 20c, Sir Edward Hawke, Royal
George. 30c, Lord Nelson, H.M.S. Victory.
65c, Adm. Sir George Cockburn, H.M.S.
Albion. 95c, Adm. Sir David Beatty, H.M.S.
Indefatigable. $2, 18th century naval gunner,
cannons.

1985, Apr. 17
666 A115 20c multicolored   3.25 2.25
667 A115 30c multicolored   3.50 3.25
668 A115 65c multicolored   5.25 4.50
669 A115 95c multicolored   6.50 7.00
       Nos. 666-669 (4)   18.50 17.00

Souvenir Sheet
670 A115 $2 multicolored   6.25 6.25

Intl.
Youth
Year
A116

Anniversaries: 25c, Return of Halley's
Comet, 1986. 35c, Mark Twain (1835-1910),
Mississippi river boat. 50c, Jakob Grimm
(1785-1863), Hansel & Gretel, vert. 95c,
Grimm, Rumpelstiltskin, vert. $2, Twain,
Grimm, portraits.

1985, May 17
671 A116 25c multicolored   1.75   .55
672 A116 35c multicolored   2.75   .70
673 A116 50c multicolored   3.25 1.00
674 A116 95c multicolored   4.50 2.25
       Nos. 671-674 (4)   12.25 4.50

Souvenir Sheet
675 A116 $2 multicolored   6.00 6.00

Queen Mother,
85th
Birthday — A117

Designs: 30c, Queen Mother outside Clarence House, vert. 50c, Visiting Biggin Hill Airfield by helicopter. $1.10, 80th birthday por-
trait, vert. $2, With Prince Charles at the 1968
Garter Ceremony, Windsor Castle, vert.

1985, July 15
676 A117 30c multicolored   1.00 1.00
677 A117 50c multicolored   1.50 1.50
678 A117 $1.10 multicolored   3.50 3.50
       Nos. 676-678 (3)   6.00 6.00

Souvenir Sheet
679 A117 $2 multicolored   5.00 5.00

George Frideric   Johann Sebastian
Handel — A118   Bach — A119

Handel or Bach and: 4c, King George II,
Zadok the Priest music, 1727. 10c, Queen
Caroline, Funeral Anthem, 1737. 15c, Bas-
soon, Invention No. 3 in D Major. 40c, Natural
horn, Invention No. 3 in D Major. 50c, King
George I, Water Music, 1714. 60c, Viola
d'amore, Invention No. 3 . . . 95c, Clavichord,
Invention No. 3 . . . $1.10, Queen Anne, Or la
Tromba from Rinaldo. No. 688, Handel, por-
trait. No. 689, Bach, portrait.

1985, July 17   Perf. 15
680 A118 4c multicolored   .70   .55
681 A118 10c multicolored   1.10   .55
682 A119 15c multicolored   1.10   .50
683 A119 40c multicolored   2.25 1.00
684 A119 50c multicolored   3.00 2.50
685 A119 60c multicolored   2.75 1.25
686 A119 95c multicolored   3.25 2.50
687 A118 $1.10 multicolored   5.25 5.00
       Nos. 680-687 (8)   19.40 13.85

Souvenir Sheets

688	A118	$2 multicolored	7.25	7.25
689	A119	$2 multicolored	5.25	5.00

Motorcycle Centenary — A120

Flag of US, UK, Fed. Rep. of Germany or Japan and: 8c, 1915 dual cylinder Harley-Davidson. 25c, 1950 Thunderbird Triumph. 55c, 1985 BMW K100RS. $1.20, 1985 Honda 1100 Shadow. $2, 1885 Daimler Single Track, vert.

1985, Sept. 4			**Perf. 14**	
690	A120	8c multicolored	1.00	.40
691	A120	25c multicolored	2.10	1.00
692	A120	55c multicolored	3.25	2.50
693	A120	$1.20 multicolored	5.00	7.75
		Nos. 690-693 (4)	11.35	11.65

Souvenir Sheet

694	A120	$2 multicolored	6.25	6.25

Pirates of the Caribbean — A121

Disneyland, 30th Anniv.: No. 695, Fate of Capt. Kidd. No. 696, Pirates imprisoned. No. 697, Bartholomew Roberts, church-going pirate. No. 698, Buccaneers in battle. No. 699, Bride auction. No. 700, Plunder. No. 701, Singing pirates. No. 702, Blackbeard. No. 703, Henry Morgan. No. 704, Mary Read, Anne Bonney.

1985, Oct. 4		**Litho.**	**Perf. 14**	
695	A121	1c multicolored	.35	.35
696	A121	1c multicolored	.35	.35
697	A121	2c multicolored	.35	.35
698	A121	2c multicolored	.35	.35
699	A121	3c multicolored	.35	.35
700	A121	3c multicolored	.35	.35
701	A121	35c multicolored	2.25	.90
702	A121	75c multicolored	4.25	4.75
703	A121	$1.10 multicolored	4.75	5.50
		Nos. 695-703 (9)	13.35	13.25

Souvenir Sheet

704	A121	$2.50 multicolored	9.25	9.25

Girl Guides, 75th Anniv. A122

Uniforms of Turks and Caicos and: 10c, Papua New Guinea and China brownies. 40c, Surinam and Korea brownies. 70c, Australia and Canada girl guides. 80c, West Germany and Israel girl guides.

1985, Nov. 4				
705	A122	10c multicolored	1.10	.75
706	A122	40c multicolored	2.75	2.10
707	A122	70c multicolored	3.75	4.50
708	A122	80c multicolored	3.75	4.75
		Nos. 705-708 (4)	11.35	12.10

Souvenir Sheet

709	A122	$2 Anniv. emblem	5.00	5.00

Grand Turk Chapter, 35th anniv.

World Wildlife Fund A123

Map of the Islands — A124

Turks & Caicos ground iguanas.

1986, Nov. 20			**Perf. 14**	
710	A123	8c multicolored	2.50	1.25
711	A123	10c multicolored	2.50	1.25
712	A123	20c multicolored	4.25	2.50
713	A123	35c multicolored	9.75	8.50
		Nos. 710-713 (4)	19.00	13.50

Souvenir Sheet

714	A124	$2 multicolored	19.00	19.00

A125

Wedding pictures.

1986, Dec. 19		**Litho.**	**Perf. 14**	
715	A125	35c Couple	1.25	1.25
716	A125	65c Sarah in coach	2.25	2.25
717	A125	$1.10 Couple, close-up	4.00	4.00
		Nos. 715-717 (3)	7.50	7.50

Souvenir Sheet

718	A125	$2 In Westminster Abbey	7.00	7.00

Wedding of Prince Andrew and Sarah Ferguson.

Christmas — A126

Illuminations by miniaturist Giorgio Giulio Clovio (1498-1578) from the Farnese Book of Hours: 35c, Prophecy of the Birth of Christ to King Achaz. 50c, The Annunciation. 65c, The Circumcision. 95c, Adoration of the Kings. $2, The Nativity, from the Townley Lectionary.

1987, Dec. 9		**Litho.**	**Perf. 14**	
719	A126	35c multicolored	1.50	.85
720	A126	50c multicolored	2.25	2.10
721	A126	65c multicolored	2.75	2.75
722	A126	95c multicolored	4.00	4.50
		Nos. 719-722 (4)	10.50	10.20

Souvenir Sheet

723	A126	$2 multicolored	8.00	9.25

Accession of Queen Victoria to the Throne of England, 150th Anniv. A127

Ships and memorials: 8c, HMS Victoria, Victoria Cross. 35c, SS Victoria, coin. 55c, Victoria & Albert I, Great Britain No. 1. 95c, Victoria & Albert II, Victoria Public Library, Turks & Caicos. $2, Bark Victoria.

1987, Dec. 24				
724	A127	8c multicolored	3.75	1.60
725	A127	35c multicolored	3.75	3.25
726	A127	55c multicolored	4.25	4.25
727	A127	95c multicolored	5.25	7.00
		Nos. 724-727 (4)	17.00	16.10

Souvenir Sheet

728	A127	$2 multicolored	11.00	11.00

US Constitution Bicentennial — A128

Designs: 10c, NJ state flag. 35c, Freedom of Worship, vert. 65c, US Supreme Court, vert. 80c, John Adams, vert. $2, George Mason, vert.

1987, Dec. 31				
729	A128	10c multicolored	.25	.25
730	A128	35c multicolored	.75	.75
731	A128	65c multicolored	2.00	2.00
732	A128	80c multicolored	3.00	3.00
		Nos. 729-732 (4)	6.00	6.00

Souvenir Sheet

733	A128	$2 multicolored	4.00	4.50

Discovery of America, 500th Anniv. (in 1992) A129

4c, Caravel, first sighting of land, Oct. 12, 1492. 25c, Columbus meets with Indians, Oct. 14. 70c, Fleet anchored in harbor, Oct. 15. $1, Landing, Oct. 16. $2, Nina, Pinta and Santa Maria.

1988, Jan. 20				
734	A129	4c multicolored	.80	.50
735	A129	25c multicolored	1.50	.95
736	A129	70c multicolored	4.50	5.00
737	A129	$1 multicolored	4.50	5.00
		Nos. 734-737 (4)	11.30	11.45

Souvenir Sheet

738	A129	$2 multicolored	8.00	8.00

Sea Scouts Salute Jamboree and Australia A130

Australia Bicent.: 8c, Arawak artifact, scouts exploring cave on Middle Caicos, vert. 35c, Santa Maria, scouts rowing to Hawks Nest. 65c, Scouts diving to explore a sunken Spanish galleon, vert. 95c, Plantation worker cutting sisal, scouts exploring plantation ruins. $2, Splashdown of Friendship 7, piloted by John Glenn, Feb. 20, 1962, vert.

1988, Feb. 12		**Litho.**	**Perf. 14**	
739	A130	8c multicolored	.35	.35
740	A130	35c shown	1.00	1.00
741	A130	65c multicolored	1.90	1.90
742	A130	95c multicolored	2.75	2.75
		Nos. 739-742 (4)	6.00	6.00

Souvenir Sheet

743	A130	$2 multicolored	5.25	5.75

Nos. 581, 583 and 590 Ovptd. "40th WEDDING ANNIVERSARY / H.M. QUEEN ELIZABETH II / H.R.H. THE DUKE OF EDINBURGH"

1988, Mar. 14		**Litho.**	**Perf. 14**	
744	A103	10c multicolored	.25	.25
745	A103	25c multicolored	.75	.75
746	A103	$2 multicolored	6.00	6.00
		Nos. 744-746 (3)	7.00	7.00

A131

1988, Aug. 29			**Litho.**	
747	A131	8c Soccer	.75	.40
748	A131	30c Yachting	1.50	1.50
749	A131	70c Cycling	4.75	4.00
750	A131	$1 Running	3.75	4.75
		Nos. 747-750 (4)	10.75	10.65

Souvenir Sheet

751	A131	$2 Swimming	5.00	5.00

1988 Summer Olympics, Seoul.

A132

Billfish Tournament: 8c, Passenger jet, fishing boat and fisherman reeling-in giant swordfish. 10c, Photographing prize catch. 70c, Fishing boat, lighthouse. $1, Blue marlin. $2, Sailfish.

1988, Sept. 5			**Litho.**	
752	A132	8c multicolored	1.40	.35
753	A132	10c multicolored	.70	.35
754	A132	70c multicolored	3.00	3.25
755	A132	$1 multicolored	3.50	.40
		Nos. 752-755 (4)	8.60	4.35

Souvenir Sheet

756	A132	$2 multicolored	6.00	6.00

Christmas A133

Paintings by Titian: 15c, Madonna and Child with St. Catherine and the Infant John the Baptist, c. 1530. 25c, Madonna with a Rabbit, c. 1526. 35c, Virgin and Child with Sts. Stephen, Jerome and Mauritius, c. 1520. 40c, The Gypsy Madonna, c. 1510. 50c, The Holy Family and a Shepherd, c. 1510. 65c, Madonna and Child, c. 1510. $3, Madonna and Child with St. John the Baptist and St. Catherine, c. 1530. No. 764, Adoration of the Magi, c. 1560. No. 765, The Annunciation, c. 1560.

1988, Oct. 24			**Litho.**	
757	A133	15c multicolored	.40	.40
758	A133	25c multicolored	.60	.60
759	A133	35c multicolored	.85	.85
760	A133	40c multicolored	.95	.95
761	A133	50c multicolored	1.25	1.25
762	A133	65c multicolored	1.50	1.50
763	A133	$3 multicolored	7.00	7.00
		Nos. 757-763 (7)	12.55	12.55

Souvenir Sheets

764	A133	$2 multicolored	5.00	5.00
765	A133	$2 multicolored	5.00	5.00

Visit of Princess Alexandra, 1st Cousin of Queen Elizabeth II — A134

Various portraits and: 70c, Government House. $1.40, Map. $2, Flora, vert.

1988, Nov. 14　　Litho.　　Perf. 14
766　A134　70c multicolored　　　4.50　3.75
767　A134　$1.40 multicolored　　10.00　10.50

Souvenir Sheet

768　A134　$2 multicolored　　　16.00　16.00

Arms Type of 1970 Without Inscription
Perf. 14½x15
1988, Dec. 15　　Litho.　　Unwmk.
769　A35　$10 multicolored　　　20.00　20.00

Pre-Columbian Societies and Their Customs — A135

UPAE and discovery of America anniv. emblems and: 10c, Hollowing-out tree to make a canoe, vert. 50c, Body painting and statue. 65c, Three islanders with body paint. $1, Canoeing, vert. $2, Petroglyph.

1989, May 15　　Litho.　　Perf. 14
770　A135　10c multicolored　　　.40　.40
771　A135　50c multicolored　　　1.60　1.60
772　A135　65c multicolored　　　2.00　2.00
773　A135　$1 multicolored　　　3.25　3.25
　　　Nos. 770-773 (4)　　　7.25　7.25

Souvenir Sheet

774　A135　$2 multicolored　　　8.00　8.25

Discovery of America 500th anniv. (in 1992).

Souvenir Sheet

Lincoln Memorial, Washington, D.C. — A136

1989, Nov. 17　　Litho.　　Perf. 14
775　A136　$1.50 multicolored　　5.25　5.25
World Stamp Expo '89.

Miniature Sheets

American Presidential Office, 200th Anniv. — A137

US presidents, historic events and monuments.
No. 776: a, Jackson, early train. b, Van Buren, origins of baseball and Moses Fleetwood Walker, 1st black to play professional baseball. c, Harrison, Harrison's "Keep the Ball Rollin'" slogan and parade. d, Tyler, annexation of Texas, 1845. e, Polk, 1st US postage stamps (#2), 1847, and discovery of

gold in California, 1849. f, Taylor, Mexican-American War, 1847.
No. 777: a, Hayes, end of Civil War reconstruction. b, Garfield, Garfield leading Union soldiers in the Battle of Shiloh. c, Arthur, opening of the Brooklyn Bridge, 1883. d, Cleveland, Columbian Exposition, 1893 (US #245). e, Benjamin Harrison, Pan-American Union building, map. f, McKinley, Spanish-American War (Rough Riders Monument, by Solon Borglum).
No. 778: a, Hoover, 1933 Olympic Games, Los Angeles and Lake Placid (American sprinter Ralph Metcalf and Norwegian figure skater Sonja Henie). b, Franklin Delano Roosevelt, Roosevelt's support of the March of Dimes (dime, 1946). c, 150th anniv. of inauguration of Washington, New York World's Fair, 1939. d, Truman, founding of the U.N., 1945. e, Eisenhower, invasion of Normandy, 1944. f, Kennedy, Apollo 11 mission, 1969.

1989, Nov. 19　　　　Perf. 14
776　　Sheet of 6　　　　15.00　15.00
　a.-f. A137 50c any single　　2.40　2.40
777　　Sheet of 6　　　　15.00　15.00
　a.-f. A137 50c any single　　2.40　2.40
778　　Sheet of 6　　　　15.00　15.00
　a.-f. A137 50c any single　　2.40　2.40

Fraser is incorrectly spelled "Frazer" on No. 778c.

Christmas — A138

Religious paintings by Giovanni Bellini: 15c, Madonna and Child. 25c, The Madonna of the Shrubs. 35c, The Virgin and Child. 40c, The Virgin and Child with a Greek Inscription. 50c, The Madonna of the Meadow. 65c, The Madonna of the Pear. 70c, The Virgin and Child, diff. $1, Madonna and Child, diff. No. 787, The Madonna with John the Baptist and Another Saint. No. 788, The Virgin and Child Enthroned.

1989, Dec. 18
779　A138　15c multicolored　　　.55　.55
780　A138　25c multicolored　　　.85　.85
781　A138　35c multicolored　　　1.25　1.25
782　A138　40c multicolored　　　1.50　1.50
783　A138　50c multicolored　　　1.75　1.75
784　A138　65c multicolored　　　2.25　2.25
785　A138　70c multicolored　　　2.50　2.50
786　A138　$1 multicolored　　　7.00　7.00
　　　Nos. 779-786 (8)　　　17.65　17.65

Souvenir Sheets

787　A138　$2 multicolored　　　8.00　8.00
788　A138　$2 multicolored　　　8.00　8.00

Souvenir Sheet

1st Moon Landing, 20th Anniv. — A139

Designs: a, Liftoff. b, Eagle lunar module on Moon's surface. c, Aldrin obtaining soil samples. d, Neil Armstrong walking on Moon. e, Columbia and Eagle in space.

1990, Jan. 8
789　　Sheet of 5　　　　8.50　8.50
　a.-e. A139 50c any single　　1.60　1.60

Flowers — A140

1990, Jan. 11　　Litho.　　Perf. 14
790　A140　8c　Zephyranthes rosea　　　.25　.25
791　A140　10c　Sophora tomentosa　　.25　.25
792　A140　15c　Coccoloba uvifera　　.35　.35
793　A140　20c　Encyclia gracilis　　.50　.50
794　A140　25c　Tillandsia streptophylla　.60　.60
795　A140　30c　Maurandella antirrhiniflora　.70　.70
796　A140　35c　Tillandsia balbisiana　.85　.85
797　A140　50c　Encyclia rufa　1.25　1.25
798　A140　65c　Aechmea lingulata　1.50　1.50
799　A140　80c　Asclepias curassavica　1.90　1.90
800　A140　$1　Caesalpinia bahamensis　2.40　2.40
801　A140　$1.10　Capparis cynophal-lophora　2.75　2.75
802　A140　$1.25　Stachytarpheta jamaicensis　3.00　3.00
803　A140　$2　Cassia biflora　4.75　4.75
804　A140　$5　Clusia rosea　12.00　12.00
805　A140　$10　Opuntia bahamana　24.00　24.00
　　　Nos. 790-805 (16)　　57.05　57.05

1994　　　　　　　　Perf. 12
790a　A140　8c　　　.25　.25
791a　A140　10c　　　.25　.25
792a　A140　15c　　　.35　.35
793a　A140　20c　　　.50　.50
794a　A140　25c　　　.60　.60
795a　A140　30c　　　.70　.70
796a　A140　35c　　　.85　.85
797a　A140　50c　　　1.25　1.25
798a　A140　65c　　　1.50　1.50
799a　A140　80c　　　1.90　1.90
800a　A140　$1　　　2.40　2.40
801a　A140　$1.10　　2.75　2.75
802a　A140　$1.25　　3.00　3.00
803a　A140　$2　　　4.75　4.75
804a　A140　$5　　　12.00　12.00
805a　A140　$10　('95)　24.00　24.00
　　　Nos. 790a-805a (16)　57.05　57.05

Birds A141

1990, Feb. 19
806　A141　10c　Yellow-billed cuckoo　1.40　.80
807　A141　15c　White-tailed tropic bird　1.60　.80
808　A141　20c　Kirtland's warbler　2.00　1.10
809　A141　30c　Yellow-crowned night heron　2.50　1.10
810　A141　50c　West Indian tree duck　3.50　1.60
811　A141　80c　Yellow-bellied sapsucker　4.25　3.50
812　A141　$1　American kestrel　5.75　6.50
813　A141　$1.40　Mockingbird　5.50　4.25
　　　Nos. 806-813 (8)　26.50　19.65

Souvenir Sheets

814　A141　$2　Osprey　12.50　12.50
815　A141　$2　Yellow warbler　12.50　12.50

Fish A142

1990, Feb. 12　　Litho.　　Perf. 14
816　A142　8c　Queen parrotfish　.30　.30
817　A142　10c　Queen triggerfish　.30　.30
818　A142　25c　Sergeant major　.70　.70
819　A142　40c　Spotted goatfish　1.10　1.10
820　A142　50c　Neon goby　1.40　1.40
821　A142　75c　Nassau grouper　2.10　2.10
822　A142　80c　Jawfish　2.25　2.25
823　A142　$1　Blue tang　2.75　2.75
　　　Nos. 816-823 (8)　10.90　10.90

Souvenir Sheets

824　A142　$2　Butter hamlet　9.00　9.00
825　A142　$2　Queen angelfish　9.00　9.00

Butterflies A143

1990, Mar. 19
826　A143　15c　White peacock　1.00　.70
827　A143　25c　Cloudless sulphur　1.25　.90
828　A143　35c　Mexican fritillary　1.60　1.10
829　A143　40c　Fiery skipper　1.75　1.25
830　A143　50c　Chamberlain's sulphur　1.75　1.50
831　A143　65c　Pygmy blue　2.10　2.10
832　A143　90c　Dusky swallow-tail　3.50　4.25
833　A143　$1　Antillean dagger wing　3.50　4.25
　　　Nos. 826-833 (8)　16.45　16.05

Souvenir Sheets

834　A143　$2　Thomas's blue　9.00　9.00
835　A143　$2　9 Queen species　9.00　9.00

Nos. 826, 831 and 833 vert.

America Issue A144

Fish, UPAE and discovery of America 500th anniv. emblems.

1990, Apr. 2
836　A144　10c　Rock beauty　.80　.50
837　A144　15c　Coney　.90　.65
838　A144　25c　Red hind　1.25　.85
839　A144　50c　Banded butterflyfish　1.75　1.75
840　A144　60c　French angelfish　2.40　2.10
841　A144　75c　Blackbar soldierfish　2.75　3.00
842　A144　90c　Stoplight parrotfish　3.00　3.50
843　A144　$1　French grunt　3.25　3.75
　　　Nos. 836-843 (8)　16.10　16.10

Souvenir Sheets

844　A144　$2　Gray angelfish　5.25　5.25
845　A144　$2　Blue chromis　5.25　5.25

Penny Black, 150th Anniv. — A145

British Pillar Boxes — A146

25c, 1p essay in blue, without letters. 35c, Letter Box #1, 1855. 50c, Penfold Box, 1866. 75c, Great Britain #3, essay. $1, 2p blue essay. $1.25, Air mail box, 1935. #852, Great Britain #1. #853, K type box, 1979.

1990, May 3　　Litho.　　Perf. 14
846　A145　25c　bluish blk　1.40　.90
847　A146　35c　gray & pale brn　1.00　1.00
848　A145　50c　gray & dk blue　1.40　1.40
849　A146　75c　red brown　3.00　2.25
850　A145　$1　dk blue　3.75　3.75
851　A146　$1.25　gray & blue　3.00　4.50
　　　Nos. 846-851 (6)　13.55　13.80

Souvenir Sheets

852　A145　$2　black　5.75　5.75
853　A146　$2　blk & red brn　7.25　7.25

Stamp World London '90.

Queen Mother, 90th Birthday — A147

1990, Aug. 20   Litho.   Perf. 14
854	A147	10c multicolored	.55	.50
855	A147	25c multi, diff.	1.10	.80
856	A147	75c multi, diff.	2.00	2.00
857	A147	$1.25 multi, diff.	3.25	3.75
		Nos. 854-857 (4)	6.90	7.05

Souvenir Sheet
858	A147	$2 multi, diff.	7.00	7.00

Birds A148

1990, Sept. 24   Litho.   Perf. 14
859	A148	8c Stripe-headed tanager, vert.	1.25	.90
860	A148	10c Black-whiskered vireo	1.25	.90
861	A148	25c Blue-grey gnat-catcher	1.60	.90
862	A148	40c Lesser scaup	3.25	1.90
863	A148	50c White-cheeked pintail	3.25	1.90
864	A148	75c Common stilt	3.75	3.75
865	A148	80c Common oyster-catcher, vert.	3.75	4.50
866	A148	$1 Tricolored heron	4.50	5.25
		Nos. 859-866 (8)	22.60	20.00

Souvenir Sheets
867	A148	$2 Bahama wood-star	6.25	6.25
868	A148	$2 American coot	6.25	6.25

Christmas A149

Different details from paintings by Rubens: 10c, 50c, 75c, No. 876, Triumph of Christ over Sin and Death. 35c, 45c, 65c, $1.25, No. 877, St. Theresa Praying for the Souls in Purgatory. Nos. 876-877 show entire painting.

1990, Dec. 17   Litho.   Perf. 14
869	A149	10c multicolored	.45	.25
870	A149	35c multicolored	1.50	1.25
871	A149	45c multicolored	1.60	1.50
872	A149	50c multicolored	1.90	1.60
873	A149	65c multicolored	2.75	2.10
874	A149	75c multicolored	3.00	2.75
875	A149	$1.25 multicolored	4.50	4.50
		Nos. 869-875 (7)	15.70	13.95

Souvenir Sheets
876	A149	$2 multicolored	9.00	9.00
877	A149	$2 multicolored	9.00	9.00

1992 Summer Olympics, Barcelona — A150

1991, Jan. 17
878	A150	10c Kayaking	.25	.25
879	A150	25c Track	.80	.80
880	A150	75c Pole vault	2.25	2.25
881	A150	$1.25 Javelin	3.75	3.75
		Nos. 878-881 (4)	7.05	7.05

Souvenir Sheet
882	A150	$2 Baseball	10.50	11.50

No. 878 inscribed Canoeing.

Voyages of Discovery A151

Designs: 5c, Henry Hudson, 1611. 10c, Roald Amundsen (airship), 1926. 15c, Amundsen (ship), 1906. 50c, USS Nautilus, 1958. 75c, Robert Scott, 1911. $1, Richard Byrd, Floyd Bennett, 1926. $1.25, Lincoln Ellsworth, 1935. $1.50, Cook, 1772-75. No. 891, The Nina. No. 892, The search for land.

1991, Apr. 15   Litho.   Perf. 14
883	A151	5c multicolored	1.10	.70
884	A151	10c multicolored	1.10	.70
885	A151	15c multicolored	1.60	1.00
886	A151	50c multicolored	2.10	1.50
887	A151	75c multicolored	3.75	2.75
888	A151	$1 multicolored	4.00	3.50
889	A151	$1.25 multicolored	5.75	6.75
890	A151	$1.50 multicolored	6.00	7.75
		Nos. 883-890 (8)	25.40	24.65

Souvenir Sheets
891	A151	$2 multicolored	8.00	8.00
892	A151	$2 multicolored	8.00	8.00

Discovery of America, 500th anniv. (in 1992).

Butterflies A152

1991, May 13   Litho.   Perf. 14
893	A152	5c White peacock	.35	.35
894	A152	25c Orion	1.05	1.05
895	A152	35c Gulf fritillary	1.40	1.40
896	A152	45c Caribbean buck-eye	1.90	1.90
897	A152	55c Flambeau	2.25	2.25
898	A152	65c Malachite	2.60	2.60
899	A152	70c Florida white	3.00	3.00
900	A152	$1 Great southern white	4.00	4.00
		Nos. 893-900 (8)	16.55	16.55

Souvenir Sheets
901	A152	$2 Giant hairstreak	8.50	8.50
902	A152	$2 Orange-barred sulphur	8.50	8.50

Extinct Animals A153

1991, June 3
903	A153	5c Protohy-drochoerus	.35	.35
904	A153	10c Phororhacos	.35	.35
905	A153	15c Prothylacynus	.55	.55
906	A153	50c Borhyaena	1.75	1.75
907	A153	75c Smilodon	2.75	2.75
908	A153	$1 Thoatherium	3.75	3.75
909	A153	$1.25 Cuvieronius	4.75	4.75
910	A153	$1.50 Toxodon	5.75	5.75
		Nos. 903-910 (8)	20.00	20.00

Souvenir Sheets
911	A153	$2 Mesosaurus	9.00	9.00
912	A153	$2 Astrapotheri-um	9.00	9.00

Royal Family Birthday, Anniversary
Common Design Type

1991   Litho.   Perf. 14
913	CD347	10c multicolored	.70	.35
914	CD347	25c multicolored	.95	.80
915	CD347	35c multicolored	1.25	.95
916	CD347	45c multicolored	2.75	1.50
917	CD347	50c multicolored	3.00	1.90
918	CD347	65c multicolored	2.25	2.25
919	CD347	80c multicolored	2.75	3.00
920	CD347	$1 multicolored	3.50	4.25
		Nos. 913-920 (8)	17.15	15.00

Souvenir Sheets
921	CD347	$2 Elizabeth, Philip	6.25	6.75
922	CD347	$2 Diana, sons, Charles	8.25	8.25

10c, 45c, 50c, $1, No. 922, Charles and Diana, 10th wedding anniv., issued: July 29. Others, Queen Elizabeth II, 65th birthday, issued: June 8.
For overprints see Nos. 1020-1022.

Mushrooms — A154

10c, Pluteus chrysophlebius. 15c, Leucopaxillus gracillimus. 20c, Marasmius haematocephalus. 35c, Collybia subpruinosa. 50c, Marasmius atrorubens, vert. 65c, Leucocoprinus birnbaumii, vert. $1.10, Trogia cantharelloides, vert. $1.25, Boletellus cubensis, vert. No. 931, Gerronema citrinum. No. 932, Pyrrhoglossum pyrrhum, vert.

1991, June 24   Litho.   Perf. 14
923	A154	10c multicolored	.35	.35
924	A154	15c multicolored	.55	.55
925	A154	20c multicolored	.70	.70
926	A154	35c multicolored	1.25	1.25
927	A154	50c multicolored	1.75	1.75
928	A154	65c multicolored	2.25	2.25
929	A154	$1.10 multicolored	4.00	4.00
930	A154	$1.25 multicolored	4.50	4.50
		Nos. 923-930 (8)	15.35	15.35

Miniature Sheets
931	A154	$2 multicolored	7.50	7.75
932	A154	$2 multicolored	7.50	7.75

Paintings by Vincent Van Gogh — A155

Paintings: 15c, Weaver Facing Left, with Spinning Wheel. 25c, Head of a Young Peasant with Pipe, vert. 35c, The Old Cemetery Tower at Nuenen, vert. 45c, Cottage at Nightfall. 50c, Still Life with Open Bible. 65c, Lane at the Jardin du Luxembourg. 80c, The Pont du Carrousel and the Louvre. $1, Vase with Poppies, Cornflowers, Peonies and Chrysanthemums, vert. No. 941, Entrance to the Public Park. No. 942, Plowed Field.

1991, Aug. 26   Perf. 13
933	A155	15c multicolored	.65	.65
934	A155	25c multicolored	1.10	1.10
935	A155	35c multicolored	1.50	1.50
936	A155	45c multicolored	2.10	2.10
937	A155	50c multicolored	2.40	2.40
938	A155	65c multicolored	3.00	3.00
939	A155	80c multicolored	3.75	3.75
940	A155	$1 multicolored	4.00	4.00
		Nos. 933-940 (8)	19.00	19.00

Size: 107x80mm
Imperf
941	A155	$2 multicolored	8.50	8.50
942	A155	$2 multicolored	8.50	8.50

Phila Nippon '91 A156

Japanese steam locomotives.

1991, Nov. 4   Litho.   Perf. 14
943	A156	8c Series 8550	.60	.60
944	A156	10c C 57	.60	.60
945	A156	45c Series 4110	1.90	1.25
946	A156	50c C 55	1.90	1.25
947	A156	65c Series 6250	2.75	2.75
948	A156	80c E 10	3.00	3.00
949	A156	$1 Series 4500	3.25	3.50
950	A156	$1.25 C 11	4.25	4.25
		Nos. 943-950 (8)	18.25	17.20

Souvenir Sheets
951	A156	$2 C 62	6.50	6.50
952	A156	$2 C 58	6.50	6.50

Christmas A157

Details or entire paintings by Gerard David: 8c, Adoration of the Shepherds. 15c, Virgin and Child Enthroned with Two Angels. 35c, The Annunciation (outside wings). 45c, The Rest on the Flight into Egypt. 50c, The Rest on the Flight into Egypt, diff. 65c, Virgin and Child with Angels. 80c, The Adoration of the Shepherds, diff. $1.25, The Perussis Altarpiece. No. 961, The Adoration of the Kings. No. 962, The Nativity.

1991, Dec. 23   Perf. 12
953	A157	8c multicolored	.40	.40
954	A157	15c multicolored	.65	.65
955	A157	35c multicolored	1.40	1.40
956	A157	45c multicolored	1.75	1.75
957	A157	50c multicolored	2.10	2.10
958	A157	65c multicolored	3.50	2.50
959	A157	80c multicolored	3.25	3.25
960	A157	$1.25 multicolored	5.00	5.00
		Nos. 953-960 (8)	18.05	17.05

Souvenir Sheets
Perf. 14½
961	A157	$2 multicolored	6.50	6.50
962	A157	$2 multicolored	6.50	6.50

Boy Scouts A160

No. 968, Member of Boy Scout Service Corps at New York World's Fair, 1964-65. No. 969, Lord Robert Baden-Powell, vert. $2, Silver Buffalo Award.

1992, July 6   Litho.   Perf. 14
968	A160	$1 multicolored	4.50	4.50
969	A160	$1 multicolored	4.50	4.50

Souvenir Sheet
970	A160	$2 multicolored	8.50	8.50

17th World Scout Jamboree, Korea.

Anniversaries and Events — A161

Designs: 25c, Astronaut releasing communications satellite. 50c, Tree with dead side, healthy side. 65c, Emblems, globe, food products. 80c, Fish in polluted, clean water. $1, Runners, Lions Intl. emblem. $1.25, Orbiting quarantine facility modules. No. 977, Planned orbital transfer vehicle for Mars. No. 977A, Industrial pollution, clean beach.

1992-93   Litho.   Perf. 14
971	A161	25c multicolored	1.50	1.50
972	A161	50c multicolored	1.75	1.75
973	A161	65c multicolored	4.25	4.25
974	A161	80c multicolored	2.50	2.50
975	A161	$1 multicolored	5.00	5.00
976	A161	$1.25 multicolored	7.00	7.00
		Nos. 971-976 (6)	22.00	22.00

Souvenir Sheets
977	A161	$2 multicolored	10.00	10.00
977A	A161	$2 multicolored	10.00	10.00

Intl. Space Year (#971, 976-977). Earth Summit, Rio de Janeiro (#972, 974, 977A).

Intl. Conf. on Nutrition, Rome (#973). Lions Intl., 75th anniv. (#975).
Issued: #972, 974, 977A, 1/93; others, 12/92.

Queen Elizabeth II's Accession to the Throne, 40th Anniv.
Common Design Type

1992, Feb. 6		**Litho.**	*Perf. 14*	
978 CD348	10c multicolored		.70	.70
979 CD348	20c multicolored		1.40	1.40
980 CD348	25c multicolored		1.50	1.50
981 CD348	35c multicolored		1.50	1.50
982 CD348	50c multicolored		2.25	2.25
983 CD348	65c multicolored		2.75	2.75
984 CD348	80c multicolored		2.75	2.75
985 CD348	$1.10 multicolored		3.25	3.25
	Nos. 978-985 (8)		16.10	16.10

Souvenir Sheets

986 CD348	$2 Queen at left, boat dock		7.50	7.50
987 CD348	$2 Queen at right, shoreline		7.50	7.50

Spanish Art — A162

Paintings: 8c, St. Monica, by Luis Tristan. 20c, 45c, The Vision of Ezekiel: The Resurrection of the Flesh (different details) by Francisco Collantes. 50c, The Martyrdom of St. Philip, by Jose de Ribera. 65c, St. John the Evangelist, by Juan Ribalta. 80c, Archimedes by Jose de Ribera. $1, St. John the Baptist in the Desert by de Ribera. $1.25, The Martyrdom of St. Philip (detail), by de Ribera. No. 996, The Baptism of Christ by Juan Fernandez Navarrete. No. 997, Battle between Christians and Moors at El Sotillo, by Francisco de Zurbaran.

1992, May 26		**Litho.**	*Perf. 13*	
988 A162	8c multicolored		.25	.25
989 A162	20c multicolored		.70	.70
990 A162	45c multicolored		1.75	1.75
991 A162	50c multicolored		1.75	1.75
992 A162	65c multicolored		2.25	2.25
993 A162	80c multicolored		3.00	3.00
994 A162	$1 multicolored		3.75	3.75
995 A162	$1.25 multicolored		4.50	4.50
	Nos. 988-995 (8)		17.95	17.95

Size: 95x120mm
Imperf

996 A162	$2 multicolored		8.50	8.50
997 A162	$2 multicolored		8.50	8.50

Granada '92.

Discovery of America, 500th Anniv. A163

Commemorative coins, scenes of first voyage: 10c, Nina, ship. 15c, Pinta, ship. 20c, Santa Maria, Columbus' second coat of arms. 25c, Fleet at sea, ships. 30c, Landfall, sailing ship. 35c, Setting sail, Columbus departing. 50c, Columbus sighting New World, Columbus. 65c, Columbus exploring Caribbean, ship. 80c, Claiming land for Spain, Columbus, priest and cross. $1.10, Columbus exchanging gifts with native, Columbus, native.
No. 1008, Coins like #998-1000. No. 1009, Coins like #1004, 1006-1007.

1992, Oct.		**Litho.**	*Perf. 14*	
998 A163	10c multicolored		.70	.70
999 A164	15c multicolored		1.10	1.10
1000 A164	20c multicolored		1.10	1.10
1001 A164	25c multicolored		1.50	1.50
1002 A164	30c multicolored		1.50	1.50
1003 A164	35c multicolored		1.75	1.75
1004 A164	50c multicolored		2.00	2.00
1005 A164	65c multicolored		3.00	3.00
1006 A164	80c multicolored		3.00	3.00
1007 A164	$1.10 multicolored		3.25	3.25
	Nos. 998-1007 (10)		18.90	18.90

Souvenir Sheets

1008 A164	$2 multicolored		8.50	8.50
1009 A164	$2 multicolored		8.50	8.50

Christmas A164

Details or entire paintings by Simon Bening: 8c, Nativity. 15c, Circumcision. 35c, Flight to Egypt. 50c, Massacre of the Innocents.
By Dirk Bouts: 65c, The Annunciation. 80c, The Visitation. $1.10, The Adoration of the Angels. $1.25, The Adoration of the Wise Men. No. 1018, The Virgin and Child. No. 1019, The Virgin Seated with the Child.

1992, Nov.		**Litho.**	*Perf. 13½x14*	
1010 A164	8c multicolored		.55	.55
1011 A164	15c multicolored		1.10	1.10
1012 A164	35c multicolored		1.60	1.60
1013 A164	50c multicolored		2.00	2.00
1014 A164	65c multicolored		2.75	2.75
1015 A164	80c multicolored		3.25	3.25
1016 A164	$1.10 multicolored		3.75	3.75
1017 A164	$1.25 multicolored		3.75	3.75
	Nos. 1010-1017 (8)		18.75	18.75

Souvenir Sheets

1018 A164	$2 multicolored		8.50	8.50
1019 A164	$2 multicolored		8.50	8.50

Nos. 915, 918 & 921 Ovptd. in Red or Black

1993, Mar. 20		**Litho.**	*Perf. 14*	
1020 CD347	35c on #915		2.75	2.75
1021 CD347	65c on #918		5.75	5.75

Souvenir Sheet

1022 CD347	$2 on #921 (Bk)		10.00	10.00

Miniature Sheet

Coronation of Queen Elizabeth II, 40th Anniv. — A165

Designs: a, 15c, Chalice and paten from royal collection. b, 50c, Official coronation photograph. c, $1, Coronation ceremony. d, $1.25, Queen, Prince Philip.
$2, New Portrait.

1993, June 2		**Litho.**	*Perf. 13½x14*	
1023 A165	Sheet, 2 ea #a.-d.		16.00	16.00

Souvenir Sheet
Perf. 14

1024 A165	$2 multicolored		9.00	9.00

No. 1024 contains one 28x42mm stamp.

Christmas A166

Details or entire woodcut, Mary, Queen of the Angels, by Durer: 8c, 20c, 35c, $1.25.
Details or entire paintings by Raphael: 50c, $1, Virgin and Child with St. John the Baptist. 65c, The Canagiani Holy Family. 80c, The Holy Family with the Lamb.
Each $2: No. 1033, Mary, Queen of the Angels, by Durer. No. 1034, The Canagiani Holy Family, diff., by Raphael.

Perf. 13½x14, 14x13½

1993, Dec.			**Litho.**	
1025-1032 A166	Set of 8		18.00	18.00

Souvenir Sheets

1033-1034 A166	Set of 2		13.00	13.00

Dinosaurs A167

8c, Omphalosaurus. 15c, Coelophysis. 20c, $2 (#1043), Triceratops. 35c, $2 (#1044), Dilophosaurus. 50c, Pterodactylus. 65c, Elasmosaurus. 80c, Stegosaurus. $1.25, Euoplocephalus.

1993, Nov. 15		**Litho.**	*Perf. 14*	
1035-1042 A167	Set of 8		10.00	10.00

Souvenir Sheets

1043-1044 A167	Set of 2		17.00	17.00

Birds A168

Designs: 10c, Killdeer. 15c, Yellow-crowned night heron, vert. 35c, Northern mockingbird. 50c, Eastern kingbird, vert. 65c, Magnolia warbler. 80c, Cedar waxwing, vert. $1.10, Ruby-throated hummingbird. $1.25, Painted bunting, vert. No. 1053, American kestrel. No. 1054, Ruddy duck.

1993, Dec.				
1045 A168	10c multicolored		.50	.50
1046 A168	15c multicolored		.75	.75
1047 A168	35c multicolored		1.90	1.90
1048 A168	50c multicolored		2.50	2.50
1049 A168	65c multicolored		3.50	3.50
1050 A168	80c multicolored		4.00	4.00
1051 A168	$1.10 multicolored		5.50	5.50
1052 A168	$1.25 multicolored		6.25	6.25
	Nos. 1045-1052 (8)		24.90	24.90

Souvenir Sheets

1053 A168	$2 multicolored		8.50	8.50
1054 A168	$2 multicolored		8.50	8.50

Fish A169

Designs: 10c, Bluehead wrasse. 20c, Honeycomb cowfish. 25c, Glasseye snapper. 35c, Spotted drum. 50c, Jolthead porgy. 65, Smallmouth grunt. 80c, Peppermint bass. $1.10, Indigo hamlet.
Each $2: No. 1063, Bonnethead shark. No. 1064, Sharpnose shark.

1993, Dec. 15				
1055-1062 A169	Set of 8		9.50	9.50

Souvenir Sheets

1063-1064 A169	Set of 2		10.00	10.00

1994 World Cup Soccer Championships, US — A170

Designs: 8c, Segio Goycoechea, Argentina. 10c, Bado Illgner, Germany. 50c, Nico Claesen, Belgium. 65c, West German team. 80c, Cameroun team. $1, Santin, Francescoli, Uruguay; Cuciuffo, Argentina. $1.10, Sanchez, Mexico.
Each $2: No. 1072, Imre Garaba, Hungary, vert. No. 1073, Pontiac Silverdome.

1994, Sept. 26		**Litho.**	*Perf. 14*	
1065-1071 A170	Set of 7		12.50	12.50

Souvenir Sheets

1072-1073 A170	Set of 2		9.00	9.00

Mushrooms — A171

Designs: 5c, Xerocomus guadelupae, vert. 10c, Volvariella volvacea, vert. 35c, Hygrocybe atrosquamosa. 50c, Pleurotus ostreatus. 65c, Marasmius pallescens. 80c, Coprinus plicatilis, vert. $1.10, Bolbitius vitellinus. $1.50, Pyroglossum lilaceipes, vert.
Each $2: No. 1082, Lentinus edodes. No. 1083, Russula cremeolilacina, vert.

1994, Oct. 10				
1074-1081 A171	Set of 8		12.00	12.00

Souvenir Sheets

1082-1083 A171	Set of 2		11.50	11.50

Christmas A172

Illustrations from French Book of Hours: 25c, The Annunciation. 50c, The Visitation. 65c, Annunciation to the Shepherds. 80c, The Nativity. $1, Flight into Egypt.
$2, The Adoration of the Magi.

1994, Dec. 5		**Litho.**	*Perf. 14*	
1084-1088 A172	Set of 5		14.00	14.00

Souvenir Sheet

1089 A172	$2 multicolored		8.00	8.00

Butterflies A173

Designs: 15c, Dryas julia. 20c, Urbanus proteus. 25c, Colobura dirce. 50c, Papilio homerus. 65c, Chiodes catillus. 80c, Eurytides zonaria. $1, Hypolymnas misippus. $1.25, Phoebis avellaneda.
Each $2: No. 1098, Eurema adamsi. No. 1099, Morpho peleides.

1994, Dec. 12
1090-1097 A173 Set of 8   14.00 14.00
Souvenir Sheets
1098-1099 A173 Set of 2   10.00 10.00

D-Day,
50th
Anniv.
A174

Designs: 10c, Gen. Montgomery, British landing on Juno Beach. 15c, Adm. Sir Bertram Ramsay, British commandos at Sword Beach. 35c, Gun crew aboard HMS Belfast. 50c, Montgomery, Eisenhower, Tedder review battle scene. 65c, Gen. Eisenhower, 101st Airborne Div. paratroopers. 80c, Gen. Omar Bradley, US landings on Omaha Beach. $1.10, Second wave of US troops on D-Day. $1.25, Supreme Commander Eisenhower presents Operation Overload.
Each $2: No. 1108, Eisenhower, Montgomery seated at table. No. 1109, Beachhead secured.

1994, Dec. 19
1100-1107 A174 Set of 8   12.00 12.00
Souvenir Sheets
1108-1109 A174 Set of 2   9.50 9.50

Orchids
A175

Designs: 8c, Cattleya deckeri. 20c, Epidendrum carpophorum. 25c, Epidendrum ciliare. 50c, Encyclia phoenicea. 65c, Bletia patula. 80c, Brassia caudata. $1, Brassavola nodosa. $1.25, Bletia purpurea.
Each $2: No. 1118, Ionopsis utricularioides. No. 1119, Vanilla planifolia.

1995, Jan. 5
1110-1117 A175 Set of 8   12.00 12.00
Souvenir Sheets
1118-1119 A175 Set of 2   11.00 11.00

Miniature Sheet of 12

PHILAKOREA '94 — A176

Jurassic marine reptiles: a, Elasmosaurus. b, Plesiosaurus. c, Ichthyosaurus. d, Arcfielon. e, Askeptosaurus. f, Macroplata. g, Ceresiosaurus. h, Lipoleurodon. i, Henodus. j, Muraenosaurus. k, Placodus. l, Kronosaurus.

1995, Jan. 23
1120 A176 35c #1120a-1120 l 10.50 10.50

First
Manned
Moon
Landing,
25th
Anniv.
A177

Designs: 10c, Apollo XI in flight. 20c, Simulated moon landing. 25c, Painting, Astronauts on the Moon, by Kovales. 35c, First foot, footprint on moon. 50c, Aldrin, solar wind experiment. 65c, Armstrong, Aldrin setting up flag on moon. 80c, Command module Columbia in Lunar orbit. $1.10, Recovery of Apollo XI in Pacific.

Each $2: No. 1129, Lift-off at Cape Canaveral, vert. No. 1130, Moon rock on display in Houston.

1995, Jan. 9   Litho.   Perf. 14
1121-1128 A177 Set of 8   9.50 9.50
Souvenir Sheets
1129-1130 A177 Set of 2   9.50 9.50

Intl. Olympic
Committee,
Cent. — A178

Summer, Winter Olympic events: 8c, Fencing. 10c, Speed skating. 15c, Diving. 20c, Cycling. 25c, Ice hockey. 35c, Figure skating. 50c, Soccer. 65c, Bobsled. 80c, Super giant slalom. $1.25, Equestrian.
Each $2: #1141, Gymnastics. #1142, Downhill skiing.

1995, Feb. 6
1131-1140 A178 Set of 10   17.00 17.00
Souvenir Sheets
1141-1142 A178 Set of 2   11.50 11.50

Domestic
Cats
A179

Various cats, kittens: 15c, 20c, 35c, 50c, 65c, 80c, $1, $1.25.
Each $2: No. 1151, Two sleeping. No. 1152, Kitten, ladybugs in flowers.

1995, July 3   Litho.   Perf. 14
1143-1150 A179 Set of 8   17.00 17.00
Souvenir Sheets
1151-1152 A179 Set of 2   12.00 12.00

Birds — A180

A180a

10c, Belted kingfisher. 15c, Clapper rail. 20c, American redstart. 25c, Roseate tern. 35c, Purple gallinule. 45c, Ruddy turnstone. 50c, Barn owl. 60c, Brown booby. 80c, Great blue heron. $1, Antillean nighthawk. $1.25, Thick-billed vireo. $1.40, American flamingo. $2, Wilson's plover. $5, Blue-winged teal. $10, Reddish egret.

1995, Aug. 2   Litho.   Perf. 13
1153   A180   10c multi   .25   .25
1154   A180   15c multi   .40   .40
1155   A180   20c multi   .55   .55
1156   A180   25c multi   .70   .70
1157   A180   35c multi   .95   .95
1158   A180   45c multi   1.25 1.25
1159   A180   50c multi   1.40 1.40
1160   A180   60c multi   1.75 1.75
1161   A180   80c multi   2.25 2.25
1162   A180 $1 multi   2.75 2.75
1163   A180 $1.25 multi   3.50 3.50
1164   A180 $1.40 multi   3.75 3.75
1165   A180 $2 multi   5.50 5.50
1166   A180 $5 multi   13.50 13.50
1166A A180a $10 multi   27.50 27.50
Nos. 1153-1166A (15)   66.00 66.00

Queen
Mother, 95th
Birthday
A181

No. 1167: a, Drawing. b, Wearing crown jewels. c, Formal portrait. d, Blue dress with pearls.
$2, Green blue outfit.

1995, Aug. 4   Perf. 13½x14
1167 A181 50c Block or strip of
             4, #a.-d.   9.00 9.00
Souvenir Sheet
1168 A181 $2 multicolored   9.00 9.00
No. 1167 was issued in sheets of 8 stamps.

VE Day,
50th
Anniv.
A182

Designs: 10c, "Big Three" meet at Yalta. 15c, Allied war prisoners released. 20c, American, Soviets meet at Elbe River. 25c, Death of Franklin D. Roosevelt. 60c, US 9th Army confirms cease fire. 80c, New York City celebrates VE Day. $1, Nuremberg War Crimes trials begin.
$2, Big Ben, US Capitol, St. Basil's Cathedral.

1995, Aug. 14   Litho.   Perf. 14
1169-1175 A182 Set of 7   11.00 11.00
Souvenir Sheet
1176 A182 $2 multicolored   6.00 6.00

Miniature Sheet of 9

Singapore
'95 — A183

Diving equipment, each 60c: No. 1177a, Wm. James, scuba, 1825. b, Rouquayrol apparatus, 1864. c, Fluess oxygen rebreathing apparatus, 1878. d, Armored diving suit, 1900. e, Jim Janett explores sunken Lusitania in Peress armored diving suit, 1935. f, Cousteau-Gagnan aqualung, 1943. g, Underwater camera, 1955. h, Sylvia Earle dives to 1,520 ft. in Jim suit, 1979. i, Spider propeller-driven rigid suit, 1984.
Each $2: No. 1178, Helmet diver, 1935. No. 1179, Jacques-Yves Cousteau.

1995, Sept. 1   Perf. 14½
1177 A183 Sheet of 9, #a.-i. 15.00 15.00
Souvenir Sheets
1178-1179 A183 Set of 2   10.00 10.00

Christmas
A184

Details or entire paintings, by Piero di Cosimo (1462-1521): 20c, Madonna and Child with Young St. John. 25c, Adoration of the Child. 60c, Madonna and Child with Young St. John, St. Margaret, and An Angel. $1, Madonna and Child with An Angel.

$2, Madonna and Child with Angels and Saints.

1995, Dec. 29   Litho.   Perf. 14
1180-1183 A184 Set of 4   9.00 9.00
Souvenir Sheet
1184 A184 $2 multicolored   10.50 10.50

UN, 50th Anniv. — A185

Designs: 15c, Rights of women and children. 60c, Peace. 80c, Human rights. $1, Education.
Each $2: No. 1189, Flags of nations forming "50." No. 1190, Tractor, portions of UN, FAO emblems.

1996, Feb. 26   Litho.   Perf. 14
1185-1188 A185 Set of 4   6.25 6.25
Souvenir Sheets
1189-1190 A185 Set of 2   10.00 10.00

Queen
Elizabeth II,
70th
Birthday
A186

No. 1191: a, Portrait. b, Wearing blue hat. c, In uniform, on horseback.
$2, As younger woman wearing white and yellow hat.

1996, Apr. 21   Litho.   Perf. 13½x14
1191 A186 80c Strip of 3, #a.-c. 5.50 5.50
Souvenir Sheet
1192 A186 $2 multicolored   4.75 4.75
No. 1191 was issued in sheets of 9 stamps.

History of
Underwater
Exploration
A187

No. 1193, each 55c: a, Glaucus, God of Divers, 2500BC. b, Alexander the Great decends to ocean bottom, 332BC. c, Salvage diver, 1430. d, Borelli's rebreathing device, 1680. e, Edmond Halley's diving bell, 1690. f, John Lethbridge's diving machine, 1715. g, Klingert's diving apparatus, 1789. h, Drieberg's triton, 1808. i, Seibe's diving helmet, 1819.
No. 1194, each 60c: a, Jim Jarrat in "Iron Man" armored diving suit explores Lusitania, 1935. b, Cousteau, team excavate first shipwreck using scuba gear, 1952. c, Oldest shipwreck ever found, coast of Turkey, 1959. d, Swedish warship Vasa raised, 1961. e, Mel Fisher discovers Spanish galleon Atocha, 1971. f, Whydah, first pirate ship found, is discovered by Barry Clifford, 1984. g, Dr. Robert Ballard, using robot sub Argo finds battleship Bismarck, 1989. h, Radeau "Land Tortoise" scuttled in 1758 during French and Indian War found in Lake George, NY, 1991. i, Deep-diving nuclear submarine recovers ancient Roman shipwreck cargo, 1994.
Each $2: No. 1195, Arab diver Issa, 12th cent. No. 1196, Pearl diver in Caribbean, 1498. No. 1197, Diver in Newtsuit investigates Edmund Fitzgerald. No. 1198, Submarine Alvin explores Titanic, 1985.

1996, May 13   Litho.   Perf. 14
1193 A187 Sheet of 9, #a.-i. 16.00 16.00

1194 A187 Sheet of 9, #a.-i. 12.00 12.00

Souvenir Sheets

1195-1198 A187 Set of 4 20.00 20.00

CHINA '96 (Nos. 1193, 1195-1196). CAPEX '96 (Nos. 1194, 1197-1198).

1996 Summer Olympics, Atlanta A188

Olympic gold medals for: No. 1199, Equestrian. No. 1200, Cycling. No. 1201, Fencing. No. 1202, Gymnastics. No. 1203, Hurdles. No. 1204, Pole vault. No. 1205, Sprints. No. 1206, Swimming. No. 1207, Diving. No. 1208, Running.

1996, May 27 **Perf. 13½**

1199-1208 A188 55c Set of 10 11.50 11.50

1208a Sheet of 10, #1199-1208 11.50

Nos. 1199-1208 issued in sheets as well as in No. 1208a.

A189   A190

James A.G.S. McCartney (1945-80), 1st Chief Minister of Turks & Caicos Islands.

1996, July 8 **Litho.** **Perf. 14**

1209 A189 60c multicolored 1.25 1.25

Ministerial Government, 20th anniv. No. 1209 was issued in sheets of 9.

1996, Sept. 8 **Litho.** **Perf. 14**

Working Dogs: No. 1210: a, Space research. b, Racing. c, Rescue. d, Military. e, Sporting. f, Companion. g, Hearing ear. h, Sled. i, Police. j, Guarding. k, Watch. l, Security.

Each $2: No. 1211, Guide. No. 1212, Sheep dog.

1210 A190 25c Sheet of 12, #a.-l. 13.00 13.00

Souvenir Sheets

1211-1212 A190 Set of 2 13.00 13.00

Winnie the Pooh, Christmas A191

Designs: 15c, Pooh trying to stay awake. 20c, Piglet, star. 35c, Ribbons and bows. 50c, Jingle bells. 60c, "Pooh loves Christmas." 80c, "Big hearts come in bouncy packages." $1, Santa Pooh. $1.25, "My most favorite."

No. 1221, Piglet, cookie. No. 1222, Piglet placing star atop tree.

1996, Nov. 25 **Litho.** **Perf. 13½x14**

1213-1220 A191 Set of 8 17.00 17.00

Souvenir Sheets

1221 A191 $2 multicolored 7.50 7.50

1222 A191 $2.60 multicolored 9.50 9.50

Flowers — A192

No. 1223: a, Giant milkweed. b, Geiger tree. c, Passion flower. d, Hibiscus.

No. 1224: a, Yellow elder. b, Prickly poppy. c, Frangipani. d, Seaside mahoe.

Each $2: No. 1225, Chain of love. No. 1226, Firecracker.

1997, Feb. 10 **Litho.** **Perf. 14**

1223 A192 20c Strip or block of 4, #a.-d. 3.25 3.25

1224 A192 60c Strip or block of 4, #a.-d. 4.75 4.75

Souvenir Sheets

1225-1226 A192 Set of 2 9.50 9.50

Nos. 1223-1224 were each issued in sheets of 8 stamps.

A193

UNICEF, 50th Anniv.: a, Dove flying right. b, Three children. c, Dove flying left. d, Boy with dog, girl holding cat.

1997, Mar. 24 **Litho.** **Perf. 14**

1227 A193 60c Sheet of 4, #a.-d. 8.00 8.00

Souvenir Sheets

UNESCO, 50th Anniv. — A194

Canterbury Cathedral: No. 1228, View from rear. No. 1229, Interior view.

1997, Mar. 24 **Litho.** **Perf. 14**

1228 A194 $2 multicolored 5.25 5.25

1229 A194 $2 multicolored 5.25 5.25

Queen Elizabeth II, Prince Philip, 50th Wedding Anniv. A195

Designs: a, Queen waving. b, Royal arms. c, Queen, Prince riding in car. d, Prince, Queen seated. e, Windsor Castle. f, Prince Philip. $2, Wedding portrait.

1997, Apr. 21 **Litho.** **Perf. 14**

1230 A195 60c Sheet of 6, #a.-f. 12.00 12.00

Souvenir Sheet

1231 A195 $2 multicolored 9.00 9.00

Heinrich von Stephan (1831-97), Founder of UPU A196

Portrait of Von Stephan and: No. 1232: a, British mail coach, 1700's. b, UPU emblem. c, Space shuttle, future transport.

$2, Von Stephan, Hemerodrome, messenger of ancient Greece.

1997, July 1 **Litho.** **Perf. 14**

1232 A196 50c Sheet of 3, #a.-c. 6.00 6.00

Souvenir Sheet

1233 A196 $2 multicolored 5.50 5.50

PACIFIC 97.

Underwater Exploration A197

No. 1234: a, Edgerton camera taking photos at 6,000 ft., 1954. b, Conshelf Habitat, 1963. c, Sealab II, 1965. d, Research Habitat, Tektite, 1970. e, Discovery of Galapagos Volcanic Rift, 1974. f, Epaulard, robot survey craft, 1979. g, Sea life discovered thriving in undersea oil field, 1995. h, Deep flight, 1996, one-man research vessel. i, Sea ice is studied from above, under sea, Okhotsk Tower, off Japan, 1996.

Each $2: No. 1235, Coelacanth. No. 1236, John Williamson makes first underwater movies, 1914.

1997, Aug. 21 **Litho.** **Perf. 14**

1234 A197 20c Sheet of 9, #a.-i. 8.00 8.00

Souvenir Sheets

1235-1236 A197 Set of 2 10.00 10.00

Stampshow 97.

Christmas A198

Entire paintings or details: 15c, Adoration of an Angel, by Studio of Fra Angelico. 20c, Scenes from the Life of St. John the Baptist, by Master of Saint Severin. 35c, Archangel Gabriel, by Masolino de Panicale. 50c, 60c, Jeremiah with Two Angels, by Gherardo Starnina (diff. angels). 80c, The Annunciation, by Giovanni di Palo di Grazia. $1, The Annunciation, by Carlo di Bracceso. $1.25, The Nativity, by Benvenuto di Giovanni Guasta.

Each $2: No. 1245, The Wilton Diptych (right panel), by unknown English or French artist, c. 1395. No. 1246, Adoring Angels, from The Journey of the Magi, by Benozzo Gozzoli.

1997, Dec. 8 **Litho.** **Perf. 14**

1237-1244 A198 Set of 8 12.00 12.00

Souvenir Sheets

1245-1246 A198 Set of 2 10.50 10.50

World Wildlife Fund — A199

Snapper: a, Blackfin. b, Dog. c, Cubera. d, Mahogany.

1998, Feb. 24 **Litho.** **Perf. 14**

1247 A199 25c Block of 4, #a.-d. 3.75 3.75

No. 1247 was issued in sheets of 16 stamps. Intl. Year of the Reef.

Marine Life — A200

Underwater photographs: 20c, Spotted flamingo tongue. 50c, Feather duster. 60c, Squirrel fish. 80c, Queen angelfish. $1, Barracuda. $1.25, Fairy basslet.

Each $2: No. 1254, Rough file clam. No. 1255, Spotted cleaning shrimp.

1998, May 1 **Litho.** **Perf. 14**

1248-1253 A200 Set of 6 13.00 13.00

Souvenir Sheets

1254-1255 A200 Set of 2 9.50 9.50

A201   A202

Stylized designs showing symbol for earth, water, and — No. 1256: a, Dove. b, Crab. c, Fish. d, Clover leaf.

$2, Symbol for earth and water.

1998, July 30 **Litho.** **Perf. 14**

1256 A201 50c Sheet of 4, #a.-d. 7.00 7.00

Souvenir Sheet

1257 A201 $2 multicolored 6.50 6.50

Intl. Year of the Ocean.

Royal Air Force, 80th Anniv.
Common Design Type Re-Inscribed

Designs: 20c, SE 5A. 50c, Sopwith Camel. 60c, Supermarine Spitfire. 80c, Avro Lancaster. $1, Panavia Tornado. $1.25, Hawker Hurricane.

Each $2: No. 1264, Hawker Siddeley Harrier. No. 1265, Avro Vulcan.

1998, Aug. 18 **Litho.** **Perf. 14**

1258-1263 CD350 Set of 6 16.00 16.00

Souvenir Sheets

1264-1265 CD350 Set of 2 16.00 16.00

1998, July 30 **Litho.** **Perf. 14**

Anniversaries and Events: 20c, University of the West Indies, 50th anniv. 60c, UNESCO, World Summit Program. 80c, Universal Declaration of Human Rights. $1, John Glenn's return to space.

$2, NASA Space Shuttle leaving launching pad.

1266-1269 A202 Set of 4 6.25 6.25

Souvenir Sheet

1270 A202 $2 multicolored 5.50 5.50

A203

1998, Aug. 31
1271 A203 60c multicolored 2.25 2.25
Diana, Princess of Wales (1961-97). No. 1271 was issued in sheets of 6.

A204

Paintings by Sister Thomasita Fessler — #1272: a, Magi's Visit. b, Flight Into Egypt. c, Wedding Feast. d, Maria. e, Annunciation & Visitation. f, Nativity. $2, Queen of Mothers.

1998, Nov. 30   Litho.   Perf. 14
1272 A204 50c Sheet of 6,
    #a.-f.   10.50 10.50
Souvenir Sheet
1273 A204 $2 multicolored 5.50 5.50
Christmas. Nos. 1272e-1272f are each 58x48mm.

Coral Gardens
A205

No. 1274: a, Flamingos in flight. b, Sailboats. c, Seagulls, lighthouse. d, House along shore, seagulls. e, Pillar coral, yellowtail snapper (f). f, Eliptical star coral. g, Porkfish. h, Spotted eagle ray. i, Large ivory coral. j, Mustard hill coral, shy hamlet. k, Blue crust coral. l, Fused staghorn coral. m, Queen angelfish, massive starlet coral. n, Pinnate spiny sea fan. o, Knobby star coral, squirrelfish. p, Lowridge cactus coral, juvenile porkfish. q, Orange telesto coral. r, Spanish hogfish (q), Knobby ten-ray star coral. s, Boulder brain coral, clown wrasse. t, Rainbow parrotfish, regal sea fan. u, Great star coral, bluestriped grunt. v, Stinging coral, blue tang. w, Lavender thin finger coral. x, Juvenile french grunt (w), brilliant sea fingers.
Each $2: No. 1275, Sea fan. No. 1276, Elkhorn coral.

1999, June 7   Litho.   Perf. 14¼x14½
1274 A205 20c Sheet of 24,
    #a.-x.   24.00 24.00
Souvenir Sheets
1275-1276 A205 Set of 2 19.00 19.00

Wedding of Prince Edward and Sophie Rhys-Jones — A206

Portraits — #1277: a, Couple facing forward. b, Edward. c, Sophie. d, Couple walking arm in arm.
Each $2: No. 1278, Couple facing forward. No. 1279, Couple facing each other.

1999, June 19   Litho.   Perf. 14
1277 A206 60c Sheet of 4,
    #a.-d.   7.50 7.50
Souvenir Sheets
1278-1279 A206 Set of 2 12.00 12.00

Queen Mother (b. 1900)
A207

Designs: a, At age 7. b, At age 19. c, At wedding. d, With daughters. e, With King George VI during World War II. f, In 1958. g, At age 60. h, In 1970. i, With Princes Charles and William, 1983. j, Current photograph.

1999, Aug. 4   Litho.   Perf. 13½x13¾
1280 A207 50c Sheet of 10,
    #a.-j.   19.00 19.00
Stamp inscription on No. 1280f is incorrect. No. 1280 was reissued in 2002 with added inscription in margin, "Good Health and Happiness to her Majesty The Queen Mother on her 101st Birthday." Value, $19.

2nd World Underwater Photography Competition Winners
A208

No. 1281: a, 10c, Painted tunicates (8th place). b, 20c, Peacock flounder (7th). c, 50c, Squirt anemone shrimps (6th). d, 60c, Juvenile drum (5th). e, 80c, Batwing coral crab (4th). f, $1, Moon jellyfish (3rd).
Each $2: No. 1282, Christmas tree worms (2nd). No. 1283, Longhorn nudibranch (1st).

1999, Oct. 11   Litho.   Perf. 14¼x13¾
1281 A208 Sheet of 6, #a.-f.   11.00 11.00
    g.   As No. 1281, with corrected
        pictures   6.50 6.50
    Issued: No. 1281g, 11/6/00.
On No. 1281, the illustrations for the 10c and 20c stamps are incorrect, with the 10c stamp inscribed "Painted tunicates," but depicting a peacock flounder, and the 20c stamp inscribed "Peacock flounder," but depicting painted tunicates. The pictures were switched on No. 1281g, making the inscriptions match the pictures.

Souvenir Sheets
Perf. 13¾
1282-1283 A208 Set of 2 16.00 16.00
Nos. 1282-1283 each contain one 50x38mm stamp.

Christmas
A209

Paintings by Anthony Van Dyck: 20c, The Mystic Marriage of Saint Catherine. 50c, Rest on the Flight into Egypt. No. 1286, $2, Holy Family with Saints John and Elizabeth. No. 1287, The Madonna of the Rosary.

1999, Dec. 7   Perf. 13¾
1284-1286 A209 Set of 3 10.50 10.50
Souvenir Sheet
1287 A209 $2 multicolored 10.50 10.50

Millennium
A210

Perf. 14½x14¼
1999, Nov. 15   Litho.
1288 A210 20c silver & multi .80 .80
1289 A210 $1 gold & multi 4.00 4.00

Millennium
A211

Globe, clock and: No. 1290: a, London. b, Turks & Caicos Islands. c, New York. d, Rome. e, Jerusalem. f, Paris.
Each $2: No. 1291, Flag of Islands. No. 1292, Arms of Islands.

2000, Jan. 18   Litho.   Perf. 14x13¾
1290 A211 50c Sheet of 6,
    #a.-f.   12.00 12.00
Souvenir Sheets
1291-1292 A211 Set of 2 18.00 18.00

Mushrooms — A212

No. 1293, vert.: a, Pholiota squarroides. b, Psilocybe squamosa. c, Spathularia velutipes. d, Russula. e, Clitocybe clavipes. f, Boletus frostii.
No. 1294, Strobilurus conigenoides. No. 1295, Stereum ostrea.

2000, July 6   Litho.   Perf. 14
1293 A212 50c Sheet of 6, #a-
    f   10.00 10.00
Souvenir Sheets
1294-1295 A212 $2 Set of 2 13.00 13.00

Souvenir Sheet

2000 Summer Olympics, Sydney — A213

No. 1296: a, Johan Gabriel Oxenstierna. b, Javelin. c, Aztec Stadium, Mexico City and Mexican flag. d, Ancient Greek runners.

2000, Sept. 25
1296 A213 50c Sheet of 4, #a-d 8.00 8.00

Birds
A214

Designs: No. 1297, Chickadee. No. 1298, Scrub turkey. No. 1299, Sickle-bill gull. No. 1300: a, Egret. b, Tern. c, Osprey. d, Great blue heron. e, Pelican. f, Bahama pintail. No. 1301, Flamingo, vert. No. 1302, Macaw, vert.

2000, Oct. 2
1297-1299 A214 50c Set of 3 5.50 5.50
1300 A214 60c Sheet of 6, #a-
    f   12.50 12.50
Souvenir Sheets
1301-1302 A214 $2 Set of 2 15.00 15.00

Dogs and Cats — A215

No. 1303, 60c: a, Airedale terrier. b, Beagle. c, Dalmatian. d, Chow chow. e, Chihuahua. f, Pug.
No. 1304, 80c: a, Egyptian mau. b, Manx. c, Burmese. d, Korat. e, Maine coon cat. f, American shorthair.
No. 1305, $2, Collie. No. 1306, $2, Devon rex.

2000, Nov. 13   Litho.   Perf. 14
Sheets of 6, #a-f
1303-1304 A215 Set of 2 24.00 24.00
Souvenir Sheets
1305-1306 A215 Set of 2 12.00 12.00

Battle of Britain, 60th Anniv.
A216

Designs: No. 1307, 50c, Douglas Robert Stewart Bader. No. 1308, 50c, Alan Christopher "Al" Deere. No. 1309, 50c, James Edgar "Johnny" Johnson. No. 1310, 50c, Edgar James "Cobber" Kain. No. 1311, 50c, James Harry "Ginger" Lacey. No. 1312, 50c, Air Vice-marshal Trafford Leigh Mallory. No. 1313, 50c, Adolph Gysbert "Sailor" Malan. No. 1314, Air Vice-marshal Keith Park.
No. 1315, each 50c: a, Winston Churchill. b, Barrage balloon. c, Heinkel He-111 Casa 2 111E. d, Soldier's farewell kiss to son. e, Hawker Hurricane. f, Dr, Jocelyn Henry Temple Peakins, clergyman in Home Guard. g, RAF fighter pilots scramble after an alert. h, Civilian volunteers scan the skies.
No. 1316, $2, Churchill, British flag. No. 1317, $2, London children.

2000, Dec. 4   Perf. 14
Stamps + labels
1307-1314 A216 Set of 8 14.00 14.00
1315 A216 Sheet of 8, #a-h 14.00 14.00
Souvenir Sheets
1316-1317 A216 Set of 2 13.00 13.00

Butterflies — A217

No. 1318, 50c: a, Clorinde. b, Blue night. c, Small lace-wing. d, Mosaic. e, Monarch. f, Grecian shoemaker.
No. 1319, 50c: a, Giant swallowtail. b, Common morpho. c, Tiger pierid. d, Banded king shoemaker. e, Figure-of-eight. f, Polydamas swallowtail.
No. 1320, $2, Orange-barred sulphur. No. 1321, $2, White peacock.

2000, Dec. 11   **Litho.**
Sheets of 6, #a-f
1318-1319 A217 Set of 2 24.00 24.00
Souvenir Sheets
1320-1321 A217 Set of 2 15.00 15.00

Ships
A218

Designs: No. 1322, 60c, Neptune. No. 1323, 60c, Eagle. No. 1324, 60c, Gloria. No. 1325, 60c, Clipper ship, vert.
No. 1326, 60c: a, Viking long ship. b, Henri Grace à Dieu. c, Golden Hind. d, Endeavor. e, Anglo-Norman. f, Libertad.
No. 1327, 60c: a, Northern European cog. b, Carrack. c, Mayflower. d, Queen Anne's Revenge. e, Holkar. f, Amerigo Vespucci.
No. 1328, $2, USS Constitution, vert. No. 1329, $2, Denmark, vert.

2001, May 15   **Litho.**   **Perf. 14**
1322-1325 A218 Set of 4 9.25 9.25
Sheets of 6, #a-f
1326-1327 A218 Set of 2 27.50 27.50
Souvenir Sheets
1328-1329 A218 Set of 2 18.00 18.00

Whales
A219

Designs: No. 1330, 50c, Beluga. No. 1331, 50c, Killer. No. 1332, 50c, Dwarf sperm. No. 1333, 50c, Shortfin pilot.
No. 1334, 50c: a, Bowhead. b, Two killer. c, Pygmy sperm. d, Right. e, Sperm. f, California gray.
No. 1335, 50c: a, Narwhal. b, One killer (in air). c, Bryde's. d, Belugas. e, Sperm (and starfish). f, Pilot.
No. 1336, $2, Cuvier's beaked. No. 1337, $2, Humpback (with calf).

2001, May 15
1330-1333 A219 Set of 4 9.50 9.50
Sheets of 6, #a-f
1334-1335 A219 Set of 2 27.00 27.00
Souvenir Sheets
1336-1337 A219 Set of 2 18.00 18.00

UN Women's Human Rights Campaign — A220

Designs: 60c, Woman. 80c, Woman, bird, torch.

2001, June 18   **Litho.**   **Perf. 14**
1338-1339 A220 Set of 2 7.00 7.00

Phila Nippon '01 — A221

Designs: No. 1340, 60c, Autumn Moon in Mirror, by Suzuki Harunobu. No. 1341, 60c, Rikaku II as a Fisherman, by Hirosada. No. 1342, 60c, Musical Party, by Hishikawa Moronobu. No. 1343, 60c, Kannon and Four Farmers, by H. Gatto. No. 1344, 60c, Rain in Fifth Month, by Kunisada I. No. 1345, 60c, The Lives of Women, by Kuniyoshi Utagawa.

2001, July 30   **Perf. 12x12¼**
1340-1345 A221 Set of 6 12.00 12.00

Queen Victoria (1819-1901) — A222

No. 1346, 60c, oval frames: a, Wearing white headcovering. b, Wearing crown as young woman. c, Wearing black hat. d, Wearing crown as old woman.
No. 1347, 60c, rectangular frames: a, Wearing white headcovering. b, Holding flowers. c, Wearing white dress. d, Wearing crown, white dress with blue sash.
No. 1348, $2, Brown orange background. No. 1349, $2, Holding umbrella.

2001, July 2   **Perf. 14**
Sheets of 4, #a-d
1346-1347 A222 Set of 2 19.00 19.00
Souvenir Sheets
1348-1349 A222 Set of 2 14.00 14.00

Queen Elizabeth II, 75th Birthday — A223

No. 1350: a, In pink hat. b, With crown looking left. c, In green hat. d, With crown looking forward. e, In red orange hat. f, With crown and veil.
$2, Wearing robe.

2001, July 2
1350 A223 60c Sheet of 6, #a-f 14.50 14.50
Souvenir Sheet
1351 A223 $2 multi 8.00 8.00

Butterflies — A224

Designs: 10c, Cuban mimic. 15c, Gundlach's swallowtail, vert. 20c, Graphium androcles. 25c, Eastern black swallowtail. 35c, Papilio velvois, vert. 45c, Schaus swallowtail, vert. 50c, Pipevine swallowtail, vert. 60c, Euploea mniszecki, vert. 80c, Poey's black swallowtail, vert. $1, Graphium encelades, vert. $1.25, Jamaican ringlet. $1.40, Eastern tiger swallowtail. $2, Graphium milon, vert. $5, Palamedes swallowtail. $10, Zebra swallowtail.

Perf. 14x14¾, 14¾x14
2001, Sept. 27
1352	A224	10c multi	.30	.30
1353	A224	15c multi	.35	.35
1354	A224	20c multi	.45	.45
1355	A224	25c multi	.55	.55
1356	A224	35c multi	.80	.80
1357	A224	45c multi	1.00	1.00
1358	A224	50c multi	1.10	1.10
1359	A224	60c multi	1.40	1.40
1360	A224	80c multi	1.75	1.75
1361	A224	$1 multi	2.25	2.25
1362	A224	$1.25 multi	2.75	2.75
1363	A224	$1.40 multi	3.25	3.25
1364	A224	$2 multi	4.75	4.75
1365	A224	$5 multi	11.00	11.00
1366	A224	$10 multi	22.50	22.50
		Nos. 1352-1366 (15)	54.20	54.20

25c, 35c, $5, $10 exist dated "2003." Value, set $32.50.

Reign of Queen Elizabeth II, 50th Anniv. — A225

No. 1367: a, Crossing Place Trail, Middle Caicos. b, Wades Green Plantation, North Caicos. c, Underwater scenery, Grand Turk. d, St. Thomas Anglican Church, Grand Turk. e, Ripsaw band, Grand Turk. f, Basketweaving.
No. 1368: a, Visit of Princess Royal, 1960. b, Visit of Queen Elizabeth II, 1966. c, Visit of Princess Alexandra, 1988. d, Visit of Duke of

Edinburgh, 1993. e, Visit of Prince Andrew, 2000.
No. 1369: a, Salt Industry, 1952-62. b, Space splashdown, 1962-72. c, Ministerial government system, 1972-82. d, Quincentennial of Columbus' landfall, 1982-92. e, National Museum, 1992-2002.

2002, June 1   **Litho.**   **Perf. 14¼**
1367 Sheet of 6 4.25 4.25
a.-f. A225 25c Any single .70 .70
Perf. 13¾
1368 Sheet of 5 8.75 8.75
a.-e. A225 60c Any single 1.75 1.75
Perf. 13¾x14¼
1369 Sheet of 5 11.00 11.00
a.-e A225 80c Any single 2.10 2.10

No. 1368 contains five 31x31mm stamps; No. 1369 contains five 30x34mm stamps.

20th World Scout Jamboree, Thailand — A226

No. 1370: a, Scout with mallet and chisel. b, Scout with rifle. c, Scout hanging on rope above water. d, Scouts and lantern.
$2, Handicapped Scouts.

2002, July 15   **Perf. 14**
1370 A226 80c Sheet of 4, #a-d 9.50 9.50
Souvenir Sheet
1371 A226 $2 multi 6.00 6.00

Intl. Year of Ecotourism — A227

No. 1372, vert.: a, Humpback whale. b, Water sports. c, Regattas. d, Queen angelfish. e, Manta ray. f, Turtle.
$2, Jojo dolphin.

2002, July 15
1372 A227 60c Sheet of 6, #a-f 12.50 12.50
Souvenir Sheet
1373 A227 $2 multi 6.25 6.25

No. 1372 contains six 28x42mm stamps.

Intl. Year of Mountains — A228

No. 1374: a, Devil's Peak, South Africa. b, Mt. Drakensburg, South Africa. c, Mt. Blanc, France. d, Roan Mountain, US. e, Mt. Sefton, New Zealand. f, Mt. Cook, New Zealand. $2, Northwest Highlands, Scotland.

2002, July 22
1374 A228 80c Sheet of 6, #a-
f   14.00 14.00
Souvenir Sheet
1375 A228 $2 multi   6.25 6.25

United We Stand — A229

2002, Aug. 5
1376 A229 50c multi   1.50 1.50
Printed in sheets of 4.

Insects and Birds — A230

No. 1377, 60c: a, Hawk moth. b, Burnet moth. c, Mammoth wasp. d, Branch-boring beetle. e, Flower mantid, Pseudocrebotra species. f, Flower mantid, Creobroter species.
No. 1378, 60c: a, Sooty tern. b, Magnificent frigatebird. c, American white pelican. d, Northern shoveler. e, Baltimore oriole. f, Roseate spoonbill.
No. 1379, $2, Tiphiid wasp. No. 1380, $2, Greater flamingo.

2002, Aug. 12   *Perf. 14*
Sheets of 6, #a-f
1377-1378 A230 Set of 2   22.50 22.50
Souvenir Sheets
1379-1380 A230 Set of 2   12.00 12.00

Queen Mother Elizabeth (1900-2002) — A231

No. 1381: a, Without hat. b, With hat.

2002, Oct. 21
1381 A231 80c Sheet, 2 each
#a-b   10.00 10.00

First Nonstop Solo Transatlantic Flight, 75th Anniv. — A232

No. 1382: a, Charles Lindbergh's early exploits as a barnstormer. b, Lindbergh standing in front of Spirit of St. Louis. c, Spirit of St. Louis. d, Take-off from Roosevelt Field. e, Crossing the Atlantic. f, Arrival and welcome in Paris.

2002, Nov. 18   Litho.   Perf. 14
1382 A232 60c Sheet of 6, #a-
f   11.50 11.50

Pres. John F. Kennedy (1917-63) — A233

No. 1383 — Portrait color: a, Orange brown. b, Red violet. c, Greenish gray. d, Blue violet. e, Purple. f, Dull brown.

2002, Nov. 18
1383 A233 60c multi   11.50 11.50

Christmas A234

Designs: 20c, Madonna and Child, by Giovanni Bellini, vert. 25c, Adoration of the Magi, by Correggio. 60c, Transfiguration of Christ, by Bellini, vert. 80c, Polyptych of St. Vincent Ferrer, by Bellini, vert. $1, Miraculous Mass, by Simone Martini, vert.
$2, Christ in Heaven with Four Saints, by Domenico Ghirlandaio.

2002, Nov. 25
1384-1388 A234 Set of 5   8.00 8.00
Souvenir Sheet
1389 A234 $2 multi   6.00 6.00

Japanese Art — A235

Designs: 25c, Nagata no Taro Nagamune, by Kuniyoshi Utagawa. 35c, Danjuro Ichikawa VII, by Kunisada Utagawa. 60c, Nagata no Taro Nagamune, by Kuniyoshi Utagawa, diff. $1, Nagata no Taro Nagamune, by Kuniyoshi Utagawa, diff.
No. 1394 — Scroll of Actors, by Chikanobu Toyohara and others: a, Smiling man holding fan. b, Man holding sword at mouth. c, Man holding sword vertically. d, Man with tree branch above head.
$2, Two Women by a River, by Chikanobu Hashimoto.

2003, June 17   Litho.   Perf. 14¼
1390-1393 A235 Set of 4   4.50 4.50
1394 A235 80c Sheet of 4, #a-d 6.50 6.50
Souvenir Sheet
1395 A235 $2 multi   4.00 4.00

Rembrandt Paintings A236

Designs: 25c, Portrait of a Young Man Resting His Chin on His Hand. 50c, A Woman at an Open Door. No. 1398, $1, The Return of the Prodigal Son. No. 1399, $1, Portrait of an Elderly Man.
No. 1400: a, Nicolaas van Bambeeck. b, Agatha Bas, Wife of Nicolaas van Bambeeck. c, Portrait of a Man Holding His Hat. d, Saskia in a Red Hat.
$2, Christ Driving the Money Changers from the Temple.

Perf. 14¼, 13¼ (#1400)
2003, June 17
1396-1399 A236 Set of 4   5.50 5.50
1400 A236 60c Sheet of 4, #a-d 5.00 5.00
Souvenir Sheet
1401 A236 $2 multi   4.00 4.00

Paintings by Joan Miró — A237

Designs: 25c, Portrait of a Young Girl. 50c, Table with Glove. 60c, Self-portrait, 1917. $1, The Farmer's Wife.
No. 1406: a, Portrait of Ramon Sunyer. b, Self-portrait, 1919. c, Portrait of a Spanish Dancer. d, Portrait of Joana Obrador.
No. 1407, Flowers and Butterfly. No. 1408, Still Life of the Coffee Grinder, horiz.

2003, June 17   *Perf. 14¼*
1402-1405 A237 Set of 4   4.75 4.75
1406 A237 80c Sheet of 4, #a-d 6.50 6.50
Imperf
Size: 104x83mm
1407 A237 $2 multi   4.00 4.00
Size: 83x104mm
1408 A237 $2 multi   4.00 4.00

Caribbean Community, 30th Anniv. — A238

2003, July 4   *Perf. 14*
1409 A238 60c multi   1.25 1.25

Tanya Streeter, World Champion Freediver — A239

No. 1410: a, Wearing wetsuit in water. b, Diving underwater, portrait. c, Wearing bathing suit at shore. d, Standing in front of map. e, Holding on to diving apparatus.

2003, July 15
1410 A239 20c Sheet of 5, #a-e 2.00 2.00

Coronation of Queen Elizabeth II, 50th Anniv. — A240

No. 1411: a, Wearing crown and white robe. b, Wearing lilac dress. c, Wearing tiara and red dress.
$2, Wearing hat and blue cape. $5, Profile portrait.

2003, Aug. 25
1411 A240 80c Sheet of 3, #a-
c   5.00 5.00
Souvenir Sheets
1412-1413 A240 Set of 2   14.00 14.00

Prince William, 21st Birthday — A241

No. 1414: a, Portrait in blue. b, Pink background. c, Purple background.
$2, Dark blue background.

2003, Aug. 25
1414 A241 $1 Sheet of 3, #a-c   6.00 6.00
Souvenir Sheet
1415 A241 $2 multi   4.00 4.00

Tour de France Bicycle Race,
Cent. — A242

No. 1416: a, Eddy Merckx, 1974. b, Bernard Thévenet, 1975. c, Lucien Van Impe, 1976. d, Thévenet, 1977.
$2, Bernard Hinault, 1979.

2003, Aug. 25   Perf. 13¾x14¼
1416 A242 $1 Sheet of 4, #a-d   8.00 8.00
Souvenir Sheet
1417 A242 $2 multi   4.00 4.00

Powered Flight, Cent. — A243

No. 1418: a, Vought F4U Corsair. b, Messerschmidt Me 262. c, A6M. d, Hawker Hurricane.
$2, Supermarine Spitfire Mk IX.

2003, Aug. 25   Perf. 14
1418 A243 60c Sheet of 4, #a-d   5.00 5.00
Souvenir Sheet
1419 A243 $2 multi   4.00 4.00

German Teddy Bears — A244

No. 1420, vert.: a, Bear with red and yellow uniform. b, Bear with dress. c, Bear with violin case. d, Bear with sword.
$2, Bear on beer mug.

2003, Aug. 25   Perf. 12x12¼
1420 A244 50c Sheet of 4, #a-d   4.00 4.00
Souvenir Sheet
Perf. 12¼x12
1421 A244 $2 multi   4.00 4.00

Butterflies   50¢
A245

Designs: 50c, Papilio thersites. 60c, Papilio andraemon. 80c, Papilio pelaus. $1, Consul hippona.
$2, Papilio pelaus, diff.

2003, Nov. 17   Perf. 14
1422-1425 A245   Set of 4   6.00 6.00
Souvenir Sheet
1426 A245 $2 multi   4.00 4.00

Orchids
A246

Designs: 50c, Laelia anceps. 60c, Laelia briegeri. 80c, Laelia fidelensis. $1, Laelia cinnabarina.
$2, Laelia rubescens.

2003, Nov. 17
1427-1430 A246   Set of 4   6.00 6.00
Souvenir Sheet
1431 A246 $2 multi   4.00 4.00

Dogs   50¢
A247

Designs: 50c, Beagle. 60c, Sabueso Espanol, vert. 80c, Basset hound, vert. $1, Jack Russell terrier, vert.
$2, Dachshund.

2003, Nov. 17
1432-1435 A247   Set of 4   6.00 6.00
Souvenir Sheet
1436 A247 $2 multi   4.00 4.00

Cats
A248

Designs: 50c, Persian. 60c, Cymric. 80c, Main Coon, vert. $1, Tiffany.
$2, Kurile Island bobtail.

2003, Nov. 17
1437-1440 A248   Set of 4   6.00 6.00
Souvenir Sheet
1441 A248 $2 multi   4.00 4.00

Christmas
A249

Paintings: 25c, Madonna of the Harpies, by Andrea del Sarto. 60c, Madonna and Child with St. John, by del Sarto. 80c, Madonna and Child with St. Joseph and St. Peter Martyr, by del Sarto. $1, Madonna and Child with the Angels, by del Sarto.
$2, Montefeltro Altarpiece, by Piero della Francesca.

2003, Nov. 24   Perf. 14¼
1442-1445 A249   Set of 4   5.50 5.50
Souvenir Sheet
1446 A249 $2 multi   4.00 4.00

Marine Life — A250

Photographs from underwater photography contest: Nos. 1447, 1452a, 25c, Golden Rough Head Blennie, by Rand McMeins. Nos. 1448, 1452b, 50c, Octopus at Night, by Marc Van Driessche. Nos. 1449, 1452c, 60c, Sea Turtle, by Mike Nebel. Nos. 1450, 1452d, 80c, Juvenile Octopus, by Amber Blecker. Nos. 1451, 1452e, $1, School of Horse Eye Jacks, by Blecker.
$2, Coral Reef, by Keith Kaplan, vert.

Perf. 12, 12¾ (#1452)
2006, June 1   Litho.
Stamps With Thin "Shadow" Frame
1447-1451 A250   Set of 5   6.50 6.50
Miniature Sheet
Stamps With Thick "Shadow" Frame
1452 A250   Sheet of 5, #a-e   6.50 6.50
Souvenir Sheet
1453 A250 $2 multi   4.00 4.00

Washington 2006 World Philatelic Exhibition. (Nos. 1452-1453). The perforation tips at the tops of the stamps on Nos. 1452a-1452e are all white, gradiating to blue on the lower halves of the stamps, while the perforation tips on Nos. 1447-1451 show other colors. The shadow frames at the bottom of Nos 1452a-1452e are 1mm thick and about ½mm thick on Nos. 1447-1451. The distances between the bottom of the denomination and the top of the country name differ on Nos. 1452a-1452e from those found on Nos. 1447-1451. No. 1447 has incorrect spelling, "Ruogh," in inscription, while No. 1452a has word correctly spelled as "Rough."

Queen Elizabeth II, 80th
Birthday — A251

No. 1454 — Various depictions of Queen Elizabeth II: a, 50c. b, 60c. c, 80c. d, $1.
$6, Wearing crown.

2006, Sept. 12   Litho.   Perf. 13½
1454 A251   Sheet of 4, #a-d   6.00 6.00
Souvenir Sheet
1455 A251 $6 multi   12.00 12.00

Christmas — A252

The Birth of Christ and Adoration of the Shepherds, by Peter Paul Rubens: Nos. 1456, 1460a, 25c, Praying shepherd. Nos. 1457, 1460b, 60c, Infant Jesus. Nos. 1458, 1460c, 80c, Heads of two shepherds. Nos. 1459, 1460d, $1, Virgin Mary.
$6, Our Lady, The Christ Child and Saints, by Rubens, vert.

2006, Dec. 27   Perf. 13¼x13½
Stamps With Painting Title
1456-1459 A252   Set of 4   5.50 5.50
Stamps Without Painting Title
1460 A252   Sheet of 4, #a-d   5.50 5.50
Souvenir Sheet
Perf. 13½x13¼
1461 A252 $6 multi   12.00 12.00

Shells — A253

Designs: 10c, Cymatium muricinum. 15c, Tellina radiata. 20c, Tonna maculosa. 25c, Leucozonia nassa. 35c, Trachycardium magnum. 45c, Papyridea soleniformis. 50c, Epitonium lamellosum. 60c, Astraea brevispina. 80c, Bulla striata. $1, Murex margaritensis. $1.25, Chama macerophylla. $1.40, Vasum capitellum. $2, Coralliophila abbreviata. $5, Trachycardium isocardia. $10, Oliva reticularis.

2007, June 11   Litho.   Perf. 12¾
1462 A253 10c multi   .30   .30
1463 A253 15c multi   .35   .35
1464 A253 20c multi   .50   .50
1465 A253 25c multi   .60   .60
1466 A253 35c multi   .85   .85
1467 A253 45c multi   1.10 1.10
1468 A253 50c multi   1.20 1.20
1469 A253 60c multi   1.50 1.50
1470 A253 80c multi   1.90 1.90
1471 A253 $1 multi   2.25 2.25
1472 A253 $1.25 multi   3.00 3.00
1473 A253 $1.40 multi   3.50 3.50
1474 A253 $2 multi   4.75 4.75
1475 A253 $5 multi   12.00 12.00
1476 A253 $10 multi   24.00 24.00
    Nos. 1462-1476 (15) 57.80 57.80

Christmas
A254

Paintings: 25c, The Virgin and Child, by Carlo Maratta. 60c, The Adoration of the Magi, by Vincent Malo. 80c, The Annunciation, by Robert Campin, horiz. $1, The Adoration of the Magi, by Giovanni di Paolo, horiz. $6, The Adoration of the Magi, by Quentin Massys.

Perf. 14¼x14¾, 14¾x14¼

2007, Dec. 10
1477-1480 A254   Set of 4   5.50 5.50

Souvenir Sheet
Perf. 14
1481 A254 $6 multi   12.00 12.00

No. 1481 contains one 28x42mm stamp.

Worldwide Fund for Nature (WWF) — A255

No. 1482 — Red-tailed hawk: a, Pair on fenceposts. b, Adults and chicks at nest. c, Adults on hill and in flight. d, Head of hawk.

2007, Dec. 24   **Perf. 13¼**
1482 Horiz. strip of 4   6.00   6.00
a.-d A255 50c Any single   1.50   1.50
e.   Souvenir sheet, 2 each #a-d 15.00 15.00

Wedding of Queen Elizabeth II and Prince Philip, 60th Anniv. — A256

No. 1483, vert.: a, Couple, country name in purple. b, Queen, country name in purple. c, Queen, country name in blue. d, Couple, country name in blue. e, Couple, country name in black. f, Queen, country name in black.
$6, Couple on balcony.

2007, Dec. 28   **Perf. 13¼**
1483 A256 $1 Sheet of 6, #a-f 12.00 12.00
Souvenir Sheet
1484 A256 $6 multi   12.00 12.00

Princess Diana (1961-97) — A257

No. 1485 — Various photographs as shown.
$6, Princess Diana wearing hat.

2007, Dec. 28
1485 A257 $1 Sheet of 4, #a-d 8.00 8.00
Souvenir Sheet
1486 A257 $6 multi   12.00 12.00

Pope Benedict XVI — A258

2008, Sept. 15   Litho.   Perf. 13¼
1487 A258 75c multi   1.50 1.50
Printed in sheets of 8.

Scouting, Cent. (in 2007) — A259

No. 1488, horiz.: a, Fleur-de-lis, silhouette of Lord Robert Baden-Powell and flags of Tanzania, United States and Colombia on top row. b, Dove, silhouette of fleur-de-lis and green, light green and red national Scouting emblem at UL. c, As "b," with orange, brown and dark green national Scouting emblem at UL. d, As "a," with flags of Israel, Canada, Chile and Macedonia on second row. e, As "a," with flags of Taiwan, Luxembourg and Philippines on top row. f, As "b," with Israel Scouting emblem at UL.
$6, Lord Baden-Powell.

2008, Sept. 23
1488 A259 80c Sheet of 6, #a-
      f   9.75 9.75
Souvenir Sheet
1489 A259 $6 multi   12.00 12.00

Space Exploration, 50th Anniv. (in 2007) — A260

No. 1490 — International Space Station: a, With solar panels under silhouette of Queen. b, With solar panels touching nose of Queen. c, With solar panels spread horizontally. d, With solar panels running to UL from Queen's chest.
$6, International Space Station, diff.

2008, Sept. 23
1490 A260 $1 Sheet of 4, #a-d 8.00 8.00
Souvenir Sheet
1491 A260 $6 multi   12.00 12.00

Marine Life A261

Photographs from underwater photography contest: 25c, Arrow Crab, by Garin Bescoby. 60c, Trumpet Fish, by Karin Nargis. 80c, Sting Ray, by Barbara Shively. $1, Giant Anemone, by Roddy Mcleod.
$6, Red Banded Lobster, by Jayne Baker.

2008, Nov. 25   Litho.   Perf. 13¼
1492-1495 A261   Set of 4   5.50 5.50
1495a Souvenir sheet, #1492-
       1495   5.50 5.50
Souvenir Sheet
1496 A261 $6 multi   12.00 12.00

Christmas
A262

Paintings: 25c, The Nativity, by Philippe de Champaigne. 60c, Mystic Nativity, by Sandro Botticelli. 80c, The Virgin in a Rose Arbor, by Stefan Lochner. $1, The Adoration of the Shepherds, by Francisco Zurbaran.
$6, The Virgin with Angels, by William Bouguereau.

2008, Nov. 25   **Perf. 14x14¾**
1497-1500 A262   Set of 4   5.50 5.50
Souvenir Sheet
1501 A262 $6 multi   12.00 12.00

WAR TAX STAMPS

Regular Issue of 1913-16 Overprinted

1917   Wmk. 3   Perf. 14
Black Overprint at Bottom of Stamp
MR1 A10 1p carmine   .25   1.75
a.   Double overprint   200.00 275.00
b.   "TAX" omitted
c.   Pair, one without ovpt. 700.00
MR2 A10 3p violet, yel   1.40   5.75
a.   Double overprint   110.00

Black Overprint at Top or Middle of Stamp

1917
MR3 A10 1p carmine   .25   1.40
a.   Inverted overprint   55.00
b.   Double overprint   65.00 77.50
c.   Pair, one without over-
       print   650.00
MR4 A10 3p violet, yel   .70   2.00
a.   Double overprint   50.00 60.00
b.   Dbl. ovpt., one inverted 375.00

Same Overprint in Violet or Red

1918-19
MR5 A10 1p car (V) ('19)   .50   4.50
a.   Double overprint   24.00
b.   "WAR" omitted   200.00
MR6 A10 3p violet, yel (R) 15.00 45.00
a.   Double overprint   375.00

Regular Issue of 1913-16 Overprinted in Black

1918
MR7 A10 1p carmine   .25   1.75
MR8 A10 3p violet, yel   4.50   5.00

Same Overprint in Red

1919
MR9 A10 3p violet, yel   .25   2.75

Regular Issue of 1913-16 Overprinted in Black

MR10 A10 1p carmine   .25   1.10
a.   Double overprint   160.00 190.00
MR11 A10 3p violet, yel   .35   3.00

Regular Issue of 1913-16 Overprinted

MR12 A10 1p carmine   .25   2.75
a.   Double overprint   100.00
MR13 A10 3p violet, yel   .55   3.00

The bottom two rows of this setting show the words "War" and "Tax" about 1mm farther apart.

CAICOS

Catalogue values for all unused stamps in this country are for Never Hinged items.

Turks & Caicos Nos. 360, 364, 366, 369, 371-373 Ovptd. with Black Bar and "CAICOS ISLANDS"

Unwmk.
1981, July 24   Litho.   Perf. 14
1 A69 1c Indigo hamlet   .25   .25
2 A69 5c Spanish grunt   .25   .25
3 A69 8c Foureye butter-
        lyfish   .25   .25
4 A69 20c Queen angelfish .40   .40
5 A69 50c Fairy basslet   .85   .85
6 A69 $1 Clown wrasse   1.75 1.75
7 A69 $2 Stoplight parrotfish 3.25 3.25
        Nos. 1-7 (7)   7.00 7.00

Common Design Types pictured following the introduction.

Royal Wedding Issue
Common Design Type
Turks & Caicos Nos. 486-489 Ovptd. with Black Bar and "Caicos Islands"

1981, July 24
8 CD331a 35c Charles & Di-
          ana   .30   .30
9 CD331a 65c Kensington
          Palace   .60   .60
10 CD331a 90c Prince Charles .85 .85
          Nos. 8-10 (3)   1.75 1.75
Souvenir Sheet
11 CD331 $2 Glass coach   4.50 4.50

Roulette x Imperf. (#12a), Imperf. (#12b)
1981, Oct. 29
Self-Adhesive
12 Souvenir booklet   27.50
a.   A88a Pane, 3 each 20c, Diana,
     $1, Charles)   15.00
b.   A88a Pane of 1 $2, Couple 10.00

Nos. 8-11 exist with overprint in all capital letters, values about the same. Nos. 8-10, in both overprint types, also exist in sheets of 5 plus label in changed colors, perf. 12.

Hawksbill turtle C1

1983-84   **Perf. 14**
13 C1 8c Diver with lobster
        and conch shell   .40   .40
14 C1 10c shown   .40   .40
15 C1 20c Stone idol, Ara-
        wak Indians   .90   .90
16 C1 35c Sloop construc-
        tion   1.40 1.40
17 C1 50c Marine biology 2.00 2.00
18 C1 95c 707 Jetliner   4.25 4.25
19 C1 $1.10 15th cent. Span-
        ish ship   4.75 4.75
20 C1 $2 British soldier,
        Fort St. George   8.50 8.50
21 C1 $3 Pirates Anne Bon-
        ny, Calico Jack   13.00 13.00
        Nos. 13-21 (9)   35.60 35.60

Issued: #13-19, 6/6/83; #20-21, 5/18/84.
For overprints see Nos. 47-49.

Christmas Type of Turks and Caicos
Walt Disney characters in Santa Claus is Coming to Town.

1983, Nov. 7   Perf. 11

22	A104	1c Chip 'n Dale	.50	.50
23	A104	1c Goofy & Patch	.50	.50
24	A104	2c Morty, Ferdie & Pluto	.50	.50
25	A104	2c Morty	.50	.50
26	A104	3c Donald, Huey, Dewey & Louie	.50	.50
27	A104	3c Goofy & Louie	.50	.50
28	A104	50c Uncle Scrooge	3.25	3.25
29	A104	70c Mickey Mouse & Ferdie	4.50	4.50
30	A104	$1.10 Pinocchio, Jiminy Cricket and Figaro	6.25	6.25
		Nos. 22-30 (9)	17.00	17.00

Souvenir Sheet
Perf. 13½x14

31	A104	$2 Morty & Ferdie, fireplace	7.50	7.50

Drawings by Raphael — C2

1984 Summer Olympics, Los Angeles — C3

Designs: 35c, Leda and the Swan. 50c, Study of Apollo for Parnassus. 95c, Study of two figures for The Battle of Ostia. $1.10, Study for the Madonna of the Goldfinch. $2.50, The Garvagh Madonna.

1983, Dec. 15   Perf. 14

32	C2	35c multicolored	1.25	1.25
33	C2	50c multicolored	1.75	1.75
34	C2	95c multicolored	3.25	3.25
35	C2	$1.10 multicolored	3.75	3.75
		Nos. 32-35 (4)	10.00	10.00

Souvenir Sheet

36	C2	$2.50 multicolored	8.00	8.00

500th birth anniv. of Raphael.

1984, Mar. 1

37	C3	4c High jump	.25	.25
38	C3	25c Archery	.50	.50
39	C3	65c Cycling	1.40	1.40
40	C3	$1.10 Soccer	2.40	2.40
		Nos. 37-40 (4)	4.55	4.55

Souvenir Sheet

41	C3	$2 Show jumping, horiz.	5.00	5.00

Easter — C4

Walt Disney characters: 35c, Horace Horsecollar, Clarabelle Cow. 45c, Mickey, Minnie & Chip. 75c, Gyro Gearloose, Chip 'n Dale. 85c, Mickey, Chip 'n Dale. $2.20, Donald sailing with nephews.

1984, Apr. 15   Perf. 14x13½

42	C4	35c multicolored	1.40	1.40
43	C4	45c multicolored	1.60	1.60
44	C4	75c multicolored	2.75	2.75
45	C4	85c multicolored	3.50	3.50
		Nos. 42-45 (4)	9.25	9.25

Souvenir Sheet

46	C4	$2.20 mulitcolored	7.00	7.00

Nos. 18-19 Ovptd. with emblem and "Universal Postal Union 1874-1984"

1984, June 19   Perf. 14

47	C1	95c multicolored	2.00	2.00
48	C1	$1.10 multicolored	2.50	2.50

No. 20 Ovptd. "AUSIPEX 1984"

1984, Aug. 22

49	C1	$2 multicolored	4.75	4.75

Columbus' First Landfall — C5

1984, Sept. 21

50	C5	10c Sighting manatees	1.00	1.00
51	C5	70c Fleet	4.50	4.50
52	C5	$1 West Indies landing	6.50	6.50
		Nos. 50-52 (3)	12.00	12.00

Souvenir Sheet

53	C5	$2 Fleet, map	4.75	4.75

Columbus' first landing, 492nd anniv.

Christmas C6

Walt Disney characters: 20c, Santa Claus, Donald and Mickey. 35c, Donald at refrigerator. 50c, Donald, Micky riding toy train. 75c, Donald carrying presents. $1.10, Huey, Louie, Dewey and Donald singing carols. $2, Donald as Christmas tree.

Perf. 13½x14, 12x12½ (75c)
1984, Nov. 26

54	C6	20c multicolored	1.10	1.10
55	C6	35c multicolored	2.00	2.00
56	C6	50c multicolored	2.75	2.75
57	C6	75c multicolored	4.25	4.25
58	C6	$1.10 multicolored	6.25	6.25
		Nos. 54-58 (5)	16.35	16.35

Souvenir Sheet
Perf. 13½x14

59	C6	$2 multicolored	6.25	6.25

No. 57 printed in sheets of 8.

Audubon Birth Bicentenary — C7

1985, Feb. 12   Perf. 14

60	C7	20c Thick-billed vireo	1.10	1.10
61	C7	35c Black-faced grassquit	2.00	2.00
62	C7	50c Pearly-eyed thrasher	2.75	2.75
63	C7	$1 Greater Antillean bullfinch	5.50	5.50
		Nos. 60-63 (4)	11.35	11.35

Souvenir Sheet

64	C7	$2 Stripe-headed tanagers	6.25	6.25

No. 64 exists imperf.

Intl. Youth Year — C8

1985, May 8

65	C8	16c Education	.35	.35
66	C8	35c Health	.80	.80
67	C8	70c Love	1.50	1.50
68	C8	90c Peace	1.90	1.90
		Nos. 65-68 (4)	4.55	4.55

Souvenir Sheet

69	C8	$2 Peace dove, child	5.00	5.00

UN 40th anniv.

Intl. Civil Aviation Org., 40th Anniv. C9

1985, May 26

70	C9	35c DC-3	2.50	2.50
71	C9	75c Convair 440	5.00	5.00
72	C9	90c TCNA Islander	6.00	6.00
		Nos. 70-72 (3)	13.50	13.50

Souvenir Sheet

73	C9	$2.20 Hang glider	5.75	5.75

Queen Mother, 85th Birthday Type of Turks & Caicos

1985, July 7

74	A117	35c Wearing green hat	1.25	1.25
75	A117	65c With Princess Anne, horiz.	2.00	2.00
76	A117	95c Wearing white hat	3.25	3.25
		Nos. 74-76 (3)	6.50	6.50

Souvenir Sheet

77	A117	$2 Inspecting guardsmen	6.50	6.50

Mark Twain, 150th Birth Anniv. — C10

Walt Disney characters in Tom Sawyer, Detective (Intl. Youth Year): 8c, Mickey and Goofy as Tom and Huck reading reward poster. 35c, Meeting Jake Dunlap. 95c, Spying on Jubiter Dunlap. $1.10, With Pluto finding body. No. 86, Unmasking Jubiter Dunlap.

Walt Disney characters portraying Six Soldiers of Fortune (The Brothers Grimm, Bicent.): 16c, Donald receiving his meager pay. 25c, Donald meets Horace Horsecollar as strong man. 65c, Donald meets Mickey the marksman. $1.35, Goofy wins footrace against Princess Daisy. No. 87, Soldiers with sack of gold.

1985, Dec. 5   Perf. 14x13½

78	C10	8c multicolored	.30	.30
79	C10	16c multicolored	.45	.45
80	C10	25c multicolored	.70	.70
81	C10	35c multicolored	1.00	1.00
82	C10	65c multicolored	1.75	1.75
83	C10	95c multicolored	2.60	2.60
84	C10	$1.10 multicolored	3.25	3.25
85	C10	$1.35 multicolored	4.00	4.00
		Nos. 78-85 (8)	14.05	14.05

Souvenir Sheet

86	C10	$2 multicolored	8.00	8.00
87	C10	$2 multicolored	8.00	8.00

Stamps are no longer being produced for Caicos.

TURKS ISLANDS

'tərks 'i-ləndz

LOCATION — West Indies, at the southern extremity of the Bahamas
GOVT. — Former dependency of Jamaica
POP. — 2,000 (approx.)
CAPITAL — Grand Turk

In 1848 the Turks Islands together with the Caicos group, lying to the northwest, were made a British colony. In 1873 the Colony became a dependency under the government of Jamaica although separate stamp issues were continued. Postage stamps inscribed Turks and Caicos Islands have been used since 1900.

12 Pence = 1 Shilling

Values for unused stamps are for examples with original gum as defined in the catalogue introduction. Very fine examples of Nos. 1-42 will have generally rough perforations that cut into the design on one or more sides due to the narrow spacing of the stamps on the plates and imperfect perforating methods. Stamps with perfs clear of the design on all four sides are extremely scarce and will command substantially higher prices.

Because of the printing and imperfect perforating methods, stamps are often found scissor separated. Prices will not be adversely affected on those stamps where the scissor cut does not remove the perforations.

Watermark

Wmk. 5 — Small Star

Queen Victoria — A1

Perf. 11½ to 13

			Engr.	
1867		Unwmk.		
1	A1	1p rose	67.50	67.50
2	A1	6p gray black	110.00	140.00
3	A1	1sh slate blue	105.00	67.50
		Nos. 1-3 (3)	282.50	275.00

Perf. 11 to 13x14 to 15

			Wmk. 5	
1873-79				
4	A1	1p lake	57.50	57.50
5	A1	1p dull red ('79)	62.50	67.50
a.		Horiz. pair, imperf. btwn.	25,000.	
b.		Perf. 11-12	1,100.	
6	A1	1sh violet	5,750.	2,250.

Stamps offered as No. 6 are often examples from which the surcharge has been removed.

Stamps of 1867-79 Surcharged in Black

a

b

c

d

e

12 settings of the ½p, 9 of 2½p, and 6 of 4p.

1881   Unwmk.   Perf. 11 to 13

7	(a)	½p on 6p gray blk	95.00	160.00
7A	(b)	½p on 6p gray blk	90.00	140.00
8	(b)	½p on 1sh slate bl	130.00	190.00
a.		Double surcharge	7,500.	

8B (c) ½p on 1sh slate bl — 11,000.
c. Without fraction bar

Perf. 11 to 13x14 to 15
Wmk. 5
9 (a) ½p on 1p dull red — 150.00 200.00
a. Double surcharge
10 (b) ½p on 1p dull red — 55.00 90.00
11 (c) ½p on 1p dull red — 210.00 275.00
a. Double surcharge — 4,250.
12 (d) ½p on 1p dull red — 260.00
a. Without fraction bar — 1,150.
b. Double surcharge
13 (e) ½p on 1p dull red — 600.00
14 ½p on 1sh violet — 175.00 225.00
a. Double surcharge — 4,000.
15 (b) ½p on 1sh violet — 140.00 225.00
a. Without fraction bar — 625.00
16 (c) ½p on 1sh violet — 105.00 190.00

f · g

h

Perf. 11 to 13
Unwmk.
17 (f) 2½p on 6p gray blk — 9,500.
18 (g) 2½p on 6p gray blk — 425.00 450.00
a. Horiz. pair, imperf. between — 19,000.
b. Double surcharge — 9,500.
19 (h) 2½p on 6p gray blk — 225.00 400.00
a. Double surcharge — 9,500.

i · j

Perf. 11 to 13x14 to 15
Wmk. 5
20 (i) 2½p on 1sh violet — 2,600.
21 (h) 2½p on 1sh violet — 625.00 950.00
22 (j) 2½p on 1sh violet — 9,500.

k · l

m · n

Perf. 11 to 13
Unwmk.
24 (k) 2½p on 6p gray blk — 9,500.
25 (k) 2½p on 1sh slate bl — 15,000.
26 (l) 2½p on 1sh slate bl — 1,500.
27 (m) 2½p on 1sh slate bl — 2,200.
a. Without fraction bar — 8,000.
28 (n) 2½p on 1sh slate bl — 6,500.

o

Perf. 11 to 13x14 to 15
Wmk. 5
29 (l) 2½p on 1p dull red — 600.00
30 (o) 2½p on 1p dull red — 1,350.
31 (l) 2½p on 1sh violet — 850.00
a. Double surcharge of "½" — 4,000.
32 (o) 2½p on 1sh violet — 1,350.
b. Double surcharge of "½" — 5,750.

p · q

r

Perf. 11 to 13
Unwmk.
33 (p) 4p on 6p gray black — 95.00 140.00
34 (q) 4p on 6p gray black — 375.00 475.00
35 (r) 4p on 6p gray black — 475.00 350.00

Examples of No. 33 with top of "4" painted in are sometimes offered as No. 35.

Perf. 11 to 13x14 to 15
Wmk. 5
36 (r) 4p on 1p dull red — 950.00 625.00
a. Inverted surcharge — 3,250.
37 (p) 4p on 1p dull red — 850.00 550.00
a. Inverted surcharge
38 (q) 4p on 1sh violet — 450.00 625.00
39 (q) 4p on 1sh violet — 2,750.

Wmk. Crown and C C (1)

1881		Engr.		Perf. 14
40	A1	1p brown red	77.50	105.00

a. Diagonal half used as ½p on cover
41 A1 6p olive brown — 120.00 175.00
42 A1 1sh slate green — 190.00 140.00
Nos. 40-42 (3) — 387.50 420.00

A2

1881 **Typo.**
43 A2 4p ultramarine — 155.00 67.50

1882-95 **Engr.** **Wmk. 2**
44 A1 1p orange brn ('83) — 100.00 35.00
a. Half used as ½p on cover — 5,000.
45 A1 1p car lake ('89) — 3.50 2.25
46 A1 6p yellow brn ('89) — 4.00 4.50
47 A1 1sh black brn ('87) — 5.50 4.00
a. 1sh deep brown — 5.50 4.00

Typo.
Die A
48 A2 ½p dull green ('85) — 5.00 5.00
a. ½p blue green ('82) — 20.00 27.50
49 A2 2½p red brown ('82) — 35.00 14.00
50 A2 4p gray ('84) — 32.00 3.50
a. Half used as 2p on cover — 5,000.

Die B
51 A2 ½p gray green ('94) — 3.50 2.00
52 A2 2½p ultra ('93) — 3.50 2.75
53 A2 4p dk vio & bl ('95) — 11.00 15.00

For descriptions of dies A and B see "Dies of British Colonial Stamps" in table of contents.

1887 **Engr.** **Perf. 12**
54 A1 1p carmine lake — 14.00 3.25

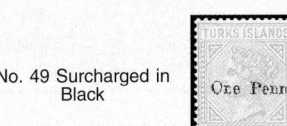

No. 49 Surcharged in Black

1889
55 A2 1p on 2½p red brn — 11.00 13.50
a. Double surcharge
b. Double surcharge, one inverted
c. "One" omitted — 1,800.
d. Half used as ½p on cover — 5,500.

No. 55c caused by the misplacement of the surcharge. Stamps also exist from the same sheet reading "Penny One."

No. 50 Surcharged in Black

Two types of surcharge:
Type I — Upper bar continuous across sheet.
Type II — Upper bar breaks between stamps.

1893
56 A2 ½p on 4p gray (I) — 165.00 155.00
a. Type II — 3,250. 1,450.

This surcharge exists in five settings.

A3

1894 **Typo.**
57 A3 5p olive grn & carmine — 9.00 21.00
a. Diag. half used as 2½p on cover — 5,000.

TUVALU
tü-'vä-ˌü

LOCATION — A group of islands in the Pacific Ocean northeast of Australia.
GOVT. — Independent state in the British Commonwealth
AREA — 9½ sq. mi.
POP. — 10,588 (1999 est.)
CAPITAL — Funafuti

Tuvalu, formerly Ellice Islands, consists of nine islands.

Australian dollar

Catalogue values for all unused stamps in this country are for Never Hinged items.

Watermark

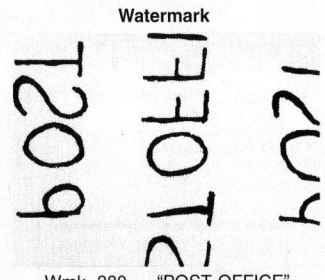

Wmk. 380 — "POST OFFICE"

Gilbert and Ellice Islands Types of 1971
Overprinted "TUVALU" and Bar in Violet Blue or Silver (35c)
Wmk. 373

1976, Jan. 1		Litho.		Perf. 14
1	A18	1c	1.25	.60
2	A19	2c	1.60	.85
a.		Wmk. 314 sideways	240.00	25.00
b.		Wmk. 314 upright	1,500.	140.00
3	A19	3c Wmk. 314	2.50	1.25
a.		Wmk. 373	.80	.55
4	A19	4c	1.60	.90
5	A19	5c Wmk. 314	1.60	1.25
6	A18	6c	1.60	.85
7	A18	8c Wmk. 314	1.60	1.25
8	A19	10c Wmk. 314	1.60	1.60
9	A18	15c	2.50	1.00
10	A19	20c	1.60	1.25
11	A19	25c Wmk. 314	10.50	3.50
a.		Wmk. 373	.90	.75
12	A19	35c	2.50	1.40
13	A18	50c	1.60	1.25
a.		Wmk. 314	47.50	22.50
14	A18	$1	1.60	1.60
a.		Wmk. 314	110.00	70.00
15	A18	$2	2.10	1.60
		Nos. 1-15 (15)	35.75	20.15

Men from Gilbert and Ellice — A1

Designs: 10c, Map of Gilbert and Ellice Islands, vert. 35c, Gilbert and Ellice canoes.

1976, Jan. 1 **Wmk. 373**
16 A1 4c multicolored — .60 .75
17 A1 10c multicolored — .80 .90
18 A1 35c multicolored — 1.10 1.25
Nos. 16-18 (3) — 2.50 2.90

Separation of the Gilbert and Ellice Islands.

50c Coin and Octopus — A2

New coinage: 10c, 10c-coin and red-dyed crab. 15c, 20c-coin and flyingfish. 35c, $1-coin and green turtle.

Wmk. 373
1976, Apr. 21 **Litho.** **Perf. 14**
19 A2 5c bister & multi — .30 .30
20 A2 10c ultra & multi — .85 .65
21 A2 15c blue & multi — 1.25 .80
22 A2 35c lt green & multi — 2.25 1.40
Nos. 19-22 (4) — 4.65 3.15

Map of Niulakita, Leathery Turtle — A3

2c, Map of Nukulaelae and sleeping mat. 4c, Map of Nui and talo vegetable. 5c, Map of Nanumanga and grass dancing skirt. 6c, Map of Nukufetau and coconut crab. 8c, Map of Funafuti and banana tree. 10c, Map of Tuvalu Islands. 15c, Map of Niutao and flyingfish. 20c, Map of Vaitupu and maneapa (house). 25c, Map of Nanumea and palu fish hook. No. 33, 35c, Te Ano Game, horiz. No. 34, 50c, Canoe pole fishing, horiz. No. 35, $1, Reef fishing by flare, horiz. No. 36, $2, House, horiz. No. 37, $5, Colony Ship M.V. Nivanga, horiz.

1976 **Wmk. 373** **Litho.** **Perf. 13½**
23-37 A3 Set of 15 — 65.00 18.00

Issue dates: $5, Sept. 1; others July 1.
See #58-70. For overprints see #85-91.

New Testament A5

Designs: 20c, Lotolelei Church, Nanumea. 25c, Kelupi Church, Nui. 30c, Mataloa o Tuvalu Church, Vaitupu. 35c, Palataiso o Keliso Church, Nanumanga.

Perf. 14x14½
1976, Oct. 6 **Litho.** **Wmk. 373**
38-42 A5 Set of 5 — 8.50 6.00

Christmas 1976. Printed in sheets of 10 stamps and 2 labels.

Prince Philip Carried Ashore at
Vaitupu — A6

Designs: 15c, Queen and Prince Philip on
Buckingham Palace balcony. 50c, Queen
Leaving Buckingham Palace for coronation.

1977, Feb. 9   Litho.   Perf. 13½x14
43	A6	15c multicolored	1.75	1.50
44	A6	35c multicolored	2.25	2.50
45	A6	50c multicolored	3.50	3.50
a.		Souv. sheet, #43-45, perf. 15	9.00	9.00
		Nos. 43-45 (3)	7.50	7.50

25th anniv. of the reign of Elizabeth II.

Health (Microscope) — A7

20c, Education (blackboard). 30c, Fruit
growing (palm). 35c, Map of South Pacific
Territory.

1977, May 4   Litho.   Perf. 13½x14
46	A7	5c lilac & multi	.70	.50
47	A7	20c orange & multi	.70	.50
48	A7	30c yellow grn & multi	.70	.50
49	A7	35c lt blue & multi	1.10	.65
		Nos. 46-49 (4)	3.20	2.15

South Pacific Commission, 30th anniv.

Swearing-in Ceremony and Scout
Emblem — A8

Designs (Scout Emblem and): 20c, Scouts
in outrigger canoe. 30c, Scouts under sun
shelter. 35c, Lord Baden-Powell.

Perf. 13½x14
1977, Aug. 10   Litho.   Wmk. 373
50	A8	5c multicolored	.65	.65
51	A8	20c multicolored	.65	.65
52	A8	30c multicolored	1.00	1.00
53	A8	35c multicolored	1.00	1.00
		Nos. 50-53 (4)	3.30	3.30

Scouting in Tuvalu (Ellice Islands), 50th
anniv.

Hurricane Beach and Coral — A9

Designs: 20c, Boring apparatus on "Porpoise," vert. 30c, Map of islands showing line
of dredgings to prove Darwin's theory, vert.
35c, Charles Darwin and "Beagle."

Perf. 13½
1977, Nov. 2   Unwmk.   Litho.
54	A9	5c multicolored	.75	.75
55	A9	20c multicolored	.75	.75
56	A9	30c multicolored	1.10	.90
57	A9	35c multicolored	1.10	.90
		Nos. 54-57 (4)	3.70	3.30

1896-97 Royal Soc. of London Expeditions
to explore coral reefs by dredging and boring.

Types of 1976

Designs: 30c, Fatele, local dance. 40c,
Screw pine. Others as before.

1977-78   Unwmk.   Perf. 13½
58	A3	1c multicolored	.35	.35
59	A3	2c multicolored	.35	.35
60	A3	4c multicolored	.35	.35
61	A3	5c multicolored	.35	.35
62	A3	6c multicolored	.35	.35
63	A3	8c multicolored	.35	.35
64	A3	10c multicolored	.35	.35
66	A3	20c multicolored	2.50	1.75
67	A3	25c multicolored	1.75	.60
68	A4	30c multicolored	.70	.70
69	A4	40c multicolored	.95	1.00
70	A4	$5 multicolored	7.00	7.00
		Nos. 58-70 (12)	15.35	13.50

Issued: #58, 61, 63-64, 67, 1977; others,
1978.

Pacific
Pigeon — A10

Wild Birds of Tuvalu: 20c, Reef heron. 30c,
Fairy tern. 40c, Lesser frigate bird.

Perf. 14x13½
1978, Jan. 25   Litho.   Unwmk.
73	A10	8c lilac & multi	1.60	.90
74	A10	20c ocher & multi	2.00	1.25
75	A10	30c dull green & multi	2.50	1.75
76	A10	40c brt green & multi	2.50	2.00
		Nos. 73-76 (4)	8.60	5.90

Lawedua — A11

Ships: 20c, Tug Wallacia. 30c, Freighter
Cenpac Rounder. 40c, Pacific Explorer.

1978, Apr. 5   Unwmk.   Perf. 13½x14
77	A11	8c multicolored	.25	.25
78	A11	20c multicolored	.45	.35
79	A11	30c multicolored	.65	.45
80	A11	40c multicolored	.75	.65
		Nos. 77-80 (4)	2.10	1.70

Canterbury Cathedral — A12

Designs: 30c, Salisbury Cathedral. 40c,
Wells Cathedral. $1, Hereford Cathedral.

1978, June 2   Litho.   Perf. 13½x14
81	A12	8c multicolored	.25	.25
82	A12	30c multicolored	.25	.25
83	A12	40c multicolored	.25	.25
84	A12	$1 multicolored	.65	.65
a.		Souv. sheet, #81-84, perf. 15	1.25	1.25
		Nos. 81-84 (4)	1.40	1.40

25th anniv. of coronation of Elizabeth II.
#81-84 were also issued in bklt. panes of 2.

Types of 1976 Overprinted:
"INDEPENDENCE 1ST OCTOBER
1978"

1978, Oct. 1   Litho.   Perf. 13½
85	A3	8c multicolored	.25	.25
86	A3	10c multicolored	.25	.25
87	A3	15c multicolored	.25	.25
88	A3	20c multicolored	.25	.25
89	A4	30c multicolored	.25	.25
90	A4	35c multicolored	.25	.25
91	A4	40c multicolored	.30	.30
		Nos. 85-91 (7)	1.80	1.80

Independence, Oct. 1, 1978. Overprint in 3
lines on vert. stamps, 1 line on horiz.

White
Frangipani — A13

Wild Flowers: 20c, Zephyrantes rosea. 30c,
Gardenia taitensis. 40c, Clerodendron inerme.

1978, Oct. 4   Unwmk.   Perf. 14
92	A13	8c multicolored	.25	.25
93	A13	20c multicolored	.25	.30
94	A13	30c multicolored	.35	.40
95	A13	40c multicolored	.50	.70
		Nos. 92-95 (4)	1.35	1.65

Squirrelfish — A14

Fish: 2c, Yellow-banded goatfish. 4c, Imperial angelfish. 5c, Rainbow butterfly. 6c, Blue
angelfish. 8c, Blue striped snapper. 10c,
Orange clownfish. 15c, Chevroned coralfish.
20c, Fairy cod. 25c, Clown triggerfish. 30c,
Long-nosed butterfly. 35c, Yellowfin tuna. 40c,
Spotted eagle ray. 45c, Black-tipped rock cod.
50c, Hammerhead shark. 70c, Lionfish, vert.
$1, White-barred triggerfish, vert. $2, Beaked
coralfish, vert. $5, Tiger shark, vert.

1979, Jan. 24   Litho.   Perf. 14
96	A14	1c multicolored	.25	.25
97	A14	2c multicolored	.25	.25
98	A14	4c multicolored	.25	.25
99	A14	5c multicolored	.25	.25
100	A14	6c multicolored	.25	.25
101	A14	8c multicolored	.25	.25
102	A14	10c multicolored	.25	.25
103	A14	15c multicolored	.25	.25
104	A14	20c multicolored	.25	.25
105	A14	25c multicolored	.25	.25
106	A14	30c multicolored	.25	.25
107	A14	35c multicolored	.30	.30
108	A14	40c multicolored	.35	.35
108A	A14	45c multicolored	1.90	1.25
109	A14	50c multicolored	.55	.55
110	A14	70c multicolored	.60	.60
111	A14	$1 multicolored	.80	.80
112	A14	$2 multicolored	1.90	1.90
113	A14	$5 multicolored	4.50	4.50
		Nos. 96-113 (19)	13.65	13.00

No. 108A issued June 16, 1981.
#101, 104, 106, 108 and #102, 105, 107,
108A were also issued in booklet panes of 4.
For surcharge & overprints see #150, O1-
O19.

Capt. Cook
A15

Designs: 30c, Flag raising on new island.
40c, Observation of transit of Venus. $1, Death
of Capt. Cook.

1979, Feb. 14   Perf. 14x14½
114	A15	8c multicolored	.25	.25
115	A15	30c multicolored	.25	.25
116	A15	40c multicolored	.25	.25
117	A15	$1 multicolored	.40	.40
a.		Strip of 4, #114-117	2.75	2.75

Bicentenary of death of Capt. James Cook
(1728-1779). Nos. 114-117 printed se-tenant
horizontally in sheets of 12 (4x3) with gutters
between horizontal rows.

Grumman Goose over
Nukulaelae — A16

Grumman Goose over: 20c, Vaitupu. 30c,
Nui. 40c, Funafuti.

1979, May 16   Litho.   Perf. 14x13½
118	A16	8c multicolored	.35	.35
119	A16	20c multicolored	.35	.35
120	A16	30c multicolored	.45	.55
121	A16	40c multicolored	.65	.65
		Nos. 118-121 (4)	1.80	1.90

Inauguration of internal air service.

Hill, Tuvalu No. 16, Letterbox, London,
1855 — A17

Hill, Stamps of Tuvalu and: 40c, No. 17,
Penny Black. $1, No. 18, mail coach.

1979, Aug. 20   Litho.   Perf. 13½x14
122	A17	30c multicolored	.30	.30
123	A17	40c multicolored	.30	.30
124	A17	$1 multicolored	.75	.75
a.		Souvenir sheet of 3, #122-124	1.90	1.90
		Nos. 122-124 (3)	1.35	1.35

Sir Rowland Hill (1795-1879), originator of
penny postage.

Boy — A18

Designs: Children of Tuvalu.

1979, Oct. 20   Litho.   Perf. 14
125	A18	8c multicolored	.25	.25
126	A18	20c multicolored	.25	.25
127	A18	30c multicolored	.30	.30
128	A18	40c multicolored	.35	.35
		Nos. 125-128 (4)	1.15	1.15

International Year of the Child.

Cowry
Shells
A19

1980, Feb.   Litho.   Perf. 14
129	A19	8c Cypraea Argus	.35	.35
130	A19	20c Cypraea scurra	.35	.35
131	A19	30c Cypraea carneola	.45	.45
132	A19	40c Cypraea aurantium	.60	.60
		Nos. 129-132 (4)	1.75	1.75

Philatelic Bureau, Funafuti, Tuvalu No. 28, Arms, London 1980 Emblem — A20

Coat of Arms, London 1980 Emblem and: 20c, Gilbert and Ellice #41, Nukulaelae cancel, Tuvalu #24. 30c, US airmail cover. $1, Map of Tuvalu.

1980, Apr. 30   Litho.   Perf. 13½x14
133	A20	10c multicolored	.30	.30
134	A20	20c multicolored	.30	.30
135	A20	30c multicolored	.35	.35
136	A20	$1 multicolored	.95	.95
a.		Souvenir sheet of 4, #133-136	2.25	2.25
		Nos. 133-136 (4)	1.90	1.90

London 80 Intl. Stamp Exhib., May 6-14.

Queen Mother Elizabeth, 80th Birthday — A21

1980, Aug. 14   Litho.   Perf. 14
137 A21 50c multicolored   .50 .50

Issued in sheets of 10 plus 2 labels.

Aethaloessa Calidalis — A22

1980, Aug. 20   Litho.   Perf. 14
138	A22	8c shown	.25	.25
139	A22	20c Parotis suralis	.25	.25
140	A22	30c Dudua aprobola	.35	.35
141	A22	40c Decadarchis simulans	.50	.50
		Nos. 138-141 (4)	1.35	1.35

Air Pacific Heron (First Regular Air Service to Tuvalu, 1964) — A23

Aviation Anniversaries: 20c, Hawker Siddeley 748 (air service to Tuvalu). 30c, Sunderland Flying Boat (War time service to Funafuti, 1945. 40c, Orville Wright and Flyer (Wright brothers' first flight, 1903).

1980, Nov. 5   Litho.   Perf. 14
142	A23	8c multicolored	.25	.25
143	A23	20c multicolored	.25	.25
144	A23	30c multicolored	.35	.25
145	A23	40c multicolored	.50	.45
		Nos. 142-145 (4)	1.35	1.20

Hypolimnas Bolina Elliciana — A24

1981, Feb. 3   Litho.   Perf. 14½
146	A24	8c shown	.35	.35
147	A24	20c Hypolimnas, diff.	.40	.40
148	A24	30c Hypolimnas, diff.	.50	.50
149	A24	40c Junonia vallida	.85	.85
		Nos. 146-149 (4)	2.10	2.10

No. 109 Surcharged

1981, Feb. 24   Litho.   Perf. 14
150 A14 45c on 50c multicolored   .60 .60

Elizabeth, 1809 A25

Wmk. 373
1981, May 13   Litho.   Perf. 14
151	A25	10c shown	.25	.25
152	A25	25c Rebecca, 1819	.25	.25
153	A25	35c Independence II, 1821	.35	.35
154	A25	40c Basilisk, 1872	.45	.45
155	A25	45c Royalist, 1890	.50	.50
156	A25	50c Olivebank, 1920	.65	.65
		Nos. 151-156 (6)	2.45	2.45

See Nos. 216-221, 353-356, 410-413.

Prince Charles, Lady Diana, Royal Yacht Charlotte A25a

Prince Charles and Lady Diana — A25b

Wmk. 380
1981, July 10   Litho.   Perf. 14
157	A25a	10c Couple, Carolina	.25	.25
a.		Blkt. pane of 4, perf. 12, unwmkd.	.60	
158	A25b	10c Couple	.40	.40
159	A25a	45c Victoria and Albert III	.25	.25
160	A25b	45c like #158	.50	.50
a.		Blkt. pane of 2, perf. 12, unwmkd.	1.00	
161	A25a	$2 Britannia	1.00	1.00
162	A25b	$2 like #158	2.75	2.75
		Nos. 157-162 (6)	5.15	5.15

Royal wedding. Issued in sheets of 7 (6 design A25a; 1 design A25b). Set of 3 $12. For surcharges see Nos. B1-B2.

Souvenir Sheet

1981, Dec.   Litho.   Perf. 12
163 A25b $1.50 Couple   1.00 1.00

Admission to UPU — A26

Wmk. Harrison's, London
1981, Nov. 19   Engr.   Perf. 14½x14
164	A26	70c dark blue	.50	.50
165	A26	$1 dark red brown	.75	.75
a.		Souv. sheet of 2, #164-165, unwmkd.	2.00	2.00

Amatuku Maritime School — A27

1982, Feb. 17   Litho.   Perf. 13½x14
166	A27	10c Map	.35	.35
167	A27	25c Motorboat	.35	.35
168	A27	35c School, dock	.45	.45
169	A27	45c Flag, ship	.65	.65
		Nos. 166-169 (4)	1.80	1.80

A27a

Wmk. 380
1982, May 19   Litho.   Perf. 14
170	A27a	10c Caroline of Brandenburg-Ansbach, 1714	.25	.25
171	A27a	45c Brandenburg-Ansbach arms	.25	.25
172	A27a	$1.50 Diana	1.00	1.00
		Nos. 170-172 (3)	1.50	1.50

21st birthday of Princess Diana, July 1.

#170-172 Overprinted: "ROYAL BABY"
1982, July 14   Litho.   Perf. 14
173	A27a	10c multicolored	.30	.30
174	A27a	45c multicolored	.30	.30
175	A27a	$1.50 multicolored	.90	.90
		Nos. 173-175 (3)	1.50	1.50

Birth of Prince William of Wales, June 21.

Scouting Year — A28

1982, Aug. 18
176	A28	10c Emblems	.25	.25
177	A28	25c Campfire	.40	.35
178	A28	35c Parade	.55	.40
179	A28	45c Scout	.70	.45
		Nos. 176-179 (4)	1.90	1.45

Visit of Queen Elizabeth II and Prince Philip — A29

1982, Oct. 26   Litho.   Perf. 14
180	A29	25c Arms, Duke of Edinburgh's Personal Standard	.25	.25
181	A29	45c Flags	.50	.50
182	A29	50c Queen Elizabeth II, maps	.55	.55
a.		Souvenir sheet of 3, #180-182	1.50	1.50
		Nos. 180-182 (3)	1.30	1.30

Handicrafts — A30

1c, Fisherman's hat, lures, hooks. 2c, Cowrie shell handbags. 5c, Wedding & baby food baskets. 10c, Canoe model. 15c, Women's sun hats. 20c, Climbing rope. 25c, Pandanus baskets. 30c, Tray, coconut stands. 35c, Pandanus pillows, shell necklaces. 40c, Round baskets, fans. 45c, Reef sandals, fish trap. 50c, Rat trap, vert. 60c, Waterproof boxes,

vert. $1, Pump drill, adze, vert. $2, Fisherman's hat, canoe bailers, vert. $5, Fishing rod, lures, scoop nets, vert.

1983-84   Litho.   Perf. 14
183	A30	1c multicolored	.35	.25
184	A30	2c multicolored	.35	.25
185	A30	5c multicolored	.35	.25
186	A30	10c multicolored	.35	.25
186A	A30	15c multicolored	2.50	2.75
187	A30	20c multicolored	.35	.25
188	A30	25c multicolored	.35	.25
188A	A30	30c multicolored	2.25	2.25
189	A30	35c multicolored	.50	.40
190	A30	40c multicolored	.35	.55
191	A30	45c multicolored	.40	.65
192	A30	50c multicolored	.50	.70
192A	A30	60c multicolored	3.25	2.25
193	A30	$1 multicolored	.50	.70
194	A30	$2 multicolored	.70	.85
195	A30	$5 multicolored	1.10	1.25
		Nos. 183-195 (16)	14.15	13.85

Issued: 15c, 1984; others, 3/14/83.
For surcharges & overprints see #207, 230, O20-O32.

Commonwealth Day — A31

Wmk. 373
1983, Mar. 14   Litho.   Perf. 14
196	A31	20c Fishing industry	.35	.25
197	A31	35c Traditional dancing	.35	.30
198	A31	45c Satellite view	.45	.40
199	A31	50c First container ship	.60	.50
		Nos. 196-199 (4)	1.75	1.45

Dragonflies — A32

1983, May 25   Wmk. 380
200	A32	10c Pantala flavescens	.25	.25
201	A32	35c Anax guttatus	.65	.65
202	A32	40c Tholymis tillarga	.75	.75
203	A32	50c Diplacodes bipunctata	.85	.85
		Nos. 200-203 (4)	2.50	2.50

Boys Brigade Centenary — A33

1983, Aug. 10   Wmk. 373
204	A33	10c Running, emblem	.30	.30
205	A33	35c Canoeing	.65	.65
206	A33	$1 Officer, boys	1.50	1.50
		Nos. 204-206 (3)	2.45	2.45

No. 193 Surcharged in Black
1983, Aug. 26   Wmk. 380
207 A30 60c on $1 multi   1.00 .60

First Manned Flight Bicentenary — A34

1983, Sept. 21   Wmk. 373
208	A34	25c Montgolfier balloon, vert.	.40	.40
209	A34	35c McKinnon Turbo Goose	.50	.50
210	A34	45c Beechcraft Super King Air 200	.60	.60

211 A34 50c Double Eagle II Balloon, vert. .70 .70
　a. Souvenir sheet of 4, #208-211 3.00 3.00
　　Nos. 208-211 (4) 2.20 2.20

World Communications Year — A35

1983, Nov. 18 **Wmk. 380**
212 A35 25c Conch Shell Trumpet, vert. .25 .25
213 A35 35c Radio Operator, vert. .40 .40
214 A35 45c Teleprinter .55 .55
215 A35 50c Transmitting station .60 .60
　　Nos. 212-215 (4) 1.80 1.80

Ship Type of 1981
1984, Feb. 16 **Wmk. 380**
216 A25 10c Titus, 1897 .25 .25
217 A25 20c Malaita, 1905 .25 .25
218 A25 25c Aymeric, 1906 .30 .30
219 A25 35c Anshun, 1965 .40 .40
220 A25 45c Beaverbank, 1970 .50 .50
221 A25 50c Benjamin Bowring, 1981 .65 .65
　　Nos. 216-221 (6) 2.35 2.35

Leaders of the World
Large quantities of some Leaders of the World issues were sold at a fraction of face value when the printer was liquidated.

Historic Locomotives — A36

Perf. 12½x13
1984, Feb. 29 **Unwmk.**
Se-tenant Pairs, #a.-b.
　a. — Side and front views.
　b. — Action scene.
222 A36 1c Class GS-4, US, 1941 .25 .25
223 A36 15c AD-60, Australia, 1952 .30 .30
224 A36 40c C38, Australia, 1943 .90 .90
225 A36 60c Achilles England, 1892 1.25 1.25
　　Nos. 222-225 (4) 2.70 2.70

See Nos. 235-246, 291-294, 320-323.

No. 191 Surcharged
Wmk. 380
1984, Feb. 1 **Litho.** **Perf. 14**
230 A30 30c on 45c multi .60 .60

For overprint see No. O25.

Beach Flowers A38

1984, May 30
231 A38 25c Ipomoea pes-caprae .40 .40
232 A38 45c Ipomoea macrantha .60 .60
233 A38 50c Triumfetta procumbens .80 .80
234 A38 60c Portulaca quadrifida 1.00 1.00
　　Nos. 231-234 (4) 2.80 2.80

Train Type of 1984
1984 **Litho.** **Perf. 12½x13**
Se-tenant Pairs, #a.-b.
　a. — Side and front views.
　b. — Action scene.
235 A36 1c Class 9700, Japan, 1897 .40 .40
236 A36 10c Casey Jones, US, 1896 .40 .40
237 A36 15c Class 231C/K, France, 1909 .40 .40
238 A36 15c Triplex, US, 1914 .40 .40
239 A36 20c Class 370, Gt. Britain, 1981 .40 .40
240 A36 25c Class 4F, Gt. Britain, 1924 .50 .50
241 A36 30c Class 640, Italy, 1907 .60 .60
242 A36 40c Tornado, Gt. Britain, 1888 .80 .80
243 A36 50c Broadlands, Gt. Britain, 1967 1.00 1.00
244 A36 60c Locomotion, Gt. Britain, 1825 1.25 1.25
245 A36 $1 C57, Japan, 1937 2.00 2.00
246 A36 $1 Class 4500, France, 1906 2.00 2.00
　　Nos. 235-246 (12) 10.15 10.15

Issued: #235, 237, 241, 245, 10/4; others, 6/27.

15th South Pacific Forum A38a

1984, Aug. 21 **Litho.** **Perf. 14**
255 A38a 60c National flag .55 .55
256 A38a 60c Tuvalu crest .55 .55

Ausipex '84 A38b

1984, Aug. 21 **Perf. 14**
257 A38b 60c Exhib. emblem .55 .55
258 A38b 60c Royal Exhibi. Building .55 .55

A. Shrewsbury Playing Cricket — A39

Cricket players in action or portrait.

1984, Nov. 5 **Litho.** **Perf. 12½**
Se-tenant Pairs #a.-b.
259 A39 5c shown .35 .35
260 A39 30c H. Verity 1.00 1.00
261 A39 50c E.H. Hendren 1.00 1.00
262 A39 60c J. Briggs 1.25 1.25
　　Nos. 259-262 (4) 3.60 3.60

Drawings, Christmas 1984 — A40

1984, Nov. 14 **Litho.** **Perf. 14½x14**
267 A40 15c By Eli Faalata .30 .30
268 A40 40c By Toakai Niutao .40 .40
269 A40 50c By Falesa Teuila .50 .50
270 A40 60c By Piuani Talie .65 .65
　　Nos. 267-270 (4) 1.85 1.85

Classic Automobiles — A41

Sketch listed first followed by angled view.

1984, Dec. 7 **Litho.** **Perf. 12½x13**
Se-tenant Pairs, #a.-b.
　a. — Side and front views.
　b. — Action scene.
271 A41 1c Morris Minor, 1949 .50 .50
272 A41 15c Studebaker Avanti, 1963 .50 .50
273 A41 50c Chevrolet International Six, 1929 1.25 1.25
274 A41 $1 Allard J2, 1950 2.50 2.50
　　Nos. 271-274 (4) 4.75 4.75

See Nos. 299-302, 332-339, 396-396E, 414-425.

John J. Audubon — A42

#279a, Common flicker. #279b, Say's phoebe. #280a, Townsend's warbler. #280b, Bohemian waxwing. #281a, Prothonotary warbler. #281b, Worm-eating warbler. #282a, Broad-winged hawk. #282b, Northern harrier.

1985, Feb. 12 **Litho.** **Perf. 12½**
279 A42 1c Pair, #a.-b. .40 .40
280 A42 25c Pair, #a.-b. .80 .80
281 A42 50c Pair, #a.-b. 1.60 1.60
282 A42 70c Pair, #a.-b. 2.00 2.00
　　Nos. 279-282 (4) 4.80 4.80

Birds and Eggs A43

1985, Feb. 27 **Perf. 14**
287 A43 15c Black-naped tern .60 .35
288 A43 40c Black noddy 1.25 .85
289 A43 50c White-tailed tropic-bird 1.60 .95
290 A43 60c Sooty tern 2.00 1.25
　　Nos. 287-290 (4) 5.45 3.40

Train Type of 1984
1985, Mar. 19 **Perf. 12½**
Se-tenant Pairs, #a.-b.
　a. — Side and front views.
　b. — Action scene.
291 A36 5c Churchward, U.K. .35 .35
292 A36 10c Class K.F., China .35 .35
293 A36 30c Class 99.77, East Germany .90 .90
294 A36 $1 Pearson, U.K. 3.00 3.00
　　Nos. 291-294 (4) 4.60 4.60

Automobile Type of 1984
1985, Apr. 3
Se-tenant Pairs, #a.-b.
　a. — Side and front views.
　b. — Action scene.
299 A41 1c Rickenbacker, 1923 .50 .50
300 A41 20c Detroit-Electric, 1914 .50 .50

301 A41 50c Packard Clipper, 1941 1.25 1.25
302 A41 70c Audi Quattro, 1982 1.90 1.90
　　Nos. 299-302 (4) 4.15 4.15

World War II Aircraft A44

1985, May 29 **Litho.** **Perf. 14**
307 A44 15c Curtiss P-40N 1.75 1.00
308 A44 40c Consolidated B-24D Liberator 2.00 1.50
309 A44 50c Lockheed PV-1 Ventura 2.00 2.25
310 A44 60c Douglas C-54 Skymaster 2.00 2.25
　a. Souvenir sheet of 4, #307-310 7.00 7.00
　　Nos. 307-310 (4) 7.75 7.00

Queen Mother, 85th Birthday — A45

#310a, Facing right. #310b, Facing left. #311a, 317a, Facing right. #311b, 317b, Facing front. #312a, 316a, Waving to crowd. #312b, 316b, Facing front. #313a, Facing front. #313b, Facing left. #314a, As a young woman. #314b, as Queen Consort.

1985-86 **Litho.** **Perf. 12½**
311 A45 5c Pair, #a.-b. .45 .45
312 A45 30c Pair, #a.-b. .70 .70
313 A45 60c Pair, #a.-b. 1.40 1.40
314 A45 $1 Pair, #a.-b. 2.10 2.10
　　Nos. 311-314 (4) 4.65 4.65

Souvenir Sheets
315 A45 $1.20 #a.-b. 2.50 2.50
316 A45 $2 #a.-b. 6.25 6.25
317 A45 $3 #a.-b. 8.75 8.75

Issued: #316-317, 6/10/86; others, 7/4/85.

Train Type of 1984
1985, Sept. 18
Se-tenant Pairs, #a.-b.
　a. — Side and front views.
　b. — Action scene.
320 A36 10c 1936 Green Arrow, U.K. .40 .40
321 A36 40c 1982 G.M. (EMD) SD-50, US 1.10 1.10
322 A36 65c 1932 DRG Flying Hamburger, Germany 1.50 1.50
323 A36 $1 1908 JNR Class 1070, Japan 1.60 1.60
　　Nos. 320-323 (4) 4.60 4.60

Girl Guides, 75th Anniv. — A46

1985, Aug. 28 **Litho.** **Perf. 15**
328 A46 15c Playing guitar .35 .25
329 A46 40c Camping .70 .70
330 A46 50c Flag bearer .85 .85
331 A46 60c Guides' salute 1.00 1.00
　a. Souvenir sheet of 4, #328-331 3.25 3.25
　　Nos. 328-331 (4) 2.90 2.80

Car Type of 1984
5c, 1929 Cord L-29, US. 10c, 1932 Horch 670 V-12, Germany. 15c, 1901 Lanchester, UK. 35c, 1950 Citroen 2 CV, France. 40c, 1957 MGA, UK. 55c, 1962 Ferrari 250-GTO, Italy. $1, 1932 Ford V-8, US. $1.50, 1977 Aston Martin-Lagonda, UK.

1985, Oct. 8   *Perf. 12½*
a. — Side and front views.
b. — Action scene.
332-339 A41 Set of 8 pairs   7.75   7.75

Crabs
A47

1986, Jan. 7   *Perf. 15*
348 A47 15c Stalk-eyed ghost   .40   .40
349 A47 40c Red and white
        painted   1.10   1.10
350 A47 50c Red-spotted   1.25   1.25
351 A47 60c Red hermit   1.60   1.60
    Nos. 348-351 (4)   4.35   4.35

Souvenir Sheet of 2

Events — A48

#352a, American and Soviet flags, chess board & knight. #352b, Rotary Intl. emblem.

1986, Mar. 19   Litho.   *Perf. 13x12½*
352 A48 $3 #a.-b.   8.00   8.00

Fischer and Karpov, world chess champions; Rotary Intl., 80th anniv.
No. 352 exists with plain or decorated border.

Ship Type of 1981
1986, Apr. 14   *Perf. 15*
353 A25 15c Messenger of
        Peace   .35   .35
354 A25 40c John Wesley   .90   .90
355 A25 50c Duff   1.10   1.10
356 A25 60c Triton   1.25   1.25
    Nos. 353-356 (4)   3.60   3.60

Queen Elizabeth II, 60th
Birthday — A49

Various portraits.

1986, Apr. 21   *Perf. 12½*
357 A49 10c multicolored   .40   .40
358 A49 90c multicolored   .60   .60
359 A49 $1.50 multicolored   1.00   1.00
360 A49 $3 multi, vert.   2.00   2.00
    Nos. 357-360 (4)   4.00   4.00
Souvenir Sheet
361 A49 $4 multicolored   4.50   4.50

Peace
Corps,
25th
Anniv.
A50

1986, May 22   *Perf. 14*
362 A50 50c multicolored   1.00   1.00
For overprint see No. 374.

A51

1986, May 22   *Perf. 14x13½*
363 A51 60c multicolored   .90   .90
AMERIPEX '86.

A52

Players and teams.

1986, June 30   Litho.   *Perf. 15*
364 A52 1c So. Korea   .25   .25
365 A52 5c France   .25   .25
366 A52 10c W. Germany,
        1974   .25   .25
367 A52 40c Italy   .45   .45
Size: 60x40mm
Perf. 13x12½
368 A52 60c W. Germany vs.
        Holland, 1974   .55   .55
369 A52 $1 Canada   .95   .95
370 A52 $2 No. Ireland   2.10   2.10
371 A52 $3 England   2.75   2.75
    Nos. 364-371 (8)   7.55   7.55
Souvenir Sheets
372 A52 $1.50 like #369   2.10   2.10
373 A52 $2.50 like #370   3.50   3.50

1986 World Cup Soccer Championships. Nos. 366 and 368 picture emblem; others picture character trademark.

No. 362 Ovptd. with STAMPEX '86 Emblem
1986, Aug. 4   Litho.   *Perf. 14*
374 A50 50c multicolored   .70   .70

A53

Wedding of Prince Andrew and Sarah
Ferguson — A54

#381a, Andrew, vert. #381b, Couple, vert. #382a, Andrew. #382b, Princess Diana, Sarah.
Perf. 12½
1986, July 18   Litho.   Unwmk.
381 A53 60c Pair, #a.-b.   1.00   1.00
382 A53 $1 Pair, #a.-b.   2.00   2.00
Souvenir Sheet
Perf. 13x12½
383 A54 $6 Newlyweds   5.00   5.00
No. 382a pictures Westminster Abbey in LR. For overprints see Nos. 389-390.

Geckos
A55

1986, July 30   Litho.   *Perf. 14*
384 A55 15c Mourning gecko   .40   .30
385 A55 40c Oceanic stump-toed   1.40   1.10
386 A55 50c Azure-tailed skink   1.75   1.40
387 A55 60c Moth skink   2.50   1.90
    Nos. 384-387 (4)   6.05   4.70

Souvenir Sheet

South
Pacific
Forum,
15th
Anniv.
A56

Flags and maps: a, Australia. b, Cook Islands. c, Micronesia. d, Fiji. e, Kiribati. f, Nauru. g, New Zealand. h, Niue. i, Papua New Guinea. j, Solomon Islands. k, Tonga. l, Tuvalu. m, Vanuatu. n, Western Samoa.

Wmk. 380
1986, Aug. 4   *Perf. 15*
388   Sheet of 14 + label   9.00   9.00
a.-n.   A56 40c any single   .60   .60
No. 388 has center label picturing Executive Committee headquarters, Suva, Fiji.

Nos. 381-382 Ovptd. "Congratulations to T.R.H. The Duke & Duchess of York" in Silver
1986   Unwmk.   *Perf. 12½*
389 A53 60c Pair, #a.-b.   1.75   1.75
390 A53 $1 Pair, #a.-b.   2.75   2.75
    Exist tete-beche.

Car Type of 1984
15c, 1953 Cooper, UK. 40c, 1964 Rover 2000, UK. 50c, 1930 Ruxton, US. 60c, 1950 Jowett Jupiter, UK. 90c, 1964 Cobra Daytona Coupe, US. $1.50, 1903 Packard Model F "Old Pacific," US.
1986, Oct.   Litho.   *Perf. 12½*
Se-tenant Pairs, #a.-b.
a. — Side and front views.
b. — Action scene.
391-396 A41 Set of 6 pairs   7.75   7.75

Marine
Life
A57

1986, Nov. 5   Unwmk.   *Perf. 14*
397 A57 15c Sea star   1.10   1.10
398 A57 40c Pencil urchin   1.90   1.90
399 A57 50c Fragile coral   2.10   2.10
400 A57 60c Pink coral   2.40   2.40
    Nos. 397-400 (4)   7.50   7.50

See Nos. 465-468, 524-527.

Souvenir Sheets

Statue of Liberty, Cent. — A58

Various views of the statue.

1986, Nov. 24
401 A58 $1.25 multicolored   1.10   1.10
402 A58 $1.50 multicolored   1.50   1.50
403 A58 $1.80 multicolored   1.90   1.90
404 A58 $2 multicolored   2.10   2.10
405 A58 $2.25 multicolored   2.40   2.40
406 A58 $2.50 multicolored   2.50   2.50
407 A58 $3 multicolored   3.25   3.25
408 A58 $3.25 multicolored   3.50   3.50
409 A58 $3.50 multicolored   4.00   4.00
    Nos. 401-409 (9)   22.25   22.25

Ships Type of 1981
1987, Feb. 4   Unwmk.   *Perf. 14*
410 A25 15c Southern Cross IV   1.00   1.00
411 A25 40c John Williams VI   2.25   2.25
412 A25 50c John Williams IV   2.40   2.40
413 A25 60c M.S. Southern
        Cross   2.40   2.40
    Nos. 410-413 (4)   8.05   8.05

Car Type of 1984
1c, 1938 Talbot-Lago, France. 2c, 1930 Dupont Model G, US. 5c, 1950 Riley RM, U.K. 10c, 1915 Chevrolet Baby Grand, US. 20c, 1968 Shelby Mustang GT 500 KR, US. 30c, 1952 Ferrari 212 Export Barchetta, Italy. 40c, 1912 Peerless Model 48-Six, US. 50c, 1954 Sunbeam Alpine, U.K. 60c, 1969 Matra-Ford MS80, France. 70c, 1934 Squire 1-Litre, U.K. 75c, 1931 Talbot 105, U.K. $1, 1928 Plymouth Model Q, US.

Perf. 12½
1987, May 7   Litho.   Unwmk.
Se-tenant Pairs, #a.-b.
a. — Side and front views.
b. — Action scene.
414-425 A41 Set of 12 pairs,
        #a.-b.   8.75   8.75
425c   Souv. sheet of 2   4.50   4.50

Ferns — A59

1987, July 7   Wmk. 380   *Perf. 14*
438 A59 15c Nephrolepis
        saligna   .25   .25
439 A59 40c Asplenium nidus   .85   .85
440 A59 50c Microsorum
        scolopendria   1.10   1.10
441 A59 60c Pteris tripartita   1.25   1.25
    Nos. 438-441 (4)   3.45   3.45
Souvenir Sheet
442 A59 $1.50 Psilotum nudum   3.25   3.25

A60

#443a, 444b, 445a, 456b, Flowers, all diff. #443b, 444a, 445b, 456a, Woman wearing fou, all diff.

1987, Aug. 12 Wmk. 380
443	A60	15c	Pair, #a.-b.	.50	.50
444	A60	40c	Pair, #a.-b.	1.25	1.25
445	A60	50c	Pair, #a.-b.	1.50	1.50
446	A60	60c	Pair, #a.-b.	2.00	2.00
			Nos. 443-446 (4)	5.25	5.25

Crayfish and Coconut Crabs A61

Wmk. 380
1987, Nov. 11 Litho. *Perf. 14*
451	A61	40c	Coconut crabs	1.50	1.10
452	A61	50c	Painted crayfish	1.90	1.40
453	A61	60c	Ocean crayfish	2.10	1.75
			Nos. 451-453 (3)	5.50	4.25

Photograph of Queen Victoria, 1897, by Downey — A62

60c, Elizabeth and Philip on their wedding day, 1947. 80c, Elizabeth, Charles, Philip, c. 1950. $1, Elizabeth, Anne, 1950. $2, Elizabeth, 1970. $3, Elizabeth, children, 1950.

1987, Nov. 20 Unwmk. *Perf. 15*
454-458	A62		Set of 5	6.00 6.00

Souvenir Sheet
459		A62	$3 red org & blk	5.25 5.25

Accession of Queen Victoria to the throne of England, sesquicentennial; wedding of Queen Elizabeth II and Prince Philip, 40th anniv.

16th World Scout Jamboree, Australia, 1987-88 — A63

Jamboree and Australia bicentennial emblems plus: 40c, Aborigine, Ayer's Rock. 60c, Capt. Cook, by Dance, and HMS Endeavor. $1, Scout and Scout Park Arch. $1.50, Koala and kangaroo. $2.50, Lord and Lady Baden-Powell.

Perf. 13x12½
1987, Dec. 2 Litho. Unwmk.
460	A63	40c	multicolored	.55	.55
461	A63	60c	multicolored	.80	.80
462	A63	$1	multicolored	1.50	1.50
463	A63	$1.50	multicolored	2.10	2.10
			Nos. 460-463 (4)	4.95	4.95

Souvenir Sheet
464	A63	$2.50	multicolored	3.75	3.75

Marine Life Type of 1986
Unwmk.
1988, Feb. 29 Litho. *Perf. 15*
465	A57	15c	Spanish dancer	.65	.35
466	A57	40c	Hard corals	1.60	.75
467	A57	50c	Feather stars	1.90	.95
468	A57	60c	Staghorn corals	2.25	1.10
			Nos. 465-468 (4)	6.40	3.15

Birds A64

1988, Mar. 2 *Perf. 15*
469	A64	5c	Jungle fowl	.25	.25
470	A64	10c	White tern	.25	.25
471	A64	15c	Brown noddy	.25	.25
472	A64	20c	Phoenix petrel	.25	.25
473	A64	25c	Pacific golden plover	.25	.25
474	A64	30c	Crested tern	.30	.30
475	A64	35c	Sooty tern	.35	.35
476	A64	40c	Bristle-thighed curlew	.40	.40
477	A64	45c	Eastern bar-tailed godwit	.45	.45
478	A64	50c	Reef heron	.50	.50
479	A64	55c	Greater frigatebird	.55	.55
480	A64	60c	Red-footed booby	.65	.65
481	A64	70c	Red-necked stint	.75	.75
482	A64	$1	New Zealand long-tailed cuckoo	1.25	1.25
483	A64	$2	Red-tailed tropicbird	2.25	2.25
484	A64	$5	Banded rail	5.50	5.50
			Nos. 469-484 (16)	14.20	14.20

For overprints see Nos. 676-679, 796-799, O33-O48.

Intl. Red Cross and Red Crescent Organizations, 125th Annivs. — A65

Perf. 12½
1988, May 9 Litho. Unwmk.
485	A65	15c	Jean-Henri Dunant	.30	.30
486	A65	40c	Junior Red Cross	.35	.35
487	A65	50c	Care for the handicapped	.55	.55
488	A65	60c	First aid training	.60	.60
			Nos. 485-488 (4)	1.80	1.80

Souvenir Sheet
489	A65	$1.50	Lecture	1.90	1.90

A66

Voyages of Capt. Cook — A67

Designs: 20c, HMS *Endeavour* (starboard side). 40c, *Endeavour* (stern). 50c, Landing, Tahiti, 1769, vert. 60c, Maori chief, vert. 80c, *Resolution* and native Hawaiian sail ship. $1, Cook, by Sir Nathaniel Dance-Holland (1735-1811), vert. $2.50, Antarctic icebergs surrounding the *Resolution*.

1988, June 15 Litho. *Perf. 12½*
490-495	A66		Set of 6	5.75 5.75

Souvenir Sheet
496		A67	$2.50 shown	10.00 10.00

Fungi — A68

1988, July 25 Litho. *Perf. 15*
497	A68	40c	Ganoderma applanatum	1.25	1.25
498	A68	50c	Pseudoepicoccum cocos	1.50	1.50
499	A68	60c	Rigidoporus zonalis	1.75	1.75
500	A68	90c	Rigidoporus microporus	2.50	2.50
			Nos. 497-500 (4)	7.00	7.00

See Nos. 520-523.

1988 Summer Olympics, Seoul — A69

Perf. 12½
1988, Aug. 19 Litho. Unwmk.
501	A69	10c	Rifles, target	.40	.40
502	A69	20c	Judo	.65	.65
503	A69	40c	One-man kayak	1.50	1.50
504	A69	60c	Swimming	2.25	2.25
505	A69	80c	Yachting	2.75	2.75
506	A69	$1	Balance beam	4.00	4.00
			Nos. 501-506 (6)	11.55	11.55

Natl. Independence, 10th Anniv. — A70

Wmk. 380
1988, Sept. 28 Litho. *Perf. 14*
507	A70	60c	Queen Elizabeth in boat	1.10	1.10
a.			Souvenir sheet of 1	1.10	1.10
508	A70	90c	In sedan chair	1.60	1.60
a.			Souvenir sheet of 1	1.60	1.60
509	A70	$1	shown	1.90	1.90
a.			Souvenir sheet of 1	1.90	1.90
510	A70	$1.20	Seated at dais	2.40	2.40
a.			Souvenir sheet of 1	2.40	2.40
			Nos. 507-510 (4)	7.00	7.00

Nos. 507-508 and 510 vert.

Christmas — A71

Unwmk.
1988, Dec. 5 Litho. *Perf. 14*
511	A71	15c	Mary	.40	.40
512	A71	40c	Christ child	1.00	1.00
513	A71	60c	Joseph	1.50	1.50
			Nos. 511-513 (3)	2.90	2.90

Souvenir Sheet
514	A71	$1.50	Heraldic angel	2.75	2.75

Palm-frond or Pandanus-leaf Skirts — A72

1989, Mar. 31 Litho. *Perf. 14*
515	A72	40c	multi	1.00	1.00
516	A72	50c	multi, diff.	1.25	1.25
517	A72	60c	multi, diff.	1.50	1.50
518	A72	90c	multi, diff.	2.10	2.10
			Nos. 515-518 (4)	5.85	5.85

Souvenir Sheet
519	A72	$1.50	multi, vert.	3.50	3.50

Fungi Type of 1988
1989, May 24 Litho. *Perf. 14*
520	A68	40c	Trametes muelleri	1.25	1.25
521	A68	50c	Pestalotiopsis palmarum	2.50	2.50
522	A68	60c	Trametes cingulata	3.00	3.00
523	A68	90c	Schizophyllum commune	4.75	4.75
			Nos. 520-523 (4)	11.50	11.50

Marine Life Type of 1986
1989, July 31 Litho. *Perf. 14*
524	A57	40c	Pennant coralfish	1.90	1.90
525	A57	50c	Anemone fish	2.40	2.40
526	A57	60c	Batfish	2.75	2.75
527	A57	90c	Threadfin coralfish	5.00	5.00
a.			Miniature sheet of 4, #524-527	12.00	12.00
			Nos. 524-527 (4)	12.05	12.05

Souvenir Sheet

Maiden Voyage of M.V. *Nivaga II*, 1988 — A73

1989, Oct. 9 Litho. *Perf. 14*
528	A73	$1.50 multicolored	5.75 5.75

Christmas — A74

Elizabeth II 60th Birthday Type

1986, Apr. 21 *Perf. 13x12½, 12½x13*
51	A49	5c Scarf	.30	.30
52	A49	40c Tiara	.35	.35
53	A49	$2 Bareheaded	1.40	1.40
54	A49	$4 Tiara, vert.	3.50	3.50
		Nos. 51-54 (4)	5.55	5.55

Souvenir Sheet
55	A49	$5 Blue hat	4.25	4.25

For overprints see Nos. 65-69.

Royal Wedding Type of 1986

#58a, Couple, vert. #58b, Andrew, vert. #59a, Andrew, parents. #59b, Andrew.

1986, July 22
58	A53	60c Pair, #a.-b.	1.25	1.25
59	A53	$1 Pair, #a.-b.	2.00	2.00

Souvenir Sheet
60	A56	$4 Wedding ceremony	4.75	4.75

Nos. 58-59 Ovptd. in Silver
"Congratulations to T.R.H. The Duke &
Duchess of York"

1986, Oct. 28
61	A53	60c Pair, #a.-b.	1.75	1.75
62	A53	$1 Pair, #a.-b.	3.25	3.25

Nos. 51-55 Ovptd. in Gold
"40th WEDDING ANNIVERSARY OF
H.M. QUEEN ELIZABETH II"

1987, Oct. 15
65	A49	5c multicolored	.25	.25
66	A49	40c multicolored	.40	.40
67	A49	$2 multicolored	2.00	2.00
68	A49	$4 multicolored	4.00	4.00
		Nos. 65-68 (4)	6.65	6.65

Souvenir Sheet
69	A49	$5 multicolored	6.25	6.25

NUKULAELAE

Locomotive Type of 1984
Perf. 12½x13

1984-86   Litho.   Unwmk.
Se-tenant Pairs, #a.-b.
a. — Side and front views.
b. — Action scene.
Tuvalu Design A36
1		5c 1891 Calbourne Class 02, UK	.25	.25
2		5c 1912 K.P.E.V. Class T18, Germany	.25	.25
3		10c 1942 SNCF Class 141P, France	.25	.25
4		10c 1962 Class 47, UK	.25	.25
5		15c 1941 Union Pacific Big Boy, US	.25	.25
6		15c 1955 DRB 83-10, Germany	.25	.25
7		20c 1940 S.N.C.F. 160-A-1, France	.45	.45
8		25c 1901 Class AEG High Speed Railcar, Germany	.50	.50
9		25c 1839 Albion Railroad Samson, Canada	.50	.50
10		40c 1907 Saint Class, UK	.90	.90
11		40c 1900 Nord De Glehn Atlantic, France	.90	.90
12		40c 1851 Folkstone Class, UK	.90	.90
13		50c 1914 J.N.R. Class 8620, Japan	1.10	1.10
14		50c 1936 Class 8F, UK	1.10	1.10
15		80c 1857 Shannon, UK	1.90	1.90
16		$1 1948 Class A1, UK	2.40	2.40
17		$1 1955 E.A.R. Class 59, Kenya	2.40	2.40
18		$1 1897 V.R. Class Na, Australia	2.40	2.40
19		$1 1859 Undine Class, UK	2.40	2.40
20		$1.50 1935 Turbomotive, UK	3.50	3.50
		Nos. 1-20 (20)	22.85	22.85

Issued: #1, 5, 10, 16, 5/23; #2, 7, 11, 17, 12/12; #3, 8, 13, 18, 3/24/85; #4, 6, 9, 12, 14, 15, 19-20, 7/11/86.
1986 stamps not inscribed "Leaders of the World."

Cricket Players Type of 1984
1984, Aug. 8   *Perf. 13x12½*
Se-tenant Pairs, #a.-b.
21	A39	5c D.B. Close	.25	.25
22	A39	15c G. Boycott	.30	.30
23	A39	30c D.L. Bairstow	.80	.80
24	A39	$1 T.G. Evans	2.25	2.25
		Nos. 21-24 (4)	3.60	3.60

Automobile Type of 1984
1985   *Perf. 12½x13*
Se-tenant Pairs, #a.-b.
a. — Side and front views.
b. — Action scene.
Tuvalu Design A41
25		5c 1924 Bugatti Type 35, France	.30	.30
26		10c 1908 Sizaire-Naudin, France	.30	.30
27		25c 1965 Sunbeam Tiger, UK	.55	.55
28		35c 1907 Napier 60HP Touring Car, UK	.75	.75
29		35c 1975 BMW 2002 Tll, Germany	.75	.75
30		50c 1910 Austro-Daimler Prince Henry, Austria	1.10	1.10
31		50c 1927 La Salle, US	1.10	1.10
32		70c 1901 Oldsmobile Curved Dash Buckboard	1.50	1.50
33		75c 1955 Rover 90, UK	1.60	1.60
34		$1 1948 Chrysler Town & Country	1.90	1.90
		Nos. 25-34 (10)	9.85	9.85

Issue dates: #25, 28, 30, 32, Feb. 8; #26-27, 29, 31, 33-34, July 23.

Dogs — A8

#35a, Hungarian vizsla. #35b, Bearded collie. #36a, Bernese mountain dog. #36b, Boxer. #37a, Labrador retriever. #37b, Shetland sheepdog. #38a, Welsh springer spaniel. #38b, Scottish terrier.

1985, Apr. 30
35	A8	5c Pair, #a.-b.	.25	.25
36	A8	20c Pair, #a.-b.	.40	.40
37	A8	50c Pair, #a.-b.	1.00	1.00
38	A8	70c Pair, #a.-b.	1.50	1.50
		Nos. 35-38 (4)	3.15	3.15

Queen Mother Type of 1985

Hat: #47a, Purple. #47b, Blue. #48a, 52a, Tiara. #48b, 52b, Lavender. #49a, 53a, Pink. #49b, 53b, Dark blue. #50a, Light purple. #50b, Light blue. #51a, As young girl. #51b, Lace.

1985-86
47	A45	5c Pair, #a.-b.	.25	.25
48	A45	25c Pair, #a.-b.	.45	.45
49	A45	85c Pair, #a.-b.	1.60	1.60
50	A45	$1 Pair, #a.-b.	2.00	2.00
		Nos. 47-50 (4)	4.30	4.30

Souvenir Sheets of 2
51	A45	$1.20 #a.-b.	2.25	2.25
52	A45	$1.20 #a.-b.	1.75	1.75
53	A45	$3.50 #a.-b.	6.00	6.00

Issued: #46-51, 9/4; #52-53, 1/8/86.

Elizabeth II 60th Birthday Type
1986, Apr. 21   *Perf. 13x12½, 12½x13*
54	A49	10c White hat	.25	.25
55	A49	$1 As young woman	.75	.75
56	A49	$1.50 In orange dress	1.10	1.10
57	A49	$3 Tiara, vert.	2.00	2.00
		Nos. 54-57 (4)	4.10	4.10

Souvenir Sheet
58	A49	$4 In brown dress	4.25	4.25

Royal Wedding Type of 1986
#61a, Andrew, vert. #61b, Couple, vert. #62a, Sarah Ferguson and Princess Diana. #62b, Andrew.

1986, July 23   *Perf. 12½x13, 13x12½*
61	A53	60c Pair, #a.-b.	1.10	1.10
62	A53	$1 Pair, #a.-b.	1.75	1.75

Souvenir Sheet
63	A56	$4 Sarah in wedding dress	4.75	4.75

Nos. 61-62 Ovptd. in Silver
"Congratulations to T.R.H. The Duke &
Duchess of York"

1986, Oct. 28
64	A53	60c Pair, #a.-b.	2.00	2.00
65	A53	$1 Pair, #a.-b.	3.25	3.25

Queen Elizabeth II 40th Wedding Anniv. Type of Nanumaga
1987, Oct. 15   *Perf. 15*
68	A5	15c Queen Victoria	.25	.25
69	A5	35c Princesses Margaret and Elizabeth	.50	.50
70	A5	60c Elizabeth holding Princess Anne	.75	.75
71	A5	$1.50 Elizabeth, Philip	2.10	2.10
72	A5	$1.75 Elizabeth wearing tiara	2.40	2.40
		Nos. 68-72 (5)	6.00	6.00

Souvenir Sheet
73	A5	$3 Elizabeth	4.00	4.00

Queen Victoria's accession to the throne, sesquicentennial.

VAITUPU

Automobile Type of 1984
Perf. 12½x13

1984-85   Litho.   Unwmk.
Se-tenant Pairs, #a.-b.
a. — Side and front views.
b. — Action scene.
Tuvalu Design A41
1		5c 1961 Lotus Elite, UK	.25	.25
2		15c 1950 MG TD Midget, UK	.25	.25
3		15c 1932 Hillman Minx, UK	.25	.25
4		15c 1905 White Model E Steam Car, US	.25	.25
5		25c 1935 Auburn Supercharged 851, US	.40	.40
6		25c 1981 Renault RE20, France	.40	.40
7		30c 1928 Lea-Francis Hyper	.50	.50
8		30c 1940 Packard Darrin	.50	.50
9		30c 1938 Graham, US	.50	.50
10		40c 1968 Chevrolet Camaro	.70	.70
11		40c 1957 Renault Dauphine-Gordini, France	.70	.70
12		50c 1930 Packard Eight	.90	.90
13		50c 1926 Miller Special, US	.90	.90
14		60c 1950 Healey Silverstone, UK	1.10	1.10
15		60c 1970 De Tomaso Pantera, Italy	1.10	1.10
16		$1 1927 Bentley 3-Liter, UK	1.75	1.75
		Nos. 1-16 (16)	10.45	10.45

Issued: #2, 5, 7, 12, Mar. 19; #1, 3, 6, 8, 10, 13-14, 16, Dec. 12; #4, 9, 11, 15, Apr. 4, 1985.

British Monarchs Type of Nanumaga
1984, July 18   *Perf. 13x12½*
Se-tenant Pairs, #a.-b.
17	A2	1c Richard III	.25	.25
18	A2	5c Charles I	.25	.25
19	A2	15c Charles I, diff.	.25	.25
20	A2	40c Richard III, diff.	.75	.75
21	A2	50c Charles I, diff.	.90	.90
22	A2	$1 Charles I, diff.	1.75	1.75
		Nos. 17-22 (6)	4.15	4.15

Locomotive Type of 1984
1985-87   *Perf. 12½x13*
Se-tenant Pairs, #a.-b.
a. — Side and front views.
b. — Action scene.
Tuvalu Design A36
23		5c 1929 D.R.G. V3201, Germany	.25	.25
24		10c 1841 G.W.R. Leo Class, UK	.25	.25
25		10c 1937 New York Central Railroad Class J3a	.25	.25
26		15c 1949 Richmond, Fredericksburg & Potomac Railroad Class E8	.30	.30
27		25c 1845 Columbine, UK	.55	.55
28		25c 1954 BR Class 2MT, UK	.55	.55
29		25c 1980 Amtrak Class AEM-7	.55	.55
30		35c 1981 Via Rail LRC Class MPA-27a, Canada	.75	.75
31		45c 1983 British Columbia Railway Class GF6C	.95	.95
32		50c 1888 D&H Class B, India	1.10	1.10
33		60c 1936 D.R. Class 45, Germany	1.25	1.25
34		65c 1904 Northern Pacific Railway Class W, US	1.40	1.40
35		80c 1855 W. & A. R.R. General, US	1.75	1.75
36		85c 1938 Chicago & North Western Railway Class E-4	1.90	1.90
37		$1 1911 J.N.R. Class 9020 Mallet, Japan	2.25	2.25
38		$1 1977 Chicago Regional Transportation Authority Class F40	2.25	2.25
		Nos. 23-38 (16)	16.30	16.30

Issued: #24, 27, 32-33, 3/7/85; #23, 28, 35, 37, 1/16/86; #25-26, 29-31, 34, 36, 38, 9/10/87.
1986 and 1987 stamps not inscribed "Leaders of the World."

A9

Butterfly illustrations by Roger V. Vigurs: #39a, Marpesia petreus. #39b, Pseudolycaena marsyas. #40a, Charaxes jasius. #40b, Junonia coenia. #41a, Palaeochrysophanus hippothoe. #41b, Sticopthalma camadeva. #42a, Phoebis avellaneda. #42b, Apatura iris.

1985, Mar. 12   *Perf. 13x12½*
39	A9	5c Pair, #a.-b.	.25	.25
40	A9	15c Pair, #a.-b.	.30	.30
41	A9	50c Pair, #a.-b.	1.00	1.00
42	A9	75c Pair, #a.-b.	1.60	1.60
		Nos. 39-42 (4)	3.15	3.15

Queen Mother Type of 1985

Hat: #51a, 57a, Light blue. #51b, 57b, White. #52a, Tiara. #52b, Lavender. #53a, 56a, Violet. #53b, 56b, Green. #54a, Blue. #54b, Pink. #55a, Looking up. #55b, Looking forward.

1985-86
51	A45	15c Pair, #a.-b.	.25	.25
52	A45	40c Pair, #a.-b.	.75	.75
53	A45	65c Pair, #a.-b.	1.10	1.10
54	A45	95c Pair, #a.-b.	1.90	1.90
		Nos. 51-54 (4)	4.00	4.00

Souvenir Sheets of 2
55	A45	$1.10 #a.-b.	2.75	2.75
56	A45	$2 #a.-b.	3.00	3.00
57	A45	$2.50 #a.-b.	4.00	4.00

Issued: #51-55, 8/28; 56-57, 1/8/86.

Elizabeth II 60th Birthday Type
1986, Apr. 21   *Perf. 13x12½, 12½x13*
58	A49	5c Green hat	.25	.25
59	A49	60c As young woman	.25	.25
60	A49	$2 Flowered hat	.95	.95
61	A49	$3.50 Tiara, vert.	1.60	1.60
		Nos. 58-61 (4)	3.05	3.05

Souvenir Sheet
62	A49	$5 Straw hat	4.50	4.50

For overprints see Nos. 72-76.

Royal Wedding Type of 1986
#65a, Andrew, vert. #65b, Sarah Ferguson, vert. #66a, Charles, Andrew. #66b, Couple.

1986, July 18   *Perf. 12½x13, 13x12½*
65	A53	60c Pair, #a.-b.	1.10	1.10
66	A53	$1 Pair, #a.-b.	1.75	1.75

Souvenir Sheet
67	A56	$4 Newlyweds	4.50	4.50

Nos. 65-66 Ovptd. in Silver
"Congratulations to T.R.H. The Duke &
Duchess of York"

1986, Oct. 28
68	A53	60c Pair, #a.-b.	2.25	2.25
69	A53	$1 Pair, #a.-b.	3.50	3.50

Nos. 58-62 Ovptd. in Gold
"40th WEDDING ANNIVERSARY OF
H.M. QUEEN ELIZABETH II"

1987, Oct. 15   *Perf. 13x12½, 12½x13*
72	A49	5c multicolored	.25	.25
73	A49	60c multicolored	.75	.75
74	A49	$2 multicolored	2.50	2.50
75	A49	$3 multicolored	3.75	3.75
		Nos. 72-75 (4)	7.25	7.25

Souvenir Sheet
76	A49	$5 multicolored	5.75	5.75

UBANGI-SHARI

ü-ˈbaŋ͵gē ˈshär-ē

(Ubangi-Shari-Chad)

LOCATION — In Western Africa, north of the equator
GOVT. — French Colony
AREA — 238,767 sq. mi.
POP. — 833,916
CAPITAL — Bangui

In 1910 French Congo was divided into the three colonies of Gabon, Middle Congo and Ubangi-Shari and officially named "French Equatorial Africa." Under that name in 1934 the group, with the territory of Chad included, became a single administrative unit. See Gabon.

100 Centimes = 1 Franc

Stamps of
Middle
Congo
Ovptd. in
Black

1915-22   Unwmk.   Perf. 14x13½
Chalky Paper

1	A1	1c ol gray & brn	.35	.35
a.		Double overprint	225.00	
b.		Imperf.	67.50	
2	A1	2c violet & brn	.35	.35
3	A1	4c blue & brn	.65	.80
4	A1	5c dk grn & bl	.70	.85
5	A1	50c yel & bl ('22)	1.20	1.60
6	A1	10c carmine & bl	1.20	1.20
7	A1	10c dp grn & bl grn ('22)	1.20	1.60
8	A1	15c brn vio & rose	2.00	2.40
9	A1	20c brown & blue	4.00	4.75

No. 8 is on ordinary paper

Overprinted

10	A2	25c blue & grn	2.00	2.40
11	A2	25c bl grn & gray ('22)	1.60	1.60
12	A2	30c scarlet & grn	1.60	2.00
13	A2	30c dp rose & rose ('22)	1.20	1.60
14	A2	35c vio brn & bl	5.50	6.50
15	A2	40c dl grn & brn	6.50	7.25
16	A2	45c vio & red	6.50	7.25
17	A2	50c bl grn & red	6.00	6.75
18	A2	50c blue & grn ('22)	1.60	1.60
19	A2	75c brown & bl	14.50	16.00
20	A3	1fr dp grn & vio	14.50	16.00
21	A3	2fr vio & gray grn	16.50	19.00
22	A3	5fr blue & rose	45.00	47.50
		Nos. 1-22 (22)	134.25	149.35

For surcharges see Nos. B1-B2.

Middle
Congo of
1907-22
Ovptd. in
Black or
Red

1922

23	A1	1c violet & grn	.80	1.20
a.		Overprint omitted	190.00	210.00
b.		Imperf.	45.00	
24	A1	2c grn & salmon	.85	1.20
25	A1	4c ol brn & brn	1.20	1.60
a.		Overprint omitted	225.00	
26	A1	5c indigo & rose	1.20	1.60
27	A1	10c dp grn & gray grn	2.00	2.40
28	A1	15c lt red & dl bl	2.00	2.40
29	A1	20c choc & salmon	5.75	6.50

Overprinted

30	A2	25c vio & salmon	8.00	9.50
31	A2	30c rose & pale rose	3.50	4.00
32	A2	35c vio & grn	5.00	5.50
33	A2	40c ind & vio (R)	5.00	5.50
34	A2	45c choc & vio	5.00	5.50
35	A2	50c dk bl & pale bl	3.25	4.00
36	A2	60c on 75c vio, *pnksh*	4.00	4.75
37	A2	75c choc & sal	5.75	7.25
38	A3	1fr grn & dl bl (R)	10.50	13.00
a.		Overprint omitted	325.00	
39	A3	2fr grn & salmon	13.50	16.00
40	A3	5fr grn & ol brn	24.00	27.50
		Nos. 23-40 (18)	101.30	119.40

Nos. 23-29
with
Additional
Ovpt. in
Black, Blue
or Red

1924-33

41	A1	1c vio & grn (Bl)	.35	.55
a.		"OUBANGUI CHARI" omitted	160.00	160.00
42	A1	2c grn & sal (Bl)	.40	.65
a.		"OUBANGUI CHARI" omitted	160.00	160.00
b.		Double overprint	175.00	
43	A1	4c ol brn & brn (Bl)	.40	.65
a.		Double overprint (Bl + Bk)	200.00	
b.		"OUBANGUI CHARI" omitted	180.00	
44	A1	5c ind & rose	.40	.65
a.		"OUBANGUI CHARI" omitted	150.00	
45	A1	10c dp grn & gray grn	.80	.95
46	A1	10c red org & bl ('25)	.95	1.05
47	A1	15c sal & dl bl	.90	.95
48	A1	15c sal & dl bl (Bl) ('26)	1.20	1.60
49	A1	20c choc & salmon (Bl)	1.20	1.60

On Nos. 41-49 the color in ( ) refers to the overprint "Afrique Equatoriale Française."

Overprinted

50	A2	25c vio & salmon (Bl)	.85	.85
a.		Imperf.		
51	A2	30c rose & pale rose (Bl)	.80	1.20
52	A2	30c choc & red ('25)	.90	.95
a.		"OUBANGUI CHARI" omitted	160.00	
53	A2	30c dk grn & grn ('27)	1.60	2.00
54	A2	35c vio & grn (Bl)	.85	1.20
a.		"OUBANGUI CHARI" omitted	525.00	
55	A2	40c ind & vio (Bl)	.85	1.20
56	A2	45c choc & vio (Bl)	1.20	1.60
57	A2	50c dk bl & pale bl (R)	.80	.80
58	A2	50c gray & bl vio ('25) (R)	1.60	1.75
59	A2	60c on 75c dk vio, *pnksh* (R)	.60	.65
60	A2	65c org brn & bl ('28)	1.60	2.00
61	A2	75c choc & sal (Bl)	2.00	2.40
62	A2	75c dp bl & lt bl ('25) (R)	1.20	1.60
a.		"OUBANGUI CHARI" omitted	160.00	
63	A2	75c rose & dk brn ('28)	2.50	2.75
64	A2	90c brn red & pink ('30)	5.00	5.50
65	A3	1fr grn & ind (Bk + Bl) ('25)	.95	1.10
66	A3	1fr grn & ind (R + Bl)	1.60	2.40
67	A3	1.10fr bister & bl ('28)	3.25	4.00
68	A3	1.25fr mag & lt grn ('33)	9.50	11.00
69	A3	1.50fr ultra & bl ('30)	7.25	8.00
70	A3	1.75fr dk brn & dp buff ('33)	12.00	13.50

71	A3	2fr grn & red	1.60	2.40
a.		"OUBANGUI CHARI" omitted	1,875.	1,200.
72	A3	3fr red vio ('30)	5.75	6.50
73	A3	5fr grn & ol brn	5.25	6.50
		Nos. 41-73 (33)	76.10	90.50

On Nos. 65, 66 the first overprint color refers to OUBANGUI CHARI.
For surcharges see Nos. 74-81.

Types of 1924 Issue Surcharged with New Values in Black or Red

1925-26

74	A3	65c on 1fr vio & ol	2.00	2.40
a.		"65" omitted	160.00	
75	A3	85c on 1fr vio & ol	2.00	2.40
a.		"AFRIQUE EQUATORIALE FRANCAISE" omitted	160.00	
b.		Double surcharge	180.00	
76	A3	1.25fr on 1fr dk bl & ultra (R) ('26)	1.45	1.75
a.		"1f25" omitted	190.00	125.00

Bars cover old denomination on No. 76.

Types of 1924 Issue Surcharged with New Values and Bars

1927

77	A2	90c on 75c brn red & rose red	2.40	3.25
78	A3	1.50fr on 1fr ultra & bl	2.40	3.25
79	A3	3fr on 5fr org brn & dl red	3.50	4.00
80	A3	10fr on 5fr ver & vio	19.00	21.00
81	A3	20fr on 5fr ind & gray	30.00	35.00
		Nos. 77-81 (5)	57.30	66.50

Common Design Types pictured following the introduction.

Colonial Exposition Issue
Common Design Types

1931   Engr.   Perf. 12½
Name of Country Typo. in Black

82	CD70	40c deep green	5.50	5.50
83	CD71	50c violet	5.50	5.50
84	CD72	90c red orange	5.50	5.50
a.		Imperf.	130.00	
85	CD73l	1.50fr dull blue	5.50	5.50
		Nos. 82-85 (4)	22.00	22.00

SEMI-POSTAL STAMPS

Regular
Issue of
1915
Surcharged

1916   Unwmk.   Perf. 14x13½
Chalky Paper

B1	A1	10c + 5c car & blue	3.25	3.50
a.		Inverted surch.	180.00	
b.		Double surcharge	180.00	
c.		Double surch., one invtd.	130.00	130.00
d.		Vertical surcharge	140.00	140.00
e.		No period under "C"	20.00	20.00

Regular
Issue of
1915
Surcharged
in Carmine

B2	A1	10c + 5c car & blue	2.00	2.40

POSTAGE DUE STAMPS

Postage Due Stamps of
France Overprinted

1928   Unwmk.   Perf. 14x13½

J1	D2	5c light blue	1.60	2.00
J2	D2	10c gray brown	2.00	2.40
J3	D2	20c olive green	2.00	2.40
J4	D2	25c bright rose	2.00	2.40
J5	D2	30c light red	2.00	2.40
J6	D2	45c blue green	2.00	2.40
J7	D2	50c brown violet	2.75	3.25
J8	D2	60c yellow brown	3.25	3.50

J9	D2	1fr red brown	4.00	4.75
J10	D2	2fr orange red	6.50	7.25
J11	D2	3fr bright violet	6.50	7.25
		Nos. J1-J11 (11)	34.60	40.00

Landscape
D3

Emile Gentil — D4

1930   Typo.

J12	D3	5c dp bl & olive	.85	1.20
J13	D3	10c dk red & brn	1.20	1.60
J14	D3	20c green & brn	1.20	1.60
J15	D3	25c lt bl & brn	1.60	2.00
J16	D3	30c bis brn & Prus bl	2.75	3.25
J17	D3	45c Prus bl & ol	3.50	4.00
J18	D3	50c red vio & brn	6.00	6.75
J19	D3	60c gray lil & bl blk	6.50	7.25
J20	D4	1fr bis brn & bl blk	6.00	6.75
J21	D4	2fr violet & brown	6.50	8.00
J22	D4	3fr dp red & brn	8.00	9.50
		Nos. J12-J22 (11)	44.10	51.90

Stamps of Ubangi-Shari were replaced in 1936 by those of French Equatorial Africa.

UGANDA

ü-'gan-də

LOCATION — East Africa, at the Equator and separated from the Indian Ocean by Kenya and Tanzania
GOVT. — Independent state
AREA — 91,343 sq. mi.
POP. — 21,619,700 (1999 est.)
CAPITAL — Kampala

Stamps of 1898-1902 were replaced by those issued for Kenya, Tanganyika and Uganda. Uganda became independent October 9, 1962.

Cowries (50 = 4 Pence)
16 Annas = 1 Rupee (1896)
100 Cents = 1 Shilling (1962)

Catalogue values for unused stamps in this country are for **Never Hinged** items, beginning with Scott 79 in the regular postage section and Scott J1 in the postage due section.

Unused values for Nos. 2-68 are for stamps without gum. Very fine examples will be evenly cut and will show at least two full typewritten framelines.

A1

A2

Nos. 1-53 were produced with a typewriter by Rev. Ernest Millar of the Church Missionary Society. They were 20-26mm wide, with nine stamps in a horizontal row. Later two more were added to each row, and the stamps became narrower, 16-18mm.
Rev. Millar got a new typewriter in 1895, and the stamps he typed on it have a different appearance. A violet ribbon in the machine, inserted late in 1895, resulted in Nos. 35-53.
Nos. 1-53 are on thin, tough, white paper, laid horizontally with traces of a few vertical lines.
Forgeries of Nos. 1-53 are known.

Without Gum
Wide Letters
Typeset on Thin Laid Paper
Stamps 20 to 26mm wide

1895		**Unwmk.**		**Imperf.**
1	A1	10(c) black	5,750.	3,750.
2	A1	20(c) black	7,000.	1,900.
3	A1	30(c) black	1,900.	1,800.
4	A1	40(c) black	5,750.	2,100.
5	A1	50(c) black	1,550.	1,300.
6	A1	60(c) black	2,650.	2,400.

Surcharged with New Value in Black, Pen-written

9	A1	10 on 30(c) black	8,000.
10	A1	10 on 50(c) black	6,000.
11	A1	15 on 10(c) black	8,000.
12	A1	15 on 20(c) black	7,250.
13	A1	15 on 40(c) black	8,000.
14	A1	15 on 50(c) black	8,000.
15	A1	25 on 50(c) black	8,000.
16	A1	50 on 60(c) black	8,000.

Stamps 16 to 18mm wide

17	A1	5(c) black	3,500.	1,375.
18	A1	10(c) black	3,500.	1,700.
19	A1	15(c) black	2,100.	1,600.
20	A1	20(c) black	3,500.	1,600.
a.	Vertically laid paper			8,000.
21	A1	25(c) black	1,575.	1,600.
22	A1	30(c) black	9,000.	9,000.
23	A1	40(c) black	8,500.	8,500.
24	A1	50(c) black	4,000.	5,750.
25	A1	60(c) black	8,000.	9,000.

Narrow Letters
Stamps 16 to 18mm wide

26	A2	5(c) black	1,375.
27	A2	10(c) black	1,500.
28	A2	15(c) black	1,500.
29	A2	20(c) black	1,175.
30	A2	25(c) black	1,275.
31	A2	30(c) black	1,575.
32	A2	40(c) black	1,375.
33	A2	50(c) black	1,500.
34	A2	60(c) black	2,000.

35	A2	5(c) violet	700.	700.
36	A2	10(c) violet	650.	700.
37	A2	15(c) violet	950.	650.
38	A2	20(c) violet	450.	350.
39	A2	25(c) violet	1,600.	1,500.
40	A2	30(c) violet	2,100.	1,050.
41	A2	40(c) violet	1,900.	1,500.
42	A2	50(c) violet	1,900.	1,575.
43	A2	100(c) violet	3,250.	3,750.

As a favor to a philatelist, 35c and 45c denominations were made in black and violet. They were not intended for postal use and no rate called for those denominations.

A3

A4

1896

44	A3	5(c) violet	700.	1,100.
45	A3	10(c) violet	800.	650.
46	A3	15(c) violet	700.	375.
47	A3	20(c) violet	325.	200.
48	A3	25(c) violet	600.	950.
49	A3	30(c) violet	650.	1,150.
50	A3	40(c) violet	850.	1,150.
51	A3	50(c) violet	700.	900.
52	A3	60(c) violet	1,600.	2,250.
53	A3	100(c) violet	1,500.	2,250.

Overprinted "L" in Black

1896	**Typeset**		**White Paper**
54	A4	1a black (thin "1")	200.	190.
a.	Small "O" in "POSTAGE"	1,500.	1,150.
55	A4	2a black	115.	140.
a.	Small "O" in "POSTAGE"	525.	600.
56	A4	3a black	275.	350.
a.	Small "O" in "POSTAGE"	1,600.	1,900.
57	A4	4a black	115.	175.
a.	Small "O" in "POSTAGE"	575.	

Yellowish Paper

58	A4	8a black	210.	275.
a.	Small "O" in "POSTAGE"		1,500.	1,700.
59	A4	1r black	425.	475.
a.	Small "O" in "POSTAGE"		2,000.	
60	A4	5r black	37,500.	37,500.

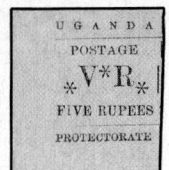
A4a

Without Overprint
White Paper

61	A4a	1a black (thin "1")	125.00	110.00
a.	Small "O" in "POSTAGE"		700.00	625.00
62	A4a	1a black (thick "1")	21.00	27.50
a.	Small "O" in "POSTAGE"		90.00	110.00
63	A4a	2a black	29.00	35.00
a.	Small "O" in "POSTAGE"		110.00	140.00
64	A4a	3a black	30.00	40.00
a.	Small "O" in "POSTAGE"		130.00	175.00
65	A4a	4a black	30.00	37.50
a.	Small "O" in "POSTAGE"		110.00	140.00

Yellowish Paper

66	A4a	8a black	35.00	40.00
a.	Small "O" in "POSTAGE"		140.00	175.00
67	A4a	1r black	87.50	110.00
a.	Small "O" in "POSTAGE"		350.00	450.00
68	A4a	5r black	300.00	400.00
a.	Small "O" in "POSTAGE"		850.00	1,050.

A5

Queen Victoria — A6

1898-1902 Engr. Wmk. 2 Perf. 14

69	A5	1a red	3.50	3.25
70	A5	1a car rose ('02)	2.25	1.40
71	A5	2a brown	5.25	8.50
72	A5	3a gray	16.00	35.00
73	A5	4a dark green	13.00	15.00
74	A5	8a olive gray	11.00	30.00

Wmk. 1

75	A6	1r ultra	50.00	50.00
76	A6	5r brown	85.00	115.00
	Nos. 69-76 (8)		186.00	258.15

A7

1902 Wmk. 2 Black Overprint

77	A7	½a yellow green	2.25	1.60
a.	Inverted overprint		2,100.	
b.	Double overprint		2,400.	
c.	Pair, one without overprint		4,750.	

Red Overprint

78	A7	2½a dark blue	3.25	3.50
a.	Double overprint		750.00	

Catalogue values for unused stamps in this section, from this point to the end of the section, are for **Never Hinged** items.

Ripon Falls and Speke Monument A8

Wmk. 314

1962, July 28		**Engr.**		**Perf. 14**
79	A8	30c vermilion & blk	.30	.30
80	A8	50c violet & blk	.30	.30
81	A8	1.30sh green & blk	.55	.55
82	A8	2.50sh ultra & blk	2.00	2.00
	Nos. 79-82 (4)		3.15	3.15

Cent. of the discovery of the source of the Nile by John Hanning Speke.

Independent State

Murchison Falls — A9

Mulago Hospital, X-Ray Service A10

Designs: 10c, Tobacco growing. 15c, Coffee growing. 20c, Ankole cattle. 30c, Cotton growing. 50c, Mountains of the Moon. 1.30sh, Rubaga and Namirembe Cathedrals and Kibuli Mosque. 2sh, Makerere College and students. 5sh, Copper mining. 10sh, Cement factory. 20sh, Parliament.

Perf. 14½x14, 14x14½

1962, Oct. 9		**Photo.**		**Unwmk.**
83	A9	5c Prus green	.25	.60
84	A9	10c red brown	.25	.60
85	A9	15c grn, blk & car	.25	.60
86	A9	20c bister & pur	.25	.60
87	A9	30c brt blue	.25	.60
88	A9	50c bluish grn & blk	.25	.60
89	A10	1sh bl grn, sep & red	.25	.60
90	A10	1.30sh pur & ocher	.40	.60
91	A10	2sh grnsh bl, blk & dk car	.50	.75
92	A10	5sh dk green & blk	1.25	1.50
93	A10	10sh red brn & slate	2.50	3.25
94	A10	20sh blue & pale brn	7.00	8.50
	Nos. 83-94 (12)		13.40	18.80

Uganda's independence, Oct. 9, 1962.

Crowned Crane — A11

1965, Feb. 20 Photo. Perf. 14½

95	A11	30c bl grn, blk, yel & red	.40	.25
96	A11	1sh30c ultra, blk, yel & red	1.10	.70

Intl. Trade Fair at Lugogo Stadium, Kampala, Feb. 20-28.

Black Bee-eater A12

African Jacana A13

Arms of Uganda and Birds: 15c, Orange weaver. 20c, Narina trogon. 30c, Sacred ibis. 40c, Blue-breasted kingfisher. 50c, Whale-headed stork. 65c, Black-winged red bishop. 1sh, Ruwenzori turaco. 1.30sh, African fish eagle. 2.50sh, Great blue turaco. 5sh, Lilac-breasted roller. 10sh, Black-collared lovebird. 20sh, Crowned crane.

Perf. 14½x14, 14x14½
1965, Oct. 9 Photo. Unwmk.
Birds in Natural Colors
Size: 17x21mm, 21x17mm

97	A12	5c lt vio bl & blk	.30	.35
98	A13	10c dull blue & red	.30	.35
99	A12	15c dk brown & org	.30	.35
100	A13	20c bister & brt grn	.30	.35
101	A13	30c hn brn & blk	2.00	.35
102	A12	40c lt yel grn & red	1.25	.55
103	A13	50c dp pur & gray	.35	.35
104	A13	65c gray & brick red	2.75	1.75

Perf. 14½
Size: 41x25mm, 25x41mm

105	A13	1sh lt blue & blk	.70	.35
106	A12	1.30sh yel & red brn	7.00	.35
107	A13	2.50sh brt yel grn & blk	5.50	.55
108	A12	5sh lil gray & vio bl	8.50	3.50
109	A13	10sh lt brown & blk	13.50	9.25
110	A13	20sh olive grn & blk	25.00	30.00
	Nos. 97-110 (14)		67.75	48.40

Parliament Building — A14

13th Commonwealth Parliamentary Assoc. Conf.: 30c, Animal carvings from entrance hall of Uganda Parliament. 50c, Arms of Uganda. 2.50sh, Parliament Chamber.

1967, Oct. 26 Perf. 14½

111	A14	30c multicolored	.25	.25
112	A14	50c multicolored	.25	.25
113	A14	1.30sh multicolored	.35	.30
114	A14	2.50sh multicolored	.70	.60
	Nos. 111-114 (4)		1.55	1.40

Cordia
Abyssinica
A15

Black-galled
Acacia
A16

Flowers: 10c, Grewia similis. 15c, Cassia didymobotrya. 20c, Coleus barbatus. 30c, Ochna ovata. 40c, Ipomoea spathulata (morning glory). 50c, Spathodea nilotica (flame tree). 60c, Oncoba spinosa. 70c, Carissa edulis. 1.50sh, Clerodendrum myricoides (blue butterfly bush). 2.50sh, Acanthus arboreus. 5sh, Kigelia aethiopium (sausage tree). 10sh, Erythrina abyssinica (Uganda coral). 20sh, Monodora myristica.

Perf. 14½x14

1969, Oct. 9		**Photo.**	**Unwmk.**	
115	A15	5c multicolored	.25	.25
116	A15	10c multicolored	.25	.25
117	A15	15c multicolored	.25	.25
118	A15	20c multicolored	.25	.25
119	A15	30c multicolored	.25	.25
120	A15	40c gray & multi	.25	.25
121	A15	50c tan & multi	.25	.25
122	A15	60c multicolored	.25	.25
123	A15	70c multicolored	.25	.25

Perf. 14

124	A16	1sh multicolored	.35	.25
125	A16	1.50sh multicolored	.55	.25
126	A16	2.50sh multicolored	.70	.25
127	A16	5sh multicolored	1.25	.25
128	A16	10sh multicolored	3.00	.55
129	A16	20sh tan & multi	7.75	1.25
		Nos. 115-129 (15)	15.85	5.05

Values of Nos. 124-129 are for canceled-to-order stamps. Cancellations were printed on Nos. 128-129. Postally used examples sell for higher prices.

Nos. 125-126, 129 Surcharged

1975, Sept. 29		**Photo.**	**Perf. 14**	
130	A16	2sh on 1.50sh multi	1.25	1.60
131	A16	3sh on 2.50sh multi	25.00	32.50
132	A16	40c on 20sh multi	10.00	13.00
		Nos. 130-132 (3)	36.25	47.10

Millet — A17

Ugandan Crops: 20c, Sugar cane. 30c, Tobacco. 40c, Onions. 50c, Tomatoes. 70c, Tea. 80c, Bananas. 1sh, Corn. 2sh, Pineapple. 3sh, Coffee. 5sh, Oranges. 10sh, Peanuts. 20sh, Cotton. 40sh, Beans.

1975, Oct. 9 Photo. Perf. 14x14½
Size: 21x17mm
Multicolored, Name Panel as follows

133	A17	10c lt brown	.25	.25
134	A17	20c blue	.25	.25
135	A17	30c vermilion	.25	.25
136	A17	40c lilac	.25	.25
137	A17	50c olive	.25	.25
138	A17	70c brt green	.25	.25
139	A17	80c purple	.25	.25

Perf. 14½
Size: 41x25mm

140	A17	1sh ocher	.25	.25
141	A17	2sh slate	.25	.25
142	A17	3sh blue	.40	.40
143	A17	5sh yellow green	.50	.55
144	A17	10sh brown red	1.00	1.10
145	A17	20sh rose lilac	2.10	2.25
146	A17	40sh orange	4.00	4.25
		Nos. 133-146 (14)	10.25	10.80

See #195-198. For surcharge & overprints see #175, 203-206, 227-244, 253-257.

Communications Type of Tanzania 1976

Designs: 50c, Microwave tower. 1sh, Cordless switchboard and operators, horiz. 2sh, Telephones of 1880, 1930 and 1976. 3sh, Message switching center, horiz.

1976, Apr. 15 Litho. Perf. 14½

147	A6a	50c blue & multi	.25	.25
148	A6a	1sh red & multi	.25	.25
149	A6a	2sh yellow & multi	.35	.25
150	A6a	3sh multicolored	.50	.40
a.		Souvenir sheet of 4	1.75	1.75
		Nos. 147-150 (4)	1.35	1.15

Telecommunications development in East Africa. No. 150a contains 4 stamps similar to Nos. 147-150 with simulated perforations.

Olympics Type of Tanzania 1976

Designs: 50c, Akii Bua, Ugandan hurdler. 1sh, Filbert Bayi, Tanzanian runner. 2sh, Steve Muchoki, Kenyan boxer. 3sh, Olympic torch, flags of Kenya, Tanzania and Uganda.

1976, July 5 Litho. Perf. 14½

151	A6b	50c blue & multi	.25	.25
152	A6b	1sh red & multi	.25	.25
153	A6b	2sh yellow & multi	.45	.40
154	A6b	3sh blue & multi	.70	.60
a.		Souv. sheet of 4, #151-154, perf. 13	7.00	5.00
		Nos. 151-154 (4)	1.65	1.50

21st Olympic Games, Montreal, Canada, July 17-Aug. 1.

Railway Type of Tanzania 1976

Designs: 50c, Tanzania-Zambia Railway. 1sh, Nile Bridge, Uganda. 2sh, Nakuru Station, Kenya. 3sh, Class A locomotive, 1896.

1976, Oct. 4 Litho. Perf. 14

155	A6c	50c lilac & multi	.25	.25
156	A6c	1sh emerald & multi	.40	.25
157	A6c	2sh brt rose & multi	.80	.45
158	A6c	3sh yellow & multi	1.25	.65
a.		Souv. sheet, #155-158, perf 13	3.50	3.50
		Nos. 155-158 (4)	2.70	1.60

Rail transport in East Africa.

Fish Type of Tanzania 1977

1977, Jan. 10 Litho. Perf. 14½

159	A6d	50c Nile perch	.25	.25
160	A6d	1sh Tilapia	.30	.25
161	A6d	3sh Sailfish	.85	.60
162	A6d	5sh Black marlin	1.25	1.00
a.		Souvenir sheet of 4, #159-162	6.00	5.50
		Nos. 159-162 (4)	2.65	2.10

Festival Type of Tanzania 1977

Festival Emblem and: 50c, Masai tribesmen bleeding cow. 1sh, Dancers from Uganda. 2sh, Makonde sculpture, Tanzania. 3sh, Tribesmen skinning hippopotamus.

1977, Jan. 15 Perf. 13½x14

163	A6e	50c multicolored	.25	.25
164	A6e	1sh multicolored	.25	.25
165	A6e	2sh multicolored	.45	.40
166	A6e	3sh multicolored	.70	.60
a.		Souvenir sheet of 4, #163-166	2.60	2.25
		Nos. 163-166 (4)	1.65	1.50

2nd World Black and African Festival, Lagos, Nigeria, Jan. 15-Feb. 12.

Rally Type of Tanzania 1977

Safari Rally Emblem and: 50c, Automobile passing through village. 1sh, Winner at finish line. 2sh, Car passing through washout. 5sh, Car, elephants and Mt. Kenya.

1977, Apr. 5 Litho. Perf. 14

167	A6f	50c multicolored	.25	.25
168	A6f	1sh multicolored	.25	.25
169	A6f	2sh multicolored	.45	.30
170	A6f	5sh multicolored	1.10	.85
a.		Souvenir sheet of 4, #167-170	2.50	2.50
		Nos. 167-170 (4)	2.05	1.65

25th Safari Rally, Apr. 7-11.

Church Type of Tanzania 1977

Designs: 50c, Rev. Canon Apolo Kivebulaya. 1sh, Uganda Cathedral. 2sh, Early grass-topped Cathedral. 5sh, Early tent congregation, Kigezi.

1977, June 30 Litho. Perf. 14

171	A6g	50c multicolored	.25	.25
172	A6g	1sh multicolored	.25	.25
173	A6g	2sh multicolored	.40	.30
174	A6g	5sh multicolored	1.00	.75
a.		Souvenir sheet of 4, #171-174	2.00	2.00
		Nos. 171-174 (4)	1.90	1.55

Church of Uganda, centenary.

Type of 1975 Surcharged with New Value and 2 Bars

1977, Aug. 22 Photo. Perf. 14x14½

175	A17	80c on 60c bananas	.50	.25

No. 175 was not issued without surcharge.

Wildlife Type of Tanzania 1977

Wildlife Fund Emblem and: 50c, Pancake tortoise. 1sh, Nile crocodile. 2sh, Hunter's hartebeest. 3sh, Red colobus monkey. 5sh, Dugong.

1977, Sept. 26 Litho. Perf. 14x13½

176	A6h	50c multicolored	.30	.25
177	A6h	1sh multicolored	.50	.40
178	A6h	2sh multicolored	2.25	1.00
179	A6h	3sh multicolored	3.25	1.40
180	A6h	5sh multicolored	3.25	2.50
a.		Souvenir sheet of 4, #177-180	8.50	6.00
		Nos. 176-180 (5)	9.55	5.55

Endangered species.

Soccer Type of Tanzania

Soccer Cup and: 50c, Soccer scene and Joe Kadenge. 1sh, Mohammed Chuma receiving trophy, and his portrait. 2sh, Shot on goal and Omari S. Kidevu. 5sh, Backfield defense and Polly Ouma.

1978, May 3 Litho. Perf. 14x13½

181	A8a	50c green & multi	.25	.25
182	A8a	1sh lt brown & multi	.25	.25
183	A8a	2sh lilac & multi	.40	.30
184	A8a	5sh dk blue & multi	1.10	.75
a.		Souvenir sheet of 4, #181-184	2.25	2.25
		Nos. 181-184 (4)	2.00	1.55

World Soccer Championships, Argentina, June 1-25.
See Nos. 203-206.

Crop Type of 1975

Designs as before.

1978, June Litho. Perf. 14½
Size: 41x25mm
Multicolored, Name Panel as follows

195	A17	5sh blue	.25	.25
196	A17	10sh rose lilac	.50	.50
197	A17	20sh brown	1.00	1.00
198	A17	40sh deep orange	2.10	2.10
		Nos. 195-198 (4)	3.85	3.85

Shot Put
A18

1978, July 10 Litho. Perf. 14

199	A18	50c shown	.25	.25
200	A18	1sh Broad jump	.25	.25
201	A18	2sh Running	.40	.40
202	A18	5sh Boxing	1.00	1.00
a.		Souv. sheet, #199-202, perf 12	2.75	2.75
		Nos. 199-202 (4)	1.90	1.90

Commonwealth Games, Edmonton, Canada, Aug. 3-12.
For overprints see Nos. 249-252.

Soccer Type of 1978 Inscribed: "WORLD CUP 1978"

Designs: 50c, Backfield defense and Polly Ouma. 2sh, Shot on goal and Omari S. Kidevu. 5sh, Soccer scene and Joe Kadenge. 10sh, Mohammed Chuma receiving trophy, and his portrait.

1978, Sept. 11 Litho. Perf. 14x13½

203	A8a	50c dk blue & multi	.25	.25
204	A8a	2sh lilac & multi	.45	.35
205	A8a	5sh green & multi	1.00	.90
206	A8a	10sh lt brown & multi	2.00	1.75
a.		Souv. sheet of 4, #203-206, perf. 12	4.00	4.00
		Nos. 203-206 (4)	3.70	3.25

World Cup Soccer Championship winners.

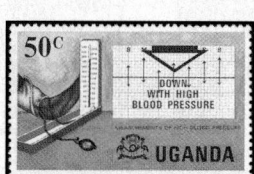

Blood Pressure Gauge and
Chart — A19

1978, Sept. 25 Litho. Perf. 14

207	A19	50c shown	.25	.25
208	A19	1sh Heart	.25	.25
209	A19	2sh Retina	.40	.35
210	A19	5sh Kidneys	1.00	.95
a.		Souvenir sheet of 4, #207-210	2.75	2.75
		Nos. 207-210 (4)	1.90	1.80

World Health Day and Hypertension Month.

Cattle
Unloaded
from
Plane
A20

Flyer 1 and: 1.50sh, "Islander" on runway, Kampala. 2.70sh, Coffee loaded on transport jet. 10sh, Concorde.

1978, Dec. 16

211	A20	1sh multicolored	.25	.25
212	A20	1.50sh multicolored	.25	.25
213	A20	2.70sh multicolored	.45	.40
214	A20	10sh multicolored	1.90	1.40
a.		Souvenir sheet of 4, #211-214	3.00	3.00
		Nos. 211-214 (4)	2.85	2.30

75th anniversary of 1st powered flight.
For overprints see Nos. 258-261.

Elizabeth II Leaving Owen Falls
Dam — A21

Designs: 1.50sh, Coronation regalia. 2.70sh, Coronation ceremony. 10sh, Royal family on balcony of Buckingham Palace.

1979, Mar. 1 Litho. Perf. 12½x12

215	A21	1sh multicolored	.25	.25
216	A21	1.50sh multicolored	.25	.25
217	A21	2.70sh multicolored	.35	.30
218	A21	10sh multicolored	1.40	1.10
a.		Souvenir sheet of 4, #215-218	2.40	2.40
		Nos. 215-218 (4)	2.25	1.90

25th anniv. of coronation of Elizabeth II.
For overprints see Nos. 245-248.

Bishop
Joseph
Kiwanuka
A22

Designs: 1.50sh, Lubaga Cathedral. 2.70sh, Ugandan pilgrims and St. Peter's, Rome. 10sh, Friar Lourdel-Mapeera, missionary.

1979, Feb. 15 Perf. 14

219	A22	1sh multicolored	.25	.25
220	A22	1.50sh multicolored	.25	.25
221	A22	2.70sh multicolored	.35	.30
222	A22	10sh multicolored	1.40	1.10
a.		Souvenir sheet of 4, #219-222	2.40	2.40
		Nos. 219-222 (4)	2.25	1.90

Ugandan Catholic Church, centenary.
See No. 274. For overprints see Nos. 262-265.

Child Receiving Vaccination — A23

IYC Emblem and: 1.50sh, Handicapped children playing. 2.70sh, Ugandan IYC emblem. 10sh, Teacher and pupils.

1979, July 16 Litho. Perf. 14

223	A23	1sh multicolored	.25	.25
224	A23	1.50sh multicolored	.25	.25
225	A23	2.70sh multicolored	.25	.25
226	A23	10sh multicolored	1.10	.90
a.		Souvenir sheet of 4, #223-226	2.00	2.00
		Nos. 223-226 (4)	1.85	1.65

International Year of the Child.
For overprints see Nos. 266-269.

Nos. 133-146, 195-198, 215-218
Overprinted: "UGANDA / LIBERATED / 1979"

1979, July 12 Photo. Perf. 14x14½
Size: 21x17mm

227	A17	10c multicolored	.25	.25
228	A17	20c multicolored	.25	.25
229	A17	30c multicolored	.25	.25
230	A17	40c multicolored	.25	.25
231	A17	50c multicolored	.25	.25
232	A17	70c multicolored	.25	.25
233	A17	80c multicolored	.25	.25

Perf. 14½
Size: 41x25mm

234	A17	1sh multicolored	.25	.25
235	A17	2sh multicolored	.25	.25
236	A17	3sh multicolored	.40	.30
237	A17	5sh multicolored	.55	.45
238	A17	10sh multicolored	1.10	.90
239	A17	20sh multicolored	2.25	2.00
240	A17	40sh multicolored	4.50	3.75
		Nos. 227-240 (14)	11.05	9.65

1979 Litho. Perf. 14½
Multicolored, name panel as follows

241	A17	5sh blue	.75	.55
242	A17	10sh rose lilac	1.40	1.10
243	A17	20sh brown	2.60	2.25
244	A17	40sh deep orange	5.25	4.50
		Nos. 241-244 (4)	10.00	8.40

1979, July 12 Litho. Perf. 12½x12

245	A21	1sh multicolored	.25	.25
246	A21	1.50sh multicolored	.25	.25
247	A21	2.70sh multicolored	.25	.25
248	A21	15sh on 10sh multi	1.60	1.10
a.		Souvenir sheet of 4	3.00	
		Nos. 245-248 (4)	2.35	1.85

No. 248a contains Nos. 245-247 and a 15sh in design of No. 218. Issued Aug. 1.

Nos. 199-202; 203, 204-206; 211-214; 219-222, 223-226 Overprinted: "UGANDA LIBERATED 1979"

1979, Aug. 1 Litho. Perf. 14

249	A18	50c multicolored	.25	.25
250	A18	1sh multicolored	.25	.25
251	A18	2sh multicolored	.35	.25
252	A18	5sh multicolored	.85	.75

Type A17 Issue of Kenya

1979, Aug. 1 Perf. 14x13½

253	A17	50c multi	.25	.25
255	A17	2sh multi (#204)	.30	.25
256	A17	5sh multi	.85	.70
257	A17	10sh multi	1.75	1.40

Overprint exists on No. 183.

1979, Aug. 1 Perf. 14

258	A20	1sh multicolored	.25	.25
259	A20	1.50sh multicolored	.30	.25
260	A20	2.70sh multicolored	.60	.50
261	A20	10sh multicolored	2.10	1.75

1979, Aug. 1

262	A22	1sh multicolored	.25	.25
263	A22	1.50sh multicolored	.25	.25
264	A22	2.70sh multicolored	.45	.40
265	A22	10sh multicolored	1.60	1.40

1979, Aug. 16

266	A23	1sh multicolored	.25	.25
267	A23	1.50sh multicolored	.25	.25
268	A23	2.70sh multicolored	.50	.45
269	A23	10sh multicolored	1.75	1.60
a.		Souvenir sheet of 4, #266-269	2.75	2.75
		Nos. 249-269 (20)	13.40	11.70

ITU Emblem, Radio Waves A24

1979, Sept. 11

270	A24	1sh lt gray & multi	.25	.25
271	A24	1.50sh orange & multi	.25	.25
272	A24	2.70sh yellow & multi	.25	.25
273	A24	10sh blue & multi	.90	.75
		Nos. 270-273 (4)	1.65	1.50

50th anniv. of Intl. Radio Consultative Committee (CCIR) of the ITU.

No. 222a Redrawn and Inscribed: FREEDOM OF WORSHIP DECLARED
Souvenir Sheet

1979, Sept. Perf. 12

274		Sheet of 4	2.25	2.25
a.		A22 1sh No. 219	.25	.25
b.		A22 1.50sh No. 220	.25	.25
c.		A22 2.70sh No. 221	.35	.35
d.		A22 10sh No. 222	1.40	1.25

In top panel of margin scrolls and coat of arms have been replaced by inscription.

A25

1979, Nov. 12 Litho. Perf. 14

275	A25	1sh #110	.25	.25
276	A25	1.50sh #112	.25	.25
277	A25	2.70sh #94	.40	.35
278	A25	10sh #69	1.50	1.25
a.		Souvenir sheet of 4, #275-278	2.25	2.25
		Nos. 275-278 (4)	2.40	2.10

Sir Rowland Hill (1795-1879), originator of penny postage.
For overprints see Nos. 293-296.

Thomson's Gazelle — A26

Designs: 10c, Impalas. 20c, Large-spotted genet. 50c, Bush babies. 80c, Wild hunting dogs. 1sh, Lions. 1.50sh, Mountain gorillas. 2sh, Zebras. 2.70sh, Leopards. 3.50sh, Black rhinoceroses. 5sh, Defassa waterbucks. 10sh, African black buffaloes. 20sh, Hippopotami. 40sh, African elephants.

1979, Dec. 3 Litho. Perf. 14
No Date Imprint Below Design
Size: 21x17mm

279	A26	10c multicolored	.25	.25
280	A26	20c multicolored	.25	.25
281	A26	30c multicolored	.25	.25
282	A26	50c multicolored	.25	.25
283	A26	80c multicolored	.25	.25

Size: 39x25mm

284	A26	1sh multicolored	.25	.25
a.		Imprint "1982"	.60	.25
285	A26	1.50sh multicolored	.25	.25
286	A26	2sh multicolored	.25	.25
a.		Imprint "1982"	.80	.40
287	A26	2.70sh multicolored	.30	.30
288	A26	3.50sh multicolored	.40	.35
289	A26	5sh multicolored	.60	.55
a.		Imprint "1982"	.80	.80
290	A26	10sh multicolored	1.10	1.00
291	A26	20sh multicolored	2.50	2.10
292	A26	40sh multicolored	5.25	4.25
		Nos. 279-292 (14)	12.15	10.55

Nos. 284, 286, 289 reissued inscribed 1982. See Nos. 400-406. For surcharges see Nos. 386-392.

Nos. 275-278a Overprinted: "LONDON 1980"

1980, May 6 Litho. Perf. 14

293	A25	1sh multicolored	.25	.25
294	A25	1.50sh multicolored	.25	.25
295	A25	2.70sh multicolored	.40	.35
296	A25	10sh multicolored	1.40	1.40
a.		Souvenir sheet of 4, #293-296	2.25	2.25
		Nos. 293-296 (4)	2.30	2.25

London 80 Intl. Stamp Exhib., May 6-14.

Paul Harris Wheeling Rotary Cart A27

1980, Aug. Litho. Perf. 14

297	A27	1sh Rotary emblem, vert.	.25	.25
298	A27	20sh shown	2.10	1.60
a.		Souvenir sheet of 2, #297-298	3.00	3.00

Rotary International, 75th anniversary.

Soccer, Flags of Olympic Participants, Flame — A28

1980, Dec. 29 Litho. Perf. 14

299	A28	1sh shown	.25	.25
300	A28	2sh Relay race	.25	.25
301	A28	10sh Hurdles	.80	.80
302	A28	20sh Boxing	1.60	1.60
		Nos. 299-302 (4)	2.90	2.90

Souvenir Sheet

303		Sheet of 4	3.00	3.00
a.		A28 2.70sh like #299	.25	.25
b.		A28 3sh like #300	.25	.25
c.		A28 5sh like #301	.40	.35
d.		A28 25sh like 302	2.10	1.75

22nd Summer Olympic Games, Moscow, July 19-Aug. 3.

Nos. 299-303 Overprinted with Sport, Winner and Country

1980, Dec. 29

304	A28	1sh multicolored	.25	.25
305	A28	2sh multicolored	.25	.25
306	A28	10sh multicolored	.80	.80
307	A28	20sh multicolored	1.60	1.60
		Nos. 304-307 (4)	2.90	2.90

Souvenir Sheet

308		Sheet of 4	3.00	3.00
a.		A28 2.70sh like #304	.25	.25
b.		A28 3sh like #305	.25	.25
c.		A28 5sh like #306	.40	.35
d.		A28 25sh like #307	2.10	1.75

Souvenir Sheet

Christ in the Storm on the Sea of Galilee, by Rembrandt — A29

1980, Dec. 31 Imperf.

309	A29	25sh multicolored	7.00	6.00

Christmas 1980.

Heinrich von Stephan and UPU Emblem A30

1981, June 2 Litho. Perf. 14

310	A30	1sh shown	.25	.25
311	A30	2sh UPU headquarters	.40	.30
312	A30	2.70sh Mail plane, 1935	.50	.40
313	A30	10sh Mail train, 1927	1.75	1.50
a.		Souvenir sheet of 4, #310-313	4.00	4.00
		Nos. 310-313 (4)	2.90	2.45

Von Stephan (1831-97), UPU founder.

Common Design Types pictured following the introduction.

Royal Wedding Issue
Common Design Type

1981 Litho. Perf. 14

314	CD331a	10sh Couple	.25	.25
a.		10sh on 1sh	.25	.25

315	CD331a	50sh Tower of London	.30	.25
a.		50sh on 5sh	.30	.25
316	CD331a	200sh Prince Charles	1.50	1.25
a.		200sh on 20sh	1.50	1.25
		Nos. 314-316 (3)	2.05	1.75
		Nos. 314a-316a (3)	2.05	1.75

Souvenir Sheet

317	CD331	250sh Royal mews	1.50	1.50
a.		250sh on 25sh, light orange	1.50	1.50

Royal wedding. Issue dates: surcharges, July 13; others, July 29. Nos. 314-316 also issued in sheets of 5 plus label, perf. 12, in changed colors.
For overprints see Nos. 342-345.

Sleeping Woman Before Green Shutters, by Picasso — A31

Picasso Birth Centenary: 20sh, Bullfight. 30sh, Nude Asleep on a Landscape. 200sh, Interior with a Girl Drawing. 250sh, Minotaur.

1981, Sept. 21 Litho. Perf. 14

318	A31	10sh multicolored	.25	.25
319	A31	20sh multicolored	.35	.30
320	A31	30sh multicolored	.50	.40
321	A31	200sh multicolored	3.50	2.75

Size: 120x146mm
Imperf

322	A31	250sh multicolored	5.00	4.00
		Nos. 318-322 (5)	9.60	7.70

Intl. Year of the Disabled A32

1981, Dec. Perf. 15

323	A32	1sh Sign language	.25	.25
324	A32	10sh Teacher in wheelchair	.25	.25
325	A32	50sh Retarded children	.80	.65
326	A32	200sh Blind man	3.25	2.60
a.		Souvenir sheet of 4, #323-326	5.75	5.00
		Nos. 323-326 (4)	4.55	3.75

1982 World Cup Soccer A33

Designs: Various soccer players.

1982, Jan. 11 Litho. Perf. 14

327	A33	1sh multicolored	.25	.25
328	A33	10sh multicolored	.25	.25
329	A33	50sh multicolored	.85	.75
330	A33	200sh multicolored	3.50	3.00
		Nos. 327-330 (4)	4.85	4.25

Souvenir Sheet

331	A33	250sh World Cup	4.50	4.50

TB Bacillus Centenary — A34

1982, June 14 Litho.

332	A34	1sh Koch	.35	.30
333	A34	10sh Microscope	.60	.35
334	A34	50sh Inoculation	2.75	1.40

335 A34 100sh Virus under microscope   5.75 2.75
Nos. 332-335 (4)   9.45 4.80
Souvenir Sheet
336 A34 150sh Medical School   6.50 4.00

Peaceful
Uses of
Outer
Space
A35

1982, May 17   Litho.   Perf. 15
337 A35   5sh Mpoma Satellite
Earth Station   .35   .35
338 A35 10sh Pioneer II   .35   .35
339 A35 50sh Columbia space
shuttle   1.60 1.40
340 A35 100sh Voyager II, Saturn 3.25 2.75
Nos. 337-340 (4)   5.55 4.85
Souvenir Sheet
341 A35 150sh Columbia shuttle 5.25 4.50

Nos. 314-317 Overprinted: "21st
BIRTHDAY / HRH Princess of Wales /
JULY 1 1982"

1982, July 7   Perf. 14
342 CD331 10sh multicolored   .25   .25
343 CD331 50sh multicolored   .55   .45
344 CD331 200sh multicolored   2.25 1.75
Nos. 342-344 (3)   3.05 2.45
Souvenir Sheet
345 CD331 250sh multicolored   4.50 4.00

Also issued in sheets of 5 + label in
changed colors, perf. 12x12½.

20th Anniversary of Independence
A 150sh souvenir sheet showing the
Coat of Arms was not issued.

Hornbill — A36

1982, July 12
346 A36   1sh shown   .25   .25
347 A36 20sh Superb starling   .70   .60
348 A36 50sh Bateleur eagle   1.60 1.40
349 A36 100sh Saddle-bill
stork   3.50 2.90
Nos. 346-349 (4)   6.05 5.15
Souvenir Sheet
350 A36 200sh Laughing dove   12.50 11.00

Scouting
Year
A37

1982, Aug. 23
351 A37   5sh Scouts   .45   .45
352 A37 20sh Trophy presen-
tation   .95   .75
353 A37 50sh Helping disabled   2.40 2.10
354 A37 100sh First aid instruction   4.75 4.25
Nos. 351-354 (4)   8.55 7.55
Souvenir Sheet
355 A37 150sh Baden-Powell   6.00 5.25

For overprints see Nos. 376-380.

Franklin D. Roosevelt (1882-
1945) — A38

Roosevelt and Washington: 50sh, 200sh,
Inaugurations. No. 358, Mount Vernon. No.
359, Hyde Park.

1982, Sept.   Litho.
356 A38 50sh multicolored   .70   .60
357 A38 200sh multicolored   2.75 2.40
Souvenir Sheets
358 A38 150sh multicolored   2.00 1.90
359 A38 150sh multicolored   2.00 1.90

Italy's
Victory
in 1982
World
Cup
A39

1982, Oct.   Litho.   Perf. 14½
359A A39 10sh Players   .25   .25
359B A39 200sh Team   3.00 3.00
Souvenir Sheet
359C A39 250sh Globe   3.00 3.00

A39a

1983, Mar. 14   Litho.   Perf. 14
360 A39a   5sh Dancers   .25   .25
361 A39a 20sh Traditional currency   .30   .30
362 A39a 50sh Village   .70   .70
363 A39a 100sh Drums   1.40 1.40
Nos. 360-363 (4)   2.65 2.65
Commonwealth Day.

St. George
and the
Dragon, by
Raphael
A40

1983, Apr.
364 A40   5sh shown   .25   .25
365 A40 20sh St. George and
the Dragon,
1505   .35   .35
366 A40 50sh Moses Parts
the Red Sea   .90   .90
367 A40 200sh Expulsion of
Heliodorus   3.25 3.25
Nos. 364-367 (4)   4.75 4.75
Souvenir Sheet
368 A40 250sh Leo the Great
and Attila,
1513   3.25 3.25

A41

7th Non-aligned Summit
Conference — A42

1983, Aug. 15   Litho.   Perf. 14½
369 A41   5sh multicolored   .25   .25
370 A42 200sh multicolored   2.00 2.00

African
Elephants
and World
Wildlife
Emblem
A43

5sh, Three adults with elephant bones.
10sh, Three adults walking. 30sh, Elephants
standing in water hole. 70sh, Adults with calf.

1983, Aug. 22   Perf. 15
371 A43   5sh multicolored   1.25 1.25
372 A43 10sh multicolored   2.00 2.00
373 A43 30sh multicolored   4.75 4.75
374 A43 70sh multicolored   12.00 12.00
Nos. 371-374 (4)   20.00 20.00

Nos. 371-374 were reprinted in 1990, perf
14. Value $25.

Souvenir Sheet
375 A43 300sh Zebras, vert.   8.00 7.00

No. 375 does not have the WWF emblem.
See Nos. 948-953.

Nos. 351-355 Overprinted or
Surcharged: "BOYS BRIGADE
CENTENARY 1883-1983"

1983, Sept. 19   Litho.   Perf. 14
376 A37   5sh multicolored   .25   .25
377 A37 20sh multicolored   .25   .25
378 A37 50sh multicolored   .55   .55
379 A37 400sh on 100sh multi   4.50 4.50
Nos. 376-379 (4)   5.55 5.55
Souvenir Sheet
380 A37 150sh multicolored   1.75 1.75

World Communications Year — A44

Designs: 20sh, Mpoma Satellite Earth Station. 50sh, Railroad, Computer Operator.
70sh, Filming Lions. 100sh, Pilots, Radio
Communications. 300sh, Communications
Satellite.

1983, Oct. 3   Litho.   Perf. 15
381 A44 20sh multicolored   .25   .25
382 A44 50sh multicolored   .80   .80
383 A44 70sh multicolored   1.10 1.10
384 A44 100sh multicolored   1.60 1.60
Nos. 381-384 (4)   3.75 3.75
Souvenir Sheet
385 A44 300sh multicolored   3.50 3.50

Nos. 279, 281-285, 289 Surcharged

1983, Nov. 7   Perf. 14
386 A26 100sh on 10c multi
387 A26 135sh on 1sh multi
388 A26 175sh on 30c multi
389 A26 200sh on 50c multi
390 A26 400sh on 80c multi
391 A26 700sh on 5sh multi
392 A26 1000sh on 1.50sh
Nos. 386-392 (7)   18.00 18.00

World
Food Day
A45

Christmas — A46

1983, Dec. 12   Litho.   Perf. 14
395 A46 10sh Navitity   .25   .25
396 A46 50sh Sheperds and
Angel   .40   .40
397 A46 175sh Flight into Egypt 1.25 1.25
398 A46 400sh Angels Blowing
Trumpets   3.00 3.00
Nos. 395-398 (4)   4.90 4.90
Souvenir Sheet
399 A46 300sh Three Kings   2.25 2.25

Animal Type of 1979
1983, Dec. 19
400 A26 100sh like No. 284   .70   .70
401 A26 135sh like No. 285   .85   .85
402 A26 175sh like No. 286   1.00 1.00
403 A26 200sh like No. 287   1.40 1.40
404 A26 400sh like No. 288   3.00 3.00
405 A26 700sh like No. 292   4.75 4.75
406 A26 1000sh like No. 291   6.50 6.50
Nos. 400-406 (7)   18.20 18.20

1984
Summer
Olympics
A48

1983   Perf. 14½
417 A48   5sh Ruth Kyalisiima   .25   .25
418 A48 115sh Javelin   .50   .50
419 A48 155sh Wrestling   .65   .65
420 A48 175sh Rowing   .85   .85
Nos. 417-420 (4)   2.25 2.25
Souvenir Sheet
421 A48 500sh Akii-Bua   2.40 2.40

For overprints see Nos. 458-462.

Intl. Civil
Aviation
Org., 40th
Anniv.
A49

1984, Sept.
422 A49   5sh Passenger service   .55   .55
423 A49 115sh Cargo service   1.90 1.90
424 A49 155sh Police airwing   2.75 2.75
425 A49 175sh Soroti Flying
School plane   4.00 4.00
Nos. 422-425 (4)   9.20 9.20
Souvenir Sheet
426 A49 250sh Hot air balloon 5.00 5.00

Butterflies
A50

1984, Oct.   Litho.   Perf. 14½
427 A50   5sh Silver-barred
Charaxes   .35   .35
428 A50 115sh Western Em-
peror Swal-
lowtail   2.75 2.75
429 A50 155sh African Giant
Swallowtail   3.75 3.75
430 A50 175sh Blue Salamis   4.50 4.50
Nos. 427-430 (4)   11.35 11.35
Souvenir Sheet
431 A50 250sh Veinted Yellow   5.50 5.00

Freshwater Fish — A51

1985		**Litho.**		**Perf. 15**
432	A51	5sh Nothobranchi-us taeni-opygus	.55	.55
433	A51	10sh Bagrus dogmac	.80	.55
434	A51	50sh Polypterus senegalus	1.50	.45
435	A51	100sh Clarias	1.50	.45
436	A51	135sh Mormyrus kannume	2.50	1.40
437	A51	175sh Synodontis victoriae	2.50	2.40
438	A51	205sh Haplochromis brownae	2.50	2.75
439	A51	400sh Lates niloticus	2.50	3.00
440	A51	700sh Protopterus aethiopicus	2.50	3.50
441	A51	1000sh Barbus rad-cliffii	2.50	3.50
442	A51	2500sh Malapterus electricus	3.00	4.75
		Nos. 432-442 (11)	22.35	23.30

Issued: #432-435, 437-441, 4/1; #436, 442, 6/10.

For overprints see Nos. 490-494.

Easter A52

1985, May 13		**Litho.**		**Perf. 14**
443	A52	5sh The Last Supper	.55	.55
444	A52	115sh Jesus confronts doubting Thomas	1.75	1.75
445	A52	155sh Crucifixion	1.90	2.50
446	A52	175sh Pentecost	2.50	3.25
		Nos. 443-446 (4)	6.70	8.05

Souvenir Sheet

447	A52	250sh Last prayer in garden	1.25	1.25

UN Child Survival Campaign A53

1985, July 1				
448	A53	5sh Mother breastfeeding	.40	.40
449	A53	115sh Growth monitorization	2.10	2.10
450	A53	155sh Immunization	2.75	2.75
451	A53	175sh Oral rehydration therapy	3.25	3.25
		Nos. 448-451 (4)	8.50	8.50

Souvenir Sheet

452	A53	500sh Expectant Moth-er, food	6.00	6.00

Audubon Birth Bicent. — A54 / UN Decade for Women — A56

1985, July				
453	A54	115sh Acrocephalus schoe-nobaenus	2.10	1.75
454	A54	155sh Ardeola ibis	2.50	1.90
455	A54	175sh Galerida gris-tata	2.10	2.50

456	A54	500sh Aythya fuligu-la	3.50	5.00
		Nos. 453-456 (4)	10.20	11.15

Souvenir Sheet

457	A54	1000sh Strix aluco	11.50	11.50
		See Nos. 469-473.		

Nos. 417-421 Ovptd. or Surcharged with Winners Names, Medals and Countries in Gold

Gold medalists: 5sh, Benita Brown-Fitzger-ald, US, 100-meter hurdles. 115sh, Árto Haerkoenen, Finland, javelin. 155sh, Atsuji Miyahara, Japan, 115-pound Greco-Roman wrestling. 100sh, West Germany, quadruple sculls. 1200sh, Edwin Moses, US, 400-meter hurdles.

1985, July				**Perf. 15**
458	A48	5sh multicolored	.25	.25
459	A48	115sh multicolored	.35	.35
460	A48	155sh multicolored	.50	.50
461	A48	175sh on 175sh multi	3.00	3.00
		Nos. 458-461 (4)	4.10	4.10

Souvenir Sheet

462	A48	1200sh on 500sh multi	3.50	3.50

1985		**Litho.**		**Perf. 14**

5sh, Natl. Women's Day, Mar. 8. 115sh, Girl Guides 75th anniv., horiz. 155sh, Mother The-resa, 1979 Nobel Peace Prize laureate. 1000sh, Queen Mother. #467, Queen Mother inspecting troops. #468, like 115sh, horiz.

463	A56	5sh multicolored	.25	.25
464	A56	115sh multicolored	1.75	1.60
465	A56	155sh multicolored	2.90	2.50
466	A56	1000sh multicolored	1.40	1.75
		Nos. 463-466 (4)	6.30	6.10

Souvenir Sheets

467	A56	1000sh multicolored	3.50	3.50
468	A56	1500sh multicolored	5.00	5.00

Issued: #466-467, Aug. 21; others, Nov. 1.

Audubon Type of 1985

1985, Dec. 23				**Perf. 12½x12**
469	A54	5sh Rock ptarmi-gan	.65	.40
470	A54	155sh Sage grouse	2.25	2.00
471	A54	175sh Lesser yellow-legs	2.25	2.50
472	A54	500sh Brown-head-ed cowbird	3.75	4.50
		Nos. 469-472 (4)	8.90	9.40

Souvenir Sheet
Perf. 14

473	A54	1000sh Whooping crane	9.50	9.50

UN, 40th Anniv. A57

Designs: 10sh, Forest resources, vert. 180sh, UN Peace-keeping Force. 200sh, Emblem, UN Development Project. 250sh, Intl. Peace Year. 2000sh, Natl., UN flags, vert. 2500sh, Flags, UN Building, New York, vert.

1986, Feb.				**Perf. 15**
474	A57	10sh multicolored	.25	.25
475	A57	180sh multicolored	.35	.35
476	A57	200sh multicolored	.45	.45
477	A57	250sh multicolored	.55	.55
478	A57	2000sh multicolored	4.25	4.25
		Nos. 474-478 (5)	5.85	5.85

Souvenir Sheet

479	A57	2500sh multicolored	3.25	3.25

1986 World Cup Soccer Championships, Mexico — A58

Various soccer plays.

1986, Mar.				**Perf. 14**
480	A58	10sh multicolored	.30	.30
481	A58	180sh multicolored	1.00	.60
482	A58	250sh multicolored	1.10	.75
483	A58	2500sh multicolored	6.25	7.00
		Nos. 480-483 (4)	8.65	8.65

Souvenir Sheet

484	A58	3000sh multicolored	6.00	6.00

No. 484 contains vert. stamp.
For overprints see Nos. 514-518.

Halley's Comet — A60

Designs: 50sh, Arecibo radio telescope, Puerto Rico, and Tycho Brahe (1546-1601), Danish astronomer. 100sh, Recovery of Astronaut John Glenn, US space capsule, Caribbean, 1962. 140sh, Adoration of the Magi, 1301, by Giotto (1276-1337). 2500sh, Sighting, 1835, Davy Crockett at The Alamo.

1986, Mar.		**Litho.**		**Perf. 14**
485	A59	50sh multicolored	.30	.25
486	A59	100sh multicolored	.45	.25
487	A59	140sh multicolored	.70	.45
488	A59	2500sh multicolored	5.50	6.75
		Nos. 485-488 (4)	6.95	7.70

Souvenir Sheet

489	A60	3000sh multicolored	7.50	7.50

For overprints see Nos. 519-523.

Nos. 437, 439-442 and 468 Ovptd. "NRA LIBERATION / 1986" in Silver or Black

1986, Apr.				**Perf. 15**
490	A51	175sh multi	1.50	1.25
490A	A51	400sh multi	2.75	2.75
491	A51	700sh multi	4.00	4.00
492	A51	1000sh multi (Bk)	4.50	4.50
493	A51	2500sh multi (Bk)	7.00	8.25
		Nos. 490-493 (5)	19.75	20.75

Souvenir Sheet
Perf. 14

494	A56	1500sh multi (Bk)	5.75	4.75

No. 494 ovptd. in one line in margin. A 400sh also exists with silver overprint. All stamps exist with overprint colors transposed.

Queen Elizabeth II, 60th Birthday
Common Design Type

1986, Apr. 21				**Perf. 14**
495	CD339	100sh At London Zoo, c. 1938	.25	.25
496	CD339	140sh At the races, 1970	.25	.25
497	CD339	2500sh San-dringham, 1982	4.25	4.25
		Nos. 495-497 (3)	4.75	4.75

Souvenir Sheet

498	CD339	3000sh Engagement, 1947	4.75	4.75

AMERIPEX '86 — A61

1986, May 22				**Perf. 15**
499	A61	50sh Niagara Falls	.30	.30
500	A61	100sh Jefferson Memo-rial	.30	.30
501	A61	250sh Liberty Bell	.50	.50
502	A61	1000sh The Alamo	1.90	1.90

503	A61	2500sh George Wash-ington Bridge	4.50	4.50
		Nos. 499-503 (5)	7.50	7.50

Souvenir Sheet

504	A61	3000sh Grand Canyon	3.75	3.75
		Statue of Liberty, cent.		

A62

Statue of Liberty, Cent. — A63

Tall ships, Operation Sail: 50sh, Gloria, Colombia, vert. 100sh, Mircea, Romania, vert. 140sh, Sagres II, Portugal. 2500sh, Gazela Primero, US.

1986, July				**Perf. 14**
505	A62	50sh multicolored	.75	.60
506	A62	100sh multicolored	1.00	.60
507	A62	140sh multicolored	1.75	1.25
508	A62	2500sh multicolored	7.75	9.25
		Nos. 505-508 (4)	11.25	11.70

Souvenir Sheet

509	A63	3000sh multicolored	4.50	4.50

Royal Wedding Issue, 1986
Common Design Type

Designs: 50sh, Prince Andrew and Sarah Ferguson. 140sh, Andrew and Princess Anne. 2500sh, At formal affair. 3000sh, Couple diff. Nos. 510-512 horiz.

1986, July 23				
510	CD340	50sh multicolored	.25	.25
511	CD340	140sh multicolored	.25	.25
512	CD340	2500sh multicolored	4.00	4.75
		Nos. 510-512 (3)	4.50	5.25

Souvenir Sheet

513	CD340	3000sh multicolored	5.00	5.00

Nos. 480-484 Ovptd. or Surcharged "WINNERS Argentina 3 W. Germany 2" in Gold in 2 or 3 Lines

1986, Sept. 15		**Litho.**		**Perf. 14**
514	A58	50sh on 10sh multi	.25	.25
515	A58	180sh multicolored	.25	.25
516	A58	250sh multicolored	.30	.30
517	A58	2500sh multicolored	3.75	3.25
		Nos. 514-517 (4)	4.55	4.05

Souvenir Sheet

518	A58	3000sh multicolored	6.00	6.00

Nos. 485-489 Ovptd. with Halley's Comet Emblem

1986, Oct. 15		**Litho.**		**Perf. 14**
519	A59	50sh multicolored	.35	.35
520	A59	100sh multicolored	.60	.40
521	A59	140sh multicolored	.80	.70
522	A59	2500sh multicolored	7.25	8.25
		Nos. 519-522 (4)	9.00	9.70

Souvenir Sheet

523	A60	3000sh multicolored	6.50	6.50

Christian
Martyrs
A64

Designs: 50sh, St. Kizito. 150sh, St. Kizito educating Ganda converts. 200sh, Execution of Bishop James Hannington. 1000sh, Mwanga's execution of converts, cent. 1500sh, King Mwanga sentencing Christians to death.

1986, Oct. 15

524	A64	50sh multicolored	.25	.25
525	A64	150sh multicolored	.25	.25
526	A64	200sh multicolored	.50	.50
527	A64	1000sh multicolored	2.00	2.00
		Nos. 524-527 (4)	3.00	3.00

Souvenir Sheet

528	A64	1500sh multicolored	2.25	2.25

A65

Christmas — A66

Paintings by Albrecht Durer and Titian: 50sh, Madonna of the Cherries. 150sh, Madonna and Child, vert. 200sh, Assumption of the Virgin, vert. 2500sh, Praying Hands, vert. No. 533, Adoration of the Magi. No. 534, Presentation of the Virgin in the Temple.

1986, Nov. 26   Litho.   Perf. 14

529	A65	50sh multicolored	.25	.25
530	A65	150sh multicolored	.55	.25
531	A65	200sh multicolored	.75	.30
532	A65	2500sh multicolored	5.50	7.00
		Nos. 529-532 (4)	7.05	7.80

Souvenir Sheets

533	A66	3000sh multicolored	5.25	5.25
534	A66	3000sh multicolored	5.25	5.25

Birds and
Animals
A67

1987   Perf. 15

535	A67	2sh Red-billed firefinch	.40	.35
536	A67	5sh African pygmy kingfisher	.55	.35
537	A67	10sh Scarlet-chested sunbird	.80	.35
538	A67	25sh White rhinoceros	1.25	.95
539	A67	35sh Lion	1.25	1.25
540	A67	45sh Cheetahs	1.50	1.75
541	A67	50sh Cordon bleu	1.75	2.10
542	A67	100sh Giant eland	2.75	3.50
		Nos. 535-542 (8)	10.25	10.60

Souvenir Sheets

543	A67	150sh Carmine bee-eaters	4.75	4.75
544	A67	150sh Cattle egret, zebra	4.75	4.75

Issue dates: Nos. 535-537, 541, 543, Nov. 2; Nos. 538-540, 542-544, July 22.

Transportation Innovations — A68

1987, Aug. 14

545	A68	2sh Eagle, 1987	.30	.30
546	A68	3sh Bremen, 1928	.30	.30
547	A68	5sh Winnie Mae, 1933	.35	.35
548	A68	10sh Voyager, 1986	.50	.50
549	A68	15sh Chanute bi-plane glider, 1896	.80	.80
550	A68	25sh Norge, 1926	1.10	1.10
551	A68	35sh Curtis biplane, USS Pennsylvania, 1911	1.75	1.75
552	A68	45sh Freedom 7, 1961	2.00	2.00
553	A68	100sh Concorde, 1976	5.75	6.75
		Nos. 545-553 (9)	12.85	13.85

1988
Summer
Olympics,
Seoul
A69

Flags and athletes.

1987, Oct. 5   Perf. 14½x14

554	A69	5sh Torch bearer	.25	.25
555	A69	10sh Swimming	.30	.30
556	A69	50sh Cycling	1.40	1.40
557	A69	100sh Gymnastic rings	2.75	2.75
		Nos. 554-557 (4)	4.70	4.70

Souvenir Sheet

558	A69	150sh Boxing	4.25	4.50

A70

Natl. Independence, 25th
Anniv. — A71

1987, Oct. 8

559	A70	5sh shown	.25	.25
560	A70	10sh Mulago Hispital	.45	.45
561	A70	25sh Independence Monument	1.00	1.00
562	A70	50sh High Court	1.90	1.90
		Nos. 559-562 (4)	3.60	3.60

Souvenir Sheet

563	A71	100sh shown	3.25	3.25

A72

Science and Space — A73

Designs: 5sh, Hippocrates, father of modern medicine, caduceus and surgeons. 25sh, Albert Einstein and Theory of Relativity equation. 35sh, Sir Isaac Newton and Optics Theory. 45sh, Karl Benz (1844-1929), German engineer, automobile pioneer, and the Velocipede, Mercedes-Benz sports coupe and manufacturers' emblems.

1987, Nov. 2   Perf. 14½x14

564	A72	5sh multicolored	.70	.70
565	A72	25sh multicolored	2.75	2.75
566	A72	35sh multicolored	3.25	3.25
567	A72	45sh multicolored	4.00	4.00
		Nos. 564-567 (4)	10.70	10.70

Souvenir Sheet
Perf. 14x14½

568	A73	150sh shown	6.00	6.00

Birds — A74

1987, Nov. 2   Litho.   Perf. 14

569	A74	5sh Golden-backed weaver	.75	.75
570	A74	10sh Hoopoe	1.60	1.40
571	A74	15sh Red-throated bee-eater	1.75	1.40
572	A74	25sh Lilac-breasted roller	2.25	1.90
573	A74	35sh Pygmy goose	2.50	2.10
574	A74	45sh Scarlet-chested sunbird	2.75	2.75
575	A74	50sh Crowned crane	2.75	2.75
576	A74	100sh Long-tailed fiscal shrike	5.00	5.00
		Nos. 569-576 (8)	19.35	18.05

Souvenir Sheets

577	A74	150sh African barn owl, horiz.	5.00	5.00
578	A74	150sh African fish-eagle, horiz.	5.00	5.00

14th World Boy Scout Jamboree,
Australia, 1987-88 — A75

Activities: 5sh, Stamp collecting, Uganda Nos. 84 and 116. 25sh, Planting trees, Natl. flag. 35sh, Canoeing on Lake Victoria. 45sh, Hiking and camping. 150sh, Logo of 1987 jamboree and natl. Boy Scout organization emblem.

1987, Nov. 20

579	A75	5sh multicolored	.30	.30
580	A75	25sh multicolored	1.25	1.25
581	A75	35sh multicolored	1.75	1.75
582	A75	45sh multicolored	2.10	2.10
		Nos. 579-582 (4)	5.40	5.40

Souvenir Sheet

583	A75	150sh multicolored	5.00	5.00

Christmas
A76

The life of Christ and the Virgin pictured on bas-reliefs, c. 1250, and a tapestry from France: 5sh, The Annunciation. 10sh, The Nativity. 50sh, Flight into Egypt. 100sh, The Adoration of the Magi. 150sh, The Mystic Wine Tapestry.

1987, Dec. 18

584	A76	5sh multicolored	.25	.25
585	A76	10sh multicolored	.25	.25
586	A76	50sh multicolored	1.60	1.75
587	A76	100sh multicolored	3.00	3.50
		Nos. 584-587 (4)	5.10	5.75

Souvenir Sheet

588	A76	150sh multicolored	5.00	5.00

Locomotives — A77

Designs: 5sh, Class 12 2-6-2T light shunter. 10sh, Class 92 1Co-Co1 diesel electric. 15sh, Class 2-8-2. 25sh, Class 2-6-2T light shunter. 35sh, Class 4-8-0. 45sh, Class 4-8-2. 50sh, Class 4-8-4+4-8-4 Garratt. 100sh, Class 87 1Co-Co1 diesel electric. No. 597, Class 59 4-8-2+2-8-4 Garratt. No. 598, Class 31 2-8-4.

1988, Jan. 18

589	A77	5sh multicolored	.25	.25
590	A77	10sh multicolored	.45	.45
591	A77	15sh multicolored	.70	.65
592	A77	25sh multicolored	1.00	1.00
593	A77	35sh multicolored	1.60	1.25
594	A77	45sh multicolored	2.00	1.75
595	A77	50sh multicolored	2.10	1.90
596	A77	100sh multicolored	5.00	3.00
		Nos. 589-596 (8)	13.10	10.25

Souvenir Sheets

597	A77	150sh multicolored	5.25	5.25
598	A77	150sh multicolored	5.25	5.25

Minerals — A78

1988, Jan. 18

599	A78	1sh Columbite-tantalite	.25	.25
600	A78	2sh Galena	.25	.25
601	A78	5sh Malachite	.25	.25
602	A78	10sh Cassiterite	.35	.35
603	A78	35sh Ferberite	1.50	1.50
604	A78	50sh Emerald	2.00	2.00
605	A78	100sh Monazite	3.75	3.75
606	A78	150sh Microcline	6.00	6.00
		Nos. 599-606 (8)	14.35	14.35

1988
Summer
Olympics,
Seoul
A79

1988, May 16   Litho.   Perf. 14

607	A79	5sh Hurdles	.30	.30
608	A79	25sh High jump	.55	.75
609	A79	35sh Javelin	.60	.75
610	A79	45sh Long jump	.85	1.00
		Nos. 607-610 (4)	2.30	2.80

Souvenir Sheet

611	A79	150sh Medals, five-ring emblem	2.25	2.25

For overprints see Nos. 651-655.

Flowers
A80

1988, July 28   Litho.   Perf. 15

612	A80	5sh	Spathodea campanulata	.60	.25
613	A80	10sh	Gloriosa simplex	.60	.25
614	A80	20sh	Thevetica peruviana, vert.	.80	.60
615	A80	25sh	Hibiscus schizopetalus	.80	.80
616	A80	35sh	Aframomum sceptrum	.80	.85
617	A80	45sh	Adenium obesum	.80	1.10
618	A80	50sh	Kigelia africana, vert.	1.00	1.40
619	A80	100sh	Clappertonia ficifolia	1.50	2.25

Nos. 612-619 (8)   6.90 7.50

Souvenir Sheets

620	A80	150sh	Costus spectabiis	3.50 3.50
621	A80	150sh	Canarina abyssinica, vert.	3.50 3.50

Intl. Red Cross, 125th Anniv. A81

1988, Oct. 28   Litho.   Perf. 14

622	A81	10sh	"AIDS"	.30 .30
623	A81	40sh	Immunize children	1.00 1.00
624	A81	70sh	Relief distribution	2.10 2.10
625	A81	90sh	First aid	2.75 2.75

Nos. 622-625 (4)   6.15 6.15

Souvenir Sheet

626 A81 150sh Jean-Henri Dunant, vert.   3.25 3.25

Paintings by Titian — A82

Designs: 10sh, Portrait of a Lady, c. 1508. 20sh, Portrait of a Man, 1507. 40sh, Portrait of Isabella d'Este, c. 1534. 50sh, Portrait of Vincenzo Mosti, 1520. 70sh, Pope Paul III Farnese, c. 1545. 90sh, Violante, 1515. 100sh, Lavinia, Titian's Daughter, c. 1565. 250sh, Portrait of Dr. Parma, c. 1515. No. 635, The Speech of Alfonso D'Avalos, c. 1540. No. 636, Cain and Abel.

1988, Oct. 31   Perf. 14

627	A82	10sh	multicolored	.25 .25
628	A82	20sh	multicolored	.40 .40
629	A82	40sh	multicolored	.60 .60
630	A82	50sh	multicolored	.75 .75
631	A82	70sh	multicolored	.85 .85
632	A82	90sh	multicolored	1.00 1.00
633	A82	100sh	multicolored	1.25 1.25
634	A82	250sh	multicolored	2.40 2.40

Nos. 627-634 (8)   7.50 7.50

Souvenir Sheets

635	A82	350sh	multicolored	4.75 4.75
636	A82	350sh	multicolored	4.75 4.75

Game Preserves — A83

Designs: 10sh, Giraffes, Kidepo Valley Natl. Park. 25sh, Zebras, Lake Mburo Natl. Park. 100sh, African buffalo, Murchison Falls Natl. Park. 250sh, Pelicans, Queen Elizabeth Natl. Park. 350sh, Roan antelopes, Lake Mburo Natl. Park.

1988, Nov. 18   Litho.   Perf. 14

637	A83	10sh	multicolored	.45 .25
638	A83	25sh	multicolored	1.60 .65
639	A83	100sh	multicolored	3.25 3.50
640	A83	250sh	multicolored	9.00 11.00

Nos. 637-640 (4)   14.30 15.40

Souvenir Sheet

641 A83 350sh multicolored   4.50 4.50

WHO 40th Anniv., Alma Ata Declaration 10th Anniv. — A84

1988, Dec. 1

642	A84	10sh	Primary health care	.25 .25
643	A84	25sh	Mental health	.45 .45
644	A84	45sh	Rural health care	.75 .75
645	A84	100sh	Dental care	1.75 1.75
646	A84	200sh	Postnatal care	3.25 3.25

Nos. 642-646 (5)   6.45 6.45

Souvenir Sheet

647 A84 350sh Conference Hall, Alma-Ata, USSR 4.25 4.25

Miniature Sheet

Christmas, Mickey Mouse 60th Birthday — A85

Walt Disney characters: No. 648a, Santa Claus. b, Goofy. c, Mickey Mouse. d, Huey at conveyor belt. e, Dewey packing building blocks. f, Donald Duck. g, Chip-n-Dale. h, Louie at conveyor belt controls. No. 649, Preparing reindeer for Christmas eve flight. No. 650, Mickey loading sleigh with toys, horiz.

1988, Dec. 2   Perf. 13½x14, 14x13½

648		Sheet of 8	10.00 10.00
a.-h.	A85 50sh any single		.80 .80

Souvenir Sheets

649	A85	350sh	multicolored	5.75 5.75
650	A85	350sh	multicolored	5.75 5.75

Nos. 607-611 Ovptd. or Surcharged to Honor Olympic Winners
5sh: "110 M HURDLES / R. KINGDOM / USA"
25sh: "HIGH JUMP / G. AVDEENKO / USSR"
35sh: "JAVELIN / T. KORJUS / FINLAND"
300sh: "LONG JUMP / C. LEWIS / USA"

1989, Jan. 30   Litho.   Perf. 14

651	A79	5sh	multicolored	.25 .25
652	A79	25sh	multicolored	.30 .30
653	A79	35sh	multicolored	.35 .35
654	A79	300sh on 45sh multi		3.25 3.25

Nos. 651-654 (4)   4.15 4.15

Souvenir Sheet

655 A79 350sh on 150sh multi   5.00 5.00

1990 World Cup Soccer Championships, Italy — A86

Various action scenes.

1989, Apr. 24   Litho.   Perf. 14

656	A86	10sh	multi, vert.	.35 .35
657	A86	25sh	multicolored	.55 .55
658	A86	75sh	multicolored	1.60 1.60
659	A86	200sh	multi, vert.	4.00 4.00

Nos. 656-659 (4)   6.50 6.50

Souvenir Sheet

660 A86 300sh multicolored   4.50 4.50

Mushrooms — A87

1989, Aug. 14   Litho.   Perf. 14

661	A87	10sh	Suillus granulatus	.60 .60
662	A87	15sh	Omphalotus olearius	.75 .75
663	A87	45sh	Oudemansiella radicata	1.50 1.50
664	A87	50sh	Clitocybe nebularis	1.50 1.50
665	A87	60sh	Macrolepiota rhacodes	1.60 1.60
666	A87	75sh	Lepista nuda	1.90 1.90
667	A87	150sh	Suillus luteus	3.50 3.50
668	A87	200sh	Agaricus campestris	3.75 3.75

Nos. 661-668 (8)   15.10 15.10

Souvenir Sheets

669	A87	350sh	Schizophyllum commune	8.00 8.00
670	A87	350sh	Bolbitius vitellinus	8.00 8.00

"The Thirty-six Views of Mt. Fuji" — A88

Prints by Hokusai (1760-1849): 10sh, Fuji and the Great Wave off Kanagawa. 15sh, Fuji from Lake Suwa. 20sh, Fuji from Kajikazawa. 60sh, Fuji from Shichirigahama. 90sh, Fuji from Ejiri in Sunshu. 120sh, Fuji Above Lightning. 200sh, Fuji from Lower Meguro in Edo. 250sh, Fuji from Edo. No. 679, The Red Fuji from the Foot. No. 680, Fuji from Umezawa.

1989, May 15   Litho.   Perf. 14x13½

671	A88	10sh	multicolored	.35 .35
672	A88	15sh	multicolored	.35 .35
673	A88	20sh	multicolored	.35 .35
674	A88	60sh	multicolored	.90 .90
675	A88	90sh	multicolored	1.40 1.40
676	A88	120sh	multicolored	2.00 2.00
677	A88	200sh	multicolored	3.25 3.25
678	A88	250sh	multicolored	4.00 4.00

Nos. 671-678 (8)   12.60 12.60

Souvenir Sheets

679	A88	500sh	multicolored	6.25 6.25
680	A88	500sh	multicolored	6.25 6.25

Hirohito (1901-1989), Showa emperor, and Akihito, Heisei emperor of Japan.

PHILEXFRANCE '89 — A89

1989, July 7   Litho.   Perf. 14

681	A89	20sh	No. 1	.60 .60
682	A89	70sh	No. 10	1.50 1.50
683	A89	100sh	No. 48	1.75 1.75

684	A89	250sh	No. 67	3.50 3.50
a.	Souvenir sheet of 4, #681-684		11.00 11.00

Nos. 681-684 (4)   7.35 7.35

No. 684a sold for 500sh.

2nd All African Scout Jamboree, Aug. 3-15 — A90

1989, Aug. 3   Litho.   Perf. 14

685	A90	10sh	Fatal child ailments	.35 .35
686	A90	70sh	Raising poultry	1.75 1.75
687	A90	90sh	Immunization	2.10 2.10
688	A90	100sh	Brick-making	2.10 2.10

Nos. 685-688 (4)   6.30 6.30

Souvenir Sheet

689 A90 500sh Natl. emblem, vert.   5.75 5.75

Scouting, 75th anniv.
For surcharges see Nos. 1301-1304.

Miniature Sheet

Wildlife at Waterhole — A91

Designs: a, Saddle-billed stork. b, White pelican. c, Marabou stork. d, Egyptian vulture, giraffes. e, Bateleur eagle, antelope. f, African elephant. g, Giraffe. h, Goliath heron. i, Black rhinoceros, zebras. j, Zebras, oribi. k, African fish eagle. l, Hippopotamus. m, Black-backed jackal, white pelican. n, Cape buffalo. o, Olive baboon. p, Bohor reedbuck. q, Lesser flamingo, serval. r, Shoebill stork. s, Crowned crane. t, Impala. No. 691, Lion. No. 692, Long-crested eagle.

1989, Sept. 12   Perf. 14½x14

690		Sheet of 20	22.00 22.00
a.-t.	A91 30sh any single		.60 .60

Souvenir Sheets

691	A91	500sh	multicolored	5.75 5.75
692	A91	500sh	multicolored	5.75 5.75

1st Moon Landing, 20th Anniv. — A92   Butterflies — A93

Quotations and scenes from the Apollo 11 mission.

1989, Oct. 20   Litho.   Perf. 14

693	A92	10sh	Launch vehicle, Moon	.30 .30
694	A92	20sh	Eagle lower stage on Moon	.30 .30
695	A92	30sh	Columbia	.55 .55
696	A92	50sh	Eagle landing	.75 .75
697	A92	70sh	Aldrin on Moon	1.10 1.10
698	A92	250sh	Armstrong on ladder	3.75 3.75
699	A92	300sh	Eagle ascending	4.25 4.25
700	A92	350sh	Aldrin, diff.	5.00 5.00

Nos. 693-700 (8)   16.00 16.00

Souvenir Sheets

701	A92	500sh Liftoff	5.25	5.25
702	A92	500sh Parachute landing	5.25	5.25

Nos. 693-697 and 699 horiz.

1989, Nov. 13   "UGANDA" in Black

703	A93	5sh Ioalus pallene	.65	.65
704	A93	10sh Hewitsonia boisduvali	.70	.70
705	A93	20sh Euxanthe wakefeildi	1.10	1.10
706	A93	30sh Papilio echerioides	1.25	1.25
707	A93	40sh Acraea semivitrea	1.40	1.40
708	A93	50sh Colotis antevippe	1.40	1.40
709	A93	70sh Acraea perenna	1.75	1.75
710	A93	90sh Charaxes cynthia	1.75	1.75
711	A93	100sh Euphaedra neophroa	1.75	1.75
712	A93	150sh Cymothoe beckeri	2.25	2.25
713	A93	200sh Vanessula milca	2.25	2.25
714	A93	400sh Mimacraea marshalli	3.25	3.25
715	A93	500sh Axiocerses amanga	3.50	3.50
716	A93	1000sh Precis hierta	4.50	4.50
		Nos. 703-716 (14)	27.50	27.50

See Nos. 826-839 for "UGANDA" in blue.

Explorers of Africa A94

Designs: 10sh, John Speke (1827-64), satellite view of Lake Victoria. 25sh, Sir Richard Burton (1821-90), satellite view of Lake Tanganyika. 40sh, Richard Lander (1804-34), bronze ritual figure of the Bakota tribe. 90sh, Rene Caillie (1799-1838), mosque. 125sh, Dorcas gazelle and Sir Samuel Baker (1821-93), discoverer of Lake Albert. 150sh, Phoenician galley and Necho II (d. 595 B.C.), king of Egypt credited by Herodotus with sending an expedition to circumnavigate Africa. 250sh, Vasco da Gama (c. 1460-1524), 1st European to sail around the Cape of Good Hope, and caravel. 300sh, Sir Henry Stanley (1841-1904), discoverer of Lake Edward, and Lady Alice . No. 725, Dr. David Livingstone (1813-73), discoverer of Victoria Falls, and steam launch Ma-Robert. No. 726, Mary Kingsley (1862-1900), ethnologist, and tail-spot climbing perch.

1989, Nov. 15   Litho.   Perf. 14

717	A94	10sh multicolored	.40	.40
718	A94	25sh multicolored	.45	.45
719	A94	40sh multicolored	.75	.75
720	A94	90sh multicolored	1.60	1.60
721	A94	125sh multicolored	2.25	2.25
722	A94	150sh multicolored	2.75	2.75
723	A94	250sh multicolored	4.50	4.50
724	A94	300sh multicolored	5.50	5.50
		Nos. 717-724 (8)	18.20	18.20

Souvenir Sheets

725	A94	500sh multicolored	6.50	6.50
726	A94	500sh multicolored	6.50	6.50

Anniversaries and Events — A95

1989, Dec. 12

727	A95	10sh Bank emblem	.30	.30
728	A95	20sh Satellite dishes, arrows	.30	.30
729	A95	75sh Nehru	2.40	2.40
730	A95	90sh Pan-American Dixie Clipper	2.40	2.40
731	A95	100sh Locomotion, Stephenson	2.40	2.40
732	A95	150sh Concorde cockpit	3.75	3.50
733	A95	250sh Wapen von Hamburg, Leopoldus Primus	3.75	3.50
734	A95	300sh Concorde cockpit, crew	4.75	4.75
		Nos. 727-734 (8)	20.05	19.55

Souvenir Sheets

735	A95	500sh Storming of the Bastille	6.00	6.00
736	A95	500sh Emperor Frederick I Barbarossa, charter	6.00	6.00

African Development Bank 25th anniv. (10sh); World Telecommunications Day, May 17 (20sh); Birth cent. of Jawaharlal Nehru, 1st prime minister of independent India (75sh); 1st scheduled transatlantic airmail flight, 50th anniv. (90sh); 175th anniv. of the invention of the 1st steam locomotive by George Stephenson and opening of the Stockton & Darlington Railway in 1825 (100sh); 1st test flight of the Concorde, 20th anniv. (150sh, 300sh); Port of Hamburg, 800th anniv. (250sh, No. 736); and French revolution bicent. (No. 735).

Christmas — A96

Orchids — A97

Religious paintings by Fra Angelico: 10sh, Madonna and Child. 20sh, Adoration of the Magi. 40sh, Virgin and Child Enthroned with Saints. 75sh, The Annunciation. 100sh, St. Peter Martyr triptych center panel. 150sh, Virgin and Child Enthroned with Saints, diff. 250sh, Virgin and Child Enthroned. 350sh, Annalena Altarpiece. No. 745, Bosco ai Frati Altarpiece. No. 746, Madonna and Child with Twelve Angels.

1989, Dec. 18

737	A96	10sh multicolored	.25	.25
738	A96	20sh multicolored	.25	.25
739	A96	40sh multicolored	.55	.55
740	A96	75sh multicolored	.90	.90
741	A96	100sh multicolored	1.10	1.10
742	A96	150sh multicolored	1.50	1.50
743	A96	250sh multicolored	2.10	2.10
744	A96	350sh multicolored	2.40	2.40
		Nos. 737-744 (8)	9.05	9.05

Souvenir Sheets

745	A96	500sh multicolored	4.00	4.00
746	A96	500sh multicolored	4.00	4.00

1989, Dec. 18

747	A97	10sh Aerangis kotschyana	.25	.25
748	A97	15sh Angraecum infundibulare	.25	.25
749	A97	45sh Cyrtorchis chailluana	.60	.60
750	A97	50sh Aerangis rhodosticta	.65	.65
751	A97	100sh Eulophia speciosa	1.25	1.25
752	A97	200sh Calanthe sylvatica	2.75	2.75
753	A97	250sh Vanilla imperialis	3.25	3.25
754	A97	350sh Polystachya vulcanica	4.50	4.50
		Nos. 747-754 (8)	13.50	13.50

Souvenir Sheets

755	A97	500sh Ansellia africana	5.75	5.75
756	A97	500sh Ancistrochilus rothschildianus	5.75	5.75

For overprints see Nos. 782-786A.

EXPO '90, Osaka — A98

Flowering trees.

1990, Apr. 17   Litho.   Perf. 14

757	A98	10sh Thevetia peruviana	.30	.30
758	A98	20sh Acanthus eminens	.30	.30
759	A98	90sh Gnidia glauca	.80	.80

760	A98	150sh Oncoba spinosa	1.10	1.10
761	A98	175sh Hibiscus rosa-sinensis	1.25	1.25
762	A98	400sh Jacaranda mimosifolia	2.00	2.00
763	A98	500sh Erythrina abyssinica	2.25	2.25
764	A98	700sh Bauhinia purpurea	2.50	2.50
		Nos. 757-764 (8)	10.50	10.50

Souvenir Sheets

765	A98	1000sh Delonix regia	6.75	6.75
766	A98	1000sh Cassia didymobatrya	6.75	6.75

World War II Milestones — A99

Designs: 5sh, Allies penetrate west wall, Dec. 3, 1944. 10sh, VE Day, May 8, 1945. 20sh, US forces capture Okinawa, June 22, 1945. 75sh, DeGaulle named commander of all Free French forces, Apr. 4, 1944. 100sh, US troops invade Saipan, June 15, 1944. 150sh, Allied troops launch Operation Market Garden, Sept. 17, 1944. 200sh, Gen. MacArthur returns to Philippines, Oct. 20, 1944. 300sh, US victory at Coral Sea, May 8, 1942. 350sh, First battle of El Alamein, July 1, 1942. 500sh, Naval battle at Guadalcanal, Nov. 12, 1942. 1000sh, Battle of Britain.

1990, June 8   Litho.   Perf. 14

767	A99	5sh multicolored	.35	.35
768	A99	10sh multicolored	.35	.35
769	A99	20sh multicolored	.35	.35
770	A99	75sh multicolored	.75	.75
771	A99	100sh multicolored	1.00	1.00
772	A99	150sh multicolored	1.50	1.50
773	A99	200sh multicolored	2.00	2.00
774	A99	300sh multicolored	3.25	3.25
775	A99	350sh multicolored	3.50	3.50
776	A99	500sh multicolored	5.00	5.00
		Nos. 767-776 (10)	18.05	18.05

Souvenir Sheet

777	A99	500sh multicolored	7.50	7.50

Queen Mother, 90th Birthday — A100

1990, July 5

778		250sh Hands clasped	1.00	1.00
779		250sh Facing left	1.00	1.00
780		250sh Holding dog	1.00	1.00
a.		A100 Strip of 3, #778-780	4.25	4.25
		Nos. 778-780 (3)	3.00	3.00

Souvenir Sheet

781	A100	1000sh like No. 778	4.25	4.25

Nos. 747-754 Ovptd. in Silver

Nos. 755-756 Ovptd. in Silver in Sheet Margin

1990   Litho.   Perf. 14

782	A97	10sh on No. 747	1.00	1.00
782A	A97	15sh on No. 748	1.00	1.00
782B	A97	45sh on No. 749	1.50	1.50
783	A97	50sh on No. 750	1.50	1.50
783A	A97	100sh on No. 751	1.90	1.90
784	A97	200sh on No. 752	2.50	2.50
785	A97	250sh on No. 753	2.50	2.50
785A	A97	350sh on No. 754	3.00	3.00
		Nos. 782-785A (8)	14.90	14.90

Souvenir Sheet

786	A97	500sh on No. 755	6.00	6.00
786A	A97	500sh on No. 756	6.00	6.00

Issue dates: 15sh, 45sh, 100sh, 350sh, No. 786A, Nov.; others, July 30.

Pan African Postal Union, 10th Anniv. A101

Designs: 750sh, UN Conference on the least developed countries, Paris, Sept. 3-14.

1990, Aug. 3   Litho.   Perf. 14

787	A101	80sh multicolored	1.40	1.40

Souvenir Sheet

788	A101	750sh multicolored	4.75	4.75

Great Britain No. O1 — A102

Designs: 50sh, Canada #12. 100sh, Baden #4b. 150sh, Switzerland #3L1. 200sh, US #C3a. 300sh, Western Australia #1. 500sh, Uganda #29. 600sh, Great Britain #2. No. 797, Uganda #29. No. 798, Sir Rowland Hill.

1990, Aug. 6   Litho.   Perf. 14

789	A102	25sh multicolored	.35	.35
790	A102	50sh multicolored	.65	.65
791	A102	100sh multicolored	1.25	1.25
792	A102	150sh multicolored	1.50	1.50
793	A102	200sh multicolored	1.75	1.75
794	A102	300sh gray & black	2.25	2.25
795	A102	500sh multicolored	2.50	2.50
796	A102	600sh multicolored	2.50	2.50
		Nos. 789-796 (8)	12.75	12.75

Souvenir Sheets
Size: 108x77mm

797	A102	1000sh multicolored	6.25	6.25

Size: 119x85mm

798	A102	1000sh scarlet & blk	6.25	6.25

Penny Black, 150th anniversary. Nos. 797-798, Stamp World London '90.

Birds A103

1990, Sept. 3   Litho.   Perf. 14

799	A103	10sh African jacana	.90	.90
800	A103	15sh Ground hornbill	.90	.90
801	A103	45sh Kori bustard, vert.	1.10	1.10
802	A103	50sh Secretary bird	1.10	1.10
803	A103	100sh Egyptian geese	1.75	1.75
804	A103	300sh Goliath heron, vert.	3.00	3.00
805	A103	500sh Ostrich, vert.	4.00	4.00
806	A103	650sh Saddlebill stork, vert.	4.25	4.25
		Nos. 799-806 (8)	17.00	17.00

Souvenir Sheets

807 A103 1000sh Volturine
guinea fowl,
vert. 5.75 5.75
808 A103 1000sh Lesser flamingo, vert. 5.75 5.75

World Cup Soccer Championships,
Italy — A104

Players from various national teams.

1990, Sept. 24
809 A104 50sh Cameroun .30 .30
810 A104 100sh Egypt .60 .60
811 A104 250sh Ireland 1.50 1.50
812 A104 600sh West Germany 3.75 3.75
Nos. 809-812 (4) 6.15 6.15

Souvenir Sheets
813 A104 1000sh Sweden 5.25 5.25
814 A104 1000sh Scotland 5.25 5.25

WHO, Promote Better Health — A105

Walt Disney characters in scenes promoting improved health: 10sh, Mickey, Minnie Mouse having a good breakfast. 20sh, Huey, Dewey and Louie looking before crossing street. 50sh, Mickey, Donald Duck against smoking. 90sh, Mickey saving Donald from choking. 100sh, Mickey, Goofy using seat belts. 250sh, Mickey, Minnie avoiding drugs. 500sh, Donald, Daisy exercising. 600sh, Mickey showing bicycle safety. No. 823, Mickey, friends at doctor's office. No. 824, Mickey, friends walking.

1990, Oct. 19   Litho.   Perf. 13½x13
815 A105 10sh multicolored .30 .30
816 A105 20sh multicolored .30 .30
817 A105 50sh multicolored .45 .45
818 A105 90sh multicolored .75 .75
819 A105 100sh multicolored .85 .85
820 A105 250sh multicolored 1.90 1.90
821 A105 500sh multicolored 4.25 4.25
822 A105 600sh multicolored 5.00 5.00
Nos. 815-822 (8) 13.80 13.80

Souvenir Sheets
823 A105 1000sh multicolored 6.00 6.00
824 A105 1000sh multicolored 6.00 6.00

Butterfly Type of 1989
"Uganda" in Blue

1990-92   Litho.   Perf. 14
826 A93 10sh like #704 .65 .65
827 A93 20sh like #705 .75 .75
  a. Imprint "1991" .85 .75
828 A93 30sh like #706 .75 .75
829 A93 40sh like #707 .75 .75
830 A93 50sh like #708 1.00 1.00
831 A93 70sh like #709 1.00 1.00
832 A93 90sh like #710 1.10 1.10
833 A93 100sh like #711 1.10 1.10
  a. Imprint "1991" 1.20 1.10
834 A93 150sh like #712 1.50 1.50
835 A93 200sh like #713 1.90 1.90
  a. Imprint "1991" 1.90 1.90
836 A93 400sh like #714 2.25 2.25
837 A93 500sh like #715 2.25 2.25
838 A93 1000sh like #716 4.50 4.50
839 A93 2000sh like #716 11.00 11.00
  a. Imprint "1991" 5.50 5.50
840 A93 3000sh Euphaedra
eusemoides 13.50 13.50
841 A93 4000sh Acraea natali-
ca 14.50 14.50
842 A93 5000sh Euphaedra
themis 14.50 14.50
Nos. 826-842 (17) 73.00 73.00

Issue dates: 10sh, 20sh, 30sh, 40sh, 70sh, 90sh, 100sh, 150sh, 200sh, 2000sh, 11/90. 50sh, 400sh, 500sh, 1000sh, 11/4/91. 3000sh, 4000sh, 10/9/92.

Nos. 826-829, 831-835, 839-839C do not have a year date imprint below design. Nos. 830, 836-838 are inscribed "1991" below design.

Christmas
A106

Details from paintings by Rubens: 10sh, 500sh, The Baptism of Christ. 20sh, 150sh, 400sh, St. Gregory the Great and Other Saints. 100sh, Saints Nereus, Domitilla and Achilleus. 300sh, Saint Augustine. No. 853, Victory of Eucharistic Truth Over Heresy, horiz. No. 854, Triumph of Faith, horiz.

1990, Dec. 17   Litho.   Perf. 14
845 A106 10sh multicolored .25 .25
846 A106 20sh multicolored .25 .25
847 A106 100sh multicolored .90 .90
848 A106 150sh multicolored 1.25 1.25
849 A106 300sh multicolored 2.00 2.00
850 A106 400sh multicolored 2.10 2.10
851 A106 500sh multicolored 2.25 2.25
852 A106 600sh multicolored 2.50 2.50
Nos. 845-852 (8) 11.50 11.50

Souvenir Sheets
853 A106 1000sh multicolored 6.25 6.25
854 A106 1000sh multicolored 6.25 6.25

Natl. Census A107

Design: 1000sh, Counting on fingers, houses, people.

1990, Dec. 28   Litho.   Perf. 14
855 A107 20sh multicolored 1.00 1.00

Souvenir Sheet
856 A107 7.25 7.25

Wetlands
Fauna — A108

No. 857:a, Damselfly. b, Purple gallinule. c, Sitatunga. d, Purple heron. e, Bushpig. f, Vervet monkey. g, Long reed frog. h, Malachite kingfisher. i, Marsh mongoose. j, Painted reed frog. k, Jacana. l, Charaxes butterfly. m, Nile crocodile. n, Herald snake. o, Dragonfly. p, Lungfish.
No. 858, Nile monitor, horiz.

1991, Jan. 1   Litho.   Perf. 14
857 A108 70sh Sheet of 16,
#a.-p. 17.00 17.00

Souvenir Sheet
858 A108 1000sh multi 9.50 9.50

Fish
A109

Designs: 10sh, Haplochromis limax. 20sh, Notobranchius palmqvisti. 40sh, Distichodus affinis. 90sh, Haplochromis sauvagei. 100sh, Aphyosemion calliurum. 350sh, Haplochromis johnstoni. 600sh, Haplochromis dichrourus. 800sh, Hemichromis bimaculatus. No. 867, Haplochromis sp. No. 868, Aphyosemion striatum.

1991, Jan. 18   Litho.   Perf. 14
859 A109 10sh multicolored .30 .30
860 A109 20sh multicolored .30 .30
861 A109 40sh multicolored .30 .30
862 A109 90sh multicolored .55 .55
863 A109 100sh multicolored .65 .65
864 A109 350sh multicolored 1.60 1.60
865 A109 600sh multicolored 3.25 3.25
866 A109 800sh multicolored 4.00 4.00
Nos. 859-866 (8) 10.95 10.95

Souvenir Sheets
867 A109 1000sh multicolored 7.50 7.50
868 A109 1000sh multicolored 7.50 7.50

1992 Summer
Olympics,
Barcelona — A110

1991, Feb. 25   Litho.   Perf. 14
869 A110 20sh Women's hur-
dles .30 .30
870 A110 40sh Long jump .30 .30
871 A110 125sh Table tennis .90 .90
872 A110 250sh Soccer 2.00 2.00
873 A110 500sh 800-meter race 3.75 3.75
Nos. 869-873 (5) 7.25 7.25

Souvenir Sheets
874 A110 1200sh Women's
4x100-meter
relay, horiz. 7.00 7.00
875 A110 1200sh Opening ceremony, horiz. 7.00 7.00

Trains
A111

Designs: 10sh, 10th Class, Zimbabwe. 20sh, 12th Class, Zimbabwe. 80sh, Tribal class, Tanzania and Zambia. 200sh, 4-6-0 Type, Egypt. 300sh, Mikado, Sudan. 400sh, Mountain class Garrat, Uganda. 500sh, Mallet Type, Uganda. 1000sh, 5 F 1 Electric locomotive, South Africa. No. 884, 4-8-2 Type, Zimbabwe. No. 885, Atlantic type, Egypt. No. 886, 4-8-2 Type, Angola. No. 887, Mallet Compound Type, Natal.

1991, Apr. 2   Litho.   Perf. 14
876 A111 10sh multicolored .35 .35
877 A111 20sh multicolored .35 .35
878 A111 80sh multicolored .60 .60
879 A111 200sh multicolored 1.75 1.75
880 A111 300sh multicolored 2.50 2.50
881 A111 400sh multicolored 3.25 3.25
882 A111 500sh multicolored 4.00 4.00
883 A111 1000sh multicolored 7.75 7.75
Nos. 876-883 (8) 20.55 20.55

Souvenir Sheets
884 A111 1200sh multicolored 5.75 5.75
885 A111 1200sh multicolored 5.75 5.75
886 A111 1200sh multicolored 5.75 5.75
887 A111 1200sh multicolored 5.75 5.75

Even though Nos. 886-887 have the same issue date as Nos. 876-885, their dollar value was lower when they were released.

Phila Nippon '91 — A112

Walt Disney characters in Japan: 10sh, Scrooge McDuck celebrating Ga-No-Iwai. 20sh, Mickey removes shoes before entering Minnie's home. 70sh, Cartman Goofy leading horse. 80sh, Daisy, Minnie exchange gifts. 300sh, Minnie kneels at entrance to home. 400sh, Mickey, Donald in volcanic sand bath. 500sh, Clarabelle Cow enjoys incense burning. 1000sh, Mickey, Minnie writing New Year cards. No. 896, Mickey, Donald and Goofy in public bath. No. 897, Mickey and friends playing Japanese music.

1991, May 29   Litho.   Perf. 14x13½
888 A112 10sh multicolored .25 .25
889 A112 20sh multicolored .25 .25
890 A112 70sh multicolored .45 .45
891 A112 80sh multicolored .50 .50
892 A112 300sh multicolored 1.90 1.90
893 A112 400sh multicolored 2.40 2.40
894 A112 500sh multicolored 3.25 3.25
895 A112 1000sh multicolored 6.00 6.00
Nos. 888-895 (8) 15.00 15.00

Souvenir Sheets
896 A112 1200sh multicolored 7.50 7.50
897 A112 1200sh multicolored 7.50 7.50

17th World Scout Jamboree,
Korea — A113

Designs: 20sh, Lord Baden-Powell. 80sh, Scouts collecting stamps. 100sh, Scout encampment, NY World's Fair, 1939. 150sh, Cover of 1st Scout Handbook. 300sh, Cooking over campfire. 400sh, Neil Armstrong, Edwin Aldrin, 1st scouts on moon. 500sh, Hands raised for Scout Pledge. 1000sh, Statue to Unknown Scout, Gilwell Park, England. No. 906, William D. Boyce, Lord Baden-Powell, Rev. L. Hadley. No. 907, 17th Jamboree Emblem.

1991, May 27   Perf. 14
898 A113 20sh multicolored .30 .30
899 A113 80sh multicolored .45 .45
900 A113 100sh multicolored .55 .55
901 A113 150sh grn & blk .80 .80
902 A113 300sh multicolored 1.60 1.60
903 A113 400sh multicolored 2.25 2.25
904 A113 500sh multicolored 2.75 2.75
905 A113 1000sh multicolored 5.25 5.25
Nos. 898-905 (8) 13.95 13.95

Souvenir Sheets
906 A113 1200sh multicolored 7.50 7.50
907 A113 1200sh cream & blk 7.50 7.50

For surcharge see No. 1305.

Paintings by Vincent Van
Gogh — A114

Paintings: 10sh, Snowy Landscape with Arles in the Background. 20sh, Peasant Woman Binding Sheaves, vert. 60sh, The Drinkers. 80sh, View of Auvers. 200sh, Mourning Man, vert. 400sh, Still Life: Vase with Roses. 800sh, The Raising of Lazarus. 1000sh, The Good Samaritan, vert. No. 916, First Steps. No. 917, Village Street and Steps in Auvers with Figures.

1991, June 26   Litho.   Perf. 13½
908 A114 10sh multicolored .25 .25
909 A114 20sh multicolored .25 .25
910 A114 60sh multicolored .30 .30
911 A114 80sh multicolored .40 .40
912 A114 200sh multicolored 1.00 1.00
913 A114 400sh multicolored 2.00 2.00
914 A114 800sh multicolored 4.00 4.00
915 A114 1000sh multicolored 5.00 5.00
Nos. 908-915 (8) 13.20 13.20

Size: 102x76mm
Imperf
916 A114 1200sh multicolored 7.00 7.00
917 A114 1200sh multicolored 7.00 7.00

Royal Family Birthday, Anniversary
Common Design Type

1991, July 5   Litho.   Perf. 14
918 CD347 20sh multi .30 .30
919 CD347 70sh multi .45 .45
920 CD347 90sh multi .70 .70
921 CD347 100sh multi .75 .75
922 CD347 200sh multi 1.40 1.40
923 CD347 500sh multi 3.25 3.25

924	CD347	600sh multi	4.25	4.25
925	CD347	1000sh multi	6.75	6.75
	Nos. 918-925 (8)		17.85	17.85

Souvenir Sheets

| 926 | CD347 | 1200sh Elizabeth, Philip | 6.25 | 6.25 |
| 927 | CD347 | 1200sh Sons, Diana, Charles | 7.75 | 7.75 |

20sh, 100sh, 200sh, 1000sh, No. 927, Charles and Diana, 10th wedding anniversary. Others, Queen Elizabeth II, 65th birthday.

Charles de Gaulle, Birth Cent. A115

Designs: 20sh, Portrait, vert. 70sh, Liberation of Paris, 1944, vert. 90sh, With King George VI, 1940, vert. 100sh, Reviewing Free French forces, 1940. 200sh, Making his appeal on BBC, 1940. 500sh, In Normandy, 1944. 600sh, At Albert Hall, 1940. 1000sh, Becoming President of France, 1959, vert. No. 936, Entering Paris, 1944, vert. No. 937, With Eisenhower, 1942.

1991, July 15   Perf. 14

928	A115	20sh multicolored	.25	.25
929	A115	70sh multicolored	.35	.35
930	A115	90sh multicolored	.45	.45
931	A115	100sh multicolored	.50	.50
932	A115	200sh multicolored	1.00	1.00
933	A115	500sh multicolored	2.50	2.50
934	A115	600sh multicolored	3.00	3.00
935	A115	1000sh multicolored	5.00	5.00
	Nos. 928-935 (8)		13.05	13.05

Souvenir Sheets

| 936 | A115 | 1200sh multicolored | 6.00 | 6.00 |
| 937 | A115 | 1200sh multicolored | 6.00 | 6.00 |

Mushrooms A116

Designs: 20sh, Volvariella bingensis. 70sh, Agrocybe broadwayi. 90sh, Camarophyllus olidus. 140sh, Marasmius arborescens. 180sh, Marasmiellus subcinereus. 200sh, Agaricus campestris. 500sh, Chlorophyllum molybdites. 1000sh, Agaricus bingensis. No. 946, Leucocoprinus cepaestipes, horiz. No. 947, Laccaria lateritia, horiz.

1991, July 19   Litho.   Perf. 14

938	A116	20sh multicolored	.30	.30
939	A116	70sh multicolored	.50	.50
940	A116	90sh multicolored	.65	.65
941	A116	140sh multicolored	1.00	1.00
942	A116	180sh multicolored	1.25	1.25
943	A116	200sh multicolored	1.40	1.40
944	A116	500sh multicolored	4.00	4.00
945	A116	1000sh multicolored	8.00	8.00
	Nos. 938-945 (8)		17.10	17.10

Souvenir Sheets

| 946 | A116 | 1200sh multicolored | 6.50 | 6.50 |
| 947 | A116 | 1200sh multicolored | 6.50 | 6.50 |

World Wildlife Type of 1983

1991, Aug. 1

948	A43	100sh as No. 371	1.00	1.00
949	A43	140sh as No. 372	1.40	1.40
950	A43	200sh as No. 373	1.90	1.90
951	A43	600sh as No. 374	5.50	5.50
	Nos. 948-951 (4)		9.80	9.80

Souvenir Sheets

Perf. 13x12½

| 952 | A43 | 1200sh Giraffe | 11.00 | 11.00 |
| 953 | A43 | 1200sh Rhinoceros | 11.00 | 11.00 |

World Wildlife Fund. Nos. 952-953 do not have the WWF emblem.

Flowers in Royal Botanical Gardens, Kew — A118

No. 954: a, Cypripedium calceolus. b, Rhododendron thomsonii. c, Ginkgo biloba. d, Magnolia campbellii. e, Wisteria sinensis. f, Clerodendrum ugandense. g, Eulophia horsfallii. h, Aerangis rhodosticta. i, Abelmoschus moschatus. j, Gloriosa superba. k, Carissa edulis. l, Ochna kirkii. m, Canarina abyssinica. n, Nymphaea caerulea. o, Ceropegia succulenta. p, Strelitzia reginae. q, Strongylodon macrobotrys. r, Victoria amazonica. s, Orchis militaris. t, Sophora microphylla.

No. 955 — Royal Botanic Gardens, Melbourne, Australia: a, Anigozanthos manglesii. b, Banksia grandis. c, Clianthus formosus. d, Gossypium sturtianum. e, Callistemon lanceolatus. f, Saintpaulia ionantha. g, Calodendrum capense. h, Aloe ferox. i, Bolusanthus speciousus. j, Lithops schwantesii k, Protea repens. l, Plumbago capensis. m, Clerodendrum thomsoniae. n, Thunbergia alata. o, Schotia latifolia. p, Epacris impressa. q, Acacia pycnantha. r, Telopea speciosissima. s, Wahlenbergia gloriosa. t, Eucalyptus globulus.

No. 956, The Pagoda, Kew. No. 957, Temple of the Winds, Melbourne.

1991, Nov. 25   Litho.   Perf. 14½

| 954 | A118 | 100sh Sheet of 20, #a.-t. | 17.00 | 17.00 |
| 955 | A118 | 90sh Sheet of 20, #a.-t. | 11.00 | 11.00 |

Souvenir Sheets

| 956 | A118 | 1400sh multicolored | 9.50 | 9.50 |
| 957 | A118 | 1400sh multicolored | 7.00 | 7.00 |

No. 956 contains one 30x38mm stamp.

While Nos. 955 and 957 have the same issue date as Nos. 954 and 956, their dollar value was lower when released. Numbers have been reserved for additional values in this set.

Christmas A120

Paintings by Piero Della Francesca: 20sh, Madonna with Child and Angels. 50sh, The Baptism of Christ. 80sh, Polyptych of Mercy. 100sh, The Madonna of Mercy. 200sh, The Legend of the True Cross: The Annunciation. 500sh, Pregnant Madonna. 1000sh, Polyptych of St. Anthony: The Annunciation. 1500sh, The Nativity. No. 968, The Brera Altarpiece. No. 969, Polyptych of St. Anthony.

1991, Dec. 18   Litho.   Perf. 12

960	A120	20sh multicolored	.25	.25
961	A120	50sh multicolored	.25	.25
962	A120	80sh multicolored	.40	.40
963	A120	100sh multicolored	.50	.50
964	A120	200sh multicolored	1.00	1.00
965	A120	500sh multicolored	2.50	2.50
966	A120	1000sh multicolored	5.00	5.00
967	A120	1500sh multicolored	7.50	7.50
	Nos. 960-967 (8)		17.40	17.40

Souvenir Sheets

Perf. 14½

| 968 | A120 | 1800sh multicolored | 9.00 | 9.00 |
| 969 | A120 | 1800sh multicolored | 9.00 | 9.00 |

Boy Scouts A121

Designs: 20sh, Boy Scout Monument, Silver Bay, NY and Ernest Thompson Seton, first chief scout. 50sh, Tree house and Daniel Beard, Boy Scout pioneer, vert. 1500sh, Boy Scout emblem.

1992, Jan. 6   Litho.   Perf. 14

| 970 | A121 | 20sh multicolored | .50 | .50 |
| 971 | A121 | 50sh multicolored | .65 | .65 |

Souvenir Sheet

| 972 | A121 | 1500sh multicolored | 7.50 | 7.50 |

YMCA-Boy Scouts partnership, Lord Robert Baden-Powell, 50th death anniv. in 1991 (#970) and 17th World Scout Jamboree, Korea (#971-972).

A number has been reserved for an additional value in this set.

Balloons A122

Balloons: a, Modern Hot Air. b, Sport. c, Pro Juventute. d, Blanchard's. e, Nadar's Le Geant. f, First trans-Pacific balloon crossing. g, Montgolfier's. h, Paris, Double Eagle II, used in first trans-Atlantic balloon crossing. i, Tethered.

1992, Jan. 6   Litho.   Perf. 14

| 974 | A122 | 200sh Sheet of 9, #a.-i. | 10.50 | 10.50 |

Japanese Attack on Pearl Harbor, 50th Anniv. (in 1991) A123

Designs: a, Japanese bombers attack USS Vestal. b, Japanese Zero fighter. c, Zeros over burning USS Arizona. d, Battleship Row, USS Nevada under way. e, Japanese Val dive bomber. f, US Dauntless dive bomber attacking Hiryu, g, Japanese planes over Midway Island. h, US Buffalo fighter plane. i, US Wildcat fighters over carrier. j, USS Yorktown and Hammann torpedoed by Japanese submarine.

1992, Jan. 6   Perf. 14½x15

| 975 | A123 | 200sh Sheet of 10, #a.-j. | 13.50 | 13.50 |

Battle of Midway, 50th anniv. (#975f-975j). Inscription for No. 975i incorrectly describes fighters as Hellcats.

Anniversaries and Events — A124

Designs: 400sh, Glider No. 8. 500sh, Man breaking pieces from Berlin Wall. 700sh, Portrait of Mozart and scene from "The Magic Flute." 1200sh, Electric locomotive.

1992, Jan. 6   Litho.   Perf. 14

976	A124	400sh multicolored	2.00	2.00
977	A124	500sh multicolored	2.50	2.50
978	A124	700sh multicolored	8.25	8.25
	Nos. 976-978 (3)		12.75	12.75

Souvenir Sheet

| 979 | A124 | 1200sh multicolored | 6.00 | 6.00 |

Otto Lillienthal, hang glider, cent. (in 1991) (#976). Brandenburg Gate, Bicent. (#977), Wolfgang Amadeus Mozart, death bicent. (#978), Trans-Siberian Railway, cent. (#979).

Walt Disney Characters on World Tour — A125

Designs: 20sh, Safari surprise in Africa. 50sh, Pluto's tail of India. 80sh, Donald's calypso beat in Caribbean. 200sh, Goofy pulling rickshaw in China. 500sh, Minnie, Mickey on camel in Egypt. 800sh, Wrestling, Japanese style. 1000sh, Goofy bullfighting in Spain. 1500sh, Mickey scoring in soccer game. No. 988, Daisy singing opera in Germany. No. 989, Mickey and Pluto as Cossack dancers in Moscow.

1992, Feb.   Perf. 13

980	A125	20sh multi	.30	.30
981	A125	50sh multi	.30	.30
982	A125	80sh multi	.30	.30
983	A125	200sh multi	.70	.70
984	A125	500sh multi	1.75	1.75
985	A125	800sh multi	3.00	3.00
986	A125	1000sh multi	3.50	3.50
987	A125	1500sh multi	5.25	5.25
	Nos. 980-987 (8)		15.10	15.10

Souvenir Sheets

| 988 | A125 | 2000sh multi, vert. | 7.50 | 7.50 |
| 989 | A125 | 2000sh multi, vert. | 7.50 | 7.50 |

Queen Elizabeth II's Accession to the Throne, 40th Anniv.

Common Design Type

1992, Feb. 6   Litho.   Perf. 14

990	CD348	100sh multi	.50	.50
991	CD348	200sh multi	1.00	1.00
992	CD348	500sh multi	2.50	2.50
993	CD348	1000sh multi	5.00	5.00
	Nos. 990-993 (4)		9.00	9.00

Souvenir Sheets

| 994 | CD348 | 1800sh Queen, waterfalls | 9.00 | 9.00 |
| 995 | CD348 | 1800sh Queen, dam | 9.00 | 9.00 |

Dinosaurs A126

1992, Apr. 8   Litho.   Perf. 14

996	A126	50sh Kentrosaurus	.35	.35
997	A126	200sh Iguanodon	.65	.65
998	A126	250sh Hypsilophodon	1.25	1.25
999	A126	300sh Brachiosaurus	1.00	1.00
1000	A126	400sh Peloneustes	1.75	1.75
1001	A126	500sh Pteranodon	1.60	1.60
1002	A126	800sh Tetralophodon	2.50	2.50
1003	A126	1000sh Megalosaurus	4.50	4.50
	Nos. 996-1003 (8)		13.60	13.60

Souvenir Sheets

| 1004 | A126 | 2000sh like #1003 | 7.50 | 7.50 |
| 1005 | A126 | 2000sh like #998 | 7.50 | 7.50 |

Nos. 1004-1005 printed in continuous design.

While Nos. 997, 999, 1001-1002, 1005 have the same release date as Nos. 996, 998, 1000, 1003-1004, their value in relation to the dollar was lower when they were released.

Easter A127

Paintings: 50sh, The Entry into Jerusalem (detail), by Giotto. 100sh, Pilate and the Watch from psalter of Robert de Lisle. 200sh, The Kiss of Judas (detail), by Giotto. 250sh, Christ Washing the Feet of the Disciples, illumination from Life of Christ. 300sh, Christ Seized in the Garden from Melissande Psalter. 500sh, Doubting Thomas, illumination from Life of Christ. 1000sh, The Marys at the Tomb (detail), artist unknown. 2000sh, The Ascension, from 14th century Florentine illuminated manuscript.

Limoge enamels: No. 1014, Agony at Gethsemane. No. 1015, The Piercing of Christ's Side.

1992

1992		**Litho.**	**Perf. 13½x14**	
1006	A127	50sh multi	.30	.30
1007	A127	100sh multi	.40	.40
1008	A127	200sh multi	.85	.85
1009	A127	250sh multi	.95	.95
1010	A127	300sh multi	1.10	1.10
1011	A127	500sh multi	1.90	1.90
1012	A127	1000sh multi	3.75	3.75
1013	A127	2000sh multi	7.75	7.75
	Nos. 1006-1013 (8)		17.00	17.00

Souvenir Sheets

1014	A127	2500sh multi	7.75	7.75
1015	A127	2500sh multi	7.75	7.75

Musical Instruments A128

1992, July 20		**Litho.**	**Perf. 14**	
1016	A128	50sh Adungu	.25	.25
1017	A128	100sh Endingidi	.35	.35
1018	A128	200sh Akogo	.75	.75
1019	A128	250sh Nanga	.85	.85
1020	A128	300sh Engoma	1.00	1.00
1021	A128	400sh Amakondere	1.40	1.40
1022	A128	500sh Akaky-		
		enkye	1.75	1.75
1023	A128	1000sh Ennanga	3.50	3.50
	Nos. 1016-1023 (8)		9.85	9.85

Discovery of America, 500th Anniv. A129

Designs: 50sh, World map, 1486. 100sh, Map of Africa, 1508. 150sh, New World, 1500. 200sh, Nina, astrolabe. 600sh, Quadrant, Pinta. 800sh, Hour glass. 900sh, 15th century compass. 2000sh, World map, 1492. No. 1032, 1490 Map by Henricus Martellus, 1490. No. 1033, Sections of 1492 globe.

1992, July 24		**Litho.**	**Perf. 14**	
1024	A129	50sh multi	.30	.30
1025	A129	100sh multi	.30	.30
1026	A129	150sh multi	.30	.30
1027	A129	200sh multi	.85	.85
1028	A129	600sh multi	2.50	2.50
1029	A129	800sh multi	3.25	3.25
1030	A129	900sh multi	3.50	3.50
1031	A129	2000sh multi	2.75	2.75
	Nos. 1024-1031 (8)		13.75	13.75

Souvenir Sheets

1032	A129	2500sh multi, vert.	7.25	7.25
1033	A129	2500sh multi	5.00	5.00

World Columbian Stamp Expo '92, Chicago.
While Nos. 1024-1026, 1031 and 1033 have the same issue date as Nos. 1027-1030 and 1032, their value in relation to the dollar was lower when they were released.

Hummel Figurines — A130   1992 Summer Olympics, Barcelona — A131

No. 1042: a, Like #1034. b, Like #1035. c, Like #1036. d, Like #1037.
No. 1043: a, Like #1039. b, Like #1038. c, Like #1040. d, Like #1041.

1992, Aug. 28		**Litho.**	**Perf. 14**	
1034	A130	50sh Little Laun-dry Girl	.25	.25
1035	A130	200sh Scrub Girl	.80	.80
1036	A130	250sh Sweeper Girl	.90	.90
1037	A130	300sh Little Moth-er	1.10	1.10

1038	A130	600sh Little Moun-taineer	1.60	1.60
1039	A130	900sh Little Knit-ter	2.25	2.25
1040	A130	1000sh Little Cow-boy	2.75	2.75
1041	A130	1500sh Little As-tronomer	5.50	5.50
	Nos. 1034-1041 (8)		15.15	15.15

Souvenir Sheets

1042	A130	500sh Sheet of 4, #a.-d.	7.25	7.25
1043	A130	500sh Sheet of 4, #a.-d.	7.25	7.25

While Nos. 1034, 1038-1040, 1043 have the same release date as Nos. 1035-1037, 1041-1042, their value in relation to the dollar was lower when they were released.

1992		**Litho.**	**Perf. 14**	
1044	A131	50sh Javelin	.35	.35
1045	A131	100sh High jump, horiz.	.35	.35
1046	A131	200sh Pentathlon (Fencing)	.65	.65
1047	A131	250sh Volleyball	.80	.80
1048	A131	300sh Women's platform diving	1.00	1.00
1049	A131	500sh Team cy-cling	1.60	1.60
1050	A131	1000sh Tennis	3.25	3.25
1051	A131	2000sh Boxing, horiz.	6.50	6.50
	Nos. 1044-1051 (8)		14.50	14.50

Souvenir Sheets

1052	A131	2500sh Baseball	7.50	7.50
1053	A131	2500sh Basketball	7.50	7.50

Wild Animals A132

1992, Sept. 25		**Litho.**	**Perf. 14**	
1054	A132	50sh Spotted hy-ena	.25	.25
1055	A132	100sh Impala	.25	.25
1056	A132	200sh Giant forest hog	.45	.45
1057	A132	250sh Pangolin	.55	.55
1058	A132	300sh Golden monkey	.70	.70
1059	A132	800sh Serval	1.75	1.75
1060	A132	1000sh Bush genet	2.25	2.25
1061	A132	3000sh Defassa waterbuck	6.75	6.75
	Nos. 1054-1061 (8)		12.95	12.95

Souvenir Sheets

1062	A132	2500sh Mountain gorilla	6.50	6.50
1063	A132	2500sh Hippopota-mus	6.50	6.50

Birds — A133

Designs: 20sh, Red necked falcon. 30sh, Yellow-billed hornbill. 50sh, Purple heron. 100sh, Regal sunbird. 150sh, White-brown robin chat. 200sh, Shining-blue kingfisher. 250sh, Great blue turaco. 300sh, Emerald cuckoo. 500sh, Abyssinian roller. 800sh, Crowned crane. 1000sh, Doherty's bush shrike. 2000sh, Splendid glossy starling. 3000sh, Little bee eater. 4000sh, Red-headed lovebird.

1992, Aug.		**Litho.**	**Perf. 15x14**	
1064	A133	20sh multi	.25	.25
1065	A133	30sh multi	.25	.25
1066	A133	50sh multi	.25	.25
1067	A133	100sh multi	.25	.25
1068	A133	150sh multi	.30	.30
1069	A133	200sh multi	.40	.40
1070	A133	250sh multi	.50	.50
1071	A133	300sh multi	.55	.55
1072	A133	500sh multi	1.00	1.00
1073	A133	800sh multi	1.60	1.60
1074	A133	1000sh multi	2.00	2.00
1075	A133	2000sh multi	4.00	4.00
1076	A133	3000sh multi	6.00	6.00
1076A	A133	4000sh multi	8.00	8.00
	Nos. 1064-1076A (14)		25.35	25.35

Issued: 3000sh, Oct.; others, Aug.?

Walt Disney's Goofy, 60th Anniv. — A134

Scenes from Disney animated films: 50sh, Hawaiian Holiday, 1937, vert. 100sh, The Nifty Nineties, 1941, vert. 200sh, Mickey's Fire Bri-gade, 1935, vert. 250sh, The Art of Skiing, 1941. 300sh, Mickey's Amateurs, 1937. 1000sh, Boat Builders, 1938. 1500sh, The Olympic Champ, 1942, vert. 2000sh, The Olympic Champ, 1942, vert. No. 1085, Goofy and Wilbur, 1939. No. 1086, Goofy's family tree, vert.

			Perf. 13½x14, 14x13½	
1992, Nov. 2			**Litho.**	
1077	A134	50sh multi	.25	.25
1078	A134	100sh multi	.25	.25
1079	A134	200sh multi	.50	.50
1080	A134	250sh multi	.65	.65
1081	A134	300sh multi	.80	.80
1082	A134	1000sh multi	2.50	2.50
1083	A134	1500sh multi	4.00	4.00
1084	A134	2000sh multi	5.25	5.25
	Nos. 1077-1084 (8)		14.20	14.20

Souvenir Sheets

1085	A134	3000sh multi	7.50	7.50
1086	A134	3000sh multi	7.50	7.50

Souvenir Sheet

UN Headquarters, New York City — A135

1992, Oct. 28		**Litho.**	**Perf. 14**	
1087	A135	2500sh multi	7.50	7.50

Postage Stamp Mega Event '92, NYC.

Christmas A136

Details or entire paintings by Zurbaran: 50sh, The Annunciation (angel at left). 200sh, The Annunciation (angel at right). 250sh, The Virgin of the Immaculate Conception. 300sh, The Virgin of the Immaculate Conception (detail). 800sh, 900sh, The Holy Family with Saints Anne, Joachim and John the Baptist (800sh, entire, 900sh, detail). 1000sh, Adora-tion of the Magi (entire). 2000sh, Adoration of the Magi. No. 1096, The Virgin of the Immacu-late Conception (Virgin with arms out-stretched). No. 1097, The Virgin of the Immac-ulate Conception (Virgin with arms folded).

1992, Nov. 16		**Litho.**	**Perf. 13½x14**	
1088	A136	50sh multi	.30	.30
1089	A136	200sh multi	.50	.50
1090	A136	250sh multi	.70	.70
1091	A136	300sh multi	.85	.85
1092	A136	800sh multi	2.25	2.25
1093	A136	900sh multi	2.50	2.50
1094	A136	1000sh multi	2.75	2.75
1095	A136	2000sh multi	5.50	5.50
	Nos. 1088-1095 (8)		15.35	15.35

Souvenir Sheets

1096	A136	2500sh multi	7.50	7.50
1097	A136	2500sh multi	7.50	7.50

World Health Organization — A137

Anniversaries and Events — A138

Designs: 50sh, Improving household food security. 200sh, Continue to breastfeed. 250sh, At four months old, give breast milk and soft food. No. 1101, Drink water from a safe and protected source. No. 1102, Jupiter, Voyager 2. No. 1103, Mother holding baby. No. 1104, Impala. No. 1105, Zebra. No. 1106, Count Ferdinand von Zeppelin, zeppelin. 2000sh, Neptune, Voyager 2. 3000sh, Count Zeppelin, zeppelin, diff. No. 1109, Voyager 2, Jupiter, diff. No. 1110, Wart hog. No. 1111, Doctor examining child, Lions Intl. emblem. No. 1112, Count Zeppelin, balloon.

1992		**Litho.**	**Perf. 14**	
1098	A137	50sh multi	.25	.25
1099	A137	200sh multi	.40	.40
1100	A137	250sh multi	.50	.50
1101	A137	300sh multi	.60	.60
1102	A138	300sh multi	1.40	1.40
1103	A137	800sh multi	1.60	1.60
1104	A138	800sh multi	3.25	3.25
1105	A138	1000sh multi	3.75	3.75
1106	A138	1000sh multi	2.00	2.00
1107	A138	2000sh multi	9.75	9.75
1108	A138	3000sh multi	6.00	6.00
	Nos. 1098-1108 (11)		29.50	29.50

Souvenir Sheets

1109	A138	2500sh multi	7.75	7.75
1110	A138	2500sh multi	7.75	7.75
1111	A138	2500sh multi	7.75	7.75
1112	A138	2500sh multi	7.75	7.75

WHO (#1098-1101, 1103). Intl. Space Year (#1102, 1107, 1109). Earth Summit, Rio de Janeiro (#1104-1105, 1110). Count Zeppelin, 75th anniv. of death (#1106, 1108, 1112). Lions Intl., 75th anniv. (#1111).
Issue dates: Nos. 1098-1103, 1106, 1109, 1112, Nov.; others, Dec.

1993 Visit of Pope John Paul II to Uganda A139

A139a

Designs: 50sh, Cathedral in Kampala, site of Papal Mass, Kampala, hands releasing doves. 200sh, Site of Papal Mass, Pope. 250sh, Ugandan man, Pope. 300sh, Three Ugandan Catholic leaders, Pope. 800sh, Pope waving, Ugandan map and flag. 900sh, Ugandan woman, Pope wearing mitre. 1000sh, Pope, Ugandan flag, site of Papal Mass. 2000sh, Ugandan flag, Pope waving. No. 1121, Pope at door of airplane, vert. No. 1122, Pope delivering message at podium, vert.
No. 1123, Pope John Paul II. No. 1124, Pope with hands raised.

1993, Feb. 1 — Litho. — Perf. 14

1113	A139	50sh multi	.30	.30
1114	A139	200sh multi	.50	.50
1115	A139	250sh multi	.60	.60
1116	A139	300sh multi	.70	.70
1117	A139	800sh multi	1.75	1.75
1118	A139	900sh multi	1.90	1.90
1119	A139	1000sh multi	2.25	2.25
1120	A139	2000sh multi	4.50	4.50
		Nos. 1113-1120 (8)	12.50	12.50

Souvenir Sheets

1121	A139	3000sh multi	7.25	7.25
1122	A139	3000sh multi	7.25	7.25

Embossed
Perf. 12

1123	A139a	5000sh gold	30.00	30.00

Souvenir Sheet
Imperf

1124	A139a	5000sh gold	30.00	30.00

Miniature Sheet

Louvre Museum, Bicent. A140

Details or entire paintings by Rembrandt: No. 1125a, Self-Portrait with an Easel. b, Birds of Paradise. c, The Beef Carcass. d, The Supper at Emmaus. e, Hendrickje Stoffels. f, Titus, Son of the Artist. g, The Holy Family (left). h, The Holy Family (right).
2500sh, Philosopher in Meditation, horiz.

1993, Apr. 5 — Litho. — Perf. 12

1125	A140	500sh Sheet of 8, #a.-h. + label	11.25	11.25

Souvenir Sheet
Perf. 14½

1126	A140	2500sh multi	7.00	7.00

Dogs A141

1993, May 28 — Litho. — Perf. 14

1127	A141	50sh Afghan hound	.45	.45
1128	A141	100sh Newfoundland	.45	.45
1129	A141	200sh Siberian huskies	.80	.80
1130	A141	250sh Briard	1.00	1.00
1131	A141	300sh Saluki	1.40	1.40
1132	A141	800sh Labrador retriever, vert.	3.50	3.50
1133	A141	1000sh Greyhound	4.00	4.00
1134	A141	1500sh Pointer	6.50	6.50
		Nos. 1127-1134 (8)	18.10	18.10

Souvenir Sheets

1135	A141	2500sh Cape hunting dog	11.00	11.00
1136	A141	2500sh Norwegian elkhound	11.00	11.00

Miniature Sheet

Coronation of Queen Elizabeth II, 40th Anniv. — A142

No. 1137: a, 50sh, Official coronation photograph. b, 200sh, Orb, Rod of Equity & Mercy. c, 500sh, Queen during coronation ceremony.

d, 1500sh, Queen Elizabeth II, Princess Margaret.
2500sh, The Crown, by Grace Wheatley, 1959.

1993, June 2 — Litho. — Perf. 13½x14

1137	A142	Sheet, 2 each #a.-d.	13.50	13.50

Souvenir Sheet
Perf. 14

1138	A142	2500sh multicolored	7.50	7.50

No. 1138 contains one 28x42mm stamp.

Miniature Sheet

Taipei '93 — A143

Funerary objects: No. 1139a, Tomb guardian god. b, Civil official. c, Tomb guardian god, diff. d, Civil official, diff. e, Chimera. f, Civil official, diff.
2500sh, Statue of Sacred Mother, Ceremonial Hall, Taiyuan, Shanxi.

1993, Sept. 22 — Litho. — Perf. 14x13½

1139	A143	600sh Sheet of 6, #a.-f.	8.50	8.50

Souvenir Sheet

1140	A143	2500sh multicolored	8.00	8.00

With Bangkok '93 Emblem

Thai sculpture: No. 1141a, Standing Buddha, 13th-15th cent. b, Crowned Buddha, 13th cent. c, Thepanom, 15th cent. d, Crowned Buddha, 12th cent. e, Four-armed Avalokitesvara, 9th cent. f, Lop Buri standing Buddha, 13th cent.
2500sh, Buddha, interior of Wat Mahathat.

1993, Sept. 22

1141	A143	600sh Sheet of 6, #a.-f.	8.50	8.50

Souvenir Sheet

1142	A143	2500sh multicolored	8.00	8.00

With Indopex '93 Emblem

Japanese Wayang Puppets, Indonesia: No. 1143a, Bupati karma, Prince of Wangga. b, Rahwana. c, Sondjeng Sandjata. d, Raden Damar Wulan. e, Klitik figure. f, Hanaman. 2500sh, Candi Mendut in Kedu Plain, Java, Indonesia.

1993, Sept. 22 — Litho. — Perf. 13½x14

1143	A143	600sh Sheet of 6, #a.-f.	8.50	8.50

Souvenir Sheet

1144	A143	2500sh multicolored	8.00	8.00

A144   A145

1993, Oct. 1 — Litho. — Perf. 14

1145	A144	50sh Gutierrez, Voeller	.35	.35
1146	A144	200sh Tomas Brolin	.60	.60
1147	A144	250sh Gary Lineker	.75	.75
1148	A144	300sh Munoz, Butragueno	.85	.85
1149	A144	800sh Carlos Valderrama	2.40	2.40
1150	A144	900sh Diego Maradona	2.55	2.55
1151	A144	1000sh Pedro Troglio	3.00	3.00
1152	A144	2000sh Enzo Scifo	6.00	6.00
		Nos. 1145-1152 (8)	16.50	16.50

Souvenir Sheets

1153	A144	2500sh Brazil coaches	7.25	7.25
1154	A144	2500sh De Napoli, Skuhravy, horiz.	7.25	7.25

1994 World Cup Soccer Championships, US.

1993, Nov. 3 — Perf. 14

Cathedrals of the World: 50sh, York Minster, England. 100sh, Notre Dame, Paris. 200sh, Little Metropolis, Athens. 250sh, St. Patrick's, New York. 300sh, Ulm, Germany. 800sh, St. Basil's, Moscow. 1000sh, Roskilde, Denmark. 2000sh, Seville, Spain. No. 1163, Namirembe, Uganda. No. 1163A, St. Peter's, Vatican City.

1155	A145	50sh multi	.35	.35
1156	A145	100sh multi	.35	.35
1157	A145	200sh multi	.65	.65
1158	A145	250sh multi	.70	.70
1159	A145	300sh multi	.95	.95
1160	A145	800sh multi	2.50	2.50
1161	A145	1000sh multi	3.25	3.25
1162	A145	2000sh multi	6.25	6.25
		Nos. 1155-1162 (8)	15.00	15.00

Souvenir Sheets

1163	A145	2500sh multi	7.50	7.50
1163A	A145	2500sh multi	7.50	7.50

Christmas A146

Details or entire woodcut, The Virgin with Carthusian Monks, by Durer: 50sh, 200sh, 300sh, 2000sh.
Details or entire paintings by Raphael: 100sh, 800sh, Sacred Family. 250sh, The Virgin of the Rose. 1000sh, Holy Family (Virgin with Beardless Joseph).
No. 1172, 2500sh, The Virgin with Carthusian Monks, by Durer. No. 1173, 2500sh, Sacred Family, by Raphael.

1993, Nov. 19 — Litho. — Perf. 13½x14

1164-1171	A146	Set of 8	13.50	13.50

Souvenir Sheets

1172-1173	A146	Set of 2	16.00	16.00

Mickey Mouse, Friends with Dinosaurs — A147

Disney characters depicted with: 50sh, Stegosaurus. 100sh, Pterandom. 200sh, Mamenchisaurus. 250sh, Rock painting. 300sh, Dino "sails." 500sh, Diplodocus. 800sh, Mamenshisaurus, diff. 1000sh, Triceratops.
No. 1182, 2500sh, Tyrannosaurus rex, Mickey. No. 1183, 2500sh, Minnie, Mickey, mamenchisaurus, diff.

1993, Dec. 22 — Litho. — Perf. 14x13½

1174-1181	A147	Set of 8	14.00	14.00

Souvenir Sheets

1182-1183	A147	Set of 2	13.00	13.00

Rinderpest Campaign A148

Picasso (1881-1973) A149

1993, Dec. 29 — Perf. 14

1184	A148	200sh multicolored	1.00	1.00

1993, Dec. 29

Paintings: 100sh, Woman in Yellow, 1907. 250sh, Gertrude Stein, 1906. 2500sh, Woman by a Window, 1956.

1185-1186	A149	Set of 2	1.50	1.50

Souvenir Sheet

1187	A149	2500sh multicolored	8.00	8.00

Copernicus (1473-1543) — A150

Telescopes: 500sh, Early. 1000sh, Modern. 2500sh, Copernicus.

1993, Dec. 29

1188-1189	A150	Set of 2	4.50	4.50

Souvenir Sheet

1190	A150	2500sh multicolored	8.00	8.00

Polska '93 — A151

Paintings: 800sh, Creation of the World, by S. I. Witkiewicz par J. Gloqowski, 1921. 1000sh, For the Right to Work, by Andrezej Strumillo, 1952. 2500sh, Temptation of St. Anthony I, by S. I. Witkiewicz (1908-21), horiz.

1993, Dec. 29

1191-1192	A151	Set of 2	5.75	5.75

Souvenir Sheet

1193	A151	2500sh multicolored	7.00	7.00

World Meteorological Day — A152

Fruits and Crops — A153

Designs: 50sh, Weather station, horiz. 200sh, Observatory at Meteorological Training School, Entebbe. 250sh, Satellite receiver at National Meteorological Center, horiz. 300sh, Reading temperatures, National Center, Entebbe, horiz. 400sh, Automatic weather station. 800sh, Destruction by hail storm, horiz. 2500sh, Barograph, horiz.

1993, Dec. 29

1194-1199	A152	Set of 6	10.50	10.50

Souvenir Sheet

1200	A152	2500sh multicolored	8.25	8.25

1993, Dec. 29

Designs: 50sh, Passiflora edulis. 100sh, Helianthus annus. 150sh, Musa sapientum. 200sh, Vanilla fragrans. 250sh, Ananas comosus. 300sh, Artocarpus heterophyllus. 500sh, Sorghum bicolor. 800sh, Zea mays.
No. 1209, 2000sh, Sesamum indicum. No. 1210, 2000sh, Coffea canephora.

1201-1208	A153	Set of 8	9.25	9.25

Souvenir Sheets

1209-1210	A153	Set of 2	12.50	12.50

Automotive Anniversaries — A154

No. 1211: a, 1903 Model A Ford, Henry Ford. b, Model T Snowmobile at 1932 Winter Olympics, Jack Shea. c, Lee Iacocca, Ford Mustang at New York World's Fair. d, Jim Clark, Lotus-Ford winning 1965 Indianapolis 500 race.
No. 1212: a, 1994 Mercedes Benz S600 Coupe. b, 1955 Mercedes Benz W196 Grand Prix Champion car, Juan Manuel Fangio. c, 1938 Mercedes Benz W125 road speed record holder, Rudolph Caracciola. d, Carl Benz, 1893 Benz Viktoria.
No. 1213, Carl Benz, vert. No. 1214, Henry Ford, vert.

1994, Jan. 18   Litho.   Perf. 14

1211	A154	700sh Strip of 4, #a.-d.	6.50	6.50
1212	A154	800sh Strip of 4, #a.-d.	7.50	7.50

Souvenir Sheets

1213	A154	2500sh multicolored	6.00	6.00
1214	A154	2500sh multicolored	6.00	6.00

First Ford motor, cent. (#1211, #1214). First Benz four-wheel car, cent. (#1212, #1213).

A155

Hong Kong '94 — A156

Stamps, religious shrines, Repulse Bay: No. 1215, Hong Kong #531. No. 1216, #1163.
Snuff boxes, Qing Dynasty: No. 1217a, Glass painted enamel with pavilion. b, Porcelain with floral design. c, Porcelain with quail design. d, Porcelain with openwork design. e, Agate with pair of dogs. f, Agate with man on donkey.

1994, Feb. 18   Litho.   Perf. 14

1215	A155	500sh multicolored	.90	.90
1216	A155	500sh multicolored	.90	.90
a.		Pair, #1215-1216	1.75	1.75

Miniature Sheet

1217	A156	200sh Sheet of 6, #a.-f.	3.75	3.75

Nos. 1215-1216 issued in sheets of 5 pairs. No. 1216a is continuous design.
New Year 1994 (Year of the Dog) (#1217e).

Miniature Sheet

1994 World Cup Soccer Championships, US — A157

Designs: No. 1218a, Georges Grun, Belgium. b, Oscar Ruggeri, Argentina. c, Frank Rijkaard, Holand. d, Magid "Tyson" Musisi, Uganda. e, Donald Keeman, Holland. f, Igor Shallmov, Russia.
No. 1219, 2500sh, RFK Stadium, Washington DC. No. 1220, 2500sh, Ruud Gullit, Holland.

1994, June 27   Litho.   Perf. 14

1218	A157	500sh Sheet of 6, #a.-f.	9.75	9.75

Souvenir Sheets

1219-1220	A157	Set of 2	11.00	11.00

Heifer Project Intl., 50th Anniv. A158

1994, June 29   Litho.   Perf. 14

1221	A158	100sh multicolored	2.25	2.25

Moths — A159   Native Crafts — A160

Designs: 100sh, Lobobunaea goodii. 200sh, Bunaeopsis hersilia. 300sh, Rufoglanis rosea. 350sh, Acherontia atropos. 400sh, Rohaniella pygmaea. 450sh, Euchloron megaera. 500sh, Epiphora rectifascia. 1000sh, Polyphychus coryndoni.
Lobobunaea goodii: No. 1230, 2500sh, Wings down. No. 1231, 2500sh, Wings extended.

1994, July 13

1222-1229	A159	Set of 8	8.25	8.25

Souvenir Sheets

1230-1231	A159	Set of 2	12.00	12.00

1994, July 18

Designs: 100sh, Wood stool. 200sh, Wood & banana fiber chair. 250sh, Raffia & palm leaves basket. 300sh, Wool tapestry showing tree planting. 450sh, Wool tapestry showing hair grooming. 500sh, Wood sculpture, drummer. 800sh, Decorated gourds. 1000sh, Lady's bag made from bark cloth.
No. 1240, 2500sh, Raffia baskets. No. 1241, 2500sh, Papyrus hats.

1232-1239	A160	Set of 8	7.75	7.75

Souvenir Sheets

1240-1241	A160	Set of 2	11.00	11.00

Cats — A161   ILO, 75th Anniv. — A162

Cat, historic landmark: 50sh, Turkish angora, Blue Mosque, Turkey, horiz. 100sh, Japanese bobtail, Mt. Fuji, Japan, horiz. 200sh, Norwegian forest cat, windmill, Holland, horiz. 300sh, Egyptian mau, pyramids, Egypt. 450sh, Rex, Stonehenge, England. 500sh, Chartreux, Eiffel Tower, France, horiz. 1000sh, Burmese, Shwe Dagon Pagoda, Burma. 1500sh, Maine coon, Pemaquid Point Lighthouse, Maine.
No. 1250, 2500sh, Russian blue, horiz. No. 1251, 2500sh, Manx, horiz.

1994, July 22

1242-1249	A161	Set of 8	13.50	13.50

Souvenir Sheets

1250-1251	A161	Set of 2	16.00	16.00

1994, July 29

1252	A162	350sh multicolored	1.60	1.60

PHILAKOREA '94 — A163

Designs: 100sh, Eight story Sari pagoda, Paekyangsa. 350sh, Ch'omsongdae (Natl. treasure). 1000sh, Pulguksa Temple exterior. 2500sh, Bronze mural, Pagoda Park, Seoul.

1994, Aug. 8

1253-1255	A163	Set of 3	3.00	3.00

Souvenir Sheet

1256	A163	2500sh multicolored	5.00	5.00

Intl. Year of the Family A164

1994, Aug. 11

1257	A164	100sh multicolored	1.00	1.00

D-Day, 50th Anniv. A165

Designs: 300sh, Mulberry Harbor pierhead moves into position. 1000sh, Mulberry Harbor floating bridge lands armor.
2500sh, Ships, Mulberry Harbor.

1994, Aug. 11

1258	A165	300sh multicolored	.85	.85
1259	A165	1000sh multicolored	2.75	2.75

Souvenir Sheet

1260	A165	2500sh multicolored	7.25	7.25

A166

Intl. Olympic Committee, Cent. — A167

Designs: 350sh, John Akii-bua, Uganda, 100-meter hurdles, 1972. 900sh, Heike Herkel, Germany, high jump, 1992.

2500sh, Aleksei Urmanov, Russia, figure skating, 1994.

1994, Aug. 11

1261	A166	350sh multicolored	.70	.70
1262	A167	900sh multicolored	1.75	1.75

Souvenir Sheet

1263	A166	2500sh multicolored	5.00	5.00

First Manned Moon Landing, 25th Anniv. A168

No. 1264 — Project Mercury astronauts: a, 50sh, Alan B. Shepard, Jr., Freedom 7. b, 100sh, M. Scott Carpenter, Aurora 7. c, 200sh, Virgil I. Grissom, Liberty Bell 7. d, 300sh, L. Gordon Cooper, Jr., Faith 7. e, 400sh, Walter M. Schirra, Jr., Sigma 7. f, 500sh, Donald K. Slayton, Apollo-Soyuz, 1975. g, John H. Glenn, Jr., Friendship 7.
3000sh, Apollo 11 anniv. emblem.

1994, Aug. 11

1264	A168	Sheet of 7, #a.-g, + 2 labels	10.00	10.00

Souvenir Sheet

1265	A168	3000sh multicolored	10.00	10.00

A169

Disney's The Lion King — A169a

No. 1266: a, Baby Simba. b, Mufasa, Simba. c, Young Simba, Nala. d, Timon. e, Rafiki. f, Pumbaa. g, Hyenas. h, Scar. i, Zazu.
No. 1267: a, Rafiki, Mufasa. b, Rafiki, Mufasa, Sarabi. c, Rafiki, Simba. d, Scar, Zazu. e, Rafiki seeing vision. f, Simba, Scar. g, Simba, Nala. h, Simba trying on mane. i, Simba, Nala, Zazu.
No. 1268: a, Scar plots evil plan. b, Mufasa rescues Simba. c, Destroying Mufasa. d, Simba escaping hyenas. e, Timon, Pumbaa, Simba. f, Simba, Timon, Pumbaa sing Hakuna Matata. g, Rafiki. h, Simba, Nala. i, Simba seeing reflection.
No. 1269, 2500sh, Simba, Timon. No. 1270, 2500sh, Characters of the Lion King, vert. No. 1271, 2500sh, Simba's colorful animal kingdom.
No. 1271A, Mufasa, Simba. No. 1271B, Mufasa, Simba on back, standing on rock. Illustration A169a reduced.

Perf. 14x13½, 13½x14

1994, Sept. 30

1266	A169	100sh Sheet of 9, #a.-i.	2.75	2.75
1267	A169	200sh Sheet of 9, #a.-i.	5.75	5.75
1268	A169	250sh Sheet of 9, #a.-i.	7.50	7.50
Nos. 1266-1268 (3)			16.00	16.00

Souvenir Sheets

1269-1271	A169	Set of 3	24.00	24.00

Litho. & Embossed

Perf. 11½

1271A	A169a	5000sh gold	
1271B	A169a	5000sh gold	

Sierra Club, Cent. — A170

No. 1272, horiz.: a, 200sh, Cheetahs. b, 250sh, Cheetah kittens. c, 300sh, African wild dog. d, 500sh, African wild dog. e, 600sh, Grevy's zebra. f, 800sh, Chimpanzee. g, 1000sh, Grevy's zebra.

No. 1273: a, 100sh, Chimpanzee. b, 200sh, Chimpanzee. c, 250sh, African wild dog. d, 300sh, Cheetah. e-f, 500sh, 600sh, Gelada baboon. g, 800sh, Grevy's zebra. h, 1000sh, Gelada baboon.

1994, Nov. 9
| 1272 | A170 | Sheet of 7, #a.-g. + label | 9.00 | 9.00 |
| 1273 | A170 | Sheet of 8, #a.-h. | 9.25 | 9.25 |

ICAO, 50th Anniv. A171

Designs: 100sh, Entebbe Intl. Airport terminal building. 250sh, Entebbe control tower.

1994, Nov. 14   Litho.   Perf. 14
| 1274 | A171 | 100sh multicolored | .90 | .90 |
| 1275 | A171 | 250sh multicolored | 1.60 | 1.60 |

Environmental Protection — A172

Designs: 100sh, Stop poaching. 250sh, Waste disposals. 350sh, Overfishing is a threat. 500sh, Deforestation.

1994, Nov. 15
| 1276-1279 | A172 | Set of 4 | 4.00 | 4.00 |

Christmas A173

Paintings: 100sh, Adoration of the Christ Child, by Fillipino Lippi. 200sh, The Holy Family Rests on the Flight into Egypt, by Annibale Carracci. 300sh, Madonna with Christ Child ant St. John, by Piero di Cosimo. 350sh, The Conestabile Madonna, by Raphael. 450sh, Madonna and Child with Angels, after Antonio Rossellino. 500sh, Madonna and Child with St. John, by Raphael. 900sh, Madonna and Child, by Luca Signorelli. 1000sh, Madonna with the Child Jesus, St. John and an Angel, in style of Pier Francesco Fiorentino.

No. 1288, 2500sh, The Madonna of the Magnificat, by Sandro Botticelli. No. 1289, 2500sh, Adoration of the Magi, by Fra Angelico & Filippo Lippi.

1994, Dec. 5   Litho.   Perf. 13½x14
| 1280-1287 | A173 | Set of 8 | 10.00 | 10.00 |
| **Souvenir Sheets** |
| 1288-1289 | A173 | Set of 2 | 12.50 | 12.50 |

Tintoretto (1518-94) A174

Details or entire paintings: 100sh, Self-portrait. 300sh, A Philosopher. 400sh, The Creation of the Animals, horiz. 450sh, The Feast of Belshazzar, horiz. 500sh, The Raising of the Brazen Serpent. 1000sh, Elijah Fed by the Angel.

No. 1296, 2000sh, Finding of Moses. No. 1297, 2000sh, Moses Striking Water from a Rock.

1995, Feb. 7   Litho.   Perf. 13½
| 1290-1295 | A174 | Set of 6 | 6.50 | 6.50 |
| **Souvenir Sheets** |
| 1296-1297 | A174 | Set of 2 | 10.00 | 10.00 |

Birds A175

No. 1298: a, White-faced tree duck. b, European shoveler. c, Hartlaub's duck. d, Milky eagle-owl. e, Avocet. f, African fish eagle. g, Spectacled weaver. h, Black-headed gonolek. i, Great crested grebe. j, Red-knobbed coot. k, Woodland kingfisher. l, Pintail. m, Squacco heron. n, Purple gallinule. o, African darter. p, African jacana.

No. 1299, 2500sh, Fulvous tree duck. No. 1300, 2500sh, Pygmy goose.

1995, Apr. 24   Litho.   Perf. 14
| 1298 | A175 | 200sh Sheet of 16, #a.-p. | 13.50 | 13.50 |
| **Souvenir Sheets** |
| 1299-1300 | A175 | Set of 2 | 12.00 | 12.00 |

Nos. 685-688, 906 Surcharged

1995, June 1   Litho.   Perf. 14
1301	A90	100sh on #688 multi	.25	.25
1302	A90	450sh on 70sh #686	1.25	1.25
1303	A90	800sh on 90sh #687	2.00	2.00
1304	A90	1500sh on 10sh #685	3.75	3.75
		Nos. 1301-1304 (4)	7.25	7.25
Souvenir Sheet
1305	A113	2500sh on 1200sh multi	6.00	6.00

UN, 50th Anniv. — A176

Designs: 1000sh, Hands releasing butterflies, dragonfly, dove.
No. 1308, Infant's hand holding adult's finger.

1995, July 6   Litho.   Perf. 14
| 1306 | A176 | 450sh shown | 1.25 | 1.25 |
| 1307 | A176 | 1000sh multicolored | 2.75 | 2.75 |
| **Souvenir Sheet** |
| 1308 | A176 | 2000sh multicolored | 4.50 | 4.50 |

FAO, 50th Anniv. — A177

No. 1309 — Corn huskers: a, 350sh, Young woman. b, 500sh, Old woman, girl. c, 1000sh, Woman with baby on back.
2000sh, Boy beside bore well for livestock, irrigation.

1995, July 6
| 1309 | A177 | Strip of 3, #a.-c. | 4.00 | 4.00 |
| **Souvenir Sheet** |
| 1310 | A177 | 2000sh multicolored | 4.50 | 4.50 |

A178

End of World War II, 50th Anniv. A179

No. 1311: a, Russian 152mm gun fires into center of Berlin. b, Soviets capture Moltke Bridge. c, Emperor William Memorial Church, now war memorial. d, Brandenburg Gate falls to Russian tanks. e, US B-17's continue to devastate industrial Germany. f, Soviet tanks enter Berlin. g, Hitler's chancellery lies in ruins. h, Reichstag burns.

Flags of countries each forming "VJ:" No. 1312a, Australia. b, Great Britain. c, New Zealand. d, US. e, China. f, Canada.

No. 1313, Waving Soviet flag from atop building in Berlin. No. 1314, US flag, combat soldier.

1995, July 6
| 1311 | A178 | 500sh Sheet of 8, #a.-h. + label | 10.50 | 10.50 |
| 1312 | A179 | 600sh Sheet of 6, #a.-f. + label | 8.00 | 8.00 |
| **Souvenir Sheets** |
| 1313 | A178 | 2500sh multi | 6.50 | 6.50 |
| 1314 | A179 | 2500sh multi | 7.00 | 7.00 |

No. 1313 contains one 56x42mm stamp.

Rotary Intl., 90th Anniv. — A180

Rotary emblem and: No. 1315, Paul Harris. No. 1316, Natl. flag.

1995, July 6   Litho.   Perf. 14
| 1315 | A180 | 2000sh multicolored | 4.50 | 4.50 |
| **Souvenir Sheet** |
| 1316 | A180 | 2000sh multicolored | 4.50 | 4.50 |

Queen Mother, 95th Anniv. A181

No. 1317: a, Drawing. b, Waving. c, Formal portrait. d, Green blue outfit.
2500sh, Pale blue outfit.

1995, July 6   Perf. 13½x14
| 1317 | A181 | 500sh Block or strip of 4, #a.-d. | 7.00 | 7.00 |
| **Souvenir Sheet** |
| 1318 | A181 | 2500sh multicolored | 6.75 | 6.75 |

No. 1317 was issued in sheets of 8 stamps.
Sheets of Nos. 1317-1318 exist with with black border and text "In Memoriam/1900-2002" in sheet margins.

Dinosaurs A182

Designs: 150sh, Veloceraptor. 200sh, Psittacosaurus. 350sh, Dilophosaurus. 400sh, Kentrosaurus. 500sh, Stegosaurus. 1500sh, Pterodaustro.

No. 1325, vert: a, Archaeopteryx. b, Quetzalcoatlus. c, Pteranodon (b, d). d, Brachiosa (g, h). e, Tsintaosaur. f, Allosaur (g-h). g, Tyranosaur (f, i-k). h, Apatosaur (l). i, Giant dragonfly. j, Dimorphodon. k, Triceratops (l). l, Compsognathus.

No. 1326, 2000sh, Parasaurolophus. No. 1327, 2000sh, Shunosaurus.

1995, July 15   Perf. 14
| 1319-1324 | A182 | Set of 6 | 9.00 | 9.00 |
| 1325 | A182 | 300sh Sheet of 12, #a.-l. | 11.00 | 11.00 |
| **Souvenir Sheets** |
| 1326-1327 | A182 | Set of 2 | 10.50 | 10.50 |

Reptiles — A183

1995   Litho.   Perf. 14x15
1328		50sh Rough scaled bush viper	.25	.25
1329		100sh Pygmy python	.25	.25
1330		150sh Three horned chameleon	.30	.30
1331		200sh African rock python	.40	.40
1332		350sh Nile monitor	.70	.70
1333		400sh Savannah monitor	.85	.85
1334		450sh Bush viper	.95	.95
1335		500sh Nile crocodile	1.00	1.00
Size: 38x24mm
Perf. 14
1336		700sh Bell's hinged tortoise	1.40	1.40
1337		900sh Rhinoceros viper	1.90	1.90
1338		1000sh Gaboon viper	2.00	2.00
1339		2000sh Spitting cobra	4.00	4.00
1340		3000sh Leopard tortoise	6.25	6.25
1341		4000sh Puff adder	8.25	8.25
1341A		5000sh Common house gecko	10.00	10.00
1341B		6000sh Dwarf chameleon	12.00	12.00
1341C		10,000sh Boomslang	20.00	20.00
		Nos. 1328-1341C (17)	70.50	70.50

Issued: 5000sh, 6000sh, 10,000sh, 11/20; others, 8/21.
Compare with Nos. 1550-1552.

Nsambya Church A184

Designs: 450sh, Namilyango College. 500sh, Intl. Cooperative Alliance, cent. 1000sh, UN Volunteers, 25th anniv.

1995, Sept. 7 Litho. Perf. 14
1342-1345 A184 Set of 4   4.50 4.50
Mill Hill Missionaries in Uganda, cent. (#1342-1343).

Scenic Landscapes & Waterfalls of Uganda — A185

Designs: No. 1346, 50sh, Bwindi Forest. No. 1347, 50sh, Sipi Falls, vert. No. 1348, 100sh, Karamoja. No. 1349, 100sh, Murchison Falls. No. 1350, 450sh, Sunset, Lake Mburo Natl. Park. No. 1351, 450sh, Bujagali Falls. No. 1352, 500sh, Sunset, Gulu District. No. 1353, 500sh, Two Falls, Murchison. No. 1354, 900sh, Kabale District. No. 1355, 900sh, Falls, Rwenzoris, vert. No. 1356, 1000sh, Rwenzori Mountains. No. 1357, 1000sh, Falls, Rwenzoris, diff., vert.

1995, Sept. 14
1346-1357 A185 Set of 12   12.50 12.50

1996 Summer Olympics, Atlanta A186

Athletes: 50sh, Peter Rono, runner. 350sh, Reiner Klimke, dressage. 450sh, German cycling team. 500sh, Grace Birungi, runner. 900sh, Francis Ogola, track. 1000sh, Nyakana Godfrey, welter-weight boxer.
No. 1364, 2500sh, Rolf Dannenberg, discus, vert. No. 1365, 2500sh, Sebastian Coe, runner.

1995, Sept. 21
1358-1363 A186 Set of 6   7.25 7.25
Souvenir Sheets
1364-1365 A186 Set of 2   11.00 11.00

Domestic Animals A187

No. 1366: a, Peafowl (e). b, Pouter pigeon. c, Rock dove. d, Rouen duck. e, Guinea fowl. f, Donkey. g, Shetland pony. h, Palomino. i, Pigs. j, Border collie. k, Merino sheep. l, Milch goat. m, Black dutch rabbit. n, Lop rabbit. o, Somali cat (p). p, Asian cat.
No. 1367, 2500sh, Saddle bred horses. No. 1368, 2500sh, Oxen.

1995, Oct. 2
1366 A187 200sh Sheet of 16,
  #a.-p.   12.00 12.00
Souvenir Sheets
1367-1368 A187 Set of 2   13.00 13.00

Boy Scouts at Immunization Centers — A188

Designs: 150sh, Dressing children for weighing, vert. 350sh, Helping mothers carry children, vert. 450sh, Checking health cards. 800sh, Assisting in immunization. 1000sh, Weighing children, vert.

1995, Oct. 18 Litho. Perf. 14
1369-1373 A188 Set of 5   6.00 6.00

Establishment of Nobel Prize Fund, Cent. — A189

No. 1374, 300sh: a, Hideki Yukawa, physics, 1949. b, F.W. DeKlerk, peace, 1993. c, Nelson Mandela, peace, 1993. d, Odysseus Elytis, literature, 1979. e, Ferdinand Buisson, peace, 1927. f, Lev Landau, physics, 1962. g, Halldor Laxness, literature, 1955. h, Wole Soyinka, literature, 1986. i, Desmond Tutu, peace, 1984. j, Susumu Tonegawa, physiology or medicine, 1987. k, Louis de Broglie, physics, 1929. l, George Seferis, literature, 1963.
No. 1375, 300sh: a, Hermann Staudinger, chemistry, 1953. b, Fritz Haber, chemistry, 1918. c, Bert Sakmann, physiology or medicine, 1991. d, Adolf O.R. Windaus, chemistry, 1928. e, Wilhelm Wien, physics, 1911. f, Ernest Hemingway, literature, 1954. g, Richard M. Willstätter, chemistry, 1915. h, Stanley Cohen, physiology or medicine, 1986. i, J. Hans D. Jensen, physics, 1963. j, Otto H. Warburg, physiology or medicine, 1931. k, Heinrich O. Wieland, chemistry, 1927. l, Albrecht Kossel, physiology or medicine, 1910.
No. 1376, 2000sh, Werner Forssmann, physiology or medicine, 1956. No. 1377, 2000sh, Nelly Sachs, literature, 1966.

1995, Oct. 31
Sheets of 12, #a-l
1374-1375 A189 Set of 2   18.00 18.00
Souvenir Sheets
1376-1377 A189 Set of 2   10.00 10.00

Christmas A190

Details or entire paintings of the Madonna and Child, by: 150sh, Hans Holbein the Younger. 350sh, Procaccini. 500sh, Pisanello. 1000sh, Crivelli. 1500sh, Le Nain.
No. 1383, 2500sh, The Holy Family, by Andrea Del Sarto. No. 1384, 2500sh, Madonna and Child, by Bellini.

1995, Nov. 30 Litho. Perf. 13½x14
1378-1382 A190 Set of 5   7.75 7.75
Souvenir Sheets
1383-1384 A190 Set of 2   10.00 10.00

Orchids — A191

Designs: 150sh, Ansellia africana. 450sh, Satyricum crassicaule. 500sh, Polystachya cultriformis. 800sh, Disa erubescens.
No. 1389: a, Aerangis iuteoalba. b, Satyrium sacculatum. c, Bolusiella maudiae. d, Habenaria attenuata. e, Cyrtorchis arcuata. f, Eulophia angolensis. g, Tridactyle bicaudata. h, Eulophia horsfallii. i, Diaphananthe fragrantissima.
No. 1390, 2500sh, Diaphananthe pulchella. No. 1391, 2500sh, Rangaeris amaniensis.

1995, Dec. 8 Perf. 14
1385-1388 A191 Set of 4   6.00 6.00
Miniature Sheet
1389 A191 350sh Sheet of 9,
  #a.-i.   14.00 14.00
Souvenir Sheets
1390-1391 A191 Set of 2   12.00 12.00

New Year 1996 (Year of the Rat) A192

Rat eating: a, Purple grapes. b, Radishes. c, Corn. d, Squash.
2000sh, Green grapes.

1996, Jan. 29 Litho. Perf. 14
1392 A192 350sh Block of 4,
  #a.-d.   2.75 2.75
  e. Miniature sheet, No. 1392   2.75 2.75
Souvenir Sheet
1393 A192 2000sh multicolored   4.00 4.00
No. 1392 issued in sheets of 16 stamps.

Miniature Sheet

Wildlife A193

No. 1394: a, 150sh, Wild dogs. b, 200sh, Fish eagle. c, 250sh, Hippopotamus. d, 350sh, Leopard. e, 400sh, Lion. f, 450sh, Lioness. g, 500sh, Meerkat. h, 550sh, Black rhinoceros. No. 1395: a, 150sh, Gorilla. b, 200sh, Cheetah. c, 250sh, Elephant. d, 350sh, Thomson's gazelle. e, 400sh, Crowned crane. f, 450sh, Sattlebill. g, 500sh, Vulture. h, 550sh, Zebra. No. 1396, 2000sh, Giraffe, vert. No. 1397, 2000sh, Gray heron.

1996, Mar. 27 Litho. Perf. 14
1394 A193 Sheet of 8, #a.-h.   6.25 6.25
1395 A193 Sheet of 8, #a.-h.   6.75 6.75
Souvenir Sheets
1396-1397 A193 Set of 2   9.50 9.50

Disney Characters on the Orient Express — A194

Designs: 50sh, From London to Constantinople via Calais. 100sh, From Paris to Athens. 150sh, Ticket for the Pullman. 200sh, Pullman Corridor. 250sh, Dining car. 300sh, Staff beyond reproach. 600sh, Fun in the Pullman. 700sh, 1901 Unstoppable train enters the buffet in Frankfurt station. 800sh, 1929 passage

detained five days by snowstorm. 900sh, Filming "Murder on the Orient Express."
No. 1408, 2500sh, Donald Duck in engine. No. 1409, 2500sh, Mickey, Goofy, Minnie waving from back of train.

1996, Apr. 15 Perf. 14x13½
1398-1407 A194 Set of 10   12.50 12.50
Souvenir Sheets
1408-1409 A194 Set of 2   13.00 13.00

Paintings by Qi Baishi (1864-1957) A195

No. 1410: a, 50sh, Autumn Pond. b, 100sh, Partridge and Smartweed. c, 150sh, Begonias and Mynah. d, 200sh, Chrysanthemums, Cocks and Hens. e, 250sh, Crabs. f, 300sh, Wisterias and Bee. g, 350sh, Smartweed and Ink-drawn Butterflies. h, 400sh, Lotus and Mandarin Ducks. i, 450sh, Lichees and Locust. j, 500sh, Millet and Preying Mantis.
No. 1411: a, Locust, flowers. b, Crustaceans.

1996, May 8 Litho. Perf. 15x14
1410 A195 Sheet of 10, #a.-j.   8.00 8.00
Souvenir Sheet
Perf. 14
1411 A195 800sh Sheet of 2,
  #a.-b.   7.50 7.50
No. 1411 contains two 48x34mm stamps. The captions on Nos. 1410c and 1410d are transposed.
CHINA '96, 9th Asian Intl. Philatelic Exhibition.
See Nos. 1475-1476.

Queen Elizabeth II, 70th Birthday — A196

No. 1412: a, Portrait. b, As young woman, wearing crown jewels. c, Wearing red hat, coat.
2000sh, Portrait, diff.

1996, July 10 Perf. 13½x14
1412 A196 500sh Strip of 3,
  #a.-c.   5.25 5.25
Souvenir Sheet
1413 A196 2000sh multicolored   5.00 5.00
No. 1412 was issued in sheets of 9 stamps.

Jerusalem, 3000th Anniv. — A197

No. 1414: a, 300sh, Knesset Menorah. b, 500sh, Jerusalem Theater. c, 1000sh, Israel Museum.
2000sh, Grotto of the Nativity.

1996, July 10   **Perf. 14**
1414 A197   Sheet of 3, #a.-c.   4.50   4.50
Souvenir Sheet
1415 A197 2000sh multicolored   4.50   4.50
For overprint see Nos. 1556-1557.

Radio, Cent.
A198

Entertainers: 200sh, Ella Fitzgerald. 300sh, Bob Hope. 500sh, Nat "King" Cole. 800sh, Burns & Allen.
2000sh, Jimmy Durante.

1996, July 10   **Perf. 13½x14**
1416-1419 A198   Set of 4   3.50   3.50
Souvenir Sheet
1420 A198 2000sh multicolored   4.00   4.00

Mushrooms
A199

No. 1421: a, 150sh, Coprinus disseminatus. b, 300sh, Caprinus radians. c, 350sh, Hygrophorus coccineus. d, 400sh, Marasmius siccus. e, 450sh, Cortinarius collinitus. f, 500sh, Cortinarius cinnabarinus. g, 550sh, Coltricia cinnamomea. h, 1000sh, Mutinus elegans.
No. 1422, 2500sh, Inocybe soroia. No. 1423, 2500sh, Flammulina velutipes.

1996, June 24   **Perf. 14**
1421 A199   Sheet of 8, #a.-h.   7.50   7.50
Souvenir Sheets
1422-1423 A199   Set of 2   10.00   10.00

Butterflies
A200

No. 1424: a, 50sh, Catopsilia philea. b, 100sh, Dione vanillae. c, 150sh, Metemorpha dido. d, 200sh, Papilio sesotris. e, 250sh, Papilio neophilus. f, 300sh, Papilio thoas. g, 350sh, Diorina periander. h, 400sh, Morpho cipris. i, 450sh, Catonephele numilia. j, 500sh, Heliconius doris. k, 550sh, Prepona antimache. l, 600sh, Eunica alcmena.
No. 1425, 2500sh, Caligo martia. No. 1426, 2500sh, Heliconius doris.

1996, June 26
1424 A200   Sheet of 12, #a.-l.   8.50   8.50
Souvenir Sheets
1425-1426 A200   Set of 2   10.00   10.00

UNICEF, 50th Anniv. A201

Designs: 450sh, Two children. 500sh, Two children wearing hats. 550sh, Boy in classroom.
2000sh, Mother and child, vert.

1996, July 10   **Litho.**   **Perf. 14**
1427-1429 A201   Set of 3   3.75   3.75
Souvenir Sheet
1430 A201 2000sh multicolored   4.00   4.00

UNESCO, 50th Anniv. — A202

Natl. Parks: 450sh, Darien, Panama. 500sh, Los Glaciares, Argentina. 550sh, Tubbatha Reef Marine Park, Philippines.
2500sh, Rwenzori Mountains, Uganda.

1996, July 10
1431-1433 A202   Set of 3   4.50   4.50
Souvenir Sheet
1434 A202 2500sh multicolored   6.00   6.00

Trains — A203

No. 1435: a, Loco Type B.B.B., Japan, 1968. b, Stephenson's "Rocket," 1829. c, "Austria," 1843. d, 19th cent. type. e, Loco Anglo-Indian, India, 1947. f, Type CoCo DB, Germany.
No. 1436: a, "Lady of Lynn," Great Western, England. b, Chinese type, 1930. c, Meyer-Ritson, Chile. d, Union Pacific "Centennial," US. e, "581" Japanese Natl. Railway, Japan, 1968. f, Co.Co. Series "120" DB, Germany.
No. 1437, 2500sh, Mallard, Great Britain. No. 1438, 2500sh, "99" Type 1-5-0, Germany.

1996, July 25
1435 A203 450sh Sheet of 6, #a.-f.   5.50   5.50
1436 A203 550sh Sheet of 6, #a.-f.   6.50   6.50
Souvenir Sheets
1437-1438 A203   Set of 2   10.00   10.00

Uganda Post Office, Cent. A204

Designs: 150sh, Emblem. 450sh, Post bus service. 500sh, Modern mail transportation means. 550sh, "100," #48, #59.

1996, Aug. 30   **Litho.**   **Perf. 14**
1439-1442 A204   Set of 4   6.00   6.00

Fruits A205

Designs: 150sh, Mango, vert. 350sh, Orange, vert. 450sh, Paw paw, vert. 500sh, Avocado, vert. 550sh, Watermelon.

1996, Oct. 8   **Litho.**   **Perf. 14**
1443-1447 A205   Set of 5   5.50   5.50

Christmas A206

Details or entire paintings: 150sh, Annunciation, by Lorenzo Di Credi. 350sh, Madonna of the Loggia (detail), by Botticelli. 400sh, Virgin in Glory with Child and Angels, by Lorenzetti P. 450sh, Adoration of the Child, by Filippino Lippi. 500sh, Madonna of the Loggia, by Botticelli. 550sh, The Strength, by Bottticelli.
No. 1454, 2500sh, Holy Allegory, by Giovanni Bellini, horiz. No. 1455, 2500sh, The Virgin on the Throne with Child and Saints, by Ghirlandaio, horiz.

1996, Nov. 18   **Perf. 13½x14**
1448-1453 A206   Set of 6   5.75   5.75
Souvenir Sheets
     Perf. 14x13½
1454-1455 A206   Set of 2   10.00   10.00

Sylvester Stallone in Movie, "Rocky III" — A207

1996, Nov. 21   **Litho.**   **Perf. 14**
1456 A207 800sh Sheet of 3   6.00   6.00

1996 Summer Olympic Games, Atlanta A208

Scenes from first Olympic Games in US, St. Louis, 1904: 350sh, Steamboat race, stadium. 450sh, Boxer George Finnegan. 500sh, Quadriga race (ancient games). 800sh, John Flanagan, hammer throw, vert.

1996, Dec. 8   **Set of 4**
1457-1460 A208   5.00   5.00

Traditional Attire — A209

Designs: 150sh, Western region, vert. 350sh, Karimo Jong women, vert. 450sh, Ganda. 500sh, Acholi.
No. 1465, vert. — Headdresses: a, Acholi. b, Alur. c, Bwola dance. d, Madi. e, Karimojong. f, Karimojong with feathers.

1997, Jan. 2
1461-1464 A209   Set of 4   4.00   4.00
1465 A209 300sh Sheet of 6, #a.-f.   5.00   5.00

New Year 1997 (Year of the Ox) A210

Paintings of oxen: Nos. 1466a, 1467b, Walking left. Nos. 1466b, 1467b, Calf nursing. Nos. 1466c, 1467d, Calf lying down, adult. Nos. 1466d, 1467c, Adult lying down.
1500sh, Calf, vert.

1997, Jan. 24   **Litho.**   **Perf. 14**
1466 A210   350sh Strip of 4, #a.-d.   4.00   4.00
1467 A210   350sh Sheet of 4, #a.-d.   4.00   4.00
Souvenir Sheet
1468 A210 1500sh multicolored   4.00   4.00
No. 1466 was issued in sheets of 4 vert. strips.

World Wildlife Fund — A211

No. 1469 — Rothschild's giraffe: a, Running. b, One bending neck across another's back. c, Head up close. d, Young giraffe, adult facing opposite directions.
2500sh, like #1469d, horiz.

1997, Feb. 12
1469 A211   300sh Strip of 4, #a.-d.   3.75   3.75
Souvenir Sheet
1470 A211 2500sh multicolored   6.50   6.50
No. 1469 was issued in sheets of 4 strips with each strip in a different order.
No. 1470 does not have the WWF emblem.

Souvenir Sheet

Mural from Tomb in Xian — A212

1996, May 8   **Litho.**   **Perf. 14**
1471 A212 500sh multicolored   3.00   3.00
China '96. No. 1471 was not available until March 1997.

Promulgation of the Constitution, Oct. 8, 1995 — A213

Designs: 150sh, shown. 350sh, Scroll. 550sh, Closed book, vert.

1997, Feb. 25   **Perf. 14x13½**
1472-1474 A213   Set of 3   3.00   3.00

Paintings Type of 1996

No. 1475 — Paintings by Wu Changshuo (1844-1927): a, 50sh, Red Plum Blossom and Daffodil. b, 100sh, Peony. c, 150sh, Rosaceae. d, 200sh, Pomegranate. e, 250sh, Peach, Peony, and Plum Blossom. f, 300sh, Calyx canthus. g, 350sh, Chrysanthemum. h, 400sh, Calabash. i, 450sh, Chrysanthemum, diff. j, 500sh, Cypress tree.
No. 1476: a, 550sh, Litchi. b, 1000sh, Water lily.

1997, Mar. 5   **Perf. 14x15**
1475 A195   Sheet of 10, #a.-j.   6.50   6.50

Souvenir Sheet
Perf. 14

1476 A195 Sheet of 2, #a.-b.   3.50 3.50

Hong Kong '97. No. 1476 contains two 51x38mm stamps.

Summer Olympic Winners — A214

No. 1477: a, 150sh, Sohn Kee-chung, marathon, 1936. b, 200sh, Walter Davis, high jump, 1952. c, 250sh, Roland Matthes, swimming, 1968. d, 300sh, Akii Bua, 400m hurdles, 1972. e, 350sh, Wolfgang Nordwig, pole vault, 1972. f, 400sh, Wilma Rudolph, 4x100m relay, 1960. g, 450sh, Abebe Bikila, marathon, 1964. h, 500sh, Edwin Moses, 400m hurdles, 1984. i, 550sh, Randy Williams, long jump, 1972.

No. 1478: a, 150sh, Bob Hayes, 100m, 1964. b, 200sh, Rod Milburn, 110m hurdles, 1972. c, 250sh, Filbert Bayi, running, 1976. d, 300sh, H. Kipchoge Keino, steeple chase, 1972. e, 350sh, Ron Ray, running, 1976. f, 400sh, Joe Frazier, boxing, 1976. g, 450sh, Carl Lewis, 100m race, 1984. h, 500sh, Gisela Mauermayer, discus, 1936. i, 550sh, Dietmar Mogenburg, high jump, 1984.

1997, Mar. 3   Litho.   *Perf. 14*
Sheets of 9, #a-i

1477-1478 A214   Set of 2   15.00 15.00

No. 1478h is inscribed shot put in error.

Disney's "Toy Story" — A215

No. 1479, vert.: a, Woody. b, Buzz Lightyear. c, Bo Peep. d, Hamm. e, Slinky. f, Rex.
No. 1480: a, Woody on Andy's bed. b, "Get this wagon train a-movin." c, Bo Peep, blocks. d, Buzz Lightyear. e, Slinky, Rex. f, Woody hides. g, Buzz, Woody. h, Rex, Slinky, Buzz. i, Buzz, Woody on bed.
No. 1481: a, Woody telling Buzz he's sheriff. b, Green Army on alert. c, Woody, Buzz compete. d, Woody sights alien. e, Buzz ponders fate. f, "The Cla-a-a-a-a-w." g, Intergalactic emergency. h, Buzz, Woody argue at gas station. i, Buzz, Woody give chase.
No. 1482, 2000sh, Woody spots an intruder, vert. No. 1483, 2000sh, Andy's toys, vert. No. 1484, 2000sh, Buzz Lightyear in space, vert.

1997, Apr. 2   *Perf. 14x13½, 13½x14*
1479 A215 100sh Sheet of 6,
#a.-f.   2.75 2.75
1480 A215 150sh Sheet of 9,
#a.-i.   6.00 6.00
1481 A215 200sh Sheet of 9,
#a.-i.   7.25 7.25
Souvenir Sheets
1482-1484 A215   Set of 3   20.00 20.00

Man in Space
A216

No. 1484A: b, Pioneer 10. c, Voyager 1. d, Viking Orbiter. e, Pioneer, Venus 1. f, Mariner 9. g, Galileo Entry Probe. h, Mariner 10. i, Voyager 2.
No. 1485: a, Sputnik 1. b, Apollo. c, Soyuz. d, Intelsat 1. e, Manned maneuvering unit. f, Skylab. g, Telstar 1. h, Hubble telescope.
No. 1486, Space shuttle Challenger. No. 1486A, Mars Viking Lander Robot.

1997, Apr. 16   Litho.   *Perf. 14*
1484A A216 250sh Sheet of 8,
#b.-i.   5.00 5.00
1485 A216 300sh Sheet of 8,
#a.-h.   5.50 5.50
Souvenir Sheet
1486 A216 2000sh multicolored 4.75 4.75
1486A A216 2000sh multicolored 5.00 5.00

No. 1486 contains one 34x61mm stamp, No. 1486A one 61x35mm stamp.

Deng Xiaoping (1904-97), Chinese Leader — A217

Designs: a, 500sh. b, 550sh. c, 1000sh. 2000sh, Portrait, diff.

1997, May 9
1487 A217   Sheet of 3, #a.-c.   5.00 5.00
Souvenir Sheet
1488 A217 2000sh multicolored   5.00 5.00

Environmental Protection — A218

No. 1489: a-d, Various water hyacinths.
No. 1490: a, Buffalo. b, Uganda kob. c, Guinea fowl. d, Malibu stork.
2500sh, Gorilla.

1997, May 14
1489 A218 500sh Sheet of 4,
#a.-d.   4.50 4.50
1490 A218 550sh Sheet of 4,
#a.-d.   5.00 5.00
Souvenir Sheet
1491 A218 2500sh multicolored   5.50 5.50

Queen Elizabeth II, Prince Philip, 50th Wedding Anniv.
A219

No. 1492: a, Queen. b, Royal arms. c, Queen in purple outfit, Prince. d, Prince, Queen in white hat. e, Buckingham Palace. f, Prince Philip.
2000sh, Queen in wedding dress.

1997, June 2   Litho.   *Perf. 14*
1492 A219 200sh Sheet of 6,
#a.-f.   6.75 6.75
Souvenir Sheet
1493 A219 2000sh multicolored   4.50 4.50

Paul E. Harris (1868-1947), Founder of Rotary, Intl. — A220

Designs: 1000sh, Combating hunger, Harris. 2500sh, First Rotarians, Gustavus H. Loehr, Sylvester Schiele, Hiram E. Shorey, Paul E. Harris.

1997, June 2
1494 A220 1000sh multicolored 3.00 3.00
Souvenir Sheet
1495 A220 2500sh multicolored 5.00 5.00

Heinrich von Stephan (1831-97)
A221

No. 1496 — Portrait of Von Stephan and: a, Chinese post boat. b, UPU emblem. c, Russian special post.
2500sh, Von Stephan, French postman on stilts.

1997, June 2
1496 A221   800sh Sheet of 3,
#a.-c.   4.75 4.75
Souvenir Sheet
1497 A221 2500sh multicolored   5.00 5.00

PACIFIC 97.

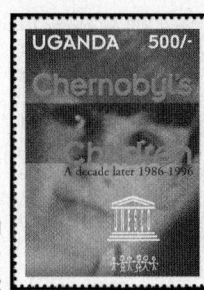

Chernobyl Disaster, 10th Anniv.
A222

Designs: 500sh, UNESCO. 700sh, Chabad's Children of Chernobyl.

1997, May 21   Litho.   *Perf. 14x13½*
1498 A222 500sh multicolored   1.50 1.50
1499 A222 700sh multicolored   2.00 2.00

1998 Winter Olympic Games, Nagano
A223

Designs: 350sh, Men's slalom, vert. 450sh, Two-man bobsled, vert. 800sh, Women's slalom. 2000sh, Men's speed skating.
No. 1504: a, Ski jumping. b, Giant slalom. c, Cross-country skiing. d, Ice hockey. e, Man, pairs figure skating. f, Woman, pairs figure skating.
No. 1505, 2500sh, Downhill skiing. No. 1506, 2500sh, Women's figure skating.

1997, June 23   Litho.   *Perf. 14*
1500-1503 A223   Set of 4   7.25 7.25
1504 A223 500sh Sheet of 6,
#a.-f.   6.25 6.25
Souvenir Sheets
1505-1506 A223   Set of 2   10.00 10.00

Makerere University, 75th Anniv. — A224

Designs: 150sh, Main building, administration block. 450sh, East African School of Librarianship, vert. 500sh, Buyana stock farm. 550sh, Ceramic dish, School of Architectural and Fine Arts.

1997, July 31   *Perf. 14x13½, 13½x14*
1507-1510 A224   Set of 4   4.00 4.00

Mahatma Gandhi (1869-1948)
A225

Various portraits.

1997, Oct. 5   Litho.   *Perf. 14*
1511 A225 600sh multicolored   2.50 2.50
1512 A225 700sh multicolored   2.75 2.75
Souvenir Sheet
1513 A225 1000sh multicolored   4.50 4.50

1998 World Cup Soccer Championships, France — A226

No. 1514, vert: a, 200sh, Fritz Walter, Germany. b, 300sh, Daniel Passarella, Argentina. c, 450sh, Dino Zoff, Italy. d, 500sh, Bobby Moore, England. e, 600sh, Diego Maradona, Argentina. f, 550sh, Franz Beckenbauer, West Germany.
No. 1515 — Argentina vs. West Germany, Mexico City, 1986: a, d, e, f, h, Action scenes. b, Azteca Stadium. c, Argentine player holding World Cup. g, Argentina team picture.
No. 1516 — Top tournament scorers: a, Paulo Rossi. b, Mario Kempes. c, Gerd Muller. d, Grzegorz Lato. e, Ademir. f, Eusebio Ferreica da Silva. g, Salvatore (Toto) Schillaci. h, Leonidas da Silva. i, Gary Lineker.
No. 1517, 2000sh, England, 1966. No. 1518, 2000sh, W. Germany, 1990.

1997, Oct. 3   Litho.   *Perf. 14*
1514 A226   Sheet of 6, #a.-f.   5.50 5.50
1515 A226 250sh Sheet of 8,
#a.-h.   5.00 5.00
1516 A226 250sh Sheet of 9,
#a.-i. + label   5.00 5.00
Souvenir Sheets
1517-1518 A226   Set of 2   8.50 8.50

Diana, Princess of Wales (1961-97)
A227

1997, Dec. 1
1519 A227   60sh multicolored   2.00 2.00

No. 1519 was issued in sheets of 6.

Christmas
A228

Sculpture, entire paintings or details: 200sh, Putto and Dolphin, by Andrea del Verrocchio. 300sh, The Fall of the Rebel Angels, by Pieter Bruegel the Elder. 400sh, The Immaculate

Conception, by Murillo. 500sh, Music-making Angel, by Rosso Fiorentino. 600sh, Cupid and Psyche, by Adolphe-William Bouguereau. 700sh, Cupid and Psyche, by Antonio Canova.

No. 1526, 2500sh, Virgin, Angels from The Assumption of the Virgin, by El Greco. No. 1527, 2500sh, Angel from The Assumption of the Virgin, by El Greco.

1997, Dec. 1
1520-1525 A228 Set of 6   5.50 5.50
Souvenir Sheets
1526-1527 A228 Set of 2   10.00 10.00

New Year 1998 (Year of the Tiger) A229

Various paintings of tigers: No. 1528: a, Looking backward. b, Jumping. c, Lying, looking forward. d, Lying, mouth open. 1500sh, On cliff.

1998, Jan. 16   Litho.   Perf. 13½
1528 A229 350sh Sheet of 4,
            #a.-d.   3.25 3.25
Souvenir Sheet
1529 A229 1500sh multicolored   3.00 3.00

Tourist Attractions — A230

Designs: 300sh, Namugongo Martyrs Shrine, vert. 400sh, Kasubi Tombs. 500sh, Tourist boat, Kazinga Channel. 600sh, Elephant. 700sh, Bujagali Falls, Jinja.

1998, Feb. 6   Litho.   Perf. 14
1530-1534 A230 Set of 5   6.00 6.00

Mother Teresa (1910-97) — A231

No. 1535: a-h, Various portraits. 2000sh, With Diana, Princess of Wales (1961-97).

1998, Feb. 9   Litho.   Perf. 14
1535 A231 300sh Sheet of 8,
            #a.-h.   6.75 6.75
Souvenir Sheet
1536 A231 2000sh multicolored 6.00 6.00

Nos. 1535a, 1535d-1535e, 1535h are each 22x36mm.

UNICEF in Uganda, 30th Anniv. A232

Designs: 300sh, "Support for children with disabilities." 400sh, "Safeguard children

against polio." 600sh, "Sanitation... responsibility for all." 700sh, "Children's right to basic education."

1998, Mar. 6   Perf. 13½x14
1537-1540 A232 Set of 4   5.50 5.50

Dinosaurs — A233

Designs, horiz: 300sh, Pteranodon. 400sh, Diplodocus. 500sh, Lambeosaurus. 600sh, Centrosaurus. 700sh, Parasaurolophus.

No. 1546: a, Cetiosaurus. b, Brontosaurus. c, Brachiosaurus. d, Deinonychus. e, Dimetrodon. f, Megalosaurus.

No. 1547, 2500sh, Tyrannosaurus. No. 1548, 2500sh, Iguanodon.

1998, Mar. 24   Litho.   Perf. 14
1541-1545 A233 Set of 5   5.50 5.50
1546 A233 600sh Sheet of 6,
            #a.-f.   8.00 8.00
Souvenir Sheets
1547-1548 A233 Set of 2   12.00 12.00

Nos. 1547-1548 each contain one 43x57mm stamp.

Writers — A234

No. 1549: a, Rita Dove. b, Mari Evans. c, Sterling A. Brown. d, June Jordan. e, Stephen Henderson. f, Zora Neale Hurston.

1998, Apr. 6
1549 A234 300sh Sheet of 6,
            #a.-f.   4.25 4.25

Reptiles — A235

Designs: 300sh, Armadillo girdled lizard. 600sh, Spotted sandveld lizard. 700sh, Bell's ringed tortoise.

1998, Apr. 21   Perf. 13½
1550 A235 300sh multicolored   .75   .75
1551 A235 600sh multicolored 1.50 1.50
1552 A235 700sh multicolored 1.75 1.75
     Nos. 1550-1552 (3)   4.00 4.00

Compare with Nos. 1328-1335.

Mickey Mouse, 70th Birthday — A236

No. 1553 — Scenes from cartoon, "Runaway Brain:" a, Mickey afraid of shadow. b, Mickey petting Pluto, newspaper. c, Mickey playing computer game, Pluto. d, Mickey, Minnie running. e, Mickey as target of experiment. f, Minnie being held captive by Pete on top of skyscraper. g, Mickey throwing lasso. h, Mickey surrounding Pete with rope. i, Mickey, Minnie holding onto rope above skyscrapers.

No. 1554, 3000sh, Mickey, Minnie embracing on top of skyscraper. No. 1555, 3000sh, Mickey, Minnie kissing on raft, vert.

1998, May 4   Litho.   Perf. 14x13½
1553 A236 400sh Sheet of 9,
            #a.-i.   10.50 10.50
Souvenir Sheets
1554-1555 A236 Set of 2   14.00 14.00

Nos. 1414-1415 Ovptd.

1998, May 13   Litho.   Perf. 14
1556 A197 Sheet of 3, #a.-c.
            (#1414)   4.00 4.00
Souvenir Sheet
1557 A197 2000sh multi (#1415) 4.50 4.50

Sheet margins of Nos. 1556-1557 each contain additional overprint, "ISRAEL 98 — WORLD STAMP EXHIBITION/TEL-AVIV 13-21 MAY 1998."

Sailing Ships A237

No. 1558, 1000sh: a, Fishing schooner. b, Chesapeake oyster boat. c, Java Sea schooner.

No. 1559, 1000sh: a, Santa Maria, 15th cent. galleon. b, Mayflower, 15th cent. galleon. c, Bark.

No. 1560, 3000sh, Boat with lateen sails. No. 1561, 3000sh, Thames River barge, vert.

1998, June 2   Litho.   Perf. 13x13½
Sheets of 3, #a-c + Label
1558-1559 A237 Set of 2   13.00 13.00
Souvenir Sheets
1560-1561 A237 Set of 2   13.00 13.00

Nos. 1560-1561 are continuous designs.

Aircraft A238

No. 1562: a, US F4F Wildcat. b, Japanese Zero. c, British Spitfire. d, British Harrier. e, S3A Viking. f, US Corsair.

No. 1563: a, Dornier Do-X transatlantic flyer, 1929. b, German Zucker mail rocket, 1930. c, X-15 Rocket Plane, 1955. d, Goddard's Rocket, 1930's. e, Wright brothers' flight, 1903. f, 160R Sikorsky helicopter, 1939.

No. 1564, 2500sh, P40 Tomahawk. No. 1565, 2500sh, SH346 Seabat.

1998, July 24   Litho.   Perf. 14
1562 A238 500sh Sheet of 6,
            #a.-f.   7.00 7.00
1563 A238 600sh Sheet of 6,
            #a.-f.   8.25 8.25
Souvenir Sheets
1564-1565 A238 Set of 2   12.00 12.00

Flowers of the Mediterranean — A239

No. 1566, vert: a, Onosma. b, Rhododendron luteum. c, Paeonia mascula. d, Geranium macorrhizum. e, Cyclamen graecum. f, Lilium

rhodopaedum. g, Narcissus pseudonarcissus. h, Paeonia rhodia. i, Aquilegia amaliae.

No. 1567: a, Paeonia peregrina. b, Muscari comutatum. c, Sternbergia. d, Dianthus. e, Verbascum. f, Aubrieta gracilis. g, Galanthus nivalis. h, Campanula incurva. i, Crocus sieberi.

No. 1568, 2000sh, Paeonia parnassica, vert. No. 1569, 2000sh, Pancratium maritimum, vert.

1998, Sept. 23   Litho.   Perf. 14
1566 A239 300sh Sheet of 9,
            #a.-i.   5.50 5.50
1567 A239 600sh Sheet of 9,
            #a.-i.   11.00 11.00
Souvenir Sheets
1568-1569 A239 Set of 2   9.00 9.00

Christmas A240

Birds: 300sh, Bohemian waxwing. 400sh, House sparrow. 500sh, Black-capped chickadee. 600sh, Eurasian bullfinch. 700sh, Painted bunting. 1000sh, Northern cardinal.

No. 1576, 2500sh, Winter wren, vert. No. 1577, 2500sh, Red-winged blackbird, vert.

1998, Dec. 3   Litho.   Perf. 14
1570-1575 A240 Set of 6   7.00 7.00
Souvenir Sheets
1576-1577 A240 Set of 2   11.00 11.00

Diana, Princess of Wales (1961-97) A241

1998, Dec. 28   Litho.   Perf. 14½
1578 A241 700sh multicolored 2.00 2.00

Picasso A242

Paintings: 500sh, Woman Reading, 1935, vert. 600sh, Portrait of Dora Maar, 1937, vert. 700sh, Des Moiselles D'Avignon, 1907.

2500sh, Night Fishing at Antibes, 1939, vert.

1998, Dec. 28   Perf. 14½x13, 13x14½
1579-1581 A242 Set of 3   3.75 3.75
Souvenir Sheet
1582 A242 2500sh multicolored 5.25 5.25

Gandhi — A243

1998, Dec. 28   Perf. 14
1583 A243 600sh Portrait   5.25 5.25
Souvenir Sheet
1584 A243 2500sh Family portrait, horiz. 6.75 6.75

No. 1583 was issued in sheets of 4.

1998 World Scouting Jamboree, Chile — A244

No. 1585: a, Cub Scouts greet Pres. Eisenhower, Georgia, 1956. b, Uncle Dan Beard at 90th birthday party, 1990. c, Future Vice President Hubert Humphrey leads South Dakota troop, 1934.
2000sh, Young scout, tamed beaver, vert.

1998, Dec. 28
1585 A244 700sh Sheet of 3,
#a.-c.   6.00 6.00
Souvenir Sheet
1586 A244 2000sh multicolored   4.00 4.00

New Year 1999 (Year of the Rabbit) A245

No. 1587 — Rabbits: a, White. b, With carrot. c, Brown & white. e, Black & white.

1999, Jan. 4
1587 A245 350sh Sheet of 4,
#a.-d.   3.75 3.75
Souvenir Sheet
1588 A245 1500sh Rabbit, diff.   3.75 3.75

Uganda Post Office A246

1999, Jan. 18
1589 A246 300sh multicolored   1.75 1.75

Traditional Hairstyles — A247

Hairstyle, region: 300sh, Iru, Bairu. 500sh, Enshunju, Bahima. 550sh, Elemungole, Karamojong. 600sh, Longo, Langi. 700sh, Ekikuura, Bahima.

1999, Feb. 1
1590-1594 A247 Set of 5   6.00 6.00

Marine Life A248

No. 1595: a, Wolfish. b, Equal sea star. c, Purple sea urchin. d, Mountain crab.
No. 1596: a, Blue marlin. b, Arctic tern. c, Common dolphin. d, Blacktip shark. e, Manta ray. f, Blackedge moray. g, Loggerhead turtle. h, Sailfin tang. i, Two-spotted octopus.
No. 1597, 2500sh, Sea nettle jellyfish. No. 1598, 2500sh, Decatopecten striatus.

1999, Mar. 15 Litho. **Perf. 14**
1595 A248 500sh Sheet of 4,
#a.-d.   4.00 4.00

1596 A248 500sh Sheet of 9,
#a.-i.   10.00 10.00
Souvenir Sheets
1597-1598 A248 each   9.50 9.50
Intl. Year of the Ocean.

Intl. Year of the Elderly A249

Designs: 300sh, Income generating activity. 500sh, Learning from each other. 600sh, Leisure time for the aged. 700sh, Distributing food to the aged.

1999, July 19 Litho. **Perf. 13x13½**
1599-1602 A249 Set of 4   5.25 5.25

First Manned Moon Landing, 30th Anniv. — A250

No. 1603: a, Apollo 11 launch. b, Apollo 11 command and service modules. c, Edwin E. Aldrin, Jr. on lunar module ladder. d, Saturn V ready to launch. e, Lunar module descending. f, Aldrin on moon.
No. 1604: a, Freedom 7. b, Gemini 4. c, Apollo 11 command and service modules, diff. d, Vostok 1. e, Saturn V. f, Lunar module on moon.
No. 1605, 3000sh, Aldrin with scientific experiment. No. 1606, 3000sh, Command module re-entry.

1999, Nov. 24 Litho. **Perf. 13¾**
1603 A250 600sh Sheet of 6,
#a.-f.   6.50 6.50
1604 A250 700sh Sheet of 6,
#a.-f.   7.50 7.50
Souvenir Sheets
1605-1606 A250 Set of 2   13.50 13.50

Queen Mother (b. 1900) — A251

No. 1607: a, With stole. b, At wedding. c, With tiara (black and white photo). d, With tiara (color photo).
3000sh, Visiting Cambridge, 1961.

1999, Nov. 24 **Perf. 14**
1607 A251 1200sh Sheet of 4,
#a.-d.   10.00 10.00
Souvenir Sheet
Perf. 13¾
1608 A251 3000sh multi   7.50 7.50
No. 1608 contains one 38x51mm stamp.

Hokusai Paintings A252

No. 1609: a, Dragon Flying Over Mount Fuji (dragon). b, Famous Poses From the Kabuki Theater (one figure). c, Kitsune No Yomeiri. d, Dragon Flying Over Mount Fuji (Mount Fuji). e, Famous Poses From the Kabuki Theater (two figures). f, Girl Holding Cloth.
3000sh, Japanese Spaniel.

1999, Nov. 24 Litho. **Perf. 13¾**
1609 A252 700sh Sheet of 6,
#a.-f.   7.50 7.50
Souvenir Sheet
1610 A252 3000sh multicolored   6.00 6.00

Birds — A253

Designs: 300sh, African penduline tit. 1000sh, Yellow-fronted tinkerbird. 1200sh, Zebra waxbill. 1800sh, Sooty anteater chat.
No. 1615: a, Gray-headed kingfisher. b, Green-headed sunbird. c, Speckled pigeon. d, Gray parrot. e, Barn owl. f, Gray crowned crane. g, Shoebill. h, Black heron.
No. 1616: a, Scarlet-chested sunbird. b, Lesser honeyguide. c, African palm swift. d, Swamp flycatcher. e, Lizard buzzard. f, Osprey. g, Cardinal woodpecker. h, Pearl-spotted owlet.
No. 1617: a, Fox's weaver. b, Chin-spot flycatcher. c, Blue swallow. d, Purple-breasted sunbird. e, Knob-billed duck. f, Red-collared widowbird. g, Ruwenzori turaco. h, African cuckoo hawk.
No. 1618, 3000sh, Four-banded sandgrouse. No. 1619, 3000sh, Paradise whydah.

1999, Dec. 6 **Perf. 14**
1611-1614 A253 Set of 4   9.75 9.75
1615 A253 500sh Sheet of 8,
#a.-h.   9.00 9.00
1616 A253 600sh Sheet of 8,
#a.-h.   10.50 10.50
1617 A253 700sh Sheet of 8,
#a.-h.   12.50 12.50
Souvenir Sheets
1618-1619 A253 Set of 2   14.00 14.00

Primates — A254

Designs: 300sh, L'hoesti monkey. 400sh, Blue monkey. 500sh, Patas monkey. 600sh, Red-tailed monkey. 700sh, Black and white colobus. 1000sh, Mountain gorilla. 2500sh, Olive baboon.

1999, Nov. 19 Litho. **Perf. 13½x14**
1620-1625 A254 Set of 6   6.75 6.75
Souvenir Sheet
1626 A254 2500sh multicolored   5.25 5.25

Butterflies A255

Designs: 300sh, Epiphora bauhiniae, vert. 400sh, Phylloxiphia formosa. 500sh, Bunaea alcinoe, vert. 600sh, Euchloron megaera. 700sh, Argema mimosae, vert. 1800sh, Denephila nerii.
3000sh, Lobobunaea angasana.

Perf. 13½x13¼, 13¼x13½
2000, Jan. 19   **Litho.**
1627-1632 A255 Set of 6   9.00 9.00
Souvenir Sheet
1633 A255 3000sh multi   7.50 7.50

A256   A257

UPU, 125th anniv. (in 1999): 600sh, Postman, two women, girl. 700sh, Woman, girl, mail box. 1200sh, Postman in horse-drawn wagon.

2000, Jan. 28 Litho. **Perf. 14**
1634-1636 A256 Set of 3   5.25 5.25

2000, Feb. 18
No. 1637, 600sh — Orchids: a, Angraecum eichcerianum. b, Angraecum leonis. c, Arpophyllum giganteum. d, Bulbophyllum barbigerum. e, Angraecum ciryamae. f, Aerangis ellisii. g, Disa umiflora. h, Eulophia alta. i, Ancistrochilius stylosa.
No. 1638, 600sh: a, Eulophia paivenna. b, Ansellia gigantea. c, Anglaecopsis gracillima. d, Bonatea steudneri. e, Bulbophyllum falcatum. f, Aerangis citrata. g, Eulophiella elisabethae. h, Aerangis rhodosticta. i, Angraecum scottianum.
No. 1639, 700sh: a, Grammangis ellisii. b, Eulophia stenophylia. c, Oeoniella polystachys. d, Cymbidiella humblotti. e, Polystachya bella. f, Vanilla polycepis. g, Eulophileea roemplerana. h, Habenaria englerana. i, Ansellia frallana.
No. 1640, 700sh: a, Eulophia orthoplectra. b, Cirrhopetalum umbellatum. c, Eulophiella rolfei. d, Eulophia porphyroglossa. e, Eulopia petersii. f, Cyrtorchis arcuata. g, Eurychone rothschildiana. h, Eulophia quartiniana. i, Eulophia stenophylia (one flower).
No. 1641, 3000sh, Polystachya tayloriana, horiz. No. 1642, 3000sh, Ancistrochilus rothschildianus, horiz. No. 1643, 3000sh, Calanthe corymbosa, horiz. No. 1644, 3000sh, Cymbidiella rhodochila, horiz.

Sheets of 9, #a.-i.
1637-1638 A257 Set of 2   19.50 19.50
1639-1640 A257 Set of 2   24.00 24.00
Souvenir Sheets
1641-1644 A257 Set of 4   20.00 20.00

Butterflies — A258

Designs: 300sh, Short-tailed admiral. 400sh, Guineafowl. 1200sh, Club-tailed charaxes. 1800sh, Cymothoe egesta.
No. 1649: a, Charaxes anrticlea. b, Epitola posthumus. c, Beautiful monarch. d, Blue-banded nymph. e, Euxanthe crossleyi. f, African map. g, Western blue charaxes. h, Noble.
No. 1650: a, Green-veined charaxes. b, Ansorge's leaf butterfly. c, Crawshay's sapphire blue. d, Palla ussheri. e, Friar. f, Blood-red cymothoe. g, Mocker. h, Charaxes eupale.

No. 1651: a, Aeraea pseudolycia. b, Veined yellow. c, Buxton's hairstreak. d, Iolaus isomenias. e, Veined swallowtail. f, Figtree blue. g, Scarlet tip. h, Precis octavia.
No. 1652, 3000sh, African monarch. No. 1653, 3000sh, Kigezi swordtail.

2000, May 24		Litho.	Perf. 14	
1645-1648	A258	Set of 4	7.25	7.25
1649	A258	500sh Sheet of 8,		
		#a-h	7.50	7.50
1650	A258	600sh Sheet of 8,		
		#a-h	7.50	7.50
1651	A258	700sh Sheet of 8,		
		#a-h	8.50	8.50

Souvenir Sheets

1652-1653	A258	Set of 2	10.50	10.50

The Stamp Show 2000, London (Nos. 1649-1653).

Popes — A259

No. 1654: a, Agapetus II (946-55). b, Alexander II (1061-73). c, Anastasius IV (1153-54). d, Benedict VIII (1012-24). e, Benedict VII (974-83). f, Calixtus II (1119-24).
No. 1655, Celestine III (1191-98).

2000, June 28			Perf. 13¾
1654	A259	900sh Sheet of 6,	
		#a-f	13.50 13.50

Souvenir Sheet

1655	A259	3000sh multi	6.75 6.75

Monarchs — A260

No. 1655A: b, Philip II of France (1180-1223). c, Richard I of England (1189-99). d, William I of England (1066-87).
No. 1656: a, Boris III of Bulgaria (1918-43). b, Holy Roman Emperor Charles V (1519-58). c, Pedro II of Brazil (1831-89). d, Empress Elizabeth of Austria (1854-98). e, Francis Joseph of Austria (1848-1916). f, Frederick I of Bohemia (1619-20).
No. 1657, Mutesa I of Buganda (1191-98). No. 1657A, Cwa II Kabaleega.

2000, June 28			Perf. 13¾
1655A	A260	900sh Sheet of 3,	
		#b-d	4.75 4.75
1656	A260	900sh Sheet of 6,	
		#a-f	8.50 8.50

Souvenir Sheets

1657	A260	3000sh multi	5.25 5.25
1657A	A260	3000sh multi	5.25 5.25

Millennium — A261

No. 1658 — Highlights of 1850-1900: a, Opening of Japan. b, First safe elevator. c, Bessemer process of steel production. d, Florence Nightingale establishes nursing as a profession. e, Louis Pasteur proposes germ theory of disease. f, First oil well drilled. g, Charles Darwin publishes The Origin of Species. h, Gregor Mendel discovers laws of heredity. i, Alfred Nobel invents dynamite. j, Suez Canal opens. k, Invention of the telephone. l, Invention of the electric light. m, World's time zones established. n, Invention of the electric motor. o, Motion pictures appear. p, US Civil War (57x37mm). q, Restoration of the Olympic Games.
Illustration reduced.

2000, June 28		Perf. 12¾x12½
1658	A261	300sh Sheet of 17,
		#a-q + label 8.00 8.00

Millennium — A262

Designs: 300sh, Education for all. 600sh, Nile River. 700sh, Non-traditional exports. 1800sh, Tourism.

2000, July 24		Perf. 14½
1659-1662	A262	Set of 4 6.00 6.00

Common Market for Eastern and Southern Africa A263

Designs: 500sh, Border checkpoint before and after COMESA treaty. 1400sh, Open border checkpoint.

2000, July 24		
1663-1664	A263	Set of 2 2.50 2.50

Modern British Commonwealth, 50th Anniv. — A264

Designs: 600sh, Flags. 1200sh, Map.

2000, July 24		
1665-1666	A264	Set of 2 2.25 2.25

Trains A265

Designs: 300sh, Kenya Railways A 60 Class 4-8-2+2-8-4. 400sh, Mozambique Railways Baldwin 2-8-0. 600sh, Uganda Railways 73 Class German locomotive. 700sh, South Africa Railways Baby Garratt. 1200sh, Uganda Railways 82 Class French locomotive. 1400sh, East Africa Railway Beyer Garratt 4-8-2+2-8-4. 1800sh, Rhodesian Railways 2-8-2+2-8-2 Beyer Garratt. 2000sh, East African Railways Garratt.
No. 1675, 700sh: a, Uganda Railways 36 Class German locomotive. b, South African Railways Class 19D 4-8-2. c, Algeria Railways Garratt 4-8-2+2-8-4. d, Cameroon Railways French locomotive. e, South Africa railways electric freight locomotive. f, Rhodesia Railways 14A Class 2-8-2. g, British-built Egyptian railways locomotive. h, Uganda Railways 73 Class German locomotive, diff.
No. 1676, 700sh: a, 36 Class German locomotive (no counrtry specified). b, Rhodesian Railways 12th Class locomotive. c, Rhodesian Railways Garratt. d, 62 Class German locomotive. e, South Africa Railways Beyer Garratt. f, Sudan Railways locomotive. g, Nigerian Railways locomotive. h, 4-8-0 South Africa Railways.
No. 1677, 3500sh, East African Railways locomotive. No. 1678, 3500sh, Rhodesian Railways Alco 2-8-0. No. 1679, 3500sh, Egyptian State Railways 4-8-2.

2000, Aug. 14		Perf. 14
1667-1674	A265	Set of 8 11.00 11.00

Sheets of 8, #a-h

1675-1676	A265	Set of 2 14.00 14.00

Souvenir Sheets

1677-1679	A265	Set of 3 13.50 13.50

Nos. 1677-1679 each contain one 56x42mm stamp.

Christmas — A266

Artwork by: 300sh, Drateru Fortunate Oliver, vert. 400sh, Brenda Tumwebaze. 500sh, Joseph Mukiibi, vert. 600sh, Paul Serunjogi. 700sh, Edward Maswere. 1200sh, Ndeba Harriet. 1800sh, Jude Kasagga, vert.
No. 1687, 3000sh, Nicole Kwiringira, vert. No. 1688, 3000sh, Michael Tinkamanyire, vert.

2000, Dec. 14		Litho.	Perf. 14
1680-1686	A266	Set of 7	7.00 7.00

Souvenir Sheets

1687-1688	A266	Set of 2 7.50 7.50

New Year 2001 (Year of the Snake) — A267

No. 1689: a, Snake with tongue out. b, Snake wrapped around person. c, Snake with open mouth. d, Snake hanging from branch.

2001, Jan. 5		
1689	A267	600sh Sheet of 4,
		#a-d 3.00 3.00

Souvenir Sheet

1690	A267	2500sh shown 3.25 3.25

Wildlife — A268

No. 1691: a, Bongo, horiz. b, Black rhinoceros, horiz. c, Leopard.
No. 1692, 3000sh, Parrot. No. 1693, 3000sh, Mountain gorillas, horiz.

Perf. 13¼x13¾, 13¾x13¼			
2001, Feb. 5			
1691	A268	600sh Strip of 3, #a-c 2.25 2.25

Souvenir Sheets

1692-1693	A268	Set of 2 7.50 7.50

Holy Year 2000 — A269

Designs: 300sh, Holy Family. 700sh, Madonna and Child. 1200sh, Nativity, horiz.

2001, Apr. 4		Litho.	Perf. 13¼
1694-1696	A269	Set of 3	2.75 2.75

East African School of Library and Information Science, Makerere University, Kampala — A270

Nairobi University, Kenya — A271

Universities and Flags on Map — A272

Design: 1200sh, Nkrumah Hall, University of Dar es Salaam, Tanzania.

2001, Apr. 23			
1697	A270	300sh multi	.40 .40
1698	A271	400sh multi	.50 .50
1699	A270	1200sh multi	1.50 1.50
1700	A272	1800sh multi	2.25 2.25
	Nos. 1697-1700 (4)		4.65 4.65

World Meteorological Organization, 50th Anniv. (in 2000) — A273

Designs: 300sh, Anemometer, vert. 2000sh, Tropical sun recorder.

2001, May 28

1701-1702	A273	Set of 2	3.00	3.00

UN High Commissioner for Refugees — A274

Designs: 300sh, Ensure crop production. 600sh, Ensure community participation. 700sh, Ensure improved skills. 1800sh, Ensure improved health and water services.

2001, June 15

1703-1706	A274	Set of 4	4.25	4.25

Phila Nippon '01, Japan — A275

Designs: 600sh, Kikunojo Segawa I and Danjuro Ichikawa as Samurai, by Kiyonobu II. 700sh, Kamezo Tchimura as a Warrior, by Kiyohiro. 1000sh, Danjuro Ichikawa as Shirobei, by Kiyomitsu. 1200sh, Actor Sangoro Arashi, by Shunsho. 1400sh, Koshiro Matsumoto IV as Sukenari Juro, by Kiyonaga. 2000sh, Pheasant on Pine Branch, by Kiyomasu II.
3500sh, Tale of Ise, by Eishi.

2001, Aug. 1   **Litho.**   **Perf. 14**

1707-1712	A275	Set of 6	8.75	8.75

Souvenir Sheet

1713	A275	3500sh multi		4.50	4.50

Cats and Dogs — A276

Designs: 400sh, Tabby British shorthair. 900sh, Turkish cat.
No. 1716, 600sh, horiz.: a, Blue and cream shorthair. b, Manx. c, Angora. d, Red and white British shorthair. e, Turkish cat, diff. f, Egyptian mau.
No. 1717, 1400sh, horiz.: a, Red tabby shorthair. b, Japanese bobtail. c, Siamese. d, Tabby Persian. e, Black and white Persian. f, Blue Russian.
No. 1718, 3500sh, Blue-eyed British shorthair. No. 1719, 3500sh, Calico American shorthair.

2001, Aug. 23

1714-1715	A276	Set of 2	1.60	1.60

Sheets of 6, #a-f

1716-1717	A276	Set of 2	15.00	15.00

Souvenir Sheets

1718-1719	A276	Set of 2	9.00	9.00

2001, Aug. 23

Designs: 1100sh, German shepherd. 1200sh, Irish setter.
No. 1722, 700sh, horiz.: a, Rottweiler. b, Flat-coated retriever. c, Samoyed. d, Poodle. e, Maltese. f, Irish terrier.
No. 1723, 1300sh, horiz: a, English sheepdog. b, German shepherd, diff. c, Great Dane. d, Boston terrier. e, Bull terrier. f, Australian terrier.
No. 1724, 3500sh, Bloodhound. No. 1725, 3500sh, Pointer, horiz.

1720-1721	A276	Set of 2	3.00	3.00

Sheets of 6, #a-f

1722-1723	A276	Set of 2	15.00	15.00

Souvenir Sheets

1724-1725	A276	Set of 2	9.00	9.00

APS Stampshow, Chicago (#1723).

Royal Navy Submarines, Cent. — A277

No. 1726, vert.: a, HMS Tribune. b, HMS Royal Oak. c, HMS Invincible. d, HMS Dreadnought. e, HMS Ark Royal. f, HMS Cardiff.

2001, Aug. 27

1726	A277	1000sh Sheet of 6, #a-f	7.50	7.50

Souvenir Sheet

1727	A277	3500sh HMS Triad	4.50	4.50

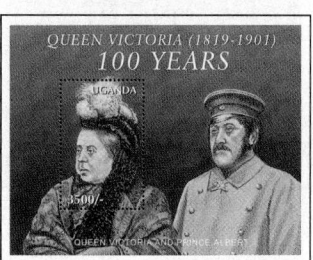

Queen Victoria (1819-1901) — A278

No. 1728: a, Wearing tiara. b, Wearing white head covering, looking right. c, Wearing black hat. d, Wearing red dress with blue sash. e, Wearing white head covering, looking left. f, With hand on chin.
3500sh, Wearing black, hat, diff.

2001, Aug. 27

1728	A278	1000sh Sheet of 6, #a-f	7.50	7.50

Souvenir Sheet

1729	A278	3500sh multi	4.50	4.50

Queen Elizabeth II, 75th Birthday — A279

No. 1730: a, In 1926. b, In 1931. c, In 1939. d, In 1955. e, In 1963. f, In 1999.
3500sh, Wearing cap.

2001, Aug. 27

1730	A279	1000sh Sheet of 6, #a-f	7.50	7.50

Souvenir Sheet

1731	A279	3500sh multi	4.50	4.50

Toulouse-Lautrec Paintings — A280

No. 1732: a, Woman Combing Her Hair. b, The Toilette. c, The English Girl at the Star in Le Havre.
3500sh, Ambassadeurs: Aristide Bruant.

2001, Aug. 27   **Litho.**   **Perf. 13¾**

1732	A280	1500sh Sheet of 3, #a-c	5.75	5.75

Souvenir Sheet

1733	A280	3500sh multi	4.50	4.50

Monet Paintings — A281

No. 1734, horiz.: a, Storm, Belle-Ile Coast. b, The Manneporte, Etretat. c, The Rocks at Pourville, Low Tide. d, The Wild Sea.
3500sh, Sunflowers.

2001, Aug. 27

1734	A281	1200sh Sheet of 4, #a-d	6.00	6.00

Souvenir Sheet

1735	A281	3500sh multi	4.50	4.50

Year of Dialogue Among Civilizations A282

Perf. 13¾x13¼

2001, Nov. 16   **Litho.**

1736	A282	3000sh multi	3.75	3.75

Intl. Volunteers Year A283

Designs: 300sh, Ebola outbreak. 700sh, Save life, donate blood. 2000sh, Collective effort for clean water.

2001, Nov. 16   **Perf. 13¼x13¾**

1737-1739	A283	Set of 3	3.75	3.75

Mushrooms — A284

Designs: 300sh, Amanita excelsa. 500sh, Coprinus cinereus. 600sh, Scleroderma aurantium. 700sh, Armillaria mellea. 1200sh, Leopiota procera. 2000sh, Flammulina velutipes.
3000sh, Amanita phalloides.

2001, Nov. 26   **Perf. 14½**

1740-1745	A284	Set of 6	6.75	6.75

Souvenir Sheets

1746	A284	3000sh multi	3.75	3.75
1746A	A284	3000sh multi	3.75	3.75

Christmas — A285

Musical instruments: 400sh, Single skin long drum. 800sh, Animal horn trumpet, horiz. 1000sh, Bugisu clay drum. 1200sh, Musical bow. 1400sh, Pan pipes. 2000sh, Log xylophones, horiz.
No. 1753, 3500sh, Eight-stringed giant bow harp. No. 1754, Nativity scene, horiz.

2001   **Perf. 13¾x13¼, 13¼x13¾**

1747-1752	A285	Set of 6	8.50	8.50

Souvenir Sheets

1753-1754	A285	Set of 2	9.00	9.00

New Year 2002 (Year of the Horse) — A286

No. 1755: a, White horse facing left. b, Dark brown and gray brown horse facing right with all feet on ground. c, Tan and brown horse facing right, with two feet raised.
3000r, Rearing horse.

2002, May 8   **Litho.**   **Perf. 14x14¼**

1755	A286	1200sh Sheet of 3, #a-c	4.50	4.50

Souvenir Sheet

1756	A286	3000sh multi	3.75	3.75

Historic Sites of East Africa A287

Designs: 400sh, Namugongo Shrine Church, Uganda. 800sh, Maruhubi Palace Ruins, Zanzibar, Tanzania. 1200sh, Kings' Burial Grounds, Mparo, Uganda. 1400sh, Old Law Courts, Mombasa, Kenya, vert.

2002, May 8   *Perf. 14½*
1757-1760 A287   Set of 4   4.75 4.75

Reign of Queen Elizabeth II, 50th Anniv. — A288

No. 1761: a, Wearing blue dress. b, Wearing blue and red hat. c, Without hat. d, Wearing blue hat.
3500sh, Wearing brown hat.

2002, June 17   *Perf. 14¼*
1761 A288 1500sh Sheet of 4,
    #a-d   7.50 7.50
    Souvenir Sheet
1762 A288 3500sh multi   4.50 4.50

8th Intl. Interdisciplinary Congress on Women, Kampala — A289

Designs: 400sh, Women, building. 1200sh, Makerere University arms, vert.

   Perf. 13¼x13¾, 13¾x13¼
2002, July 8
1763-1764 A289   Set of 2   2.00 2.00

United We Stand — A290

2002, July 15   *Perf. 13¾x13¼*
1765 A290 1500sh multi   1.90 1.90
    Printed in sheets of 4.

Intl. Year of Mountains — A291

No. 1766: a, Tateyama, Japan. b, Mt. Nikko, Japan. c, Mt. Hodaka, Japan.
3500sh, Mt. Fuji, Japan.

2002, July 15   *Perf. 13¼x13¾*
1766 A291 2000sh Sheet of 3,
    #a-c   7.50 7.50
    Souvenir Sheet
1767 A291 3500sh multi   4.50 4.50

2002 Winter Olympics, Salt Lake City — A292

Designs: No. 1768, 1200sh, Cross-country skiing. No. 1769, 1200sh, Ski jumping.

2002, July 15   *Perf. 13¾x13¼*
1768-1769 A292   Set of 2   3.00 3.00
1769a   Souvenir sheet, #1768-
    1769   3.00 3.00

20th World Scout Jamboree, Thailand — A293

No. 1770: a, Scout in forest, 1930s. b, Scout saluting. c, Scouts hiking. d, Scout badge.
3500sh, Lord Robert Baden-Powell.

2002   *Perf. 13¼x13¾*
1770 A293 1400sh Sheet of 4,
    #a-d   7.00 7.00
    Souvenir Sheet
    Perf. 13¾x13¼
1771 A293 3500sh multi   4.50 4.50

Mammals, Insects, Flowers and Mushrooms — A294

Designs: 400sh, Ceratotherium simum. 800sh, Macrotermes subhyalinus. No. 1774, 1200sh, Gloriosa superba. 1400sh, Cyptotrama asprata.
No. 1776, 1000sh, horiz. — Insects: a, Nudaurelia cytherea. b, Locusta migratoria. c,

Anacridium aegyptium. d, Sternotomis bohemanni. e, Papilio dardanus. f, Mantis polyspilota.
No. 1777, 1000sh, horiz. — Mushrooms: a, Termitomyces microcarpus. b, Agaricus trisulphuratus. c, Macrolepiota zeyheri. d, Lentinus stupeus. e, Lentinus sajor-caju. f, Lentinus velutinus.
No. 1778, 1200sh, horiz. — Flowers: a, Canarina eminii. b, Vigna unguiculata. c, Gardenia ternifolia. d, Canavalia rosea. e, Hibiscus calyphyllus. f, Nymphaea lotus.
No. 1779, 1200sh, horiz. — Mammals: a, Kobus kob. b, Alcelaphus buselaphus. c, Damaliiscus lunatus. d, Papio anubis. e, Panthera leo. f, Phacochoerus africanus.
No. 1780, 4000sh, Glossina austeni, horiz. No. 1781, 4000sh, Podoscypha parvula, horiz. No. 1782, 4000sh, Abutilon grandiflorum, horiz. No. 1783, 4000sh, Kobus ellipsiprymnus.

2002, Nov. 6   Litho.   *Perf. 14*
1772-1775 A294   Set of 4   4.75 4.75
    Sheets of 6, #a-f
1776-1779 A294   Set of 4   35.00 35.00
    Souvenir Sheets
1780-1781 A294   Set of 4   20.00 20.00

A295

Pres. John F. Kennedy (1917-63) — A296

Various photos.

2002, Dec. 30
1784 A295 1200sh Sheet of 4,
    #a-d   6.00 6.00
1785 A296 1400sh Sheet of 4,
    #a-d   7.00 7.00

A297

Pres. Ronald Reagan — A298

Various photos.

2002, Dec. 30
1786 A297 1200sh Sheet of 4,
    #a-d   6.00 6.00
1787 A298 1400sh Sheet of 4,
    #a-d   7.00 7.00

A299

Princess Diana (1961-97) — A300

2002, Dec. 30
1788 A299 1200sh Sheet of 4,
    #a-d   6.00 6.00
1789 A300 2000sh Sheet of 4,
    #a-d   10.00 10.00

New Year 2003 (Year of the Ram) — A301

No. 1790: a, Ram on stage. b, Ram on hill. c, Ram on hill, six ram's heads. d, Six rams. e, Ram in field. f, Ram on mountainside.

2003, Feb. 1   *Perf. 14¼x14*
1790 A301 1000sh Sheet of 6,
    #a-f   7.50 7.50

Japanese Art — A302

Designs: 400sh, Beauty Arranging Her Hair, by Eisen Keisai. 1000sh, Geishas, by Tsukimaro Kitagawa. 1200sh, Woman Behind a Screen, by Chikanobu Toyohara. 1400sh, Geishas, by Kitagawa, diff.

No. 1795: a, Scene in a Villa (basin in foreground), by Kinichika Toyohara. b, Scene in a Villa (screen at left), by Kunichika Toyohara. c, Visiting a Flower Garden (two people), by Kunisada Utagawa. d, Visiting a Flower Garden (one person), by Utagawa.
5000sh, Woman and Children, by Chikakazu.

2003, May 26   **Litho.**   *Perf. 14¼*
1791-1794 A302   Set of 4   5.00 5.00
1795 A302 1200sh Sheet of 4,
   #a-d   6.00 6.00
Souvenir Sheet
1796 A302 5000sh multi   6.25 6.25

Rembrandt
Paintings
A303

Designs: 400sh, Jacob Blessing the Sons of Joseph. 1000sh, A Young Woman in Profile With Fan. 1200sh, The Apostle Peter Kneeling. 1400sh, The Painter Hendrick Martensz Sorgh.
No. 1801: a, Portrait of Margaretha de Geer. b, Portrait of a White Haired Man. c, Portrait of Nicolaes Ruts. d, Portrait of Catrina Hooghsaet.
5000sh, Joseph Accused by Potiphar's Wife.

2003, May 26
1797-1800 A303   Set of 4   5.00 5.00
1801 A303 1400sh Sheet of 4,
   #a-d   7.00 7.00
Souvenir Sheet
1802 A303 5000sh multi   6.25 6.25

Paintings of Joan Miró — A304

Designs: 400sh, Group of Personages in the Forest. 800sh, Nocturne. 1200sh, The Smile of a Tear. 1400sh, Personage Before the Sun.
No. 1807, vert: a, Man's Head III. b, Catalan Peasant by Moonlight. c, Woman in the Night. d, Seated Woman.
No. 1808, 3500sh, Self-portrait II. No. 1809, 3500sh, Woman with Three Hairs, Birds and Constellations.

2003, May 26   *Perf. 14¼*
1803-1806 A304   Set of 4   4.75 4.75
1807 A304 1400sh Sheet of 4,
   #a-d   7.00 7.00
Imperf
Size: 103x82mm
1808-1809 A304   Set of 2   8.75 8.75

Buganda Princess Katrina-Sarah
Ssangalyambogo, 2nd
Birthday — A305

Princess and: 400sh, Bulange (government office building). 1200sh, Twekobe (palace), vert. 1400sh, Drummer, vert.

Perf. 13x13¼, 13¼x13
2003, June 16
1810-1812 A305   Set of 3   3.75 3.75

Coronation of Queen Elizabeth II, 50th
Anniv. — A306

No. 1813: a, As toddler. b, As young woman, wearing flowered hat. c, Wearing robe and feathered hat.
3500sh, Wearing crown.

2003, July 15   *Perf. 14*
1813 A306 2000sh Sheet of 3,
   #a-c   7.50 7.50
Souvenir Sheet
1814 A306 3500sh multi   4.50 4.50

Prince William, 21st Birthday — A307

No. 1815: a, Wearing cap. b, Wearing blue striped shirt. c, Wearing white shirt.
5000sh, With hand on chin.

2003, July 15
1815 A307 2000sh Sheet of 3,
   #a-c   7.50 7.50
Souvenir Sheet
1816 A307 5000sh multi   6.25 6.25

General Motors Automobiles — A308

No. 1817, 1200sh — Cadillacs: a, 1979 Seville Elegante. b, 1998 Eldorado Touring Coupe. c, 2002 Escalade. d, 1983 Seville Elegante.
No. 1818, 1400sh — Corvettes: a, 1970. b, 1972. c, 1982 Collector Edition. d, 1977.
No. 1819, 3500sh, Cadillac Eldorado convertible, 1950s. No. 1820, 3500sh, 1982 Collector Edition Corvette, diff.

2003, July 15   *Perf. 14¼*
Sheets of 4, #a-d
1817-1818 A308   Set of 2   13.00 13.00
Souvenir Sheets
1819-1820 A308   Set of 2   8.75 8.75

Millennium Development
Goals — A309

Designs: No. 1821, 400sh, Promote gender equity and empower women. No. 1822, 400sh, Improve maternal health. 600sh, Ensure environmental sustainability. 1000sh, Reduce child mortality. No. 1825, 1200sh, Eradicate extreme poverty and hunger. No. 1826, 1200sh, Combat HIV, AIDS, malaria and other diseases. 1400sh, Achieve universal primary education. 2000sh, Develop a global partnership for development.

2003, Oct. 24   *Perf. 14½*
1821-1828 A309   Set of 8   10.50 10.50

Dances and
Costumes — A310

Dances: 400sh, Entogoro. 800sh, Karimojong. 1400sh, Teso.
No. 1832 — Costumes: a, Kiga. b, Acholi. c, Karimojong. d, Ganda.

2003, Nov. 10   *Perf. 14*
1829-1831 A310   Set of 3   3.25 3.25
1832 A310 1200sh Sheet of 4,
   #a-d   6.00 6.00

Christmas — A311

Dances: 300sh, Journey to Bethlehem. 400sh, Shepherds and angels. 1200sh, Nativity. 1400sh, Adoration of the Magi.
3000sh, Holy Family.

2003, Nov. 10
1833-1836 A311   Set of 4   4.25 4.25
Souvenir Sheet
1837 A311 3000sh multi   3.75 3.75

All-Africa Conference on Assuring
Food and Nutrition Security in Africa
by 2020, Kampala — A312

Map of Africa, food basket, Intl. Food Policy Research Institute emblem and: 400sh, Boy. 1400sh, Boy, diff.

2004, Aug. 31   **Litho.**   *Perf. 14¼*
1838-1839 A312   Set of 2   2.25 2.25

Straight Talk Foundation — A313

Child and: 400sh, "Pioneers in Adolescent Health Communication." 1200sh, "Communication for Better Adolescent Health," vert.

2004, Sept. 22
1840-1841 A313   Set of 2   2.00 2.00

Campaign Against Child
Labor — A314

Inscriptions: 400sh, "Stop Child Domestic Labor." 2000sh, "Keep the Community Informed."

2004, Sept. 22
1842-1843 A314   Set of 2   3.00 3.00

Rotary International, Cent. (in
2005) — A315

Rotary emblem and: 400sh, "Celebrate Rotary." 1200sh, "A Century of Service / A New Century of Success," vert.

2004, Sept. 22
1844-1845 A315   Set of 2   2.00 2.00

New Year 2005 (Year of the
Rooster) — A316

No. 1846 — Rooster shades: a, Blue. b, Orange. c, Purple. d, Red.
5000sh, Yellow.

2005, Apr. 4   **Litho.**   *Perf. 14*
1846 A316 1200sh Sheet of 4,
   #a-d   6.00 6.00
Souvenir Sheet
1847 A316 5000sh multi   6.25 6.25

Fight Against
Tuberculosis,
HIV and
Leprosy — A317

WHO emblem and: No. 1848, 400sh, Ill man in blanket. No. 1849, 400sh, Doctor holding arm of ill man. No. 1850, 400sh, Mother and infant. No. 1851, 400sh, Infant in blanket. No. 1852, 400sh, Leper with artificial leg. No. 1853, 400sh, Leper wearing crucifix.

2005, May 31   *Perf. 13x12¾*
1848-1853 A317   Set of 6   3.00 3.00

Flowering
Plants — A318

Designs: 100sh, Clerodendrum sp. 400sh, Calliandra haematocephala. 600sh, Asteraceae compositae. 850sh, Angraecum sp. 900sh, Delonix regia. 1100sh, Bidens grantii. 1200sh, Musa sapientum. 1400sh, Begonia coccinea. 1600sh, Impatiens walleriana. 2000sh, Strelitzia reginae. 5000sh, Tecomaria capensis. 6000sh, Ixora hybrida. 10,000sh, Datura suaveolens. 20,000sh, Cucurbita pepo.

**   Perf. 12¾x13½**
2005, June 22   Litho.
1854	A318	100sh multi	.25	.25
1855	A318	400sh multi	.45	.45
1856	A318	600sh multi	.70	.70
1857	A318	850sh multi	1.00	1.00
1858	A318	900sh multi	1.10	1.10
1859	A318	1100sh multi	1.25	1.25
1860	A318	1200sh multi	1.40	1.40
1861	A318	1400sh multi	1.60	1.60
1862	A318	1600sh multi	1.90	1.90
1863	A318	2000sh multi	2.40	2.40
1864	A318	5000sh multi	5.75	5.75
1865	A318	6000sh multi	7.00	7.00
1866	A318	10,000sh multi	11.50	11.50
1867	A318	20,000sh multi	23.00	23.00
		Nos. 1854-1867 (14)	59.30	59.30

Fish
A319

Designs: 400sh, Synodontis afrofischeri. 600sh, Protopterus aethiopicus. 1100sh, Clarias gariepinus. 1200sh, Rastrineobola agentea. 1600sh, Bagrus docmac. 2000sh, Schilbe mystus.
No. 1874: a, Mormyrus kannume. b, Barbus jacksonni. c, Bagrus docmac, diff. d, Labeo victorianus.

2005, Oct. 6   Litho.   *Perf. 13¼*
1868-1873 A319   Set of 6   8.75 8.75
Souvenir Sheet
1874 A319 1000sh Sheet of 4,
          #a-d   5.00 5.00

Western Union in Africa, 10th
Anniv. — A320

Designs: 400sh, Map of Africa, olive branches. 1600sh, Globe. 2000sh, Globe and flags, vert.

2006, July 20   Litho.   *Perf. 14¼*
1875-1877 A320   Set of 3   5.00 5.00

Bank of Uganda,
40th
Anniv. — A321

Designs: 400sh, Bank emblem. 600sh, Bank emblem, building, wildlife. 1600sh, Bank emblem, Tilapia nilotica. 2000sh, Bank emblem, mountain gorilla.

2006, Oct. 3   *Perf. 13¼*
1878-1881 A321   Set of 4   5.75 5.75

Wetlands
A322

Designs: 400sh, Cattle and herdsman at water, Ramsar Convention emblem. 1600sh, People and birds near stream. 2000sh, Fishermen at Lake George.

2006   *Perf. 13x13½*
1882-1884 A322   Set of 3   5.00 5.00

2007 Commonwealth Heads of
Government Meeting,
Kampala — A323

Flag of Uganda and: 400sh, Commonwealth Heads of Government Meeting emblem. 1600sh, Boniface Kiprop, runner. 2000sh, Dorcas Inzikuru, runner. 5000sh, Arms of Uganda, vert.

2007, Nov. 27   Litho.   *Perf. 13x13½*
1885-1888 A323   Set of 4   10.50 10.50

24th UPU
Congress,
Geneva — A324

People in native costumes: No. 1889, Karimojong man.
No. 1890: a, Omwenda women. b, Ebibaraho man. c, Kikoyi women. d, Kanzu men. e, Gomesi women.

2007, Dec. 7   Litho.   *Perf. 13¼x13*
1889 A324 1600sh multi   1.90 1.90
1890 A324 1600sh Horiz. strip of
          5, #a-e   9.50 9.50
The UPU Congress was moved from Nairobi, Kenya, to Geneva because of political unrest.

Miniature Sheet

2008 Summer Olympics,
Beijing — A325

No. 1891: a, Javelin. b, Running. c, Boxing. d, Swimming.

2008, June 18   *Perf. 12*
1891 A325 1000sh Sheet of 4,
          #a-d   5.00 5.00

Worldwide Fund for Nature
(WWF) — A326

No. 1892 — Spotted hyena: a, Running. b, With pack, devouring prey. c, Adult and juveniles. d, Two juveniles.

2008, June 18   *Perf. 13¼*
1892   Strip of 4   5.00 5.00
a.-d. A326 1000sh Any single   1.25 1.25
e.   Sheet of 8, 2 each #1892a-
          1892d   10.00 10.00

Reign of
Aga
Khan,
50th
Anniv.
(in 2007)
A327

Designs: No. 1893, 400sh, Diamond Trust Building. No. 1894, 400sh, Kampala Serena Hotel. No. 1895, 400sh, Jubilee Insurance Company Building.
No. 1896: a, School children (madrasa program). b, Ismaili Jamatkhana, Kampala. c, Aga Khan High School (educational services). d, Air Uganda airplane. e, Dam (Bujagali hydropower project).

2008, Sept. 30   Litho.   *Perf. 14½*
1893-1895 A327   Set of 3   1.50 1.50
1896 A327 1100sh Horiz. strip of
          5, #a-e   6.50 6.50

Peony
A328

2009, Apr. 10   Litho.   *Perf. 13¼*
1897 A328 1600sh multi   1.50 1.50
Printed in sheets of 8 + central label.

Miniature Sheet

China 2009 World Stamp Exhibition,
Luoyang — A329

No. 1898 — Tourist attractions in China: a, Longmen Grottoes, Luoyang. b, Bridge over

Pearl River, Guangzhou. c, Twin Temples on Fir Lake, Guilin. d, Yu Yuan Garden, Shanghai.

2009, Apr. 10   *Perf. 12*
1898 A329 1000sh Sheet of 4,
          #a-d   3.75 3.75

Miniature Sheet

Pres. Abraham Lincoln (1809-
65) — A330

No. 1899 — Photographs of Lincoln taken in: a, 1857 (wearing vest). b, 1864. c, 1863. d, 1857 (without vest).

2009, Apr. 10   *Perf. 13¼*
1899 A330 2000sh Sheet of 4,
          #a-d   7.50 7.50

Miniature Sheet

Inauguration of US Pres. Barack
Obama — A331

No. 1900: a, Pres. Obama and wife, Michelle, balustrade over heads. b, Pres. Obama with blue striped tie, window at left. c, Pres. Obama with red and gold tie, balustrade above head. d, As "b," window above head. e, As "c," White House portico lamp above head. f, As "a," windows over heads.

2009, Apr. 10   *Perf. 11½x11¼*
1900 A331 2000sh Sheet of 6,
          #a-f   11.00 11.00

Miniature Sheets

A332

Michael Jackson (1958-2009),
Singer — A333

No. 1901: a, Wearing tan jacket, no microphone shown. b, Wearing blue and white shirt, no microphone shown. c, Wearing blue jacket, with microphone. d, Wearing tan jacket, with microphone.

No. 1902: a, Facing right, microphone at mouth. b, Holding microphone on stand. c, Behind microphone on stand. d, Facing left, microphone at mouth.

2009   **Perf. 13¼x13**
1901 A332 2000sh Sheet of 4,
     #a-d   8.50 8.50
1902 A333 2000sh Sheet of 4,
     #a-d   8.50 8.50

The printer of Nos. 1901-1902 claims the stamps were issued June 25, the day Michael Jackson died. The editors doubt this claim.

Chinese Aviation, Cent. — A334

No. 1903: a, Q-5. b, Q-5C. c, JH-7A. d, JH-7 on ground. 4000sh, JH-7 in flight.

2009, Nov. 12   **Perf. 14¼**
1903 A334 2000sh Sheet of 4,
    #a-d   8.50 8.50
Souvenir Sheet
1904 A334 4000sh multi   4.25 4.25

Aeropex 2009, Beijing. No. 1903 contains four 42x33mm stamps.

Miniature Sheet

Princess Diana (1961-97) — A335

No. 1905 — Princess Diana: a, Wearing black and white hat. b, Wearing pink hat. c, Wearing white blouse. d, Holding flowers.

2010, Feb. 15   **Perf. 11½**
1905 A335 2000sh Sheet of 4,
    #a-d   8.00 8.00

Miniature Sheet

Pope John Paul II (1920-2005) — A336

No. 1906 — Pope John Paul II: a, 400sh, Greeting crowd. b, 1600sh, With arms raised. c, 2000sh, Standing in front of painting. d, 4000sh, With hand on chest.

2010, June 24
1906 A336   Sheet of 4, #a-d   7.25 7.25

Souvenir Sheet

Boy Scouts of America, Cent. — A337

No. 1907 — Emblem of: a, National Scout Jamboree. b, Philmont Scout Ranch, Cimarron, New Mexico. c, Florida High Adventure Sea Base.

2010, Oct. 14   **Perf. 13½**
1907 A337 3000sh Sheet of 3,
    #a-c   8.00 8.00

Miniature Sheets

A338

Pope Benedict XVI — A339

No. 1908 — Various photographs of Pope Benedict XVI with denomination at upper right: a, 400sh. b, 1600sh. c, 2000sh. d, 4000sh.
No. 1909 — Various photographs of Pope Benedict XVI with denomination at upper left: a, 400sh. b, 1600sh. c, 2000sh. d, 4000sh.

2011, Feb. 25   **Perf. 12**
1908 A338   Sheet of 4, #a-d   6.75 6.75
1909 A339   Sheet of 4, #a-d   6.75 6.75

Miniature Sheets

2010 World Cup Soccer Championships, South Africa — A340

No. 1910 — Team from: a, 400sh, Algeria. b, 400sh, South Africa. c, 1600sh, Ghana. d, 1600sh, Nigeria. e, 3000sh, Ivory Coast. f, 3000sh, Cameroun.
No. 1911 — Team from: a, 900sh, Italy. b, 900sh, Brazil. c, 1100sh, Japan. d, 1100sh, New Zealand. e, 4000sh, Australia. f, 4000sh, United States.

2011, Feb. 25   **Litho.**   **Perf. 12**
Sheets of 6, #a-f
1910-1911 A340   Set of 2   18.50 18.50

Disease Prevention A341

Inscriptions: 400sh, Treat livestock against nagana. 900sh, Treat humans against sleeping sickness, horiz. 1600sh, War against tsetse flies in Uganda, horiz. 3000sh, Empower communities against trypanosomiasis, horiz.

2011, Jan. 18   **Perf. 13x13½, 13½x13**
1912-1915 A341   Set of 4   5.25 5.25

Souvenir Sheet

New Year 2011 (Year of the Rabbit) — A342

No. 1916: a, Rabbit standing on hind legs. b, Rabbit leaping.

2011, Feb. 1   **Perf. 12**
1916 A342 2000sh Sheet of 2,
    #a-b   3.50 3.50

Wedding of Prince William and Catherine Middleton — A343

No. 1917 — Stamps with blue panels: a, 600sh, Bride standing. b, 2500sh, Couple.
No. 1918 — Stamps with red panels: a, 600sh, Bride in coach. b, 2500sh, Couple waving.

2011, Apr. 29   **Perf. 13¼x13**
Pairs, #a-b
1917-1918 A343   Set of 2   5.25 5.25

Nos. 1917-1918 each were printed in sheets containing two pairs. Nos. 1917-1918 could not have been issued on the stated day of issue, as the stamps show photographs of the wedding that day.

A344

A345

A346

A347

A348

A349

A350

A351

A352

A353

A354

A355

A356

A357

A358

A359

A360

A361

A362

Gorillas
A363

2011, June 18   *Perf. 14½*

1919		Block of 10	3.00	3.00
a.	A344	400sh multi	.30	.30
b.	A345	400sh multi	.30	.30
c.	A346	400sh multi	.30	.30
d.	A347	400sh multi	.30	.30
e.	A348	400sh multi	.30	.30
f.	A349	400sh multi	.30	.30
g.	A350	400sh multi	.30	.30
h.	A351	400sh multi	.30	.30
i.	A352	400sh multi	.30	.30
j.	A352	400sh multi	.30	.30
1920		Vert. strip of 5	4.00	4.00
a.	A354	1000sh multi	.80	.80
b.	A355	1000sh multi	.80	.80
c.	A356	1000sh multi	.80	.80
d.	A357	1000sh multi	.80	.80
e.	A358	1000sh multi	.80	.80

1921		Vert. strip of 5	6.25	6.25
a.	A359	1600sh multi	1.25	1.25
b.	A360	1600sh multi	1.25	1.25
c.	A361	1600sh multi	1.25	1.25
d.	A362	1600sh multi	1.25	1.25
e.	A363	1600sh multi	1.25	1.25
		Nos. 1919-1921 (3)	13.25	13.25

Pan-African Postal Union, 30th anniv. (in 2010).

SEMI-POSTAL STAMPS

> Catalogue values for all unused stamps in this section are for never Hinged items.

PAPU (Pan African Postal Union), 18th Anniv. — SP1

1998, Jan. 18   **Litho.**   *Perf. 14*

B1	SP1	300sh +150sh Mountain gorilla	1.10 1.10

POSTAGE DUE STAMPS

> Catalogue values for unused stamps in this section are for Never Hinged items.

Type of Kenya, 1967
Perf. 14x13½

1967, Jan. 3   **Litho.**   Unwmk.

J1	D1	5c red	.25	4.00
J2	D1	10c green	.25	4.00
J3	D1	20c dark blue	.25	5.00
J4	D1	30c reddish brown	.45	6.50
J5	D1	40c red lilac	.65	7.25
J6	D1	1sh orange	2.00	18.00
		Nos. J1-J6 (6)	3.85	44.75

1970, Mar. 31   *Perf. 14x15*

J1a	D1	5c red	.25	1.25
J2a	D1	10c green	.25	1.25
J3a	D1	20c dark blue	.30	4.25
J4a	D1	30c reddish brown	.40	5.00
J5a	D1	40c red lilac	.60	6.00
		Nos. J1a-J5a (5)	1.80	17.75

1973   *Perf. 15*

J1b	D1	5c red	.25	1.25
J2b	D1	10c green	.25	1.25
J3b	D1	20c dark blue	.70	3.25
J4b	D1	30c reddish brown	.95	4.75
J5b	D1	40c red lilac	1.60	7.25
J6b	D1	1sh orange	4.00	13.00
		Nos. J1b-J6b (6)	7.75	30.75

Nos. J1-J6 Overprinted in Black: "LIBERATED / 1979"

1979, Dec.   **Litho.**   *Perf. 14*

J7	D1	5c red	.25	.70
J8	D1	10c green	.25	.70
J9	D1	20c violet blue	.25	.70
J10	D1	30c reddish brown	.25	1.00
J11	D1	40c red lilac	.25	1.00
J12	D1	1sh orange	.70	1.25
		Nos. J7-J12 (6)	1.95	5.35

Wildlife — D2

1985, Mar. 11   **Litho.**   *Perf. 15x14*

J13	D2	5sh Lion	.25	.95
J14	D2	10sh African buffalo	.25	.95
J15	D2	20sh Kob antelope	.60	1.40
J16	D2	40sh Elephant	1.25	2.10
J17	D2	50sh Zebra	1.25	2.10
J18	D2	100sh Rhinoceros	1.75	3.50
		Nos. J13-J18 (6)	5.35	11.00

UKRAINE

yü-ˈkrän

LOCATION — In southeastern Europe, bordering on the Black Sea
GOVT. — Republic
AREA — 231,900 sq. mi.
POP. — 48,760,474 (2001)
CAPITAL — Kyiv

Following the collapse of the Russian Empire, a national assembly met at Kyiv and declared the Ukrainian National Republic on Jan. 22, 1918. During three years of civil war, the Ukrainian army, as well as Bolshevik, White Russian, Allied and Polish armies, fought back and forth across the country. By November, 1920, Ukraine was finally occupied by Soviet forces, and Soviet stamps were used from that time, until the recreation of the independent Ukraine on Aug. 24, 1991.

200 Shahiv = 100 Kopiyok (Kopecks)
= 1 Karbovanets (Ruble)
100 Shahiv = 1 Hryvnia
100 Kopiyok = 1 Karbovanets (1992)
100 Kopiyok = 1 Hryvnia   (1996)

> Catalogue values for unused stamps in this country are for Never Hinged items, beginning with Scott 100 in the regular postage section, Scott B9 in the semi-postal section, and Scott F1 in the registration section.

Watermarks

Wmk. 116 —
Crosses and Circles

Wmk. 399

Republic's Trident Emblem — A1

Ukrainian Peasant — A2

Allegorical Ukraine — A3

Trident — A4

Inscription of Value — A5

1918, July   **Typo.**   *Imperf.*
Thin Paper

1	A1	10sh buff	.35	.40
2	A2	20sh brown	.35	.40
3	A3	30sh ultra	.35	.40
a.		30sh blue	2.75	6.50
4	A4	40sh green	.35	.40
5	A5	50sh red	.35	.40
		Nos. 1-5 (5)	1.75	2.00

The stamps of this issue exist perforated or pin-perforated unofficially.

Forgeries of this set exist on a very thin, glossy paper.

These designs were earlier (April, 1918) utilized for money tokens, printed on thin cardboard, perforated 11½, and bearing an inscription on the reverse "Circulates on par with coins" in Ukrainian. These tokens exist favor canceled but were not postage stamps. Value uncanceled, $6 each.

Stamps of Russia Overprinted in Violet, Black, Blue, Red, Brown or Green

This trident-shaped emblem was taken from the arms of the Grand Prince Volodymyr and adopted as the device of the Ukrainian Republic.

In the early months of independence, Russian stamps were commonly used, but the influx of large quantities of stamps from Russia made it necessary to take measures to protect postal revenue. In August, 1918, local post offices were ordered to send their existing stocks of Russian stamps to regional centers, where they were overprinted with the trident arms. Unoverprinted Russian stamps were declared invalid after October 1, although they were often accepted for use.

This overprint was handstamped, typographed or lithographed. It was applied in various cities in the Ukraine and there are numerous types.

> Nos. 6-47 represent the basic Russian stamps that received these overprints. Values are for the most common overprint variety.
>
> For a detailed listing of these overprints, see the *Scott Classic Specialized Catalogue of Stamps and Covers 1840-1940.*

The basic Russian stamps to which Trident overprints were applied

A8

A9

A11

A12

A13

A14

A15

On Stamps of 1902-03

1918		**Wmk. 168**		**Perf. 13½**
6	A12	3½r black & gray	75.00	75.00
7	A12	7r black & yellow	75.00	75.00

On Stamps of 1909-18
Lozenges of Varnish on Face
Perf. 14, 14½x15
Unwmk.

8	A14	1k orange	.25	.35
9	A14	2k green	.25	.35
10	A14	3k red	.25	.35
11	A15	4k carmine	.25	.35
12	A14	5k claret	.25	.35
13	A14	7k light blue	.25	.35
14	A15	10k dark blue	.25	.35
15	A14	14k blue & rose	.25	.35
16	A11	15k red brn & bl	.25	.35
17	A8	20k blue & car	.25	.35
18	A11	25k grn & gray vio	.40	.50
19	A11	35k red brn & grn	.25	.35
20	A8	50k violet & grn	.25	.35
21	A11	70k brown & org	.25	.35

Perf. 13½

22	A9	1r lt brn, brn & org	.50	.75
23	A12	3½r mar & lt grn	1.00	2.50
24	A13	5r dk bl, grn & pale bl	7.00	11.00
25	A12	7r dk grn & pink	8.00	12.00
26	A13	10r scar, yel & gray	12.00	18.00
		Nos. 6-26 (21)	182.15	199.30

On Stamps of 1917
Perf. 14, 14½x15

27	A14	10k on 7k light blue	.75	1.00
28	A11	20k on 14k bl & rose	.75	1.00

On Stamps of 1917-18
Imperf

29	A14	1k orange	.25	.35
30	A14	2k gray green	.25	.35
31	A14	3k red	.25	.35
32	A15	4k carmine	.25	.35
33	A14	5k claret	.90	1.50
34	A11	15k red brn & bl	.25	.35
35	A8	20k bl & car	.75	1.50
36	A11	25k grn & gray vio	60.00	—
37	A11	35k red brn & grn	.25	.35
38	A8	50k violet & grn	.30	.35
39	A11	70k brown & org	.25	.35
40	A9	1r pale brn, brn & red org	.25	.60
41	A12	3½r mar & lt grn	1.00	2.50
42	A13	5r dk bl, grn & pale bl	1.50	3.00
43	A12	7r dk grn & pink	2.50	4.00
44	A13	10r scar, yel & gray	70.00	85.00
		Nos. 29-44 (16)	138.95	100.90

On Russia Nos. AR1-AR3

		Wmk. 171		**Litho.**
		Perf. 14, 14½x14¾		
45	PF1	1k red, *buff*	5.00	25.00
46	PF1	5k green, *buff*	20.00	200.00
47	PF1	10k brown, *buff*	35.00	350.00
		Nos. 45-47 (3)	60.00	495.00

Nos. 45-47 were used and accepted as postage stamps during stamp shortages.

The trident overprint was applied by favor to Russia Nos. 88-104, 110-111, the Romanov issue.

For surcharges see Russian Offices in the Turkish Empire Nos. 320-339.

A6

1919, Jan.				**Litho.**
48	A6	20h red & green	10.00	25.00

Because of its high face value, No. 48 was used primarily on money transfer forms or parcel receipts. Used value is for a postally used example.

Nos. 1 and 5 Surcharged

1919, Feb.		**Unwmk.**		**Imperf.**
49	A1	35k on 10sh buff	9.00	20.00
50	A5	70k on 50sh red	70.00	50.00
a.		Surcharge inverted		60.00

Nos. 49 and 50 were originally believed to have been created by the Soviets in the Ukraine in April, 1919, but more recent research seems to indicate that they were created by the White (Don) Army operating in eastern Ukraine at the request of the Ukrainian government. Correctly franked covers have been recorded from the February-June 1919 period.

Excellent forged surcharges exist.

Ukrainian Soviet Socialist Republic

During 1920/1921, hyperinflation of the ruble created a desperate need for stamps to pay ever-rising postal rates. Many Russian cities and districts surcharged existing stocks of Russian stamps in needed denominations for provisional use.

In June 1920 the national government of the Soviet Ukrainian Republic authorized the Kharkiv post office to create such surcharges for use in the Kharkiv region and in adjacent oblasts. Both unoverprinted Russian stamps and stamps bearing the regional trident overprints of Katerynoslav, Kharkiv and Kyiv were surcharged to raise their face value 100-fold. They were sold at 236 post offices in the Ukraine from June 1920 through Feb. 1921.

In Feb. 1922 three Russian postal savings stamps were surcharged for provisional use by the Kyiv post office, at the direction of the central government. As with the Kharkiv surcharges, these stamps were distributed over a wide area within the country.

KHARKIV ISSUE
Ukrainian and Russian Stamps Handstamp Surcharged

Ukrainian trident overprinted issues and unoverprinted Russian stamps revalued 100-fold by changing denominations from kopecks to rubles.

Two types of overprint: type I, Cyrillic RUB (not including periods) 9.5mmx6.5mm; type II, 8.5mmx6.5mm.

Number of basic Ukrainian or Russian stamp shown in parentheses.

1920, June
Type I Reading Upward
On Katerynoslav Trident Ovpt. Issue of 1918

51	A11	15k red brown & blue (#16a)	75.00	75.00

Kharkiv Trident Ovpt. Issue of 1918

52	A14	1k orange (#8b)	100.00	60.00
a.		Surcharge reading downward	150.00	150.00
53	A14	2k green (#9b)	100.00	65.00
54	A14	3k red (#10b)	80.00	40.00

55	A11	15k red brn & blue (#16b)	40.00	35.00
56	A8	20k blue & car (#17b)	200.00	175.00
a.		Surcharge reading downward	300.00	300.00
57	A11	20k on 14k blue & rose (#28b)	170.00	190.00
		Imperf		
58	A14	1k orange (#29b)	75.00	75.00
a.		Surcharge reading downward	120.00	120.00
59	A14	2k green (#30b)	250.00	250.00
60	A14	3k red (#31b)	40.00	40.00

On Kyiv Trident Ovpt. Issue of 1918

No. 61   No. 63

On Kyiv II Overprint

61	A14	1k orange (#8f)	40.00	40.00
		Imperf		
62	A14	1k orange (#29f)	40.00	50.00
a.		Surcharge reading downward	—	—

On Kyiv III Overprint

63	A14	3k red (#31g)	15.00	20.00

On Russian Arms Issue of 1909-18

No. 64

64	A14	1k orange (#73)	50.00	50.00
65	A14	2k green (#74)	10.00	15.00
a.		Surcharge reading downward	15.00	20.00
66	A14	3k red (#75)	10.00	15.00
a.		Surcharge reading downward	25.00	20.00
67	A15	4k red (#76)	325.00	
68	A14	5k claret (#77)	7.00	6.00
a.		Surcharge reading downward	20.00	20.00
69	A15	10k dk blue (#79)	15.00	15.00
a.		Surcharge reading downward	90.00	100.00
70	A11	15k red brn & blue (#81)	7.00	6.00
a.		Surcharge reading downward	10.00	10.00
71	A8	20k blue & car (#82)	10.00	6.00
a.		Surcharge reading downward	15.00	12.00
		Imperf		
72	A14	1k orange (#119)	50.00	36.00
a.		Surcharge reading downward	100.00	100.00
73	A14	2k green (#120)	45.00	55.00
74	A14	3k red (#121)	30.00	36.00
75	A14	5k claret (#123)	9.00	7.00
a.		Surcharge reading downward	25.00	25.00
76	A11	15k red brn & blue (#125)	120.00	130.00
a.		Surcharge reading downward	—	—

Type II Reading Upward
On Kharkiv Trident Ovpt. Issue of 1918

No. 79a

77	A14	3k red (#31b)	35.00	40.00

On Kyiv Trident Ovpt. Issue of 1918

78	A14	1k orange (#29f)	20.00	25.00

On Russian Arms Issue of 1919-18
Perf. 14x14½

79	A14	2k green (#74)	6.00	7.00
a.		Surcharge reading downward	12.00	12.00
80	A14	5k claret (#77)	8.00	7.00
a.		Surcharge reading downward	15.00	12.00
81	A15	10k dk blue (#79)	18.00	18.00
a.		Surcharge reading downward	100.00	115.00
82	A11	15k red brn & blue (#81)	8.00	7.00
a.		Surcharge reading downward	12.00	10.00

83	A8	20k blue & car (#82)	8.00	7.00
		Imperf		
84	A14	2k green (#120)	50.00	60.00

KYIV ISSUE

Russian Postal Savings Stamps Handstamp Surcharged

1922, Feb.			**Wmk. 171**
85	7500 (r) on 5k, green, *buff*	50.00	50.00
a.	Surcharge reading downward	60.00	55.00
86	8000 (r) on 5k, green, *buff*	150.00	90.00
a.	Surcharge reading downward	180.00	150.00
87	15000 (r) on 10k, brown, *buff*	300.00	150.00
a.	Surcharge reading downward	450.00	250.00

Nos. 85-87 are normally found on stamps watermarked with a vertical diamond pattern (Wmk. 171) but also exist on paper watermarked sideways, with both upward and downward-reading surcharges. These are rare and are worth approximately 8 times the values shown.

Nos. 1-5 surcharged in grivni (hryven) with the Polish eagle were sold as Polish occupation issues. They are of private origin.

Nos. 1-3 and 5 overprinted diagonally as above ("South Russia") are believed to be of private origin.

A lithographed set of 14 stamps (1h-200h) of these types, perf. 11½, was prepared in 1920, but never placed in use. Value, set $5.

All values exist imperf., some with inverted centers. Trial printings exist on various papers, including inverted, multiple, omitted and misaligned center vignettes. These are from the printer's waste.

This set handstamped "VILNA UKRAINA / 1921" and 6 values additionally overprinted "DOPLATA" are of private origin.

In 1923 the Ukrainian government-in-exile in Warsaw prepared an 11-value set, consisting of the 10h, 20h and 40h denominations of the unissued 1920 set surcharged and overprinted with the Cyrillic "UPP," supposedly intended as a Field Post issue for a planned invasion of the Ukraine. The invasion never occurred, and the stamps were never issued. Value $15.

For German stamps overprinted "Ukraine" see Russia Nos. N29-N48.

Catalogue values for unused stamps in this section, from this point to the end of the section, are for Never Hinged items.

Cossacks in Ukraine, 500th Anniv. — A20

Design: No. 101, Ukrainian emigrants to Canada.

1992, Mar. 1   Litho.   Perf. 12
100 A20 15k multicolored   1.25 1.25
101 A20 15k multicolored   1.25 1.25

Ukrainian emigration to Canada, centennial (No. 101). Dated 1991.

Mykola V. Lysenko (1842-1912), Composer — A21

1992, Mar. 22   Perf. 13
102 A21 100k multicolored   1.25 1.25

Numerous trident overprints on Soviet stamps exist. Many of them are legitimate local issues and were in official use. Locally produced stamps also exist.

Ukrainian Girl — A22

1992   Litho.   Perf. 12x12½
118 A22 50k bright blue   .25 .25
119 A22 70k bister   .25 .25
121 A22 1kb yellow green   .25 .25
122 A22 2kb purple   .25 .25
124 A22 5kb blue   .25 .25
126 A22 10kb red   .50 .50
128 A22 20kb green   2.50 2.50
130 A22 50kb brown   3.00 3.00
Nos. 118-130 (8)   7.25 7.25

Issued: Nos. 124, 126, 128, 130, 5/16; 118-119, 121-122, 6/17.

Mykola I. Kostomarov (1817-1885), Writer — A23

1992, May 16   Photo.   Perf. 12x11½
133 A23 20k olive green   1.25 1.25

1992 Summer Olympics, Barcelona
A24   A25

1992, July 25   Litho.   Perf. 13
134 A24 3kb yel green & multi   .65 .65
135 A25 4kb multicolored   .85 .85
136 A24 5kb buff & multi   1.10 1.10
Nos. 134-136 (3)   2.60 2.60

World Forum of Ukrainians, Kyiv — A26

1992, Aug. 19   Litho.   Perf. 13
137 A26 2kb multicolored   1.25 1.25

Declaration of Independence from the Soviet Union — A27

1992, Aug. 19   Perf. 13½x13
138 A27 2kb multicolored   1.25 1.25

Souvenir Sheet

Union of Ukrainian Philatelists, 25th Anniv. — A28

1992, Aug. 19   Perf. 12
139 A28 2kb multicolored   2.10 2.10

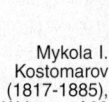

Intl. Letter Writing Week A29

1992, Oct. 4   Perf. 13x13½
140 A29 5kb multicolored   .70 .70

World Congress of Ukrainian Lawyers, Kyiv — A30

1992, Oct. 18   Litho.   Perf. 13
141 A30 15kb multicolored   1.25 1.25

Ukrainian Diaspora in Austria A31

Perf. 13½x14½
1992, Nov. 27   Litho.
142 A31 5kb multicolored   1.40 1.40

Embroidery A32

1992, Nov. 16   Litho.   Perf. 11½x12
143 A32 50k black & orange   1.40 1.40

Mohyla Academy, Kyiv, 360th Anniv. A33

1992, Nov. 27   Litho.   Perf. 12x12½
144 A33 1.50kb multicolored   1.40 1.40

Souvenir Sheet

Ukrainian Medal Winners, 1992 Summer Olympics, Barcelona — A34

1992, Dec. 14   Litho.   Perf. 14
145 A34 10kb multicolored   4.00 4.00

Coats of Arms — A35

1993, Feb. 15   Litho.   Perf. 14x13½
148 A35 3kb Lviv   1.75 1.75
150 A35 5kb Kyiv   2.75 2.75
See No. 292.

Cardinal Joseph Slipyj (1892-1984) A36

1993, Feb. 17   Litho.   Perf. 14x13½
166 A36 15kb multicolored   3.00 3.00

1st Vienna-Cracow-Lviv-Kyiv Air Mail Flight, 75th Anniv. — A37

1993, Mar. 31   Perf. 13½x14
167 A37 35kb Biplane   1.30 1.30
168 A37 50kb Jet   1.90 1.90

Easter A39

1993, Apr. 18   Litho.   Perf. 13½
169 A39 15kb multicolored   1.25 1.25

UN Declaration of Human Rights, 45th Anniv. — A40

Design: 5kb, Country Wedding in Lower Austria, by Ferdinand Georg Waldmuller.

Perf. 14½x13½
1993, June 11   Litho.
170 A40 5kb multicolored   3.00 3.00

A41   A41a

A41b   A41c

A41d   A41e

A41f

A41g

A41h

Villagers at Work: 50kb, #177, Reaper with scythe. 100kb, #185, Ox carts. #173A, 200kb, 500kb, Reaper with sickle. #173B, Farmer with oxen. 150kb, 300kb, #184, Shepherd. #183, Bee keeper. #184A, Fisherman. #186, Potter. (Illustrations A41a-A41h help identify the Cyrillic characters, not the designs.)

Perf. 12x12½, 14 (#174, 180, 182, 184)

1993-98				Litho.	
171	A41	50kb	green	.40	.40
172	A41	100kb	blue	.40	.40
173	A41c	(100kb)	brown	.50	.50
174	A41e	(100kb)	magenta	.60	.60
175	A41	150kb	red	.40	.40
176	A41	200kb	orange	.50	.50
177	A41d	(250kb)	green	.50	.50
178	A41	300kb	violet	.50	.50
179	A41	500kb	brown	.50	.50
180	A41f	(1800kb)	org brn	.50	.50
181	A41a	(5000kb)	red	2.50	2.50
182	A41g	(5300kb)	blue	1.25	1.25
183	A41h	(10,000kb)	blue	1.00	1.00
a.		Perf. 14		7.00	7.00
184	A41h	(17,000kb)	red brn	2.25	2.25
		Nos. 171-184 (14)		11.80	11.30

Nos. 174, 181 issued for domestic letter rate; Nos. 177, 180 for letters within the Commonwealth of Independent States; Nos. 183-184 for mail abroad, surface and airmail. Actual amounts sold for varied with inflation. No. 183a sold for 30k on date of issue and was used for the domestic rate.

Issued: 50, 100, 150, 200, 300, 500kb, 12/18/93; #181, 183a, 5/28/94; #173, 177, 7/2/94; #174, 182, 10/15/94; #180, 184, 11/12/94; #183, 12/30/98.

Famine Deaths, 60th Anniv. — A42

1993, Sept. 12   Litho.   Perf. 12
188 A42 75kb brown   1.40 1.40

First Ukrainian Postage Stamp, 75th Anniv. A43

1993, Oct. 9
189 A43 100kb blue & brown   1.40 1.40
Stamp Day.

Liberation of Kyiv, 50th Anniv. A44

1993, Nov. 6   Litho.   Perf. 12
190 A44 75kb multicolored   1.25 1.25

A45

1994, Jan. 15   Litho.   Perf. 12
191 A45 200kb black & red   1.25 1.25
Agapit, Kyivan Rus physician, Middle Ages.

A46

Endangered species: No. 192, Erythronium dens, canis. No. 193, Cypripedium calceolus.

1994, Feb. 19   Perf. 12x12½
192 A46 200kb multicolored   1.30 1.30
193 A46 200kb multicolored   1.30 1.30

Independence Day — A47

1994, Sept. 3   Litho.   Imperf.
194 A47 5000kb multicolored 1.50 1.50
No. 194 has simulated perforations.

Kyiv University A47a

Litho. & Engr.
1994, Sept. 24   Perf. 13x13½
194A A47a 10,000kb multi   1.00 1.00
Souvenir Sheet
Perf. 12½x13
194B A47a 25,000kb multi   2.50 2.50
No. 194B contains one 40x27mm stamp.

Liberation of Soviet Areas, 50th Anniv. A48

Battle maps and: a, Katyusha rockets, liberation of Russia. b, Fighter planes, liberation of Ukraine. c, Combined offensive, liberation of Belarus.

1994, Oct. 8   Litho.   Perf. 12½x12
195 A48 500kb Block of 3, #a.-c.,
          + label   1.50 1.50
See Russia No. 6213, Belarus No. 78.

Excavation of Trypillia culture, Cent. — A49

1994, Dec. 17   Litho.   Perf. 12x12½
196 A49 4000kb multicolored .50 .50

1st Books Printed in Ukrainian, 500th Anniv. — A50

1994, Dec. 17   Perf. 13½
197 A50 4000kb multicolored .50 .50

Sofiyivka Natural Park, Bicent. A51

1994, Dec. 17   Perf. 12½x12
198 A51 5000kb multicolored .75 .75

Ilya Y. Repin (1844-1930), Painter — A52

1994, Dec. 17   Perf. 12x12½
199 A52 4000kb multicolored .50 .50

City of Uzhhorod, 1100th Anniv. — A53

1995, Jan. 28   Litho.   Perf. 12
200 A53 5000kb multicolored .60 .60

Ivan Franko (1856-1916), Writer — A54

Ivan Puliuj (1845-1918), Physicist — A55

No. 203, Lesia Ukrainka (1871-1913), poet.

1995, Feb. 2   Perf. 13½
201 A54 3000kb multicolored .70 .70
202 A55 3000kb multicolored .80 .80
203 A54 3000kb multicolored .70 .70
     Nos. 201-203 (3)   2.20 2.20

Falco Peregrinus — A56

1995, Apr. 15   Litho.   Perf. 12
204 A56 5000kb shown   .50 .50
205 A56 10,000kb Grus grus   1.00 1.00

Maksym T. Rylskyi (1895-1964), Writer — A57

1995, Apr. 15   Perf. 13½x14
206 A57 50,000kb multicolored 2.00 2.00

End of World War II, 50th Anniv. — A58

1995, May 9   Litho.   Perf. 13½
207 A58 100,000kb multicolored 2.25 2.25

Artek, Intl. Children's Camp A59

1995, June 16   Litho.   Perf. 13½
208 A59 5000kb multicolored .75 .75

Famous Writers A60

Design: 1000kb, Ivan Kotliarevskyi (1769-1838), depiction of his poem, "Eneida." 3000kb, Taras Shevchenko (1814-61), his book, "Kobzar."

1995, July 8
209 A60 1000kb multicolored .50 .50
210 A60 3000kb multicolored .50 .50

Hetman Petro Konashevych-
Sahaidachny — A61

1995, July 22   Litho.   Perf. 13½
211 A61 30,000kb multicolored   1.00 1.00

Arms of
Luhansk — A62

1995   Litho.   Perf. 13½
212 A62 10,000kb shown   .50 .50
213 A62 10,000kb Chernihiv   1.50 1.50

Issued: No. 212, 9/15; No. 213, 10/22.

Hetman Bohdan Khmelnytsky
(Khmelnytskyi; 1593?-1657) — A63

1995, Sept. 23   Litho.   Perf. 12½x12
214 A63 40,000kb multi   1.10 1.10

Hetman Ivan Mazepa (1640?-
1709) — A64

1995, Oct. 14   Perf. 13½
215 A64 30,000kb multi   1.60 1.60

A65   A66

1995, Oct. 14
216 A65 50,000kb multi   2.00 2.00

European Nature Protection Year.

1995, Oct. 22
217 A66 50,000kb multi   1.60 1.60

Intl. Children's Day.

UN, 50th
Anniv.
A67

1995, Oct. 24   Perf. 12x12½
218 A67 50,000kb multi   1.60 1.60

A68   A69

1995, Dec. 9   Perf. 13½
219 A68 50,000kb multi   1.40 1.40

Ivan Karpenko-Karyi, playwright, actor.

1995, Dec. 9
220 A69 50,000kb multi   1.75 1.75

Mikhailo Hrushevskyi, 1st Ukrainian
president.

P. Safarik (1795-1861), Writer — A70

1995, Dec. 27
221 A70 30,000kb green   1.40 1.40

Trolleybus   Streetcar
A71   A72

City Bus — A73

1995, Dec. 27   Litho.   Perf. 14
No Year Date
222 A71 (1000kb) blue violet   .25 .25
  a. Imprint "2003"   1.25 1.25
  b. Imprint "2005"   1.25 1.25
  c. Imprint "2006"   1.25 1.25
223 A72 (2000kb) green   2.75 2.75
224 A73 (3000kb) red   1.00 .80
  a. Imprint "2006"   .25 .25
    Nos. 222-224 (3)   4.00 3.80

The postal rate that No. 223 paid was
sharply increased greatly affecting the cost of
the stamp at the post offices.
Imprinted values issued: #222a, 2003;
#222b, 12/1/05; #222c, 2/3/06. #224a,
9/28/06.

Taras Shevchenko University
Astronomical Observatory, Kyiv, 150th
Anniv. — A74

a, 20,000 l, Early astronomical instruments.
b, 30,000 l, Telescope. c, 50,000 l, Observatory, sun.

1996, Jan. 13   Perf. 12
225 A74   Strip of 3, #a.-c.   2.40 2.40

1994 Winter Olympics,
Lillehammer — A75

Medalists: a, 40,000kb, Valentina Tserbe,
bronze, biathlon. b, 50,000kb, Oksana Bayul,
gold, figure skating.

1996, Jan. 13
226 A75   Sheet of 2, #a.-b.   2.25 2.50

Ahatanhel   Kharkiv Zoo,
Krymskyi (1871-   Cent. — A77
1942),
Writer — A76

1996, Jan. 15   Perf. 13½
227 A76 20,000kb bister & brown   .90 .90

1996, Mar. 23   Perf. 12½x12
228 A77 20,000kb multicolored   .80 .80

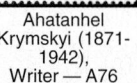

Ivan S. Kozlovskyi
(1900-93), Opera
Singer — A78

1996, Mar. 23   Perf. 13½
229 A78 20,000kb multicolored   .50 .50

Motion
Pictures,
Cent.
A79

Oleksandr Dovzhenko, film maker, house.

1996, Mar. 23   Perf. 12½x12
230 A79 4000kb multicolored   .90 .90

No. 230 was issued se-tenant with two
labels showing scenes from films.

Chernobyl Nuclear
Disaster, 10th
Anniv. — A80

1996, Apr. 26   Litho.   Perf. 13½
231 A80 20,000kb multicolored   .90 .90

Symyrenko
Family
A81

Vasyl Fedorovych (1835-1915), Volodymyr
Levkovych (1891-1938), Levko Platonovych
(1855-1920).

1996, May 25
232 A81 20,000kb multicolored   .90 .90

Vasil Stefanyk (1871-1936),
Writer — A82

1996, June 29
233 A82 20,000kb multicolored   .90 .90

Mykola M. Myklukho-Maklai (1846-88),
Explorer, Philologist — A83

Litho. & Engr.
1996, July 17   Perf. 13½
234 A83 40,000kb multicolored   1.50 1.50

1996 Summer
Olympic Games,
Atlanta — A84

Modern
Olympic
Games,
Cent.
A85

1996, July 19   Litho.   Perf. 13½
235 A84 20,000kb Wrestling   .60 .60
236 A84 40,000kb Handball   1.25 1.25
237 A85 40,000kb Greek ath-
    letes   1.75 1.75
    Nos. 235-237 (3)   3.60 3.60
Souvenir Sheet
Perf. 12
238 A84 100,000kb Gymnast   2.25 2.25

Independence,   First Ukrainian
5th Anniv. — A86   Satellite, "Sich-
    1" — A87

1996, Aug. 24   Perf. 13½
239 A86 20,000kb multicolored   .70 .70

1996, Aug. 31
240 A87 20,000kb multicolored   .80 .80

Locomotives — A88

Designs: 20,000kb, Steam, class OD. 40,000kb, Diesel class 2 TE-116.

1996, Aug. 31
241 A88 20,000kb multicolored .80 .80
242 A88 40,000kb multicolored 1.50 1.50
a. Pair, #241-242 2.75 2.75

Airplanes Designed by O.K. Antonov (1906-84) A89

No. 243, Glider A-15, portrait of Antonov. No. 244, AN-2. No. 245, AN-124. No. 246, AN-225.

1996, Sept. 14
243 A89 20,000kb multicolored 1.00 1.00
244 A89 20,000kb multicolored 1.00 1.00
245 A89 40,000kb multicolored 1.00 1.00
246 A89 40,000kb multicolored 1.00 1.00
a. Block of 4, #243-246 4.00 4.00

Ivan Piddubnyi (1871-1949), Wrestler — A90

1996, Nov. 16
247 A90 40k multicolored 1.20 1.20

First Ukrainian Antarctic Expedition A91

1996, Nov. 23
248 A91 20k multicolored 3.25 3.25

A92 A93

Flowers: 20k, Leontopodium alpinum. 40k, Narcissus anqustifolius.

1996, Nov. 23
249 A92 20k multicolored .75 .75
250 A92 40k multicolored 1.10 1.10
a. Pair, #249-250 + label 2.10 2.10

1996, Dec. 7   Litho.   Perf. 13½
251 A93 20k multicolored .80 .80

UNESCO, 50th anniv.

Viktor S. Kosenko, Composer, Birth Cent. A94

1996, Dec. 21   Litho.   Perf. 13½
252 A94 20k multicolored .60 .60

St. Sophia's Cathedral, Kyiv — A95

Illinska (St. Elijah) Church, Subotiv A96

St. George Church, Drohobych A97

#256, Troitska Cathedral, Novomoskovsk.

1996, Dec. 25
253 A95 20k multicolored .50 .50
254 A96 20k multicolored .50 .50
255 A97 20k multicolored .50 .50
256 A97 20k multicolored .50 .50
a. Block of 4, #253-256 2.50 2.50

UNICEF, 50th Anniv. A98

1996, Dec. 31
257 A98 20k multicolored .75 .75

Petro Mohyla (1596-1647), Metropolitan of Kyiv — A99

1996, Dec. 31
258 A99 20k multicolored .75 .75

Wild Animals — A100

1997, Mar. 22   Litho.   Perf. 13½
259 A100 20k Lynx lynx 1.00 1.00
260 A100 20k Ursos arctos 1.00 1.00
a. Pair, #259-260 + label 3.00 3.00

Cathedral of the Exaltation of the Holy Cross, Poltava, 17th Cent. A101

Designs: No. 262, St. George's Cathedral, Lviv, 18th cent. No. 263, Protection Fortified Church, Sutkivtsi, 14-15th cent.

1997, Apr. 19   Litho.   Perf. 13½
261 A101 20k multicolored 1.00 1.00
262 A101 20k multicolored 1.00 1.00
263 A101 20k multicolored 1.00 1.00
Nos. 261-263 (3) 3.00 3.00

Legendary Founders of Kyiv — A101a

Europa: a, Kyi (holding staff and shield) and Shchek (holding sword). b, Khoriv (holding sword, leaning on shield) and sister, Lybid.

1997, May 6 Litho. & Engr. Perf. 13
264 A101a 40k Sheet of 2, #a.-b. 10.00 10.00

4th Natl. Philatelic Exhibition, Cherkasy A102

Design: Statue of Taras Shevchenko, stamps, exhibition hall.

1997, May 17   Litho.   Perf. 13½
265 A102 10k multicolored .90 .90

Yurii V. Kondratiuk (1897-1942), Space Pioneer — A103

1997, June 21   Perf. 12½x12
266 A103 20k multicolored .90 .90

Constitution, 1st Anniv. — A104

1997, June 28   Perf. 13½
267 A104 20k multicolored .80 .80

Midsummer Festival of Ivan Kupalo — A104a

1997, July 5   Litho.   Perf. 13½
268 A104a 20k multicolored .75 .75

Princess Olha A105   Sultana Roksoliana A106

1997, July 12   Litho.   Perf. 13½
269 A105 40k multicolored 1.40 1.25
270 A106 40k multicolored 1.40 1.25

First Ukrainian Emigration to Argentina, Cent. A107

Design: Monument to poet Taras Shevchenko, Buenos Aires.

1997, Aug. 16   Litho.   Perf. 13½
271 A107 20k multicolored .90 .90

For Exceptional Service — A108

Order of Yaroslav the Wise — A109

Medals for: No. 273, Military Service. 30k, Bravery. 40k, Order of Bohdan Khmelnytsky. No. 276, Honored Service.
No. 277: a, Medal hanging from chain. b, 8-point star.

Litho. & Engr.   Perf. 13½
272 A108 20k multicolored 1.40 1.40
273 A108 20k multicolored 1.40 1.40
274 A108 30k multicolored 2.10 2.10
275 A108 40k multicolored 2.75 2.75
276 A108 60k multicolored 4.00 4.00
a. Strip of 5, #272-276 15.00 15.00

Souvenir Sheet   Perf. 13
277 A109 60k Sheet of 2, #a.-b. 9.00 9.00

Nos. 277a-277b are each 35x50mm.

Hetman — A110

No. 278, Dmytro "Baida" Vyshnevetskyj (?-1563), boats, archers. No. 279, Pylyp Orlyk (1672-1742), Stockholm harbor, crowd in Thessaloniki street.

1997, Sept. 13 Litho. *Perf. 12½x12*
278 A110 20k multicolored   1.10 1.10
279 A110 20k multicolored   1.10 1.10

See Nos. 357-358, 376-377, 412-413, 449-451, 510-511.

Solomiia Krushelnytska (Salomea Krusceniski, 1872-1952), Actress, Singer — A111

1997, Sept. 23 Litho. *Perf. 13½*
280 A111 20k multicolored   .95 .95

Airplanes A112

Designs: 20k, Antonov An-74 TK-200. 40k, Antonov An-38-100.

1997, Oct. 30
281 A112 20k multicolored   .60 .60
282 A112 40k multicolored   1.40 1.40

Ships A113

1997, Dec. 6 Litho. *Perf. 13½*
283 A113 20k Zavyietnyj, 1903   .60 .60
284 A113 40k Serhii Korolev, 1970, Academician   1.40 1.40

A114

1997, Dec. 6 Litho. *Perf. 12x12½*
285 A114 40k multi + label   1.75 1.75

Participation of Ukrainian astronaut in US space shuttle mission.

A115

Vasyl Krychevskyi (1872-1952), painter, architect.

1997, Dec. 20 *Perf. 13½*
286 A115 10k multicolored   .75 .75

Christmas — A116

1997, Dec. 20
287 A116 20k multicolored   1.00 1.00

Traditional Handicrafts A117

Region: #288, Rooster, Dnipropetrovsk. #289, Vest, Chernivtsi. #290, Ram, Poltava. #291, Molded design, Ivano-Frankivsk.

1997, Dec. 20
288 A117 20k multicolored   .75 .75
289 A117 20k multicolored   .75 .75
290 A117 40k multicolored   1.25 1.25
291 A117 40k multicolored   1.25 1.25
      Nos. 288-291 (4)   4.00 4.00

                    Perf. 11½
288a   20k   .75 .75
289a   20k   .75 .75
290a   40k   1.25 1.25
291a   40k   1.25 1.25
    b. Sheet, 2 each #288a-291a 8.00 8.00

Nos. 288-291 have colored border. Nos. 288a-291a do not.

Arms Type of 1993

Arms of Transcarpathia (Zakarpattya).

1997, Dec. 30 Litho. *Perf. 13½*
292 A35 20k multicolored   .90 .90

A118   A119

Wildlife: a, 20k, Skylark. b, 40k, White-tailed eagle. c, 20k, Black stork. d, 40k, Long-eared hedgehog. e, 20k, Garden dormouse. f, 40k, Wild boar.

1997, Dec. 30 Litho. *Perf. 11½*
293 A118 Sheet of 6, #a.-f.   5.00 5.00

Litho. & Engr.

1997, Dec. 27 *Perf. 13½*
294 A119 60k multicolored   1.10 1.10

Hryhorii Skovoroda (1722-94), philosopher.

A120   A121

1998, Jan. 6 Litho. *Perf. 13½*
295 A120 20k multicolored   1.50 1.00

Volodymyr Sosiura (1898-1965), poet.

1998, Feb. 14 Litho. *Perf. 13½*
296 A121 20k Figure skating   .75 .75
297 A121 20k Biathlon   .75 .75

1998 Winter Olympic Games, Nagano.

Bilhorod Dnistrovskyi Fortress, 2500th Anniv. — A122

1998, Apr. 21 Litho. *Perf. 13½*
298 A122 20k multicolored   .90 .90

UKRFILEKS 98 Natl. Philatelic Exhibition, Sevastopol — A123

Design: Frigate, "Hetman Sahaidachnyi."

1998, Apr. 28 Litho. *Perf. 13½*
299 A123 30k multi + label   .90 .90

European Bank of Reconstruction and Development — A124

Obverse, reverse of Ukrainian coins: a, 1k, Gold, 11th cent. b, 1k, Silver, 11th cent. c, 60k, 500h St. Sophia Cathedral gold coin. d, 60k, 200h Taras Shevchenko gold coin. e, 30k, 1,000,000k Bohdan Khmelnytsky silver coin. f, 30k, 10h Petro Mohyla silver coin.

Litho. & Engr.

1998, May 8 *Perf. 13½*
300 A124 Sheet of 6, #a.-f.   11.00 11.00

Ivan Kupalo Natl. Festival — A125

1998, May 16 Litho. *Perf. 13½*
301 A125 40k multicolored   2.50 2.50

Europa.

Souvenir Sheet

Askania Nova Nature Preserve, Cent. — A126

a, 40k, Deer. b, 60k, Przewalski horses.

1998, May 16 Litho. *Perf. 11½*
302 A126 Sheet of 2, #a.-b.   4.00 4.00

Paintings from Lviv Picture Gallery — A127

Designs: No. 303, Portrait of Maria Theresa, by J.E. Liotard. No. 304, Man with a Cello, by Gerard von Honthorst. 40k, Madonna and Child, 17th cent. Lviv School. 1.20h, Madonna and Child and Two Saints, by 16th cent. Italian school.

1998, June 20 *Perf. 13½*
303 A127 20k multicolored   .40 .40
304 A127 20k multicolored   .40 .40
305 A127 40k multicolored   .80 .80
    a. Strip of 3, #303-305   2.00 2.00

Souvenir Sheet

306 A127 1.20h multicolored   2.25 2.25

Souvenir Sheet

Polytechnical Institute, Kyiv, Cent. — A128

1998, June 27 Litho. *Perf. 11½*
307 A128 1h multicolored   4.00 4.00

Askold & Dyr A129

Litho. & Engr.

1998, July 4 *Perf. 13½*
308 A129 3h multi + label   5.00 5.00

Hetman Bohdan Khmelnytsky A130

Designs: a, 30k, Battle scene, denomination LR. b, 2k, Portrait of Khmelnytsky. c, 30k, Battle scene, denomination LL. d, 40k, denomination LR. e, 60k, Battle scene. f, 40k, Battle scene, denomination LL.

1998, July 25 Litho. & Engr.
309 A130 Sheet of 6, #a.-f.   8.00 8.00

Ukrainian uprising, 350th anniv.

Town of
Halych,
1100th
Anniv.
A131

1998, Aug. 1 **Litho.**
310 A131 20k multicolored .70 .70

Queen Anna
Yaroslavna (1024?-75)
A132

1998, Aug. 8
311 A132 40k multicolored 1.00 1.00

Yurii Lysianskyi (1773-1837),
Explorer — A133

1998, Aug. 13
312 A133 40k multicolored 1.40 1.40

Natalia Uzhvii (1898-1986), Stage
Actress — A134

1998, Sept. 8 **Litho.** **Perf. 13½**
313 A134 40k multicolored 1.25 1.25

Polytechnical Institute, Kyiv,
Cent. — A135

Designs: 10k, W.L. Kirpichov, first president.
No. 315, E.O. Paton, bridge. No. 316, S.P.
Timoschenko, mathematical formula. 30k, Igor
I. Sikorsky, biplane. 40k, Sergei P. Korolev,
rocket, satellite.

1998, Sept. 10 **Perf. 12½x12**
314 A135 10k multicolored .60 .60
315 A135 20k multicolored .60 .60
316 A135 20k multicolored .60 .60
317 A135 30k multicolored 1.10 1.10
318 A135 40k multicolored 1.25 1.25
 a. Strip of 5, #314-318 4.75 4.75

A136 A137

1998, Sept. 19 **Litho.** **Perf. 13½**
319 A136 10k multicolored .75 .75

World Post Day.

1998, Sept.19
320 A137 20k multicolored .75 .75

Ukrainian book, 1000th anniv.

Church
Architecture
A138

Designs: No. 321, Church of the Transfiguration, Chernihiv, 11th cent. No. 322, Church of
the Holy Protection, Kharkiv, 17th cent.

1998, Sept. 21
321 A138 20k multicolored .90 .70
322 A138 20k multicolored .90 .70

World
Wildlife
Fund
A139

Branta ruficollis: a, f, 20k, Adults. b, g, 30k,
Female on nest. c, h, 40k, Female with goslings. d, i, 60k, Adults, goslings.

1998, Oct. 10 **Litho.** **Perf. 13½**
323 A139 Block of 4, #a.-d. 3.00 3.00
 e. Block of 4, perf. 11½, #f.-i. 3.50 3.50
 j. Sheet of 2, #323e 7.00 7.00

Antonov
Airplanes
A140

1998, Nov. 28 **Litho.** **Perf. 13½**
324 A140 20k Antonov 140 .65 .65
325 A140 40k Antonov 70 .85 .85

Hetman Type of 1997

Design: Petro Doroshenko (1627-98).

1998, Nov. 28 **Litho.** **Perf. 12½x12**
326 A141 20k multicolored .80 .80

Borys D. Hrinchenko (1863-1910),
Writer — A142

1998, Dec. 4 **Litho.** **Perf. 13½**
327 A142 20k multicolored 1.50 1.50

Christmas — A143

1998, Dec. 11
328 A143 30k multicolored 1.50 1.00

Ukrainians
in Australia,
50th Anniv.
A144

1998, Dec. 20
329 A144 40k multicolored 1.00 1.00

Illintsi
Meteor
Impact
Area
A145

1998, Dec. 25
330 A145 40k multicolored 1.25 1.25

Universal
Declaration of
Human Rights,
50th
Anniv. — A146

Paintings of various flowers by Kateryna
Bilokur (1900-61): 30k, 1940. 50k, 1959.

1998, Dec. 25
331 A146 30k multicolored .75 .75
332 A146 50k multicolored 1.20 1.20
 a. Pair, #331-332 +label 2.00 2.00

Serhii Paradzhanov (1924-90), Film
Director — A147

1999, Feb. 27 **Litho.** **Perf. 13½**
333 A147 40k multi + label 1.30 1.30

Volodymyr
Ivasiuk
(1949-79),
Composer
A148

1999, Mar. 4
334 A148 30k multicolored .50 .50

Scythian
Gold
A149

1999, Mar. 20
335 A149 20k Clasp .40 .40
336 A149 40k Boar .65 .65
337 A149 50k Young elk .85 .85
338 A149 1h Necklace 1.40 1.40
 a. Block of 4, #335-338 3.50 3.50

Spring Easter
Dance — A150

1999, Apr. 7
339 A150 30k multicolored .50 .50

A151

Synevyr Natl. Park: a, 50k, Wooden monuments on bank of Tereblyia River. b, 1h,
Thymallus thymallus, river scene.

1999, Apr. 24
340 A151 Pair, #a.-b. 3.00 3.00

Europa.

A152

1999, May 13
341 A152 40k multicolored .80 .80

Panas Myrnyi (1849-1920), writer.

Honoré de Balzac (1799-1850),
Writer — A153

1999, May 20
342 A153 40k multicolored .80 .80

Council of
Europe,
50th Anniv.
A154

1999, May 22
343 A154 40k multicolored .80 .80

Aleksandr Pushkin
(1799-1837),
Poet — A155

1999, June 6
344 A155 40k + label .80 .80

Sailboats — A156

No. 345: a, Bark (Baidak), double sails, one
man at tiller. b, Cossack (Chaika), single sail,
rowers.

1999, June 26
345 A156 30k Pair, #a.-b. 1.25 1.25

Souvenir Sheet

Yaroslav the Wise — A157

1999, July 2 Litho. Perf. 11½
346 A157 1.20h multicolored 2.50 2.50

Principality of Halytsko-Volynskyi,
800th Anniv. — A158

1999, July 27 Perf. 13½
347 A158 50k multicolored 1.50 1.00

A159 A160

Designs: a, 30k, Icon of St. George. b, 60,
Girl in a Red Hat, by O.O. Murashko.

1999, July 27
348 A159 Pair, #a.-b. + label 2.00 1.50
Natl. Museum of Art, Cent.

1999, Aug. 7
349 A160 30k Bee on flower 1.00 1.00
Bee keeping in Ukraine.

A161 A162

1999, Aug. 14 Litho. Perf. 13½
350 A161 30k multicolored .65 .65
UPU, 125th anniv.

1999, Aug. 14
351 A162 30k multicolored .80 .80
Poltava, 1100th anniv.

Presidential
Medals — A163

Designs: 30k, Order of Princess Olga.
No. 353: a, Medal with trident. b, Medal with
star.

1999, Aug. 17 Litho. & Engr.
352 A163 30k multicolored .80 .80
Souvenir Sheet of 2
353 A163 2.50h #a.-b. 8.00 8.00
No. 353 contains two 35x50mm stamps.

Polish-Ukrainian Cooperation in Nature
Conservation — A164

a, Cervus elaphus. b, Felis silvestris.

1999, Sept. 22 Litho. Perf. 13½
354 A164 1.40h Pair, #a.-b. 3.50 2.00
See Poland Nos. 3477-3478.

National
Bank — A165

1999, Sept. 28 Litho. & Engr.
355 A165 3h multicolored 4.00 3.00
Souvenir Sheet
356 A165 5h multicolored 6.75 5.50

Hetman Type of 1997

Designs: No. 357, Ivan Vyhovskyi (d. 1664),
cavalry in water. No. 358, Pavlo Polubotok
(1660-1724), ships in water.

1999 Litho. Perf. 12¼x12
357 A110 30k multi .90 .90
358 A110 30k multi .90 .90
Issued: No. 357, 11/20; No. 358, 12/22.

A166

Christmas
A167

1999, Nov. 26 Wmk. 399 Perf. 13½
359 A166 30k multi .50 .50
Unwmk.
360 A167 60k multi 1.00 1.00

Children's Art — A168

a, Spacecraft, alien creatures. b, Elephant in
space. c, Rocket and space car on planet.

1999, Nov. 30 Unwmk. Perf. 11½
361 A168 10k Strip of 3, #a.-c. 3.00 3.00

Fauna
A169

Designs: a, 40k, Desmana moschata. b,
60k, Gyps fulvus. c, 40k, Lucanus cervus.

1999, Dec. 9 Perf. 13½
362 A169 Strip of 3, #a.-c. 2.25 2.25

Church of St. Andrew, Kyiv — A170

1999, Dec. 12
363 A170 60k multi + label 2.00 2.00

Mushrooms
A171

Designs: a, 30k, Armillariella mellea. b, 30k,
Paxillus atrotomentosus. c, 30k, Pleurotus
ostratus. d, 40k, Cantharellus cibarius. e, 60k,
Agaricus campester.

1999, Dec. 15 Perf. 11½
364 A171 Sheet of 5, #a.-e., +
label 4.00 4.00

New Year 2000 — A172

1999, Dec. 18 Perf. 13½
365 A172 50k multi + label 2.00 2.00

Motor Vehicles — A173

a, Kraz-65032 truck. b, Tavriia Nova car.

1999, Dec. 18 Litho.
366 A173 30k Pair, #a.-b. 1.50 1.00

Works of Maria Prymachenko — A174

Denomination colors: a, Green. b, Violet.

1999, Dec. 22
367 A174 30k Pair, #a.-b., + central label 1.50 1.00

Halshka
Hulevychivna,
Philanthropist
A175

1999, Dec. 25 Perf. 13½
368 A175 30k multi .80 .80

Zoogeographic Endowment
Fund — A176

Animals from: a, 10k, Carpathian Reserve.
b, 30k, Polissia Reserve. c, 40k, Kaniv
Reserve. d, 60k, Trakhtemyriv Reserve. e, 1h,
Askaniia-Nova Reserve (ram, birds). f, 1h,
Kara-Dag Reserve (birds).

1999, Dec. 28 Perf. 11½
369 A176 Sheet of 6, #a.-f. 5.50 4.00

Christianity, 2000th Anniv. — A177

Designs: a, Mother of God mosaic, St. Sofia Cathedral, Kyiv, 11th cent. b, Christ Pantocrator fresco, Church of the Savior's Transfiguration, Polotsk, Belarus, 12th cent. c, Volodymyr Madonna, Tretiakov Gallery, Moscow, 12th cent.

2000, Jan. 5   Litho.   Perf. 11½
Souvenir Sheet
370 A177 80k Sheet of 3, #a.-c.   5.00 4.25

Opera and Ballet Theaters — A178

No. 371: a, National Academic, Kyiv. b, Odessa State, Odessa. c, Kharkov State Academic, Kharkov. d, Ivan Franko State Academic, Lviv.

2000, Jan. 29   Litho.   Perf. 11½
371 A178 40k Sheet of 4, #a.-d.   5.00 5.00

Kyiv Bridges — A179

No. 372: a, 10k, Moscow Bridge. b, 30k, Y. O. Paton Bridge. c, 40k, Pedestrian park bridge. d, 60k, Subway bridge.

2000, Jan. 29   Perf. 12¼x12
372 A179 Block of 4, #a.-d.   3.00 3.00
Souvenir Sheet

Peresopnytsia Gospel — A180

2000, Feb. 8   Perf. 11½
373 A180 1.50h multi   2.50 2.40

A181   A182

2000, Feb. 11   Perf. 13½
374 A181 30k multi   1.50 .60
Oksana Petrusenko (1900-40), opera singer

2000, Feb. 18
375 A182 40k multi   1.25 1.25
Marusia Churai, 17th cent. singer

Hetman Type of 1997
Designs: No. 376, Danylo Apostol (1654-1734), church, burning castle. No. 377, Ivan Samoylovych (d. 1690), tent, winter scene.

2000   Perf. 12¼x12
376 A110 30k multi   1.00 1.00
377 A110 30k multi   1.00 1.00
Issued: No. 376, 2/22; No. 377, 3/3.

World Meteorological Organization, 50th Anniv. — A183

2000, Mar. 10   Litho.   Perf. 13½
378 A183 30k multi   1.00 1.00

Europa, 2000
Common Design Type
2000, Mar. 29   Litho.   Perf. 13½
379 CD17 3h multi   4.50 3.00

Souvenir Sheets

Easter Eggs — A184

No. 380: a, 30k, Egg with black and red star design, Podillia region. b, 30k, Flower egg, Chernihiv region. c, 30k, Egg with leaf design, Kyiv region. d, 30k, Egg with green, white and yellow geometric design, Odesa region. e, 70k, Egg with reindeer design, Hutsulshchyna region. f, 70k, Egg with cross design, Volyn region.

2000, Apr. 28   Perf. 11½
380 A184 Sheet of 6, #a-f   5.25 3.50

Stamp Exhibitions — A185

No. 381: a, Woman in native costume, Austria #2. b, Man in native costume, Great Britain #1.

2000, May 20
381 A185 80k Sheet of 2, #a-b   3.00 2.50
WIPA 2000 Stamp Exhibition, Vienna; The Stamp Show 2000, London.

Donetsk Oblast — A186

City of Kyiv — A187

2000   Perf. 12¼x12
382 A186 30k multi   .80 .80
383 A187 30k multi   .80 .80
Regional and administrative areas.
Issued: No. 382, 5/26; No. 383, 5/28.

6th Natl. Philatelic Exhibition, Donetsk — A188

2000, May 28   Litho.   Perf. 12¼x12
384 A188 30k multi   .80 .80

City of Ostroh, 900th Anniv. — A189

2000, June 16   Litho.   Perf. 13½
385 A189 30k multi   .80 .80

2000 Summer Olympics, Sydney — A190

2000, June 26
386 A190 30k High jump   .50 .50
387 A190 30k Boxing   .50 .50
388 A190 70k Yachting   .85 .85
389 A190 1h Rhythmic gymnastics   1.50 1.50
Nos. 386-389 (4)   3.35 3.35

Petro Prokopovych (1775-1850), Apiarist — A191

2000, July 12   Litho.   Perf. 13½
390 A191 30k multi   .70 .70

Shipbuilding — A192

2000, July 14
391 A192 Pair   1.75 1.75
a.   40k Ship St. Paul   .65 .65
b.   70k Ship St. Nicholas   1.00 1.00

Tetiana Pata (1884-1976), Artist — A193

No. 392: a, Leafy Plants with Flowers, 1950s. b, Viburnum Berries and Bird, 1957.

2000, July 21
392 A193 Horiz. pair, #a-b + central label   1.00 1.00
a.-b.   40k Any single   .45 .45

Dubno, 900th Anniv. — A194

2000, July 28
393 A194 30k multi   .60 .60

Harvest Festival — A195

2000, Aug. 4
394 A195 30k multi   .65 .65
Souvenir Sheet

Presidential Symbols — A196

Designs: a, Flag. b, Mace. c, Seal. d, Badge.

2000, Aug. 18   Litho.   Perf. 11½
395 A196 60k Sheet of 4, #a-d   5.00 4.00

Regional and Administrative Areas

Volynska Oblast — A197

Autonomous Republic of
Crimea — A198

2000   **Perf. 12¼x12**
396 A197 30k multi   .55 .55
397 A198 30k multi   .65 .65

Issued: No. 396, 8/23; No. 397, 10/20.

Kyiv Post Office, 225th Anniv. — A199

2000, Sept. 3   **Perf. 11½**
398 A199 30k multi   .60 .60

Endangered Amphibians — A200

No. 399: a, 30k, Trituris vulgaris. b, 70k, Salamandra salamandra.

2000, Sept. 8   **Perf. 13½**
399 A200 Pair, #a-b   1.75 1.40

Yurij
Drohobych
(1450-94),
Writer
A201

2000, Sept. 12
400 A201 30k multi   .70 .70

Souvenir Sheet

Carpathian National Park — A202

No. 401: a, Mt. Breskul, 1911 meters. b, Mt. Hoberla, 2061 meters.

2000, Sept. 15   **Perf. 11½**
401 A202 80k Sheet of 2, #a-b   5.00 4.00

Flowers — A203

Designs: a, Marigolds. b, Chamomiles. c, Hollyhocks. d, Poppies. e, Periwinkles. f, Cornflowers. g, Morning glories. h, Martagon lilies. i, Peonies. j, Bluebells.

2000, Oct. 6
402 A203 30k Sheet of 10, #a-j   7.50 6.00

Children's Folk Tales — A204

Designs: a, "Ivasyk and Telesyk," (boy in boat, witch). b, "The Crooked Duck," (couple with duck). c, "The Cat and the Rooster."

2000, Nov. 3
403   30k Horiz. strip of 3   2.00 1.60
a.-c. A204 Any single   .50 .50

New
Year
2001
A205

2000, Nov. 24
404 A205 30k multi   .70 .70

St. Onufrius Church, Lviv — A206   Church of Christ's Birth, Velyke — A207

Design: 70k, Church of the Resurrection, Sumy.

2000, Dec. 8   **Perf. 13½**
405 A206 30k multi   .55 .55
406 A207 30k multi   .55 .55
407 A207 70k multi   1.10 1.10
  Nos. 405-407 (3)   2.20 2.20

Souvenir Sheet

St. Vladimir (c. 956-1015), Kyivan Prince — A208

2000, Dec. 15   **Perf. 11½**
408 A208 2h multi   4.50 3.00

Dmytro Rostovskyi (1651-1709), Religious Leader — A209

2001, Jan. 16   **Litho.**   **Perf. 13½**
409 A209 75k multi   1.40 1.00

Love — A210

2001, Jan. 26
410 A210 30k multi   .80 .80

Souvenir Sheet

Prince Danylo Romanovych (1201-64) — A211

2001, Feb. 1   **Perf. 11½**
411 A211 3h multi   5.00 4.00

Hetman Type of 1997

Designs: 30k, Yuryi Khmelnytski (1641-85), as monk in Turkish prison, Kamianets-Podilskyi fortifications. 50k, Mykhailo Khanenko (1620-80), leading troops, relinquishing power.

2001, Feb. 20   **Perf. 12¼x12**
412-413 A110 Set of 2   1.25 1.25

Invention of the Telephone, 125th Anniv. A212

2001, Mar. 6   **Perf. 13½**
414 A212 70k multi   1.00 1.00

Children's Art — A213

Art by: 10k, Alyna Nochvaj. 30k, Olyia Pynych. 40k, Dasha Chemberzhi.

2001, Mar. 7   **Perf. 11½**
415-417 A213 Set of 3   1.60 1.60

Hollyhocks A214   Marigolds A215

Sunflower A216   Viburnum Opulus Berries A217

Wheat — A218

2001, Apr. 4   **Litho.**   **Perf. 13¾**
418 A214 (10k) multi   .25 .25
419 A215 (30k) multi   .25 .25
420 A216 (71k) multi   .50 .50
  b. Imprint "2003"   3.00 3.00
  c. Imprint "2004"   2.50 2.50
421 A217 (2.66h) multi   1.75 .85
  b. Imprint "2003"   2.50 2.50
  c. Imprint "2004"   2.00 2.00
  d. Imprint "2006"   2.50 2.50
422 A218 (3.65h) multi   2.50 1.00
  b. Imprint "2003"   3.75 3.75
  c. Imprint "2004"   3.75 3.75
  d. Imprint "2005"   2.50 2.50
  e. Imprint "2006"   2.50 2.50
  Nos. 418-422 (5)   5.25 2.85

2006, Oct. 9   **Perf. 11½**
    Dated 2006
418a A214 (10k) multi   1.10 1.10
419a A215 (30k) multi   1.10 1.10
420a A216 (71k) multi   1.25 1.25
421a A217 (2.66h) multi   4.50 4.50
422a A218 (3.65h) multi   6.00 6.00
  Nos. 418a-422a (5)   13.95 13.95

Nos. 418a-422a were issued only in No. F2b. See Nos. 453-454, 466-468, 515, 572, 606-609.

Folktales — A219

No. 423: a, The Fox and Wolf (fox on sleigh, fish). b, The Mitten (bear, fox, wolf, rabbit mouse, frog). c, Sirko the Dog (wolf with bottle, dog).

2001, Apr. 14   **Perf. 13½**
423 A219 30k Horiz. strip of 3, #a-c   1.40 1.40

Ships — A220

No. 424: a, 20k, Twelve Apostles. b, 30k, Three Priests.

2001, Apr. 20
424 A220 Horiz. pair, #a-b   1.25 1.25

Europa — A221

Fish, jellyfish, seaweed: a, 28x40mm. b, 56x40mm.

2001, Apr. 27
425 A221 1h Horiz. pair, #a-b   3.00 3.00

Holy Trinity
A222

2001, May 15
426 A222 30k multi   .70 .70

Souvenir Sheet

Apiculture — A223

No. 427: a, Bee on flower. b, Plant cutting, jar of honey, bowl of pollen, jars. c, Worker on honeycomb. d, Queen. e, Hive. f, Drone.

2001, May 22   Perf. 11½
427 A223 50k Sheet of 6, #a-f   6.50 6.00

Souvenir Sheet

Kyievo-Pecherska Monastery, 950th Anniv. — A224

2001, May 25
428 A224 1.50h multi   2.25 2.25

Visit of
Pope John
Paul II, June
23-27
A225

2001, June 15   Perf. 13½
429 A225 3h multi   2.75 2.50

Regional and Administrative Areas

Zakarpatska Oblast — A226

Kharkivska Oblast — A227

Chernihivska Oblast — A228

Kirovohradska Oblast — A229

2001   Litho.   Perf. 12¼x12
430 A226 30k multi   .70 .70
431 A227 30k multi   .70 .70
432 A228 30k multi   .70 .70
433 A229 30k multi   .70 .70
    Issued: No. 430, 6/29; No. 431, 8/18; No. 432, 9/21; No. 433, 9/22.

Souvenir Sheet

Icons From Khanenko Art
Museum — A230

No. 434: a, 20k, Virgin and Child, 28x40mm. b, 30k, St. John the Baptist, 28x40mm. c, Saints Serhyi and Bacchus, 56x40mm.

2001, July 12   Litho.   Perf. 11½
434 A230 Sheet of 3, #a-c   2.25 1.90

Endangered
Species
A231

No. 435: a, Milvus milvus. b, Scirtopoda telum.

2001, July 24   Perf. 13
435 A231 1h Vert. pair, #a-b   1.75 1.75

Dmytro Bortnianskyi (1751-1825),
Composer — A232

2001, July 26
436 A232 20k multi   .50 .50

Soccer — A233

2001, Aug. 10
437 A233 50k multi   .70 .70

Souvenir Sheet

Independence, 10th Anniv. — A234

2001, Aug. 15   Perf. 11½
438 A234 3h multi   3.25 3.25

7th Natl. Philatelic Exhibition,
Dnipropetrovsk — A235

2001, Oct. 7   Litho.   Perf. 12¼x12
439 A235 30k multi   .65 .65

Year of Dialogue
Among Civilizations
A236

2001, Oct. 9   Perf. 13
440 A236 70k multi   1.25 1.25

Souvenir Sheet

Black Sea Marine Life — A237

No. 441: a, 30k, Seahorses. b, 70k, Dolphins, birds.

2001, Oct. 19   Perf. 11½
441 A237 Sheet of 2, #a-b   2.40 2.40

Christmas — A238

2001, Nov. 9   Perf. 12¼x12
442 A238 30k multi   .85 .85

St. Nicholas
A239

2001, Nov. 16   Perf. 13
443 A239 30k multi   .75 .75

Happy New
Year — A240

2001, Nov. 23
444 A240 30k multi   .75 .75

Poets — A241

No. 445: a, Taras Shevchenko (1814-61), Ukrainian poet. b, Akakii Tsereteli (1840-1915), Georgian poet.

2001, Dec. 19
445 A241 40k Horiz. pair, #a-b   1.00 1.00
    See Georgia No. 276.

Regional Costumes

Kyivshchyna Region — A242

Chernihivshchyna Region — A243

Poltavshchyna Region — A244

No. 446: a, 20k, Two women. b, 50k, Man and woman.
No. 447: a, 20k, Musicians and girl. b, 50k, Bride and groom, boy.
No. 448: a, 20k, Priest and family. b, 50k, Two women.

2001, Dec. 20   Perf. 13¼
446 A242 Horiz. pair, #a-b   .60 .60
447 A243 Horiz. pair, #a-b   .60 .60
448 A244 Horiz. pair, #a-b   .60 .60
c.   Souvenir sheet, #446-448, perf.
     11½   2.00 2.00
     Nos. 446-448 (3)   1.80 1.80

Hetman Type of 1997

Designs: No. 449, 40k, Pavlo Teteryia (d. 1670) holding scepter, people in town, horsemen and carriage heading for town. No. 450, 40k, Demyian Mnohohrishnyi, receiving scepter, boats in river. No. 451, 40k, Ivan Briukhovetskyi (d. 1668), battle scenes.

2002, Jan. 17   Perf. 12¼x12
449-451 A110 Set of 3   1.60 1.60

Scythian Military History — A245

No. 452: a, Archer on horseback. b, Swordsman in battle. c, Commander on horseback, warrior. d, Female warrior.

2002, Jan. 29 **Perf. 13**
452 A245 40k Block of 4, #a-d   1.50 1.50

Flower Type of 2001 and

Periwinkle — A246

2002	Litho.		Perf. 13¾
	Year imprint		
453	A246 5k multi, "2002"	.50	.50
a.	Perf. 11½, dated "2006"	1.50	1.50
b.	As #453, dated "2004"	.75	.75
c.	As #453, dated "2005"	.75	.75
d.	As #453, dated "2006"	.75	.75
454	A214 10k multi, "2002"	.50	.50
a.	Perf. 11½, dated "2006"	1.50	1.50
b.	As #454, dated "2003"	.75	.75
c.	As #453, dated "2005"	.75	.75
d.	As #453, dated "2006"	.75	.75

Issued: #453, 2/1; #453b, 7/19/04; #453c, 2005; #453d, 12/1/05; #454, 2/26; #454b, 2003; #454c, #2005; #454d, 12/1/05. Nos. 453a-454a, 10/9/06. Nos. 453a-454a were issued only in No. F2b.

Sporting Achievements — A247

Designs: No. 455, 40k, Zhanna Pintusevich-Block winning 100-meter dash at 2001 World Track and Field Championships. No. 456, 40k, Swimmer at 2000 Summer Olympics.

2002, Feb. 15 **Perf. 13**
455-456 A247 Set of 2   .90 .90

Regional and Administrative Areas

Kyivska Oblast — A248

2002, Feb. 18 **Perf. 12¼x12**
457 A248 40k multi   .50 .50

Shipbuilding — A249

No. 458: a, Frigate Sizopol and coast. b, Brigantine Perseus.

2002, Feb. 22 **Perf. 13½**
458 A249 40k Horiz. pair, #a-b   .80 .80

Issuance of First Stamp After Independence, 10th Anniv. — A250

2002, Mar. 1
459 A250 40k No. 100   .80 .80

Leonid Hlibov (1827-93), Writer — A251

2002, Mar. 4 **Litho.** **Perf. 13¼**
460 A251 40k multi   .50 .50

Ruslan Ponomariov, Winner of 16th World Chess Championships — A252

2002, Mar. 29 **Perf. 13½**
461 A252 3.50h multi   2.00 2.00

Souvenir Sheet

Europa — A253

No. 462: a, Lion. b, Tiger, horiz.

2002, Apr. 4 **Perf. 11½**
462 A253 1.75h Sheet of 2, #a-b   4.25 4.25

Palm Sunday — A254

2002, Apr. 19 **Perf. 13½**
463 A254 40k multi   .45 .45

Worldwide Fund for Nature (WWF) — A255

Various views of Elaphe situla: a, 40k. b, 70k. c, 80k. d, 2.50h.

2002, May 25 **Perf. 13½**
464 A255 Block of 4, #a-d   2.50 2.50
  e. Perf. 11½   3.50 3.50

Souvenir Sheet

Opera and Ballet Theaters — A256

No. 465: a, Donetsk (tree at center). b, Dnipropetrovsk (trees at side).

2002, May 31 **Perf. 11½**
465 A256 1.25h Sheet of 2, #a-b   2.25 2.25

Flower Type of 2001 and

Blue Cornflower A257   Lilac A258

2002	Litho.		Perf. 13¾
	Year Imprint		
466	A215 30k multi, "2002"	.50	.50
a.	Perf. 11½, dated "2002"	1.75	1.75
b.	As #466, dated "2003"	.70	.70
c.	As #466, dated "2004"	.70	.70
d.	As #466, dated "2005"	.70	.70
e.	As #466, dated "2006"	.70	.70
467	A257 45k multi, "2002"	.50	.50
a.	Perf. 11½, dated "2006"	1.75	1.75
b.	As #467, dated "2003"	.70	.70
c.	As #467, dated "2004"	.70	.70
d.	As #467, dated "2005"	.70	.70
e.	As #467, dated "2006"	.70	.70
468	A258 (80k) multi, "2002"	.80	.80
a.	Perf. 11½, dated "2006"	2.50	2.50
b.	As #468, dated "2003"	1.00	1.00
c.	As #468, dated "2004"	1.00	1.00

Issued: Issued: #466, 6/1/02; #466b4/17/03; #466c, 1/22/04; #466d, 2/3/05; #466e, 12/1/05. #467, 9/19/02; #467b, 4/17/03; #467c, 2/6/04; #467d, 4/29/05; #467e, 3/3/06. #468, 7/5/02; #468b, 2003; #468c, 7/19/04. Nos. 466a-468a issued 10/9/06. Nos. 466a-468a were issued only in No. F2b.

Regional and Administrative Areas

Luhanska Oblast — A259

Chernivetska Oblast — A260

Odeska Oblast — A261

Cherkaska Oblast — A262

Sumska Oblast — A263

2002			Perf. 12¼x12
469	A259 40k multi	.50	.50
470	A260 40k multi	.50	.50
471	A261 45k multi	.50	.50
472	A262 45k multi	.50	.50
473	A263 45k multi	.50	.50
	Nos. 469-473 (5)	2.50	2.50

Issued: No. 469, 6/2; No. 470, 6/27; No. 471, 9/20. No. 472, 10/9; No. 473, 10/21.

Endangered Species A264

No. 474: a, Phalacrocorax aristotelis. b, Phocoena phocoena.

2002, June 14 **Litho.** **Perf. 13**
474 A264 70k Pair, #a-b   1.10 1.10

Mykola Leontovich (1877-1921), Composer — A265

2002, June 21 **Perf. 13½**
475 A265 40k multi   .50 .50

Souvenir Sheet

Black Sea Nature Reserve — A266

No. 476: a, Haematopus ostralegus (40x28mm). b, Larus genei (40x28mm). c, Iris pumila (22x26mm). d, Numenius arquata (26x22mm). e, Charadrius alexandrinus (26x22mm).

2002, July 13 **Perf. 11½**
476 A266 50k Sheet of 5, #a-e   3.00 2.50

Folk Tales — A267

No. 477: a, Fox and Pancake. b, Mr. Cat. c, Speckled Chicken.

2002, July 19   **Perf. 14¼x14**
477 A267 40k Horiz. strip of 3,
   #a-c   .80   .80

Art of Hanna Sobachko-
Shostak — A268

No. 478: a, Cage for Starlings, 1963 (peach
background). b, Vase with Flowers, 1964 (red
background). c, Chamomile Flowers, 1964
(yellow background).

2002, Aug. 9   **Perf. 14x14¼**
478   Horiz. strip of 3   .90   .90
a.-c. A268 45k Any single   .30   .30

Space Pioneers — A269

Designs: 40k, Yurii V. Kondratiuk (1897-
1942). 45k, Mykhailo Yianhel (1911-71). 50k,
Mykola Kybalchych (1853-81). 70k, Serhii
Korolov (1907-66).

2002, Aug. 23   **Perf. 12¼x12**
479-482 A269   Set of 4   1.60   1.60
See Nos. 500-503.

Marine Life — A270

No. 483: a, Phoca caspica. b, Huso huso
ponticus.

2002, Sept. 6   **Perf. 14x14¼**
483 A270 75k Horiz. pair, #a-b   1.25   1.25
See Kazakhstan No. 386.

Khotyn, 1000th Anniv. — A271

2002, Sept. 21   **Perf. 12¼x12**
484 A271 40k multi   .55   .55

Odesaphil 2002
Stamp Exhibition,
Odesa — A272

2002, Oct. 5   **Litho.**   **Perf. 14¼x14**
485 A272 45k multi   .50   .50

Paintings of Kyiv by Taras Shevchenko
(1814-61) — A273

Designs: 45k, Askold's Tomb. 75k, Dnieper
River Shoreline. 80k, St. Alexander's Church.

    Perf. 13¾x14½
2002, Nov. 15   **Litho.**
486-488 A273   Set of 3   1.40   1.40
See Nos. 516-519, 548-551, 590-593

Happy New
Year — A274

2002, Nov. 22   **Perf. 14x14¼**
489 A274 45k multi   .70   .70

Regional Costumes

Vinychyna Region — A275

Cherkashchyna Region — A276

Ternopilska Region — A277

No. 490: a, Family, rainbow. b, Family, fruit
tree.
No. 491: a, Four girls holding hands. b,
Couple gathering crops.
No. 492: a, Priest blessing family. b, People
with Easter baskets.

2002, Dec. 6   **Perf. 13¼**
490 A275 45k Horiz. pair, #a-b   .55   .55
491 A276 45k Horiz. pair, #a-b   .55   .55
492 A277 45k Horiz. pair, #a-b   .55   .55
c.   Souvenir sheet, #490-492, perf.
   11½   1.75   1.75
Nos. 490-492 (3)   1.65   1.65

Folk Tales — A278

No. 493: a, Koza-Dezera (cow on bridge). b,
The Straw Bull. c, The Fox and Crane.

2003, Jan. 17   **Litho.**   **Perf. 14¼x14**
493 A278 45k Horiz. strip of 3,
   #a-c   .75   .75

Speed
Skating
— A279

2003, Jan. 24   **Perf. 14x14¼**
494 A279 65k multi   .60   .60

Military History — A280

No. 495: a, War with Goths, 4th cent. (soldier with spear and shield) b, Battles with
Huns, 5th cent. (archer). c, Balkan campaigns,
6th cent. (soldier with hatchet). d, Battles with
the Avars, 6th cent. (soldier with spears).

2003, Feb. 7
495 A280 45k Block of 4, #a-d   1.10   1.10

Shipbuilding — A281

No. 496: a, Steamship Grozny (denomination at left. b, Steamship Odessa (denomination at right).

2003, Feb. 14
496 A281 1h Horiz. pair, #a-b   1.25   1.25

Mikola Arkas (1853-1909),
Composer — A282

2003, Feb. 21
497 A282 45k multi   .50   .50

Souvenir Sheet

Javorivsky National Nature
Park — A283

No. 498: a, 1h, Alcede atthis (32x44mm). b,
1h, Cypripedium calceolus (36x41mm). c,
1.50h, Eudia pavonia, horiz. (44x32mm)

2003, Mar. 3   **Perf. 11½**
498 A283   Sheet of 3, #a-c   3.00   3.00

Europa — A284

Poster by Oleksiy Shtanko: a, Virgin Mary
with dove. b, Guardian angel.

2003, Mar. 21   **Perf. 11½**
499 A284 1.75h Horiz. pair, #a-b   3.50   3.50
c.   Booklet pane, 2 #499 + central
   label   6.25   —
   Complete booklet, #499c   6.25   —

Space Pioneers Type of 2002

Designs: 45k, Olkeksandr Zasiadko (1779-
1837). 65k, Kostyantin Konstantinov (1817-

---

71). 70k, Valyntyn Hlushko (1908-89). 80k,
Volodymyr Chelomei (1914-84).

2003, Apr. 11   **Litho.**   **Perf. 13¾x14½**
500-503 A269   Set of 4   1.60   1.60

Ukrainian Red Cross Society, 85th
Anniv. — A285

2003, Apr. 18
504 A285 45k multi   .50   .50

Regional and Administrative Areas

Dnipropetrovska Oblast — A286

Lvivska Oblast — A287

Khmelnytska Oblast — A288

Mykolayivska Oblast — A289

Zaporizhiya Oblast — A290

2003
505 A286 45k multi   .50   .50
506 A287 45k multi   .50   .50
507 A288 45k multi   .50   .50
508 A289 45k multi   .50   .50
509 A290 45k multi   .50   .50
Nos. 505-509 (5)   2.50   2.50

Issued: No. 505, 4/21; No. 506, 5/8; No.
507, 9/26; No. 508, 10/4; No. 509, 10/11.

Hetman Type of 1997

Designs: No. 510, 45k, Ivan Skoropadskiy
(1646-1722) wearing robe, serfs in field, subjects bowing. No. 511, 45k, Kyrylo Rozumov-
skiy (1728-1803) holding scepter, attack of
palace, palace ruins.

2003, May 22
510-511 A110   Set of 2   .75   .75

Souvenir Sheet

Volodymyr Monomakh (1053-1125),
Grand Prince of Kyiv — A291

2003, May 28   **Perf. 11½**
512 A291 3.50h multi   1.90 1.90

Owls — A292

No. 513: a, Bubo bubo. b, Strix uralensis. c, Strix aluco. d, Strix nebulosa. e, Glaucidium passerinum. f, Aegolius funereus. g, Otus scops. h, Athene noctua. i, Tyto alba. j, Asio otus. k, Asio flammeus. l, Surnia ulula. Size of # 513e-513h: 25x27mm; others: 25x36mm.

2003, June 14
513 A292 45k Sheet of 12, #a-l   7.00 3.50

Oleksandr Myshuha (1853-1922), Opera Singer — A293

2003, June 20   **Perf. 13¼**
514 A293 45k multi   .55 .55

Sweet Pea — A294

2003, July 4   **Perf. 13¾**
Year Imprint
515 A294 65k multi, "2003"   .90 .90
  a. Perf. 11½, dated "2006"   2.50 2.50
  b. As #515, dated "2004"   2.00 2.00
  c. As #515, dated "2005"   1.25 1.25

Issued: #515b, 2/6/04; #515c, 2/1/05.
No. 515a issued 10/9/06. No. 515a was issued only in No. F2b.

Paintings Type of 2002

Paintings of Kyiv: No. 516, 45k, Podil, by Mykhailo Sazhyn, 1840. No. 517, 45k, Kyiv-Pecherska Monastery, by Vasyl Timm, 1857. No. 518, 45k, Ruins of St. Irene Monastery, by Sazhyn, 1846. No. 519, 45k, View of Old City from Yaroslav Embankment, by Timm, 1854.

2003, July 18   **Perf. 13¾x14½**
516-519 A273 Set of 4   1.40 1.40

Customs and Traditions — A295

No. 520: a, Celebration of the Harvest (Church, flowers and insects). b, Ascension (Church, fruit).

2003, July 25   **Perf. 14¼x14**
520 A295 45k Horiz. pair, #a-b   .55 .55

Borys Hmyryia (1903-69), Composer A296

2003, Aug. 5   **Perf. 14x14¼**
521 A296 45k multi   .55 .55

Souvenir Sheet

Manyiavskyi Monastery — A297

No. 522: a, Denomination at LL. b, Denomination at LR.

2003, Aug. 15   **Perf. 11x11½**
522 A297 1.25h Sheet of 2, #a-b   1.40 2.00

Yevpatoriya, 2500th Anniv. — A298

2003, Aug. 29   **Perf. 13¾x14½**
523 A298 45k multi   .55 .55

Ancient Trade Routes — A299

No. 524: a, Arrival of Scandinavian seamen in rowboat, coin of Danish King Svend Estridsen. b, Silver coin of Prince Volodymyr Sviatoslavovych, Slavic warship with sail.

2003, Sept. 17   **Perf. 11½**
524 A299 80k Vert. pair, #a-b, +   central label   .90 .90
  c. Booklet pane, #524   3.75 —
  d. Booklet pane, #524a   2.50 —
  e. Booklet pane, #524b   2.50 —
     Complete booklet, #524c, 524d, 524e   9.00

Hryhoryi Kvitka-Osnovyianenko (1778-1843), Writer — A300

2003, Nov. 14 Litho.   **Perf. 14¼x14**
525 A300 45k multi   .55 .55

Famine of 1932-33 — A301

2003, Nov. 21   **Perf. 13¾x14½**
526 A301 45k multi   .40 .40

Christmas A302

Litho. with Foil Application
2003, Nov. 25   **Perf. 13¼x13½**
527 A302 45k multi   1.00 1.00

New Year's Greetings A303

2003, Nov. 25 Litho.   **Perf. 13½**
528 A303 45k multi   1.00 1.00

Regional Costumes

Kharkiv Region — A304

Sumy Region — A305

Donetsk Region — A306

No. 529: a, Women, religious icons. b, Family, lute.
No. 530: a, Woman, men. b, Group of women.
No. 531: a, Family, sled. b, Workers in field.

2003, Dec. 19   **Perf. 13¼**
529 A304 45k Horiz. pair, #a-b   1.00 1.00
530 A305 45k Horiz. pair, #a-b   1.00 1.00
531 A306 45k Horiz. pair, #a-b   1.00 1.00
  c. Souvenir sheet, #529-531, perf. 11½   3.00 3.00

Unification of Ukraine and Western Ukraine, 85th Anniv. — A307

2004, Jan. 22 Litho.   **Perf. 13¾x14½**
532 A307 45k multi   .40 .40

Stanislav Ludkevych (1879-1979), Composer A308

2004, Jan. 24   **Perf. 13¼**
533 A308 45k multi   .40 .40

Possessions of Hetman Bohdan Khmelnytsky — A309

No. 534: a, Flag. b, Mace. c, Cap. d, Chalice decorated with leaves. e, Tankard. f, Sword.

Litho. With Foil Application
2004, Jan. 29   **Perf. 11½**
534 A309 45k Sheet of 6, #a-f   2.50 2.50

Shipbuilding — A310

No. 535: a, 1h, Oil tanker Kriti Amber (55x26mm). b, 2.50h, Anti-submarine ship Mikolayiv (55x29mm). c, 3.50h Aircraft carrier Admiral Kuznetzov (55x40mm).

2004, Feb. 21   Litho.   Perf. 11½
535 A310   Sheet of 3, #a-c   5.00 5.00

Regional and Administrative Areas

Ternopilska Oblast — A311

2004, Mar. 3   Perf. 13¾x14½
536 A311 45k multi   .50 .50

Membership in UNESCO, 50th Anniv. — A312

2004, Mar. 19   Perf. 14¼x14
537 A312 45k multi   .50 .50

Butterflies — A313

No. 538: a, 45k, Endromis versicolora. b, 75k, Smerinthus ocellatus. c, 80k, Catocala fraxini. d, 2.60h, Apatura ilia. e, 3.50h, Papilio machaon.

2004, Mar. 26   Perf. 8
538 A313   Sheet of 5, #a-e   4.50 7.00

Famous Ukrainians A314

Designs: No. 539, 45k, Serhyi Lyfar (1904-86), ballet dancer and choreographer. No. 540, 45k, Maria Zankovetska (1854-1934), actress. No. 541, 45k, Mykhaylo Maksymovych (1804-73), historian.

2004   Litho.   Perf. 14x14¼
539-541 A314   Set of 3   1.25 1.25

Issued: No. 539, 4/2, Nos. 540-541, 7/23.
See Nos. 574-575, 613-614, 641, 655-656, 750-751, 757-758.

Zenit-1 Rocket A315

2004, Apr. 14
542 A315 45k multi   .55 .55

European Weight Lifting Championships, Kyiv — A316

2004, Apr. 20
543 A316 65k multi   .60 .60

Miniature Sheet

Europa — A317

No. 544: a, 45k, Lastivchyne Hnizdo (22x33mm). b, 75k, Carpathian Mountains (22x33mm). c, 2.61h, Khotyn Castle (29x33mm). d, 3.52h, Pecherska Lavra (39x28mm).

2004, Apr. 23   Perf. 11½
544 A317   Sheet of 4, #a-d   6.50 6.50

UEFA (European Football Union), 50th Anniv. — A318

2004, May 17   Perf. 14¼x14
545 A318 3.52h multi   2.00 2.00

FIFA (Fédération Internationale de Football Association), Cent. — A319

No. 546: a, 45k, Player #11. b, 75k, Player #6. c, 80k, Fan. d, 2.61h, Two women players.

2004, May 17   Perf. 13¼
546 A319   Block of 4, #a-d   2.50 2.50

Symon Petlura (1879-1926), Political Leader — A320

2004, May 21
547 A320 45k multi   .50 .50

Painting Type of 2002

Designs: No. 548, 45k, Kiev with St. Andrew's Church, by unknown artist, 1889. No. 549, 45k, Fountain Near the Golden Gate, by Petro Levchenko, 1910. No. 550, 45k, Spring in Kurenivka, by Abram Manevych, 1914-15. No. 551, 45k, St. Michael's Cathedral From the South, by Mykola Burachek, 1919.

2004, June 11   Perf. 13¾x14½
548-551 A273   Set of 4   1.25 1.25

Folktales — A321

No. 552: a, The Cat. b, Ivasyk Telesyk. c, The Fat Man.

2004, June 18   Perf. 14¼x14
552 A321 45k Horiz. strip of 3, #a-c   .90 .90

2004 Summer Olympics, Athens A322

2004, June 26   Perf. 14x14¼
553 A322 2.61h multi   1.40 1.40

Regional and Administrative Areas

Rovenska Oblast — A323

Khersonska Oblast — A324

Poltavska Oblast — A325

2004   Perf. 13¾x14½
554 A323 45k multi   .55 .55
555 A324 45k multi   .55 .55
556 A325 45k multi   .55 .55

Issued: No. 554, 7/16; No. 555, 8/20; No. 556, 9/22.

Balaklava, 2500th Anniv. — A327

Perf. 13¾x14½
2004, Aug. 14   Litho.
557 A327 45k multi   .55 .55

Kharkiv, 350th Anniv. — A328

2004, Aug. 20   Perf. 14¼x14
558 A328 45k multi   .55 .55

Bridges — A329

No. 559: a, Inhulskyi Bridge (open drawbridge). b, Darnytska Bridge (three arches above roadway). c, B. M. Preobrazhenskoho Bridge (arches below roadway). d, Southern Buh Bridge (swing bridge).

2004, Aug. 25   Perf. 13¾x14½
559 A329 45k Block of 4, #a-d   1.25 1.25

No. 194B Surcharged

Litho. & Engr.
2004, Sept. 15   Perf. 12½x13
560 A47a 2.61h on 25,000kb
   multi   1.50 1.50

Taras Shevchenko University, 170th anniv.

Kirovohrad, 250th Anniv. — A330

Perf. 13¾x14¼
2004, Sept. 17   Litho.
561 A330 45k multi   .55 .55

Military History — A331

No. 562: a, Infantryman of Prince Oleg, 10th cent. b, National militia, 11th-12th cent. c, Archer on horseback, 12th cent. d, Cavalryman for Danylo Halyts, 13th cent.

2004, Oct. 15   Perf. 14x14¼
562 A331 45k Block of 4, #a-d   1.50 1.50

Miniature Sheet

Birds of the Danube Nature
Reserve — A332

No. 563: a, 45k, Cygnus olor. b, 75k,
Phalacrocorax pygmaeus. c, 80k, Egretta
alba. d, 2.61h, Anser anser. e, 3.52h, Platalea
leucordia.

2004, Oct. 26   **Perf. 11½**
563 A332   Sheet of 5, #a-e   4.50 6.00

Khartron
Control
Systems in
Space
A333

1516 Battle Between Cossacks and
Tartars Using Fiery Projectiles
A334

2004, Nov. 12   **Perf. 14x14¼**
564 A333   45k multi   .55   .55
565 A334   45k multi   .55   .55

Christmas
A335

No. 566: a, Magi facing right ("2" in background). b, Magi facing left ("5" in background). c, Nativity ("0" in background).

Litho. With Foil Application
2004, Nov. 26   **Perf. 13¼**
566   Horiz. strip of 4, #a-b, 2
           #c   1.00 1.00
a.-c.   A335 45k Any single, gold & multi .25   .25

Numbers in background of strip of 4 read
"2005."

New Year's
Greetings
A336

No. 567: a, Santa Claus, large trees at left
("2" in background). b, Santa Claus, large
trees at right ("5" in background). c, Tree and
gifts ("0" in background).

2004, Nov. 26
567   Horiz. strip of 4, #a-b,
           2 #c   1.00 1.00
a.-c.   A336 45k Any single, silver &
           multi   .25   .25

Numbers in background of strip of 4 read
"2005."

Ukrainian and Iranian Aircraft — A337

No. 568: a, Antonov-140, Ukraine (denomination at left). b, Iran-140, Iran (denomination
at right).

2004, Nov. 30   Litho.   Perf. 11½
568   Horiz. pair + central la-
           bel   1.10 1.00
a.-b.   A337 80k Either single   .50   .50
           See Iran No.

Regional Costumes

Lvivshchyna Region — A338

Ivano-Frankivshchyna Region — A339

Hutsulshchyna Region — A340

No. 569: a, Family, rooster. b, Family,
pitcher.
No. 570: a, Musicians. b, Dancers at
wedding.
No. 571: a, Men, child, lamb. b, Family,
cradle.

2004, Dec. 10   **Perf. 13¼**
569 A338   60k Horiz. pair, #a-b   .70   .70
570 A339   60k Horiz. pair, #a-b   .70   .70
571 A340   60k Horiz. pair, #a-b   .70   .70
c.   Miniature sheet, #569-571, perf.
           11½   2.10 2.10

Poppy — A341

2005, Jan. 14   Litho.   Perf. 13¾
Date Imprint
572 A341   1h multi, "2005"   1.00 1.00
a.   Perf. 11½, dated "2006"   2.50 2.50
b.   As #572, dated "2006"   1.00 1.00

No. 572b issued 5/23/06.
No. 572a issued 10/9/06. No. 572a was
issued only in No. F2b.

November - December 2004 Protests
Against Rigged Elections — A342

2005, Jan. 23   **Perf. 11½**
573 A342   45k multi   .45   .45

Printed in sheets of 7 + label.

Famous Ukrainians Type of 2004

Design: No. 574, Pavlo Virskyi (1905-75),
choreographer. No. 575, Volodymyr Vyn-
nychenko (1880-1951), writer and statesman.

2005   Litho.   Perf. 14x14¼
574 A314   45k multi   .45   .45
575 A314   45k multi   .45   .45

Issued. No. 574, 2/4; No. 575, 7/15.

Miniature Sheet

Moths — A343

No. 576: a, 45k, Acherontia atropos. b, 75k,
Catocala sponsa. c, 80k, Staurophora celsia.
d, 2.61h, Marumba quercus. e, 3.52h, Saturnia
pyri.

2005, Feb. 11   **Perf. 11½**
576 A343   Sheet of 5, #a-e   4.50 4.50

Regional and Administrative Areas

Vinnytska Oblast — A344

Sevastopol City — A345

Ivano-Frankivska Oblast — A346

Zhitomyrska Oblast — A347

2005   **Perf. 13¾x14½**
577 A344   45k multi   .45   .45
578 A345   45k multi   .45   .45
579 A345   45k multi   .45   .45
580 A347   70k multi   .55   .55
           Nos. 577-580 (4)   1.90 1.90

Issued: No. 577, 2/23; No. 578, 6/11; No.
579, 7/16; 70k, 9/10.

Paintings by Ivan Aivazovskyi — A348

No. 581: a, Sea — Koktebel, 1853. b, Towers on the Rock Near the Bosporus, 1859.

2005, Mar. 4   Litho.   Perf. 14x14¼
581   Horiz. pair, #a-b, +
           central label   .90   .90
a.-b.   A348 45k Either single   .45   .45

The Shepherd, by Heorhyi Yakutovych
(1930-2000) — A349

Litho. & Engr.
2005, Mar. 26   **Perf. 11½**
582 A349   3.52h silver & gray
           blue   2.00 2.00

Cosmos-1
Satellite
A350

Zenit-2
Rocket
A351

Designs: No. 585, Dnepr rocket. No. 586,
Cyclone-3 rocket.

2005, Apr. 12   Litho.   Perf. 14x14¼
583 A350   45k shown   .45   .45
584 A351   45k shown   .45   .45
585 A351   45k multi   .45   .45
586 A351   45k multi   .45   .45
           Nos. 583-586 (4)   1.80 1.80

A352

End of World War II, 60th
Anniv. — A353

2005   **Perf. 14x14¼**
587 A352   45k multi   .45   .45

Souvenir Sheet
Perf. 11½
588 A353 80k multi .80 .80

Issued: 45k, 4/22; 80k, 5/7. No. 587 issued in sheets of 8 + central label.

Ninth Intl. Philatelic Exhibition, Kyiv — A354

2005, May 17   **Perf. 13¾x14½**
589 A354 45k multi .45 .45

Painting Type of 2002
Paintings of Kyiv: 45k, New Street, by Serhyi Shyshko, 1966. 75k, Park in Winter, by Shyshko, 1960. 80k, Sacred Sophia, by Yuryi Khymych, 1965. 1h, Khreshchatyk Boulevard, by Khymych, 1967, vert.

Perf. 13¾x14½, 14½x13¾
2005, May 18
590-593 A273 Set of 4 2.50 2.50

Ruslana, Winner of 2004 Eurovision Song Contest — A355

Logo for 2005 Eurovision Song Contest A356

2005, May 19   **Perf. 11½**
594 A355 45k multi .45 .45
595 A356 2.50h multi 1.75 1.75

Europa — A357

Nos. 596 and 597: a, 2.61h, Bowl of borscht, beets, onions, garlic, tomatoes, pepper, beans, lard, parsley and dill. b, 3.52h, Lidded tureen, cabbage, carrots, onion, garlic, pepper.

2005, May 20   **Perf. 11½**
Stamp Size: 45x32mm
596 A357 Horiz. pair, #a-b 3.50 3.50
Booklet Stamps
Stamp Size: 40x27mm
Perf. 14x14¼
597 A357 Horiz. pair, #a-b 6.00 6.00
c. Booklet pane, 2 #597 12.00
Complete booklet, #597c 12.00

Complete booklet sold for 19.38h.

Development of the Cyrillic Alphabet — A358

Litho. & Embossed
2005, May 21   **Perf. 14¼x14**
598 A358 45k multi .45 .45

Souvenir Sheet

Flora and Fauna in Karadazkyi Nature Reserve — A359

No. 599: a, 45k, Falco cherrug (33x40mm). b, 70k, Ascalaphus macaronius (29x35mm). c, 2.50h, Tursiops truncatus ponticus (33x33mm). d, 3.50h, Martes foina (49x33mm).

2005, July 28   **Litho.**   **Perf. 11½**
599 A359 Sheet of 4, #a-d 4.25 4.25

World Summit on the Information Society, Tunis A360

2005, Aug. 12   **Perf. 14x14¼**
600 A360 2.50h multi 1.40 1.40

Series Ov Locomotive — A361

Series C Locomotive — A362

Series Shch Locomotive — A363

Series Ye Locomotive — A364

2005, Aug. 31
601 A361 70k multi .50 .50
602 A362 70k multi .50 .50
603 A363 70k multi .50 .50
604 A364 70k multi .50 .50
Nos. 601-604 (4) 2.00 2.00

Nos. 601-604 were each printed in sheets of 11 + label.

Sumy, 350th Anniv. — A365

2005, Sept. 2
605 A365 45k multi .45 .45

Nasturtium A366

Water Lily A367

Violets — A368

Wild Rose — A369

2005   **Perf. 13¾**
Date imprint
606 A366 25k multi .45 .45
a. Perf. 11½, dated "2006" .75 .75
b. As #606, dated "2006" 1.00 1.00
607 A367 70k multi .90 .90
a. Perf. 11½, dated "2006" 1.00 1.00
b. As #607, dated "2006" .90 .90
608 A368 (1.53h) multi 1.50 1.50
a. Perf. 11½, dated "2006" 4.00 4.00
b. As #608, dated "2006" 1.50 1.50
609 A369 (2.55h) multi 2.50 2.50
a. Perf. 11½, dated "2006" 5.00 5.00
b. As #609, dated "2006" 2.50 2.50
Nos. 606-609 (4) 5.35 5.35

Issued: #606, 9/8/05; #606b, 2/7/06. #607, 9/12/05; #607b, 2/7/06. #608, 12/16/05; #608b, 9/28/06. #609,11/25/05; 609a, 6/5/06. Nos. 606a-609a issued 10/9/06. Nos. 606a-609a were issued only in No. F2b.

Horses — A370

No. 610: a, Novoolexandrivskyi heavy draft horse (brown horse facing left with four-line inscription). b, Orlov-Rostopchin (white horse). c, Ukrainian riding horse (brown horse facing left with three-line inscription). d, Thoroughbred (brown horse facing right).

2005, Sept. 15   **Perf. 11½**
610 A370 70k Block of 4, #a-d 1.60 1.60

"Safety - Green Light" A371

"Give a Helping Hand" A372

"No to Drugs" A373

2005, Oct. 14   **Perf. 14x14¼**
611 Horiz. strip of 3 1.60 1.60
a. A371 70k multi .50 .50
b. A372 70k multi .50 .50
c. A373 70k multi .50 .50

Military History — A374

No. 612: a, Commander Bobrok Volnyets at Battle of Kulikovo, 1380. b, Artillerymen and riflemen, 14th-15th cent. c, Knight Ivanko Sushyk at Grunwald, 1410. d, Prince Konstiantyn Ostrozkyi at Orsha, 1512.

2005, Oct. 22
612 A374 70k Block of 4, #a-d 1.60 1.60

Famous Ukrainians Type of 2004
Designs: No. 613, Dmytro Yiavornytskyi (1855-1940), historian. No. 614, Oleg Antonov (1906-84), aircraft designer.

2005-06   **Litho.**
613 A314 70k multi .60 .60
614 A314 70k multi .60 .60

Issued: #613, 11/7; #614, 2/7/06.

Christmas A375

Litho. With Foil Application
2005, Nov. 11   **Perf. 13¼**
615 A375 70k multi .55 .55

New Year's Day — A376

2005, Nov. 11   **Litho.**
616 A376 70k multi .55 .55

St. Barbara's Church, Vienna, Austria — A377

2005, Dec. 9   **Perf. 14¼x14**
617 A377 75k multi + label .75 .75

Lviv National Museum, Cent. — A378

No. 618: a, Archangel Michael, by unknown artist (denomination at right). b, Dalmatynka, by Teofil Kopystynskyi (denomination at left).

2005, Dec. 13   **Litho.**
618 A378 70k Horiz. pair, #a-b, + central label 1.10 1.10

Regional Costumes

Zhytomyrshchyna Region — A379

Rivnenshchyna Region — A380

Volyn Region — A381

No. 619: a, Family and dog, St. Basil's Day. b, Man and woman, St. Zosyma's Day.

No. 620: a, People with animals, St. George's Day. b, Men, women and musician, Sts. Peter and Paul's Day.

No. 621: a, People with buckets, Annunciation Day. b, Family and cat, St. Nicholas's Day.

2005, Dec. 20   *Perf. 13¼*
619 A379 70k Horiz. pair, #a-b   .85   .85
620 A380 70k Horiz. pair, #a-b   .85   .85
621 A381 70k Horiz. pair, #a-b   .85   .85
  c.   Miniature sheet, #619-621, perf.
        11½   3.75 3.75

Europa Stamps, 50th Anniv. — A382

Designs: Nos. 622a, 623a, 1.30h, 50th anniversary emblem. Nos. 622a, 622b, 2.50h, CEPT emblem.

2006, Jan. 5   Litho.   Perf. 13¼
With Names of Designers at Right of Stamps
622 A382 Vert. pair, #a-b   2.25 2.25

Souvenir Sheet
Without Names of Designers at Right of Stamps
Perf. 11½
623 A382 Sheet of 2, #a-b   2.25 2.25

Art by Hryhoryi Narbut (1886-1920) — A383

Litho. & Engr.
2006, Mar. 10   *Perf. 11½*
624 A383 3.33h multi   2.10 2.10
        Printed in sheets of 11 + label.

Miniature Sheet

Traditional Women's
Headdresses — A384

No. 625: a, Drawing of woman wearing fur hat. b, Woman, facing left, wearing black hat with brown ribbon. c, Drawing of woman facing left, wearing undecorated head covering. d, Woman wearing large floral head covering. e, Woman wearing red kerchief. f, Woman wearing small floral head covering. g, Woman wearing white kerchief with red dots. h, Woman wearing brown kerchief with knot in front. i, Drawing of woman, facing right, wearing undecorated head covering. j, Woman wearing floral headcovering with thin black edge. k, Woman wearing kerchief with floral pattern. l, Woman wearing small floral head covering with ribbon.

2006, Mar. 30   Litho.   Perf. 11½
625 A384 70k Sheet of 12, #a-l 5.00 5.00

Coronas-1
Satellite
A385

Designs: No. 627, Welding in space. No. 628, International observation of Halley's Comet.

2006, Apr. 12   *Perf. 14x14¼*
Color of Panel Denomination Panel
626 A385 85k gray   .80   .80
627 A385 85k red brown   .80   .80
628 A385 85k dark brown   .80   .80
        Nos. 626-628 (3)   2.40 2.40

Europa — A386

Designs: Nos. 629a, 630a, 2.50h, Earth and Saturn. Nos. 629b, 630b, 3.50h, Earth and Jupiter.

2006, Apr. 28   *Perf. 11½*
Top Cyrillic Inscription in Black
629 A386 Horiz. pair, #a-b   3.50 3.50
Top Cyrillic Inscription in Red
630 A386 Booklet pane of 2,
           #a-b + 2 labels   8.00 8.00
    Complete booklet, #630   8.00

    Nos. 630a-630b are 52x26mm. No. 630 sold for 11.52h.

2006 World Cup Soccer
Championships, Germany — A387

Designs: 2.50k, Ukrainian soccer players. 3.50k, Soccer ball.

2006, May 4
631-632 A387   Set of 2   4.50 4.50

Georgia,
Ukraine,
Azerbaijan
and
Moldova
Summit,
Kiev
A388

2006, May 23   *Perf. 14x14¼*
633 A388 70k multi   .65   .65

Paintings of Kiev — A389

Designs: No. 634, 70k, Zaborovskyi Gate, by Boris Tulin, 1987 (shown). No. 635, 70k, Olha Basystiuk Sings, by Tulin, 1987. No. 636, 70k, Kiev-Peherska Lavra, by Oleksandr Hubarev, 1990. No. 637, 70k, Andrew's Alley, by Hubarev, 1983.

2006, May 24   *Perf. 13¾x14¼*
634-637 A389   Set of 4   2.40 2.40

Souvenir Sheet

Lviv, 750th Anniv. — A390

No. 638 — View of Lviv, 1618 and: a, 70k, Coat of arms (38x31mm). b, 2.50h, Coin (69x31mm).

2006, June 16   *Perf. 11½*
638 A390 Sheet of 2, #a-b   2.10 2.10

Miniature Sheet

Fauna of Shatskyi National
Park — A391

No. 639: a, Lanius excubitor (28x40mm). b, Lynx lynx (33x35mm). c, Anguilla anguilla (41x29mm). d, Bufo calamita (28x29mm). e, Mustela erminea (45x29mm).

2006, July 14
639 A391 70k Sheet of 5, #a-e 3.25 3.25

Miniature Sheet

Cossack Leaders — A392

No. 640: a, Ivan Bohun (denomination at UL). b, Ivan Honta (denomination at UR). c, Ivan Pidkova (denomination at LL). d, Ivan Sirko (denomination at LR).

Litho. & Engr. With Foil Application
2006, Aug. 18
640 A392 3.50h Sheet of 4, #a-d 8.50 8.50

Famous Ukrainians Type of 2004
    Design: Ivan Franko (1856-1916), writer.

2006, Aug. 27   Litho.   Perf. 14x14¼
641 A314 70k multi   .65   .65

Series L Locomotive — A393

Series SO Locomotive — A394

Series YS Locomotive — A395

Series FD Locomotive — A396

2006, Sept. 15
642 A393 70k multi   .65   .65
643 A394 70k multi   .65   .65
644 A395 70k multi   .65   .65
645 A396 70k multi   .65   .65
        Nos. 642-645 (4)   2.60 2.60

Each stamp printed in sheets of 11 + label.

Tenth Natl. Philatelic Exhibition,
Lviv — A397

2006, Oct. 6   Litho. & Embossed
646 A397 70k multi   .65   .65

Miltary History — A398

No. 647: a, Cossack-siroma, 16th-17th cent. b, Naval campaigns of 16th-18th cents. c, Khmelnychna national liberation movement (soldiers aiming guns), 17th cent. d, Haidamachnya national liberation movement (soldier with sword), 17th cent.

2006, Nov. 3   Litho.   Perf. 14x14¼
647 A398 70k Block of 4, #a-d   2.60 2.60

Horses in Sports — A399

No. 648: a, Dressage. b, Horse racing. c, Harness racing. d, Show jumping.

2006, Nov. 17   Perf. 11½
648 A399 70k Block of 4, #a-d   2.60 2.60

Printed in sheets containing two each of Nos. 648a-648d.

St. Nicholas's Day — A400

No. 649: a, Children following angel. b, Angel and St. Nicholas.

Litho. With Foil Application
2006, Nov. 17   Perf. 13¼
649 A400 70k Horiz. pair, #a-b   1.00 1.00

Christmas — A401

2006, Nov. 24   Perf. 14¼x14
650 A401 70k multi   .65 .65

Lviv, 750th Anniv. A402

Litho. & Engr.
2006, Dec. 1   Perf. 14x13¾
651 A402 3.50h multi   2.75 2.75

Printed in sheets of 10 + 5 labels. See Austria No. 2075.

Regional Costumes

Zaporizhzha Region — A403

Khersonshchyna Region — A404

Odeshchyna Region — A405

No. 652: a, People with flags, candle, and swords, St. Michael's Day. b, People and horses, Assumption Day.
No. 653: a, Women and spinning wheel, St. Catherine's Day. b, Men and oxen, St. Elias's Day.
No. 654: a, People and pig, St. Barbara and St. Sava's Day. b, People and fish, St. Boris and St. Hlib's Day.

2006, Dec. 15   Litho.   Perf. 13¼
652 A403 70k Horiz. pair, #a-b   .75 .75
653 A404 70k Horiz. pair, #a-b   .75 .75
654 A405 70k Horiz. pair, #a-b   .75 .75
c.   Miniature sheet, #652-654, perf. 11½   2.25 2.25

Famous Ukrainians Type of 2004

Designs: No. 655, 70k, Metropolitan Ivan Ohienko (1882-1972). No. 656, 70k, Igor Stravinsky (1882-1971), composer.

2007   Litho.   Perf. 14x14¼
655-656 A314   Set of 2   1.40 1.40

Issued: No. 655, 1/12; No. 656, 6/8.

Conjoined Pots A406

Candelabra A407

Clay Bull A408

Inkwell A409

Mug — A410

Rag Doll — A411

Folk decorative art: 3k, Horse figurine. 5k, Whistle. 10k, Jug. 50k, Spinning wheel. 60k, Demijohn. 70k, Circular water container. 85k, Ladle. 1h, Decorated cup with handle. 2h, Pitcher with handle.

2007   Litho.   Perf. 13¾
Date Imprint

657	A406	1k multi,		
		"2007"	.25	.25
a.		Imprint "2007-II"	.25	.25
658	A406	3k multi,		
		"2007"	.25	.25
a.		Imprint "2007-II"	.25	.25
b.		Imprint "2008"	.50	.50
659	A406	5k multi,		
		"2007"	.25	.25
a.		Imprint "2007-II"	.25	.25
b.		Imprint "2008"	.25	.25
c.		Imprint "2008-II"	.50	.50
d.		Imprint "2008-III"	.50	.50
e.		Imprint "2010"	.40	.40
f.		Imprint "2010-II"	.25	.25
g.		Imprint "2011"	.25	.25
660	A406	10k multi,		
		"2007"	.25	.25
a.		Imprint "2007-II"	.25	.25
b.		Imprint "2008"	.50	.50
c.		Imprint "2008-II"	.50	.50
d.		Imprint "2008-III"	.50	.50
e.		Imprint "2008-IV"	.50	.50
f.		Imprint "2009"	.25	.25
g.		Imprint "2010"	.50	.50
h.		Imprint "2010-II"	.50	.50
i.		Imprint "2011"	.25	.25
j.		Imprint "2011-II"	.25	.25
661	A406	50k multi,		
		"2007"	.40	.40
a.		Imprint "2007-II"	.40	.40
b.		Imprint "2008"	.50	.50
c.		Dated "2009"	.50	.50
d.		Imprint "2009-II"	.50	.50
e.		Imprint "2010"	.75	.75
f.		Imprint "2010-II"	.75	.75
g.		Imprint "2011"	.25	.25
h.		Imprint "2011-II"	.25	.25
662	A406	60k multi,		
		"2007"	.50	.50
a.		Imprint "2008"	.50	.50
b.		Imprint "2008-II"	.75	.75
663	A406	70k multi,		
		"2007"	.50	.50
a.		Imprint "2007-II"	.50	.50
b.		Imprint "2008"	.75	.75
c.		Imprint "2008-II"	.75	.75
d.		Imprint "2008-III"	.75	.75
664	A406	85k multi,		
		"2007"	.75	.75
a.		Imprint "2007-II"	.75	.75
b.		Imprint "2008"	.90	.90
665	A406	1h multi,		
		"2007"	.75	.75
a.		Imprint "2007-II"	.75	.75
b.		Imprint "2008"	.80	.80
c.		Imprint "2008-II"	.80	.80
d.		Imprint "2009"	.80	.80
e.		Imprint "2009-II"	.80	.80
f.		Imprint "2010"	.85	.85
g.		Imprint "2010-II"	.85	.85
h.		Imprint "2011"	.25	.25
666	A407	(1.52h) multi,		
		"2007"	.80	.80
a.		Imprint "2007-II"	.80	.80
b.		Imprint "2008"	1.00	1.00
c.		Imprint "2010"	.75	.75
d.		Imprint "2011"	.60	.60
667	A406	2h multi,		
		"2007"	1.40	1.40
a.		Imprint "2007-II"	1.40	1.40
b.		Imprint "2008"	1.40	1.40
c.		Imprint "2008-II"	2.00	2.00
d.		Dated "2009"	1.40	1.40
e.		Imprint "2009-II"	1.50	1.50
f.		Imprint "2010"	1.50	1.50
g.		Imprint "2010-II"	1.50	1.50
h.		Imprint "2010-III"	1.50	1.50
i.		Imprint "2011"	.75	.75
j.		Imprint "2011-II"	.75	.75
668	A408	(2.48h) multi,		
		"2007"	1.25	1.25
a.		Imprint "2007-II"	1.25	1.25
b.		Imprint "2008"	1.25	1.25
669	A409	(3.33h) multi,		
		"2007"	1.75	1.75
a.		Imprint "2007-II"	1.75	1.75
b.		Imprint "2008"	1.75	1.75
670	A410	(3.79h) multi,		
		"2007"	2.00	2.00
a.		Imprint "2008"	2.00	2.00
b.		Imprint "2011"	2.00	2.00
671	A411	(10.10h) multi,		
		"2007"	5.25	5.25
a.		Imprint "2007-II"	5.25	5.25
b.		Imprint "2008"	5.25	5.25
c.		Imprint "2011"	5.25	5.25
		Nos. 657-671 (15)	16.35	16.35

Issued: #657, 4/14/07; #657a, 12/07. #658, 4/14/07; #658a,9/6/07; #658b, 2008. #659, 3/16/07; #659a, 9/8/07; #659b, 2/08; #659c, 9/27/08; #659d, 10/27/08; #659e, 3/24/10; #659f, 8/13/10; # 659g, 6/7/11. #660, 4/14/07; #660a, 11/16/07; #660b, 4/18/08; #660c, 5/30/08; #660d, 9/5/08; #660e, 2008; #660f, 9/7/09; #660g, 2/8/10; #660h, 8/13/10; #660i-660j, 6/7/11. #661, 1/26/07; #661a, 5/07; #661b, 8/22/08; #661c, 6/10/09; #661d, 9/7/09; #661e, 2/8/10; No. 661f, 8/13/10; #661g-661h, 6/7/11. #662, 1/26/07; #662a, 6/18/08; #662b, 8/22/08. #663, 1/26/07; #663a, 9/6/07; #663b, 4/11/08; #663c, 5/30/08; #663d, 7/28/08. #664, 1/26/07; #664a, 8/13/07; #664b, 8/22/08. #665, 4/6/07; #665a, 12/07; #665b, 7/26/08; #665c, 2008; #665d, 665e, 2009; #665f, 2/8/10; #665g, 8/13/10; #665h, 6/7/11. #666, 4/6/07; #666a, 10/24/07; #666b, 10/21/08; #666c, 8/13/10; #666d, 6/7/11. #667, 3/16/07; #667a, 10/24/07; #667b, 667c, 9/27/08; #667d, 7/16/09; #667e, 9/7/09; #667f, 2/8/10; #667g, 3/24/10; #667h, 2010; #667i-667j, 6/7/11. #668, 4/6/07; #668a, 11/16/07; #668b, 10/17/08. #669, 4/14/07; #669a, 12/07; #669b, 11/08. #670, 3/16/07; #670a, 11/8/08; #670b, 6/7/11. #671, 3/16/07; #671a, 11/16/07; #671b, 11/8/08; #671c, 6/7/11.

For surcharges, see Nos. 803-804. See Nos. 720, 764, 817-820.

St. Michael's Cathedral, Adelaide, Australia — A412

2007, Feb. 9   Perf. 13¼
672 A412 3.35k multi + label   1.75 1.75

Souvenir Sheet

Taras Shevchenko (1814-61), Poet — A413

No. 673: a, 2.50h, Drawing of Shevchenko's house, poem (66x40mm). b, 3.35k, Shevchenko (36x40mm).

Litho. With Foil Application
2007, Feb. 23   Perf. 11½
673 A413   Sheet of 2, #a-b   3.75 3.75

Wedding Rings — A414

Flowers — A415

Pechersk Lavra Monastery, Kiev — A416

Oranta Monument — A417

2007, Mar. 1   Litho.   Perf. 11½
674 A414 70k multi + label   1.75 1.75
675 A415 70k multi + label   1.75 1.75
676 A416 70k multi + label   1.75 1.75
677 A417 70k multi + label   1.75 1.75
    Nos. 674-677 (4)   7.00 7.00

Nos. 674-676 were printed in sheets of 22 stamps + 22 labels that could be personalized, and sold for 60.60h per sheet. No. 677 was printed in sheets of 18 stamps + 18 labels that could be personalized, and sold for 54.60h per sheet. Labels shown are generic.

Space Exploration A418

Designs: No. 678, 70k, Leonid Kadeniuck, first Ukrainian cosmonaut. No. 679, 70k, Sea Launch rocket lifting off.

2007, Apr. 12   **Perf. 14x14¼**
678-679 A418 Set of 2   .80   .80

Europa — A419

Nos. 680 and 681: a, 2.50h, Scout emblem, neckerchief and "100." b, 3.35h, Scouts.

2007, Apr. 28   **Perf. 14x14¼**
       Stamp Size: 40x28mm
680 A419   Horiz. pair, #a-b   3.50   3.50
       Stamp Size: 45x33mm
         Perf. 11½
681 A419   Booklet pane of 2,
      #a-b   7.50   —
    Complete booklet, #681   7.50

Scouting, cent. No. 681 sold for 11.52h.

Paintings of Kiev — A420

Designs: No. 682, 70k, Sunny Day, Yaroslaviv Val, by Vitalii Petrovskyi, 1997. No. 683, 70k, Street of Recollections, by Tetiana Kuhai, 2004 (red panel), vert. No. 684, 70k, Kiev Walk, by Yulia Kuznietsova, 2004 (lilac panel), vert. No. 685, 70k, Snowing, by Maria Lashkevych, 2007.

    Perf. 13¾x14½, 14½x13¾
2007, May 18
682-685 A420 Set of 4   2.60   2.60

      Miniature Sheets

Dogs — A421

Cats — A422

No. 686: a, Pug. b, Irish setter. c, Alaskan malamute. d, Basset hound. e, Bull mastiff. f, American cocker spaniel.
No. 687: a, American shorthair. b, Sphynx. c, Scottish fold. d, Snowshoe. e, Russian blue. f, Somali.

2007, June 15   **Perf. 11½**
686 A421 70k Sheet of 6, #a-f   3.25   3.25
687 A422 70k Sheet of 6, #a-f   3.25   3.25

Roman Shukhevych (1907-50), Military Leader — A423

2007, June 29   **Perf. 14x14¼**
688 A423 70k multi   .65   .65

TE1 Diesel Locomotive — A424

TE2 Diesel Locomotive — A425

TE3 Diesel Locomotive — A426

TE7 Diesel Locomotive — A427

2007, July 13   **Litho.**   **Perf. 14x14¼**
689 A424 70k multi   .65   .65
690 A425 70k multi   .65   .65
691 A426 70k multi   .65   .65
692 A427 70k multi   .65   .65
    Nos. 689-692 (4)   2.60   2.60

Each stamp printed in sheets of 11 + label.

      Miniature Sheet

Wedding Headdresses — A428

No. 693: a, Woman facing right wearing floral headdress with gray ribbon behind head. b, Woman facing left wearing gathered fabric headdress with broad red headband. c, Woman facing left wearing floral headdress with broad red ribbon at back. d, Woman facing right wearing ribboned floral headdress. e, Woman facing forward wearing tall red headdress with black and white spots. f, Woman wearing fabric headdress. g, Woman wearing headdress with wide floral ring above smaller floral rings. h, Man wearing hat and jacket with high collar. i, Woman facing left wearing tall

floral headdress covering ear. j, Man wearing tall hat and collarless shirt with decorated front. k, Woman wearing headdress with one floral ring above broad red headband. l, Man wearing hat with chinstrap.

2007, Aug 23   **Litho.**   **Perf. 11½**
693 A428 70k Sheet of 12, #a-l   5.75   5.75

Dnieper River Fish Preservation — A429

No. 694: a, Acipenser gueldenstaedtii. b, Zingel zingel.

2007, Sept. 6
694   Horiz. pair + central label   2.50   2.50
  a.   A429 1.50h multi   1.00   1.00
  b.   A429 2.50h multi   1.50   1.50

    See Moldova No. 569.

Pereyaslav Khmelnytskyi, 1100th Anniv. — A430

2007, Sept. 16   **Perf. 14x14¼**
695 A430 70k multi   .65   .65

Worldwide Fund for Nature (WWF) — A431

No. 696 — Pelecanus onocrotalus: a, 70k, In flight. b, 1.50h, In water. c, 2.50h, Two birds. d, 3.50h, One bird standing.

2007, Sept. 20   **Perf. 14x14¼**
696 A431   Block of 4, #a-d   4.25   4.25
  e.   Miniature sheet, 4 each
     #696a-696d, perf. 11½, + 4
     labels   17.00   17.00

      Souvenir Sheet

Launch of Sputnik 1, 50th Anniv. — A432

2007, Oct. 4   **Perf. 11½**
697 A432 3.33h multi   2.00   2.00

      Miniature Sheets

A433

Peasant Houses — A434

No. 698 — House from: a, Podillya, with ox cart in front. b, Kiev, with couple, cat and pumpkins in front. c, Lemkivschyna, with horse and ducks in front. d, Hutsulschyna, with horse in front. e, Volyn, with wheat sheaves in front. f, Slobozhanschyna, with sunflowers at sides of house.
No. 699 — House from: a, Polissya, with basket weavers and horse in front. b, Khorolschyna, with children rolling hoop in front. c, Bukovyna, with couple in doorway. d, Boikivschyna, with dog and people carrying bundles of sticks in front. e, Poltava, people threshing grain in front. f, Lower Dnieper area, with man with fishing net in front.

2007, Oct. 24
698 A433 70k Sheet of 6, #a-f   3.75   3.75
699 A434 70k Sheet of 6, #a-f   3.75   3.75

Christmas and New Year's Day — A435

No. 700: a, Angels in sled. b, Angels with Christmas tree.

   Litho. With Foil Application
2007, Nov. 16   **Perf. 13½**
700 A435 70k Horiz. pair, #a-b   .85   .85

Christmas and New Year's Day — A436

2007, Nov. 23   **Perf. 11½**
701 A436 1h multi + label   2.75   2.75

Printed in sheets of 18 stamps + 18 labels that could be personalized.

2012 European Soccer Championships, Poland and Ukraine — A437

2007, Dec. 22
702 A437 3.33h multi   2.10   2.10

    Regional Costumes

Khmelnytska Region — A438

Bukovyna Region — A439

Zakarpatyia Region — A440

No. 703: a, Potter and carolers, Christmas. b, People celebrating St. Simeon's Day, horses.

No. 704: a, Woman holding cross, man, woman, fruit basket, St. Ephrosinia's Day. b, Man holding violin, women and children, Ascension Day.

No. 705: a, Men and blacksmith holding mugs, Kuzma and Demyan Day. b, People near cross and candle, Easter.

2007, Dec. 22   Litho.   Perf. 13¼
703	A438	70k Horiz. pair, #a-b	.80	.80
704	A439	70k Horiz. pair, #a-b	.80	.80
705	A440	70k Horiz. pair, #a-b	.80	.80
c.		Miniature sheet, #703-705, perf. 11½	2.40	2.40

Aries — A441

Taurus — A442

Gemini — A443   Cancer — A444

Leo — A445   Virgo — A446

Libra — A447   Scorpio — A448

Sagittarius
A449

Capricorn
A450

Aquarius — A451   Pisces — A452

2008, Jan. 18   Perf. 14¼x14
706	A441	1h multi	.90	.90
707	A442	1h multi	.90	.90
708	A443	1h multi	.90	.90
709	A444	1h multi	.90	.90
710	A445	1h multi	.90	.90
711	A446	1h multi	.90	.90
712	A447	1h multi	.90	.90
713	A448	1h multi	.90	.90
714	A449	1h multi	.90	.90
715	A450	1h multi	.90	.90
716	A451	1h multi	.90	.90
717	A452	1h multi	.90	.90
		Nos. 706-717 (12)	10.80	10.80

2008 Summer Olympics,
Beijing — A453

No. 718: a, 1h, Archery. b, 1.30h, Fencing. c, 2.47h, Cycling. d, 3.33h, Rowing.

Litho. With Foil Application
2008, Jan. 26   Perf. 11½
718	A453	Block of 4, #a-d	4.50	4.50

Roses and Hearts — A454

2008, Feb. 6   Litho.   Perf. 11½
719	A454	1h multi + label	2.00	2.00

Printed in sheets of 22 stamps + 22 labels that could be personalized that sold for 69.90h. Label shown is generic.

Folk Decorative Art Type of 2007

Design: Carved pipe.

2008, Feb. 15   Litho.   Perf. 13¾
720	A406	30k multi, "2008"	.25	.25
a.		Imprint "2008-II"	.25	.25
b.		Imprint "2009"	.50	.50
c.		Imprint "2009-II"	.50	.50
d.		Imprint "2010"	.75	.75
e.		Imprint "2010-II"	.90	.90
f.		Imprint "2011"	.25	.25

Issued: No. 720a, 7/26/08; No. 720b, 7/16/09; No. 720c, 2009; No. 720d, 2/1/10; No. 720e, 8/13/10. No. 720f, 6/7/11.

Paintings by
Taras
Shevchenko
(1814-61)
A455

Designs: 1h, Gypsy Fortune Teller. 1.52h, Kateryna. 2.47h, Self-portrait.

Litho. With Foil Application
2008, Feb. 23   Perf. 11½
721-723	A455	Set of 3	3.00	3.00

Europa — A456

No. 724 — Letter writers with: a, 2.47h, Quill pen. b, 3.33h, Computer.

2008, Mar. 12   Litho.   Perf. 13¼
724	A456	Horiz. pair, #a-b	3.50	3.50

A booklet containing two 37x30mm perf. 11½ stamps like Nos. 724a-724b sold for 12.84h.

Nicolay Gogol (1809-52),
Writer — A457

No. 725: a, 1.52h, Gogol, gun, quill pen and inkwell, pipe. b, 2.47h, Taras Bulba on horseback.

2008, Mar. 21   Perf. 14x14¼
725	A457	Pair, #a-b	2.50	2.50

Easter — A458

Litho. With Foil Application
2008, Apr. 11   Perf. 13¼
726	A458	1h multi	.90	.90

Miniature Sheet

18th and 19th Century Decorative
Clocks — A459

No. 727: a, French mantle clock with clock as chariot wheel, 19th cent. (33x33mm). b, Russian mantle clock with nymphs, 19th cent. (33x33mm). c, French mantle clock with nude woman and nymphs on goats, 19th cent. (33x33mm). d, French clock by Charles Baltazar with blue green frame and nymph on top, 18th cent. (33x45mm). e, French clock with woman with shield on top, 18th cent. (33x45mm). f, German clock with woman trumpeter on top, 18th cent. (33x45mm). g, English clock with landscape above face, 18th cent. (33x45mm). h, Austrian clock with pillars at sides, 19th cent. (33x45mm). i, French mantle clock with birds at top, 19th cent. (33x45mm).

Litho. With Foil Application
2008, Apr. 18   Perf. 11½
727	A459	1h Sheet of 9, #a-i	5.50	5.50

Miniature Sheets

Dogs — A460

Cats — A461

No. 728: a, Smooth-haired dachshund. b, American bulldog. c, Rottweiler. d, Chow chow. e, Schnauzer. f, German shepherd.

No. 729: a, Persian. b, Selkirk Rex. c, Exotic shorthair. d, Burmese. e, Siamese. f, Kuril Island bobtail.

2008, May 16   Litho.
728	A460	1r Sheet of 6, #a-f	3.75	3.75
729	A461	1r Sheet of 6, #a-f	3.75	3.75

Miniature Sheet

Crimean Nature Reserve — A462

No. 730: a, Aegypius monachus (31x38mm). b, Cranes and swans (36x31mm). c, Cervus elaphus (47x31mm). d, Silene jailensis and insect (31x31mm).

2008, June 18
730	A462	1h Sheet of 4, #a-d	2.60	2.60

Souvenir Sheets

Ukrainian Postage Stamps, 90th
Anniv. — A463

No. 731: a, 2.47h, Ukraine #1. b, 3.33h, Ukraine #2.

No. 732: a, 1h, Ukraine #4. b, 2.47h, Ukraine #5. c, 3.33j, Ukraine #3.

2008, July 4
| 731 | A463 | Sheet of 2, #a-b, + 2 labels | 3.50 | 3.50 |
| 732 | A463 | Sheet of 3, #a-c, + label | 4.25 | 4.25 |

Souvenir Sheet

Myhailivskyi Monastery, 900th Anniv. — A464

2008, July 11
| 733 | A464 | 3.33h multi | 2.10 | 2.10 |

TEP10 Diesel Locomotive — A465

2TE10L Diesel Locomotive — A466

M62 Diesel Locomotive — A467

TE109 Diesel Locomotive — A468

2008, Aug. 8   *Perf. 14x14¼*
734	A465	1h multi	.60	.60
735	A466	1h multi	.60	.60
736	A467	1h multi	.60	.60
737	A468	1h multi	.60	.60
		Nos. 734-737 (4)	2.40	2.40

Each stamp printed in sheets of 11 + label.

Christmas Carols — A469

Songs of Spring — A470

Songs of the Cossacks A471

Songs of the Chumaks A472

2008, Sept. 5   *Perf. 13½*
738	A469	1h multi	.60	.60
739	A470	1h multi	.60	.60
740	A471	1h multi	.60	.60
741	A472	1h multi	.60	.60
		Nos. 738-741 (4)	2.40	2.40

Ukrainian musical heritage.

Jewelry — A473

No. 742: a, 2.47h, Earring, 12th-13th cent. b, 3.33h, Pendant, 19th cent.

2008, Sept. 18   *Perf. 11½*
| 742 | A473 | Horiz. pair, #a-b, + central label | 3.50 | 3.50 |

See Azerbaijan No. 885.

Ukrainian and Swedish Military and Political Alliances of 17th and 18th Centuries A474

Litho. With Foil Application
2008, Oct. 1
| 743 | A474 | 1h multi | .80 | .80 |

A475

Ninth Natl. Philatelic Exhibition, Chernivtsi — A476

2008, Oct. 3   **Litho.**   *Perf. 14x14¼*
| 744 | A475 | 1h multi | .80 | .80 |

         Perf. 11½
| 745 | A476 | 1h multi + label | 4.50 | 4.50 |

No. 745 was printed in sheets of 10 stamps + 10 labels that could be personalized that sold for 88.38h. Label shown is generic.

Chernivtsi, 600th Anniv. A477

2008, Oct. 4   *Perf. 14x14¼*
| 746 | A477 | 1h multi | .80 | .80 |

Sacking of Baturyn, 300th Anniv. — A478

2008, Oct. 24   *Perf. 14¼x14*
| 747 | A478 | 1h multi | .80 | .80 |

Christmas — A479

New Year's Day — A480

Litho. With Foil Application
2008, Nov. 21   *Perf. 11½*
| 748 | A479 | 1h multi | .80 | .80 |
| 749 | A480 | 1h multi | .80 | .80 |

Famous Ukrainians Type of 2004
Designs: No. 750, 1h, Marko Vovchok (1833-1907), writer. No. 751, 1h, Vyachyslav Chornovil (1937-99), politician.

2008   **Litho.**   *Perf. 14x14¼*
| 750-751 | A314 | Set of 2 | 1.60 | 1.60 |

Issued: No. 750, 11/28; No. 751, 12/24.

Miniature Sheet

Headdresses — A481

No. 752: a, Woman facing right wearing brown and red headdress and red necklace. b, Woman facing forward wearing white headdress wrapping under chin. c, Woman facing left with headdress with blue-tipped tassels above eyes. d, Woman facing right wearing white headdress. e, Woman facing forward wearing brown, red and green headdress and red necklace. f, Woman facing forward wearing white, red and green headdress, denomination in white. g, Woman wearing headdress and laurel wreath. h, Woman wearing white, gray and red headdress. i, Woman facing left wearing white, red and green headdress with floral pattern over red striped forehead band. j, Man wearing brown hat. k, Woman facing forward wearing headdress with lace trim on forehead. l, Man wearing black and red hat.

2008, Dec. 10   *Perf. 11½*
| 752 | A481 | 1h Sheet of 12, #a-l | 7.75 | 7.75 |

Regional Costumes

Crimea Region — A482

Dnipropetrovshchyna Region — A483

Luhanshchyna Region — A484

No. 753: a, People with grapes, Feast of the Transfiguration. b, Baby being christened.
No. 754: a, Bride and groom receiving crowns. b, Three women at Harvest Festival.
No. 755: a, Musicians, Feast of Saints Cyril and Methodius. b, People and church on hill, Feast of the Miracle Worker.

2008, Dec. 25   **Litho.**   *Perf. 13¼*
753	A482	1h Horiz. pair, #a-b	.80	.80
754	A483	1h Horiz. pair, #a-b	.80	.80
755	A484	1h Horiz. pair, #a-b	.80	.80
c.		Miniature sheet, #753-755, perf. 11½	2.40	2.40
		Nos. 753-755 (3)	2.40	2.40

Stephan Bandera (1909-59), Nationalist Leader — A485

2009, Jan. 1
756 A485 1h multi   .65 .65

Famous Ukrainians Type of 2004

Designs: 1h, Stepan Rudanskyi (1834-73), poet. 2.20h, Sholem Aleichem (1859-1916), writer.

2009   **Perf. 14x14¼**
757-758 A314 Set of 2   1.40 1.40
Issued: No. 757, 1/17; No. 758, 2/18.

Souvenir Sheet

Kiev Zoo, Cent. — A486

2009, Feb. 20 Litho.   Perf. 11½
759 A486 3.20h multi   1.40 1.40

Paintings by Taras Shevchenko A487

Designs: No. 760, 1.50h, Portrait of I. I. Lyzohub, 1846-47. No. 761, 1.50h, Portrait of E. V. Keikuatova, 1847. No. 762, 1.50h, Village Family, 1843, horiz.

Litho. With Foil Application
2009, Mar. 9
760-762 A487 Set of 3   1.75 1.75
Nos. 760-762 each were printed in sheets of 11 + label.

Preservation of Polar Regions — A488

No. 763: a, Academician Vernadskiy Antarctic Station. b, Iceberg.

2009, Mar. 18
763 A488 3.30h Pair, #a-b   2.75 2.75
Printed in sheets containing 4 of each stamp and a central label.

Folk Art Type of 2007
Designs: Tile depicting Cossack on horse.

2009, Mar. 25   Litho.   Perf. 13¾
764 A406 1.50h multi   .60 .60
a.   Imprint "2009-II"   .75 .75
b.   Imprint "2010"   .75 .75

---

c.   Imprint "2010-II"   .75 .75
d.   Imprint "2011"   .55 .55
e.   Imprint "2011-II"   .55 .55
Issued: No. 764a, 7/16; Nos. 764b, 764c, 2010. Nos. 764d, 764e, 6/7/11.

Souvenir Sheet

Nikolai Gogol (1809-52), Writer — A489

No. 765: a, 1.50h, Scene from "Night Before Christmas." b, 2.20h, Gogol.

Litho. With Foil Application
2009, Apr. 1   **Perf. 11½**
765 A489 Sheet of 2, #a-b   1.50 1.50

Europa — A490

No. 766: a, Telescope and star chart. b, Map of solar system, Galileo Galilei and his telescope.

2009, Apr. 17 Litho.   Perf. 13¾x14¼
Size: 52x25mm
766   Horiz. pair   3.00 3.00
a.   A490 3.75h multi   1.25 1.25
b.   A490 5.25h multi   1.75 1.75
Intl. Year of Astronomy. A booklet containing a pane with a pair of 57x28mm perf. 11½ stamps like Nos. 766a-766b sold for 18.42h. Value, $8.

Architecture in China and Ukraine A491

No. 767: a, Stork Tower, Shanghai. b, Golden Gate, Kiev.

2009, Aug. 14   **Perf. 11½**
767   Horiz. pair + central la-
        bel   3.75 3.75
a.   A491 3.85h multi   1.60 1.60
b.   A491 5.40h multi   2.00 2.00

Miniature Sheet

Gorgany Game Reserve — A492

No. 768: a, Tetrao urogallus (40x37mm). b, Pinus cembra (30x47mm). c, Arnica montana (40x40mm). d, Felis silvestris (57x30mm).

2009, Sept. 29
768 A492 1.50h Sheet of 4, #a-d 2.50 2.50

Electric Locomotive VL26 — A493

Electric Locomotive VL41 — A494

Diesel Locomotive 2TE116 — A495

Diesel Locomotive 2TE121 — A496

2009, Oct. 22   **Perf. 13¾x14¼**
769 A493 1.50h multi   .60 .60
770 A494 1.50h multi   .60 .60
771 A495 1.50h multi   .60 .60
772 A496 1.50h multi   .60 .60
        Nos. 769-772 (4)   2.40 2.40

Miniature Sheet

Lighthouses — A497

No. 773: a, Kyz-Aulskyi Lighthouse (blue top). b, Luparivskyi Front Lighthouse (base with vertical red and white stripes). c, Yaltinskyi Lighthouse (white, with hexagonal base). d, Vorontsovskyi Lighthouse (red top). e, Sarych Lighthouse (white, with circular base). f, Berdianskyi Lower Lighthouse (base with horizontal red and white stripes).

2009, Oct. 30   **Perf. 11½**
773 A497 1.50h Sheet of 6, #a-f 3.75 3.75

Ukrainian Supreme Liberation Council, 65th Anniv. — A498

2009, Nov. 27   **Perf. 14¼x14**
774 A498 1.50h multi   .65 .65

A499

A500

A501

Songs — A502

2009, Nov. 27   **Perf. 11½**
775 A499 1.50h multi   .75 .75
776 A500 1.50h multi   .75 .75
777 A501 2h multi   .90 .90
778 A502 2h multi   .90 .90
        Nos. 775-778 (4)   3.30 3.30

Christmas A503

New Year 2010 — A504

Litho. With Foil Application
2009, Dec. 9   **Perf. 11½**
779 A503 1.50h multi   .65 .65
                                Perf. 13¾x14¼
780 A504 1.50h multi   .65 .65

White Sukholimanskiy Grapes and Vineyard — A505

White Muscat Grapes, Sailboat and Vineyard — A506

2009, Dec. 15   Litho.   Perf. 11½
781 A505 1.50h multi   .65 .65
782 A506 1.50h multi   .65 .65

Narodny Rukh
(People's
Movement) Party,
20th Anniv. — A507

2009, Dec. 19   **Perf. 13¾**
783 A507 1.50h multi   .65 .65

Miniature Sheet

Minerals — A508

No. 784: a, 1.50h, Quartz. b, 1.90h, Native
sulphur. c, 2h, Topaz. d, 2.20h, Beryl. e, 3.30h,
Tiger's eye. f, 4.85h, Kertschenite.

Litho. & Embossed
2009, Dec. 23   **Perf. 11½**
784 A508 Sheet of 6, #a-h   7.00 7.00

2010 Winter Olympics,
Vancouver — A509

No. 785: a, 1.50h, Cross-country skiing. b,
1.50h, Biathlon. c, 2h, Freestyle skiing. d, 2h,
Luge.

Litho. With Foil Application
2010, Feb. 5   **Perf. 11½**
785 A509 Horiz. strip of 4, #a-d 3.50 3.50

Souvenir Sheet

Taras Shevchenko (1814-61),
Poet — A510

No. 786: a, 1.50h, Woman at butter churn,
poem (66x40mm). b, 2h, Self-portrait
(36x40mm).

2010, Mar. 9
786 A510 Sheet of 2, #a-b   1.75 1.75

Souvenir Sheet

Constitution of Pylyp Orlik, 300th
Anniv. — A511

2010, Mar. 29   Litho.
787 A511 1.50h multi   .85 .85

Victory in World
War II, 65th
Anniv. — A512

2010, Apr. 15   **Perf. 13¼**
788 A512 1.50h multi   .85 .85

Souvenir Sheets

Prepared But Unissued Postage
Stamps of Ukrainian National
Republic, 90th Anniv. — A513

No. 789: a, 1.50h, Unissued 1h stamp. b,
1.50h, Unissued 10h stamp. c, 2h, Unissued
2h stamp. d, 2h, Unissued 15h stamp.
No. 790: a, 1.50h, Unissued 20h stamp. b,
1.50h, Unissued 40h stamp. c, 2h, Unissued
30h stamp. d, 2h, Unissued 50h stamp.

2010, Apr. 22   **Perf. 11½**
Sheets of 4, #a-d, + Label
789-790 A513 Set of 2   6.50 6.50

Europa — A514

Nos. 791 and 792 — Scenes from children's
books: a, 2.20h, Mare's Head. b, 3.30h, Gold
Shoe.

Litho. With Foil Application
2010, Apr. 30   **Perf. 13¼**
791 A514 Horiz. pair, #a-b   2.50 2.50
                                            Perf. 11½
792 A514 Booklet pane of 2,
             #a-b, + central label 5.00   —
     Complete booklet, #792   5.00
Nos. 792a and 792b are 43x41mm. No. 792
sold for 10.50h.

Famous Ukrainians Type of 2004
Designs: 1h, Oleksandr Potebnia (1835-91),
linguiot. 1.50h, Mykola Pyrohov (1810 81),
surgeon.

2010   Litho.   **Perf. 14x14¼**
793 A314 1h multi   .65 .65
794 A314 1.50h multi   .85 .85
     Issued: No. 793, 9/10; No. 794, 6/2.

Wladimir
and Vitali
Klitschko,
Boxers
A515

2010, June 8
795 A515 1.50h multi   .85 .85

Flowers — A516

Litho. With Foil Application
2010, Aug. 11   **Perf. 13¼x13½**
796 A516 (1.50h) multi + label   3.75 3.75
No. 796 was printed in sheets of 10 stamps
+ 10 labels that could be personalized that
sold for 105h. The label shown is generic.

DE1 Electric Locomotive — A517

DC3 Electric Locomotive — A518

TEM103 Diesel Locomotive — A519

TEP150 Diesel Locomotive — A520

2010, Sept. 4   Litho.   **Perf. 14x14¼**
797 A517   1h multi   .45 .45
798 A518   1.50h multi   .60 .60
799 A519   2h multi   .85 .85
800 A520   2h multi   .85 .85
         Nos. 797-800 (4)   2.75 2.75
Nos. 797-800 each printed in sheets of 11 +
label.

Sculptures by Johann Georg
Pinsel — A521

No. 801: a, 1.50h, Mother of God. b, 2h,
Angel.

2010, Sept. 8   **Perf. 13¼**
801 A521 Horiz. pair, #a-b   1.40 1.40

Miniature Sheet

National Technical University Kharkhiv
Polytechnical Institute, 125th
Anniv. — A522

No. 802: a, 1.50h, O. M. Beketov (1862-
1941), architect. b, 1.50h, P. P. Kopniaev
(1867-1932), electrical engineer. c, 1.50h, O.
M. Liapunov (1857-1918), mathematician. d,
1.50h, E. I. Orlov (1865-1944), chemical engineer. e, 1.50h, M. D. Pylchykov (1857-1908),
physicist. f, 1.50h, V. M. Khrushchov (1882-
1941), electrical engineer. g, 2h, V. L.
Kyrpychov (1845-1913), mechanical engineer.
h, 2h, M. M. Beketov (1827-1911), chemist. i,
2h, L. D. Landau (1908-68), theoretical physicist. j, 2m, P. M. Mukhachov (1861-1935),

engineer. k, 2h, V. A. Stieklov (1863-1926),
mathematician.

2010, Sept. 16   **Perf. 11½**
802 A522 Sheet of 11, #a-k, +
             label   8.00 8.00

Nos. 657a, 658a, 658b
Surcharged

Methods and Perfs As Before
2010, Oct. 6
803 A406 1.50h on 3k #658a   1.25 1.25
   a.   A406 1.50h on 3k #658b   1.25 1.25
804 A406 2h on 1k #657a   1.75 1.75

Miniature Sheet

Lighthouses — A523

No. 805: a, 1.50h, Tendrivskyi Lighthouse
(with two horizontal black bands). b, 1.50h,
Pavlovskyi Fort Lighthouse (hexagonal with
brown vertical stripe). c, 1.50h, Khersoneskyi
Lighthouse (round white lighthouse with ten
windows). d, 2h, Sanzhiiskyi Lighthouse (hexagonal white lighthouse with two windows). e,
2h, Tarkhankutskyi Lighthouse (round white
lighthouse with four windows). f, 2h, Illichivskyi
Lighthouse (with horizontal red bands).

2010, Oct. 8   Litho.   **Perf. 11½**
805 A523 Sheet of 6, #a-f   4.50 4.50

Leaders of Cossack
Rebellions — A524

No. 806: a, 1.50h, Kryshtof Kosynskyi
(1545-93). b, 2h, Bohdan Mykoshynskyi.

2010, Oct. 15   **Perf. 14x14¼**
806 A524 Block of 2, #a-b, + 2
             labels   1.40 1.40

Military History — A525

No. 807: a, 1.50h, Danubian Sich (country
name in brown). b, 1.50h, Cossack regiments
of 1812 (country name in blue). c, 2h, Defense
of Sevastopol (country name in blue). d, 2h,
Ataman Yakiv Kukharenko on horse (country
name in brown).

2010, Oct. 29
807 A525 Block of 4, #a-d   3.00 3.00

Hetman Pavlo Polubotok (1660-1724) — A526

Litho. With Foil Application
2010, Oct. 29
808 A526 1.50h multi .65 .65

Miniature Sheet

Kiev Metro, 50th Anniv. — A527

No. 809: a, 1.50h, Dorohzhychi Station escalators. b, 1.50h, Train. c, 2h, Lukianivska Station exterior. d, 2h, Tunnel under construction.

2010, Nov. 3   Litho.   Perf. 11½
809 A527   Sheet of 4, #a-d   3.00 3.00

Cabernet Sauvignon Grapes and Estate — A528

2010, Dec. 17
810 A528 1.50h multi .65 .65

Miniature Sheet

Fauna of Sviati Hory National Park — A529

No. 811: a, 1h, Zerynthia polyxena (38x30mm). b, 1.50h, Luscinia svecica (38x30mm). c, 1.50h, Lutra lutra (38x37mm). d,2h, Emys orbicularis (38x37mm).

2010, Dec. 28
811 A529   Sheet of 4, #a-d   2.50 2.50

Signing of the Universal Declaration of Human Rights, 60th Anniv. A530

2010, Dec. 31   Perf. 14x14¼
812 A530 1.50h multi .65 .65

Miniature Sheet

Minerals — A531

No. 813: a, 1.50h, Syngenite (brown mineral). b, 1.50h, Amber. c, 1.50h, Labradorite (black and red mineral). d, 2h, Carpathite (black arnd brown mineral). e, 2h, Agate (mineral with rings). f, 2h, Rhodonite (red and gray mineral).

Litho. & Embossed
2010, Dec. 31   Perf. 11½
813 A531   Sheet of 6, #a-f   4.50 4.50

First Man in Space, 50th Anniv. — A532

2011, Apr. 12   Litho.   Perf. 14x14¼
814 A532 6h multi   2.25 2.25

Georgy Beregovoi (1921-95), Cosmonaut — A533

2011, Apr. 16   Perf. 14¼x14
815 A533 2.20h multi   .75 .75

Kazashka Katya, Painting by Taras Shevchenko (1814-61) A534

Litho. With Foil Application
2011, May 21   Perf. 11½
816 A534 1.50h multi   .60 .60

Folk Decorative Art Type of 2007

Designs: 1.90h, Tobacco pouch. 2.20h, Powder flask. 6h, Bandura. 7h, Bowl with lid.

2011   Litho.   Perf. 13¾
817 A406 1.90h multi .75 .75
818 A406 2.20h multi .85 .85
819 A406 6h multi 2.40 2.40
820 A406 7h multi 2.75 2.75
Nos. 817-820 (4) 6.75 6.75

Issued: Nos. 817-820, 6/7.

Leaders of Cossack Rebellions — A535

No. 821: a, 1.50h, Hryhorii Loboda. b, 2h, Severyn Nalyvaiko.

2011, June 9   Perf. 14x14¼
821 A535   Block of 2, #a-b, + 2 labels   1.40 1.40

Ukrainian Constitution, 15th Anniv. — A536

Litho. & Embossed With Foil Application
2011, June 17   Perf. 11½
822 A536 6h multi   2.25 2.25

Miniature Sheet

Farmhouse and Animals — A537

No. 823: a, 1.50h, Cat. b, 1.50h, Birds. c, 1.50h, Pig. d, 2h, Cow. e, 2h, Dog.

2011, June 25   Litho.
823 A537   Sheet of 5, #a-e   3.50 3.50

Personalized Stamp — A538

Litho. With Foil Application
2011, June 25   Perf. 11½
824 A538 (1.50h) multi + label   3.00 3.00

No. 824 was printed in sheets of 18 + 18 labels that could be personalized. The label shown, depicting the national arms and posthorns, is the generic label image.

Trains — A539

Designs: 1.50h, Diesel train DPL1. 1.90h, Diesel train, DEP 02. 2.20h, Electric train EPL 2T. 6h, Electric train EPL 9T.

2011, July 5   Litho.   Perf. 14x14¼
825-828 A539   Set of 4   4.50 4.50

First Flight of Dirigible "Kiev," Cent. — A540

2011, Aug. 5
829 A540 2.20h multi   .90 .90

Emigration of Ukrainians to Brazil, 120th Anniv. — A541

2011, Aug. 24   Perf. 14¼x14
830 A541 2.20h multi   .90 .90

Independence, 20th Anniv. — A542

Litho. With Foil Application
2011, Aug. 24   Perf. 14x14¼
831 A542 2.20h multi   .90 .90

"The Snow Queen" Fairy Tale — A543

No. 832: a, 1.50h, Snow Queen in horse-drawn sleigh flying above town (43x26mm). b, 6h, Crow and girl (26x26mm).

2011, Sept. 1   Litho.   Perf. 11½
832 A543   Horiz. pair, #a-b   2.75 2.75

12th Natl. Philatelic Exhibition, Odessa A544

2011, Sept. 9   Perf. 14x14¼
833 A544 4.30h multi   1.75 1.75

Miniature Sheet

Prepared but Unissued Ukrainian National Republic Stamps, 90th Anniv. — A545

No. 834: a, 1.50h, Unissued 5h stamp. b, 1.50h, Unissued 3h stamp. c, 2h, Unissued 60h stamp. d, 2h, Unissued 80h stamp. e, 6h, Unissued 100h stamp. f, 7h, Unissued 200h stamp.

2011, Sept. 12   Perf. 11½
834 A545   Sheet of 6, #a-f   7.50 7.50

Tetiana Markus (1921-43), Anti-Nazi
Resistance Fighter — A546

2011, Sept. 21   *Perf. 14x14¼*
835 A546 1.50h multi   .55   .55

Babi Yar
Massacres, 70th
Anniv. — A547

2011, Sept. 29   *Perf. 13¼*
836 A547 2.20h multi   .90   .90

Motion Picture *Natalka Poltavka,* 75th
Anniv. — A548

No. 837: a, 1.50h, People. b, 6h, Woman.

Litho. With Foil Application
2011, Sept. 30   *Perf. 14x14¼*
837 A548 Horiz. pair, #a-b   2.75 2.75

Lvov National University, 350th
Anniv. — A549

2011, Oct. 11   **Litho.**   *Perf. 11½*
838 A549 1.50h multi   .55   .55

Regional Communications
Commonwealth, 20th Anniv. — A550

2011, Oct. 14
839 A550 1.90h multi   .75   .75

Mykhailo
Yanhel (1911-
71), Missile
Designer
A551

2011, Oct. 25   *Perf. 13¼*
840 A551 1.50h multi   .55   .55

St.
Sophia's
Cathedral,
Kyiv,
1000th
Anniv.
A553

No. 842: a, Painting above three arches. b,
Round ceiling painting.

Litho. With Foil Application
2011, Nov. 18   *Perf. 11½*
842   Horiz. pair + central label 3.00 3.00
a. A553 1.90h multi   .75   .75
b. A553 6h multi   2.25   2.25

Miniature Sheet

Amphibians — A554

No. 843: a, 1.80h, Pelophylax esculentus. b,
1.80h, Hyla arborea. c, 2.20h, Pelophylax les-
sonae. d, 2.20h, Rana dalmantina. e, 4.30h,
Pelophylax ridibundus.

2011, Nov. 22   **Litho.**
843 A554   Sheet of 5, #a-e   4.50 4.50

Miniature Sheet

Spring — A555

No. 844: a, 1.80h, Bird on flower branch
held by woman (30x40mm). b, 1.80h, Bare
trees, white flowers and pond (30x21mm). c,
1.80h, Purple and yellow flowers (24x32mm).
d, 1.90h, Cut flowers held by woman
(30x40mm). e, 2.20h, Purple flowers
(30x40mm). f, 6h, White flowers (30x40mm).

Litho. With Foil Application
2011, Nov. 25
844 A555   Sheet of 6, #a-f   5.75 5.75

Traminer Grapes and
Vineyard — A556

Aligoté Grapes and Vineyard — A557

2011, Nov. 30   **Litho.**
845 A556 1.90h multi   .70   .70
846 A557 4.30h multi   1.60   1.60

Campaign
Against AIDS,
30th
Anniv. — A558

2011, Dec. 1   *Perf. 13¼*
847 A558 1.80h multi   .65   .65

Europa — A561

No. 850: a, 2.20h, Bird-shaped opening in
forest canopy. b, 4.30h, Star in opening in
snow-covered forest canopy.

2011, Dec. 20   **Litho.**   *Perf. 13¼*
850 A561 Horiz. pair, #a-b   2.40 2.40
     Intl. Year of Forests.

Christmas and New Year's
Greetings — A562

No. 851: a, Grandfather Frost with bag of
toys. b, People outside of church.

2011, Dec. 23   *Perf. 11½*
851 A562 1.80h Horiz. pair, #a-b 1.40 1.40

Miniature Sheet

Water Mills — A563

No. 852 — Various mills: a, 1.80h. b, 2.20h.
c, 6.50h. d, 7.70h.

2011, Dec. 28
852 A563   Sheet of 4, #a-d   6.75 6.75

SEMI-POSTAL STAMPS

Ukrainian Soviet Socialist Republic

"Famine" — SP1

Taras H.
Shevchenko
SP2

"Death" Stalking
Peasant — SP3

"Ukraine"
Distributing
Food — SP4

Perf. 14½x13½, 13½x14½
1923, June   **Litho.**   **Unwmk.**
B1   SP1   10k + 10k gray bl &
                blk   1.00   5.50
B2   SP2   20k + 20k vio brn &
                org brn   1.00   5.50
B3   SP3   90k + 30k db & blk,
                straw   1.00   5.50
B4   SP4   150k + 50k red brn &
                blk   1.00   5.50
     Nos. B1-B4 (4)   4.00 22.00

Imperf., Pairs
B1a SP1   10k + 10k   100.00 120.00
B2a SP2   20k + 20k   100.00 120.00
B3a SP3   90k + 30k   100.00 120.00
B4a SP4   150k + 50k   100.00 120.00

The values of these stamps are in
karbovanets, which by 1923 converted to
rubles at 100 to 1.

Wmk. 116
Same Colors
B5   SP1   10k + 10k   50.00 70.00
B6   SP2   20k + 20k   50.00 70.00
a.   Imperf., pair   2,500.
B7   SP3   90k + 30k   50.00 70.00
B8   SP4   150k + 50k   50.00 70.00
     Nos. B5-B8 (4)   200.00 280.00

┌─────────────────────────────────┐
│ **Catalogue values for unused** │
│ **stamps in this section, from this** │
│ **point to the end of the section, are** │
│ **for Never Hinged items.**   │
└─────────────────────────────────┘

Charity and
Health
Fund — SP5

1994, Jan. 15   **Litho.**   *Perf. 12*
B9   SP5 150kb +20kb multi   1.25   .65

Third Natl.
Philatelic
Exhibition,
Lviv — SP6

1995, Sept. 23   **Litho.**   *Perf. 13½*
B10 SP6 50,000kb +5000kb multi 1.50 1.50

Souvenir Sheet

Zymnenska Icon of Madonna and Child — SP7

1999, Sept. 4   Litho.   Perf. 11½
B11 SP7 1.20h +10k multicolored 3.50 3.50
Intl. Year of the Elderly.

REGISTRATION STAMPS

Catalogue values for unused stamps in this section are for Never Hinged items.

Trident — R1

2001, Apr. 1   Litho.   Perf. 13¾
F1 R1 (10.84h) multi 8.00 7.25
a. Imprint "2003" 9.00 7.25
b. Perf. 11½, dated "2006" 7.25 7.25

Issued: No. F1a, 1/28/03; No. F1b, 10/9/06. No. F1b was issued only in No. F2c.

Trident With Frame — R2

2005-06   Litho.   Perf. 13¾
F2 R2 (10.10h) multi 7.00 7.00
a. Imprint "2006" 7.00 7.00
b. Perf. 11½, dated "2006" 7.00 7.00
c. Sheet of 18, #418a-422a, 453a-454a, 466a-468a, 515a, 572a, 606a-609a, F1b, F2b 25.00 25.00

Issued: No. F2, 10/28/05; No. F2a, 2/7/06; No. F2b, 10/9/06. No. F2b was issued only in No. F2c. No. F2c sold for 35.41h and exists imperf.

MILITARY STAMPS

COURIER FIELD POST ISSUE

Nos. 1-5, 48 Surcharged

1920, Aug. 26
M1 A1 10h on 10sh buff 20.00 —
a. Inverted surcharge 80.00
M2 A2 10h on 20sh brown 40.00 —
M3 A3 10h on 30sh ul-
          tramarine 50.00
M4 A4 10h on 40sh green 55.00
a. Inverted surcharge 215.00
M5 A5 10h on 50sh red 50.00
M6 A1 20h on 10sh buff 55.00
M7 A2 20h on 20sh brown 15.00
a. Inverted surcharge 60.00
M8 A3 20h on 30sh ul-
          tramarine 40.00
a. Inverted surcharge 160.00
M9 A4 20h on 40sh green 40.00
M10 A5 20h on 50sh red 40.00
a. Inverted surcharge 160.00
M11 A1 40h on 10sh buff 200.00
M12 A2 40h on 20sh brown 100.00

M13 A3 40h on 30sh ul-
          tramarine 400.00 —
M14 A4 40h on 40sh green 200.00 —
M15 A5 40h on 50sh red 400.00 —
M16 A6 40h on 20hr red &
          green — —

Nos. M1-M16 were prepared to facilitate communications between the Ukrainian government-in-exile at Tarnow, Poland, and its military units in the field.

Only two examples of No. M16 are known, one unused and one used on cover.

Forged surcharges and cancellations exist.

UMM AL QIWAIN

'um-al-kĭ-'wĭn

LOCATION — Oman Peninsula, Arabia, on Arabian Gulf
GOVT. — Sheikdom under British protection
AREA — 300 sq. mi.
POP. — 5,700

Umm al Qiwain is one of six Persian Gulf sheikdoms to join the United Arab Emirates which proclaimed independence Dec. 2, 1971. See United Arab Emirates.

100 Naye Paise = 1 Rupee
100 Dirham = 1 Riyal (1967)

Catalogue values for all unused stamps in this country are for Never Hinged items.

Sheik Ahmed bin Rashid al Mulla and Gazelles — A1

Photogravure and Lithographed
1964, June 29   Unwmk.   Perf. 14
Size: 35x22mm
1   A1 1np shown .25 .25
2   A1 2np Snake .25 .25
3   A1 3np Hyena .25 .25
4   A1 4np Conspicuous trig-
          gerfish .25 .25
5   A1 5np Fish .25 .25
6   A1 10np Silver angelfish .30 .25
7   A1 15np Palace .30 .25
8   A1 20np Umm al Qiwain .30 .25
9   A1 30np Tower .35 .30
Size: 42x26mm
10 A1 40np as 1np .35 .30
11 A1 50np as 2np .45 .35
12 A1 70np as 3np .75 .40
13 A1 1r as 4np 1.00 .50
14 A1 1.50r as 4np 1.25 .65
15 A1 2r as 10np 1.75 .90
Size: 52x33mm
16 A1 3r as 15np 3.00 2.00
17 A1 5r as 20np 5.25 3.25
18 A1 10r as 30np 9.00 6.00
    Nos. 1-18 (18) 25.30 16.65

National Stadium, Tokyo, and Discobolus — A2

Designs: 1r, 2r, National Stadium, Tokyo. 1.50r, Indoor swimming arena. 3r, Komazawa Gymnasium. 4r, Stadium entrance.

1964, Nov. 25   Photo.   Perf. 14
19 A2 50np multi .30 .25
20 A2 1r multi .50 .25
21 A2 1.50r multi .65 .25
22 A2 2r multi 1.00 .25
23 A2 3r multi 1.25 .45

---

24 A2 4r multi 2.50 .85
25 A2 5r multi 3.25 1.00
    Nos. 19-25 (7) 9.45 3.30

18th Olympic Games, Tokyo, Oct. 10-25, 1964. Perf. and imperf. souvenir sheets contain 4 stamps similar to #22-25 in changed colors. Size: 145x115mm.

A3

Designs: 10np, Pres. Kennedy's funeral cortege leaving White House. 15np, Mrs. Kennedy with children, and Robert Kennedy following coffin. 50np, Horse-drawn caisson. 1r, Presidents Truman and Eisenhower, and Margaret Truman Daniels. 2r, Pres. Charles de Gaulle, Emperor Haile Selassie, Chancellor Ludwig Erhart, Sir Alec Douglas-Home and King Frederick IX. 3r, Kennedy family on steps of St. Matthew's Cathedral. 5r, Honor guard at tomb. 7.50r, Portrait of Pres. John F. Kennedy.

Perf. 14½
1965, Jan. 20   Unwmk.   Photo.
Black Design with Gold Inscriptions
Size: 29x44mm
26 A3 10np pale blue .25 .25
27 A3 15np pale yellow .25 .25
28 A3 50np pale green .30 .25
29 A3 1r pale pink .60 .35
30 A3 2r pale green 1.00 .45
Size: 33x51mm
31 A3 3r pale gray 1.75 .65
32 A3 5r pale blue 3.00 .90
33 A3 7.50r pale yellow 4.00 1.50
    Nos. 26-33 (8) 11.15 4.60

Pres. John F. Kennedy. A souvenir sheet contains 2 stamps similar to Nos. 32-33 with pale green (5r) and pale salmon (7.50r) backgrounds, size: 29x44mm. Size of sheet: 114x70mm.

A4

Designs: 10d, Astronaut on Moon. 20d, Landing module approaching moon. 30d, Apollo XII on launching pad. 50d, Commanders Charles Conrad, Jr., Alan L. Bean, Richard F. Gordon, Jr., earth and moon, horiz. 75d, Earth and Apollo XII, horiz. 1r, Sheik Ahmed, rocket and lunar landing module, horiz.

1969, Nov. 19   Litho.   Perf. 14½
34 A4 10d multi .25
35 A4 20d multi .35
36 A4 30d multi .45
37 A4 50d emerald & multi .65
38 A4 75d purple & multi 1.00
39 A4 1r dk bl & multi 1.75
    Nos. 34-39 (6) 4.35

US Apollo XII moon landing mission, 11/14-24/69.
Two imperf. souvenir sheets of 3 exist, containing stamps similar to Nos. 34-36 and Nos. 37-39.

A5

1970, May 29   Litho.   Perf. 14
40 A5 10d James A. Lovell .25
41 A5 30d Fred W. Haise, Jr. .40
42 A5 50d John L. Swigert, Jr. .90
a. Souv. sheet of 3, #40-42 2.00
    Nos. 40-42 (3) 1.55

Safe return of the crew of Apollo 13.

A6

Designs: 5d, 1.25r, EXPO '70 Emblem. 10d, 20d, Japanese Pavilion.

1970, Aug. 14   Litho.   Perf. 13½x14
43 A6 5d yellow & multi .25
44 A6 10d blue & multi .35
45 A6 20d red & multi .45
48 A6 1.25r red & multi .90
    Nos. 43-48 (4) 1.95

EXPO '70 Intl. Exhib., Osaka, Japan, Mar. 15-Sept. 13, 1970.
A 40d and 1r, showing the Emperor and Empress of Japan, and a souvenir sheet containing these and Nos. 43-45, 48 were prepared, but not issued.

A7

Uniforms: 10d, Private, North Lancashire Regiment. 20d, Royal Navy seaman. 30d, Officer, North Lancashire (Loyal) Regiment. 50d, Private, York and Lancaster Regiment. 75d, Royal Navy officer. 1r, Officer, York and Lancaster Regiment.

1970, Oct. 12   Litho.   Perf. 14½x14
49 A7 10d multi .25
50 A7 20d multi .35
51 A7 30d multi .55
a. Souv. sheet of 3, #49-51 2.75
52 A7 50d buff & multi .90
53 A7 75d multi 1.25
54 A7 1r buff & multi 1.75
a. Souv. sheet of 3, #52-54 4.00
    Nos. 49-54 (6) 5.05

British landings on the Trucial Coast, 150th anniv.
Stamps of Umm al Qiwain were replaced in 1972 by those of United Arab Emirates.

AIR POST STAMPS

Type of Regular Issue, 1964
Photogravure and Lithographed
1965   Unwmk.   Perf. 14
Size: 42x26mm
C1 A1 15np as #1 .25 .25
C2 A1 25np as #2 .25 .25
C3 A1 35np as #3 .25 .25
C4 A1 50np as #4 .60 .25
C5 A1 75np as #5 1.10 .30
C6 A1 1r as #6 1.40 .40

Size: 52x33mm

C7	A1	2r as #7	2.25	.55
C8	A1	3r as #8	3.25	.75
C9	A1	5r as #9	4.50	1.25
		Nos. C1-C9 (9)	13.85	4.25

Issued: #C7-C9, Nov. 6; others, Oct. 18.

AIR POST OFFICIAL STAMPS

Type of Regular Issue, 1964
Photogravure and Lithographed
1965, Dec. 22   Unwmk.   *Perf. 14*
Size: 42x26mm

CO1	A1	75np as #6	1.00	.30

Size: 52x33mm

CO2	A1	2r as #7	2.50	.75
CO3	A1	3r as #8	3.75	1.00
CO4	A1	5r as #9	5.00	1.50
		Nos. CO1-CO4 (4)	12.25	3.55

OFFICIAL STAMPS

Type of Regular Issue, 1964
Photogravure and Lithographed
1965, Dec. 22   Unwmk.   *Perf. 14*
Size: 42x26mm

O1	A1	25np as #1	.35	.25
O2	A1	40np as #2	.45	.25
O3	A1	75np as #3	.75	.25
O4	A1	75np as #4	1.00	.30
O5	A1	1r as #5	1.25	.35
		Nos. O1-O5 (5)	3.80	1.40

UNITED ARAB EMIRATES

yu-ˌnī-təd ˈar-əb i-ˈmiˌəˌr-əts

(Trucial States)

LOCATION — Arabia, on Arabian Gulf
GOVT. — Federation of sheikdoms
AREA — 32,300 sq. mi.
POP. — 2,377,453 (1995)
CAPITAL — Abu Dhabi

The UAE was formed Dec. 2, 1971, by the union of Abu Dhabi, Ajman, Dubai, Fujeira, Sharjah and Umm al Qiwain. Ras al Khaima joined in Feb. 1972.

1,000 Fils = 1 Dinar
100 Fils = 1 Dirham (1973)

Catalogue values for all unused stamps in this country are for Never Hinged items.

Abu Dhabi Nos. 56-67 Overprinted

1972, Aug.   Litho.   Unwmk.   *Perf. 14*

1	A10	5f multicolored	3.25	3.25
2	A10	10f multicolored	3.25	3.25
3	A10	25f multicolored	5.00	5.00
4	A10	35f multicolored	6.50	6.50
5	A10	50f multicolored	11.00	11.00
6	A10	60f multicolored	12.00	12.00
7	A10	70f multicolored	16.00	16.00
8	A10	90f multicolored	20.00	20.00
9	A11	125f multicolored	65.00	65.00
10	A11	150f multicolored	90.00	90.00
11	A11	500f multicolored	210.00	210.00
12	A11	1d multicolored	400.00	400.00
		Nos. 1-12 (12)	842.00	842.00

The overprint differs.
#1-12 were used in Abu Dhabi. #2-3 were placed on sale later in Dubai & Sharjah.

Map and Flag of UAE A1

Almagta Bridge, Abu Dhabi — A2

Designs: 10f, Like 5f. 15f, 35f, Coat of arms of UAE (eagle). 75f, Khor Fakkan, Sharjah. 1d, Steel Clock Tower, Dubai. 1.25d, Buthnah Fort, Fujeira. 2d, Alfalaj Fort, Umm al Qiwain. 3d, Khor Khwair, Ras al Khaima. 5d, Palace of Sheik Rashid bin Humaid al Nuaimi, Ajman. 10d, Sheik Zaid bin Sultan al Nahayan, Abu Dhabi.

1973, Jan. 1   Unwmk.   *Perf. 14½*
Size: 41x25mm

13	A1	5f multicolored	.25	.25
14	A1	10f multicolored	.25	.25
15	A1	15f blue & multi	.50	.25
16	A1	35f olive & multi	.75	.30

Perf. 14x15
Size: 45x29½mm

17	A2	65f multicolored	1.25	1.25
18	A2	75f multicolored	1.75	1.25
19	A2	1d multicolored	2.00	1.25
20	A2	1.25d multicolored	4.25	2.00
21	A2	2d multicolored	50.00	12.50
22	A2	3d multicolored	10.00	7.25
23	A2	5d multicolored	11.00	7.50
24	A2	10d multicolored	25.00	16.00
		Nos. 13-24 (12)	107.00	50.05

For surcharge see No. 68.

Festival Emblem A3

1973, Mar. 27   Litho.   *Perf. 13½x14*

25	A3	10f shown	7.50	.35
26	A3	1.25d Trophy	18.50	11.00

National Youth Festival, Mar. 27.

Pedestrian Crossing in Dubai — A4

35f, Traffic light school crossing sign, vert. 1.25d, Traffic policemen with car & radio, vert.

1973, Apr. 1   *Perf. 13½x14, 14x13½*

27	A4	35f green & multi	4.00	1.75
28	A4	75f blue & multi	7.50	3.50
29	A4	1.25d violet & multi	13.00	6.00
		Nos. 27-29 (3)	24.50	11.25

Traffic Week, Apr. 1-7.

Human Rights Flame and People — A5

1973, Dec. 10   Litho.   *Perf. 14½x14*

30	A5	35f blue, blk & org	1.50	.95
31	A5	65f red, blk & org	5.25	2.00
32	A5	1.25d olive, blk & org	9.75	4.00
		Nos. 30-32 (3)	16.50	6.95

25th anniversary of the Universal Declaration of Human Rights.

UPU and Arab Postal Union Emblems — A6

1974, Aug. 5   Litho.   *Perf. 14x14½*

33	A6	25f multicolored	2.00	1.00
34	A6	60f emerald & multi	3.25	1.75
35	A6	1.25d lt brown & multi	6.75	4.50
		Nos. 33-35 (3)	12.00	7.25

Centenary of Universal Postal Union.

Health Care — A7

Education — A8

Designs: 65f, Construction. 1.25d, UAE flag, UN and Arab League emblems.

1974, Dec. 2   Litho.   *Perf. 13½*

36	A7	10f multicolored	1.10	.40
37	A8	35f multicolored	3.00	1.00
38	A8	65f blue & brown	3.25	1.50
39	A8	1.25d multicolored	7.00	3.25
		Nos. 36-39 (4)	14.35	6.15

Third National Day.

Arab Man and Woman Holding Candle over Book — A9

Man and Woman Reading Book — A10

1974, Dec. 27   *Perf. 14x14½, 14½x14*

40	A9	35f deep ultra & multi	2.75	.60
41	A10	65f orange brn & multi	3.25	1.25
42	A10	1.25d gray & multi	6.75	2.50
		Nos. 40-42 (3)	12.75	4.35

World Literacy Day.

Oil De-gassing Station — A11

50f, Off-shore drilling platform. 100f, Underwater storage tank. 125f, Oil production platform.

1975, Mar. 10   Litho.   *Perf. 13x13½*

43	A11	25f multicolored	1.50	.55
44	A11	50f multicolored	3.25	1.00
45	A11	100f multicolored	8.00	2.50
46	A11	125f multicolored	11.00	3.00
a.	Souvenir sheet of 4, #43-46		40.00	30.00
		Nos. 43-46 (4)	23.75	7.05

9th Arab Petroleum Conference.

Three stamps to commemorate the 2nd Gulf Long Distance Swimming Championship were prepared in June, 1975, but not issued. Value $500.

Jabal Ali Earth Station — A12

Jabal Ali Earth Station: 35f, 65f, Communications satellite over globe.

1975, Nov. 8   Litho.   *Perf. 13*

47	A12	15f multicolored	1.25	.35
48	A12	35f multicolored	3.00	.65
49	A12	65f multicolored	5.00	1.10
50	A12	2d multicolored	11.00	4.00
		Nos. 47-50 (4)	20.25	6.10

Various Scenes — A13

Sheik Hamad,
Fujeira
Ruler — A14

Supreme Council Members (Sheikdom rulers): 60f, Sheik Rashid bin Humaid al Naimi, Ajman. 80f, Sheik Ahmed bin Rashid al Mulla, Umm al Qiwain. 90f, Sheik Sultan bin Mohammed al Qasimi, Sharjah. 1d, Sheik Saqr bin Mohammed al Qasimi, Ras al Khaima. 140f, Sheik Rashid bin Said al Maktum, Dubai. 5d, Sheik Zaid bin Sultan al Nahayan, Abu Dhabi.

1975, Dec. 2   Litho.   Perf. 14

51	A13	10f multicolored	.85 .25
52	A14	35f multicolored	2.25 .90
53	A14	60f multicolored	3.25 1.75
54	A14	80f multicolored	4.50 2.75
55	A14	90f multicolored	5.25 3.00
56	A14	1d multicolored	5.50 3.50
57	A14	140f multicolored	7.75 4.50
58	A14	5d multicolored	32.50 18.00
		Nos. 51-58 (8)	61.85 34.65

Fourth National Day.

Students and Lamp of Learning — A15

Arab Literacy Day: 15f, Lamp of learning.

1976, Feb. 8   Litho.   Perf. 14

59	A15	15f orange & multi	.75 .35
60	A15	50f ultra & multi	2.50 1.00
61	A15	3d multicolored	12.00 7.75
		Nos. 59-61 (3)	15.25 9.10

Children Crossing Street — A16

Traffic Week: 15f, Traffic lights and signals, vert. 80f, Road and traffic lights.

Perf. 14½x14, 14x14½

1976, Apr. 1   Litho.

62	A16	15f brt blue & multi	2.50 1.25
63	A16	80f blue & multi	9.25 4.50
64	A16	140f ocher & multi	18.00 10.00
		Nos. 62-64 (3)	29.75 15.75

Waves and Ear Phones, ITU Emblem, Coat of Arms — A17

1976, May 17   Litho.   Perf. 14

65	A17	50f gray grn & multi	1.50 .65
66	A17	80f pink & multi	3.00 1.25
67	A17	2d tan & multi	6.50 3.25
		Nos. 65-67 (3)	11.00 5.15

International Telecommunications Day.

No. 18 Surcharged

1976   Litho.   Perf. 14x15

68	A2	50f on 75f multi	75.00 24.00

Coat of Arms — A18

1976, Aug. 15   Litho.   Perf. 11½

69	A18	5f dull rose	.35 .25
70	A18	10f golden brown	.35 .25
71	A18	15f orange	.50 .40
72	A18	35f dull red brn	.75 .25
73	A18	50f bright lilac	1.00 .50
74	A18	60f bister	1.25 .60
75	A18	80f yellow green	1.50 .70
76	A18	90f ultra	2.00 .80
77	A18	1d blue	2.25 .80
78	A18	140f olive green	3.50 1.50
79	A18	150f rose violet	5.25 2.00
80	A18	2d slate	5.50 2.25
81	A18	5d blue green	13.00 6.25
82	A18	10d lilac rose	24.00 14.00
		Nos. 69-82 (14)	61.20 30.55

See Nos. 91-104.

Sheik Zaid — A19

1976, Dec. 12   Litho.   Perf. 13

83	A19	15f rose & multi	6.00 .60
84	A19	140f blue & multi	12.00 5.00

5th National Day.

Symbolic Falcon and Globe — A20

1976, Dec. 15   Perf. 14x13½

85	A20	80f yellow & multi	6.00 1.50
86	A20	2d red & multi	11.00 6.00

International Falconry Congress, Abu Dhabi, Dec. 1976.

A21

1976, Dec. 30   Litho.   Perf. 13

87	A21	50f multicolored	5.00 1.50
88	A21	80f multicolored	10.00 3.00

Mohammed Ali Jinnah (1876-1948), 1st Governor General of Pakistan.

A22

APU emblem, members' flags.

1977, Apr. 12   Litho.   Perf. 13½x14

89	A22	50f multicolored	6.00 1.50
90	A22	80f multicolored	9.00 3.50

Arab Postal Union, 25th anniversary.

Arms Type of 1976

1977, July 25   Litho.   Perf. 11½

91	A18	5f dull rose & blk	.40 .35
92	A18	10f gldn brn & blk	.40 .35
93	A18	15f dull org & blk	.55 .45
94	A18	35f lt brown & blk	1.40 .50
95	A18	50f brt lilac & blk	1.60 .55
96	A18	60f bister & blk	1.75 .60
97	A18	80f yel grn & blk	1.75 .60
98	A18	90f ultra & blk	2.75 .95
99	A18	1d blue & blk	4.00 1.40
100	A18	140f ol grn & blk	6.00 1.90
101	A18	150f rose vio & blk	6.50 2.25
102	A18	2d slate & blk	10.00 3.25
103	A18	5d bl grn & blk	22.50 8.25
104	A18	10d lil rose & bl	37.50 24.50
		Nos. 91-104 (14)	97.10 45.90

Man Reading Book, UAE Arms, UN Emblem A23

1977, Sept. 8   Litho.   Perf. 14x13½

105	A23	50f green, brn & gold	3.50 .80
106	A23	3d blue & multi	12.50 5.50

International Literacy Day.

A set of three stamps for the 6th Natl. Day was withdrawn from sale on the day of issue, Dec. 2, 1977. Value, $850.

Post Horn and Sails — A24

1979, Apr. 14   Photo.   Perf. 12x11½

107	A24	50f multicolored	1.25 1.00
108	A24	5d multicolored	8.50 6.00

Gulf Postal Organization, 2nd Conf., Dubai.

Arab Achievements — A25

1980, Mar. 22   Litho.   Perf. 14x14½

109	A25	50f multicolored	.75 .50
110	A25	140f multicolored	2.25 1.25
111	A25	3d multicolored	4.50 2.75
		Nos. 109-111 (3)	7.50 4.50

9th National Day — A26

1980, Dec. 2   Litho.   Perf. 13½

112	A26	15f multicolored	.60 .35
113	A26	50f multicolored	2.00 1.00
114	A26	80f multicolored	2.50 1.50
115	A26	150f multicolored	3.75 2.25
		Nos. 112-115 (4)	8.85 5.10

Souvenir Sheet

Perf. 13½x14

116	A26	3d multicolored	15.00 15.00

Family on Graph — A27

1980, Dec. 15

117	A27	15f shown	.80 .35
118	A27	80f Symbols	2.75 1.25
119	A27	90f like #118	3.50 2.25
120	A27	2d like #117	7.25 5.00
		Nos. 117-120 (4)	14.30 8.85

1980 population census.

Hegira (Pilgrimage Year) — A28

1980, Dec. 18   Perf. 14x13½

121	A28	15f multicolored	.50 .25
122	A28	80f multicolored	2.00 1.25
123	A28	90f multicolored	2.75 1.50
124	A28	140f multicolored	4.25 2.50
		Nos. 121-124 (4)	9.50 5.50

Souvenir Sheet

125	A28	2d multicolored	11.50 11.50

No. 125 contains one 36x57mm stamp.

OPEC Emblem — A29

1980, Dec. 21   Perf. 14

126	A29	50f Men holding OPEC emblem, vert.	1.25 .50
127	A29	80f like #126	2.00 1.25
128	A29	90f shown	2.25 1.50
129	A29	140f like #128	4.00 2.25
		Nos. 126-129 (4)	9.50 5.50

Souvenir Sheet

130	A29	3d like #128	18.00 18.00

Traffic Week — A30

15f, 80f, Crossing guard, students, traffic light. 50f, 5d, Crossing guard, traffic light and signs.

1981, Mar. 26		**Litho.**		**Perf. 14½**
131	A30	15f multicolored	.65	.30
132	A30	50f multicolored	1.25	.75
133	A30	80f multicolored	2.50	1.50
134	A30	5d multicolored	11.00	7.50
		Nos. 131-134 (4)	15.40	10.05

Size of Nos. 131 and 133: 25½x35mm.

10th Natl. Day — A31

1981, Dec. 2		**Litho.**		**Perf. 15x14**
135	A31	25f Cogwheel	.75	.40
136	A31	150f Soldiers	5.00	2.50
137	A31	2d UN emblem	6.50	3.00
		Nos. 135-137 (3)	12.25	5.90

Intl. Year of the Disabled — A32

Perf. 14½x14, 14x14½

1981, Dec. 26				**Litho.**
138	A32	25f Couple	.75	.35
139	A32	45f Man in wheel-chair, vert.	1.50	1.10
140	A32	150f like #139	5.00	2.50
141	A32	2d like #138	7.50	3.25
		Nos. 138-141 (4)	14.75	7.20

Natl. Arms — A33

1982-86				
142	A33	5f multicolored	.25	.25
143	A33	10f multicolored	.25	.25
144	A33	15f multicolored	.25	.25
145	A33	25f multicolored	.25	.25
145A	A33	35f multicolored	.25	.25
146	A33	50f multicolored	.40	.40
147	A33	75f multicolored	.60	.60
148	A33	100f multicolored	.90	.90
149	A33	110f multicolored	1.00	1.00
150	A33	125f multicolored	1.50	1.40
151	A33	150f multicolored	1.75	1.25
151A	A33	175f multicolored	2.00	1.25

Size: 23x27mm
Perf. 13

152	A33	2d multicolored	2.25	1.60
152A	A33	250f multicolored	2.40	1.40
153	A33	3d multicolored	3.50	1.90
154	A33	5d multicolored	6.00	3.25
155	A33	10d multicolored	13.00	8.25
156	A33	20d multicolored	24.50	13.50
157	A33	50d multicolored	50.00	24.50
		Nos. 142-157 (19)	111.05	62.45

Issued: 35f, 175f, 250f, 12/15/84; 50d, 2/6/86; others, 3/7/82.

6th Arab Gulf Soccer Championships — A34

1982, Apr. 4		**Litho.**		**Perf. 14**
167	A34	25f Emblem, flags	1.25	.60
168	A34	75f Eagle, soccer ball, stadium, vert.	3.25	2.40
169	A34	125f Players, vert.	4.25	3.00
170	A34	3d like 75f, vert.	9.25	7.75
		Nos. 167-170 (4)	18.00	13.75

2nd Disarmament Meeting A35

1982, Oct. 24		**Litho.**		**Perf. 13x13½**
171	A35	25f multicolored	.65	.30
172	A35	75f multicolored	2.00	2.25
173	A35	125f multicolored	3.50	2.40
174	A35	150f multicolored	4.00	3.00
		Nos. 171-174 (4)	10.15	7.95

11th Natl. Day — A36

Designs: 25f, 150f, Skyscraper, communications tower, natl. crest, castle turret, open book, flag. 75f, 125f, Sun, bird, vert.

1982, Dec. 2		**Litho.**		**Perf. 14½**
175	A36	25f multicolored	.60	.40
176	A36	75f multicolored	2.40	1.60
177	A36	125f multicolored	3.25	2.25
178	A36	150f multicolored	3.75	2.75
		Nos. 175-178 (4)	10.00	7.00

A37

1983, Dec. 20		**Litho.**		**Perf. 14x14½**
179	A37	25f multicolored	.80	.30
180	A37	150f multicolored	3.50	1.60
181	A37	2d multicolored	5.00	3.00
182	A37	3d multicolored	7.00	3.75
		Nos. 179-182 (4)	16.30	8.65

World Communications Year.

A38

Arab Literacy Day: 25f, 75f, Oil lamp, open Koran. 35f, 3d, Scribe.

1983, Jan. 8		**Litho.**		**Perf. 14½**
183	A38	25f multicolored	42.50	60.00
184	A38	35f multicolored	1.50	.80
185	A38	75f multicolored	42.50	55.00
186	A38	3d multicolored	10.00	5.00

Nos. 183 and 185 withdrawn from sale on day of issue because of an error in Koranic inscription.

INTELSAT, 20th Anniv. — A39

1984, Nov. 24		**Litho.**		**Perf. 14½**
187	A39	2d multicolored	5.50	5.00
188	A39	2.50d multicolored	8.00	7.00

13th Natl. Day A40

Flag, portrait of an Emir and building or view from each capital.

1984, Dec. 2				**Perf. 14½x13½**
189	A40	1d Building, pavilion	2.50	1.50
190	A40	1d Fortress, cannon	2.50	1.50
191	A40	1d Port, boats	2.50	1.50
192	A40	1d Fortress	2.50	1.50
193	A40	1d Oil refinery	2.50	1.50
194	A40	1d Building, garden	2.50	1.50
195	A40	1d Oil well, palace	2.50	1.50
		Nos. 189-195 (7)	17.50	10.50

Tidy Week — A41

1985, Mar. 15				**Perf. 12½**
196	A41	5d multicolored	11.50	10.00

A42

1985, Sept. 10				**Perf. 13½x14½**
197	A42	2d multicolored	7.00	4.50
198	A42	250f multicolored	10.00	6.50

World Junior Chess Championships, Sharjah, Sept. 10-27.

14th Natl. Day — A43

1985, Dec. 2				**Perf. 14x13½**
199	A43	50f multicolored	.75	.55
200	A43	3d multicolored	7.00	4.50

Population Census — A44

1985, Dec. 16				
201	A44	50f multicolored	1.10	.55
202	A44	1d multicolored	3.00	1.40
203	A44	3d multicolored	7.75	3.50
		Nos. 201-203 (3)	11.85	5.45

Intl. Youth Year A45

1985, Dec. 23				**Perf. 14½**
204	A45	50f Silhouettes, sapling, vert.	1.00	.65
205	A45	175f Globe, open book	3.00	1.60
206	A45	2d Youth carrying world, vert.	3.75	2.25
		Nos. 204-206 (3)	7.75	4.50

Women and Family Day — A46

1986, Mar. 21				**Perf. 13½**
207	A46	1d multicolored	1.50	1.00
208	A46	3d multicolored	4.50	3.25

General Postal Authority, 1st Anniv. A47

Designs: 50f, 250f, Posthorn, map, natl. flag, globe. 1d, 2d, Emblem, globe, vert.

1986, Apr. 1				
209	A47	50f multicolored	.60	.50
210	A47	1d multicolored	1.25	.80
211	A47	2d multicolored	3.25	2.25
212	A47	250f multicolored	3.50	2.75
		Nos. 209-212 (4)	8.60	6.30

United Arab Shipping Co., 10th Anniv. A48

1986, Aug. 20				**Perf. 13x13½**
213	A48	2d shown	4.50	2.75
214	A48	3d Ship's bow, vert.	5.50	3.75

A49

1986, Sept. 1				**Perf. 13½x13**
215	A49	250f multicolored	4.25	1.65
216	A49	3d multicolored	5.25	1.90

Emirates Telecommunications Corp., Ltd., 10th anniv.

Hawk — A50

A51

1986, Sept. 9 Photo. *Perf. 15x14*
Booklet Stamps
Background Color

217	A50	50f pale green	.75	.75
218	A50	75f pink	1.25	1.25
219	A50	125f gray	2.00	2.00
a.		Bklt. pane, 75f, 125f, 2 50f	8.00	
		Nos. 217-219 (3)	4.00	4.00

1986, Oct. 25 *Perf. 13½*

220	A51	50f Jet, camel	1.75	1.25
221	A51	175f Jet	5.50	4.25

Emirates Airlines, 1st anniv.

State Crests, GCC Emblem A52

1986, Nov. 2 *Perf. 13*

222	A52	50f shown	.80	.60
222A	A52	175f like no. 223	2.75	2.25
223	A52	3d Tree, emblem	4.50	4.25
		Nos. 222-223 (3)	8.05	7.10

Gulf Cooperation Council supreme council 7th session, Abu Dhabi, Nov. 1986. No. 222A incorrectly inscribed "1.75f."

15th Natl. Day — A53

1986, Dec. 2 Litho. *Perf. 13½*

224	A53	50f shown	1.10	.55
225	A53	1d like 50f	2.50	1.60
226	A53	175f Flag, emblem	4.50	2.75
227	A53	2d like 175f	4.50	3.25
		Nos. 224-227 (4)	12.60	8.15

27th Chess Olympiad, Dubai — A54

1986, Nov. 14 *Perf. 12½*

228	A54	50f Skyscraper, vert.	1.40	.90
229	A54	2d shown	5.50	4.50
230	A54	250f Tapestry, diff.	7.00	5.50
a.		Souv. sheet, #228-230, perf 13	22.50	22.50
		Nos. 228-230 (3)	13.90	10.80

No. 230a exists imperf. Value, $35.

Arab Police Day — A55

1986, Dec. 18 *Perf. 13½*

231	A55	50f multicolored	1.75	1.00
232	A55	1d multicolored	3.00	2.50

A56

1987, Mar. 15

233	A56	50f multicolored	1.75	1.00
234	A56	1d multicolored	3.00	2.50

Municipalities and Environment Week.

A57

1987, Apr. 10

235	A57	200f multicolored	3.50	3.50
236	A57	250f multicolored	4.00	4.00

UAE Flight Information Region, 1st anniv.

A58

1987, May 25

237	A58	50f Water	1.00	1.00
238	A58	2d Solar energy, oil well	8.50	8.50

Conservation.

A59

1987, June 23

239	A59	1d multicolored	1.75	1.75
240	A59	3d multicolored	4.50	4.50

United Arab Emirates University, 10th anniv.

1st Shipment of Crude Oil from Abu Dhabi, 25th Anniv. — A60

1987, July 4 *Perf. 13*

241	A60	50f Oil rig	.80	.80
242	A60	1d Drilling well, vert.	1.90	1.90
243	A60	175f Crew, drill	3.00	3.00
244	A60	2d Oil tanker	3.25	3.25
		Nos. 241-244 (4)	8.95	8.95

Arab Palm Tree and Date Day — A61

1987, Sept. 15 Litho. *Perf. 14x15*

245	A61	50f shown	.90	.90
246	A61	1d Tree, fruit, diff.	1.60	1.60

A62

1987, Nov. 21 Litho. *Perf. 13x13½*

247	A62	2d multicolored	3.00	3.00
248	A62	250f multicolored	3.50	3.50

Intl. Year of Shelter for the Homeless.

A63

1987, Dec. 15 *Perf. 13½*

249	A63	1d multicolored	2.00	2.00
250	A63	2d multicolored	4.50	4.50

Salim Bin Ali Al-Owais (b. 1887), poet.

UN Child Survival Campaign A64

Abu Dhabi Intl. Airport, 6th Anniv. A65

1987, Oct. 25 Litho. *Perf. 13*

251	A64	50f Growth monitoring	.60	.50
252	A64	1d Immunization	1.25	1.00
253	A64	175f Oral rehydration therapy	2.00	1.75
254	A64	2d Breast feeding, horiz.	2.25	1.90
		Nos. 251-254 (4)	6.10	5.15

1988, Jan. 2

255	A65	50f Control tower	.85	.85
256	A65	50f Terminal interior	.85	.85
257	A65	100f Aircraft over airport	2.00	2.00
258	A65	100f Aircraft at gates	2.00	2.00
		Nos. 255-258 (4)	5.70	5.70

Natl. Arts Festival A66

1988, Mar. 21 Litho. *Perf. 13½*

259	A66	50f multicolored	1.25	1.25
260	A66	250f multicolored	3.75	3.75

Youth Cultural Festival A67

Winning children's drawings of a design contest sponsored by the Ministry of Education and the Sharjah Cultural and Information Department.

Perf. 13x13½, 13½x13

1988, May 25 Litho.

261	A67	50f Net fisherman	.75	.50
262	A67	1d Woman	1.40	1.25
263	A67	1.75d Youth as flower	2.25	2.00
264	A67	2d Recreation	2.75	2.50
		Nos. 261-264 (4)	7.15	6.25

Palestinian Uprising — A68

1988, June 28 Litho. *Perf. 13½*

265	A68	2d multicolored	2.75	2.25
266	A68	250f multicolored	3.50	2.75

A69

Banks — A70

1988, July 16 Litho. *Perf. 13½*

267	A69	50f multicolored	2.50	2.50
268	A70	50f multicolored	2.50	2.50

Abu Dhabi Natl. Bank, Ltd., 20th anniv. (No. 267); Natl. Bank of Dubai, Ltd., 25th anniv. (No. 268).

Port Rashid, Dubai, 16th Anniv. — A71

1988, Aug. 31 Litho. *Perf. 13½*

269	A71	50f Ground transportation	.60	.60
270	A71	1d Piers	1.25	1.25
271	A71	175f Ship at dock	2.50	2.50
272	A71	2d Ship, unloading cranes	2.75	2.75
		Nos. 269-272 (4)	7.10	7.10

1988 Summer Olympics, Seoul — A72

1988, Sept. 17 **Perf. 15x14½**
273 2d Swimming   3.25 3.25
274 250f Cycling   4.00 4.00
  a. A72 Pair, #273-274   7.50 7.50

Ras Al Khaima Natl. Museum, 1st Anniv. — A74

1988, Nov. 19 **Litho.** **Perf. 14**
275 A74 50f Vase, vert.   .75   .55
276 A74 3d Gold crown   3.25 2.25

18th Arab Scout Conference, Nov. 29-Dec. 3, Abu Dhabi — A75

1988, Nov. 29 **Perf. 12½**
277 A75 1d multicolored   1.20 1.20

10th Arbor Day — A76

Perf. 13½x13, 13x13½
1989, Mar. 6 **Litho.**
278 A76 50f Ghaf, vert.   .60   .60
279 A76 100f Palm   1.25 1.25
280 A76 250f Dahlia blossom 2.75 2.75
  Nos. 278-280 (3)   4.60 4.60

Sharjah Intl. Airport, 10th Anniv. — A77

1989, Apr. 21 **Litho.** **Perf. 13½**
281 A77 50f multicolored   .90   .90
282 A77 100f multicolored 2.10 2.10

Postal Service, 80th Anniv. — A78

1989, Aug. 19 **Litho.** **Perf. 13x13½**
283 A78 50f Seaplane   1.00 1.00
284 A78 3d Ship   6.50 6.50

Al-Ittihad Newspaper, 20th Anniv. — A79

1989, Oct. 20 **Litho.** **Perf. 13½**
285 A79 50f multicolored   .75   .75
286 A79 1d Al Ittihad Press 1.25 1.25

Gulf Investment Corporation, 5th Anniv. — A80

1989, Nov. 25
287 A80 50f multicolored   .75   .75
288 A80 2d multicolored   3.25 3.25

Child on Crutches, Hands — A81

Designs: 2d, Crouched youth, cracked earth, bread in hand, horiz.

1989, Dec. 5 **Perf. 15x14, 14x15**
289 A81 2d multicolored   2.75 2.75
290 A81 250f shown   3.25 3.25
Intl. Volunteer's Day, Red Crescent Soc.

Bank Building — A82

1989, Dec. 20 **Perf. 13½**
291 A82 50f Emblem, architecture   .75   .75
292 A82 1d shown   1.25 1.25
Commercial Bank of Dubai, Ltd., 20th Anniv.

Astrolabe, Manuscript Page and Ship of Bin Majid, 15th Cent. Navigator and Writer A83

1989, Dec. 25 **Perf. 13x13½, 13½x13**
293 A83 1d shown   1.25 1.25
294 A83 3d Ship, page, vert. 4.25 4.25
Heritage revival.

A84   Falcon — A85

1990, Jan. 17 **Perf. 13½**
295 A84 50f multicolored   .75   .75
296 A84 1d multicolored   1.90 1.90
3rd Al Ain festival.

1990, Feb. 17 **Litho.** **Perf. 11½**
Granite Paper
297 A85 5f multicolored   .25   .25
298 A85 20f multicolored   .25   .25
299 A85 25f multicolored   .25   .25
301 A85 50f multicolored   .45   .40
302 A85 100f multicolored 2.25 1.25
303 A85 150f multicolored 3.75 1.75
304 A85 175f multicolored 4.00 2.00

Size: 21x26mm
Perf. 11½x12
306 A85 2d multicolored   5.50   3.00
307 A85 250f multicolored 6.00   3.25
309 A85 3d multicolored   7.75   3.75
310 A85 5d multicolored   11.00   6.50
311 A85 10d multicolored 22.50 13.00
312 A85 20d multicolored 37.50 22.50
313 A85 50d multicolored 100.00 60.00
  Nos. 297-313 (14)   201.45 118.15
See also Nos. 726A-726G.

A86

1990, Mar. 10 **Litho.** **Perf. 13½**
316 A86 50f multicolored   .60   .60
317 A86 250f multicolored 2.50 2.50
Children's cultural festival.

A87

1990, Aug. 5 **Litho.** **Perf. 14x15**
318 A87 175f shown   1.90 1.90
319 A87 2d Starving child 2.50 2.50
Red Crescent Society.

Dubai Chamber of Commerce and Industry, 25th Anniv. A88

1990, July 1 **Perf. 13**
320 A88 50f multicolored   .75   .75
321 A88 1d multicolored   1.50 1.50

World Cup Soccer Championships, Italy — A89

UAE emblem, character trademark and: 1d, Leaning Tower of Pisa, desert, vert. 2d, Soccer ball, vert. 250f, Circle of flags. 3d, Map, vert.

1990, June 8 **Perf. 13½**
322 A89 50f multicolored   .75   .75
323 A89 1d multicolored   1.50 1.50
324 A89 2d multicolored   3.00 3.00
325 A89 250f multicolored 4.00 4.00
  Nos. 322-325 (4)   9.25 9.25

Souvenir Sheet
Perf. 12½
326 A89 3d multicolored   7.00 7.00

A90

1990, Sept. 22 **Litho.** **Perf. 13½**
327 A90 50f shown   .75   .75
328 A90 1d Emblem, 30 years 2.25 2.25
329 A90 175f Emblem, drop of oil 3.50 3.50
  Nos. 327-329 (3)   6.50 6.50
Organization of Petroleum Exporting Countries (OPEC), 30th anniv.

A91

Flowers.

1990, Aug. 25 **Perf. 14x14½**
330 A91 50f Argyrolobeum roseum   .90   .90
331 A91 50f Lamranthus roseus   .90   .90
332 A91 50f Centavrea pseudo sinaica .90 .90
333 A91 50f Calotropis procera   .90   .90
  a. Souvenir sheet of 4, #330-333 4.50 4.50
334 A91 50f Nerium oleander   .90   .90
335 A91 50f Catharanthus roseus   .90   .90
336 A91 50f Hibiscus rosa sinensis 4.00 4.00
337 A91 50f Bougainvillea glabra 4.00 4.00
  a. Souvenir sheet of 4, #334-337 17.00 17.00
  Nos. 330-337 (8)   13.40 13.40

A92

1990, Oct. 8 **Litho.** **Perf. 13**
338 A92 50f Water pollution .50   .50
339 A92 3d Air pollution   3.25 3.25
Environmental pollution.

A93

1990, Dec. 2   *Perf. 13½*
340 A93 50f shown   .50 .50
341 A93 175f Bank building,
              horiz.   3.25 3.25
    Central Bank, 10th anniv.

Intl. Conference
on High Salinity
Tolerant
Plants — A94

1990, Dec. 8   *Perf. 13x13½*
342 A94 50f Tree   .50 .50
343 A94 250f Water, trees   2.75 2.75

Grand
Mosque, Abu
Dhabi — A95

2d, Al Jumeirah Mosque, Dubai, vert.

Perf. 13½x13, 13x13½
1990, Nov. 26
344 A95 1d multicolored   1.10 1.10
345 A95 2d multicolored   4.50 4.50

A96

1991, Jan. 16 Litho. Perf. 13x13½
346 A96 50f multicolored   1.00 1.00
347 A96 2d multicolored   2.50 2.50
    Abu Dhabi Intl. Fair.

A97

1991, May 17 Litho. Perf. 14x13½
348 A97 2d multicolored   3.00 3.00
349 A97 3d multicolored   4.50 4.50
    World Telecommunications Day.

A98

1991, June 18   *Perf. 13½*
350 A98 1d Sheikh Saqr Mosque 1.50 1.50
351 A98 2d King Faisal Mosque 3.25 3.25

Children's
Paintings
A99

Designs: 50f, Celebration. 1d, Women waving flags. 175f, Women playing blind-man's
buff. 250f, Women dancing for men.

1991, July 15 Litho. Perf. 14x13½
352 A99 50f multicolored   .60 .45
353 A99 1d multicolored   1.40 1.00
354 A99 175f multicolored 2.50 2.25
355 A99 250f multicolored 3.00 2.50
    Nos. 352-355 (4)   7.50 6.20

Fish
A100

1991, Aug. 5 Litho. Perf. 13½x14
356 A100 50f Yellow marked but-
              terflyfish   .60 .60
357 A100 50f Golden trevally .60 .60
358 A100 50f Two banded porgy .60 .60
359 A100 50f Red snapper   .60 .60
360 A100 1d Three banded
              grunt   1.25 1.25
361 A100 1d Rabbit fish   1.25 1.25
362 A100 1d Black bream   1.25 1.25
363 A100 1d Greasy grouper 1.25 1.25
    a. Min. sheet of 8, #356-363 8.50 8.50
    Nos. 356-363 (8)   7.40 7.40

A101

Intl. Aerospace Exhibition, Dubai: 175f, Jet
fighter over Dubai Intl. Airport. 2d, Fighter silhouette over airport.

1991, Nov. 3 Litho. Perf. 13½
364 A101 175f multicolored 2.25 2.25
365 A101 2d multicolored   2.50 2.50

A102

Sheikh Rashid Bin Said Al Maktum (1912-
90), Ruler of Dubai and: 50f, Airport, vert.
175f, City skyline, vert. 2d, Waterfront, satellite
dish.

1991, Oct. 7   *Perf. 13*
366 A102 50f multicolored   .50 .50
367 A102 1d multicolored   1.10 1.10
368 A102 175f multicolored 2.00 2.00
369 A102 2d multicolored   2.25 2.25
    Nos. 366-369 (4)   5.85 5.85

A103

1991, Oct. 8 Litho. Perf. 13½
370 A103 50f multicolored   .75 .75
371 A103 1d multicolored   1.75 1.75
    Civil Defense Day.

A104

A105

A106

20th Natl. Day — A107

#374, Emir at left, fortress, cannon. #377,
Fortress on rocky outcropping. #378, Emir at
right, fortress, cannon. 3d, Sheikh Said bin
Sultan al Nahayan, Defense Forces.

1991, Dec. 2 Litho. Perf. 13
372 A104 75f multicolored 1.20 1.20
373 A105 75f multicolored 1.20 1.20
374 A105 75f multicolored 1.20 1.20
375 A106 75f multicolored 1.20 1.20
376 A107 75f multicolored 1.20 1.20
377 A107 75f multicolored 1.20 1.20
378 A107 75f multicolored 1.20 1.20

Imperf
Size: 70x90mm
378A A107 3d multicolored 8.00 8.00
    Nos. 372-378A (8)   16.40 16.40

On Nos. 372-378 portions of the design
were applied by a thermographic process producing a shiny, raised effect.

A108

1991, Nov. 16   *Perf. 13½*
379 A108 50f lt green & multi .45 .45
380 A108 3d orange & multi 3.75 3.75
    Gulf Cooperaton Council, 10th anniv.

A109

1992, Jan. 15 Litho. Perf. 13½
381 A109 175f pink & multi 2.20 2.20
382 A109 250f lt blue & multi 2.50 2.50
    Abu Dhabi National Oil Co., 20th anniv.

Al-Jahli
Castle Al-
Ain
A110

1992, Apr. 20 Litho. Perf. 13½
383 A110 2d multicolored   2.00 2.00
384 A110 250f multicolored 60.00 60.00
    Expo '92, Seville.
No. 384 was withdrawn because of poor
rendition of Arabic word for "postage."

A111

Mosques: 50f, Sheikh Rashid bin Humaid al
Nuaimi, Ajman. 1d, Sheikh Ahmed Bin Rashid
Al Mualla, Umm Al Quwain.

1992, Mar. 26   *Perf. 14x13½*
385 A111 50f multicolored   .80 .80
386 A111 1d multicolored   1.60 1.60
    See Nos. 417-418.

A112

1992, Apr. 20   *Perf. 13½x13*
387 A112 1d shown   1.75 1.75
388 A112 3d Ear with hearing aid 4.00 4.00
    Week of the deaf child.

Zayed Seaport, 20th Anniv. — A113

1992, June 28 Litho. Perf. 13½
389 A113 50f Aerial view   .50 .50
390 A113 1d Cargo transport 1.25 1.25
391 A113 175f Ship docked   2.25 2.25
392 A113 2d Map   2.50 2.50
    Nos. 389-392 (4)   6.50 6.50

1992 Summer
Olympics,
Barcelona
A114

1992, July 25 Litho. Perf. 14x13½
393 A114 50f Yachting   .50 .50
394 A114 1d Running   1.00 1.00
395 A114 175f Swimming   2.00 2.00
396 A114 250f Cycling   2.25 2.25
    Nos. 393-396 (4)   5.75 5.75

Souvenir Sheet
396A A114 3d Equestrian   5.75 5.75

Children's
Paintings
A115

1992, Aug. 15   **Perf. 13½x14**
397 A115 50f Playing soccer   .50   .50
398 A115   1d Playing in field   1.00 1.00
399 A115   2d Playground   2.25 2.25
400 A115 250f Children among
                    trees   3.00 3.00
        Nos. 397-400 (4)   6.75 6.75

Intl. Bank of
United Arab
Emirates, 15th
Anniv. — A116

Design: 175f, Bank emblem.

Litho. & Embossed
1992, Sept. 9   **Perf. 11**
401 A116 50f gold & multi   .75   .75
        Size: 35x41mm
              Perf. 11½
402 A116 175f lake, gold & vio   2.25 2.25

Traditional Musical
Instruments — A116a

1992, Oct. 17   Litho.   Perf. 13½
402A A116a 50f Tambourah,
                    vert.   .60   .60
402B A116a 50f Oud, vert.   .60   .60
402C A116a 50f Rababah,
                    vert.   1.25 1.25
   g.   Sheet, #402A-402C, perf.
             12¾   3.50 3.50
402D A116a   1d Mizmar,
                    shindo   2.50 2.50
402E A116a   1d Tabel, hibban   2.50 2.50
402F A116a   1d Marwas, duff   2.50 2.50
   h.   Sheet, #402D-402F, perf.
             12¾   7.25 7.25
        Nos. 402A-402F (6)   9.95 9.95

Camels
A117

Designs: 50f, Race. 1d, Used for transportation, vert. 175f, Harnessed for obtaining water
from well. 2d, Roaming free, vert.

1992, Dec. 23   Litho.   Perf. 13½
403 A117 50f multicolored   .50   .30
404 A117   1d multicolored   1.25 .70
405 A117 175f multicolored   2.50 1.25
406 A117   2d multicolored   2.75 1.50
        Nos. 403-406 (4)   7.00 3.75

A118

1992, Dec. 21
407 A118 50f multicolored   1.25 1.25
408 A118   2d yellow & multi   5.50 5.50

Gulf Cooperation Council, 13th session.

A119

1993, Jan. 28   Litho.   Perf. 13½
409 A119   2d shown   2.50 2.50
410 A119 250f Building, fishing
                    boat   4.25 4.25

Dubai Creek Golf and Yacht Club.

A120

1993, Jan. 16
411 A120 50f Golf, horiz.   .75   .75
412 A120   1d Fishing   1.50 1.50
413 A120   2d Boating, horiz.   3.00 3.00
414 A120 250f Motor vehicle
              touring, horiz.   3.75 3.75
        Nos. 411-414 (4)   9.00 9.00

Tourism.

A121

1993, Mar. 27   Litho.   Perf. 14x13½
415 A121 50f violet & multi   1.00 1.00
416 A121   3d red brown & multi   4.00 4.00

Natl. Youth Festival.

Mosque Type of 1992
1993, Feb. 16   **Perf. 13½**
   50f, Thabit bin Khalid Mosque, Fujeira. 1d,
Sharq al Morabbah Mosque, Al Ain.

417 A111 50f multicolored   1.25 1.25
418 A111   1d multicolored   2.50 2.50

Shells
A122

1993, Apr. 3   Litho.   Perf. 13
419 A122 25f Conus textile   .35   .35
420 A122 50f Pinctada
                    radiata   .50   .50
421 A122 100f Murex scolopax   1.00 1.00
422 A122 150f Natica pulicaris   1.50 1.50

423 A122 175f Lambis truncata
                    sebae   2.25 2.25
424 A122 200f Cardita bicolor   2.50 2.50
425 A122 250f Cypraea
                    grayana   3.00 3.00
426 A122 300f Cymatium
                    trilineatum   4.00 4.00
        Nos. 419-426 (8)   15.10 15.10

Campaign
Against
Drugs
A123

Design: 1d, Skull, drugs, vert.

1993, Aug. 21   Litho.   Perf. 13½
427 A123 50f multicolored   1.60 1.60
428 A123   1d multicolored   2.25 2.25

A124

Natl. Bank of Abu Dhabi, 25th Anniv.: 50f,
Abu Dhabi skyline, bank emblem. 1d, Bank
emblem. 175f, Bank building, emblem. 2d,
Skyline, emblem, diff.

Litho. & Typo.
1993, Sept. 15   **Perf. 11½**
429 A124 50f silver & multi   .55   .55
430 A124   1d silver & multi   1.10 1.10
431 A124 175f silver & multi   2.50 2.50
432 A124   2d silver & multi   2.75 2.75
        Nos. 429-432 (4)   6.90 6.90

A125

Dubai Ports Authority: 50f, Aerial view of
port. 1d, Loading cargo. 2d, Aerial view, diff.
250f, Globe.

1993, Nov. 10   Litho.   Perf. 13½
433 A125 50f purple & multi   .60   .60
434 A125   1d green & multi   1.50 1.50
435 A125   2d orange & multi   3.00 3.00
436 A125 250f pink & multi   3.75 3.75
        Nos. 433-436 (4)   8.85 8.85

Natl. Day
A126

Children's paintings: 50f, Soldiers saluting
flag. 1d, Two women sitting, one standing,
flag, vert. 175f, Flag, boat. 2d, Flags atop castle tower.

1993, Dec. 2   Litho.   Perf. 13½
437 A126 50f multicolored   .60   .60
438 A126   1d multicolored   1.50 1.50
439 A126 175f multicolored   2.75 2.75
440 A126   2d multicolored   3.00 3.00
        Nos. 437-440 (4)   7.85 7.85

Archaeological Discoveries — A127

Designs: 50f, Tomb. 1d, Rectangular artifact. 175f, Animal-shaped artifact. 250f, Bowl.

1993, Dec. 15   **Perf. 14x13½**
441 A127 50f multicolored   .60   .60
442 A127   1d multicolored   1.40 1.40
443 A127 175f multicolored   2.50 2.50
444 A127 250f multicolored   3.25 3.25
        Nos. 441-444 (4)   7.75 7.75

10th
Childrens'
Festival,
Sharjah
A128

Children's paintings: 50f, Children with balloons, flags. 1d, Children playing, three trees.
175f, Child with picture, girls with balloons. 2d,
House, children playing outdoors.

1994, Mar. 19   Litho.   Perf. 13x13½
445 A128 50f green & multi   .60   .60
446 A128   1d blue & multi   1.50 1.50
447 A128 175f red violet & multi   2.50 2.50
448 A128   2d carmine & multi   2.75 2.75
        Nos. 445-448 (4)   7.35 7.35

Arabian
Horses
A129

50f, Brown horse on hind feet, vert. 1d,
White horse. 175f, Head of brown horse, vert.
250f, Head of white and brown horse.

1994, Jan. 25   Perf. 13x13½, 13½x13
449 A129 50f multicolored   .60   .60
450 A129   1d multicolored   1.50 1.50
451 A129 175f multicolored   2.50 2.50
452 A129 250f multicolored   3.25 3.25
        Nos. 449-452 (4)   7.85 7.85

10th
Conference
of Arab
Towns,
Dubai
A130

              Perf. 13x13½, 13½x13
1994, May 15   **Litho.**
453 A100 50f Map, city, vert.   .55   .55
454 A130   1d shown   2.25 2.25

Pilgrimage to
Mecca — A131

1994, Apr. 29   Litho.   Perf. 13x13½
455 A131 50f shown   .75   .75
456 A131   2d Holy Ka'aba   3.00 3.00

Intl. Year of the Family
A132

Intl. Olympic Committee, Cent. A133

Arab Housing Day — A134

Writers Assoc., 10th Anniv. — A135

1994, June 15   **Perf. 13x13½**
457 A132 1d multicolored   1.40 1.40
458 A133 1d multicolored   1.40 1.40
    Perf. 13½x13
459 A134 1d multicolored   1.40 1.40
460 A135 1d multicolored   1.40 1.40
   Nos. 457-460 (4)   5.60 5.60

Archaeological Finds, Al Qusais, Dubai — A136

Designs: 50f, Lidded pitcher, vert. 1d, Pointed-handle pitcher. 175f, Pitcher, arm-shaped handle. 250f, Short round vase.

1994, Aug. 16   **Litho.**   **Perf. 13½**
461 A136 50f multicolored   .55 .55
462 A136 1d multicolored   1.30 1.30
463 A136 175f multicolored   2.20 2.20
464 A136 250f multicolored   3.00 3.00
   Nos. 461-464 (4)   7.05 7.05

Environmental Protection — A137

Designs: 50f, Arabian leopard. 1d, Gordon's wildcat. 2d, Caracal. 250f, Sand cat.

1994, Oct. 10   **Litho.**   **Perf. 13½**
465 A137 50f multicolored   .60 .60
466 A137 1d multicolored   1.60 1.60
467 A137 2d multicolored   3.50 3.50
468 A137 250f multicolored   4.25 4.25
   Nos. 465-468 (4)   9.95 9.95

12th Arab Gulf Soccer Championships, Abu Dhabi — A138

1994, Nov. 3   **Litho.**   **Perf. 13½**
469 A138 50f Ball, emblem, vert.   .55 .55
470 A138 3d Soccer players   3.75 3.75

Birds A139

50f, Merops orientalis. 175f, Halcyon chloris. 2d, Dromas ardeola. 250f, Coracias benghalensis. 3d, Phoenicopterus ruber.

1994, Dec. 12
471 A139 50f multicolored   .60 .60
472 A139 175f multicolored   3.25 3.25
473 A139 2d multicolored   3.50 3.50
474 A139 250f multicolored   5.50 5.50
   Nos. 471-474 (4)   12.85 12.85
   Souvenir Sheet
475 A139 3d multi, vert.   8.00 8.00

Archaeological Finds, Mulaiha, Sharjah — A140

Designs: 50f, Front of carved horse, vert. 175f, Ancient coin, vert. 2d, Inscription on metal, vert. 250f, Inscription on stone.

1995, Jan. 25   **Litho.**   **Perf. 13½**
476 A140 50f multicolored   .55 .55
477 A140 175f multicolored   2.25 2.25
478 A140 2d multicolored   3.00 3.00
479 A140 250f multicolored   3.25 3.25
   Nos. 476-479 (4)   9.05 9.05

Natl. Dances A141

1995, Feb. 14
480 A141 50f Al-Naashat   .50 .50
481 A141 175f Al-Ayaalah   2.10 2.10
482 A141 2d Al-Shahhoh   2.40 2.40
   Nos. 480-482 (3)   5.00 5.00

A142

1995, Mar. 19   **Litho.**   **Perf. 13½**
483 A142 50f Helicopters   .50 .50
484 A142 1d Emblem   1.50 1.50
485 A142 175f Warships, horiz.   2.75 2.75
486 A142 2d Artillery, horiz.   3.25 3.25
   Nos. 483-486 (4)   8.00 8.00
Intl. Defense Exhibition & Conf., Abu Dhabi.

A143

1995, Mar. 22
487 A143 1d Arab League emblem   1.25 1.25
488 A143 2d FAO emblem   2.75 2.75
489 A143 250f UN emblem   3.50 3.50
   Nos. 487-489 (3)   7.50 7.50
50th Anniv. of Arab League, FAO & UN.

General Post Office Authority, 10th Anniv. — A144

1995, Apr. 1
490 A144 50f multicolored   .75 .75

First Gulf Cooperation Council Philatelic Exhibition, Abu Dhabi — A145

1995, Apr. 11   **Litho.**   **Perf. 13½**
491 A145 50f multicolored   .75 .75

Traditional Games, Ajman Museum — A146

50f, Boy with hoop, stick. 175f, Girl on swing. 2d, Boy, girl playing stick game within marked boundary. 250f, Two girls playing game with stones.

1995, Aug. 28   **Litho.**   **Perf. 13½x13**
492 A146 50f multicolored   .45 .45
493 A146 175f multicolored   1.90 1.90
494 A146 2d multicolored   2.25 2.25
495 A146 250f multicolored   2.50 2.50
   Nos. 492-495 (4)   7.10 7.10

A147

Birds: 50f, Falco naumanni. 175f, Phalacrocorax nigrogularis. 2d, Cursorius cursor. 250f, Upupa epops.

1995, Sept. 25
496 A147 50f multicolored   .55 .55
497 A147 175f multicolored   2.10 2.10
498 A147 2d multicolored   2.50 2.50
499 A147 250f multicolored   2.75 2.75
   Nos. 496-499 (4)   7.90 7.90
   See Nos. 528-532.

A148

Natl. Census: 50f, Stylized family, building. 250f, Mosque, skyscrapers, stylized family.

1995, Nov. 20
500 A148 50f multicolored   .50 .50
501 A148 250f multicolored   2.50 2.50

National Day A149

Children's paintings: 50f, People wearing feathered headdresses, palm trees, building. 175f, Girls with flags, balloons, flowers. 2d, Trees, family in front of house holding balloons, flags. 250f, Groups of children along street watching parade of cars.

1995, Dec. 2   **Perf. 13x13½**
502 A149 50f multicolored   .45 .45
503 A149 175f multicolored   1.25 1.25
504 A149 2d multicolored   1.40 1.40
505 A149 250f multicolored   1.75 1.75
   Nos. 502-505 (4)   4.85 4.85

Environmental Protection — A150

1996, Jan. 25   **Litho.**   **Perf. 13x13½**
506 A150 50f Dugong dugon   .50 .50
507 A150 2d Delphinus delphis   1.50 1.50
508 A150 3d Megaptera novae-angliae   2.25 2.25
   a.   Souvenir sheet, #506-508   4.75 4.75
   Nos. 506-508 (3)   4.25 4.25

A151

1996, Feb. 27   **Perf. 13½**
509 A151 50f shown   .50 .50
510 A151 3d Building, beach   2.75 2.75
Hobie Cat 16 World Sailing Championships.

A152

Archaelogical Finds, Fujeira Museum: 50f, Two-handled pitcher. 175f, Kettle. 250f, Bracelet. 3d, Metal ornament, horiz.

1996, Apr. 15
511	A152	50f multicolored	.50	.50
512	A152	175f multicolored	1.25	1.25
513	A152	250f multicolored	2.25	2.25
514	A152	3d multicolored	2.75	2.75
		Nos. 511-514 (4)	6.75	6.75

1996 Summer Olympic Games, Atlanta A153

Perf. 13½x14, 14x 13½
1996, July 19 — *Litho.*
515	A153	50f Shooting	.50	.50
516	A153	1d Cycling, vert.	.80	.80
517	A153	250f Running, vert.	2.00	2.00
518	A153	350f Swimming	2.50	2.50
		Nos. 515-518 (4)	5.80	5.80

Women's Union, 21st Anniv. A154

Perf. 14x13½, 13½x14
1996, Aug. 15
519	A154	50f Emblem, vert.	.50	.50
520	A154	3d shown	2.75	2.75

A155

1996, Sept. 15 — *Perf. 14x13½*
521	A155	1d shown	.75	.75
522	A155	250f Soccer player	2.00	2.00

11th Asian Soccer Cup Championship.

A156

UN Campaign Against Illegal Use of Drugs: 50f, World with snake around it. 3d, Half of man's face, half of skull, hypodermic needle, pills.

1996, Oct. 15 — *Perf. 13½*
523	A156	50f multicolored	.75	.75
524	A156	3d multicolored	2.75	2.75

Sheikh Saeed Al-Maktoum House, Cent. — A157

Designs: 250f Sheikh Saeed, close-up view of house. 350f, Overall view of house.

1996, Nov. 12 — *Litho.* — *Perf. 13x13½*
525	A157	50f multicolored	.50	.50
526	A157	250f multicolored	1.75	1.75
527	A157	350f multicolored	2.50	2.50
		Nos. 525-527 (3)	4.75	4.75

Bird Type of 1995
Designs: 50f, Pterocles exustus. 150f, Otus brucei. 250f, Hypocolus ampelinus. 3d, Irania gutturalis. 350f, Falco concolor.

1996, Nov. 18 — *Perf. 14x13½*
528	A147	50f multicolored	.35	.35
529	A147	150f multicolored	1.25	1.25
530	A147	250f multicolored	2.25	2.25
531	A147	3d multicolored	3.00	3.00
532	A147	350f multicolored	3.25	3.25
		Nos. 528-532 (5)	10.10	10.10

Children's Paintings A158

50f, Face. 1d, Boats. 250f, Flowers. 350f, Woman in long dress, palm tree, tent.

Perf. 14x13½, 13½x14
1996, Nov. 19
533	A158	50f multi, vert.	.35	.35
534	A158	1d multi	.80	.80
535	A158	250f multi, vert.	2.25	2.25
536	A158	350f multi, vert.	2.75	2.75
		Nos. 533-536 (4)	6.15	6.15

Sheik Zaid bin Sultan al Nahayan, Accession to the Throne of Abu Dhabi, 30th Anniv. A158a

A159

Sheik and: 50f, 250f, Flowers. 1d, 350f, Date palm.

1996, Dec. 2 — *Photo.* — *Perf. 12*
537	A158a	50f red & multi	.40	.40
538	A158a	1d olive & multi	.65	.65
539	A158a	250f purple & multi	1.60	1.60
540	A158a	350f gray & multi	2.25	2.25
		Nos. 537-540 (4)	4.90	4.90

Photo. & Embossed
Imperf
Size: 90x70mm
541	A159	5d On horseback, gazelles	5.00	5.00

Anniversaries A160

Photo. & Embossed
1996, Dec. 2 — *Perf. 12*
542	A160	50f red violet & multi	.30	.30
543	A160	1d silver & multi	1.40	1.40

Sheik Zaid bin Sultan al Nahayan's accession to the throne of Abu Dhabi, 30th anniv., Creation of United Arab Emirates, 25th anniv.

Natl. Day, 25th Anniv. — A161

50f, 150f, Seven rulers of United Arab Emirates. 1d, 3d, Heraldic eagle, national flag. 5d, Score of Natl. Anthem.

1996, Dec. 2 — *Granite Paper*
544	A161	50f green & multi	.70	.70
545	A161	1d multicolored	1.25	1.25
546	A161	150f tan & multi	1.60	1.60
547	A161	3d multicolored	3.25	3.25
		Nos. 544-547 (4)	6.80	6.80

Photo. & Embossed
Imperf
Size: 70x90mm
547A	A161	5d multicolored	5.50	5.50

Butterflies A162

1997, Jan. 28 — *Litho.* — *Perf. 14x13½*
548	A162	50f Agrodiaetus loewii	.60	.60
549	A162	1d Papilio machaon	1.25	1.25
550	A162	150f Orithya	1.90	1.90
551	A162	250f Chrysippus	3.25	3.25
		Nos. 548-551 (4)	7.00	7.00

Dubai Shopping Festival A163

1997, Feb. 22 — *Litho.*
552	A163	50f shown	.50	.50
553	A163	250f Shopping bag, vert.	2.50	2.50

Intl. Defense Exhibition & Conference A164

50f, Helicopter airlifting jeep. 1d, Emblem. 250f, Artillery, emblem. 350f, Ships, emblem.

1997, Mar. 16 — *Litho.* — *Perf. 13½*
554	A164	50f multicolored	.50	.50
555	A164	1d multicolored	.85	.85
556	A164	250f multicolored	2.25	2.25
557	A164	350f multicolored	3.25	3.25
		Nos. 554-557 (4)	6.85	6.85

Emirates Bank Group, 20th Anniv. — A165

Perf. 13¾x13¼
1997, Mar. 23 — *Litho.*
568	A165	50f multi	.55	.55
569	A165	1d buff & multi	1.20	1.20
a.		Souv. sheet, #568-569, imperf.	6.00	6.00

No. 569a sold for 5d.

Technical Education and National Development Conference A166

1997, Apr. 6 — *Perf. 13¾x13¼*
570	A166	50f shown	.75	.75
571	A166	250f Emblem	2.75	2.75

Sharjah Heritage A167

Designs: 50f, Coins. 3d, Museum.

1997, June 17 — *Litho.* — *Perf. 13½*
572	A167	50f multicolored	.75	.75
573	A167	3d multicolored	3.25	3.25

Emirates Philatelic Association A168

Perf. 13¾x13¼, 13¼x13¾
1997, June 24 — *Litho.*
574	A168	50f shown	.50	.50
575	A168	250f Stamps, horiz.	2.50	2.50

Children's Paintings A169

50f, Cats. 1d, Children playing. 250f, Children, moon, vert. 3d, Abstract.

1997, Sept. 15 — *Litho.* — *Perf. 13½*
576	A169	50f multicolored	.55	.55
577	A169	1d multicolored	.95	.95
578	A169	250f multicolored	2.25	2.25
579	A169	3d multicolored	3.00	3.00
		Nos. 576-579 (4)	6.75	6.75

Reunion, by Sheikha Hassan Maktoum al Maktoum — A170

Mindscape, by Sarah Majid al Futtaim
A170a

Blue Musings, by Maha Abdulla Al
Mazroui — A170b

The
Pause,
by
Khulood
Mattar
Rashid
A170c

The Seas I, by   Still Life, by
Sheikha Sawsan   Sheikha Bodour
Abdulaziz Al   Sultan Al Qasimi
Qasimi — A170d   A170e

The Opening, by Tina Ahmed and
Others — 170f

1997, Oct. 25   Litho.   Perf. 13¾
580	A170	50f multi	.65	.65
581	A170a	50f multi	.65	.65
582	A170b	50f multi	.65	.65
583	A170c	50f multi	.65	.65
584	A170d	50f multi	.65	.65
585	A170e	50f multi	.65	.65
		Nos. 580-585 (6)	3.90	3.90

Imperf
586	A170f	5d multi	7.50	7.50

Intl.
Aerospace
Exhibition,
Dubai
A171

Perf. 13½x13¾
1997, Nov. 16   Litho.
587	A171	250f Jet fighter	3.00	3.00
588	A171	3d VTOL airplane	3.75	3.75

26th
National
Day
A172

Sheikh Zaid bin Sultan al Nahayan and: 50f,
Gardens. 1d, Trees and mountains. 150f,
Water, trees and mountains. 250f, Roadway.

1997, Dec. 2   Litho.   Perf. 13½x13¾
589	A172	50f multi	.45	.45
590	A172	1d multi	.75	.75
591	A172	150f multi	1.20	1.20
592	A172	250f multi	1.75	1.75
		Nos. 589-592 (4)	4.15	4.15

3rd Afro-
Arab Trade
Fair
A173

Perf. 13x13¼, 13¼x13
1997, Dec. 6   Litho.
593	A173	150f Emblem, vert.	1.25	1.25
594	A173	350f Handshake	2.75	2.75

Arthropods
A174

50f, Blepharopsis mendica. 150f, Galeodes
sp. 250f, Crocothemis arythraea. 350f,
Xylocopa aestuans.

1998, Feb. 25   Litho.   Perf. 13¼
595	A174	50f multicolored	.55	.55
596	A174	150f multicolored	1.50	1.50
597	A174	250f multicolored	2.50	2.50
598	A174	350f multicolored	3.25	3.25
		Nos. 595-598 (4)	7.80	7.80

ISAF World Sailing
Championship — A175

Various sailboats.

Perf. 13¼x13, 13x13¼
1998, Mar. 2   Litho.
599	A175	50f multi, vert.	.45	.45
600	A175	1d multi	1.25	1.25
601	A175	250f multi	2.10	2.10
602	A175	3d multi, vert.	3.00	3.00
		Nos. 599-602 (4)	6.80	6.80

A176

Triple Intl. Defense Exhibition & Conf., Abu
Dhabi: 50f, Combat soldiers in protective gear,
horiz. 1d, Emblem over world map, skyline of
Abu Dhabi. 150f, Electronic gear. 350f, Missile
battery, electronic warfare components.

1998, Mar. 15   Litho.   Perf. 13½
603	A176	50f multicolored	.45	.45
604	A176	1d multicolored	1.25	1.25
605	A176	150f multicolored	2.10	2.10
606	A176	350f multicolored	3.00	3.00
		Nos. 603-606 (4)	6.80	6.80

A177

1998, Apr. 20   Litho.   Perf. 13½
607	A177	50f shown	.50	.50
608	A177	3d Emblem, monument	3.75	3.75

Sharjah, 1998 Arab cultural capital.

World
Environment
Day — A178

1998, May 17   Litho.   Perf. 13½
609	A178	1d Landscape, oryx	1.75	1.75
610	A178	350f multicolored	3.00	3.00

Henna
A179

Various designs painted on hands.

1998, Sept. 9   Litho.   Perf. 13½
611	A179	50f multicolored	.60	.60
612	A179	1d multicolored	.90	.90
613	A179	150f multicolored	1.40	1.40
614	A179	2d multicolored	1.75	1.75
615	A179	250f multicolored	2.25	2.25
616	A179	3d multicolored	2.75	2.75
		Nos. 611-616 (6)	9.65	9.65

Art — A180

1998, Oct. 20   Litho.   Perf. 13½
617	A180	50f Fish	.50	.50
618	A180	1d shown	.95	.95
619	A180	250f Mosque, palm trees, vert.	2.25	2.25
620	A180	350f Door, jar	3.25	3.25
		Nos. 617-620 (4)	6.95	6.95

27th
National
Day
A181

1998, Dec. 2   Litho.   Perf. 13x13½
621	A181	50f Mountain road	.45	.45
622	A181	350f Boat, city skyline	4.25	4.25

Flowers — A182

Designs: 25f, Indigofera arabica. 50f,
Centaureum pulchellum. 75f, Lavandula citri-
odora. 1d, Taverniera glabra. 150f, Convolvu-
lus deserti. 2d, Capparis spinosa. 250f,
Rumex vesicrius. 3d, Anagallis arvensis. 350f,
Tribulus arabicus. 5d, Reichardia tinitana.

1998, Dec. 8   Litho.   Perf. 13¼x13¾
623	A182	25f multicolored	.25	.25
624	A182	50f multicolored	.45	.45
625	A182	75f multicolored	.60	.60
626	A182	1d multicolored	.80	.80
627	A182	150f multicolored	1.25	1.25
628	A182	2d multicolored	1.60	1.60
629	A182	250f multicolored	2.10	2.10
630	A182	3d multicolored	2.50	2.50
631	A182	350f multicolored	2.75	2.75
632	A182	5d multicolored	4.00	4.00
		Nos. 623-632 (10)	16.30	16.30

Arthropods
A183

50f, Anthia duodecimguttata. 150f, Daphnis
nerii. 250f, Acorypha glaucopsis. 350f,
Androctonus crassicauda.

1999, Mar. 15   Litho.   Perf. 13½x14
633	A183	50f multicolored	.60	.60
634	A183	150f multicolored	1.40	1.40
635	A183	250f multicolored	2.75	2.75
636	A183	350f multicolored	4.25	4.25
		Nos. 633-636 (4)	9.00	9.00

Intl. Day for
Monuments
and Sites
A184

1999, Apr. 18   Litho.   Perf. 13x13½
637	A184	150f shown	1.50	1.50
638	A184	250f Fort	2.75	2.75

UPU, 125th
Anniv. — A185

1999   Litho.   Perf. 13½x13
639	A185	50f shown	1.00	1.00
640	A185	350f Emblem, "125"	2.75	2.75

Imperf
Size: 90x70mm
641	A185	5d Hemispheres	6.00	6.00

Environmental Protection — A186

Marine life: 50f, Lamprometra klunzingeri.
150f, Pelagia noctiluca. 250f, Hexabranchus
sanguineus. 3d, Siphonochalina siphonella.

1999, Nov. 3   Litho.   Perf. 13½x14
642	A186	50f multi	.60	.60
643	A186	150f multi	2.00	2.00
644	A186	250f multi	3.25	3.25
645	A186	3d multi	3.75	3.75
		Nos. 642-645 (4)	9.60	9.60

Handicrafts
A187

Designs: 50f, Lacemaking. 1d, Embroidery. 250f, Woman with wickerwork. 350f, Finished wickerwork.

1999, Nov. 8   **Perf. 14x13½**
646 A187 50f multi .60 .60
647 A187 1d multi 1.40 1.40
648 A187 250f multi 3.50 3.50
649 A187 350f multi 5.50 5.50
     Nos. 646-649 (4) 11.00 11.00

14th Pro World Ten-pin Bowling Championships A188

Designs: 50f, Emblem. 250f, Bowler, pins, Abu Dhabi skyline.

1999, Nov. 16 Litho. Perf. 14x13½
650-651 A188 Set of 2 3.25 3.25

Children's Art — A189

Art by: 50f, Nooran Khaleefa. 1d, Khawla Al Hawal. 150f, Khawla Salem. 250f, Fatimah Ibrahim.

1999, Dec. 15 Perf. 13x13½
652-655 A189 Set of 4 5.75 5.75

Millennium A190

Falcon and "2000" in: 50f, Gray and silver. 250f, Blue and gold.

1999, Dec. 22 Perf. 13½x13
656-657 A190 Set of 2 2.75 2.75

Dubai Ports and Customs, Cent. A191

50f, Old building. 3d, Modern building.

2000, Jan. 26 Perf. 13x13½
658-659 A191 Set of 2 3.75 3.75

Intl. Desertification Conference, Dubai — A192

2000, Feb. 12 Perf. 13½x13
660 A192 250f multi 2.50 2.50

Environmental Protection — A193

Designs: 50f, Palm trees, Al Gheel. 250f, Aggah Beach.

2000, Feb. 29 Litho. Perf. 13x13½
661 A193 50f multi .50 .50
662 A193 250f multi 2.25 2.25

2000 Summer Olympics, Sydney A194

Emblem and: 50f, Swimmer. 2d, Runner. 350f, Shooter.

2000, Sept. 16 Litho. Perf. 13x13½
663-665 A194 Set of 3 4.25 4.25

Dubai Intl. Holy Koran Award — A195

50f, Medal on ribbon of flags. 250f, Sheikh Zaid bin Sultan al Nahayan and UAE flag.

2000, Sept. 23 Perf. 13½x13
666-667 A195 Set of 2 4.25 4.25

World Meteorological Organization, 50th Anniv. — A196

Designs: 50f, Barometer and modern map. 250f, Gauge's pointer and old map .

2000
668-669 A196 Set of 2 4.25 4.25

Expansion of Dubai Intl. Airport A197

Denominations: 50f, 350f.

2000, Nov. 4 Litho. Perf. 13x13½
670-671 A197 Set of 2 5.75 5.75

Development and Environment A198

Designs: 50f, Smile. 250f, Flower. 3d, Heart as leaf. 350f, Heart as globe.

2001, Mar. 20 Litho. Perf. 13¼x13
672-675 A198 Set of 4 10.00 10.00

Dubai Millennium, Winner of 2000 Dubai World Cup A199

Designs: 3d, Horse's head. 350f, Horse at track.

2001, Mar. 24 Perf. 13x13¼
676-677 A199 Set of 2 9.50 9.50

Sultan Bin Ali Al Owais (1925-2000), Poet — A200

Designs: 50f, Calligraphy. 1d, Portrait.

2001, Apr. 30 Perf. 13¼x13
678-679 A200 Set of 2 3.75 3.75

Arab Bank for Investment and Foreign Trade, 25th Anniv. — A201

Designs: 50f, Emblem. 1d, Emblem, diff.

2001, July 7 Litho. Perf. 13¼x13
680-681 A201 Set of 2 2.75 2.75

7th GCC Postage Stamp Exhibition, Dubai — A202

2001, July 10
682 A202 50f multi 1.75 1.75

Traditional Boats A203

Designs: 50f, Shahoof. 250f, Bagarah. 3d, Sam'aa. 350f, Jalboot.

2001, Aug. 25 Perf. 14x13¼
683-686 A203 Set of 4 10.00 10.00

Year of Dialogue Among Civilizations A204

Designs: 50f, Emblem. 250f, Branch with multicolored leaves.

2001, Oct. 9 Perf. 13¼x13
687-688 A204 Set of 2 3.75 3.75

Emirates Post A205

Falcons and inscription: 50f, Changing. 250f, Growing. 3d, Achieving.

2001, Sept. 15 Perf. 13x13¼
689-691 A205 Set of 3 7.50 7.50

Children's Art — A206

Designs: 1d, Mosque. 250f, Boatbuilding. 3d, Man pouring coffee, vert. 350f, Falconry.

Perf. 14x13¼, 13¼x14
2001, Nov. 12 Litho.
692-695 A206 Set of 4 10.50 10.50

Unification of Armed Forces, 25th Anniv. — A207

2001, Dec. 30 Perf. 13¼x13
696 A207 1d multi 2.75 2.75

Intl. Water Resources and Management Conference, Dubai — A208

2002, Feb. 2
697 A208 50f multi 2.00 2.00

UAE University, 25th Anniv. — A209

Background colors: 50f, Blue. 1d, Red.

2002, Mar. 25 Perf. 13¼x14
698-699 A209 Set of 2 2.75 2.75

Arabian
Saluki
A210

Various salukis: 50f, 150f, 250f, 3d.

2002, Apr. 29 Litho. Perf. 13½x13¼
700-703 A210 Set of 4   14.00 14.00

Emirates Post, 1st
Anniv. — A211

"1" and: 50f, Ring of text. 3d, Emblem.

2002, May 29   Perf. 13¼x13
704 A211 50f blue   2.00 2.00
Souvenir Sheet
Perf. 14¼
705 A211 3d multi   11.50 11.50
No. 705 contains one 45x35mm stamp.

Rashid Bin
Salim Al-
Suwaidi Al-
Khadhar
(1905-80),
Poet
A212

Designs: 50f, Text. 250f, Portrait.

2002, July 17 Litho. Perf. 13½x13¼
706-707 A212 Set of 2   6.50 6.50

Children's
Creativity
A213

Designs: 50f, Antelope and boat, by Amna
al-Bloushi. 1d, Children, by Fahd al-Habsi. 2d,
Earth holding flower, by Hana Mohammed.
250f, Fish, by Hatem al-Dhaheri. 3d, Child
holding Earth, by Abdulla Ridha. 350f, Stick
figures, by Yousef al-Sind. 5d, Emblem of
Latifa Bint Mohammed Award for Childhood
Creativity (29x39mm).

Perf. 13x13¼, 13¼x13 (5d)
2002, Oct. 9
708-714 A213 Set of 7   17.50 17.50

Sheikh
Hamdan Bin
Rashid Al-
Maktoum
Award for
Medical
Sciences
A214

Designs: 50f, Award, emblem, sand dunes.
250f, Caduceus, map.

2002, Oct. 21   Perf. 13x13¼
715-716 A214 Set of 2   4.75 4.75

31st National
Day — A215

Landmarks in the Emirates: Nos. 717, 724a,
50f, Ajman. Nos. 718, 724b, 50f, Sharjah. Nos.
719, 724c, 50f, Dubai. Nos. 720, 724d, 50f,
Abu Dhabi. Nos. 721, 724e, 50f, Ras al
Khaima. Nos. 722, 724f, Fujeira. Nos. 723,
724g, Umm al Qiwain.

2002, Dec. 2 Litho. Perf. 13¼x14
717-723 A215 Set of 7   7.50 7.50
Souvenir Sheet
Litho. & Embossed
Imperf
724   Sheet of 7   7.50 7.50
a.-g.   A215 50f Any single   1.00 1.00
No. 724 sold for 5d.

Thuraya Satellite
Communications
A216

Denominations: 25f, 250f.

2002   Litho.   Perf. 14
725-726 A216 Set of 2   2.75 2.75
Issued: 25f, 1/27; 250f, 1/6.

Falcon Type of 1990
2003-04   Litho.   Perf. 11½
Granite Paper
726A A85 125f multi   .90   .90
Size: 21x26mm
Perf. 11½x11¾
726B A85 225f multi   1.50 1.50
726C A85 275f multi   2.00 2.00
726D A85 325f multi   2.75 2.75
726E A85 375f multi   1.90 1.90
726F A85   4d multi   2.25 2.25
726G A85   6d multi   3.00 3.00
        Nos. 726A-726G (7)   14.30 14.30
Issued: 125f, 2/23; 225f, 11/24/04; 275f,
325f, 375f, 4/13; 4d, 6d, 9/16.

Items in Al
Ain National
Museum
A217

Designs: 50f, Jar from Hili tombs. 275f, Pottery from Umm an-Nar tombs. 4d, Bronze axe.
6d, Soapstone vessel.

2003, Feb. 25   Perf. 14x13½
727-730 A217 Set of 4   11.50 11.50

National
Bank of
Dubai, 40th
Anniv. A218

Panel color: 50f, Blue. 4d, Orange. 6d, Red.

2003, Apr. 15 Litho. Perf. 14x13¼
731-733 A218 Set of 3   10.50 10.50

Miniature Sheet

Wildlife — A218a

No. 733A: b, Arabian leopard. c, Blanford's
fox. d, Caracal. e, Cheetah. f, Gordon's wild
cat. g, Striped hyena. h, Jackal. i, White-tailed
mongoose. j, Ruppell's fox. k, Sand cat. l,
Small spotted genet. m, Arabian wolf.

2003, June 10 Litho. Perf. 14½
733A A218a 50f Sheet of 12, #b-
      m   8.00 8.00

Coins
A219

Designs: 50f, Dirham of Caliph Al Walid bin
Abdul Malik. 125f, Arab Sasanian Dirham of
Caliph Abdul Malik Bin Marwan. 275f, Dinar of
Al Mustansir Billah Al Fatimi. 375f, Dinar of
Caliph Abdul Malik bin Marwan.
5d, Dirham of Caliph Muhammed Al Ameen
to mark election of Mousa Al Natiq Bilhaq.

2003, July 20 Litho. Perf. 13¼x13¾
734-737 A219 Set of 4   7.50 7.50
Size: 106x73mm
Imperf
738   A219 5d multi   20.00 20.00

Sheikh Zaid
bin Sultan
al Nahayan,
37th Anniv.
of
Accession
as Ruler of
Abu Dhabi
A220

Sheikh Zaid and: 50f, Camel and sand
dune. 175f, Modern buildings.

2003, Aug. 6 Litho.   Perf. 13
739-740 A220 Set of 2   2.75 2.75

World Youth Soccer Championships,
United Arab Emirates — A221

2003, Sept. 7   Perf. 13x13¼
741   A221 375f multi   3.75 3.75

World Bank
Boards of
Governors Annual
Meetings,
Dubai — A222

Emblem and: 50f, Emirates Tower. 175f, Falcon. 275f, Mosque domes, horiz. 375f, Dhow.
5d, English and Arabic text.

Perf. 13¼x13, 13x13¼
2003, Sept. 23   Litho.
742-745 A222 Set of 4   8.50 8.50
Imperf
Size: 118x74mm
746   A222 5d multi   6.75 6.75

Peace
A223

Dove and: 50f, Zakharafs. 225f, Door and
wind tower. 275f, Columns. 325f, Water taxi.

2003, Oct. 1   Perf. 13x13¼
747-750 A223 Set of 4   9.50 9.50

Traditional
Housing
A224

Designs: 50f, Palm frond house. 175f, Mud
house. 275f, Stone house. 325f, Tent.

2003, Oct. 20   Perf. 13½x14
751-754 A224 Set of 4   10.00 10.00

Falcons — A225

Designs: 50f, Peregrine falcon. 125f, Hybrid
gyr-peregrine falcon. 275f, Gyrfalcon. 375f,
Saker falcon.

2003, Nov. 17   Perf. 13¼x14
755-758 A225 Set of 4   5.75 5.75

Poetry of
Saeed Bin
Ateej Al
Hamli
(1875-1919)
A226

Poetry: 125f, Four short lines. 175f, Four
long lines.

2003, Dec. 29   Perf. 13x13¼
759-760 A226 Set of 2   3.25 3.25

Mohammed Bin
Saeed Bin
Ghubash (1899-
1969), Religious
Scholar — A227

Designs: 50f, Portrait. 175f, Books.

2004, Apr. 5 Litho. Perf. 13¼x14
761-762 A227 Set of 2   3.25 3.25

Fourth Family
Meeting — A228

Color of hands: 375f, Orange. 4d, Purple.

2004, Apr. 19
763-764 A228   Set of 2   5.25 5.25

FIFA (Fédération Internationale de
Football Association), Cent. — A229

2004, May 21   Litho.   Perf. 13x13¼
765 A229 375f multi   2.75 2.75

Handicrafts by
Special Needs
Persons — A230

Designs: 50f, Handcrafted vase. 125f, Painting. 275f, Framed branch. 5d, Pottery artwork.

2004, June 29   Perf. 13¼x13
766-769 A230   Set of 4   5.25 5.25

2004 Summer
Olympics,
Athens
A231

Olympic rings and: 50f, Track athlete. 125f,
Rifle shooter. 275f, Swimmer. 375f, 2004 Athens Olympics emblem, torch bearer.

2004, Aug. 13   Litho.   Perf. 13x13¼
770-773 A231   Set of 4   4.50 4.50

Endangered or Extinct Persian Gulf
Marine Life — A232

Designs: 50f, Black finless porpoise. 175f,
Serranidae. 275f, Whale shark. 375f,
Dugongidae.

2004, Sept. 26   Perf. 14
774-777 A232   Set of 4   4.75 4.75
777a   Booklet pane, 2 each #774-
          777   9.50 —
          Complete booklet, #777a 9.50

Operation
Emirates Solidarity
for Mine
Clearance in
South
Lebanon — A233

Flags and: 275f, Person clearing mines.
375f, Map, people clearing mines, horiz.

2004, Oct. 25   Perf. 13x12¾, 12¾x13
778-779 A233   Set of 2   3.50 3.50

Sheik Dr. Sultan bin
Mohammed al-
Qassimi, Ruler of
Sharjah — A234

Color of denomination: 50f, Orange brown.
125f, Green. 275f, Red brown. 4d, Blue.

2004, Nov. 30   Perf. 13½x14
780-783 A234   Set of 4   4.75 4.75

Traditional
Women's
Clothing — A235

Designs: 50f, Drawers. 125f, Robe. 175f,
Gown. 225f, Jalabia. 275f, Scarf. 375f,
Yashmak.

2004, Dec. 29   Litho.   Perf. 14
784-789 A235   Set of 6   6.75 6.75
789a   Booklet pane, #784-789 6.75 6.75
          Complete booklet, #789a 6.75

Dubai
Aluminum,
25th Anniv.
A236

Designs: 50f, Smelting complex. 275f,
Smelting complex, sheikhs (brown background). 375f, Like 275f, blue background.

2005, Jan. 8   Perf. 13
790-792 A236   Set of 3   4.00 4.00

10th Dubai
Shopping
Festival — A237

Designs: 50f, Emblem. 125f, Emblem, diff.
275f, Emblem and "10," green background.
375f, Emblem and "10," red background.

2005, Jan. 12   Perf. 13¼x13
793-796 A237   Set of 4   4.50 4.50

2nd Intl.
Gathering of
Scouting and
Belonging,
Sharjah — A238

Designs: 50f, Emblem. 375f, Scouts and
truck.

2005, Apr. 1   Litho.   Perf. 13¼x14
797-798 A238   Set of 2   2.40 2.40

Shaikha Fatima Bint Mubarak,
Women's Rights Activist — A239

2005, Apr. 10   Perf. 14½
799 A239 50f multi   .30 .30

Al
Majedi
Bin
Dhaher,
17th
Century
Poet
A240

Poetry and: 50f, Sand. 175f, Bricks.

2005, May 30   Litho.   Perf. 14½
800-801 A240   Set of 2   1.25 1.25

Reptiles
A241

Designs: 50f, Agama. 125f, Desert monitor.
225f, Sand lizard. 275f, Dune sand gecko.
375f, Spiny-tailed lizard. 5d, Sand skink.

2005, Aug. 2   Perf. 13¾
802-807 A241   Set of 6   8.50 8.50
807a   Booklet pane, #802-807 8.50
          Complete booklet, #807a 8.50

Accession of Sheik Khalifa Bin Zayed
Al Nahyan, 1st Anniv. — A242

Sheik Khalifa: 50f, With a child. 175f, With
another sheik. 275f, With another sheik, diff.
375f, Kissing sheik.

2005, Nov. 3   Litho.   Perf. 14x13¼
808-811 A242   Set of 4   4.75 4.75
811a   Sheet of 4, #808-811   5.50 5.50

No. 811a sold for 10d.

2005
Census — A243

Emblem at: 50f, Bottom. 375f, Left, horiz.

Perf. 13¼x13, 13x13¼
2005, Nov. 10
812-813 A243   Set of 2   2.40 2.40

Desert
Plants
A244

Designs: 50f, Leptadenia pyrotechnica.
125f, Lycium shawii. 225f, Calotropis procera.
275f, Prosopis cineraria. 325f, Zizyphus spina-
christi. 375f, Acacia tortilis.

2005, Nov. 27   Litho.   Perf. 13½
814-819 A244   Set of 6   7.50 7.50
819a   Booklet pane, #814-819 7.50
          Complete booklet, #819a 7.50

34th National
Day — A245

Children's art: 50f, Flower in Arabic script,
by Shaimaa Mohammed Al Halabi. 125f, Ring
of children, by Muaz Jamal Ahmed Hassan,
horiz. 275f, Hands, by Pithani Srinidhi. 375f,
Doves, flag and plants, by Lina Abu Baker
Mukhtar, horiz.

2005, Dec. 2   Perf. 14¼
820-823 A245   Set of 4   4.50 4.50

Pearl
Diving
Tools
A246

Designs: 50f, F'ttam (nose clip). 125f, Al
Khabet (finger protectors). 175f, Al Dayeen
(basket). 275f, Sea rock (diver's weight). 375f,
Diver's outfit.

2005, Dec. 21   Perf. 14
824-828 A246   Set of 5   5.50 5.50

A souvenir sheet containing Nos. 824-828
with pearl halves affixed to each stamp sold for
100d.

Gulf Cooperation Council Day for Autistic Children — A247

2006, Apr. 4   Litho.   Perf. 13
829 A247 4d multi   2.25 2.25

Souvenir Sheet

Hamad Bin Khalifa Abu Shehab (1932-2002), Poet — A248

No. 830: a, 1d, Head. b, 2d, Hands, poetry in Arabic text.

2006, Apr. 26   Perf. 14¼
830 A248 Sheet of 2, #a-b   1.75 1.75

A249

Gulf Cooperation Council, 25th Anniv. — A250

Litho. with Foil Application
2006, May 25   Perf. 14
831 A249 1d multi   .55 .55

Imperf
Size: 165x105mm
832 A250 5d multi   2.75 2.75

See Bahrain Nos. 628-629, Kuwait Nos. 1646-1647, Oman Nos. 477-478, Qatar Nos. 1007-1008, and Saudi Arabia No. 1378.

Dubai Police, 50th Anniv. — A251

2006, June 1   Perf. 13¼x13
833 A251 1d multi   .55 .55

19th Asian Stamp Exhibition, Dubai A252

Designs: 1d, shown. 4d, Four towers.

Litho. With Foil Application
2006, June 24   Perf. 13¾
834-835 A252 Set of 2   2.75 2.75

Dubai Intl. Holy Koran Award, 10th Anniv. A253

2006, July 24   Litho.   Perf. 14x13½
836 A253 1d multi   .55 .55

Al Raha Beach Developments — A254

Designs: 1d, Khor Al Raha. 2d, Al Lissaily. 350f, Al Wateed (40x40mm). 4d, Al Bandar (40x40mm).

2006, Sept. 18   Litho.   Perf. 13
837-840 A254 Set of 4   5.75 5.75

UPU Strategy Conference, Dubai — A255

Designs: 1d, Green arrows. 4d, Blue and green arrows.

Litho. & Embossed
2006, Sept. 27   Perf. 14x13½
841-842 A255 Set of 2   2.75 2.75

12th Gulf Cooperation Council Postage Stamp Exhibition A256

2006, Nov. 13   Litho.   Perf. 13¼x13
843 A256 1d multi   .55 .55

35th National Day — A257

2006, Dec. 1
844 A257 1d multi   .55 .55

A souvenir sheet containing one stamp sold for 10d.

Sheikh Mohammed bin Rashid al Maktoum, Prime Minister — A258

Sheikh Mohammed: 1d, Wearing kaffiyeh. 4d, Wearing polo helmet (44x53mm).

Litho. With 3-Dimensional Plastic Affixed
2006, Dec. 2   Serpentine Die Cut 9
Self-Adhesive
845-846 A258 Set of 2   2.75 2.75

Gazelles A259

Designs: 1d, Tahr. 2d, Sand gazelle. 3d, Mountain gazelle. 350f, Arabian oryx.

2006, Nov. 29   Litho.   Perf. 14
847-850 A259 Set of 4   5.25 5.25
850a   Souvenir sheet, #847-850   5.25 5.25

Intl. Volunteers Day A260

Man giving items to: 2d, Two children. 4d, Three children.

2006, Dec. 5   Perf. 13x13¼
851-852 A260 Set of 2   3.25 3.25

Women's Jewelry A261

Designs: 1d, Mariya um alnairat. 150f, Mortasha. 2d, Shaghab bu shouk. 3d, Shahid ring. 350f, Bushuq. 4d, Tassah.

2006, Dec. 31   Perf. 13x13¼
853-858 A261 Set of 6   8.25 8.25
858a   Booklet pane, #853-858   8.25
          Complete booklet, #858a   8.25

Falcon — A262

2007, Jan. 31   Perf. 13¼x13
Background Color
859 A262 1d buff   .55 .55
860 A262 150f gray   .85 .85
861 A262 2d lilac   1.10 1.10
862 A262 3d yellow   1.60 1.60
863 A262 350f yel green 1.90 1.90
864 A262 4d pink   2.25 2.25
865 A262 5d blue vio   2.75 2.75
     Nos. 859-865 (7)   11.00 11.00

Booklet Stamps
Self-Adhesive
Serpentine Die Cut 12½
Background Color
865A A262 1d buff   .55 .55
865B A262 150f gray   .85 .85
865C A262 2d lilac   1.10 1.10
865D A262 3d yellow   1.60 1.60
865E A262 350f yel green 1.90 1.90
865F A262 4d pink   2.25 2.25
865G A262 5d blue vio   2.75 2.75
h.   Booklet pane, #865A-865G   11.00 —
      Complete booklet, #865Gh   11.00
      Nos. 865A-865G (7)   11.00 11.00

See No. 937. Compare with Nos. 959-965.

Dubai Tennis Championships A263

Background colors: 1d, Orange. 3d, Red violet.

2007, Feb. 19   Perf. 14
866-867 A263 Set of 2   2.25 2.25

18th Arabian Gulf Soccer Cup Championships, Abu Dhabi — A264

Arabian Gulf Cup with frame in: 1d, Red. 3d, Green.

2007, May 9   Litho.   Perf. 14x13¾
868-869 A264 Set of 2   2.25 2.25
869a   Souvenir sheet, #868-869   5.50 5.50

No. 869a sold for 10d.

Etisalat (Telecommunications Company), 30th Anniv. — A265

Denomination color: 1d, Blue. 3d, Orange red. 350f, Purple. 4d, Red.

2007, May 17   **Perf. 13x13¼**
870-873 A265   Set of 4   6.25 6.25
Each stamp has a die cut opening.

Souvenir Sheet

World Blood Donor Day — A266

No. 874 — World Blood Donor Day emblem and: a, 1d, Heart. b, 3d, Blood drop.

2007, June 14   **Perf. 13**
874   A266   Sheet of 2, #a-b   2.25 2.25

Sheikh Ahmed Mohamed Hasher Al Maktoum, UAE's First Olympic Gold Medalist — A267

2007, July 17   **Perf. 14x13½**
875   A267   3d multi   1.75 1.75

A268

Emirates Bank, 30th Anniv. A269

Perf. 14x13¾ (A268), 14 (A269)
2007, Aug. 28
876   A268   1d blue & multi   .55 .55
877   A269   150f blue & multi   .85 .85
878   A268   3d brn & multi   1.75 1.75
879   A269   350f brn & multi   1.90 1.90
   a.   Souvenir sheet, #876-879   8.25 8.25
     Nos. 876-879 (4)   5.05 5.05

No. 879a sold for 15d.

Emirates Banks Association, 25th Anniv. — A270

2007, Oct. 4   **Perf. 13¾**
880 A270 1d red & bis brn   .55 .55

Abu Dhabi Islamic Bank, 10th Anniv. — A271

Differing backgrounds with denominations of: 1d, 150f, 2d, 3d.

2007, Nov. 8   **Litho.**   **Perf. 14¼**
881-884 A271   Set of 4   4.25 4.25
  884a   Souvenir sheet, #881-884   4.25 4.25

Abu Dhabi Police, 50th Anniv. — A272

Litho. With Foil Application
2007, Nov. 14   **Perf. 13¼x14**
885 A272 1d multi   .55 .55

Children's Art — A273

Designs: Nos. 886, 892, Woman and two men in prayer. Nos. 887, 893, Woman presenting gift to another woman, vert. Nos. 888, 894, Children facing mosque. Nos. 889, 895, Hands holding child giving item to woman, vert. Nos. 890, 896, Child helping man across street. Nos. 891, 897, Child helping handicapped person, vert.

2007, Nov. 29   **Litho.**   **Perf. 14**
886 A273   1d multi   .55 .55
887 A273   150f multi   .85 .85
888 A273   2d multi   1.10 1.10
889 A273   3d multi   1.75 1.75
890 A273   350f multi   1.90 1.90
891 A273   4d multi   2.25 2.25
     Nos. 886-891 (6)   8.40 8.40
Booklet Stamps
Self-Adhesive
Die Cut Perf. 11¼x12, 12x11¼
892 A273   1d multi   .55 .55
893 A273   150f multi   .85 .85
894 A273   2d multi   1.10 1.10
895 A273   3d multi   1.75 1.75
896 A273   350f multi   1.90 1.90
897 A273   4d multi   2.25 2.25
   a.   Complete booklet, #892-897   8.50
     Nos. 892-897 (6)   8.40 8.40

Complete booklet is stapled in center with one stamp per page and with the center leaf of the booklet having stamps on both sides.

Souvenir Sheet

Sheikh Mohammed Al Khazraji (1919-2006), Chief Justice — A274

No. 898: a, 1d, Facing right. b, 3d, Facing forward.

2007, Dec. 9   **Perf. 13½x13¾**
898 A274   Sheet of 2, #a-b   2.25 2.25

Al Abbas Group, 40th Anniv. A275

Denominations: 1d, 150f, 2d, 3d.

2007, Dec. 16   **Perf. 14¼**
899-902 A275   Set of 4   4.25 4.25

Al Rostamani Group, 50th Anniv. A276

Background colors: 1d, Gray. 150f, Prussian blue.

2007, Dec. 23   **Perf. 13x13¼**
903-904 A276   Set of 2   1.40 1.40

Union Properties, 20th Anniv. A277

Designs: 1d, Emblem. 150f, F1 Theme Park, Dubai, horiz. 2d, Uptown. 3d, Green community, horiz.

Perf. 13¼x13½, 13½x13¼
2007, Dec. 27
905-908 A277   Set of 4   4.25 4.25
  908a   Souvenir sheet, #905-908   8.50 8.50

No. 908a sold for 15d.

Federal National Council, 36th Anniv. A278

2008, Feb. 12   **Perf. 13¼**
909 A278 1d multi   .55 .55

National Bank of Abu Dhabi, 40th Anniv. A279

"40" and: 1d, Yellow panel at top. 150f, Yellow panel at top. 225d, White panel at top. 4d, White panel at top.

2008, Feb. 13   **Perf. 13**
910-913 A279   Set of 4   4.75 4.75
  913a   Souvenir sheet, #910-913   8.25 8.25

No. 913a sold for 15d.

Municipality and Planning Department of Ajman — A280

Emblems of: 1d, Municipality and Planning Department. 150f, Ajman Urban Planning Conference. 2d, E-services. 4d, Geographic Information Systems.

2008, Mar. 24   **Litho.**   **Perf. 13¼**
914-917 A280   Set of 4   4.75 4.75
  917a   Souvenir sheet, #914-917,
          perf. 13¼x14¼   8.25 8.25

No. 917a sold for 15d.

Souvenir Sheet

Hamdan Bin Rashid Al Maktoum Award for Distinguished Academic Performance — A281

No. 918: a, 1d, Emblem and "10." b, 2d, Rashid Al Maktoum, emblem.

2008, Apr. 1   **Perf. 13¼**
918 A281   Sheet of 2, #a-b   1.75 1.75

Traditional Souqs — A282

Marketplaces: 1d, Spice Souq, Dubai. 150f, Al Arsa Souq, Sharjah. 2d, Gold Souq, Dubai. 3d, Old Souq, Abu Dhabi.

Litho. & Embossed
2008, Apr. 20   **Perf. 13½x13¼**
919-922 A282   Set of 4   4.25 4.25

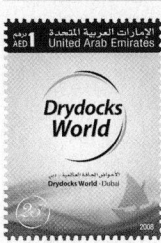

Drydocks World, 25th Anniv. — A283

Designs: 1d, Shown. 4d, Emblem, dhow, horiz.

Perf. 13¼x13, 13x13¼
2008, June 4 **Litho.**
923-924 A283 Set of 2 2.75 2.75

Sharjah Intl. Airport, 75th Anniv. — A284

2008, July 7 **Perf. 13½**
925 A284 1d multi .55 .55

2008 Summer Olympics, Beijing A285

Emblem of Beijing Olympics, emblems of five sports and: 1d, Yellow orange background. 4d, Olympic torch, vert. 475f Olympic torch, diff., vert. 550f, Red violet background. 10d, Olympic torch, vignettes of Nos. 926-929.

2008, Aug. 4 **Perf. 14x13¼, 13¼x14**
926-929 A285 Set of 4 8.50 8.50
Size: 120x120mm
Imperf
930 A285 10d multi 5.50 5.50

Gulf News, 30th Anniv. — A286

Background color: 1d, Blue. 150f, Maroon. 225f, Orange.

2008, Sept. 30 **Perf. 13½x13¼**
Granite Paper
931-933 A286 Set of 3 2.60 2.60
A souvenir sheet containing Nos. 931-933 sold for 15d.

Souvenir Sheet

Arab Postal Day — A287

No. 934 — Emblem and: a, 1d, World map, pigeon. b, 225f, Camel caravan.

Litho. & Silkscreened With Foil Application
2008, Oct. 10
934 A287 Sheet of 2, #a-b 1.75 1.75

Miniature Sheets

Date Varieties — A288

No. 935: a, Abuman. b, Jash Hamad. c, Msalli.
No. 936, vert.: a, Farth. b, Mirzaban. c, Abukibal. d, Salani.

2008, Oct. 22 **Litho.** **Perf. 13x13¼**
935 A288 1d Sheet of 3, #a-c 1.75 1.75
Perf. 13¼x13
936 A288 1d Sheet of 4, #a-d 2.25 2.25

Falcon Type of 2007 Inscribed "Priority"
Litho. & Embossed
2008, Dec. 2 **Perf. 13¼x14**
Background Color
937 A262 2d vermilion 1.10 1.10

Center for Documentaion and Research, 40th Anniv. — A289

Designs: 1d, Building. 4d, Sheikhs and crowd of people. 10d, Sheikhs, vert.

2008, Dec. 2 **Litho.** **Perf. 14¼**
939 A289 1d multi .55 .55
940 A289 4d multi 2.25 2.25
Miniature Sheet
Litho With 3-Dimensional Plastic Affixed
Self-Adhesive
Serpentine Die Cut 9
941 A289 10d multi 5.50 5.50

Eid Al Adha — A290

Designs: 1d, Al Eidiya. 3d, Eid prayers.

Litho. With Foil Application
2008, Dec. 6 **Perf. 13¾**
942-943 A290 Set of 2 2.25 2.25
943a Souvenir sheet, #942-943 3.25 3.25
No. 943a sold for 6d.

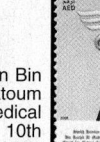

Sheikh Hamdan Bin Rashid Al Maktoum Award for Medical Science, 10th Anniv. — A291

Designs: 1d, Award. 2d, Special Recognition Award. 3d, Sheikh Hamdan Bin Rashid Al Maktoum, award. 4d, 10th anniversary emblem.

2008, Dec. 15 **Litho.** **Perf. 13¼**
944-947 A291 Set of 4 5.50 5.50
947a Souvenir sheet, #944-947 8.25 8.25
No. 947a sold for 15d.

Dubai Duty Free, 25th Anniv. — A292

Designs: 1d, 25th anniversary emblem in gray. 2d, 25th anniversary emblem in red. 3d, Dubai Duty Free shop. 4d, Shop, diff.

2008, Dec. 20 **Litho.** **Perf. 13¼x13**
948-951 A292 Set of 4 5.50 5.50
951a Souvenir sheet, #948-951 5.50 5.50

Universal Declaration of Human Rights, 60th Anniv. — A293

Color of top panel: 1d, Red brown. 4d, Orange and yellow.

Perf. 13¾x13½
2008, Dec. 31 **Litho.**
952-953 A293 Set of 2 2.75 2.75
953a Souvenir sheet, #952-953 3.25 3.25
No. 953a sold for 6d.

Second Arab Stamp Exhibition, Dubai — A294

Serpentine Die Cut 12½
2009, Mar. 5 **Litho. & Embossed**
Self-Adhesive
Printed on Clear Plastic Film
954 A294 1d multi .55 .55
No. 954 has white backing paper.

Emirates Center for Strategic Studies and Research (ECSSR), 15th Anniv. A295

Designs: 1d, Books published by ECSSR. 150f, UAE Federation Library. 2d, Media monitoring room. 4d, ECSSR Building.

2009, Mar. 26 **Litho.** **Perf. 13¼**
Granite Paper
955-958 A295 Set of 4 4.75 4.75
958a Souvenir sheet, #955-958 5.50 5.50
No. 958a sold for 10d.

Falcon Type of 2007 Redrawn
2009, Apr. 2 **Litho.** **Perf. 13¼x13**
Background Color
959 A262 25f black .25 .25
960 A262 1d dark buff .55 .55
961 A262 150f brownish gray .80 .80
962 A262 2d gray lilac 1.10 1.10
963 A262 10d orange 5.50 5.50
964 A262 20d lt greenish blue 11.00 11.00
965 A262 50d dark green 27.50 27.50
Nos. 959-965 (7) 46.70 46.70

Nos. 959-965 are dated 2009 and lack the buff curved line to the left of the Arabic country name found on Nos. 859-865. Denominations for Nos. 960 and 962 use "AED" rather than the "Dh." or "Dhs." used on Nos. 859 and 861.

Rashid Bin Tannaf (1910-99), Poet — A296

Rashid Bin Tannaf: 1d, Wearing kaffiyeh. 4d, Without kaffiyeh.

2009, Apr. 30 **Perf. 13¼**
Granite Paper
966-967 A296 Set of 2 2.75 2.75
A souvenir sheet containing Nos. 966-967 sold for 15d.

Discovery of Umm An Nar Culture, 50th Anniv. A297

Umm An Nar tomb with background color of: 1d, Red brown. 150f, Brown. 4d, Olive green.

2009, June 28 **Perf. 13x13¼**
968-970 A297 Set of 3 3.75 3.75

Jerusalem, Capital of Arab Culture — A298

2009, Aug. 3 **Perf. 13¼x13**
971 A298 2d multi 1.10 1.10

Postal Services in the Emirates, Cent. — A299

Covers bearing: 1d, Pakistan Nos. 1, 2, 5 and 12. 150f, Trucial States No. 4, Oman Nos. 21 and 52. 4f, United Arab Emirates No. 3, Dubai Nos. 80 and 83, and Sharjah stamp. 5d, Withdrawn United Arab Emirates National Day stamp of 1977.
10d, Various India stamps.

2009, Aug. 19   **Perf. 13¼**
Granite Paper
972-975 A299 Set of 4   6.25 6.25
Souvenir Sheet
976 A299 10d multi   5.50 5.50

38th
National
Day
A300

2009, Dec. 2   **Perf. 13**
977 A300 1d multi   .55 .55

FIFA 2009 Club World Cup Soccer
Championships, Abu Dhabi — A301

Designs: 1d, Shown. 10d, Similar to 1d, with
United Arab Emirates flag at right.

2009, Dec. 19   **Perf. 13¾**
978 A301 1d multi   .55 .55
Souvenir Sheet
Perf. 13
979 A301 10d multi   5.50 5.50

No. 979 contains one 40x40mm stamp.

Securities and Commodities Authority,
10th Anniv. — A302

Emblem and: 1d, Numerals and squares.
2d, Text on computer screen, graphs. 3d,
Emirates Securities Market trading board. 5d,
Falcon and numerals.

2010, Feb. 1   **Perf. 13**
Granite Paper
980-983 A302 Set of 4   6.00 6.00

A souvenir sheet containing No. 983 sold for
15d.

Emirates
Aluminum,
3rd Anniv.
A303

Designs: 1d, Emblem. 2d, Hand holding
frame with picture of smelting complex. 3d,
Falcon, horse. 5d, United Arab Emirates flag.

2010, Feb. 24   **Perf. 13x14¼**
984-987 A303 Set of 4   6.00 6.00
987a   Souvenir sheet, #984-987,
     perf. 14¼   8.25 8.25

No. 987a sold for 15d.

United Arab
Emirates
Pavilion, Expo
2010, Shanghai
A304

Pavilion: 1d, In daylight. 550f, At dusk.

Litho. With Foil Application
2010, May 13   **Perf. 13¼x13**
988-989 A304   Set of 2   3.75 3.75

Diplomatic Relations Between United
Arab Emirates and Republic of Korea,
30th Anniv. — A305

No. 990: a, 1d, Flag of United Arab Emirates
and air-conditioning tower. b, 550f, Flag of
South Korea and Mt. Amisan Chimney,
Gyeongbokgung Palace.

2010, June 17   **Litho.**   **Perf. 13x13¼**
990 A305   Horiz. pair, #a-b   3.75 3.75

See South Korea No. 2337.

Jebel Ali Free
Zone, 25th
Anniv.
A306

Designs: 1d, Zone in 1986. 2d, Zone in
1997. 3d, Zone in 2009. 4d, 25th anniversary
emblem.

2010, June 30   **Perf. 13¼x13½**
991-994 A306   Set of 4   5.50 5.50
994a   Sheet of 4, #991-994, perf.
     14¼x13½   8.25 8.25

No. 994a sold for 15d.

Souvenir Sheet

2010 Youth Olympics,
Singapore — A307

2010, Aug. 19   **Perf. 13¾**
995 A307 475f multi   2.60 2.60

Sheikh Zayed
Grand
Mosque — A308

Designs: 1d, Mosque. 5d, Mosque, horiz.
25d, Mosque, diff., horiz.

Perf. 13½x13¼, 13¼x13½
2010, Aug. 29   **Litho.**
996-997 A308   Set of 2   3.25 3.25
Litho. & Embossed With Foil
Application
Imperf
Size:145x110mm
998 A308 25d gold & multi   14.00 14.00

Old Schools — A309

Designs: 1d, Al Nehyania School, Abu
Dhabi. 150f, Al Ahmadiya School, Dubai. 4d,
Al Eslah School, Sharjah.

Perf. 13½x13¾
2010, Sept. 19   **Litho.**
999-1001 A309   Set of 3   3.75 3.75

A souvenir sheet containing Nos. 999-1001
sold for 15d.

Organization of the Petroleum
Exporting Countries, 50th
Anniv. — A310

2010, Sept. 27   **Perf. 13**
1002 A310 1d multi   .55 .55

World Post
Day
A311

Designs: 1d, Dove holding envelope. 550f,
Universal Postal Union emblem.

2010, Oct. 9   **Perf. 13¼x13**
1003-1004 A311   Set of 2   3.75 3.75

Miniature Sheet

Sea Birds — A312

No. 1005: a, 1d, Black-headed gull. b, 150f,
Crab plover. c, 2d, Gray heron ardea. d, 3d,
Sooty gull. e, 450f, Socotra cormorant. f, 550f,
Caspian gull.

2010, Nov. 4   **Litho.**   **Perf. 13**
Granite Paper
1005 A312   Sheet of 6, #a-f, +
     label   9.50 9.50

DP World
Marine
Terminal
Operators
A313

DP World emblem and various port scenes:
1d, 2d, 3d, 4d.

2010, Nov. 9   **Perf. 14¼x13¾**
Granite Paper
1006-1009 A313 Set of 4   5.50 5.50
1009a   Sheet of 4, #1006-1009   8.25 8.25

No. 1009a sold for 15d.

Yas Marina Racing Circuit, Abu
Dhabi — A314

Designs: 1d, Race car on track. 550f,
Grandstands.

2010, Nov. 14   **Perf. 13¼x13**
1010-1011 A314 Set of 2   3.75 3.75

Watani
(National
Identity)
A315

Designs: 1d, Four stylized fingerprints. 150f,
Map of United Arab Emirates composed of fingerprints, vert.

2010, Dec. 2   **Perf. 13x13½, 13½x13**
1012-1013 A315 Set of 2   1.40 1.40

39th National Day — A316

Nos. 1014 and 1015 — Winning designs in
children's stamp design contest: a, Four automobiles, people waving flags and signs. b,
Children with flags around grills. c, Flag of
United Arab Emirates, tower. d, Four people,
flags, towers. e, Children with balloons. f, Flag
and "December 2."

2010, Dec. 2   **Perf. 13**
1014 A316 1d Sheet of 6, #a-f   3.25 3.25
Stamp Size: 35x26mm
Self-Adhesive
Serpentine Die Cut 12¾
1015 A316 1d Booklet pane of
     12, 2 each #a-f   6.50 6.50

Ghaf
Tree — A317

2011, Mar. 31   **Perf. 13¼**
1016 A317 1d green   .55 .55

A souvenir sheet containing No. 1016 and a
4d stamp with a ghaf tree seed and a plastic
netting affixed to it sold for 40d.

17th Gulf
Cooperation
Council
Postage
Stamp
Exhibition,
Abu
Dhabi — A318

2011, Apr. 4   **Perf. 13**
1017 A318 150f multi   .85 .85

Miniature Sheet

31st Session of the Gulf Cooperation
Council Supreme Council, Abu
Dhabi — A319

No. 1018 — Various buildings and: a, King
Abdullah, flag of Saudi Arabia. b, Sheikh
Khalifa, flag of United Arab Emirates. c,
Sheikh Sabah, flag of Kuwait. d, King Hamad,
flag of Bahrain. e, Sheikh Hamad, flag of
Qatar. f, Sultan Qaboos, flag of Oman.

2011, Apr. 5   **Perf. 13½x13¾**
1018 A319 150f Sheet of 6, #a-f 5.00 5.00

Fifth Gulf Federation for Cancer
Control Conference, Sharjah — A320

2011, May 31 Litho. Perf. 14x13½
Granite Paper
1019 A320 1d multi   .55 .55

Emblem of
Sheikha
Fatima Bint
Mubarak
A321

Litho. With Foil Application
2011, July 24   **Perf. 13**
1020 A321 1d multi   .55 .55

Al Bidyah
Mosque,
Fujeira — A322

Designs: 1d, Archway. 150f, Mosque
exterior.
15d, Mosque exerior, wall carving.

2011, Aug. 27 Litho. Perf. 14x14¼
1021 A322 1d multi   .55 .55
1022 A322 150f multi   .85 .85

Litho. & Embossed
Imperf
Size: 130x80mm
1023 A322 15d multi   8.25 8.25

No. 1023 contains one 40x40mm perforated
label.

Fauna of Bu
Tinah
Island — A323

Designs: No. 1024, 1d, Dugong (35x35mm).
No. 1025, 1d, One fish (35x35mm). No. 1026,
1d, Three fish (35x35mm). No. 1027, 1d, Crab
(35x35mm). No. 1028, 1d, Bird (35x35mm).
No. 1029, 1d, Coral (35x35mm). No. 1030, 1d,
Coral (48x30mm). No. 1031, 1d, Dolphin
(48x30mm). No. 1032, 1d, Flamingos
(48x30mm). No. 1033, 1d, Sea turtle
(48x30mm).
15d, Sea turtle, dugong, dolphins, coral,
crab, birds.

Perf. 13¼, 13¼x13½ (#1030-1033)
2011, Nov. 30   **Litho.**
1024-1033 A323 Set of 10 5.50 5.50
Size: 120x70mm
Imperf
1034 A323 15d multi   8.25 8.25

40th National Day — A324

2011, Dec. 2   **Perf. 13½x13¾**
Granite Paper
1035 A324 1d multi   .55 .55

UPPER SENEGAL & NIGER

ˈə-pər ˌse-nə-gäl and ˈnī-jər

LOCATION — In Northwest Africa,
north of French Guinea and Ivory
Coast
GOVT. — A former French Colony
AREA — 617,600 sq. mi.
POP. — 2,474,142
CAPITAL — Bamako

In 1921 the name of this colony was
changed to French Sudan and postage
stamps so inscribed were placed in use.

100 Centimes = 1 Franc

Gen. Louis
Faidherbe
A1

Oil Palms — A2

Dr. N.
Eugène
Ballay — A3

Perf. 14x13½
1906-07   Unwmk.   Typo.
Name of Colony in Red or Blue
1	A1	1c slate	2.00	2.00
2	A1	2c brown	2.75	2.40
3	A1	4c brn, *gray bl*	6.50	2.75
4	A1	5c green	7.25	3.25
5	A1	10c car (B)	7.25	3.25
6	A1	15c vio ('07)	5.00	5.50
7	A2	20c bluish gray	6.50	6.50
8	A2	25c bl, *pnksh*	20.00	5.00
9	A2	30c vio brn, *pnksh*	8.25	6.50
10	A2	35c blk, *yellow*	6.50	5.50
11	A2	40c car, *az* (B)	10.50	10.00
12	A2	45c brn, *grnsh*	12.50	13.00
13	A2	50c dp vio	12.50	13.00
14	A2	75c bl, *org*	12.50	13.50
15	A3	1fr blk, *azure*	29.00	32.50
16	A3	2fr bl, *pink*	52.50	60.00
17	A3	5fr car, *straw* (B)	110.00	120.00
		Nos. 1-17 (17)	311.50	304.65

Camel with
Rider — A4

1914-17   **Perf. 13½x14**
18	A4	1c brn vio & vio	.35	.50
19	A4	2c gray & brn vio	.35	.50
20	A4	4c black & blue	.35	.50
21	A4	5c yel grn & bl grn	1.05	.60
22	A4	10c red org & rose	2.75	2.40
23	A4	15c choc & org ('17)	2.00	1.25
24	A4	20c brn vio & blk	2.40	2.40
25	A4	25c ultra & bl	2.00	1.60
26	A4	30c ol brn & brn	2.00	2.40
27	A4	35c car rose & vio	3.25	2.75
28	A4	40c gray & car rose	2.50	1.60
29	A4	45c bl & ol brn	2.40	2.40
30	A4	50c black & green	2.75	3.25
31	A4	75c org & ol brn	2.75	3.25
32	A4	1fr brown & brn vio	2.75	3.25
33	A4	2fr green & blue	3.25	4.00
34	A4	5fr violet & black	13.00	15.00
		Nos. 18-34 (17)	45.90	47.65

See Burkina Faso for types of this issue that
escaped overprinting.
For surcharge see No. B1.

SEMI-POSTAL STAMP

Regular Issue of
1914 Surcharged in
Red

1915   Unwmk.   Perf. 13½x14
B1 A4 10c + 5c red orange &
        rose   2.40 2.40

POSTAGE DUE STAMPS

Natives — D1   D2

1906 Unwmk. Typo. Perf. 14x13½
J1	D1	5c green, *greenish*	4.00	4.00
J2	D1	10c red brown	8.25	8.00
J3	D1	15c dark blue	11.50	11.50
J4	D1	20c black, *yellow*	15.00	7.50
J5	D1	50c violet	27.50	30.00
J6	D1	60c black, *buff*	22.50	24.00
J7	D1	1fr black, *pinkish*	40.00	45.00
		Nos. J1-J7 (7)	128.75	130.00

1914
J8	D2	5c green	1.25	1.60
J9	D2	10c rose	1.60	2.00
J10	D2	15c gray	1.60	2.00
J11	D2	20c brown	1.60	2.00
J12	D2	30c blue	2.40	2.75
J13	D2	50c black	2.00	2.40
J14	D2	60c orange	7.25	8.00
J15	D2	1fr violet	7.25	8.00
		Nos. J8-J15 (8)	24.95	28.75

Stamps of Upper Senegal and Niger were
superceded in 1921 by those of French
Sudan.

UPPER SILESIA

ˈə-pər sī'lē-zhˌē-ˌə

LOCATION — Formerly in eastern Germany and prior to World War I a part of Germany.

A plebiscite held under the terms of the Treaty of Versailles failed to determine the status of the country, the voting resulting about equally in favor of Germany and Poland. Accordingly, the League of Nations divided the territory between Germany and Poland.

100 Pfennig = 1 Mark
100 Fennigi = 1 Marka

Plebiscite Issues

A1

Perf. 14x13½

1920, Feb. 20		Typo.	Unwmk.	
1	A1	2½pf slate	.40	.80
2	A1	3pf brown	.40	.85
3	A1	5pf green	.30	.80
4	A1	10pf dull red	.40	.90
5	A1	15pf violet	.25	.80
6	A1	20pf blue	.25	.80
a.		Imperf. pair	275.00	—
b.		Half used as 10pf on cover		110.00
7	A1	50pf violet brn	4.75	8.00
8	A1	1m claret	5.00	11.00
9	A1	5m orange	5.00	11.00
		Nos. 1-9 (9)	16.75	34.95
		Set, never hinged	52.00	

Black Surcharge

Pf.	Pf.	Pf.	Pf.
I	II	III	IV

10	A1	5pf on 15pf vio (I)	160.00	525.00
		Never hinged	400.00	
a.		Type II		
b.		Type III		
c.		Type IV	13.00	
11	A1	5pf on 20pf blue (I)	1.10	3.25
		Never hinged	2.75	
a.		Type II	1.25	3.75
b.		Type III	1.60	4.00
c.		Type IV	2.00	5.00

Red Surcharge

Pf.	Pf.	Pf.	Pf.
I	II	III	IV

12	A1	10pf on 20pf bl (I)	1.10	3.25
		Never hinged	2.75	
a.		Type II	1.10	3.25
b.		Type III	1.10	3.25
c.		Type IV	1.10	3.25
d.		Imperf.	60.00	240.00

Black Surcharge

50	50	50	50	50
Pf.	Pf.	Pf.	Pf.	Pf.
Type I	Type II	Type III	Type IV	Type V

13	A1	50pf on 5m org (I),	22.50	52.50
		shiny ovpt.		
		Never hinged	160.00	
a.		Type II	24.00	55.00
b.		Type III	26.00	87.50
c.		Type IV	26.00	87.50
d.		Type V	40.00	120.00
e.		Type I, matte ovpt.	35.00	87.50

Nos. 10-13 are found with many varieties including surcharges inverted, double and double inverted.

Dove with Olive Branch Flying over Silesian Terrain — A2

A3

1920, Mar. 26		Typo.	Perf. 13½x14	
15	A2	2½pf gray	.30	.80
16	A2	3pf red brown	.30	.80
17	A2	5pf green	.30	.80
18	A2	10pf dull red	.30	.80
19	A2	15pf violet	.30	.80
20	A2	20pf blue	.30	2.00
21	A2	25pf dark brown	.30	.80
22	A2	30pf orange	.30	.80
23	A2	40pf olive green	.30	2.00

Perf. 14x13½

24	A3	50pf gray	.40	.80
25	A3	60pf blue	.40	1.60
26	A3	75pf deep green	1.10	2.00
27	A3	80pf red brown	1.10	1.10
28	A3	1m claret	1.10	.80
29	A3	2m dark brown	.80	.80
30	A3	3m violet	.80	.80
31	A3	5m orange	2.75	4.50
		Nos. 15-31 (17)	11.15	22.00
		Set, never hinged	56.00	

Nos. 18-28 Overprinted in Black or Red

Plébiscite 20 mars 1921.

1921, Mar. 20				
32	A2	10pf dull red	4.00	10.00
33	A2	15pf violet	4.00	10.00
34	A2	20pf blue	5.50	14.00
35	A2	25pf dk brn (R)	12.00	32.50
36	A2	30pf orange	10.00	20.00
37	A2	40pf olive grn (R)	11.00	20.00

Overprinted

Plébiscite 20 mars 1921.

38	A3	50pf gray (R)	11.00	27.50
39	A3	60pf blue	12.00	22.50
40	A3	75pf deep green	12.00	27.50
a.		75pf blue green	1,650.	1,850.
41	A3	80pf red brown	20.00	35.00
42	A3	1m claret	24.00	65.00
		Nos. 32-42 (11)	125.50	284.00
		Set, never hinged	625.00	

Inverted or double overprints exist on Nos. 32-33, 35-40. Counterfeit overprints exist.

Type of 1920 and Surcharged

10 M

1922, Mar.				
45	A3	4m on 60pf ol grn	.80	2.00
46	A3	10m on 75pf red	1.25	2.75
47	A3	20m on 80pf orange	6.50	16.00
		Nos. 45-47 (3)	8.55	20.75
		Set, never hinged	32.00	

Stamps of the above design were a private issue not recognized by the Inter-Allied Commission of Government. Value, set of 7, $65 unused, $225 never hinged, $225 used.

OFFICIAL STAMPS

German Stamps of 1905-20 Handstamped in Blue

1920, Feb.	Wmk. 125	Perf. 14, 14½		
		On Stamps of 1906-19		
O1	A22	2pf gray	1.10	1.25
O3	A22	2½pf gray	.55	.65
O4	A16	3pf brown	.55	.65
O5	A16	5pf green	.55	.65
O6	A22	7½pf orange	.55	.65
O7	A16	10pf car rose	.55	.65
O8	A22	15pf dk violet	.55	.65
O9	A16	20pf blue violet	.55	.65
O10	A16	25pf org & blk, yel	8.00	6.50
O11	A16	30pf org & blk, buff	.55	.65
O12	A22	35pf red brown	.55	.65
O13	A16	40pf lake & blk	.55	.65
O14	A16	50pf vio & blk, buff	.55	.65
O15	A16	60pf magenta	.55	.65
O16	A16	75pf green & blk	.55	.65
O17	A16	80pf lake & blk, rose	6.50	8.00
O18	A17	1m car rose	1.10	1.25
O19	A21	2m gray blue	5.25	6.50

On National Assembly Stamps of 1919-20

O25	A23	10pf car rose	.90	1.10
O26	A24	15pf choc & bl	1.60	2.00
O27	A25	25pf green & red	3.25	4.00
O28	A25	30pf red vio & red	2.50	3.00

On Semi-Postal Stamps of 1919

O30	A16	10pf + 5pf carmine	6.50	8.00
O31	A22	15pf + 5pf dk vio	6.50	8.00
		Nos. O1-O31 (24)	50.35	58.05

Red Handstamp

O5a	A16	5pf	10.00	14.00
O8a	A22	15pf	6.50	10.00
O9a	A16	20pf	6.50	10.00
O13a	A16	40pf	20.00	30.00
O16a	A16	75pf	20.00	30.00
O26a	A24	15pf	1.10	1.25
		Nos. O5a-O26a (6)	64.10	95.25

Values of Nos. O1-O31 are for reprints made with a second type of handstamp differing in minor details from the original (example: period after "S" is round instead of the earlier triangular form). Originals are scarce. Counterfeits exist.

Germany No. 65C with this handstamp is considered bogus by experts.

Local Official Stamps of Germany, 1920, Overprinted

C. G. H. S.

1920, Apr.			Perf. 14	
O32	LO2	5pf green	.30	1.00
O33	LO3	10pf carmine	.30	1.00
O34	LO4	15pf violet brn	.30	1.00
O35	LO5	20pf deep ultra	.30	1.00
O36	LO6	30pf orange, buff	.30	1.00
O37	LO7	50pf violet, buff	.80	3.00
O38	LO8	1m red, buff	6.50	15.00
		Nos. O32-O38 (7)	8.80	23.00

Same Overprint on Official Stamps of Germany, 1920-21

1920-21				
O39	O1	5pf green	1.00	8.00
O40	O2	10pf carmine	.25	1.00
O41	O3	15pf violet brn	.25	1.00
O42	O4	20pf deep ultra	.25	1.00
O43	O5	30pf orange, buff	.25	1.00
O44	O6	40pf carmine rose	.25	1.00
O45	O7	50pf violet, buff	.25	1.00
O46	O8	60pf red brown	.25	1.00
O47	O9	1m red, buff	.25	1.00
O48	O10	1.25m dk blue, yel	.25	1.00
O49	O11	2m dark blue	7.25	12.00
O50	O12	5m brown, yel	.25	1.00
1922, Feb.			Wmk. 126	
O51	O11	2m dark blue	.25	1.00
		Nos. O39-O51 (13)	11.00	31.00

This overprint is found both horizontal, reading upright or inverted, and vertical, reading up or down. These variations generally command no premium over the values above.

The overprint also exists on most values double and double, one inverted, in the above formats, as well as at a 45 degree angle, upreading and downreading, either upright or inverted. These varieties generally sell for 25-100 percent over the value of normal examples.

URUGUAY

ˈyur-ə-ˌgwā

LOCATION — South America, between Brazil and Argentina and bordering on the Atlantic Ocean
GOVT. — Republic
AREA — 68,037 sq. mi.
POP. — 3,137,668 (1996)
CAPITAL — Montevideo

120 Centavos = 1 Real
8 Reales = 1 Peso
100 Centesimos = 1 Peso (1859)
1000 Milesimos = 1 Peso (1898)

Watermarks

Wmk. 90 — Large Sun and RA

Wmk. 187 — R O in Diamond

Wmk. 188 — REPUBLICA O. DEL URUGUAY

Wmk. 189 — Caduceus

Wmk. 227 — Greek Border and REPUBLICA O. DEL URUGUAY in Alternate Curved Lines

Wmk. 327 — Coat of Arms

Wmk. 332 — Large Sun and R O U

Catalogue values for unused stamps in this country are for Never Hinged items, beginning with Scott 534 in the regular postage section, Scott B5 in the semipostal section, Scott C113 in the airpost section, Scott CB1 in the airpost semi-postal section, Scott E9 in the special delivery section, and Scott Q64 in the parcel post section.

CARRIER ISSUES
Issued by Atanasio Lapido, Administrator-General of Posts

A1   A1a
"El Sol de Mayo"
Unwmk.

1856, Oct. 1		**Litho.**		**Imperf.**
1	A1	60c blue	450.	450.
2	A1	80c green	500.	500.
3	A1	1r vermilion	400.	400.

1857, Oct. 1
3B	A1a	60c blue	2,750.	—

Nos. 1-3B were spaced very closely on the stone. Very fine examples will have clear margins on three sides and touching or slightly cut into the frames on the fourth (consult the grading illustrations in the catalogue introduction). All genuinely used examples are pen canceled. Certification by a recognized authority is recommended.

Stamps with tiny faults, such as small thin spots, sell for about 75% of the values of sound examples.

See Nos. 410-413, 771A.

A2

1858, Mar.
4	A2	120c blue	550.00	550.00
c.		Tête bêche pair	—	
5	A2	180c green	120.00	175.00
c.		Thick paper	500.00	
d.		Tête bêche pair	—	
6	A2	240c dull ver	150.00	1,500.
c.		180c in stone of 240c	—	
d.		Thick paper (dull ver)	—	
e.		240c setenant with a vacant space	5,000.	
		Nos. 4-6 (3)	820.00	2,225.

Nos. 4-6e have been extensively forged. Certification by a recognized authority is recommended.

GOVERNMENT ISSUES

A3   A4

1859, June 26 — **Thin Numerals**
7	A3	60c lilac	45.00	35.00
a.		60c gray lilac	50.00	35.00
8	A3	80c orange	300.00	60.00
a.		80c yellow	450.00	75.00
9	A3	100c brown lake	100.00	70.00
a.		100c brown rose	120.00	100.00
10	A3	120c blue	55.00	30.00
a.		120c slate blue	75.00	25.00
11	A3	180c green	22.00	25.00
12	A3	240c vermilion	90.00	90.00
		Nos. 7-12 (6)	612.00	310.00

1860 — **Thick Numerals**
13	A4	60c dull lilac	25.00	12.00
a.		60c gray lilac	25.00	12.00
b.		60c brown lilac	30.00	18.00
c.		60c red lilac	120.00	60.00
d.		As "a," fine impression (1st printing)	70.00	40.00
14	A4	80c yellow	50.00	25.00
a.		80c orange	100.00	27.50
15	A4	100c rose	100.00	55.00
a.		100c carmine	110.00	55.00
16	A4	120c blue	42.50	25.00
17	A4	180c yellow grn	425.00	375.00
a.		180c deep green	425.00	450.00
		Nos. 13-17 (5)	642.50	492.00

No. 13 was first printed (1860) in sheets of 192 (16x12) containing 24 types. The impressions are very clear; paper is whitish and of better quality than that of the later printings. In the 1861-62 printings, the layout contains 12 types and the subjects are spaced farther apart.

Coat of Arms — A5

1864, Apr. 13
18	A5	6c rose	12.00	10.00
a.		6c carmine	40.00	30.00
b.		6c red	40.00	30.00
c.		6c brick red	40.00	30.00
20	A5	6c salmon	300.00	500.00
21	A5	8c green	22.00	22.00
a.		Tête bêche pair	775.00	
22	A5	10c yellow	30.00	25.00
a.		10c ocher	30.00	25.00
23	A5	12c blue	15.00	12.00
a.		12c dark blue	25.00	18.00
b.		12c slate blue	30.00	20.00

No. 20, which is on thicker paper, was never placed in use.

Stamps of 1864 Surcharged in Black

1866, Jan. 1
24	A5	5c on 12c blue	26.00	55.00
a.		5c on 12c slate blue	30.00	60.00
b.		Inverted surcharge	150.00	
c.		Double surcharge	150.00	
d.		Pair, one without surcharge	150.00	
e.		Triple surcharge	55.00	
25	A5	10c on 8c brt grn	26.00	55.00
a.		10c on 8c dl grn	26.00	55.00
b.		Tête bêche pair	300.00	
c.		Double surcharge	150.00	
26	A5	15c on 10c ocher	26.00	85.00
a.		15c on 10c yellow	26.00	85.00
b.		Inverted surcharge	150.00	
c.		Double surcharge	150.00	
27	A5	20c on 6c rose	35.00	85.00
a.		20c on 6c rose red	37.50	75.00
b.		Inverted surcharge	150.00	
c.		Double surcharge	150.00	
d.		Pair, one without surcharge	150.00	
28	A5	20c on 6c brick red	350.00	
a.		Double surcharge	400.00	
		Nos. 24-27 (4)	113.00	280.00

Many counterfeits exist.
No. 28 was not issued.

Coat of Arms and Numeral of Value — A7

A8   A8a

A8b   A8c

Type I

Type II

ONE CENTESIMO:
Type I — The wavy lines behind "CENTESIMO" are clear and distinct. Stamps 4mm apart.
Type II — The wavy lines are rough and blurred. Stamps 3mm apart.

1866, Jan. 10 — **Imperf.**
29	A7	1c black (type II)	5.00	7.50
a.		1c black (type I)	5.00	7.50
30	A8	5c blue	5.00	2.50
a.		5c dull blue	5.00	2.50
b.		5c ultramarine	32.50	7.50
c.		Numeral with white flag	25.00	12.00
d.		"ENTECIMOS"	25.00	12.00
e.		"CENTECIMO"	25.00	12.00
f.		"CENTECIMOS" with small "S"	25.00	12.00
g.		Pelure paper	100.00	100.00
h.		Thick paper		
31	A8a	10c yellow green	17.50	6.00
a.		10c blue green	17.00	6.00
b.		"I" of "CENTECIMOS" omitted	27.50	14.00
c.		"CENIECIMOS"	27.50	14.00
d.		"CENTRCIMOS"	27.50	14.00
32	A8b	15c orange yel	26.00	11.00
a.		15c yellow	26.00	11.00
33	A8c	20c rose	30.00	11.00
a.		20c lilac rose	30.00	11.00
b.		Thick paper	35.00	15.00
		Nos. 29-33 (5)	83.50	38.00

See Nos. 34-38. For overprint see No. O11.

Engraved plates were prepared for Nos. 30 to 33 but were not put in use. The stamps were printed from lithographic transfers from the plate. In 1915 a few reprints of the 15c were made from the engraved plate by a California philatelic society, each sheet being numbered and signed by officers of the society; then the plate was defaced.

1866-67 — **Perf. 8½ to 13½**
34	A7	1c black	5.00	20.00
35	A8	5c blue	5.00	1.00
a.		5c dark blue	5.00	1.00
b.		Numeral with white flag	15.00	8.00
c.		"ENTECIMOS"	15.00	8.00
d.		"CENTECIMO"	15.00	8.00
e.		"CENTECIMOS" with small "S"	15.00	8.00
f.		Pelure paper	90.00	20.00
36	A8a	10c green	12.00	4.00
a.		10c yellow green	14.00	4.00
b.		"CENIECIMOS"	20.00	10.00
c.		"I" of "CENTECIMOS" omitted	20.00	10.00
d.		"CENTRCIMOS"	20.00	10.00
e.		Pelure paper	90.00	20.00
37	A8b	15c orange yel	21.00	6.00
a.		15c yellow	21.00	6.00
b.		Thin paper	25.00	10.00
38	A8c	20c rose	25.00	10.00
a.		20c brown rose	25.00	10.00
b.		Thin paper	30.00	15.00
c.		Thick paper	30.00	15.00
		Nos. 34-38 (5)	68.00	41.00

A9   A10

A11

A12

1877-79 Engr. Rouletted 8

39	A9	1c red brown	.70	.50
40	A10	5c green	.70	.60
a.		Thick paper	5.00	2.50
41	A11	10c vermilion	1.10	.60
42	A11	20c bister	1.20	.60
43	A11	50c black	9.00	3.50
43A	A12	1p blue ('79)	45.00	25.00
		Nos. 39-43A (6)	57.70	30.70

The first printing of the 1p had the coat of arms smaller with quarterings reversed. These "error" stamps were not issued, and all were ordered burned. One example is known to have been in a celebrated Uruguayan collection and a few others exist.

See No. 44. For overprints and surcharges see Nos. 52-53, O1-O8, O10, O19.

1880, Nov. 10 Engr. Rouletted 6

44	A9	1c brown	.40	.40
a.		Imperf., pair	10.00	
b.		Rouletted 12½	2.50	

Joaquin Suárez — A13

1881, Aug. 25 Perf. 12½

45	A13	7c blue	1.75	1.75
a.		Imperf., pair	9.00	9.00

For overprint see No. O9.

Devices from Coat of Arms
A14   A14a

1882, May 15

46	A14	1c green	1.25	1.25
a.		1c yellow green	4.00	2.00
b.		Imperf., pair	13.00	
47	A14a	2c rose	1.00	.75
a.		Imperf., pair	15.00	

These stamps bear numbers from 1 to 100 according to their position on the sheet. Counterfeits of Nos. 46 and 47 are plentiful. See Nos. 1132-1133. For overprints see Nos. 54, O12-O13, O20.

Coat of Arms
A15   A16

Gen. Máximo   General José
Santos — A17   Artigas — A18

Perf. 12, 12x12½, 12x13, 13x12
1883, Mar. 1

48	A15	1c green	1.25	1.00
49	A16	2c red	1.50	1.25
50	A17	5c blue	2.50	1.75
51	A18	10c brown	3.00	2.10
		Nos. 48-51 (4)	8.25	6.10

Imperf., Pairs

48a	A15	1c	7.00
49a	A16	2c	7.00
50a	A17	5c	6.50
51a	A18	10c	11.00

For overprints see Nos. O14-O18.

No. 40 Overprinted in Black

1883, Sept. 24 Rouletted 8

52	A10	5c green	1.00	.75
a.		Double overprint	15.00	15.00
b.		Overprint reading down	6.00	6.00
c.		"Provisorio" omitted	7.00	7.00
d.		"1883" omitted	4.50	4.50

No. 52 with overprint in red is a color essay.

No. 41 Surcharged in Black

1884, Jan. 15

53	A11	1c on 10c ver	.50	.50
a.		Small figure "1"	4.25	4.25
b.		Inverted surcharge	4.25	4.25
c.		Double surcharge	8.00	5.00

No. 47 Overprinted in Black

Perf. 12½

54	A14a	2c rose	.75	.75
a.		Double overprint	14.00	
b.		Imperf., pair	40.00	

A22

A23

Thick Paper
1884, Jan. 25 Litho. Unwmk.

55	A22	5c ultra	2.00	1.00
a.		Imperf., pair	7.50	4.00

Thin Paper
Perf. 12½, 13 and Compound

56	A23	5c blue	1.50	.70
a.		Imperf., pair	14.00	

For overprints see Nos. O21-O22.

A24

A24a

A24b

Artigas — A25

Santos — A26

A27

A28

1884-88 Engr. Rouletted 8

57	A24	1c gray	.80	.50
58	A24	1c olive	.75	.40
59	A24	1c green	.65	.40
60	A24a	2c vermilion	.40	.25
60A	A24a	2c rose ('88)	.40	.25
61	A24b	5c deep blue	.80	.30
61A	A24b	5c blue, blue	2.00	.85
62	A24b	5c violet ('86)	.50	.25
63	A24b	5c lt bl ('88)	.50	.25
64	A25	7c dk brown	2.00	.85
65	A25	7c org ('88)	2.00	.75
66	A26	10c olive brn	.80	.35
67	A27	20c red violet	2.00	1.00
68	A27	20c bis brn ('88)	2.00	1.00
69	A28	25c gray violet	4.00	1.50
70	A28	25c ver ('88)	3.00	1.00
		Nos. 57-70 (16)	22.60	9.90

Water dissolves the blue in the paper of No. 61A.

For overprints see Nos. 73, 98-99, O23-O34, O36-O39, O61.

A29

A30

1887, Oct. 17 Litho. Rouletted 9

71	A29	10c lilac	2.50	1.25
a.		10c gray lilac	3.00	1.25

For overprint see No. O40.

1888, Jan. 1 Engr. Rouletted 8

72	A30	10c violet	.60	.25

For overprint see No. O35.

No. 62 Overprinted in Black

1889, Oct. 14

73	A24b	5c violet	.40	.40
a.		Inverted overprint	8.00	6.00
b.		Inverted "A" for "V" in "Provisorio"	4.00	4.00

No. 73 with overprint in red is a color essay.

Coat of   Numeral of
Arms — A32   Value — A33

A34

A35

A36

A37

Justice
A38

Mercury
A39

A40

Perf. 12½ to 15½ and Compound
1889-1901 Engr.

74	A32	1c green	.50	.25
a.		Imperf., pair	13.00	
75	A32	1c dull bl ('94)	.50	.25
76	A33	2c rose	.50	.25
77	A33	2c red brn ('94)	.55	.25
78	A33	2c org ('99)	.55	.25
79	A34	5c dp blue	.50	.25
80	A34	5c rose ('94)	.55	.25
81	A35	7c bister brn	1.00	.30
82	A35	7c green ('94)	4.75	2.75
83	A35	7c car ('00)	4.00	1.75
84	A36	10c blue grn	3.50	.85
a.		Printed on both sides	20.00	
85	A36	10c org ('94)	3.25	.60
86	A37	20c orange	2.50	.60
87	A37	20c brown ('94)	4.75	1.75
88	A37	20c lt blue ('00)	2.75	.40
a.		20c greenish blue	3.00	.40
89	A38	25c red brown	3.25	.85
90	A38	25c ver ('94)	6.75	3.50
91	A38	25c bis brn ('01)	3.75	.50
92	A39	50c lt blue	7.50	5.00
93	A39	50c lilac ('94)	11.00	5.50
94	A39	50c car ('01)	6.75	1.00
95	A40	1p lilac	18.00	5.00
96	A40	1p lt hlue ('94)	25.00	7.00
97	A40	1p dp grn ('01)	20.00	2.25
a.		Imperf., pair	30.00	
		Nos. 74-97 (24)	132.15	41.35

For surcharges and overprints see Nos. 100-101, 142, 180, 185, C1-C3, O41-O60, O89-O91, O108-O109.

Nos. 59 and 62 Overprinted in Red

a   b

1891-92 Rouletted 8

98	A24 (a)	1c green ('92)	.40	.40
a.		Inverted overprint	6.00	6.00
b.		Double overprint	7.75	2.75
c.		Double ovpt., one invtd.	3.00	2.50
d.		"PREVISORIO"	4.00	4.00
99	A24b (b)	5c violet	.25	.25
a.		"1391"	4.00	2.75
b.		Double overprint	4.00	2.75
c.		Inverted overprint	4.00	2.75
d.		Double ovpt., one invtd.	5.00	3.00

Nos. 86 and 81 Surcharged in Black or Red

c   d

Perf. 12½ to 15½ and Compound
1892

100	A37 (c)	1c on 20c org (Bk)	.40	.40
a.		Inverted surcharge	3.00	3.00
101	A35 (d)	5c on 7c bis brn (R)	.40	.40
a.		Inverted surcharge	1.00	1.00
b.		Double surcharge, one invtd.	3.00	3.00
c.		Double surcharge	3.00	3.00
d.		Vertical surcharge	10.00	
e.		"PREVISORIO"	3.00	3.00
f.		"Cinco" omitted	4.50	

No. 101 with surcharge in green is a color essay.

Several surcharge errors of date and misspelling of "Centésimos" exist. Value $15.

A45

A46

Arms
A47

Peace
A48

1892   **Engr.**
102 A45 1c green .50 .25
103 A46 2c rose .50 .25
104 A47 5c blue .50 .25
105 A48 10c orange 2.00 .85
    Nos. 102-105 (4) 3.50 1.60

Issued: 1c, 2c, 3/9; 5c, 4/19; 10c, 12/15.

Liberty
A49

Arms
A50

1894, June 2
106 A49 2p carmine 27.50 17.00
107 A50 3p dull violet 27.50 17.00

Gaucho
A51

Solis Theater
A52

Locomotive
A53

Bull's Head
A54

Ceres — A55

Sailing
Ship — A56

Liberty — A57

Mercury — A58

Coat of
Arms — A59

Montevideo
Fortress — A60

Cathedral in
Montevideo
A61

Perf. 12 to 15½ and Compound
1895-99
108 A51 1c bister .50 .25
109 A51 1c slate bl ('97) .50 .25
 a. Printed on both sides 14.00
110 A52 2c blue .50 .25
111 A52 2c claret ('97) .50 .25
112 A53 5c red .50 .25
113 A53 5c green ('97) .65 .25
 a. Imperf., pair 3.50
114 A53 5c grnsh bl ('99) 1.00 .40
115 A54 7c deep green 7.75 2.50
116 A54 7c orange ('97) 3.50 1.25
117 A55 10c brown 2.00 .50
118 A56 20c green & blk 7.00 .85
119 A56 20c cl & blk ('97) 4.75 .60
120 A57 25c red brn & blk 5.50 1.50
 a. Center inverted 2,000.
121 A57 25c pink & bl ('97) 3.50 .60
122 A58 50c blue & blk 7.00 3.50
123 A58 50c grn & brn ('97) 5.00 1.25
124 A59 1p org brn & blk 14.00 5.50
125 A59 1p yel brn & bl ('97) 9.50 3.50
126 A60 2p violet & grn 32.50 20.00
127 A60 2p bis & car ('97) 9.50 2.00
128 A61 3p carmine & blue 32.50 20.00
129 A61 3p lil & car ('97) 12.50 2.50
    Nos. 108-129 (22) 160.65 67.95

All values of this issue exist imperforate but they were not issued in that form.
For overprints and surcharges see Nos. 138-140, 143, 145, 147, O62-O78.

President Joaquin Suárez
A62   A63

Statue of President
Suárez — A64

Perf. 12½ to 15 and Compound
1896, July 18
130 A62 1c brown vio & blk .25 .25
131 A63 5c pale bl & blk .25 .25
132 A64 10c lake & blk 1.00 .30
    Nos. 130-132 (3) 1.50 .80

Dedication of Pres. Suárez statue.
For overprints and surcharge see Nos. 133-135, 144, 146, 152, O79-O81.

Same Overprinted in Red

e

f

1897, Mar. 1
133 A62 (e) 1c brn vio & blk .40 .40
 a. Inverted overprint 6.00 6.00
134 A63 (e) 5c pale blue & blk .50 .40
 a. Inverted overprint 9.50 6.00
135 A64 (f) 10c lake & blk 1.00 .60
 a. Inverted overprint 12.00 9.50
 b. Double overprint 7.50
    Nos. 133-135 (3) 1.90 1.40

"Electricity" — A68

1897-99   **Engr.**
136 A68 10c red 1.75 .40
137 A68 10c red lilac ('99) .75 .50

For overprints see Nos. 141, O82-O83.

Regular Issues
Overprinted in Red or Blue

1897, Sept. 26
138 A51 1c slate bl (R) .80 .60
 a. Inverted overprint 4.75 4.75
139 A52 2c claret (Bl) 1.25 1.25
 a. Inverted overprint 4.75 4.75
140 A53 5c green (Bl) 1.75 1.60
 a. Inverted overprint 7.75 7.75
141 A68 10c red (Bl) 2.75 2.75
 a. Inverted overprint 17.00 17.00
    Nos. 138-141 (4) 6.55 6.20

Commemorating the Restoration of Peace at the end of the Civil War.
Issue for use only on the days of the National Fête, Sept. 26-28, 1897.

Regular Issues
Surcharged in Black, Blue or Red

1898, July 25
142 A32 ½c on 1c bl (Bk) .40 .40
 a. Inverted surcharge 3.00 3.00
143 A51 ½c on 1c bis (Bl) .40 .40
 a. Inverted surcharge 3.00
 b. Double surcharge 2.50
144 A62 ½c on 1c brn vio & blk (R) .40 .40
145 A52 ½c on 2c blue (Bk) .40 .40
146 A63 ½c on 5c pale bl & blk (R) .40 .40
 a. Double surcharge 6.25
147 A54 ½c on 7c dp grn (R) .40 .40
    Nos. 142-147 (6) 2.40 2.40

The 2c red brown of 1894 (#77) was also surcharged like #142-147 but was not issued. Value $12.

Liberty — A69

Statue of
Artigas — A70

1898-99   **Litho.**   **Perf. 11, 11½**
148 A69 5m rose .25 .25
149 A69 5m purple ('99) .25 .25

1899-1900 Engr. Perf. 12½, 14, 15
150 A70 5m lt blue .25 .25
151 A70 5m orange ('00) .25 .25

No. 135 With
Additional Surcharge
in Black

1900, Dec. 1
152 A64 5c on 10c lake & blk .50 .25
 a. Black bar covering "1897" omitted 15.00

Cattle — A72

Girl's
Head — A73

Shepherdess — A74

Perf. 13½ to 16 and Compound
1900-10   **Engr.**
153 A72 1c yellow green .40 .25
154 A73 5c dull blue .80 .25
155 A73 5c slate grn ('10) .80 .25
156 A74 10c gray violet 1.00 .25
    Nos. 153-156 (4) 3.00 1.00

For surcharges and overprints see Nos. 179, 184, O84, O86, O88, O106-O107.

Eros and
Cornucopia
A75

Basket of Fruit
A76

1901, Feb. 11
157 A75 2c vermilion .50 .25
158 A76 7c brown orange 1.75 .25

For surcharges and overprints see Nos. 197-198, O85, O87, O105.

General
Artigas — A78

Cattle — A79

Eros — A80

Cow — A81

Shepherdess
A82

Numeral
A83

Justice — A84

1904-05   **Litho.**   **Perf. 11½**
160 A78 5m orange .40 .25
 a. 5m yellow .40
161 A79 1c green .50 .25
 a. Imperf., pair 3.50
162 A80 2c dp orange .25 .25
 a. 2c orange red .25 .25
 b. Imperf., pair 3.00
163 A81 5c blue .80 .25
 a. Imperf., pair 3.50
164 A82 10c dk violet ('05) .50 .25
165 A83 20c gray grn ('05) 2.50 .50
166 A84 25c olive bis ('05) 3.25 .80
    Nos. 160-166 (7) 8.20 2.55

For overprints see Nos. 167-169, O92-O98, O101-O103.

Overprinted Diagonally
in Carmine or Black

1904, Oct. 15
167 A79 1c green (C) .40 .40
168 A80 2c deep orange (Bk) .65 .40
169 A81 5c dark blue (C) 1.25 .60
 Nos. 167-169 (3) 2.30 1.40

End of the Civil War of 1904. In the first overprinting, "Paz 1904" appears at a 50-degree angle; in the second, at a 63-degree angle.

A85 A86

1906, Feb. 23 Litho. Unwmk.
170 A85 5c dark blue 1.10 .25
 a. Imperf., pair 6.00

1906-07
171 A86 5c deep blue .30 .30
172 A86 7c orange brn ('07) .70 .50
173 A86 50c rose 5.00 1.25
 Nos. 171-173 (3) 6.00 2.05

Cruiser "Montevideo" — A87

1908, Aug. 23 Typo. Rouletted 13
174 A87 1c car & dk grn 2.00 1.50
175 A87 2c green & dk grn 2.00 1.50
176 A87 5c org & dk grn 2.00 1.50
 Nos. 174-176 (3) 6.00 4.50

Center Inverted
174a A87 1c 300.00 300.00
175a A87 2c 300.00 300.00
176a A87 5c 300.00 300.00
 Nos. 174a-176a (3) 900.00 900.00

Imperf., Pairs
174b A87 1c 30.00
175b A87 2c 30.00
176b A87 5c 30.00

Independence of Uruguay, declared Aug. 25, 1825. Counterfeits exist.
For surcharges and overprints see Nos. 186, O99-O100, O104, O110.

View of the Port of Montevideo — A88

Wmk. 187
1909, Aug. 24 Engr. Perf. 11½
177 A88 2c lt brown & blk 1.25 1.00
178 A88 5c rose red & blk 1.25 1.00

Issued to commemorate the opening of the Port of Montevideo, Aug. 25, 1909.

Nos. 156, 91
Surcharged

Perf. 14 to 16
1909, Sept. 13 Unwmk.
179 A74 8c on 10c dull vio .75 .25
 a. "Contesimos" 4.00 2.00
180 A38 23c on 25c bis brn 1.75 .60

Centaur — A89

Wmk. 187
1910, May 22 Engr. Perf. 11½
182 A89 2c carmine red .60 .40
183 A89 5c deep blue .60 .40

Cent. of Liberation Day, May 25, 1810.
The 2c in deep blue and 5c in carmine red were prepared for collectors.

Stamps of 1900-06 Surcharged

g h

i

Perf. 14 to 16, 11½
1910, Oct. 6 Unwmk.
Black Surcharge
184 A72 (g) 5m on 1c yel grn .25 .25
 a. Inverted surcharge 4.50 3.75
Dark Blue Surcharge
185 A39 (h) 5c on 50c dull red .40 .25
 a. Inverted surcharge 4.50 4.50
Blue Surcharge
186 A86 (i) 5c on 50c rose .80 .45
 a. Double surcharge 20.00
 b. Inverted surcharge 10.00 8.75
 Nos. 184-186 (3) 1.45 .95

Artigas
A90

"Commercial Progress"
A91

1910, Nov. 21 Engr. Perf. 14, 15
187 A90 5m dk violet .25 .25
188 A90 1c dp green .25 .25
189 A90 2c orange red .25 .25
190 A90 5c dk blue .25 .25
191 A90 8c gray blk .40 .25
192 A90 20c brown .60 .25
193 A91 23c dp ultra 2.75 .40
194 A91 50c orange 4.00 1.25
195 A91 1p scarlet 7.50 1.25
 Nos. 187-195 (9) 16.25 4.40

See Nos. 199-210. For overprints see Nos. 211-213, O118-O124.

Symbolical of the
Posts — A92

1911, Jan. 6 Wmk. 187 Perf. 11½
196 A92 5c rose car & blk .80 .60

1st South American Postal Cong., at Montevideo, Jan. 1911.

No. 158 Surcharged
in Red or Dark Blue

Perf. 14 to 16
1911, May 17 Unwmk.
197 A76 2c on 7c brn org (R) .40 .40
198 A76 5c on 7c brn org (Bl) .40 .25
 a. Inverted surcharge 8.50 8.50

Centenary of the battle of Las Piedras, won by the forces under Gen. Jose Gervasio Artigas, May 8, 1811.

Types of 1910

FOUR AND FIVE CENTESIMOS:
Type I — Large numerals about 3mm high.
Type II — Small numerals about 2¼mm high.

1912-15 Typo. Perf. 11½
199 A90 5m violet .25 .25
 a. 5m purple .25 .25
200 A90 5m magenta .25 .25
 a. 5m dull rose .25 .25
201 A90 1c green ('13) .25 .25
202 A90 2c brown org .25 .25
203 A90 2c rose red ('13) .25 .25
 a. 2c deep red ('14) .25 .25
204 A90 4c org (I) ('14) .25 .25
 a. 4c orange (II) ('15) .25 .25
 b. 4c yellow (II) ('13) .25 .25
205 A90 5c dull bl (I) .40 .25
 a. 5c blue (II) .40 .25
206 A90 8c ultra ('13) .50 .25
207 A90 20c brown ('13) 1.40 .25
 a. 20c chocolate 1.40 .25
208 A91 23c dk blue ('15) 3.50 .60
209 A91 50c orange ('14) 3.50 1.50
210 A91 1p vermilion ('15) 10.50 1.25
 Nos. 199-210 (12) 21.30 5.60

Stamps of 1912-15
Overprinted

CENTENARIO
DE LAS
INSTRUCCIONES
DEL
AÑO XIII

1913, Apr. 4
211 A90 2c brown orange .85 .50
 a. Inverted overprint 5.00 4.50
212 A90 4c yellow .85 .50
213 A90 5c blue .85 .50
 Nos. 211-213 (3) 2.55 1.50

Cent. of the Buenos Aires Cong. of 1813.

Liberty
Extending
Peace to the
Country — A93

1918, Jan. 3 Litho.
214 A93 2c green & red .85 .50
215 A93 5c buff & blue .85 .50

Promulgation of the Constitution.

Statue of
Liberty, New
York Harbor
A94

Harbor of
Montevideo
A95

Perf. 14, 15, 13½
1919, July 15 Engr.
217 A94 2c carmine & brn .55 .25
218 A94 4c orange & brn .55 .25
219 A94 5c blue & brn .80 .40
220 A94 8c org brn & ind .80 .40
221 A94 20c ol bis & blk 2.00 .80
222 A94 23c green & blk 4.00 1.25
 Nos. 217-222 (6) 8.70 3.35

Peace at end of World War I.
Perf 13½ used only on 2c, 20c, 23c.

1919-20 Litho. Perf. 11½
225 A95 5m violet & blk .25 .25
226 A95 1c green & blk .25 .25
227 A95 2c red & blk .25 .25
228 A95 4c orange & blk .35 .25
229 A95 5c ultra & slate .40 .25
230 A95 8c gray bl & blk .50 .25
231 A95 20c brown & blk 1.60 .35
232 A95 23c green & brn 2.75 .65
233 A95 50c brown & blue 5.00 2.00
234 A95 1p dull red & bl 10.00 3.00
 Nos. 225-234 (10) 21.35 7.50

For overprints see Nos. O125-O131.

José Enrique
Rodó — A96

Mercury — A97

1920, Feb. 28 Engr. Perf. 14, 15
235 A96 2c car & blk .55 .40
236 A96 4c org & bl .65 .50
237 A96 5c bl & brn .75 .55
 Nos. 235-237 (3) 1.95 1.45

Issued to honor José Enrique Rodó, author.
For surcharges see Nos. P2-P4.

1921-22 Litho. Perf. 11½
238 A97 5m lilac .25 .25
239 A97 5m gray blk ('22) .25 .25
240 A97 1c lt grn .25 .25
241 A97 1c vio ('22) .25 .25
242 A97 2c fawn .40 .25
243 A97 2c red ('22) .40 .25
244 A97 3c bl grn ('22) .60 .25
245 A97 4c orange .40 .25
246 A97 5c ultra .50 .25
247 A97 5c choc ('22) .60 .25
248 A97 12c ultra ('22) 2.40 .60
249 A97 36c ol grn ('22) 7.75 2.75
 Nos. 238-249 (12) 14.05 5.85

See Nos. 254-260. For overprint and surcharge see Nos. E1, P1.

Dámaso A.
Larrañaga (1771-
1848), Bishop,
Writer, Scientist and
Physician — A98

1921, Dec. 10 Unwmk.
250 A98 5c slate 1.25 1.00

Mercury Type of 1921-22
1922-23 Wmk. 188
254 A97 5m gray blk .25 .25
255 A97 1c violet ('23) .25 .25
 a. 1c red violet .25 .25
256 A97 2c pale red .25 .25
257 A97 2c deep rose ('23) .30 .25
259 A97 5c yel brn ('23) .65 .25
260 A97 8c salmon pink ('23) 1.00 .90
 Nos. 254-260 (6) 2.70 2.15

Equestrian Statue of Artigas — A99

Unwmk.

1923, Feb. 26   Engr.   Perf. 14
264 A99 2c car & sepia .40 .25
265 A99 5c vio & sepia .40 .25
266 A99 12c blue & sepia .40 .25
Nos. 264-266 (3) 1.20 .75

Southern Lapwing A100

Battle Monument A101

Perf. 12½, 11½x12½

1923, June 25   Litho.   Wmk. 189
Size: 18x22½mm
267 A100 5m gray .25 .25
268 A100 1c org yel .25 .25
269 A100 2c lt vio .25 .25
270 A100 3c gray grn .40 .25
271 A100 5c lt bl .40 .25
272 A100 8c rose red .80 .50
273 A100 12c dp bl .80 .50
274 A100 20c brn org 2.00 .50
275 A100 36c emerald 4.00 1.75
276 A100 50c orange 6.75 2.75
277 A100 1p brt rose 32.50 20.00
278 A100 2p lt grn 47.50 20.00
Nos. 267-278 (12) 95.90 47.25

See #285-298, 309-314, 317-323, 334-339. For surcharges and overprints see Nos. 345-348, O132-O148, P5-P7.

1923, Oct. 12   Wmk. 188   Perf. 11½
279 A101 2c dp grn .55 .40
280 A101 5c scarlet .55 .40
281 A101 12c dk bl .55 .40
Nos. 279-281 (3) 1.65 1.20

Unveiling of the Sarandi Battle Monument by José Luis Zorrilla, Oct. 12, 1923.

"Victory of Samothrace" — A102

Unwmk.

1924, July 29   Typo.   Perf. 11
282 A102 2c rose 20.00 10.00
283 A102 5c mauve 20.00 10.00
284 A102 12c brt bl 20.00 10.00
Nos. 282-284 (3) 60.00 30.00

Olympic Games. Sheets of 20 (5x4). Five thousand sets of these stamps were printed on yellow paper for presentation purposes. They were not on sale at post offices. Value for set, $650.

Lapwing Type of 1923
First Redrawing
Imprint: "A. BARREIRO Y RAMOS"

1924, July 26   Litho.   Perf. 12½, 11½
Size: 17¼x21½mm
285 A100 5m gray blk .25 .25
286 A100 1c fawn .25 .25
287 A100 2c rose lil .30 .25
288 A100 3c gray grn .25 .25
289 A100 5c chalky blue .25 .25
290 A100 8c pink .50 .25
291 A100 10c turq blue .40 .25
292 A100 12c slate blue .50 .25
293 A100 15c lt vio .50 .25
294 A100 20c brown .75 .30
295 A100 36c salmon 3.00 .70
296 A100 50c greenish gray 5.00 2.00
297 A100 1p buff 12.00 4.00
298 A100 2p dl vio 20.00 10.00
Nos. 285-298 (14) 43.95 19.25

Landing of the 33 "Immortals" Led by Juan Antonio Lavalleja — A103

Perf. 11, 11½

1925, Apr. 19   Wmk. 188
300 A103 2c salmon pink & blk 1.40 .80
301 A103 5c lilac & blk 1.40 .80
302 A103 12c blue & blk 1.40 .80
Nos. 300-302 (3) 4.20 2.40

Cent. of the landing of the 33 Founders of the Uruguayan Republic.

Legislative Palace — A104

Perf. 11½

1925, Aug. 24   Unwmk.   Engr.
303 A104 5c vio & blk 1.25 .80
304 A104 12c bl & blk 1.25 .80

Dedication of the Legislative Palace.

General Fructuoso Rivera — A105

Wmk. 188

1925, Sept. 24   Litho.   Perf. 11
305 A105 5c light red .50 .40

Centenary of Battle of Rincón. See No. C9.

Battle of Sarandí A106

1925, Oct. 12   Perf. 11½
306 A106 2c bl grn 1.25 1.00
307 A106 5c dl vio 1.25 1.00
308 A106 12c dp bl 1.25 1.00
Nos. 306-308 (3) 3.75 3.00

Centenary of the Battle of Sarandi.

Lapwing Type of 1923
Second Redrawing
Imprint: "Imprenta Nacional"

1925-26   Perf. 11, 11½, 10½
Size: 17½x21¾mm
309 A100 5m gray blk 1.00 .25
310 A100 1c dl vio 1.25 .25
311 A100 2c brt rose 1.60 .25
312 A100 3c gray grn 1.25 .40
313 A100 5c dl bl ('26) 2.00 .25
314 A100 12c slate blue 4.00 .40
Nos. 309-314 (6) 11.10 1.80

The design differs in many small details from that of the 1923-24 issues. These stamps may be readily identified by the imprint and perforation.

Lapwing Type of 1923
Third Redrawing
Imprint: "Imp. Nacional" at center

1926-27   Perf. 11, 11½, 10½
Size: 17½x21¾mm
317 A100 5m gray .40 .25
318 A100 1c lt vio ('27) 2.40 .55
319 A100 2c red 1.75 .40
320 A100 3c gray grn 2.40 .65
321 A100 5c lt bl .75 .25

322 A100 8c pink ('27) 3.50 .80
323 A100 36c rose buff 8.00 4.00
Nos. 317-323 (7) 19.20 6.90

These stamps may be distinguished from preceding stamps of the same design by the imprint.

Philatelic Exhibition Issue

Post Office at Montevideo A107

Unwmk.

1927, May 25   Engr.   Imperf.
330 A107 2c green 4.75 3.50
a. Sheet of 4 20.00 20.00
331 A107 5c dull red 4.75 3.50
a. Sheet of 4 20.00 20.00
332 A107 8c dark blue 4.75 3.50
a. Sheet of 4 20.00 20.00
Nos. 330-332 (3) 14.25 10.50

Printed in sheets of 4 and sold at the Montevideo Exhibition. Lithographed counterfeits exist.

Lapwing Type of 1923
Fourth Redrawing
Imprint: "Imp. Nacional" at right

1927, May 6   Litho.   Wmk. 188
Size: 17¾x21¾mm
334 A100 1c gray vio .40 .25
335 A100 2c vermilion .40 .25
336 A100 3c gray grn .80 .35
337 A100 5c blue .40 .25
338 A100 8c rose 3.00 .80
339 A100 20c gray brn 4.00 1.60
Nos. 334-339 (6) 9.00 3.50

The design has been slightly retouched in various places. The imprint is in italic capitals and is placed below the right numeral of value.

No. 292 Surcharged in Red

Inauguración Ferrocarril SAN CARLOS à ROCHA 14/1/1928
5 cts. 5

1928, Jan. 13   Unwmk.   Perf. 11½
345 A100 2c on 12c slate blue 2.00 2.00
346 A100 5c on 12c slate blue 2.00 2.00
347 A100 10c on 12c slate blue 2.00 2.00
348 A100 15c on 12c slate blue 2.00 2.00
Nos. 345-348 (4) 8.00 8.00

Issued to celebrate the inauguration of the railroad between San Carlos and Rocha.

General Rivera — A108

1928, Apr. 19   Engr.   Perf. 12
349 A108 5c car rose .50 .35

Centenary of the Battle of Las Misiones.

Artigas (7 dots in panels below portrait.) — A109

Imprint: "Waterlow & Sons. Ltd., Londres"

Perf. 11, 12½, 13x13½, 12½x13, 13x12½

1928-43   Size: 16x19½mm
350 A109 5m black .25 .25
350A A109 5m org ('43) .25 .25
351 A109 1c dk vio .25 .25
352 A109 1c brn vio ('34) .25 .25
352A A109 1c vio bl ('43) .25 .25
353 A109 2c brn vio .25 .25
353A A109 2c brn red ('43) .25 .25

354 A109 3c bister .25 .25
355 A109 3c dp grn ('32) .25 .25
355A A109 3c brt grn ('43) .25 .25
356 A109 5c red .25 .25
357 A109 5c ol grn ('33) .25 .25
357A A109 5c dl pur ('43) .25 .25
358 A109 7c car ('32) .25 .25
359 A109 8c dk bl .25 .25
360 A109 8c brn ('33) .25 .25
361 A109 10c orange .25 .25
362 A109 10c red org ('32) .60 .40
363 A109 12c dp bl ('32) .40 .25
364 A109 15c dl bl .40 .25
365 A109 17c dk vio ('32) .80 .25
366 A109 20c ol brn .65 .25
367 A109 20c red brn ('33) 1.25 .50
368 A109 24c car rose .90 .35
369 A109 24c yel ('33) .80 .40
370 A109 36c ol grn ('33) 1.40 .50
371 A109 50c gray 2.40 1.25
372 A109 50c blk ('33) 3.50 1.60
373 A109 50c blk brn ('33) 3.00 1.25
374 A109 1p yel grn 7.00 4.00
Nos. 350-374 (30) 27.35 15.50

1929-33   Perf. 12½
Size: 22 to 22½x28½ to 29½mm
375 A109 1p ol brn ('33) 6.00 4.00
376 A109 2p dk grn 17.00 9.00
377 A109 2p dl red ('32) 20.00 16.00
378 A109 3p dk bl 25.00 17.00
379 A109 3p blk ('32) 23.00 20.00
380 A109 4p violet 28.00 17.00
381 A109 4p dk ol grn ('32) 23.00 20.00
382 A109 5p car brn 32.50 23.00
383 A109 5p red org ('32) 30.00 20.00
384 A109 10p lake ('33) 92.50 70.00
385 A109 10p dp ultra ('33) 92.50 70.00
Nos. 375-385 (11) 389.50 286.00

See Nos. 420-423, 462. See type A135.

Equestrian Statue of Artigas — A110

1928, May 1
386 A110 2p Prus bl & choc 16.00 7.75
387 A110 3p dp rose & blk 23.00 12.00

Symbolical of Soccer Victory — A111

Gen. Eugenio Garzón — A112

1928, July 29
388 A111 2c brn vio 16.00 9.25
389 A111 5c dp red 16.00 9.25
390 A111 8c ultra 16.00 9.25
Nos. 388-390 (3) 48.00 27.75

Uruguayan soccer victories in the Olympic Games of 1924 and 1928. Printed in sheets of 20, in panes of 10 (5x2).

1928, July 29   Imperf.
391 A112 2c red 1.40 1.40
a. Sheet of 4 6.50 6.50
392 A112 5c yel grn 1.40 1.40
a. Sheet of 4 6.50 6.50
393 A112 8c dp bl 1.40 1.40
a. Sheet of 4 6.50 6.50
Nos. 391-393 (3) 4.20 4.20

Dedication of monument to Garzon. Issued in sheets of 4. Lithographed counterfeits exist.

Black River Bridge A113

Gauchos Breaking a Horse — A114

Peace A115

Montevideo A116

Liberty and Flag of Uruguay A117

Liberty with Torch and Caduceus A118

Statue of Artigas A124

Artigas Dictating Instructions for 1813 Congress A119

Seascape A120

Montevideo Harbor, 1830 — A121

Liberty and Coat of Arms A122

Montevideo Harbor, 1930 — A123

1930, June 16   *Perf. 12½, 12*

394	A113	5m gray blk	.25	.25
395	A114	1c dk brn	.25	.25
396	A115	2c brn rose	.25	.25
397	A116	3c yel grn	.25	.25
398	A117	5c dk bl	.25	.25
399	A118	8c dl red	.35	.25
400	A119	10c dk vio	.50	.35
401	A120	15c bl grn	.65	.50
402	A121	20c indigo	.80	.65

403	A122	24c red brn	1.10	.80
404	A123	50c org red	3.00	2.00
405	A124	1p black	6.00	3.00
406	A124	2p bl vio	14.00	8.50
407	A124	3p dk red	20.00	14.00
408	A124	4p red org	23.00	19.00
409	A124	5p lilac	35.00	22.50
		Nos. 394-409 (16)	105.65	72.80

Cent. of natl. independence and the promulgation of the constitution.

Type of 1856 Issue
Values in Centesimos
Wmk. 227

1931, Apr. 11   Litho.   *Imperf.*

410	A1	2c gray blue	3.00	2.00
a.		Sheet of 4	15.00	15.00
411	A1	8c dull red	3.00	2.00
a.		Sheet of 4	15.00	15.00
412	A1	15c blue black	3.00	2.00
a.		Sheet of 4	15.00	15.00

Wmk. 188

413	A1	5c light green	3.00	2.00
a.		Sheet of 4	15.00	15.00
		Nos. 410-413 (4)	12.00	8.00

Sold only at the Philatelic Exhibition, Montevideo, Apr. 11-15, 1931. Issued in sheets of 4.

Juan Zorrilla de San Martin, Uruguayan Poet — A125

1932, June 6   Unwmk.   *Perf. 12½*

414	A125	1½c brown violet	.25	.25
415	A125	3c green	.25	.25
416	A125	7c dk blue	.25	.25
417	A125	12c lt blue	.40	.25
418	A125	1p deep brown	20.00	13.00
		Nos. 414-418 (5)	21.15	14.00

Semi-Postal Stamp No. B2 Surcharged

1932, Nov. 1   *Perf. 12*

419	SP1	1½c on 2c + 2c dp grn	.35	.35

Artigas Type of 1928
Imprint: "Imprenta Nacional" at center

1932-35   Litho.   *Perf. 11, 12½*
Size: 15¾x19¼mm

420	A109	5m lt brown ('35)	.25	.25
421	A109	1c pale violet ('35)	.25	.25
422	A109	15m black	.25	.25
423	A109	5c bluish grn ('35)	.50	.25
		Nos. 420-423 (4)	1.25	1.00

Gen. J. A. Lavalleja A126

Flag of the Race and Globe A127

1933, July 12   Engr.   *Perf. 12½*

429	A126	15m brown lake	.25	.25

Perf. 11, 11½, 11x11½

1933, Aug. 3   Litho.

430	A127	3c blue green	.50	.25
431	A127	5c rose	.50	.25
432	A127	7c lt blue	.50	.25
433	A127	8c dull red	1.00	.55
434	A127	12c deep blue	.65	.25
435	A127	17c violet	1.75	.80
436	A127	20c red brown	3.50	1.60
437	A127	24c yellow	3.50	1.75
438	A127	36c orange	5.00	2.40
439	A127	50c olive gray	5.50	3.00
440	A127	1p bister	13.00	6.25
		Nos. 430-440 (11)	35.40	17.35

Raising of the "Flag of the Race" and of the 441st anniv. of the sailing of Columbus from Palos, Spain, on his first voyage to America.

Sower A128

Juan Zorrilla de San Martin A129

1933, Aug. 28   Unwmk.   *Perf. 11½*

441	A128	3c blue green	.25	.25
442	A128	5c dull violet	.40	.25
443	A128	7c lt blue	.40	.25
444	A128	8c deep red	.80	.50
445	A128	12c ultra	2.00	1.00
		Nos. 441-445 (5)	3.85	2.25

3rd Constituent National Assembly.

1933, Nov. 9   Engr.   *Perf. 12½*

446	A129	7c slate	.25	.25

Albatross Flying over Map of the Americas — A130

1933, Dec. 3   Typo.   *Perf. 11½*

447	A130	3c green, blk & brn	2.75	2.00
448	A130	7c furq bl, brn & blk	1.60	.80
449	A130	12c dk bl, gray & ver	2.40	1.60
450	A130	17c ver, gray & vio	5.00	2.75
451	A130	20c yellow, bl & grn	6.00	3.50
452	A130	36c red, blk & yel	7.75	5.50
		Nos. 447-452 (6)	25.50	16.15

7th Pan-American Conf., Montevideo. Issued in sheets of 6. Value $200. For overprints see Nos. C61-C62.

General Rivera — A131

1934, Feb.   Engr.   *Perf. 12½*

453	A131	3c green	.25	.25

Stars Representing the Three Constitutions — A132

1934, Mar. 23   Typo.

454	A132	3c yellow grn & grn	.60	.40
455	A132	7c org red & red	.60	.40
456	A132	12c ultra & black	2.00	.80

Perf. 11½

457	A132	17c brown & rose	2.50	1.25
458	A132	20c yellow & gray	3.50	1.60
459	A132	36c dk vio & bl grn	3.50	1.60
460	A132	50c black & blue	7.00	3.25
461	A132	1p dk car & vio	16.00	6.75
		Nos. 454-461 (8)	35.70	16.05

First Year of Third Republic.

Artigas Type of 1928
Imprint: "Barreiro & Ramos S. A."

1934, Nov. 28   Litho.

462	A109	50c brown black	6.00	2.50

"Uruguay" and "Brazil" Holding Scales of Justice A133

Florencio Sánchez A134

1935, May 30   Unwmk.   *Perf. 11*

463	A133	5m brown	.80	.40
464	A133	15m black	.40	.25
465	A133	3c green	.40	.25
466	A133	7c orange	.40	.25
467	A133	12c ultra	.80	.60
468	A133	50c yellow green	4.00	2.50
		Nos. 463-468 (6)	6.80	4.25

Visit of President Vargas of Brazil.

1935, Nov. 7

469	A134	3c green	.25	.25
470	A134	7c brown	.25	.25
471	A134	12c blue	.55	.35
		Nos. 469-471 (3)	1.05	.85

Florencio Sanchez (1875-1910), author.

Artigas (6 dots in panels below portrait) — A135

Imprint: "Imprenta Nacional" at center

1936-44   *Perf. 11, 12½*

474	A135	5m org brn ('37)	.25	.25
475	A135	5m lt brown ('39)	.25	.25
476	A135	1c lt violet ('37)	.25	.25
477	A135	2c dk brown ('37)	.25	.25
478	A135	2c green ('39)	.25	.25
479	A135	5c brt blue ('37)	.25	.25
480	A135	5c bluish grn ('39)	.40	.25
481	A135	12c dull blue ('38)	.40	.25
482	A135	20c fawn	1.40	.35
482A	A135	20c rose ('44)	1.00	.40
483	A135	50c brown black	3.00	.80

Size: 21½x28½mm

483A	A135	1p brown	8.50	3.00
483B	A135	2p blue	14.00	12.00
483C	A135	3p gray black	20.00	16.00
		Nos. 474-483C (14)	50.20	34.55

See Nos. 488, and 576. See type A109.

Power Dam on Black River — A136

1937-38

484	A136	1c dull violet	.25	.25
485	A136	10c blue	.50	.25
486	A136	15c rose	1.25	.65
487	A136	1p choc ('38)	6.25	2.50
		Nos. 484-487 (4)	8.25	3.65

Imprint: "Imprenta Nacional" at right

1938

488	A135	1c bright violet	.40	.25

International Law Congress, 1889 — A137

1939, July 16   Litho.   *Perf. 12½*

489	A137	1c brown orange	.25	.25
490	A137	2c dull green	.25	.25
491	A137	5c rose ver	.25	.25

492	A137	12c dull blue	.65 .40
493	A137	50c lt violet	2.50 1.50
		Nos. 489-493 (5)	3.90 2.65

50th anniversary of the Montevideo Congress of International Law.

Artigas
A138   A138a

1939-43   Litho.   Unwmk.
Size: 15¾x19mm

494	A138	5m dl brn org ('40)	.25 .25
495	A138	1c lt blue	.25 .25
496	A138	2c lt violet	.25 .25
497	A138	5c violet brn	.25 .25
498	A138	8c rose red	.25 .25
499	A138	10c green	.50 .25
500	A138	15c dull blue	1.25 .60

Size: 24x29½mm

501	A138	1p dull brn ('41)	2.50 1.00
502	A138	2p dl rose vio ('40)	7.00 3.00
503	A138	4p orange ('43)	9.25 4.00
504	A138	5p ver ('41)	14.00 6.00
		Nos. 494-504 (11)	35.75 16.10

See No. 578.

Redrawn: Horizontal lines in portrait background

1940-44
Size: 17x21mm

505	A138a	5m brn org ('41)	.25 .25
506	A138a	1c lt blue	.25 .25
507	A138a	2c lt violet ('41)	.25 .25
508	A138a	5c violet brn	.25 .25
509	A138a	8c sal pink ('44)	.25 .25
510	A138a	10c green ('41)	.40 .25
511	A138a	50c olive bis ('42)	6.25 1.75
511A	A138a	50c yel grn ('44)	4.75 1.75
		Nos. 505-511A (8)	12.65 5.00

See Nos. 568-575, 577, 601, 632, 660-661. For surcharges see Nos. 523, 726.

Juan Manuel   Francisco
Blanes, Artist   Acuna de
A139   Figueroa
                  A140

1941, Aug. 11   Engr.   Perf. 12½

512	A139	5m ocher	.25 .25
513	A139	1c henna brown	.25 .25
514	A139	2c green	.25 .25
515	A139	5c rose carmine	.60 .25
516	A139	12c deep blue	1.25 .60
517	A139	50c dark violet	4.75 3.25
		Nos. 512-517 (6)	7.35 4.85

1942, Mar. 18   Unwmk.

518	A140	1c henna brown	.25 .25
519	A140	2c deep green	.25 .25
520	A140	5c rose carmine	.25 .25
521	A140	12c deep blue	1.00 .40
522	A140	50c dark violet	3.25 2.50
		Nos. 518-522 (5)	5.00 3.65

Issued in honor of Francisco Acuna de Figueroa, author of the National anthem.

No. 506 Surcharged in
Red

1943, Jan. 27

523	A138a	5m on 1c lt bl	.25 .25

Coat of   Clio — A142
Arms — A141

1943, Mar. 12   Litho.

524	A141	1c on 2c dl vio brn (R)	.25 .25
525	A141	2c on 2c dl vio brn (V)	.25 .25
a.		Inverted surcharge	20.00 20.00

Nos. 524-525 are unissued stamps surcharged. See Nos. 546-555, Q67, Q69, Q74-Q76.

1943, Aug. 24

526	A142	5m lt violet	.25 .25
527	A142	1c lt ultra	.25 .25
528	A142	2c brt rose	.50 .25
529	A142	5c buff	.50 .25
		Nos. 526-529 (4)	1.50 1.00

100th anniversary of the Historic and Geographic Institute of Uruguay.

Swiss Colony
Monument — A143

Overprinted and Surcharged in
Various Colors

1944, May 18

530	A143	1c on 3c dull grn (R)	.25 .25
531	A143	5c on 7c brn red (B)	.25 .25
532	A143	10c on 12c dk bl (Br)	.65 .25
		Nos. 530-532 (3)	1.15 .75

Founding of the Swiss Colony, 50th anniv.

YMCA Seal — A144

1944, Sept. 8

533	A144	5c blue	.25 .25

100th anniv. of the YMCA.

> Catalogue values for unused stamps in this section, from this point to the end of the section, are for **Never Hinged** items.

"La Educación   José Pedro
del Pueblo"   Varela
A145   A146

A147

Monument
A148

Perf. 11½

1945, June 13   Litho.   Unwmk.

534	A145	5m brt green	.25 .25
535	A146	1c dp brown	.25 .25

Perf. 12½

536	A147	2c rose red	.25 .25
537	A148	5c blue	.25 .25
a.		Perf. 11½	.25 .25
		Nos. 534-537 (4)	1.00 1.00

José Pedro Varela, author, birth cent.

Santiago   Silvestre
Vazquez   Blanco
A149   A150

Eduardo   Bruno
Acevedo   Mauricio de
A151   Zabala
               A152

José Pedro   José
Varela — A153   Ellauri — A154

Gen. Luis de
Larrobla — A155

**Engraved (5m, 5c, 10c);
Lithographed**
1945-47   Perf. 10½, 11, 11½, 12½

538	A149	5m purple ('46)	.25 .25
539	A150	1c yel brn ('46)	.25 .25
540	A151	2c brown vio	.25 .25
541	A152	3c grn & dp grn ('47)	.25 .25
542	A153	5c brt carmine	.25 .25
543	A154	10c ultra	.40 .25
544	A155	20c dp grn & choc ('47)	1.25 .50
		Nos. 538-544 (7)	2.90 2.00

No. C86A
Surcharged in
Blue

1946, Jan. 9   Perf. 12½

545	AP7	20c on 68c pale vio brn	1.25 .60

Inauguration of the Black River Power Dam. See No. C120.

Type A141 Overprinted

1946-51   Unwmk. Litho.   Perf. 12½

546	A141	5m orange ('49)	.25 .25
a.		Inverted overprint	
547	A141	2c dl vio brn ('47)	.25 .25
548	A141	3c green	.25 .25
549	A141	5c ultra ('51)	.25 .25
550	A141	10c orange brn	.35 .25
551	A141	20c dk green	.65 .25
552	A141	50c brown	2.00 1.00
553	A141	3p lilac rose	7.00 4.50
		Nos. 546-553 (8)	11.00 7.00

Type A141 Surcharged

1947-48

554	A141	2c on 5c ultra ('48)	.25 .25
555	A141	3c on 5c ultra	.25 .25

Statue of   Bust of José
Ariel — A158   Enrique
                 Rodó — A159

Bas-relief
A160

Bas-relief
A161

Perf. 12½

1948, Jan. 30   Unwmk.   Engr.
Center in Orange Brown

556	A158	1c grnsh gray	.25 .25
557	A159	2c purple	.25 .25
558	A160	3c green	.25 .25
559	A161	5c red violet	.25 .25
560	A160	10c dp orange	.35 .25
561	A161	12c ultra	.40 .25
562	A158	20c rose violet	.80 .25
563	A159	50c dp carmine	2.50 .90
		Nos. 556-563 (8)	5.05 2.65

Dedication of the Rodó monument.

View of the Port,
Paysandú — A162

Arms of
Paysandú
A163

1948, Oct. 9   Litho.

564	A162	3c blue green	.25 .25
565	A163	7c ultra	.40 .25

Exposition of Industry and Agriculture, Paysandú, October-November 1948.

Santa Lucia River Highway Bridge A164

1948, Dec. 10

566	A164	10c dark blue	.80	.25
567	A164	50c green	2.50	1.00

Redrawn Artigas Types of 1940, 1936, 1939

1948-51		**Litho.**	**Perf. 12½**	
568	A138a	5m gray ('49)	.25	.25
569	A138a	1c rose vio ('50)	.25	.25
570	A138a	2c orange	.25	.25
571	A138a	2c choc ('50)	.25	.25
572	A138a	3c blue green	.25	.25
572A	A138a	7c violet blue	.25	.25
573	A138a	8c rose car ('49)	.25	.25
574	A138a	10c orange brn ('51)	.25	.25
575	A138a	12c blue ('51)	.25	.25
576	A135	20c violet	.30	.25
577	A138a	20c rose pink ('51)	.55	.25

Size: 18x21¾mm

578	A138	1p lilac rose ('51)	1.10	.25
		Nos. 568-578 (12)	4.20	3.00

Nos. 571-572A also exist perf. 11.

Plowing A165

Mounted Cattle Herder A166

1949, Apr. 29   Unwmk.   Perf. 12½

579	A165	3c green	.25	.25
580	A166	7c blue	.40	.25

4th Regional American Conf. of Labor, 1949.

Cannon, Rural and Urban Views — A167

1950, Oct. 11   Litho.

581	A167	1c lilac rose	.25	.25
582	A167	3c green	.25	.25
583	A167	7c deep blue	.25	.25
		Nos. 581-583 (3)	.75	.75

200th anniv. of the founding of Cordón, a district of Montevideo.

Symbolical of Soccer Matches — A168

1951, Mar. 20   Perf. 12½, 11

584	A168	3c green	1.00	.25
585	A168	7c violet blue	2.25	.80

4th World Soccer Championship, Rio de Janeiro.

Gen. José Artigas — A169

Flight of the People A170

1c, 2c, 5c, Various equestrian portraits of Artigas. 7c, Dictating instructions. 8c, In congress. 10c, Artigas' flag. 14c, At the citadel. 20c, Arms of Artigas. 50c, In Paraguay. 1p, Bust.

Engraved and Photogravure

1952, Jan. 7		**Unwmk.**	**Perf. 13½**	
586	A169	5m slate	.25	.25
587	A169	1c bl & blk	.25	.25
588	A169	2c pur & red brn	.25	.25
589	A170	3c aqua & dk brn	.25	.25
590	A170	5c red org & blk	.25	.25
591	A170	7c ol & blk	.30	.25
592	A170	8c car & blk	.40	.25
593	A170	10c choc, brt ultra & crim	.40	.25
594	A169	14c dp bl	.40	.25
595	A169	20c org yel, dp ultra & car	.90	.25
596	A169	50c org brn & blk	1.75	.40
597	A169	1p bl gray & cit	3.25	1.25
		Nos. 586-597 (12)	8.65	4.15

Centenary (in 1950) of the death of Gen. José Artigas.

Plane and Stagecoach A171

1952, Oct. 9		**Photo.**	**Perf. 13½x13**	
598	A171	3c bl grn	.25	.25
599	A171	7c blk brn	.25	.25
600	A171	12c ultra	.30	.25
		Nos. 598-600 (3)	.80	.75

75th anniv. (in 1949) of the UPU.

Redrawn Artigas Type of 1940-44

1953, Feb. 23	**Litho.**	**Perf. 11**	
	Size: 24x29½mm		
601	A138a	2p fawn	11.00	8.50

Franklin D. Roosevelt — A172

1953, Apr. 9		**Engr.**	**Perf. 13½**	
602	A172	3c green	.25	.25
603	A172	7c ultra	.25	.25
604	A172	12c blk brn	.40	.25
		Nos. 602-604 (3)	.90	.75

5th Postal Cong. of the Americas & Spain.

Ceibo, Natl. Flower — A173   Horse Breaking — A174

Legislature Building A175

"Island of Seals" (Southern Sea Lions) — A176   Fair Entrance — A177

Designs: 2c, 10c, 5p, Ombu tree. 3c, 50c, Passion Flower. 7c, 3p, Montevideo fortress. 12c, 2p, Outer gate, Montevideo.

Perf. 13x13½, 13½x13, 12½x13, 13x12½

Photo. (5m, 3c, 20c, 50c); Engr.

1954, Jan. 14			**Unwmk.**	
605	A173	5m multi	.25	.25
606	A174	1c car & blk	.25	.25
607	A174	2c brn & grn	.25	.25
608	A173	3c multi	.25	.25
609	A175	5c pur & red brn	.25	.25
610	A173	7c brn & grn	.25	.25
611	A176	8c car & ultra	.40	.25
612	A174	10c org & grn	.35	.25
613	A175	12c dp ultra & dk brn	.25	.25
614	A174	14c rose lil & blk	.25	.25
615	A173	20c grn, brn, gray & car	.70	.25
616	A173	50c car & multi	2.00	.25
617	A175	1p car & red brn	2.50	1.00
618	A175	2p car & blk brn	4.00	1.60
619	A173	3p lil & grn	4.75	2.00
620	A176	4p dp brn & dp ultra	13.00	5.00
621	A174	5p vio bl & grn	10.00	4.00
		Nos. 605-621 (17)	39.70	16.60

For surcharges see Nos. 637-639, 750, C299.

1956, Jan. 19		**Litho.**	**Perf. 11**	
622	A177	3c pale olive green	.25	.25
623	A177	7c blue	.25	.25
		Nos. 622-623,C166-C168 (5)	2.90	1.60

First Exposition of National Products.

José Batlle y Ordonez, Birth Centenary A178

Design: 7c, Full length portrait.

Perf. 13½

1956, Dec. 15		**Wmk. 90**	**Photo.**	
624	A178	3c rose red	.25	.25
625	A178	7c sepia	.25	.25
		Nos. 624-625,C169-C172 (6)	3.10	1.90

Same Surcharged with New Values

1957-58				
626	A178	5c on 3c ('58)	.25	.25
627	A178	10c on 7c	.25	.25
a.		Surcharge inverted	25.00	25.00

Diver — A179   Eduardo Acevedo — A180

Design: 10c, Swimmer at start, horiz.

Perf. 10½, 11½

1958, Feb. 15		**Litho.**	**Unwmk.**	
628	A179	5c brt bl grn	.25	.25
629	A179	10c brt bl	.35	.25

14th South American swimming meet, Montevideo.

1958, Mar. 19			**Perf. 11½, 10½**	
630	A180	5c lt ol grn & blk	.25	.25
631	A180	10c ultra & blk	.25	.25

Eduardo Acevedo (1856-1948), lawyer, legislator, minister of foreign affairs, birth cent.

Redrawn Artigas Type of 1940-44

1958, Sept. 25	**Litho.**	**Perf. 11**	
632	A138a	5m blue	.25	.25

Baygorria Hydroelectric Works — A181

1958, Oct. 30		**Unwmk.**	**Perf. 11**	
633	A181	5c yel grn & blk	.25	.25
634	A181	10c brn org & blk	.25	.25
635	A181	1p bl gray & blk	.65	.25
636	A181	2p rose & blk	1.25	.55
		Nos. 633-636 (4)	2.40	1.30

Nos. 608, 610 and 605 Surcharged Similarly to

Photogravure and Engraved

1958-59			**Perf. 13x13½**	
637	A173	5c on 3c multi ('59)	.30	.25
638	A173	10c on 7c brn & grn	.30	.25
639	A173	20c on 5m multi	.30	.25
		Nos. 637-639 (3)	.90	.75

Gabriela Mistral — A182   Carlos Vaz Ferreira — A183

Wmk. 327

1959, July 6		**Litho.**	**Perf. 11½**	
640	A182	5c green	.25	.25
641	A182	10c dark blue	.25	.25
642	A182	20c red	.25	.25
		Nos. 640-642 (3)	.75	.75

Gabriela Mistral, Chilean poet and educator.

1959, Sept. 3			**Perf. 11**	
643	A183	5c blk & lt bl	.25	.25
644	A183	10c blk & ocher	.25	.25
645	A183	20c blk & ver	.25	.25
646	A183	50c blk & vio	.35	.25
647	A183	1p blk & grn	.55	.25
		Nos. 643-647 (5)	1.65	1.25

Ferreira (1872-1958), educator and author.

A184   A185

Wmk. 332

1960, May 16		**Litho.**		***Perf. 12***
648	A184	3c red lil & blk	.25	.25
649	A184	5c dp vio & blk	.25	.25
650	A184	10c brt bl & blk	.25	.25
651	A184	20c chocolate & blk	.30	.25
652	A184	1p gray & blk	.45	.25
653	A184	2p org & blk	1.10	.25
654	A184	3p olive grn & blk	1.75	.40
655	A184	4p yel brn & blk	2.25	.75
656	A184	5p brt red & blk	2.75	.75
		Nos. 648-656 (9)	9.35	3.40

Dr. Martin C. Martinez (1859-1940), statesman.

1960, June 6		**Wmk. 332**		***Perf. 12***
657	A185	10c Uprooted oak emblem	.25	.25

Issued to publicize World Refugee Year, July 1, 1959-June 30, 1960. See No. C207.

Revolutionists and Cabildo, Buenos Aires — A186

1960, Nov. 4		**Litho.**		***Perf. 12***
658	A186	5c bl & blk	.25	.25
659	A186	10c bl & ocher	.25	.25
		Nos. 658-659,C208-C210 (5)	1.60	1.25

150th anniv. of the May Revolution of 1810.

Redrawn Artigas Type of 1940-44

1960-61		**Wmk. 332**		***Perf. 11***
660	A138a	2c gray	.25	.25
661	A138a	50c brn ('61)	.25	.25

Gen. Manuel Oribe (1796?-1857), Revolutionary Leader, Pres. of Uruguay (1835-38) — A187

1961, Mar. 4		**Litho.**		***Perf. 12***
671	A187	10c brt bl & blk	.25	.25
672	A187	20c bis & blk	.30	.25
673	A187	40c grn & blk	.30	.25
		Nos. 671-673 (3)	.85	.75

Cavalry Charge A188

1961, June 12		**Wmk. 332**		***Perf. 12***
674	A188	20c bl & blk	.25	.25
675	A188	40c emer & blk	.40	.25

150th anniversary of the revolution.

Welfare, Justice and Education — A189   Gen. José Fructuoso Rivera — A190

1961, Aug. 14		**Wmk. 322**		***Perf. 12***
676	A189	2c bister & lilac	.40	.25
677	A189	5c bister & orange	.40	.25
678	A189	10c bister & scarlet	.40	.25
679	A189	20c bister & yel grn	.40	.25
680	A189	50c bister & light vio	.40	.25
681	A189	1p bister & blue	.40	.25
682	A189	2p bister & citron	1.10	.25
683	A189	3p bister & gray	1.50	.65
684	A189	4p bister & light bl	2.50	.80
685	A189	5p bister & chocolate	2.75	1.25
		Nos. 676-685 (10)	10.25	4.45

Inter-American Economic and Social Conference of the Organization of American States, Punta del Este, August, 1961. See Nos. C233-C244.

Wmk. 332

1962, May 29		**Litho.**		***Perf. 12***
686	A190	10c brt red & blk	.25	.25
687	A190	20c bis & blk	.25	.25
688	A190	40c grn & blk	.25	.25
		Nos. 686-688 (3)	.75	.75

Issued to honor Gen. José Fructuoso Rivera (1790-1854), first President of Uruguay.

Spade, Grain, Swiss "Scarf" and Hat — A191

1962, Aug. 1		**Wmk. 332**		***Perf. 12***
689	A191	10c bl, blk & car	.25	.25
690	A191	20c lt grn, blk & car	.25	.25
		Nos. 689-690,C245-C246 (4)	1.30	1.10

Swiss Settlement in Uruguay, cent.

Bernardo Prudencio Berro — A192

1962, Oct. 22		**Litho.**		***Perf. 12***
691	A192	10c grnsh bl & blk	.25	.25
692	A192	20c yel brn & blk	.25	.25

Pres. Bernardo P. Berro (1803-1868).

Damaso Larrañaga A193

1963, Jan. 24		**Wmk. 332**		***Perf. 12***
693	A193	20c lt bl grn & dk brn	.25	.25
694	A193	40c tan & dk brn	.25	.25

Damaso Antonio Larranaga (1771-1848), teacher, writer and founder of National Library.

Rufous-bellied Thrush — A194

Birds: 50c, Rufous ovenbird. 1p, Chalk-browed mockingbird. 2p, Rufous-collared sparrow.

1963, Apr. 1		**Wmk. 332**		***Perf. 12***
695	A194	2c rose, brn & blk	.25	.25
696	A194	50c lt brn & blk	.85	.25
697	A194	1p tan, brn & blk	2.10	.25
698	A194	2p lt brn, blk & gray	4.00	.80
		Nos. 695-698 (4)	7.20	1.55

Thin frame on No. 696, no frame on No. 698.

UPAE Emblem A195

1963, May 31				**Litho.**
699	A195	20c ultra & blk		.50	.25
		Nos. 699,C252-C253 (3)	1.00	.75

50th anniv. of the founding of the Postal Union of the Americas and Spain, UPAE. For surcharge see No. C321.

Wheat Emblem — A196

1963, July 8		**Wmk. 332**		***Perf. 12***
700	A196	10c grn & yel	.25	.25
701	A196	20c brn & yel	.30	.25
		Nos. 700-701,C254-C255 (4)	1.15	1.10

FAO "Freedom from Hunger" campaign.

Anchors — A197

1963, Aug. 16				
702	A197	10c org & vio	.25	.25
703	A197	20c dk red & gray	.30	.25
		Nos. 702-703,C256-C257 (4)	1.35	1.15

Voyage around the world by the Uruguayan sailing vessel "Alferez Campora," 1960-63.

Large Intestine, Congress Emblem A198

1963, Dec. 9				**Litho.**
704	A198	10c lt grn, blk & dk car	.25	.25
705	A198	20c org, yel, blk & dk car	.30	.25

1st Uruguayan Proctology Cong., Montevideo, Dec. 9-15.

Red Cross Centenary Emblem A199

Imprint: "Imp. Nacional"

1964, June 5		**Wmk. 332**		***Perf. 12***
706	A199	20c blue & red	.25	.25
707	A199	40c gray & red	.30	.25

Centenary of International Red Cross. No. 706 exists with imprint missing. Value $4.

Luis Alberto de Herrera A200

1964, July 22		**Litho.**		**Unwmk.**
708	A200	20c dl grn, bl & blk	.25	.25
709	A200	40c lt bl, bl & blk	.25	.25
710	A200	80c yel org, bl & blk	.25	.25
711	A200	1p lt vio, bl & blk	.45	.25
712	A200	2p gray, bl & blk	.65	.50
		Nos. 708-712 (5)	1.85	1.50

Herrera (1873-1959), leader of Herrerista party and member of National Government Council.

Nile Gods Uniting Upper and Lower Egypt (Abu Simbel) A201

1964, Oct. 30		**Wmk. 332**		***Perf. 12***
713	A201	20c multi	.25	.25
		Nos. 713,C266-C267 (3)	1.80	1.00

UNESCO world campaign to save historic monuments in Nubia. See No. C267a.

Pres. John F. Kennedy A202

1965, Mar. 5		**Wmk. 327**		***Perf. 11½***
714	A202	20c gold, emer & blk	.25	.25
a.		Gold omitted		
715	A202	40c gold, redsh brn & blk	.30	.25
a.		Gold omitted		
		Nos. 714-715,C269-C270 (4)	1.55	1.50

Tete Beche Pair of 1864, No. 21a A203

1965, Mar. 19		**Wmk. 332**		***Perf. 12***
716	A203	40c black & green	.25	.25

1st Rio de la Plata Stamp Show, sponsored jointly by the Argentine and Uruguayan philatelic associations, Montevideo, Mar. 19-28. See No. C271.

Benito Nardone A204

40c, Benito Nardone before microphone.

1965, Mar. 25   Litho.
717 A204 20c blk & emer   .30 .25
718 A204 40c blk & emer, vert.   .35 .25

1st anniversary of the death of Benito Nardone, president of the Council of Government.

Artigas Quotation — A205

40c, Artigas bust, quotation. 80c, José Artigas.

Perf. 12x11½
1965, May 17   Litho.   Wmk. 327
719 A205 20c bl, yel & red   .25 .25
720 A205 40c vio bl, cit & blk   .25 .25
721 A205 80c brn, yel, red & bl   .35 .25
   Nos. 719-721, C273-C275 (6)   2.50 1.75

José Artigas (1764-1850), leader of the independence revolt against Spain.

Soccer A206

Designs: 40c, Basketball. 80c, Bicycling. 1p, Woman swimmer.

1965, Aug. 3   Litho.   Wmk. 327
722 A206 20c grn, org & blk   .30 .25
723 A206 40c hn brn, cit & blk   .30 .25
724 A206 80c gray, red & blk   .30 .25
725 A206 1p bl, yel grn & blk   .30 .25
   Nos. 722-725, C276-C281 (10)   5.50 3.45

18th Olympic Games, Tokyo, 10/10-25/64.

No. 572A Surcharged in Red

1965   Unwmk.   Perf. 12½
726 A138a 10c on 7c vio bl   .25 .25

No. B5 Srchd.

1966, Jan. 25   Wmk. 327   Perf. 11½
727 SP2 4c on 5c + 10c grn & org   .25 .25

Association of Uruguayan Architects, 50th anniv.

Winston Churchill A207

Wmk. 332
1966, Apr. 29   Litho.   Perf. 12
728 A207 40c car, dp ultra & brn   .30 .25

Sir Winston Spencer Churchill, statesman and World War II leader. See No. C284.

Arms of Rio de Janeiro and Sugar Loaf Mountain A208

1966, June 9   Litho.   Wmk. 332
729 A208 40c emer & brn   .25 .25

400th anniversary of the founding of Rio de Janeiro. See No. C285.

Army Engineer — A209   Daniel Fernandez Crespo — A210

1966, June 17   Litho.
730 A209 20c blk, red, vio bl & yel   .25 .25

50th anniversary of the Army Engineers Corps.

1966, Sept. 16   Wmk. 332   Perf. 12
Portraits: No. 732, Washington Beltran. No. 733, Luis Batlle Berres.

731 A210 20c lt bl & blk   .25 .25
732 A210 20c lt bl & dk brn   .25 .25
733 A210 20c brick red & blk   .25 .25
   Nos. 731-733 (3)   .75 .75

Issued to honor political leaders.

Old Printing Press — A211

1966, Oct. 14   Photo.   Perf. 12
734 A211 20c tan, grnsh gray & dk brn   .25 .25

50th anniversary of State Printing Office.

Fireman A212

1966   Litho.
735 A212 20c red & blk   .50 .25

Issued to publicize fire prevention. Printed with alternating red and black labels inscribed: "Prevengase del fuego! Del pueblo y para el pueblo."

No. 716 Overprinted in Red: "Segunda Muestra y / Jornadas Rioplatenses / de Filatelia / Abril 1966 / Centenario del Sello / Escudito Resellado"

1966, Nov. 4
736 A203 40c blk & grn   .25 .25

2nd Rio de la Plata Stamp Show, Buenos Aires, Apr. 1966, and cent. of Uruguay's 1st surcharged issue. See No. C298.

General Leandro Gomez — A213

#738, Gen. Juan Antonio Lavalleja. #739, Aparicio Saravia, revolutionary, on horseback.

Wmk. 332
1966, Nov. 24   Litho.   Perf. 12
737 A213 20c slate, blk & dp bl   .30 .25
738 A213 20c red, blk & bl   .30 .25
739 A213 20c blue & blk, horiz.   .30 .25
   Nos. 737-739 (3)   .90 .75

Montevideo Planetarium A214

1967, Jan. 13   Wmk. 332   Perf. 12
740 A214 40c pink & blk   .30 .25

10th anniv. of the Montevideo Municipal Planetarium. See No. C301.

Sunflower, Cow and Emblem — A215   Church of San Carlos — A216

1967, Jan. 13   Litho.
741 A215 40c dk brn & yel   .30 .25

Young Farmers' Movement, 20th anniv.

1967, Apr. 17   Wmk. 332   Perf. 12
742 A216 40c lt bl, blk & dk red   .40 .25

Bicentenary of San Carlos.

Eduardo Acevedo A217

1967, Apr. 17   Litho.
743 A217 20c grn & brn   .25 .25
744 A217 40c org & grn   .30 .25

Issued to honor Eduardo Acevedo, lawyer, legislator and Minister of Foreign Affairs.

Arms of Carmelo A218   José Enrique Rodó A219

1967, Aug. 11   Litho.   Perf. 12
745 A218 40c lt & dk bl & ocher   .30 .25

Founding of Carmelo, 150th anniv.

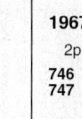

1967, Oct. 6   Wmk. 332   Perf. 12
2p, Portrait of Rodó and sculpture, horiz.

746 A219 1p gray, brn & blk   .30 .25
747 A219 2p rose claret, blk & tan   .30 .25

50th anniversary of the death of José Enrique Rodó, author.

Senen M. Rodriguez and Locomotive A220

1967, Oct. 26   Litho.   Perf. 12
748 A220 2p ocher & dk brn   .40 .25

Centenary of the founding of the first national railroad company.

Child and Map of Americas A221   Cocoi Heron A222

1967, Nov. 10   Wmk. 332   Perf. 12
749 A221 1p vio & red   .30 .25

Inter-American Children's Institute, 40th anniv.

No. 610 Surcharged in Red

Perf. 13x13½
1967, Nov. 10   Engr.   Unwmk.
750 A173 1p on 7c brn & grn   .25 .25

1968-70   Wmk. 332   Litho.   Perf. 12
Birds: 1p, Great horned owl. 3p, Brown-headed gull, horiz. No. 754, White-faced tree duck, horiz. No. 754A, Black-tailed stilts. 5p, Wattled jacanas, horiz. 10p, Snowy egret, horiz.

751 A222 1p dl yel & brn   2.00 .40
752 A222 2p bl grn & blk   2.00 .40
753 A222 3p org, gray & blk ('69)   1.50 .35
754 A222 4p brn, tan & blk   3.25 .60
754A A222 4p ver & blk ('70)   1.50 .35
755 A222 5p lt red brn, blk & yel   3.75 .60
756 A222 10p lil & blk   6.75 .80
   Nos. 751-756 (7)   20.75 3.50

Concord Bridge, Presidents of Uruguay, Brazil A223

1968, Apr. 3
757 A223 6p brown   .30 .25

Opening of Concord Bridge across the Uruguay River by Presidents Jorge Pacheco Areco of Uruguay and Arthur Costa e Silva of Brazil.

Soccer Player and
Trophy — A224

1968, May 29   **Litho.**
758 A224 1p blk & yel   .30   .25

Victory of the Penarol Athletic Club in the Intercontinental Soccer Championships of 1966.

St. John
Bosco,
Symbols of
Education
and Industry
A225

1968, July 31   **Wmk. 332**   *Perf. 12*
759 A225 2p brn & blk   .25   .25

75th anniv. of the Don Bosco Workshops of the Salesian Brothers.

Sailors'
Monument,
Montevideo
A226

Designs: 6p, Lighthouse and buoy, vert. 12p, Gunboat "Suarez" (1860).

1968, Nov. 12   **Litho.**   *Perf. 12*
760 A226   2p gray ol & blk   .25   .25
761 A226   6p lt grn & blk   .25   .25
762 A226   12p brt bl & blk   .25   .25
   Nos. 760-762,C340-C343 (7)   2.15   1.75

Sesquicentennial of National Navy.
For surcharge see No. Q101.

Oscar D.
Gestido
A227

1968, Dec. 6   **Wmk. 332**   *Perf. 12*
763 A227 6p brn, dp car & bl   .25   .25

First anniversary of the death of President Oscar D. Gestido.

Gearwheel,
Grain and
Two Heads
A228

1969, Mar. 17   **Litho.**   *Perf. 12*
764 A228 2p blk & ver   .25   .25

25th anniversary of Labor University.

Bicyclists
A229

1969, Mar. 21   **Wmk. 332**
765 A229 6p dk bl, org & emer   .30   .25

1968 World Bicycle Championships. See No. C347.

Gymnasts
and Club
Emblem
A230

1969, May 8   **Wmk. 332**   *Perf. 12*
766 A230 6p blk & ver   .30   .25

75th anniversary of L'Avenir Athletic Club.

Baltasar Brum
(1883-1933)
A231

Former presidents: No. 768, Tomas Berreta (1875-1947).

1969   **Litho.**   *Perf. 12*
767 A231 6p rose red & blk   .25   .25
768 A231 6p car rose & blk   .25   .25

Fair Emblem — A232

1969, Aug. 15   **Wmk. 332**   *Perf. 12*
769 A232 2p multi   .25   .25

Issued to publicize the 2nd Industrial World's Fair, Montevideo, 1970.

Diesel
Locomotive
A233

Design: No. 771, Old steam locomotive and modern railroad cars.

1969, Sept. 19   **Litho.**   **Wmk. 332**
770 A233 6p car, blk & ultra   .40   .25
771 A233 6p car, blk & ultra   .40   .25
   e.   Pair, #770-771   .80   .80

Centenary of Uruguayan railroads. No. 771e has continuous design and label between pairs.
For surcharges see Nos. Q102-Q103.

Souvenir Sheet

Diligencia Issue, 1856 — A233a

1969, Oct. 1   **Imperf.**
771A A233a   Sheet of 3   10.00   10.00
   b.   60p blue   2.50   2.50
   c.   80p green   3.25   3.25
   d.   100p red   3.75   3.75

Stamp Day 1969. No. 771A contains stamps similar to No. 1-3, with denominations in pesos.
No. 771A was re-issued Apr. 15, 1972, with black overprint for 15th anniv. of 1st Lufthansa flight from Uruguay to Germany and the Munich Olympic Games. Value $30.

"Combat" and Sculptor Belloni — A234

1969, Oct. 22   **Wmk. 332**   *Perf. 12*
772 A234 6p olive, slate grn & blk   .40   .25

José L. Belloni (1882-), sculptor.

Reserve
Officers'
Training
Center
Emblem
A235

Design: 2p, Training Center emblem, and officer in uniform and as civilian.

1969, Nov. 5   **Litho.**
773 A235 1p yel & dk bl   .25   .25
774 A235 2p dk brn & lt bl   .25   .25

Reserve Officers' Training Center, 25th anniv.

Map of Americas
and Sun — A236

Stylized
Pine — A237

1970, Apr. 20   **Wmk. 332**   *Perf. 12*
775 A236 10p dp bl & gold   .40   .25

11th meeting of the governors of the Inter-American Development Bank, Punta del Este.

1970, May 14
776 A237 2p red, blk & brt grn   .35   .25
2nd National Forestry and Wood Exhibition.

Artigas'
Ancestral
Home in
Sauce
A238

1970, June 18   **Wmk. 332**   *Perf. 12*
777 A238 15p ver, ultra & blk   .40   .25

Map of
Uruguay,
Sun and
Sea
A239

1970, July 8   **Litho.**
778 A239 5p greenish blue   .35   .25

Issued for tourist publicity.

EXPO '70
Emblem, Mt.
Fuji and
Uruguay
Coat of
Arms
A240

EXPO '70 Intl. Exhibition, Osaka, Japan, 3/15-9/13: No. 780, Geisha. No. 781, Sun Tower. No. 782, Youth pole.

1970, Aug. 5   **Wmk. 332**   *Perf. 12*
779 A240 25p grn, slate bl & yel   .40   .40
780 A240 25p org, slate bl & grn   .40   .40
781 A240 25p yel, slate bl & pur   .40   .40
782 A240 25p pur, slate bl & org   .40   .40
   a.   Block of 4, #779-782   1.60   1.60

Cobbled Street in
Colonia del
Sacramento
A241

1970, Oct. 21   **Litho.**   *Perf. 12*
783 A241 5p blk & multi   .35   .25

290th anniv. of the founding of Colonia del Sacramento, the 1st European settlement in Uruguay.

Mother and Son
by Edmundo Prati
in Salto — A242

1970, Nov. 4   **Litho.**
784 A242 10p grn & blk   .45   .30

Issued to honor mothers.

URUEXPO
Emblem
A243

1970, Dec. 9   **Wmk. 332**   *Perf. 12*
785 A243 15p bl, brn org & vio   .40   .40

URUEXPO '70, National Philatelic Exposition, Montevideo, Sept. 26-Oct. 4.

Children Holding Hands, and
UNESCO Emblem — A244

Children's Drawings: No. 786, Two girls holding hands, vert. No. 788, Boy sitting at school desk, vert. No. 789, Astronaut and monster.

1970, Dec. 29   **Litho.**   *Perf. 12½*
786 A244 10p multi   .35   .35
787 A244 10p multi   .35   .35
788 A244 10p dp car & multi   .35   .35
789 A244 10p bl & multi   .35   .35
   a.   Block of 4, #786-789 + 2 labels   1.60   1.60

International Education Year.

Alfonso Espinola (1845-1905), Physician, Professor and Philanthropist A245

1971, Jan. 13   Wmk. 332   *Perf. 12*
790 A245 5p dp org & blk   .35 .25

Exposition Poster — A246

1971   *Litho.*   *Perf. 12*
791 A246 15p multi   .35 .25
Uruguay Philatelic Exposition, 1971, Montevideo, March 26-Apr. 19.

5c Coin of 1840, Obverse A247

1971, Apr. 16   Wmk. 332   *Perf. 12*
792 A247 25p bl, brn & blk   .60 .60
793 A247 25p bl, brn & blk   .50 .50
a.   Pair, #792-793   1.40 1.40
Numismatists' Day.

Domingo Arena, Lawyer and Journalist — A248

1971, May 3   Wmk. 332   *Perf. 12*
794 A248 5p dk car   .30 .25

National Anthem A249

1971, May 19   *Litho.*
795 A249 15p bl, blk & yel   .40 .40

José F. Arias, Physician — A250

1971, May 25   Wmk. 332   *Perf. 12*
796 A250 5p sepia   .30 .25

Eduardo Fabini, Bar from "Campo" A251

1971, June 2   *Litho.*
797 A251 5p dk car rose & blk   .40 .40
Eduardo Fabini (1882-1950), composer, and 40th anniversary of first radio concert.

José E. Rodó, UPAE Emblem A252

1971, July 15   Wmk. 332   *Perf. 12*
798 A252 15p ultra & blk   .35 .25
José Enrique Rodó (1871-1917), writer, first Uruguayan delegate to Congress of the Postal Union of the Americas and Spain.

Water Cart and Faucet A253

1971, July 17
799 A253 5p ultra & multi   .30 .25
Centenary of Montevideo's drinking water system.

Sheep and Cloth A254

Design: 15p, Sheep, cloth and bale of wool.

1971, Aug. 7
800 A254 5p grn & gray   .25 .25
801 A254 15p dk bl, grnsh bl & gray   .30 .25
Wool Promotion.

José Maria Elorza and Merilin Sheep A255

1971, Aug. 10
802 A255 5p lt bl, grn & blk   .30 .25
José Maria Elorza, developer of the Merilin sheep.

Criollo Horse A256

1971, Aug. 11
803 A256 5p blk, gray bl & org   .35 .25

Bull and Ram A257

1971, Aug. 13
804 A257 20p red, grn, blk & gold   .45 .35
Centenary of Rural Association of Uruguay; 19th International Cattle Breeding Exposition, and 66th National Cattle Championships at Prado, Aug. 1971.

Symbol of Liberty and Order A258

20p, Policemen, flag of Uruguay and emblem.

1971
805 A258 10p gray, blk & bl   .30 .25
806 A258 20p dk bl, blk, lt bl & gold   .35 .25
To honor policemen killed on duty. Issue dates: 10p, Sept. 9; 20p, Nov. 4.

10p Banknote of 1896 — A259

Design: No. 808, Reverse of 10p note.

1971, Sept. 23
807 A259 25p dl grn, gold & blk   .50 .50
808 A259 25p dl grn, gold & blk   .50 .50
a.   Pair, #807-808 + label   1.25 1.25
75th anniversary of Bank of the Republic.

Farmer and Arms of Durazno A260

1971, Oct. 11
809 A260 20p gold, bl & blk   .30 .25
Sesquicentennial of the founding of Durazno.

Emblem and Laurel — A261

1971, Oct. 20
810 A261 10p vio bl, gold & red   .30 .25
Winners of Liberator's Cup, American Soccer Champions, 1971.
For surcharge see No. 825.

Voter Casting Ballot — A262

Design: 20p, Citizens voting, horiz.

1971, Nov. 22   Wmk. 332   *Perf. 12*
811 A262 10p bl & blk   .30 .25
812 A262 20p bl & blk   .30 .25
Universal, secret and obligatory franchise.

Map of Uruguay on Globe A263

1971, Dec. 23
813 A263 20p lt bl & vio brn   .40 .25
7th Littoral Expo., Paysandu, 3/26-4/11.

Juan Lindolfo Cuestas — A264

1971, Dec. 27
814 A264 10p shown   .25 .25
815 A264 10p Julio Herrera y Obes   .25 .25
816 A264 10p Claudio Williman   .25 .25
817 A264 10p José Serrato   .25 .25
818 A264 10p Andres Martinez Truebá   .25 .25
a.   Horiz. strip of 5, #814-818   1.50 1.50
Presidents of Uruguay.

Souvenir Sheet

Uruguay No. 4, Cathedral of Montevideo and Plaza de la Constitucion — A265

1972, Jan. 17   *Imperf.*
819 A265 120p brn, bl & dp rose   1.00 1.00
Stamp Day 1971 (release date delayed). See Nos. 834-835, 863.

Bartolomé Hidalgo — A266

1972, Feb. 28   *Perf. 12*
820 A266 5p lt brn, blk & red   .35 .25
Bartolomé Hidalgo (1788-1822), Uruguayan-Argentine poet.

Missa Solemnis, by
Beethoven — A267

1972, Apr. 20   Litho.   Wmk. 332
822 A267 20p lil, emer & blk   .35 .25
12th Choir Festival of Eastern Uruguay.

Dove and
Wounded
Bird — A268

1972, May 9
823 A268 10p ver & multi   .35 .25
To honor Dionision Disz (age 9), who died
saving his sister.

Columbus Arch,
Colon — A269

1972, June 21
824 A269 20p red, bl & blk   .35 .25
Centenary of Colon, now suburb of
Montevideo.

No. 810 Surcharged in Silver

(Surcharge 69mm wide)

1972, June 30
825 A261 50p on 10p multi   .35 .25
Winners of the 1971 Intl. Soccer Cup.

Tree
Planting — A270

1972, Aug. 5   Wmk. 332   Perf. 12
826 A270 20p grn & blk   .35 .25
Afforestation program.

"Collective
Housing" — A271

1972, Sept. 30   Litho.
827 A271 10p dp bl & multi   .35 .25
Publicity for collective housing plan.

Amethyst
A272

Uruguayan Gem Stones: 9p, Agate. 15p,
Chalcedony.

1972, Oct. 7
828 A272 5p gray & multi   .50 .50
829 A272 9p gray bl & multi   .50 .50
830 A272 15p gray grn & multi   .60 .60
    Nos. 828-830 (3)   1.60 1.60

Uniform of
1830 — A273

Design: 20p, Lancer.

1972, Nov. 21   Litho.
831 A273 10p multi   .35 .25
832 A273 20p rose red & multi   .35 .25

Red
Cross and
Map of
Uruguay
A274

1972, Dec. 11   Wmk. 332   Perf. 12
833 A274 30p multi   .40 .25
75th anniv. of the Uruguayan Red Cross.

Stamp Day Type of 1972
Souvenir Sheets

Designs: 200p, Coat of arms type of 1864
similar to Nos. 18, 20-21, but 60p, 60p and
80p. 220p, Similar to Nos. 22-23, but 100p and
120p.

1972, Dec. 20   Imperf.
834 A265 200p multi   1.25 .60
835 A265 220p multi   1.50 .75
Stamp Day 1972. 1st printed cancellations,
200th anniv., #834; Decree establishing regular postal service, cent., #835.

Scales of
Justice,
Olive
Branch
A275

1972, Dec. 27   Wmk. 332   Perf. 12
836 A275 10p gold, dk & lt bl   .30 .25
Civil Rights Law for Women, 25th anniv.

Gen. José
Artigas
A276

Hand Holding Cup;
Grain, Map of
Americas
A277

1972-74   Wmk. 332   Litho.   Perf. 12
837 A276 5p yel ('74)   .25 .25
838 A276 10p dk bis ('74)   .25 .25
839 A276 15p emer ('74)   .25 .25
840 A276 20p lilac ('73)   .25 .25
841 A276 30p lt bl ('73)   .25 .25
842 A278 4Up dp org ('73)   .25 .25
843 A276 50p ver ('73)   .25 .25
844 A276 75p ap grn ('73)   .25 .25
845 A276 100p emerald ('73)   .25 .25
846 A276 150p choc ('73)   .25 .25
847 A276 200p dk bl ('73)   .45 .30
848 A276 250p pur ('73)   .50 .35
849 A276 500p gray ('73)   1.25 .60
849A A276 1000p blue ('73)   2.50 1.25
    Nos. 837-849A (14)   7.20 5.00

For surcharges see Nos. 929-932.

1973, Jan. 9
850 A277 30p rose red, yel & blk   .30 .25
Intl. Institute for Agricultural Research, 39th
anniv.

Elbio Fernandez
and José P.
Varela — A278

1973, Jan. 16
851 A278 10p dl grn, gold & blk   .30 .25
Society of Friends of Public Education, cent.

Map of
Americas,
"1972" and
Columbus
A279

1973, Jan. 30
852 A279 50p purple   .30 .25
Tourist Year of the Americas 1972.

Carlos
Maria
Ramirez,
Scales
and
Books
A280

1973, Feb. 15
853 A280 10p shown   .25 .25
854 A280 10p Justino Jimenez
            de Arechaga   .25 .25
855 A280 10p Juan Andres Ra-
            mirez   .25 .25
856 A280 10p Justino E. Jimenez
            de Arechaga   .25 .25
    a. Horiz. strip, #853-856 + label   1.25 1.25
Professorship of Constitutional Rights, cent.

Provincial
Map of
Uruguay
A281

1973, Feb. 27   Litho.   Perf. 12½x12
857 A281 20p bl & multi   .40 .25
See No. 1167.

Francisco
de los
Santos
A282

1973, May 16   Wmk. 332   Perf. 12
858 A282 20p grn & blk   .35 .25
Soldiers' Day and Battle of Piedras. Santos
was a courier who went through enemy lines.

**No. C319 Surcharged with New Value
and: "HOMENAJE AL 4 CENTENARIO
DE CORDOBA . ARGENTINA . 1973"**
1973, May 9   Litho.   Imperf.
            Souvenir Sheet
859 AP57 100p on 5p multi   1.00 1.00
Founding of Cordoba in Argentina, 400th
anniv.

Friar, Indians,
Church — A283

1973, July 25   Perf. 12
860 A283 20p lt ultra, pur & blk   .30 .25
Villa Santo Domingo Soriano, first Spanish
settlement in Uruguay.

Symbolic
Fish
A284

1973, Aug. 15
861 A284 100p bl & multi   .50 .25
First station of Oceanographic and Fishery
Service, Montevideo.

A285

Sun over flower in Italian colors.

1973, Sept.
862 A285 100p multi   .30 .25
Italian Chamber of Commerce of Uruguay.

Stamp Day Type of 1972
Souvenir Sheet

Design: 240p, Thin numeral sun type of 1859 and street scene.

Wmk. 332
1973, Oct. 1   Litho.   Imperf.
863 A265 240p grn, org & blk   1.50 1.50
Stamp Day 1973.

Herrera — A286

1973, Nov. 12   Perf. 12
866 A286 50p gray, brn & dk brn   .30   .25
Centenary of the birth of Luis Alberto de Herrera.

Emblem of Social Coordination Volunteers A287

Wmk. 352
1973, Nov. 19   Litho.   Perf. 12
867 A287 50p bl & multi   .35   .25
Festival of Nations, Montevideo.

Arm with Arteries and Heart A288

1973, Nov. 22
868 A288 50p blk, red & pink   .30   .25
3rd Cong. of the Pan-American Federation of Blood Donors, Montevideo, Nov. 23-25.

Madonna, by Rafael Perez Barradas — A289

1973, Dec. 10   Litho.   Wmk. 332
869 A289 50p grn, gray & yel grn   .40   .25
Christmas 1973.

Nicolaus Copernicus — A290

1973, Dec. 26   Litho.
870 A290 50p grn & multi   .45   .25
500th anniversary of the birth of Nicolaus Copernicus (1473-1543), Polish astronomer.

Praying Hands and Andes — A291

75p, Statue of Christ on mountain, and flower.

1973, Dec. 26   Litho.
871 A291 50p blk, lt grn & ultra   .25   .25
872 A291 75p bl, blk & org   .30   .25
Survival and rescue of victims of airplane crash.

OAS Emblem and Map of Americas A292

1974, Jan. 14   Wmk. 332   Perf. 12
873 A292 250p gray & multi   .75   .40
25th anniversary of the Organization of American States (OAS).

Scout Emblems and Flame A293

1974, Jan. 21
874 A293 250p multi   .75   .40
1st Intl. Boy Scout Games, Montevideo, 1974.

Hector Suppici Sedes and Car — A294

1974, Jan. 28   Perf. 12
875 A294 50p sep, grn & blk   .40   .25
70th anniversary of the birth of Hector Suppici Sedes (1903-1948), automobile racer.

Three Gauchos — A295

1974, Mar. 20   Litho.   Wmk. 332
876 A295 50p multi   .35   .25
Centenary of the publication of "Los Tres Gauchos Orientales" by Antonio D. Lussich.

Rifle, Target and Swiss Flag A296

1974, Apr. 2
877 A296 100p multi   .35   .25
Centenary of the Swiss Rifle Association.

Map of Uruguay and Compass Rose A297

1974, Apr. 23   Litho.
878 A297 50p multi   .35   .25
Military Geographical Service.

Montevideo Stadium Tower — A298

Design: 75p, Soccer player, Games' emblem, horiz. 1000p, similar to 75p.

1974, May 7   Wmk. 332   Perf. 12
879 A298   50p multi   .25   .25
880 A298   75p multi   .25   .25
881 A298 1000p multi   22.50 8.50
World Cup Soccer Championship, Munich, June 13-July 7.
No. 881 had limited distribution. A souvenir sheet of one No. 881 was not valid for postage.

Tourism — A299

Wmk. 332
1974, June 6   Litho.   Perf. 12
882 A299 1000p multicolored   35.00 35.00
No. 882 had limited distribution.

Old and New School and Founders A300

1974, May 21
883 A300 75p black & bister   .35   .25
Centenary of the Osimani-Llerena Technical School at Salto, founded by Gervasio Osimani and Miguel Llerena.

Gardel and Score — A301

Wmk. 332
1974, June 24   Litho.   Perf. 12
884 A301 100p multi   .50   .25
Carlos Gardel (1887-1935), singer and motion picture actor. See No. 1173.

Volleyball and Net — A302

1974, July 11   Wmk. 332   Perf. 12
885 A302 200p lil, yel & blk   .50   .25
First anniversary of Women's Volleyball championships, Montevideo, 1973.

"Protect your Heart" — A303

1974, July 24   Litho.
886 A303 75p ol grn, yel & red   .35   .25
Heart Foundation publicity.

Portrait and Statue — A304

1974, Aug. 5
887 A304 75p dk & lt bl   .30   .25
Centenary (in 1973) of the founding of San José de Mayo by Eusebio Vidal.

A305

A306

Artigas statue, Buenos Aires, flags of Uruguay and Argentina.

1974, Aug. 13   **Perf. 12½**
888 A305 75p multi   .35 .25
Unveiling of Artigas monument, Buenos Aires.

1974, Sept. 24 Wmk. 332 Perf. 12
889 A306 100p Radio tower and
           waves   .35 .25
50th anniv. of Broadcasting in Uruguay.

URUEXPO 74 Emblem — A307

URUEXPO Emblem and Old Map of
Montevideo Bay — A308

1974
890 A307 100p blk, dk bl & red .25 .25
891 A308 300p sepia, red & grn .60 .60
URUEXPO 74 Philatelic Exhibition, 10th anniversary of Philatelic Circle of Uruguay (100p) and 250th anniversary of fortification of Montevideo.
Issue dates: 100p, Oct. 1; 300p, Oct. 19.

Letters
and UPU
Emblem
A309

UPU Cent.: 200p, UPU emblem, letter, and globe.

1974, Oct. 9
892 A309 100p lt bl & multi .25 .25
893 A309 200p lil, blk & gold .35 .25
  Nos. 892-893,C395-C396 (4) 2.60 2.50
A 1000p souvenir sheet was not valid for postage. Value $45.

Artigas
Statue
and Map
of
Lavalleja
A310

1974, Oct. 17   **Perf. 12**
894 A310 100p ultra & multi .40 .25
Unveiling of Artigas statue in Minas, Lavalleja.

Ship in
Dry Dock,
Arsenal's
Emblem
A312

1974, Nov. 15 Litho. Wmk. 332
896 A312 200p multi   .40 .30
Centenary of Naval Arsenal, Montevideo.

Globe Hydrogen Balloon — A313

1974, Nov. 20
897 A313 100p shown   .25 .25
898 A313 100p Farman biplane .25 .25
899 A313 100p Castaibert mono-
           plane   .25 .25
900 A313 100p Bleriot mono-
           plane   .25 .25
  a. Strip of 4, #897-900   1.50 1.50
901 A313 150p Military and civil-
           ian pilots' em-
           blems   .25 .25
902 A313 150p Nieuport biplane .25 .25
903 A313 150p Breguet-Bidon
           fighter   .25 .25
904 A313 150p Caproni bomber .25 .25
  a. Strip of 4, #901-904   1.50 1.50
  Nos. 897-904 (8)   2.00 2.00
Aviation pioneers.

Sugar Loaf Mountain and Summit
Cross — A314

1974, Nov. 30
905 A314 150p multi   .35 .25
Cent. of the founding of Sugar Loaf City.

Adoration of the Kings — A315

1974   **Perf. 12**
906 A315 100p shown   .30 .25
907 A315 150p Three Kings   .30 .25
  Nos. 906-907,C400 (3)   1.20 .75
Christmas 1974. See No. C401. Issue dates: 100p, Dec. 17; 150p, Dec. 19.

Nike, Fireworks,
Rowers and Club
Emblem — A316

1975, Jan. 27 Litho. Wmk. 332
908 A316 150p gray & multi   .40 .25
Centenary of Montevideo Rowing Club.

Treaty Signing, by José Zorilla de San
Martin — A317

1975, Feb. 12   **Perf. 12**
909 A317 100p multi   .40 .25
Commercial Treaty between Great Britain and Uruguay, 1817.

Rose — A318

1975, Mar. 18 Litho. Wmk. 332
910 A318 150p multi   .70 .40
Bicentenary of city of Rosario.

"The Oath of the 33," by Juan M.
Blanes — A319

1975, Apr. 16   **Perf. 12**
911 A319 150p gold & multi   .40 .25
Sesquicentennial of liberation movement.

Ship, Columbus
and Ancient
Map — A320

1975, Oct. 9   Litho.   Wmk. 332
912 A320 1p gray & multi   1.60 1.00
Hispanic Stamp Day.

Leonardo Olivera and Santa Teresa
Fort — A321

Artigas as
Young
and Old
Man
A322

1975   Litho.   Wmk. 332   Perf. 12
913 A321 10c org & multi   .30 .25
914 A322 50c vio bl & multi .70 .40
Sesquicentennial of the capture of Fort Santa Teresa (10c) and of Uruguay's declaration of independence (50c).
Issue dates: 10c, Oct. 20; 50c, Oct. 17.

Battle of Rincon, by Diogenes
Hequet — A323

#916, Artigas' Home, Ibiray, Paraguay. 25c, Battle of Sarandi, by J. Manuel Blanes.

1975   **Litho.**
915 A323 15c ol & blk   .30 .25
916 A323 15c ol & multi   .30 .25
917 A323 25c ol & multi   .50 .30
  Nos. 915-917 (3)   1.10 .80
Uruguayan independence. Nos. 915 and 917, 150th anniversary of Battles of Rincon and Sarandi. No. 916, 50th anniversary of school at Artigas mansion.
Issued: #915, 10/23; #916, 11/18; #917, 11/28.

"En
Familia,"
by
Sanchez
A324

Florencio Sanchez A325

Plays by Sanchez: #919, Barranca Abajo. #920, M'Hijo el Doctor. #921, Canillita.

1975, Oct. 31   Wmk. 332   Perf. 12

918	A324	20c gray, red & blk	.35	.25
919	A324	20c bl, grn & blk	.35	.25
920	A324	20c red, bl & blk	.35	.25
921	A324	20c grn, gray & blk	.35	.25
922	A325	20c multi	.35	.25
a.		Block of 5 stamps + 4 labels	2.75	2.75

Florencio Sanchez (1875-1910), dramatist, birth centenary. Nos. 918-922 printed se-tenant in sheets of 30 stamps and 20 labels.

Maria Eugenia Vaz Ferreira A326

Design: No. 924, Julio Herrera y Reissig.

1975

923	A326	15c yel, blk & brn	.30	.25
924	A326	15c org, blk & maroon	.30	.25

Maria Eugenia Vaz Ferreira (1875-1924), poetess, and Julio Herrera y Reissig (1875-1910), poet, birth anniversaries.
Issue dates: #923, Dec. 9; #924, Dec. 29.

A327

Virgin and Child — A328

Fireworks — A329

1975

925	A327	20c bl & multi	.50	.50
926	A328	30c blk & multi	.75	.75
927	A329	60c multi	1.50	1.50
		Nos. 925-927 (3)	2.75	2.75

Christmas 1975.
Issued: 20c, 12/16; 30c, 12/15; 60c, 12/11.

Col. Lorenzo Latorre (1840-1916), Pres. of Uruguay (1876-80) A330

1975, Dec. 30   Perf. 12

928	A330	15c multi	.30	.25

Nos. 840, 842-843, 849A Surcharged

1975

929	A276	10c on 20p lilac	.25	.25
930	A276	15c on 40p orange	.25	.25
931	A276	50c on 50p ver	.45	.45
932	A276	1p on 1000p blue	.95	.95
		Nos. 929-932 (4)	1.90	1.90

There are two surcharge types for Nos. 929 and 930. Values are the same.

Ariel, Stars, Book and Youths A331

1976, Jan. 12   Litho.   Wmk. 332

933	A331	15c grn & multi	.30	.25

75th anniversary of publication of "Ariel," by Jose Enrique Rodo (1872-1917), writer.

Water Sports — A332

1976, Mar. 12   Litho.   Wmk. 332

934	A332	30c multi	.35	.25

23rd South American Swimming, Diving and Water Polo Championships.

Telephone A333

1976, Apr. 9   Perf. 12

935	A333	83c multi	.60	.30

Centenary of first telephone call by Alexander Graham Bell, Mar. 10, 1876.

"Plus Ultra" and Columbus' Ships — A334

1976, May 10   Litho.   Perf. 12

936	A334	63c gray & multi	.70	.30

Flight of Dornier "Plus Ultra" from Spain to South America, 50th anniversary.

A335   A336

Dornier "Wal" and Boeing 727, hourglass.

1976, May 24

937	A335	83c gray & multi	.80	.30

Lufthansa German Airline, 50th anniv.

1976, June 3   Perf. 11½

Designs: 10c, Olympics. 15c, Telephone, cent. 25c, UPU, cent., UN #2. 50c, World Cup Soccer Championships, Argentina, 1978.

938	A336	10c shown	1.75	.60
939	A336	15c multicolored	1.75	.60
940	A336	25c multicolored	1.75	.60
941	A336	50c multicolored	1.75	.60
		Nos. 938-941 (4)	7.00	2.40

Nos. 938-941 had limited distribution. A souvenir sheet containing one each, Nos. 938-941, was not valid for postage. Value $35.

Louis Braille A340

1976, June 7

942	A340	60c blk & brn	1.00	.40

Sesquicentennial of the invention of the Braille system of writing for the blind by Louis Braille (1809-1852).

Signing of US Declaration of Independence A341

1976, June 21

943	A341	1.50p multi	2.75	2.25

American Bicentennial.

The Candombe, by P. Figari — A342

Wmk. 332

1976, July 29   Litho.   Perf. 12

944	A342	30c ultra & multi	.35	.25

Abolition of slavery, sesquicentennial.

Gen. Fructuoso Rivera Statue A343

1976, Aug. 2

945	A343	5p on 10p multi	4.50	2.25

No. 945 was not issued without surcharge.

General Accounting Office — A344

Wmk. 332

1976, Aug. 24   Litho.   Perf. 12

946	A344	30c bl, blk & brn	.35	.25

National General Accounting Office, sesquicentennial.

Old Pump, Emblem and Flame — A345

1976, Sept. 6

947	A345	20c red & blk	.40	.25

First official fire fighting service, centenary.

Southern Lapwing A346   Mburucuya Flower A347

Spearhead A348   Figurine A349

La Yerra, by J. M. Blanes A350   The Gaucho, by Blanes A351

Artigas — A352

Designs: 15c, Ceibo flower.

1976-79   Litho.   Wmk. 332   Perf. 12

948	A346	1c violet	.25	.25
949	A347	5c lt grn	.25	.25
950	A347	15c car rose	.25	.25
951	A348	20c gray	.25	.25
952	A349	30c gray blue	.25	.25
953	A352	45c brt bl ('79)	.25	.25
954	A350	50c grnsh bl ('77)	.25	.25
955	A351	1p dk brn ('77)	.50	.25
956	A352	1p brt yel ('79)	.25	.25
957	A352	1.75p bl grn ('79)	.40	.30
958	A352	1.95p gray ('79)	.40	.30
959	A352	2p dl grn ('77)	1.10	.40
960	A352	2p lil rose ('79)	.50	.35
961	A352	2.65p vio ('79)	.50	.40
962	A352	5p dk bl	3.50	2.00
963	A352	10p brn ('77)	6.75	2.00
		Nos. 948-963 (16)	15.65	8.00

"Diligencia" Uruguay No. 1 — A353

Wmk. 332
1976, Sept. 26   Litho.   Perf. 12
964 A353 30c bister, red & blue   .40   .25
Philatelic Club of Uruguay, 50th anniv.

Games'
Emblem — A354

1976, Oct. 26   Litho.   Perf. 12
965 A354 83c gray & multi   1.00   .50
5th World University Soccer Championships.

World Cup Soccer Championships,
Argentina — A355

Anniversaries and Events: 30c, 1976 Summer Olympics, Montreal. 50c, Viking spacecraft. 80c, Nobel prizes, 75th anniv.

1976, Nov. 12   Perf. 12
966 A355 10c multicolored   1.75   .85
967 A355 30c multicolored   1.75   .85
968 A355 50c multicolored   1.75   .85
969 A355 80c multicolored   1.75   .85
    Nos. 966-969 (4)   7.00   3.40

Nos. 966-969 had limited distribution.
See Nos. C424-C425.

Eye and
Spectrum
A356

1976, Nov. 24
970 A356 20c blk & multi   .50   .25
Foresight prevents blindness.

Map of Montevideo, 1748 — A357

45c, Montevideo Harbor, 1842. 70c, First settlers, 1726. 80c, Coin with Montevideo arms, vert. 1.15p, Montevideo's first coat of arms, vert.

Wmk. 332
1976, Dec. 30   Perf. 12
971 A357 30c multi   .40   .25
972 A357 45c multi   .55   .25
973 A357 70c multi   .70   .35
974 A357 80c multi   1.00   .35
975 A357 1.15p multi   1.60   .45
    Nos. 971-975 (5)   4.25   1.65
Founding of Montevideo, 250th anniversary.

Symbolic
of Flight
A358

1977, May 7   Litho.   Perf. 12
976 A358 80c multi   .75   .50
50th anniversary of Varig airlines.

Artigas Mausoleum — A359

1977, June 17   Litho.   Perf. 12
977 A359 45c multi   .50   .30

A360

1977, July 5   Wmk. 332
978 A360 45c Map of Uruguay,
    arch   .45   .30
Centenary of Salesian Brothers' educational system in Uruguay.

A361

Anniversaries and events: 20c, Werner Heisenberg, Nobel Prize for Physics. 30c, World Cup Soccer Championships, Uruguay Nos. 282, 390. 50c, Lindbergh's trans-Atlantic flight, 50th anniv. 1p, Rubens 400th birth anniv.

1977, July 21
979 A361 20c shown   2.25   1.40
980 A361 30c multicolored   2.25   1.40
981 A361 50c multicolored   2.25   1.40
982 A361 1p multicolored   2.25   1.40
    a.   Strip, 2 ea #979-982 + 2 labels
    Nos. 979-982 (4)   9.00   5.60

Nos. 979-982 had limited distribution.
A souvenir sheet containing Nos. 979-982, imperf., was not valid for postage. It sold for 8p. See Nos. C426-C427.

Children — A362

1977, Aug. 10   Litho.   Perf. 12
983 A362 45c multi   .50   .30
Interamerican Children's Inst., 50th anniv.

"El Sol de
Mayo"
A363

1977, Oct. 1   Litho.   Perf. 12
984 A363 45c multi   .60   .60
Stamp Day 1977.

Windmills — A364

1977, Sept. 29   Wmk. 332
985 A364 70c yel, car & blk   .75   .35
Spanish Heritage Day.

Souvenir Sheet

View of Sans (Barcelona), by
Barradas — A365

1977, Oct. 7   Litho.   Perf. 12
986 A365   Sheet of 2   6.50   6.50
    a.-b.   5p, single stamp   3.00   3.00
ESPAMER '77 Philatelic Exhibition, Barcelona, Oct. 7-13.

Planes,
UN
Emblem,
Globe
A366

1977, Oct. 17
987 A366 45c multi   .35   .25
30th anniv. of Civil Aviation Organization.

Holy
Family — A367

Santa Claus — A368

1977, Dec. 1   Wmk. 332
988 A367 45c multi   .25   .25
989 A368 70c blk, yel & red   .25   .25
Christmas 1977.

Map of
Rio Negro
Province
A369

1977, Dec. 16
990 A369 45c multi   .75   .30
Rio Negro Dam; development of argiculture, livestock and beekeeping. See Nos. 1021-1033.

Mail Collection
A370

1977, Dec. 21
991 A370 50c shown   .30   .25
992 A370 50c Mail truck   .30   .25
993 A370 50c Post office
    counter   .30   .25
994 A370 50c Postal boxes   .30   .25
995 A370 50c Mail sorting   .30   .25
996 A370 50c Pigeonhole sort-
    ing   .30   .25
997 A370 50c Route sorting
    (seated carriers)   .30   .25
998 A370 50c Home delivery   .30   .25
999 A370 50c Special delivery
    (motorcyclists)   .30   .25
1000 A370 50c Airport counter   .30   .25
    a.   Strip of 10, #991-1000   7.50   7.50
Uruguayan postal service, 150th anniv.

Edison's Phonograph, 1877 — A371

1977, Dec. 30
1001 A371 50c vio brn & yel   .75   .30
Centenary of invention of the phonograph.

"R",
Rainbow
and
Emblem
A372

1977, Dec. 30   Wmk. 332
1002 A372 50c multi   .30   .25
World Rheumatism Year.

Emblem
and
Diploma
A373

1978, Mar. 27   Litho.   Perf. 12
1003 A373 50c multi   .35   .25
50th anniversary of Military College.

Erhard Schon by Albrecht Durer
(1471-1528) — A374

Painting: 50c, Self-Portrait by Peter Paul
Rubens (1577-1640).

1978, June 13   **Perf. 12½**
1004 A374   25c blk & brn   1.25 1.00
1005 A374   50c brn & blk   2.00 1.50
Nos. 1004-1005 had limited distribution.
See Nos. C430-C432.

Map and Arms of Artigas
Department — A375

                          Wmk. 332
1978, June 16   Litho.   Perf. 12
1006 A375   45c multi   .40 .25

Souvenir Sheet

Anniversaries — A376

Designs: 2p, Papilio thoas. No. 1007b,
"100." No. 1007c, Argentina '78 emblem and
globes. 5p, Model T Ford.

                          Wmk. 332
1978, Aug. 24   Litho.   Perf. 12
1007 A376   Sheet of 4   18.00 18.00
  a.   2p multi   1.75 1.75
  b.   4p multi   3.50 3.50
  c.   4p multi   3.50 3.50
  d.   5p multi   4.25 4.25
75th anniv. of 1st powered flight; URUEXPO
'78 Phil. Exhib.; Parva Domus social club,
cent.; 11th World Cup Soccer Championship,
Argentina, June 1-25; Ford motor cars, 75th
anniv.

Visiting Angels, by Solari — A377

Designs (Details from No. 1008b): No.
1008a, Second angel. No. 1008c, Third angel.

1978, Sept. 13   Unwmk.
1008   Strip of 3   2.00 2.00
  a. A377 1.50p, 19x30mm   .40 .40
  b. A377 1.50p, 38x30mm   .40 .40
  c. A377 1.50p, 19x30mm   .40 .40
Solari, Uruguayan painter.

Bernardo
O'Higgins
A378

#1010, José de San Martin and monument.

1978   Wmk. 332
1009 A378   1p multi   .35 .25
1010 A378   1p multi   .35 .25
Benardo O'Higgins (1778-1842 and José de
San Martin (1778-1850), South American
liberators.
   Issued: #1009, Sept. 13; #1010, Oct. 10.

Telephone
Dials
A379

1978, Sept. 25
1011 A379   50c multi   .40 .25
Automation of telephone service.

Symbolic
Stamps
A380

Iberian Tile
Pattern — A381

1978, Oct. 31
1012 A380   50c multi   .30 .25
1013 A381   1p multi   .30 .25
Stamp Day (50c) and Spanish heritage (1p).

Boeing
727
A382

1978, Nov. 27
1014 A382   50c multi   .60 .25
Inauguration of Boeing 727 flights by
PLUNA Uruguayan airlines, Nov. 1978.

Angel Blowing Horn — A383

1978, Dec. 7
1015 A383   50c multi   .25 .25
1016 A383   1p multi   .35 .25
Christmas 1978.

A384   A385

1978, Dec. 15   Perf. 12½
1017 A384   1p Flag flying on Pla-
             za of the Nation   .35 .25

          Wmk. 332
1978, Dec. 27   Litho.   Perf. 12
1018 A385   1p blk, red & yel   .30 .25
Horacio Quiroga (1868-1928), short story
writer.

Arch,
Olympic
Rings,
Lake
Placid and
Moscow
Emblems
A386

7p, Olympic Rings, Lake Placid '80 emblem.

1979, Apr. 28   Litho.   Perf. 12
1019 A386   5p multi   2.00 1.40
1020 A386   7p multi   2.25 1.00
81st Session of Olympic Organizing Committee, Apr. 3-8 (5p), and 13th Winter Olympic
Games, Lake Placid, NY, Feb. 12-24.

          Souvenir Sheets
1021   Sheet of 4   35.00 35.00
  a. A386 3p similar to #1019
  b. A386 5p Olympic rings
  c. A386 7p Rider looking back
  d. A386 10p Rider facing forward
1022   Sheet of 4   35.00 35.00
  a. A386 3p similar to #1020
  b. A386 5p Uruguay '79
  c. A386 7p World Chess Olym-
            pics '78
  d. A386 10p Sir Rowland Hill,
            Great Britain stamp
No. 1022d shows Great Britain No. 836, but
with 11p denomination. No. 1021c-1021d have
continuous design.
Nos. 1021-1022 had limited distribution.
Except for No. 1022d, singles were sold for
postal use in 1980. Nos. 1021-1022 exist
imperf.

Map and
Arms of
Paysandu
A387

Map and Arms of
Maldonado
A388

1979-81
1023 A387   45c shown   .40 .40
1024 A387   45c Salto   .40 .40
1025 A387   45c shown   .40 .40
1026 A387   45c Cerro Largo   .40 .40
1027 A387   50c Treinta y Tres   .40 .40
1028 A387   50c Durazno ('80)   .40 .40
1029 A388   2p Rocha ('81)   .40 .40
1030 A388   2p Flores   .40 .40
   Nos. 1023-1030 (8)   3.20 3.20
          See No. 990.

Sapper with
Pickax,
1837 — A389

Army Day: No. 1039, Artillery man with cannon, 1830.

1979, May 18   Litho.   Perf. 12
1038 A389   5p multi   1.90 1.00
1039 A389   5p multi   1.90 1.00

Madonna
and Child
by Durer
A390

Anniversaries and events: 80c, World Cup
Soccer Championships, Spain. 1.30p, Sir
Rowland Hill, Greece No. 117.

1979, June 18   Perf. 12
1040 A390   70c brn & gray   6.50 3.25
1041 A390   80c multicolored   5.00 2.75
1042 A390   1.30p multicolored   5.00 2.75
   Nos. 1040-1042 (3)   16.50 8.75
Nos. 1040-1042 had limited distribution.
Issued in sheets of 24 containing 6 blocks of
4 with margin around. See #C437-C438.

Salto
Dam
A391

1979, June 19
1043 A391   2p multi   .60 .30

Crandon
Institute
Emblem,
Grain
A392

1979, July 19
1044 A392   1p vio bl & bl   .30 .25
Crandon Institute (private Methodist school),
centenary.

IYC Emblem,
Smiling
Kites — A393

Cinderella
A394

1979
1045 A393 2p multi .60 .25
1046 A394 2p multi .60 .25

International Year of the Child. Issue dates:
No. 1045, July 23; No. 1046, Aug. 29.

Uruguay Coat of Arms 150th
Anniversary — A395

1979, Sept. 6
1047 A395 8p multi 3.00 1.40

Virgin and
Child — A396

Wmk. 332
1979, Nov. 19 Litho. Perf. 12
1048 A396 10p multi 2.75 1.60

Christmas 1979; Intl. Year of the Child.

Symbols, by
Torres-Garcia
A397

1979, Nov. 12
1049 A397 10p yel & blk 3.00 1.60

J. Torres-Garcia (1874-1948), painter.

UPU and Brazilian Postal
Emblems — A398

1979, Oct. 11
1050 A398 5p multi 1.25 .80

18th UPU Congress, Rio, Sept.-Oct.

Dish Antenna and Sun — A400

Perf. 12x11½
1979, Nov. 26 Litho. Wmk. 332
1052 A400 10p multi 3.00 1.25

Telecom '79, 3rd World Telecommunications
Exhibition, Geneva, Sept. 20-26.

Spanish Heritage
Day — A401

1979, Dec. 3 Perf. 12
1053 A401 10p multi 2.75 1.60

Silver
Coin
Centenary
A402

Designs: Obverse and reverse of coins in
denominations matching stamps.

1979, Dec. 26
1054 A402 10c multi .25 .25
1055 A402 20c multi .25 .25
1056 A402 50c multi .25 .25
1057 A402 1p multi .45 .25
Nos. 1054-1057 (4) 1.20 1.00

Souvenir Sheet

Security
Agent — A403

1980, Jan. 10
1058 Sheet of 4 3.50 3.50
a. A403 1p Police emblem .30 .30
b. A403 2p shown .50 .50
c. A403 3p Policeman, 1843 .75 .75
d. A403 4p Cadet, 1979 1.00 1.00

Police force sesquicentennial.

Light Bulb, Thomas Edison — A404

1980, Jan. 18
1059 A404 2p multi .75 .35

Centenary of electric light (1979).

Bass and
Singer — A405

1980, Jan. 30
1060 Sheet of 4 3.00 3.00
a. A405 2p Radio waves .65 .65
b. A405 2p shown .65 .65
c. A405 2p Ballerina .65 .65
d. A405 2p Television waves .65 .65

Performing Arts Society, 50th anniversary.

Stamp
Day — A406

1980, Feb.
1061 A406 1p multi .45 .25

La Leyenda
Patria — A407

1980, Feb. 26
1062 A407 1p multi .30 .25

Printers'
Association,
50th
Anniversary
A408

1980, Feb.
1063 A408 1p multi .35 .25

Lufthansa Cargo Container Service
Inauguration — A409

1980, Apr. 12 Unwmk. Perf. 12½
1064 A409 2p multi .60 .25

Conf. Emblem,
Banners — A410

1980, Apr. 28 Wmk. 332 Perf. 12
1065 A410 2p multi .60 .35

8th World Hereford Conf., Punta del Este
and Livestock Exhib., Prado/Montivideo.

Man, Woman and
Birds — A411

1980 Litho. Perf. 12
1066 A411 1p multi .50 .25

International Year of the Child (1979).

Latin-American Lions, 9th
Forum — A412

1980, May 6 Wmk. 332 Perf. 12
1067 A412 1p multi .50 .25

Souvenir Sheet

Army Day, May 18 — A413

1980, May 16
1068 Sheet of 4 5.00 5.00
a. A413 2p Rifleman, 1814 1.00 1.00
b. A413 2p Cavalry officer, 1830 1.00 1.00
c. A413 2p Private Liberty Dragoons,
1826 1.00 1.00
d. A413 2p, Artigas Militia officer,
1815 1.00 1.00

Arms of
Colonia — A414

Colonia,
1680
A415

1980, June 17　Litho.　Perf. 12
1069 A414 50c multi　　　1.50　.25
Souvenir Sheet
1070　Sheet of 4　　　　1.60　1.60
 a. A415 1p shown　　　.30　.30
 b. A415 1p 1680, diff.　.30　.30
 c. A415 1p 1980　　.30　.30
 d. A415 1p 1980, diff.　.30　.30

 Colonia, 300th anniversary.

Rotary Emblem
on Globe — A416

1980, July 8
1071 A416 5p multi　　　1.50　.90

 Rotary International, 75th anniversary.

Hand Putting Out
Cigarette — A417

1980, Sept. 8　　　Photo.
1072 A417 1p multi　　　.40　.25

 World Health Day and anti-smoking
campaign.

Artigas — A418

Wmk. 332
1980-85　Litho.　Perf. 12½
1073 A418　10c blue ('81)　.25　.25
1074 A418　20c orange　　.25　.25
1075 A418　50c red　　　.25　.25
1076 A418　60c yellow　　.25　.25
1077 A418　1p gray　　　.55　.25
1078 A418　2p brown　　1.00　.30
1079 A418　3p brt grn　　1.75　.35
1080 A418　4p brt bl ('82)　2.10　.45
1081 A418　5p green ('82)　1.10　.25
1082 A418　6p brt org ('85)　.40　.25
1083 A418　7p lil rose ('82)　5.00　.75
1084 A418　10p blue ('82)　2.00　.35
1085 A418　12p blk ('85)　1.10　.25
1086 A418　15.50p emer ('85)　1.50　.30
1087 A418　20p dk vio ('82)　4.25　.75
1088 A418　30p lt brn ('82)　6.50　.75
1089 A418　50p gray bl ('82)　11.00　1.90
 Nos. 1073-1089 (17)　39.25　7.90

Christmas
1980
A419

1980, Dec. 15　Litho.　Perf. 12
1090 A419 2p multi　　　.75　.25

Constitution Title Page — A420

1980, Dec. 23　　Perf. 12½
1091 A420 4p brt bl & gold　1.25　.65
 Sesquicentennial of Constitution.

A421

1980, Dec. 30　　　Perf. 12
1092 A421　5p Montevideo
   Stadium　　2.00　1.00
1093 A421　5p Soccer gold
   cup　　　2.00　1.00
Size: 25x79mm
1094 A421 10p Flags　　2.00　1.00
 a. Souv. sheet of 3, #1092-
  1094　　　10.50　10.50
 Nos. 1092-1094 (3)　6.00　3.00

 Soccer　Gold　Cup　Championship,
Montevideo.

A422

1981, Jan. 27
1095 A422 2p multi　　　.70　.25

 Spanish Heritage Day.

UPU Membership Centenary — A423

1981, Feb. 6
1096 A423 2p multi　　　.70　.25

Alexander von
Humboldt (1769-
1859), German
Explorer and
Scientist — A424

1981, Feb. 19
1097 A424 2p multi　　　.70　.25

Intl. Education Congress and Fair,
Montevideo (1980) — A425

1981, Mar. 31
1098 A425 2p multi　　　.60　.25

Hand Holding
Gold Cup — A426

1981, Apr. 8
1099 A426 2p multi　　　.60　.25
1100 A426 5p multi　　　1.40　.50

 1980 victory in Gold Cup Soccer
Championship.

Eighth Notes on
Map of
Americas — A427

1981, Apr. 28
1101 A427 2p multi　　　.60　.25
 Inter-American Institute of Musicology, 40th
anniv.

World Tourism Conference, Manila,
Sept. 27, 1980 — A428

Wmk. 332
1981, June 1　Litho.　Perf. 12
1102 A428 2p multi　　　.60　.25

Inauguration of PLUNA Flights to
Madrid — A429

1981, May 12
1103 A429　2p multi　　.40　.25
1104 A429　5p multi　　.95　.45
1105 A429　10p multi　　1.90　.95
 Nos. 1103-1105 (3)　3.25　1.65

Army
Day — A430

Wmk. 332
1981, May 18　Litho.　Perf. 12
1106 A430 2p Cavalry soldier,
   1843　　　.70　.25
1107 A430 2p Infantryman, 1843　.70　.25

Natl. Atomic
Energy
Commission, 25th
Anniv. — A431

1981, July 20
1108 A431 2p multi　　　.70　.25

Europe-South American Soccer
Cup — A432

1981, Aug. 4
1109 A432 2p multi　　　.90　.25

Stone Tablets, Salto Grande
Excavation — A433

1981, Sept. 10
1110 A433 2p multi　　　.70　.25

10th Lavalleja
Week — A434

1981, Oct. 3
1111 A434 4p multi　　　1.40　.45

Intl. Year
of the
Disabled
A435

Wmk. 332
1981, Oct. 26　Litho.　Perf. 12
1112 A435 2p multi　　　.60　.25

UN Environmental Law Meeting
Montevideo, Oct. 28-Nov. 6 — A436

1981, Oct. 28
1113 A436 5p multi   1.40 .45

A437

1981, Oct. 13
1114 A437 2p multi   .70 .25

50th anniv. of ANCAP (Natl. Administration
of Combustible Fuels, Alcohol and Cement).

Souvenir Sheets

Uruguay 81 Intl. Philatelic
Exhibition — A438

No. 1114A: b, Copa de Oro trophy. c, Soc-
cer player kicking ball.
No. 1115: a, Chess pieces. b, Prince
Charles and Lady Diana, flags of Uruguay and
Great Britain.

Wmk. 332
1981, Nov. 23   Litho.   Perf. 12
1114A A438 5p Sheet of 2, #b-
        c   23.00 23.00
1115   A438 5p Sheet of 2, #a-
        b   25.00 25.00

1982 World Cup Soccer Championships,
Spain (No. 1114Ac), World Chess Championships, Atlanta (No. 1115a); Wedding of Prince
Charles and Lady Diana (No. 1115b). Nos.
1114A-1115 exist imperf., which were not valid
for postage.

Topographical Society
Sesequicentennial — A439

1981, Dec. 5   Perf. 12
1116 A439 2p multi   .75 .25
        See No. 1407.

Bank of Uruguay, 85th Anniv. — A440

1981, Dec. 17   Perf. 12½
1117 A440 2p multi   .60 .25

Palmar Dam — A441

1981, Dec. 22   Perf. 12
1118 A441 2p multi   .75 .25

Christmas
1981
A442

1981, Dec. 23
1119 A442 2p multi   .60 .25

Pres. Joaquin
Suarez
Bicentenary
A443

1982, Mar. 15
1120 A443 5p multi   1.60 .50

Artillery Captain,
1872, Army
Day — A444

Wmk. 332
1982, May 18   Litho.   Perf. 12
1121 A444 3p shown   1.00 .25
1122 A444 3p Florida Battalion,
            1865   1.00 .25
        See Nos. 1136-1137.

Cent. (1981) of
Pinocchio, by
Carlo
Collodi — A445

1982, June 17
1123 A445 2p multi   .70 .25

2nd UN
Conference on
Peaceful Uses
of Outer
Space,
Vienna, Aug.
9-21 — A446

1982, June 3
1124 A446 3p multi   1.25 .70

World
Food Day
A447

1982
1125 A447 2p multi   .65 .25

25th Anniv. of Lufthansa's Uruguay-
Germany Flight — A448

1982, Apr. 14   Unwmk.   Perf. 12½
1126 A448 3p Lockheed L-1049-
            G Super Constel-
            lation   1.00 .40
1127 A448 7p Boeing 747   2.25 .80

American Air
Forces
Cooperation
System — A449

1982, Apr. 14   Wmk. 332   Perf. 12
1128 A449 10p Emblem   2.75 .80

Juan Zorilla de San Martin (1855-
1931), Painter — A450

1982, Aug. 18   Perf. 12½
1129 A450 3p Self-portrait   .80 .40

165th Anniv. of Natl. Navy — A451

1982, Nov. 15   Perf. 12
1130 A451 3p Navy vessel
            Capitan Miranda   1.00 .40

Natl. Literacy   Stamp
Campaign — A452   Day — A453

1982, Nov. 30
1131 A452 3p multi   .80 .35

1982, Dec. 23   Perf. 12½
1132 A453 3p like #46   .40 .25
1133 A453 3p like #47   .40 .25
    a.   Pair, #1132-1133   1.40 1.40

These stamps bear numbers from 1 to 100
according to their position on the sheet.

Christmas 1982 — A454

1983, Jan. 4   Perf. 12
1134 A454 3p multi   .60 .25

Eduardo Fabini (1882-1950),
Composer — A455

1983, May 10
1135 A455 3p gold & brn   .60 .25

Army Day Type of 1982

1983, May 18
1136 A444 3p Military College
          cadet, 1885   .45 .25
1137 A444 3p 2nd Cavalry Regi-
          ment officer,
          1885   .45 .25

Visit of King Juan Carlos and Queen
Sofia of Spain, May — A456

1983, May 20   **Unwmk.**
1138 A456 3p Santa Maria, globe .85 .40
1139 A456 7p Profiles, flags   1.90 .80
          Size of No. 1138: 29x39mm.

Brasiliana '83
Emblem — A457

80th Anniv. of
First Automobile
in
Uruguay — A458

Opening of UPAE
Building,
Montevideo
A459

Jose Cuneo
(1887-1977),
Painter — A460

1982
World
Cup
A461

Graf Zeppelin Flight Over Montevideo,
50th Anniv. (1984) — A462

J.W. Goethe (1749-1832), 150th
Death Anniv. — A463

First
Space
Shuttle
Flight
A464

1983   Litho.   Wmk. 332   Perf. 12
1140 A457 3p multi   1.00 1.00
1141 A458 3p multi   1.00 1.00
1142 A459 3p multi   1.00 1.00
1143 A460 3p multi   1.00 1.00
  a.   Souvenir sheet of 4   6.00 6.00
1144 A461 7p multi   1.50 1.50
1145 A462 7p multi   1.50 1.50
1146 A463 7p multi   1.50 1.50
1147 A464 7p multi   1.50 1.50
  a.   Souvenir sheet of 4   10.00 10.00
     Nos. 1140-1147 (8)   10.00 10.00

No. 1143a contains stamps similar to Nos.
1140-1143. No. 1147a stamps similar to Nos.
1144-1147. Nos. 1143a and 1147a for
URUEXPO '83 and World Communications
Year.
   Issued: #1142, 6/8; #1143, 1146, 9/29;
#1143a, 1147a, 6/9; #1140, 7/22; #1144,
12/13; #1146, 9/20; #1145, 12/8.

Bicentenary of
City of
Minas — A465

Wmk. 332
1983, Oct. 17   Litho.   Perf. 12
1148 A465 3p Founder   .65 .25

World Communications Year — A466

1983, Nov. 30
1149 A400 0p multi   .40 .25

Garibaldi
Death
Centenary
A467

1983, Dec. 5
1150 A467 7p multi   1.00 .40

Christmas
1983
A468

Lithographed and Embossed
(Braille)
1983, Dec. 21   Perf. 12½
1151 A468 4.50p multi   .75 .25

50th Anniv. of Automatic
Telephones — A469

1983, Dec. 27   Perf. 12
1152 A469 4.50p multi   .60 .25

Simon
Bolivar,
Battle
Scene
A470

Wmk. 332
1984, Mar. 28   Litho.   Perf. 12
1153 A470 4.50p brn & gldn brn 1.10 .40

Gen. Leandro
Gomez — A471

1984, Jan. 2
1154 A471 4.50p multi   .50 .25

American
Women's
Day — A472

1984, Feb. 18
1155 A472 4.50p Flags, emblem   .50 .25

Reunion
Emblem
A473

1984, Mar. 23
1156 A473 10p multi   1.00 .45
   Intl. Development Bank Governors, 25th
annual reunion, Punta del Este.

50th
Anniv. of
Radio
Club of
Uruguay
(1983)
A474

1984, Apr. 11
1157 A474 7p multi   .65 .30

A475

1984, Feb. 7   Litho.   Perf. 12
1158 A475 4.50p multi   .50 .25
   Intl. Maritime Org., 25th anniv.

A476

1984, May 2   Litho.   Perf. 12
1159 A476 4.50p multi   .50 .25
   1930 World Soccer Championships,
Montevideo.

Department of San Jose de Mayo,
200th Anniv. — A477

1984, May 9   Litho.   Perf. 12
1160 A477 4.50p multi   .50 .25

Tourism,
50th
Anniv.
A478

1984, May 15   Litho.   Perf. 12
1161 A478 4.50p multi   .50 .25

Military Uniforms — A479

1984, June 19   Litho.   Perf. 12
1162 A479 4.50p Artillery Regiment, 1895   .55   .25
1163 A479 4.50p Cazadores, 2nd battalion   .55   .25

Artigas on the Plains — A480

1984, July 2   Litho.   Perf. 12
1164 A480 4.50p bl & blk   .45   .25
1165 A480 8.50p bl & redsh brn   .85   .40

A. Penarol Soccer Club A481

1984, Aug. 21   Litho.   Perf. 12
1166 A481 4.50p Championship trophy   .55   .25

Provincial Map Type of 1973
1984, Sept. 21   Litho.   Perf. 12
1167 A281 4.50p multi   .50   .25

Childrens Council, 50th Anniv. A482

1984, Oct. 11   Litho.   Perf. 12
1168 A482 4.50p multi   .50   .25

Christmas A483

1984   Litho.   Perf. 12
1169 A483 6p multi   .70   .30

A484

1985, Feb. 13   Litho.   Perf. 12
1170 A484 4.50p multi   .50   .25
1st Jr. World Basketball Championships.

Don Bruno Mauricio de Zabala, 300th Birth Anniv. — A485

1985, Apr. 16   Litho.   Perf. 12
1171 A485 4.50p multi   .60   .25

Intl. Olympic Committee, 90th Anniv. — A486

Design: Olympic rings, Los Angeles and Sarajevo 1984 Games emblems.

1985, May 22   Perf. 12½
1172 A486 12p multi   1.00   .50

Carlos Gardel, (1890-1935), Entertainer A487

1985, June 21   Perf. 12
1173 A487 6p lt gray, red brn & bl   .50   .25

Catholic Circle of Workers, Cent. — A488

Wmk. 332
1985, June 21   Litho.   Perf. 12
1174 A488 6p Cross, clasped hands   .30   .25

Icarus, by Hans Erni — A489

1985, July   Photo.   Wmk. 332
1175 A489 4.50p multi   .50   .25
Intl. Civil Aviation Org., 40th anniv.

American Air Forces Cooperation System, 25th Anniv. — A490

1985, July
1176 A490 12p Emblem, flags   .50   .25

FUNSA, Natl. Investment Funds Corp., 50th Anniv. — A491

1985, July 31   Litho.   Wmk. 332
1177 A491 6p multi   .30   .25

Intl. Youth Year A492

1985, Aug. 28
1178 A492 12p mar & blk   .40   .25

Installation of Democratic Government — A493

1985, Aug. 30
1179 A493 20p brt pur, yel ocher & dk grnsh bl   1.10   .45

Intl. Book Fair — A494

1985
1180 A494 20p multi   .80   .35

Military School, Cent. A495

1985, Nov. 29   Litho.   Perf. 12
1181 A495 10p multi   .40   .25

Department of Flores, Cent. — A496

1985, Dec. 9
1182 A496 6p Map, arms   .40   .25

Christmas 1985 A497

1985, Dec. 23
1183 A497 10p multi   .40   .25
1184 A497 22p multi   .60   .30

Day of Hispanic Solidarity — A498

1985, Dec. 27
1185 A498 12p Isabel Monument   .50   .25

3rd Inter-American Agricultural Congress — A499

Wmk. 332
1986, Jan. 7   Photo.   Perf. 12
1186 A499 12p blk, dl yel & red   .60   .30

UPU Day A500

1986, Jan. 14   Litho.   Perf. 12
1187 A500 15.50p multi   .55   .25

1985 Census A501

1986, Jan. 21
1188 A501 10p multi   .35   .25

Conaprole, 50th Anniv. — A502

1986, Jan. 25
1189 A502 10p gold, brt ultra & bl   .50   .25

UN, 40th Anniv. A503

Wmk. 332
1986, Feb. 26   Litho.   Perf. 12
1190 A503 20p multi   .60   .25

Brokers and Auctioneers Assoc., 50th Anniv. — A504

1986, Mar. 19
1191 A504 10p multi   .35   .25

Gen. Manuel Ceferino Oribe (1792-1857), President — A505

Portraits: Nos. 1196, 1200, 2p, 7p, 15p, 20p, Oribe. Nos. 1195, 1209, 1211, 3p, Lavalleja. Nos. 1199, 1208, 1210, 30p, 100p, 200p, Artigas. No. 1198, 17p, 22p, 26p, 45p, 75p, Rivera.

1986-89   Perf. 12½
1192 A505 1p dl grn   .25   .25
1193 A505 2p scarlet   .25   .25
1194 A505 3p ultra   .25   .25
1195 A505 5p dark blue   .25   .25
1196 A505 5p violet blue   .25   .25
1197 A505 7p tan   .25   .25
1198 A505 10p lilac rose   .30   .25
1199 A505 10p brt green   .25   .25
1200 A505 10p bluish grn   .25   .25
1201 A505 15p dull blue   .25   .25
1202 A505 17p deep blue   .30   .25
1203 A505 20p light brown   .25   .25
1204 A505 22p violet   .25   .25
1205 A505 26p olive blk   .35   .25
1206 A505 30p pale org   .35   .25
1207 A505 45p dark red   .35   .25
1208 A505 50p dp bis   .65   .45
1209 A505 50p bright pink   .25   .25
1210 A505 60p dark gray   .90   .45
1211 A505 60p orange   .25   .25
1211A A505 75p red orange   .35   .25
1211B A505 100p dl red brn   1.40   .60
1211C A505 200p brt yel grn   2.00   .75
   Nos. 1192-1211C (23)   10.20 7.00

The 22p is airmail.
Issued: 1p, 7p, 4/18; #1195, 30p, 6/16; #1198, 22p, 9/24; #1208, 8/5; 100p, 7/2; 2p, 6/16/87; 3p, #1210, 8/14/87; #1199, 17p, 8/4/87; 26p, 9/2/87; 15p, 9/9/88; 45p, 12/20/88; 200p, 10/19/88; #1211A, 5/19/89; #1211, 7/27/89; #1196, 1203, 8/15/89; #1209, 12/12/89; #1200, 1989.
See Nos. 1321-1329.

Italian Chamber of Commerce in Uruguay — A506

1986, May 5   Perf. 12
1212 A506 20p multi   .75   .25

A507

1986, May 28   Photo.   Perf. 12
1213 A507 20p multi   .60   .30
1986 World Cup Soccer Championships, Mexico.

A508

Wmk. 332
1986, May 19   Litho.   Perf. 12
1214 A508 10p multi   .60   .30
Genocide of the Armenian people, 71st anniv.

A509

1986, June 16
1215 A509 10p multi   .30   .25
El Dia Newspaper, cent.

A510

1986, July 14
1216 A510 20p Garcia, Peruvian flag   .40   .25
State visit of Pres. Alan Garcia of Peru.

Simon Bolivar, Gen. Sucre, Map A511

1986, July 24
1217 A511 20p multi   .65   .25
State visit of Pres. Jaime Lusinchi of Venezuela.

State Visit of Pres. Jose Sarney of Brazil — A512

1986, July 31
1218 A512 20p multi   .40   .25

Zelmar Michelini, Assassinated Liberal Senator — A513

1986, Aug. 21
1219 A513 10p vio bl & rose lake   .30   .25

B'nai B'rith of Uruguay, 50th Anniv. A514

1986, Sept. 10
1220 A514 10p red, gold & red brn   .70   .30

General Agreement on Tariffs & Trade (GATT) Committee Meeting, Punta del Este — A515

1986, Sept. 15
1221 A515 10p multi   .50   .25

Scheduled Flights between Uruguay and Spain, 40th Anniv. — A516

1986, Sept. 22
1222 A516 20p multi   .60   .30

Fish Exports A517

1986, Oct. 1
1223 A517 20p multi   .60   .30

Wool Exports A518

1986, Oct. 15
1224 A518 20p multi   .60   .30

Pres. Blanco, Natl. and Dominican Flags A519

1986, Oct. 29
1225 A519 20p multi   .35   .25
State visit of Pres. Salvador Jorge Blanco of the Dominican Republic.

State Visit of Pres. Sandro Pertini of Italy — A520

1986, Oct. 31
1226 A520 20p grn & buff   .30   .25

State Visit of Pres. Raul Alfonsin of Argentina A521

1986, Nov. 10
1227 A521 20p multi   .40   .25

Hispanic Solidarity Day A522

Design: Felipe and Santiago, the patron saints of Montevideo, and cathedral.

Wmk. 332
1987, Jan. 12   Litho.   Perf. 12
1228 A522 10p rose lake & blk   .60   .30

JUVENTUS, 50th Anniv. (in 1986) — A523

1987, Jan. 28
1229 A523 10p brt yel, blk & ultra   .40   .25
Juventus, a Catholic sports, culture and leisure organization.

Hector Gutierrez
Ruiz (1934-1976),
Politician — A524

Intl. Symposium
on Science and
Technology
A525

1987, Feb. 23
1230 A524 10p brn & deep mag .25 .25
1231 A525 20p multi .30 .25

Ruiz represented Uruguay at an earlier science and technology symposium.

Visit of Pope
John Paul II to La
Plata
Region — A526

1987, Mar. 31
1232 A526 50p blk & deep org 1.00 .50

Dr. Jose F. Arias
(1885-1985),
Founder of the
University of
Crafts — A527

1987, Apr. 28
1233 A527 10p multi .30 .25

Jewish
Community in
Uruguay, 70th
Anniv. — A528

1987, July 8
1234 A528 10p blk, org & brt bl .70 .30

Pluna
Airlines,
50th
Anniv. (in
1986)
A529

1987, Sept. 16
1235 A529 10p Dragon Fly .40 .25
1236 A529 20p Douglas DC-3 .50 .25
1237 A529 25p Vickers Viscount .60 .25
1238 A529 30p Boeing 707 .80 .30
Nos. 1235-1238 (4) 2.30 1.05

Artigas
Antarctic
Station
A530

1987, Sept. 28
1239 A530 20p multi .70 .30

Uruguay
Mortgage
Bank,
75th
Anniv.
A531

1987, Oct. 14
1240 A531 26p multi .40 .25

Exports — A532

1987, Oct. 28
1241 A532 51p Beef .85 .40
1242 A532 51p Milk products .85 .40

Christmas 1987 — A533

1987, Dec. 21
1243 A533 17p Nativity, vert. .45 .25
1244 A533 66p shown .85 .50

State Visit of
Jose Napoleon
Duarte, President
of El
Salvador — A534

1988, Jan. 12
1245 A534 20p brt olive grn &
Prus blue .30 .25

VARIG Airlines,
60th Anniv. (in
1987) — A535

1988, Feb. 9
1246 A535 66p blk, blue & brt yel 1.10 1.10

Post Office
Stamp
Foundation
A536

Wmk. 332
1988, Feb. 9 Litho. Perf. 12
1247 A536 30p on 10+5p brt
blue, blk & yel .60 .30
No. 1247 not issued without surcharge.

Intl. Peace
Year
A537

1988, Feb. 11
1248 A537 10p multi .30 .25

Euskal Erria, 75th
Anniv. (in
1987) — A538

1988, Mar. 9
1249 A538 66p multi .70 .40

Basque-Uruguayan diplomatic relations.

Air Force,
75th
Anniv.
A539

1988, Mar. 11
1250 A539 17p multi .35 .25

Interamerican
Children's
Institute, 60th
Anniv. — A540

Wmk. 332
1988, Mar. 28 Litho. Perf. 12
1251 A540 30p apple grn, blk &
grn .70 .30

State Hydroelectric Works (UTE), 75th
Anniv. — A541

1988, Apr. 20
1252 A541 17p shown .25 .25
1253 A541 17p Baygorria Dam .25 .25
1254 A541 51p Gabriel Terra
Dam .70 .30
1255 A541 51p Constitucion Dam .70 .30
1256 A541 66p Dams on map 1.00 .45
Nos. 1252-1256 (5) 2.90 1.55
Dated 1987.

Postal Union of America and Spain
(UPAE), 75th Anniv. (in 1987)
A542

1988, May 10
1257 A542 66p multi .65 .45

Israel,
40th
Anniv.
A543

1988, May 17
1258 A543 66p lt ultra & blk .65 .35

Postal Messenger of Peace — A544

1988, May 24
1259 A544 66p multi .65 .35

Portrait, La
Cumparsita
Tango — A545

1988, June 7
1260 A545 17p Parade, horiz. .45 .25
1261 A545 51p Score 1.40 .55

Gerardo H. Matos Rodrigues, composer.

Firemen,
Cent. — A546

1988, June 21
1262 A546 17p Pablo Banales,
founder .40 .25
1263 A546 26p Fireman, 1900 .45 .25
1264 A546 34p Emblem, horiz. .60 .30
1265 A546 51p Merry Weather
fire engine,
1907, horiz. .90 .45
1266 A546 66p Fire pump,
1888, horiz. 1.40 .65
Size: 44x24 ½mm
1267 A546 100p Ladder truck,
1921 2.25 1.10
Nos. 1262-1267 (6) 6.00 3.00

Capitan Miranda Trans-world Voyage,
Cent. — A547

1988, July 28
1268 A547 30p multi   .40 .25

Exports
A548

1988
1269 A548 30p Citrus fruit   .35 .25
1270 A548 45p Rice   .70 .25
1271 A548 55p Footwear   .80 .30
1272 A548 55p Leather and furs   .80 .35
     Nos. 1269-1272 (4)   2.65 1.15

Issued: 30p, #1272, 9/14; 45p, #1271, 8/23.

Natl. Museum of
Natural History,
150th
Anniv. — A549

30p, *Usnea densirostra* fossil. 90p, *Toxodon platensis* bone, Quaternary period.

1988, Sept. 20
1273 A549 30p blk, yel & red brn   .60 .30
1274 A549 90p blk, ultra & beige   1.40 .65
     a.   Pair, #1273-1274   3.00 3.00

Battle of Carpinteria, 150th Anniv. (in
1986) — A550

1988, Nov. 23
1275 A550 30p multi   .30 .25
   Horiz. row contains two stamps, label, then
two more stamps.

A551

1988, Dec. 21
1276 A551 115p multi   1.00 1.00
   Christmas.

A552

Paintings: a, *Manolita Pina, 1920*, by J. Torres Garcia. b, *78 Squares and Rectangles*, by J.P. Costigliolo. c, Print publicizing an exhibition of works by Pedrero Figari, 1945. d, *Self-portrait, 1947*, by J. Torres Garcia.

1988, Dec. 27
1277   Block or strip of 4 + label   4.50 4.50
   a.-d. A552 115p any single   1.00 .65
   No. 1277 can be collected as a vert. or
horiz. strip of 4, or block of 4, with label.

Spanish
Heritage
Day
A553

1989, Jan. 9
1278 A553 90p multi   .75 .40
1279 A553 115p multi   1.10 .50

Armenian
Organization
Hnchakian,
Cent. — A554

Wmk. 332
1989, June 7   Litho.   Perf. 12
1280 A554 210p red, yel & blue   1.75 .70

French Revolution,
Bicentennial — A555

1989, July 3
1281 A555 50p Plumb line,
                frame   .35 .25
1282 A555 50p Liberty tree   .35 .25
1283 A555 210p Eye in sunburst   1.40 .45
1284 A555 210p Liberty   1.40 .45
     Nos. 1281-1284 (4)   3.50 1.40

Use Postal Codes — A556

1989, July 25
1285 A556 50p Montevideo
                Dept. map   .35 .25
1286 A556 210p National map,
                vert.   1.10 .40

3rd Pan
American Milk
Congress
A557

1989, Aug. 24
1287 A557 170p sky blue & ultra   1.10 .45

A558

Wmk. 332
1989, Aug. 29   Photo.   Perf. 12
1288 A558 170p multicolored   .85 .30
   Joaquin Jose da Silva Xavier.

A559

1989, Aug. 31
1289 A559 210p blk, red & bl   1.00 .35
   Inter-Parliamentary Union Conf., London.

FAO Emblem, Map, Citrus
Slice — A560

1989, Sept. 11
1290 A560 180p multicolored   .80 .35
   8th Conf., Intergovernmental Group on Citrus Fruits.

UN Decade for the Disabled — A561

1989, Oct. 4
1291 A561 50p shown   .35 .25
1292 A561 210p Disabled people   .95 .40

America
Issue — A562

Nacurutu artifact and UPAE emblem.

1989, Oct. 11   Perf. 12½
1293 A562 60p multicolored   1.00 .40
1294 A562 180p multicolored   2.50 1.10

City of Pando, Bicentennial — A563

1989, Dec. 27   Litho.   Perf. 12
1295 A563 60p multicolored   .30 .25

Christmas
A564

1989, Dec. 19
1296 A564 70p Virgin of Trienta
                y Tres   .45 .25
1297 A564 210p Barradas, horiz.   1.10 .45

Charity Hospital, Bicent. (in
1988) — A565

1990, Jan. 23   Wmk. 332
1298 A565 60p multicolored   .70 .70

Provincial
Arms and
Maps
A566

1990
1299 A566 70p Soriano   .40 .40
1300 A566 70p Florida, vert.   .45 .45
1301 A566 90p Canelones   .50 .50
1302 A566 90p Lavalleja, vert.   .50 .50
1303 A566 90p San Jose, vert.   .50 .50
1304 A566 90p Rivera   .50 .50
     Nos. 1299-1304 (6)   2.85 2.85
          Dated 1989.

Writers — A567

Designs: a, Luisa Luisi (1883-1940). b, Javier de Viana (1872-1926). c, Delmira Agustini (1886-1914). d, J. Zorrilla de San Martin (1855-1931). e, Alfonsina Storni (1892-1938). f, Julio Casal (1889-1954). g, Juana de Ibarbourou (1895-1979). h, Carlos Roxlo (1861-1926).

1990, Mar. 20

1320	Block of 8 + 2 labels	6.00	6.00
a.-b.	A567 60p any single	.35	.35
c.-d.	A567 75p any single	.40	.40
e.-f.	A567 170p any single	1.00	1.00
g.-h.	A567 210p any single	1.25	1.25

Printed in sheets of 4 blocks of 4 separated by vert. and horiz. rows of 5 labels. Position of denomination varies to form border around each block. Dated 1989.

Portraits Type of 1986

25p, 30p, Lavalleja. 60p, 90p, Rivera. 100p, 150p, 300p, 500p, 1000p, Artigas.

1990		**Litho.**	**Wmk. 332**	**Perf. 12½**
1321	A505	25p orange	.30	.25
1322	A505	30p ultra	.30	.25
1323	A505	60p purple	.30	.25
1324	A505	90p org red	.60	.30
1325	A505	100p brown	.45	.35
1326	A505	150p dk blue green	.90	.50
1327	A505	300p blue	1.50	1.00
1328	A505	500p orange red	2.50	1.00
1329	A505	1000p red	5.00	3.00
	Nos. 1321-1329 (9)		11.85	6.90

Issued: 30p, 60p, 7/17; 90p, 3/24; 150p, 6/22; 300p, 7/5; 500p, 3/22; 1000p, 7/24.

A568

1990, Apr. 3 **Perf. 12**
1346 A568 70p multicolored .40 .40
City of Mercedes, bicent. Dated 1989.

A569

1990, Apr. 24
1347 A569 210p multicolored 1.10 1.10
Intl. Agricultural Development Fund, 10th anniv. Dated 1989.

Traffic Safety — A570

Designs: a, Bus, car. b, Don't drink and drive. c, Cross on the green light. d, Obey traffic signs.

1990, May 28
1348 A570 70p Block of 4, #a.-d. 1.10 1.10

General Artigas A571

1990, June 18
1349 A571 60p red & blue .45 .45

A572

1990, June 26
1350 A572 70p multicolored .40 .40
Intl. Mothers' Day. Dated 1989.

A573

Treaty of Montevideo, 1889: a, Gonzalo Ramirez. b, Ildefonso Garcia. c, Flags at left. d, Flags at right.

1990, July 10
1351 A573 60p Block of 4, #a.-d. 1.40 1.40
Nos. 1351c-1351d printed in continuous design. Dated 1989.

Microphone, Tower — A574

b, Newspaper boy. c, Television camera. d, Books.

1990, Sept. 26
1352 A574 70p Block of 4, #a.-d. 2.00 2.00

Carlos Federico Saez (1878-1901) — A575

Portraits: b, Pedro Blanes Viale (1879-1926). c, Edmundo Prati (1889-1970). d, Jose L. Zorrilla de San Martin (1891-1975).

1990, Dec. 26

1353	Block of 4	3.50	3.50
a.-b.	A575 90p any single	.50	.50
c.-d.	A575 210p any single	1.10	1.10

Prevent Forest Fires — A576

Wmk. 332
1990, Oct. 26 **Litho.** **Perf. 12**
1354 A576 70np multicolored 2.00 2.00

America Issue — A577

1990, Nov. 6
1355 A577 120p Odocoileus bezoarticus .80 .80
1356 A577 360p Peltophorum dubium, vert. 2.75 2.75

Army Corps of Engineers, 75th Anniv. — A578

1991, Jan. 21
1357 A578 170p multicolored 1.00 1.00

The Nativity by Brother Juan B. Maino — A579

1990, Dec. 24
1358 A579 170p bister & multi 1.00 1.00
1359 A579 830p silver & multi 4.75 4.75

Organization of American States, Cent. (in 1989) A580

Wmk. 332
1991, Mar. 21 **Litho.** **Perf. 12**
1360 A580 830p bl, blk & yel 4.50 4.50

Prevention of AIDS — A581

1991, Mar. 8
1361 A581 170p bl & multi 1.00 1.00
1362 A581 830p grn & multi 4.75 4.75

Carnival — A582

1991, Feb. 19
1363 A582 170p multicolored 1.00 1.00

Education — A583

Expanding youth's horizons: a, Stone ax, megalithic monument. b, Wheel, pyramids. c, Printing press, solar system. d, Satellite, diagram.

Wmk. 332
1991, Apr. 23 **Litho.** **Perf. 12**

1364	Block of 4	3.00	3.00
a.-b.	A583 120p any single	.40	.40
c.-d.	A583 330p any single	1.25	1.25

Natl. Cancer Day — A584

1991, June 17
1365 A584 360p red & black 1.10 1.10

A585

Exports of Uruguay — A586

Perf. 12½x13, 13x12½
1991 Litho. Wmk. 332
1366 A585 120p Textiles .40 .40
1367 A586 120p Clothing .50 .35
1368 A585 400p Semiprecious
stones, granite 1.40 1.40
Nos. 1366-1368 (3) 2.30 2.15

Issued: #1366, 400p, 4/23; #1367, 6/26.

7th Pan American Maccabiah
Games — A587

1991, July 4   Perf. 12½x13
1369 A587 1490p multicolored 6.00 6.00

Dornier Wal, Route Map — A588

1991, July 5   Perf. 12
1370 A588 1510p multicolored 5.00 5.00
Espamer '91.

Entrance to
Sacramento
Colony
A589

Railroads and Trains: 540p, 825p, First locomotive, 1869. 600p, like 360p. 800p, Entrance
to Sacramento Colony. 1510p, 2500p, Horse-
drawn streetcar.

Wmk. 332
1991-2002 Litho. Perf. 12
1378 A589 360p ol bis & yel .95 .60
1378A A589 540p dk bl &
gray 1.40 .95
1379 A589 600p brn, yel &
blk .95 .85
1379A A589 800p grn & yel
grn .95 .95
1379B A589 825p bl, gray &
blk 1.40 1.25
1380 A589 1510p ol bis &
emer 4.25 3.00
1382 A589 2500p ol bis, emer & blk 3.50 3.00
Nos. 1378-1382 (7) 13.40 10.60

Issued: 360p, 540p, 1510p, July 19; 825p,
Feb. 11, 1992; 2500p, May 20, 2002; 600p,
June 18, 1992; 800p, Feb. 9, 1993.
For surcharges, see Nos. 2011B, 2057-
2059.

Sagrada
Family
College,
Cent. — A590

College of the
Immaculate
Heart of Mary,
Cent. — A591

Wmk. 332
1991, June 26 Litho. Perf. 12
1383 A590 360p multicolored .75 .75
1384 A591 1370p multicolored 3.00 3.00

Constitutional Oath — A592

1991, July 17
1385 A592 360p multicolored .90 .90

Swiss
Confederation,
700th
Anniv. — A593

1991, Aug. 1   Perf. 13x12½
1386 A593 1510p multicolored 5.25 5.25
Souvenir Sheet
Perf. 12
1387 A593 3000p multicolored 11.00 11.00

Photography, 150th Anniv. — A594

Perf. 12½x13
1991, Sept. 12 Litho. Wmk. 332
1388 A594 1370p multi 3.00 3.00

Actors Society
of Uruguay,
50th
Anniv. — A595

1991, Aug. 24   Perf. 12
1389 A595 450p blk & red 1.10 1.10

CREA (Agriculture Association), 25th
Anniv. — A596

1991, Sept. 14   Perf. 12½x13
1390 A596 450p multicolored 1.10 1.10

Whitbread
Around the World
Race — A597

1991, Aug. 20   Perf. 13x12½
1391 A597 1510p multicolored 3.75 3.75

Amerigo Vespucci (1454-
1512) — A598

America Issue: 450p, First landing at River
Plate, 1602, vert.

1991, Oct. 11   Perf. 12
1392 A598 450p yel & brn 1.00 1.00
1393 A598 1740p ol & brn 3.50 3.50

Automobiles — A599

Designs: 350p, Gladiator, 1902. 1370p,
E.M.F., 1909. 1490p, Renault, 1912. 1510p,
Clement-Bayard, 1903, vert.

1991, Oct. 18 Perf. 12½x13, 13x12½
1394 A599 360p multicolored .85 .85
1395 A599 1370p multicolored 3.00 3.00
1396 A599 1490p multicolored 3.00 3.00
1397 A599 1510p multicolored 3.50 3.50
Nos. 1394-1397 (4) 10.35 10.35

Team Nacional Montevideo, Winners
of Toyota and Europe-South America
Soccer Cups — A600

Wmk. 332
1991, Nov. 8 Litho. Perf. 12
1398 A600 450p shown 1.00 1.00
1399 A600 450p Emblem, trophy,
vert. 1.00 1.00

Margarita Xirgu (1888-1969),
Actress — A601

1991, Oct. 4
1400 A601 360p yel & brn 1.00 1.00

INTERPOL,
60th Congress
A602

1991, Oct. 30
1401 A602 1740p multicolored 3.50 3.50

Maria Auxiliadora Institute,
Cent. — A603

1991, Nov. 11
1402 A603 450p multicolored 1.10 1.10

Technological Laboratory, 25th
Anniv. — A604

1991, Nov. 11
1403 A604 1570p dk bl & lt bl 3.00 3.00

The Table by Zoma Baitler — A605

1991, Oct. 18
1404 A605 360p multicolored 1.00 1.00

World
Food Day
A606

1991, Oct. 16   Perf. 12½x13
1405 A606 1740p multicolored 3.50 3.50

Ships
A607

Designs: a, Steam yacht, Gen. Rivera. b, Coast Guard cutter, Salto. c, Cruiser, Uruguay. d, Tanker, Pte. Oribe.

Wmk. 332
1991, Oct. 4   Litho.   Perf. 12
1406   Block of 4   10.00 10.00
a.-b. A607 450p any single   1.25 1.25
c.-d. A607 1570p any single   3.50 3.50

Topographical Society Type of 1981
1991, Dec. 3   Perf. 12½
1407 A439 550p multi   .85   .85
     Topographical Society, 160th anniv.

World AIDS Day — A608

1991, Dec. 1
1408 A608 550p bl, blk & brt yel 1.10 1.10
1409 A608 2040p lt grn, blk & lil 3.75 3.75

Export Industries A609

Wmk. 332
1991, Mar. 20   Litho.   Perf. 12½
1410 A609 120p multicolored   .40   .40

Christmas A610

1991, Dec. 24   Perf. 12
1411 A610 550p Angel   .90   .90
1412 A610 2040p Adoration of
           the Angels   3.00 3.00

Muscians — A611

Designs: a, Juan de Dios Filiberto. b, Pintin Castellanos. c, Francisco Canaro. d, Anibal Troilo.

Wmk. 332
1992, Jan. 20   Photo.   Perf. 12
1413 A611 450p Block of 4, #a-d 3.50 3.50

Patricio Aylwin, Pres. of Chile — A612

Perf. 11½x12
1992, Mar. 23   Litho.   Unwmk.
1415 A612 550p multicolored   .85   .85

Penarol, Winners of Liberator's Cup in Club Soccer — A612a

Perf. 13x12½
1992, May 29   Litho.   Wmk. 332
1415A A612a 600p yel & blk   1.00 1.00
Souvenir Sheet
Perf. 12
1415B A612a 3000p yel & blk   4.50 4.50

La Paz City, 120th Anniv. — A612b

1992, May 25   Perf. 13x12½
1415C A612b 550p multicolored   .85   .85

World No-Smoking Day — A613

Wmk. 332
1992, May 31   Litho.   Perf. 12
1416 A613 2500p multicolored   3.75 3.75

United Nations World Health Day A614

Wmk. 332
1992, July 28   Litho.   Perf. 13
1417 A614 2500p bl, lt bl & red 3.75 3.75

Mercosur A615

1992, Aug. 5   Photo.   Perf. 12
1418 A615 2500p multicolored   3.50 3.50

Olymphilex '92, Barcelona — A616

Wmk. 332
1992, Aug. 8   Photo.   Perf. 12
1419 A616 2900p multicolored   4.00 4.00

Discovery of America, 500th Anniv. — A617

Perf. 11½x12, 12x11½
1992, Oct. 10   Litho.   Unwmk.
1420 A617 700p Ship, masts,
           vert.   1.25 1.25
1421 A617 2900p Globe, ship   4.00 4.00

Jose Pedro Varela Natl. Teachers College, 50th Anniv. A618

1992, Oct. 22   Perf. 12x11½
1422 A618 700p multicolored   .85   .85

22nd Regional FAO Conference — A619

Designs: 2500p, Emblems. 2900p, Emblems, children with food basket.

1992, Sept. 28
1423 A619 2500p multicolored   3.00 3.00
1424 A619 2900p multicolored   3.50 3.50
     Intl. Conf. on Nutrition, Rome, Italy (#1424).

Cesar Vallejo (1892-1938), Poet — A620

1992, Sept. 30
1425 A620 2500p brn & dk brn   3.00 3.00

A621

1992, Oct. 26   Perf. 11½x12
1426 A621 700p gray, red & blk   .85   .85
     Assoc. of Wholesalers and Retailers, cent.

A622

Perf. 11½x12
1992, Oct. 10   Litho.   Unwmk.
1427 A622 700p black, blue &
           grn   1.25 1.25
     Monument to Columbus, cent.

A623

Ruins and lighthouse, Colonia del Sacramento.

1992, Oct. 10
1428 A623 700p multicolored   1.25 1.25
     Discovery of America, 500th anniv.

A624

1992, Oct. 19
1429 A624 700p red lil, rose lil &
           blk   1.25 1.25
     Columbus Philanthropic Society, cent.

A625

1992, Oct. 19
1430 A625 2900p multicolored   3.50 3.50
Judaism in the Americas, 500th anniv.

A626

1992, Oct. 30
1431 A626 2900p multicolored   3.50 3.50
Lebanon Society of Uruguay, 50th anniv.

Pan American Health Organization,
90th Anniv. — A627

Perf. 12x11½
1992, Dec. 15   Litho.   Unwmk.
1432 A627 3200p blk, bl & yel   3.50 3.50

22nd Lions Club Forum for Latin
America and the Caribbean — A628

1992, Dec. 2
1433 A628 2700p multicolored   3.00 3.00

Christmas
A629

1992, Dec. 1   Perf. 11½x12
1434 A629 800p Nativity scene   1.00 1.00
1435 A629 3200p Star in sky   3.50 3.50

General
Manuel
Oribe,
Birth
Bicent.
A630

Designs: No. 1436, Oribe, Oriental College.
No. 1437, Oribe in military dress uniform, vert.

Perf. 12x11½, 11½x12
1992, Dec. 8   Litho.   Unwmk.
1436 A630 800p multicolored   1.00 1.00
1437 A630 800p multicolored   1.00 1.00

Logosofia, 60th Anniv. — A631

1992, Dec. 29   Perf. 12x11½
1438 A631 800p blue & yellow   1.00 1.00

Immigrants'
Day — A632

1992, Dec. 4   Perf. 11½x12
1439 A632 800p black & green   1.00 1.00

ANDEBU, 70th Anniv. — A633

Caritas
of
Uruguay,
30th
Anniv.
A634

1992, Dec. 22 Photo. Perf. 12x11½
1440 A633 2700p Satellite   3.00 3.00
1441 A634 3200p Map, huts by
                        water   3.50 3.50

A635

1992, Dec. 18   Perf. 11½x12
1442 A635 800p brown & yellow   1.00 1.00
Jose H. Molaguero S. A., 50th anniv.

A636

1993, Mar. 1   Litho.   Unwmk.
1443 A636 80c multicolored   .90 .90
Wilson Ferreira Aldunate.

Economic Science and Accountancy
College, Cent. — A637

Perf. 12x11½
1993, Apr. 15   Photo.   Unwmk.
1444 A637 1p multicolored   1.10 1.10

Souvenir Sheet

Polska '93, Intl. Philatelic
Exhibition — A638

a, Lech Walesa. b, Pope John Paul II.

1993, May 3   Perf. 11½x12
1445 A638 2p Sheet of 2, #a.-b.   5.00 5.00

A639   A639a

A639b

A639c   A639d

A639e   A639f

    A639h

A639g   A639h

Design A639g shows the Postal Administration Tower.

ONE PESO (Letter Box — A639):
Type I — "Bugon vecinal 1879" 21½mm, letter box 23½mm high.
Type II — "Bugon vecinal 1879" 22mm, letter box 22½mm high.
Type III — "Bugon vecinal 1879" 19½mm,
letter box 21mm high.
There are other differences among the three
types.

Perf. 12½, 12 (#1449, 1465)
1993-99   Litho.   Wmk. 332
1446	A639	50c gray ol & yel	.30	.30
1447	A639	1p lt brn & yel		
		(I)	.50	.50
a.		Type II	.60	.60
b.		Type III, unwatermarked	.35	.35
c.		Type III, photo., unwmkd.	.35	.35
1448	A639a	1p org yel & bl	1.00	1.00
1449	A639b	1p org & bl	.65	.65
1450	A639c	(1.20p) blue	.70	.70
1451	A639c	(1.40p) green	.75	.75
1452	A639d	1.40p yel & bl	.75	.75
1453	A639c	(1.60p) red	1.25	1.25
1454	A639	1.80p bl & yel	1.40	1.40
1455	A639c	(1.80p) brown	1.25	1.25
1456	A639c	(2p) gray	1.25	1.25
1457	A639c	(2.30p) lilac	1.60	1.60
1458	A639	2.60p bl, yel &		
		grn	1.60	1.60
1459	A639e	(2.60p) grn & yel	1.60	1.60
1460	A639e	(2.90p) bl & yel	1.60	1.60
1460A	A639e	(3p) gray & brt		
		yel grn	1.00	1.00
b.		Unwmkd.	1.00	1.00
1461	A639e	(3.10p) red &		
		pink	1.10	1.10
1462	A639e	(3.20p) rose brn		
		& lt brn	3.25	3.25
1462A	A639e	(3.50p) pur & lt		
		bl	—	—
1462B	A639e	(3.80p) brt blue	1.60	1.60
1463	A639e	(4p) bis & yel,		
		litho.	1.25	1.25
1464	A639f	5p bl & yel, perf.		
		12½	2.50	2.50
1465	A639g	6p blue & blk	1.75	1.75
1465A	A639f	7p blue & yel	3.25	3.25
1465B	A639	7.50p vio & yel	3.75	3.75
1465C	A639h	8p bl & yel	3.75	3.75

Nos. 1446-1462, 1463-1465C
(24)   37.80 37.80

The design of Nos. 1460A, 1462-1463 does
not include "PORTE MINIMO." There are
minor design differences between #1464 and
1465A.
  Issued: #1448, 4/15/93; #1450, 8/2/93;
#1451, 12/1/93; #1452, 1/4/94; #1453, 4/4/94;
#1455, 8/1/94; #1454 8/9/94; #1449, 10/3/94;
1456, 12/1/94. #1457, 4/1/95; #1458, (2.60p)
50c, #1447, 8/27/96; #1460, (3.10p),
(3.50p), 4/1/96; 7.50p, 5/21/96; 5p, 1997;
(3.80p), 5/9/97; #1463, 8/1/97; 6p, 8/13/97;
(3.50p), 7/28/98; (3p), 2/1/99. #1460Ab, 1999.
  For surcharges, see Nos. 2056, 2106, 2186,
2269.

Interior Fire
Service, 50th
Anniv. — A640

Perf. 11½x12
1993, May 28   Litho.   Unwmk.
1466 A640 1p multicolored   1.00 1.00

15th Congress of
UPAEP — A641

1993, June 21
1467 A641 3.50p multicolored   3.25 3.25

Uruguayan Navy, 175th Anniv. — A642

Sailing ship, Pedro Campbell, first admiral.

Perf. 12x11½
1993, June 28   Litho.   Wmk. 332
1468 A642 1p multicolored   1.10 1.10

Intl. University Society, 25th
Anniv. — A643

1993, July 2
1469 A643 1p multicolored   1.10 1.10

Automobile Club of Uruguay, 75th
Anniv. — A644

1993, July 19   Photo.   Unwmk.
1470 A644 3.50p 1910
Hupmobile   3.25 3.25

Uruguay Battalion in UN Peacekeeping
Force, Cambodia — A645

Perf. 12x11½
1993, Aug. 6   Litho.   Unwmk.
1471 A645 1p multicolored   1.10 1.10

Souvenir Sheet

Brasiliana '93 — A646

World Cup Soccer Champions: a, Uruguay,
1930, 1950. b, Brazil, 1958, 1962, 1970.
1993, July 28   Perf. 11½x12
1472 A646 2.50p Sheet of 2, #a.-
b.   7.50 7.50

State Television Channel 5, 30th
Anniv. — A647

1993, Aug. 19   Perf. 12x11½
1473 A647 1.20p multicolored   1.10 1.10

ANDA,
60th
Anniv.
A648

Perf. 12½
1993, Sept. 24   Litho.   Unwmk.
1474 A648 1.20p multicolored   1.10 1.10

Natl.
Police
Academy,
50th
Anniv.
A649

1993, Sept. 24
1475 A649 1.20p multicolored   1.40 1.40

Newspaper Diario
El Pais, 75th
Anniv. — A650

Perf. 12½
1993, Sept. 30   Litho.   Unwmk.
1476 A650 1.20p multicolored   1.40 1.40

Latin American Conference on Rural
Electrification — A651

1993, Oct. 11
1477 A651 3.50p multicolored   3.25 3.25

B'nai
B'rith,
150th
Anniv.
A652

1993, Oct. 13
1478 A652 3.70p multicolored   3.50 3.50

A653   Fauna — A654

1993   Photo.   Wmk. 332   Perf. 12½
1482 A653 20c Seriema bird   .55 .25
1484 A653 30c Dragon bird   .75 .25
1486 A653 50c Anteaters,
horiz.   1.25 .40
1492 A654 1.20p Giant armadillo   1.50 1.25
Nos. 1482-1492 (4)   4.05 2.15
Issued: 1.20p, 8/3/93; 20c, 30c, 50c,
10/22/93.
This is an expanding set. Numbers may
change.
For surcharges, see Nos. 2011A, 2055,
2150, 2185.

America
Issue
A655

Perf. 12½
1993, Oct. 6   Litho.   Unwmk.
1504 A655 1.20p Caiman latirostris   1.25 1.25
1505 A655 3.50p Athene cunicularia, vert.   3.75 3.75

Souvenir Sheet

Whitbread Trans-Global Yacht
Race — A656

1993, Oct. 22   Perf. 11½x12
1506 A656 5p multicolored   4.25 4.25

Beatification of
Mother Francisca
Rubatto — A657

1993, Oct. 29   Wmk. 332   Perf. 12
1507 A657 1.20p multicolored   1.25 1.25

Intl. Year of
Indigenous
People — A658

Perf. 13x12½
1993, Oct. 29
1508 A658 3.50p multicolored   3.00 3.00

Rotary Club of
Montevideo, 75th
Anniv. — A658a

Perf. 12½
1993, Nov. 10   Litho.   Unwmk.
1508A A658a 3.50p dk bl & bis   3.50 3.50

Rhea
Americana
A659

America
Issue
A655

1993, Dec. 20   Litho.   Perf. 12
1509 A659 20c shown   .80 .35
1510 A659 20c With chicks   .90 .40
1511 A659 50c Head   1.40 .75
1512 A659 50c Two walking   1.40 .75
Nos. 1509-1512 (4)   4.50 2.25
World Wildlife Fund.

Children's
Rights
Day
A660

1994, Jan. 4   Perf. 12½
1513 A660 1.40p multicolored   1.25 1.25

Independence of Lebanon, 50th
Anniv. — A661

1993, Nov. 22
1514 A661 3.70p multicolored   2.75 2.75

Eduardo Victor
Haedo — A662

1993, Nov. 24
1515 A662 1.20p multicolored   1.10 1.10

Christmas
A663

1993, Dec. 7
1516 A663 1.40p shown   1.00 1.00
1517 A663 4p Nativity, diff.   3.00 3.00

Intl. AIDS
Day — A664

1993, Dec. 1
1518 A664 1.40p multicolored   1.90 1.90

Souvenir Sheets

Anniversaries & Events — A665

Designs: No. 1519a, Switzerland #3L1, 1913 Swiss private air mail stamp. b, Germany #C40, Uruguay #C426c. c, Uruguay #C372, US #C76. d, Uruguay #C282a, US #C104.
No. 1520a, Switzerland Types A1, A2. b, Switzerland #B541.

1993, Nov. 18
1519 A665 1p #a.-d. 11.00 11.00
1520 A665 2.50p #a.-b. 11.00 11.00
Swiss postage stamps, 150th anniv. (#1519a, 1520). Dr. Hugo Eckener, 125th anniv. of birth (#1519b). First man on moon, 25th anniv. (#1519c). 1994 World Cup Soccer Championships, US (#1519d).
Nos. 1519-1520 exist imperf. Value $30.

17th Inter-American Naval Conference — A666

1994, Mar. 21 Litho. Perf. 12½
1521 A666 3.70p multicolored 3.00 3.00

A667

1994, Mar. 11 Perf. 12½
1522 A667 4p multicolored 3.25 3.25
5th World Sports Congress, Punta del Este.

A668

Unwmk.
1994, Apr. 4 Litho. Perf. 12
1523 A668 3.90p multicolored 2.75 2.75
Latin America Youth Organization, 7th conference.

A669

1994, Apr. 18
1524 A669 4.30p multicolored 3.75 3.75
4th World Congress on Merino Wool.

A670

1994, Apr. 28 Perf. 12½
1525 A670 4.30p multicolored 3.25 3.25
ILO, 75th anniv.

Miniature Sheet

1994 Winter Olympic Medal Winners — A671

Designs: a, Katja Seizinger. b, Markus Wasmeier. c, Vreni Schneider. d, Gustav Weder.

1994, May 6 Perf. 12
1526 A671 1.25p Sheet of 4,
#a.-d. 10.00 10.00
No. 1526 exists demonitized and imperf on paper with watermark 322. This item was sold with No. 1526 and has a matching serial number.

Miniature Sheet

1994 World Cup Soccer Championships, US — A672

a, Soccer ball, flags of Uruguay, Brazil. b, Ball, flags of Italy, Argentina. c, Ball, flags of Germany, Great Britain. d, Olympic Rings.

1994, May 16
1527 A672 1.25p Sheet of 4,
#a.-d. 10.00 10.00
Uruguay, Olympic soccer gold medalists, 1924-1928 (#1527d).
See note after No. 1526.

Clemente Estable (1894-1976), Biologist — A673

1994, May 23 Litho. Perf. 12½
1528 A673 1.60p olive & black 1.40 1.40

Electoral Court, 70th Anniv. — A674

1994, June 7
1529 A674 1.60p multicolored 1.40 1.40

Natl. Commission to Prevent Tapeworms — A675

Perf. 12½
1994, June 17 Litho. Unwmk.
1530 A675 1.60p multicolored 1.50 1.50

Souvenir Sheet

Cesareo L. Berisso, First Aviator to Land at Natl. Airport, Carrasco — A676

1994, June 21 Perf. 12
1531 A676 5p multicolored 3.75 3.75

Intl. Cooperatives, 150th Anniv. — A677

1994, July 1 Perf. 12½
1532 A677 4.30p multicolored 3.00 3.00

Commission on Integration of Regional Electricity, 30th Anniv. — A678

1994, July 8
1533 A678 1.60p multicolored 1.10 1.10

Abate Pierre A679

Perf. 12½
1994, Aug. 5 Litho. Unwmk.
1534 A679 4.80p multicolored 3.25 3.25

Intl. Year of the Family A680

1994, July 28
1535 A680 4.80p multicolored 3.25 3.25

The Man of Lugano, by Goffredo Sommavilla (1850-1944) — A681

Perf. 12½
1994, Aug. 15 Litho. Unwmk.
1536 A681 4.80p multicolored 3.25 3.25

First Manned Moon Landing, 25th Annvi. A682

1994, July 20
1537 A682 3p multicolored 3.00 3.00

Intl. Olympic Committee, Cent. — A683

1994, Aug. 23
1538 A683 4.80p multicolored 3.50 3.50

Elbio Fernandez School, 125th Anniv. A684

Perf. 12½
1994, Aug. 29   Litho.   Unwmk.
1539 A684 1.80p multicolored   1.25 1.25

A685

1994, Sept. 10   Perf. 12
1540 A685 1.80p black & blue   1.25 1.25
Gral. Aparicio Saravia, 90th Death Anniv.

A686

1994, Sept. 30   Perf. 12½
1541 A686 4.80p multicolored   3.00 3.00
6th Latin American Urban Congress.

General Assoc. of Uruguayan Authors, 65th Anniv. — A687

Perf. 12½
1994, Sept. 26   Litho.   Unwmk.
1542 A687 1.80p multicolored   1.10 1.10

America Issue A688

1994, Oct. 10
1543 A688 1.80p Stagecoach   1.50 1.50
1544 A688 4.80p Paddle steamer   4.00 4.00

A689

Perf. 12½
1994, Oct. 28   Litho.   Unwmk.
1545 A689 2p multicolored   1.25 1.25
Assoc. of Directors of Marketing, 50th anniv.

A690

1994, Nov. 25
1546 A690 2p multicolored   1.25 1.25
YMCA in Uruguay, 85th anniv.

Lottery, 55th Anniv. A691

1994, Nov. 21
1547 A691 2p multicolored   1.25 1.25

First Intl. Seminar to Promote Roads in Uruguay, Punta del Este A692

1994, Oct. 14
1548 A692 2p multicolored   1.25 1.25

Uruguayan Press Assoc., 50th Anniv. — A693

1994, Oct. 24
1549 A693 2p multicolored   1.25 1.25

Miniature Sheet

Natl. Mint, 150th Anniv. A694

Portions of old coin press and: a, Mint building. b, 1844 Copper coin. c, 1844 Silver coin. d, Montevideo silver peso.

1994, Oct. 17   Perf. 12
1550 A694 1.50p Sheet of 4, #a.-
    d.   9.00 9.00
No. 1550 exists demonitized and imperf. on paper with watermark 332. This item was sold with No. 1550 and has matching serial numbers.

Miniature Sheet

Natl. Navy A695

Ships: a, ROU Uruguay, ROU Artigas. b, ROU Fortuna. c, ROU Uruguay. d, ROU Cte. Pedro Campbell.

1994, Nov. 15
1551 A695 1.50p Sheet of 4, #a.-
    d.   8.00 8.00

Latin American Peace Movement, 25th Anniv. — A696

1994, Nov. 15   Perf. 12½
1552 A696 4.30p multicolored   2.75 2.75

4th Conference of the Latin American and Caribbean Organization of High Fiscal Entities, Montevideo — A697

1994, Dec. 5
1553 A697 5.50p multicolored   3.50 3.50

Christmas A698

1994, Dec. 2
1554 A698   2p shown   1.25 1.25
1555 A698 5.50p Star, tree, house   3.25 3.25

Uruguayan Red Cross & Red Crescent Societies, 75th Anniv. — A699

Perf. 12½
1994, Dec. 20   Litho.   Unwmk.
1556 A699 5p multicolored   2.75 2.75

City Post Office — A700

1995-97   Litho.   Wmk. 332   Perf. 12
1557 A700 20c yellow green   .50 .50
1565 A700 10p brown   6.75 6.75
1566 A700 10p dark brown   3.75 3.75
Unwmk.
1566A A700 10p claret & black   3.75 3.75
    Nos. 1557-1566A (4)   14.75 14.75
Issued: 20c, 1/11/95; 10p, 5/21/96; #1566, 1566A, 1997.
Denomination has no decimal places on Nos. 1566-1566A.
This is an expanding set. Number may change.

Naval Aviation, 70th Anniv. A704

Perf. 12½
1995, Feb. 7   Litho.   Unwmk.
1567 A704 2p multicolored   1.50 1.50

World Tourism Organization — A705

Designs: No. 1568, Ranch house, sheep herders. No. 1569, Water recreation park. No. 1570, Native wildlife. No. 1571, Beach resort.

1995, Feb. 13
1568 A705 5p multicolored   3.25 3.25
1569 A705 5p multicolored   3.25 3.25
1570 A705 5p multicolored   3.25 3.25
1571 A705 5p multicolored   3.25 3.25
    Nos. 1568-1571 (4)   13.00 13.00

17th World Conference of Lifeguard Services — A706

1995, Feb. 15
1572 A706 5p multicolored   3.00 3.00

Rotary Intl., 90th Anniv. A707

1995, Feb. 22
1573 A707 5p multicolored   3.00 3.00

ICAO, 50th Anniv. A708

1995, Mar. 14
1574 A708 5p multicolored   2.75 2.75

Pietro Mascagni (1863-1945), Composer — A709

Perf. 12½
1995, Mar. 30   Litho.   Unwmk.
1575 A709 5p multicolored   2.75 2.75

Miniature Sheet

Butterflies — A710

Designs: a, Phoebis neocypris. b, Diogas erippus. c, Euryades duponcheli. d, Automeris coresus.

1995, June 15   Litho.   Perf. 12½
1576 A710 5p Sheet of 4, #a.-
    d.   12.00 12.00

Wild Dog
A711

1995, May 17   Litho.   Perf. 12½
1577 A711 2.30p multicolored   1.50 1.50

America Cup
Soccer
Championships
A712

Game scenes, flags of participating countries, match sites: a, Paysandu. b, Rivera. c, Ball (no site). d, Montevideo. e, Maldonado.

1995, July 4
1578 A712 2.30p Strip of 5, #a.-
    e.   6.50 6.50

No. 1578 is a continuous design.

FAO, 50th
Anniv. — A713

1995, July 7
1579 A713 5.50p multicolored   3.00 3.00

UN Peace-Keeping Missions — A714

1995, July 14   Litho.   Perf. 12½
1580 A714 2.30p multicolored   1.75 1.75

Visit of Italy's Pres. Oscar Luigi Scalfaro A715

1995, July 21
1581 A715 5.50p multicolored   3.00 3.00

A716

1995, July 24
1582 A716 5p multicolored   3.00 3.00
    Rotary Intl., 90th anniv.

A717

1995, Sept. 22
1583 A717 2.60p multicolored   1.60 1.60
    Jose Pedro Varela, 150th birth anniv.

Miniature Sheet

Shells — A718

a, Zidona dufresnei. b, Boccinanops duartei. c, Dorsanum moniliferum. d, Olivancillaria uretai.

1995, Aug. 4
1584 A710 5p Sheet of 4, #a.-
    d.   20.00 20.00

America Issue A719

Designs: 3p, Dicksonia sellowiana, vert. 6p, Chrysocyon brachyurus.

Unwmk.
1995, Oct. 10   Litho.   Perf. 12
1585 A719 3p multicolored   2.00 2.00
1586 A719 6p multicolored   3.50 3.50

Carlos Gardel, Musician A720

1995, Sept. 4   Perf. 12½
1587 A720 5.50p blue & black   3.25 3.25

Flowers — A721

Designs: a, Notocactus roseinflorus. b, Verbena chamaedryfolia. c, Bauhinia candicans. d, Tillandsia aeranthos. e, Eichhornia crassipes.

1995, Sept. 12
1588 A721 3p Strip of 5, #a.-e. 10.00 10.00

Miniature Sheet

Uruguay's Artigas Antarctic Scientific Research Base, 10th Anniv. — A722

Designs: a, 2.50p, Albatross. b, 4p, Fairchild FAU572. c, 4p, ROU Vanguard. d, 2.50p, PTS/M Amphibian transporter.

1995, Oct. 13
1589 A722 Sheet of 4, #a.-d.   12.00 12.00

Uruguayan Antarctic Institute, 20th anniv.
No. 1589 exists demonitized and imperf. on paper with watermark 332. This item was sold with No. 1589 and has matching serial numbers.

Holocaust Memorial — A723

1995, Sept. 27   Litho.   Perf. 13x12½
1590 A723 6p multicolored   6.00 6.00

UN, 50th Anniv. — A724

1995, Oct. 24   Litho.   Perf. 12
1591 A724 6p multicolored   3.75 3.75

Early Locomotives — A725

No. 1592, Beyer & Peacock, 1876. No. 1593, Criollo, 1895. No. 1594, Beyer & Peacock, 1910.

1995, Nov. 7
1592 A725 3p multicolored   2.00 2.00
1593 A725 3p multicolored   2.00 2.00
1594 A725 3p multicolored   2.00 2.00
    Nos. 1592-1594 (3)   6.00 6.00

Uruguayan Navy, 178th Anniv. — A726

No. 1595, Sailing ship, Artiguista. No. 1596, ROU Pte. Rivera. No. 1597, ROU Montevideo.

1995, Nov. 15   Perf. 12½
1595 A726 3p multicolored   2.00 2.00
1596 A726 3p multicolored   2.00 2.00
1597 A726 3p multicolored   2.00 2.00
    Nos. 1595-1597 (3)   6.00 6.00

Motion Pictures, Cent. A727

1995, Dec. 13
1598 A727 6p Lumiere Brothers   4.00 4.00

A728

Christmas A729

1995, Dec. 15
1599 A728 2.90p multicolored   1.50 1.50
1600 A729 6.50p multicolored   3.50 3.50

Modern Olympic Games, Cent. A730

Designs: a, Equestrian event, Atlanta 1996. b, Ski jumper, Nagano 1988. c, Torch bearer, Sydney 2000. d, Skier, Salt Lake City 2002.

1996, Jan. 30   Litho.   Perf. 12½
1601 A730 2.50p Sheet of 4, #a.-
       d.   9.50 9.50

Latin America Philatelic Exposition.
No. 1601 exists demonitized and imperf. on paper with watermark 332. This item was sold with No. 1601 and has matching serial numbers.

Carnival Personalities A732

1996, Feb. 16   Litho.   Perf. 12½
1603 A732 2.90p Rosa Luna   1.50 1.50
1604 A732 2.90p Pepino   1.50 1.50
1605 A732 2.90p Santiago Luz   1.50 1.50
     Nos. 1603-1605 (3)   4.50 4.50

Golf in Uruguay A733

Designs: a, Cantegril Country Club. b, Cerro Golf Club. c, Fay Crocker. d, Lago Golf Club. e, Golf Club of Uruguay.

1996, Feb. 27
1606 A733 2.90p Strip of 5,
       #a.-e.   12.00 12.00

No. 1606 was issued in sheets of 25 stamps.

Famous People, Events A734

Designs: a, Statue, Cardinal Barbieri (1892-1979). b, Yitzhak Rabin (1922-95), Nobel Peace Prize. c, Soccer players, First World Cup Soccer Championship, Grand Park Central, July 13, 1930. d, Robert Stolz (1880-1975), composer.

1996, Mar. 8
1607 A734 2.50p Sheet of 4, #a.-
       d.   7.00 7.00

Philatelic Academy of Uruguay. The Stamp of Today, SODRE TV Chanel 5, 10th anniv.

Montevideo, Capital of Latin American Culture — A735

1996, Mar. 5
1608 A735 2.90p Solis Theater,
       1837   1.50 1.50
   a. Booklet pane of 3   6.00
       Complete booklet, #1608a 6.00

General Census A736

1996, Apr. 29
1609 A736 3.20p multicolored   1.50 1.50

1998 World Cup Soccer Championships, France — A737

a, Player in early uniform, Olympic champions, 1924-28, world cup champions, 1930-50, older trophy. b, Trophy, player. d, Two children playing, UNICEF emblem, soccer emblems. e, Olympic rings, two players, eliminations for Atlanta '96.

1996, Apr. 10
1610 A737 2.50p Sheet of 4, #a.-
       d.   7.50 7.50

Latin America Philatelic Exposition.
No. 1610 exists demonitized and imperf. on paper with watermark 332. This item was sold with No. 1610 and has matching serial numbers.

Bones from Indian Burial Grounds — A738

1996, Apr. 18
1611 A738 3.20p multicolored   1.75 1.75

Alfredo Zitarrosa (1936-89), Guitarist A739

1996, Mar. 15   Perf. 12
1612 A739 3p multicolored   1.50 1.50

Prehistoric Animals — A740

Designs: a, Glyptodon claripes. b, Macrauchenia patachonica. c, Toxodon platensis. d, Glossotherium robustum. e, Titanosaurus.

1996, Apr. 18   Perf. 12½
1613 A740 3.20p Strip of 5,
       #a.-e.   10.00 10.00

No. 1613 was issued in sheets of 25 stamps.

Taking Care of Planet Earth, Everyone's Responsibility, by Soraya Campanella — A741

Unwmk.
1996, June 5   Litho.   Perf. 12
1614 A741 3.20p multicolored   1.75 1.75

Souvenir Sheet

Calidris Canutus — A742

1996, May 28   Perf. 12½
1615 A742 12p multicolored   11.00 11.00

CAPEX '96.

Early Methods of Transportation — A743

Designs: a, 1912 Dion-Buton omnibus. b, 1928 Ford Model A. c, 1940 Raleigh bicycle. d, 1926 Magirus firetruck. e, 1917 Hotchkiss ambulance.

1996, May 21
1616 A743 3.20p Strip of 5,
       #a.-e.   10.00 10.00

No. 1616 was issued in sheets of 25 stamps.

Sailing Ships A744

Designs: a, Our Lady of Encina, 1726. b, San Francisco. c, Ships of E. Moreau. d, Bold Lady. e, Our Lady of the Light.

1996, June 17   Litho.   Perf. 12½
1617 A744 3.20p Strip of 5, #a.-
       e.   8.50 8.50

No. 1617 was issued in sheets of 25 stamps.

Landscape in Las Flores, by Carmelo de Arzadun — A745

1996, July 15   Litho.   Perf. 12½
1618 A745 3.50p multicolored   1.50 1.50

Jewish Community in Uruguay, 80th Anniv. — A746

1996, July 29
1619 A746 7.50p multicolored   4.00 4.00

A747

Scientists from Uruguay A748

No. 1620, Enrique Legrand (1861-1939). No. 1621, Victor Bertullo (1919-79). No. 1622, Tomas Beno Hirschfeld (1939-86). No. 1623, Miguel C. Rubino (1886-1945).

1996, July 30
1620 A747 3.50p multicolored   1.90 1.90
1621 A747 3.50p multicolored   1.90 1.90
1622 A748 3.50p multicolored   1.90 1.90
1623 A748 3.50p multicolored   1.90 1.90
     Nos. 1620-1623 (4)   7.60 7.60

Bank of Uruguay, Cent. — A749

1996, Sept. 9   Perf. 12
1624 A749 3.50p 10p note   1.60 1.60
   a. Booklet pane, #1624   2.50
1625 A749 3.50p 500p note   1.60 1.60
   a. Booklet pane, #1625   2.50
       Complete bklt., #1624a, 1625a 5.00

Souvenir Sheet

Otto Lilienthal (1848-1896) — A750

1996, Aug. 30
1626 A750 12p multicolored   6.50 6.50

AEROFILA '96.

Scientists A751

No. 1627, Albert Einstein. No. 1628, Aristotle. No. 1629, Isaac Newton.

1996, Sept. 3   Perf. 12½
1627 A751 7.50p multicolored   4.00 4.00
1628 A751 7.50p multicolored   4.00 4.00
1629 A751 7.50p multicolored   4.00 4.00
     Nos. 1627-1629 (3)   12.00 12.00

National Heritage — A752

Designs: No. 1630, Map of Gorriti Island showing locations of Spanish forts, 18th cent. No. 1631, Narbona Church, 18th cent.

1996, Sept. 12   Litho.   Unwmk.
1630 A752 3.50p multicolored   1.60 1.60
1631 A752 3.50p multicolored   1.60 1.60

Rural Assoc., 125th Anniv. A753

1996, Sept. 20   Perf. 12½x13
1632 A753 3.50p multicolored   1.50 1.50

Marine Life A754

a, Carchardon carcharias. b, Alopias vulpinus. c, Notorynchus cepedianus. d, Squatina dumerili.

1996, Sept. 23
1633 A754 3.50p Sheet of 4, #a.-d.   8.00 8.00

Istanbul '96.

Sports Champions from Uruguay — A755

Designs: a, Angel Rodriguez, boxing, 1917. b, Leandro Noli, cycling, 1939. c, Eduardo G. Risso, rowing, 1948. d, Estrella Puente, javelin, 1949. e, Oscar Moglia, basketball, 1956.

1996, Oct. 1
1634 A755 3.50p Strip of 5, #a.-e.   9.50 9.50

Traditional Costumes A756

America issue: 3.50p, Gaucho. 7.50p, Woman of the campana.

1996, Oct. 11   Perf. 13x12½
1635 A756 3.50p multicolored   2.00 2.00
1636 A756 7.50p multicolored   3.75 3.75

3rd Space Conference of the Americas — A757

1996, Nov. 4   Wmk. 332   Perf. 12
1637 A757 3.50p multicolored   2.10 2.10

Comic Strips, Cent. A758

"Peloduro," by Julio E. Suarez.

1996, Nov. 7
1638 A758 4p multicolored   2.25 2.25

Health Institute, Cent. A759

1996, Nov. 20
1639 A759 4p multicolored   1.75 1.75

Church of the 7th Day Adventists in Uruguay, Cent. — A760

Wmk. 332
1996, Nov. 26   Litho.   Perf. 12½
1640 A760 3.50p multicolored   1.60 1.60

Felix de Azara (1746-1811), Naturalist — A761

1996, Nov. 20   Perf. 12
1641 A761 4p multicolored   2.25 2.25

Fish A762

Designs: No. 1642, Cynolebia nigripinnis. No. 1643, Cynolebia viarius.

Unwmk.
1997, Feb. 24   Litho.   Die Cut
Self-Adhesive
1642 A762 4p multicolored   1.90 1.90
1643 A762 4p multicolored   1.90 1.90

Popular Festivals A763

#1644, Natl. Folklore Festival, Durazno. #1645, Traditional Gaucho Festival, Tacuarembo.

1997   Wmk. 332   Perf. 12½
1644 A763 4p multi   2.25 2.25
1645 A763 4p multi, vert.   2.25 2.25

Issued: #1644, 1/30; #1645, 3/10.
See Nos. 1653-1656.

Mushrooms — A764

Designs: a, Tricholoma nudum. b, Agaricus xanthodermus. c, Russula sardonia. d, Microsporum canis. e, Polyporus versicolor.

1997, Feb. 7
1646 A764 4p Strip of 5, #a.-e.   12.00 12.00
No. 1646 was issued in sheets of 25 stamps.

Ports A765

No. 1647, Colonia. No. 1648, Punta del Este. No. 1649, Santiago Vázquez. No. 1650, Buceo.

1997, Feb. 28   Litho.   Die Cut
Self-Adhesive
1647 A765 4p multicolored   2.00 2.00
1648 A765 4p multicolored   2.00 2.00
1649 A765 4p multicolored   2.00 2.00
1650 A765 4p multicolored   2.00 2.00
Nos. 1647-1650 (4)   8.00 8.00

Artigas' Lancers, Bicent. A766

1997, Mar. 10   Wmk. 332   Perf. 12½
1651 A766 4p multicolored   2.00 2.00

Military Academy, 50th Anniv. — A767

1997, Mar. 13
1652 A767 4p multicolored   2.00 2.00

Popular Festivals Type of 1997

Coat of arms and: No. 1653, Performers under outdoor pavilion, Beer Week. No. 1654, Ruben Lena, bridge, river, Olimar River Festival, vert. No. 1655, Guitar, man on horse, Festival de Minas Y Abril. No. 1656, Family around person on horseback, Roosevelt Park.

1997   Litho.
1653 A763 5p multicolored   2.50 2.50
1654 A763 5p multicolored   2.50 2.50

1655 A763 5p multicolored   2.50 2.50
Die Cut
Unwmk.
Self-Adhesive
1656 A763 5p multicolored   2.50 2.50
Nos. 1653-1656 (4)   10.00 10.00

Lions Intl. (#1656). Issued: #1653, 3/23; #1654, 3/24; #1655, 4/26; #1656, 3/21.

United Mobile Coronary Unit (UCM), 20th Anniv. A768

1997, Apr. 4   Unwmk.   Die Cut
Self-Adhesive
1657 A768 5p multicolored   2.50 2.50

UNICEF, 50th Anniv. — A769

1997, Apr. 8   Die Cut
Self-Adhesive
1658 A769 5p multicolored   2.50 2.50

Lighthouses A770

Various birds and: a, Anchorena Tower, 1920. b, Farallón Lighthouse, 1870. c, José Ignacio Lighthouse, 1877. d, Santa Maria Lighthouse, 1874. e, Vigía Tower, 18th cent.

1997, Apr. 22   Die Cut
Self-Adhesive
1659 A770 5p Strip of 5, #a.-e.   15.00 15.00

Prehistoric Animals A771

Designs: a, Devincenzia gallinali. b, Smilodon populator. c, Mesosaurus tenuidens. d, Doedicurus clavicaudatus. e, Artigasia magna.

1997, May 5   Die Cut
Self-Adhesive
1660 A771 5p Strip of 5, #a.-e.   15.00 15.00

A772

Ecclesiastical Provinces — A772a

#1661, Church, diocese of Salto. #1662, Church, diocese of Melo. #1663, Bishop Jacinto Vera, 1st bishop of Montevideo. #1664, Msgr. Mariano Soler, 1st archbishop of Montevideo.

Wmk. 332
1997, May 9   Litho.   Perf. 12½
1661 A772   5p multicolored   3.00 3.00
1662 A772   5p multicolored   3.00 3.00
1663 A772a 5p multicolored   3.00 3.00
1664 A772a 5p multicolored   3.00 3.00
    Nos. 1661-1664 (4)   12.00 12.00

Youth Stamp Collecting A773

Designs: a, 2p, Boy, "Philately?" b, 2p, Boy thinking of stamps. c, 2p, Girl with soccer ball, boy. d, 1p, Boy looking at stamps in album. e, 1p, Boy with tongs and magnifying glass.

1997, May 25   Unwmk.
1665 A773 Strip of 5, #a.-e.   5.00 5.00

PACIFIC 97 — A774

1997, May 29   Perf. 12
1666 A774 10p Rynchops niger   5.00 5.00

Maccio Theater of San Jose, 85th Anniv. A775

1997, June 5   Wmk. 332   Perf. 12½
1667 A775 5p multicolored   2.50 2.50

Inter-American Institute of Children, 70th Anniv. — A776

1997, June 9   Unwmk.
1668 A776 5p multicolored   2.50 2.50

Colony of Sacramento — A777

1997, July 4
1669 A777 5p multicolored   2.50 2.50

Punta del Este, 90th Anniv. A778

1997, July 1
1670 A778 5p multicolored   2.50 2.50

Uruguayan Comics — A779

Scenes from comics by: No. 1671, Julio E. Suarez (Peloduro). No. 1672, Geoffrey Foladori.

Perf. 12½
1997, June 30   Litho.   Unwmk.
1671 A779 5p multicolored   1.75 1.75
1672 A779 5p multicolored   1.75 1.75

Zionism, Cent. A780

Design: Theodor Herzl (1860-1904), founder of Zionist movement.

1997, July 17
1673 A780 5p multicolored   3.00 3.00

Children's Painting A781 — Geranoaetus Melanoleucus A782

1997, July 21   Litho.   Die Cut
Self-Adhesive
1674 A781 15p multicolored   10.00 10.00
1675 A782 25p multicolored   16.00 16.00
  a.   Type II ('04)   4.50 4.50

Type I stamps have printer's name at right, designer's name at left, and have an eagle's head that is rounder, with its edge making a sharper angle with the right margin than on type II. Type II stamps have the printer's name at left and the designer's name at right.

No. 1675a issued 2004. No. 1675a also exists dated "2005."

Nos. 1674, 1675 exist dated 1999.

See Nos. 1840, 1850, 1853, 1855.

Isolation of Acetylsalicylic Acid from Willow Trees, Cent. — A783

1997, Aug. 12   Litho.   Perf. 12½
1676 A783 6p multicolored   2.00 2.00
  a.   Booklet pane of 2   6.50
       Complete booklet, #1676a 6.50

Department of Salto — A784

1997, Aug. 26
1677 A784 6p multicolored   2.00 2.00

Felix Mendelssohn (1809-47) — A785

No. 1679, Johannes Brahms (1833-97).

1997, Sept. 1
1678 A785 6p multicolored   1.90 1.90
1679 A785 6p multicolored   1.90 1.90
  a.   Pair, #1678-1679   4.25 4.25

Natural History Museum of Montevideo, 160th Anniv. — A786

Designs: a, Lucas Kraguevich, paleontologist. b, Jose Arechavaleta, botanist. c, Garibaldi J. Devincenzi, zoologist. d, Antonio Taddei, archaelogist.

1997, Sept. 3
1680 A786 6p Strip of 4, #a.-d.   7.50 7.50

Mercosur (Common Market of Latin America) A787

1997, Sept. 26   Perf. 12
1681 A787 11p multicolored   3.75 3.75

See Argentina, No. 1975; Bolivia No. 1019; Brazil, No. 2646; Paraguay, No. 2564.

Souvenir Sheet

Passiflora Coerulea — A788

1997, Sept. 26   Perf. 12½
1682 A788 15p multicolored   5.00 5.00

1st Philatelic Exhibition of Mercosur countries.

Heinrich von Stephan (1831-97) A789

1997, Oct. 9
1683 A789 11p multicolored   3.75 3.75

Souvenir Sheet

Spanish-Uruguayan Monument — A790

1997, Oct. 9
1684 A790 15p Monument   5.00 5.00

Philatelic Exhibition, Spain 1997.

America Issue — A791

Designs: 6p, Woman carrying mail. 11p, Man delivering letters.

1997, Oct. 10
1685 A791 6p multicolored   2.00 2.00
1686 A791 11p multicolored   3.75 3.75

Artigas Scientific Base, Antarctica — A792

1997, Oct. 15   Perf. 12
1687 A792 6p Pygoscelis papua 3.50 3.50

Painting, by Domingo Laporte (1855-1928) — A793

1997, Oct. 21   Perf. 12½
1688 A793 6p multicolored   2.00 2.00

Galicia House, 80th Anniv. A794

1997, Oct. 24
1689 A794 6p multicolored   2.00 2.00

3rd Intl. Congress of Aeronautical and Space History, Montevideo — A795

Perf. 12½
1997, Oct. 27   Litho.   Unwmk.
1690 A795 6p Arme 2 Biplane   2.00 2.00

1st Biennial Interparliamentary Exhibition of MERCOSUR Paintings, Montevideo — A796

1997, Oct. 28
1691 A796 11p multicolored   3.50 3.50

Souvenir Sheet

Pope John Paul II, Holy Year 2000 — A797

1997, Nov. 7
1692 A797 10p multicolored   8.00 8.00

Third Intl. Assembly Punta del Este, and of arrival of first Polish colonists at River Plate, cent.

Uruguayan Navy, 180th Anniv. — A798

1997, Nov. 14
1693 A798 6p multicolored   2.00 2.00

Shanghai '97 Intl. Stamp and Coin Exhibition A799

No. 1694: a, 3.50p, Front and back of 1 peso coin. b, 3.50p, Chinese flag, Hong Kong

harbor, flower, junk. c, 4p, Michael Schumacher, Formula 1 driving champion, Ferrari. d, 4p, Sojourner on Mars, Pathfinder Mission.
No. 1695: a, 3.50p, Martina Hingis, 1997 Wimbledon Ladies' champion. b, 3.50p, Jan Ullrich, 1997 Tour de France winner. c, 4p, Soccer players, 1998 World Cup Soccer Championship, France. d, 4p, Ski jumper, 1998 Winter Olympic Games, Nagano.

1997, Nov. 19
1694 A799 Sheet of 4, #a.-d.   6.00 6.00
1695 A799 Sheet of 4, #a.-d.   6.00 6.00

Christmas A800

1997, Nov. 20
1696 A800 6p Magi   2.00 2.00
1697 A800 11p Madonna & Child   3.50 3.50

Uruguayan Sportsmen — A801

Designs: a, Adesio Lombardo, Olympic bronze medalist, basketball, Helsinki, 1952. b, Guillermo Douglas, Olympic bronze medalist, single sculls, Rome, 1932. c, Obdulio Varela, soccer player on 1950 World Cup championship team. d, Atilio Francois, silver medalist, 1947 World Cycling Championships, Paris. e, Juan López Testa, South American 100 meters champion, 1947.

1997, Nov. 26
1698 A801 6p Strip of 5, #a.-e. 10.00 10.00

Mevifil '97, 1st Intl. Exhibition of Philatelic Audio-Visual and Computer Systems — A802

1997, Dec. 1   Perf. 12
1699 A802 11p multicolored   3.50 3.50

INDEPEX '97 A803

Early vehicles, inventors: a, 1st Land Rover, 1947. b, Henry Ford (1863-1947), Model A. c, Robert Bosch (1861-1942), inventor of automotive components. d, Rudolf Diesel (1858-1913), patented first diesel engine, 1897.

1997, Dec. 8   Perf. 12½
1700 A803 6p Strip of 4, #a.-d.   8.00 8.00

Naval Academy of Uruguay, 90th Anniv. A804

1997, Dec. 12
1701 A804 6p multicolored   2.00 2.00

Supreme Court of Uruguay, 90th Anniv. A805

1997, Dec. 12
1702 A805 6p multicolored   2.00 2.00

Uruguayan Post Office, 170th Anniv. — A806

1997, Dec. 19
1703 A806 6p multicolored   2.00 2.00

MEVIR (Movement for Eradication of Unsanitary Rural Housing), 90th Anniv. — A807

Design: Homes, Dr. A. Gallinal, logo.

1997, Dec. 26
1704 A807 6p multicolored   2.00 2.00

Construction Projects — A808

a, Preparation. b, Planning. c, Execution.

1997, Dec. 29   Perf. 12
1705 A808 6p Strip of 3, #a.-c.   6.00 6.00
    d.   Booklet pane, #1705   7.25
           Complete booklet, #1705d   7.25

Souvenir Sheet

1897 Revolution, Cent. — A809

Design: Gen. Antonio "Chiquito" Saravia and Col. Diego Lamas.

1997, Dec. 30   Perf. 12½
1706 A809 15p multicolored   5.00 5.00

Painting by Héctor Ragni (b. 1898) — A810

1998, Feb. 6
1707 A810 6p multicolored   2.00 2.00

Naval Station, Montevideo — A811

1998, Feb. 13
1708 A811 6p multicolored   2.00 2.00

Native Trees — A812

a, Butia capitata. b, Grove of butia capitata. c, Grove of phytolacca dioica. d, Phytolacca dioica.

1998, Mar. 20   Perf. 12
1709 A812 6p Block of 4, #a.-d.   7.50 7.50

Museum of Humor — A813

Cartoons: No. 1710, by Oscar Abín. No. 1711, by Emilio Cortinas.

1998, Mar. 13   Perf. 12½
1710 A813 6p multicolored   2.00 2.00
1711 A813 6p multicolored   2.00 2.00
    a.   Pair, #1710-1711   4.00 4.00

Wilson Ferreira Aldunate (1919-88) A814

1998, Mar. 17   Perf. 12
1712 A814 6p multicolored   2.00 2.00

Fossilized Animals — A815

Designs: a, Testudinites sellowi. b, Proborhyaena gigantea. c, Propachyrucos schiaffinos. d, Stegomastodon platensis.

1998, Mar. 26
1713 A815 6p Block of 4, #a.-d.   8.00 8.00

Israel '98, State of Israel, 50th Anniv. — A816

1998, Mar. 31   *Perf. 12*
1714 A816 12p multicolored   5.00 5.00

Birds — A820

a, Plyborus plancus. b, Cygnus melancoryphus. c, Platalea ajaja. d, Theristicus caudatus.

1998, Apr. 30
1718 A820 6p Block of 4, #a.-d.   9.00 9.00

Organization of American States, 50th Anniv. — A821

1998, Apr. 14 Litho.   *Perf. 12¾x12½*
1719 A821 12p multi   4.25 4.25

61st World Congress of Sports Journalism A822

1998, Apr. 21 Litho.   *Perf. 12*
1720 A822 6p multicolored   2.00 2.00

Land Settlement Institute, 50th Anniv. — A823

1998, Apr. 22 Litho.   *Perf. 12¾x12½*
1721 A823 6p multi   1.60 1.60

Souvenir Sheet

Intl. Topical Philatelic Exhibition, Nueva Helvecia — A824

Cross and: a, 3.50p, Switzerland #5, Uruguay #1. b, 3.50p, Obverse and reverse of Euro coin. c, 4p, Olympic rings and mountain. d, 4p, Space station.

1998, May 12   *Perf. 12½x12¾*
1722 A824 Sheet of 4, #a.-d.   5.00 5.00
    Swiss Republic, bicent.

Souvenir Sheet

Whales — A825

a, 3.50p, Balaeneoptera physalus (b). b, 3.50p, Balaeneoptera acutorostrata. c, 4p, Megaptera novaeangliae (d). d, 4p, Eubalaena australis (c).

1998, May 15 Litho.   *Perf. 12½*
1723 A825 Sheet of 4, #a.-d.   7.50 7.50
    Ambiente '98, Maia, Portugal; Intl. Year of the Ocean; Expo '98, Lisbon.

1983 Labor Day Democracy Demonstrations — A826

1998, May 27 Litho.   Wmk. 332
    Perf. 12¼x12¾
1724 A826 6p brn & blk   1.75 1.75
    See Nos. 1740, 1775.

Street Cars — A827

Historic Montevideo trams: a, English "La Comercial," 1906. b, German Transatlantica Co., 1907. c, Transatlantica, 1908. d, Transatlantica double decker, 1916.

1998, May 29 Litho.   *Perf. 12*
1725 A827 6p Block of 4, #a.-d.   7.50 7.50

Juvalux '98 — A828

Wildcats: a, Felis colocola. b, Felis pardalis. c, Felis wiedil. d, Panthera onca.

    Unwmk.
1998, June 18 Litho.   *Perf. 12*
1726 A828 6p Block of 4, #a.-d.   8.50 8.50

Ships A829

a, "Sirius." b, Gunboat "18 de Julio." c, Transport, "Maldonado." d, "Instituto de Pesca No. 1."

1998, June 25 Litho.   *Perf. 12*
1727 A829 6p Block of 4, #a.-d.   7.50 7.50

Jesuit Mission Church, Calera de las Huérfanas A830

    Perf. 12½x12¾
1998, July 24 Litho.   **Unwmk.**
1728 A830 12p multi   3.50 3.50

Monument to the Peace of 1872, San José de Mayo, 125th Anniv. — A831

1998, July 31   *Perf. 12¾x12½*
1729 A831 6p multi   2.00 2.00

155mm Artillery Unit No. 5, Cent. A832

1998, Aug. 7   *Perf. 12½x12¾*
1730 A832 6p multi   2.00 2.00

Butterflies — A833

1998, Aug. 14 Litho.   *Perf. 12*
1731 A833 6p Eacles imperialis   3.00 3.00
1732 A833 6p Protoparce lucetius   3.00 3.00
   a.   Pair, #1731-1732   6.00 6.00

First Monument to José Artigas, San José de Mayo, Cent. — A834

    Perf. 12¾x12½
1998, Aug. 24   **Litho.**
1733 A834 6p multi   2.00 2.00

A835

1998, Aug. 28
1734 A835 6p multi   2.00 2.00
    Dr. Mauricio López Lombo (1918-93), zoo founder.

A836

1998, Aug. 31
1735 A836 6p multi   2.00 2.00
Falleri-Balzo Music Conservatory, Montevideo, cent.

José Fernández Vergara (1810-1906), Founder of Pueblo Vergara — A837

1998, Sept. 8
1736 A837 6p multi   2.00 2.00

Souvenir Sheet

El Pais Newspaper, 80th Anniv. — A838

1998, Sept. 14   *Perf. 12½x12¾*
1737 A838 12p multi   4.50 4.50

Collective Medical Assistance Institute, 145th Anniv. — A839

1998, Sept. 24   *Perf. 12¾x12½*
1738 A839 6p multi   2.00 2.00

Postal Link Between Montevideo and Corunna, Spain, 230th Anniv. — A840

1998, Sept. 24
1739 A840 12p multi   4.50 4.50
Espamer '98, Buenos Aires.

Labor Day Type
6p, March of the Social and Cultural Assoc. of Public School Students, 9/25/83.

Perf. 12½x12¾
1998, Sept. 25   **Wmk. 332**
1740 A826 6p brn & blk   2.00 2.00

Iberoamericana '98 Philatelic Exhibition, Maia, Portugal — A841

Airplanes: a, Junkers J52. b, Spad VII. c, Ansaldo SVA-10. d, Neybar.

Unwmk.
1998, Oct. 2   Litho.   *Perf. 12*
1741 A841 6p Block of 4, #a.-d.   7.50 7.50

Death of Chilean Pres. Salvador Allende, 25th Anniv. A842

Perf. 12¼x12¾
1998, Oct. 2   Litho.   Unwmk.
1742 A842 12p multi   3.75 3.75

50th Anniv. of Enrique Rodríguez Fabregat (1885-1976) as UN Commissioner for Palestine — A843

1998, Oct. 5   *Perf. 12¾x12½*
1743 A843 6p multi   2.00 2.00

Radio Carve, 70th Anniv. A844

1998, Oct. 7   Litho.   *Perf. 12½x12¾*
1744 A844 6p multi   2.00 2.00

World Post Day A845

1998, Oct. 9   Litho.   *Perf. 12½x12¾*
1745 A845 12p multi   3.75 3.75
Ilsapex '98, Johannesburg.

America Issue — A846

Famous women: 6p, Julia Guarino (1897-1985), first woman architect in South America. 12p, Dr. Paulina Luisi (1875-1950).

1998, Oct. 9   Litho.   *Perf. 12*
1746 A846 6p multi   2.00 2.00
1747 A846 12p multi   4.00 4.00

Assoc. of Inland Pharmacies, 50th Anniv. — A847

1998, Oct. 10   *Perf. 12½x12¾*
1748 A847 6p multi   2.00 2.00

Postal Services A847a

Serpentine Die Cut 11¼
1998, Oct. 15   Litho.   Unwmk.
Self-Adhesive
1748A A847a 25p multi   7.50 7.50
Exists dated 1999.

Classic Vehicles — A848

Designs: a, 1950 Lancia fire engine. b, 1946 Maserati San Remo. c, 1954 Alfa Romeo trolley bus. d, 1936 Fiat Topolino.

1998, Oct. 23   Litho.   *Perf. 12*
1749 A848 6p Block of 4, #a.-d.   8.50 8.50
Italia'98.

Artists A849

Designs: No. 1750, Sculpture, "Motherhood," and self-portrait of Nerses Ounanian (1920-57). No. 1751, Illustrations from book "Piquín y Chispita," by Serafín J. Garcia (1905-85), vert. No. 1752, Musical score by Héctor M. Artola (1903-82), vert.

Perf. 12½x12¾, 12¾x12½
1998, Oct. 27   Litho.
1750 A849 6p multi   1.90 1.90
1751 A849 6p multi   1.90 1.90
1752 A849 6p multi   1.90 1.90
   Nos. 1750-1752 (3)   5.70 5.70

Juvenalia '98 — A850

1998, Oct. 30   Litho.   *Perf. 12¾x12½*
1753 A850 6p multi   2.00 2.00

Souvenir Sheet

Uruguay-Germany Philatelic Exhibition, Montevideo — A851

Designs: a, 3.50p, Zeppelin cover, Zeppelin NT. b, 3.50p, Germany #1592, Germany Berlin #9N584, German Democratic Republic #2791, mail box. c, 4p, Brandenburg Gate, Volkswagen Beetle, Konrad Adenauer. d, 4p, Airplane, German mark note and coin.

1998, Nov. 6 Litho.   *Perf. 12½x12¾*
1754 A851 Sheet of 4, #a.-d.   4.50 4.50
IBRA '99, 150th anniv. of German stamps (#1754a, 1754b), 50th anniv. of Federal Republic of Germany (#1754c), 50th anniv. of German mark (#1754d).

16th Congress of Expenditure Control Boards — A852

1998, Nov. 9
1755 A852 12p blue & silver   3.75 3.75

Uruguayan Chamber of Industries, Cent. — A853

1998, Nov. 9
1756 A853 6p multi   2.00 2.00

Flowers A854

Serpentine Die Cut 11¼
1998-99   **Litho.**
Self-Adhesive
1757 A854 1p Oxalis pudica,
           "98" date   .30   .30
   a. "99" in inscription   .30   .30
   b. "2000" in inscription   .30   .30
   c. "2001" in inscription   .30   .30
   d. "2002" in inscription   .30   .30
1760 A854 4p Oxalis pudica
           (white)   1.00 1.00
1761 A854 5p Oxalis pudica
           (purple)   .80   .80
1762 A854 6p Eugenia
           uniflora   1.75 1.75
1763 A854 7p Eugenia
           uniflora   1.75 1.75
1765 A854 9p Eugenia
           uniflora   5.50 5.50
1766 A854 10p Aechmea
           recurvata,
           "98" date   2.75 2.75
   a. "99" in inscription   2.75 2.75
   b. "2002" in inscription   2.75 2.75
1770 A854 14p Acca sellowi-
           ana   3.75 3.75
1771 A854 50p Acca sellowi-
           ana   9.50 9.50
   Nos. 1757-1771 (9)   27.10 27.10

Issued: 7p, 2/4/99; 4p, 12/23/99; 14p, 8/6/99; 1p, 6p, 10p, 50p, 1998. 9p, 1999. 5p, 2/19/02.

Reprints issued: #1757a, 12/7/99; #1757b, 12/15/00; #1757c, 2/24/01; #1757d, 5/22/02. #1766a, 12/7/99; #1766b, 2/8/02.

Christmas — A855

Designs: 6p, The Virgin's Descent to Reward St. Ildefons' Writings (detail), by El Greco. 12p, St. Peter's Tears (detail), by Bartolomé Esteban Murillo.

1998, Nov. 23   Litho.   *Perf. 12*
1772 A855 6p multi   1.75 1.75
1773 A855 12p multi   3.50 3.50

Paso Del Molina Neighborhood of Montevideo, 250th Anniv. — A856

1998, Nov. 26   *Perf. 12½x12¾*
1774 A856 6p multi   2.00 2.00

Labor Day Type
6p, Proclamation at the Obelisk, 11/27/83.

Perf. 12¼x12¾
1998, Nov. 27   Litho.   Wmk. 332
1775 A826 6p brn & blk   2.00 2.00

Morosoli Cultural Awards — A857

Perf. 12¾x12½
1998, Nov. 27   Litho.   Unwmk.
1776 A857 6p multi   2.00 2.00

Universal Declaration of Human Rights, 50th Anniv. — A858

1998, Dec. 10   *Perf. 12½x12¾*
1777 A858 6p multi   2.00 2.00

Uruguayan Olympic Committee, 75th Anniv. — A859

1998, Dec. 15   *Perf. 12*
1778 A859 6p multi   2.00 2.00

Uruguayan Sportsmen A860

Designs: a, Juan Lopez (1907-83), soccer coach. b, Hector Scarone (1899-1967), soccer player. c, Leandro Gomez Harley (1902-79), basketball player, hurdler. d, Liberto Corney (1905-55), boxer.

1998, Dec. 15   *Perf. 12¾x12½*
1779 A860 6p Block of 4, #a.-d.   7.50 7.50

Famous Uruguayans — A861

Designs: No. 1780: Dr. Roberto Caldeyro Barcia (1921-96), physiologist. No. 1781, Dr. José Verocay (1876-1923), pathologist. No. 1782, Dr. José L. Duomarco (1905-85), medical researcher.

Perf. 12¼x12¾
1998, Dec. 18   Litho.   Unwmk.
1780 A861 6p multi   1.75 1.75
1781 A861 6p multi   1.75 1.75
1782 A861 6p multi   1.75 1.75
      Nos. 1780-1782 (3)   5.25 5.25

Emile Zola's "J'accuse" Letter, Cent. (in 1998) A862

1999, Jan. 4   Litho.   *Perf. 12½x12¾*
1783 A862 14p multicolored   4.00 4.00

Las Cañas Resort, Fray Bentos A863

1999, Feb. 26
1784 A863 7p multicolored   2.25 2.25

Rio de la Plata Boundary Treaty, 25th Anniv. A864

1999, Mar. 15
1785 A864 7p multicolored   2.25 2.25

Famous Uruguayans — A865

Designs: No. 1786, Joaquin Torres Garcia (1874-1949), painter. No. 1787, Luis Ernesto Aroztegui (1930-94), textile artist. No. 1788, Juan José Morosoli (1899-1957), writer.

1999, Mar. 26
1786 A865 7p multicolored   2.50 2.50
1787 A865 7p multicolored   2.50 2.50
1788 A865 7p multicolored   2.50 2.50
      Nos. 1786-1788 (3)   7.50 7.50

Birds and Flowering Trees A866

a, Psidium cattleianum, Pipraeidea melanonota. b, Tabebuia ipe, Chlorostilbon aureoventris. c, Duranta repens, Tangara preciosa. d, Citharexylum montevidense, Tachuris rubigastra.

1999, Apr. 14   Litho.   *Perf. 12¼x12¾*
1789 A866 7p Block of 4, #a.-d.   7.50 7.50

Carriages A867

Designs: a, Break de chasse. b, Mylord. c, Coupé trois quarts. d, Break de champ.

1999, Apr. 29   Litho.   *Perf. 12½x12¾*
1790 A867 7p Block of 4, #a.-d.   7.50 7.50

National Soccer Team, Cent. — A868

Designs: a, B. Céspedes, M. Nebel, C. Céspedes, team's first field. b, H. Castro, P. Cea, A. Ciocca, team flag. c, R. Porta, A García, S. Gambetta, team headquarters.

1999, May 5   Litho.   *Perf. 12*
1791 A868 7p Strip of 3, #a.-c.   6.25 6.25
      Complete booklet, #1791   7.25

Children's Millennium Stamp Design Contest Winners A869

Designs: a, By Stefani Andrea Furtado. b, By Pilar Trujillo. c, By Lucia Lavie. d, By Cecilia Chopitea.

1999, May 6   Litho.   *Perf. 12½x12¾*
1792 A869 7p Block of 4, #a.-d.   7.50 7.50

Jorge Chebataroff (1909-84), Geographer, Botanist — A870

1999, May 14
1793 A870 7p multicolored   2.00 2.00

Formation of Infantry Brigade No. 1, 60th Anniv. A871

Paintings: No. 1794, Infantry Battalion No. 2 at Battle of Montecaseros, 1852. No. 1795, Infantry Brigade No. 1 at Battle of Estero Bellaco, 1866. No. 1796, Infantry Battalion No. 1 at Battle of Boquerón, 1866.

1999, May 18
1794 A871 7p multicolored   1.90 1.90
1795 A871 7p multicolored   1.90 1.90
1796 A871 7p multicolored   1.90 1.90
      Nos. 1794-1796 (3)   5.70 5.70

Villa de la Restauracion, 150th Anniv. — A872

1999, May 24   *Perf. 12¾x12½*
1797 A872 7p multicolored   2.00 2.00

Souvenir Sheet

Barcelona, Spain Soccer Team, Cent. — A873

1999, May 28   Litho.   *Perf. 12½x12¾*
1798 A873 15p multi   4.25 4.25

1st Festival of Film Critics, Montevideo A874

1999, June 2   *Perf. 12¾x12¼*
Booklet Stamp
1799 A874 7p multi   2.00 2.00
a.   Booklet pane, 2 #1799   4.00
      Complete booklet, #1799a   4.00

Philex France 99 A875

Horses: a, Arabian. b, Quarter horse. c, Thoroughbred. d, Shetland pony.

Perf. 12½x12¾
1999, June 10   Litho.
1800 A875 7p Block of 4, #a.-d.   7.50 7.50

Publication "Marcha," 60th
Anniv. — A876

Perf. 12¼x12¾

1999, June 23   **Litho.**
1801 A876 7p multi   2.00 2.00

Permanent Home
for "Espacio
Ciencia" Science
Exhibits — A877

1999, July 2   **Perf. 12¾x12¼**
1802 A877 7p multi   2.00 2.00

Artigas
Antarctic
Scientific
Base,
25th
Anniv.
A878

1999, July 12   **Perf. 12¼x12¾**
1803 A878 7p multi   2.25 2.25

Republic
of
Uruguay
University,
150th
Anniv.
A879

1999, July 19
1804 A879 7p yel & blk   2.00 2.00

UNESCO
Regional Office,
50th
Anniv. — A880

1999, July 20   **Perf. 12¾x12¼**
1805 A880 7p multi   2.00 2.00

The Last Charruas — A881

a, One seated, one standing. b, Two seated.

1999, July 22 Litho. Perf. 12¾x12½
1806 A881 7p Pair, #a.-b.   4.25 4.25

Souvenir Sheet

Millennium — A882

a, 3.50p, Apollo space program. b, 3.50p,
Soccer players, 2000 Olympic Games, Sydney. c, 4p, Centenary of Zeppelins. d, 4p,
#C60.

1999, July 30 Litho. Perf. 12½x12¾
1807 A882 Sheet of 4, #a.-d.   7.50 7.50
UPU, 125th anniv., Bangkok 2000, Espana
2000, WIPA 2000, Hanover World's Fair.

El Galpón
Theater,
Montevideo, 50th
Anniv. — A883

1999, Aug. 3   **Perf. 12¾x12¼**
1808 A883 7p multi   2.00 2.00

China 1999 World Philatelic
Exhibition — A884

Sea planes: a, Piper J-3. b, Short
Sunderland.

1999, Aug. 18   **Perf. 12¼x12¾**
1809 A884 7p Pair, #a.-b.   4.00 4.00

Dogs — A885

Designs: a, Cocker spaniel. b, German
shepherd. c, Dalmatian. d, Basset hound.

Perf. 12¾x12½
1999, Aug. 24   **Litho.**
1810 A885 7p Block of 4, #a.-d.   7.50 7.50

Insects &
Flowers
A886

a, Halictidae, Oxalis sp. b, Apanteles sp.,
Epidendrum paniculosum. c, Metabolosia
univita, Baccharis trimera. d, Compositae,
Cantarido.

Perf. 12½x12¾
1999, Sept. 10   **Litho.**
1811 A886 7p Block of 4, #a.-d.   7.50 7.50

A887

Uruguayan Artists: No. 1812, Orlando
Aldama (1904-87), writer. No. 1813, Julio Martínez Oyanguren (1901-73), guitarist.

Perf. 12¾x12½
1999, Sept. 13   **Litho.**
1812 A887 7p multi   1.90 1.90
1813 A887 7p multi   1.90 1.90

A888

Perf. 12¾x12¼
1999, Sept. 18   **Litho.**
1814 A888 7p multi   1.90 1.90
Cultural heritage of Mercosur countries.

First Uruguayan Participation in
Olympics, Paris, 1924 — A889

Designs: a, Poster, medal. b, Medal, medal-
winning soccer team.

1999, Sept. 30   **Perf. 12¼x12¾**
1815 A889 7p Pair, #a.-b.   4.00 4.00

Intl. Year
of Older
Persons
A890

1999, Oct. 1 Litho. Perf. 12¼x12¾
1816 A890 7p multi   2.00 2.00

Philatelic Witches Sabbath, by
Mariano Barbasán — A891

1999, Oct. 1   **Perf. 12**
1817 A891 7p multi   2.00 2.00
Stamp Day.

America Issue, A
New Millennium
Without
Arms — A892

7p, Arms in trash can. 14p, Earth, satellites.

1999, Oct. 6   **Perf. 13¾x12¼**
1818 A892 7p multi   2.00 2.00
1819 A892 14p multi   4.00 4.00

Inter-American Development Bank,
40th Anniv. — A893

1999, Oct. 6   **Perf. 12¼x12¾**
1820 A893 7p multi   2.00 2.00

Winner of
Older
Person's
Stamp
Design
Contest
A894

1999, Oct. 8
1821 A894 7p multi   2.00 2.00

El Ceibo
Society,
50th
Anniv.
A895

1999, Oct. 8
1822 A895 7p multi   2.00 2.00

Third Intl.
Conference of
Ministers for
Sports, Punta
del
Este — A896

1999, Oct. 13   **Perf. 12**
1823 A896 7p multi   2.00 2.00

Souvenir Sheets

Official Service of Broadcasting,
Television and Entertainment — A897

No. 1824: a, 4p, Television cameraman. b, 4p, Building. c, 3p, Radio studio. d, 3p, Film cameraman.

No. 1825: a, 4p, Symphony orchestra. b, 4p, Chamber music group. c, 3p, Chorus. d, 3p, Ballet dancers.

1999, Oct. 22   **Perf. 12¼x12¾**
1824 A897   Sheet of 4, #a.-d.   4.25 4.25
1825 A897   Sheet of 4, #a.-d.   4.25 4.25

Uruguayan Standards Institute, 60th Anniv. — A898

1999, Nov. 3
1826 A898 7p multi   2.00 2.00

A899

1999, Nov. 3   **Perf. 12¾x12¼**
1827 A899 7p multi   2.00 2.00

Vice-President Hugo Batalla (1926-98).

A900

Cover of 4/29/29 Mundo Uruguayo magazine.

1999, Nov.12
1828 A900 7p multi   2.00 2.00

Exhibition of art and design from the 1920s, Blanes Museum, Montevideo.

Millennium — A901

No. 1829 — Various buildings and: a, "1999." b, "2000."

1999, Nov. 23   **Litho.**   **Perf. 12**
1829 A901 3.50p Pair, #a.-b.   2.00 2.00

Celmar Poumé (1924-83), Cartoonist A902

1999, Nov. 26   **Perf. 12¾x12¼**
1830 A902 7p multi   2.00 2.00

Christmas A903

9p, Tree with ornaments. 18p, Carolers.

Perf. 12¼x12¾, 12¾x12¼
1999, Dec. 3
1831 A903   9p multi   2.25 2.25
1832 A903   18p multi, vert.   4.50 4.50

Tannat Wines, 20th Anniv. — A904

1999, Dec. 9   **Perf. 12**
1833 A904 9p shown   3.00 3.00
1834 A904 9p Wine drinker   3.00 3.00

New Maldonado Department Governmental Building — A905

1999, Dec. 11   **Perf. 12¼x12¾**
1835 A905 9p multi   3.00 3.00

Types of 1997 and

Crow's Gorge Nature Reserve A907

Chilean Lapwing — A908

Design: 2p, Penitente Waterfall, vert. 5p, Chilean Lapwing (*Vanellus chilensis*). 10p, Crow's Gorge Nature Reserve. No. 1841, Gruta del Palacio, vert. 100p, Sierra de los Caracoles.

Serpentine Die Cut 11¼, Die Cut (#1836A, 1840, 1850, 1853)
2000-06   **Litho.**
Self-Adhesive
1836   A907   2p multi, "2001"   .30   .30
   a.   Dated "2002"   .30   .30
1836A A908   5p multi   .45   .45
1837   A907   10p multi   .85   .85
1838   A907   11p multi   2.00 2.00
1840   A781   20p multi, "2000"   4.50 4.50
   a.   Dated "2001"   4.50 4.50
1841   A907   20p multi, "2001"   5.00 5.00
   a.   Dated "2006"   5.00 5.00
1850   A782   32p multi   7.25 7.25
1853   A782   80p multi   18.00 18.00
1854   A907   100p multi   14.00 14.00
1855   A782   100p multi   7.50 7.50
1855A A782   100p multi   7.50 7.50
   Nos. 1836-1855A (11)   67.35 67.35

Issued: 32p, 1/20. No. 1840, 80p, 12/12. 11p, 3/16/01. No. 1841, 4/26/01. 2p, 8/1/01. No. 1854, 2/13/02. No. 1855, 10/5/04. 5p, 12/1/06; 10p, 10/18/06; 100p, 9/26/06. This is an expanding set. Numbers may change.

No. 1855 has straight numerals in denomination. No. 1855A has slanted numerals.

50th Anniv of Artistic Career of Carlos Páez Vilaró — A916

2000, Jan. 15   **Litho.**   **Perf. 12**
1856 A916 9p multi   3.00 3.00

Orchids — A917

No. 1857: a, 5p, Laelia purpurata. b, 4p, Cattleya corcovado. c, 4p, Cattleya sp. "hybrid." d, 5p, Laelia tenebrosa.

2000, Mar. 3
1857 A917   Block of 4, #a.-d.   6.50 6.50

Lighthouses — A918

No. 1858: a, 5p, Isla de Flores, 1828. b, 4p, Punta del Este, 1860. c, 4p, Cabo Polonio, 1881. d, 5p, Punta Brava, 1876.

2000, Mar. 14
1858 A918   Block of 4, #a.-d.   7.50 7.50

Carlos Quijano (1900-84), Economics Journalist — A919

2000, Mar. 30   **Perf. 12¼x12¾**
1859 A919 9p multi   3.00 3.00

The Gold Rush, Starring Charlie Chaplin, 75th Anniv. A920

2000, Apr. 7   **Litho.**   **Perf. 12¼x12¾**
1860 A920 18p multi   5.75 5.75

Lubrapex 2000 Stamp Show, Brazil.

El Cordón Neighborhood of Montevideo, 250th Anniv. — A921

2000, Apr. 10   **Litho.**   **Perf. 12¼x12¾**
1861 A921 9p multi   3.00 3.00

Mural "Espina de la Cruz," by Children of Mercedes — A922

a, 5p, Branches. b, 4p, Two red flowers.

2000, Apr. 26   **Perf. 12¼x12**
1862 A922   Pair, #a-b   3.00 3.00

Francisco García y Santos (1856-1921), Government Official — A923

2000, May 2   **Perf. 12¾x12¼**
1863 A923 9p multi   3.00 3.00

Uruguayan Notaries Assoc., 125th Anniv. — A924

2000, May 9   **Litho.**   **Perf. 12¾x12¼**
1864 A924 9p multi   3.00 3.00

Intl. Museum Day — A925

2000, May 18   **Litho.**   **Perf. 12¾x12¼**
1865 A925 9p multi   3.00 3.00

Stampin' the Future Children's Stamp Design Contest Winners — A926

Artwork by: a, 5p, Helena Perez. b, 4p, Maria Pia Pereyra. c, 4p, Virginia Regueiro. d, 5p, Blanca E. Lima.

2000, June 2   Litho.   Perf. 12
1866 A926   Block of 4, #a-d   5.75 5.75

Club Soriano, 90th Anniv. A927

2000, June 9   Litho.   Perf. 12¼x12¾
1867 A927   9p multi   3.00 3.00

Antonio Rupenian, Founder of Radio Armenia — A928

2000, June 16   Perf. 12¾x12¼
1868 A928   18p multi   5.25 5.25

"1900 Generation" Writers, Cent. — A929

Perf. 12¾x12¼
2000, June 22   Litho.
1869 A929   9p multi   3.00 3.00

Cacti — A930

No. 1870: a, 5p, Notocactus ottonis. b, 4p, Echinopsis multiplex.

2000, July 4   Perf. 12¼
1870 A930   Horiz. pair, #a-b   3.00 3.00

Uruguayan Soccer Association, Cent. — A931

No. 1871: a, 5p, Players marching. b, 4p, Team photo. c, 4p, Stadium, World Cup. d, 5p, Players in action, World Cup.

2000, July 14   Litho.   Perf. 12¼x12
1871 A931   Block of 4, #a-d   8.75 8.75

Opera Anniversaries — A932

No. 1872: a, 9p, Scene from Carmen, composer Georges Bizet. b, 9p, Scene from Tosca, composer Giacomo Puccini.

2000, July 20
1872 A932   Pair, #a-b   5.75 5.75
Carmen, 125th anniv.; Tosca, cent.

Latin American Integration Association, 20th Anniv. — A933

2000, Aug. 11   Perf. 12¾x12¼
1873 A933   18p multi   5.75 5.75

Naval Aviation, 75th Anniv. A934

2000, Aug. 18   Perf. 12¼x12¾
1874 A934   9p multi   3.00 3.00

ORT, 120th Anniv. A935

2000, Aug. 28
1875 A935   9p multi   3.00 3.00

Luis de la Robla (1780-1844), First Postmaster General — A936

2000, Aug. 28   Perf. 12¾x12¼
1876 A936   9p multi   3.00 3.00

Gonzalo Rodriguez (1971-99), Race Car Driver — A937

a, 9p, Rodriguez, dark blue car. b, 9p, Rodriguez holding trophy, light blue car.

2000, Sept. 11   Perf. 12x12¼
1877 A937   Pair, #a-b   6.25 6.25

Gen. José Artigas (1764-1850) A938

2000, Sept. 22   Litho.   Perf. 12¼
1878 A938   9p multi + label   3.00 3.00

España 2000 Intl. Philatelic Exhibition — A939

Birds: a, 5p, Donacospiza albifrons. b, 4p, Geositta cunicularia. c, 4p, Phacellodomus striaticollis. d, 5p, Cacicus chrysopterus.

2000, Sept. 27   Perf. 12
1879 A939   Block of 4, #a-d   7.00 7.00

Soka Gakkai International, 25th Anniv. — A940

2000, Oct. 2   Perf. 12¼x12¾
1880 A940   18p multi   6.00 6.00

America Issue, Fight Against AIDS — A941

No. 1881: a, 9p, Tic-tac-toe game with condoms and crosses. b, 18p, Syringe and red ribbon.

2000, Oct. 10   Perf. 12¼
1881 A941   Horiz. pair, #a-b   8.00 8.00

Mercosur Cultural Heritage Day — A942

2000, Oct. 14   Perf. 12¾x12¼
1882 A942   18p multi   6.00 6.00

Dragon, by Luis Mazzey (1895-1983) — A943

2000, Oct. 19   Perf. 12¼x12¾
1883 A943   9p multi   3.00 3.00

Fire Fighters A944

Designs: No. 1884, 9p, At car crash. No. 1885, 9p, Searching for victims, vert.

Perf. 12¼x12¾, 12¾x12¼
2000, Oct. 26
1884-1885 A944   Set of 2   8.00 8.00

Prof. Julio Ricaldoni (1906-93), Structural Engineer A945

2000, Nov. 13   Perf. 12¼x12¾
1886 A945   9p multi   3.00 3.00
29th Conference on Structural Engineering, Punta del Este.

Training Ship "Capitan Miranda," 70th Anniv. A946

2000, Nov. 15
1887 A946   9p multi   3.00 3.00

Holy Roman Emperor Charles V (1500-58) A947

2000, Nov. 22   Litho.
1888 A947   22p multi   6.00 6.00

Christmas A948

Designs: 11p, Fireworks. 22p, Holy Family.

2000, Dec. 1
1889-1890 A948 Set of 2 9.00 9.00

Sarandi del Yi, 125th Anniv. — A949

2000, Dec. 14 Perf. 12¾x12¼
1891 A949 11p multi 3.25 3.25

Forest Fire Prevention Service A950

2001, Feb. 9 Litho. Perf. 12½x12¾
1892 A950 11p multi 3.50 3.50

Amphibians and Reptiles — A951

No. 1893: a, Phyllomedusa iheringii. b, Acanthochelys spixii. c, Phrynops hilarii. d, Scinax sqalirostris.

2001, Feb. 15 Perf. 12
1893 A951 11p Block of 4, #a-d 14.00 14.00

Paysandú Rowing Club, Cent. A952

2001, Feb. 28 Perf. 12½x12¾
1894 A952 11p multi 3.25 3.25

17th Congress of Latin American Confederation of Congress Organizers A953

2001, Mar. 2 Perf. 12¾x12½
1895 A953 11p multi 3.00 3.00

City of Belén, Bicent. — A954

2001, Mar. 14
1896 A954 11p multi 2.75 2.75

David, by Michelangelo, 500th Anniv. — A955

2001, Mar. 22
1897 A955 22p multi 6.00 6.00

Uruguayan Society of Performers, 50th Anniv. — A956

2001, Mar. 26 Perf. 12½x12¾
1898 A956 11p multi 3.00 3.00

Casal Catalá, 75th Anniv. — A957

2001, Apr. 20 Perf. 12¾x12½
1899 A957 11p multi 3.00 3.00

Universidad Mayor de la República Engineering Faculty, 85th Anniv. — A958

2001, Apr. 30
1900 A958 11p blue 3.25 3.25

Rodolfo V. Tálice (1899-1999), Biologist — A959

2001, May 2 Perf. 12½x12¾
1901 A959 11p multi 3.50 3.50

Montevideo Lions Club, 50th Anniv. — A960

2001, May 14 Perf. 12¾x12½
1902 A960 11p multi 3.50 3.50

Invention of the Telephone, 125th Anniv. A961

2001, May 22 Perf. 12½x12¾
1903 A961 22p multi 6.00 6.00

Snakes — A962

No. 1904: a, Philodryas olfersii. b, Bothrops alternatus.

2001, May 28 Perf. 12
1904 A962 11p Horiz. pair, #a-b 7.00 7.00

Juan Manuel Blanes (1830-1901), Painter — A963

2001, June 8 Litho. Perf. 12½x12¾
1905 A963 11p multi 2.75 2.75

Start of Pediatrics Teaching by Dr. Luis Morquio, Cent. — A964

2001, June 15 Perf. 12¾x12½
1906 A964 11p multi 2.75 2.75

The Ring of the Nibelung, by Richard Wagner — A965

No. 1907: a, The Rhinegold (El Oro del Rin). b, The Valkyrie (La Walquiria). c, Siegfried (Sigfrido). d, The Twilight of the Gods (El Ocaso de los Dioses).

2001, June 29 Perf. 12
1907 A965 11p Block of 4, #a-d 8.50 8.50

Intl. Organization for Migration, 50th Anniv. — A966

2001, July 5 Perf. 12¾x12½
1908 A966 22p blue & black 5.00 5.00

Thomas Alva Edison (1847-1931) A967

2001, July 12
1909 A967 22p multi 5.00 5.00

Laying of Foundation Stone for Montevideo Port, Cent. — A968

2001, July 18 Perf. 12½x12¾
1910 A968 11p multi 3.00 3.00

Fowl — A969

No. 1911: a, New Hampshire. b, Orpington-Buff. c, Araucanas. d, Leghorn-Light brown.

2001, July 30 Perf. 12
1911 A969 11p Block of 4, #a-d 8.00 8.00

Moby Dick, by Herman Melville, 150th Anniv. — A970

2001, Aug. 2 Perf. 12¾x12½
1912 A970 22p multi 5.00 5.00

Bernardo González Pecotche (1901-63), Founder of Logosophy A971

2001, Aug. 7   *Perf. 12*
1913 A971 11p multi   3.00 3.00

First Concorde Flight, 25th Anniv. A972

2001, Aug. 10   *Perf. 12½x12¾*
1914 A972 22p multi   6.00 6.00

Rose Varieties — A973

No. 1915: a, Louis Philippe. b, Souvenir de Mme. Léonie Viennot. c, Kronenbourg. d, Lady Hillingdon.

2001, Aug. 16   *Perf. 12*
1915 A973 11p Block of 4, #a-d   10.00 10.00

Apiculture — A974

No. 1916: a, Apiculturists. b, Bee on flower.

2001, Sept. 12
1916 A974 12p Horiz. pair, #a-b   7.00 7.00

Town of Dolores, Bicent. — A975

2001, Sept. 21   *Perf. 12¾x12½*
1917 A975 12p multi   2.75 2.75

Uruguay Philatelic Club, 75th Anniv. A976

Sun and inscription: No. 1918, 12p, "75 Años." No. 1919, 12p, "1er Presidente / Dr. Miguel A. Paez Formoso."

2001, Sept. 26   *Perf. 12½x12¾*
1918-1919 A976   Set of 2   6.50 6.50

America Issue - UNESCO World Heritage Sites — A977

Buildings from Historic Quarter of Colonia del Sacramento: a, 12p, Basilica del Santisimo. b, 24p, San Benito de Palermo Chapel.

2001, Sept. 28   *Perf. 12*
1920 A977   Horiz. pair, #a-b   9.50 9.50

Carlos Amoretti, 50th Anniv. as Artist A978

2001, Oct. 2   *Perf. 12½x12¾*
1921 A978 12p multi   3.00 3.00

Town of Sauce, 150th Anniv. — A979

2001, Oct. 12   *Perf. 12¾x12½*
1922 A979 12p multi   5.00 5.00

Uruguay - Japan Diplomatic Relations, 80th Anniv. A980

     Perf. 12¼x12¾
2001, Sept. 24   *Litho.*
1923 A980 24p multi   6.00 6.00

Prevention of Illegal Drug Use A981

2001, Oct. 16
1924 A981 12p multi   3.00 3.00

Year of Dialogue Among Civilizations A982

2001, Oct. 23   *Perf. 12¾x12¼*
1925 A982 24p multi   7.00 7.00

Honorary Committee for Fighting Cancer — A983

2001, Oct. 29
1926 A983 12p multi   3.00 3.00

Ultimas Noticias Newspaper, 20th Anniv. — A984

2001, Oct. 31
1927 A984 12p multi   2.75 2.75

Sauce Basketball Club, 50th Anniv. A985

2001, Nov. 9   *Perf. 12¼x12¾*
1928 A985 12p multi   3.75 3.75

Blood Donor's Day — A986

2001, Nov. 12   *Perf. 12¾x12¼*
1929 A986 12p multi   2.75 2.75

Juan Zorilla de San Martín (1855-1931), Writer — A987

2001, Nov. 13   *Perf. 12¼x12¾*
1930 A987 12p multi   2.75 2.75

Uruguayan Navy's Hydrographic Ship "Oyarvide" — A988

2001, Nov. 14
1931 A988 12p multi   3.25 3.25

Uruguayan Visit of Rotary Intl. President Richard King and Wife Cherie — A989

2001, Nov. 20   *Perf. 12¾x12¼*
1932 A989 24p multi   5.00 5.00

Peñarol Athletic Club, 110th Anniv. — A990

2001, Nov. 22   *Perf. 12*
1933 A990 12p multi   2.75 2.75

Julio Sosa (1926-64), Tango Singer — A991

2001, Nov. 26   *Perf. 12¾x12¼*
1934 A991 12p multi   2.75 2.75

José Nasazzi (1901-68), Soccer Player — A992

2001, Nov. 29
1935 A992 12p multi   2.75 2.75

Christmas — A993

Paintings of Adoration of the Shepherds, by: 12p, José Ribera. 24p, Anton Raphael Mengs.

2001, Dec. 6
1936-1937 A993   Set of 2   7.00 7.00

Church of San
Carlos,
Bicent. — A994

2001, Dec. 7
1938 A994 12p multi 2.75 2.75

National Museum of Visual Arts, 90th
Anniv. — A995

2001, Dec. 12 *Perf. 12*
1939 A995 12p multi 3.50 3.50

State Insurance
Bank, 90th
Anniv. — A996

2001, Dec. 20 *Perf. 12¾x12¼*
1940 A996 12p multi 2.75 2.75

Guettarda Uruguensis — A997

2001, Dec. 21 *Perf. 12¼x12¾*
1941 A997 24p multi 5.00 5.00

St. Josemaría Escrivá de Balaguer
(1902-75) — A998

Balaguer and quotes: a, "El trabajo es. . ." b,
"Quieres de verdad. . ." c, "La santidad. . ." d,
"Que busques. . ."

2002, Jan. 9 *Perf. 12*
1942 A998 12p Block of 4, #a-
d 10.00 10.00

Uruguayan Association of Directors of
Carnivals and Folk Festivals, 50th
Anniv. — A999

Feet of: a, Ringmaster. b, Clown. c, Acrobat.

2002, Mar. 8 **Litho.** *Perf. 12½*
Self-Adhesive
1943 Booklet pane of 3 5.00 5.00
a.-b. A999 6p Either single 1.25 1.25
c. A999 12p black 2.50 2.50
Booklet, #1943 6.00 6.00

Christianity in
Armenia,
1700th Anniv.
A1000

2002, Apr. 23 *Perf. 12*
1944 A1000 12p multi 2.50 2.50

New Year 2003
(Year of the
Horse) — A1001

2002, May 14 *Perf. 12¾x12¼*
1945 A1001 24p multi 4.50 4.50

2002 World Cup Soccer
Championships, Japan and
Korea — A1002

No. 1946: a, Flags, soccer ball, and field
(38mm diameter). b, Soccer players, years of
Uruguayan championships.

2002, May 21 *Perf. 12¾*
1946 A1002 12p Horiz. pair, #a-b 4.00 4.00

See Argentina No. 2184, Brazil No. 2840,
France No. 2891, Germany No. 2163 and Italy
No. 2526.

Book
Day — A1003

2002, May 24 *Perf. 12¾x12¼*
1947 A1003 12p multi 2.25 2.25

Inter-American Children's Institute,
75th Anniv. — A1004

2002, June 10 *Perf. 12¼x12¾*
1948 A1004 12p multi 2.25 2.25

Department of Tacuarembó, 165th
Anniv. — A1005

2002, June 14
1949 A1005 12p multi 2.25 2.25

Cerro de Montevideo Lighthouse,
Bicent. — A1006

Designs: 12p, Old lighthouse. 24p, New
lighthouse, vert.

Perf. 12¼x12¾, 12¾x12¼
2002, June 24
1950-1951 A1006 Set of 2 5.00 5.00

Villa Constitución, 150th
Anniv. — A1007

2002, July 11 *Perf. 12¼x12¾*
1952 A1007 12p multi 2.00 2.00

"We Are
United"
A1008

2002, July 17
1953 A1008 6p multi 1.00 1.00
Printed in sheets of 3 + label. Value $4.

Natural
Uruguay
A1009

2002, July 22 **Litho.**
1954 A1009 24p blue & orange 3.25 3.25

Montevideo Botanical
Gardens,
Cent. — A1010

No. 1955: a, Botanical Gardens building,
Erythrina cristigalli. b, Rhodophiala bifida. c,
Prof. Atilio Lombardo and Tillandsia arequitae.
d, Heteropterys dumetorum.

2002, July 31 *Perf. 12*
1955 Horiz. strip of 4 7.00 7.00
a.-d. A1010 12p Any single 1.60 1.60

Montevideo
Wanderers Soccer
Team,
Cent. — A1011

2002, Aug. 1 *Perf. 12¾x12¼*
1956 A1011 12p black 2.00 2.00

Sportsmen — A1012

Designs: No. 1957, 12p, Lorenzo Fernán-
dez, soccer player. No. 1958, 12p, Josè Lean-
dro Andrade, soccer player. No. 1959, 12p,
Alvaro Gestido, soccer player. No. 1960, 12p,
César L. Gallardo, fencer. No. 1961, 12p,
Pedro Petrone, soccer player.

2002, Aug. 16 *Perf. 12¼x12¾*
1957-1961 A1012 Set of 5 8.50 8.50

Elvis Presley
(1935-77)
A1013

2002, Aug. 19 *Perf. 12¾x12¼*
1962 A1013 24p multi 3.00 3.00

Agustín Bisio
(1894-1952),
Poet — A1014

2002, Aug. 30 *Perf. 12¾x12¼*
Self-Adhesive
1963 A1014 12p multi 2.00 2.00

City of Artigas,
150th
Anniv. — A1015

2002, Sept. 12 *Perf. 12¾x12¼*
Self-Adhesive
1964 A1015 12p multi 2.00 2.00

Uruguayan Cooperative Society of Bus Services, 65th Anniv. — A1016

2002, Sept. 16   *Perf. 12¼x12¾*
1965 A1016 12p multi   2.00 2.00

Psychoanalysis, Cent. — A1017

2002, Sept. 20   *Perf. 12*
1966 A1017 12p multi   2.00 2.00

24th Latin American Psychoanalysis Congress, Montevideo.

Horacio Arredondo (1888-1967), Historical Preservationist, and San Miguel Fort — A1018

2002, Sept. 20   *Perf. 12¼x12¾*
1967 A1018 12p multi   2.00 2.00

Paso del Rey Barracks Natl. Historic Monument — A1019

2002, Sept. 23   *Perf. 12*
1968 A1019 12p multi   2.00 2.00

Intl. Year of Ecotourism — A1020

2002, Sept. 24   *Litho.*
1969 A1020 12p multi   2.00 2.00

Uruguayan Postal Services, 175th Anniv. — A1021

Designs: No. 1970, Postal Services headquarters, Montevideo. No. 1971, Letter box.

2002, Oct. 9   *Perf. 12¾x12¼*
1970 A1021 12p multi   2.00 2.00

Souvenir Sheet
Imperf
1971 A1021 12p multi   2.00 2.00

First Equestrian Statue of Brig. Gen. Juan Antonio Lavalleja, Cent. — A1022

2002, Oct. 11   *Perf. 12¾x12¼*
1972 A1022 12p multi   2.00 2.00

America Issue — Youth, Education and Literacy A1023

"ANALFABETISMO" in: 12p, Word search puzzle. 24p, Bowl of alphabet soup.

2002, Oct. 16   *Perf. 12¼x12¾*
1973-1974 A1023 Set of 2   5.00 5.00

Christmas A1024

2002, Nov. 4   *Perf. 12¾x12¼*
1975 A1024 12p multi   2.00 2.00

Association of Uruguayan Pharmacies, 65th Anniv. — A1025

2002, Nov. 8   *Litho.*
1976 A1025 12p multi   2.00 2.00

Tannat Wine — A1026

2002, Nov. 13
1977 A1026 12p multi   2.00 2.00

Uruguayan Navy, 185th Anniv. — A1027

2002, Nov. 13   *Perf. 13½*
1978 A1027 12p multi   2.00 2.00

National Organ and Tissue Bank, 25th Anniv. A1028

2002, Nov. 15
1979 A1028 12p multi   2.00 2.00

Taxis in Uruguay, Cent. A1029

2002, Nov. 25   *Perf. 12¼x12¾*
1980 A1029 12p multi   2.00 2.00

Brig. Gen. Manuel Oribe (1792-1857) A1030

2002, Nov. 28   *Perf. 12¾x12¼*
1981 A1030 12p multi   2.00 2.00

George Harrison (1943-2001), Rock Musician A1031

2002, Nov. 29   *Perf. 13½*
1982 A1031 24p multi   4.50 4.50

Pan-American Health Organization, Cent. — A1032

2002, Dec. 2
1983 A1032 12p multi   2.00 2.00

Uruguayan Participation in U.N. Peace Keeping Missions, 50th Anniv. — A1033

2002, Dec. 6   *Perf. 12¼x12¾*
1984 A1033 12p multi   2.00 2.00

Alfredo Testoni (1919-2000), Artist — A1034

2002, Dec. 9   *Perf. 13½*
1985 A1034 12p multi   2.00 2.00

Mercosur A1035

Designs: 12p, Ship and coastline. 24p, Beach.

2002, Dec. 12
1986-1987 A1035 Set of 2   5.00 5.00

Battle of Ituzaingó, 175th Anniv. A1036

2002, Dec. 17   *Litho.*
1988 A1036 12p multi   2.00 2.00

Battle of Juncal, 175th Anniv. A1037

2002, Dec. 17
1989 A1037 12p multi   2.00 2.00

Village of Juanicó, 130th Anniv. A1038

2002, Dec. 23   *Perf. 12¼x12¾*
1990 A1038 12p multi   2.00 2.00

Uruguay
on World
Map
A1039

2003, Jan. 17 Litho. Perf. 12¼x12¾
1991 A1039 12p multi 2.00 2.00

Busqueda
Weekly,
30th Anniv.
A1040

2003, Jan. 29
1992 A1040 12p multi 2.00 2.00

Water Goddess
Iemanja — A1041

2003, Jan. 29 Perf. 12¾x12¼
1993 A1041 12p multi 2.00 2.00

Uruguay - People's Republic of China
Diplomatic Relations, 15th
Anniv. — A1042

2003, Jan. 31 Perf. 12
1994 A1042 12p multi 2.00 2.00

New Year 2003
(Year of the
Ram) — A1043

2003, Feb. 7 Perf. 12¾x12¼
1995 A1043 5p multi .75 .75

Explorers
A1044

Explorers and maps of their voyages: a,
Christopher Columbus, 4th voyage, 1502. b,
Juan Díaz de Solís, 1516. c, Sebastian Cabot,
1526-30. d, Hernando Arias de Saavedra,
1597-1618.

2003, Feb. 14 Perf. 12
1996 Horiz. strip of 4 5.25 5.25
a.-d. A1044 12p Any single 1.25 1.25

Communications Services Regulatory
Union, 2nd Anniv. — A1045

2003, Feb. 21 Perf. 12¼x12¾
1997 A1045 12p multi 1.75 1.75

Intl. Women's
Day — A1046

2003, Mar. 7 Perf. 12¾x12¼
1998 A1046 12p multi 1.75 1.75

City of
Treinta y
Tres, 150th
Anniv.
A1047

2003, Mar. 10 Perf. 12¼x12¾
1999 A1047 12p multi 1.75 1.75

Butterflies — A1048

No. 2000: a, Heliconius erato. b, Junonia
evarete. c, Dryadula phaetusa. d, Parides
perrhebus.

2003, Mar. 18 Perf. 12
2000 A1048 12p Block of 4, #a-d 9.00 9.00

First
Presidency of
José Batlle y
Ordóñez,
Cent. — A1049

No. 2001 — Batlle y Ordóñez: a, Wearing
overcoat. b, Wearing presidential sash. c, With
head on hand. d, Wearing white jacket.

2003, Mar. 25 Perf. 12
2001 Horiz. strip of 4 4.00 4.00
a.-d. A1049 12p Any single 1.00 1.00

Rural
Women's
Crafts
A1050

No. 2002: a, Basket weaving. b, Knitting. c,
Pottery making. d, Food canning. e, Jewelry
making.

2003, Mar. 23 Litho. Perf. 12
2002 Horiz. strip of 5 6.50 6.50
a.-e. A1050 12p Any single 1.25 1.25

Farruco's
Chapel — A1051

2003, Apr. 4 Litho. Perf. 12¾x12¼
2003 A1051 12p multi 1.75 1.75

Natural
Foods
A1052

2003, Apr. 9 Perf. 12¼x12¾
2004 A1052 12p multi 1.75 1.75

Cerros
Azules
Caiman
Farm
A1053

Serpentine Die Cut 11¼
2003, Apr. 10 Self-Adhesive
2005 A1053 12p multi 1.75 1.75

Memorial to 1972
Airplane Crash in
the
Andes — A1054

2003, Apr. 22 Perf. 12¾x12¼
2006 A1054 12p multi 1.75 1.75

Military
Center — A1055

2003, May 21
2007 A1055 12p multi 1.75 1.75

May 18,
1811
Military
Museum,
150th
Anniv.
A1056

2003, May 26 Perf. 12
2008 A1056 12p multi 1.75 1.75

Casa de Ximénes and Las Bóvedas,
Montevideo Historical District — A1057

2003, May 30 Perf. 12¼
2009 A1057 14p multi 2.00 2.00

Wilson Ferreira Aldunate (1919-88),
Politician — A1058

No. 2010: a, Brown background. b, Green
background. c, Dark violet background, text at
right. d, Light violet background, text at left.

2003, June 16 Litho. Perf. 12
2010 A1058 14p Block of 4, #a-d 6.25 6.25

Olympic
Soccer
Gold
Medal,
75th
Anniv.
A1059

2003, June 18
2011 A1059 14p multi 1.60 1.60

Nos. 1382, 1492 Overprinted in Gold

**Methods, Perfs and Watermarks as
Before**
2003, June 18
2011A A654 (14p) on 1.20p 1.50 1.50
  #1492
  Complete booklet of 10 15.00
2011B A589 (36p) on 2500p 4.50 4.50
  #1382
  Complete booklet of 10 45.00

Compare No. 2011A with No. 2055.

Richard Anderson College, 70th Anniv. — A1060

2003, July 15
2012 A1060 14p multi   1.75 1.75

Santa Isabel del Paso de los Toros, Cent. — A1061

2003, July 17
2013 A1061 14p multi   1.75 1.75

National Association of Affiliates, 70th Anniv. — A1062

2003, July 24
2014 A1062 14p multi   1.75 1.75

Jesús María College, Carrasco, 50th Anniv. — A1063

2003, Aug. 4
2015 A1063 14p multi   1.75 1.75

Philatelic Academy of Uruguay, 25th Anniv. A1064

2003, Aug. 5
2016 A1064 14p multi   1.75 1.75

Palacio Heber A1065

2003, Aug. 14
2017 A1065 14p multi   1.75 1.75

Parva Domus Magna Quies, 125th Anniv. — A1066

2003, Aug. 15
2018 A1066 14p multi   1.75 1.75

Security Dept. Commission of Interior Ministry, 4th Anniv. — A1067

2003, Aug. 18
2019 A1067 14p multi   1.75 1.75

First International Victory of Uruguayan Soccer Team, Cent. — A1068

2003, Sept. 12   *Perf. 12½x12¾*
2020 A1068 14p multi   1.75 1.75

Lauro Ayestarán (1913-66), Musicologist — A1069

2003, Sept. 19   *Perf. 12*
2021 A1069 14p multi   1.75 1.75

Asociacion Española Primera de Socorros Mutuos Hospital, 150th Anniv. A1070

2003, Sept. 19   *Perf. 12½x12¾*
2022 A1070 14p multi   1.75 1.75

Dr. Manuel Quintela Clinical Hospital, 50th Anniv. A1071

2003, Sept. 23   *Perf. 12*
2023 A1071 14p multi   1.75 1.75

Society of Friends of Public Education, 135th Anniv. — A1072

2003, Sept. 24
2024 A1072 14p multi   1.75 1.75

Association of Uruguayan Newspaper Reporters, 45th Anniv. — A1073

2003, Sept. 29   *Perf. 12½x12¾*
2025 A1073 14p multi   1.75 1.75

Pres. Fructoso Rivera (c. 1788-1854) A1074

2003, Oct. 1   *Perf. 12*
2026 A1074 14p multi   2.50 2.50

Naval Club, 75th Anniv. A1075

2003, Oct. 1   *Perf. 12½x12¾*
2027 A1075 14p multi   1.75 1.75

Malos Pensamientos Radio Program — A1076

2003, Oct. 3
2028 A1076 14p multi   1.75 1.75

Successes in Intl. Events by Milton Wynants, Cyclist — A1077

2003, Oct. 7   *Perf. 12¾x12½*
2029 A1077 14p multi   1.75 1.75

Ente Nazionale Assistenza Sociale in Uruguay, 50th Anniv. — A1078

2003, Oct. 9   *Perf. 12½x12¾*
2030 A1078 14p multi   1.75 1.75

City of Cardona, Cent. — A1079

2003, Oct. 10   *Perf. 12*
2031 A1079 14p multi   1.75 1.75

Construction League of Uruguay, 84th Anniv. — A1080

2003, Oct. 14   *Perf. 12¾x12½*
2032 A1080 14p multi   1.75 1.75

María Tsakos Foundation, 25th Anniv. — A1081

2003, Oct. 15
2033 A1081 14p multi   1.75 1.75

America Issue — Flora and Fauna A1082

Designs: 14p, Prosopis affinis. 36p, Agouti paca paca.

2003, Oct. 22   *Perf. 12½x12¾*
2034-2035 A1082   Set of 2   5.25 5.25

Independence of Lebanon, 60th Anniv. — A1083

2003, Oct. 24
2036 A1083 14p olive grn & red   1.75 1.75

Souvenir Sheet

Masons in Uruguay, 147th Anniv. — A1084

2003, Oct. 29   **Perf. 12¾x12½**
2037 A1084 14p multi   1.75 1.75

Cacho Bochinche Television Show, 30th Anniv. A1085

2003, Oct. 29   **Perf. 12½x12¾**
2038 A1085 14p multi   1.75 1.75

Morenada, 50th Anniv. — A1086

2003, Oct. 29
2039 A1086 14p multi   1.75 1.75

Brig. Gen. Juan A. Lavalleja (c. 1786-1853) A1087

2003, Oct. 30   **Perf. 12**
2040 A1087 14p multi   1.75 1.75

Souvenir Sheet

Election of Pope John Paul II, 25th Anniv. — A1088

No. 1089 — Uruguayan flag and: a, Pope John Paul II, Vatican arms. b, Polish eagle, map of Latin America.

2003, Oct. 31
2041 A1088 12p Sheet of 2, #a-b 3.50 3.50

Union of Latin American Polish Societies and Organizations, 10th anniv. (#2041b).

Souvenir Sheet

2006 World Cup Soccer Championships, Germany — A1089

No. 2042 — World Cup trophy and: a, Uruguayan flag, J. A. Schiaffino. b, German flag, Fritz Walter.

2003, Oct. 31
2042 A1089 12p Sheet of 2, #a-b 3.50 3.50

Christmas A1090

2003, Nov. 7   **Perf. 12¾x12½**
2043 A1090 14p multi   1.75 1.75

Italian Chamber of Commerce of Uruguay, 120th Anniv. A1091

2003, Nov. 10   **Perf. 12½x12¾**
2044 A1091 14p multi   1.75 1.75

Visit of Manuel Fraga Iribarne, President of Spanish Autonomous Community of Galicia — A1092

2003, Nov. 10
2045 A1092 14p multi   1.75 1.75

San Gregorio de Polanco, 150th Anniv. A1093

2003, Nov. 14
2046 A1093 14p multi   1.75 1.75

United Biblical Society, Bicent. A1094

2003, Nov. 24
2047 A1094 14p multi   1.75 1.75

R.O.U. Paysandu A1095

2003, Nov. 25   **Perf. 12**
2048 A1095 14p multi   1.75 1.75

University Culture Foundation, 35th Anniv. — A1096

2003, Nov. 28
2049 A1096 14p multi   1.75 1.75

Uruguayan Air Force, 50th Anniv. A1097

2003, Dec. 4
2050 A1097 14p multi   1.75 1.75

Visit of Mirko Tremaglia, Italian Minister for Italians Abroad — A1098

2003, Dec. 15
2051 A1098 14p multi   1.75 1.75

Mercosur A1099

Designs: 14p, Horn. 36p, Silver stirrup.

2003, Dec. 16
2052-2053 A1099   Set of 2   7.00 7.00

Powered Flight, Cent. A1100

2003, Dec. 19
2054 A1100 14p multi   1.75 1.75

Nos. 1378, 1382, 1458 and 1492 Surcharged in Black or Blue Violet

j

k

Methods and Perfs. as Before

2004			**Wmk. 332**	
2055	A654(j)	1p on 1.20p		
		#1492	.40	.40
2056	A639(j)	2p on 2.60p		
		#1458 (BV)	.40	.40
2057	A589(k)	5p on 2500p		
		#1382	.60	.60
2058	A589(k)	10p on 360p #1378	1.00	1.00
2059	A589(k)	50p on 825p		
		#1379B	5.00	5.00
	Nos. 2055-2059 (5)		7.40	7.40

Issued: Nos. 2055-2056, 1/19; Nos. 2057-2058, 2/16; No. 2059, 3/23. Obliterator on Nos. 2055 and 2056 covers the centesimos portion of the denomination.

Compare No. 2055 with No. 2011A.

Birds — A1101

No. 2060: a, Puffinius gravis. b, Macronectes halli. c, Daption capense. d, Diamedea melanophrys.

Unwmk.
2004, Jan. 22   **Litho.**   **Perf. 12**
2060 A1101 14p Block of 4, #a-d 8.25 8.25

Isla de Lobos Lighthouse A1102

No. 2061: a, Isla de Flores Lighthouse. b, Farallon Lighthouse. c, La Panela Lighthouse. d, Banco Ingles Floating Lighthouse.

2004, Feb. 10   **Litho.**   **Perf. 12**
2061 A1102 10p Block of 4, #a-d 4.00 4.00
2062 A1102 14p shown 1.50 1.50

Abitab, 10th Anniv. — A1103

Unwmk.
2004, Feb. 12   **Litho.**   **Perf. 12**
2063 A1103 14p multi 1.60 1.60

National Naval Prefecture, 175th
Anniv. — A1104

2004, Feb. 20   Litho.   *Perf. 12*
2064 A1104 14p multi   1.60 1.60

Maté Containers — A1105

No. 2065: a, Maté de Cáliz. b, Maté de Plata
Colonial. c, Maté de Calabaza.

2004, Mar. 4
2065 A1105 5p Strip of 3, #a-c   1.75 1.75

33 Orientales Mechanized Infantry
Battalion No. 10, Cent. — A1106

2004, Mar. 12
2066 A1106 14p multi   1.60 1.60

Intl.
Water
Day
A1107

2004, Mar. 25
2067 A1107 14p multi   1.60 1.60

Regional Energy
Integration
Commission,
40th
Anniv. — A1108

2004, Mar. 25
2068 A1108 14p multi   1.60 1.60

Grenadier
Guards, 80th
Anniv. — A1109

2004, Apr. 1
2069 A1109 14p multi   1.60 1.60

Expansion of La Teja
Refinery — A1110

2004, Apr. 2
2070 A1110 14p multi   1.60 1.60

Florida
Infantry
Batallion
No. 1,
175th
Anniv.
A1111

2004, Apr. 16
2071 A1111 14p multi   1.60 1.60

Tribute to Servicemen — A1112

2004, May 26
2072 A1112 14p multi   1.60 1.60

Medicinal
Plants — A1113

No. 2073: a, Malva sylvestris. b, Achyrocline
satureioides, c, Baccharis trimera. d, Mentha x
piperita.

2004, June 3
2073   Strip of 4   11.00 11.00
a.-d. A1113 36p Any single   2.75 2.75

Map and Arms of Montevideo
Department — A1114

2004, June 17
2074 A1114 14p multi   1.60 1.60
a.   Booklet pane of 2   3.50   —
          Complete booklet, #2074a 3.50

No. 2074a sold for 35p.

Carlos Gardel
(1890-1935),
Singer — A1115

2004, June 24   Litho.   *Perf. 12*
2075 A1115 14p multi   1.60 1.60

Campaign
Against Illegal
Drugs — A1116

2004, June 25   Litho.   *Perf. 12*
2076 A1116 14p multi   1.60 1.60

Renán Rodríguez, Politician — A1117

2004, Aug. 10
2077 A1117 14p multi   1.60 1.60

Maimonides
(1135-1204),
Philosopher
A1118

2004, Aug. 12
2078 A1118 16p multi   1.75 1.75

Galician Center, Montevideo, 125th
Anniv. — A1119

2004, Aug. 30
2079 A1119 16p multi   1.75 1.75

1904 Battles of Gen. Aparicio
Saravia — A1120

No. 2080 — Battle of: a, Illescas. b, Fray-
Marcos. c, Paso del Parque. d, Masoller.

2004, Sept. 8
2080   Block of 4   4.00 4.00
a.-d. A1120 10p Any single   1.00 1.00

Highway
Patrol,
50th
Anniv.
A1121

2004, Sept. 15   *Perf. 12½x12¾*
2081 A1121 16p multi   1.75 1.75

Joaquín Torres García (1874-1949),
Painter — A1122

2004, Sept. 19
2082 A1122 16p multi   1.75 1.75

Magisterial Cooperative, 75th
Anniv. — A1123

2004, Sept. 22
2083 A1123 16p multi   1.75 1.75

Army Administrative Corps,
Cent. — A1124

2004, Sept. 22
2084 A1124 16p multi   1.75 1.75

FIFA (Fédération Internationale de
Football Association), Cent. — A1125

2004, Oct. 5   *Perf. 12*
2085 A1125 37p multi   3.75 3.75

Uruguay - Republic of Korea
Diplomatic Relations, 40th
Anniv. — A1126

2004, Oct. 7
2086 A1126 16p multi   1.75 1.75

Montevideo Cathedral,
Bicent. — A1127

2004, Oct. 19 Litho. Perf. 12
2087 A1127 16p multi   1.75 1.75

Montevideo Council Building — A1128

2004, Oct. 22 Litho. Perf. 12
2088 A1128 16p multi   1.75 1.75

Tomás Toribio
House — A1129

2004, Oct. 22
2089 A1129 16p multi   1.75 1.75

America Issue - Environmental
Protection — A1130

Dirty and clean: 16p, Water. 37p, Birds.

2004, Oct. 26
2090-2091 A1130 Set of 2   5.75 5.75

Armored Infantry Batallion No. 13,
Cent. — A1131

2004, Nov. 16
2092 A1131 16p multi   1.75 1.75

Corner
Store,
18th
Cent.
A1132

2004, Nov. 22
2093 A1132 16p multi   1.75 1.75

PriceWaterhouseCoopers in Uruguay,
85th Anniv. — A1133

2004, Dec. 7
2094 A1133 16p multi   1.75 1.75

Review of Court
Clerks,
Cent. — A1134

2004, Dec. 8
2095 A1134 16p multi   1.75 1.75

Christmas
A1135

2004, Dec. 14
2096 A1135 16p multi   1.75 1.75

Water
Conservation
A1136

2004, Dec. 21
2097 A1136 37p multi   4.00 4.00

Souvenir Sheet

Punta del Este — A1137

2004, Dec. 27
2098 A1137 16p multi   1.75 1.75

1912 Orenstein & Kopell
Locomotive — A1138

Serpentine Die Cut 11¼
2004, Dec. 28
Self-Adhesive
2099 A1138 30p multi   3.50 3.50

Rotary
International,
Cent. — A1139

2005, Feb. 23 Litho. Perf. 12
2100 A1139 37p multi   6.00 6.00

Bridges — A1140

No. 2101: a, Chuy del Tacuari Bridge. b,
Barra Bridge, Maldonado. c, Mauá Bridge
Yaguarón River. d, Castells Bridge, Víboras.

2005, Mar. 18
2101 A1140 16p Block of 4, #a-d 8.25 8.25

Ninth Meeting of Latin American
Energy Regulators — A1141

2005, Apr. 5
2102 A1141 16p multi   1.75 1.75

"Liberating Dragoons" Ninth
Mechanized Cavalry Regiment,
Cent. — A1142

2005, Apr. 11
2103 A1142 16p multi   1.75 1.75

Armenian
Genocide, 90th
Anniv. — A1143

2005, Apr. 25
2104 A1143 16p multi   1.75 1.75

Fingerprint Analysis in Uruguay,
Cent. — A1144

2005, Apr. 26
2105 A1144 16p multi   1.75 1.75

No. 1446 Surcharged

Wmk. 332
2005, May 27 Perf. 12½
2106 A639 2p on 50c #1446   .35   .35

Fountains
A1145

Designs: No. 2107, 10p, Constitution Plaza
Fountain. No. 2108, 10p, Botanical Garden
Fountain. No. 2109, 10p, Athlete's Fountain,
Rodó Park. 37p, Cordier Fountain, Prado,
horiz.

2005, June 8 Litho. Perf. 12
2107-2110 A1145 Set of 4   7.00 7.00

Catholic
Circle,
120th
Anniv.
A1146

2005, June 9
2111 A1146 16p multi   2.00 2.00

SOS
Children's
Villages,
45th
Anniv.
A1147

2005, June 23
2112 A1147 16p multi   2.00 2.00

St. John
the
Baptist
College,
75th
Anniv.
A1148

2005, June 24
2113 A1148 16p multi   2.00 2.00

Souvenir Sheet

Death of Pope John Paul II and
Election of Pope Benedict
XVI — A1149

No. 2114: a, Cross and statue of Pope John
Paul II, Montevideo. b, Pope Benedict XVI.

Perf. 12x11¾
2005, July 15   Litho.   Unwmk.
2114 A1149 10p Sheet of 2, #a-b 2.50 2.50

Medical
Association
Assistance
Center, 70th
Anniv. — A1150

2005   Perf. 12
2115 A1150 16p multi   2.00 2.00
**Inscribed "Correos Uruguay" at
Right**
Perf. 12¾x12½
2116 A1150 16p multi   2.00 2.00
    Issued: No. 2115, 7/19; No. 2116, 8/4.

Seminary
College,
125th
Anniv.
A1151

Designs: No. 2117, 16p, St. Ignatius of
Loyola, college building. No. 2118, 16p, College building.

2005, July 29   Perf. 12
2117-2118 A1151 Set of 2   3.50 3.50

General Liber Seregni (1916-
2004) — A1152

No. 2119 — Inscriptions: a, Vocacion. b,
Comienzo. c, Liberacion. d, Reconocimiento.

2005
2119 A1152 16p Block of 4, #a-
          d   8.00 8.00
    e. Booklet pane, #2119   8.50   —
        Complete booklet, #2119e 10.00
    Issued: No. 2119, 8/1; No. 2119e, 10/11.

Pope John
Paul II (1920-
2005)
A1153

CORREOS URUGUAY $37

2005, Aug. 11   Perf. 13½x13¾
2120 A1153 37p multi   4.25 4.25

Europa
Stamps,
50th
Anniv.
A1154

Designs: 16p, Landscape, by C. De
Arzadun, Spain #1263. 37p, The Emus, by De
Arzadun, Spain, #1126, vert.

Perf. 13¾x13½, 13½x13¾
2005, Aug. 11   Litho.
2121-2122 A1154 Set of 2   6.00 6.00

Urutem 2005
Philatelic
Exhibition
A1155

2005, Aug. 15   Litho.   Perf. 12
2123 A1155 16p multi   2.00 2.00

Legislative
Palace, 80th
Anniv.
A1156

2005, Aug. 24   Litho.   Perf. 12
2124 A1156 16p multi   2.00 2.00

Estadio Centenario, 75th
Anniv. — A1157

Children's art: No. 2125, $16, Stadium, by
Jonatan Belón. No. 2126, 16p, "75" made with
flag and soccer field, by Sofía Arca.

2005, Aug. 30
2125-2126 A1157 Set of 2   3.25 3.25

Carlos Solé, Soccer
Broadcaster — A1158

2005, Sept. 20
2127 A1158 16p multi   2.00 2.00

World Cup Soccer Championships,
75th Anniv. — A1159

Designs: No. 2128, 16p, Parade of athletes.
No. 2129, 16p, Handshake before match. No.
2130, 16p, Awarding of World Cup. 37p, Flags
of Germany and Uruguay, emblem of 2006
World Cup Soccer Championships, Germany.

2005, Oct. 3
2128-2131 A1159 Set of 4   8.50 8.50

44th Congress of Intl. Congress and
Convention Association,
Montevideo — A1160

No. 2132: a, Fish sun and buildings. b,
Association emblem.

2005, Nov. 4   Litho.   Perf. 12
2132 A1160 8p Horiz. pair, #a-b 2.00 2.00

Uruguay River Fish — A1161

No. 2133: a, Rhamdia sapo. b, Odontesthes
bonariensis. c, Hoplias malabaricus. d,
Pygocentrus nattereri.

2005, Nov. 22
2133 A1161 16p Block of 4, #a-d 6.75 6.75

El Escolar Magazine, 50th
Anniv. — A1162

2005, Nov. 23
2134 A1162 16p multi   2.00 2.00

Customhouse Brokers Association,
70th Anniv. — A1163

2005, Nov. 25
2135 A1163 16p multi   2.00 2.00

Detail From Mural, Oficios, by Julio
Alpuy — A1164

2005, Dec. 1
2136 A1164 16p multi   2.00 2.00

Writers — A1165

Designs: 16p, Juan Zorilla de San Martin
(1855-1931). 37p, Constancio C. Vigil (1876-
1954).

2005, Dec. 9
2137-2138 A1165 Set of 2   5.50 5.50

Commercial and Industrial Center of
Salto, Cent. — A1166

2005, Dec. 12
2139 A1166 16p multi   2.00 2.00

Central
Español
Soccer
Team,
Cent.
A1167

2005, Dec. 12
2140 A1167 16p multi   2.00 2.00

Christmas — A1168

2005, Dec. 12
2141 A1168 16p multi   2.00 2.00

Montevideo Atheneum, 137th Anniv. — A1169

2005, Dec. 14 **Litho.**
2142 A1169 16p multi 2.00 2.00

1924 Paris Olympics, 80th Anniv. (in 2004) A1170

Designs: No. 2143, 16p, Andrés Mazali, soccer gold medalist. No. 2144, 16p, Juan Pedro Cea, soccer gold medalist. No. 2145, 16p, Alfredo Ghierra, soccer gold medalist. 37p, Urn showing soccer players, vert.

2005, Dec. 20 **Perf. 12**
2143-2146 A1170 Set of 4 8.75 8.75

America Issue, Fight Against Poverty — A1171

Designs: 16p, Children, teacher and school. 37p, Men with shovel.

2005, Dec. 22
2147-2148 A1171 Set of 2 5.50 5.50

Capitán Miranda, 75th Anniv. — A1172

No. 2149: a, Capitán Miranda in 1930. b, Capitán Miranda in 2005. c, Capt. Francisco P. Miranda (1869-1925). d, Crests of ships Capitán Miranda, Cádiz, and Montevideo.

2005, Dec. 28
2149 A1172 16p Block of 4, #a-d 7.00 7.00

No. 1492 Surcharged in Brown

2005? Photo. Wmk. 332 Perf. 12½
2150 A654 1p on 1.20p #1492 .50 .50

Obliterator on No. 2150 covers the "20" of original denomination. Compare with Nos. 2055 and 2011A.

Maldonado, 250th Anniv. — A1173

Designs: No. 2151, 16p, San Fernando Cathedral. No. 2152, 16p, Dragoon Quarters.

2006, Feb. 22 **Litho.** **Perf. 12**
2151-2152 A1173 Set of 2 3.50 3.50

Alfredo Zitarrosa (1936-89), Singer — A1174

Zitarrosa and: No. 2153, 16p, Guitar, violin. No. 2154, 16p, Guitar, violin, vert.

2006, Mar. 10
2153-2154 A1174 Set of 2 3.50 3.50

Solís Theater, 150th Anniv. — A1175

2006, Mar. 28
2155 A1175 16p multi 2.00 2.00

Diario Español Newspaper, Cent. — A1176

2006, May 15
2156 A1176 16p multi 2.00 2.00

Public Enterprise Day — A1177

2006, May 19
2157 A1177 16p black 2.00 2.00

Assassinated Politicians — A1178

Designs: No. 2158, 16p, Héctor Gutiérrez Ruiz (1934-76). No. 2159, 16p, Zelmar Michelini (1924-76). No. 2160, 16p, Michelini and Gutiérrez Ruiz.

2006, June 1
2158-2160 A1178 Set of 3 5.00 5.00

SODRE Symphonic Orchestra, 75th Anniv. — A1179

2006, June 20
2161 A1179 16p black 2.00 2.00

Masons in Uruguay, 150th Anniv. — A1180

2006, Aug. 15
2162 A1180 16p multi 2.00 2.00

Horse Breeds — A1181

No. 2163: a, Appaloosa. b, Percheron. c, Belgian Heavy Draft. d, Criollo.

2006, Aug. 18
2163 A1181 16p Block of 4, #a-d 6.75 6.75

First Uruguayan Postage Stamps, 150th Anniv. — A1182

2006, Sept. 29
2164 A1182 16p multi 2.00 2.00

Eladio Dieste (1917-2000), Architect — A1183

2006, Oct. 3
2165 A1183 16p multi 2.00 2.00

Syndical Unification Congress, 40th Anniv. — A1184

No. 2166: a, Marchers with banner. b, Marchers with flag.

2006, Oct. 3
2166 A1184 16p Horiz. pair, #a-b 3.50 3.50

Diplomatic Relations Between Uruguay and the Sovereign Military Order of Malta, 40th Anniv. A1185

2006, Oct. 4
2167 A1185 16p multi 2.00 2.00

Paysandú, 250th Anniv. — A1186

2006, Oct. 12
2168 A1186 16p multi 2.00 2.00

Dr. Washington Beltrán (1914-2003), Politician A1187

2006, Oct. 25
2169 A1187 16p multi 2.00 2.00

16th Ibero-American Summit, Montevideo — A1188

2006, Nov. 1 **Litho.** **Perf. 12**
2170 A1188 37p multi 4.25 4.25

Salto, 250th Anniv. A1189

2006, Nov. 7 **Litho.** **Perf. 12**
2171 A1189 16p multi 2.00 2.00

Channel 10, 50th Anniv. — A1190

2006, Nov. 8   **Litho.**   *Perf. 12*
2172 A1190 16p multi   2.00 2.00

America Issue, Energy Conservation — A1191

No. 2173: a, 16p, Screw-in fluorescent light bulbs. b, 37p, Solar panels.

2006, Nov. 17   **Litho.**   *Perf. 12*
2173 A1191   Horiz. pair, #a-b   6.00 6.00

Sports A1192

Designs: No. 2174, 16p, Indoor soccer. No. 2175, 16p, Handball. No. 2176, 16p, Rugby. No. 2177, 16p, Tennis.

2006, Nov. 30
2174-2177 A1192   Set of 4   6.75 6.75

Christmas A1193

2006, Dec. 7
2178 A1193 37p multi   4.00 4.00

Musical Instruments A1194

Designs: 15p, Guitar. 37p, Drum, horiz.

2006, Dec. 11
2179-2180 A1194   Set of 2   5.50 5.50

Ocean Liners and Ports — A1195

No. 2181: a, Queen Mary 2, Montevideo. b, Costa Fortuna, Montevideo. c, Zuiderman, Montevideo. d, Star Princess, Punta del Este.

2006, Dec. 18
2181 A1195 37p Block of 4,
   #a-d   18.00 18.00

Uruguayan Lottery, 150th Anniv. — A1196

2006, Dec. 22   **Litho.**   *Perf. 12*
2182 A1196 15p multi   1.75 1.75

Optimist Class Yacht World Championships — A1197

2006, Dec. 28   **Litho.**   *Perf. 12*
2183 A1197 37p multi   4.50 4.50

Uruguay Post Emblem A1198

Serpentine Die Cut 11¼
2006, Dec. 29   **Litho.**
    Self-Adhesive
2184 A1198 15p multi   1.75 1.75

No. 1492 Surcharged in Golden Brown

No. 1454 Surcharged in Black and Silver

Methods, Perfs, and Watermarks As Before
2007, Jan. 24
2185 A654 1p on 1.20p #1492   .60 .60
2186 A639 2p on 1.80p #1454   .60 .60
   Compare No. 2185 with Nos. 2011A, 2055 and 2150.

Punta del Este, Cent. — A1199

Unwmk.
2007, Jan. 26   **Litho.**   *Perf. 12*
2187 A1199 37p multi   4.25 4.25

José Nasazzi Children's Soccer Cup — A1200

2007, Feb. 5   **Litho.**   *Perf. 12*
2188 A1200 15p multi   1.75 1.75

Julia Arévalo (1898-1985), Politician — A1201

2007, Mar. 8   **Litho.**   *Perf. 12*
2189 A1201 15p multi   1.75 1.75

Souvenir Sheet

Ministry of Transportation and Public Works, Cent. — A1202

No. 2190: a, 5p, Highway construction crew. b, 10p, Airplanes at airport. c, 15p, Bridge.

2007, Mar. 12   **Litho.**   *Perf. 12¼*
2190 A1202   Sheet of 3, #a-c   2.50 2.50

Colón Soccer Club, Cent. A1203

2007, Mar. 12   **Litho.**   *Perf. 12*
2191 A1203 15p multi   1.75 1.75

Campaign Against Dengue Fever — A1204

Serpentine Die Cut 11¼
2007, Mar. 28
    Self-Adhesive
2192 A1204 15p multi   1.75 1.75

National Cadastre, Cent. A1205

2007, Apr. 12   *Perf. 12*
2193 A1205 15p multi   1.75 1.75

Regional Art Meeting A1206

2007, June 8
2194 A1206 15p multi   1.75 1.75

Shells — A1207

No. 2195: a, 5p, Aequipecten tehuelchus. b, 5p, Trophon pelseneeri. c, 10p, Americominella duartei. d, 10p, Conus clenchi.

2007, June 26
2195 A1207   Block of 4, #a-d   4.00 4.00

Giuseppe Garibaldi (1807-82), Italian Leader — A1208

Designs: 15p, Ship, Garibaldi on horseback. 37p, Garibaldi, ship.

2007, July 4
2196-2197 A1208   Set of 2   6.00 6.00
   See Brazil Nos. 3021-3022.

Guichón, Cent. — A1209

2007, July 13
2198 A1209 15p multi   2.00 2.00

Souvenir Sheet

La Estrella del Sur Publication, Bicent. — A1210

2007, July 19 *Perf. 12½x12¾*
2199 A1210 15p multi   2.00 2.00

Agronomy Faculties, Cent. — A1211

2007, July 30
2200 A1211 15p multi   2.00 2.00

Scouting, Cent. — A1212

Children's drawings: No. 2201, 15p, Scout emblem, by Victoria Ferrer. No. 2202, 15p, Scouts at Flag Ceremony, by Paula Barrios. No. 2203, horiz.: a, Knot, Lord Robert Baden-Powell and Duke of Connaught. b, Knot, International Scout emblem patch.

2007, Aug. 9 *Perf. 12*
2201-2202 A1212   Set of 2   3.75 3.75
Souvenir Sheet
2203 A1212 25p Sheet of 2, #a-b 6.00 6.00

Three Musicians in Primary Colors, by José Gurvich (1927-74) A1213

2007, Aug. 17
2204 A1213 15p multi   1.75 1.75

Diplomatic Relations Between Uruguay and Guatemala, Cent. — A1214

No. 2205: a, 15p, Santa Catarina Arch, Antigua, Guatemala. b, 37p, City gate, Colonia del Sacramento, Uruguay.

2007, Sept. 3 *Litho.* *Perf. 12½x12¾*
2205 A1214   Horiz. pair, #a-b   6.00 6.00
See Guatemala No. 583.

German College and High School, Montevideo, 150th Anniv. A1215

No. 2206: a, Anniversary emblem. b, Children's drawing of girl and colors of flags of Germany and Uruguay.

2007, Sept. 5 *Perf. 12*
2206   Horiz. pair + central label   3.50 3.50
   a.-b.   A1215 15p Either single   1.75 1.75

Occupations — A1216

Designs: 1p, Peanut vendor. 7p, Knife grinder, vert. 10p, Organ grinder, vert. 25p, Barber, vert. 50p, Druggist, vert.

Serpentine Die Cut 11¼
2007, Oct. 6
   Self-Adhesive
2207 A1216   1p multi   .25 .25
2208 A1216   7p multi   .80 .80
2209 A1216   10p multi   1.10 1.10
2210 A1216   25p multi   2.75 2.75
2211 A1216   50p multi   5.50 5.50
   Nos. 2207-2211 (5)   10.40 10.40
See Nos. 2253, 2282, 2290, 2292-2295, B13.

Marine Mammal Conservation — A1217

2007, Oct. 12 *Die Cut*
   Self-Adhesive
2212 A1217 37p multi   4.50 4.50

Butterflies — A1218

No. 2213: a, 5p, Eurybia lycisca. b, 10p, Catagramma excelsior pastazza. c, 15p, Agrias claudina. d, 20p, Marpesia marcella.

2007, Oct. 26 *Perf. 12½x12¾*
2213 A1218   Block of 4, #a-d   6.00 6.00

Torrijos - Carter Panama Canal Treaties, 30th Anniv. A1219

2007, Nov. 5 *Perf. 12*
2214 A1219 37p multi   4.50 4.50

America Issue, Education For All A1220

Designs: 15p, Rectangles. 37p, Squares and rectangles.

2007, Nov. 22
2215-2216 A1220   Set of 2   7.00 7.00

Naval School, Cent. — A1221

2007, Dec. 5 *Perf. 12x11¾*
2217 A1221 12p multi   1.75 1.75

Diplomatic Relations Between Uruguay and Russia, 150th Anniv. — A1223

No. 2218: a, 12p, Sacred Heart of Jesus Sanctuary, Uruguay. b, 37p, St. Basil's Cathedral, Russia.

2007, Dec. 21 *Litho.* *Perf. 12*
2218 A1223   Horiz. pair, #a-b + central label   6.00 6.00

Christmas A1224

2007, Dec. 21
2219 A1224 12p multi   1.75 1.75

Architecture A1225

Designs: 12p, House, by Julio Vilamajó. 37p, Joaquín Torres García Building, by Carlos Ott.

2007, Dec. 28
2220-2221 A1225   Set of 2   6.00 6.00

Nelly Goitiño (1924-2007), Actress and Director — A1226

2008, Mar. 24 *Litho.* *Perf. 12*
2222 A1226 12p multi   1.25 1.25

Natl. Association of Milk Producers, 75th Anniv. — A1227

2008, Apr. 23 *Litho.* *Perf. 12*
2223 A1227 12p multi   1.25 1.25

Israel, 60th Anniv. A1228

2008, May 8
2224 A1228 37p multi + label   3.75 3.75

Diplomatic Relations Between Uruguay and the People's Republic of China, 20th Anniv. — A1229

Designs: No. 2225, 12p, Terracotta warriors, China. No. 2226, 12p, The Three Chiripás, painting by J. M. Blaines.

2008, May 19 *Litho.* *Perf. 12*
2225-2226 A1229   Set of 2   2.50 2.50

Dr. Juan J. Crottogini (1908-96), Gynecologist A1230

2008, May 27 *Litho.* *Perf. 12*
2227 A1230 12p multi   1.25 1.25

Souvenir Sheet

Uruguayan Artisans Association, 25th Anniv. — A1231

2008, May 29   *Perf. 12½x12¾*
2228 A1231 12p multi   1.25 1.25

Discount Bank, 50th Anniv. — A1232

2008, June 4   *Perf. 12*
                        Self-Adhesive
2229 A1232 12p multi   1.25 1.25

Intl. Day Against Child Labor — A1233

2008, June 12
2230 A1233 12p multi   1.25 1.25

Birds
A1234

Designs: 12p, Piranga flava. 37p, Cyanocorax chrysops, vert.

2008, June 20
2231-2232 A1234   Set of 2   5.25 5.25

Salvador Allende (1908-73), President of Chile — A1235

2008, June 26
2233 A1235 37p multi   4.00 4.00

Francisco Gómez House, 120th Anniv. as Montevideo Government Building
A1236

2008, July 11   *Perf. 12*
2234 A1236 12p multi   1.25 1.25

Hospital Centenaries — A1237

Designs: No. 2235, 12p, Dr. Raul Amorin Cal Hospital, Florida. No. 2236, 12p, Central Hospital of the Armed Forces. No. 2237, 12p, Pereira Rossell Hospital Center.

2008, July 15
2235-2237 A1237   Set of 3   3.75 3.75

2008 Summer Olympics, Beijing — A1238

No. 2238: a, 2p, Pole vault. b, 5p, Cycling. c, 10p, Swimming. d, 20p, Kayaking.

2008, July 22
2238 A1238   Block of 4, #a-d   4.00 4.00

Intl. Swimming Federation (FINA), Cent. A1239

2008, July 22
2239 A1239 37p multi   4.00 4.00

Club Español, Montevideo, 130th Anniv. A1240

**2008, Aug. 28   Litho.   *Perf. 12*
2240 A1240 12p multi   1.25 1.25

Carlos Vaz Ferreira (1872-1958), Philosopher — A1241

**2008, Sept. 25   Litho.   *Perf. 12*
2241 A1241 12p multi   1.25 1.25

Latin American and Caribbean Coalition — A1242

2008, Sept. 25
2242   Horiz. strip of 3   3.75 3.75
  a. A1242 10p Three people   .95   .95
  b. A1242 12p Three people, diff.   1.25 1.25
  c. A1242 15p Four people   1.40 1.40

Souvenir Sheet

Intl. Polar Year — A1243

No. 1243: a, Skuas. b, Arctocephalus gazella.

2008, Oct. 7
2243 A1243 20p Sheet of 2, #a-b   3.75 3.75

America Issue, National Festivals A1244

Designs: 12p, Guitarist, dancers. 37p, Dancer, costumed drummers.

Perf. 12¾x12½, 12 (37p)
2008, Oct. 24
2244-2245 A1244   Set of 2   4.25 4.25

Dr. Roberto De Bellis (1938-2007), Hematologist — A1245

2008, Oct. 29   *Perf. 12*
2246 A1245 12p multi   1.10 1.10

José "Pepe" Sasía, Soccer Player A1246

**2008, Nov. 20   Litho.   *Perf. 12*
2247 A1246 12p multi   1.00 1.00

Flowers
A1247

Designs: 1p, Sagittaria montevidensis. 2p, Lantana camara. 10p, Calliandra parvifolia. 17p, Erythrina crista-galli. 25p, Prunus subcoriacea.

**2008-09   Litho.   *Die Cut*
                        Self-Adhesive
2248 A1247   1p multi   .25   .25
2249 A1247   2p multi   .25   .25
2250 A1247 10p multi   .85   .85
  a.   Dated "2009"   .90   .90
2251 A1247 17p multi   1.40 1.40
2252 A1247 25p multi   2.10 2.10
    Nos. 2248-2252 (5)   4.85 4.85

Issued: 1p, 2p, 3/12/09; 10p, 25p, 11/28; 17p, 12/18.
No. 2250a, 5/15/09.
See Nos. 2265-2266, 2287.

Occupations Type of 2007
2008, Dec. 7   *Die Cut*
                        Self-Adhesive
2253 A1216 8p Pasta makers   .65   .65

Ministry of Foreign Affairs, 180th Anniv. — A1248

**2008, Dec. 10   Litho.   *Perf. 12*
2254 A1248 37p multi   3.00 3.00

Christmas — A1249

2008, Dec. 24
2255 A1249 12p multi   1.00 1.00

National Flag, 180th Anniv. A1250

2008, Dec. 29
2256 A1250 37p multi   3.00 3.00

Pres. Baltasar Brum (1883-1933) — A1251

2009, Mar. 4   *Perf. 12½x12¾*
2257 A1251 12p multi   1.00 1.00

Delmira Agustini (1886-1914), Poet — A1252

2009, Mar. 26
2258 A1252 12p multi   1.00 1.00

Miguelete, Cent. — A1253

2009, Mar. 27   *Perf. 12¾x12½*
2259 A1253 12p multi   1.00 1.00

Fray Bentos, 150th Anniv. — A1254

2009, Apr. 15   *Litho.*   *Perf. 12*
2260 A1254 12p multi   1.00 1.00

City of Florida, 200th Anniv. — A1255

2009, Apr. 24   *Perf. 12¾x12½*
2261 A1255 12p multi   1.00 1.00

Carnival Costume Designed by Juan Mascheroni — A1256

2009, May 28   *Die Cut*
Self-Adhesive
2262 A1256 37p multi   3.25 3.25

Souvenir Sheet

Intl. Year of Astronomy — A1257

No. 2263: a, 10p, Intl. Year of Astronomy emblem. b, 12p, Galileo Galilei at Inquisition. c, 25p, Head of Galileo.

2009, June 4   *Perf. 12*
2263 A1257   Sheet of 3, #a-c   4.25 4.25

Juan Carlos Onetti (1909-94), Writer — A1258

2009, July 1   *Perf. 12½x12¾*
2264 A1258 12p multi   1.10 1.10

Flowers Type of 2008-09

Designs: 30p, Tessaria absinthioides. 50p, Eichhornia crassipes.

2009, July 14   *Die Cut*
Self-Adhesive
2265 A1247 30p multi   2.60 2.60
2266 A1247 50p multi   4.25 4.25

Souvenir Sheet

Port of Montevideo, Cent. — A1259

2009, July 21   *Perf. 12*
2267 A1259 37p multi   3.25 3.25

Charles Darwin (1809-82), Naturalist — A1260

No. 2268: a, 12p, Head of Darwin, evolution of humans. b, 37p, HMS Beagle.

2009, Aug. 31
2268 A1260   Horiz. pair, #a-b   4.50 4.50

No. 1454 Surcharged

Method, Perf. and Watermark As Before
2009, Sept. 10
2269 A639 1p on 1.80p #2269   .25 .25
    Obliterator covers the centisimos portion of the denomination.

Acipenser Gueldenstaedtii and Caviar — A1262

Unwmk.
2009, Sept. 30   *Litho.*   *Perf. 12*
2271 A1262 37p multi   3.50 3.50

Intl. Labor Organization, 90th Anniv. — A1263

2009, Oct. 7
2272 A1263 37p multi   3.75 3.75

Butterflies and Birds — A1264

No. 2273: a, Hamadryas amphione. b, Anartia amathea. c, Tachuris rubrigasta. d, Colaptes melanochloros.

2009, Oct. 13
2273 A1264 12p Block of 4, #a-d 4.75 4.75

America Issue, Traditional Games A1265

Designs: 12p, Hand holding stone for Taba. 37p, Taba Game, painting by Juan Manuel Blanes.

2009, Oct. 23   *Perf. 12½x12¾*
2274-2275 A1265   Set of 2   4.75 4.75

Government House Museum, 10th Anniv. — A1266

2009, Nov. 6   *Perf. 12*
2276 A1266 12p multi + label   1.25 1.25

Christmas A1267

2009, Nov. 17   *Perf. 12¾x12½*
2277 A1267 12p multi   1.25 1.25

Exports — A1268

Designs: 10p, Vegetables. 25p, Fruits.

2009, Nov. 19   *Die Cut*
Self-Adhesive
2278 A1268 10p multi   1.00 1.00
2279 A1268 25p multi   2.60 2.60

Inter-American Development Bank, 50th Anniv. — A1269

2009, Nov. 24   *Perf. 12¾x12½*
2280 A1269 37p multi   3.75 3.75

Christian Youth Association (YMCA) in Uruguay, Cent. — A1270

2009, Nov. 25
2281 A1270 12p multi   1.25 1.25

Occupations Type of 2007
2009, Nov. 27   *Die Cut*
Self-Adhesive
2282 A1216 8p Grocer, vert.   .80 .80

Chauffeur's Protection Center, Montevideo, Cent. — A1271

2009, Dec. 3   *Perf. 12½x12¾*
2283 A1271 12p multi   1.25 1.25

Souvenir Sheet

Battle of the River Plate, 70th Anniv. — A1272

No. 2284: a, 10p, HMS Ajax. b, 12p, HMSNZ Achilles. c, 15p, HMS Exeter.

2009, Dec. 16   *Perf. 12*
2284 A1272   Sheet of 3, #a-c   3.75 3.75

Official Service of Broadcasting, Television and Entertainment, 80th Anniv. — A1273

2009, Dec. 18   *Perf. 12¾x12½*
2285 A1273 37p multi   3.75 3.75

Alba Roballo (1908-96), Politician — A1274

2010, Mar. 8   **Litho.**   *Perf. 12*
2286 A1274 12p multi   1.25 1.25

Flowers Type of 2008-09
2010, Apr. 12   *Die Cut*
Self-Adhesive
2287 A1247 12p Erithrina crista-galli   1.25 1.25

Historic Hotels — A1275

Designs: No. 2288, 12p, Gran Hotel Concordia, Salto. No. 2289, 12p, Hotel Colón, Piriápolis.

2010, May 26   *Perf. 12¾x12½*
2288-2289 A1275   Set of 2   2.50 2.50

Occupations Type of 2007
Designs: 5p, Street vendor with basket, vert. 7p, Candy vendor, vert. 10p, Shoemaker, vert. 17p, Cuarteador (man on horseback), vert. 25p, Fish vendor, vert. 30p, Ice cream vendor with pushcart.

2010   **Litho.**   *Die Cut*
Self-Adhesive
2290 A1216 5p multi   .55 .55
2291 A1216 7p multi   .70 .70
2292 A1216 10p multi   1.10 1.10
2293 A1216 17p multi   1.75 1.75
2294 A1216 25p multi   2.40 2.40
2295 A1216 30p multi   3.00 3.00
   Nos. 2290-2295 (6)   9.50 9.50

Issued: 5p, 10p, 5/27; 17p, 30p, 8/10; 25p, 8/19; 7p, 10/20.

First Russians in Uruguay, 150th Anniv. — A1276

Perf. 12¾x12½
2010, June 11   **Litho.**
2296 A1276 37p multi   3.75 3.75

Decade of Peace — A1277

2010, June 30
2297 A1277 12p multi   1.25 1.25

Souvenir Sheet

Frédéric Chopin (1810-49), Composer — A1278

No. 2298: a, 12p, Chopin. b, 37p, Piano.

2010, July 21   *Perf. 12*
2298 A1278   Sheet of 2, #a-b   4.75 4.75

Diplomatic Relations Between Uruguay and Romania, 75th Anniv. — A1279

2010, July 23   *Perf. 12¾x12½*
2299 A1279 37p multi   3.75 3.75

Asturian Center, Montevideo, Cent. — A1280

2010, Aug. 28
2300 A1280 37p multi   3.75 3.75

Sporting Club Uruguay, Cent. A1281

2010, Sept. 1   **Litho.**   *Perf. 12*
2301 A1281 12p multi   1.25 1.25

Diplomatic Relations Between Uruguay and Greece, 135th Anniv. — A1282

2010, Sept. 8   **Litho.**   *Perf. 12*
2302 A1282 37p multi   3.75 3.75

Florencio Sánchez (1875-1910), Playwright — A1283

2010, Sept. 17   *Perf. 12¼x12¾*
2303 A1283 12p multi   1.25 1.25

Restoration of Democracy in Uruguay, 25th Anniv. — A1284

Perf. 12¾x12½
2010, Sept. 21   **Litho.**
2304 A1284 12p multi   1.25 1.25

Mario Benedetti (1920-2009), Writer — A1285

No. 2305 — Benedetti at: a, Right. b, Left.

2010, Sept. 25   *Perf. 12½x12¾*
2305 A1285 12p Horiz. pair, #a-b   2.40 2.40
   c.   Booklet pane of 2, #2305a-2305b   3.00 —
     Complete booklet, #2305c   3.00
   No. 2305c sold for 30p.

Flowers and Birds — A1286

No. 2306: a, Bauhinia forficata var. pruinosa. b, Furnarius rufus. c, Guira guira. d, Passiflora coerulea.

2010, Sept. 30
2306 A1286 12p Block of 4, #a-d   4.75 4.75

Uruguay as Antarctic Treaty Consultative Member, 25th Anniv. — A1287

2010, Oct. 8   **Litho.**   *Perf. 12½x12¾*
2307 A1287 37p multi   3.75 3.75

Christmas A1288

2010, Oct. 29   *Perf. 12¾x12½*
2308 A1288 12p multi   1.25 1.25

America Issue — A1289

No. 2309 — Flag of Uruguay and: a, 12p, National anthem. b, 37p, National coat of arms.

2010, Nov. 8
2309 A1289   Horiz. pair, #a-b   5.00 5.00

Blue Uniform of Uruguay Soccer Team, Cent. A1290

No. 2310: a, Team of 1910. b, Team of 2010, emblem of 2010 World Cup Soccer Tournament, South Africa (84x30mm).

2010, Nov. 15   *Perf. 12½x12¾*
2310   Horiz. pair   2.50 2.50
   a.-b.   A1290 12p Either single   1.25 1.25

Cruise Ships and Their Ports of
Call — A1291

No. 2311: a, MSC Lirica, Punta del Este. b,
Veendam, Montevideo. c, Silver Whisper,
Punta del Este and Casapueblo. d, Splendour
of the Seas, Punta del Este and Isla de Lobos.

2010, Nov. 19   **Perf. 12**
2311 A1291 37p Block of 4,
    #a-d   15.00 15.00

Souvenir Sheet

First Airplane Flights in Uruguay,
Cent. — A1292

No. 2312 — Airplane and: a, Armand
Prevost, pilot of Dec. 7, 1910 flight. b,
Bartolomeo Cattaneo, pilot of Dec. 16, 1910
flight.

2010, Nov. 30   **Perf. 12¾x12½**
2312 A1292 37p Sheet of 2, #a-
    b, + central la-
    bel   7.50 7.50

El Telégrafo
Newspaper,
Paysandu,
Cent. — A1293

2010, Dec. 9   **Perf. 12¾x12½**
2313 A1293 12p multi   1.25 1.25

Socialist
Party of
Uruguay,
Cent.
A1294

2010, Dec. 10   **Perf. 12½x12¾**
2314 A1294 12p multi   1.25 1.25

Paintings by Eduardo Vernazza (1910-
91) — A1295

Paintings by Carmelo Arden Quin
(1913-2010) — A1296

No. 2315: a, "Gato con Botas," - Ballet
Ruso. b, Personaje Femenino - Opera Chia
(Dan).
No. 2316: a, Couronnes I. b, Dualité - Peri-
ode Indienne.

2010, Dec. 22   **Perf. 12¾x12½**
2315 A1295 12p Horiz. pair, #a-b 2.40 2.40
     Perf. 12½x12¾
2316 A1296 12p Horiz. pair, #a-b 2.40 2.40

Independence, 200th
Anniv. — A1297

2011, Jan. 3   **Die Cut**
     Self-Adhesive
2317 A1297 1p multi   .25 .25

Artisan
Crafts — A1298

Designs: 2p, Baskets, thistles and cattails.
No. 2319, Handbag, wool (lana). No. 2320,
Iron toy car (hierro). 12p, Wooden sheep,
wood. 20p, Silver container. 22p, Bamboo
sculpture, bamboo. 37p, Ceramic pot. 44p,
Wire sculpture. 200p, Leather basket, cow.

2011   **Die Cut**
     Self-Adhesive
2318 A1298   2p multi   .25 .25
2319 A1298   10p multi   1.10 1.10
2320 A1298   10p multi   1.10 1.10
2321 A1298   12p multi   1.25 1.25
2322 A1298   20p multi   2.10 2.10
2323 A1298   22p multi   2.25 2.25
2324 A1298   37p multi   4.00 4.00
     Size: 27x19mm
2325 A1298   44p multi   4.75 4.75
     Size: 42x30mm
2326 A1298   200p multi   22.00 22.00
     Nos. 2318-2326 (9)   38.80 38.80

Issed: 2p, 1/31; No. 2319, 37p, 3/23; No.
2320, 22p, 12/15; 12p, 20p, 4/12; 44p, 5/13;
200p, 5/6.

25th Gaucho Culture Festival,
Tacuarembó — A1299

No. 2327: a, Cauldron, meat on grill. b,
Bola, gaucho on horse. c, Spurs, gaucho on
horse.

2011, Feb. 3   **Perf. 12**
2327   Horiz. strip of 3   3.75 3.75
   a.-c.   A1299 12p Any single   1.25 1.25
Uruguayan Independence, bicent.

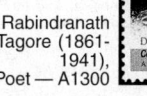

Rabindranath
Tagore (1861-
1941),
Poet — A1300

2011, Feb. 16   **Perf. 12¾x12½**
2328 A1300 37p multi   4.00 4.00
Indipex 2011 Intl. Philatelic Exhibition, New
Delhi.

Battle of Las Piedras, by Juan Luis
and Juan Manuel Blanes — A1301

2011, Feb. 25
2329 A1301 12p multi   1.25 1.25
Uruguayan Army, Uruguayan Independence, bicent.

Cry of Asencio, Bicent. — A1302

No. 2330: a, 12p, Hand on sword, hand on
knife, spears. b, 37p, Bearded man with spear,
horse, hand on knife.

2011, Feb. 28
2330 A1302   Horiz. pair, #a-b   5.00 5.00
Uruguayan Independence, bicent.

Gen. Leandro
Gómez (1811-65)
A1303

2011, Mar. 3   **Perf. 12¾x12½**
2331 A1303 12p multi   1.25 1.25

Souvenir Sheet

Las Llamadas, by Carlos Páez
Vilaró — A1304

2011, Mar. 4   **Litho.**
2332 A1304 37p multi   4.00 4.00

Famous Women — A1305

Designs: No. 2333, 12p, Petrona Rosende
(1787-1862), writer. No. 2334, 12p, Josefa
Oribe (1789-1835), independence supporter.

2011, Mar. 8   **Perf. 12**
2333-2334 A1305   Set of 2   2.50 2.50
Uruguayan Independence, bicent.

Uruguay No.
196 — A1306

2011, Mar. 23   **Perf. 12¾x12½**
2335 A1306 37p multi   4.00 4.00
Postal Union of the Americas, Spain and
Portugal (UPAEP), cent.

Planeta
Building,
Atlántida
A1307

2011, Apr. 8   **Perf. 12½x12¾**
2336 A1307 12p multi   1.25 1.25
Atlántida, cent.

Mother's
Day — A1308

2011, May 11   **Die Cut**
     Self-Adhesive
2337 A1308 12p multi   1.25 1.25

Monte
Carlo TV
Channel
4, 50th
Anniv.
A1309

2011, May 11   **Perf. 12½x12¾**
2338 A1309 12p multi   1.25 1.25

Battle of Las Piedras, Bicent. — A1310

2011, May 12   **Perf. 12**
2339 A1310 12p multi   1.25 1.25
Uruguayan Independence, bicent.

2011 Copa
América Soccer
Tournament,
Argentina
A1311

2011, June 15   **Perf. 12¾x12½**
2340 A1311 37p multi   4.00 4.00

Aitona, by
Ignacio
Iturria
A1312

2011, June 29   **Perf. 12½x12¾**
2341 A1312 12p multi   1.40 1.40
Basque Center, Montevideo, cent.

Campaign Against Human
Immunodeficiency Virus, 30th
Anniv. — A1313

2011, June 30   **Perf. 12¾x12½**
2342 A1313 12p multi   1.40 1.40

Natl. Physical Education Commission,
Cent. — A1314

2011, July 20   **Perf. 12½x12¾**
2343 A1314 12p multi   1.25 1.25

Uruguay,
Champions of
2011 Copa
América
Soccer
Tournament
A1315

No. 2344: a, Cristian Rodriguez. b, Alvaro
Pereira. c, Abel Hernández. d, Luis Suárez. e,
Nicolás Lodeiro. f, Sebastián Abreu. g, Diego
Pérez. h, Fernando Muslera. i, Diego Forlán. j,
Team manager Washington Tabárez. k, Edin-
son Cavani. l, Sebastián Eguren. m, Martín
Cáceres. n, Diego Godín. o, Egidio Arévalo. p,
Alvaro González. q, Maximiliano Pereira. r,
Juan Castillo. s, Diego Lugano. t, Walter Gar-
gano. u, Mauricio Victorino. v, Andrés Scotti.
w, Martín Silva. x, Sebastián Coates.

2011, Aug. 11   **Perf. 12**
2344   Sheet of 24   16.00 16.00
a.-x. A1315 6p Any single   .65 .65

Intl. Year of Forests — A1316

2011, Sept. 21   **Litho.**
2345 A1316 12p multi   1.25 1.25

America Issue,
Mailboxes
A1317

Designs: 12p, Cylindrical mailbox, Avenida
18 de Julio, Montevideo. 37p, Rectangular
mailbox, Plaza Independecia, Montevideo.

2011, Sept. 30   **Perf. 12¾x12½**
2346-2347 A1317   Set of 2   5.00 5.00

Diplomatic Relations Between Japan
and Uruguay, 90th Anniv. — A1318

2011, Oct. 5   **Perf. 12**
2348 A1318 37p multi + label   3.75 3.75

La Redota (Exodus of Gen. José
Artigas and Supporters),
Bicent. — A1319

2011, Oct. 13
2349 A1319 12p multi   1.25 1.25
Uruguayan Independece, bicent.

Souvenir Sheet

China Zorrilla, Actress — A1320

2011, Oct. 18   **Perf. 12½x12¾**
2350 A1320 37p multi   3.75 3.75

Whale Watching — A1321

No. 2351 — Eubalaena australis: a, 12p,
Tail above surface near boat. b, 12p, Tail below
water. c, 37p, At water's surface near land. d,
37p, Diving underwater.

2011, Nov. 16   **Litho.**
2351 A1321   Block of 4, #a-d 10.00 10.00

Isla de Flores National Park — A1322

2011, Nov. 16   **Perf. 12**
2352 A1322 12p multi   1.25 1.25

Cruise Ships — A1323

No. 2353: a, Seabourn Sojourn near José
Batlle y Ordonez Power Plant. b, Asuka II near
Joaquín Torres García Telecommunications
Tower. c, Costa Victoria in Port of Montevideo.
d, AIDAcara near Cerro de Montevideo.

2011, Nov. 22
2353 A1323 37p Block of 4,
    #a-d   15.00 15.00

PLUNA Airlines, 75th Anniv. — A1324

2011, Nov. 22
2354 A1324 12p multi   1.25 1.25

Tango
Musicians
A1325

No. 2355: a, César Zagnoli (1911-2002). b,
Juan D'Arienzo (1900-76). c, Donato Racciatti
(1918-2000).

Perf. 12½x12¾
2011, Nov. 30   **Litho.**
2355   Horiz. strip of 3   3.75 3.75
a.-c. A1325 12p Any single   1.25 1.25

Christmas — A1326

2011, Dec. 7   **Perf. 12**
2356 A1326 12p multi   1.25 1.25

Souvenir Sheet

Intl. Year of Chemistry — A1327

2011, Dec. 9   **Perf. 12½x12¾**
2357 A1327 37p multi   3.75 3.75

Diplomatic Relations Between Uruguay
and the Czech Republic and Slovakia,
90th Anniv. — A1328

2011, Dec. 13   **Perf. 12**
2358 A1328 37p multi   3.75 3.75

Paintings
A1329

Designs: No. 2359, Formas, by María
Freire. No. 2360, Composición 17 de Julio -
1968, by Freire, vert.
No. 2361, vert.: a, Crepúsculo, by Vicente
Martín. b, Dama con Mandolina, by Martín.

2011, Dec. 19   **Perf. 12½x12¾**
2359 A1329 12p multi   1.25 1.25
    Perf. 12¾x12½
2360 A1329 12p multi   1.25 1.25
2361   Horiz. pair   2.50 2.50
a.-b. A1329 12p Either single   1.25 1.25
    Nos. 2359-2361 (3)   5.00 5.00

Intl. Year of
People of
African
Descent
A1330

"Año Internacional
de los Afrodescendientes"

Paintings by Mary Porto Casas: 12p, La Lancera. 37p, Mandela, horiz.

		2011, Dec. 27		**Perf. 12**
2362-2363	A1330	Set of 2	5.00	5.00

State Insurance Bank, Cent. — A1331

2011, Dec. 27
2364	A1331	12p multi	1.25	1.25

Independence, 200th Anniv. — A1332

No. 2365: a, Indigenous man with headband holding stick. b, Man of African descent with hat and gun.

2011, Dec. 28   **Litho.**
2365	A1332	12p Horiz. pair, #a-b	2.50	2.50

SEMI-POSTAL STAMPS

Indigent Old
Man — SP1

1930, Nov. 13   **Engr.**   **Perf. 12**
B1	SP1	1c + 1c dark violet	.30	.30
B2	SP1	2c + 2c deep green	.30	.30
B3	SP1	5c + 5c red	.45	.45
B4	SP1	8c + 8c gray violet	.45	.45
		Nos. B1-B4 (4)	1.50	1.50

The surtax on these stamps was for a fund to assist the aged.
For surcharge see No. 419.

> Catalogue values for unused stamps in this section, from this point to the end of the section, are for Never Hinged items.

Dam, Child
and Rising
Sun — SP2

Wmk. 327

1959, Sept. 29   **Litho.**   **Perf. 11½**
B5	SP2	5c + 10c green & org	.25	.25
B6	SP2	10c + 10c dk bl & org	.25	.25
B7	SP2	1p + 10c purple & org	.50	.50
		Nos. B5-B7,CB1-CB2 (3)	1.00	1.00

National recovery. For surcharges see Nos. 727, Q100.

Souvenir Sheet

Taipei '96, Intl. Philatelic
Exhibition — SP3

Unwmk.
1996, Oct. 21   **Litho.**   **Perf. 12**
B8	SP3	7p +3p multi	8.00	8.00

Gen. Artigas Central Railway Station, Montevideo, Cent. — SP4

a, Baldwin, 1889. b, Hudswell Clarke, 1895. c, Luis Andreoni, engineer. d, Hawthorn Leslie, 1914. e, General Electric, 1954.

       Perf. 12½
1997, July 15   **Litho.**   **Unwmk.**
B9	SP4	4p +1p, Strip of 5, #a.-e.	12.00	12.00

Diana, Princess
of Wales (1961-
97) — SP5

Designs: No. B10, In protective clothing. No. B11, In blue blouse. No. B12, In white.

1998, Jan. 15   **Litho.**   **Perf. 12½**
B10	SP5	2p +1p multi	2.50	2.50
B11	SP5	2p +1p multi	2.50	2.50

Souvenir Sheet
       Perf. 12
B12	SP5	12p +3p multi	15.00	15.00

No. B12 contains one 35x50mm stamp.

Occupations Type of 2008
Serpentine Die Cut 11¼
2007, Nov. 18   **Litho.**
     Self-Adhesive
B13	A1216	5p +2p Baker	.90	.90

AIR POST STAMPS

No. 91 Overprinted in
Dark Blue, Red or
Green

1921-22   **Unwmk.**   **Perf. 14**
C1	A38	25c bister brn (Bl)	17.50	14.00
a.		Black overprint	800.00	800.00
C2	A38	25c bister brn (R)	6.50	5.00
a.		Inverted overprint	100.00	100.00
C3	A38	25c bister brn (G)		
		('22)	6.50	5.00
		Nos. C1-C3 (3)	30.50	24.00

This overprint, on No. C3, also exists in light yellow green. Value, $85 unused and used.
No. C1a was not issued. Some authorities consider it an overprint color trial.

AP2

Wmk. 188
1924, Jan. 2   **Litho.**   **Perf. 11½**
C4	AP2	6c dark blue	2.50	2.00
C5	AP2	10c scarlet	3.50	3.00
C6	AP2	20c deep green	5.00	5.00
		Nos. C4-C6 (3)	11.00	10.00

Heron — AP3

1925, Aug. 24   **Perf. 12½**
Inscribed "MONTEVIDEO"
C7	AP3	14c blue & blk	30.00	14.00

Inscribed "FLORIDA"
C8	AP3	14c blue & blk	30.00	14.00

These stamps were used only on Aug. 25, 1925, the cent. of the Assembly of Florida, on letters intended to be carried by airplane between Montevideo and Florida, a town 60 miles north. The stamps were not delivered to the public but were affixed to the letters and canceled by post office clerks. Later uncanceled stamps came on the market.

One authority believes Nos. C7-C8 served as registration stamps on these two attempted special flights.

Gaucho Cavalryman at Rincón — AP4

1925, Sept. 24   **Perf. 11**
C9	AP4	45c blue green		15.00

Centenary of Battle of Rincon. Used only on Sept. 24. No. C9 was affixed and canceled by post office clerks.

Albatross — AP5

1926, Mar. 3   **Wmk. 188**   **Imperf.**
C10	AP5	6c dark blue	1.50	1.50
C11	AP5	10c vermilion	2.00	2.00
C12	AP5	20c blue green	2.50	2.50
C13	AP5	25c violet	4.00	4.00
		Nos. C10-C13 (4)	10.00	10.00

Excellent counterfeits exist.

1928, June 25   **Perf. 11**
C14	AP5	10c green	2.50	2.00
C15	AP5	20c orange	4.00	3.00
C16	AP5	30c indigo	4.00	3.00
C17	AP5	38c green	7.00	6.00
C18	AP5	40c yellow	8.00	6.00
C19	AP5	50c violet	9.00	7.00
C20	AP5	76c orange	17.00	15.00
C21	AP5	1p red	20.00	18.00
C22	AP5	1.14p indigo	45.00	40.00
C23	AP5	1.52p yellow	70.00	65.00

C24	AP5	1.90p violet	90.00	75.00
C25	AP5	3.80p red	200.00	150.00
		Nos. C14-C25 (12)	476.50	390.00

Counterfeits of No. C25 exist.

1929, Aug. 23   **Unwmk.**
C26	AP5	4c olive brown	2.50	2.00

The design was redrawn for Nos. C14-C26. The numerals are narrower, "CENTS" is 1mm high instead of 2½mm and imprint letters touch the bottom frame line.

Pegasus
AP6

1929-43   **Engr.**   **Perf. 12½**
     Size: 34x23mm
C27	AP6	1c red lilac		
		('30)	.40	.40
C28	AP6	1c dk blue		
		('32)	.40	.40
C29	AP6	2c yellow ('30)	.40	.40
C30	AP6	2c olive grn		
		('32)	.40	.40
C31	AP6	4c Prus blue		
		('30)	.70	.70
C32	AP6	4c car rose		
		('32)	.70	.70
C33	AP6	6c dull vio		
		('30)	.70	.70
C34	AP6	6c red brown		
		('32)	.70	.70
C35	AP6	8c red orange	3.00	2.50
C36	AP6	8c gray ('30)	4.00	3.00
C36A	AP6	8c brt green		
		('43)	2.50	2.00
C37	AP6	16c indigo	.50	.50
C38	AP6	16c rose ('30)	3.25	3.00
C39	AP6	24c claret	4.25	3.50
C40	AP6	24c brt violet		
		('30)	3.00	2.50
C41	AP6	30c bister	3.00	2.75
C42	AP6	30c dk green		
		('30)	2.00	1.50
C43	AP6	40c dk brown	5.50	5.00
C44	AP6	40c yel org		
		('30)	6.00	5.00
C45	AP6	60c blue green	5.00	3.25
C46	AP6	60c emerald		
		('30)	8.50	7.00
C47	AP6	60c dp orange		
		('31)	3.00	2.00
C48	AP6	80c dk ultra	8.00	7.00
C49	AP6	80c green ('30)	15.00	12.00
C50	AP6	90c light blue	8.00	6.00
C51	AP6	90c dk olive		
		grn ('30)	15.00	12.00
C52	AP6	1p car rose		
		('30)	10.00	7.50
C53	AP6	1.20p olive grn	22.00	20.00
C54	AP6	1.20p dp car		
		('30)	30.00	26.00
C55	AP6	1.50p red brown	25.00	20.00
C56	AP6	1.50p blk brn		
		('30)	20.00	15.00
C57	AP6	3p deep red	40.00	35.00
C58	AP6	3p ultra ('30)	30.00	25.00
C59	AP6	4.50p black	75.00	55.00
C60	AP6	4.50p violet ('30)	45.00	35.00
C60A	AP6	10p dp ultra		
		('43)	17.00	12.00
		Nos. C27-C60A (36)	417.90	335.40

See Nos. C63-C82. For surcharges see Nos. C106-C112, C114.

Nos. 450, 452 Overprinted in Red

1934, Jan. 1   **Perf. 11½**
C61	A130	17c ver, gray &		
		vio	20.00	15.00
a.		Sheet of 6	140.00	
b.		Gray omitted	150.00	
c.		Double overprint	150.00	
C62	A130	36c red, blk & yel	20.00	15.00
a.		Sheet of 6	140.00	

7th Pan-American Conference, Montevideo.

Pegasus Type of 1929

1935   **Engr.**   **Perf. 12½**

Size: 31½x21mm

C63	AP6	15c dull yellow	2.50	2.00
C64	AP6	22c brick red	1.50	1.40
C65	AP6	30c brown violet	2.50	2.00
C66	AP6	37c gray lilac	1.40	1.00
C67	AP6	40c rose lake	2.00	1.40
C68	AP6	47c rose	4.00	3.50
C69	AP6	50c Prus blue	1.40	.80
C70	AP6	52c dp ultra	4.00	3.50
C71	AP6	57c grnsh blue	2.00	1.75
C72	AP6	62c olive green	1.75	.80
C73	AP6	87c gray green	5.00	4.00
C74	AP6	1p olive	3.50	2.25
C75	AP6	1.12p brown red	3.50	2.25
C76	AP6	1.20p bister brn	15.00	12.00
C77	AP6	1.27p red brown	15.00	13.00
C78	AP6	1.62p rose	10.00	9.00
C79	AP6	2p brown rose	17.00	14.00
C80	AP6	2.12p dk slate grn	17.00	14.00
C81	AP6	3p dull blue	15.00	13.00
C82	AP6	5p orange	60.00	60.00
		Nos. C63-C82 (20)	184.05	161.65

Counterfeits exist.
For surcharges, see Nos. C106-C112.

Power Dam on
Black
River — AP7

Imprint: "Imp. Nacional" at center

1937-41   **Litho.**

C83	AP7	20c lt green ('38)	5.50	4.00
C84	AP7	35c red brown	8.00	6.50
C85	AP7	62c blue grn ('38)	.80	.30
C86	AP7	68c yel org ('38)	2.00	1.50
C86A	AP7	68c pale vio brn ('41)	1.75	.70
C87	AP7	75c violet	7.50	5.00
C88	AP7	1p dp pink ('38)	2.50	1.75
C89	AP7	1.38p rose ('38)	25.00	20.00
C90	AP7	3p dk blue ('40)	17.00	12.00
		Nos. C83-C90 (9)	70.05	51.75

Imprint at left

C91	AP7	8c pale green ('39)	.60	.50
C92	AP7	20c lt green ('38)	2.00	1.50

For surcharge and overprint see Nos. 545, C120.

Plane over
Sculptured
Oxcart — AP8

1939-44   **Perf. 12½**

C93	AP8	20c slate	.50	.40
C94	AP8	20c lt violet ('43)	.80	.80
C95	AP8	20c blue ('44)	.60	.40
C96	AP8	35c red	1.00	.80
C97	AP8	50c brown org	1.00	.30
C98	AP8	75c deep pink	1.10	.25
C99	AP8	1p dp blue ('40)	3.25	.60
C100	AP8	1.38p brt vio	5.50	2.25
C101	AP8	1.38p yel org ('44)	5.00	4.00
C102	AP8	2p blue	8.00	1.40
a.		Perf. 11	7.00	1.10
C103	AP8	5p rose lilac	10.00	2.25
C104	AP8	5p rose grn ('44)	15.00	7.00
C105	AP8	10p rose ('40)	100.00	65.00
		Nos. C93-C105 (13)	151.75	85.45

Counterfeits exist. These differ in design detail and are perfed other than 12.
For surcharges see Nos. C116-C119.

Nos. C68,
C71, C75,
C73, C77-C78,
C80
Surcharged in
Red or Black

1944, Nov. 22

C106	AP6	40c on 47c	1.00	1.00
C107	AP6	40c on 57c (R)	1.00	1.00
C108	AP6	74c on 1.12p	1.00	1.00

C109	AP6	79c on 87c	2.00	2.00
C110	AP6	79c on 1.27p	3.00	3.00
C111	AP6	1.20p on 1.62p	2.00	2.00
C112	AP6	1.43p on 2.12p (R)	2.00	2.00
		Nos. C106-C112 (7)	12.00	12.00

**Catalogue values for unused
stamps in this section, from this
point to the end of the section, are
for Never Hinged items.**

Legislature
Building
AP9

Unwmk.

1945, May 11 **Engr.** **Perf. 11**

C113	AP9	2p ultra	4.75	2.00

Type of
1929, Srchd.
in Violet

1945, Aug. 14   **Perf. 12½**

C114	AP6	44c on 75c brown	1.25	.55

Allied Nations' victory in Europe.

"La Eolo"
AP10

1945, Oct. 31   **Perf. 11**

C115	AP10	8c green	2.00	1.00

Nos. C97 and
C101 Srchd. in
Violet, Black or
Blue

1945-46   **Perf. 12½**

C116	AP8	14c on 50c (V) ('46)	1.00	.50
a.		Inverted surcharge	37.50	
C117	AP8	23c on 1.38p	1.00	.50
a.		Inverted surcharge	75.00	
C118	AP8	23c on 50c	1.00	.50
a.		Inverted surcharge	75.00	
C119	AP8	1p on 1.38p (Bl)	1.00	.50
a.		Inverted surcharge	75.00	
		Nos. C116-C119 (4)	4.00	2.00

Victory of the Allied Nations in WWII.

No. C85
Overprinted in
Black

1946, Jan. 9

C120	AP7	62c blue green	2.00	1.00

Issued to commemorate the inauguration of the Black River Power Dam.

AP11

Black Overprint

1946-49   **Litho.**

C121	AP11	8c car rose	.25	.25
a.		Inverted overprint		

C122	AP11	50c brown	.55	.25
a.		Double overprint	25.00	
C123	AP11	1p lt bl	1.25	.40
C124	AP11	2p ol ('49)	3.50	2.00
C125	AP11	3p lil rose	5.25	3.00
C126	AP11	5p rose car	9.50	6.00
		Nos. C121-C126 (6)	20.30	11.90

Four-Motored
Plane — AP12

National
Airport
AP13

1947-49   **Perf. 11½, 12½**

C129	AP12	3c org brn ('49)	.25	.25
C130	AP12	8c car rose ('49)	.25	.25
C131	AP12	14c ultra	.50	.30
C132	AP12	23c emerald	.25	.25
C133	AP13	1p car & brn ('49)	1.25	.40
C134	AP13	3p ultra & brn ('49)	2.75	1.60
C135	AP13	5p grn & brn ('49)	8.00	4.00
C136	AP13	10p lil rose & brn	12.00	6.00
		Nos. C129-C136 (8)	25.25	13.05

Counterfeits exist, perf 11¼. Design size of genuine stamps is 34½x24mm, while forgeries are 33½x23½mm.
See Nos. C145-C164. For surcharges see Nos. C206, Q94.

AP14

Black Overprint

1948, June 9   **Perf. 12½**

C137	AP14	12c blue	.25	.25
C138	AP14	24c Prus grn	.50	.25
C139	AP14	36c slate blue	.55	.35
		Nos. C137-C139 (3)	1.30	.85

School of
Architecture,
University of
Uruguay
AP15

Designs: 27c, Medical School. 31c, Engineering School. 36c, University.

1949, Dec. 7

C141	AP15	15c carmine	.25	.25
C142	AP15	27c chocolate	.25	.25
C143	AP15	31c dp ultra	.40	.25
C144	AP15	36c dull green	.60	.35
		Nos. C141-C144 (4)	1.50	1.10

Founding of the University of Uruguay, cent.

Plane Type of 1947-49

1952-59 **Unwmk.** **Perf. 11, 12½**

C145	AP12	10c blk ('54)	.25	.25
C146	AP12	10c lt red ('58)	.25	.25
a.		Imperf., pair	30.00	
C147	AP12	15c org brn	.25	.25
a.		Vert. pair, imperf btwn.	42.50	
C148	AP12	20c lil rose ('54)	.30	.25
C149	AP12	21c purple	.40	.25
C150	AP12	27c yel grn ('57)	.40	.25
C151	AP12	31c chocolate	.55	.25
C152	AP12	36c ultra	.40	.25
C153	AP12	36c blk ('58)	.40	.25
C154	AP12	50c lt bl ('57)	.65	.50
C155	AP12	50c bl blk ('58)	.50	.25
C156	AP12	62c dl sl bl ('53)	.70	.50
C157	AP12	65c rose ('53)	.70	.50
C158	AP12	84c org ('59)	1.00	.70
C159	AP12	1.08p vio brn	1.60	.80
C160	AP12	2p Prus bl	2.50	1.40
C161	AP12	3p red org	3.25	1.75
C162	AP12	5p dk gray grn	6.75	4.00
C163	AP12	5p gray ('57)	3.50	2.50
C164	AP12	10p dp grn ('55)	17.00	12.50
		Nos. C145-C164 (20)	41.35	27.65

Planes and
Show
Emblem
AP16

Unwmk.

1956, Jan. 5 **Litho.** **Perf. 11**

C166	AP16	20c ultra	.60	.40
C167	AP16	31c olive grn	.70	.30
C168	AP16	36c car rose	1.10	.40
		Nos. C166-C168 (3)	2.40	1.10

First Exposition of National Products.

Type of Regular Issue and

José
Batlle y
Ordóñez
AP17

Designs: 10c, Full-face portrait without hand. 36c, Portrait facing right.

Perf. 13½

1956, Dec. 15 **Wmk. 90** **Photo.**

C169	A178	10c magenta	.50	.25
C170	A178	20c grnsh blk	.50	.25
C171	AP17	31c brown	.60	.40
C172	A178	36c bl grn	1.00	.50
		Nos. C169-C172 (4)	2.60	1.30

Stamp of 1856 and
Stagecoach — AP18

1956, Dec. 15   **Litho.**

C173	AP18	20c grn, bl & pale yel	.70	.40
C174	AP18	31c brn, bl & lt bl	.80	.40
C175	AP18	36c dp claret & bl	1.40	.40
		Nos. C173-C175 (3)	2.90	1.20

1st postage stamps of Uruguay, cent.

Flags of 21
American
Nations — AP19   Men and Torch of
Freedom — AP20

Perf. 11, 11½ (No. C177)

1958, June 19   **Unwmk.**

C176	AP19	23c blue & blk	.50	.25
C177	AP19	34c green & blk	.70	.25
C178	AP19	44c cerise & blk	.80	.40
		Nos. C176-C178 (3)	2.00	.90

Organization of American States, 10th anniv.

1958, Dec. 10   **Perf. 11**

C179	AP20	23c blk & blue	.40	.25
C180	AP20	34c blk & yel grn	.60	.25
C181	AP20	44c blk & org red	1.00	.45
		Nos. C179-C181 (3)	2.00	.95

10th anniversary of the signing of the Universal Declaration of Human Rights.

"Flight" from Monument to Fallen Aviators — AP21

1959		**Litho.**		**Perf. 11**
		Size: 22x37½mm		
C182	AP21	3c bis brn & blk	.35	.25
C183	AP21	8c brt lil & blk	.35	.25
C184	AP21	38c black	.35	.25
C185	AP21	50c citron & blk	.35	.25
C186	AP21	60c vio & blk	.35	.25
C187	AP21	90c ol grn & blk	.40	.25
C188	AP21	1p blue & blk	.50	.25
C189	AP21	2p ocher & blk	1.75	.55
C190	AP21	3p grn & blk	2.00	.95
C191	AP21	5p vio brn & blk	2.50	1.50
C192	AP21	10p dp rose car & blk	8.00	4.25
		Nos. C182-C192 (11)	16.90	9.00

See Nos. C211-C222. For surcharge see No. Q97.

Alberto Santos-Dumont — AP22

1959, Feb. 13		**Wmk. 327**		**Perf. 11½**
C193	AP22	31c multi	.60	.25
C194	AP22	36c multi	.60	.25

Airplane flight of Alberto Santos-Dumont, Brazilian aeronaut, in 1906 in France.

Girl and Waves AP23

Designs: 38c, 60c, 1.05p, Compass and map of Punta del Este.

1959, Mar. 6				**Perf. 11½**
C195	AP23	10c ocher & lt bl	.30	.25
C196	AP23	38c grn & bis	.30	.25
C197	AP23	60c lilac & bister	.45	.25
C198	AP23	90c red org & grn	.60	.25
C199	AP23	1.05p blue & bister	.90	.55
		Nos. C195-C199 (5)	2.55	1.55

50th anniv. of Punta del Este, seaside resort.

Torch, YMCA Emblem and Chrismon AP24

Wmk. 327

1959, Dec. 22		**Litho.**		**Perf. 11½**
C200	AP24	38c emer, blk & gray	.50	.25
C201	AP24	50c bl, blk & gray	.50	.25
C202	AP24	60c red, blk & gray	.70	.50
		Nos. C200-C202 (3)	1.70	1.00

50th anniv. of the YMCA in Uruguay.

José Artigas and George Washington AP25

Refugees and WRY Emblem AP26

1960, Mar. 2				**Perf. 11½x12**
C203	AP25	38c red & blk	.30	.25
C204	AP25	50c brt bl & blk	.40	.25
C205	AP25	60c dp grn & blk	.65	.25
		Nos. C203-C205 (3)	1.35	.75

Pres. Eisenhower's visit to Uruguay, Feb. 1960.

No. C204 exists imperforate, but was not regularly issued in this form.

No. C150 Surcharged

1960, Apr. 8		**Unwmk.**		**Perf. 11**
C206	AP12	20c on 27c yel grn	.50	.25
a.		Perf. 12½	.50	.25

1960, June 6		**Wmk. 332**		
		Size: 24x35mm		
C207	AP26	60c brt lil rose & blk	.50	.25

World Refugee Year, 7/1/59-6/30/60.

Type of Regular Issue, 1960

Wmk. 332

1960, Nov. 4		**Litho.**		**Perf. 12**
C208	A186	38c bl & ol grn	.30	.25
C209	A186	50c bl & ver	.30	.25
C210	A186	60c bl & pur	.50	.25
		Nos. C208-C210 (3)	1.10	.60

Type of 1959 Redrawn with Silhouette of Airplane Added

1960-61		**Litho.**		**Perf. 12**
C211	AP21	3c blk & pale vio	.30	.25
C212	AP21	20c blk & crimson	.30	.25
C213	AP21	38c blk & pale bl	.30	.25
C214	AP21	50c blk & buff	.30	.25
C215	AP21	60c blk & dp grn	.40	.25
C216	AP21	90c blk & rose	.45	.25
C217	AP21	1p blk & gray	.60	.25
C218	AP21	2p blk & yel grn	.85	.25
C219	AP21	3p blk & red lil	1.10	.25
C220	AP21	5p blk & org ver	1.60	.50
C221	AP21	10p blk & yel	3.50	1.60
C222	AP21	20p blk & dk bl ('61)	7.50	3.25
		Nos. C211-C222 (12)	17.20	7.60

Pres. Gronchi and Flag Colors AP27

1961, Apr. 17		**Wmk. 332**		**Perf. 12**
C223	AP27	90c multi	.45	.25
C224	AP27	1.20p multi	.55	.25
C225	AP27	1.40p multi	.60	.40
		Nos. C223-C225 (3)	1.60	.90

Visit of President Giovanni Gronchi of Italy to Uruguay, April, 1961.

Carrasco National Airport AP28

1961, May 16		**Wmk. 332**		**Perf. 12**
		Building in Gray		
C226	AP28	1p lt vio	.30	.25
C227	AP28	2p ol gray	.70	.25
C228	AP28	3p orange	1.25	.40
C229	AP28	4p purple	1.50	.50
C230	AP28	5p aqua	2.00	.70
C231	AP28	10p lt ultra	4.00	1.25
C232	AP28	20p maroon	6.00	2.50
		Nos. C226-C232 (7)	15.75	5.85

Type of Regular "CIES" Issue, 1961

1961, Aug. 3		**Litho.**		**Wmk. 332**
C233	A189	20c blk & org	.40	.25
C234	A189	45c blk & grn	.40	.25
C235	A189	50c blk & gray	.40	.25
C236	A189	90c blk & plum	.40	.25
C237	A189	1p blk & dp rose	.50	.25
C238	A189	1.40p blk & lt vio	.60	.25
C239	A189	2p blk & bister	.70	.25
C240	A189	3p blk & lt bl	1.10	.30
C241	A189	4p blk & yellow	1.50	.55
C242	A189	5p blk & blue	2.00	.85
C243	A189	10p blk & yel grn	3.50	1.50
C244	A189	20p blk & dp pink	7.50	2.75
		Nos. C233-C244 (12)	19.00	7.70

Swiss Flag, Plow, Wheat Sheaf AP29

1962, Aug. 1		**Wmk. 332**		**Perf. 12**
C245	AP29	90c car, org & blk	.30	.25
C246	AP29	1.40p car, bl & blk	.50	.35

Cent. of the Swiss Settlement in Uruguay.

Red-crested Cardinal — AP30

Birds: 45c, White-capped tanager, horiz. 90c, Vermilion flycatcher. 1.20p, Great kiskadee, horiz. 1.40p, Fork-tailed flycatcher.

1962, Dec. 5		**Litho.**		**Perf. 12**
C247	AP30	20c gray, blk & red	.30	.25
C248	AP30	45c multi	.60	.25
C249	AP30	90c crim rose, blk & lt brn	1.25	.25
C250	AP30	1.20p lt bl, blk & yel	1.60	.25
C251	AP30	1.40p blue & sepia	2.40	.30
		Nos. C247-C251 (5)	6.15	1.30

No frame on #C248, thin frame on #C251. See #C258-C263. For surcharge see #C320.

Type of Regular UPAE Issue, 1963

1963, May 31		**Wmk. 332**		**Perf. 12**
C252	A195	45c bluish grn & blk	.25	.25
C253	A195	90c magenta & blk	.25	.25

Freedom from Hunger Type of Regular Issue

1963, July 9		**Wmk. 332**		**Perf. 12**
C254	A196	90c red & yel	.25	.25
C255	A196	1.40p violet & yel	.35	.35

"Alferez Campora" AP31

1963, Aug. 16				**Litho.**
C256	AP31	90c dk grn & org	.30	.25
C257	AP31	1.40p ultra & yel	.50	.40

Voyage around the world by the Uruguayan sailing vessel "Alferez Campora," 1960-63.

Bird Type of 1962

Birds: 1p, Glossy cowbird (tordo). 2p, Yellow cardinal. 3p, Hooded siskin. 5p, Sayaca tanager. 10p, Blue and yellow tanager. 20p, Scarlet-headed marsh-bird. All horizontal.

1963, Nov. 15		**Wmk. 332**		**Perf. 12**
C258	AP30	1p vio bl, blk & brn org	.80	.25
C259	AP30	2p lt brn, blk & yel	1.60	.30
C260	AP30	3p yel, brn & blk	2.40	.50
C261	AP30	5p emer, bl grn & blk	4.00	.70
C262	AP30	10p multi	8.00	1.25
C263	AP30	20p gray, org & blk	20.00	7.75
		Nos. C258-C263 (6)	36.80	10.75

Frame on Nos. C260-C263.

Pres. Charles de Gaulle AP32

2.40p, Flags of France and Uruguay.

1964, Oct. 9		**Litho.**		**Perf. 12**
C264	AP32	1.50p multi	.50	.25
C265	AP32	2.40p multi	1.25	.35

Charles de Gaulle, Pres. of France, Oct. 1964.

Submerged Statue of Ramses II — AP33

Design: 2p, Head of Ramses II.

1964, Oct. 30		**Litho.**		**Wmk. 332**
C266	AP33	1.30p multi	.30	.25
C267	AP33	2p bis, red brn & brt bl	1.25	.50
a.		Souv. sheet of 3, #713, C266-C267, imperf.	2.50	2.50

UNESCO world campaign to save historic monuments in Nubia.

National Flag AP34

1965, Feb. 18		**Wmk. 332**		**Perf. 12**
C268	AP34	50p gray, dk bl & yel	8.50	4.00

Kennedy Type of Regular Issue

1965, Mar. 5		**Wmk. 327**		**Perf. 11½**
C269	A202	1.50p gold, lil & blk	.30	.30
C270	A202	2.40p gold, brt bl & blk	.70	.70

Issue of 1864, No. 23 — AP35

6c, 8c, 10c denominations of 1864 issue.

Wmk. 332

1965, Mar. 19		**Litho.**		**Perf. 12**
C271		Sheet of 10	4.50	4.50
		"URUGUAY" at bottom		
a.	AP35	1p blue & black	.35	.35
b.	AP35	1p brick red & black	.35	.35
c.	AP35	1p green & black	.35	.35
d.	AP35	1p ocher & black	.35	.35
e.	AP35	1p carmine & black	.35	.35

"URUGUAY" at top

f.	AP35 1p blue & black	.35	.35
g.	AP35 1p brick red & black	.35	.35
h.	AP35 1p green & black	.35	.35
i.	AP35 1p ocher & black	.35	.35
j.	AP35 1p carmine & black	.35	.35

1st Rio de la Plata Stamp Show, sponsored jointly by the Argentine and Uruguayan philatelic associations, Montevideo, Mar. 19-28. No. C271 contains two horizontal rows of stamps and two rows of labels; Nos. C271a-C271e are in first row, Nos. C271f-C271j in second row. Adjacent labels in top and bottom rows.

For overprint see No. C298.

National Arms — AP36

1965, Apr. 30   Wmk. 332   Perf. 12
C272 AP36 20p multi   2.50 1.10

Type of Regular Issue and

Artigas Monument AP37

Designs: 1.50p, Artigas and wagontrain. 2.40p, Artigas quotation.

Perf. 11½x12, 12x11½
1965, May 17   Litho.   Wmk. 327
C273 AP37 1p multi   .25 .25
C274 A205 1.50p multi   .50 .25
C275 A205 2.40p multi   .90 .50
      Nos. C273-C275 (3)   1.60 .95

José Artigas (1764-1850), leader of the independence revolt against Spain.

Olympic Games Type of Regular Issue

Olympic Games Type of Regular Issue

Designs: 1p, Boxing. 1.50p, Running. 2p, Fencing. 2.40p, Sculling. 3p, Pistol shooting. 20p, Olympic rings.

1965, Aug. 3   Litho.   Perf. 12x11½
C276 A206 1p red, gray & blk   .25 .25
C277 A206 1.50p emer, bl & blk   .25 .25
C278 A206 2p dk car, bl & blk   .50 .25
C279 A206 2.40p lt ultra, org & blk .70 .35
C280 A206 3p lil, yel & blk   1.00 .50
C281 A206 20p dk vio bl, pink & lt bl 1.60 .85
      Nos. C276-C281 (6)   4.20 2.35

Souvenir Sheet

Designs: 5p, Stamp of 1924, No. 284. 10p, Stamp of 1928, No. 389.

C282 Sheet of 2   3.00 3.00
  a. 5p buff, blue & black   .95 .95
  b. 10p blue, black & rose red 1.40 1.40

18th Olympic Games, Tokyo, 10/10-25/64.

ITU Emblem and Satellite AP38

1966, Jan. 25   Wmk. 332   Perf. 12
C283 AP38 1p bl, bluish blk & ver .50 .25

Cent. of the ITU (in 1965).

Winston Churchill — AP39

1966, Apr. 29   Wmk. 332   Perf. 12
C284 AP39 2p car, brn & gold   .50 .25

Rio de Janeiro Type of Regular Issue

1966, June 9   Wmk. 332   Perf. 12
C285 A208 80c dp org & brn   .40 .25

International Cooperation Year Emblem AP40

1966, June 9   Litho.
C286 AP40 1p bluish grn & blk   .40 .25

UN International Cooperation Year.

President Zalman Shazar of Israel AP41

1966, June 21   Wmk. 327
C287 AP41 7p multi   1.00 .30

Visit of Pres. Zalman Shazar of Israel.

Crested Screamer — AP42

1966, July 7   Wmk. 327   Perf. 12
C288 AP42 100p bl, blk, red & gray 10.50 2.25

Jules Rimet Cup, Soccer Ball and Globe AP43

1966, July 11   Litho.
C289 AP43 10p dk pur, org & lil   1.00 .30

World Cup Soccer Championship, Wembley, England, July 11-30.

Bulls AP44

1966   Wmk. 327, 332 (10p)
C290 AP44 4p Hereford   .25 .25
C291 AP44 6p Holstein   .25 .25
C292 AP44 10p Shorthorn   .70 .25
C293 AP44 15p Aberdeen Angus   1.25 .35
C294 AP44 20p Norman   2.25 .55

C295 AP44 30p Jersey   3.00 .85
C296 AP44 50p Charolais   5.00 1.50
      Nos. C290-C296 (7)   12.70 4.00

Issued to publicize Uruguayan cattle. Issued: 4p, 50p, 8/13; 6p, 30p, 8/29; 10p, 15p, 20p, 9/26.

Boiso Lanza, Early Plane and Space Capsule AP45

1966, Oct. 14   Litho.   Perf. 12
C297 AP45 25p ultra, blk & lt bl 1.10 .50

Issued to honor Capt. Juan Manuel Boiso Lanza, pioneer of military aviation.

No. C271 Overprinted in Black

1966, Nov. 4   Wmk. 332
C298 Sheet of 10   4.50 4.50

"URUGUAY" at bottom
  a.-e. AP35 1p each   .35 .35
"URUGUAY" at top
  f.-j. AP35 1p each   .35 .35

2nd Rio de la Plata Stamp Show, Buenos Aires, Apr. 1966, sponsored by the Argentine and Uruguayan philatelic associations, and for the cent. of Uruguay's 1st surcharged issue. The addition of black numerals makes the designs resemble the surcharged issue of 1866, Nos. 24-28.

Labels in top row are overprinted "SEGUNDA MUESTRA 1966," in bottom row "SEGUNDAS JORNADAS 1966" and "CENTENARIO DEL SELLO / ESCUDITO RESELLADO" in both rows. One label each in top and bottom rows is overprinted "BUENOS AIRES / ABRIL 1966."

No. 613 Surcharged in Dark Blue

Perf. 12½x13
1966, Dec. 17   Engr.   Unwmk.
C299 A175 1p on 12c   .50 .25

Philatelic Club of Uruguay, 40th anniv.

Dante Alighieri — AP46   Planetarium Projector — AP47

Wmk. 332
1966, Dec. 27   Litho.   Perf. 12
C300 AP46 50c sepia & bister   .55 .25

Dante Alighieri (1265-1321), Italian poet.

1967, Jan. 13   Wmk. 332   Perf. 12
C301 AP47 5p dl bl & blk   .80 .30

Montevideo Municipal Planetarium, 10th anniv.

Archbishop Makarios and Map of Cyprus AP48

1967, Feb. 14   Wmk. 332   Perf. 12
C302 AP48 6.60p rose lil & blk .50 .25

Visit of Archbishop Makarios, president of Cyprus, Oct. 21, 1966.

Dr. Albert Schweitzer Holding Fawn — AP49

1967, Mar. 31   Litho.   Wmk. 332
C303 AP49 6p grn, blk, brn & sal .85 .85

Albert Schweitzer (1875-1965), medical missionary.

Corriedale Ram AP50

Various Rams: 4p, Ideal. 5p, Romney Marsh. 10p, Australian Merino.

1967, Apr. 5
C304 AP50 3p red org, blk & gray 1.75 .25
C305 AP50 4p emer, blk & gray   1.75 .25
C306 AP50 5p ultra, blk & gray   1.75 .25
C307 AP50 10p yel, blk & gray   1.75 .50
      Nos. C304-C307 (4)   7.00 1.25

Uruguayan sheep raising.

Flag of Uruguay and Map of the Americas AP51

1967, Apr. 8
C308 AP51 10p dk gray, bl & gold .85 .25

Meeting of American Presidents, Punta del Este, Apr. 10-12.

Numeral Stamps of 1866, Nos. 30-31 AP52

Design: 6p, Nos. 32-33; diff. frame.

Wmk. 332
1967, May 10   Litho.   Perf. 12
C309 AP52 3p bl, yel grn & blk   .45 .25
  a. Souvenir sheet of 4   1.50 1.50
C310 AP52 6p bis, dp rose & blk .55 .30
  a. Souvenir sheet of 4   2.50 2.50

Cent. of the 1866 numeral issue. Nos. C309a-C310a each contain 4 stamps similar to Nos. C309 and C310 respectively (the arrangement of colors differs in the souvenir sheets).

Ansina, Portrait by
Medardo
Latorre — AP53

1967, May 17
C311 AP53 2p gray, dk bl & red   .50 .25
   Issued to honor Ansina, servant of Gen.
José Artigas.

Plane
Landing
AP54

1967, May 30
C312 AP54 10p red, bl, blk & yel   .70 .25
   30th anniv. (in 1966) of PLUNA Airline.

Shooting for
Basket — AP55

Basketball Game — AP56

   Basketball Players in Action: No. C314,
Driving (ball shoulder high). No. C315, About
to pass (ball head high). No. C316, Ready to
pass (ball held straight in front). No. C317,
Dribbling with right hand.

1967, June 9
C313 AP55 5p multi   .40 .25
C314 AP55 5p multi   .40 .25
C315 AP55 5p multi   .40 .25
C316 AP55 5p multi   .40 .25
C317 AP55 5p multi   .40 .25
   a. Strip of 5, Nos. C313-C317   2.50 2.50
   Souvenir Sheet
C318 AP56 10p org, brt grn & blk 2.50 2.50
   5th World Basketball Championships, Mon-
tevideo, May 1967.
   For overprint see No. C349.

José Artigas, Manuel Belgrano, Flags
of Uruguay and Argentina — AP57

Wmk. 332
1967, June 19   Litho.   Imperf.
C319 AP57 5p bl, grn & yel   1.50 1.50
   3rd Rio de la Plata Stamp Show, Montevideo, Uruguay, June 18-25.
   For surcharge see No. 859.

   **Nos. C248 and C252 Surcharged in
Gold**
1967, June 22   Perf. 12
C320 AP30 5.90p on 45c multi   .45 .25
C321 A195 5.90p on 45c multi   .45 .25

Don Quixote and Sancho Panza,
Painted by Denry Torres — AP58

1967, July 10
C322 AP58 8p bister brn & brn   .60 .25
   Issued in honor of Miguel de Cervantes
Saavedra (1547-1616), Spanish novelist.
   For surcharge see No. C356.

Stone Axe — AP59

   Designs: 15p, Headbreaker stones. 20p,
Spearhead. 50p, Birdstone. 75p, Clay pot.
100p, Ornitholite (ritual sculpture), Balizas,
horiz. 150p, Lasso weights (boleadores).
200p, Two spearheads.

1967-68   Wmk. 332   Perf. 12
C323 AP59 15p gray & blk   .30 .25
C324 AP59 20p gray & blk   .30 .25
C325 AP59 30p gray & lt gray   .70 .25
C326 AP59 50p gray & blk   1.00 .25
C327 AP59 75p brn & blk   1.60 .35
C328 AP59 100p gray & blk   2.25 .70
C329 AP59 150p gray & blk
                           ('68)   2.50 .70
C330 AP59 200p gray & blk
                           ('68)   4.00 1.50
   Nos. C323-C330 (8)   12.65 4.25

Railroad
Crossing
AP60

1967, Dec. 4
C331 AP60 4p blk, yel & red   .50 .25
   10th Pan-American Highway Congress,
Montevideo.

Lions Emblem and
Map of South
America — AP61

1967, Dec. 29
C332 AP61 5p pur, yel & emer   .70 .25
   50th anniversary of Lions International.

Boy Scout
AP62

1968, Jan. 24   Litho.
C333 AP62 9p sepia & brick red   .75 .30
   Issued in memory of Robert Baden-Powell,
founder of the Boy Scout organization.

Sun, UN Emblem and Transportation
Means — AP63

1968, Feb. 29   Wmk. 332   Perf. 12
C334 AP63 10p gray, yel, lt & dk
                           bl   .50 .25
   Issued for International Tourist Year.

Octopus
AP64

   Marine Fauna: 20p, Silversides. 25p, Chara-
cin. 30p, Catfish, vert. 50p, Squid, vert.

1968   Wmk. 332   Perf. 12
C335 AP64 15p lt grn, bl & blk   1.00 .25
C336 AP64 20p brn, grn & bl   1.00 .25
C337 AP64 25p multi   1.50 .25
C338 AP64 30p bl, grn & blk   1.75 .50
C339 AP64 50p dp org, grn & dk
                           bl   2.75 .65
   Nos. C335-C339 (5)   8.00 1.90
Issued: 30p, 50p, 10/10; 15p, 20p, 25p, 11/5.

   Navy Type of Regular Issue
   Designs: 4p, Naval Air Force. 6p, Naval
arms. 10p, Signal flags, vert. 20p, Corsair
(chartered by General Artigas).

1968, Nov. 12   Litho.
C340 A226 4p bl, blk & red   .30 .25
C341 A226 6p multi   .30 .25
C342 A226 10p lt ultra, red & yel   .30 .25
C343 A226 20p ultra & blk   .50 .25
   Nos. C340-C343 (4)   1.40 .80

Rowing
AP65

1969, Feb. 11   Wmk. 332   Perf. 12
C344 AP65 30p shown   .60 .25
C345 AP65 50p Running   1.00 .35
C346 AP65 100p Soccer   1.75 .55
   Nos. C344-C346 (3)   3.35 1.15
   19th Olympic Games, Mexico City, 10/12-
27/68.

   Bicycling Type of Regular Issue
   Designs: 20p, Bicyclist and globe, vert.

1969, Mar. 21   Wmk. 332   Perf. 12
C347 A229 20p bl, pur & yel   .60 .25

"EFIMEX
68" and
Globe
AP66

1969, Apr. 10   Wmk. 332   Perf. 12
C348 AP66 20p dk grn, red & bl   .90 .25
   EFIMEX '68, International Philatelic Exhibi-
tion, Mexico City, Nov. 1-9, 1968.

   No. C318 Overprinted with Names of
Participating Countries, Emblem, Bars,
etc. and "CAMPEONATO MUNDIAL
DE VOLEIBOL"
1969, Apr. 25
   Souvenir Sheet
C349 AP56 10p org, brt grn & blk 1.10 1.10
   Issued to commemorate the World Volley-
ball Championships, Montevideo, Apr. 1969.

Book, Quill and
Emblem — AP67

1969, Sept. 16   Litho.   Perf. 12
C350 AP67 30p grn, org & blk   .75 .25
   10th Congress of Latin American Notaries.

Automobile Club
Emblem — AP68

1969, Oct. 7   Wmk. 332   Perf. 12
C351 AP68 10p ultra & red   .50 .25
   50th anniv. (in 1968) of the Uruguayan Automobile Club.

ILO Emblem
AP69

1969, Oct. 29   Litho.   Perf. 12
C352 AP69 30p dk bl grn & blk   .60 .25
   50th anniv. of the ILO.

Exhibition
Emblem — AP70

1969, Nov. 15   Wmk. 332   Perf. 12
C353 AP70 20p ultra, yel & grn   .60 .25
   ABUEXPO 69 Philatelic Exhibition, San
Pablo, Brazil, Nov. 15-23.

Rotary
Emblem and
Hemispheres
AP71

1969, Dec. 6   Perf. 12
C354 AP71 20p ultra, bl & bis   1.00 .30
   South American Regional Rotary Confer-
ence and the 50th anniv. of the Montevideo
Rotary Club.

Dr. Luis Morquio — AP72

1969, Dec. 22   Litho.   Wmk. 332
C355 AP72 20p org red & brn   .50   .25
Centenary of the birth of Dr. Luis Morquio, pediatrician.

No. C322 Surcharged "FELIZ AÑO 1970 / 6.00 / PESOS"

1969, Dec. 24
C356 AP58 6p on 8p bis brn & brn   .50   .25
Issued for New Year 1970.

Mahatma Gandhi and UNESCO Emblem AP73

1970, Jan. 26   Wmk. 332   Perf. 12
C357 AP73 100p lt bl & brn   5.00   .90
Mohandas K. Gandhi (1869-1948), leader in India's fight for independence.

Evaristo C. Ciganda — AP74   Giuseppe Garibaldi — AP75

1970, Mar. 10   Litho.
C358 AP74 6p brt grn & brn   .50   .25
Ciganda, author of the 1st law for teachers' pensions, birth cent.

1970, Apr. 7   Unwmk.   Perf. 12
C359 AP75 20p rose car & pink   .70   .25
Centenary of Garibaldi's command of foreign legionnaires in the Uruguayan Civil War.

Fur Seal AP76

Designs: 20p, Rhea, vert. 30p, Common tegu (lizard). 50p, Capybara. 100p, Mulita armadillo. 150p, Puma. 200p, Nutria.

1970-71   Wmk. 332   Perf. 12
C361 AP76 20p pur, emer & blk   1.25   .25
C362 AP76 30p emer, yel & blk   1.25   .30
C363 AP76 50p dl yel & brn   2.50   .50
C365 AP76 100p org, sep & blk   3.25   .75
C366 AP76 150p emer & brn   2.50   .85
C367 AP76 200p brt rose, brn & blk ('71)   6.00   2.25
C368 AP76 250p gray, bl & blk   7.00   2.25
    Nos. C361-C368 (7)   23.75   7.15

Soccer and Mexican Flag AP77

1970, June 2   Litho.   Perf. 12
C369 AP77 50p multi   1.10   .50
9th World Soccer Championships for the Jules Rimet Cup, Mexico City, 5/30-6/21.

"U N" and Laurel — AP78

1970, June 26   Wmk. 332   Perf. 12
C370 AP78 32p dk bl & gold   .60   .25
25th anniversary of the United Nations.

Eisenhower and US Flag — AP79

1970, July 14   Litho.
C371 AP79 30p gray, vio bl & red 1.00   .25
Issued in memory of Gen. Dwight David Eisenhower, 34th Pres. of US (1890-1969).

Neil A. Armstrong Stepping onto Moon — AP80

1970, July 21
C372 AP80 200p multi   5.00   1.50
1st anniv. of man's 1st landing on the moon.

Flag of the "Immortals" — AP81

1970, Aug. 24   Wmk. 332   Perf. 12
C373 AP81 500p bl, blk & red   7.00   7.00
The 145th anniversary of the arrival of the 33 "Immortals," the patriots, who started the revolution for independence.

Congress Emblem with Map of South America AP82

1970, Sept. 16   Unwmk.   Perf. 12
C374 AP82 30p bl, dk bl & yel   .80   .25
Issued to publicize the 5th Pan-American Congress of Rheumatology, Punta del Este.

Souvenir Sheet

Types of First Air Post Issue — AP83

1970, Oct. 1   Wmk. 332   Perf. 12½
C375 AP83 Sheet of 3   3.00   3.00
    a.   25p brown (Bl)   .90   .90
    b.   25p brown (R)   .90   .90
    c.   25p brown (G)   .90   .90
Stamp Day. #C375 contains 3 stamps similar to #C1-C3, but with denominations in pesos.

Flags of ALALC Countries — AP84

1970, Nov. 23   Litho.   Perf. 12
C376 AP84 22p multi   .75   .25
For the Latin-American Association for Free Trade (Asociación Latinoamericana de Libre Comercio).

Yellow Fever, by J. M. Blanes AP85

1971, June 8   Wmk. 332   Perf. 12
C377 AP85 50p blk, dk red brn & yel   .80   .35
Juan Manuel Blanes (1830-1901), painter.

Racial Equality, UN Emblem AP86

1971, June 28   Litho.
C378 AP86 27p blk, pink & bis   .65   .25
Intl. Year Against Racial Discrimination.

Congress Emblem with Maps of Americas AP87

1971, July 6   Wmk. 332   Perf. 12
C379 AP87 58p dl grn, blk & org 1.00   .40
12th Pan-American Congress of Gastroenterology, Punta del Este, Dec. 5-10, 1971.

Committee Emblem AP88

1971, Nov. 29
C380 AP88 30p bl, blk & yel   .85   .25
Inter-governmental Committee for European Migration.

Llama and Mountains AP89

1971, Dec. 30
C381 AP89 37p multi   1.00   .40
EXFILIMA '71, Third Inter-American Philatelic Exposition, Lima, Peru, Nov. 6-14.

Munich Olympic Games Emblem — AP90

Designs (Munich '72 Emblem and): 100p, Torchbearer. 500p, Discobolus.

1972, Feb. 1   Perf. 11½x12
C382 AP90 50p blk, red & org   .35   .25
C383 AP90 100p multi   .65   .40
C384 AP90 500p multi   3.50   2.00
    Nos. C382-C384 (3)   4.50   2.65
20th Olympic Games, Munich, 8/26-9/11.

Retort and WHO Emblem — AP91

1972, Feb. 22   Perf. 12
C385 AP91 27p multi   .70   .25
50th anniversary of the discovery of insulin by Frederick G. Banting and Charles H. Best.

Ship with Flags Forming Sails — AP92

1972, Mar. 6   Wmk. 332
C386 AP92 37p multi   .70   .25
Stamp Day of the Americas.

1924 and 1928 Gold Medals, Soccer — AP93

Design: 300p, Olympic flag, Motion and Munich emblems, vert.

1972, June 12   Litho.   Perf. 12
C387 AP93 100p bl & multi   .75 .75
C388 AP93 300p multi   2.25 2.25

20th Olympic Games, Munich, 8/26-9/11.

Cross AP94

1972, Aug. 10
C389 AP94 37p vio & gold   .45 .25

Dan A. Mitrione (1920-70), slain US official.

Interlocking Squares and UN Emblem — AP95

1972, Aug. 16
C390 AP95 30p gray & multi   .60 .25

3rd UN Conf. on Trade and Development (UNCTAD III), Santiago, Chile, Apr.-May 1972.

Brazil's "Bull's-eye," 1843 — AP96

Wmk. 332
1972, Aug. 26   Litho.   Perf. 12
C391 AP96 50p grn, yel & bl   .60 .25

4th Inter-American Philatelic Exhibition, EXFILBRA, Rio de Janeiro, Aug. 26-Sept. 2.

Map of South America, Compass Rose — AP97

1972, Sept. 28
C392 AP97 37p multi   .45 .25

Uruguay's support for extending territorial sovereignty 200 miles into the sea.

Adoration of the Kings and Shepherds, by Rafael Perez Barradas — AP98

1972, Oct. 12
C393 AP98 20p lemon & multi + label   .65 .25

Christmas 1972 and first biennial exhibition of Uruguayan painting, 1970.

WPY Emblem AP99

Wmk. 332
1974, Aug. 20   Litho.   Perf. 12
C394 AP99 500p gray & red   1.10 .70

World Population Year 1974.

Soccer, Olympics and UPU Emblems AP100

Anniversaries and events: No. C398a, 17th UPU Congress, Lausanne. No. C398b, World Soccer Federation, 1st South American president. No. C398c, 1976 Summer and Winter Olympics, Innsbruck and Montreal.

1974, Aug. 30
C395 AP100 200p grn & multi   1.00 1.00
C396 AP100 300p org & multi   1.00 1.00
C397 AP100 500p multicolored   9.00 9.00
Souvenir Sheet
C398   Sheet of 3   70.00 70.00
a.-c.   AP100 500p any single 20.00 20.00

Centenary of Universal Postal Union. Nos. C397-C398 had limited distribution.

Mexico No. O1 and Mexican Coat of Arms AP101

Wmk. 332
1974, Oct. 15   Litho.   Perf. 12
C399 AP101 200p multi   .60 .25

EXFILMEX '74 5th Inter-American Philatelic Exhibition, Mexico City, Oct. 26-Nov. 3.

Christmas Type of 1974

240p, Kings following star. 2500p, Virgin & Child.

1974
C400 A315 240p multi   .60 .25
Miniature Sheet
C401 A315 2500p multi   5.00 5.00

Issued: 240p, Dec. 27; 2500p, Dec. 31.

Spain No. 1, Colors of Spain and Uruguay — AP102

1975, Mar. 4
C402 AP102 400p multi   .70 .25

Espana 75, International Philatelic Exhibition, Madrid, Apr. 4-13.

Souvenir Sheet

Nos. C253, 893 and C402 — AP103

Wmk. 332
1975, Apr. 4   Litho.   Perf. 12
C403 AP103 Sheet of 3   6.50 6.50
a.   1000p No. C253   2.00 2.00
b.   1000p No. 893   2.00 2.00
c.   1000p No. C402   2.00 2.00

Espana 75 Intl. Phil. Exhib., Madrid, Apr. 4-13.

1976 Summer & Winter Olympics, Innsbruck & Montreal AP104

1975, May 16   Perf. 12
C404 AP104 400p shown   1.00 .60
C405 AP104 600p Flags, Olympic rings   1.50 .95

Souvenir Sheets
C406   Sheet of 2   42.50 42.50
a.   AP104 500p Montreal emblem 12.50 12.50
b.   AP104 1000p Innsbruck emblem 27.50 27.50
C407   Sheet of 2   42.50 42.50
a.   AP104 500p Emblems, horiz. 12.50 12.50
b.   AP104 1000p Flags, horiz.   27.50 27.50

Nos. C404-C407 had limited distribution.

Floor Design for Capitol, Rome AP105

1975, Aug. 15
C408 AP105 1p multi   1.50 1.50

500th birth anniversary of Michelangelo Buonarroti (1475-1564), Italian sculptor, painter and architect.

Apollo-Soyuz Space Mission, USA & Uruguay Independence — AP106

Anniversaries and events: 15c, Apollo-Soyuz spacecraft. 20c, Apollo-Soyuz spacecraft. 25c, Artigas monument, vert. 30c, George Washington, Pres. Artigas. No. C412, Early Aircraft, vert. No. C413a, Apollo spacecraft, astronauts. No. C413c, US and Uruguayan Declarations of Independence. No. C413c, Modern aircraft. No. C413d, UN Secretaries General. No. C414c, Boiso Lanza, aviation pioneer. 1p, Flags of UN and Uruguay.

1975, Sept. 29
C409 AP106 10c multicolored   1.10 .85
C410 AP106 15c multicolored   1.60 1.25
C411 AP106 25c multicolored   2.00 1.40
C412 AP106 50c multicolored   2.75 1.75
    Nos. C409-C412 (4)   7.45 5.25
Souvenir Sheets
C413   Sheet of 4   42.50 42.50
a.-d. AP106 40c any single   9.00 9.00
C414   Sheet of 4   42.50 42.50
a.   AP106 20c multicolored   1.75 1.75
b.   AP106 30c multicolored   4.25 4.25
c.   AP106 50c multicolored   7.25 7.25
d.   AP106 1p multicolored   16.00 16.00

Nos. C409-C414 had limited distribution.

Sun, Uruguay No. C59 and other Stamps — AP108

Wmk. 332
1975, Oct. 13   Litho.   Perf. 12
C415 AP108 1p blk, gray & yel 3.25 1.60

Uruguayan Stamp Day.

Montreal Olympic Emblem and Argentina '78 — AP109   **Flags of US and Uruguay — AP110**

UPU and UPAE Emblems AP111

Wmk. 332
1975, Oct. 14   Litho.   Perf. 11½
C416 AP109 1p multi   2.00 .70
C417 AP110 1p multi   2.00 .70
C418 AP111 1p multi   2.00 .70
a.   Souvenir sheet of 3   22.50 22.50
    Nos. C416-C418 (3)   6.00 2.10

EXFILMO '75 and ESPAMER '75 Stamp Exhibitions, Montevideo, Oct. 10-19. No. C418a contains 3 stamps similar to Nos. C416-C418, 2p each.

Ocelot
AP112

Orchid: #C416, Oncidium bifolium.

1976, Jan.   Litho.   Perf. 12
C419 AP112 50c vio bl & multi   .85   .35
C420 AP112 50c emer & multi   .85   .35

Souvenir Sheets

Olympics, Soccer, Telecommunications
and UPU — AP113

1976, June 3   Perf. 11½
C422 Sheet of 3   55.00 55.00
  a. AP113 30c Soccer player   6.50   6.50
  b. AP113 70c Alexander Graham
      Bell   15.00 15.00
  c. AP113 1p UPU emblem, UN
      #5   22.50 22.50
C423 Sheet of 3   55.00 55.00
  a. AP113 40c Discus thrower   6.50   6.50
  b. AP113 60c Telephone, cent. 10.00 10.00
  c. AP113 2p UPU emblem, UN
      #11   27.50 27.50

Nos. C422-C423 had limited distribution.

Anniversaries and Events Type of 1976
Souvenir Sheets

20c, Frederick Passy, Henri Dunant. 35c, Nobel prize, 75th anniv. 40c, Viking spacecraft. 60c, 1976 Summer Olympics, Montreal. 75c, US space missions. 90c, 1976 Summer Olympics, diff.
World Cup Soccer Championships, Argentina: 1p, Uruguay, 1930 champions. 1.50p, Uruguay, 1950 champions.

1976, Nov. 12   Perf. 12
C424 Sheet of 4   40.00 40.00
  a. A355 20c multicolored   2.75   2.75
  b. A355 40c multicolored   5.00   5.00
  c. A355 60c multicolored   7.25   7.25
  d. A355 1.50p multicolored   17.50 17.50
C425 Sheet of 4   40.00 40.00
  a. A355 35c multicolored   5.50   5.50
  b. A355 75c multicolored   7.75   7.75
  c. A355 90c multicolored   8.75   8.75
  d. A355 1p multicolored   11.00 11.00

Nos. C424-C425 had limited distribution.

Nobel Prize Type of 1977
Souvenir Sheets

Anniversaries and events: 10c, World Cup Soccer Championships. 40c, Victor Hess, Nobel Prize in Physics. 60c, Max Plank, Nobel Prize in Physics. 80c, Graf Zeppelin. Concorde. 90c, Virgin and Child by Rubens. 1.20p, World Cup Soccer Championships, diff. 1.50p, Eduardo Bonilla, Count von Zeppelin. 2p, The Nativity by Rubens.

1977, July 21
C426 Sheet of 4   35.00 35.00
  a. A361 10c multicolored   1.00   1.00
  b. A361 60c multicolored   4.00   4.00
  c. A361 80c multicolored   6.00   6.00
  d. A361 2p multicolored   14.00 14.00
C427 Sheet of 4   35.00 35.00
  a. A361 40c multicolored   2.50   2.50
  b. A361 90c multicolored   6.50   6.50
  c. A361 1.20p multicolored   7.50   7.50
  d. A361 1.50p multicolored   11.00 11.00

Nos. C426-C427 had limited distribution.

Uruguay
Natl.
Postal
System,
150th
Anniv.
AP114

1977, July 27
C428 AP114 8p multicolored   12.00 12.00

Souvenir Sheet
C429 AP114 10p multicolored 17.00 17.00

No. C428, imperf., was not valid for postage. Souvenir sheets sold in the package with No. C429 were not valid for postage.
For overprint see No. C435.

Paintings Type of 1978

Paintings: 1p, St. George Slaying Dragon by Durer. 1.25p, Duke of Lerma by Rubens. No. 432a, Madonna and Child by Durer. No. 432b, Holy Family by Rubens. No. 432c, Flight from Egypt by Francisco de Goya (1746-1828).

1978, June 13   Perf. 12½
C430   A374 1p brn & blk   4.25   4.25
C431   A374 1.25p blk & brn   4.50   4.50

Souvenir Sheet
C432   Sheet of 3   19.00 19.00
  a.-c. A374 1p any single   5.25   5.25

Nos. C430-C432 had limited distribution.

Souvenir Sheet

ICAO, 30th Anniv. and 1st Powered
Flight, 75th Anniv. — AP115

Designs: a, Concorde, Dornier DO-x. b, Graf Zeppelin, Wright Brothers' Flyer. c, Space shuttle and De Pinedo's plane.

1978, June 13
C433   Sheet of 3   25.00 25.00
  a.-c. AP115 1p any single   6.50   6.50

No. C433 had limited distribution.

Souvenir Sheet

World Cup Soccer Championships,
Argentina — AP116

1978, June 13   Perf. 12
C434   Sheet of 3   55.00 55.00
  a. AP116 50c multicolored   5.00   5.00
  b. AP116 1.50p multicolored 13.50 13.50
  c. AP116 2p multicolored   20.00 20.00

No. C434 had limited distribution.

No. C428 Overprinted in Black

1978, Aug. 28
C435 AP114 8p multicolored   7.50   3.00

No. C435 had limited distribution.

Madonna and Child Type of 1979

Various Madonna and Child etchings by Albrecht Dürer with Intl. Year of the Child emblem at: a, UL. b, UR.

Wmk. 332

1979, June 18   Litho.   Perf. 12½
C436 A390 1.50p Sheet of 2,
                      #a-b   26.00 26.00

No. C436 had limited distribution.

Boiso
Lanza,
Wright
Brothers
AP117

75th anniv. of powered flight.

1979, June 18   Perf. 12½
C437 AP117 1.80p multicolored 3.50   1.50

No. C437 had limited distribution.
Issued in sheet of 24 containing 6 blocks of 4r with margin around. See Nos. 1040-1042.

Souvenir Sheet

1982 World Cup Soccer
Championships, Spain — AP118

1979, June 18   Perf. 12
C438 AP118 Sheet of 3   40.00 40.00
  a. 50c Jules Rimet cup   3.00   3.00
  b. 2.50p Uruguay flag   12.50 12.50
  c. 3p Espana '82   17.00 17.00

No. C438 had limited distribution.

Souvenir Sheet

Rowland Hill Cent. — AP119

1979, June 18
C439 AP119 Sheet of 2   40.00 40.00
  a. 2p Uruguay #1, C1   20.00 20.00
  b. 2p Great Britain #1, 836 20.00 20.00

No. C439 had limited distribution.

AIR POST SEMI-POSTAL STAMPS

> Catalogue values for unused stamps in this section are for Never Hinged items.

Type of Semi-Postal Stamps, 1959
Wmk. 327

1959, Dec. 29   Litho.   Perf. 11½
CB1 SP2 38c + 10c brown & org   .30   .30
CB2 SP2 60c + 10c gray grn &
              org   .50   .50

Issued for national recovery.

SPECIAL DELIVERY STAMPS

No. 242 Overprinted

1921, Aug.   Unwmk.   Perf. 11½
E1   A97 2c fawn   .70   .25
  a.   Double overprint   4.25

Caduceus — SD1

Imprint: "IMP. NACIONAL."
1922, Dec. 2   Litho.   Wmk. 188
Size: 21x27mm

E2   SD1 2c light red   .50   .25

1924, Oct. 1

E3   SD1 2c pale ultra   .50   .25

1928   Unwmk.   Perf. 11

E4   SD1 2c light blue   .50   .25

Imprint: "IMPRA. NACIONAL."
1928-36   Wmk. 188
Size: 16½x19½mm.

E5   SD1 2c black, *green*   .25   .25

Unwmk.

E6   SD1 2c blue green ('29) .25   .25

Perf. 11½, 12½
E7 SD1 2c blue ('36) .25 .25
Nos. E5-E7 (3) .75 .75

1944, Oct. 23 **Perf. 12½**
E8 SD1 2c salmon pink .25 .25

> Catalogue values for unused stamps in this section, from this point to the end of the section, are for Never Hinged items.

1947, Nov. 19
E9 SD1 2c red brown .25 .25

No. E9 Surcharged in Black

$ 0 05
MENSAJERIAS

1957, Oct. 30
E10 SD1 5c on 2c red brown .25 .25

LATE FEE STAMPS

Galleon and Modern Steamship — LF1

Wmk. Crossed Keys in Sheet
1936, May 18   Litho.   Perf. 11
I1 LF1 3c green .25 .25
I2 LF1 5c violet .25 .25
I3 LF1 6c blue green .25 .25
I4 LF1 7c brown .25 .25
I5 LF1 8c carmine .50 .50
I6 LF1 12c deep blue .65 .65
Nos. I1-I6 (6) 2.15 2.15

POSTAGE DUE STAMPS

D1

1902 Unwmk. Engr. Perf. 14 to 15
Size: 21¼x18½mm
J1 D1 1c blue green .50 .25
J2 D1 2c carmine .50 .25
J3 D1 4c gray violet .80 .25
J4 D1 10c dark blue 1.25 .25
J5 D1 20c ocher 2.00 .80
Nos. J1-J5 (5) 5.05 1.80

Surcharged in Red

PROVISORIO
UN cent'mo.

1904
J6 D1 1c on 10c dk bl 1.00 1.00
a. Inverted surcharge 10.00 10.00

1913-15   Litho.   Perf. 11½
Size: 22½x20mm
J7 D1 1c lt grn .60 .25
J8 D1 2c rose red .60 .25
J9 D1 4c dl vio .80 .25
J10 D1 6c dp brn 1.00 .40
Size: 21¼x19mm
J11 D1 10c dl bl 1.00 .40
Nos. J7-J11 (5) 4.00 1.55

Imprint: "Imprenta Nacional"
1922   Size: 20x17mm
J12 D1 1c bl grn .25 .25
J13 D1 2c red .25 .25
J14 D1 3c red brn .50 .25
J15 D1 4c brn vio .30 .25
J16 D1 5c blue .50 .25
J17 D1 10c gray grn .50 .25
Nos. J12-J17 (6) 2.30 1.50

1926-27   Wmk. 188   Perf. 11
Size: 20x17mm
J18 D1 1c bl grn ('27) .50 .25
J19 D1 3c red brn ('27) .50 .25
J20 D1 5c slate blue .50 .25
J21 D1 6c light brown .50 .50
Nos. J18-J21 (4) 2.00 1.25

1929   Unwmk.   Perf. 10½, 11
J22 D1 1c blue green .25 .25
J23 D1 10c gray green .50 .25

Figure of Value Redrawn (Flat on sides)
1932   Wmk. 188
J24 D1 6c yel brn .50 .25

Imprint: "Casa A. Barreiro Ramos S. A."
1935 Unwmk. Litho. Perf. 12½
Size: 20x17mm
J25 D1 4c violet .50 .25
J26 D1 5c rose .50 .25

Type of 1935
Imprint: "Imprenta Nacional" at right
1938
J27 D1 1c blue green .25 .25
J28 D1 2c red brown .25 .25
J29 D1 3c deep pink .25 .25
J30 D1 4c light violet .25 .25
J31 D1 5c blue .25 .25
J32 D1 8c rose .25 .25
Nos. J27-J32 (6) 1.50 1.50

OFFICIAL STAMPS

Regular Issues Handstamped in Black, Red or Blue

Many double and inverted impressions exist of the handstamped overprints on Nos. O1-O83. Prices are the same as for normal stamps or slightly more.

On Stamps of 1877-79
1880-82   Unwmk.   Rouletted 8
O1 A9 1c red brown 4.00 3.50
O2 A10 5c green 3.00 2.50
O3 A11 20c bister 3.25 3.25
O4 A11 50c black 22.00 22.00
O5 A12 1p blue 22.00 22.00
Nos. O1-O5 (5) 54.25 53.25

On No. 44   Rouletted 6
O6 A9 1c brown ('81) 6.00 6.00

On Nos. 43-43A   Rouletted 8
O7 A11 50c black (R) 17.00 16.00
O8 A12 1p blue (R) 22.50 20.00

On Nos. 45, 41, 37a   Perf. 12½
O9 A13 7c blue (R) ('81) 4.25 3.25
Rouletted 8
O10 A11 10c ver (Bl) 2.00 2.00
Perf. 13½
O11 A8b 15c yellow (Bl) 5.00 4.50

On Nos. 46-47
1883   Perf. 12½
O12 A14 1c green 6.50 6.50
O13 A14a 2c rose 9.50 9.50

On Nos. 50-51
Perf. 12½, 12x12½, 13
O14 A17 5c blue (R) 4.00 4.00
a. Imperf., pair 4.50
O15 A18 10c brown (Bl) 6.50 6.50
a. Imperf., pair 6.00

No. 48 Handstamped

FRANCO

1884   Perf. 12½
O16 A15 1c green 35.00 32.50

Overprinted Type "a" in Black
On Nos. 48-49
1884   Perf. 12, 12x12½, 13
O17 A15 1c green 35.00 32.50
O18 A16 2c red 12.00 9.50

On Nos. 53-56   Rouletted 8
O19 A11 1c on 10c ver 2.00 1.60
a. Small "1" (No. 53a) 5.00

Perf. 12½
O20 A14a 2c rose 6.50 6.50
O21 A22 5c ultra 6.50 6.50
O22 A23 5c blue 5.00 2.00
Nos. O17-O22 (6) 67.00 58.60

On Stamps of 1884-88
1884-89   Rouletted 8
O23 A24 1c gray 12.00 5.00
O24 A24 1c green ('88) 2.50 1.60
O25 A24 1c olive grn 3.25 1.75
O26 A24a 2c vermilion 1.00 .60
O27 A24a 2c rose ('88) 2.25 1.25
O28 A24b 5c slate blue 2.25 1.25
O29 A24b 5c slate bl, bl 6.50 5.00
O30 A24b 5c violet ('88) 6.50 5.00
O31 A24b 5c lt blue ('89) 6.50 5.00
O32 A25 7c dk brown 3.25 1.60
O33 A25 7c orange ('89) 3.25 2.25
O34 A26 10c olive brn 2.00 .90
O35 A26 10c violet ('89) 16.00 9.50
O36 A27 20c red violet 3.00 1.60
O37 A27 20c bister brn ('89) 16.00 7.00
O38 A28 25c gray violet 3.50 2.50
O39 A28 25c vermilion ('89) 16.00 7.00
Nos. O23-O39 (17) 105.75 59.30

The OFICIAL handstamp, type "a," was also applied to No. 73, the 5c violet with "Provisorio" overprint, but it was not regularly issued.

On No. 71
1887   Rouletted 9
O40 A29 10c lilac 5.00
No. O40 was not regularly issued.

On Stamps of 1889-1899
Perf. 12½ to 15 and Compound
1890-1900
O41 A32 1c green .80 .25
O43 A32 1c blue ('95) 2.00 2.00
O44 A33 2c rose .80 .25
O45 A33 2c red brn ('95) 2.50 2.50
O46 A33 2c orange ('00) .80 .80
O47 A34 5c deep blue 1.50 1.50
O48 A34 5c rose ('95) 2.00 2.00
O49 A35 7c bister brown 1.25 .80
O50 A35 7c green ('95) 25.00
O51 A36 10c blue green 1.25 .80
O52 A36 10c orange ('95) 25.00
O53 A37 20c orange 1.25 .80
O54 A37 20c brown ('95) 25.00
O55 A38 25c red brown 1.25 .80
O56 A38 25c ver ('95) 55.00
O57 A39 50c lt blue 4.50 4.50
O58 A39 50c lilac ('95) 5.50 5.50
O59 A40 1p lilac 7.00 5.00
O60 A40 1p lt blue ('95) 40.00 22.50
Nos. O50, O52, O54, O56 and O60 were not regularly issued.

On No. 99
1891   Rouletted 8
O61 A24b 5c violet 1.50 1.25
a. "1391" 9.00

On Stamps of 1895-99
Perf. 12½ to 15 and Compound
1895-1900
O62 A51 1c bister .60 .60
O63 A51 1c slate blue ('97) 1.25 .55
O64 A52 2c blue .25 .25
O65 A52 2c claret ('97) 1.25 .55
O66 A53 5c red .80 .55
O67 A53 5c green ('97) 1.25 .55
O68 A53 5c grnsh blue ('00) .95 .75
O69 A54 7c deep green .50 .50
O70 A55 10c brown .50 .50
O71 A56 20c green & blk .80 .80
O72 A56 20c claret & blk ('97) 4.50 2.25
O73 A57 25c red brn & blk .80 .80
O74 A57 25c pink & bl ('97) 4.50 2.25
O75 A58 50c blue & blk .95 .95
O76 A58 50c grn & brn ('97) 5.75 2.75
O77 A59 1p org brn & blk 4.75 4.75
O78 A59 1p yel brn & bl ('97) 9.25 5.75
a. Inverted overprint
Nos. O62-O78 (17) 38.65 25.10

On Nos. 133-135
1897, Sept.
O79 A62 1c brown vio & blk 1.25 1.00
O80 A63 5c pale bl & blk 1.75 1.00
O81 A64 10c lake & blk 1.75 1.10
Nos. O79-O81 (3) 4.75 3.10

On Nos. 136-137
Perf. 12½ to 15 and Compound
1897-1900
O82 A68 10c red 2.50 1.50
O83 A68 10c red lilac ('00) 1.25 1.25

Regular Issue of 1900-01 Overprinted

OFICIAL

1901   Perf. 14 to 16
O84 A72 1c yellow green .50 .25
O85 A75 2c vermilion .65 .25
O86 A73 5c dull blue .65 .25
O87 A76 7c brown orange .90 .50
O88 A74 10c gray violet .95 .55
O89 A37 20c lt blue 8.00 4.00
O90 A38 25c bister brown 1.60 .80
O91 A40 1p deep green 10.50 6.00
a. Inverted overprint 12.50 8.00
Nos. O84-O91 (8) 23.75 12.60

Most of the used official stamps of 1901-1928 have been punched with holes of various shapes, in addition to the postal cancellations.

Regular Issue of 1904-05 Overprinted

OFICIAL

1905   Perf. 11½
O92 A79 1c green .50 .25
O93 A80 2c orange red .50 .25
O94 A81 5c deep blue .50 .25
O95 A82 10c dark violet 1.00 .40
O96 A83 20c gray green 3.25 1.00
a. Inverted overprint
O97 A84 25c olive bister 2.25 .80
Nos. O92-O97 (6) 8.00 2.95

Regular Issues of 1904-07 Overprinted

OFICIAL

1907, Mar.
O98 A79 1c green .25 .25
O99 A86 5c deep blue .25 .25
O100 A86 7c orange brown .25 .25
O101 A82 10c dark violet .25 .25
O102 A83 20c gray green .40 .35
a. Inverted overprint 4.00
O103 A84 25c olive bister .50 .40
O104 A86 50c rose .95 .70
Nos. O98-O104 (7) 2.85 2.45

Regular Issues of 1900-10 Overprinted

OFICIAL 1910

1910, July 15   Perf. 14½ to 16
O105 A75 2c vermilion 8.75 4.00
O106 A73 5c slate green 5.25 3.00
O107 A74 10c gray violet 2.75 1.25
O108 A37 20c grnsh blue 2.75 1.25
O109 A38 25c bister brown 4.50 2.40
Perf. 11½
O110 A86 50c rose 6.00 2.50
a. Inverted overprint 20.00 15.00
Nos. O105-O110 (6) 30.00 14.40

Peace—O1

1911, Feb. 18   Litho.
O111 O1 2c red brown .40 .25
O112 O1 5c dark blue .40 .40
O113 O1 8c slate .40 .65
O114 O1 20c gray brown .55 .95

O115 O1 23c claret .80 .95
O116 O1 50c orange 1.60 1.25
O117 O1 1p red 4.00 1.50
Nos. O111-O117 (7) 8.15 5.95

Regular Issue of
1912-15 Overprinted

1915, Sept. 16
O118 A90 2c carmine .55 .40
O119 A90 5c dark blue .55 .40
O120 A90 8c ultra .55 .40
O121 A90 20c dark brown 1.25 .50
O122 A91 23c dark blue 4.00 3.50
O123 A91 50c orange 6.00 3.50
O124 A91 1p vermilion 8.00 4.00
Nos. O118-O124 (7) 20.90 12.70

Regular Issue of 1919
Overprinted

1919, Dec. 25
O125 A95 2c red & black .80 .40
a. Inverted overprint 3.50
O126 A95 5c ultra & blk .95 .40
O127 A95 8c gray bl & lt brn .95 .40
a. Inverted overprint 3.50
O128 A95 20c brown & blk 2.00 .80
O129 A95 23c green & brn 2.00 .80
O130 A95 50c brown & bl 4.00 2.00
O131 A95 1p dull red & bl 10.00 4.00
a. Double overprint 15.00
Nos. O125-O131 (7) 20.70 8.80

Regular Issue of 1923
Overprinted

1924 **Wmk. 189** **Perf. 12½**
O132 A100 2c violet .25 .25
O133 A100 5c light blue .25 .25
O134 A100 12c deep blue .30 .25
O135 A100 20c buff .40 .25
O136 A100 36c blue green 1.75 .50
O137 A100 50c orange 3.50 2.50
O138 A100 1p pink 6.25 5.00
O139 A100 2p lt green 12.00 10.00
Nos. O132-O139 (8) 24.70 19.75

Same Overprint on Regular Issue of
1924

1926-27 **Unwmk.** **Imperf.**
O140 A100 2c rose lilac .40 .25
O141 A100 5c pale blue .65 .25
O142 A100 8c pink ('27) .80 .25
O143 A100 12c slate blue .95 .25
O144 A100 20c brown 2.00 .40
O145 A100 36c dull rose 3.25 .95
Nos. O140-O145 (6) 8.05 2.35

Regular Issue of 1924
Overprinted

1928 **Perf. 12½**
O146 A100 2c rose lilac 1.50 .95
O147 A100 8c pink 1.50 .50
O148 A100 10c turq blue 2.00 .50
Nos. O146-O148 (3) 5.00 1.95

Since 1928, instead of official stamps, Uruguay has used envelopes with "S. O." printed on them, and stamps of many issues which are punched with various designs such as star or crescent.

NEWSPAPER STAMPS

No. 245 Surcharged

1922, June 1 **Unwmk.** **Perf. 11½**
P1 A97 3c on 4c orange .40 .40
a. Inverted surcharge 9.50 9.50
b. Double surcharge 2.50 2.50

Nos. 235-237
Surcharged

1924, June 1 **Perf. 14½**
P2 A96 3c on 2c car & blk .40 .40
P3 A96 6c on 4c red org & bl .40 .40
P4 A96 9c on 5c bl & brn .40 .40
Nos. P2-P4 (3) 1.20 1.20

Nos. 288, 291, 293 Overprinted or
Surcharged in Red

1926 **Imperf.**
P5 A100 3c gray green .80 .25
a. Double overprint 1.00 1.00
P6 A100 9c on 10c turq bl .95 .40
a. Double surcharge 1.00 1.00
P7 A100 15c light violet 1.25 .50
Nos. P5-P7 (3) 3.00 1.15

PARCEL POST STAMPS

Mercury — PP1

Imprint: "IMPRENTA NACIONAL"
Perf. 11½
1922, Jan. 15 **Litho.** **Unwmk.**
Size: 20x29½mm
Inscribed "Exterior"
Q1 PP1 5c grn, *straw* .25 .25
Q2 PP1 10c grn, *bl gray* .40 .25
Q3 PP1 20c grn, *rose* 2.10 .55
Q4 PP1 30c grn, *grn* 2.10 .25
Q5 PP1 50c grn, *blue* 3.50 .40
Q6 PP1 1p grn, *org* 5.25 1.60
Nos. Q1-Q6 (6) 13.60 3.30

Inscribed "Interior"
Q7 PP1 5c grn, *straw* .25 .25
Q8 PP1 10c grn, *bl gray* .25 .25
Q9 PP1 20c grn, *rose* 1.00 .25
Q10 PP1 30c grn, *grn* 1.40 .25
Q11 PP1 50c grn, *blue* 2.25 .35
Q12 PP1 1p grn, *org* 6.00 1.25
Nos. Q7-Q12 (6) 11.15 2.60

Imprint: "IMP. NACIONAL"
Inscribed "Exterior"
1926, Jan. 20 **Perf. 11½**
Q13 PP1 20c grn, *rose* 1.75 .50

Inscribed "Interior"
Perf. 11
Q14 PP1 5c grn, *yellow* .40 .25
Q15 PP1 10c grn, *bl gray* .50 .25
Q16 PP1 20c grn, *rose* 1.00 .25
Q17 PP1 30c grn, *bl grn* 1.75 .40
Nos. Q13-Q17 (5) 5.40 1.65

Inscribed "Exterior"
1926 **Perf. 11½**
Q18 PP1 5c blk, *straw* .40 .25
Q19 PP1 10c blk, *bl gray* .65 .25
Q20 PP1 20c blk, *rose* 1.75 .25

Inscribed "Interior"
Q21 PP1 5c blk, *straw* .40 .25
Q22 PP1 10c blk, *bl gray* .50 .25
Q23 PP1 20c blk, *rose* 1.00 .25
Q24 PP1 30c blk, *bl grn* 1.75 .40
Nos. Q18-Q24 (7) 6.45 1.90

PP2 PP3

Perf. 11, 11½
1927, Feb. 22 **Wmk. 188**
Q25 PP2 1c dp bl .25 .25
Q26 PP2 2c lt grn .25 .25
Q27 PP2 4c violet .25 .25
Q28 PP2 5c red .25 .25
Q29 PP2 10c dk brn .40 .25
Q30 PP2 20c rose .65 .40
Nos. Q25-Q30 (6) 2.05 1.65

See Nos. Q35-Q38, Q51-Q54.

1928, Nov. 20 **Perf. 11**
Size: 15x20mm
Q31 PP3 5c blk, *straw* .25 .25
Q32 PP3 10c blk, *gray blue* .25 .25
Q33 PP3 20c blk, *rose* .50 .25
Q34 PP3 30c blk, *green* .80 .25
Nos. Q31-Q34 (4) 1.80 1.00

Type of 1927 Issue
1929-30 **Unwmk.** **Perf. 11, 12½**
Q35 PP2 1c violet .25 .25
Q36 PP2 1c ultra ('30) .25 .25
Q37 PP2 2c bl grn ('30) .25 .25
Q38 PP2 5c red ('30) .25 .25
Nos. Q35-Q38 (4) 1.00 1.00

Nos. Q35-Q38, and possibly later issues, occasionally show parts of a papermaker's watermark.

PP4

1929, July 27 **Wmk. 188** **Perf. 11**
Q39 PP4 10c orange .50 .50
Q40 PP4 15c slate blue .50 .50
Q41 PP4 20c ol brn .50 .50
Q42 PP4 25c rose red 1.00 .50
Q43 PP4 50c dark gray 2.00 1.00
Q44 PP4 75c violet 8.00 6.00
Q45 PP4 1p gray green 7.50 3.00
Nos. Q39-Q45 (7) 20.00 12.00

For overprints see Nos. Q57-Q63.

Ship and Numeral of
Train — PP5 Value — PP6

1938-39 **Unwmk.** **Perf. 12½**
Q46 PP5 10c scarlet .40 .25
Q47 PP5 20c dk bl .60 .25
Q48 PP5 30c lt vio ('39) .95 .25
Q49 PP5 50c green 1.75 .25
Q50 PP5 1p brn org 2.50 1.10
Nos. Q46-Q50 (5) 6.20 2.10

See Nos. Q70-Q73, Q80, Q88-Q90, Q92-Q93, Q95.

Type of 1927 Redrawn
1942-55? **Litho.** **Perf. 12½**
Q51 PP2 1c vio ('55) .25 .25
Q52 PP2 2c bl grn .25 .25
Q54 PP2 5c lt red ('44) .25 .25

The vertical and horizontal lines of the design have been strengthened, the "2"

---

redrawn, etc. No. Q51 has oval "O" in CENTESIMO, 2¼mm from frame line at right; No. Q35 has round "O" 1¾mm from frame line.

1943, Apr. 28 **Engr.**
Q55 PP6 1c dk car rose .25 .25
Q56 PP6 2c grnsh blk .25 .25

Parcel Post
Stamps of
1929
Overprinted in
Black

1943, Dec. 15 **Wmk. 188** **Perf. 11**
Q57 PP4 10c orange 1.00 .50
Q58 PP4 15c slate blue 1.00 .50
Q59 PP4 20c olive brn 1.00 .50
Q60 PP4 25c rose red 1.50 1.00
Q61 PP4 50c dk gray 2.50 2.00
Q62 PP4 75c violet 5.00 4.00
Q63 PP4 1p gray grn 8.00 4.50
Nos. Q57-Q63 (7) 20.00 13.00

Catalogue values for unused stamps in this section, from this point to the end of the section, are for **Never Hinged** items.

Bank of the University — PP8
Republic — PP7

Perf. 12½
1945, Sept. 5 **Litho.** **Unwmk.**
Q64 PP7 1c green .25 .25
Q65 PP8 2c brt vio .25 .25

See Nos. Q77-Q79, Q84.

Custom House — PP9

1946, Dec. 11 **Perf. 11½**
Q66 PP9 5c yel brn & bl .25 .25

Type A141 Overprinted
in Red

1946, Dec. 27 **Perf. 12½**
Q67 A141 1p light blue .95 .25

See Nos. Q69, Q76.

Mail Coach — PP11

1946, Dec. 23
Q68 PP11 5p red & ol brn 12.00 5.00

Type A141 Overprinted in Black

1947
Q69 A141 2c dull violet brn .25 .25
See Nos. Q74-Q76.

Type of 1938
1947-52 Unwmk. Perf. 12½
Q70 PP5 5c brown org ('52) .25 .25
Q71 PP5 10c violet .25 .25
Q72 PP5 20c vermilion .40 .25
Q73 PP5 30c blue .55 .25
Nos. Q70-Q73 (4) 1.45 1.00

Type of 1947
1948-49 Black Overprint
Q74 A141 1c rose lilac ('49) .25 .25
Q75 A141 5c ultra .25 .25
Q76 A141 5p rose carmine 4.00 1.75
Nos. Q74-Q76 (3) 4.50 2.25

Types of 1945
1950
Q77 PP8 1c vermilion .25 .25
Q78 PP7 2c chalky blue .25 .25

1952 Perf. 11
Q79 PP7 10c blue green .25 .25

Type of 1938-39
1954 Perf. 12½
Q80 PP5 20c carmine .25 .25

Custom House — PP13

1p, State Railroad Administration Building.

1955 Unwmk. Litho. Perf. 12½
Q81 PP13 5c brown .25 .25
Q82 PP13 1p light ultra 2.10 1.60
See Nos. Q83, Q85-Q86, Q96. For surcharge see No. Q87.

Types of 1945 and 1955
Design: 20c, Solis Theater.

1956-57 Perf. 11
Q83 PP13 5c gray ('57) .30 .25
Q84 PP7 10c lt olive grn .25 .25
Q85 PP13 20c yellow .25 .25
Q86 PP13 20c lt red brn ('57) .25 .25
Nos. Q83-Q86 (4) 1.05 1.00

No. Q83 Surcharged with New Value in Red
1957
Q87 PP13 30c on 5c gray .25 .25

Type of 1938-39
1957-60 Wmk. 327 Perf. 11
Q88 PP5 20c lt blue ('59) .25 .25
Unwmk.
Q89 PP5 30c red lilac .25 .25
Perf. 12½
Q90 PP5 1p dk blue ('60) .50 .50
Nos. Q88-Q90 (3) 1.00 1.00
Nos. Q88 and Q93 are in slightly larger format-17¼x21mm instead of 16x19½mm.

National Printing Works PP14

1960, Mar. 23 Wmk. 327 Perf. 11
Q91 PP14 30c yellow green .25 .25

Type of 1938-39
1962-63 Wmk. 332 Perf. 11
Q92 PP5 50c slate green .25 .25
Perf. 10½
Q93 PP5 1p blue grn ('63) .50 .50

No. C158 Surcharged

1965 Unwmk. Perf. 11
Q94 AP12 5p on 84c orange .35 .25
For use on regular and air post parcels.

Types of 1938-55
1p, State Railroad Administration Building.
1966 Litho. Perf. 10½
Q95 PP5 10c blue green .25 .25
Wmk. 327
Q96 PP13 1p brown .25 .25

No. C184 Surcharged in Red

1966 Unwmk. Perf. 11
Q97 AP21 1p on 38c black .25 .25

Plane and Bus — PP15

Design: 20p, Plane facing left and bus; "Encomiendas" on top.

Wmk. 332
1969, July 8 Litho. Perf. 12
Q98 PP15 10p blk, crim & bl grn .25 .25
Q99 PP15 20p bl, blk & yel .40 .25

No. B7 Surcharged

1971, Feb. 3 Wmk. 327 Perf. 11½
Q100 SP2 60c on 1p + 10c 1.25 .60

No. 761 Surcharged in Red

1971, Nov. 12 Wmk. 332 Perf. 12
Q101 A226 60c on 6p lt grn & blk .45 .25

Nos. 770-771 Surcharged

1972, Nov. 6 Litho. Perf. 12
Q102 A233 1p on 6p multi (#770) 1.40 .55
Q103 A233 1p on 6p multi (#771) 1.40 .55
a. Pair, #Q102-Q103 3.00 1.10
See note after No. 771.

Parcels and Arrows PP16

Old Mail Truck PP17

Designs: Early means of mail transport.

1974 Wmk. 332 Litho. Perf. 12
Q104 PP16 75p shown .25 .25
Q105 PP17 100p shown .40 .25
Q106 PP17 150p Steam engine .95 .95
Q107 PP17 300p Side-wheeler .90 .55
Q108 PP17 500p Plane 1.40 .80
Nos. Q104-Q108 (5) 3.90 2.80
Issue dates: 75p, Feb. 13; others, Mar. 6.

UZBEKISTAN

ˌuz-ˌbe-ki-'stan

LOCATION — Central Asia, bounded by Kazakhstan, Turkmenistan, Tajikistan, Afghanistan and Kyrgyzstan
GOVT. — Independent republic, member of the Commonwealth of Independent States
AREA — 172,741 sq. mi.
POP. — 25,155,064 (2001 est.)
CAPITAL — Tashkent (Toshkent)

With the breakup of the Soviet Union on Dec. 26, 1991, Uzbekistan and ten former Soviet republics established the Commonwealth of Independent States.

100 Kopecks = 1 Ruble
100 Tiyin = 1 Sum

Catalogue values for all unused stamps in this country are for Never Hinged items.

Princess Nadira (1792-1842) — A1

Perf. 11½x12
1992, May 7 Unwmk. Photo.
1 A1 20k multicolored .35 .35

Melitaea Acreina A2

1992, Aug. 31 Litho. Perf. 12
2 A2 1r multicolored .30 .30

Independence from Soviet Union, 1st Anniv. — A3

1992, Sept. 25 Photo. Perf. 12
3 A3 1r multicolored .30 .30

Khiva Mosque, 19th Cent. — A4

1992, Oct. 20 Perf. 11½
4 A4 50k multicolored .30 .30

Samarkand — A5

1992, Oct. 28 Litho. Perf. 13x13½
5 A5 10r multicolored .60 .60
Winner of 1992 Aga Khan Award for Architecture.

Samovar, 19th Cent. — A6

1992, Nov. 20 Perf. 12x11½
6 A6 50k multicolored .35 .35

Fauna A7

Designs: 1r, Teratoscincus scincus. No. 8, Naja oxiana. No. 9, Ondatra zibethica, vert. 3r, Pandion haliaetus, vert. 5r, Remiz pendulinus, vert. 10r, Dryomys nitedula, vert. 15r, Varanus griseus. 20r, Cervus elaphus baktrianus.

1993, Mar. 12 Litho. Perf. 12
7 A7 1r multicolored .25 .25
8 A7 2r multicolored .25 .25
9 A7 2r multicolored .25 .25
10 A7 3r multicolored .25 .25
11 A7 5r multicolored .25 .25
12 A7 10r multicolored .45 .45
13 A7 15r multicolored .75 .75
Nos. 7-13 (7) 2.45 2.45
Souvenir Sheet
14 A7 20r multicolored 1.00 1.00

Russia Nos. 4596-4600, 5838, 5841-5843, 5984 Surcharged in Vio Bl, Brt Bl, Bl, Red, Blk and Grn

a

Methods and perfs as before 1993

15	A2765	2r on 1k (#5838, BB)	.60	.60
16	A2138	8r on 4k (#4599, BI)	.55	.55
17	A2138	15r on 2k (#4597)	4.50	4.50
18	A2765	15r on 2k (#5984)	4.50	4.50
19	A2765	15r on 3k (#5839, R)	4.50	4.50
20	A2765	15r on 4k (#4520, V)	4.50	4.50
21	A2765	15r on 4k (#5840, R)	4.50	4.50
22	A2765	15r on 5k (#5841)	4.50	4.50
23	A2139	15r on 6k (#4600, R)	4.50	4.50
24	A2765	15r on 7k (#5985a, R)	4.50	4.50
25	A2765	15r on 10k (#5842)	4.50	4.50
26	A2765	15r on 15k (#5843, R)	4.50	4.50
27	A2138	20r on 4k (#4599, Bk)	.75	.75
28	A2139	30r on 3k (#4598, G)	.75	.75
28A	A2138	100r on 1k (#4596, R)	.90	.90
29	A2138	500r on 1k (#4596, BI)	5.25	5.25
		Nos. 15-29 (16)	53.80	53.80

No. 18 exists imperf.

Flag and Coat of Arms — A8

Perf. 12x12½, 11½x12 (#33)

1993, June 10   Litho.

30	A8	8r multicolored	.30	.30
31	A8	15r multicolored	.35	.35
33	A8	50r multicolored	.85	.85
34	A8	100r multicolored	2.00	2.00
		Nos. 30-34 (4)	3.50	3.50

No. 33 is 19x26½mm.

Flowers — A9

1993, Sept. 10   Perf. 12

38	A9	20r Dianthus uzbekistanicus	.25	.25
39	A9	20r Colchicum kesselringii	.25	.25
40	A9	25r Crocus alatavicus	.30	.30
41	A9	25r Salvia bucharica	.00	.30
42	A9	30r Tulipa kaufmanniana	.35	.35
43	A9	30r Tulipa greigii	.35	.35
		Nos. 38-43 (6)	1.80	1.80

Souvenir Sheet

| 44 | A9 | 50r Tulip | 1.00 | 1.00 |

Coat of Arms — A10

1994-95   Litho.   Perf. 12

45	A10	1t green	.25	.25

Perf. 11½x12

| 46 | A10 | 75s claret | .35 | .35 |

Issued: 1t, 3/20/95; 75s, 7/2.

1995   Litho.   Perf. 14

| 47 | A10 | 2s green | 1.00 | 1.00 |

Size: 20x33mm

48	A10	3s carmine	1.00	1.00
49	A10	6s carmine	1.50	1.50
49A	A10	15s blue	2.25	2.25

Denomination Shown with Decimal

50	A10	3s carmine	.35	.35
51	A10	6s blue	1.50	1.50
		Nos. 45-51 (8)	8.20	8.20

Issued: 15s, 12/26; others, 4/18.
See Nos. 151A-154, 167-171, 228-237, 405-415.

Statue of Tamerlane, Tashkent — A10a

1994, Sept. 1   Litho.   Perf. 12½x12

| 52 | A10a | 20t multicolored | .40 | .40 |

Bakhouddin, 675th Anniv. — A11

1994, Aug. 1   Perf. 12½x12

| 55 | A11 | 100s multi + label | .50 | .50 |

Souvenir Sheet

President's Cup Intl. Tennis Tournament, Tashkent — A12

1994, June 3   Perf. 12x12½

| 56 | A12 | 500s multicolored | 1.25 | 1.25 |

Ulugh Beg (1394-1449), Astronomer — A13

30t, Portals of Samarkand. 35t, Portals of Bukhara. 40t, Globe, astrolabe. 45t, Statue. 60t, Portrait.

1994, Sept. 15   Litho.   Perf. 12x12½

57	A13	30t multi + label	.30	.30
58	A13	35t multi + label	.30	.30
59	A13	40t multi + label	.30	.30
60	A13	45t multi + label	.70	.70
		Nos. 57-60 (4)	1.60	1.60

Souvenir Sheet

| 61 | A13 | 60t multicolored | 1.40 | 1.40 |

Russia Nos. 4596, 5113, 5839, 5840, 5843, 5984 Surcharged in Red Violet or Red

b

Methods and perfs as before 1995, Jan.

61A	A2138(a)	2s on 1k (#4596, R)	1.50	1.50
61B	A2765(a)	2s on 3k (#5839, R)	1.50	1.50
61C	A2765(b)	200s on 2k (#5984)	1.50	1.50
61D	A2765(b)	200s on 4k (#5840)	1.50	1.50
61E	A2436(b)	200s on 5k (#5113)	1.50	1.50
61F	A2765(b)	200s on 15k (#5843)	1.50	1.50
		Nos. 61A-61F (6)	9.00	9.00

No. 61C exists imperf.

Souvenir Sheet

End of World War II, 50th Anniv. — A14

1995, May 8   Litho.   Perf. 12

| 62 | A14 | 20s multicolored | 3.00 | 3.00 |

Souvenir Sheet

UPU — A15

1995, Sept. 21

| 63 | A15 | 20s multicolored | 2.50 | 2.50 |

Capra Falconeri A16

1995, Aug. 15   Perf. 12½

64	A16	6s shown	.90	.50
65	A16	10s Three on mountain	1.50	.75
66	A16	10s Up close	1.50	.75
67	A16	15s Lying down	2.25	1.25
		Nos. 64-67 (4)	6.15	3.25

World Wildlife Fund.

Intl. Tennis Tournament, Tashkent '95 — A17

1995, Aug. 25   Perf. 14

| 68 | A17 | 10s multicolored | 2.25 | 2.25 |

Silk Road Architecture A19

Designs: 6s, Mosque, 15th cent. No. 71, Blue-domed mosque, ruins, 15th cent. No. 72, Mosque with 4 minarets, 19th cent. No. 73, Cylindrical-style mosque, 19th cent. 20s, Map of mosque sites, camel, mosque.

1995, Aug. 28   Litho.   Perf. 12x12½

70	A19	6s multicolored	1.25	1.25
71	A19	10s multicolored	2.50	2.50
72	A19	10s multicolored	2.50	2.50
73	A19	15s multicolored	3.75	3.75
		Nos. 70-73 (4)	10.00	10.00

Souvenir Sheet

| 74 | A19 | 20s multicolored | 6.00 | 6.00 |

Folktales — A20

6s, Man wrestling with creature, woman spilling bowls. #76, Man looking at stork, nest of eggs. #77, Women watching man cut into watermelon full of gold coins. #78, Creature carrying woman. 15s, Man holding beads, parrot.

1995, Aug. 24

75	A20	6s multi + label	1.90	1.90
76	A20	10s multicolored	2.75	2.75
77	A20	10s multicolored	2.75	2.75
78	A20	10s multicolored	2.75	2.75
79	A20	15s multicolored	4.00	4.00
		Nos. 75-79 (5)	14.15	14.15

Moths A21

6s, Karanasa abramovi. #81, Colias romanovi. #82, Parnassius delphius. #83, Neohipparchia fatua. #84, Chasara staudingeri. #85, Colias wiskotti. 15s, Parnassius tianschanicus. 20s, Colias christophi.

1995, Oct. 10   Perf. 12½x12

80	A21	6s multicolored	1.40	1.40
81	A21	10s multicolored	2.25	2.25
82	A21	10s multicolored	2.25	2.25
83	A21	10s multicolored	2.25	2.25
84	A21	10s multicolored	2.25	2.25
85	A21	10s multicolored	2.25	2.25
86	A21	15s multicolored	3.00	3.00
		Nos. 80-86 (7)	15.65	15.65

Souvenir Sheet

| 87 | A21 | 20s multicolored | 3.75 | 3.75 |

Aircraft A22

1995, Oct. 10

88	A22	6s JIN-2	1.10	1.10
89	A22	10s IL-76	1.75	1.75
90	A22	10s KA-22	1.75	1.75
91	A22	10s AN-8	1.75	1.75
92	A22	10s AN-22	1.75	1.75
93	A22	10s AN-12	1.75	1.75
94	A22	15s IL-114	2.50	2.50
		Nos. 88-94 (7)	12.35	12.35

Souvenir Sheet

| 95 | A22 | 20s like No. 94 | 3.75 | 3.75 |

Wildlife from Tashkent Zoo — A23

Designs: 6s, Camelus ferus. No. 97, Aegupius monachus. No. 98, Ursus arctos isabellinus. No. 99, Zebra. No. 100, Macaca mulatta. No. 101, Pelecanus crispus. 15s, Loxodonta africana.

20s, Capra falconeri.

1995, Nov. 30			Perf. 12x12½	
96	A23	6s multicolored	1.10	1.10
97	A23	10s multicolored	1.75	1.75
98	A23	10s multicolored	1.75	1.75
99	A23	10s multicolored	1.75	1.75
100	A23	10s multicolored	1.75	1.75
101	A23	10s multicolored	1.75	1.75
102	A23	15s multicolored	2.50	2.50
	Nos. 96-102 (7)		12.35	12.35

Souvenir Sheet

103	A23	20s multicolored	3.25	3.25

Wild Animals A24

Designs: 10s, Ovis ammon bocharensis. No. 105, Ovis ammon severtzov. No. 106, Cervus elaphus bactrianus. No. 107, Capra sibirica. No. 108, Ovis ammon karelini. No. 109, Ovis ammon cycloceros. 20s, Saiga tatarica.

25s, Gazella subgutturosa.

1996, Feb. 16			Perf. 12½x12	
104	A24	10s multicolored	1.25	1.25
105	A24	15s multicolored	1.90	1.90
106	A24	15s multicolored	1.90	1.90
107	A24	15s multicolored	1.90	1.90
108	A24	15s multicolored	1.90	1.90
109	A24	15s multicolored	1.90	1.90
110	A24	20s multicolored	2.75	2.75
	Nos. 104-110 (7)		13.50	13.50

Souvenir Sheet

111	A24	25s multicolored	3.50	3.50

Painting A25

1995, Oct.		Litho.	Perf. 12x12½	
112	A25	15s multicolored	1.75	1.75

Souvenir Sheet

Save the Aral Sea — A26

a, 15s, Felis caracal. b, 15s, Salmo trutta aralensis. c, 20s, Hyaena hyaena. d, 20t,

Pseudoscaphirynchus kaufmanni. e, 25t, Aspiolucius esocinus.

1996, May 15			Perf. 14	
113	A26	Sheet of 5, #a.-e.	5.50	5.50

See Kazakhstan #145, Kyrgyzstan #107, Tadjikistan #91, Turkmenistan #52.

1996 Summer Olympic Games, Atlanta A27

1996, June 23		Litho.	Perf. 12½x12	
114	A27	6s Soccer	.60	.60
115	A27	10s Equestrian event	1.25	1.25
116	A27	15s Boxing	1.75	1.75
117	A27	20s Cycling	2.50	2.50
	Nos. 114-117 (4)		6.10	6.10

Souvenir Sheet

Tamerlane (1336-1405) — A28

1996, Aug. 31		Litho.	Perf. 14	
118	A28	20s multicolored	4.50	4.50
a.	Inscribed "1336-1404," perf 12x12½		6.00	6.00

Issued: No. 118a, 8/9/96.

Souvenir Sheet

Independence Day — A29

1996, Aug. 27		Litho.	Perf. 12x12½	
119	A29	20s multicolored	2.50	2.50

Tashkent Tennis Cup Championship A30

1996, Sept. 2		Litho.	Perf. 14	
121	A30	12s green	8.00	8.00

A31   A32

1996, Sept. 18			Perf. 14	
122	A31	15s Faijzulla Khodjaev	6.00	6.00

1996, Oct. 14		Litho.	Perf. 14	
123	A32	15s black & buff	6.00	6.00

Abdurauf Fitrat (1886-1996).

Futuristic Space Travel — A33

9s, Shuttle-type vehicle. #126, Vehicle in front of sun. #127, Sun's rays, vehicle traveling left. #128, Large vehicle, sun in distance. #129, Saucer-shaped vehicle landing on planet. 25s, Two men in cockpit.

30s, Two different space vehicles.

1997, Mar. 17				
124	A33	9s multi, vert.	1.00	1.00
125	A33	15s shown	1.50	1.50
126	A33	15s multi	1.50	1.50
127	A33	15s multi	1.50	1.50
128	A33	15s multi, vert.	1.50	1.50
129	A33	15s multi, vert.	1.50	1.50
130	A33	25s multi, vert.	2.25	2.25
	Nos. 124-130 (7)		10.75	10.75

Souvenir Sheet

131	A33	30s multi, vert.	6.00	6.00

Fairy Tales A34

#132, Genie. #133, Bird. #134, Child holding mirror in front of couple. #135, Ape. #136, Face of creature, horse. #137, Large bird attacking deer. 30s, Two people kneeling before throne.

35s, Man on horse.

1997, Apr. 18				
132	A34	15s multicolored	1.10	1.10
133	A34	15s multicolored	1.10	1.10
134	A34	20s multicolored	1.40	1.40
135	A34	20s multicolored	1.40	1.40
136	A34	25s multicolored	1.60	1.60
137	A34	25s multicolored	1.60	1.60
138	A34	30s multicolored	2.25	2.25
	Nos. 132-138 (7)		10.45	10.45

Souvenir Sheet

139	A34	35s multicolored	6.50	6.50

Abdulhamid Sulaymon, Birth Cent. — A35

1997, June 20				
140	A35	6s lilac, black & gray	2.00	2.00

Pantera Pardus Tullianus A36

Designs: No. 142, Yawning. No. 143, Stretching. 25s, Walking on fallen tree. 30s, With mouth open.

1997, May 28				
141	A36	9s multicolored	.95	.95
142	A36	15s multicolored	1.75	1.75
143	A36	15s multicolored	1.75	1.75
144	A36	25s multicolored	3.25	3.25
	Nos. 141-144 (4)		7.70	7.70

Souvenir Sheet

145	A36	30s multicolored	3.75	3.75

No. 145 contains one 30x40mm stamp.

Sites on Silk Road A37

In Bukhara: No. 146, Ancient citadel. No. 147, Tomb of Ismail Samani. No.

In Khiva: No. 148, Minaret, vert. No. 149, Fortress wall with open door.

No. 150, Mosque, Bukhara. No. 151, Minaret, Khiva, diff., vert.

1997		Litho.	Perf. 14	
146	A37	15s multicolored	2.50	2.50
147	A37	15s multicolored	2.50	2.50
148	A37	15s multicolored	2.50	2.50
149	A37	15s multicolored	2.50	2.50
	Nos. 146-149 (4)		10.00	10.00

Souvenir Sheets

150	A37	30s multicolored	3.00	3.00
151	A37	30s multicolored	3.00	3.00

Issued: Nos. 146-147, 150, 10/7; Nos. 148-149, 151, 10/8.

Arms Type of 1994 Redrawn

1998		Litho.	Perf. 14	
		Size: 14x22mm		
151A	A10	2s green	.40	.40
152	A10	3s carmine, "1998"	1.25	1.25
a.	Dated "1999"		.50	.50
153	A10	6s green, "1998"	3.00	3.00
a.	Dated "1999"		.70	.70
153A	A10	12s green	2.75	2.75
153B	A10	15s red	1.75	1.75
154	A10	45s blue	4.25	4.25
	Nos. 151A-154 (6)		13.40	13.40

Nos. 152-154 have country name "O'ZBEKISTON" at top and "POCHTA 1998" at bottom.

Issued: 6s, 2/25; 12s, 15s, 45s, 3/25; 2s, 4/16; 3s, 4/17.

Intl. Tennis Tournament, Tashkent A38

Emblem and: No. 155, President's Cup. No. 156, Tennis player. No. 157, Camel.

1997		Litho.	Perf. 14	
155	A38	6s blue & grn	3.00	3.00
156	A38	6s blue & grn	3.00	3.00
157	A38	6s blue & grn	3.00	3.00
	Nos. 155-157 (3)		9.00	9.00

Automobiles — A39

a, 9s, Tico. b, 12s, Damas. c, 15s, Nexia.

1997, Sept. 19   Litho.   Perf. 14
158 A39 Block of 3, #a.-c. + label   6.00 6.00

Tennis
Tournament
A40

Sharq Taronlalari
Intl. Music
Festival
A41

1998, Aug. 17   Litho.   Perf. 14
159 A40 15s multicolored   1.50 1.50

1998, July 15
160 A41 15s multicolored   1.00 1.00

Berdaq
Monument
A42

Kamoliddin
Behzod, Poet
A43

1998, Aug. 17
161 A42 15s blue & brown   1.00 1.00

1998, Aug. 17
162 A43 15s multicolored   1.40 1.40

Imam Al-Buxorily
A44

Ahmad Al-
Fargoni
A45

1998, June 26
163 A44 15s multicolored   1.00 1.00

1998, June 26
164 A45 15s multicolored   1.50 1.50

Folktales — A46

Designs: a, 8s, Woman holding baby. b,
10s, "Alpomish" over rainbow. c, 15s, Three
men seated before fire. d, 15s, Man talking to
man with sword. e, 18s, Man riding horse. f,
18s, Knight with longbow, squire with arrow. g,
20s, Swordmaker at work. h, 20s, Man fighting
lion. i, 25s, Man, woman walking arm in arm.

1998, Nov. 27   Litho.   Perf. 14
165 A46 Sheet of 9, #a.-i.   7.50 7.50

No. 165 is a continuous design.

Arms Type of 1994 Redrawn
1999-2001   Litho.   Perf. 14
Size: 14x23mm
167 A10 5s blue green,
          "2000"   .50 .50
  a. Dated "2004"   .50 .50
  b. Dated "2005"   .50 .50
168 A10 6s green   1.00 1.00
168A A10 10s dk green   .50 .50
  d. 10s emerald, dated "2004" .50 .50
168B A10 15s lt blue   .85 .85
168C A10 17s dk blue   .90 .90
169 A10 30s blue   1.00 1.00
170 A10 40s rose, "2000"   1.00 1.00
  b. Dated "2001"   .90 .90
170A A10 45s rose   1.75 1.75
  c. 45s carmine, dated "2001" 2.10 2.10
171 A10 60s rose car   1.75 1.75
          Nos. 167-171 (9)   9.25 9.25

Issued: 6s, 3/22/99. 15s, 17s, 30s, 45s,
12/5/00. 5s, 60s, 1/17/01; No. 168A, 40s,
2/5/01. No. 168Ad, 6/15/04.
Nos. 167-171 have country name
"O'ZBEKISTON" at top and "POCHTA" and
year at bottom. Stamps issued in 2001 are
inscribed "2000".
No. 168 is inscribed "6 so'm." No. 153 is
inscribed "6-00."

Trains — A47

Locomotives: #172, OV steam, 1897-1917.
#173, EA steam, 1931-35. 28s, FD steam,
1931-41. 36s, SO steam, 1934-52. #176, VL-
22 electric. #177, KCh. 69s, TEP-6.

1999, May 11   Litho.   Perf. 14
172 A47 18s multicolored   .70 .70
173 A47 18s multicolored   .70 .70
174 A47 28s multicolored   1.00 1.00
175 A47 36s multicolored   1.10 1.10
176 A47 56s multicolored   2.00 2.00
177 A47 56s multicolored   2.00 2.00
178 A47 69s multicolored   2.25 2.25
          Nos. 172-178 (7)   9.75 9.75

A48

Designs: 18s, Horse rearing.
No. 180, horiz.: a, 36s, Robed rider on
horse. b, 28s, White horse. c, 69s, Jockey on
race horse.
75s, Black horse, horiz.

1999, May 25
179 A48 18s multicolored   3.00 3.00
180 A48 Vert. strip of 3, #a.-
          c.   8.00 8.00
Souvenir Sheet
181 A48 75s multicolored   6.50 6.50

No. 180 printed in sheets of 8 stamps containing 2 strips and one each of Nos. 180a and
180c.

A49

Story of Badal Qorachi — #182: a, 18s,
Woman, deer. b, 18s, Two archers on horses.
c, 28s, Archer on horse. d, 36s, White giant. e,
56s, Black giant. f, 56s, Troll, cat, bones. g,
Man, woman.
75s, Woman on sofa, demon, horiz.

1999, June 8
182 A49 Sheet of 7, #a.-g. + la-
          bel   7.50 7.50
Souvenir Sheet
183 A49 75s multicolored   3.25 3.25

A50

A51

Reptiles: No. 184, Trapelus sanguinolentus.
No. 185, horiz.: a, 18s, Eremias arguta. b,
18s, Vipera ursinii. c, 28s, Phrynocephalus
mystaceus. d, 36s, Agkistrodon halys. e, 56s,
Eumeces schneideri. f, 69s, Vipera lebetina.
75s, Two lizards, horiz.

1999, June 22
184 A50 56s multicolored   1.25 1.25
185 A50 Sheet of 6, #a.-f. 6.25 6.25
Souvenir Sheet
186 A50 75s multicolored   3.75 3.75

1999, July 7
187 A51 45s light green & black 1.60 1.60
UPU, 125th anniv.

A52

1999, July 21
188 A52 30s green & claret 1.25 1.25
Muhammadrizo Erniyozbek ogli-Ogahiy, poet.

A53

Birds of Prey: No. 189, Circaetus qallicus.
No. 190, Falco tinnunculus. No. 191, Aquila
chrysaetos. No. 192, Gyps fulvus. 36s, Falco
cherrug. 56s, Gypaetus barbatus. 60s, Pandion haliaetus.
75s, Bird, hatchlings.

1999, Oct. 22   Litho.   Perf. 14x13¾
189 A53 15s multi   .80 .80
190 A53 15s multi   .80 .80
191 A53 18s multi   1.00 1.00
192 A53 18s multi   1.00 1.00
193 A53 36s multi   1.40 1.40
194 A53 56s multi   2.00 2.00
195 A53 60s multi   2.25 2.25
          Nos. 189-195 (7) 9.25 9.25
Souvenir Sheet
196 A53 75s multi   5.00 5.00

A54

Soccer.
1999, Nov. 8
197 A54 15s Two players   .65 .65
198 A54 18s Two players, diff. .65 .65
199 A54 28s Two players, diff. .85 .85
200 A54 28s Player, goalie   .85 .85
201 A54 36s Player, goalie,
          diff.   1.50 1.50
202 A54 56s Two players, diff. 1.75 1.75
203 A54 69s Two players, diff. 2.25 2.25
          Nos. 197-203 (7)   8.50 8.50
Souvenir Sheet
Perf. 13¾x14
204 A54 75s Two players,
          horiz.   4.00 4.00

A55

Prehistoric Animals: a, 28s, Meqaneura. b,
28s, Mesosaurus. c, 36s, Rhamphorhynchus.
d, 36s, Styracosaurus albertensis. e, 56s,
Trachodon annectens. f, 56s, Tarbosaurus
bataar. g, 69s, Arsinoitherium. h, 75s,
Phororhacos.

1999, Dec. 13   Litho.   Perf. 14x13¾
205 A55 Sheet of 8, #a.-h.   12.00 12.00

Uzbek
National
Circus — A56

28s, Woman and lion. # 207, 36s, Acrobat
with bow and arrow. #208, 36s, Acrobat. #209,
56s, Clown on horse. #210, 56s, Two riders on
horse. 69s, Wire walker.
100s, Woman, camels, llamas, horiz.

2000. Jan. 4   Perf. 14
206 A56 28s multi   .95 .95
207 A56 36s multi   .95 .95
208 A56 36s multi   .95 .95
209 A56 56s multi   1.90 1.90
210 A56 56s multi   1.90 1.90
211 A56 69s multi   2.25 2.25
          Nos. 206-211 (6)   8.90 8.90
Souvenir Sheet
212 A56 100s multi   3.25 3.25

Horses — A57

Designs: 69s, Horses pulling carriage.
No. 214: a, 36s, Horse in dressage competi-
tion. b, 36s, Horse jumping fences. c, 56s,
Horses in race. d, 56s, Horse jumping steeple-
chase fence. e, 75s, Horse with sulky. f, 75s,
Race winner.

2000, Feb. 1
213 A57 69s multi   1.60 1.60
214 A57 Sheet of 6, #a.-f. 9.00 9.00

Ajiniyoz Qo'siboy,
Poet — A58

2000, Mar. 31   Litho.   Perf. 14
215 A58 28s multi   1.25 1.25

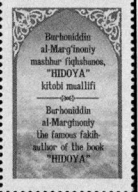

Famous Uzbek Writers — A59

Designs: No. 216, 60s, Burhoniddin al
Marg'inoniy. No. 217, 60s, Imam Abu mansur
al-Moturidiy, horiz.

2000, Oct. 24
Stamp + label
216-217 A59   Set of 2   3.25 3.25

UN High Commissioner for Refugees,
50th Anniv. — A60

2000, Dec. 11
218 A60 125s multi + label   2.25 2.25

Bats
A61

Designs: 15s, Tadarida teniotis. 30s,
Otonycteris hemrichi. 45s, Nyctalus lasi-
opterus, vert. 50s, Muotis frater, vert. 60s, Rhinolophus hipposideros, vert. 90s, Barbastella
leucomelas, vert. 125s, Nyctalus noctula, vert.
160s, Unidentified bat, vert.

2001, Feb. 23   Perf. 13¾x14, 14x13¾
219-225 A61   Set of 7   8.25 8.25
Souvenir Sheet
226 A61 160s multi   4.50 4.50

Dated 2000.

Native
Costumes — A62

2001, Feb. 26   Perf. 14x13¾
227   Horiz. strip of 5 + label 6.00 6.00
  a. A62 45s multi   .50   .50
  b. A62 50s multi, diff.   .60   .60
  c. A62 60s multi, diff.   .70   .70
  d. A62 90s multi, diff.   1.00 1.00
  e. A62 125s multi, diff.   1.50 1.50

Dated 2000.

Arms Type of 1994 Redrawn
2001-05   Litho.   Perf. 14
Size: 14x23mm
228 A10 15s emerald   .70   .70
229 A10 17s dull green   .70   .70
230 A10 20s dull green   .70   .70
231 A10 25s bright blue   .70   .70
232 A10 30s sky blue   .70   .70
232A A10 30s green   .90   .90
  a.   Dated "2004"   .90   .90
  b.   light green, dated "2005" .90   .90
233 A10 33s gray blue   .90   .90
234 A10 45s red   1.25 1.25
235 A10 50s rose   1.40 1.40
236 A10 60s rose pink   1.75 1.75
237 A10 100s rose, "2001"   2.10 2.10
  a.   Dated "2003"   .85   .85
      Nos. 228-237 (11)   11.80 11.80

Issued: 15s, 17s, 25s, 33s, 50s, 60s, 100s,
4/3; 20s, 30s, 4/11; 45s, 6/22. No. 232A,
5/26/03; No. 232Aa, 6/15/04; No. 232Ab,
3/25/05. No. 237a, 5/26/03.

Ali Shir Nava'i (1441-
1501), Poet — A63

2001, Apr. 11
238   Horiz. strip of 5 + label 8.25 8.25
  a. A63 60s Hayrat ul-abror   1.00 1.00
  b. A63 70s Farhod va Shirin   1.00 1.00
  c. A63 85s Layli va Majnun   1.25 1.25
  d. A63 90s Sab'ai sayyora   1.25 1.25
  e. A63 125s Saddi Iskandariy   1.75 1.75

World Environment
Day — A64

2001, June 20
239 A64 100s multi   2.10 2.10

Avesto,
2700th
Anniv. — A65

2001, June 20
240 A65 160s multi   3.25 3.25

Souvenir Sheet

Termiz, 2500th Anniv. — A66

2001, June 20
241 A66   175s multi   4.00 4.00

Souvenir Sheet

Independence, 10th Anniv. — A67

2001, June 20
242 A67 175s multi   4.25 4.25

Souvenir Sheet

Regional Communications
Cooperation — A68

2001, June 20
243 A68 175s multi   3.75 3.75

10th Anniv. of Independence Issue

Vertical Label

Horizontal
Label

Tourist
Hotel — A69

Monuments — A70

Inauguration of Pres. Islam
Karimov — A71

Pres.
Karimov at
United
Nations
A72

Pres.
Karimov at
Istanbul
Summit
A73

Hirmon
A74

Silk
Cocoons
A75

Fergana
Refinery
A76

Power
Station
A77

Daewoo
Auto
Factory
A78

Securities
Exchange
A79

Kamchik
Tunnel
A80

Pres. Karimov and US Pres. Clinton A81

Pres. Karimov and Russian Pres. Vladimir Putin A82

Pres. Karimov and Japanese Emperor Akihito A83

Pres. Karimov and Chinese Pres. Jiang Zemin A84

Pres. Karimov and German Chancellor Gerhard Schröder A85

Pres. Karimov and French Pres. Jacques Chirac A86

Pres. Karimov and British Prime Minister John Major A87

Pres. Karimov and Iranian Pres. Ali Mohammad Khatami — A88

Pres. Karimov and Egyptian Pres. Hosni Mubarak A89

Pres. Karimov and Italian Pres. Carlos Ciampi A90

Pres. Karimov and Indian Pres. Kocheril Narayanan A91

Pres. Karimov and Pope John Paul II — A92

Textile Workers A93

Shurtan Gas Complex — A94

Muborak Refinery — A95

Oil Pipeline — A96

Solar Collector A97

Soldiers with Flag A98

Missiles A99

Soldiers Training A100

Kurash Sports Complex A101

New Year's Celebration — A102

Mother and Child — A103

Wedding A104

Bukhara Refinery — A105

Nuclear Power Plant — A106

A70 Designs: No. 245, Zahriddin Bobur Monument. No. 246, Amir Temur Monument. No. 247, Al-Motorudi Monument. No. 248, Al-Marginoniy Monument. No. 249, Jaloliddin Manguberdi Monument. No. 250, Al-Bukhoriy Monument. No. 273, Alisher Navoi Monument. No 274, Berdaq Monument. No. 284, Alpomish Monument. No. 288, Al-Fargoni Monument.

2001 Litho. Perf. 14x13¾, 13¾x14
Stamp + Label with Same Orientation

244	A69	60s multi	.50	.50
245	A70	60s multi	.50	.50
246	A70	70s multi	.50	.50
247	A70	75s multi	.50	.50
248	A70	75s multi	.50	.50
249	A70	85s multi	.70	.70
250	A70	90s multi	.70	.70
251	A71	90s multi	.70	.70
252	A72	90s multi	.70	.70
253	A73	90s multi	.70	.70
254	A74	90s multi	.70	.70
255	A75	90s multi	.70	.70
256	A76	90s multi	.70	.70
257	A77	90s multi	.70	.70
258	A78	90s multi	.70	.70
259	A79	90s multi	.70	.70
260	A80	90s multi	.70	.70
261	A81	95s multi	.80	.80
262	A82	95s multi	.80	.80
263	A83	95s multi	.80	.80
264	A84	95s multi	.80	.80
265	A85	95s multi	.80	.80
266	A86	95s multi	.80	.80
267	A87	95s multi	.80	.80
268	A88	95s multi	.80	.80
269	A89	95s multi	.80	.80
270	A90	95s multi	.80	.80
271	A91	95s multi	.80	.80
272	A92	95s multi	.80	.80
273	A70	115s multi	1.00	1.00
274	A70	115s multi	1.00	1.00
275	A93	115s multi	1.00	1.00
276	A94	115s multi	1.00	1.00
277	A95	115s multi	1.00	1.00
278	A96	115s multi	1.00	1.00
279	A97	115s multi	1.00	1.00
280	A98	115s multi	1.00	1.00
281	A99	115s multi	1.00	1.00
282	A100	115s multi	1.00	1.00
283	A101	115s multi	1.00	1.00
284	A70	125s multi	1.00	1.00
285	A102	125s multi	1.00	1.00
286	A103	125s multi	1.00	1.00
287	A104	125s multi	1.00	1.00
288	A70	160s multi	1.25	1.25
289	A105	160s multi	1.25	1.25
290	A106	160s multi	1.25	1.25

Nos. 244-290 (47)   39.25   39.25

Nos. 244-290 were each printed in sheets of 2 stamps and 2 labels.
See No. 363.

Uzbekistan Arms — A107

Uzbekistan Flag — A108

Motor Vehicles A109

Central Bank Building — A110

Bank Association Building — A111

Tashkent Khokimiyat Building A112

Central
Trade
Center
Building
A113

Shurtan
Gas
Complex
A114

Shurtan
Gas
Complex
A115

Couple
with Baby
A116

Children
A117

Farm Equipment
A118

Airplanes
A119

Constitution
A120

Majlis Hall — A121

Gold
Ingots and
Coins
A122

Muruntay
Gold Mine
A123

Independence Day
Celebrations — A124

Independence Day
Celebrations — A125

A109 Designs: No. 292a, Nexia. No. 292b, Damas. No. 293a, Tico. No. 293b, Matiz.
A118 Designs: No. 298a, Case 2022 cotton picker. No. 298b, SHR-100 tractor.
A119 Designs: No. 299a, IL-76 MF cargo plane. No. 299b, IL-114-100 passenger plane.

291	Pair with central label	1.50	1.50
a.	A107 90s multi	.75	.75
b.	A108 90s multi	.75	.75
292	Pair with central label	1.50	1.50
a.-b	A109 90s Any single	.75	.75
293	Pair with central label	1.50	1.50
a.-b.	A109 90s multi	.75	.75
294	Pair with central label	1.50	1.50
a.	A110 90s multi	.75	.75
b.	A111 90s multi	.75	.75
295	Pair with central label	1.50	1.50
a.	A112 90s multi	.75	.75
b.	A113 90s multi	.75	.75
296	Pair with central label	2.25	2.25
a.	A114 115s multi	1.10	1.10
b.	A115 115s multi	1.10	1.10
297	Pair with central label	2.25	2.25
a.	A116 125s multi	1.10	1.10
b.	A117 125s multi	1.10	1.10
298	Pair with central label	2.50	2.50
a.-b.	A118 160s Any single	1.25	1.25
299	Pair with central label	1.75	1.75
a.	A119 90s multi	.75	.75
b.	A119 115s multi	.95	.95
300	Pair with central label	1.50	1.50
a.	A120 90s multi	.90	.90
b.	A121 60s multi	.50	.50
301	Pair with central label	1.75	1.75
a.	A122 115s multi	.90	.90
b.	A123 90s multi	.60	.60
302	Pair with central label	1.75	1.75
a.	A124 125s multi	.95	.95
b.	A125 90s multi	.70	.70
	Nos. 291-302 (12)	21.25	21.25

Nos. 291-302 printed in sheets of four stamps and two labels (two pairs).
See Nos. 361-362, 364-366, 371.

Theater
A126

Theater
A127

Theater
A128

Medals — A129

Combine
A130

Combine
A131

Pres.
Karimov
and
Farmers
A132

Soldier
Taking
Oath
Before
Flag
A133

Man and
Soldier
Embracing
A134

Frontier
Guards
and Dog
A135

Athletes — A136

Soldiers in
Formation
A137

Diver
Training
A138

Decontamination Training — A139

Modern Architecture — A140

Armed Forces — A141

Archaeology — A142

High School — A143

Uzbekistan on World Map — A144

A129 Designs: No. 304a, Dostelik. No. 304b, I Darajali "Shon-Sharaf." No. 304c, II Darajali "Shon-Sharaf." No. 305a, I Darajali Sog'lom Avlod Uchun. No. 305b, II Darajali

Sog'lom Avlod Uchun. No. 305c, Mehnat Shuhrati. No. 306a, Jaloliddin Manguberdi. No. 306b, Buyuk Xizmatlari Uchun. No. 306c, El-Yurt Hurmati. No. 307a, Oltin Yildiz. No. 307b, Mustaqillik. No. 307c, Amir Temur.

A136 Designs: No. 310a, Muhammadqodir Abdullayev. No. 310b, Lina Cheryazova. No. 310c, Artur Grigoryan. No. 312a, 160s, Armen Bagdasarov. No. 312b, 160s, Rustam Qosimjonov. No. 312c, 115s, Otabek Kosimov. No. 312d, 115s, Iroda To'laganova. No. 312e, 100s, Dilshod Muxtorov. No. 312e, 115s, Oksana Chusovitina.

No. 313: a, Temuriylar Tarixi Muzeyi (Amir Temur Museum). b, Oqsaroy. c, Olly Majlis. d, Motamsaro Ona (Monument to Grieving Mother). e, Shahidlar Xotirasi (Respect Monument). f, Interkontinental mehmonxonasi (Intercontinental Hotel). g, Milliy Bank (National Bank). h, Yunusobod Sport Majmuasi (Yunusobod Sport Complex).

No. 314: a, 60s, Infantrymen, tank. b, 70s, Airplane and crew. c, 80s, Helicopter and crew. d, 90s, Soldier directing tank with flags. e, 90s, Minesweeper. f, 115s, Soldiers in classroom. g, 160s, Tanks. h, 60s, Artillery.

No. 315: a, 75s, Pot. b, 75s, Artifact with arch. c, 75s, Artifact with hole at top and side. d, 80s, Broken pot. e, 80s, Anthropomorphic figure with arms. f, 80s, Buddha. g, 80s, Costumed figure. h, 80s, Disk. i, 80s, Anthropomorphic figure missing arm. j, 80s, Box. k, 80s, Face.

303	Strip of 3 + label	1.90	1.90
a.	A126 90s multi	.60	.60
b.	A127 90s multi	.60	.60
c.	A128 90s multi	.60	.60
304	Strip of 3 + label	3.25	3.25
a.-c.	A129 160s Any single	1.00	1.00
305	Strip of 3 + label	3.25	3.25
a.-c.	A129 160s Any single	1.00	1.00
306	Strip of 3 + label	3.25	3.25
a.-c.	A129 160s Any single	1.00	1.00
307	Strip of 3 + label	3.25	3.25
a.-c.	A129 160s Any single	1.00	1.00
308	Strip of 3 + label	3.25	3.25
a.	A130 160s multi	1.00	1.00
b.	A131 160s multi	1.00	1.00
c.	A132 160s multi	1.00	1.00
309	Strip of 3 + label	2.25	2.25
a.	A133 60s multi	.45	.45
b.	A134 80s multi	.60	.60
c.	A135 90s multi	.70	.70
310	Strip of 3 + label	3.00	3.00
a.	A136 160s multi	1.25	1.25
b.-c.	A136 115s Any single	.85	.85
311	Block of 3 + label	2.25	2.25
a.	A137 115s multi	.80	.80
b.	A138 80s multi	.60	.60
c.	A139 70s multi	.50	.50
	Nos. 303-311 (9)	25.65	25.65

Sheets

312	A136 Sheet of 6, #a-f, + 3 labels	5.50	5.50
313	A140 115s Sheet of 8, #a-h, + label	7.50	7.50
314	A141 Sheet of 8, #a-h, + label	5.50	5.50
315	A142 Sheet of 11, #a-k, + label	6.50	6.50

Souvenir Sheets

316	A143 160s multi	2.00	2.00
317	A144 175s multi	2.25	2.25

Labels have same orientation as stamps and are at left side of strips on Nos. 303-310, and at UR on No. 311. No. 312 contains three different labels.
See No. 370.

Commonwealth of Independent States, 10th Anniv. — A145

2001, Nov. 8   Perf. 13¾x14
318 A145 60s multi   1.40 1.40

Artwork of Oral Tansiqboyev — A146

No. 319: a, 100s, Mening Qo'shig'im (My Song). b, 125s, Angren-Qo'qon Tog'yo'li (Angren-Kokand Mountain Road).

2001, Nov. 8
319 A146   Pair, #a-b, with central label   5.00 5.00

Flowers — A147

Designs: 45s, Zygophyllum bucharicum. 50s, Viola hissarica. 60s, Bergenia hissarica. 70s, Eremurus hilariae. 85s, Salvia korolkowii. 90s, Lamyropappus schakaptaricus. 145s, Punica granatum.
175s, Undescribed flowers.

2002, May 10   Litho.   Perf. 14x13¾
320-326 A147   Set of 7   8.00 8.00
Souvenir Sheet
327 A147 175s multi   3.00 3.00

Hominids — A148

No. 328: a, 40s, Dryopithecus maior. b, 45s, Homo erectus modjokertensis. c, 50s, Pithecanthropus erectus. d, 60s, Australopithecus afarensis. e, 70s, Zinjanthropus boisei. f, 85s, Homo sapiens neanderthalensis. g, 90s, Sinanthropus pekinensis. h, 125s, Protanthropus heidelbergensis. i, 160s, Homo sapiens fossilis.

2002, May 10   Perf. 13¾x14
328 A148   Sheet of 9, #a-i, + 3 labels   10.00 10.00

Protection of Ozone Layer — A149

2002, June 7   Litho.   Perf. 13¾x14
329 A149 40s multi   1.60 1.60

Souvenir Sheet

City of Shahrisabz, 2700th Anniv. — A150

2002, June 14   Perf. 14
330 A150 30s multi   1.50 1.50

Uzbek Sports A151

Designs: 45s, Chavgon. 50s, Poyga. 60s, Kamondan otish. 70s, Qiz quvmoq. 85s, Ro'molcha olish. 90s, Kurash. 145s, Uloq. 175s, Ro'molcha olish, diff.

2002, July 26   Perf. 13¾x14
331-337 A151   Set of 7   7.00 7.00
Souvenir Sheet
338 A151 175s multi   2.75 2.75

Ancient Coins — A152

No. 339: a, 30s, Silver tetradrachm of Eucratides I c. 171-135 BC, obverse. b, 45s, As "a," reverse. c, 60s, Silver coin of Buxoro, obverse. d, 90s, As "c," reverse. e, 125s, Silver miri of Tamerlane, 1370-1405, obverse. f, 160s, As "e," reverse.

2002, Aug. 1
339 A152   Block of 6, #a-f   7.00 7.00
See Nos. 367-369.

City of Nukus, 70th Anniv. — A153

2002, Oct. 2
340 A153 100s multi   1.60 1.60

Iris Varieties — A154

Designs: 15s, Qoraqum. 30s, Solnechniy zaychik. 45s, Simfoniya. 50s, Chimyon. 60s, Ikar. 90s, Babye leto. 125s, Toshkent. 160s, Askiya.

2002, Oct. 2   Perf. 14x13¾
341-347 A154   Set of 7   7.00 7.00
Souvenir Sheet
348 A154 160s multi   3.00 3.00

Uzbekistan postal officials have declared the following items as "illegal":
Sheets of eight stamps depicting Trains (4 different sheets with denominations of 56s, 75s, 95s and 125s);
Sheets of six stamps with various denominations depicting Birds (2 different), Animals, Year of the Snake, Chiroptera, Lizards, Chess;
Sheets of one label and five stamps with various denominations depicting Perissodactyla;
Souvenir sheets of one depicting Trains (8 different 36s sheets, 4 different 56s sheets, 2 different 75s sheets).

G'afur G'ulom (1903-66), Poet — A155

2003, May 4   Litho.   Perf. 13¾x14
349 A155 1000s brown   8.00 8.00

European Bank Annual Meeting Issue

Vertical Label

Horizontal Label

National Bank, Tashkent — A156

Kaltaminor Minaret, Khiva — A157

Aloqabank, Tashkent A158

Pres Karimov and European Bank for Reconstruction and Development Pres. Jean Lemierre — A159

Islamkhodja Minaret, Khiva — A160

East Gates, Khiva — A161

Samanid Museum, Bukhara — A162

Ark, Bukhara — A163

Women's Traditional Dress — A164

Women's Traditional Dress — A165

Women's Traditional Dress — A166

Women's Traditional Dress — A167

Women's Traditional Dress — A168

A157 Designs: 630s, Gumbazi Sayyidon Mausoleum, Shahrisabz. 920s, Go'ri Amir Mausoleum, Samarqand. 970s, Chorminor Madrasasi, Bukhara. 1330s, Registon, Samarqand, horiz.

2003, May 4 Perf. 14x13¾, 13¾x14
Stamp + Label with Same Orientation

350	A156	520s	multi	6.25 6.25
351	A157	520s	multi	6.25 6.25
352	A157	630s	multi	7.25 7.25
353	A157	920s	multi	11.00 11.00
354	A157	970s	multi	12.00 12.00
355	A158	970s	multi	12.00 12.00
356	A157	1330s	multi	15.00 15.00
357	A158	1330s	multi	15.00 15.00
358		Horiz. pair with central label		14.00 14.00
a.	A160 580s multi			6.25 6.25
b.	A161 520s multi			6.25 6.25
359		Horiz. pair with central label		21.00 21.00
a.	A162 1170s multi			12.50 12.50
b.	A163 630s multi			7.00 7.00
360		Horiz. strip of 5 with flanking label		27.50 27.50
a.	A164 240s multi			2.75 2.75
b.	A165 320s multi			4.00 4.00
c.	A166 520s multi			6.25 6.25
d.	A167 580s multi			6.25 6.25
e.	A168 630s multi			7.25 7.25

Types of 2001-02
Stamp + Label with Same Orientation

361	A110 520s multi		6.25 6.25
362	A111 580s multi		6.25 6.25
363	Horiz. pair with central label		14.00 14.00
a.	A74 170s multi		2.00 2.00
b.	A93 920s multi		11.00 11.00
364	Horiz. pair with central label		9.75 9.75
a.	A107 240s multi		2.75 2.75
b.	A108 520s multi		6.25 6.25
365	Horiz. pair with central label		10.00 10.00
a.	A114 630s multi		7.25 7.25
b.	A115 240s multi		2.75 2.75
366	Horiz. pair with central label		10.00 10.00
a.	A122 520s multi		6.25 6.25
b.	A123 320s multi		4.00 4.00
367	Horiz. pair with flanking label		14.00 14.00
a.	A152 520s Like #339a		6.25 6.25
b.	A152 520s Like #339b		6.25 6.25
368	Horiz. pair with flanking label		14.00 14.00
a.	A152 580s Like #339c		6.25 6.25
b.	A152 580s Like #339d		6.25 6.25
369	Horiz. pair with flanking label		15.00 15.00
a.	A152 630s Like #339e		7.25 7.25
b.	A152 630s Like #339f		7.25 7.25
370	A140 Sheet of 8 + central label		60.00 60.00
a.	520s Like #313a		6.25 6.25
b.	970s Like #313b		12.00 12.00
c.	580s Like #313c		6.25 6.25
d.	630s Like #313d		7.25 7.25
e.	320s Like #313e		4.00 4.00
f.	320s Like #313f		7.25 7.25
g.	920s Toshkent shahar hokimiyati (mayor's house)		11.00 11.00

h.	240s Like #313h	2.75 2.75

Type of 2001 Redrawn
371	Horiz. pair with central label		19.00 19.00
a.	A109 630s Like #292a		7.25 7.25
b.	A109 970s Like #293b		12.00 12.00
	Nos. 350-371 (22)		325.50 325.50

Famous Men — A169

Designs: 125s, Komil Yormatov, film director. 500s, Jo'raxon Sultonov, singer.

2003, July 8 Perf. 13¾x14
372-373 A169 Set of 2 5.50 5.50

Birds — A170

Designs: No. 374, 100s, Ciconia ciconia asiatica. No. 375, 100s, Ciconia nigra. No. 376, 125s, Platalea leucorodia. No. 377, 125s, Phoenicopterus ruber.

2003, Sept. 17 Perf. 14x13¾
374-377 A170 Set of 4 6.75 6.75

Caps — A171

Designs: No. 378, 100s, Kula-tung. No. 379, 100s, Erkaklar do'ppisi. No. 380, 100s, Bayram do'ppisi. No. 381, 125s, Ayollar do'ppisi. No. 382, 125s, Ayollar taxya-do'ppisi. No. 383, 155s, Erkaklar do'ppisi, diff. No. 384, 155s, Bolalar bayram do'ppisi.

2003, Oct. 7
378-384 A171 Set of 7 11.00 11.00

Paintings — A172

No. 385: a, Tong. Onalik, by R. Ahmedov. b, Baxt, by S. Ayitbayev.

2003, Nov. 19
385 A172 970s Horiz. pair, #a-b 13.00 13.00
See Kazakhstan No. 434.

Abuxoliq G'ijdvoniy, Bukhara, 900th Anniv. — A173

2003, Nov. 28 Perf. 13¾x14
386 A173 125s multi + label 2.25 2.25

Souvenir Sheet

2004 Summer Olympics, Athens — A174

2004, June 15 Litho. Perf. 14x13¾
387 A174 205s multi 3.00 3.00

Ma'murjon Uzoqov (1904-63), Singer — A175

Abdulla Qodiriy (1894-1938), Writer — A176

2004, Oct. 11 Perf. 14
388 A175 100s lt blue & blk 1.50 1.50
389 A176 125s lt blue & blk 1.75 1.75

Grapes — A177

Designs: 60s, Kaltak. No. 391, 100s, Oq husayni. No. 392, 100s, Kattaqo'rg'on. No. 393, 125s, Echkemar. No. 394, 125s, Qizil Xurmoni. 155s, Qora Andijon. 210s, Parkent.

2004, Oct. 11 Perf. 14x13¾
390-396 A177 Set of 7 12.00 12.00

Jewelry of 19th and 20th Centuries A178

Inscriptions: 60s, Tumor, Samarqand. No. 398, 100s, Tumor, Toshkent. No. 399, 100s, Qi'ltiqtumor, Qo'qon. No. 400, 125s, Tumor, Buxoro. No. 401, 125s, Bo'yintumor, Toshkent.

155s, Qo'ltiqtumor, Buxoro. 210s, Tumor, Bux-oro, diff.

2004, Oct. 18
397-403 A178 Set of 7   14.00 14.00

Kitab State Geological Reserve, 25th Anniv. — A179

2004, Dec. 1
404 A179 100s multi + label   2.00 2.00

Arms Type of 1994 Redrawn
2004-06 **Litho.** **Perf. 14**
Size: 14x23mm

405	A10	35s green	.25	.25
406	A10	60s green	.35	.35
a.		light green, dated "2005"	.35	.35
407	A10	65s green	.40	.40
408	A10	125s dark blue	.60	.60
409	A10	200s red	.85	.85
410	A10	250s blue	1.10	1.10
411	A10	290s red	1.25	1.25
412	A10	350s blue	1.50	1.50
413	A10	430s red	1.75	1.75
414	A10	2500s red	10.00	10.00
415	A10	3700s blue	14.00	14.00
		Nos. 405-415 (11)	32.05	32.05

Issued: No. 406, 6/15; Nos. 406a, 408, 4/15/05; others, 1/5/06. Nos. 405, 407, 409-415 are dated "2005," though issued in 2006.

Oybek (1905-68), Writer — A180

2005, Apr. 25 **Litho.** **Perf. 14x13¾**
416 A180 125s multi   1.90 1.90

Miniature Sheet

End of World War II, 60th Anniv. — A181

No. 417: a, 60s, Veterans at war memorial. b, 60s, Child with balloon at memorial. c, 100s, Sculptures. d, 100s, Child looking at memorial. e, 125s, Veterans looking at airplane sculpture. f, 125s, Woman passing soldiers. g, 155s, Soldier and floral display. h, 155s, Man looking at scrapbook.

2005, May 6
417 A181 Sheet of 8, #a-h, + central label   8.50 8.50

Tashkent University of Information Technologies, 50th Anniv. — A182

2005, May 25 **Perf. 13¾x14**
418 A182 125s multi + label   1.90 1.90

Qarshi, 2700th Anniv. — A183

2005, Aug. 1
419 A183 125s multi   1.25 1.25

Doves — A184

No. 420: a, 85s, Qopqon-chinni. b, 85s, Ruyan. c, 100s, Novvoti. d, 100s, Oq kaptar. e, 125s, Juk. f, 125s, Chelkar. g, 155s, Udi. h, 155s, Gulsor.
210s, Buxoro kaptari.

2005, Sept. 15
420 A184 Sheet of 8, #a-h   9.00 9.00

Souvenir Sheet
421 A184 210s multi   3.00 3.00

Miniature Sheet

Toreutic Art — A185

No. 422: a, 60s, Teapot with ribbed ornamentation. b, 60s, Teapot with round ornamentation. c, 100s, Teapot, diff. d, 125s, Teapot, diff. 155s, Teapot-samovar. 340s, Teapot with square lid.

2005, Oct. 25
422 A185 Sheet of 6, #a-f   7.50 7.50

Ma'mun Academy, 1000th Anniv. — A186

2005, Dec. 15 **Perf. 13¾x14**
423 A186 430s multi   3.25 3.25

Paintings A187

Designs: No. 424, 200s, Ko'i, by V. I. Yenin. No. 425, 200s, Osuda Kun, by B. Boboyev, vert. No. 426, 250s, Samarqand, Navro'z, by G. Abdurahmanov, vert. No. 427, 250s, Qo'qondagi Choyxona, by J. Umarbekov, vert. No. 428, 300s, Oqtosh, by R. Ahmedov, vert. No. 429, 300s, Yoz, by Y. P. Melnikov, vert. 350s, Kuz, by N. Qo'ziboyev, vert.

2006, Jan. 3 **Perf. 13¾x14, 14x13¾**
424-430 A187 Set of 7   10.00 10.00

Dated 2005.

Rustam Qosimjonov, Intl. Chess Federation World Champion — A188

2006, Jan. 5 **Perf. 13¾x14**
431 A188 200s multi   1.25 1.25

Dated 2005.

Medalists at 2004 Summer Olympics, Athens — A189

Designs: No. 432, 200s, Artur Taymazov, 120kg freestyle wrestling gold medalist. No. 433, 200s, Aleksandr Doxturushvili, 74kg Greco-Roman wrestling gold medalist. 250s, Magomed Ibragimov, 96kg freestyle wrestling silver medalist. 350s, O'tkir Haydarov and Bahodir Sultonov, 81kg and 54kg boxing bronze medalists, horiz.

2006, Jan. 5 **Perf. 14x13¾, 13¾x14**
432-435 A189 Set of 4   5.50 5.50

Dated 2005.

2006 Winter Olympics, Turin — A190

Designs: 1540s, Skiing. 2155s, Figure skating.

2006, May 19 **Litho.** **Perf. 14x13¾**
436-437 A190 Set of 2   13.50 13.50

Musical Instruments A191

Designs: 200s, Tanbur and Qashqar rubobi. 250s, Surnay and Tor. 290s, Surnay and Doira. 350s, Nay and Dutor. 410s, G'ijjak. 430s, Nog'om. 580s, Tanbur and Chang.

2006, May 19 Set of 7   10.00 10.00
438-444 A191

Dogs A192

Designs: 350s, Labrador retriever. 540s, Cocker spaniel. 600s, German shepherd. 780s, Asian sheepdog. 1150s, Collie and German shepherd.

2006, May 19 **Perf. 13¾x14**
445-448 A192 Set of 4   9.00 9.00

Souvenir Sheet
449 A192 1150s multi   4.00 4.00

Souvenir Sheet

2006 World Cup Soccer Championships, Germany — A193

2006, May 19 **Perf. 14x13¾**
450 A193 720s multi   3.50 3.50

Fish — A194

No. 451: a, 45s, Salmo trutta aralensis. b, 90s, Acipenser nudiventris. c, 250s, Pseudos-caphirhynchus kaufmanni. d, 300s, Barbus brachycephalus.
1010s, Aspiolucius esocinus.

2006, July 10 **Perf. 13¾x14**
451 A194 Sheet of 4, #a-d   3.50 3.50

Souvenir Sheet
452 A194 1010s multi   4.25 4.25

Bell Tower,
Tashkent
A195

Alisher Navoiy
Theater
A196

2006, Aug. 10   *Perf. 14x13¾*
453 A195 55s green   .50   .50
          Perf. 13¾x14
454 A196 90s emerald   .60   .60
 See Nos. 543, 545, 548, 597, 599. Compare
with Type A249.

Butterflies
A197

Designs: 45s, Papilio alexanor. 90s, Parnassius mnemosyne. 200s, Parnassius apollonius. 250s, Parnassius maximinus. 300s, Parnassius honrathi. No. 460, 350s, Hypermnestra helios. No. 461, 350s, Parnassius charltonius.
 1010s, Parnassius actius.

2006, Aug. 10   *Perf. 13¾x14*
455-461 A197 Set of 7   6.50 6.50
          Souvenir Sheet
462 A197 1010s multi   4.75 4.75

15th Anniv. of Independence Issue

THE 15TH YEAR OF THE
INDEPENDENCE OF UZBEKISTAN

Horizontal Label

THE 15th
YEAR OF THE
INDEPENDENCE OF
UZBEKISTAN

Vertical Label

Pres. Islam Karimov and Indian Prime
Minister Manmohan Singh — A198

School and Children, Kokand — A199

House of Children's Creativity — A200

Senate Chamber — A201

Emblem of 2005 Intl. Cotton Fair,
Tashkent, and Cotton Boll — A202

Pres. Karimov and People's Republic
of China Chairman Hu Jintao — A203

Pres. Karimov and Latvian Pres. Vaire
Vike-Fraiberg — A204

Qungirot Soda Factory — A205

Leaders at Shanghai Cooperation
Organization Summit,
Tashkent — A206

Cement
Factory
A207

Railroad Construction — A208

Pres. Karimov and Graduates of
Vaseda University — A209

Monument of Independence and
Humanism — A210

Mine — A211

Bronze Smelter — A212

Festival — A213

Daewoo Nexia DOHC — A214

Kurash
A215

Intl. Kurash
Association
Medal
A216

Pres. Karimov and Cotton
Pickers — A217

Pres. Karimov and Cotton
Pickers — A218

Pres. Karimov and Farmers — A219

Roads — A220

Textiles — A221

Military — A222

Sports — A223

A198 Designs — Pres. Karimov and: No. 466, Malaysian King Tuanku Syed Sirajuddin. No. 470, Writer Said Akhmad. No. 474, Slovenian Pres. Janez Drnovsek. No. 477, Russian Pres. Vladimir Putin. No. 480, South Korean Pres. Roh Moo-hyun. No. 483, Uzbek labor leader.

A200 Designs: No. 469, Humanism Arch. No. 478, Medical School, Margilan. No. 484, Tashkent Railway Station. No. 486, Senate Building.

A206 Design: No. 482, Leaders at Euro-Asian Economic Union meeting.

A207 Design: No. 481, Angren Coal Mine.

A213 Design: No. 489b, 90s, Festival, diff.

A214 Design: No. 490b, 200s, Daewoo Damas II.

A215 Designs: No. 491b, 90s, Kurash, diff. No. 491c, 100s, Kurash, diff.

A216 Designs: No. 492b, 580s, FILA Wrestling medal. No. 492c, 720s, National Olympic Committee medal.

No. 494: a, 90s, Winding mountain road. b, 180s, Road construction. c, 55s, Highway.

No. 495: a, 410s, Workers and textile mill machinery. b, 580s, Women holding skeins of thread. c, 250s, Textile mill machinery.

No. 496: a, 410s, Soldiers in joint Uzbekistan-Russia anti-terrorism exercises, flags. b, 100s, Graduation of cadets. c, 250s, Soldiers at desks.

No. 497: a, 580s, Pres. Karimov and student athletes. b, 45s Stadium. c, 55s, Swimming meet. d, 90s, Athletes with medals. e, 200s, Karate. f, 250s, Soccer. g, 100s, Synchronized swimming. h, 290s, Equestrian event.

Perf. 13¾x14, 14x13¾

2006, Aug. 25

Stamp + Label With Same Orientation

463	A198	45s multi	.60	.60
464	A199	45s multi	.60	.60
465	A200	45s multi	.60	.60
466	A198	55s multi	.60	.60
467	A201	90s multi	.60	.60
468	A202	90s multi	.60	.60
469	A200	95s multi	.60	.60
470	A198	100s multi	.60	.60
471	A203	200s multi	1.00	1.00
472	A204	200s multi	1.00	1.00
473	A205	200s multi	1.00	1.00
474	A198	250s multi	1.25	1.25
475	A206	250s multi	1.25	1.25
476	A207	250s multi	1.25	1.25
477	A198	290s multi	1.50	1.50
478	A200	290s multi	1.50	1.50
479	A208	290s multi	1.50	1.50
480	A198	350s multi	1.50	1.50
481	A207	350s multi	1.50	1.50
482	A206	410s multi	2.00	2.00
483	A198	430s multi	2.10	2.10
484	A200	430s multi	2.10	2.10
485	A209	580s multi	3.00	3.00

486	A200	720s multi	3.75	3.75
487	A210	1010s multi	5.25	5.25
		Nos. 463-487 (25)	37.25	37.25

Pairs

488		Horiz. pair with central label	1.20	1.20
a.	A211	45s multi	.60	.60
b.	A212	45s multi	.60	.60
489		Horiz. pair with central label	1.20	1.20
a.	A213	45s multi	.60	.60
b.	A213	45s multi	.60	.60
490		Horiz. pair with central label	2.50	2.50
a.	A214	290s multi	1.50	1.50
b.	A214	200s multi	1.00	1.00
		Nos. 488-490 (3)	4.90	4.90

Strips

491		Strip of 3 + label	3.25	3.25
a.	A215	430s multi	2.10	2.10
b.	A215	90s multi	.60	.60
c.	A215	100s multi	.60	.60
492		Strip of 3 + label	9.00	9.00
a.	A216	410s multi	2.00	2.00
b.	A216	580s multi	3.00	3.00
c.	A216	720s multi	3.75	3.75
493		Strip of 3 + label	3.00	3.00
a.	A217	200s multi	1.00	1.00
b.	A218	250s multi	1.25	1.25
c.	A219	90s multi	.60	.60
		Nos. 491-493 (3)	15.25	15.25

Sheets

494	A220	Sheet of 3, #a-c, + label	1.60	1.60
495	A221	Sheet of 3, #a-c, + label	6.00	6.00
496	A222	Sheet of 3, #a-c, + label	3.75	3.75
497	A223	Sheet of 8, #a-h, + label	8.25	8.25
		Nos. 494-497 (4)	19.60	19.60

Nos. 463-475, 477-480, 482-486 were printed in sheets of 2 stamps and 2 labels. Nos. 476, 481 and 487 were printed in sheets of 5 stamps and 5 labels. Nos. 488-490 were printed in sheets of 4 stamps and 2 labels (2 pairs).

National Flag, 15th Anniv. — A224

2006, Nov. 1   **Perf. 13¾x14**
498   A224   600s multi + label   2.50   2.50

Miniature Sheet

Intl. Year of Deserts and Desertification — A225

No. 499: a, 45s, Oxyura leucocephala. b, 250s, Haliaeetus albicilla. c, 350s, Phalcrocorax pygmaeus. d, 350s, Marmaronetta angustirostris.

2006, Nov. 1
499   A225   Sheet of 4, #a-d   5.00   5.00

Roses — A226

Designs: 45s, Rosa divina. 90s, Rosa maracandica. 250s, Rosa persica. 350s, Rosa vassilczencoi.
600s, Rosa divina, diff.

2006, Nov. 1   **Perf. 14x13¾**
500-503   A226   Set of 4   4.25   4.25
Souvenir Sheet
504   A226   600s multi   2.00   2.00

Souvenir Sheet

Year of Charity and Medical Workers — A227

2006, Nov. 17   **Perf. 13¾x14**
505   A227   720s multi   2.75   2.75

Souvenir Sheet

Regional Communications Commonwealth, 15th Anniv. — A228

2006, Nov. 17
506   A228   1010s multi   4.75   4.75

2006 Asian Games, Doha, Qatar A229

Designs: 90s, High jump. 250s, Tennis. No. 509, 350s, Basketball. No. 510, 350s, Soccer.

2006, Dec. 27   **Litho.**   **Perf. 13¾x14**
507-510   A229   Set of 4   4.75   4.75

Diplomatic Relations Between Uzbekistan and People's Republic of China, 15th Anniv. — A230

2006, Dec. 29
511   A230   200s multi   1.25   1.25

Admission to the United Nations, 15th Anniv. — A231

2007, Mar. 1
512   A231   410s multi   1.75   1.75

Souvenir Sheet

Spring Festival — A232

2007, Mar. 1   **Perf. 14x13¾**
513   A232   1440s multi   5.75   5.75

2007 Winter Asian Games, Changchun, People's Republic of China — A233

Designs: 250s, Figure skating. 350s, Skiing.

2007, Mar. 1
514-515   A233   Set of 2   3.00   3.00

Abdulla Qahhor (1907-68), Writer — A234

No. 516: a, 350s, Scene from "Shohi So'zana." b, 420s, Qahhor.

2007, May 31   **Perf. 13¾x14**
516   A234   Horiz. pair, #a-b   3.25   3.25

Souvenir Sheets

A235

A236

A237

Architecture — A238

No. 517: a, 200s, Norbo'tabiy Madrasasi (madrassa). b, 410s, Daxmai Shohon Maqbarasi (mausoleum). c, 430s, Xudoyorxon Saroyi (palace).

No. 518: a, 250s, Modarixon Madrasasi (madrassa). b, 420s, Mir Arab Madrasasi (madrassa). c, 430s, Chor Bakr Me'moriy Majmuasi (mausoleum).

No. 519: a, 90s, Qo'shdarvoza (city gate). b, 250s, Muhammad Rahimxon Madrasasi (madrassa). c, 1010s, Pahlavon Mahmud Maqbarasi (mausoleum).

No. 520: a, 300s, Yunusxon Maqbarasi (mausoleum). b, 350s, Baroqxon Madrasasi (madrassa). c, Abulqosim Madrasasi (madrassa).

2007, May 31   Perf. 13¾x14, 14x13¾
517	A235	Sheet of 3, #a-c, + label	4.50	4.50
518	A236	Sheet of 3, #a-c, + label	4.50	4.50
519	A237	Sheet of 3, #a-c, + label	5.50	5.50
520	A238	Sheet of 3, #a-c, + label	5.50	5.50
		Nos. 517-520 (4)	20.00	20.00

Margilan, 2000th Anniv. — A239

2007, June 30   Perf. 14x13¾
521	A239	350s multi	1.40	1.40

Quddus Muhammadiy (1907-99), Poet — A240

2007, July 30   Perf. 13¾x14
522	A240	410s light blue & blk	1.60	1.60

Berries A241

Designs: 100s, Fragaria. 250s, Ribes nigrum. 580s, Rubus idaeus. 720s, Grossularia reclinata.

2007, July 30   Litho.
523-526	A241	Set of 4	6.75	6.75

Jewelry — A242

Designs: 300s, Yarim tirnoq. 350s, Ko'krak do'zi, horiz. 670s, Shovkala, horiz. 720s, Bodomoy.

2007, July 30   Perf. 14x13¾, 13¾x14
527-530	A242	Set of 4	8.25	8.25

Miniature Sheets

Samarqand, 2750th Anniv. — A243

No. 531: a, 45s, Registon Maydoni, Ulug'bel Madrasasi. b, 55s, Registon Maydoni, Sherdor Madrasasi. c, 100s, Registon Maydoni, Tillakori Madrasasi. d, 180s, Amir Temur Maqbarasi, Umumiy Ko'rinishi. e, 200s, Bibixonim Masjidi. f, 250s, Ruhobod Maqbarasi. g, 490s, Registon Maydoni, Umumiy Ko'rinishi. h, 720s, Shohisinda Majmuasi, Qo'shgumbazli Maqbara.

No. 532, vert.: a, 90s, Imom al-Moturidiy Maqbarasi. b, 100s, Imom Buxoriy Maqbarasi. c, 180s, Amir Temur Maqbarasi Kirish Peshtoqi. d, 200s, Amir Temur Haykali (statue). e, 410s, Bibixonim Maqbarasi. f, 680s, Shohizinda Majmuasi. g, 700s, Bibixonim Masjidi Kirish Peshtoqi. h, 1150s, Shohizinda Majmuasi, Tuman Oqo Maqbarasi.

2007, July 30   Perf. 13¾x14
531	A243	Sheet of 8, #a-h, + central label	8.00	8.00
		Perf. 14x13¾		
532	A243	Sheet of 8, #a-h, + central label	14.00	14.00

Acinonyx Jubatus A244

Designs: 90s, Leaping. 490s, Resting. 680s, Walking. 780s, Standing. 1440s, Adult with juvenile, vert.

2007, Oct. 3   Perf. 13¾x14
533-536	A244	Set of 4	7.25	7.25
		Souvenir Sheet		
		Perf. 14x13¾		
537	A244	1440s multi	5.25	5.25

Souvenir Sheet

Tashkent Subway, 30th Anniv. — A245

No. 538: a, 540s, Train and system map. b, 780s, Subway emblem and station entrance.

2007, Nov. 20   Perf. 14x13¾
538	A245	Sheet of 2, #a-b	5.00	5.00

Constitution, 15th Anniv. — A246

2007, Dec. 5   Litho.
539	A246	600s multi	2.25	2.25

Miniature Sheet

Zahiruddin Muhammad Babur (1483-1530), Founder of Mughal Dynasty — A247

No. 540 — Inscriptions: a, 200s, Boburning toj kiyib Farg'ona taxtiga chiqishi (Coronation). b, 250s, Boburning Samarqandliklar tomonidan tantana bilan kutib olinishi (Samarqand people welcome Babur). c, 350s, Bobur Hirotda Sulton Huseyn xonadonida (Babur at Sultan Hussein's house). d, 350s, Bengaliya elchisi Bobur qabulida (Babur receives Bengal ambassador). e, 350s, Babur. f, 410s, Qobul qal'asining qamaldan ozod etilishi (Babur freeing Kabul fortress). g, 490s, Bobur Dehli atrofidagi maqbaralarni ziyorat qilmoqda (Babur views Delhi mausoleum). h, 540s, Qobul atrofidagi Xo'ja Seyoron chashmasi (Xo'ja Seyoron Spring near Kabul). i, 680s, Bobur Mon Sing va Bikramojit saroylarini tomosha qilmoqda (Babur views Man Singh and Bikramajit Palaces).

2008, Feb. 13
540	A247	Sheet of 9, #a-i	12.50	12.50

National Academic Drama Theater — A248

Alisher Navoiy Theater — A249

2008, Feb. 28   Perf. 13¾x14
541	A248	45s blue	.55	.55
542	A249	90s dark green	.55	.55

No. 542 has thicker lettering than No. 454.

Architecture Types of 2006-08

2008   Litho.   Perf. 13¾x14, 14x13¾
543	A195	30s green	.35	.35
544	A249	75s dark green	.35	.35
545	A195	85s dark green	.35	.35
546	A248	100s red	.35	.35
547	A249	150s dark green	.45	.45
548	A195	160s green	.45	.45
549	A248	200s red	.55	.55
550	A249	250s blue	.75	.75
551	A249	310s dark green	.90	.90
552	A248	350s blue	1.00	1.00
		Nos. 543-552 (10)	5.50	5.50

Issued: 75s, 85s, 150s, 310s, 350s, 4/1; 30s, 7/15; 100s, 11/25; 160s, 200s, 250s, 4/1. See Nos. 598, 600-601.

Yahyo Gulomov (1908-77), Archaeologist A250

2008, June 25   Litho.   Perf. 13¾x14
553	A250	150s multi	.65	.65

2008 Summer Olympics, Beijing A251

Designs: 150s, Judo. 200s, Boxing. 250s, Running. 310s, Rhythmic gymnastics, vert.

Perf. 13¾x14, 14x13¾
2008, June 25
554-557	A251	Set of 4	6.00	6.00

Flowers — A252

Designs: 150s, Cousinia butkovii. 200s, Cousinia dshisakensis. 250s, Cousinia adenophora. 310s, Cousinia angreni.

2008, June 25   Perf. 14x13¾
558-561	A252	Set of 4	3.00	3.00

Intl. Swimming Federation (FINA), Cent. — A253

No. 562: a, 310s, Water polo. b, 450s, Synchronized swimming.
No. 563: a, 620s, Diving. b, 750s, Freestyle swimming.

2008, July 24   Perf. 14x13¾
Horiz. Pairs, #a-b, + Central Label
562-563	A253	Set of 2	7.75	7.75

Souvenir Sheet

Navoi, 50th Anniv. — A254

No. 564: a, 930s, Farkhad monument, Culture Palace. b, 1250s, Gold bars.

2008, Oct. 22   **Perf. 13¾x14**
564 A254   Sheet of 2, #a-b, + 2 labels   7.75 7.75

Writers — A255

Designs: 620s, Maqsud Shayxzoda (1908-67). 750s, Mirzakalon Ismoiliy (1908-86).

2008, Nov. 5
565-566 A255   Set of 2   4.25 4.25

Men's Traditional Costumes A256

2008, Dec. 31   **Perf. 14x13¾**
567   Horiz. strip of 4 + label   9.50 9.50
   a.   A256 310s Joma   1.00 1.00
   b.   A256 350s Yaktak   1.10 1.10
   c.   A256 750s Erkalar liboslari   2.50 2.50
   d.   A256 1250s Joma, diff.   4.50 4.50

Louis Braille (1809-52), Educator of the Blind — A257

2009, Feb. 2   **Litho.**   **Perf. 13¾x14**
568 A257 620s multi   2.00 2.00

Intl. Year of Astronomy — A258

No. 569: a, 350s, Observatory of Sultan Ulugh Beg, Samarkand. b, 750s, Statue of Ulugh Beg.

2009, Mar. 22   **Perf. 14x13¾**
569 A258   Horiz. pair, #a-b, + central label   3.50 3.50

Birds A259

2009, Apr. 8   **Perf. 13¾x14**
570   Horiz. strip of 4   6.00 6.00
   a.   A259 310s Rufibrenta ruticollis   .90 .90
   b.   A250 350s Cygnus cygnus   1.00 1.00
   c.   A259 620s Aythya nyroca   1.75 1.75
   d.   A259 750s Anser erythropus   2.25 2.25

A260

A261

A262

A263

A264

Children's Art — A265

2009, June 1   **Perf. 13¾x14**
571 A260 200s multi   .60 .60
572 A261 200s multi   .60 .60
573 A262 200s multi   .60 .60
     Perf. 14x13¾
574 A263 200s multi   .60 .60
575 A264 200s multi   .60 .60
576 A265 200s multi   .60 .60
     Nos. 571-576 (6)   3.60 3.60

2010 Youth Olympic Games, Singapore A266

Designs: 450s, Basketball. 750s, Soccer, horiz.

2009, July 1   **Perf. 14x13¾, 13¾x14**
577-578 A266   Set of 2   3.75 3.75

Miniature Sheet

Tashkent, 2200th Anniv. — A267

No. 579: a, 310s, Majlis Building (Oliy Majlis binosi). b, 310s, Senate Building (Senat binosi). c, 350s, Intl. Business Center (Xalqaro biznes markazi). d, 350s, Temurids History Museum (Temuriylar tarixi davlat muzeyi). e, 620s, Turkistan Palace (Turkiston saroyi). f, 620s, Madrassa (Hazrat Imom majmuasi Baroqxon madrasasi). g, 750s, Museum of Victims of Oppression. h, 750s, Map of Great Silk Road.

2009, Aug. 17   **Perf. 13¾x14**
579 A267   Sheet of 8, #a-h   12.00 12.00

Cities Along the Great Silk Road — A268

Designs: 350s, Khiva. 750s, Madrassa, Tashkent. 1250s, Samarkand Gate, Bukhara.

2009, Oct. 9   **Perf. 14x13¾**
580-581 A268   Set of 2   3.00 3.00
     Souvenir Sheet
582 A268 1250s multi   3.50 3.50

Theater Types of 2009

2009, Dec. 1   **Litho.**   **Perf. 13¾x14**
583 A248 450s red   1.40 1.40
584 A249 600s blue   1.60 1.60

Circus Performers A269

Designs: 450s, Two women on horse. 600s, Three women on two horses. 1200s, Three women on horse.

2009, Dec. 28   **Perf. 14x13¾**
585-587 A269   Set of 3   6.25 6.25

Carpet Designs A270

No. 588: a, Samarqand, 19th cent. b, Andijon, 20th cent.

No. 589: a, Bukhara, 19th cent. b, Tashkent, 20th cent.

2009, Dec. 28   **Perf. 13¾x14**
588   Horiz. pair + central label   4.00 4.00
   a.   A270 450s multi   1.00 1.00
   b.   A270 1200s multi   3.00 3.00
589   Horiz. pair + central label   4.00 4.00
   a.   A270 600s multi   1.50 1.50
   b.   A270 1000s multi   2.50 2.50

Endangered Flora — A271

Designs: 450s, Fritillaria eduardii. 1200s, Iridodictyum winklerii.

2010, Jan. 26   **Perf. 14x13¾**
590-591 A271   Set of 2   4.50 4.50

Tashkent Zoo Animals — A272

Designs: 450s, Macaca sinica. 800s, Macaca fascicularis. 1000s, Mandrillus sphinx. 1650s, Lemur catta, horiz.

2010, Feb. 12   **Perf. 14x13¾**
592-594 A272   Set of 3   3.00 3.00
     Souvenir Sheet
     Perf. 13¾x14
595 A272 1650s multi   2.25 2.25

Amir Temur Monument, Shahrisabz — A273

Qarshi Railroad Station A274

2010, Mar. 29   **Perf. 13¾x14**
596   Horiz. pair + central label 2.60 2.60
   a.   A273 800s multi   1.00 1.00
   b.   A274 1200s multi   1.60 1.60
     Sites in Kashkadarya Vilayet.

Architecture Types of 2006-08

2010, Apr. 1   *Perf. 14x13¾, 13¾x14*
597	A195	25s green	.25	.25
598	A248	100s green	.25	.25
599	A195	110s green	.25	.25
600	A248	125s green	.25	.25
601	A248	200s green	.25	.25

Nos. 597-601 (5)   1.25 1.25

Endangered Birds — A275

Designs: 400s, Chettusia gregaria. 800s, Myophonus coeruleus. 1000s, Tichodroma muraria. 1200s, Grus leucogeranus. 1900s, Cygnus olor.

2010, Apr. 15   *Perf. 14x13¾*
602-605 A275 Set of 4   4.25 4.25

Souvenir Sheet
606 A275 1900s multi   2.40 2.40

No. 606 contains one 37x52mm stamp.

43rd Annual Meeting of the Asian Development Bank Board of Governors Issue

Horizontal Label

Vertical Label

Combine A276

Irrigation Canal A277

Bukhara Oil Refinery A278

Fergana Oil Refinery A279

Tractor Trailer A280

Train A281

Poytaxt Business Center A282

Uzbekistan Forum — A283

Sitorai Mohi Xosa Palace, Bukhara A284

Hazrati Imam Complex, Tashkent A285

Majlis A286

Conservatory Building — A287

Arch A288

Tashkent Business Center A289

Senate Building A290

White Palace A291

Highway Cloverleaf A292

Highway and Bridge A293

Two Highways A294

Bridge Over Highway A295

Seamstresses — A296

Pottery Shop A297

Water Polo A298

Parade of Competitors at Yunusabad Sports Complex — A299

Construction Vehicles — A300

Railway Bridge A301

Daewoo Automobile Plant — A302

Tashkent Tractor Factory A303

Students in Laboratory — A304

Children in Computer Class A305

Flag of Uzbekistan — A306

Coat of Arms A307

Bank Association
Building — A308

Central Bank
Building — A309

Man and Woman
in Traditional
Clothes — A310

Man , Woman
and Child in
Traditional
Clothes — A311

Infant and
Nurse — A312

Surgeons in
Operating
Room — A313

2010, Apr. 15   *Perf. 13¾x14*

607	Horiz. pair + central label	2.25	2.25
a.	A276 800s multi	1.00	1.00
b.	A277 1000s multi	1.25	1.25
608	Horiz. pair + central label	2.25	2.25
a.	A278 800s multi	1.00	1.00
b.	A279 1000s multi	1.25	1.25
609	Horiz. pair + central label	2.50	2.50
a.	A280 800s multi	1.00	1.00
b.	A281 1200s multi	1.50	1.50
610	Horiz. pair + central label	2.50	2.50
a.	A282 800s multi	1.00	1.00
b.	A283 1200s multi	1.50	1.50
611	Horiz. pair + central label	2.50	2.50
a.	A284 800s multi	1.00	1.00
b.	A285 1200s multi	1.50	1.50
612	Horiz. pair + central label	2.50	2.50
a.	A286 800s multi	1.00	1.00
b.	A287 1200s multi	1.50	1.50

613	Horiz. pair + central label	2.50	2.50
a.	A288 800s multi	1.00	1.00
b.	A289 1200s multi	1.50	1.50
614	Horiz. pair + central label	2.50	2.50
a.	A290 800s multi	1.00	1.00
b.	A291 1200s multi	1.50	1.50
615	Horiz. pair + central label	2.50	2.50
a.	A292 900s multi	1.10	1.10
b.	A293 1100s multi	1.40	1.40
616	Horiz. pair + central label	2.50	2.50
a.	A294 900s multi	1.10	1.10
b.	A295 1100s multi	1.40	1.40
617	Horiz. pair + central label	2.60	2.60
a.	A296 900s multi	1.10	1.10
b.	A297 1200s multi	1.50	1.50
618	Horiz. pair + central label	2.60	2.60
a.	A298 900s multi	1.10	1.10
b.	A299 1200s multi	1.50	1.50
619	Horiz. pair + central label	2.75	2.75
a.	A300 1000s multi	1.25	1.25
b.	A301 1200s multi	1.50	1.50
620	Horiz. pair + central label	2.75	2.75
a.	A302 1000s multi	1.25	1.25
b.	A303 1200s multi	1.50	1.50
621	Horiz. pair + central label	2.75	2.75
a.	A304 1000s multi	1.25	1.25
b.	A305 1200s multi	1.50	1.50
622	Horiz. pair + central label	2.75	2.75
a.	A306 1000s multi	1.25	1.25
b.	A307 1200s multi	1.50	1.50

Perf. 14x13¾

623	Horiz. pair + central label	2.50	2.50
a.	A308 800s multi	1.00	1.00
b.	A309 1200s multi	1.50	1.50
624	Horiz. pair + central label	2.60	2.60
a.	A310 900s multi	1.10	1.10
b.	A311 1200s multi	1.50	1.50
625	Horiz. pair + central label	2.60	2.60
a.	A312 900s multi	1.10	1.10
b.	A313 1200s multi	1.50	1.50
	Nos. 607-625 (19)	48.40	48.40

Miniature Sheet

Victory in World War II, 65th
Anniv. — A314

No. 626: a, 400s, Young people giving flowers to veterans. b, 800s, Ceremony at Grieving Mother Monument. c, 1000s, Soldier, women and children. d, 1200s, Celebratory ceremony with soldiers.

2010, May 9   *Perf. 13¾x14*
626	A314	Sheet of 4, #a-d	4.25	4.25

2010 Youth
Olympics,
Singapore
A315

2010, July 12   *Perf. 14x13¾*
627	A315 800s multi	1.00	1.00

Uzbekistan-China Gas
Pipeline — A316

2010, July 15   **Litho.**
628	A316 250s multi	.30	.30

Miniature Sheet

19th Century Copperware — A317

No. 629: a, 400s, Bucket, Central Asia. b, 800s, Bowl and pitcher, Khiva. c, 1000s, Pitcher and warming plate, Kokand. d, 1200s, Tray and pitcher, Khiva and Bukhara.

2010, Aug. 25   *Perf. 13¾x14*
629	A317	Sheet of 4, #a-d	4.25	4.25

Tulips — A318

Designs: 400s, Tulipa micheliana. 800s, Tulipa dasystemon. No. 632, 1000s, Tulipa lehmaniana. No. 633, 1200s, Tulipa bifloriformis.
No. 634: a, 1000s, Three Tulipa dasystemon. b, 1900s, One Tulipa dasystemon, rock.

2010, Sept. 27   *Perf. 14x13¾*
630-633	A318	Set of 4	4.25	4.25

Souvenir Sheet
634	A318	Sheet of 2, #a-b	3.75	3.75

Fish
A319

Designs: 800s, Pterois volitans. No. 636, 1000s, Trichogaster leeri. 1200s, Carassius auratus.
No. 638: a, 1000s, Pterophyllum scalare. b, 1900s, Trichogaster leeri, diff.

2010, Oct. 9   *Perf. 13¾x14*
635-637	A319	Set of 3	3.75	3.75

Souvenir Sheet
638	A319	Sheet of 2, #a-b	3.75	3.75

16th Asian Games, Guangzhou,
China — A320

2010, Oct. 25   **Litho.**
639	A320 800s multi	1.00	1.00

Protection of
Polar Regions
and
Glaciers — A321

2010, Oct. 25   *Perf. 14x13¾*
640	A321 900s multi	1.10	1.10

Bobur Monument, Andijon — A322

Olympic
Sports
College,
Andijon
A323

2010, Dec. 30   *Perf. 13¾x14*
641	Horiz. pair + central label	2.60	2.60
a.	A322 900s multi	1.10	1.10
b.	A323 1200s multi	1.50	1.50

Sites in Andijon Vilayet.

Soyib Xo'jayev
(1910-82),
Actor — A324

2010, Dec. 30   *Perf. 14x13¾*
642	A324 900s multi	1.10	1.10

Seventh Asian
Winter Games,
Astana and
Almaty — A325

Designs: 800s, Figure skater. 900s, Freestyle skier.

2011, Jan. 5
643-644	A325	Set of 2	2.10	2.10

Flowers — A326

Designs: 800s, Lagochilus vevedenskyi. 900s, Echinops babtagensis. No. 647, 1000s, Saxifraga hirculus. 1200s, Nathaliella alaica.
No. 649: a, 1000s, Eremus korolkovii, plant 21mm tall. b, 1900s, Eremus korolkovii, plant 37mm tall.

2011, Mar. 31
645-648 A326 Set of 4   4.75 4.75
Souvenir Sheet
649 A326 Sheet of 2, #a-b   3.50 3.50

Miniature Sheet

Carved Wood Items — A327

No. 650: a, 800s, Table, 1983. b, 900s,
Round covered box, 1984. c, 1000s, Lavh,
1990. d, 1200s, Decorative pumpkin, 1985.

2011, Apr. 12   **Perf. 13¾x14**
650 A327 Sheet of 4, #a-d   4.75 4.75

A328

A329

A330

Children's
Art — A331

2011, June 1
651 A328 500s multi   .60 .60
652 A329 500s multi   .60 .60
653 A330 500s multi   .60 .60
654 A331 500s multi   .60 .60
    Nos. 651-654 (4)   2.40 2.40

Independence, 20th Anniv. Issue

Vertical Label

Horizontal
Label

Navoiyazot Gas
Tanks — A332

Maxam-Chirchiq
Fertilizer
Plant — A333

Wedding
Hall,
Termez
A334

Archaeological Museum,
Termez — A335

Plaza,
Urgench
A336

Al-Xorazmi Monument,
Urgench — A337

Theater,
Bukhara
A338

Monument, Bukhara — A339

Jokorgi
Kenes
Building,
Nukus
A340

Berdaq
Museum,
Nukus
A341

Sports Complex, Namangan — A342

Aloqabank Building,
Namangan — A343

Daewoo Automotive Plant — A344

Captiva, Epica and Spark
Automobiles, Car Dealership — A345

Highway
Cloverleaf
A346

Highway
Overpass
A347

Regional
Pre-natal
Center,
Gulistan
A348

Denausky Medical Association
Hospital — A349

Independence Day
Celebrations — A350

Ballet
Dancers
A351

High
Jumper
Svetlana
Radzivil
A352

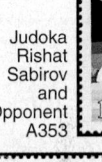

Judoka
Rishat
Sabirov
and
Opponent
A353

Zarafshansky
Gold Mining
Complex — A354

Bekabadsky
Metallurgical
Complex — A355

Wedding Hall, Samarkand — A356

Concert Hall, Samarkand — A357

Academic Lyceum, State University,
Karshi — A358

Fergana Branch of Tashkent University
of Information Technology — A359

Youth
Center,
Andijan
A360

College
of Light
Industry,
Andijan
A361

Worker at Control Center of MTS-
Uzbekistan Company — A362

Uztelecom Control Center — A363

Textile
Factory,
Bukhara
A364

Gulistansky Textile Factory — A365

Talimarzhdansky Power Plant — A366

Sogdiana Substation — A367

Kungradsky Soda Factory — A368

Shurtangas Oil Pumps — A369

Mountains in Winter — A370

Mountains in Spring — A371

Gissar
National
Park
A372

Gissar
National
Park
A373

Uzbekistan Forum, Tashkent — A374

Educational Center, Tashkent — A375

Buildings,
Kokand
A376

Park
Gazebos,
Kokand
A377

Isuzu Automotive Factory,
Samarqand — A378

Isuzu
Truck
A379

Bodomzor Subway Station — A380

Train on Tashguzar-Baysun-
Kumkurgan Bridge — A381

Eski
Machit
Dancers
A382

Musicians
With
Karnays
A383

National Library and Monument to
Amir Temura — A384

Perf. 14x13¾ (#655, 666), 13¾x14

2011, Aug. 29			Litho.	
655		Horiz. pair + central label	2.40	2.40
a.	A332	800s multi	.95	.95
b.	A333	1200s multi	1.40	1.40
656		Horiz. pair + central label	2.40	2.40
a.	A334	800s multi	.95	.95
b.	A335	1200s multi	1.40	1.40
657		Horiz. pair + central label	2.40	2.40
a.	A336	800s multi	.95	.95
b.	A337	1200s multi	1.40	1.40
658		Horiz. pair + central label	2.40	2.40
a.	A338	800s multi	.95	.95
b.	A339	1200s multi	1.40	1.40
659		Horiz. pair + central label	2.40	2.40
a.	A340	800s multi	.95	.95
b.	A341	1200s multi	1.40	1.40
660		Horiz. pair + central label	2.40	2.40
a.	A342	800s multi	.95	.95
b.	A343	1200s multi	1.40	1.40
661		Horiz. pair + central label	2.40	2.40
a.	A344	800s multi	.95	.95
b.	A345	1200s multi	1.40	1.40
662		Horiz. pair + central label	2.40	2.40
a.	A346	800s multi	.95	.95
b.	A347	1200s multi	1.40	1.40
663		Horiz. pair + central label	2.40	2.40
a.	A348	800s multi	.95	.95
b.	A349	1200s multi	1.40	1.40
664		Horiz. pair + central label	2.40	2.40
a.	A350	800s multi	.95	.95
b.	A351	1200s multi	1.40	1.40
665		Horiz. pair + central label	2.40	2.40
a.	A352	800s multi	.95	.95
b.	A353	1200s multi	1.40	1.40
666		Horiz. pair + central label	2.50	2.50
a.	A354	900s multi	1.10	1.10
b.	A355	1200s multi	1.40	1.40
667		Horiz. pair + central label	2.50	2.50
a.	A356	900s multi	1.10	1.10
b.	A357	1200s multi	1.40	1.40
668		Horiz. pair + central label	2.50	2.50
a.	A358	900s multi	1.10	1.10
b.	A359	1200s multi	1.40	1.40
669		Horiz. pair + central label	2.50	2.50
a.	A360	900s multi	1.10	1.10
b.	A361	1200s multi	1.40	1.40
670		Horiz. pair + central label	2.50	2.50
a.	A362	900s multi	1.10	1.10
b.	A363	1200s multi	1.40	1.40
671		Horiz. pair + central label	2.50	2.50
a.	A364	900s multi	1.10	1.10
b.	A365	1200s multi	1.40	1.40
672		Horiz. pair + central label	2.50	2.50
a.	A366	900s multi	1.10	1.10
b.	A367	1200s multi	1.40	1.40
673		Horiz. pair + central label	2.50	2.50
a.	A368	900s multi	1.10	1.10
b.	A369	1200s multi	1.40	1.40
674		Horiz. pair + central label	2.50	2.50
a.	A370	900s multi	1.10	1.10
b.	A371	1200s multi	1.40	1.40
675		Horiz. pair + central label	2.50	2.50
a.	A372	900s multi	1.10	1.10
b.	A373	1200s multi	1.40	1.40
676		Horiz. pair + central label	2.75	2.75
a.	A374	1000s multi	1.25	1.25
b.	A375	1200s multi	1.40	1.40
677		Horiz. pair + central label	2.75	2.75
a.	A376	1000s multi	1.25	1.25
b.	A377	1200s multi	1.40	1.40
678		Horiz. pair + central label	2.75	2.75
a.	A378	1000s multi	1.25	1.25
b.	A379	1200s multi	1.40	1.40
679		Horiz. pair + central label	2.75	2.75
a.	A380	1000s multi	1.25	1.25
b.	A381	1200s multi	1.40	1.40
680		Horiz. pair + central label	2.75	2.75
a.	A382	1000s multi	1.25	1.25
b.	A383	1200s multi	1.40	1.40

Litho. & Embossed With Foil Application
Perf. 14
681 A384 15,000s multi   17.50 17.50
  Nos. 655-681 (27)   82.65 82.65

Souvenir Sheet

Regional Communications Commonwealth, 20th Anniv. — A385

2011, Nov. 1   Litho.   **Perf. 14x13¾**
682 A385 2000s multi   2.25 2.25

Campaign Against AIDS, 30th Anniv. — A386

2011, Dec. 16
683 A386 900s multi   1.00 1.00

VANUATU

ˌvan-ˌwä-'tü

LOCATION — Island group in south Pacific Ocean northeast of New Caledonia
GOVT. — Republic
AREA — 5,700 sq. mi.
POP. — 189,036 (1999 est.)
CAPITAL — Port Vila

The Anglo-French condominium of New Hebrides (Vol. 5) became the independent state of Vanuatu July 30, 1980.

Hebrides franc Vatu (1981)

Catalogue values for all unused stamps in this country are for Never Hinged items.

Erromango Is. and Kaori Tree — A44

Designs: 10fr, Archipelago and man making copra. 15fr, Espiritu Santo Island and cattle. 20fr, Efate Island and Post Office, Vila. 25fr, Malakula Island and headdresses. 30fr, Aoba and Maewo Islands and pig tusks. 35fr, Pentecost Island and land diving. 40fr, Tanna Island and Prophet John Frum's Red Cross. 50fr, Shepherd Island and canoe with sail. 70fr, Banks Island and dancers. 100fr, Ambrym Island and carvings. 200fr, Aneityum Island and decorated baskets. 500fr, Torres Islands and fishing with bow and arrow.

Wmk. 373
1980, July 30   Litho.   **Perf. 14**
280 A44 5fr multicolored .25 .25
281 A44 10fr multicolored .25 .25
282 A44 15fr multicolored .35 .30
283 A44 20fr multicolored .45 .40

284 A44 25fr multicolored .55 .45
285 A44 30fr multicolored .70 .60
286 A44 35fr multicolored .80 .65
287 A44 40fr multicolored .80 .75
288 A44 50fr multicolored .85 .90
289 A44 70fr multicolored 1.60 1.25
290 A44 100fr multicolored 1.60 1.00
291 A44 200fr multicolored 1.75 1.75
292 A44 500fr multicolored 3.25 3.75
  Nos. 280-292 (13) 13.20 12.30

Inscribed in French
Unwmk.
280a A44 5fr multicolored .50 .25
281a A44 10fr multicolored .65 .25
282a A44 15fr multicolored .75 .65
283a A44 20fr multicolored .80 .75
284a A44 25fr multicolored .90 .85
285a A44 30fr multicolored .90 1.00
286a A44 35fr multicolored 1.00 1.25
287a A44 40fr multicolored 1.40 1.40
288a A44 50fr multicolored 1.60 1.60
289a A44 70fr multicolored 2.25 2.25
290a A44 100fr multicolored 2.40 2.50
291a A44 200fr multicolored 2.75 4.25
292a A44 500fr multicolored 6.25 8.25
  Nos. 280a-292a (13) 22.15 25.25

Rotary Emblem — A52   Kiwanis Emblem — A53

1980, Sept. 16   Wmk. 373
293 A52 10fr Emblem, horiz. .25 .25
294 A52 40fr shown .75 .75

Inscribed in French
Unwmk.
293a A52 10fr multicolored .25 .25
294a A52 40fr multicolored .95 .95
75th anniv. of Rotary Intl. and 8th anniv. of Port Vila Rotary Club (40fr).

1980, Sept. 16   Wmk. 373
295 A53 10fr shown .25 .25
296 A53 40fr Emblem, horiz. 1.00 1.00

Inscribed in French
Unwmk.
295a A53 10fr multicolored .25 .25
296a A53 40fr multicolored 1.00 1.00
New Zealand District Kiwanis Convention, Port Vila, Sept. 16-18.

Christmas A54

Paintings: 10fr, Virgin and Child, by Michael Pacher. 15fr, Virgin and Child, by Hans Memling. 30fr, Rest on the Flight to Egypt, by Adriaen van der Werff.

1980, Nov. 12   Wmk. 373
297 A54 10fr multicolored .25 .25
298 A54 15fr multicolored .30 .30
299 A54 30fr multicolored .65 .65
  Nos. 297-299 (3) 1.20 1.20

Erythrura Trichroa — A55

1980, July 30 [heading area]

1981, Feb. 18
300 A55 10fr shown .60 .30
301 A55 20fr Chalcophaps indica 1.10 .70
302 A55 30fr Pachycephala pectoralis 1.60 1.10
303 A55 40fr Ptilinopus tannensis 2.10 1.40
  Nos. 300-303 (4) 5.40 3.50

Duke of Edinburgh's 60th Birthday — A56

1981, June 10   **Perf. 14x14½**
304 A56 15v Tribesman, portrait .25 .25
305 A56 25v Portrait .30 .30
306 A56 35v Family .45 .45
307 A56 45v shown .60 .60
  Nos. 304-307 (4) 1.60 1.60

Common Design Types
pictured following the introduction.

Royal Wedding Issue
Common Design Type
1981, July 29
308 CD331 15v Bouquet .25 .25
309 CD331 45v Charles .55 .55
310 CD331 75v Couple .80 .80
  Nos. 308-310 (3) 1.60 1.60

First Anniv. of Independence — A57

1981, July 19
311 A57 15v Map, flag, vert. .25 .25
312 A57 25v Emblem .25 .25
313 A57 45v Anthem .60 .60
314 A57 75v Arms, vert. .80 .80
  Nos. 311-314 (4) 1.90 1.90

Christmas A58

Designs: Children's drawings.

Wmk. 373
1981, Nov. 11   Litho.   **Perf. 14**
315 A58 15v Three kings .25 .25
316 A58 25v Girl holding lamb, vert. .35 .35
317 A58 35v Butterfly-angel .50 .50
318 A58 45v Gift bearer, vert. .70 .70
  a. Souvenir sheet, #315-318 2.50 2.50
  Nos. 315-318 (4) 1.80 1.80

Broadbills — A59

1982, Feb. 8   **Perf. 14½x14**
319 A59 15v shown .75 .75
320 A59 20v Rainbow lorries 1.00 1.00
321 A59 25v Buff-bellied flycatchers 1.25 1.25
322 A59 45v Fantails 2.25 2.25
  Nos. 319-322 (4) 5.25 5.25

Orchids — A60

Perf. 14x13½, 13½x14
1982, June 15
323 A60 1v Flickengeria comata .25 .70
324 A60 2v Calanthe triplicata .30 .75
325 A60 10v Dendrobium sladei .35 .40
326 A60 15v Dendrobium mohlianum .50 .35
327 A60 20v Dendrobium macrophyllum .60 .40
328 A60 25v Dendrobium purpureum .95 .70
329 A60 30v Robiquetia mimus 1.10 1.10
330 A60 35v Dendrobium mooreanum 1.25 1.25
331 A60 45v Spathoglottis plicata 1.50 1.40
332 A60 50v Dendrobium seemannii 1.75 1.75
333 A60 75v Dendrobium conanthum 2.75 2.75
334 A60 100v Dendrobium macranthum 3.25 2.75
335 A60 200v Coelogyne lamellata 4.00 4.25
336 A60 500v Bulbophyllum longiscapum 7.75 9.25
  Nos. 323-336 (14) 26.30 27.80
Nos. 330-333, 336 horiz.
For surcharges see Nos. 383, 512, 551-554, 586-589A, B1.

Scouting Year A61

Wmk. 373
1982, Sept. 1   Litho.   **Perf. 14**
337 A61 15v Around campfire .45 .45
338 A61 20v First aid .50 .50
339 A61 25v Signal tower .65 .65
340 A61 45v Building raft 1.40 1.40
341 A61 75v Scout sign 2.00 2.00
  Nos. 337-341 (5) 5.00 5.00

Christmas — A62

Details from Nativity painting. 35v, 45v horiz.

1982, Nov. 16
342 A62 15v multicolored .40 .40
343 A62 25v multicolored .65 .65
344 A62 35v multicolored .95 .95
345 A62 45v multicolored 1.25 1.25
  a. Souvenir sheet of 4, #342-345 4.25 4.25
  Nos. 342-345 (4) 3.25 3.25

Hypolimnas Octocula A63

1983, Jan. 17   **Perf. 14½**
346 Pair 2.75 2.10
  a. A63 15v shown 1.25 .95
  b. A63 15v Euploea sylvester 1.25 .95
347 Pair 3.25 2.75
  a. A63 20v Polyura sacco 1.50 1.25
  b. A63 20v Papilio canopus 1.50 1.25

348   Pair   4.25   3.00
a. A63 25v Parantica pumila   2.00 1.50
b. A63 25v Luthrodes cleotas   2.00 1.50
Nos. 346-348 (3)   10.25 7.85

A64

1983, Mar. 14   *Perf. 13½x14*
349 A64 15v Pres. Sokomanu   .40 .40
350 A64 20v Fisherman   .45 .45
351 A64 25v Herdsman, cattle   .50 .50
352 A64 75v Flags, map   1.10 1.10
Nos. 349-352 (4)   2.45 2.45

Commonwealth Day. 20v, 75v inscribed in French.

Economic Zone — A65

a, Thunnus albacares. b, Map. c, Matthew Isld. d, Hunter Isld. e, Epinephelus morrhua, etelis carbunculus. f, Katsuwonus pelamis.

Perf. 14x13½
1983, May 23   **Litho.**   **Wmk. 373**
353   Sheet of 6   5.00 5.00
a.-f. A65 25v multicolored   .80 .80

Manned Flight Bicentenary — A66

Balloons or Airships: 15v, Montgolfiere, 1783. 20v, J.A.C. Charles 1st hydrogen balloon, 1783. 25v, Blanchard & Jeffries 1st English Channel crossing, 1785. 35v, H. Giffard's 1st mechanically powered airship, 1852. 40v, Renard and Krebs' airship, 1884. 45v, Graf Zeppelin's 1st transworld flight, 1929.

1983, Aug. 4   **Litho.**   *Perf. 14*
354 A66 15v multi, vert.   .40 .40
355 A66 20v multi, vert.   .45 .45
356 A66 25v multi, vert.   .60 .60
357 A66 35v multi   .80 .80
358 A66 40v multi   .90 .90
359 A66 45v multi   1.10 1.10
Nos. 354-359 (6)   4.25 4.25

For overprint see No. 372.

World Communications Year — A67

1983, Oct. 10   **Litho.**   **Wmk. 373**
360 A67 15v Mail transport, Bauerfield Airport   .30 .30
361 A67 20v Switchboard operator   .45 .45
362 A67 25v Telex operator   .65 .65
363 A67 45v Satellite earth station   1.10 1.10
a. Souv. sheet of 4, #360-363 + 3 labels   6.50 6.50
Nos. 360-363 (4)   2.50 2.50

No. 363a issued for WCY and 75th anniv. of New Hebrides stamps.

Local Fungi — A68

1984, Jan. 9   **Litho.**   *Perf. 14*
364 A68 15v Cymatoderma elegans, vert.   1.10 1.10
365 A68 25v Lignosus rhinoceros, vert.   1.25 1.25
366 A68 35v Stereum ostrea   2.00 2.00
367 A68 45v Ganoderma boninenze, vert.   2.50 2.50
Nos. 364-367 (4)   6.85 6.85

Lloyd's List Issue
Common Design Type
1984, Apr. 30   **Litho.**   *Perf. 14½x14*
368 CD335 15v Port Vila   .40 .40
369 CD335 20v Induna   .55 .55
370 CD335 25v Air Vanuatu jet   .70 .70
371 CD335 45v Brahman Express   1.25 1.25
Nos. 368-371 (4)   2.90 2.90

No. 359 Overprinted "UPU CONGRESS / HAMBURG"
1984, June 11   **Wmk. 373**   *Perf. 14*
372 A66 45v multicolored   1.10 1.10

Cattle A69

1984, July 3   **Litho.**   *Perf. 14*
373 A69 15v Charolais   .40 .40
374 A69 25v Charolais-Afrikaner   .60 .60
375 A69 45v Friesian   1.10 1.10
376 A69 75v Charolais-Brahman   1.90 1.90
Nos. 373-376 (4)   4.00 4.00

Ausipex '84 — A70

Ships.
1984, Sept. 7
377 A70 25v Makambo   .90 .65
378 A70 45v Rockton   1.60 1.25
379 A70 100v Waroonga   3.00 4.75
a. Souvenir sheet of 3, #377-379   5.50 5.75
Nos. 377-379 (3)   5.50 6.65

Christmas A71

1984, Nov. 19   **Litho.**   **Wmk. 373**
380 A71 25v Father Christmas, child in hospital   .60 .35
381 A71 45v Nativity   1.10 .90
382 A71 75v Father Christmas, children   1.75 1.75
Nos. 380-382 (3)   3.45 3.00

No. 323 Surcharged

1985, Jan. 22   **Litho.**   *Perf. 14x13½*
383 A60 5v on 1v multi   2.00 1.25

Ceremonial Dance Costumes — A71a

Audubon Birth Bicent. — A72

1985, Jan. 22   *Perf. 14*
384 A71a 20v Ambrym Island   .40 .40
385 A71a 25v Pentecost Island   .60 .60
386 A71a 45v Women's Grade Ceremony, S.W. Malakula   1.00 1.00
387 A71a 75v Same, men's   1.50 1.50
Nos. 384-387 (4)   3.50 3.50

Wmk. 373
1985, Mar. 26   **Litho.**   *Perf. 14*
Peregrine falcons.
388 A72 20v multicolored   1.25 1.25
389 A72 35v multicolored   1.50 1.50
390 A72 45v multicolored   1.75 1.75
391 A72 100v multicolored   3.00 3.00
Nos. 388-391 (4)   7.50 7.50

Queen Mother 85th Birthday
Common Design Type
Perf. 14½x14
1985, June 7   **Wmk. 384**
392 CD336 5v Wedding photo   .30 .30
393 CD336 20v 80th birthday celebration   .55 .55
394 CD336 35v At Ancona, Italy   .70 .70
395 CD336 55v Holding Prince Henry   1.10 1.10
Nos. 392-395 (4)   2.65 2.65

Souvenir Sheet
396 CD336 100v At Covent Garden Opera   3.50 3.50

EXPO '85, Tsukuba — A73

35v, Mala naval patrol boat. 45v, Japanese fishing fleet, Port Vila. 55v, Mobile Force Band. 100v, Prime Minister Walter H. Lini.
1985, July 26   **Wmk. 373**   *Perf. 14*
397 A73 35v multicolored   .80 .50
398 A73 45v multicolored   1.00 .75
399 A73 55v multicolored   1.10 .90
400 A73 100v multicolored   1.25 1.90
a. Souvenir sheet of 4, #397-400   5.25 5.25
Nos. 397-400 (4)   4.15 4.05

Natl. independence, 5th anniv.

Intl. Youth Year A74

Children's drawings.
1985, Sept. 16   **Wmk. 373**   *Perf. 14*
401 A74 20v Alain Lagaliu   .65 .65
402 A74 30v Peter Obed   .75 .75
403 A74 50v Mary Estelle   1.25 1.25
404 A74 100v Abel M rani   2.10 2.10
Nos. 401-404 (4)   4.75 4.75

Natl. and UN Flags, Map A75

1985, Sept. 24   **Litho.**   *Perf. 14*
405 A75 45v multicolored   1.25 1.10
Admission of Vanuatu to UN, 4th anniv.

Sea Slugs — A76

1985, Nov. 11   **Wmk. 373**   *Perf. 14½*
406 A76 20v Chromodoris elisa bethina   .60 .60
407 A76 35v Halgerda aurantiomaculata   1.10 1.10
408 A76 55v Chromodoris kuniei   1.60 1.60
409 A76 100v Notodoris minor   3.00 3.00
Nos. 406-409 (4)   6.30 6.30

Nos. 407-408 horiz. See Nos. 497-500.

Scuba Diving — A77

1986, Jan. 22   **Wmk. 384**   *Perf. 14*
410 A77 30v shown   1.10 .65
411 A77 35v Volcanic eruption   1.25 .70
412 A77 55v Land diving   1.25 1.10
413 A77 100v Wind surfing   1.60 2.50
Nos. 410-413 (4)   5.20 4.95

See No. 479.

Queen Elizabeth II 60th Birthday
Common Design Type
Designs: 20v, With Prince Charles and Princess Anne, 1951. 35v, At christening of Prince William, the Music Room, Buckhingham Palace, 1982. 45v, State visit, 1985. 55v, State visit to Mexico, 1974. 100v, Visiting Crown Agents' offices, 1983.

1986, Apr. 21   **Litho.**   *Perf. 14x14½*
414 CD337 20v scar, blk & sil   .40 .40
415 CD337 35v ultra & multi   .70 .70
416 CD337 45v green & multi   .80 .80
417 CD337 55v violet & multi   1.00 1.00
418 CD337 100v multicolored   1.90 1.90
Nos. 414-418 (5)   4.80 4.80

For overprints & surcharges see #465-469, B2-B6.

AMERIPEX '86 — A78

1986, May 19   **Wmk. 373**   *Perf. 14*
419 A78 45v SS President Coolidge   1.50 .80
420 A78 55v As troop ship, 1942   1.75 1.00
421 A78 135v Site of sinking, 1942   3.00 2.50
a. Souvenir sheet of 3, #419-421   6.25 6.25
Nos. 419-421 (3)   6.25 4.30

Halley's
Comet
A79

1986, June 23   Wmk. 384   Perf. 14½
422	A79	30v	Comet, deity statue	1.40 1.40
423	A79	45v	Family sighting comet	1.60 1.60
424	A79	55v	Comet over SW Pacific	1.90 1.90
425	A79	100v	Edmond Halley, manuscript	2.50 2.50
			Nos. 422-425 (4)	7.40 7.40

Coral
A80

1986, Oct. 27   Wmk. 373   Perf. 14
426	A80	20v	Daisy	.85 .85
427	A80	45v	Organ pipe	1.90 1.90
428	A80	55v	Sea fan	2.25 2.25
429	A80	135v	Soft	5.50 5.50
			Nos. 426-429 (4)	10.50 10.50

Intl.
Peace
Year
A81

1986, Nov. 3   Litho.   Perf. 14
430	A81	30v	Children of the world	.75 .75
431	A81	45v	Child praying	1.25 1.25
432	A81	55v	UN building, negotiators	1.50 1.50
433	A81	135v	Peoples working in harmony	3.75 3.75
			Nos. 430-433 (4)	7.25 7.25

Automotives
A82

1987, Jan. 22
434	A82	20v	Datsun 240Z, 1969	.40 .40
435	A82	45v	Model A Ford, 1927	.80 .80
436	A82	55v	Unic, 1924-25	.95 .95
437	A82	135v	Citroen DS19, 1975	2.25 2.25
			Nos. 434-437 (4)	4.40 4.40

IRHO
Coconut
Research
Station, 25th
Anniv.
A83

1987, May 13   Perf. 14½x14
438	A83	35v	Nursery	.75 .75
439	A83	45v	Cocos nucifera tree	1.10 1.10
440	A83	100v	Cocos nucifera fruit	1.75 1.75
441	A83	135v	Station	2.25 2.25
			Nos. 438-441 (4)	5.85 5.85

Fish — A84

Perf. 14x14½
1987, July 15   Wmk. 384
442	A84	1v	Cirrhitichthys aprinus	.25 .25
443	A84	5v	Zanclus cornutus	.25 .25
444	A84	10v	Canthigaster cinctus	.25 .25
445	A84	15v	Amphiprion rubrocinctus	.35 .35
446	A84	20v	Acanthurus lineatus	.50 .50
447	A84	30v	Thalassoma hardwicki	.65 .65
448	A84	35v	Anthias tuka	.70 .70
449	A84	40v	Adioryx microstomus	.80 .80
450	A84	45v	Balistoides conspicillum	1.00 1.00
451	A84	50v	Xyrichtys taeniouris	1.10 1.10
452	A84	55v	Hemitaurich-thys polyepis	1.25 1.25
453	A84	65v	Pterois volitans	1.40 1.40
454	A84	100v	Paracirrhites forsteri	2.50 2.50
455	A84	300v	Balistapus undulatus	6.75 6.75
456	A84	500v	Chaetodon ephippium	9.25 9.25
			Nos. 442-456 (15)	27.00 27.00

Insects
A85

1987, Sept. 22   Wmk. 373   Perf. 14
457	A85	45v	Xylotrupes gideon	1.25 1.25
458	A85	55v	Phyllodes imperialis	1.40 1.40
459	A85	65v	Cyphogaster	1.90 1.90
460	A85	100v	Othreis fullonia	2.75 2.75
			Nos. 457-460 (4)	7.30 7.30

Christmas
Carols — A86

1987, Nov. 10   Perf. 13½x14
461	A86	20v	Away in a Manger	.45 .45
462	A86	45v	Once in Royal David's City	1.00 1.00
463	A86	55v	While Shepherds Watched Their Flocks	1.25 1.25
464	A86	65v	We Three Kings of Orient Are	1.50 1.50
			Nos. 461-464 (4)	4.20 4.20

Nos. 414-418 Ovptd. in Silver:
"40TH WEDDING ANNIVERSARY"

Perf. 14x14½
1987, Dec. 9   Litho.   Wmk. 384
465	CD337	20v	scar, blk & sil	.60 .60
466	CD337	35v	ultra & multi	.75 .75
467	CD337	45v	green & multi	1.00 1.00
468	CD337	55v	violet & multi	1.10 1.10
469	CD337	100v	multicolored	1.90 1.90
			Nos. 465-469 (5)	5.35 5.35

World
Wildlife
Fund — A87

Dugongs.

1988, Feb. 29   Perf. 13x13½
470	A87	5v	Mother, calf	1.25 .45
471	A87	10v	Adult	2.00 .45
472	A87	20v	Two adults	2.50 1.25
473	A87	45v	Herd	4.50 3.25
			Nos. 470-473 (4)	10.25 5.40

Australia
Bicentennial
A88

Burns Philip emblem, bicent. emblem and
steamships.

1988, May 18   Wmk. 373   Perf. 12
474	A88	20v	S.S. Tambo	.45 .45
475	A88	45v	S.S. Induna	.95 .95
476	A88	55v	S.S. Morinda	1.10 1.10
477	A88	65v	S.S. Marsina	1.25 1.25
			Nos. 474-477 (4)	3.75 3.75

Capt. James Cook
(1728-1779),
Explorer — A89

Perf. 14 on 2 or 3 Sides
1988, July 29   Wmk. 384
478	A89	45v	black & red	1.10 1.10

SYDPEX '88. No. 478 printed in panes of 10
plus 5 center labels picturing a map of Vanuatu, HMS Resolution, exhibition emblem, HMS
Endeavour or a map of Australia.

Tourism Type of 1986
Souvenir Sheet
Wmk. 373
1988, Aug. 24   Litho.   Perf. 14
479		Sheet of 2		4.50 4.50
	a.	A77 55v like No. 412		1.10 1.10
	b.	A77 100v like No. 413		2.25 2.25

EXPO '88. Nos. 479a-479b are dated 1988
and "Vanuatu" is inscribed in violet blue.

1988 Summer
Olympics,
Seoul — A90

1988, Sept. 19   Perf. 13½x14
480	A90	20v	Boxing	.30 .30
481	A90	45v	Track events	.85 .85
482	A90	55v	Signing Olympic agreement	1.00 1.00
483	A90	65v	Soccer	1.25 1.25
			Nos. 480-483 (4)	3.40 3.40

Souvenir Sheet
484	A90	150v	Tennis	4.00 4.00

Intl. Tennis Federation, 75th anniv. (150v).

Lloyds of London, 300th Anniv.
Common Design Type

Designs: 20v, Lloyds new building, 1988.
55v, Cargo ship Shirrabank, horiz. 65v, Adela,
horiz. 145v, Excursion steamer General Slocum on fire in New York Harbor, 1904.

1988, Oct. 25   Wmk. 384   Perf. 14
485	CD341	20v	multicolored	.55 .55
486	CD341	55v	multicolored	1.40 1.40
487	CD341	65v	multicolored	1.50 1.50
488	CD341	145v	multicolored	3.75 3.75
			Nos. 485-488 (4)	7.20 7.20

FAO — A91

Perf. 14½x14, 14x14½
1988, Nov. 14
489	A91	45v	Tending crops	1.10 1.10
490	A91	55v	Fishing, vert.	1.25 1.25
491	A91	65v	Animal husbandry, vert.	1.25 1.25
492	A91	120v	Produce market	1.60 1.60
			Nos. 489-492 (4)	5.20 5.20

Christmas
A92

Carols: 20v, Silent Night, Holy Night. 45v,
Angels From the Realms of Glory. 65v, O
Come All Ye Faithful. 155v, In That Poor Stable How Charming Jesus Lies.

1988, Dec. 1   Litho.   Perf. 14½x14
493	A92	20v	multicolored	.50 .50
494	A92	45v	multicolored	.80 .80
495	A92	65v	multicolored	.90 .90
496	A92	155v	multicolored	2.40 2.50
			Nos. 493-496 (4)	4.60 4.70

Marine Life Type of 1985

Shrimp.

1989, Feb. 1   Perf. 14
497	A76	20v	Periclimenes brevicarpalis	.50 .50
498	A76	45v	Lysmata grabhami	1.25 1.25
499	A76	65v	Rhynchocinetes	1.60 1.60
500	A76	150v	Stenopus hispidus	3.25 3.25
			Nos. 497-500 (4)	6.60 6.60

Economic &
Social
Commission
for Asia and
the Pacific
(ESCAP)
A93

Perf. 12x12½
1989, Apr. 5   Litho.   Wmk. 373
501	A93	20v	Consolidated Catalina	1.25 1.25
502	A93	45v	Douglas DC-3	1.75 1.75
503	A93	55v	Embraer EMB110 Bandeirante	1.90 1.90
504	A93	200v	Boeing 737-300	6.00 6.00
			Nos. 501-504 (4)	10.90 10.90

Inauguration of the Sydney-Noumea-Espiritu Santo Service, 1948 (20v).

PHILEXFRANCE '89 — A94

Exhibition emblem and: No. 505a, Porte de
Versailles Hall Number 1. No. 505b, Eiffel
Tower. No. 506, Revolt of French Troops,
Nancy, 1790.

1989, July 5   Wmk. 373   Perf. 12
505	A94		Pair	6.50 6.50
a.-b.		100v any single		3.00 3.00

Souvenir Sheet
Perf. 14
Wmk. 384
506	A94	100v	multicolored	2.75 2.75

French revolution, bicent.

Moon Landing, 20th Anniv.
Common Design Type

Apollo 17: 45v, Command module in space.
55v, Harrison Schmitt, Gene Cerman and Ron
Evans. 65v, Mission emblem. 120v, Liftoff.
100v, Recovery of Apollo 11 crew after
spashdown.

1989, July 20   Wmk. 384   Perf. 14
Size of Nos. 508-509: 29x29mm
507	CD342	45v	multicolored	1.75 1.75
508	CD342	55v	multicolored	1.75 1.75
509	CD342	65v	multicolored	2.00 2.00
510	CD342	120v	multicolored	3.50 3.50
			Nos. 507-510 (4)	9.00 9.00

Souvenir Sheet
511	CD342	100v	multicolored	3.25 3.25

No. 324
Surcharged

Perf. 14x13½
1989, Oct. 18   Litho.   Wmk. 373
512 A60 100v on 2v multi   6.75 6.75

STAMPSHOW '89, Melbourne.

World
Stamp
Expo
'89 — A95

Perf. 14x13½
1989, Nov. 6   Litho.   Wmk. 384
513 A95 65v New Hebrides
          #256   4.50 4.50

Souvenir Sheet
514   Sheet of 2   11.50 11.50
  a. A95 65v New Hebrides #254   4.00 4.00
  b. A95 100v The White House
      (detail)   6.00 6.00

A96

Flora.

Perf. 12½x12
1990, Jan. 5   Wmk. 373
515 A96 45v Alocasia macror-
          rhiza   1.10 1.10
516 A96 55v Acacia spirorbis   1.25 1.25
517 A96 65v Metrosideros col-
          lina   1.50 1.50
518 A96 145v Hoya australis   3.50 3.50
      Nos. 515-518 (4)   7.35 7.35

A97

Stamp World London '90 Exhibition emblem
and simulated stamps or stamps on stamps:
45v, Kava (simulated stamps). 65v, Luganville
P.O. exterior, interior (simulated stamps).
100v, Propeller plane, 19th cent. packet (simulated stamps). 150v, New Hebrides #187-188,
first day cancellation. 200v, Great Britain #1,
Vanuatu #281.

1990, Apr. 30   Perf. 13x13½
519 A97 45v multicolored   1.10 1.10
520 A97 65v multicolored   1.75 1.75
521 A97 100v multicolored   2.50 2.50
522 A97 200v multicolored   4.50 4.50
      Nos. 519-522 (4)   9.85 9.85

Souvenir Sheet
523 A97 150v multicolored   8.50 8.50

Penny Black, 150th anniv. No. 523 margin
pictures first day cancel and cachet.

Independence, 10th Anniv. — A98

25v, Natl. Council of Women Emblem. 50v,
Pres. Frederick Kalomuana Timakata. 55v,
Preamble to Constitution. 65v, Vanuaaku Pati
flag. 80v, Reserve Bank. 150v, Prime Minister
Walter H. Lini.

1990, July 30   Perf. 14
524 A98 25v multicolored   .50 .50
525 A98 50v multicolored   1.10 1.10
526 A98 55v multicolored   1.25 1.25
527 A98 65v multicolored   1.40 1.40
528 A98 75v multicolored   1.75 1.75
      Nos. 524-528 (5)   6.00 6.00

Souvenir Sheet
529 A98 150v multi   6.75 6.75

Miniature Sheet

Charles De Gaulle (1890-1970) — A99

Wmk. 373
1990, Nov. 22   Litho.   Perf. 14
530   Sheet, 2 ea #530c-530f
            + 2 labels   26.50 26.50
  a. A99 20v At Bayeux, after D-day
           landing   4.75 4.75
  b. A99 25v Alsace, 1945   4.75 4.75
  c. A99 30v Portrait   1.90 1.90
  d. A99 45v Spitfire, Biggin Hill,
           1942   2.10 2.10
  e. A99 55v Casablanca, 1943   2.25 2.25
  f. A99 65v Day of Glory, Paris,
           1944   2.40 2.40

Christmas — A100

1990, Dec. 5   Perf. 13
531   Strip of 5   6.00 6.00
  a. A100 25v Angel facing right   .60 .60
  b. A100 50v Shepherds   .90 .90
  c. A100 65v Nativity   1.00 1.00
  d. A100 70v The Three Kings   1.10 1.10
  e. A100 80v Angel facing left   1.10 1.10

Butterflies
A101

Perf. 14x14½
1991, Jan. 9   Wmk. 384
532 A101 25v Parthenos sylvia   .85 .85
533 A101 55v Euploea leucos-
           tictos   1.60 1.60
534 A101 80v Lampides
           boeticus   2.25 2.25
535 A101 150v Danaus plexippus   4.25 4.25
      Nos. 532-535 (4)   8.95 8.95

Art
Festival — A102

Wmk. 373
1991, May 2   Litho.   Perf. 13½
536 A102 25v Dance   .60 .60
537 A102 65v Weaving   1.60 1.60
538 A102 80v Carving   2.10 2.10
539 A102 150v Music   3.75 3.75
      Nos. 536-539 (4)   8.05 8.05

Elizabeth & Philip, Birthdays
Common Design Types
Wmk. 384
1991, June 17   Litho.   Perf. 14½
540 CD345 65v multicolored   1.10 1.10
541 CD346 70v multicolored   1.25 1.25
  a. Pair, #540-541 + label   3.00 3.00

Phila Nippon
'91 — A103

Birds: 50v, White-collared kingfisher. 55v,
Green palm lorikeet. 80v, Scarlet robin. 100v,
Pacific swallow. 150v, Reef heron.

Wmk. 373
1991, Nov. 15   Litho.   Perf. 14½
542 A103 50v multicolored   1.25 1.25
543 A103 55v multicolored   1.25 1.25
544 A103 80v multicolored   1.90 1.90
545 A103 100v multicolored   2.25 2.25
      Nos. 542-545 (4)   6.65 6.65

Souvenir Sheet
546 A103 150v multicolored   4.50 4.50

Fight
Against
AIDS
A104

Designs: 25v, Multiple partners, unsafe sex
can spread AIDS. 65v, AIDS victim and care
giver. 80v, AIDS kills, shark. 150v, Children's
playground.

1991, Nov. 29   Wmk. 384   Perf. 14
547 A104 25v multicolored   .75 .75
548 A104 65v multicolored   1.40 1.40
549 A104 80v multicolored   1.75 1.75
550 A104 150v multicolored   3.25 3.25
      Nos. 547-550 (4)   7.15 7.15

Nos. 324-326 &
329 Surcharged

Perf. 14x13½
1991, June 12   Litho.   Wmk. 373
551 A60 20v on 2v #324   .85 .85
552 A60 60v on 10v #325   2.50 2.50
553 A60 70v on 15v #326   3.00 3.00
554 A60 80v on 30v #329   3.25 3.25
      Nos. 551-554 (4)   9.60 9.60

**Queen Elizabeth II's Accession to
the Throne, 40th Anniv.**
Common Design Type
1992, Feb. 6   Wmk. 384   Perf. 14
555 CD349 20v multicolored   .40 .40
556 CD349 25v multicolored   .50 .50
557 CD349 60v multicolored   1.10 1.10
558 CD349 65v multicolored   1.25 1.25
Wmk. 373
559 CD349 70v multicolored   1.25 1.25
      Nos. 555-559 (5)   4.50 4.50

New Hebrides Participation in World
War II — A105

Designs: 50v, Grumman F4F-4 Wildcat.
55v, Douglas SBD-3 Dauntless. 65v, Consolidated PBY-5A Catalina. 80v, USS Hornet.
200v, Vought-Sikorsky OS2U-3.

Perf. 13½x14
1992, May 22   Litho.   Wmk. 373
560 A105 50v multicolored   2.75 2.75
561 A105 55v multicolored   2.75 2.75
562 A105 65v multicolored   3.00 3.00
563 A105 80v multicolored   4.25 4.25
      Nos. 560-563 (4)   12.75 12.75

Souvenir Sheet
564 A105 200v multicolored   14.00 14.00

World Columbian Stamp Expo, Chicago
(No. 564).
See Nos. 590-594, 664-667.

Vanuatu's Membership in the World
Meteorological Organization, 10th
Anniv. — A106

Designs: 25v, Meteorological station, Port
Vila. 60v, Cyclone near Vanuatu seen by Japanese satellite GMS 4. 80v, Weather chart
showing cyclone. 105v, Cyclone warning
broadcast by radio.

1992, June 20   Perf. 14
565 A106 25v multicolored   .65 .65
566 A106 60v multicolored   1.60 1.60
567 A106 80v multicolored   2.10 2.10
568 A106 105v multicolored   2.25 2.25
      Nos. 565-568 (4)   6.60 6.60

1992 Melanesian Cup — A107

1992, July 20   Perf. 13½x14
569 A107 20v Soccer team, tro-
           phy   .60 .60
570 A107 65v Soccer players   1.50 1.50
571 A107 70v Men's track   1.75 1.75
572 A107 80v Women's track   1.75 1.75
      Nos. 569-572 (4)   5.60 5.60

1992 Summer Olympics, Barcelona (#571-
572).
For surcharges see Nos. 621-622.

World Food
Day — A108

Designs: 20v, "Breast is best." 70v, Central
Hospital, Port Vila. 80v, "Give your children a
healthy future." 150v, Nutritious food.

1992, Oct. 16   Wmk. 384   Perf. 14
573 A108 20v green & brown   .50 .50
574 A108 70v brown & green   1.25 1.25
575 A108 80v green & brown   1.50 1.50
576 A108 150v brown & green   2.75 2.75
      Nos. 573-576 (4)   6.00 6.00

Turtles
A109

1992, Dec. 15   *Perf. 14x14½*
577	A109	55v Leatherback turtle	2.10	2.10
578	A109	65v Loggerhead turtle	2.40	2.40
579	A109	70v Hawksbill turtle	3.25	3.25
580	A109	80v Green turtle	4.25	4.25
		Nos. 577-580 (4)	12.00	12.00

Souvenir Sheet
581	A109	200v Green turtle hatchlings	9.00	9.00

Hibiscus — A110

Designs: 25v, Light pink hibiscus rosa-sinensis. 55v, Hibiscus tiliaceus. 80v, Red hibiscus rosa-sinensis. 150v, Dark pink hibiscus rosa-sinensis.

Wmk. 384
1993, Mar. 3   **Litho.**   *Perf. 14*
582	A110	25v multicolored	.55	.55
583	A110	55v multicolored	1.25	1.25
584	A110	80v multicolored	1.60	1.60
585	A110	150v multicolored	3.00	3.00
		Nos. 582-585 (4)	6.40	6.40

Nos. 331, 333-335 Surcharged

Perf. 13½x14, 14x13½
1993, Apr. 21   **Wmk. 373**
586	A60	40v on 45v #331	1.10	1.10
587	A60	55v on 75v #333	1.50	1.50
588	A60	65v on 100v #334	1.75	1.75
589	A60	150v on 200v #335	4.25	4.25
		Nos. 586-589 (4)	8.60	8.60

Size and location of surcharge varies.

No. 326 Surcharged

1993, June 1
589A	A60	20v on 35v #326	8.00	8.00

World War II Type of 1992

20v, Grumman F6F-3 Hellcat. 55v, Lockheed P-38F Lightning. 65v, GrummanTBF-1 Avenger. 80v, USS Essex. 200v, Douglas C-47 Dakota.

1993, June 30   *Perf. 13½*
590	A105	20v multicolored	.90	.90
591	A105	55v multicolored	2.50	2.50
592	A105	65v multicolored	3.00	3.00
593	A105	80v multicolored	3.75	3.75
		Nos. 590-593 (4)	10.15	10.15

Souvenir Sheet
594	A105	200v multicolored	11.00	11.00

Island Scenes
A111

Designs: 5v, Iririki Island, Port Vila. 10v, Iririki Island, yachts. 15v, Court House, Port Vila. 20v, Two girls, Pentecost Island. 25v, Women dancers, Tanna Island. 30v, Market, Port Vila. 45v, Man with canoe, Erakor Island, vert. 50v, Coconut trees, Champagne Beach. 55v, Coconut trees, North Efate Islands. 60v, Fish (Banks Group). 70v, Sea fan, Tongoa Island, vert. 75v, Espiritu Santo Island. 80v, Sailboat at sunset, Port Vila Bay, vert. 100v, Mele Waterfall, vert. 300v, Yasur Volcano, Tanna Island, vert. 500v, Erakor Island.

1993, July 7   *Perf. 14x14½, 14½x14*
595	A111	5v multicolored	.25	.25
596	A111	10v multicolored	.25	.25
597	A111	15v multicolored	.30	.30
598	A111	20v multicolored	.40	.40
599	A111	25v multicolored	.45	.45
600	A111	30v multicolored	.55	.50
601	A111	45v multicolored	.80	.80
602	A111	50v multicolored	.90	.90
603	A111	55v multicolored	1.00	1.00
604	A111	60v multicolored	1.10	1.10
605	A111	70v multicolored	1.25	1.25
606	A111	75v multicolored	1.40	1.40
a.		Souvenir sheet, #596, 603, 604, 606 ('94)	4.75	4.75
607	A111	80v multicolored	1.40	1.40
608	A111	100v multicolored	1.75	1.75
609	A111	300v multicolored	5.25	5.25
610	A111	500v multicolored	8.75	8.75
		Nos. 595-610 (16)	25.80	25.75

No. 606a, Philakorea '94 International Stamp Exhibition.
For surcharges see Nos. 619-620, 742-745A, 745D.

Shells — A112

Wmk. 373
1993, Sept. 15   **Litho.**   *Perf. 14½*
611	A112	55v Trochus niloticus	1.60	1.60
612	A112	65v Lioconcha castrensis	2.10	2.10
613	A112	80v Turbo petholatus	2.50	2.50
614	A112	150v Pleuroploca trapezium	4.75	4.75
		Nos. 611-614 (4)	10.95	10.95

See Nos. 632-635, 654-657.

Louvre Museum, Bicent. A113

Paintings by De La Tour: 25v, St. Joseph the Carpenter. 55v, The Newborn. 80v, Adoration of the Shepherds (detail). 150v, Adoration of the Shepherds (entire).

Wmk. 373
1993, Nov. 10   **Litho.**   *Perf. 14*
615	A113	25v multicolored	.60	.60
616	A113	55v multicolored	1.25	1.25
617	A113	80v multicolored	1.90	1.90
618	A113	150v multicolored	4.00	4.00
		Nos. 615-618 (4)	7.75	7.75

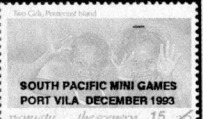

Nos. 570, 572, 598, 600 Surcharged

1993, Dec. 6   **Litho.**   **Wmk. 373**
Perfs. as Before
619	A111	15v on 20v #598	.35	.35
620	A111	25v on 30v #600	.50	.50
621	A107	55v on 65v #570	1.25	1.25
622	A107	70v on 80v #572	1.50	1.50
		Nos. 619-622 (4)	3.60	3.60

Service Organizations A114   Intl. Year of the Family A115

Hong Kong '94: 25v, Kiwanis Intl., Charity Races, vert. 60v, Lions Intl. Twin Otter on mercy mission. 75v, Rotary Intl. fighting malaria, vert. 150v, Red Cross blood donar service. 200v, Emblems of service organizations.

Perf. 14x15, 15x14
1994, Feb. 18   **Litho.**   **Wmk. 373**
623	A114	25v multicolored	.50	.50
624	A114	60v multicolored	1.40	1.40
625	A114	75v multicolored	1.60	1.60
626	A114	150v multicolored	3.00	3.00
		Nos. 623-626 (4)	6.50	6.50

Souvenir Sheet
627	A114	200v multicolored	4.25	4.25

1994, Mar. 2   *Perf. 14*
628	A115	25v vio & rose brn	.50	.50
629	A115	60v ver & dk grn	1.25	1.25
630	A115	90v green & sepia	1.75	1.75
631	A115	150v brn & vio bl	3.00	3.00
		Nos. 628-631 (4)	6.50	6.50

Shell Type of 1993
1994, May 31   **Litho.**   *Perf. 12*
632	A112	60v Cyprea argus	1.60	1.60
633	A112	70v Conus marmoreus	1.90	1.90
634	A112	85v Lambis chiragra	2.50	2.50
635	A112	155v Chicoreus brunneus	4.50	4.50
		Nos. 632-635 (4)	10.50	10.50

Tourism — A116

Designs: a, 25v, Slit gong (drum), traditional hut. b, 75v, Volcano, boats. c, 90v, Sailboats, airplane, green palm lorikeet. d, 200v, Helicopter, woman with tray of fruit.

1994, July 27   **Litho.**   *Perf. 13½*
636	A116	Strip of 4, #a.-d.	9.50	9.50

Anemonefish — A117

1994, Aug. 16   **Litho.**   *Perf. 12*
637	A117	55v Pink	2.50	2.50
638	A117	70v Clark's	3.25	3.25
639	A117	80v Red & black	3.50	3.50
640	A117	140v Orange-fin	6.50	6.50
a.		Souvenir sheet of 1	6.50	6.50
		Nos. 637-640 (4)	15.75	15.75

Philakorea '94 (#640a).

ICAO, 50th Anniv. — A118

Designs: 25v, 1950 Qantas Catalina. 60v, 1956 Tai Douglas DC3. 75v, 1966 New Herbrides Airways Drover. 90v, 1994 Air Vanuatu Boeing 737.

1994, Dec. 7
641	A118	25v multicolored	.70	.70
642	A118	60v multicolored	2.00	2.00
643	A118	75v multicolored	2.25	2.25
644	A118	90v multicolored	3.00	3.00
		Nos. 641-644 (4)	7.95	7.95

Hibiscus A119

1995, Feb. 1   **Litho.**   *Perf. 12*
645	A119	25v The Path	.55	.55
646	A119	60v Old Frankie	1.40	1.40
647	A119	90v Fijian white	2.10	2.10
648	A119	200v Surf rider	4.75	4.75
		Nos. 645-648 (4)	8.80	8.80

Lizards A120

Designs: 25v, Emoia nigromarginata. 55v, Nactus multicarinatus. 70v, Lepidodactylus. 80v, Emoia caerulocauda. 140v, Emoia sanfordi.

1995, Apr. 12
649	A120	25v multicolored	.60	.60
650	A120	55v multicolored	1.40	1.40
651	A120	70v multicolored	1.75	1.75
652	A120	80v multicolored	2.00	2.00
653	A120	140v multicolored	3.50	3.50
		Nos. 649-653 (5)	9.25	9.25

Shell Type of 1993
1995, June 1
654	A112	25v Epitonium scalare	.70	.70
655	A112	55v Strombus latissimus	1.60	1.60
656	A112	90v Conus bullatus	2.50	2.50
657	A112	200v Pterynotus pinnatus	5.75	5.75
		Nos. 654-657 (4)	10.55	10.55

Anniversaries — A121

Designs: 25v, Girls wearing traditional head pieces. 55v, Stylized picture of natives dancing, vert. 60v, Children, doves, natl. flag, UN flag, vert. 75v, Embroidered tapestry of native, vert. 90v, Troops parading. 140v, Group in traditional ceremony.

Perf. 14x13½, 13½x14
1995, July 28   **Litho.**
658	A121	25v multicolored	.55	.55
659	A121	55v multicolored	1.25	1.25
660	A121	60v multicolored	1.25	1.25
661	A121	75v multicolored	1.75	1.75
662	A121	90v multicolored	1.90	1.90

663	A121	140v multicolored	3.00	3.00
a.		Souvenir sheet of 1	4.75	4.75
		Nos. 658-663 (6)	9.70	9.70

UN, 50th anniv. (#660). Singapore 95 (#663a). Others, independence, 15th anniv.

World War II Type of 1992

1995, Sept. 1　　Litho.　　Perf. 12½

664	A105	60v SB2C Helldiver	2.50	2.50
665	A105	70v Spitfire Mk VIII	2.75	2.75
666	A105	75v F4U-1A Corsair	2.75	2.75
667	A105	80v PV1 Ventura	3.25	3.25
		Nos. 664-667 (4)	11.25	11.25

Souvenir Sheet
Perf. 13½

667A	A105	140v Japanese surrender, USS Missouri	8.50	8.50

No. 667A for Singapore 95.

Artifacts — A122

Ambae money mat and: a, 25v, Rambaramp mortuary effigy, Malakula. b, 60v, Wusi pot, Espiritu Santo. c, 75v, Slit gong, Efate Island. d, 90v, Tapa cloth, Erromango Island. Nos. 668a, 668f, like No. 668d.

1995, Nov. 22　Litho.　Perf. 13½x13

668	A122	Strip of 4, #a.-d.	7.50	7.50
e.		90v Perf. 14	2.25	2.25
f.		Souvenir sheet #668e	3.50	3.50

No. 668f, 9th Asian Intl. Philatelic Exhibition, Beijing.
Issued: Nos. 668e, 668f, Dec. 1995.
See No. 720.

Fishing
A123

1996, Feb. 1　　Litho.　　Perf. 14

669	A123	55v Cast net	1.25	1.25
670	A123	75v Reef	1.50	1.50
671	A123	80v Deep water, vert.	1.60	1.60
672	A123	140v Game, vert.	3.00	3.00
		Nos. 669-672 (4)	7.35	7.35

Flying
Foxes
A124

No. 673, Notopteris macdonaldi, facing left. No. 674, Pteropus anetianus, green leaves on tree, vert. No. 675, Pteropus anetianus, diff., vert. No. 676, Notopteris macdonaldi, diff.
No. 677, vert: a, 90v, Pteropus tonganus. b, 140v, Pteropus tonganus, diff.

1996, Apr. 3　　Litho.　　Perf. 14

673	A124	25v multicolored	.95	.75
674	A124	25v multicolored	.95	.75
675	A124	25v multicolored	.95	.75
676	A124	25v multicolored	.95	.75
		Nos. 673-676 (4)	3.80	3.00

Souvenir Sheet

677	A124	Sheet of 2, #a.-b.	6.00	6.00

World Wildlife Fund (Nos. 673-676). 9th Asian Intl. Philatelic Exhibition (No. 677).

UNICEF,
50th
Anniv.
A125

Unwmk.
1996, June 5　　Litho.　　Perf. 14

678	A125	55v Immunizations	1.40	1.40
679	A125	60v Breast feeding	1.60	1.60

Radio,
Cent.
A126

60v, Airplane, radio signal. 75v, Radio Vanuatu. 80v, Guglielmo Marconi. 90v, Ship, radio signal.

1996, June 5　　　　　　Perf. 14½

680	A126	60v multicolored	1.25	1.25
681	A126	75v multicolored	1.50	1.50
682	A126	80v multicolored	1.60	1.60
683	A126	90v multicolored	1.90	1.90
a.		Block of 4, #680-683	8.00	8.00

Modern Olympic Games,
Cent. — A127

Designs: 25v, Marie Kapalu, Tawai Keiruan, Baptiste Firiam, Tava Kalo, 1996 athletes from Vanuatu. 70v, 1996 Athletes in training. 75v, 1950's Athletes. 200v, 1896 Athletes.

1996, July 17　　Litho.　　Perf. 14

684	A127	25v multicolored	.50	.50
685	A127	70v multicolored	1.50	1.50
686	A127	75v multicolored	1.50	1.50
687	A127	200v multicolored	4.50	4.50
		Nos. 684-687 (4)	8.00	8.00

Christmas
A128

Children of various races holding candles in front of churches: a, 25v, Presbyterian, Roman Catholic. b, 60v, Church of Christ. c, 75v, 7th Day Adventist, Apostolic. d, 90v, Anglican.

1996, Sept. 11　　Litho.　　Perf. 14

688	A128	Strip of 4, #a.-d.	5.50	5.50

No. 688 is a continuous design.

Hibiscus
A129

1996, Nov. 13　　Litho.　　Perf. 13½

689	A129	25v Lady Cilento	.60	.60
690	A129	60v Kinchen's Yellow	1.50	1.50
691	A129	90v D.J. O'Brien	2.10	2.10
692	A129	200v Cuban Variety	4.50	4.50
a.		Sheet of 2, #689, #692	7.00	7.00
		Nos. 689-692 (4)	8.70	8.70

Hong Kong '97. No. 692a issued 2/12/97.

Diving
A130

Designs: 70v, Coral Garden. 75v, Lady of the President Coolidge. 90v, "Boris," Queensland grouper. 140v, Wreck of the President Coolidge.

1997, Jan. 15　Litho.　Perf. 14½x14

693	A130	70v multicolored	1.50	1.50
694	A130	75v multicolored	1.50	1.50
695	A130	90v multicolored	1.90	1.90
696	A130	140v multicolored	3.00	3.00
a.		Souvenir sheet, #694, 696	7.00	7.00
b.		Souvenir sheet, #693-696	14.00	14.00
		Nos. 693-696 (4)	7.90	7.90

Pacific '97 (#696a).

Birds
A131

25v, Sharp-tailed sandpiper. 55v, Crested tern. 60v, Little pied cormorant. 75v, Brown booby. 80v, Reef heron. 90v, Red-tailed tropic bird.

1997, June 4　　Litho.　Perf. 13½x14

697	A131	25v multi	.70	.70
698	A131	55v multi	1.40	1.40
699	A131	60v multi	1.50	1.50
700	A131	75v multi	1.75	1.75
701	A131	80v multi, vert.	1.75	1.75
702	A131	90v multi, vert.	2.10	2.10
		Nos. 697-702 (6)	9.20	9.20

Air
Vanuatu,
10th Anniv.
A132

Designs: 25v, Pilot at controls. 60v, Airplane being serviced, cargo loaded. 90v, Serving drinks to passengers. 200v, Passengers leaving plane upon arrival at Vanuatu.

1997, Apr. 2　　　　Perf. 14½x14

703	A132	25v multicolored	.55	.55
704	A132	60v multicolored	1.40	1.40
705	A132	90v multicolored	2.10	2.10
706	A132	200v multicolored	4.50	4.50
		Nos. 703-706 (4)	8.55	8.55

No. 704 is 81x31mm.

Thomas A. Edison (1847-
1931) — A133

Designs: 60v, Light bulb, Edison. 70v, Hydro dam, Santo. 200v, Port Vila by dusk.

1997, Aug. 27　　Litho.　　Perf. 12

707	A133	60v multicolored	1.25	1.25
708	A133	70v multicolored	1.50	1.50
709	A133	200v multicolored	4.25	4.25
a.		Block of 3, #707-709 + label	8.75	8.75

No. 709 is 80x30mm.

Fish — A134

Designs: 25v, Yellow-faced angelfish. 55v, Flame angelfish. 60v, Lemonpeel angelfish. 70v, Emperor angelfish. 140v, Multi-barred angelfish.

1997, Nov. 12　Litho.　Perf. 14x13½

710	A134	25v multicolored	.50	.50
711	A134	55v multicolored	1.25	1.25
712	A134	60v multicolored	1.40	1.40
713	A134	70v multicolored	1.50	1.50
714	A134	140v multicolored	3.00	3.00
		Nos. 710-714 (5)	7.65	7.65

Architecture
in Vanuatu
A135

Designs: 30v, Fale-Espiritu Santo. 65v, Natl. Cultural Center. 80v, University of the South Pacific. 200v, Chief's Nakamal.

1998, Feb. 11　Litho.　Perf. 14½x14

715	A135	30v multicolored	.55	.55
716	A135	65v multicolored	1.25	1.25
717	A135	80v multicolored	1.40	1.40
718	A135	200v multicolored	3.50	3.50
		Nos. 715-718 (4)	6.70	6.70

Diana, Princess of Wales (1961-97)
Common Design Type

Various portraits: a, 75v. b, 85v. c, 145v.

1998, Mar. 31　Litho.　Perf. 14½x14

718A	CD355	95v multicolored	1.75	1.75

Sheet of 4

719	CD355	#a.-c., 718A	9.75	9.75

No. 719 sold for 400v + 50v, with surtax from international sales being donated to The Diana, Princess of Wales Memorial Fund and surtax from national sales being donated to designated local charity.

Artifacts Type of 1995

Tribal masks: a, 30v, South West Malakula. b, 65v, North Ambrym. c, 75v, Gana Island Banks. d, 85v, Uripiv Island, Malakula. e, 95v, Vao Island, Malakula, and Central South Pentecost.

1998, June 3　　Litho.　　Perf. 14½

720	A122	Strip of 5, #a.-e.	8.75	8.75

Butterflies — A136

30v, Danaus plexippus. 60v, Hypolimnas bolina. 65v, Eurema hecabe. 75v, Nymphalidae. 95v, Precis villida. 205v, Tirumala hamata.

1998, July 23　　Litho.　　Die Cut
Self-Adhesive

721	A136	30v multicolored	.65	.65
722	A136	60v multicolored	1.40	1.40
723	A136	65v multicolored	1.60	1.60
724	A136	75v multicolored	1.90	1.90
725	A136	95v multicolored	2.25	2.25
726	A136	205v multicolored	4.00	4.00
a.		Souvenir sheet of 1	6.00	6.00
		Nos. 721-726 (6)	11.80	11.80

Singpex '98 (#726a).

Volcanoes — A137

30v, Yasur, Tanna. 60v, Marum & Benbow, Ambrym. 75v, Gaua. 80v, Lopevi. 145v, Ambae.

1998, Oct. 23   Litho.   Perf. 15x14

728	A137	30v multicolored	.55	.55
729	A137	60v multicolored	1.10	1.10
730	A137	75v multicolored	1.40	1.40
731	A137	80v multicolored	1.40	1.40
732	A137	145v multicolored	2.75	2.75
		Nos. 728-732 (5)	7.20	7.20

Early Explorers A138

Explorer, ship: 34v, Pedro Fernandez de Quiros, San Pedro y Paulo, 1606. 73v, Louis-Antoine de Bougainville, Boudeuse, 1768. 84v, Capt. James Cook, HMS Resolution, 1774. 90v, Jean-Fancois de Galaup de la Perousse, Astrolabe, 1788. 96v, Jules Sebastien-Cesar Dumont d'Urville, Astrolabe, "1788."

1999, Feb. 17   Litho.   Perf. 14

733	A138	34v multicolored	.60	.60
734	A138	73v multicolored	2.00	2.00
735	A138	84v multicolored	2.25	2.25
a.		Souv. sheet, #733-735	4.50	4.50
736	A138	90v multicolored	2.25	2.25
737	A138	96v multicolored	2.40	2.40
a.		Souv. sheet, #734, 736-737	6.75	6.75
		Nos. 733-737 (5)	9.50	9.50

No. 735a was released for Australia '99 World Stamp Expo on 3/19/99; No. 737a for PhilexFrance 99.

Birds — A139

34v, Vanuatu kingfisher. 67v, Shining cuckoo. 73v, Peregrine falcon. 107v, Rainbow lorikeet.

1999, May 12   Litho.   Perf. 14

738	A139	34v multicolored	.90	.90
739	A139	67v multicolored	1.60	1.60
		Booklet, 5 #739	11.00	
740	A139	73v multicolored	1.90	1.90
741	A139	107v multicolored	2.75	2.75
a.		Sheet of 1	6.00	6.00
b.		Sheet of 1 with China 1999 emblem in margin	7.50	7.50
		Nos. 738-741 (4)	7.15	7.15

Issued: #741b, 8/18.

Nos. 601, 603-605, 607, 608 Surcharged

Perf. 14½x14, 14x14½
1998-2000   Litho.

742	A111	1v on 100v #608	.25	.25
742A	A111	2v on 45v #601	.25	.25
743	A111	2v on 55v #603	.25	.25
744	A111	3v on 60v #604	.25	.25
744A	A111	3v on 75v #606	.25	.25

745	A111	4v on 45v #601	.25	.25
745A	A111	5v on 70v #605		
745B	A111	34v on 20v #598	.50	.50
745C	A111	67v on 300v #609	1.00	1.00
745D	A111	73v on 80v #607		
		Nos. 742-745D (10)	3.00	3.00

Issued: No. 742, No. 742A, 743, 744, 745, 745A, 12/18/98; No. 744A, 4/27/99; Nos. 745B, 745C, 745D, 2/17/00.

Ceremonial Dancers — A140

1v, Banks Islands. 2v, Small Nambas, Laman-Malakula. 3v, Small Nambas, Malakula. 5v, Smol Bag Theatre. 107v, South West Bay, Malakula. 200v, Big Nambas, Malakula. 500v, Pentacost.

1999, July 14   Perf. 14

746	A140	1v multicolored	.25	.25
747	A140	2v multicolored	.25	.25
748	A140	3v multicolored	.25	.25
749	A140	5v multicolored	.25	.25
750	A140	107v multicolored	1.90	1.90
751	A140	200v multicolored	3.75	3.75
752	A140	500v multicolored	9.25	9.25
		Nos. 746-752 (7)	15.90	15.90

See Nos. 788-791.

Poisonous Fish — A141

Designs: 34v, Pterois antennata. 84v, Pterois antennata, diff. 90v, Pterois volitans. 96v, Pterois volitans, diff.

1999, Oct. 13   Litho.   Perf. 14¼

753	A141	34v multi	.90	.90
754	A141	84v multi	2.10	2.10
755	A141	90v multi	2.50	2.50
756	A141	96v multi	2.75	2.75
		Nos. 753-756 (4)	8.25	8.25

Millennium A142

Designs: a, 34v, Fish. b, 68v, Girl, land diver, vert. c, 84v, Fetish, vert. d, 90v, Bird, flowers. e, 96v, Man with conch shell.

1999, Dec. 1   Perf. 14½

757	A142	Sheet of 5, #a.-e.	8.50	8.50

Souvenir Sheet

Queen Mother, 100th Birthday — A143

a, 107v, As child. b, 100v, As old woman.

Litho. with Foil Application
2000, May 22   Perf. 13¼

758	A143	Sheet of 2, #a-b	6.00	6.00

The Stamp Show 2000, London.

Intelsat A144

Designs: 10v, Launch vehicle. 34v, Port Vila ground station. 100v, Intelsat 802 over Vanuatu. 225v, Intelsat and Tam Tam drum.

Litho. with Foil Application
2000, June 21   Die Cut Perf. 10
Self-Adhesive

759-762	A144	Set of 4	8.50	8.50
762a		Souvenir sheet, #760, 762	6.50	6.50

World Stamp Expo 2000, Anaheim (#762a).

Independence, 20th Anniv., UN Peace Year — A145

Artwork: 34v, Abstract painting by Sero Kuautonga. 67v, Tapa cloth by Moses Pita. 73v, Tapestry by Juliet Pita. 84v, Natora wood carving by Emmannuel Watt. 90v, Watercolor by Joseph John.

2000, July 29 Litho. Perf. 13¾x13¼

763-767	A145	Set of 5	9.50	9.50
		Booklet, 5 #764	8.00	

2000 Summer Olympics, Sydney — A146

Designs: 56v, Runner. 67v, Weight lifter. 90v, High jumper. 96v, Boxer.

2000, Sept. 15   Perf. 13¼x13

768-771	A146	Set of 4	7.00	7.00
		Booklet, 5 #769	7.50	

Dolphins — A147

34v, Common. 73v, Spotted. 84v, Spinner. 107v, Bottlenose.

2000, Nov. 30   Litho.   Perf. 12½

772-775	A147	Set of 4	8.00	8.00
775a		Souvenir sheet, #774-775	7.00	7.00

Hong Kong 2001 Stamp Exhibition (#775a).

Birds — A148

Designs: 35v, Cardinal honeyeater. 60v, Vanuatu white-eye. 90v, Santo Mountain starling. 100v, Royal parrotfinch. 110v, Vanuatu Mountain honeyeater.

2001, Feb. 1   Litho.   Perf. 14

776-780	A148	Set of 5	12.00	12.00
780a		Horiz. strip, #776-780	12.00	12.00

Exports — A149

Designs: 35v, Vanilla. 75v, Cacao. 90v, Coffee. 110v, Copra.

2001, Apr. 11   Perf. 13¼x13

781-784	A149	Set of 4	8.25	8.25

Whales A150

Designs: 60v, Sperm. 80v, Humpback, vert. 90v, Blue.

Perf. 14½x14¾, 14¾x14½

2001, July 18   Litho.

785-787	A150	Set of 3	7.50	7.50
787a		Souvenir sheet, #785-787, perf. 14½	7.50	7.50

See New Caledonia No. 874.

Ceremonial Dancers Type of 1999

Designs: 35v, Snake dance, Banks Islands, horiz. 100v, Toka Dance, Tanna, horiz. 300v, Rom Dance, Ambryn, horiz. 1000v, Brasive Dance, Futuna, horiz.

2001, Sept. 12 Litho. Perf. 13x13¼

788	A140	35v multi	.90	.90
789	A140	100v multi	2.50	2.50
790	A140	300v multi	7.50	7.50

Litho. With Foil Application

791	A140	1000v multi	24.00	24.00
		Nos. 788-791 (4)	34.90	34.90

Sand Drawings — A151

Various sand drawings and: a, Four people on beach. b, Man standing in canoe in water. c, Man sitting on canoe, man rowing canoe. d, Canoe, shelter.

Perf. 12¾x13½

2001, Nov. 28   Litho.

792	A151	60v multi	1.00	1.00
792A	A151	90v multi	1.50	1.50
792B	A151	110v multi	1.90	1.90
792C	A151	135v multi	2.40	2.40
d.		Horiz. strip of 4 + central label	9.00	9.00

Intl. Year of
Ecotourism
A152

Designs: Nos. 793, 798a, 35v, Mount Yasur, Pentecost Island land diver, dancers. Nos. 794, 798b, 60v Dancers, man making kava. Nos. 795, 798c, 75v, Siri Falls, flowers, birds, vert. Nos. 796, 798d, 110v, Kayakers, scuba diver, vert. Nos. 797, 798e, 135v, Beach bungalows, tourists.

2002, Jan. 30   Litho.   Perf. 14
Stamps + Label
793-797 A152   Set of 5   10.50 10.50
Souvenir Sheet
Without Labels
Perf. 14½x14¾
798 A152   Sheet of 5, #a-e   10.50 10.50

Nos. 793, 794, and 797 are 38x26mm and Nos. 795-796 are 26x38mm, while Nos. 798a, 798b, and 798e are 37x25mm and Nos. 798c-798d are 25x37mm.

Horses
A153

Designs: 35v, Working horses. 60v, Cattle roundup. 75v, Horse racing. 80v, Tourism and horses. 200v, Wild Tanna horse.

2002, Mar. 27   Perf. 14¾x14
799-803 A153   Set of 5   10.00 10.00
803a   Souvenir sheet of 1   5.00   5.00
803b   Souvenir sheet of 1 with Phi-
          lakorea 2002 emblem   5.00   5.00

Issued: No. 803b, 7/31/02.

Soccer
A154

Designs: 35v, Children's soccer. 80v, Under 17 soccer. 110v, Women's soccer. 135v, International soccer.

2002, May 31   Litho.   Perf. 13¾
804-807 A154   Set of 4   8.50   8.50
Value is for stamps with surrounding selvage.

Reforestation — A155

No. 808: a, Girl with seedling of Artocarpus atilis. b, Boy and man planting seedling of Endospermum medullosum. c, Canoe carver with Gyrocarpus americanus log. d, Mother and child with Dracontomelon vitiense fruit.

Serpentine Die Cut
2002, July 31   Litho.
Self-Adhesive
808   Horiz. strip of 4   8.00
a.   A155 35v multi   .95   .95
b.   A155 60v multi   1.60   1.60
c.   A155 90v multi   2.25   2.25
d.   A155 110v multi   3.00   3.00

Dugongs
A156

Designs: 35v, Pair nuzzling. 75v, Pair swimming. 80v, One swimming. 135v, One on ocean floor.

2002, Sept. 25   Litho.   Perf. 13¾
812-815 A156   Set of 4   7.50   7.50
815a   Souvenir sheet, #814-815 8.50   8.50

Orchids — A157

Designs: 35v, Dendrobium gouldii. 60v, Dendrobium polysema. 90v, Dendrobium spectabile. 110v, Flickingeria comata.

2002, Nov. 27   Litho.   Perf. 13¼
816-819 A157   Set of 4   7.50   7.50

Year of
Cattle — A158

Cattle Breeds: 35v, Limousin. 80v, Charolais. 110v, Simmental. 135v, Red Brahman.

2003, Jan. 29   Perf. 13
820-823 A158   Set of 4   8.50   8.50

Pentecost
Island Land
Divers — A159

Designs: 35v, Diver on platform. 80v, Diver in air. 110v, Dancers, platform. 200v, Diver and platform (35x90mm).

2003, Mar. 26   Perf. 13¾x13¼
824-827 A159   Set of 4   11.50 11.50
827a   Souvenir sheet of 1   6.25   6.25

Snorkeling
A160

Various people snorkeling: 35v, 80v, 90v, 110v, 135v. 80v and 90v are vert.

2003, May 28   Litho.   Perf. 13¾
828-832 A160   Set of 5   9.00   9.00
832a   Souvenir sheet, #828-832,
          perf. 13¼   10.00 10.00

Natanggura
Palm — A161

Half of palm nut and: 35v, Man planting palm tree, carved dolphins. 80v, Man weaving thatch for roof, carved turtle. 90v, Carver, carved lizard. 135v, Carvers, carved fish.

2003, July 23   Perf. 13¾x13¼
833-836 A161   Set of 4   7.00   7.00

Opening of
Underwater Post
Office in May
2003 — A162

2003, Sept. 24   Perf. 13¾
837 A162 90v multi   2.50   2.50

Sea
Horses — A163

Designs: 60v, Hippocampus kuda. 90v, Hippocampus histrix. 200v, Hippocampus bargibanti.

2003, Sept. 24
838-840 A163   Set of 3   7.25   7.25
840a   Souvenir sheet of 1   4.50   4.50

Moths
A164

Designs: 35v, Daphnis hypothous. 90v, Hippotion celerio. 110v, Euchromia creusa. 135v, Eudocima salaminia.

2003, Nov. 26   Perf. 13½
841-844 A164   Set of 4   8.00   8.00

Activities at
Underwater Post
Office — A165

Designs: 35v, Workers placing mail in bag. 80v, Swimmer placing mail in mail box. 110v, Swimmer at counter. 220v, Clerk at counter, swimmer near mail box.

2004, Jan. 30   Perf. 13¾x13½
845-848 A165   Set of 4   9.75   9.75
848a   Souvenir sheet of 1   5.75   5.75

2004 Hong Kong Stamp Expo (#848a).

Starfish
A166

Designs: 35v, Protoreaster nodulosus. 60v, Linckia laevigata. 90v, Fromia monilis. 250v, Echinaster callosus.

Serpentine Die Cut
2004, Apr. 28   Litho.
Self-Adhesive
849-852 A166   Set of 4   10.00 10.00

Red-tailed
Tropicbird
A167

Designs: 35v, Adult and juvenile. 50v, Adult and chick, vert. 75v, Adult flying above juvenile, vert. 135v, Adult in flight. 200v, Adult pair.

2004, July 14   Litho.   Perf. 13¾
853-857 A167   Set of 5   12.50 12.50
857a   Souvenir sheet, #853-857,
          perf. 13½   12.50 12.50

Musket Cove to Port Vila Yacht Race,
25th Anniv. — A168

Various yachts: 35v, 80v, 90v, 200v. 80v and 200v are vert.

2004, Sept. 18   Perf. 14¼
858-861 A168   Set of 4   12.00 12.00
861a   Souvenir sheet of 1   6.25   6.25

See Fiji Nos. 1024-1027

Miniature Sheet

Marine Life — A169

No. 862: a, Red and black anemonefish. b, Longfin bannerfish. c, Goldman's sweetlips. d, Green turtle. e, Clark's anemonefish. f, Harlequin sweetlips. g, Yellowtail coris. h, Emperor angelfish. i, Hairy red hermit crab, leaf oyster. j, Spotfin lionfish. k, Yellow-lipped sea krait. l, Clam.

Serpentine Die Cut 13¼
2004, Nov. 24   Litho.
Self-Adhesive
862 A169 35v Sheet of 12, #a-l 13.50 13.50

Christmas
A170

Serpentine Die Cut 13
2004, Nov. 24
Self-Adhesive
863 A170 80v multi   2.75 2.75

Sunsets
A171

Designs: 60v, Sailboat. 80v, Man with raised arm, vert. 90v, Sailboats, vert. 135v, Man blowing conch shell.

2005, Jan. 19 *Perf. 14x14½, 14½x14*
864-867 A171 Set of 4   11.00 11.00

Miniature Sheet

Lapita People — A172

No. 868: a, 50v, Man holding tool, vert. b, 70v, People cleaning fish. c, 110v, People tending fire and carrying animal to fire. d, 200v, Women making baskets, mother and child, vert.

2005, Mar. 2   *Perf. 13¼*
868 A172 Sheet of 4, #a-d   12.50 12.50

Pacific Explorer 2005 World Stamp Expo, Sydney.

Volcano
Post
A173

Mail box on Mount Yasur and: 35v, Five tourists. 80v, Native woman. 100v, Three postal workers. 250v, Postal worker removing mail.

2005, May 31 Litho. *Perf. 14x14¼*
869-872 A173 Set of 4   10.00 10.00
872a   Souvenir sheet of 1   6.00 6.00

Souvenir Sheet

Independence, 25th Anniv. — A174

No. 873: a, 35v, Vanuatu natives celebrating. b, 50v, Soldiers raising Vanuatu flag, 1980. c, 400v, Children and statue of family.

2005, July 30 Litho.   *Perf. 13*
873 A174 Sheet of 3, #a-c   15.00 15.00

Miniature Sheet

Corals — A175

No. 874: a, Lace coral. b, Star coral. c, Sun coral (Tubastraea sp.). d, Plate coral. e, Brown anthelia. f, Bubble coral. g, Flowerpot coral. h, Cup coral. i, Daisy coral. j, Sun coral (Tubastraea diaphana). k, Mushroom-feather coral. l, Sun coral (Tubastraea micrantha).

Serpentine Die Cut 13½x13¼
2005, Sept. 7   Litho.
Self-Adhesive
874 A175 35v Sheet of 12, #a-l 13.00 13.00

Landscapes — A176

Designs: 80v, Horse and rider on beach. 90v, Palm trees. 110v, Waterfall. 135v, Harbor.

2005, Nov. 16 Litho. *Perf. 14¼x14*
875-878 A176 Set of 4   13.00 13.00

Miniature Sheet

Reef Shells — A177

No. 879: a, Crocus clam. b, Pearl oyster. c, Gold-ringer cowrie. d, Cock-a-comb oyster. e, Tiger cowrie. f, Textile cone. g, Marlinspike. h, Vibex bonnet. i, Erosa cowrie. j, Scorpion conch. k, Honey cowrie. l, Umbilical ovula.

Serpentine Die Cut 13½
2006, Feb. 8
Self-Adhesive
879 A177 35v Sheet of 12, #a-l 13.00 13.00

Queen Elizabeth II, 80th Birthday
A178

Queen: 50v, As young woman in Army uniform. 100v, Without hat. No. 882, 110v, With blue hat. No. 883, 200v, With yellow hat.
No. 884: a, 110v, Like 100v. b, 200v, Like No. 882.

2006, Apr. 21 Litho.   *Perf. 14*
With White Frames
880-883 A178 Set of 4   9.00 9.00
Souvenir Sheet
Without White Frames
884 A178 Sheet of 2, #a-b   6.50 6.50

Souvenir Sheet

Arrival in Vanuatu of Pedro Fernandez de Quiros, 400th Anniv. — A179

2006, May 10   *Perf. 13¼*
885 A179 350v multi   8.00 8.00

2006 World Cup Soccer Championships, Germany — A180

Various soccer players, 2006 World Cup emblem on soccer jersey: 35v, 80v, 110v, 135v.

2006, June 9 Litho. *Die Cut*
Self-Adhesive
886-889 A180 Set of 4   7.50 7.50
889a   Souvenir sheet, #886-889 7.50 7.50

Flowers
A181

Designs: 5v, Passiflora foetida. 10v, Hibiscus rosa-sinensis. 20v, Cereus undatus. 40v, Strelitzia reginae. 50v, Spathodea campanulata. 70v, Delonix regia. 90v, Hibiscus hilaceus. 100v, Nymphaea sp. 150v, Plumeria obtusa. 500v, Allamanda cathartica. 1000v, Thunbergia grandiflora.

Serpentine Die Cut 11¾
2006, July 1
Self-Adhesive
890 A181 5v multi   .25 .25
891 A181 10v multi   .25 .25
892 A181 20v multi   .35 .35
893 A181 40v multi   .70 .70
894 A181 50v multi   .90 .90
895 A181 70v multi   1.25 1.25
896 A181 100v multi   1.75 1.75
897 A181 150v multi   2.75 2.75
898 A181 500v multi   9.00 9.00
899 A181 1000v multi   18.00 18.00
Inscribed "International Post" at Left
900 A181 5v multi   .25 .25
901 A181 10v multi   .25 .25
902 A181 20v multi   .35 .35
903 A181 50v multi   .90 .90
904 A181 90v multi   1.60 1.60
905 A181 100v multi   1.75 1.75
906 A181 500v multi   9.00 9.00
907 A181 1000v multi   18.00 18.00
   Nos. 890-907 (18)   67.30 67.30

Miniature Sheet

Worldwide Fund for Nature (WWF) — A182

No. 908: a, 70v, Giant grouper and coral. b, 90v, Giant grouper and smaller fish. c, 100v, Juvenile giant groupers. d, 150v, Giant grouper, smaller fish, diff.

2006, Oct. 4 Litho.   *Perf. 13¼*
908 A182 Sheet, 2 each #a-d 15.00 15.00

Shipwreck of the SS President Coolidge — A183

Designs: 90v, Diver, corals. 100v, Divers, fish. 130v, Shipwreck, fish. 150v, Ship sinking, sailors leaving ship (85x30mm).
No. 913: a, 90v, Like #909. b, 100v, Like #910. c, 130v, Like #911. d, 150v, Like #912.

2006, Nov. 29 Litho.   *Perf. 13¼*
Stamps Inscribed "International Post"
909-912 A183 Set of 4   10.00 10.00
Souvenir Sheet
Stamps Without "International Post"
913   A183 Sheet of 4, #a-d 10.00 10.00

Reef Heron
A184

Reef heron: 10v, With wings extended. 20v, Standing on land, vert. 50v, With fish in bill, vert. 70v, Head. 250v, Chicks.

2007, Feb. 9   *Perf. 14½*
914-918 A184 Set of 5   8.50 8.50
918a   Souvenir sheet, #914-918 8.50 8.50

Diving at Million Dollar Point
A185

Designs: Nos. 919, 923a, 90v, Divers near submerged jeep. Nos. 920, 923b, 100v, Divers near submerged truck, vert. (42x60mm). Nos. 921, 923c, 130v, Diver, diff. Nos. 922, 923d, 150v, Diver, lionfish.

2007, Apr. 18   *Perf. 13¼*
Stamps Inscribed "International Post"
919-922 A185 Set of 4   10.00 10.00
Souvenir Sheet
Stamps Without "International Post"
923   A185 Sheet of 4, #a-d 10.00 10.00

Fruit — A186

Designs: 30v, Bananas. 40v, Watermelon. 70v, Limes. 100v, Papayas. 250v, Coconuts.

2007, June 27 *Serpentine Die Cut*
Self-Adhesive
924-928 A186 Set of 5   11.00 11.00

James A. Michener (1907-97), Writer
A187

Michener: 40v, With pen. 90v, At typewriter. 130v, With island natives. 350v, Holding book.

2007, Aug. 22   **Perf. 14½**
929-932 A187   Set of 4   13.00 13.00

Banded
Iguana — A188

Designs: 50v, Two iguanas, two flowers. 70v, Iguana on branch. 100v, Iguana. 250v, Iguana on flower bud.

Serpentine Die Cut 15
2007, Nov. 7   **Litho.**
Self-Adhesive
933-936 A188   Set of 4   11.00 11.00
936a   Souvenir sheet, #935-936 8.50 8.50

Air Vanuatu, 20th Anniv. — A189

Designs: 40v, Three airplanes at airport. 90v, Boeing 737-800. 130v, Boeing 737-300. 180v, Twin Otter. 250v, ATR 42.

2007-08   **Serpentine Die Cut 15**
937 A189 40v multi   .85   .85
938 A189 90v multi   1.90 1.90
939 A189 130v multi   2.75 2.75
940 A189 180v multi   3.75 3.75
941 A189 250v multi   5.25 5.25
       Nos. 937-941 (5)   14.50 14.50

First flight of Boeing 737-800 (#938). Issued: 40v, 130v, 180v, 250v, 11/23; 90v, 1/17/08.

Coconut
Crabs
A190

Crab on: 60v, Beach. 500v, Tree, vert.

Perf. 13½x13¼, 13¼x13½
2008, Feb. 20   **Litho.**
942-943 A190   Set of 2   14.00 14.00
943a   Souvenir sheet, #942-943 14.00 14.00

Miniature Sheet

2008 Summer Olympics,
Beijing — A191

No. 944: a, 10v, Archery. b, 40v, Athletics. c, 60v, Table tennis. d, 90v, Weight lifting.

2008, June 18   **Litho.**   **Perf. 12**
944 A191   Sheet of 4, #a-d   5.00 5.00

Underwater Post Office — A192

Designs: 40v, Underwater postal workers carrying sacks of mail, fish with postcard. 80v, Postal worker, fish with letters. 100v, Postal workers in raft, fish with mail. 200v, Underwater post office, fish and marine life with letters.

2008, July 30   **Litho.**   **Die Cut**
Self-Adhesive
945-948 A192   Set of 4   9.50 9.50

Tourism — A193

Scenes and website addresses of: No. 949, 90v, Vanuatu Tourism. No. 950, 90v, Breakas Beach Resort. No. 951, 90v, Iririki Island Resort and Spa. No. 952, 90v, Le Lagon Resort. No. 953, 90v, The Melanesian Hotel. No. 954, 90v, Le Meridien Resort Spa and Casino. No. 955, 90v, Sebel Hotel.

2008, Aug. 27   **Perf. 15x14¾**
949-955 A193   Set of 7   14.00 14.00

Miniature Sheet

Nudibranchs — A194

No. 956: a, Risbecia tryoni. b, Phyllidia coelestis. c, Flabellina rubrolineata. d, Chromodoris lochi. e, Chromodoris elisabethina. f, Jorunna funebris. g, Glossodoris rufomarginata. h, Phyllidia ocellata. i, Chromodoris geometrica. j, Phyllidia madangensis. k, Hexabranchus sanguineus. l, Glossodoris atromarginata.

Serpentine Die Cut 13¼
2008, Oct. 8
Self-Adhesive
956 A194 40v Sheet of 12, #a-l 10.00 10.00

Birds — A195

Designs: 45v, Eastern reef heron. 100v, Great crested tern. 130v, White-tailed tropicbird. 250v, Fairy tern.

2008, Nov. 26   **Litho.**   **Perf. 14½x15**
957-960 A195   Set of 4   10.50 10.50
960a   Souvenir sheet of 1 #960 5.50 5.50

Romance in Vanuatu — A196

Couples in Vanuatu, website addresses for: No. 961, 90v, Bride and groom wearing flowers (Events Vanuatu). No. 962, 90v, Bride and groom with wine glasses (Events Vanuatu). No. 963, 90v, Man and woman sitting on beach (Air Vanuatu). No. 964, 90v, Man and woman sitting on chaise lounges (Breakas Beach Resort). No. 965, 90v, Man and woman at table (White Grass Ocean Resort).

2009, Jan. 28   **Litho.**   **Die Cut**
Self-Adhesive
961-965 A196   Set of 5   7.75 7.75

Mystery (Inyeug)
Island — A197

Designs: Nos. 966, 970a, 90v, Boat dock. Nos. 967, 970b, 100v, Snorkelers and boat, horiz. Nos. 968, 970c, 130v, Sailboat and trees, horiz. Nos. 969, 970d, 200v, Man and woman on outrigger canoe on beach.

2009, Mar. 28   **Litho.**   **Perf. 14**
Stamps Inscribed "International Post"
966-969 A197   Set of 4   9.25 9.25
Souvenir Sheet
Stamps Without "International Post"
970 A197   Sheet of 4, #a-d   9.25 9.25

Peonies
A198

2009, Apr. 10   **Litho.**   **Perf. 13¼**
971 A198 100v multi   1.90 1.90
       Printed in sheets of 8.

Plumeria Flowers — A199

Various plumeria flowers: 90v, 100v, 130v, 150v.

2009, May 14   **Perf. 14½x14**
972-975 A199   Set of 4   9.00 9.00

Souvenir Sheet

Hong Kong 2009 Intl. Stamp
Exhibition — A200

2009, May 14   **Perf. 13½**
976 A200   Sheet of 2, Pitcairn
            Islands #685a,
            Vanuatu #976a   6.25 6.25
a.   150v Two pandas   3.00 3.00

No. 976 sold for 310v and New Zealand $5, and is identical to Pitcairn Islands No. 685.

Souvenir Sheet

First Contact Between Russia and
Vanuatu, 200th Anniv. — A201

No. 977 — Map and: a, 130v, Russian Admiral V. M. Golovnin. b, 350v, Russian ship, "Diana."

2009, July 28   **Perf. 13¼**
977 A201   Sheet of 2, #a-b   9.50 9.50

Charles Darwin (1809-82),
Naturalist — A202

No. 978 — Darwin, birds and: a, Tortoises. b, Iguanas.

2009, Sept. 2   **Perf. 13¼x13½**
978 A202   200v Horiz. pair, #a-b,
            + central label   8.00 8.00

Worldwide Fund for Nature
(WWF) — A203

No. 979 — Beach thick-knee: a, Adult on nest, bird in flight. b, Adult and chick on ground, two birds in flight. c, Two adults at water's edge, bird in flight. d, Adult on beach, bird in flight.

2009, Nov. 25   **Litho.**   **Perf. 13¼**
979   Horiz. strip of 4   9.00 9.00
a. A203 50v multi   1.10 1.10
b. A203 90v multi   1.90 1.90
c. A203 130v multi   2.75 2.75
d. A203 150v multi   3.25 3.25

No. 979 was printed in sheets containing two strips.

VANUATU

Souvenir Sheet

New Year 2010 (Year of the Tiger) — A204

2010, Feb. 14   *Perf. 13¼*
980 A204 250v multi   5.25 5.25

Miniature Sheet

Butterflies — A205

No. 981: a, Calopsilia pomona. b, Papilio godeffroyi. c, Hypolimnas octocula. d, Doleschallia bisaltide. e, Acraea andromacha. f, Danaus affinis.

2010, Apr. 14   *Die Cut*
Self-Adhesive
981 A205 100v Sheet of 6, #a-f   12.50 12.50

Tourism — A206

Designs: 40v, Dugong off Epi Island. 140v, Snake Dance, Banks Island, horiz. 160v, Iririki Resort, Efate Island. 190v, Mt. Yasur Volcano, Tanna Island, horiz.

Perf. 13¼x13¾, 13¾x13¼
2010, Apr. 30
982 A206 40v multi   .85 .85
   a.   Perf. 14   .85 .85

Inscribed "International Post" at Left

983 A206 140v multi   3.00 3.00
984 A206 160v multi   3.25 3.25
985 A206 190v multi   4.00 4.00
   Nos. 982-985 (4)   11.10 11.10

Miniature Sheet
Perf. 14
986   Sheet of 4, #982a, 986a-986c   11.50 11.50
   a.   A206 140v Like #983, without "International Post" at left   3.00 3.00
   b.   A206 160v Like #984, without "International Post" at left   3.25 3.25
   c.   A206 190v Like #985, without "International Post" at left   4.00 4.00

Expo 2010, Shanghai (#986).

Cats — A207

Color of cat: 10v, White. 100v, Black and white. 160v, Brown and white. 190v, Gray and white.

2010, July 14   *Perf. 14½x14*
987-990 A207   Set of 4   9.50 9.50

Souvenir Sheet

2010 Youth Olympics, Singapore — A208

2010, Aug. 14   *Perf. 13¼*
991 A208 500v multi   10.00 10.00

"Smile With Us" A209

Designs: No. 992, 20v, Man, statues in background. No. 993, 20v, Two women. No. 994, 20v, Three children. No. 995, 20v, Fish. No. 996, 20v, Dugong. No. 997, 100v, Woman. No. 998, 100v, Divers at Underwater Post Office. No. 999, 100v, Island. No. 1000, 100v, Dolphin. No. 1001, 100v, Airplane.

2010, Dec. 15   *Perf. 13½*
992-1001 A209   Set of 10   12.50 12.50
996a   Horiz. strip of 5, #992-996   2.00 2.00
1001a   Horiz. strip of 5, #997-1001a   10.50 10.50

Turtles A210

No. 1002: a, Green turtles, "International Post" at left. b, Green turtles, "International Post" at right. c, Hawksbill turtle, "International Post" at left. d, Hawksbill turtles, "International Post" at right.

2011, Jan. 26   *Perf. 13½x13¼*
1002   Horiz. strip of 4 + central label   8.50 8.50
   a.-d.   A210 100v Any single   2.10 2.10

Tanna Coffee — A211

Designs: No. 1003, 100v, Short black. No. 1004, 100v, Long black. 140v, Latte. 160v, Cappuccino.

2011, Mar. 23   *Perf. 14½x14*
1003-1006 A211   Set of 4   11.00 11.00

Worldwide Fund for Nature (WWF) — A212

No. 1007 — Massena's lorikeet: a, Bird facing left. b, Bird on branch. c, Two birds on branch. d, Bird on palm frond.

2011, May 25   *Litho.*   *Perf. 14*
1007   Horiz. strip of 4   9.50 9.50
   a.   A212 40v multi   .90 .90
   b.   A212 60v multi   1.40 1.40
   c.   A212 140v multi   3.25 3.25
   d.   A212 160v multi   3.75 3.75
   e.   Sheet of 8, 2 each #1007a-1007d   19.00 19.00

Green and Golden Bell Frog — A213

Designs: 45v, Frog on branch. 70v, Frog in flower. 140v, Three frogs in flower. 200v, Frog on cut branch.

2011, July 27   *Perf. 14¼*
1008-1011 A213   Set of 4   10.50 10.50
1011a   Souvenir sheet of 2, #1010-1011   7.75 7.75

SEMI POSTAL STAMPS

No. 324 Surcharged

Nos. 414-418 Surcharged

Wmk. 373 (No. B1), 384
Perf. 14x13½, 14x14½

1987, May 12   *Litho.*
B1 A60   20v +10v on 2v   1.40 1.40
B2 CD337   20v +10v   1.40 1.40
B3 CD337   35v +15v   2.40 2.40
B4 CD337   45v +20v   2.75 2.75
B5 CD337   55v +25v   5.25 5.25
B6 CD337   100v +50v   5.75 5.75
   Nos. B1-B6 (6)   18.95 18.95

Old value of #B1 obliterated by 2 horizontal bars. Surcharge indicated by text "Surcharge +10."

VATICAN CITY

ˈva-ti-kən ˈsi-tē

LOCATION — Western Italy, directly outside the western boundary of Rome
GOVT. — Independent state subject to certain political restrictions under a treaty with Italy
AREA — 108.7 acres

POP. — 870 (1999 est.)

100 Centesimi = 1 Lira
100 Cents = 1 Euro (2002)

Catalogue values for unused stamps in this country are for Never Hinged items, beginning with Scott 68 in the regular postage section, Scott C1 in the airpost section, Scott E3 in the special delivery section, and Scott J7 in the postage due section.

Watermarks

Wmk. 235 — Crossed Keys   Wmk. 277 — Winged Wheel

Papal Arms — A1   Pope Pius XI — A2

Unwmk.
1929, Aug. 1   *Engr.*   *Perf. 14*
Surface-Colored Paper
1   A1   5c dk brn & pink   .25 .25
2   A1   10c dk grn & lt grn   .25 .35
3   A1   20c violet & lilac   .70 .60
4   A1   25c dk bl & lt bl   .85 .70
5   A1   30c indigo & yellow   1.00 .80
6   A1   50c ind & sal buff   1.50 .80
7   A1   75c brn car & gray   2.00 1.40

Photo.
White Paper
8   A2   80c carmine rose   1.50 .45
9   A2   1.25 l dark blue   2.50 1.00
10   A2   2 l olive brown   5.00 2.00
11   A2   2.50 l red orange   4.00 3.50
12   A2   5 l dk green   5.00 11.00
13   A2   10 l olive blk   10.00 15.00
   Nos. 1-13,E1-E2 (15)   67.55 63.85
   Set, never hinged   240.00

The stamps of Type A1 have, in this and subsequent issues, the words "POSTE VATICANE" in rows of colorless letters in the background.

For surcharges and overprints see Nos. 14, 35-40, 61-67, J1-J6, Q1-Q13.

No. 5 Surcharged in Red

1931, Oct. 1
14   A1   25c on 30c ind & yel   2.25 2.00
   Never hinged   10.00

Arms of Pope Pius XI — A5   Vatican Palace and Obelisk — A6

Vatican
Gardens — A7

Pope
Pius XI
A8

St.
Peter's
Basilica
A9

1933, May 31   Engr.   Wmk. 235

19	A5	5c copper red	.25	.25
a.		Imperf., pair	250.00	400.00
20	A6	10c dk brn & blk	.25	.25
21	A6	12½c dp grn & blk	.25	.25
22	A6	20c orange & blk	.25	.25
a.		Vertical pair imperf. between and at bottom	650.00	
23	A6	25c dk olive & blk	.25	.25
a.		Imperf., pair	200.00	300.00
24	A7	30c blk & dk brn	.25	.25
25	A7	50c vio & dk brn	.25	.25
26	A7	75c brn red & dk brn	.25	.25
27	A7	80c rose & dk brn	.25	.25
28	A8	1 l violet & blk	6.50	6.50
29	A8	1.25 l dk bl & blk	19.00	11.50
30	A8	2 l dk brn & blk	45.00	32.50
31	A8	2.75 l dk vio & blk	60.00	80.00
32	A9	5 l blk brn & dk grn	.25	.25
33	A9	10 l dk bl & dk grn	.25	.30
34	A9	20 l blk & dp grn	.30	.40
		Nos. 19-34,E3-E4 (18)	134.25	134.60
		Set, never hinged	540.00	

Nos. 8-13 Surcharged in
Black

No. 36

No. 36a

1934, June 16   Unwmk.

35	A2	40c on 80c	47.50	20.00
36	A2	1.30 l on 1.25 l	200.00	100.00
a.		Small figures "30" in "1.30"	22,500.	16,000.
		Never hinged	27,500.	
37	A2	2.05 l on 2 l	260.00	32.50
a.		No comma btwn. 2 & 0	400.00	40.00
		Never hinged	1,200.	
38	A2	2.55 l on 2.50 l	160.00	275.00
a.		No comma btwn. 2 & 5	200.00	475.00
		Never hinged	600.00	
39	A2	3.05 l on 5 l	525.00	475.00
40	A2	3.70 l on 10 l	475.00	725.00
a.		No comma btwn. 3 & 7		
		Nos. 35-40 (6)	1,667.	1,627.
		Set, never hinged	4,000.	

A second printing of Nos. 36-40 was made
in 1937. The 2.55 l and 3.05 l of the first printing and 1.30 l of the second printing sell for
more.

The status of No. 40a has been questioned.
The editors would like to examine an authenticated example of this variety.

Forged surcharges of Nos. 35-40 are
plentiful.

Tribonian
Presenting
Pandects to
Justinian I
A10

Pope
Gregory IX
Promulgating
Decretals
A11

1935, Feb. 1   Photo.

41	A10	5c red orange	4.50	4.50
42	A10	10c purple	4.50	4.50
43	A10	25c green	25.00	35.00
44	A11	75c rose red	65.00	60.00
45	A11	80c dark brown	55.00	42.50
46	A11	1.25 l dark blue	65.00	52.50
		Nos. 41-46 (6)	219.00	199.00
		Set, never hinged	1,045.	

Intl. Juridical Congress, Rome, 1934.

Doves and
Bell — A12

Allegory of
Church and
Bible — A13

St. John
Bosco — A14

St. Francis de
Sales — A15

1936, June 22

47	A12	5c blue green	1.50	1.50
48	A13	10c black	1.50	1.50
49	A14	25c yellow green	45.00	15.00
50	A12	50c rose violet	1.50	1.50
51	A13	75c rose red	47.50	60.00
52	A14	80c orange brn	2.50	3.00
53	A15	1.25 l dark blue	2.75	3.00
54	A15	5 l dark brown	2.75	7.50
		Nos. 47-54 (8)	105.00	93.00
		Set, never hinged	495.00	

Catholic Press Conference, 1936.

Crypt of St.
Cecilia in
Catacombs
of St.
Calixtus
A16

Basilica of Sts. Nereus and Achilleus
in Catacombs of St. Domitilla
A17

1938, Oct. 12   Perf. 14

55	A16	5c bister brown	.30	.30
56	A16	10c deep orange	.30	.30
57	A16	25c deep green	.35	.35
58	A17	75c deep rose	7.50	7.50
59	A17	80c violet	20.00	20.00
60	A17	1.25 l blue	29.00	29.00
		Nos. 55-60 (6)	57.45	57.45
		Set, never hinged	200.00	

Intl. Christian Archaeological Congress,
Rome, 1938.

Interregnum Issue

Nos. 1-7 Overprinted
in Black

1939, Feb. 20   Perf. 14

61	A1	5c dk brn & pink	26.00	7.50
62	A1	10c dk grn & lt grn	.75	.25
63	A1	20c violet & lilac	.75	.25
64	A1	25c dk bl & lt bl	3.25	5.00
65	A1	30c indigo & yellow	1.25	.25
a.		Pair, one without ovpt.	2,400.	
66	A1	50c indigo & sal buff	1.25	.25
67	A1	75c brn car & gray	1.25	.25
		Nos. 61-67 (7)	34.50	13.75
		Set, never hinged	135.00	

Catalogue values for unused
stamps in this section, from this
point to the end of the section, are
for Never Hinged items.

Coronation of Pope
Pius XII — A18

1939, June 2   Photo.

68	A18	25c green	3.00	.40
69	A18	75c rose red	.70	.70
70	A18	80c violet	8.50	4.00
71	A18	1.25 l deep blue	.70	.70
		Nos. 68-71 (4)	12.90	5.80

Coronation of Pope Pius XII, Mar. 12, 1939.

Arms of Pope
Pius XII — A19

Pope Pius XII
A20   A21

Wmk. 235

1940, Mar. 12   Engr.   Perf. 14

72	A19	5c dark carmine	.25	.25
73	A20	1 l purple & blk	.25	.25
74	A21	1.25 l slate bl & blk	.25	.25
a.		Imperf., pair	450.00	500.00
75	A20	2 l dk brn & blk	1.40	.85
76	A21	2.75 l dk rose vio & blk	2.00	1.75
		Nos. 72-76 (5)	4.15	3.35

See Nos. 91-98. For surcharges see Nos.
102-109.

A22

Picture of Jesus inscribed "I have Compas-
sion on the Multitude."

1942, Sept. 1   Photo.   Unwmk.

77	A22	25c dk blue green	.25	.25
78	A22	80c chestnut brown	.25	.25
79	A22	1.25 l deep blue	.25	.25
		Nos. 77-79 (3)	.75	.75

See Nos. 84-86, 99-101.

A23

Consecration of Archbishop Pacelli by Pope
Benedict XV.

1942, Jan. 16

80	A23	25c myr grn & gray grn	.25	.25
81	A23	80c dk brn & yel grn	.25	.25
82	A23	1.25 l sapphire & vio bl	.25	.25
a.		Name and value panel omitted		
83	A23	5 l vio blk & gray blk	.25	.25
		Nos. 80-83 (4)	1.00	1.00

25th anniv. of the consecration of Msgr.
Eugenio Pacelli (later Pope Pius XII) as Archbishop of Sardes.

Type of 1942
Inscribed MCMXLIII

1944, Jan. 31

84	A22	25c dk blue green	.25	.25
85	A22	80c chestnut brown	.25	.25
86	A22	1.25 l deep blue	.25	.25
		Nos. 84-86 (3)	.75	.75

Raphael
Sanzio — A24

Designs: 80c, Antonio da Sangallo. 1.25 l,
Carlo Maratti. 10 l, Antonio Canova.

1944, Nov. 21   Wmk. 235   Photo.

87	A24	25c olive & green	.30	.25
88	A24	80c cl & rose vio	.60	.25
a.		Dbl. impression of center	750.00	
89	A24	1.25 l bl vio & dp bl	.60	.25
a.		Imperf., pair	650.00	900.
90	A24	10 l bister & ol brn	1.25	.75
		Nos. 87-90 (4)	2.75	1.50

400th anniv. of the Pontifical Academy of
the Virtuosi of the Pantheon.

Types of 1940

1945, Mar. 5   Engr.   Unwmk.

91	A19	5c gray	.25	.25
a.		Imperf., pair	200.00	
92	A19	30c brown	.25	.25
a.		Imperf., pair	120.00	
93	A19	50c dark green	.25	.25
94	A21	1 l brown & blk	.25	.25
95	A21	1.50 l rose car & blk	.25	.25
a.		Imperf., pair	325.00	
96	A21	2.50 l dp ultra & blk	.25	.25
97	A20	5 l rose vio & blk	.25	.25
98	A20	20 l gray grn & blk	.25	.30
		Nos. 91-98,E5-E6 (10)	2.60	2.65

Nos. 91-96 exist in pairs imperf. between,
some vertical, some horizontal. Value, each
$150.

Pair imperf. vertically exist of 30c and 50c
(value $50), and of 5 lire (value $90).

Type of 1942
Inscribed MCMXLIV
Wmk. 277

1945, Sept. 12   Photo.   Perf. 14

99	A22	1 l dk blue green	.25	.25
100	A22	3 l dk carmine	.25	.25
a.		Jesus image omitted	100.00	100.00
101	A22	5 l deep ultra	.25	.25
		Nos. 99-101 (3)	.75	.75

Nos. 99-101 exist in pairs imperf. between,
both horizontal and vertical. Value, each $140.

Pairs imperf. horizontally exist of 3 lire
(value $50) and 5 lire (value $60).

Nos. 91 to 98 Surcharged with New
Values and Bars in Black or Blue

Two types of 25c on 30c:
I — Surcharge 16mm wide.
II — Surcharge 19mm wide.

Two types of 1 l on 50c:
I — Surcharge bars 5mm wide.
II — Bars 4mm wide.

1946, Jan. 9   Unwmk.   Perf. 14

102	A19	20c on 5c	.25	.25
103	A19	25c on 30c (I)	.25	.25
a.		Type II	.40	.25
b.		Inverted surcharge (II)	350.00	350.00
104	A19	1 l on 50c (I)	.25	.25
a.		Type II	5.00	3.50
105	A21	1.50 l on 1 l (Bl)	.25	.25
a.		Double surcharge	175.00	
106	A21	3 l on 1.50 l	.25	.25
107	A21	5 l on 2.50 l	.40	.25
108	A20	10 l on 5 l	1.10	.55
109	A20	30 l on 20 l	3.25	1.50
	Nos. 102-109,E7-E8 (10)		14.50	7.05

Nos. 102, 105-109 exist in horizontal pairs, imperf. between. Value, each $150.
Vertical pairs imperf. between exist of Nos. 102, 106-107 (value, each $150) and of No. 104a (value $250).
Nos. 102, 104-108 exist in pairs imperf. vertically or horizontally, or both. Value $40 to $60.
Nos. 102-108 exist in pairs, one without surcharge. Value, Nos. 102-105, each $150; Nos. 106-108, each $200.

St. Vigilio
Cathedral,
Trent — A28

St. Angela
Merici — A29

Designs: 50c, St. Anthony Zaccaria. 75c, St. Ignatius of Loyola. 1 l, St. Cajetan Thiene. 1.50 l, St. John Fisher. 2 l, Christoforo Cardinal Madruzzi. 2.50 l, Reginald Cardinal Pole. 3 l, Marcello Cardinal Cervini. 4 l, Giovanni Cardinal del Monte. 5 l, Emperor Charles V. 10 l, Pope Paul III.

Perf. 14, 14x13½

1946, Feb. 21   Photo.   Unwmk.
Centers in Dark Brown

110	A28	5c olive bister	.25	.25
111	A29	25c purple	.25	.25
112	A29	50c brown orange	.25	.25
113	A29	75c black	.25	.25
114	A29	1 l dk violet	.25	.25
115	A29	1.50 l red orange	.25	.25
116	A29	2 l yellow green	.25	.25
117	A29	2.50 l deep blue	.25	.25
118	A29	3 l brt carmine	.25	.25
119	A29	4 l ocher	.25	.25
120	A29	5 l brt ultra	.25	.25
121	A29	10 l dp rose car	.25	.25
	Nos. 110-121,E9-E10 (14)		3.50	3.50

Council of Trent (1545-63), 400th anniv.
Vertical pairs imperf. between exist of Nos. 110-111, 114, 116-117 (value, each $150); Nos. 113, 119 (value, each $100); Nos. 115, 118 (value, each $75).
Horizontal pairs imperf. between exist of #121 (value $200); #113, 117 (value $150).

Basilica of St.
Agnes — A40

Basilica of
the Holy
Cross in
Jerusalem
A41

Pope
Pius XII
A42

Basilicas: 3 l, St. Clement. 5 l, St. Prassede. 8 l, St. Mary in Cosmedin. 16 l, St. Sebastian. 25 l, St. Lawrence. 35 l, St. Paul. 40 l, St. Mary Major.

Perf. 14, 14x13½

1949, Mar. 7   Photo.   Wmk. 235

122	A40	1 l dark brown	.25	.25
123	A40	3 l violet	.25	.25
124	A40	5 l deep orange	.25	.25
a.		Perf. 14x13½	15.00	4.50
125	A40	8 l dp blue grn	.25	.25

Perf. 14, 13½x14

126	A41	13 l dull green	6.00	5.00
127	A41	16 l dk olive brn	.25	.25
a.		Perf. 14	.75	.25
128	A41	25 l car rose	4.75	.65
129	A41	35 l red violet	26.00	12.00
a.		Perf. 13½x14	55.00	8.25
130	A41	40 l blue	.25	.25
a.		Perf. 13½x14	.25	.25

Engr.
Perf. 14

131	A42	100 l sepia	3.00	3.00
	Nos. 122-131,E11-E12 (12)		89.25	45.40

All values come in two perfs except the 100 l.

Jesus Giving St.
Peter the Keys to
Heaven — A43

Cathedrals of St.
Peter, St. Paul, St.
John Lateran and
St. Mary
Major — A44

Pope Boniface VIII
Proclaiming Holy
Year in
1300 — A45

Pope Pius XII in
Ceremony of
Opening the Holy
Door — A46

Wmk. 277

1949, Dec 21   Photo.   Perf. 14

132	A43	5 l red brn & brn	.25	.25
133	A44	6 l ind & yel brn	.25	.25
134	A45	8 l ultra & dk grn	.75	.35
135	A46	10 l green & slate	.25	.25
136	A43	20 l dk grn & red brn	1.25	.25
137	A44	25 l sepia & dp blue	.60	.25
138	A45	30 l grnsh blk & rose lil	1.50	1.00
139	A46	60 l blk brn & brn rose	1.00	1.00
	Nos. 132-139 (8)		5.85	3.60

Holy Year, 1950.

Palatine Guard and
Statue of St.
Peter — A47

1950, Sept. 12

140	A47	25 l sepia	8.25	2.50
141	A47	35 l dark green	3.25	2.50
142	A47	55 l red brown	1.90	2.50
	Nos. 140-142 (3)		13.40	7.50

Centenary of the Palatine Guard.

Pope Pius XII
Making
Proclamation
A48

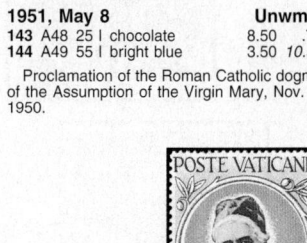

Crowd at St.
Peter's
Basilica — A49

1951, May 8   Unwmk.

143	A48	25 l chocolate	8.50	.75
144	A49	55 l bright blue	3.50	10.50

Proclamation of the Roman Catholic dogma of the Assumption of the Virgin Mary, Nov. 1, 1950.

A50

Pope
Pius X — A51

Perf. 14x13½

1951, June 3   Photo.   Wmk. 235
Background of Medallion in Gold

145	A50	6 l	purple	.25 .25
146	A50	10 l	Prus green	.25 .25
147	A51	60 l	blue	5.50 5.50
148	A51	115 l	brown	15.00 15.00
		Nos. 145-148 (4)		21.00 21.00

Council of Chalcedon A52

Pope Leo I Remonstrating with Attila the Hun — A53

1951, Oct. 31   Engr.   Perf. 14x13½

149	A52	5 l	dk gray green	.50 .25
a.		Pair, imperf. horiz.		350.00
150	A53	25 l	red brown	3.00 1.75
a.		Horiz. pair, imperf. btwn.		700.00 700.00
151	A52	35 l	carmine rose	8.00 3.00
152	A53	60 l	deep blue	22.50 10.00
153	A52	100 l	dark brown	30.00 25.00
		Nos. 149-153 (5)		64.00 40.00

Council of Chalcedon, 1500th anniv.

No. 126 Surcharged with New Value and Bars in Carmine

1952, Mar. 15   Perf. 14

154	A41	12 l on 13 l dull grn		1.75 1.00
a.		Perf. 13½x14		1.75 1.00
b.		Pair, one without surcharge		300.00 300.00

Roman States Stamp and Stagecoach — A54

1952, June 9   Engr.   Perf. 13

155	A54	50 l	sep & dp bl, cr	5.00 3.25
a.		Souvenir sheet		140.00 100.00

1st stamp of the Papal States, cent. #155a contains 4 stamps similar to #155, with papal insignia and inscription in purple. Singles from the souvenir sheet differ slightly from #155. The colors are closer to black and blue, and the cream tone of the paper is visible on the back.

St. Maria Goretti — A55

St. Peter — A56

Perf. 13½x14

1953, Feb. 12   Photo.   Wmk. 235

156	A55	15 l	dp brown & vio	4.25 2.00
157	A55	35 l	dp rose & brn	3.25 2.00

Martyrdom of St. Maria Goretti, 50th anniv.

Perf. 13½x13, 14

1953, Apr. 23   Engr.

Designs: 5 l, Pius XII and Roman sepulcher. 10 l, St. Peter and Tomb of the Apostle. 12 l, Sylvester I and Constantine Basilica. 20 l, Julius II and Bramante's plans. 25 l, Paul III and the Apse. 35 l, Sixtus V and dome. 45 l, Paul V and facade. 60 l, Urban VIII and the

---

canopy. 65 l, Alexander VII and colonnade. 100 l, Pius VI and the sacristy.

158	A56	3 l	dk red brn & blk	.25 .25
159	A56	5 l	slate & blk	.25 .25
160	A56	10 l	dk green & blk	.25 .25
161	A56	12 l	chestnut & blk	.25 .25
162	A56	20 l	violet & blk	.25 .25
163	A56	25 l	dk brown & blk	.25 .25
164	A56	35 l	dk carmine & blk	.25 .25
165	A56	45 l	olive brn & blk	.25 .25
166	A56	60 l	dk blue & blk	.25 .25
167	A56	65 l	car rose & blk	.25 .25
168	A56	100 l	rose vio & blk	.25 .25
		Nos. 158-168,E13-E14 (13)		3.35 3.25

St. Clare of Assisi — A57

Unwmk.

1953, Aug. 12   Photo.   Perf. 13

169	A57	25 l	aqua, yel brn & vio brn	2.00 1.00
170	A57	35 l	brn red, yel brn & vio brn	14.00 9.00

Death of St. Clare of Assisi, 700th anniv.

Virgin Mary and St. Bernard A58

1953, Nov. 10

171	A58	20 l	ol grn & dk vio brn	.75 .50
172	A58	60 l	brt bl & ol grn	7.25 4.00

Death of St. Bernard of Clairvaux, 800th anniv.

Peter Lombard Medal — A59

1953, Dec. 29

173	A59	100 l	lil rose, bl, dk grn & yel	32.50 20.00

Peter Lombard, Bishop of Paris 1159.

Pope Pius XI and Vatican City — A60

1954, Feb. 12   Wmk. 235

174	A60	25 l	bl, red brn & cr	1.25 1.00
175	A60	60 l	yel brn & dp bl	3.00 2.50

Signing of the Lateran Pacts, 25th anniv.

Pope Pius IX A61

Portraits: (At left) - 6 l, 20 l, Pope Pius IX. (At right) — 4 l, 12 l, 35 l, Pope Pius XII.

1954, May 26   Engr.   Perf. 13

176	A61	3 l	violet	.25 .25
177	A61	4 l	carmine	.25 .25
178	A61	6 l	plum	.25 .25
179	A61	12 l	blue green	1.00 .25

180	A61	20 l	red brown	.90 .85
181	A61	35 l	ultra	2.25 2.25
		Nos. 176-181 (6)		4.90 4.10

Marian Year; centenary of the dogma of the Immaculate Conception.

St. Pius X — A62

1954, May 29   Photo.
Colors (except background): Yellow and Plum

182	A62	10 l	dark brown	.25 .25
183	A62	25 l	violet	2.50 1.25
184	A62	35 l	dk slate gray	4.25 2.50
		Nos. 182-184 (3)		7.00 4.00

Canonization of Pope Pius X, May 20, 1954. #182-184 exist imperf. Value, each pair $800.

Basilica of St. Francis of Assisi A63

1954, Oct. 1   Photo.   Perf. 14

185	A63	20 l	dk vio gray & cr	2.00 1.75
186	A63	35 l	dk brown & cream	1.50 1.40

Consecration of the Basilica of St. Francis of Assisi, 200th anniv.

St. Augustine A64

1954, Nov. 13

187	A64	35 l	blue green	1.00 .90
188	A64	50 l	redsh brown	1.90 1.75

1600th birth anniv. of St. Augustine.

Madonna of the Gate of Dawn, Vilnius — A65

1954, Dec. 7

189	A65	20 l	pink & multi	1.00 .75
190	A65	35 l	blue & multi	7.50 3.75
191	A65	60 l	multicolored	12.50 5.75
		Nos. 189-191 (3)		21.00 10.25

Issued to mark the end of the Marian Year.

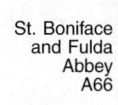

St. Boniface and Fulda Abbey A66

1955, Apr. 28   Engr.   Perf. 13

192	A66	10 l	grnsh gray	.25 .25
193	A66	35 l	violet	.60 .60
a.		Imperf., pair		100.00
194	A66	60 l	brt blue green	.70 .70
		Nos. 192-194 (3)		1.55 1.55

1200th death anniv. of St. Boniface.

Pope Sixtus II and St. Lawrence A67

Pope Nicholas V A68

Wmk. 235

1955, June 27   Photo.   Perf. 14

195	A67	50 l	carmine	3.75 2.00
196	A67	100 l	deep blue	2.50 2.00

Fra Angelico (1387-1455), painter. Design is from a Fra Angelico fresco.

1955, Nov. 28

197	A68	20 l	grnsh bl & ol brn	.25 .25
198	A68	35 l	rose car & ol brn	.35 .25
199	A68	60 l	yel grn & ol brn	.70 .35
		Nos. 197-199 (3)		1.30 .85

Death of Pope Nicholas V, 500th anniv.

St. Bartholomew and Church of Grottaferrata A69

Capt. Gaspar Roust A70

1955, Dec. 29

200	A69	10 l	brown & gray	.25 .25
201	A69	25 l	car rose & gray	.80 .30
202	A69	100 l	dk green & gray	2.00 1.50
		Nos. 200-202 (3)		3.05 2.05

900th death anniv. of St. Bartholomew, abbot of Grottaferrata.

1956, Apr. 27   Engr.   Perf. 13

6 l, 50 l, Guardsman. 10 l, 60 l, Two drummers.

203	A70	4 l	dk carmine rose	.25 .25
204	A70	6 l	deep orange	.25 .25
205	A70	10 l	deep ultra	.25 .25
206	A70	35 l	brown	.55 .40
207	A70	50 l	violet	.75 .60
208	A70	60 l	blue green	.85 .65
		Nos. 203-208 (6)		2.90 2.40

450th anniv. of the Swiss Papal Guard.

St. Rita of Cascia — A71

Pope Paul III Confirming Society of Jesus — A72

1956, May 19   Photo.   Perf. 14

209	A71	10 l	gray green	.25 .25
210	A71	25 l	olive brown	.60 .60
211	A71	35 l	ultra	.45 .45
		Nos. 209-211 (3)		1.30 1.30

500th death anniv. of St. Rita of Cascia.

1956, July 31   Engr.   Perf. 13

212	A72	35 l	dk red brown	.55 .55
213	A72	60 l	blue gray	1.10 1.10

400th death anniv. of St. Ignatius of Loyola, founder of the Society of Jesus.

St. John of
Capistrano
A73

1956, Oct. 30 *Perf. 14*
214 A73 25 l slate blk & grn 2.25 1.25
215 A73 35 l dk brn car & brn 1.00 .75

5th cent. of the death of St. John of Capistrano, leader in the war against the Turks.

Black Madonna of
Czestochowa — A74

St. Domenico
Savio — A75

1956, Dec. 20
216 A74 35 l dk blue & blk .25 .25
217 A74 60 l green & ultra .60 .55
218 A74 100 l brn & dk car rose 1.00 .85
Nos. 216-218 (3) 1.85 1.65

300th anniv. of the proclamation of the Madonna of Czestochowa as "Queen of Poland."

1957, Mar. 21 Wmk. 235 Perf. 13½

6 l, 60 l, Sts. Domenico Savio and John Bosco.

219 A75 4 l red brown .25 .25
220 A75 6 l brt carmine .25 .25
221 A75 25 l green .25 .25
222 A75 60 l ultra 1.40 1.10
Nos. 219-222 (4) 2.15 1.85

Death cent. of St. Domenico Savio.

Cardinal
Capranica
and College
A76

Design: 10 l, 100 l, Pope Pius XII.

1957, June 27 Engr. Perf. 13
223 A76 5 l dk carmine rose .25 .25
224 A76 10 l pale brown .25 .25
225 A76 35 l grnsh black .25 .25
226 A76 100 l ultra .50 .50
Nos. 223-226 (4) 1.25 1.25

500th anniv. of Capranica College, oldest seminary in the world.

Pontifical
Academy of
Science
A77

1957, Oct. 9 Photo. Perf. 14
227 A77 35 l dk blue & green .55 .55
228 A77 60 l brown & ultra .80 .55

Pontifical Academy of Science, 20th anniv.

Mariazell
A78

High
Altar — A79

1957, Nov. 14 Engr. Perf. 13½
229 A78 5 l green .25 .25
230 A79 15 l slate .25 .25
231 A78 60 l ultra .70 .25
232 A79 100 l violet .90 .85
Nos. 229-232 (4) 2.10 1.60

Mariazell shrine, Austria, 800th anniv.

Apparition of the
Virgin
Mary — A80

Designs: 10 l, 35 l, Sick man and basilica. 15 l, 100 l, St. Bernadette.

Perf. 13x14
1958, Feb. 21 Wmk. 235
233 A80 5 l dark blue .25 .25
234 A80 10 l blue green .25 .25
235 A80 15 l reddish brown .25 .25
236 A80 25 l rose carmine .25 .25
237 A80 35 l gray brown .25 .25
238 A80 100 l violet .25 .25
Nos. 233-238 (6) 1.50 1.50

Centenary of apparition of the Virgin Mary at Lourdes and the establishment of the shrine.

Pope
Pius XII — A81

Statue of Pope
Clement XIII by
Canova — A82

60 l, 100 l, Vatican pavilion at Brussels fair.

1958, June 19 Engr. Perf. 13
239 A81 35 l claret .30 .25
Perf. 13x14
240 A81 60 l fawn .55 .55
241 A81 100 l violet 1.75 1.25
242 A81 300 l ultra 1.40 1.10
a. Souvenir sheet of 4, #239-242 20.00 15.00
Nos. 239-242 (4) 4.00 3.15

Universal and Intl. Exposition, Brussels.

1958, July 2 Perf. 14

Statues: 10 l, Clement XIV. 35 l, Pius VI. 100 l, Pius VII.

243 A82 5 l brown .25 .25
244 A82 10 l carmine rose .25 .25
245 A82 35 l blue gray .25 .25
246 A82 100 l dark blue .85 .85
Nos. 243-246 (4) 1.60 1.60

Antonio Canova (1757-1822), sculptor.

Interregnum Issue

St. Peter's Keys and Papal
Chamberlain's Insignia — A83

Wmk. 235
1958, Oct. 21 Photo. Perf. 14
247 A83 15 l brn blk, yel 1.40 1.00
248 A83 25 l brown black .25 .25
249 A83 60 l brn blk, pale vio .25 .25
Nos. 247-249 (3) 1.90 1.25

Pope John
XXIII — A84

Design: 35 l, 100 l, Coat of Arms.

1959, Apr. 2 Photo. Perf. 14
250 A84 25 l car rose, bl & buff .25 .25
251 A84 35 l multicolored .25 .25
252 A84 60 l rose car, bl & ocher .25 .25
253 A84 100 l multicolored .25 .25
Nos. 250-253 (4) 1.001.00

Coronation of Pope John XXIII, 11/4/58.

Pope
Pius XI — A85

1959, May 25 Wmk. 235 Perf. 14
254 A85 30 l brown .25 .25
255 A85 100 l violet blue .25 .25

Lateran Pacts, 30th anniversary.

 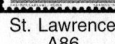

St. Lawrence
A86

Radio Tower and
Archangel Gabriel
A87

Portraits of Saints: 25 l, Pope Sixtus II. 50 l, Agapitus. 60 l, Filicissimus. 100 l, Cyprianus. 300 l, Fructuosus.

1959, May 25
256 A86 15 l red, brn & yel .25 .25
257 A86 25 l lilac, brn & yel .25 .25
258 A86 50 l Prus bl, blk & yel .25 .25
259 A86 60 l ol grn, brn & bis .25 .25
260 A86 100 l maroon, brn & yel .25 .25
261 A86 300 l bis brn & dk brn .50 .35
Nos. 256-261 (6) 1.75 1.60

Martyrs of Emperor Valerian's persecutions.

1959, Oct. 27 Photo. Perf. 14
262 A87 25 l rose, org yel & dk brn .25 .25
263 A87 60 l multicolored .25 .25

2nd anniv. of the papal radio station, St. Maria di Galeria.

St. Casimir,
Palace and
Cathedral,
Vilnius
A88

1959, Dec. 14 Engr. Wmk. 235
264 A88 50 l brown .25 .25
265 A88 100 l dull green .25 .25

500th anniv. (in 1958) of the birth of St. Casimir, patron saint of Lithuania.

Nativity by
Raphael — A89

1959, Dec. 14 Engr. Perf. 13½
266 A89 15 l dark gray .25 .25
267 A89 25 l magenta .25 .25
268 A89 60 l bright ultra .25 .25
Nos. 266-268 (3) .75 .75

St.
Antoninus — A90

25 l, 110 l, St. Antoninus preaching.

Perf. 13x14
1960, Feb. 29 Wmk. 235
269 A90 15 l ultra .25 .25
270 A90 25 l turquoise .25 .25
271 A90 60 l brown .30 .25
272 A90 110 l rose claret .60 .35
Nos. 269-272 (4) 1.40 1.10

5th cent. of death of St. Antoninus, bishop of Florence.

Transept of Lateran
Basilica — A91

1960, Feb. 29 Photo. Perf. 14
273 A91 15 l brown .25 .25
274 A91 60 l black .40 .25

Roman Diocesan Synod, February, 1960.

Flight into Egypt
by Fra
Angelico — A92

Designs: 10 l, 100 l, St. Peter Giving Alms to the Poor, by Masaccio. 25 l, 300 l, Madonna of Mercy, by Piero della Francesca.

1960, Apr. 7 Wmk. 235 Perf. 14
275 A92 5 l green .25 .25
276 A92 10 l gray brown .25 .25
277 A92 25 l deep carmine .25 .25
278 A92 60 l lilac .25 .25
279 A92 100 l ultra 1.90 1.50
280 A92 300 l Prus green .65 .40
Nos. 275-280 (6) 3.55 2.90

World Refugee Year, 7/1/59-6/30/60.

Cardinal Sarto's
Departure from
Venice — A93

35 l, Pope John XXIII praying at coffin of Pope Pius X. 60 l, Body of Pope Pius X returning to Venice.

1960, Apr. 11   Engr.   Perf. 13½
281 A93 15 l brown .25 .25
282 A93 35 l rose carmine .60 .60
283 A93 60 l Prus green 1.25 .85
 Nos. 281-283 (3) 2.10 1.70

Return of the body of Pope Pius X to Venice.

Feeding the Hungry A94

"Acts of Mercy," by Della Robbia: 10 l, Giving drink to the thirsty. 15 l, Clothing the naked. 20 l, Sheltering the homeless. 30 l, Visiting the sick. 35 l, Visiting prisoners. 40 l, Burying the dead. 70 l, Pope John XXIII.

1960, Nov. 8   Photo.   Perf. 14
Centers in Brown
284 A94 5 l red brown .25 .25
285 A94 10 l green .25 .25
286 A94 15 l slate .25 .25
287 A94 20 l rose carmine .25 .25
288 A94 30 l violet blue .25 .25
289 A94 35 l violet brown .25 .25
290 A94 40 l red orange .25 .25
291 A94 70 l ocher .25 .25
 Nos. 284-291,E15-E16 (10) 2.50 2.50

Holy Family by Gerard van Honthorst A95

1960, Dec. 6   Wmk. 235   Perf. 14
292 A95 10 l slate grn & slate blk .25 .25
293 A95 15 l sepia & ol blk .25 .25
294 A95 70 l grnsh bl & dp bl .30 .25
 Nos. 292-294 (3) .80 .75

St. Vincent de Paul — A96

Designs: 70 l, St. Louisa de Marillac. 100 l, St. Louisa and St. Vincent.

1960, Dec. 6
295 A96 40 l dull violet .25 .25
296 A96 70 l dark gray .30 .25
297 A96 100 l dk red brown .70 .30
 Nos. 295-297 (3) 1.25 .80

Death of St. Vincent de Paul, 300th anniv.

St. Meinrad — A97

1961, Feb. 28   Perf. 14
298 A97 30 l dark gray .45 .25
299 A97 40 l lt violet 1.50 .40
300 A97 100 l brown 1.50 .85
 Nos. 298-300 (3) 3.45 1.50

Death of St. Meinrad, 1,100th anniv.; Einsiedeln Abbey, Switzerland.

Pope Leo the Great Defying Attila — A98

Wmk. 235
1961, Apr. 6   Photo.   Perf. 14
301 A98 15 l rose brown .25 .25
302 A98 70 l Prus green .25 .25
303 A98 300 l brown black 1.75 .55
 Nos. 301-303 (3) 2.25 1.05

Death of Pope Leo the Great (St. Leo Magnus), 1,500th anniv. The design is from a marble bas-relief in St. Peter's Basilica.

St. Paul Arriving in Rome, 61 A.D. — A99

10 l, 30 l, Map showing St. Paul's journey to Rome. 20 l, 200 l, First Basilica of St. Paul, Rome.

1961, June 13   Wmk. 235   Perf. 14
304 A99 10 l Prus green .25 .25
305 A99 15 l dl red brn & gray .25 .25
306 A99 20 l red org & gray .25 .25
307 A99 30 l blue .25 .25
308 A99 75 l org brn & gray .30 .30
309 A99 200 l blue & gray 1.60 1.10
 Nos. 304-309 (6) 2.90 2.40

Arrival of St. Paul in Rome, 1,900th anniv.

1861 and 1961 Mastheads A100

70 l, Editorial offices. 250 l, Rotary press.

1961, July 4
310 A100 40 l red brn & blk .25 .25
311 A100 70 l blue & blk .40 .30
312 A100 250 l yellow & blk 1.90 1.10
 Nos. 310-312 (3) 2.55 1.65

Centenary of L'Osservatore Romano, Vatican's newspaper.

St. Patrick's Purgatory, Lough Derg — A101

10 l, 40 l, St. Patrick, marble sculpture.

Wmk. 235
1961, Oct. 6   Photo.   Perf. 14
313 A101 10 l buff & slate grn .25 .25
314 A101 15 l blue & sepia .25 .25
315 A101 40 l yellow & bl grn .25 .25
316 A101 150 l Prus bl & red brn .70 .50
 Nos. 313-316 (4) 1.45 1.25

Death of St. Patrick, 1,500th anniv.

Arms of Roncalli Family — A102

Designs: 25 l, Church at Sotto il Monte. 30 l, Santa Maria in Monte Santo, Rome. 40 l, Church of San Carlo al Corso, Rome (erroneously inscribed with name of Basilica of Sts. Ambrosius and Charles, Milan). 70 l, Altar, St. Peter's, Rome. 115 l, Pope John XXIII.

1961, Nov. 25
317 A102 10 l gray & red brn .25 .25
318 A102 25 l ol bis & sl grn .25 .25
319 A102 30 l vio bl & pale pur .25 .25
320 A102 40 l lilac & dk blue .25 .25
321 A102 70 l gray grn & org brn .30 .25
322 A102 115 l choc & slate .70 .45
 Nos. 317-322 (6) 2.00 1.70

80th birthday of Pope John XXIII.

"The Adoration" by Lucas Chen — A103

1961, Nov. 25   Center Multicolored
323 A103 15 l bluish green .25 .25
324 A103 40 l gray .25 .25
325 A103 70 l pale lilac .30 .25
 Nos. 323-325 (3) .80 .75

Christmas.

Draining of Pontine Marshes Medal by Pope Sixtus V, 1588 — A104

40 l, 300 l, Map of Pontine Marshes showing 18th cent. drainage under Pope Pius VI.

1962, Apr. 6   Wmk. 235   Perf. 14
326 A104 15 l dark violet .25 .25
327 A104 40 l rose carmine .25 .25
328 A104 70 l brown .25 .25
329 A104 300 l dull green .65 .40
 Nos. 326-329 (4) 1.40 1.15

WHO drive to eradicate malaria.

"The Good Shepherd" A105

Wheatfield (Luke 10:2) — A106

1962, June 2   Photo.
330 A105 10 l lilac & black .25 .25
331 A106 15 l blue & ocher .25 .25
332 A105 70 l lt green & blk .25 .30
333 A106 115 l fawn & ocher 1.25 1.10
334 A105 200 l brown & black 2.00 1.40
 Nos. 330-334 (5) 4.00 3.30

Issued to honor the priesthood and to stress its importance as a vocation.
"The Good Shepherd" is a fourth-century statue in the Lateran Museum, Rome.

St. Catherine of Siena — A107

Paulina M. Jaricot — A108

1962, June 12
335 A107 15 l brown .25 .25
336 A107 60 l brt violet .30 .25
337 A107 100 l blue .60 .40
 Nos. 335-337 (3) 1.15 .90

Canonization of St. Catherine of Siena, 500th anniv. The portrait is from a fresco by Il Sodoma, Church of St. Dominic, Siena.

1962, July 5   Portrait Multicolored
338 A108 15 l pale violet .25 .25
339 A108 50 l dull green .25 .25
340 A108 150 l gray .80 .50
 Nos. 338-340 (3) 1.30 1.00

Paulina M. Jaricot (1799-1862), founder of the Society for the Propagation of the Faith.

Sts. Peter and Paul A109

Design: 40 l, 100 l, "The Invincible Cross," relief from sarcophagus.

Wmk. 235
1962, Sept. 25   Photo.   Perf. 14
341 A109 20 l lilac & brown .25 .25
342 A109 40 l lt brown & blk .25 .25
343 A109 70 l bluish grn & brn .25 .25
344 A109 100 l sal pink & blk .25 .25
 Nos. 341-344 (4) 1.00 1.00

6th Congress of Christian Archeology, Ravenna, Sept. 23-28.

"Faith" by Raphael — A110

Designs: 10 l, "Hope." 15 l, "Charity." 25 l, Arms of Pope John XXIII and emblems of the Four Evangelists. 30 l, Ecumenical Congress meeting in St. Peter's. 40 l, Pope John XXIII on throne. 60 l, Statue of St. Peter. 115 l, The Holy Ghost as a dove (symbolic design).

Photo.; Center Engr. on 30 l
1962, Oct. 30
345 A110 5 l brt blue & blk .25 .25
346 A110 10 l green & blk .25 .25
347 A110 15 l ver & sepia .25 .25
348 A110 25 l ver & slate .25 .25
349 A110 30 l lilac & blk .25 .25
350 A110 40 l dk carmine & blk .25 .25
351 A110 60 l dk grn & dp org .25 .25
352 A110 115 l crimson .25 .25
 Nos. 345-352 (8) 2.00 2.00

Vatican II, the 21st Ecumenical Council of the Roman Catholic Church, which opened Oct. 11, 1962. Nos. 345-347 show "the Three Theological Virtues" by Raphael.

Nativity Scene A111

Set in India, following a design by Marcus Toano.

1962, Dec. 4   Center Multicolored
353 A111 10 l gray .25 .25
354 A111 15 l brown .25 .25
355 A111 90 l dull green .30 .25
  Nos. 353-355 (3) .80 .75

Miracle of the Loaves and Fishes by Murillo — A112

Pope John XXIII — A113

Design: 40 l, 200 l, "The Miraculous Catch of Fishes" by Raphael.

Wmk. 235
1963, Mar. 21   Photo.   Perf. 14
356 A112 15 l brn & dk brn .25 .25
357 A112 40 l rose red & blk .25 .25
358 A112 100 l blue & dk brn .25 .25
359 A112 200 l bl grn & blk .25 .25
  Nos. 356-359 (4) 1.00 1.00

FAO "Freedom from Hunger" campaign.

1963, May 8
360 A113 15 l red brown .25 .25
361 A113 160 l black .40 .25

Awarding of the Balzan Peace Prize to Pope John XXIII.

Interregnum Issue

Keys of St. Peter and Papal Chamberlain's Insignia — A114

1963, June 15   Wmk. 235   Perf. 14
362 A114 10 l dk brown .25 .25
363 A114 40 l dk brown, yel .25 .25
364 A114 100 l dk brown, vio .25 .25
  Nos. 362-364 (3) .75 .75

Pope Paul VI — A115

Design: 40 l, 200 l, Arms of Pope Paul VI.

1963, Oct. 16   Engr.   Perf. 13x14
365 A115 15 l black .25 .25
366 A115 40 l carmine .25 .25
367 A115 115 l redsh brown .25 .25
368 A115 200 l slate blue .40 .25
  Nos. 365-368 (4) 1.15 1.00

Coronation of Pope Paul VI, June 30, 1963.

St. Cyril — A116

Designs: 70 l, Map of Hungary, Moravia and Poland, 16th century. 150 l, St. Methodius.

Wmk. 235
1963, Nov. 22   Photo.   Perf. 14
369 A116 30 l violet black .25 .25
370 A116 70 l brown .30 .25
371 A116 150 l rose claret .40 .25
  Nos. 369-371 (3) .95 .75

1100th anniv. of the beginning of missionary work among the Slavs by Sts. Cyril and Methodius. The pictures of the saints are from 16th century frescoes in St. Clement's Basilica, Rome.

African Nativity Scene — A117

1963, Nov. 22
372 A117 10 l brn & pale brn .25 .25
373 A117 40 l ultra & brown .25 .25
374 A117 100 l gray olive & brn .25 .25
  Nos. 372-374 (3) .75 .75

The design is after a sculpture by the Burundi artist Andreas Bukuru.

Church of the Holy Sepulcher, Jerusalem A118

15 l, Pope Paul VI. 25 l, Nativity Church, Bethlehem. 160 l, Well of the Virgin Mary, Nazareth.

1964, Jan. 4   Wmk. 235   Perf. 14
375 A118 15 l black .25 .25
376 A118 25 l rose brown .25 .25
377 A118 70 l brown .25 .25
378 A118 160 l ultra .25 .25
  Nos. 375-378 (4) 1.00 1.00

Visit of Pope Paul VI to the Holy Land, Jan. 4-6.

St. Peter from Coptic Church at Wadi-es-Sebua, Sudan — A119

Design: 20 l, 200 l, Trajan's Kiosk, Philae.

1964, Mar. 10   Photo.
379 A119 10 l ultra & red brn .25 .25
380 A119 20 l multicolored .25 .25
381 A119 70 l gray & red brn .25 .25
382 A119 200 l gray & multi .25 .25
  Nos. 379-382 (4) 1.00 1.00

UNESCO world campaign to save historic monuments in Nubia.

Pietà by Michelangelo A120

Designs: 15 l, 100 l, Pope Paul VI. 250 l, Head of Mary from Pietà.

1964, Apr. 22   Wmk. 235   Perf. 14
383 A120 15 l violet blue .25 .25
384 A120 50 l dark brown .25 .25
385 A120 100 l slate blue .25 .25
386 A120 250 l chestnut .25 .25
  Nos. 383-386 (4) 1.00 1.00

New York World's Fair, 1964-65.

Isaiah by Michelangelo A121

1964, June 16   Engr.   Perf. 13½x14
387 A121 10 l Michelangelo, after Jacopino del Conte .25 .25
388 A121 25 l Isaiah .25 .25
389 A121 30 l Delphie Sibyl .25 .25
390 A121 40 l Jeremiah .25 .25
391 A121 150 l Joel .25 .25
  Nos. 387-391 (5) 1.25 1.25

Michelangelo Buonarroti (1475-1564). Designs are from the Sistine Chapel.

The Good Samaritan A122

Perf. 14x13½
1964, Sept. 22   Engr.   Wmk. 235
392 A122 10 l red brown & red .25 .25
393 A122 30 l dark blue & red .25 .25
394 A122 300 l gray & red .25 .25
  Nos. 392-394 (3) .75 .75

Cent. (in 1963) of the founding of the Intl. Red Cross.

Birthplace of Cardinal Nicolaus Cusanus A123

Design: 200 l, Cardinal's sepulcher, Church of San Pietro in Vincoli, Rome.

1964, Nov. 16   Wmk. 235
395 A123 40 l dull blue grn .25 .25
396 A123 200 l rose red .30 .25

German cardinal Nicolaus Cusanus (Nicolaus Krebs of Kues) (1401-1464).

Japanese Nativity Scene by Kimiko Koseki — A124

1964, Nov. 16   Photo.   Perf. 14
397 A124 10 l multicolored .25 .25
  a. Yellow omitted
398 A124 15 l black & multi .25 .25
399 A124 135 l bister & multi .25 .25
  Nos. 397-399 (3) .75 .75

Pope Paul VI and Map of India and Southeast Asia — A125

Designs: 15 l, Pope Paul VI at prayer. 25 l, Eucharistic Congress altar, Bombay, horiz. 60 l, Gateway of India, Bombay, horiz.

1964, Dec. 2
400 A125 15 l dull violet .25 .25
401 A125 25 l green .25 .25
402 A125 60 l brown .25 .25
403 A125 200 l dull violet .25 .25
  Nos. 400-403 (4) 1.00 1.00

Trip of Pope Paul VI to India, Dec. 2-5, 1964.

Uganda Martyrs — A126

Various groups of Martyrs of Uganda.

Perf. 13½x14
1965, Mar. 16   Engr.   Wmk. 235
404 A126 15 l Prus green .25 .25
405 A126 20 l brown .25 .25
406 A126 30 l ultra .25 .25
407 A126 75 l black .25 .25
408 A126 100 l rose red .25 .25
409 A126 160 l violet .25 .25
  Nos. 404-409 (6) 1.50 1.50

Canonization of 22 African martyrs, 10/18/64.

Dante by Raphael — A127

Designs: 40 l, Dante and the 3 beasts at entrance to the Inferno. 70 l, Dante and Virgil at entrance to Purgatory. 200 l, Dante and Beatrice in Paradise. (40 l, 70 l, 200 l, by Botticelli.)

Photogravure and Engraved
1965, May 18   Perf. 13½x14
410 A127 10 l bis brn & dk brn .25 .25
411 A127 40 l rose & dk brn .25 .25
412 A127 70 l lt grn & dk brn .25 .25
413 A127 200 l pale bl & dk brn .25 .25
  Nos. 410-413 (4) 1.00 1.00

Birth of Dante Alighieri, 700th anniv.

St. Benedict by Perugino A128

Pope Paul VI Addressing UN Assembly A129

Design: 300 l, View of Monte Cassino.

1965, July 2   Photo.   Perf. 14
414 A128 40 l brown .... .25 .25
415 A128 300 l dark green .... .30 .25

Conferring of the title Patron Saint of Europe upon St. Benedict by Pope Paul VI; restoring of the Abbey of Monte Cassino.

1965, Oct. 4   Wmk. 235   Perf. 14
30 l, 150 l, UN Headquarters and olive branch.
416 A129 20 l brown .... .25 .25
417 A129 30 l sapphire .... .25 .25
418 A129 150 l olive green .... .25 .25
419 A129 300 l rose violet .... .25 .25
    Nos. 416-419 (4) 1.00 1.00

Visit of Pope Paul VI to the UN, NYC, Oct. 4.

Peruvian Nativity Scene A130

Cartographer A131

1965, Nov. 25   Engr.   Perf. 13½x14
420 A130 20 l rose claret .... .25 .25
421 A130 40 l red brown .... .25 .25
422 A130 200 l gray green .... .25 .25
    Nos. 420-422 (3) .... .75 .75

1966, Mar. 8   Photo.   Perf. 14
Designs: 5 l, Pope Paul VI. 10 l, Organist. 20 l, Painter. 30 l, Sculptor. 40 l, Bricklayer. 55 l, Printer. 75 l, Plowing farmer. 90 l, Blacksmith. 130 l, Scholar.
423 A131 5 l sepia .... .25 .25
424 A131 10 l violet .... .25 .25
425 A131 15 l brown .... .25 .25
426 A131 20 l gray green .... .25 .25
427 A131 30 l brown red .... .25 .25
428 A131 40 l Prus green .... .25 .25
429 A131 55 l dark blue .... .25 .25
430 A131 75 l dk rose brown .... .25 .25
431 A131 90 l carmine rose ..... .25 .25
432 A131 130 l black .... .25 .25
    Nos. 423-432,E17-E18 (12) ... 3.00 3.00

The Pope's portrait is from a bas-relief by Enrico Manfrini; the arts and crafts designs are bas-reliefs by Mario Rudelli from the chair in the Pope's private chapel.

King Mieszko I and Queen Dabrowka A132

Designs: 25 l, St. Adalbert (Wojciech) and Cathedrals of Wroclaw and Gniezno. 40 l, St. Stanislas, Skalka Church, Wawel Cathedral and Castle, Cracow. 50 l, Queen Jadwiga (Hedwig), Holy Gate with Our Lady of Mercy, Vilnius, and Jagellon University Library, Cracow. 150 l, Black Madonna of Czestochowa, cloister and church of Bright Mountain, Czestochowa, and St. John's Cathedral, Warsaw. 220 l, Pope Paul VI blessing students and farmers.

Perf. 14x13½
1966, May 3   Engr.   Wmk. 235
433 A132 15 l black .... .25 .25
434 A132 25 l violet .... .25 .25
435 A132 40 l brick red .... .25 .25
436 A132 50 l claret .... .25 .25
437 A132 150 l slate blue ...... .25 .25
438 A132 220 l brown .... .25 .25
    Nos. 433-438 (6) 1.50 1.50

Millenium of Christianization of Poland.

Pope John XXIII Opening Vatican II Council A133

Nativity, Sculpture by Scorzelli A134

Designs: 15 l, Ancient Bible on ornate display stand. 55 l, Bishops celebrating Mass. 90 l, Pope Paul VI greeting Patriarch Athenagoras I. 100 l, Gold ring given to participating bishops. 130 l, Pope Paul VI carried in front of St. Peter's.

1966, Oct. 11   Photo.   Perf. 14
439 A133 10 l red & black ...... .25 .25
440 A133 15 l brown & green ... .25 .25
441 A133 55 l blk & brt rose ... .25 .25
442 A133 90 l slate grn & blk .. .25 .25
443 A133 100 l green & ocher ... .25 .25
444 A133 130 l orange brn & brn .25 .25
    Nos. 439-444 (6) 1.50 1.50

Conclusion of Vatican II, the 21st Ecumenical Council of the Roman Catholic Church, Dec. 8, 1965.

1966, Nov. 24   Wmk. 235   Perf. 14
445 A134 20 l plum .... .25 .25
446 A134 55 l slate green ..... .25 .25
447 A134 225 l yellow brown ... .25 .25
    Nos. 445-447 (3) .... .75 .75

St. Peter, Fresco, Catacombs, Rome — A135

Cross, People and Globe — A136

Designs: 20 l, St. Paul, fresco from Catacombs, Rome. 55 l, Sts. Peter and Paul, glass painting, Vatican Library. 90 l, Baldachin by Bernini, St. Peter's, Rome. 220 l, Interior of St. Paul's, Rome.

Perf. 13½x14
1967, June 15   Photo.   Unwmk.
448 A135 15 l multi .... .25 .25
449 A135 20 l multi .... .25 .25
450 A135 55 l multi .... .25 .25
451 A135 90 l multi .... .25 .25
452 A135 220 l multi .... .25 .25
    Nos. 448-452 (5) 1.25 1.25

Martyrdom of the Apostles Peter and Paul, 1,900th anniv.

1967, Oct. 13   Wmk. 235   Perf. 14
453 A136 40 l carmine rose .... .25 .25
454 A136 130 l brt blue .... .25 .25

3rd Congress of Catholic Laymen, Rome, Oct. 11-18.

Sculpture of Shepherd Children of Fatima — A137

Designs: 50 l, Basilica at Fatima. 200 l, Pope Paul VI praying before statue of Virgin of Fatima.

1967, Oct. 13   Perf. 13½x14
455 A137 30 l multi .... .25 .25
456 A137 50 l multi .... .25 .25
457 A137 200 l multi .... .25 .25
    Nos. 455-457 (3) .... .75 .75

Apparition of the Virgin Mary to 3 shepherd children at Fatima, 50th anniv.

Christmas Issue

Nativity, 9th Century Painting on Wood — A138

1967, Nov. 28   Photo.   Unwmk.
458 A138 25 l purple & multi ... .25 .25
459 A138 55 l gray & multi ..... .25 .25
460 A138 180 l green & multi ... .25 .25
    Nos. 458-460 (3) .... .75 .75

Pope Paul VI — A139

Holy Infant of Prague — A140

Designs: 55 l, Monstrance from fresco by Raphael. 220 l, Map of South America.

1968, Aug. 22   Wmk. 235   Perf. 14
461 A139 25 l blk & dk red brn .. .25 .25
462 A139 55 l blk, gray & ocher . .25 .25
463 A139 220 l blk, lt bl & sep .. .25 .25
    Nos. 461-463 (3) .... .75 .75

Visit of Pope Paul VI to the 39th Eucharistic Congress in Bogotá, Colombia, Aug. 22-25.

Engraved and Photogravure
1968, Nov. 28   Perf. 13½x14
464 A140 20 l plum & pink ...... .25 .25
465 A140 50 l vio & pale vio .... .25 .25
466 A140 250 l dk bl & lt bluish
          gray .... .25 .25
    Nos. 464-466 (3) .... .75 .75

The Resurrection, by Fra Angelico de Fiesole — A141

Easter Issue
Perf. 13½x14
1969, Mar. 6   Engr.   Wmk. 235
467 A141 20 l dk carmine & buff .25 .25
468 A141 90 l green & buff ..... .25 .25
469 A141 180 l ultra & buff .... .25 .25
    Nos. 467-469 (3) .... .75 .75

Common Design Types pictured following the introduction.

Europa Issue
Common Design Type
Perf. 13½x14
1969, Apr. 28   Photo.   Wmk. 235
Size: 36½x27mm
470 CD12 50 l gray & lt brn .... .25 .25
471 CD12 90 l vermilion & lt brn .25 .25
472 CD12 130 l olive & lt brn ... .25 .25
    Nos. 470-472 (3) .... .75 .75

Pope Paul VI with African Children — A142

Designs: 55 l, Pope Paul VI and African bishops. 250 l, Map of Africa with Kampala, olive branch and compass rose.

Perf. 13½x14
1969, July 31   Photo.   Wmk. 235
473 A142 25 l bister & brown .... .25 .25
474 A142 55 l dk red & brown ... .25 .25
475 A142 250 l multicolored .... .25 .25
    Nos. 473-475 (3) .... .75 .75

Visit of Pope Paul VI to Uganda, 7/31-8/2.

Pope Pius IX — A143

Designs: 50 l, Chrismon, emblem of St. Peter's Circle. 220 l, Pope Paul VI.

Perf. 13½x14
1969, Nov. 18   Engr.   Wmk. 235
476 A143 30 l red brown .... .25 .25
477 A143 50 l dark gray .... .25 .25
478 A143 220 l deep plum ..... .25 .25
    Nos. 476-478 (3) .... .75 .75

Centenary of St. Peter's Circle, a lay society dedicated to prayer, action and sacrifice.

Mt. Fuji and EXPO '70 Emblem — A144

EXPO '70 Emblem and: 25 l, EXPO '70 emblem. 40 l, Osaka Castle. 55 l, Japanese Virgin and Child, by Domoto in Osaka Cathedral. 90 l, Christian Pavilion.

1970, Mar. 16   Photo.   Unwmk.
479 A144 25 l gold, red & blk ... .25 .25
480 A144 40 l red & multi ...... .25 .25
481 A144 55 l brown & multi ... .25 .25
482 A144 90 l gold & multi ..... .25 .25
483 A144 110 l blue & multi .... .25 .25
    Nos. 479-483 (5) 1.25 1.25

EXPO '70 Intl. Exhibition, Osaka, Japan, Mar. 15-Sept. 13.

Centenary Medal, Jesus Giving St. Peter the Keys — A145

Designs: 50 l, Coat of arms of Pope Pius IX. 180 l, Vatican I Council meeting in St. Peter's, obverse of centenary medal.

Engr. & Photo.; Photo. (50 l)
1970, Apr. 29   Perf. 13x14
484 A145 20 l orange & brown ... .25 .25
485 A145 50 l multicolored ..... .25 .25
486 A145 180 l ver & brn .... .30 .25
    Nos. 484-486 (3) .... .80 .75

Centenary of the Vatican I Council.

Christ, by Simone Martini A146

25 l, Christ with Crown of Thorns, by Rogier van der Weyden. 50 l, Christ, by Albrecht Dürer. 90 l, Christ, by El Greco. 180 l, Pope Paul VI.

1970, May 29   Photo.   Perf. 14x13
487	A146	15 l gold & multi	.25	.25
488	A146	25 l gold & multi	.25	.25
489	A146	50 l gold & multi	.25	.25
490	A146	90 l gold & multi	.25	.25
491	A146	180 l gold & multi	.25	.25
		Nos. 487-491 (5)	1.25	1.25

Ordination of Pope Paul VI, 50th anniv.

Adam, by Michelangelo; UN Emblem — A147

UN Emblem and: 90 l, Eve, by Michelangelo. 220 l, Olive branch.

1970, Oct. 8   Photo.   Perf. 13x14
492	A147	20 l multi	.25	.25
493	A147	90 l multi	.25	.25
494	A147	220 l multi	.25	.25
		Nos. 492-494 (3)	.75	.75

25th anniversary of the United Nations.

Pope Paul VI — A148

Designs: 55 l, Holy Child of Cebu, Philippines. 100 l, Madonna and Child, by Georg Hamori, Darwin Cathedral, Australia. 130 l, Cathedral of Manila. 220 l, Cathedral of Sydney.

1970, Nov. 26   Photo.   Unwmk.
495	A148	25 l multi	.25	.25
496	A148	55 l multi	.25	.25
497	A148	100 l multi	.25	.25
498	A148	130 l multi	.25	.25
499	A148	220 l multi	.25	.25
		Nos. 495-499 (5)	1.25	1.25

Visit of Pope Paul VI to the Far East, Oceania and Australia, Nov. 26-Dec. 5.

Angel Holding Lectern — A149

Sculptures by Corrado Ruffini: 40 l, 130 l, Crucified Christ surrounded by doves. 50 l, like 20 l.

1971, Feb. 2   Perf. 13x14
500	A149	20 l multicolored	.25	.25
501	A149	40 l dp orange & multi	.25	.25
502	A149	50 l purple & multi	.25	.25
503	A149	130 l multicolored	.25	.25
		Nos. 500-503 (4)	1.00	1.00

Intl. year against racial discrimination.

Madonna and Child by Francesco Ghissi — A150

Paintings: Madonna and Child, 40 l, by Sassetta (Stefano di Giovanni); 55 l, Carlo Crivelli; 90 l, by Carlo Maratta. 180 l, Holy Family, by Ghisberto Ceracchini.

1971, Mar. 26   Photo.   Perf. 14
504	A150	25 l gray & multi	.25	.25
505	A150	40 l gray & multi	.25	.25
506	A150	55 l gray & multi	.25	.25
507	A150	90 l gray & multi	.25	.25
508	A150	180 l gray & multi	.25	.25
		Nos. 504-508 (5)	1.25	1.25

St. Dominic, Sienese School — A151

Portraits of St. Dominic: 55 l, by Fra Angelico. 90 l, by Titian. 180 l, by El Greco.

1971, May 25   Unwmk.   Perf. 13x14
509	A151	25 l multi	.25	.25
510	A151	55 l multi	.25	.25
511	A151	90 l multi	.25	.25
512	A151	180 l multi	.25	.25
		Nos. 509-512 (4)	1.00	1.00

St. Dominic de Guzman (1170-1221), founder of the Dominican Order.

St. Stephen, from Chasuble, 1031 — A152

180 l, Madonna as Patroness of Hungary, 1511.

1971, Nov. 25
513	A152	50 l multi	.25	.25
514	A152	180 l black & yellow	.30	.25

Millenium of the birth of St. Stephen (975?-1038), king of Hungary.

Bramante A153

Designs: 25 l, Bramante's design for dome of St. Peter's. 130 l, Design for spiral staircase.

1972, Feb. 22   Engr.   Perf. 13½x14
515	A153	25 l dull yellow & blk	.25	.25
516	A153	90 l dull yellow & blk	.25	.25
517	A153	130 l dull yellow & blk	.25	.25
		Nos. 515-517 (3)	.75	.75

Bramante (real name Donato d'Agnolo; 1444-1514), architect.

St. Mark in Storm, 12th Century Mosaic — A154

Map of Venice, 1581 — A155

Design: 180 l, St. Mark's Basilica, Painting by Emilio Vangelli.

Unwmk.
1972, June 6   Photo.   Perf. 14
518	A154	25 l lt brown & multi	.25	.25
519	A155	Block of 4	1.00	.60
a.-d.		50 l, UL, UR, LL, LR, each	.25	.25
520	A154	180 l lt blue & multi	1.10	.65
a.		Souvenir sheet, #518-520	2.50	2.50
		Nos. 518-520 (3)	2.35	1.50

UNESCO campaign to save Venice.

Gospel of St. Matthew, 13th Century, French A156

Illuminated Initials from: 50 l, St. Luke's Gospel, Biblia dell'Aracoeli 13th century, French. 90 l, Second Epistle of St. John, 14th century, Bologna. 100 l, Apocalypse of St. John, 14th century, Bologna. 130 l, Book of Romans, 14th century, Central Italy.

1972, Oct. 11   Perf. 14x13½
521	A156	30 l multi	.25	.25
522	A156	50 l multi	.25	.25
523	A156	90 l multi	.25	.25
524	A156	100 l multi	.25	.25
525	A156	130 l multi	.35	.25
		Nos. 521-525 (5)	1.35	1.25

Intl. Book Year. Illustrations are from illuminated medieval manuscripts.

Luigi Orione A157

Design: 180 l, Lorenzo Perosi and music from "Hallelujah."

1972, Nov. 28   Photo.   Perf. 14x13½
526	A157	50 l rose, lilac & blk	.25	.25
527	A157	180 l orange, grn & blk	.30	.25

Secular priests Luigi Orione (1872-1940), founder of CARITAS, Catholic welfare organization; and Lorenzo Perosi (1872-1956), composer.

Cardinal Bessarion A158

40 l, Reading Bull of Union between the Greek and Latin Churches, 1439, from bronze door of St. Peter's. 130 l, Coat of arms from tomb, Basilica of Holy Apostles, Rome.

Perf. 13x14
1972, Nov. 28   Wmk. 235   Engr.
528	A158	40 l dull green	.25	.25
529	A158	90 l carmine	.25	.25
530	A158	130 l black	.25	.25
		Nos. 528-530 (3)	.75	.75

Johannes Cardinal Bessarion (1403?-1472), Latin Patriarch of Constantinople, who worked for union of the Greek and Latin Churches. Portrait by Cosimo Rosselli in Sistine Chapel.

Eucharistic Congress Emblem — A159

Designs: 75 l, Head of Mary (Pietá), by Michelangelo. 300 l, Melbourne Cathedral.

1973, Feb. 27   Photo.   Unwmk.
531	A159	25 l violet & multi	.25	.25
532	A159	75 l olive & multi	.25	.25
533	A159	300 l multicolored	.50	.40
		Nos. 531-533 (3)	1.00	.90

40th Intl. Eucharistic Congress, Melbourne, Australia, Feb. 18-25.

St. Teresa — A160

Designs: 25 l, St. Teresa's birthplace, Alençon. 220 l, Lisieux Basilica.

1973, May 23   Engr. & Photo.
534	A160	25 l black & pink	.25	.25
535	A160	75 l black & yellow	.25	.25
536	A160	220 l black & lt blue	.40	.25
		Nos. 534-536 (3)	.90	.75

St. Teresa of Lisieux and of the Infant Jesus (1873-1897), Carmelite nun.

Copernicus A161

Designs: 20 l, 100 l, View of Torun.

1973, June 19   Engr.   Perf. 14
537	A161	20 l dull green	.25	.25
538	A161	50 l brown	.25	.25
539	A161	100 l lilac	.25	.25
540	A161	130 l dark blue	.30	.25
		Nos. 537-540 (4)	1.05	1.00

Nicolaus Copernicus (1473-1543), Polish astronomer.

St. Wenceslas A162

1973, Sept. 25   Photo.   Perf. 14
541 A162 20 l shown   .25 .25
542 A162 90 l Arms of Prague
                  Diocese   .25 .25
543 A162 150 l Spire of Prague
                  Cathedral   .25 .25
544 A162 220 l St. Adalbert   .35 .25
    Nos. 541-544 (4)   1.10 1.00

Millenium of Prague Latin Episcopal See.

St. Nerses Shnorali — A163

25 l, Church of St. Hripsime. 90 l, Armenian khatchkar, a stele with cross and inscription.

Engr. & Litho.
1973, Nov. 27   Perf. 13x14
545 A163 25 l tan & dk brown   .25 .25
546 A163 90 l lt violet & blk   .25 .25
547 A163 180 l lt green & sepia   .35 .25
    Nos. 545-547 (3)   .85 .75

Armenian Patriarch St. Nerses Shnorali (1102-1173).

Noah's Ark, Rainbow and Dove (Mosaic) — A164

Design: 90 l, Lamb drinking from stream, and Tablets of the Law (mosaic).

1974, Apr. 23   Litho.   Perf. 13x14
548 A164 50 l gold & multi   .25 .25
549 A164 90 l gold & multi   .30 .25

Centenary of the Universal Postal Union.

"And There was Light" — A165

Designs: 25 l, Noah's Ark, horiz. 50 l, The Annunciation. 90 l, Nativity (African). 180 l, Hands holding grain (Spanish inscription: The Lord feeds his people), horiz. Designs chosen through worldwide youth competition in connection with 1972 Intl. Book Year.

Perf. 13x14, 14x13
1974, Apr. 23   Photo.
550 A165 15 l brown & multi   .25 .25
551 A165 25 l yellow & multi   .25 .25
552 A165 50 l blue & multi   .25 .25
553 A165 90 l green & multi   .25 .25
554 A165 180 l rose & multi   .25 .25
    Nos. 550-554 (5)   1.25 1.25

"The Bible: the Book of Books."

St. Thomas Aquinas Teaching — A166

Designs: 50 l, Students (left panel). 220 l, Students (right panel). Designs from a painting in the Convent of St. Mark in Florence, by an artist from the School of Fra Angelico.

Sizes: 50 l, 220 l, 20x36mm, 90 l, 26x36mm

Engr. & Litho.
1974, June 18   Unwmk.   Perf. 13x14
555 A166 50 l dk brown & gold   .25 .25
556 A166 90 l dk brown & gold   .25 .25
557 A166 220 l dk brown & gold   .40 .25
    a. Strip of 3, #555-557   .70 .55

St. Thomas Aquinas (1225-1274), scholastic philosopher.

St. Bonaventure A167

Woodcuts: 40 l, Civita Bagnoregio. 90 l, Tree of Life (13th century).

1974, Sept. 26   Photo.   Perf. 13x14
558 A167 40 l gold & multi   .25 .25
559 A167 90 l gold & multi   .25 .25
560 A167 220 l gold & multi   .30 .25
    Nos. 558-560 (3)   .80 .75

St. Bonaventure (Giovanni di Fidanza; 1221-1274), scholastic philosopher.

Christ, St. Peter's Basilica — A168

Pope Paul VI Giving his Blessing — A169

Holy Year 1975: 10 l, Christus Victor, Sts. Peter and Paul. 30 l, Christ. 40 l, Cross surmounted by dove. 50 l, Christ enthroned. 55 l, St. Peter. 90 l, St. Paul. 100 l, St. Peter. 130 l, St. Paul. 220 l, Arms of Pope Paul VI. Designs of 10 l, 25 l, are from St. Peter's; 30 l, 40 l, from St. John Lateran; 50 l, 55 l, 90 l, from St. Mary Major; 100 l, 130 l, from St. Paul outside the Walls.

1974, Dec. 19   Photo.   Perf. 13x14
561 A168 10 l multi   .25 .25
562 A168 25 l multi   .25 .25
563 A168 30 l multi   .25 .25
564 A168 40 l multi   .25 .25
565 A168 50 l multi   .25 .25
566 A168 55 l multi   .25 .25
567 A168 90 l multi   .25 .25
568 A168 100 l multi   .25 .25
569 A168 130 l multi   .25 .25
570 A169 220 l multi   .25 .25
571 A169 250 l multi   .30 .25
    Nos. 561-571 (11)   2.80 2.75

Pentecost, by El Greco — A170

1975, May 22   Engr.   Perf. 13x14
572 A170 300 l car rose & orange   .60 .40

Fountain, St. Peter's Square — A171

Fountains of Rome: 40 l, Piazza St. Martha, Apse of St. Peter's. 50 l, Borgia Tower and St. Peter's. 90 l, Belvedere Courtyard. 100 l, Academy of Sciences. 200 l, Galleon.

Litho. & Engr.
1975, May 22   Perf. 14
573 A171 20 l buff & blk   .25 .25
574 A171 40 l pale violet & blk   .25 .25
575 A171 50 l salmon & blk   .25 .25
576 A171 90 l pale citron & blk   .25 .25
577 A171 100 l pale green & blk   .25 .25
578 A171 200 l pale blue & blk   .30 .25
    Nos. 573-578 (6)   1.55 1.50

European Architectural Heritage Year.

Miracle of Loaves and Fishes, Gilt Glass A172

Designs: 150 l, Painting of Christ, from Comodilla Catacomb. 200 l, Raising of Lazarus. All works from 4th century.

Perf. 14x13½
1975, Sept. 25   Photo.   Unwmk.
579 A172 30 l multi   .25 .25
580 A172 150 l brown & multi   .25 .25
581 A172 200 l green & multi   .45 .30
    Nos. 579-581 (3)   .95 .80

9th Intl. Congress of Christian Archaeology.

Investiture of First Librarian Bartolomeo Sacchi by Pope Sixtus IV A173

Designs: 100 l, Pope Sixtus IV and books in old wooden press, from Latin Vatican Codex 2044, vert. 250 l, Pope Sixtus IV visiting Library, fresco in Hospital of the Holy Spirit. Design of 70 l is from fresco by Melozzo di Forli in Vatican Gallery.

Perf. 14x13½, 13½x14
1975, Sept. 25   Litho. & Engr.
582 A173 70 l gray & lilac   .25 .25
583 A173 100 l lt yellow & grn   .25 .25
584 A173 250 l gray & red   .55 .30
    Nos. 582-584 (3)   1.05 .80

Founding of the Vatican Apostolic Library, 500th anniv.

Mt. Argentario Monastery A174

St. Paul of the Cross, by Giovanni Della Porta — A175

Design: 300 l, Basilica of Sts. John and Paul and burial chapel of Saint.

1975, Nov. 27   Photo.   Perf. 14x13½
585 A174 50 l multi   .25 .25
586 A175 150 l multi   .25 .25
587 A174 300 l multi   .45 .25
    Nos. 585-587 (3)   .95 .75

Bicentenary of death of St. Paul of the Cross, founder of the Passionist religious order in 1737.

Praying Women, by Fra Angelico — A176

International Women's Year: 200 l, Seated women, by Fra Angelico.

1975, Nov. 27   Perf. 13½x14
588 A176 100 l multi   .25 .25
589 A176 200 l multi   .40 .25

Virgin and Child in Glory, by Titian A177

Design: 300 l, The Six Saints, by Titian. Designs from "The Madonna in Glory with the Child Jesus and Six Saints."

1976, May 13   Engr.   Perf. 14x13½
590 A177 100 l rose magenta   .25 .25
591 A177 300 l rose magenta   .50 .40
    a. Pair, #590-591   .75 .60

Titian (1477-1576), painter.

A178

Designs: 150 l, Eucharist, wheat and globe. 200 l, Hands Holding Eucharist. 400 l, Hungry mankind reaching for the Eucharist.

1976, July 2   Photo.   Perf. 13½x14
592 A178 150 l gold, red & bl   .25 .25
593 A178 200 l gold & blue   .25 .25
594 A178 400 l gold, grn & brn   .40 .40
    Nos. 592-594 (3)   .90 .90

41st Intl. Eucharistic Congress, Philadelphia, PA, Aug. 1-8.

A179

Details from Transfiguration by Raphael: 30 l, Moses Holding Tablets. 40 l, Transfigured Christ. 50 l, Prophet Elijah with book. 100 l, Apostles John and Peter. 150 l, Group of women. 200 l, Landscape.

1976, Sept. 30 Photo. Perf. 13½x14
595	A179	30 l	ocher & multi	.25 .25
596	A179	40 l	red & multi	.25 .25
597	A179	50 l	violet & multi	.25 .25
598	A179	100 l	multicolored	.25 .25
599	A179	150 l	green & multi	.25 .25
600	A179	200 l	ocher & multi	.35 .25
	Nos. 595-600 (6)			1.60 1.50

St. John's Tower A180

Roman Views: 100 l, Fountain of the Sacrament. 120 l, Fountain at entrance to the gardens. 180 l, Basilica, Cupola of St. Peter's and Sacristy. 250 l, Borgia Tower and Sistine Chapel. 300 l, Apostolic Palace and Courtyard of St. Damasius.

Litho. & Engr.
1976, Nov. 23 Perf. 14
601	A180	50 l	gray & black	.25 .25
602	A180	100 l	salmon & dk grn	.25 .25
603	A180	120 l	citron & dk grn	.25 .25
604	A180	180 l	pale gray & blk	.25 .25
605	A180	250 l	yellow & brn	.25 .25
606	A180	300 l	pale lilac & mag	.30 .25
	Nos. 601-606 (6)			1.55 1.50

The Lord's Creatures A181

70 l, Brother Sun. 100 l, Sister Moon and Stars. 130 l, Sister Water. 170 l, Praise in infirmities and tribulations. 200 l, Praise for bodily death. Designs are illustrations by Duilio Cambellotti for "The Canticle of Brother Sun," by St. Francis.

1977, Mar. 10 Photo. Perf. 14x13½
607	A181	50 l	multi	.25 .25
608	A181	70 l	multi	.25 .25
609	A181	100 l	multi	.25 .25
610	A181	130 l	multi	.25 .25
611	A181	170 l	multi	.25 .25
612	A181	200 l	multi	.25 .25
	Nos. 607-612 (6)			1.50 1.50

St. Francis of Assisi, 750th death anniv.

Sts. Peter and Paul A182

Design: 350 l, Pope Gregory XI and St. Catherine of Siena. Designs are after fresco by Giorgio Vasari.

1977, May 20 Engr. Perf. 14
613	170 l	black		.30 .25
614	350 l	black		.50 .30
a.	A182 Pair, #613-614			.85 .60

Return of Pope Gregory XI from Avignon, 600th anniv.

Dormition of the Virgin — A183

Design: 400 l, Virgin Mary in Heaven. Both designs after miniatures in Latin manuscripts, Vatican Library.

1977, July 5 Photo. Perf. 13½x14
615	A183	200 l	multi	.30 .25
616	A183	400 l	multi	.55 .30

Feast of the Assumption.

The Nile Deity, Roman Sculpture — A184

Sculptures: 120 l, Head of Pericles. 130 l, Roman Couple Joining Hands. 150 l, Apollo Belvedere, head. 170 l, Laocoon, head. 350 l, Apollo Belvedere, torso.

1977, Sept. 29 Perf. 14x13½
617	A184	50 l	multi	.25 .25
618	A184	120 l	multi	.25 .25
619	A184	130 l	multi	.25 .25
620	A184	150 l	multi	.25 .25
621	A184	170 l	multi	.25 .25
622	A184	350 l	multi	.30 .30
	Nos. 617-622 (6)			1.55 1.55

Classical sculptures in Vatican Museums.

Creation of Man and Woman — A185

Designs: 70 l, Three youths in the furnace. 100 l, Adoration of the Kings. 130 l, Raising of Lazarus. 200 l, The Good Shepherd. 400 l, Chrismon, Cross, sleeping soldiers (Resurrection). Designs are bas-reliefs from Christian sarcophagi, 250-350 A.D., found in Roman excavations.

1977, Dec. 9 Photo. Perf. 14x13½
623	A185	50 l	multi	.25 .25
624	A185	70 l	multi	.25 .25
625	A185	100 l	multi	.25 .25
626	A185	130 l	multi	.25 .25
627	A185	200 l	multi	.25 .25
628	A185	400 l	multi	.35 .25
	Nos. 623-628 (6)			1.60 1.50

Madonna with the Parrot and Rubens Self-portrait A186

1977, Dec. 9 Perf. 13½x14
629	A186	350 l	multi	.50 .50

Peter Paul Rubens (1577-1640).

Pope Paul VI, by Lino Bianchi Barriviera A187

Design: 350 l, Christ's Face, by Pericle Fazzini and arms of Pope Paul VI.

1978, Mar. 9 Photo. Perf. 14
630	A187	350 l	multi	.50 .30
631	A187	400 l	multi	.50 .40

80th birthday of Pope Paul VI.

Pope Pius IX (1792-1878) A188

Designs: 130 l, Arms of Pope Pius IX. 170 l, Seal of Pius IX, used to sign definition of Dogma of Immaculate Conception.

Litho. & Engr.
1978, May 9 Perf. 13x14
632	A188	130 l	multi	.25 .25
633	A188	170 l	multi	.30 .25
634	A188	200 l	multi	.35 .25
	Nos. 632-634 (3)			.90 .75

Interregnum Issues

Keys of St. Peter and Papal Chamberlain's Insignia
A189   A190

1978, Aug. 23 Photo. Perf. 14
635	A189	120 l	purple & lt green	.30 .25
636	A189	150 l	purple & salmon	.35 .25
637	A189	200 l	purple & yellow	.35 .25
	Nos. 635-637 (3)			1.00 .75

1978, Oct. 12 Photo. Perf. 14
638	A190	120 l	black & multi	.25 .25
639	A190	200 l	black & multi	.25 .25
640	A190	250 l	black & multi	.25 .25
	Nos. 638-640 (3)			.75 .75

Pope John Paul I, Pope from Aug. 26 to Sept. 28, 1978 — A191

Pope John Paul I: 70 l, Sitting on his throne. 250 l, Walking in Vatican garden. 350 l, Giving blessing, horiz.

1978, Dec. 11 Perf. 13x14, 14x13
641	A191	70 l	multi	.25 .25
642	A191	120 l	multi	.25 .25
643	A191	250 l	multi	.30 .30
644	A191	350 l	multi	.40 .40
	Nos. 641-644 (4)			1.20 1.20

Arms of Pope John Paul II A192

Designs: 250 l, Pope John Paul II raising hand in blessing. 400 l, Jesus giving keys to St. Peter.

Litho. & Engr.
1979, Mar. 22 Perf. 14x13
645	A192	170 l	black & multi	.25 .25
646	A192	250 l	black & multi	.30 .30
647	A192	400 l	black & multi	.55 .45
	Nos. 645-647 (3)			1.10 1.00

Inauguration of pontificate of Pope John Paul II.

Martyrdom of St. Stanislas A193   St. Basil the Great Instructing Monk A194

Designs: 150 l, St. Stanislas appearing to the people. 250 l, Gold reliquary, 1504, containing saint's head. 500 l, View of Cracow Cathedral.

1979, May 18 Photo. Perf. 14
648	A193	120 l	multi	.25 .25
649	A193	150 l	multi	.25 .25
650	A193	250 l	multi	.35 .30
651	A193	500 l	multi	.75 .65
	Nos. 648-651 (4)			1.60 1.45

900th anniversary of martyrdom of St. Stanislas (1030-1079), patron saint of Poland.

Engr. & Photo.
1979, June 25 Perf. 13½x14
St. Basil the Great, 16th cent. of death: 520 l, St. Basil the Great visiting the sick.
652	A194	150 l	multi	.25 .25
653	A194	520 l	multi	.85 .70

Father Secchi, Solar Protuberance, Spectrum and Meteorograph — A195

Father Angelo Secchi (1818-1878), astronomer, solar protuberance, spectrum and: 220 l, Spectroscope. 300 l, Telescope.

Litho. & Engr.
1979, June 25   *Perf. 14x13½*
654 A195 180 l multi   .25 .25
655 A195 220 l multi   .35 .30
656 A195 300 l multi   .40 .30
    Nos. 654-656 (3)   1.00 .85

Vatican City A196

Papal Arms and Portraits: 70 l, Pius XI. 120 l, Pius XII. 150 l, John XXIII. 170 l, Paul VI. 250 l, John Paul I. 450 l, John Paul II.

1979, Oct. 11   **Photo.**   *Perf. 14x13½*
657 A196   50 l multi   .25 .25
658 A196   70 l multi   .25 .25
659 A196 120 l multi   .25 .25
660 A196 150 l multi   .25 .25
661 A196 170 l multi   .25 .25
662 A196 250 l multi   .30 .30
663 A196 450 l multi   .65 .50
    Nos. 657-663 (7)   2.20 2.05

Vatican City State, 50th anniversary.

Infant, by Andrea Della Robbia, IYC Emblem — A197

IYC Emblem and Della Robbia Bas Reliefs, Hospital of the Innocents, Florence.

Engr. & Photo.
1979, Nov. 27   *Perf. 13½x14*
664 A197   50 l multi   .25 .25
665 A197 120 l multi   .25 .25
666 A197 200 l multi   .30 .25
667 A197 350 l multi   .50 .40
    Nos. 664-667 (4)   1.30 1.15

International Year of the Child.

Abbot Desiderius Giving Codex to St. Benedict — A198

Illuminated Letters and Illustrations, Codices, Vatican Apostolic Library: 100 l, St. Benedict writing the Rule. 150 l, Page from the Rule. 220 l, Death of St. Benedict. 450 l, Montecassino (after painting by Paul Bril).

1980, Mar. 21   **Photo.**   *Perf. 14x13½*
668 A198   80 l multi   .25 .25
669 A198 100 l multi   .25 .25
670 A198 150 l multi   .25 .25
671 A198 220 l multi   .30 .30
672 A198 450 l multi   .60 .55
    Nos. 668-672 (5)   1.65 1.60

St. Benedict of Nursia (patron saint of Europe), 1500th birth anniversary.

Bernini, Medallion Showing Baldacchino in St. Peter's — A199

Gian Lorenzo Bernini (1598-1680), Architect (Self-portrait and Medallion): 170 l, St. Peter's Square with third wing (never built). 250 l, Bronze chair, Doctors of the Church. 350 l, Apostolic Palace stairway.

1980, Oct. 16   **Litho.**   *Perf. 14x13½*
673 A199   80 l multicolored   .25 .25
674 A199 170 l multicolored   .25 .25
675 A199 250 l multicolored   .35 .30
676 A199 350 l multicolored   .55 .35
    Nos. 673-676 (4)   1.40 1.15

St. Albertus Magnus on Mission of Peace — A200

1980, Nov. 18   **Litho.**   *Perf. 13½x14*
677 A200 300 l shown   .40 .30
678 A200 400 l As bishop   .55 .40

St. Albertus Magnus, 700th death anniv.

Communion of the Saints — A201

1980, Nov. 18   *Perf. 14x13½*
679 A201 250 l shown   .35 .25
680 A201 500 l Christ and saints   .65 .60

Feast of All Saints.

Guglielmo Marconi and Pope Pius XI, Vatican Radio Emblem, Vatican Arms A202

Designs: 150 l, Microphone, Bible text. 200 l, St. Maria di Galeria Radio Center antenna, Archangel Gabriel statue. 600 l, Pope John Paul II.

1981, Feb. 12   **Photo.**   *Perf. 14x13½*
681 A202 100 l shown   .25 .25
682 A202 150 l multicolored   .25 .25
683 A202 200 l multicolored   .30 .25
684 A202 600 l multicolored   .80 .65
    Nos. 681-684 (4)   1.60 1.40

Vatican Radio, 50th anniversary.

Virgil Seated at Podium, Vergilius Romanus — A203

1981, Apr. 23   **Litho.**   *Perf. 14*
685 A203 350 l multicolored   .75 .65
686 A203 600 l multicolored   1.40 1.10

2000th birth anniversary of Virgil. Issued in sheets of 16 stamps plus 9 labels.

Congress Emblem A204

Congress Emblem and: 150 l, Virgin appearing to St. Bernadette. 200 l, Pilgrims going to Lourdes. 500 l, Bishop and pilgrims.

1981, June 22   **Photo.**
687 A204   80 l multicolored   .25 .25
688 A204 150 l multicolored   .25 .25
689 A204 200 l multicolored   .30 .30
690 A204 500 l multicolored   .60 .60
    Nos. 687-690 (4)   1.40 1.40

42nd Intl. Eucharistic Congress, Lourdes, France, July 16-23.

Intl. Year of the Disabled A205

1981, Sept. 29   **Photo.**   *Perf. 14x13½*
691 A205 600 l multicolored   .90 .80

Jan van Ruusbroec, Flemish Mystic, 500th Birth Anniv. — A206

Litho. & Engr.
1981, Sept. 29   *Perf. 13½x14*
692 A206 200 l shown   .35 .35
693 A206 300 l Portrait   .45 .45

1980 Journeys of Pope John Paul II — A207

1981, Dec. 3   **Photo.**   *Perf. 13½x14½*
694 A207   50 l Papal arms   .25 .25
695 A207 100 l Map of Africa   .25 .25
696 A207 120 l Crucifix   .25 .25
697 A207 150 l Baptism   .25 .25
698 A207 200 l African bishop   .25 .25
699 A207 250 l Visiting sick   .30 .30
700 A207 300 l Notre Dame, France   .40 .40
701 A207 400 l UNESCO speech   .50 .50
702 A207 600 l Christ of the Andes, Brazil   .90 .90
703 A207 700 l Cologne Cathedral, Germany   1.00 1.00
704 A207 900 l John Paul II   1.10 1.10
   a.   Complete booklet, 8 each #694, 695, 698, 699 ('82)   27.50
    Nos. 694-704 (11)   5.45 5.45

700th Death Anniv. of St. Agnes of Prague — A208

Designs: 700 l, Handing order to Grand Master of the Crosiers of the Red Star. 900 l, Receiving letter from St. Clare.

1982, Feb. 16   **Photo.**   *Perf. 13½x14*
705 A208 700 l multicolored   1.00 1.00
706 A208 900 l multicolored   1.10 1.10

Pueri Cantores A209   St. Teresa of Avila (1515-1582) A210

Luca Della Robbia (1400-1482), Sculptor: No. 708, Pueri Cantores, diff. No. 709, Virgin in Prayer (44x36mm).

Photo. & Engr.
1982, May 21   *Perf. 14*
707 A209 1000 l multicolored   1.25 1.10
708 A209 1000 l multicolored   1.25 1.10
709 A209 1000 l multicolored   1.25 1.10
   a.   Strip of 3, #707-709   4.00 3.50

1982, Sept. 23   **Photo.**

Sketches of St. Teresa by Riccardo Tommasi-Ferroni.

710 A210   200 l multicolored   .25 .25
711 A210   600 l multicolored   .80 .80
712 A210 1000 l multicolored   1.25 1.25
    Nos. 710-712 (3)   2.30 2.30

Christmas A211

Nativity Bas-Reliefs: 300 l, Wit Stwosz, Church of the Virgin Mary, Cracow. 450 l, Enrico Manfrini.

Photo. & Engr.
1982, Nov. 23   *Perf. 14*
713 A211 300 l multicolored   .45 .45
714 A211 450 l multicolored   .65 .65

400th Anniv. of Gregorian Calendar — A212

Sculpture Details, Tomb of Pope Gregory XIII, St. Peter's Basilica.

1982, Nov. 23   **Engr.**   *Perf. 13½x14*
715 A212 200 l Surveying the globe   .25 .25
716 A212 300 l Receiving Edict of Reform   .40 .40
717 A212 700 l Presenting edict   .90 .90
   a.   Souvenir sheet of 3, #715-717   2.50 2.50
    Nos. 715-717 (3)   1.55 1.55

Souvenir Sheets

CITTÀ DEL VATICANO

THE VATICAN COLLECTIONS: THE PAPACY AND ART · USA 1983

The Papacy and Art, US 1983
Exhibition — A213

1983, Mar. 10   Litho.   Perf. 13½x14
718		Sheet of 6		3.25 2.00
a.	A213 100 l	Greek Vase	.25	.25
b.	A213 200 l	Italian vase	.35	.25
c.	A213 250 l	Female terra-cotta bust	.50	.30
d.	A213 300 l	Marcus Aurelius bust	.55	.35
e.	A213 350 l	Bird fresco	.65	.45
f.	A213 400 l	Pope Clement VIII vestment	.75	.45

1983, June 14   Litho.   Perf. 13½x14
719		Sheet of 6		3.50 3.50
a.	A213 100 l	Horse's head, Etruscan terra cotta	.25	.25
b.	A213 200 l	Horseman, Greek fragment	.25	.25
c.	A213 300 l	Male head, Etruscan	.30	.25
d.	A213 400 l	Apollo Belvedere head	.50	.25
e.	A213 500 l	Moses, Roman fresco	.55	.35
f.	A213 1000 l	Madonna and Child, by Bernardo Daddi	1.25	.70

1983, Nov. 10   Litho.   Perf. 13½x14
720		Sheet of 6		4.00 4.00
a.	A213 150 l	Greek cup, Oedipus and the Sphinx	.25	.25
b.	A213 200 l	Etruscan bronze statue of a child	.30	.25
c.	A213 350 l	Emperor Augustus marble statue	.40	.25
d.	A213 400 l	Good Shepherd marble statue	.55	.30
e.	A213 500 l	St. Nicholas Saving a ship by G. da Fabriano	.70	.40
f.	A213 1200 l	The Holy face by G. Rouault	1.50 1.00

Vatican Collection: The Papacy and Art - US 1983 exhibition, New York, Chicago, San Francisco.

Extraordinary Holy Year, 1983-84 (1950th Anniv. of Redemption) A214

Sketches by Giovanni Hajnal.

1983, Mar. 10   Photo. & Engr.
721	A214 300 l	Crucifixion	.45	.30
722	A214 350 l	Christ the Redeemer	.55	.40
723	A214 400 l	Pope	.45	.45
724	A214 2000 l	Holy Spirit	2.75 2.75
		Nos. 721-724 (4)	4.20 3.90

Theology, by Raphael (1483-1517) A215

Allegories, Room of the Segnatura.

1983, June 14
725	A215 50 l	shown	.25	.25
726	A215 400 l	Poetry	.60	.60
727	A215 500 l	Justice	.70	.70
728	A215 1200 l	Philosphy	1.75 1.75
		Nos. 725-728 (4)	3.30 3.30

Gregor Johann Mendel (1822-1884), Biologist — A216

Phases of pea plant hybridization.

Photo. & Engr.
1984, Feb. 28   Perf. 14x13½
729	A216 450 l	multicolored	.60	.45
730	A216 1500 l	multicolored	2.00 1.50

St. Casimir of Lithuania (1458-1484) — A217

1984, Feb. 28   Perf. 14
731	A217 550 l	multicolored	.90	.55
732	A217 1200 l	multicolored	2.00 1.25

Pontifical Academy of Sciences — A218

1984, June 18   Litho. & Engr.
733	A218 150 l	shown	.25	.25
734	A218 450 l	Secret Archives	.65	.55
735	A218 850 l	Apostolic Library	.85	.65
736	A218 1500 l	Observatory	2.25 1.75
		Nos. 733-736 (4)	4.00 3.20

Papal Journeys A218a

1984-85   Photo.   Perf. 13½x14½
737	A218a 50 l	Pakistan	.25	.25
738	A218a 100 l	Philippines	.25	.25
739	A218a 150 l	Guam	.30	.25
740	A218a 250 l	Japan	.45	.30
741	A218a 300 l	Alaska	.55	.50
742	A218a 400 l	Africa	.80	.50
743	A218a 450 l	Portugal	.90	.60
a.		Bklt. pane, 4 ea #738, 741-743 + 4 labels ('85)	10.00
		Complete booklet, #743a	10.00
744	A218a 550 l	Grt. Britain	1.10	.70
745	A218a 1000 l	Argentina	2.00 1.40
746	A218a 1500 l	Switzerland	3.00 1.90
747	A218a 2500 l	San Marino	4.00 3.25
748	A218a 4000 l	Spain	8.00 5.25
		Nos. 737-748 (12)	21.60 15.15

Issued: Nos. 737-748, 10/2/84; No. 743a, 3/14/85.

St. Damasus I (b. 304) A219

St. Damasus I and: 200 l, Sepulchre of Sts. Marcellinus and Peter. 500 l, Epigraph of St. Januarius. 2000 l, Basilica, Church of the Martyrs Simplicius, Faustinus and Beatrice.

1984, Nov. 27   Photo.   Perf. 14x13½
749	A219 200 l	multicolored	.35	.25
750	A219 500 l	multicolored	.90	.60
751	A219 2000 l	multicolored	3.75 2.25
		Nos. 749-751 (3)	5.00 3.10

St. Methodius (d. 885) — A220

St. Methodius and: 500 l, Madonna and Christ. 600 l, St. Cyril, carrying the body of St. Clement I. 1700 l, Sts. Benedict and Cyril, patrons of Europe.

Photo. & Engr.
1985, May 7   Perf. 13½x14
752	A220 500 l	multicolored	.90	.50
753	A220 600 l	multicolored	1.10	.60
754	A220 1700 l	multicolored	3.25 1.60
		Nos. 752-754 (3)	5.25 2.70

St. Thomas More (1477-1535) — A221

St. Thomas More (from a portrait by Hans Holbein) and: 250 l, map of British Isles. 400 l, Frontispiece of Utopia. 2000 l, Frontispiece of Domenico Regi's biography of More.

Litho. & Engr.
1985, May 7   Perf. 14x13½
755	A221 250 l	multicolored	.45	.25
756	A221 400 l	multicolored	.80	.40
757	A221 2000 l	multicolored	3.75 2.00
		Nos. 755-757 (3)	5.00 2.65

St. Gregory VII (c. 1020-85) A222

Designs: 150 l, Eagle from Byzantine door, St. Paul's Basilica, Rome. 450 l, St. Gregory blessing. 2500 l, Sarcophagus.

Perf. 13½x14, 14x13½
1985, June 18   Photo.
758	A222 150 l	multi, vert.	.25	.25
759	A222 450 l	multi, vert.	.75	.45
760	A222 2500 l	multicolored	4.00 2.50
		Nos. 758-760 (3)	5.00 3.20

43rd Intl. Eucharistic Congress — A223

Emblem, host, cross and: 100 l, Outline map of Africa. 400 l, Altar and Assembly of Bishops. 600 l, African chalice. 2300 l, African Christian family.

Photo. & Engr.
1985, June 18   Perf. 13½x14
761	A223 100 l	multicolored	.25	.25
762	A223 400 l	multicolored	.60	.40
763	A223 600 l	multicolored	.90	.55
764	A223 2300 l	multicolored	3.50 2.00
		Nos. 761-764 (4)	5.25 3.20

Concordat Agreement Ratification A224

1985, Oct. 15   Photo.   Perf. 14x13½
765	A224 400 l	Papal arms, map of Italy	.65	.35

Coaches A225

1985, Oct. 15   Litho. & Engr.
766	A225 450 l	dp lil rose & int bl	.75	.35
767	A225 1500 l	brt bl & dp lil rose	2.00 1.40
a.		Souvenir sheet of 2, #766-767, perf. 13½x12½	3.25 3.25

Italia '85.

Intl. Peace Year 1986 — A226

Biblical and gospel texts: 50 l, Isaiah 2:4. 350 l, Isaiah 52:7. 450 l, Matthew 5:9. 650 l, Luke 2:14. 2000 l, Message for World Peace, speech of Pope John Paul II, Jan. 1, 1986.

1986, Apr. 14   Photo.   Perf. 14
768	A226 50 l	multicolored	.25	.25
769	A226 350 l	multicolored	.55	.30
770	A226 450 l	multicolored	.80	.40
771	A226 650 l	multicolored	1.10	.60
772	A226 2000 l	multicolored	3.50 2.00
		Nos. 768-772 (5)	6.20 3.55

Vatican City — A227

1986, Apr. 14   Perf. 13½x14
773	A227	Block of 6	6.75 3.00
a.-f.		550 l, any single	1.10	.50

UNESCO World Heritage Campaign. No. 773 has continuous design.

Patron Saints of the Sick — A228

Designs: No. 774, St. Camillus de Lellis rescuing invalid during Tiber flood, by Pierre Subleyras (1699-1749). No. 775, St. John of God with invalids, by Gomez Moreno (1834-1918). 2000 l, Pope John Paul II visiting the sick.

Litho. & Engr.

1986, June 12   *Perf. 13½x14*

774	A228	700 l	multicolored	1.25	.60
775	A228	700 l	multicolored	1.25	.60
776	A228	2000 l	multicolored	3.50	1.90
	Nos. 774-776 (3)			6.00	3.10

Pontifical Academy of Sciences, 50th Anniv. A229

School of Athens (details), by Raphael: 1500 l, Scribes. 2500 l, Students learning math.

Litho. & Engr.

1986, Oct. 2   *Perf. 14x13½*

777	A229	1500 l	multicolored	2.75	1.50
778	A229	2500 l	multicolored	4.25	2.50

Conversion of St. Augustine (354-430) in 387 — A230

Religious art: 300 l, St. Augustine reading St. Paul's Epistles, fresco by Benozzo Gozzoli (1420-1498), Church of St. Augustine, San Gimignano. 400 l, Baptism of St. Augustine, painting by Bartolomeo di Gentile (1470-1534), Vatican Art Gallery. 500 l, Ecstasy of St. Augustine, fresco by Benozzo Gozzoli, Church of St. Augustine. 2200 l, St. Augustine, detail of Disputa del Sacramento, fresco by Raphael (1483-1520), Room of the Segnatura, Apostolic Palace.

1987, Apr. 7   **Photo.**   *Perf. 13½x14*

779	A230	300 l	multicolored	.50	.30
780	A230	400 l	multicolored	.70	.45
781	A230	500 l	multicolored	.85	.50
782	A230	2200 l	multicolored	3.75	2.25
	Nos. 779-782 (4)			5.80	3.50

A231

Seals: 700 l, Church of Riga, 1224-1269. 2400 l, Marian Basilica of the Assumption, Aglona, 1780.

1987, June 2   **Photo.**   *Perf. 13½x14*

783	A231	700 l	multicolored	1.40	.95
784	A231	2400 l	multicolored	4.75	3.25

Christianization of Latvia, 800th anniv.

Christianization Anniversaries A232

Designs: 200 l, Christ, statue in the Lithuanian Chapel, Vatican Crypt. 700 l, Two Angels and Our Lady Holding the Body of Christ, by a Lithuanian artist. 3000 l, Lithuanian shrine.

1987, June 2   *Perf. 13½x14*

785	A232	200 l	multicolored	.30	.25
786	A232	700 l	multicolored	1.10	.75
787	A232	3000 l	multicolored	4.50	3.00
	Nos. 785-787 (3)			5.90	4.00

Christianization of Lithuania, 600th anniv.

OLYMPHILEX '87, Rome, Aug. 29-Sept. 9 — A233

Details of mosaic from the Baths of Caracalla: 400 l, Judge. 500 l, Athlete. 600 l, Athlete, diff. 2000 l, Athlete, diff.

Litho. & Engr.

1987, Aug. 29   *Perf. 14*

788	A233	400 l	multicolored	.65	.45
789	A233	500 l	multicolored	.85	.55
790	A233	600 l	multicolored	1.00	.65
791	A233	2000 l	multicolored	3.25	2.25
	Nos. 788-791 (4)			5.75	3.90

Souvenir Sheet

792	Sheet of 4 + 4 labels		5.75	5.75
a.	A233 400 l like No. 788		.65	.65
b.	A233 500 l like No. 789		.80	.80
c.	A233 600 l like No. 780		1.00	1.00
d.	A233 2000 l		3.25	3.25

Stamps from souvenir sheet have a Greek border in blue surrounding vignettes (pictured). Nos. 788-791 have single line border in blue. No. 792 has 4 labels picturing the papal arms, a goblet, a crown and the exhibition emblem.

Inauguration of the Philatelic and Numismatic Museum — A235

Designs: 400 l, Philatelic department, Vatican City, No. 1. 3500 l, Numismatic department, 1000-lire coin of 1986.

1987, Sept. 29   **Photo.**   *Perf. 14x13½*

793	A235	400 l	multicolored	.60	.45
794	A235	3500 l	multicolored	5.50	3.75

Journeys of Pope John Paul II, 1985-86 A236

Designs: 50 l, Venezuela, Peru, Ecuador and Trinidad & Tobago, 1985. 250 l, The Netherlands, Luxembourg, Belgium, 1985. 400 l, Togo, Ivory Coast, Cameroun, Central Africa, Zaire, Kenya and Morocco, 1985. 500 l, Liechtenstein, 1986. 4000 l, Bangladesh, Singapore, Fiji, New Zealand, Australia and Seychelles, 1986.

1987, Oct. 27   **Photo.**   *Perf. 14x13½*

795	A236	50 l	multicolored	.25	.25
796	A236	250 l	multicolored	.65	.45
797	A236	400 l	multicolored	1.10	.70
798	A236	500 l	multicolored	1.25	.85
799	A236	600 l	multicolored	1.60	1.00
800	A236	700 l	multicolored	1.90	1.25
801	A236	2500 l	multicolored	6.75	4.50
802	A236	4000 l	multicolored	11.00	7.25
	Nos. 795-802 (8)			24.50	16.25

A237

Transfer of St. Nicholas Relics from Myra to Bari, 900th anniv.: 500 l, Arrival of relics at Bari. 700 l, Act of charity, three improverished women. 3000 l, Miraculous rescue of ship.

1987, Dec. 3   *Perf. 13½x14*

803	A237	500 l	multicolored	2.00	1.25
804	A237	700 l	multicolored	3.00	2.00
805	A237	3000 l	multicolored	12.50	8.00
	Nos. 803-805 (3)			17.50	11.25

St. Nicholas of Bari (c. 270-352), bishop of Myra. Legend of Santa Claus originated because of his charitable works. Printed in sheets of 8 + 16 se-tenant labels picturing Santa Claus.

A238

Children and: 500 l, Sister of the Institute of the Daughters of Mary Help of Christians. 1000 l, St. John Bosco. 2000 l, Salesian lay brother. Printed in a continuous design.

1988, Apr. 19   **Photo.**

806	Strip of 3			5.25	4.00
a.	A238 500 l multicolored			.70	.50
b.	A238 1000 l multicolored			1.50	1.00
c.	A238 2000 l multicolored			3.00	2.00

St. John Bosco (1815-1888), educator.

A239

1988, June 16   **Photo.**   *Perf. 13½x14*

807	A239	50 l	Annunciation	.25	.25
808	A239	300 l	Nativity	.40	.25
809	A239	500 l	Pentecost	.65	.40
810	A239	750 l	Assumption	1.10	.60
811	A239	1000 l	Mother of the Church	1.40	.80
812	A239	2400 l	Refuge of Sinners	3.25	1.90
	Nos. 807-812 (6)			7.05	4.20

Marian Year, 1987-88.

A240

Baptism of the Rus' of Kiev, Millennium: 450 l, "Prince St. Vladimir the Great," from a 15th cent. icon. 650 l, Cathedral of St. Sophia, Kiev. 2500 l, "Mother of God in Prayer," from a mosaic at the cathedral.

1988, June 16

813	A240	450 l	multicolored	.75	.45
814	A240	650 l	multicolored	1.00	.65
815	A240	2500 l	multicolored	3.75	2.25
	Nos. 813-815 (3)			5.50	3.35

Paintings by Paolo Veronese (1528-1588) — A241

Designs: 550 l, Marriage of Cana (Madonna and Christ) the Louvre, Paris. 650 l, Self-portrait of the Artist, Villa Barbaro of Maser, Treviso. 3000 l, Marriage of Cana (woman and two men).

Perf. 13½x14, 14x13½

1988, Sept. 29   **Photo. & Engr.**

816	A241	550 l	multicolored	.80	.45
817	A241	650 l	multi, horiz.	.95	.55
818	A241	3000 l	multicolored	4.25	2.50
	Nos. 816-818 (3)			6.00	3.50

Christmas A242

Luke 2:14 and: 50 l, Angel facing LR. 400 l, Angel facing UR. 500 l, Angel facing LL. 550 l, Shepherds. 850 l, Nativity. 1500 l, Magi.

1988, Dec. 12   **Photo.**   *Perf. 13½x14*

819	A242	50 l	multicolored	.25	.25
820	A242	400 l	multicolored	.60	.30
821	A242	500 l	multicolored	.70	.35
822	A242	550 l	multicolored	.80	.40
823	A242	850 l	multicolored	1.25	.60
824	A242	1500 l	multicolored	2.25	1.00
	Nos. 819-824 (6)			5.85	2.90

Souvenir Sheet

825	Sheet of 6		5.75	5.75
a.	A242 50 l gold & multi		.25	.25
b.	A242 400 l gold & multi		.60	.30
c.	A242 500 l gold & multi		.70	.35
d.	A242 550 l gold & multi		.80	.40
e.	A242 850 l gold & multi		1.25	.60
f.	A242 1500 l gold & multi		2.25	1.00

No. 825 has continuous design.

Feast of the Visitation, 600th Anniv. — A243

Illuminations: 550 l, The Annunciation. 750 l, The Visitation (Virgin and St. Elizabeth). 2500 l, Mary, Elizabeth and infants.

1989, May 5   **Photo.**   *Perf. 13½x14*

826	A243	550 l	multicolored	.80	.40
827	A243	750 l	multicolored	1.10	.55
828	A243	2500 l	multicolored	3.75	1.90
	Nos. 826-828 (3)			5.65	2.85

Souvenir Sheet

Gregorian Egyptian Museum, 150th Anniv. — A244

Designs: 400 l, Apis. 650 l, Isis and Apis dicephalous bust. 750 l, Statue of the physician Ugiahorresne. 2400 l, Pharaoh Mentuhotep.

Litho. & Engr.

1989, May 5   *Perf. 14x13½*

829	Sheet of 4		6.00	6.00
a.	A244 400 l multicolored		.55	.30
b.	A244 650 l multicolored		.90	.50
c.	A244 750 l multicolored		1.10	.55
d.	A244 2400 l multicolored		3.25	1.75

A245

Birds from engravings by Eleazar Albin in *Histoire Naturelle des Oiseaux*, 1750.

1989, June 13   **Photo.**   **Perf. 12**
Granite Paper

830	A245	100 l Parrot	.25	.25
831	A245	150 l Green wood- pecker	.25	.25
832	A245	200 l Crested and common wrens	.25	.25
833	A245	350 l Kingfisher	.45	.25
834	A245	500 l Red grosbeak of Virginia	.65	.30
835	A245	700 l Bullfinch	.90	.45
836	A245	1500 l Lapwing plover	2.00	1.00
837	A245	3000 l French teal	4.00	2.00
		Nos. 830-837 (8)	8.75	4.75

A246

Symbols of the Eucharist.

Photo. & Engr.
1989, Sept. 29   **Perf. 13½x14**

838	A246	550 l shown	.80	.40
839	A246	850 l multi, diff.	1.25	.65
840	A246	1000 l multi, diff.	1.50	.75
841	A246	2500 l multi, diff.	3.75	1.90
		Nos. 838-841 (4)	7.30	3.70

44th Intl. Eucharistic Cong., Seoul, Oct. 5-8.

Ecclesiastical Hierarchy in the US, Bicent. — A247

Designs: 450 l, Basilica of the Assumption of the Blessed Virgin Mary, Baltimore. 1350 l, John Carroll (1735-1815), 1st bishop of Baltimore and the US. 2400 l, Cathedral of Mary Our Queen, Baltimore.

1989, Nov. 9   **Photo.**   **Perf. 12**

842	A247	450 l multicolored	.65	.40
843	A247	1350 l multicolored	2.00	1.25
844	A247	2400 l multicolored	3.50	2.00
		Nos. 842-844 (3)	6.15	3.65

Papal Journeys 1988 A248

Papal arms, Pope John Paul II and maps: 50 l, Uruguay, Bolivia, Peru and Paraguay, May 7-19. 550 l, Austria, June 23-27. 800 l, Zimbabwe, Botswana, Lesotho, Swaziland and Mozambique, Sept. 10-19. 1000 l, France, Oct. 8-11. 4000 l, Pastoral visits in Italy, 1978-1988.

1989, Nov. 9   **Perf. 14x13½**

845	A248	50 l multicolored	.25	.25
846	A248	550 l multicolored	.80	.50
847	A248	800 l multicolored	1.10	.70
848	A248	1000 l multicolored	1.50	.90
849	A248	4000 l multicolored	5.75	3.50
		Nos. 845-849 (5)	9.40	5.85

St. Angela Merici (c. 1474-1540) A249

Designs: 700 l, The vision of the mystical stair, Prophecy of the Ursulines. 800 l, Evangelical counsel. 2800 l, Ursulines mission continued.

1990, Apr. 5   **Photo.**   **Perf. 13½x14**

850	A249	700 l multicolored	1.25	.80
851	A249	800 l multicolored	1.40	.95
852	A249	2800 l multicolored	4.75	3.25
		Nos. 850-852 (3)	7.40	5.00

Caritas Intl., 40th Anniv. A250

Designs: 450 l, Abraham. 650 l, Three visitors. 800 l, Abraham and Sarah. 2000 l, Three visitors at Abraham's table.

1990, June 5   **Photo.**   **Perf. 12x11½**
Granite Paper

853	A250	450 l multicolored	.75	.45
854	A250	650 l multicolored	1.10	.70
855	A250	800 l multicolored	1.25	.85
856	A250	2000 l multicolored	3.25	2.00
		Nos. 853-856 (4)	6.35	4.00

Souvenir Sheet

857		Sheet of 4	6.00	6.00
a.		A250 450 l like #853	.65	.50
b.		A250 650 l like #854	1.00	.65
c.		A250 800 l like #855	1.25	.85
d.		A250 2000 l like #856	3.00	2.00

Nos. 853-856 have a single line border in gold. Nos. 857a-857d have no border line.

No. 857 with "Pro Terremotati 1997" overprinted in sheet margin exists in limited quantities, sold for 8000 l to assist earthquake victims in Umbria and Marche, but was not officially issued by Vatican postal authorities. Value $25.

A251

1990, June 5   **Perf. 13½x14**

858	A251	300 l Ordination of St. Willibrord	.50	.30
859	A251	700 l Stay in Antwerp	1.10	.70
860	A251	3000 l Leaving belongings, death	4.75	3.25
		Nos. 858-860 (3)	6.35	4.25

1300th anniv. of ministry of St. Willibrord.

A252

Diocese of Beijing-Nanking, 300th Anniv.: 500 l, Lake Beijing. 750 l, Church of the Immaculate Conception, Beijing, 1650. 1500 l, Lake Beijing, diff. 2000 l, Church of the Redeemer, Beijing, 1703.

1990, Oct. 2

861	A252	500 l multicolored	.70	.45
862	A252	750 l multicolored	1.10	.70
863	A252	1500 l multicolored	2.25	1.40
864	A252	2000 l multicolored	2.75	1.90
		Nos. 861-864 (4)	6.80	4.45

Christmas A253

Details from painting by Sebastiano Mainardi.

1990, Nov. 27   **Photo.**   **Perf. 13**

865	A253	50 l Choir of Angels	.25	.25
866	A253	200 l St. Joseph	.30	.30
867	A253	650 l Holy Child	1.10	1.10
868	A253	750 l Madonna	1.25	1.25
869	A253	2500 l Nativity scene, vert.	4.00	4.00
		Nos. 865-869 (5)	6.90	6.90

Paintings of the Sistine Chapel — A254

Different details from lunettes: 50 l, 100 l, Eleazar. 150 l, 250 l, Jacob. 350 l, 400 l, Josiah. 500 l, 650 l, Asa. 800 l, 1000 l, Zerubbabel. 2000 l, 3000 l, Azor.

1991, Apr. 9   **Photo.**   **Perf. 11½**
Granite Paper

870	A254	50 l multicolored	.25	.25
871	A254	100 l multicolored	.25	.25
a.		Booklet pane of 6	.75	
872	A254	150 l multicolored	.25	.25
a.		Booklet pane of 6	1.25	
873	A254	250 l multicolored	.35	.35
874	A254	350 l multicolored	.45	.45
875	A254	400 l multicolored	.50	.50
876	A254	500 l multicolored	.70	.70
877	A254	650 l multicolored	.90	.90
a.		Booklet pane of 6	5.50	
		Complete booklet, #871a, 872a, 877a	7.50	
878	A254	800 l multicolored	1.00	1.00
879	A254	1000 l multicolored	1.40	1.40
880	A254	2000 l multicolored	2.75	2.75
881	A254	3000 l multicolored	4.00	4.00
		Nos. 870-881 (12)	12.80	12.80

Encyclical Rerum Novarum, Cent. A255

Arms of Pope Leo XIII and: 600 l, Title page of Encyclical. 750 l, Allegory of Church's interest in workers, employers. 3500 l, Pope Leo XIII (1878-1903).

1991, May 23   **Engr.**   **Perf. 14x13½**

882	A255	600 l blue & dk grn	.90	.90
883	A255	750 l sage grn & rose car	1.10	1.10
884	A255	3500 l brt pur & dk bl	5.25	5.25
		Nos. 882-884 (3)	7.25	7.25

Vatican Observatory, Cent. — A256

Designs: 750 l, Astrograph for making photographic sky map, 1891. 1000 l, Zeiss Double Astrograph, Lake Castelgandolfo, 1935, horiz. 3000 l, New telescope, Vatican Observatory, Mt. Graham, Arizona, 1991.

Perf. 11½x12, 12x11½
1991, Oct. 1   **Photo.**
Granite Paper

885	A256	750 l multicolored	1.10	1.10
886	A256	1000 l multicolored	1.50	1.50
887	A256	3000 l multicolored	4.50	4.50
		Nos. 885-887 (3)	7.10	7.10

Canonization of St. Bridget, 600th Anniv. — A257

Designs: 1500 l, Receiving Madonna's revelations. 2000 l, Receiving Christ's revelations.

1991, Oct. 1   **Perf. 12½x13**

888	A257	1500 l multicolored	2.25	2.25
889	A257	2000 l multicolored	3.25	3.25

Journeys of Pope John Paul II, 1990 — A258

Pope John Paul II and: 200 l, Cathedral of Immaculate Conception, Ouagadougou, Burkina Faso. 550 l, St. Vitus' Cathedral, Prague. 750 l, Our Lady of Guadalupe's Basilica, Mexico. 1500 l, Ta' Pinu Sanctuary, Gozo. 3500 l, Cathedral of Christ the King, Gitega, Burundi.

Litho. & Engr.
1991, Nov. 11   **Perf. 13½x14**

890	A258	200 l green & multi	.30	.30
891	A258	550 l org brn & multi	.85	.85
892	A258	750 l claret & multi	1.10	1.10
893	A258	1500 l dk brn & multi	2.25	2.25
894	A258	3500 l grn bl & multi	5.50	5.50
		Nos. 890-894 (5)	10.00	10.00

West Africa, Jan. 25-Feb. 1 (200 l); Czechoslovakia, Apr. 21-22 (550 l); Mexico, Curacao, May 6-14 (750 l); Malta, May 25-27 (1500 l); Tanzania, Burundi, Rwanda, Ivory Coast, Sept. 1-10 (3500 l).

A259

Special Assembly for Europe of Synod of Bishops: 300 l, Colonnade of St. Peter's Basilica. 500 l, St. Peter's Basilica and Square. 4000 l, Colonnade of St. Peter's Basilica, Apostolic Palace.

1991, Nov. 11   **Engr.**   **Perf. 12½x13**

895	A259	300 l olive & blk	.45	.45
896	A259	500 l olive & blk	.80	.80
897	A259	4000 l olive & blk	6.00	6.00
a.		Strip of 3, #895-897	8.00	8.00

No. 897a has continous design.

A260

Discovery and Evangelization of America, 500th Anniv.: 500 l, Christopher Columbus. 600 l, Saint Peter Claver. 850 l, La Virgen de los Reyes Catolicos. 1000 l, Bishop Bartolome de las Casas. 2000 l, Father Junipero Serra.

Charts: 1500 l, New World. 2500 l, Old World.

1992, Mar. 24   Photo.   Perf. 11½x12
Granite Paper
898	A260	500 l multicolored	.75	.75
899	A260	600 l multicolored	.90	.90
900	A260	850 l multicolored	1.25	1.25
901	A260	1000 l multicolored	1.50	1.50
902	A260	2000 l multicolored	3.00	3.00
		Nos. 898-902 (5)	7.40	7.40

Souvenir Sheet
Perf. 12
903	A260	Sheet of 2	6.00	6.00
a.		1500 l multicolored	2.25	2.25
b.		2500 l multicolored	3.75	3.75

Piero Della Francesca (d. 1492), Painter — A261

Frescoes: 300 l, 750 l (detail), Our Lady of Childbirth. 1000 l, 3000 l (detail), Resurrection.

1992, May 15   Photo.   Perf. 13½x14
904	A261	300 l multicolored	.40	.40
905	A261	750 l multicolored	1.10	1.10
906	A261	1000 l multicolored	1.40	1.40
907	A261	3000 l multicolored	4.25	4.25
		Nos. 904-907 (4)	7.15	7.15

St. Giuseppe Benedetto Cottolengo (1786-1842) A262

St. Giuseppe Benedetto Cottolengo: 650 l, Comforting the sick. 850 l, With Little House of Divine Providence.

1992, May 15   Perf. 11½x12
Granite Paper
908	A262	650 l multicolored	1.00	1.00
909	A262	850 l multicolored	1.40	1.40

A263

Plants of the New World: a, Frumentum indicum. b, Solanum pomiferum. c, Opuntia. d, Cacaos, cacavifera. e, Solanum tuberosum, capsicum, mordens. f, Ananas sagitae folio.

1992, Sept. 15   Photo.   Perf. 11½x12
Granite Paper
910		Block of 6	7.50	7.50
a.-f.	A263	850 l any single	1.25	1.25

A264

1992, Oct. 12   Perf. 12½x13
911	A264	700 l multicolored	1.00	1.00

4th General Conference of the Latin American Episcopacy.

Christmas A265

Mosaics from Basilica of St. Maria Maggiore, Rome: 600 l, The Annunciation. 700 l, Nativity. 1000 l, Adoration of the Magi. 1500 l, Presentation to the Temple.

1992, Nov. 24   Photo.   Perf. 11½
Granite Paper
912	A265	600 l multicolored	.90	.90
913	A265	700 l multicolored	1.00	1.00
914	A265	1000 l multicolored	1.40	1.40
915	A265	1500 l multicolored	2.10	2.10
		Nos. 912-915 (4)	5.40	5.40

St. Francis Healing Man from Ilerda, by Giotto di Bondone (1266-1337) — A266

1993, Jan. 9   Litho.   Perf. 13½x14
916	A266	1000 l multi + label	1.25	1.25

Prayer Meeting for Peace in Europe, Assisi.

Architecture of Vatican City and Rome — A267

Buildings: 200 l, St. Peter's Basilica, Vatican City. 300 l, St. John Lateran Basilica, Rome. 350 l, St. Mary Major's Basilica, Rome. 500 l, St. Paul's Basilica, Rome. 600 l, Apostolic Palace, Vatican. 700 l, Lateran Apostolic Palace, Rome. 850 l, Papal Palace, Castel Gandolfo. 1000 l, Chancery Palace, Rome. 2000 l, Palace of the Propagation of the Faith, Rome. 3000 l, St. Calixtus Palace, Rome.

1993, Mar. 23   Photo.   Perf. 12x11½
Granite Paper
917	A267	200 l multicolored	.25	.25
a.		Booklet pane of 4	1.10	
918	A267	300 l multicolored	.40	.40
a.		Booklet pane of 4	1.60	
919	A267	350 l multicolored	.50	.50
a.		Booklet pane of 4	2.00	
920	A267	500 l multicolored	.65	.65
a.		Booklet pane of 4	2.75	
		Complete booklet, #917a, 918a, 919a, 920a	7.50	
921	A267	600 l multicolored	.80	.80
922	A267	700 l multicolored	.95	.95
923	A267	850 l multicolored	1.10	1.10
924	A267	1000 l multicolored	1.40	1.40
925	A267	2000 l multicolored	2.75	2.75
926	A267	3000 l multicolored	4.00	4.00
		Nos. 917-926 (10)	12.80	12.80

A268

Congress emblem, Vatican arms and: 500 l, Cross, grape vines. 700 l, Cross, hands breaking bread. 1500 l, Hands lifting chalice. 2500 l, Wheat, banner.

1993, May 22   Litho.   Perf. 14x13½
927	A268	500 l multicolored	.60	.60
928	A268	700 l multicolored	.90	.90
929	A268	1500 l multicolored	1.90	1.90
930	A268	2500 l multicolored	3.00	3.00
		Nos. 927-930 (4)	6.40	6.40

45th Intl. Eucharistic Congress, Seville.

A269

Traditio Legis Sarcophagus, St. Peter's Basilica: a, 200 l, Sacrifice of Isaac. b, 750 l, Apostle Peter receiving law from Jesus, Apostle Paul. c, 3000 l, Christ watching servant pouring water on Pilate's hands.

1993, May 22   Engr.   Perf. 13½x14
931	A269	Triptych, #a.-c.	5.00	5.00

Ascension Day, May 20.

Contemporary Art — A270

Europa: 750 l, Crucifixion, by Felice Casorati (1886-1963). 850 l, Rouen Cathedral, by Maurice Utrillo (1883-1955).

1993, Sept. 29   Photo.   Perf. 13
932	A270	750 l multicolored	.95	.95
933	A270	850 l multicolored	1.00	1.00

Death of St. John of Nepomuk, 600th Anniv. — A271

2000 l, Buildings in Prague, Charles Bridge.

1993, Sept. 29   Litho.   Perf. 13½x14
934	A271	1000 l multicolored	1.25	1.25
935	A271	2000 l multicolored	2.50	2.50

Travels of Pope John Paul II — A272

Visits to: 600 l, Senegal, Gambia, Guinea. 1000 l, Angola, St. Thomas and Prince. 5000 l, Dominican Republic.

1993, Nov. 23   Photo.   Perf. 12x11½
Granite Paper
936	A272	600 l multicolored	.70	.70
937	A272	1000 l multicolored	1.25	1.25
938	A272	5000 l multicolored	5.75	5.75
		Nos. 936-938 (3)	7.70	7.70

Hans Holbein the Younger (1497?-1543), Painter — A273

Details or entire paintings: 700 l, 1000 l, Madonna of Solothurn. 1500 l, Self-portrait.

Litho. & Engr.
1993, Nov. 23   Perf. 13½x14
939	A273	700 l multicolored	.85	.85
940	A273	1000 l multicolored	1.25	1.25
941	A273	1500 l multicolored	1.75	1.75
		Nos. 939-941 (3)	3.85	3.85

Synod of Bishops, Special Assembly for Africa A274

Designs: 850 l, Stylized crosier, dome with cross, vert. 1000 l, Crucifix, dome of St. Peter's Basilica, crosiers, African landscape.

Perf. 12½x13, 13x12½
1994, Apr. 8   Photo.
942	A274	850 l multicolored	1.10	1.10
943	A274	1000 l multicolored	1.25	1.25

The Restored Sistine Chapel — A275

Frescoes, by Michelangelo: Creation of the Sun and Moon: No. 944, Sun. No. 945, God pointing toward moon. Creation of Man: No. 946, Adam, No. 947, God. Original Sin: No. 948, Adam, Eve taking apple from serpent. No. 949, Adam, Eve forced from Garden of Eden. The Flood: No. 950, People on dry ground. No. 951, People on stone outcropping.
4000 l, Detail of Last Judgment, Christ and the Virgin.

1994, Apr. 8   Photo.   Perf. 11½
944		350 l multicolored	.40	.40
945		350 l multicolored	.40	.40
a.	A275	Pair, #944-945	.80	.80
946		500 l multicolored	.60	.60
947		500 l multicolored	.60	.60
a.	A275	Pair, #946-947	1.25	1.25
948		1000 l multicolored	1.25	1.25
949		1000 l multicolored	1.25	1.25
a.	A275	Pair, #948-949	2.50	2.50
950		2000 l multicolored	2.50	2.50
951		2000 l multicolored	2.50	2.50
a.	A275	Pair, 950-951	5.00	5.00
		Nos. 944-951 (8)	9.50	9.50

Souvenir Sheet
Perf. 12
952	A275	4000 l multicolored	5.00	5.00

No. 952 contains one 36x54mm stamp.

European Inventions, Discoveries — A276

Europa: 750 l, Progess from wheel to atom traced by white thread. 850 l, Galileo in center of solar system, scientific instruments.

1994, May 31   Litho.   Perf. 13x13½
953	A276	750 l multicolored	.95	.95
954	A276	850 l multicolored	1.10	1.10

Intl. Year of the
Family — A277

Stained glass: 400 l, God creating man and
woman. 750 l, Family under names of four
Evangelists. 1000 l, Parents teaching son.
2000 l, Young man comforting elderly couple.

1994, May 31   Photo.   Perf. 13x14
955 A277 400 l multicolored   .50 .50
956 A277 750 l multicolored   .95 .95
957 A277 1000 l multicolored 1.25 1.25
958 A277 2000 l multicolored 2.50 2.50
    Nos. 955-958 (4)   5.20 5.20

Giovanni da Montecorvino (1247-
1328), Missionary — A278

1994, Sept. 27   Litho.   Perf. 14
959 A278 1000 l multicolored 1.40 1.40

Evangelization of China, 700th anniv.

13th Intl.
Convention of
Christian
Archaeology,
Split,
Croatia — A279

Mosaics from Euphrasian Basilica, Paren-
tium, Croatia, 6th Cent.: 700 l, Bishop
Euphrasius, Archdeacon Claudius, Claudius'
son. 1500 l, Madonna and Child, two angels.
3000 l, Christ, Apostles Peter & Paul.

1994, Sept. 27   Perf. 13x14
960 A279 700 l multicolored 1.00 1.00
961 A279 1500 l multicolored 2.00 2.00
962 A279 3000 l multicolored 4.25 4.25
    Nos. 960-962 (3)   7.25 7.25

Travels of Pope John Paul II — A280

Designs: 600 l, Benin, Uganda, Sudan.
700 l, Albania. 1000 l, Spain. 2000 l, Jamaica,
Mexico, US. 3000 l, Lithuania, Latvia, Estonia.

1994, Nov. 18   Engr.   Perf. 13
963 A280 600 l multicolored   .85 .85
964 A280 700 l multicolored 1.00 1.00
965 A280 1000 l multicolored 1.40 1.40
966 A280 2000 l multicolored 2.75 2.75
967 A280 3000 l multicolored 4.25 4.25
    Nos. 963-967 (5)   10.25 10.25

Christmas
A281

The Nativity, by Il Tintoretto: 700 l, The Holy
Family. No. 969, The Holy Family, two women.
No. 970, Adoration of the shepherds.

1994, Nov. 18   Photo.   Perf. 11½
Granite Paper
968 A281 700 l multicolored 1.00 1.00
    Size: 45x27mm
969 A281 1000 l multicolored 1.40 1.40
970 A281 1000 l multicolored 1.40 1.40
    a. Pair, #969-970   2.80 2.80
    Nos. 968-970 (3)   3.80 3.80

Peace and
Freedom
A282

1995, Mar. 25   Photo.   Perf. 14x13
971 A282 750 l shown   .90 .90
972 A282 850 l Hands clasp,
              dove   1.00 1.00
    Europa.

Shrine of
Loreto, 700th
Anniv. — A283

Details of artworks from vaults of Sacristy:
600 l, St. Mark's, Angel with chalice, by
Melozzo da Forli. 700 l, St. Mark's, Angel with
lamb, by da Forli. 1500 l, 2500 l, St. John's,
Music making angels, by Luca Signorelli.
No. 977, Marble carving showing Holy
House of Loreto.

1995, Mar. 25   Perf. 11½
973 A283 600 l multicolored   .70 .70
974 A283 700 l multicolored   .80 .80
975 A283 1500 l multicolored 1.75 1.75
976 A283 2500 l multicolored 3.00 3.00
    Nos. 973-976 (4)   6.25 6.25
    Souvenir Sheet
977 A283 3000 l multicolored 3.50 3.50

No. 977 contains one 36x36mm stamp.

Radio,
Cent.
A284

Designs: 850 l, Guglielmo Marconi, transmitting equipment. 1000 l, Archangel Gabriel,
Pope John Paul II, Marconi broadcasting station, Vatican City.

1995, June 8   Photo.   Perf. 14
978 A284 850 l multicolored 1.00 1.00
979 A284 1000 l multicolored 1.25 1.25

See Germany No. 1990, Ireland Nos. 973-
974, Italy Nos. 2038-2039, San Marino Nos.
1336-1337.

A285

European Nature Conservation Year
(Scenes in Vatican Gardens & Castel
Gandolfo: 200 l, Fountain of the Triton, arches
of rhyncospernum jasminoides. 300 l, Avenue
of roses, Palazzo Barberini. 400 l, Statue of
Apollo Citaredo. 550 l, Ruins of Domitian's
Villa, Avenue of roses. 750 l, Acer negundo,

Viale dell'Osservatorio. 1500 l, Belvedere garden. 2000 l, Fountain of the Eagle, Quercus
ilex. 3000 l, Avenue of cypresses, equestrian
statue.

1995, June 8   Perf. 12
Granite Paper
980 A285 200 l multicolored   .25 .25
981 A285 300 l multicolored   .35 .35
    a. Booklet pane of 3   1.00
982 A285 400 l multicolored   .50 .50
    a. Booklet pane of 3   1.50
983 A285 550 l multicolored   .70 .70
    a. Booklet pane of 3   2.25
984 A285 750 l multicolored   .90 .90
    a. Booklet pane of 3   2.75
        Complete booklet, #981a,
        982a, 983a, 984a   7.50
985 A285 1500 l multicolored 1.90 1.90
986 A285 2000 l multicolored 2.50 2.50
987 A285 3000 l multicolored 3.75 3.75
    Nos. 980-987 (8)   10.85 10.85

A286

Paintings of peace, by Paolo Guiotto: 550 l,
Small hearts flying from large heart. 750 l,
Stylized faces. 850 l, Doves in flight. 1250 l,
Lymph reaching to smallest branches. 2000 l,
Explosion of colors, people.

1995, Oct. 3   Photo.   Perf. 13½x13
988 A286 550 l multicolored   .70 .70
989 A286 750 l multicolored   .95 .95
990 A286 850 l multicolored 1.10 1.10
991 A286 1250 l multicolored 1.50 1.50
992 A286 2000 l multicolored 2.50 2.50
    Nos. 988-992 (5)   6.75 6.75

    UN, 50th anniv.

A287

St. Anthony of Padua (1195-1231): 750 l, St.
John of God (1495-1550). 3000 l, St. Philip
Neri (1515-95).

Litho. & Engr.
1995, Oct. 3   Perf. 13½x14
993 A287 500 l green & brown .65 .65
994 A287 750 l violet & green .95 .95
995 A287 3000 l magenta &
              black   3.75 3.75
    Nos. 993-995 (3)   5.35 5.35

A288

Scenes depicting life of Jesus Christ from
illuminated manuscripts: 400 l, The Annunciation. 850 l, Nativity. 1250 l, Flight into Egypt.
2000 l, Jesus among the teachers.

1995, Nov. 20   Photo.   Perf. 12x11½
Granite Paper
996 A288 400 l multicolored   .50 .50
997 A288 850 l multicolored 1.10 1.10
998 A288 1250 l multicolored 1.60 1.60
999 A288 2000 l multicolored 2.50 2.50
    Nos. 996-999 (4)   5.70 5.70

    Towards the Holy Year 2000.

Travels of
Pope John
Paul II
A289

Designs: 1000 l, Giving greeting in Croatia,
statue of Blessed Lady, Zagreb Cathedral.
2000 l, In Italy, lighthouse in Genoa, Orvieto
Cathedral, Valley of Temples in Agrigento.

1995, Nov. 20   Litho.   Perf. 14½x14
1000 A289 1000 l multicolored 1.25 1.25
1001 A289 2000 l multicolored 2.50 2.50

Religious
Anniversaries
A290

Designs: 1250 l, Angel holding crosses,
Union of Brest-Litovsk, 400th anniv. 2000 l,
Cross with branches, Latin episcopal mitre,
Byzantine mitre, Union of Uzhorod, 350th
anniv.

1996, Mar. 16   Photo.   Perf. 13½x14
1002 A290 1250 l multicolored 1.60 1.60
1003 A290 2000 l multicolored 2.50 2.50

A291

Marco Polo's Return from China,
700th Anniv. — A292

Designs from miniatures, Bodleian Library,
Oxford: 350 l, Marco Polo delivering Pope
Gregory X's letter to Great Khan. 850 l, Great
Khan dispensing alms to poor in Cambaluc.
1250 l, Marco Polo receiving golden book from
Great Khan. 2500 l, Marco Polo in Persia listening to story of three Kings who go to Beth-
lehem to adore Jesus. 2000 l, Stylized portrait of Marco Polo drawn
from first printed edition of "Il Milione."

1996, Mar. 15   Perf. 11½
Granite Paper
1004 A291 350 l multicolored .45 .45
1005 A291 850 l multicolored 1.10 1.10
1006 A291 1250 l multicolored 1.60 1.60
1007 A291 2500 l multicolored 3.25 3.25
    Nos. 1004-1007 (4)   6.40 6.40
    Souvenir Sheet
    Perf. 12x11½
1008 A292 2000 l black   2.50 2.50

A293

Famous Women: 750 l, Gianna Baretta Molla (1922-62), physician. 850 l, Sister Edith Stein (1891-1942).

1996, May 7   Engr.   Perf. 13x14
1009 A293 750 l blue   1.00 1.00
1010 A293 850 l brown   1.10 1.10

A294

Modern Olympic Games, Cent.: a, Statue of athlete. b, Athlete's torso. c, Hand. d, Statue of athlete reaching upward. e, Hercules.

1996, May 7   Photo.   Perf. 13
1011   Strip of 5   8.00 8.00
a.-e. A294 1250 l any single   1.60 1.60

Ordination of Pope John Paul II, 50th Anniv.
A295

Designs: 500 l, Wawel Cathedral, Krakow. 750 l, Pope John Paul II giving blessing. 1250 l, Basilica of St. John Lateran, Rome.

1996, Oct. 12   Litho.   Perf. 14
1012 A295 500 l multicolored   .65 .65
1013 A295 750 l multicolored   1.00 1.00
1014 A295 1250 l multicolored   1.60 1.60
       Nos. 1012-1014 (3)   3.25 3.25

Life of Jesus Christ from Illuminated Manuscripts
A296

Designs: 550 l, Baptism of Jesus at River Jordan. 850 l, Temptation in the desert. 1500 l, Cure of the leper. 2500 l, Jesus the teacher.

1996, Oct. 12   Photo.   Perf. 12x11½
1015 A296 550 l multicolored   .75 .75
1016 A296 850 l multicolored   1.10 1.10
1017 A296 1500 l multicolored   2.00 2.00
1018 A296 2500 l multicolored   3.25 3.25
       Nos. 1015-1018 (4)   7.10 7.10

Christmas — A297

Nativity, by Murillo (1618-82).

1996, Nov. 20   Litho.   Perf. 13½
1019 A297 750 l multicolored   1.00 1.00

St. Celestine V (1215-96)
A298

#1021, St. Alfonso Maria De'Liguori (1696-1787).

1996, Nov. 20   Perf. 13½x14
1020 A298 1250 l multicolored   1.60 1.60
1021 A298 1250 l multicolored   1.60 1.60

Travels of Pope John Paul II, 1995
A299

Designs: 250 l, Jan. 11-21, Philippines, Papua New Guinea, Australia, Sri Lanka. 500 l, May 20-22, Czech Republic, Poland. 750 l, June 3-4, Belgium. 1000 l, June 30-July 3, Slovakia. 2000 l, Sept. 14-20, Cameroun, South Africa, Kenya. 5000 l, Oct. 4-9, UN headquarters, NY, US.

1996, Nov. 20   Perf. 14x13½
1022 A299 250 l blue & multi   .35 .35
1023 A299 500 l blue green & multi .65 .65
1024 A299 750 l green & multi   1.00 1.00
1025 A299 1000 l brown & multi   1.25 1.25
1026 A299 2000 l gray & multi   2.50 2.50
1027 A299 5000 l pink & multi   6.75 6.75
       Nos. 1022-1027 (6)   12.50 12.50

Papal Carriages and Automobiles
A300

Designs: 50 l, Touring carriage. 100 l, Graham Paige. 300 l, Festive traveling carriage. 500 l, Citroen Lictoria VI. 750 l, Grand touring carriage. 850 l, Mercedes Benz. 1000 l, Festive half carriage. 1250 l, Mercedes Benz 300SEL. 2000 l, Touring carriage, diff. 4000 l, Fiat "Pope mobile."

1997, Mar. 20   Photo.   Perf. 12
Granite Paper
1028 A300 50 l multicolored   .25 .25
1029 A300 100 l multicolored   .25 .25
a.   Booklet pane of 4   .75
1030 A300 300 l multicolored   .35 .35
a.   Booklet pane of 4   1.40
1031 A300 500 l multicolored   .60 .60
a.   Booklet pane of 4   2.50
1032 A300 750 l multicolored   .90 .90
a.   Booklet pane of 4   3.75
      Complete booklet, #1029a,
       1030a, 1031a, 1032a   8.50
1033 A300 850 l multicolored   1.00 1.00
1034 A300 1000 l multicolored   1.10 1.10
1035 A300 1250 l multicolored   1.50 1.50
1036 A300 2000 l multicolored   2.25 2.25
1037 A300 4000 l multicolored   4.75 4.75
       Nos. 1028-1037 (10)   12.95 12.95

A301

Swiss Guard: 750 l, Guard in traditional attire. 850 l, Guard in armor with sword in front of iron gate.

1997, Mar. 20   Litho.   Perf. 13½
1038 A301 750 l multicolored   .90 .90
1039 A301 850 l multicolored   1.00 1.00
a.   Strip of 2 + 2 labels   1.90 1.90

Europa.

A302

1997, Apr. 23   Engr.   Perf. 14
1040 A302 850 l deep violet   1.00 1.00

St. Adalbert (956-997). See Germany No. 1964, Poland No. 3337, Czech Republic No. 3012, Hungary No. 3569.

A303

"Looking at the Classics," Museum Exhibition — A304

Pictures from texts of Latin and Greek classics: 500 l, Aristotle observing and describing various species from man to insect, from his "De Historia Animalium." 750 l, Bacchus riding dragon, from "Metamorphoses" by Ovid. 1250 l, General haranguing his soldiers, from "Iliad" by Homer. 2000 l, Hannibal leaving Canne, two horsemen, foot soldier, from "Ab Urbe Condita" by Titus Livius.
Masks from "Comedies," by Terrence: No. 1045: a, Man, woman. b, Two women. c, Two men.

1997, Apr. 23   Photo.   Perf. 14
1041 A303 500 l multicolored   .60 .60
1042 A303 750 l multicolored   .90 .90
1043 A303 1250 l multicolored   1.50 1.50
1044 A303 2000 l multicolored   2.40 2.40
       Nos. 1041-1044 (4)   5.40 5.40

Perf. 13½
1045 A304 1000 l Sheet of 3, #a.-c.   3.50 3.50

A305

46th Intl. Eucharistic Congress, Wroclaw, Poland: 650 l, Elements of the Eucharist, chalice, consecrated Host, arms of Wroclaw. 1000 l, The Last Supper, fish, Congress emblem. 1250 l, Wroclaw Cathedral, sheaf of wheat, holy spirit descending on church. 2500 l, "IHS" symbol of Christ on cross, doves, world with two hands on it.

1997, May 27   Photo.   Perf. 13
1046 A305 650 l multicolored   .75 .75
1047 A305 1000 l multicolored   1.10 1.10
1048 A305 1250 l multicolored   1.40 1.40
1049 A305 2500 l multicolored   2.75 2.75
       Nos. 1046-1049 (4)   6.00 6.00

A306

1997, Sept. 15   Litho.   Perf. 13x14
1050 A306 900 l multicolored   1.00 1.00

Pope Paul VI (1897-1978).
No. 1050 was printed se-tenant with 4 labels.

St. Ambrose (d. 397) — A307

1997, Sept. 15   Photo.   Perf. 13x14
1051 A307 800 l multicolored   .90 .90

Towards the Holy Year 2000 — A308

Illustrations of Christ's miracles: 400 l, Healing of paralyzed man. 800 l, Calming of the tempest. 1300 l, Multiplication of bread and fish. 3600 l, Peter's confession and conferment of primacy.

1997, Sept. 15   Perf. 12
Granite Paper
1052 A308 400 l multicolored   .45 .45
1053 A308 800 l multicolored   .90 .90
1054 A308 1300 l multicolored   1.90 1.90
1055 A308 3600 l multicolored   4.25 4.25
       Nos. 1052-1055 (4)   7.50 7.50

1996 Travels of Pope John Paul II — A309

Designs: 400 l, Central & South America, Feb. 5-12. 900 l, Tunisia, Apr. 14. 1000 l, Slovenia, May 17-19. 1300 l, Germany, June 21-23. 2000 l, Hungary, Sept. 6-7. 4000 l, France, Sept. 19-22.

1997, Nov. 11   Litho.   Perf. 14x13½
1056 A309 400 l multicolored   .50 .50
1057 A309 900 l multicolored   1.00 1.00
1058 A309 1000 l multicolored   1.25 1.25
1059 A309 1300 l multicolored   1.50 1.50
1060 A309 2000 l multicolored   2.25 2.25
1061 A309 4000 l multicolored   4.75 4.75
       Nos. 1056-1061 (6)   11.25 11.25

Christmas — A310

Detail from "The Nativity," by Benozzo Gozzoli (1420-97).

1997, Nov. 11   Photo.   *Perf. 14*
1062 A310 800 l multicolored   .95 .95

Feasts of Sts. Peter and Paul, June 29th — A311

1998, Mar. 24   Photo.   *Perf. 13*
1063 A311 800 l St. Peter   .90 .90
1064 A311 900 l St. Paul   1.00 1.00

Europa.

The Popes of the Holy Years 1300-1525 A312

Designs: 200 l, Boniface VIII, 1300. 400 l, Clement VI, 1350. 500 l, Boniface IX, 1390, 1400. 700 l, Martin V, 1423. 800 l, Nicholas V, 1450. 900 l, Sixtus IV, 1475. 1300 l, Alexander VI, 1500. 3000 l, Clement VII, 1525.

1998, Mar. 24   Litho.   *Perf. 14*
1065 A312 200 l multicolored   .25 .25
1066 A312 400 l multicolored   .45 .45
1067 A312 500 l multicolored   .60 .60
1068 A312 700 l multicolored   .80 .80
1069 A312 800 l multicolored   .90 .90
1070 A312 900 l multicolored   1.00 1.00
1071 A312 1300 l multicolored   1.50 1.50
1072 A312 3000 l multicolored   3.50 3.50
   Nos. 1065-1072 (8)   9.00 9.00

Nos. 1065-1072 were each printed se-tenant with a label picturing the respective papal arms.
See Nos. 1095-1102, 1141-1150.

A313

Litho. & Engr.
1998, May 19   *Perf. 13½x14*
1073 A313 900 l Face on Shroud   1.00 1.00
1074 A313 2500 l Cathedral of Turin   2.75 2.75

Exposition of the Shroud of Turin.

A314

Frescoes of Angels, by Melozzo da Forli (1438-94), Basilica of Sts. Apostles, Rome: Angels playing various musical instruments.

1998, May 19   Photo.   *Perf. 12*
Granite Paper
1075 A314 450 l multicolored   .60 .60
1076 A314 650 l multicolored   .75 .75
1077 A314 800 l multicolored   .90 .90
1078 A314 1000 l multicolored   1.10 1.10
1079 A314 1300 l multicolored   1.50 1.50
1080 A314 2000 l multicolored   2.25 2.25
   Nos. 1075-1080 (6)   7.10 7.10

Towards Holy Year 2000 A315

Episodes from the Life of Christ: 500 l, Triumphal entry into Jerusalem. 800 l, Washing of the feet. 1300 l, The Last Supper. 3000 l, Crucifixion.

1998, May 19   *Perf. 12*
Granite Paper
1081 A315 500 l multicolored   .60 .60
1082 A315 800 l multicolored   .90 .90
1083 A315 1300 l multicolored   1.50 1.50
1084 A315 3000 l multicolored   3.25 3.25
   Nos. 1081-1084 (4)   6.25 6.25

Italia '98 A316

1998, Oct. 23   Photo.   *Perf. 14*
1085 A316 800 l Pope John Paul II   1.00 1.00
   Complete booklet, 5 #1085   6.00

See Italy No. 2259 and San Marino No. 1430.

The Good Shepherd — A317   Christian Sculptures — A318

1998, Oct. 25   *Perf. 12 Vert.*
Granite Paper
Booklet Stamp
1086 A317 900 l multicolored   1.10 1.10
  a.   Booklet pane of 5   5.50
   Complete booklet, #1086a   5.50

Italia '98.

1998, Oct. 25   *Perf. 12*
Designs: a, 600 l, Peter's denial. b, 900 l, Praying woman. c, 1000 l, Christ and the Cyrenean. 2000 l, Christ with the Cross and Two Apostles.

Granite Paper
1087 A318 Sheet of 4, #a.-d.   5.50 5.50

Italia '98. Margin is embossed.

Christmas — A319

1998, Dec. 1   Litho.   *Perf. 14x13½*
1088 A319 800 l multicolored   1.00 1.00

See Croatia No. 381.

1997 Travels of Pope John Paul II — A320

Designs: 300 l, Sarajevo, 4/12-13/97. 600 l, Prague, 4/25-27/97. 800 l, Beirut, 5/10-11/97. 900 l, Poland, 5/21-6/10/97. 1300 l, Paris, 8/21-24/97. 5000 l, Rio de Janeiro, 10/2-6/97.

1998, Dec. 1   *Perf. 12½*
1089 A320 300 l brown   .35 .35
1090 A320 600 l green   .70 .70
1091 A320 800 l brown   1.00 1.00
1092 A320 900 l violet blue   1.10 1.10
1093 A320 1300 l org brn   1.60 1.60
1094 A320 5000 l org brn   6.00 6.00
   Nos. 1089-1094 (6)   10.75 10.75

Popes of the Holy Years Type of 1998
Popes: 300 l, Julius III, 1550. 600 l, Gregory XIII, 1575. 800 l, Clement VIII, 1600. 900 l, Urban VIII, 1625. 1000 l, Innocent X, 1650. 1300 l, Clement X, 1675. 1500 l, Innocent XII, 1700. 2000 l, Benedict XIII, 1725.

1999, Mar. 23   Litho.   *Perf. 14*
1095 A312 300 l multicolored   .35 .35
1096 A312 600 l multicolored   .65 .65
1097 A312 800 l multicolored   .90 .90
1098 A312 900 l multicolored   1.00 1.00
1099 A312 1000 l multicolored   1.10 1.10
1100 A312 1300 l multicolored   1.40 1.40
1101 A312 1500 l multicolored   1.60 1.60
1102 A312 2000 l multicolored   2.25 2.25
   Nos. 1095-1102 (8)   9.25 9.25

Nos. 1095-1102 were each printed se-tenant with a label picturing the respective papal arms.

Flowers from Vatican Gardens and Papal Villa, Castelgandolfo A321

Europa: 800 l, John Paul II Rose. 900 l, Water lilies.

1999, Mar. 23   Litho.   *Perf. 12½x13*
1103 A321 800 l multicolored   .90 .90
1104 A321 900 l multicolored   1.00 1.00
  a.   Pair, #1103-1104 + label   1.90 1.90

Padre Pio de Pietrelcina (1887-1968) — A322

#1106: a, 1st church, San Giovanni Rotondo. b, New church, San Giovanni Rotondo. c, Like #1105.

1999, Apr. 27   Litho.   *Perf. 14x13*
1105 A322 800 l multicolored   .90 .90
Souvenir Sheet
Perf. 13x13½
1106 A322 Sheet of 3   2.10 2.10
  a.   300 l multi, vert.   .35 .35
  b.   600 l multi, vert.   .70 .70
  c.   900 l multi   1.00 1.00

Nos. 1106a-1106b are 30x40mm, No. 1106c is 60x40mm.

A323

Holy Places in Palestine — A324

Nos. 1107-1111: 19th cent. watercolors, Pontifical Lateran University Library.
Map of Holy Land from "Geographia Blaviana," 17th cent — #1112: a, Mediterranean Sea, denomination, LL. b, Mediterranean Sea, denomination LR. c, Red Sea, Holy Land. d, Inscription indentifying map.

1999, May 25   Photo.   *Perf. 11½*
Granite Paper
1107 A323 200 l Bethlehem   .25 .25
1108 A323 500 l Nazareth   .55 .55
1109 A323 800 l Lake of Tiberias   .85 .85
1110 A323 900 l Jerusalem   1.00 1.00
1111 A323 1300 l Mount Tabor   1.40 1.40
   Nos. 1107-1111 (5)   4.05 4.05
Perf. 12x11¾
1112 A324 1000 l Sheet of 4, #a.-d.   4.25 4.25

Towards Holy Year 2000 A325

Events from life of Christ: 400 l, Deposition from the Cross. 700 l, Resurrection. 1300 l, Pentecost. 3000 l, Last Judgement.

1999, May 25   *Perf. 12x11¾*
Granite Paper
1113 A325 400 l multicolored   .45 .45
1114 A325 700 l multicolored   .75 .75
1115 A325 1300 l multicolored   1.40 1.40
1116 A325 3000 l multicolored   3.25 3.25
   Nos. 1113-1116 (4)   5.85 5.85

Kosovo 1999 — A326

1999, May 25   *Perf. 12¼*
Granite Paper
1117 A326 3600 l black   4.00 4.00

Proceeds from sale of stamp benefits victims of the fighting in Kosovo.

1998 Travels of
Pope John Paul
II — A327

600 l, Cuba, June 21-26. 800 l, Nigeria, Mar.
21-23. 900 l, Austria, June 19-21. 1300 l, Croatia, Oct. 2-4. 2000 l, Italy, Oct. 20.

1999, Oct. 12   Litho.   Perf. 14x13½
1118	A327	600 l	multicolored	.70	.70
1119	A327	800 l	multicolored	.90	.90
1120	A327	900 l	multicolored	1.00	1.00
1121	A327	1300 l	multicolored	1.50	1.50
1122	A327	2000 l	multicolored	2.25	2.25
		Nos. 1118-1122 (5)		6.35	6.35

Council of
Europe, 50th
Anniv. — A328

1999, Oct. 12   Photo.   Perf. 11¾
Granite Paper
1123	A328	1200 l	multicolored	1.40	1.40

Christmas
A329

The Birth of Christ, by Giovanni di Pietro:
500 l, Joseph (detail). 800 l, Christ (detail).
900 l, Mary (detail). 1200 l, Entire painting.

Perf. 13¼x12½
1999, Nov. 24   Litho.
1124	A329	500 l	multi	.50	.50
1125	A329	800 l	multi	.80	.80
1126	A329	900 l	multi	.90	.90
1127	A329	1200 l	multi	1.25	1.25
		Nos. 1124-1127 (4)		3.45	3.45

Opening of
the Holy
Door for
Holy Year
2000
A330

Various panels of Holy Door. Stamps on No.
1100 lack white border.

1999, Nov. 24   Photo.   Perf. 11¾x12
Granite Paper
1128	A330	200 l	multi	.25	.25
1129	A330	300 l	multi	.30	.30
1130	A330	400 l	multi	.40	.40
1131	A330	500 l	multi	.50	.50
1132	A330	600 l	multi	.60	.60
1133	A330	800 l	multi	.75	.75
1134	A330	1000 l	multi	1.00	1.00
1135	A330	1200 l	multi	1.25	1.25
		Nos. 1128-1135 (8)		5.05	5.05

Souvenir Sheet
1136	Sheet of 8, #a.-h.		5.25	5.25
a.	A330 200 l Like #1128		.25	.25
b.	A330 300 l Like #1129		.30	.30
c.	A330 400 l Like #1130		.40	.40
d.	A330 500 l Like #1131		.50	.50
e.	A330 600 l Like #1132		.60	.60
f.	A330 800 l Like #1133		.80	.80
g.	A330 1000 l Like #1134		1.00	1.00
h.	A330 1200 l Like #1135		1.25	1.25

Holy Year
2000 — A331

Designs: 800 l, St. Peter's Basilica. 1000 l,
Basilica of St. John Lateran. 1200 l, Basilica of
St. Mary Major. 2000 l, Basilica of St. Paul.

2000, Feb. 4   Photo.   Perf. 11¾
Granite Paper
1137	A331	800 l	multi	.75	.75
1138	A331	1000 l	multi	1.00	1.00
1139	A331	1200 l	multi	1.25	1.25
1140	A331	2000 l	multi	2.00	2.00
		Nos. 1137-1140 (4)		5.00	5.00

Popes of the Holy Year Type of 1998

Designs: 300 l, Benedict XIV, 1750. 400 l,
Pius VI, 1775. 500 l, Leo XII, 1825. 600 l, Pius
IX, 1875. 700 l, Leo XIII, 1900. 800 l, Pius XI,
1925. 1200 l, Pius XII, 1950. 1500 l, Paul VI,
1975. No. 1149, John Paul II with miter, 2000.
No. 1150, John Paul II with hand on chin,
2000.

2000, Feb. 4   Litho.   Perf. 13¾
1141	A312	300 l	multi + label	.30	.30
1142	A312	400 l	multi + label	.40	.40
1143	A312	500 l	multi + label	.50	.50
1144	A312	600 l	multi + label	.60	.60
1145	A312	700 l	multi + label	.70	.70
1146	A312	800 l	multi + label	.75	.75
1147	A312	1200 l	multi + label	1.25	1.25
1148	A312	1500 l	multi + label	1.50	1.50
1149	A312	2000 l	multi + label	2.00	2.00
		Nos. 1141-1149 (9)		8.00	8.00

Souvenir Sheet
1150	A312	2000 l	multi	2.00	2.00

No. 1150 contains one label.

Christianity
in Iceland,
1000th
Anniv.
A332

2000, Feb. 4   Perf. 13¼x13¾
1151	A332	1500 l	multi	1.50	1.50

See Iceland Nos. 900-901.

Europa, 2000
Common Design Type
2000, May 9   Litho.   Perf. 13¼x13
1152	CD17	1200 l	multi	1.25	1.25

Printed in sheets of 10, with left and right
side selvage of Priority Mail etiquettes.

Pope John Paul
II, 80th
Birthday — A333

800 l, Pope. 1200 l, Black Madonna of
Jasna Gora. 2000 l, Pope's silver cross.

2000, May 9   Engr.   Perf. 13x12¾
1153	A333	800 l	purple	.75	.75
1154	A333	1200 l	dark blue	1.25	1.25
1155	A333	2000 l	green	2.00	2.00
		Nos. 1153-1155 (3)		4.00	4.00

See Poland Nos. 3520-3522.

Restored Sistine Chapel
Frescoes — A334

Designs: 500 l, The Calling of St. Peter and
St. Andrew, by Domenico Ghirlandaio. 1000 l,
The Trials of Moses, by Sandro Botticelli.
1500 l, The Donation of the Keys, by Pietro
Perugino. 3000 l, The Worship of the Golden
Calf, by Cosimo Rosselli.

Perf. 11½x11¾
2000, May 9   Photo.   Blue Frame
Granite Paper
1156	A334	500 l	multi	.50	.50
1157	A334	1000 l	multi	1.00	1.00
1158	A334	1500 l	multi	1.50	1.50
1159	A334	3000 l	multi	3.00	3.00
		Nos. 1156-1159 (4)		6.00	6.00

See Nos. 1172-1175, 1215-1218.

20th World Youth
Day — A335

Various photos of Pope John Paul II and
youth.

Perf. 13¾x13¼
2000, June 19   Litho.
Color of Cross
1160	A335	800 l	red	.80	.80
1161	A335	1000 l	green	1.00	1.00
1162	A335	1200 l	violet	1.10	1.10
1163	A335	1500 l	orange	1.50	1.50

Booklet Stamp
Self-Adhesive
Serpentine Die Cut 12
1164	A335	1000 l	green	1.00	1.00
a.	Booklet of 4 + 4 labels			4.00	
	Nos. 1160-1164 (5)			5.40	5.40

47th Intl.
Eucharistic
Congress
A336

2000, June 19   Perf. 13x12½
1165	A336	1200 l	multi	1.10	1.10

Beatification of
Pope John
XXIII — A337

2000, Sept. 1   Photo.   Perf. 13¼x14
1166	A337	1200 l	multi	1.10	1.10

1999 Travels of
Pope John Paul
II — A338

#1167: a, Mexico, 1/22-28. b, Romania, 5/7-
9. c, Poland, 6/17. d, Slovenia, 9/19. e, India
and Georgia, 11/5-9.

2000, Sept. 1   Perf. 11¾
Granite Paper
1167		Horiz. strip of 5		4.50	4.50
a.-e.	A338 1000 l Any single			.90	.90

Christmas
A339

Frescoes in Basilica of St. Francis, Assisi,
by Giotto: 800 l, Nativity. 1200 l, Infant Jesus.
1500 l, Mary. 2000 l, Joseph.

2000, Nov. 7   Photo.   Perf. 11¾x11½
Granite Paper
1168-1171	A339	Set of 4		5.00	5.00

**Sistine Chapel Restoration Type of
2000**

Paintings: 800 l, The Baptism of Christ, by
Pietro Perugino. 1200 l, The Passage of the
Red Sea, by Biagio d'Antonio. 1500 l, The
Punishment of Korah and the Stoning of
Moses and Aaron, by Sandro Botticelli. 4000 l,
The Sermon on the Mount, by Cosimo
Rosselli.

Perf. 11½x11¾
2001, Feb. 15   Photo.
Granite Paper
Red Frame
1172-1175	A334	Set of 4		7.00	7.00

Christian
Conversion of
Armenia, 1700th
Anniv. — A340

Scenes from illuminated code of 1569:
1200 l, St. Gregory prepares to give King Tiridates human features. 1500 l, St. Gregory
makes Agatangel write history of Armenians.
2000 l, St. Gregory and King Tiridates meet
Emperor Constantine and Pope Sylvester I.

2001, Feb. 15   Perf 11¾
Granite Paper
1176-1178	A340	Set of 3		4.50	4.50

Year of Dialogue
Among
Civilizations
A341

2001, May 22   Litho.   Perf. 14¼x14
1179	A341	1500 l	multi	1.40	1.40

Europa — A342

Designs: 800 l, Hands holding water above earth. 1200 l, Hand catching water.

2001, May 22		Perf. 13½x13¼	
1180-1181	A342	Set of 2	1.75 1.75

Giuseppe Verdi (1813-1901), Composer A343

Verdi and: 800 l, Score from Nabucco. 1500 l, Costumes from Aida. 2000 l, Scenery from Othello.

2001, May 22		Perf. 13¼x14¼	
1182-1184	A343	Set of 3	3.75 3.75

2000 Travels of Pope John Paul II — A344

Designs: 500 l, Mount Sinai, Feb. 26. 800 l, Mount Nebo, Mar. 20. 1200 l, The Last Supper, Mar. 23. 1500 l, Holy Sepulchre, Mar. 26. 5000 l, Fatima, May 12.
3000 l, Western Wall.

2001, Sept. 25		Litho.	Perf. 13¼	
1185-1189	A344	Set of 5		8.50 8.50

Souvenir Sheet
Perf. 13¼x14

1190	A344	3000 l multi	2.75 2.75

No. 1190 contains one 35x26mm stamp.

Remission of Debts of Poor Countries A345

Various panels by Carlo di Camerino: 200 l, 400 l, 800 l, 1000 l, 1500 l.

2001, Sept. 25		Photo.	Perf. 13	
1191-1195	A345	Set of 5		3.75 3.75

Giuseppe Toniolo Institute for Higher Studies, 80th Anniv. — A346

Litho. & Embossed

2001, Nov. 22			Perf. 12¾	
1196	A346	1200 l red & blue		1.10 1.10

Etruscan Museum Gold Objects — A347

Designs: 800 l, Parade fibula. 1200 l, Earrings. 1500 l, Vulci fibula. 2000 l, Head of Medusa.

2001, Nov. 22		Photo.	Perf. 13½	
1197-1200	A347	Set of 4		5.25 5.25

Christmas A348

Artwork by Egino G. Weinert: 800 l, The Annunciation. 1200 l, The Nativity. 1500 l, Adoration of the Magi.

2001, Nov. 22		Litho.	Perf. 13x13¼	
1201-1203	A348	Set of 3		3.25 3.25
1202a		Booklet pane of 4 + 4 etiquettes		4.50
		Booklet, #1202a		4.50

100 Cents = 1 Euro (€)

Depictions of Virgin Mary in Vatican Basilica — A349

Designs: 8c, Our Lady of Women in Labor. 15c, Our Lady with People Praying. 23c, Our Lady at the Tomb of Pius XII. 31c, Our Lady of the Fever. 41c, Our Lady of the Slap. 52c, Mary Immaculate. 62c, Our Lady Help of Christians. 77c, Virgin of the Deesis. €1.03, L'Addolorata. €1.55, Presentation of Mary at the Temple.

2002, Mar. 12		Litho.	Perf. 13¼x13	
1204	A349	8c multi	.25	.25
1205	A349	15c multi	.35	.35
1206	A349	23c multi	.55	.55
1207	A349	31c multi	.75	.75
1208	A349	41c multi	1.00	1.00
1209	A349	52c multi	1.20	1.20
1210	A349	62c multi	1.50	1.50
1211	A349	77c multi	1.80	1.80
1212	A349	€1.03 multi	2.40	2.40
1213	A349	€1.55 multi	3.50	3.50
		Nos. 1204-1213 (10)	13.30	13.30

Pontifical Ecclesiastical Academy, 300th Anniv. — A350

No. 1214: a, Pope Clement XI. b, Academy building (46x33mm). c, Pope John Paul II.

2002, Mar. 12		Engr.	Perf. 13¼x13	
1214	A350	Horiz. strip of 3	5.50	5.50
a.-c.		77c Any single	1.80	1.80

Sistine Chapel Restoration Type of 2000

Designs: 26c, The Temptation of Christ, by Sandro Botticelli. 41c, The Last Supper, by Cosimo Rosselli. 77c, Moses' Journey in Egypt, by Pietro Perugino. €1.55, The Last Days of Moses, by Luca Signorelli.

Perf. 11½x11¾

2002, June 13			Photo.

Granite Paper

1215-1218	A334	Set of 4	7.00 7.00

Europa — A351

Christ and the Circus, by Aldo Carpi: 41c, Entire painting. 62c, Detail.

2002, June 13		Perf. 13¼	
1219-1220	A351	Set of 2	2.40 2.40

Roman States Postage Stamps, 150th Anniv. — A352

Designs: 41c, Regina Viarum, Roman States #11. 52c, Cassian Way, Roman States #25. €1.03, Vatican walls, Vatican City #2. €1.55, St. Peter's Basilica.

2002, June 13		Perf. 13x13¼	
1221-1223	A352	Set of 3	4.50 4.50

Souvenir Sheet
Perf.

1224	A352	€1.55 multi	3.60 3.60

No. 1224 contains one 31mm diameter stamp.

St. Leo IX (1002-54), Pope A353

Designs: 41c, Portrait. 62c, In procession, receiving papal miter. €1.29, Reading from scroll, as prisoner of Normans.

2002, Sept. 26		Litho.	Perf. 13x13¼	
1225-1227	A353	Set of 3		5.50 5.50

Cimabue (1240-1302), Artist — A354

Designs: 26c, Crucifix. 62c, Jesus Christ. 77c, Virgin Mary. €1.03, St. John.

2002, Sept. 26		Photo.	Perf. 13¼x14	
1228-1231	A354	Set of 4		6.25 6.25

Nativity, by Pseudo Ambrogio di Baldese — A355

2002, Nov. 21		Photo.	Perf. 13	
1232	A355	41c multi		.95 .95

See New Zealand No. 1834.

2001 Travels of Pope John Paul II — A356

Designs: 41c, Greece, Syria and Malta, May 4-9. 62c, Ukraine, June 23-27. €1.55, Armenia and Kazakhstan, Sept. 22-27.

2002, Nov. 21		Litho.	Perf. 13x13¼	
1233-1235	A356	Set of 3	6.00 6.00	
1234a		Booklet pane, 4 #1234 + 4 etiquettes	5.75	
		Booklet, #1234a	5.75	

A357

Pontificate of John Paul II, 25th Anniv. — A358

No. 1236: a, Election as Pope, 1978. b, In Poland, 1979. c, In France, 1980. d, Assassination attempt, 1981. e, At Fatima, Portugal, 1982. f, Extraordinary Holy Year, 1983. g, At Quirinale Palace, Rome, 1984. h, World Youth Day, 1985. i, At synagogue, Rome, 1986. j, Pentecost vigil, 1987. k, At European Parliament, Strasbourg, France, 1988. l, Meeting with Mikhail Gorbachev, 1989. m, At Guinea-Bissau leper colony, 1990. n, At European Bishops' Synod, 1991. o, Publication of Catechism of the Catholic Church, 1992. p, Praying for the Balkans in Assisi, 1993. q, At Sistine Chapel, 1994. r, At UN Headquarters for 50th anniv. celebrations, 1995. s, In Germany, 1996. t, In Sarajevo, Bosnia & Herzegovina, 1997. u, In Cuba, 1998. v, Opening Holy Doors, 1999. w, World Youth Day, 2000. x, Closing Holy Doors, 2001. y, Addressing Italian Parliament, 2002.

2003, Mar. 20		Litho.	Perf. 13x13¼	
1236		Sheet of 25	24.00 24.00	
a.-y.	A357	41c Any single	.95	.95

Etched on Silver Foil
Die Cut Perf. 12½x13
Self-Adhesive

1237	A358	€2.58 Pope John Paul II	8.00 8.00

Cancels can be easily removed from No. 1237.
See Poland Nos. 3668-3669.

Martyrdom of St. George, 1700th Anniv. A359

2003, May 6		Litho. & Engr.	Perf. 13	
1238	A359	62c multi		1.50 1.50

Europa — A360

Poster art for: 41c, 1975 Holy Year. 62c, Exhibition of Slav codices, incunabula and rare books at Sistine Hall, 1985.

2003, May 6   Litho.   Perf. 13¼x13
1239-1240 A360   Set of 2   2.40 2.40

Masterpieces by Beato Angelico in Niccolina Chapel — A361

Designs: 41c, Diaconal Consecration of St. Lawrence. 62c, St. Stephen Preaching. 77c, Trial of St. Lawrence. €1.03, Stoning of St. Stephen.

2003, May 6   Photo.   Perf. 13¼
1241-1244 A361   Set of 4   6.50 6.50

Beatification of Mother Teresa of Calcutta — A362

Perf. 13½x13¼
2003, Sept. 23   Litho.
1245 A362 41c multi + label   .95 .95
Printed in sheets of 5 + 5 different labels.

19th Century Artists — A363

Designs: 41c, Blessed Are the Pure at Heart, by Paul Gauguin. 62c, The Pietà, by Vincent van Gogh.

Perf. 13¼x13½
2003, Sept. 23   Photo.
1246 A363 41c multi   .95 .95
1247 A363 62c multi   1.50 1.50
a.   Booklet pane of 4 + 4 eti-
      quettes   6.00   —
      Complete booklet, #1247a   6.00

Animals in Vatican Basilica Art A364

Designs: 21c, Dragon. 31c, Camel. 77c, Horse. €1.03, Leopard.

2003, Sept. 23
1248-1251 A364   Set of 4   5.50 5.50

Canonization of Josemaría Escrivá de Balaguer, Oct. 6, 2003 — A365

2003, Nov. 18   Litho.   Perf. 14x13¼
1252 A365 41c multi   1.00 1.00

2002 Travels of Pope John Paul II — A366

Designs: 62c, Bulgaria and Azerbaijan, May 22-26. 77c, Canada, Guatemala and Mexico, July 23-Aug. 2. €2.07, Poland, Aug. 16-19.

2003, Nov. 18   Perf. 13x13¼
1253-1255 A366   Set of 3   8.50 8.50

Christmas A367

2003, Nov. 18
Stamp With White Border
1256 A367 41c multi   1.00 1.00
Souvenir Sheet
Stamp Without White Border
1257 A367 41c multi   1.00 1.00
Death of Pope Paul VI, 25th anniv. (#1257).

St. Pius V (1504-72) A368

Altarpiece by Grazio Cossoli in Chapel of the Rosary, Santa Croce di Bosco Marengo: 4c, Detail depicting St. Pius V and flag. €2, Entire altarpiece.

Litho. & Silk Screened
2004, Mar. 18   Perf. 13¼x13
1258-1259 A368   Set of 2   5.00 5.00

2003 Travels of Pope John Paul II — A369

Designs: 60c, Spain, May 3-4. 62c, Bosnia & Herzegovina, June 22. 80c, Croatia, June 5-9. €1.40, Slovakia, Sept. 11-14.

2004, Mar. 18   Litho.
1260-1263 A369   Set of 4   8.50 8.50

EMISSIONE CONGIUNTA

Papal Visits to Poland — A370

No. 1264, 45c: a, Pope with hand on chin. b, Pope praying. c, Pope carrying crucifix. d, Pope with crucifix against head.
No. 1265, 62c: a, Pope holding crucifix, diff. b, Pope with arm raised. c, Pope, wearing white, seated. d, Pope, wearing red cape, seated.

Litho. (Labels Litho. & Embossed)
2004, Mar. 18
Sheets of 4, #a-d, + 8 Labels
1264-1265 A370   Set of 2   10.50 10.50

Children AIDS Victims — A371

2004, June 3   Photo.   Perf. 13¼x13
1266 A371 45c multi + label   1.10 1.10
Printed in sheets of 6 + 6 stamp-sized labels (with different text) and 1 large central label.

Europa — A372

Paintings of: 45c, Men on horses. 62c, People in garden.

2004, June 3   Litho.   Perf. 12¾x13¼
1267-1268 A372   Set of 2   2.60 2.60

Flags and One-Euro Coins — A373

2004, June 3   Litho.   Perf. 13½
1269 A373 4c Austria   .25 .25
1270 A373 8c Belgium   .25 .25
1271 A373 15c Finland   .35 .35
1272 A373 25c France   .60 .60
1273 A373 30c Germany   .70 .70
1274 A373 40c Greece   .95 .95
1275 A373 45c Vatican City   1.10 1.10
1276 A373 60c Ireland   1.40 1.40
1277 A373 62c Italy   1.50 1.50
1278 A373 70c Luxembourg   1.75 1.75
1279 A373 80c Monaco   1.90 1.90
1280 A373 €1 Netherlands   2.40 2.40
1281 A373 €1.40 Portugal   3.50 3.50
1282 A373 €2 San Marino   4.75 4.75
1283 A373 €2.80 Spain   6.75 6.75
    Nos. 1269-1283 (15)   28.15 28.15

48th Intl. Eucharistic Congress A374

Designs: 45c, Hands breaking bread over chalice. 65c, Hand raising eucharist.

2004, Sept. 16   Litho.   Perf. 13x13¼
1284-1285 A374   Set of 2   2.75 2.75

Contemporary Religious Art in Vatican Museum Collection — A375

Designs: 45c, Still Life with Bottles, by Giorgio Morandi. 60c, The Fall of an Angel, by Marino Marini. 80c, Landscape with Houses, by Ezio Pastorio. 85c, Tuscan Countryside, by Giulio Cesare Vinzio.

2004, Sept. 16   Photo.   Perf. 14x13¼
1286 A375 45c multi   1.10 1.10
1287 A375 60c multi   1.50 1.50
a.   Perf. 13½x13¼   1.50 1.50
b.   Booklet pane of 4 #1287a + 4
      etiquettes   6.00   —
      Complete booklet, #1287b   6.00
1288 A375 80c multi   2.00 2.00
1289 A375 85c multi   2.10 2.10
    Nos. 1286-1289 (4)   6.70 6.70

Petrarch (1304-74), Poet A376

2004, Nov. 18   Photo.   Perf. 13¼x13
1290 A376 60c multi   1.60 1.60

Christmas A377

2004, Nov. 18   Litho.   Perf. 13¼
1291 A377 80c multi   2.25 2.25

Interregnum Issue

Arms of St. Peter and Papal Chamberlain's Insignia — A378

Inscription colors: 60c, Blue. 62c, Red. 80c, Green.

2005, Apr. 12   Litho.   Perf. 13½x13
1292-1294   A378   Set of 3   5.25 5.25

Pope Benedict XVI — A379

Pope Benedict XVI wearing: 45c, Stole. 62c, White vestments. 80c, Miter.

2005, June 2   Litho.   Perf. 13¼x13
1295-1297   A379   Set of 3   4.75 4.75
Coronation of Pope Benedict XVI, Apr. 19, 2005.

20th World Youth Day A380

2005, June 2
1298   A380   62c multi   1.50 1.50
See Germany No. 2343.

Europa A381

Ceramic plates depicting fish painted by Pablo Picasso with background colors of: 62c, Orange. 80c, Blue.

2005, June 2   Perf. 12½
1299-1300   A381   Set of 2   3.50 3.50

Ratification of Modifications to Italy-Vatican Concordat, 20th Anniv. — A382

Arms of Vatican City and Italy and: 45c, Pen. €2.80, Map.

2005, June 9   Photo.   Perf. 13¼
1301-1302   A382   Set of 2   8.00 8.00
See Italy Nos. 2677-2678.

Resurrection of Christ, by Perugino — A383

Various painting details: 60c, 62c, 80c, €1. €2.80, Jesus Christ.

2005, June 9   Perf. 14x13¼
1303-1306   A383   Set of 4   7.50 7.50

Souvenir Sheet
Perf. 13¼x13¾
1307   A383   €2.80 multi   6.75 6.75
No. 1307 contains one 29x60mm stamp.

Dinner at Emmaus, by Primo Conti A384

2005, Nov. 10   Litho.   Perf. 13x13¼
1308   A384   62c multi   1.50 1.50
Eleventh General Assembly of the Synod of Bishops.

2004 Journeys of Pope John Paul II — A385

Designs: 45c, Bern, Switzerland, June 5-6. 80c, Lourdes, France, Aug. 14-15. €2, Loreto, Italy, Sept. 5.

2005, Nov. 10
1309-1311   A385   Set of 3   7.75 7.75

The Annunciation, by Raphael — A386

Designs: Nos. 1312, 1314a, Drawing of Angel, Painting of Virgin Mary. Nos. 1313, 1314b, Painting of Angel, drawing of Virgin Mary.

Litho. & Engr.
2005, Nov. 10   Perf. 13x13¼
1312   A386   62c multi   1.50 1.50
1313   A386   €1 multi   2.40 2.40
Souvenir Sheet
1314   A386   €1.40 Sheet of 2, #a-b   6.75 6.75
See France No. 3153.

Swiss Papal Guards, 500th Anniv. A387

Designs: 62c, Guard and drummers. 80c, Guards and St. Peter's Basilica.

2005, Nov. 22   Litho.   Perf. 14x14¼
1315-1316   A387   Set of 2   3.50 3.50
Nos. 1315-1316 each issued in sheets of 6. See Switzerland Nos. 1224-1225.

Christmas A388

Details from Adoration of the Shepherds, by François Le Moyne: 45c, Shepherds and sheep. 62c, Angel. 80c, Madonna and Child.

2005, Nov. 22   Perf. 13¼x13
1317-1319   A388   Set of 3   4.50 4.50
1319a   Booklet pane of 4 #1319   7.50
               Complete booklet, #1319a   7.50

Europa A389

Designs: 62c, Praying hands, church, mosque and synagogue. 80c, Handshake, classroom.

2006, Mar. 16   Litho.   Perf. 13x13¼
1320-1321   A389   Set of 2   3.50 3.50

Jesuits A390

Designs: 45c, Blessed Peter Faber (1506-46). 60c, St. Ignatius of Loyola (1491-1556). €2, St. Francis Xavier (1506-52).

2006, Mar. 16
1322-1324   A390   Set of 3   7.50 7.50

Andrea Mantegna (c. 1430-1506), Painter A391

Designs: 60c, Madonna and Child. 85c, Saints Gregory and John the Baptist. €1, Saints Peter and Paul.
No. 1328 — San Zeno Polyptych: a, Country name at right. b, Country name at left.

2006, Mar. 16   Photo.   Perf. 12¾
1325-1327   A391   Set of 3   6.00 6.00
Souvenir Sheet
Perf. 13¼x13
1328   A391   €1.40 Sheet of 2, #a-b   6.75 6.75
No. 1328 contains two 21x37mm stamps.

Wolfgang Amadeus Mozart (1756-91), Composer A392

Litho. & Engr.
2006, June 22   Perf. 14x14¼
1329   A392   80c multi   2.10 2.10

2005 Travels of Pope Benedict XVI — A393

Designs: 62c, National Eucharistic Congress, Bari, Italy, May 21-29. €1.40, World Youth Day, Cologne, Germany, Aug. 16-21.

2006, June 22   Litho.   Perf. 13¼x13
1330-1331   A393   Set of 2   5.25 5.25

St. Peter's Basilica, 500th Anniv. — A394

No. 1332, 45c — 1506 medallion depicting: a, Allegory of architecture (denomination at LL). b, Architect Donato Bramante (denomination at UR).
No. 1333, 60c — 1506 medallion depicting: a, Pope Julius II (denomination at LL). b, Bramante's plan for St. Peter's Basilica (denomination at UR).

Litho. & Embossed
2006, June 22   Perf. 14
Horiz. Pairs, #a-b
1332-1333   A394   Set of 2   5.50 5.50

Intl. Year of Deserts and Desertification — A395

Designs: 62c, Flowers, child on parched earth. €1, Trees, child and cattle.

2006, Oct. 12   Litho.   Perf. 13½x13¼
1334-1335   A395   Set of 2   4.25 4.25

Diplomatic Relations Between Vatican City and Singapore, 25th Anniv. — A396

Designs: 85c, Merlion and St. Peter's Basilica. €2, Flags of Singapore and Vatican City.

2006, Oct. 12   Perf. 13½x13
1336-1337   A396   Set of 2   7.25 7.25
See Singapore Nos. 1232-1233.

Vatican Musum, 500th Anniv. A397

Heads from Laocoon sculpture: 60c, Son of Laocoon. 65c, Laocoon. €1.40, Son of Laocoon, diff.
€2.80, Laocoon, horiz.

Litho. & Embossed
2006, Oct. 12 **Perf. 13x13¼**
1338-1340 A397 Set of 3   6.75 6.75
Souvenir Sheet
Perf. 13 Horiz.
1341 A397 €2.80 multi   7.00 7.00
No. 1341 contains one 80x30mm stamp.

Christmas
A398

Stained glass from Pope's private chapel: 60c, Shepherds. 65c, Holy Family. 85c, Magi and Star of Bethlehem.

2006, Oct. 12 Litho. Perf. 13¼x13
1342-1344 A398 Set of 3   5.25 5.25
1343a   Booklet pane of 4 #1343   6.50 —
            Complete booklet, #1343a   6.50

St. Francis of Paola (1416-1507) — A399

Details from sculpture: 60c, Head of St. Francis. €1, Angel.

2007, Mar. 16 Litho. Perf. 13x13¼
1345-1346 A399 Set of 2   4.25 4.25

Pope Benedict XVI, 80th Birthday — A400

Pope Benedict XVI: 60c, Wearing zucchetto. 65c, Without head covering. 85c, Wearing miter.

2007, Mar. 16 **Perf. 13¼x13**
Stamp + Label
1347-1349 A400 Set of 3   5.75 5.75

Europa
A401

Designs: 60c, Scouts reading map, Scout holding chick. 65c, Scouts around campfire.

2007, June 12 **Perf. 13x13¼**
1350-1351 A401 Set of 2   3.50 3.50
Scouting, cent.

Christian Museum, 250th Anniv. A402

Designs: 85c, Gilded glass depicting Saints Peter and Paul, silver vase. €2, Bronze lamp with monogram of Christ, silver bottle.

2007, June 12
1352-1353 A402 Set of 2   7.75 7.75

Carlo Goldoni (1707-93), Playwright A403

Goldoni and: 60c, Bridge, man, harlequin. 85c, Church, man, woman. €2.80, Goldoni holding book.

2007, June 12 Perf. 13x13¼
1354-1355 A403 Set of 2   4.00 4.00
Souvenir Sheet
Perf. 13
1356 A403 €2.80 multi   7.75 7.75
No. 1356 contains one 45x33mm stamp and was sold with side portions of the sheet folded to produce an effect like a theater curtain.

New Philatelic and Numismatic Museum — A404

No. 1357: a, Vatican City #37, 576, 1013, 1296. b, Four Vatican City coins.

Litho. & Embossed
2007, Sept. 20 **Perf. 14**
1357 A404 60c Horiz. pair, #a-b 3.50 3.50

Treaty of Rome, 50th Anniv. A405

Stars and: 15c, Atomium, Brussels. 30c, Eiffel Tower, Paris. 60c, Brandenburg Gate, Berlin. 65c, Plaza, Rome. €1, Castle, Luxembourg. €4, Buildings and bridges, Amsterdam. €2.80, Mother and child.

2007, Sept. 20 Litho. Perf. 13x13¼
1358-1363 A405 Set of 6   19.00 19.00
Souvenir Sheet
Perf. 13x13¼ on 2 Sides
1364 A405 €2.80 multi   8.00 8.00
No. 1364 contains one 40x37mm stamp.

St. Elizabeth of Hungary (1207-31) A406

2007, Nov. 20 **Perf. 13¾**
1365 A406 65c multi   1.90 1.90

2006 Travels of Pope Benedict XVI — A407

Travels: 60c, Poland, May 25-28. 65c, Valencia, Spain, July 8-9. 85c, Germany, Sept. 9-14. €1.40, Turkey, Nov. 28-Dec. 1.

2007, Nov. 20 **Perf. 13¼x13**
1366-1369 A407 Set of 4   10.50 10.50
Booklet Stamp
Self-Adhesive
1370 A407 85c Like #1368   2.50 2.50
a.   Booklet pane of 4   10.00

Christmas
A408

Vatican arms and nave paintings in St. Andrew's Church, Luqa, Malta, by Giuseppe Calì: 60c, Madonna and Child. 65c, Holy Family with Women and Young Girl. 85c, Infant Jesus and Young Girl.

2007, Nov. 20
1371-1373 A408 Set of 3   6.25 6.25
See Malta Nos. 1319-1321.

Europa
A409

Designs: 60c, Envelope with cachet and cancels. 85c, Handwritten letter, Pope Benedict XVI.

2008, Mar. 6 Litho. Perf. 13¾
1374-1375 A409 Set of 2   4.50 4.50

Sistine Chapel Paintings by Michelangelo, 500th Anniv. — A410

Designs: 5c, Libyan. 10c, Eritrean. 25c, Delphic Sibyl. 60c, Sibyl Cumana. 65c, Daniel. 85c, Jonah. €2, Ezekiel. €5, Zaccharias.

2008, Mar. 6 **Perf. 13x13¼**
1376 A410 5c multi   .25   .25
1377 A410 10c multi   .30   .30
1378 A410 25c multi   .75   .75
1379 A410 60c multi   1.90 1.90
1380 A410 65c multi   2.00 2.00
1381 A410 85c multi   2.60 2.60
1382 A410 €2 multi   6.25 6.25
1383 A410 €5 multi   15.50 15.50
       Nos. 1376-1383 (8)   29.55 29.55

23rd World Youth Day A411

2008, May 15 Litho. Perf. 13¾
1384 A411 €1 multi   3.25 3.25

Visit of Pope Benedict XVI to United Nations — A412

2008, May 15
1385 A412 €1.40 multi   4.50 4.50

49th Eucharistic Congress, Quebec — A413

Designs: 60c, Wedding at Cana, Washing of the Feet, Last Supper. 85c, Crucifixion, Resurrection, Disciples of Emmaus.

2008, May 15 **Perf. 13¾x13¼**
1386-1387 A413 Set of 2   4.75 4.75

Apparition of the Virgin Mary at Lourdes, 150th Anniv. — A414

Designs: 65c, Pilgrims at Lourdes. 85c, Virgin Mary, Lourdes.

2008, May 15 Litho. Perf. 13x13¼
1388-1389 A414 Set of 2   7.50 7.50
Nos. 1388-1389 each were printed in sheets of 4.

2007 Travels of Pope Benedict XVI — A415

Travels: 66c, Brazil, May 9-14. 85c, Austria, Sept. 7-9.

Litho. & Engr.
2008, Sept. 17 **Perf. 12¾**
1390-1391 A415 Set of 2   4.25 4.25

Pauline Year — A416

Designs: 60c, Conversion of St. Paul. 65c, St. Paul preaching. 85c, St. Paul imprisoned.

2008, Sept. 17 Litho. Perf. 13¼x13
1392-1394 A416 Set of 3   6.00 6.00

Postal Convention Between Vatican City and Sovereign Military Order of Malta
A417

2008, Nov. 13   **Litho.**   *Perf. 13¾*
1395 A417   €2.50 multi + label   6.50 6.50

Andrea Palladio (1508-80), Architect — A418

Designs: 65c, San Giorgio Maggiore Church, Venice. 85c, Villa Rotonda, Vicenza, Italy.
€2.80, Palladio.

2008, Nov. 13   *Perf. 13¼x14*
1396-1397 A418   Set of 2   4.00 4.00
Souvenir Sheet
1398 A418   €2.80 multi   7.25 7.25

Christmas A419

Designs: 60c, Adoration of the Magi, by Raphael. 65c, Nativity, by Albrecht Dürer.

2008, Nov. 13   **Litho.**   *Perf. 13x13¼*
1399-1400 A419   Set of 2   3.25 3.25
Booklet Stamp
Self-Adhesive
Serpentine Die Cut 12½
1401   A419 60c multi   1.60 1.60
  a.   Booklet pane of 4   6.50

See Germany Nos. B1008-B1009.

Gibraltar Shrine to Our Lady of Europe, 700th Anniv. — A420

2009, Feb. 10   **Litho.**   *Perf. 14x14¾*
1402 A420 85c multi   2.25 2.25

Printed in sheets of 4. See Gibraltar No. 1182.

A421

Vatican City State, 80th Anniv. — A422

Popes: No. 1403, 65c, Pius XI. No. 1404, 65c, Pius XII. No. 1405, 65c, John XXIII. No. 1406, 65c, Paul VI. No. 1407, 65c, John Paul I. No. 1408, 65c, John Paul II. No. 1409, Benedict XVI.
€2.80, Vatican City map.

2009, Feb. 10   *Perf. 13½x14*
1403-1409 A421   Set of 7   11.50 11.50
Souvenir Sheet
1410 A422   €2.80 gray & blk   7.25 7.25

Europa A423

Paintings from Astronomical Observations series by Donato Creti: 60c, The Sun. 65c, Saturn.

2009, May 20   **Litho.**   *Perf. 14¼*
1411-1412 A423   Set of 2   3.50 3.50

Intl. Year of Astronomy.

St. Frances of Rome (1384-1440) — A424

Designs: 85c, St. Frances healing a poor man with an injured arm. €1, Miracle of the grapes.

2009, May 20   *Perf. 13¼*
1413-1414 A424   Set of 2   5.25 5.25

World Book and Copyright Day — A425

Pontifical Biblical Institute, Cent. — A426

75th Intl. Federationo of Library Associations and Institutions General Conference, Milan — A427

2009, May 20   *Perf. 14x14¾*
1415 A425   60c multi   1.75 1.75
1416 A426   85c multi   2.40 2.40
1417 A427   €1.40 multi   4.00 4.00
  Nos. 1415-1417 (3)   8.15 8.15

Guglielmo Cardinal Massaja (1809-89), Missionary in Africa — A428

2009, Sept. 23   **Litho.**   *Perf. 13¾*
1418 A428 60c brown   1.75 1.75

2008 Travels of Pope Benedict XVI
A429

Travels: 65c, France, Sept. 12-15. 85c, United States, Apr. 15-21. €1, Australia, July 12-21.

2009, Sept. 23
1419-1421 A429   Set of 3   7.50 7.50

A430

A431

The Disputation of the Holy Sacrament, by Raphael, 500th Anniv. — A432

Designs: Nos. 1422-1424, Various painting details. €3.30, Entire painting.

2009, Sept. 23   *Perf. 14*
1422 A430   65c multi   1.90 1.90
1423 A431   65c multi   1.90 1.90
1424 A432   65c multi   1.90 1.90
  Nos. 1422-1424 (3)   5.70 5.70

Souvenir Sheet
Perf. 13¾
1425 A432   €3.30 multi   9.75 9.75
No. 1425 contains one 35x50mm stamp.

Italian Language Day — A433

2009, Oct. 21   **Photo.**   *Perf. 13¼x13*
1426 A433 60c multi + label   1.90 1.90

Printed in sheets of 5 + 5 labels. See Italy No. 2966; San Marino No. 1801.

Composers — A434

Designs: 65c, George Frideric Handel (1685-1759). 85c, Joseph Haydn (1732-1809). €5, Felix Mendelssohn Bartholdy (1809-47).

2009, Oct. 24   **Litho.**   *Perf. 14¾x14*
1427-1429 A434   Set of 3   19.50 19.50

Convocation of Second Vatican Council, 50th Anniv. — A435

Litho. & Embossed
2009, Nov. 4   *Perf. 14*
1430 A435 60c multi   1.90 1.90

Louis Braille (1809-52), Educator of the Blind A436

2009, Nov. 4   *Perf. 14¾x14*
1431 A436 65c multi   2.00 2.00

Christmas A437

Madonna and Child Enthroned with Two Angels and Saints Joachim and Anne, by Francesco Melanzio: 60c, Detail. 65c, Entire painting.

2009, Nov. 4   **Litho.**   *Perf. 12½*
1432 A437 60c multi   1.90 1.90
1433 A437 65c multi   2.00 2.00
  a.   Booklet pane of 4   8.00 8.00
   Complete booklet, #1433a   8.00

Easter — A438

Litho. & Engr.

2010, Mar. 5   **Perf. 13x12¾**
1434 A438 65c multi   1.75 1.75

Sandro Botticelli (1445-1510), Painter — A439

Details of Sistine Chapel paintings: 60c, Women from *The Temptation of Christ.* 85c, Woman holding walking stick from *The Life of Moses.* €1.45, Woman carrying basket on head from *The Life of Moses.*

2010, Mar. 5   **Litho.**   **Perf. 13¾x13½**
1435-1437 A439   Set of 3   7.75 7.75

The Deposition, by Caravaggio (1573-1610) A440

2010, June 22   **Litho.**   **Perf. 13¼x14**
1438 A440 65c multi   1.75 1.75

Europa A441

Illustrations from *The Bible Narrated for Children:* 60c, Adam and Eve in the Garden of Eden. 65c, Jesus and children.

2010, June 22   **Perf. 13**
1439-1440 A441   Set of 2   3.25 3.25

Sacerdotal Year — A442

Designs: €1.40, St. John Vianney (1786-1859) and priests. €1.50, The Good Shepherd, sheep and wolf.

2010, June 22   **Perf. 13¾x13½**
1441-1442 A442   Set of 2   7.25 7.25

Father Matteo Ricci (1552-1610), Missionary to China — A443

Designs: 5c, Ricci and Xu Guangqi, Chinese court official. €3.30, Ricci.

2010, June 22   **Perf. 14¾x14**
1443-1444 A443   Set of 2   8.50 8.50

Pope Leo XIII (1810-1903) A444

2010, Sept. 20   **Litho.**   **Perf. 14¾x14**
1445 A444 65c multi   1.90 1.90

Composers A445

Designs: 65c, Frédéric Chopin (1810-49). €1, Robert Schumann (1810-56). €4.40, Chopin and Schumann, horiz. (65x16mm).

2010, Sept. 20   **Perf. 13x12¾**
1446 A445   65c multi   1.90 1.90
1447 A445   €1 multi   2.75 2.75
    Perf. 12¾ at Top
1448 A445   €4.40 multi + label 12.50 12.50
    Nos. 1446-1448 (3)   17.15 17.15

Reopening of the Vatican Library A446

Designs: 65c, Crucified Christ. 85c, Sts. Cosmas and Damian. €3.90, Medallion depicting Pope Sixtus V, vert.

2010, Sept. 20   **Perf. 14x13½**
1449 A446   65c multi   1.90 1.90
1450 A446   85c multi   2.40 2.40
    Imperf
1451 A446   €3.90 multi   11.00 11.00
    Nos. 1449-1451 (3)   15.30 15.30

No. 1451 is printed as a miniature book made up of two pieces of paper of different sizes. Both pieces of paper are printed on both sides, and are glued together. The cover of the book is the longer of the two pieces of paper, and is folded into three parts. The stamp, the front cover of the book, is the middle part of this piece of paper. The gum, applied to the left of the stamp, becomes the book's back cover when the longer piece of paper is folded. The title page of *De Nuptiis Philologiae et Mercurii* is to the right of the stamp, and is the book's first page. Text and illustrations are on the reverse of this picture and the stamp, and another picture depicting text and the seal of the Vatican Library is printed on the back of the gum. The second piece of paper, folded in half to constitute four pages of the book, has text and illustrations, and is glued to the back of longer sheet where the fold between the stamp and the photo is found. Values are for the complete item.

Approval of the Franciscan Rule, 800th Anniv. — A447

2010, Nov. 15   **Litho.**   **Perf. 12¾**
1452 A447 65c multi   1.90 1.90

Writers — A448

Scenes from works by: 60c, Anton Chekhov (1860-1904). 65c, Leo Tolstoy (1828-1910).

2010, Nov. 15   **Perf. 14¼x14¾**
1453-1454 A448   Set of 2   3.50 3.50

2009 Travels of Pope Benedict XVI A449

Travels: 10c, Cameroun and Angola, Mar. 17-23. 65c, Holy Land, May 8-15. 85c, Czech Republic, Sept. 26-28.

2010, Nov. 15   **Perf. 13x13¼**
1455-1457 A449   Set of 3   4.50 4.50
    See Israel No. 1837.

Christmas A450

Paintings: 60c, The Birth of Jesus, by Gheorghe Tattarascu. 65c, The Nativity and Adoration of the Shepherds, by the School of Murillo.

2010, Nov. 15   **Perf. 13¼**
1458 A450 60c multi   1.75 1.75
1459 A450 65c multi   1.90 1.90

Booklet Stamps
Self-Adhesive
Serpentine Die Cut 12½

1460 A450 60c multi   1.75 1.75
  a.   Booklet pane of 4   7.00
1461 A450 65c multi   1.90 1.90
  a.   Booklet pane of 4   7.75

    See Romania Nos. 5218-5219.

Easter A451

2011, Mar. 21   **Perf. 12¾**
1462 A451 75c multi   2.25 2.25

Father Eusebio Kino (1645-1711), Missionary in Mexico — A452

2011, Mar. 21   **Perf. 14¼x14¾**
1463 A452 €1.60 maroon & black   4.75 4.75

A453

Unification of Italy, 150th Anniv. — A454

Designs: No. 1464, 60c, Milan Cathedral and Lombardy-Venetia #6. No. 1465, 60c, Modena Cathedral and Modena #3. No. 1466, 60c, Uffizi Gallery, Palazzo Vecchio, Florence and Tuscany #4. No. 1467, 60c, San Carlo Square, Turin and Sardinia #1. No. 1468, 60c, Mt. Vesuvius and Naples, Two Sicilies #3, 13. No. 1469, 60c, Baptistry, Parma and Parma #4.
€1.50, Piazza del Popolo, Rome.

2011, Mar. 21   **Perf. 12½**
1464-1469 A453   Set of 6   10.50 10.50
    Souvenir Sheet
1470 A454 €1.50 multi   4.50 4.50
    See Italy No. 3046.

Beatification of Pope John Paul II — A455

2011, Apr. 12   **Perf. 13**
1471 A455 75c multi   2.25 2.25
    Printed in sheets of 6. See Poland No. 4009.

World Youth Day, Madrid — A456

2011, June 21   **Perf. 14x13½**
1472 A456   75c multi   2.10 2.10
    See Spain No. 3797.

Europa — A457

Detail from The Journey of Moses into Egypt, by Perugino: a, 60c, "Europa" at UL. b, 75c, "Europa" at UR.

2011, June 21   **Perf. 13¾**
1473 A457 Horiz. pair, #a-b   4.00 4.00
Intl. Year of Forests.

Ordination of Pope Benedict XVI, 60th Anniv. — A458

Designs: No. 1474, 75c, Shell, photograph from ordination as priest, June 29, 1951. No. 1475, 75c, Bear, photograph from installation as bishop, May 28, 1977. No. 1476, 75c, St. Corbinian, photograph from installation as cardinal, June 27, 1977. No. 1477, 75c, Papal arms, photograph from installation as pope, Apr. 19, 2005.

2011, June 21   **Perf. 13½x13¾**
1474-1477 A458 Set of 4   8.50 8.50

Miniature Sheet

L'Osservatore Romano (Official Vatican Newspaper), 150th Anniv. — A459

No. 1478 — Front pages of newspaper announcing election of Pope: a, Leo XIII. b, Pius X. c, Benedict XV. d, Pius XI. e, Pius XII. f, John XXIII. g, Paul VI. h, John Paul I. i, John Paul II. j, Benedict XVI.

2011, June 21   **Perf. 14x14¾**
1478 A459 60c Sheet fo 10, #a-j   17.00 17.00

Mater et Magistra, Encyclical by Pope John XXIII, 50th Anniv. A460

2011, Sept. 2   **Perf. 13¾**
1479 A460 60c multi   1.75 1.75

Room of Heliodorus Frescoes by Raphael, 500th Anniv. — A461

Details from The Expulsion of Heliodorus from the Temple. 75c, Left side of fresco. €1.60, Right side of fresco.

2011, Sept. 2   **Perf. 14¼**
1480-1481 A461 Set of 2   6.50 6.50

Rudjer Boskovic (1711-87), Astronomer, and Dome of St. Peter's Basilica — A462

2011, Sept. 13
1482 A462 €3.30 multi   9.00 9.00
See Croatia No. 810.

Composers A463

Designs: 75c, Franz Liszt (1811-86). €1.60, Gustav Mahler (1860-1911).

2011, Nov. 18 Litho. Perf. 14x14¾
1483-1484 A463 Set of 2   6.50 6.50

2010 Travels of Pope Benedict XVI A464

Travels: 60c, Malta, Apr. 17-18. 75c, Portugal, May 11-14. €1.40, Cyprus, June 4-6. €1.60, United Kingdom, Sept. 16-19. €2, Spain, Nov. 6-7.

2011, Nov. 18   **Perf. 13¼**
1485-1489 A464 Set of 5   17.00 17.00

Christmas A465

Designs: 60c, Madonna and Child, Saints Benedict and Francis. 75c, Infant Jesus and animals.

2011, Nov. 18   **Perf. 13¼**
1490 A465 60c multi   1.75 1.75
1491 A465 75c multi   2.00 2.00

Booklet Stamp
Self-Adhesive
Serpentine Die Cut 12½x12¼
1492 A465 75c multi   2.00 2.00
a.   Booklet pane of 4   8.00

Easter — A466

2012, Mar. 1   **Perf. 14¼x14¾**
1493 A466 75c multi   2.00 2.00

Father Christopher Clavius (1538-1612), Mathematician and Astronomer A467

2012, Mar. 1   **Perf. 14¼**
1494 A467 €1.60 black & red   4.25 4.25

Madonna of Foligno, by Raphael A468

Sistine Madonna, by Raphael A469

2012, Mar. 1   **Perf. 13¼**
1495 A468 60c multi   1.60 1.60
1496 A469 75c multi   2.00 2.00

Souvenir Sheets
1497 A468 €1.40 multi   3.75 3.75
1498 A469 €2.40 multi   6.50 6.50
See Germany No. 2666.

St. Joan of Arc (c. 1412-31) — A470

Litho. & Engr.
2012, May 11   **Perf. 13**
1499 A470 75c multi   2.00 2.00
See France No.

Seventh World Meeting of Families, Milan — A471

2012, May 11 Litho. Perf. 13¼x14
1500 A471 €1.50 multi   4.00 4.00

Europa — A472

Designs: No. 1501, 75c, Dome of St. Peter's Basilica. No. 1502, 75c, Dove in stained-glass window, St. Peter's Basilica.

2012, May 11
1501-1502 A472 Set of 2   4.00 4.00

50th Intl. Eucharistic Congress, Dublin A473

Designs: 75c, Celtic cross from the Rock of Cashel, Tipperary, Ireland. €1, Ardagh Chalice.

2012, May 11   **Perf. 14¾x14**
1503-1504 A473 Set of 2   4.75 4.75

SEMI-POSTAL STAMPS

Holy Year Issue

Cross and Orb
SP1   SP2

1933 Unwmk. Engr. Perf. 13x13½

B1	SP1	25c + 10c green	4.00	4.00
B2	SP1	75c + 15c scarlet	6.50	12.50
B3	SP2	80c + 20c red brown	24.00	18.00
B4	SP2	1.25 l + 25c ultra	7.50	13.50
	Nos. B1-B4 (4)		42.00	48.00
	Set, never hinged		160.00	

Catalogue values for unused stamps in this section, from this point to the end of the section, are for Never Hinged items.

Shrine of Our Lady of Mentorella, Italy, 1500th Anniv. — SP3

2010, Mar. 5 Litho. Perf. 14¼x14¾

B5	SP3	65c +20c multi	2.25	2.25

Printed in sheets of 6. Surtax for Haitian earthquake relief.

AIR POST STAMPS

Catalogue values for unused stamps in this section are for Never Hinged items.

Statue of St. Peter AP1

Dove of Peace over Vatican AP2

Elijah's Ascent into Heaven AP3

Our Lady of Loreto and Angels Moving the Holy House AP4

Wmk. 235

1938, June 22 Engr. Perf. 14

C1	AP1	25c brown	.30	.25
C2	AP2	50c green	.30	.25
C3	AP3	75c lake	.30	.30
C4	AP4	80c dark blue	.30	.45
C5	AP1	1 l violet	.75	.50
C6	AP2	2 l ultra	1.50	.80
C7	AP3	5 l slate blk	3.25	1.90
C8	AP4	10 l dk brown vio	3.25	1.90
	Nos. C1-C8 (8)		9.95	6.35

Dove of Peace Above St. Peter's Basilica — AP5

House of Our Lady of Loreto — AP6

Birds Circling Cross — AP7

1947, Nov. 10 Photo.

C9	AP5	1 l rose red	.25	.25
C10	AP6	4 l dark brown	.25	.25
C11	AP5	5 l brt ultra	.25	.25
C12	AP7	15 l brt purple	2.25	2.10
C13	AP6	25 l dk blue green	5.00	2.75
C14	AP7	50 l dk gray	7.00	5.25
C15	AP7	100 l red orange	30.00	9.00
	Nos. C9-C15 (7)		45.00	19.85

Nos. C13-C15 exist imperf. Value, each pair $1,000.

Archangel Raphael and Young Tobias AP8

1948, Dec. 28 Engr. Perf. 14

C16	AP8	250 l sepia	55.00	10.00
C17	AP8	500 l ultra	585.00	375.00
	Set, hinged		440.00	

Angels and Globe AP9

1949, Dec. 3

C18	AP9	300 l ultra	30.00	12.50
C19	AP9	1000 l green	150.00	82.50
	Set, hinged		95.00	

UPU, 75th anniversary.

Franciscus Gratianus AP10

Dome of St. Peter's Basilica AP11

1951, Dec. 20 Perf. 14x13

C20	AP10	300 l deep plum	350.00	220.00
C21	AP10	500 l deep blue	45.00	20.00
	Set, hinged		240.00	

Publication of unified canon laws, 800th anniv.

1953, Aug. 10 Perf. 13

C22	AP11	500 l chocolate	35.00	9.00
C23	AP11	1000 l deep ultra	105.00	20.00
	Set, hinged		47.50	

See Nos. C33-C34.

Archangel Gabriel by Melozzo da Forli — AP12

Obelisk of St. John Lateran — AP13

Archangel Gabriel: 10 l, 35 l, 100 l, Annunciation by Pietro Cavallini. 15 l, 50 l, 300 l, Annunciation by Leonardo da Vinci.

1956, Feb. 12 Wmk. 235

C24	AP12	5 l gray black	.25	.25
C25	AP12	10 l blue green	.25	.25
C26	AP12	15 l deep orange	.25	.25
C27	AP12	25 l dk car rose	.25	.25
C28	AP12	35 l carmine	.25	.25
C29	AP12	50 l olive brown	.25	.25
C30	AP12	60 l ultra	2.75	2.25
C31	AP12	100 l orange brown	.25	.25
C32	AP12	300 l deep violet	.50	.25
	Nos. C24-C32 (9)		5.00	4.25

Type of 1953

1958 Perf. 13½

C33	AP11	500 l grn & bl	7.50	4.00
	a. Perf. 14	grn	1,200.	700.00
C34	AP11	1000 l dp mag	.75	.75
	a. Perf. 14		.75	.75

1959, Oct. 27 Engr. Perf. 13½x14

Obelisks, Rome: 10 l, 60 l, St. Mary Major. 15 l, 100 l, St. Peter. 25 l, 200 l, Piazza del Popolo. 35 l, 500 l, Trinita dei Monti.

C35	AP13	5 l dull violet	.25	.25
C36	AP13	10 l blue green	.25	.25
C37	AP13	15 l dk brown	.25	.25
C38	AP13	25 l slate grn	.25	.25
C39	AP13	35 l ultra	.25	.25
C40	AP13	50 l yellow grn	.25	.25
C41	AP13	60 l rose carmine	.25	.25
C42	AP13	100 l bluish black	.25	.25
C43	AP13	200 l brown	.25	.25
C44	AP13	500 l orange brn	.30	.25
	Nos. C35-C44 (10)		2.55	2.50

Archangel Gabriel by Filippo Valle — AP14

1962, Mar. 13 Wmk. 235

C45	AP14	1000 l brown	1.25	.75
C46	AP14	1500 l dark blue	1.75	1.25

Jet over St. Peter's Cathedral AP15

Designs: 40 l, 200 l, Radio tower and statue of Archangel Gabriel (like A87). 90 l, 500 l, Aerial view of St. Peter's Square and Vatican City.

1967, Mar. 7 Photo. Perf. 14

C47	AP15	20 l brt violet	.25	.25
C48	AP15	40 l black & pink	.25	.25
C49	AP15	90 l sl bl & dk gray	.25	.25
C50	AP15	100 l black & salmon	.25	.25
C51	AP15	200 l vio blk & gray	.25	.25
C52	AP15	500 l dk brn & lt brn	.25	.25
	Nos. C47-C52 (6)		1.50	1.50

Archangel Gabriel by Fra Angelico — AP16

1968, Mar. 12 Engr. Perf. 13½x14

C53	AP16	1000 l dk car rose, *cr*	1.00	.75
C54	AP16	1500 l black, *cr*	1.75	1.50

St. Matthew, by Fra Angelico AP17

The Evangelists, by Fra Angelico from Niccolina Chapel: 300 l, St. Mark. 500 l, St. Luke. 1000 l, St. John.

Engr. & Photo. Perf. 14x13½

1971, Sept. 30 Unwmk.

C55	AP17	200 l blk & pale grn	.25	.25
C56	AP17	300 l black & bister	.25	.25
C57	AP17	500 l black & salmon	.85	.60
C58	AP17	1000 l black & pale lil	1.00	.75
	Nos. C55-C58 (4)		2.35	1.85

AP18

Seraph, mosaic from St. Mark's Basilica, Venice.

Litho. & Engr.

1974, Feb. 21 Perf. 13x14

C59	AP18	2500 l multicolored	2.50	2.00

AP19

Last Judgment, by Michelangelo: 500 l, Angel with Trumpet. 1000 l, Ascending figures. 2500 l, Angels with trumpets.

Litho. & Engr.

1976, Feb. 19 Perf. 13x14

C60	AP19	500 l sal, bl & brn	1.25	1.10
C61	AP19	1000 l sal, bl & brn	1.50	1.10
C62	AP19	2500 l sal, bl & brn	2.00	1.50
	Nos. C60-C62 (3)		4.75	3.70

Radio Waves, Antenna, Papal Arms AP20

1978, July 11 Engr. Perf. 14x13

C63	AP20	1000 l multicolored	1.00	.70
C64	AP20	2000 l multicolored	2.00	1.40
C65	AP20	3000 l multicolored	3.00	1.90
	Nos. C63-C65 (3)		6.00	4.00

10th World Telecommunications Day.

Pope John Paul II Shaking Hands, Arms of Dominican Republic AP21

Litho. & Engr.

1980, June 24 Perf. 14x13½

C66	AP21	200 l shown	.25	.25
C67	AP21	300 l Mexico	.30	.30
C68	AP21	500 l Poland	.60	.60
C69	AP21	1000 l Ireland	1.10	1.10
C70	AP21	1500 l US	1.75	1.75
C71	AP21	2000 l UN	2.00	2.00

C72 AP21 3000 l with Dimitrios
I, Turkey 3.50 3.50
Nos. C66-C72 (7) 9.50 9.50

Issued: 3000 l, Sept. 18; others June 24.

World Communications Year — AP22

Designs: 2000 l, Moses Explaining The Law to the People by Luca Signorelli. 5000 l, Paul Preaching in Athens, Tapestry of Raphael design.

1983, Nov. 10 *Perf. 14*
C73 AP22 2000 l multicolored 3.00 3.00
C74 AP22 5000 l multicolored 6.75 6.75

Journeys of Pope John Paul II, 1983-84 AP23

Designs: 350 l, Central America, the Caribbean, 1983. 450 l, Warsaw Cathedral, Our Lady of Czestochowa, Poland, 1983. 700 l, Statue of Our Lady, Lourdes, France, 1983. 1000 l, Mariazell Sanctuary, St. Stephen's Cathedral, Austria, 1983. 1500 l, Asia, the Pacific, 1984. 2000 l, Einsiedeln Basilica, St. Nicholas of Flue, Switzerland, 1984. 2500 l, Quebec's Notre Dame Cathedral, five crosses of the Jesuit martyrs, Canada, 1984. 5000 l, Saragossa, Spain, Dominican Republic and Puerto Rico, 1984.

1986, Nov. 20 *Photo.* *Perf. 14x13½*
C75 AP23 350 l multicolored .50 .50
C76 AP23 450 l multicolored .65 .65
C77 AP23 700 l multicolored 1.00 1.00
C78 AP23 1000 l multicolored 1.50 1.50
C79 AP23 1500 l multicolored 2.25 2.25
C80 AP23 2000 l multicolored 3.25 3.25
C81 AP23 2500 l multicolored 4.00 4.00
C82 AP23 5000 l multicolored 8.00 8.00
Nos. C75-C82 (8) 21.15 21.15

Papal Journeys Type of 1986
Designs: 450 l, Horseman, shepherdess, St. Peter's Basilica, Cathedral of Santiago in Chile, and the Sanctuary of Our Lady of Lujan, Argentina. 650 l, Youths and the Cathedral of Speyer, Federal Republic of Germany. 1000 l, St. Peter's Basilica, Altar of Gdansk, flowers and thorns. 2500 l, Crowd and American skyscrapers. 5000 l, Tepee at Fort Simpson, Canada, and American Indians.

1988, Oct. 27 *Photo.* *Perf. 14x13½*
C83 AP23 450 l multicolored .65 .65
C84 AP23 650 l multicolored .95 .95
C85 AP23 1000 l multicolored 1.50 1.50
C86 AP23 2500 l multicolored 3.50 3.50
C87 AP23 5000 l multicolored 7.25 7.25
Nos. C83-C87 (5) 13.85 13.85

Uruguay, Chile and Argentina, Mar. 30-Apr. 14, 1987 (450 l); Federal Republic of Germany, Apr. 30-May 4, 1987 (650 l); Poland, June 8-14, 1987 (1000 l); US, Sept. 10-19, 1987 (2500 l); and Canada, Sept. 20, 1987 (5000 l).

Journeys of Pope John Paul II, 1989 AP24

1990, Nov. 27 *Photo.* *Perf. 12*
Granite Paper
C88 AP24 500 l Africa .80 .80
C89 AP24 1000 l Scandinavia 1.60 1.60
C90 AP24 3000 l Santiago de Compostela, Spain 5.00 5.00
C91 AP24 5000 l Asia 8.00 8.00
Nos. C88-C91 (4) 15.40 15.40

Madagascar, Reunion, Zambia and Malawi, Apr. 28-May 6 (500 l); Norway, Iceland, Finland, Denmark and Sweden, June 1-10 (1000 l); Korea, Indonesia and Mauritius, Oct. 6-16 (5000 l).

Travels of Pope John Paul II, 1991 AP25

1992, Nov. 24 *Photo.* *Perf. 14*
C92 AP25 500 l multicolored .65 .65
C93 AP25 1000 l multicolored 1.40 1.40
C94 AP25 4000 l multicolored 5.25 5.25
C95 AP25 6000 l multicolored 8.00 8.00
Nos. C92-C95 (4) 15.30 15.30

Portugal, May 10-13 (500 l); Poland, June 1-9 (1000 l); Poland, Hungary, Aug. 13-20 (4000 l); Brazil, Oct. 12-21 (6000 l).

SPECIAL DELIVERY STAMPS

Pius XI SD1

Unwmk.
1929, Aug. 1 *Photo.* *Perf. 14*
E1 SD1 2 l carmine rose 18.00 11.50
E2 SD1 2.50 l dark blue 15.00 14.50

For overprints see Nos. Q14-Q15.

Catalogue values for unused stamps in this section, from this point to the end of the section, are for Never Hinged items.

Aerial View of Vatican City SD2

1933, May 31 **Wmk. 235** **Engr.**
E3 SD2 2 l rose red & brn .35 .35
E4 SD2 2.50 l dp blue & brn .35 .55

1945, Mar. 2 **Unwmk.**
E5 SD2 3.50 l dk car & ultra .30 .30
E6 SD2 5 l ultra & green .30 .30

Nos. E5 and E6 Surcharged with New Values and Bars in Black
1945, Dec. 29
E7 SD2 6 l on 3.50 l dk car & ultra 4.25 1.75
E8 SD2 12 l on 5 l ultra & grn 4.25 1.75

Vertical pairs imperf. between exist of No. E7 (value $150) and No. E8 (value $200).

Bishop Matteo Giberti SD3

Design: 12 l, Gaspar Cardinal Contarini.

1946, Feb. 21 **Photo.**
Centers in Dark Brown
E9 SD3 6 l dark green .25 .25
E10 SD3 12 l copper brown .25 .25

See note after No. 121.
#E9-E10 exist imperf and part perf.

St. Peter's Basilica SD5

Design: 80 l, Basilica of St. John.

1949, Mar. 7 **Wmk. 235** **Perf. 14**
E11 SD5 40 l slate gray 10.50 3.25
a. Perf. 13½x14 21.00 7.50
E12 SD5 80 l chestnut brown 37.50 20.00
a. Perf. 13½x14 40.00 22.50

St. Peter and His Tomb — SD6

85 l, Pius XII and Roman sepulcher.

Perf. 13½x13, 14
1953, Apr. 23 **Engr.**
E13 SD6 50 l blue grn & dk brn .25 .25
E14 SD6 85 l dp orange & dk brn .35 .25

Arms of Pope John XXIII SD7

1960 **Photo.** **Perf. 14**
E15 SD7 75 l red & brown .25 .25
E16 SD7 100 l dk blue & brown .25 .25

Pope Paul VI by Enrico Manfrini — SD8

Design: 150 l, Papal arms.

1966, Mar. 8 **Wmk. 235** **Perf. 14**
E17 SD8 150 l black brown .25 .25
E18 SD8 180 l brown .25 .25

POSTAGE DUE STAMPS

Nos. 1-3 Overprinted in Black and Brown

1931, Oct. 1 **Unwmk.** **Perf. 14**
J1 A1 5c dk brown & pink .35 .60
a. Double frame
J2 A1 10c dk grn & lt grn .35 .60
a. Frame omitted 4,000.

J3 A1 20c violet & lilac 1.50 2.00

No. 5 Surcharged

J4 A1 40c on 30c indigo & yel 2.00 4.75

Nos. 10-11 Surcharged

J5 A2 60c on 2 l olive brn 32.50 24.00
J6 A2 1.10 l on 2.50 l red org 6.50 18.00
Nos. J1-J6 (6) 43.20 49.95
Set, never hinged 235.00

In addition to the surcharges, #J4-J6 are overprinted with ornamental frame as on #J1-J3.

No. J5 is valued in the grade of fine.

Catalogue values for unused stamps in this section, from this point to the end of the section, are for Never Hinged items.

Papal Arms
D1   D2

Unwmk.
1945, Aug. 16 **Typo.** *Perf. 14*
J7 D1 5c black & yellow .25 .25
J8 D1 20c black & lilac .25 .25
J9 D1 80c black & salmon .25 .25
J10 D1 1 l black & green .25 .25
J11 D1 2 l black & blue .25 .25
J12 D1 5 l black & gray .25 .25
a. Imperf., pair 125.00 125.00
Nos. J7-J12 (6) 1.50 1.50

A second type of Nos. J7-J12 exists, in which the colored lines of the background are thicker.

The 20c and 5 lire exist in horizontal pairs imperf. vertically. Value, each $100.

The 20c exists in horizontal pairs imperf. between. Value $275.

Perf. 13½x13
1954, Apr. 30 **Wmk. 235** **Engr.**
J13 D2 4 l black & rose .25 .25
J14 D2 6 l black & green .30 .30
J15 D2 10 l black & yellow .25 .25
J16 D2 20 l black & blue .45 .30
J17 D2 50 l black & ol brn .25 .25
J18 D2 70 l black & red brn .25 .25
Nos. J13-J18 (6) 1.75 1.60

Papal Arms — D3

Photo. & Engr.
1968, May 28 **Wmk. 235** *Perf. 14*
J19 D3 10 l black, *grysh bl* .25 .25
J20 D3 20 l black, *pale bl* .25 .25
J21 D3 50 l black, *pale lil rose* .25 .25
J22 D3 60 l black, *gray* .25 .25
J23 D3 100 l black, *dull yel* .25 .25
J24 D3 180 l black, *bluish lil* .25 .25
Nos. J19-J24 (6) 1.50 1.50

PARCEL POST STAMPS

Nos. 1-7 Overprinted

1931		Unwmk.		Perf. 14	
Q1	A1	5c dk brown & pink		.25	.45
Q2	A1	10c dk grn & lt grn		.25	.45
Q3	A1	20c violet & lilac		6.00	2.10
Q4	A1	25c dk bl & lt bl		9.00	4.75
Q5	A1	30c indigo & yel		6.00	4.75
Q6	A1	50c indigo & sal buff		6.00	4.75
Q7	A1	75c brn car & gray		1.25	4.75
a.		Inverted overprint		600.00	

Nos. 8-13 Overprinted

Q8	A2	80c carmine rose		.90	4.75
Q9	A2	1.25 l dark blue		1.25	4.75
Q10	A2	2 l olive brown		.90	4.75
a.		Inverted overprint		600.00	750.00
Q11	A2	2.50 l red orange		1.50	4.75
a.		Double overprint		650.00	
b.		Inverted overprint		1,200.	
Q12	A2	5 l dark green		1.50	4.75
Q13	A2	10 l olive black		1.25	4.75
a.		Double overprint		950.00	

Nos. E1-E2
Overprinted
Vertically

Q14	SD1	2 l carmine rose		1.25	4.75
Q15	SD1	2.50 l dark blue		1.25	4.75
a.		Inverted overprint		650.00	
		Nos. Q1-Q15 (15)		38.55	60.00
		Set, never hinged		160.00	

VENEZUELA

ˌve-nə-ˈzwā-lə

LOCATION — Northern coast of South America, bordering on the Caribbean Sea
GOVT. — Republic
AREA — 352,143 sq. mi.
POP. — 23,203,466 (1999 est.)
CAPITAL — Caracas

100 Centavos = 8 Reales = 1 Peso
100 Centesimos = 1 Venezolano (1879)
100 Centimos = 1 Bolivar (1880)

Watermark

Wmk. 346

Catalogue values for unused stamps in this country are for Never Hinged items, beginning with Scott 743 in the regular postage section, Scott B2 in the semi-postal section, Scott C709 in the airpost section, and Scott E1 in the special delivery section.

Coat of Arms — A1

Fine Impression
No Dividing Line Between Stamps

Unwmk.

1859, Jan. 1	**Litho.**		**Imperf.**
1	A1 ½r yellow	23.00	9.25
a.	½r orange	27.00	11.00
b.	Greenish paper	225.00	
2	A1 1r blue	325.00	20.00
a.	Half used as ½r on cover		7,500.
3	A1 2r red	42.50	15.00
a.	2r dull rose red	55.00	17.00
b.	Half used as 1r on cover		1,250.
c.	Greenish paper	225.00	140.00
	Nos. 1-3 (3)	390.50	44.25

Coarse Impression

1859-62		**Thick Paper**	
4	A1 ½r orange ('61)	12.00	4.00
a.	½r yellow ('59)	500.00	30.00
b.	½r olive yellow	750.00	35.00
c.	Bluish paper	575.00	
d.	½r dull rose (error)	250,000.	350,000.
5	A1 1r blue ('62)	20.00	12.50
a.	1r pale blue	35.00	15.00
b.	1r dark blue	35.00	15.00
c.	Half used as ½r on cover		7,500.
d.	Bluish paper	200.00	
6	A1 2r red ('62)	30.00	20.00
a.	2r dull rose	42.50	20.00
b.	Tête bêche pair	10,000.	
c.	Half used as 1r on cover		400.00
d.	Bluish paper	225.00	
	Nos. 4-6 (3)	62.00	36.50

In the fine impression, the background lines of the shield are more sharply drawn. In the coarse impression, the shading lines at each end of the scroll inscribed "LIBERTAD" are usually very heavy. Stamps of the coarse impression are closer together, and there is usually a dividing line between them.

Nos. 1-3 exist on thick paper and on bluish paper. Nos. 1-6 exist on pelure paper.

The greenish paper varieties (Nos. 1b and 3c) and the bluish paper varieties were not regularly issued.

Arms — A2   Eagle — A3

1862			**Litho.**
7	A2 ¼c green	20.00	110.00
8	A2 ½c dull lilac	30.00	190.00
	½c violet	40.00	210.00
9	A2 1c gray brown	42.50	225.00
	Nos. 7-9 (3)	92.50	525.00

Counterfeits are plentiful. Forged cancellations abound on Nos. 7-17.

1863-64			
10	A3 ½c pale red ('64)	55.00	125.00
a.	½c red	60.00	125.00
11	A3 1c slate ('64)	62.50	160.00
12	A3 ½r orange	7.75	3.50
13	A3 1r blue	17.00	8.50
a.	1r pale blue	30.00	13.00
b.	Half used as ½r on cover		750.00
14	A3 2r green	23.00	20.00
a.	2r deep yellow green	30.00	20.00
b.	Quarter used as ½r on cover		7,500.
c.	Half used as 1r on cover		2,000.

Counterfeits exist.

Redrawn

1865			
15	A3 ½r orange	4.00	2.50

The redrawn stamp has a broad "N" in "FEDERACION." "MEDIO REAL" and "FEDERACION" are in thin letters. There are 52 instead of 49 pearls in the circle.

No. 15 in yellow is a postal forgery.

A4   Simón Bolívar — A5

1865-70			
16	A4 ½c yel grn ('67)	200.00	300.00
17	A4 1c bl grn ('67)	200.00	250.00
18	A4 ½r brn vio (thin paper)	9.25	2.00
19	A4 ½r lil rose ('70)	9.25	2.50
a.	½r brownish rose	9.25	3.00
b.	Tête bêche pair	110.00	150.00
20	A4 1r vermilion	42.50	15.00
a.	Half used as ½r on cover		500.00
21	A4 2r yellow	160.00	77.50
a.	Half used as 1r on cover		3,000.
	Nos. 16-21 (6)	621.00	647.00

This issue is known unofficially rouletted. Postal forgeries exist of the ½r.
One quarter of #21 used as ½r is a postal forgery.
For overprints see Nos. 37-48.

Overprinted in Very Small Upright Letters "Bolivar Sucre Miranda — Decreto de 27 de Abril de 1870", or "Decreto de 27 de Junio 1870" in Slanting Letters

(The "Junio" overprint is continuously repeated, in four lines arranged in two pairs, with the second line of each pair inverted.)

Un	1	Siete	7
Dos	2	Nueve	9
Tres	3	Quince	15
Cuatro	4	Veinte	20
Cinco	5	Cincuenta	50

1871-76			**Litho.**
22	A5 1c yellow	1.50	.40
a.	1c orange	2.10	.45
b.	1c brown orange ('76)	2.10	.30
c.	1c pale buff ('76)	2.10	.45
d.	Laid paper	1.00	.75
23	A5 2c yellow	2.00	.45
a.	2c orange	4.00	.45
b.	2c brown orange	3.50	.75
c.	2c pale buff ('76)	3.50	.45
d.	Laid paper	3.50	.55
e.	Frame inverted	4,000.	3,000.
24	A5 3c yellow	3.00	.75
a.	3c orange	3.00	1.40
b.	3c pale buff ('76)	5.50	1.75
25	A5 4c yellow	4.00	.75
a.	4c orange	4.50	1.25
b.	4c brown orange ('76)	4.50	1.25
c.	4c buff ('76)	4.50	1.25
26	A5 5c yellow	4.00	.75
a.	5c orange	4.00	.90
b.	5c pale buff ('76)	4.00	.90
c.	Laid paper	7.50	.90
27	A5 1r rose	4.00	2.00
a.	1r pale red	4.00	2.00
b.	Laid paper	6.00	2.50
c.	Half used as ½r on cover		1,500.
28	A5 2r rose	4.50	2.00
a.	2r pale red	4.50	2.00
b.	Laid paper	12.00	2.50
29	A5 3r rose	6.00	2.00
a.	3r pale red	6.00	2.00
30	A5 5r rose	5.75	1.00
a.	5r pale red	5.75	1.00
31	A5 7r rose	22.50	4.00
a.	7r pale red	22.50	4.00
32	A5 9r green	22.50	4.25
a.	9r olive green	22.50	6.00
33	A5 15r green	55.00	8.50
a.	15r gray green ('76)	55.00	8.50
b.	Frame inverted	8,000.	6,500.
34	A5 20r green	77.50	20.00
a.	Laid paper	110.00	35.00
35	A5 30r green	375.00	110.00
a.	30r gray green ('76)	600.00	160.00
b.	Double overprint		
36	A5 50r green		1,200. 300.00
a.	50r gray green ('76)		
	Nos. 22-34 (13)	212.25	46.85
	Nos. 22-35 (14)	587.25	156.85

These stamps were made available for postage and revenue by official decree, and were the only stamps sold for postage in Venezuela from Mar., 1871 to Aug., 1873.

Due to lack of canceling handstamps, the majority of stamps were canceled with pen marks. Fiscal cancellations were also made with the pen. The values quoted are for pen-canceled stamps.

Different settings were used for the different overprints. Stamps with the upright letters were issued in 1871. Those with the slanting letters in one double line were issued in 1872-73. Those with the slanting overprint in two double lines were issued starting in 1874 from several different settings, those of 1877-78 showing much coarser impressions of the design than the earlier issues. The 7r and 9r are not known with this overprint. Stamps on laid paper (1875) are from a separate setting.

Stamps and Types of 1866-67
Overprinted in Two Lines of Very
Small Letters Repeated Continuously

Overprinted
"Estampillas de Correo — Contrasena"

1873, July 1			
37	A4 ½r pale rose	70.00	13.00
a.	½r rose	70.00	13.00
b.	Inverted overprint	175.00	75.00
c.	Tête bêche pair	3,000.	2,000.
38	A4 1r vermilion	85.00	25.00
a.	Inverted overprint		
b.	Half used as ½r on cover		5,500.
39	A4 2r yellow	300.00	125.00
a.	Inverted overprint		
b.	Half used as 1r on cover		12,000.
	Nos. 37-39 (3)	455.00	163.00

Overprinted
"Contrasena —
Estampillas de Correo"

1873, Nov.			
40	A4 1c gray lilac	30.00	32.50
a.	Inverted overprint	6.50	17.00
41	A4 2c green	125.00	90.00
a.	Inverted overprint	40.00	50.00
b.	As "a," half used as 1c on cover		7,500.
42	A4 ½r rose	72.50	13.00
a.	Inverted overprint	30.00	4.00
b.	½r pink	60.00	11.00
43	A4 1r vermilion	85.00	23.00
a.	Inverted overprint	35.00	9.00
b.	Half used as ½r on cover		300.00
44	A4 2r yellow	325.00	160.00
a.	Inverted overprint	110.00	50.00
b.	Half used as 1r on cover		10,000.
	Nos. 40-44 (5)	637.50	318.50

Overprinted
"Contrasena —
Estampilla de Correos"

1875			
45	A4 ½r rose	85.00	10.00
a.	Inverted overprint	125.00	25.00
b.	Double overprint	160.00	90.00
46	A4 1r vermilion	160.00	15.00
a.	Inverted overprint	200.00	80.00
b.	Tête bêche pair	3,500.	3,000.
c.	Half used as ½r on cover		3,500.

Overprinted
"Estampillas de correo — Contrasena"

1876-77			
47	A4 ½r rose	77.50	9.25
a.	½r pink	65.00	7.50
b.	Inverted overprint	65.00	7.50
c.	Both lines of overprint read "Contrasena"	75.00	17.50
d.	Both lines of overprint read "Estampillas de correo"	75.00	17.50
e.	Double overprint	125.00	35.00
48	A4 1r vermilion ('77)	92.50	23.00
a.	Inverted overprint	85.00	24.00
b.	Tête bêche pair	2,250.	2,500.
c.	Half used as ½r on cover		

On Nos. 47 and 48 "correo" has a small "c" instead of a capital. Nos. 45 and 46 have the overprint in slightly larger letters than the other stamps of the 1873-76 issues.

Simón Bolívar
A6   A7

Overprinted
"Decreto de 27 Junio 1870"
Twice, One Line Inverted

1879			**Imperf.**
49	A6 1c yellow	4.00	1.00
a.	1c orange	5.00	1.50
b.	1c olive yellow	5.50	1.75
50	A6 5c yellow	3.50	.50
a.	5c orange	2.50	.75
b.	Double overprint	20.00	10.00
51	A6 10c blue	5.00	.50
52	A6 30c blue	7.75	1.00
53	A6 50c blue	7.75	1.00
54	A6 90c blue	40.00	12.00
55	A7 1v rose red	77.50	18.00
56	A7 3v rose red	130.00	55.00
57	A7 5v rose red	225.00	77.50
	Nos. 49-57 (9)	500.50	166.50

In 1879 and the early part of 1880 there were no regular postage stamps in Venezuela and the stamps inscribed "Escuelas" were permitted to serve for postal as well as revenue purposes. Postally canceled stamps are extremely scarce. Values quoted are for stamps with cancellations of banks or business houses or with pen cancellations. Stamps with pen marks removed are sometimes offered as unused stamps, or may have fraudulent postal cancellations added.

Nos. 49-57 exist without overprint. These are proofs.

A8   A9

1880			**Perf. 11**
58	A8 5c yellow	1.50	.50
a.	5c orange	1.50	.50
b.	Printed on both sides	150.00	85.00
59	A8 10c yellow	2.50	.60
a.	10c orange	2.50	.60
60	A8 25c yellow	2.50	.60
a.	25c orange	2.75	.70
b.	Printed on both sides	110.00	52.50
c.	Impression of 5c on back	175.00	90.00
61	A8 50c yellow	4.75	.80
a.	50c orange	5.25	.85
b.	Half used as 25c on cover		
c.	Printed on both sides	150.00	90.00
d.	Impression of 25c on back	150.00	90.00
62	A9 1b pale blue	12.00	1.40
63	A9 2b pale blue	17.00	1.75
64	A9 5b pale blue	40.00	5.75
a.	Half used as 2½b on cover		
65	A9 10b rose red	200.00	70.00
66	A9 20b rose red	1,200.	200.00
67	A9 25b rose red	5,000.	500.00
	Nos. 58-65 (8)	280.25	81.40

See note on used values below No. 57.

Bolívar — A10

1880 Litho. Perf. 11
Thick or Thin Paper

68	A10	5c blue	15.00	7.25
a.		Printed on both sides	225.00	140.00
69	A10	10c rose	20.00	12.00
a.		10c carmine	20.00	12.00
b.		Double impression	90.00	75.00
c.		Horiz. pair, imperf. btwn.	75.00	75.00
70	A10	10c scarlet	20.00	12.00
a.		Horiz. pair, imperf. btwn.	75.00	75.00
71	A10	25c yellow	15.00	7.25
b.		Thick paper	20.00	10.00
72	A10	50c brown	92.50	40.00
a.		50c deep brown	92.50	.40
b.		Printed on both sides	225.00	140.00
c.		Half used as 25c on cover		5,000.
73	A10	1b green	140.00	50.00
a.		Horiz. pair, imperf. btwn.	300.00	300.00
		Nos. 68-73 (6)	302.50	128.50

Nos. 68 to 73 were used for the payment of postage on letters to be sent abroad and the Escuelas stamps were then restricted to internal use.

Counterfeits of this issue exist in a great variety of shades as well as in wrong colors. They are on thick and thin paper, white or toned, and imperf. or perforated 11, 12 and compound. They are also found tête bêche. Counterfeits of Nos. 68 to 72 inclusive have a diagonal line across the "S" of "CENTS" and a short line from the bottom of that letter to the frame below it. Originals of No. 73 show parts of a frame around "BOLIVAR."

Simón Bolívar
A11 A12

A13 A14

A15

1882, Aug. 1 Engr. Perf. 12

74	A11	5c blue	.70	.35
75	A12	10c red brown	.70	.35
76	A13	25c yellow brown	1.00	.40
a.		Printed on both sides	50.00	27.50
77	A14	50c green	2.40	.70
a.		Half used as 25c on cover		500.00
78	A15	1b violet	3.25	1.75
		Nos. 74-78 (5)	8.05	3.55

Nos. 75-78 exist imperf. Value, set $32.50.
See Nos. 88, 92-95. For surcharges and overprints see Nos. 100-103, 108-112.

A16 A17

A18 A19

A20 A21

A22 A23

1882-88

79	A16	5c blue green	.25	.25
80	A17	10c brown	.25	.25
81	A18	25c orange	.25	.25
82	A19	50c blue	.25	.25
83	A20	1b vermilion	.25	.25
84	A21	3b dull vio ('88)	.25	.25
85	A22	10b dark brn ('88)	1.25	.80
86	A23	20b plum ('88)	1.50	.95
		Nos. 79-86 (8)	4.25	3.25

By official decree, dated Apr. 14, 1882, stamps of types A11 to A15 were to be used for foreign postage and those of types A16 to A23 for inland correspondence and fiscal use.
Issue date: Nos. 79-83, Aug. 1.
See Nos. 87, 89-91, 96-99. For surcharges and overprints see Nos. 104-107, 114-122.

1887-88 Litho. Perf. 11

87	A16	5c gray green	.25	.25
88	A13	25c yellow brown	42.50	15.00
89	A18	25c orange	.40	.35
90	A20	1b orange red ('88)	3.50	.75
		Nos. 87-90 (4)	46.65	16.35

Perf. 14

91	A16	5c gray green	70.00	22.50

Stamps of type A16, perf. 11 and 14, are from a new die with "ESCUELAS" in smaller letters. Stamps of the 1887-88 issue, perf. 12, and a 50c dark blue, perf. 11 or 12, are believed by experts to be from printer's waste.
Counterfeits of No. 91 have been made by perforating printers waste of No. 96.

Rouletted 8

92	A11	5c blue	40.00	17.00
93	A13	25c yel brown	15.00	10.00
94	A14	50c green	15.00	10.00
95	A15	1b purple	30.00	20.00
		Nos. 92-95 (4)	100.00	57.00

1887-88

96	A16	5c green	.25	.25
97	A18	25c orange	.25	.25
98	A19	50c dark blue	.70	.70
99	A21	3b purple ('88)	3.00	3.00
a.		On overfranked cover		1,000.
		Nos. 96-99 (4)	4.20	4.20

The so-called imperforate varieties of Nos. 92 to 99, and the pin perforated 50c dark blue, type A19, are believed to be from printer's waste.

Stamps of 1882-88
Handstamp
Surcharged in Violet

1892 Perf. 12

100	A11	25c on 5c blue	40.00	40.00
101	A12	25c on 10c red brn	16.00	16.00
102	A13	1b on 25c yel brn	16.00	16.00
103	A14	1b on 50c green	20.00	20.00
		Nos. 100-103 (4)	92.00	92.00

See note after No. 107.

1892

104	A16	25c on 5c bl grn	10.00	6.00
105	A17	25c on 10c brown	10.00	6.00
106	A18	1b on 25c orange	15.00	12.00
107	A19	1b on 50c blue	23.00	12.00
		Nos. 104-107 (4)	58.00	36.00

Counterfeits of this surcharge abound.

Stamps of 1882-88
Overprinted in Red or
Black

1893

108	A11	5c blue (R)	.55	.25
a.		Inverted overprint	3.25	3.25
b.		Double overprint	16.00	16.00
109	A12	10c red brn (Bk)	.90	.90
a.		Inverted overprint	4.00	4.00
b.		Double overprint	16.00	16.00
110	A13	25c yel brn (R)	.80	.50
a.		Inverted overprint	5.25	5.25
b.		Double overprint	16.00	16.00
c.		25c yel brn (Bk)	500.00	500.00
111	A14	50c green (R)	1.25	.80
a.		Inverted overprint	5.25	5.25
b.		Double overprint	27.50	27.50
112	A15	1b pur (R)	3.00	1.20
a.		Inverted overprint	10.00	10.00
		Nos. 108-112 (5)	6.50	3.65

1893

114	A16	5c bl grn (R)	.25	.25
a.		Inverted overprint	3.25	3.25
b.		Double overprint	5.25	5.25
115	A17	10c brn (R)	.25	.25
a.		Inverted overprint	3.25	3.25
116	A18	25c org (R)	.25	.25
a.		Inverted overprint	3.25	3.25
117	A18	25c org (Bk)	5.75	2.75
a.		Inverted overprint	8.25	5.00
118	A19	50c blue (R)	.25	.25
a.		Inverted overprint	3.25	3.25
119	A20	1b ver (Bk)	.60	.40
a.		Inverted overprint	4.00	4.00
120	A21	3b dl vio (R)	.90	.40
a.		Double overprint	8.25	8.25
121	A22	10b dk brn (R)	3.50	2.25
a.		Double overprint	10.00	10.00
b.		Inverted overprint	20.00	20.00
122	A23	20b plum (Bk)	3.00	3.00
a.		Double overprint	10.00	20.00
b.		Inverted overprint		
		Nos. 114-122 (9)	14.75	9.80

Counterfeits exist.

Simón Bolívar
A24 A25

1893 Engr.

123	A24	5c red brn	.90	.25
124	A24	10c blue	3.25	1.25
125	A24	25c magenta	15.00	.50
126	A24	50c brn vio	4.25	.55
127	A24	1b green	5.75	1.25
		Nos. 123-127 (5)	29.15	3.80

Many shades exist in this issue, but their values do not vary.

1893

128	A25	5c gray	.25	.25
129	A25	10c green	.25	.25
130	A25	25c blue	.25	.25
131	A25	50c orange	.25	.25
132	A25	1b red vio	.25	.25
133	A25	3b red	.55	.25
134	A25	10b dl vio	.90	.80
135	A25	20b red brn	4.25	2.75
		Nos. 128-135 (8)	6.95	5.05

By decree of Nov. 28, 1892, the stamps inscribed "Correos" were to be used for external postage and those inscribed "Instruccion" were for internal postage and revenue purposes.
For surcharge see No. 230.

After July 1, 1895, stamps inscribed "Escuelas" or "Instruccion" were no longer available for postage. Stamps of design A25 in shades different than those listed were printed after 1895.

Landing of
Columbus
A26

1893 Perf. 12

136	A26	25c magenta	11.00	.60

4th cent. of the discovery of the mainland of South America, also participation of Venezuela in the Intl. Exhib. at Chicago in 1893.

Map of
Venezuela
A27

1896 Litho.

137	A27	5c yel grn	3.00	2.75
a.		5c apple green	3.00	2.75
138	A27	10c blue	4.00	3.00
139	A27	25c yellow	4.00	5.50
a.		25c orange	4.00	5.50
b.		Tête bêche pair	125.00	125.00
140	A27	50c rose red	52.50	27.00
a.		50c red	52.50	52.50
b.		Tête bêche pair	375.00	375.00
141	A27	1b violet	40.00	27.00
		Nos. 137-141 (5)	103.50	65.25

Gen. Francisco Antonio Gabriel de Miranda (1752-1816).
These stamps were in use from July 4 to Nov. 4, 1896. Later usage is known.
There are many forgeries of this issue. They include faked errors, imperforate stamps and many tête bêche. The paper of the originals is thin, white and semi-transparent. The gum is shiny and crackled. The paper of the reprints is often thick and opaque. The gum is usually dull, smooth, thin and only slightly adhesive.

Bolívar — A28

1899-1901 Engr.

142	A28	5c dk grn	1.00	.25
143	A28	10c red	1.25	.40
144	A28	25c blue	1.50	.55
145	A28	50c gray blk	2.00	1.00
146	A28	50c org ('01)	1.75	.50
147	A28	1b yel grn	32.50	15.00
149	A28	2b orange	375.00	225.00
		Nos. 142-147,149 (7)	415.00	242.70

Stamps of 1899
Overprinted in Black

1900

150	A28	5c dk grn	1.25	.40
a.		Inverted overprint	4.75	4.75
151	A28	10c red	1.25	.40
a.		Inverted overprint	6.50	6.50
b.		Double overprint	10.50	10.50
152	A28	25c blue	7.75	1.25
a.		Inverted overprint	13.00	13.00
153	A28	50c gray blk	4.00	.55
a.		Inverted overprint	12.00	12.00
154	A28	1b yel grn	1.75	.80
a.		Double overprint	13.00	13.00
b.		Inverted overprint	12.00	12.00
155	A28	2b orange	2.75	2.25
a.		Inverted overprint	35.00	35.00
b.		Double overprint	32.50	32.50
		Nos. 150-155 (6)	18.75	5.65

Initials are those of R. T. Mendoza.
Counterfeit overprints exist, especially of inverted and doubled varieties.

Bolivar Type of 1899-
1903 Overprinted

1900

156	A28	5c dk grn	200.00	200.00
157	A28	10c red	200.00	200.00
158	A28	25c blue	350.00	175.00
159	A28	50c yel orange	23.00	1.60
160	A28	1b slate	1.25	1.00
a.		Without overprint	4,000.	—
		Nos. 156-160 (5)	774.25	577.60

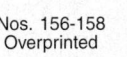

Nos. 156-158
Overprinted

1900, Aug. 14

161	A28	5c green	7.75	.55
162	A28	10c red	7.00	1.00
163	A28	25c blue	7.75	1.00
		Nos. 161-163 (3)	22.50	2.55

Inverted Overprint

161a	A28	5c	9.25	6.50
162a	A28	10c	9.25	6.50
163a	A28	25c	12.00	7.25
		Nos. 161a-163a (3)	30.50	20.25

Overprint exists on each value without "Castro" or without "1900."

Type of 1893
Surcharged

1904, Jan. — Perf. 12

230	A25	5c on 50c green	.80	.60
a.		"Vele"	23.00	23.00
b.		Surcharge reading up	1.00	.50
c.		Double surcharge	18.00	18.00

Gen. José de   Pres. Cipriano
Sucre — A35   Castro — A37

1904-09 — Engr.

231	A35	5c bl grn	.50	.25
232	A35	10c carmine	.55	.25
233	A35	15c violet	.90	.40
234	A35	25c dp ultra	6.50	.40
235	A35	50c plum	1.00	.50
236	A35	1b plum	1.10	.50
		Nos. 231-236 (6)	10.55	2.30

Issue date: 15c, Dec. 1909. Others, July 1, 1904.

1905, July 5 — Litho. — Perf. 11½

245	A37	5c vermilion	3.25	3.25
a.		5c carmine	5.00	5.00
246	A37	10c dark blue	5.50	4.25
247	A37	25c yellow	2.00	1.50
		Nos. 245-247 (3)	10.75	9.00

National Congress. Issued for interior postage only. Valid only for 90 days.
Various part-perforate varieties of Nos. 245-247 exist. Value, $15-$30.

Liberty — A38

1910, Apr. 19 — Engr. — Perf. 12

249	A38	25c dark blue	13.00	.60

Centenary of national independence.

Francisco de   Rafael
Miranda   Urdaneta
A39   A40

Bolívar — A41

1911 — Litho. — Perf. 11½x12

250	A39	5c dp grn	.50	.25
251	A39	10c carmine	.50	.25
252	A40	15c gray	5.75	.40
253	A40	25c dp bl	3.25	.60
a.		Imperf., pair	40.00	50.00
254	A41	50c purple	3.50	.40
255	A41	1b yellow	3.50	1.50
		Nos. 250-255 (6)	17.00	3.40

The 50c with center in blue was never issued although examples were postmarked by favor.
The centers of Nos. 250-255 were separately printed and often vary in shade from the rest of the design. In a second printing of the 5c and 10c, the entire design was printed at one time.

Redrawn

1913

255A	A40	15c gray	3.50	2.25
255B	A40	25c deep blue	2.00	.65
255C	A41	50c purple	2.00	.65
		Nos. 255A-255C (3)	7.50	3.55

The redrawn stamps have two berries instead of one at top of the left spray; a berry has been added over the "C" and "S" of "Centimos"; and the lowest leaf at the right is cut by the corner square.

Simón Bolívar
A42   A43

1914, July — Engr. — Perf. 13½, 14, 15

256	A42	5c yel grn	37.50	.55
257	A42	10c scarlet	35.00	.50
258	A42	25c dark blue	5.75	.25
		Nos. 256-258 (3)	78.25	1.30

Printed by the American Bank Note Co.

Different frames.

1915-23 — Perf. 12

259	A43	5c green	4.25	.25
260	A43	10c vermilion	10.00	.60
261	A43	10c claret ('22)	10.00	.90
262	A43	15c dull ol grn	9.25	.60
263	A43	25c ultra	6.50	.25
a.		25c blue	13.00	.60
264	A43	40c dull green	23.00	11.50
265	A43	50c dp violet	6.50	.80
266	A43	50c ultra ('23)	17.00	4.75
267	A43	75c lt blue	57.50	23.00
a.		75c greenish blue	57.50	23.00
268	A43	1b dark gray	35.00	5.25
		Nos. 259-268 (10)	179.00	47.90

See Nos. 269-285. For surcharges see Nos. 307, 309-310.

Type of 1915-23 Issue
Printed by Waterlow & Sons, Ltd.
Re-engraved

1924-39 — Perf. 12½

269	A43	5c orange brn	.55	.25
a.		5c yellow brown	.55	.25
b.		Horiz. pair, imperf. between	25.00	40.00
270	A43	5c green ('39)	12.00	1.00
271	A43	7½c yel grn ('39)	1.25	.40
272	A43	10c dk green	.25	.25
273	A43	10c dk car ('39)	4.00	.25
274	A43	15c olive grn	2.25	.50
275	A43	15c brown ('27)	.30	.25
276	A43	25c ultra	2.25	.25

277	A43	25c red ('28)	.25	.25
a.		Horiz. pair, imperf. btwn.	50.00	85.00
278	A43	40c dp blue ('25)	.55	.25
279	A43	40c slate bl ('39)	7.75	1.25
280	A43	50c dk blue	.55	.25
281	A43	50c dk pur ('39)	7.75	.85
282	A43	1b black	.55	.25
283	A43	3b yel org ('25)	1.75	.95
284	A43	3b red org ('39)	12.00	4.25
285	A43	5b dull vio ('25)	16.00	8.50
		Nos. 269-285 (17)	70.00	19.95

Perf. 14

269c	A43	5c	7.00	2.00
272a	A43	10c	7.00	2.00
274a	A43	15c	8.25	2.75
276a	A43	25c	12.00	4.75
280a	A43	50c	35.00	14.00
282a	A43	1b	42.50	27.00
		Nos. 269c-282a (6)	111.75	52.50

The re-engraved stamps may readily be distinguished from the 1915 issue by the perforation and sometimes by the colors. The designs differ in many minor details which are too minute for illustration or description.

Bolívar
and Sucre
A44

Perf. 11½x12, 12

1924, Dec. 1 — Litho.

286	A44	25c grayish blue	2.75	.55

Redrawn

286A	A44	25c ultra	3.50	.85

Centenary of the Battle of Ayacucho.
The redrawn stamp has a whiter effect with less shading in the faces. Bolívar's ear is clearly visible and the outline of his aquiline nose is broken.

A45   A46

Revenue Stamps Surcharged in Black or Red

1926 — Perf. 12, 12½

287	A45	5c on 1b ol grn	.65	.40
a.		Double surcharge	8.00	8.00
b.		Pair, one without surcharge	12.00	12.00
c.		Inverted surcharge	8.00	8.00
288	A46	25c on 5c dk brn (R)	.65	.40
a.		Inverted surcharge	8.00	8.00
b.		Double surcharge	8.00	8.00

View of Ciudad
Bolívar and
General J.V.
Gómez — A47

1928, July 21 — Litho. — Perf. 12

289	A47	10c deep green	1.00	.65
a.		Imperf., pair	40.00	

25th anniversary of the Battle of Ciudad Bolívar and the foundation of peace in Venezuela.

Simón Bolívar
A48   A49

1930, Dec. 9

290	A48	5c yellow	1.00	.35
291	A48	10c dark blue	1.00	.25
292	A48	25c rose red	1.00	.25
		Nos. 290-292 (3)	3.00	.85

Imperf., Pairs

290a	A48	5c	5.25	5.25
291a	A48	10c	6.50	6.50
292a	A48	25c	10.50	10.50

Death centenary of Simón Bolívar (1783-1830), South American liberator.
Nos. 290-292 exist part-perforate, including pairs imperf. between, imperf. horiz., imperf. vert. Value range, $6-12.

Various Frames
Bluish Winchester Security Paper

1932-38 — Engr. — Perf. 12½

293	A49	5c violet	.50	.25
294	A49	7½c dk green ('37)	1.00	.40
295	A49	10c green	.60	.25
296	A49	15c yellow	1.50	.25
297	A49	22½c dp car ('38)	3.50	.50
298	A49	25c red	1.25	.25
299	A49	37½c ultra ('36)	4.50	2.00
300	A49	40c indigo	4.50	.25
301	A49	50c olive grn	4.50	.40
302	A49	1b lt blue	6.00	.70
303	A49	3b brown	40.00	13.00
304	A49	5b yellow brn	50.00	17.00
		Nos. 293-304 (12)	117.85	35.25

For surcharges see Nos. 308, 318-319, C223.

Arms of
Bolívar — A50

1933, July 24 — Litho. — Perf. 11

306	A50	25c brown red	3.00	2.40
a.		Imperf., pair	32.50	32.50

150th anniv. of the birth of Simón Bolívar. Valid only to Aug. 21.

Stamps of 1924-32
Surcharged in Black
— (Blocks of
Surcharge in Color
of stamps)

1933

307	A43	7½c on 10c grn	.50	.25
a.		Double surcharge	2.50	2.50
b.		Inverted surcharge	4.25	4.25
308	A49	22½c on 25c (#298)	2.00	.85
309	A43	22½c on 25c (#277)	1.50	1.50
a.		Double surcharge	10.00	10.00
310	A43	37½c on 40c dp bl	2.00	.95
a.		Double surcharge	11.50	11.50
b.		Inverted surcharge	10.00	10.00
		Nos. 307-310 (4)	6.00	3.55

Nurse and   River
Child — A51   Scene — A52

Gathering Cacao
Pods — A53

Cattle
Raising
A54

Plowing
A55

Perf. 11, 11½ or Compound
1937, July 1   Litho.
311	A51	5c deep violet	.55	.35
312	A52	10c dk slate grn	.55	.25
313	A53	15c yellow brn	1.00	.55
314	A51	25c cerise	1.00	.35
315	A54	50c yellow grn	6.50	4.25
316	A55	3b red orange	12.00	7.75
317	A51	5b lt brown	23.00	15.00
		Nos. 311-317 (7)	44.60	28.50

Nos. 311-317 exist imperforate. Value for set $75. Nos. 311-315 exist in pairs, imperf. between; value range, $20-$30.
For overprints and surcharges see Nos. 321-324, 345, 376-377, 380-384.

No. 300 Surcharged in Black

1937, July   Perf. 12½
318	A49	25c on 40c indigo	7.75	.95
a.		Double surcharge	16.00	16.00
b.		Inverted surcharge	13.00	13.00
c.		Triple surcharge	32.50	32.50

No. 300 Surcharged

319	A49	25c on 40c indigo	440.00	350.00
a.		Double surcharge		

A56

1937, Oct. 28   Litho.   Perf. 10½
320	A56	25c blue	1.25	.45

Acquisition of the Port of La Guaira by the Government from the British Corporation, June 3, 1937. Exists imperf. See Nos. C64-C65.
A redrawn printing of No. 320, with top inscription beginning "Nacionalización . . ." was prepared but not issued. Value, $40.
For surcharge see No. 385.

Stamps of 1937 Overprinted in Black

1937, Dec. 17   Perf. 11, 11½
321	A51	5c deep violet	5.75	3.25
322	A52	10c dk slate grn	1.75	.75
a.		Inverted overprint	13.00	13.00

323	A51	25c cerise	1.50	.55
a.		Inverted overprint	16.00	16.00
324	A55	3b red orange	375.00	225.00
		Nos. 321-324 (4)	384.00	229.55

Part-perforate pairs exist of Nos. 321-322 and 324. Value range, $12.50 to $125.
See Nos. C66-C78.

Gathering Coffee
Beans — A57

Simón
Bolívar — A58

Post Office,
Caracas — A59

1938   Engr.   Perf. 12
325	A57	5c green	.40	.25
326	A57	5c deep green	.40	.25
327	A58	10c car rose	.70	.25
328	A58	10c dp rose	.70	.25
329	A59	15c dk violet	1.40	.25
330	A59	15c olive grn	.85	.25
331	A58	25c lt blue	.40	.25
332	A58	25c dk blue	.40	.25
333	A58	37½c dk blue	8.50	4.00
334	A58	37½c lt blue	2.75	.85
335	A59	40c sepia	20.00	7.75
336	A59	40c black	17.00	7.75
337	A57	50c olive grn	27.50	7.75
338	A57	50c dull violet	9.25	.85
339	A58	1b dp brown	12.00	5.50
340	A58	1b black brown	17.00	1.50
341	A57	3b orange	92.50	50.00
342	A59	5b black	15.00	7.75
		Nos. 325-342 (18)	226.75	95.70

See Nos. 400, 412.

Teresa
Carreño — A60

Bolívar
Statue — A61

1938, June 12   Perf. 11¼x12
343	A60	25c blue	5.75	.60

Teresa Carreno, Venezuelan pianist, whose remains were repatriated Feb. 14, 1938.
For surcharge see No. 386.

1938, July 24   Perf. 12
344	A61	25c dark blue	6.50	.60

"The Day of the Worker."
For surcharge see No. 387.

Type of 1937 Surcharged in Black

1938   Litho.   Perf. 11, 11½
345	A51	40c on 5b lt brn	8.50	4.50
a.		Inverted surcharge	21.00	21.00

Gen. José I. Paz
Castillo, Postmaster of
Venezuela, 1859 — A62

1939, Apr. 19   Engr.   Perf. 12½
348	A62	10c carmine	2.50	.70

80th anniv. of the first Venezuelan stamp.

View of
Ojeda
A63

1939, June 24   Photo.
349	A63	25c dull blue	9.25	.75

Founding of city of Ojeda.

Cristóbal
Mendoza
A64

Diego
Urbaneja
A65

1939, Oct. 14   Engr.   Perf. 13
350	A64	5c green	.40	.25
351	A64	10c dk car rose	.40	.25
352	A64	15c dull lilac	1.00	.25
353	A64	25c brt ultra	.80	.25
354	A64	37½c dark blue	15.00	6.25
355	A64	50c lt olive grn	16.00	4.00
356	A64	1b dark brown	6.50	3.50
		Nos. 350-356 (7)	40.10	14.75

Mendoza (1772-1839), postmaster general.

1940-43   Perf. 12
357	A65	5c Prus green	.55	.25
357A	A65	7½c dk bl grn ('43)	.80	.30
358	A65	15c olive	.95	.30
359	A65	37½c deep blue	1.50	.70
360	A65	40c violet blue	1.10	.35
361	A65	50c violet	6.50	1.75
362	A65	1b dk violet brn	3.50	.90
363	A65	3b scarlet	9.50	3.75
		Nos. 357-363 (8)	24.40	8.30

See Nos. 399, 408, 410-411. For surcharges see Nos. 396, C226.

Battle of
Carabobo,
1821 — A67

1940, June 13
365	A67	25c blue	6.75	.80

Birth of General JoséAntonio Páez, 150th anniv.

"Crossing the
Andes" by Tito
Salas — A68

1940, June 13
366	A68	25c dark blue	6.75	.80

Death cent. of General Francisco Santander.

Monument and
Urn containing
Ashes of Simón
Bolívar — A69

Bed where Simón
Bolívar was
Born — A70

Designs: 15c, "Christening of Bolivar" by Tito Salas. 20c, Bolivar's birthplace, Caracas. 25c, "Bolivar on Horseback" by Salas. 30c, Patio of Bolivar House, Caracas. 37½c, Patio of Bolivar's Birthplace. 50c, "Rebellion of 1812" by Salas.

1940-41
367	A69	5c turq green	.25	.25
368	A70	10c rose pink	.25	.25
369	A69	15c olive	.60	.25
370	A70	20c blue ('41)	1.00	.25
371	A69	25c lt blue	.60	.25
372	A70	30c plum ('41)	1.50	.25
373	A70	37½c dk blue	3.00	1.00
374	A70	50c purple	2.00	.50
		Nos. 367-374 (8)	9.20	3.00

110th anniv. of the death of Simón Bolívar.
See Nos. 397, 398, 403, 405-407, 409. For surcharges see Nos. 375, 401-402, C224, C237-C238.

No. 371 Surcharged In Black

1941
375	A69	20c on 25c lt blue	.60	.25
a.		Inverted surcharge	10.00	10.00

Nos. 311-312 Overprinted in Black

1941   Perf. 11½
376	A51	5c deep violet	2.00	.50
a.		Double overprint	10.00	8.25
b.		Vert. pair, imperf. btwn.	14.00	14.00
c.		Inverted overprint	20.00	16.00
377	A52	10c dk slate grn	1.00	.30
a.		Double overprint	13.00	13.00

Symbols of
Industry
A77

Caracas
Cathedral
A78

1942, Dec. 17   Litho.   Perf. 12
378	A77	10c scarlet	1.00	.25
a.		Imperf., pair	22.50	22.50

Grand Industrial Exposition, Caracas.

1943   Engr.
379	A78	10c rose carmine	.75	.25

See No. 404.

Stamps of 1937
Overprinted in Black

1943
			Perf. 11, 11½	
380	A51	5c deep violet	16.00	9.50
381	A52	10c dk slate grn	6.00	4.00
382	A54	50c yellow green	8.00	4.50
383	A55	3b red orange	45.00	22.00
		Nos. 380-383 (4)	75.00	40.00

Issued for sale to philatelists & sold only in sets.

Stamps of 1937-38
Surcharged in Black

1943
			Perf. 11½, 10½, 12	
384	A51	20c on 25c cerise	30.00	30.00
385	A56	20c on 25c blue	77.50	77.50
386	A60	20c on 25c dk blue	15.00	15.00
387	A61	20c on 25c dk blue	15.00	15.00
a.		Inverted surcharge	42.50	42.50
		Nos. 384-387 (4)	137.50	137.50

Issued for sale to philatelists & sold only in sets.

Souvenir Sheet

A79

1944, Aug. 22   Litho.   *Perf. 12*
Flags in Red, Yellow, Blue & Black
388	A79	Sheet of 4	35.00	35.00
a.		5c Prussian green	3.00	.80
b.		10c rose	4.50	.80
c.		20c ultramarine	4.50	1.75
d.		1b rose lake	6.00	2.25

80th anniv. of Intl. Red Cross and 37th anniv. of Venezuela's joining.
No. 388 exists imperf. Value $60.

Antonio José de
Sucre — A80

1945, Mar. 3   Engr.   Unwmk.
389	A80	5c orange yellow	2.10	1.10
390	A80	10c dark blue	3.25	1.75
391	A80	20c rose pink	4.25	1.75
		Nos. 389-391,C206-C215 (13)	33.55	22.30

Birth of Antonio de Sucre, 150th anniv.

Andrés   Gen. Rafael
Bello — A81   Urdaneta — A82

1946, Aug. 24
392	A81	20c deep blue	.65	.35
393	A82	20c deep blue	.65	.35
		Nos. 392-393,C216-C217 (4)	3.50	1.20

80th anniversary of the death of Andrés Bello (1780?-1865), educator and writer, and the centenary of the death of Gen. Rafael Urdaneta.

Allegory of the
Republic — A83

1946, Oct. 18   Litho.   *Perf. 11½*
394	A83	20c greenish blue	.80	.35
		Nos. 394,C218-C221 (5)	5.60	3.85

Anniversary of Revolution of October, 1945. Exists imperf.

Anti-tuberculosis Institute,
Maracaibo — A84

1947, Jan. 12
395	A84	20c ultra & yellow	.80	.35
		Nos. 395,C228-C231 (5)	6.90	5.15

12th Pan-American Health Conf., Caracas, Jan. 1947. Exists imperf. and part perf.

No. 362 Surcharged in
Green

396	A65	15c on 1b dk vio brn	.70	.30
a.		Inverted surcharge	6.00	5.00
		Nos. 396,C223-C227 (6)	30.50	23.95

Types of 1938-40

1947   Engr.
397	A69	5c green	.25	.25
398	A70	30c black	1.00	.50
399	A65	40c red violet	.95	.25
400	A59	5b deep orange	40.00	18.00
		Nos. 397-400 (4)	42.20	19.00

In 1947 a decree authorized the use of 5c and 10c revenue stamps of the above type for franking correspondence. Other denominations were also used unofficially.
For surcharges see Nos. 876-883.

Nos. 398 and 373
Surcharged in Red

1947   Unwmk.   *Perf. 12*
401	A70	5c on 30c black	.40	.25
a.		Inverted surcharge	5.00	5.00
402	A70	5c on 37½c dk bl	.45	.25
a.		Inverted surcharge	5.00	5.00

Types of 1938-43

1947-48
403	A69	5c brt ultra	.25	.25
404	A78	10c red	.25	.25
405	A69	15c rose car	.50	.25
406	A69	25c violet	.40	.25
407	A70	30c dk vio brn ('48)	.50	.25
408	A70	40c orange ('48)	.50	.25
409	A70	50c olive green	.95	.25
410	A65	1b deep blue	1.75	.25
411	A65	3b gray	3.50	.90
412	A59	5b chocolate	13.00	5.00
		Nos. 403-412 (10)	21.60	7.90

M. S.
Republica
de
Venezuela
A85

Imprint: "American Bank Note Company"

1948-50   Engr.   *Perf. 12*
413	A85	5c blue	.25	.25
414	A85	7½c red org ('49)	.70	.40
a.		Booklet pane of 20		
415	A85	10c car rose	.55	.25
a.		Booklet pane of 10		
416	A85	15c gray ('50)	.55	.25
417	A85	20c sepia	.40	.25
418	A85	25c violet ('49)	.55	.25
419	A85	30c orange ('50)	3.75	2.25
420	A85	37½c brown ('49)	1.75	1.40
421	A85	40c olive ('50)	2.50	1.75
422	A85	50c red violet ('49)	.70	.25
423	A85	1b gray green	1.75	.55
		Nos. 413-423 (11)	13.45	7.85

Grand Colombian Merchant Fleet. See Nos. 632-634, C256-C271, C554-C556. For surcharges see Nos. 450-451.

Santos
Michelena — A86

1949, Apr. 25   *Perf. 12½*
424	A86	5c ultra	.25	.25
425	A86	10c carmine	.40	.25
426	A86	20c sepia	1.60	.60
427	A86	1b green	5.75	3.00
		Nos. 424-427,C272-C277 (10)	16.50	9.70

Centenary of the death of Santos Michelena, Finance Minister, and the 110th anniversary of the Postal Convention of Bogota.

Christopher
Columbus — A87

1949-50   Engr.
428	A87	5c deep ultra	.45	.25
429	A87	10c carmine	1.50	.50
430	A87	20c dark brown	1.75	.60
431	A87	1b green	4.75	2.10
		Nos. 428-431,C278-C283 (10)	18.45	8.65

450th anniversary (in 1948) of Columbus' discovery of the American mainland.
Issued: 5c, 10c, 1949; 20c, 1b, Jan. 1950.

Arms of
Venezuela
A88

1948
432	A88	5c blue	1.40	.70
433	A88	10c red	1.75	.80

The 20c and 1b, type A88, and six similar air post stamps were prepared but not issued. Value, set of 8, about $125.

Gen. Francisco de
Miranda — A89

1950, Mar. 28   Unwmk.   *Perf. 12*
434	A89	5c blue	.25	.25
435	A89	10c green	.40	.25
436	A89	20c sepia	.85	.35
437	A89	1b rose carmine	4.00	1.75
		Nos. 434-437 (4)	5.50	2.60

Bicentenary of birth of General Francisco de Miranda.

Map and   Alonso de
Population   Ojeda — A91
Chart — A90

1950, Sept. 1
438	A90	5c blue	.25	.25
439	A90	10c gray	.25	.25
440	A90	15c green	.25	.25
441	A90	25c green	.45	.25
442	A90	30c red	.55	.25
443	A90	50c violet	1.10	.45
444	A90	1b red brown	2.75	1.40
		Nos. 438-444,C302-C310 (16)	12.00	7.50

8th National Census of the Americas.

1950, Dec. 18   Photo.   *Perf. 11½*
445	A91	5c deep blue	.25	.25
446	A91	10c deep red	.30	.25
447	A91	15c slate gray	.35	.25
448	A91	20c ultra	1.40	.55
449	A91	1b blue green	5.50	2.75
		Nos. 445-449 (5)	7.80	4.05
		Nos. 445-449,C316-C321 (11)	15.65	7.80

450th anniversary (in 1949) of the discovery of the Gulf of Maracaibo.

Nos. 414 and 420 Surcharged in Black

1951   Unwmk.   *Perf. 12*
450	A85	5c on 7½c red org	.30	.25
451	A85	10c on 37½c brn	.30	.25
a.		Inverted surcharge	16.00	16.00

Telegraph Stamps
Surcharged in
Black or Red

1951, June   Engr.
Grayish Security Paper
452	5c on 5c brown	.25	.25
453	10c on 10c green	.25	.25
454	20c on 1b blk (R)	.50	.25

455	25c on 25c carmine		.65	.25
456	30c on 2b ol grn (R)		.90	.70
	Nos. 452-456 (5)		2.55	1.70

The 5c and 10c surcharges include quotation marks on each line and values are expressed "Bs. 0.05" etc.

Bolivar Statue, New York — A92

1951, July 13   *Perf. 12*

457	A92	5c green	.25	.25
458	A92	10c car rose	.40	.25
459	A92	20c ultra	.40	.25
460	A92	30c slate gray	.50	.25
461	A92	40c deep green	.70	.25
462	A92	50c red brown	1.50	.50
463	A92	1b gray black	4.75	2.50
	Nos. 457-463 (7)		8.50	4.25
	Nos. 457-463,C322-C329 (15)		21.65	9.50

Relocation of the equestrian statue of Simon Bolivar in NYC, Apr. 19, 1951.

Arms of Carabobo and "Industry" — A93

1951   Unwmk.   Photo.   *Perf. 11½*

464	A93	5c green	.25	.25
465	A93	10c red	.25	.25
466	A93	15c brown	1.40	.25
467	A93	20c ultra	2.00	.25
468	A93	25c orange brn	2.25	.25
469	A93	30c blue	5.00	2.00
470	A93	35c purple	19.00	16.00
	Nos. 464-470 (7)		30.05	19.00

Issue dates: 5c, 10c, Oct. 8; others, Oct. 29.

Arms of Zulia and "Industry"

471	A93	5c green	.25	.25
472	A93	10c red	.95	.25
473	A93	15c brown	2.10	.95
474	A93	20c ultra	2.75	1.25
475	A93	50c brown org	16.00	12.00
476	A93	1b dp gray grn	5.50	2.10
477	A93	5b rose violet	12.00	8.00
	Nos. 471-477 (7)		39.50	24.70

Issued: 5c, 10c, Sept. 8; others, Sept. 20.

Arms of Anzoategui and Globe

478	A93	5c green	.25	.25
479	A93	10c red	.25	.25
480	A93	15c brown	2.25	1.00
481	A93	20c ultra	3.75	.25
482	A93	40c red orange	7.75	3.75
483	A93	45c rose violet	22.50	1.25
484	A93	3b blue gray	8.75	4.25
	Nos. 478-484 (7)		45.40	10.85

Issue date: Nov. 9.

Arms of Caracas and Buildings

485	A93	5c green	1.25	.25
486	A93	10c red	1.75	.25
487	A93	15c brown	4.25	1.00
488	A93	20c ultra	8.50	1.00
489	A93	25c orange brn	11.50	2.25
490	A93	30c blue	11.00	2.50
491	A93	35c purple	110.00	62.50
	Nos. 485-491 (7)		148.25	69.65

Issued: 5c, 10c, June 20; others, Aug. 6.

Arms of Tachira and Agricultural Products

492	A93	5c green	.25	.25
493	A93	10c red	.95	.25
494	A93	15c brown	1.75	.60
495	A93	20c ultra	4.25	1.10
496	A93	50c brown org	260.00	3.25
497	A93	1b dp gray grn	4.25	1.50
498	A93	5b dull purple	10.50	6.00
	Nos. 492-498 (7)		281.90	12.85

Issue date: Aug. 9.

Arms of Venezuela and Statue of Simon Bolivar

499	A93	5c green	1.00	.25
500	A93	10c red	.85	.25
501	A93	15c brown	7.50	1.50
502	A93	20c ultra	7.50	1.00
503	A93	25c orange brn	12.50	2.75

504	A93	30c blue	12.50	2.75
505	A93	35c purple	65.00	50.00
	Nos. 499-505 (7)		106.85	58.40

Issue date: Aug. 6.

1952

Arms of Miranda and Agricultural Products

506	A93	5c green	.25	.25
507	A93	10c red	.25	.25
508	A93	15c brown	1.75	.25
509	A93	20c ultra	1.90	.25
510	A93	25c orange brn	2.50	1.10
511	A93	30c blue	4.25	1.90
512	A93	35c purple	26.00	18.00
	Nos. 506-512 (7)		36.80	21.80

Arms of Aragua and Stylized Farm

513	A93	5c green	.25	.25
514	A93	10c red	.25	.25
515	A93	15c brown	1.90	.25
516	A93	20c ultra	1.90	.25
517	A93	25c orange brn	4.25	1.10
518	A93	30c blue	4.25	1.90
519	A93	35c purple	22.50	17.50
	Nos. 513-519 (7)		35.20	21.30

Issue date: 20c, 30c, Mar. 24.

Arms of Lara, Agricultural Products and Rope

520	A93	5c green	.25	.25
521	A93	10c red	.25	.25
522	A93	15c brown	1.00	.25
523	A93	20c ultra	2.40	.25
524	A93	25c orange brn	2.75	1.75
525	A93	30c blue	5.25	1.40
526	A93	35c purple	21.00	13.00
	Nos. 520-526 (7)		32.80	16.95

Issue date: 20c, 30c, Mar. 24.

Arms of Bolivar and Stylized Design

527	A93	5c green	.25	.25
528	A93	10c red	.25	.25
529	A93	15c brown	.95	.25
530	A93	20c ultra	2.10	.25
531	A93	40c red orange	8.00	2.75
532	A93	45c rose violet	20.00	14.00
533	A93	3b blue gray	9.50	6.25
	Nos. 527-533 (7)		40.95	23.80

Issue date: 20c, Mar. 24.

Arms of Sucre, Palms and Seascape

534	A93	5c green	.25	.25
535	A93	10c red	.25	.25
536	A93	15c brown	2.40	.25
537	A93	20c ultra	2.40	.25
538	A93	40c red orange	8.00	2.10
539	A93	45c rose violet	27.50	17.50
540	A93	3b blue gray	7.00	4.75
	Nos. 534-540 (7)		47.70	25.15

Arms of Trujillo Surrounded by Stylized Tree

541	A93	5c green	.25	.25
542	A93	10c red	.25	.25
543	A93	15c brown	2.50	.25
544	A93	20c ultra	2.50	.60
545	A93	50c brown orange	15.00	7.25
546	A93	1b dp gray green	3.50	1.25
547	A93	5b dull purple	9.00	4.50
	Nos. 541-547 (7)		32.90	14.20

1953-54

Map of Delta Amacuro and Ship

548	A93	5c green	.25	.25
549	A93	10c red	.25	.25
550	A93	15c brown	.90	.25
551	A93	20c ultra	1.50	.25
552	A93	40c red orange	4.75	3.00
553	A93	45c rose violet	22.50	13.50
554	A93	3b blue gray	6.00	4.50
	Nos. 548-554 (7)		36.05	21.80

Arms of Falcon and Stylized Oil Refinery

555	A93	5c green	.25	.25
556	A93	10c red	.25	.25
557	A93	15c brown	1.40	.25
558	A93	20c ultra	1.40	.25
559	A93	50c brown orange	7.25	3.50
560	A93	1b dp gray grn	4.50	2.75
561	A93	5b dull purple	13.50	7.25
	Nos. 555-561 (7)		28.45	14.30

Issue date: 20c, Feb. 13.

Arms of Guarico and Factory

562	A93	5c green	.25	.25
563	A93	10c red	.25	.25
564	A93	15c brown	1.10	.25
565	A93	20c ultra	1.25	.25
566	A93	40c red orange	6.50	4.00
567	A93	45c rose violet	16.00	7.75
568	A93	3b blue gray	6.50	3.50
	Nos. 562-568 (7)		31.75	16.05

Issue date: 20c, Feb. 13.

Arms of Merida and Church

569	A93	5c green	.25	.25
570	A93	10c red	.25	.25
571	A93	15c brown	.85	.25
572	A93	20c ultra	2.10	.25
573	A93	50c brown orange	9.00	4.00

574	A93	1b dp gray green	2.50	1.75
575	A93	5b dull purple	9.00	5.25
	Nos. 569-575 (7)		23.85	11.80

Issue date: 20c, Feb. 2.

Arms of Monagas and Horses

576	A93	5c green	.25	.25
577	A93	10c red	.25	.25
578	A93	15c brown	1.10	.25
579	A93	20c ultra	1.60	.90
580	A93	40c red orange	7.50	2.75
581	A93	45c rose violet	22.50	13.50
582	A93	3b blue gray	9.25	7.50
	Nos. 576-582 (7)		42.35	25.25

Arms of Portuguesa and Forest

583	A93	5c green	.25	.25
584	A93	10c red	.25	.25
585	A93	15c brown	.65	.25
586	A93	20c ultra	1.40	.25
587	A93	50c brown org	7.25	4.75
588	A93	1b dp gray grn	1.90	.80
589	A93	5b dull purple	8.00	5.25
	Nos. 583-589 (7)		19.60	11.60

Issue date: 5c, 10c, Feb. 2.

Map of Amazonas and Orchid

590	A93	5c green	1.40	.25
591	A93	10c red	1.40	.25
592	A93	15c brown	3.00	.25
593	A93	20c ultra	8.50	.85
594	A93	40c red orange	10.00	3.00
595	A93	45c rose violet	16.00	7.75
596	A93	3b blue gray	24.00	8.50
	Nos. 590-596 (7)		64.30	20.70

Issue date: Jan. 1954.

Arms of Apure, Horse and Bird

597	A93	5c green	.25	.25
598	A93	10c red	.25	.25
599	A93	15c brown	1.60	.25
600	A93	20c ultra	8.50	.25
601	A93	50c brown org	11.00	8.50
602	A93	1b dp gray grn	3.50	3.00
603	A93	5b dull purple	21.00	12.00
	Nos. 597-603 (7)		46.00	24.30

Issue date: Jan. 1954.

Arms of Barinas, Cow and Horse

604	A93	5c green	.25	.25
605	A93	10c red	.25	.25
606	A93	15c brown	.55	.25
607	A93	20c ultra	3.75	.55
608	A93	50c brown org	4.50	2.75
609	A93	1b dp gray grn	1.10	.55
610	A93	5b dull purple	10.00	5.00
	Nos. 604-610 (7)		20.30	9.45

Issue date: Jan. 1954.

Arms of Cojedes and Cattle

611	A93	5c green	.25	.25
612	A93	10c red	.25	.25
613	A93	15c brown	.25	.25
614	A93	20c ultra	.25	.25
615	A93	25c orange brown	4.00	1.10
616	A93	30c blue	6.25	1.75
617	A93	35c purple	7.75	6.25
	Nos. 611-617 (7)		18.80	9.90

Issue date: Dec. 17, 1953.

Arms of Nueva Esparta and Fish

618	A93	5c green	.25	.25
619	A93	10c red	.25	.25
620	A93	15c brown	1.40	.25
621	A93	20c ultra	1.60	.25
622	A93	40c red orange	7.25	2.75
623	A93	45c rose vio	17.50	10.00
624	A93	3b blue gray	8.00	5.50
	Nos. 618-624 (7)		36.15	19.05

Issue date: Jan. 1954.

Arms of Yaracuy and Tropical Foliage

625	A93	5c green	1.50	.25
626	A93	10c red	.25	.25
627	A93	15c brown	1.10	.25
628	A93	20c ultra	1.75	.25
629	A93	25c orange brn	2.50	1.10
630	A93	30c blue	2.75	.95
631	A93	35c purple	6.50	4.25
	Nos. 625-631 (7)		16.30	7.10
	Nos. 464-631 (168)		1,264.	514.15

Issue date: Jan. 1954.
See Nos. C338-C553.

Ship Type of 1948-50, Redrawn

Coil Stamps
Imprint: "Courvoisier S.A."

1952   Unwmk.   Photo.   *Perf. 11½x12*

632	A85	5c green	1.50	.25
633	A85	10c car rose	2.50	.25
634	A85	15c gray	9.00	.25
	Nos. 632-634,C554-C556 (6)		22.50	1.50

Juan de Villegas and Cross of Father Yepez — A94

Virgin of Coromoto and Child — A95

1952, Sept. 14   *Perf. 11½*

635	A94	5c green	.25	.25
636	A94	10c red	1.25	.25
637	A94	20c dk gray bl	1.90	.60
638	A94	40c dp org	9.00	3.50
639	A94	50c brown	4.75	2.00
640	A94	1b violet	9.00	2.40
	Nos. 635-640 (6)		26.15	9.00
	Nos. 635-640,C557-C564 (14)		38.00	13.80

Founding of the city of Barquisimeto by Juan de Villegas, 400th anniv.

1952-53   *Perf. 11½x12*

Size: 17x26mm

641	A95	1b rose pink	8.00	1.25

Size: 26½x41mm

642	A95	1b rose pink ('53)	6.00	1.25

Size: 36x55mm

643	A95	1b rose pink ('53)	2.75	.95
	Nos. 641-643 (3)		16.75	3.45

300th anniv. of the appearance of the Virgin Mary to a chief of the Coromoto Indians.
Issue date: No. 641, Oct. 6.

Telegraph Stamps Surcharged in Black or Red

1952, Nov. 24   Engr.   *Perf. 12*

Grayish Security Paper

644		5c on 25c car	.30	.25
645		10c on 1b blk (R)	.30	.25

Surcharged

1952, Dec.

646		20c on 25c car	.35	.25
647		30c on 2b ol grn	2.10	1.40
648		40c on 1b blk (R)	.85	.45
649		50c on 3b red org	2.75	1.60
	Nos. 646-649 (4)		6.05	3.70

Post Office, Caracas — A96

1953-54   Unwmk.   *Perf. 13x12½*   Photo.

650	A96	5c green	.25	.25
a.		Bklt. pane of 10		
651	A96	7½c brt green	.35	.25
652	A96	10c rose carmine	.25	.25
a.		Bklt. pane of 10		
653	A96	15c gray	.40	.25
654	A96	20c ultra	.40	.25
655	A96	25c magenta	.40	.25
656	A96	30c blue	1.90	.25
657	A96	35c brt red vio	.85	.25
658	A96	40c orange	1.25	.40
659	A96	45c violet	1.90	.65
660	A96	50c red orange	1.25	.40
	Nos. 650-660 (11)		9.05	3.45

Issued: 20c, 30c, 45c, 3/11; 7½c, 25c, 6/53; 5c, 10c, 2/54; 15c, 1954.
See Nos. C565-C575, C587-C589.

Type of 1953-54 Inscribed "Republica de Venezuela"

A96a

1955

661	A96a	5c green		.25	.25
662	A96a	10c rose car		.25	.25
663	A96a	15c gray		.25	.25
664	A96a	20c ultra		.25	.25
665	A96a	30c blue		.65	.40
666	A96a	35c brt red vio		.65	.25
667	A96a	40c orange		1.00	.25
668	A96a	45c violet		1.25	.50
		Nos. 661-668 (8)		4.55	2.40
		Nos. 661-668,C597-C606 (18)		13.65	6.55

Arms of Valencia and Industrial Scene — A97

Coat of Arms — A98

1955, Mar. 26   Engr.   Perf. 12

669	A97	5c brt grn		.25	.25
670	A97	20c ultra		.40	.25
671	A97	25c reddish brn		.65	.25
672	A97	50c vermilion		1.00	.25
		Nos. 669-672,C590-C596 (11)		5.10	2.75

Founding of Valencia del Rey, 400th anniv.

1955, Dec. 9   Unwmk.   Perf. 11½

673	A98	5c green		1.10	.25
674	A98	20c ultra		3.75	.25
675	A98	25c rose car		3.00	.25
676	A98	50c orange		3.75	.25
		Nos. 673-676,C607-C612 (10)		19.90	3.50

1st Postal Convention, Caracas, 2/9-15/54.

Book and Map of the Americas — A99

Simon Bolivar — A100

1956   Photo.   Perf. 11½
Granite Paper

677	A99	5c lt grn & bluish grn		.25	.25
678	A99	10c lil rose & rose vio		.25	.25
679	A99	20c ultra & dk bl		.25	.25
680	A99	25c gray & lil gray		.55	.25
681	A99	30c lt bl & bl		.55	.25
682	A99	40c bis brn & brn		.65	.25
683	A99	50c ver & red brn		1.40	.65
684	A99	1b lt pur & vio		2.25	1.10
		Nos. 677-684 (8)		6.15	3.25
		Nos. 677-684,C629-C635 (15)		10.80	5.15

Book Festival of the Americas, 11/15-30/56.

Engraved, Center Embossed

1957-58   Unwmk.   Perf. 13½

685	A100	5c brt bl grn		.25	.25
686	A100	10c red		.25	.25
687	A100	20c lt slate bl		.40	.25
688	A100	25c rose lake		.40	.25
689	A100	30c vio blue		.50	.25
690	A100	40c red orange		.75	.25
691	A100	50c orange yel		1.10	.55
		Nos. 685-691 (7)		3.65	2.05
		Nos. 685-691,C636-C642 (14)		7.40	3.45

150th anniv. of the Oath of Monte Sacro and the 125th anniv. of the death of Simon Bolivar (1783-1830).
Issued: 10c, 50c, 1958; others, 11/15/57.

Hotel Tamanaco, Caracas A101

1957-58   Engr.   Perf. 13

692	A101	5c green		.25	.25
693	A101	10c carmine		.25	.25
694	A101	15c black		.25	.25
695	A101	20c dark blue		.30	.25
696	A101	25c dp claret		.30	.25
697	A101	30c dp ultra		.50	.25
698	A101	35c purple		.30	.25
699	A101	40c orange		.40	.25
700	A101	45c rose violet		.50	.25
701	A101	50c yellow		.70	.25
702	A101	1b dk slate grn		1.10	.45
		Nos. 692-702 (11)		4.85	2.95
		Nos. 692-702,C643-C657 (26)		14.65	7.30

Issued: 5c, 10c, Oct. 10, 1957; others, 1958.
For surcharge see No. 878.

Main Post Office, Caracas — A102

1958, May 14   Litho.   Perf. 14

703	A102	5c emerald		.25	.25
704	A102	10c rose red		.25	.25
705	A102	15c gray		.25	.25
706	A102	20c lt bl		.25	.25
707	A102	35c red lilac		.25	.25
708	A102	45c brt vio		1.25	.85
709	A102	50c yellow		.30	.25
710	A102	1b lt ol grn		.75	.40
		Nos. 703-710 (8)		3.55	2.75
		Nos. 703-710,C658-C670 (21)		15.80	10.85

See Nos. 748-750, C658-C670, C786-C792.
For surcharges see Nos. 865, C807, C856-C861.

Main Post Office, Caracas A103

1958, Nov. 17   Engr.   Perf. 11½x12

711	A103	5c green		.25	.25
712	A103	10c rose red		.40	.25
713	A103	15c black		.60	.25
		Nos. 711-713,C671-C673 (6)		2.45	1.50

Arms of Merida — A104

1958, Oct. 9   Photo.   Perf. 14x13½

714	A104	5c green		.25	.25
715	A104	10c bright red		.25	.25
716	A104	15c greenish gray		.25	.25
717	A104	20c blue		.25	.25
718	A104	25c magenta		.45	.25
719	A104	30c violet		.25	.25
720	A104	35c light purple		.30	.25
721	A104	40c orange		.65	.25
722	A104	45c deep rose lilac		.35	.25
723	A104	50c bright yellow		.55	.25
724	A104	1b gray green		1.60	.55
		Nos. 714-724 (11)		5.15	3.05
		Nos. 714-724,C674-C689 (27)		13.90	7.50

400th anniversary of the founding of the city of Merida. For surcharge see No. 873.

Arms of Trujillo, Bolivar Monument and Trujillo Hotel — A105

1959, Nov. 17   Unwmk.   Perf. 14

725	A105	5c emerald		.25	.25
726	A105	10c rose		.25	.25
727	A105	15c gray		.25	.25
728	A105	20c blue		.25	.25
729	A105	25c brt pink		.35	.25
730	A105	30c lt ultra		.50	.25
731	A105	35c lt pur		.50	.25
732	A105	45c rose lilac		.65	.35
733	A105	50c yellow		.65	.25
734	A105	1b lt ol grn		1.60	.85
		Nos. 725-734 (10)		5.25	3.20
		Nos. 725-734,C690-C700 (21)		10.95	5.95

Founding of the city of Trujillo, 400th anniv.

Stadium A106

1959 Mar. 10   Litho.   Perf. 13½

735	A106	5c brt grn		.35	.25
736	A106	10c rose pink		.35	.25
737	A106	20c blue		.60	.25
738	A106	30c dk bl		.70	.25
739	A106	50c red lilac		1.10	.25
		Nos. 735-739 (5)		3.10	1.25
		Nos. 735-739,C701-C705 (10)		5.55	2.45

8th Central American and Caribbean Games, Caracas, Nov. 29-Dec. 14, 1958.
#735-739 exist imperf. Value, pair $25.

Stamp of 1859, Mailman and José Ignacio Paz Castillo A107

1959, Sept. 15   Engr.   Perf. 13½x14

740	A107	25c org yel		.50	.25
741	A107	50c blue		.50	.25
742	A107	1b rose red		1.25	.45
		Nos. 740-742,C706-C708 (6)		3.90	1.85

Stamp of 1859 and: 50c, Mailman on horseback and Jacinto Gutierrez. 1b, Plane, train and Miguel Herrera.

1959, Sept. 15   Engr.   Perf. 13½x14

Centenary of Venezuelan postage stamps.

> **Catalogue values for unused stamps in this section, from this point to the end of the section, are for Never Hinged items.**

Alexander von Humboldt — A108

1960, Feb. 9   Unwmk.   Perf. 13½

743	A108	5c grn & yel grn		.35	.25
744	A108	30c vio bl & vio		1.40	.35
745	A108	40c org & brn org		1.75	.55
		Nos. 743-745,C709-C711 (6)		7.25	2.05

Centenary of the death of Alexander von Humboldt, German naturalist and geographer.

Post Office Type of 1958

1960, July   Litho.   Perf. 14

748	A102	25c yellow		.25	.25
749	A102	30c light blue		.25	.25
750	A102	40c fawn		.55	.25
		Nos. 748-750 (3)		1.05	.75

Newspaper, 1808, and View of Caracas, 1958 — A109

1960, June 6   Litho.   Perf. 14

751	A109	10c rose & blk		.40	.25
752	A109	20c lt blue & blk		.65	.25
753	A109	35c lilac & blk		1.40	1.00
		Nos. 751-753,C712-C714 (6)		8.70	3.75

150th anniv. (in 1958) of the 1st Venezuelan newspaper, Gazeta de Caracas.

Agustin Codazzi A110

1960, June 15   Engr.   Unwmk.

754	A110	5c brt green		.25	.25
755	A110	15c gray		1.10	.25
756	A110	20c blue		.85	.25
757	A110	45c purple		1.10	.50
		Nos. 754-757,C715-C720 (10)		9.35	3.70

Centenary (in 1959) of the death of Agustin Codazzi, geographer.
For surcharges see Nos. 869, C884.

National Pantheon — A111

Pantheon in Bister

1960, May 9   Litho.

758	A111	5c emerald		.25	.25
759	A111	20c brt blue		.60	.25
760	A111	25c light olive		.95	.25
761	A111	30c dull blue		1.10	.30
762	A111	40c fawn		1.60	.55
763	A111	45c lilac		1.50	.55
		Nos. 758-763 (6)		6.00	2.15
		Nos. 758-763,C721-C734 (20)		27.95	7.75

For surcharges see Nos. C894-C895.

Andres Eloy Blanco, Poet (1896-1955) A112

1960, May 21   Unwmk.   Perf. 14
Portrait in Black

764	A112	5c emerald		.30	.25
765	A112	30c dull blue		.40	.25
766	A112	50c yellow		.85	.30
		Nos. 764-766,C735-C737 (6)		5.25	1.85

For surcharge see No. C874.

Independence Meeting of April 19, 1810, Led by Miranda — A113

1960, Aug. 19   Litho.   Perf. 13½
Center Multicolored

767	A113	5c brt green		.50	.25
768	A113	20c blue		1.40	.35
769	A113	30c violet blue		1.75	.45
		Nos. 767-769,C738-C740 (6)		8.10	2.35

150th anniversary of Venezuela's Independence.

See Nos. 812-814, C804-C806. For surcharge see No. C893.

Drilling for Oil — A114

1960, Aug. 26   Engr.   Perf. 14
770 A114 5c grn & slate grn   2.75   .95
771 A114 10c dk car & brn   .90   .35
772 A114 15c gray & dull pur   1.25   .45
   Nos. 770-772,C741-C743 (6)   8.40   3.00

Issued to publicize Venezuela's oil industry.

Luisa Cáceres de Arismendi A115

Unwmk.
1960, Oct. 21   Litho.   Perf. 14
Center Multicolored
773 A115 20c light blue   1.75   .50
774 A115 25c citron   1.00   .40
775 A115 30c dull blue   1.90   .70
   Nos. 773-775,C744-C746 (6)   10.35   3.65

Death of Luisa Càceres de Arismendi, 94th anniv.

José Antonio Anzoategui — A116

1960, Oct. 29   Engr.
776 A116 5c emerald & gray ol   .45   .25
777 A116 15c ol gray & dl vio   .65   .25
778 A116 20c blue & gray vio   .90   .25
   Nos. 776-778,C747-C749 (6)   4.80   2.05

140th anniversary (in 1959) of the death of General José Antonio Anzoategui.

Antonio José de Sucre — A117

Unwmk.
1960, Nov. 18   Litho.   Perf. 14
Center Multicolored
779 A117 10c deep rose   .50   .25
780 A117 15c gray brown   .60   .30
781 A117 20c blue   .85   .40
   Nos. 779-781,C750-C752 (6)   6.00   2.45

130th anniversary of the death of General Antonio José de Sucre.

Bolivar Peak, Merida — A118

Designs: 15c, Caroni Falls, Bolivar. 35c, Guacharo caves, Monagas.

1960, Mar. 22   Perf. 14
782 A118 5c emerald & grn   1.25   1.25
783 A118 15c gray & dk gray   4.00   4.00
784 A118 35c rose lil & lil   3.50   3.50
   Nos. 782-784,C753-C755 (6)   15.50   15.50

Buildings and People — A119

1961   Litho.   Unwmk.
Building in Orange
785 A119 5c emerald   .25   .25
786 A119 10c carmine   .25   .25
787 A119 15c gray   .25   .25
788 A119 20c blue   .25   .25
789 A119 25c lt red brown   .25   .25
790 A119 30c dull blue   .25   .25
791 A119 35c red lilac   .35   .25
792 A119 40c fawn   .55   .25
793 A119 45c brt violet   .70   .30
794 A119 50c yellow   .55   .25
   Nos. 785-794 (10)   3.65   2.55

1960 national census. See #C756-C770. For surcharge see No. 866.

Rafael Maria Baralt — A120

1961, Mar. 11   Engr.   Perf. 14
795 A120 5c grn & slate grn   .25   .25
796 A120 15c gray & dull red brn   .50   .25
797 A120 35c rose lilac & lt vio   .75   .25
   Nos. 795-797,C771-C773 (6)   4.30   1.95

Rafael Maria Baralt, statesman, death cent.

Yellow-headed Parrot — A121

1961, Sept. 6   Litho.   Perf. 14½
798 A121 30c shown   1.25   .50
799 A121 40c Snowy egret   1.90   .50
800 A121 50c Scarlet ibis   3.00   .90
   Nos. 798-800,C776-C778 (6)   9.55   4.25

Juan J. Aguerrevere — A122

1961, Oct. 21   Unwmk.   Perf. 14
801 A122 25c dark blue   .25   .25
   a.   Souvenir sheet, imperf.   2.50   2.50

Centenary of the founding of the Engineering Society of Venezuela, Oct. 28, 1861.
No. 801a sold for 1b.
No. 801a exists with "Valor: Bs 1,00" omitted at lower left corner. Value, $7.

Battle of Carabobo, 1821 — A123

1961, Dec. 1   Perf. 14
Center Multicolored
802 A123 5c emerald & blk   .25   .25
803 A123 40c brown & blk   .60   .25
   Nos. 802-803,C779-C784 (8)   15.10   5.00

140th anniversary of Battle of Carabobo.

Oncidium Papilio Lindl. — A124

Orchids: 10c, Caularthron bilamellatum. 20c, Stanhopea Wardii Lodd. 25c, Catasetum pileatum. 30c, Masdevallia tovarensis. 35c, Epidendrum Stamfordianum Batem, horiz. 50c, Epidendrum atropurpureum Willd. 3b, Oncidium falcipetalum Lindl.

Perf. 14x13½, 13½x14
1962, May 30   Litho.   Unwmk.
Orchids in Natural Colors
804 A124 5c black & orange   .25   .25
805 A124 10c blk & brt grnsh bl   .25   .25
806 A124 20c black & yel grn   .55   .25
807 A124 25c black & lt blue   .80   .25
808 A124 30c black & olive   .90   .25
809 A124 35c black & yellow   1.00   .30
810 A124 50c black & gray   1.10   .35
811 A124 3b black & vio   6.75   2.75
   Nos. 804-811 (8)   11.60   4.65
   Nos. 804-811,C794-C803 (18)   28.10   10.10

For surcharges see Nos. 872, C885-C887.

Independence Type of 1960
Signing Declaration of Independence.

1962, June 11   Perf. 13½
Center Multicolored
812 A113 5c emerald   .30   .25
813 A113 20c blue   .50   .25
814 A113 25c yellow   .75   .30
   a.   Souv. sheet, #812-814, imperf   4.00   4.00
   Nos. 812-814,C804-C806 (6)   5.85   2.10

150th anniv. of the Venezuelan Declaration of Independence, July 5, 1811.
No. 814a sold for 1.50b.

Shot Put A125

1962, Nov. 30   Litho.   Perf. 13x14
815 A125 5c shown   .30   .25
816 A125 10c Soccer   .30   .25
817 A125 25c Swimming   .40   .25
   a.   Souv. sheet, #815-817, imperf   3.50   3.50
   Nos. 815-817,C808-C810 (6)   3.95   2.20

1st Natl. Games, Caracas, 1961. The stamps are arranged so that two pale colored edges of each stamp join to make a border around blocks of four.
No. 817a sold for 1.40b.
For surcharge see No. C899.

Vermilion Cardinal — A126

Malaria Eradication Emblem, Mosquito and Map — A127

Birds: 10c, Great kiskadee. 20c, Glossy black thrush. 25c, Collared trogons. 30c, Swallow tanager. 40c, Long-tailed sylph. 3b, Black-necked stilt.

1962, Dec. 14   Perf. 14x13½
Birds in Natural Colors, Black Inscription
818 A126 5c brt yellow grn   .25   .25
819 A126 10c violet blue   .25   .25
820 A126 20c lilac rose   .50   .25
821 A126 25c dull brown   .60   .25
822 A126 30c lemon   .75   .25
823 A126 40c lilac   1.00   .30
824 A126 3b fawn   7.00   3.00
   Nos. 818-824 (7)   10.35   4.55
   Nos. 818-824,C811-C818 (15)   27.95   11.45

For surcharges see Nos. 868, C880-C882.

Lithographed and Embossed
Perf. 13½x14
1962, Dec. 20   Wmk. 346
825 A127 50c brown & black   .80   .30

WHO drive to eradicate malaria. See Nos. C819-C819a.

White-tailed Deer A128

Designs: 10c, Collared peccary. 35c, Collared titi (monkey). 50c, Giant Brazilian otter. 1b, Puma. 3b, Capybara.

Perf. 13½x14
1963, Mar. 13   Litho.   Unwmk.
Multicolored Center; Black Inscriptions
826 A128 5c green   .25   .25
827 A128 10c orange   .25   .25
828 A128 35c red lilac   .25   .25
829 A128 50c blue   .55   .25
830 A128 1b rose brown   2.75   1.40
831 A128 3b yellow   5.50   3.50
   Nos. 826-831 (6)   9.55   5.90
   Nos. 826-831,C820-C825 (12)   23.75   11.00

For surcharges see #870-871, C888-C889.

Fisherman and Map of Venezuela A129

Cathedral of Bocono A130

1963, Mar. 21
832 A129 25c pink & ultra   .25   .25
   Nos. 832,C826-C827 (3)   1.60   1.05

FAO "Freedom from Hunger" campaign.

1963, May 30   Wmk. 346
833 A130 50c brn, red & grn, *buff*   .75   .25

400th anniversary of the founding of Bocono. See No. C828.

St. Peter's Basilica, Rome A131

1963, June 11   Perf. 14x13½
834 A131 35c dk bl, brn & buff   .45   .25
835 A131 45c dk grn, red brn & buff   .50   .25
    Nos. 834-835,C829-C830 (4)   3.75 1.35

Vatican II, the 21st Ecumenical Council of the Roman Catholic Church.

National Flag — A132

1963, July 29   Unwmk.   Perf. 14
836 A132 30c gray, red, yel & bl   1.00   .25

Centenary of Venezuela's flag and coat of arms. See No. C831.

Lake Maracaibo Bridge — A133

Perf. 13½x14
1963, Aug. 24   Wmk. 346
837 A133 30c blue & brown   .45   .25
838 A133 35c bluish grn & brn   .50   .25
839 A133 80c blue grn & brn   1.10   .45
    Nos. 837-839,C832-C834 (6)   6.65 2.55

Opening of bridge over Lake Maracaibo. For surcharge see No. 875.

Map, Soldier and Emblem — A134

1963, Sept. 10   Unwmk.
840 A134 50c red, bl & grn, *buff*   .75   .25

25th anniversary of the armed forces. See No. C835. For surcharge see No. C862.

Dag Hammarskjold and World Map — A135

Perf. 14x13½
1963, Sept. 25   Unwmk.
841 A135 25c dk bl, bl grn & ocher   .35   .25
842 A135 55c grn, grnsh bl & ocher   1.40   .40
    Nos. 841-842,C836-C837 (4)   4.60 1.85

"1st" anniv. of the death of Dag Hammarskjold, Secretary General of the UN, 1953-61.

See #C837a. For surcharges see #867, C875-C876.

Dr. Luis Razetti — A136

1963, Oct. 10   Litho.
843 A136 35c blue, ocher & brn   .60   .25
844 A136 45c mag, ocher & brn   .90   .25
    Nos. 843-844,C838-C839 (4)   5.60 2.40

Dr. Luis Razetti, physician, birth cent.

Dr. Francisco A. Risquez — A137

Design: 20c, Dr. Carlos J. Bello.

1963, Dec. 31   Perf. 11½x12
845 A137 15c multicolored   .25   .25
846 A137 20c multicolored   .30   .25
    Nos. 845-846,C840-C841 (4)   2.05 1.20

Cent. of the Intl. Red Cross.

Oil Field Workers — A138

10c, Oil refinery. 15c Crane & building construction. 30c, Cactus, train & truck. 40c, Tractor.

1964, Feb. 5   Litho.   Perf. 14x13½
847 A138   5c multi   .25   .25
848 A138 10c multi   .25   .25
849 A138 15c multi   .30   .25
850 A138 30c multi   .50   .25
851 A138 40c multi   .55   .25
    Nos. 847-851 (5)   1.85 1.25
    Nos. 847-851,C842-C846 (10)   3.35 2.10

Department of Industrial Development, cent.

Pedro Gual — A139

1964, Mar. 20   Unwmk.   Perf. 14
852 A139 40c lt olive green   .60   .25
853 A139 50c lt red brown   .80   .30
    Nos. 852-853,C847-C848 (4)   3.50 1.45

Pedro Gual (1784-1862), statesman.

Carlos Arvelo — A140

1964, Apr. 17   Engr.   Perf. 14x13½
854 A140 1b dull bl & gray   1.75   .55

Centenary of the death of Dr. Carlos Arvelo (1784-1862), chief physician of Bolivar's revolutionary army, director of Caracas Hospital, rector of Central University and professor of pathology.

For surcharge see No. 874.

Foundry Ladle and Molds A141

1964, May 22   Perf. 14x13½
855 A141 20c multicolored   .40   .25
856 A141 50c multicolored   .75   .25
    Nos. 855-856,C849-C850 (4)   4.00 1.45

Orinoco Steel Mills.

Romulo Gallegos, Novelist, 80th Birthday — A142

Unwmk.
1964, Aug. 3   Litho.   Perf. 12
857 A142   5c dk & lt green   .25   .25
858 A142 10c bl & pale bl   .25   .25
859 A142 15c dk & lt red lil   .40   .25
    Nos. 857-859,C852-C854 (6)   2.90 1.55

Angel Falls, Bolivar State A143

Tourist Publicity: 10c, Tropical landscape, Sucre State. 15c, San Juan Peaks, Guarico. 30c, Net fishermen, Anzoategui. 40c, Mountaineer, Merida.

1964, Oct. 22   Perf. 13½x14
860 A143   5c multi   .25   .25
861 A143 10c multi   .25   .25
862 A143 15c multi   .25   .25
863 A143 30c multi   .55   .25
864 A143 40c multi   .80   .25
    Nos. 860-864 (5)   2.10 1.25

Issues of 1958-64 Surcharged in Black, Dark Blue or Lilac

RESELLADO   VALOR   Bs. 0,05

1965
865 A102   5c on 1b (#710)   .60   .25
866 A119 10c on 45c (#793)   .25   .25
867 A135 15c on 55c (#842)   .25   .25
868 A126 20c on 3b (#824)   .25   .25
869 A110 25c on 45c (#757) (DB)   .25   .25
870 A128 25c on 1b (#830)   .40   .25
871 A128 25c on 3b (#831)   .45   .25
872 A124 25c on 3b (#811) (L)   .25   .25
873 A104 30c on 1b (#724)   .40   .25
874 A140 40c on 1b (#854)   .90   .25
875 A133 60c on 80c (#839)   1.25   .40
    Nos. 865-875 (11)   5.25 2.90

Lines of surcharge arranged variously; old denomination obliterated with bars on Nos. 867, 870-872. See Nos. C856-C899.

Revenue Stamps of 1947 Surcharged in Red or Black

CORREOS   RESELLADO   VALOR   Bs. 0,05

Imprint: "American Bank Note Co."

1965   Engr.   Perf. 12, 13½ (No. 882)
876 R1   5c on 5c emerald   .25   .25
877 R1   5c on 20c red brn   .25   .25
878 R1 10c on 10c brn ol   .25   .25
879 R1 15c on 40c grn   .25   .25

880 R1 20c on 3b dk bl (R)   .40   .25
881 R1 25c on 5b vio bl (R)   .80   .35
882 R1 25c on 5b vio bl (R) (Imprint: "Bundesdruckerei Berlin")   .40   .25
883 R1 60c on 3b dk bl (R)   1.00   .35
    Nos. 876-883 (8)   3.60 2.20

Type R1 is illustrated above No. 401.

John F. Kennedy and Alliance for Progress Emblem A144

1965, Aug. 20   Photo.   Perf. 12x11½
884 A144 20c gray   .50   .25
885 A144 40c bright lilac   .80   .25
    Nos. 884-885,C900-C901 (4)   3.65 1.40

Map of Venezuela and Guiana by Codazzi, 1840 — A145

Maps of Venezuela and Guiana: 15c, by Juan M. Restrepo, 1827, horiz. 40c, by L. de Surville, 1778.

1965, Nov. 5   Litho.   Perf. 13½
886 A145   5c multi   .25   .25
887 A145 15c multi   .40   .25
888 A145 40c multi   .70   .25
    a.   Souv. sheet, #886-888, imperf   8.00 8.00
    Nos. 886-888,C905-C907 (6)   3.45 1.65

Issued to publicize Venezuela's claim to part of British Guiana.

No. 888a sold for 85c.

Protesilaus Leucones — A146

Various Butterflies in Natural Colors Black Inscriptions

1966, Jan. 25   Litho.   Perf. 13½x14
889 A146 20c lt olive grn   1.25   .25
890 A146 30c lt yellow grn   2.50   .25
891 A146 50c yellow   3.75   .30
    Nos. 889-891,C915-C917 (6)   14.50 2.30

Ship and Map of Atlantic Ocean A147

1966, Mar. 10   Litho.   Perf. 13½x14
892 A147 60c brown, bl & blk   2.25   .70

Bicentenary of the first maritime mail.

"El Carite" Dance — A148

Various Folk Dances

Perf. 14x13½

1966, Apr. 5   Litho.   Unwmk.
893 A148   5c gray & multi   .25   .25
894 A148   10c orange & multi   .25   .25
895 A148   15c lemon & multi   .40   .25
896 A148   20c lilac & multi   .50   .25
897 A148   25c brt pink & multi   .70   .35
898 A148   35c yel grn & multi   .80   .40
    Nos. 893-898,C919-C924 (12)   11.80 4.70

Type of Air Post Stamps and

Arturo Michelena, Self-portrait A149

Paintings: 1b, Penthesileia, battle scene. 1.05b, The Red Cloak.

Perf. 12½x12, 12x12½

1966, May 12   Litho.   Unwmk.
899 A149   95c sepia & buff   .90   .65
900 AP74   1b multi   1.10   .65
901 AP74   1.05b multi   1.40   .65
    Nos. 899-901,C927-C929 (6) 7.05 3.60

Arturo Michelena (1863-1898), painter. Miniature sheets of 12 exist.

Construction Worker and Map of Americas — A150

Designs: 20c, as 10c. 30c, 65c, Labor monument. 35c, Machinery worker and map of Venezuela. 50c, Automobile assembly line.

1966, July 6   Litho.   Perf. 14x13½
902 A150   10c yellow & blk   .25   .25
903 A150   20c lt grnsh bl & blk   .30   .25
904 A150   30c lt blue & vio   .30   .25
905 A150   35c lemon & olive   .45   .25
906 A150   50c brt rose & claret   .60   .30
907 A150   65c salmon pink & brn   .80   .50
    Nos. 902-907 (6)   2.70 1.65

2nd Conference of Ministers of Labor of the Organization of American States.

Velvet Cichlid A151

1966, Aug. 31   Litho.   Perf. 13½x14
908 A151   15c shown   .30   .25
909 A151   25c Perch cichlid   .40   .25
910 A151   45c Piranha   1.00   .35
    Nos. 908-910,C933-C935 (6) 6.50 2.20

Nativity — A152

1966, Dec. 9   Litho.   Perf. 13½x14
911 A152   65c violet & blk   1.10   .40
    Christmas 1966.

Satellite, Radar, Globe, Plane and Ship A153

1966, Dec. 28   Perf. 13½x14
912 A153   45c multi   .80   .30
    Ministry of Communications, 30th anniv.

Rubén Dario — A154

1967   Litho.
913 A154   70c gray bl & dk bl   1.40   .65
    Rubén Dario (pen name of Felix Rubén Garcia Sarmiento, 1867-1916), Nicaraguan poet, newspaper correspondent and diplomat.

Old Building and Arms, University of Zulia A155

Perf. 13½x14

1967, Apr. 21   Litho.   Unwmk.
914 A155   80c gold, blk & car   1.40   .65
    University of Zulia founding, 75th anniv.

Front Page and Printing Press — A156

1968, June 27 Photo. Perf. 14x13½
915 A156   1.50b emer, blk & brn   2.00   .80
    Newspaper Correo del Orinoco, 150th anniv.

Boll Weevil A157

Insect Pests: 20c, Corn borer, vert. 90c, Tobacco caterpillar.

Perf. 14x13½, 13½x14

1968, Aug. 30   Litho.
916 A157   20c multicolored   .50   .25
917 A157   75c olive & multi   1.50   .25
918 A157   90c multicolored   2.10   .35
    Nos. 916-918,C989-C991 (6) 7.10 1.60

Guayana Substation A158

Designs: 45c, Guaira River Dam, horiz. 50c, Macagua Dam and power plant, horiz. 80c, Guri River Dam and power plant.

1968, Nov. 8   Litho.
919 A158   15c fawn & multi   .25   .25
920 A158   45c dl yel & multi   .75   .25
921 A158   50c bl grn & multi   1.10   .35
922 A158   80c blue & multi   1.60   .75
    Nos. 919-922 (4)   3.70 1.60
    Electrification program.

House and Piggy Bank A159

1968, Dec. 6   Litho.   Perf. 13½x14
923 A159   45c blue & multi   .80   .35
    National Savings System.

Nursery and Child Planting Tree A160

Designs: 15c, Child planting tree (vert.; this design used as emblem on entire issue). 30c, Waterfall, vert. 45c, Logging. 55c, Fields and village, vert. 75c, Palambra (fish).

Perf. 14x13½, 13½x14

1968, Dec. 19   Litho.
924 A160   15c multicolored   .35   .25
925 A160   20c multicolored   .35   .25
926 A160   30c multicolored   .40   .25
927 A160   45c multicolored   .55   .25
928 A160   55c multicolored   1.25   .35
929 A160   75c multicolored   .85   .25
    Nos. 924-929 (6)   3.75 1.60
    Nos. 924-929,C1000-C1005 (12) 10.55 4.05

Issued to publicize nature conservation.

Colorada Beach, Sucre A161

Designs: 45c, Church of St. Francis of Yare, Miranda. 90c, Stilt houses, Zulia.

1969, Jan. 24   Perf. 13½x14
930 A161   15c multicolored   .25   .25
931 A161   45c multicolored   .85   .25
932 A161   90c multicolored   1.25   .75
    Nos. 930-932,C1006-C1008 (6) 3.80 3.85

Tourist publicity. For souvenir sheet see No. C1007a.

Bolivar Addressing Congress of Angostura — A162

1969, Feb. 15   Litho.   Perf. 11
933 A162   45c multicolored   .80   .35
    Sesquicentennial of the Congress of Angostura (Ciudad Bolivar).

Martin Luther King, Jr. — A163

1969, Apr. 1   Litho.   Perf. 13½
934 A163   1b bl, red & dk brn   1.00   .30
    Rev. Dr. Martin Luther King, Jr. (1929-1968), American civil rights leader and recipient of the Nobel Peace Prize, 1964.

Tabebuia A164

Trees: 65c, Erythrina poeppigiana. 90c, Platymiscium.

1969, May 30   Litho.   Perf. 13½x14
935 A164   50c multicolored   .75   .25
936 A164   65c gray & multi   1.00   .25
937 A164   90c pink & multi   1.50   .40
    Nos. 935-937,C1009-C1011 (6) 5.35 1.65

Issued to publicize nature conservation.

Still Life with Pheasant, by Rojas — A165

Paintings by Cristobal Rojas (1858-1890): 25c, On the Balcony, vert. 45c, The Christening. 50c, The Empty Place (family). 60c, The Tavern. 1b, Man's Arm, vert.

Perf. 14x13½, 13½x14

1969, June 27   Litho.   Unwmk.
Size: 32x42mm, 42x32mm
938 A165   25c gold & multi   .25   .25
939 A165   35c gold & multi   .55   .25
940 A165   45c gold & multi   .90   .30
941 A165   50c gold & multi   1.00   .35
942 A165   60c gold & multi   1.40   .45

Perf. 11
Size: 26x53mm
943 A165   1b gold & multi   1.90   .70
    Nos. 938-943 (6)   6.00 2.30

ILO Emblem A166

1969, July 28   Perf. 13½
944 A166   2.50b fawn & blk   2.50 1.50
    50th anniv. of the ILO.

Charter and Coat of Arms A167

Industrial Complex A168

1969, Aug. 26   Litho.   Perf. 13½
945 A167 45c ultra & multi   .85 .30
946 A168 1b multicolored   1.25 .40

Industrial development.

House with Arcade, Carora — A169

Designs: 25c, Ruins of Pastora Church. 55c, Chapel of the Cross. 65c, House of Culture.

1969, Sept. 8   Perf. 13x14½
947 A169 20c multicolored   .25 .25
948 A169 25c multicolored   .40 .25
949 A169 55c multicolored   .90 .30
950 A169 65c multicolored   1.25 .45
        Nos. 947-950 (4)   2.80 1.25

400th anniversary of city of Carora.

Simon Bolivar in Madrid — A170

Designs: 10c, Bolivar's wedding, Madrid, 1802, horiz. 35c, Bolivar monument. Madrid.

Perf. 13½x14, 14x13½
1969, Oct. 28   Litho.
951 A170 10c multicolored   .25 .25
952 A170 15c brn red & blk   .45 .25
953 A170 35c multicolored   .60 .25
  a.   Souvenir sheet of 2   2.50 2.50
        Nos. 951-953 (3)   1.30 .75

Bolivar's sojourn in Spain. No. 953a contains 2 imperf. stamps similar to Nos. 952-953 with simulated perforation. Sold for 75c.

"Birds in the Woods" — A171

Design: 45c, "Children in Summer Camp." Both designs are after children's paintings.

1969, Dec. 12   Litho.   Perf. 12½
954 A171 5c emerald & multi   .25 .25
955 A171 45c red & multi   .90 .40

Issued for Children's Day.

Map of Great Colombia A172

1969, Dec. 16   Litho.   Perf. 11½
956 A172 45c multicolored   .70 .25

150th anniversary of the founding of the State of Great Colombia.

St. Anthony's, Clarines A173

Churches: 30c, Church of the Conception, Caroni. 40c, St. Michael's, Burbusay. 45c, St. Anthony's, Maturin. 75c, St. Nicholas, Moruy. 1b, Coro Cathedral.

1970, Jan. 15   Perf. 14
957 A173 10c pink & multi   .25 .25
958 A173 30c emerald & multi   .30 .25
959 A173 40c yellow & multi   .65 .25
960 A173 45c gray bl & multi   .90 .30
  a.   Souvenir sheet of 1, imperf.   2.00 2.00
961 A173 75c yellow & multi   1.25 .45
962 A173 1b orange & multi   1.50 .55
        Nos. 957-962 (6)   4.85 2.05

Colonial architecture.
No. 960a sold for 75c.

A174

Design: Seven Hills of Valera.

1970, Feb. 13   Litho.   Perf. 13x14½
963 A174 95c multicolored   1.25 .40

Sesquicentennial of the city of Valera.

A175

Flowers: 20c, Monochaetum Humboldtianum. 25c, Symbolanthus vasculosis. 45c, Cavedishia splendens. 1b, Befaria glauca.

1970, July 29   Litho.   Perf. 14x13½
964 A175 20c multicolored   .50 .25
965 A175 25c multicolored   .80 .25
966 A175 45c multicolored   1.10 .40
967 A175 1b multicolored   1.60 .55
        Nos. 964-967,C1049-C1052 (4)   4.00 1.45

Battle of Boyaca, by Martin Tovar y Tovar A176

1970, Aug. 7   Perf. 13½x14
968 A176 30c multicolored   .50 .25

150th anniversary of Battle of Boyaca.

Our Lady of Belén de San Mateo — A177

Designs: 35c, Pastoral Cross of Archbishop Silvestre Guevera y Lira, 1867. 40c, Our Lady of Valle. 90c, Virgin of Chiquinquira. 1b, Our Lady of Socorro de Valencia.

1970, Sept. 1   Perf. 14x13½
969 A177 35c gray & multi   .60 .25
970 A177 40c gray & multi   .70 .25
971 A177 60c gray & multi   1.00 .40
  a.   Souvenir sheet of 1, imperf.   1.75 1.75
972 A177 90c gray & multi   1.25 .55
973 A177 1b gray & multi   1.60 .65
        Nos. 969-973 (5)   5.15 2.10

The designs are from sculptures and paintings in various Venezuelan churches.
No. 971a sold for 75c.

Venezuela No. 22 and EXFILCA Emblem — A178

Designs: 20c, EXFILCA emblem and flags of participating nations, vert. 70c, Venezuela No. C13 and EXFILCA emblem, vert.

1970, Nov. 28   Litho.   Perf. 11
974 A178 20c yellow & multi   .40 .25
975 A178 25c dk blue & multi   .45 .25
976 A178 70c brown & multi   .90 .40
  a.   Souvenir sheet of 1, imperf.   1.75 1.75
        Nos. 974-976 (3)   1.75 .90

EXFILCA 70, 2nd Interamerican Philatelic Exhibition, Caracas, Nov. 27-Dec. 6. No. 976a is a hexagon with each side 50mm long. Sold for 85c.

Guardian Angel, by Juan Pedro Lopez — A179

1970, Dec. 1   Litho.   Perf. 14½x13½
977 A179 45c dull yellow & multi   .70 .30

Christmas 1970.

Jet and 1920 Plane A180

1970, Dec. 10   Perf. 13x14
978 A180 5c blue & multi   .30 .25

Venezuelan Air Force, 50th anniversary.

Question Mark Full of Citizens — A181

1971, Apr. 30   Litho.   Perf. 14x13½
Light Green, Red & Black
979   Block of 4   4.00 2.25
  a.   A181 30c frame T & T   .95 .45
  b.   A181 30c frame T & R   .95 .45
  c.   A181 30c frame L & B   .95 .45
  d.   A181 30c frame B & R   .95 .45

National Census, 1971. Sheet of 20 contains 5 No. 979 and 5 blocks of 4 labels. See No. C1054.

Battle of Carabobo A182

1971, June 21   Perf. 13½x14
980 A182 2b blue & multi   2.10 1.25

Sesquicentennial of Battle of Carabobo.

Map of Federal District — A183

State maps. 25c, 55c, 85c, 90c, vert.

1971   Litho.   Perf. 13½x14, 14x13½
981 A183 5c shown   .40 .25
982 A183 15c Monagas   .40 .25
983 A183 20c Nueva Esparta   .40 .25
984 A183 25c Portuguesa   .40 .25
985 A183 45c Sucre   .45 .25
986 A183 55c Tachira   .55 .25
987 A183 65c Trujillo   .65 .25
988 A183 75c Yaracuy   .75 .30
989 A183 85c Zulia   .95 .30
990 A183 90c Amazonas   1.50 .30
991 A183 1b Federal Dependencies   1.60 .55
        Nos. 981-991 (11)   8.05 3.20
        Nos. 981-991,C1035-C1048 (25)   19.20 6.85

Issued: 5c, 7/15; 15c, 20c, 8/16; 25c, 45c, 9/15; 55c, 65c, 10/15; 75c, 85c, 11/15; 90c, 1b, 12/15.

Madonna and Child A184   Luis Daniel Beauperthuy A185

Design: #993, Madonna & Jesus in manger.

1971, Dec. 1   Perf. 11
992 A184 25c multicolored   .60 .25
993 A184 25c multicolored   .60 .25
  a.   Pair, #992-993   1.25 .60

Christmas 1971. Printed checkerwise.

1971, Dec. 10   Perf. 14x13½
994 A185 1b vio bl & multi   1.25 .60

Dr. Luis Daniel Beauperthuy, scientist.

Globe in Heart Shape — A186

1972, Apr. 7 Litho. Perf. 14x13½
995 A186 1b red, ultra & blk   1.00 .60

"Your heart is your health," World Health Day 1972.

Flags of Americas and Arms of Venezuela A187

Designs: 4b, Venezuelan flag. 5b, National anthem. 10b, Araguaney, national tree. 15b, Map, North and South America. All show flags of American nations in background.

1972, May 16 Litho. Perf. 14x13½
996	A187	3b multicolored	4.00	1.00
997	A187	4b multicolored	4.25	1.75
998	A187	5b multicolored	4.75	2.25
999	A187	10b multicolored	9.00	3.00
1000	A187	15b multicolored	13.00	4.25
		Nos. 996-1000 (5)	35.00	12.25

"Venezuela in America."

Parque Central Complex A188

#1002, Front view ("Parque Central" on top). #1003, Side view ("Parque Central" at right).

1972, July 25 Perf. 11½
1001	A188	30c yellow & multi	.25	.25
1002	A188	30c blue & multi	.25	.25
1003	A188	30c red & multi	.25	.25
a.		Strip of 3, #1001-1003	1.40	1.40

Completion of "Parque Central" middle-income housing project, Caracas.

Mahatma Gandhi — A189

1972, Oct. 2 Litho. Perf. 13½x14
1004 A189 60c multicolored   .75 .40

103rd birthday of Mohandas K. Gandhi (1869-1948), leader in India's fight for independence, advocate of non-violence.

Children Playing Music — A190

Christmas: #1006, Children roller skating.

1972, Dec. 5 Litho. Perf. 13½x14
1005	30c multicolored		.25	.25
1006	30c multicolored		.25	.25
a.	A190 Pair, #1005-1006		1.00	1.00

Indigo Snake A191

Snake: 15c, South American chicken snake. 25c, Venezuelan lance-head. 30c, Coral snake. 60c, Casabel rattlesnake. 1b, Boa constrictor.

1972, Dec. 15 Litho. Perf. 13½x14
1007	A191	10c black & multi	.50	.35
1008	A191	15c black & multi	.50	.35
1009	A191	25c black & multi	.70	.35
1010	A191	30c black & multi	.80	.35
1011	A191	60c black & multi	1.50	.40
1012	A191	1b black & multi	2.25	.60
		Nos. 1007-1012 (6)	6.25	2.40

Copernicus — A192

Designs: 5c, Model of solarcentric system. 15c, Copernicus' book "De Revolutionibus."

1973, Feb. 19 Litho. Perf. 13½x14
1013	5c multicolored		.25	.25
1014	10c multicolored		.35	.25
1015	15c multicolored		.50	.25
a.	A192 Strip of 3, #1013-1015		1.10	.90

Sun — A193

Designs: Planetary system.

Size: 26½x29mm

1973 Litho. Perf. 13½
1016	A193	5c shown	.25	.25
1017	A193	5c Earth	.25	.25
1018	A193	20c Mars	.55	.25
1019	A193	20c Saturn	.40	.25
1020	A193	30c Asteroids	.45	.25
1021	A193	40c Neptune	.55	.25
1022	A193	50c Venus	.80	.40
1023	A193	60c Jupiter	.95	.45
1024	A193	75c Uranus	1.10	.55
1025	A193	90c Pluto	1.40	.80
1026	A193	90c Moon	2.00	.80
1027	A193	1b Mercury	2.25	.95

Size: 27x55mm
Perf. 12
1028	A193	10c Orbits and Saturn	.25	.25
1029	A193	15c Sun, Mercury, Venus, Earth	.40	.25
1030	A193	15c Jupiter, Uranus, Neptune, Pluto	.45	.25
a.		Strip of 3, #1028-1030	1.10	1.10
		Nos. 1016-1030 (15)	12.05	6.20

10th anniversary of Humboldt Planetarium. No. 1030a has continuous design showing solar system.
Issue dates: Nos. 1016, 1018, 1021, 1023-1025, Mar. 15; others Mar. 30.

OAS Emblem, Map of Americas — A194

1973, Apr. 30 Litho. Perf. 13½x14
1031 A194 60c multicolored   .55 .30

Organization of American States, 25th anniv.

José Antonio Paez — A195

Street of the Lancers, Puerto Cabello — A196

Designs: 10c, Paez in uniform. 30c, Paez and horse, from old print. 2b, Paez at Battle of Centauro, horiz. 10c, 2b are after contemporary paintings.

1973 Perf. 14x13½, 13½x14
1032	A195	10c gold & multi	.25	.25
1033	A195	30c red, blk & gold	.35	.25
1034	A195	50c bl, vio bl & dk brn	.60	.35
1035	A196	1b multicolored	1.25	.60
1036	A195	2b gold & multi	2.10	1.25
		Nos. 1032-1036 (5)	4.55	2.70

Gen. José Antonio Paez (1790-1873), leader in War of Independence, President of Venezuela. The 1b for the sesquicentenary of the fall of Puerto Cabello.
Issue dates: Nos. 1033-1034, May 6; Nos. 1032, 1036, June 13; No. 1035, Nov. 8.

José P. Padilla, Mariano Montilla, Manuel Manrique — A197

1b, Naval battle. 2b, Line-up for naval battle.

1973, July 27 Litho. Perf. 12½
1037	A197	50c multicolored	.35	.25
1038	A197	1b multicolored	1.00	.45
1039	A197	2b multicolored	2.00	1.00
		Nos. 1037-1039 (3)	3.35	1.70

150th anniv. of the Battle of Maracaibo.

Bishop Ramos de Lora — A198

1973, Aug. 1 Photo. Perf. 14x13½
1040 A198 75c gold & dk brn   .60 .25

Sesquicentennial of the birth of Ramos de Lora (1722-1790), first Bishop of Merida de Maracaibo and founder of the Colegio Seminario, the forerunner of the University of the Andes.

Plane, Ship, Margarita Island — A199

1973, Sept. 8 Litho. Perf. 14x13½
1041 A199 5c multicolored   .25 .25

Establishment of Margarita Island as a free port.

Map of Golden Road and Waterfall — A200

Designs (Road Map and): 10c, Scarlet macaw. 20c, Church ruins. 50c, 60c, Indian mountain sanctuary. 90c, Colonial church. 1b, Flags of Venezuela and Brazil.

1973, Oct. 1 Litho. Perf. 13
1042	A200	5c black & multi	.25	.25
1043	A200	10c black & multi	.25	.25
1044	A200	20c black & multi	.80	.25
1045	A200	50c black & multi	.85	.35
1046	A200	60c black & multi	.85	.35
1047	A200	90c black & multi	1.30	.40
1048	A200	1b black & multi	1.60	.55
		Nos. 1042-1048 (7)	5.90	2.40

Completion of the Golden Road from Santa Elena de Uairen, Brazil, to El Dorado, Venezuela.
Issued: 50c, 60c, Oct. 30; others Oct. 1.

Gen. Paez Dam and Power Station — A201

1973, Oct. 14 Perf. 14x13½
1049 A201 30c multicolored   .40 .25

Opening of the Gen. José Antonio Paez Dam and Power Station.

Child on Slide — A202

Designs: No. 1051, Fairytale animals. No. 1052, Children's book. No. 1053, Children disembarking from plane for vacation.

1973, Dec. 4   Litho.   Perf. 12
1050	A202	10c multicolored	.30	.25
1051	A202	10c multicolored	.30	.25
1052	A202	10c multicolored	.30	.25
1053	A202	10c multicolored	.30	.25
		Nos. 1050-1053 (4)	1.20	1.00

Children's Foundation Festival.

King Following Star — A203

Christmas: No. 1055, Two Kings.

1973, Dec. 5   Litho.   Perf. 14x13½
1054		30c multicolored	.55	.25
1055		30c multicolored	.55	.25
a.	A203	Pair, #1054-1055	1.25	1.25

Regional Map of Venezuela A204

1973, Dec. 13   Perf. 13½x14
1056	A204	25c multicolored	.40	.25

Introduction of regionalization.

Handicraft A205

Designs: 35c, Industrial park. 45c, Cog wheels and chimney.

1973, Dec. 18   Perf. 14x13½
1057	A205	15c blue & multi	.25	.25
1058	A205	35c multicolored	.30	.25
1059	A205	45c yellow & multi	.50	.25
		Nos. 1057-1059 (3)	1.05	.75

Progress in Venezuela and jobs for the handicapped.

Map of Carupano and Revelers — A206

1974, Feb. 22   Perf. 13½x14
1060	A206	5c multicolored	.30	.25

10th anniversary of Carupano Carnival.

Congress Emblem — A207

1974, May 20   Litho.   Perf. 13½
1061	A207	50c multicolored	.55	.25

9th Venezuelan Engineering Congress, Maracaibo, May 19-25.

Waves and "M" A208

Designs: Under-water photographs of deep-sea fish and marine life.

1974, June 20   Litho.   Perf. 12½
1062	A208	15c multicolored	.45	.25
1063	A208	35c multicolored	.70	.25
1064	A208	75c multicolored	.85	.30
1065	A208	80c multicolored	.85	.40
		Nos. 1062-1065 (4)	2.85	1.20

3rd UN Conference on the Law of the Sea, Caracas, June 20-Aug. 29.

Pupil and New School — A209

"Pay your Taxes" Campaign: 10c, 15c, 20c, like 5c. 25c, 30c, 35c, 40c, Suburban housing development. 45c, 50c, 55c, 60c, Highway and overpass. 65c, 70c, 75c, 80c, Playing field (sport). 85c, 90c, 95c, 1b, Operating room. All designs include Venezuelan coat of arms, coins and banknotes.

1974   Perf. 13½
1066	A209	5c blue & multi	.25	.25
1067	A209	10c ultra & multi	.25	.25
1068	A209	15c violet & multi	.25	.25
1069	A209	20c lilac & multi	.25	.25
1070	A209	25c multicolored	.25	.25
1071	A209	30c multicolored	.50	.25
1072	A209	35c multicolored	.25	.25
1073	A209	40c olive & multi	.40	.25
1074	A209	45c multicolored	.40	.25
1075	A209	50c green & multi	.40	.25
1076	A209	55c multicolored	.70	.40
1077	A209	60c multicolored	.55	.30
1078	A209	65c bister & multi	1.30	.60
1079	A209	70c multicolored	.60	.25
1080	A209	75c multicolored	.70	.30
1081	A209	80c brown & multi	.70	.30
1082	A209	85c ver & multi	.70	.30
1083	A209	90c multicolored	.85	.30
1084	A209	95c multicolored	1.50	.95
1085	A209	1b multicolored	.85	.40
		Nos. 1066-1085 (20)	11.65	6.60

Bolivar at Battle of Junin A210

1974, Aug. 6   Litho.   Perf. 13½x14
1086	A210	2b multicolored	2.00	1.00

Sesquicentennial of the Battle of Junin.

Globe and UPU Emblem — A211

50c, Postrider, sailing ship, steamer and jet.

1974, Oct. 9   Perf. 12
1087	A211	45c dk blue & multi	.45	.25
1088	A211	50c black & multi	.55	.25

Centenary of Universal Postal Union.

Rufino Blanco-Fombona — A212

Portraits of Blanco-Fombona and his books.

1974, Oct. 16   Litho.   Perf. 12½
1089	A212	10c gray & multi	.25	.25
1090	A212	30c yellow & multi	.25	.25
1091	A212	45c multicolored	.45	.25
1092	A212	90c buff & multi	.70	.35
		Nos. 1089-1092 (4)	1.65	1.10

Centenary of the birth of Rufino Blanco-Fombona (1874-1944), writer.

Children A213

1974, Nov. 29   Litho.   Perf. 13½
1093	A213	70c blue & multi	.60	.25

Children's Foundation Festival.

General Sucre — A214

Globe with South American Map and Flags — A215

Battle of Ayacucho — A216

1b, Map of South America with battles marked.

1974, Dec. 9   Perf. 14x13½, 13½x14
1094	A214	30c multicolored	.25	.25
1095	A215	50c multicolored	.40	.25
1096	A215	1b multicolored	.85	.40
1097	A216	2b multicolored	1.75	.85
		Nos. 1094-1097 (4)	3.25	1.85

Sesquicentennial of the Battle of Ayacucho.

Adoration of the Shepherds, by J. B. Mayno — A217

1974, Dec. 16   Photo.   Perf. 14x13½
1098		30c Shepherd	.35	.30
1099		30c Madonna & Child	.35	.30
a.	A217	Pair, #1098-1099	1.00	1.00

Christmas 1974.

Road Building, 1905 and El Ciempies Overpass, 1972 — A219

Designs: 20c, 1b, Jesus Muñoz Tebar, first Minister of Public Works. 25c, Bridges on Caracas-La Guaira Road, 1912 and 1953. 40c, View of Caracas, 1874 and 1974. 70c, Tucacas Railroad Station, 1911, and projected terminal, 1974. 80c, Anatomical Institute, Caracas, 1911, and Social Security Hospital, 1969. 85c, Quininari River Bridge, 1804, and Orinoco River Bridge, 1967.

1974, Dec. 18   Litho.   Perf. 12½
1100	A219	5c ultra & multi	.25	.25
1101	A219	20c ocher & blk	.30	.25
1102	A219	25c blue & multi	.35	.25
1103	A219	40c yellow & multi	.35	.25
1104	A219	70c green & multi	1.75	.30
1105	A219	80c multicolored	1.40	.35
1106	A219	85c orange & multi	1.75	.35
1107	A219	1b red & black	1.90	.60
		Nos. 1100-1107 (8)	8.05	2.60

Centenary of the Ministry of Public Works.

Women and IWY Emblem — A220

1975, Oct. 8   Litho.   Perf. 13½x14
1108	A220	90c multicolored	.60	.35

International Women's Year.

Scout Emblem and Tents — A221

1975, Nov. 11   Litho.   Perf. 13½x14
1109 A221 20c multicolored   .25   .25
1110 A221 80c multicolored   .60   .30

14th World Boy Scout Jamboree, Lille-hammer, Norway, July 29-Aug. 7.

Adoration of the Shepherds — A222

1975, Dec. 5   Litho.   Perf. 13½x14
1111 30c multicolored   .40   .40
1112 30c multicolored   .40   .40
  a. A222 Pair, #1111-1112   1.00 1.00

Christmas 1975.

Bolivar's Tomb — A224

Design: 1.05b, National Pantheon.

1976, Feb. 2   Engr.   Perf. 14x13½
1113 A224 30c gray & ultra   .25   .25
1114 A224 1.05b sepia & car   .60   .30

Centenary of National Pantheon.

Bolivia Flag Colors A225

1976, Mar. 22   Litho.   Perf. 13½
1115 A225 60c multicolored   .50   .25

Sesquicentennial of Bolivia's independence.

Aerial Map Survey — A226

1976, Apr. 8   Perf. 13½x12½
1116 A226 1b black & vio bl   .75   .35

Natl. Cartographic Institute, 40th anniv.

Gen. Ribas' Signature A227

José Felix Ribas A228

1976, Apr. 26   Photo.   Perf. 12½x13
1117 A227 40c red & green   .35   .25

Perf. 13½
1118 A228 55c multicolored   .45   .25

Gen. José Felix Ribas (1775-1815), independence hero, birth bicentenary.

Musicians of the Chacao School, by Armandio Barrios — A229

Lamas's Colophon A230

1976, May 13   Litho.   Perf. 13½
1119 A229 75c multicolored   1.25   .80

Photo.   Perf. 12½x13
1120 A230 1.25b buff, red & gray .70   .35

José Angel Lamas (1775-1814), composer, birth bicentenary.

Bolivar, by José Maria Espinoza — A231

1976   Engr.   Perf. 12
Size: 18x22½mm
1121 A231 5c green   .25   .25
1122 A231 10c lilac rose .25   .25
1123 A231 15c brown   .25   .25
1124 A231 20c black   .25   .25
1125 A231 25c yellow   .25   .25
1126 A231 30c violet bl   .25   .25
1127 A231 45c dk purple   .25   .25
1128 A231 50c orange   .25   .25
1129 A231 65c blue   .35   .25
1130 A231 1b vermilion   .45   .35

Size: 26x32mm
Perf. 12x11½
1131 A231 2b gray   .90   .35
1132 A231 3b violet blue 1.40 .55
1133 A231 4b yellow   1.75 .75
1134 A231 5b orange   2.10 1.00
1135 A231 10b dull purple 5.00 2.00
1136 A231 15b blue   7.25 2.75
1137 A231 20b vermilion   9.25 3.75
  Nos. 1121-1137 (17)   30.45 13.75

Issued: 5c-1b, May 17; 2b-20b, July 15.

Coil Stamps
1978, May 22   Perf. 13½ Horiz.
Size: 18x22½mm
1138 A231 5c green   .25   .25
1139 A231 10c lilac rose .25   .25
1140 A231 15c brown   .25   .25
1141 A231 20c black   .25   .25
1142 A231 25c yellow   .25   .25
1143 A231 30c violet blue .25   .25
1144 A231 45c dk purple   .25   .25
1144A A231 50c orange   .25   .25
1144B A231 65c blue   .25   .25
1144C A231 1b vermilion   .40   .25
  Nos. 1138-1144C (10)   2.65 2.50

Black control number on back of every fifth stamp.
See Nos. 1305-1307, 1362-1366, 1401-1409, 1482, 1484, 1487, 1490. Compare with designs A405-A406.

Maze A232

Central University A233

Faculty Emblems A234

1976, June 1   Litho.   Perf. 12½x13
1145 A232 30c multicolored   .25   .25
1146 A233 50c yel, org & blk   .35   .25
1147 A234 90c black & yellow   .70   .45
  Nos. 1145-1147 (3)   1.30   .95

Central University of Venezuela, 250th anniv.

"Unity" — A235

Designs: 45c, 1.25b, similar to 15c.

1976, June 29   Litho.   Perf. 12½
1148 A235 15c multicolored   .25   .25
1149 A235 45c multicolored   .35   .25
1150 A235 1.25b multicolored   .70   .45
  Nos. 1148-1150 (3)   1.30   .95

Amphictyonic Cong. of Panama, Sesqui.

Washington, US Bicent. Emblem A236

US Bicentennial Emblem and: No. 1152, Jefferson. No. 1153, Lincoln. No. 1154, F. D. Roosevelt. No. 1155, J. F. Kennedy.

1976, July 4   Engr.   Perf. 14
1151 A236 1b red brn & blk   .70   .35
1152 A236 1b green & blk   .70   .35
1153 A236 1b purple & blk   .70   .35
1154 A236 1b blue & blk   .70   .35
1155 A236 1b olive & blk   .70   .35
  Nos. 1151-1155 (5)   3.50 1.75

American Bicentennial.

Valve — A237

Computer drawings of valves & pipelines.

1976, Nov. 8   Photo.   Perf. 12⅓½x14
1156 A237 10c multicolored   .25   .25
1157 A237 30c multicolored   .25   .25
1158 A237 35c multicolored   .25   .25
1159 A237 40c multicolored   .25   .25
1160 A237 55c multicolored   .25   .25
1161 A237 90c multicolored   .45   .25
  Nos. 1156-1161 (6)   1.70 1.50

Nationalization of the oil industry.

Nativity, by Barbaro Rivas — A238

1976, Dec. 1   Litho.   Perf. 13x14
1162 A238 30c multicolored   .50   .30

Christmas 1976.

Ornament A239

Lithographed and Embossed
1976, Dec. 15   Perf. 14x13½
1163 A239 60c yellow & black   .50   .25

Declaration of Bogota (economic agreements of Andean countries), 10th anniv.

Coat of Arms of Barinas — A240

1977, May 25   Photo.   Perf. 12½x13
1164 A240 50c multicolored   .50   .50

400th anniv. of the founding of Barinas.

Crucified Christ, Patron Saint of La Grita — A241

1977, Aug. 6   Litho.   Perf. 13
1165 A241 30c multicolored   .30   .25

Founding of La Grita, 400th anniv. (in 1976).

Symbolic City — A242

1977, Aug. 26   Litho.   Perf. 13½
1166 A242 1b multicolored   .65   .30

450th anniversary of the founding of Coro.

Communications Symbols — A243

1977, Sept. 30   Litho.   Perf. 13½x14
1167 A243 85c multicolored   .65   .25

9th Interamerican Postal and Telecommunications Staff Congress, Caracas, Sept. 26-30.

Cable Connecting
with TV, Telephone
and Circuit
Box — A244

1977, Oct. 12   Litho.   Perf. 14
1168 A244 95c multicolored   .65   .25
Inauguration of Columbus underwater cable
linking Venezuela and the Canary Islands.

"Venezuela"
A245

Designs: "Venezuela" horizontal on 50c,
1.05b; reading up on 80c, 1.25b; reading down
on 1.50b.

1977, Nov. 26   Photo.   Perf. 13½x13
1169 A245 30c brt yel & blk   .25   .25
1170 A245 50c dp org & blk   .35   .25
1171 A245 80c gray & blk   .60   .25
1172 A245 1.05b red & blk   .65   .25
1173 A245 1.25b yel & blk   .80   .25
1174 A245 1.50b gray & blk   1.00   .25
      Nos. 1169-1174 (6)   3.65 1.60
Iron industry nationalization, 1st anniv.

Juan Pablo   Nativity, Colonial
Duarte — A246   Sculpture — A247

1977, Dec. 8   Engr.   Perf. 11x13
1175 A246 75c black & lilac   .55   .25
Duarte (1813-76), leader in liberation
struggle.

1977, Dec. 15   Litho.   Perf. 13
1176 A247 30c green & multi   .30   .25
Christmas 1977.

OPEC
Emblem — A248

1977, Dec. 20
1177 A248 1.05b brt & lt bl & blk   .60   .25
50th Conference of Oil Producing and
Exporting Countries, Caracas.

Bicyclist
A249

1978, Jan. 16   Litho.   Perf. 13½x13
1178 A249 5c Racing bicy-
            clists   .25   .25
1179 A249 1.25b shown   .80   .25
World Bicycling Championships, San Cristobal, Tachira, Aug. 22-Sept. 4.

Profiles
A250

1978, Apr. 21   Litho.   Perf. 13½x14
1180 A250 70c blk, gray & lil   .40   .25
Language Day.
Issued in tete-beche pairs. Value $1.25.

Magnetic
Computer
Tape and
Satellite
A251

1978, May 17   Litho.   Perf. 14
1184 A251 75c violet blue   .50   .25
10th World Telecommunications Day.

"1777-1977" — A252

Goya's Carlos
III as Computer
Print — A253

1978, June 23   Litho.   Perf. 12
1185 A252 30c multicolored   .25   .25
1186 A253 1b multicolored   .55   .25
200th anniversary of Venezuelan unification.

Bolivar Bicentenary

Juan Vicente Bolivar y Ponte, Father
of Simon Bolivar — A254

1978, July 24   Engr.   Perf. 12½
1187 A254 30c emerald & blk   .25   .25
1188 A254 1b multicolored   .55   .25

Bs. 2,50   Tito Salas - El Juramento del Monte Sacro - Fragmento - 1930 - Panteón Nacional

The Oath on Monte Sacro, Rome, by
Tito Salas — A255

Designs: 30c, Bolivar as infant in nurse-
maid's arms (detail from design of No. 1189).
No. 1189, Baptism of the Liberator, by Tito
Salas, 1929.

Souvenir Sheet
Litho.
Perf. 14
1189 A255 Sheet of 5   40.00 40.00
  a.   50c, single stamp   1.50 1.50

1978, Dec. 17   Engr.   Perf. 12½
Designs: 30c, Bolivar at 25. 1b, Simon Rodriguez. No. 1192, shown. (Bolivar's tutor).
1190 A254 30c multicolored   .25   .25
1191 A254 1b rose red & blk   .45   .25

Souvenir Sheet
Litho.
Perf. 14
1192 A255 Sheet of 5   24.00 24.00
  a.   50c, single stamp   1.10 1.10
Size of souvenir sheet stamps: 20x24mm.
Size of #1189: 154x130mm; #1192:
130x155mm.

1979, July 24   Engr.   Perf. 12½
Designs: 30c, Alexander Sabes Petion,
president of Haiti. 1b, Bolivar's signature.
No. 1195: a, Partial map of Jamaica, horiz.
b, Partial map of Jamaica, vert. c, Bolivar,
1816. d, Luis Brion. e, Petion.
1193 A254 30c org, vio & blk   .30   .25
1194 A254 1b red org & blk   .45   .25

Souvenir Sheet
Litho.
Perf. 14
1195 A255 Sheet of 5   4.00 4.00
  a.-e. 50c, any single   .35   .35
Size of souvenir sheet stamps: 26x20,
20x26mm.

1979, Dec. 17   Engr.   Perf. 12½
Designs: 30c, Bolivar. 1b, Slave. No. 1198,
Freeing of the Slaves, by Tito Salas. (30c, 1b,
details from design of No. 1198.)
1196 A254 30c multicolored   .25   .25
1197 A254 1b multicolored   .30   .25

Souvenir Sheet
Litho.
Perf. 14
1198 A255 Sheet of 5   6.50 6.50
  a.   50c, single stamp   1.10 1.10
Simon Bolivar, birth centenary. Size of souvenir sheet stamps: 22x28mm.
See Nos. 1228-1230, 1264-1266, 1276-
1284, 1294-1296, 1317-1322.

"T" and   Symbolic
"CTV" — A256   Design — A257

Designs: Different arrangement of letters "T"
and "CTV" for "Confederacion de Trabajeros
Venezolanos."

1978, Sept. 27   Photo.   Perf. 13x13½
1199   Strip of 5   .90   .90
  a.-e. A256 30c, single stamp   .25   .25
1200   Strip of 5   1.90 1.90
  a.-e. A256 95c, single stamp   .30   .25
Workers' Day.

1978, Oct. 3   Litho.   Perf. 14
1201 A257 50c dark brown   .65   .30
Rafael Rangel, physician and scientist, birth
cententary.

Drill Head,
Tachira Oil
Field
Map — A258

"P" as
Pipeline
A259

1978, Nov. 2   Litho.   Perf. 13½
1202 A258 30c multicolored   .25   .25
1203 A259 1.05b multicolored   .55   .25
Centenary of oil industry.

Star — A260

1978, Dec. 6   Litho.   Perf. 14
1204 A260 30c multicolored   .30   .25
Christmas 1978.

"P T" — A261

1979, Feb. 8   Litho.   Perf. 12½
1205 A261 75c black & red   .30   .25
Creation of Postal and Telegraph Institute.

"Dam Holding
Back Water"
A262

1979, Feb. 15   Photo.   Perf. 13½
1206 A262 2b silver, gray & blk   .90   .45
Guri Dam, 10th anniversary.

San Martin, by E. J. Maury — A263

60c, San Martin, by Mercedes. 70c, Monument, Guayaquil. 75c, San Martin's signature.

1979, Feb. 25   Litho.   Perf. 12½x13
1207 A263 40c blue, blk & yel   .25   .25
1208 A263 60c blue, blk & yel   .25   .25
1209 A263 70c blue, blk & yel   .35   .25
1210 A263 75c blue, blk & yel   .35   .25
      Nos. 1207-1210 (4)   1.20 1.00
José de San Martin (1778-1850), South
American liberator.

"Rotary" — A264

1979, Aug. 7   Litho.   Perf. 14x13½
1211 A264 85c gold & blk   .40   .25
Rotary Club of Caracas, 50th anniversary.

Our Lady of Coromoto Appearing to Children
A265

Engraved and Lithographed
1979, Aug. 23   *Perf. 13*
1212 A265 55c black & dp org   .30 .25
Canonization of Our Lady of Coromoto, 25th anniv.

London Residence, Coat of Arms, Miranda — A266

1979, Oct. 23   **Litho.**   *Perf. 14½x14*
1213 A266 50c multicolored   .30 .25
Francisco de Miranda (1750-1816), Venezuelan independence fighter.

O'Leary, Maps of South America and United Kingdom A267

1979, Nov. 6
1214 A267 30c multicolored   .30 .25
Daniel O'Leary (1801-1854), general, writer.

A268   A269

IYC Emblem and: 79c, Boy holding nest. 80c, Boys in water, bridge.

1979, Nov. 20   **Litho.**   *Perf. 14½x14*
1215 A268 70c lt blue & blk   .25 .25
1216 A268 80c multicolored   .30 .25
International Year of the Child.

1979, Dec. 1   **Litho.**   *Perf. 13*
1217 A269 30c multicolored   .30 .25
Christmas 1979.

Caudron Bomber, EXFILVE Emblem A270

EXFILVE Emblem and: No. 1219, Stearman biplane. No. 1220, UH-1H helicopter. No. 1221, CF-5 jet fighter.

1979, Dec. 15   *Perf. 11x11½*
1218 A270 75c multicolored   .25 .25
1219 A270 75c multicolored   .25 .25
1220 A270 75c multicolored   .25 .25
1221 A270 75c multicolored   .25 .25
   a.   Block of 4, #1218-1221   1.25 .60
Venezuelan Air Force, 59th anniv.; EXFILVE 79, 3rd Natl. Philatelic Exhibition, Dec. 7-17.

IPOSTEL Emblem, World Map A271

1979, Dec. 27   *Perf. 11½*
1222 A271 75c multicolored   .30 .25
Postal and Telegraph Institute, introduction of new logo.

Queen Victoria, Hill — A272

1980, Feb. 13   **Litho.**   *Perf. 12½*
1223 A272 55c multicolored   .30 .25
Sir Rowland Hill (1795-1879), originator of penny postage.

Dr. Augusto Pi Suner, Physiologist, Birth Centenary — A273

1980, Mar. 14   **Litho.**   *Perf. 11½*
1224 A273 80c multicolored   .40 .25

Spanish Seed Leaf — A274   Juan Lovera (1778-1841), Artist — A275

Lithographed and Engraved
1980, Mar. 27   *Perf. 13*
1225 A274 50c multicolored   .50 .25
Pedro Loefling (1729-56), Swedish botanist.

1980, May 25   **Litho.**   *Perf. 13½*
1226 A275 60c blue & dp org   .25 .25
1227 A275 75c violet & org   .30 .25

Bolivar Types of 1978
30c, Signing of document. 1b, House of Congress. #1230, Angostura Congress, by Tito Salas.

1980, July 24   **Engr.**   *Perf. 12½*
1228 A254 30c multicolored   .25 .25
1229 A254 1b multicolored   .40 .25

Souvenir Sheet
Litho.
Perf. 14
1230 A255   Sheet of 5   4.00 4.00
   a.   50c, single stamp   .25 .25
Simon Bolivar (1783-1830), revolutionary. Size of souvenir sheet stamps: 25x20mm, 20x25mm.

Dancing Girls, by Armando Reveron — A276

1980, Aug. 17   **Litho.**   *Perf. 13*
1231 A276 50c shown   .25 .25
Size: 25x40mm
1232 A276 65c Portrait   .55 .30
Armando Reveron (1889-1955), artist.

Bernardo O'Higgins — A277

Lithographed and Engraved
1980, Aug. 22   *Perf. 13x14*
1233 A277 85c multicolored   .75 .30
Bernardo O'Higgins (1776-1842), Chilean soldier and statesman.

School Ship Simon Bolivar A278

Frigate Mariscal Sucre A279

Perf. 11½ (#1234), 11x11½
1980, Sept. 13   **Litho.**
1234 A278 1.50b shown   1.25 .40
1235 A279 1.50b shown   1.25 .40
1236 A279 1.50b Submarine Picua   1.25 .40
1237 A279 1.50b Naval Academy   1.25 .40
   Nos. 1234-1237 (4)   5.00 1.60
"Picuda" is misspelled on stamp.

Workers Holding OPEC Emblem A280

20th Anniv. of OPEC (Organization of Petroleum Exporting Countries): #1239, Emblem.

1980, Sept. 14   **Litho.**   *Perf. 12x11½*
1238 A280 1.50b multicolored   .65 .30
1239 A280 1.50b multicolored   .65 .30

Death of Simon Bolivar A281

1980, Dec. 17   **Litho.**   *Perf. 11x11½*
1240 A281 2b multicolored   1.60 .50
Simon Bolivar, 150th anniversary of death.

A282

Lithographed and Engraved
1980, Dec. 17   *Perf. 13x12½*
1241 A282 2b multicolored   .90 .40
Gen. José Antonio Sucre, 150th anniv. of death.

A283

1980, Dec. 19   **Litho.**   *Perf. 14x13½*
1242 A283 1b Nativity by Rubens   .50 .35
Christmas 1980.

Helen Keller's Initials (Written and Braille) — A284

Lithographed and Embossed
1981, Feb. 12   *Perf. 12½*
1243 A284 1.50b multicolored   .65 .35
Helen Keller (1880-1968), blind and deaf writer and lecturer.

John Baptiste de la Salle — A285   San Felipe City, 250th Anniv. — A286

1981, May 15   **Litho.**   *Perf. 11½x11*
1244 A285 1.25b multicolored   .55 .25
Christian Brothers' 300th anniv.

1981, May 1   *Perf. 11½*
1245 A286 3b multicolored   1.10 .50

Municipal Theater of Caracas Centenary A287

1981, June 28   **Litho.**   *Perf. 12*
1246 A287 1.25b multicolored   2.00 .35

A288

1981, Sept. 15   Litho.   Perf. 11½
1247 A288 2b multicolored   .60   .25
UPU membership centenary.

A289

1981, Oct. 14   Litho.
1248 A289 1b multicolored   .45   .25
11th natl. population and housing census.

A290

1981, Dec. 3   Litho.   Perf. 11½
1249 A290 95c multicolored   .45   .25
9th Bolivar Games, Barquismeto.

19th
Cent.
Bicycle
A291

1981, Dec. 5   Photo.   Perf. 13x14
1250 A291   1b shown   .55   .35
1251 A291 1.05b Locomotive,
                  1926   .55   .35
1252 A291 1.25b Buick, 1937   .95   .50
1253 A291 1.50b Coach   1.25   .60
      Nos. 1250-1253 (4)   3.30 1.80
    See Nos. 1289-1292, 1308-1311.

Christmas
1981
A292

1981, Dec. 21   Litho.   Perf. 11½
1254 A292 1b multicolored   .35   .25

50th Anniv. of
Natural Science
Society — A293

1982, Jan. 21   Perf. 11½
1255 A293   1b Mt. Autana   .45   .25
1256 A293 1.50b Sarisarinama   .70   .40
1257 A293   2b Guacharo Cave   .90   .45
      Nos. 1255-1257 (3)   2.05 1.10

20th Anniv.
of
Constitution
A294

1982, Jan. 28   Photo.   Perf. 13x13½
1258 A294 1.85b gold & blk   .90   .35

A295   A296

1982, Feb. 19   Litho.   Perf. 13½
1259 A295 3b multicolored   1.40   .60
20th anniv. of agricultural reform.

1982, Mar. 12   Litho.   Perf. 13½
1260 A296 1b blue & dk blue   .45   .25
Jules Verne (1828-1905), science fiction
writer.

Natl.
Anthem
Centenary
(1981)
A297

1982, Mar. 26   Perf. 11½
1261 A297 1b multicolored   .65   .25

1300th Anniv. of   6th Natl. 5-
Bulgaria   Year Plan,
A298   1981-85
                      A299

1982, June 2   Litho.   Perf. 13½
1262 A298 65c multicolored   .35   .35

1982, June 11
1263 A299 2b multicolored   .45   .25

Bolivar Types of 1978
1982, July 24   Engr.   Perf. 12½
1264 A254 30c Juan José
                 Rondon   .30   .30
1265 A254   1b José Antonio
                 Anzoategui   .30   .30
Souvenir Sheet
Litho.   Perf. 14
1266 A255   Sheet of 5   4.50 4.50
  a.-e.   50c, any single   .30   .30
  Single stamps of No. 1266 show details
from Battle of Boyaca, by Martin Tovar y Tovar.
Size of souvenir sheet stamps: 19x26mm,
26x19mm.

Cecilio Acosta
(1818-1881),
Writer — A299a

1982, Aug. 13   Litho.   Perf. 11½
1266F A299a 3b multicolored   .65   .35

Aloe
A300

1982, Oct. 14   Photo.   Perf. 13
1267 A300 1.05b shown   .75   .40
1268 A300 2.55b Tortoise   1.90   .40
1269 A300 2.75b Tara amarilla
                  tree   2.10   .40
1270 A300   3b Guacharo bird   2.50   .45
      Nos. 1267-1270 (4)   7.25 1.65

Andres Bello (1781-1865), Statesman
and Reformer — A301

1982, Nov. 20   Litho.   Perf. 12
1271 A301 1.05b multicolored   .45   .25
1272 A301 2.55b multicolored   .95   .30
1273 A301 2.75b multicolored   .95   .30
1274 A301   3b multicolored   1.25   .35
      Nos. 1271-1274 (4)   3.60 1.20

Christmas
1982 — A302

Design: Holy Family creche figures by Francisco J. Cardozo, 18th cent.

Photogravure and Engraved
1982, Dec. 7   Perf. 13½
1275 A302 1b multicolored   .25   .25

Bolivar Types of 1978
1982-83   Engr.   Perf. 12½
1276 A254 30c Victory Monu-
                 ment, Carabobo   .25   .25
1277 A254 30c Monument to the
                 Meeting plaque   .25   .25
1278 A254 30c Antonio de Sucre   .25   .25
1279 A254   1b Jose Antonio
                 Paez   .35   .35
1280 A254   1b Sword hilt, 1824   .35   .35
1281 A254   1b Guayaquil Monu-
                 ment   .35   .25
      Nos. 1276-1281 (6)   1.80 1.50
Souvenir Sheets
Litho.   Perf. 14
1282 A255   Sheet of 5   5.00 5.00
  a.-e.   50c, any single   .30   .30
1283 A255   Sheet of 5   5.00 5.00
  a.-e.   50c, any single   .30   .30
1284 A255   Sheet of 5   5.00 5.00
  a.-e.   50c, any single   .30   .30
  No. 1282: Battle of Carabobo by Martin
Tovar y Tovar; No. 1283, Monument to the
Meeting; No. 1284, Battle of Ayacucho, by
Martin Tovar y Tovar.
  Issue dates: Nos. 1276-1277, 1279, 1281-
1283, Dec. 17; others, Apr. 18, 1983.

Gen. Jose Francisco
Bermudez — A303

Antonio
Nicolas
Briceno,
Liberation
Hero
A304

Perf. 13x13½, 15x14
1982, Dec. 23   Litho.
1285 A303 3b multicolored   1.60   .50
1286 A304 3b multicolored   1.60   .50

25th Anniv.
of 1958
Reforms
A305

1983, Jan. 23   Perf. 10½x10
1287 A305 3b multicolored   1.00   .45

A306

1983, Mar. 20   Photo.   Perf. 13½x13
1288 A306 4b olive & red   1.00   .45
25th anniv. of Judicial Police Technical Dept.

Transportation Type of 1981
Perf. 13½x14½
1983, Mar. 28   Photo.
1289 A291 75c Lincoln, 1923   1.10   .45
1290 A291 80c Locomotive, 1889   1.10   .45
1291 A291 85c Willys truck, 1927 1.40   .45
1292 A291 95c Cleveland motor-
                 cycle, 1920   1.40   .45
      Nos. 1289-1292 (4)   5.00 1.80

A307

1983, May 17   Photo.   Perf. 13x12½
1293 A307 2.85b multicolored   .65   .40
World Communications Year.

Bolivar Types of 1978
  Designs: 30c; Flags of Colombia, Peru,
Chile, Venezuela, and Buenos Aires. 1b;
Equestrian Statue of Bolivar.

Photo. & Engr. (#1294), Engr.
(#1295)
1983, July 25   Perf. 12½
1294 A254 30c multicolored   .35   .25
1295 A254   1b multicolored   .40   .25

Souvenir Sheet
Litho.
Perf. 14

1296	A255	Sheet of 5	5.00	4.75
a.-e.		50c, any single	.25	.25

Single stamps of No. 1296 show details of "The Liberator on the Silver Mountain of Potosi" Size of souvenir sheet stamps, 20x25mm.

9th Pan-American Games
A308   A309

Designs: #1303a, baseball. b, cycle wheel. c, boxing glove. d, soccer ball. e, target.

Lithographed and Engraved
1983, Aug. 25   Perf. 13

1297	A308	2b shown	.40	.25
1298	A308	2b Swimming	.40	.25
1299	A308	2.70b Cycling	.50	.40
1300	A308	2.70b Fencing	.50	.40
1301	A308	2.85b Runners	.55	.50
1302	A308	2.85b Weightlifting	.55	.50
		Nos. 1297-1302 (6)	2.90	2.30

Souvenir Sheet

1303		Sheet of 5	16.00	16.00
a.-e.	A309	1b, any single	16.00	16.00

#1303 for Copan '83. Size: 167x121mm.

25th Anniv. of Cadafe (State Electricity Authority) — A310

1983, Oct. 27   Litho.   Perf. 14

1304	A310	3b multicolored	1.40	.65

Redrawn Bolivar Type of 1976
1983, Sept. 29   Engr.   Perf. 12
Size: 26x32mm

1305	A231	25b blue green	11.50	5.50
1306	A231	30b brown	13.50	6.75
1307	A231	50b brt rose lilac	20.00	11.50
		Nos. 1305-1307 (3)	45.00	23.75

Transportation Type of 1981

Various views of Caracas Metro.

1983, Dec.   Photo.   Perf. 13½x14½

1308	A291	55c multicolored	.70	.45
1309	A291	75c multicolored	.70	.45
1310	A291	95c multicolored	.70	.45
1311	A291	2b multicolored	1.50	.65
		Nos. 1308-1311 (4)	3.60	2.00

Christmas 1983
A311

1983, Dec. 1   Litho.   Perf. 13x14

1312	A311	1b Nativity	.35	.35

Scouting Year (1982)
A312

Lithographed and Engraved
1983, Dec. 14   Perf. 12½x13

1313	A312	2.25p Pitching tent	.55	.35
1314	A312	2.55b Planting tree	.55	.35
1315	A312	2.75b Mountain climbing	.60	.35
1316	A312	3b Camp site	.60	.35
		Nos. 1313-1316 (4)	2.30	1.40

Bolivar Types of 1978

Designs: No. 1317, Title page of "Opere de Raimondo Montecuccoli" (most valuable book in Caracas University Library). No. 1318, Pedro Gual, Congress of Panama delegate, 1826. No. 1319, Jose Maria Vargas (b. 1786), University of Caracas pres. No. 1320, José Faustino Sanchez Carrion, Congress of Panama delegate, 1826.

1984   Engr.   Perf. 12½

1317	A254	30c multicolored	.25	.25
1318	A254	30c multicolored	.25	.25
1319	A254	1b multicolored	.25	.25
1320	A254	1b multicolored	.25	.25
		Nos. 1317-1320 (4)	1.00	1.00

Souvenir Sheets
Litho.
Perf. 14

1321	A255	Sheet of 5	4.75	4.50
a.-e.		50c, any single	.30	.30
1322	A255	Sheet of 5	5.25	5.25
a.-e.		50c, any single	.30	.30

Single stamps of No. 1321 show details of Arts, Science and Education, fresco by Hector Poleo; 1322, Map of South America, 1829. Size of souvenir sheet stamps: 20x30mm; 27x20mm.

Issued: #1317, 1319, 1321, 1/19; others, 1/20.

Radio Waves — A313

1984, Jan. 30   Litho.   Perf. 14x13

1323	A313	2.70b multicolored	.55	.25

Radio Club of Venezuela, 50th anniv.

Intelligentsia for Peace — A314

1984, Jan. 31

1324	A314	1b Doves	.25	.25
1325	A314	2.70b Profile	.55	.25
1326	A314	2.85b Flower, head	.55	.25
		Nos. 1324-1326 (3)	1.35	.75

President Romulo Gallegos (1884-1969)
A315

Gallegos: No. 1327, Portrait as a young man in formal dress. No. 1328, Portrait, 1948.

1984-85   Litho.   Perf. 11½

1327	A315	1.70b royal bl, dl bl, beige & blk	.65	.40
1328	A315	1.70b ocher, org brn & buff	.65	.40

Issued: #1327, 10/12/84; #1328, 1/18/85.
See Nos. 1335-1336.

Pan-American Union of Engineering Associations, 18th Convention
A316

1984, Oct. 28

1329	A316	2.55b pale buff, dk bl	.65	.25

Christmas 1984
A317

1984, Dec. 3

1330	A317	1b multicolored	.35	.25

Pope John Paul II, Statue of the Virgin of Caracas
A318

1985, Jan. 26   Litho.   Perf. 12

1331	A318	1b multicolored	1.40	.45

Papal visit, 1985.

Pascua City Bicent.
A319

1985, Feb. 10

1332	A319	1.50b multicolored	.55	.35

Dr. Mario Briceno-Iragorry (b. 1897), Historian — A320

1985, Oct.   Litho.   Perf. 12

1333	A320	1.25b silver & ver	.45	.25

Natl. St. Vincent de Paul Soc., Cent. — A321

1985, July

1334	A321	1b dk ol bis, ver & buff	.40	.25

Gallegos Memorial Type of 1984-85

Designs: Gallegos, diff.

1985, Aug. 8

1335	A315	1.70b gray grn, dk gray grn & dl gray grn	.30	.25
1336	A315	1.70b grn, sage grn & dl grn	.30	.25
		Dated 1984.		

Latin American Economic System, 10th Anniv.
A322

1985, Aug. 15

1337	A322	4b black & red	2.00	.85

Miniature Sheet

Virgin Mary, Birth Bimillennium — A323

Statues: a, Virgin of the Divine Shepherd. b, Chiquinquira Madonna. c, Coromoto Madonna. d, Valley Madonna. e, Virgin of Perpetual Succor. f, Virgin of Peace. g, Immaculate Conception Virgin. h, Soledad Madonna. i, Virgin of Consolation. j, Nieves Madonna.

1985, Sept. 9

1338		Sheet of 10	6.00	6.00
a.-j.	A323	1b, any single	.40	.25

OPEC, 25th Anniv.
A324

1985, Sept. 13

1339	A324	6b multicolored	1.50	.80

Opening of the Museum of Contemporary Art, Caracas — A325

1985, Oct. 24   Perf. 13½

1340	A325	3b multicolored	.80	.45
		Dated 1983.		

UN, 40th Anniv.
A326

1985, Nov. 15   Perf. 12

1341	A326	10b brt blue & ver	2.25	1.40

Intl. Youth
Year
A327

1985, Nov. 26
1342 A327 1.50b multicolored   .45 .25

Christmas 1985 — A328

Nativity: a, Sheperds. b, Holy Family, Magi.
Se-tenant in a continuous design.

1985, Dec. 2
1343 A328 Pair   1.75 1.75
 a.-b.   2b, any single   .85 .25

Dr. Luis Maria
Drago (b.
1859),
Politician
A329

1985, Dec. 20   *Perf. 13½*
1344 A329 2.70b tan, ver & sepia   .70 .50
                Dated 1984.

Miniature Sheet

Natl. Oil Industry, 10th Anniv. — A330

Designs: a, Industry emblem. b, Isla Oil
Refinery. c, Bariven oil terminal. d, Pequiven
refinery. e, Corpoven drilling rig. f, Maraven
offshore rig. g, Intevep labs. h, Meneven refinery. i, Lagoven refinery. j, Emblem, early drilling rig.

1985, Dec. 13   *Perf. 12*
1345   Sheet of 10   12.00 12.00
 a.-b. A330 1b multi   .25 .25
 c.-d. A330 2b multi   .55 .25
 e.-f. A330 3b multi   1.00 .35
 g.-h. A330 4b multi   1.25 .40
 i.-j. A330 5b multi   1.50 .50

Simon Bolivar
Memorial
Coins — A331

1985, Dec. 18
1346 A331   2b multicolored   .50 .35
1347 A331 2.70b multicolored   .70 .45
1348 A331   3b multicolored   .80 .50
        Nos. 1346-1348 (3)   2.00 1.30
                Dated 1984.

Guayana Development Corp., 25th
Anniv. — A332

1985, Dec. 27
1349 A332 2b Guayana City   .50 .40
1350 A332 3b Orinoco Steel Mill   .85 .50
1351 A332 5b Raul Leoni-Guri
             Hydro-electric
             Dam   1.40 .90
        Nos. 1349-1351 (3)   2.75 1.80

Bicentenario del Nacimiento
del Dr. José María Vargas

A333

Dr. Jose Vargas (1786-1854) — A334

Designs: No. 1352a, Handwriting and signature. b, Portrait, 1874, by Martin Tovar y Tovar.
c, Statue, Palace of the Academies. d, Flags,
EXFILBO '86 emblem. e, Vargas do Caracas
Hospital. f, Frontispiece of lectures manual,
1842. g, Portrait, 1986, by Alirio Palacios. h,
Gesneria vargasii. i, Bolivar-Vargas commemorative medal, 1955, 6th Natl. Medical Sciences Cong. j, Portrait, anonymous, 19th cent.
  No. 1353a, Portrait, facing front. b, Portrait,
facing left, Nos. 1352a, 1352d, 1352e, 1352h
and 1352i have horizontal vignettes.

Miniature Sheet
1986, Mar. 10   Litho.   *Perf. 12*
1352   Sheet of 10   11.00 11.00
 a.-j.   A333 3b, any single   .90 .40

Souvenir Sheet
Imperf
1353   Sheet of 2   13.50 13.50
 a.-b.   A334 15b, any single   6.00 1.00
   EXFILBO '86, Mar. 10-17, Caracas, 1st
Bolivarian exhibition.

Youths
Painting
School Wall
A335

1986, May 12   *Perf. 12*
1354 A335 3b shown   .75 .35
1355 A335 5b Repairing desk   1.25 .35
  Founding and maintenance of educational
institutions.

Francisco
Miranda's
Work for
American
Liberation,
Bicent.
(1981)
A336

Lithographed and Engraved
1986, Apr. 18   *Perf. 13*
1356 A336 1.05b multicolored   .25 .25
                Dated 1983.

INDULAC,
45th Anniv.
A337

1986, June 27   Litho.   *Perf. 12*
1357 A337 2.55b Milk trucks,
             vert.   .50 .25
1358 A337 2.70b Map, vert.   .60 .25
1359 A337 3.70b Milk processing
             plant   .70 .25
        Nos. 1357-1359 (3)   1.80 .75
  Industria Lactea (INDULAC), Venezuelan
milk processing company.

Miniature Sheet

Viasa Venezuelan Airlines, 25th
Anniv. — A338

a, Commemorative coin. b, Douglas DC-8
ascending. c, DC-8 taxiing. d, Boeing 747 in
flight. e, DC-10 tails. f, Map of hemispheres. g,
DC-10 taking off. h, Rear of DC-10 & DC8 on
runway. i, DC-9 over mountains. j, Crew in
cockpit.

1986, Aug. 11   Litho.   *Perf. 12*
1360   Sheet of 10   9.00 9.00
 a.-e.   A338 3b, any single   .55 .40
 f.-j.   A338 3.25b, any single   .60 .40

Miniature Sheet

Romulo Betancourt (1908-1981),
President — A339

a, i, Portrait with natl. flag. b, j, Seated in
armchair, smoking pipe. c, h, Wearing hat,
text. d, f, Wearing sash of office. e, g, Reading.

1986, Sept. 28
1361   Sheet of 10   10.00 10.00
 a.-e.   A339 2.70b, any single   .50 .25
 f.-j.   A339 3b, any single   .60 .25

Redrawn Bolivar Type of 1976
1986, Sept. 29   Litho.   *Perf. 12½*
1362 A231 25c red   .45 .35
1363 A231 50c blue   .45 .35
1364 A231 75c pink   .45 .35
1365 A231 1b orange   .45 .35
1366 A231 2b brt yellow grn   .55 .35
        Nos. 1362-1366 (5)   2.35 1.75
  Nos. 1362-1366 inscribed Armitano.
  For surcharges see Nos. 1453-1464.

Re-opening of
Zulia University,
40th
Anniv. — A340

1986, Sept. 29
1367 A340 2.70b shown   .45 .35
1368 A340 2.70b Library entrance .45 .35
 a.   Pair, #1367-1368   .90 .90

11th Congress of Architects,
Engineers and Affiliated
Professionals — A341

1986, Oct. 3
1369 A341 1.40b multicolored   .25 .25
1370 A341 1.55b multicolored   .25 .25
 a.   Pair, #1369-1370   .60 .60

Fauna
and
Flora
A342

1986, Sept. 12   Photo.   *Perf. 13½*
1371 A342 70c Priodontes
              maximus   .70 .60
1372 A342 85c Espeletia
              angustifolia   .70 .60
1373 A342 2.70b Crocodylus in-
              termedius   .70 .60
1374 A342   3b Brownea gran-
              diceps   .90 .65
        Nos. 1371-1374 (4)   3.00 2.45

Miniature Sheet

State Visit of Pope John
Paul II — A343

1986, Oct. 22   *Perf. 12*
1375   Sheet of 10   7.50 7.50
 a.   A343 1b, mountains   .25 .25
 b.   A343 2b Bridge   .40 .25
 c.   A343 3b Kissing the ground .50 .25
 d.   A343 3b Statue of Our Lady .50 .25
 e.   A343 4b Crosier, buildings .70 .25
 f.   A343 5.25b Waterfall   .95 .30

  #1375 contains 2 each #1375a-1375b,
1375e-1375f and one each #1375c-1375d.

Miniature Sheet

Children's Foundation, 20th
Anniv. — A344

Children's drawings: a, Three children. b, Hearts, children, birds. c, Child, animals. d, Animals, house. e, Landscape. f, Child, flowers on table. g, Child holding ball. h, Children, birds. i, Lighthouse, port. j, Butterfly in flight.

1986, Nov. 10
1376	Sheet of 10	5.50	5.50
a.-e.	A344 2.55b, any single	.40	.25
f.-j.	A344 2.70b, any single	.40	.25

Christmas — A345

Creche figures carved by Eliecer Alvarez.

1986, Nov. 10
1377	2b shown	.35	.25
1378	2b Virgin and child	.35	.25
a.	A345 Pair, #1377-1378	.75	.75

City Police,
25th Anniv.
A346

Emblem and: a, Emergency medical aid, helicopter. b, Security at sporting event. c, Bar code. d, Cadets in front of police academy. e, Motorcycle police.

1986, Dec. 10
1379	Strip of 5	4.00	4.00
a.-e.	A346 2.70b, any single	.50	.25

Folk Art
A347

Lithographed and Engraved
1987, Jan. 31   *Perf. 13*
1380	A347 2b Musical instrument	.60	.25
1381	A347 2b Fabric	.60	.25
1382	A347 3b Ceramic pot	.80	.25
1383	A347 3b Basket work	.80	.25
	Nos. 1380-1383 (4)	2.80	1.00

Dated 1983. Nos. 1380, 1382 show Pre-Hispanic art.

Discovery of the Tubercle Bacillus by
Robert Koch, Cent. (in 1982)
A348

Lithographed and Engraved
1987, Feb. 27   *Perf. 14x14½*
1384	A348 2.55b multicolored	1.60	.25

Dated 1983.

Miniature Sheet

Easter 1987 — A349

Paintings and sculpture: a, Arrival of Jesus in Jerusalem. b, Christ at the Column. c, Jesus of Nazareth. d, The Descent. e, The Solitude. f, The Last Supper. g, Christ Suffering. h, The Crucifixion. i, Christ Entombed. j, The Resurrection.

1987, Apr. 2   **Litho.**   *Perf. 12*
1385	Sheet of 10	17.50	17.50
a.-e.	A349 2b, any single	1.00	.25
f.-j.	A349 2.25b, any single	1.10	.25

World
Neurochemistry
Congress — A350

3b, Bolivar and Bello, outdoor sculpture by Marisol Escobar. 4.25b, Retinal neurons.

1987, May 8   **Litho.**   *Perf. 12*
1386	A350 3b multicolored	.50	.25
1387	A350 4.25b multicolored	.70	.25
a.	Pair, #1386-1387	3.00	3.00

Miniature Sheet

Tourism — A351

Hotels: a, f, Barquisimeto Hilton. b, g, Lake Hotel Intercontinental, Maracaibo. c, h, Macuto Sheraton, Caraballeda. d, i, Melia Caribe, Caraballeda. e, j, Melia, Puerto la Cruz.

1987, May 29   **Litho.**   *Perf. 12*
1388	Sheet of 10	13.00	13.00
a.-e.	A351 6b, any single	.70	.25
f.-j.	A351 6.50b, any single, diff.	.70	.25

Natl. Institute of Canalization, 35th
Anniv. — A352

1987, June 25   **Litho.**   *Perf. 12*
1389	A352	2b Map of Amazon territory waterways	.25	.25
1390	A352	4.25b Apure and Bolivar states waterways	.35	.25
g.		Pair, #1389-1390	1.00	1.00

Vicente Emilio Sojo (1887-1974),
Composer — A352a

2b, Academy of Fine Arts, Caracas. 4b, Sojos directing choir. 5b, Hymn to Bolivar score. 6b, Sojo, score on blackboard. 7b, Portrait, signature.

1987, July 1   **Litho.**   *Perf. 12*
1390A	Strip of 5	37.50	37.50
b.	A352a 2b tan & sepia	1.25	1.25
c.	A352a 4b tan & sepia	2.00	1.40
d.	A352a 5b tan & sepia	2.00	1.40
e.	A352a 6b tan & sepia	3.25	2.00
f.	A352a 7b tan & sepia	4.00	2.00

Printed in sheets of 10 containing two strips of five, black control number (UR).

Simon
Bolivar
University,
20th Anniv.
A353

Designs: a, Bolivar statue by Roca Rey, 1973. b, Outdoor sculpture of solar panels by Alejandro Otero, 1972. c, Rectory, 1716. d, Laser. e, Owl, sculpture, 1973.

1987, July 9   **Litho.**   *Perf. 12*
1391	Strip of 5	15.00	15.00
a.	A353 2b multicolored	.50	.25
b.	A353 3b multicolored	.75	.25
c.	A353 4b multicolored	1.00	.25
d.	A353 5b multicolored	1.25	.50
e.	A353 6b multicolored	1.50	.50

Miniature Sheet

Ministry of Transportation and
Communication — A354

Designs: a, Automobiles. b, Ship. c, Train, Cathedral. d, Letters, telegraph key. e, Communication towers. f, Highway. g, Airplane. h, Locomotive, rail caution signs. i, Satellite dish. j, Satellite in orbit.

1987, July 16
1392	Sheet of 10	9.00	9.00
a.-e.	A354 2b any single	.25	.25
f.-j.	A354 2.25b any single	.25	.25

Nos. 1392a and 1392f, 1392b and 1392g, 1392c and 1392h, 1392d and 1392i, 1392e and 1392j have continuous designs.

Miniature Sheet

Venezuela Navigation Company, 70th
Anniv. — A355

Designs: a, Corporate headquarters. b, Fork lift. c, Ship's Superstructure. d, Engine room. e, The Zulia. f, The Guarico. g, Ship's officer on the bridge. h, Bow of supertanker. i, Loading dock. j, Map of sea routes.

1987, July 31   **Litho.**   *Perf. 12*
1393	Sheet of 10	6.25	6.25
a.-b.	A355 2b, any single	.25	.25
c.-d.	A355 3b, any single	.25	.25

e.-f. A355 4b, any single	.30	.25
g.-h. A355 5b, any single	.40	.25
i.-j. A355 6b, any single	.45	.25

Nos. 1393a, 1393c, 1393e, 1393g and 1393i in vertical strip; No. 1393b, 1393d, 1393f, 1393h and 1393j in vertical strip.

Miniature Sheet

Natl. Guard, 50th Anniv. — A356

a, f, Air-sea rescue. b, g, Traffic control. c, h, Environment and nature protection. d, i, Border control. e, j, Industrial security.

1987, Aug. 6

1394	Sheet of 10	40.00	40.00
a.-e.	A356 2b, any single	.75	.25
f.-j.	A356 4b, any single	1.50	.50

Discovery of America, 500th Anniv. (in 1992) A357

20th cent. paintings (details): 2b, Departure from Port of Palos, by Jacobo Borges. 7b, Discovery of America, by Tito Salas. 11.50b, El Padre de las Casas, Protector of the Indians, by Salas. 12b, Trading in Venezuela at the Time of the Conquest, by Salas. 12.50b, Defeat of Guaicaipuro, by Borges.

1987, Oct.   Litho.   Perf. 12

1395	Strip of 5	11.00	11.00
a.	A357 2b multi	.25	.25
b.	A357 7b multi	.60	.30
c.	A357 11.50b multi	1.00	.45
d.	A357 12b multi	1.10	.55
e.	A357 12.50b multi	1.25	.55

Christmas 1987 — A358

Paintings and sculpture representing the Spanish Colonial School, 18th cent.: 2b, *The Annunciation,* by Juan Pedro Lopez (1724-1787). 3b, *Nativity,* by Jose Francisco Rodriguez (1767-1818). 5.50b, *Adoration of the Magi,* anonymous. 6b, *Flight into Egypt,* by Lopez.

1987, Nov. 17   Litho.   Perf. 12

1396	Block of 4	6.75	6.75
a.	A358 2b multi	.25	.25
b.	A358 3b multi	.30	.25
c.	A358 5.50b multi	.50	.30
d.	A358 6b multi	.60	.30

Miniature Sheet

Sidor Mills, 25th Anniv. — A359

Natl. steel production: a-d, Exterior view of steel plant (in a continuous design). e, Tower bearing the SIDOR emblem. f, Furnaces and molten steel flowing down gutters. g, Pooring steel rods. h, Slab mill. i, Steel rod production, diff. j, Anniv. emblem.

1987, Nov. 23

1397	Sheet of 10	11.00	11.00
a.	A359 2b multi	.25	.25
b.	A359 6b multi	.80	.40
c.	A359 7b multi	.95	.50
d.	A359 11.50b multi	1.50	.75
e.	A359 12b black	1.75	.80
f.	A359 2b multi	.25	.25
g.	A359 6b multi	.80	.40
h.	A359 7b multi	.95	.50
i.	A359 11.50b multi	1.50	.75
j.	A359 12b multi	1.75	.80

Meeting of 8 Latin American Presidents, 1st Anniv. — A360

1987, Nov. 26

1398	A360 6b multi	.80	.40

Pequiven Petrochemical Co., 10th Anniv. — A361

1987, Dec. 1

1399	Strip of 5	7.75	7.75
a.	A361 2b Plastics	.25	.25
b.	A361 6b Refined oil products	.60	.30
c.	A361 7b Fertilizers	.70	.30
d.	A361 11.50b Installations	1.10	.55
e.	A361 12b Expansion	1.25	.60

St. John Bosco (1815-88) A362

Portrait of Bosco and: 2b, Map, children. 3b, National Church, Caracas. 4b, Vocational training (printer's apprentice). 5b, Church of Mary Auxiliadora. 6b, Missionary school (nun teaching children).

1987, Dec. 8

1400	Strip of 5	4.00	4.00
a.	A362 2b multi	.25	.25
b.	A362 3b multi	.30	.25
c.	A362 4b multi	.40	.25
d.	A362 5b multi	.45	.25
e.	A362 6b multi	.60	.30

Redrawn Bolivar Type of 1976

1987, Dec. 31   Litho.   Perf. 12½

1401	A231 3b emerald grn	.35	.25
1402	A231 4b gray	.50	.25
1403	A231 5b vermilion	.65	.25
1404	A231 10b dark olive bister	1.50	.50
1405	A231 15b rose claret	2.50	.90
1406	A231 20b bright blue	3.00	1.10
1407	A231 25b olive bister	4.00	1.75
1408	A231 30b dark violet	4.75	1.90
1409	A231 50b carmine	7.75	3.00
	Nos. 1401-1409 (9)	25.00	9.90

Nos. 1401-1409 inscribed Armitano.

29th Assembly of Inter-American Development Bank Governors — A363

1988, Mar. 18   Litho.   Perf. 12

1410	A363 11.50b multi	1.50	.80

Miniature Sheet

Republic Bank, 30th Anniv. — A364

Bank functions and finance projects: a, Personal banking at branch. b, Capital for labor. c, Industrial projects. d, Financing technology. e, Exports and imports. f, Financing agriculture. g, Fishery credits. h, Dairy farming development. i, Construction projects. j, Tourism trade development.

1988, Apr. 11

1411	Sheet of 10	10.00	10.00
a.-e.	A364 2b any single	.35	.25
f.-j.	A364 6b any single	.50	.25

No. 1411 contains two strips of five.

Anti-Polio Campaign Day of Victory, May 25 — A365

Design: Polio victims pictured on bronze relief, Rotary and campaign emblems.

1988, May 20   Litho.   Perf. 12

1412	A365 11.50b multi	1.40	.65

Carlos Eduardo Frias (1906-1986), Founder of the Natl. Publicity Industry — A366

1988, May 27   Litho.   Perf. 12

1414	A366 Pair	4.00	4.00
a.	4b multi	.35	.25
b.	10b multi	.75	.45

Publicity Industry, 50th anniv.

Venalum Natl. Aluminum Corp., 10th Anniv. — A367

Designs: 2b, Factory interior. 6b, Electric smelter. 7b, Aluminum pipes. 11.50b, Aluminum blocks moved by crane. 12b, Soccer team, aluminum equipment on playing field.

1988, June 10

1415	Strip of 5	9.00	9.00
a.	A367 2b multi	.30	.25
b.	A367 6b multi	.80	.25
c.	A367 7b multi	.90	.25
d.	A367 11.50b multi	1.50	.55
e.	A367 12b multi	1.50	.55

Nature Conservation — A368

Birds: 2b, Carduelis cucullata. 6b, Eudocimus ruber. 11.50b, Harpia harpyja. 12b, Phoenicopterus ruber ruber. 12.50b, Pauxi pauxi.

1988, June 17   Litho.   Perf. 12

1416	Strip of 5	6.00	6.00
a.	A368 2b multi	.25	.25
b.	A368 6b multi	.60	.25
c.	A368 11.50b multi	1.10	.45
d.	A368 12b multi	1.25	.40
e.	A368 12.50b multi	1.25	.45

Army Day — A369

Military uniforms: a, Simon Bolivar in dress uniform, 1828. b, Gen.-in-Chief Jose Antonio Paez in dress uniform, 1821. c, Liberation Army division gen., 1810. d, Brig. gen., 1820. e, Artillery corpsman, 1836. f, Alferez Regiment parade uniform, 1988. g, Division Gen. No. 1 dress uniform, 1988. h, Line Infantry Regiment, 1820. i, Promenade Infantry, 1820. j, Light Cavalry, 1820.

1988, June 20

1417	Sheet of 10	15.00	15.00
a., f.	A369 2b multi	.30	.25
b., g.	A369 6b multi	.75	.25
c., h.	A369 7b multi	.90	.25
d., i.	A369 11.50b multi	1.50	.45
e., j.	A369 12b multi	1.60	.45

Scabbard, Sword and Signature A370

Paintings by Tito Salas: 4.75b, *The General's Wedding.* 6b, Portrait. 7b, *Battle of Valencia.* 12b, *Retreat from San Carlos.*

1988, July 1   Litho.   Perf. 12

1418	Strip of 5	7.50	7.50
a.	A370 2b shown	.35	.25
b.	A370 4.75b multi	.65	.25
c.	A370 6b multi	.75	.25
d.	A370 7b multi	1.25	.30
e.	A370 12b multi	2.75	.45

General Rafael Urdaneta (b. 1788).

General Santiago Marino (b. 1788), by Martin Tovar y Tovar — A371

1988, July
1419 A371 4.75b multi   .65 .35

1988 Summer Olympics, Seoul — A372

1988, Aug. 2
1420 A372 12b multi   1.40 .70

Electric Industry, Cent. A373

Buildings, 1888: 2b, 1st Office. 4.75b, Jaime Carrillo and electrical plant. 10b, Bolivar Plaza. 11.50b, Baralt Theater. 12.50b, Central Thermoelectric Plant, Ramon Lagoon, 1988.

1988, Oct. 25   Litho.   Perf. 12
1421   Strip of 5   6.50 6.50
  a. A373 2b multi   .25 .25
  b. A373 4.75b multi   .40 .25
  c. A373 10b multi   .80 .35
  d. A373 11.50b multi   .90 .45
  e. A373 12.50b multi   1.00 .45

Christmas — A374

Designs: 4b, Nativity (left side), by Tito Salas, 1936. 6b, Christ child, anonymous, 17th cent. 15b, Nativity (right side).

1988, Dec. 9
1422   4b multi   .40 .25
1423   6b multi   .70 .30
1424   15b multi   1.90 .90
  a. A374 Strip, #1423, 2 ea #1422, 1424   3.50 3.50

Miniature Sheet

Marian Year — A375

Icons: a, Our Lady of Copacabana, Bolivia. b, Our Lady of Chiquinquira, Colombia. c, Our Lady of Coromoto, Venezuela. d, Our Lady of the Clouds, Ecuador. e, Our Lady of Antigua, Panama. f, Our Lady of the Evangelization, Peru. g, Our Lady of Lujan, Argentina. h, Our Lady of Altagracia, Dominican Republic. i, Our Lady of Aparecida, Brazil. j, Our Lady of Guadalupe, Mexico.

1988, Aug. 15   Litho.   Perf. 12
1425   Sheet of 10   12.50 12.50
  a.-e. A375 4.75b any single   .50 .25
  f.-j. A375 6b any single   .55 .35

Juan Manuel Cagigal Observatory, Cent. — A376

Designs: 2b, Bardou refracting telescope. 4.75b, Universal theodolite AUZ-27. 6b, Bust of Cagigal. 11.50b, Boulton cupola and night sky over Caracas in September. 12b, Satellite photographing Hurricane Allen.

1989, Sept. 5
1426   Strip of 5   6.75 6.75
  a. A376 2b multicolored   .25 .25
  b. A376 4.75b multicolored   .45 .25
  c. A376 6b multicolored   .60 .30
  d. A376 11.50b multicolored   1.00 .50
  e. A376 12b multicolored   1.10 .60

Comptroller-General's Office, 50th Anniv. — A377

1988, Oct. 14   Litho.   Perf. 12
1427 A377 10b multi   1.10 .60

Portrait of Founder Juan Pablo Rojas Paul, by Cristobal Rojas, 1890 — A378

1989, Oct. 21   Litho.   Perf. 12
1428 A378   6b Commemorative medal   .60 .35
1429 A378 6.50b shown   .65 .35
  a. Pair, #1428-1429   1.50 1.50

Natl. History Academy, cent.

Portrait of Ricardo A379

Paintings: No. 1430, Simon Bolivar and Dr. Mordechay Ricardo. No. 1430A, The Octagon. Nos. 1430-1430A printed in continuous design completing the painting *The Liberator in Curacao*, by John de Pool.

1989, Jan. 27   Litho.   Perf. 12
1430   A379   10b multi   .75 .40
1430A A379   10b multi   .75 .40
1430B A379 11.50b shown   1.10 .50
  c. Strip of 5, #1430B, 2 ea #1430-1430A   9.25 9.25

Convention with Holy See, 25th Anniv. — A380

Designs: a, Raul Leoni, constitutional president, 1964-69. b, Cardinal Quintero, archbishop of Caracas, 1960-80. c, Arms of Cardinal Lebrun, archbishop of Caracas since 1980. d, Arms of Luciano Storero, titular archbishop of Tigimma. e, Pope Paul VI.

1989, May 4   Litho.   Perf. 12
1431   Strip of 5   5.00 5.00
  a.-b. A380 4b any single   .40 .25
  c.-d. A380 12b any single   1.00 .75
  e. A380 16b any single   1.40 1.00

Bank of Venezuela, Cent. A381

Designs: a, *Cocoa Harvest*, by Tito Salas, 1946. b, *Teaching a Boy How to Grow Coffee*, by Salas, 1946. c, Bank headquarters, Caracas. d, Archive of the Liberator, Caracas. e, Aforestation campaign (seedling). f, Aforestation campaign (five youths planting seedlings). g, 50-Bolivar bank note (left side). h, 50-Bolivar bank note (right side). i, 500-Bolivar bank note (left side). j, 500-Bolivar bank note (right side).

1989, Aug. 1
1432   Sheet of 10   12.50 12.50
  a.-f. A381 4b any single   .35 .25
  g.-j. A381 8b any single   .85 .50

Nos. 1432g-1432h and 1432i-1432j printed in continuous designs.

America Issue — A382

UPAE emblem and pre-Columbian votive bisque artifacts: 6b, Vessel. 24b, Statue of a man.

1989
1433 A382   6b multicolored   .80 .25
1434 A382   24b multicolored   3.50 1.75
  a. Pair, #1433-1434   5.00 5.00

Christmas A383

a, Shepherds, sheep. b, Angel appears to 3 shepherds. c, Holy Family. 12b, Two witnesses. 15b, Adoration of the kings.

1989   Litho.   Perf. 12
1435   Strip of 5   11.50 11.50
  a. A383 5b shown   .40 .25
  b.-c. A383 6b any single   .45 .25
  d. A383 12b multicolored   1.00 .45
  e. A383 15b multicolored   1.10 .60

Miniature Sheets

Bank of Venezuela, 20th Anniv. — A384

Tree and arms: No. 1436: a, Tabebuia chrysantha, national. b, Ceiba pentandra, Federal District. c, Myrospermum frutescens, Anzoategui. d, Pithecellobium saman, Aragua. e, Cedrela odorata, Barinas. f, Diptenyx punctata, Bolivar. g, Licania pyrofolia, Apure. h, Sterculia apetala, Carabobo.

No. 1437: a, Tabebuia rosea, Cojedes. b, Prosopis juliflora, Falcon. c, Copernicia tectorum, Guarico. d, Erythrina poeppigiana, Merida. e, Brawnea leucantha, Miranda. f, Mauritia flexuosa, Monagas. g, Malpighia glabra, Lara. h, Guaicum officinale, Nueva Esparta.

No. 1438: a, Swietenia macrophylla, Portuguesa. b, Platymiscium diadelphum, Sucre. c, Prumnopitys montana de Laub, Tachira. d, Roystonea venezuelana, Yaracuy. e, Cocos nucifera, Zulia. f, Hevea benthamiana, Federal Territory of Amazonas. g, Erythrina fusca, Trujillo. h, Rhizophora mangle, Territory of the Amacuro Delta.

1990, June 27   Litho.   Perf. 12
1436   Sheet of 8 + 2 labels   22.50 22.50
  a.-f. A384 10b any single   .65 .35
  g. A384 40b multicolored   2.50 1.25
  h. A384 50b multicolored   3.25 1.60
1437   Sheet of 8 + 2 labels   22.50 22.50
  a.-f. A384 10b any single   .65 .35
  g. A384 40b multicolored   2.50 1.25
  h. A384 50b multicolored   3.25 1.60
1438   Sheet of 8 + 2 labels   22.50 22.50
  a.-f. A384 10b any single   .65 .35
  g. A384 40b multicolored   2.50 1.25
  h. A384 50b multicolored   3.25 1.60

Central Bank of Venezuela, 50th Anniv. A385

Designs: a, Santa Capilla Headquarters, 1943. b, Headquarters, 1967. c, Left half of 500b Bank Note, 1940. d, Right half of 500b Bank Note, 1940. e, Sun of Peru decoration, 1825. f, Medals Ayacucho, 1824, Boyaca, 1820 and Liberators of Quito, 1822. g, Swords of Peru, 1825. h, Cross pendant, Bucaramanga, 1830. i, Medallion of George Washington, 1826. j, Portrait of Gen. O'Leary.

1990, Oct. 15
1439   Sheet of 10   15.00 15.00
  a.-f. A385 10b any single   .70 .40
  g.-h. A385 15b any single   1.00 .50
  i. A385 40b multicolored   2.75 1.40
  j. A385 50b multicolored   3.50 1.75

University of Zulia, Cent. A386

Designs: a, Dr. Francisco Ochoa, founder. b, Dr. Jesus E. Lossada, President, 1946-47. c, Soil conservation. d, Developing alternative automotive fuels. e, Organ transplants.

1990, Sept. 18   Litho.   Perf. 12
1440   Strip of 5   8.00 8.00
  a.-b. A386 10b any single   .50 .30
  c.-d. A386 15b any single   .75 .35
  e. A386 20b multicolored   1.10 .55

Christmas A387

Paintings: a, St. Joseph and Child by Juan Pedro Lopez. b, The Nativity by Lopez. c, The Return from Egypt by Matheo Moreno. d, The Holy Family by unknown artist. e, The Nativity (oval painting) by Lopez.

1990, Nov. 25
1441   Strip of 5   7.50 7.50
  a.-c. A387 10b any single   .50 .30
  d.-e. A387 20b any single   1.10 .55

OPEC, 30th
Anniv. — A388

a, Globe. b, Square emblem. c, Circular emblem. d, Diamond emblem. e, Flags.

1990, Dec. 21   **Litho.**   **Perf. 12**
1442   Strip of 5   8.00   8.00
a.-b.   A388 10b any single   .70   .40
  c.   A388 20b multicolored   1.50   .75
  d.   A388 30b multicolored   2.10   1.00
  e.   A388 40b multicolored   2.75   1.50

America
Issue — A389

1990, Dec. 12   **Litho.**   **Perf. 12**
1443   A389 10b Lake dwelling   1.50   .65
1444   A389 40b Coastline   4.00   2.25
  a.   Pair, #1443-1444   6.00   6.00

Exfilve '90, Caracas — A389a

Designs: 40b, Bank of Venezuela 1000b note. 50b, Bank of Caracas 100b note.

1990, Nov. 16   **Litho.**   **Imperf.**
1444B   A389a 40b multicolored   3.50   3.50
1444C   A389a 50b multicolored   4.50   4.50

No. 1444B, Bank of Venezuela, cent. No. 1444C, Bank of Caracas, cent.

St. Ignatius of
Loyola (1491-
1556)
A390

Designs: a, Jesuit quarters, Caracas. b, Death mask. c, Statue by Francisco de Vergara, 18th century. d, Statue of Our Lady of Montserrat, 11th century.

1991, Apr. 12   **Litho.**   **Perf. 12**
1445   Strip of 4 + label   12.50   12.50
a.-b.   A390 12b any single   .55   .30
  c.   A390 40b multicolored   2.00   .90
  d.   A390 50b multicolored   2.25   1.10

Venezuelan-American Cultural Center,
50th Anniv. — A391

Designs: a, Elisa Elvira Zuloaga (1900-1980), painter & engraver. b, Gloria Stolk (1912-1979), writer. c, Caroline Lloyd (1924-1980), composer. d, Jules Waldman (1912-

1990), publisher. e, William Coles (1908-1978), attorney.

1991, July 4   **Litho.**   **Perf. 12**
1446   Strip of 5   12.50   12.50
a.-c.   A391 12b any single   .55   .30
  d.   A391 40b multicolored   2.00   1.00
  e.   A391 50b multicolored   2.25   1.10

Miniature Sheet

Orchids — A392

Designs: No. 1447a, 12b, Acineta alticola. b, 12b, Brassavola nodosa. c, 12b, Brachionidium brevicaudatum. d, 12b, Bifrenaria maguirei. e, 12b, Odontoglossum spectatissimum. f, 12b, Catasetum macrocarpum. g, 40b, Mendocella jorisiana. h, 40b, Cochleanthes discolor. i, 50b, Maxillaria splendens. j, 50b, Pleurothallis dunstervillei. No. 1448, Cattleya violacea.

1991, Aug. 22   **Litho.**   **Perf. 12**
1447   A392   Sheet of 10,
     #a.-j.   18.00   18.00

Souvenir Sheet
1448   A392 50b multicolored   18.00   18.00

No. 1448 contains one 42x37mm stamp. No. 1447 exists imperf. Value $45.
See Nos. 1499-1500, 1508-1509.

Democratic Action Party, 50th
Anniv. — A393

Designs: a, People voting. b, Agricultural reform. c, Students and teachers. d, Nationalization of the petroleum industry.

1991, Sept. 13   **Litho.**   **Perf. 12**
1449   A393 12b Block of 4, #a.-d.   3.25   3.25

America
Issue
A394

1991, Oct. 24
1450   A394 12b Terepaima Chief   .60   .30
1451   A394 40b Paramaconi Chief   2.40   1.50
  a.   Pair, #1450-1451   3.50   3.50

Nos. 1450-1451 also exist imperf.

Children's Foundation, 25th
Anniv. — A395

Children's drawings: a, 12b, Children in house. b, 12b, Playground. c, 12b, Carnival. d, 12b, Woman and girl walking by pond. e, 12b, Boy in hospital. f, 12b, Five children around tree. g, 40b, Two girls in colorful room. h, 40b, Classroom. i, 50b, Three children. j, 50b, Four children dancing.

1991, Oct. 31   **Litho.**   **Perf. 12**
1452   A395   Sheet of 10, #a.-j.   17.00   17.00

Nos. 1362-1364
Surcharged

1991   **Litho.**   **Perf. 12½**
1453   A231   5b on 25c red   .30   .25
1454   A231   5b on 75c pink   .30   .25
1455   A231   10b on 25c red   .55   .30
1456   A231   10b on 75c pink   .55   .30
1457   A231   12b on 50c blue   .70   .40
1458   A231   12b on 75c pink   .70   .40
1459   A231   20b on 50c blue   1.10   .55
1460   A231   20b on 75c pink   1.10   .55
1461   A231   40b on 50c blue   2.10   1.10
1462   A231   40b on 75c pink   2.10   1.10
1463   A231   50b on 50c blue   2.75   1.40
1464   A231   50b on 75c pink   2.75   1.40
   Nos. 1453-1464 (12)   15.00   8.00

Christmas
A396

Children's art work: a, 10b, Wise men. b, 12b, Holy Family. c, 20b, Statues of Holy Family. d, 25b, Shepherds. e, 30b, Holy Family, cow, donkey.

1991, Nov. 14   **Litho.**   **Perf. 12**
1465   A396   Strip of 5, #a.-e.   6.75   6.75

Souvenir Sheet

Exfilve '91, Caracas — A397

1991, Nov. 29   **Litho.**   **Perf. 12**
1466   A397 50b No. 136   3.50   3.50

Discovery of
America,
500th Anniv.
(in 1992)
A398

a, 12b, Coat of arms of Columbus. b, 12b, Santa Maria. c, 12b, Map by Juan de la Cosa. d, 40b, Sighting land. e, 50b, Columbus with Queen Isabella and King Ferdinand II.

1991, Dec. 12   **Litho.**   **Perf. 12**
1468   A398   Strip of 5, #a.-e.   6.25   6.25

1992, Mar. 15

Designs: No. 1469a, 12b, Emblem for discovery of America Commission. b, 12b, Venezuelan pavillion, Expo '92. c, 12b, 15th century map of Spain. d, 12b, Portrait of Columbus, by Susy Dembo. e, 12b, Encounter, by Ivan Jose Rojas. f, 12b, 0x500 America, by Annella Armas. g, 40b, Imago-Mundi, by Alessandro Grechi. h, 40b, Long Journey, by Gloria Fiallo. i, 50b, Playa Dorado, by Carlos Riera. j, 50b, Irminaoro, by Erasmo Sanches Cedeno. No. 1470, Untitled work, by Muaricio Sanchez.

1469   A398   Sheet of 10,
     #a.-j.   18.00   18.00
1470   A398 50b multicolored   4.50   4.50

Expo '92, Seville. No. 1470 contains one 38x42mm stamp.

Protection of Nature — A399

Turtles: No. 1471a, Geochelone carbonaria, facing left. b, Geochelone carbonaria, facing right. c, Podocnemis expansa, facing left. d, Podocnemis expansa, swimming.

1992, June 12   **Litho.**   **Perf. 12**
1471   A399 12b Block of 4, #a.-d.   10.00   6.00

World Wildlife Fund.
No. 1471 also exists imperf.

Miniature Sheet

Beatification of Josemaria
Escriva — A400

Designs: a, 18b, Teaching in Venezuela, 1975. b, 18b, Celebrating mass. c, 18b, Parents, Jose Escriva and Dolores Albas. d, 18b, Text with autograph. e, 18b, Kissing feet of Madonna. f, 18b, Commemorative medallion. g, 60b, With Pope Paul VI. h, 60b, At desk, writing. i, 75b, Portrait. j, 75b, Portrait in St. Peter's Square, 1992.

1992, Oct. 2   Litho.   Perf. 12
1472 A400   Sheet of 10, #a.-j.   18.00 18.00

Electrification
of Southern
Regions
A401

Designs: a, 12b, Roof of native hut. b, 12b, Transmission lines and towers. c, 12b, Horses running through pond. d, 40b, Workmen under tower. e, 50b, Baskets, crafts.

1992, July 15   Litho.   Perf. 12
1473 A401   Strip of 5, #a.-e.   6.00 6.00

Miniature Sheet

Artwork, by
Mateo
Manaure — A402

Color of background: a, 12b, Red. b, 12b, Red violet. c, 12b, Gray. d, 12b, Violet brown. e, 40b, Brown. f, 40b, Blue. g, 50b, Blue violet. h, 50b, Black.

1993, July 23
1474 A402   Sheet of 8, #a.-h. +
2 labels   8.50 8.50

Bank of Maracaibo, 110th anniv.

Discovery of
America, 500th
Anniv. — A403

Paintings: a, 18b, The Third Trip, by Elio Caldera. b, 60b, Descontextura, by Juan Pablo Nascimiento.

1992, Nov. 20   Litho.   Perf. 12
1476 A403   Pair, #a.-b.   4.00 4.00

Christmas
A404

Artwork by Lucio Rivas: a, 18b, Adoration of the Shepherds. b, 75b, Adoration of the Magi. 100b, Flight into Egypt.

1992, Dec. 3   Litho.   Perf. 12
1477 A404   Pair, #a.-b.   3.50 3.50

Souvenir Sheet
1478 A404   100b multicolored   4.00 4.00

No. 1478 contains one 42x38mm stamp.

Redrawn Bolivar Type of 1976 and

A405   A406

Designs: 5b, Natl. Pantheon. 10b, Victory Monument, Carabobo. 20b, Jose Antonio Paez. 25b, Luisa Caceres de Arismendi. 35b, Ezequiel Zamora. 40b, Cristobal Mendoza. #1490, Central University. #1491, Jose Felix Ribas. #1494, Manuel Piar. 200b, Simon Bolivar.

1993-94   Litho.   Perf. 12½
Size: 18x22mm
1479	A405	1b silver	.35	.25
1480	A405	2b greenish blue	.35	.25
1482	A231	5b red	.35	.25
1484	A231	10b violet	.35	.25
1487	A231	20b olive green	.75	.35
1488	A405	25b red brown	.55	.45
1488A	A405	35b brt yel grn	.85	.55
1489	A405	40b lt blue	.90	.65
1490	A231	50b orange	2.00	.85
1491	A405	50b lilac rose	1.25	.90
1493	A406	100b brown	4.00	2.00
1494	A405	100b dark blue	2.50	1.40
1496	A405	200b brown	5.00	2.75
		Nos. 1479-1496 (13)	19.20	10.90

Nos. 1479-1493 inscribed Armitano.
See Nos. 1548-1562.

Orchid Type of 1991
Miniature Sheet

Designs: a, 20b, Cattleya percivaliana. b, 20b, Anguloa ruckeri. c, 20b, Chondrorhyncha flaveola. d, 20b, Stenia pallida. e, 20b, Zygosepalum lindeniae. f, 20b, Maxillaria triloris. g, 80b, Stanhopea wardii. h, 80b, Oncidium papilio. i, 100b, Oncidium hastilabium. j, 100b, Sobralia cattleya. 150b, Polycycnis muscifera.

1993, Apr. 1   Litho.   Perf. 12
1499 A392   Sheet of 10, #a.-j.   18.00 18.00

Souvenir Sheet
1500 A392   150b multicolored   7.50 7.50

Miniature Sheet

Settlement of Tovar Colony, 150th
Anniv. — A408

Designs: a, 24b, Woman. b, 24b, Children. c, 24b, Catholic Church, 1862. d, 24b, Statue of St. Martin of Tours, 1843. e, 24b, Fruits and vegetables. f, 24b, School, 1916. g, 80b, Home of founder, Augustin Codazzi, 1845. h, 80b, House of colony director, Alexander Benitz, 1845. i, 100b, Breidenbach Mill, 1860. j, 100b, Parade.

1993, Apr. 12   Litho.   Perf. 12
1501 A408   Sheet of 10, #a.-j.   18.00 18.00

Miniature Sheet

19th Pan-American Railways
Conference — A409

Designs: a, 24b, Tucacas steam locomotive. b, 24b, Halcon steam locomotive on Las Mostazas Bridge, 1894. c, 24b, Maracaibo locomotive. d, 24b, Tender, rail cars, Palo Grande Station. e, 24b, Fiat diesel locomotive, 1957. f, 24b, GP-9-L diesel locomotive, 1957. g, 80b, GP-15-L diesel locomotive, 1982. h, 80b, Metro subway train, Caracas. i, 100b, Electric locomotive. j, 100b, Passenger cars of electric train.

1993, May 25   Litho.   Perf. 12
1502 A409   Sheet of 10, #a.-j.   22.50 22.50

Nos. 1502c-1502d, 1502i-1502j are continuous designs.

A410   A411

World Day to Stop Smoking: a, 24b, Shown. b, 80b, "No smoking" emblem.

1993, May 27   Litho.   Perf. 12½x12
1503 A410   Pair, #a.-b.   4.00 4.00

1993, Oct. 7   Litho.   Perf. 12

America Issue: a, 24b, Amazona barbadensis. b, 80b, Ara macao.
1504 A411   Pair, #a.-b.   6.75 6.75

Miniature Sheets

Native
Indians — A412

Designs: No. 1505a, 1b, Two Yanomami children with painted bodies, spear. b, 1b, Yanomami woman preparing food. c, 40b, Two Panare children performing in Katyayinto ceremony. d, 40b, Panare man with nose flute. e, 40b, Taurepan man in canoe. f, 40b, Taurepan girl weaving. g, 40b, Piaroa woman with infant. h, 40b, Piaroa dancers wearing war masks. i, 100b, Hoti man blowing flute. j, 100b, Hoti woman carrying baby, basket over back.
150b, Child blowing traditional whistle.

1993, Nov. 25   Litho.   Perf. 12
1505 A412   Sheet of 10, #a.-j.   12.00 12.00

Souvenir Sheet
1506 A412   150b multicolored   4.50 4.50

Christmas
A413

Nativity scene: a, f, 24b, Joseph. b, g, 24b, Madonna and Child. c, h, 24b, Shepherd boy, wise man holding gift, lambs. d, i, 80b, Wise man with hands folded, boy. e, j, 100b, Wise man presenting gift, boy with hands folded.

1993, Nov. 30
1507 A413   Sheet of 10, #a.-j.   15.00 15.00

Nos. 1507f-1507j are black, magenta & buff.

Orchid Type of 1991
Miniature Sheet

Designs: a, 35b, Chrysocycnis schlimii. b, 35b, Galeandra minax. c, 35b, Oncidium falcipetalum. d, 35b, Oncidium lanceanum. e, 40b, Sobralia violacea linden. f, 40b, Sobralia infundibuligera. g, 80b, Mendoncella burkei. h, 80b, Phragmipedium caudatum. i, 100b, Phragmipedium kaieteurum. j, 100b, Phragmipedium kaieteurum. j, 200b, Stanhopea grandiflora.
150b, Epidendrum elongatum.

1994, May 19   Litho.   Perf. 12
1508 A392   Sheet of 10, #a.-j.   18.00 18.00

Souvenir Sheet
1509 A392   150b multicolored   3.75 3.75

No. 1509 contains one 42x37mm stamp.

Miniature Sheet of 10

FEDECAMARAS (Federal Council of Production & Commerce Associations), 50th Anniv. — A414

a, 35b; f, 80b, Anniversary emblem. b, 35b; e, 80b, Luis Gonzalo Marturet (1914-64), 1st president. c, 35b; d, 80b, FEDECAMARAS emblem.

1994, July 17   Litho.   Perf. 12
1510 A414   #c, f, 2 ea #a-b, d-e   13.50 13.50

Judicial
Service
A415

1994, Sept. 13   Litho.   Perf. 12
1511 A415 100b multicolored   1.75 1.75

Miniature Sheet

Christmas — A416

Paintings: a, 35b, g, 80b, The Nativity, by follower of Jose Lorenzo de Alvarado. b, 35b, h, 80b, Birth of Christ, 19th cent. c, 35b, i, 80b, The Nativity, diff., by follower of Jose Lorenzo de Alvarado. d, 35b, j, 80b, Adoration of the Magi, 17th cent.. e, 35b, f, 80b, Birth of Christ, by School of Tocuyo.

1994, Dec. 1
1512 A416   Sheet of 10, #a.-j.   13.50 13.50

Miniature Sheet

Antonio Jose de Sucre (1795-1830) — A417

Designs: No. 1513a, 25b, Portrait. b, 25b, Dona Mariana Carcelen Y Larrea Marquesa de Solanda. c, 35b, Top of equestrian monument. d, 35b, Bottom of monument. e, 40b, Painting of Battle of Pichincha, mountains at top. f, 40b, Painting of Battle of Pichincha, battle scent. g, 80b, Painting of Battle of Ayacucho, soldiers on horseback. h, 80b, Painting of Battle of Ayacucho, dead soldiers. i, 100b, Painting of Surrender at Ayachucho, general signing document. j, 100b, Painting of Surrender at Ayachucho, seated general at right.
150b, Portion of mural, Carabobo, by Pedro Centeno Vallenilla.

1995, Feb. 2
1513 A417   Sheet of 10, #a.-j.   13.50 13.50
Souvenir Sheet
1514 A417 150b multicolored   3.50 3.50

Postal Transportation — A418

a, 35b, Post office van. b, 80b, Airplane.

1995, Mar. 22   Litho.   Perf. 12
1515 A418   Pair, #a.-b.   2.50 2.50

No. 1515 issued in sheets of 10 stamps.

Miniature Sheet

St. Jean-Baptiste de La Salle (1651-1719), Educator — A419

Denomination LR: a, 100b, Portrait. b, 35b, Students with microscope, academic education. c, 35b, Soccer players, sports education. d, 35b, Scouts at camp, citizenship education. e, 80b, La Salle College, Caracas.
Denomination LL: f, like #1516e. g, like #1516d. h, like #1516b. i, like #1516c. j, like #1516a.

1995, May 15
1516 A419   Sheet of 10, #a.-j.   11.00 11.00

Miniature Sheet

Founding of Salesian Order, Cent. — A420

Designs: a, 35b, St. John Bosco (1815-88), priest with child. b, 35b, Lonely child, Madonna and Child. c, 35b, Man running machine tool. d, 35b, Young men working with electronic instruments. e, 35b, Baseball game. f, 35b, Basketball game. g, 80b, People working in fields. h, 80b, Man looking at chili peppers. i, 100b, Young tribal natives receiving religious training. j, 100b, Tribal native.

1995, Apr. 26
1517 A420   Sheet of 10, #a.-j.   11.00 11.00

Miniature Sheet

Orchids — A421

Designs: a, 35b, Maxillaria guareimensis. b, 35b, Paphinia lindeniana. c, 50b, Catasetum longifolium. d, 50b, Anguloa clowesii. e, 35b, Coryanthes biflora. f, 35b, Catasetum pileatum. g, 80b, Maxillaria histrionica. h, 80b, Sobralia ruckeri. i, 35b, Mormodes convolutum. j, 35b, Huntleya lucida.
150b, Catasetum barbatum.

1995, May 31   Litho.   Perf. 12
1518 A421   Sheet of 10, #a.-j.   12.00 12.00
Souvenir Sheet
1519 A421 150b multicolored   3.50 3.50

No. 1519 contains one 42x36mm stamp.
See #1534-1535, 1563-1564, 1587-1588.

CAF (Andes
Development
Corporation),
25th
Anniv. — A422

1995, June 7
1520 A422 80b multicolored   1.50 1.50

Miniature Sheet

Beatification of Mother Maria of San Jose — A423

Designs: a, 35b, In formal habit. b, 35b, Pope John Paul II. c, 35b, As young woman distributing Bibles. d, 35b, Doing embroidery work. e, 35b, Statue of Madonna, altar. f, 35b, Kneeling in devotions. g, 80b, Walking with Sisters in hospital. h, 80b, With patient in hospital. i, 100b, Working with children. j, 100b, Helping person seated along road.

1995, July 2
1521 A423 Sheet of 10, #a.-j. 11.00 11.00
   Nos. 1521a-1521b, 1521c-1521d, 1521e-1521f, 1521g-1521h, 1521i-1521j are each continuous designs.

UN, 50th Anniv. — A424

Designs: a, People from different countries unfurling UN flag. b, Emblem on UN flag.

1995, June 26
1522 A424 50b Pair, #a.-b.   3.25 3.25

Gen. José Gregorio Monagas (1795-1858), President, Liberator of the Slaves — A425

a, Portrait. b, Slave family with opened chains.

1995, July 26   Litho.   Perf. 12
1523 A425 50b Pair, #a.-b.   2.00 2.00

Slave Rebellion, Bicent. — A426

Jose Leonardo Chirino and: a, Liberty leading the people (after Delacroix). b, Revolutionaries with weapons.

1995, Aug. 16
1524 A426 50b Pair, #a.-b.   2.25 2.25

Venezuelan Red Cross, Cent. A427

Designs: a, 100b, Red Cross flag. b, 80b, Carlos J. Bello Hospital. c, 35b, Surgery scene. d, 35b, Rescue workers carrying victim. e, 35b, Care givers with child.

1995, Aug. 30
1525 A427 Strip of 5, #a.-e.   5.50 5.50

America Issue A428

Environmental protection: a, 35b, Trees, lake. b, 80b, Flowers, hillside.

1995, Sept. 13   Litho.   Perf. 12
1526 A428 Pair, #a.-b.   2.50 2.50

No. 1526 was issued in sheets of 10 stamps.
   No. 1526 exists in two types: the heavy border at top is above "America" only: the heavy line extends over the denomination. Values the same.

Miniature Sheet

Native Aboriginals — A429

No. 1527: a, 25b, Kuana man seated on post. b, 25b, Kuana woman using stones to do laundry. c, 35b, Guahibo people, one playing flute. d, 35b, Guahibo shaman with child. e, 50b, Uruak man with tree branch. f, 50b, Uruak woman cooking. g, 80b, Warao woman spinning twine. h, 80b, Warao man, woman in boat. i, 100b, Bari men with bows, arrows. j, 100b, Bari man rubbing sticks to make fire.
150b, Young boy with bird.

1995, Oct. 18
1527 A429   Sheet of 10,
                 #a.-j.   16.00 16.00
   Souvenir Sheet
1528 A429 150b multicolored   5.00 5.00
   See Nos. 1541-1542.

Miniature Sheet

Electricity in Caracas, Cent. — A430

Designs: a, 35b, Ricardo Zuloaga, early pioneer. b, 35b, Early electric plant. c, 35b, Substation. d, 35b, 1908 Electric trams. e, 35b, Electric lampposts mandated by Congress, 1908. f, 35b, Lampposts, Bolivar Plaza. g, 80b, Electrical repairman. h, 80b, Lighted cross, Avila. i, 100b, Teresa Carreño Cultural Complex. j, 100b, Ricardo Zuloaga main generator plant.

1995, Nov. 6
1529 A430 Sheet of 10, #a.-j. 11.00 11.00

Miniature Sheet

Christmas — A431

Designs: a, 35b, The Annunciation. b, 35b, Being turned away at the inn. c, 100b, Birth of Christ in the stable. d, 35b, Angel appearing to shepherds. e, 35b, Three Magi. f, 40b, Christmas pageant. g, 40b, Children skating. h, 100b, Christmas presents. i, 40b, Women preparing food for holidays. j, 40b, Children, mother preparing food for holidays.

1995, Nov. 15
1530 A431 Sheet of 10, #a.-j. 10.00 10.00
   Nos. 1530f-1530g, and 1530i-1530j are each continuous designs.

Miniature Sheet

Petroleum Industries of South America (PDVSA), 20th Anniv. — A432

a, 35b, PDVSA emblem, 7 petroleum company emblems. b, PDVSA emblem, 6 petroleum company emblems. c, 80b, Oil derrick. d, 80b, Refinery. e, 35b, Oil tanker crossing under bridge. f, 35b, Worker, orimulsion tanks. g, 35b, Two people examining carbon. h, 35b, Semi truck hauling petrochemicals. i, 35b, Filling station. j, 35b, Gas storage tanks.

1995, Dec. 13   Litho.   Perf. 12
1531 A432 Sheet of 10, #a.-j. 11.00 11.00

Miniature Sheet

Town of El Tocuyo, 450th Anniv. — A433

Designs: a, 35b, City arms. b, 35b, Workers in sugar cane field. c, Church of Our Lady of Immaculate Conception. d, Statue of Madonna inside church. e, 35b, Ruins of Temple of Santa Domingo. f, 35b, House of Culture. g, 80b, Cactus, vegetation. h, 80b, Cactus up close. i, 100b, Dancers with swords. j, 100b, Man playing guitar.

1995, Dec. 5
1532 A433 Sheet of 10, #a.-j. 11.00 11.00

Miniature Sheet

Vist of Pope John Paul II — A434

Statues of various saints, Pope and: a, 25b, Children. b, 25b, Man, woman. c, 40b, Man, woman, baby. d, 40b, Elderly man. e, 50b, Woman, boy. f, 50b, Sick person. g, 60b, Man in prison. h, 60b, Working man. i, 100b, People of various career fields. j, 100b, Priests, nuns.
200b, Pope John Paul II holding crucifix.

1996, Jan. 26
1533 A434   Sheet of 10,
                 #a.-j.   12.00 12.00
   Souvenir Sheet
1533K A434 200b multicolored 6.50 6.50

Orchid Type of 1995

Designs: a, Epidendrum fimbriatum. b, Myoxanthus reymondii. c, Catasetum pileatum. d, Ponthieva maculata. e, Maxillaria triloris. f, Scaphosepalum breve. g, Cleistes

rosea. h, Maxillaria sophronitis. i, Catasetum discolor. j, Oncidium ampliatum.
200b, Odontoglossum naevium.

1996, May 31   Litho.   Perf. 12
1534 A421   60b Sheet of 10,
#a.-j.   11.00 11.00
Souvenir Sheet
1535 A421   200b multicolored   6.50 6.50

1996 Summer Olympic Games, Atlanta A435

Designs: a, Emblem of Olympic Committee. b, Swimmer. c, Boxer. d, Cyclist. e, Medal winners.

1996, June 28   Litho.   Perf. 12
1536 A435   130b Strip of 5, #a.-e. 9.00 9.00
No. 1536 was issued in a sheet of 10 stamps.

Maiquetia Intl. Airport, 25th Anniv. A436

Designs: a, Symbol of automation. b, Map of airport flight routes. c, La Guaira Airdrome, 1929. d, Maiqueitia Airport, 1944. e, Simon Bolivar Airport, 1972. f, Interior view of terminal. g, Airport police, control tower. h, Airport firetruck. i, Airplane at terminal, Simon Bolivar Airport. j, Airplane on taxiway, Simon Bolivar Airport.

1996, Aug. 4
1537 A436   80b Sheet of 10,
#a-j   12.50 12.50

America Issue A437

Traditional costumes: a, 60b, Women's. b, 130b, Men's.

1996, Sept. 10
1538 A437   Pair, #a.-b.   3.25 3.25
No. 1538 was issued in sheets of 10 stamps.

Mario Briceño-Iragorry (1897-1958) — A438

Portraits: a, As young man, Trujillo, 1913. b, At University of Mérida, 1919. c, As politician, 1944. d, As writer, 1947. e, As older man, Caracas, 1952.

1996, Sept. 24
1539 A438   80b Strip of 5, #a.-e. 6.50 6.50
No. 1539 was issued in sheets of 10 stamps.

Caracas Rotary Club, 70th Anniv. — A439

1996, Oct. 3
1540 A439   50b multicolored   .75 .75
No. 1540 was issued in sheets of 10.

Native Aboriginal Type of 1995
Designs: a, 80b, Yukpa boy working in garden. b, 80b, Paraujanos girl carrying fruit. c, 80b, Kinaroes man, woman bundling cattails. d, 80b, Motilon man with bananas. e, 80b, Chaque mother carrying infant on back. f, 100b, Guajiros man, young woman fixing hair. g, 100b, Mucuchi man carrying pack on back. h, 100b, Mape man with bow and arrow. i, 100b, Macoa working with grain, painted faces. j, 100b, Yaruros man weaving.
200b, Woman breastfeeding infant.

1996, Oct. 11
1541 A429   Sheet of 10, #a.-j.   13.50 13.50
Souvenir Sheet
1542 A429   200b multicolored   3.25 3.25

Souvenir Sheet

Taipei '96, Intl. Philatelic Exhibition — A440

1996, Oct. 21   Litho.   Perf. 12
1543 A440   200b Ara chloroptera   7.50 7.50

José Gregorio Hernández (1864-1908), Physician — A441

a, As young boy. b, As student, anatomy drawing. c, Praying, Madonna statue. d, Thinking of the needy. e, In research study. f, As professor of university. g, Comforting sick patient. h, Empty chair at academy. i, Vargas Hospital, statue, portrait of Hernández. j, Hospital named after Hernández, statue.
200b, Portrait of Hernández.

1996, Oct. 26   Litho.   Perf. 12
1544 A441   60b Sheet of 10,
#a.-j.   7.00 7.00
Souvenir Sheet
1545 A441   200b multicolored   2.75 2.75
No. 1545 contains one 42x36mm stamp.

Christmas A442

Designs: a, 60b, Child setting up Nativity scene. b, 60b, Three men with guitars,

woman. c, 60b, Rooster, people making music. d, 60b, People with painted faces dancing, singing. e, 60b, Men, woman playing drums, instruments. f, 80b, Exchanging gifts of food. g, 80b, Family at table, looking at gift of food. h, 80b, Child in hammock, presents. i, 80b, Parading replica of infant Jesus. j, 80b, Kissing feet of Christ Child.

1996, Nov. 7
1546 A442   Sheet of 10, #a.-j.   6.50 6.50

Andrés Eloy Blanco (1896-1955), Politician, Writer A443

Designs: a, As adolescent. b, As Caracas city official, government building. c, With family. d, With democratic founders. e, As politician, building. f, As President of Constituent Assembly, building. g, As "Poet of Pueblo." h, Lincoln Memorial, as Chancellor of the Republic. i, Author of writings on Spain, sailing ship. j, Map of Spain, sailing ships, conquistador on horseback.

1997, Feb. 17   Litho.   Perf. 12
1547 A443   100b Sheet of 10,
#a.-j.   9.00 9.00

Simon Bolivar (1783-1830) — A444

1997, Mar. 7   Litho.   Perf. 13½x13
1548 A444   15b olive   .25   .25
1549 A444   20b brown org   .25   .25
1550 A444   40b dark brown   .40   .40
1551 A444   50b rose claret   .60   .60
1552 A444   70b deep violet   .85   .85
1553 A444   90b deep blue   1.25 1.25
1554 A444   200b dp grn bl   2.25 2.25
1555 A444   300b dp bl grn   3.00 3.00
1556 A444   400b gray   4.50 4.50
1557 A444   500b pale sepia   5.25 5.25
1558 A444   600b pale brown   5.75 5.75
1559 A444   800b pale vio brn   7.25 7.25
1560 A444   900b slate blue   7.50 7.50
1561 A444   1000b dk org brn   8.00 8.00
1562 A444   2000b olive bister   15.00 15.00
    Nos. 1548-1562 (15)   62.10 62.10

Orchid Type of 1995
Designs: a, Phragmipedium lindleyanum. b, Zygosepalum labiosum. c, Acacallis cyanea. d, Maxillaria camaridii. e, Scuticaria steelei. f, Aspasia variegata. g, Comparettia falcata. h, Scapyglottis stellata. i, Maxillaria ruffescens. j, Vanilla pompona.
250b, Rodriguezia lanceolata.

1997, May 30   Perf. 12
1563 A421   165b Sheet of 10,
#a.-j.   15.00 15.00
Souvenir Sheet
1564 A421   250b multicolored   3.50 3.50
No. 1564 contains one 42x37mm stamp.

Independence Conspiracy of Gual and España, Bicent. — A445

#1565, José María España, proclamation for independence being read. #1566, España under arrest. #1567, Manuel Gual, soldiers. #1568, Gual fleeing through door, sailing ship, standing on Trinidad. #1569, Revolutionary flag, sailing ship.

1997, July 16
1565 A445   165b multicolored   1.50 1.50
1566 A445   165b multicolored   1.50 1.50
   a.   Pair, #1565-1566   3.00 3.00
1567 A445   165b multicolored   1.50 1.50
   a.   Pair, #1566-1567   3.00 3.00
1568 A445   165b multicolored   1.50 1.50
   a.   Pair, #1567-1568   3.00 3.00

1569 A445   165b multicolored   1.50 1.50
   a.   Pair, #1565, 1569   3.00 3.00
   b.   Pair, #1568-1569   3.00 3.00
Printed in sheet of 10 containing one each #1566a, 1567a, 1568a, 1569a-1569b. Value $16.

Treaty of Tlatelolco Banning Use of Nuclear Weapons in Latin America, 30th Anniv. A446

Various stylized designs representing devastation resulting from use of nuclear weapons: a.-e., White inscriptions. f.-j., Black inscriptions.

1997, July 31
1570 A446   140b Sheet of 10,
#a.-j.   15.00 15.00

Stories for Children A447

"The Rabbit and the Tiger:" a, Rabbit, tiger carrying satchel. b, Watching rat figure digging. c, Watching turtle on his back. d, Rabbit. e, Rat in net, rabbit. f, Tiger, house, rat. g, Bird, rat, rabbit, bee, beehive. h, Rabbit, turtle. i, Tiger with stick over shoulder. j, Tiger with mouth open, bees.
250b, Rabbit, tiger.

1997, Aug. 7
1571 A447   55b Sheet of 10,
#a.-j.   8.00 8.00
Souvenir Sheet
1572 A447   250b multicolored   3.25 3.25
No. 1572 contains one 42x37mm stamp.
The reverse of Nos. 1571a-1571j are each inscribed with parts of the childrens' story.

Unexpected Adventures of a Postman A448

America Issue: 110p, Giving letter to woman with dog. 280p, With motor scooter in rain.

1997, Aug. 29   Litho.   Perf. 12
1573 A448   110p multicolored   1.50 1.50
1574 A448   280p multicolored   3.00 3.00
   a.   Pair, #1573-1574   7.25 7.25
No. 1574a was issued in sheets of 10 stamps.

Villa of Anauco Villa, Bicent. A449

Designs: a, Inscription. b, Main entrance. c, Entrance corridor. d, Interior patio. e, Exterior corridor leading to kitchen. f, Kitchen. g, Stairs leading to balcony. h, Coach house. i, Stable. j, Outside stable, water trough.

1997, Sept. 23
1575 A449   110b Sheet of 10,
#a.-j.   11.00 11.00

Independence in India, 50th Anniv. — A450

Designs: a, 165b, Jawaharlal Nehru. b, 200b, Sardar Patel, flag. c, 165b, Congressional building. d, 200b, Gandhi. e, 165b, Purification at the Ganges. f, 200b, Rabindranath Tagore. g, 165b, Motion picture industry. h, 200b, Traditional music. i, 165b, Insat-1B meteorological satellite. j, 200b, Use of modern technology.
250b, Minarets of Taj Majal.

1997, Oct. 2
1576 A450 Sheet of 10, #a.-j. 20.00 20.00
Souvenir Sheet
1577 A450 250b multicolored 3.25 3.25

Heinrich von Stephan (1831-97) A451

a, 110b, Portrait. b, 280b, UPU emblem.

1997, Oct. 9   Litho.   Perf. 12
1578 A451 Pair, #a.-b. 3.75 3.75

Wicker-work A452

No. 1579: a, Red basket, Ye'Kuana. b, With handles, Ye'Kuana. c, Round, Ye'Kuana. d, Tray, Panare. e, Backpack, Pemon. f, With carrying strap, Yanomami. g, Round (dk brown), diff., Ye'Kuana. h, Tray, Ye'Kuana. i, Oval tray, Panare. j, Wide mouth, Warao.
250b, Square box with lid, Ye'Kuana.

1997, Oct. 24   Perf. 12
1579 A452 140b Sheet of 10, #a.-j. 15.00 15.00
Souvenir Sheet
1580 A452 250b multicolored 4.00 4.00
No. 1580 contains one 42x37mm stamp.

Christmas A453

a, Annunciation. b, Mary, St. Elizabeth. c, No room at the inn. d, Nativity. e, Annunciation to shepherds. f, Adoration of the shepherds. g, Magi following star. h, Adoration of the Magi. i, Presentation of Christ child in temple. j, Flight into Egypt.

1997, Oct. 31
1581 A453 110b Sheet of 10, #a.-j. 11.00 11.00

7th Summit of Latin American Chiefs of State and Government, Isla de Margarita A454

a, 165b, j, 200b, Social justice. b, 165b, i, 200b, Free elections. c, 165b, h, 200b, Summit emblem. d, 165b, g, 200b, Truthful information. e, 165b, f, 200b, Human rights.

1997, Nov. 5
1582 A454 Sheet of 10, #a.-j. 18.00 18.00

Diocese of Zulia, Cent. A455

Churches: a, Convent. b, Church of St. Ann. c, Reliquary, Chiquinquira. d, Basilica of Chiquinquira and St. John of God. e, Church, Aranza. f, Cathedral, Maracaibo. g, Cathedral, Machiques. h, Archbishop's seal. i, Cathedral, Cabimas. j, Cathedral of the Virgin, San Carlos.

1997, Dec. 16
1583 A455 110b Sheet of 10, #a.-j. 10.00 10.00

Democracy in Venezuela, 40th Anniv. — A456

Designs: a, Commemorative emblem. b, Popular decision. c, Public education. d, Social development. e, Freedom of expression. f, Capital, constitution. g, Popular culture. h, Civil rights. i, Environmental protection. j, Social and civic participation.

1998, Feb. 19   Litho.   Perf. 12
1584 A456 110b Sheet of 10, #a.-j. 12.00 12.00

Discovery of Margarita Island, 500th Anniv. — A457

Map of Margarita Islands and: a, 200b, Angel Rock. b, 265b, Christopher Columbus, ship. c, 200b, Simon Bolivar. d, 200b, Pearl diver. e, 265b, Statue of the Virgin del Valle, church. f, 100b, Mending fish net, fishermen in boats. g, 200b, Gen. Santiago Marino. h, 100b, Petronila Mata, cannon. i, 200b, Gen. Juan Bautista Arismendi. j, 100b, Parrot.
250b, Women weeping at the Lagoon of Martyrs, horiz.

1998, Mar. 26   Litho.   Perf. 12
1585 A457 Sheet of 10, #a.-j. 17.00 17.00
Souvenir Sheet
1586 A457 250b multicolored 3.25 3.25
No. 1586 contains one 42x37mm stamp.

Orchid Type of 1995
a, Oncidium orthostates. b, Epidendrum praetervisum. c, Odontoglossum schilleranum. d, Bletia lansbergii. e, Caularthron bicornutum. f, Darwiniera bergoldii. g, Houlletia tigrina. h, Pleurothallis acuminata. i, Elleanthus lupulinus. j, Epidendrum ferrugineum.
250b, Pleurothallis immersa.

1998, May 29
1587 A421 185b Sheet of 10, #a.-j. 18.00 18.00
Souvenir Sheet
1588 A421 250b multicolored 3.25 3.25
No. 1588 contains one 42x37mm stamp.

Henri Pittier Natl. Park, 60th Anniv. — A458

Fauna: a, 140b, Crax pauxi. b, 150b, Spizaetus ornatus. c, 200b, Touit collaris. d, 200b, Trogon collaris. e, 350b, Cyanocorax yncas. f, 140b, Tersina viridis. g, 150b, Phyllomedusa trinitatis. h, 200b, Morpho peleides. i, 200b, Acrocinus longimanus. j, 350b, Dynastes hercules.

1998, July 17
1589 A453 Sheet of 10, #a.-j. 20.00 20.00

Comptroller General of the Republic, 60th Anniv. — A459

Designs: a, 140b, Gumersindo Torres Millet, founding Comptroller. b, 140b, Luis Antonio Pietri Yépez, first Comptroller of the democracy. c, 140b, View of capitol dome. d, 140b, Colors of flag (service to society). e, 200b, Simon Bolivar, coins. f, 200b, Various numbers on green background. g, 350b, Newspaper headlines (inform the public). h, 350b, Statue of justice (uphold law). i, 350b, Text of duties of the Comptroller General. j, 350b, Emblem, the 6th Assembly of the Latin American and Caribbean States Comptrollers.

1998, July 29
1590 A459 Sheet of 10, #a.-j. 20.00 20.00

Organization of the American States (OAS), 50th Anniv. — A460

a, 140b, Logo of the anniversary. b, 140b, OAS emblem. c, 350b, Flags forming double helix, US flag at center left. d, 150b, Deactivating land mine. e, 150b, Defending human rights. f, 200b, Simon Bolivar. g, 200b, Scroll, quill pen, inkwell. h, 350b, Flags forming double helix, Venezuelan flag at center right. i, 200b, Road sign with map of Americas. j, 200b, Mountain climbers.

1998, July 30
1591 A460 Sheet of 10, #a.-j. 8.00 8.00

Expo '98, Lisbon A461

Designs: a, 140b, Bird, turtle, crab. b, 140b, Fishermen throwing net from boat. c, 150b, Seashells, turtle. d, 150b, Fish. e, 200b, Marine life, denomination, UR. f, 200b, Marine life, denomination LR. g, 200b, Man riding through river on horse. h, 200b, Cattle in river, monkey. i, 350b, Two sea birds. j, 350b, Monkey, waterfall, flower.

1998, July 31
1592 A461 Sheet of 10, #a.-j. 20.00 20.00

18th Central American and Caribbean Games, Maracaibo A462

Figures: a, 150b, Running. b, 200b, Playing basketball. c, 150b, Bowling. d, 200b, Boxing. e, 150b, Cycling. f, 200b, Fencing. g, 150b, Performing gymnastics. h, 200b, Weight lifting. i, 150b, Swimming. j, 200b, Playing tennis.

1998, Aug. 4
1593 A462 Sheet of 10, #a.-j. 15.00 15.00

Discovery of Venezuela, 500th Anniv. — A463

Designs: a, 350b, Christopher Columbus. b, 200b, Juan de la Cosa (1460?-1510), map. c, 200b, Huts built on stilts in water. d, 150b, Women of three different races. e, 140b, 13th cent. artifact. f, 350b, Alonso de Ojeda (1465-1515), map. g, 200b, Detail of map of Jodocus Hondius. h, 200b, Modern city. i, 150b, Various people of modern Venezuela. j, 140b, Statues of Catholic king and queen.

1998, Aug. 10
1594 A463 Sheet of 10, #a.-j. 18.00 18.00

Landing of Christoper Columbus, and Exploration of Amerigo Vespucci, 500th Anniv. A464

1998, Aug. 12
1595 A464 400b multicolored 3.50 3.50
See Italy No. 2252.

Treaty of Amazon Cooperation, 20th Anniv. A465

Designs: a, Casiquiare River, denomination LR. b, Casiquiare River, denomination LL. c, Bactris gasipaes. d, Neblinaria celiae. e, Paracheidon axelrodi. f, Dendrobates leucomelas. g, Nocthocrax urumatum. h, Speothos venaticus. i, Cocuy mountain. j, Neblina Mountains.

1998, Aug. 20
1596 A465 200b Sheet of 10,
#a.-j.   18.00 18.00

Children's Story — A466

Cockroach Martinez and Perez Rat: a, Cockroach. b, Burro. c, Parrot. d, Insects with camera, pad. e, Cat. f, Cockroach, pig. g, Goat. h, Cockroach, rat. i, Rat. j, Cockroach, bird.
350b, Cockroach.

1998, Aug. 21 **Litho.** *Perf. 12*
1597 A466 130b Sheet of 10,
#a.-j.   10.00 10.00
Souvenir Sheet
1598 A466 350b multicolored   4.00 4.00

State of Israel, 50th Anniv. — A467

a, 350b, Menorah. b, 350b, Moses, Ten Commandments. c, 200b, Theodore Herzl. d, 200b, King David. e, 140b, Blowing of Shofar. f, 350b, Torah. g, 350b, Praying at Wailing Wall. h, 200b, David Ben Gurion. i, 200b, Knesset. j, 140b, Book Museum.

1998, Sept. 15
1599 A467 Sheet of 10, #a.-j. 20.00 20.00

Souvenir Sheet

Comptroller General, 60th Anniv. — A468

1998, Sept.
1600 A468 480b multicolored   4.50 4.50

UPU, 125th Anniv. A469

a, 100b, Customer at window, clerks at left. b, 100b, Scanning bar code, woman at right. c, 100b, Electronic mail. d, 100b, Hybrid mail. e, 100b, Business mail. f, 300b, Like "a," clerks at right. g, 300b, Like "b," woman at left. h, 300b, Like "c," large monitor at right. i, 300b, Like "d," woman at right. j, 300b, Like "e," building with stacks at left.

1998, Sept. 29
1601 A469 Sheet of 10, #a.-j.   10.00 10.00

Legendary Caciques A470

a, Caruao. b, Manaure. c, Guacamayo. d, Tapiaracay. e, Mamacuri. f, Maniacuare. g, Mara. h, Chacao. i, Tamanaco. j, Tiuna.
500b, Indian.

1998, Oct. 9
1602 A470 420b Sheet of 10,
#a.-j.   22.50 22.50
Souvenir Sheet
1603 A470 500b multicolored   4.00 4.00

Evangelism in Venezuela, 500th Anniv. A471

No. 1604: a, 100b, Fr. Francisco de Córdoba, Fr. Juan Garcés. b, 100b, Fr. Matías Ruíz Blanco. c, 100b, Fr. Vincente de Requejada. d, 100b, Fr. José Gumilla. e, 100b, Fr. Antonio Gonzáles de Acuña. f, 300b, Fr. Pedro de Córdoba. g, 300b, Fr. Francisco de Pamplona. h, 300b, Fr. Bartolomé Díaz. i, 300b, Fr. Filipe Salvador Gilij. j, 300b, Don Mariano Martí.
350b, Emblem of Papal Nuncio.

1998, Oct. 24 **Litho.** *Perf. 12*
1604 A471 Sheet of 10, #a.-j. 13.50 13.50
Souvenir Sheet
1605 A471 350b multicolored   3.50 3.50
No. 1605 contains one 42x37mm stamp.

Special Olympics, 30th Anniv. A472

180b: a, Carrying torch. b, Giving hug. c, Soccer players. d, Girl holding small flag. e, Girl performing gymnastics.
420b: f, Swimmer. g, Coach walking with athletes. h, Hitting volleyball. i, Participants cheering. j, Coach instructing girl in softball.

1998, Oct. 30 **Litho.** *Perf. 12*
1606 A472 Sheet of 10, #a.-j. 15.00 15.00

Christmas A473

Children standing in front of windows — 180b: a, Girl holding sparkler. b, Boy holding artist's brush, ornament. c, Girl with kite. d, Boy with pinwheel. e, Girls playing musical instruments.
420b: f, Boy on wagon. g, Girl with yo-yo, doll. h, Boy with bell. i, Girl with spool and thread. j, Boy on skateboard.

1998, Nov. 4
1607 A473 Sheet of 10, #a.-j.   15.00 15.00

America Issue — A474

Famous women: a, 180b, Teresa de la Parra (1889-1936), writer. b, 420b, Teresa Carreño (1853-1917), pianist.

1998, Nov. 23
1608 A474 Pair, #a.-b.   3.00 3.00

William H. Phelps (1875-1965), Ornithologist A475

Portrait of Phelps and — 200b: a, Cephalopterus ornatus. b, Topaza pella. c, Grallaria excelsa phelpsi. d, Chrysolampis mosquitus. e, Tangara xanthogastra phelpsi.
300b: f, Radio transmitter. g, Mt. Phelps. h, Baseball and glove. i, Phelps Library. j, Cash register.

1998, Dec. 4
1609 A475 Sheet of 10, #a.-j.   16.00 16.00

Msgr. Jesús Manuel Jáuregui Moreno (1848-1905) A476

Designs: a, Portrait as younger man. b, Christ on the cross. c, Our Mother of Angels Church. d, Madonna and Child. e, Portrait as older man.

1999, Jan. 30 **Litho.** *Perf. 12*
1610 A476 500b Strip of 5,
#a.-e.   12.00 12.00

Holy Sacrament for the Consecration of the Republic of Venezuela, Cent. A477

No. 1612: a, Man, elderly woman. b, Priest. c, Ostensorium (top). d, Boy with basketball, girl. e, Man, woman holding baby. f, Lady doctor. g, Woman. h, Ostensorium (base). i, Soldier. j, Native man holding spear.
500b, portrait of priest holding the Host.

1999, June 16 **Litho.** *Perf. 12*
1611 A477 250b Sheet of 10,
#a.-j.   12.00 12.00
Souvenir Sheet
1612 A477 500b multicolored   2.25 2.25
No. 1612 contains one 42x37mm stamp.

Souvenir Sheet

Andino Parliament, 20th Anniv. — A478

1999 **Litho.** *Perf. 12*
1613 A478 500b multi   2.25 2.25

Christmas A479

a, 500b, Betrothal of Joseph, Mary. b, 500b, Annunciation. c, 500b, Elizabeth, Mary. d, 500b, The search for lodging in Bethlehem. e, 500b, Birth of Jesus. f, 300b, Vision of the shepherds. g, 300b, Magi following star. h, 300b, Adoration of the Magi. i, 300b, Flight into Egypt. j, 300b, Slaughter of the innocents.

1999, Nov. 5 *Perf. 12x12¼*
1614 A479 Sheet of 10, #a.-j. 20.00 20.00

Souvenir Sheet

Expo 2000, Hanover — A480

2000, July 8 **Litho.** *Perf. 12*
1615 A480 650b multi   4.00 4.00

2nd Summit of Heads of State and Government of OPEC Countries — A481

No. 1616 — Sites in Venezuela: a, 300b, Angel Falls. b, 300b, Llanos, Cojedes. c, 300b, Quebrada Jaspe. d, 300b, Morichal Largo. e, 300b, Auyantepuy, Carrao River. f, 400b, Lake Maracaibo. g, 400b, Humboldt Peak. h, 400b, Mochima. i, 400b, Morichal Largo River. j, 400b, Auyantepuy, from Uruyen.
No. 1617, 550b: a, Saudi Arabia. b, Algeria. c, United Arab Emirates. d, Indonesia. e, Iraq. f, Iran. g, Kuwait. h, Libya. i, Nigeria. j, Qatar.

2000, Sept. 26 Litho. *Perf. 12*
Sheets of 10, #a-j
1616-1617 A481 Set of 2 60.00 60.00

Christmas — A482

No. 1618: a, 300b, Angel and "Gloria." b, 300b, Angel and "a." c, 650b, Angel and "Dios." d, 300b, Angel and "en los." e, 300b, Angel and "Cielos." f, 300b, Shepherd and lamb. g, 550b, Joseph. h, 650b, Jesus. i, 550b, Mary. j, 300b, Woman with water jar.

2000, Nov. 29
1618 A482 Sheet of 10, #a-j 24.00 24.00

America Issue, A New Millennium Without Arms — A483

No. 1619: a, 300b, Finger in gun barrel. b, 650b, Man in heaven.

2000, Dec. 14
1619 A483 Vert. pair, #a-b 5.50 5.50

Educational Building and Endowment Foundation, 25th Anniv. — A484

No. 1620 — School buildings in: a, Caracas. b, Vargas State. c, Portuguesa State. d, Mérida State. e, Yaracuy State.

2001, May 9 Litho. *Perf. 12*
1620 Horiz. strip of 5 9.00 0.00
a.-c. A484 300b Any single 1.60 1.60
d.-e. A484 400b Any single 2.10 2.10

Orchids — A485

No. 1621: a, 200b, Galeottia jorisiana. b, 200b, Lycaste longipetala. c, 300b, Coryanthes albertinae. d, 300b, Hexisea bidentata. e, 400b, Lycaste macrophylla. f, 400b, Masdevallia maculata. g, 550b, Ada aurantiaca. h,

550f, Kefersteinia graminea. i, 550b, Sobralia liliastrum. j, 550b, Gongora maculata. 650b, Masdevallia tovarensis.

2001, May 25
1621 A485 Sheet of 10, #a-j 24.00 24.00
Souvenir Sheet
1622 A485 650b multi 4.00 4.00

Blessed Josemaría Escrivá de Balaguer (1902-75), Founder of Opus Dei — A486

No. 1623: a, 300b, Portrait. b, 300b, Bell of Nuestra Senora de los Angeles Church. c, 300b, Figure of Infant Jesus. d, 300b, Escrivá with men. e, 550b, Escrivá with women. f, 550f, Escrivá receiving doctorate, 1972. g, 550b, Escrivá with children, 1975. h, 300b, Commemorative plaque, Caracas Cathedral. i, 550b, Color portrait. j, 300b, Beatification ceremony, St. Peter's Square, Vatican City.

2001, June 8
1623 A486 Sheet of 10, #a-j 25.00 25.00

Battle of Carabobo, 180th Anniv. A487

No. 1624: a, Thomas I. Ferriar. b, Bolívar in Buenavista, by Martín Tovar y Tovar. c, Quote by Simón Bolívar. d, Commemorative column. e, Pedro Camejo. f, José Antonio Páez, by Tovar y Tovar. g, Santiago Mariño, by Tovar y Tovar. h, Simón Bolívar, by M. Eberstein. i, Manuel Cedeño, by Tito Salas. j, Ambrosio Plaza, by Salas.

2001, June 22
1624 A487 Sheet of 10 27.50 27.50
a.-e. A487 400b Any single 1.25 1.25
f.-j. A487 600b Any single 1.75 1.75

Christmas — A488

Holy Family and angel with: a, 200b, Clarinet. b, 200b, Guitar. c, 220b, Lute. d, 220b, Trumpet. e, 280b, Violin. f, 280b, Harp. g, 400b, Bagpipes. h, 400b, Pan pipes. i, 500b, Drum. j, 500b, Stringed instrument.

2001, Nov. 30 Litho. *Perf. 12*
1625 A488 Sheet of 10, #a-j 18.00 18.00

Navigational Signaling, 160th Anniv. — A489

Navigational aids: a, Margarita Aqueduct buoy. b, BNFA buoy. c, Punta Brava lighthouse. d, Punta Macolla lighthouse. e, Los Roques lighthouse. f, Isla Redonda lighthouse. g, Punta Faragoza lighthouse. h, Punta Ballena lighthouse. i, Punta Tigre lighthouse. j, Recalada de Güiria lighthouse.

2002, May 10 Litho. *Perf. 12*
1626 Sheet of 10 15.00 15.00
a.-b. A489 300b Either single .75 .75
c.-f. A489 450b Any single 1.10 1.10
g.-j. A489 500b Any single 1.25 1.25

Symbolic Incorporation of Guacaipuro into National Pantheon — A490

No. 1627: a, Tiaora and Caycape, sisters of Guacaipuro. b, Guacaipuro defeats Pedro de Miranda. c, Guacaipuro defeated by Juan Rodriguez Suárez. d, Killing in the gold mines. e, Death of Juan Rodriguez Suárez. f, Guacaipuro's escape from cabin fire. g, Death of Guacaipuro. h, Urquía, companion of Guacairpuro. i, Baruta, first son of Guacaipuro. j, Guacaipuro, Cacique of the Teques and Caracas people.

2002, Oct. 29 Litho. *Perf. 12*
1627 Sheet of 10 11.00 11.00
a. A490 200b multi .45 .45
b-g. A490 300b any single .65 .65
h. A490 350b multi .75 .75
i. A490 400b multi .85 .85
j. A490 500b multi 1.00 1.00

Mission Robinson — A491

No. 1628: a, Toddler. b, Boy reading. c, Simón Bolívar and torch. d, Simón "Robinson" Rodriguez, Bolívar's teacher. e, Rodriguez

and Eiffel Tower. f, Bolívar and flag. g, Bolívar and Rodriguez reading. h, Bolívar standing and Rodriguez seated. i, Rodriguez, men and women reading. j, Indians reading.

2003, Sept. 19 Litho. *Perf. 12x12¼*
1628 A491 Sheet of 10 7.50 7.50
a.-d. 300b Any single .35 .35
e.-f. 400b Either single .50 .50
g.-j. 500b Any single .65 .65

Agricultural, Fishery and Forestry Fund (FONDAFA) — A492

No. 1629: a, Cattle drive. b, Farmer plowing field. c, Row of tractors. d, Farmer tending crops. e, Corn in field. f, Boats. g, Ear of corn. h, Farmer in tractor in field. i, Cacao pods. j, Cacao beans.

2003, Nov. 7 *Perf. 12*
1629 A492 Sheet of 10 7.00 7.00
a.-f. 300b Any single .35 .35
g.-h. 400b Either single .50 .50
i.-j. 500b Either single .65 .65

National Urban Development Fund (FONDUR), 28th Anniv. — A493

No. 1630: a, Barinas. b, Portuguesa. c, Carabobo. d, Miranda. e, Sucre. f, Trujillo. g, Táchira. h, Vargas. i, FONDUR emblem. j, Lara.

2003, Dec. 16 Litho. *Perf. 14¼*
1630 A493 Sheet of 10 6.00 6.00
a.-f. 300b Any single .45 .45
g.-h. 400b Either single .65 .65
i.-j. 500b Either single .85 .85

Natl. Urban Transportation Fund
(FONTUR), 12th Anniv. — A494

No. 1631: a, Av. Uruguay, Lara. b, Carretera
del Páramo, Merida. c, Av. Cumanan-
Cumanacoa, Sucre. d, Carratera Santa Lucia,
Barinas. e, Francissco Fajardo Expressway,
Caracas. f, Students. g, Paraiso Tunnel,
Caracas. h, VIVEX Module. i, Row of buses. j,
Av. Cruz Paredes, Barinas.

2003, Dec. 18	Litho.	Perf. 14¼
1631 A494	Sheet of 10	6.50 6.50
a.-c.	300b Any single	.45 .45
d.-f.	400b Any single	.60 .60
g.-j.	500b Any single	.80 .80

Natl. Telecommunications Commission
(CONATEL) — A495

No. 1632: a, Three Amazonian children, two
dogs and hammock. b, Caracas and mountain. c, Amazonian children with spears. d,
Snow-covered Bolivar Peak. e, Amazonian
child in canoe aiming arrow. f, Medina Beach.
g, Amazonian children aiming arrows skyward.
h, Angel Falls. i, Amazonian children making
baskets. j, Coro Dunes.

2003, Dec. 23	Litho.	Perf. 12
1632 A495	Sheet of 10	7.50 7.50
a.-d.	300b Any single	.50 .50
e.-f.	400b Either single	.70 .70
g.-h.	500b Either single	.90 .90
i.-j.	600b Either single	1.00 1.00

Foundation for the Development of
Community and Municipal
Reconstruction (FUNDACOMUN),
42nd Anniv. — A496

No. 1633: a, Miranda. b, Trujillo. c, Mérida.
d, Falcón. e, Vargas. f, Esparta. g, Caracas,
denomination at left. h, Caracas, denomination at right. i, Barinas. j, Lara.

2004, Mar. 10	Litho.	Perf. 12
1633 A496	Sheet of 10	6.50 6.50
a.-c.	300b Any single	.45 .45
d.-f.	400b Any single	.65 .65
g.-j.	500b Any single	.70 .70

Barrio Adentro Mission — A497

No. 1634: a, Houses on hillside, people in
doorway. b, Woman, house, ladder, people in
alley. c, Woman, mother and child. d, Family,
children. e, Boys playing baseball, boat. f,
People near fence, man with cap. g, Man,
sand dunes. h, Man with guitar, cows. i, Mountain, woman, cross and statue. j, Indians, river.

2004, Mar. 24	Perf. 12
1634 A497	Sheet of 10	12.00 12.00
a.-b.	300b Either single	.35 .35
c.-f.	500b Any single	.55 .55
g.	750b multi	.90 .90
h.-i.	1500b Either single	1.75 1.75
j.	1700b multi	1.90 1.90

Souvenir Sheet

Design: 1000b, Man pushing wheelbarrow,
horiz.

1634K A497	1000b multi	2.75 2.75

No. 1634K contains one 41x36mm stamp.

National Housing Institute
(INAVI) — A498

No. 1635: a, Apartment block 6, El Silencio.
b, El Pilar. c, Central section of apartment
block 1, El Silencio. d, La Quiboreña. e, Apartment block 7, El Silencio. f, Santa Ana. g,
Apartment block 144, El Silencio. h, La
Quiracha. i, Architectural drawings of Caracas
buildings. j, Los Peregrinos.

2004, May 28	Litho.	Perf. 12
1635 A498	Sheet of 10	6.00 6.00
a.-c.	300b Any single	.40 .40
d.-f.	400b Any single	.60 .60
g.-j.	500b Any single	.70 .70

National Aquatic Areas and Islands
Institute (INEA) — A499

No. 1636: a, INEA emblem. b, INEA emblem
and headquarters. c, Marine firefighters,
boats. d, Firetruck, marine firefighter moving
drum. e, Sunken tugboat Gran Roque. f,
Underwater view of Gran Roque. g, Tugboats.
h, Large ships at port. i, Starfish, religious
statue. j, Boats and birds.

2004, June 15		
1636 A499	Sheet of 10	11.00 11.00
a.-b.	300b Either single	.45 .45
c.-f.	500b Any single	.80 .80
g.	6000b multi	.85 .85
h.	1000b multi	1.40 1.40
i.	1500b multi	2.25 2.25
j.	1700b multi	2.50 2.50

A500

Latin American Parliament, 40th
Anniv. — A501

No. 1637: a, Latin American Parliament
emblem, 40th anniversary emblem. b, 40th
anniversary emblem. c, Latin American Parlia-
ment flag and 40th anniversary emblem. d,
Flags of member nations. e, Flags and Andrés
Townsend Ezcurra. f, Flags and Luis Beltrán
Prieto Figueroa. g, Flags and Nelson
Carneiro. h, Plenary meeting room, Vene-
zuela. i, Assembly hall, Sao Paolo. j, Latin
American Parliament Building, Sao Paolo.
No. 1638: a, Latin American Parliament
emblem, 40th Anniversary emblem. c,
Mérida Session emblem. d, Charter of Social
Rights. e, Flags and map of Latin America. f,
Flag and map of Panama. g, Táchira Session
emblem. h, Bird with ball and chain (social

debt). i, Simón Bolivar. j, Constitutional
Hypothesis.

2004, July 12		
1637 A500	Sheet of 10	11.00 11.00
a.-c.	300b Any single	.40 .40
d.-e.	450b Either single	.60 .60
f.-g.	500b Either single	.75 .75
h.-i.	1500b Either single	2.10 2.10
j.	1700b multi	2.25 2.25
1638 A501	Sheet of 10	11.00 11.00
a.-c.	300b Any single	.40 .40
d.-e.	450b Either single	.60 .60
f.-g.	500b Either single	.75 .75
h.-i.	1500b Either single	2.10 2.10
j.	1700b multi	2.25 2.25

CVG Edelca, 40th Anniv. — A502

No. 1639: a, Macagua Hydroelectric Station
and Dam,, Ciudad Guayana. b, Electric trans-
mission towers and lines. c, Electrical power
equipment. d, Room, Guri. e, Native people. f,
Guri Hydroelectric Station and Dam. g, Street-
lights near Macagua Hydroelectric Station and
Dam. h, Solar tower, by Alejandro Otero. i,
Dam, Ecomuseum, Caroní. j, Gran Sabana.
No. 1640, Guri Hydroelectric Station and
Dam.

2004, July 29		
1639 A502	Sheet of 10	8.50 8.50
a.-b.	300b Either single	.40 .40
c.	400b multi	.60 .60
d.-g.	500b Any single	.70 .70
h.	600b multi	.80 .80
i.	1000b multi	1.25 1.25
j.	1500b multi	2.10 2.10

Souvenir Sheet

1640 A502	1000b multi	3.25 3.25

No. 1640 contains one 41x36mm stamp.

United Nations Population
Fund — A503

No. 1641 — Inscriptions: a, Los y las
adolescentes . . . b, El comporttmiento . . . c,
Las niñas tienen . . . d, Los seres humanos . . .
e, Promovamos el empoderamiento . . . f, Los
derechjos reproductivos . . . g, Por una
maternidad sin riesgo. h, El derecho al desar-
rollo . . . i, Eliminemos la violencia . . . j, El
condón protege vidas.

2004, Sept. 15

1641	A503	Sheet of 10	11.00	11.00
a.-d.		500b Any single	.70	.70
e.-j.		1000b Any single	1.25	1.25

National Parks Institute (INPARQUES) — A504

No. 1642 — Parks and: a, Food. b, Education. c, Recreation. d, Water. e, Landscapes. f, Biodiversity. g, Conservation. h, Electricity. i, Tourism. j, Ethnic people.

2004, Oct. 11　Litho.　Perf. 14¼x14½

1642	A504	Sheet of 10	8.50	8.50
a.-b.		300b Either single	.40	.40
c.		400b multi	.50	.50
d.-g.		500b Any single	.70	.70
h.		600b multi	.80	.80
i.		1000b multi	1.40	1.40
j.		1500b multi	2.10	2.10

National Tax and Customs Administration (SENIAT) — A505

No. 1643 — Inscriptions: a, Aporte a la educación, cultura y deporte (children). b, Aporte a la salud. c, Dile no al contrabando. d, Con tus tributos . . . e, Aporte a la educación, cultura y deporte (baseball players). f, Construcción de futuras . . . g, Aporte a la vialidad. h, Bienvenidos a un país . . . i, Aporte a la educación, cultura y deporte (building and palm tree). j, Aporte a la educación, cultura y deporte (modern building and sculpture).

2004, Oct. 15　Litho.　Perf. 12

1643	A505	Sheet of 10	11.00	11.00
a.-d.		500b Any single	.70	.70
e.-j.		1000b Any single	1.25	1.25

A506

Banco Federal — A507

No. 1644: a, Cerro El Avila, Caracas, 1945. b, Nuevo Circo, Caracas, 1970. c, Plaza Venezuela, Caracas, 1943. d, Sculpture by Francisco Narváez, Caracas, 1940. e, Baralt Theater, Maracaibo, 1883. f, Los Próceres, Caracas, 1956. g, El Paraíso Horse Track, Caracas, 1908. h, Bullfighter Luis Sánchez Olivares, Caracas, 1950. i, Funicular, Mérida, 1954. j, Angel Falls, Bolivar State, 1937. k, Banco Federal emblem, gold star. l, Banco Federal Building (sepia). m, Lake Bridge, Maracaibo, 1962. n, Virgin of Coromoto (sepia). o, El Silencio, Caracas, 1945.

No. 1645: a, San Fernando de Apure Church. b, Caracas Cathedral. c, Coro Cathedral. d, Santa Inés de Cumaná Cathedral. e, Our Lady of Chiquinquirá Basilica. f, Our Lady of Coromoto Basilica. g, St. Rose of Lima Church, Ortíz. h, Mérida Cathedral. i, Our Lady of the Assumption Cathedral. j, San Cristóbal Cathedral. k, Banco Federal emblem, silver star. l, Banco Federal Building (full color). m, Barquisimeto Cathedral. n, Virgin of Coromoto (full color). o, Valencia Cathedral.

2005, Jan. 20　Litho.　Perf. 14¼x14½

1644	A506	Sheet of 15	13.00	13.00
a.-e.		300b Any single	.40	.40
f.-h.		400b Any single	.55	.55
i.-j.		600b Either single	.80	.80
k.-l.		750b Either single	1.10	1.10
m.-n.		1000b Either single	1.40	1.40
o.		1700b multi	2.25	2.25
1645	A507	Sheet of 15	13.00	13.00
a.-e.		300b Any single	.40	.40
f.-h.		400b Any single	.55	.55
i.-j.		600b Either single	.80	.80
k.-l.		750b Either single	1.10	1.10
m.-n.		1000b Either single	1.40	1.40
o.		1700b multi	2.25	2.25

Christmas — A508

No. 1646 — Creche figures from various states: a, Bolívar. b, Falcón. c, Mérida. d, Aragua. e, Miranda. f, Miranda, diff. g, Falcón, diff. h, Zulia. i, Bolívar, diff. j, Trujillo.

2004, Dec. 23　　　　Perf. 12

1646	A508	Sheet of 10	10.00	10.00
a.-b.		300b Either single	.45	.45
c.-d.		400b Either single	.55	.55
e.		600b multi	.80	.80
f.-g.		750b Either single	1.00	1.00
h.-i.		1000b Either single	1.40	1.40
j.		1700b multi	2.25	2.25

Souvenir Sheet

Incan and Modern Mail Deliverers — A509

2004　　　　　　　　Perf. 12

1647	A509 1000b multi	2.75	2.75

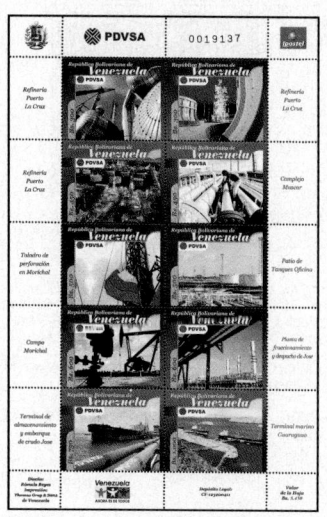

Petróleos de Venezuela, S. A. — A510

No. 1648: a, Crane above turbines, Puerto La Cruz Refinery. b, Night view of tower Puerto La Cruz Refinery. c, Aerial view of Puerto La Cruz refinery. d, Man inspecting pipes. e, Crane and Venezuelan flag. f, Storage tanks. g, Oil wells. h, Refinery towers. i, Oil tanker and pipes. j, Tankers at Guaraguao Marine Terminal.

2004, Nov. 24　Litho.　Perf. 14¼

1648	A510	Sheet of 10	7.50	7.50
a.-b.		300b Either single	.45	.45
c.-d.		450b Either single	.60	.60
e.-f.		500b Either single	.65	.65
g.-h.		600b Either single	.85	.85
i.		750b multi	1.10	1.10
j.		1000b multi	1.40	1.40

Mountains — A511

Designs: No. 1649, Bolivar Peak, Venezuela. No. 1650, Mt. Damavand, Iran.

2004　　Litho.　　Perf. 13

1649	A511 1700b multi	2.40	2.40
1650	A511 1700b multi	2.40	2.40
a.	Horiz. pair, #1649-1650	5.00	5.00

No. 1650 has "Republica Bolivariana de Venezuela" overprinted in black over vignette. No. 1650 exists without overprint.

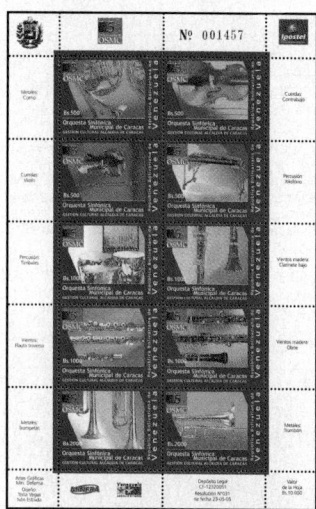

Caracas Municipal Symphony Orchestra, 25th Anniv. — A512

No. 1651: a, French horns. b, Bass (in blue) and bow. c, Violin and bow. d, Marimba. e, Timpani. f, Clarinets. g, Flutes. h, Oboes. i, Trumpets. j, Trombone.

2005　　　　　　　　Perf. 12

1651	A512	Sheet of 10	15.00	15.00
a.-d.		500b Any single	.65	.65
e.-h.		1000b Any single	1.40	1.40
i.-j.		2000b Either single	2.75	2.75

16th World Youth and Student Festival — A513

No. 1652: a, Festival emblems from 1947-59. b, Festival emblems from 1962-2005. c, Festival emblem and joined arms. d, Festival emblem and text of Simón Bolívar's Vow of Monte Sacro. e, Festival emblem and Bolívar with outstretched arm, signature of Bolívar. f, Festival emblem and broken chain. g, Festival emblem, Bolívar. h, Festival emblem, dove. i, Festival emblem, dove, globe and hands. j, Festival emblem and hands.

1000b, Festival emblem and Bolívar with outstretched arm, horiz.

2005, Aug. 5　Litho.　Perf. 12

1652	A513	Sheet of 10	7.50	7.50
a.-d.		300b Any single	.45	.45
e.-i.		500b Any single	.65	.65
j.		1500b multi	2.10	2.10

Souvenir Sheet
Perf. 12x11¾

1653	A513 1000b multi	3.25	3.25

No. 1653 contains one 41x36mm stamp.

IPOSTEL — A514

No. 1654: a, IPOSTEL emblem, flag, Caracas Post Office. b, Postal vans. c, IPOSTEL emblem on envelope, Caracas Post Office. d, Postal motorcycles. e, Carmelitas Post Office. f, Airplane, postal bicycles. g, Falcón Post Office. h, Mail carriers. i, Zulia Post Office. j, Postal workers in San Martín.

No. 1655: a, Man, IPOSTEL emblem, letters. b, Postal worker, mail sacks. c, Mail on conveyor belt. d, Mail carriers with parcels. e, Postal workers sorting mail. f, Postal workers at Ribas Mission. g, Mail sacks. h, Doctor, medical equipment at Barrio Adentro Mission. i, Postal worker and postal machinery. j, Forklift and Mercal emblem.

2005, Oct. 10   **Perf. 12**
1654	A514	Sheet of 10	13.50	13.50
a.-b.		300b Either single	.45	.45
c.-d.		400b Either single	.50	.50
e.-f.		600b Either single	.80	.80
g.-i.		1700b Any single	2.25	2.25
j.		2000b multi	2.75	2.75
1655	A514	Sheet of 10	13.50	13.50
a.-b.		300b Either single	.45	.45
c.-d.		400b Either single	.50	.50
e.-f.		600b Either single	.80	.80
g.-i.		1700b Any single	2.25	2.25
j.		2000b multi	2.75	2.75

Central Bank of Venezuela, 65th Anniv. — A515

No. 1656: a, Bank emblem. b, Caracas branch. c, Maracaibo branch. d, Venezuela Mint. e, Children's economic educational program. f, Numismatic Museum. g, Plaza Juan Pedro López. h, Gold bars. i, Bank notes and printing plates. j, Coins.

2005, Oct. 20   **Perf. 12½x13½**
1656	A515	Sheet of 10	12.50	12.50
a.-b.		300b Either single	.45	.45
c.-d.		400b Either single	.50	.50
e.-f.		600b Either single	.80	.80
g.-h.		1500b Either single	2.00	2.00
i.-j.		1700b Either single	2.25	2.25

Christmas — A516

No. 1657 — Angel with: a, h, Long-necked stringed instrument with bow. b, j, Lute. c, Harp. d, g, Maracas. e, i, Stringed instrument with bow. f, Horn.

2005, Dec. 1   **Perf. 12**
1657	A516	Sheet of 10	12.00	12.00
a.-c.		400b Any single	.55	.55
d.-f.		600b Any single	.85	.85
g.-h.		1000b Either single	1.40	1.40
i.		1500b multi	2.10	2.10
j.		2000b multi	3.00	3.00

National Guard — A517

No. 1658: a, Villa Zoila. b, Troops and building with ornate roof. c, Troops and automobiles. d, Troops saluting. e, Helicopter. f, Troops in inflatable raft. g, Three guardsmen at industrial site. h, Two guardsmen inspecting boxes. i, Guardsman with drug-sniffing dog. j, Guardsman, children.

2006, Feb. 23
1658	A517	Sheet of 10	12.50	12.50
a.-d.		300b Any single	.45	.45
e.-f.		400b Either single	.50	.50
g.-h.		1500b Either single	2.00	2.00
i.-j.		2000b Either single	2.75	2.75

Banco Guayana, 50th Anniv. — A518

No. 1659 — Shimaraña people: a, People with painted faces. b, Archer and man with spear. c, Canoes on water. d, Women near dock. e, Man in canoe, woman's face. f, Children. g, Bow fishermen. h, Men, child, waterfall. i, Child. j, Women, dancer and river.

2006, Mar. 16
1659	A518	Sheet of 10	15.00	15.00
a.-b.		300b Either single	.45	.45
c.-f.		500b Any single	.65	.65
g.-h.		1700b Either single	2.40	2.40
i.-j.		2000b Either single	2.75	2.75

National Tax and Customs Administration (SENIAT) — A519

No. 1660 — Customs buildings in: a, Valencia. b, Puerto Cabello. c, Paraguachón. d, Santa Elena de Uairén. e, Maiquetia (in day). f, Maiquetia (at night). g, Ureña. h, Táchira. i, Barcelona. j, La Guaira.

2006, Mar. 22
1660	A519	Sheet of 10	12.50	12.50
a.-b.		400b Either single	.50	.50
c.-d.		500b Either single	.65	.65
e.-f.		700b Either single	.90	.90
g.-h.		1000b Either single	1.25	1.25
i.-j.		2000b Either single	2.75	2.75

Carauchi Hydroelectric Dam Project — A520

No. 1661: a, Dam at night. b, Aerial view of dam. c, Worker at dam. d, Power lines. e, Aerial view of dam, water flowing to right. f, Aerial view of dam, water flowing straight ahead, descriptive text at left. g, Control tower. h, Spillway. i, Electrical substation. j, Control room.

No. 1662 — Rescued animals: a, Iguana iguana. b, Caluromys philander. c, Paleosuchus palpebrosus. d, Geochelone carbonaria. e, Cebus olivaceus. f, Choloepus didactylus. g, Tupinambis teguixin. h, Lora bejuca. i, Coendou prehensilis. j, Tamandua tetradactyla.

No. 1663, Aerial view of dam, water flowing straight ahead, descriptive text at top.

2006, Apr. 6
1661	A520	Sheet of 10	16.50	16.50
a.-b.		300b Either single	.45	.45
c.-f.		1000b Any single	1.40	1.40
g.-h.		1500b Either single	2.10	2.10
i.-j.		2000b Either single	3.00	3.00
1662	A520	Sheet of 10	16.50	16.50
a.-b.		300b Either single	.45	.45
c.-f.		1000b Any single	1.40	1.40
g.-h.		1500b Either single	2.10	2.10
i.-j.		2000b Either single	3.00	3.00

Souvenir Sheet
1663	A520	1000b multi	3.25	3.25

No. 1663 contains one 42x37mm stamp.

141st Extraordinary Meeting of OPEC — A521

No. 1664 — Petroleum facilities, meeting emblem and: a, "OPEP". b, Flag of United Arab Emirates flag. c, Flag of Libya. d, Flag of Iraq. e, Flag of Saudi Arabia. f, Flag of Indonesia. g, Flag of Nigeria. h, Flag of Algeria. i, Flag of Iran. j, Flag of Qatar. k, Flag of Venezuela. l, Flag of Kuwait.

2006, June 1
1664		Sheet of 12	15.00	15.00
a.-b.	A521	300b Either single	.45	.45
c.-h.	A521	500b Any single	.65	.65
i.-j.	A521	1500b Either single	2.10	2.10
k.-l.	A521	2000b Either single	2.75	2.75

Caracas Mass Transit — A522

No. 1665: a, Train on Yellow line. b, Yellow line station. c, Plaza Venezuela Station. d, Three trains. e, Train switches. f, Line 4 Tunnel. g, Metro bus. h, Control room. i, Construction of Line 4 Nuevo Circo Station. j, Art by Jesús Soto, Chacaíto Station.

2006, July 2

1665	A522	Sheet of 10	20.00 20.00
a.-b.		300b Either single	.50 .50
c.-d.		500b Either single	.70 .70
e.-f.		1500b Either single	2.25 2.25
g.-j.		2000b Any single	3.00 3.00

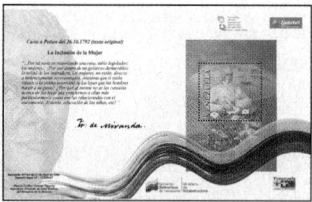

Francisco de Miranda
University — A523

No. 1666, vert.: a, Miranda on horse. b, Miranda facing left. c, Nose, mouth and hand of Miranda. d, Statue of Miranda, Venezuelan flag. e, Miranda holding flag. f, Miranda at Venezuelan independence ceremonies. g, Miranda. h, Statues of Miranda. i, Miranda facing right. j, Miranda writing letter, ship.
No. 1667, Like #1666j.

2006, July 28

1666	A523	Sheet of 10	14.00 14.00
a.-d.		300b Any single	.50 .50
e.-f.		500b Either single	.70 .70
g.-h.		1500b Either single	2.25 2.25
i.-j.		2000b Either single	3.00 3.00

Souvenir Sheet

1667	A523	1500b multi	1.40 1.40

No. 1666 contains ten 35x45mm stamps.

Children's Art — A524

No. 1668: a, Flag of Liberty, by Elimar Sanchez. b, Miranda (Miranda and broken chain), by Gabriel Solano. c, Miranda and Catalina, by Elikarina Sánchez. d, Musical Aspects of Miranda (G clef), by Josmelys Díaz. e, Miranda Playing, by Nasser Sultan. f, Miranda and His Dreams, by Cynthia Urbina. g, Flag of Miranda, by Janem Sultan. h, Miranda Thinking, by Luis Miguel Martínez. i, Miranda and His Family, by Vianny Gonella. j, Diary of Miranda, by José A. Martínez.

2006

1668	A524	Sheet of 10	14.00 14.00
a.-d.		300b Any single	.50 .50
e.-f.		500b Either single	.70 .70
g.-h.		1500b Either single	2.25 2.25
i.-j.		2000b Either single	3.00 3.00

Souvenir Sheet

CVG EDELCA, 43rd Anniv. — A525

2006

1669	A525	3500b multi	5.00 5.00

Central University, Caracas — A526

No. 1670: a, Exterior of Engineering Library. b, Interior of Engineering Library. c, Electrical Engineering Building. d, School of Engineering, Metallurgy and Material Sciences, Sculpture by Harry Abend. e, School of Civil Engineering. f, School of Chemical Engineering, Petroleum and Geology, Mines and Geophysics. g, Mural by Alejandro Otero at School of Engineering. h, Machinery at Institute of Materials and Structural Models. i, Fluid Mechanics Institute. j, Aulas Auditorium.

2006

1670	A526	Sheet of 10	27.50 27.50
a.-d.		400b Any single	.50 .50
e.-f.		600b Either single	.80 .80
g.-h.		3000b Either single	4.00 4.00
i.-j.		5000b Either single	7.00 7.00

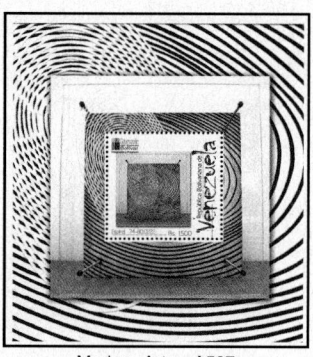

Modern Art — A527

No. 1671: a, Esfera Japón. b, Biface Naranja. c, Repetición y Progresión. d, Repetición Optica No. 2. e, Composición Dinámica. f, Muro Optico. g, Pardelas Interferentes. h, Espiral. i, Ambivalencia Dicembre. j, Estructura Cinética.
1500b, Espiral, diff.

2006

1671	A527	Sheet of 10	10.00 10.00
a.-b.		300b Either single	.50 .50
c.-f.		500b Any single	.70 .70
g.-j.		1000b Any single	1.50 1.50

Souvenir Sheet

1672	A527	1500b multi	3.25 3.25

No. 1671 contains ten 45x35mm stamps.

Transportation — A528

No. 1673: a, Airplane in flight. b, Simón Bolívar Intl. Airport, Maiquetía. c, Highway, Ayacucho. d, Highway, Barquisimeto. e, José Antonio Páez Highway. f, Caracas — La Guaira Viaduct. g, Line 3, Caracas Metro. h, Line 4, Caracas Metro. i, Maracaibo Metro. j, Teques Metro. k, Valencia Metro. l, Caracas — Tuy Medio tram.

2006

1673	A528	Sheet of 12	22.50 22.50
a.-g.		300b Any single	.50 .50
h.-j.		2000b Any single	3.00 3.00
k.-l.		3000b Either single	4.25 4.25

A529

Christmas — A530

No. 1674: a, Musicians. b, Toy. c, Top. d, Holiday table setting. e, Food. f, Letter to Baby Jesus. g, Illuminated cross. h, Yo-yo. i, Yo-yo, top and toy. j, Envelope with Holy Family.
No. 1675: a, Nativity. b, Food. c, Letter to Baby Jesus. d, IPOSTEL emblem with Holy Family.

2006

1674	A529	Sheet of 10	14.00 14.00
a.-b.		300b Either single	.45 .45
c.-d.		450b Either single	.60 .60
e.-f.		550b Either single	.75 .75
g.-h.		1000b Either single	1.40 1.40
i.		2000b multi	2.75 2.75
j.		3000b multi	4.00 4.00
1675	A529	Sheet of 4	5.25 5.25
a.-b.		300b Either single	.45 .45
c.		1000b multi	1.40 1.40
d.		2000b multi	2.75 2.75

Miniature Sheets

A531

A532

2007 Copa America Soccer
Tournament, Venezuela — A533

No. 1676: a, Mascot Guaky and soccer ball. b, City University Olympic Stadium, Caracas. c, José E. Pachencho Stadium, Maracaibo. d, Metropolitan Stadium, Lara. e, Agustín Tovar "La Carolina" Stadium, Barinas. f, General J. A. Anzoátegui Stadium, Puerto La Cruz. g, Cachamay Total Entertainment Center, Ciudad Guayana. h, Metropolitan Stadium, Mérida. i, Monumental Stadium, Maturín. j,

Multisport Stadium, Pueblo Nuevo San Cristóbal.

No. 1677 — Mascots: a, Guaky Jugador. b, Guaky Inspector. c, Guaky Bombero. d, Guaky Doctor. e, Guaky Futbolista. f, Guaky Obrero. g, Guaky Sembrador. h, Guaky Militar. i, Guaky Policia. j, Guaky Jugador, diff.

No. 1678 — Mascot Guaky and emblem of soccer governing body of: a, Venezuela. b, Brazil. c, Argentina. d, Mexico. e, Colombia. f, Chile. g, Peru. h, Uruguay. i, Ecuador. j, Bolivia. k, Paraguay. l, United States.

2007, June 18   Litho.   Perf. 12

1676	A531	Sheet of 10	20.00	20.00
a.-b.		300b Either single	.40	.40
c.-f.		400b Any single	.55	.55
g.-h.		2000b Either single	2.75	2.75
i.		3000b multi	3.75	3.75
j.		5000b multi	6.75	6.75
1677	A532	Sheet of 10	20.00	20.00
a.-b.		300b Either single	.40	.40
c.-f.		400b Any single	.55	.55
g.-h.		2000b Either single	2.75	2.75
i.		3000b multi	3.75	3.75
j.		5000b multi	6.75	6.75
1678	A533	Sheet of 12	20.00	20.00
a.-d.		300b Any single	.40	.40
e.-h.		400b Any single	.50	.50
i.-j.		2000b Either single	2.40	2.40
k.		3000b multi	3.50	3.50
l.		5000b multi	6.00	6.00
		Nos. 1676-1678 (3)	60.00	60.00

Intelligence and Prevention Service (DISIP), 38th Anniv. — A534

No. 1679 — DISIP emblem and: a, El Helicoide (Headquarters Building), denomination in red, "Venezuela" in dark blue. b, Model of El Helicoide, denomination in dark blue, "Venezuela" in orange. c, Model of El Helicoide, denomination in yellow. d, El Helicoide being built, denomination in red, "Venezuela" in green. e, Cupola of El Helicoide, denomination in orange. f, Auditorium of El Helicoide, denomination in light blue, "Venezuela" in red. g, El Helicoide, denomination in green. h, El Helicoide, denomination in red. i, Garden outside El Helicoide. j, Plaza Bolívar.

3500b, El Helicoide, denomination in yellow.

2007, June 21

1679	A534	Sheet of 10	20.00	20.00
a.-f.		300b Any single	.40	.40
g.-h.		2000b Either single	2.75	2.75
i.		3000b multi	3.75	3.75
j.		5000b multi	6.75	6.75
		Souvenir Sheet		
1680	A534	3500b multi	5.00	5.00

No. 1680 contains one 42x37mm stamp.

Miniature Sheet

Simón Bolívar Center, Caracas — A535

No. 1681: a, Muses de los Niños. b, Juan Pablo II buildings. c, Torres del Silencio. d, Palacio de Justicia. e, Parque Central building. f, Museo de Arte Contemporaneo de Caracas. g, Avenida Bolívar. h, Paseo Vargas. i, Teresa Carreño Theater. j, Cristobal Rojas.

2007, July 19

1681	A535	Sheet of 10	20.00	20.00
a.-d.		300b Any single	.40	.40
e.-f.		450b Either single	.55	.55
g.-h.		2000b Either single	2.75	2.75
i.		3000b multi	3.75	3.75
j.		5000b multi	6.75	6.75

Miniature Sheet

Christmas — A536

No. 1682 — Art: a, Resplendent God, by Hugo Rivero. b, Creole Christmas, by Vidalia González. c, Christmas Door, by Soccoro Peraza. d, Christmas, wood carvings by Orlando Campos. e, Christmas, wood carving by Tomás Flores. f, Christmas Wish, by Alberto Allup. g, St. Joseph, Virgin and Child, by Baldomero Higuera. h, Christmas, by Edgar Vegas. i, Holy Family, by Margarita Pérez de Lamanna. j, Merry Christmas, by Ana Teresa Pesce.

2007, Dec. 10

1682	A536	Sheet of 10	12.50	12.50
a.-d.		500b Any single	.65	.65
e.-h.		1000b Any single	1.40	1.40
i.-j.		1500b Either single	1.95	1.95

Miniature Sheet

Venezuelan Institute for Scientific Investigations (IVIC) — A537

No. 1683 — IVIC emblem and: a, Quimbiotec Blood Products Plant. b, Beatriz Roche Children's Band. c, Academic medal. d, Cubagua gargoyle. e, Advance Studies Center graduates. f, Bolívar and Bello Plaza. g, Molecular model. h, Investigative laboratory. i, Marcel Roche Library. j, Samuel Robinson Apartments.

2007, Dec. 14

1683	A537	Sheet of 10	15.00	15.00
a.-d.		500b Any single	.65	.65
e.-h.		1000b Any single	1.40	1.40
i.-j.		2000b Either single	2.75	2.75

Miniature Sheet

Coins and Banknotes of Revalued Currency — A538

No. 1685: a, Coins and banknotes. b, 1 centimo coin. c, 5 centimo coin. d, 10 centimo coin. e, 12½ centimo coin. f, 25 centimo coin. g, 50 centimo coin. h, 1 bolivar coin. i, Francisco de Miranda and Inia geoffrensis from 2 bolivar banknote. j, Pedro Camejo and Priodontes maximus from 5 bolivar banknote. k, Guaicaipuro and Harpia harpyja from 10 bolivar banknote. l, Luisa Cáceres de Arismendi and Eretmochelys imbricata from 20 bolivar banknote. m, Simón Rodríguez and Tremarctos ornatus from 50 bolivar banknote. n, Simon Bolivar and Carduelis cucullata from 100 bolivar banknote.

2008, May 7   Litho.   Perf. 12

1685	A538	Sheet of 14	13.50	13.50
a.-d.		40c Any single	.45	.45
e.-f.		50c Either single	.50	.50
g.-h.		60c Either single	6.00	6.00

i.-j.		1b Either single	1.00	1.00
k.-l.		1.50b Either single	1.50	1.50
m.-n.		2b Either single	2.10	2.10

Miniature Sheet

2008 Summer Olympics, Beijing — A539

No. 1686: a, Swimming. b, Weight lifting. c, Women's wrestling. d, Fencing.

2008, June 20   Perf. 12

1686	A539	1b Sheet of 4, #a-d	4.50	4.50

Miniature Sheet

Sites in Caracas — A540

No. 1687: a, Palacio de las Academias. b, Sabana Grande Boulevard. c, Plaza El Venezolano. d, Abra Solar. e, Carmelitas Post Office. f, Plaza O'Leary. g, City Hall (Palacio Municipal). h, Reflecting pool (Paseo Monumental Los Próceres). i, Casona Anauco Arriba. j, Plaza Bolívar.

3b, Reflecting pool (Paseo Monumental Los Próceres).

2008, Oct. 9   Litho.   Perf. 12

1687	A540	Sheet of 10	21.00	21.00
a.-b.		30c Either single	.35	.35
c.-d.		40c Either single	.45	.45
e.-f.		60c Either single	.60	.60
g.-h.		1.50b Either single	1.50	1.50
i.		5b multi	5.25	5.25
j.		10b multi	10.00	10.00
		Souvenir Sheet		
1688	A540	3bmulti	3.00	3.00

Miniature Sheet

Portraits of Simon Bolivar — A541

No. 1689 — Portraits by: a, José M. Espinosa. b, Pierre Colf. c, Tito Salas. d, José Gil de Castro. e, Angel Zeballos. f, Gil de Castro, diff. g, Salas, diff. h, Juan Lovera. i, Unknown artist. j, Salas, diff. k, Salas, diff. l, Daniel Hernández.

2008   Litho.   Perf. 12

1689	A541	Sheet of 12	21.00	21.00
a.-d.		30c Any single	.35	.35
e.-g.		50c Any single	.50	.50
h.-j.		1.50b Any single	1.50	1.50
k.		3b multi	3.25	3.25
l.		10b multi	10.00	10.00

Miniature Sheet

Christmas — A542

No. 1690: a, Four people wearing hats, baby. b, Children giving letters to baby Jesus. c, Woman in kitchen. d, Family eating holiday meal. e, Boy and girl with toys. f, Boys flying kite. g, Choir and musicians. h, Three children at small creche. i, Musicians. j, Children playing, house decorated with Christmas lights.

2008, Dec. 1	Litho.	Perf. 12	
1690 A542	Sheet of 10	13.00	13.00
a.-c.	30c Any single	.30	.30
d.-e.	40c Either single	.40	.40
f.-g.	1b Either single	.95	.95
h.	2b multi	1.90	1.90
i.	3b multi	2.75	2.75
j.	5b multi	4.75	4.75

Miniature Sheet

Simón Bolívar Satellite — A543

No. 1691: a, Parts of satellite. b, Arm of satellite folded up. c, Satellite on scaffolds. d, Scaffolds and sign. e, Launch pad. f, Satellite dishes. g, Lift-off. h, Satellite dishes and control building. i, Satellite dish and control room. j, Satellite in space.

2009, Jan. 8			
1691 A543	Sheet of 10	18.50	18.50
a.-b.	30c Either single	.30	.30
c.-d.	60c Either single	.55	.55
e.-f.	1b Either single	.95	.95
g.	2b multi	1.90	1.90
h.-i.	3b Either single	2.75	2.75
j.	8b multi	7.50	7.50

Miniature Sheet

Protection of Children on the Internet — A544

No. 1692: a, Two boys at laptop computer. b, Two children at desktop computers. c, Man at computer. d, Two children at laptop computer, diff. (children at right). e, Two boys at laptop computer, diff. (Children at left). f, Child at computer with adult watching. g, Group of children in computer classroom. h, Boy with finger at ear near computer. i, Man and woman in field with computer. j, Laptop computer showing children on screen.

2009, May 15			
1692 A544	Sheet of 10	16.00	16.00
a.-b.	30c Either single	.30	.30
c.-f.	50c Any single	.45	.45
g.-h.	2b Either single	1.90	1.90
i.	4b multi	3.75	3.75
j.	6.50b multi	6.00	6.00

Francisco de Miranda (1750-1816), Revolutionist in Venezuela and France — A545

2009, Oct. 15			
1693 A545	1.50b multi	1.40	1.40
a.	Souvenir sheet of 1, imperf.	1.40	1.40

See France No. 3729.

Miniature Sheets

Venezuelan Declaration of Independence, 200th Anniv. (in 2011) — A546

A547

Miniature Sheet

Signers of the Venezuelan Declaration of Independence — A548

No. 1694: a, Part 7 of Declaration of Independence. b, Part 8. c, Part 9. d, Part 4. e, Part 5. f, Part 6. g, Part 2. h, Part 3. i, Part 1. j, Signatures. k, Signatures, diff. l, Simon Bolivar and map of North and South America.

No. 1695: a, Francisco de Miranda. b, Francisco Hernández. c, Salvador Delgado. d, Juan José de Maya. e, Juan Antonio Díaz Argote. f, Felipe Fermín Paul. g, Manuel Vicente Maya. h, Juan Toro. i, Francisco Policarpo Ortiz. j, Gabriel Pérez de Pagola. k, José María Ramírez. l, Fernando Toro.

No. 1696: a, Gabriel de Ponte. b, Lino de Clemente. c, Ramón Ignacio Méndez. d, Francisco Javier Ustáriz. e, Isidoro Antonio López Méndez. f, El Marqués del Toro. g, Juan Antonio Rodríguez Domínguez. h, José de Sata y Busy. i, José Vicente de Unda. j, Antonio Nicolás Briceño.

2009		Litho.	Perf. 12	
1694 A546		Sheet of 12	21.00	21.00
a.-c.		30c Any single	.30	.30
d.-f.		50c Any single	.45	.45
g.-h.		1b Either single	.95	.95
i.-j.		2b Either single	1.90	1.90
k.		3.50b multi	3.25	3.25
l.		9.50b multi	9.00	9.00
1695 A547		Sheet of 12	21.00	21.00
a.-c.		30c Any single	.30	.30
d.-f.		50c Any single	.45	.45
g.-h.		1b Either single	.95	.95
i.-j.		2b Either single	1.90	1.90
k.		3.50b multi	3.25	3.25
l.		9.50b multi	9.00	9.00
1696 A548		Sheet of 10	21.00	21.00
a.		30c multi	.30	.30
b.-c.		50c Either single	.45	.45
d.-f.		1b Any single	.95	.95
g.-h.		2b Either single	1.90	1.90
i.		3.50b multi	3.25	3.25
j.		9.50b multi	9.00	9.00
		Nos. 1694-1696 (3)	63.00	63.00

Miniature Sheets

History of the Venezuelan Flag — A549

No. 1697 — Flag from: a, 1797. b, 1800. c, 1806 (Sun and Moon). d, 1806 (yellow, blue and red stripes). e, 1810. f, 1811. g, 1817 (7 stars). h, 1817 (8 stars). i, 1819. j, 1821 (arms in upper left corner).

No. 1698 — Flag from: a, 1821. b, 1830. c, 1836. d, 1859 (7 stars). e, 1859 (20 stars). f, 1863. g, 1905. h, 1930. i, 1954. j, 2006.

2009		Litho.	Perf. 12	
1697 A549		Sheet of 10	13.00	13.00
a.-b.		40c Either single	.40	.40
c.		50c multi	.45	.45
d.		60c multi	.55	.55
e.-f.		1b Either single	.95	.95
g.-h.		2b Either single	1.90	1.90
i.-j.		3b Either single	2.75	2.75
1698 A549		Sheet of 10	13.00	13.00
a.-b.		40c Either single	.40	.40
c.		50c multi	.45	.45
d.		60c multi	.55	.55
e.-f.		1b Either single	.95	.95
g.-h.		2b Either single	1.90	1.90
i.-j.		3b Either single	2.75	2.75

Miniature Sheets

History of the Venezuelan Coat of Arms — A550

No. 1699 — Arms from: a, 1591. b, 1811 (sun and banner). c, 1811 (dated 19 Abril de 1810). d, 1811 (dated 1811). e, 1812 (with 7 stars). f, 1812 (eagle with shield). g, 1819. h, 1821 (with eagle). i, 1821 (fasces and cornucopias). j, 1822.

No. 1700 — Arms from: a, 1830. b, 1834. c, 1836. d, 1856. e, 1863. f, 1871. g, 1905. h, 1930. i, 1954. j, 2006.

2009		Litho.	Perf. 12	
1699 A550		Sheet of 10	13.00	13.00
a.-b.		40c Either single	.40	.40
c.		50c multi	.45	.45
d.		60c multi	.55	.55
e.-f.		1b Either single	.95	.95
g.-h.		2b Either single	1.90	1.90
i.-j.		3b Either single	2.75	2.75
1700 A550		Sheet of 10	13.00	13.00
a.-b.		40c Either single	.40	.40
c.		50c multi	.45	.45
d.		60c multi	.55	.55
e.-f.		1b Either single	.95	.95
g.-h.		2b Either single	1.90	1.90
i.-j.		3b Either single	2.75	2.75

Miniature Sheet

Ayacucho Library, 35th Anniv. — A551

No. 1701 — Map color: a, Bister. b, Dark green. c, Dark blue. d, Lilac. e, Gray brown. f, Light blue. g, Yellow. h, Apple green. i, Brownish lilac. j, Gray.

2009		Litho.	Perf. 12	
1701 A551		Sheet of 10	19.00	19.00
a.-d.		30c Any single	.30	.30
e.-f.		2b Either single	1.90	1.90
g.-h.		0.50b Either single	3.25	3.25
i.-j.		4b Either single	3.75	3.75

Miniature Sheet

Christmas — A552

No. 1702 — Religious art by: a, Lidoska Pirela. b, Miguel MarSán. c, Thays Arteaga. d, Gustavo Martínez. e, Orlando Campos. f, Daniel Sanseviero. g, Hugo Rivero. h, Edgar Vegas. i, Liliana Benítez. j, Alberto Allup.

2009				
1702 A552		Sheet of 10	16.00	16.00
a.-d.		30c Any single	.30	.30
e.-g.		50c Any single	.45	.45

h.	3.10b multi	3.00	3.00
i.	4.20b multi	4.00	4.00
j.	6.50b multi	6.25	6.25

Miniature Sheets

A553

Signers of the Venezuelan Declaration
of Independence — A554

No. 1703: a, Juan Germán Roscio. b, Fernando Peñalver. c, Martín Tovar Ponte. d, Ignacio Fernández. e, José Angel Alamo. f, Luis Ignacio Mendoza. g, Nicolás de Castro. h, Ignacio Ramón Briceño. i, Francisco Javier Yánes. j, Gabriel de Alcalá.

No. 1704: a, Mariano de la Cova. b, Juan Bermúdez. c, Francisco Isnardi. d, Manuel Plácido Maneiro. e, Juan Pablo Pacheco. f, José Luis Cabrera. g, Manuel Palacio. h, Juan Nepomuceno Quintana. i, Luis José de Cazorla. j, Francisco Javier de Mayz.

2009			***Perf. 12***
1703	A553 Sheet of 10	20.00	20.00
a.-b.	30c Either single	.30	.30
c.	50c multi	.45	.45
d.-f.	1b Any single	.95	.95
g.-h.	2b Either single	1.90	1.90
i.	3.50b multi	3.25	3.25
j.	9.50b multi	9.00	9.00
1704	A554 Sheet of 10	19.50	19.50
a.-b.	30c Either single	.30	.30
c.-d.	50c Either single	.45	.45
e.-f.	1b multi	.95	.95
g.-h.	2b Either single	1.90	1.90
i.	3.50b multi	3.25	3.25
j.	9.50b multi	9.00	9.00

Miniature Sheet

Bolivarian Militia — A555

No. 1705 — General Command Building: a, Domed and crenellated tower. b, Columns and balcony. c, Flag above main entrance. d, Round crenellated tower in foreground. e, Round crenellated tower in background. f, Rectangular tower. g, Columns and Plaza of Honor. h, Militia members, round crenellated tower in background. i, Building. j, Building and flag.

2010, Apr. 21			
1705	A555 Sheet of 10	16.50	16.50
a.-c.	1b Any single	.45	.45
d.-f.	2b Any single	.95	.95
g.-h.	4.50b Either single	2.10	2.10
i.	6b multi	2.75	2.75
j.	10.50b multi	5.00	5.00

Miniature Sheet

Prominent Figures of the First
Republic of Venezuela — A556

No. 1706: a, Juan Germán Roscio (1763-1821). b, José Félix Ribas (1775-1815). c, Francisco Espejo (1758-1814). d, Isidoro Lópex Méndez (1751-1814). e, Lino de Clemente (1767-1834). f, José Félix Sosa (1773-1814). g, Martín Tovar Ponte (1772-1843). h, Francisco Javier Ustáriz (1772-1814). i, Francisco Salias (1785-1834). j, José Cortés de Madariaga (1766-1826).

2010, Apr. 28			
1706	A556 Sheet of 10	17.50	17.50
a.-b.	1b Either single	.45	.45
c.-f.	2.50b Any single	1.25	1.25
g.-i.	4b Any single	1.90	1.90
j.	12b multi	5.75	5.75

Manuela Sáenz (c. 1797-1856),
Mistress of Simón Bolívar — A557

2010, May 24

1707	A557 2.50b multi	1.25	1.25

See Ecuadoe No. 2007.

Miniature Sheet

Scenes From Independence Day
Military Parade — A558

No. 1708: a, National flag (Bandera Nacional). b, Athletes on float (Atletas). c, Women from cultural group wearing yellow and green dresses (Agrupaciones Culturales). d, People from cultural group wearing masks, red and white costumes (Agrupaciones Culturales). e, Women from cultural group wearing headdresses and white blouses (Agrupaciones Culturales). f, Indigenous people (Etnias Indígenas). g, People carrying flags (Estandartes FANB). h, Two uniformed men and white horse (Réplica de la Espada del Libertador). i, Soldiers from Venezuela Military Academy marching (Academia Militar de Venezuela). j, Sailors from Naval School (Escuela Naval). k, Students from Military Aviation School (Escuela de Aviación Militar). l, Students from National Guard Officer's Training School (EFOFAC). m, Students from Military Technical School (Escuela Técnica Militar). n, Male members of Bolivarian Militia wearing red pants (Milicia Bolivariana). o, Female members of Bolivarian Militia wearing white boots (Milicia Bolivariana). p, Rural militia (Milicia Campesina). q, AMX-30 tank. r, C-90 Escorpión tank. s, Dragón 300 armored fighting vehicle. t, E-11 Urutu armored personnel carrier. u, Oto Melara armored personnel carrier. v, Sultán tank. w, AMX-13 tank. x, Tank of Mechanized Infantry with banner (Infantería Mecanizada del Ejército). y, Members of Brazil delegation. z, Members of Cuba delegation. aa, Members of Bolivia delegation. ab, Members of Nicaragua delegation. ac, Members of Argentina delegation. ad, Members of Ecuador delegation. ae, Members of Belarus delegation. af, Members of Dominican Republic delegation. ag, Members of Parachute battalion (Batallón de Paracaidistas). ah, Members of Caribbean Batallion (Batallón de Caribes). ai, Members of Forest Batallion (Batallón de Selva). aj, Special Forces wearing jungle camouflage with hoods (Fuerzas Especiales). ak, Special Forces members, man with black ski cap at right (Fuerzas Especiales). al, Special Forces members with open mouths and camouflage painted faces, white gun straps (Fuerzas Especiales). am, Special Forces members wearing red berets (Fuerzas Especiales). an, Special Forces members with fully-painted faces, black gun straps (Fuerzas Especiales). ao, Sukhoi 30MK2 jet. ap, F-16 jet. aq, K-8 jet. ar, MI-26T Panare helicopter. as, MI-35M Caribe helicopter. at, MI-17V5 Pemón helicopter. au, Sikorsky AS-61D helicopter. av, Mounted sqadron (Escuadrón de Caballería).

2010, Aug. 9

1708	Sheet of 48	17.00	17.00
a.-x.	A558 30c Any single	.25	.25
y.-av.	A558 1b Any single	.45	.45

Organization of Petroleum Exporting
Countries (OPEC), 50th
Anniv. — A559

No. 1709 — Paintings: a, Sembradores, by Ender Cepeda. b, Y Por Fin Nos Tocó Un Chorrito de Petróleo, by Soccorro Salinas. c, Cartografía Soberana, by Saúl Huerta. d, Serie Atardecer en Campos Petroleros, by Ernesto León. e, Como Caída del Cielo, by Rosa Contreras. f, Marea, by Morella Jurado. g, Julio, by Omar Carreño. h, Del Reventón al Barril Dorado, by Gabriel Bracho. i, Petróleo Nuestro de Cada Día, by Manuel Quintana Castillo. j, El Pozo y Las Ocho Estrellas, by Paúl Del Río.

12p, 50th anniversary emblem, horiz.

2010, Sept. 14			
1709	Sheet of 10	17.50	17.50
a.-c.	30c Any single	.25	.25
d.-e.	50c Either single	.25	.25
f.-g.	3b Either single	1.40	1.40
h.	8b multi	3.75	3.75
i.-j.	10b Either single	4.75	4.75
Souvenir Sheet			
1710	A559 12b multi	5.75	5.75

No. 1710 contains one 42x37mm stamp.

Miniature Sheet

Central Bank of Venezuela Art
Collection, 70th Anniv. — A560

No. 1711 — Paintings: a, Venezuela, by Armando Reverón. b, Formas en Equilibio N-1, by Angel Hurtado. c, Bananeros, by Camille Pissarro. d, La Pareja, by Armando Barrias. e, Left half of El Avila Visto Desde el Country Club (trees at left), by Manuel Cabré. f, Right half of El Avila Visto Desde el Country Club (trees at right), by Cabré.

2010, Nov. 24			
1711	A560 Sheet of 6	19.00	19.00
a.-b.	30c Either single	.25	.25
c.	5b multi	2.40	2.40
d.	8b multi	3.75	3.75
e.-f.	12.50b Either single	6.00	6.00

Miniature Sheet

Christmas — A561

No. 1712: a, Nativity. b, Satellite over the three Magi. c, Musicians. d, Cable car, buildings on mountainside, children playing. e, Woman and man at market. f, Fireworks over building. g, Teacher and children in school room, boy working at computer. h, Father and son opening Christmas gift. i, Father and son outside of candy store. j, Child on blanket in plaza, people, bus.

2010, Dec. 7			
1712	A561 Sheet of 10	18.50	18.50
a.-c.	30c Any single	.25	.25
d.-e.	60c Either single	.30	.30
f.-g.	4.50b Either single	2.10	2.10
h.	6.50b multi	3.00	3.00
i.-j.	10b Either single	4.75	4.75

Miniature Sheet

Venezuelan Antarctic Program — A562

No. 1713: a, Members of first expedition, 2008. b, Scientists taking measurements. c, Members of third expedition, 2010. d, Line of expedition members in snowstorm. e, Iceberg adrift. f, Antarctic base buildings, iceberg. g, Members of second expedition, 2009. h, Giant petrel. i, Penguins and ship, Barrientos Island. j, Whale at surface.

2010, Dec. 21			***Perf. 12¼x12***
1713	A562 Sheet of 10	19.00	19.00
a.-b.	30c Either single	.25	.25
c.-d.	40c Either single	.25	.25
e.-f.	60c Either single	.30	.30
g.	6.50b multi	3.00	3.00
h.-i.	8.50b Either single	4.00	4.00
j.	13.50b multi	6.25	6.25

America Issue (National
Symbols) — A563

2011, Feb. 21		***Perf. 14¼***
1714	A563 2b multi	.95 .95

Miniature Sheet

Army Day — A564

No. 1715 — Uniform of: a, Batallón Bravos de Apure. b, Guardia de Honor del Libertador. c, Soldado Llanero. d, Batallón de Rifles. e, Batallón Tiradores de la Guardia. f, Cazadores Britanicos. g, Dragones de la Guardia. h, Husares de Páez. i, General de División Patriota. j, Campaña del Libertador.

2011, June 27			***Perf. 12***
1715	A564 Sheet of 10	18.00	18.00
a.-b.	30c Either single	.25	.25
c.-e.	40c Any single	.25	.25
f.-g.	1.50b Either single	.70	.70
h.	6.50b multi	3.00	3.00
i.	10b multi	4.75	4.75
j.	15.60b multi	7.25	7.25

Reunion of the Patriotic Society, by Tito Salas — A565

The Pantheon of Heroes, by Arturo Michelena — A566

No. 1717: a, Woman in black dress at right (left fifth of painting). b, Three men seated on bench at right, man at lectern in foreground (fourth fifth of painting). c, Bearded man standing at right (right fifth of painting). d, Woman with white dress in foreground at table (second fifth of painting). e, As "a." f, As "b." g, Three men seated on bench at left, lectern in foreground (middle fifth of painting). h, As "d." i, As "b." j, As "g."

2011, June 27		Perf. 12	
1716	A565	Sheet of 10	22.50	22.50
a.-c.		30c Any single	.25	.25
d.-e.		60c Either single	.30	.30
f.		1.50b multi	.70	.70
g.-h.		8.50b Either single	4.00	4.00
i.-j.		12.50b Either single	6.00	6.00
Souvenir Sheet				
1717	A566	18b multi	8.50	8.50

SEMI-POSTAL STAMPS

A 5c green stamp of the Cruzada Venezolana Sanitaria Social portraying Simon Bolivar was overprinted "EE. UU. DE VENEZUELA CORREOS" in 1937.

It is stated that 50,000 stamps without control numbers on back were sold by post offices and 147,700 with control numbers on back were offered for sale by the Society at eight times face value.

Bolívar Funeral Carriage SP1

Unwmk.				
1942, Dec. 17		**Engr.**	**Perf. 12**	
B1	SP1	20c + 5c blue	6.00	.65

Cent. of the arrival of Simón Bolívar's remains in Caracas. The surtax was used to erect a monument to his memory. See Nos. CB1-CB2.

> **Catalogue values for unused stamps in this section, from this point to the end of the section, are for Never Hinged items.**

Red Cross Nurse — SP2

1975, Dec. 15		**Litho.**	**Perf. 14**	
B2	SP2	30c + 15c multi	.40	.25
B3	SP2	50c + 25c multi	.60	.40

Surtax for Venezuelan Red Cross.

Carmen América Fernandez de Leoni — SP3

Children in Home — SP4

1976, June 7		**Litho.**	**Perf. 13½**	
B4	SP3	30c + 15c multi	.30	.25
B5	SP4	50c + 25c multi	.50	.35

Surtax was for the Children's Foundation, founded by Carmen América Fernandez de Leoni in 1966.

Patient — SP5

1976, Dec. 8		**Litho.**	**Perf. 14**	
B6	SP5	10c + 5c multi	.25	.25
B7	SP5	30c + 10c multi	.25	.25

Surtax was for Anti-tuberculosis Society.

AIR POST STAMPS

Air post stamps of 1930-42 perforated "GN" (Gobierno Nacional) were for official use.

Airplane and Map of Venezuela
AP1　　　　AP2

1930		**Unwmk.　Litho.**	**Perf. 12**	
C1	AP1	5c bister brn	.25	.25
C2	AP1	10c yellow	.25	.25
a.		10c salmon	32.50	32.50
C3	AP1	15c gray	.25	.25
C4	AP1	15c lilac	.25	.25
C5	AP1	40c olive grn	.25	.25
a.		40c slate blue	40.00	
b.		40c slate green	40.00	
C6	AP1	75c dp red	.30	.25
C7	AP1	1b indigo	.45	.25
C8	AP1	1.20b blue grn	.70	.25
C9	AP1	1.70b dk blue	.90	.45
C10	AP1	1.90b blue grn	.90	.50
C11	AP1	2.10b dk blue	1.75	.50
C12	AP1	2.30b vermilion	1.75	.50
C13	AP1	2.50b dk blue	1.75	.50
C14	AP1	3.70b blue grn	1.75	1.10
C15	AP1	10b dull vio	5.25	2.40
C16	AP1	20b gray grn	8.00	4.50
Nos. C1-C16 (16)			24.75	12.70

Nos. C1-C16 exist imperforate or partly perforated. See Nos. C119-C126.
Issued: 10b, 6/8; 20b, 6/16; others, 4/5.

Bluish Winchester Security Paper

1932, July 12		**Engr.**	**Perf. 12½**	
C17	AP2	5c brown	.40	.25
C18	AP2	10c org yel	.40	.25
C19	AP2	15c gray lilac	.40	.25
C20	AP2	25c violet	.40	.25
C21	AP2	40c ol grn	.80	.25
C22	AP2	70c rose	.55	.25
C23	AP2	75c red org	1.00	.25
C24	AP2	1b dk bl	1.10	.25
C25	AP2	1.20b green	2.25	.85
C26	AP2	1.70b red brn	4.50	.55
C27	AP2	1.80b ultra	2.25	.35
C28	AP2	1.90b green	5.50	3.50
C29	AP2	1.95b blue	6.50	2.75
C30	AP2	2b blk brn	4.00	2.25
C31	AP2	2.10b blue	9.25	5.50
C32	AP2	2.30b red	4.00	2.25
C33	AP2	2.50b dk bl	5.50	1.40
C34	AP2	3b dk vio	5.50	.85
C35	AP2	3.70b emerald	7.75	5.50
C36	AP2	4b red org	5.50	1.40
C37	AP2	5b black	6.50	2.25
C38	AP2	8b dk car	13.00	4.50
C39	AP2	10b dk vio	25.00	7.75
C40	AP2	20b grnsh slate	55.00	20.00
Nos. C17-C40 (24)			167.05	63.65

Pairs imperf. between exist of the 1b (value $150); the 25c and 4b (value $300 each).

Air Post Stamps of 1932 Surcharged in Black

1937, June 4				
C41	AP2	5c on 1.70b red brn	11.00	7.00
C42	AP2	10c on 3.70b emer	11.00	7.00
C43	AP2	15c on 4b red org	5.00	3.50
C44	AP2	25c on 5b blk	5.00	3.50
C45	AP2	1b on 8b dk car	4.00	3.50
C46	AP2	2b on 2.10b bl	30.00	23.00
Nos. C41-C46 (6)			66.00	47.50

Various varieties of surcharge exist, including double and triple impressions. No. C43 exists in pair imperf. between; value $30 unused, $50 used.

Allegory of Flight AP3

Allegory of Flight AP4

National Pantheon at Caracas AP5

Airplane — AP6

AP7

Perf. 11, 11½ and Compound

1937, July 1			**Litho.**	
C47	AP3	5c brn org	.30	.40
C48	AP4	10c org red	.25	.25
C49	AP5	15c gray blk	.60	.40
C50	AP6	25c dk vio	.60	.40
C51	AP4	40c yel grn	1.10	.55
C52	AP3	70c red	1.10	.40
C53	AP5	75c bister	2.50	1.30
C54	AP3	1b dk gray	1.50	.55
C55	AP4	1.20b pck grn	6.50	4.25
C56	AP3	1.80b dk ultra	3.25	2.00
C57	AP5	1.95b lt ultra	10.00	7.75
C58	AP6	2b chocolate	4.25	2.75
C59	AP6	2.50b gray bl	11.50	11.50
C60	AP4	3b lt vio	6.50	4.50
C61	AP6	3.70b rose red	11.50	15.00
C62	AP5	10b red vio	25.00	15.00
C63	AP3	20b gray	30.00	23.00
Nos. C47-C63 (17)			116.45	90.00

All values exist imperf, and all except the 3.70b part-perf.
Counterfeits exist.
For overprints & surcharges see Nos. C66-C78, C114-C118, C164-C167, C169-C172, C174-C180.

1937, Oct. 28			**Perf. 11**	
C64	AP7	70c emerald	1.40	.55
C65	AP7	1.80b ultra	2.25	1.00

Acquisition of the Port of La Guaira by the Government from the British Corporation, June 3, 1937. Exist imperf.
A redrawn printing of #C64-C65, with lower inscription beginning "Nacionalización . ." was prepared but not issued. Value, $40 each.
For overprints see Nos. C168, C173.

Air Post Stamps of 1937 Overprinted in Black

1937, Dec. 17			**Perf. 11, 11½**	
C66	AP4	10c org red	1.00	.70
a.		Inverted overprint	15.00	12.00
C67	AP6	25c dk vio	2.00	1.00
C68	AP6	40c yel grn	2.00	1.40
C69	AP3	70c red	1.50	1.00
a.		Inverted overprint	15.00	14.00
b.		Double overprint	20.00	16.00
C70	AP3	1b dk gray	2.00	1.40
a.		Inverted overprint	16.00	13.00
b.		Double overprint	13.00	
C71	AP4	1.20b pck grn	30.00	20.00
a.		Inverted overprint	77.50	
C72	AP3	1.80b dk ultra	5.75	2.40
C73	AP5	1.95b lt ultra	7.75	4.25
a.		Inverted overprint	60.00	40.00
C74	AP6	2b chocolate	50.00	23.00
a.		Inverted overprint	100.00	90.00
b.		Double overprint	82.50	82.50
C75	AP6	2.50b gray bl	50.00	19.00
a.		Double overprint	70.00	
b.		Inverted overprint	100.00	82.50
C76	AP4	3b lt vio	30.00	12.00
C77	AP5	10b red vio	72.50	40.00
C78	AP3	20b gray	77.50	47.50
a.		Double overprint	150.00	150.00
Nos. C66-C78 (13)			332.00	173.65

Counterfeit overprints exist on #C77-C78.

View of La Guaira AP8

National Pantheon AP9

Oil Wells AP10

1938-39		**Engr.**	**Perf. 12**	
C79	AP8	5c green	1.00	.50
C80	AP8	5c dk grn	.25	.25
C81	AP9	10c car rose	1.40	.80
C82	AP9	10c scarlet	.25	.25
C83	AP8	12½c dull vio	.60	.55
C84	AP10	15c slate vio	3.00	1.25
C85	AP10	15c dk bl	.85	.25
C86	AP8	25c dk bl	3.00	1.25
C87	AP8	25c bis brn	.25	.25
C88	AP10	30c vio ('39)	2.00	.25
C89	AP9	40c dk vio	3.50	1.25
C90	AP9	40c redsh brn	2.50	.25

C91	AP8	45c Prus grn ('39)	1.00	.25
C92	AP9	50c blue ('39)	1.25	.25
C93	AP10	70c car rose	.85	.25
C94	AP8	75c bis brn	6.00	2.00
C95	AP10	75c ol bis	1.40	.25
C96	AP10	90c red org ('39)	1.00	.25
C97	AP9	1b ol & bis	7.00	2.75
C98	AP9	1b dk vio	1.25	.25
C99	AP10	1.20b orange	20.00	5.75
C100	AP10	1.20b green	2.00	.55
C101	AP8	1.80b ultra	2.00	.55
C102	AP9	1.90b black	5.50	2.75
C103	AP8	1.95b lt bl	4.25	2.50
C104	AP8	2b ol gray	45.00	15.00
C105	AP8	2b car rose	1.75	.70
C106	AP9	2.50b red brn	45.00	20.00
C107	AP9	2.50b orange	10.00	2.75
C108	AP10	3b bl grn	20.00	4.75
C109	AP10	3b ol gray	5.50	2.00
C110	AP8	3.70b gray blk	7.75	5.50
C111	AP10	5b red brn ('39)	7.75	2.00
C112	AP9	10b vio brn	20.00	2.40
C113	AP10	20b red org	57.50	25.00
		Nos. C79-C113 (35)	292.35	105.55

See Nos. C227a, C235-C236, C254-C255.
For surcharge see No. C227.

Nos. C51, C56, C58-C59, C61
Surcharged

1938, Apr. 15   *Perf. 11, 11½*

C114	AP3	5c on 1.80b	.85	.60
a.		Inverted surcharge	12.50	7.50
C115	AP6	10c on 2.50b	3.00	1.40
a.		Inverted surcharge	10.00	7.50
C116	AP6	15c on 2b	1.40	1.10
C117	AP4	15c on 40c	1.75	1.40
C118	AP4	40c on 3.70b	3.50	3.25
		Nos. C114-C118 (5)	10.50	7.75

Plane & Map Type of 1930
White Paper; No Imprint

1938-39   Engr.   *Perf. 12½*

C119	AP1	5c dk grn ('39)	.25	.25
C120	AP1	10c org yel ('39)	.55	.25
C121	AP1	12½c rose vio ('39)	1.10	.85
C122	AP1	15c dp bl	.95	.25
C123	AP1	25c brown	1.10	.25
C124	AP1	40c olive ('39)	2.75	.40
C125	AP1	70c rose car ('39)	20.00	7.75
C126	AP1	1b dk bl ('39)	7.75	3.00
		Nos. C119-C126 (8)	34.45	13.00

Monument to Sucre — AP11

Monuments at Carabobo
AP12   AP13

1938, Dec. 23   *Perf. 13½*

C127	AP11	20c brn blk	.80	.30
C128	AP12	30c purple	1.20	.30
C129	AP13	45c dk bl	1.75	.25
C130	AP11	50c lt ultra	1.50	.25
C131	AP13	70c dk car	26.00	7.50
C132	AP12	90c red org	2.50	.75
C133	AP13	1.35b gray blk	3.00	1.00
C134	AP11	1.40b slate gray	12.00	2.75
C135	AP12	2.25b green	6.00	2.00
		Nos. C127-C135 (9)	54.75	15.10

For surcharge see No. C198.

Simón Bolívar and Carabobo Monument AP14

1940, Mar. 30   *Perf. 12*

C136	AP14	15c blue	.75	.25
C137	AP14	20c olive bis	.75	.25
C138	AP14	25c red brn	2.75	.40
C139	AP14	40c blk brn	2.25	.25
C140	AP14	1b red lilac	5.00	.55
C141	AP14	2b rose car	11.00	1.40
		Nos. C136-C141 (6)	22.50	3.10

"The Founding of Grand Colombia" AP15

1940, June 13

C142	AP15	15c copper brown	1.25	.45

Founding of the Pan American Union, 50th anniv.

Statue of Simón Bolívar, Caracas — AP16

1940-44

C143	AP16	5c dk grn ('42)	.25	.25
C144	AP16	10c scar ('42)	.25	.25
C145	AP16	12½c dull purple	.75	.30
C146	AP16	15c blue ('43)	.50	.25
C147	AP16	20c bis brn ('44)	.50	.25
C148	AP16	25c bis brn ('42)	.50	.25
C149	AP16	30c dp vio ('43)	.50	.25
C150	AP16	40c blk brn ('43)	.65	.25
C151	AP16	45c turq grn ('43)	.65	.25
C152	AP16	50c blue ('44)	.65	.25
C153	AP16	70c rose pink	2.00	.30
C154	AP16	75c ol bis ('43)	7.75	1.60
C155	AP16	90c red org ('43)	1.25	.30
C156	AP16	1b dp red lil ('42)	.65	.25
C157	AP16	1.20b dp yel grn ('43)	2.50	.70
C158	AP16	1.35b gray blk ('42)	10.50	3.50
C159	AP16	2b rose pink ('43)	2.00	.25
C160	AP16	3b ol blk ('43)	3.25	.75
C161	AP16	4b black	2.50	.75
C162	AP16	5b red brn ('44)	20.00	8.00
		Nos. C143-C162 (20)	57.60	19.00

See Nos. C232-C234, C239-C253. For surcharges see Nos. C225, C873.

Nos. C48, C50-C65 Overprinted

Resellado 1943

Perf. 11, 11½ & Compound
1943, Dec. 21

C164	AP4	10c orange red	2.00	.90
C165	AP4	25c dk violet	2.00	.90
C166	AP4	40c yellow grn	2.00	.90
C167	AP3	70c red	2.00	.90
C168	AP7	70c emerald	2.00	.90
C169	AP5	75c bister	2.00	.90
C170	AP3	1b dk gray	2.00	.90
C171	AP4	1.20b peacock grn	5.00	1.60
C172	AP3	1.80b dk ultra	5.00	1.60
C173	AP7	1.80b dk ultra	5.00	2.50
C174	AP4	1.95b lt ultra	6.00	3.25
C175	AP6	2b chocolate	6.00	3.25
C176	AP5	2.50b gray blue	5.00	3.25
C177	AP4	3b lt violet	6.00	3.25
C178	AP5	3.70b rose red	52.50	45.00
C179	AP5	10b red violet	12.00	10.00
C180	AP3	20b gray	27.50	20.00
		Nos. C164-C180 (17)	144.00	100.00
		Set, never hinged	175.00	

Issued for sale to philatelists. Nos. C164-C169 were sold only in sets.
Nearly all are known with invtd. ovpt.

Flags of Venezuela and the Red Cross — AP17
Baseball Players — AP18

1944, Aug. 22   Litho.   *Perf. 12*
Flags in red, yellow, blue and black

C181	AP17	5c gray green	.25	.25
C182	AP17	10c magenta	.25	.25
C183	AP17	20c brt blue	.25	.25
C184	AP17	30c violet bl	.35	.25
C185	AP17	40c chocolate	.50	.25
C186	AP17	45c apple green	.50	.45
C187	AP17	90c orange	1.25	.45
C188	AP17	1b gray black	3.00	.45
		Nos. C181-C188 (8)	6.35	2.60
		Set, never hinged	9.50	

80th anniv. of the Intl. Red Cross and 37th anniv. of Venezuela's joining the organization. Nos. C181-C188 exist imperf. and part perf.

1944, Oct. 12
"AEREO" in dark carmine

C189	AP18	5c dull vio brn	.30	.25
C190	AP18	10c gray green	.50	.25
C191	AP18	20c ultra	.50	.25
C192	AP18	30c dull rose	1.00	.40
C193	AP18	45c rose violet	2.00	.70
C194	AP18	90c red orange	3.50	1.40
C195	AP18	1b dark gray	4.00	1.40
C196	AP18	1.20b yellow grn	9.25	7.25
C197	AP18	1.80b ocher	12.00	9.25
		Nos. C189-C197 (9)	33.05	21.15
		Set, never hinged	42.50	

7th World Amateur Baseball Championship Games, Caracas.
Nos. C189-C197 exist imperf, and all but 1b exist part perf. Various errors of "AEREO" overprint exist.

No. C134 Surcharged in Black
Habilitado 1944 VALE Bs. 0.30

1944, Nov. 17   *Perf. 13½*

C198	AP11	30c on 1.40b	.50	.50
a.		Double surcharge	35.00	35.00
b.		Inverted surcharge	13.50	13.50

Charles Howarth — AP19

1944, Dec. 21   Unwmk.   *Perf. 12*

C199	AP19	5c black	.25	.25
C200	AP19	10c purple	.25	.25
C201	AP19	20c sepia	.35	.35
C202	AP19	30c dull green	.40	.35
C203	AP19	1.20b bister	1.90	1.60
C204	AP19	1.80b deep ultra	4.50	3.25
C205	AP19	3.70b rose	3.25	3.25
		Nos. C199-C205 (7)	10.90	9.30
		Set, never hinged	18.00	

Cent. of founding of 1st cooperative shop in Rochdale, England, by Charles Howarth.
Nos. C199-C205 exist imperf. and part perf.

Antonio José de Sucre — AP20

1945, Mar. 3   Engr.

C206	AP20	5c orange	.25	.25
C207	AP20	10c violet	.25	.25
C208	AP20	20c grnsh blk	.25	.25
C209	AP20	30c brt green	.25	.25
C210	AP20	40c olive	1.10	1.10
C211	AP20	45c black brn	1.60	1.10
C212	AP20	90c redsh brn	2.10	1.10
C213	AP20	1b dp red lil	2.10	1.10
C214	AP20	1.20b black	6.25	5.25
C215	AP20	2b yellow	10.00	7.25
		Nos. C206-C215 (10)	24.15	17.90
		Set, never hinged	30.00	

150th birth anniv. of Antonio Jose de Sucre, Grand Marshal of Ayacucho.

Type of 1946
1946, Aug. 24   *Perf. 12*

C216	A81	30c Bello	1.10	.25
C217	A82	30c Urdaneta	1.10	.25
		Set, never hinged	2.75	

Allegory of Republic — AP23

Perf. 11½
1946, Oct. 18   Litho.   Unwmk.

C218	AP23	15c dp violet bl	.40	.25
C219	AP23	20c bister brn	.40	.25
C220	AP23	30c dp violet	.50	.25
C221	AP23	1b brt rose	3.50	2.75
		Nos. C218-C221 (4)	4.80	3.60
		Set, never hinged	6.25	

Anniversary of the Revolution of October, 1945. Exist imperf. and part perf.

Nos. 297, 371, C152 and 362 Surcharged in Black
J. R. G. AEREO Vale Bs. 0.15 1946

1947, Jan.   *Perf. 12*

C223	A49	10c on 22½c dp car	.25	.25
a.		Inverted surcharge	4.00	4.00
C224	A69	15c on 25c lt bl	.40	.25
C225	AP16	20c on 50c blue	.40	.25
a.		Inverted surcharge	5.00	5.00
C226	A65	70c on 1b dk vio brn	.75	.45
a.		Inverted surcharge	4.00	4.00

Type of 1938 Surcharged in Black

J. R. G. AEREO Vale Bs. 20 1946

C227	AP10	20b on 20b org red	28.00	22.50
a.		Surcharge omitted	92.50	40.00
		Nos. C223-C227 (5)	29.80	23.70
		Set, never hinged	40.00	

"J. R. G." are the initials of "Junta Revolucionaria de Gobierno."
Also exist: 20c on #C143, 10c on #371.

Anti-tuberculosis Institute, Maracaibo — AP24

1947, Jan. 12   Litho.
Venezuela Shown on Map in Yellow

C228	AP24	15c dark blue	.45	.35
C229	AP24	20c dark brown	.45	.35
C230	AP24	30c violet	.45	.35
C231	AP24	1b carmine	4.75	3.75
		Nos. C228-C231 (4)	6.10	4.80
		Set, never hinged	8.00	

12th Pan-American Health Conf., Caracas, Jan. 1947.

Nos. C228-C231 exist imperf., part perf. and with yellow omitted.

Types of 1938-40

1947, Mar. 17   Engr.

C232	AP16	75c orange	7.50	4.50
C233	AP16	1b brt ultra	.70	.25
C234	AP16	3b red brown	17.50	8.00
C235	AP10	5b scarlet	15.00	5.00
C236	AP9	10b violet	20.00	7.50
		Nos. C232-C236 (5)	60.70	25.25
		Set, never hinged	85.00	

On Nos. C235 and C236 the numerals of value are in color on a white tablet.

No. 370 Surcharged in Black

1947, June 20

C237	A70	5c on 20c blue	.40	.25
C238	A70	10c on 20c blue	.40	.25
a.		Inverted surcharge	5.00	5.00
		Set, never hinged	1.00	

Types of 1938-44

1947-48   Engr.

C239	AP16	5c orange	.25	.25
C240	AP16	10c dk green	.25	.25
C241	AP16	12½ bister brn	.45	.45
C242	AP16	15c gray	.25	.25
C243	AP16	20c violet	.25	.25
C244	AP16	25c dull green	.25	.25
C245	AP16	30c brt ultra	.45	.25
C246	AP16	40c green ('48)	.25	.25
C247	AP16	45c vermicion	.45	.25
C248	AP16	50c red violet	.25	.25
C249	AP16	70c dk car	1.00	.45
C250	AP16	75c purple ('48)	.65	.25
C251	AP16	90c black	1.00	.30
C252	AP16	1.20b red brn ('48)	1.25	.50
C253	AP16	3b dp blue	1.75	.50
C254	AP10	5b olive grn	9.25	5.00
C255	AP9	10b yellow	8.25	4.75
		Nos. C239-C255 (17)	26.25	14.45
		Set, never hinged	35.00	

On Nos. C254 and C255 the numerals of value are in color on a white tablet.
Issue dates: 5c, 10c, Oct. 8. 15c, Dec. 2, 40c, 75c, 1.20b, May 10, 1948. Others, Oct. 27, 1947.

M. S. Republica de Venezuela — AP25

Imprint: "American Bank Note Company"

1948-50   Unwmk.   Perf. 12

C256	AP25	5c red brown	.25	.25
C257	AP25	10c deep green	.25	.25
C258	AP25	15c brown	.25	.25
C259	AP25	20c violet brn	.35	.25
C260	AP25	25c brown black	.35	.25
C261	AP25	30c olive green	.35	.25
C262	AP25	45c blue green	.65	.35
C263	AP25	50c gray black	1.00	.55
C264	AP25	70c orange	1.75	.55
C265	AP25	75c brt ultra	3.00	.75
C266	AP25	90c car lake	1.75	1.10
C267	AP25	1b purple	2.40	1.10
C268	AP25	2b gray	2.50	1.75
C269	AP25	3b emerald	9.75	5.50
C270	AP25	4b deep blue	4.50	5.50
C271	AP25	5b orange red	18.00	8.25
		Nos. C256-C271 (16)	47.10	27.55

Issued to honor the Grand-Colombian Merchant Fleet. See Nos. C554-C556.
Issued: 5c, 10c, 15c, 25c, 30c, 1b, 7/9/48; 45c, 75c, 5b, 5/11/50; others, 3/9/49.
For surcharges see Nos. C863-C864.

Santos Michelena AP26

1949, Apr. 25

C272	AP26	5c orange brn	.25	.25
C273	AP26	10c gray	.25	.25
C274	AP26	15c red orange	.50	.50
C275	AP26	25c dull green	1.00	.80
C276	AP26	30c plum	1.00	.80
C277	AP26	1b violet	5.50	3.00
		Nos. C272-C277 (6)	8.50	5.60

See note after No. 427.

Christopher Columbus AP27

1948-49   Unwmk.   Perf. 12½

C278	AP27	5c brown ('49)	.30	.25
C279	AP27	10c gray	.30	.30
C280	AP27	15c orange ('49)	.65	.30
C281	AP27	25c green ('49)	1.25	.65
C282	AP27	30c red vio ('49)	1.50	.95
C283	AP27	1b violet ('49)	6.00	2.75
		Nos. C278-C283 (6)	10.00	5.20

See note after No. 431.

AP28   AP29

Symbols of global air mail.

1950   Perf. 12

C284	AP28	5c red brown	.25	.25
C285	AP28	10c dk green	.25	.25
C286	AP28	15c olive brn	.25	.25
C287	AP28	25c olive gray	.40	.30
C288	AP28	30c olive grn	.55	.30
C289	AP28	50c black	.40	.25
C290	AP28	60c brt ultra	1.10	.60
C291	AP28	90c carmine	1.40	.75
C292	AP28	1b purple	1.90	.50
		Nos. C284-C292 (9)	6.50	3.45
		Set, never hinged	10.50	

75th anniv. of the UPU.
Issue dates: 5c, Jan. 28. Others, Feb. 19.

Foliage in Yellow

Araguaney, Venezuelan national tree.

1950, Aug. 25   Photo.   Perf. 11½

C293	AP29	5c orange brn	.25	.25
C294	AP29	10c blue grn	.25	.25
C295	AP29	15c deep plum	.50	.25
C296	AP29	25c dk gray grn	4.50	1.25
C297	AP29	30c red orange	4.75	1.60
C298	AP29	50c dark gray	2.75	.40
C299	AP29	60c deep blue	4.50	.80
C300	AP29	90c red	7.00	1.60
C301	AP29	1b rose violet	8.00	2.00
		Nos. C293-C301 (9)	32.50	8.40
		Set, never hinged	160.00	

Issued to publicize Forest Week, 1950.

Census Type of 1950

1950, Sept. 1   Engr.   Perf. 12

C302	A90	5c olive gray	.25	.25
C303	A90	10c green	.25	.25
C304	A90	15c olive green	.25	.25
C305	A90	25c gray	.45	.45
C306	A90	30c orange	.65	.30
C307	A90	50c lt brown	.45	.25
C308	A90	60c ultra	.45	.25
C309	A90	90c rose carmine	1.40	.65
C310	A90	1b violet	2.25	1.75
		Nos. C302-C310 (9)	6.40	4.40

Signing Act of Independence — AP31

1950, Nov. 17

C311	AP31	5c vermilion	.60	.25
C312	AP31	10c red brown	.60	.25
C313	AP31	15c violet	.85	.25
C314	AP31	30c brt blue	1.10	.40
C315	AP31	1b green	5.50	2.40
		Nos. C311-C315 (5)	8.65	3.55

200th anniversary of the birth of Gen. Francisco de Miranda.

Alonso de Ojeda Type of 1950

1950, Dec. 18   Photo.   Perf. 11½

C316	A91	5c orange brn	.25	.25
C317	A91	10c cerise	.30	.25
C318	A91	15c black brn	.55	.25
C319	A91	25c violet	.60	.30
C320	A91	30c orange	1.25	.50
C321	A91	1b emerald	5.00	2.50
		Nos. C316-C321 (6)	7.95	4.05

Bolivar Statue Type of 1951

1951, July 13   Engr.   Perf. 12

C322	A92	5c purple	.70	.25
C323	A92	10c dull green	.80	.25
C324	A92	20c olive gray	.80	.25
C325	A92	25c olive green	.90	.25
C326	A92	30c vermilion	1.25	.55
C327	A92	40c lt brown	1.25	.55
C328	A92	50c gray	3.00	1.00
C329	A92	70c orange	4.50	2.50
		Nos. C322-C329 (8)	13.20	5.60

Queen Isabella I — AP34

1951, Oct. 12   Photo.   Perf. 11½

C330	AP34	5c dk green & buff	.45	.25
C331	AP34	10c dk red & cream	.45	.25
C332	AP34	20c dp blue & gray	.75	.25
C333	AP34	30c dk blue & gray	.75	.25
a.		Souv. sheet of 4, #C330-C333	14.00	15.00
		Nos. C330-C333 (4)	2.40	1.00

500th anniv. of the birth of Queen Isabella I of Spain.

Bicycle Racecourse — AP35

1951, Dec. 18   Engr.   Perf. 12

C334	AP35	5c green	.80	.25
C335	AP35	10c rose carmine	.80	.25
C336	AP35	20c redsh brown	1.00	.70
C337	AP35	30c dk blue	1.30	1.00
a.		Souv. sheet, #C334-C337	20.00	24.00
		Nos. C334-C337 (4)	3.90	2.20

3rd Bolivarian Games, Caracas, Dec. 1951.

Arms of Carabobo and "Industry" — AP36

1951   Photo.   Perf. 11½

C338	AP36	5c blue green	2.50	1.10
C339	AP36	7½c gray green	3.25	1.90
C340	AP36	10c car rose	2.50	1.10
C341	AP36	15c dark brown	3.25	1.10
C342	AP36	20c gray blue	3.50	1.10
C343	AP36	30c deep blue	9.50	1.60
C344	AP36	45c magenta	4.75	1.60
C345	AP36	60c olive brown	9.00	3.50
C346	AP36	90c rose brown	20.00	11.00
		Nos. C338-C346 (9)	58.25	24.00

Issue date: Oct. 29.

Arms of Zulia and "Industry"

C347	AP36	5c blue green	1.25	.60
C348	AP36	10c car rose	1.25	.60
C349	AP36	15c dark brown	1.90	.60
C350	AP36	30c deep blue	12.50	4.00
C351	AP36	60c olive brown	7.50	1.25
C352	AP36	1.20b brown car	25.00	16.00
C353	AP36	3b blue gray	8.75	2.40
C354	AP36	5b purple brn	12.50	6.25
C355	AP36	10b violet	20.00	12.50
		Nos. C347-C355 (9)	90.65	44.20

Issued: 5b, 9/8; 5c, 3b, 10b, 10/8; others, 10/29.

Arms of Anzoategui

C356	AP36	5c blue green	1.50	.85
C357	AP36	10c car rose	1.50	.85
C358	AP36	15c dk brown	2.00	.85
C359	AP36	25c sepia	2.40	.85
C360	AP36	30c deep blue	6.25	3.50
C361	AP36	50c henna brn	6.25	1.75
C362	AP36	60c olive brn	9.00	1.10
C363	AP36	1b purple	11.00	3.50
C364	AP36	2b violet gray	19.00	7.75
		Nos. C356-C364 (9)	58.90	21.00

Issue date: Nov. 9.

Arms of Caracas and Buildings

C365	AP36	5c blue green	2.75	1.10
C366	AP36	7½c gray green	8.00	3.50
C367	AP36	10c car rose	1.90	1.10
C368	AP36	15c dk brown	19.00	2.50
C369	AP36	20c gray blue	12.50	2.50
C370	AP36	30c deep blue	21.00	4.75
C371	AP36	45c magenta	12.50	2.75
C372	AP36	60c olive brn	42.50	5.75
C373	AP36	90c rose brn	25.00	20.00
		Nos. C365-C373 (9)	145.15	43.95

Issue date: Aug. 6.

Arms of Tachira and Agricultural Products

C374	AP36	5c blue green	.90	.90
C375	AP36	10c car rose	.90	.90
C376	AP36	15c dk brown	2.50	.90
C377	AP36	30c deep blue	32.50	3.75
C378	AP36	60c olive brn	26.00	3.75
C379	AP36	1.20b brown car	26.00	18.00
C380	AP36	3b blue gray	8.50	3.75
C381	AP36	5b purple brn	15.00	7.75
C382	AP36	10b violet	20.00	15.00
		Nos. C374-C382 (9)	132.30	54.70

Issue date: Aug. 9.

Arms of Venezuela and Bolivar Statue

C383	AP36	5c blue green	1.75	.90
C384	AP36	7½c gray grn	4.50	2.75
C385	AP36	10c car rose	13.50	.90
C386	AP36	15c dk brown	10.00	2.75
C387	AP36	20c gray blue	13.50	2.25
C388	AP36	30c deep blue	24.50	4.75
C389	AP36	45c magenta	11.00	2.00
C390	AP36	60c olive brn	50.00	10.00
C391	AP36	90c rose brn	32.50	22.50
		Nos. C383-C391 (9)	161.25	48.80

Issue date: Aug. 6.

1952

Arms of Miranda and Agricultural Products

C392	AP36	5c blue green	1.00	.70
C393	AP36	7½c gray grn	1.75	1.00
C394	AP36	10c car rose	1.00	.70
C395	AP36	15c dark brown	2.10	.70
C396	AP36	20c gray blue	3.00	.85
C397	AP36	30c deep blue	6.00	1.40
C398	AP36	45c magenta	5.50	.70
C399	AP36	60c olive brn	10.50	1.90
C400	AP36	90c rose brn	45.00	27.50
		Nos. C392-C400 (9)	75.85	35.45

Issue date: 7½c, 15c, 20c, 30c, Mar. 24.

Arms of Aragua and Stylized Farm

C401	AP36	5c blue green	2.50	.90
C402	AP36	7½c gray grn	2.25	1.25
C403	AP36	10c car rose	1.25	.90
C404	AP36	15c dk brown	7.75	1.10
C405	AP36	20c gray blue	3.75	1.10
C406	AP36	30c deep blue	11.00	1.25
C407	AP36	45c magenta	8.50	1.10
C408	AP36	60c olive brn	18.00	1.75
C409	AP36	90c rose brn	67.50	35.00
		Nos. C401-C409 (9)	122.50	44.35

Issue date: 7½c, 15c, 20c, 30c, Mar. 24.

Arms of Lara, Agricultural Products and Rope

C410	AP36	5c blue green	2.25	.80
C411	AP36	7½c gray grn	2.00	1.10
C412	AP36	10c car rose	1.10	.80

C413	AP36	15c dk brown	3.50	.80
C414	AP36	20c gray blue	5.50	.80
C415	AP36	30c deep blue	11.00	1.60
C416	AP36	45c magenta	5.50	1.40
C417	AP36	60c olive brn	11.00	2.50
C418	AP36	90c rose brn	60.00	40.00
		Nos. C410-C418 (9)	101.85	49.80

Issue date: 7½c, 15c, 20c, Mar. 24.

Arms of Bolivar and Stylized Design

C419	AP36	5c blue		
		green	11.50	1.25
C420	AP36	10c car rose	1.00	.70
C421	AP36	15c dark		
		brown	1.75	.70
C422	AP36	25c sepia	1.40	.70
C423	AP36	30c deep blue	8.00	3.25
C424	AP36	50c henna brn	5.40	1.40
C425	AP36	60c olive brn	9.00	1.75
C426	AP36	1b purple	8.00	1.40
C427	AP36	2b violet gray	18.00	6.25
		Nos. C419-C427 (9)	64.05	17.40

Issue date: 15c, 30c, Mar. 24.

Arms of Sucre, Palms and Seascape

C428	AP36	5c blue		
		green	1.00	.65
C429	AP36	10c car rose	.65	.65
C430	AP36	15c dk brown	1.40	.65
C431	AP36	25c sepia	27.50	.65
C432	AP36	30c deep blue	9.25	2.75
C433	AP36	50c henna brn	4.25	1.00
C434	AP36	60c olive brn	5.25	2.10
C435	AP36	1b purple	6.75	1.60
C436	AP36	2b violet gray	15.00	7.50
		Nos. C428-C436 (9)	71.05	17.55

Issue date: 15c, 30c, Mar. 24.

Arms of Trujillo Surrounded by Stylized Tree

C437	AP36	5c blue		
		green	11.00	.70
C438	AP36	10c car rose	.80	.40
C439	AP36	15c dk brown	3.00	.40
C440	AP36	30c deep blue	13.50	2.25
C441	AP36	60c olive brn	9.75	2.10
C442	AP36	1.20b rose red	8.75	5.00
C443	AP36	3b blue gray	4.25	3.10
C444	AP36	5b purple brn	9.25	3.50
C445	AP36	10b violet	16.00	8.25
		Nos. C437-C445 (9)	76.30	25.70

Issue date: 5c, 30c, Mar. 24.

1953-54
Map of Delta Amacuro and Ship

C446	AP36	5c bl grn	1.25	.85
C447	AP36	10c car		
		rose	.85	.85
C448	AP36	15c dk brn	1.90	.96
C449	AP36	25c sepia	2.75	1.25
C450	AP36	30c dp bl	11.00	3.25
C451	AP36	50c hn brn	5.50	1.25
C452	AP36	60c ol brn	8.25	2.50
C453	AP36	1b purple	10.50	3.50
C454	AP36	2b vio		
		gray	17.50	13.00
		Nos. C446-C454 (9)	59.50	27.41

Issue date: 15c, 30c, Feb. 13.

Arms of Falcon and Stylized Oil Refinery

C455	AP36	5c bl grn	1.00	.50
C456	AP36	10c car		
		rose	.50	.50
C457	AP36	15c dk brn	1.00	.50
C458	AP36	30c dp bl	8.25	2.25
C459	AP36	60c ol brn	6.25	1.75
C460	AP36	1.20b rose		
		red	7.75	7.25
C461	AP36	3b bl gray	8.25	4.50
C462	AP36	5b pur		
		brn	13.50	9.25
C463	AP36	10b violet	13.50	10.50
		Nos. C455-C463 (9)	60.00	37.00

Issue date: 10c, 15c, 30c, Feb. 13.

Arms of Guarico and Factory

C464	AP36	5c blue		
		grn	1.10	.80
C465	AP36	10c car		
		rose	.80	.80
C466	AP36	15c dk brn	1.75	.80
C467	AP36	25c sepia	2.50	1.10
C468	AP36	30c dp bl	11.00	4.25
C469	AP36	50c hn brn	5.50	1.75
C470	AP36	60c ol brn	6.25	2.50
C471	AP36	1b purple	11.00	2.50
C472	AP36	2b vio		
		gray	16.00	8.25
		Nos. C464-C472 (9)	55.90	22.75

Issue date: 15c, 30c, Feb. 13.

Arms of Merida and Church

C473	AP36	5c bl grn	.95	.80
C474	AP36	10c car		
		rose	.80	.80
C475	AP36	15c dk brn	1.50	.80
C476	AP36	30c dp bl	14.00	3.25
C477	AP36	60c ol brn	7.00	1.90
C478	AP36	1.20b rose		
		red	12.00	7.00
C479	AP36	3b bl gray	7.00	3.25

C480	AP36	5b pur		
		brn	13.50	7.00
C481	AP36	10b violet	19.00	12.00
		Nos. C473-C481 (9)	75.75	36.80

Issue date: 10c, Feb. 2.

Arms of Monagas and Horses

C482	AP36	5c bl grn	1.10	.85
C483	AP36	10c car		
		rose	.85	.85
C484	AP36	15c dk brn	1.75	.85
C485	AP36	25c sepia	1.25	.85
C486	AP36	30c dp bl	16.00	4.25
C487	AP36	50c hn brn	6.50	2.10
C488	AP36	60c ol brn	7.50	2.10
C489	AP36	1b purple	11.00	2.75
C490	AP36	2b vio		
		gray	9.50	7.50
		Nos. C482-C490 (9)	60.95	22.10

Issue date: 10c, Feb. 2.

Arms of Portuguesa and Forest

C491	AP36	5c bl grn	4.00	1.25
C492	AP36	10c car		
		rose	.95	.95
C493	AP36	15c dk brn	2.40	.95
C494	AP36	30c dp bl	12.00	5.50
C495	AP36	60c ol brn	8.75	2.25
C496	AP36	1.20b rose		
		red	20.00	12.00
C497	AP36	3b bl gray	7.00	4.00
C498	AP36	5b pur		
		brn	12.50	7.00
C499	AP36	10b violet	18.00	15.00
		Nos. C491-C499 (9)	85.60	48.90

Issue date: 5c, 10c, 30c, Feb. 2.

Map of Amazonas and Orchid

C500	AP36	5c bl grn	9.25	2.10
C501	AP36	10c car		
		rose	2.10	2.10
C502	AP36	15c dk brn	9.25	2.10
C503	AP36	25c sepia	9.25	2.10
C504	AP36	30c dp bl	47.50	4.75
C505	AP36	50c hn brn	37.50	8.25
C506	AP36	60c ol brn	47.50	8.25
C507	AP36	1b purple	190.00	27.50
C508	AP36	2b vio		
		gray	75.00	32.50
		Nos. C500-C508 (9)	437.10	89.65

Issue date: Jan. 1954

Arms of Apure, Horse and Bird

C509	AP36	5c bl grn	1.60	.80
C510	AP36	10c car		
		rose	.80	.80
C511	AP36	15c dk brn	1.60	.80
C512	AP36	30c dp bl	6.25	2.75
C513	AP36	60c ol brn	5.75	1.40
C514	AP36	1.20b brn		
		car	9.75	7.00
C515	AP36	3b bl gray	5.75	3.00
C516	AP36	5b pur		
		brn	11.50	5.50
C517	AP36	10b violet brn	16.00	11.50
		Nos. C509-C517 (9)	59.00	33.55

Issue date: Jan. 1954.

Arms of Barinas, Cow and Horse

C518	AP36	5c bl grn	.50	.50
C519	AP36	10c car		
		rose	.50	.50
C520	AP36	15c dk brn	1.90	.50
C521	AP36	30c dp		
		blue	6.50	2.50
C522	AP36	60c ol brn	6.50	1.25
C523	AP36	1.20b brn		
		car	9.00	4.75
C524	AP36	3b bl gray	5.75	3.50
C525	AP36	5b pur		
		brn	9.75	3.25
C526	AP36	10b violet	14.00	10.00
		Nos. C518-C526 (9)	54.40	26.75

Issue date: Jan. 1954.

Arms of Cojedes and Cattle

C527	AP36	5c bl grn	7.75	1.10
C528	AP36	7½c gray		
		grn	2.00	1.10
C529	AP36	10c car		
		rose	.60	.60
C530	AP36	15c dk brn	.60	.60
C531	AP36	20c gray bl	1.50	.60
C532	AP36	30c dp		
		blue	10.50	1.50
C533	AP36	45c mag	3.75	.90
C534	AP36	60c ol brn	7.75	1.25
C535	AP36	90c rose		
		brn	9.25	5.25
		Nos. C527-C535 (9)	43.70	12.90

Issue date: Dec.

Arms of Nueva Esparta and Fish

C536	AP36	5c bl grn	1.25	.65
C537	AP36	10c car		
		rose	.65	.65
C538	AP36	15c dk brn	2.10	.65
C539	AP36	25c sepia	3.50	.85
C540	AP36	30c dp bl	7.50	1.60
C541	AP36	50c hn brn	7.50	1.60
C542	AP36	60c ol brn	7.50	1.00
C543	AP36	1b purple	11.00	2.50

C544	AP36	2b vio		
		gray	15.00	7.50
		Nos. C536-C544 (9)	56.00	17.00

Issue date: Jan. 1954.

Arms of Yaracuy and Tropical Foliage

C545	AP36	5c bl grn	2.00	.75
C546	AP36	7½c gray		
		grn	24.50	22.50
C547	AP36	10c car		
		rose	1.10	.75
C548	AP36	15c dk brn	2.25	.75
C549	AP36	20c gray bl	3.75	.75
C550	AP36	30c dp bl	7.50	1.90
C551	AP36	45c mag	5.25	1.10
C552	AP36	60c ol brn	5.25	1.90
C553	AP36	90c rose		
		brn	14.00	9.50
		Nos. C545-C553 (9)	65.60	39.90
		Nos. C338-C553 (216)	2,271.	841.61

Issue date: Jan. 1954.

Ship Type of 1948-50 Redrawn
● Coil Stamps
Imprint: "Courvoisier S.A."

1952 Unwmk. Perf. 12x11½

C554	AP25	5c rose brn	2.00	.25
C555	AP25	10c org red	3.25	.25
C556	AP25	15c ol brn	4.25	.25
		Nos. C554-C556 (3)	9.50	.75

Barquisimeto Type of 1952

1952, Sept. 14 Photo. Perf. 11½

C557	A94	5c blue green	.25	.25
C558	A94	10c car rose	.25	.25
C559	A94	20c dk blue	.40	.25
C560	A94	25c black brn	.60	.25
C561	A94	30c ultra	.75	.25
C562	A94	40c brown org	3.50	1.50
C563	A94	50c dk ol grn	1.40	.40
C564	A94	1b purple	4.75	2.00
		Nos. C557-C564 (8)	11.90	5.15

Caracas Post Office Type of 1953-54

1953, Mar. 11 Perf. 12½

C565	A96	7½c yellow grn	.25	.25
C566	A96	15c dp plum	.25	.25
C567	A96	20c slate	.25	.25
C568	A96	25c sepia	.50	.25
C569	A96	40c plum	.50	.25
C570	A96	45c rose vio	.50	.25
C571	A96	50c red orange	.75	.25
C572	A96	70c dk sl grn	1.50	.75
C573	A96	75c dp ultra	5.25	1.10
C574	A96	90c brown org	1.25	.60
C575	A96	1b violet blue	1.25	.60
		Nos. C565-C575 (11)	12.25	4.80

See Nos. C587-C589, C597-C606.

Simon Rodriguez AP39

Quotation from Bolivar's Manifesto of 1824 AP40

1954, Feb. 28 Perf. 11½

C576	AP39	5c blue green	1.50	.25
C577	AP39	10c car rose	2.10	.25
C578	AP39	20c gray blue	2.75	.25
C579	AP39	45c magenta	4.00	1.50
C580	AP39	65c gray green	13.50	6.00
		Nos. C576-C580 (5)	23.85	8.25

Centenary of the death of Simon Rodriguez, scholar and tutor of Bolivar.

1954, Mar. 1 Unwmk.

C581	AP40	15c blk & brn buff	.25	.25
C582	AP40	25c dk red brn &		
		gray	3.50	.25
C583	AP40	40c dk red brn &		
		red org	2.50	.25
C584	AP40	65c black & blue	6.00	3.25
C585	AP40	80c dk red brn &		
		rose	4.75	2.50
C586	AP40	1b pur & rose lil	9.75	1.90
		Nos. C581-C586 (6)	26.75	8.40

10th Inter-American Conf., Caracas, Mar. 1954.

P.O. Type of 1953

1954, Feb. Photo. Perf. 12½

C587	A96	5c orange	.25	.25
C588	A96	30c red brown	2.50	1.25
C589	A96	60c bright red	2.50	1.60
		Nos. C587-C589 (3)	5.25	3.10

Valencia Arms Type of 1955

1955, Mar. 26 Engr. Perf. 12

C590	A97	5c blue green	.25	.25
C591	A97	10c rose pink	.25	.25
C592	A97	20c ultra	.25	.25
C593	A97	25c gray	.25	.25
C594	A97	40c violet	.45	.25
C595	A97	50c vermilion	.45	.25
C596	A97	60c olive green	.90	.25
		Nos. C590-C596 (7)	2.80	1.75

P.O. Type of 1953 Inscribed: "Republica de Venezuela"

1955 Photo. Perf. 12½

C597	A96a	5c orange	.25	.25
C598	A96a	10c olive brn	.25	.25
C599	A96a	15c deep plum	.25	.25
C600	A96a	20c slate	.40	.25
C601	A96a	30c red brn	.40	.25
C602	A96a	40c plum	1.10	.80
C603	A96a	45c rose violet	1.10	.60
C604	A96a	70c dk slate grn	2.75	1.25
C605	A96a	75c deep ultra	1.90	.75
C606	A96a	90c brown org	1.00	.40
		Nos. C597-C606 (10)	9.40	4.65

Caracas Arms Type of 1955

1955, Dec. 9 Unwmk. Perf. 11½

C607	A98	5c yellow org	.25	.25
C608	A98	15c claret brn	.25	.25
C609	A98	25c violet blk	.25	.25
C610	A98	40c red	1.90	.25
C611	A98	50c red orange	1.90	.25
C612	A98	60c car rose	3.75	1.25
		Nos. C607-C612 (6)	8.30	2.50

University Hospital, Caracas AP43

5c, 10c, 15c, 70c, O'Leary School, Barinas. 25c, 30c, 80c, University Hospital, Caracas. 40c, 45c, 50c, 1b, Caracas-La Guaira Highway. 60c, 65c, 75c, 2b, Towers of Simon Bolivar Center.

1956-57 Unwmk. Perf. 11½

C613	AP43	5c orange	1.10	.85
C614	AP43	10c sepia	1.10	.85
C615	AP43	15c claret brown	1.10	.85
C616	AP43	20c dark blue	1.10	.85
C617	AP43	25c gray black	1.10	.85
C618	AP43	30c henna brown	1.25	.85
C619	AP43	40c bright crimson	2.00	.85
C620	AP43	45c brown violet	1.25	.85
C621	AP43	50c deep orange	2.50	.85
C622	AP43	60c olive green	2.50	.85
C623	AP43	65c bright blue	4.00	.85
C624	AP43	70c blue green	4.25	1.10
C625	AP43	75c ultra	4.50	1.60
C626	AP43	80c carmine rose	5.00	.90
C627	AP43	1b plum	3.00	1.10
C628	AP43	2b dark car rose	6.25	3.25
		Nos. C613-C628 (16)	42.00	17.30

Issued: 20c, 40c, 45c, 50c, 1b, 11/5/56; others, 1957.

Book and Flags of American Nations — AP44

1956-57 Granite Paper

C629	AP44	5c orange & brn	.25	.25
C630	AP44	10c brn & pale brn	.25	.25
C631	AP44	20c blue & sapphire	.25	.25
C632	AP44	25c gray vio & gray	.55	.25
C633	AP44	40c rose red & pale		
		pur	.75	.25
C634	AP44	45c vio brn & gray		
			1.00	.25
C635	AP44	60c olive & gray ol	1.90	1.00
		Nos. C629-C635 (7)	4.95	2.50

Book Festival of the Americas, 11/15-30/56.
Issued: 5c, 40c, 11/15; others, 2/7/57.

Bolivar Type of 1957-58
Engraved; Center Embossed

1957-58		Unwmk.	Perf. 13½	
C636	A100	5c orange	.25	.25
C637	A100	10c olive gray	.25	.25
C638	A100	20c blue	.55	.25
C639	A100	25c gray black	.60	.25
C640	A100	40c rose red	.55	.25
C641	A100	45c rose lilac	.65	.25
C642	A100	65c yellow brn	1.10	.45
	Nos. C636-C642 (7)		3.95	1.95

Issued: 45c, 1958; others, Nov. 15, 1957.

Tamanaco Hotel Type of 1957-58

1957-58		Engr.	Perf. 13	
C643	A101	5c dull yellow	.25	.25
C644	A101	10c brown	.25	.25
C645	A101	15c chocolate	.25	.25
C646	A101	20c gray blue	.25	.25
C647	A101	25c sepia	.25	.25
C648	A101	30c violet bl	.25	.25
C649	A101	40c car rose	.30	.25
C650	A101	45c claret	.35	.25
C651	A101	50c red org	.35	.25
C652	A101	60c yellow grn	.70	.25
C653	A101	65c orange brn	1.75	.80
C654	A101	70c slate	1.00	.40
C655	A101	75c grnsh blue	1.10	.50
C656	A101	1b dk claret	1.10	.50
C657	A101	2b dk gray	1.75	.60
	Nos. C643-C657 (15)		9.90	5.30

Issue dates: 5c, 10c, Oct. 10; others, 1958.
For surcharge see No. C878.

Post Office Type of 1958

1958, May 14		Litho.	Perf. 14	
C658	A102	5c dp yellow	.25	.25
C659	A102	10c brown	.25	.25
C660	A102	15c red brn	.25	.25
C661	A102	20c lt blue	.25	.25
C662	A102	25c lt gray	.25	.25
C663	A102	30c lt ultra	.25	.25
C664	A102	40c brt yel grn	.25	.25
C665	A102	50c red orange	.25	.25
C666	A102	60c rose pink	.25	.25
C667	A102	65c red	.30	.25
C668	A102	90c violet	.40	.25
C669	A102	1b lilac	.50	.25
C670	A102	1.20b bister brn	9.50	6.00
	Nos. C658-C670 (13)		12.95	9.00

See Nos. C786-C792. For surcharges see Nos. C856-C861.

Post Office Type of 1958
Coil Stamps

1958		Engr.	Perf. 11½x12	
C671	A103	5c deep yellow	.25	.25
C672	A103	10c brown	.35	.25
C673	A103	15c dark brown	.60	.25
	Nos. C671-C673 (3)		1.20	.75

Merida Type of 1958

1958, Oct. 9		Photo.	Perf. 13½	
C674	A104	5c orange yellow	.25	.25
C675	A104	10c gray brown	.25	.25
C676	A104	15c dull red brn	.25	.25
C677	A104	20c chalky blue	.25	.25
C678	A104	25c brown gray	.25	.25
C679	A104	30c violet bl	.25	.25
C680	A104	40c rose car	.35	.25
C681	A104	45c brt lilac	.35	.25
C682	A104	50c red orange	.45	.25
C683	A104	60c lt olive grn	.40	.25
C684	A104	65c hennna brn	1.25	.50
C685	A104	70c gray black	.70	.40
C686	A104	75c brt grnsh bl	1.40	.70
C687	A104	80c brt vio bl	.90	.40
C688	A104	90c blue green	.90	.40
C689	A104	1b lilac	1.00	.50
	Nos. C674-C689 (16)		9.20	5.40

Trujillo Type of 1959

1958, Nov. 17		Photo.	Perf. 14	
C690	A105	5c orange yel	.25	.25
C691	A105	10c lt brown	.25	.25
C692	A105	15c redsh brown	.25	.25
C693	A105	20c lt blue	.25	.25
C694	A105	25c pale gray	.35	.25
C695	A105	30c lt vio blue	.35	.25
C696	A105	40c brt yel grn	.40	.25
C697	A105	50c red orange	.40	.25
C698	A105	60c lilac rose	.60	.35
C699	A105	65c vermilion	1.90	.85
C700	A105	1b lilac	1.10	.50
	Nos. C690-C700 (11)		6.10	3.55

Emblem — AP45

1959, Mar. 10		Litho.	Perf. 13½	
C701	AP45	5c yellow	.35	.25
C702	AP45	10c red brown	.35	.25
C703	AP45	15c orange	.40	.25
C704	AP45	30c gray	.65	.40
C705	AP45	50c green	.70	.45
	Nos. C701-C705 (5)		2.45	1.60

8th Central American and Caribbean Games, Caracas, Nov. 29-Dec. 14, 1958. Exist imperf. Value, pair $25.

Stamp Centenary Type of 1959

Stamp of 1859 and: 25c, Mailman and José Ignacio Paz Castillo. 50c, Mailman on horseback and Jacinto Gutierrez. 1b, Plane, train and Miguel Herrera.

1959, Sept. 15		Engr.	Perf. 13½	
C706	A107	25c orange yel	.30	.25
C707	A107	50c blue	.45	.25
C708	A107	1b rose red	.90	.45
	Nos. C706-C708 (3)		1.65	.95

> Catalogue values for unused stamps in this section, from this point to the end of the section, are for Never Hinged items.

Alexander von Humboldt Type of 1960

1960, Feb. 9			Unwmk.	
C709	A108	5c ocher & brn	.35	.25
C710	A108	20c brt bl & turq bl	1.40	.25
C711	A108	40c ol & ol grn	2.00	.50
	Nos. C709-C711 (3)		3.75	1.00

Newspaper Type of 1960

1960, June 11		Litho.	Perf. 14	
C712	A109	5c yellow & blk	2.75	1.10
C713	A109	15c lt red brn & blk	1.40	.40
C714	A109	65c salmon & blk	2.10	.75
	Nos. C712-C714 (3)		6.25	2.25

Agustin Codazzi Type of 1960

1960, June 15			Engr.	
C715	A110	5c yel org & brn	.25	.25
C716	A110	10c brn & dk brn	.25	.25
C717	A110	25c gray & blk	.70	.25
C718	A110	30c vio bl & sl	.95	.25
C719	A110	50c org brn & brn	1.50	.50
C720	A110	70c gray ol & ol gray	2.40	.95
	Nos. C715-C720 (6)		6.05	2.45

For surcharge see No. C884.

National Pantheon Type of 1960

1960, May 9			Litho.	
		Pantheon in Bister		
C721	A111	5c dp bister	.25	.25
C722	A111	10c red brown	.30	.25
C723	A111	15c fawn	.35	.25
C724	A111	20c lt blue	.55	.25
C725	A111	25c gray	3.00	.30
C726	A111	30c lt vio bl	3.00	.50
C727	A111	40c brt yel grn	.55	.25
C728	A111	45c lt violet	.85	.25
C729	A111	60c deep pink	1.10	.35
C730	A111	65c salmon	1.10	.35
C731	A111	70c gray	1.50	.50
C732	A111	75c chalky blue	4.50	.85
C733	A111	80c lt ultra	2.25	.70
C734	A111	1.20b bister brn	2.75	1.00
	Nos. C721-C734 (14)		22.05	6.05

For surcharges see Nos. C894-C895.

Andres Eloy Blanco Type of 1960

1960, May 21			Perf. 14	
		Portrait in Black		
C735	A112	20c blue	.50	.25
C736	A112	75c grnsh blue	1.60	.40
C737	A112	90c brt violet	1.60	.40
	Nos. C735-C737 (3)		3.70	1.05

For surcharge see No. C874.

Independence Type of 1960

1960, Aug. 19		Litho.	Perf. 13½	
		Center Multicolored		
C738	A113	50c orange	1.10	.35
C739	A113	75c brt grnsh blue	1.60	.50
C740	A113	90c purple	1.75	.45
	Nos. C738-C740 (3)		4.45	1.30

Oil Refinery
AP46

Unwmk.

1960, Aug. 26		Engr.	Perf. 14	
C741	AP46	30c dk bl & sl bl	.75	.25
C742	AP46	40c yel grn & ol	1.25	.45
C743	AP46	50c org & red brn	1.50	.60
	Nos. C741-C743 (3)		3.50	1.30

Issued to publicize Venezuela's oil industry.

Luisa Cáceres de Arismendi Type of 1960

1960, Oct. 21		Litho.	Perf. 14	
		Center Multicolored		
C744	A115	5c bister	.95	.35
C745	A115	10c redsh brown	1.75	.75
C746	A115	60c rose carmine	3.00	.95
	Nos. C744-C746 (3)		5.70	2.05

José Antonio Anzoategui Type of 1960

1960, Oct. 29			Engr.	
C747	A116	25c gray & brown	.85	.25
C748	A116	40c yel grn & ol gray	.85	.60
C749	A116	45c rose cl & dl pur	1.10	.45
	Nos. C747-C749 (3)		2.80	1.30

Antonio José de Sucre Type of 1960
Unwmk.

1960, Nov. 18		Litho.	Perf. 14	
		Center Multicolored		
C750	A117	25c gray	.90	.35
C751	A117	30c violet blue	1.40	.50
C752	A117	50c brown orange	1.75	.65
	Nos. C750-C752 (3)		4.05	1.50

Type of Regular Issue, 1960

Designs: 30c, Bolivar Peak. 50c, Caroni Falls. 65c, Guacharo caves.

1960, Mar. 22			Perf. 14	
C753	A118	30c vio bl & blk bl	2.25	2.25
C754	A118	50c brn org & brn	2.25	2.25
C755	A118	65c red org & red brn	2.25	2.25
	Nos. C753-C755 (3)		6.75	6.75

Cow's Head, Grain, Man and Child
AP47

Arms of San Cristobal
AP48

1961, Feb. 6		Litho.	Unwmk.	
		Cow and Inscription in Black		
C756	AP47	5c yellow	.25	.25
C757	AP47	10c brown	.25	.25
C758	AP47	15c redsh brn	.25	.25
C759	AP47	20c dull blue	.25	.25
C760	AP47	25c gray	.25	.25
C761	AP47	30c violet bl	.25	.25
C762	AP47	40c yellow grn	.30	.25
C763	AP47	45c lilac	.35	.25
C764	AP47	50c orange	.40	.25
C765	AP47	60c cerise	.45	.25
C766	AP47	65c red orange	.60	.25
C767	AP47	70c gray	.90	.30
C768	AP47	75c brt grnsh bl	.85	.25
C769	AP47	80c brt violet	.85	.25
C770	AP47	90c violet	1.25	.40
	Nos. C756-C770 (15)		7.45	3.95

9th general census & 3rd agricultural census. Issued: 5-15c, 30c, 60-65c, 75-80c, 2/6; others, 4/6.
For surcharges see Nos. C865-C866.

Rafael Maria Baralt Type of 1961

1961, Mar. 1		Engr.	Perf. 14	
C771	A120	25c gray & sepia	.80	.35
C772	A120	30c dk blue & vio	.90	.35
C773	A120	40c yel grn & ol grn	1.10	.50
	Nos. C771-C773 (3)		2.80	1.20

1961, Apr. 10			Litho.	
		Arms in Original Colors		
C774	AP48	5c orange & blk	.25	.25
C775	AP48	55c yel grn & blk	.85	.30

400th anniversary of San Cristobal.
For surcharge see No. C879.

Bird Type of 1961

Birds: 5c, Troupial. 10c, Golden cock of the rock. 15c, Tropical mockingbird.

1961, Sept. 6		Unwmk.	Perf. 14½	
C776	A121	5c multicolored	1.60	1.10
C777	A121	10c multicolored	.80	.60
C778	A121	15c multicolored	1.00	.65
	Nos. C776-C778 (3)		3.40	2.35

Charge, Battle of Carabobo — AP49

1961, Dec. 1		Litho.	Perf. 14	
		Center Multicolored		
C779	AP49	50c black & ultra	.75	.25
C780	AP49	1.05b black & org	1.75	.50
C781	AP49	1.50b blk & lil rose	2.00	.50
C782	AP49	1.90b black & lilac	2.50	1.00
C783	AP49	2b black & gray	3.25	1.00
C784	AP49	3b black & grnsh bl	4.00	1.25
	Nos. C779-C784 (6)		14.25	4.50

140th anniversary of Battle of Carabobo. For surcharges see Nos. C867-C870.

Arms of Cardinal Quintero
AP50

1962, Mar. 1			Unwmk.	
C785	AP50	5c lilac rose	.40	.25
a.	Souv. sheet of 1, imperf.		4.00	3.50

1st Venezuelan Cardinal, José Humberto Quintero.
No. C785a, issued Mar. 23, sold for 1b.

Post Office Type of 1958

1962, Apr. 12		Litho.	Perf. 13½x14	
C786	A102	35c citron	.30	.25
C787	A102	55c gray olive	.45	.25
C788	A102	70c bluish green	.75	.30
C789	A102	75c brown orange	.90	.25
C790	A102	80c fawn	.90	.35
C791	A102	85c deep rose	1.40	.50
C792	A102	95c lilac rose	.95	.45
	Nos. C786-C792 (7)		5.65	2.35

For surcharges see Nos. C856-C861.

Archbishop Rafael Arias Blanco — AP51

1962, May 10			Perf. 10½	
C793	AP51	75c red lilac	.80	.30

4th anniversary (in 1961) of the anti-communist pastoral letter of the Archbishop of Caracas, Rafael Arias Blanco.

Orchid Type of 1962

Orchids: 5c, Oncidium volvox. 20c, Cycnoches chlorochilon. 25c, Cattleya Gaskelliana. 30c, Epidendrum difforme, horiz. 40c, Catasetum callosum Lindl, horiz. 50c, Oncidium bicolor Lindl. 1b, Brassavola nodosa Lindl, horiz. 1.05b, Epidendrum lividum Lindl. 1.50b, Schomburgkia undulata Lindl. 2b, Oncidium zebrinum.

		Perf. 14x13½, 13½x14		
1962, May 30		Litho.	Unwmk.	
		Orchids in Natural Colors		
C794	A124	5c blk & lt grn	.25	.25
C795	A124	20c black	.25	.25
C796	A124	25c black & fawn	.60	.25
C797	A124	30c black & pink	.55	.25
C798	A124	40c black & yel	.60	.25
C799	A124	50c black & lil	.85	.25
C800	A124	1b blk & pale rose	1.10	.40
C801	A124	1.05b blk & dp org	3.50	1.10

C802 A124 1.50b blk & pale
vio 4.00 1.25
C803 A124 2b blk & org brn 5.00 1.75
Nos. C794-C803 (10) 16.70 6.00
For surcharges see Nos. C885-C887.

Independence Type of 1960

Signing Declaration of Independence.

1962, June 11 *Perf. 13½*
Center Multicolored
C804 A113 55c olive .60 .25
C805 A113 1.05b brt rose 2.10 .55
C806 A113 1.50b purple 1.60 .50
a. Souv. sheet of 3, #C804-C806,
imperf. 5.00 5.00
Nos. C804-C806 (3) 4.30 1.30

No. C806a, issued Oct. 13, sold for 4.10b.
A buff cardboard folder exists with impressions of Nos. 812-814, C804-C806. Perforation is simulated. Sold for 5.60b. Value $10.
For surcharge see No. C893.

No. 710 Surcharged in Rose Carmine:
"BICENTENARIO DE UPATA 1762-
1962 RESELLADO AEREO VALOR
Bs. 2,00"

1962, July 7 *Perf. 13½x14*
C807 A102 2b on 1b lt ol grn 2.50 1.10

Upata, a village in the state of Bolivar, 200th anniv.

National Games Type of 1962

Perf. 13x14
1962, Nov. 30 **Unwmk.** **Litho.**
C808 A125 40c Bicycling .50 .30
C809 A125 75c Baseball .70 .35
C810 A125 85c Woman athlete 1.75 .80
a. Souv. sheet of 3, #C808-C810
imperf. 4.75 4.25
Nos. C808-C810 (3) 2.95 1.45

See note after No. 817.
No. C810a sold for 3b.
For surcharge see No. C899.

Bird Type of 1962

Birds: 5c, American kestrel. 20c, Black-bellied tree duck, horiz. 25c, Amazon kingfisher. 30c, Rufous-tailed chachalaca. 50c, Black-and-yellow troupial. 55c, White-naped nightjar. 2.30b, Red-crowned woodpecker. 2.50b, Black-moustached quail-dove.

1962, Dec. 14 *Perf. 14x13½, 13½x14*
**Birds in Natural Colors;
Black Inscription**
C811 A126 5c car rose .25 .25
C812 A126 20c brt blue .60 .25
C813 A126 25c lt gray .70 .25
C814 A126 30c lt olive .75 .25
C815 A126 50c violet 1.25 .35
C816 A126 55c dp orange 2.10 .50
C817 A126 2.30b dl red brn 6.00 2.50
C818 A126 2.50b orange yel 6.00 3.00
Nos. C811-C818 (8) 17.65 7.35

For surcharges see Nos. C880-C882.

Malaria
Eradication
Emblem, Mosquito
and Map — AP52

Lithographed and Embossed
Perf. 13½x14
1962, Dec. 20 **Wmk. 346**
C819 AP52 30c green & blk .75 .35
a. Souv. sheet of 2, #825, C819,
imperf. 4.00 4.00

WHO drive to eradicate malaria. No. C819a sold for 2b.

Animal Type of Regular Issue

5c, Spectacle bear, vert. 40c, Paca. 50c, Three-toed sloths. 55c, Great anteater. 1.50b, South American tapirs. 2b, Jaguar.

**Multicolored Center; Black
Inscriptions**
Perf. 14x13½, 13½x14
1963, Mar. 13 **Litho.** **Unwmk.**
C820 A128 5c yellow .25 .25
C821 A128 40c brt green .80 .25
C822 A128 50c lt violet 1.10 .30
C823 A128 55c brown olive 1.40 .40

C824 A128 1.50b gray 4.00 1.60
C825 A128 2b ultra 6.75 2.50
Nos. C820-C825 (6) 14.30 5.30
For surcharges see Nos. C888-C889.

Freedom from Hunger Type of 1963

40c, Map, shepherd. 75c, Map, farmer.

1963, Mar. 21
C826 A129 40c lt yel grn & dl red .45 .30
C827 A129 75c yellow & brown .90 .50

Arms of
Bocono — AP53

1963, May 30 **Wmk. 346**
C828 AP53 1b multicolored 2.00 .55

400th anniversary of the founding of Bocono.
For surcharge see No. C892.

Papal and
Venezuelan
Arms
AP54

1963, June 11 *Perf. 14x13½*
Arms Multicolored
C829 AP54 80c light green 1.40 .35
C830 AP54 90c gray 1.40 .50

Vatican II, the 21st Ecumenical Council of the Roman Catholic Church.
For surcharges see Nos. C871-C872.

Arms of
Venezuela — AP55

1963, July 29 **Unwmk.** **Perf. 14**
C831 AP55 70c gray, red, yel &
bl 1.25 .50

Cent. of Venezuela's flag and coat of arms.
For surcharge see No. C883.

Lake
Maracaibo
Bridge
AP56

Wmk. 346
1963, Aug. 24 **Litho.** **Perf. 14**
C832 AP56 90c grn, brn & ocher 1.60 .50
C833 AP56 95c blue, brn & och 1.60 .60
C834 AP56 1b ultra, brn & och 1.40 .50
Nos. C832-C834 (3) 4.60 1.60

Opening of bridge over Lake Maracaibo.
For surcharges see Nos. C897-C898.

Armed Forces Type of 1963

1963, Sept. 10 **Unwmk.**
C835 A134 1b red & bl, *buff* 2.40 1.00
For surcharge see No. C862.

Hammarskjold Type of 1963

1963, Sept. 25 **Unwmk.** **Perf. 14**
C836 A135 80c dk bl, lt ultra &
ocher 1.25 .50
C837 A135 90c dk bl, bl & ocher 1.60 .70
a. Souv. sheet of 4, #841-842,
C836-C837, imperf. 5.25 5.25

No. C837a sold for 3b.
For surcharges see Nos. C875-C876.

Dr. Luis Razetti,
Physician, Birth
Cent. — AP57

1963, Oct. 10 **Engr.**
C838 AP57 95c dk blue & mag 2.00 .90
C839 AP57 1.05b dk brn & grn 2.10 1.00
For surcharges see Nos. C890-C891.

Red Cross Type of 1963

Designs: 40c, Sir Vincent K. Barrington. 75c, Red Cross nurse and child.

1963, Dec. 31 **Litho.** **Perf. 11½x12**
C840 A137 40c multicolored .55 .30
C841 A137 75c multicolored .95 .40

Development Type of 1964

Designs: 5c, Loading cargo. 10c, Tractor and corn. 15c, Oil field workers. 20c, Oil refinery. 50c, Crane and building construction.

1964, Feb. 5 **Unwmk.** *Perf. 14x13½*
C842 A138 5c multicolored .25 .25
C843 A138 10c multicolored .25 .25
C844 A138 15c multicolored .25 .25
C845 A138 20c multicolored .25 .25
C846 A138 50c multicolored .50 .25
Nos. C842-C846 (5) 1.50 1.25

Cent. of the Dept. of Industrial Development and to publicize the Natl. Industrial Expo.

Pedro Gual Type of 1964

1964, Mar. 20 *Perf. 14x13½*
C847 A139 75c dull blue green .85 .30
C848 A139 1b bright pink 1.25 .40

Blast Furnace and
Map of
Venezuela — AP58

Arms of Ciudad
Bolivar — AP59

1964, May 22 **Litho.** *Perf. 13½x14*
C849 AP58 80c multi 1.25 .45
C850 AP58 1b multi 1.60 .50

Issued to publicize the Orinoco steel mills.

1964, May 22 *Perf. 10½*
C851 AP59 1b multi 1.75 .95

Bicentenary of Ciudad Bolivar.

AP60

1964, Aug. 3 **Unwmk.** *Perf. 11½*
C852 AP60 30c bister brn & yel .45 .25
C853 AP60 40c plum & pink .65 .25
C854 AP60 50c brn & tan .90 .30
Nos. C852-C854 (3) 2.00 .80

80th birthday of novelist Romulo Gallegos.

AP61

1964, Nov. 11 **Litho.** *Perf. 14x13½*
C855 AP61 1b orange & dk vio 1.50 .65

Eleanor Roosevelt and 15th anniv. (in 1963) of the Universal Declaration of Human Rights.
For surcharge see No. C896.

Issues of 1947-64 Surcharged
in Black, Dark Blue, Red, Carmine or
Lilac with New Value and:
"RESELLADO / VALOR"

1965
C856 A102 5c on 55c
(#C787) .55 .25
C857 A102 5c on 70c
(#C788) .55 .25
C858 A102 5c on 80c
(#C790) .55 .25
C859 A102 5c on 85c
(#C791) .55 .25
C860 A102 5c on 90c
(#C668) .55 .25
C861 A102 5c on 95c
(#C792) .55 .25
C862 A134 5c on 1b (#C835) .75 .25
C863 AP25 10c on 3b (#C269)
(C) .55 .25
C864 AP25 10c on 4b (#C270)
(C) .95 .25
C865 AP47 10c on 70c
(#C767) (C) .60 .25
C866 AP47 10c on 90c
(#C770) (C) .55 .25
C867 AP49 10c on 1.05b
(#C780) .80 .25
C868 AP49 10c on 1.90b
(#C782) .55 .25
C869 AP49 10c on 2b (#C783) .60 .25
C870 AP49 10c on 3b (#C784) .60 .25
C871 AP54 10c on 80c
(#C829) .55 .25
C872 AP54 10c on 90c
(#C830) .55 .25
C873 AP16 15c on 3b (#C253) .60 .25
C874 A112 15c on 90c
(#C737) .55 .25
C875 A135 15c on 80c
(#C836) .55 .25
C876 A135 15c on 90c
(#C837) .55 .25
C877 AP59 15c on 1b (#C851) .60 .25
C878 A101 20c on 2b (#C657)
(R) .75 .25
C879 AP48 20c on 55c
(#C775) (DB) .60 .25
C880 A126 20c on 55c
(#C816) .80 .25
a. 25c on 55c (#C816)
C881 A126 20c on 2.30b
(#C817) .60 .25
C882 A126 20c on 2.50b
(#C818) .80 .25
C883 AP55 20c on 70c
(#C831) .80 .25
C884 A110 25c on 70c
(#C720) (DB) .85 .25
C885 A124 25c on 1.05b
(#C801) (L) .60 .25
C886 A124 25c on 1.50b
(#C802) (L) .60 .25
C887 A124 25c on 2b (#C803)
(L) .80 .25
C888 A128 25c on 1.50b
(#C824) .80 .25
C889 A128 25c on 2b (#C825) .80 .25
C890 AP57 25c on 95c
(#C838) .75 .25
C891 AP57 25c on 1.05b
(#C839) .80 .25
C892 AP53 30c on 1b (#C828) 1.00 .25
C893 A113 40c on 1.05b
(#C805) (DB) .80 .25
C894 A111 50c on 65c
(#C730) (DB) .55 .25
C895 A111 50c on 1.20b
(#C734) (DB) 1.00 .25
C896 AP61 50c on 1b (#C855) .60 .25
C897 AP56 60c on 90c
(#C832) 1.40 .40
C898 AP56 60c on 95c
(#C833) 1.10 .25
C899 A125 75c on 85c
(#C810) 1.25 .40
Nos. C856-C899 (44) 31.25 11.30

Lines of surcharge arranged variously on Nos. C856-C899. Old denominations obliterated with bars on Nos. C862, C871-C873, C875-C877, C883, C885-C887, C889, C892, C896-C898. Vertical surcharge on Nos. C865-C866, C871-C872, C874, C878, C896.

Kennedy Type of 1965

1965, Aug. 20 Photo. *Perf. 12x11½*
C900 A144 60c lt grnsh bl   1.10   .40
C901 A144 80c red brn   1.25   .50

Medical Federation Emblem — AP62

1965, Aug. 24 Litho. *Perf. 13½x14*
C902 AP62 65c red org & blk   1.60   .75

20th anniversary of the founding of the Medical Federation of Venezuela.

Unisphere and Venezuela Pavilion AP63

1965, Aug. 31 *Perf. 14x13½*
C903 AP63 1b multi   1.25   .35

New York World's Fair, 1964-65.

Andrés Bello (1780?-1865), Educator and Writer — AP64

Perf. 14x13½
1965, Oct. 15 Litho. Unwmk.
C904 AP64 80c dk brn & org   1.50   .75

Map Type of 1965

Maps of Venezuela and Guiana: 25c, Map of Venezuela and Guiana by J. Cruz Cano, 1775. 40c, Map stamp of 1896 (No. 140). 75c, Map by the Ministry of the Exterior, 1965 (all horiz.).

1965, Nov. 5 *Perf. 13½*
C905 A145 25c multi   .45   .25
C906 A145 40c multi   .65   .25
C907 A145 75c multi   1.00   .40
  a. Souv. sheet of 3, #C905-
      C907, imperf.   14.00 14.00
  Nos. C905-C907 (3)   2.10   .90

#C907a, issued June 7, 1966, sold for 1.65b.

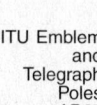

ITU Emblem and Telegraph Poles AP65

1965, Nov. 19 Litho. *Perf. 13½x14*
C908 AP65 75c blk & ol grn   1.00   .40

Cent. of the ITU.

Simon Bolivar and Quotation AP66

1965, Dec. 9 *Perf. 14x13½*
C909 AP66 75c lt bl & dk brn 1.00   .40

Sesquicentennial of Bolivar's Jamaica letter, Sept. 6, 1815.

Children Riding Magic Carpet and Three Kings on Camels — AP67

1965, Dec. 16 *Perf. 13½x14*
C910 AP67 70c yel & vio bl   1.50   .75

Children's Festival, 1965 (Christmas).

Fermin Toro — AP68

1965, Dec. 22 *Perf. 14x13½*
C911 AP68 1b blk & org   1.10   .35

Death centenary of Fermin Toro (1808-1865), statesman and writer.

Winston Churchill — AP69

1965, Dec. 29 *Perf. 14½x13*
C912 AP69 1b lilac & blk   1.50   .55

Sir Winston Spencer Churchill (1874-1965), statesman and World War II leader.

ICY Emblem, Arms of Venezuela and UN Emblem AP70

1965, Dec. 30 *Perf. 13½x14*
C913 AP70 85c gold & vio blk 1.50   .55

International Cooperation Year, 1965.

OAS Emblem and Map of America — AP71

1965, Dec. 31 *Perf. 14x13½*
C914 AP71 50c bl, blk & gold 1.25   .40

Organization of American States, 75th anniv.

Butterfly Type of 1966
Butterfly Type of 1966

1966, Jan. 25 Litho. *Perf. 13½x14*
Various Butterflies in Natural Colors; Black Inscriptions
C915 A146 65c lilac   1.75   .40
C916 A146 85c blue   2.50   .50
C917 A146 1b salmon pink   2.75   .60
  Nos. C915-C917 (3)   7.00   1.50

Farms of 1936 and 1966 — AP72

1966, Mar. 1 *Perf. 14x13½*
C918 AP72 55c blk, yel & emer 1.10   .40

30th anniversary of the Ministry for Agriculture and Husbandry.

Dance Type of 1966
Various folk dances.

1966, Apr. 5 Litho. *Perf. 14*
C919 A148 40c bl & multi   1.00   .35
C920 A148 50c multi   1.10   .40
C921 A148 60c vio & multi   .80   .25
C922 A148 70c multi   1.90   .50
C923 A148 80c red & multi   2.00   .65
C924 A148 90c ocher & multi 2.10   .80
  Nos. C919-C924 (6)   8.90   2.95

Title Page "Popule Meus" AP73

1966, Apr. 15 *Perf. 13½x14*
C925 AP73 55c yel grn, blk & bis .80 .45
C926 AP73 95c dp mag, blk &
                      bis   1.00   .60

150th anniv. (in 1964) of the death of José Angel Lamas, composer of natl. anthem.

Circus Scene, by Michelena — AP74

Paintings by Michelena: 1b, Miranda in La Carraca. 1.05b, Charlotte Corday.

Perf. 12x12½
1966, May 12 Litho. Unwmk.
C927 AP74 95c multi   1.00   .55
C928 AP74 1b multi   1.25   .55
C929 AP74 1.05b multi   1.40   .55
  Nos. C927-C929 (3)   3.65   1.65

Cent. of the birth of Arturo Michelena (1863-1898), painter. Miniature sheets of 12 exist. See Nos. 900-901.

Abraham Lincoln — AP75

1966, May 31 *Perf. 13½x14*
C930 AP75 1b gray & blk   1.25   .75

Dr. José Gregorio Hernandez AP76

1966, July 29 Litho. *Perf. 14x13½*
C931 AP76 1b brt bl & vio bl 1.60   .65

Centenary (in 1964) of the birth of Dr. José Gregorio Hernandez, physician.

Dr. Manuel Dagnino and Hospital AP77

1966, Aug. 16 Litho. *Perf. 13½x14*
C932 AP77 1b sl grn & yel grn 1.50   .55

Founding of Chiquinquira Hospital, cent.

Fish Type of 1966
Fish: 75c, Pearl headstander, vert. 90c, Swordtail characine. 1b, Ramirez's dwarf cichlid.

Perf. 14x13½, 13½x14
1966, Aug. 31
C933 A151 75c multi   1.60   .45
C934 A151 90c grn & multi   1.60   .45
C935 A151 1b multi   1.60   .45
  Nos. C933-C935 (3)   4.80   1.35

Rafael Arevalo Gonzalez — AP78

1966, Sept. 13 Litho. *Perf. 13½x14*
C936 AP78 75c yel bis & blk 1.40   .55

Centenary of the birth of Rafael Arevalo Gonzalez, journalist.

Simon Bolivar, 1816 — AP79

Bolivar Portraits: 25c, 30c, 35c, by José Gil de Castro, 1825. 40c, 50c, 60c, Anonymous painter, 1825. 80c, 1.20b, 4b, Anonymous painter, c. 1829.

Imprint: "Bundesdruckerei Berlin 1966"

1966		**Multicolored Center**	
C937	AP79	5c lem & blk	.25	.25
C938	AP79	10c lt ol grn & blk	.25	.25
C939	AP79	20c grn & blk	.25	.25
C940	AP79	25c salmon & blk	.25	.25
C941	AP79	30c pink & blk	.25	.25
C942	AP79	35c dl rose & blk	.30	.25
C943	AP79	40c bis brn & blk	.25	.25
C944	AP79	50c org brn & blk	.45	.25
C945	AP79	60c brn red & blk	.45	.25
C946	AP79	80c brt bl & blk	.90	.35
C947	AP79	1.20b dl bl & blk	1.40	.65
C948	AP79	4b vio bl & blk	4.50	2.75
	Nos. C937-C948 (12)		9.50	6.00

Issued to honor Simon Bolivar.
Issue dates: Nos. C937-C939, Aug. 15; Nos. C940-C942, Sept. 29; others, Oct. 14. See Nos. C961-C972.

"Justice" — AP80

1966, Nov. 3   Litho.   Perf. 14x13½
C949 AP80 50c pale lil & red lil   1.00   .40
50th anniversary of the Academy of Political and Social Sciences.

Angostura Bridge, Orinoco River — AP81

1967, Jan. 6   Litho.   Perf. 13½x14
C950 AP81 40c multi   .50   .25
Issued to commemorate the opening of the Angostura Bridge over the Orinoco River.

Pavilion of Venezuela AP82

1967, Apr. 28   Litho.   Perf. 11x13½
C951 AP82 1b multi   1.25   .40
EXPO '67, International Exhibition, Montreal, Apr. 28-Oct. 27, 1967.

Statue of Chief Guaicaipuro AP83

Constellations over Caracas, 1567 and 1967 — AP84

Designs: 45c, Captain Francisco Fajardo. 55c, Diego de Losada, the Founder. 65c, Arms of Caracas. 90c, Map of Caracas, 1578. 1b, Market on Plaza Mayor, 1800.

1967   Litho.   Perf. 14x13½, 13½x14
C952 AP83 15c multi   .25   .25
C953 AP83 45c gold, car & brn   .45   .25
C954 AP83 55c multi   .55   .25
C955 AP84 60c blk, ultra & sil   .60   .25
C956 AP83 65c multi   .80   .30
C957 AP84 90c multi   .95   .35
C958 AP84 1b multi   1.10   .45
Nos. C952-C958 (7)   4.70   2.10
400th anniv. of the founding of Caracas (1st issue). See Nos. C977-C982 (2nd issue).
Two souvenir sheets each contain single stamps similar to Nos. C952-C953, but with simulated perforation. Sold for 1b each. Size: 80x119mm. Value $45 each.
Issued: 55c, 65c, July 28; others, July 12.

Gen. Francisco Esteban Gomez — AP85

1967, July 31   Litho.   Perf. 14x13½
C959 AP85 90c multi   1.25   .55
150th anniversary, Battle of Matasiete.

Juan Vicente González — AP86

1967, Oct. 18   Litho.   Perf. 14x13½
C960 AP86 80c ocher & blk   1.25   .40
Centenary of the death (in 1866) of Juan Vicente González, journalist.

Bolivar Type of 1966
Imprint: "Druck Bruder Rosenbaum. Wien"

1967-68   Litho.   Perf. 13½x14
Multicolored Center
C961 AP79 5c lemon & blk   .25   .25
C962 AP79 10c lemon & blk   .25   .25
C963 AP79 20c grn & blk   .35   .25
C964 AP79 25c salmon & blk   .30   .25
C965 AP79 30c pink & blk   .35   .25
C966 AP79 35c dl rose & blk   .35   .25
C967 AP79 40c bis brn & blk   .60   .25
C968 AP79 50c org brn & blk   4.75   .35
C969 AP79 60c brn red & blk   2.10   .90
C970 AP79 80c brt bl & blk   1.25   .50
C971 AP79 1.20b dl bl & blk   1.75   .35
C972 AP79 4b vio bl & blk   4.75   1.90
Nos. C961-C972 (12)   17.05   5.75
Issue dates: 20c, 30c, 50c, Nov. 24; 5c, 25c, 40c, Feb. 5, 1968; others, Aug. 28, 1967.

Child with Pinwheel AP87

1967, Dec. 15   Litho.   Perf. 14x13½
C973 AP87 45c multi   .60   .25
C974 AP87 75c multi   .80   .30
C975 AP87 90c multi   1.00   .35
Nos. C973-C975 (3)   2.40   .90
Children's Festival.

Madonna with the Rosebush, by Stephan Lochner AP88

1967, Dec. 19
C976 AP88 1b multi   1.60   .70
Christmas 1967.

Palace of the Academies, Caracas — AP89

Views of Caracas: 50c, St. Theresa's Church, vert. 70c, Federal Legislature. 75c, University City. 85c, El Pulpo highways crossing. 2b, Avenida Libertador.

1967, Dec. 28   Perf. 13½x14, 14x13½
C977 AP89 10c multi   .25   .25
C978 AP89 50c lil & multi   .35   .25
C979 AP89 70c multi   .65   .25
C980 AP89 75c multi   .75   .25
C981 AP89 85c multi   .80   .30
C982 AP89 2b multi   2.25   .85
Nos. C977-C982 (6)   5.05   2.15
400th anniv. of Caracas (2nd issue).

Dr. José Manuel Nuñez Ponte (1870-1965), Educador — AP90

1968, Mar. 8   Litho.   Perf. 14
C983 AP90 65c multi   .75   .35

De Miranda and Printing Press AP91

Designs (Miranda Portraits and): 35c, Parliament, London. 45c, Arc de Triomphe, Paris. 70c, Portrait, vert. 80c, Portrait bust and Venezuelan flags, vert.

Perf. 13½x14, 14x13½
1968, June 20   Litho.
C984 AP91 20c yel brn, grn & brn   .35   .25
C985 AP91 35c multi   .55   .25
C986 AP91 45c lt bl & multi   1.00   .40
C987 AP91 70c multi   1.25   .35
C988 AP91 80c multi   1.50   .55
Nos. C984-C988 (5)   4.65   1.80
General Francisco de Miranda (1750?-1816), revolutionist, dictator of Venezuela.

Insect Type of 1968
Insect Pests: 5c, Red leaf-cutting ant, vert. 15c, Sugar cane beetle, vert. 20c, Leaf beetle.

Perf. 14x13½, 13½x14
1968, Aug. 30   Litho.
C989 A157 5c multi   .50   .25
C990 A157 15c multi   1.00   .25
C991 A157 20c gray & multi   1.50   .25
Nos. C989-C991 (3)   3.00   .75

Three Keys — AP92

1968, Oct. 17   Litho.   Perf. 14x13½
C992 AP92 95c yel, vio & dk grn   1.40   .50
Natl. Comptroller's Office, 30th anniv.

Fencing — AP93

Designs: 5c, Pistol shooting, vert. 15c, Running. 75c, Boxing. 5b, Sailing, vert.

Perf. 14x13½, 13½x14
1968, Nov. 6   Litho.   Unwmk.
C993 AP93 5c vio, bl & blk   .50   .30
C994 AP93 15c multi   .60   .30
C995 AP93 30c yel grn, dk grn & blk   .75   .30
C996 AP93 75c multi   1.40   .40
C997 AP93 5b multi   5.25   1.90
Nos. C993-C997 (5)   8.50   3.20
19th Olympic Games, Mexico City, 10/12-27.

Holy Family, by Francisco José de Lerma — AP94

1968, Dec. 4   Litho.   Perf. 14x13½
C998 AP94 40c multi   .75   .25
Christmas 1968.

Dancing Children and Stars — AP95

1968, Dec. 13   Litho.   Perf. 14x13½
C999 AP95 80c vio & org   1.10   .50
Issued for the 5th Children's Festival.

Conservation Type of 1968
Designs: 15c, Marbled wood-quail, vert. 20c, Water birds, vert. 30c, Woodcarvings and tools, vert. 90c, Brown trout. 95c, Valley and road. 1b, Red-eyed vireo feeding young bronzed cowbird.

Perf. 13½x14, 14x13½
1968, Dec. 19   Litho.
C1000 A160 15c multi   .45   .35
C1001 A160 20c multi   .45   .35
C1002 A160 30c multi   .55   .35
C1003 A160 90c multi   1.50   .45
C1004 A160 95c multi   2.25   .65
C1005 A160 1b multi   1.60   .55
Nos. C1000-C1005 (6)   6.80   2.70

Tourist Type of 1969
Designs: 15c, Giant cactus and desert, Falcon. 30c, Hotel Humboldt, Federal District. 40c, Cable car and mountain peaks, Merida.

1969, Jan. 24   Perf. 13½x14
C1006 A161 15c multi   .35   .25
C1007 A161 30c multi   .35   .25
a.   Souv. sheet of 2, #931, C1007, imperf.   2.10   2.10
C1008 A161 40c multi   .75   2.10
Nos. C1006-C1008 (3)   1.45   2.60

Tree Type of 1969
Trees: 5c, Cassia grandis. 20c, Triplaris caracasana. 25c, Samanea saman.

1969, May 30   Litho.   Perf. 13½x14
C1009 A164 5c lt grn & multi   .50   .25
C1010 A164 20c org & multi   .75   .25
C1011 A164 25c lt vio & multi   .85   .25
Nos. C1009-C1011 (3)   2.10   .75

Alexander von Humboldt, by Joseph Stieler — AP96

1969, Sept. 12   Photo.   Perf. 14
C1012   AP96 50c multi   .80   .25

Alexander von Humboldt (1769-1859), naturalist and explorer.

Map of Maracaibo, 1562 — AP97

20c, Ambrosio Alfinger, Alfonso Pacheco, Pedro Maldonado, horiz. 40c, Maracaibo coat of arms. 70c, University Hospital. 75c, Monument to the Indian Mara. 1b, Baralt Square, horiz.

Perf. 13½x13, 13x13½
1969, Sept. 30   Litho.
C1013   AP97 20c lil & multi   .35   .25
C1014   AP97 25c org & multi   .40   .25
C1015   AP97 40c multi   .45   .25
C1016   AP97 70c grn & multi   1.00   .35
C1017   AP97 75c brn & multi   1.25   .40
C1018   AP97 1b multi   1.40   .50
        Nos. C1013-C1018 (6)   4.85 2.00

400th anniversary of Maracaibo.

Astronauts Neil A. Armstrong, Edwin E. Aldrin, Jr., Michael Collins and Moonscape AP98

1969, Nov. 18   Litho.   Perf. 12½
C1019   AP98 90c multi   1.60   .65
   a.   Souv. sheet of 1, imperf. 3.25 3.25

See note after US No. C76.

Virgin with the Rosary, 17th Century AP99

Christmas: 80c, Holy Family, Caracas, 18th Cent.

1969, Dec. 1   Litho.   Perf. 12½
C1020   AP99 75c gold & multi   .90   .35
C1021   AP99 80c gold & multi   1.10   .45
   a.   Pair, #C1020-C1021   2.40 2.40

Simon Bolivar, 1819, by M. N. Bate — AP100

Bolivar Portraits: 45c, 55c, like 15c. 65c, 70c, 75c Drawing by Francois Roulin, 1828. 85c, 90c, 95c, Charcoal drawing by José María Espinoza, 1828. 1b, 1.50b, 2b, Drawing by Espinoza, 1830.

1970, Mar. 16   Litho.   Perf. 14x13½
C1022   AP100 15c multi   .25   .25
C1023   AP100 45c bl & multi   .45   .25
C1024   AP100 55c org & multi   .60   .25
C1025   AP100 65c multi   .60   .30
C1026   AP100 70c bl & multi   .70   .40
C1027   AP100 75c org & multi   .95   .40
C1028   AP100 85c multi   1.10   .45
C1029   AP100 90c bl & multi   1.10   .45
C1030   AP100 95c org & multi   1.25   .50
C1031   AP100 1b multi   1.25   .50
C1032   AP100 1.50b bl & multi   1.40   .55
C1033   AP100 2b multi   3.00 1.75
        Nos. C1022-C1033 (12) 12.65 6.00

Issued to honor Simon Bolivar (1783-1830), liberator and father of his country.

General Antonio Guzmán Blanco and Dr. Martin J. Sanabria AP101

1970, June 26   Litho.   Perf. 13
C1034   AP101 75c brt grn & multi .80   .35

Free obligatory elementary education, cent.

Map of Venezuela with Claim to Part of Guyana — AP102

State map and arms. 55c, 90c, vert.

Perf. 13½x14, 14x13½
1970-71   Litho.
C1035   AP102 5c shown   .35   .25
C1036   AP102 15c Apure   .35   .25
C1037   AP102 20c Aragua   .40   .25
C1038   AP102 20c Anzoategui   .45   .25
C1039   AP102 25c Barinas   .45   .25
C1040   AP102 25c Bolivar   .45   .25
C1041   AP102 45c Carabobo   .65   .25
C1042   AP102 55c Cojedes   .70   .25
C1043   AP102 65c Falcon   .75   .25
C1044   AP102 75c Guárico   .90   .25
C1045   AP102 85c Lara   1.10   .30
C1046   AP102 90c Mérida   1.10   .30
C1047   AP102 1b Miranda   1.10   .40
C1048   AP102 2b Delta
                 Amacuro
                 Territory   2.40   .95
        Nos. C1035-C1048 (14) 11.15 4.45

Issued: 5c, 7/15; 15c, #C1037, 1/18; #C1038-C1039, 2/15/71; #C1040, 45c, 3/15/71; 55c, 65c, 4/15; 75c, 85c, 5/15/71; 90c, 1b, 6/15/71; 2b, 7/15/71.

Flower Type of 1970

Flowers: 20c, Epidendrum secundum. 25c, Oyedaea verbesinoides. 45c, Heliconia villosa. 1b, Macleania nitida.

1970, July 29   Litho.   Perf. 14x13½
C1049   A175 20c multi   .50   .25
C1050   A175 25c multi   .60   .25
C1051   A175 45c multi   1.50   .35
C1052   A175 1b multi   1.90   .45
        Nos. C1049-C1052 (4) 4.50 1.30

Caracciolo Parra Olmedo AP104

1970, Nov. 16   Photo.   Perf. 12½
C1053   AP104 20c bl & multi   .30   .25

Sesquicentennial of birth of Caracciolo Parra Olmedo (1819-1900), professor of law, rector of University of Merida.

Census Chart — AP105

1971, Apr. 30   Litho.   Perf. 13½x14
C1054   Block of 4   5.00 2.50
   a.   AP105 70c, frame L & T   .90   .35
   b.   AP105 70c, frame T & R   .90   .35
   c.   AP105 70c, frame L & B   .90   .35
   d.   AP105 70c, frame B & R   .90   .35

See note after No. 979.

Cattleya Gaskelliana — AP106

Orchids: 20c, Cattleya percivaliana, vert. 75c, Cattleya mossiae, vert. 90c, Cattleya violacea. 1b, Cattleya lawrenciana.

Perf. 14x13½, 13½x14
1971, Aug. 25
C1055   AP106 20c blk & multi   .55   .25
C1056   AP106 25c blk & multi   .80   .25
C1057   AP106 75c blk & multi   1.50   .50
C1058   AP106 90c blk & multi   2.10   .80
C1059   AP106 1b blk & multi   2.25   .90
        Nos. C1055-C1059 (5)   7.20 2.70

40th anniversary of Venezuelan Society of Natural History. Issued in sheets of 5 stamps and one label with Society emblem in blue. Value $37.50.

Draft of Constitution Superimposed on Capitol AP107

1971, Dec. 29   Litho.   Perf. 13½
C1060   AP107 90c multi   .80   .40

Anniversary of 1961 Constitution.

AIR POST SEMI-POSTAL STAMPS

King Vulture SPAP1

Unwmk.
1942, Dec. 17   Engr.   Perf. 12
CB1   SPAP1 15c + 10c org brn   2.25   .60
CB2   SPAP1 30c + 5c violet   2.25   .75
      Set, never hinged   7.50

See note after No. B1.

SPECIAL DELIVERY STAMPS

Catalogue values for unused stamps in this section are for Never Hinged items.

SD1   SD2

Perf. 12½
1949, Mar. 9   Unwmk.   Engr.
E1   SD1 30c red   .60   .30

Wmk. 116
1961, Apr. 7   Litho.   Perf. 13½
E2   SD2 30c orange   .55   .25

REGISTRATION STAMPS

Bolívar — R1

1899, May   Unwmk. Engr.   Perf. 12
F1   R1 25c yellow brown   3.00 2.50

No. F1 Overprinted like Nos. 150-155
1900
F2   R1 25c yellow brown   1.50 1.50
   a.   Inverted overprint   22.50 22.50
   b.   Double overprint   30.00 30.00

Counterfeit overprints exist, especially of the varieties.

OFFICIAL STAMPS

Coat of Arms — O1

Lithographed, Center Engraved
1898, May 1   Unwmk.   Perf. 12
O1   O1 5c bl grn & blk   .80   .55
O2   O1 10c rose & blk   .95   .85
O3   O1 25c bl & blk   1.50 1.40
O4   O1 50c yel & blk   2.50 2.25
O5   O1 1b vio & blk   2.75 2.50
     Nos. O1-O5 (5)   8.50 7.55

Nos. O4 and O5
Handstamp
Surcharged in
Magenta or Violet

1899, Nov.

O6	O1	5c on 50c yel & blk	4.75	4.50
O7	O1	5c on 1b vio & blk	20.00	18.00
O8	O1	25c on 50c yel & blk	20.00	18.00
O9	O1	25c on 1b vio & blk	12.00	11.00
	Nos. O6-O9 (4)		56.75	51.50

Inverted Surcharge

O6a	O1	5c on 50c	15.00	15.00
O7a	O1	5c on 1b	40.00	40.00
O8a	O1	25c on 50c	32.50	32.50
O9a	O1	25c on 1b	32.50	32.50
	Nos. O6a-O9a (4)		120.00	120.00

Nos. O6-O9 exist with double surcharge.
Value each $18.50-$37.50.
Many of the magenta overprints have
become violet. There are intermediate
shades.
Counterfeit overprints exist.

Coat of Arms — O3

1900   Litho., Center Engr.

O14	O3	5c bl grn & blk	.40	.40
O15	O3	10c rose & blk	.55	.55
O16	O3	25c bl & blk	.55	.55
O17	O3	50c yel & blk	.55	.55
O18	O3	1b dl vio & blk	.65	.65
	Nos. O14-O18 (5)		2.70	2.70

O4   No Stars Above
                 Shield — O5

Imprint: "American Bank Note Co.,
N.Y."

1904, July   Engr.

O19	O4	5c emerald & blk	.25	.25
O20	O4	10c rose & blk	.65	.65
O21	O4	25c blue & blk	.65	.65
O22	O4	50c red brn & blk	4.25	4.25
a.		50c claret & black	4.25	4.25
O23	O4	1b red brn & blk	2.00	2.00
a.		1b claret & black	2.00	2.00
	Nos. O19-O23 (5)		7.80	7.80

1912   Lithographed in Caracas

O24	O5	5c grn & blk	.55	.30
O25	O5	10c car & blk	.55	.30
O26	O5	25c dk bl & blk	.55	.30
O27	O5	50c pur & blk	.55	.40
a.		Center double	19.00	
O28	O5	1b yel & blk	1.30	.80
	Nos. O24-O28 (5)		3.50	2.10

Perforated Initials

After 1925, Venezuela's official
stamps consisted of regular postage
stamps, some commemoratives and air
post stamps of 1930-42 punched with
"GN" (Gobierno Nacional) in large perforated initials.

LOCAL STAMPS FOR THE PORT OF CARUPANO

In 1902 Great Britain, Germany and
Italy, seeking compensation for revolutionary damages, established a block-
ade of La Guaira and seized the custom
house. Carúpano, a port near Trinidad,
was isolated and issued the following
provisionals. A treaty effected May 7,

1903, referred the dispute to the Hague
Tribunal.

A1

A2

1902   Typeset   Imperf.

1	A1	5c purple, *orange*	27.00	
2	A2	10c black, *orange*	40.00	
a.		Tête bêche pair	82.50	
3	A1	25c purple, *green*	32.50	
4	A1	50c green, *yellow*	80.00	
5	A1	1b blue, *rose*	100.00	
	Nos. 1-5 (5)		279.50	

A3

1902

6	A3	1b black, *yellow*	200.00	
a.		Tête bêche pair		

A4

1903   Handstamped

7	A4	5c carmine, *yellow*	40.00	40.00
8	A4	10c green, *yellow*	92.50	92.50
9	A4	25c green, *orange*	45.00	45.00
10	A4	50c blue, *rose*	45.00	45.00
11	A4	1b violet, *gray*	45.00	45.00
12	A4	2b carmine, *green*	45.00	45.00
13	A4	5b violet, *blue*	45.00	45.00
	Nos. 7-13 (7)		357.50	357.50

Dangerous counterfeits exist of Nos. 1-13.

LOCAL STAMPS FOR THE STATE OF GUAYANA

Revolutionary
Steamship
"Banrigh" — A1

Control Mark

Control Mark on Block of 4

1903   Typo.   Perf. 12

1	A1	5c black, *gray*	19.00	19.00
2	A1	10c black, *orange*	47.50	47.50
3	A1	25c black, *pink*	19.00	19.00
4	A1	50c black, *blue*	30.00	30.00
5	A1	1b black, *straw*	25.00	25.00
	Nos. 1-5 (5)		140.50	140.50

Nos. 1-5 can be found with or without the
illustrated control mark which covers four
stamps.
Counterfeits include the 10c and 50c in red
and are from different settings from the originals. They are on papers differing in colors
from the originals. All 5c on granite paper are
bogus.

Coat of
Arms
A2

1903

11	A2	5c black, *pink*	40.00	
12	A2	10c black, *orange*	50.00	
13	A2	25c black, *gray blue*	40.00	
a.		25c black, *blue*	40.00	
14	A2	50c black, *straw*	40.00	
15	A2	1b black, *gray*	30.00	
	Nos. 11-15 (5)		200.00	

Postally used examples are very scarce, as
are examples having 9 ornaments in horizontal borders. Nos. 11-15 pen canceled sell for
same values as unused.
See note on controls after No. 5.
Counterfeits exist of Nos. 11-15. Stamps
with 10 ornaments in horizontal borders are
counterfeits.
Nos. 1-5, 11-15 were issued by a group of
revolutionists and had a limited local use. The
dates on the stamps commemorate the declaration of Venezuelan independence and a
compact with Spain against Joseph
Bonaparte.

VIET NAM

vē-'et-'näm

LOCATION — In eastern Indo-China
GOVT. — Kingdom
AREA — 123,949 sq. mi.
POP. — 77,311,210 (1999 est.)
CAPITAL — Hanoi

Viet Nam, which included the former
French territories of Tonkin, Annam and
Cochin China, became an Associated
State of the French Union in 1949. The
Communist Viet Minh obtained control
of Northern Viet Nam in 1954, and the
republic of South Viet Nam was estab-
lished in October, 1955.

100 Cents (Xu) = 1 Piaster (Dong)

Catalogue values for unused
stamps in this country are for
Never Hinged items, beginning
with Scott 27 in the regular postage section, Scott B2 in the semi-
postal section, Scott C1 in the airpost section, Scott J1 in the postage due section, and Scott M1 in
the military section.

Bongour
Falls,
Dalat — A1

Emperor Bao-
Dai — A2

Designs: 20c, 2pi, 10pi, Imperial palace,
Hué. 30c, 15pi, Lake, Hanoi. 50c, 1pi, Temple,
Saigon.

Perf. 13x13½, 13½x13
Unwmk.

1951, June 6-Oct. 23   Photo.

1	A1	10c olive green	.25	.25
2	A1	20c deep plum	.25	.25
3	A1	30c blue	.30	.40
4	A1	50c red	.50	.25
5	A1	60c brown	.40	.25
6	A1	1pi chestnut brn	.40	.25
7	A2	1.20pi yellow brn	4.00	5.00
8	A1	2pi purple	1.50	.25
9	A2	3pi dull blue	4.00	.25
10	A1	5pi green	5.00	.70
11	A1	10pi crimson	16.00	1.00
12	A1	15pi red brown	75.00	6.00
13	A2	30pi blue green	45.00	7.00
	Nos. 1-13 (13)		152.60	21.85
	Set, never hinged		250.00	

Souvenir booklets exist comprising five
gummed sheets of 1 containing Nos. 1, 2, 6, 9,
12, together with commemorative inscriptions.
Value, $150.

Empress Nam-   Globe and
Phuong   Lightning Bolt
A3   A4

1952, Aug. 15   Perf. 12½

14	A3	30c dk pur, yel & brn	.60	.35
15	A3	50c blue, yel & brn	1.25	.65
16	A3	1.50pi ol grn, yel & brn	2.40	.30
	Nos. 14-16 (3)		4.25	1.30
	Set, never hinged		8.00	

For surcharge see No. B1.

1952, Aug. 24   Engr.   Perf. 13

17	A4	1pi greenish blue	2.50	1.75
	Never hinged		9.00	

Viet Nam's admission to the ITU, 1st anniv.

Coastal
Scene and
UPU
Emblem
A5

1952, Sept. 12

18	A5	5pi red brown	2.75	1.25
	Never hinged		4.75	

Viet Nam's admission to the UPU, 1st anniv.

Bao-Dai
and Pagoda
of
Literature,
Hanoi — A6

1952, Nov. 10   Perf. 12

19   A6 1.50pi rose violet   2.50   .50
       Never hinged   4.50

39th birthday of Emperor Bao-Dai.

Crown Prince Bao-
Long in Annamite
Costume — A7

70c, 80c, 100pi, Prince in Annamite costume. 90c, 20pi, 50pi, Prince in Western
uniform.

1954, June 15   Perf. 13

20   A7 40c aqua   .25   .25
21   A7 70c claret   .25   .25
22   A7 80c black brown   .25   .30
23   A7 90c dark green   .40   .80
24   A7 20pi rose pink   1.25 2.25
25   A7 50pi violet   4.00 7.00
26   A7 100pi blue violet   6.00 10.00
       Nos. 20-26 (7)   12.40 20.85
Set, never hinged, brown
  gum   20.00
Set, never hinged, white
  gum   50.00

REPUBLIC OF VIET NAM

(South Viet Nam)

(Viet Nam Cong Hoa)

GOVT. — Republic
AREA — 66,280 sq. mi.
POP. — 19,600,000 (est. 1973)
CAPITAL — Saigon

> Catalogue values for unused
> stamps in this section, from this
> point to the end of the section, are
> for Never Hinged items. Because
> of the tropical conditions, never
> hinged stamps must also be free
> of wrinkles, toning, and any other
> disturbance.

Mythological Turtle — A8

Unwmk.

1955, July 20   Engr.   Perf. 13

27   A8 30c claret   2.50   .25
28   A8 50c dark green   6.00 1.50
29   A8 1.50pi bright blue   6.00   .60
       Nos. 27-29 (3)   14.50 2.35

Refugees on Raft — A9

1955, Oct. 11

30   A9 70c crimson rose   1.00   .25
31   A9 80c brown violet   3.00   .40
32   A9 10pi indigo   6.00   .55
33   A9 20pi vio, red brn &
            org   19.00   .80
34   A9 35pi dk bl, blk brn &
            yel   35.00 4.00
35   A9 100pi dk grn, brn vio
            & org   80.00 7.25
       Nos. 30-35 (6)   144.00 13.25

1st anniv. of the flight of the North
Vietnamese.

No. 34 is inscribed "Chiên-Dich-Huynh-Dê"
(Operation Brotherhood) below design. See
No. 54.

Post Office,   Pres. Ngo Dinh
Saigon — A10   Diem — A11

1956, Jan. 10   Perf. 12

36   A10 60c bluish green   1.90   .25
37   A10 90c violet   3.50   .40
38   A10 3pi red brown   6.75   .60
       Nos. 36-38 (3)   12.15 1.25

5th anniv. of independent postal service.
For overprints see Nos. 51-53.

1956   Engr.   Perf. 13x13½

39   A11 20c orange ver   .40   .25
40   A11 30c rose lilac   .75   .25
41   A11 50c brt carmine   .40   .25
42   A11 1pi violet   .80   .25
43   A11 1.50pi violet   1.60   .25
44   A11 3pi black brown   1.60   .25
45   A11 4pi dark blue   2.40   .25
46   A11 5pi red brown   3.25   .25
47   A11 10pi blue   3.75   .30
48   A11 20pi gray black   10.00   .65
49   A11 35pi green   29.00 1.50
50   A11 100pi brown   60.00 5.50
       Nos. 39-50 (12)   113.95 9.95

Nos. 36-38
Overprinted

1956, Aug. 6   Perf. 12

51   A10 60c bluish green   1.10   .45
52   A10 90c violet   2.50   .45
53   A10 3pi red brown   3.25   .90
       Nos. 51-53 (3)   6.85 1.80

The overprint reads: "Government Post
Office Building."

No. 34 Overprinted

1956, Aug. 6

54   A9 35pi dk bl, blk brn & yel 12.00 6.00

Bamboo — A12   Children — A13

1956, Oct. 26 Litho. Perf. 13x13½

55   A12 50c scarlet   .95   .25
56   A12 1.50pi rose violet 1.25   .25
57   A12 2pi brt green   1.60   .30
58   A12 4pi deep blue   4.25   .45
       Nos. 55-58 (4)   8.05 1.25

1st anniv. of the Republic.

1956, Nov. 7   Engr.   Perf. 13½x14

59   A13 1pi lilac rose   .80   .25
60   A13 2pi blue green   1.25   .25
61   A13 6pi purple   2.00   .25
62   A13 35pi violet blue   11.00 4.00
       Nos. 59-62 (4)   15.05 4.75

"Operation Brotherhood."

Hunters on   Loading Cargo
Elephants   A15
A14

Design: 90c, 2pi, 3pi, Mountain dwelling.

1957, July 7   Photo.   Perf. 13

63   A14 20c yellow grn & pur 1.25   .25
64   A14 30c bister & dp mag   1.50   .25
65   A14 90c yel grn & dk brn 1.75   .25
66   A14 2pi green & ultra   2.40   .25
67   A14 3pi blue vio & brn   3.00   .75
       Nos. 63-67 (5)   9.90 1.75

1957, Oct. 21   Perf. 13½x13

68   A15 20c rose violet   .25   .25
69   A15 40c lt olive grn   .25   .25
70   A15 50c lt carmine rose   .50   .25
71   A15 2pi ultra   1.60   .25
72   A15 3pi brt green   2.25   .25
       Nos. 68-72 (5)   4.85 1.25

9th Colombo Plan Conference, Saigon.

Torch, Map and   Farmers, Tractor
Constitution   and Village
A16   A17

1957, Oct. 26   Litho. Perf. 13x13½

73   A16 50c black, green & sal   .25   .25
74   A16 80c black, brt bl & mag .25   .25
75   A16 1pi black, bl grn & brt
            car   .50   .25
76   A16 4pi blk, ol grn & fawn   .70   .25
77   A16 5pi blk, grnsh bl & cit 1.00   .35
78   A16 10pi black, ultra & rose 2.10 .55
       Nos. 73-78 (6)   4.80 1.90

Republic of South Viet Nam, 2nd anniv.

1958, July 7   Engr.   Perf. 13½

79   A17 50c yellow green   .40   .25
80   A17 1pi deep violet   .60   .25
81   A17 2pi ultra   1.25   .25
82   A17 10pi brick red   2.50   .90
       Nos. 79-82 (4)   4.75 1.65

4th anniv. of the government of Ngo Dinh
Diem.

Girl and   A19
Lantern — A18

1958, Sept. 27

83   A18 30c yellow   .45   .25
84   A18 50c dk carmine rose   .50   .25
85   A18 2pi dp carmine   .60   .25
86   A18 3pi blue green   1.25   .25
87   A18 4pi lt olive green   2.10   .25
       Nos. 83-87 (5)   4.90 1.25

Children's Festival.

1958, Oct. 26   Perf. 13½

88   A19 1pi dull red brown   .60   .25
89   A19 2pi bluish green   .75   .25
90   A19 4pi rose carmine   1.10   .25
91   A19 5pi rose lilac   2.40   .75
       Nos. 88-91 (4)   4.85 1.50

Issued for United Nations Day.

> Most South Viet Nam stamps from
> 1958 onward exist imperforate in
> issued and trial colors, and also in
> small presentation sheets in issued
> colors.

UNESCO Building,   Torch and UN
Paris — A20   Emblem — A21

1958, Nov. 3   Perf. 12½x13

92   A20 50c ultra   .55   .25
93   A20 2pi bright red   .70   .25
94   A20 3pi lilac rose   1.40   .25
95   A20 6pi violet   2.25   .55
       Nos. 92-95 (4)   4.90 1.30

UNESCO Headquarters in Paris opening,
11/3.

1958, Dec. 10   Engr.   Perf. 13½

96   A21 50c dark blue   .25   .25
97   A21 1pi brown carmine   .45   .25
98   A21 2pi yellow green   .75   .25
99   A21 6pi rose violet   1.60   .65
       Nos. 96-99 (4)   3.05 1.40

Signing of the Universal Declaration of
Human Rights, 10th anniv.

Cathedral of
Hué — A22

Thien Mu
Pagoda,
Hué — A23

National
Museum
A24

50c, 2pi, Palace of Independence, Saigon.

1958-59   Perf. 13½

100 A22 10c dk blue gray   .25   .25
101 A23 30c green ('59)   .60   .25
102 A24 40c dk green ('59)   .85   .25
103 A24 50c green ('59)   .85   .25
104 A24 2pi grnsh blue ('59) 2.50   .25
105 A23 4pi dull purple ('59) 2.75 .40
106 A24 5pi dk carmine ('59) 3.00   .40
107 A22 6pi orange brown   4.25   .50
       Nos. 100-107 (8)   15.05 2.55

Trung Sisters
on Elephants
A25

1959, Mar. 14   **Photo.**   **Perf. 13**
108 A25 50c multicolored   1.25   .25
109 A25 2pi ocher, grn & bl   2.50   .25
110 A25 3pi emerald, vio & bis   4.00   .25
111 A25 6pi multicolored   7.50   .80
   Nos. 108-111 (4)   15.25 1.55

Sisters Trung Trac and Trung Nhi who resisted a Chinese invasion in 40-44 A.D.

Symbols of Agrarian Reforms A26

1959, July 7   **Engr.**   **Perf. 13**
112 A26 70c lilac rose   .60   .25
113 A26 2pi dk grn & Prus bl   .70   .25
114 A26 3pi olive   1.25   .25
115 A26 6pi dark red & red   2.50   .70
   Nos. 112-115 (4)   5.05 1.45

5th anniv. of Ngo Dinh Diem's presidency.

Diesel Engine and Map of North and South Viet Nam — A27

1959, Aug. 7
116 A27 1pi lt violet & grn   1.25   .25
117 A27 2pi gray & green   1.40   .25
118 A27 3pi grnsh bl & grn   1.90   .25
119 A27 4pi maroon & grn   3.25   .45
   Nos. 116-119 (4)   7.80 1.20

Re-opening of the Saigon-Dongha Railroad.

Volunteer Road Workers A28

1959, Oct. 26
120 A28 1pi org brn, ultra & grn   .95   .25
121 A28 2pi violet, org & grn   1.25   .25
122 A28 4pi dk bl, bl & bis   3.00   .45
123 A28 5pi bister, brn & ocher   3.00   .65
   Nos. 120-123 (4)   8.20 1.60

4th anniv. of the constitution, stressing communal development.

Boy Scout — A29

1959, Dec.   **Engr.**   **Perf. 13**
124 A29 3pi brt yellow grn   .50   .25
125 A29 4pi deep lilac rose   1.25   .25
126 A29 8pi dk brn & lil rose   2.25   .50
127 A29 20pi Prus bl & bl grn   5.50 1.00
   Nos. 124-127 (4)   9.50 2.00

National Boy Scout Jamboree.

Symbols of Family and Justice A30

1960
128 A30 20c emerald   .40   .25
129 A30 30c brt grnsh blue   .50   .25
130 A30 2pi orange & maroon   1.10   .25
131 A30 6pi car & rose vio   4.20   .75
   Nos. 128-131 (4)   6.20 1.50

Issued to commemorate the family code.

Refugee Family and WRY Emblem A31

1960, Apr. 7   **Engr.**   **Perf. 13**
132 A31 50c brt lilac rose   .40   .25
133 A31 3pi brt green   .70   .25
134 A31 4pi scarlet   .85   .40
135 A31 5pi dp violet blue   1.25   .55
   Nos. 132-135 (4)   3.20 1.45

World Refugee Year, 7/1/59-6/30/60.

Henri Dunant — A32

1960, May 8   **Cross in Carmine**
136 A32 1pi dark blue   .70   .25
137 A32 3pi green   2.25   .25
138 A32 4pi crimson rose   2.25   .25
139 A32 6pi dp lilac rose   2.75   .70
   Nos. 136-139 (4)   7.95 1.70

Centenary (in 1959) of the Red Cross idea.

Model Farm A33

1960, July 7   **Perf. 13**
140 A33 50c ultra   .50   .25
141 A33 1pi dark green   .60   .25
142 A33 3pi orange   1.25   .35
143 A33 7pi bright pink   2.40   .50
   Nos. 140-143 (4)   4.75 1.35

Establishment of communal rice farming.

Girl With Basket of Rice and Rice Plant A34

1960, Nov. 21
144 A34 2pi emerald & green   1.00   .25
145 A34 4pi blue & ultra   2.25   .65

Conf. of the UN FAO, Saigon, Nov. 1960.

Map and Flag of Viet Nam — A35

1960, Oct. 26   **Engr.**   **Perf. 13**
146 A35 50c grnsh bl, car & yel   .55   .25
147 A35 1pi ultra, car & yel   .75   .25
148 A35 3pi purple, car & yel   1.25   .25
149 A35 7pi yel grn, car & yel   2.25   .40
   Nos. 146-149 (4)   4.80 1.15

Fifth anniversary of the Republic.

Agricultural Development Center, Tractor and Plow — A36

1961, Jan. 3   **Perf. 13**
150 A36 50c red brown   .45   .25
151 A36 70c rose lilac   .85   .25
152 A36 80c rose red   .95   .25
153 A36 10pi bright pink   4.75   .60
   Nos. 150-153 (4)   7.00 1.35

Plant and Child — A37   Pres. Ngo Dinh Diem — A38

1961, Mar. 23   **Perf. 13**
154 A37 70c light blue   .45   .25
155 A37 80c ultra   .55   .25
156 A37 4pi olive bister   .75   .25
157 A37 7pi grnsh bl & yel grn   2.00   .50
   Nos. 154-157 (4)   3.75 1.25

Child protection.

1961, Apr. 29   **Perf. 13**
158 A38 50c brt ultra   .60   .25
159 A38 1pi red   1.00   .25
160 A38 2pi lilac rose   2.00   .25
161 A38 4pi brt violet   4.00   .25
   Nos. 158-161 (4)   7.60 1.00

Second term of Pres. Ngo Dinh Diem.

Boy, Girl and Flaming Torch A39

1961, July 7   **Engr.**   **Perf. 13**
162 A39 50c red   .25   .25
163 A39 70c bright pink   .65   .25
164 A39 80c ver & maroon   .80   .25
165 A39 8pi dp claret & mag   2.25   .70
   Nos. 162-165 (4)   3.95 1.45

Issued for Youth Day.

Saigon-Bien Hoa Highway Bridge — A40

1961, July 28
166 A40 50c yellow green   .55   .25
167 A40 1pi orange brown   .80   .25
168 A40 2pi dark blue   1.25   .25
169 A40 5pi brt red lilac   2.40   .25
   Nos. 166-169 (4)   5.00 1.00

Opening of Saigon-Bien Hoa Highway.

Alexandre de Rhodes A41

1961, Sept. 5
170 A41 50c rose carmine   .35   .25
171 A41 1pi claret   .50   .25
172 A41 3pi bister brown   .55   .25
173 A41 6pi emerald   1.60   .30
   Nos. 170-173 (4)   3.00 1.05

Alexandre de Rhodes (1591-1660), Jesuit missionary who introduced Roman characters to express the Viet Nam language.

Young Man with Torch, Sage, Pagoda — A42   Temple Dedicated to Confucius — A43

1961, Oct. 26   **Perf. 13**
174 A42 50c orange ver   .40   .25
175 A42 1pi brt green   .85   .25
176 A42 3pi rose red   1.00   .25
177 A42 8pi rose lilac & brn   3.25   .40
   Nos. 174-177 (4)   5.50 1.15

Moral Rearmament of Youth Movement.

1961, Nov. 4   **Engr.**
178 A43 1pi brt green   .60   .25
179 A43 2pi rose red   .90   .25
180 A43 5pi olive   2.50   .50
   Nos. 178-180 (3)   4.00 1.00

15th anniversary of UNESCO.

Earth Scraper Preparing Ground for Model Village — A44   Man Fighting Mosquito and Emblem — A45

1961, Dec. 11   **Perf. 13**
181 A44 50c dark green   .60   .25
182 A44 1pi Prus bl & car lake   .70   .25
183 A44 2pi olive grn & brn   .90   .25
184 A44 10pi Prus blue   3.25   .35
   Nos. 181-184 (4)   5.45 1.10

Agrarian reform program.

1962, Apr. 7   **Perf. 13**
185 A45 50c brt lilac rose   .45   .25
186 A45 1pi orange   .65   .25
187 A45 2pi emerald   .85   .25
188 A45 6pi ultra   2.00   .65
   Nos. 185-188 (4)   3.95 1.40

WHO drive to eradicate malaria.

Postal Check Center, Saigon — A46   Madonna of Vang — A47

1962, May 15   **Engr.**   **Perf. 13**
189 A46 70c dull green   .25   .25
190 A46 80c chocolate   .40   .25
191 A46 4pi lilac rose   1.25   .25
192 A46 7pi rose red   3.00   .55
   Nos. 189-192 (4)   4.90 1.30

Inauguration of postal checking service.

1962, July 7
193	A47	50c violet & rose red	.40	.25
194	A47	1pi red brn & indigo	.55	.25
195	A47	2pi brown & rose car	1.00	.25
196	A47	8pi green & dk blue	5.25	.40
		Nos. 193-196 (4)	7.20	1.15

Catholic shrine of the Madonna of Vang.

Armed Guards and Village A48

1962, Oct. 26
197	A48	50c bright red	.55	.25
198	A48	1pi yellow green	.85	.25
199	A48	1.50pi lilac rose	1.10	.25
200	A48	7pi ultra	3.00	.65
		Nos. 197-200 (4)	5.50	1.40

"Strategic village" defense system.

Gougah Waterfall, Dalat — A49

1963, Jan. 3
201	A49	60c orange red	1.25	.25
202	A49	1pi bluish black	2.00	.25

62nd birthday of Pres. Ngo Dinh Diem; Spring Festival.

Trung Sisters' Monument and Vietnamese Women — A50

1963, Mar. 1   **Engr.**
203	A50	50c green	.25	.25
204	A50	1pi dk carmine rose	.50	.25
205	A50	3pi lilac rose	.60	.25
206	A50	8pi violet blue	1.75	.60
		Nos. 203-206 (4)	3.10	1.35

Issued for Women's Day.

Farm Woman with Grain A51

1963, Mar. 21   **Perf. 13**
207	A51	50c red	.50	.25
208	A51	1pi dk car rose	.55	.25
209	A51	3pi lilac rose	.80	.25
210	A51	8pi violet	1.40	.50
		Nos. 207-210 (4)	3.25	1.25

FAO "Freedom from Hunger" campaign.

Common Defense Emblem — A52   Emblem — A53

1963, July 7   **Engr.**   **Perf. 13**
211	A52	30c bister	.65	.25
212	A52	50c lilac rose	.80	.25
213	A52	3pi brt green	1.25	.25
214	A52	8pi red	2.10	.35
		Nos. 211-214 (4)	4.80	1.10

Common defense effort. The inscription says: "Personalism-Common Progress."

1963, Oct. 26   **Perf. 13**
215	A53	50c rose red	.40	.25
216	A53	1pi emerald	.65	.25
217	A53	4pi purple	1.40	.25
218	A53	5pi orange	2.50	.95
		Nos. 215-218 (4)	4.95	1.70

The fighting soldiers of the Republic.

Centenary Emblem and Map — A54

1963, Nov. 17   **Engr.**
Cross in Deep Carmine
219	A54	50c Prus blue	.50	.25
220	A54	1pi deep carmine	1.00	.25
221	A54	3pi orange yellow	1.40	.25
222	A54	6pi brown	3.25	.55
		Nos. 219-222 (4)	6.15	1.30

Centenary of International Red Cross.

Constitution and Scales — A55

1963, Dec. 10   **Perf. 13**
223	A55	70c orange	.25	.25
224	A55	1pi brt rose	.50	.25
225	A55	3pi green	.65	.25
226	A55	8pi ocher	1.75	.50
		Nos. 223-226 (4)	3.15	1.25

15th anniv. of the Universal Declaration of Human Rights.

Danhim Hydroelectric Station — A56

1964, Jan. 15   **Engr.**
227	A56	40c rose red	.65	.25
228	A56	1pi bister brown	.65	.25
229	A56	3pi violet blue	.95	.25
230	A56	8pi olive green	1.75	.70
		Nos. 227-230 (4)	4.00	1.45

Inauguration of the Danhim Hydroelectric Station.

Compass Rose, Barograph and UN Emblem — A58

South Vietnamese Gesturing to North Vietnamese; Map — A59

1964, Mar. 23   **Engr.**
235	A58	50c bister	.25	.25
236	A58	1pi vermilion	.40	.25
237	A58	1.50pi rose claret	.60	.25
238	A58	10pi emerald	1.90	.70
		Nos. 235-238 (4)	3.15	1.45

4th World Meteorological Day, Mar. 23.

1964, July 20   **Perf. 13**
239	A59	30c dk grn, ultra & mar	1.60	.25
240	A59	50c dk car rose, yel & blk	1.60	.25
241	A59	1.50pi dk bl, dp org & blk	1.60	.50
		Nos. 239-241 (3)	4.80	1.00

10th anniv. of the Day of National Grief, July 20, 1954, when the nation was divided into South and North Viet Nam.

Hatien Beach — A60

1964, Sept. 7   **Engr.**   **Perf. 13½**
242	A60	20c bright ultra	.50	.50
243	A60	3pi emerald	1.75	.55

Revolutionists and "Nov. 1" — A61

Designs: 80c, Soldier breaking chain. 3pi, Broken chain and date: "1-11 1963," vert.

1964, Nov. 1   **Engr.**   **Perf. 13**
244	A61	50c red lilac & indigo	.65	.25
245	A61	80c violet & red brn	.70	.25
246	A61	3pi dk blue & red	1.10	.70
		Nos. 244-246 (3)	2.45	1.20

Anniv. of November 1963 revolution.

Temple, Saigon A62

Designs: 1pi, Royal tombs, Hué. 1.50pi, Fishermen and sailboats at Phan-Thiet beach. 3pi, Temple, Gia-Dhin.

1964-66   **Perf. 13**
Size: 35½x26mm
247	A62	50c fawn, grn & dl vio	.70	.25
248	A62	1pi olive bis & ind	1.10	.25
249	A62	1.50pi ol gray & dk sl	1.00	.25
250	A62	3pi vio, dk sl grn & cl	2.00	.50
		Nos. 247-250 (4)	4.80	1.25

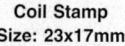

Coil Stamp
Size: 23x17mm
250A	A62	1pi ol bis & ind ('66)	6.00	3.50

Issue date: Nos. 247-250, Dec. 2, 1964.

Hung Vuong and Au Co with their Children A63

1965, Apr.   **Engr.**   **Perf. 13**
251	A63	3pi car lake & org red	1.50	.45
252	A63	100pi brown vio & vio	19.00	3.50

Mythological founders of Viet Nam, c. 2000 B.C.

ITU Emblem, Insulator and TV Mast — A64

1965, May 17   **Engr.**
253	A64	1pi olive, dp car & bister	.75	.25
254	A64	3pi henna brn, car & lil	1.75	.45

ITU, centenary.

Buddhist Wheel of Life and Flames — A65

1.50pi, Wheel, lotus blossom and world map, horiz. 3pi, Wheel and Buddhist flag.

Inscribed: "Phat-Giao" (Buddhism)

1965, May 15   **Perf. 13**
255	A65	50c dark carmine	1.50	.25
256	A65	1.50pi dk blue & ocher	1.50	.25
257	A65	3pi org brn & dk brn	2.25	.35
		Nos. 255-257 (3)	5.25	.85

Anniversary of Buddha's birth.

ICY Emblem and Women of Various Races — A66

1965, June 26
258	A66	50c bluish blk & bis	1.00	.25
259	A66	1pi dk brn & brn	1.00	.25
260	A66	1.50pi dark red & gray	1.60	.45
		Nos. 258-260 (3)	3.60	.95

International Cooperation Year.

Ixora — A67

Flowers: 80c, Orchid. 1pi, Chrysanthemum. 1.50pi, Lotus, horiz. 3pi, Plum blossoms.

1965, Sept. 10   Engr.   Perf. 13
261 A67 70c grn, slate grn & red .40 .25
262 A67 80c dk brn, lil & sl grn .55 .25
263 A67 1pi dk blue & yellow .70 .25
264 A67 1.50pi sl grn, dl grn & gray 1.00 .25
265 A67 3pi slate grn & org 2.10 .55
    Nos. 261-265 (5) 4.75 1.55

Student, Dormitory and Map of Thu Duc — A68

1965, Oct. 15   Perf. 13
266 A68 50c dark brown .25 .25
267 A68 1pi bright green .25 .25
268 A68 3pi crimson .75 .25
269 A68 7pi dark blue violet 2.00 .65
    Nos. 266-269 (4) 3.25 1.40

Issued to publicize higher education.

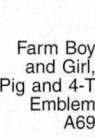
Farm Boy and Girl, Pig and 4-T Emblem A69

4pi, Farm boy with chicken, village and 4-T flag.

1965, Nov. 25   Engr.   Perf. 13
270 A69 3pi emerald & dk red 1.50 .25
271 A69 4pi dull violet & plum 2.50 .50

10th anniv. of the 4-T Clubs and the National Congress of Young Farmers.

Basketball A70

Designs: 1pi, Javelin. 1.50pi, Hand holding torch, athletic couple. 10pi, Pole vault.

1965, Dec. 14   Engr.   Perf. 13
272 A70 50c dk car & brn org .60 .25
273 A70 1pi org & red brn .75 .25
274 A70 1.50pi brt green 1.10 .25
275 A70 10pi red lil & brn org 3.00 .75
    Nos. 272-275 (4) 5.45 1.50

Radio Tower — A71

Radio tower, telephone dial, map of Viet Nam.

1966, Apr. 24   Engr.   Perf. 13
276 A71 3pi brt blue & brn .45 .25
277 A71 4pi purple, red & blk .55 .25

Saigon microwave station.

Loading Hook and Globe — A72

1966, June 22   Engr.   Perf. 13
278 A72 3pi gray & dk car rose .40 .25
279 A72 4pi olive & dk purple .60 .25
280 A72 6pi brt grn & dk blue 1.00 .35
    Nos. 278-280 (3) 2.00 .85

Appreciation of the help given by the free world.

Hands Reaching for Persecuted Refugees A73

1966, July 20
281 A73 3pi brn, vio brn & olive .50 .25
282 A73 7pi claret, vio brn & dk pur 1.25 .25

Refugees from communist oppression.

Paper Soldiers, Votive Offering A74

Designs: 1.50pi, Man and woman making offerings. 3pi, Floating candles in paper boats. 5pi, Woman burning paper offerings.

1966, Aug. 30   Engr.   Perf. 13
283 A74 50c red, blk & bis brn .75 .25
284 A74 1.50pi brown, emer & grn 1.25 .25
285 A74 3pi rose red & lake 1.75 .25
286 A74 5pi org brn, bis & dk brn 2.50 .40
    Nos. 283-286 (4) 6.25 1.15

Wandering Souls Festival.

Oriental Two-string Violin A75

Vietnamese Instruments: 3pi, Woman playing 16-string guitar. 4pi, Musicians playing two-string guitars. 7pi, Woman and boy playing flutes.

1966   Engr.   Perf. 13
Size: 35½x26mm
287 A75 1pi brown red & brn .95 .25
288 A75 3pi rose lilac & pur .95 .25
289 A75 4pi rose brown & brn 1.60 .30
290 A75 7pi dp blue & vio bl 3.50 .50
    Nos. 287-290 (4) 7.00 1.30

Coil Stamp
Size: 23x17mm
290A A75 3pi rose lil & pur 5.00 3.50
    b. Booklet pane of 5 50.00
        Complete booklet, 2 #290Ab 100.00

Nos. 287-290 were issued Sept. 28. Complete booklet contains two vertical strips of 5 with selvage at either end. These strips were also sold loose without booklet cover.

WHO Building, Geneva, and Flag — A76

Designs: 50c, WHO Building and emblem, horiz. 8pi, WHO flag and building.

1966, Oct. 12
291 A76 50c purple & carmine .25 .25
292 A76 1.50pi red brn, vio bl & blk .25 .25
293 A76 8pi grnsh bl, vio bl & brn 2.50 1.10
    Nos. 291-293 (3) 3.00 1.60

Opening of WHO Headquarters, Geneva.

Hand Holding Spade, and Soldiers A77

Soldier and Workers — A78

Designs: 1.50pi, Flag, workers. 4pi, Soldier and cavalryman.

1966, Nov. 1   Engr.   Perf. 13
294 A77 80c dull brn & red brn .40 .25
295 A77 1.50pi car rose, yel & brn .85 .25
296 A78 3pi brown & slate grn .85 .25
297 A78 4pi lilac, black & brn 3.00 .35
    Nos. 294-297 (4) 5.10 1.10

3rd anniv. of the revolution against the government of Pres. Ngo Dinh Diem.

Symbolic Tree and UNESCO Emblem — A79

Designs: 3pi, Globe and olive branches. 7pi, Symbolic temple, horiz.

1966, Dec. 15   Engr.   Perf. 13
298 A79 1pi pink, brn & dk car 1.10 .25
299 A79 3pi dp bl, grn & brn org 1.10 .25
300 A79 7pi grnsh bl, dk bl & red 2.75 .65
    Nos. 298-300 (3) 4.95 1.15

20th anniv. of UNESCO.

Bitter Melon A80

1967, Jan. 12   Engr.   Perf. 13
301 A80 50c Cashew, vert. 1.40 .25
302 A80 1.50pi shown 2.10 .25
303 A80 3pi Sweetsop 2.40 .25
304 A80 20pi Areca nuts 6.00 .55
    Nos. 301-304 (4) 11.90 1.30

Phan-Boi-Chau — A81

Designs: 20pi, Phan-Chau-Trinh portrait and addressing crowd.

1967, Mar. 24   Engr.   Perf. 13
305 A81 1pi mar, red brn & dk brn .75 .25
306 A81 20pi vio, slate grn & blk 2.00 .80

Issued to honor Vietnamese patriots.

Woman Carrying Produce A82

Labor Day: 1pi, Market scene. 3pi, Two-wheeled horse cart. 8pi, Farm scene with water buffalo.

1967, May 1   Engr.   Perf. 13
307 A82 50c vio bl, dk bl & ultra .25 .25
308 A82 1pi sl grn & dull pur .25 .25
309 A82 3pi dk carmine .60 .25
310 A82 8pi brt car rose & pur 1.25 .60
    Nos. 307-310 (4) 2.35 1.35

Potter, Vases and Lamp — A83

Weavers and Potters A84

Designs: 1.50pi, Vase and basket. 35d, Bag and lacquerware.

1967, July 22   Engr.   Perf. 13
311 A83 50c red brn, grn & ultra .25 .25
312 A83 1.50pi grnsh bl, car & blk .55 .25
313 A84 3pi red, vio & org brn 1.40 .25
314 A84 35pi bis brn, blk & dk red 4.25 .85
    Nos. 311-314 (4) 6.45 1.60

Issued to publicize Vietnamese handicrafts.

Wedding Procession A85

1967, Sept. 18   Engr.   Perf. 13
315 A85 3pi rose cl, dk vio & red 1.25 .35

Symbols of Stage, Music and Art — A86

Litho. & Engr.
1967, Oct. 27   Perf. 13
316 A86 10pi bl gray, blk & red 1.50 .25

Issued to publicize the Cultural Institute.

"Freedom and Justice" A87

Balloting A88

"Establishment of Democracy" — A89

1967, Nov. 1   **Photo.**
317 A87 4pi mag, brn & ocher .95 .25
318 A88 5pi brown, yel & blk 1.25 .25
319 A89 30pi dl lil, indigo & red 3.50 .65
    Nos. 317-319 (3) 5.70 1.15
National Day; general elections.

Pagoda and Lions Emblem A90

1967, Dec. 5   **Photo.**   **Perf. 13½x13**
320 A90 3pi multicolored 1.75 .50
50th anniversary of Lions International.

Teacher with Pupils and Globe — A91

1967, Dec. 10   **Perf. 13x13½**
321 A91 3pi tan, blk, yel & car 1.75 .40
International Literacy Day, Sept. 8, 1967.

Tractor and Village — A92

Rural Construction Program: 9pi, Bulldozer and home building. 10pi, Wheelbarrow, tractor and new building. 20pi, Vietnamese and Americans working together.

1968, Jan. 26   **Photo.**   **Perf. 13½**
322 A92 1pi multicolored .25 .25
323 A92 9pi lt blue & multi 1.00 .25
324 A92 10pi multicolored 1.60 .30
325 A92 20pi yel, red lil & blk 2.10 .45
    Nos. 322-325 (4) 4.95 1.25

WHO Emblem — A93

1968, Apr. 7   **Photo.**   **Perf. 13½**
326 A93 10pi gray grn, blk & yel 2.00 1.00
WHO, 20th anniversary.

Flags of Viet Nam's Allies — A94

Designs: 1.50pi, Flags surrounding SEATO emblem. 3pi, Flags, handclasp, globe and map of Viet Nam. 50pi, Flags and handclasp.

1968, June 22   **Photo.**   **Perf. 13½**
327 A94 1pi multicolored .60 .25
328 A94 1.50pi multicolored 1.25 .25
329 A94 3pi multicolored 2.40 .25
330 A94 50pi multicolored 7.75 .95
    Nos. 327-330 (4) 12.00 1.70
Issued to honor Viet Nam's allies.

Three-wheeled Truck and Tractor — A95

Private Property Ownership: 80c, Farmer, city man and symbols of property. 2pi, Three-wheeled cart, taxi and farmers. 30pi, Taxi, three-wheeled cart and tractor in field.

Inscribed: "HUU-SAN-HOA CONG-NHAN VA NONG-DAN"

1968, Nov. 1   **Photo.**   **Perf. 13½**
331 A95 80c multicolored .25 .25
332 A95 2pi steel blue & multi .25 .25
333 A95 10pi orange brn & multi 1.10 .45
334 A95 30pi gray blue & multi 3.50 1.25
    Nos. 331-334 (4) 5.10 2.20

Human Rights Flame — A96

Men of Various Races — A97

1968, Dec. 10   **Photo.**   **Perf. 13½**
335 A96 10pi multicolored .90 .30
336 A97 16pi purple & multi 1.75 .35
International Human Rights Year.

UNICEF Emblem, Mother and Child — A98

6pi, Children flying kite with UNICEF emblem.

1968, Dec. 11
337 A98 6pi multicolored 1.00 .50
338 A98 16pi multicolored 2.00 .80

Workers and Train — A99

1.50pi, 3pi, Crane, train, map of Viet Nam.

1968, Dec. 15
339 A99 1.50pi multicolored 1.00 .25
340 A99 3pi org, vio bl & grn 1.10 .25
341 A99 9pi multicolored 1.50 .25
342 A99 20pi multicolored 2.75 .50
    Nos. 339-342 (4) 6.35 1.25
Reopening of Trans-Viet Nam Railroad.

Farm Woman — A100

Vietnamese Women: 1pi, Merchant. 3pi, Nurses, horiz. 20pi, Three ladies.

1969, Mar. 23   **Engr.**   **Perf. 13**
343 A100 50c vio bl, lil & ocher .25 .25
344 A100 1pi grn, bis & dk brn .25 .25
345 A100 3pi brown, blk & bl .55 .25
346 A100 20pi lilac & multi 2.50 1.00
    Nos. 343-346 (4) 3.55 1.75

Soldiers and Civilians A101

Family Welcoming Soldier A102

1969, June 1   **Photo.**   **Perf. 13**
347 A101 2pi multicolored .25 .25
348 A102 50pi multicolored 3.25 .75
Pacification campaign.

Man Reading Constitution, Scales of Justice A103

Voters, Torch and Scales A104

1969, June 9
349 A103 1pi yel org, yel & blk .25 .25
350 A104 20pi multicolored 3.00 .50
Constitutional democracy. Phrase on both stamps: "Democratic and Governed by Law."

Mobile Post Office — A105

Mobile Post Office: 3pi, Window service. 4pi, Child with letter. 20pi, Crowd at window and postmark: "15, 12, 67."

1969, July 10
351 A105 1pi multicolored .25 .25
352 A105 3pi multicolored .60 .25
353 A105 4pi multicolored .75 .25
354 A105 20pi ocher & multi 1.50 .50
    Nos. 351-354 (4) 3.10 1.25
Installation of the first mobile post office in Viet Nam.

Mnong-gar Woman A106

1pi, Djarai woman. 50pi, Bahnar man.

1969, Aug. 29   **Photo.**   **Perf. 13**
355 A106 1pi brt pink & multi .90 .25
356 A106 6pi sky blue & multi 2.10 .25
357 A106 50pi gray & multi 9.00 .50
    Nos. 355-357 (3) 12.00 1.00
Ethnic minorities in Viet Nam.

Civilians Becoming Soldiers A107

General Mobilization: 3pi, Bayonet training. 5pi, Guard duty. 10pi, Farewell.

1969, Sept. 20
Inscribed: "TONG BONG VIEN"
358 A107 1.50pi orange & multi .80 .25
359 A107 3pi purple & multi 1.75 .25
360 A107 5pi blk, red & ocher 2.50 .25
361 A107 10pi pink & multi 3.50 .35
    Nos. 358-361 (4) 8.55 1.10

ILO Emblem and Globe — A108

1969, Oct. 29   **Photo.**   **Perf. 13**
362 A108 6pi blue grn, blk & gray .60 .25
363 A108 20pi red, blk & gray 1.90 .25
ILO, 50th anniversary.

Pegu House Sparrow — A109

Birds: 6pi, Moluccan munia. 7pi, Great hornbill. 30pi, Old world tree sparrow.

1970, Jan. 15   **Photo.**   **Perf. 12½x14**
364 A109 2pi blue & multi 1.00 .35
365 A109 6pi orange & multi 3.00 .70
366 A109 7pi org brn & multi 4.00 .70
367 A109 30pi blue & multi 14.00 2.10
    Nos. 364-367 (4) 22.00 3.85

Burning House and Family — A110

Design: 20pi, Family fleeing burning house and physician examining child.

1970, Jan. 31   Photo.   Perf. 13
368 A110 10pi multicolored   1.25 .25
369 A110 10pi multicolored   2.00 .30

Mau Than disaster, 1968.

Vietnamese Costumes — A111

Traditional Costumes: 1pi, Man, woman and priest. 2pi, Seated woman with fan. 100pi, Man and woman.

Inscribed: "Y-PHUC CO TRUYEN"

1970, Mar. 13   Photo.   Perf. 13
370 A111 1pi lt brown & multi   .25 .25
371 A111 2pi pink & multi   .25 .25
372 A111 3pi ultra & multi   .25 .25
373 A111 100pi multicolored   8.00 2.00
    Nos. 370-373 (4)   8.75 2.75

Issued for the Trung Sisters' Festival.

Building Workers, Pagodas and Bridge A112

Rebuilding of Hué: 20pi, Concrete mixers and scaffolds.

1970, June 10   Litho. & Engr.
374 A112 6pi multicolored   1.00 .25
375 A112 20pi rose lil, brn & bis   1.50 .50

Plower in Rice Field — A113

1970, Aug. 29   Perf. 13
376 A113 6pi multicolored   1.75 .45

"Land to the Tiller" agricultural reform program.

New Building and Scaffold A114

Construction Work — A115

1970, Sept. 15   Engr.   Perf. 13
377 A114 8pi pale ol & brn org   1.25 .25
378 A115 16pi brn, indigo & yel   2.75 .90

Reconstruction after 1968 Tet Offensive.

Productivity Year Emblem A116

1970, Oct. 3
379 A116 10pi multicolored   1.75 .45

Asian Productivity Year.

Nguyen-Dinh-Chieu — A117

1970, Nov. 16   Engr.   Perf. 13½
380 A117 6pi dull vio, red & brn   1.25 .25
381 A117 10pi grn, red & dk brn   2.00 .25

Nguyen-Dinh-Chieu (1822-1888), poet.

Education Year Emblem — A118

Litho. & Engr.
1970, Nov. 30   Perf. 13
382 A118 10pi pale brn, yel & blk   1.75 .65

International Education Year.

Parliament Building A119

Design: 6pi, Senate Building.

1970, Dec.
383 A119 6pi lt bl, cit & dk brn   .75 .25
384 A119 10pi multicolored   1.50 .25

6pi issued Dec. 8 for the 6th Cong.; 10pi issued Dec. 9 for the 9th General Assembly of the Asian Interparliamentary Union.

Dancers — A120

Designs: Various Vietnamese dancers and musicians. 6pi and 7pi horizontal.

1971, Jan. 12
385 A120 2pi ultra & multi   .85 .25
386 A120 6pi pale green & multi   2.40 .25
387 A120 7pi pink & multi   2.75 .25
388 A120 10pi brown org & multi   3.00 .45
    Nos. 385-388 (4)   9.00 1.20

For surcharge see No. 500.

Farmers and Law — A121

Agrarian Reform Law: 3pi, Tractor and law, dated 26.3.1970. 16pi, Farmers, people rejoicing and law book.

1971, Mar. 26   Engr.   Perf. 13
389 A121 2pi vio bl, dk brn & dl
            org   .25 .25
    a.   Dated "1970"   30.00
390 A121 3pi pale grn, brn & dk
            bl   .80 .25
391 A121 16pi multicolored   3.50 .25
    Nos. 389-391 (3)   4.55 .75

No. 389 is dated "1971."

For surcharge see No. 482.

Courier on Horseback A122

Design: 6pi, Mounted courier with flag.

Engr. & Photo.
1971, June 6   Perf. 13
392 A122 2pi violet & multi   .50 .25
393 A122 6pi tan & multi   2.25 .25

Postal history.

Military and Naval Operations on Vietnamese Coast — A123

1971, June 19
394 A123 3pi multi + label   1.00 .25
395 A123 40pi multi + label   5.00 .65

Armed Forces Day.

Deer — A124

1971, Aug. 20   Engr.
396 A124 9pi shown   1.25 .25
397 A124 30pi Tiger   3.75 .70

Rice Harvest A125

30pi, Threshing and winnowing rice and rice plants. 40pi, Bundling and carrying rice.

Litho. & Engr.
1971, Sept. 28   Perf. 13
398 A125 1pi multicolored   .25 .25
399 A125 30pi sal pink, dk pur &
            blk   3.00 .25
400 A125 40pi sepia, yel & grn   3.50 .30
    Nos. 398-400 (3)   6.75 .80

For surcharge see No. 496.

Inauguration of UPU Building, Bern — A126

1971, Nov. 9   Engr.   Perf. 13
401 A126 20pi green & multi   2.50 .75

Fish — A127

Various Fish; 2pi vertical.

1971, Nov. 16   Photo. & Engr.
402 A127 2pi multicolored   2.00 .25
403 A127 10pi violet & multi   4.00 .25
404 A127 100pi lilac & multi   27.50 2.40
    Nos. 402-404 (3)   33.50 2.90

Mailman and Woman on Water Buffalo A128

Rural Mail: 10pi, Bird carrying letter. 20pi, Mailman with bicycle delivering mail to villagers.

Inscribed: "PHAT TRIEN BUU-CHINH NONG THON"

1971, Dec. 20   Engr.   Perf. 13
405 A128 5pi multicolored   .65 .25
406 A128 10pi multicolored   1.10 .25
407 A128 20pi multicolored   2.00 .65
    Nos. 405-407 (3)   3.75 1.15

Trawler Fishermen, and Fish — A129

Publicity for Fishing Industry: 7pi, Net fishing from boat. 50d, Trawler with seine.

1972, Jan. 2   Engr.   Perf. 13
408 A129 4pi pink, blk & blue   .40 .25
409 A129 7pi lt blue, blk & red   .65 .25
410 A129 50pi multicolored   3.50 1.60
    Nos. 408-410 (3)   4.55 2.10

King Quang Trung (1752-1792) — A130

1972, Jan. 28   Perf. 13½
411 A130 6pi red & multi   1.10 .25
    a.   Booklet pane of 10   100.00
412 A130 20pi black & multi   3.50 .50

No. 411a is imperf. horizontally.

Road Workers A131

1972, Feb. 4
413 A131 3pi multicolored   .50 .25
414 A131 8pi multicolored   1.50 .25

Community development.

Rice Farming A132

1972, Mar. 26   Engr.   Perf. 13½
415 A132 1pi shown   .25 .25
416 A132 10pi Wheat farming   2.00 .25

Farmers' Day.

Plane over Dalat — A133

1972, Apr. 18   Engr. & Photo.
417 A133 10pi shown   2.00 .25
418 A133 10pi over Ha-tien   2.00 .25
419 A133 10pi over Hue   2.00 .25
420 A133 10pi over Saigon   2.00 .25
    a.   Block of 4, #417-420   18.00 3.25
421 A133 25pi like No. 417   4.50 .25
422 A133 25pi like No. 418   4.50 .25

423	A133	25pi like No. 419	5.00	.25
424	A133	25pi like No. 420	5.00	.25
a.		Block of 4, #421-424	40.00	8.00
		Nos. 417-424 (8)	27.00	2.00

20 years Air Viet Nam.

Scholar
A134

20pi, Teacher, pupils. 50pi, Scholar, scroll.

1972, May 5 Engr. & Litho.

425	A134	5pi multicolored	.40	.25

Engr.

426	A134	20pi lt green & multi	1.75	.50
427	A134	50pi pink & multi	4.75	.70
		Nos. 425-427 (3)	6.90	1.45

Ancient letter writing art.

Armed
Farmer — A135

6pi, Civilian rifleman & Self-defense Forces emblem, horiz. 20pi, Man, woman training with rifles.

Engr. & Litho.

1972, June 15 Perf. 13

428	A135	2pi brt rose & multi	1.25	.25
429	A135	6pi multicolored	2.00	.25
430	A135	20pi lt violet & multi	2.75	.25
		Nos. 428-430 (3)	6.00	.75

Civilian Self-defense Forces.

Hands
Holding
Safe — A136

1972, July 10

431	A136	10pi lt blue & multi	1.75	.25
432	A136	25pi lt green & multi	3.25	.40

Treasury Bonds campaign.

Frontier
Guard — A137

Soldier Helping
Wounded
Man — A138

Designs: 10pi, 3 guards and horse, horiz. 40pi, Marching guards, horiz.

Engr. & Litho.

1972, Aug. 14 Perf. 13

433	A137	10pi olive & multi	1.00	.25
434	A137	30pi buff & multi	2.50	.30
435	A137	40pi lt blue & multi	3.25	.55
		Nos. 433-435 (3)	6.75	1.10

Historic frontier guards.

1972, Sept. 1

Designs: 16pi, Soldier on crutches and flowers. 100pi, Veterans' memorial, map and flag.

436	A138	9pi olive & multi	1.00	.35
437	A138	16pi yellow & multi	1.40	.35
438	A138	100pi lt blue & multi	7.50	1.40
		Nos. 436-438 (3)	9.90	2.10

For surcharge see No. 483.

Tank,
Memorial,
Flag and
Map — A139

Soldiers and Map of
Viet Nam — A140

1972, Nov. 25 Litho. Perf. 13

439	A139	5pi multicolored	8.00	.25
440	A140	10pi ultra & multi	12.00	.25

Victory at Binh-Long.

Book Year
Emblem and
Globe — A141

Designs: 4pi, Emblem, books circling globe. 5pi, Emblem, books and globe.

1972, Nov. 30

441	A141	2pi dp carmine & multi	1.00	.25
442	A141	4pi blue & multi	1.60	.25
443	A141	5pi yellow bister & multi	2.50	.25
		Nos. 441-443 (3)	5.10	.75

International Book Year.

Liberated
Vietnamese
Family — A142

Soldiers Raising
Vietnamese
Flag — A143

1973, Feb. 18 Litho. Perf. 13

444	A142	10pi yellow & multi	2.25	.25

To celebrate the 200,000th returnee.

1973, Feb. 24 Litho. Perf. 13

Design: 10pi, Victorious soldiers and map of demilitarized zone, horiz.

445	A143	3pi lilac & multi	1.75	.25
446	A143	10pi yellow grn & multi	2.25	.25

Victory at Quang Tri.

Satellite,
Storm over
Viet
Nam — A144

1973, Mar. 23 Litho. Perf. 12½x12

447	A144	1pi lt blue & multi	1.25	.25

World Meteorological Day.
For surcharge see No. 497.

Farmers with
Tractor,
Symbol of
Law — A145

Farmer
Plowing with
Water Buffalos
A146

Pres. Thieu
Holding
Agrarian
Reform
Law
A147

1973, Mar. 26 Litho. Perf. 12½x12

448	A145	2pi lt green & multi	3.00	.60
449	A146	5pi orange & multi	3.00	.60

Perf. 11

450	A147	10pi blue & multi	120.00	30.00
		Nos. 448-450 (3)	126.00	31.20

3rd anniv. of the agrarian reform law; 5-year plan for rural development.
Value for No. 450 is for stamp with first day cancel. Commercially used examples are worth substantially more.
See No. 475.

INTERPOL
Emblem and
Headquarters
A148

2pi, INTERPOL emblem. 25pi, INTERPOL emblem, side view of Headquarters.

1973, Apr. 8 Litho. Perf. 12½x12

451	A148	1pi olive & multi	.25	.25
452	A148	2pi yellow & multi	.25	.25
453	A148	25pi ocher, lilac & brn	4.75	.25
		Nos. 451-453 (3)	5.25	.75

Intl. Criminal Police Org., 50th anniv.
For surcharge see No. 498.

ITU Emblem
and Waves
A149

2pi, Globe and waves. 3pi, ITU emblem.

1973, May 17

454	A149	1pi dull blue & multi	.40	.25
455	A149	2pi brt blue & multi	.85	.25
456	A149	3pi orange & multi	1.25	.25
		Nos. 454-456 (3)	2.50	.75

World Telecommunications Day.
For surcharge see No. 499.

Globe, Hand
Holding
House — A150

Men Building
Pylon — A151

Design: 10pi, Fish in net, symbols of agriculture, industry and transportation.

1973, Nov. 6 Litho. Perf. 12x12½

457	A150	8pi gray & multi	1.00	.25
458	A150	10pi vio bl, blk & gray	1.25	.25
459	A151	15pi blk, org & lil rose	2.10	.40
		Nos. 457-459 (3)	4.35	.90

National development.
For surcharge see No. 514.

Water Buffalos
A152

1973, Dec. 20 Litho. Perf. 12½x12

460	A152	5pi shown	1.50	.50
461	A152	10pi Water buffalo	2.50	.25

Human Rights
Flame, Three
Races
A153

Design: 100pi, Human Rights flame, scales and people, vert.

1973, Dec. 29 Perf. 12½x12, 12x12½

462	A153	15pi ultra & multi	1.00	.25
463	A153	100pi green & multi	3.25	.50

25th anniv. of Universal Declaration of Human Rights.

"25" and WHO
Emblem
A154

Design: 15pi, WHO emblem, diff.

1973, Dec. 31 Perf. 12½x12

464	A154	8pi orange, bl & brn	1.00	.25
465	A154	15pi lt brn, bl & brt pink	1.50	.25

25th anniversary of WHO.
For surcharge see No. 515.

Sampan
Ferry
A155

Design: 10pi, Sampan ferry (different).

1974, Jan. 13 Litho. Perf. 14x13½

466	A155	5pi lt blue & multi	1.75	.25
467	A155	10pi yellow grn & multi	2.50	.70

Sampan ferry women.

Soldiers of 7
Nations
A156

American War
Memorial
A157

Map of South Viet Nam and Allied Flags — A158

Design: No. 469, Soldiers and flags of South Viet Nam, Korea, US, Australia New Zealand, Thailand and Philippines. Same flags shown on 8pi and 60pi.

1974, Jan. 28   Perf. 12½x12, 12x12½
468 A156 8pi multicolored   .65   .25
469 A156 15pi lt brown & multi   1.40   .25
470 A157 15pi multicolored   1.40   .25
471 A158 60pi multicolored   4.00   .25
    Nos. 468-471 (4)   7.45 1.00

In honor of South Viet Nam's allies. For surcharge see No. 516.

Trung Sisters on Elephants Fighting Chinese A159

1974, Feb. 27 Litho. Perf. 12½x12
472 A159 8pi green, citron & blk 1.50   .25
473 A159 15pi dp orange & multi   2.00   .25
474 A159 80pi ultra, pink & blk   3.75   .25
    Nos. 472-474 (3)   7.25   .75

Trung Trac and Trung Nhi, queens of Viet Nam, 39-43 A.D. Day of Vietnamese Women.

Pres. Thieu Type of 1973 and

Farmers Going to Work — A160

Woman Farmer Holding Rice — A161

1974, Mar. 26 Litho. Perf. 14
475 A147 10pi blue & multi   1.50   .25
        Perf. 12½x12, 12x12½
476 A160 20pi yellow & multi   1.50   .25
477 A161 70pi blue & multi   12.00 1.50
    Nos. 475-477 (3)   15.00 2.00

Agriculture Day. Size of No. 475 is 31x50mm, No. 450 is 34x54mm and printed on thick paper. No. 475 has been extensively redrawn and first line of inscription in bottom panel changed to "26 THANG BA."

Value for No. 477 is for stamp with first day cancel. Commercially used examples are worth substantially more.

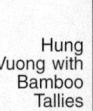

Hung Vuong with Bamboo Tallies A162

Flag Inscribed: Hung Vuong, Founder of Kingdom A163

1974, Apr. 2   Perf. 14x13½
478 A162 20pi yellow & multi   1.60   .45
479 A163 100pi olive & multi   5.50   .80

Hung Vuong, founder of Vietnamese nation and of Hồng-Bang Dynasty (2879-258 B.C.).

National Library A164

New National Library Building: 15pi, Library, right facade and Phoenix.

1974, Apr. 14
480 A164 10pi orange, brn & blk   1.25   .55
481 A164 15pi multicolored   1.50   .75

Nos. 391 and 437 Surcharged with New Value and Two Bars in Red

1974   Perf. 13
482 A121 25pi on 16pi multi   10.00 2.75
483 A138 25pi on 16pi multi   5.00 2.25

Memorial Tower, Saigon — A165

Globe, Crane Lifting Crate — A167

Crane with Flags, Globe and Map of Viet Nam — A166

Perf. 12x12½, 12½x12
1974, June 22   Litho.
484 A165 10pi blue & multi   .75   .25
485 A166 20pi multicolored   1.75   .30
486 A167 60pi yellow & multi   5.50   .35
    Nos. 484-486 (3)   8.00   .90

International Aid Day.

Sun and Views of Saigon, Dalat Hué A168

Cau-Bong Bridge, Nha Trang A169

Thien-Mu Pagoda, Hué — A170

1974, July 12 Perf. 14x13½, 13½x14
487 A168 5pi blue & multi   1.10   .45
488 A169 10pi blue & multi   1.10   .45
489 A170 15pi yellow & multi   1.90   .45
    Nos. 487-489 (3)   4.10 1.35

Tourist publicity.

Rhynchostylis Gigantea — A171

Orchids: 20pi, Cypripedium caliosum, vert. 200pi, Dendrobium nobile.

1974, Aug. 18
490 A171 10pi blue & multi   .35   .25
491 A171 20pi yellow & multi   .40   .25
492 A171 200pi bister & multi   6.50 1.25
    Nos. 490-492 (3)   7.25 1.75

Hands Passing Letter, UPU Emblem A172

UPU Emblem and Woman — A173

UPU Cent.: 30pi, World map, bird, UPU emblem.

Perf. 12½x12, 12x12½
1974, Oct. 9
493 A172 20pi ultra & multi   .30   .25
494 A172 30pi orange & multi   .65   .30
495 A173 300pi gray & multi   4.25 1.25
    Nos. 493-495 (3)   5.20 1.80

Nos. 398, 447, 451, 454, 387 Surcharged with New Value and Two Bars in Red

1974-75
496 A125 25pi on 1pi multi   16.00
497 A144 25pi on 1pi multi   16.00
498 A148 25pi on 1pi multi   16.00
499 A149 25pi on 1pi multi   22.50
500 A120 25pi on 7pi multi   19.00
    Nos. 496-500 (5)   89.50

Issued: #496, 498, 1/1/75; others, 11/18/74.

Hien Lam Pavilion, Hué A174

Throne, Imperial Palace, Hué A175

Water Pavilion, Hué A176

1975, Jan. 5 Litho. Perf. 14x13½
501 A174 25pi multicolored   1.50   .25
502 A175 30pi multicolored   2.25   .25
503 A176 60pi multicolored   2.75   .50
    Nos. 501-503 (3)   6.50 1.00

Historic sites.

Symbol of Youth, Children Holding Flower — A177

Family and Emblem A178

1975, Jan. 14   Perf. 11½
504 A177 20pi blue & multi   3.50   .30
        Perf. 12½x12
505 A178 70pi yellow & multi   3.50   .35

Intl. Conf. on Children & Natl. Development.

Unicorn Dance A179

Boy Lighting Firecracker A180

Bringing New Year Gifts and Wishes — A181

Perf. 14x13½, 13½x14
1975, Jan. 26   Litho.
506 A179 20pi multicolored   2.50   .25
507 A180 30pi blue & multi   3.00   .30
508 A181 100pi bister & multi   7.00   .50
    Nos. 506-508 (3)   12.50 1.05

Lunar New Year, Tet.

A182

A183

A184

Designs: 25pi, Military chief from play "San Hau." 40pi, Scene from "Tam Ha Nam Duong." 100pi, Warrior Luu-Kim-Dinn.

1975, Feb. 23
509	A182	25pi rose & multi	1.25	.45
510	A183	40pi lt green & multi	2.00	.45
511	A184	100pi violet & multi	6.75	.75
		Nos. 509-511 (3)	10.00	1.65

National theater.

Produce, Map of Viet Nam, Ship — A185

Irrigation Project A186

1975, Mar. 26   Litho.   Perf. 12½x12
512	A185	10pi multicolored	1.75	.25
513	A186	50pi multicolored	5.25	.30

Agriculture Day; 5th anniv. of Agrarian Reform Law.

Nos. 457, 464, 468 Surcharged with New Value and Two Bars in Red

1975
514	A150	10pi on 8pi multi	30.00	10.00
515	A154	10pi on 8pi multi	19.00	6.00
516	A156	25pi on 8pi multi	9.00	4.00
		Nos. 514-516 (3)	58.00	20.00

In the 1980's a number of South Viet Nam stamps appeared on the market. These apparently had been printed before the collapse of the Republic but saw no postal use. These include, but are not limited to, sets of two for western electric and for rural electric, one each for history, library, New Year and cows, a set of three for transportation and a set of four for economic development.

SEMI-POSTAL STAMPS

Type of 1952 Surcharged in Carmine

Perf. 12x12½
1952, Nov. 10   Unwmk.
B1	A3	1.50pi + 50c bl, yel & brn	4.00	3.25
		Never hinged	10.00	

The surtax was for the Red Cross.

Catalogue values for unused stamps in this section, from this point to the end of the section, are for Never Hinged items. Because of the tropical conditions, never hinged stamps must also be free of wrinkles, toning, and any other disturbance.

Sabers and Flag — SP1

1952, Dec. 21   Engr.   Perf. 13
B2	SP1	3.30pi + 1.70pi dp claret	2.50	1.10

The surtax was for the Wounded Soldiers' Aid Organization.

X-ray Camera and Patient SP2

1960, Aug. 1   Perf. 13
B3	SP2	3pi + 50c bl grn & red	1.50	.90

The surtax was for the Anti-Tuberculosis Foundation.

AIR POST STAMPS

Catalogue values for unused stamps in this section, from this point to the end of the section, are for Never Hinged items. Because of the tropical conditions, never hinged stamps must also be free of wrinkles, toning, and any other disturbance.

AP1

AP2

Perf. 13½x12½
1952-53   Unwmk.   Photo.
C1	AP1	3.30pi dk brn red & pale yel grn	1.00	.50
C2	AP1	4pi brown & yellow	1.50	.25
C3	AP1	5.10pi dk vio bl & pink	1.50	.40
C4	AP2	6.30pi yellow & car	1.50	.50
		Nos. C1-C4 (4)	5.50	1.65

Issued: #C2, 11/24/53; others, 3/8/52.

Dragon AP3

Fish — AP4

1952, Sept. 3   Engr.   Perf. 13
C5	AP3	40c red	1.40	.35
C6	AP3	70c green	2.40	.50
C7	AP3	80c ultra	2.40	.50
C8	AP3	90c brown	2.40	.50
C9	AP4	3.70pi deep magenta	5.25	.75
		Nos. C5-C9 (5)	13.85	2.60

Nos. C5-C9 exist imperforate in a souvenir booklet. Value, $175.

South Viet Nam

Phoenix — AP5

1955, Sept. 7
C10	AP5	4pi violet & lil rose	3.25	.60

Crane Carrying Letter AP6

1960, Dec. 20.   Perf. 13
C11	AP6	1pi olive	.90	.35
C12	AP6	4pi green & dk blue	2.10	.35
C13	AP6	5pi ocher & purple	2.50	.50
C14	AP6	10pi deep magenta	4.50	1.10
		Nos. C11-C14 (4)	10.00	2.30

POSTAGE DUE STAMPS

Catalogue values for unused stamps in this section, from this point to the end of the section, are for Never Hinged items. Because of the tropical conditions, never hinged stamps must also be free wrinkles, toning, and any other disturbance.

Temple Lion D1

Dragon D2

Perf. 13x13½
1952, June 16   Typo.   Unwmk.
J1	D1	10c red & green	.85	.25
J2	D1	20c green & yellow	1.10	.25
J3	D1	30c purple & orange	1.40	.25
J4	D1	40c dk grn & sal rose	1.90	.25
J5	D1	50c dp carmine & gray	2.50	.30
J6	D1	1pi blue & silver	4.25	.25
		Nos. J1-J6 (6)	12.00	1.55

South Viet Nam

1955-56
J7	D2	2pi red vio & org	.40	.25
J8	D2	3pi violet & grnsh bl	.55	.25
J9	D2	5pi violet & yellow	.60	.25
J10	D2	10pi dk green & car	.90	.25
J11	D2	20pi red & brt grn ('56)	2.00	.50
J12	D2	30pi brt grn & yel ('56)	3.00	1.00
J13	D2	50pi dk red brn & yel ('56)	6.00	2.00
J14	D2	100pi pur & yel ('56)	12.00	6.00
		Nos. J7-J14 (8)	25.45	10.50

Nos. J11-J14 inscribed "BUU-CHINH" instead of "TIMBRE-TAXE."

Atlas Moth — D3

Design: 3pi, 5pi, 10pi, Three butterflies.

1968, Aug. 20   Photo.   Perf. 13½x13
J15	D3	50c multicolored	3.00	.50
J16	D3	1pi multicolored	3.00	.50
J17	D3	2pi multicolored	6.00	.50
J18	D3	3pi multicolored	8.00	.50
J19	D3	5pi multicolored	14.00	.50
J20	D3	10pi multicolored	18.00	.50
		Nos. J15-J20 (6)	52.00	3.00

Nos. J15-J18 Surcharged with New Value and Two Bars in Red

1974, Oct. 1
J21	D3	5pi on 3pi multi		.75
J22	D3	50c on 50c multi		.75
J23	D3	40pi on 1pi multi		2.75
J24	D3	60pi on 2pi multi		3.25
		Nos. J21-J24 (4)		7.50

MILITARY STAMPS

Catalogue values for unused stamps in this section, from this point to the end of the section, are for Never Hinged items. Because of the tropical conditions, never hinged stamps must also be free wrinkles, toning, and any other disturbance.

Soldier Guarding Village M1

Rouletted 7½
1961, June   Unwmk.   Litho.
M1	M1	och, brn, dk grn & blk	4.00	1.00

1961, Sept.   Typo.
M2	M1	org yel, dk grn & brn	4.00	1.00

Bottom inscription on No. M1 is black, brown on No. M2.

Battle and Refugees M2

1969, Feb. 22   Litho.   Imperf.
M3	M2	red & green	65.00	
a.		Booklet pane of 10	700.00	

VIET NAM, DEMOCRATIC REPUBLIC

(North Viet Nam)

LOCATION — In eastern Indo-China
GOVT. — Republic
AREA — 61,293 sq. mi.
POP. — 18,800,000 (1968 est.)
CAPITAL — Hanoi

Beginning in 1946, the Communist Viet Minh fought the French in a guerrilla war that ended with the French defeat at Dien Bien Phu in 1954. In an agreement signed in Geneva on July 21, 1954, Viet Nam was partitioned at the 17th parallel. The government in Hanoi controlled the north, and engaged in another protracted military campaign against American and South Vietnamese forces that led to the official reunification of the country under Communist control on July 2, 1976.

100 cents = 1 Dong
100 Xu = 1 Dong (1959)

> All stamps are without gum unless otherwise indicated. Values for stamps with gum are for Never Hinged items.

Watermark

Wmk. 376 — "R de C"

VIET MINH ISSUES

Stamps and Types of Indo-China Overprinted or Surcharged
Printing Methods and Perfs as Before

1945-46   **Without Gum**
No. 236 Overprinted
"VIET NAM DAN CHU CONG HOA"

1L1	A41	1pi yel grn (Yersin)	8.00

Nos. 238-239 (Rhodes) Overprinted
"VIET NAM DAN CHU CONG HOA"
with "VN" & "IXIXIXIXIX" Obliterators
Perf. 11 ½

1L2	A43	15c dk vio brn, perf.		
		11½		1.25
a.		Perf. 12		1.25
b.		Perf. 11½, green overprint		2.50
1L3	A43	30c org brn, perf.		
		11½		1.00
a.		Perf. 13½		2.00
b.		Perf. 12		15.00

No. 242 Overprinted
"VIET NAM DAN CHU CONG HOA"
with "VN" & "VN.VN" Obliterators

1L4	A44	50c dl red (Athlete)	7.00

No. 241 Overprinted
"VIET NAM DAN CHU CONG HOA"
with "VN" & "XXXX" Obliterators

1L5	A44	10c dk vio brn & yel (Athlete)	18.00

Nos. 218-222 (Petain) Overprinted
"VIET NAM DAN CHU CONG HOA"
with "Buu-Chinh" and Wavy Line Obliterators

1L6	A32	3c olive brn, perf.		
		11½		1.75
a.		Perf. 12x14		5.00
b.		Perf. 14		15.00
1L7	A32	6c rose red		1.00
1L8	A32	10c dull grn (R)		5.00
1L9	A32	40c dk bl (R)		3.00
1L10	A32	40c slate bl (R)		3.00
		Nos. 1L6-1L10 (5)		13.75

Nos. 245-246 and Type (Pavie) Overprinted "VIET NAM DAN CHU CONG-HOA" with "BUU-CHINH" and Wavy Line & "VN" Obliterators

1L11	A46	4c org yel	1.50
1L12	A46	10c dl grn	1.50
1L13	A46	20c dark red	1.25
		Nos. 1L11-1L13 (3)	4.25

No. 165A Overprinted
"VIET NAM DAN CHU CONG HOA"
with "BUU CHINH" and Slanted Lines Obliterator

1L14	A22	25c dk bl (Planting Rice, R), top line 18 mm wide		1.00
a.		Top line 20 mm wide		60.00

Nos. 1L14-1L14a issued with gum.

No. 232 (Courbet) Overprinted
"VIET NAM DAN CHU CONG HOA DOC-LAP TU-DO HANH-PHUC"

1L15	A39	3c lt brn	1.00
1L16	A39	6c car rose	2.00

No. 261 (Lagree) Overprinted
Vertically "VIET NAM DAN CHU CONG-HOA DOC-LAP TU-DO HANH-PHUC" with "BUU-CHINH" & "III" Obliterator

1L17	A52	40c brt bl	1.50

Nos. 253-255 (Doumer) Overprinted
"VIET-NAM DOC-LAP TU-DO HANH-PHUC BUU-CHINH"
with Wavy Line Obliterators

1L18	A50	2c red vio	1.50
1L19	A50	4c lt brn	1.25
1L20	A50	10c yel grn	1.50
		Nos. 1L18-1L20 (3)	4.25

Nos. 217, 256-258 (Petain, Charner) Overprinted "VIET-NAM DOC-LAP TU-DO HANH-PHUC BUU-CHINH" with "VN" and Wavy Line Obliterators

1L21	A32	1c blk brn	2.00
1L22	A51	10c green	1.75
1L23	A51	20c brn red	1.75
1L24	A51	1pi pale yel grn	7.50
		Nos. 1L21-1L24 (4)	13.00

No. 230 and Type (Genouilly)
Overprinted "VIET-NAM DOC-LAP TU-DO HANH-PHUC BUU-CHINH" with "X" Obliterator

1L25	A37	5c dull brown	1.50
1L26	A37	6c carmine rose	5.00

No. 210-212 (Sihanouk) Surcharged with New Value & "X" Obliterators

1L27	A28	5d on 1c red org (Bl)		12.50
1L28	A28	10d on 6c violet (R)		15.00
1L29	A28	15d on 25c dp ultra (R)		15.00
		Nos. 1L27-1L29 (3)		42.50

Nos. 225-226 (Sihanouk) Surcharged with New Value with Wavy Line and Straight Line Obliterators

1L30	A34	50xu on 1c brown	3.00
1L31	A35	2d on 6c car rose	20.00

Nos. 213-214 (Elephant) Surcharged with New Value, "VIET NAM DAN CHU CONG-HOA," Wavy Line and Straight Line Obliterators

1L32	A29	2d on 3c reddish brn (G)	12.50
1L33	A29	4d on 6c crim (G)	12.50

Nos. 247-248 (Pasquier) Surcharged Vertically with New Value, "VIET NAM DAN CHU CONG-HOA," Wavy Line & "X" Obliterators

1L34	A47	1d on 5c brn vio	4.00

1L35	A47	2d on 10c dl grn	6.50

No. B30 Surcharged with New Value, "VIET NAM DAN CHU CONG HOA" "Binh-si Bi-nan," Wavy Line Obliterator

1L36	SP7	5d on 15c+60c brn vio (Cathedral)	25.00

Nos. 259-260 (Lagree) Surcharged Vertically with New Value, "VIET-NAM DAN CHU CONG HOA BUU-CHINH," Wavy Line & "VN" Obliterators

1L37	A52	30xu on 1c dl gray brn (R)	1.75
1L38	A52	3d on 15c dl rose vio	

Nos. 243-244 (La Grandiere) Surcharged with New Value, "VIET-NAM DAN CHU CONG HOA BUU CHINH," Wavy Line Obliterator

1L39	A45	1d on 5c dk brn (Bl)	12.50
1L40	A45	4d on 1c dull brn	3.00

Surcharged with New Value, "VIET-NAM Dan chu Cong hoa BUU-CHINH," Wavy & Straight Line Obliterators

1L41	A42	30xu on 15c brn vio (Garnier, R)	2.50

No. 242 (Garnier) Surcharged with New Value, "VIET-NAM DAN CHU CONG HOA BUU-CHINH," Wavy & Straight Line Obliterators

1L42	A42	5d on 1c dull ol bis	5.00

Nos. 249-252 (De Lanessan, Van Vollenhoven) Surcharged with New Value, "VIET-NAM DAN CHU CONG HOA BUU CHINH," Straight Line Obliterators

1L43	A49	50xu on 1c dl gray brn		3.00
1L44	A48	60xu on 1c ol brn		4.50
1L45	A48	1.60d on 10c green		14.00
1L46	A49	3d on 15c dl rose vio (Bl)		4.50
		Nos. 1L43-1L46 (4)		26.00

Nos. B30-B31 (Cathedral) Surcharged with New Value, "VIET NAM DAN CHU CONG HOA CUU-DOI," Wavy Line Obliterators

1L47	SP7	2d on 15c+60c brn vio	22.50
1L48	SP7	3d on 40c+1.10pi blue	22.50

No. 234 (Yersin) Surcharged with Added Value, "VIET-NAM DAN CHU CONG HOA Bao Anh," and Straight Line obliterators

1L49	A41	+2d on 6c car rose	9.00

No. 233 (Behaine) Surcharged with Added Value, "VIET-NAM DAN-CHU CONG-HOA Binh si bi nan," Wavy Line, "V" & "N" Obliterators

1L50	A40	+3d on 20c dull red	5.00

No. 215 (Saigon Fair) Surcharged with Added Value, "VIET-NAM DAN CHU CONG HOA Chong nan mu chu" & Wavy Line

1L51	A30	+4d on 6c car rose	9.00

No. 229 (Natl. Revolution) Surcharged with Added Value, "VIET-NAM DAN-CHU CONGHOA Doi song moi," and "X" Obliterator

1L52	A36	+4d on 6c car rose	6.50

Nos. 213-214 Surcharged with Added Value, "VIET-NAM DAN-CHU CONG-HOA Quoc-Phong" and Wavy Line in Blue

1L53	A29	+5d on 3c reddish brown	17.50
1L54	A29	+10d on 6c crimson	17.50

Nos. 216, 224 Surcharged with "VIET NAM DAN CHU CONG HOA DAN-SINH" & Straight Lines

1L55	A31	30xu +3d on 6c (Nam-Phuong)		3.75
		Perf. 13½		
1L56	A33	30xu +3d on 6c (Bao-Dai)		3.75
a.		Perf. 12		50.00

Ho Chi Minh

VM1   VM2

1946   Litho.   Unwmk.   ***Perf. 11½***
Without Gum

1L57	VM1	1h green	.50
1L58	VM1	3h rose	.50
1L59	VM1	9h yellow bister	.50

With Added Inscription "+PHU THU CUU-QUOC"

1L60	VM1	4h +6h Prussian blue	1.50
1L61	VM1	6h +9h brown violet	1.50
		Nos. 1L57-1L61 (5)	4.50

1948   Typo.   ***Perf. 7 Rough***
Thin, Rough, Brown Paper

1L62	VM2	2d brown	22.50
1L63	VM2	5d red	22.50

For surcharge and overprints see Nos. 50, O6-O7.

DEMOCRATIC REPUBLIC OF VIET NAM

> From 1945-2002, all stamps are without gum unless otherwise indicated. Values for stamps with gum are for Never Hinged items.

Many North Vietnamese stamps are roughly perforated, especially issues before 1958.

Ho Chi Minh, Map of Vietnam
A1

1951-55   Unwmk.   Litho.   ***Imperf.***

1	A1	100d brown	26.00	10.00
a.		Perf. 11¼ ('55)	35.00	9.00
2	A1	100d green	25.00	10.00
a.		Perf. 11¼ ('55)	35.00	9.00
		Perf. 11¼		
3	A1	200d red	30.00	10.00
a.		Imperf. ('55)	27.50	9.00
		Nos. 1-3 (3)	81.00	30.00

Nos. 1-3 printed on thin semi-transparent paper.
Nos. 1-3 used values are for cto. Postally used examples are worth about 5 times these values.
Counterfeits exist.
For surcharges, see Nos. 9-14, 36-38, and note before No. J1.

Blacksmith — A2

1953-55   ***Perf. 11¼***

4	A2	100d violet	4.00	3.00
5	A2	500d brown	6.00	8.00
		Issued: 100d, 6/53. 500d, 2/55.		

Georgi Malenkov, Ho Chi Minh, Mao Tse-tung and Flags — A3

1954-55   **Perf. 11¼**
6	A3	50d brown & red,		
		brnish	25.00	35.00
7	A3	100d red	25.00	30.00
8	A3	100d yellow & red,		
		brnish	37.50	37.50
		Nos. 6-8 (3)	87.50	102.50

Issued: 50d, 10/54; #7, 1/54; #8, 4/55.
No. 7 printed on thin, white paper.

Nos. 1-3 Surcharged in Red or Blue

1954, Oct.   **Imperf.**
9	A1	10d on 100d brown	22.50	32.50
10	A1	10d on 100d green	22.50	32.50

Perf. 11
11	A1	20d on 200d red		
		(Bl)	22.50	42.50
		Nos. 9-11 (3)	67.50	107.50

Nos. 1-3 Surcharged in Black, Red or Blue

1954, Oct.   **Imperf.**
12	A1	10d on 100d brown		
		(Bk, R or Bl)	26.00	35.00
13	A1	10d on 100d green		
		(Bk, R or Bl)	26.00	35.00

Perf. 11
14	A1	20d on 200d red (Bk or Bl)	60.00	75.00
		Nos. 12-14 (3)	112.00	145.00

Nos. 9-14 exist with counterfeit surcharges, counterfeit surcharges on counterfeit stamps, and with fantasy surcharges.

Victory at Dien Bien Phu A4

1954-56   **Perf. 11¼**
17	A4	10d red brn & yel brn	25.00	30.00
a.		Imperf	110.00	110.00
18	A4	50d red & org yel	25.00	30.00
a.		Imperf	25.00	40.00
19	A4	150d brown & blue	25.00	35.00
a.		Imperf	25.00	40.00
		Nos. 17-19 (3)	75.00	95.00

Issued: Imperfs, 10/54; others, 1956. See #O5.
Used values for Nos. 17-19 are for postally used examples. The 10d exists cto, perf or imperf. Value about 1/10 those shown above.

Liberation of Hanoi — A5

1955, Jan. 1   **Perf. 11½**
20	A5	10d lt blue & bl	10.00	8.00
21	A5	50d dk grn & grn	10.00	8.00
22	A5	150d rose & brn red	20.00	12.00
		Nos. 20-22 (3)	40.00	28.00

Nos. 20-22 used values are for postally used examples. Cto stamps are worth about $1 each.

Land Reform A6

1955-56   **Perf. 11¼**
23	A6	5d lt green	18.00	8.50
24	A6	10d gray	18.00	8.50
25	A6	20d orange	18.00	8.50
26	A6	50d rose	18.00	8.50
27	A6	100d lt brown	37.50	32.50
		Nos. 23-27 (5)	109.50	66.50

Issued: 100d, 12/55; 20d, 50d, 2/56; others, 6/56. See Nos. O8-O9.

Return of Government to Hanoi — A7

1956, Mar. 1   **Perf. 11¼**
28	A7	1000d violet	32.50	25.00
29	A7	1500d dk blue	32.50	25.00
30	A7	2000d turquoise	85.00	67.50
31	A7	3000d blue green	160.00	210.00
		Nos. 28-31 (4)	310.00	327.50

Counterfeits exist, often imperf and offered as proofs.

Re-opening of Hanoi-China Railroad — A8

1956, Mar. 1
32	A8	100d dark blue	40.00	16.00
33	A8	200d blue green	40.00	16.00
34	A8	300d violet	40.00	32.50
35	A8	500d lilac brown	40.00	65.00
		Nos. 32-35 (4)	160.00	129.50

Counterfeits exist, often imperf and offered as proofs.

Nos. 1-3 Surcharged

1954, Oct.   **Imperf.**
36	A1	10d on 100d brown	35.00	50.00
37	A1	10d on 100d green	35.00	50.00

Perf. 11
38	A1	20d on 200d red	35.00	50.00
		Nos. 36-38 (3)	105.00	150.00

Nos. 36-38 exist with counterfeit surcharges, counterfeit surcharges on counterfeit stamps, and with fantasy surcharges.

Tran Dang Ninh (1910-55), Guerrilla Leader A9

1956, July   **Litho.**   **Perf. 11¼**
39	A9	5d bl grn & pale grn	5.00	2.40
40	A9	10d lilac & rose	5.00	2.40
41	A9	20d gr brn & dk gray	7.75	3.00
42	A9	100d dk blue pale bl	7.75	3.00
		Nos. 39-42 (4)	25.50	10.80

Nos. 39-42 used values are for cto. Postally used value, set $14.

Mac Thi Buoi (1927-51), Guerrilla Leader A10

1956, Nov. 3   **Perf. 11½**
43	A10	1000d rose & lilac rose	100.00	100.00
44	A10	2000d brown & bister	100.00	100.00
45	A10	4000d bl grn & green	150.00	100.00
46	A10	5000d ultra & lt blue	300.00	400.00
		Nos. 43-46 (4)	650.00	700.00

Nos. 43-46 used values are for postally used. Cto value, set $100.
Counterfeits exist, often imperf and offered as proofs.

Bai Thuong Dam — A11

1956-58   **Perf. 11¼**
47	A11	100d vio bl & lil brn	10.00	1.90
a.		Perf 13	10.00	1.60
48	A11	200d lilac & gr grn	10.00	2.25
a.		Perf 13	10.00	1.90
49	A11	300d rose & lil brn	20.00	3.25
a.		Perf 13	20.00	2.75
		Nos. 47-49 (3)	40.00	7.40

Nos. 47-49 used values are for cto. Postally used copies are worth about 10 times these values.
Issued: #47-49, 12/15/56; #47a-49a, 1958.

No. 1L63 Surcharged

1956, Dec.   **Typo.**   **Perf. 7 Rough**
50	VM2	50d on 5d dp red,		
		brnish	90.00	100.00

Reprints and counterfeits exist.

Nam Dinh Textile Mill — A13

1957, Mar.   **Litho.**   **Perf. 12½**
51-53	A13	100d, 200d, 300d, set of 3	27.50	3.75
51a		Perf. 11½	7.50	7.50

Nos. 51-53 used values are for cto. Postally used value, set $15.
No. 51 also exists perf 11½x12½, imperf and imperf by perf 11½.

Ho Chi Minh — A14

1957   **Perf. 12½**
54-57	A14	20d, 60d, 100d, 300d, set of 4	30.00	21.00

Issued: 20d, 60d, 12/13; others, 5/19.

Fourth World Trade Union Congress, Leipzig A15

1957, Aug. 1   **Perf. 12½**
58	A15	300d red violet	10.00	3.00

See Nos. O17-O20.

Democratic Republic, 12th Anniv. A16

1957, Sept. 2   **Perf. 13**
59-60	A16	20d, 100d, set of 2	17.50	9.75

Presidents Voroshilov, Ho Chi Minh — A17

1957, Nov. 7   **Perf. 12½**
61-63	A17	100d, 500d, set of 1000d, 3	47.50	37.50

Russian revolution, 40th anniv.

Anti-illiteracy Campaign — A18

1958, Jan. 6   **Perf. 12½**
64-66	A18	50d, 150d, 1000d, set of 3	30.00	21.00

A19   A20

1958, Mar. 8
67-68	A19	150d, 500d, set of 2	30.00	22.50

Physical education.

1958, May 1
69-70	A20	50d, 150d, set of 2	10.00	6.00

May Day.

Fourth Intl. Congress of Democratic Women, Vienna A21

1958, May   **Typo.**
71   A21 150d blue   8.00 7.25

A22

A22a

A22: #72, 150d, #75, 2000d, Basket, lace & cup, vert.
A22a: #73, 150d, #74, 1000d, Potter.

1958   **Litho.**
72-75 A22, A22a Set of 4   25.00 21.00
Arts & Crafts Fair, Hanoi.
Issued: Nos. 72, 75, 6/26; others, 8/19.

Building the Reunification Railway — A23

1958, July 20
76-77 A23 50d, 150d, set of 2   8.00 3.25

August Revolution, 13th Anniv. A24

1958, Aug. 19
78-79 A24 150d, 500d, set of 2   7.00 5.75

Resistance Movement in South Viet Nam, 13th Anniv. A25

1958, Sept. 23
80-81 A25 50d, 150d, set of 2   12.00 5.75

A26

1958, Oct.
82   A26 150d grnsh blue & blk   3.00 1.50
Tran Hung Dao (1253-1300).

A27

Hanoi Engineering Plant.

1958, Nov. 7   **Engr.**   **Perf. 11½**
83   A27 150d brown   3.50 1.40

Mutual Aid Teams — A28

1958, Nov. 7
84-85 A28 150d, 500d, set of 2   12.00 4.50

Ngoc Son Temple (Temple of Jade) — A29

1958, Dec. 1   **Photo.**   **Perf. 12**
86-87 A29 150d, 2000d, set of 2   32.50 11.00

Rattanware Cooperative A30

1958, Dec. 31
88   A30 150d greenish blue   3.50 1.25

Ha Long Bay — A31

1959, Feb. 8
89-90 A31 150d, 350d, set of 2   7.00 3.25

Cam Pha Coal Mines — A32

1959, Mar. 3   **Engr.**   **Perf. 11½**
91   A32 150d blue   5.00 .75

Trung Sisters — A33

1959, Mar. 14   **Litho.**   **Perf. 11**
92-93 A33 5xu, 8xu, set of 2   9.00 6.25

World Peace Movement, 10th Anniv. — A34

1959, Apr. 15
94   A34 12xu purple, *rose*   2.50 .60

Xuan Quang Dam A35

1959, May 1
95-96 A35 6xu, 12xu, set of 2   8.50 1.50

Phu Loi Massacre A36

1959, May 15
97-98 A36 12xu, 20xu, set of 2   7.00 1.75

Hien Luong Bridge — A37

1959, July 20
99   A37 12xu black & carmine   3.00 1.50

Me Tri Radio Station — A38

1959, Aug. 10
100-101 A38 3xu, 12xu, set of 2   5.00 1.40

Sports A39

Designs: 1xu, Shooting. 6xu, Swimming. 12xu, Wrestling.

1959, Sept. 2
102-104 A39 Set of 3   8.00 3.00
Size of No. 103 is 43x31mm.

People's Republic of China, 10th Anniv. — A40

1959, Oct. 1
105 A40 12xu multicolored   5.00 .70

Fruits — A41

Designs: 3xu, Coconuts. 12xu, Bananas. 30xu, Pineapple.

1959, Nov. 20
106-108 A41 Set of 3   8.00 3.50

People's Army, 15th Anniv. A42

1959, Dec. 22
109 A42 12xu multicolored   3.50 1.60

A43   A44

1960, Jan. 6
110-111 A43 2xu, 12xu, set of 2 5.50 3.00
Vietnamese Workers' Party, 30th Anniv.

1960, Jan. 6
Ethnic costumes: 2xu, Ede. 10xu, Meo. No. 114, 12xu, Tay. No. 115, 12xu, Thai.
112-115 A44 Set of 4   9.00 7.00

Census A45

Designs: 1xu, People. 12xu, Transmitting tower, dam, buildings, workers.

1960, Feb. 20
116-117 A45 Set of 2   4.00 2.75
No. 117 is 37x26mm.

Intl. Women's Day, 50th Anniv. A46

1960, Mar. 8
118 A46 12xu multicolored 2.50 1.75

A47   A48

1960, Apr. 5
119-120 A47 4xu, 12xu, set of 2   62.50 30.00
Hung Vuong Temple.

1960, Apr. 22
121-122 A48 5xu, 12xu, set of 2   6.50
121a   Souv. sheet of 1, olive brown & blue, imperf.   75.00
Lenin. No. 121a exists on brownish paper.

Election of National Assembly Delegates — A49

1960, May 3   *Perf. 11*
123 A49 12xu multicolored, *rose* 2.00 1.60

A50   A51

1960, May 8
124-125 A50 8xu, 12xu, set of 2   6.00 1.50
Viet Nam Red Cross.

1960, May 19
Ho Chi Minh, 70th Birthday: Nos. 128, 130, Ho with children.
126 A51 4xu green & purple
127 A51 12xu pink & brown
128 A51 12xu multicolored
Nos. 126-128 (3)   8.00 3.00

Souvenir Sheets
Imperf
129 A51 10xu yel bis & brn, *rose*   8.00
130 A51 10xu multicolored   7.00
No. 128 is 25x39mm.

New Constitution A52

1960, July 7
131 A52 12xu lemon & gray 3.00 1.50

National Day, 15th Anniv. A53

1960, Sept. 2
132-133 A53 4xu, 12xu, set of 2 7.50 7.00

Development — A54

Designs: No. 134, Classroom. No. 135, Plowing. No. 136, Factory.

1960, Sept. 2
134-136 A54 12xu Set of 3   13.50

3rd Vietnamese Communist Party Congress — A55

1960, Sept. 4
137-138 A55 1xu, 12xu, set of 2 6.50 3.00

World Federation of Trade Unions, 15th Anniv. — A56

1960, Oct. 3
139 A56 12xu black & vermilion 5.00 4.25

Hanoi, 950th Anniv. A57

1960, Oct. 10   **Litho.**   *Perf. 11*
140-141 A57 8xu, 12xu, set of 2   6.75 2.75
141a   Souv. sheet of 1, imperf.   13.00 12.00
No. 141a exists on brownish paper.

15 Years' Achievements Exhibition — A58

1960, Oct. 20
142-143 A58 2xu, 12xu, set of 2 4.00 2.10

World Federation of Democratic Youth, 15th Anniv. — A59

1960, Nov. 10
144 A59 12xu multicolored 3.50 3.00

Trade Unions, 2nd Natl. Congress A60

1961, Feb. 10
145 A60 12xu multicolored, *rose* 2.50 1.25

Vietnamese Women's Union, 3rd Natl. Congress — A61

1961, Mar. 8   **Tinted Paper**
146-147 A61 6xu, 12xu, set of 2 4.50 1.60

Animals — A62   Ly Tu Trong — A63

Designs: 12xu, Rusa unicolor. 20xu, Helarctos malynus. 50xu, Elephas maximus. 1d, Hylobates leucogenys.

1961, Mar. 8
148-151 A62 Set of 4   30.00 13.00
Imperf., #148-151   60.00 60.00

1961, Mar. 18
152-153 A63 2xu, 12xu, set of 2 3.75 2.10
Youth Labor Union, 3rd Congress.

Young Pioneers, 20th Anniv. — A64

1961, May 2
154-155 A64 1xu, 12xu, set of 2 4.00 2.25

Intl. Red Cross — A65

1961, May 8
156-157 A65 6xu, 12xu, set of 2 6.00 2.75

Intl. Children's Day — A66

1961, June 1
158-159 A66 4xu, 12xu, set of 2 6.00 3.00

Yuri Gagarin's Space Flight A67

1961, June 15
160-161 A67 6xu, 12xu, set of 2   24.00 10.50
Imperf., #160-161   27.50

Hanoi, Hue and Saigon A68

1961, July 20
162-163 A68 12xu, 3d, set of 2 11.00 8.50

A69   A70

1961, July 20
164-165 A69 12xu, 2d, set of 2 10.00 2.75
Imperf., #164-165   —
Reunification campaign.

1961, Aug. 21
166-167 A70 2xu, 12xu, set of 2 5.00 2.00
Geological exploration.

Savings Campaign A71

1961, Aug. 21
168-169 A71 3xu, 12xu, set of 2 5.00 1.50

Ancient Towers — A72

Designs: 6xu, Thien Mu, Hue. 10xu, Pen Brush, Bac Ninh. No. 172, 12xu, Binh Son, Vinh Phuc. No. 173, 12xu, Cham, Phan Rang.

1961, Sept. 12
170-173 A72 Set of 4   10.00 3.75
  Imperf., #170-173   24.00

A73

6xu, 12xu, Gherman Titov's Space Flight.

1961, Oct. 17
174-175 A73 Set of 2   8.00 3.75
  Imperf., #174-175   12.00

A74

1961, Oct. 17
176 A74 12xu vermilion & black 3.50 2.40
22nd Communist Party Congress, Moscow.

Port of Haiphong — A75

1961, Nov. 7
177-178 A75 5xu, 12xu, set of 2 9.50 3.00

A76

Musicians: No. 179, 12xu, Flutist. No. 180, 12xu, Cymbalist. 30xu, Dancer with fan. 50xu, Guitarist.

1961, Nov. 18   Perf. 13½
179-182 A76 Set of 4   16.00 14.00
  Imperf., #179-182   20.00
182a   Souvenir sheet, #179-182   50.00

Stamps on No. 182a are se-tenant and perfed on outside edges of the strip of 4.

5th World Trade Union Congress, Moscow A77

1961, Dec. 4   Perf. 11
183 A77 12xu dp red lil & gray 2.00 .80

Natl. Resistance, 15th Anniv. A78

1961, Dec. 4
184-185 A78 4xu, 12xu, set of 2 2.25 2.00

Tet Holiday — A79

Designs: 6xu, Sow, piglets. 12xu, Poultry.

1962, Jan. 16   Litho.
186-187 A79 Set of 2   9.00 6.00

Tet Tree-Planting Festival — A80

1962, Jan. 16
188-189 A80 12xu, 40xu, set of 2 4.00

Crops — A81

Designs: 2xu, Camellia sinensis. 6xu, Illicium verum. No. 192, 12xu, Coffea arabica. No. 193, 12xu, Ricinus communis. 30xu, Rhus succedanea.

1962, Mar. 1
190-194 A81 Set of 5   15.00 6.00

Folk Dances — A82

Designs: No. 195, 12xu, Rong Chieng. No. 196, 12xu, Bamboo. 30xu, Hat. 50xu, Parasol.

1962, Mar. 20 Photo.   Perf. 11½x12
195-198 A82 Set of 4   20.00 6.00
  Imperf., #195-198   25.00
  Souvenir Sheet
199 A82 30xu like #195   15.00

First Five Year Plan — A83

Designs: 1xu, Kim Lien Apartments, Hanoi. 3xu, State farm. 8xu, Natl. Institute of Hydraulics.

1962, Apr. 10   Litho.   Perf. 11
200-202 A83 Set of 3   4.00 4.00

A84   A85

Flowers: No. 203, 12xu, Hibiscus rosa sinensis. No. 204, 12xu, Plumeria acutifolia. 20xu, Chrysanthemum indicum. 30xu, Nelumbium nuciferum. 50xu, Ipomoea pulchella.

Perf. 12½x11½
1962, Apr. 10   Photo.
203-207 A84 Set of 5   21.00 9.25
  Imperf., #203-207   30.00
206a   Souvenir sheet of 1   12.00

1962, May 4 Litho.   Perf. 11
208 A85 12xu multicolored 3.00 3.00
3rd Natl. Heroes of Labor Congress.

Harrow A86

Dai Lai Lake A87

1962, May 25
209-210 A86-A87 6xu, 12xu, set of 2 4.00 4.00

Visit by Gherman Titov A88

Titov: 12xu, Waving at children. 20xu, Receiving medal from Ho Chi Minh. 30xu, Wearing space suit.

1962, June 12
211-213 A88 Set of 3   8.00 6.50
  Imperf., #211-213   12.00

Anti-Malaria Campaign A89

1962, July 9
214-216 A89 8xu, 12xu, 20xu, set of 3 7.50 3.00

War for Reunification — A90

1962, July 20
217 A90 12xu multicolored 2.50 1.25

Ba Be Lake — A91

Design: No. 219, Ban Gioc Falls, vert.

1962, Aug. 14
218-219 A91 12xu Set of 2 4.00 3.25

A stamp picturing a weight lifter exists, but was not released. Value $200.

King Quang Trung (1752-92) A92   Nguyen Trai (1380-1442) A93

1962, Sept. 16
220-221 A92 3xu, 12xu, set of 2 3.50 2.50

1962, Sept. 19
222-223 A93 3xu, 12xu, set of 2 3.50

Food Crops A94

Designs: 1xu, Peanuts. 4xu, Beans. 6xu, Sweet potatoes. 12xu, Corn. 30xu, Cassava.

1962, Oct. 10
224-228 A94 Set of 5   9.00 3.75
  Imperf., #224-228

Animal Husbandry A95

Designs: 2xu, Feeding poultry. No. 230, 12xu, Feeding pigs. No. 231, 12xu, Cattle grazing. No. 232, 12xu, Tending water buffalo.

1962, Nov. 28
229-232 A95 Set of 4   8.00 3.50

A stamp commemorating the 45th anniversary of the Russian Revolution exists, but was not issued. Value $200.

First Five
Year Plan
A96

#233, Evening classes. #234, Clearing land.

1962, Dec. 28
233-234 A96 12xu Set of 2   5.00 2.00

Flights of
Vostok 3
and
4 — A97

12xu, Pavel Popovich, Vostok 4. 20xu, Andrian Nikolayev, Vostok 3. 30xu, Rockets lifting-off, vert.

1962, Dec. 28   *Perf. 11*
235-237 A97 Set of 3   6.00 2.75
  Imperf., #235-237   12.00

Guerrilla   Hoang Hoa Tham
A98   (1846-1913)
                   A99

1963, Jan. 15
238-239 A98 5xu, 12xu, set of 2 4.00 1.50

1963, Feb. 10
240-241 A99 6xu, 12xu, set of 2 3.75 1.40

A100

First Five
Year Plan
A100a

Designs: No. 242, Fertilizing rice paddy. No. 243, Lam Thao superphosphate plant.

1963, Feb. 25
242-243 A100-A100a 12xu Set of
         2   3.50 1.50

Karl Marx — A101

1963, Mar. 14
244-245 A101 3xu, 12xu, set of 2 3.25 1.50
  Nos. 244-245 are printed on greenish and rose toned paper respectively.

Fidel Castro,
Vietnamese
Soldiers
A102

1963, Apr. 17
246 A102 12xu multicolored   3.25 1.00

May
Day
A103

1963, May 8
247 A103 12xu multicolored   3.25 1.00

A104   Intl. Red Cross,
                Cent. — A105

Design: No. 249, Child, syringe.

1963, May 8
248 A104 12xu grn, blk & red
249 A104 12xu grn, red & blk
250 A105 20xu multicolored
         Nos. 248-250 (3) 7.00

Mars 1 Spacecraft — A106

6xu, 12xu (#252), Mars 1 approaching Mars. 12xu (#253), 20xu, Mars 1 entering orbit, vert.

1963, May 21
251-254 A106 Set of 4   9.00 5.00
  Imperf., #251-254   20.00

Fishing
Industry
A107

Designs: No. 255, Trawler, offshore fish. No. 256, Freshwater fish.

1963, July 3
255-256 A107 12xu Set of 2   10.50 6.00

Ho Chi Minh,
Nguyen Van
Hien — A108

1963, July 20
257 A108 12xu multicolored   2.50 1.75

Flights
of Vostok
3, 4
A109

Designs: 12xu, Rockets in orbit. 20xu, Nikolayev. 30xu, Popovich.

1963, Aug. 11
258-260 A109 Set of 3   7.00 6.00
  Imperf., #258-260   13.00

First Five
Year Plan
for
Chemical
Industry
A110

Designs: 3xu, Viet Tri Insecticide Factory. 12xu, Viet Tri Chemical Factory.

1963, Aug. 11
261-262 A110 Set of 2   3.75 2.00

Fish
A111

Designs: No. 263, 12xu, Cyprinus carpio. No. 264, 12xu, Myloharyngodon piceus. No. 265, 12xu, Hypophthalmichthys molitrix. 20xu, Ophiocephalus caqua. 30xu, Tilapia mossambica.

1963, Sept. 10
263-267 A111 Set of 5   17.00 7.75
  Imperf., #263-267   24.00
  a.   Souvenir Sheet 0f 1, #266 67.50

A112

Birds: #268, 12xu, Francolinus stephenson. #269, 12xu, Acridotheres cristatellus. #270, 12xu, Halcyon smyrneusis. 20xu, Diardigallus diardi, horiz. 30xu, Egretta. 40xu, Psittacula alexandri.

Perf. 11½x12, 12x11½
1963, Oct. 15   Photo.
268-273 A112 Set of 6   35.00 15.00
  Imperf., #268-273   55.00

Souvenir Sheet
274 A112 50xu Sheet of 1,
         like #272   100.00

A113

1963, Oct. 20 Litho.   *Perf. 11*
275 A113 12xu multicolored   2.00 1.00
  World Federation of Trade Unions Congress for Viet Nam.

GANEFO
Games
A114

#276, 12xu, Swimming. #277, 12xu, Volleyball, vert. #278, 12xu, Soccer, vert. 30xu, High jump.

1963, Nov. 10
276-279 A114 Set of 4   5.00 5.00
  Imperf., #276-279   8.50

A115   A116

Flowers: 6xu, Rauwolfia verticillata. No. 281, 12xu, Sophora japonica. No. 282, 12xu, Fibraurea tinctoria. No. 283, 12xu, Chenopodium ambrosioides. 20xu, Momordica cochinchinensis.

1963, Dec. 3
280-284 A115 Set of 5   7.50 3.75
  Imperf., #280-284   10.00

1963, Dec. 20
285 A116 12xu multicolored   2.50 1.00
  World Day for Viet Nam.

A117

First Five-Year
Plan — A118

6xu, Molten cast iron. #287, 12xu, Thai Nguyen Steel & Iron Works. #288, 12xu, Power lines.

1964, Jan. 25   Litho.
286-288 A117-A118 Set of 3 4.50 1.75

Intl. Quiet Sun
Year — A119

1964, Jan. 25
289-290 A119 12xu, 50xu, set
         of 2   5.00 3.00
  Imperf., #289-290   20.00

Flights of Vostok 5 and 6 A120

#291, 12xu, Rockets in orbit. #292, 12xu, Valery Bykovsky. 30xu, Valentina Tereshkova.

1964, Mar. 25
291-293 A120 Set of 3   6.00 5.00
     Imperf., #291-293   14.00

A stamp commemorating the anniversary of the founding of the People's Democratic Republic of Korea was printed but not issued.

A121   A122

Flowers: No. 294, 12xu, Persica vulgaris. No. 295, 12xu, Hibiscus mutabilis. No. 296, 12xu, Passiflora hispida. No. 297, 12xu, Saraca dives. 20xu, Michelia champaca. 30xu, Camellia amplexicaulis.

1964, Apr. 10   **Perf. 11½x12**
294-299 A121 Set of 6   13.00 5.00
     Imperf., #294-299   15.00

1964, Apr. 27   **Perf. 11**
Costumes: 6xu, Peasant, 19th cent. No. 301, 12xu, Woman wearing large hat, 19th cent. No. 302, 12xu, Woman carrying hat.

300-302 A122 Set of 3   5.00 3.00

Battle of Dien Bien Phu, 10th Anniv. A123

Designs: 3xu, Artillery. 6xu, Machine gun emplacement. Nos. 305, 307c, Bomb disposal. Nos. 306, 307d, Farmer on tractor.

1964, May 7
303 A123 3xu red & black
304 A123 6xu blue & black
305 A123 12xu yel org & blk
306 A123 12xu red lilac & black
     Nos. 303-306
          (4)   7.50 6.00
     Imperf., #303-306   13.00

Souvenir Sheet
Imperf

307   Sheet of 4   17.00
 a.   A123 3xu orange & black
 b.   A123 6xu yellow green & black
 c.   A123 12xu red, black & orange
 d.   A123 12xu blue & black

Ham Rong Bridge — A124

1964, May 17
308 A124 12xu multicolored   2.50 1.00

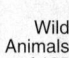

Wild Animals A125

Designs: No. 309, 12xu, Panthera tigris, vert. No. 310, 12xu, Pseudaxis axis, vert. No. 311, 12xu, Tapirus indicus. 20xu, Bubalus bubalis. 30xu, Rhinoceros bicornis. 40xu, Bibos banteng.

1964, June 2   **Perf. 10½**
309-314 A125 Set of 6   16.00 13.00
     Imperf., #309-314   25.00

Geneva Agreement on Viet Nam, 10th Anniv. A126

Intl. Labor Federation Committee United with People of South Viet Nam — A127

1964, July 20   **Perf. 11**
315-316 A126-A127 12xu Set of
          2   3.00 1.50

Nam Bac Ninh Pumping Station A128

1964, Aug. 25
317 A128 12xu blue gray & black 1.75 .80

Liberation of Hanoi, 10th Anniv. — A129

6xu, People cheering soldiers in truck. 12xu, Construction, hammerhead crane.

1964, Oct. 10
318-319 A129 Set of 2   3.50 2.50

Natl. Defense Games — A130

Designs: 5xu, Rowing. No. 321, 12xu, Parachuting, vert. No. 322, 12xu, Gliders, vert. No. 323, 12xu, Shooting.

1964, Oct. 18
320-323 A130 Set of 4   6.50 2.50

Fruits — A131

Designs: No. 324, 12xu, Mangifera indica. No. 325, 12xu, Guarcinia mangostana. No. 326, 12xu, Nephelium litchi. 20xu, Anona squamosa. 50xu, Citrus medica.

1964, Oct. 31 Photo. Perf. 11½x12
324-328 A131 Set of 5   10.00 3.75
     Imperf., #324-328   15.00

World Solidarity Conference — A132

Designs: a, Ba Dinh Hall. b, Vietnamese soldier shaking hands with foreign people. c, Fist, planes, submarine.

1964, Nov. 25 Litho. Perf. 11
329 A132 12xu Strip of 3, #a.-c. 6.50 3.25

People's Army, 20th Anniv. A133

Designs: No. 330, Soldiers, flag. No. 331a, Coast guards. No. 331b, Mounted border guards, vert.

1964, Dec. 22
330 A133 12xu multicolored
331 A133 12xu Pair, #a.-b.
     Nos. 330-331 (2)   5.00 1.25

Cuban Revolution, 6th Anniv. — A134

Designs: a, Vietnamese, Cuban flags. b, Cuban revolutionaries.

1965, Jan. 1
332 A134 12xu Pair, #a.-b.   4.50 3.00

Economic & Cultural Development of Mountain Region — A135

Designs: 2xu, 3xu, Women pollinating corn. 12xu, Girls walking to school.

1965, Jan. 1
333-335 A135 Set of 3   3.00 2.50
     Imperf., #333-335

A136

Vietnamese Worker's Party, 35th Anniv. — A137

Politicians: No. 336a, Le Hong Phong. b, Tran Phu. c, Hoang Van Thu. d, Ngo Gia Tu. e, Nguyen Van Cu.
No. 337a, Party flag. b, Worker, soldier.

1965   Litho.   Perf. 11
336 A136 6xu Strip of 5, #a.-e.
337 A137 12xu Pair, #a.-b.   5.00 4.75
     Issued: No. 336, 2/3; No. 337, 1/30.

Transportation Ministers Conference, Hanoi — A138

12xu, 30xu, Nguyen Van Troi, locomotive.

1965, Mar. 23
338-339 A138 Set of 2   8.50 2.00
     Imperf., #338-339

Vignette on No. 339 is mirror image of No. 338.

Flight of Voskhod 1 — A139

20xu, Cosmonauts Komarov, Feoktistov, Yegorov, rocket, globe. 1d, Cosmonauts, rocket.

1965, Mar. 30
340-341 A139 Set of 2   9.00 9.00
     Imperf., #340-341   11.00

Lenin, 95th Birth Anniv. A140

1965, Apr. 22   Litho.
342-343 A140 8xu, 12xu, set of 2 4.00 1.00

A141

1965, May 19
344-345 A141 6xu, 12xu, set of 2 3.00 1.90
Ho Chi Minh, 75th birthday.

A142

1965, May 19
346 A142 12xu multicolored 3.00 2.00
Afro-Asian Conference, 10th anniv.

Trade Union Conference, Hanoi — A143

Designs: No. 347, Workers solidarity. No. 348, Soldiers, vert. No. 349, Naval battle.

1965, June 2
347-349 A143 12xu Set of 3 4.50 1.50

Wild Animals — A144

Designs: No. 350, 12xu, Martes flavigula. No. 351, 12xu, Chrotogale owstoni. No. 352, 12xu, Manis pentadactyla. No. 353, 12xu, Presbytis delacouri, vert. 20xu, Petaurista lylei, vert. 50xu, Nycticebus pygmaeus, vert.

1965, June 24 Photo. Perf. 12
350-355 A144 Set of 6 17.00 5.50
　　Imperf., #350-355 25.00

A145

1965, July 1 Perf. 11½x11
356 A145 12xu multicolored 3.50 .50
6th Socialist Postal Ministers Conference.

A146

Nguyen Van Troi (1940-64). Denominations: 12xu, 50xu, 4d.

1965, July 20 Litho. Perf. 11
357-359 A146 Set of 3 9.00 6.00

A147

Insects — A148

Designs: No. 360, 12xu, Tessaratoma papillosa. No. 361, 12xu, Rhynchocoris humeralis. No. 362, 12xu, Poeciliocoris latus.
　　No. 363, 12xu, Tosena melanoptera. 20xu, Cicada. 30xu, Fulgora candelaria.

1965, July 24 Photo.
360-362 A147 Set of 3
363-365 A148 Set of 3
　　Nos. 360-365 (6) 12.00 7.00
　　Imperf., #360-365 18.00

August Revolution, 20th Anniv. A149

1965, Aug. 19 Litho.
366-367 A149 6xu, 12xu, set of 2 3.00 1.75

Crustaceans — A150

Designs: No. 368, 12xu, Penaeus indicus. No. 369, 12xu, Scylla serrata. No. 370, 12xu, Metapenaeus joyneri. No. 371, 12xu, Neptunus. 20xu, Palinurus japonicus. 50xu, Uca marionis.

1965, Aug. 19
368-373 A150 Set of 6 19.00 8.00
　　Imperf., #368-373 21.00

500th US Warplane Shot Down — A151

1965, Aug. 30
374 A151 12xu gray green & lilac 7.00 5.50

A152

Completion of 1st Five-Year Plan — A153

#375, Foundry worker. #376, Electricity, irrigation. #377, Public health, education. #378, Students, children playing. #379, Factory worker. #380, Agricultural workers.

1965
375-377 A152 12xu Set of 3 3.50 1.75
378-380 A153 12xu Set of 3 3.50 1.75
　　Imperf., #375-380
Issued: #375-377, 9/2; #378-380, 12/25.

Nghe An, Ha Tinh Uprising, 35th Anniv. — A154

1965, Sept. 12
381-382 A154 10xu, 12xu, set of 2 2.50 1.65
　　Imperf., #381-382

Friendship Between Viet Nam, People's Republic of China, 16th Anniv. — A155

Designs: No. 383, Youth holding flags, Friendship Gate. No. 384, Children waving flags, walking through Gate, vert.

1965, Oct. 1
383-384 A155 12xu Set of 2 10.00 1.75

Flight of Voskhod 2 — A156

#385, 12xu, Konstantin Tsiolkovsky, Sputnik I. #386, 12xu, Voskhod 2, A. Leonov, P.

Belyayev. #387, 50xu, Yuri Gagarin. #388, 50xu, Leonov walking in space.

1965, Oct. 5
385-388 A156 Set of 4 8.00 3.25
　　Imperf., #385-388

A157

Norman R. Morrison, US anti-war demonstration.

1965, Nov. 22
389 A157 12xu black & red 3.00 1.25

A158

Nguyen Du (1765-1820), poet: No. 390, 12xu, Birthplace. No. 391, 12xu, Museum. 20xu, Volume of poems entitled Kieu. 1d, Scene from Kieu.

1965, Nov. 25
390-393 A158 Set of 4 6.00 5.00

A159

Designs: No. 394, 12xu, Ho Chi Minh. No. 395, 12xu, Karl Marx. No. 396, 12xu, Lenin. 50xu, Frederich Engels.

Litho. & Engr. (#394), Litho.
1965, Nov. 28 Perf. 11½
394-397 A159 Set of 4 6.00 6.00
Nos. 395-397 have white border.

Butterflies A160

#398, 12xu, Cethosia cyane. #399, 12xu, Zelides sarpedon. #400, 12xu, Cethosia. #401, 12xu, Apatura ambica. 20xu, Papilio paris. 30xu, Tros aristolochiae.

1965, Nov. 28 Litho. Perf. 11
398-403 A160 Set of 6 24.00 6.50
　　Imperf., #398-403 65.00

South Viet Nam Natl. Liberation Front,
5th Anniv. — A161

1965, Dec. 20
404   A161   12xu lilac   2.50 1.25
     Imperf.

1st General Elections, 20th
Anniv. — A162

1966, Jan. 6
405   A162   12xu black & red   2.50 1.25

A163   A164

Orchids: No. 406, 12xu, Vanda teres. No.
407, 12xu, Dendrobium meschatum. No. 408,
12xu, Dendrobium nobile. No. 409, 12xu, Dendrobium crystallinum. 20xu, Vandopsis
gigantea. 30xu, Dendrobium.

1966, Jan. 10   *Perf. 12*
406-411   A163   Set of 6   14.00 5.50
     Imperf., #406-411   25.00

1966, Jan. 18   *Perf. 11*
412   A164   12xu multicolored   2.50 1.00
     Imperf.
     New Year 1966 (Year of the Horse).

Reptiles
A165

#413, 12xu, Physignathus cocincinus. #414,
12xu, Gekko gecko. #415, 12xu, Trionyx
sinensis. #416, 12xu, Testudo elongata. 20xu,
Varanus salvator. 40xu, Eretmochelys
imbricata.

1966, Feb. 25   *Perf. 12x11½*
413-418   A165   Set of 6   12.00 6.00
     Imperf., #413-418   20.00

Natl.
Sports
A166

Designs: No. 419, Archery. No. 420, Wrestling. No. 421, Spear fighting.

1966, Mar. 25   *Perf. 11*
419-421   A166   12xu Set of 3   5.00 2.75

6xu, 12xu, 1d stamps for running,
swimming and shooting were printed
but not issued.

Youth Labor
Union, 35th
Anniv. — A167

1966, Mar. 26
422   A167   12xu multicolored   2.00 2.00

1000th US Warplane Shot
Down — A168

1966, Apr. 29
423   A168   12xu multicolored   7.50 4.00

May
Day — A169

1966, May 1
424   A169   6xu multicolored   2.00   .65

Defending Con Co Island — A170

1966, June 1
425   A170   12xu multicolored   2.50 1.50

A171

1966, June 1
426   A171   12xu red & black   1.75 1.00
     Young Pioneers, 25th anniv.

A172

Designs: 3xu, View of Yenan. 12xu, Ho Chi
Minh, Mao Tse-Tung.

1966, July 1
427-428   A172   Set of 2   6.00 1.00
     Imperf., #427-428

Chinese Communist Party, 45th anniv.

A173

Luna 9: 12xu, Flight path to moon. 50xu, In
lunar orbit.

1966, Aug. 5
429-430   A173   Set of 2   6.50 2.50
     Imperf., #429-430   10.00

A174

1966, Oct. 10
431   A174   12xu multicolored   10.00 3.00
**With Additional Inscription: "NGAY
14.10.1966"**
431A   A174   12xu multicolored   15.00 3.75
     Imperf., #431-431A

1500th US warplane shot down.

Victory in Dry Season
Campaign — A175

Designs: 1xu, 12xu (No. 433), Woman guerrilla carrying guns. 12xu (No. 434), Soldier
escorting prisoners of war.

1966, Oct. 15
432-434   A175   Set of 3   5.00 2.25
     Imperf., #432-434
     See also No. 618A.

Vietnamese
Women's
Union, 20th
Anniv.
A176

1966, Oct. 20
435   A176   12xu orange & black   2.25   .70
     Imperf.

Birds
A177

Designs: No. 436, 12xu, Pitta moluccensis.
No. 437, 12xu, Psarisomus dolhousiae. Nos.
438, 12xu, Alcedo atthis, vert. No. 439, 12xu,
Oriolus chinensis, vert. 20xu, Upupa epops,
vert. 30xu, Oriolus traillii.

1966, Oct. 31   *Perf. 12x12½, 12½x12*
436-441   A177   Set of 6   12.00 5.00
     Imperf., #436-441   25.00

GANEFO Asian
Games — A178

Designs: No. 442, Soccer. No. 443, Shooting. No. 444, Swimming. No. 445, Running.

1966, Nov. 25   *Perf. 11*
442-445   Set of 4   7.00 4.00
     Imperf., #442-445   11.00
443a   A178   12xu Pair, #442-443   5.00
445a   A178   30xu Pair, #444-445   5.00
     Nos. 443a, 445a (4)   10.00

Ho Chi Minh's Appeal for Natl.
Resistance, 20th Anniv. — A179

Designs: No. 446, Flags, workers. No. 447,
Soldiers, workers, ships.

1967, Jan. 30
446-447   A179   12xu Set of 2   2.25 1.75
     See Nos. 501-504.

Rice
Harvest
A180

1967, Jan. 30
448   A180   12xu multicolored   1.75 1.40

Bamboo
A181

No. 449, 12xu, Bambusa arundinaceu. No.
450, 12xu, Arundinaria rolleana. No. 451,
12xu, Arundinaria racemosa. No. 452, 12xu,
Bambusa bingami. 30xu, Bambusa nutans.
50xu, Dendrocalamus patellaris.

1967, Feb. 2   *Perf. 12x11½*
449-454   A181   Set of 6   9.00 7.25
     Imperf., #449-454   12.00

Wild Animals — A182

Designs: No. 455, 12xu, Cuon rutilans. No. 456, 12xu, Arctictis binturong. No. 457, 12xu, Arctonyx collaris. 20xu, Viverra zibetha. 40xu, Macaca speciosa. 50xu, Neofelis nebulosa.

1967, Mar. 26	Litho.	Perf. 12	
455-460 A182	Set of 6	11.00	6.00
	Imperf., #455-460	13.00	

2000th US Aircraft Shot Down — A183

1967, June 7		Perf. 11	
461-462 A183	6xu, 12xu, set of 2	8.00	6.50

Fish A184

#463, 12xu, Saurida filamentosa. #464, 12xu, Scomberomorus niphonius. #465, 12xu, Haplogenys mucronatus. 20xu, Lethrinus haematopterus. 30xu, Formio niger. 50xu, Lutianus erythropterus.

1967, July 25		Perf. 12	
463-468 A184	Set of 6	11.00	9.75
	Imperf., #463-468	13.00	

A185　　　　A186

Launch of 1st Chinese ballistic missile: 12xu, Missile, flag, agricultural scene. 30xu, Missile, Gate of Heavenly Peace.

1967, July 25		Perf. 11	
469-470 A185	Set of 2	9.00	3.00
	Imperf., #469-470		

1967, Oct. 15

Russian October Revolution, 50th anniv.: 6xu, Lenin, revolutionary soldiers. No. 472a, 12xu, Lenin, armed mob. No. 472b, 12xu, Lenin, Marx, Vietnamese soldiers. 20xu, Cruiser Aurora.

1967, Oct. 15			
471-473 A186	Set of 4	4.00	3.00

No. 472 is printed se-tenant.

2500th US Warplane Shot Down — A187

Design: No. 475, Plane in flames, vert.

1967, Nov. 6			
474-475 A187	12xu Set of 2	8.00	7.00

1st Chinese Hydrogen Bomb Test — A188

Designs: 12xu, Atomic symbol, Gate of Heavenly Peace. 20xu, Chinese lantern, atomic symbol, dove.

1967, Nov. 20			
476-477 A188	Set of 2	7.50	3.00
	Imperf., #476-477	35.00	

No. 477 is 30x35mm.

A189

#478, 12xu, Rifle fire from trenches. #479, 12xu, Militia with captured US pilot. #480, 12xu, Factory anti-aircraft unit. #481, 12xu, Naval anti-aircraft unit. 20xu, Aerial dog-fight. 30xu, Heavy anti-aircraft battery.

1967, Dec. 19		Perf. 12	
478-483 A189	Set of 6	6.00	4.75

Chickens — A190

Designs: No. 484, 12xu, White spotted cock, hen. No. 485, 12xu, Black hens. No. 486, 12xu, Bantam cock, hen. No 487, 12xu, Bantam cock. 20xu, Fighting cocks. 30xu, Exotic hen. 40xu, Hen, chicks from Ho region. 50xu, Dong Cao's cock, hen.

1968, Feb. 29			
484-491 A190	Set of 8	11.00	5.00
	Imperf., #484-491	17.50	

Victories of 1966-67 — A191

No. 492: a, Soldier attacking US tank. b, Gunner firing on US ships. c, Burning stockade. d, Soldier firing mortar.
No. 493: a, Attacking US artillery. b, Escorting US prisoners. c, Interrogating refugees. d, Civilian demonstration.

1968, Mar. 5		Perf. 11	
492-493 A191	12xu, 2 blocks of 4	6.00	6.00
	Imperf., #492-493		

Maxim Gorki (1868-1936) — A192

1968, Mar. 5			
494 A192	12xu brown & black	1.75	.80
	Imperf.		

Roses — A193

Designs: No. 495, 12xu, Pale red. No. 496, 12xu, Orange. No. 497, 12xu, Pink. 20xu, Yellow. 30xu, Dark red. 40xu, Lilac.

1968, Apr. 25	Photo.	Perf. 11½x12	
495-500 A193	Set of 6	9.00	9.00
	Imperf., #495-500	15.00	

Ho Chi Minh's Appeal for Resistance Type

Values and colors: No. 501, 6xu, greenish blue and yellow. No. 502, 12xu, vermilion. No. 503, 12xu, bright blue. No. 504, 12xu, brownish lilac.

1968, Apr. 25	Litho.	Perf. 11	
	Size: 25x17mm		
501-504 A179	6xu, 12xu Set of 4	6.00	3.00
	Imperf., #501-504		

Ho Chi Minh, Flag A195

1968, May 19			
505 A195	12xu brown & red	2.75	.60
	Imperf.		

Karl Marx — A196

1968, May 19			
506 A196	12xu olive grn & blk	1.75	.50

3000th US Warplane Shot Down A197

#507: a, 12xu, Anti-aircraft machine gunners. b, 12xu, Women firing anti-aircraft gun.
#508: a, 40xu, Vietnamese plane shooting down US plane. b, 40xu, Anti-aircraft missile.

1968, May 19

1968, May 19			
507-508 A197	Set of 2 pairs	12.00	8.50
	Imperf., #507-508		

Handicrafts — A198

6xu, Rattan products. #510, 12xu, Ceramics. #511, 12xu, Bamboo products. 20xu, Ivory carving. 30xu, Lacquerware. 40xu, Silverware.

1968, July 5		Perf. 12	
509-514 A198	Set of 6	6.50	6.00
	Imperf., #509-514	15.00	

Martial Arts A199

Designs: No. 515, 12xu, Saber fencing. No. 516, 12xu, Stick fighting. No. 517, 12xu, Dagger fighting. 30xu, Unarmed combat. 40xu, Chinese war sword fighting. 50xu, Duel with swords, shields.

1968, Nov. 1			
515-520 A199	Set of 6	10.00	9.00
	Imperf., #515-520	16.00	

Architecture — A200

Designs: No. 521, 12xu, Khue Van tower, vert. No. 522, 12xu, Bell tower, Keo pagoda, vert. 20xu, Covered bridge, Thay pagoda. 30xu, One-pillar pagoda, Hanoi, vert. 40xu, Gateway, Ninh Phuc pagoda. 50xu, Tay Phuong pagoda.

1968, Nov. 5			
521-526 A200	Set of 6	6.00	5.75
	Imperf., #521-526	10.00	

Foreign Solidarity with Viet Nam — A201

#527, 12xu, Latin American guerrilla, vert. #528, 12xu, Cuban, Vietnamese militia. 20xu, Asian, African, Latin American soldiers, vert.

1968, Dec. 15	Wmk. 376	Perf. 12½	
	With Gum		
527-529 A201	Set of 3	4.00	3.00

Scenes of War A202

Artworks: No. 530, 12xu, Defending the mines. No. 531, 12xu, Plowman with rifle, vert. 30xu, Repairing railway track. 40xu, Wreckage of US aircraft.

1968, Dec. 15 Wmk. 376 Perf. 12½
With Gum
530-533 A202 Set of 4   4.50 3.75

Victories in South Viet Nam — A203

#534, 12xu, Tay Nguyen throwing grenade. #535, 12xu, Gun crews, Tri Thien. #536, 12xu, Nam Ngai shooting down US aircraft. 40xu, Insurgents, Tay Ninh, destroyed US armor. 50xu, Guerrillas preparing bamboo spike booby traps.

1969, Feb. 16 Unwmk. Perf. 11½
534-538 A203 Set of 5   6.00 6.00

Timber Industry A204

Designs: 6xu, Loading timber trucks. No. 540, 12xu, Log raft running rapids. No. 541, 12xu, Launch towing log raft. No. 542, 12xu, Elephant hauling timber. No. 543, 12xu, Forest protection. 20xu, Water buffalo hauling log. 30xu, Hauling logs by overhead cable.

1969, Apr. 10
539-545 A204 Set of 7   7.50 4.00
Imperf., #539-545   15.00

Scenes of War — A205

Designs: No. 546, 12xu, Young guerrilla. No. 547, 12xu, Scout on patrol. 20xu, Female guerrilla, vert. 30xu, Halt at way station. 40xu, After a skirmish. 50xu, Liberated hamlet.

Perf. 12½x11½, 11½x12½
1969, July 20
546-551 A205 Set of 6   8.00 5.50
Imperf., #546-551   15.00

Tet Offensive Battles — A206

Designs: 8xu, 12xu (No. 553), Ben Tre. No. 554, 12xu, Mortar crew, Khe Sanh, vert. No. 555, 12xu, Two soldiers, flag, Hue, vert. No.

556, 12xu, Soldier running toward US Embassy, Saigon, vert.

1969, July 31 Perf. 11
552-556 A206 Set of 5   3.50 2.25
Imperf., #552-556

Liberation of Hanoi, 15th Anniv. A207

#557, Soldier with flamethrower. #558, Children constructing toy buildings.

1969, Oct. 10
557-558 A207 12xu Set of 2   3.50 1.75
Imperf., #557-558

A208

1969, Oct. 10
559 A208 12xu brn, blk & red   3.00 .80
Imperf.

Bertrand Russell Intl. War Crimes Tribunal, Stockholm and Roskilde.

A209

Fruits: No. 560, 12xu, Papaya. No. 561, 12xu, Grapefruit. 20xu, Tangerines. 30xu, Oranges. 40xu, Lychee nuts. 50xu, Persimmons.

1969, Nov. 20 Perf. 12
560-565 A209 Set of 6   5.50 2.75
Imperf., #560-565   8.50

Viet Nam Labor Party, 40th Anniv. — A210

Designs: No. 566, Nguyen Ai Quoc. No. 567, Ho Chi Minh. No. 568, Le Hong Phong. No. 569, Tran Phu. No. 570, Nguyen Van Cu.

1970, Feb. 3 Perf. 11
566-570 A210 12xu Set of 5   4.00 3.25
Imperf., #566-570

Nos. 568-570 are 40x25mm. Nos. 566-567 issued in vert. or horiz. se-tenant pairs. Nos. 568-570 issued in horizontal strips of 3.

Children's Activities — A211

Designs: No. 571, 12xu, Playing with toys. No. 572, 12xu, Three boys at kindergarten. No. 573, 20xu, Tending a garden. No. 574, 20xu, Tending water buffaloes. 30xu, Feeding chickens. 40xu, Piano, violin duet. 50xu, Flying model airplane. 60xu, Walking to school.

1970, Mar. 8 Perf. 12
571-578 A211 Set of 8   6.50 6.50
For overprints see Nos. 2181-2188.

Lenin, Birth Centenary A212

Designs: 12xu, Making speech. 1d, Portrait.

1970, Apr. 22 Perf. 11
579-580 A212 Set of 2   4.00 3.75
Imperf., #579-580

Shells A213

No. 581, 12xu, On con lon. No. 582, 12xu, Oc xa cu. 20xu, Oc tien. 1d, Oc tu va.

1970, Apr. 26 Perf. 12½x12
581-584 A213 Set of 4   6.50 6.00
Imperf., #581-584   11.50

Ho Chi Minh — A214

12xu (#585, 588c, 588g), In 1930 (full face, no beard). 12xu (#586, 588b, 588f), In 1945 (facing right, beard). 2d, 6xu, (#587, 588a, 588e), In 1969 (full face, beard).

1970, May 19 Perf. 11
585-587 A214 Set of 3   4.75 4.50
Imperf., #585-587
Souvenir Sheets of 3
Imperf
588 Types of #585-587, #a.-c.,
     orange background   8.00
588D Types of #585-587, #e.-g.,
     pale lilac background   8.00

Stamps in souvenir sheets have white backgrounds. The 6xu stamp is larger than the 2d stamp. Nos. 588a and 588e, 588c and 588g are different colors.

Vietcong Flag A215

1970, June 6
589 A215 12xu multicolored   2.25 .75
Formation of Revolutionary Provisional Government of South Viet Nam, 1st anniv.

Fruits and Vegetables A216

#590, 12xu, Watermelon. #591, 12xu, Pumpkin. 20xu, Cucumber. 50xu, Zucchini. 1d, Melon.

1970, July 15 Perf. 12
590-594 A216 Set of 5   4.50 4.50
Imperf., #590-594   12.00

Consumer Industries — A217

#595, Coal miners, truck. #596, Power linesman, vert. #597, Textile worker, soldier, vert. #598, Stoker, power plant, vert.

Perf. 12x11½, 11½x12
1970, Aug. 25 Litho. & Engr.
595-598 A217 12xu Set of 4   4.00 4.00

Agriculture A218

1970, Aug. 25 Litho. Perf. 11
599 A218 12xu multicolored   2.50 .75

Democratic Republic of Viet Nam, 25th Anniv. — A219

Famous people: #600, 12xu, Vo Thi Sau facing firing squad. #601, 12xu, Nguyen Van Troi, captors. #602, 12xu, Phan Din Giot attacking pillbox. #603, 12xu, Ho Chi Minh. 20xu, Nguyen Viet Xuan, troops in battle. 1d, Nguyen Van Be attacking tank with mine.

1970, Sept. 2
600-605 A219 Set of 6   5.25 4.75
Imperf., #600-605

No. 603 is 41x28mm.

Indo-Chinese People's Summit Conf. — A220

1970, Oct. 25
606 A220 12xu multicolored   2.50 .70
Imperf.

Bananas
A221

Designs: No. 607, 12xu, Tay. No. 608, 12xu, Tieu. 50xu, Ngu. 1d, Mat.

1970, Oct. 25   **Perf. 12**
607-610 A221   Set of 4   7.00 4.00
   Imperf., #607-610   13.00

Friedrich Engels — A222

1970, Nov. 28   **Perf. 11**
611-612 A222 12xu, 1d, set of 2   2.50 2.00

Snakes
A223

Designs: 12xu, Akistrodon ciatus. 20xu, Calliophis macclellandii. 50xu, Bungarus faciatus. 1d, Trimeresurus gramineus.

1970, Nov. 30 Photo. Perf. 12x11½
613-616 A223   Set of 4   6.00 5.00
   Imperf., #613-616   20.00

Natl. Liberation Front of South Viet Nam, 10th Anniv. — A224

Design: 6xu, Mother and child, flag, vert.

1970, Dec. 20 Litho. Perf. 11
617-618 A224   Set of 2   2.50 1.65
   Imperf., #617-618

Victory Type of 1966
1971, Apr. 10
618A A175 2xu black & orange   2.50 .70

Launching of 1st Chinese Satellite, 1st Anniv. — A225

1971, Apr. 10
619-620 A225 12xu, 50xu Set of 2   6.50 2.00
   Imperf., #619-620

Ho Chi Minh
A226

Denominations: 1xu, 3xu, 10xu, 12xu.

1971, May 19
621-624 A226   Set of 4   3.00 1.75
   Imperf., #621-624
624a   Souvenir sheet of 1, imperf.   6.00
No. 624a contains one 52x52mm stamp.

Tay Son Uprising, Bicent. — A227

1971, June 1
625-626 A227 6xu, 12xu, set of 2 3.00 1.65
   Imperf., #625-626

Marx, Music for The Internationale — A228

1971, June 20   **Perf. 12½**
627 A228 12xu org, blk & red   3.25 .75
   Imperf.
Paris Commune, cent.

Hai Thuong Lan Ong, Physician, 250th Birth Anniv.
A229

1971, July 1
628-629 A229 12xu, 50xu Set of 2   3.50 2.00
   Imperf., #628-629

Statues from Tay Phuong Pagoda
A230

Designs: No. 630, 12xu, Vasumitri. No. 631, 12xu, Kapimala. No. 632, 12xu, Dhikaca. No. 633, 12xu, Sangkayasheta. 30xu, Bouddha Nandi. 40xu, Rahulata. 50xu, Sangha Nandi. 1d, Cakyamuni.

1971, July 30 Photo. Perf. 12
630-637 A230   Set of 8   13.00 13.00
   Imperf., #630-637   30.00

Ho Chi Minh Working Youth Union, 40th Anniv.
A231

1971, Sept. 7 Litho. Perf. 11
638 A231 12xu multicolored   2.00 .75
   Imperf.

Flight of Luna 16 — A232

Luna 16: No. 639a, 12xu, Return from Moon. No. 639b, 12xu, Flight to Moon. 1d, On Moon.

1971, Sept. 17
639-640 A232   Set of 3   4.00 3.50
   Imperf., #639-640   22.50
No. 639 is se-tenant.

Flight of Luna 17 A233

Designs: No. 641, 12xu, Landing on Moon, vert. No. 642 12xu, On Moon. 1d, Lunakhod 1 crossing lunar crevasse.

1971, Oct. 15
641-643 A233   Set of 3   5.00 5.00
   Imperf., #641-643   18.00

Five Tigers
A234

Folk paintings: No. 644, 12xu, White tiger. No. 645, 12xu, Red tiger. No. 646, 12xu, Yellow tiger. 40xu, Green tiger. 50xu, Black tiger. 1d, Five tigers.

1971, Nov. 25   **Perf. 12**
644-649 A234   Set of 6   10.00 6.00
   Imperf., #644-649   18.00
   Size: 90x119mm
     Imperf
650 A234 1d multicolored   14.00

Chinese Communist Party, 50th Anniv.
A235

1971, Dec. 1   **Perf. 11**
651 A235 12xu multicolored   1.90 .50

Mongolian People's Republic, 50th Anniv. — A236

1971, Dec. 25
652 A236 12xu multicolored   1.90 .50

Folk Engravings from Dong Ho — A237

#653a, 12xu, Traditional wrestling. #653b, 12xu, Drum procession. #654a, 12xu, Gathering coconuts, vert. #654b, 12xu, Jealousy, vert. 40xu, Wedding of mice. 50xu, Frog school.

1972, Jan. 30
653-656 A237   Set of 6   10.00 9.00
   Imperf., #653-656   10.00
No. 653 is tete-beche.
The 30xu in design of #654a is a proof.

3rd Natl. Trade Unions Congress A238

Designs: 1xu, Workers facing right. 12xu, Workers facing left.

1972, May 1
657-658 A238   Set of 2   2.25 1.25
   Imperf., #657-658

Natl. Resistance, 25th Anniv. — A239

Designs: No. 659, Munitions worker. No. 660, Soldier in battle. No. 661, Woman in paddy field. No. 662, Text of Ho Chi Minh's appeal.

1972, May 5
659-662 A239 12xu Set of 4   3.50 1.75
   Imperf., #659-662   20.00

Ho Chi Minh's Birthplace A240

Design: No. 664, Home in Hanoi.

1972, May 19
663-664 A240 12xu Set of 2   2.50 1.75
Imperf., #663-664   5.00

A241

1972, June 20
665-666 A241 12xu Set of 2   7.00 2.50
Imperf., #665-666

3500th US warplane shot down. Added inscription on No. 666 reads "NGAY 20.4.1972."

A242

Georgi Dimitrov (1882-1949), Bulgarian politician: No. 668, Dimitrov at Leipzig Court, 1933.

1972, Aug. 15
667-668 A242 12xu Set of 2   2.50 1.50
Imperf., #667-668   5.00

Birds — A243

Designs: No. 669, 12xu, Lobivanellus indicus. No. 670, 12xu, Anas falcata. 30xu, Bubulcus ibis. 40xu, Gallicrex cinerea. 50xu, Prophyria porphyrio. 1d, Leptoptilos dubius.

1972, Oct. 12   **Perf. 12**
669-674 A243 Set of 6   10.00 8.00
Imperf., #669-674   22.50

A244

4000th US warplane shot down: No. 676, Gunner holding rocket.

1972, Oct. 19   **Perf. 11**
675-676 A244 12xu Set of 2   8.00 1.75
Imperf., #675-676   9.00

A245

Tay Nguyen folk dances: #677, 12xu, Drum. #678, 12xu, Umbrella. #679, 12xu, Shield. 20xu, Horse. 30xu, Ca Dong. 40xu, Rice pounding. 50xu, Khaen. 1d, Cham rong.

1972, Dec. 1   **Perf. 12**
677-684 A245 Set of 8   7.00 6.25
Imperf., #677-684   10.00

Flight of Soyuz 11 A246

Designs: 12xu, Soyuz 11 docking with Salyut laboratory. 1d, Soyuz 11 cosmonauts.

1972, Dec. 30   **Perf. 11**
685-686 A246 Set of 2   3.00 2.75
Imperf., #685-686   18.00

Wild Animals — A247

Designs: 12xu, Cuon alpinus. 30xu, Panthera pardus. 50xu, Felis bengalensis. 1d, Lutra lutra.

1973, Feb. 15   **Perf. 12½**
687-690 A247 Set of 4   7.00 5.00
Imperf., #687-690   27.50

Copernicus A248

Copernicus and: No. 691a, 12xu, Armillary sphere. No. 691b, 12xu, Sun. 30xu, Signature, vert.

1973, Feb. 17   **Perf. 11**
691-692 A248 Set of 3   3.50 3.00
Imperf., #691-692

Engravings on Ngoc Lu Bronze Drums — A249

Designs: No. 693, Drummers (Nha Danh Trong). No. 694, Pounding rice (Nha Gia Gao). No. 695, Dancers (Mua). No. 696, War canoe (Thuyen). No. 697, Birds (Chim, Thu).

1973, Apr. 12
693-697 A249 12xu Set of 5   4.50 4.50
Imperf., #693-697

Wild Animals — A250

Designs: 12xu, Tragulus javanicus. 30xu, Capricornis sumatraensis. 50xu, Sus scrofa. 1d, Moschus moschiferus.

1973, May 25   **Perf. 12x12½**
698-701 A250 Set of 4   5.00 5.00
Imperf., 698-701   13.00

Birds A251

#702, 12xu, Pycnonotus jocosus. #703, 12xu, Megalurus palustris. 20xu, Capsychus saularis. 40xu, Rhipidura albicollis. 50xu, Parus major. 1d, Zosterops japonica.

1973, July 15   **Perf. 12**
702-707 A251 Set of 6   7.00 4.00
Imperf., 702-707   15.00

Disabled Soldiers
A252   A252a

1973, July 27   **Perf. 11**
708-709 A252, A252a 12xu Set of 2   3.00
Imperf., #708-709

Three Readiness Youth Movement A253

Designs: No. 710, Road building. No. 711, Open-air class. No. 712, On the march.

1973, Sept. 2
710-712 A253 12xu Set of 3   2.50 1.25
Imperf., #710-712

Democratic People's Republic of Korea, 25th Anniv. — A254

1973, Sept. 9
713 A254 12xu multicolored   1.75 .40
Imperf.

4181st US Warplane Shot Down A255

Designs: No. 714, 12xu, US B-52 hit by air attack. No. 715, 12xu, US B-52, fighter crashing over Haiphong Harbor. No. 716, 12xu, Anti-aircraft battery. 1d, Aircraft wreckage caught in fishing net.

1973, Oct. 10
714-717 A255 Set of 4   9.00 3.75
Imperf., #714-717

Flowers — A256

6xu, 12xu (#719), Chrysanthemum (Cuc). #720, 12xu, Rose. #721, 12xu, Dahlia. #722, 12xu, Chrysanthemum (Bach mi). #723, 12xu, Chrysanthemum (Dai doa).

1974, Jan. 15
718-723 A256 Set of 6   40.00
Imperf., #718-723   70.00

No. 718 may not have been officially released.

Elephants A257

#724, 12xu, Hauling logs. #725, 12xu, War elephant. 40xu, Setting logs in place. 50xu, Circus elephant. 1d, Carrying war supplies.

1974, Feb. 10   **Perf. 11½**
724-728 A257 Set of 5   7.50 7.00
Imperf., #724-728   14.00

Victory at Dien Bien Phu, 20th Anniv. — A258

Designs: a, Dien Bien Phu soldier's badge. b, Soldier waving victory flag.

1974, May 7   **Perf. 11**
729 A258 12xu Pair, #a.-b.   2.50 .70
Imperf.   5.00

Three Responsibilities Women's Movement — A259

Designs: a, Armed worker, peasant. b, Female textile worker.

1974, June 1
730 A259 12xu Pair, #a.-b.   2.50 1.50
    Imperf.

A260

Chrysanthemums: No. 731, 12xu, Brown. No. 732, 12xu, Yellow (Vang). 20xu, Ngoc Khong Tuoc. 30xu, White. 40xu, Kim. 50xu, Hong mi. 60xu, Gam. 1d, Lilac.

1974, June 20   *Perf. 12x12½*
731-738 A260 Set of 8   7.00 4.00
    Imperf., #731-738   11.00

A261

Industrial plants: No. 739, 12xu, Corchorus capsularis. No. 740, 12xu, Cyperus tojet jormis. 30xu, Morus alba.

1974, Aug. 15   *Perf. 11*
739-741 A261 Set of 3   3.75 2.25
    Imperf., #739-741   10.00

Liberation of Hanoi, 20th Anniv. — A262

Designs: a, Woman laying bricks. b, Soldier holding child waving flag.

1974, Oct. 10
742 A262 12xu Pair, #a.-b.   2.50 .80

Solidarity with Chilean Revolution A263

Designs: No. 743, Pres. Salvador Allende, flag. No. 744, Pablo Neruda, poet.

1974, Oct. 15
743-744 A263 12xu Set of 2   2.50 .70
    Imperf., #743-744   5.00

Marine Life — A264

Designs: No. 745, 12xu, Rhizostoma. No. 746, 12xu, Loligo. 30xu, Haleotis. 40xu, Pteria martensii. 50xu, Sepia officinalis. 1d, Palinurus japonicus.

1974, Oct. 25   *Perf. 12½*
745-750 A264 Set of 6   7.00 2.50
    Imperf., #745-750   12.00

People's Republic of Albania, 30th Anniv. — A265

Designs: a, Natl. arms. b, Albanian, Vietnamese flags, women.

1974, Nov. 29   *Perf. 11*
752 A265 12xu Pair, #a.-b.   2.25 .75
    Imperf.

Paris Agreement on Vietnam, 2nd Anniv. — A266

Designs: No. 753, Intl. Conference on Viet Nam in session, 5-line inscription. No. 754, Signing of Paris Agreement, 4-line inscription.

1975, Jan. 27
753-754 A266 12xu Set of 2   2.50 .75
    Imperf.

Medicinal Plants — A267

Designs: No. 755, 12xu, Costus speciosus. No. 756, 12xu, Curcuma zedoaria. No. 757, 12xu, Rosa laevigata. 30xu, Erythrina indica. 40xu, Lilium brownii. 50xu, Hibiscus sagittifolius. 60xu, Papaver somniferum. 1d, Belamcanda chinensis.

1975, Feb. 2   *Perf. 11½x12*
755-762 A267 Set of 8   8.00 8.00
    Imperf., #755-762   12.50

Vietnamese Labor Party, 45th Anniv. — A268

Designs: No. 763, 12xu, Tran Phu. No. 764, 12xu, Le Hong Phong. No. 765, 12xu, Nguyen Van Cu. No. 766, 12xu, Ngo Gia Tu. 60xu, Ho Chi Minh in 1924, vert.

1975, Feb. 3   *Perf. 11*
763-767 A268 Set of 5   2.75 2.00
    Imperf., #763-767   10.00

A269

Fruit: No. 768, 12xu, Achras sapota. No. 769, 12xu, Persica vulgaris. 20xu, Eugenia jambos. 30xu, Chrysophyllum cainito. 40xu, Lucuma mamosa. 50xu, Prunica granitum. 60xu, Durio ziberthinus. 1d, Prunus salicina.

1975, Apr. 25   *Perf. 12x12½*
768-775 A269 Set of 8   6.50 5.00
    Imperf., 768-775   12.00

A270

1975, May 19   *Perf. 11*
776-777 A270 12xu, 60xu, set
                              of 2   3.50 1.25
    Imperf., #776-777   10.00

Ho Chi Minh, 85th birthday.

People's Republic of Poland, 30th Anniv. A271

1975, July 5
778-781 A271 1xu, 2xu, 3xu,
              12xu, set of 4   3.00
    Imperf., #778-781

Flags A272

Natl. Arms — A273

Flag of North Viet Nam and: No. 782, Draped flag. No. 783, Flag with star & cresent. No. 784, DDR flag and handshake.

1975
782-785 A272-A273 12xu Set of
                              4   7.00
    Imperf., #782-784

People's Republic of China, 25th anniv. (#782), Republic of Algeria, 20th anniv. (#783), German Democratic Republic, 25th anniv. (#784), liberation of Hungary, 30th anniv. (#785).
Issued: No. 782, 7/5. Nos. 783-785, 8/15.

Independence, 30th Anniv. — A274

#786, Flag. #787, Natl. arms. #788-789, Ho Chi Minh proclaiming independence.

1975, Sept. 2
786-788 A274 12xu Set of 3   3.50 1.25
        Souvenir Sheet
            Imperf
789   A274 20xu multicolored 22.50
No. 789 contains one 45x30mm stamp.

Reptiles A275

#790, 12xu, Dermochelys coriacea. #791, 12xu, Physignathus cocincinus. 20xu, Hydrophis brookii. 30xu, Platysternum megacephalum. 40xu, Leiolepis belliana. 50xu, Python molurus. 60xu, Naja hannah. 1d, Draco maculatus.

1975, Nov. 25   *Perf. 12*
790-797 A275 Set of 8   9.00 7.00
    Imperf., #790-797   20.00

Butterflies — A276

#798, 12xu, Pathysa antiphates. #799, 12xu, Danaus plexippus. 20xu, Cynautocera papilionaria. 30xu, Maenas salaminia. 40xu, Papilio machaon. 50xu, Ixias pyrene. 60xu, Eusemia vetula. 1d, Eriboea.

1976, Jan. 6
798-805 A276 Set of 8   9.00 9.00
    Imperf., #798-805   25.00

No. 799 misspelled "Danais."

Lan Hoang Thao Orchid A277

1976, Jan. 25   *Perf. 11*
806-807 A277 6xu, 12xu, set of 2 5.00 1.75

See Nos. 854-855.

Wild Animals A278

#808, 12xu, Callosciurus erythraeus. #809, 12xu, Paguma larvata. 20xu, Macaca mulatta. 30xu, Hystrix hodgsoni. 40xu, Nyctereutes procyonoides. 50xu, Selenarctos thibetanus. 60xu, Panthera pardus. 1d, Cynocephalus variegatus.

1976, Mar. 20   *Perf. 12*
808-815 A278 Set of 8   7.00 2.50
   Imperf., #808-815   15.00

1st Elections to Unified Natl. Assembly A279

6xu (#816), Map, hand placing ballot in ballot box. 6xu (#817), 12xu, Map, voters.

1976, Apr. 10   *Perf. 11*
816-818 A279 Set of 3   3.50 1.25
   Imperf., #816-818

Size of Nos. 817-818 is 35x22mm.
Identical stamps inscribed "Mien Nam Viet Nam" are National Front issues. Same values.

Unified Natl. Assembly, 1st Session A280

Design: 12xu, Inscribed "Doc Lap Thong Nhat Chu Nghia Xa Hoi."

1976, June 24
819-820 A280 6xu, 12xu, set of 2 2.50   .80

Identical stamps inscribed "Mien Nam Viet Nam" are National Front issues. Same values.

A281

1976, June 24   *Perf. 12x12½*
821 A281 12xu multicolored   1.50 .40
Reunification of Viet Nam.

A282

Orchids: No. 822, 12xu, Habenaria rhodocheila. No. 823, 12xu, Dendrobium devonianum. 20xu, Dendrobium tortile. 30xu, Doritis pulcherrima. 40xu, Dendrobium farmeri. 50xu, Dendrobium aggregatum. 60xu, Eria pannea. 1d, Paphiopedilum concolor.

1976, June 24   *Perf. 12*
822-829 A282 Set of 8   9.00 2.00
   Imperf., #822-829   15.00

DEMOCRATIC REPUBLIC OF VIET NAM
(After Unification)

AREA — 128,000 sq. mi.
POP. — 77,311,210 (1999 est.)
CAPITAL — Hanoi

Vietnamese Red Cross, 30th Anniv. — A283

1976, July 27   *Perf. 11*
830 A283 12xu multicolored   2.50 .80
   Imperf.

Fish — A284

#831, 12xu, Lutjanus sebae. #832, 12xu, Dampieria melanotaenia. 20xu, Therapon theraps. 30xu, Amphiprion bifasciatus. 40xu, Abudefduf sexfasciatus. 50xu, Heniochus acuminatus. 60xu, Amphiprion macrostoma. 1d, Symphorus spilurus.

1976, Aug. 15   *Perf. 12*
831-838 A284 Set of 8   6.00 4.75
   Imperf., #831-838   10.00

Viet Nam Worker's Party, 4th Natl. Congress A285

1976, Nov. 12   *Perf. 11*
839-844 A285 2, 3, 5, 10, 12, 20xu, set of 6   3.50 2.50

Viet Nam Communist Party, 4th Natl. Congress — A286

Designs: a, Agriculture, industry. b, Ho Chi Minh, worker, farmer, soldier, scientist.

Design size 24.5mmx35mm

1976, Dec. 10
845 A286 12xu Pair, #a.-b.   2.50 .80
   Imperf.
   See Nos. 951-954.

Unification of Viet Nam — A287

1976, Dec. 14
846-847 A287 6xu, 12xu, set of 2 2.50   .80
   Imperf., #846-847   4.50

General Offensive, 1975 — A288

Designs: 2xu, 50xu, Liberation of Buon Me Thuot. 3xu, 1d, Tanks liberating Da Nang. 6xu, 2d, Tank, soldiers liberating Presidential palace, Saigon.

1976, Dec. 14
848-853 A288 Set of 6   4.50 4.50

Lan Hoang Thao Orchid Type of 1976 Inscribed "VIET NAM" and "1976"

1976, Dec.   Litho.   *Perf. 11*
854-855 A277 6xu, 12xu Set of 2   45.00 15.00

Dragonflies — A289

#856, 12xu, Ho. #857, 12xu, Bao. 20xu, Canh dom. 30xu, Nuong. 40xu, Suoi. 50xu, Canh vang. 60xu, Canh khoang. 1d, Canh den.

1977, Jan. 25   *Perf. 12*
856-863 A289 Set of 8   7.00 1.50
   Imperf., #856-863   15.00

A290

Rare Birds: 12xu (#864), 60xu, Buceros bicornis. 12xu (#865), Ptilolaemus tickelli. 20xu, Berenicornis comatus. 30xu, Aceros undulatus. 40xu, Anthracoceros malabaricus. 50xu, Anthracoceros malayanus. 1d, Aceros nipalensis.

1977, Apr. 15
864-871 A290 Set of 8   6.00 2.75
   Imperf., #864-871   10.00

A291

Bronze drum and: 4xu, Thang Long Tower. 5xu, Map. 12xu, Lotus blossom. 50xu, Flag.

1977, Apr. 25   *Perf. 11*
872-875 A291 Set of 4   4.50 2.00
   Imperf., #872-875

Natl. Assembly general elections, 1st anniv.

Beetles A292

#876, 12xu, Black-spotted (Dom den). #877, 12xu, Yellow-spotted (Lang vang). 20xu, Veined (Van gach). 30xu, Green (Nhung xanh). 40xu, Green-spotted (Hoa xanh). 50xu, Black (Van den). 60xu, Leopard skin (Da bao). 1d, Nine-spotted (Chin cham).

1977, June 15   *Perf. 12½x12*
876-883 A292 Set of 8   7.00 1.75
   Imperf., #876-883   13.50

Wildflowers A293

Designs: No. 884, 12xu, Thevetia peruviana. No. 885, 12xu, Broussonetia papvrifera. 20xu, Aleurites montana. 30xu, Cerbera manghes. 40xu, Cassia multijuga. 50xu, Cassia nodosa. 60xu, Hibiscus schizopetalus. 1d, Lagerstroesnia speciosa.

1977, Aug. 19   *Perf. 12x12½*
884-891 A293 Set of 8   5.00 1.75
   Imperf., #884-891   10.00

A294   A295

Dahlias: 6xu (#892), 12xu (#894), Pink. 6xu (#893), 12xu (#895), Orange.

1977, Sept. 10   *Perf. 11*
892-895 A294 Set of 4   4.00 1.75
   See Nos. 921-924.

1977, Sept. 10
Children drawing map of unified Viet Nam. Denominations: 4xu, 5xu, 10xu, 12xu, 30xu each have different colored border.
896-900 A295 Set of 5   5.00 5.00

Goldfish A296

Designs: No. 901, 12xu, Dong nai. No. 902, 12xu, Velvet (Hoa nhung). 20xu, Blue Chinese (Tau xanh). 30xu, Dragon-eyed (Mat bong). 40xu, Cam trang. 50xu, Five-colored (Ngu sac). 60xu, Dong nai. 1d, Thap cam.

1977, Oct. 20   *Perf. 12*
901-908 A296 Set of 8   7.50 2.00
   Imperf., #901-908   13.00

A297

Russian October Revolution, 60th anniv.: 12xu (No. 909, olive background), 12xu (No. 910, blue background), Ho Chi Minh, Lenin banner. 50xu, Mother holding child with flag. 1d, Workers, farmers, Moscow Kremlin, cruiser Aurora.

1977, Nov. 7
909-912 A297 Set of 4   3.25 2.50

A298

Songbirds: 12xu, Gracula religiosa. No. 914, 20xu, Garrulax canorus. No. 915, 20xu, Streptopelia chinensis. 30xu, Linius schach. 40xu, Garrulax formosus. 50xu, Garrulax chinensis. 60xu, Acridotheres cristatellus. 1d, Garrulax yersini.

1978, Jan. 25
913-920 A298 Set of 8   6.00 1.75
        Imperf., #913-920   12.00

Cultivated Flower Type of 1977

5xu, 10xu, Sunflower. 6xu, 12xu, Pansy.

1978, Mar. 20   Perf. 11
921-924 A294 Set of 4   4.25 2.40

Intl. Children's Day (June 1977) — A299

1978, Mar. 20
925 A299 12xu multicolored   1.75 .40

Sports A300

#926, 12xu, Discus. #927, 12xu, Long jump. 20xu, Hurdles. 30xu, Hammer throw. 40xu, Shot put. 50xu, Javelin. 60xu, Running. 1d, High jump.

1978, Apr. 10   Perf. 11½
926-933 A300 Set of 8   4.50 2.00
        Imperf., #926-933   10.00

A301

4th Viet Nam Trade Union Cong.: #934, Trade Union emblem. #935, Ho Chi Minh, workers.

1978, May 1   Perf. 11
934-935 A301 10xu Set of 2   2.50 .80

A302

10xu, Ho Chi Minh conducting orchestra. 12xu, Ho Chi Minh's mausoleum, horiz.

1978, May 15
936-937 A302 Set of 2   2.25 .80
        No. 937 is 39x23mm.

Young Pioneers' Cultural Palace, Hanoi — A303

1978, May 29
938 A303 10xu multicolored   1.50 .40
        Intl. Children's Day.

Sculptures from Tay Phuong Pagoda — A304

Designs: No. 939, 12xu, Sanakavasa. No. 940, 12xu, Parsva. No. 941, 12xu, Punyasas. No. 942, 20xu, Kumarata. No. 943, 20xu, Nagarjuna. 30xu, Yayata. 40xu, Cadiep. 50xu, Ananda. 60xu, Buddhamitra. 1d, Asvagmosa.

1978, July 1   Perf. 12
939-948 A304 Set of 10   7.00 3.00
        Imperf., #939-948   20.00

Cuban Revolution, 25th Anniv. — A305

1978, July 20   Perf. 11
949-950 A305 6xu, 12xu Set of 2 2.50 .80

Types of 1976

6xu (No. 951), 12xu (No. 953), like #845a. 6xu (No. 952), 12xu (No. 952), like #845b.

Design size 18.5mmx23mm
1978, Aug. 15
951-954 A286 Set of 4   4.00 2.00

Space Exploration, 20th Anniv. — A306

#955, 12xu, Sputnik. #956, 12xu, Venus 1. 30xu, Spacecraft docking. 40xu, Molniya 1. 60xu, Soyuz. 2d, Cosmonauts Gubarev, Grechko.

1978, Aug. 28   Perf. 12½x12
955-960 A306 Set of 6   5.00 1.75
        Imperf., #955-960   10.00

World Telecommunications Day — A307

Designs: a, Printed circuit. b, ITU emblem.

1978, Sept. 25   Perf. 11
962 A307 12xu Pair, #a.-b.   2.50 .80
        Imperf.   18.00

20th Congress of Socialist Postal Ministers — A308

1978, Sept. 25
963 A308 12xu multicolored   1.50 .40

Chrysanthemums — A309

No. 964, 12xu, Tim. No. 965, 12xu, Kim tien. 20xu, Hong. 30xu, Van tho. 40xu, Vang. 50xu, Thuy tim. 60xu, Vang mo. 1d, Nau do.

1978, Oct. 1   Perf. 12
964-971 A309 Set of 8   5.50 2.00
        Imperf., #964-971   12.00

Dinosaurs A310

Designs: No. 972, 12xu, Plesiosaurus. No. 973, 12xu, Brontosaurus. 20xu, Iguanodon.

30xu, Tyrannosaurus rex. 40xu, Stegosaurus. 50xu, Mosasaurus. 60xu, Triceratops. 1d, Pteranodon.

1979, Jan. 1 Litho.   Perf. 11½
972-979 A310 Set of 8   10.00 2.00
        Imperf., #972-979   17.00
        No. 977 misspelled "Mozasaurus."

A311

1979, Jan. 1   Perf. 11
980 A311 12xu multicolored   1.50 .40
        Imperf.   5.00
        Socialist Republic of Cuba, 20th anniv.

A312

Quang Trung's victory over the Chinese, 190th Anniv.: #981, Battle plan. #982, Quang Trung.

1979, Feb. 1
981-982 A312 12xu Set of 2   2.50 .80
    a. Perf 12, #981-982   20.00

Albert Einstein, Physicist A313

Designs: No. 983, 12xu, Einstein. No. 984, 60xu, Equation, sun, planets.

1979, Mar. 14
983-984 A313 12xu, 60xu, set of 2 7.00 1.50

Domestic Animals — A314

10xu, Ram. 12xu, Ox. 20xu, Ewe, lamb. 30xu, White water buffalo, vert. 40xu, Cow. 50xu, Goat. 60xu, Water buffalo, calf. 1d, Young goat, vert.

1979, Mar. 20   Perf. 12
985-992 A314 Set of 8   5.00 1.50
        Imperf., #985-992   9.00

Five Year Plan (1976-80) — A315

#993, 998, Map, emblem. #994, 999, Factory worker. #995, 1000, Peasant woman, tractor. #996, 1001, Soldier. #997, 1002, Man, atom, compass.

1979   *Perf. 11*
993-997 A315 6xu Set of 5
998-1002 A315 12xu Set of 5
1000a   *Perf. 12*
   Nos. 993-1002 (10)   10.00
Issued: Nos. 993-997, 5/1. Nos. 998-1002, 6/1. Nos. 993, 996-1002 on toned paper.

Philaserdica '79, Intl. Stamp Exhibition, Sofia, Bulgaria A316

1979, May 27   *Perf. 12*
1003-1004   12xu, 30xu, set of 2   2.50   .80

Intl. Year of the Child — A317

2xu, Ho Chi Minh, children. 20xu, Nurse, mother, child. 50xu, Children with glider, painting supplies. 1d, Girls of different races.

1979, June 1   *Perf. 11*
1005-1008 A317 Set of 4   4.00 3.00

Ornamental Birds — A318

#1009, 12xu, Lophura diardi. #1010, 12xu, Tragopan temminckii. 20xu, Phasianus colchicus. 30xu, Lophura edwardsi. 40xu, Lophura nycthemera, vert. 50xu, Polyplectron germaini, vert. 60xu, Rheinhardia ocellata, vert. 1d, Pavo muticus, vert.

1979, June 16   *Perf. 12*
1009-1016 A318 Set of 8   7.50 2.10
   Imperf., #1009-1016   12.00

Orchids A319

Designs: No. 1017, 12xu, Dendrobium heterocacpum. No. 1018, 12xu, Cymbidium hybridum. 20xu, Rhynchostylis gigantea. 30xu, Dendrobium mobile. 40xu, Aerides falcatum. 50xu, Paphiopedilum callosum. 60xu, Vanda teres. 1d, Dendrobium phalaenopsis.

1979, Aug. 10   *Perf. 12*
1017-1024 A319 Set of 8   7.50 1.75
   Imperf., #1017-1024   13.00

Cats A320

Designs: No. 1025, 12xu, Meo tam the. No. 1026, 12xu, Meo muop, vert. 20xu, Meo khoang, vert. 30xu, Meo dom van. 40xu, Meo

muop dom, vert. 50xu, Meo vang, vert. 60xu, Meo xiem. 1d, Meo van am.

1979, Nov. 10
1025-1032 A320 Set of 8   6.50 3.00
   Imperf., #1025-1032   13.00

Vietnamese People's Army, 25th Anniv. — A321

a, People greeting soldiers. b, Frontier guards.

1979, Dec. 22   *Perf. 11*
1033 A321 12xu Pair, #a.-b.   2.00 2.00

Roses — A322

Designs: 1xu, 12xu (No. 1036), Red, pink roses. 2xu, 12xu (No. 1037), Single pink rose.

1980, Jan. 1
1034-1037 A322 Set of 4   5.00 2.00
   See Nos. 1084-1085.

Aquatic Flowers A323

#1038, 12xu, Nelumbium nuciferum. #1039, 12xu, Nymphala stellata. 20xu, Ipomola reptans. 30xu, Nymphoides indicum. 40xu, Jussiala repens. 50xu, Eichhornia crassipes. 60xu, Monochoria voginalis. 1d, Nelumbo nucifera.

1980, Jan. 15   *Perf. 12½*
1038-1045 A323 Set of 8   4.75 2.25
   Imperf., #1038-1045   9.00

Vietnamese Communist Party, 50th Anniv. — A324

Designs: No. 1046a, Ho Chi Minh proclaiming independence, 1945. No. 1046b, Peasants with banner, improvised weapons. No. 1047a, Map, soldiers, tanks storming palace. No. 1047b, Soldiers waving flag at Dien Bien Phu. 2d, Ho Chi Minh, soldiers and workers.

1980, Feb. 3   *Perf. 11*
1046 A324 12xu Pair, #a.-b.
1047 A324 20xu Pair, #a.-b.
1048 A324 2d multicolored
   Nos. 1046-1048 (5)   4.00 4.00

Lenin, 110th Anniv. of Birth A325

1980, Apr. 22   *Perf. 12*
1049-1051 A325 6xu, 12xu, 1d, set of 3   3.25 2.00

1980 Summer Olympics, Moscow A326

#1052, 12xu, Hurdles. #1053, 12xu, Running. 20xu, Team handball. 30xu, Soccer. 40xu, Wrestling. 50xu, Gymnastics, horiz. 60xu, Swimming, horiz. 1d, Sailing, horiz.

1980, May 1   *Perf. 12x12½, 12½x12*
1052-1059 A326 Set of 8   6.00 1.75
   Imperf., #1052-1059   10.00

A327

Ho Chi Minh, 90th anniv. of birth: 12xu, In 1924. 40xu, As president.

1980, May 19   *Perf. 11*
1060-1061 A327 Set of 2   2.25 1.25

A328

1980, June 15
1062 A328 5xu multicolored   1.25 .40
   Intl. Children's Day.

Intercosmos '80, Soviet-Vietnamese Space Mission — A329

Designs: No. 1063, 12xu, Cosmonauts. No. 1064, 12xu, Soyuz 37 atop booster. 20xu, Soyuz 37. 40xu, Soyuz docking with Salyut space station. 1d, Soyuz firing retro-rockets. 2d, Parachute landing. 3d, Cosmonauts, Soyuz-Salyut station.

1980, July 24   *Perf. 12x12½*
1063-1068 A329 Set of 6   5.50 1.00
          10.00
Souvenir Sheet
1069 A329 3d multicolored   8.00
   Imperf.   9.00

Saltwater Fish — A330

Designs: No. 1070, 12xu, Rhincodon typus. No. 1071, 12xu, Galeocerdo cuvier. 20xu, Orectolobus japonicus. 30xu, Heterodontus zebra. 40xu, Dasyatis uarnak. 50xu, Pristis microdon. 60xu, Sphyrna lewini. 1d, Myliobatis tobijei.

1980, Aug. 1   *Perf. 12*
1070-1077 A330 Set of 8   6.50 1.75
   Imperf., #1070-1077   14.00

A331   A332

Post and Telecommunications Office, 35th Anniv.: 12xu, Ho Chi Minh reading newspaper. 20xu, Ho Chi Minh talking on telephone. 50xu, Kim Dong carrying bird in cage. 1d, Dish antenna.

1980, Aug. 15   *Litho.*   *Perf. 12½*
1078-1081 A331 Set of 4   3.50 3.00

1980, Aug. 25   *Perf. 11, 12 (#1083)*
Natl. Telecommunications Day: No. 1082, Telephone switchboard operator. No. 1083, Train, map.

1082-1083 A332 12xu Set of 2   2.75 1.60

Rose Type of 1980
No. 1084, Pink. No. 1085, Red and pink.

1980, Aug. 25   *Perf. 11*
Size: 20x24mm
1084-1085 A322 12xu Set of 2   4.25 1.40
   For surcharge see No. 1385.

Republic of Vietnam, 35th Anniv. — A333

Designs: No. 1086, 12xu, Ho Chi Minh. No. 1087, 12xu, Natl. arms. 40xu, Pac Bo Cave. 1d, Source of Lenin River, horiz.

1980, Sept. 2   *Perf. 12½*
1086-1089 A333 Set of 4   4.00 4.00

A334

Natl. emblems: 6xu, Arms. No. 1091, 12xu, Flag, horiz. No. 1092, 12xu, Anthem.

1980, Sept. 20   *Perf. 12*
1090-1092 A334 Set of 3   3.50

A335

Nguyen Trai, 600th birth anniv.: 12xu, Nguyen Trai. 50xu, Books, horiz. 1d, Ho Chi Minh reading commemorative stele, Con Son.

1980, Oct. 6   *Perf. 11*
1093-1095 A335 Set of 3   3.50 3.50
For surcharge see No. 1386.

A336

Natl. Women's Union, 50th Anniv.: #1096, Ho Chi Minh, women. #1097, Group of 4 women.

1980, Oct. 20
1096-1097 A336 12xu Set of 2   2.25 .80

A337

Flowers: No. 1098, 12xu, Ipomoea pulchella. No. 1099, 12xu, Biguoniaceae venusta. 20xu, Petunia hybrida. 30xu, Trapaeolum majus. 40xu, Thunbergia grandiflora. 50xu, Anlamanda cathartica. 60xu, Campsis radicans. 1d, Bougainivillaea spectabilis.

1980, Nov. 20   *Perf. 12½*
1098-1105 A337 Set of 8   6.25 1.50
    Imperf., #1098-1105   10.00

Ornamental Fish — A338

Designs: No. 1106, 12xu, Betta splendens. No. 1107, 12xu, Symphysodon aequifasciata. 20xu, Poecilobrycon eques. 30xu, Gyrinocheilus aymonieri. 40xu, Barbus tetrazona. 50xu, Pterophyllum eimekei. 60xu, Xiphophorus helleri. 1d, Trichopterus sumatranus.

1981, Jan. 15   *Perf. 12*
1106-1113 A338 Set of 8   6.25 6.25
    Imperf., #1106-1113   10.00

26th Soviet Communist Party Congress A339

20xu, Rocket, book. 50xu, Young people, flag.

1981, Feb. 23   *Perf. 11*
1114-1115 A339 Set of 2   3.25 2.00

Animals from Cuc Phuona Natl. Forest — A340

#1116, 12xu, Hylobates concolor. #1117, 12xu, Macaca speciosa. 20xu, Selenarctos thibetanus. 30xu, Cuon alpinus. 40xu, Sus scrofa. 50xu, Cervus unicolor. 60xu, Panthera pardus. 1d, Panthera tigris.

1981, Apr. 10   *Perf. 12½x12*
1116-1123 A340 Set of 8   8.00 1.75
    Imperf., #1116-1123   13.00

Doves A341

#1124, 12xu, Treron sieboldi. #1125, 12xu, Ducula aenea, vert. 20xu, Streptopelia tranquebarica, vert. 30xu, Macropygia unchall, vert. 40xu, Ducula badia, vert. 50xu, Treron apicauda. 60xu, Chalcophaps indica. 1d, Seimun treron seimundi.

1981, June 5   *Perf. 12*
1124-1131 A341 Set of 8   6.75 4.00
    Imperf., #1124-1131   10.00

Nectar-sucking Birds — A342

Designs: No. 1132, 20xu, Aethopyga siparaja. No. 1133, 20xu, Anthreptes singalensis. 30xu, Aethopyga saturata. 40xu, Aethopyga gouldiae. No. 1136, 50xu, Nectarinia chalcostetha. No. 1137, 50xu, Nectarinia hypogrammica. 60xu, Nectarinia sperata. 1d, Aethopyga nipalensis.

1981, Aug. 5   *Perf. 12½x12*
1132-1139 A342 Set of 8   5.00 1.75
    Imperf., #1132-1139   10.00

A343   A343a

1981, Aug. 5   *Perf. 11*
1140 A343 12xu Lotus flower   5.00

1981, Aug. 5

Design: Factory militiawoman.
1140A A343a 12xu yel & multi   20.00
    See Nos. M30-M31.

A344   A345

Fruit: No. 1141, 20xu, Elaeagnus latifolia. No. 1142, 20xu, Fortunella japonica. 30xu, Nephelium lappaceum. 40xu, Averrhoa bilimbi. No. 1145, 50xu, Ziziphus mauritiana. No. 1146, 50xu, Fragaria vesca. 60xu, Bouea oppositifolia. 1d, Syzygium aqueum.

1981, Oct. 12   *Perf. 12*
1141-1148 A344 Set of 8   5.75 1.75
    Imperf., #1141-1148   10.00

1981, Nov. 15   *Perf. 11*

Planting trees: No. 1149, Ho Chi Minh. No. 1150, Three people.
1149-1150 A345 30xu Set of 2   2.00 1.00
    Tree planting festival.

Bulgaria, 1300th Anniv. A346

1981, Dec. 9   *Perf. 11*
1151-1153 A346 30xu, 50xu, 2d, set of 3   4.00 4.00

Wild Animals — A347

Designs: No. 1154, 30xu, Orangutan. No. 1155, 30xu, Bison bonasus. No. 1156, 40xu, Kangaroo. No. 1157, 40xu, Hippopotamus. No. 1158, 50xu, Rhinoceros sondaicus. No. 1159, 50xu, Giraffe. 60xu, Zebra. 1d, Lion.

1981, Dec. 9   *Perf. 12½x12*
1154-1161 A347 Set of 8   5.00 2.00
    Imperf., #1154-1161   9.00

A348

World Food Day: 30xu, 50xu, Woman holding sheaf of rice. 2d, FAO emblem, horiz.

1982, Jan. 26   *Perf. 11*
1162-1164 A348 Set of 3   3.00

A349

1982, Feb. 19
1165-1166 A349 50xu, 5d, set of 2   3.75 3.75
    10th World Trade Unions Congress, Havana, Cuba.

5th Vietnamese Communist Party Congress — A350

Designs: No. 1167, 30xu, Ho Chi Minh. No. 1168, 30xu, Hammer, sickle. No. 1169, 30xu, Worker, dam. 50xu, Women harvesting rice. 1d, Ho Chi Minh.

1982, Feb. 15
1167-1170 A350 Set of 4   4.50 2.00
      Imperf
      Size: 99x61 mm
1171 A350 1d multicolored   60.00

Bees & Wasps A351

Designs: No. 1172, 20xu, Ong bove. No. 1173, 20xu, Ong van xanh. 30xu, To vo nau. 40xu, Ong vang. No. 1176, 50xu, Ong dau nau. No. 1177, 50xu, To vo xanh. 60xu, Ong bau. 1d, Ong mat.

1982, Feb. 25   *Perf. 12*
1172-1179 A351 Set of 8   5.00 2.00
    Imperf., #1172-1179   10.00

Soccer A352

#1180, 30xu, 3 players. #1181, 30xu, 2 players. #1182, 40xu, Striped background. #1183, 40xu, grass background. #1184, 50xu, Vertically striped background. #1185, 50xu, Horizontally striped background. 60xu, 1d, Various soccer scenes.

1982, Apr. 15
1180-1187 A352 Set of 8   5.00 2.00
    Imperf., #1180-1187   10.00
    For overprints see Nos. 2142-2149.

A353

A354

Vietnamese Red Cross, 35th Anniv.: 1d, Red Cross emblem.

1982, May 15   **Perf. 11**
1188-1189 A353 Set of 2   2.50

1982, May 19   **Perf. 12**
5th Natl. Women's Congress: No. 1191, Congress emblem, three women.

1190-1191 A354 12xu Set of 2   2.50

A355

Birds of Prey: No. 1192, 30xu, Microhierax melanoleucos. No. 1193, 30xu, Falco tinnunculus. 40xu, Aviceda leuphotes. No. 1195, 50xu, Icthyophaga nana. No. 1196, 50xu, Milvus korschun. 60xu, Neohierax harmandi, horiz. No. 1198, 1d, Elanus caeruleus, horiz. No. 1199, 1d, Circaetus gallicus.

1982, June 1
1192-1199 A355 Set of 8   8.00 2.25
   Imperf., #1192-1199   12.00

A356

1982, June 1   **Perf. 11**
1200-1201 A356 30xu, 3d, set of 2   4.00

Georgi Dimitrov (1882-1949), Bulgarian Communist leader.

Dahlias
A357

Designs (last word or two of Vietnamese inscription): No. 1202, 30xu, Da cam. No. 1203, 30xu, Do. 40xu, Canh se. No. 1205, 50xu, Do nhung. No. 1206, 50xu, Vang. 60xu, Do tuoi. No. 1208, 1d, Bien. No. 1209, 1d, Trang. Various flowers.

1982, July 15   **Perf. 12x12½**
1202-1209 A357 Set of 8   7.00 2.25
   Imperf., #1202-1209   12.00

1982 World Cup Soccer Championships, Spain — A358

#1210, 50xu, Ball at bottom right. #1211, 50xu, Ball at right in air. #1212, 50xu, Ball at bottom center. #1213, 1d, 1 player. #1214, 1d, 3 players. 2d, 2 players.

1982, July 15   **Perf. 12x12½**
1210-1215 A358 Set of 6   6.00 6.00
   Imperf., #1210-1215   10.00

A359

1982, July 25   **Perf. 11**
1216 A359 30xu Natl. defense   1.50   .80
     See No. M32.

A360

1982, Aug. 15
1217 A360 30xu multicolored   1.50
Cuban victory at Giron (Bay of Pigs), 20th anniv.

World Environment Day — A361

#1219, Ho Chi Minh, children planting tree.

1982, Aug. 15
1218-1219 A361 30xu Set of 2   3.00
   Imperf., #1218-1219   40.00

A362

1982, Sept. 20
1220 A362 30xu multicolored   1.50   .80
Rabindranath Tagore (1861-1941), poet.

A363

Insects: No. 1221, 30xu, Catacanthus incarnatus. No. 1222, 30xu, Sycanus falleni. 40xu, Nezara viridula. No. 1224, 50xu, Lohita grandis. No. 1225, 50xu, Helcomeria spinosa. 60xu, Chrysocoris stollii. No. 1227, 1d, Pterygamia srayi. No. 1228, 1d, Tiarodes ostentans.

1982, Sept. 25   **Perf. 12x12½**
1221-1228 A363 Set of 8   6.00 2.00
   Imperf., #1221-1228   11.50

Russian Revolution, 65th Anniv. — A364

Design: No. 1230, Lenin, workers.

1982, Nov. 7   **Perf. 11**
1229-1230 A364 30xu Set of 2   2.00

9th South East Asian Games, New Delhi, India A365

#1231, 30xu, Table tennis. #1232, 30xu, Swimming. 1d, Wrestling. 2d, Shooting.

1982, Nov. 19
1231-1234 A365 Set of 4   4.75

Fish
A366

Designs: No. 1235, 30xu, Samaris cristatus. No. 1236, 30xu, Tephrinectes sinensis. No. 1237, 40xu, Psettodes erumei. No. 1238, 40xu, Zebrias zebra. No. 1239, 50xu, Cynoglossus puncticeps. No. 1240, 50xu, Pardachirus pavoninus. 60xu, Brachirus orientalis. 1d, Psettina iijimae.

1982, Dec. 15   **Perf. 12**
1235-1242 A366 Set of 8   6.00 1.75
   Imperf., #1235-1242   13.00

Socialist Ideals — A367

#1243, 30xu, Agriculture. #1244, 30xu, Industry. 1d, Natl. defense. 2d, Health & education.

1982, Dec. 25   **Perf. 11**
1243-1246 A367 Set of 4   5.50

Founding of Soviet Union, 60th Anniv. A368

1982, Dec. 30
1247 A368 30xu multicolored   2.50   .80

Sampans
A369

Designs: 30xu, Docked. 50xu, With striped sails. 1d, Sampans on Red River. 3d, With white sails. 5d, With patched sail. 10d, Fast sampan, horiz.

1983, Jan. 10   **Perf. 12½**
1248-1253 A369 Set of 6   6.00
   Imperf., #1248-1253   15.00

Locomotives — A370

30xu, Class 231-300. 50xu, Class 230-000. 1d, Class 140-601. 2d, Class 241-000. 3d, Class 141-500. 5d, Class 150-000. 8d, Class 40-300.

1983, Feb. 20   **Perf. 13**
1254-1260 A370 Set of 7   7.50
   Imperf., #1254-1260   15.00

1st Manned Balloon Flight, Bicent. A371

Balloons: 30xu, Montgolfier. 50xu, Yellow. 1d, CA-11. 2d, Hot-air. 3d, Over harbor. 5d, Le Geant. 8d, Ascending. 10d, Montgolfier, diff.

1983, Mar. 25   **Litho.**   **Perf. 12½**
1261-1267 A371 Set of 7   8.00
   Imperf., #1261-1267   15.00
     Souvenir Sheet
     Perf. 13
1268 A371 10d Sheet of 1   5.50

No. 1268 contains one 32x40mm stamp.

Discovery of Tubercle Bacillus,
Cent. — A372

1983, Mar. 25   *Perf. 11*
1269 A372 5d multicolored   3.00

Laos-Cambodia-Viet Nam
Summit — A373

1983, Mar. 25
1270-1271 A373 50xu, 5d Set of
     2   2.75

Cosmonauts — A374

Designs: 30xu, Gubarev, Remek. No. 1273,
50xu, Klimuk, Hermaszewski. No. 1274, 50xu,
Bykovsky, Jahn. No. 1275, 1d, Rukavishnikov,
Ivanov. No. 1276, 1d, Farcas, Kubasov. No.
1277, 2d, Mendez, Romanenko. No. 1278, 2d,
Gorbatko, Tuan. 5d, Dzhanibekov, Gurragcha.
8d, Popov, Prunariu. No. 1281, Gagarin.

1983, Apr. 1   *Perf. 12½x12*
1272-1280 A374 Set of 9   6.50
    Imperf., #1272-1280   12.00
Souvenir Sheet
1281 A374 10d multicolored   6.00
   No. 1281 contains one 36x28mm stamp.

Reptiles
A375

Designs: No. 1282, 30xu, Teratolepis fasciata. No. 1283, 30xu, Chamaeleo jacksoni.
No. 1284, 50xu, Uromastyx acanthinurus. No.
1285, 80xu, Heloderma suspectum. 1d,
Cameleo menle. 2d, Amphibolurus barbatus.
5d, Chlamydosaurus kingi. 10d, Phrynosoma
coronatum.

1983, Apr. 5   *Perf.*
1282-1289 A375 Set of 8   7.50
    Imperf., #1282-1289   13.00

Raphael (1483-
1520),
Painter — A375a

Designs: 30xu, Virgin Mother Seated on
Chair. 50xu, Granduca, the Virgin Mother. 1d,
Sistine Madonna. 2d, Marriage of Maria. 3d,

The Gardener. 5d, Woman with Veil. 8d, 10d,
Self-Portrait.

1983, Apr. 30   *Perf. 12½*
1289A-1289G A375a Set of 7   7.50
    Imperf., #1289A-1289G   10.00
Souvenir Sheet
Perf. 13
1289H A375a 10d multicolored   12.00

Chess
Pieces — A376

Designs: 30xu, Vietnamese pawns. 50xu,
Indian elephant. 1d, Scottish knight, bishop.
2d, Indian elephant, diff. 3d, Knight. 5d, Sailing
ship. 8d, Jester, elephant. 10d, Modern
pawns.

1983, May 9   *Perf. 13*
1290-1296 A376 Set of 7   6.50
    Imperf., #1290-1296   17.00
Souvenir Sheet
1297 A376 10d multicolored   7.25
   No. 1297 contains one 28x36mm stamp.

Souvenir Sheet

TEMBAL '83 World Stamp Exhibition,
Basel — A377

1983, May 21   *Perf. 13*
1298 A377 10d multicolored   5.00 5.00

1984 Summer
Olympics, Los
Angeles
A378

Designs: 30xu, Long jump. 50xu, Running.
1d, Javelin. 2d, High jump, horiz. 3d, Hurdles,
horiz. 5d, Shot put. 8d, Pole vault. 10d,
Discus.

1983, June 13   **Litho.**   *Perf. 13*
1299-1305 A378 Set of 7   7.50
Souvenir Sheet
1306 A378 10d Sheet of 1   6.25
   No. 1306 contains one 32x40mm stamp.
   The issuance of this set has been
questioned.

Souvenir Sheet

Brasiliana '83, Rio de Janeiro — A379

1983, July 20   *Perf. 13*
1307 A379 10d Rhamphastos
     toco   6.00 5.00

Butterflies
A380

Designs: No. 1308, 30xu, Leptocircus
meges. No. 1309, 30xu, Terias hecabe. No.
1310, 40xu, Zetides agamemnon. No. 1311,
40xu, Nyctalemon patroclus. No. 1312, 50xu,
Papilio chaon. No. 1313, 50xu, Precis almana.
60xu, Thauria lathyi. 1d, Kallima inachus.

1983, July 30   **Litho.**   *Perf. 12*
1308-1315 A380 Set of 8   8.00
    Imperf., #1308-1315   13.50

Souvenir Sheet

Bangkok '83 — A381

1983, Aug. 4   *Perf. 13*
1316 A381 10d multicolored   10.00 10.00

Karl Marx
(1818-1883)
A382

1983, Oct. 10   *Perf. 11*
1317-1318 A382 50xu, 10d, set
     of 2   5.00
    Imperf., #1317-1318   50.00

Phu Dong Sports Festival — A383

1983, Oct. 10
1319-1320 A383 30xu, 1d, Set of
     2   2.75

World
Food Day
A384

Design: 50xu, Infant, fish. 4d, Family.

1983, Oct. 10   *Perf. 12½*
1321-1322 A384 Set of 2   2.50
    Imperf., #1321-1322   7.00

Mushrooms
A385

#1323, 50xu, Flammulina velutipes. #1324,
50xu, Pleurotus ostreatus. #1325, 50xu,
Cantharellus cibarius. #1326, 50xu, Coprinus
atramentarius. 1d, Volvariella volvacea. 2d,
Agaricus silvaticus. 5d, Morchella esculenta.
10d, Amanita caesarea.

1983, Oct. 10   *Perf. 12x12½*
1323-1330 A385 Set of 8   11.00 8.00
    Imperf., #1323-1330   14.50

   For overprints see Nos. 2150-2157.

World Communications Year — A386

50xu, Letter carrier. 2d, Mail sorting room.
8d, Switchboard operators. #1334, 10d, Radio
operator, antenna. #1335, 10d, Telephone, letter, dish antenna, ship.

1983, Oct. 30   *Perf. 12½*
1331-1334 A386 Set of 4   5.75
Souvenir Sheet
Perf. 13
1335 A386 10d Sheet of 1   3.00

5th Natl. Trade Unions
Congress — A387

50xu, Woman with flowers, Vietnam-Soviet
Union Friendship Cultural Building. 2d, 30d,
Welder.

1983, Nov. 16   *Perf. 11*
1336-1338 A387 Set of 3   7.50

Water Birds
A388

Designs: No. 1339, 50xu, Ciconia nigra. No. 1340, 50xu, Ardea cinerea. No. 1341, 50xu, Ardea purpurea. No. 1342, 50xu, Ibis leucocephalus. 1d, Grus grus. 2d, Platalea minor. 5d, Nycticorax nycticorax. 10d, Anastomus oscitans.

1983, Nov. 20 Perf. 12x12½
1339-1346 A388 Set of 8 9.00 5.00
　Imperf., #1339-1346 16.00

No. 1343 inscribed "Grus grue."

World Peace Conference, Prague — A389

Designs: 50xu, Shown. 3d, 5d, 20d, Hands, globe, dove.

1984, Jan. 15 Perf. 11
1347-1350 A389 Set of 4 9.00

1984 Winter Olympics, Sarajevo, Yugoslavia — A390

#1351, 50xu, Cross-country skiing, vert. #1352, 50xu, Biathlon, vert. 1d, Speed skating, vert. 2d, Bobsled, vert. 3d, Hockey. 5d, Ski jumping. 6d, Slalom skiing. 10d, Pairs figure skating.

1984, Jan. 30 Perf. 12½
1351-1357 A390 Set of 7 5.00
　Imperf., #1351-1357 15.00
Souvenir Sheet
1358 A390 10d multicolored 4.50

No. 1358 contains one 40x32mm stamp.

Soviet Union-Vietnamese Projects, 1978-83 — A391

Designs: 20xu (No. 1359), 4d, Hoa Binh Hydro-electric project. 20xu (No. 1360), Vietnamese-Soviet Cultural Palace. 50xu, Thang Long Bridge.

1984, Jan. 31 Perf. 11
With Gum
1359-1362 A391 Set of 4 55.00

Endangered Animals — A392

Designs: No. 1363, 50xu, Felis marmorata. No. 1364, 50xu, Panthera tigris. No. 1365, 50xu, Panthera pardus. No. 1366, 50xu, Hylobates lar. No. 1367, 1d, Nycticebus coucang. No. 1368, 2d, Elephas indidus. No. 1369, 2d, Bos gaurus.

1984, Feb. 26 Perf. 12½x12
1363-1369 A392 Set of 7 5.00
　Imperf., #1363-1369 14.00

A393

Wildflowers: No. 1370, 50xu, Banhinia variegata. No. 1371, 50xu, Caesalpinia pulcherrima. 1d, Cassia fistula. 2d, Delonix regia. 3d, Artagotrys uncinatus. 5d, Corchorus olitorius. 8d, Banhinia grandiflora.

1984, Mar. 15 Perf. 12x12½
1370-1376 A393 Set of 7 5.50
　Imperf., #1370-1376 11.00
Souvenir Sheet
1377 A393 10d Delonix regia 4.50

Location of inscriptions differs on Nos. 1373, 1377.

A394

Orchids: No. 1378, 50xu, Cymbidium. No. 1379, 50xu, Brasse cattleya. 1d, Cattleya Dianx. 2d, Cymbidium, diff. 3d, Cymbidium hybridum. 5d, Phoenix winged orchids. 8d, Yellow Queen orchids.

1984, Mar. 28 Perf. 13
1378-1384 A394 Set of 7 9.50
　Imperf., #1378-1384 17.00

Nos. 1085, 1093 Surcharged

a　　　　b

1984, Apr. 25 Perfs. as before
1385 A322(a) 50xu on 12xu
　　　　#1085 10.00
1386 A335(b) 50xu on 12xu
　　　　#1093 10.00

Souvenir Sheet

Espana '84, Madrid — A395

1984, Apr. 27 Perf. 12½
1387 A395 10d Ciconia ciconia 5.50

Victory at Dien Bien Phu, 30th Anniv. A396

#1388, 50xu; #1395, 10d, Ho Chi Minh, generals, battle map. #1389, 50xu, Troops, truck. 1d, Civilians carrying provisions. 2d, Man-hauling artillery. 3d, Anti-aircraft battery. 5d, Troops attacking enemy base. 8d, Troops waving flag.

1984, May 7 Perf. 12½
1388-1394 A396 Set of 7 4.50
Souvenir Sheet
1395 A396 10d multicolored 4.50

Souvenir Sheet

UPU Congress, Hamburg '84 — A397

1984, June 19 Perf. 13
1396 A397 10d Junkers JU-52
　　　3M 5.00

Fish
A398

Designs: No. 1397, 30xu, Cypselurus spilopterus. No. 1398, 30xu, Ostracion cornutus. 50xu, Diodon hystrix. 80xu, Chelmon rostratus. 1d, Antennarius tridens. 2d, Pterois russelli. 5d, Mola mola. 10d, Minous monodactylus.

1984, June 25 Litho. Perf. 12
1397-1404 A398 Set of 8 7.25
　Imperf., #1397-1404 11.50

Ornamental Fish — A399

Designs: No. 1405, 50xu, Trichogaster trichopterus. No. 1406, 50xu, Brachydanio rerio. 1d, Macropodus opercularis. 2d, Gymnocorymbus ternetzi. 3d, Hyphessobrycon serpae. 5d, Labeo bicolor. 8d, Batta splendens.

1984, June 29 Perf. 12½
1405-1411 A399 Set of 7 6.00
　Imperf., #1405-1411 11.50

Vietnamese Trade Union Movement, 55th Anniv. — A400

Designs: No. 1412a, 50xu, House at 15 Hang Non St., Hanoi. No. 1412b, 50xu, Nguyen Duc Canh, vert. 1d, Striking workers. 2d, Ho Chi Minh visiting factory. 3d, Hanoi Mechanical Engineering plant. 5d, Intl. trade union movement.

1984, July 20 Perf. 11
1412-1416 A400 Set of 6 4.50
Souvenir Sheet
Imperf
1417 A400 2d like #1414 11.00

No. 1412 printed se-tenant. No. 1417 contains one 45x38mm stamp.

Rock Formations, Ha Long Bay — A401

#1418, 50xu, Hang-Bo Nau. #1419, 50xu, Nui Yen Ngua. #1420, 50xu, Hon Dua. #1421, 50xu, Hang Con Gai. #1422, 1d, Hon Coc. #1423, 1d, Hon Ga Choi. 2d, Hon Dinh Huong. 3d, Hon Su Tu. 5d, Hon Am. 8d, Nui Bai Tho.

1984, July 30 Perf. 12½x12
1418-1427 A401 Set of 10 7.00
　Imperf., #1418-1427 13.50

Dinosaurs — A402

#1428, 50xu, Styracosaurus. #1429, 50xu, Diplodocus. #1430, 1d, Corythosaurus. #1431, 1d, Rhamphyorhynchus. 2d, Seymouria. 3d, Allosaurus. 5d, Dimetrodon. 8d, Brachiosaurus.

1984, Aug. 30
1428-1435 A402 Set of 8 13.50
　Imperf., #1428-1435 15.00

Viet Nam-Laos-Cambodia Friendship — A403

1984, Aug. 30 Perf. 11
1436-1437 A403 50xu, 10d, set
　　　　of 2 6.00

Souvenir Sheet

Ausipex '84, Melbourne,
Australia — A404

1984, Sept. 20   *Perf. 13*
1438 A404 10d Koala   12.00

Viet Nam-
Cambodia
Friendship
Agreement, 5th
Anniv. — A405

50xu, 3d, People, pagoda, statue. 50d,
Dancers.

1984, Sept. 30   *Perf. 11*
1439-1441 A405 Set of 3   12.00

Liberation
of Hanoi,
30th
Anniv.
A406

Designs: 50xu, Thang Long Bridge. 1d,
Khue Van Gateway. 2d, Ho Chi Minh
mausoleum.

1984, Oct. 5
1442-1444 A406 Set of 3   4.00

Vintage Automobiles — A407

#1445, 50xu, Vis-a-Vis, vert. #1446, 50xu,
Duc. 1d, Tonneau. 2d, Double phaeton. 3d,
Landaulet. 5d, Torpedo. 6d, Coupe de Ville.

1984, Oct. 30 *Perf. 12½x13, 13x12½*
1445-1451 A407 Set of 7   5.00
            Imperf., #1445-1451   11.50

Lenin (1870-
1924)
A408

Paintings of Lenin: 50xu, At his desk. 1d,
Standing with revolutionaries. 3d, Speaking at
factory. 5d, Meeting with farmers.

1984, Nov. 15   *Perf. 12x12½*
1452-1455 A408 Set of 4   3.00
            Imperf., #1452-1455   6.75

UNICEF
A409

Paintings: 30xu, Woman, soldiers. 50xu,
Mother, children. 1d, Miner, family. 3d, Young
girl, vert. 5d, Children playing on ground. 10d,
Women, child, vert.

1984, Dec. 7   *Perf. 12*
1456-1461 A409 Set of 6   5.50
            Imperf., #1456-1461   10.00

A410   A411

50xu, 30d. Frontier Forces, 25th anniv.

1984, Dec. 15   *Perf. 11*
1462-1463 A410 Set of 2   11.00
            Imperf., #1462-1463
            See No. M39.

1984, Dec.   *Perf. 12½x12*
Flora and Fauna: 20xu, Bubalus bubalis.
30xu, Felis marmorata. No. 1466, 50xu, Hibiscus rosa-sinensis. No. 1467, 50xu, Ailurus
fulgens. No. 1468, 50xu, Rosa centifolia. No.
1469, 50xu, Betta splendens. No. 1470, 1d,
Chrysanthemum sinense. No. 1471, 1d,
Nymphaea ampla. No. 1472, 1d, Pelecanus
onocrotalus. No. 1473, 1d, Panthera tigris. No.
1474, 2d, Nycticebus coucang. No. 1475, 2d,
Macaca fascicularis. No. 1476, 2d, Dalia coccinea. 5d, Gekko gecko. 10d, Rhytidoceros
bicornis.

1464-1478 A411 Set of 15   12.50
            Imperf., #1464-1478   15.00

No. 1466 inscribed "Hybiscus." No. 1470
inscribed "Chrysanthemun."

A412   A413

1985   *Perf. 11*
1479-1480 A412 3d, 5d, set of 2   2.75
            Imperf., #1479-1480   30.00

New Year 1985 (Year of the Buffalo).
Issued: 3d, 1/21; 5d, 4/30.

1985, Apr. 26   *Perf. 11*
1481 A413 2d Ho Chi Minh   1.10

Vietnamese Communist Party, 55th anniv.

Military
Victory in
South Viet
Nam, 10th
Anniv.
A414

Designs: 1d, Soldiers advancing forward.
2d, 10d, Ho Chi Minh, tank, soldiers. 4d, Construction worker. 5d, Map, women.

1985, Apr. 30   *Perf. 12½*
1482-1485 A414 Set of 4   4.50
Souvenir Sheet
Perf. 13
1486 A414 10d multicolored   3.75

Cactus
A415

Designs: No. 1487, 50xu, Echinocereus
knippelianus. No. 1488, 50xu, Lemaireocereus
thurberi. 1d, Notocactus haselbergii. 2d,
Parodia chrysacanthion. 3d, Pelecyphora
pseudopectinata. 5d, Rebutia frebrighii. 8d,
Lobivia aurea.

1985, Apr. 30   *Perf. 11½*
1487-1493 A415 Set of 7   7.25
            Imperf., #1487-1493   15.00

Vietnamese People's Army, 40th
Anniv. — A416

Designs: No. 1494, 50xu, Ho Chi Minh. No.
1495, 50xu, Taking oath on flag. 1d, Anti-aircraft missile. 2d, Soldiers, civilians working
together. 3d, Tank entering grounds of presidential palace, Saigon. 5d, Soldier demonstrating use of rifle. 8d, Officers, soldiers, map.
10d, Four soldiers representing branches of
military.

1985, May 6   *Perf. 12½*
1494-1500 A416   Set of 7   5.50
Souvenir Sheet
1501   A416 10d multicolored 4.00

End of World War
II, 40th
Anniv. — A417

Designs: 1d, 10d, Victory Monument. 2d,
Vietnamese soldier. 4d, Dove, falling American eagle. 5d, Child, doves.

1985, May 7   *Perf. 12x12½*
1502-1505 A417 Set of 4   4.00
            Imperf., #1502-1505   15.00
Souvenir Sheet
1506 A417 10d multicolored   3.25

Liberation of
Haiphong, 30th
Anniv. — A418

Designs: 2d, Long Chau Lighthouse. 5d, An
Duong Bridge, horiz.
10d, To Hieu (1912-44), vert.

1985, May 13   *Perf. 11*
1507-1508 A418 Set of 2   2.50

Souvenir Sheet
Imperf
1509 A418 10d multicolored   3.50

Ho Chi Minh, 95th Birth
Anniv. — A419

Ho Chi Minh: 1d, At battlefield. 2d, Reading.
4d, 10d, Portrait, vert. 5d, Writing.

1985, May 19   *Perf. 12½*
1510-1513 A419 Set of 4   4.00
Souvenir Sheet
Perf. 13
1514 A419 10d multicolored   5.00
No. 1514 contains one 30x36mm stamp.

Motorcycles, Cent. — A420

Designs: No. 1515, 1d, 1895, Germany. No.
1516, 1d, 1898 tricycle, France. No. 1517, 2d,
1913 Harley-Davidson, US. No. 1518, 2d,
1918 Cleveland, US. 3d, 1935 Simplex, US.
4d, 1984 Minarelli, Italy. 6d, 1984 Honda,
Japan. 10d, 1984 Honda racing bike.

1985, June 28   *Perf. 13*
1515-1521 A420 Set of 7   5.50
            Imperf., #1515-1521   14.00
Souvenir Sheet
1522 A420 10d multicolored   5.00
No. 1522 contains one 32x40mm stamp.

Argentina '85, Buenos Aires — A421

Wild animals: No. 1523, 1d, Aptenodytes
pennati, vert No. 1524, 1d, Doliohotis
patagonum, vert. No. 1525, 2d, Panthera
onca. No. 1526, 2d, Hydrochoerys capibara.
3d, Peterocnemia pennata, vert. 4d, Priodontes giganteus. 6d, Voltur gryphus. 10d,
Lama glama, horiz.

1985, July 5   *Perf. 12½*
1523-1529 A421 Set of 7   10.00
            Imperf., #1523-1529   18.00
Souvenir Sheet
With Gum
Perf. 13
1530 A421 10d multicolored   12.50
No. 1530 contains one 40x32mm stamp.

12th World
Youth and
Students
Festival,
Moscow
A422

No. 1531, 2d, Youth carrying flags, globe.
No. 1532, 2d, Workers, power transmission
lines. 4d, Lighthouse, coastal defense. 5d, Intl.
festival.

1985, July 27   *Perf. 12½*
1531-1534 A422   Set of 4   5.00
    Imperf., #1531-1534   17.50

Souvenir Sheet
With Gum
Perf. 13

1535 A422   10d like #1531   5.00

Marine Life
A423

#1536, 30xu, Nadoa tuberculata. #1537, 30xu, Luidia maculata. #1538, 30xu, Stichopus chloronotus. #1539, 30xu, Holothuria monacaria. #1540, 40xu, Astropyga radiata. #1541, 40xu, Astropecten scoparius. #1542, 40xu, Linckia laevigata.

1985, July 30   *Perf. 12*
1536-1542 A423   Set of 7   8.00
    Imperf., #1536-1542   19.00

Socialist
Republic of Viet
Nam, 40th
Anniv. — A424

Designs: 2d, Construction. 3d, Hands shaking, doves. 5d, Flag, military forces. No. 1567, 10d, Flag, Ho Chi Minh.

1985, Aug. 28   *Perf. 12½*
1543-1546 A424   Set of 4   4.50
    Imperf., #1543-1546   20.00

Souvenir Sheet
Perf. 13

1547 A424   10d like #1543   4.00
   No. 1547 contains one 32x40mm stamp.

Vietnamese Police Force, 40th
Anniv. — A425

1985, Aug. 30   *Perf. 11*
1548 A425   10d multicolored   4.00
       See No. M41.

1st Natl.
Sports
Festival
A426

Designs: 5d, Gymnastics. 10d, Gymnastics, running, swimming.

1985, Aug. 30
1549-1550 A426   Set of 2   4.50

German Railways, 150th
Anniv. — A427

Various locomotives: #1551, 1d, Facing left. #1552, 1d, Facing right. #1553, 2d, Facing left. #1554, 2d, Facing right. 3d, 4d, 6d.

1985, Sept. 13   *Perf. 12½*
1551-1557 A427   Set of 7   6.25
    Imperf., #1551-1557   10.00

Souvenir Sheet
With Gum
Perf. 13

1558 A427   10d multicolored   4.50
   No. 1558 contains one 32x40mm stamp.

Vietnamese Geological Survey, 30th
Anniv. — A428

#1559, Drilling rigs. #1560, Aerial survey.

1985, Oct. 5   *Perf. 11*
1559-1560 A428   1d Set of 2   2.75

Italia '85
A429

Vintage Italian cars: No. 1561, 1d, 1922 Alfa Romeo. No. 1562, 1d, 1932 Bianchi Berlina. No. 1563, 2d, 1928 Isotta Fraschini. No. 1564, 2d, 1930 Bugatti. No. 1565, 3d, 1912 Itala. 4d, 1934 Lancia Augusta. 6d, 1927 Fiat Convertable (top up). 10d, 1927 Fiat Convertable (top down).

1985, Oct. 25   *Perf. 13*
1561-1567 A429   Set of 7   5.50
    Imperf., #1561-1567   17.50

Souvenir Sheet
With Gum

1568 A429   10d multicolored   6.00
   No. 1568 contains one 40x32mm stamp.

Whales
A430

Designs: No. 1569, 1d, Balaenoptera musculus. No. 1570, 1d, Balaena borealis. No. 1571, 2d, Orcinus orca. No. 1572, 2d, Delphinus. 3d, Megaptera boops. 4d, Balaenoptera physalus. 6d, Eubalaena glacialis.

1985, Nov. 15
1569-1575 A430   Set of 7   8.50
    Imperf., #1569-1575   20.00

1986 World Cup Soccer
Championships, Mexico City — A431

Various soccer plays: No. 1576, 1d, From behind goal. No. 1577, 1d, Goalie from side. No. 1578, 2d, From behind goal. No. 1579, 2d, From in front of goal, vert. 3d, vert. 4d, vert. 6d, vert.

1985, Nov. 30
1576-1582 A431   Set of 7   5.00
                  10.00

Souvenir Sheet
Perf. 13

1583 A431   10d multicolored   5.00
   No. 1583 contains one 40x32mm stamp.

People's
Democratic
Republic of
Laos, 10th
Anniv. — A432

a, Woman, dove. b, Woman dancing, natl. arms.

1985, Dec. 2   *Perf. 11*
1584 A432   1d Pair, #a.-b.   3.00

Traditional Musical
Instruments — A433

#1585, 1d, Stone chimes. #1586, 1d, Large bronze drum. #1587, 2d, Flutes. #1588, 2d, Large red drum. 3d, Monochord. 4d, Moon-shaped lute. 6d, Vietnamese two-string violin.

1985, Dec. 5   *Perf. 12½x12*
1585-1591 A433   Set of 7   5.75

A434

Socialist Republic of Viet Nam, 40th Anniv.: No. 1592, 10d, Industry. No. 1593, 10d, Agriculture. 20d, Public health. 30d, Education.

1985, Dec. 15   *Perf. 11*
1592-1595 A434   Set of 4   30.00

A435

1986, Jan. 6   *Litho.*   *Perf. 11*
1596-1597 A435   50xu, 1d Set of 2   2.25
     1st Natl. Elections, 40th anniv.

A436

1986, Jan. 6
1598 A436   1d multicolored   1.50
       UN 40th anniv.

A437

Halley's Comet: No. 1599, 2d, Edmond Halley. No. 1600, 2d, Isaac Newton. 3d, Rocket, flags. 5d, Comet.

1986, Feb. 24   *Perf. 12½*
1599-1602 A437   Set of 4   5.00
    Imperf., #1599-1602   10.00

A438

Soviet Communist Party, 27th Congress: 50xu, Kremlin, map. 1d, Lenin banner.

1986, Feb. 25   *Perf. 11*
1603-1604 A438   Set of 2   2.50
    Imperf., #1603-1604   40.00

A439

1986, Mar. 1
1605 A439   1d Map of Battle of
           Xuong Giang   1.75
     Le Loi, 600th birth anniv.

1986 World
Cup Soccer
Championships,
Mexico
City — A440

Various soccer players in action: No. 1606, 1d, Viet Nam at left. No. 1607, 1d, Viet Nam at right. 2d, Viet Nam at left. No. 1609, 3d, Viet Nam at left. No. 1610, 3d, Viet Nam at right. No. 1611, 5d, Viet Nam at left. No. 1612, 5d, Viet Nam at right.

1986, Mar. 3   *Perf. 12½*
1606-1612 A440 Set of 7   5.50
    Imperf., #1606-1612   9.00
Souvenir Sheet
Perf. 13
1613 A440 10d multicolored   4.75
   No. 1613 contains one 40x32mm stamp.

1st Manned Space Flight, 25th Anniv. A441

#1614, 1d, Konstantin Tsiolkovsky. #1615, 1d, Rocket on transporter. 2d, Yuri Gagarin. #1617, 3d, Valentina Tereshkova, vert. #1618, 3d, Alexei Leonov. #1619, 5d, Apollo-Soyuz, crews. #1620, 5d, Soyuz, Salut space station. 10d, Cosmonauts, vert.

1986, Apr. 12   *Perf. 13*
1614-1620 A441 Set of 7   5.50
    Imperf., #1614-1620   10.00
Souvenir Sheet
1621 A441 10d multicolored   5.00
   No. 1621 contains one 32x40mm stamp.

Ernst Thalmann (1886-1944), German Politician — A442

1986, Apr. 16   *Perf. 11*
1622 A442 2d red & black   1.50

May Day — A443

1986, May 1
1623-1624 A443 1d, 5d, set of 2   2.25

Vancouver Expo '86 — A444

Airplanes: No. 1625, 1d, Hawker Hart. No. 1626, 1d, Curtiss Jenny. 2d, PZL-P23. No. 1628, 3d, Yakovlev Yak-11. No. 1629, 3d, Fokker Dr.1. No. 1630, 5d, Boeing P-12 (1920). No. 1631, 5d, Nieuport-Delage NiD.29C1 (1929).

1986, May 12   *Perf. 13*
1625-1631 A444 Set of 7   5.50
    Imperf., #1625-1631   8.00

Dam-Strengthening Committee, 40th Anniv. — A445

1986, May 22   *Perf. 11*
1632 A445 1d carmine   1.50

Bonsai — A446

Designs: No. 1633, 1d, Ficus glomerata. No. 1634, 1d, Ficus benjamina. 2d, Ulmus tonkinensis. No. 1636, 3d, Persica vulgaris. No. 1637, 3d, Streblus asper. No. 1638, 5d, Pinus khasya. No. 1639, 5d, Podocarpus macrophyllus. 10d, Serissa foetida, horiz.

1986, June 16   *Perf. 12x12½*
1633-1639 A446 Set of 7   6.00
    Imperf., #1633-1639   15.00
Souvenir Sheet
Perf. 12½x12
1640 A446 10d multicolored   4.75

Domestic Cats — A447

Various cats (Background colors): No. 1641, 1d, blue green. No. 1642, 1d, red. 2d, blue. No. 1644, 3d, brown. No. 1645, 3d, blue. No. 1646, 5d, violet. No. 1647, 5d, red, vert.

Perf. 13x12½, 12½x13
1986, June 16
1641-1647 A447 Set of 7   7.50
    Imperf., #1641-1647   16.00

Traditional Houses A448

Designs: No. 1648, 1d, Thai den. No. 1649, 1d, Nung. 2d, Thai trang. No. 1651, 3d, Tay. No. 1652, 3d, Hmong. No. 1653, 5d, Dao. No. 1654, 5d, Tay nguyen, vert.

Perf. 12½x12, 12x12½
1986, June 20
1648-1654 A448 Set of 7   6.00
    Imperf., #1648-1654   13.50
Souvenir Sheet
Perf. 12x12½
1655 A448 10d like #1654   3.50

Postal Service, 40th Anniv. — A449

Designs: No. 1656, 2d, Telecommunications. No. 1657, 2d, Map, letter carrier. 4d, Soldiers, Nguyen Thi Nghia. 5d, Dish antenna.

1986, Aug. 15   *Perf. 13*
1656-1659 A449 Set of 4   3.25
    Imperf., #1656-1659   22.50

A450

Birds: No. 1660, 1d, Merops apiaster. No. 1661, 1d, Cissa chinensis. 2d, Pteruthius erythropterus. No. 1663, 3d, Garrulax leucolophus. No. 1664, 3d, Psarisomus dalhousiae, horiz. No. 1665, 5d, Cyanopica cyanus, horiz. No. 1666, 5d, Motacilla alba. 10d, Copsychus malabaricus.

1986, Aug. 28   *Perf. 13*
1660-1666 A450 Set of 7   5.00
    Imperf., #1660-1666   12.00
Souvenir Sheet
Perf. 12½
1667 A450 10d multicolored   5.25
   No. 1667 contains one 32x40mm stamp. Stockholmia '86.

A451

Domestic fowl: No. 1668, 1d, Plymouth Rock. No. 1669, 1d, Maleagris gallopavo. No. 1670, 2d, Ri. No. 1671, 2d, White Plymouth rock. No. 1672, 3d, Leghorn. No. 1673, 3d, Rhode Island red. No. 1674, 3d, Rhode ri. 5d, Gray Plymouth rock hen.

1986, Sept. 15   *Perf. 12x12½*
1668-1675 A451 Set of 8   6.00
    Imperf., #1668-1675   13.50

11th Intl. Trade Unions Congress — A452

1986, Sept. 16   *Perf. 12½*
1676 A452 1d blue & red   1.50

Artifacts, Hung-Voung Period — A453

Designs: No. 1677, 1d, Seated figure, vert. No. 1678, 1d, Knife hilt in form of female figure, vert. 2d, Bronze axe. No. 1680, 3d, Bronze axe, diff. No. 1681, 3d, Bronze bowl. No. 1682, 5d, Bronze pot (round). No. 1683, 5d, Bronze vase (open top).

1986, Oct. 15   *Perf. 12x12½, 12½x12*
1677-1683 A453 Set of 7   5.00
    Imperf., #1677-1683   11.00
Souvenir Sheet
Perf. 12½x12½
1684 A453 10d like #1677   4.25

Vietnamese Red Cross, 40th Anniv. — A454

1986, Oct. 20   *Perf. 12½*
1685 A454 3d rose & greenish blue   1.50

Sailing Ships — A455

Various sail and oar-powered ships (sail colors): #1686, 1d, bl, grn, yel. #1687, 1d, org. 2d, yel. #1689, 3d, pur & red. #1690, 3d, bl. #1691, 5d, bl, brn, org. #1692, 5d, org.

Perf. 12½x12, 12½x13 (#1688)
1986, Oct. 20
1686-1692 A455 Set of 7   6.00
   No. 1688 is 38x47mm.

Butterflies — A456

Designs: No. 1693, 1d, Catopsilia scylla. No. 1694, 1d, Euploea midamus. 2d, Appias nero. No. 1696, 3d, Danaus chrysippus. No. 1697, 3d, Papilio polytes stichius. No. 1698, 5d, Euploea diocletiana. No. 1699, 5d, Charaxes polyxena.

1986, Nov. 11   *Perf. 12½*
1693-1699 A456 Set of 7   6.00
    Imperf., #1693-1699   13.00
   No. 1696 misspelled "Danais."

Vietnamese Communist Party, 6th
Congress — A457

1d, Construction projects. 2d, Natl. defense.
4d, Ho Chi Minh. 5d, Intl. cooperation.

1986, Nov. 20		Perf. 11
1700-1703	A457 Set of 4	5.50
1700a-1703a	Perf. 12½	50.00
1702b	Perf. 11x12½	27.50

Souvenir Sheet
Imperf

1704	A457 10d like #1700	4.50

Insects
A458

Designs: No. 1705, 1d, Poecilocoris
nepalensis. No. 1706, 1d, Bombus america-
norum. 2d, Romalea microptera. No. 1708, 3d,
Chalcocoris rutilans. No. 1709, 3d,
Chrysocoris sellatus. No. 1710, 5d, Paran-
threne palmi. No. 1711, 5d, Crocisa crucifera.
10d, Anabrus simplex.

1986, Nov. 30		Perf. 12½
1705-1711	A458 Set of 7	5.50
	Imperf., #1705-1711	12.50

Souvenir Sheet

1712	A458 10d multicolored	5.00

No. 1712 contains one 32x40mm stamp.

Intl. Peace
Year — A459

1986, Dec. 7		Perf. 11
1713-1714	A459 1d, 3d, set of 2	3.50

Handicrafts — A460

Designs: No. 1715, 1d, Round dish. No.
1716, 1d, Rattan handbag. 2d, Rattan foot
stool. No. 1718, 3d, Bamboo hand basket. No.
1719, 3d, Muong pannier. No. 1720, 5d, Rattan basket with shoulder straps. No. 1721, 5d,
Rattan basket with lid. 10d, Tall rattan basket.

1986, Dec. 10		Perf. 11½
1715-1721	A460 Set of 7	5.00
	Imperf., #1715-1721	9.00

Souvenir Sheet

1722	A460 10d multicolored	3.50

A461

1986, Dec. 18		Perf. 11
1723	A461 2d blue green & fawn	1.50

Natl. Resistance, 40th anniv.

A462

Endangered flora: No. 1724, 1d, Fokienia
hodginsii. No. 1725, 1d, Amentotaxus yunnanensis. 2d, Pinus kwangtungensis. No.
1727, 3d, Taxus chinensis. No. 1728, 3d,
Cupressus torulosa. No. 1729, 5d,
Ducampopinus krempfii. No. 1730, 5d, Tsuga
yunnanensis. 10d, Abies nukiangensis.

1986, Dec. 26		Perf. 12x12½
1724-1730	A462 Set of 7	5.00
	Imperf., #1724-1730	12.00

Souvenir Sheet

1731	A462 10d multicolored	4.25

Elephants — A463

#1732, 1d, Two elephants. #1733, 1d,
Female, calf. #1734, 3d, Elephant. #1735, 1d,
Elephant facing, vert. #1736, 5d, Man riding
elephant, vert. #1737, 5d, Four elephants.

1986, Dec. 30		Perf. 12½
1732-1737	A463 Set of 6	7.50
	Imperf., #1732-1737	15.00

No. 1737 is 68x27mm.

Vietnamese
Legends
A464

Designs: a, Son Tinh. b, My Nuong. c-e,
Battle between Mountain Genie and Water
Genie. f-h, Celebration.

1987, Jan. 20		Perf. 12
1738	A464 3d Strip of 8, #a.-h.	7.00
	Imperf.	13.50

New Year 1987
(Year of the
Cat) — A465

1987, Jan. 25		Perf. 11
1739	A465 3d red lilac	1.50

Natl.
Events
A466

Ho Chi Minh and: 10d, August revolution,
Aug. 19, 1945. 20d, Proclaiming independence, Sept. 9, 1945. 30d, Victory at Dien
Bien Phu, July 7, 1954. 50d, Capture of Saigon, Apr. 30, 1975.

1987, Apr. 10		Perf. 11
1740-1743	A466 Set of 4	6.25

A467

Champa art: 3d, Temple, Da Nang. 10d,
Tower, Na Trang. 15d, Temple, Da Nang (side
view). 20d, Dancing girl. 25d, Bust of woman.
30d, Girl playing flute. 40d, Dancing girl, diff.

1987, June 30		Perf. 12x12½
1744-1750	A467 Set of 7	7.25
	Imperf., #1744-1750	9.50

Souvenir Sheet

1751	A467 50d like #1749	4.00

A468

Various flowering cacti: 5d, 10d, 15d, 20d,
25d, 30d, 40d.

1987, July 10		Perf. 12½
1752-1758	A468 Set of 7	5.00

Souvenir Sheet
Perf. 13

1759	A468 50d multicolored	5.00

Global Population Reaches 5
Billion — A469

1987, July 11		Perf. 13
1760	A469 5d multicolored	1.75

World Wildlife
Fund — A470

Designs: No. 1761, 5d, Concolor gibbon.
No. 1762, 5d, Douc monkeys. 15d, Black concolor gibbon. 40d, Douc monkey.

1987, July 15		Perf. 12½
1761-1764	A470 Set of 4	10.00 3.50
	Imperf., #1761-1764	40.00

A471

Western high plateau costumes: 5d, Male
Bana. No. 1766, 20d, Female Bana. No. 1767,
20d, Female Gia Rai. No. 1768, 30d, Male Gia
Rai. No. 1769, 30d, Male Ede. 40d, Female
Ede.

1987, July 25		Perf. 12x12½
1765-1770	A471 Set of 6	6.25
	Imperf., #1765-1770	12.50

A472

1987, July 27		Perf. 13
1771	A472 5d multicolored	1.60

Day of the Invalids, 40th anniv.

Postal
Trade
Union,
40th
Anniv.
A473

Designs: 5d, Letter carrier, jet, truck, train.
30d, Switchboard operator.

1987, Aug. 30		
1772-1773	A473 Set of 2	2.10

A474

Paintings by Picasso: No. 1774, 3d, *The Three Musicians*. No. 1775, 20d, War. No. 1776, 20d, Peace. No. 1777, 30d, Child with Dove, vert. No. 1778, 30d, Portrait of Gertrude Stein, vert. 40d, Guernica. 50d, Child as Harlequin.

1987, Oct. 1　　　　　**Perf. 12½**
1774-1779　A474　Set of 6　　5.75
　Imperf., #1774-1779　　　12.00
Souvenir Sheet
1780　A474　50d multicolored　5.00
　No. 1779 is 44x27mm. No. 1780 contains one 40x32mm stamp.

Coral — A475

Designs: 5d, Epanouis. 10d, Acropora. 15d, Rhizopsammia. 20d, Acropora, diff. 25d, Alcyone, 30d, Corollum. 40d, Cristatella.

1987, Oct. 3　　　　　**Perf. 12x12½**
1781-1787　A475　Set of 7　　7.50
　Imperf., #1781-1787　　　12.50

Intl. Year for Housing for the Homeless
A476

1987, Oct. 5　　　　　**Perf. 13**
1788　A476　5d greenish bl & blk　1.50

Russian Revolution, 70th Anniv. — A477

Designs: 5d, 65d, Industry, agriculture. 20d, Lenin. 30d, Construction. 50d, Ho Chi Minh.

1987, Oct. 6　　　　　**Perf. 13**
1789-1792　A477　Set of 4　　3.50
Souvenir Sheet
1793　A477　65d multicolored　4.00

Hafnia '87
A478

Seaplanes: 5d, PBY-5. 10d, LeO H-246. 15d, Dornier DO-18. 20d, Short Sunderland. 25d, Rohrbach Rostra. 30d, Chetverikov ARK-3. 40d, CANT Z-509. 50d, Curtiss H-16.

1987, Oct. 12　　　　　**Perf. 13**
1794-1800　A478　Set of 7　　5.00
　Imperf., #1794-1800　　　12.50
Souvenir Sheet
1801　A478　50d multicolored　4.50
　No. 1801 contains one 40x32mm stamp.

Czechoslovakia-Viet Nam Friendship Agreement, 10th Anniv. — A479

10d, Handshake. 50d, Flags, buildings.

1987, Oct. 31
1802-1803　A479　Set of 2　　3.25
　Imperf., 1802-1803　　　17.50

Viet Nam-Soviet Union Cooperation — A480

Designs: 5d, Industry. 50d, Buildings.

1987, Nov. 3
1804-1805　A480　Set of 2　　3.50

Mushrooms
A481

Designs: 5d, Polyporellus squamosus. 10d, Clitocybe geotropa. 15d, Tricholoma terreum. 20d, Russula aurata. 25d, Collybia fusipes. 30d, Cortinarius violaceus. 40d, Boletus aereus.

1987, Nov. 10　　　　　**Perf. 12½**
1806-1812　A481　Set of 7　　5.00
　Imperf., #1806-1812　　　11.50

Peace
A482

1987, Nov. 30　　　　　**Perf. 13**
1813　A482　10d multicolored　1.40

Afro-Asian Solidarity Committee (AAPSO), 30th Anniv. — A483

10d, Hands, dove. 30d, Map, hands, vert.

1987, Nov. 30
1814-1815　A483　Set of 2　　2.25
　Imperf., #1814-1815　　　20.00

Victory Over US Bombing Campaign, 15th Anniv. — A484

Designs: 10d, B-52 wreckage. 30d, Children with flowers, wreckage.

1987, Dec. 26
1816-1817　A484　Set of 2　　2.75
　Imperf., #1816-1817　　　27.50

Productivity
A485

Designs: 5d, Consumer goods. 20d, Agriculture. 30d, Export products.

1987, Dec. 30
1818-1820　A485　Set of 3　　3.25

Hoang Sa, Truong Sa Islands
A486

Designs: 10d, Ship, sailor. 100d, Maps.

1988, Jan. 19
1821-1822　A486　Set of 2　　5.25

Roses — A487

Various roses: 5d, 10d, 15d, 20d, 25d, 30d, 40d.

1988, Jan. 20　　　　　**Perf. 12½**
1823-1829　A487　Set of 7　　6.00
　Imperf., #1823-1829　　　15.00
Souvenir Sheet
Perf. 13
1830　A487　50d multicolored　5.00

Tropical Fish
A488

Designs: 5d, Red betta splendens. 10d, Labeo bicolor. 15d, Puntis tetrazona. 20d, Brachydania albolineatus. 25d, Puntis conchonius. 30d, Betta splendens, diff. 40d, Botia leontei.

1988, Jan. 20　　　　　**Perf. 13**
1831-1837　A488　Set of 7　　5.00
　Imperf., #1831-1837　　　12.00

Intl. Red Cross, Red Crescent, 125th Anniv. — A489

1988, Feb. 17
1838　A489　10d multicolored　1.25

Battle of Bach Dang, 700th Anniv.
A490

80d, Fleet of ships. 200d, Battle scene.

1988, Apr. 8
1839-1840　A490　Set of 2　　5.00

Tourism
A491

5d, One-pillar pagoda. 10d, Bach Dang River. 15d, Thien Mu Tower, Hue. 20d, Ngu Hanh Mountain, Da Nang. 25d, Nha Trang beach. 30d, Pren Waterfalls. 40d, Market, Ben Thanh. 50d, Cleft Rocks, Quang Ninh.

1988, Apr. 20　　　　　**Perf. 12½x12**
1841-1847　A491　Set of 7　　5.50　5.50
　Imperf., #1841-1847　　　10.00
Souvenir Sheet
1848　A491　50d multicolored　3.50

Water Lilies — A492

Designs: 5d, Nymphaea lotus. No. 1850, 10d, Nymphaea pubescens. No. 1851, 10d, Nymphaea nouchali. No. 1852, 20d, Nymphaea rubra. No. 1853, 20d, Nymphaea gigantea. 30d, Nymphaea laydekeri. 50d, Nymphaea capensis.

1988, Apr. 20　　　　　**Perf. 12x12½**
1849-1855　A492　Set of 7　　5.75
　Imperf., #1849-1855　　　12.50

Offshore Oil Drilling — A493

1988, Apr. 28　　　　　**Perf. 13**
1856　A493　1000d multicolored　9.00

A494

Parrots: No. 1857, 10d, Ara araruna. No. 1858, 10d, Psittacula himalayana. No. 1859, 20d, Aprosmictus erythropterus. No. 1860, 20d, Ara chloroptera. No. 1861, 30d, Ara militaris. No. 1862, 30d, Psittacula alexandri. 50d, Loriculus vernalis. 80d, Ara chloroptera, diff.

1988, May 5   *Perf. 12x12½*
1857-1863 A494   Set of 7   6.00
    Imperf., #1857-1863   16.00
Souvenir Sheet
1864 A494   80d multicolored   4.00

A495   A496

Membership in Council of Mutual Economic Assistance, 10th Anniv.: 200d, Map. 300d, Headquarters building.

1988, May 29   *Perf. 13*
1865-1866 A495   Set of 2   6.50

1988, June 1
1867 A496   60d multicolored   1.40
    Vaccinations against disease.

Problems of Peace and Socialism Magazine, 30th Anniv. — A497

1988, July 20
1868 A497   20d multicolored   1.25

A498

1988, Aug. 20
1869 A498   150d multicolored   2.00
    Pres. Ton Duc Thang, birth cent.

A499

6th Vietnamese Trade Union Congress: 50d, Emblem. 100d, Workers.

1988, Aug. 28
1870-1871 A499   Set of 2   2.25

Children's Paintings A500

#1872, 10d, My Family. #1873, 10d, My House. #1874, 20d, Fishing. #1875, 20d, Flying Kites. #1876, 30d, Girl playing guitar, animals. #1877, 30d, Children in rain, vert. 50d, Girl holding dove, vert. 80d, Family, diff., vert.

Perf. 12½x12, 12x12½
1988, Sept. 25
1872-1878 A500   Set of 7   6.00   1.60
    Imperf., #1872-1878   11.50
Souvenir Sheet
Perf. 12x12½
1879 A500   80d multicolored   4.00

Hydroelectric Plants — A501

Designs: 2000d, Tri An. 3000d, Hoa Binh.

1988, Sept. 27   *Perf. 13*
1880-1881 A501   Set of 2   11.00

A502   A503

1988, Nov. 3   *Perf. 13½x13*
1882 A502   50d multicolored   2.00
    Viet Nam-USSR Friendship Agreement, 10th anniv.

1988, Dec. 27
    Designs: 100d, Fidel Castro. 300d, Flags, Vietnamese, Cuban people.
1883-1884 A503   Set of 2   2.25
    Cuban revolution, 30th anniv.

Wild Animals A504

Designs: No. 1885, 10d, Bos banteng. No. 1886, 10d, Bos gaurus. No. 1887, 20d, Axis porcinus. No. 1888, 20d, Tapirus indicus. No. 1889, 30d, Capricornis sumatrensis. No. 1890, 30d, Sus scrofa. 50d, Bubalus bubalus. 80d, Rhinoceros sodaicus.

1988, Dec. 30   *Perf. 12½*
1885-1891 A504   Set of 7   5.00
    Imperf., #1885-1891   15.00
Souvenir Sheet
1892 A504   80d multicolored   7.25
    Imperf.   20.00

Locomotives — A505

Designs: No. 1893, 20d, Kiha 80, Japan. No. 1894, 20d, LRC, Canada. No. 1895, 20d, Hitachi, Japan. No. 1896, 20d, BL-85, USSR. No. 1897, 30d, RC-1, Sweden. No. 1898, 30d, DR-1A, USSR. 50d, T3-136, USSR. 80d, SCNF Z6400.

1988, Dec. 30   *Perf. 13*
1893-1899 A505   Set of 7   5.00
    Imperf., #1893-1899   12.50
Souvenir Sheet
1900 A505   80d multicolored   4.75
    Imperf.   7.00
    No. 1900 contains one 40x32mm stamp.

A506

Fruits, vegetables: No. 1901, 10d, Lagenaria siceraria. No. 1902, 10d, Momordica charantia. No. 1903, 20d, Solanum melongena. No. 1904, 20d, Cucurbita moschata. No. 1905, 30d, Luffa cylindrica. No. 1906, 30d, Benincasa hispida. 50d, Lycopercicon esculentum.

1988, Dec. 30   *Perf. 12x12½*
1901-1907 A506   Set of 7   5.50
    Imperf., #1901-1907   10.50

A507

Various project spacecraft: No. 1908, 10d, Mars. No. 1909, 10d, Moon. No. 1910, 20d, Saturn. No. 1911, 20d, Inter-planetary. No. 1912, 30d, Venus. No. 1913, 30d, Earth orbital space station. 50d, Cosmos house. 80d, Lander docking with orbiter.

1988, Dec. 30   *Perf. 13*
1908-1914 A507   Set of 7   4.75
    Imperf., #1908-1914   17.00
Souvenir Sheet
1915 A507   80d multicolored   4.75
    Cosmos Day.
    No. 1915 contains one 32x40mm stamp.

Shells A508

Designs: No. 1916, 10d, Conus miles. No. 1917, 10d, Strombus lentiginosus. No. 1918, 20d, Nautilus. No. 1919, 20d, Bursa rana. No. 1920, 30d, Turbo petholatus. No. 1921, 30d, Oliva erythros. 50d, Mitra eriscopalis. 80d, Tonna tessellata.

1988, Dec. 30   *Perf. 12½x12*
1916-1922 A508   Set of 7   5.75
    Imperf., #1916-1922   13.50
Souvenir Sheet
1923 A508   80d multicolored   5.00

India '89 — A509

Butterflies: No. 1924, 50d, Anaea echemus. No. 1925, 50d, Ascia monuste. No. 1926, 50d, Juniona evarete. No. 1927, 100d, Phoebis avellaneda. No. 1928, 100d, Eurema proterpia. 200d, Papilio palamedes. 300d, Danaus plexippus. 400d, Parides gundlachiamus.

1989, Jan. 7   *Perf. 12½*
1924-1930 A509   Set of 7   6.50
    Imperf., #1924-1930   11.00
Souvenir Sheet
1931 A509   400d multicolored   4.75
    No. 1931 contains one 40x32mm stamp. Nos. 1924-1930 printed with se-tenant label.

Natl. Day of Cambodia, 10th Anniv. — A510

Designs: 100d, Soldiers, women working in field. 500d, Viet Nam-Cambodia friendship.

1989, Jan. 7   *Perf. 13x13½*
1932-1933 A510   Set of 2   2.75
    Imperf., #1932-1933   21.00

India '89 — A511

Designs: No. 1934, 100d, Science, technology. No. 1935, 100d, Agriculture, industry. 300d, Asoka pillar. 600d, Nehru (1889-1964).

1989, Jan. 20   *Perf. 13*
1934-1937 A511   Set of 4   3.00

Battle of Dong Da, Bicent. — A512

Designs: 100d, Festival. 1000d, Quang Trung defeating Qing invaders.

1989, Feb. 10   *Perf. 13*
1938-1939 A512   Set of 2   3.00

Inter-Parliamentary Union, Cent. — A513

Designs: 100d, Vietnamese membership, 10th anniv. 200d, Centennial emblem.

1989, Mar. 1
1940-1941 A513   Set of 2   2.25

Fishing Boats — A513a

Boats from: No. 1942, 10d, Quang Nam. No. 1943, 10d, Quang Tri. No. 1944, 20d, Thua Thien. No. 1945, 20d, Da Nang (sail furled). No. 1946, 30d, Da Nang (under sail). No. 1947, 30d, Quang Tri (under sail). 50d, Hue.

1989, Mar. 20　　　　　　**Perf. 12½x12**
1942-1948 A513a Set of 7　　5.50
　　Imperf., #1942-1948　　12.00

Helicopters — A514

#1949, 10d, Kamov KA-26. #1950, 10d, Boeing Vertol 234. #1951, 20d, Mil MI-10(V10). #1952, 20d, MBB BO 105. #1953, 30d, Kawasaki Hughes 369HS. #1954, 30d, Bell 206B Jet Ranger. 50d, Mil MI-8. 80d, Puma SA330.

1989, Apr. 12　　　　　　**Perf. 12½**
1949-1955 A514 Set of 7　　4.75
　　Imperf., #1949-1955　　14.00
Souvenir Sheet
1956 A514 80d multicolored　　3.00
　　Imperf.　　10.00
No. 1956 contains one 40x32mm stamp.

Bicycles
A515

#1957, 10d, Bowden Spacelander. #1958, 10d, Rabasa Derbi. #1959, 20d, Huffy. #1960, 20d, Rabasa Derbi. #1961, 30d, VMX-PL. #1962, 30d, Premier. 50d, Columbia RX5.

1989, May 1　　　　　　**Perf. 13**
1957-1963 A515 Set of 7　　5.50
　　Imperf., #1957-1963　　10.00

Turtles — A516

No. 1964, 10d, Cuora trifasciata. No. 1965, 10d, Testudo elegans. No. 1966, 20d, Eretmochelys imbricata. No. 1967, 20d, Platysternon megacephalum. No. 1968, 30d, Dermochelys coriacea. No. 1969, 30d, Chelonia mydas. 50d, Caretta caretta. 80d, Caretta caretta, diff.

1989, May 1　　　　　　**Perf. 12½**
1964-1970 A516 Set of 7　　7.00
　　Imperf., #1964-1970　　13.50
Souvenir Sheet
1971 A516 80d multicolored　　6.00
　　Imperf.　　17.00
Finlandia '88 (#1971).

Poisonous Snakes — A517

Designs: No. 1972, 10d, Trimeresurus popeorum. No. 1973, 10d, Trimeresurus mucrosquamatus. No. 1974, 20d, Bungarus fasciatus. No. 1975, 20d, Bungarus candidus. No. 1976, 30d, Calliophis maclellandii. No. 1977, 30d, Ancistrodon acutus. 50d, Ophiophagus hannah, vert.

1989, May 1
1972-1978 A517 Set of 7　　5.75
　　Imperf., #1972-1978　　13.50

Pairs Figure Skating — A518

Various figure skaters: No. 1979, 10d, "Viet Nam" at left. No. 1980, 10d, "Viet Nam" at right. No. 1981, 20d, "Viet Nam" at left. No. 1982, 20d, "Viet Nam" at right, horiz. No. 1983, 30d, "Viet Nam" at left. No. 1984, 30d, "Viet Nam" at right, horiz. 50d, "Viet Nam" at left, horiz.

1989, May 29　　　　　　**Perf. 13**
1979-1985 A518 Set of 7　　5.00
　　Imperf., #1979-1985　　11.00
Souvenir Sheet
With Gum
1986 A518 80d multi, horiz.　　4.25
No. 1986 contains one 40x32mm stamp.

A519　　　　　　A520

1989, June 5　　　　　　**Perf. 13**
1987 A519 100d buff　　1.40
Post & Telecommunications.

1989, July 1　　　　　　**Perf. 12**
Ceramics, Li-Tran Period: 50d, Pitcher. No. 1989, 100d, Dowl. No. 1990, 100d, Jug. 200d, Jug, diff. 300d, Vase.

1988-1992 A520 Set of 5　　3.75
　　Imperf., #1988-1992　　10.00

Legend of Giong
A521

Designs: 50d, Mother nursing infant. No. 1994, 100d, Giong meets imperial messenger. No. 1995, 100d, Giong riding iron horse, people following. 200d, Giong pulling up bamboo trees. 300d, Giong flying into sky.

1989, July 1　　　　　　**Perf. 12½x12**
1993-1997 A521 Set of 5　　3.50
　　Imperf., #1993-1997　　7.25

French Revolution, Bicent. — A522

Designs: 100d, Emblem. 500d, Liberty leading the people, after Delacroix.

1989, July 14　　　　　　**Perf. 13½x13**
1998-1999 A522 Set of 2　　2.50

PHILEXFRANCE '89 — A523

Paintings: No. 2000, 50d, Oath of the Tennis Court, by David. No. 2001, 50d, Capture of Louis XVI, horiz. No. 2002, 50d, Liberty, Equality, Fraternity, horiz. No. 2003, 100d, Storming the Bastille. No. 2004, 100d, Death of Marat, by David. 200d, Child and Rabbit, by Prud'hon. 300d, Slave Market, by Gerome, horiz. 400d, Liberty Leading the People, by Delacroix.

1989, July 14　　　　　　**Perf. 13**
2000-2006 A523 Set of 7　　5.00
　　Imperf., #2000-2006　　10.00
Souvenir Sheet
2007 A523 400d multicolored　　3.75
No. 2007 contains one 33x44mm stamp.

1989 World Cup Soccer
Championships, Italy — A524

Soccer plays: No. 2008, 50d, Dribbling. No. 2009, 50d, Tackling. No. 2010, 50d, Goalie. No. 2011, 100d, Dribbling, diff. No. 2012, 100d, Dribbling, diff., vert. 200d, Preparing to kick, vert. 300d, Heading ball, vert. 400d, Heading ball, diff., vert.

Perf. 13x12½, 12½x13
1989, Aug. 27
2008-2014 A524 Set of 7　　4.50
　　Imperf., #2008-2014　　11.00
Souvenir Sheet
Perf. 13
2015 A524 400d multicolored　　3.50
No. 2015 contains one 32x40mm stamp.

Dogs
A525

#2016, 50d, Dachshund. #2017, 50d, Beagle. #2018, 50d, English setter, vert. #2019, 100d, German short-haired pointer, vert. #2020, 100d, Basset hounds. 200d, German sheperd, vert. 300d, Beagle, diff.

1989, Aug. 20　　　　　　**Perf. 12½**
2016-2022 A525 Set of 7　　5.50
　　Imperf., #2016-2022　　10.00
No. 2020 is 68x28mm.

Horses
A526

#2023, 50d, Tennessee Walking. #2024, 50d, Appaloosa. #2025, 50d, Tersky. #2025, 100d, Kladruber. #2026, 100d, Welsh cob. 200d, Pinto. 300d, Pony and bridle.

1989, Sept. 23　　　　　　**Perf. 13**
2023-2029 A526 Set of 7　　5.50
　　Imperf., #2023-2029　　12.50
No. 2029 is 68x28mm.

Flowers — A527

No. 2030, 50d, Paphiopedilum siamense. No. 2031, 50d, Fuchsia fulgens. No. 2032, 100d, Hemerocallis fulva. No. 2033, 100d, Gloriosa superba. 200d, Strelitzia reginae. 300d, Iris.

1989, Sept. 23　　　　　　**Perf. 12½**
2030-2035 A527 Set of 6　　5.50　2.00
　　Imperf., #2030-2035　　11.50

German Democratic Republic, 40th Anniv. — A528

1989, Oct. 7　　　　　　**Perf. 13**
2036 A528 200d multicolored　　1.40

Immunization Campaign — A529

#2037, Woman receiving vaccination. #2038, Child receiving oral vaccine. #2039, Clinic.

1989, Oct. 20
2037-2039 A529 100d Set of 3　　2.75

Drawings of Everyday Life, 19th Cent. — A530

Designs: 50d, Assembling plow. No. 2041, 100d, Harrowing. No. 2042, 100d, Irrigating. 200d, Fertilizing. 300d, Harvesting.

1989, Oct. 28   *Perf. 12x12½*
2040-2044 A530 Set of 5   3.75 2.40
   Imperf. #2040-2044   8.50

Horse Paintings,
by Xu Beihong
(1895-1953)
A531

Various horses: 100d, 200d, 300d, 500d horiz., 800d, 1000d, 1500d.

1989, Dec. 22   *Perf. 13*
2045-2051 A531 Set of 7   5.75
   Imperf., #2045-2051   9.00

Imperf

Size: 117x72mm

2052 A531 2000d multicolored   7.50
   Imperf.   14.00

Vietnamese Communist Party, 60th
Anniv. — A532

Designs: 100d, Ho Chi Minh, tank. 500d, Workers, refinery, field.

1990, Feb. 3   *Litho.*   *Perf. 13*
2053-2054 A532 Set of 2   3.50
   Imperf., #2053-2054   6.50

Ducks — A533

a, 100d, Anas platyrhynchos hybrid. b, 300d, Anas penelope. c, 500d, Anas platyrhynchos. d, 1000d, Anas erythrorhyncha. e, 2000d, Anas platyrhynchos, diff. f, 3000d, Anas undulata.

1990, Feb. 15
2055 A533 Block of 6, #a.-f.   4.75

Trucks
A534

100d, Mack. 200d, Volvo F89. 300d, Tatra 915 S1. 500d, Hino KZ30000. 1000d, Iveco. 2000d, Leyland DAF Super Comet. 3000d, Kamaz 53212.

1990, Feb. 20
2056-2062 A534 Set of 7   4.00 1.50
   Imperf., #2056-2062   6.25

Architectural Sites, Hue — A535

#2063, 100d, Tu Duc's Mausoleum. #2064, 100d, Hien Nhon Arch. 200d, Ngo Mon Gate. 300d, Thien Mu Temple. 400d, Palace, gateway.

1990, Feb. 20   *Perf. 12½x12*
2063-2066 A535 Set of 4   3.25
   Souvenir Sheet
2067 A535 400d multicolored   3.75

Goldfish — A536

100d, Bulging-eyed, horiz. 300d, Telescopic-eyed, horiz. 500d, Red-headed, horiz. 1000d, Double-tailed. 2000d, Rainbow. 3000d, Comet.

1990, Mar. 20   *Perf. 13*
2068-2073 A536 Set of 6   4.50 1.25
   Imperf., #2068-2073   7.50

Paintings
A537

London '90: 100d, Antonia Zarate, by Goya. 200d, Girl Holding a Paper Fan, by Renoir. 300d, Janet Grizel, by John Russell. 500d, Love Untieing the Belt of Beauty, by Sir Joshua Reynolds. 1000d, Portrait of a Woman, by George Romney. 2000d, Portrait of Madame Ginoux, by Van Gogh. 3000d, Woman in Blue, by Gainsborough. 3500d, Woman in a Straw Hat, by Van Gogh.

1990, Apr. 10
2074-2080 A537 Set of 7   4.50 1.50
   Imperf., #2074-2080   9.00
   Souvenir Sheet
2081 A537 3500d multicolored   3.50 1.60

1990 World Cup Soccer
Championships, Italy — A538

Various soccer players in action: 100d, 200d, 300d, 500d, 1000d, 2000d, 3000d.

1990, Apr. 19
2082-2088 A538 Set of 7   4.00
   Imperf., #2082-2088   20.00
   Souvenir Sheet
2089 A538 3500d multicolored   3.25
No. 2089 contains one 32x40mm stamp. For overprints see Nos. 2189-2196.

Cats — A539

Various cats: 100d, horiz., 200d, 300d, horiz., 500d, 1000d, horiz., 2000d, 3000d.

1990, May 5
2090-2096 A539 Set of 7   5.00
   Souvenir Sheet
2097 A539 3500d multicolored   4.00
   Imperf.   5.00
No. 2097 contains one 44x33mm stamp. Belgica '90 (#2097).

Dogs — A540

Various dogs: 100d, 200d, 300d, 500d, 1000d, 2000d, 3000d.

1990, May 15
2098-2104 A540 Set of 7   4.25
   Souvenir Sheet
2105 A540 3500d Collies   3.25
   Imperf.   7.50
New Zealand '90.

Ho Chi Minh
(1890-1969)
A541

Ho Chi Minh and: 100d, Lenin. 300d, Soldiers waving flag. 500d, Hand holding rifle, dove. 1000d, Map. 2000d, Child, dove. 3000d, Stylized globe. 3500d, Flag.

1990, May 17   *Perf. 13*
2106-2111 A541 Set of 6   3.75
   Imperf., #2106-2111   6.00
   Souvenir Sheet
   Perf. 12½x13
2112 A541 3500d multicolored   4.25
No. 2112 contains one 33x44mm stamp.

Dinosaurs — A542

100d, Gorgosaurus. 500d, Ceratosaurus. 1000d, Ankylosaurus. 2000d, Ankylosaurus, diff. 3000d, Edaphosaurus.

1990, June 1   *Perf. 13*
2113-2117 A542 Set of 5   5.25 2.25

Columbus' Discovery of America,
500th Anniv. — A543

Designs: 50d, Fleet. No. 2119, 100d, Columbus presenting gifts to natives. No. 2120, 100d, Columbus, priest at Rabida. No. 2121, 100d, Columbus at Court of Ferdinand, Isabella. No. 2122, 200d, Map of Caribbean. No. 2123, 200d, Columbus, arms. 300d, Map of Atlantic. 500d, Teotihuacan pot.

1990, June 10   *Perf. 12½*
2118-2124 A543 Set of 7   5.75
   Imperf. #2118-2124   20.00
   Souvenir Sheet
2125 A543 500d multicolored   3.50
No. 2125 contains one 40x32mm stamp. For overprints see Nos. 2313-2320.

Sailing
Ships
A544

Designs: 100d, Viking longship. 500d, Caravel. No. 2128, 1000d, Carrack, 14th-15th cent. No. 2129, 1000d, Flit. No. 2130, 1000d, Carrack, 15th cent., vert. 2000d, Galleon, vert. 3000d, Galleon, diff. 4200d, Egyptian barge.

1990, June 10   *Perf. 13*
2126-2132 A544 Set of 7   5.75
   Imperf., #2126-2132   10.50
   Souvenir Sheet
   Perf. 13x12½
2133 A544 4200d multicolored   5.25
No. 2133 contains one 44x33mm stamp.

11th Asian
Games,
Beijing — A545

Designs: 100d, High jump. 200d, Basketball. 300d, Table tennis. 500d, Volleyball. 1000d, Rhythmic gymnastics. 2000d, Tennis. 3000d, Judo. 3500d, Hurdles.

1990, June 20   *Perf. 13*
2134-2140 A545 Set of 7   5.00 3.25
   Imperf., #2134-2140   12.00
   Souvenir Sheet
   Perf. 12½x13
2141 A545 3500d multicolored   3.75
No. 2141 contains one 33x44mm stamp.

Nos. 1180-1187 Ovptd. in Red, Green
and Black

1990, June 22   *Perf. 12*
2142-2149 A352 Set of 8   10.00
1990 World Cup Soccer Championships, Italy.

Nos. 1323-1330
Ovptd. in Black
and Red

1990, June 22   *Perf. 12x12½*
2150-2157 A385 Set of 8   10.00
Tourism.

Modern Ships
A546

100d, Freighter. 300d, Container ship. 500d, Cruise ship. 1000d, Liquified natural gas tanker. 2000d, Ro-Ro ship. 3000d, Ferry.

1990, July 20   **Perf. 13**
2158-2163　A546　Set of 6　　5.00
　　Imperf., #2158-2163　　7.50

Post & Telecommunications Dept., 45th Anniv. — A547

Designs: 100d, Dove, ship, plane. 1000d, Satellite antenna.

1990, Aug. 15   **Perf. 13x13½**
2164-2165　A547　Set of 2　　2.00
　　Imperf., #2164-2165　　4.00

Socialist Republic of Viet Nam, 45th Anniv. — A548

Designs: 100d, Flag, construction projects. 500d, Map, tank, soldiers. 1000d, "VI," ship, communications network. 3000d, Workers, oil rigs. 3500d, Ho Chi Minh.

1990, Sept. 1   **Perf. 13**
2166-2169　A548　Set of 4　　4.50
　　Imperf., #2166-2169　　6.50
Souvenir Sheet
Perf. 12½x13
2170　A548　3500d multicolored　　3.00
　　No. 2170 contains one 33x44mm stamp. Sixth Vietnamese Communist Party Congress (#2168).

Airships
A549

Designs: 100d, Henry Gifford, 1871. 200d, Lebandy, 1910. 300d, Graf Zeppelin. 500d, R-101, 1930. 1000d, Soviet, 1936. 3000d, Tissandier, 1883. 3500d, US Navy. 3500d, "Zodiac," 1931.

1990, Sept. 10   **Perf. 12½**
2171-2177　A549　Set of 7　　5.00
　　Imperf., #2171-2177　　9.50
Souvenir Sheet
2178　A549　3500d multicolored　　2.50 1.00
　　No. 2178 contains one 40x32mm stamp. Helvetia '90, Stamp World London '90.

Fable of Thach Sanh — A550

Designs: a, 100d, Thach Sanh carrying bundles of wood. b, 300d, Ly Thong. c, 500d, Thach Sanh killing python. d, 1000d, Thach Sanh shooting arrow at eagle. e, 2000d, Thach Sanh in prison. f, 3000d, Thach Sanh, princess.

1990, Sept. 20   **Perf. 13**
2179　A550　Block of 6, #a.-f.　　6.00
　　Imperf.　　8.00

Asian-Pacific Postal Training Center, 20th Anniv. — A551

1990, Sept. 25
2180　A551　150d multicolored　　1.25

Nos. 571-578 Ovptd. with Red Cross in Red and "FOR THE FUTURE GENERATION" in various Languages in Black

Language: No. 2181, 12xu, Japanese. No. 2182, 12xu, Italian. No. 2183, 20xu, German. No. 2184, 20xu, Vietnamese. 30xu, English. 40xu, Russian. 50xu, French. 60xu, Spanish.

1990, Sept. 25   **Perf. 12**
2181-2188　A211　Set of 8　　10.00
　　Position of overprint varies.
　　Use of these stamps at stated face value is unlikely.

Nos. 2082-2089 Ovptd.

1990, Sept. 25   **Perf. 13**
2189-2195　A538　Set of 7　　10.00
Souvenir Sheet
2196　A538　3500d multicolored　　8.00

Vietnamese Women's Federation, 60th Anniv. — A552

Designs: 100d, Woman carrying rifle. 500d, Women working in field, laboratory.

1990, Oct. 10
2197-2198　A552　Set of 2　　2.50
　　Imperf., #2197-2198　　5.00

Correggio (1494-1534), Painter — A553

Various paintings of the Madonna and Child: No. 2199, 50xu, shown. No. 2200, 50xu, diff. 1d, 2d, 3d, 5d, 6d.

1990, Nov. 13   **Perf. 12½**
2199-2205　A553　Set of 7　　5.50
Souvenir Sheet
2206　A553　10d multicolored　　5.50
　　No. 2206 contains one 32x40mm stamp. Dated "1984." Use of these stamps at stated face value is unlikely.

Protection of Forests — A554

Designs: 200d, Water conservation, healthy forest. 1000d, SOS, prevent forest fires.

1990, Nov. 15   **Perf. 13**
2207-2208　A554　Set of 2　　3.50
　　Imperf., #2207-2208　　7.00

A555

Poisonous mushrooms: 200d, Amanita pantherina. 300d, Amanita phalloides. 1000d, Amanita virosa. 1500d, Amanita muscaria. 2000d, Russula emetica. 3000d, Boletus satanas.

1991, Jan. 21
2209-2214　A555　Set of 6　　5.50
　　Imperf., #2209-2214　　9.50

A555a

1992 Summer Olympics, Barcelona: 200d, Sailing. 300d, Boxing. 400d, Cycling. 1000d, High jump. 2000d, Equestrian. No. 2220, 3000d, Judo. No. 2221, 3000d, Wrestling, horiz. 5000d, Soccer, horiz.

1991, Jan. 31
2215-2221　A555a　Set of 7　　4.00
　　Imperf., #2215-2221　　7.00
Souvenir Sheet
2222　A555a　5000d multicolored　　3.00
　　Imperf., #2222　　5.00
　　No. 2222 contains one 44x33mm stamp.

Nguyen Binh Khiem (1491-1585), Writer — A556

1991, Feb. 15
2223　A556　200d multicolored　　1.50
　　Imperf.　　3.25

Discovery of America, 500th Anniv. — A557

Sailing ships: 200d, Marisiliana. No. 2225, 400d, Venetian. No. 2226, 400d, Cromster, vert. No. 2227, 2000d, Nina. No. 2228, 2000d, Pinta. 3000d, Howker, vert. 5000d, Santa Maria.
6500d, Portrait of Columbus.

1991, Feb. 22
2224-2230　A557　Set of 7　　5.75
　　Imperf., #2224-2230　　6.00
Souvenir Sheet
2231　A557　6500d multicolored　　3.50
　　Imperf.　　7.00

Golden Heart Charity — A558

Women wearing traditional costumes: 200d, 500d, 1000d, 5000d.

1991, Feb. 26
2232-2235　A558　Set of 4　　3.75
　　Imperf., #2232-2235　　7.50

Sharks A559

Designs: 200d, Carcharhinus melanopterus. 300d, Carcharhinus amblyrhynchos. 400d, Triakis semifasciata. 1000d, Sphyrna mokarran. 2000d, Triaenodon obesus. No. 2241, 3000d, Carcharias taurus. No. 2242, 3000d, Carcharhinus leucas.

1991, Apr. 6
2236-2242　A559　Set of 7　　9.00
　　Imperf., #2236-2242　　13.00

Endangered Birds — A560

World Wildlife Fund: 200d, Grus vipio. 300d, Grus antigone chick, vert. 400d, Grus japonensis, vert. 1000d, Grus antigone, adults, vert. 2000d, Grus nigricollis, vert. No. 2248, 3000d, Balearica regulorum, vert. No. 2249, 3000d, Bugeranus leucogerranus.

1991, Apr. 20
2243-2249　A560　Set of 7　　10.00 3.50
　　Imperf., #2243-2249　　20.00

Shellfish A561

Designs: 200d, 1000d, 2000d, Palinurus, all diff. 300d, Alpheus bellulus. 400d, Periclemenes brevicarpalis. No. 2255, 3000d, Astacus. No. 2256, 3000d, Palinurus, diff.

1991, Apr. 20
2250-2256 A561 Set of 7   5.00 1.75
   Imperf., #2250-2256   10.00

Young Pioneers, 50th Anniv. — A562

Designs: 200d, shown. 400d, UN Convention on Children's Rights.

1991, May 15
2257-2258 A562 Set of 2   2.50
   Imperf., #2257-2258   4.50

Rally Cars A563

#2259, 400d, Lada. #2260, 400d, Nissan. 500d, Ford Sierra RS Cosworth. 1000d, Suzuki. 2000d, Mazda 323 4WD. #2264, 3000d, Lancia. #2265, 3000d, Peugeot. 5000d, Peugeot 405.

1991, May 24
2259-2265 A563 Set of 7   5.50
   Imperf., #2259-2265   6.50

Souvenir Sheet
2266 A563 5000d multicolored   4.00
   Imperf.   5.00

No. 2266 contains one 44x33mm stamp.

Locomotives — A564

#2267, 400d, Puffing Billy, 1811, vert. #2268, 400d, Fusee, 1829, vert. 500d, Stevens, 1825. 1000d, Crampton #80, 1852. 2000d, Locomotion, 1825. #2272, 3000d, Saint-Lo, 1844. #2273, 3000d, Coutances, 1855. 5000d, Atlantic, 1843.

1991, May 25
2267-2273 A564 Set of 7   5.50
   Imperf., #2267-2273   8.00

Souvenir Sheet
2274 A564 5000d multicolored   3.75
   Imperf.   6.50

No. 2274 contains one 33x44mm stamp.

Frogs A565

World Wildlife Fund: 200d, Dendrobates leucomelas. 400d, Rana esculenta. 500d, Mantella aurantiaca. 1000d, Dendrobates tinctorius. 2000d, Hyla halowelli. No. 2280, 3000d, Agalychnis callidryas. No. 2281, 3000d, Hyla aurea.

1991, June 12
2275-2281 A565 Set of 7   10.00 3.50
   Imperf., #2275-2281   25.00

7th Vietnamese Communist Party Congress A566

Designs: 200d, Ho Chi Minh, buildings. 300d, Workers. 400d, Mother, children.

1991, June
2282-2284 A566 Set of 3   1.50
   Imperf., #2282-2284   4.50

Vietnamese Communist Party, 60th Anniv. — A566a

1991, June 24   Litho.   Perf. 13
2284A A566a 100d red   2.00

1992 Winter Olympics, Albertville A567

Designs: 200d, Speed skating, vert. 300d, Free-style skiing, vert. 400d, Bobsled. 1000d, Biathlon. 2000d, Slalom skiing. No. 2290, 3000d, Cross-country skiing, vert. No. 2291, 3000d, Ice dancing, vert. 5000d, Hockey, vert.

1991, July 15
2285-2291 A567 Set of 7   5.50
   Imperf., #2285-2291   5.50

Souvenir Sheet
2292 A567 5000d multicolored   2.50
   Imperf.   5.00

No. 2292 contains one 33x44mm stamp.

Prehistoric Animals — A568

Designs: a, 200d, Arsinoitherium zitteli. b, 500d, Elephas primigenius. c, 1000d, Baluchitherium. d, 2000d, Deinotherium giganteum. e, 3000d, Brontops. f, 3000d, Uinatherium.

1991, July 26
2293 A568 Block of 6, #a.-f.   4.50
   Imperf., #2293   6.50

A569

Golden Heart Charity: 200d, Eye, folded hands. 3000d, Tennis player in wheelchair.

1991, July 27
2294-2295 A569 Set of 2   2.00

A570

Chess pieces: 200d, Pawn. 300d, Knight. 1000d, Rook. 2000d, Queen. No. 2300, 3000d, Bishop. No. 2301, 3000d, King. 5000d, Pawn, Knight, King.

1991, Aug. 20
2296-2301 A570 Set of 6   5.50
   Imperf., #2296-2301   6.75

Souvenir Sheet
2302 A570 5000d multicolored   3.25
   Imperf.   5.00

No. 2302 contains one 33x44mm stamp.

PHILANIPPON '91 — A571

Butterflies: 200d, Attacus atlas. 400d, Morpho cypris. 500d, Troides rotschildi. No. 2306, 1000d, Papilio demetrius. No. 2307, 1000d, Vanessa atalanta. 3000d, Papilio weiskei. 5000d, Apatura ilia substituta. 5500d, Heliconius melpomene.

1991, Aug. 29
2303-2309 A571 Set of 7   4.50
   Imperf., #2303-2309   5.00

Souvenir Sheet
2310 A571 5500d multicolored   4.50
   Imperf.   7.00

No. 2310 contains one 44x33mm stamp.

Post and Telecommunications Research Institute, 25th Anniv. — A572

1991, Aug.
2311 A572 200d multicolored   1.40
   Imperf.   4.50

Souvenir Sheet
2312 A572 3500d Communications network, horiz.   2.50
   Imperf.   5.00

No. 2312 contains one 44x33mm stamp.

Nos. 2118-2125 Ovptd. in Red

1992, Jan. 15   Perf. 12½
2313-2319 A543 Set of 7   7.50

Souvenir Sheet
2320 A543 500d multicolored   4.50

7th Vietnamese Communist Party Congress A574

200d, Workers, industry, agriculture, atomic energy symbol. 2000d, Map of Asia, hands clasped.

1992, Feb. 3   Litho.   Perf. 13
2322-2323 A574 Set of 2   2.25

1992 Winter Olympics, Albertville — A575

Designs: 200d, Biathlon. 2000d, Hockey. 4000d, Slalom skiing. 5000d, Pairs figure skating. 6000d, Downhill skiing.

1992, Feb. 5
2324-2328 A575 Set of 5   4.50

Miniature Sheet

Columbus' Discovery of America, 500th Anniv. — A576

Designs: a, 4000d, Columbus, flag. b, 6000d, Columbus, natives. c, 8000d, Aboard ship. d, 3000d, Two sailing ships. e, 400d, Columbus' fleet setting sail.
11,000d, Columbus with Ferdinand and Isabella.

1992, Feb. 12
2329 A576 #a.-f. + label   4.25
   Imperf

Size: 102x70mm
2330 A576 11,000d multicolored   3.75

Airplanes — A577

Designs: 400d, Tupolev TU-154M. 500d, Concorde. 1000d, Airbus A-320. 3000d, Airbus A340-300. 4000d, Boeing Dash 8-400. 5000d, Boeing 747-200. 6000d, McDonnell-Douglas MD-11CF.

1992, Mar. 6   Perf. 13
2331-2337 A577 Set of 7   4.25

A578

Intl. Decade for Natural Disaster Reduction: 400d, Storm system, weather forecasting equipment. 4000d, Man taking water depth readings.

1992, Mar. 23
2338-2339 A578 Set of 2   2.00

A579

1992 Summer Olympics, Barcelona: 400d, Archery. 600d, Volleyball. 1000d, Wrestling. 3000d, Fencing. 4000d, Running. 5000d, Weight lifting. 6000d, Field hockey. 10,000d, Basketball.

1992, Mar. 28
2340-2346 A579 Set of 7   3.75
Souvenir Sheet
2347 A579 10,000d multicolored   3.00
No. 2347 contains one 32x43mm stamp.

Motorcycles — A580

Designs: 400d, 5000d, Suzuki 500F. 500d, Honda CBR 600F. 1000d, Honda HRC 500F. 3000d, Kawasaki 250F, vert. 4000d, Suzuki RM 250F, vert. 6000d, BMW 1000F. 10,000d, Suzuki RM 250F, diff.

1992, Apr. 8
2348-2354 A580 Set of 7   4.50
Souvenir Sheet
2355 A580 10,000d multicolored   3.50
No. 2355 contains one 33x44mm stamp.

Intl. Space Year A581

400d, Space shuttle launch, vert. 500d, Launch of shuttle Columbia, vert. 3000d, Columbia in space. 4000d, Space station, shuttle Hermes. 5000d, Shuttle Hermes. 6000d, Astronauts, Hubble space telescope, vert.

1992, Apr. 12
2356-2361 A581 Set of 6   4.25

Saigon Post Office, Cent. A582

200d, Main entrance. 10,000d, Facade.

1992, Apr. 30   *Perf. 13*
2362 A582 200d multicolored   1.00
Souvenir Sheet
Perf. 13½
2363 A582 10,000d multicolored   3.00
No. 2363 contains one 43x32mm stamp.

European Cup Soccer Championships A583

Various soccer players in action: 200d, 2000d, 4000d, 5000d, 6000d.

1992, May 14   *Perf. 13*
2364-2368 A583 Set of 5   5.00
Souvenir Sheet
2369 A583 9000d multicolored   3.50
No. 2369 contains one 44x33mm stamp.

Spanish Paintings A584

Designs: 400d, Childhood of the Virgin, by Zurbaran. 500d, Woman with a Jug, by Murillo. 1000d, Portrait of Maria Aptrickaia, by Velazquez. 3000d, Holy Family with St. Katherine, by de Ribera. 4000d, Madonna and Child with Saints Agnes and Thekla, by El Greco. 5000d, Woman with a Jug, by Goya. 6000d, The Naked Maja, by Goya, horiz. 10,000d, Three Women, by Picasso, horiz.

1992, May 30
2370-2376 A584 Set of 7   4.25
Souvenir Sheet
2377 A584 10,000d multicolored   3.50
No. 2377 contains one 44x33mm stamp. Expo '92, Seville (#2377).

UN Conference on Environmental Protection, 20th Anniv. — A585

Designs: 200d, Clean, polluted water. 4000d, Graph comparing current development pattern with environmentally safe pattern.

1992, June 1
2378-2379 A585 Set of 2   2.00

A586   Flowers — A587

Lighthouses: 200d, Cu Lao Xanh. 3000d, Can Gio. 5000d, Vung Tau. 6000d, Long Chau.

1992, June 14   *Perf. 13½x13*
2380-2383 A586 Set of 4   10.00
Genoa '92.

1992, June 28   *Perf. 13*
Designs: 200d, Citrus maxima. 2000d, Nerium indicum. 4000d, Ixora coccinea. 5000d, Cananga oborata. 6000d, Cassia surattensis.
2384-2388 A587 Set of 5   4.50

Birds — A588

Designs: 200d, Ducula spilorrhoa. 2000d, Petrophassa ferruginea. 4000d, Columba livia. 5000d, Lopholaimus antarcticus. 6000d, Streptopelia senegalensis, horiz.

1992, July 3
2389-2393 A588 Set of 5   4.50

Rodents — A589

Designs: 200d, 500d, Cavia porcellus, horiz. 3000d, Hystrix indica, horiz. 4000d, Gerbillus gerbillus. 5000d, Petaurista petaurista. 6000d, Oryctolagus cuniculus.

1992, July 26
2394-2399 A589 Set of 6   4.50

Disabled Soldiers Day, 45th Anniv. A590

1992, July 27
2400 A590 200d multicolored   1.00

3rd Phu Dong Games A591

1992, Aug. 1
2401 A591 200d multicolored   1.00

Betta Splendens — A592

Various fish: 200d, 500d, 3000d, 4000d, 5000d, 6000d.

1992, Aug. 15
2402-2407 A592 Set of 6   4.50

1984 Summer Olympics, Los Angeles A592a

Designs: No. 2407A, 50xu, Gymnastics. No. 2407B, 50xu, Soccer, vert. 1d, Wrestling. 2d, Volleyball, vert. 3d, Hurdles. 5d, Basketball, vert. 8d, Weight lifting. 10d, Running, vert.

1992, Sept. 1   Litho.   Perf. 12½
2407A-2407G A592a Set of 7 5.00 5.00
Souvenir Sheet
2407H A592a 10d multi   5.00 5.00
Nos. 2407A-2407G were prepared in 1984 but were not released at that time, because of Viet Nam's boycott of the 1984 Summer Olympics.

Intl. Planned Parenthood Federation, 40th Anniv. — A593

Designs: 200d, Map showing member's locations, vert. 4000d, Anniv. emblem, map.

1992, Oct. 1
2408-2409 A593 Set of 2   2.00

Hanoi Medical School, 90th Anniv. A594

Designs: 200d, Medical students. 5000d, Alexandre Yersin, school.

1992, Nov. 20
2410-2411 A594 Set of 2   2.50

SOS Children's Villages — A595

Designs: 200d, Adult sheltering child. 5000d, Women, children inside house.

1992, Dec. 22
2412-2413 A595 Set of 2   2.00

17th Southeast Asian Games,
Singapore — A596

1993, Jan. 1
2414 A596 200d multicolored   1.00

Bees
A597

Designs: 200d, Apis dorsata. 800d, Apis
koschevnikovi. 1000d, Apis laboriosa. 2000d,
Apis cerana japonica. 5000d, Apis cerana cerana. 10,000d, Apis mellifera, vert.

1993, Jan. 15
2415-2420 A597 Set of 6   5.50

Fable of Tam
Cam — A598

Designs: 200d, Returning from river. 800d,
Vision of old man by goldfish pool. 1000d,
With unsold rice at market. 3000d, Trying on
slipper for prince. 4000d, Rising from lotus
flower. 10,000d, Royal couple.

1993, Jan. 18
2421-2426 A598 Set of 6   6.50

New Year
1993 (Year of
the Rooster)
A599

200d, 5000d, Rooster, hen and chicks.

1993, Jan. 20
2427-2428 A599 Set of 2   2.50

Medicinal
Plants
A600

Designs: 200d, Atractylodes macrocephala.
No. 2430, 1000d, Lonicera japonica. No. 2431,
1000d, Quisqualis indica. 3000d, Rehmannia
glutinosa. 12,000d, Gardenia jasminoides.

1993, Feb. 27
2429-2433 A600 Set of 5   5.50

Communications
A601

200d, Map, communications equipment.
2500d, Map, Hong Kong-Sri Racha Cable
route.

1993, Mar. 1
2434-2435 A601 Set of 2   1.75

Asian
Animals
A602

200d, Ailuropoda melanoleuca. 800d,
Panthera tigris. 1000d, Elephas maximus.
3000d, Rhinoceros unicornis. 4000d, Hylobates leucogenys. #2441, 10,000d, Neofelis
nebulosa. #2442, 10,000d, Bos sauveli.

1993, Mar. 10
2436-2441 A602 Set of 6   6.50
Souvenir Sheet
Perf. 13½
2442 A602 10,000d multicolored   4.00

1994 World Cup Soccer
Championships, U.S. — A603

Various soccer players in action.

1993, Mar. 30   *Perf. 13*
2443-2445 A603 200d, 1500d,
                 7000d, set of
                 3   3.00

Transportation — A604

Designs: 200d, Wheelbarrow. 800d, Buffalo
cart. 1000d, Rickshaw, top up. 2000d, Rickshaw with passenger. 5000d, Rickshaw, top
down. 10,000d, Horse-drawn carriage.

1993, Apr. 6
2446-2451 A604 Set of 6   5.00

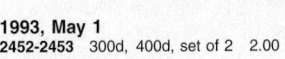

500Kv Electricity
Lines — A605

1993, May 1
2452-2453 300d, 400d, set of 2   2.00

Polska
'93 — A606

Paintings: 200d, Sunflowers, by Van Gogh.
No. 2455, 1000d, Young Woman, by Mogidi-
liani. No. 2456, 1000d, Couple in Forest, by
Rousseau. 5000d, Harlequin with Family, by
Picasso. No. 2458, 10,000d, Female Model,
by Matisse, horiz. No. 2459, 10,000d, Portrait
of Dr. Gachet, by Van Gogh.

1993, May 7   *Perf. 13*
2454-2458 A606 Set of 5   5.00
Souvenir Sheet
Perf. 12½
2459 A606 10,000d multicolored   5.00
No. 2459 contains one 32x43mm stamp.

Da Lat,
Cent.
A607

Orchids: 400d, Paphiopedilum hirsutissimum. No. 2461, 1000d, Paphiopedilum mali-
poense. No. 2462, 1000d, Paphiopedilum gratrixianum.   12,000d,   Paphiopedilum
hennisianum.

1993, June 15   *Perf. 13*
2460-2463 A607 Set of 4   5.00

Asian Architecture — A608

Landmark buildings from: 400d, Thailand,
vert. 800d, Indonesia, vert. 1000d, Singapore,
vert. No. 2467, 2000d, Malaysia. No. 2468,
2000d, Cambodia. 6000d, Laos. 8000d,
Brunei.
10,000d, Thai Binh, Viet Nam, vert.

1993, July 10   Litho.
2464-2470 A608 Set of 7   4.75
Souvenir Sheet
Perf. 14x13½
2471 A608 10,000d multicolored   4.00 4.00

7th Trade Union Congress — A608a

Designs: 400d, Industry, communications.
5000d, Hand holding hammer, doves, flowers.

1993, July 28 Litho. *Perf. 13*
2471A-2471B A608a Set of 2   4.50

Crabs
A609

Designs: 400d, Scylla serrata. 800d, Portunus sanguinotentus. 1000d, Charybdis
bimaculata. 2000d, Paralithodes brevipes.
5000d, Portunus pelagicus. 10,000d, Lithodes
turritus.

1993, July 30
2472-2477 A609 Set of 6   7.00

Stamp
Day
A610

5000d, Hand holding stamped envelope.

1993, Aug. 15
2478-2479 A610 Set of 2   2.25

Miniature Sheet

Tennis — A611

Women tennis players: a, 400d. c, 1000d.
Male tennis players: b, 1000d. d, 12,000d.

1993, Sept. 20
2480 A611 #a.-d. + 2 labels   5.50

A613

Costumes: 400d, Lo Lo. 800d, Thai. 1000d,
Dao Do. 2000d, H'mong. 5000d, Kho Mu. No.
2488, 10,000d, Kinh.
No. 2489, 10,000d, Precious gem stones.

1993, Oct. 1   *Perf. 13*
2483-2488 A613 Set of 6   4.00
Souvenir Sheet
Perf. 13½
2489 A613 10,000d multicolored   5.25

Bangkok '93. Issued: Nos. 2483-2488,
10/1/93. No. 2489, 10/10/93.
No. 2489 contains one 43x32mm stamp.

A614

New Year 1994 (Year of the Dog): Various dogs.

1994, Jan. 1
2490-2491 A614 400d, 6000d,
                set of 2   2.50
    Imperf., #2490-2491   4.00

Flowers
A615

#2492, 400d, Prunus persica. #2493, 400d, Chrysanthemum morifolium. #2494, 400d, Rosa chinensis. 15,000d, Delonix regia.

1994
2492-2495 A615 Set of 4   5.50

    Issued: #2492, 1/4; 15,000d, 4/3; #2493, 7/30; #2494, 10/10.

Chess
A616

Designs: 400d, Anatoly Karpov. 1000d, Gary Kasparov. 2000d, Bobby Fischer. 4000d, Emanuel Lasker. No. 2500, 10,000d, Jose Capablanca.
    No. 2501, 10,000d, King.

1994, Jan. 20
2496-2500 A616 Set of 5   4.50
    Imperf., #2496-2500   8.00
Souvenir Sheet
2501 A616 10,000d multicolored   3.25
    Imperf.   5.25

Hong Kong
'94 — A617

Festivals: 400d, Hoi Lim. 800d, Cham. 1000d, Tay Nguyen. 12,000d, Nam Bo.

1994, Feb. 18
2502-2505 A617 Set of 4   4.00
    Imperf., #2502-2505   6.75

A618

Various opera masks: 400d, 500d, 2000d, 3000d, 4000d, 7000d.

1994, Mar. 15
2506-2511 A618 Set of 6   4.75
    Imperf., #2506-2511   8.50

A619

Various gladiolus hybridus: 400d, 2000d, 5000d, 8000d.

1994, Mar. 30
2512-2515 A619 Set of 4   3.75
    Imperf., #2512-2515   6.75

Japanese Paintings — A620

Paintings by: 400d, Utamaro. 500d, Harunobu. 1000d, Hokusai. 2000d, Hiroshige. 3000d, Hokusai, diff. 4000d, Utamaro, diff. 8000d, Choki.

1994, Apr. 9
2516-2522 A620 Set of 7   6.50
    Imperf., #2516-2522   11.00

Insects — A621

Designs: 400d, Cicindela aurulenta. 1000d, Harmonia octomaculata. 6000d, Cicindela tennipes. 7000d, Collyris.

1994, Apr. 20
2523-2526 A621 Set of 4   4.00
    Imperf., #2523-2526   6.75

Victory at Dien Bien Phu, 40th Anniv.
A622

Designs: 400d, Soldiers dragging equipment. 3000d, Celebration.

1994, Apr.
2527-2528 A622 Set of 2   1.00
    Imperf., #2527-2528   1.75

Newspaper "Young Pioneers," 40th Anniv.
A623

1994, May 15   *Perf. 13x13½*
2529 A623 400d red & black   .50

Crocodiles — A625

Designs: 400d, Crocodylus porosus. 600d, Alligator mississippiensis. 2000d, Crocodylus niloticus. 3000d, Alligator sinensis. 4000d, Caiman yacare. 9000d, Crocodylus johnsoni. 10,000d, Caiman crocodilus.

1994, June 1   *Perf. 13x13½*
2532-2537 A625 Set of 6   5.00
    Imperf., #2532-2537   7.50
Souvenir Sheet
        Perf. 13½
2538 A625 10,000d multicolored   3.50
    Imperf.   6.00
    No. 2538 contains one 43x32mm stamp.

1994 World Cup Soccer Championships, US — A626

Various soccer players in action: 400d, 600d, 1000d, 2000d, 3000d, 11,000d.

1994, June 15   *Perf. 13*
2539-2544 A626 Set of 6   4.75
    Imperf., #2539-2544   8.25
Souvenir Sheet
        Perf. 13½
2545 A626 10,000d multicolored   3.25
    Imperf.   4.75
    No. 2545 contains one 32x43mm stamp.

Yersin's Discovery of Plague Bacillus, Cent.
A627

1994, June   *Perf. 13x13½*
2546 A627 400d multicolored   .75

UPU, 120th Anniv.
A629

Designs: 400d, UPU emblem, "120." 5000d, World map. 10,000d, UPU emblem, "P," vert.

1994, Aug. 1   *Perf. 13*
2551-2552 A629 Set of 2   1.50
Souvenir Sheet
        Perf. 14x13½
2553 A629 10,000d multicolored   4.25

PHILAKOREA '94 — A630

Birds: 400d, Numenius arquata. 600d, Oceanites oceanicus. 1000d, Fregata minor. 2000d, Morus capensis. 3000d, Lunda cirrhata. 11,000d, Larus belcheri. 10,000d, Collocalia fuciphaga.

1994, Aug. 16   *Perf. 13x13½*
2554-2559 A630 Set of 6   5.00
Souvenir Sheet
        Perf. 13½
2560 A630 10,000d multicolored   4.00
    No. 2560 contains one 43x32mm stamp.

A631

Bamboo: 400d, Bambusa blumeana. 1000d, Phyllostachys aurea. 2000d, Bambusa vulgaris. 4000d, Tetragonocalamus quadrangularis. 10,000d, Bambusa venticosa.

1994, Aug. 17   *Perf. 13½x13*
2561-2565 A631 Set of 5   5.00
    Singpex '94.

A632

Various bridges: 400d, 900d, 8000d.

1994, Sept. 20   *Perf. 13x13½*
2566-2568 A632 Set of 3   2.75

Children's Future
A634

Designs: 400d+100d, Boy helping girl in wheelchair with kite. 2000d, Children dancing, vert.

1994, Oct. 2   *Litho.*   *Perf. 13*
2572-2573 A634 Set of 2   1.25

A636

People's Army, 50th Anniv.: 400d, People in formation. 1000d, Soldiers, battle map. 2000d, Ho Chi Minh, child. 4000d, Anti-aircraft battery.

1994, Dec. 22
2576-2579 A636 Set of 4   2.25

A637

Intl. Olympic Committee, Cent.: 400d, Flags. 6000d, Pierre de Coubertin.

1994, June 25   *Perf. 13*
2580-2581 A637 Set of 2   2.75

ICAO, 50th Anniv.
A638

Jets: 400d, In flight. 3000d, On ground.

1994, Dec. 7
2582-2583 A638 Set of 2   1.25

Trams
A639

Designs: 400d, With overhead conductor. 900d, Paris tram. 8000d, Philadelphia mail.

1994, Oct. 10   Litho.   Perf. 13x13½
2584-2586 A639 Set of 3   2.25

Liberation of Hanoi, 40th Anniv. A640

Designs: 400d, Greeting soldiers. 2000d, Workers, students, modern technology.

1994, Oct. 10
2587-2588 A640 Set of 2   .80

New Year 1995 (Year of the Boar) A641

Stylized boars: 400d, Adult, five young. 8000d, One eating.

1995, Jan. 2   Litho.   Perf. 13
2589-2590 A641 Set of 2   2.50

A642

Birds: No. 2591, 400d, Pluvialis apricaria, horiz. No. 2592, 400d, Philetairus socius, horiz. No. 2593, 400d, Oxyruncus cristatus, horiz. No. 2594, 400d, Pandion haliaetus. No. 2595, 5000d, Cariama cristata.

1995, Jan. 20   Perf. 13x13½, 13½x13
2591-2595 A642 Set of 5   2.00

A number has been reserved for a souvenir sheet with this set.

A643

Traditional women's attire: 400d, Young women, bicycle. 3000d, Bride. 5000d, Girl in formal dress holding hat.

1995, Feb. 1   Perf. 13
2597-2599 A643 Set of 3   2.50

Vietstampex '95 — A644

1995, Feb. 18
2600 A644 5500d multicolored   2.00

Owls — A645

Designs: 400d, Ketupa zeylonensis. 1000d, Strix aluco. 2000d, Strix nebulosa. 5000d, Strix seloputo. 10,000d, Otus leucotis. 12,500d, Tyto alba.

1995, Mar. 1   Perf. 13½x13
2601-2605 A645 Set of 5   5.00

Souvenir Sheet
Perf. 14x13½
2606 A645 12,500d multicolored   5.50
     Imperf.   6.75

Fish A646

Designs: 400d, Pomacanthus arcuatus. 1000d, Rhinecanthus rectangulus. 2000d, Pygoplites diacanthus. 4000d, Pomacanthus ciliaris. 5000d, Balistes vetula. 9000d, Balistes conspicillum.

1995, Mar. 20   Perf. 13
2607-2612 A646 Set of 6   4.25

Lenin, 125th Birth Anniv. — A647

1995, Apr. 22   Litho.   Perf. 13
2613 A647 400d red & black   .45

End of World War II, 50th Anniv. A648

1995, May 2   Litho.   Perf. 13
2614 A648 400d multicolored   1.00

A649

1996 Summer Olympics, Atlanta: 400d, Hammer throw. 3000d, Cycling. 4000d, Running. 10,000d, Pole vault. 12,500d, Basketball.

1995, Apr. 5   Litho.   Perf. 13
2615-2618 A649 Set of 4   4.00
Souvenir Sheet
2619 A649 12,500d multicolored   3.50

A650

Various balloons: 500d, 1000d, 2000d, 3000d, 4000d, 5000d, 7000d.

1995, May 5
2620-2626 A650 Set of 7   6.50
Finlandia '95, Intl. Philatelic Exhibition, Helsinki.

Miniature Sheets

Tapirus Indicus — A651

No. 2627a, 400d, With young. b, 1000d, Facing left. c, 2000d, Walking right. d, 4000d, Mouth open, left. No. 2528a, 4000d, Facing right. b, 4000d, Eating leaves. c, 5000d, In water. d, 6000d, Head protruding out of water.

1995, Apr. 25
2627 A651 Sheet of 4, #a.-d.   5.00
2628 A651 Sheet of 4, #a.-d.   5.50
World Wildlife Fund (#2627).

Miniature Sheet

Parachutes — A652

No. 2629: a, 400d, One parachutist descending from sky. b, 2000d, Two descending. c, 3000d, One about to touch ground. d, 9000d, Three men on ground with open parachute.

1995, May 24
2629 A652 Sheet of 4, #a.-d.   4.00

Rhododendrons — A653

Designs: 400d, Fleuryi. 1000d, Sulphoreum. 2000d, Sinofalconeri. 3000d, Lyi. 5000d, Ovatum. 9000d, Tanastylum.

1995, June 30
2630-2635 A653 Set of 6   4.50

Miniature Sheet

Native Folktale — A654

a, 400d, Brothers and their parents. b, 1000d, Mother saying farewell to her departing sons. c, 3000d, One brother is transformed into a statue. d, 10,000d, Both brothers transformed into statues.

1995, July 20   Litho.   Perf. 13
2636 A654 Sheet of 4, #a.-d.   4.25

A655

400d, Statue of a woman holding child. 3000d, Three women of different races, emblem, horiz.

1995, Aug. 5
2637-2638 A655 Set of 2   1.00
Women's Federation of Viet Nam: 65th anniv. (#2637), 1995 Intl. Women's Conf., Beijing (#2638).

A656

1995, July 26
2639 A656 400d multicolored   .35
Admission to Assoc. of Southeast Asian Nations (ASEAN).

Natl.
Day — A657

#2640, 400d, Ho Chi Minh, people waving flags, dove of peace. #2641, 400d, Ho Chi Minh holding child. #2642, 1000d, Communist symbol, bridge, electrical wire, Ho Chi Minh Mausoleum. #2643, 1000d, Ho Chi Minh, silhouettes of soldiers, building with flags flying. #2644, 2000d, Soldiers, natl. flag. #2645, 2000d, Antenna, satellite dish, van, olive branch, people on motorcycles.

1995, Aug. 14
2640-2645 A657　Set of 6　　3.00

Viet Nam Labor Party, 65th anniv. (No. 2640). Ho Chi Minh, 105th birth anniv. (No. 2641). Evacuation of French troops from North Viet Nam, 40th anniv. (No. 2642). End of war in Viet Nam, 20th anniv. (No 2643). Natl. army, 50th anniv. (No. 2644). Post and Telecommunications Service, 50th anniv. (No. 2645).

Sir Rowland Hill (1795-1879)
A658

Design: 4000d, Hill, "penny black."

1995, Aug. 15
2646 A658　4000d multicolored　　1.25

Natl. Sports Games — A659

1995, Aug. 30
2647 A659　400d multicolored　　.50

Singapore '95 — A660

Orchids: 400d, Paphiopedilum druryi. 2000d, Dendrobium orcraceum. 3000d, Vanda. 4000d, Cattelya. 5000d, Paphiopedilum hirsutissimum. 6000d, Christenosia vietnamica haeger.
12,500d, Angraecum sesquipedale.

1995, Sept. 1
2648-2653 A660　Set of 6　　6.50

Souvenir Sheet
2654 A660　12,500d multicolored　　5.50

No. 2654 contains one 32x43mm stamp.

Asian Sites — A661

Designs: 400d, Buildings, monuments, tombs, Hue, Viet Nam. 3000d, Walkway over water, Trung Quoc. 4000d, Temple, Macao. 5000d, Kowloon, Hong Kong. 6000d, Pagoda, Dai Bac.

1995, Sept. 6
2655-2659 A661　Set of 5　　4.75

UN, 50th Anniv. A662

1995, Oct. 10
2660 A662　2000d multicolored　　.75

Total Solar Eclipse, Oct. 10, 1995
A663

1995, Dec. 23　Litho.　Perf. 13
2661 A663　400d multicolored　　1.00

Paintings of Women
A664

Designs: 400d, Woman in white dress, flowers, by To Ngoc Van (1906-54) (4-1). 2000d, Washing hair, by Tran Van Can (1906-94) (4-2). 6000d, Standing beside vase of flowers, by To Ngoc Van (4-3). 8000d, Two women, by Tran Van Can (4-4).

1995, Nov. 15　Litho.　Perf. 13
2662-2665 A664　Set of 4　　3.75

New Year 1996 (Year of the Rat) — A665

Stylized rats: 400d, One carrying fan, one riding horse. 8000d, Four carrying one in palanquin.
13,000d, Marching in parade, carrying banner.

1996, Jan. 2　Litho.　Perf. 13
2666 A665　400d multicolored　　.20
2667 A665　8000d multicolored　　1.75

Souvenir Sheet
2668 A665　13,000d multi, vert.　　2.75

No. 2668 contains one 32x43mm stamp.

Dinosaurs — A666

Designs: 400d, Tsintaosaurus. 1000d, Archaeopteryx. 2000d, Psittacosaurus. 3000d, Hypsilophodon. 13,000d, Parasaurolophus.

1996, Mar. 6
2669-2673 A666　Set of 5　　4.50

Kingfishers A667

Designs: 400d, Halcyon smyrnensis. 1000d, Megaceryle alcyon. 2000d, Alcedo Atthis. 4000d, Halcyon coromanda. 12,000d, Ceryle rudis.

1996, Mar. 11
2674-2678 A667　Set of 5　　4.50

Flowers A668

Various flowers: No. 2679, 400d, brown (5-1). No. 2680, 400d, claret (5-2). No. 2681, 400d, green (5-3). No. 2682, 400d, blue (5-4). No. 2683, 5000d, red (5-5), vert.

Perf. 13x13½, 13½x13
1996, Jan. 10　　　　　Litho.
2679-2683 A668　Set of 5　　1.25

8th Vietnamese Communist Party Congress — A669

Designs: 400d, Ho Chi Minh (2-1). 3000d, Stylized dove, satellite dish, electrical towers, hammer & sickle, building, olive branch (2-2).

1996, Feb. 3　　　　　Perf. 13
2684-2685 A669　Set of 2　　.75

Asian Sites — A670

Monuments and statues in: 400d, Hanoi. 2000d, Thailand. 3000d, Bhubanesvar, India. 4000d, Kyoto, Japan. 10,000d, Borobudur, Java.

1996, Feb. 10　Litho.　Perf. 13
2686-2690 A670　Set of 5　　4.50

See Nos. 2773-2777.

Statues — A671

Various statues of men in traditional costumes of early warriors: 400d, 600d, 1000d, 2000d, 3000d, 5000d, 6000d, 8000d.

1996　　Litho.　Perf. 13½x13
2691-2698 A671　Set of 8　　5.50

Central Committee, 50th Anniv. — A672

1996, May 22　　　　Perf. 13
2699 A672　400d multicolored　　.30

UNICEF, 50th Anniv. A673

Designs: 400d, Children of different races, cultures. 7000d, Plant, emblem, water droplets containing representations of education, drinking water, medicine, food.

1996, May 15
2700-2701 A673　Set of 2　　1.75

Red Cross of Viet Nam, 50th Anniv. A674

1996, May 8　　　　Perf. 13½
2702 A674　3000d Quotation, Ho Chi Minh　　.75

A675

Traditional Musical Instruments: a, 400d, Mandolin. b, 3000d, Bow and string instrument. c, 4000d, Square-shaped guitar-like instrument. d, 9000d, Zither.

1996, Apr. 24　　　Perf. 13½x13
2703 A675　Sheet of 4, #a.-d.　　3.50

China '96 Intl. Philatelic Exhibition.

A676

Insects: 400d, Cincindela japonica. 500d, Calodema wallacei. 1000d, Mylabris oculata. 4000d, Chrysochroa buqueti. 5000d, Ophioniea nigrofasciata. 12,000d, Carabus tauricus.

1996, May 20　　　　Perf. 13
2704-2709 A676　Set of 6　　5.00

1996 Summer Olympic Games, Atlanta A677

Designs: 2000d, Soccer. 4000d, Sailing. 5000d, Field hockey.

1996, July 8
2710-2712 A677 Set of 3 2.75

Euro '96, European Soccer Championships, Great Britain — A678

Designs: a, 400d, Net, goalie. b, 8000d, Player making shot on goal.

1996, June 1
2713 A678 Pair, #a.-b. 2.00

No. 2713 is a continuous design.

Aircraft A679

400d, Airbus A320. 1000d, AN-72. 2000d, MD-11F. 6000d, RJ-85. 10,000d, B747-400F. 13,000d, Space shuttle carried by Boeing 747.

1996, June 1
2714-2718 A679 Set of 5 4.50
Souvenir Sheet
Perf. 13½
2719 A679 13,000d multicolored 2.75

Stamp Day A680

1996, Aug. 15	**Perf. 13**
2720 A680 400d No. 1L57 (1-1) .30

Paintings by Nguyen Sáng (1923-88) A681

400d, Woman, vase of flowers (2-1). 8000d, Soldiers returning from battle (2-2).

1996, Sept. 10	**Perf. 13**
2721-2722 A681 Set of 2 2.00

Hue School, Cent. — A682

400d, Women walking beside entrance (2-1). 3000d, View of portals, building (2-2).

1996, Sept. 5
2723-2724 A682 Set of 2 .75

Mushrooms A683

Designs: 400d, Aleuria aurantia. 500d, Morchella conica. 1000d, Anthurus archeri. 4000d, Laetiporus serlphureus. 5000d, Filoboletus manipularis. 12,000d, Tremiscus helvelloides.

1996, Aug. 26	**Litho.**	**Perf. 13**
2725-2730 A683 Set of 6 5.25

Wild Animals — A684

Designs: a, 400d, Pygathrix nemacus. b, 2000d, Panthera tigris. c, 4000d, Rhinoceros sondaicus. d, 10,000d, Balearica regulorum.

1996, Oct. 10	**Litho.**	**Perf. 13**
2731 A684 Sheet of 4, #a.-d. 3.75

Taipei '96.

Campaign Promoting Iodized Salt — A685

1996, Nov. 2	**Litho.**	**Perf. 13**
2732 A685 400d multicolored .55

Natl. Liberation Movement, 50th Anniv. — A686

1996, Dec. 19
2733 A686 400d multicolored .40

Fruit — A687

Designs: No. 2734, Hylocereus undatus. No. 2735, Durio zibethinus. No. 2736, Persea americana. No. 2737, Garcinia mangostana. No. 2738, Nephelium lappaceum.

1997, Jan. 2	**Perf. 13x13½**
2734-2738 A687 400d Set of 5 .75

New Year 1997 (Year of the Ox) — A688

Stylized oxen: 400d, Adult, calf. 8000d, Adult.

1997, Jan. 8	**Litho.**	**Perf. 13**
2739-2740 A688 Set of 2 2.00

8th Vietnamese Communist Party Congress — A689

1997, Feb. 3
2741 A689 400d multicolored .40

Goldfish A690

Various carassius auratus: 400d, 1000d, 5000d, 7000d, 8000d.

1997, Feb. 5
2742-2746 A690 Set of 5 4.00
Souvenir Sheet
Perf. 13½x14
2747 A690 14,000d multicolored 3.00

No. 2747 contains one 43x32mm stamp. Hong Kong '97 (#2747).

Sculptures from Ly Dynasty — A691

Designs: 400d, Serpents in round figure, vert. 1000d, Dragon head, vert. 3000d, People playing instruments. 5000d, Gargoyle. 10,000d, Dragon-head bowl.

1997, Mar. 5
2748-2752 A691 Set of 5 4.50

Scenes — A692

Designs: 400d, Lake, people in park, Hà Tay. 5000d, Footbridge over river, Lai Chau. 7000d, Houses, fog, trees, Lào Cai.

1997, Mar. 20
2753-2755 A692 Set of 3 3.00

Huynh Thuc Khang (1876-1947) A693

1997, Apr. 21	**Litho.**	**Perf. 13½x13**
2756 A693 400d multi .35

Disabled People in Sports — A694

1000d, Tennis. 6000d, Shooting.

1997, Apr. 27	**Perf. 13**
2757-2758 A694 Set of 2 1.60

Wild Animals A695

400d, Chrotogale owstoni. 3000d, Lutra lutra. 4000d, Callosciurus erythraeus. 10,000d, Felis bangalensis.

1997, May 2
2759-2762 A695 Set of 4 3.75

A696

1997, May 19
2763 A696 400d Women's Union .50

A697

Lilium longiflorum (Lilies): 400d, Red. 1000d, White. 5000d, Pink & white. 10,000d, Orange.

1997, Apr. 15　　Litho.　　Perf. 13
2764-2767　A697　Set of 4　　　3.50

PACIFIC 97 — A698

Suspension bridges: 400d, Golden Gate, San Francisco. 5000d, Raippaluoto. 10,000d, Seto.

1997, May 12
2768-2770　A698　Set of 3　　　3.25

Children
A699

400d, UN Convention on the Rights of the Child. 5000d, Breast milk is better.

1997, June 1　　Litho.　　Perf. 13
With Gum
2771-2772　A699　Set of 2　　1.25　1.25

Asian Sites Type of 1996

Designs: 400d, Pagoda, Hanoi, Viet Nam. 1000d, Ruins of Persepolis, Iran. 3000d, Statue of woman, Iraq. 5000d, Sacred Rock, Kyaikto, Burma. 10,000d, Statue of Buddha lying down, Sr. Lanka.

1997, June 20　　Litho.　　Perf. 13
2773-2777　A670　Set of 5　　　4.25

Women's
Costumes
A700

Various costumes: 400d, Woman holding umbrella, San Chay. 2000d, Woman sewing, wearing jacket tied with sash, Dao quain trang. 5000d, Woman pumping water from well provided by UNICEF, Phù Lá. 10,000d, Woman holding hands in air, Kho Me.

1997, July 8
2778-2781　A700　Set of 4　　　3.75

A701

1997, July 11
2782　A701　400d multicolored　　.50
Prevention of AIDS.

A702

1997, Aug. 8　　Litho.　　Perf. 13
2783　A702　400d multicolored　　.35
ASEAN, 30th anniv.

Monument to War Martyrs & Invalids,
50th Anniv. — A703

1997, July 25
2784　A703　400d multicolored　　.35　.35

Hibiscus — A704

a, 1000d, Hibiscus rosa sinensis. b, 3000d, Hibiscus schizopetalus. c, 5000d, Hibiscus syriacus (pink). d, 9000d, Hibiscus syriacus (yellow).

1997, Aug. 1
2785　A704　Sheet of 4, #a.-d.　　3.75　3.75

A705

1997, Aug. 26　　Litho.　　Perf. 13
2786　A705　400d multicolored　　.40　.40
Post and Telecommunications Union, 50th anniv.

A706

Sea horses: 400d, 1000d, Hippocampus (diff.). 3000d, Hippocampus guttulatus. 5000d, Hippocampus kelloggi. 6000d, Hippocampus japonicus. 7000d, Hippocampus hippocampus.

1997, Sept. 4
2787-2792　A706　Set of 6　　　4.75　4.75

19th Southeast
Asian
Games — A707

1997, Oct. 11　　Litho.　　Perf. 13
2793　A707　5000d multicolored　　1.25　1.25

Handicrafts
A708

Designs: No. 2794, 400d, Lamp. No. 2795, 400d, Two baskets. No. 2796, 400d, Swan-shaped basket. No. 2797, 400d, Deer-shaped basket. 2000d, Basket with handle,

1998, Jan. 1　　Litho.　　Perf. 13
2794-2798　A708　Set of 5　　1.10　1.10

7th Francophone Summit,
Hanoi — A709

1997, Sept. 24　　Litho.　　Perf. 13½x13
2799　A709　5000d multicolored　　2.75　2.75

Birds
A710

400d, Syrmaticus ellioti. 3000d, Lophura diardi. 5000d, Phasianus cholchicus. 6000d, Chrysolophus amherstiae. 8000d, Polyplectron germaini. 14,000d, Lophura imperialis.

1997, Oct. 15　　　　Perf. 13
2800-2804　A710　Set of 5　　4.75　4.75
Souvenir Sheet
Perf. 13½
2805　A710　14,000d multicolored　2.75　2.75
No. 2805 contains one 43x30mm stamp.

New Year
1998 (Year of
the Tiger)
A711

Stylized tigers: 400d, Adult with young. 8000d, Adult.

1998, Jan. 5　　　　Perf. 13
2806-2807　A711　Set of 2　　2.00　2.00

Sites in
Vietnam
A712

Designs: No. 2808, 400d, Rocks, lake, Ninh Thuan. No. 2809, 400d, Lake, cavern, Quang Binh. 10,000d, Village of Quang Nam.

1998, Feb. 2
2808-2810　A712　Set of 3　　2.10　2.10

Communist
Manifesto, 150th
Anniv. — A713

1998, Feb. 3
2811　A713　400d multicolored　　.40　.40

Bonsai
A714

#2812, 400d, Limonia acidissima. #2813, 400d, Deeringia polysperma. #2814, 400d, Pinus merkusii, vert. 4000d, Barringtonia acutangula, vert. 6000d, Ficus elastica, vert. 10,000d, Wrightia religiosa, vert.
No. 2818, Adenium obesum.

1998, Mar. 2
2812-2817　A714　Set of 6　　4.25　4.25

Souvenir Sheet
Perf. 13½
2818 A714 14,000d multicolored 2.50 2.50
No. 2818 contains one 43x32mm stamp.

Tet Offensive, 30th Anniv. — A715

1998, Jan. 30 **Litho.** **Perf. 13**
2819 A715 400d multicolored .40 .40

Opera — A716

Designs: a, 400d, Thi kính bi oan. b, 1000d, Thi mẫu lên chúa. c, 2000d, Thi mẫu-gia nô. d, 4000d, Thi me dóp-Xa trúong. e, 6000d, Thi kính bi phat va. f, 9000d, Thi kính xin sua.

1998, Apr. 20
2820 A716 Sheet of 6, #a.-f 4.50 4.50

Raptors A717

Designs: No. 2821, 400d, Pernis apivorus. No. 2822, 400d, Spizaetus ornatus. No. 2823, 400d, Accipter gentilis. 3000d, Buteo buteo. 5000d, Circus melanoleucas. 12,000d, Haliaeetus albicilla.

1998, May 4 **Litho.** **Perf. 13**
2821-2826 A717 Set of 6 4.25 4.25

Ho Chi Minh City (Saigon), 300th Anniv. — A718

400d, Tank, natl. flag, Ho Chi Minh as young man, building. 5000d, Monument to Ho Chi Minh, symbols of industry, communications, and transportation.

1998, Apr. 30
2827-2828 A718 Set of 2 1.10 1.10

Orchids A719

Designs: 400d, Paphiopedilum appletonianum. 6000d, Paphiopedilum helenae.

1998, May 18 **Litho.** **Perf. 13½**
2829-2830 A719 Set of 2 2.00 2.00

Children's Paintings A720

UNICEF: 400d, Children, mother in front of home. 5000d, Children on playground.

1998, June 1 **Perf. 13**
2831-2832 A720 Set of 2 1.25 1.25

1998 World Cup Soccer Championships, France — A721

Various soccer plays: 400d, 5000d, 7000d.

1998, June 10
2833-2835 A721 Set of 3 2.50 2.50

Sculptures of the Tran Dynasty A722

Ornate designs: No. 2836, 400d, Serpent. No. 2837, 400d, Two people. 1000d, Shown. 8000d, Person. 9000d, Face.

1998, June 15 **Litho.** **Perf. 13**
2836-2840 A722 Set of 5 3.50 3.50

Martial Arts A723

1998, July 13
2841 A723 2000d multicolored .70 .70

Intl. Year of the Ocean A724

1998, Aug. 1 **Litho.** **Perf. 13**
2842 A724 400d multicolored 1.00 1.00

Stamp Day — A725

1998, Aug. 15
2843 A725 400d Bell's telephone .40 .40

Ton Duc Thang (1888-1980) A726

1998, Aug. 20
2844 A726 400d multicolored .40 .40

Moths A727

Designs: No. 2845, 400d, Antheraea helferi. No. 2846, 400d, Attacus atlas. 4000d, Argema mittrei, vert. 10,000d, Argema maenas, vert.

1998, Aug. 22
2845-2848 A727 Set of 4 3.25 3.25

Paintings by Te Bach Thach (Qi Baishi; 1863-1957) A728

Various paintings: 400d, Dragonfly & Lotus. 1000d, Chrysanthemum, Cock & Hens. 2000d, Shrimps, 1948. 4000d, Crabs. 6000d, Lotus & Mandarin Ducks. 9000d, Shrimps, 1949.

1998, Sept. 16
2849-2854 A728 Set of 6 4.25 4.25

Legend of the Lake A729

Designs: No. 2855, Turtle with sword leading boat. No. 2856, Lake.

1998, Oct. 10
2855-2856 A729 400d Set of 2 .70 .70

Le Thanh Tong (1442-1497) — A730

1998, Oct. 12
2857 A730 400d multicolored .40 .40

Souvenir Sheet

Italia '98, Intl. Philatelic Exhibition — A731

Milan Cathedral.

1998, Oct. 6 **Perf. 13½**
2858 A731 16,000d multicolored 3.25 3.25

8th Trade Union Congress A732

1998, Oct. 15 **Litho.** **Perf. 13**
2859 A732 400d multicolored .40 .40

Quy Nhon City, 396th Anniv., Binh Dinh Province, Cent. — A733

1998, Oct. 20
2860 A733 400d multicolored .40 .40

Buoi-Chu Van An Secondary School, 90th Anniv. — A734

Designs: 400d, Students outside school. 5000d, Students listening to speaker.

1998, Nov. 20
2861-2862 A734 Set of 2 1.25 1.25

6th ASEAN Congress, Hanoi — A735

1998, Dec. **Litho.** **Perf. 13**
2863 A735 1000d multicolored .75 .75

Cuban Revolution, 40th Anniv. (in 1999) — A736

1998, Dec. Litho. **Perf. 13**
2864 A736 400d multicolored .30 .30

A737

Paintings: 400d, Birds, tree, flowers (Spring). 1000d, Flowers, ducks (Summer). 3000d, Flowers, rooster (Fall). 12,000d, Tree, flowers, deer & fawn (Winter).

1999, Jan. 4 Litho. **Perf. 13½x13**
2865-2868 A737 Set of 4 3.50 3.50

A738

New Year 1999 (Year of the Cat): 400d, Cat holding tree branch. 8000d, Two cats. 13,000d, Kittens, ball.

1999, Jan. 6 **Perf. 13½**
2869-2870 A738 Set of 2 1.75 1.75
Souvenir Sheet
2871 A738 13,000d multicolored 2.50 2.50
No. 2871 contains one 32x43mm stamp.

Kites — A739

400d, Large bird with long tail. 5000d, Crescent-shaped. 7000d, Bird with long legs.

1999 Litho. **Perf. 13½x13**
2872-2874 A739 Set of 3 2.25 2.25

Australia '99, World Stamp Expo A740

Various sailing vessels: #2875, 400d, (4-1). #2876, 400d, (4-2). 7000d, (4-3). 9000d, (4-4).

1999, Mar. 10 Litho. **Perf. 13**
2875-2878 A740 Set of 4 3.00 3.00

Medicinal Plants A741

Designs: No. 2879, 400d, Kaempferia galanga. No. 2880, 400d, Tacca chantrieri, vert. No. 2881, Alpinia galanga, vert. 6000d, Typhonium trilobatum, vert. 13,000d, Asarum maximum, vert.

1999, Mar. 15
2879-2883 A741 Set of 5 3.75 3.75

Opera Masks A742

Various masks: 400d (6-1). 1000d (6-2). 2000d (6-3). 5000d (6-4). 6000d (6-5). 10,000d (6-6).

1999, Apr. 16 **Perf. 13½**
2884-2889 A742 Set of 6 4.25 4.25

IBRA'99, World Philatelic Exhibition, Nuremberg A743

Octopuses: No. 2890, 400d, Octopus gibertianus. No. 2891, 400d, Philonexis catenulata. 4000d, Paroctopus yendol. 12,000d, Octopus vulgaris.

1999, Apr. 20
2890-2893 A743 Set of 4 3.00 3.00

Landscape Paintings of Southern Viet Nam — A744

#2894, 400d, Sun over lake, Cà Mau. #2895, 400d, Rocks protruding out of water, Kien Giang. 12,000d, Traditional huts, Bac Lieu.

1999, May 4 **Perf. 13**
2894-2896 A744 Set of 3 2.25 2.25

Asia-Pacific Telecommunity, 20th Anniv. — A745

1999, May 10 Litho. **Perf. 13x13¼**
2897 A745 400d multi .50 .50

Woodpeckers A746

Designs: 400d, Chrysocolaptes lucidus. 1000d, Picumnus innominatus. 3000d, Picus rabieri. 13,000d, Blythipicus pyrrhotis.

1999, May 18 Litho. **Perf. 13**
2898-2901 A746 Set of 4 3.00 3.00

UNICEF A747

Designs: 400d, Girl, hand. 5000d, Boy carrying factory.

1999, June 1 Litho. **Perf. 13**
2902-2903 A747 Set of 2 1.00 1.00

Architecture of Late 19th and Early 20th Centuries — A748

Designs: No. 2904, 400d, Government Office Building, Hanoi (3-1). No. 2905, 400d, History Museum, Ho Chi Minh City (3-2). 12,000d, Duc Ba Cathedral (3-3). 15,000d, Theater, Hanoi.

1999, June 10 **Perf. 13**
2904-2906 A748 Set of 3 2.25 2.25
Souvenir Sheet
Perf. 13½x14
2907 A748 15,000d multi 2.75 2.75
PhilexFrance '99 (No. 2907). No. 2907 contains one 44x32mm stamp.

Intl. Day to Stop Drug Abuse A749

1999, June 24 Litho. **Perf. 13**
2908 A749 400d multicolored .35 .35

Da Rang Bridge, Phu Yen A750

1999, July 1 Litho. **Perf. 13**
2909 A750 400d multi .40 .40

Le Dynasty Sculptures — A751

Designs: No. 2910, 1000d, Man Against Tiger (5-1). No. 2911, 1000d, Phoenix (5-2). 3000d, Playing Chess, vert. (5-3). 7000d, Hostler, vert. (5-4). 9000d, Dragon (5-5).

1999, July 1
2910-2914 A751 Set of 5 3.75 3.75

Birth of World's Six Billionth Person — A752

1999, Aug. 2
2915 A752 400d multi .35 .35

Chinese Landscapes — A753

Designs: 400d, Park, Beijing (4-1). 2000d, Scenic overlook, Anhwei (4-2). 3000d, Park, Shandong, (4-3). 10,000d, Park, Beijing, diff. (4-4). 14,000d, Great Wall of China.

1999, Aug. 16 **Perf. 13**
2916-2919 A753 Set of 4 3.00 3.00
Souvenir Sheet
Perf. 13½x14
2920 A753 14,000d multi 2.50 2.50
China 1999 World Philatelic Exhibition (No. 2920). No. 2920 contains one 43x32mm stamp.

Boat Races A754

Races from regions: 400d, North (3-1). 2000d, Central (3-2). 10,000d, South (3-3).

1999, Sept. 10 **Perf. 13**
2921-2923 A754 Set of 3 2.25 2.25

Women's Costumes A755

Various costumes. #2924, 400d (3-1). #2925, 400d (3-2). #2926, 12,000d (3-3).

1999, Sept. 10
2924-2926 A755 Set of 3 2.25 2.25

Buffalo
Fighting
Festivals
A756

Fighting buffaloes: 400d, (2-1). 5000d, (2-2).

1999, Sept. 15
2927-2928 A756 Set of 2   1.00 1.00

Ngo Quyen (898-944),
General — A757

1999, Oct. 21
2929 A757 400d multi   .35 .35

Nguyen Van
Sieu (1799-
1872), Teacher,
Writer — A758

1999, Nov. 2   Litho.   Perf. 13
2930 A758 400d multi   .35 .35

Tran Xuan Soan (1849-1923), Anti-
colonial Leader — A759

1999, Nov. 24
2931 A759 400d multi   .35 .35

United Nations Development
Program — A760

Designs: 400d, Mother and child, farmer,
fisherman. 8000d, Villagers, buildings.

1999, Dec. 3
2932-2933 A760 Set of 2   1.75 1.75

Viet Nam in the
20th
Century — A761

Designs; No. 2934, 400d, Founding of Viet
Nam Communist Party (6-1). No. 2935, 400d,
Ho Chi Minh's declaration of country's inde-
pendence (6-2). No. 2936, 1000d, Conquest

of South Viet Nam (6-3). No. 2937, 1000d,
People, dam, high tension wire tower, atom (6-
4). 8000d, People, satellite, satellite dish, dam,
high tension wire tower (6-5). 12,000d, Organizations Viet Nam belongs to (6-6).

2000, Jan. 1   Litho.   Perf. 13
2934-2939 A761 Set of 6   3.75 3.75
2939a   Sheet, #2934-2939, without
gum   4.00 4.00

New Year
2000 (Year of
the Dragon)
A762

Dragon: 400d, Facing right (2-1). 8000d,
Facing right (2-2).

2000, Jan. 3   Perf. 13½
With Gum
2940-2941 A762 Set of 2   1.75 1.75

Intl. Year of
Culture and
Peace
A763

2000, Jan. 18   With Gum
2942 A763 400d multi   .35 .35

Viet Nam Communist Party, 70th
Anniv. — A764

#2943, Ho Chi Minh (1890-1969), Pres. (8-
1). #2944, Tran Phu (1904-31), 1st Gen. Sec.
(8-2). #2945, Le Hong Phong (1902-42), Gen.
Sec. (8-3). #2946, Ha Huy Tap (1902-41),
Gen. Sec. (8-4). #2947, Nguyen Van Cu
(1912-41), Gen. Sec. (8-5). #2948, Truong
Chinh (1907-88), Gen. Sec. (8-6). #2949, Le
Duan (1907-86), Gen. Sec. (8-7). #2950,
Nguyen Van Linh (1915-98), Gen. Sec. (8-8).

2000, Feb. 2   Perf. 13
With Gum
2943-2950 A764 400d Set of 8   1.50 1.50

Cockfighting — A765

Postures: No. 2951, 400d, Song long cuoc
(4-1). No. 2952, 400d, Long vu da dao (4-2).
7000d, Song long phuong hoang (4-3). 9000d,
Nhan o giap chien (4-4).

2000, Feb. 8   Litho.   Perf. 13
2951-2954 A765 Set of 4   3.50 3.50
Imperf., #2951-2954   5.75

Bangkok
2000
Stamp
Exhibition
A766

Palanquins: 400d, Imperial court roofed palanquin (3-1). 7000d, Palanquin without roof (3-
2). 8000d, Roofed palanquin (3-3).
15,000d, Palanquin in procession.

2000, Mar. 10   With Gum
2955-2957 A766 Set of 3   3.25 3.25
Souvenir Sheet
2958 A766 15,000d multi   3.25 3.25

Legend of Lac Long
Quan and Au
Co — A767

Designs: No. 2959, 400d, Lang Long Quan
and Au Co marry (6-1). No. 2960, 400d, Au
Co, gives birth to 100 sons (6-2). 500d, Au Co
takes 50 children to forest (6-3). 3000d, Lac
Long Quan takes 50 children to sea (6-4).
4000d, Eldest son, Hung Vuong ascends to
throne (6-5). 11,000d, Vietnamese ethnic
groups as descendents (6-6).

2000, Apr. 4   Perf. 13½
2959-2964 A767 Set of 6   4.00 4.00

Souvenir Sheet

The Stamp Show 2000,
London — A768

No. 2965 — Fire engines: a, 400d, Iveco
Magirus, Germany. b, 1000d, Hino, Japan. c,
5000d, ZIL 103E, Russia. d, 12,000d, FPS.32
Camiva, France.

2000, May 15   Perf. 13
2965 A768 Sheet of 4, #a-d   3.50 3.50

Worldwide
Fund for
Nature
A769

Pseudoryx nghetinhensis: No. 2966, 400d,
Head, vine (4-1). No. 2967, 400d, In grass (4-
2). 5000d, Near pond (4-3). 10,000d, Head,
mountains (4-4).

2000, May 18   Perf. 13½
With Gum
2966-2969 A769 Set of 4   4.50 4.50
2969a   Sheet, 2 each #2966-2969   9.75 9.75

Ho Chi Minh
(1890-1969)
A770

2000, May 19   Perf. 13
With Gum
2970 A770 400d multi   .35 .35

World Stamp
Expo 2000,
Anaheim
A771

Water puppets: No. 2971, 400d, Chu teu (6-
1). No. 2972, 400d, Fairy (6-2). No. 2973,
400d, Man plowing field (6-3). 3000d, Female
peasant (6-4). 9000d, Drummer (6-5).
11,000d, Fisherman (6-6).

2000, June 28   Perf. 13½
2971-2976 A771 Set of 6   4.50 4.50

50th Vietnam
Youth
Volunteers'
Day — A772

2000, July 15   Perf. 13
With Gum
2977 A772 400d multi   .35 .35

Phu
Dong
Natl.
Youth
Sports
Festival
A773

2000, July 20   With Gum
2978 A773 400d multi   .35 .35

Fish
A774

Designs: No. 2979, 400d, Cephalopholis
miniatus (6-1). No. 2980, 400d, Pomacanthus
imperator (6-2). No. 2981, 400d, Epinephelus
merra (6-3). 4000d, Zancius cornutus, vert. (6-
4). 6000d, Chaetodon ephippium, vert. (6-5).
12,000d, Heniochus acuminatus, vert. (6-6).
15,000d, Chaetodon lunula.

2000, Aug. 7   Perf. 13
2979-2984 A774 Set of 6   4.00 4.00
Souvenir Sheet
Perf. 13½x13¾
2985 A774 15,000d multi   2.75 2.75

Post and
Telegraph
Dept.,
55th
Anniv.
A775

2000, Aug. 15   Perf. 13
With Gum
2986 A775 400d multi   .35 .35

People's Police, 50th Anniv. A776

Designs: 400d, Ho Chi Minh, five policemen. 2000d, Policeman checking documents, vert.

2000, Aug. 19   **Litho.**   **Perf. 13**
With Gum
2987-2988   A776   Set of 2   .55   .55

Gen. Nguyen Tri Phuong, 200th Anniv. of Birth — A777

2000, Aug. 31   **Perf. 13½**
With Gum
2989   A777   400d multi   .35   .35

UN Right of the Child Conference, 10th Anniv. — A778

Emblem and: 400d, Boy and girl. 5000d, Five children, vert.

2000, Sept. 8   **Perf. 13**
2990-2991   A778   Set of 2   1.25   1.25

2000 Summer Olympics, Sydney — A779

Designs: 400d, Running. 6000d, Shooting. 7000d, Taekwondo, vert.

2000, Sept. 15
2992-2994   A779   Set of 3   2.25   2.25

Gen. Tran Hung Dao, 700th Anniv. of Death. — A780

2000, Sept. 17   **With Gum**
2995   A780   400d multi   .35   .35

Birds — A781

Designs: No. 2996, 400d, Leiothrix argentauris. No. 2997, 400d, Pitta ellioti. No. 2998, 400d, Pomatorinus ferruginosus. 5000d,

---

Dicrurus paradiceus, vert. 7000d, Melanochlora sultanea, vert. 10,000d, Stachyris striolata, vert.

2000, Sept. 28   **Perf. 13½**
2996-3001   A781   Set of 6   4.50   4.50
Souvenir Sheet
Perf. 13½x13¾
3002   A781   15,000d   Trena puella   2.75   2.75

No. 3002 contains one 42x31mm stamp. España 2000 Intl. Philatelic Exhibition (No. 3002).

Vietnam Philately Association, 40th Anniv. — A782

2000, Oct. 6   **Perf. 13**
With Gum
3003   A782   400d   No. 821   .35   .35

Farmer's Association, 70th Anniv. — A783

2000, Oct. 14   **With Gum**
3004   A783   400d multi   .35   .35

Women's Union, 70th Anniv. A784

2000, Oct. 14   **With Gum**
3005   A784   400d multi   .35   .35

Hanoi, 000th Anniv. A785

Designs: 400d, Building, and Ly Thai To, founder of Hanoi. 3000d, Temple, two people, monuments. 10,000d, Peasants with goods, building. 15,000d, People and doves.

2000, Oct. 15   **Perf. 13**
3006-3008   A785   Set of 3   2.25   2.25
Souvenir Sheet
Perf. 13½x13¾
3009   A785   15,000d multi   2.75   2.75

Bats — A786

Designs: No. 3010, 400d, Scotomanes ornatus. No. 3011, 400d, Pteropus lylei. 2000d, Rhinolophus paradoxolophus. 6000d,

---

Eonycteris spelaea. 11,000d, Cynopterus sphinx.

2000, Oct. 16   **Perf. 13**
3010-3014   A786   Set of 5   3.25   3.25

Fatherland Front, 70th Anniv. — A787

2000, Oct. 18   **With Gum**
3015   A787   400d multi   .35   .35

6th Natl. Emulation Congress A788

Designs: 400d, People at work. 3000d, Symbols of industry, vert.

2000, Nov. 10   **With Gum**
3016-3017   A788   Set of 2   .90   .90

Flowers A789

Designs: 400d, Oxyspora sp. 5000d, Melanstoma villosa, vert.

2000, Nov. 15   **Perf. 13½**
With Gum
3018-3019   A789   Set of 2   1.25   1.25

Hon Khoai Uprising, 60th Anniv. A790

2000, Dec. 13   **Perf. 13**
With Gum
3020   A790   400d multi   .35   .35

Advent of New Millennium A791

2001, Jan. 1   **With Gum**
3021   A791   400d multi   .35   .35

New Year 2001 (Year of the Snake) A792

Snake and: 400d, Pink flowers. 8000d, Yellow flowers.

2001, Jan. 1   **Perf. 13½**
With Gum
3022-3023   A792   Set of 2   1.60   1.60

Hong Kong 2001 Stamp Exhibition — A793

Fish: 400d, Toxotes microlepis. 800d, Cosmocheilus harmandi. 2000d, Anguilla bicolor pacifica. 3000d, Chitala ornata. 7000d, Megalops cyprinoides. 8000d, Probarbus jullieni.

2001, Jan. 18   **Litho.**   **Perf. 13**
3024-3029   A793   Set of 6   3.50   3.50

Nobel Prize, Cent. A794

2001, Jan. 27   **Perf. 13½**
With Gum
3030   A794   400d multi   .35   .35

Four Seasons — A795

No. 3031: a, 400d, Peach blossoms and birds (spring). b, 800d, Cotton rose and pheasant (summer). c, 4000d, Chrysanthemum and phoenix (autumn). d, 10,000d, Pine tree and cranes (winter).

2001, Feb. 1   **Perf. 13¼x13**
With Gum
3031   A795   Sheet of 4, #a-d   2.75   2.75

Wild Fruits — A796

Designs: No. 3032, 400d, Rubus cochinchinensis. No. 3033, 400d, Rhizophora mucronata. No. 3034, 400d, Podocarpus neriifolius. No. 3035, 400d, Magnolia pumila. 15,000d, Taxus chinensis.

2001, Feb. 8   **Perf. 13½**
With Gum
3032-3036   A796   Set of 5   2.60   2.60

Landscapes — A797

Designs: No. 3037, 400d, Co Tien Mountain (3-1). No. 3038, 400d, Dong Pagoda, Yen Tu

Mountain (3-2). 10,000d, King Dinh Temple (3-3).

2001, Feb. 23   *Perf. 13*
3037-3039 A797   Set of 3   2.00 2.00

Nhan Dan Newspaper, 50th Anniv. — A798

2001, Mar. 11   **With Gum**
3040 A798 400d multi   .35 .35

Rubies Found in Tan Huong A799

Designs: 400d, 1960-gram ruby. 6000d, 2160-gram "Viet Nam Star."

2001, Mar. 20   **With Gum**
3041-3042 A799   Set of 2   1.10 1.10

Ho Chi Minh Youth Union, 70th Anniv. — A800

2001, Mar. 26   **Litho.**   *Perf. 13*
     With Gum
3043 A800 400d multi   .35 .35

9th Communist Party Congress — A801

Designs: 400d, Ho Chi Minh, flag, map (2-1). 3000d, Hammer and sickle, Ngoc Lu bronze drum head, symbols of technology, vert (2-2).

2001, Apr. 18   **With Gum**
3044-3045 A801   Set of 2   .55 .55

Fauna in Cat Tien Natl. Park — A802

Designs: 400d, Arborophila davidi (4-1). 800d, Stichophthalma uemurai (4-2). 3000d, Rhinoceros sondaicus (4-3). 5000d, Crocodylus siamensis (4-4).

2001, Apr. 30   *Perf. 13½*
3046-3049 A802   Set of 4   2.25 2.25

Mushrooms A803

Designs: No. 3050, 400d, Phallus indusiatus (7-1). No. 3051, 400d, Aseroe arachnoidea (7-2). No. 3052, 400d, Phallus tenuis (7-3). 2000d, Phallus impudicus (7-4). 5000d, Phallus rugulosus (7-5). 6000d, Simblum periphragmoides (7-6). 7000d, Mutinus bambusinus (7-7).

2001, May 2
3050-3056 A803   Set of 7   4.00 4.00

A number has been reserved for a souvenir sheet for this set.

Mushrooms Type of 2001

Design: 13,000d,   Pseudocolus schellenbergiae.

2001, May 2   **Litho.**   *Perf. 13½x13¾*
3057 A803 13,000d multi   2.75 2.75

No. 3057 contains one 42x31mm stamp.

Ho Chi Minh Young Pioneer's League, 60th Anniv. — A804

2001, May 15   **Litho.**   *Perf. 13*
     With Gum
3058 A804 400d multi   .35 .35

Viet Minh Front, 60th Anniv. A805

2001, May 19   **With Gum**
3059 A805 400d multi   .35 .35

Campaign Against Smoking — A806

2001, May 30   *Perf. 13¼x13½*
     With Gum
3060 A806 800d multi   .45 .45

Children A807

Designs: 400d, Two children, UNICEF emblem. 5000d, Five children, UN emblem.

2001, June 1   *Perf. 13½*
3061-3062 A807   Set of 2   1.10 1.10

Children's safety day (#3061); UN Special Session on Children, Washington, DC (#3062).

Diesel Locomotives — A808

Designs: No. 3063, 400d, D18E (6-1). No. 3064, 400d, D4H (6-2). 800d, D11H (6-3). 2000d, D5H (6-4). 6000d, D9E (6-5). 7000d, D12E (6-6).

2001, June 5   *Perf. 13*
3063-3068 A808   Set of 6   3.50 3.50
     Souvenir Sheet
     Perf. 13½x13¾
3069 A808 13,000d D11H, diff.   2.75 2.75

No. 3069 contains one 43x32mm stamp.

Orchids A809

Designs: No. 3070, 800d, Vanda sp. (6-1). No. 3071, 800d, Dendrobium lowianum (6-2). No. 3072, 800d, Phajus wallichii (6-3). No. 3073, 800d, Habenaria medioflexa (6-4). No. 3074, 800d, Arundina graminifolia, vert. (6-5). 12,000d, Calanthe clavata, vert. (6-6).

Perf. 13½x13¼, 13¼x13½

2001, July 5
     With Gum
3070-3075 A809   Set of 6   3.25 3.25

Phila Nippon '01 — A810

Butterflies: No. 3076, 800d, Troides aeacus (6-1). No. 3077, 800d, Inachis io (6-2). No. 3078, 800d, Ancyluris formosissima (6-3). 5000d, Cymothoe sanguris (6-4). 7000d, Taenaris selene (6-5). 10,000d, Trogonoptera brookiana (6-6).

13,000d, Atrophaneura horishanus, vert.

2001, July 16   *Perf. 13½x13¼*
3076-3081 A810   Set of 6   4.00 4.00
     Souvenir Sheet
     Perf. 13¾x13½
3082 A810 13,000d multi   2.75 2.75

No. 3082 contains one 32x42mm stamp.

2002 World Cup Soccer Championships, Japan and Korea — A811

No. 3083: a, 800d, Player with red shirt. b, 3000d, Player with white shirt.

2001, July 24   *Perf. 13*
     With Gum
3083 A811   Horiz. pair, #a-b   .90 .90

Musical Instruments — A812

Designs: No. 3084, 800d, Ho gáo (6-1). No. 3085, 800d, Kenh (6-2). No. 3086, 800d, Dàn tú, vert. (6-3). 2000d, Dàn t'rung, vert. (6-4). 6000d, Trong kinang, vert . (6-5). 9000d, Tính tau, vert. (6-6).

Perf. 13x13¼, 13¼x13

2001, Aug. 4   **Litho.**
3084-3089 A812   Set of 6   3.25 3.25

Year of Dialogue Among Civilizations — A813

2001, Oct. 9   **Litho.**   *Perf. 13¼x13½*
     With Gum
3090 A813 800d multi   .45 .45

Tran Huy Lieu (1901-69), Writer — A814

2001, Nov. 5   *Perf. 13x12¾*
     With Gum
3091 A814 800d multi   .45 .45

Nam Cao (1917-51), Writer A815

2001, Nov. 30   *Perf. 13x13¼*
     With Gum
3092 A815 800d multi   .45 .45

A816   A817

2001   *Perf. 13½*
     With Gum
3093 A816   800d multi   .25 .25
3094 A817   3000d multi   .65 .65

New Year 2002 (Year of the Horse) A818

Horse facing: 800d, Right. 8000d, Left. 14,000d, Horse galloping.

2002, Jan. 2   *Perf. 13½*
With Gum
3095-3096 A818   Set of 2   1.40   1.40
Souvenir Sheet
Perf. 13½x13¼
3097 A818 14,000d multi   2.75   2.75
No. 3097 contains one 42x31mm stamp.

Opera Costumes
A819

Designs: No. 3098, 1000d, Giáp Tuong Nam (6-1). No. 3099, 1000d, Giáp Tuong Nu (6-2). 2000d, Giáp Tuong Phan Dien (6-3). 3000d, Long Chan (6-4). 5000d, Giáp Tuong Phien (6-5). 9000d, Lung Xiem Quan Giáp (6-6).

2002, Jan. 15   *Perf. 13*
3098-3103 A819   Set of 6   3.25   3.25

Vo Thi Sáu, Heroine, 50th Anniv. of Death A820

2002, Jan. 23   *Perf. 13x13¼*
3104 A820 1000d multi   .45   .45

Program Implementation of 9th Communist Party Congress
A821

Designs: 800d, Map, satellite, buildings, dam, power lines, bridge, computer keyboard (2-1). 3000d, Flag, building, doves, people (2-2).

2002, Feb. 1   *Perf. 13¼x13*
With Gum
3105-3106 A821   Set of 2   .90   .90

Cacti — A822

Designs: No. 3107, 1000d, Echinocereus albatus (5-1). No. 3108, 1000d, Echinocereus delaetii (5-2). No. 3109, 1000d, Cylindropuntia bigelowii (5-3). 5000d, Echinocereus triglochidatus (5-4). 10,000d, Epiphyllum truncatum (5-5).

2002, Feb. 18   *Perf. 13¼x13½*
3107-3111 A822   Set of 5   3.00   3.00

Victor Hugo (1802-85), French Writer
A823

2002, Feb. 26   *Perf. 13x13¼*
With Gum
3112 A823 1000d multi   .45   .45

A824

2002   Litho.   *Perf. 13x13¼*
With Gum
3113 A824 800d multi   .45   .45

Birds — A825

Designs: 600d, Actinodura sodangorum (6-1). No. 3115, 800d, Garrulax ngoclinhensis (6-2). No. 3116, 800d, Garrulax pectoralis (6-3). No. 3117, 800d, Pomatorhinus hypoleucos (6-4). Minla ignotincta (6-5). 8000d, Minla cyanouroptera (6-6).

2002, Mar. 15   Litho.   *Perf. 13½*
With Gum
3114-3119 A825   Set of 6   2.75   2.75

Landscapes
A826

Designs: No. 3120, 800d, Ganh Son, Binh Thuan (3-1). No. 3121, 800d, Dawn over Tung Estuary, Quang Tri (3-2). 10,000d, Sa Huynh Harbor, Quang Ngai (3-3).

2002, Mar. 15   **With Gum**
3120-3122 A826   Set of 3   2.00   2.00

Primates — A827

Designs: 600d, Trachypithecus poliocephalus (8-1). 800d, Trachypithecus delacouri (8-2). 1000d, Rhinopithecus avunculus (8-3). 2000d, Pygathrix cinerea (8-4). 4000d, Nomascus concolor (8-5). 5000d, Trachypithecus laotum hatinhensis (8-6). 7000d, Trachypithecus phayrei (8-7). 9000d, Pygathrix nemaeus (8-8).

2002, Apr. 10
3123-3130 A827   Set of 8   4.50   4.50
3130a   Souvenir sheet, #3123-3130 + label   4.50   4.50

Bui Thi Xuan, 200th Anniv. of Death — A828

2002, Apr. 13   *Perf. 13*
With Gum
3131 A828 1000d multi   .45   .45

Souvenir Sheet

2002 World Cup Soccer Championships, Japan and Korea — A829

Color of player or players: a, 1000d, Blue. b, 2000d, Red. c, 5000d, Red violet. d, 7000d, Green.

2002, June 1   Litho.
With Gum
3132 A829   Sheet of 4, #a-d   2.75   2.75

Flowers — A830

Designs: 600d, Paphiopedilum concolor (7-1). 800d, Sterculia lanceolata (7-2). 1000d, Schefflera alongensis (7-3). 2000d, Hibiscus tiliaceus (7-4). 3000d, Mussaenda glabra (7-5). 5000d, Boniodendron parviflorum (7-6). 9000d, Bauhinia ornata.

2002, June 5
3133-3139 A830   Set of 7   3.25   3.25

Chau Van Liem, Communist Party Leader, Cent. of Birth — A831

2002, June 28   Litho.   *Perf. 13*
With Gum
3140 A831 800d multi   .45   .45

Stamp Day — A832

2002, July 1   *Perf. 13x12¾*
With Gum
3141 A832 800d multi + label   .45   .45

Tay Nguyen Province
A833

2002, July 10   Litho.   *Perf. 13*
With Gum
3142 A833 800d multi   .25   .25

Soft-shell Turtles
A834

Designs: 800d, Pelochelys bibroni (4-1). 2000d, Pelodiscus sinensis. 5000d, Palea steindachneri. 9000d, Trionyx cartilagineus.

2002, July 15   Litho.   *Perf. 13½*
3143-3146 A834   Set of 4   2.60   2.60
3146a   Souvenir sheet, 2 each #3143-3146   5.25   5.25

Viet Nam — Laos Diplomatic Relations, 40th Anniv.
A835

2002, July 18   *Perf. 13*
With Gum
3147 A835 800d multi   .45   .45

Civil Aircraft
A836

Designs: 800d, Super King Air B200 in air (4-1). 2000d, Fokker 70 (4-2). 3000d, ATR-72 (4-3). 8000d, Boeing 767-300 (4-4). 14,000d, Super King Air B200 on ground.

2002, Aug. 1   *Perf. 13*
With Gum
3148-3151 A836   Set of 4   2.25   2.25
Souvenir Sheet
Perf. 13½x13¾
3152 A836 14,000d multi   2.25   2.25

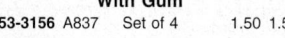

Autumn Festival Lanterns
A837

Designs: No. 3153, 800d, Den Ong Sao (4-1). No. 3154, 800d, Den Ong Su (4-2). 2000d, Den Con Tho Om Trang (4-3). 7000d, Den Xep (4-4).

2002, Aug. 16   *Perf. 13½*
With Gum
3153-3156 A837   Set of 4   1.50   1.50

Viet Nam Posts and Telecommunications Trade Union, 55th Anniv. — A838

2002, Aug. 23   **Perf. 13**
With Gum
3157 A838 800d multi   .35   .35

Bridges — A839

Designs: No. 3158, 800d, Cau Long Bien (4-1). No. 3159, 800d, Cau Song Han (4-2). 2000d, Cau Truong Tien (4-3). 10,000d, Cau My Thuan (4-4).

2002, Sept. 27   **Perf. 13x13¼**
With Gum
3158-3161 A839   Set of 4   2.00   2.00

Communist Party's Ideology and Culture Commission, 72nd Anniv. — A840

2002, Oct. 10   **Perf. 13**
With Gum
3162 A840 800d multi   .35   .35

Hanoi Medical University, Cent. A841

2002, Nov. 15   **With Gum**
3163 A841 800d multi   .35   .35

Teachers' Day — A842

2002, Nov. 20   **With Gum**
3164 A842 800d multi   .35   .35

New Year 2003 (Year of the Ram) — A843

Various goats with background colors of: 800d, Rose pink (2-1). 8000d, Orange (2-2).

2002, Dec. 15   **Perf. 13½**
With Gum
3165-3166 A843   Set of 2   1.25   1.25

Viet Nam — South Korea Diplomatic Relations, 10th Anniv. — A844

Pagoda from: No. 3167, 800d, Viet Nam (2-1). No. 3168, 800d, South Korea (2-2).

2002, Dec. 21   **Perf. 13**
With Gum
3167-3168 A844   Set of 2   .65   .65

Starting with the 2003 issues, stamps are gummed unless otherwise indicated.

Landscapes — A845

Designs: 800d, Rung Cao Su, Bình Phuoc (3-1). 3000d, Ao Bà Om, Trà Vinh (3-2). 7000d, Mot nhanh song Rach Gam-Xoài Mút, Tien Giang (3-3).

2003, Feb. 1   **Litho.**   **Perf. 13**
3169-3171 A845   Set of 3   1.40   1.40

Viet Nam Culture Program, 60th Anniv. — A846

2003, Feb. 3
3172 A846 800d multi   .30   .30

Viet Nam Cinema Association, 50th Anniv. — A847

2003, Mar. 1
3173 A847 1000d multi   .30   .30

Khanh Hoa Province, 350th Anniv. A848

2003, Mar. 25
3174 A848 800d multi   .30   .30

Cycle Rickshaws A849

Cycle rickshaws from: 800d, Hanoi. 3000d, Ho Chi Minh City. 8000d, Haiphong.

2003, Apr. 1
3175-3177 A849   Set of 3   1.60   1.60

Adventures of the Cricket — A850

2003, May 1   **Perf. 13¼x13½**
3178   Horiz. strip of 6   2.60   2.60
  a.   A850 800d Toi là út...   .25   .25
  b.   A850 1000d Chang bao...   .25   .25
  c.   A850 2000d Toi an han...   .25   .25
  d.   A850 3000d Toi và Trui...   .40   .40
  e.   A850 5000d Mot ngày...   .65   .65
  f.   A850 8000d Tu nay the...   1.00   1.00

Animals in Ba Vi National Park — A851

Designs: No. 3179, 800d, Manis pentadactyla (4-1). No. 3180, 800d, Petaurista petaurista (4-2). 5000d, Selenarctos thibetanus (4-3). 10,000d, Capricornis suma-traensis (4-4).

2003, June 5   **Perf. 13½**
3179-3182 A851   Set of 4   2.25   2.25

22nd South East Asian Games, Viet Nam — A852

Designs: 800d, Soccer (4-1). 2000d, Hurdles (4-2). 3000d, Kayaking (4-3). 7000d, Wrestling (4-4).
10,000d, Games emblem, mascot, stadium.

2003, July 1   **Perf. 13**
3183-3186 A852   Set of 4   1.75   1.75
Souvenir Sheet
Perf. 13½x13¾
3187 A852 10,000d multi   1.25   1.25

Camellias — A854

Designs: 800d, Camellia petelotii (4-1). 1000d, Camellia rubriflora (4-2). 5000d, Camellia vietnamensis (4-3). 6000d, Camellia gilberti (4-4).

2003, Sept. 1   **Perf. 13½**
3189-3192 A854   Set of 4   1.75   1.75
Bangkok 2003 World Philatelic Exhibition.

Orchids A855

Designs: 800d, Paphiopedilum dianthum (2-1). 8000d, Pleione bulbocodioides (2-2).

2003, Oct. 1   **Perf. 13**
3193-3194 A855   Set of 2   1.10   1.10

Asian Elephants A856

Designs: 800d, Elephant with trunk extended (4-1). 1000d, Elephants and riders (4-2). 2000d, Elephant with trunk down (4-3). 8000d, Two elephants (4-4)

2003, Oct. 1   **Perf. 13½**
3195-3198 A856   Set of 4   1.50   1.50
3198a   Miniature sheet, 2 each
    #3195-3198   3.00   3.00

My Son World Heritage Site — A857

Various ruins: 800d, (3-1). 3000d, (3-2). 8000d (3-3).
10,000d, Temple (43x32mm).

2003, Dec. 1   **Perf. 13x13¼**
3199-3201 A857   Set of 3   1.50   1.50
Souvenir Sheet
Perf. 13½x13¾
3202 A857 10,000d multi   1.25   1.25

New Year 2004 (Year of the Monkey) A858

Monkeys and: 800d, Apple tree (2-1). 8000d, Palm leaf (2-2).

2003, Dec. 1   **Perf. 13½**
3203-3204 A858   Set of 2   1.10   1.10

Ninth Congress of Viet Nam Federation of Trade Unions — A853

2003, July 28   **Perf. 13**
3188 A853 800d multi   .30   .30

Ngo Gia Tu (1908-35), Leader of 1926 Strike — A859

2003, Dec. 30 *Perf. 13¼x13*
3205 A859 800d multi .30 .30

Congratulations A860

Designs: 800d, Flowers (2-1). 8000d, Bird with envelope (2-2).

2004, Jan. 1 *Perf. 13 Syncopated*
3206-3207 A860 Set of 2 1.10 1.10

Shells A861

Designs: 800d, Murex trocheli (3-1). 3000d, Murex haustellum (3-2). 8000d, Chicoreus ramosus (3-3).

2004, Feb. 1 *Perf. 13*
3208-3210 A861 Set of 3 1.50 1.50

Bamboo Lamps — A862

Various lamps with background colors of: 400d, Yellow (3-1). 1000d, Pale green (3-2). 7000d, Buff (3-3).

Perf. 13 Syncopated
2004, Mar. 1 *Litho.*
3211-3213 A862 Set of 3 1.10 1.10
See Nos. 3352-3363.

Hué, UNESCO World Heritage Site — A863

Designs: 800d, Pavilion of Edicts (3-1). 4000d, Ngo Mon Gate (3-2). No. 3216, 8000d, Hien Lam Pavilion (3-3). No. 3217, 8000d, Thai Hoa Palace.

2004, Apr. 1 *Perf. 13*
Stamp + Label
3214-3216 A863 Set of 3 1.75 1.75
Souvenir Sheet
Perf. 13½x13¾
3217 A863 8000d multi 1.00 1.00
No. 3217 contains one 42x31mm stamp.

Tran Phu (1904-31), Communist Leader — A864

2004, May 1 *Perf. 13*
3218 A864 800d multi .30 .30

Battle of Dien Bien Phu, 50th Anniv. A865

Designs: 800d, Soldier, flowers (2-1). 5000d, Dancer, flowers. 8000d, Three dancers, flowers.

2004, May 4 *Perf. 13*
3219-3220 A865 Set of 2 .75 .75
Souvenir Sheet
Perf. 13½x13¾
3221 A865 8000d multi 1.00 1.00

FIFA (Fédération Internationale de Football Association), Cent. — A866

2004, May 21 *Perf. 13*
3222 A866 800d multi .30 .30

Thieu Nien Newspaper, 50th Anniv. — A867

2004, June 1
3223 A867 800d multi .30 .30

Bonsai — A868

Designs: 800d, Ficus microcarpa (4-1). 2000d, Premna serratifolia (4-2). 3000d, Ficus pilosa (4-3). 8000d, Ficus religiosa (4-4).

2004, July 1
3224-3227 A868 Set of 4 1.75 1.75
2004 World Stamp Championship, Singapore.

2004 Summer Olympics, Athens — A869

Designs: 800d, Hurdles (4-1). 1000d, Swimming, horiz. (4-2). 6000d, Shooting, horiz. (4-3). 7000d, Taekwondo (4-4).

2004, Aug. 1
3228-3231 A869 Set of 4 1.90 1.90

Naming of Country as Viet Nam, Bicent. A870

Designs: 800d, Citadel, Hué, lotus flower (2-1). 5000d, Ho Chi Minh, flag (2-2).

2004, Sept. 2 Set of 2 .75 .75
3232-3233 A870

World Summit on the Information Society, Geneva — A871

2004, Oct. 9
3234 A871 1000d multi .30 .30

Liberation of Hanoi From French, 50th Anniv. — A872

2004, Oct. 10
3235 A872 800d multi .30 .30

Dak Lak Province, Cent. — A873

2004, Nov. 22
3236 A873 800d multi .30 .30

Hoi An, UNESCO World Heritage Site — A874

Designs: 800d, Chua Cau. 8000d, Hoi Quán Phúc Kien.

Perf. 13¼x13¾ Syncopated
2004, Dec. 1
3237 A874 800d multi .30 .30
Souvenir Sheet
Perf. 13½x13¾
3238 A874 8000d multi 1.00 1.00
No. 3238 contains one 42x31mm stamp.

New Year 2005 (Year of the Rooster) A875

Designs: 800d, Rooster (2-1). 8000d, Hen and chicks.

2004, Dec. 15 *Perf. 13*
3239-3240 A875 Set of 2 1.10 1.10
3240a Souvenir sheet, #3239-3240 1.10 1.10

Viet Nam Communist Party, 75th Anniv. — A876

2005, Feb. 3
3241 A876 800d multi .30 .30

Gia Lai Province A877

Perf. 13¼x13¾ Syncopated
2005, Mar. 16 *Litho.*
3242 A877 800d multi .25 .25

Nha Trang Bay — A878

Designs: 800d, Boat near shore (2-1). 8000d, Road near shore (2-2).

2005, Apr. 2 *Perf. 13x12¾*
Stamp + Label
3243-3244 A878 Set of 2 1.10 1.10

Worldwide Fund for Nature (WWF) A879

Various views of Chrotogale owstoni: 800d, (4-1). 3000d, (4-2). 5000d, (4-3). 8000d, (4-4).

2005, May 2 *Perf. 13½*
3245-3248 A879 Set of 4 3.25 3.25
3248a Souvenir sheet, #3245-3248, perf. 13x13½ 3.50 3.50

Liberation of Haiphong, 50th Anniv. — A880

Designs: 800d, Burning airplanes at Cat Bi Airport, Haiphong harbor (2-1). 5000d, Nam Trieu Port (2-2).

2005, May 6   **Perf. 13x12¾**
Stamp + Label
3249-3250 A880   Set of 2   .75 .75

People's Police, 60th Anniv.
A881

Medals and: 800d, Marching police, statue of Ho Chi Minh (2-1). 10,000d, Police helping civilians (2-2).

2005, Aug. 10   **Perf. 13**
3251-3252 A881   Set of 2   1.40 1.40

Posts and Telecommunications Dept., 60th Anniv. — A882

2005, Aug. 15   **Perf. 13**
Background Color
3253 A882 800d beige   .25 .25
Souvenir Sheet
Perf. 13½x13¾
3254 A882 8000d gray   1.00 1.00

August Revolution, 60th Anniv. — A883

Crowd with flags in: 1000d, Hanoi (3-1). 2000d, Hué (3-2). 4000d, Saigon (3-3).

2005, Aug. 19   **Perf. 13**
3255-3257 A883   Set of 3   .90 .90
3257a   Souvenir sheet, #3255-
            3257   .90 .90

Traditional Dress and Houses of Ethnic Groups — A884

No. 3258: a, Ba-na (54-1). b, Bo Y (54-2). c, Brau (54-3). d, Bru-Van Kieu (54-4). e, Cham (54-5). f, Cho-ro (54-6). g, Chu-ru (54-7). h, Chut (54-8). i, Co (54-9). j, Cong (54-10). k, Co-ho (54-11). l, Co Lao (54-12). m, Co-tu (54-13). n, Dao (54-14). o, E-de (54-15). p, Gia-rai (54-16). q, Giay (54-17). r, Gie-Trieng (54-18). s, Ha Nhi (54-19). t, Hoa (54-20). u, Hre (54-21). v, Khang (54-22). w, Khmer (54-23). x, Kho-mu (54-24). y, Kinh (54-25). z, La Chi (54-26). aa, La Ha (54-27). ab, La Hu (54-28). ac, Lao (54-29). ad, Lo Lo (54-30). ae, Lu (54-31). af, Ma (54-32). ag, Mang (54-33). ah, Mnong (54-34). ai, Mong (54-35). aj, Muong (54-36). ak, Ngai (54-37). al, Nung (54-38). am, O Du (54-39). an, Pa Then (54-40). ao, Phu La (54-41). ap, Pu Peo (54-42). aq, Ra-glai (54-43). ar, Ro-mam (54-44). as, San Chay (54-45). at, San Diu (54-46). au, Si La (54-47). av, Ta-oi (54-48). aw, Tay (54-49). ax, Thai (54-50). ay, Tho (54-51). az, Xinh-mun (54-52). ba, Xo-dang (54-53). bb, Xtieng (54-54).

Perf. 13¾x13¼ Syncopated
2005, Aug. 30
3258   Sheet of 54 + 2 labels 5.50 5.50
a.-bb.   A884 800d Any single   .25   .25
          Complete booklet, #3258a-
          3258bb   5.50

Thang Long (Hanoi), 1000th Anniv.
A885

People reenacting battles and: 800d, Statue of Gen. Quang Trung, building (3-1). 5000d, Statue of Independence Fighters, building (3-2). No. 3261, 8000d, Statue of Victory Against B-52's, Long Bien Bridge (3-3).

No. 3262, Government officials on dais in Ba Dinh Square.

2005, Oct. 10   **Litho.**   **Perf. 13**
3259-3261 A885   Set of 3   1.75 1.75
Souvenir Sheet
Perf. 13½x13¾
3262 A885 8000d multi   1.00 1.00

New Year 2006 (Year of the Dog) A886

Designs: 800d, Dog and puppies (2-1). 8000d, Dog (2-2).

2005, Dec. 1   **Perf. 13**
3263-3264 A886   Set of 2   1.10 1.10
3264a   Souvenir sheet, #3263-
            3264   1.10 1.10

National Coat of Arms, 50th Anniv.
A887

2006, Jan. 14   **Perf. 13**
3265 A887 1000d multi   .25 .25

10th Vietnamese Communist Party Congress
A888

2006, Feb. 3
3266 A888 800d multi   .25 .25

Prime Minister Pham Van Dong (1906-2000) — A889

2006, Mar. 1
3267 A889 800d multi   .25 .25

Wolfgang Amadeus Mozart (1756-91), Composer — A890

2006, Mar. 1
3268 A890 2000d multi   .25 .25

Léopold Senghor (1906-2001), First President of Senegal — A891

2006, Mar. 20   **Litho.**   **Perf. 13**
3269 A891 800d multi   .25 .25

BirdLife International
A892

Designs: 800d, Lophura edwardsi (5-1). 2000d, Arborophila davidi (5-2). 3000d, Lophura hatinhensis (5-3). 5000d, Polyplectron germaini (5-4, 49x23mm). 8000d, Rheinardia ocellata (5-5, 49x23mm).

Perf. 13¼x14 Syncopated, 13¼x13½ Syncopated (#3273-3274)
2006, Apr. 1
3270-3274 A892   Set of 5   2.40 2.40
3274a   Souvenir sheet, #3270-
            3274   2.40 2.40

2006 World Cup Soccer Championships, Germany — A893

Designs: 800d, One player (1-2). 10,000d, Two players (2-2).

2006, May 1   **Litho.**   **Perf. 13¼x13**
3275-3276 A893   Set of 2   1.40 1.40

Phong Nha - Ke Bang National Park World Heritage Site — A894

Designs: 800d, Bi Ky Cave (3-1). 4000d, Xuyen Son Cave (3-2). 8000d, Nuoc Moc Stream (3-3). 12,000d, Tien Cave, vert.

2006, June 1   **Perf. 13x12¾**
3277-3279 A894   Set of 3   1.60 1.60
Souvenir Sheet
Perf. 13¾x13½
3280 A894 12,000d multi   1.50 1.50

No. 3280 contains one 32x43mm stamp.

Animals in Ben En Botanical Gardens
A895

Designs: 800d, Nycticebus bengalensis (4-1). 1000d, Neofelis nebulosa, horiz. (4-2). 7000d, Cuon alpinus, horiz. (4-3). 10,000d, Nomascus leucogenys (4-4). 12,000d, Physignathus cocincinus, horiz.

2006, July 1   **Perf. 13¼x13, 13x13¼**
3281-3284 A895   Set of 4   2.40 2.40
Souvenir Sheet
Perf. 13½x13¾
3285 A895 12,000d multi   1.50 1.50

Flowers — A896

Designs: 800d, Momordica cochinchinensis (4-1). 3000d, Telosma cordata (4-2). 5000d, Momordica charantia (4-3). 8000d, Luffa cylindrica (4-4).

2006, Aug. 1   **Perf. 13**
3286-3289 A896   Set of 4   2.10 2.10

Asia-Pacific Economic Cooperation Summit — A897

2006, Sept. 16
3290 A897 8000d multi   1.00 1.00

Cooperation Between Viet Nam and European Union — A898

2006, Oct. 1   **Perf. 13x13¼**
3291 A898 800d multi   .25   .25

New Year 2007 (Year of the Pig) A899

Designs: 800d, Pig and piglets (2-1). 8000d, Pig (2-2).

2006, Dec. 15   **Perf. 13**
3292-3293 A899   Set of 2   1.10 1.10

Tran Te Xuong (1870-1907),
Poet — A900

2007, Jan. 20　Litho.　Perf. 13x13¼
3294　A900　1000d multi　　　.25　.25

Implementation of
Resolutions of 10th
Communist Party
Congress — A901

Perf. 13½x13¼ Syncopated
2007, Feb. 3
3295　A901　800d multi　　　.25　.25

Truong Chinh (1907-88), General
Secretary of Communist Party — A902

2007, Feb. 9　　　　Perf. 13x13¼
3296　A902　800d multi　　　.25　.25

Le Duan (1907-86), First Secretary of
Communist Party — A903

2007, Apr. 7
3297　A903　800d multi　　　.25　.25

Dugong Dugon — A904

Various depictions of Dugong dugon: 800d,
(4-1). 1000d, (4-2). 7000d, (4-3). 9000d, (4-4).

2007, Aug. 1　Litho.　Perf. 13
3298-3301　A904　Set of 4　　2.25　2.25

Association of South East Asian
Nations (ASEAN), 40th Anniv. — A905

Designs: No. 3302, 800d, Secretariat Building, Bandar Seri Begawan, Brunei (10-1). No.
3303, 800d, National Museum of Cambodia
(10-2). No. 3304, 800d, Fatahillah Museum,
Jakarta, Indonesia (10-3). No. 3305, 800d,
Typical house, Laos (10-4). No. 3306, 800d,
Malayan Railway Headquarters Building,
Kuala Lumpur, Malaysia (10-5). No. 3307,
800d, Yangon Post Office, Myanmar (Burma)

(10-6). No. 3308, 800d, Malacañang Palace,
Philippines (10-7). No. 3309, 800d, National
Museum of Singapore (10-8). No. 3310, 800d,
Vimanmek Mansion, Bangkok, Thailand (10-
9). No. 3311, 800d, Presidential Palace,
Hanoi, Viet Nam (10-10).

2007, Aug. 8　Litho.　Perf. 13x13¼
3302-3311　A905　Set of 10　　1.00　1.00
3311a　Miniature sheet of 10, #3302-
　　　3311　　　　　　　1.00　1.00

See Brunei No. 607, Burma No. 370, Cambodia No. 2339, Indonesia Nos. 2120-2121,
Laos Nos. 1717-1718, Malaysia No. 1170,
Philippines Nos. 3103-3105, Singapore No.
1265, and Thailand No. 2315.

Tay
Nguyen
Tribal
Gongs
A906

Various tribal members using gongs: 800d,
(3-1). 5000d, (3-2). 8000d, (3-3).
12,000d, Man holding gong.

2007, Nov. 21　Litho.　Perf. 13x13¼
3312-3314　A906　Set of 3　　1.75　1.75
Souvenir Sheet
3314A　A906　12,000d multi　　1.50　1.50

New Year
2008 (Year
of the
Rat) — A907

Designs: 800d, Rat at left (2-1). 8000d, Rat
at right (2-2).

2007, Dec. 1　　　　Perf. 13½
3315-3316　A907　Set of 2　　1.10　1.10

Ho Chi Minh
(1890-1969)
A908

Perf. 13¼x13½
2007, Dec. 31　　　　Litho.
3317　A908　1000d dk red & pink　.25　.25
3318　A908　3000d dk & lt green　.40　.40
3319　A908　4000d dk & lt blue　.50　.50
　　　Nos. 3317-3319 (3)　　1.15　1.15

Vietnamese Cuisine — A909

Designs: 800d, Nem rán (2-1). 9000d, Pho
bò (2-2).

2008, Feb. 1　　　　Perf. 13x13¼
3320-3321　A909　Set of 2　　1.25　1.25

Orchids
A910

Designs: 800d, Calanthe densiflora (4-1).
2000d, Ludisia discolor (4-2). 6000d,
Spathoglottis affinis (4-3). 8000d, Calanthe
argenteo-striata (4-4).

2008, Mar. 1　Litho.　Perf. 13½
3322-3325　A910　Set of 4　　2.10　2.10

2008 Summer Olympics,
Beijing — A911

Designs: 800d, Wushu (4-1). 3000d, Swimming (4-2). 5000d, Taekwondo (4-3). 9000d,
Canoeing (4-4).

Perf. 14x13½ Syncopated
2008, Mar. 15　　　　Litho.
3326-3329　A911　Set of 4　　2.25　2.25

Cyprinus Carpio — A912

Various depictions of Cyprinus carpio: 800d,
(3-1). 6000d, (3-2). 8000d, (3-3).

2008, Apr. 1　　　　Perf. 13
3330-3332　A912　Set of 3　　1.90　1.90

Vinasat-1
Satellite
A913

2008, Apr. 19　　　　Perf. 13½
3333　A913　800d multi　　　.25　.25

Vietnamese Court Music, UNESCO
Masterpiece of Intangible
Heritage — A914

Inscriptions: 800d, Dai nhac, Bien khanh (3-
1). 4000d, Tieu nhac, Dàn Nguyet và Nhi (3-
2). 8000d, Luc cúng hoa dang, Kèn Bóp và
Sáo (3-3).
9000d, Dai nhac trong le te.

2008, June 3　Litho.　Perf. 13x12¾
3334-3336　A914　Set of 3　　1.60　1.60
Souvenir Sheet
Perf. 13x12¾ Syncopated
3337　A914　9000d multi　　1.10　1.10

No. 3337 contains one 40x28mm stamp.

Tran Quy Cáp (1870-1908),
Progressive Movement Leader — A915

2008, June 8　Litho.　Perf. 13
3338　A915　1000d multi　　　.25　.25

Binh
Thuan
Province
A916

2008, Sept. 1　　　　Perf. 13x12¾
3339　A916　800d multi　　　.25　.25

Seascapes of France and Viet
Nam — A917

Designs: 800d, Strait of Bonifacio, France
(2-1). 14,000d, Along Bay, Viet Nam (2-2).

2008, Oct. 15
3340-3341　A917　Set of 2　　1.75　1.75
See France Nos. 3519-3520.

Lady Trieu's
Rebellion, A.D.
248 — A918

Perf. 13¼x13½ Syncopated
2008, Oct. 20
3342　A918　1000d multi　　　.25　.25

Flowers
A919

Designs: 800d, Ceiba chodatii (2-1).
10,000d, Nelumbo nucifera (2-2).

2008, Oct. 25　　　　Perf. 13
3343-3344　A019　Set of 2　　1.40　1.40
See Argentina Nos. 2508-2509.

Fruit — A920

Designs: 2000d, Durio zibetinus (2-1).
8000d, Hylocereus undatus (2-2).

2008, Nov. 18　Litho.　Perf. 13½
3345-3346　A920　Set of 2　　1.25　1.25
See Singapore Nos. 1352-1353.

New Year 2009 (Year of the Ox) — A921

Designs: 2000d, Ox (2-1). 9000d, Ox and calf (2-2).

2008, Dec. 1   Litho.   Perf. 13½
3347-3348 A921   Set of 2   1.40 1.40
3348a   Souvenir sheet,
                   #3347-3348   1.40 1.40

Nguyen Khuyen (1835-1909), Poet — A922

2009, Feb. 2   Litho.   Perf. 13¼x13
3349 A922 2000d multi   .25 .25

Charles Darwin (1809-82), Naturalist A923

2009, Feb. 12   Perf. 13
3350 A923 2000d multi   .25 .25

Border and Coast Guard's Day — A924

2009, Mar. 3   Perf. 13¼x13
3351 A924 2000d multi   .25 .25

Bamboo Lamps Type of 2004
Perf. 13 Syncopated
2009, May 15   Litho.
Background Color
Design of No. 3211
3352 A862 1200d yellow (12-
            1)   .25 .25
3353 A862 2000d lt green
            (12-2)   .25 .25
3354 A862 2500d blue (12-3)   .30 .30
3355 A862 4500d gray blue
            (12-4)   .50 .50
Design of No. 3212
3356 A862 5000d gray green
            (12-5)   .55 .55
3357 A862 6500d brn vio
            (12-6)   .75 .75
3358 A862 9500d violet (12-
            7)   1.10 1.10
3359 A862 10,500d red (12-8)   1.25 1.25
Design of No. 3213
3360 A862 13,500d fawn (12-
            9)   1.50 1.50
3361 A862 14,500d brn yel
            (12-10)   1.75 1.75
3362 A862 17,500d drab (12-
            11)   2.00 2.00
3363 A862 18,500d olive grn
            (12-12)   2.10 2.10
      Nos. 3352-3363 (12)   12.30 12.30

Opening of the Ho Chi Minh Trail, 50th Anniv. A925

2009, May 19   Perf. 13
3364 A925 2000d multi   .25 .25

Praying Mantises A926

Designs: 1500d, Mantis religiosa (2-1). 12,500d, Tenodera aridiforia (2-2).

2009, July 1   Litho.   Perf. 13½
3365-3366 A926 Set of 2   1.60 1.60

Rhododendrons — A927

Designs: 500d, Rhododendron fortunei (4-1). 1200d, Rhododendron simsii (4-2). 4500d, Rhododendron sp. (4-3). 14,500d, Enkianthus quinqueflorus (4-4).

Perf. 13¼x13¾ Syncopated
2009, Aug. 1
3367-3370 A927 Set of 4   2.40 2.40

Fish A928

Designs: 2000d, Botia macracanthus (4-1). 3000d, Trichopsis pumila (4-2). 6500d, Cynolebias elongatus (4-3). 10,500d, Centropyge flavissima (4-4). 14,500d Scleropages formosus.

2009, Sept. 1   Perf. 13
3371-3374 A928 Set of 4   2.50 2.50
Souvenir Sheet
Perf. 13½x13¾
3375 A928 14,500d multi   1.75 1.75

New Year 2010 (Year of the Tiger) A929

Tiger: 2000d, Walking (2-1). 8500d, Sitting (2-2).

2009, Dec. 1   Litho.   Perf. 13x13¼
3376-3377 A929 Set of 2   1.25 1.25

Viet Nam Communist Party, 80th Anniv. — A930

2010, Feb. 2   Litho.   Perf. 13¼x13
3378 A930 2000d multi   .25 .25

Frédéric Chopin (1810-49), Composer — A931

2010, Feb. 22   Litho.   Perf. 13
3379 A931 2000d multi   .25 .25

Intl. Women's Day A932

2010, Mar. 8   Litho.   Perf. 13x13¼
3380 A932 3000d multi   .35 .35

Pres. Ho Chi Minh (1890-1969), A933

2010, May 16   Litho.   Perf. 13
3381 A933 2000d multi   .25 .25

BirdLife International — A934

Birds: 2000d, Tringa guttifer. 6500d, Calidris pygmeus. 8500d, Larus saundersi. 14,500d, Rynchops albicollis.

2010, May 25   Litho.   Perf. 13x13¼
3382-3384 A934 Set of 3   1.90 1.90
Souvenir Sheet
Perf. 13½x13¾
3385 A934 14,500d multi   1.60 1.60

Nguyen Huu Tho (1910-96), Acting President — A935

2010, July 10   Perf. 13x13¼
3386 A935 2000d multi   .25 .25

Ta Quang Buu (1910-86), Minister of Higher and Secondary Professional Education — A936

2010, July 23
3387 A936 2000d multi   .25 .25

Fairy Lilies — A937

Designs: 3500d, Zephyranthes carinata. 10,500d, Zephyranthes ajax.

Perf. 14x13½ Syncopated
2010, July 30
3388-3389 A937 Set of 2   1.50 1.50
Bangkok 2010 Intl. Philatelic Exhibition.

Worldwide Fund for Nature (WWF) — A938

Prionailurus viverrinus: 2000d, At water's edge, facing right. 2500d, In water with fish in mouth. 4500d, Standing on rocks, facing left. 10,500d, Sitting.

2010, Aug. 1   Litho.   Perf. 13
3390-3393 A938 Set of 4   2.10 2.10
3393a   Miniature sheet of 8, 2
                 each #3390-3393   4.25 4.25

Hanoi, 1000th Anniv. A939

Dragon and: 2000d, Banner, Hanoi Flag Tower. 2500d, Quan Chuong City Gate, National Conference Center, apartment buildings. 4500d, Long Biên Bridge, Nhât Tân Bridge. 6500d, Hanoi Train Station, Noi Bài Airport.
14,000d, Highways, graduate, computer operators, vert.

2010, Oct. 2   Perf. 13x13¼
3394-3397 A939 Set of 4   1.60 1.60
Souvenir Sheet
Perf. 13¾x13½
3398 A939 14,000d multi   1.50 1.50

Viet Nam Stamp Association, 50th Anniv. — A940

2010, Oct. 3   Perf. 13x13¼
3399 A940 2000d multi   .25 .25

Viet Nam Membership in Association
of South East Asian Nations (ASEAN),
15th Anniv. — A941

2010, Oct. 27
3400 A941 8500d multi   .90   .90

New Year
2011 (Year
of the
Cat) — A942

Cat: 2000d, Sitting. 10,500d, Lying down.

2010, Dec. 1   *Perf. 13½*
3401-3402 A942 Set of 2   1.40 1.40

Diplomatic
Relations
Between
Viet Nam
and Cuba,
50th Anniv.
A943

2010, Dec. 2
3403 A943 2000d multi   .25   .25

11th Congress
of Vietnamese
Communist
Party — A944

2011, Jan. 5   *Perf. 13¼x13*
3404 A944 2000d multi   .25   .25

UNESCO
Intangible
Heritage Quan
Ho Bac Ninh
Folk
Songs — A945

Singers: 3000d, Two men with umbrella, two
women with hats. 4500d, Two men and two
women seated, horiz. 10,500d, Two men with
umbrella in boat, two women holding hats.
12,500d, Men and women in boat, horiz.

2011, Jan. 15 *Perf. 13¼x13, 13x13¼*
3405-3407 A945 Set of 3   1.90 1.90
Souvenir Sheet
Perf. 13½x13¾
3408 A945 12,500d multi   1.40 1.40

Fauna in
Ba Be
National
Park
A948

Designs: 2000d, Muntiacus muntjac (4-1).
3500d, Gorsachius magnificus (4-2). 6000d,
Acanthosaura lepidogaster (4-3). 8500d, Pyx-
idea mouhoti (4-4).
14,500d, Catopuma temminckii.

2011, May 15 *Litho.* *Perf. 13*
3411-3414 A948 Set of 4   2.00 2.00
Souvenir Sheet
Perf. 13½x13¾
3515 A948 14,500d multi   1.40 1.40

Ho Chi Minh 's Departure From Viet
Nam, Cent. — A949

2011, June 5   *Perf. 13*
3416 A949 2000d multi   .25   .25

Ernest
Hemingway
(1899-1961),
Writer
A950

2011, July 2   *Perf. 13½*
3417 A950 10,500d multi   1.10 1.10

Dragonflies
A951

Designs: 2000d, Lyriothemis mortoni (4-1).
2500d, Trithemis aurora (4-2). 6500d, Rhy-
othemis obsolescens (4-3). 10,500d, Icti-
nogomphus decoratus (4-4).

2011, July 11   *Perf. 13½*
3418-3421 A951 Set of 4   2.10 2.10
PhilaNippon '11 Intl. Philatelic Exhibition,
Yokohama.

Tran Van Giau (1911-2010),
Revolutionary Activist — A952

2011, Sept. 6   *Perf. 13*
3422 A952 2000d multi   .25   .25

Decade for
Road
Safety — A953

Designs: 2000d, Traffic light, police officer
teaching students traffic signs (2-1). 6500d,
People crossing street in crosswalk (2-2).

2011, Oct. 1   *Litho.*
3423-3424 A953 Set of 2   .85   .85

Mikhail Lomonosov (1711-65),
Scientist — A954

2011, Nov. 19
3425 A954 8500d multi   .80   .80

New
Year
2012
(Year of
the
Dragon)
A955

Dragon with background color of: 2000d,
Bright pink (2-1). 10,500d, Olive green (2-2).

2011, Dec. 1   *Perf. 13x13¼*
3426-3427 A955 Set of 2   1.25 1.25

One-Pillar   Keo Pagoda, Vu
Pagoda,   Thu — A957
Hanoi — A956

Bridge Pagoda, Hoi An — A958

Perf. 13¾x13½ Syncopated
2012, Jan. 16
3428 A956 2000d rose carmine   .25   .25
3429 A956 3000d green   .30   .30
3430 A957 3500d brn orange   .35   .35
3431 A957 4500d red lilac   .45   .45
Perf. 13½x13¾ Syncopated
3432 A958 6500d blue   .65   .65
3433 A958 10,500d red   1.00 1.00
      Nos. 3428-3433 (6)   3.00 3.00

Ao Dais — A959

Designs: 2500d, Woman in brown ao dai
with hat (4-1). 3000d, Woman in orange ao
dai, woman in red ao dai (4-2). 6000d, Woman
in red ao dai holding hat, woman in blue ao dai
(4-3). 10,500d, Woman in blue ao dai standing, woman in purple ao dai seated (4-4).

2012, Mar. 8   *Perf. 13*
3434-3437 A959 Set of 4   2.25 2.25

SEMI-POSTAL STAMPS

World Communications Year — SP1

#B1, Hands holding envelope with ITU
emblem. #B2, Satellite dish antenna.

Unwmk.
1983, Nov. 1 *Litho.* *Perf. 11*
B1-B2 SP1 50xu +10xu Set of 2 3.75

AIR POST STAMP

AP1

Unwmk.
1959, Nov. 20 *Litho.* *Perf. 11*
C1 AP1 20xu blue & black   10.00 7.75

POSTAGE DUE STAMPS

Democratic Republic of Viet Nam
Nos. 1-4 exist with handstamps of "TT"
in a diamond. It is unclear to the editors
if these stamps were used.

D1

1955   *Typo.*   *Perf. 11½*
J14 D1 50d brown & yellow   15.00 9.00

D2

1958, Dec. 1　　Litho.　　Perf. 12½
J15　D2　10d purple & red
J16　D2　20d orange & aqua
J17　D2　100d gray blue & red
J18　D2　300d olive grn & red
　Nos. J15-J18 (4)　　　　15.00 14.00

MILITARY STAMPS

M1

Perf. 12½
1958, May 1　Litho.　Unwmk.
M1　M1　multicolored　　　15.00 9.00

Invalids in
Field
Paddy
M2

1959-60　　Litho.　　Perf. 11
M2　M2　org brn & brown
M3　M2　grey blue & olive
　Nos. M2-M3 (2)　　　11.50 4.50
　Issued: No. M2, 3/14/59; No. M3, 7/27/60.

Soldier, Train — M3

1959, July 1
M4　M3　bluish green　　　5.00 1.90

Frontier
Guard — M4

1961, Jan. 3
M5　M4　multicolored　　15.00 9.75

Naval
Patrol
M5

1962, June 15
M6　M5　multicolored　　　5.75 3.25

Military Medal,
Invalid's
Badge — M6

1963, Sept. 10
M7　M6　12xu multicolored　4.50 3.75

Rifleman
M7

1964, Aug.
M8　M7　multicolored　　　5.00 4.00

Rifleman Jumping
Wall — M8

1965
M9　M8　red & black
M10　M8　yellow green & black
　Nos. M9-M10 (2)　　9.00 6.25
　Issued: No. M9, 7/1; No. M10, 12/25.

Soldier,
Guerrilla
Woman
M9

1966-67
M11　M9　greenish blue & vio bl　9.00 7.00
Redrawn with two boats at right
M12　M9　olive & brown bl　13.50 10.50
　Issued: #M11, Sept. 25, 1966; #M12, 1967.

Badge of
People's
Army — M10

1967, Oct. 7
M13　M10　multicolored　　2.75 .75

M11

1968, Nov. 10
M14　M11　lilac　　　　3.00 .40

M12

1969, Nov. 15
M15　M12　red & brown red　2.00 .75

M13

1971, Apr. 27
M16　M13　yellow, brown & red　2.00 .75

Nguyen
Van Be
M14

Design: No. M18, Nguyen Viet Xuan.

1971, Oct. 30　　　　Perf. 11
M17　M14　multicolored　　1.75 .60
**　　　　　　Perf. 12½**
M18　M14　black, pink & buff　2.50 1.10
M19　M14　black & green　　2.50 1.10

M15

M16

1973, Dec. 20　　　　Perf. 11
M20　M15　blue, black & buff　1.25
　a.　Perf. 12½　　　　　4.50
M22　M16　olive, red & black　1.25
　a.　Perf. 12½　　　　　4.50

Disabled
Veteran in
Factory
M17

No. M24, Invalid's Badge, open book, vert.

1976, July 27
M23-M24　M17　Set of 2　　3.50 .25

Soldier,　　　　　Pilot — M19
Map — M18

1976, Oct. 21
M25　M18　red & black　　　1.25

1978
　No. M27, Tank driver. No. M28, Seaman.
M26-M28　M19　Set of 3　　5.00 2.00
　Issued: No. M26, 6/3; others, 10/10.

M20

Designs: a, Pilot. b, Badge of People's
Army.

1979, Dec. 22
M29　M20　Vertical pair, #a.-b.　3.50

Types A343a, A359 and

Ho Chi
Minh — M21

#M30, Factory militiawoman. #M31, Soldier,
woman pointing. #M32, Militiawoman.

1981, Aug. 5
M30　A343a　salmon & multi　1.25 .75
M31　A343a　green & multi　　1.25 .75
M32　A359　blue & multi　　1.25 .75
M33　M21　blue & tan　　　1.25 .75
　Nos. M30-M33 (4)　　5.00 3.00
　Size of No. M32: 13x18mm.

M22

1982, Nov. 9
M34　M22　pink & greenish blue　1.75 1.00

M23

1983, Apr. 30
M35　M23　multicolored　　2.25 1.10

Victory at Dien Bien Phu, 30th Anniv. M24

1984, May 5   **Litho.**
M37   M24   multicolored   1.75

Disabled Soldier Teaching Class — M25

1984, Nov. 10
M38   M25   tan & brown   1.25

Frontier Forces Type of 1984
1984, Dec. 15
M39   A410   multicolored   1.50

M26

1984, Dec. 22
M40   M26   multicolored   2.50

Policemen and Women M27

1985, Aug. 30
M41   M27   multicolored   2.00

M28

1986, Oct. 1
M42   M28   olive brown & black   1.50   .75

M29

1987, Sept. 23
M43   M29   carmine and tan   2.00   1.00

OFFICIAL STAMPS

Harvesting Rice — O1

Denominations in grams or kilograms of rice. Dated 1952.

Perf. 11¼
1953, July   **Litho.**   **Unwmk.**
O1   O1   600g rose   6.00   3.00
O2   O1   1kg ol brown   6.50   4.00
O3   O1   2kg orange   9.00   7.00
O4   O1   5kg gray   15.00   12.00
   Nos. O1-O4 (4)   36.50   26.00

Dien Bien Phu Type of 1954
1954-56   **Perf. 11**
O5   A4   600g sepia & ocher   18.00   12.50

   No. O5 exists perf 6, Value $60; and also imperf, Value $18.
   Issued: #O5, 10/54; perf 6, 12/54; imperf, 1956.

Nos. 1L62-1L63 Overprinted

1955   **Typo.**   **Perf. 7 Rough**
O6-O7   VM2   100g on 2d, 100g on 5d, set of 2   475.00

Land Reform Type of 1955-56
Inscribed "SU VU" Above Value
1955   **Litho.**   **Perf. 11**
O8-O9   A6   40d, 80d, set of 2   35.00   32.50

Cu Chinh Lan (1930-1952) O3

Denominations: 20d, 80d, 100d, 500d, 1000d, 2000d, 3000d.

1956, June   **Litho.**   **Perf. 11½**
O10-O16   O3   Set of 7   275.00   250.00

4th World Trade Union Congress
Type of 1957
Inscribed "SU VU" Above Value
1957, Aug. 1   **Perf. 12½**
O17-O20   A15   20d, 40d, 80d, 100d, set of 4   20.00   16.00

One-Pillar Pagoda — O4

1957-58
O21   O4   150d green and brown
O22   O4   150d orange and slate
   Nos. O21-O22 (2)   26.00   11.00

   Nos. O21-O22 exist with and without imprint and designer's name. Issued: No. O21, 12/22/57; No. O22, 3/12/58.

Craft Fair, Hanoi — O5

1958, May 30
O23-O24   O5   150d, 200d, set of 2   8.00   6.00

1st World Congress of Young Workers, Prague — O6

1958, June 26
O25   O6   150d lt olive green & red   3.50   1.75

Soldier, Factory, Crops — O7

1958, Aug. 19
O26-O28   O7   50, 150, 200d, set of 3   11.00   7.00

Opening of New Hanoi Stadium O8

1958, Dec. 31
O29-O32   O8   10d, 20d, 80d, 150d, set of 4   9.50   4.75

Planting Rice — O9

1962, Sept. 1   **Perf. 11**
O33-O35   O9   3, 6, 12xu, set of 3   3.00   2.50

Rural Mail Service O10

1966, July 1   **Perf. 11**
O36-O37   O10   3xu, 6xu, set of 2   3.00   1.00

VIRGIN ISLANDS

ˈvər-jən ˈī-ləndz

LOCATION — West Indies, southeast of Puerto Rico
GOVT. — British colony
AREA — 59 sq. mi.
POP. — 19,107 (1997)
CAPITAL — Road Town

   The British Virgin Islands constituted one of the presidencies of the former Leeward Islands colony until it became a colony itself in 1956. For many years stamps of Leeward Islands were used concurrently.
   The Virgin Islands group is divided between Great Britain and the United States. See Danish West Indies.

    12 Pence = 1 Shilling
    20 Shillings = 1 Pound
    100 Cents = 1 Dollar (1951)
    100 Cents = 1 US Dollar (1962)

> **Catalogue values for unused stamps in this country are for Never Hinged items, beginning with Scott 88 in the regular postage section and Scott O1 in the officials section.**

Values for unused stamps are for examples with original gum as defined in the catalogue introduction. However, Nos. 1-2c are valued without gum as the vast majority of examples are found thus.

Virgin and Lamps — A1   St. Ursula — A2

A3   A4

1866   **Litho.**   **Unwmk.**   **Perf. 12**
Toned or White Paper
1   A1   1p green   50.00   65.00
  a.   Toned paper   52.50   65.00
  c.   Perf. 15x12, toned paper   12,000.   7,750.
2   A3   6p rose   65.00   100.00
  a.   Large "V" in "VIRGIN"   300.00   400.00
  b.   White paper   100.00   120.00
  c.   As "a," white paper   410.00   525.00

   Examples offered as No. 1c frequently have forged perfs.

1867-70   **Perf. 15**
3   A1   1p blue grn ('70)   65.00   75.00
4   A1   1p yel grn ('68)   80.00   80.00
  a.   Toned paper   92.50   85.00
5   A2   4p lake, *buff*   45.00   65.00
  a.   4p lake, *rose*   55.00   75.00
6   A3   6p rose   650.00   650.00
  a.   Toned paper ('68)   325.00   375.00
7   A4   1sh rose & blk   300.00   400.00
  a.   Toned paper   300.00   400.00
  b.   Double lined frame   300.00   400.00
  c.   As "b," bluish paper   300.00   400.00

Colored Margins
8   A4   1sh rose & blk   70.00   82.50
  a.   White paper   80.00   90.00
  b.   Bluish paper   825.00   1,000.
  c.   Central figure omitted   225,000.
   Nos. 3-8 (6)   1,210.   1,352.

   Examples of No. 8c have perfs. trimmed on one or two sides.

1878   **Wmk. 1**   **Perf. 14**
9   A1   1p green   90.00   110.00

   See #16-17, 19-20. For surcharge see #18.

Queen Victoria — A5

1880   **Typo.**
10   A5   1p green   80.00   95.00
11   A5   2½p red brown   110.00   130.00

1883-84   **Wmk. 2**
12   A5   ½p yellow   92.50   92.50
13   A5   ½p green   6.00   13.00
  a.   Imperf., pair   1,750.
14   A5   1p rose   32.50   37.50
15   A5   2½p ultra ('84)   3.00   17.50
   Nos. 12-15 (4)   134.00   160.50

   No. 13a probably is a plate proof.

1887   **Litho.**
16   A2   4p brick red   40.00   70.00
  a.   4p brown red   50.00   80.00
17   A3   6p violet   19.00   50.00

No. 8 Handstamp
Surcharged in Violet

1888		Unwmk.		Perf. 15
18	A4	4p on 1sh dp rose & blk, toned paper	140.00	175.00
a.		Double surcharge	8,500.	
b.		Inverted surcharge	55,000.	
c.		White paper	200.00	250.00

1889		Wmk. 2		Perf. 14
19	A1	1p carmine	2.75	8.25
20	A4	1sh brown	50.00	80.00
a.		1sh black brown	90.00	110.00

St. Ursula
with Sheaf of
Lilies
A7

Edward VII
A8

1899				Engr.
21	A7	½p yellow grn	3.75	.60
a.		"PFNNY"	92.50	140.00
b.		"F" without cross bar	92.50	140.00
c.		Horiz. pair, imperf. between	13,000.	
22	A7	1p red	4.75	2.75
23	A7	2½p ultra	13.00	3.00
24	A7	4p chocolate	4.50	20.00
a.		"PENCE"	825.	1,200.
25	A7	6p dark violet	5.50	3.50
26	A7	7p slate green	11.00	6.50
27	A7	1sh ocher	25.00	37.50
28	A7	5sh dark blue	80.00	95.00
		Nos. 21-28 (8)	147.50	168.85

1904		Typo.		Wmk. 3
29	A8	½p violet & bl grn	1.00	.60
30	A8	1p violet & scar	3.25	.55
31	A8	2p violet & bis	7.75	4.75
32	A8	2½p violet & ultra	3.00	2.75
33	A8	3p violet & blk	4.75	3.25
34	A8	6p violet & brn	3.50	3.25
35	A8	1sh green & scar	5.50	6.50
36	A8	2sh6p green & blk	32.50	72.50
37	A8	5sh green & ultra	62.50	87.50
		Nos. 29-37 (9)	123.75	181.65

Numerals of 2p, 3p, 1sh and 2sh6p of type A8 are in color on plain tablet.

George V — A9

Die I

For description of dies I and II see "Dies of British Colonial Stamps" in Table of Contents.

1913				Ordinary Paper
38	A9	½p green	1.90	5.00
39	A9	1p scarlet	2.75	17.50
a.		1p orange	57.50	32.50
40	A9	2p gray	5.00	30.00
41	A9	2½p ultra	6.50	11.00

Chalky Paper

42	A9	3p vio, yel	3.25	8.00
43	A9	6p dl vio & red vio	7.50	16.00
44	A9	1sh blk, green	3.75	11.00
45	A9	2sh6p blk & red, bl	57.50	60.00
46	A9	5sh grn & red, yel	42.50	140.00
		Nos. 38-46 (9)	130.65	298.50

Numerals of 2p, 3p, 1sh and 2sh6p of type A9 are in color on plain tablet.

Die II

1921				Wmk. 4
47	A9	½p green	8.50	45.00
48	A9	1p carmine	6.00	29.00

For overprints see Nos. MR1-MR2.

Colony Seal — A10

1922				Wmk. 3
49	A10	3p violet, yel	1.10	21.00
50	A10	1sh black, emerald	1.00	17.50
51	A10	2sh6p blk & red, bl	7.25	14.00
52	A10	5sh grn & red, yel	42.50	125.00
		Nos. 49-52 (4)	51.85	177.50

1922-28				Wmk. 4
53	A10	½p green	1.25	3.50
54	A10	1p rose red	.80	.80
55	A10	1p violet ('27)	1.40	4.75
56	A10	1½p rose red ('27)	2.10	3.25
57	A10	1½p fawn ('28)	2.25	1.90
58	A10	2p gray	1.40	7.75
59	A10	2½p ultra	3.25	24.00
60	A10	2½p orange ('23)	1.75	2.10
61	A10	3p dl vio, yel ('28)	3.25	15.00
62	A10	5p dl lil & ol grn	7.75	60.00
63	A10	6p dl vio & red vio	2.10	9.00
a.		6p brown lilac & red violet	2.10	9.00
64	A10	1sh blk, emer ('28)	3.50	19.00
65	A10	2sh6p blk & red, bl ('28)	27.50	62.50
66	A10	5sh grn & red, yel ('23)	27.50	95.00
		Nos. 53-66 (14)	85.80	308.55

The ½, 1, 2 and 2½p are on ordinary paper, the others on chalky.
Numerals of 1½p of type A10 are in color on plain tablet.

Common Design Types pictured following the introduction.

Silver Jubilee Issue
Common Design Type

1935, May 6		Engr.		Perf. 11x12
69	CD301	1p car & dk blue	1.25	6.00
70	CD301	1½p black & ultra	1.25	5.50
71	CD301	2½p ultra & brn	3.25	5.00
72	CD301	1sh brn vio & ind	18.00	26.00
		Nos. 69-72 (4)	23.75	42.50
		Set, never hinged	30.00	

Coronation Issue
Common Design Type

1937, May 12				Perf. 11x11½
73	CD302	1p dark carmine	.40	1.50
74	CD302	1½p brown	.40	1.50
75	CD302	2½p deep ultra	.40	.75
		Nos. 73-75 (3)	1.20	3.75
		Set, never hinged	2.00	

King George VI and
Seal of the
Colony — A11

1938-47		Photo.		Perf. 14
76	A11	½p green	.90	.90
77	A11	1p scarlet	1.25	1.00
78	A11	1½p red brown	1.50	1.25
79	A11	2p gray	1.50	1.25
80	A11	2½p ultra	2.00	1.50
81	A11	3p orange	1.25	1.00
82	A11	6p deep violet	3.50	1.00
83	A11	1sh olive bister	2.50	2.00
84	A11	2sh6p sepia	11.00	5.00
85	A11	5sh rose lake	11.00	6.00
86	A11	10sh brt blue ('47)	5.50	11.00
87	A11	£1 gray blk ('47)	6.50	25.00
		Nos. 76-87 (12)	48.40	56.90
		Set, never hinged	70.00	

Catalogue values for unused stamps in this section, from this point to the end of the section, are for Never Hinged items.

Peace Issue
Common Design Type

1946, Nov. 1		Engr.		Wmk. 4
				Perf. 13½x14
88	CD303	1½p red brown	.25	.25
89	CD303	3p orange	.25	.25

Silver Wedding Issue
Common Design Types

1949, Jan. 3		Photo.		Perf. 14x14½
90	CD304	2½p brt ultra	.35	.35

Engr.; Name Typo.
Perf. 11½x11

| 91 | CD305 | £1 gray black | 18.50 | 21.00 |

UPU Issue
Common Design Types

Engr.; Name Typo. on Nos. 93 & 94

1949, Oct. 10			Perf. 13½, 11x11½
92	CD306	2½p ultra	.40	.75
93	CD307	3p deep orange	1.25	2.00
94	CD308	6p red lilac	.50	.40
95	CD309	1sh olive	.45	.40
		Nos. 92-95 (4)	2.60	3.55

University Issue
Common Design Types

1951		Engr.		Perf. 14x14½
96	CD310	3c red brn & gray blk	.40	.40
97	CD311	12c purple & black	1.10	1.10

Map of the
Islands
A12

1951, Apr. 2		Wmk. 4		Perf. 14½x14
98	A12	6c red orange	.50	1.00
99	A12	12c purple	.75	.50
100	A12	24c olive grn	.65	1.00
101	A12	$1.20 carmine	2.50	1.50
		Nos. 98-101 (4)	4.40	4.00

Restoration of the Legislative Council, 1950.

Sombrero
Lighthouse — A13

Map of Jost
van
Dyke — A14

Designs: 3c, Sheep. 4c, Map, Anegada. 5c, Cattle. 8c, Map, Virgin Gorda. 12c, Map, Tortola. 24c, Badge of the Presidency. 60c, Dead Man's Chest. $1.20, Sir Francis Drake Channel. $2.40, Road Town. $4.80, Map, Virgin Islands.

1952, Apr. 15		Perf. 12½x13, 13x12½		
102	A13	1c gray black	.40	2.00
103	A14	2c deep green	.85	.25
104	A14	3c choc & gray blk	.45	1.25
105	A14	4c red	.70	1.60
106	A14	5c gray blk & rose lake	1.40	.70
107	A13	8c ultra	.85	1.25
108	A14	12c purple	1.25	1.60
109	A13	24c dk brown	1.00	.25
110	A14	60c blue & ol grn	4.00	11.00
111	A14	$1.20 ultra & blk	6.00	12.00
112	A14	$2.40 hn brn & dk grn	15.00	16.00
113	A14	$4.80 rose car & bl	19.00	19.00
		Nos. 102-113 (12)	50.90	66.90

Coronation Issue
Common Design Type

1953, June 2				Perf. 13½x14
114	CD312	2c dk green & blk	.40	.65

Map of
Tortola — A15

Brown
Pelican
A16

Designs: 1c, Virgin Islands sloop. 2c, Nelthrop Red Poll bull. 3c, Road Harbor. 4c, Mountain travel. 5c, St. Ursula. 8c, Beach scene. 12c, Boat launching. 24c, White Cedar tree. 60c, Skipjack tuna. $1.20, Treasury Square. $4.80, Magnificent frigatebird.

			Perf. 13x12½	
1956, Nov. 1		Engr.		Wmk. 4
115	A15	½c claret & blk	.45	.25
116	A15	1c dk bl & grnsh bl	1.90	1.10
117	A15	2c black & ver	.40	.25
118	A15	3c olive & brt bl	.40	.45
119	A15	4c blue grn & brn	.45	.45
120	A15	5c gray	.50	.25
121	A15	8c dp ultra & org	.75	.65
122	A15	12c car & brt ultra	2.50	1.10
123	A15	24c dull red & grn	1.25	1.00
124	A15	60c yel org & dk bl	10.00	12.00
125	A15	$1.20 car & yel grn	2.75	11.00

		Perf. 12x11½		
126	A16	$2.40 vio brn & dl yel	37.50	20.00
127	A16	$4.80 grnsh bl & dk brn	40.00	20.00
		Nos. 115-127 (13)	98.85	68.50

Types of 1956
Surcharged

		Perf. 13x12½		
1962, Dec. 10				Wmk. 314
128	A15	1c on ½c	.25	.25
129	A15	2c on 1c	1.25	.25
130	A15	3c on 2c	.25	.25
131	A15	4c on 3c	.25	.25
132	A15	5c on 4c	.25	.25
133	A15	8c on 8c	.35	.35
134	A15	10c on 12c	.45	.45
135	A15	12c on 24c	.65	.65
136	A15	25c on 60c	3.25	1.25
137	A15	70c on $1.20	.70	3.25

		Perf. 12x11½		
138	A16	$1.40 on $2.40	12.50	21.00
139	A16	$2.80 on $4.80	12.50	16.00
		Nos. 128-139 (12)	32.65	44.20

Freedom from Hunger Issue
Common Design Type

1963, June 4		Photo.		Perf. 14x14½
140	CD314	25c lilac	.50	.50

Red Cross Centenary Issue
Common Design Type
Wmk. 314

1963, Sept. 2		Litho.		Perf. 13
141	CD315	2c black & red	.25	.25
142	CD315	25c ultra & red	.90	.90

Shakespeare Issue
Common Design Type

1964, Apr. 23		Photo.		Perf. 14x14½
143	CD316	10c ultramarine	.45	.45

Bonito — A17

Map of Tortola
Island — A18

2c, Seaplane at Soper's Hole. 3c, Brown pelican. 4c, Dead Man's Chest (mountain). 5c,

Road Harbor. 6c, Fallen Jerusalem Island. 8c, The Baths, Virgin Gorda. 10c, Map of Virgin Islands. 12c, Ferry service, Tortola—St. Thomas. 15c, The Towers. 25c, Plane at Beef Island Airfield. $1, Virgin Gorda Island. $1.40, Yachts, Tortola. $2.80, Badge.

Perf. 13x12½

			Engr.	Wmk. 314	
1964, Nov. 2					
144	A17	1c gray ol & dk bl		.35	2.40
145	A17	2c rose red & ol		.35	.45
146	A17	3c grnsh bl & sep		4.25	2.40
147	A17	4c carmine & blk		1.10	2.40
148	A17	5c green & blk		.90	1.60
149	A17	6c orange & blk		.35	1.40
150	A17	8c pink & blk		.35	1.00
151	A17	10c lt violet & mar		1.60	.45
152	A17	12c vio bl & Prus grn		2.75	3.50
153	A17	15c gray & yel grn		.45	3.50
154	A17	25c pur & yel grn		15.00	3.50

Perf. 13x13½
Size: 27x30½mm

155	A18	70c bister brn & blk		5.25	8.00
156	A18	$1 red brn & yel grn		4.25	3.50
157	A18	$1.40 pink & blue		27.50	16.00

Perf. 11½x12
Size: 27x37mm

158	A18	$2.80 rose lilac & blk		27.50	16.00
		Nos. 144-158 (15)		91.95	66.10

For surcharges & overprints see Nos. 173-175, 190-191.

ITU Issue
Common Design Type

Perf. 11x11½

		Litho.	Wmk. 314	
1965, May 17				
159	CD317	4c yellow & bl grn	.25	.25
160	CD317	25c blue & org yel	.80	.80

Intl. Cooperation Year Issue
Common Design Type

		Wmk. 314	Perf. 14½	
1965, Oct. 25				
161	CD318	1c blue grn & cl	.25	.25
162	CD318	25c lt violet & grn	.65	.65

Churchill Memorial Issue
Common Design Type

1966, Jan. 24 Photo. Perf. 14
Design in Black, Gold and Carmine Rose

163	CD319	1c brt blue	.25	.25
164	CD319	2c green	.25	.25
165	CD319	10c brown	.40	.40
166	CD319	25c violet	1.00	1.00
		Nos. 163-166 (4)	1.90	1.90

Royal Visit Issue
Common Design Type

		Litho.	Perf. 11x12	
1966, Feb. 22				
167	CD320	4c violet blue	.25	.25
168	CD320	70c dk car rose	2.25	2.25

Stamps of 1866 — A19

Designs: 5c, R.M.S. Atrato, 1866. 25c, Beechcraft mail plane on Beef Island Airfield and 6p stamp (No. 2). 60c, Landing mail at Road Town, 1866, and 1p stamp (No. 1).

Perf. 12½x13

		Wmk. 314		
1966, Apr. 25				
169	A19	5c grn, yel, red & blk	.25	.25
170	A19	10c yel, grn, red, blk & rose	.25	.25
171	A19	25c lt grn, bl, red, blk & rose	.85	.85
172	A19	60c bl, red, blk, & grn	1.75	1.75
		Nos. 169-172 (4)	3.10	3.10

Centenary of Virgin Islands postage stamps.

Nos. 155, 157-158 Surcharged with New Value and Two Bars

Perf. 13x12½, 11½x12

		Engr.	Wmk. 314	
1966, Sept. 15				
173	A18	50c on 70c	2.00	2.00
174	A18	$1.50 on $1.40	4.00	4.00
175	A18	$3 on $2.80	4.00	4.00
		Nos. 173-175 (3)	10.00	10.00

UNESCO Anniversary Issue
Common Design Type

		Litho.	Perf. 14	
1966, Dec. 1				
176	CD323	2c "Education"	.25	.25
177	CD323	12c "Science"	.30	.30
178	CD323	60c "Culture"	.95	.95
		Nos. 176-178 (3)	1.50	1.50

Map and Seal of Virgin Islands A20

Wmk. 314

		Photo.	Perf. 14½	
1967, Apr. 18				
179	A20	2c gold, grn & org	.25	.25
180	A20	10c gold, rose red, grn & org	.25	.25
181	A20	25c gold, red brn, grn & org	.25	.25
182	A20	$1 gold, bl, grn & org	.85	.85
		Nos. 179-182 (4)	1.60	1.60

Introduction of new constitution.

Map of Virgin Islands, Bermuda and C.S. Mercury — A21

10c, Communications center, Chalwell, Virgin Islands. 50c, Cable ship Mercury.

		Wmk. 314	Perf. 14½	
1967, Sept. 14				
183	A21	4c green & multi	.25	.25
184	A21	10c dp plum & multi	.25	.25
185	A21	50c bister & multi	.70	.70
		Nos. 183-185 (3)	1.20	1.20

Completion of the Bermuda-Tortola, Virgin Islands, telephone link.

Blue Marlin A22

Designs: 10c, Sergeant fish (cobia). 25c, Peto fish (Wahoo). 40c, Fishing boat, map of Virgin Islands and fishing records.

Perf. 12½x12

		Photo.	Wmk. 314	
1968, Jan. 2				
186	A22	2c multicolored	.25	.25
187	A22	10c multicolored	.30	.30
188	A22	25c multicolored	.60	.60
189	A22	40c multicolored	1.00	1.00
		Nos. 186-189 (4)	2.15	2.15

Game fishing in Virgin Islands waters

Nos. 151 and 154 Overprinted: "1968 / INTERNATIONAL / YEAR FOR / HUMAN RIGHTS"

		Engr.	Perf. 13x12½	
1968, July 1				
190	A17	10c lt violet & maroon	.25	.25
191	A17	25c purple & green	.45	.45

Martin Luther King, Bible and Sword A23

		Litho.	Perf. 14	
1968, Oct. 15				
192	A23	4c dl org, vio & blk	.35	.35
193	A23	25c dl org, gray grn & blk	.50	.65

Martin Luther King, Jr. (1929-68), American civil rights leader.

DHC-6 Twin Otter A24

Designs: 10c, Hawker Siddeley 748. 25c, Hawker Siddeley Heron. $1, Badge from cap of Royal Engineers.

		Unwmk.	Perf. 14	
1968, Dec. 16				
194	A24	2c brn red & multi	.25	.60
195	A24	10c grnsh bl, blk & red	.25	.25
196	A24	25c ultra, lt bl, org & blk	.40	.25
197	A24	$1 green & multi	1.75	2.00
		Nos. 194-197 (4)	2.65	3.35

Opening of enlarged Beef Island Airport.

Long John Silver and Jim Hawkins — A25

Scenes from Treasure Island: 10c, Jim's escape from the pirates, horiz. 40c, The fight with Israel Hands. $1, Treasure trove, horiz.

Perf. 13½x13, 13x13½

		Photo.	Wmk. 314	
1969, Mar. 18				
198	A25	4c dp car & multi	.40	.25
199	A25	10c multicolored	.45	.25
200	A25	40c ultra & multi	.55	.65
201	A25	$1 black & multi	1.25	2.25
		Nos. 198-201 (4)	2.65	3.40

Robert Louis Stevenson (1850-94). The Virgin Islands were used as the setting for "Treasure Island."

Tourist and Rock Grouper — A26

Tourist Publicity: 10c, Yachts in Road Harbor, Tortola, horiz. 20c, Tourists on beach in Virgin Gorda National Park, horiz. $1, Pipe organ cactus and woman tourist.

		Litho.	Perf. 12½	
1969, Oct. 20				
202	A26	2c multicolored	.25	.55
203	A26	10c multicolored	.25	.25
204	A26	20c multicolored	.35	.25
205	A26	$1 multicolored	1.75	2.00
		Nos. 202-205 (4)	2.60	3.05

Carib Canoe A27

Ships: 1c, Santa Maria. 2c, H.M.S. Elizabeth Bonaventure. 3c, Dutch buccaneer, 1660. 4c, Thetis (1827 merchant ship). 5c, Henry Morgan's ship. 6c, Frigate Boreas. 8c, Schooner L'Eclair, 1804. 10c, H.M.S. Formidable. 12c, H.M.S. Nymph burning. 15c, Packet Windsor Castle fighting French privateer. 20c, Frigate Astrea, 1808. 50c, H.M.S. Rhone. $1, Tortola sloop. $2, H.M.S. Frobisher. $3, Booker Line Viking (cargo ship) $5, Hydrofoil Sun Arrow.

Wmk. 314 Sideways

			Perf. 14½	
1970, Feb. 16				
206	A27	½c brn & ocher	.25	.25
207	A27	1c bl, lt grn & vio	.25	.25
208	A27	2c red brn, org & gray	.25	.25
209	A27	3c ver, bl & brn	.25	.25
210	A27	4c brn, bl & vio bl	.25	.25
211	A27	5c grn, pink & blk	.25	.25
212	A27	6c lil, grn & blk	.25	.25
213	A27	8c lt ol, yel & brn	.30	.30
214	A27	10c ocher, bl & brn	.35	.40
215	A27	12c sep, yel & dp cl	.50	.60
216	A27	15c org, grnsh bl & brn	.45	.45
217	A27	25c bl, grnsh gray & pur	.65	.85
218	A27	50c rose car, lt grn & brn	1.40	1.60
219	A27	$1 brn, sal pink & dk grn	2.75	3.25
220	A27	$2 gray & red	5.50	6.75
221	A27	$3 brn, ol bis & dk bl	8.50	10.50
222	A27	$5 lil & gray	14.00	17.00
		Nos. 206-222 (17)	36.15	43.55

For overprints see Nos. 235-236.

		Wmk. 314 Upright		
1973, Oct. 17				
206a	A27	½c	.85	5.75
209a	A27	3c	2.00	2.25
210a	A27	4c	2.00	4.25
211a	A27	5c	2.00	2.10
214a	A27	10c	2.40	2.40
215a	A27	15c	3.25	3.25
		Nos. 206a-215a (6)	12.50	20.00

Wmk. 314 Sideways

			Perf. 13½	
1974, Nov. 11				
207a	A27	1c	1.25	1.90
214b	A27	10c	2.25	2.10
215b	A27	12c	2.25	3.00
216a	A27	15c	3.25	3.00
		Nos. 207a-216a (4)	9.00	10.00

"A Tale of Two Cities," by Dickens A28

Charles Dickens: 10c, "Oliver Twist." 25c, "Great Expectations."

		Litho.	Perf. 14½	
1970, May 4				
223	A28	5c blk, gray & pink	.25	.25
224	A28	10c blk, pale yel grn & blue	.40	.35
225	A28	25c blk, yel & lt yel grn	.65	.95
		Nos. 223-225 (3)	1.30	1.55

Hospital Visitor A29

10c, Girl Scouts receiving 1st aid training at lake side. 25c, Red Cross & Virgin Islands coat of arms.

		Wmk. 314	Perf. 14	
1970, Aug. 10				
226	A29	4c multicolored	.25	.25
227	A29	10c multicolored	.55	.25
228	A29	25c multicolored	1.25	1.10
		Nos. 226-228 (3)	2.05	1.60

Centenary of British Red Cross.

Mary Read — A30

Pirates: 10c, George Lowther. 30c, Edward Teach (Blackbeard). 60c, Henry Morgan.

1970, Nov. 16   Wmk. 314   Perf. 14

229	A30	½c dp rose & multi	.25	.25
230	A30	10c blue grn & multi	.50	.50
231	A30	30c ultra & multi	1.40	1.40
232	A30	60c multicolored	1.90	1.90
		Nos. 229-232 (4)	4.05	4.05

Children Spelling out "UNICEF" A31

1971, Dec. 13

233	A31	15c tan & multi	.25	.25
234	A31	30c lt blue & multi	.50	.50

25th anniv. of UNICEF.

Nos. 210 and 217 Dated "1972" and Overprinted: "VISIT OF / H.R.H. / THE / PRINCESS MARGARET"

1972, Mar. 7   Perf. 14½

235	A27	4c multicolored	.25	.25
236	A27	25c multicolored	.60	.60

Seaman, 1800 — A32

10c, Boatswain, 1787-1807. 30c, Captain, 1795-1812. 60c, Admiral in full dress uniform, 1787-95.

1972, Mar. 17   Perf. 14x13½

237	A32	½c yellow & multi	.25	.25
238	A32	10c brt pink & multi	.40	.40
239	A32	30c orange & multi	1.10	1.10
240	A32	60c blue & multi	2.50	2.50
		Nos. 237-240 (4)	4.25	4.25

INTERPEX, 14th Intl. Stamp Exhib., NYC, Mar. 17-19.

Silver Wedding Issue, 1972
Common Design Type

Design: Queen Elizabeth II, Prince Philip, sailfish and "Sir Winston Churchill" yacht.

1972, Nov. 24   Photo.   Perf. 14x14½

241	CD324	15c ultra & multi	.30	.30
242	CD324	25c Prus blue & multi	.30	.30

Allison Tuna A33

1972, Dec. 12   Litho.   Perf. 13½x14

243	A33	½c Wahoo	.25	.25
244	A33	½c Blue marlin	.25	.25
a.		Horiz. or vert. pair, #243-244	.25	.25
245	A33	15c shown	.50	.50
246	A33	25c White marlin	.80	.80
247	A33	50c Sailfish	1.40	1.40
248	A33	$1 Dolphin	3.50	3.50
a.		Souvenir sheet of 6, #243-248	14.00	14.00
		Nos. 243-248 (6)	6.70	6.70

Game fish.

Lettsom House and Medal — A34

Themes from Quaker History: ½c, Dr. John Coakley Lettsom, vert. 15c, Dr. William Thornton, vert. 30c, US Capitol, Washington, DC,

and Dr. Thornton who designed it. $1, Library Hall, Philadelphia, and William Penn.

1973, Mar. 9   Litho.   Perf. 13½

249	A34	½c rose & multi	.25	.25
250	A34	10c multicolored	.25	.25
251	A34	15c multicolored	.30	.30
252	A34	30c ultra & multi	.55	.55
253	A34	$1 multicolored	1.60	1.60
		Nos. 249-253 (5)	2.95	2.95

INTERPEX, 15th Intl. Phil. Exhib., NYC, Mar. 9-11.

Hummingbirds on 1c Coin — A35

Coins and Beach Scenes: 5c, Zenaida doves. 10c, Kingfisher. 25c, Mangrove cuckoos. 50c, Brown pelicans. $1, Magnificent frigate birds.

1973, June 30   Wmk. 314   Perf. 14½

254	A35	1c orange & multi	.25	.45
255	A35	5c lt blue & multi	.75	.25
256	A35	10c pale ultra & multi	1.10	.25
257	A35	25c yellow & multi	1.40	.25
258	A35	50c lt violet & multi	1.60	1.60
259	A35	$1 ultra & multi	2.00	3.00
		Nos. 254-259 (6)	7.10	5.80

New Virgin Islands coinage.

Princess Anne's Wedding Issue
Common Design Type

1973, Nov. 16   Wmk. 314   Perf. 14

260	CD325	5c citron & multi	.25	.25
261	CD325	50c blue grn & multi	.40	.40

Virgin and Child, by Bernardino Pintoricchio A36

Arms of French Minesweeper Canopus A37

Christmas (Paintings of the Virgin and Child by): 3c, Lorenzo Credi. 25c, Carlo Crivelli. 50c, Bernardino Luini.

1973, Dec. 7   Perf. 14x14½

262	A36	½c lt green & multi	.25	.25
263	A36	3c rose & multi	.25	.25
264	A36	25c ocher & multi	.50	.50
265	A36	50c lt blue & multi	.95	.95
		Nos. 262-265 (4)	1.95	1.95

1974, Mar. 22   Wmk. 314   Perf. 14

266	A37	5c shown	.25	.25
267	A37	18c USS Saginaw	.40	.40
268	A37	25c HMS Rothesay	.50	.50
269	A37	50c HMCS Ottawa	1.00	1.00
a.		Souvenir sheet of 4, #266-269	3.00	3.00
		Nos. 266-269 (4)	2.15	2.15

INTERPEX Phil. Exhib., NYC, Mar. 22-24.

Famous Explorers — A38

1974, Aug. 19   Perf. 14½

270	A38	5c Columbus	.30	.30
271	A38	10c Sir Walter Raleigh	.40	.40
272	A38	25c Sir Martin Frobisher	.45	.45
273	A38	40c Sir Francis Drake	.85	.85
a.		Souvenir sheet of 4, #270-273	2.50	2.50
		Nos. 270-273 (4)	2.00	2.00

Sea Shells A39

1974, Sept. 30   Perf. 13x13½

274	A39	5c Trumpet triton	.45	.45
275	A39	18c West Indian murex	1.00	1.00
276	A39	25c Bleeding tooth	1.25	1.25
277	A39	75c Virgin Island latirus	3.00	3.00
a.		Souvenir sheet of 4, #274-277	7.25	7.25
		Nos. 274-277 (4)	5.70	5.70

St. Mary, Aldermanbury, London, — A40

Design: 50c, St. Mary, Fulton, Missouri.

1974, Nov. 30   Wmk. 373   Perf. 14

278	A40	10c multicolored	.25	.25
279	A40	50c multicolored	.50	.50
a.		Souvenir sheet of 2, #278-279	1.00	1.00

Sir Winston Churchill (1874-1965).

Figurehead from "Boreas" — A41

Figureheads: 18c, The Golden Hind. 40c, Crowned lion from the "Superb." 85c, Warrior, from the "Formidable."

Perf. 13½x13

1975, Mar. 14   Wmk. 314

280	A41	5c multicolored	.25	.25
281	A41	18c multicolored	.55	.55
282	A41	40c multicolored	.75	.75
283	A41	85c multicolored	1.50	1.50
a.		Souv. sheet of 4, #280-283, perf. 14	3.50	3.50
		Nos. 280-283 (4)	3.05	3.05

INTERPEX, 17th Phil. Exhib., NYC, Mar. 14-16.

Rock Beauty A42

Designs: Fish.

1975   Wmk. 373   Perf. 14
Inscribed "1975" Below Design

284	A42	½c shown	.25	.25
285	A42	1c Squirrelfish	.55	.65
286	A42	3c Queen trigger-fish	1.50	1.75
287	A42	5c Blue angelfish	.35	.45
288	A42	8c Stoplight par-rotfish	.35	.45
289	A42	10c Queen angel-fish	.35	.45
290	A42	12c Nassau grouper	.55	.65
291	A42	13c Blue tang	.55	.65
292	A42	15c Sergeant major	.55	.65
293	A42	18c Jewfish	1.25	1.50
294	A42	20c Bluehead wrasse	.75	.95
295	A42	25c Gray angelfish	1.60	1.90
296	A42	60c Glasseye snap-per	1.90	2.40
297	A42	$1 Blue chromis	2.75	3.25
298	A42	$2.50 French angel-fish	4.50	5.50
299	A42	$3 Queen par-rotfish	6.25	7.25

300	A42	$5 Four-eye butter-flyfish	6.75	8.00
		Nos. 284-300 (17)	30.75	36.70

Issue dates: $5, Aug. 15. Others, June 16.

1977
Inscribed "1977" Below Design

284a	A42	½c multicolored	.55	.55
287a	A42	5c multicolored	1.00	1.00
288a	A42	8c multicolored	1.00	1.00
289a	A42	10c multicolored	1.00	1.00
290a	A42	12c multicolored	1.40	1.40
291a	A42	13c multicolored	1.40	1.40
292a	A42	15c multicolored	1.40	1.40
294a	A42	20c multicolored	2.00	2.00
		Nos. 284a-294a (8)	9.75	9.75

St. Georges Parish School A43

Designs: 25c, Legislative Council Building. 40c, Mace and gavel of Legislative Council. 75c, Scroll with dates of historical events.

1975, Nov. 27   Litho.   Wmk. 373

301	A43	5c ultra & multi	.25	.25
302	A43	25c green & multi	.35	.35
303	A43	40c ocher & multi	.45	.45
304	A43	75c blue & multi	.60	.60
		Nos. 301-304 (4)	1.65	1.65

Restoration of Legislative Council, 25th anniv.

Copper Mine Point A44

Historic Sites: 18c, Dr. Thornton's Ruin, Pleasant Valley. 50c, Callwood distillery. 75c, The Dungeon.

1976, Mar. 12   Litho.   Perf. 14½

305	A44	5c red & multi	.25	.25
306	A44	18c red & multi	.30	.30
307	A44	50c red & multi	.60	.60
308	A44	75c red & multi	.85	.85
		Nos. 305-308 (4)	2.00	2.00

Massachusetts Brig Hazard — A45

Designs: 22c, American Privateer Spy. 40c, Continental Navy Frigate Raleigh. 75c, Frigate Alliance and HMS Trepasy.

1976, May 29   Wmk. 373   Perf. 14

309	A45	8c multicolored	.35	.35
310	A45	22c multicolored	.75	.55
311	A45	40c multicolored	1.40	1.10
312	A45	75c multicolored	2.75	2.00
a.		Souvenir sheet of 4, #309-312	9.00	9.00
		Nos. 309-312 (4)	5.25	3.90

American Bicentennial.

Government House, Tortola — A46

Designs: 15c, Government House, St. Croix, vert. 30c, Flags of US and British Virgin Islands, vert. 75c, Arms of British and US Virgin Islands.

1976, Oct. 29   **Litho.**   *Perf. 14*
313	A46	8c green & multi	.25	.25
314	A46	15c green & multi	.25	.25
315	A46	30c green & multi	.35	.35
316	A46	75c green & multi	.75	.75
		Nos. 313-316 (4)	1.60	1.60

US and British Virgin Islands Friendship Day, 5th anniversary.

Holy Bible — A47

8c, Queen visiting Agricultural Station, Tortola, 1966. 60c, Presentation of Holy Bible.

1977, Feb. 7   *Perf. 14x13½*
317	A47	8c silver & multi	.25	.25
318	A47	30c silver & multi	.25	.25
319	A47	60c silver & multi	.45	.45
		Nos. 317-319 (3)	.95	.95

25th anniv. of the reign of Elizabeth II.
For overprints see Nos. 324-326.

Virgin Islands Chart, 1739 — A48

18th Century Maps of Virgin Islands: 22c, 1758. 30c, 1775. 75c, 1779.

1977, June 12   **Wmk. 373**   *Perf. 13½*
320	A48	8c multicolored	.35	.25
321	A48	22c multicolored	.70	.60
322	A48	30c multicolored	.95	.85
323	A48	75c multicolored	2.00	2.00
		Nos. 320-323 (4)	4.00	3.70

Type of 1977 Inscribed "ROYAL VISIT"

Designs: 5c, Queen visiting Agricultural Station, Tortola, 1966. 25c, Holy Bible. 50c, Presentation of Holy Bible.

1977, Oct. 26   **Litho.**   *Perf. 14x13½*
324	A47	5c yel brn & multi	.25	.25
325	A47	25c dk blue & multi	.30	.30
326	A47	50c purple & multi	.50	.50
		Nos. 324-326 (3)	1.05	1.05

Caribbean visit of Queen Elizabeth II.

Divers Checking Equipment — A49

Tourist publicity: 5c, Cup coral inside bow of "Rhone." 8c, Sponge growing on superstructure of "Rhone." 22c, Sponge and cup coral. 30c, Scuba diver searching for sponges in cave. 75c, Marine life.

1977, Dec. 15   **Wmk. 373**   *Perf. 13½*
327	A49	½c multicolored	.25	.25
328	A49	5c multicolored	.25	.25
329	A49	8c multicolored	.25	.25
330	A49	22c multicolored	.70	.70
331	A49	30c multicolored	.95	.95
332	A49	75c multicolored	1.75	1.75
		Nos. 327-332 (6)	4.15	4.15

Corals A50

1978, Feb. 10   *Perf. 14*
333	A50	8c Fire	.35	.35
334	A50	15c Staghorn	.55	.55
335	A50	40c Brain	1.00	1.00
336	A50	75c Elkhorn	2.10	2.10
		Nos. 333-336 (4)	4.00	4.00

Elizabeth II Coronation Anniversary Issue

Common Design Types

Souvenir Sheet

1978, June 2   **Unwmk.**   *Perf. 15*
337		Sheet of 6	2.75	2.75
a.		CD326 50c Falcon of the Plantagenets	.40	.40
b.		CD327 50c Elizabeth II	.40	.40
c.		CD328 50c Iguana	.40	.40

No. 337 contains 2 se-tenant strips of Nos. 337a-337c, separated by horizontal gutter.

Lignum Vitae A51

Flowering Trees: 22c, Ginger thomas. 40c, Dog almond. 75c, White cedar.

1978, Sept. 4   **Litho.**   *Perf. 13x13½*
338	A51	8c multicolored	.35	.35
339	A51	22c multicolored	.55	.55
340	A51	40c multicolored	.75	.75
341	A51	75c multicolored	1.10	1.10
a.		Souvenir sheet of 4, #338-341	2.75	2.75
		Nos. 338-341 (4)	2.75	2.75

Eurema Lisa A52

Butterflies: 22c, Dione vanillae. 30c, Heliconius charitonius. 75c, Hemiargus hanno.

1978, Dec. 4   **Wmk. 373**   *Perf. 14*
342	A52	5c multicolored	.35	.25
343	A52	22c multicolored	1.25	1.00
a.		Sheet of 9, 6 #342, 3 #343	5.00	5.00
344	A52	30c multicolored	1.60	1.40
345	A52	75c multicolored	4.00	3.50
		Nos. 342-345 (4)	7.20	6.15

Spiny Lobsters A53

Conservation: 15c, Iguana, vert. 22c, Hawksbill turtle. 75c, Black coral, vert.

1979, Feb. 10   *Litho.*
346	A53	5c multicolored	.25	.25
347	A53	15c multicolored	.45	.45
348	A53	22c multicolored	.80	.80
349	A53	75c multicolored	1.75	1.75
a.		Souvenir sheet of 4, #346-349	4.50	4.50
		Nos. 346-349 (4)	3.25	3.25

Strawberry Cactus — A54

Native Cacti: 5c, Snowy cactus. 13c, Barrel cactus. 22c, Tree cactus. 30c, Prickly pear. 75c, Dildo cactus.

1979, May 7   **Wmk. 373**   *Perf. 14*
350	A54	½c multicolored	.25	.25
351	A54	5c multicolored	.25	.25
352	A54	13c multicolored	.40	.40
353	A54	22c multicolored	.55	.55
354	A54	30c multicolored	.60	.60
355	A54	75c multicolored	1.10	1.10
		Nos. 350-355 (6)	3.15	3.15

West Indies Girl and Church — A55

Children and IYC Emblem: 10c, African boy and dancers. 13c, Asian girl and children playing. $1, European girl and bicycle.

1979, July 9   *Perf. 14x14½*
356	A55	5c multicolored	.25	.25
357	A55	10c multicolored	.25	.25
358	A55	13c multicolored	.25	.25
359	A55	$1 multicolored	.60	.60
a.		Souvenir sheet of 4, #356-359	1.50	1.50
		Nos. 356-359 (4)	1.35	1.35

International Year of the Child.

No. 118 — A56

Rowland Hill's Signature and: 13c, Virgin Islands No. 11, horiz. 75c, Unissued Great Britain 2d stamp, 1910, horiz. $1, Virgin Islands No. 8c.

1979, Oct. 1   **Photo.**   *Perf. 13½*
360	A56	5c multicolored	.25	.25
361	A56	13c multicolored	.25	.25
362	A56	75c multicolored	.85	.85
		Nos. 360-362 (3)	1.35	1.35

Souvenir Sheet

363	A56	$1 multicolored	1.00	1.00

Sir Rowland Hill (1795-1879), originator of penny postage.
For overprints see Nos. 389-390.

Pencil Urchin — A57

"1979" or "1980" Below Design

1979-80   **Litho.**   *Perf. 14*
364	A57	½c Calcified algae	.25	.25
365	A57	1c Purple-tipped sea anemone	.25	.25
366	A57	3c Starfish	.25	.25
367	A57	5c shown	.25	.25
368	A57	8c Triton's trumpet	.25	.25
369	A57	10c Christmas tree worms	.25	.25
370	A57	13c Flamingo tongue snails	.25	.25
371	A57	15c Spider crab	.35	.35
372	A57	18c Sea squirts	.35	.35
373	A57	20c True tulip	.40	.40
374	A57	25c Rooster tail conch	.50	.55
375	A57	30c Fighting conch	.70	.75
376	A57	60c Mangrove crab	1.50	*1.60*
377	A57	$1 Coral polyps	2.25	2.40
378	A57	$2.50 Peppermint shrimp	5.50	6.00
379	A57	$3 West Indian murex	6.75	7.25
380	A57	$5 Carpet anemone	11.50	12.50
		Nos. 364-380 (17)	31.55	33.90

Issued: 5, 8, 10, 15, 20, 25c, $2.50, $3, 12/17/79; others, 4/1/80. Date of year of issue below design.
For overprints see Nos. O1-O15.

"1982" Below Design

1982, Aug. 27   **Chalky Paper**
367a	A57	5c multicolored	.75	.75
368a	A57	8c multicolored	.75	.75
370a	A57	13c multicolored	1.50	1.50
371a	A57	15c multicolored	1.50	1.50
373a	A57	20c multicolored	1.25	1.25
375a	A57	30c multicolored	2.00	2.00
		Nos. 367a-375a (6)	7.75	7.75

Rotary Athletic Meet, Tortola, Emblem A58

1980, Mar. 3   **Litho.**   *Perf. 13½x14*
381	A58	8c shown	.25	.25
382	A58	22c Paul P. Harris	.25	.25
383	A58	60c Mount Sage National Park	.55	.55
384	A58	$1 Anniversary emblem	1.00	1.00
a.		Souvenir sheet of 4, #381-384	2.50	2.50
		Nos. 381-384 (4)	2.05	2.05

Rotary International, 75th anniv.

Brown Booby, London 1980 Emblem A59

1980, May 6   **Wmk. 373**   *Perf. 14*
385	A59	20c shown	.35	.35
386	A59	25c Magnificent frigatebird	.45	.45
387	A59	50c White-tailed tropic bird	.70	.70
388	A59	75c Brown pelican	.95	.95
a.		Souvenir sheet of 4, #385-388	3.00	3.00
		Nos. 385-388 (4)	2.45	2.45

London 80 Intl. Stamp Exhib., May 6-14.

Nos. 361-362 Overprinted

1980, July 7   **Photo.**   *Perf. 13½*
389	A56	13c multicolored	.25	.25
390	A56	75c multicolored	.80	.80

Sir Francis Drake — A60

1980, Sept. 26   **Litho.**   *Perf. 14½*
391	A60	8c shown	.50	.50
392	A60	15c Queen Elizabeth I	.80	.80
393	A60	30c Drake knighted	.95	.95
394	A60	75c Golden Hinde	2.00	2.00
a.		Souvenir sheet of 4, #391-394	4.50	4.50
		Nos. 391-394 (4)	4.25	4.25

400th anniv. of circumnavigation of the world.

Jost Van Dyke A61

1980, Dec. 1   Wmk. 373   Perf. 14

395	A61	2c shown	.25	.25
396	A61	5c Peter Island	.25	.25
397	A61	13c Virgin Gorda	.25	.25
398	A61	22c Anegada	.35	.35
399	A61	30c Norman Island	.40	.40
400	A61	$1 Tortola	1.25	1.25
a.		Souvenir sheet of 1	1.75	1.75
		Nos. 395-400 (6)	2.75	2.75

Dancing Lady — A62

1981, Mar. 3   Litho.   Perf. 11

401	A62	5c shown	.35	.35
402	A62	20c Love in the mist	.40	.40
403	A62	22c Red pineapple	.40	.40
404	A62	75c Dutchman's pipe	1.10	1.10
405	A62	$1 Maiden apple	1.40	1.40
		Nos. 401-405 (5)	3.65	3.65

Royal Wedding Issue
Common Design Type

1981, July 22   Litho.   Perf. 14

406	CD331	10c Bouquet	.25	.25
407	CD331	35c Charles, Queen Mother	.40	.40
408	CD331	$1.25 Couple	1.25	1.25
		Nos. 406-408 (3)	1.90	1.90

#406-408 each se-tenant with decorative label.

Duke of Edinburgh's Awards, 25th Anniv. — A63

1981, Sept. 16   Wmk. 373   Perf. 14

409	A63	10c Stamp collecting	.25	.25
410	A63	15c Running	.25	.25
411	A63	50c Camping	.60	.60
412	A63	$1 Duke of Edinburgh	1.25	1.25
		Nos. 409-412 (4)	2.35	2.35

Intl. Year of the Disabled A64

1981, Oct. 19   Litho.   Perf. 14

413	A64	15c Children	.30	.30
414	A64	20c Fort Charlotte Children's Center	.40	.40
415	A64	30c Playing music	.50	.50
416	A64	$1 Center, diff.	1.60	1.60
		Nos. 413-416 (4)	2.80	2.80

A65   A66

Virgin and Child (Christmas): Details from Adoration of the Shepherds, by Rubens. 50c, horiz.

1981, Nov. 30   Litho.   Perf. 14

417	A65	5c multicolored	.25	.25
418	A65	15c multicolored	.25	.25
419	A65	30c multicolored	.50	.50
420	A65	$1 multicolored	2.00	2.00
		Nos. 417-420 (4)	3.00	3.00

Souvenir Sheet

421	A65	50c multicolored	2.50	2.50

1982, Apr. 15   Litho.   Perf. 14x14½

Hummingbirds on local flora.

422	A66	15c Green-throated carib, erythrina	.50	.50
423	A66	30c Same, bougainvillea	1.00	1.00
424	A66	35c Antillean crested hummingbird, granadilla passiflora	1.25	1.25
425	A66	$1.25 Same, hibiscus	3.75	3.75
		Nos. 422-425 (4)	6.50	6.50

10th Anniv. of Lions Club of Tortola — A67

1982, May 3   Perf. 13½x14

426	A67	10c Helping disabled	.25	.25
427	A67	20c Headquarters	.35	.35
428	A67	30c Map	.50	.50
429	A67	$1.50 Emblem	2.50	2.50
a.		Souvenir sheet of 4, #426-429	4.50	4.50
		Nos. 426-429 (4)	3.60	3.60

Princess Diana Issue
Common Design Type

1982, July 1   Litho.   Perf. 14

430	CD333	10c Arms	.25	.25
431	CD333	35c Diana	.55	.55
432	CD333	50c Wedding	.75	.75
433	CD333	$1.50 Portrait	2.50	2.50
		Nos. 430-433 (4)	4.05	4.05

10th Anniv. of Air BVI (Natl. Airline) A68

1982, Sept. 10   Wmk. 373   Perf. 14

434	A68	10c Douglas DC-3	.30	.30
435	A68	15c Britten-Norman Islander	.55	.55
436	A68	60c Hawker-Siddeley	2.40	2.40
437	A68	75c Planes	2.75	2.75
		Nos. 434-437 (4)	6.00	6.00

Scouting Year A69

1982, Nov. 18

438	A69	8c Emblem, Flag raising	.25	.25
439	A69	20c Cub scout, nature study	.40	.40
440	A69	50c Kayak, sea scout	1.00	1.00

441	A69	$1 Camp Brownsea Is., Baden-Powell	2.00	2.00
		Nos. 438-441 (4)	3.65	3.65

Commonwealth Day — A70

1983, Mar. 14   Perf. 13½x14

442	A70	10c Legislature in session	.25	.25
443	A70	30c Wind surfing	.50	.50
444	A70	35c Globe	.60	.60
445	A70	75c Flags	1.25	1.25
		Nos. 442-445 (4)	2.60	2.60

Nursing Week A71

1983, May 9   Litho.   Perf. 14½

446	A71	10c Florence Nightingale (1820-1910), vert.	.50	.50
447	A71	30c Nurse, assistant, vert.	1.25	1.25
448	A71	60c Public health	2.50	2.50
449	A71	75c Peebles Hospital	3.25	3.25
		Nos. 446-449 (4)	7.50	7.50

Boat Building A72

1983, July 25   Perf. 14

450	A72	15c First stage	.40	.40
451	A72	25c 2nd stage	.60	.60
452	A72	50c Launching	1.25	1.25
453	A72	$1 First voyage	2.50	2.50
a.		Souvenir sheet of 4, #450-453	5.00	5.00
		Nos. 450-453 (4)	4.75	4.75

Manned Flight Bicentenary — A73

1983, Sept. 15   Wmk. 373   Perf. 14

454	A73	10c Grumman Goose	.25	.25
455	A73	30c De Havilland Heron	.55	.55
456	A73	60c EMB Bandeirante	1.25	1.25
457	A73	$1.25 Hawker-Siddeley 748	2.25	2.25
		Nos. 454-457 (4)	4.30	4.30

Christmas — A74

Raphael Paintings.

1983, Nov. 7   Litho.   Perf. 14½

458	A74	8c Madonna & Child with Infant Baptist	.25	.25
459	A74	15c La Belle Jardiniere	.30	.30
460	A74	50c Madonna del Granduca	.95	.95
461	A74	$1 Terranuova Madonna	1.90	1.90
a.		Souvenir sheet of 4, #458-461	4.25	4.25
		Nos. 458-461 (4)	3.40	3.40

World Chess Federation, 60th Anniv. — A75

1984, Feb. 20   Litho.   Perf. 14

462	A75	10c Local tournament	.60	.60
463	A75	35c Chess pieces, vert.	1.90	1.90
464	A75	75c 1980 Olympiad, Winning board, vert.	4.50	4.50
465	A75	$1 Gold medal	7.00	7.00
		Nos. 462-465 (4)	14.00	14.00

Lloyd's List Issue
Common Design Type

1984, Apr. 16   Litho.   Perf. 14½x14

466	CD335	15c Port Purcell, Tortola	.35	.35
467	CD335	25c Boeing 747	.65	.65
468	CD335	50c Shipwreck of RMS Rhone	1.25	1.25
469	CD335	$1 Booker Viking	2.75	2.75
		Nos. 466-469 (4)	5.00	5.00

Souvenir Sheet

UPU Congress — A76

1984, May 16   Wmk. 373   Perf. 14

470	A76	$1 Emblem, jet, mailboat	3.50	3.50

1984 Summer Olympics A77

1984, July 3

471	A77	15c Runners	.40	.40
472	A77	15c Runner	.40	.40
a.		Pair, #471-472	1.25	1.25
473	A77	20c Wind surfers	.50	.50
474	A77	20c Wind surfer	.50	.50
a.		Pair, #473-474	1.50	1.50
475	A77	30c Yachts	.75	.75
476	A77	30c Yacht	.75	.75
a.		Pair, #475-476	2.25	2.25
		Nos. 471-476 (6)	3.30	3.30

Souvenir Sheet

477	A77	$1 Torch bearer, vert.	2.75	2.75

Festival (Slavery Abolition Sesquicentennial) — A78

Designs: No. 478: a, Steel band. b, Calypso dancers. c, Dancers (men). d, Woman in traditional dress. e, Parade float.

No. 479 (Sail color of boat(s) in foreground): a, Green & white. b, Red & white, white, purple & white. c, white, yellow & white, blue & white. d, Yellow, red & white. e, Purple & white, white.

Nos. 478 and 479 each in continuous design.

1984, Aug. 14   **Perf. 13½x14**
478   Strip of 5, Parade   1.50 1.50
  a.-e. A78 10c, any single   .25   .25
479   Strip of 5, Regatta   3.75 3.75
  a.-e. A78 30c, any single   .60   .60

Local
Boats
A79

1984, Nov. 15   Wmk. 373   Perf. 13
480 A79 10c Sloop   .30   .30
481 A79 35c Fishing boat   1.25 1.25
482 A79 60c Schooner   2.25 2.25
483 A79 75c Cargo boat   2.75 2.75
  a.   Souvenir sheet of 4, #480-483 6.75 6.75
       Nos. 480-483 (4)   6.55 6.55

Four stamps picturing Michael Jackson were printed. The designs were not acceptable to the Virgin Islands so they were not issued. A number of stamps had been distributed in advance for publicity purposes.

New
Coinage
A80

1985, Jan. 15   Litho.   Perf. 14½
484 A80   1c Hawksbill Turtle   .25   .25
485 A80   5c Bonito   .25   .25
486 A80 10c Great Barricuda   .25   .25
487 A80 25c Blue Marlin   .80   .80
488 A80 50c Dolphin   1.60 1.60
489 A80 $1   Spotfin Butterfly
               Fish   3.00 3.00
  a.   Miniature sheet of 6, #484-489 6.50 6.50
       Nos. 484-489 (6)   6.15 6.15

Birds — A81

1985, July 3   Wmk. 373   Perf. 14
490 A81   1c Boatswain bird   .25   .30
491 A81   2c Night gaulin   .25   .30
492 A81   5c Rain bird   .25   .30
493 A81   8c Mockingbird   .25   .30
494 A81 10c Chinchary   .30   .40
495 A81 12c Wild pigeon   .40   .50
496 A81 15c Bittlin   .60   .55
497 A81 18c Black witch   .55   .65
498 A81 20c Pond shakey   .65   .75
499 A81 25c Killy-killy   .80   .90
500 A81 30c Thrushie   1.00 1.25
501 A81 35c Marmi dove   1.10 1.40
502 A81 40c Little gaulin   1.40 1.75
503 A81 50c Ground dove   1.60 2.00
504 A81 60c Blue gaulin   2.50 2.75
505 A81 $1   Pimleco   4.00 4.50
506 A81 $2   White booby   8.00 9.00
507 A81 $3   Cow bird   11.00 12.00
508 A81 $5   Turtle dove   18.00 21.00
       Nos. 490-508 (19)   52.80 60.60

For overprints see Nos. O16-O34.

1987, Oct. 28   Wmk. 384
494a A81 10c   .50   .50
496a A81 15c   .75   .75
498a A81 20c   1.10 1.10
499a A81 25c   1.25 1.25
501a A81 35c   1.75 1.75
505a A81 $1   5.25 5.25
507a A81 $3   15.00 15.00
       Nos. 494a-507a (7)   25.60 25.60

Queen Mother,
85th
Birthday — A82

Portraits.

1985, Aug. 26   Litho.   Perf. 12½
509 A82 10c Facing right   .25   .25
510 A82 10c Facing left   .25   .25
511 A82 25c Facing right   .45   .45
512 A82 25c Facing left   .45   .45
513 A82 50c Facing right   .90   .90
514 A82 50c Facing forward   .90   .90
515 A82 75c Facing forward   1.25 1.25
516 A82 75c Facing forward   1.25 1.25
       Nos. 509-516 (8)   5.70 5.70

Souvenir Sheets
1985-86   Litho.   Perf. 13x12½
517   Sheet of 2   3.50 3.50
  a.-b. A82 $1 dull grn & multi   1.75 1.75
518   Sheet of 2   3.50 3.50
  a.-b. A82 $1 orange & multi   1.60 1.60
519   Sheet of 2   8.50 8.50
  a.-b. A82 $2.50 dl yel & multi   4.25 4.25

Issued: #517, 12/18/85; #518-519, 2/18/86.
For overprints see Nos. 528-531.

Audubon Birth
Bicent. — A83

1985, Dec. 17   Perf. 15
520 A83   5c Seaside sparrow   .25   .25
521 A83 30c Passenger pigeon   .60   .60
522 A83 50c Yellow-breasted
               chat   1.00 1.00
523 A83 $1   American kestrel   2.00 2.00
       Nos. 520-523 (4)   3.85 3.85

Cruise
Ships
A84

1986, Jan. 27
524 A84 35c Flying Cloud   .80   .80
525 A84 50c Newport Clipper   1.25 1.25
526 A84 75c Cunard Countess   1.90 1.90
527 A84 $1   Sea Goddess   2.75 2.75
       Nos. 524-527 (4)   6.70 6.70

Nos. 511-512,
515-516 Ovptd.

1986, Apr. 17   Litho.   Perf. 12½
528 A82 25c on No. 511   .50   .50
529 A82 25c on No. 512   .50   .50
530 A82 75c on No. 515   1.75 1.75
531 A82 75c on No. 516   1.75 1.75
       Nos. 528-531 (4)   4.50 4.50

Queen Elizabeth II, 60th
Birthday — A85

Perf. 13x12½, 12½x13
1986, Apr. 21   Litho.
532 A85 12c Portrait, 1958   .25   .25
533 A85 35c Maundy service   .30   .30
534 A85 $1.50 Contemporary
               photograph   1.10 1.10
535 A85 $2   Canberra, 1982,
               vert.   1.50 1.50
       Nos. 532-535 (4)   3.15 3.15

Souvenir Sheet
536 A85 $3   Contemporary
               photograph, diff.   6.00 6.00

Stamps with blue ribbons and frames omitted were from stock sold when the printer was liquidated.

Wedding of Prince Andrew and Sarah
Ferguson — A86

1986, July 23   Perf. 12½
537 A86 35c Couple, vert.   .50   .50
538 A86 35c Sarah, vert.   .50   .50
539 A86 $1   Andrew   1.50 1.50
540 A86 $1   Sarah, diff.   1.50 1.50
       Nos. 537-540 (4)   4.00 4.00

Stamps of the same denomination exist se-tenant.
Nos. 537-540 overprinted "Congratulations to T.R.H. The Duke & Duchess of York" were not issued.

Traditional Rum Production — A87

1986, July 30   Perf. 14
541 A87 12c Harvesting sugar
               cane   .50   .50
542 A87 40c Grinding   2.00 2.00
543 A87 60c Distillery   3.25 3.25
544 A87 $1   Transport   5.25 5.25
       Nos. 541-544 (4)   11.00 11.00

Souvenir Sheet
545 A87 $2   Up Spirits cere-
               mony, 19th cent.   9.50 9.50

Souvenir Sheet

Wedding of Prince Andrew and Sarah
Ferguson — A88

1986, Oct. 15   Litho.   Perf. 13x12½
546 A88 $4   multicolored   5.00 5.00

Cable-Laying Ships — A89

1986, Oct. 15   Wmk. 380   Perf. 12½
547 A89 35c Sentinel   .70   .70
548 A89 35c Retriever   .70   .70
  a.   Pair, #547-548   1.40 1.40
549 A89 60c Cable Enterprise   1.25 1.25
550 A89 60c Mercury   1.25 1.25
  a.   Pair, #549-550   2.50 2.50
551 A89 75c Recorder   1.50 1.50
552 A89 75c Pacific Guardian   1.50 1.50
  a.   Pair, #551-552   3.00 3.00
553 A89 $1   Great Eastern   2.00 2.00
554 A89 $1   Cable Venture   2.00 2.00
  a.   Pair, #553-554   4.00 4.00
       Nos. 547-554 (8)   10.90 10.90

Souvenir Sheets
555   Sheet of 2   1.40 1.40
  a.-b. A89 40c, like #547-548   .70   .70
556   Sheet of 2   1.75 1.75
  a.-b. A89 50c, like #549-550   .90   .90
557   Sheet of 2   2.75 2.75
  a.-b. A89 80c, like #551-552   1.40 1.40
558   Sheet of 2   5.25 5.25
  a.-b. A89 $1.50, like #553-554   2.50 2.50

Cable and wireless in the islands, 20th anniv.

Souvenir Sheets

Statue of Liberty, Cent. — A90

Various views of the statue.

1986, Dec. 15   Litho.   Perf. 14
559 A90 50c multicolored   .75   .75
560 A90 75c multicolored   1.25 1.25
561 A90 90c multicolored   1.40 1.40
562 A90 $1   multicolored   1.60 1.60
563 A90 $1.25 multicolored   2.00 2.00
564 A90 $1.50 multicolored   2.40 2.40
565 A90 $1.75 multicolored   2.75 2.75
566 A90 $2   multicolored   3.00 3.00
567 A90 $2.50 multicolored   4.00 4.00
       Nos. 559-567 (9)   19.15 19.15

A91

Shipwrecks — A92

1987, Apr. 15 — Perf. 14

572	A91	12c Spanish galleon, 18th cent.	.85	.85
573	A91	35c HMS Astrea, 1808	2.40	2.40
574	A91	75c RMS Rhone, 1867	4.75	4.75
575	A91	$1.50 SS Rocus, 1929	10.00	10.00
		Nos. 572-575 (4)	18.00	18.00

Souvenir Sheet

576	A92	$2.50 Brig Volvart, 1918	19.00	19.00

Natl. Flags, Outline Maps — A93

Botanical Gardens — A94

1987, May 28

577	A93	10c Montserrat	.25	.25
578	A93	15c Grenada	.60	.60
579	A93	20c Dominica	.85	.85
580	A93	25c St. Kitts-Nevis	1.10	1.10
581	A93	35c St. Vincent and Grenadines	1.40	1.40
582	A93	50c Virgin Isls.	2.10	2.10
583	A93	75c Antigua & Barbuda	3.00	3.00
584	A93	$1 St. Lucia	4.25	4.25
		Nos. 577-584 (8)	13.55	13.55

11th Meeting of the Organization of Eastern Caribbean States.

1987, Aug. 12 — Wmk. 384

585	A94	12c Spider lily	.75	.75
586	A94	35c Barrel cactus	2.25	2.25
587	A94	$1 Wild plantain	6.25	6.25
588	A94	$1.50 Little butterfly orchid	9.25	9.25
		Nos. 585-588 (4)	18.50	18.50

Souvenir Sheet

589	A94	$2.50 White cedar	6.25	6.25

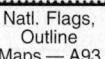

Postal Service Bicent. A95

Designs: 10c, 18th Cent. packet, #7 canceled "A13." 20c, Map of the islands, #22 canceled "A91." 35c, Tortola Post Office and Customs House, and #5 canceled "Tortola De 20 61." $1.50, Mail plane and #154 canceled "Road town No 2 64 Tortola W.I." $2.50, Late 19th cent. steam packet and #10 canceled "A Tortola Ap 12 70."

1987, Dec. 17 — Litho. — Perf. 14½

590	A95	10c multicolored	.75	.75
591	A95	20c multicolored	1.50	1.50
592	A95	35c multicolored	2.50	2.50
593	A95	$1.50 multicolored	10.50	10.50
		Nos. 590-593 (4)	15.25	15.25

Souvenir Sheet

594	A95	$2.50 multicolored	8.00	8.00

Paintings by Titian — A96

10c, Salome, 1512. 12c, Man with the Glove, c. 1520-22. 20c, Fabrizio Salvaresio, 1558. 25c, Daughter of Roberto Strozzi, 1542.

40c, Pope Julius II. 50c, Bishop Ludovico Beccadelli, 1552. 60c, Philip II. $1, Empress Isabella of Portugal, 1548. #603, Emperor Charles V at Muhlberg, 1548. #604, Pope Paul III & His Grandsons, 1546.

Perf. 13½x14 — Unwmk.

595	A96	10c multicolored	.35	.35
596	A96	12c multicolored	.50	.50
597	A96	20c multicolored	.80	.80
598	A96	25c multicolored	1.00	1.00
599	A96	40c multicolored	1.75	1.75
600	A96	50c multicolored	2.10	2.10
601	A96	60c multicolored	2.75	2.75
602	A96	$1 multicolored	4.75	4.75
		Nos. 595-602 (8)	14.00	14.00

Souvenir Sheet

603	A96	$2 multicolored	8.25	8.25
604	A96	$2 multicolored	8.25	8.25

1st Annual Open Chess Tournament — A97

35c, Pawn & Transporter aircraft over Sir Francis Drake Channel. $1, King & Jose Raul Capablanca (1888-1942), Cuban chess master and world champion from 1921-27. $2, Match scene.

1988, Aug. 25 — Unwmk. — Perf. 14

605	A97	35c multicolored	4.00	4.00
606	A97	$1 multicolored	11.50	11.50

Souvenir Sheet

607	A97	$2 multicolored	13.00	13.00

1988 Summer Olympics, Seoul A98

1988, Sept. 8

608	A98	12c Hurdling	.65	.65
609	A98	20c Windsurfing	1.10	1.10
610	A98	75c Basketball	4.00	4.00
611	A98	$1 Tennis	5.25	5.25
		Nos. 608-611 (4)	11.00	11.00

Souvenir Sheet

612	A98	$2 Running	5.50	5.50

Intl. Red Cross, 125th Anniv. A99

Safety warnings and steps in administering cardiopulmonary resuscitation (CPR): 12c, "Don't swim alone." 30c, "No swimming during electrical storms." 60c, "Don't eat before swimming." $1, "Proper equipment for boating." No. 617a, Turn victim on back. No. 617b, Position victim's chin in breathing passages are not blocked. No. 617c, Mouth-to-mouth resuscitation. No. 617d, Chest compressions. Nos. 617a-617d vert.

1988, Sept. 26

613	A99	12c multicolored	.65	.65
614	A99	30c multicolored	1.60	1.60
615	A99	60c multicolored	3.00	3.00
616	A99	$1 multicolored	5.25	5.25
		Nos. 613-616 (4)	10.50	10.50

Souvenir Sheet

617		Sheet of 4	8.75	8.75
a.-d.		A99 50c any single	1.10	1.10

#617a-617d has a continuous design.

Visit of Princess Alexandra — A100

World Wildlife Fund — A101

Various photographs of the princess.

1988, Nov. 9 — Litho. — Perf. 14

618	A100	40c shown	2.00	2.00
619	A100	$1.50 multi, diff.	8.00	8.00

Souvenir Sheet

620	A100	$2 multi, diff.	9.00	9.00

1988, Nov. 15

Brown pelicans, *Pelecanus Occidentalis*.

621	A101	10c Pelican in flight	1.50	1.50
622	A101	12c Perched	1.75	1.75
623	A101	15c Close-up of head	2.00	2.00
624	A101	35c Swallowing fish	4.75	4.75
		Nos. 621-624 (4)	10.00	10.00

Reptiles, Marine Mammals and Birds — A102

20c, Anegada rock iguana. 40c, Virgin gorda dwarf gecko. 60c, Hawksbill turtle. $1, Humpback whale. #629, Northern shoveler, American widgeon & ring-necked ducks. #630, Trunk turtle.

1988, Nov. 15

625	A102	20c multicolored	1.50	1.50
626	A102	40c multicolored	2.75	2.75
627	A102	60c multicolored	4.25	4.25
628	A102	$1 multicolored	7.00	7.00
		Nos. 625-628 (4)	15.50	15.50

Souvenir Sheets

629	A102	$2 multicolored	10.50	10.50
630	A102	$2 multicolored	8.00	8.00

Spring Regatta A103

Various yachts.

1989, Apr. 7 — Litho. — Perf. 14

631	A103	12c multi, diff., vert.	.50	.50
632	A103	40c shown	1.50	1.50
633	A103	75c multi, diff., vert.	2.50	2.50
634	A103	$1 multi, diff.	3.50	3.50
		Nos. 631-634 (4)	8.00	8.00

Souvenir Sheet

635	A103	$2 multi, diff., vert.	8.75	8.75

Pre-Columbian Societies and Their Customs — A104

1989, May 18

636	A104	10c Hammock	.45	.45
637	A104	20c Making a fire	.95	.95
638	A104	25c Carvers	1.10	1.10
639	A104	$1.50 Arawak family	7.50	7.50
		Nos. 636-639 (4)	10.00	10.00

Souvenir Sheet

640	A104	$2 Ritual	10.00	10.00

Discovery of America 500th anniv. (in 1992).

1st Moon Landing, 20th Anniv. A105

Highlights of the Apollo 11 mission: 15c, Lunar surface, mission emblem. 30c, Buzz Aldrin conducting solar wind experiment. 65c, Raising American flag. $1, Recovery of crew after splashdown. $2, Portrait of crew.

1989, Sept. 28 — Litho. — Perf. 14

641	A105	15c multicolored	1.00	1.00
642	A105	30c multicolored	1.75	1.75
643	A105	65c multicolored	3.50	3.50
644	A105	$1 multicolored	5.75	5.75
		Nos. 641-644 (4)	12.00	12.00

Souvenir Sheet — Perf. 13½x14

645	A105	$2 multicolored	9.50	9.50

No. 645 contains one 37x46mm stamp.

Methodist Church, 200th Anniv. A106

Designs: 12c, Black Harry, Nathaniel Gilbert preaching. 25c, Book symbolizing role of the church in education. 35c, East End Methodist Church, 1810. $1.25, John Wesley, modern youth choir. $2, Thomas Coke.

1989, Oct. 24 — Perf. 14

646	A106	12c multicolored	.55	.55
647	A106	25c multicolored	1.25	1.25
648	A106	35c multicolored	1.75	1.75
649	A106	$1.25 multicolored	6.00	6.00
		Nos. 646-649 (4)	9.55	9.55

Souvenir Sheet

650	A106	$2 multicolored	8.00	8.00

1990 World Cup Soccer Championships, Italy — A107

Various athletes.

1989, Nov. 6

651	A107	5c shown	.70	.70
652	A107	10c multi, diff.	.70	.70
653	A107	20c multi, diff.	1.50	1.50
654	A107	$1.75 multi, diff.	11.50	11.50
		Nos. 651-654 (4)	14.40	14.40

Souvenir Sheet

655	A107	$2 Natl. team	11.00	11.00

Princess Alexandra, Sunset House — A108

British Virgin Islands

Stamp World London 90

Royal Yacht Britannia — A109

b, Princess Margaret, Government House. c, Hon. Angus Ogilvy, Little Dix Bay Hotel. d, Princess Diana & her children, Necker Island Resort.

1990, May 3   Litho.   Perf. 14
656   Min. sheet of 4   11.50 11.50
 a.-d.   A108 50c any single   1.10   1.10

Souvenir Sheet
657   A109 $2 multicolored   8.50   8.50

Stamp World London '90.

Audubon's Shearwater — A110

1990, May 15
658   A110   5c shown   .25   .25
659   A110   12c Red-necked
                pigeon   .40   .40
660   A110   20c Common galli-
                nule   .70   .70
661   A110   25c Green heron   .90   .90
662   A110   40c Yellow warbler   1.40   1.40
663   A110   60c Smooth-billed
                ani   2.25   2.25
664   A110 $1 Antillean
                crested hum-
                mingbird   3.50   3.50
665   A110 $1.25 Black-faced
                grassquit   4.50   4.50
        Nos. 658-665 (8)   13.90 13.90

Souvenir Sheets
666   A110 $2 Egg of royal
                tern   5.50   5.50
667   A110 $2 Egg of red-
                billed tropic-
                bird   5.50   5.50

Blue
Tang
A111

1990, June 18
668   A111   10c shown   .50   .50
669   A111   35c Glasseye   1.90   1.90
670   A111   50c Slippery Dick   2.75   2.75
671   A111 $1 Porkfish   5.50   5.50
        Nos. 668-671 (4)   10.65 10.65

Souvenir Sheet
672   A111 $2 Yellowtail snap-
                per   8.00   8.00

A112

1990, Aug. 30   Litho.   Perf. 14
673   A112   12c multicolored   .40   .40
674   A112   25c multi, diff.   .85   .85
675   A112   60c multi, diff.   2.25   2.25
676   A112 $1 multi, diff.   4.00   4.00
        Nos. 673-676 (4)   7.50   7.50

Souvenir Sheet
677   A112 $2 multi, diff.   6.00   6.00

Queen Mother, 90th birthday.

A113

Various soccer players.

1990, Dec. 10   Litho.   Perf. 14
678   A113   12c multicolored   .50   .50
679   A113   20c multi, diff.   .90   .90
680   A113   50c multi, diff.   2.10   2.10
681   A113 $1.25 multi, diff.   5.50   5.50
        Nos. 678-681 (4)   9.00   9.00

Souvenir Sheet
682   A113 $2 multi, diff.   7.50   7.50

World Cup Soccer Championships, Italy.

1992 Summer Olympics, Barcelona A114

1990, Dec. 20   Litho.   Perf. 14
683   A114   12c multicolored   .65   .65
684   A114   40c Yachting   2.10   2.10
685   A114   60c Hurdles   3.25   3.25
686   A114 $1 Show jumping   5.50   5.50
        Nos. 683-686 (4)   11.50 11.50

Souvenir Sheet
687   A114 $2 Windsurfing   6.50   6.50

Copper
Mine
Ruins
A115

1991, Mar. 1   Litho.   Perf. 14
688   A115   10c Cyathea
                arborea, vert.   .40   .40
689   A115   25c shown   1.10   1.10
690   A115   35c Mt. Healthy
                windmill ruin,
                vert.   1.75   1.75
691   A115 $2 Baths, Virgin
                Gorda   8.75   8.75
        Nos. 688-691 (4)   12.00 12.00

National Park Trust.

Flowers — A116

1991-92   Litho.   Perf. 14
No Date Imprint Below Design
692   A116   1c Haiti Haiti   .25   .25
693   A116   2c Lobster claw   .25   .25
694   A116   5c Frangipani   .25   .25
695   A116   10c Autograph tree   .25   .25
696   A116   12c Yellow alla-
                manda   .25   .25
697   A116   15c Lantana   .40   .40
698   A116   20c Jerusalem thorn   .55   .55
699   A116   25c Turk's cap   .65   .65

700   A116   30c Swamp immor-
                telle   .75   .75
701   A116   35c White cedar   .85   .85
702   A116   40c Mahoe tree   1.00   1.00
703   A116   45c Pinguin   1.10   1.10
704   A116   50c Christmas
                orchid   1.25   1.25
 a.   Perf 12   2.00   2.00
705   A116   70c Lignum vitae   1.75   1.75
706   A116 $1 African tulip tree 2.50   2.50
 a.   Perf 12   3.25   3.25
707   A116 $2 Beach morning
                glory   5.00   5.00
 a.   Perf 12   6.50   6.50
708   A116 $3 Organ pipe cac-
                tus   7.25   7.25
 a.   Perf 12½x11½   10.00 10.00
709   A116 $5 Tall ground
                orchid   12.50 12.50
710   A116 $10 Ground orchid   24.00 24.00
        Nos. 692-710 (19)   60.80 60.80

Issued: 1c-$5, 5/1/91; $10, 5/92; Nos. 704a, 706a, 707a, 708a, 8/95.
For overprints see Nos. O37-O51.

1995, June 1   Wmk. 373 Sideways
Inscribed "1995" Below Design
695b A116   10c multicolored   .60   1.60
697b A116   15c multicolored   .80   .50
700b A116   30c multicolored   .85   .60
701b A116   35c multicolored   1.00   .65
703b A116   45c multicolored   1.20   1.00
704b A116   50c multicolored   2.75   2.10
707b A116 $2 multicolored   3.75   6.00
709b A116 $5 multicolored   10.50 14.00
        Nos. 695b-709b (8)   21.45 26.45

Butterflies — A117

1991, June 28   Litho.   Perf. 14
711   A117   5c Cloudless
                sulphur   .50   .50
712   A117   10c Flambeau   .50   .50
713   A117   15c Caribbean
                buckeye   .85   .85
714   A117   20c Gulf fritillary 1.25   1.25
715   A117   25c Polydamus
                swallowtail   1.40   1.40
716   A117   30c Little sulphur 1.75   1.75
717   A117   35c Zebra   2.10   2.10
718   A117 $1.50 Malachite   8.75   8.75
        Nos. 711-718 (8)   17.10 17.10

Souvenir Sheets
719   A117 $2 Monarch,
                horiz.   10.00 10.00
720   A117 $2 Red rim,
                horiz.   10.00 10.00

Voyages of Discovery A118

Ships of explorers: 12c, Ferdinand Magellan, 1519-1521. 50c, Rene-Robert de la Salle, 1682. 75c, John Cabot, 1497-1498. $1, Jacques Cartier, 1534. $2, Columbus' ship, 1493 woodcut, vert.

1991, Sept. 20   Litho.   Perf. 14
721   A118   12c multicolored   .60   .60
722   A118   50c multicolored   2.50   2.50
723   A118   75c multicolored   4.00   4.00
724   A118 $1 multicolored   5.25   5.25
        Nos. 721-724 (4)   12.35 12.35

Souvenir Sheet
725   A118 $2 multicolored   10.50 10.50

Vincent Van Gogh (1853-1890), Painter — A119

Paintings: 15c, Cottage with Decrepit Barn and Stooping Woman. 30c, Paul Gauguin's Armchair, vert. 75c, Breton Women. $1, Vase with Red Gladioli, vert. $2, The Dance Hall in Arles (detail).

1991, Nov. 1   Perf. 13
726   A119   15c multicolored   .90   .90
727   A119   30c multicolored   1.75   1.75
728   A119   75c multicolored   4.50   4.50
729   A119 $1 multicolored   6.25   6.25
        Nos. 726-729 (4)   13.40 13.40

Souvenir Sheet
730   A119 $2 multicolored   13.00 13.00

Christmas A120

Entire paintings or details by Quinten Massys: 15c, The Virgin and Child Enthroned. 30c, The Virgin and Child Enthroned, diff. 60c, The Adoration of the Magi. $1, Virgin in Adoration. No. 735, The Virgin Standing with Angels. No. 736, The Adoration of the Magi.

1991, Dec. 12   Litho.   Perf. 12
731   A120   15c multicolored   .85   .85
732   A120   30c multicolored   1.90   1.90
733   A120   60c multicolored   3.75   3.75
734   A120 $1 multicolored   6.00   6.00
        Nos. 731-734 (4)   12.50 12.50

Souvenir Sheets
Perf. 14½
735   A120 $2 multicolored   6.75   6.75
736   A120 $2 multicolored   6.75   6.75

Mushrooms — A121

1992, Jan. 15   Perf. 14
737   A121   12c Agaricus
                bisporus, vert. 1.00   1.00
738   A121   30c Lentinus edodes 2.25   2.25
739   A121   45c Hyrocybe
                acutoconica,
                vert.   3.50   3.50
740   A121 $1 Gymnopilus
                chrysopellus   7.25   7.25
        Nos. 737-740 (4)   14.00 14.00

Souvenir Sheet
741   A121 $2 Pleurotus os-
                treatus   11.50 11.50

Queen Elizabeth II's Accession to the Throne, 40th Anniv.
Common Design Type
1992, Feb. 6   Litho.   Perf. 14
742   CD348 12c multicolored   .40   .40
743   CD348 45c multicolored   1.50   1.50
744   CD348 60c multicolored   2.10   2.10
745   CD348 $1 multicolored   3.50   3.50
        Nos. 742-745 (4)   7.50   7.50

Souvenir Sheet
746   CD348 $2 multicolored   8.00   8.00

Discovery of America, 500th Anniv. A122

10c, Queen Isabella. 15c, Columbus' fleet. 20c, Columbus' second coat of arms. 30c, Landing Monument on Watling Island, Columbus' signature. 45c, Columbus. 50c, Flag of Ferdinand & Isabella, Columbus landing on Watling Island. 70c, Convent at La Rabida. $1.50, Replica of Santa Maria at New York World's Fair, 1964-65. #755, Columbus' 2nd fleet. #756, Map.

1992, May 26   Litho.   Perf. 14

747	A122	10c multi, vert.	.50	.50
748	A122	15c multi	.70	.70
749	A122	20c multi, vert.	.95	.95
750	A122	30c multi	1.25	1.25
751	A122	45c multi, vert.	1.75	1.75
752	A122	50c multi	2.10	2.10
753	A122	70c multi, vert.	3.00	3.00
754	A122	$1.50 multi	6.75	6.75
		Nos. 747-754 (8)	17.00	17.00

Souvenir Sheet

755	A122	$2 multicolored	8.00	8.00
756	A122	$2 multicolored	8.00	8.00

1992 Summer Olympics, Barcelona — A123

1992, Aug.   Litho.   Perf. 14

757	A123	15c Basketball	.85	.85
758	A123	30c Tennis	1.90	1.90
759	A123	60c Volleyball	3.75	3.75
760	A123	$1 Soccer	6.00	6.00
		Nos. 757-760 (4)	12.50	12.50

Souvenir Sheet

761	A123	$2 Olympic flame	11.00	11.00

Ministerial Government, 25th Anniv. — A124

Designs: 12c, Social progress and development. 15c, Map of Virgin Islands. 45c, Administration complex. $1.30, International finance.

1993, Apr.   Litho.   Perf. 14

762	A124	12c multicolored	.40	.40
763	A124	15c multicolored	.45	.45
764	A124	45c multicolored	1.40	1.40
765	A124	$1.30 multicolored	4.25	4.25
		Nos. 762-765 (4)	6.50	6.50

Tourism A125

15c, Swimming from anchored yacht. 30c, Sailboat. 60c, Scuba diver in pink wetsuit. $1, Snorkelers, anchored boat.
#770: a, Trimaran, vert. b, Scuba diver, vert.

1993, Apr.   Litho.   Perf. 14

766	A125	15c multi	.50	.50
767	A125	30c multi, vert.	1.25	1.25
768	A125	60c multi	2.75	2.75
769	A125	$1 multi, vert.	4.50	4.50
		Nos. 766-769 (4)	9.00	9.00

Souvenir Sheet

770	A125	$1 Sheet of 2, #a.-		
		b.	9.00	9.00

Miniature Sheet

Coronation of Queen Elizabeth II, 40th Anniv. A126

No. 771: a, 12c, Official coronation photograph. b, 45c, Dove atop Rod of Equity and

Mercy. c, 60c, Royal family. d, $1, Recent color photo.

1993, June 2   Litho.   Perf. 13½x14

771	A126	Sheet, 2 each #a.-		
		d.	14.00	14.00

A souvenir sheet containing a $2 stamp was not an authorized issue. Value $17.

Discovery of Virgin Islands, 500th Anniv. A127

3c, Ferdinand and Isabella supporting Columbus. 12c, Departure of Columbus. 15c, Departure of second voyage. 25c, Arms, flag of British Virgin Islands. 30c, Columbus, Santa Maria. 45c, Columbus' second fleet at sea. 60c, Rowing ashore. $1, Landing of Columbus. #781, Natives watching ships. #782, Columbus, two ships of his fleet.

1993, Sept. 24   Litho.   Perf. 14

773	A127	3c multicolored	.30	.30
774	A127	12c multicolored	.40	.40
775	A127	15c multicolored	.55	.55
776	A127	25c multicolored	.85	.85
777	A127	30c multicolored	1.10	1.10
778	A127	45c multicolored	1.50	1.50
779	A127	60c multicolored	2.10	2.10
780	A127	$1 multicolored	3.50	3.50
		Nos. 773-780 (8)	10.30	10.30

Souvenir Sheets

781	A127	$2 multicolored	5.25	5.25
782	A127	$2 multicolored	5.25	5.25

Secondary Education and Library Services, 50th Anniv. — A128

Designs: 5c, Historical documents. 10c, Sporting activities. 15c, Stanley W. Nibbs, educator, vert. 20c, Bookmobile. 30c, Norwell E. Harrigan, educator, vert. 35c, Public library's annual summer program. 70c, Text. $1, High school.

Perf. 14x13½, 13½x14

1993, Dec.   Litho.

783	A128	5c multicolored	.45	.45
784	A128	10c multicolored	.45	.45
785	A128	15c multicolored	.65	.65
786	A128	20c multicolored	.95	.95
787	A128	30c multicolored	1.40	1.40
788	A128	35c multicolored	1.60	1.60
789	A128	70c multicolored	3.00	3.00
790	A128	$1 multicolored	4.50	4.50
		Nos. 783-790 (8)	13.00	13.00

Anegada Ground Iguana — A129

5c, Crawling right. 10c, Head up to right. 15c, View from behind. 45c, Head up to left. $2, Head.

1994, Jan.   Litho.   Perf. 14

791	A129	5c multicolored	.90	.90
792	A129	10c multicolored	.90	.90
793	A129	15c multicolored	1.25	1.25
794	A129	45c multicolored	4.00	4.00
		Nos. 791-794 (4)	7.05	7.05

Souvenir Sheet

795	A129	$2 multicolored	6.25	6.25

World Wildlife Fund.

Rotary Club of Virgin Islands, 25th Anniv. A130

Designs: 15c, Disaster relief airlift. 45c, Kids, Sea "Kats." 50c, Donated hospital equipment. 90c, Paul P. Harris (1868-1947), founder of Rotary Intl.

1994, June 3   Litho.   Perf. 14

796	A130	15c multicolored	.65	.65
797	A130	45c multicolored	1.75	1.75
798	A130	50c multicolored	2.10	2.10
799	A130	90c multicolored	3.50	3.50
		Nos. 796-799 (4)	8.00	8.00

Miniature Sheet of 6

First Manned Moon Landing, 25th Anniv. — A131

Designs: No. 800a, Anniversary emblem. b, Lunar landing training vehicle. c, Apollo 11 lift-off, July 16, 1969. d, Lunar module Eagle in flight. e, Moon landing site approached by Eagle. f, 1st step on Moon, July 20, 1969. No. 801, Mission patch, crew signatures.

1994, Sept. 30   Litho.   Perf. 14

800	A131	50c #a.-f.	15.00	15.00

Souvenir Sheet

801	A131	$2 multicolored	10.50	10.50

A132

Previous champions: 15c, Argentina, 1978. 35c, Italy, 1982. 50c, Argentina, 1986. $1.30, W. Germany, 1990.
$2, US flag, World Cup trophy, horiz.

1994, Dec. 16   Litho.   Perf. 14

802	A132	15c multicolored	.90	.90
803	A132	35c multicolored	2.10	2.10
804	A132	50c multicolored	3.00	3.00
805	A132	$1.30 multicolored	7.50	7.50
		Nos. 802-805 (4)	13.50	13.50

Souvenir Sheet

806	A132	$2 multicolored	11.50	11.50

1994 World Cup Soccer Championships, US.

UN, 50th Anniv.
Common Design Type

Designs: 15c, Peugeot P4 all-purpose light vehicle. 30c, Foden medium tanker. 45c, Sisu all-terrain vehicle. $2, Westland Lynx AH7 helicopter.

Wmk. 373

1995, Oct. 24   Litho.   Perf. 14

807	CD353	15c multicolored	.50	.50
808	CD353	30c multicolored	1.00	1.00
809	CD353	45c multicolored	1.75	1.75
810	CD353	$2 multicolored	6.75	6.75
		Nos. 807-810 (4)	10.00	10.00

A133

Anegada Flamingos.

Wmk. 373

1995, Nov. 15   Litho.   Perf. 13

811	A133	15c Juveniles	.50	.50
812	A133	20c Adults	.75	.75
813	A133	60c Adult feeding	2.25	2.25
814	A133	$1.45 Adult feeding chick	5.50	5.50
		Nos. 811-814 (4)	9.00	9.00

Souvenir Sheet

815	A133	$2 Chicks	7.00	7.00

Christmas — A134

Children's paintings: 12c, House with palm trees. 50c, Santa in boat. 70c, Red house, Christmas tree, presents. $1.30, Dove of peace.

Wmk. 384

1995, Dec. 1   Litho.   Perf. 14

816	A134	12c multicolored	.60	.60
817	A134	50c multicolored	2.40	2.40
818	A134	70c multicolored	3.25	3.25
819	A134	$1.30 multicolored	6.25	6.25
		Nos. 816-819 (4)	12.50	12.50

Island Scenes A135

Designs: 15c, Seine fishing. 35c, Sandy Spit, Jost Van Dyke. 90c, Map of Jost Van Dyke. $1.50, Foxy's wooden boat regatta.

Perf. 13½x13

1996, Feb. 14   Litho.   Wmk. 373

820	A135	15c multicolored	.60	.60
821	A135	35c multicolored	1.40	1.40
822	A135	90c multicolored	3.25	3.25
823	A135	$1.50 multicolored	5.75	5.75
		Nos. 820-823 (4)	11.00	11.00

See Nos. 892-896.

Queen Elizabeth II, 70th Birthday
Common Design Type

Queen in various attire, scenes of Virgin Islands: 10c, Government House, Tortola. 30c, Legislative Council Chambers. 45c, Road Harbor. $1.50, Map of Virgin Islands. $2, Wearing royal crown.

Perf. 13½x14

1996, Apr. 22   Litho.   Wmk. 373

824	CD354	10c multicolored	.25	.25
825	CD354	30c multicolored	.90	.90
826	CD354	45c multicolored	1.40	1.40
827	CD354	$1.50 multicolored	4.00	4.00
		Nos. 824-827 (4)	6.55	6.55

Souvenir Sheet
Perf. 13x13½

828	CD354	$2 multicolored	5.25	5.25

Modern Olympic Games, Cent. A136

Wmk. 373

1996, May 22   Litho.   Perf. 13

829	A136	20c Hurdles	.65	.65
830	A136	35c Volleyball	1.25	1.25
831	A136	50c Swimming	1.60	1.60
832	A136	$1 Sailing	3.50	3.50
		Nos. 829-832 (4)	7.00	7.00

CAPEX '96 — A137

Vintage automobiles: 15c, 1934 Mercedes-Benz 500KA Cabriolet. 40c, 1934 Citroen 12. 60c, 1932 Cadillac V-8 Sport Phaeton. $1.35, 1934 Rolls Royce Phantom II. $2, 1932 Ford Sport Coupe.

Wmk. 373

1996, June 8   Litho.   Perf. 13½

833	A137	15c multicolored	.40	.40
834	A137	40c multicolored	1.10	1.10
835	A137	60c multicolored	2.00	2.00
836	A137	$1.35 multicolored	4.00	4.00
		Nos. 833-836 (4)	7.50	7.50

Souvenir Sheet

837	A137	$2 multicolored	5.00	5.00

UNICEF, 50th Anniv. A138

Goals of UNICEF for the year 2000: 10c, Educate the child. 15c, Children first. 30c, Children have rights. 45c, No more polio.

Perf. 14x14½

1996, Sept. 16   Litho.   Wmk. 373

838	A138	10c multicolored	.50	.50
839	A138	15c multicolored	.75	.75
840	A138	30c multicolored	1.75	1.75
841	A138	45c multicolored	2.50	2.50
		Nos. 838-841 (4)	5.50	5.50

Girl Guiding in Virgin Islands, 25th Anniv. — A139

Designs: 10c, Rainbows, arts and crafts. 15c, Brownies, community service. 30c, Guides, campfire. 45c, Rangers, H.M. Queen's birthday parade. $2, Lady Baden-Powell, world chief guide.

Wmk. 373

1996, Dec. 30   Litho.   Perf. 13½

842	A139	10c multicolored	.25	.25
843	A139	15c multicolored	.45	.45
844	A139	30c multicolored	.75	.75
845	A139	45c multicolored	1.10	1.10
846	A139	$2 multicolored	4.75	4.75
		Nos. 842-846 (5)	7.30	7.30

Game Fish A140

1997, Jan. 6   Wmk. 384   Perf. 14

847	A140	1c Mackerel	.25	.25
848	A140	10c Wahoo	.25	.25
849	A140	15c Barracuda	.35	.35
850	A140	20c Tarpon	.50	.50
851	A140	25c Tiger shark	.60	.60
852	A140	35c Sailfish	.85	.85
853	A140	40c Dolphin	.95	.95
854	A140	50c Blackfin tuna	1.25	1.25
855	A140	60c Yellowfin tuna	1.50	1.50
856	A140	75c Kingfish	1.75	1.75

857	A140	$1.50 White marlin	3.50	3.50
a.		Souvenir sheet of 1, wmk. 373	4.50	4.50
858	A140	$1.85 Amberjack	4.50	4.50
859	A140	$2 Bonito	4.75	4.75
860	A140	$5 Bonefish	12.00	12.00
861	A140	$10 Blue marlin	24.00	24.00
		Nos. 847-861 (15)	57.00	57.00

No. 857a, Hong Kong '97.
See Nos. 1020-1023.

Queen Elizabeth II and Prince Philip, 50th Wedding Anniv. — A141

#862, Prince with horse. #863, Queen Elizabeth II. #864, Queen riding in open carriage. #865, Prince Philip. #866, Queen holding hat down, Prince. #867, Prince Charles on polo pony.
$2, Queen, Prince riding in open carriage, horiz.

Wmk. 373

1997, July 10   Litho.   Perf. 13

862		30c multicolored	.70	.70
863		30c multicolored	.70	.70
a.	A141	Pair, #862-863	1.75	1.75
864		45c multicolored	1.00	1.00
865		45c multicolored	1.00	1.00
a.	A141	Pair, #864-865	2.50	2.50
866		70c multicolored	1.50	1.50
867		70c multicolored	1.50	1.50
a.	A141	Pair, #866-867	4.00	4.00
		Nos. 862-867 (6)	6.40	6.40

Souvenir Sheet

868	A141	$2 multicolored	7.00	7.00

Crabs A142

Wmk. 373

1997, Sept. 11   Litho.   Perf. 13

869	A142	12c Fiddler	.40	.40
870	A142	15c Coral	.60	.60
871	A142	35c Blue	1.50	1.50
872	A142	$1 Giant hermit	4.50	4.50
		Nos. 869-872 (4)	7.00	7.00

Souvenir Sheet

873	A142	$2 Arrow	7.00	7.00

Orchids A143

Designs: a, 20c, Psychilis macconnelliae. b, 50c, Tolumnia prionochila. c, 60c, Tetramicra canaliculata. d, 75c, Liparis elata.
$2, Dendrobium crumenatum, vert.

Wmk. 373

1997, Nov. 26   Litho.   Perf. 14

874	A143	Strip of 4, #a.-d.	7.00	7.00

Souvenir Sheet

875	A143	$2 multicolored	6.00	6.00

World Voyage of Sir Francis Drake A144

Portions of map and: No. 876: a, Francis Drake. b, Drake Coat of Arms. c, Queen Elizabeth I. d, Christopher & Marigold. e, Golden Hinde. f, Swan. g, Cacafuego. h, Elizabeth. i, Maria. j, Drake's Astrolabe. k, Golden Hinde beakhead. l, 16th cent. compass rose.

$2, Modern ship named, "Sir Francis Drake."

1997, Dec. 13   Perf. 14½

876	A144	40c Sheet of 12, #a.-l.	18.00	18.00

Souvenir Sheet

877	A144	$2 multicolored	7.00	7.00

Diana, Princess of Wales (1961-97)
Common Design Type

Portraits: a, 15c. b, 45c. c, 70c. d, $1.

Perf. 14½x14

1998, Mar. 31   Litho.   Wmk. 373

878	CD355	Sheet of 4, #a.-d.	5.75	5.75

No. 878 sold for $2.30 + 20c, with surtax from international sales being donated to the Princess Diana Memorial Fund and surtax from national sales being donated to designated local charity.

Royal Air Force, 80th Anniv.
Common Design Type of 1993 Reinscribed

Designs: 20c, Fairey IIIF. 35c, Supermarine Scapa. 50c, Westland Sea King HAR3. $1.50, BAe Harrier GR7.
No. 883: a, Curtiss H.12 Large America. b, Curtiss JN-4A. c, Bell Airacobra. d, Boulton-Paul Defiant.

Perf. 13½x14

1998, Apr. 1   Litho.   Wmk. 373

879	CD350	20c multicolored	.50	.50
880	CD350	35c multicolored	1.00	1.00
881	CD350	50c multicolored	1.50	1.50
882	CD350	$1.50 multicolored	4.50	4.50
		Nos. 879-882 (4)	7.50	7.50

Souvenir Sheet

883	CD350	75c Sheet of 4, #a.-d.	8.75	8.75

Marine Life — A145

Designs: 15c, Fingerprint cyphoma. 30c, Long spined sea urchin. 45c, Split crown feather duster worm. $1, Upside down jelly. $2, Giant anemone.

1998, May 20   Wmk. 384   Perf. 14½

884	A145	15c multicolored	.65	.65
885	A145	30c multicolored	1.40	1.40
886	A145	45c multicolored	2.10	2.10
887	A145	$1 multicolored	4.50	4.50
		Nos. 884-887 (4)	8.65	8.65

Souvenir Sheet

888	A145	$2 multicolored	8.00	8.00

No. 888 is a continuous design.

Childrens' Art Festival A146

Island Scenes Type of 1996

Designs: 12c, Salt pond. 30c, Shipwreck, HMS Rhone. 70c, Traditional house. $1.45, Salt Island.
$2, Gathering salt.

1998, Oct. 28

892	A135	12c multicolored	.50	.50
893	A135	30c multicolored	1.00	1.00
894	A135	70c multicolored	2.25	2.25
895	A135	$1.45 multicolored	5.25	5.25
		Nos. 892-895 (4)	9.00	9.00

Souvenir Sheet

896	A135	$2 multicolored	5.50	5.50

Wmk. 373

1998, Aug. 25   Litho.   Perf. 14

889	A146	30c Girl in yellow & red, vert.	.85	.85
890	A146	45c Dancer, vert.	1.40	1.40
891	A146	$1.30 shown	3.75	3.75
		Nos. 889-891 (3)	6.00	6.00

Anniversaries and Events — A147

5c, Classes in computer training, woodworking, electronics. 15c, Students playing musical instruments. 30c, Chapel, Mona Campus, Jamaica. 45c, Plaque on wall, university crest. 50c, Dr. John Coakley Lettsom, map of Little Jost Van Dyke island. $1, Crest of the Medical Society of London, building.

Wmk. 384

1998, Dec. 14   Litho.   Perf. 14

897	A147	5c multicolored	.25	.25
898	A147	15c multicolored	.40	.40
899	A147	30c multicolored	.90	.90
900	A147	45c multicolored	1.25	1.25
901	A147	50c multicolored	1.50	1.50
902	A147	$1 multicolored	2.75	2.75
		Nos. 897-902 (6)	7.05	7.05

Comprehensive education in Virgin Islands, 30th anniv. (#897-898). University of West Indies, 50th anniv. (#899-900). Founding of the Medical Society of London by Dr. John Coakley Lettsom, 225th anniv. (#901-902).

Lizards A148

Designs: 5c, Rock iguana. 35c, Pygmy gecko. 60c, Slippery back skink. $1.50, Wood slave gecko.
No. 907: a, Doctor lizard. b, Yellow-bellied lizard. c, Man lizard. d, Ground lizard.

Perf. 14½x14

1999, Apr. 30   Litho.   Wmk. 373

903	A148	5c multicolored	.30	.30
904	A148	35c multicolored	1.10	1.10
905	A148	60c multicolored	2.00	2.00
906	A148	$1.50 multicolored	4.75	4.75
		Nos. 903-906 (4)	8.15	8.15

Sheet of 4

907	A148	75c #a.-d.	9.00	9.00

Wedding of Prince Edward and Sophie Rhys-Jones
Common Design Type

Perf. 13¾x14

1999, June 15   Litho.   Wmk. 384

908	CD356	20c Separate portraits	.45	.45
909	CD356	$3 Couple	7.25	7.25

1st Manned Moon Landing, 30th Anniv.
Common Design Type

Designs: 10c, Apollo 11 on launch pad. 40c, Second stage fires. 50c, Artist's rendition of Apollo 11 on moon. $2, Astronauts transfer to lunar module.
$2.50, Looking at earth from moon.

Perf. 14x13¾

1999, July 20   Litho.   Wmk. 384

910	CD357	10c multicolored	.25	.25
911	CD357	40c multicolored	1.10	1.10
912	CD357	50c multicolored	1.40	1.40
913	CD357	$2 multicolored	5.50	5.50
		Nos. 910-913 (4)	8.25	8.25

Souvenir Sheet
Perf. 14

914	CD357	$2.50 multicolored	6.75	6.75

No. 914 contains one 40mm circular stamp.

Shells — A149

Designs: 25c, Measle cowrie. 35c, West Indian top shell. 75c, Zigzag scallop. $1, West Indian fighting conch.

No. 919: a, 5c, Sunrise tellin. b, 10c, King helmet. c, 25c, Like No. 915. d, 35c, Like No. 916. e, 75c, Like No. 917. f, $1, Like No. 918.

Wmk. 373

1999, Nov. 1   Litho.   Perf. 14¼
915 A149 25c multi .90 .90
916 A149 35c multi 1.50 1.50
917 A149 75c multi 3.00 3.00
918 A149 $1 multi 3.75 3.75
919 A149 Strip of 6, #a.-f. 10.00 10.00
    Nos. 915-919 (5) 19.15 19.15

Vignette extends to the top perforations on Nos. 915-918, but does not on stamps from No. 919.

Christmas A150

Churches: 20c, Zion Hill Methodist. 35c, Fat Hogs Bay Seventh Day Adventist. 50c, Ruins of Kingstown St. Philip's Anglican. $1, Road Town St. William's Catholic.

Perf. 13¼x13

1999, Dec. 16   Litho.   Wmk. 373
920 A150 20c multi .45 .45
921 A150 35c multi .80 .80
922 A150 50c multi 1.10 1.10
923 A150 $1 multi 2.40 2.40
    Nos. 920-923 (4) 4.75 4.75

British Monarchs — A151

a, Henry VII. b, Lady Jane Grey. c, Charles I. d, William III. e, George III. f, Edward VII.

Wmk. 373

2000, Feb. 29   Litho.   Perf. 14
924 A151 60c Sheet of 6, #a.-f. 9.00 9.00

The Stamp Show 2000, London.

Prince William, 18th Birthday
Common Design Type

William: 20c, As toddler, on chest. 40c, As toddler, standing. 50c, With ski cap & goggles. 60c, Wearing suits & striped shirts. $1, Wearing sweater & bow tie.

Perf. 14¼x13¾, 13¾x14¼

2000, June 21   Litho.   Wmk. 373
Stamps With White Border
925 CD359 20c multi .45 .45
926 CD359 40c multi, vert. .90 .90
927 CD359 50c multi, vert. 1.25 1.25
928 CD359 $1 multi 2.40 2.40
    Nos. 925-928 (4) 5.00 5.00

Souvenir Sheet
Stamps Without White Border
Perf. 14¼
929 Sheet of 5 7.25 7.25
    a. CD359 20c multi .40 .40
    b. CD359 40c multi .80 .80
    c. CD359 50c multi 1.00 1.00
    d. CD359 60c multi 1.25 1.25
    e. CD359 $1 multi 2.00 2.00

Queen Mother, 100th Birthday — A152

Various photos. Frame color: 15c, Lilac. 35c, Light green. 70c, Pink. $1.50, Light blue.

Wmk. 373
2000, Aug. 4   Litho.   Perf. 13¾
930-933 A152 Set of 4 9.00 9.00

Flowering Plants and Trees — A153

10c, Red hibiscus. 15c, Pink oleander. 35c, Yellow bell. 50c, Yellow & white frangipani. 75c, Flamboyant. $2, Bougainvillea.

2000, Sept. 7   Perf. 13½x13¾
934-939 A153 Set of 6 10.50 10.50

Millennium — A154

Virgin Islands history: 5c, Site of Emancipation Proclamation. 20c Nurse Mary Louise Davies. 30c, Cheyney University, US, founded by Richard Humphries. 45c, Enid Leona Scatliffe, former chief education officer. 50c, H. Lavity Stoutt Community College. $1 Sir J. Olva Georges. $2, Victoria Cross of Pvt. Samuel Hodge, vert.

Wmk. 373
2000, Nov. 16   Litho.   Perf. 14
940-945 A154 Set of 6 6.75 6.75
Souvenir Sheet
946 A154 $2 multi 5.50 5.50

Restoration of the Legislative Council, 50th Anniv. — A155

Virgin Islands Councilmen: 10c, Dr. Q. William Osbourne & Arnando Scatliffe. 15c, H. Robinson O'Neal & A. Austin Henley. 20c, Wilfred W. Smith & John C. Brudenell-Bruce. 35c, Howard R. Penn & I. G. Fonseca. 50c, Carlton L. de Castro & Theodolph H. Faulkner. 60c, Willard W. Wheatley. $1, H. Lavity Stoutt.

2000, Nov. 22
947-953 A155 Set of 7 9.00 9.00

Souvenir Sheet

New Year 2001 (Year of the Snake) — A156

No. 954: a, 50c, White-crowned dove. b, 50c, Bar-tailed cuckoo dove.

2001, Feb. 1   Perf. 14½
954 A156 Sheet of 2, #a-b 4.50 4.50

Hong Kong 2001 Stamp Exhibition.

Visiting Royal Navy Ships A157

Designs: 35c, HMS Wistaria, 1923-30. 50c, HMS Dundee, 1934-35. 60c, HMS Eurydice, 1787. 75c, HMS Pegasus, 1787. $1, HMS Astrea, 1807. $1.50 HM Yacht Britannia, 1966.

Wmk. 373
2001, Sept. 28   Litho.   Perf. 14
955-960 A157 Set of 6 14.00 14.00

Nobel Prizes, Cent. — A158

Nobel laureates: 10c, Fridtjof Nansen, Peace, 1922. 20c, Albert Einstein, Physics, 1921. 25c, Sir Albert Lewis, Economics, 1979. 40c, Saint-John Perse, Literature, 1960. 70c, Mother Teresa, Peace, 1979. $2, Christian Lous Lange, Peace, 1921.

2001, Oct. 5
961-966 A158 Set of 6 13.00 13.00

Reign Of Queen Elizabeth II, 50th Anniv. Issue
Common Design Type

Designs: Nos. 967, 971a, 15c, Princess Elizabeth in uniform. Nos. 968, 971b, 50c, In 1977. Nos. 969, 971c, 60c, Holding flowers. Nos. 970, 971d, 75c, In 1996. No. 971e, $1, 1955 portrait by Annigoni (38x50mm).

Perf. 14¼x14½, 13¾ (#971e)
2002, Feb. 6   Litho.   Wmk. 373
With Gold Frames
967-970 CD360 Set of 4 7.50 7.50
Souvenir Sheet
Without Gold Frames
971 CD360 Sheet of 5, #a-e 11.00 11.00

Reptiles in Guinness Book Of World Records A159

Designs: 5c, Estuarine crocodile. 20c, Reticulated python. 30c, Komodo dragon. 40c, Boa constrictor. $1, Dwarf caiman. $2, Sphaerodactylus parthenopion. $1.50, Head of Sphaerodactylus parthenopion.

Perf. 13¼x13
2002, June 10   Litho.   Wmk. 373
972-977 A159 Set of 6 13.00 13.00
    977a Sheet of 6, #972-977 13.00 13.00
Souvenir Sheet
978 A159 $1.50 multi 7.50 7.50

Queen Mother Elizabeth (1900-2002)
Common Design Type

Designs: 20c, Wearing tiara (black and white photograph). 60c, Wearing dark blue hat. $2, Wearing hat (black and white photograph). Nos. 982, 983b, $3, Wearing pink hat.

Perf. 13¾x14¼
2002, Aug. 5   Litho.   Wmk. 373
With Purple Frames
979-982 CD361 Set of 4 14.50 14.50
Souvenir Sheet
Without Purple Frames
Perf. 14½x14¼
983 CD361 Sheet of 2, #a-b 12.50 12.50

Royal Navy Ships A160

Designs: 20c, HMS Invincible and HMS Argo. 35c, HMS Boreas and HMS Solebay. 50c, HMS Coventry. $3, HMS Argyll.

Wmk. 373
2002, Aug. 30   Litho.   Perf. 14
984-987 A160 Set of 4 10.00 10.00

Island Scenes Type of 1996

Designs: 5c, Spring Bay. 40c, Devils Bay. 60c, The Baths. 75c, St. Thomas Bay. $1, Savannah and Pond Bay. $2, Trunk Bay.

2002, Sept. 13
988-993 A135 Set of 6 10.00 10.00

West Indian Whistling Duck — A161

Designs: Nos. 994, 998a, 10c, Duckling and eggs. Nos. 995, 998b, 35c, Duck standing on rock, vert. Nos. 996, 998c, 40c, Duck in water, vert. Nos. 997, 998d, 70c, Two ducks. No. 998e, $2, Duck's head.

Perf. 14¼x13¾, 13¾x14¼
2002, Dec.   Wmk. 373
Stamps With Brown Border
994-997 A161 Set of 4 3.75 3.75
Souvenir Sheet
Stamps Without Brown Border
Perf. 14¼x14½ (Horiz. stamps), 14½ (Vert. stamps)
998 A161 Sheet of 5, #a-e 8.50 8.50

Birdlife International.

Anniversaries and Events — A162

No. 999, 10c: a, Sprinters. b, Cyclists.
No. 1000, 35c: a, Laser class sailboats. b, Women's long jump.
No. 1001, 50c: a, Bareboat class sailboats. b, Racing Cruiser class sailboats.
No. 1002, $1.35: a, Carlos and Esme Downing, founders of Island Sun newspaper. b, Island Sun newspaper and emblem.

Wmk. 373
2003, Mar. 13   Litho.   Perf. 13½
Horiz. pairs, #a-b
999-1002 A162 Set of 4 13.00 13.00

2002 Commonwealth Games (#999); Admission to Olympic Games, 20th anniv. (#1000); Spring Regatta, 30th anniv. (#1001); Island Sun newspaper, 40th anniv. (#1002).

Head of Queen Elizabeth II
Common Design Type
Wmk. 373
2003, June 2   Litho.   Perf. 13¾
1003 CD362 $5 multi 10.00 10.00

Coronation of Queen Elizabeth II, 50th Anniv.
Common Design Type

Designs: Nos. 1004, 1006a, 15c, Queen in gown. Nos. 1005, 1006b, $5, Royal Family on Buckingham Palace balcony.

Perf. 14¼x14½
2003, June 2   Wmk. 373
Vignettes Framed, Red Background
1004-1005 CD363 Set of 2 12.50 12.50
Souvenir Sheet
Vignettes Without Frame, Purple Panel
1006 CD363 Sheet of 2, #a-b 12.50 12.50

Prince William, 21st Birthday
Common Design Type

Designs: 50c, William in polo uniform at right. $2, William on polo pony at left.

Wmk. 373
2003, June 21 Litho. Perf. 14¼
With Gray Frames
| 1007 | CD364 | 50c multi | 1.25 | 1.25 |
| 1008 | CD364 | $2 multi | 4.75 | 4.75 |

Without Gray Frames
1009		Horiz. pair	6.00	6.00
a.		CD364 50c multi	1.25	1.25
b.		CD364 $2 multi	4.75	4.75
		Nos. 1007-1009 (3)	12.00	12.00

Powered Flight, Cent. — A163

Designs: 15c, Douglas DC-4. 20c, Boeing Stearman "Kaydet." 35c, B-25 J Mitchell. 40c, F-4B Phantom. 70c, CH-47 Chinook helicopter. $2, AH-64 Apache helicopter.

Perf. 13¼x13¾
2003, Nov. 15 Litho. Wmk. 373
Stamp + Label
| 1010-1015 | A163 | Set of 6 | 8.50 | 8.50 |

Christmas — A164

Details from Arrival of the English Ambassadors, by Vittore Carpaccio: 20c, Men standing near railing and pillar. 40c, Men, ships in background. $2.50, Seated man.
No. 1019a (36x36mm), Kneeling man delivering message.

Perf. 13¾x13½
2003, Dec. 15 Litho. Wmk. 373
| 1016-1018 | A164 | Set of 3 | 8.00 | 8.00 |

Souvenir Sheet
| 1019 | A164 | Sheet, #1016-1018, 1019a | 4.00 | 4.00 |
| a. | | $1 multi, perf. 13½x13¼ | 2.00 | 2.00 |

Game Fish Type of 1997
Serpentine Die Cut 12½ on 3 Sides
2004, July 1 Litho. Unwmk.
Self-Adhesive
Booklet Stamps
Size: 21x17mm
1020	A140	15c Barracuda	.30	.30
a.		Booklet pane of 4	1.20	
1021	A140	20c Tarpon	.40	.40
a.		Booklet pane of 4	1.60	
1022	A140	35c Sailfish	.70	.70
a.		Booklet pane of 4	2.80	
		Complete booklet, #1020a, 1022a	4.00	
1023	A140	40c Dolphin	.80	.80
a.		Booklet pane of 3 + label	2.40	
		Complete booklet, #1021a, 1023a	5.25	
		Nos. 1020-1023 (4)	2.20	2.20

Fruit — A165

2004, July 20 Wmk. 373 Perf. 13¾
Inscribed "2004" Below Design
1024	A165	15c Pomegranates	.30	.30
1025	A165	20c Cashews	.40	.40
1026	A165	35c Tamarinds	.70	.70
1027	A165	40c Soursop	.80	.80
1028	A165	50c Mangos	1.00	1.00
1029	A165	$2 Guavaberries	4.00	4.00
1030	A165	$5 Mamee apples	10.00	10.00
		Nos. 1024-1030 (7)	17.20	17.20
		See Nos. 1042-1049.		

2007
Inscribed "2007" Below Design
1025a	A165	20c multicolored	.40	.40
1026a	A165	35c multicolored	.70	.70
1028a	A165	50c multicolored	1.00	1.00
1029a	A165	$2 multicolored	4.00	4.00
		Nos. 1025a-1029a (4)	6.10	6.10

Virgin Islands Festival, 50th Anniv. — A166

Designs: 10c, Parade. 60c, Horse race. $1, Kayak race. $2.35, Festival Queen.

Wmk. 373
2004, Oct. 26 Litho. Perf. 13¼
| 1031-1034 | A166 | Set of 4 | 8.25 | 8.25 |

Sports — A167

Designs: 75c, Women soccer players. $1, Runner.

2004, Dec. 30 Perf. 14
| 1035-1036 | A167 | Set of 2 | 3.50 | 3.50 |
FIFA (Fédération Internationale de Football Association), cent.; 2004 Summer Olympics, Athens.

Caribbean Endemic Bird Festival A168

Designs: 5c, Black and white warbler. 25c, Worm-eating warbler. 35c, Yellow warbler. 50c, Prothonotary warbler.
No. 1041: a, 10c, Prairie warbler. b, 15c, Yellow-rumped warbler. c, 40c, Black-throated blue warbler. d, 60c, Cape May warbler. e, 75c, Northern parula. f, $2.75, Palm warbler.

Wmk. 373
2005, July 8 Litho. Perf. 13¾
| 1037-1040 | A168 | Set of 4 | 2.40 | 2.40 |
| 1041 | A168 | Miniature sheet, #1037-1040, 1041a-1041f | 12.00 | 12.00 |

Fruit Type of 2004
2005, Aug. 25 Wmk. 373
Inscribed "2005" Below Design
1042	A165	1c Hog plum	.25	.25
a.		Inscribed "2007"	.25	.25
1043	A165	10c Coco plum	.25	.25
1044	A165	25c Sugar apple	.50	.50
1045	A165	60c Papaya	1.25	1.25
1046	A165	75c Custard apple	1.50	1.50
1047	A165	$1 Otaheite gooseberry	2.00	2.00
1048	A165	$1.50 Guava	3.00	3.00
1049	A165	$10 Passion fruit	20.00	20.00
		Nos. 1042-1049 (8)	28.75	28.75

Pope John Paul II (1920-2005) A169

Wmk. 373
2005, Aug. 18 Litho. Perf. 14
| 1050 | A169 | 75c multi | 1.50 | 1.50 |

Worldwide Fund for Nature (WWF) — A170

Various depictions of Virgin Islands tree boa: 20c, 30c, 70c, $1.05.

Wmk. 373
2005, Sept. 15 Litho. Perf. 14
| 1051-1054 | A170 | Set of 4 | 4.50 | 4.50 |
| 1054a | | Miniature sheet, 2 each #1051-1054 | 9.00 | 9.00 |

Battle of Trafalgar, Bicent. — A171

Designs: 5c, HMS Colossus. 25c, HMS Boreas. 75c, HMS Victory. $3, Admiral Horatio Nelson, vert.
$2.50, HMS Colossus and French ship.

2005, Oct. 18 Perf. 14x14¾, 14¾x14
| 1055-1058 | A171 | Set of 4 | 8.25 | 8.25 |

Souvenir Sheet
Perf. 13½
| 1059 | A171 | $2.50 multi | 5.00 | 5.00 |
No. 1059 contains one 44x44mm stamp.

Christmas A172

Flora: 15c, Century plant. 35c, Poinsettia, horiz. 60c, Inkberry. $2.50, Snow on the mountain, horiz.

2005, Nov. 3 Perf. 14¾x14, 14x14¾
| 1060-1063 | A172 | Set of 4 | 7.25 | 7.25 |

Anniversaries A173

Designs: 20c, Social Security, 25th anniv. 40c, ZBVI radio station, 40th anniv. 50c, Beef Island Airstrip, 50th anniv. $1, Rotary International, cent.

Wmk. 373
2005, Nov. 16 Litho. Perf. 13¾
| 1064-1067 | A173 | Set of 4 | 4.25 | 4.25 |

Queen Elizabeth II, 80th Birthday A174

Queen: 15c, As young woman, in uniform. 75c, Wearing white hat. No. 1070, $1.50, Wearing large earrings. No. 1071, $2, Wearing gray hat with large brim.
No. 1072: a, $1.50, Like 75c. b, $2, Like #1070.

Perf. 14¼x14
2006, July 17 Litho. Wmk. 373
Stamps With White Frames
| 1068-1071 | A174 | Set of 4 | 9.00 | 9.00 |

Souvenir Sheet
Stamps Without White Frames
| 1072 | A174 | Sheet of 2, #a-b | 7.00 | 7.00 |

Red Cross Buildings A175

Designs: 20c, New building. $3, Previous building.

Wmk. 373
2007, Aug. 1 Litho. Perf. 14
| 1073-1074 | A175 | Set of 2 | 6.50 | 6.50 |

Royal Air Force, 90th Anniv. A176

Designs: 18c, Supermarine Spitfire. 20c, Avro Lancaster. 35c, Douglas C-47 Dakota. 60c, Handley Page Halifax. $1.25 Westland Lysander.
$2.50, Spitfire patrolling D-Day beaches.

Wmk. 373
2008, Apr. 1 Litho. Perf. 14
| 1075-1079 | A176 | Set of 5 | 5.25 | 5.25 |

Souvenir Sheet
| 1080 | A176 | $2.50 multi | 5.00 | 5.00 |

Princess Diana (1961-97) A177

Princess Diana in: 60c, Black dress. $3.50, Red dress.

2008, Apr. 7 Perf. 13¾
| 1081 | A177 | 60c multi | 1.25 | 1.25 |

Souvenir Sheet
Perf. 14¼
| 1082 | A177 | $3.50 multi | 7.00 | 7.00 |
No. 1082 contains one 42x57mm stamp.

Rev. Charles Wesley (1707-88), Hymn Writer — A178

Designs: 20c, Arms. 50c, Wesley. $1.75, Wesley, diff.

2008, May 1 Perf. 14
| 1083-1085 | A178 | Set of 3 | 5.00 | 5.00 |

2008 Summer Olympics, Beijing A179

Designs: 15c, Bamboo, runner. 18c, Dragon, yachting. 20c, Lanterns, runner. $1, Fish, yachting.

2008, Aug. 1 — Perf. 13½
1086-1089 A179 Set of 4 — 3.25 3.25

Ministerial Government — A180

Arms and: 18c, Mace in House of Assembly, mace head. 35c, House of Assembly, entrance arch. 60c, Henry O. Creque, Ivan Dawson. $2, Paul Wattley, Terrance B. Lettsome.

2008, Aug. 21 — Perf. 14x14¾
1090-1093 A180 Set of 4 — 6.25 6.25

End of World War I, 90th Anniv. — A181

Designs: 75c, Sanctuary Wood Cemetery, Ypres, Belgium. 80c, Somme Battlefield, France, horiz. 90c, Lone Pine Cemetery, Gallipoli, Turkey, horiz. $1, War Memorial, Vauquois, France. $1.15, Theipval Memorial, France, horiz. $1.25, Menin Gate, Ypres, Belgium, horiz.
$2, Wreath of Remembrance.

Wmk. 406
2008, Sept. 16 Litho. Perf. 14
1094-1099 A181 Set of 6 — 12.00 12.00
Souvenir Sheet
1100 A181 $2 multi — 4.00 4.00

J. R. O'Neal Botanic Gardens — A182

Designs: 20c, Climbing pandanus. 35c, True aloe. 50c, Crown of thorns. $1, Red-eared slider (turtle). $2.50, Fountain.

Wmk. 373
2009, Mar. 27 Litho. Perf. 14
1101-1104 A182 Set of 4 — 4.25 4.25
Souvenir Sheet
1105 A182 $2.50 multi — 5.00 5.00

Ships and Explorers A183

Designs: 15c HMS Ark Royal. 20c, Whydah. 60c, Santa Maria. 70c, RMS Rhone. 90c, Golden Hind. $1.95, HMY Britannia.
$2, Christopher Columbus, vert.

Wmk. 406
2009, May 25 Litho. Perf. 14
1106-1111 A183 Set of 6 — 9.00 9.00
Souvenir Sheet
1112 A183 $2 multi — 4.00 4.00

Naval Aviation, Cent. A184

Victoria Cross recipients: 18c, Lieutenant Robert Hampton Gray. 35c, Lieutenant Commander Eugene Esmonde. 60c, Flight Squadron Lieutenant Rex Warneford. 90c, Squadron Commander Richard Bell Davies.
$2, HMS Illustrious.

2009, June 30
1113-1116 A184 Set of 4 — 4.25 4.25
Souvenir Sheet
1117 A184 $2 multi — 4.00 4.00
Nos. 1113-1116 each were printed in sheets of 8 + central label.

Space Exploration A185

Designs: 50c, Goddard Rocket Shop, Roswell, New Mexico, 1940. 75c, Vertol VZ-2, 1960. $1, Apollo 11 on launch pad, 1969. $1.25, Space Shuttle flight STS-126 on launch pad, 2008. $2.30, Docking procedure, International Space Station.
$3, Lunar Rover on Moon, painting by Capt. Alan Bean, vert.

2009, July 20 — Perf. 13¼
1118-1122 A185 Set of 5 — 12.00 12.00
Souvenir Sheet
— Perf. 13x13¼
1123 A185 $3 multi — 6.00 6.00
No. 1123 contains one 40x60mm stamp. Nos. 1118-1122 each were printed in sheets of 6.

Coral Reefs A186

Designs: 20c, Sea turtle. 35c, Fish. 50c, Seahorse, vert. 60c, Shell. $1.50, Coral reef.

Wmk. 406
2010, Mar. 29 Litho. Perf. 12½
1124-1128 A186 Set of 5 — 6.50 6.50

Construction of New North Sound Post Office Substation A187

Designs: 20c, John E. George, Sub-postmaster. 50c, New post office substation, horiz. $2, Old post office substation, horiz.

East End Methodist Church, 200th Anniv. A188

Designs: 20c, Church bell. 50c, Church in 2010. 60c, Church in 1977. $2, Church in early 19th cent.

Wmk. 406
2010, May 3 Litho. Perf. 12½
1129-1131 A187 Set of 3 — 5.50 5.50

Wmk. 406
2010, Nov. 10 Litho. Perf. 13¼
1132-1135 A188 Set of 4 — 6.75 6.75

Sailability — A189

Various sailors and sailboats with country name and lower panels in: 5c, Dark red. 20c, Violet blue. 25c, Purple. 40c, Green. 50c, Red. $1.50, Orange red.

Wmk. 406
2011, Feb. 24 Litho. Perf. 12½
1136-1141 A189 Set of 6 — 6.00 6.00

2011 Spring Regatta A190

Various sailboats with country name and lower panels in: 15c, Green. 35c, Blue, vert. 50c, Olive green, vert. $2, Olive brown.

2011, Mar. 1
1142-1145 A190 Set of 4 — 6.00 6.00

Souvenir Sheet

Wedding of Prince William and Catherine Middleton — A191

— Perf. 14¾x14
2011, Apr. 29 Wmk. 406
1146 A191 $5 multi — 10.00 10.00

WAR TAX STAMPS

Regular Issue of 1913 Overprinted

1916-17 Wmk. 3 Perf. 14
Die I
MR1 A9 1p scarlet — .55 8.00
a. 1p carmine — 2.50 20.00
MR2 A9 3p violet, yellow — 3.50 20.00

OFFICIAL STAMPS

Catalogue values for unused stamps in this section are for Never Hinged items.

Nos. 365-368, 370-380 Overprinted "OFFICIAL" in Silver

1985, July Litho. Perf. 14
O1 A57 1c multi — .30 1.25
O2 A57 3c multi — .45 1.25
O3 A57 5c multi — .45 .45
O4 A57 8c multi — .55 .60
O5 A57 13c multi — .80 .75
O6 A57 15c multi — .80 .75
O7 A57 18c multi — .90 1.50
O8 A57 20c multi — .90 .80
O9 A57 25c multi — 1.25 2.00
O10 A57 30c multi — 1.40 1.00
O11 A57 60c multi — 2.00 2.50
O12 A57 $1 multi — 3.25 3.75
O13 A57 $2.50 multi — 5.75 8.00
O14 A57 $3 multi — 8.75 10.00
O15 A57 $5 multi — 11.50 11.50
Nos. O1-O15 (15) — 39.05 46.10

Nos. 364-380 overprinted in gold and Nos. 364, 369 overprinted in silver exist but were not issued by the Virgin Islands.

Nos. 490-508 Ovptd. "OFFICIAL"
1986 Litho. Perf. 14
O16 A81 1c multicolored — .40 .40
O17 A81 2c multicolored — .40 .40
O18 A81 5c multicolored — .40 .40
O19 A81 8c multicolored — .40 .40
O20 A81 10c multicolored — .40 .40
O21 A81 12c multicolored — .50 .50
O22 A81 15c multicolored — .60 .60
O23 A81 18c multicolored — .70 .70
O24 A81 20c multicolored — .85 .85
O25 A81 25c multicolored — 1.00 1.00
O26 A81 30c multicolored — 1.25 1.25
O27 A81 35c multicolored — 1.40 1.40
O28 A81 40c multicolored — 1.60 1.60
O29 A81 50c multicolored — 1.75 1.75
O30 A81 60c multicolored — 2.10 2.10
O31 A81 $1 multicolored — 3.50 3.50
O32 A81 $2 multicolored — 7.50 7.50
O33 A81 $3 multicolored — 11.00 11.00
O34 A81 $5 multicolored — 20.00 20.00
Nos. O16-O34 (19) — 55.75 55.75
Issue: 1, 5, 10, 15, 20-35c, $5, 7/3; others, 1/28.

Nos. 694-695, 698, 701-706, 708 Ovptd. "OFFICIAL"
1991, Sept. Litho. Perf. 14
O37 A116 5c multicolored — .25 .25
O38 A116 10c multicolored — .25 .25
O41 A116 20c multicolored — .75 .75
O44 A116 35c multicolored — 1.40 1.40
O45 A116 40c multicolored — 1.50 1.50
O46 A116 45c multicolored — 1.75 1.75
O47 A116 50c multicolored — 1.90 1.90
O48 A116 70c multicolored — 2.75 2.75
O49 A116 $1 multicolored — 3.75 3.75
O51 A116 $3 multicolored — 11.50 11.50
Nos. O37-O51 (10) — 25.80 25.80

Ovpt. on Nos. O37-O51 is 19mm long. Used values are for c-t-o copies. Nos. O37-O38, O41, O44-O49, O51 were not available unused until mid-1992. This set was never used in the Virgin Islands.

Nos. 694-695, 698, 700-706, 708 Ovptd. "OFFICIAL"
1992 Litho. Perf. 14
O55 A116 5c multicolored — .25 .25
O56 A116 10c multicolored — .25 .25
O59 A116 20c multicolored — .75 .75
O61 A116 30c multicolored — 1.25 1.25
O62 A116 35c multicolored — 1.40 1.40
O63 A116 40c multicolored — 1.50 1.50
O64 A116 45c multicolored — 1.75 1.75
O65 A116 50c multicolored — 1.90 1.90
O66 A116 70c multicolored — 2.75 2.75
O67 A116 $1 multicolored — 3.75 3.75
O69 A116 $3 multicolored — 11.50 11.50
Nos. O55-O69 (11) — 27.05 27.05
Ovpt. on Nos. O55-O56, O59, O61-O67, O69 is 15½mm long.

WALLIS & FUTUNA ISLANDS

'wä-ləs and fə-'tü-nə

'ī-lənds

LOCATION — Group of islands in the South Pacific Ocean, northeast of Fiji
GOVT. — French Overseas Territory
AREA — 106 sq. mi.
POP. — 15,129 (1999 est.)
CAPITAL — Mata-Utu, Wallis Island

100 Centimes = 1 Franc

Catalogue values for unused stamps in this country are for Never Hinged items, beginning with Scott 127 in the regular postage section, Scott B9 in the semipostal section, Scott C1 in the airpost section, and Scott J37 in the postage due section.

New Caledonia Stamps of 1905-28 Overprinted in Black or Red

			1920-28		Unwmk.		Perf. 14x13½
1	A16	1c black, *green*				.30	.30
a.		Double overprint				175.00	
2	A16	2c red brown				.30	.30
3	A16	4c blue, *org*				.50	.50
4	A16	5c green				.50	.50
5	A16	5c dull blue ('22)				.40	.55
6	A16	10c rose				.65	.65
7	A16	10c green ('22)				.90	.90
8	A16	10c red, *pink* ('25)				2.25	2.25
9	A16	15c violet				1.10	1.10
10	A17	20c gray brown				1.00	1.25
11	A17	25c blue, *grn*				1.50	1.50
12	A17	25c red, *yel* ('22)				1.00	1.00
13	A17	30c brown, *org*				1.60	2.00
14	A17	30c dp rose ('22)				1.50	1.75
15	A17	30c red orange ('25)				.85	.85
16	A17	30c lt green ('27)				2.40	3.25
17	A17	35c black, *yel* (R)				1.00	1.00
18	A17	40c rose, *grn*				1.25	1.50
19	A17	45c violet brn, *pnksh*				1.60	2.00
20	A17	50c red, *org*				1.75	2.10
21	A17	50c dark blue ('22)				2.00	2.40
22	A17	50c dark gray ('25)				2.60	3.25
23	A17	65c deep blue ('28)				6.00	6.50
24	A17	75c olive green				2.25	2.60

Nos. 113, 115-116 Overprinted

25	A18	1fr blue, *yel grn*	4.50	5.25
a.		Triple overprint	200.00	
b.		Double overprint	200.00	
c.		Pair, one stamp without overprint	525.00	
26	A18	1.10fr orange brn ('28)	6.25	7.25
27	A18	2fr carmine, *bl*	6.75	8.00
28	A18	5fr black, *org* (R)	14.50	16.50
		Nos. 1-28 (28)	66.20	77.00

No. 9 Surcharged in Various Colors

1922

29	A16	0.01c on 15c violet (Bk)	.75	.95
30	A16	0.02c on 15c violet (Bl)	.75	.95
31	A16	0.04c on 15c violet (G)	.75	.95
32	A16	0.05c on 15c violet (R)	.75	.95
		Nos. 29-32 (4)	3.00	3.80

Stamps and Types of 1920 Surcharged in Black or Red

1924-27

33	A18	25c on 2fr car, *bl*	1.00	1.00
34	A18	25c on 5fr black, *org*	1.00	1.00
35	A17	65c on 40c rose red, *grn* ('25)	1.75	2.00
36	A17	85c on 75c ol grn ('25)	1.40	1.60
37	A17	90c on 75c dp rose ('27)	2.25	2.75
38	A18	1.25fr on 1fr dp bl (R; '26)	1.10	1.40
39	A18	1.50fr on 1fr dp bl, *bl* ('27)	4.75	5.50
a.		Double surcharge	300.00	
b.		Surcharge omitted	290.00	
40	A18	3fr on 5fr red vio ('27)	7.25	8.75
a.		Surcharge omitted	240.00	
b.		Double surcharge	325.00	
41	A18	10fr on 5fr ol, *lav* ('27)	34.50	40.00
42	A18	20fr on 5fr vio rose, *yel* ('27)	42.50	47.50
		Nos. 33-42 (10)	97.50	111.50

New Caledonia Stamps and Types of 1928-40 Overprinted as in 1920

1930-40			**Perf. 13½, 14x13, 14x13½**	
43	A19	1c brn vio & indigo	.25	.25
a.		Double overprint	200.00	
44	A19	2c dk brn & yel grn	.25	.25
45	A19	3c brn vio & ind ('40)	.25	.25
46	A19	4c org & Prus grn	.25	.25
47	A19	5c Prus bl & dp ol	.30	.40
48	A19	10c gray lil & dk brn	.30	.40
49	A19	15c yel brn & dp bl	.40	.40
50	A19	20c brn red & dk brn	.60	.70
51	A19	25c dk grn & dk brn	1.10	1.25
52	A20	30c gray grn & bl	1.10	1.25
53	A20	35c Prus grn & dk grn ('38)	1.10	1.25
a.		Without overprint	200.00	
54	A20	40c brt red & olive	1.10	1.10
55	A20	45c dp bl & red org	1.10	1.25
56	A20	45c bl grn & dl grn ('40)	.90	1.00
57	A20	50c violet & brn	1.10	1.10
58	A20	55c bl vio & rose red ('38)	2.40	2.75
59	A20	60c vio bl & car ('40)	.75	.90
60	A20	60c org brn & bl	2.00	2.00
61	A20	70c dp rose & brn ('38)	1.40	1.60
62	A20	75c Prus bl & ol gray	3.00	3.00
63	A20	80c dk cl & grn ('38)	1.40	1.60
64	A20	85c green & brown ('38)	3.75	4.00
65	A20	90c dp red & brt red	2.40	2.75
66	A20	90c ol grn & rose red ('39)	1.10	1.25
67	A21	1fr dp ol & sal red	4.00	4.75
68	A21	1fr rose red & dk car ('38)	2.40	2.75
69	A21	1fr brn red & grn ('40)	.80	.80
70	A21	1.10fr dp grn & brn	34.00	37.50
71	A21	1.25fr brn red & grn ('33)	3.25	3.50
72	A21	1.25fr rose red & dk car ('39)	1.10	1.25
73	A21	1.40fr dk bl & red org ('40)	1.10	1.40
74	A21	1.50fr dp bl & bl	1.25	1.50
75	A21	1.60fr dp grn & brn ('40)	1.60	2.00
76	A21	1.75fr dk bl & red org ('33)	13.00	14.00
77	A21	1.75fr vio bl ('38)	2.40	2.75
78	A21	2fr red org & brn	1.60	1.90
79	A21	2.25fr vio bl ('39)	2.00	2.40
80	A21	2.50fr brn & lt brn ('40)	1.90	2.40
81	A21	3fr magenta & brn	1.75	2.00
82	A21	5fr dk bl & brn	2.40	2.60
83	A21	10fr vio & brn, *pnksh*	2.90	3.50
84	A21	20fr red & brn, *yel*	4.50	5.25
		Nos. 43-84 (42)	110.15	123.20

For overprints see Nos. 94-126.
For types A19 and A21 of New Caledonia, with "RF," overprinted as above, see Nos. 126A-126F.

Common Design Types pictured following the introduction.

Colonial Exposition Issue
Common Design Types
1931, Apr. 13   Engr.   Perf. 12½
Name of Country Typo. in Black

85	CD70	40c deep green	8.75	8.75
86	CD71	50c violet	8.75	8.75
87	CD72	90c red orange	8.75	8.75
88	CD73	1.50fr dull blue	8.75	8.75
		Nos. 85-88 (4)	35.00	35.00

Colonial Arts Exhibition Issue
Common Design Type
Souvenir Sheet

1937   Imperf.

89	CD78	3fr red violet	28.50	37.50
		Never hinged	45.00	

New York World's Fair Issue
Common Design Type

1939, May 10   Engr.   Perf. 12½x12

90	CD82	1.25fr carmine lake	3.00	3.00
91	CD82	2.25fr ultramarine	3.00	3.00

Petain Issue
New Caledonia Nos. 216A-216B Overprinted "WALLIS ET FUTUNA" in Lilac or Red

1941   Engr.   Perf. 12½x12

92	A21a	1fr bluish green (L)	1.40	
93	A21a	2.50fr dark blue (R)	1.40	

Nos. 92-93 were issued by the Vichy government in France, but were not placed on sale in Wallis & Futuna.
For surcharges, see Nos. B8A-B8B.

Nos. 43-69, 71, 74, 77-78, 80-84 with Additional Overprint in Black

1941-43			**Perf. 14x13½**	
94	A19	1c	2.75	2.75
95	A19	2c	2.75	2.75
96	A19	3c	95.00	95.00
97	A19	4c	3.75	3.75
98	A19	5c	3.75	3.75
99	A19	10c	3.75	3.75
100	A19	15c	3.75	3.75
101	A19	20c	5.00	5.00
102	A19	25c	5.00	5.00
103	A20	30c	5.00	5.00
104	A20	35c	3.75	3.75
105	A20	40c	4.50	4.50
106	A20	45c #55	4.50	4.50
107	A20	45c #56	100.00	100.00
108	A20	50c	3.75	3.75
109	A20	55c	82.50	82.50
110	A20	60c	3.75	3.75
111	A20	65c	3.75	3.75
112	A20	70c	3.75	3.75
113	A20	75c	5.00	5.00
114	A20	80c	3.75	3.75
115	A20	85c	4.50	4.50
116	A20	90c #65	3.75	3.75
117	A21	1fr #68	4.50	4.50
118	A21	1.25fr #71	4.50	4.50
119	A21	1.50fr	3.75	3.75
120	A21	1.75fr #77	3.75	3.75
121	A21	2fr	4.50	4.50
122	A21	2.50fr	150.00	150.00
123	A21	3fr	3.75	3.75
124	A21	5fr	8.25	8.25
125	A21	10fr	55.00	55.00
126	A21	20fr	90.00	90.00
		Nos. 94-126 (33)	685.75	685.75

Types of New Caledonia Without "RF" overprinted as in 1920

1944

126A	A19	10c gray lil & dk brn	1.10	
126B	A19	15c yel brn & dp bl	1.25	
126C	A21	1fr brn red & grn	1.90	
126D	A21	1.50fr blue	2.10	
126E	A21	10fr vio & brn, *pnksh*	2.10	
126F	A21	20fr red & brn, *yel*	2.60	
		Nos. 126A-126F (6)	11.05	

Nos. 126A-126F were issued by the Vichy government in France, but were not placed on sale in Wallis & Futuna.

Catalogue values for unused stamps in this section, from this point to the end of the section, are for Never Hinged items.

Ivi Poo, Bone Carving in Tiki Design A1

1944   Unwmk.   Photo.   Perf. 11½x12

127	A1	5c lt brown	.40	.30
128	A1	10c dp gray blue	.40	.30
129	A1	25c emerald	.40	.30
130	A1	30c dull orange	.40	.30
131	A1	40c dk slate grn	1.10	.90
132	A1	80c brown red	1.10	.90
133	A1	1fr red violet	.50	.40
134	A1	1.50fr red	.65	.40
135	A1	2fr gray black	.65	.50
136	A1	2.50fr brt ultra	.90	.65
137	A1	4fr dark purple	1.10	.90
138	A1	5fr lemon yellow	1.40	1.10
139	A1	10fr chocolate	1.80	1.40
140	A1	20fr deep green	1.90	1.50
		Nos. 127-140 (14)	12.70	9.85

Nos. 127, 129 and 136 Surcharged with New Values and Bars in Black or Carmine

1946

141	A1	50c on 5c lt brown	.90	.65
142	A1	60c on 5c lt brown	1.00	.75
143	A1	70c on 5c lt brown	1.00	.75
144	A1	1.20fr on 5c lt brown	1.10	.90
145	A1	2.40fr on 25c emerald	1.10	.90
146	A1	3fr on 25c emerald	1.10	.90
147	A1	4.50fr on 25c emerald	2.40	1.75
148	A1	15fr on 2.50fr (C)	2.50	1.75
		Nos. 141-148 (8)	11.00	8.20

Military Medal Issue
Common Design Type
Engraved and Typographed

1952, Dec. 1   Perf. 13

149	CD101	2fr multicolored	9.50	7.00

Wallis Islander A2

Unwmk.

1957, June 11   Engr.   Perf. 13

150	A2	3fr dk purple & lil rose	1.50	1.10
151	A2	9fr bl, dl lil & vio brn	2.75	2.25

Imperforates
Most Wallis and Futuna stamps from 1957 onward exist imperforate in issued and trial colors, and also in small presentation sheets in issued colors.

Flower Issue
Common Design Type

Design: 5fr, Montrouziera, horiz.

1958, Aug. 4   Photo.   Perf. 12½x12

152	CD104	5fr multicolored	4.50	2.50

Human Rights Issue
Common Design Type

1958, Dec. 10   Engr.   Perf. 13

153	CD105	17fr brt bl & dk bl	5.75	4.00

Women Making Tapa Cloth — A3

Kava Ceremony A4

17fr, Dancers. 19fr, Dancers with paddles.

1960, Sept. 19   Engr.   Perf. 13
154 A3 5fr dk brown, grn & org
  brn   1.50 1.10
155 A4 7fr dk brown & Prus
  grn   2.25 1.90
156 A4 17fr ultra, claret & grn 3.00 2.25
157 A3 19fr claret & slate   3.25 2.50
  Nos. 154-157 (4)   10.00 7.75
For No. 157 with surcharge, see No. 174.

Map of South Pacific — A4a

1962, July 18   Photo.   Perf. 13x12
158 A4a 16fr multicolored   4.50 4.00
5th South Pacific Conf., Pago Pago, 1962.

Sea Shells — A5

1962-63   Engr.   Perf. 13
Size: 22x36mm
159 A5 25c Triton   1.10 1.10
160 A5 1fr Mitra episcopalis 1.10 1.10
161 A5 2fr Cypraecassis rufa 2.10 2.10
162 A5 4fr Murex tenuspina   3.00 3.00
163 A5 10fr Oliva erythrostoma 7.00 7.00
164 A5 20fr Cyprae tigris   10.50 10.50
  Nos. 159-164,C18 (7)   37.30 31.80

Red Cross Centenary Issue
Common Design Type
1963, Sept. 2   Unwmk.   Perf. 13
165 CD113 12fr red lil, gray & car 4.00 3.50

Human Rights Issue
Common Design Type
1963, Dec. 10   Engr.
166 CD117 29fr dk red & ocher 8.00 7.50

Philatec Issue
Common Design Type
1964, Apr. 15   Unwmk.   Perf. 13
167 CD118 9fr dk sl grn, grn &
  red   3.50 3.50

Queen
Amelia and
Ship
"Queen
Amelia"
A6

1965, Feb. 15   Photo.   Perf. 12½x13
168 A6 11fr multicolored   8.00 7.50

WHO Anniversary Issue
Common Design Type
1968, May 4   Engr.   Perf. 13
169 CD126 17fr bl grn, org & lil 6.50 4.50

Human Rights Year Issue
Common Design Type
1968, Aug. 10   Engr.   Perf. 13
170 CD127 19fr dk pur, org brn &
  brt mag   3.75 3.75

Outrigger
Canoe
A7

1969, Apr. 30   Photo.   Perf. 13
171 A7 1fr multicolored   1.10 1.10
  Nos. 171,C31-C35 (6)   40.60 18.85

ILO Issue
Common Design Type
1969, Nov. 24   Engr.   Perf. 13
172 CD131 9fr orange, brn & bl 3.00 2.90

UPU Headquarters Issue
Common Design Type
1970, May 20   Engr.   Perf. 13
173 CD133 21fr lil rose, ind & ol
  bis   4.00 4.00

No. 157 Surcharged with New Value
and Two Bars
1971   Engr.   Perf. 13
174 A3 12fr on 19fr   1.25 1.25

Weight Lifting — A8

1971, Oct. 25
175 A8 24fr shown   6.00 5.25
176 A8 36fr Basketball   7.00 6.50
  Nos. 175-176,C37-C38 (4)   27.25 19.75
4th South Pacific Games, Papeete, French
Polynesia, Sept. 8-19.

De Gaulle Issue
Common Design Type
Designs: 30fr, Gen. de Gaulle, 1940. 70fr,
Pres. de Gaulle, 1970.
1971, Nov. 9   Engr.   Perf. 13
177 CD134 30fr blue & black   9.50 6.25
178 CD134 70fr blue & black 14.50 10.00

Child's
Outrigger
Canoe
A9

Designs: 16fr, Children's canoe race. 18fr,
Outrigger racing canoe.

1972, Oct. 16   Photo.   Perf. 13x12½
Size: 35½x26½mm
179 A9 14fr dk green & multi 10.00 4.25
180 A9 16fr dk plum & multi   10.00 4.25
181 A9 18fr blue & multi   15.00 6.25
  Nos. 179-181,C41 (4)   80.00 39.75
Outrigger sailing canoes.

Rhinoceros
Beetle
A10

Insects: 25fr, Cosmopolites sordidus (beetle). 35fr, Ophideres fullonica (moth). 45fr,
Dragonfly.

1974, July 29   Photo.   Perf. 13
182 A10 15fr ol & multi   3.75 2.10
183 A10 25fr ol & multi   4.50 3.00
184 A10 35fr gray bl & multi 7.00 4.00
185 A10 45fr multicolored   10.00 6.00
  Nos. 182-185 (4)   25.25 15.10

Georges Pompidou
(1911-74), Pres. of
France — A11

1975, Dec. 1   Engr.   Perf. 13
186 A11 50fr ultra & slate   8.00 5.50

Battle of Yorktown and George
Washington — A12

American Bicentennial: 47fr, Virginia Cape
Battle and Lafayette.

1976, June 28   Engr.   Perf. 13
187 A12 19fr blue, red & olive   3.00 1.40
188 A12 47fr blue, red & maroon 4.50 4.00
  For overprints see Nos. 205-206.

Conus Ammiralis — A13

Sea Shells: 23fr, Cyprae assellus. 43fr,
Turbo petholatus. 61fr, Mitra papalis.

1976, Oct. 1   Engr.   Perf. 13
189 A13 20fr multicolored   2.75 2.00
190 A13 23fr multicolored   2.75 2.00
191 A13 43fr multicolored   6.00 4.00
192 A13 61fr ultra & multi   8.50 6.50
  Nos. 189-192 (4)   20.00 14.50

Father Chanel and Poi Church — A14

32fr, Father Chanel and map of islands.

1977, Apr. 28   Litho.   Perf. 12
193 A14 22fr multicolored   2.25 1.40
194 A14 32fr multicolored   2.50 1.50
Return of the ashes of Father Chanel,
missionary.

Bowl,
Mortar and
Pestle
A15

Handicrafts: 25fr, Wooden bowls and
leather bag. 33fr, Wooden comb, club, and
boat model. 45fr, War clubs, Futuna. 69fr,
Lances.

1977, Sept. 26   Litho.   Perf. 12½
195 A15 12fr multicolored   1.30   .75
196 A15 25fr multicolored   2.00 1.00
197 A15 33fr multicolored   2.25 1.25
198 A15 43fr multicolored   3.50 1.75
199 A15 69fr multicolored   4.50 3.00
  Nos. 195-199 (5)   13.55 7.75

Post Office, Mata Utu — A16

50fr, Sia Hospital, Mata Utu. 57fr, Adminis-
tration Buildings, Mata Utu. 63fr, St. Joseph's
Church, Sigave. 120fr, Royal Palace, Mara
Utu.

1977, Dec. 12   Litho.   Perf. 13
200 A16 27fr multicolored   1.80 1.40
201 A16 50fr multicolored   2.50 1.80
202 A16 57fr multicolored   3.50 1.80
203 A16 63fr multicolored   4.50 2.75
204 A16 120fr multicolored   9.00 4.50
  Nos. 200-204 (5)   21.30 12.25

Nos. 187-188 Overprinted

1978, Jan. 20   Engr.   Perf. 13
205 A12 19fr multicolored   3.50 2.50
206 A12 47fr multicolored   7.00 4.00
Bicentenary of the arrival of Capt. Cook in
the Hawaiian Islands.

Cruiser Triomphant — A17

Warships: 200fr, Destroyers Cap des
Palmes and Chevreuil. 280fr, Cruiser
Savorgnan de Brazza.

1978, June 18   Photo.   Perf. 13x12½
207 A17 150fr multicolored   10.50 6.25
208 A17 200fr multicolored   14.00 9.00
209 A17 280fr multicolored   18.00 12.50
  Nos. 207-209 (3)   42.50 27.75
Free French warships serving in the Pacific,
1940-1944.

Solanum Seaforthianum — A18

Flowers: 24fr, Cassia alata. 29fr, Gloriosa
superba. 36fr, Hymenocallis littoralis.

1978, July 11   Photo.   Perf. 13
210 A18 16fr multicolored   1.50   .90
211 A18 24fr multicolored   1.75 1.00
212 A18 29fr multicolored   2.50 1.40
213 A18 36fr multicolored   3.50 1.80
  Nos. 210-213 (4)   9.25 5.10

Gray Egret — A19

Birds: 18fr, Red-footed booby. 28fr, Brown booby. 35fr, White tern.

1978, Sept. 5   Photo.   Perf. 13
214 A19 17fr multicolored   1.75   .90
215 A19 18fr multicolored   1.80   1.00
216 A19 28fr multicolored   2.50   1.40
217 A19 35fr multicolored   3.50   1.60
     Nos. 214-217 (4)   9.55   4.90

Traditional Patterns — A20

Designs: 55fr, Corpus Christi procession. 59fr, Chief's honor guard.

1978, Oct. 3
218 A20 53fr multicolored   3.00   1.80
219 A20 55fr multicolored   4.00   2.10
220 A20 59fr multicolored   3.50   2.50
     Nos. 218-220 (3)   10.50   6.40

Human Rights Flame A21

1978, Dec. 10   Litho.   Perf. 12½
221 A21 44fr multicolored   1.80   1.30
222 A21 56fr multicolored   2.75   1.80

30th anniversary of Universal Declaration of Human Rights.

Fishing Boat — A22

Designs: 30fr, Weighing young tuna. 34fr, Stocking young tunas. 38fr, Measuring tuna. 40fr, Angler catching tuna. 48fr, Adult tuna.

1979, Mar. 19   Litho.   Perf. 12
223 A22 10fr multicolored   .90   .50
224 A22 30fr multicolored   1.40   .90
225 A22 34fr multicolored   1.50   1.00
226 A22 38fr multicolored   2.40   1.40
227 A22 40fr multicolored   2.75   2.00
228 A22 48fr multicolored   3.75   2.00
 a.   Souv. sheet of 6, #223-228 +
          3 labels   30.00 30.00
     Nos. 223-228 (6)   12.70   7.80

Tuna tagging by South Pacific Commission. For surcharge see No. 261.

Boy with Raft and IYC Emblem — A23

Design: 58fr, Girl on horseback.

1979, Apr. 9   Photo.   Perf. 13
229 A23 52fr multicolored   2.25   1.30
230 A23 58fr multicolored   2.25   1.70

International Year of the Child.

Bombax Ellipticum — A24

64fr, Callophyllum. 76fr, Pandanus odoratissimus.

1979, Apr. 23   Litho.   Perf. 13
231 A24 50fr multicolored   2.25   1.40
232 A24 64fr multicolored   3.00   1.80
233 A24 76fr multicolored   4.25   2.50
     Nos. 231-233 (3)   9.50   5.70

Green and Withered Landscapes — A25

1979, May 28   Photo.   Perf. 13
234 A25 22fr multicolored   1.80   1.10

Anti-alcoholism campaign.

Flowers — A26

1979, July 16   Photo.   Perf. 12½x13
235 A26 20fr Crinum   .90   .65
236 A26 42fr Passiflora   2.10   1.10
237 A26 62fr Canna indica   3.00   1.75
     Nos. 235-237 (3)   6.00   3.50

See Nos. 279-281.

Swimming — A27

1979, Aug. 27   Engr.   Perf. 13
238 A27 31fr shown   2.25   1.40
239 A27 39fr High jump   3.00   1.80

6th South Pacific Games, Suva, Fiji, Aug. 27-Sept. 8.

Flower Necklaces — A28

Design: 140fr, Coral necklaces.

1979, Aug. 27   Litho.
240 A28 110fr multicolored   4.25   2.75
241 A28 140fr multicolored   5.25   3.50

Trees and Birds, by Sutita — A29

Paintings by Local Artists: 65fr, Birds and Mountain, by M. A. Pilioko, vert. 78fr, Festival Procession, by Sutita.

1979, Oct. 8   Perf. 13x12½, 12½x13
242 A29 27fr multicolored   1.40   1.10
243 A29 65fr multicolored   2.25   1.50
244 A29 78fr multicolored   4.00   2.25
     Nos. 242-244 (3)   7.65   4.85

Marine Mantis A30

Marine Life: 23fr, Hexabranchus sanguineus. 25fr, Spondylus barbatus. 43fr, Gorgon coral. 45fr, Linckia laevigata. 63fr, Tridacna squamosa.

1979, Nov. 5   Photo.   Perf. 13x12½
245 A30 15fr multicolored   1.40   .75
246 A30 23fr multicolored   1.40   .90
247 A30 25fr multicolored   1.80   1.00
248 A30 43fr multicolored   2.25   1.10
249 A30 45fr multicolored   2.40   1.25
250 A30 63fr multicolored   4.50   2.50
     Nos. 245-250 (6)   13.75   7.50

See #294-297. For surcharge see #272.

Transportation Type of 1979
1980, Feb. 29   Litho.   Perf. 13
251 AP32 1fr like No. C87   .35   .25
252 AP32 3fr like No. C88   .35   .25
253 AP32 5fr like No. C89   .40   .35
     Nos. 251-253 (3)   1.10   .85

Radio Station and Tower — A31

1980, Apr. 21   Litho.   Perf. 13
254 A31 47fr multicolored   2.75   1.40

Radio station FR3, 1st anniversary.

Jesus Laid in the Tomb, by Maurice Denis — A32

1980, Apr. 28   Perf. 13x12½
255 A32 25fr multicolored   1.80   .90

Easter 1980.

Gnathodentex Mossambicus — A33

1980, Aug. 25   Litho.   Perf. 12½x13
256 A33 23fr shown   1.40   .90
257 A33 27fr Pristipomoides fi-
             lamentosus   1.80   1.00
258 A33 32fr Etelis carbuncu-
             lus   2.50   1.40
259 A33 51fr Cephalopholis
             wallisi   3.50   2.40
260 A33 59fr Aphareus rutilans   5.75   2.75
 a.   Vert. strip of 5, Nos. 256-260   16.00 15.00

No. 228 Surcharged

1980, Sept. 29   Litho.   Perf. 12
261 A22 50fr on 48fr multi   3.00   1.80

Sydpex 80 Philatelic Exhibition, Sydney.

13th World Telecommunications Day — A34

1981, May 17   Litho.   Perf. 12½
262 A34 49fr multicolored   1.00   1.10

Pierre Curie and Laboratory Equipment — A35

1981, May 25   Litho.   Perf. 13
263 A35 56fr multicolored   2.25   1.40

Pierre Curie (1859-1906), discoverer of radioactivity.

Conus Textile
A36

Designs: Marine life.

1981, June 22   *Perf. 12½x13*
264 A36 28fr Favites   1.10   .90
265 A36 30fr Cyanophycees   1.40   .90
266 A36 31fr Ceratium vultur   1.50   .90
267 A36 35fr Amphiprion
    frenatus   2.25   1.10
268 A36 40fr shown   2.25   1.40
269 A36 55fr Comatule   2.75   1.60
  a.   Vert. strip of 6, Nos. 264-269   11.50   11.00

No. 269a is from sheet of 24.

60th Anniv. of Anti-tuberculin Vaccine
(Developed by Calmette and
Guerin) — A37

1981, July 28   *Litho.*   *Perf. 13*
270 A37 27fr multicolored   1.10   .90

Intl. Year of the
Disabled — A38

1981, Aug. 17
271 A38 42fr multicolored   2.25   1.20

No. 245 Surcharged in Red

1981, Sept.   *Photo.*   *Perf. 13x12½*
272 A30 5fr on 15fr multi   .65   .35

Thomas Edison (1847-1931) and his
Phonograph, 1878 — A39

1981, Sept. 5   *Engr.*   *Perf. 13*
273 A39 59fr multicolored   2.50   1.40

Battle of Yorktown, 1781 (American
Revolution) — A40

1981, Oct. 19   *Engr.*   *Perf. 13*
274 A40 66fr Admiral de Grasse   2.75   1.80
275 A40 74fr Sea battle, vert.   3.50   2.75

200-Mile Zone Surveillance — A41

1981, Dec. 4   *Litho.*   *Perf. 13*
276 A41 60fr Patrol boat Diep-
    poise   1.80   1.40
277 A41 85fr Protet   2.75   2.10

TB Bacillus
Centenary — A42

1982, Mar. 24   *Litho.*   *Perf. 13*
278 A42 45fr multicolored   3.00   1.40

Flower Type of 1979 in Changed Colors

1982, May 3   *Photo.*   *Perf. 12½x13*
279 A26 1fr like No. 235   .30   .25
280 A26 2fr like No. 236   .40   .25
281 A26 3fr like No. 237   .40   .30
    Nos. 279-281 (3)   1.10   .80

PHILEXFRANCE '82 Intl. Stamp
Exhibition, Paris, June 11-21 — A43

1982, May 12   *Engr.*   *Perf. 13*
282 A43 140fr like No. 25   3.50   2.75

Acanthe
Phippium
A44

Orchids and rubiaceae (83fr).

1982, May 24   *Litho.*   *Perf. 12½x13*
283 A44 34fr shown   1.10   .90
284 A44 68fr Acanthe phippium,
    diff.   2.25   1.75
285 A44 70fr Spathoglottis pacifi-
    ca   2.50   1.75
286 A44 83fr Mussaenda
    raiateensis   3.00   2.25
    Nos. 283-286 (4)   8.85   6.65

Scouting
Year
A45

1982, June 21   *Perf. 12½*
287 A45 80fr Baden-Powell   2.25   1.75

Cypraea
Talpa
A46

Porcelaines shells.

1982, June 28   *Perf. 12½x13*
288 A46 10fr shown   .30   .30
289 A46 15fr Cypraea vitellus   .70   .30
290 A46 25fr Cypraea argus   .85   .65
291 A46 27fr Cypraea carneola   1.10   .75
292 A46 40fr Cypraea mappa   1.40   1.10
293 A46 55fr Cypraea tigris   1.75   1.25
    Nos. 288-293 (6)   6.10   4.35

Marine Life Type of 1979

1982, Oct. 1   *Photo.*   *Perf. 13x12½*
294 A30 32fr Gorgones milithea   1.40   .75
295 A30 35fr Linckia laevigata   1.75   1.10
296 A30 46fr Hexabranchus
    sanguineus   2.10   1.50
297 A30 63fr Spondylus barbatus   3.00   2.25
    Nos. 294-297 (4)   8.25   5.60

St. Teresa of Jesus of Avila (1515-
1582) — A48

1982, Nov. 8   *Engr.*   *Perf. 13*
298 A48 31fr multicolored   1.40   .75
    See No. 315.

Traditional
House
A49

1983, Jan. 20   *Litho.*   *Perf. 13*
299 A49 19fr multicolored   .90   .50

Gustave Eiffel (1832-1923),
Architect — A50

1983, Feb. 14   *Engr.*   *Perf. 13*
300 A50 97fr multicolored   3.50   2.75

A51

1983, June 28   *Engr.*   *Perf. 13*
301 A51 92fr Thai dancer, 19th
    cent.   3.00   1.80
BANGKOK '83 Intl. Stamp Show, Aug. 4-13.

A52

1983, Aug. 25   *Litho.*   *Perf. 13x13½*
302 A52 20fr multicolored   .70   .50
World Communications Year.

Cone Shells
A53

1983-84   *Litho.*   *Perf. 13½x13*
303 A53 10fr Conus tulipa   .50   .30
304 A53 17fr Conus
    capitaneus   .75   .50
305 A53 21fr Conus virgo   .75   .50
306 A53 22fr Strombus lentigi-
    nosus   .65   .50
307 A53 25fr Lambis chiragra   .75   .60
308 A53 35fr Strombus
    dentatus   1.40   .75
309 A53 39fr Conus vitulinus   1.40   .90
310 A53 43fr Lambis scorpius   1.75   .90
311 A53 49fr Strombus aurisdi-
    anae   2.00   1.40
312 A53 52fr Conus
    marmoreus   1.80   1.40
313 A53 65fr Conus leopardus   2.40   1.75
314 A53 76fr Lambis crocata   3.00   1.60
    Nos. 303-314 (12)   17.15   11.10

Issued: 22, 25, 35, 43, 49, 76fr, 3/23/84;
others, 10/14/83.

No. 298 Redrawn with Espana '84 Emblem

1984, Apr. 27   *Engr.*   *Perf. 13*
315 A48 70fr multicolored   2.25   1.40

Denis Diderot
(1713-1784),
Philosopher
A54

1984, May 11
316 A54 100fr Portrait, encyclo-
    pedia title page   3.00   1.75

Nature
Protection
(Whale)
A55

1984, June 5   *Litho.*   *Perf. 13x12½*
317 A55 90fr Orcina orca   3.00   1.75

4th Pacific Arts Festival — A56

1984, Nov. 30   *Litho.*   *Perf. 13*
318 A56 160fr Islanders   3.75   2.50

Lapita
Pottery — A57

Ethno-Archaeological Museum: Excavation site, reconstructed ceramic bowl.

1985, Jan. 16   Litho.   Perf. 13
319   A57   53fr multicolored   1.50   .90

Seashells
A58

1985, Feb. 11
320   A58   2fr Nautilus pompilius   .25   .25
321   A58   3fr Murex bruneus   .25   .25
322   A58   41fr Casmaria erinaceus   1.40   .90
323   A58   47fr Conus vexillum   1.75 1.00
324   A58   56fr Harpa harpa   2.10 1.10
325   A58   71fr Murex ramosus   2.50 1.60
         Nos. 320-325 (6)   8.25 5.10

Victor Hugo,
Author (1802-
1885)
A59

1985, Mar. 7   Engr.
326   A59   89fr multicolored   3.00 1.60

Bat — A60

1985, Apr. 29   Litho.
327   A60   38fr multicolored   2.00 1.10

Intl. Youth
Year — A61

1985, May 20   Litho.   Perf. 12½x13
328   A61   64fr Children   1.75 1.10

UN, 40th Anniv. — A61a

1985, July 12   Engr.   Perf. 13
328A A61a 49fr Prus grn, dk ultra
              & red   1.50   .90

Pierre de Ronsard (1524-1585),
Poet — A62

1985, Sept. 16   Engr.   Perf. 13
329   A62   170fr brt bl, sep & brn   5.00 3.50

Dr. Albert Schweitzer — A63

1985, Nov. 22   Engr.   Perf. 13
330   A63   50fr blk, dk red lil & org
              brn   2.00 1.25

World Food
Day — A64

1986, Jan. 23   Litho.   Perf. 12½x13
331   A64   39fr Breadfruit   1.25   .75

Flamboyants — A65

1986, Feb. 13   Perf. 13x12½
332   A65   38fr multicolored   2.00 1.00

Seashells
A66

1986, Apr. 24   Litho.   Perf. 13½x13
333   A66   4fr Lambis truncata   .35   .35
334   A66   5fr Charonia tritonis   .35   .35
335   A66   10fr Oliva miniacea   .50   .35
336   A66   18fr Distorsio anus   .80   .70
337   A66   25fr Mitra mitra   1.20   .75
338   A66   107fr Conus distans   3.75 2.25
         Nos. 333-338 (6)   6.95 4.75

Also exists in se-tenant strips of 6 from sheet of 24.

1986 World Cup Soccer
Championships, Mexico — A67

1986, May 20   Perf. 13x12½
339   A67   95fr multicolored   3.25 1.80
         UNICEF.

Discovery of Horn Islands, 370th
Anniv. — A68

No. 340: a, 8fr, William Schouten, ship. b, 9fr, Jacob LeMaire, ship. c, 155fr, Map of Alo & Alofi.

1986, June 19   Engr.   Perf. 13
340   A68   Strip of 3, #a.-c.   6.50 4.75

James Watt (1736-1819), Inventor,
and Steam Engine — A69

1986, July 11
341   A69   74fr blk & dk red   2.40 1.50

Minesweeper La Lorientaise — A70

7fr, 120fr vertical.

1986, Aug. 7
342   A70   6fr shown   .70   .50
343   A70   7fr Corvette Comman-
              dant Blaison   .75   .50
344   A70   120fr Frigate Balny   4.25 2.75
         Nos. 342-344 (3)   5.70 3.75

Rose Laurel — A71

1986, Oct. 2   Litho.   Perf. 13x12½
345   A71   97fr multi   3.25 2.00

Virgin and
Child, by
Sandro
Botticelli
A72

1986, Dec. 12   Litho.   Perf. 12½x13
346   A72   250fr multicolored   7.50 4.50
         Christmas.

Butterflies — A73

1987, Apr. 2   Litho.   Perf. 12½
347   A73   2fr Papilio mon-
              trouzieri   .50   .35
348   A73   42fr Belenois java   1.25   .70
349   A73   46fr Delias ellipsis   1.40   .75
350   A73   50fr Danaus pumila   1.60   .95
351   A73   52fr Luthrodes cleotas   2.00 1.00
352   A73   59fr Precis villida   2.40 1.50
         Nos. 347-352 (6)   9.15 5.25

World Wrestling
Championships — A74

1987, May 26   Litho.   Perf. 12½
353   A74   97fr multi   3.25 1.90

For overprint see No. 360.

Seashells
A75

1987, June 24   Litho.   Perf. 13
354   A75   3fr Cymatium pileare   .35   .35
355   A75   4fr Conus textile   .35   .35
356   A75   28fr Cypraea mauritiana   1.25   .75
357   A75   44fr Bursa bubo   1.50 1.00
358   A75   48fr Cypraea tes-
              tudinaria   1.60 1.10
359   A75   78fr Cypraecassis rufa   2.75 1.50
         Nos. 354-359 (6)   7.80 5.05

Also exists in se-tenant strips of 6 from sheet of 24.

No. 353
Overprinted

1987, Aug. 29   Litho.   Perf. 12½
360   A74   97fr multicolored   3.75 2.40

OLYMPHILEX '87, Rome.

Bust of a Girl, by
Auguste Rodin
(1840-1917)
A76

1987, Sept. 15   Engr.   Perf. 13
361   A76   150fr plum   4.50 2.75

See No. 390.

World Post Day — A77

1987, Oct. 9   Litho.   Perf. 13
362 A77 116fr multicolored   3.25 1.80

Birds — A78

1987, Oct. 28   Perf. 13x12½
363 A78 6fr Anas superciliosa   .35   .35
364 A78 19fr Pluvialis dominica   .70   .50
365 A78 47fr Gallicolumba stairi   1.25   .95
366 A78 56fr Arenaria interpres   1.60 1.00
367 A78 64fr Rallus philippensis   1.75 1.10
368 A78 68fr Limosa lapponica   2.25 1.30
       Nos. 363-368 (6)   7.90 5.20

Francis Carco (1886-1958),
Poet — A79

Design: Carco and views of the Moulin de la
Galette and Place du Tertre, Paris.

1988, Jan. 29   Litho.   Perf. 13
369 A79 40fr multicolored   1.40   .95

Jean-Francois de Galaup (1741-
c.1788), Comte de La Perouse,
Explorer — A80

Design: Ships *L'Astrolabe* and *La Boussole*,
portrait of La Perouse.

1988, Mar. 21   Engr.   Perf. 13
370 A80 70fr org brn, dark blue &
          olive grn   3.25 2.40

Intl. Red Cross
and Red
Crescent
Organizations,
125th
Anniv. — A81

1988, July 4   Engr.   Perf. 13
371 A81 30fr blk, dark red & brt
          blue grn   2.00 1.00

1988 Summer Olympics, Seoul — A82

1988, Sept. 1   Engr.   Perf. 13
372 A82 11fr Javelin   .70   .50
373 A82 20fr Women's volleyball   .95   .70
374 A82 60fr Windsurfing   2.00 1.50
375 A82 80fr Yachting   2.90 1.90
a.   Souv. sheet of 4, #372-375 + 2
      labels, gutter between   8.25 8.25
      Nos. 372-375 (4)   6.55 4.60

Intl. Maritime Organization Emblem
and Frigate F727 Admiral
Charner — A83

1989, Jan. 26   Litho.   Perf. 13
376 A83 26fr multi   1.00   .70

Jean Renoir (1894-1979), Film
Director, and Scene from *The Grand
Illusion* — A84

1989, Feb. 16   Engr.   Perf. 13
377 A84 24fr brt lil rose, dark vio
          brn & brt org   1.25   .75

Antoine Becquerel (1788-1878),
Physicist — A85

Perf. 13x12½
1988, Nov. 9   Engr.   Unwmk.
378 A85 18fr blk & dark ultra   .95   .50

Futuna Hydroelectric Plant — A86

Wmk. 385
1989, Apr. 13   Litho.   Perf. 13½
379 A86 25fr multi   .95   .50

A87

Unwmk.
1988, Oct. 26   Litho.   Perf. 13
380 A87 17fr multi   .95   .50
World Post Day.

A88

1989, May 17   Perf. 12½x13
381 A88 21fr multi   .95   .50
World Telecommunications Day.

Fresco
A89

1989, June 8   Perf. 12½
382 A89 22fr multi   .95   .50

PHILEXFRANCE '89 — A90

Declaration of Human Rights and
Citizenship, Bicent. — A91

1989, July 7   Litho.   Perf. 13
383 A90 29fr multi   1.00   .70
384 A91 900fr multi   22.00 14.00
a.   Souv. sheet of 2, #383-384 +
      label   30.00 30.00
No. 384 is airmail. No. 384a sold for 1000fr.

World Cycling Championships — A92

1989, Sept. 14   Engr.   Perf. 13
385 A92 10fr blk, red brn & emer   .60   .45

World Post Day — A93

Unwmk.
1989, Oct. 18   Litho.   Perf. 13
386 A93 27fr multicolored   .95   .50

Landscape — A94

1989, Nov. 23   Litho.   Perf. 13
387 A94 23fr multicolored   .95   .70

Star of
Bethlehem
A95

1990, Jan. 9   Litho.   Perf. 12½
388 A95 44fr multicolored   1.50 1.00

Fossilized
Tortoise
A96

1990, Feb. 15   Litho.   Perf. 12½x13
389 A96 48fr multicolored   2.75 1.40

Sculpture by
Auguste Rodin
(1840-1917)
A97

1990, Mar. 15   Engr.   Perf. 13
390 A97 200fr royal blue   6.00 4.00

1990 World Cup Soccer
Championships, Italy — A98

1990, Apr. 16   Litho.
391 A98 59fr multicolored   1.60 1.10

Orchids
A99

1990, May 17   Litho.   Perf. 12½
392 A99 78fr multicolored   2.75 1.50
Mother's Day

Phaeton — A100

1990, July 16   *Perf. 13*
393 A100 300fr multicolored   8.00 4.50
394 A100 600fr Island   17.50 8.50

Moana II — A101

1990, Aug. 16   *Engr.*   *Perf. 13*
395 A101 40fr shown   1.25 .95
396 A101 50fr Moana III   1.75 1.00

Native Huts
A102

1990, Sept. 17   *Litho.*   *Perf. 13x12½*
397 A102 28fr multicolored   .95 .50

Stamp Day
A103

1990, Oct. 16   *Litho.*   *Perf. 12½*
398 A103 97fr multicolored   3.25 1.90

Wallis Island
Pirogue — A104

1990, Nov. 16   *Litho.*   *Perf. 13x12½*
399 A104 46fr multicolored   1.50 .95

Best Wishes — A105

1990, Dec. 17   *Litho.*   *Perf. 13x12½*
400 A105 100fr multicolored   3.25 1.90

Patrol Boats — A106

1991   *Engr.*   *Perf. 13*
401 A106 42fr La Moqueuse   1.40 .95
402 A106 52fr La Glorieuse   1.75 1.00

Issue dates: 42fr, Jan. 7; 52fr, Mar. 4.

A107

1991, Feb. 4   *Litho.*   *Perf. 13*
403 A107 7fr Breadfruit picker   .35 .35
404 A107 54fr Taro planter   1.60 1.00
405 A107 62fr Spear fisherman   1.75 1.20
406 A107 72fr Native warrior   2.40 1.30
407 A107 90fr Kailao dancer   3.00 1.75
   a.   Souv. sheet of 5, #403-407   10.00 10.00
     Nos. 403-407 (5)   9.10 5.60

Issued: 7fr, 9/2; 54fr, 5/13; 62fr, 4/1; 72fr, 2/4; 90fr, 11/4.
No. 407a sold for 300fr.

Doctors
Without
Borders,
20th Anniv.
A108

1991, Feb. 18   *Litho.*   *Perf. 13½*
408 A108 55fr multicolored   1.60 1.00

Ultralight Aircraft — A108a

1991, June 24
409 A108a 85fr multicolored   2.75 1.80

Portrait of Jean by Auguste Renoir
(1841-1919) — A109

1991, July 8   *Photo.*   *Perf. 12½x13*
410 A109 400fr multicolored   11.00 8.00

Litho.
Die Cut
Self-Adhesive
411 A109 400fr multicolored   11.00 8.00

Overseas Territorial Status, 30th
Anniv. — A110

1991, July 29   *Litho.*   *Perf. 13*
412 A110 102fr multicolored   2.75 1.80

Feast of the Assumption — A111

1991, Aug. 15   *Perf. 13x12½*
413 A111 30fr multicolored   1.00 .70

Amnesty
Intl., 30th
Anniv.
A113

1991, Oct. 7   *Perf. 13x12½*
414 A113 140fr bl, vio & yel   4.50 2.75

Central Bank for Economic
Cooperation, 50th Anniv. — A114

1991, Dec. 2   *Litho.*   *Perf. 13*
415 A114 10fr multicolored   .50 .35

Flowers
A115

1fr, Monette allamanda cathartica. 4fr,
Hibiscus rosa sinensis. 80fr, Ninuphar.

1991, Dec. 2   *Litho.*   *Perf. 12½x13, 13x12½*
416 A115 1fr multi   .50 .25
417 A115 4fr multi, vert.   .50 .35
418 A115 80fr multi   2.40 1.50
     Nos. 416-418 (3)   3.40 2.10

Christmas — A116

1991, Dec. 16   *Litho.*   *Perf. 13*
419 A116 60fr multicolored   2.00 1.20

Maritime Surveillance — A117

1992, Jan. 20   *Litho.*   *Perf. 13*
420 A117 48fr multicolored   2.00 1.00

1992 Winter Olympics,
Albertville — A118

1992, Feb. 17   *Litho.*   *Perf. 13*
421 A118 150fr multicolored   4.00 2.75

Canada '92, Intl. Philatelic Exposition,
Montreal — A119

1992, Mar. 25   *Engr.*   *Perf. 13*
422 A119 35fr blk, violet & red   1.25 .70

1992 Summer Olympics,
Barcelona — A120

1992, Apr. 15   *Engr.*   *Perf. 13*
423 A120 106fr bl grn, grn & bl   3.25 2.25

Granada '92, Intl. Philatelic
Exposition — A121

1992, Apr. 17   *Engr.*   *Perf. 12½x12*
424 A121 100fr multicolored   3.25 2.00

Expo '92, Seville — A122

1992, Apr. 20   *Perf. 13*
425 A122 200fr bl grn, ol & red
     brn   5.50 3.75

Chaetodon Ephippium — A123

Designs: 22fr, Chaetodon auriga. 23fr, Heniochus monoceros. 24fr, Pygoplites diacanthus. 25fr, Chaetodontoplus conspicillatus. 26fr, Chaetodon unimaculatus. 27fr, Siganus punctatus. 35fr, Zebrasoma veliferum. 45fr, Paracanthurus hepatus. 53fr, Siganus vulpinus.

1992-93		**Litho.**	**Perf. 13**	
426	A123	21fr multicolored	.70	.50
427	A123	22fr multicolored	.70	.50
428	A123	23fr multicolored	.70	.50
429	A123	24fr multicolored	.80	.70
430	A123	25fr multicolored	1.00	.70
431	A123	26fr multicolored	1.00	.70
432	A123	27fr multicolored	1.00	.80
433	A123	35fr multicolored	1.00	.80
434	A123	45fr multicolored	1.25	.95
435	A123	53fr multicolored	1.60	1.25
	Nos. 426-435 (10)		9.75	7.40

Issued: 21fr, 26fr, 5/18; 22fr, 7/27; 25fr, 7/27; 23fr, 24fr, 9/14; 35fr, 45fr, 6/21/93; 27fr, 53fr, 9/6/93.

Natives A125

a, 3 warriors. b, 2 warriors. c, Warrior, 2 boats. d, 2 spear fisherman. e, 3 fisherman.

1992, June 15   Litho.   Perf. 12
436 A125 70fr Strip of 5, #a.-e. 12.50 9.00
  f.   Souvenir sheet of 5, #a.-e. 13.00 13.00

#436 has continuous design. #436f sold for 450fr.

Support Ship, "La Garonne" A126

1992, Oct. 12   Litho.   Perf. 12
437 A126 20fr multicolored .75 .50

L'Idylle D'Ixelles, by Auguste Rodin (1840-1917) A127

1992, Nov. 17   Engr.   Perf. 13
438 A127 300fr lilac & dk blue 8.50 6.00

Miribilis Jalapa A128

1992, Dec. 7   Litho.   Perf. 12½
439 A128 200fr multicolored 5.50 3.75

Maritime Forces of the Pacific — A129

1993, Jan. 27   Litho.   Perf. 13x12½
440 A129 130fr multicolored 3.75 2.75

School Art — A130

1993, Feb. 22   Litho.   Perf. 12
441 A130 56fr multicolored 1.80 1.40

See Nos. 451-452.

Birds A131

Designs: 50fr, Rallus philippensis swindellsi. 60fr, Porphyrio porphyrio. 110fr, Ptilinopus greyi.

1993, Mar. 20   Perf. 13½
442 A131 50fr multicolored 1.60 1.00
443 A131 60fr multicolored 1.90 1.50
444 A131 110fr multicolored 3.25 1.90
  Nos. 442-444 (3) 6.75 4.40

Mother's Day A132

1993, May 30   Litho.   Perf. 12½
445 A132 95fr Hibiscus 2.75 1.75
446 A132 120fr Siale 3.50 2.75

Admiral Antoine d'Entrecasteaux (1737-1793), French Navigator — A133

1993, July 12   Engr.   Perf. 13
447 A133 170fr grn bl, red brn & blk 5.00 3.25

Taipei '93 — A134

1993, Aug. 14   Litho.   Perf. 13x12½
448 A134 435fr multicolored 12.50 10.00

Churches — A135

1993, Aug. 15   Perf. 13
449 A135 30fr Tepa, Wallis 1.00 .80
450 A135 30fr Vilamalia, Futuna 1.00 .80

School Art Type of 1993
1993   Litho.   Perf. 13x13½, 13½x13
451 A130 28fr Stylized trees .80 .55
452 A130 52fr Family, vert. 1.60 1.00

Issue dates: 28fr, Oct. 18. 52fr, Nov. 8.

Christmas A136

1993, Dec. 6   Perf. 13
453 A136 80fr multicolored 2.40 1.60

Traditional Arts and Crafts Exhibition A137

1994, Mar. 24   Litho.   Perf. 12½
454 A137 80fr multicolored 2.40 1.60

Liberation of Paris, 50th Anniv. — A138

1994, Apr. 21   Engr.   Perf. 13
455 A138 110fr black, blue & red 3.50 2.00

Satellite Communications — A139

1994, June 23   Litho.
456 A139 10fr multicolored 2.40 1.75

1994 World Cup Soccer Championships, U.S. — A140

1994, June 23
457 A140 105fr multicolored 3.25 2.00

Princesses Ouveennes, 1903 — A141

1994, July 21   Engr.   Perf. 13
458 A141 90fr blue grn, blk & red 2.50 1.50

Symbols of Playing Cards Suits — A142

1994, Aug. 25   Litho.   Perf. 13
459 A142 40fr multicolored 1.40 .70

Ultra-Light Aircraft — A143

1994, Aug. 25
460 A143 5fr multicolored .35 .35

Coconut — A144

1994, Oct. 13   Litho.   Perf. 13
461 A144 36fr multicolored 1.25 .70

Parrots
A145

1994, Nov. 17   Litho.   Perf. 13x13½
462 A145 62fr multicolored   2.00 1.25

Grand Lodge of France, Cent. — A146

1994, Nov. 24   Engr.   Perf. 13
463 A146 250fr multicolored   6.50 4.50

Preparing Traditional Meal — A147

1995, Jan. 25   Litho.   Perf. 13
464 A147 80fr multicolored   2.40 1.40

Aerial View
of Islands
A148

1995, Feb. 21   Perf. 13x13½, 13½x13
465 A148 85fr Nukulaelae   2.25 1.25
466 A148 90fr Nukufetau, vert.   2.50 1.40
467 A148 100fr Nukufotu,
                  Nukuloa   2.75 1.90
     Nos. 465-467 (3)   7.50 4.55

Mua
College — A149

1995, Apr. 11   Perf. 12
468 A149 35fr multicolored   1.10   .70

UN, 50th Anniv. — A150

1995, June 26   Litho.   Perf. 13½
469 A150 55fr multicolored   1.60 1.00

10th South Pacific Games — A151

1995, Aug. 1   Litho.   Perf. 13
470 A151 70fr multicolored   1.90 1.40

Local
Plants — A152

1995, Oct. 24   Litho.   Perf. 13½x13
471 A152 20fr Breadfruit tree   .70   .55
472 A152 60fr Tarot   1.60 1.00
473 A152 65fr Kava   2.00 1.40
     Nos. 471-473 (3)   4.30 2.95
     See Nos. 478-481, 484-485.

Tapa — A153

1995, Dec. 12   Litho.   Perf. 13
474 A153 25fr Native life, vert.   .80   .70
475 A153 26fr Fish, sea shells   1.00   .70

Mothers from the
Islands — A154

1996, Jan. 14   Litho.   Perf. 13½x13
476 A154 80fr multicolored   2.25 1.50

Golf
A155

1996, Jan. 24   Perf. 13
477 A155 95fr multicolored   3.50 2.00

Local Plant Type of 1995
1996   Litho.   Perf. 13½x13
478 A152 27fr Cananga odorata   .80   .70
479 A152 28fr Mahoaa   .90   .70
480 A152 45fr Hibiscus   1.25   .80
481 A152 52fr Ufi   1.60 1.00
     Nos. 478-481 (4)   4.55 3.20

Issued: #479, 481, 3/14; #478, 480, 6/20.

Sanglants Swamp — A156

1996, June 26   Perf. 13
482 A156 53fr multicolored   1.60 1.00

Chess — A157

1996, July 17
483 A157 110fr multicolored   3.25 2.00

Local Plant Type of 1995
Designs: 30fr, 48fr, Calladium.

1996, Sept. 17   Litho.   Perf. 13½x13
Background Color
484 A152 30fr blue green   1.00   .70
485 A152 48fr lilac   1.40   .90

Francoise Perroton,
Missionary — A158

1996, Oct. 25   Perf. 13
486 A158 50fr multicolored   1.50 1.00

UNICEF,
50th Anniv.
A159

1996, Dec. 4   Litho.   Perf. 13
487 A159 25fr multicolored   .90   .70

CPS, 50th
Anniv.
A160

1997, Feb. 6   Litho.   Perf. 13
488 A160 7fr multicolored   .35   .35

Royal
Standards
A161

1997, Feb. 14   Litho.   Perf. 13x13½
489 A161 56fr King Lavelua   1.40 1.00
490 A161 60fr King Tuiagaifo   1.40 1.00
491 A161 70fr King Tuisigave   1.90 1.00
     Nos. 489-491 (3)   4.70 3.00

Brasseur de
Kava — A162

1997, Apr. 17   Perf. 13½x13
492 A162 170fr multicolored   4.00 2.75

Island
Scenes
A163

Designs: 10fr, Old man telling stories to children seated around campfire. 36fr, Braiding
mat, vert. 40fr, Preparing "Kai'umu" (feast).

Perf. 13x13½, 13½x13
1997, May 20   Litho.
493 A163 10fr multicolored   .35   .35
494 A163 36fr multicolored   1.00   .80
495 A163 40fr multicolored   1.10   .80
     Nos. 493-495 (3)   2.45 1.95

Green
Lagoon
Turtles
A164

1997, June 18   Perf. 13x13½
496 A164 62fr Crawling ashore   1.75 1.00
497 A164 80fr Swimming   2.25 1.40

Festival of Avignon — A165

1997, July 31   Litho.   Perf. 13
498 A165 160fr multicolored   4.40 2.40

Berlin
Handicapped
Sports
Festival — A166

1997, Aug. 12
499 A166 35fr multicolored   1.10   .70

D'Uvéa Karate Club — A167

1997, Oct. 15   Litho.   Perf. 13x13½
500   A167   24fr multicolored   1.00   .50

Fight Against
AIDS — A168

1997, Dec. 1   Litho.   Perf. 13
501   A168   5fr multicolored   1.50   .35

Christmas — A169

1997, Dec. 24
502   A169   85fr Nativity   2.25   1.50

Preparation of UMU — A170

1998, Jan. 26
503   A170   800fr multicolored   16.50   11.00

Orchids — A171

70fr, Vanda T.M.A.. 85fr, Cattleya bow bells.
90fr, Arachnis. 105fr, Cattleya.

1998, Feb. 18   Litho.   Perf. 13
504   A171   70fr multi, vert.   1.90   1.00
505   A171   85fr multi   2.25   1.25
506   A171   90fr multi, vert.   2.40   1.25
507   A171   105fr multi   2.75   1.50
      Nos. 504-507 (4)   9.30   5.00

Telecom 2000 — A172

1998, Mar. 24   Litho.   Perf. 13
508   A172   7fr multicolored   .40   .40

Fishing — A173

Designs: 50fr, Fisherman casting net into
lagoon. 52fr, Fisherman sorting catch.

1998, May 26   Litho.   Perf. 13
509   A173   50fr multicolored   1.40   .70
510   A173   52fr multicolored   1.40   .70

1998 World Cup Soccer
Championships, France — A174

1998, June 10
511   A174   80fr multicolored   2.10   1.40

Insects
A175

1998, July 21   Litho.   Perf. 13x13½
512   A175   36fr Dragonfly   1.00   .50
513   A175   40fr Cicada   1.10   .70

Coral — A176

Various corals: a, 4fr. b, 5fr. c, 10fr. d, 15fr.

1998   Litho.   Perf. 13x13½
514   A176   Strip of 4, #a.-d.   1.50   1.50

52nd Autumn Philatelic Salon — A177

1998, Nov. 5   Litho.   Perf. 13½
515   A177   175fr multicolored   4.75   2.50

World Fight
Against
AIDS
A178

1998, Dec. 1   Perf. 13
516   A178   62fr multicolored   1.60   1.00

Islet of
Nuku
Taakimoa
A179

1999, Mar. 22   Litho.   Perf. 13
517   A179   130fr multicolored   3.50   1.80
      See No. 594.

Souvenir Sheet

Lagoon Life — A180

a, 20fr, Various fish. b, 855fr, Fish, diver.

1999, May 17   Litho.   Perf. 13
518   A180   Sheet of 2, #a.-b.   24.00   22.50

PhilexFrance '99, World Philatelic
Exhibition — A181

1999, July 2   Litho.   Perf. 13
519   A181   200fr multicolored   5.50   3.25

French Senate, Bicent. — A182

1999, Sept. 20   Engr.   Perf. 13
520   A182   125fr multi   3.50   2.00

Territorial Assembly Building — A183

1999, Aug. 23   Litho.
521   A183   17fr multi   .45   .35

Pandanus
A184

1999, Oct. 18
522   A184   25fr multi   .70   .45

Man
Making
Canoe
A185

1999, Nov. 8
523   A185   55fr multi   1.50   .80

French Postage Stamps, 150th
Anniv. — A186

1999, Dec. 1
524   A186   65fr Wallis & Futuna
            #86   1.75   1.00

Millennium — A187

2000, Jan. 1   Litho.   Perf. 13
525   A187   350fr multi   9.50   4.50

Mata'utu
Cathedral
A188

2000, Apr. 28   Photo.   Perf. 13x13¼
526   A188   300fr multi   8.00   3.75

Patrol Boat "La Glorieuse" — A189

2000, June 5 **Engr.** *Perf. 13x12¾*
527 A189 155fr multi   4.25 2.40

Sosefo Papilio
Makape, First
Senator — A190

2000, June 19 *Perf. 12¾x13*
528 A190 115fr multi   3.00 1.50

Overseas Broadcasting
Institute — A191

2000, July 3 *Perf. 13x12½*
529 A191 200fr multi   5.50 2.50

Taro
Cultivation
A192

2000, July 27 **Litho.** *Perf. 13*
530 A192 275fr multi   7.50 3.50

Souvenir Sheet

2000 Summer Olympics,
Sydney — A193

Traditional games, 85fr: a, Spear throwing.
b, Sailing. c, Rowing. d, Volleyball.

2000, Sept. 15 **Litho.** *Perf. 13*
531 A193 #a-d + 2 labels   9.00 9.00

8th Pacific
Arts
Festival
A194

2000, Oct. 23 *Perf. 13x13¼*
532 A194 330fr multi   9.00 4.50

Fish — A195

No. 533: a, Coryphaena hippurus. b, Caranx
melanpygyus. c, Thunnus albacares.

2000, Nov. 9 **Litho.** *Perf. 13*
533   Vert. strip of 3 + 2 la-
      bels   9.25 9.25
a.-c.   A195 115fr Any single   3.10 1.75

Canonization of St. Marcellin
Champagnat, 1st Anniv. — A196

2000, Nov. 13
534 A196 380fr multi   10.00 5.00

Talietumu Archaeological Site — A197

2000, Dec. 1 *Perf. 13x13½*
535 A197 205fr multi   5.50 2.75

Christmas
A198

2000, Dec. 25 *Perf. 13*
536 A198 225fr multi   6.00 2.75

Ship "Jacques Cartier" — A199

2001, Feb. 26 **Engr.** *Perf. 13*
537 A199 225fr multi   6.00 2.75

Campaign Against
Alcoholism
A200

2001, Mar. 14 **Litho.** *Perf. 13¼x13*
538 A200 75fr multi   2.00 1.00

Souvenir Sheet

Tapas — A201

Tapa with: a, Large diamond, shells, map of
islands. b, Triangles and diamonds. c, Scenes
of native life, fish, shells, boat. d, Overlapping
ovals.

2001, Apr. 14 *Perf. 13*
539 A201 90fr Sheet of 4, #a-d, +
      2 labels   9.75 9.75

Children's Drawings of
Flowers — A202

2001, May 31
540   Horiz. strip of 4   8.25 8.25
a.   A202 50fr multi   1.40 1.40
b.   A202 55fr multi   1.50 1.50
c.   A202 95fr multi   2.50 2.50
d.   A202 100fr multi   2.75 2.75

Territorial
Status, 40th
Anniv.
A203

2001, July 29 **Litho.** *Perf. 13*
541 A203 165fr multi   4.50 2.00

Installation
of Mediator,
1st Anniv.
A204

2001, Sept. 26
542 A204 800fr multi   22.00 10.00

Year of
Dialogue
Among
Civilizations
A205

2001, Oct. 9
543 A205 390fr multi   10.50 5.00

5th Autumn
Salon — A206

Birds: a, Dacula pacifica. b, Vini australis. c,
Tyto alba.

2001, Nov. 8
544   Vert. strip of 3 + 2
      labels   12.00 12.00
a.-c.   A206 150fr Any single   4.00 3.00

Children's
Drawings
of Fruit
A207

No. 545, 65fr: a, Custard apple (pomme
canelle). b, Breadfruit (fruit de pain).
No. 546, 65fr: a, Pineapple. b, Mango.

2001, Aug. 22 **Litho.** *Perf. 13*
Vert. Pairs, #a-b
545-546 A207   Set of 2 pairs   7.00 5.00

Tomb of Futuna King
Fakavelikele — A208

2001, Dec. 28 **Litho.** *Perf. 13*
547 A208 325fr multi   9.00 3.75

Finemui-Teesi College — A209

2002, Jan. 29   **Perf. 13x13½**
548 A209 115fr multi   3.00 1.40

Intl. Women's Day — A210

2002, Mar. 5   **Litho.**   **Perf. 13**
549 A210 800fr Queen Aloisia   22.00 10.00

Arms of Bishop Pompallier A211

2002, Apr. 19   **Engr.**   **Perf. 13¼**
550 A211 500fr multi   13.50 6.50

Uvea Firefighters A212

Serpentine Die Cut
2002, Apr. 28   **Photo.**
Self-Adhesive
551 A212 85fr multi   2.25 1.40

2002 World Cup Soccer Championships, Japan and Korea — A213

2002, May 31   **Litho.**   **Perf. 13**
552 A213 65fr multi   1.75 1.00

World Environment Day — A214

2002, June 5   **Perf. 13x13½**
553 A214 330fr multi   9.00 4.00

Traditional Buildings A215

Designs: No. 554, 50fr, Building with overhanging roof. No. 555, 50fr, Open-air shelter, vert. No. 556, 55fr, Building with two entryways. No. 557, 55fr, Building with ladder to roof, vert.

2002, Aug. 9   **Engr.**   **Perf. 13¼**
554-557 A215   Set of 4   5.75 2.50

Discovery of the Horn Islands, 1616 A216

No. 558: a, Jacob Lemaire and compass rose. b, Map of Futuna and Alofi Islands. c, William Schouten and ship.

2002, Aug. 30   **Litho.**   **Perf. 13x13¼**
558   Horiz. strip of 3   10.00 10.00
   a.-c.   A216 125fr any single   3.25 3.25
   d.   Souvenir sheet, #558   10.00 10.00

Landscapes A217

No. 559: a, Utua Bay. b, Liku Bay. c, Kingfisher at Vele. d, Aka'Aka Bay.

2002, Sept. 20
559   Horiz. strip of 4   11.50 11.50
   a.   A217 95fr multi   2.50 1.50
   b.   A217 100fr multi   2.75 1.50
   c.   A217 105fr multi   2.75 1.60
   d.   A217 135fr multi   3.50 1.75

Enygrus Bibroni — A218

2002, Oct. 28   **Litho.**   **Perf. 13¼x13**
560 A218 75fr multi   2.00 .75

Fish A219

No. 561: a, Dendrochirus biocellatus. b, Discordipina griessingeri. c, Antennacius nummifer. d, Novaculichthys taeniourus.

2002, Nov. 7   **Perf. 13x13¼**
561   Vert. strip of 4 + 3 labels   10.00 9.00
   a.-d.   A219 110fr Any single   3.00 1.75

Best Wishes A220

2002, Dec. 5
562 A220 140fr multi   3.75 1.40

Last Avro Lancaster Flight to Wallis, 40th Anniv. A221

2003, Jan. 26   **Perf. 13**
563 A221 135fr multi   3.60 1.75

St. Valentine's Day — A222

2003, Feb. 14   **Perf. 13**
564 A222 85fr multi   2.25 1.00

Introduction of the Euro, 1st Anniv. A223

2003, Feb. 17   **Perf. 12½x12¾**
565 A223 125fr multi   3.25 1.80

Values are for examples with surrounding selvage.

Alain Gerbault (1893-1941), Circumnavigator, Aboard Boat "Firecrest" — A224

2003, Mar. 6   **Engr.**   **Perf. 13¼**
566 A224 600fr grn & ol grn   16.00 8.00

Postal Art — A225

Various designs.

2003, Mar. 31   **Litho.**   **Perf. 13**
567   Horiz. strip of 5   2.40 2.40
   a.   A225 5fr multi   .25 .25
   b.   A225 10fr multi   .25 .25
   c.   A225 15fr multi   .40 .40
   d.   A225 20fr multi   .55 .25
   e.   A225 40fr multi   1.10 .40

Coral Reefs A226

Various views.

2003, Apr. 10   **Perf. 13x13¼**
568   Horiz. strip of 4   10.00 10.00
   a.   A226 95fr multi   1.75 1.75
   b.   A226 105fr multi   1.90 1.90
   c.   A226 110fr multi   2.00 2.00
   d.   A226 115fr multi   2.10 2.10

St. Pierre Chanel (1803-41), Martyred Missionary A227

2003, Apr. 28   **Engr.**   **Perf. 12¼**
569 A227 130fr multi   3.50 1.80

2003 Census — A228

2003, June 12   **Litho.**   **Perf. 13**
570 A228 55fr multi   1.50 .70

Pacific Legends A229

Legend of the Coconut Palm: 30fr, Eel. 50fr, Coconut palms, split coconut. 60fr, Split and whole coconuts. 70fr, Coconut palms and clouds.

2003, July 28   **Litho.**   **Perf. 13x13¼**
571   Horiz. strip of 4   5.75 5.75
   a.   A229 30fr multi   .80 .40
   b.   A229 50fr multi   1.40 .75
   c.   A229 60fr multi   1.60 .85
   d.   A229 70fr multi   1.90 .95
   e.   Souvenir sheet, #571a-571d   6.00 6.00

Still Life with Maori Statuette, by Paul Gauguin (1848-1903) A230

No. 573a: Study of Heads of Tahitian Women, by Gauguin.

2003   **Perf. 13**
572 A230 100fr multi   2.75 1.60
    Souvenir Sheet
573   Sheet, #572, 573a   5.50 5.50
   a.   A230 100fr multi   2.75 2.25

Issued: No. 572, 7/31; No. 573, 8/20. See New Caledonia No. 929.

Futuna Waterfalls — A231

2003, Aug. 6   **Perf. 13¼x13¼**
574 A231 115fr multi   3.00 1.75

Frigate Le
Nivose
A232

2003, Sept. 15   Engr.   Perf. 13¼
575 A232 325fr multi   8.75 4.00

Bishop Alexandre
Poncet (1884-
1973)
A233

2003, Sept. 18   Engr.   Perf. 13¼
576 A233 205fr multi   5.50 3.00

Arms of Bishop
Pierre Bataillon
(1810-77) — A234

2003, Oct. 1   Litho.   Perf. 13¼
577 A234 500fr multi   13.50 7.00

2003 Rugby
World Cup,
Australia
A235

2003, Oct. 10   Perf. 13
578 A235 65fr multi   1.75 .85

Parinari
Insularum
A236

2003, Nov. 6   Litho.   Perf. 13¼x13
579 A236 250fr multi   6.75 3.50

Goddess Havea
Hikule'o — A237

2004, Jan. 8
580 A237 85fr multi   2.25 1.40

People in
Canoe
A238

2004, Jan. 13   Perf. 13
581 A238 75fr multi   2.00 1.25

Miniature Sheet

Campaign Against Dengue
Fever — A239

No. 582: a, 5fr, Mosquito, crying man. b,
10fr, Mosquitos, man. c, 20fr, Mosquitos,
trash. d, 30fr, Mosquitos, sleeping child.

Perf. 13¼x12¾
2004, Feb. 18   Litho.
582 A239 Sheet of 4, #a-d   2.25 2.25

Badminton
A240

2004, Mar. 12   Perf. 13¼x13
583 A240 55fr multi   1.50 1.25

Kava
Drinkers
A241

2004, Mar. 31   Perf. 13x13¼
584 A241 205fr multi   5.50 4.25

Flora
A242

2004, Apr. 22   Perf. 13
585   Horiz. strip of 4 + central
           label   3.25 3.25
  a. A242 15fr Colocasia esculenta   .40   .30
  b. A242 25fr Carrica papaya   .65   .50
  c. A242 35fr Artocarpus altilus   .95   .70
  d. A242 40fr Dioscorea sp.   1.10   .80

Dispatch
Boat
Savorgnan
de Brazza
A243

Gourdou-Leseurre GL 832 Hy No. 5
and Wallis Island — A244

2004, May 12   Engr.   Perf. 13¼
586 A243 300fr multi   8.00 6.00
587 A244 380fr multi   10.25 7.75

Souvenir Sheet
Litho.
588   Sheet of 2   18.50 18.50
  a. A243 300fr multi   8.00 6.00
  b. A244 380fr multi   9.50 7.75

First flight over Wallis Island, 68th anniv.

Seaweeds — A245

2004, June 26   Litho.   Perf. 13
589   Horiz. strip of 3 + 2 al-
           ternating labels   17.50 17.50
  a. A245 105fr Turbinaria ornata   2.90 2.90
  b. A245 155fr Padina melemele   4.25 4.25
  c. A245 175fr Tubinaria concoides   4.75 4.75

Miniature Sheet

Flowers — A246

No. 590: a, Hibiscus rosa-sinensis. b,
Cananga odorata. c, Plumeria rubra. d,
Ipomeapes caprae. e, Gardenia taitensis.

Serpentine Die Cut 14
2004, June 26   Photo.
Self-Adhesive
590 A246 Sheet of 5   12.50 12.50
  a.-d.   85fr Any single   2.25 2.25
  e.   115fr multi   3.00 3.00

Salon du Timbre 2004, Paris.

Ninth
Pacific Arts
Festival,
Palau
A247

2004, July 22   Litho.   Perf. 13x13¼
591 A247 200fr multi   5.50 4.25

Pili'uli Lizard — A248

2004, July 26   Perf. 13
592 A248 100fr multi   2.75 2.10

Arms of
Monsignor Louis
Elloy (1829-78)
A249

2004, Sept. 6   Engr.   Perf. 13¼
593 A249 500fr multi   13.50 10.50

No. 517 Redrawn
2004, Nov. 10   Litho.   Perf. 13
594 A179 115fr multi   3.10 2.50

No. 594 shows a 115fr denomination below
an obliterated 130fr denomination, the denomination shown on No. 517. This new denomination is not overprinted. No. 594 also has a
2004 year date, rather than an obliterated
1999 year date.

A250

Traditional
Houses — A251

2004, Nov. 11   Perf. 13¼x13
595 A250 95fr multi   2.50 2.10
596 A251 130fr multi   3.50 3.00

Nos. 595-596 were printed in sheets containing four of each stamp plus a large central
label.

Miniature Sheet

Cone Shells — A252

No. 597: a, Conus eburneus. b, Conus
imperialis. c, Conus generalis. d, Gastridium
textile.

2005, Jan. 26   Perf. 13x13¼
597 A252 55fr Sheet of 4, #a-d   6.00 5.00

Miniature Sheet

Contes et Légendes de Wallis et Futuna

Stories and Legends — A253

No. 598: a, 65fr, Whale, bird, crab, eel, turtle. b, 65fr, Fish, octopus, dolphin, butterfly. c, 75fr, Boy, waves, G clef and musical notes. d, 75fr, Musical notes, butterflies.

			Perf. 13
2005, Jan. 31			
598	A253	Sheet of 4, #a-d	7.50 7.50

Pirogue
A254

			Perf. 13x13¼
2005, Feb. 25	Litho.		
599	A254	330fr multi	9.00 7.50

Francophone Week — A255

2005, Mar. 17			
600	A255	135fr multi	3.60 3.00

Printed in sheets of 10 + 5 labels. See New Caledonia No. 959.

Family
Budget
Inquiry
A256

			Perf. 12¾
2005, Mar. 31			
601	A256	205fr multi	5.50 4.50

Values are for stamps with surrounding selvage.

Warriors — A257

			Perf. 13½x13
2005, Apr. 19			
602		Horiz. strip of 5	3.25 3.25
a.	A257	5fr blk, red & maroon	.25 .25
b.	A257	10fr blk, bl & vio blue	.25 .25
c.	A257	20fr blk, pur & indigo	.55 .40
d.	A257	30fr blk & red	.80 .65
e.	A257	50fr blk, lt grn & emerald	1.40 1.10

Traditional
Cricket
A258

			Perf. 13
2005, May 16			
603	A258	190fr multi	5.00 4.00

Butterflies — A259

No. 604: a, 40fr, Papilio montrouzieri. b, 60fr, Danaus pumila.

			Perf. 13x13¼
2005, June 30			
604	A259	Horiz. pair, #a-b	2.75 2.75

Warrior With
Spear — A260

Serpentine Die Cut 11
2005, July 14
Booklet Stamp
Self-Adhesive

605	A260	115fr multi	3.00 2.40
a.		Booklet pane of 10	30.00

Historical Images of Wallis
Island — A261

2005, July 14	Engr.	**Perf. 13x13¼**
606		Horiz. pair + central label 9.00 9.00
a.	A261 155fr Village scene	4.25 3.25
b.	A261 175fr Family, house	4.75 3.75

First Noumea to Hihifo Flight, 58th
Anniv. — A262

2005, Aug. 19			
607	A262	380fr multi	10.00 8.00

Souvenir Sheet

Chelomia Mydas — A263

No. 608 — Green turtle: a, Adult entering water. b, Hatchlings entering water. c, Head. d, Swimming underwater.

2005, Aug. 19	Litho.	**Perf. 13x13¼**
608	A263 85fr Sheet of 4, #a-d	9.25 9.25

Arms of
Monsignor Jean
Armand Lamaze
(1833-1906)
A264

2005, Oct. 5	Engr.	**Perf. 13¼**
609	A264 500fr multi	13.50 10.00

Spattoglottis Cinguiculata — A265

2005, Oct. 30	Litho.	**Perf. 13**
610	A265 100fr multi	2.75 2.00

Printed in sheets of 10 + 5 labels.

Design of Wallis
and Futuna Islands
No. 4 — A266

Design of
Wallis and
Futuna
Islands No.
87 — A267

2005, Nov. 10	Litho.	**Perf. 13x13¼**
611	A266 150fr multi	4.00 3.00
612	A267 150fr multi	4.00 3.00

59th Autumn Philatelic Show.

Native
Child
A268

2006, Mar. 29	Litho.	**Perf. 13x13¼**
613	A268 75fr multi	2.00 1.60

Monarchical
Flags — A269

Designs: 55fr, Kingdom of Uvea. 65fr, Kingdom of Sigave. 85fr, Kingdom of Alo.

2006 Litho. ***Serpentine Die Cut 11***
Self-Adhesive
Booklet Stamps

614	A269	55fr multi	1.50 1.25
a.		Booklet pane of 10	15.00
615	A269	65fr multi	1.75 1.40
a.		Booklet pane of 10	17.50
616	A269	85fr multi	2.25 1.75
a.		Booklet pane of 10	22.50

Issued: 55fr, 6/17; 65fr, 4/18; 85fr, 3/29.

Haka Mai — A270

2006			**Perf. 13¼x13**
617	A270	190fr multi	5.00 4.25

Removal of
Christ from the
Cross, by Jean
Soane Michon
(1926-68)
A271

2006, May 31	Litho.	**Perf. 13¼x13**
618	A271 400fr multi	11.00 8.50

2006 World Cup
Soccer
Championships,
Germany
A272

2006, June 9			
619	A272	100fr multi	2.75 2.10

Mata Vai
A273

Mata Tai
A274

2006, June 17   *Perf. 13x13¼*
620 A273 140fr multi   3.75 3.00
621 A274 200fr multi   5.50 4.25

Historical Images From the 19th
Century — A275

2006, July 13   Engr.   Perf. 13x13¼
622   Horiz. pair + central la-
           bel   19.50 19.50
  a. A275 330fr Girls dancing   9.00 7.00
  b. A275 380fr Mua Church   10.00 8.00

Stamp
Day — A276

2006, Aug. 5   Litho.   Perf. 13¼x13
623 A276 150fr multi   4.00 3.25

Twin Otter Airplane "Ville de Paris",
20th Anniv. — A277

2006, Aug. 7   *Perf. 13*
624 A277 30fr multi   .80   .65

Territorial Rugby Committee — A278

2006, Sept. 9   *Perf. 12¾x13½*
625 A278 10fr multi   .25   .25

Uhilamoafa
Gravesite
A279

2006, Sept. 12   *Perf. 13x13¼*
626 A279 290fr multi   7.75 6.25

Arms of
Monsignor
Joseph Félix
Blanc (1872-
1962)
A280

2006, Oct. 5   Engr.   Perf. 13¼
627 A280 500fr multi   13.50 10.50

Tagaloa,
Polynesian
Deity — A281

2006, Nov. 8   Litho.   Perf. 13½x13
628 A281 150fr multi   4.00 3.50

Tapas
A282

No. 629: a, Tapas design (shown). b, Mako
à Ono. c, Tauasu à Leava. d, Tapas design,
diff.

Litho. & Engr.
2006, Nov. 8   *Perf. 13x13¼*
629   Vert. strip of 4 + cen-
           tral label   9.25 9.25
  a.-d. A282 85fr Any single   2.25 1.90

Souvenir Sheet

Christmas — A283

2006, Nov. 8   Litho.   Perf. 13
630 A283 225fr multi   6.00 6.00

Pio Cardinal
Taofinu'u (1923-
2006)
A284

2007, Jan. 19   Engr.   Perf. 12½x13
631 A284 800fr multi   21.50 17.50

Telemedicine
A285

2007, Feb. 28   Litho.   Perf. 13¼x13
632 A285 5fr multi   .25   .25

Audit
Office,
Bicent.
A286

2007, Mar. 19   Engr.   Perf. 13¼
633 A286 105fr multi   2.75 2.40

Woman
A287

2007, Mar. 22   Litho.   Perf. 13
634 A287 75fr multi   2.00 1.75

First Noumea-Hihifo Air Service, 50th
Anniv. — A288

2007, Apr. 30   Engr.   Perf. 13x12½
635 A288 290fr multi   6.75 6.75

Fish — A289

2007, May 22   Litho.   Perf. 12¾x13¼
636   Horiz. pair   2.00 2.00
  a. A289 40fr Eviota   .90   .90
  b. A289 50fr Trimma   1.10 1.10

Secretary
General of the
Pacific
Community, 60th
Anniv. — A290

2007, June 28   Litho.   Perf. 13
637 A290 155fr multi   3.50 3.50

Lolesio Tuita,
Javelin Thrower
A291

2007, July 30   Engr.   Perf. 12½x13
638 A291 330fr purple & red   7.50 7.50

Buildings — A292

No. 639: a, House, Tamana. b, Sanctuary of
Pierre Chanel, Poi.

2007, July 31   Engr.   Perf. 13x13¼
639   Horiz. pair with central
           label   9.00 9.00
  a. A292 190fr brown   4.25 4.25
  b. A292 200fr brown   4.75 4.75

Discovery of
Uvea Island by
Samuel Wallis,
240th
Anniv. — A293

2007, Aug. 3   *Litho.*
640 A293 225fr multi   5.25 5.25
  a.   Souvenir sheet of 1   5.50 5.50

No. 640a sold for 240fr.

Legends of
Lomipeau
A294

No. 641 — People and: a, Togitapu Island.
b, Uvea Island.

2007, Aug. 3
641   Horiz. pair   1.25 1.25
  a. A294 20fr multi   .50   .50
  b. A294 30fr multi   .75   .75

Arms of
Monsignor
Armand Olier
(1851-1911)
A295

2007, Oct. 22   Engr.   Perf. 13¼
642 A295 500fr multi   12.50 12.50

Emblem of Handisport A296

2007, Oct. 11   Photo.   Perf. 12¾
643 A296 10fr multi   .25   .25
Values are for stamps with surrounding selvage.

2007 Rugby World Cup Championships, France — A297

2007, Oct. 20   Litho.   Perf. 13
644 A297 205fr multi   5.00 5.00
Printed in sheets of 10 + label.

Dances — A298

Designs: No. 645, 100fr, Mio dance, Futuna.
No. 646, 100fr, Kailao Tokotoko dance, Wallis.

2007, Nov. 10   Litho.   Perf. 13¼x13
645-646 A298   Set of 2   5.00 5.00

Connection to the Internet, 10th Anniv. A299

2008, Mar. 3   Litho.   Perf. 13x13¼
647 A299 55fr multi   1.50 1.50
Printed in sheets of 10 + central label.

Coral Reef A300

2008, Mar. 7
648 A300 95fr multi   2.50 2.50

Islands — A301

No. 649: a, Uvea. b, Futuna and Alofi, horiz.

Perf. 13¼x13 (#649a), 13x13¼ (#649b)
2008, Mar. 7
649 A301 85fr Pair, #a-b   4.50 4.50
Printed in sheets containing four of each stamp.

Women and Hibiscus Flowers — A302

2008, Mar. 7   Perf. 13
650 A302 65fr multi   1.75 1.75
Printed in sheets of 10 + 5 labels.

2008 Summer Olympics, Beijing A303

2008, June 14   Perf. 13x13¼
651 A303 75fr multi   2.00 2.00

Intl. Year of Planet Earth — A304

2008, June 14   Perf. 13
652 A304 190fr multi   5.00 5.00
Souvenir Sheet
653 A304 200fr multi   5.25 5.25

King Tomasi Kulimoetoke II (1918-2007) A305

2008, July 29   Engr.   Perf. 13¼
654 A305 380fr orange brown   9.75 9.75

Aglaia Psilopetala A306

2008, July 30   Litho.   Perf. 13
655 A306 105fr multi   2.75 2.75

Historical Images of Futuna — A307

No. 656: a, Women braiding straw. b, Boats returning to island.

2008, July 30   Engr.   Perf. 13x13¼
656   Horiz. pair with central label   6.75 6.75
  a. A307 110fr brown   2.75 2.75
  b. A307 155fr brown   4.00 4.00

Stained-glass Windows of Lano Church — A308

Designs: 100fr, St. Theresa. 140fr, St. Peter Chanel.

2008, July 31   Litho.   Perf. 13
657-658 A308   Set of 2   6.00 6.00

Pirogue Hulls A309

Various painted pirogue hulls.

2008, Aug. 18   Perf. 13x13¼
659   Horiz. strip of 4   2.75 2.75
  a. A309 5fr multi   .25   .25
  b. A309 20fr multi   .50   .50
  c. A309 40fr multi   .95   .95
  d. A309 50fr multi   1.10 1.10

Lolesio Tuita Stadium A310

2008, Oct. 28
660 A310 55fr multi   1.25 1.25

Arms of Monsignor Alexandre Poncet (1884-1973) A311

2008, Oct. 28   Engr.   Perf. 13¼
661 A311 500fr multi   11.00 11.00

World Youth Day — A312

2008, Nov. 8   Litho.   Perf. 13¼x13
662 A312 10fr multi   .25   .25

Pigs — A313

No. 663 — Pigs on farm with denomination at: a, UL. b, UR.

2008, Nov. 8   Perf. 13x13¼
663 A313 115fr Horiz. pair, #a-b   5.00 5.00

Fifth French Republic, 50th Anniv. A314

2008, Nov. 8   Engr.   Perf. 13¼
664 A314 225fr multi   5.00 5.00

Louis Braille (1809-52), Educator of the Blind — A315

2009, Mar. 7   Engr.   Perf. 12¾x13
665 A315 330fr multi   7.50 7.50

Bougainvillea Spectabilis — A316

Flowers with background colors of: No. 666, 55fr, Black. No. 667, 55fr, Green. No. 668, 55fr, Red. No. 669, 55fr, White.

2009, May 4   Litho.   Perf. 13
666-669 A316   Set of 4   5.25 5.25

Gobies — A317

No. 670: a, Akihito futuna. b, Stiphodon rubromaculatus.

2009, May 7   Perf. 12¾x13¼
670   Horiz. pair   3.00 3.00
  a.-b. A317 65fr Either single   1.50 1.50

St. Theresa of
Lisieux (1873-97)
A318

Phil@poste at bottom in: No. 671, White
(brown border at bottom). No. 672, Black
(brown border at top).

2009, June 27   Perf. 13½x13
671 A318 140fr multi   3.25 3.25
672 A318 140fr multi   3.25 3.25

New Year 2009,
(Year of the
Ox) — A319

2009, June 30   Perf. 13¼x13
673 A319 95fr multi   2.25 2.25

Pétanque Playing
in Wallis &
Futuna
Islands — A320

2009, July 31
674 A320 105fr multi   2.50 2.50

Arms of Bishop
Michel
Darmancier
(1918-84)
A321

2009, Oct. 30   Engr.   Perf. 13¼
675 A321 500fr multi   12.50 12.50

Historical Images — A322

No. 676: a, France House. b, Army of
Wallisians.

2009, Nov. 5   Perf. 13x13¼
676   Horiz. pair + central label   9.50 9.50
a.-b. A322 190fr Either single   4.75 4.75

Man Preparing
Kava — A323

2009, Nov. 12   Litho.   Perf. 13¼x13
677 A323 115fr multi   3.00 3.00

Eiffel Tower on
Tapa
Cloth — A324

2009, Dec. 8   Perf. 13x13¼
678 A324 85fr brown & black   2.10 2.10

Wallis & Futuna
Islands as
French Overseas
Territory, 50th
Anniv. — A325

2009, Dec. 27   Engr.   Perf. 13¼
679 A325 205fr multi   5.00 5.00

Arrival of First Doctors on Futuna
Island, 50th Anniv. — A326

2010, Jan. 3   Litho.   Perf. 13
680 A326 800fr multi   18.50 18.50

Gobies — A327

2010, Feb. 19   Perf. 12¾x13¼
681   Horiz. pair   2.75 2.75
a. A327 50fr Sicyopus sasali   1.25 1.25
b. A327 65fr Stenogobius keletaona   1.50 1.50

A328

A329

A330

Coral
Reefs
A331

2010, Mar. 12   Litho.   Perf. 13x13¼
682   Horiz. strip of 4   2.40 2.40
a. A328 10fr multi   .25 .25
b. A329 20fr multi   .45 .45
c. A330 30fr multi   .70 .70
d. A331 40fr multi   .95 .95

Easter — A332

2010, Apr. 2
683 A332 135fr multi   3.25 3.25

Mother's
Day
A333

2010, May 28   Perf. 13
684 A333 105fr multi   2.25 2.25

Renewable Energy — A334

No. 685: a, Solar panels on ground. b, Solar
panels on roof.

2010, June 11
685   Horiz. pair + central label   16.50 16.50
a.-b. A334 400fr Either single   8.25 8.25

Arms of Bishop
Lolesio
Fuahea — A335

2010, July 16   Engr.   Perf. 13¼
686 A335 500fr multi   11.00 11.00

First Flight to Vele, 40th
Anniv. — A336

2010, Aug. 24   Litho.   Perf. 13¼x13
687 A336 100fr multi   2.25 2.25

Traditional Group Fishing — A337

2010, Sept. 24
688 A337 205fr brown   4.75 4.75

Depictions of the Elements — A338

No. 689: a, Water. b, Fire.

2010, Oct. 15   Perf. 13
689 A338 150fr Horiz. pair, #a-b   7.00 7.00

Christmas
A339

2010, Dec. 24   Litho.   Perf. 13
690 A339 95fr multi   2.25 2.25

Cicada — A340

2011, Jan. 17
691 A340 55fr multi   1.25 1.25

Arms of Bishop
Ghislain Marie
Raoul Suzanne
de
Rasilly — A341

2011, Feb. 19   Engr.   Perf. 13¼
692 A341 500fr multi   12.00 12.00

French Navy Ship Jacques Cartier, Relief Ship for Victims of Tropical Cyclone Tomas — A342

2011, Mar. 31   Litho.   *Perf. 13*
693 A342 600fr multi   14.50 14.50

St. Peter Chanel (1803-41) — A343

2011, Apr. 28
694 A343 75fr multi   1.75 1.75

Birds — A344

No. 695: a, 5fr, Vini australis (30x40mm). b, 20fr, Melipphage foulehaio (30x40mm). c, 115fr, Lalage maculosa futunae (60x40mm).

2011, May 28   *Perf. 13¼x13*
695 A344 Horiz. strip of 3, #a-c 3.50 3.50

SEMI-POSTAL STAMPS

French Revolution Issue
Common Design Type
Unwmk.
1939, July 5   Photo.   *Perf. 13*
Name and Value Typo. in Black

B1	CD83	45c + 25c green	19.00	*19.00*
B2	CD83	70c + 30c brown	19.00	*19.00*
B3	CD83	90c + 35c red org	19.00	*19.00*
B4	CD83	1.25fr +1fr rose pink	19.00	*19.00*
B5	CD83	2.25fr + 2fr blue	19.00	*19.00*
		Nos. B1-B5 (5)	95.00	95.00
		Set, never hinged	150.00	

New Caledonia Nos. B10 and B12 Overprinted "WALLIS ET FUTUNA" in Blue or Red, and Common Design Type

1941   Photo.   *Perf. 13½*

B6	SP2	1fr + 1fr red	2.40
B7	CD86	1.50fr + 3fr maroon	2.40
B8	SP3	2.50fr +1fr dark blue	2.40
		Nos. B6-B8 (3)	7.20
		Set, never hinged	10.00

Nos. B6-B8 were issued by the Vichy government in France, but were not placed on sale in Wallis & Futuna.

Nos. 92-93 Srchd. in Black or Red

1944   Engr.   *Perf. 12x12½*

B8A	50c + 1.50fr on 2.50fr deep blue (R)	1.90
B8B	+ 2.50fr on 1fr green	1.90

Colonial Development Fund.

Nos. B8A-B8B were issued by the Vichy government in France, but were not placed on sale in Wallis & Futuna.

> Catalogue values for unused stamps in this section, from this point to the end of the section, are for Never Hinged items.

Red Cross Issue
Common Design Type
1944   Photo.   *Perf. 14½x14*
B9 CD90 5fr + 20fr red orange 4.50 3.25

The surtax was for the French Red Cross and national relief.

AIR POST STAMPS

> Catalogue values for unused stamps in this section are for Never Hinged items.

Victory Issue
Common Design Type
Perf. 12½
1946, May 8   Unwmk.   Engr.
C1 CD92 8fr dark violet 2.50 1.90

Chad to Rhine Issue
Common Design Types
1946

C2	CD93	5fr dark violet	1.40	1.10
C3	CD94	10fr dk slate grn	1.60	1.30
C4	CD95	15fr violet brn	1.60	1.30
C5	CD96	20fr brt ultra	2.40	1.75
C6	CD97	25fr brown orange	2.75	2.10
C7	CD98	50fr carmine	4.00	2.90
		Nos. C2-C7 (6)	13.75	10.45

New Caledonia Nos. C21-C22 Overprinted in Blue

1949, July 4   *Perf. 13x12½, 12½x13*
C8 AP2 50fr yel & rose red 9.50 7.00
C9 AP3 100fr yel & red brn 15.00 12.00

The overprint on No. C9 is in three lines.

UPU Issue
Common Design Type
1949, July 4   Engr.   *Perf. 13*
C10 CD99 10fr multicolored 12.50 8.25

Liberation Issue
Common Design Type
1954, June 6
C11 CD102 3fr sepia & vio brn 12.50 8.25

Father Louis Marie Chanel — AP1

1955, Nov. 21   Unwmk.   *Perf. 13*
C12 AP1 14fr dk grn, grnsh bl & ind 4.00 1.40

Issued in honor of Father Chanel, martyred missionary to the Islands.

View of Mata-Utu, Queen Amelia and Msgr. Bataillon — AP2

33fr, Map of islands and sailing ship.

1960, Sept. 19   Engr.   *Perf. 13*
C13 AP2 21fr blue, brn & grn 5.25 4.00
C14 AP2 33fr ultra, choc & bl grn 9.00 6.00

For No. C14 with surcharge, see No. C36.

Shell Diver — AP3

1962, Sept. 20   Unwmk.   *Perf. 13*
C16 AP3 100fr bl, grn & dk red brn 21.00 15.00

Telstar Issue
Common Design Type
1962, Dec. 5
C17 CD111 12fr dk pur, mar & bl 3.50 3.50

Sea Shell Type of Regular Issue
1963, Apr. 1   Engr.
Size: 26x47mm
C18 A5 50fr Harpa ventricosa 12.50 7.00

Javelin Thrower — AP4

1964, Oct. 10   Engr.   *Perf. 13*
C19 AP4 31fr emer, ver & vio brn 22.50 14.50

18th Olympic Games, Tokyo, Oct. 10-25.

ITU Issue
Common Design Type
1965, May 17   Unwmk.   *Perf. 13*
C20 CD120 50fr multicolored 21.00 15.00

Mata-Utu Wharf — AP5

1965, Nov. 26   Engr.   *Perf. 13*
C21 AP5 27fr brt bl, sl grn & red brn 5.25 3.50

French Satellite A-1 Issue
Common Design Type

Designs: 7fr, Diamant rocket and launching installations. 10fr, A-1 satellite.

1966, Jan. 17   Engr.   *Perf. 13*
C22 CD121 7fr crim, red & car lake 4.00 4.00
C23 CD121 10fr car lake, red & crim 4.50 4.50
  a.   Strip of 2, #C22-C23 + label 9.25 9.25

French Satellite D-1 Issue
Common Design Type
1966, June 2   Engr.   *Perf. 13*
C24 CD122 10fr lake, bl grn & red 3.50 3.50

WHO Headquarters, Geneva, and Emblem — AP6

1966, July 5   Photo.   *Perf. 12½x13*
C25 AP6 30fr org, maroon & bl 3.75 3.75

New WHO Headquarters, Geneva.

Girl and Boy Reading; UNESCO Emblem — AP7

1966, Nov. 4   Engr.   *Perf. 13*
C26 AP7 50fr green, org & choc 6.25 4.25

20th anniv. of UNESCO.

Athlete and Pattern AP8

Design: 38fr, Woman ballplayer and pattern.

1966, Dec. 8   Engr.   *Perf. 13x12½*
C27 AP8 32fr bl, dp car & blk 4.75 3.00
C28 AP8 38fr emer & brt pink 6.75 4.00

2nd South Pacific Games, Nouméa, 12/8-18.

Samuel Wallis' Ship and Coast of Wallis Island — AP9

1967, Dec. 16   Photo.   *Perf. 13*
C29 AP9 12fr multicolored 8.00 4.75

Bicentenary of the discovery of Wallis Island.

Concorde Issue
Common Design Type
1969, Apr. 17   Engr.   *Perf. 13*
C30 CD129 20fr black & plum 15.00 10.00

Man Climbing Coconut Palm — AP10

32fr, Horseback rider. 38fr, Men making wooden stools. 50fr, Spear fisherman & man holding basket with fish. 100fr, Women sorting coconuts.

1969, Apr. 30   Photo.   *Perf. 13*
C31 AP10 20fr multi 3.00 1.50
C32 AP10 32fr multi 5.25 2.00
C33 AP10 38fr multi 6.00 2.50

C34 AP10 50fr multi 9.25 4.50
C35 AP10 100fr multi 16.00 7.25
　　Nos. C31-C35 (5) 39.50 17.75

No. C14 Surcharged with New Value
and Three Bars

1971 Engr. *Perf. 13*
C36 AP2 21fr on 33fr multi 5.25 4.25

Pole Vault — AP11

1971, Oct. 25 Engr. *Perf. 13*
C37 AP11 48fr shown 6.25 3.00
C38 AP11 54fr Archery 8.00 5.00

4th South Pacific Games, Papeete, French
Polynesia, Sept. 8-19.

South Pacific Commission
Headquarters, Noumea — AP12

1972, Feb. 5 Photo. *Perf. 13*
C39 AP12 44fr blue & multi 7.25 4.25
South Pacific Commission, 25th anniv.

Round House
and Festival
Emblem — AP13

1972, May 15 Engr. *Perf. 13*
C40 AP13 60fr dp car, grn &
　　　　pur 9.25 5.00
South Pacific Festival of Arts, Fiji, May 6-20.

Canoe Type of Regular Issue

Design: 200fr, Outrigger sailing canoe race,
and island woman.

1972, Oct. 16 Photo. *Perf. 13x12½*
　　　　Size: 47½x28mm
C41 A9 200fr multicolored 45.00 25.00

La Pérouse and "La
Boussole" — AP14

Explorers and their Ships: 28fr, Samuel
Wallis and "Dolphin." 40fr, Dumont D'Urville
and "Astrolabe." 72fr, Bougainville and "La
Boudeuse."

1973, July 20 Engr. *Perf. 13*
C42 AP14 22fr brn, slate & car 11.00 6.00
C43 AP14 28fr sl grn, dl red &
　　　　bl 13.50 6.00
C44 AP14 40fr brn, ind & ultra 17.50 9.25
C45 AP14 72fr brown, bl & pur 25.00 12.50
　　Nos. C42-C45 (4) 67.00 33.75

Charles de Gaulle — AP15

1973, Nov. 9 Engr. *Perf. 13*
C46 AP15 107fr brn org & dk
　　　　brn 18.00 11.00
Pres. Charles de Gaulle (1890-1970).

Red
Jasmine
AP16

Designs: Flowers from Wallis.

1973, Dec. 6 Photo. *Perf. 13*
C47 AP16 12fr shown 1.90 1.40
C48 AP16 17fr Hibiscus
　　　　tiliaceus 2.25 1.90
C49 AP16 19fr Phaeomeria
　　　　magnifica 3.00 1.90
C50 AP16 21fr Hibiscus rosa
　　　　sinensis 4.50 2.10
C51 AP16 23fr Allamanda
　　　　cathartica 4.75 2.50
C52 AP16 27fr Barringtonia 5.50 3.00
C53 AP16 39fr Flowers in vase 8.75 6.25
　　Nos. C47-C53 (7) 30.65 19.05

UPU Emblem
and Symbolic
Design — AP17

1974, Oct. 9 Engr. *Perf. 13*
C54 AP17 51fr multicolored 8.00 4.75
Centenary of Universal Postal Union.

Holy
Family,
Primitive
Painting
AP18

1974, Dec. 9 Photo. *Perf. 13*
C55 AP18 150fr multi 15.00 10.00
Christmas 1974.

Tapa Cloth — AP19

Tapa Cloth: 24fr, Village scene. 36fr, Fish &
marine life. 80fr, Marine life, map of islands,
village scene.

1975, Feb. 3 Photo. *Perf. 13*
C56 AP19 3fr multicolored .95 .65
C57 AP19 24fr multicolored 2.40 1.50
C58 AP19 36fr multicolored 4.00 2.25
C59 AP19 80fr multicolored 8.50 5.25
　　Nos. C56-C59 (4) 15.85 9.65

DC-7 in
Flight — AP20

1975, Aug. 13 Engr. *Perf. 13*
C60 AP20 100fr multicolored 7.25 5.50
First regular air service between Nouméa,
New Caledonia, and Wallis.

Volleyball
AP21

1975, Nov. 10 Photo. *Perf. 13*
C61 AP21 26fr shown 2.10 1.20
C62 AP21 44fr Soccer 3.00 1.90
C63 AP21 56fr Javelin 5.00 2.90
C64 AP21 105fr Spear fishing 10.50 6.50
　　Nos. C61-C64 (4) 20.60 12.50
5th South Pacific Games, Guam, Aug. 1-10.

Lalolalo Lake, Wallis — AP22

Landscapes: 29fr, Vasavasa, Futuna. 41fr,
Sigave Bay, Futuna. 68fr, Gahi Bay, Wallis.

1975, Dec. 1 Litho. *Perf. 13*
C65 AP22 10fr grn & multi 1.40 .95
C66 AP22 29fr grn & multi 3.00 1.75
C67 AP22 41fr grn & multi 4.50 2.40
C68 AP22 68fr grn & multi 6.25 3.75
　　Nos. C65-C68 (4) 15.15 8.85

Concorde, Eiffel Tower and Sugar Loaf
Mountain — AP23

1976, Jan. 21 Engr. *Perf. 13*
C69 AP23 250fr multi 27.50 20.00
1st commercial flight of supersonic jet Concorde from Paris to Rio, Jan. 21.
For overprint see No. C73.

Hammer Throw and Stadium — AP24

39fr, Diving, Stadium and maple leaf.

1976, Aug. 2 Engr. *Perf. 13*
C70 AP24 31fr multi 3.00 2.25
C71 AP24 39fr multi 4.75 3.50
21st Olympic Games, Montreal, Canada,
July 17-Aug. 1.

De Gaulle
Memorial
AP25

Photogravure and Embossed
1977, June 18 *Perf. 13*
C72 AP25 100fr gold & multi 10.50 7.50
5th anniversary of dedication of De Gaulle
Memorial at Colombey-les-Deux-Eglises.

No. C69 Overprinted in Dark Brown:
"PARIS NEW-YORK / 22.11.77 / 1er
VOL COMMERCIAL"

1977, Nov. 22 Engr. *Perf. 13*
C73 AP23 250fr multicolored 27.50 17.50
Concorde, 1st commercial flight, Paris-NY.

Balistes Niger — AP26

Fish: 35fr, Amphiprion akindynos. 49fr,
Pomacanthus imperator. 51fr, Zanclus
cornutus.

1978, Jan. 31 Litho. *Perf. 13*
C74 AP26 26fr multi 1.40 .75
C75 AP26 35fr multi 2.10 1.00
C76 AP26 49fr multi 2.40 1.25
C77 AP26 51fr multi 4.50 3.25
　　Nos. C74-C77 (4) 10.40 6.25

Map of Wallis and Uvea
Islands — AP27

300fr, Map of Futuna and Alofi Islands, horz.

1978, Mar. 7 Engr.
C78 AP27 300fr vio bl & grnsh
　　　　bl 17.50 12.50
C79 AP27 500fr multi 23.00 19.00

Father Bataillon, Churches on Wallis and Futuna Islands — AP28

72fr, Monsignor Pompallier, map of Wallis, Futuna and Alofi Islands, outrigger canoe.

1978, Apr. 28   Litho.   Perf. 13x12½
C80 AP28 60fr multi   2.75 1.75
C81 AP28 72fr multi   3.50 2.00
First French missionaries on Wallis and Futuna Islands.

ITU Emblem — AP29

1978, May 17   Litho.   Perf. 13
C82 AP29 66fr multi   3.50 2.25
10th World Telecommunications Day.

Nativity and Longhouse — AP30

1978, Dec. 4   Photo.   Perf. 13
C83 AP30 160fr multi   9.75 5.50
Christmas 1978.

Popes Paul VI, John Paul I, St. Peter's, Rome — AP31

37fr, Pope Paul VI. 41fr, Pope John Paul I.

Perf. 12½x13, 13x12½
1979, Jan. 31   Litho.
C84 AP31 37fr multi, vert.   2.25 1.40
C85 AP31 41fr multi, vert.   2.40 1.75
C86 AP31 105fr multi   5.00 3.50
      Nos. C84-C86 (3)   9.65 6.65
In memory of Popes Paul VI and John Paul I.

Monoplane of UTA Airlines AP32

68fr, Freighter Muana. 80fr, Hihifo Airport.

1979, Feb. 28   Perf. 13x12½
C87 AP32 46fr multi   1.50   .95
C88 AP32 68fr multi   2.00 1.50
C89 AP32 80fr multi   3.50 2.00
      Nos. C87-C89 (3)   7.00 4.45
Inter-Island transportation.
See Nos. 251-253.

France No. 67 and Eole Weather Satellite — AP33

70fr, Hibiscus & stamp similar to #25. 90fr, Rowland Hill & Penny Black. 100fr, Birds, Kano School, Japan 17th cent. & Japan #9.

1979, May 7   Photo.   Perf. 13
C90 AP33   5fr multi   1.10   .65
C91 AP33 70fr multi, vert. 3.50 1.90
C92 AP33 90fr multi   4.50 2.50
C93 AP33 100fr multi   6.00 3.75
      Nos. C90-C93 (4)   15.10 8.80
Sir Rowland Hill (1795-1879), originator of penny postage.

Cross of Lorraine and People — AP34

1979, June 18   Engr.   Perf. 13
C94 AP34 33fr multi   2.75 1.75

Map of Islands, Arms of France AP35

1979, July 19   Photo.   Perf. 13
C95 AP35 47fr multi   3.00 2.00
Visit of Pres. Valery Giscard d'Estaing of France.

Capt. Cook, Ships and Island — AP36

1979, July 28
C96 AP36 130fr multi   7.25 4.25
Capt. James Cook (1728-1779).

Telecom Emblem, Satellite, Receiving Station — AP37

1979, Sept. 20   Litho.   Perf. 13
C97 AP37 120fr multi   5.25 3.50
3rd World Telecommunications Exhibition, Geneva, Sept. 20-26.

Virgin of the Crescent Moon, by Albrecht Durer AP38

1979, Dec. 17   Engr.   Perf. 13
C98 AP38 180fr red & blk   9.25 6.25
Christmas 1979. See No. C163.

Rotary International, 75th Anniversary — AP39

1980, Feb. 29   Litho.   Perf. 13
C99 AP39 86fr multi   5.25 3.50

Rochambeau and Troops, US Flag, 1780 — AP40

1980, May 27   Engr.   Perf. 13
C100 AP40 102fr multi   5.25 3.50
Rochambeau's landing at Newport, RI (American Revolution), bicentenary.

National Day, 10th Anniversary — AP41

1980, July 15   Litho.   Perf. 13
C101 AP41 71fr multi   2.25 1.50

Transatlantic Airmail Flight, 50th Anniversary — AP42

1980, Sept. 22   Engr.   Perf. 13
C102 AP42 122fr multi   4.75 3.50

Fleming, Penicillin Bacilli — AP43

1980, Oct. 20
C103 AP43 101fr multi   4.00 2.50
Alexander Fleming (1881-1955), discoverer of penicillin, 25th death anniversary.

Charles De Gaulle, 10th Anniversary of Death — AP44

1980, Nov. 9   Engr.   Perf. 13
C104 AP44 200fr sep & dk ol
             grn   10.00 7.25

Virgin and Child with St. Catherine, by Lorenzo Lotto — AP45

1980, Dec. 20   Litho.   Perf. 13x12½
C105 AP45 150fr multi   4.50 3.50
Christmas 1980.

Alan B. Shepard and Spacecraft AP46

20th Anniv. of Space Flight: 44fr, Yuri Gagarin.

1981, May 11   Litho.   Perf. 13
C106 AP46 37fr multi   1.40   .95
C107 AP46 44fr multi   1.75 1.40

Vase of Flowers, by Paul Cezanne (1839-1906) — AP47

Design: 135fr, Harlequin, by Pablo Picasso.

1981, Oct. 22   Litho.   Perf. 12½x13
C108 AP47 53fr multi   2.25 1.40
C109 AP47 135fr multi   4.50 3.00

Espana '82 World Cup
Soccer — AP48

1981-82   Engr.   Perf. 13
C110   AP48 120fr blk, brn & grn   3.75 2.25
C110A AP48 120fr lil, brn & ol   3.75 3.00
                grn
   Issued: #C110, 11/16/81; #C110A,5/13/82.
   For overprint see No. C115.

Christmas 1981 — AP49

1981, Dec. 21   Litho.   Perf. 12½
C111 AP49 180fr multi   6.75 4.25

Tapestry,
by Pilioho
Aloi
AP50

1982, Feb. 22   Litho.   Perf. 12½x13
C112 AP50 100fr multi   4.50 2.50

Boats at Collioure, by George Braque
(1882-1963) — AP51

1982, Apr. 13   Litho.   Perf. 12½x13
C113 AP51 300fr multi   9.25 5.25

Alberto Santos-Dumont (1873-1932),
Aviation Pioneer — AP52

1982, July 24
C114 AP52 95fr multi   3.75 2.40

No. C110 Overprinted with Winner's
Name in Blue
1982, Aug. 26   Engr.   Perf. 13
C115 AP48 120fr multi   4.00 3.00
   Italy's victory in 1982 World Cup.

French Overseas Possessions Week,
Sept. 18-25 — AP53

1982, Sept. 17   Litho.
C116 AP53 105fr Beach   3.00 2.25

Day of the
Blind — AP54

1982, Oct. 18   Engr.
C117 AP54 130fr red & blue   3.75 2.00

Christmas
1982
AP55

Adoration of the Virgin, by Correggio.

1982, Dec. 20   Litho.   Perf. 12½x13
C118 AP55 170fr multi   4.50 3.00

Wind Surfing
(1984 Olympic
Event) — AP56

1983, Mar. 4   Litho.   Perf. 13
C119 AP56 270fr multi   6.50 4.75

World UPU Day — AP57

1983, Mar. 30   Litho.   Perf. 13
C120 AP57 100fr multi   2.75 1.75

Manned Flight
Bicentenary
AP58

1983, Apr. 25   Litho.   Perf. 13
C121 AP58 205fr Montgolfiere   5.75 4.00

Cat, 1926,
by Foujita
(d. 1968)
AP59

1983, May 20   Litho.   Perf. 12½x13
C122 AP59 102fr multi   3.75 2.00

Pre-Olympic
Year — AP60

1983, July 5   Engr.   Perf. 13
C123 AP60 250fr Javelin   6.50 4.50

Alfred Nobel (1833-1896) — AP61

1983, Aug. 1   Engr.   Perf. 13
C124 AP61 150fr multi   4.00 2.75

Nicephore Niepce (1765-1833),
Photography Pioneer — AP62

1983, Sept. 20   Engr.   Perf. 13
C125 AP62 75fr dk grn & rose   2.75 1.75
                vio

Raphael (1483-1520), 500th Birth
Anniv. — AP63

1983, Nov. 10   Litho.   Perf. 12½x13
C126 AP63 167fr The Triumph of
                Galatea   4.50 3.00

Pandanus
AP64

1983, Nov. 30   Litho.   Perf. 13
C127 AP64 137fr multi   4.00 3.00

Christmas
1983
AP65

1983, Dec. 22   Litho.   Perf. 12½x13
C128 AP65 200fr Sistine Madon-
                na, by
                Raphael   5.50 4.00

Steamer Commandant Bory — AP66

1984, Jan. 9   Perf. 13
C129 AP66 67fr multi   2.25 1.40

1984 Summer Olympics — AP67

1984, Feb. 3   Litho.   Perf. 13
C130 AP67 85fr Weight lifting   2.40 1.75

Frangipani
Blossoms
AP68

1984, Feb. 28   Perf. 12½
C131 AP68 130fr multi   4.00 2.25

Easter 1984 AP69

1984, Apr. 17 Litho. Perf. 12½x13
C132 AP69 190fr Descent from
the Cross 5.00 3.25

Homage to Jean Cocteau AP70

1984, June 30 Litho. Perf. 13
C133 AP70 150fr Portrait 4.00 2.90

Soano Hoatau Tiki Sculpture AP71

1984, July 26
C134 AP71 175fr multi 4.75 3.50

Portrait of Alice, by Modigliani (1884-1920) AP72

1984, Aug. 20
C135 AP72 140fr multi 3.75 2.50

Ausipex '84 — AP73

1984, Sept. 21 Litho. Perf. 12½x13
C136 AP73 180fr Pilioko Tapestry 4.00 3.00
Se-tenant with label showing exhibition
emblem.

Local Dances, by Jean Michon — AP74

1984, Oct. 11 Photo. Perf. 13
C137 AP74 110fr multi 3.50 2.00

Altar AP75

1984, Nov. 5 Litho. Perf. 13x12½
C138 AP75 52fr Mount Lulu
Chapel 1.50 1.10

Christmas 1984 — AP76

1984, Dec. 21 Litho. Perf. 13x12½
C139 AP76 260fr Tropical Nativity 7.00 4.00

Pilioko Tapestry — AP77

1985, Apr. 3 Litho. Perf. 13x12½
C140 AP77 500fr multi 13.50 6.50

The Post in 1926, by Utrillo AP78

1985, June 17 Litho. Perf. 12½x13
C141 AP78 200fr multi 6.00 4.00

Wallis Island Pirogue — AP79

1985, Aug. 9 Perf. 13
C142 AP79 350fr multi 9.50 5.00

Ship Jacques Cartier — AP80

1985, Oct. 2 Engr. Perf. 13x13½
C143 AP80 51fr Prus bl, brt bl &
dk bl 1.75 1.10

Portrait of a Young Woman, by Patrice Nielly AP81

1985, Oct. 28 Litho. Perf. 12½x13
C144 AP81 245fr multi 6.75 4.50

Nativity, by Jean Michon AP82

1985, Dec. 19 Litho. Perf. 12½x13
C145 AP82 330fr multi 10.00 6.50

Halley's Comet — AP83

1986, Mar. 6 Litho. Perf. 13
C146 AP83 100fr multi 3.25 1.75

Cure of Ars, Birth Bicent. — AP84

1986, Mar. 28 Litho. Perf. 12½x13
C147 AP84 200fr multi 5.75 4.25

French Overseas Territory Status, 25th
Anniv. — AP85

1986, July 29 Engr. Perf. 13
C148 AP85 90fr Queen Amelia 2.75 2.25
C149 AP85 137fr July 30 Law,
Journal of the
Republic 4.50 3.25
a. Strip of 2, #C148-C149 + label 7.25 6.00
Queen Amelia's request to France for pro-
tection, cent.

World Post Day — AP86

1986, Oct. 9 Litho. Perf. 13
C150 AP86 270fr multi 7.25 4.00

Statue of Liberty, Cent. — AP87

1986, Oct. 31 Engr.
C151 AP87 205fr multi 8.00 5.00

Poi Basilica, 1st Anniv. — AP88

1987, Apr. 30 Litho. Perf. 13
C152 AP88 230fr Fr. Chanel, basilica 7.00 3.75

Telstar Transmitting to Pleumeur-
Bodou, France — AP89

1987, May 17 Engr. Perf. 13
C153 AP89 200fr gray, brt bl &
brn org 7.00 3.75
World Communications Day, 25th anniv. of
Telstar.

Piccard, Bathyscaphe Trieste and Stratospheric Balloon — AP90

1987, Aug. 21   Engr.   Perf. 13
C154 AP90 135fr brt ol grn, dk bl
                    & brt bl   4.50 3.00

Auguste Piccard (1884-1962), physicist.

Arrival of First Missionary, 150th Anniv. — AP91

Design: 260fr, Monsignor Bataillon's arrival in 1837, ship and the islands.

1987, Nov. 8   Engr.   Perf. 13
C155 AP91 260fr brt blue, blk &
                    blue grn   7.50 5.00

Christmas 1987 — AP92

1987, Dec. 15   Litho.   Perf. 13x12½
C156 AP92 300fr multi   8.00 5.00

Garros and Bleriot Aircraft — AP93

1988, Feb. 18   Engr.   Perf. 13
C157 AP93 600fr multi   19.00 10.50
Roland Garros (1888-1918), aviator and tennis player.

Self-portrait with Lace Cravat, by Maurice Quentin de La Tour (1704-88) AP94

1988, Apr. 8   Litho.
C158 AP94 500fr multi   15.00 9.50

World Telecommunications Day — AP95

1988, May 5   Litho.   Perf. 12½x13
C159 AP95 100fr multi   3.00 1.90

South Pacific Episcopal Conference — AP96

1988, June 1   Litho.   Perf. 13
C160 AP96 90fr Map, bishop   2.75 1.75

Christmas — AP97

Unwmk.
1988, Dec. 15   Litho.   Perf. 13
C161 AP97 400fr multi   13.00 7.00

Royal Throne — AP98

1989, Mar. 11
C162 AP98 700fr multi   19.00 10.50

Type of 1979
Virgin of the Crescent Moon, by Albrecht Durer

1989, Dec. 21   Engr.   Perf. 13½x13
C163 AP38 800fr plum   22.00 13.00
Christmas 1989.

Clement Ader (1841-1926), Aviation Pioneer — AP100

1990, June 9   Engr.   Perf. 13
C164 AP100 56fr multicolored   2.00 1.40
First anniversary of Wallis-Tahiti air link.

Gen. Charles de Gaulle (1890-1979) — AP101

1990, Nov. 22   Perf. 12½x13
C165 AP101 1000fr multi   27.50 19.00

Father Louis Marie Chanel, 150th Death Anniv. — AP102

1991, Apr. 28   Litho.   Perf. 13
C166 AP102 235fr multicolored   6.50 4.25

French Open Tennis Championships, Cent. — AP103

1991, May 24   Engr.   Perf. 13x12½
C167 AP103 250fr blk, grn & org 8.00 5.50

Wolfgang Amadeus Mozart, Death Bicent. AP104

1991, Sept. 23   Engr.   Perf. 13
C168 AP104 500fr multicolored   15.00 9.50

World Columbian Stamp Expo '92, Chicago — AP105

1992, May 22   Litho.   Perf. 13x12½
C169 AP105 100fr multicolored   3.00 2.25

1992, July 15   Perf. 13
C170 AP105 800fr multicolored 22.00 13.00
Genoa '92.

First French Republic, Bicent. — AP106

1992, Aug. 17   Engr.   Perf. 13
C171 AP106 350fr blk, bl & red   9.75 7.50

Louvre Museum, Bicent. — AP107

1993, Apr. 12   Engr.   Perf. 13
C172 AP107 315fr blue, dk blue
                        & red   9.00 5.50

Nicolaus Copernicus, Heliocentric Solar System — AP108

1993, May 7   Engr.   Perf. 13
C173 AP108 600fr multicolored 16.00 9.25
Polska '93.

Second Year of First French Republic, Bicent. — AP109

1993, Sept. 22   Engr.   Perf. 13
C174 AP109 400fr bl, blk & red   11.00 7.50

Wallis Island Landscape — AP110

1994, Jan. 26   Litho.   Perf. 13
C175 AP110 400fr multicolored 11.00 7.50

Hong Kong '94 — AP111

1994, Feb. 18   Litho.   Perf. 14x13½
C176 AP111 700fr multicolored 19.00 12.00

South Pacific Geography
Day — AP112

1994, May 4   Litho.   Perf. 13
C177 AP112 85fr multicolored   2.50 1.75
See New Caledonia No. C259.

European Stamp
Salon,
Paris — AP113

1994, Sept. 22   Litho.   Perf. 13
C178 AP113 300fr multicolored   9.00 5.00

Antoine de Saint-Exupery (1900-44),
Aviator, Author — AP114

1994, Oct. 27   Engr.   Perf. 13
C179 AP114 800fr multicolored   22.00 15.00

Christmas
AP115

1994, Dec. 15   Litho.   Perf. 13
C180 AP115 150fr multicolored   4.00 3.00

Louis Pasteur (1822-95) — AP116

1995, Mar. 25   Litho.   Perf. 13
C181 AP116 350fr multicolored   9.50 4.75

AP117

1995, Apr. 19   Perf. 13½x13
C182 AP117 115fr multicolored   3.50 1.90
University Teacher's Training Institute of the
Pacific. See French Polynesia No. 656.

AP118

1995, May 17   Perf. 13
C183 AP118 200fr Painting of
Cocoa Nuts   5.50 3.00

Intl. Youth Year, 10th Anniv. — AP119

1995, July 25   Litho.   Perf. 13
C184 AP119 450fr multicolored   12.50 6.25

Singapore '95 — AP120

1995, Aug. 24   Litho.   Perf. 13
C185 AP120 500fr multicolored   13.50 6.75

Motion Pictures, Cent. — AP121

Lumiere Brothers, film strip.

1995, Sept. 19
C186 AP121 600fr multicolored   16.00 8.50

Charles de Gaulle (1890-
1970) — AP122

1995, Nov. 14   Engr.   Perf. 13
C187 AP122 315fr multicolored   8.50 5.50

7th Va'a (Outrigger Canoe) World
Championship, Noumea, New
Caledonia — AP123

1996, Apr. 24   Litho.   Perf. 13
C188 AP123 240fr multicolored   6.50 4.25

Sisia
College — AP124

1996, May 22   Litho.   Perf. 13½x13
C189 AP124 235fr multicolored   6.50 4.25

Radio, Cent. — AP125

1996, July 25   Engr.   Perf. 13
C190 AP125 550fr multicolored   15.00 9.25

Modern Olympic Games,
Cent. — AP126

1996, Aug. 20   Engr.   Perf. 13
C191 AP126 1000fr blk & dk bl   27.50 17.00

50th
Autumn
Stamp
Salon
AP127

1996, Oct. 24   Litho.   Perf. 13
C192 AP127 175fr multicolored   4.75 3.00

Campaign
to Control
Alcoholism
AP128

1996, Nov. 19   Perf. 13x13½
C193 AP128 260fr multicolored   7.00 4.25

Natl. Center for
Scientific
Research
AP129

1997, Mar. 14   Litho.   Perf. 13
C194 AP129 400fr Lapita pot-
tery   11.00 5.50

HIHIFO Air Service — AP130

1997, July 8   Litho.   Perf. 13
C195 AP130 130fr multicolored   3.25 2.10

Sundown Over
the
Lagoon — AP131

1997, Sept. 22   Litho.   Perf. 13½x13
C196 AP131 300fr multicolored   8.00 4.25

51st Autumn Stamp Salon — AP132

350fr, #C194, 492, 497, 486, C184, C185,
475, C192, C188, 464, 493.

1000fr, Hemispheres, #486, 475, 464, C185, C175, 493, C184, 492, C192, 497, C188, C194, Winged Victory of Samothrace.

1997, Nov. 6　　Litho.　　Perf. 13
C197 AP132 350fr multi　　9.50 4.75
Imperf
C198 AP132 1000fr multi　　27.50 24.00

Marshal Jacques Leclerc (1902-47) — AP133

1997, Nov. 28　　Litho.　　Perf. 13
C199 AP133 800fr multicolored　　22.00 11.50

Alphonse Daudet (1840-97), Writer — AP134

1997, Dec. 16　　Litho.　　Perf. 13
C200 AP134 710fr multi　　19.00 10.00

Alofi Beach — AP135

1998, Apr. 21　　Litho.　　Perf. 13
C201 AP135 315fr multicolored　　8.50 4.25

Cricket AP136

1998, Sept. 22　　Litho.　　Perf. 13x13½
C202 AP136 106fr multicolored　　2.90 1.40

Paul Gauguin (1848-1903) — AP137

1998, Oct. 27　　Litho.　　Perf. 13
C203 AP137 700fr multicolored　　19.00 9.25

Garden of Happiness — AP138

1998, Nov. 17
C204 AP138 460fr multicolored　　12.50 7.25

Polynesian Dancing AP139

1998, Dec. 15　　Litho.　　Perf. 13
C205 AP139 250fr multicolored　　6.75 3.50

Kava Porter AP140

1999, Jan. 18
C206 AP140 600fr multicolored　　16.00 8.00

Shells AP141

95fr, Epitonium scalare. 100fr, Cassis cornuta. 110fr, Charonia tritonis. 115fr, Lambis lambis.

1999, Feb. 15
C207 AP141 95fr multi, vert.　　2.50 1.75
C208 AP141 100fr multi, vert.　　2.75 1.75
C209 AP141 110fr multi　　3.00 1.75
C210 AP141 115fr multi　　3.10 1.75
　　　Nos. C207-C210 (4)　　11.35 7.00

Finemui — AP142

1999, Apr. 19　　Engr.　　Perf. 12¾
C211 AP142 900fr multicolored　　24.00 11.50

Birds of Nuku Fotu AP143

a, 10fr, Airgrettes. b, 20fr, Audubon's. c, 26fr, Fregates. d, 54fr, Paille en queue.

1999, June 14　　Litho.　　Perf. 13x13¾
C212 AP143 Strip of 4, #a.-d.　　3.00 2.50

Wind Song — AP144

1999, Nov. 22　　Engr.　　Perf. 13
C213 AP144 325fr multi　　8.75 4.50

Sunrise Over a Lagoon AP145

1999, Dec. 20　　Litho.
C214 AP145 500fr multi　　13.50 7.50

First Transport Flight to Futuna, 30th Anniv. — AP146

2000, Aug. 24　　Litho.　　Perf. 13
C215 AP146 350fr multi　　9.50 4.50

AIR POST SEMI-POSTAL STAMPS

New Caledonia Nos. CB2-CB3 overprinted "ILES WALLIS ET FUTUNA"

1942, June 22　　Engr.　　Perf. 13
CB1 SPAP1 1.50fr + 3.50fr green 2.25
CB2 SPAP1 2fr + 6fr yellow brown　　2.25

Native children's welfare fund. Nos. CB1-CB2 were issued by the Vichy government in France, but were not placed on sale in Wallis & Futuna.

Colonial Education Fund
New Caledonia No. CB4 Common Design Type overprinted "ILES WALLIS ET FUTUNA"

1942, June 22
CB3 CD86a 1.20fr + 1.00fr blue & red　　2.25

No. CB3 was issued by the Vichy government in France, but was not placed on sale in Wallis & Futuna.

POSTAGE DUE STAMPS

Postage Due Stamps of New Caledonia, 1906, Overprinted in Black or Red

1920　　Unwmk.　　Perf. 13½x14
J1 D2 5c ultra, *azure*　　1.00 1.00
J2 D2 10c brn, *buff*　　1.10 1.10
J3 D2 15c grn, *grnsh*　　1.10 1.10
J4 D2 20c blk, *yel* (R)　　1.50 1.50
　a.　Double overprint　　200.00
J5 D2 30c carmine rose　　1.50 1.50
J6 D2 50c ultra, *straw*　　2.40 2.40
J7 D2 60c olive, *azure*　　2.90 2.90
　a.　Double overprint　　200.00
J8 D2 1fr grn, *cream*　　3.75 3.75
　　　Nos. J1-J8 (8)　　15.25 15.25

Type of 1920 Issue Surcharged

1927
J9 D2 2fr on 1fr brt vio　　17.50 17.50
J10 D2 3fr on 1fr org brn　　17.50 17.50

Postage Due Stamps of New Caledonia, 1928, Overprinted as in 1920

1930
J11 D3 2c sl bl & dp brn　　.25 .25
J12 D3 4c brn red & bl grn　　.25 .25
J13 D3 5c red org & bl blk　　.25 .25
J14 D3 10c mag & Prus bl　　.25 .25
J15 D3 15c dl grn & scar　　.35 .35
J16 D3 20c maroon & ol grn　　.75 .75
J17 D3 25c bis brn & sl bl　　.75 .75
J18 D3 30c bl grn & ol grn　　1.40 1.40
J19 D3 50c lt brn & dk red　　.85 .85
J20 D3 60c mag & brt rose　　1.40 1.40
J21 D3 1fr dl bl & Prus grn　　1.40 1.40
J22 D3 2fr dk red & ol grn　　1.40 1.40
J23 D3 3fr vio & brn　　1.40 1.40
　　　Nos. J11-J23 (13)　　10.70 10.70

Postage Due Stamps of 1930 with Additional Overprint in Black

1943
J24 D3 2c sl bl & dp brn　　37.50 37.50
J25 D3 4c brn red & bl grn　　37.50 37.50
J26 D3 5c red org & bl blk　　37.50 37.50
J27 D3 10c mag & Prus bl　　37.50 37.50
J28 D3 15c dl grn & scar　　40.00 40.00
J29 D3 20c mar & ol grn　　40.00 40.00
J30 D3 25c bis brn & sl bl　　40.00 40.00
J31 D3 30c bl grn & ol grn　　40.00 40.00
J32 D3 50c lt brn & dk red　　40.00 40.00
J33 D3 60c mag & brt rose　　42.50 42.50
J34 D3 1fr dl bl & Prus grn　　42.50 42.50
J35 D3 2fr dk red & ol grn　　42.50 42.50
J36 D3 3fr violet & brn　　42.50 42.50
　　　Nos. J24-J36 (13)　　520.00 520.00

Catalogue values for unused stamps in this section, from this point to the end of the section, are for Never Hinged items.

Thalassoma Lunare — D1

Fish: 1fr, Zanclus cornutus, vert. 5fr, Amphiprion percula.

Perf. 13x13½
1963, Apr. 1　　Typo.　　Unwmk.
J37 D1 1fr yel org, bl & blk　　.95 .95
J38 D1 3fr red, grnsh bl & grn　　1.90 *2.40*
J39 D1 5fr org, bluish grn & blk　　3.00 *3.50*
　　　Nos. J37-J39 (3)　　5.85 6.85

WESTERN UKRAINE

ˈwes-tərn yü-ˈkrān

LOCATION — In Eastern Central Europe

GOVT. — A former short-lived independent State

A provisional government was established in 1918 in the eastern part of Austria-Hungary but the area later came under Polish administration.

100 Shahiv (Sotykiv) = 1 Hryvnia
100 Heller = 1 Krone

Forgeries of almost all Western Ukraine stamps are plentiful. Particularly dangerous forgeries have been noted for the Kolomyia Issue and for the First and Second Stanyslaviv Issues.

Lviv Issue

Austria Nos. 145-146, 148, 169 Overprinted

Nos. 1-4A are handstamped with an octagonal overprint that reads "ZAKHIDNO UKR. NARODNA REPUBLYKA" ("Western Ukrainian National Republic"), framing the image of a rearing crowned lion.

1918, Nov. 20

1	A37	3h	55.00	425.00
a.		Inverted overprint	150.00	
2	A37	5h light green	50.00	325.00
a.		Inverted overprint	150.00	
3	A37	10h magenta	50.00	325.00
a.		Inverted overprint	150.00	
4	A42	20h dark green	35.00	350.00
a.		Inverted overprint	150.00	
4A	A42	20h light green	240.00	900.00
		Nos. 1-4A (5)	430.00	2,325.

This issue was in circulation for only two days before Lviv was captured by the Poles on Nov. 22. No examples of Nos. 1-4A used in Lviv are known.

The Western Ukrainian National Republic (ZUNR) government evacuated to the city of Ternopil, which became the national capital. ZUNR postal operations were set up in other Western Ukrainian cities, and the Lviv Issue was used in Stanyslaviv (earliest known cancellation date, Dec. 8), Khodoriv and Kolomyia.

Nos. 1-4 exist in pairs with both normal and inverted overprints. Value $325.

Overprints in other colors (green, red and violet) are known, but these are probably proofs. Violet-black overprints are likely transitional color impressions.

Kolomyia Issue

Austria Nos. 168, 145, 147, 149 Surcharged

Kolomyia is the main town of the Pokutia region of southwestern Ukraine. Cut off from ZUNR postal officials by wartime conditions and in urgent need of basic value stamps, the Kolomyia postmaster obtained permission from the District Military Command to surcharge remaining Austrian postage stamps to either 5 or 10 sotyks, the equivalent of 5 or 10 heller. These stamps were produced on Dec. 10, under very strict security, by preparing two distinct plates (one for each value) that overprinted 25 stamps at a time (5x5 quarter sections of the Austrian 100-stamp panes). The stamps were placed on sale two days later.

1918, Dec. 12   Unwmk.   Perf. 12½

5	A42	5sot on 15h dl red	90.00	120.00
a.		Inverted overprint	600.00	725.00
b.		Double overprint	1,500.	1,600.

6	A37	10sot on 3h vio	90.00	120.00
7	A37	10sot on 6h dp org	1,650.	1,250.
8	A37	10sot on 12h lt bl	1,650.	1,500.
		Nos. 5-8 (4)	3,480.	2,990.

10 sotyk on 15 heller values are essays; only six were produced.

All inverted surcharges on Nos. 6-8 are forgeries. Double surcharges are forgeries.

First Stanyslaviv Issue

Austrian Stamps of 1916-18 Surcharged in Shahiv (shown) and Hryvnia Currency

At the end of December, 1918, the national government again moved, this time to the city of Stanyslaviv (present-day Ivano-Frankivsk). A shortage of qualified postal personnel resulted in a considerable delay in the creation of new ZUNR postage stamps. In the interim, remaining unoverprinted Austrian stamps were used. Finally, on March 18, 1919, 20 different available Austrian definitive stamps were typograph surcharged at the Weidenfeld Printing Shop in Stanyslaviv.

1919, Mar. 18

9	A37	3sh on 3h bright violet	17.00	22.50
10	A37	5sh on 5h light green	17.00	22.50
11	A37	6sh on 6h deep orange	32.50	55.00
12	A37	10sh on 10h mag	27.50	37.50
13	A37	12sh on 12h lt blue	27.50	37.50
a.		Double overprint	300.00	425.00
b.		Double overprint, one on reverse	500.00	210.00
14	A42	15sh on 15h dull red	27.50	37.50
15	A42	20sh on 20h deep green	27.50	37.50
16	A42	30sh on 30h dull violet	100.00	100.00
17	A39	40sh on 40h olive green	27.50	37.50
18	A39	50sh on 50h dark green	27.50	37.50
19	A39	60sh on 60h deep blue	27.50	37.50
20	A39	80sh on 80h orange brown	27.50	37.50
a.		Inverted overprint	300.00	425.00
21	A39	1hr on 1k car, yel	37.50	45.00
22	A40	2hr on 2k lt blue	37.50	50.00
23	A40	3hr on 3k claret (on #161)	3,250.	3,250.
24	A40	3hr on 3k car rose (on #165)	100.00	82.50
25	A40	3hr on 3k car rose (on #173)	80.00	80.00
26	A40	4hr on 4k dk grn (on #162)	600.00	700.00
27	A40	4hr on 4k yel grn (on #166)	75.00	55.00
28	A40	10hr on 10k deep violet	750.00	800.00
a.		Double overprint	3,000.	3,500.
		Nos. 9-28 (20)	5,316.	5,562.

The 25sh on 25h, type A42, in both light and dull blue shades, never received this overprint. All such stamps are fantasies.

Second Stanyslaviv Issue

The overprinting of a second issue of postage stamps in Stanyslaviv was undertaken in early May. Stamps from several different Austrian stamp series were utilized to create four distinct sets. Most of the stamps available were Austrian postage due, charity or field post stamps.

Postage Due Stamps of Bosnia, 1904 Surcharged but without Asterisks

1919, May 5

29	D1	1sh on 1h blk, red & yel	32.50	40.00
a.		Inverted overprint	100.00	65.00
b.		Double overprint	90.00	90.00
30	D1	2sh on 2h blk, red & yel	15.00	15.00
a.		Inverted overprint	85.00	150.00

31	D1	3sh on 3h blk, red & yel	17.50	35.00
a.		Inverted overprint	25.00	45.00
32	D1	4sh on 4h blk, red & yel	125.00	125.00
a.		Inverted overprint	175.00	175.00
b.		Double overprint	300.00	300.00
33	D1	5sh on 5h blk, red & yel	3,250.	3,500.
34	D1	6sh on 6h blk, red & yel	600.00	600.00
a.		Inverted overprint	900.00	900.00
b.		Double overprint	750.00	750.00
35	D1	7sh on 7h blk, red & yel	25.00	27.50
a.		Inverted overprint	37.50	42.50
36	D1	8sh on 8h blk, red & yel	25.00	30.00
a.		Inverted overprint	50.00	60.00
b.		Vertical overprint	750.00	950.00
c.		As "b," double overprint	950.00	1,100.
37	D1	10sh on 10h blk, red & yel	1,250.	1,400.
38	D1	15sh on 15h blk, red & yel	625.00	625.00
a.		Inverted overprint	750.00	800.00
39	D1	20sh on 20h blk, red & yel	6,250.	
a.		Double overprint	7,750.	17,000.
40	D1	50sh on 50h blk, red & yel	350.00	375.00
a.		Inverted overprint	550.00	600.00

Nos. 29-40 were created by overprinting Bosnian 1904 postage due stamps, which had been brought to Stanyslaviv by a Ukrainian military officer returning from the Serbian front. The same printing cliché was used as for the First Stanyslaviv Issue, but the asterisk obliterators were removed.

Most of the overprinting was made using 50-stamp panes (half of a sheet). After one half of the pane (25 positions) was overprinted, it would apparently be turned over and its second half overprinted with the same 25-position block, but as an inverted impression. After overprinting, the pane was torn into two equal 25-stamp halves.

A corrected block was utilized in overprinting, resulting in two types of surcharges on No. 29 (shahiv to shaha) and on Nos. 32, 34 and 38 (shahiv to shahi).

Same Surcharge on Austrian Military Semipostal Stamps of 1918
Perf. 12½x13

41	MSP7	10sh on 10h gray green	150.00	150.00
a.		Inverted overprint	150.00	160.00
b.		Double overprint	175.00	210.00
42	MSP8	20sh on 20h magenta	125.00	110.00
a.		Inverted overprint	125.00	120.00
b.		Double overprint	160.00	180.00
43	MSP7	45sh on 45h blue	100.00	110.00
a.		Inverted overprint	100.00	120.00

Nos. 41-43 were printed in the same manner as Nos. 29-40.

Same Surcharge on Austrian Military Stamps of 1917
Perf. 12½

44	M3	1sh on 1h grnsh blue	950.00	950.00
45	M3	2sh on 2h red orange	100.00	100.00
a.		Inverted overprint	125.00	125.00
b.		Double overprint	210.00	210.00
46	M3	3sh olive gray	175.00	190.00
a.		Inverted overprint	750.00	
47	M3	5sh on 5h olive grn	275.00	275.00
48	M3	6sh on 6h violet	150.00	175.00
49	M3	10sh on 10h org brn	900.00	1,000.
50	M3	12sh on 12h blue	550.00	600.00
a.		Inverted overprint	650.00	725.00
51	M3	15sh on 15h brt rose	500.00	600.00
a.		Inverted overprint	625.00	725.00
52	M3	20sh on 20h red brown	16.50	20.00
a.		Inverted overprint	82.50	140.00
b.		Double overprint	47.50	55.00
53	M3	25sh on 25h ultra	3,250.	3,900.
54	M3	30sh on 30h slate	1,000.	1,200.
55	M3	40sh on 40h olive bis	850.00	850.00
56	M3	50sh on 50h deep green	9.00	9.00
a.		Inverted overprint	20.00	20.00
b.		Double overprint	55.00	55.00
57	M3	60sh on 60h car rose	950.00	950.00
58	M3	80sh on 80h dull blue	47.50	47.50
a.		Inverted overprint	80.00	85.00
59	M3	90sh on 90h dk vio	950.00	1,000.
60	M4	2hr on 2k rose, straw	15.00	17.50
a.		Inverted overprint	27.50	35.00
b.		Imperforate	3,000.	
61	M4	3hr on 3k blue, grn	22.50	25.00
a.		Inverted overprint	27.50	30.00
b.		Double overprint	60.00	65.00

62	M4	4hr on 4k rose, grn	22.50	25.00
a.		Inverted overprint	50.00	30.00
b.		Double overprint	60.00	65.00
63	M4	10hr on 10k dl violet, gray	35,000.	35,000.

Two examples of No. 63 were printed, and neither was ever postally used. The "used" example was cut from a document prepared by the Western Ukrainian economic bureau (Ekonomat) to display the stamps that made up the First, Second and Third Stanyslaviv issues. The specimen stamps on this document were tied with a double-ring bureau cancel that somewhat resembles a regular double-ring postal cancellation.

About half of this issue, where several sheets were available for printing, was overprinted in the manner as Nos. 29-43.

Same Surcharge on Austrian Stamps of 1916-18, but with two upper bars

64	A38	15sh on 36h vio (on #J61)	350.00	450.00
a.		Double overprint	450.00	500.00
65	A38	50sh on 42h choc (on #J63)	5,000.	5,500.
66	A37	3sh on 3h brt violet (on #145)	190.00	190.00
67	A37	5sh on 5h lt green (on #146)	190.00	190.00
			290.00	290.00
68	A37	6sh on 6h deep org (on #147)	725.00	725.00
69	A37	10sh on 10h magenta (on #148)	210.00	210.00
a.		Inverted overprint	250.00	250.00
70	A37	12sh on 12h lt blue (on #149)	425.00	425.00
71	A38	15sh on 15h rose red (on #150)	190.00	190.00
a.		Inverted overprint	225.00	225.00
72	A42	15sh on 15h dull red (on #168)	210.00	210.00
73	A42	30sh on 30h dull violet (on #171)	190.00	190.00
a.		Double overprint	350.00	350.00
74	A39	40sh on 40h ol grn (on #154)	300.00	300.00
75	M3	50sh on 50h dp grn (on #M61)	475.00	475.00

The two bars in the surcharge were originally created to obliterate the "PORTO" on Nos. 64 and 65 but were subsequently retained for Nos. 66-75.

Third Stanyslaviv Issue

Austrian Stamps of 1916-18 Overprinted

1919, May

76	A37	3h brt violet	.50	1.00
77	A37	5h light green	.50	1.00
78	A37	6h deep orange	.50	1.00
79	A37	10h magenta	.50	1.00
80	A37	12h light blue	.50	1.00
81	A42	15h dull red	.50	1.00
82	A42	20h deep green	.50	1.00
83	A42	25h blue	.50	1.00
84	A42	30h dull vio	.50	1.00
85	A39	40h olive green	.75	1.25
86	A39	50h dark green	.75	1.25
87	A39	60h deep blue	.75	1.25
88	A39	80h orange brn	1.00	1.25
89	A39	90h red violet	1.00	1.60
90	A39	1k car, yel	1.25	4.00
91	A40	2k light blue	2.00	6.00
92	A40	3k carmine rose	2.50	7.50
93	A40	4k yellow grn	12.00	16.00
94	A40	10k deep violet	16.00	50.00
		Nos. 76-94 (19)	42.50	99.10

Issued: 3h-10h, 15h, 25h-40h, 60h-1k, 5/8; balance of set, 5/13.

A definitive set for Western Ukraine was ordered from the Austrian State Printing Office in March, 1919. Because of the time involved in designing and printing these stamps, Nos. 76-94 were overprinted in Vienna as a provisional issue and were delivered in two shipments. Because travel into and out of Stanyslaviv was becoming more difficult as the month wore on, it was not known whether or not the second shipment, which included the higher values, would arrive. Because of this, the Fourth Stanyslaviv Issue, Nos. 95-103, were overprinted locally.

Fourth Stanislaviv Issue

Austrian Military Stamps of 1917-18 Surcharged in Black

1919, May   *Perf. 12½*

95	A2	2hr on 2k rose, straw	15.00	15.00
a.		Perf 11½	130.00	150.00
96	A2	3hr on 2k rose, straw	13.00	16.00
a.		Perf 11½	130.00	160.00
97	A2	3hr on 3k grn, blue	125.00	175.00
a.		"5" instead of "3" at left in overprint	1,500.	
98	A2	4hr on 2k rose, straw	15.00	16.00
99	A2	4hr on 4k rose, grn	1,300.	1,900.
100	A2	5hr on 2k rose, straw	20.00	22.50
a.		Inverted surcharge	300.00	
101	A2	10hr on 50h dp grn (Austria type M3)	30.00	40.00
a.		Double surcharge	175.00	

Same Surcharge on Austrian Postage Due Stamps of 1916, but without Rosettes and Numerals

102	D5	1hr ultra	140.00	210.00
103	D5	5hr ultra	1,400.	2,100.

REGISTRATION STAMPS

Kolomyia Issue

RS1

Without Gum

1918-19   Unwmk.   Typeset   *Imperf.*

F1	RS1	30sot black, *rose*	250.00	175.00
F2	RS1	50sot black, *rose* ('19)	120.00	150.00

No. F1 was printed on Dec. 10 and issued Dec. 12, 1918, along with the regular Kolomyia Issue (Nos. 5-8). On Dec. 19, the ZUNR government approved an increase in the registered letter rate to 50 sotyks, effective January 1, 1919. Because of communication disruptions, the Kolomyia post office did not learn of this decree until about January 7, when it ordered new values in the higher denomination (No. F2). F1 continued to be used, usually in combination with 20h of Austrian stamps, until supplies were exhausted, at which point No. F2 was put into use. A second printing of the 50sot value was made in late March. Variations in paper color — from light pink to deep rose — as well as paper thickness occurred in the 30-sot and both of the 50-sot printings.

Nos. F1-F2a were typographed in vertical panes of five stamps by the Wilhelm Brauner Print Ship in Kolomyia.

Forgeries exist.

OCCUPATION STAMPS

Romanian Occupation of Pokutia

Only the stamps listed below were officially created. Soon after the Romanian occupation ended on Aug. 20, 1919, the C.M.T. handstamps fell into the hands of speculators, and some 37 other Austrian stamps were overprinted. None of these privately-created stamps are known on authentic covers.

Austrian Stamps Surcharged in Dark Violet Blue

1919, June 14   Unwmk.   *Perf. 12½*

On Stamps of 1916-18

N1	A37	40h on 5h lt grn	4.50	5.50
N2	A42	60h on 15h dl red	5.50	6.50
N3	A42	60h on 20h dp grn	2.25	3.25
a.		Inverted overprint	3,000.	
b.		Double overprint	25.00	
N4	A42	60h on 25h blue	12.00	13.00
a.		Inverted overprint	60.00	
b.		Double overprint	82.50	
N5	A42	60h on 30h dl vio	14.00	15.00
N6	A39	1k 20h on 50h dk grn	5.50	6.50
N7	A39	1k 20h on 60h dp bl	10.00	12.00
N8	A39	1k 20h on 1k car, yel	19.00	21.00

On Austrian Postage Due Stamps of 1910-1917

N9	D4	40h on 5h rose red	21.00	22.50
N10	D3	1k 20h on 25h carmine	175.00	350.00
N11	D4	1k 20h on 25h rose red	175.00	350.00
N12	D4	1k 20h on 30h rose red	1,400.	1,400.
N13	A38	1k 20h on 50h on 42h choc	1,500.	1,500.

Arms of Kiev

Arms of Ukraine

Arms of Galicia

First Definitive Issue, May 1919: Lithographed at the Austrian State Printing Office on unwatermarked white paper. Inscribed: "Ukrainska Narodnia Republyka Zakhidnia Oblast." ("Ukrainian National Republic Western Province"). Set of 12 values (four of each design), perf 11½ or imperf. Not issued. Value, set of 12: perf $350; imperf $550.

Second Definitive Issue, May 1919: Lithographed at the Austrian State Printing Office on unwatermarked white paper. Inscribed: "Ukrainska Narodna Respublika Z.O." ("Ukrainian National Republic W(estern) P(rovince)"). Design incorporates the heraldic arms of Ukraine (trident), Kiev (Archangel Michael) and Lviv (lion rampant). 10, 20 and 50 sotyk values imperf; 1 and 10 krone values perf 11½. Not issued. Value, set of 5, $6. Also exists on cream-colored paper.

WEST IRIAN

(Irian Barat)
(West New Guinea)

Stamps formerly listed under West Irian now appear in Volume 1, following United Nations, and Volume 3, following Indonesia.

YEMEN

'ye-mən

LOCATION — Arabian Peninsula, south of Saudi Arabia and bordering on the Red Sea
GOVT. — Republic
AREA — 204,000 sq. mi. (est.)
POP. — 16,942,230 (1999 est.)
CAPITAL — Sana'a (San'a)

40 Bogaches = 1 Imadi
40 Bogaches = 1 Riyal (1962)
100 Fils = 1 Riyal (1978)

The Yemen Arab Republic and the People's Republic of Yemen planned a 30-month unification process scheduled for completion by November 1992. While government ministries merged, both currencies remained valid.

Catalogue values for unused stamps in this country are for Never Hinged items, beginning with Scott 44 in the regular postage section, Scott C1 in the airpost section.

Watermarks

Wmk. 127 — Quatrefoils

Wmk. 258 — Arabic Characters and Y G Multiple

Wmk. 277 — Winged Wheel

For Domestic Postage

A1

Crossed Daggers and Arabic Inscriptions A2

1926   Unwmk.   Typo.   *Imperf.*
Laid Paper
Without Gum

1	A1	2½b black	60.00	60.00
2	A1	2½b black, *orange*	60.00	60.00
3	A2	5b black	60.00	60.00
		Nos. 1-3 (3)	180.00	180.00

No. 2 is known rouletted 7½ or 9.
Type A1 differs from A2 primarily in the inscription in the left dagger blade.
All come on wove paper. Beware of forgeries, especially those on wove paper.

For Foreign and Domestic Postage

Arabic Inscriptions
A3   A4

1930-31   Wmk. 127   *Perf. 14*

7	A3	½b orange ('31)	.30	.25
8	A3	1b green	.40	.30
9	A3	1b yellow grn ('31)	.35	.25
10	A3	2b olive grn	.40	.35
11	A3	2b olive brn ('31)	.35	.25
12	A3	3b dull vio ('31)	.40	.35
13	A3	4b red	.60	.50
14	A3	4b deep rose ('31)	.50	.40
15	A3	5b slate gray ('31)	.90	.50
16	A4	6b dull blue	1.25	1.00
17	A4	6b dp ultra ('31)	1.00	.75
18	A4	8b lilac rose ('31)	1.40	1.00
19	A4	10b lt brown	2.00	1.40
20	A4	10b brn org ('31)	1.75	1.00
21	A4	20b yel grn ('31)	4.50	2.50
22	A4	1i red brn & lt bl	8.00	6.00
23	A4	1i lil rose & yel grn ('31)	8.00	6.00
		Nos. 7-23 (17)	32.10	22.80

Some values exist imperforate.
For surcharges and overprints see Nos. 30, 59-62, 166-167, 169-171, 174-176, 246-246Q.

Flags of Saudi Arabia, Yemen and Iraq — A5

1939   Litho.   Wmk. 258   *Perf. 12½*

24	A5	4b dl rose & ultra	.80	.50
25	A5	6b slate bl & ultra	.80	.50
26	A5	10b fawn & ultra	1.40	.75
27	A5	14b olive & ultra	2.25	1.25

28	A5	20b yel grn & ultra	3.25	1.75
29	A5	1i claret & ultra	6.50	3.50
		Nos. 24-29 (6)	15.00	8.25

2nd anniv. of the Arab Alliance. Nos. 24-29 exist imperforate. Value set, $20.
For overprints see Nos. C29-C29D.

No. 7 Handstamped
in Black — a-b-c

Three types of surcharge
a. 11½x16mm
b. 13-13½x15½mm
c. 12x16mm
Values of surcharged stamps are for ordinary examples. Clear, legible surcharges command a premium.

1939   **Wmk. 127**   *Perf. 14*
| 30 | A3 | 4b on ½b orange | 15.00 | 12.50 |

See Nos. 44-48, 59-67, 82, 86-87.

A6

A7

1940   **Wmk. 258**   **Litho.**   *Perf. 12½*
31	A6	½b ocher & ultra	.25	.25
32	A6	1b lt grn & rose red	.25	.25
33	A6	2b bis brn & vio	.25	.25
34	A6	3b dl vio & ultra	.25	.25
35	A6	4b rose & yel grn	.35	.30
36	A6	5b dk gray grn & bis brn	.40	.35
37	A7	6b ultra & yel org	.45	.45
38	A7	8b claret & dull bl	.55	.50
39	A7	10b brn org & yel grn	.75	.75
40	A7	14b gray grn & vio	.95	.80
41	A7	18b emerald & blk	1.10	.90
42	A7	20b yel ol & cerise	1.50	1.50
43	A7	1i vio rose, yel grn & brn red	2.75	2.50
		Nos. 31-43 (13)	9.80	9.05
		Set, never hinged	20.00	

No. 36 was used as a 4b stamp in 1957.
For surcharges see Nos. 44-47.

Catalogue values for unused stamps in this section, from this point to the end of the section, are for Never Hinged items.

Nos. 31-34, 36 Handstamped Type "b" in Black

1946-51   *Perf. 12½*
44	A6	4b on ½b ('51)	3.50	2.50
45	A6	4b on 1b ('49)	4.00	3.50
46	A6	4b on 2b ('49)	4.50	3.50
47	A6	4b on 3b ('49)	4.50	3.50

1945-48   **Handstamp Type "a"**
44a	A6	4b on ½b	4.00	4.00
45a	A6	4b on 1b ('48)	4.00	3.00
46a	A6	4b on 2b ('48)	4.50	3.50
47a	A6	4b on 3b ('48)	5.00	3.50
48	A6	4b on 5b ('46)	4.00	3.00

Forged surcharges exist.

A8

1946   **Frames in Emerald**
49	A8	4b black	1.50	.85
50	A8	6b lilac rose	2.25	1.50
51	A8	10b ultra	3.25	1.90
52	A8	14b olive green	5.50	3.25
		Nos. 49-52 (4)	12.50	7.50

Opening of Mutawakkili Hospital. Exist imperforate. Value, set $15.
For overprints see Nos. 168, 172-173.

Mocha Coffee
Tree — A9

Palace,
San'a — A10

1947-58   **Unwmk.**   **Engr.**   *Perf. 12½*
53	A9	½b yellow brown	.25	.25
54	A9	1b purple	.70	.40
55	A9	2b ultra	1.40	.90
56	A10	4b red	2.25	1.25
57	A10	5b gray blue	2.50	1.50
58	A9	6b yellow green ('58)	3.50	2.00
		Nos. 53-58 (6)	10.60	6.30

No. 58 was printed in 1947 but not officially issued until June, 1958.
Additional values, prepared but not issued, were 10b, 20b and 1i, with views of palaces superimposed on flag, and palace square. These were looted from government storehouses during the 1948 revolution and a number of copies later reached collectors. Values, set: unused $20; used (cto) $15.
For surcharges see Nos. 63-65.

Admission of Yemen to the U.N.

10 postage, 5 airmail and 5 postage due stamps for the Admission of Yemen to the UN were not officially issued for use on domestic mail. Pictured on some of the stamps were Truman, Roosevelt, Churchill and the Statue of Liberty. Value, unused: 10v postage, $37; 5v air post, $22; 5v postage due, $14. Covers, scarce and all philatelic, exist to foreign destinations.

Nos. 9, 11, 12 and 15 Handstamped Type "a" in Black

1949   **Wmk. 127**   *Perf. 14*
59	A3	4b on 1b yellow grn	10.00	8.00
60	A3	4b on 2b olive brn	35.00	30.00
61	A3	4b on 3b dull vio	12.00	10.00
62	A3	4b on 5b slate gray	12.00	10.00

Handstamped type "b" are bogus.

Nos. 53-55 Handstamped Type "b" and "a"

1949   **Unwmk.**   *Perf. 12½*
63	A9(b)	4b on ½b yel brn	4.00	4.00
64	A9(a)	4b on 1b purple	5.00	5.00
a.		Handstamp type "b"	5.00	5.00
65	A9(a)	4b on 2b ultra	6.00	6.00
a.		Handstamp type "b"	6.00	6.00
b.		Handstamp 13x15mm		

Nos. J1-J2 Handstamped Type "b" in Black

1953   **Wmk. 258**
66	D1	4b on 1b org & yel grn	20.00	25.00
67	D1	4b on 2b org & yel grn	20.00	25.00
a.		Handstamp type "c"	25.00	30.00
		Nos. 59-67 (9)	124.00	123.00

Three minor types of this handstamped 4b surcharge exist. Types "a" and "b" exist inverted, double or horizontal.
Forged surcharges exist.

Parade Ground,
San'a — A13

Mosque,
San'a
A14

Designs: 5b, Flag of Yemen. 6b, Flag & eagle. 8b, Mocha coffee branch. 14b, Walled city of San'a. 20b, 1i, Ta'iz & its citadel.

1951   **Wmk. 277**   **Photo.**   *Perf. 14*
68	A13	1b dark brown	.30	.25
69	A13	2b red brown	.60	.25
70	A13	3b lilac rose	.75	.35
71	A14	5b blue & red	1.25	.60
72	A13	6b dk pur & red	1.40	.65
73	A13	8b dk bl & gray grn	1.50	.75
74	A14	10b rose lilac	1.25	.85
75	A14	14b blue green	2.25	1.00
76	A14	20b rose red	3.25	1.75
77	A14	1i violet	7.50	3.00
		Nos. 68-77 (10)	20.05	9.45
		Nos. 68-77,C3-C9 (17)	44.70	17.70

No. 71 was used as a 4b stamp in 1956. For surcharges see Nos. 82, 86-87.

Palace of the
Rock, Wadi
Dhahr — A15

Design: 20b, Walls of Ibb.

Engraved and Photogravure
1952   **Unwmk.**   *Perf. 14½, Imperf.*
78	A15	12b choc, bl & dl grn	6.00	6.00
79	A15	20b dp car, bl & brn	9.00	9.00
		Nos. 78-79,C10-C11 (4)	35.00	35.00

Flag and View of San'a (Palace in Background) — A16

1952
| 80 | A16 | 1i red brn, car & gray | 12.50 | 12.50 |

4th anniv. of the accession of King Ahmed, Feb. 18, 1948. See Nos. 81, C12-C13.

1952   **Palace in Foreground**
| 81 | A16 | 30b red brn, car & dk grn | 11.00 | 11.00 |

Victory of Mar. 13, 1948. See No. C13.

No. 69 Handstamped Type "b" in Black

1951 (?)   **Wmk. 277**   *Perf. 14*
| 82 | A13 | 4b on 2b red brown | 5.00 | 5.00 |

Forged surcharges exist. See Nos. 86-87.

Leaning Minaret,
Mosque of
Ta'iz — A17

1954   **Photo.**   **Unwmk.**
83	A17	4b deep orange	1.25	.40
84	A17	6b deep blue	2.00	.60
85	A17	8b deep blue green	2.50	1.50
		Nos. 83-85,C14-C16 (6)	19.50	6.65

Accession of King Ahmed I, 5th anniv.

Nos. 68 and 70 Handstamped Type "b" in Black

1955   **Wmk. 277**   *Perf. 14*
86	A13	4b on 1b dk brown	5.00	5.00
a.		Handstamp type "c"	20.00	10.00
87	A13	4b on 3b lilac rose	7.50	6.00

Yemen Gate,
San'a — A18

1956-57   **Wmk. 277**   *Perf. 14*
87A	A18	1b brown	1.00	.75
87B	A18	5b blue green	1.25	.75
87C	A18	10b dark blue ('57)	1.50	.85
		Nos. 87A-87C (3)	3.75	2.35

Nos. 87A-87C were prepared for official use, but issued for regular postage. The 1b and 5b were used as 4b stamps. A 20b and 1-imadi of type A18 were not issued. Value unused $25., used (CTO) $15.

Arab Postal Union Issue

Globe — A19

             Perf. 13½x13
1957-58   **Wmk. 195**   **Photo.**
88	A19	4b yellow brown	1.00	.90
89	A19	6b green ('58)	1.40	1.10
90	A19	16b violet ('58)	2.00	1.50
		Nos. 88-90 (3)	4.40	3.50

Arab Postal Union founding, July 1, 1954.

Telecommunications Issue

Globe,
Radio and
Telegraph
A20

1959, Mar.   **Wmk. 318**   *Perf. 13x13½*
| 91 | A20 | 4b vermilion | 1.75 | 1.25 |

Arab Union of Telecommunications.
Exists imperf, Value $6.

United Arab States Issue

Flags of
UAR and
Yemen
A21

1959, Mar. 13
92	A21	1b dl red brn & blk	.35	.25
93	A21	2b dk blue & blk	.45	.35
94	A21	4b sl grn, car & blk	.65	.50
		Nos. 92-94,C17-C19 (6)	6.55	5.05

First anniversary of United Arab States.
No. 94 exists imperf. Value $10.

In 1959 four special sets of stamps were distributed abroad. They honored Human Rights (4v), Yemeni stamps (6v), Automatic Telephone Service (5v) and King Ahmed's Reign (4v). They were overprinted on stamps of either the 1940 issue (type A6) or the 1931 issue (type A4). Although not regularly sold at post offices in Yemen, several values from these sets do appear on covers that passed through normal postal channels. Some values are known with inverted or doubled overprints.

Arab League Center Issue

Arab League Center, Cairo A22

Perf. 13x13½
1960, Mar. 22   Wmk. 328
95	A22	4b dull green & blk	.90 .90

Opening of the Arab League Center and the Arab Postal Museum in Cairo.
Exists imperf. Value $10.

Refugees Pointing to Map of Palestine A23

1960, Apr. 7   Photo.
96	A23	4b brown	1.10	.75
97	A23	6b yellow green	1.75	1.25

World Refugee Year, 7/1/59-6/30/60.
Exist imperf. Value, set $25.
In 1961 a souvenir sheet was issued containing a 4b gray and 6b sepia in type A18, imperf. Black marginal inscription, "YEMEN 1960," repeated in Arabic. Size: 103x85mm. Value $50.

Torch and Olympic Rings A24

1960, Dec.   Unwmk.   Perf. 14x14½
98	A24	2b black & lil rose	.55	.35
99	A24	4h black & yellow	.85	.50
100	A24	6b black & orange	1.20	.75
101	A24	8b brn blk & bl grn	2.10	1.40
102	A24	20b dk bl, org & vio	5.00	3.00
		Nos. 98-102 (5)	9.70	6.00

17th Olympic Games, Rome, 8/25-9/11.
Exist imperf. Value, set $75.
An imperf. souvenir sheet exists, containing one example of No. 99. Size: 100x60mm. Value $90.

UN Emblem Breaking Chains — A25

1961   Unwmk.   Perf. 14x14½
103	A25	1b violet	.35	.25
104	A25	2b green	.40	.30
105	A25	3b grnsh blue	.50	.35
106	A25	4b brt ultra	.55	.40
107	A25	6b brt lilac	.70	.50

108	A25	14b rose brown	1.00	.60
109	A25	20b brown	2.00	1.60
		Nos. 103-109 (7)	5.50	4.00

15th anniversary (in 1960) of UN.
Exist imperf. Value, set $14.
An imperf. souvenir sheet exists, containing one example of No. 106. Blue marginal inscription. Size: 100x60mm. Value $25.
For overprints see Nos. 137-143.

Cranes and Ship, Hodeida A26

1961, June   Litho.   Perf. 13x13½
110	A26	4b multicolored	.85	.40
111	A26	6b multicolored	1.40	.75
112	A26	16b multicolored	2.75	1.60
		Nos. 110-112 (3)	5.00	2.75

Opening of deepwater port at Hodeida.
An imperf. souvenir sheet exists, containing one each of Nos. 110-112. Size: 160x130mm. Value $7.
For overprints see Nos. 177, 180.

Alabaster Funerary Mask — A27

Designs (ancient sculptures from Marib, Sheba): 2b, Horned animal's head, symbolizing Moon God (limestone). 4b, Bronze head of an Emperor 1st or 2nd century. 8b, Statue of Emperor Dhamar Ali. 10b, Statue of a child, 2nd or 3rd century (alabaster). 12b, Stairs in court of Temple of the Moon God. 20b, Alabaster relief, boy riding monster. 1i, Woman with grapes, relief.

1961, Oct. 14   Photo.   Perf. 11½
Granite Paper
113	A27	1b salmon, blk & gray	.35	.25
114	A27	2b purple & gray	.60	.25
115	A27	4b pale brn, gray & blk	.80	.25
116	A27	8b brt pink & blk	1.00	.25
117	A27	10b yellow & blk	1.00	.35
118	A27	12b lt vio bl & blk	2.00	.50
119	A27	20b gray & blk	2.40	.60
120	A27	1i gray ol & blk	5.00	1.25
		Nos. 113-120,C20-C21 (10)	16.90	5.45

Exist imperf. Value, set (10), $25.
For overprints see Nos. 144-145, 147, 151, 153, 156-158, C24, C25.

Imam's New Palace, San'a — A28

8b, Side view of Imam's palace, San'a, horiz. 10b, Palace of the Rock (Dar al-Hajar).

1961, Nov. 15   Unwmk.
121	A28	4b black & lt bl grn	.35	.25
122	A28	8b blk, brt pink & grn	.75	.45
123	A28	10b black, sal & grn	.85	.50
		Nos. 121-123,C22-C23 (5)	3.90	2.05

Exist imperf. Value, set (5) $54.
For overprints see #148, 152, 154, C24, C25A.

Hodeida-San'a Road — A29

1961, Dec. 25   Litho.   Perf. 13½x13
124	A29	4b multicolored	.75	.25
125	A29	6b multicolored	.90	.40
126	A29	10b multicolored	1.50	.50
		Nos. 124-126 (3)	3.15	1.15

Opening of the Hodeida-San'a highway. A miniature sheet exists containing one each of Nos. 124-126, imperf. Size: 159x129mm. Value $7.
For overprints see Nos. 178-179.

Trajan's Kiosk, Philae, Nubia — A30

1962, Mar. 1   Photo.   Perf. 11x11½
127	A30	4b dk red brown	3.50	1.00
128	A30	6b blue green	6.25	2.00

Issued to publicize UNESCO's help in safeguarding the monuments of Nubia. Exist imperf. on toned paper with printer's imprint. Value, set $10.
A souvenir sheet exists, containing one each of #127-128, imperf. on white paper with printer's imprint at the bottom of the sheet. Size: 100x88½mm. Value $12.50.

Arab League Building, Cairo, and Emblem — A31

1962, Mar. 22   Perf. 13½x13
129	A31	4b dark green	.70	.25
130	A31	6b deep ultra	.85	.40

Arab League Week, Mar. 22-28.
A souvenir sheet exists, containing one each of Nos. 129-130, imperf. Size: 94x80mm. Value $3.50.
For overprints see Nos. 164-165.

Nurse, Mother and Child — A32

Designs: 4b, Nurse weighing child. 6b, Vaccination. 10b, Weighing infant.

1962, June 20   Unwmk.   Perf. 11½
131	A32	2b multicolored	.60	.25
132	A32	4b multicolored	.85	.30
133	A32	6b multicolored	1.00	.40
134	A32	10b multicolored	1.75	.50
		Nos. 131-134 (4)	4.20	1.45

Issued for Child Welfare.
Exist imperf. Value, set $8.
For overprints see Nos. 146, 149-150, 155.

Malaria Eradication Emblem — A33

1962, July 20   Perf. 13½x13
135	A33	4b black & dp org	.70	.25
136	A33	6b dk brown & grn	1.00	.40

WHO drive to eradicate malaria. An imperf. souvenir sheet contains one each of Nos. 135-136. Size: 95x79mm. Value $15.
No. 136 has laurel leaves added and inscription rearranged.
For overprints see Nos. 189-190.

Nos. 103-109 Overprinted

Perf. 14x14½
1962, Nov. 7   Photo.   Unwmk.
137	A25	1b violet	1.50	1.50
138	A25	2b green	1.50	1.50
139	A25	3b greenish blue	1.50	1.50
140	A25	4b brt ultra	1.50	1.50
141	A25	6b brt lilac	1.50	1.50
142	A25	14b rose brown	1.50	1.50
143	A25	20b brown	1.50	1.50
		Nos. 137-143 (7)	10.50	10.50

Exist imperf. and with inverted overprint.

Yemen Arab Republic
Nos. 113-123 and 131-134 Ovptd. in Dark Green or Dark Red

a

b

1963, Jan. 1   Perf. 11½
144	A27 (a)	1b No. 113 (G)	.25	.25
145	A27 (a)	2b No. 114	.25	.25
146	A32 (b)	2b No. 131	.40	.40
147	A27 (a)	4b No. 115 (G)	.40	.40
148	A28 (a)	4b No. 121	.55	.55
149	A32 (b)	4b No. 132 (G)	.55	.55
150	A32 (b)	6b No. 133	.70	.70
151	A27 (a)	8b No. 116	.70	.70
152	A28 (b)	8b No. 122 (G)	1.00	1.00
153	A27 (a)	10b No. 117	1.00	1.00
154	A28 (a)	10b No. 123	1.75	1.75
155	A32 (b)	10b No. 134 (G)	1.75	1.75
156	A27 (a)	12b No. 118	1.40	1.40
157	A27 (a)	20b No. 119	2.00	2.00
158	A27 (a)	1i No. 120	5.50	5.50
		Nos. 144-158,C24-C25A (19)	24.25	24.25

Nos. 144-158, C24-C25A exist imperf. Value, set $45.

Proclamation of the Republic
A34

UN Freedom From Hunger Campaign
A35

1963, Mar. 15   *Perf. 11x11½*
159 A34 4b shown   .55 .55
160 A34 6b Flag, tank   .85 .85
   An imperf. souvenir sheet containing Nos. 159-160 exists. Value $10.
   See Nos. C26-C28.

1963, Mar. 21   *Perf. 11½x11, 11x11½*
162 A35 4b Milk cow, horiz.   .90
163 A35 6b shown   1.25
   An imperf. souvenir sheet of 2 containing one each Nos. 162-163 exists. Value $12.
   For overprints see Nos. 219-220.

Nos. 129-130
Ovptd. in Dark Red

1963, Sept. 1   *Perf. 13½x13*
164 A31 4b dark green   7.00 7.00
165 A31 6b deep ultra   7.00 7.00

Nos. 15-16, 18-23, 50-52 Ovptd. in Black

     a   b

1963, Sept. 1
166 A3 (a) 5b No. 15   1.40 1.40
167 A4 (a) 6b No. 16   1.75 1.75
168 A4 (b) 6b No. 50   1.75 1.75
169 A4 (a) 8b No. 18   2.00 2.00
170 A4 (a) 10b No. 19   2.50 2.50
171 A4 (a) 10b No. 20   2.50 2.50
172 A8 (b) 10b No. 51   2.50 2.50
173 A8 (b) 14b No. 52   7.00 7.00
174 A4 (a) 20b No. 21   2.75 2.75
175 A4 (a) 1i No. 22   7.00 7.00
176 A4 (a) 1i No. 23   5.25 5.25
    Nos. 166-176 (11)   36.40 36.40

Nos. 111-112 and 125-126 Ovptd. in Black

       Perf. 13x13½, 13½x13
1963, Sept. 1   Litho.   Unwmk.
177 A26 6b No. 111   1.75 1.75
178 A29 6b No. 125   1.75 1.75
179 A29 10b No. 126   2.50 2.50
180 A26 16b No. 112   2.50 2.50
    Nos. 177-180 (4)   8.50 8.50
   On Nos. 178-179 the bars eliminate old inscription with text of overprint positioned below and to the right of them, on Nos. 177 and 180, the text is slightly left below the bars.
   Imperf. souvenir sheets of 2 exist containing Nos. 177 and 180 or Nos. 178-179. Value $20 each.

1st Anniv. of the Revolution — A36

     Perf. 11½x11, 11x11½
1963, Sept. 26   Photo.
186 A36 2b Flag, torch, candle, vert.   .35 .30
187 A36 4b shown   .55 .45
188 A36 6b Flag, grain, chain, vert.   .90 .70
    Nos. 186-188 (3)   1.80 1.45
   Imperf. souvenir sheet exists containing one each Nos. 186-188. Value $5.

Red Cross, Centennial — A36a

1963, October   Photo.   *Perf. 13½x13*
188A A36a ¼b bl, blk & red   .25 .25
188B A36a ⅛b lil brn, blk & red   .25 .25
188C A36a ½b ol grey, blk & red   .25 .25
188D A36a 4b vio, black & red   .75 .35
188E A36a 8b ocher, blk & red   1.00 .50
188F A36a 20b grn, blk & red   2.00 1.00
    Nos. 188A-188F (6)   4.50 2.60
   An imperf. souvenir sheet of 2 exists containing one each Nos. 188D-188E. Value $9.

Nos. 135-136
Ovptd. in Black

1963, Nov. 25   *Perf. 13½x13*
189 A33 4b black & dp orange   3.00 3.00
190 A33 6b dk brown & green   4.00 4.00

UN Declaration of Human Rights, 15th Anniv. — A37

1963, Dec. 10   *Perf. 13½*
191 A37 4b orange & dk brn vio   .55 .55
192 A37 6b blue grn & blk   .75 .75
   An imperf. souvenir sheet of 2 exists containing one each Nos. 191-192. Value $10.

Olympic Sports — A37a

1994, Mar. 30   Photo.   *Perf. 12*
192A A37a ¼b Darts   .25 .25
192B A37a ⅛b Table tennis   .25 .25
192C A37a ½b Running, vert.   .25 .25
192D A37a 1b Volleyball, vert.   .50 .40
192E A37a 1½b Soccer, vert.   .50 .40
192F A37a 4b Horse racing   .75 .50
192G A37a 20b Pole vault   1.50 1.25
   i.   Souvenir sheet of 1   3.00 3.00
192H A37a 1r Basketball, vert.   3.00 1.50
   Nos. 192F-192H are airmail. An imperf. souvenir sheet containing 1 No. 192F exists. Value $4.

Bagel Spinning and Weaving Factory Inauguration — A38

1964, Apr. 10   *Perf. 11x11½, 11½x11*
193 A38 2b Factory, bobbin, spool, cloth   .30 .25
193A A38 4b Loom machine   .40 .30
193B A38 6b Factory, spool, bolt of cloth   .55 .35
193C A38 16b shown   1.50 1.40
    Nos. 193-193C (4)   2.75 2.30
   Nos. 193-193B vert. An imperf. souvenir sheet of one exists containing No. 193C. Value $4.
   No. 193C is air mail.

Hodeida Airport Inauguration — A39

1964, Apr. 30   *Perf. 11½x11*
194 A39 4b Runway   .40 .35
194A A39 6b Runway, terminal   .55 .50
194B A39 10b Aircraft, terminal, ship at sea   .75 .55
    Nos. 194-194B (3)   1.70 1.40
   An imperf. souvenir sheet of one exists containing No. 194B. Value $3.

1964 New York World's Fair — A39a

   Designs: ¼b, 1b, 20b, Manhattan skyline, Sana'a. ⅛b, 4b, Empire State Building, minaret. ½b, 16b, Statue of Liberty, ship loading cranes.

1964, May 10   *Perf. 12*
195 A39a ¼b brown & multi   .25 .25
195A A39a ⅛b grey & multi   .25 .25
195B A39a ½b dk bl green & multi   .30 .25
195C A39a 1b dk grey & multi   .45 .35
195D A39a 4b dk grey & multi   .80 .50
195E A39a 16b brown & multi   1.50 1.00
195F A39a 20b red vio & multi   2.00 1.50
    Nos. 195-195F (7)   5.55 4.10
   Nos. 195E-195F are airmail. An imperf. souvenir sheet containing 1 No. 195F exists. Value $4.
   For overprints see Nos. 220-220F.

1964 Summer Olympic Games, Tokyo — A39b

   Designs: ¼b, 12b, Globe and flags. ⅛b, 6b, Torch. ½b, 20b, Discus thrower. 1b, Yemen flag. 1½b, 4b, Swimmers, horiz.

1964, June 1   *Perf. 12*
196 A39b ¼b multicolored   .25 .25
196A A39b ⅛b multicolored   .25 .25
196B A39b ½b multicolored   .30 .25
196C A39b 1b multicolored   .40 .30
196D A39b 1½b multicolored   .50 .35
196E A39b 4b multicolored   .85 .60
196F A39b 6b multicolored   1.00 .75
196G A39b 12b multicolored   1.75 1.25
196H A39b 20b multicolored   2.75 2.00
   i.   Souvenir sheet of 1   4.00 4.00
    Nos. 196-196H (9)   8.05 6.00
   Exist imperf. Value, set $25.
   Nos. 196E-196H are airmail.

Boy Scouts — A39c

   Designs: ¼b, 4b, Raising flag. ⅛b, 1b, 6b, Scouts, tents. ½b, 16b, Bugler. 1½b, 20b, Campfire.

1964, June 20
197 A39c ¼b multicolored   .25 .25
197A A39c ⅛b multicolored   .25 .25
197B A39c ½b multicolored   .30 .25
197C A39c 1b multicolored   .40 .30
197D A39c 1½b multicolored   .50 .35
197E A39c 4b multicolored   .85 .60
197F A39c 6b multicolored   1.00 .75
197G A39c 16b multicolored   1.75 1.25
   i.   Souvenir sheet of 1   4.00 4.00
197H A39c 20b multicolored   2.75 2.00
    Nos. 197-197H (9)   8.05 6.00
   Exist imperf. Value, set $20. An imperf. souvenir sheet containing 1 No. 197H exists. Value, $7.
   Nos. 197E-197H are airmail.

Animals — A39d

   Designs: ¼b, Baboons. ⅛b, Arabian horses. ½b, 12b, Zebu. 1b, 20b, Lions. 1½b, 4b, Gazelles.

1964, Aug. 15   Photo.   *Perf. 12x11½*
198 A39d ¼b lilac & brown   .25 .25
198A A39d ⅛b blue & dk brn   .25 .25
198B A39d ½b org & brn   .30 .25
198C A39d 1b blue & brn   .40 .30
198D A39d 1½b multicolored   .50 .35
198E A39d 4b multicolored   .85 .60
198F A39d 12b multicolored   1.00 .75
198G A39d 20b multicolored   1.75 1.25
    Nos. 198-198G (8)   5.30 4.00
   Exist imperf. Value, set $15.
   Nos. 198E-198G are airmail. See Nos. J9-J11.

Flowers — A39e

Designs: ¼b, shown. ½b, Crinum. ½b, 12b, Poinsettia. 1b, 4b, Hybrid tea. 1½b, 20b, Peppermint.

1964, Aug. 15 Photo. Perf. 11½x12

199	A39e	¼b multicolored	.25	.25
199A	A39e	½b multicolored	.25	.25
199B	A39e	½b grn, red & yel	.30	.25
199C	A39e	1b multicolored	.40	.30
199D	A39e	1½b red, grn & blk	.50	.35
199E	A39e	4b multicolored	.85	.60
199F	A39e	12b dk grn, red & yel	1.00	.75
199G	A39e	20b multicolored	1.75	1.25
		Nos. 199-199G (8)	5.30	4.00

Exist imperf. Value, set $12. Nos. 199E-199G are airmail. See Nos. J12-J14.

Sana'a Intl. Airport
Inauguration — A40

1964, Oct. 1

200	A40	1b shown	.35	.35
201	A40	2b Terminal, runway, aircraft	.35	.35
202	A40	4b like 2b	.35	.35
203	A40	8b like 1b	.70	.70
		Nos. 200-203 (4)	1.75	1.75

An imperf. souvenir sheet of two exists containing one each Nos. 202 and C30. Value $4. See No. C30.

Arab Postal Union, 10th Anniv. A41

2nd Arab Summit Conference A42

1964, Oct. 15 Perf. 13½

204	A41	4b multicolored	.75	.65

See No. C31.

1964, Nov. 30

205	A42	4b shown	.75	.65
206	A42	6b Conference emblem, map	1.00	.80

An imperf. souvenir sheet of 2 exists containing one each Nos. 205-206. Value $3. For overprints see Nos. 221-222.

2nd Anniv. of the Revolution A43

Deir Yassin Massacre A44

1964, Dec. 30

207	A43	2b Torch, map	.35	.30
208	A43	4b Revolutionary	.70	.50
209	A43	6b Flag, 2 candles, map	.70	.50
		Nos. 207-209 (3)	1.75	1.30

An imperf. souvenir sheet of one exists containing No. 209. Value $3.

Birds — A43a

Designs: ¼b, Reef Heron. ½b, Arabian red-legged partridge. ¾b, Eagle owl, vert. 1b, Hammer kop. 1½b, Yemen linnets. 4b, Hoopoes. 6b, Amethyst starlings. 8b, Bald ibis, vert. 12b, Arabian woodpecker, vert. 20b, Bateleur, vert. 1r, Bruce's green pigeon.

Perf. 15x14½, 14½x15

1965, Jan. 30 Photo.
Background Color

209A	A43a	¼b light violet	.50	.25
209B	A43a	½b brown olive	.75	.25
209C	A43a	¾b grey	.75	.25
209D	A43a	1b olive green	1.00	.40
209E	A43a	1½b rose	1.00	.40
209F	A43a	4b light blue	2.00	.75
209G	A43a	6b blue	2.00	.75
209H	A43a	8b bistre	2.00	1.00
209I	A43a	12b green	3.00	1.50
209J	A43a	20b orange	4.00	2.00
209K	A43a	1r blue green	6.00	3.00
		Nos. 209A-209K (11)	23.00	10.55

Souvenir Sheet
Imperf

209L	A43a	20b rose	15.00	15.00

Nos. 209A-209K exist imperf. Value, set $60. Nos. 209H-209L are airmail. For overprints see Nos. 221-221B.

1965, Apr. 30 Perf. 11x11½

210	A44	4b red lil & deep blue	.80	.60

See No. C32.

Intl. Telecommunications Union (ITU), Cent. — A45

1965, May 17 Perf. 11x11½, 11½x11

211	A45	4b red & pale blue, vert.	.75	.40
212	A45	6b org brn & grn	1.00	.55

A souvenir sheet of 1 exists containing #212. Value $4.

Burning of Algiers Library, 3rd Anniv. A46

1965, July 7 Perf. 11½x11

213	A46	4b sepia, red & grn	.75	.50

See No. C33.

3rd Anniv. of the Revolution A47

1965, Sept. 26

214	A47	4b Tractor, corn, grain	.75	.50
214A	A47	6b Tractor, tower, buildings	1.00	.55

An imperf. souvenir sheet of one exists containing No. 214A. Value $4.

Intl. Cooperation Year — A48

1965, Oct. 15 Perf. 11x11

215	A48	4b shown	.80	.60
215A	A48	6b UN building, New York	1.10	.65

An imperf. souvenir sheet of one exists containing No. 215A. Value $4.

Pres. John F. Kennedy — A48a

Kennedy and: Nos. 216, 216D, Rocket in flight. Nos. 216A, 216G, Launch pads. Nos. 216B-216C, Lift-off. 4b, Capsule in space. 8b, Splash down.

1965, Nov. 29 Photo. Perf. 12x11½

216	A48a	¼b multicolored	.25	.25
216A	A48a	¼b multicolored	.25	.25
216B	A48a	¼b multicolored	.25	.25
216C	A48a	½b multicolored	.25	.25
216D	A48a	½b multicolored	.25	.25
216E	A48a	4b multicolored	1.50	.75
216F	A48a	8b multicolored	2.50	1.25
216G	A48a	12b multicolored	6.00	3.00
		Nos. 216-216G (8)	11.25	6.25

Nos. 216F-216G are airmail. Imperf. souvenir sheets of Nos. 216E-216F exist. Value $5 each.

Astronauts and Cosmonauts — A48b

Spacecraft and: Nos. 217, 8b, Pavel Belyayev. Nos. 217A, 4b, Alexei Leonov. Nos. 217B, 217D, M. Scott Carpenter. Nos. 217C, 16b, Virgil I. "Gus" Grissom. No. 217H, James McDivitt, Edward White.

1965, Dec. 29 Photo. Perf. 11½x12

217	A48b	¼b multicolored	.25	.25
217A	A48b	¼b multicolored	.25	.25
217B	A48b	¼b multicolored	.25	.25
217C	A48b	½b multicolored	.25	.25
217D	A48b	½b multicolored	.25	.25
217E	A48b	4b multicolored	.75	.35
217F	A48b	8b multicolored	2.75	1.40
217G	A48b	16b multicolored	6.25	3.25
		Nos. 217-217G (8)	11.00	6.25

Souvenir Sheet
Imperf

217H	A48b	16b multicolored	12.50	12.50

Exist imperf. Value, set $15. Nos. 217E-217H are airmail. For overprints see Nos. 225-225H, 229-229D.

Nos. 162-163 Overprinted in Black

a

مكافحة الدرن
١٩٦٥
Tuberculous Campaign
1 9 6 5

b

مكافحة الدرن
١٩٦٥
TUBERCULOUS CAMPAIGN
1965

1966, Jan. 15 Perf. 11½x11, 11x11½

218	A35 (a)	4b sal rose & golden brn	1.00	.75
218A	A35 (b)	6b brt pur & yel	1.75	1.00

An imperf. souvenir sheet of two exists containing Nos. 218-218A. Value $10.

Telecommunications — A48c

Designs: No. 219, Light signals. No. 219A, Samuel F.B. Morse, telegraph. No. 219B, Early telephone. No. 219C, Philipp Reis, Thomas Edison, ealry telephone system. No. 219D, Television camera, antenna. No. 219E, Radar dish. No. 219F, Fax machine. No. 219G, Satellite.

1966, Jan. 29 Photo. Perf. 12x11½

219	A48c	¼b red & black	.25	.25
219A	A48c	¼b grnish bl & blk	.25	.25
219B	A48c	¼b yel brn & blk	.25	.25
219C	A48c	½b org red & blk	.25	.25
219D	A48c	½b violet & black	.25	.25
219E	A48c	4b yel grn & blk	.75	.35
219F	A48c	6b drab & black	1.25	.65
219G	A48c	20b blue & black	2.50	1.25
		Nos. 219-219G (8)	5.75	3.50

Nos. 219E-219G are airmail. An imperf. souvenir sheet containing 1 No. 219G exists.

Nos. 195-195F Overprinted in Black

1965 SANA'A ١٩٦٥ صنعاء

1966, Feb. 10 Photo. Perf. 12

220	A39a	¼b brown & multi	.50	.50
220A	A39a	½b grey & multi	.50	.50
220B	A39a	½b dk bl grn & multi	.60	.50
220C	A39a	1b dk grey & multi	.90	.70
220D	A39a	4b dk grcy & multi	1.00	1.00
220E	A39a	16b brown & multi	3.00	2.00
220F	A39a	20b red vio & multi	4.00	3.00
		Nos. 220-220F (7)	11.10	8.20

Nos. 220E-220F are airmail. An imperf. souvenir sheet containing 1 No. 220F exists. Value $10.

Nos. 209A-209C Overprinted in Black or Red

1966, Mar. 5 Photo. Perf. 12x11½
Background Color

221	A43a	¼b light violet	1.00	.75
221A	A43a	½b brown olive	1.00	.75
221B	A43a	¾b grey (R)	1.25	1.00
		Nos. 221-221B (3)	3.25	2.50

Nos. 205-206
Ovptd. in Red or
Black

1966, Mar. 20   *Perf. 13½*
| 222 | A42 | 4b dark green (R) | .75 | .50 |
| 222A | A42 | 6b orange brown | .85 | .55 |

An imperf. souvenir sheet of two exists containing Nos. 222-222A ovptd. in bright pink (4b) or black (6b) with additional inscription at bottom "CASABLANCA / 1965." Value $4.

Builders
of World
Peace
A49

Designs: Nos. 223, 223C, Dag Hammerskjold. Nos. 223A, 4b, John F. Kennedy. Nos. 223B, 223D, Jawaharlal Nehru. 6b, Mohammed Abdel Khaliq Hassuna. 10b, U Thant. 12b, Pope Paul VI.

1966, Mar. 25   **Photo.**   *Perf. 12*
223	A49	¼b green	.25	.25
223A	A49	¼b orange brown	.25	.25
223B	A49	¼b dark grey	.25	.25
223C	A49	½b red brown	.25	.25
223D	A49	½b violet brown	.25	.25
223E	A49	4b claret	.75	.35

Size:51x38mm
223F	A49	6b bl grn & brn	1.00	.50
223G	A49	10b blue & brown	1.25	.65
223H	A49	12b red lilac & brn	2.00	1.00
		Nos. 223-223H (9)	6.25	3.75

Exist imperf. Value, set $9. Nos. 223F-223H are airmail.

Two imperf. souvenir sheets, 4b and 8b, exist.

Domesticated Animals — A50

1966, May 5   **Photo.**   *Perf. 12½*
224	A50	¼b Rooster	.30	.25
224A	A50	¼b Rabbit	.30	.25
224B	A50	¼b Donkey	.30	.25
224C	A50	½b Cat	.40	.25
224D	A50	½b Sheep	.40	.25
224E	A50	4b Camel	1.00	.50
		Nos. 224-224E (6)	2.70	1.75

Souvenir Sheet
Imperf
| 224F | A50 | 22b Sheep, chickens, geese | 4.00 | 3.00 |

Nos. 224-224E exist imperf. Value, set $10. No. 224F is airmail.

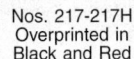

Nos. 217-217H
Overprinted in
Black and Red

Luna IX

1966, May 20   **Photo.**   *Perf. 11½x12*
225	A48b	¼b multicolored	.25	.25
225A	A48b	¼b multicolored	.25	.25
225B	A48b	¼b multicolored	.25	.25
225C	A48b	½b multicolored	.25	.25
225D	A48b	½b multicolored	.25	.25
225E	A48b	4b multicolored	.75	.35
225F	A48b	8b multicolored	2.75	1.40
225G	A48b	16b multicolored	6.25	3.25
		Nos. 225-225G (8)	11.00	6.25

Souvenir Sheet
Imperf
| 225H | A48b | 16b multicolored | 12.50 | 12.50 |

Nos. 225-225G exist imperf. Value, set $15. Nos. 225E-225H are airmail.

World Cup Soccer Championship,
London — A51

1966, May 29   **Photo.**   *Perf. 11*
Background Color
226	A51	¼b light green	.25	.25
226A	A51	¼b violet	.25	.25
226B	A51	¼b dull rose	.25	.25
226C	A51	½b green	.25	.25
226D	A51	½b orange red	.25	.25
226E	A51	4b blue	.60	.30
226F	A51	5b bistre	.75	.35
226G	A51	20b gold	2.40	1.20
		Nos. 226-226G (8)	5.00	3.10

An imperf souvenir sheet containing 1 No. 226G exists.

Traffic Day — A52

1966, June 30   *Perf. 11x11½*
| 227 | A52 | 4b green & ver | .75 | .50 |
| 228 | A52 | 6b green & ver | .85 | .55 |

Nos. 217-217D
Surcharged in
Black

Surveyor I

1966, Aug. 15   **Photo.**   *Perf. 11½x12*
229	A48b	1b on ¼b multi	1.00	1.00
229A	A48b	¼b multicolored	1.00	1.00
229B	A48b	½b multicolored	1.00	1.00
229C	A48b	½b multicolored	1.00	1.00
229D	A48b	½b multicolored	1.00	1.00
		Nos. 229-229D (5)	5.00	5.00

A53

Revolution, 6th
Anniv. — A53a

1966, Sept.   **Photo.**   *Perf. 11½*
| 230 | A53 | 2b multicolored | 2.50 | 2.00 |

Perf. 11x11¼
230A	A53a	4b multicolored	3.00	2.00
230B	A53a	6b Factory, tractor, wheat, corn	4.50	3.00
		Nos. 230-230B (3)	10.00	7.00

An imperf. souvenir sheet containing 1 each of Nos. 230A-230B exists. Value $20.

New WHO Headquarters,
Geneva — A54

WHO Headquarters, flowers and: Nos. 231, 4b, Galen (129-199). Nos. 231A, 8b, Hippocrates (460-370 BC). Nos. 231B, 16b, Ibn Sina (Avicenna) (980-1037).

1966, Nov. 1   **Litho.**   *Perf. 12½*
231	A54	¼b multicolored	.25	.25
231A	A54	¼b multicolored	.25	.25
231B	A54	¼b multicolored	.25	.25
231C	A54	4b multicolored	.50	.25
231D	A54	8b multicolored	1.00	.50
231E	A54	16b multicolored	2.00	1.00
		Nos. 231-231E (6)	4.25	2.50

Nos. 231C-231E are airmail. An imperf. souvenir sheet of 1 No. 231E exists. Value $8.

Gemini 6
and 7
Flights
A55

Designs: No. 232, Astronauts. No. 232A, Lift off. No. 232B, Spacecraft, Earth. ½b, 2b, Spacecraft in orbit. ½b, 8b, Splash down. 12b, Rendevous.

1966, Dec. 1   **Photo.**   *Perf. 12½*
Background Color
232	A55	¼b rose	.25	.25
232A	A55	¼b olive bistre	.25	.25
232B	A55	¼b blue	.25	.25
232C	A55	½b light blue	.25	.25
232D	A55	½b blue green	.25	.25
232E	A55	2b bistre	.50	.25

232F A55 8b blue   1.00 .50
232G A55 12b violet   1.50 .75
     Nos. 232-232G (8)   4.25 2.75

Nos. 232F-232G are airmail. An imperf. souvenir sheet containing 1 No. 232G exists. Value $8.

Nos. 232-232G Overprinted in Red

1966, Dec. 25   **Photo.**   *Perf. 12½*
Background Color
233	A55	¼b rose	.25	.25
233A	A55	¼b olive bistre	.25	.25
233B	A55	¼b light blue	.25	.25
233C	A55	½b light blue	.25	.25
233D	A55	½b blue green	.25	.25
233E	A55	2b bistre	.50	.25
233F	A55	8b blue	1.00	.50
233G	A55	12b violet	1.50	.75
		Nos. 233-233G (8)	4.25	2.75

Nos. 233F-233G are airmail. An imperf. souvenir sheet containing 1 No. 233G exists. Value $8.

Fruit
A56

1967, Feb. 10   **Litho.**   *Perf. 12½x12*
234	A56	¼b Figs	.25	.25
234A	A56	¼b Red apples	.25	.25
234B	A56	¼b Purple grapes	.25	.25
234C	A56	½b Dates	.25	.25
234D	A56	½b Apricots	.25	.25
234E	A56	2b Yellow apples	.60	.30
234F	A56	4b Oranges	.80	.40
234G	A56	6b Bananas	1.00	.50
234H	A56	8b Green figs	1.25	.65
234I	A56	10b Green grapes	1.50	.75
		Nos. 234-234I (10)	6.40	3.85

Exist imperf. Value, set $9. Nos. 234G-234I are airmail. See Nos. J23-J25.

Arab League
Day — A57

1967, July   **Photo.**   *Perf. 11x11½*
235	A57	4b violet & brown	.50	.25
235A	A57	6b dk violet & brown	.75	.40
235B	A57	8b violet & brown	1.25	.65
235C	A56	20b dk bl grn & brn	2.00	1.00
235D	A57	40b dk bl grn & blk	4.00	2.00
		Nos. 235-235D (5)	8.50	4.30

Gamal el-Din el-Afghani (1839-97), advocate of Arab unity.

Intl. Labor Organization (ILO) — A58

1968, Aug. Photo. Perf. 11½x11

236	A58	2b vio & dk blue	.40	.25
236A	A58	4b car & dk bl grn	.60	.30
236B	A58	6b grn & dp red lilac	1.00	.50
236C	A58	8b vio bl & ol bis	1.50	.75
		Nos. 236-236C (4)	3.50	1.80

An imperf. souvenir sheet containing 1 10b No. 236C exists. Value $6.

Agriculture — A59

1967, Sept. Photo. Perf. 11½x11

237	A59	1b multicolored	.25	.25
237A	A59	2b multicolored	.30	.25
236B	A59	4b multicolored	.35	.25
237C	A59	6b multicolored	.50	.25
237D	A59	8b multicolored	.85	.45
237E	A59	10b multicolored	1.25	.65
237F	A59	12b multicolored	1.50	.75
237G	A59	16b multicolored	1.75	.85
237H	A59	20b multicolored	2.50	1.25
237I	A59	40b multicolored	4.00	2.00
		Nos. 237-237I (10)	13.25	6.95

A set of six stamps was released in Sept. 1967 commemorating the 5th anniversary of the revolution. This issue was surcharged on Nos. 237-237E. The editors would like to examine examples of this surcharged set.

Paintings by Flemish Masters A60

Designs: ¼b, Village Wedding by Bruegel. ½b, The Doctor G. Zeile by Van Orley. ½b, H. Fourment and Her Children by Rubens. 3b, The King is Drinking by Jordaens. 6b, Self-Portrait by Van Dyck.

1967, Oct. Photo. Perf. 13½

239	A60	¼b gold & multi	.25	.25
239A	A60	½b gold & multi	.25	.25
239B	A60	½b gold & multi	.25	.25
239C	A60	3b gold & multi	.50	.25
239D	A60	6b gold & multi	1.10	.55
		Nos. 239-239D (5)	2.35	1.55

Nos. 239C-239D are airmail. An imperf. souvenir sheet containing 1 No. 239D exists. Nos. 239-239D exist imperf. with silver frames.

Flemish Painting Type

Paintings by Florentine Masters: ¼b, Portrait of a Young Man by Raphael. ½b, E. de Toledo and Her Son by A. Bronzino. ½b, Simonetta Vespucci by P. Di Cosimo. 3b, The Delphic Sibyl by Michelangelo. 6b, Spring by Botticelli.

1967, Nov. 17 Photo. Perf. 13½

240	A60	¼b gold & multi	.25	.25
240A	A60	½b gold & multi	.25	.25
240B	A60	½b gold & multi	.25	.25
240C	A60	3b gold & multi	.50	.25
240D	A60	6b gold & multi	1.10	.55
		Nos. 240-240D (5)	2.35	1.55

Nos. 240C-240D are airmail. An imperf. souvenir sheet containing 1 No. 240D exists. Nos. 240-240D exist imperf. with silver frames.

Flemish Painting Type

Paintings by Spanish Masters: ¼b, The Infanta Margarita by Velazquez. ½b, The Knock-Kneed Man by Ribera. ½b, The Beggar by Murillo. 3b, A Knight by El Greco. 6b, The Grape Gathering by Goya.

1967, Nov. 17 Photo. Perf. 13½

241	A60	¼b gold & multi	.25	.25
241A	A60	½b gold & multi	.25	.25
241B	A60	½b gold & multi	.25	.25
241C	A60	3b gold & multi	.50	.25
241D	A60	6b gold & multi	1.10	.55
		Nos. 241-241D (5)	2.35	1.55

Nos. 241C-241D are airmail. An imperf. souvenir sheet containing 1 No. 241D exists. Nos. 241-241D exist imperf. with silver frames.

1968 Winter Olympic Games, Grenoble A61

Sports: ¼b, Cross-country skiing. ½b, Figure skating. ½b, Bobsled. 3b, Ice hockey. 6b, Slalom skiing.

1967, Dec. 9 Photo. Perf. 11½

242	A61	¼b multicolored	.25	.25
242A	A61	½b multicolored	.25	.25
242B	A61	½b multicolored	.25	.25
242C	A61	3b multicolored	.50	.25
242D	A61	6b multicolored	1.10	.55
		Nos. 242-242D (5)	2.35	1.55

An imperf. souvenir sheet containing 1 No. 242D exists. Nos. 242-242D exist imperf. with different colors.

Paintings by Paul Gauguin — A62

Paintings: No. 243e, Woman in white dress. No. 243f, Woman lying on beach. No. 243g, Self-portrait. No. 243h, Nevermore. No. 243i, Girls from Pouldu. No. 243j, Girls from Bretagne. No. 243k, La Lune et la Terre. No. 243l, Angela. No. 243m, Woman. No. 243n, Two women.

1968, June Litho. Perf. 13½

243	A62	¼b Pair, #e.-f.	.40	.25
243A	A62	½b Pair, #g.-h.	.40	.25
243B	A62	½b Pair, #i.-j.	.40	.25
243C	A62	3b Pair, #k.-l.	1.00	.50
243D	A62	6b Pair, #m.-n.	2.00	1.00
		Nos. 243C-243D (5)	4.20	2.25

Nos. 243C-243D are airmail. Nos. 243-243D exist imperf. with gold frames. An imperf. souvenir sheet containing 1 No. 243D exists with either silver or gold frame.

Paintings by Gaugin Type

Paintings by Van Gogh: No. 244e, Julien Tanguy. No. 244f, Joseph Roulin. No. 244g, Sunflowers. No. 244h, Church in Auvers. No. 244i, Arnand Roulin. No. 244j, La Berceuse (Madam Roulin). No. 244k, Une Arlésienne an Mouemé. No. 244l, Marguerite Gachet at piano.. No. 244m, L'Arlésienne. No. 244n, Self-portrait.

1968, June Litho. Perf. 13½

244	A62	¼b Pair, #e.-f.	.40	.25
244A	A62	½b Pair, #g.-h.	.40	.25
244B	A62	½b Pair, #i.-j.	.40	.25
244C	A62	3b Pair, #k.-l.	1.00	.50
244D	A62	6b Pair, #m.-n.	2.00	1.00
		Nos. 244-244D (5)	4.20	2.25

Nos. 244C-244D are airmail. Nos. 244-244D exist imperf. with gold frames. An imperf. souvenir sheet containing 1 No. 244D exists with either silver or gold frame.

Paintings by Gaugin Type

Paintings by Rubens: No. 245e, Head of a little girl. No. 245f, Child's head (Holy Family detail). No. 245g, Portrait of a Negro. No. 245h, Thomas, Count of Arundel. No. 245i, Self-Portrait. No. 245j, Isabelle Brandt. No. 245k, Woman in a Hat. No. 245l, Helene Fourment. No. 245m, Rubens' sons. No. 245n, The Holy Family.

1968, June Litho. Perf. 13½

245	A62	¼b Pair, #e.-f.	.40	.25
245A	A62	½b Pair, #g.-h.	.40	.25
245B	A62	½b Pair, #i.-j.	.40	.25
245C	A62	3b Pair, #k.-l.	1.00	.50
245D	A62	6b Pair, #m.-n.	2.00	1.00
		Nos. 245-245D (5)	4.20	2.25

Nos. 245C-245D are airmail. Nos. 245-245D exist imperf. with gold frames. An imperf. souvenir sheet containing 1 No. 245D exists with either silver or gold frame.

Nos. 7-23 Overprinted in Black or Red

1968 Wmk. 127 Perf. 14

246	A3	½b on No. 7	.75
246A	A3	1b On No. 8 (R)	.75
246B	A3	1b On No. 9 (R)	.75
246C	A3	2b On No. 10 (R)	1.00
246D	A3	2b On No. 11	1.00
246E	A3	3b On No. 12	1.25
246F	A3	4b On No. 13	1.25
246G	A3	4b On No. 14	1.25
246H	A3	5b On No. 15 (R)	2.00
246I	A4	6b On No. 16 (R)	2.00
246J	A4	6b On No. 17 (R)	2.00
246K	A4	8b On No. 18	10.00
246L	A4	10b On No. 19	3.00
246M	A4	10b On No. 20	3.00
246N	A4	20b On No. 21	4.00
246O	A4	1i On No. 22	7.00
246P	A4	1i On No. 23	7.00
		Nos. 246-246P (17)	48.00

No. 246 exists with a red overprint. No. 246H is known with an inverted overprint.

Flemish Painting Type of 1967

Paintings of Horses: ¼b, Righteous Judge and Warrior of God by Hugo Van Eyck. ½b, The Virgin and the Unicorn by Zampieri (Domenichino). ½b, The Prince Baltsar Carlos by Velazquez. 3b, Roman Slave with Horses by Gericault. 6b, The Hunt by Ucello.

1968, July 10 Photo. Perf. 13½

247	A60	¼b gold & multi	.25	.25
247A	A60	½b gold & multi	.25	.25
247B	A60	½b gold & multi	.25	.25
247C	A60	3b gold & multi	.75	.35
247D	A60	6b gold & multi	1.25	.65
		Nos. 247-247D (5)	2.75	1.75

Nos. 247C-247D are airmail. An imperf. souvenir sheet containing 1 No. 247D exists. Nos. 247-247D exist imperf. with silver frames.

Flemish Painting Type of 1967

Paintings by Raphael: ¼b, La Velata. ½b, Angelo Doni. ½b, Plato and Aristotle. 3b, A Man. 6b, A Young Woman.

1968, July 10 Photo. Perf. 13½

248	A60	¼b gold & multi	.25	.25
248A	A60	½b gold & multi	.25	.25
248B	A60	½b gold & multi	.25	.25
248C	A60	3b gold & multi	.50	.25
248D	A60	6b gold & multi	1.10	.55
e.		Souvenir sheet of 1	4.00	
		Nos. 248-248D (5)	2.35	1.55

Nos. 248C-248D are airmail. An imperf. souvenir sheet of No. 248e exists. Nos. 248-248D exist imperf. with silver frames.

Flemish Painting Type of 1967

Paintings by Rembrandt: ¼b, Jan Six. ½b, Saskia. ½b, Mars. 3b, H. Stoffels. 6b, Self-portrait.

1968, July 10 Photo. Perf. 13½

249	A60	¼b gold & multi	.25	.25
249A	A60	½b gold & multi	.25	.25
249B	A60	½b gold & multi	.25	.25
249C	A60	3b gold & multi	.50	.25
249D	A60	6b gold & multi	1.10	.55
e.		Souvenir sheet of 1	4.00	
		Nos. 249-249D (5)	2.35	1.55

Nos. 249C-249D are airmail. An imperf. souvenir sheet of No. 249e exists. Nos. 249-249D exist imperf. with silver frames.

Revolution, 6th Anniversary — A63

President and: 2b, Fighters. 4b, Flag. 6b, Roses, vert.

1968, July Litho. Perf. 12¾

250	A63	2b multicolored	.40	.25
250A	A63	4b multicolored	.60	.30
250B	A63	6b multicolored	1.00	.50
		Nos. 250-250B (3)	2.00	1.05

Gold Medalists, 1968 Winter Olympic Games — A64

Various Olympic Gold Medals and: ¼b, Peggy Fleming, USA. ½b, Franco Nones, Italy. ½b, Jiri Raska, Czechosovakia. 2b, Hockey Team, USSR. 3b, Jean Claude Killy, France. 4b, Erhard Keller, Germany.

1968, Sept. 10 Litho. Perf. 13½

251	A64	¼b multicolored	.25	.25
251A	A64	½b multicolored	.25	.25
251B	A64	½b multicolored	.25	.25
251C	A64	2b multicolored	.35	.25
251D	A64	3b multicolored	.45	.25
251E	A64	4b multicolored	.60	.30
		Nos. 251-251E (6)	2.15	1.55

Nos. 251D-251E are airmail. No. 251E exists in perf. and imperf. souvenir sheets of one. Nos. 251-251E exist imperf. with light blue borders.

1968 Summer Olympic Games, Mexico City — A65

Ancient Greek art and artifacts of Mexico: ¼b, Greek man, sculpture. ½b, Woman on bull, jade mask. ½b, Three people, jaguar. 2b, Two warriors, large carving. 3b, Chariot, mask. 4b, Rider and 2 people, sculpture. No. 252F, Three warriors, Central University City Campus site.

1968, Sept. 30 Litho. Perf. 13½

252	A65	¼b multicolored	.25	.25
252A	A65	½b multicolored	.25	.25
252B	A65	½b multicolored	.25	.25
252C	A65	2b multicolored	.35	.25
252D	A65	3b multicolored	.45	.25
252E	A65	4b multicolored	.60	.30
		Nos. 251-251E (6)	2.15	1.55

Souvenir Sheet

252F	A65	4b multicolored	3.00	1.50

Nos. 252D-252F are airmail. No. 252F contains one 88x35mm stamp. Nos. 252-252F exist imperf. with silver frames.

Olympic Medals Type of 1968

Olympic Gold Medals from: ¼b, 1896, 1908, 1912. ½b, 1920, 1924. ½b, 1928, 1932. 2b, 1936, 1948, 1952. 3b, 1956, 1960, 1964. 4b, 1968, 1972.

1968, Oct. 18 Litho. Perf. 13½

253	A64	¼b multicolored	.25	.25
253A	A64	½b multicolored	.25	.25
253B	A64	½b multicolored	.25	.25
253C	A64	2b multicolored	.35	.25
253D	A64	3b multicolored	.45	.25
253E	A64	4b multicolored	.60	.30
		Nos. 253-253E (6)	2.15	1.55

Nos. 253D-253E are airmail. No. 253E exists in perf. and imperf. souvenir sheets of one. Nos. 253-253E exist imperf. with light blue borders.

Arms of Winter Olympic Games Host Cities — A66

Designs: ¼b, Ancient ski. ½b, Chamonix, 1924; St. Moritz, 1928; Lake Placid, 1932. ½b, Garmisch 1936; St. Moritz, 1948; Oslo, 1952. 2b, Cortina, 1956; Squaw Valley, 1960; Innsbruck, 1964. 3b, Grenoble, 1968. 4b,Sapporo, 1972.

			1968, Nov. 23	**Litho.**	**Perf. 13½**
254	A66	¼b multicolored		.25	.25
254A	A66	½b multicolored		.25	.25
254B	A66	½b multicolored		.25	.25
254C	A66	2b multicolored		.35	.25
254D	A66	3b multicolored		.45	.25
254E	A66	4b multicolored		.60	.30
		Nos. 254-254E (6)		2.15	1.55

Nos. 254D-254E are airmail. A perf. and imperf. souvenir sheet containing one each of Nos. 254D-254E exist. Nos. 254-254E exist perf. and imperf. with light blue borders.

Arms of Olympic Host Cities Type

Arms of Summer Olympic Games Host Cities: ¼b, Athens, 1896; London, 1908; Stockholm, 1912. ½b, Antwerp, 1920; Paris, 1924. ½b, Amsterdam, 1928; Los Angeles, 1932; Berlin, 1936. 2b, London, 1948; Helsinki, 1952. 3b, Melbourne, 1956; Rome, 1960; Tokyo, 1964. 4b, Mexico City, 1968; Munich, 1972.

			1968, Dec. 22	**Litho.**	**Perf. 13½**
255	A66	¼b multicolored		.25	.25
255A	A66	½b multicolored		.25	.25
255B	A66	½b multicolored		.25	.25
255C	A66	2b multicolored		.35	.25
255D	A66	3b multicolored		.45	.25
255E	A66	4b multicolored		.60	.30
		Nos. 255-255E (6)		2.15	1.55

Nos. 255D-255E are airmail. A perf. and imperf. souvenir sheet containing one No. 255E exists. Nos. 255-255E exist perf. and imperf. with light blue borders.

Intl. Human Rights Figures A67

Designs: ¼b, 10b, Dr. Christian Bernhard with patient, horiz. ½b, 2b, Dag Hammarskjold. ¾b, Dr. Bernhard. 1b, 4b, Rev. Martin Luther King. 6b, 14b, Robert F. and John F. Kennedy, horiz. 8b, Dr. Bernhard with heart, horiz. 12b, 16b, Dr. King and Abraham Lincoln, horiz.

			1968	**Litho.**	**Perf. 12½**
256	A67	¼b multicolored		.25	.25
256A	A67	½b multicolored		.25	.25
256B	A67	¾b multicolored		.35	.25
256C	A67	1b multicolored		.35	.25
256D	A67	2b multicolored		.40	.25
256E	A67	4b multicolored		.50	.25
256F	A67	6b multicolored		.65	.35
256G	A67	8b multicolored		.75	.35
256H	A67	10b multicolored		1.00	.50
256I	A67	12b multicolored		1.10	.55
256J	A67	14b multicolored		1.25	.65
256K	A67	16b multicolored		1.25	.65
		Nos. 256-256K (12)		8.10	4.55

Three imperf. souvenir sheets exist; a 10b with Robert and John Kennedy, a 16b with King and LIncoln and a 20b with Dr. Bernhard.

Cultural Olympiad, Mexico City — A68

Paintings in the Louvre, Paris: ¼b, Madeleine by Van Der Weyden. ½b, The Gypsy by Frans Hals. ½b, Balthasar Castiglionne by Raphael. 2b, The Lacemaker by Vermeer. 3b, Women and Child by Da Vinci. 4b, Madonna and Child by Botticelli. No. 257F, Mona Lisa by Da Vinci.

			1969, Feb. 19	**Litho.**	**Perf. 13½**
257	A68	¼b silver & multi		.25	.25
257A	A68	½b silver & multi		.25	.25
257B	A68	½b silver & multi		.25	.25
257C	A68	2b silver & multi		.35	.25
257D	A68	3b silver & multi		.45	.25
257E	A68	4b silver & multi		.60	.30
		Nos. 257-257E (6)		2.15	1.55

Souvenir Sheet

257F	A68	4b gold & multi	3.50	3.50

Nos. 257D-257F are airmail. Nos. 257-257E exist with gold frames. No. 257F exists imperf with a blue green background. No. 257C is iinscribed The Embroiderer. No. 257E is inscribed Woman and Child.

Cultural Olympiad Type

Paintings in the Uffizi Gallery, Florence: ¼b, Battista Sforza by Piero Della Francesca. ½b, Francesco delle Opere by Perugino. ½b, Francesco Maria della Rovere by Raphael. 2b, Isabel Brandt by Rubens. 3b, Don Garcia de Médicis by Bronzino. 4b, The Birth of Venus (detail) by Botticelli. No. 257F, Alegoria della Primavera by Botticelli.

			1969, Mar. 29	**Litho.**	**Perf. 13½**
258	A68	¼b gold & multi		.25	.25
258A	A68	½b gold & multi		.25	.25
258B	A68	½b gold & multi		.25	.25
258C	A68	2b gold & multi		.35	.25
258D	A68	3b gold & multi		.45	.25
258E	A68	4b gold & multi		.60	.30
		Nos. 258-258E (6)		2.15	1.55

Souvenir Sheet

258F	A68	4b gold & multi	3.50	3.50

Nos. 258D-258F are airmail. Nos. 258-258E exist with gold frames. No. 258F exists imperf with a red orange frame.

Cultural Olympiad Type

Paintings in the Prado, Madrid: ¼b, Charles the First, of England by Van Dyck. ½b, The Story of Nastaglio by Botticelli. ½b, Maria Ruthven by Van Dyck. 2b, Portrait of a Man by Dürer. 3b, Young Girl by Raphael. 2b, Self-portrait by Dürer. No. 257F, A Maja Vestida by Goya.

			1969, May 2	**Litho.**	**Perf. 13½**
259	A68	¼b silver & multi		.25	.25
259A	A68	½b silver & multi		.25	.25
259B	A68	½b silver & multi		.25	.25
259C	A68	2b silver & multi		.35	.25
259D	A68	3b silver & multi		.45	.25
259E	A68	4b silver & multi		.60	.30
		Nos. 259-259E (6)		2.15	1.55

Souvenir Sheet

259F	A68	4b gold & multi	3.50	3.50

Nos. 259D-259F are airmail. Nos. 259-259E exist with bronze frames. No. 258F exists imperf.

Discoveries of the Universe — A69

Spacecraft and Astronomers: No. 260, Vanguard, Ptolemy. No. 260A, Sputknik III, Copernicus. No. 260B, Lunik, Michelangelo. No. 260C, Explorer VI, Tycho Brahe. 3b, Lunik III, Galileo. 6b, Lunik II, Kepler. 10b, Explorer VII, Newton. 14b, Apollo 8.

			1969, May 26	**Litho.**	**Perf. 13½**
260	A69	¼b silver & multi		.25	.25
260A	A69	¼b silver & multi		.25	.25
260B	A69	½b silver & multi		.25	.25
260C	A69	½b silver & multi		.25	.25
260D	A69	3b silver & multi		.75	.35
260E	A69	6b silver & multi		1.25	.65
260F	A69	10b silver & multi		2.00	1.00
		Nos. 260-260F (7)		5.00	3.00

Souvenir Sheet

260G	A69	14b multicolored	6.00	3.00

Nos. 260E-260G are airmail. Nos. 260-260F exist imperf. with lilac-silver frames. A 14b imperf. souvenir sheet with Soyuz 4-5 and Apollo 8 exists.

Discoveries of the Universe Type

Old and New Space Travel: No. 261, Wan Pou, Pioneer IV, Pioneer V. No. 261A, Lucion di Samosa, Sputnik V, Explorer 10, Venus I. No. 261B, Cyrano de Bergerac, Mariner II, Mariner III. No. 261C, Jules Verne, Mariner V. 2b, Nicolar Kibaltchich, Zond II. 4b, Rocket Lift-off, Venus II, Venus III, Luna X. 22b, Lunar lander, Venus IV. No. 261G, Apollo 9.

			1969, July 3	**Litho.**	**Perf. 13½**
261	A69	¼b silver & multi		.25	.25
261A	A69	¼b silver & multi		.25	.25
261B	A69	½b silver & multi		.25	.25
261C	A69	½b silver & multi		.25	.25
261D	A69	2b silver & multi		.50	.35
261E	A69	4b silver & multi		.75	.35
261F	A69	22b silver & multi		2.25	1.10
		Nos. 261-261F (7)		4.50	2.80

Souvenir Sheet

261G	A69	6b multicolored	4.00	2.00

Nos. 261D-261G are airmail. Nos. 261-261F exist imperf. with gold frames. A 6b imperf. souvenir sheet with Apollo 9 and a space station exists.

Intl. Labor Organization — A70

			1969, Aug. 4	**Litho.**	**Perf. 13½**
262	A70	1b Stonemason		.25	.25
262A	A70	2b Blacksmith		.35	.25
262B	A70	3b Teacher		.50	.25
262C	A70	4b Printer		.60	.30
262D	A70	6b Polisher		.75	.35
262E	A70	8b Foundry worker		1.00	.50
262F	A70	10b Farrier		1.25	.60
		Nos. 262-262F (7)		4.70	2.50

Nos. 262D-262F are airmail. Nos. 262-262F exist imperf.

Discoveries of the Universe Type

Spacecraft: No. 263, Mercury Atlas 3, Vostok I, Vostok II, Mercury Atlas 6. No. 263A, Mercury Atlas 8, Vostok III & IV, Mercury Atlas 9, Vostok VI. No. 263B, Voskhod II, Voskhod I, Gemini 3, Gemini 4. No. 263C, Gemini 5-9. 3b, Apollo 8-9. 6b, Soyuz III, Soyuz I, Apollo 7-8. 10b, Gemini 10-12, Apollo 7. No. 263G, Vostok I, Mercury.

			1969, Aug. 25	**Litho.**	**Perf. 13½**
263	A69	¼b multicolored		.25	.25
263A	A69	¼b multicolored		.25	.25
263B	A69	½b multicolored		.25	.25
263C	A69	½b multicolored		.25	.25
263D	A69	3b multicolored		.50	.35
263E	A69	6b multicolored		1.00	.50
263F	A69	10b multicolored		1.50	.75
		Nos. 263-263F (7)		4.00	2.60

Souvenir Sheet

263G	A69	6b multicolored	6.00	3.00

Nos. 263D-263G are airmail. No. 263G contains one 82x43mm stamp. Nos. 263-263F exist imperf. with light yellow green frames. A 6b imperf. souvenir sheet with Apollo 10 exists.

Napoloen, Birth Bicentennial — A71

Napoleon: ¼b, As artillery lieutenant. ½b, As lieutenant colonel, 1792. ½b, As consul. ¾b, On his way to Augsburg. 4b, Crossing over the St. Bernard. 8b, In 1814. 10b, At the height of his career. No. 264G, At his coronation, 1804.

			1969, Sept. 16	**Litho.**	**Perf. 13½**
264	A71	¼b silver & multi		.35	.25
264A	A71	½b silver & multi		.35	.25
264B	A71	½b silver & multi		.40	.25
264C	A71	¾b silver & multi		.40	.25
264D	A71	4b silver & multi		1.50	.75
264E	A71	8b silver & multi		2.00	1.00
264F	A71	10b silver & multi		2.50	1.25
		Nos. 264-264F (7)		7.50	4.00

Souvenir Sheet

264G	A71	4b multicolored	6.00	2.00

Nos. 264D-264G are airmail. No. 264G contains one 46x69mm stamp. An imperf. 4b souvenir sheet showing a Napoleon bicentennial medal exists. Nos. 264-264F exist imperf. with lilac-silver frames.

Discoveries of the Universe Type

Lunar Research: No. 265, Soyuz IV & V, Apollo 10. No. 265A, Apollo 11. No. 265B, Planned Lunar trips. No. 265C, Lunar surface vehicles. 2b, Lunar vehicles, diff. 4b, Moon base and vehicles. 22b, Soviet lunar project, Apollo 11. No. 265G, Apollo 11.

			1969, Oct. 10	**Litho.**	**Perf. 13½**
265	A69	¼b multicolored		.25	.25
265A	A69	¼b multicolored		.25	.25
265B	A69	½b multicolored		.25	.25
265C	A69	½b multicolored		.25	.25
263D	A69	2b multicolored		.40	.25
265E	A69	4b multicolored		.60	.30
265F	A69	22b multicolored		2.00	1.00
		Nos. 265-265F (7)		4.00	2.55

Souvenir Sheet

265G	A69	14b multicolored	5.00	2.00

Nos. 265D-265G are airmail. No. 263G contains one 63x49mm stamp. Nos. 265-265F exist imperf. with light orange frames. A 14b imperf. souvenir sheet with Apollo 11 plaque and astronauts exists.

Cultural Olympiad Type

Paintings in the National Gallery, Washington, DC: ¼b, David by Del Castagno. ½b, Elena Grimaldi by Van Dyck. ½b, Girl with her Dueña by Murillo. 2b, Agostina by Corot. 3b, Ginevra Bentivoglio by Ercole Roberti. 4b, Balthasar Coymans by Frans Hals. No. 266F, Ginevra de Benci by Da Vinci.

			1969, Nov.	**Litho.**	**Perf. 13½**
266	A68	¼b lilac silver & multi		.25	.25
266A	A68	½b lilac silver & multi		.25	.25
266B	A68	½b lilac silver & multi		.25	.25
266C	A68	2b lilac silver & multi		.35	.25

266D	A68	3b lilac silver & multi	.45	.25
266E	A68	4b lilac silver & multi	.60	.30
		Nos. 266-266E (6)	2.15	1.55

Souvenir Sheet

266F	A68	4b gold & multi	4.00	2.00

Nos. 266D-266F are airmail. Nos. 266-266E exist with gold frames. No. 266F contains one 36x69mm stamp. No. 266F exists with a red background instead of blue green and also exists imperf.

Cultural Olympiad Type

Paintings in the National Gallery, London: ¼b, Portrait of a Woman by Van Der Weyden. ½b, Portrait of a Young Man by Antonello da Messina. ½b, Portrait of a Young Girl by Mabuse. 2b, The Crab Saleswoman by Hogarth. 3b, Baron Schwiter by Delacroix. 4b, Portrait of an Old Woman by Cézanne. No. 266F, Morning Promenade by Gainsborough.

1969, Dec.		Litho.	Perf. 13½	
267	A68	¼b bluish sil & multi	.25	.25
267A	A68	½b bluish sil & multi	.25	.25
267B	A68	½b bluish sil & multi	.25	.25
267C	A68	2b bluish sil & multi	.35	.25
267D	A68	3b bluish sil & multi	.45	.25
267E	A68	4b bluish sil & multi	.60	.30
		Nos. 267-267E (6)	2.15	1.55

Souvenir Sheet

267F	A68	4b gold & multi	4.00	2.00

Nos. 267D-267F are airmail. Nos. 267-267E exist with bronze frames. No. 267F contains one 35x74mm stamp. No. 267F exists with an orange yellow background instead of greenish blue and also exists imperf.

Famous French Leaders — A72

Designs: 1¾b, Clovis I. 2b, Charlemagne. 2¼b, Jeanne d'Arc. 2½b, Louis XIV. 3½b, Napoleon I. 5b, Georges Clemenceau. 6b, 10b, Charles de Gaulle.

1969		Litho.	Perf. 13½	
268	A72	1¾b gold & multi	.50	.25
268A	A72	2b gold & multi	.50	.25
268B	A72	2½b gold & multi	.50	.25
268C	A72	2½b gold & multi	.50	.25
268D	A74	3½b gold & multi	.60	.30
268E	A72	5b gold & multi	.75	.35
268F	A72	6b gold & multi	.90	.45
		Nos. 268-268F (7)	4.25	2.10

Souvenir Sheet

268G	A72	10b multicolored	6.00	2.00

Nos. 268D-268G are airmail. No. 268G contains one 50x83mm stamp. A 10b imperf. souvenir sheet exists depicting DeGaulle, Jeanne d'Arc and Napoleon. Value $6.

Art Treasures of Tutankhamen — A73

Tutankhamun: ¼b, Stone bust. ½b, Alabaster bust. ½b, Painted bust. 2b, Painted statue. 3b, Gold Mask. 4b, Painted head.

1970, May 20		Litho.	Perf. 13½	
269	A73	¼b lilac silver & multi	.25	.25
269A	A73	½b lilac silver & multi	.25	.25
269B	A73	½b lilac silver & multi	.25	.25
269C	A73	2b lilac silver & multi	.60	.30
269D	A73	3b lilac silver & multi	.75	.35
269E	A73	4b lilac silver & multi	.90	.45
		Nos. 269-269E (6)	3.00	1.85

Nos. 269D-269E are airmail. Perf. and imperf. souvenir sheets containing 1 No. 269E exist. These sheets were also overprinted in Red or Green for Roma '70. Nos. 269-269E exist imperf with silver frames.

Art Treasures Type

Treasures of Siam: ¼b, Bronze Buddha head. ½b, Stone Buddha head. ½b, Statue from Angkor. 2b, Spirit of Echiffre. 3b, King Pisei. 4b, Buddha on Naga.

1970		Litho.	Perf. 13½	
270	A73	¼b lilac silver & multi	.25	.25
270A	A73	½b lilac silver & multi	.25	.25
270B	A73	½b lilac silver & multi	.25	.25
270C	A73	2b lilac silver & multi	.60	.30
270D	A73	3b lilac silver & multi	.75	.35
270E	A73	4b lilac silver & multi	.90	.45
		Nos. 270-270E (6)	3.00	1.85

Nos. 270D-270E are airmail. Perf. and imperf. souvenir sheets containing 1 No. 270E exist. Nos. 270-270E exist imperf with silver frames.

Art Treasures Type

Treasures of Japan: Various paintings.

1970		Litho.	Perf. 13½	
271	A73	¼b lilac silver & multi	.25	.25
271A	A73	½b lilac silver & multi	.25	.25
271B	A73	½b lilac silver & multi	.25	.25
271C	A73	2b lilac silver & multi	.60	.30
271D	A73	3b lilac silver & multi	.75	.35
271E	A73	4b lilac silver & multi	.90	.45
f.		Souvenir sheet of 1, silver & multi	5.00	2.00
		Nos. 271-271E (6)	3.00	1.85

Nos. 271D-271E, 271f are airmail. No. 271f has red Expo '70 imprint in the sheet margin. Nos. 271-271E exist imperf with silver frames. No. 271f exists imperf.

Expo '70, Osaka, Japan — A74

Various traditional Japanese puppets.

1970, Mar. 15		Litho.	Perf. 13½	
272	A74	¼b gold & multi	.35	.25
272A	A74	½b gold & multi	.35	.25
272B	A74	½b gold & multi	.35	.25
272C	A74	2b gold & multi	.70	.35
272D	A74	3b gold & multi	.90	.45
272E	A74	4b gold & multi	1.10	.55
		Nos. 272-272E (6)	3.75	2.10

Nos. 272D-272E are airmail. Nos. 272-272E exist with silver frames, and imperf. with gold frames. Perf. and imperf. souvenir sheets containing 1 No. 272E exist.

World Cup Soccer Championships, Mexico — A75

1970, Apr. 4		Litho.	Perf. 13½	
273	A75	Sheet of 9+label	5.50	2.75
d.		1¾b Uruguay 1930	.50	.25
e.		2b Italy 1934	.50	.25
f.		2¼b France 1938	.50	.25
g.		2½b Brazil 1950	.50	.25
h.		3½b Switzerland 1954	.60	.30
i.		5b Sweden 1968	.60	.30
j.		7b England 1966	.70	.35
k.		8b Mexico 1970	.80	.40

Souvenir Sheets

273A	A75	4b Pele	5.00	
273B	A75	4b Beckenbauer	7.50	

Nos. 273g-273k, 273A-273B are airmail.

Opening of New UPU Headquarters, Bern, Switzerland — A76

Country Views and Europa Stamp Designs: 1½b, Austria, Luxemburg, 1956-57 designs. 1¾b, Belgium, Spain, 1958-59 designs. 2¼b, Greece, Portugal, 1960-61 designs. 2½b, Norway, Denmark, 1962-63 designs. 5b, Switzerland, Netherlands, 1964-65 designs. 7b, France, England, 1965-66 Designs. 8b, Germany, Italy, 1968-69 designs. 10b, New UPU Headquarters, 1970 design, UPU emblem.

1970, May 5		Litho.	Perf. 13½	
274	A76	Sheet of 8	4.50	2.25
b.		1½b multicolored	.40	.25
c.		1¾b multicolored	.40	.25
d.		2¼b multicolored	.40	.25
e.		2½b multicolored	.40	.25
f.		5b multicolored	.50	.30
g.		7b multicolored	.65	.30
h.		8b multicolored	.75	.35
i.		10b multicolored	1.00	.50

Souvenir Sheet

274A	A76	10b Liechtenstein 356	5.00	2.00

Nos. 274g-274i, 274A are airmail. No. 274 exists imperf with light orange borders. No. 274A contains one 50x50mm stamp. An imperf. 10b souvenir sheet showing Luxembourg 320 exists.

Apollo 12 — A77

Stages of Apollo 12 Mission: 1b, Lift-off. 1¼b, In Lunar orbit. 1½b, LM approaches landing site. 1½b, 32 hours on Lunar surface. 4b, Lift-off from the Moon. 4½b, Return to Earth. 7b, Splash down. No. 275A, Astronauts on Lunar surface.

1970, May 11		Litho.	Perf. 13½	
275	A77	Sheet of 7+label	4.50	2.25
b.		1b multicolored	.40	.25
c.		1¼b multicolored	.40	.25

---

d.		1½b multicolored	.40	.25
e.		1½b multicolored	.40	.25
f.		4b multicolored	.65	.30
g.		4½b multicolored	.75	.30
h.		7b multicolored	1.25	.65

Souvenir Sheet

275A	A77	4b multicolored	5.00	

Nos. 274f-275h, 275A are airmail. No. 275 exists imperf with yellow and gold borders. No. 275A contains one 72x56mm stamp. An imperf 4b souvenir sheet exists with the lunar scene reflected in astronaut's helmet.

World Cup Soccer Championships, Mexico — A78

1970, May 20		Litho.	Perf. 13½	
276	A78	Sheet of 6	4.00	2.00
c.		¼b Soviet team	.50	.25
d.		½b Brazilian team	.50	.25
e.		½b English team	.50	.25
f.		¾b Italian team	.50	.25
g.		4b German team	.60	.30
h.		4½b Mexican team	.60	.30

Souvenir Sheets

276A	A78	6b Stadium	5.00	
276B	A78	6b Two players	7.50	

Nos. 276g-276h, 276A-276B are airmail. Nos276A-276B each contain a 57x58mm stamp. No. 276 exists imperf. with silver borders.

A miniature sheet of 6 and two 10b souvenir sheets showing soccer players and Mexican sculptures were released 5/31/70 for the World Cup Soccer Championships in Mexico. The editors would like to examine these items.

Space '70 Interplanetary Travel — A79b

Interplanetary Stations: 1¾b, McDonnell Douglas project 1975-80. 2b, McDonnell Douglas project, diff. 2¼b, Boeing project 1980. 2½b, McDonnell Douglas project 1980-85. 5b, Earth-Moon relay station. 8b, Boeing project 1980-85. 10b, Space telescope. No. 278A, Skylab.

1970, July 21		Litho.	Perf. 13½	
278	A79b	Sheet of 7+label	4.50	2.25
b.		1¾b silver & multi	.40	.25
c.		2b silver & multi	.40	.25
d.		2¼b silver & multi	.40	.25
e.		2½b silver & multi	.40	.25
f		5b silver & multi	.60	.30
g.		8b silver & multi	.80	.40
h.		10b silver & multi	1.00	.50

Souvenir Sheet

278A	A79b	10b multicolored	5.00	

Nos. 278f-278h, 278A are airmail. No. 278 exists imperf with gold borders. No. 278A contains one 67x43mm stamp. An imperf 10b souvenir sheet exists with the a space workshop 1975 design.

Opening of New UPU Headquarters, Bern, Switzerland — A79c

New UPU Headquarters and: ½b, Post coach. 1¼b, Train. 1½b, Early mail truck. 2b, Biplane. 3½b, Zeppelin. 4½b, Jet plane. 6b, Satellite. No. 279A, Zeppelin and post coach.

1970, Aug. 25   Litho.   Perf. 13½

279	A79c	Sheet of 7+label	4.50	2.25
b.		½b silver & multi	.40	.25
c.		¼b silver & multi	.40	.25
d.		1½b silver & multi	.40	.25
e.		2b silver & multi	.40	.25
f.		3½b silver & multi	.60	.30
g.		4½b silver & multi	.80	.40
h.		6b silver & multi	1.00	.50

Souvenir Sheet

279A	A79c	6b multicolored	5.00

Nos. 279f-279h, 279A are airmail. No. 279 exists imperf with gold borders. No. 279A contains one 44x64mm stamp. An imperf 6b souvenir sheet exists with the satellite design.

Philympia London 1970 — A79d

Landmarks and stamps: ¼b, Ruins, Greece 163. ½b, Stadium, France 201. ¾b, Statue of Liberty, US719. 1b, Windsor Castle, Great Britain 274. 3b, Statue of She wolf suckling Romulus and Remus, Italy 807. 4b, Tower, Yemen 242C. No. 280A, UPU Headquarters, Germany B89.

1970, Sept. 10   Litho.   Perf. 13½

280	A79d	Sheet of 6	3.50	2.25
b.		¼b greenish silver & multi	.30	.25
c.		½b greenish silver & multi	.35	.25
d.		¾b greenish silver & multi	.40	.25
e.		1b greenish silver & multi	.50	.25
f.		3b greenish silver & multi	.85	.40
g.		4b greenish silver & multi	1.10	.55

Souvenir Sheet

280A	A79d	4b multicolored	5.00

Nos. 280g, 280A are airmail. No. 280 exists imperf with brownish silver borders. No. 280A contains one 45x51mm stamp, and also exists imperf. An imperf 4b souvenir sheet exists with Mexico C311.

Revolution, 8th Anniv. — A79e

Still Life Paintings by: No. 281b, Courbet. c, No. 281A, Linared. d, Fantin-Latour. e, Renoir, vert. f, Beert, vert.

1970, Sept. 26   Litho.   Perf. 13

281	A79e	Strip of 5	3.00	
b.-f.	A79e	¼b any single		.60

Souvenir Sheet

281A	A79e	10b multicolored	4.50

No. 281 was issued in sheets of 4 strips and also exists imperf.

Arab League, 25th Anniv. — A79f

1970, Oct. 5   Photo.   Perf. 11½x11

282	A79f	5b org, grn & dark pur	.35	—
282A	A79f	7b blue, grn & brn	.75	—
282B	A79f	16b dark olive grn, grn & chalky blue	1.75	—

A perf. souvenir sheet of one exists containing No. 282B. Value, $4.

Munich, 1972 Summer Olympic Games Host City — A79g

City Landmarks: 1b, Glyptothek. 1¾b, Wittelsbach Fountain. 2½b, Maximilianeum. 3b, National Theater. 3½b, Propylaea. 8b, Nymphenburg Castle. 10b, City Hall. No. 283A, Munich Olympic Tower, vert.

1970, Oct. 15   Litho.   Perf. 13½

283	A79g	Sheet of 7+label	4.50	2.25
b.		1b multicolored	.40	.25
c.		1¾b multicolored	.45	.25
d.		2½b multicolored	.45	.25
e.		3b multicolored	.50	.25
f.		3½b multicolored	.50	.25
g.		8b multicolored	.80	.40
h.		10b multicolored	.90	.45

Souvenir Sheet

283A	A79g	10b multicolored	3.50

Nos. 283g-283h, 283A are airmail. No. 283 exists imperf with olive inscriptions at top. No. 283A contains one 30x96mm stamp. An imperf 10b souvenir sheet exists with the Marienplatz.

Sapporo, 1972 Winter Olympic Games Host City — A79h

City Landmarks: 1½b, Sapporor City. 2½b, Olympic Skating Center. 4½b, Makomanai Indoor Ice Arena. 5b, Main Stadium. 7b, Olympic Village. 8b, Bobsled and Luge Courses. 10b, Olympic Jump Hill. No. 283A, Ski Jumper, vert.

1970, Nov. 16   Litho.   Perf. 13½

284	A79h	Sheet of 7+2 labels	4.00	2.25
b.		1½b silver & multi	.30	.25
c.		2½b silver & multi	.30	.25
d.		4½b silver & multi	.45	.25
e.		5b silver & multi	.45	.25
f.		7b silver & multi	.60	.30
g.		8b silver & multi	.60	.30
h.		10b multicolored	.80	.40

Souvenir Sheet

284A	A79h	4b multicolored	5.00

Nos. 284g-284h, 284A are airmail. No. 284 exists imperf with gold frames and inscriptions. No. 284A contains one 54x74mm stamp. An imperf 4b souvenir sheet exists with a map and speed skater.

German Olympic Medalists — A79i

Medalists: No. 285, 1896-1908 medalists. No. 285A, 1908-1932 medalists. No. 285B, 1936-1956 medalists. No. 285C, 1956-1964 medalists. No. 285D, 1968 medalists, Sapporo & Munich emblems. No. 285E, Summer Olympic medals.

1970, Dec. 15   Litho.   Perf. 13½

285	A79i	¼b red lilac & multi	.25	.25
285A	A79i	¼b red lilac & multi	.25	.25
285B	A79i	½b red lilac & multi	.25	.25
285C	A79i	½b red lilac & multi	.25	.25
285D	A79i	6b red lilac & multi	2.50	1.25
		Nos. 285-285D (5)	3.50	2.25

Souvenir Sheet

285E	A79i	6b multicolored	3.50 1.75

Nos. 285D-285E are airmail. No. 285E contains 1 54x54mm stamp and exists imperf. Nos. 285-285D exist imperf.

Gamel Abdel Nasser (1918-1970) — A79j

Nassar and: No. 286, Sukarno. No. 286A, Nehru. No. 286B, Arif. No. 286C, Hammarskjold. No. 286D, Eisenhower. No. 286E, Abdarrahman al-Iryani. No. 286F, Farmer. No. 286G, Suez Canal. No. 286H, Industrial site. No. 286I, Aswan High Dam. No. 286J, Oil field. NO. 286K, Abu Simbel. NO. 286L, World map.

1971, Jan. 6   Litho.   Perf. 11

286	A79j	¼b multicolored	.25	.25
286A	A79j	¼b multicolored	.25	.25
286B	A79j	½b multicolored	.25	.25
286C	A79j	¼b multicolored	.25	.25
286D	A79j	½b multicolored	.25	.25
286E	A79j	½b multicolored	1.00	.50
286F	A79j	1b multicolored	.35	.25
286G	A79j	2b multicolored	.40	.25
286H	A79j	5b multicolored	.50	.25
286I	A79j	7b multicolored	.65	.30
286J	A79j	10b multicolored	1.00	.50
286K	A79j	16b multicolored	1.35	.75
		Nos. 286-286K (12)	6.50	4.05

Souvenir Sheet

286L	A79i	5b multicolored	2.00 1.00

No. 286E is 85x81mm. Nos. 286F-286K are airmail. Nos. 286-286K exist imperf. A 16b imperf. souvenir sheet with a portrait of Nasser exists.

Intl. Sports Contribute to World Peace — A79k

Sports: ¼b, No. 287, Athens, Pierre de Coubertin. ½b, No. 287A, Skier, hurdler. ½b, No. 287B, Figure skater, weightlifter. 2b, Biathlon, Equestrian. 3b, Speed skater, high jump. Nos. 287E-287Ef, Ski jumping, gymnastics.

1971, Jan. 15   Litho.   Perf. 13½

287	A79k	¼b blk, yel & gold	.50	.25
287A	A79k	½b blk, grn & gold	.50	.25
287B	A79k	½b blk, pink & gold	.50	.25

287C	A79k	2b blk, pur & gold	1.00	.25
287D	A79k	3b blk, yel grn & gold	1.50	.35
287E	A79k	4b blk, blue & gold	2.00	.50
f.		Souvenir sheet of 1	5.00	1.50
		Nos. 287-287E (6)	6.00	1.85

Nos. 287D-287E are airmail. No. 287f exists imperf. Nos. 287-287E, 287f exist imperf with silver borders.

Munich, Olympic Host City — A79l

Composer, opera scenes — No. 288: ½b, Handel, Agrippina. 1¼b, Wagner, Tristan & Isolde. 1¾b, Verdi, Othello. 2¼b, Berg, Lulu. 4½b, Orff, Prometheus. 5b, Wagner, Die Meistersinger. 6b, Mozart, Marriage of Figaro. No. 288A, Richard Wagner (1813-1883), vert.

1971, Feb. 15   Litho.   Perf. 13½

288	A79l	Sheet of 7+2 labels	3.75	2.00
b.		½b multicolored	.40	.25
c.		1¼b multicolored	.40	.25
d.		1¾b multicolored	.50	.25
e.		2¼b multicolored	.50	.25
f.		4½b multicolored	.60	.30
g.		5b multicolored	.60	.30
h.		6b multicolored	.75	.35

Souvenir Sheet

288A	A79l	6b multicolored	5.00 1.50

Nos. 288g-288h, 288A are airmail. No. 288 exists with light green inscription at top. No. 288A contains one 50x56mm stamp. A 6b imperf. souvenir sheet exists with a portrait of Mozart.

Paintings in Pinakothek Gallery, Munich — A79m

Paintings — No. 289: ¼b, Sebastian by Holbein. ½b, Count Philippe by Grein. ½b, Young Man by Dürer. 1½b, O. Krel by Dürer. 2b, Susanna in the Bath by Altdorfer. 4b, C. Fugger by Amberger. 7b, C. Schuch by Leibl. No. 289A, Count Otto von Wittelsbach, horiz.

1971, Mar. 15   Litho.   Perf. 13½

289	A79m	Sheet of 7+label	4.00	
b.		¼b multicolored	.40	.25
c.		½b multicolored	.40	.25
d.		¾b multicolored	.50	.25
e.		1½b multicolored	.45	.25
f.		2b multicolored	.45	.25
g.		4b multicolored	.70	.35
h.		7b multicolored	.90	.45

Souvenir Sheet

289A	A79m	4b multicolored	5.00 2.00

Nos. 289g-289h, 289A are airmail. No. 289A contains one 66x46mm stamp. No. 288 exists imperf with inscriptions in light red. A 4b imperf. souvenir sheet exists with Suzanne in the Bath.

Art Type of 1970

Chinese Paintings: ¼b, The Hall of Green Country by Yuan Kiang. ½b, Lady at Her Dressing Table by Sou Han. ½b, The Boddhisattva Wen Tchou. 2b, Gatherer of Simples at Tchen Wei by Wou Li. 3b, Buddha by Ting Yun. 4b, Li T'ie Kouai by Yen Houei.

1971, Apr. 8   Litho.   Perf. 13½

290	A73	¼b lilac silver & multi	.25	.25
290A	A73	½b lilac silver & multi	.25	.25
290B	A73	½b lilac silver & multi	.25	.25
290C	A73	2b lilac silver & multi	.50	.25

290D	A73	3b lilac silver & multi	.75 .35
290E	A73	4b lilac silver & multi	1.00 .50
f.		Souvenir sheet of 1	5.00 1.50

Nos. 290D-290E, 290f are airmail. Stamp in No. 290f has white borders. No. 290f exists imperf.

UN, 25th Anniv. — A79n

1971, Apr. 4 Photo. Perf. 11½x11

291	A79n	5b dk ol grn, grn & dk vio	.55 .45
291A	A79n	7b bl, grn & dk bl	.90 .75

Exist imperf. Value $8.50.

Souvenir Sheet
Imperf

291B	A79n	16b multicolored	2.00 1.50

Winter Olympic Games, Sapporo — A79o

Early Winter Sports: ¼b, Woman on sled. ½b, Skier with bow. 1b, Woman on sled, diff. 1½b, Archer on ice skates. 2b, Man on ice skates. 3b, Woman on ice skates. 4b, Man on skis. No. 292A, Sapporo Games emblem, snowflakes, horiz.

1971, Apr. 15 Litho. Perf. 13¼

292	A79o	Sheet of 7+label	3.75 2.25
b.		¼b silver & multi	.40 .25
c.		½b silver & multi	.40 .25
d.		1b silver & multi	.40 .25
e.		1½b silver & multi	.50 .25
f.		2b silver & multi	.60 .30
g.		3b silver & multi	.80 .40
h.		4b silver & multi	.80 .40

Souvenir Sheet

292A	A79o	10b multicolored	5.00 1.25

Nos. 292g-292h, 292A are airmail. No. 292A contains one 66x61mm stamp. No. 292 exists imperf with grayish green borders. A 10b imperf. souvenir sheet exists with Snow Festival.

Summer Olympic Games, Munich — A79p

Early Summer Sports: ½b, Swimming. 1b, Stone throwing. 1½b, Walking, diff. 1¾b, Wrestling. 2¼b, Crossbow. 4½b, Jousting. 7b, Handball. 10b, Gymnastics. No. 293A, Stone throwing, vert.

1971, May 15 Litho. Perf. 13½

293	A79p	Sheet of 8	4.50 2.25
b.		½b gold & multi	.30 .25
c.		1b gold & multi	.30 .25
d.		1½b gold & multi	.30 .25
e.		1¾b gold & multi	.40 .25
f.		2¼b gold & multi	.40 .30
g.		4½b gold & multi	.70 .35
h.		7b gold & multi	.90 .45

i.		10b gold & multi	1.25 .65

Souvenir Sheet

293A	A79p	10b multicolored	5.00 1.50

Nos. 293g-293i, 293A are airmail. No. 293A contains one 44x78mm stamp. No. 293 exists imperf with silver borders. A 10b imperf. souvenir sheet exists with swimmers.

Conquest of Mars — A79q

Stages of Mars exploration: ¼b, Assembly of Photon rocket in Earth orbit. ½b, Lunar Base, preparations for Mars mission. ½b, Photon rocket in Lunar orbit. ¾b, Departure for Mars. 3b, In orbit around Phobos. 3½b, Three men on Mars. 6b, Upper stage of Photon rocket returns to Earth. No. 294A, Daedalus, rocket shuttle, Phobos, Mars.

1971, June 15 Litho. Perf. 13½

294	A79q	Sheet of 7+label	4.00 2.25
b.		¼b orange & multi	.40 .25
c.		½b orange & multi	.40 .25
d.		½b orange & multi	.40 .25
e.		¾b orange & multi	.40 .25
f.		3b orange & multi	.60 .30
g.		3½b orange & multi	.70 .35
h.		6b orange & multi	.90 .45

Souvenir Sheet

294A	A79q	6b multicolored	5.00 1.50

Nos. 294f-294h, 294A are airmail. No. 294A contains one 70x51mm stamp. No. 294 exists imperf with light blue borders. A 6b imperf. souvenir sheet exists with Galileo.

Ludwig van Beethoven, Birth Bicent. — A79r

Designs: No. 295h, Recital with Beethoven. No. 295i, Chamber music evening. No. 295j, Portrait of Beethoven, Schubert at piano. No. 295k, View of Bonn. No. 295l, View of Vienna. No. 295m, Beethoven's study. 1b, Birth of Beethoven. 2b, Josephine von Brunswick. 5b, Young Beethoven. 7b, 10b, 16b, Beethoven at piano, various.

1971, June 23 Litho. Perf. 12

295	A79r	Sheet of 3	1.50
h.		¼b bl, blk & grn	.50
i.		¼b org, blk & pink	.50
j.		¼b blue & multi	.50
295A	A79r	Sheet of 3+3 labels	1.50
k.		¼b multicolored	.50
l.		¼b multicolored	.50
m.		¼b multicolored	.50
295B	A79r	1b multicolored	.40
295C	A79r	2b multicolored	.50
295D	A79r	5b multicolored	.60
295E	A79r	7b multicolored	.80
295F	A79r	10b multicolored	.80
295G	A79r	16b multicolored	1.00
		Nos. 295-296G (8)	7.10

No. 295A contains 2 80x49mm stamps and 1 40x49mm stamp. Imperf. 5b and 16b souvenir sheets exist.
Nos. 295B-295G are airmail.

Art Type of 1970

Indian Paintings: ¼b, Ibrahim Adil Shah II of Bijapur. ½b, Head of Apsaras. ½b, Kamodi Ragini. 2b, Virahini. 3b, Krishna and Radha. 4b, Girls Swimming in a Lotus Pond.

1971, Apr. 8 Litho. Perf. 13½

296	A73	¼b lilac silver & multi	.25 .25
296A	A73	½b lilac silver & multi	.25 .25
296B	A73	½b lilac silver & multi	.25 .25
296C	A73	2b lilac silver & multi	.50 .25
296D	A73	3b lilac silver & multi	.75 .35
296E	A73	4b lilac silver & multi	1.00 .50
f.		Souvenir sheet of 1	5.00 1.50

Nos. 296D-296E, 296f are airmail. Stamp in No. 296f has white borders. No. 296f exists imperf.

Olympic Sailing, Kiel, Germany — A79s

Olympic sailing yachts: ¼b, 16.5m class, blue spinnaker. ½b, 5.5m class. 1¼b, 16.5m class, white spinnaker.2b, Belouga class. 3b, Flying Dutchman class. 4b, Finn class. No. 297A, Finn class, diff.

1971, Sept. 1 Litho. Perf. 13½

297	A79s	Sheet of 6	3.25 1.65
b.		¼b lilac silver & multi	.40 .25
c.		½b lilac silver & multi	.40 .25
d.		1¼b lilac silver & multi	.40 .25
e.		2b lilac silver & multi	.60 .30
f.		3b lilac silver & multi	.65 .30
g.		4b lilac silver & multi	.80 .40

Souvenir Sheet

297A	A79s	4b multicolored	5.00 1.50

Nos. 297g, 297A are airmail. No. 297A contains one 42x64mm stamp and also exists imperf. No. 297exists imperf with gold borders.

1972 Winter Olympic Games, Sapporo — A79t

Olympic Sports: ½b, Downhill skiing. ¾b, Women's figure skating. 1¼b, 2-man bobsled. 1¾b, Speed skating. 2¼b, Ski jumping. 3½b, Cross-country skiing. 6b, Pairs figure skating. No. 298A, Ski jumping, diff.

1971, Oct. 2 Litho. Perf. 13½

298	A79t	Sheet of 7+label	4.50
b.		½b silver & multi	.45
c.		¾b silver & multi	.45
d.		1¼b silver & multi	.45
e.		1¾b silver & multi	.60
f.		2¼b silver & multi	.60
g.		3½b silver & multi	.75
h.		6b silver & multi	1.00

Souvenir Sheet

298A	A79t	6b multicolored	5.00 1.25

Nos. 298g-298h, 298A are airmail. No. 298A contains one 73x50mm stamp. No. 298 exists imperf with gray violet borders. A 6b imperf. souvenir sheet exists with Sapporo emblems.

Art Type of 1970

Persian Paintings: ¼b, Murakka Gulshan. ½b, Shanname de Baisonghor. ½b, Djami al Tawarikh (drummers). 2b, Murakka Gulshan (fighting bear) . 3b, Djami al Tawarikh (kneeling). 4b, Shanname de Baisonghor (musicians).

1971, Oct. 15 Litho. Perf. 13½

299	A73	¼b lilac silver & multi	.25 .25
299A	A73	½b lilac silver & multi	.25 .25
299B	A73	½b lilac silver & multi	.25 .25
299C	A73	2b lilac silver & multi	.50 .25

299D	A73	3b lilac silver & multi	.75 .35
299E	A73	4b lilac silver & multi	1.00 .50
f.		Souvenir sheet of 1	5.00 1.50

Nos. 299D-299E, 299f are airmail. Stamp in No. 299f has white borders and exists imperf.

1972 Summer Olympic Games, Munich — A79u

Olympic Sports: ¾b, Women's hurdles. 1½b, Discus. 2½. Equestrian. 3½b, Gymnastics. 5b, Shooting. 6b, Rowing. 8b, Diving. No. 300A, Sprinter at start.

1971, Nov. 4 Litho. Perf. 13½

300	A79u	Sheet of 7+label	4.00 2.25
b.		¾b gold & multi	.40 .25
c.		1½b gold & multi	.40 .25
d.		2½b gold & multi	.50 .25
e.		3½b gold & multi	.50 .25
f.		5b gold & multi	.60 .30
g.		6b gold & multi	.60 .30
h.		8b gold & multi	.75 .35

Souvenir Sheet

300A	A79u	6b multicolored	5.00 1.25

Nos. 300g-300h, 300A are airmail. No. 300A contains one 44x59mm stamp. No. 300 exists imperf with silver gray borders. A 6b imperf. souvenir sheet exists with equestrian design.

Olympic Medalists Type of 1970 in Diamond Shape

Italian Medalists: No. 301, 1908-1924 medalists. No. 301A, 1928-1936 medalists. No. 301B, 1952-1956 medalists. No. 301C, 1960-1968 medalists. No. 301D, 1968 medalists, Sapporo, Munich emblems. No. 301E, Emblesm of Rome, Tokyo and Munich Games.

1971, Dec. 3 Litho. Perf. 13½

301	A79i	¼b silver & multi	.25 .25
301A	A79i	¼b silver & multi	.25 .25
301B	A79i	½b silver & multi	.25 .25
301C	A79i	1b silver & multi	.25 .25
301D	A79i	22b silver & multi	2.50 1.25
		Nos. 301-301D (5)	3.50 2.25

Souvenir Sheet

301E	A79i	14b multicolored	3.50 1.75

Nos. 301D-301E are airmail. No. 301E contains 1 54x54mm stamp. No. 301-301D exist imperf. with light green borders. A 14b imperf. souvenir sheet with different Olympic emblems exists.

A set of 3 stamps was released Feb. 29, 1972, commemorating the 9th anniversary of the revolution.
A set of 3 stamps was released Mar. 18, 1972, for the 25th anniversary of the Arab Postal Union.
The editors would like to examine both sets.

Olympic Medalists Type of 1970 in Diamond Shape

French Medalists: 2b, 1896-1912 medalists. 3b, 1920-1932 medalists. 4b, 1936-1964 medalists. 10b, 1968 medalists, Sapporo, Munich emblems. No. 304DE, Olympic Stadia from Tokyo, Mexico City and Munich Games.

1972, Apr. 4 Litho. Perf. 13½

304	A79i	2b bl grey & multi	.50 .25
304A	A79i	3b bl grey & multi	.60 .30
304B	A79i	4b bl grey & multi	.65 .35
304C	A79i	10b bl grey & multi	1.50 .75
		Nos. 304-304C (4)	3.25 1.65

Souvenir Sheet

304D	A79i	4b multicolored	5.00 1.50

Nos. 304B-304D are airmail. No. 304D contains 1 50x33mm stamp. No. 304-304C exist imperf. with light blue borders. A 4b imperf. souvenir sheet with different Olympic venues exists.

Art Treasures — A79x

Designs: 1b, Azure stone vase, 1583. 1¼b, Siren of the "Nautilus Cup," 1822. 1½b, Neptune vase. 1½b, Emperor Rudolph II's crown, 1602. 3b, Statue of Balthazar, 1724. 4½b, Catherine the Great's carriage, 1779. 7b, Statue of St. George.

1972, July 31   Litho.   Perf. 13x13½

305	A79x	1b bluish sil & multi	.35	.25
305A	A79x	1¼b bluish sil & multi	.35	.25
305B	A79x	1½b bluish sil & multi	.40	.25
305C	A79x	1½b bluish sil & multi	.50	.25
305D	A79x	3b bluish sil & multi	.60	.30
305E	A79x	4½b bluish sil & multi	.80	.40
305F	A79x	7b bluish sil & multi	1.00	.50
		Nos. 305-305F (7)	4.00	2.20

Nos. 305D-305F are airmail. A 6b souvenir sheet exists. The editors would like to examine it.

10th anniv. of Revolution A80

1972, Nov. 25   Photo.   Perf. 13

306	A80	7b lt blue, blk & multi	.65	.50
307	A80	10b gray, blk & multi	1.00	.65
		Nos. 306-307,C40 (3)	6.65	4.65

For surcharge see No. 318.

25th Anniv. of WHO — A81

1972, Dec. 1   Litho.

308	A81	2b lt yel grn & multi	.50	.35
308A	A81	21b sky blue & multi	1.40	1.20
308B	A81	37b red lilac & multi	2.25	2.00
		Nos. 308-308B (3)	4.15	3.55

For surcharge see No. 341A.

Burning of Al-Aqsa Mosque, 2nd Anniv. — A82

1972, Jan. 1   Photo.   Perf. 13½

309	A82	7b lt bl, blk & multi	1.50	.60
309A	A82	18b lt bl, blk & multi	2.50	1.10
		Nos. 309-309A,C41 (3)	7.00	3.70

For surcharges see Nos. 319, 341.

25th Anniv. of UNICEF — A83

1973, Jan. 15   Photo.   Perf. 13

310	A83	7b lt bl, blk & multi	1.00	.65
310A	A83	10b lt bl, blk & multi	1.50	.80
		Nos. 310-310A,C42 (3)	4.25	2.95

For surcharge see No. C46.

UPU Cent. — A84

1974, Nov. 20   Photo.   Perf. 14

311	A84	10b multicolored	.75	.40
311A	A84	30b multicolored	2.25	1.50
311B	A84	40b multicolored	3.25	1.90
		Nos. 311-311B (3)	6.25	3.80

For surcharge see No. 341B.

10th World Hunger Program A85

1975, Feb. 5   Litho.   Perf. 13½

313	A85	10b multicolored	.25	.25
314	A85	30b multicolored	.70	.70
315	A85	63b multicolored	1.25	1.25
		Nos. 313-315 (3)	2.20	2.20

12th Anniv. of Revolution A86

1975, Sept. 25

316	A86	25f Janad Mosque	.50	.35
317	A86	75f Althawra Hospital	1.00	.65

Nos. 301, 306 surcharged in Black with New Values and Bars

1975, Nov. 15   Photo.   Perf. 13½

318	A80	75f on 7b	2.00	.65
319	A82	278f on 7b	3.50	1.25
		Nos. 318-319,C46-C48 (6)	22.75	15.40

Telephone Cent. — A87

1976, Mar. 10   Litho.   Perf. 14½

320	A87	25f brt pink & blk	.65	.65
321	A87	75f lt grn & blk	2.00	2.00
322	A87	160f lt bl & blk	3.25	3.25
a.		Souvenir sheet of 1	4.00	4.00
		Nos. 320-322 (3)	5.90	5.90

No. 322a exists both perf. and imperf.

Coffee Bean Branch — A88

1976, Apr. 25   Perf. 14

323	A88	1f dull lilac	.25	.25
324	A88	3f pale gray	.25	.25
325	A88	5f lt bl grn	.25	.25
326	A88	10f bis brn	.25	.25
327	A88	25f golden brn	.25	.25
328	A88	50f brt plum	.40	.40
329	A88	75f dull pink	.70	.60

Size: 22x30mm
Perf. 14½

330	A88	1r sky blue	1.25	.70
331	A88	1.50r red lilac	1.90	1.40
332	A88	2r light grn	2.25	1.40
333	A88	5r yel org	5.00	3.00
		Nos. 323-333 (11)	12.75	8.75

For surcharges see Nos. 403-407, 592.

2nd Anniv. of Reformation Movement — A89

1976, June 13   Photo.   Perf. 12x12½

334	A89	75f Industrial Park	1.50	1.50
335	A89	135f Forestry	2.50	2.50

Souvenir Sheet

336	A89	135f Forestry	5.00	5.00

No. 336 contains one stamp (32x47mm).

14th Anniv. of Revolution — A90

Designs: 25f, Natl. Institute of Public Administration. 75f, Housing and population census. 160f, Sanaa University emblem.

1976, Sept. 26   Photo.   Perf. 12x12½

337	A90	25f buff & multi	.60	.60
338	A90	75f yel bis & multi	1.60	1.60
339	A90	160f pale grn & multi	3.00	3.00
		Nos. 337-339 (3)	5.20	5.20

Souvenir Sheet

340	A90	160f pale grn & multi	5.00	5.00

No. 340 contains one stamp (33x49mm).

No. 306 Surcharged in Black

1976

341	A82	75f on 7b	1.00	.65

Nos. 304, 312 Surcharged in Black or Red

1976   Photo.   Perf. 14

341A	A81	75f on 21b (R)	2.00	1.50
341B	A84	160f on 40b	3.00	2.50

Size and location of surcharge varies.

3rd Anniv. of Correction Movement — A91

1977   Photo.   Perf. 14

342	A91	25f Dish antenna	.45	.30
343	A91	75f Computer, technician	1.25	.65
a.		Miniature sheet of 1	4.00	4.00

15th Anniv. of September Revolution — A92

1977   Photo.   Perf. 13½

344	A92	25f Sa'ada-San'a Road	.45	.35
345	A92	75f Television, Transmitting tower	1.25	.85
346	A92	160f like 25f	2.50	2.00
a.		Souvenir sheet of 1	5.00	5.00
		Nos. 344-346 (3)	4.20	3.20

25th Anniv. of Arab Postal Union — A93   Pres. Hamdi — A94

1978   Perf. 14

347	A93	25f lt yel grn & multi	.90	.75
348	A93	60f bis & multi	2.25	1.60
a.		Miniature sheet of 1	5.00	4.50

1978   Perf. 11½

349	A94	25f dk grn & blk	.35	.35
350	A94	75f ultra & blk	1.25	1.10
351	A94	160f brn & blk	2.50	1.90
a.		Miniature sheet of 1	15.00	6.50
		Nos. 349-351 (3)	4.10	3.35

30th Anniv. of ICAO (1977) A95

1979, Nov. 15   Photo.   Perf. 13½

352	A95	75f multi	1.90	1.00
353	A95	135f multi	3.00	1.60
a.		Miniature sheet of 1	5.00	4.50

Book, World Map, Arab
Achievements — A96

1979, Dec. 1   **Perf. 14**
354 A96 25f multi   .60   .35
355 A96 75f multi   1.50   1.00
  a.   Souvenir sheet of 1   3.75   3.25

A97

1980, Jan. 1
356 A97 75f multi   1.75   1.00
357 A97 135f multi, horiz.   2.75   1.60
  a.   Miniature sheet of 1   5.00   4.50

12th World Telecommunications Day, May
17, 1979.

A98

Dome of the Rock.

1980   **Photo.**   **Perf. 14**
358 A98 5f brt bl & multi   .50   .35
359 A98 10f yel & multi   1.00   .65

Palestinian fighters and their families.

Argentina World Cup — A99

World Cup emblem and various players.

1980, Mar. 30
360 A99 25f gold & multi   .40   .40
361 A99 30f gold & multi   .40   .30
362 A99 35f gold & multi   .50   .40
363 A99 50f gold & multi   .70   .50
      Nos. 360-363,C49-C52 (8)   6.55   4.80

Issued in sheets of 8.
Exist imperf. (Value, set $20) and in souve-
nir sheets (Value, set $60).

International Year of the Child — A100

1980, Apr. 1   **Perf. 13½**
364 A100 25f Girl, bird   1.60   .50
365 A100 50f Girl, bird, diff.   2.25   .80
366 A100 75f Boy, butterfly,
                  flower   2.40   1.25
      Nos. 364-366,C53-C55 (6)   16.75   6.80

Issued in sheets of 6.
Exist imperf. (Value, set $25) and in souve-
nir sheets (Value, set $45).

World Scouting Jamboree — A101

1980, May 1   **Perf. 13½x14**
367 A101 25f Fishing   .60   .30
368 A101 35f Troup, aircraft   1.40   .50
369 A101 40f Mounted bugler,
                  flag   1.40   .50
370 A101 50f Telescope, night
                  sky   1.50   .65
      Nos. 367-370,C56-C58 (7)   13.05   5.35

Issued in sheets of 6.
Exist imperf. (Value, set $25) and in souve-
nir sheets (Value, set $50).

Argentina 1978 World Cup
Winners — A102

World cup emblem and various soccer
players.

1980, June 1   **Perf. 14**
371 A102 25f gold & multi   .45   .25
372 A102 30f gold & multi   .60   .30
373 A102 35f gold & multi   .60   .40
374 A102 50f gold & multi   .90   .40
      Nos. 371-374,C59-C62 (8)   8.05   4.35

Exist imperf. (Value, set $20) and in souve-
nir sheets (Value, set $60).

Hegira, 1400th Anniv. — A102A

Designs: 160f, Outside view.

1000, July 1   **Perf. 13½**
375 A102a 25f blk & multi   .30   .25
376 A102a 75f car rose & multi   .90   .60
377 A102a 160f blk & multi   1.90   .75
  a.   Miniature sheet of 1   4.00   4.00
       Nos. 375-377 (3)   3.10   1.60

18th Anniv.
of
September
Revolution
A103

A104

1980, Sept. 26   **Perf. 13½**
378 A103 25f multi   .35   .25
379 A104 75f multi   1.10   .65

Souvenir Sheet
380   100f multi   3.75   3.75

No. 380 contains one stamp combining
designs A103 and A104 (42x34mm).

Al Aqsa
Mosque
A105

Mosques: 25f, Al-Rawda entrance. 100f, Al-
Nabwi. 160f, Al-Haram.

1980, Nov. 6   **Photo.**   **Perf. 13½**
381 A105 25f multi   .25   .25
382 A105 75f multi   .60   .50
383 A105 100f multi   1.50   .65
384 A105 160f multi   2.00   1.00
      Nos. 381-384 (4)   4.35   2.40

Souvenir Sheet
385   160f multi   6.00   3.25

Islamic Postal Systems Week and Hegira.
No. 385 contains one stamp (109x47mm)
combining designs of Nos. 382-384.

Intl. Palestinian
Solidarity
Day — A106

1980, Nov. 29
386 A106 25f lt bl & multi   .40   .25
387 A106 75f ver & multi   1.10   .90

Inscribed 1979.

9th Arab Archaeological
Conference — A107

1981, Mar. 1   **Perf. 13½**
388 A107 75f Al Aamiriya
                  Mosque   1.10   .60
389 A107 125f Al Hadi Mosque   1.75   .85
  a.   Souvenir sheet of 2, #388-389   3.25   3.25

1980 World
Tourism
Conference,
Manila
A108

1981, Apr. 1
390 A108 25f shown   .25   .25
391 A108 75f Mosque, houses   .60   .30
392 A108 100f Columns, horiz.   .80   .45
393 A108 135f Bridge   1.10   .60
394 A108 160f View of San'a,
                  horiz.   1.40   .60
  a.   Miniature sheet of 1   4.50   4.50
       Nos. 390-394 (5)   4.15   2.20

Sir Rowland Hill (1795-1879), Postage
Stamp Inventor — A109

1981, Sept. 15   **Litho.**   **Perf. 14**
395 A109 25f Portrait, UPU
                  emblem   .60
396 A109 30f Emblem, stamp
                  of 1963   .70
397 A109 50f Portrait, stamps   1.00
398 A109 75f Portrait, globe,
                  jet   1.60
399 A109 100f Portrait, stamp
                  collection   2.25
400 A109 150f Jets, No. 322   4.00
      Nos. 395-400 (6)   10.15

Souvenir Sheets
401 A109 200f Portrait, vert.   7.50

Imperf
402 A109 200f Portrait, diff.   7.50

Nos. 398-402 are airmail.
Nos. 395-400 exist imperf. (Value, set $20)
and in souvenir sheets (Value, set $45).

Nos. 323-327 Surcharged

1981
403 A88 125f on 1f   1.00
404 A88 150f on 3f   1.25
405 A88 325f on 5f   2.75
406 A88 350f on 10f   3.25
407 A88 375f on 25f   3.50
      Nos. 403-407 (5)   11.75

20th Anniv. of Yemen Airways — A110

1983, Apr. 1   **Litho.**   **Perf. 14**
408 A110 75f yel & multi   .50   .50
409 A110 125f red & multi   .80   .80
410 A110 325f bl & multi   2.00   2.00
      Nos. 408-410 (3)   3.30   3.30

Folk Costumes — A111

1983, May 1
411	A111	50f Woman carrying waterjar	2.00
412	A111	50f Women, sheep	2.00
413	A111	50f Man, donkeys	2.00
414	A111	50f Man in town square	2.00
415	A111	75f Women, child, well	3.00
416	A111	75f Scholar	3.00
417	A111	75f Woman on beach	3.00
418	A111	75f Camel-drawn plow	3.00
		Nos. 411-418 (8)	20.00

Souvenir Sheets
419	A111	200f Woman	8.00

Imperf
420	A111	200f Man	8.00

#411-414 vert. #415-420 are airmail.
Nos. 411-418 exist imperf. (Value, set $25)
and in souvenir sheets (Value, set $60).

Sept. 26th Revolution, 20th Anniv. (1982) — A112

1983, Sept. 26   Litho.   Perf. 14
421	A112	100f Communications	1.25
422	A112	150f Literacy	1.75
423	A112	325f Educational development	3.50
a.		Souvenir sheet of 2, #422, 423	6.00
424	A112	400f Independence	5.00

World Communications Year — A113

1983, Dec. 15
425	A113	150f lt bl & multi	2.25
426	A113	325f lt grn & multi	3.50
a.		Souvenir sheet of 1	6.00

Sept. 26 Revolution, 21st Anniv. — A114

1984, Apr. 1   Litho.   Perf. 14
427	A114	100f shown	1.50
428	A114	150f Fist, statue	2.00
429	A114	325f Gate, tank	3.50
a.		Souvenir sheet of 1	6.00

Israel Aggression Day — A115

1984, Sept. 7
430	A115	150f multi	1.50
431	A115	150f multi	4.00

Size: 91x120mm
Imperf
432	A115	325f multi	25.00
		Nos. 430-432 (3)	30.50

Sept. 26 Revolution, 22nd Anniv. — A116

1985, Oct. 1
433	A116	50f Triumphal Arch	.75
434	A116	150f San'a Castle walls	1.75
435	A116	325f Stadium, Govt. Palace, San'a	3.50
a.		Souvenir sheet of 1	6.00

Intl. Anti-Apartheid Year (1978) — A117

1985, Jan. 1
436	A117	150f dp ver & multi	1.75
437	A117	325f grn & multi	3.50
a.		Souvenir sheet of 1	6.00

Intl. Civil Aviation Org., 40th Anniv. A118

1985, Sept. 20
438	A118	25f multi	.40
439	A118	50f multi	.60
440	A118	150f multi	1.50
441	A118	325f multi	3.50
a.		Souvenir sheet of 1	6.00

Arabsat Satellite, 1st Anniv. A119

1986, Apr. 15   Litho.   Perf. 14
442	A119	150f multi	2.50
443	A119	325f multi	5.50
a.		Souvenir sheet of 1	8.50

World Telecommunications, 120th Anniv. — A120

1986, May 1
444	A120	150f multi	2.50
445	A120	325f multi	5.25
a.		Souvenir sheet of 1	9.00

General People's Conference, 2nd Anniv. — A121

1986, May 1
446	A121	150f multi	2.50
447	A121	325f multi	4.50
a.		Souvenir sheet of 1	6.00

A122

1986, July 1
448	A122	150f multi	2.50
449	A122	325f multi	4.50
a.		Souvenir sheet of 1	6.00

15th Islamic Foreign Ministers' Conference, San'a, Dec. 18-22, 1984.

A123

1986, Oct. 1
450	A123	150f multi	2.50
451	A123	325f multi	4.50
a.		Souvenir sheet of 1	6.00

UN 40th anniv.

Arab League, 39th Anniv. A124

1986, Nov. 15
452	A124	150f multi	2.50
453	A124	325f multi	4.50

Natl. Arms A125

1987, Sept. 26   Litho.   Perf. 14
454	A125	100f multi	.90
455	A125	150f multi	1.25
456	A125	425f multi	3.75
a.		Souvenir sheet of 1	4.00
457	A125	450f multi	4.00
		Nos. 454-457 (4)	9.90

Sept. 26th Revolution, 25th anniv.
For surcharge see No. 593.

Intl. Youth Year (1985) A126

1987, Oct. 15   Perf. 13x13½
458	A126	150f multi	1.75
459	A126	425f multi	3.75
a.		Souvenir sheet of 1	5.00

For surcharge see No. C150.

Drilling of the Republic's First Oil Well, 1984 A127

1987, Nov. 1   Perf. 14
460	A127	150f Oil derrick	1.75
461	A127	425f Derrick, refinery	3.75
a.		Souvenir sheet of 1	5.00

For surcharge see No. C151.

General Population and Housing Census, 1986 A128

1987, Dec. 1
462	A128	150f multi	2.50
463	A128	425f multi	4.50
a.		Souvenir sheet of 1	5.50

For surcharge see No. C152.

1986 World Cup Soccer Championships, Mexico — A129

Designs: 100f, 150f, Match scenes, vert. 425f, Match scene and Pique, character trademark.

1988, Jan. 1   Litho.   Perf. 14
464	A129	100f multi	1.00
465	A129	150f multi, diff.	1.50
466	A129	425f multi	3.50
a.		Souvenir sheet of 1	5.00
		Nos. 464-466 (3)	6.00

For surcharge see No. C153.

17th Scouting Conference, San'a — A130

1988, Mar. 1   Litho.   Perf. 14
467	A130	25f Skin diving	.30
468	A130	30f Table tennis	.40
469	A130	40f Tennis	.50
470	A130	50f Two scouts, flag	.60
471	A130	60f Volleyball	.70
472	A130	100f Tug-of-war	1.00
473	A130	150f Basketball	1.50
474	A130	425f Archery	3.50
		Nos. 467-474 (8)	8.50

Souvenir Sheet
475	A130	425f Scout, emblem, hand sign	5.00

For surcharge see No. C154.

San'a Preservation — A131

1988, May 1   Litho.   Perf. 14
476	A131	25f multicolored	.40
477	A131	50f multicolored	.75
478	A131	100f multicolored	1.25
479	A131	150f multicolored	1.75

480 A131   425f multicolored   4.00
a.   Souvenir sheet of 1   5.50
     Nos. 476-480 (5)   8.15

For surcharge see No. 594.

Battle of
Hattin,
800th
Anniv. in
1987
A132

1988   **Litho.**   **Perf. 14**
482 A132   150f multicolored   2.50
483 A132   425f multicolored   6.00
a.   Souvenir sheet   9.00

For surcharge see No. C155.

Arab Telecommunication Day,
1987 — A133

1988
484 A133   100f multicolored   1.00
485 A133   150f multicolored   1.50
486 A133   425f multicolored   3.50
a.   Souvenir sheet   5.00
     Nos. 484-486 (3)   6.00

For surcharge see No. C156.

A134

Sept. 26
Revolution, 26th
Anniv. — A134a

1989, Sept. 30
487 A134   300f multicolored   1.25
488 A134   375f multicolored   1.5
489 A134a 850f multicolored   3.00
490 A134a 900f multicolored   3.50
     Nos. 487-490 (4)   9.25

A souvenir sheet containing one #488 exists.
For surcharges see Nos. 595, 605.

A135

October 14
Revolution, 25th
Anniv. — A135a

1989, Oct. 14
491 A135   300f multicolored   1.25
492 A135   375f multicolored   1.50
493 A135a 850f multicolored   3.00
494 A135a 900f multicolored   3.50
     Nos. 491-494 (4)   9.25

A souvenir sheet containing one #492 exists.
For surcharges see Nos. 596, 606.

1988
Summer
Olympics,
Seoul
A136

Game emblem and various events: 300f,
Table tennis, basketball, track, boxing. 375f,
Soccer game. 850f, Soccer, judo, vert. 900f,
Torch bearer.

1989, Nov. 10   **Litho.**   **Perf. 13x13½**
495 A136   300f multicolored   1.50
496 A136   375f multicolored   1.75
a.   Souvenir sheet   8.50
497 A136   850f multicolored   3.50
498 A136   900f multicolored   4.25
     Nos. 495-498 (4)   11.00

For surcharges see Nos. 597, 607.

Palestinian
Uprising
A137

1989, Dec. 9   **Perf. 13x13½, 13½x13**
499 A137   300f shown   2.00
500 A137   375f Flag raising,
              vert.   3.00
a.   Souvenir sheet of 1   15.00
501 A137   850f Burning barri-
              cades   5.50
502 A137   900f Man waving flag,
              vert.   7.00
     Nos. 499-502 (4)   17.50

For surcharges see Nos. 598, 608.

Arab Cooperation Council — A138

1990, Feb. 16   **Litho.**   **Perf. 13x13½**
504 A138   300f multicolored   1.00
505 A138   375f multicolored   1.25
a.   Souvenir sheet   7.50
506 A138   850f multicolored   2.75
507 A138   900f multicolored   3.00
     Nos. 504-507 (4)   8.00

For surcharges see Nos. 599, 609.

First
Exported
Oil — A139

1990, Mar. 15   **Perf. 14**
508 A139   300f multicolored   1.00
509 A139   375f multicolored   1.25
a.   Souvenir sheet   7.50
510 A139   850f multi, diff.   2.75
511 A139   900f like 850f   3.00
     Nos. 508-511 (4)   8.00

For surcharges see Nos. 600, 610.

Arab Scout
Movement,
75th Anniv.
A140

1990, June 15   **Litho.**   **Perf. 13x13½**
512 A140   300f Scouts holding
              globe   1.00
513 A140   375f like No. 512   1.25
a.   Souvenir sheet of 1   4.50
514 A140   850f Oil rig, scouts,
              globe   2.75
515 A140   900f like No. 514   3.00
     Nos. 512-515 (4)   8.00

For surcharges see Nos. 601, 611.

Arab Board for
Medical
Specializations,
10th
Anniv. — A141

1990, Apr. 15   **Photo.**   **Perf. 13½x13**
516 A141   300f brt grn & multi   1.00
517 A141   375f lt bl & multi   1.25
a.   Sheet of 1, perf. 12½   4.50
518 A141   850f lt org & multi   2.75
519 A141   900f lt vio & multi   3.00
     Nos. 516-519 (4)   8.00

For surcharges see Nos. 602, 612.

Immunization Campaign — A142

300f, 375f, Mother feeding infant, vert.

1990, May 15   **Perf. 13½x13, 13x13½**
520 A142   300f lt bl & multi   1.00
521 A142   375f lt org & multi   1.25
a.   Sheet of 1, perf. 12½   5.00
522 A142   850f lt bl grn & multi   2.75
523 A142   900f lt lake & multi   3.00
     Nos. 520-523 (4)   8.00

No. 521a contains one 26x37mm stamp.
For surcharges see Nos. 603, C157.

UN Development
Program, 40th
Anniv. — A144

1990, Oct. 24   **Litho.**   **Perf. 12**
532 A144   150f multicolored   1.00

For surcharge see No. 622.

Ducks
A145

1990, Sept. 18   **Litho.**   **Perf. 12**
533 A145   10f Pintail swimming   .25
534 A145   20f Wigeon   .25
535 A145   25f Ruddy shelduck   .25
536 A145   40f Gadwall   .30
537 A145   75f Shelduck, male   .50

538 A145   150f Shoveler   .90
539 A145   600f Teal   2.75
     Nos. 533-539 (7)   5.20
     Souvenir Sheet
540 A145   460f Pintail in flight   5.00

For surcharge see No. 623.

Moths and
Butterflies
A146

1990, Nov. 3   **Perf. 12½x12**
541 A146   5f Dirphia multicolor   .25
542 A146   20f Automeris io   .25
543 A146   25f Papilio machaon   .25
544 A146   40f Bhutanitis lid-
              derdalii   .30
545 A146   55f Prepona
              demophon
              muson   .40
546 A146   75f Agarista agricola   .50
547 A146   700f Attacus edwardsii   3.25
     Nos. 541-547 (7)   5.20
     Souvenir Sheet
     Perf. 12x12½
548 A146   460f Daphnis nerii,
              vert.   5.00

Prehistoric
Animals
A147

     Perf. 12x12½, 12½x12
1990, Nov. 27
549 A147   5f Protembolotheri-
              um, vert.   .25
550 A147   10f Diatryma, vert.   .25
551 A147   35f Mammuthus   .25
552 A147   40f Edaphosaurus   .30
553 A147   55f Dimorphodon   .40
554 A147   75f Phororhacos   .50
555 A147   700f Ichthyosaurus,
              vert.   3.25
     Nos. 549-555 (7)   5.20
     Size: 61x90mm
     Imperf
556 A147   460f Tyrannosaurus,
              vert.   4.00

A148

Various domestic cats.

1990, Dec. 26   **Perf. 12x12½**
557 A148   5f multicolored   .25
558 A148   15f multicolored   .25
559 A148   35f multicolored   .25
560 A148   55f multicolored   .35
561 A148   60f multicolored   .35
562 A148   150f multicolored   .75
563 A148   600f multicolored   2.75
     Nos. 557-563 (7)   4.95
     Size: 70x90mm
     Imperf
564 A148   460f multicolored   5.00

A149

Mushrooms.

1991, Mar. 18   Litho.   Perf. 12x12½
565	A149	50f Boletus aestivalis	.30
566	A149	60f Suillus luteus	.40
567	A149	80f Gyromitra es-	
		culenta	.50
568	A149	100f Leccinum	
		scabrum	.60
569	A149	130f Amanita muscaria	.70
570	A149	200f Boletus er-	
		ythropus	1.00
571	A149	300f Leccinum testace-	
		oscabrum	1.50
		Nos. 565-571 (7)	5.00

Size: 70x90mm
Imperf
572	A149	460f Stropharia aerugi-	
		nosa	3.00

Unified
Yemen
Republic,
1st Anniv.
A150

Designs: 300f, 375f, Eagle crest. 850f, 900f,
Hand holding flag, map, sun.

1991, May 22   Perf. 13x13½
573	A150	300f pink & multi	.60
574	A150	375f grn bl multi	.75
a.		Sheet of 1, perf. 12½	2.50
575	A150	850f lt bl & multi	1.50
576	A150	900f bl grn & multi	1.75
		Nos. 573-576 (4)	4.60

No. 574a contains one 37x27mm stamp.
For surcharges see #604, 613, 624, 627.

Unity Agreement
Signed Nov. 30,
1989 — A151

Designs: 300f, 375f, 850f, Fist, flag, map.

1991, May 22   Perf. 13½x13
577	A151	225f multicolored	.50
578	A151	300f multicolored	.60
579	A151	375f multicolored	.75
a.		Sheet of 1, perf. 12½	2.50
580	A151	650f multicolored	1.25
581	A151	850f multicolored	1.50
		Nos. 577-581 (5)	4.60

No. 579a contains one 27x37mm stamp.
For surcharges see #614, 617-619, 625.

World Anti-Smoking Day — A153

Designs: 300f, 375f, 850f, Man facing skull
smoking cigarette.

1991, May 31   Perf. 13x13½
582	A153	225f multicolored	.50
583	A153	300f multicolored	.60
584	A153	375f multicolored	.75
a.		Sheet of 1, perf. 12½	2.50

585	A153	650f multicolored	1.25
586	A153	850f multicolored	1.50
		Nos. 582-586 (5)	4.60

No. 584a contains one 36x26mm stamp.
For surcharges see Nos. 615, 620, 626.

United
Nations,
45th Anniv.
A154

1991, June 26   Perf. 13x13½
587	A154	5r multicolored	.75
588	A154	8r multicolored	1.25
589	A154	10r multicolored	1.50
590	A154	20r multicolored	2.00
		Nos. 587-590 (4)	5.50

Souvenir Sheet
Perf. 12½
591	A154	6r multicolored	2.50

No. 591 contains one 37x28mm stamp.

**Nos. 329, 456, 480, 489-490, 493-
494, 497-498, 501-502, 506-507, 510-
511, 514-515, 518-519, 523, 575-576,
581 & 586 Surcharged, "Rials"
Spelled Out**

1993, Jan. 1   Perfs., Etc. as Before
592	A88	5r on 75f #329	5.75
593	A125	8r on 425f #456	6.50
594	A131	8r on 425f #480	6.50
595	A134a	10r on 900f #490	6.50
596	A135a	10r on 900f #494	6.50
597	A136	10r on 900f #498	6.50
598	A137	10r on 900f #502	6.50
599	A138	10r on 900f #507	6.50
600	A139	10r on 900f #511	6.50
601	A140	10r on 900f #515	6.50
602	A141	10r on 900f #519	6.50
603	A142	10r on 900f #523	6.50
604	A150	10r on 900f #576	6.50
605	A134a	12r on 850f #489	7.25
606	A135a	12r on 850f #493	7.25
607	A136	12r on 850f #497	7.25
608	A137	12r on 850f #501	7.25
609	A138	12r on 850f #506	7.25
610	A139	12r on 850f #510	7.25
611	A140	12r on 850f #514	7.25
612	A141	12r on 850f #518	7.25
613	A150	12r on 850f #575	7.25
614	A151	12r on 850f #581	7.25
615	A153	12r on 850f #586	7.25
		Nos. 592-615 (24)	163.50

Size and location of surcharge varies.

Yemen (PDR)
Nos. 441, 443,
447, and Yemen
Nos. 577-578,
583 Srchd. Type
a or — c

1993   Perfs., Etc. as Before
616	A139(a)	50r on 500f	
		#447	100.00
617	A151(a)	50r on 225f	
		#577	175.00
618	A151(c)	50r on 225f	
		#577	—
a.		Pair, #617-618	
619	A151(a)	100r on 300f	
		#578	175.00
620	A153(a)	100r on 300f	
		#583	225.00
621	A139(a)	200r on 5f	
		#441	250.00
a.		3-Line surcharge	
621B	A139(a)	200r on 20f	
		#443	250.00

Size and location of surcharge varies.

1993, Sept. 1   Perfs., Etc. as Before
622	A144(a)	50r on 150f		
		#532	25.00	20.00
623	A145(a)	50r on 150f		
		#538	25.00	20.00
623A	A153(a)	505 on 225f		
		#582	300.00	200.00
624	A150(a)	50r on 375f		
		#574	27.50	20.00
625	A151(a)	50r on 375f		
		#579	27.50	25.00
626	A153(a)	50r on 375f		
		#584	27.50	25.00
627	A150(a)	100r on 300f		
		#573	50.00	25.00

Size and location of surcharge varies.
No. 623 exists with a surcharge similar to
surcharge "c."

**Yemen People's Democratic
Republic Nos. 75, 84B, 204, 208,
216, 232, 235, 244, 267, 335-336,
347, 425, 436-437, 439 & Types
Surcharged Type a and**

b

1993, Sept. 1   Perfs., Etc. as Before
628	A25(a)	8r on 110f	
		#84B	4.75
629	A63(a)	8r on 110f	
		#204	4.75
630	A64(a)	8r on 110f	
		#208	4.75
631	A66(a)	8r on 110f	
		#216	4.75
632	A72(a)	8r on 110f	
		#232	4.75
633	A74(a)	8r on 110r	
		#235	4.75
634	A76(a)	8r on 110r	
		#244	16.00
635	A86(a)	8r on 110r	
		#267	4.75
636	A105(a)	100r on 2d #347	60.00
637	A137(a)	100r on 300f	
		#439	60.00
638	A24(a)	200r on 5f #75	100.00
639	(b)	200r on 15f	
		Soyuz 10 &	
		Salyut 1	100.00
640	A105(b)	200r on 15f #335	100.00
641	(b)	200r on 20f Apol-	
		lo 8	100.00
642	A105(b)	200r on 20f #336	100.00
643	A131(a)	200r on 20f #425	240.00
644	A134(a)	200r on 75f #436	100.00
645	A135(a)	200r on 250f	
		#437	100.00

Size and location of surcharge varies.
No. 582 exists with a 50r type "b" surcharge.
No. 636 exists with a surcharge similar to
surcharge "c."
Nos. 639, 641 without surcharge have not
been listed in the Scott Catalogue.

Yemen Unity,
4th
Anniv. — A155

Various views of govt. building, San'a.

1994, Sept. 27   Litho.   Perf. 13½x14
646	A155	3r multicolored	.50
647	A155	5r multicolored	.75
648	A155	10r multicolored	1.25
649	A155	20r multicolored	2.75
		Nos. 646-649 (4)	5.25

Souvenir Sheet
650	A155	20r multi, diff.	3.00

1994 World Cup
Soccer
Championships,
US — A156

2r, Player in yellow shirt dribbling ball, vert.
6r, Player in striped shirt dribbling, vert. 10r,
Goal keeper. No. 654, Heading ball, vert.
No. 655, Tackling.

1994, Oct. 1   Perf. 14x13½, 13½x14
651	A156	2r multicolored	.50
652	A156	6r multicolored	1.25
653	A156	10r multicolored	2.00
654	A156	12r multicolored	2.50
		Nos. 651-654 (4)	6.25

Souvenir Sheet
655	A156	12r multicolored	3.50

World Day of
Environmental
Protection — A157

Perf. 14x13½, 13½x14
1995, Oct. 15   Litho.
656	A157	15r Arabian leopard	1.25
657	A157	20r Caracal lynx	1.50
658	A157	30r Guinea fowl, horiz.	2.50
		Nos. 656-658 (3)	5.25

Souvenir Sheet
659	A157	50r Partridge, horiz.	4.50

FAO, 50th
Anniv. — A158

Emblem, field, hand holding: 10r, Plant. 25r,
Seed. 30r, Fish. 50r, Grain.

1995, Oct. 16   Perf. 14x13½
660	A158	10r violet & multi	1.00
661	A158	25r claret & multi	2.00
662	A158	30r light blue & multi	2.50
		Nos. 660-662 (3)	5.50

Souvenir Sheet
663	A158	50r dark blue & multi	4.50

A159

UN, 50th anniv.: Various views of Aden
Dam.

1995, Oct. 24   Perf. 14x13½, 13½x14
664	A159	10r multi	.75
665	A159	20r multi	1.25
666	A159	25r multi, horiz.	1.50
		Nos. 664-666 (3)	3.50

Souvenir Sheet
667	A159	50r multi, horiz.	3.00

A160

Naseem Hamed Kashmem, world boxing
champion: 10r, With champion belts. 20r, Up
close. 25r, Boxing opponent, horiz. 30r, Holding up arm as winner, trainer.
50r, Boxing opponent, diff., horiz.

Perf. 14x13½, 13½x14
1995, Nov. 29
668	A160	10r multicolored	.75
669	A160	20r multicolored	1.25
670	A160	25r multicolored	1.75
671	A160	30r multicolored	2.00
		Nos. 668-671 (4)	5.75

Souvenir Sheet
672	A160	50r multicolored	3.50

Yemen Republic
Nos. 532, 538,
573-574, 579, &
584 Srchd. — a

Souvenir Sheet

CHINA '96, 9th Asian Intl. Philatelic Exhibition — A161

1996, May 18   Litho.   Perf. 11½
673 A161 80r Shanghai   4.00

1996 Summer Olympic Games, Atlanta — A162

1996, July 19   Perf. 14x13½, 13½x14
674	A162	20r Wrestling, vert.	.75
675	A162	50r High jump	1.5
676	A162	60r Running, vert.	1.75
677	A162	70r Gymnastics, vert.	2.25
678	A162	100r Judo, vert.	3.50
		Nos. 674-678 (5)	9.75

Souvenir Sheet
679 A162 150r Javelin, vert.   7.50

Landmarks A163

10r, 70r, 250r, Popular Heritage Museum, Seiyoan. 15r, 40r, 60r, 500r, Rock Palace, Wadi Dhahr, vert. 20r, 100r, 200r, Old Sana'a City. 30r, 50r, 150r, 300r, Al-Mohdhar Minaret, Tarim, vert.

Perf. 13½x14, 14x13½
1996, Sept. 26   Litho.
680	A163	10r org yel & multi	.40
681	A163	15r grn yel & multi	.45
682	A163	20r lt blue & multi	.60
683	A163	30r blue & multi	.80
684	A163	40r salmon & multi	1.00
685	A163	50r green & multi	1.25
686	A163	60r lilac & multi	1.50
687	A163	70r violet & multi	1.75
688	A163	100r yellow & multi	2.50
689	A163	150r orange & multi	3.50
690	A163	200r rose & multi	5.00
691	A163	250r gray & multi	6.25
692	A163	300r red & multi	7.50
693	A163	500r yellow & multi	12.00
		Nos. 680-693 (14)	44.50

Birds — A164

Designs: 20r, Tyto alba. 50r, Alectoris philbyi. 60r, Gypaetus barbatus. 70r, Alectoris melanocephala. 100r, Chlamydotis undulata. 150r, Ixobrychus minutus, vert.

1996, Oct. 14   Litho.   Perf. 13½x14
694	A164	20r multicolored	.40
695	A164	50r multicolored	1.00
696	A164	60r multicolored	1.20

697	A164	70r multicolored	1.40
698	A164	100r multicolored	2.00
		Nos. 694-698 (5)	6.00

Souvenir Sheet
Perf. 14x13½
699 A164 150r multicolored   3.00

Rare Plants in Yemen — A165

Designs: 20r, Parodia masii. 50r, Notocatus cristata. 60r, Adenium obesum socotranum. 70r, Dracaena cinnabari. 100r, Mammillaria erythrosperma. 150r, Parodia maasii, diff.

1996, Nov. 30   Perf. 13½x14
700	A165	20r multicolored	.40
701	A165	50r multicolored	1.00
702	A165	60r multicolored	1.20
703	A165	70r multicolored	1.40
704	A165	100r multicolored	2.00
		Nos. 700-704 (5)	6.00

Souvenir Sheet
705 A165 150r multicolored   3.00

A166

Fish: 20r, Heniochus acuminatus. 50r, 150r, Cheilinus undulatus. 60r, Zebrasoma xanthurum. 70r, Pomacanthus imperator. 100r, Pomacanthus vanthometopon.

1996, Nov. 30
706	A166	20r multicolored	.40
707	A166	50r multicolored	1.00
708	A166	60r multicolored	1.20
709	A166	70r multicolored	1.40
710	A166	100r multicolored	2.00
		Nos. 706-710 (5)	6.00

Souvenir Sheet
711 A166 150r multicolored   3.00

A167

UNICEF, 50th Anniv.: 20r, Children with books. 50r, Girls clapping hands. 60r, Mother, child. 70r, Mother, three children.
150r, Child making jewelry, horiz.

1996, Dec. 11   Perf. 14x13½
712	A167	20r multicolored	.40
713	A167	50r multicolored	1.00
714	A167	60r multicolored	1.20
715	A167	70r multicolored	1.40
		Nos. 712-715 (4)	4.00

Souvenir Sheet
Perf. 13½x14
716 A167 150r multicolored   3.00

1998 World Cup Soccer Championships, France — A168

Various soccer plays.

1998, June 10   Litho.   Perf. 13x13½
717	A168	10r multicolored	.30
718	A168	15r multicolored	.40
719	A168	35r multicolored	.75
720	A168	65r multicolored	1.25

721	A168	75r multicolored	1.50
a.		Souvenir sheet, #717-721	4.25
		Nos. 717-721 (5)	4.20

Birds A169

Designs: 10r, Ardeotis arabs. 15r, Neophron percnopterus. 35r, Coracias abyssinicus. 65r, Cinnyricinclus leucogaster. 75r, Melierax metabates.

1998, Sept. 26   Litho.   Perf. 13
| 722-726 | A169 | Set of 5 | 4.25 | 4.25 |
| 726a | | Sheet of 5, #722-726 | 4.25 | 4.25 |

Universal Declaration of Human Rights, 50th Anniv. A170

15r, Hands in air. 35r, Hands clasped in handshake. 100r, Hands reaching out.

1998, Oct. 12
| 727-729 | A170 | Set of 3 | 3.25 | 3.25 |
| 729a | | Sheet of 3, #727-729 | 3.25 | 3.25 |

First General Conference of Yemeni Immigrants (in 1999) A171

Emblem &: 60r, Dhows. 90r, Fort, camel.

2000, May 16   Litho.   Perf. 14½x14
| 730-731 | A171 | Set of 2 | 2.00 | 2.00 |
| 731a | | Souvenir sheet, #730-731 | 2.00 | 2.00 |

Tenth National Day — A172

Background colors: 30r, Light green. 50r, Rose lilac. 70r, Light blue. 150r, Orange.

2000, May 22   Perf. 14x14½
732-734 A172 Set of 3   1.60 1.60
Souvenir Sheet
735 A172 150r multi   1.60 1.60

Plants of Socotra — A173

Designs: 30r, Euphorbia abdalkuri. 70r, Dendrosicyos socotranus. 80r, Caralluma socotrana. 120r, Dracaena cinnabari. 300r, Exacum affine.

2000, July 15
736-739 A173 Set of 4   4.00 4.00
Souvenir Sheet
740 A173 300r multi   4.00 4.00

2000 Summer Olympics, Sydney — A174

Designs: 50r, Judo. 70r, Runner. 80r, Hurdler. 100r, Shooting. 300r, Tennis.

2000, Sept. 15
741-744 A174 Set of 4   4.00 4.00
Souvenir Sheet
745 A174 300r multi   4.00 4.00

Antiquities — A175

Designs: 30r, Stone idols, 3000 B.C. 70r, Statue of Ma'adi Karib, 800 B.C. 100r, Horned griffin, Royal Palace of Shabwa, 300. 120r, Statue of King of Awsan Yasduq Eil, 100 B.C. 320r, Stele with bull's head, 100 B.C., horiz.

2002, June 15   Litho.   Perf. 13x12¾
746-749 A175 Set of 4   4.25 4.25
Souvenir Sheet
Imperf
750 A175 320r multi   4.25 4.25
No. 750 contains one 41x26mm stamp.

2002 World Cup Soccer Championships, Japan and Korea — A176

Soccer players with background colors of: 30r, Bister, vert. 70r, Green. 100r, Blue, vert. 120r, Red brown, vert.
No. 755: a, Player's foot and ball. b, World Cup trophy.

2002, May 31   Perf. 13x12¾, 12¾x13
751-754 A176 Set of 4   4.25 4.25
Souvenir Sheet
Perf.
755 A176 160r Sheet of 2, #a-b   4.25 4.25
No. 755 contains two 28mm diameter stamps.

Scouting in Yemen, 75th Anniv. A177

Designs: 30r, Scout escorting man across street. 60r, Scout digging. 70r, Scouts in rowboat.
160r, Scout saluting, vert.

2002, Apr. 30   Perf. 12¾x13
756-758 A177 Set of 3   2.10 2.10
Souvenir Sheet
Perf. 13x13¼
759 A177 160r multi   2.10 2.10
No. 759 contains one 16x26mm stamp.

Palestinian
Intifada — A178

Designs: 30r, Frightened child. 60r, Bleeding child.
90r, Dome of the Rock, horiz.

2002, Apr. 27   **Perf. 13x12¾**
760-761 A178   Set of 2   1.25 1.25
Imperf
Size: 111x78mm
762 A178 90r multi   1.25 1.25

Poets — A179

Designs: Nos. 763, 30r, 765, 60r, 767a, 70r,
Hussain Al-Muhdhar (1931-2000). Nos. 764,
30r, 766, 60r, 767b, 70r, Abdullah Al-Baradony
(1929-99).

2002, June 30   Litho.   Perf. 13x12¾
763-766 A179   Set of 4   2.25 2.25
Souvenir Sheet
Perf. 13x13¼
767 A179 70r Sheet of 2, #a-b   1.75 1.75
No. 767 contains two 16x28mm stamps.

Revolution, 40th
Anniv. — A180

Background colors: 30r, Dull green. 60r,
Rose.
90r, Lilac.

2002, Sept. 26   **Perf. 13x12¾**
768-769 A180   Set of 2   1.10 1.10
Imperf
Size: 110x76mm
770 A180 90r multi   1.10 1.10

World Under-17 Soccer
Championships, Finland — A181

Various soccer players with background
color of: 30r, Red violet. 50r, Golden brown.
70r, Blue. 100r, Green.
250r, Soccer team and stadium.

2003, Aug. 13   Litho.   Perf. 12¾x13
771-774 A181   Set of 4   3.00 3.00
Imperf
Size: 109x74mm
775 A181 250r multi   3.00 3.00

Antiquities — A182

Various sculptures with background colors
of: 20r, Pale yellow. 40r, Lilac. 50r, Light
green. 150r, Pink.
260r, Black, horiz.

2003, Sept. 26   **Perf. 13x12¾**
776-779 A182   Set of 4   3.00 3.00
Souvenir Sheet
Perf. 12¾x13
780 A182 260r multi   3.00 3.00

Traditional Women's
Clothing — A183

Various women with panel colors of: 30r,
Purple. 60r, Yellow green. 70r, Dark green.
100r, Red violet. 150r, Brown.
410r, Purple background, horiz.

2003, Oct. 14   **Perf. 13x12¾**
781-785 A183   Set of 5   4.75 4.75
Souvenir Sheet
Perf. 12¾x13
786 A183 410r multi   4.75 4.75

Children's
Art — A184

Designs: 20r, Girl with flower on globe, vert.
30r, Dove over buildings, vert. 40r, Dove holding swing, vert. 50r, Children in field. 60r, Animals in field. 70r, Street and park.

2003, Oct. 15   Perf. 13x12¾, 12¾x13
787-792 A184   Set of 6   3.00 3.00

Sana'a, 2004
Arabic Cultural
Capital — A185

Various buildings with frame colors of: 30r,
White. 50r, Purple. 70r, Black. 100r, Dark
brown. 150r Red brown.
400r, Buildings, horiz.

2003, Nov. 30   **Perf. 13x12¾**
793-797 A185   Set of 5   4.50 4.50
Souvenir Sheet
Perf. 12¾x13
798 A185 400r multi   4.50 4.50

FIFA (Fédération
Internationale de
Football
Association),
Cent. — A186

2004, May 21   Litho.   Perf. 13x12¾
799 A186 100r multi   1.10 1.10
Dated 2005. Stamps did not appear in marketplace until 2005.

2004 Summer
Olympics,
Athens — A187

Designs: 70r, Running. 80r, Shooting. 100r,
Swimming.
250r, Equestrian.

2004, Aug. 13
800-802 A187   Set of 3   2.75 2.75
Souvenir Sheet
803 A187 250r multi   2.75 2.75
Dated 2005. Stamps did not appear in marketplace until 2005.

Telecommunications and
Technology — A188

Designs: 60r, Computer chips, "@" symbol,
keyboard. 70r, Computer and stylized people,
vert. 100r, Yemen Mobile emblem, vert.
400r, Like 70r, vert.

Perf. 12¾x13, 13x12¾
2004, Sept. 26
804-806 A188   Set of 3   2.50 2.50
Souvenir Sheet
807 A188 400r multi   4.50 4.50
Dated 2005. Stamps did not appear in marketplace until 2005.

Spiders
A189

No. 808: a, Tidarren argo. b, Scelidomachus
socotranus. c, Habrocestum albopunctatum.
d, Rafalus insignipalpis. e, Latrodectus hystrix.
f, Atrophothele socotrana.
300r, Like No. 808b.

2004, Oct. 14   **Perf. 12¾x13**
808   Horiz. strip of 6   3.25 3.25
   a.-f.   A189 50r Any single   .50 .50
Souvenir Sheet
809 A189 300r multi   3.25 3.25
Dated 2005. Stamps did not appear in marketplace until 2005.

Traditional Men's
Clothing — A190

Men wearing various outfits with background colors of: 50r, Light yellow. 60r, Green.
70r, Pink. 100r, Blue.
360r, Orange brown.

2004, Oct. 30   **Perf. 13x12¾**
810-813 A190   Set of 4   3.25 3.25
Souvenir Sheet
814 A190 360r multi   4.00 4.00
Dated 2005. Stamps did not appear in marketplace until 2005.

Handicrafts
A191

No. 815: a, Knife maker holding hammer. b,
Textile worker piecing fabric. c, Jeweler. d,
Weaver at loom.
3004, Like No. 815a.

2004, Nov. 30
815   Horiz. strip of 4   3.25 3.25
   a.-d.   A191 70r multi   .80 .80
Souvenir Sheet
816 A191 300r multi   3.25 3.25
Dated 2005. Stamps did not appear in marketplace until 2005.

15th National
Day — A192

Emblem and: 30r, Industrial plant. 60r, Dam
and reservoir. 70r, Man holding flag.
90r, Buildings.

2005, May 22
817-819 A192   Set of 3   1.75 1.75
Souvenir Sheet
820 A192 90r multi   1.00 1.00

United Nations,
60th
Anniv. — A193

Symbols of eight goals for a better Yemen:
No. 821, 40r, Pregnant woman and doctor.
No. 822, 40r, Woman, infant and doctor. No.
823, 40r, Woman reading book. No. 824, 40r,
Mosquito, AIDS ribbon, medicine and bottle.
No. 825, 40r, Man depositing trash in can,
tree, smiling sun. 80r, Goats, hat seller and
child. 100r, Woman, man and balance. 120r,
Handshake.
130r, UN anniversary emblem.

2005, Oct. 24   Litho.   Perf. 13x12¾
821-828 A193   Set of 8   5.50 5.50

Size: 111x83mm
Imperf

829 A193 130r multi   1.50 1.50

No. 829 contains one perforated label lacking a denomination.

Flowers
A194

Various flowers: 50r, 80r, 110r, 130r, 140r, 150r, 300r.

Perf. 13¼x13¾
2007, Sept. 26   **Litho.**
830-835 A194   Set of 6   6.75 6.75
Souvenir Sheet
836 A194 300r multi   3.00 3.00

Insects
A195

Designs: No. 837, 50r, Cheilomenes lunata yemenensis. No. 838, 50r, Pharoscymnus c-luteus. No. 839, 50r, Hippodamia variegata. No. 840, 50r, Cheilomenes propinqua vicina. No. 841, 50r, Brumoides nigrifrons. No. 842, 50r, Serangium buettikeri.
250r, Pharoscymnus c-luteus, diff.

2007, Sept. 26   **Perf. 13¾x13¼**
837-842 A195   Set of 6   3.00 3.00
Souvenir Sheet
843 A195 250r multi   2.50 2.50

Mosques
A196

Designs: 50r, Mosque of Prophethood, Hadhramaut. 80r, Al Ameria Mosque, Radaa. 100r, Queen Arwa Mosque, Jebla. 110r, Al Ashrafiah Mosque, Taiz. 120r, Al Aidarous Mosque, Aden. 200r, Al Bukiriah Mosque, Sana'a.
300r, Unidentified mosque.

2007, Oct. 14   **Perf. 13¼x13¾**
844-849 A196   Set of 6   6.75 6.75
Souvenir Sheet
850 A196 300r multi   3.00 3.00

Citadels and Castles
A197

Designs: 50r, Thulaa Citadel, Amran. 80r, Al Tawama Citadels, Hadhramaut. 100r, Serah Castle, Aden. 110r, Sumarah Castle, Ibb. 130r, Al Qahira Castle, Taiz.
300r, Unidentified castle.

2007, Oct. 14
851-855 A197   Set of 5   4.75 4.75
Souvenir Sheet
856 A197 300r multi   3.00 3.00

Marine Life
A198

Designs: 50r, Parupeneus marconema. 80r, Sarda orientalis. 100r, Carcharhinus melanopterus. 110r, Plectorhinchus schotaf. 130r, Panulirus homarus. 160r, Seriola rivoliana.
300r, Panulirus homarus, diff.

2007, Nov. 30
857-862 A198   Set of 6   6.50 6.50
Souvenir Sheet
863 A198 300r multi   3.00 3.00

Yemeni Onyx
A199

Various set and unset onyx stones: 50r, 80r, 100r, 110r, 120r, 130r, 140r, 160r.
250r, Set and unset onyx stones.

2007, Nov. 30   **Perf. 13¾x13¼**
864-871 A199   Set of 8   9.00 9.00
Souvenir Sheet
872 A199 250r multi   2.50 2.50

Natl. Day of Human Rights
A200

Globe, flag, dove, human rights emblem with background color of: 110r, Red violet. 130r, Blue.
250r, Dove and flag, vert.

2007, Dec. 10   **Perf. 13¼x13¾**
873-874 A200   Set of 2   2.40 2.40
Souvenir Sheet
Perf. 13¾x13¼
875 A200 250r multi   2.50 2.50

Yasser Arafat (1929-2004), Palestinian Leader — A201

Palestinian Authority flag and Arafat: 120r, With hand raised. 300fr, With hands not shown, horiz.

2008, Nov. 4   **Litho.**   **Perf. 13x12¾**
876 A201 120r multi   1.25 1.25
Size: 110x70mm
Imperf
877 A201 300r multi   3.00 3.00

Opening of Al-Saleh Mosque, Sana'a
A202

Mosque: 80r, Pillars, ceiling and chandeliers. 100r, Interior wall. 120r, Exterior. 300r, Exterior, diff.

2008, Nov. 22   **Perf. 12¾x13**
878-880 A202   Set of 3   3.00 3.00
Size: 109x70mm
Imperf
881 A202 300r multi   3.00 3.00

Gaza — A203

Designs: 60r, Man, boy carrying Palestinian flag. 100r, Barbed wire, children looking through hole in wall, horiz.
120r, Dove and chain.

2009, May 22   **Perf. 13¼x13, 13x13¼**
882-883 A203   Set of 2   1.60 1.60
Souvenir Sheet
884 A203 120r multi   1.25 1.25

Ancient Coins
A204

Various ancient coins: 50r, 60r, 70r, 80r, 100r, 120r. 60r and 80r are vert. 120r is 50x50mm diamond-shaped stamp.

2009, May 22   **Perf. 13x13¼, 13¼x13**
885-889 A204   Set of 5   3.75 3.75
Souvenir Sheet
Perf. 13¼
890 A204 120r multi   1.25 1.25

Ancient Jewelry — A205

Designs: 50r, Bracelet and ring. 60r, Bracelet, horiz. 80r, Necklace and earrings. 100r, Bracelets, horiz. 120r, Necklace. 140r, Bracelets, diff., horiz.
150r, Belt, horiz.

2009, May 22   **Perf. 13¼x13, 13x13¼**
891-896 A205   Set of 6   5.50 5.50
Souvenir Sheet
897 A205 150r multi   1.50 1.50

Horses
A206

Designs: 60r, Head of brown horse with white blaze. 80r, Black horse. 100r, Brown horse with white blaze. 120r, Brown horse with white mane. 140r, White horse. 150r, Head of brown horse with white blaze, diff.
200r, Dappled gray horse, vert.

2009, May 22   **Perf. 13x13¼**
898-903 A206   Set of 6   6.50 6.50
Souvenir Sheet
Perf. 13¼x13
904 A206 200r multi   2.00 2.00

Souvenir Sheet

Arab Postal Day — A207

No. 905 — Emblem and: a, World map, pigeon. b, Camel caravan.

2009, May 22   **Perf. 12¾**
905 A207 100r Sheet of 2, #a-b   2.00 2.00

National Day — A209

20th anniversary emblem and background colors of: 60r, Brown and red brown. 80r, Yellow and brown. 200r, Emblem, horiz.

2010, May 22   **Litho.**   **Perf. 13**
911-912 A209   Set of 2   3.00 3.00
Souvenir Sheet
913 A209 200r multi   4.25 4.25

2010 World Cup Soccer Championships, South Africa — A210

2010 World Cup emblem, World Cup and various South African stadiums hosting matches: 50r, 60r, 80r, 100r.
No. 918, vert.: a, 50r, 2010 World Cup emblem. b, 100r, World Cup.

2010, June 11
914-917 A210   Set of 4   7.75 7.75
Souvenir Sheet
918 A210   Sheet of 2, #a-b   4.75 4.75

Yemeni Janbiahs (Daggers)
A211

Various daggers in sheaths: 50r, 60r, 80r, 100r, 120r. 60r and 100r are vert.
200r, Dagger, diff.

2010, July 21   **Perf. 12¾**
919-923 A211   Set of 5   8.50 8.50
Souvenir Sheet
924 A211 200r multi   4.25 4.25

AIR POST STAMPS

Catalogue values for unused stamps in this section are for Never Hinged items.

Plane over San'a
AP1

YEMEN — 1459

1947 Unwmk. Engr. Perf. 12½
C1 AP1 10b bright blue — 6.00 2.00
C2 AP1 20b olive green — 10.00 2.50

Views Type of Regular Issue
6b, 8b, View of San'a. 10b, Mocha coffee tree. 12b, Palace of the Rock, Wadi Dhahr. 16b, Palace, Ta'iz. 20b, 1i, Parade Ground, San'a.

1951 Wmk. 277 Photo. Perf. 14
C3 A14 6b blue — 1.40 .50
C4 A14 8b dark brown — 1.75 .60
C5 A14 10b dark green — 2.25 1.40
C6 A13 12b dark blue — 2.50 .80
C7 A14 16b lilac rose — 3.00 .80
C8 A13 20b orange brown — 3.75 1.25
C9 A13 1i dark red — 10.00 3.00
Nos. C3-C9 (7) — 24.65 8.35

Nos. C3 and C4 were used provisionally in 1957 for registry and foreign ordinary mail.

Type of Regular Issue
Designs: 12b, Palace of the Rock, Wadi Dhahr. 20b, Walls of Ibb.

Engraved and Photogravure
1952 Unwmk. Perf. 14½, Imperf.
C10 A15 12b grnsh blk, bl & brn — 10.00 10.00
C11 A15 20b indigo, bl & brn — 10.00 10.00

Flag-and-View Type
1952
C12 A16 1i dk brn, car & brt ultra — 18.00 18.00

1952 Palace in Foreground
C13 A16 30b yel grn, car & gray — 11.00 11.00

Leaning Minaret, Mosque of Ta'iz — AP6

1954 Photo. Perf. 14
C14 AP6 10b scarlet — 3.25 .90
C15 AP6 12b dull blue — 4.00 1.25
C16 AP6 20b olive bister — 6.50 2.00
Nos. C14-C16 (3) — 13.75 4.15

Accession of King Ahmed I, 5th anniv.

Type of Regular Issue
1959 Wmk. 318 Perf. 13x13½
C17 A21 6b orange & blk — 1.00 .70
C18 A21 10b red & blk — 1.60 1.25
C19 A21 16b brt violet & red — 2.50 2.00
Nos. C17-C19 (3) — 5.10 3.95

In 1959, four values of the 1931 issue and three values of the 1930 issue overprinted Air Mail 1959 were distributed. Although these stamps were not regularly sold in Yemeni post offices, several values of these sets were used on air-mail cover going abroad. Several of these stamps exist with inverted or doubled overprints.

Antiquities of Marib Type
Designs: 6b, Columns, Temple of the Moon God. 16b, Control tower and spillway of 2,700-year-old dam of Marib.

Perf. 11½
1961, Oct. 14 Unwmk. Photo.
C20 A27 6b lt bl grn & blk — 1.00 .25
C21 A27 16b lt blue & blk — 2.75 1.50
Exist imperf.
For overprints see Nos. C24, C25.

Buildings Type
6b, Bab al-Yemen, main gate of San'a, horiz. 16b, Palace of the Rock (Dar al-Hajar).

1961, Nov. 15
C22 A28 6b blk, lt bl & grn — .55 .25
C23 A28 16b blk, rose & grn — 1.40 .60
For overprints see Nos. C24A, C25A.

Nos. C20-C23 Ovptd. Like Nos. 144-158 in Dark Red or Black
Perf. 11½
1963, Jan. 1 Photo. Unwmk.
C24 A27 (a) 6b No. C20 — .70 .70
C24A A28 (b) 6b No. C22 — .85 .85
C25 A27 (a) 16b No. C21 — 1.75 1.75
C25A A28 (a) 16b No. C23 (B) — 2.75 2.75

Proclamation of the Republic Type
1963, Mar. 15 Perf. 11x11½, 11½x11
C26 A34 8b Bayonette, torch — 1.50 1.50
C27 A34 10b Jet, torch, tank — 2.00 2.00
C28 A34 16b Flag, chain, torch — 2.75 2.75
Nos. C27-C28 horiz.
An imperf. souvenir sheet containing one No. C28 exists. Value \$10.

Nos. 25-29 Ovptd. in Black

Wmk. 258
1963, Sept. 1 Litho. Perf. 12½
C29 A5 6b slate blue & ultra — 1.50 1.50
C29A A5 10b fawn & ultra — 1.90 1.90
C29B A5 14b olive & ultra — 2.25 2.25
C29C A5 20b yel grn & ultra — 3.00 3.00
C29D A5 1i claret & ultra — 6.50 6.50
Nos. C29-C29D (5) — 15.15 15.15
Exist imperf. Value, set \$25.

Spacecraft — AP6a

Various spacecraft.

1963, Dec. 5 Photo. Perf. 13
C29E AP6a ¼b multicolored — .50 .50
C29F AP6a ⅓b multicolored — .50 .50
C29G AP6a ½b multicolored — .50 .50
C29H AP6a 4b multicolored — 1.00 1.00
C29I AP6a 20b multicolored — 5.00 5.00
Nos. C29E-C29I (5) — 7.50 7.50
Exist imperf. Value, set \$15. An imperf. souvenir sheet containing C29I also exists. Value \$7.

Nos. C29E-C29G Overprinted in Black or Red Brown

1964-1965 Photo. Perf. 13
C29J AP6a ¼b On No. C29E — 1.00 1.00
C29K AP6a ¼b On No. C29E (RB)('65) — 2.50 2.50
C29L AP6a ⅓b On No. C29F — 1.00 1.00
C29M AP6a ⅓b On No. C29F (RB)('65) — 2.50 2.50
C29N AP6a ½b On No. C29G — 1.00 1.00
Nos. C29J-C29N (5) — 8.00 8.00

Issued: Nos. C29J, C29L, C29N, 12/6/64. Others, 1965.
No. C29G was also released with a red brown overprint on May 20, 1966. The editors would like to examine an example.
Imperf. examples of Nos. C29H-C29I exist with the red borwn overprint.

San'a Intl. Airport Type
Perf. 11½x11
1964, Oct. 1 Photo. Unwmk.
C30 A40 6b Sun, buildings, air-craft — .70 .70
See note after No. 203.

APU 10th Anniv. Type
1964, Oct. 15 Perf. 13½
C31 A41 6b blue grn & blk — 1.00 .80
An imperf. souvenir sheet of one exists containing No. C31. Value \$3.

Deir Yassin Massacre Type
1965, Apr. 30 Perf. 11x11½
C32 A44 6b ver & brt org — 1.00
An imperf. souvenir sheet of one exists containing No. C32. Value \$2.50.

Library Type
1965, July 7 Perf. 11½x11
C33 A46 6b sepia, red & int blue — .85 .55
An imperf. souvenir sheet of one exists containing No. C33. Value \$2.50.

Butterflies — AP6b

Various butterflies.

1966, May 5 Photo. Perf. 12½
C33A AP6b 6b multicolored — 1.50 .75
C33B AP6b 8b multicolored — 2.00 1.00
C33C AP6b 10b multicolored — 3.00 1.50
C33D AP6b 16b multicolored — 4.00 2.00
Nos. C33A-C33D exist imperf.

1968 Winter Olympic Games, Grenoble — AP6c

1967, Nov. 11 Litho. Perf. 13¼
C33E AP6c 5b gold & multi
C33F AP6c 10b gold & multi
C33G AP6c 15b gold & multi
Exist imperf. in silver. Perf. and imperf. souvenir sheets containing one No. C33G exist in both gold and silver.

Konrad Adenauer (1876-1967) — AP6d

1968, June Litho. Perf. 11
C33H AP6d 5b gold & black
C33I AP6d 10b gold, blk & grn
C33J AP6d 15b gold, blk & blue
Exist imperf. in silver. Perf. and imperf. souvenir sheets containing one No. C33J exist in both gold and silver.

Red Crescent Organization — AP6e

1968 Litho. Perf. 11
C33K AP6e 5b gold & multi
C33L AP6e 10b gold & multi
C33M AP6e 15b gold & multi
Exist imperf. in silver. An imperf. souvenir sheet containing one No. C33M exists in silver.

Vladimir Komarov (1927-1967), Soviet Cosmonaut — AP6f

1968 Litho. Perf. 13½
C33N AP6f 5b gold & multi
C33O AP6f 10b gold & multi
C33P AP6f 15b gold & multi
Exist imperf. in silver. An imperf. souvenir sheet containing one No. C33P exists in gold.

1968 Summer Olympic Games, Mexico City — AP6g

1968, July 2 Litho. Perf. 13½
C33T AP6g 5b gold & multi
C33U AP6g 10b gold & multi
C33V AP6g 15b gold & multi
Exist imperf. in silver. Imperf. souvenir sheets containing one No. C33V exists in gold and silver.

Universal Declaration of Human
Rights, 20th Anniv. — AP6h

1968, Oct. 20　　Litho.　　Perf. 13½
C33W AP6g　5b gold & multi
C33X AP6g　10b gold & multi
C33Y AP6g　15b gold & multi

Exist imperf. in silver. An imperf. souvenir
sheet containing one No. C33Y exists in gold.

Lenin's Birth
Centenary
AP7

1970, Aug. 15　Litho.　Perf. 12x12½
C34 AP7　6b Public speech　　　1.40 1.10
C35 AP7　16b Meeting with Arab
　　　　　　delegates　　　　　3.00 1.90

8th Anniv. of the Revolution — AP8

1971, Jan. 24　　　　　　　Perf. 13
C36 AP8　5b Country estate　　　　.75
C37 AP8　7b Workers　　　　　　1.10
C38 AP8　16b Handshake, flag,
　　　　　　flowers, open
　　　　　　book　　　　　　　1.50
　　Nos. C36-C38 (3)　　　　　　3.35

A souv. sheet of 1 exists containing No.
C38. Value $5.
No. C38 was overprinted "Proclamation of
the Institution." The editors would like to
examine an example.

Nos. C33L, C33V and C33X were
surcharged in 1971. The editors would
like to examine examples.

Revolution Type

1972, Nov. 25　Photo.　Perf. 13
C40 A80　21b lilac, blk & multi　5.00 3.50

For surcharge see No. C46A.

Al-Aqsa Mosque Type

1973, Jan. 1　Photo.　Perf. 13½
C41 A82　24b lt bl, blk & multi　3.00 2.00
　a.　Min. sheet of 1, imperf.　3.00 2.00

UNICEF Type

1973, Jan. 15　Photo.　Perf. 13
C42 A83　18b lt bl, blk & multi　1.75 1.50
　a.　Min. sheet of 1, imperf.　3.25 2.50

For surcharge see No. C46.

11th Anniv.
of
Revolution
AP10

1973, Sept. 26　Photo.　Perf. 14
C43 AP10　7b Bank　　　　　　.50　.35
C44 AP10　10b Cement factory　.65　.55
C45 AP10　18b Hospital　　　1.50 1.10
　　Nos. C43-C45 (3)　　　　2.65 2.00

For surcharges see Nos. C47-C48.

**Nos. C40, C42, C43, C45
Surcharged in Black or Red with
New Value and Bars**

1975, Nov. 15
C46　A83　75f on 18b lt bl, blk
　　　　　　& multi　　　　2.50 2.50
C46A A80　75f on 21b #C40
　　　　　　(R)　　　　　5.00 4.00
C47　AP10　90f on 7b multi　5.50 2.75
C48　AP10　120f on 18b multi
　　　　　　(R)　　　　　4.25 4.25
　a.　Overprinted in black

Argentina 1978 World Cup Type

World cup emblem and various soccer
players.

1980, Mar. 30　Photo.　Perf. 14
C49 A99　60f gold & multi　　.80　.60
C50 A99　75f gold & multi　　1.00　.70
C51 A99　80f gold & multi　　1.25　.90
C52 A99　100f gold & multi　1.50 1.00
　　Nos. C49-C52 (4)　　　　4.55 3.20

Two 225f souvenir sheets exist. Value, perf.
$12, imperf. $15.

IYC Type

1980, Apr. 1　　　　　Perf. 13½
C53 A100　80f Girl, bird　　　3.00 1.25
C54 A100　100f Boy, butterfly,
　　　　　　flower　　　　3.00 1.25
C55 A100　150f Boy, butterfly,
　　　　　　flower, diff.　4.50 1.75
　　Nos. C53-C55 (3)　　　10.50 4.25

Two 200f souvenir sheets exist. Value $12
each.

Scouting Type of 1980

1980, May 1　Photo.　Perf. 13½x14
C56 A101　60f Bicycling　　　2.00　.80
C57 A101　75f Fencing　　　　2.40 1.10
C58 A101　120f Butterfly catching　3.75 1.50
　　Nos. C56-C58 (3)　　　　8.15 3.40

Two 300f souvenir sheets exist. Value $15
each.

Argentina 1978 Winners' Type

World cup emblem and various soccer
players.

1980, June 1　Photo.　Perf. 14
C59 A102　60f gold & multi　　1.00　.50
C60 A102　75f gold & multi　　1.40　.65
C61 A102　80f gold & multi　　1.50　.75
C62 A102　100f gold & multi　1.60 1.10
　　Nos. C59-C62 (4)　　　　5.50 3.00

Two 225f souvenir sheets exist. Value $12
each.

19th Anniv. of
Sept. 26th
Revolution
(1981) — AP11

1982, Jan. 25　Litho.　Perf. 14
C63 AP11　75f Map　　　　　　.45　.25
C64 AP11　125f Map in sunset　.70　.40
C65 AP11　325f Dove in natl. col-
　　　　　　ors　　　　　2.00 1.25
　a.　Souvenir sheet of 1　5.00 5.00
C66 AP11　400f Jets　　　　　2.25 1.40
　　Nos. C63-C66 (4)　　　　5.40 3.30

Al-Hasan Ibn Al-Hamadani,
Writer — AP12

1982, Feb. 1
C67 AP12　125f green & multi　1.25　.60
C68 AP12　325f blue & multi　2.75 1.40
Souvenir Sheet
C69 AP12　375f multi　　　　3.50 3.50

No. C69 contains one stamp (36x46mm).
For surcharge see No. C138.

World Food Day — AP13

Designs: No. C76a, Eggplants. No. C76b,
Tomatoes. No. C76c, Beets, peas. No. C76d,
Cauliflower, carrots. No. C77a, Dove. No.
C77b, Water birds. No. C77c, Fish. No. C77d,
Geese.

1982, Mar. 1　Litho.　Perf. 14
C70 AP13　25f Rabbits　　　　.50
C71 AP13　50f Rooster, Hens　1.00
C72 AP13　60f Turkeys　　　1.25
C73 AP13　75f Sheep　　　　1.50
C74 AP13　100f Cattle　　　2.00
C75 AP13　125f Deer　　　　2.50
　　Nos. C70-C75 (6)　　　8.75

Souvenir Sheets

C76　　Sheet of 4　　　　8.00
　a.-d. AP13 100f, any single　2.00
C77　　Sheet of 4　　　　10.00
　a.-d. AP13 125f, any single　2.50

For surcharges see Nos. C139, C144.
Nos. C70-C75 exist imperf. (Value, set $20)
and in souvenir sheets (Value, set $45).

1980
Summer
Olympics,
Moscow
AP14

1982, Apr. 1
C78 AP14　25f Gymnastics　　1.25
C79 AP14　50f Pole vault　　1.50
C80 AP14　60f Javelin　　　1.75
C81 AP14　75f Running　　　2.50
C82 AP14　100f Basketball　3.50
C83 AP14　125f Soccer　　　4.00
　　Nos. C78-C83 (6)　　　14.50

Nos. C78-C81 exist imperf. (Value, set $25)
and in souvenir sheets (Value, set $45).
Two souvenir sheets of 4 exist: 100f, picturing boxing, wrestling, canoeing, swimming
(Value $12.50), and 125f, picturing weight lift-
ing, discus, long jump, fencing (Value $15).
For surcharges see Nos. C140, C145.

Aviation — AP15

Various space and aircraft.

1982, May 21
C86 AP15　25f multi　　　　1.25
C87 AP15　50f multi　　　　1.50
C88 AP15　60f multi　　　　1.75
C89 AP15　75f multi　　　　2.50
C90 AP15　100f multi　　　3.50
C91 AP15　125f multi　　　4.00
　　Nos. C86-C91 (6)　　　14.50

Nos. C86-C91 exist imperf. (Value set, $25)
and in souvenir sheets (Value, set $45).

Two souvenir sheets of 4 exist, 100f and
125f, picturing various aircraft and satellites.
Values $12.50 and $15, respectively.
For surcharges see Nos. C141, C146.

Intl. Year of the Disabled — AP16

Designs: Nos. C94-C99, Diff. flowers.
No. C100a, Emblem, natl. flag. b, Emblem
on globe. c, Natl. colors, UN emblems. d, Disabled man, gifts, nurse.
No. C101a, Flags, globe and nurse. b, UN
emblems, natl. flag. c, Emblem, disabled man.
d, UN emblem, nurse.

1982, June 1
C94 AP16　25f multi　　　　1.25
C95 AP16　50f multi　　　　1.50
C96 AP16　60f multi　　　　1.75
C97 AP16　75f multi　　　　2.50
C98 AP16　100f multi　　　3.50
C99 AP16　125f multi　　　4.00

Souvenir Sheets

C100　　Sheet of 4　　　12.50
　a.-d. AP16 100f, any single　3.00
　　Nos. C94-C99 (6)　　　14.50
C101　　Sheet of 4　　　15.00
　a.-d. AP16 125f, any single　3.50

Nos. C94-C99 exist imperf. (Value, set $25)
and in souvenir sheets (Value, set $45).
For surcharge see No. C147.

Telecommunications Progress — AP17

Designs: 25f, FNRR communication center.
50f, Dish receivers, satellite, globe. 60f,
Broadcast towers, dish receivers. 75f, Receivers, birds over plain. 100f, Receivers, satellite,
telegraph key. No. C107, Receivers, passenger jet, Earth.
No. C108a, Receivers, Earth. b, Earth, television, flag and camera. c, Computer. d, Skyscraper, Earth, telephone.
No. C109a, Receivers, Earth, ship. b,
Communication center, bolts of energy,
receivers. c, Receivers, jet, ship, train, car,
carriage. d, Radar.

1982, July 1　Litho.　Perf. 14
C102 AP17　25f multi　　　1.00
C103 AP17　50f multi　　　1.25
C104 AP17　60f multi　　　1.50
C105 AP17　75f multi　　　2.25
C106 AP17　100f multi　　3.25
C107 AP17　125f multi　　3.75
　　Nos. C102-C107 (6)　　13.00

Souvenir Sheets

C108　　Sheet of 4　　　10.00
　a.-d. AP17 100f any single　2.50
C109　　Sheet of 4　　　12.00
　a.-d. AP17 100f any single　3.00

Nos. C102-C107 exist imperf. (Value, set
$20) and in souvenir sheets (Value, set $45).
For surcharges see Nos. C142, C148.

TB Bacillus Centenary — AP18

1982, Aug. 1   Litho.   Perf. 14
C110	AP18	25f multi	1.00
C111	AP18	50f multi	1.25
C112	AP18	60f multi	1.50
C113	AP18	75f multi	2.25
C114	AP18	100f multi	3.25
C115	AP18	125f multi	3.75
	Nos. C110-C115 (6)		13.00

Souvenir Sheets
C116		Sheet of 4, Fruit	14.00
a.		AP18 100f, any single	3.50
C117		Sheet of 4, Flowers	14.00
a.		AP18 125f, any single	3.50

Nos. C110-C115 exist imperf. (Value, set $20) and in souvenir sheets (Value, set $40). For surcharges see Nos. C143, C149.

1982 World Cup Soccer Championships, Spain — AP19

Various soccer plays.

1982, Sept. 1   Perf. 14
C118	AP19	25f multi	1.25
C119	AP19	50f multi	1.50
C120	AP19	60f multi	1.75
C121	AP19	75f multi	2.50
C122	AP19	100f multi	3.50
C123	AP19	125f multi	4.00
	Nos. C118-C123 (6)		14.50

Nos. C118-C123 exist imperf. (Value, set $25) and in souvenir sheets (Value, set $72).

Palestinian Children's Day — AP20

1982, Oct. 20
C126	AP20	75f Boy	1.50	1.00
C127	AP20	125f Girl	2.50	2.00
C128	AP20	325f Boy and girl	6.00	4.00
a.		Souvenir sheet of 1	8.00	8.00
	Nos. C126-C128 (3)		10.00	7.00

Arab Postal Union, 30th Anniv. — AP21

1982, Dec. 1
C129	AP21	75f yellow & multi	1.25	1.00
C130	AP21	125f green & multi	2.25	1.75
C131	AP21	325f magenta & multi	4.00	2.00
a.		Souvenir sheet of 1	8.00	8.00
	Nos. C129-C131 (3)		7.50	4.75

1984 Summer Olympics, Los Angeles — AP22

1984, Nov. 15
C132	AP22	20f Wrestling	.60
C133	AP22	30f Boxing	.90
C134	AP22	40f Running	1.25
C135	AP22	60f Hurdling	1.50
C136	AP22	150f Pole vault	2.25
C137	AP22	325f Javelin throw	3.50
	Nos. C132-C137 (6)		10.00

Nos. C132-C137 exist imperf. (Value, set $20) and in souvenir sheets (Value, set $45). Two souvenir sheets of four 75f stamps exist picturing water sports, gymnastics, weightlifting, shot put and discus throwing. Value $12.50 each.

No. C67 Surcharged
Nos. 459, 461, 463, 466, 474, 483, 486, 522, C73, C75, C81, C83, C89, C91, C97, C105, C107, C113 & C115 Surcharged with New Value and "AIR MAIL"

1993, Jan. 1   Perfs, etc. as Before
C138	AP12	3r on 125f #C67	
C139	AP13	3r on 125f #C75	
C140	AP14	3r on 125f #C83	
C141	AP15	3r on 125f #C91	
C142	AP17	3r on 125f #C107	
C143	AP18	3r on 125f #C115	
C144	AP13	5r on 75f #C73	
C145	AP14	5r on 75f #C81	
C146	AP15	5r on 75f #C89	
C147	AP16	5r on 75f #C97	
C148	AP17	5r on 75f #C105	
C149	AP18	5r on 75f #C113	
C150	A126	8r on 425f #459	
C151	A127	8r on 425f #461	
C152	A128	8r on 425f #463	
C153	A129	8r on 425f #466	
C154	A130	8r on 425f #474	
C155	A132	8r on 425f #483	
C156	A133	8r on 425f #486	
C157	A142	12r on 850f #522	

Size and location of surcharge varies.

POSTAGE DUE STAMPS

D1

1942   Litho.   Wmk. 258   Perf. 12½
J1	D1	1b org & yel grn	.25	.25
J2	D1	2b org & yel grn	.25	.25
J3	D1	4b org & yel grn	.45	.45
J4	D1	6b org & brt ultra	.55	.55
J5	D1	8b org & brt ultra	.80	.80
J6	D1	10b org & brt ultra	1.00	1.00
J7	D1	12b org & brt ultra	1.50	1.50
J8	D1	20b org & brt ultra	3.00	3.00
	Nos. J1-J8 (8)		7.80	7.80

Yemen had no postage due system. Nos. J1-J8 were used for regular postage. See Nos. 66-67 for surcharges.

Animals Type of Regular Issue Inscribed "Postage Due"
1964, Aug. 15   Photo.   Perf. 12x11½
J9	A39d	4b Gazelles	.90	.45
J10	A39d	12b Buffalo	2.00	1.00
J11	A39d	20b Arabian horse	3.50	1.75
	Nos. J9-J11 (3)		6.40	3.20

Flower Type of Regular Issue Inscribed "Postage Due"
1964, Sept. 1   Photo.   Perf. 11½x12
J12	A39e	4b Like No. 199C	1.40	1.00
J13	A39e	12b Like No. 199B	3.50	2.00
J14	A39e	20b Like No. 199D	5.00	3.50
	Nos. J12-J14 (3)		9.90	6.50

Nos. 209G-209K Overprinted in Black

Perf. 14x14½, 14½x15
1966, Mar. 5   Photo.
J15	A43a	6b On No. 209G	2.50	2.00
J16	A43a	8b On No. 209H	3.00	2.50
J17	A43a	12b On No. 209I	4.00	3.50
J18	A43a	20b On No. 209J	5.50	4.00
J19	A43a	1r On No. 209K	10.00	8.00
	Nos. J15-J19 (5)		25.00	20.00

A set of 3 Postage Due stamps were released May 29, 1966, in connection with the World Cup Soccer Championships in London. The editors would like to examine the set.

Fruit Type of Regular Issue Inscribed "Postage Due"
1967, Feb. 10   Litho.   Perf. 12½x12
J23	A56	6b Bananas	1.50	1.25
J24	A56	8b Figs	2.00	1.75
J25	A56	10b Green grapes	2.50	2.25
	Nos. J23-J25 (3)		6.00	5.25

Two stamps of this design were released in the late 1960s or early 1970s. While they have been called postal tax stamps, questions about their status and use exist. The editors would like more information about these stamps and would like to examine unused and on cover examples.

YEMEN, PEOPLE'S DEMOCRATIC REPUBLIC OF
ˈpē-pəls ri-ˈpə-blik of ˈye-mən

LOCATION — Southern Arabia
GOVT. — Republic
AREA — 111,074 sq. mi.
POP. — 2,030,000 (est. 1981)
CAPITAL — Aden

The People's Republic of Southern Yemen was proclaimed Nov. 30, 1967, when the Federation of South Arabia achieved independence. It consisted of the former British colony of Aden and the protectorates. The name was changed to People's Democratic Republic of Yemen on Nov. 30, 1970. See South Arabia.

The Yemen Arab Republic and the People's Republic of Yemen planned a 30-month unification process scheduled for completion by November 1992. While government ministries merged, both currencies remained valid. A civil war in 1994 delayed the merger.

1,000 Fils = 1 Dinar

People's Republic of Southern Yemen
South Arabia Nos. 3-16 Overprinted in Red or Blue

Nos. 1-10

Nos. 11-14

Perf. 14½x14
1968, Apr. 1   Photo.   Unwmk.
1	A1	5f blue	.25	.25
2	A1	10f lt vio bl	.25	.25
3	A1	15f bl grn	.25	.25
4	A1	20f green	.25	.25
5	A1	25f org brn (B)	.25	.25
6	A1	30f lemon	.25	.25
7	A1	35f red brn (B)	.35	.25
8	A1	50f rose red (B)	.45	.35
9	A1	65f lt yel grn	.60	.40
10	A1	75f rose car (B)	.80	.55
11	A2	100f multi (B)	1.25	.70
12	A2	250f multi	2.40	1.40
13	A2	500f multi (B)	4.50	2.75
14	A2	1d vio & multi	11.50	7.00
	Nos. 1-14 (14)		23.35	14.90

Globe and Flag A1

Designs: 15f, Revolutionist with broken chain and flames, vert. 50f, Aden Harbor. 100f, Cotton picking.

1968, May 25   Litho.   Perf. 13x12½
15	A1	10f multi	.25	.25
16	A1	15f multi	.25	.25
17	A1	50f multi	.75	.75
18	A1	100f multi	1.50	1.50
	Nos. 15-18 (4)		2.75	2.75

Independence Day, Nov. 30, 1967.

Girl Scouts at Campfire A2

Designs: 25f, Three Girl Scouts, vert. 50f, Three Girl Scout leaders.

Perf. 13½
1968, Sept. 21   Litho.   Unwmk.
19	A2	10f ultra & sepia	.50	.50
20	A2	25f org brn & Prus bl	.70	.70
21	A2	50f yel, bl & brn	1.50	1.50
	Nos. 19-21 (3)		2.70	2.70

Girl Scout movement in Southern Yemen, established 1966 (in Aden).

Revolutionary — A3

"Freedom-
Socialism-Unity"
A4

King of Ausan,
Alabaster Statue
A5

Design: 30f, Radfan Mountains where first
revolutionary fell.

1968, Oct. 14　　Unwmk.　　Perf. 13
22	A3	20f brn & lt bl	.30	.30
23	A3	30f grn & brn	.45	.45
24	A4	100f ver & yel	1.10	1.10
		Nos. 22-24 (3)	1.85	1.85

Revolution Day (revolution of Oct. 14, 1963).

1968, Dec. 28　　Litho.　　Perf. 13

Antiquities of Southern Yemen: 35f, African-
type sculpture of a man. 50f, Winged bull,
Assyrian-type bas-relief, horiz. 65f, Bull's
head (Moon God), alabaster plaque, 230 B.C.,
horiz.

25	A5	5f olive & bister	.25	.25
26	A5	35f maroon & lt bl	.50	.50
27	A5	50f bister & blue	1.10	1.10
28	A5	65f lt grnsh bl & lilac	1.40	1.40
		Nos. 25-28 (4)	3.25	3.25

Martyr Monument, Steamer Point, Aden.

1969, Feb. 11　　Litho.　　Perf. 13
29	A6	15f yellow & multi	.25	.25
30	A6	35f emerald & multi	.25	.25
31	A6	100f orange & multi	1.50	1.50
		Nos. 29-31 (3)	2.00	2.00

Issued for Martyr Day.

Albert Thomas Monument, Geneva, and
ILO emblem.

1969, June 1　　Litho.　　Perf. 13
32	A7	10f brt grn, blk & lt brn	.25	.25
33	A7	35f car rose, blk & lt brn	.75	.75

50th anniv. of the ILO, and to honor founder
Albert Thomas.

Classroom — A8

1969, Sept. 8　　Litho.　　Perf. 13
34	A8	35f orange & multi	.65	.65
35	A8	100f yellow & multi	1.60	1.60

International Literacy Day, Sept. 8.

Mahatma
Gandhi — A9

1969, Sept. 27　　Litho.　　Perf. 13
36	A9	35f lt ultra & vio brn	1.75	.60

Mohandas K. Gandhi (1869-1948), leader in
India's fight for independence.

Family
A10

1969, Oct. 1
37	A10	25f lt grn & multi	.75	.60
38	A10	75f car rose & multi	1.50	.90

Issued for Family Day.

UN Headquarters, NYC — A11

1969, Oct. 24　　　　　　Perf. 13
39	A11	20f rose red & multi	.60	.25
40	A11	65f emer & multi	1.25	.60

Issued for United Nations Day.

Map and Flag of Southern
Yemen — A12

40f, 50f, Tractors, flag (agricultural
progress).

1969, Nov. 30　　Litho.　　Unwmk.
Size: 41x24½mm
41	A12	15f multi	.25	.25
42	A12	35f multi	.55	.25

Size: 37x37mm
43	A12	40f blue & multi	.60	.35
44	A12	50f brown & multi	1.00	.50
		Nos. 41-44 (4)	2.40	1.35

Second anniversary of independence.

Map of Arab League Countries, Flag
and Emblem — A13

1970, Mar. 22　　Unwmk.　　Perf. 13
45	A13	35f lt bl & multi	.75	.25

25th anniversary of the Arab League.

Lenin — A14　　　Fighter — A15

1970, Apr. 22　　Litho.　　Perf. 13
46	A14	75f multi	1.50	.60

Lenin (1870-1924), Russian communist
leader.

1970, May 15

Designs: 35f, Underground soldier and
plane destroyed on ground. 50f, Fighting people hailing Arab liberation flag, horiz.

47	A15	15f grn, red & blk	.25	.25
48	A15	35f grn, bl, red & blk	.65	.55
49	A15	50f grn, blk & red	.85	.70
		Nos. 47-49 (3)	1.75	1.50

Issued for Palestine Day.

UPU Headquarters, Bern — A16

1970, May 22　　Litho.　　Perf. 13
50	A16	15f org & brt grn	.60	.25
51	A16	65f yel & car rose	1.40	.60

New UPU Headquarters in Bern.

Yemeni
Costume — A17

Regional Costumes: 15f, 20f, Women's costumes. 50f, Three men of Aden.

1970, July 2　　Litho.　　Perf. 13
52	A17	10f yel & multi	.40	.25
53	A17	15f lt lil & multi	.40	.25
54	A17	20f lt bl & multi	.65	.25
55	A17	50f multi	1.25	.45
		Nos. 52-55 (4)	2.70	1.20

Camel and Calf — A18

Designs: 25f, Goats. 35f, Arabian oryx. 65f,
Socotra dwarf cows.

1970, Aug. 31　　Litho.　　Perf. 13
56	A18	15f dk brn & multi	.40	.25
57	A18	25f car rose & multi	.70	.50
58	A18	35f ultra & multi	1.50	1.00
59	A18	65f brt grn & multi	2.40	1.50
		Nos. 56-59 (4)	5.00	3.25

A19

35f, Natl. Front Organization Headquarters.
50f, Farm worker, 1970, battle scene, 1963.

1970, Oct. 14　　Litho.　　Perf. 13
Size: 41½x29½mm
60	A19	25f multi	.50	.25

Size: 56½x27mm
61	A19	35f multi	.65	.45

Size: 41x24½mm
62	A19	50f multi	1.00	.60
		Nos. 60-62 (3)	2.15	1.30

7th anniversary of Oct. 14 Revolution.

UN Headquarters, Emblem — A20

1970, Oct. 24　　Litho.　　Perf. 13
63	A20	10f org & bl	.70	.25
64	A20	65f brt pink & bl	1.50	.80

25th anniversary of the United Nations.

**People's Democratic Republic of
Yemen**

Temples at Philae — A21

1971, Feb. 1　　Litho.　　Perf. 13½x13
65	A21	5f violet & multi	.25	.25
66	A21	35f blue & multi	.65	.40
67	A21	65f green & multi	1.60	.90
		Nos. 65-67 (3)	2.50	1.55

UNESCO campaign to save the monuments
in Nubia.

Scales,
Book and
Sword
A22

1971, Mar. 1　　　　　Perf. 13x12½
68	A22	10f brt pink & multi	.25	.25
69	A22	15f brt grn & multi	.25	.25
70	A22	35f lt ultra & multi	.65	.65
71	A22	50f rose & multi	.85	.85
		Nos. 68-71 (4)	2.00	2.00

First Constitution, 1971.

Men of 3
Races,
Human
Rights
Emblem
A23

1971, Mar. 21
72	A23	20f lt bl & multi	.25	.25
73	A23	35f grn & multi	.75	.75
74	A23	75f lt vio & multi	1.10	1.10
		Nos. 72-74 (3)	2.10	2.10

Intl. year against racial discrimination.

Map and Flag — A24

"Brothers' Blood" Tree, Socotra Island — A25

1971-77		Litho.	Perf. 13½	
75	A24	5f yel & multi	.25	.25
76	A24	10f grn & multi	.25	.25
77	A24	15f yel & multi	.25	.25
78	A24	20f org & multi	.25	.25
79	A24	25f bl & multi	.25	.25
80	A24	35f red org & multi	.35	.25
81	A24	40f vio & multi	.50	.25
82	A24	50f yel grn & multi	.75	.45
82A	A24	60f red & multi	1.50	.60
83	A24	65f pale vio & multi	.95	.65
84	A24	80f org brn & multi	1.10	.80
84A	A24	90f ol & multi	1.50	.75
		Perf. 13		
84B	A25	110f brn & multi	2.25	.95
85	A25	125f ultra & multi	1.90	1.60
86	A25	250f org & multi	3.25	2.10
87	A25	500f multi	6.75	4.00
88	A25	1d grn & multi	15.00	9.00
		Nos. 75-88 (17)	37.05	22.65

Issued: #82A, 84A-84B, 10/17/77; others, 4/1/71.

See Nos. 332-333. For surcharges see Yemen Nos. 628, 638.

Machine Gun and Map A26

Arms with Wrench and Cogwheel A27

Designs: 45f, Woman fighter and flame, horiz. 50f, Fighter, factories and rainbow.

1971, June 9		Litho.	Perf. 12½x13	
89	A26	15f multi	.25	.25
90	A26	45f green & multi	.75	.45
91	A26	50f multi	1.25	.75
		Nos. 89-91 (3)	2.25	1.45

Armed revolution in the Arabian Gulf.

1971, June 22

25f, Torch, factories, symbols. 65f, Windmill.

92	A27	15f blue & multi	.25	.25
93	A27	25f multi	.75	.55
94	A27	65f multi	1.25	.75
		Nos. 92-94 (3)	2.25	1.55

2nd anniversary of the revolution of June 22, 1969 (Corrective Movement).

A 20f picturing a fighter holding rifle and flag, with flag colors transposed, was withdrawn on day of issue.

Revolutionary Emblem — A28

40f, Map of southern Arabia & flag of republic.

1971, Sept. 26

| 95 | A28 | 10f yellow & multi | .25 | .25 |
| 96 | A28 | 40f lt grn & multi | .90 | .55 |

9th anniv. of the revolution of Sept. 26.

Gamal Abdel Nasser — A29

1971, Sept. 28		Litho.	Perf. 12½x13	
97	A29	65f multi	1.25	.75

1st anniv. of the death of Gamal Abdel Nasser (1918-1970), President of Egypt.

UNICEF Emblem, Children of the World — A30

1971, Dec. 11			Perf. 13x13½	
98	A30	15f org, car & blk	.25	.25
99	A30	40f lt ultra, car & blk	.40	.35
100	A30	50f yel grn, car & blk	.70	.55
		Nos. 98-100 (3)	1.35	1.15

25th anniv. of UNICEF.

Pigeons A31

Birds: 40f, Partridge. 65f, Partridge and guinea fowl. 100f, European kite.

1971, Dec. 22			Perf. 13½x13	
101	A31	5f bl, blk & car	.35	.25
102	A31	40f salmon & multi	1.25	.60
103	A31	65f brt grn, blk & car	3.00	1.10
104	A31	100f yel, blk & car	5.25	2.25
		Nos. 101-104 (4)	9.85	4.20

Dhow under Construction A32

Design: 80f, Dhow under sail, vert.

1972, Feb. 15		Perf. 13½x13, 13x13½		
105	A32	25f bl, brn & yel	.75	.45
106	A32	80f lt bl & multi	2.40	1.60

Band — A33

Designs: 25f, 40f, 80f, Various folk dances.

1972, Apr. 8		Litho.	Perf. 13	
107	A33	10f lt grn & multi	.25	.25
108	A33	25f org & multi	.40	.35
109	A33	40f red & multi	.80	.50
110	A33	80f blue & multi	1.50	1.00
		Nos. 107-110 (4)	2.95	2.10

Palestinian Fighter and Barbed Wire — A34

1972, May 15

111	A34	5f emerald & multi	.30	.25
112	A34	20f blue & multi	.60	.35
113	A34	65f org ver & multi	1.50	.85
		Nos. 111-113 (3)	2.40	1.45

Struggle for Palestine liberation.

Militia Women on Parade A35

Design: 25f, Policemen on parade.

1972, June 20		Litho.	Perf. 13½	
114	A35	25f lt bl & multi	.60	.25
115	A35	80f lt grn & multi	2.50	1.50
a.		Souv. sheet of 2, #114-115	9.00	9.00

Police Day. No. 115a sold for 150f.

Start of Bicycle Race A36

15f Parade of young women. 40f, Yemeni Guides & Scouts on parade. 80f, Acrobats.

1972, July 20		Litho.	Perf. 13½	
116	A36	10f lt bl & multi	.45	.25
117	A36	15f multi	.45	.25
118	A36	40f buff & multi	.90	.60
119	A36	80f lt ultra & multi	2.25	.90
		Nos. 116-119 (4)	4.05	2.00

Turtle A37

1972, Sept. 2		Litho.	Perf. 13	
120	A37	15f Shown	.90	.25
121	A37	40f Sailfish	1.25	.70
122	A37	65f Kingfish	1.50	.90
123	A37	125f Spiny lobster	3.00	1.60
		Nos. 120-123 (4)	6.65	3.45

Book Year Emblem A38

1972, Sept. 9

| 124 | A38 | 40f red, ultra & yel | .75 | .50 |
| 125 | A38 | 65f org, ultra & yel | 1.25 | .80 |

International Book Year 1972.

Farm Couple and Fields A39

1972, Nov. 23		Litho.	Perf. 13	
126	A39	10f orange & multi	.25	.25
127	A39	25f rose lilac & multi	.70	.45
128	A39	40f red & multi	1.25	.80
		Nos. 126-128 (3)	2.20	1.50

Lands Day, publicizing land reforms.

Militia — A40

20f, Soldier guarding village. 65f, Industrial, agricultural and educational progress, vert.

1972, Dec. 2		Litho.	Perf. 13	
129	A40	5f multi	.25	.25
130	A40	20f multi	.25	.25
131	A40	65f multi	1.60	1.60
a.		Souv. sheet of 3, #129-131, imperf.	4.00	4.00
		Nos. 129-131 (3)	2.10	2.10

5th anniversary of independence.

Census Chart A41

1973, Apr. 3		Litho.	Perf. 12½x13½	
132	A41	25f org, emer & ol	.25	.25
133	A41	40f rose, bl & vio	1.25	1.25

Population census 1973.

WHO Emblem and "25" — A42

1973, Apr. 7		Perf. 14x12½, 12½x14		
134	A42	5f "25" and WHO emblem, vert	.25	.25
135	A42	20f Shown	.25	.25
136	A42	125f "25" and WHO emblem	2.10	2.10
		Nos. 134-136 (3)	2.60	2.60

25th anniv. of the WHO.

Elephant Bay A43

Tourist Publicity: 20f, Taweels Tanks Reservoir, vert. 25f, Shibam Town. 100f, Al-Mohdar Mosque, Tarim.

1973, June 9		Litho.	Perf. 13	
137	A43	20f multi	.25	.25
138	A43	25f multi	.25	.25
139	A43	40f multi	1.50	1.50
140	A43	100f multi	1.75	1.75
		Nos. 137-140 (4)	3.75	3.75

Office Buildings and Slum,
Aden — A44

Design: 80f, Intersection, Aden, vert.

1973, Aug. 4　　　Litho.　　Perf. 13
141 A44 20f multi　　　　　　.25　.25
142 A44 80f multi　　　　　　1.75 1.75

Nationalization of buildings.

Army
Unit
A45

People's Army: 20f, Four marching soldiers.
40f, Sailors on parade. 80f, Tanks.

1973, Sept. 1
143 A45 10f multi　　　　　　.25　.25
144 A45 20f multi　　　　　　.25　.25
145 A45 40f multi　　　　　　1.00 1.00
146 A45 80f multi　　　　　　1.40 1.40
　　Nos. 143-146 (4)　　　2.90 2.90

FAO
Emblem,
Loading
Food
A46

Design: 80f, Workers and grain sacks.

1973, Dec. 19　　　Litho.　　Perf. 13
147 A46 20f blue & multi　　.25　.25
148 A46 80f blue & multi　　1.75 1.75

World Food Program, 10th anniversary.

Letter and
UPU
Emblem
A47

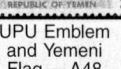

UPU Emblem　　　Map of Yemen,
and Yemeni　　　　　　UPU
Flag — A48　　　　Emblem — A49

UPU cent.: 20f, "100" formed by people,
and UPU emblem.

1974, Oct. 9　　Litho.　　Perf. 12½x13½
149 A47　5f multi　　　　　.25　.25
150 A47 20f multi　　　　　.25　.25
151 A48 40f multi　　　　　.70　.70
152 A49 125f multi　　　　1.25 1.25
　　Nos. 149-152 (4)　　　2.45 2.45

Irrigation System — A50

Progress in Agriculture: 20f, Bulldozer
pushing soil. 100f, Tractors plowing field.

1974　　　　　　Litho.　　Perf. 13
153 A50 10f multi　　　　　.25　.25
154 A50 20f multi　　　　　.25　.25
155 A50 100f multi　　　　1.50 1.50
　　Nos. 153-155 (3)　　　2.00 2.00

Lathe
Operator — A51

Industrial progress: 40f, Printers. 80f,
Women textile workers, horiz.

1975, May 1　　Litho.　　Perf. 13
156 A51 10f multi　　　　　.25　.25
157 A51 40f multi　　　　　.60　.60
158 A51 80f multi　　　　1.00 1.00
　　Nos. 156-158 (3)　　　1.85 1.85

Yemeni
Woman — A52

Designs: Various women's costumes.

1975, Nov. 15　Litho.　Perf. 11½x12
159 A52　5f blk & ocher　　.25　.25
160 A52 10f blk & vio　　　.25　.25
161 A52 15f blk & olive　　.25　.25
162 A52 25f blk & rose lil　.45　.45
163 A52 40f blk & Prus bl　.75　.75
164 A52 50f blk & org brn　1.10 1.10
　　Nos. 159-164 (6)　　　3.05 3.05

Women
Factory
Workers,
IWY
Emblem
A53

1975, Dec. 30　Litho.　Perf. 12x11½
165 A53 40f blk & salmon　.60　.60
166 A53 50f blk & yel grn　1.00 1.00

International Women's Year 1975.

Soccer Player
and
Field — A54

Designs: Different scenes from soccer.

1976, Apr. 1　Litho.　Perf. 11½x12
167 A54　5f lt bl & brn　　.25　.25
168 A54 40f yel & green　　.70　.70
169 A54 80f salmon & vio　1.10 1.10
　　Nos. 167-169 (3)　　　2.05 2.05

Rocket Take-off
from
Moon — A55

15f, Alexander Satalov. 40f, Lunokhod on
moon, horiz. 65f, Valentina Tereshkova,
rocket.

**　　Perf. 11½x12, 12x11½**
1976, Apr. 17　　　　　　Litho.
170 A55 10f multi　　　　　.25　.25
171 A55 15f multi　　　　　.25　.25
172 A55 40f multi　　　　1.00 1.00
173 A55 65f multi　　　　1.25 1.25
　　Nos. 170-173 (4)　　　2.75 2.75

Soviet cosmonauts and space program.

Traffic
Policemen
A56

1977, Apr. 16　Litho.　Perf. 14
174 A56 25f red & blk　　.60　.60
175 A56 60f yel & blk　　1.25 1.25
176 A56 75f grn & blk　　1.50 1.50
177 A56 110f dp bl & blk　2.00 2.00
　　Nos. 174-177 (4)　　　5.35 5.35

Traffic change to right side of road.

APU
Emblem — A57

1977, Apr. 12　Litho.　Perf. 13½
178 A57 20f lt bl & multi　　.25　.25
179 A57 60f gray & multi　　.80　.80
180 A57 70f lt grn & multi　1.00 1.00
181 A57 90f bl grn & multi　1.10 1.10
　　Nos. 178-181 (4)　　　3.15 3.15

Arab Postal Union, 25th anniversary.

Congress
Decree
and Red
Star
A58

Designs: 25f, Pres. Salim Rubi'a Ali, Council members Ali Nasser Muhamed and Abdul
Farta Ismail. 65f, Women's militia on parade.
95f, Aerial view of textile mill.

1977, May　　　Photo.　　Perf. 13
182 A58 25f grn, gold & dk brn　.25　.25
183 A58 35f red, gold & lt bl　　.50　.50
184 A58 65f bl, gold & lil　　1.00 1.00
185 A58 95f org, gold & grn　1.10 1.10
　　Nos. 182-185 (4)　　　2.85 2.85

Unification Congress, 1st anniversary.

Afrivoluta
Pringlei
A59

Shells: 60f, Festilyria duponti, vert. 110f,
Conus splendidulus. 180f, Cypraea
4broderipii.

1977, July 16　Litho.　Perf. 13½
186 A59 60f multi　　　　　.95　.70
187 A59 90f multi　　　　1.40　.70
188 A59 110f multi　　　2.40 1.40
189 A59 180f multi　　　3.25 2.40
　　Nos. 186-189 (4)　　　8.00 5.20

Emblem and
Flag — A60

Designs: 20f, Man with broken chain. 90f,
Pipeline, agriculture and industry. 110f, Flag,
symbolic tree and hands holding tools.

1977, Nov. 30　Litho.　Perf. 13½
190 A60　5f blk & multi　　.25　.25
191 A60 20f blk & multi　　.25　.25
192 A60 90f blk & multi　　.50　.25
193 A60 110f blk & multi　.85　.40
　　Nos. 190-193 (4)　　　1.85 1.15

10th anniversary of independence.

Dome of
the Rock
A61

1978, May 15　　　　Perf. 12
194 A61 5f multi　　　　　.70　.40

Palestinian fighters & families. See #264A.

Festival Emblem
and
"CUBA" — A62

Designs: 60f, Festival emblem. 90f, Festival emblem as flower. 110f, Festival emblem,
dove, young man and woman.

1978, June 22　Litho.　Perf. 14
195 A62　5f multi　　　　　.25　.25
196 A62 60f multi　　　　　.65　.40
197 A62 90f multi　　　　　.85　.45
198 A62 110f multi　　　1.10　.70
　　Nos. 195-198 (4)　　　2.85 1.80

11th World Youth Festival, Havana.

Silver Ornaments — A63

Designs: Various silver ornaments.

1978, July 22 Litho. Perf. 13½
199	A63	10f blk & multi	.25	.25
200	A63	15f blk & multi	.25	.25
201	A63	20f blk & multi	.25	.25
202	A63	60f blk & multi	.25	.25
203	A63	90f blk & multi	1.00	.65
204	A63	110f blk & multi	1.50	.75
		Nos. 199-204 (6)	3.50	2.40

For surcharge see Yemen No. 629.

Yemeni Musical Instruments — A64

1978, Aug. 26 Perf. 14
205	A64	35f Almarfaai	.25	.25
206	A64	60f Almizmar	.85	.25
207	A64	90f Alqnboos	1.00	.25
208	A64	110f Simsimiya	1.75	1.00
		Nos. 205-208 (4)	3.85	1.75

For surcharge see Yemen No. 630.

"V" for Vanguard
A65

1978, Oct. 11 Litho. Perf. 14
209	A65	5f multi	.25	.25
210	A65	20f multi	.25	.25
211	A65	60f multi	.40	.25
212	A65	180f multi	.85	.50
		Nos. 209-212 (4)	1.75	1.25

1st Conf. of Vanguard Party, Oct. 11-13.

Man with Palm,
Factories — A66

Designs: 10f, Palm branches, broken chains, horiz. 60f, Candle and "15." 110f, Woman and man with rifle, "15."

1978, Oct. 14
213	A66	10f multi	.25	.25
214	A66	35f multi	.25	.25
215	A66	60f multi	.45	.25
216	A66	110f multi	.75	.45
		Nos. 213-216 (4)	1.70	1.20

15th Revolution Day.
For surcharge see Yemen No. 631.

Child, Map of
Arabia and IYC
Emblem — A67

1979, Mar. 20 Litho. Perf. 13½
217	A67	15f multi	.25	.25
218	A67	20f multi	.25	.25
219	A67	60f multi	.50	.25
220	A67	90f multi	.70	.25
		Nos. 217-220 (4)	1.70	1.00

International Year of the Child.

Sickle, Star,
Tractor, Wheat
and Dove — A68

Designs: 35f, Pylon, star, compass, wheat and hammer. 60f, Students, worker and clock. 90f, Woman with raised arms, doves and star.

1979, June 22 Litho. Perf. 14
221	A68	20f multi	.25	.25
222	A68	35f multi	.25	.25
223	A68	60f multi	.40	.25
224	A68	90f multi	.55	.25
		Nos. 221-224 (4)	1.45	1.00

Corrective Movement, 10th anniversary.

Yemen
#52, Hill
A69

Hill and: 110f, Yemen #56. 250f, Aden #12.

1979, Aug. 27 Litho. Perf. 14
225	A69	90f multi	.60	.25
226	A69	110f multi	.75	.45

Souvenir Sheet
227	A69		2.25	2.25

Sir Rowland Hill (1795-1879), originator of penny postage.

Book, World Map, Arab
Achievements — A70

1979, Sept. 26 Litho. Perf. 14
228	A70	60f multi	.70	.25

Party
Emblem — A71

Cassia
Adenesis — A72

1979, Oct. 13 Perf. 14½x14
229	A71	60f multi	.70	.25

Yemeni Socialist Party, 1st anniversary.

1979, Nov. 30 Litho. Perf. 13½
Flowers: 90f, Nerium oleander. 110f, Calligonum comosum. 180f, Adenium obesium.
230	A72	20f multi	.25	.25
231	A72	90f multi	.90	.50
232	A72	110f multi	1.50	.75
233	A72	180f multi	1.90	.90
		Nos. 230-233 (4)	4.55	2.40

For surcharge see Yemen No. 632.

First Anniv. of
Iranian
Revolution — A73

1980, Feb. 12 Litho. Perf. 13½
234	A73	60f multi	1.10	1.10

Dido
A74

1980, Mar. 5 Litho. Perf. 13½
235	A74	110f shown	1.10	.50
236	A74	180f Anglia	1.60	.70
237	A74	250f India	2.25	.90
		Nos. 235-237 (3)	4.95	2.10

For surcharge see Yemen No. 633.

Basket Maker,
London 1980
Emblem — A75

1980, May 6 Litho. Perf. 14
238	A75	60f shown	.25	.25
239	A75	90f Hubble bubble pipe maker	.65	.25
240	A75	110f Weaver	.90	.55
241	A75	250f Potter	2.00	1.10
		Nos. 238-241 (4)	3.80	2.15

London 1980 Intl. Stamp Exhib., May 6-14.

Hemprich's Skink — A76

1980, May 8 Litho. Perf. 14
242	A76	20f shown	.25	.25
243	A76	35f Mole viper	.60	.25
244	A76	110f Carter's day gecko	1.50	.60
245	A76	180f Cobra	2.50	1.25
		Nos. 242-245 (4)	4.85	2.35

For surcharge see Yemen No. 634.

Misha and
Olympic
Emblem — A77

1980, July 19 Litho. Perf. 12½x12
246	A77	110f multi	1.10	.65

For overprint see No. 287.

Farmers
Armed — A78

1980, Oct. 17 Perf. 13½
247	A78	50f Armed farmers working, horiz.	.50	.25
248	A78	90f shown	.75	.50
249	A78	110f Sickle (wheat) and fist	1.00	.70
		Nos. 247-249 (3)	2.25	1.45

10th anniversary of farmers' uprising.

110th Birth
Anniversary of
Lenin — A79

1980, Nov. 7 Litho. Perf. 12
250	A79	35f multi	.50	.50

Douglas DC-3 — A80

1981, Mar. 11 Litho. Perf. 13½
251	A80	60f shown	.25	.25
252	A80	90f Boeing 707	1.50	.25
253	A80	250f DHC Dash 7	3.50	1.60
		Nos. 251-253 (3)	5.25	2.10

Democratic Yemen Airlines, 10th anniv.

Ras
Boradli
Earth
Satellite
Station
A82

1981, June 22 Litho. Perf. 12
257	A82	60f multi	.90	.65

Conocarpus
Lancifolius — A83

Supreme People's
Council, 10th
Anniv. — A84

1981, Aug. 1 Litho. Perf. 12
258	A83	90f shown	.85	.25
259	A83	180f Ficus vasta	2.00	1.10
260	A83	250f Maerua crassifolia	3.00	1.75
		Nos. 258-260 (3)	5.85	3.10

1981, Aug. 18 Litho. Perf. 15x14½
261	A84	180f multi	1.50	.90

Desert Fox — A85

1981, Sept. 26　Litho.　Perf. 14½
262 A85 50f shown　　　　　.70 .25
263 A85 90f South Arabian
　　　　　　leopard　　　　1.40 .70
264 A85 250f Ibex　　　　　3.25 1.60
　　　Nos. 262-264 (3)　　　5.35 2.55

No. 194 Redrawn

1981, Oct. 15　Litho.　Perf. 12
Size: 25x27mm
264A A61 5f multi　　　　　.45 .45
　Denomination in upper right.

Tephrosia
Apollinea — A86

1981, Nov. 30　Litho.　Perf. 13½
265 A86 50f shown　　　　　.25 .25
266 A86 90f Citrullus colo-
　　　　　　cynthis　　　　1.00 .25
267 A86 110f Aloe sqarrosa　1.40 .25
268 A86 250f Lawsonia inermis 3.50 2.00
　　　Nos. 265-268 (4)　　　6.15 2.75

For surcharge see Yemen No. 635.

Intl. Year
of the
Disabled
A87

1981, Dec. 12　Litho.　Perf. 14½
269 A87 50f multi　　　　　.25 .25
270 A87 100f multi　　　　1.00 .25
271 A87 150f multi　　　　1.50 1.00
　　　Nos. 269-271 (3)　　　2.75 1.50

TB Bacillus Centenary — A88

1982, Mar. 24　Litho.　Perf. 14½
272 A88 50f multi　　　　　1.10 .25

30th
Anniv. of
Arab
Postal
Union
A89

1982, Apr. 12　Litho.　Perf. 14
273 A89 100f multi　　　　1.25 .75

1982
World Cup
A90

Designs: Various soccer players.

1982, June 13　Litho.　Perf. 14
274 A90 50f multi　　　　　.70 .25
275 A90 100f multi　　　　1.40 .90
276 A90 150f multi　　　　2.00 1.25
277 A90 200f multi　　　　3.00 1.75
a.　Souv. sheet of 4, #274-277　7.00 7.00
　　Nos. 274-277 (4)　　　7.10 4.15

For overprints see Nos. 281-284.

60th
Anniv. of
USSR
A93

1982, Dec. 22　Litho.　Perf. 12½x12
280 A93 50f Flags, arms　　.65 .45

Nos. 274-277, 277a Ovptd. with
Emblem and "WORLD CUP /
WINNERS / 1982 / 1st ITALY / 2nd W-
GERMANY / 3rd POLAND / 4th
FRANCE" in Blue

1982, Dec. 30　Litho.　Perf. 14
281 A90 50f multi　　　　　.25 .25
282 A90 100f multi　　　　1.50 1.50
283 A90 150f multi　　　　2.25 2.25
284 A90 200f multi　　　　2.50 2.50
a.　Souvenir sheet of 4, #281-284　7.00 7.00
　　Nos. 281-284 (4)　　　6.50 6.50

Palestinian
Solidarity
A94

1983, Apr. 10　　　　Perf. 13½x14½
285 A94 50f Yasser Arafat　.25 .25
286 A94 100f Arafat, Dome of the
　　　　　　Rock　　　　3.00 3.00
a.　Souvenir sheet of 1, imperf.　3.00 3.00

No. 246 Ovptd. with TEMBAL '83
Emblem in Yellow

1983, May 21　　　　Perf. 12½x12
287 A77 110f multi　　　　4.75 4.75

World Communications Year — A95

Designs: 50f, Correspondent, postrider,
ship. 100f, Postman, coach, telegraph. No.
290, Telephones, bus. 200f, Telecommunications. No. 292, Montage.

1983, June 10　　　　Perf. 13x13½
288 A95 50f blk & brt bl　　.25 .25
289 A95 100f multi　　　　1.50 1.50
290 A95 150f multi　　　　2.40 2.40
291 A95 200f multi　　　　2.75 2.75
　　　Nos. 288-291 (4)　　　6.90 6.90
Souvenir Sheet
292 A95 150f multi　　　　3.00 3.00

Pablo Picasso (1881-1973),
Painter — A96

Paintings: No. 293, The Poor Family, 1903.
No. 294, Woman with Crow. No. 295a, The
Gourmet. No. 295b, Woman with Child on
Beach. No. 295c, Sitting Beggar. No. 296,
The Soler Family, horiz.

1983, July 25　　　　Perf. 14
293 A96 50f multi　　　　　.25 .25
294 A96 100f multi　　　　2.00 2.00
Souvenir Sheets
295　　Sheet of 3　　　13.50 13.50
a.　A96 50f multi　　　　1.75 1.75
b.　A96 100f multi　　　　4.50 4.50
c.　A96 150f multi　　　　6.50 6.50
296 A96 150f multi　　　　8.00 8.00

23rd Pre-Olympics Games,
1984 — A97

1983, July 30
297 A97 25f Show jumping　.25 .25
298 A97 50f Show jumping,
　　　　　　diff.　　　　　.25 .25
299 A97 100f Three-day event 2.50 2.50
　　　Nos. 297-299 (3)　　　3.00 3.00
Souvenir Sheets
300　　Sheet of 4　　　13.50 13.50
a.　A97 20f Bay, vert.　　　2.50 2.50
b.　A97 40f Gray, vert.　　　2.50 2.50
c.　A97 60f Bay, diff., vert.　3.25 3.25
d.　A97 80f Arabian　　　　4.50 4.50
301 A97 200f Show jumping,
　　　　　　diff., vert.　　9.75 9.75

Locomotives — A98

1983, Aug. 24　　　　Perf. 14½x15
302 A98 25f P8 steam en-
　　　　　gine, 1905　　　.25 .25
303 A98 50f 880 steam, 1915　.25 .25
304 A98 100f GT 2-4-4, 1923　4.00 4.00
　　　Nos. 302-304 (3)　　　4.50 4.50
Souvenir Sheets
305　　Sheet of 3　　　20.00 20.00
a.　A98 40f D51 steam, 1936　4.75 4.75
b.　A98 60f 45 Series, 1937　4.75 4.75
c.　A98 100f PT 47, 1948　　9.00 9.00
306 A98 200f P36, 1950　　20.00 20.00

Natl.
Revolution,
20th Anniv.
A100

1983, Oct. 15　Litho.　Perf. 13½x13
312 A100 50f shown　　　　.25 .25
313 A100 100f Flag, freedom
　　　　　　fighter　　　2.75 2.75

1st Manned
Flight,
Bicent. — A101

Balloons: 100f, La Montgolfiere prototype.
No. 316a, Lunardi's. No. 316b, Charles and
Robert's. No. 316c, Wiseman's. No. 316d,
Blanchard and Jeffries's. 200f, Five-balloon
craft.

1983, Oct. 25　　　　Perf. 14
314 A101 50f shown　　　　.25 .25
315 A101 100f multi　　　　2.50 2.50
Souvenir Sheets
316　　Sheet of 4　　　15.00 15.00
a.　A101 20f multi　　　　3.25 3.25
b.　A101 40f multi　　　　3.25 3.25
c.　A101 60f multi　　　　3.25 3.25
d.　A101 80f multi　　　　4.75 4.75
317 A101 200f multi　　　13.50 13.50

1984
Winter
Olympics,
Sarajevo
A102

1983, Dec. 28　Litho.　Perf. 14
318 A102 50f Men's downhill
　　　　　skiing　　　　.25 .25
319 A102 100f Two-man bob-
　　　　　sled　　　　2.50 2.50
Souvenir Sheets
320　　Sheet of 2　　　11.00 11.00
a.　A102 40f Ski jumping　　3.25 3.25
b.　A102 60f Figure skating　3.25 3.25
321 A102 200f Ice hockey　11.00 11.00

1984 Summer Olympics, Los
Angeles — A103

1984, Jan. 24
322 A103 25f Fencing　　　.25 .25
323 A103 50f Fencing, diff.　.25 .25
324 A103 100f Fencing, diff.　1.40 1.40
　　　Nos. 322-324 (3)　　　1.90 1.90
Souvenir Sheets
325　　Sheet of 4　　　11.00 11.00
a.　A103 20f Gymnastics　　2.75 2.75
b.　A103 40f Water polo　　2.75 2.75
c.　A103 60f Wrestling　　　2.75 2.75
d.　A103 80f Show jumping　2.75 2.75
326 A103 200f Show jumping,
　　　　　diff.　　　　11.00 11.00

Nos. 83 and 84B Surcharged with
Black Squares

1984, May 26　Litho.　Perf. 13½, 13
332 A24 50f on 65f multi
333 A25 100f on 110f multi

Fish — A105

1984, Nov. 25   Litho.   Perf. 11½

334	A105	10f Abalistes stellaris	.25	.25
335	A105	15f Caranx speciocus	.25	.25
336	A105	20f Pomadasys maculatus	.25	.25
337	A105	25f Chaetodon fasciatus	.25	.25
338	A105	35f Pomacanthus imperator	.25	.25
339	A105	50f Rastrelliger kanagurta	.25	.25
340	A105	100f Euthynnus affinis	1.25	1.25
341	A105	150f Heniochus acuminatus	1.90	1.90
342	A105	200f Pomacanthus maculosus	2.50	2.50
343	A105	250f Pterois russellii	3.25	3.25
344	A105	400f Argyrops spinifer	5.00	5.00
345	A105	500f Dasyatis uarnak	6.25	6.25
346	A105	1d Epinephalus chlorostigma	12.00	12.00
347	A105	2d Drepane longimana	25.00	25.00
		Nos. 334-347 (14)	58.65	58.65

For surcharges see Yemen Nos. 636, 640, 642.

Natl. Literacy Campaign A106

1985, Feb. 27   Perf. 12

350	A106	50f Girls writing	.25	.25
351	A106	100f Hand, fountain pen, vert.	4.25	4.25

Victory Parade, Red Square, Moscow, 1945 — A107

1985, May 9   Perf. 12x12½

352	A107	100f multi	1.50	1.50

Defeat of Nazi Germany, end of World War II, 40th anniv.

12th World Youth and Students Festival — A108

1985, Aug. 3   Perf. 12

353	A108	50f Emblem	.25	.25
354	A108	100f Hand holding emblem	4.25	4.25

UNESCO World Heritage Campaign — A109

Natl. Socialist Party, 3rd Gen. Cong. — A110

1985, Aug. 29

355	A109	50f Shibam city	.25	.25
356	A109	50f Close-up of buildings	.25	.25
357	A109	100f Windows	1.90	1.90
358	A109	100f Door	1.90	1.90
		Nos. 355-358 (4)	4.30	4.30

Nos. 355-357 horiz.

1985, Oct. 10

359	A110	25f Energy	.25	.25
360	A110	50f Industry	.25	.25
361	A110	100f Agriculture	2.25	2.25
		Nos. 359-361 (3)	2.75	2.75

UN Child Survival Campaign — A111

World Food Day — A112

1985, Nov. 28

362	A111	50f Mother feeding child	.25	.25
363	A111	50f Holding child	.25	.25
364	A111	100f Feeding child, diff.	1.90	1.90
365	A111	100f Breastfeeding	1.90	1.90
		Nos. 362-365 (4)	4.30	4.30

1986, Jan. 30

366	A112	20f Almihdar Mosque, Aden	.25	.25
367	A112	180f Palm trees	4.00	4.00

UN Food and Agriculture Org., 40th anniv.

Lenin, Red Square, Moscow A113

1986, Feb. 25   Perf. 12x12½

368	A113	75f multi	1.40	1.40
369	A113	250f multi	4.00	4.00

27th Soviet Communist Party Cong., Moscow.

Costumes Worn at the 1984 Brides Dance Festival — A114

Designs: No. 370, Bride wearing red and green costume, face markings. No. 371, Violet costume. No. 372, Veiled bride. No. 373, Unveiled bride. No. 374, Groom holding dagger. No. 375, Groom holding rifle.

1986, Feb. 27

370	A114	50f multi	.80	.80
371	A114	50f multi	.80	.80
372	A114	50f multi	.80	.80
373	A114	100f multi	1.50	1.50
374	A114	100f multi	1.50	1.50
375	A114	100f multi	1.50	1.50
		Nos. 370-375 (6)	6.90	6.90

Revolution Martyrs A115

1986, Oct. 15   Litho.   Perf. 12

376	A115	75f Abdul Fattah Ismail	1.10	1.10
377	A115	75f Ali Shayaa Hadi	1.10	1.10
378	A115	75f Saleh Musleh Kasim	1.10	1.10
379	A115	75f Ali Ahmed N. Antar	1.10	1.10
		Nos. 376-379 (4)	4.40	4.40

UN Child Survival Campaign A116

Infant Immunization Program.

1987, Apr. 7   Litho.   Perf. 12

380	A116	20f Immunizing pregnant woman	.25	.25
381	A116	75f Immunizing infant	1.00	1.00
382	A116	140f Oral immunization	1.90	1.90
383	A116	150f Infant, girl, pregnant woman	2.00	2.00
		Nos. 380-383 (4)	5.15	5.15

1st Socialist Party General Conference — A117

1987, July 30   Litho.   Perf. 12

384	A117	75fr multi	1.10	1.10
385	A117	150fr multi	2.10	2.10

October Revolution, Russia, 70th Anniv. — A118

Monuments, Ancient City of Shabwa — A119

1987, Nov. 7   Litho.   Perf. 12½x12

386	A118	250f multi	4.00	4.00

1987, Nov. 18   Perf. 12

387	A119	25f Royal palace and court	.25	.25
388	A119	75f Palace, diff.	1.10	1.10
389	A119	140f Winged lion bas-relief on stone capital	2.00	2.00
390	A119	150f The Moon, legend on bronze tablet	2.10	2.10
		Nos. 387-390 (4)	5.45	5.45

Nos. 387-388 horiz.

Natl. Independence, 20th Anniv. — A120

Designs: 5f, Students walking to school. 75f, Family, apartments. 140f, Workers, oil derrick, thermal plant. 150f, Workers, soldier, Workers' Party headquarters.

1987, Nov. 29   Perf. 12x12½

391	A120	25f multi	.25	.25
392	A120	75f multi	1.00	1.00
393	A120	140f multi	1.90	1.90
394	A120	150f multi	2.00	2.00
		Nos. 391-394 (4)	5.15	5.15

September 26th Revolution, 25th Anniv. A121

1988, Feb. 27   Litho.   Perf. 13

395	A121	75f Revolution monument, San'a	1.10	1.10

WHO, 40th Anniv. A122

1988, Apr. 7   Litho.   Perf. 12

396	A122	40f Sanitary public water supply, vert.	.45	.45
397	A122	75f No smoking	.80	.80
398	A122	140f Child immunization	1.50	1.50
399	A122	250f Health care for all by the year 2000	2.75	2.75
		Nos. 396-399 (4)	5.50	5.50

1988 Summer Olympics, Seoul A125

1988, Sept. 17   Litho.   Perf. 12x12½

406	A125	40f Weight lifting	.25	.25
407	A125	75f Running	1.00	1.00
408	A125	140f Boxing	1.90	1.90
409	A125	150f Soccer	2.00	2.00
		Nos. 406-409 (4)	5.15	5.15

1st Freedom Fighter Killed at the Liberation Front, Radfan Mountains A126

Perf. 12½x12, 12x12½

1988, Oct. 12   Litho.

410	A126	25f Freedom fighters, flag, vert.	.25	.25
411	A126	75f shown	.95	.95
412	A126	300f Anniv. emblem, vert.	4.00	4.00
		Nos. 410-412 (3)	5.20	5.20

October 14th Revolution, 25th anniv.

Indigenous Birds A127

1988, Nov. 5   *Perf. 12x12½, 12½x12*
413	A127	40f Treron waalia	.60	.60
414	A127	50f Coracias caudatus lorti, vert.	.75	.75
415	A127	75f Upupa epops, vert.	1.10	1.10
416	A127	250f Chlamydotis undulata macqueenii	3.75	3.75
		Nos. 413-416 (4)	6.20	6.20

Handicrafts — A128

Designs: 25f, Incense brazier. 75f, Cage-shaped dress form. 150f, Shell and wicker lidded basket. 250f, Wicker basket.

1988, Nov. 29   **Litho.**   *Perf. 12½x12*
417	A128	25f multi	.25	.25
418	A128	75f multi	.90	.90
419	A128	150f multi	1.75	1.75
420	A128	250f multi	3.00	3.00
		Nos. 417-420 (4)	5.90	5.90

Aden Harbor and Yemen Port Authority, Cent. A129

1988, Dec. 5   *Perf. 12x12½*
421	A129	75f Old harbor facility	1.40	1.40
422	A129	300f New facility	4.00	4.00

Preservation of San'a City, a Site on the UNESCO World Heritage List — A130

1988, Dec. 15   *Perf. 12x12½, 12½x12*
423	A130	75f shown	1.00	1.00
424	A130	250f City view, diff., vert.	3.50	3.50

World Wildlife Fund — A131

1989, May 18   **Litho.**   *Perf. 12½x12*
425	A131	20f Sand cat	1.10	.55
426	A131	25f Cat's head	1.10	.55
427	A131	50f Fennec fox	3.00	.65
428	A131	75f Fox's head	4.00	1.10
		Nos. 425-428 (4)	9.20	2.85

For surcharge see Yemen No. 643.

Military Forces — A132

Developments of the corrective movement.

1989, Aug. 15   *Perf. 12x12½*
429	A132	25f shown	.25	.25
430	A132	35f Industry	.45	.45
431	A132	40f Agriculture	.45	.45
		Nos. 429-431 (3)	1.15	1.15

June 22 Corrective Movement, 20th anniv.

Abdul Fattah Ismail — A133

1989, Aug. 28
432	A133	75f multi	.75	.75
433	A133	150f multi	1.25	1.25

50th Birthday of Abdul Fattah Ismail, 1st secretary-general of the natl. Socialist Party.

Ali Anter Yemeni Pioneer Organization, 15th Anniv. — A134

Perf. 12x12½, 12½x12

1989, Sept. 29   **Litho.**
434	A134	10f Drawing by Abeer Anwer	.25	.25
435	A134	25f Girl in pioneer uniform	.25	.25
436	A134	75f Parade, Aden	.70	.70
		Nos. 434-436 (3)	1.20	1.20

Nos. 434-435 vert.
For surcharge see Yemen No. 644.

Nehru and the Taj Mahal — A135

1989, Nov. 14   **Photo.**   *Perf. 14*
437	A135	250f blk & golden brn	2.75	2.75

Jawaharlal Nehru, 1st prime minister of independent India.
For surcharge see Yemen No. 645.

Seventy-Day Siege of San'a, 1967-68 — A136

1989, Oct. 25   **Litho.**   *Perf. 12x12½*
438	A136	150f multicolored	2.00	2.00

Coffee Plant — A137

1989, Dec. 20
439	A137	300f multicolored	4.00	4.00

For surcharge see Yemen No. 637.

Seera Rock, Aden, and the Arc de Triomphe, Paris A138

1989, Dec. 29   **Litho.**   *Perf. 12½x12*
440	A138	250f multicolored	3.25	3.25

French Revolution, bicent.

World Cup Soccer Championships, Italy — A139

Character trademark, soccer plays and flags of participants: 5f, US, Belgium, 1930. 10f, Switzerland, Holland, 1934. 20f, Italy, France, 1938. 35f, Sweden, Spain, 1950. 50f, Federal Republic of Germany, Austria, 1954. Brazil, England, 1958. 500f, Russia, Uruguay, 1962. No. 448, Soccer game.

1990, Apr. 30   **Litho.**   *Perf. 12½x12*
441	A139	5f multicolored	.25	.25
442	A139	10f multicolored	.25	.25
443	A139	20f multicolored	.25	.25
444	A139	35f multicolored	.30	.30
445	A139	50f multicolored	.35	.35
446	A139	60f multicolored	.40	.40
447	A139	500f multicolored	3.50	3.50
		Nos. 441-447 (7)	5.30	5.30

Souvenir Sheet
448	A139	340f multicolored	3.00	3.00

For surcharges see Yemen Nos. 616, 621-621B.

YUGOSLAVIA

yü-gō-'slä-vē-ə

LOCATION — Southern Europe, bordering on the Adriatic Sea
GOVT. — Republic
AREA — 39,500 sq. mi. (est)
POP. — 11,206,847 (1999 est.)
CAPITAL — Belgrade

On December 1, 1918, Bosnia and Herzegovina, Croatia, Dalmatia, Montenegro, Serbia and Slovenia united to form a kingdom which was later called Yugoslavia. A republic was proclaimed November 29, 1945. Other listings may be found under all.

100 Heller = 1 Krone (Bosnia & Herzegovina)
100 Filler = 1 Krone (Croatia-Slavonia)
100 Paras = 1 Dinar (General Issues)

Catalogue values for unused stamps in this country are for Never Hinged items, beginning with Scott 410 in the regular postage section, Scott C50 in the airpost section, Scott F1 in the registered letter section, Scott J67 in the postage due section, Scott RA1 in the postal tax section, and Scott RAJ1 in the postal tax due section.

Counterfeits exist of most of the 1918-19 overprints for Bosnia and Herzegovina, Croatia-Slavonia and Slovenia.

BOSNIA AND HERZEGOVIA

Stamps of Bosnia and Herzegovina, 1910, Overprinted or Surcharged in Black or Red

a

b

c

1918		Unwmk.		Perf. 12½	
1L1	A4(a)	3h olive green	.40	.80
1L2	A4(a)	5h dk grn (R)	.40	.40
1L3	A4(a)	10h carmine	.40	.40
1L4	A4(a)	20h dk brn (R)	.40	.40
1L5	A4(a)	25h deep blue (R)	.40	.40
1L6	A4(b)	30h green	.40	.40
1L7	A4(b)	40h orange	.40	.40
1L8	A4(b)	45h brown red	.40	.40
1L9	A4(b)	50h dull violet	.55	.80
1L10	A4(a)	60h on 50h dl vio	.40	.40
1L11	A4(b)	80h on 6h org brown	.40	.40
1L12	A4(a)	90h on 35h myr green	.40	.40
1L13	A5(c)	2k gray green	.40	.40
1L14	A4(b)	3k on 3h ol grn	2.00	2.75

1L15	A5(c)	4k on 1k mar	4.00	4.75
1L16	A4(b)	10k on 2h vio	6.00	6.75
		Nos. 1L1-1L16 (16)	17.35	20.25

Inverted and double overprints and assorted varieties exist on the stamps for Bosnia and Herzegovina.

Bosnian Girl — A1

1918		Typo.		Perf. 11½	
1L17	A1	2h ultramarine	.40	.40
1L18	A1	6h violet	.80	1.20
1L19	A1	10h rose	.40	.40
1L20	A1	20h green	.40	.40
		Nos. 1L17-1L20 (4)	2.00	2.40

Imperforate stamps of this type (A1) are newspaper stamps of Bosnia.
See Nos. 1L21-1L22, 1L43-1L45.

Bosnia and Herzegovina Nos. P1-P2 (Nos. 1L17-1L18, Imperf.) Srchd.

1918				Imperf.	
1L21	A1	3h on 2h ultra	.40	.40
a.		Double surcharge	14.00	
1L22	A1	5h on 6h violet	.40	.40
a.		Double surcharge	14.00	

Stamps of Bosnia and Herzegovina, 1906-17, Ovptd. or Srchd. in Black or Red

d

e

f

1919				Perf. 12½	
1L25	A23(d)	3h claret	.40	.80
1L26	A23(e)	5h green	.40	.40
1L27	A23(e)	10h on 6h dark gray	.40	.40
1L28	A24(d)	20h on 35h myr green	.40	.40
1L29	A23(e)	25h ultra	.40	.40
1L30	A23(e)	30h orange red	.40	.40
1L31	A24(d)	45h olive brn	.40	.40
1L32	A27(d)	45h on 80h org brown	.40	.40
a.		Perf. 11½	1.40	1.60
1L33	A24(e)	50h slate blue	100.00	100.00
1L34	A24(e)	50h on 72h dk blue (R)	.40	.40
1L35	A24(d)	60h brown violet	.40	.40
1L36	A27(e)	80h orange brown	.40	.40
a.		Perf. 11½	35.00	30.00
1L37	A27(e)	90h dark violet	.40	.40
a.		Perf. 11½	3.50	2.75
1L38	A17(f)	2k gray green	.40	.40
a.		Imperf.	35.00	
b.		Perf. 9½	4.50	5.00
1L39	A26(d)	3k car, green	.40	.55
1L40	A28(e)	4k car, green	1.75	2.50
1L41	A26(d)	5k dk vio, gray	1.75	2.75
1L42	A28(e)	10k dk vio, gray	3.25	4.00
		Nos. 1L25-1L42 (18)	112.35	115.40

Nos. 1L32, 1L36, 1L37, 1L40 and 1L42 have no bars in the overprint.
Nos. 1L25 to 1L42 exist with inverted overprint or surcharge.

Bosnia and Herzegovina Nos. P2-P4 (Nos. 1L18-1L20, Imperf.) Srchd.

1920				Imperf.	
1L43	A1	2h on 6h violet	190.00	175.00
1L44	A1	2h on 10h rose	40.00	40.00
1L45	A1	2h on 20h green	8.00	8.00
		Nos. 1L43-1L45 (3)	238.00	223.00

SEMI-POSTAL STAMPS ISSUES FOR BOSNIA AND HERZEGOVINA

Leading Blind Soldier — SP1

Wounded Soldier — SP2

Semi-Postal Stamps of Bosnia and Herzegovina, 1918 Overprinted

1918		Unwmk.		Perf. 12½, 13	
1LB1	SP1	10h greenish bl	.80	1.00
a.		Overprinted as No. 1LB2	52.50	52.50
1LB2	SP2	15h red brown	2.00	2.00
a.		Overprinted as No. 1LB1	47.50	47.50

Bosnian Semi-Postal Stamps of 1916 Overprinted like No. 1LB2

1LB3	SP1	5h green	125.00	175.00
a.		Overprinted as No. 1LB1	375.00	375.00
1LB4	SP1	10h magenta	100.00	125.00
		Nos. 1LB1-1LB4 (4)	227.80	303.00

Inverted and double overprints exist on Nos. 1LB1-1LB4.

Mail Wagon SP3

Bridge at Mostar SP4

Scene near Sarajevo — SP5

Regular Issue of Bosnia, 1906 Surcharged in Black

1919				
1LB5	SP3	10h + 10h on 40h org red	1.25	2.00
1LB6	SP4	20h + 10h on 20h dk brown	.60	1.75
1LB7	SP5	45h + 15h on 1k mar	4.75	4.75
		Nos. 1LB5-1LB7 (3)	6.60	8.50

Nos. 1LB5-1LB7 exist with surcharge inverted. Value each $7.50.

SPECIAL DELIVERY STAMPS ISSUES FOR BOSNIA AND HERZEGOVINA

Lightning

SD1

SD2

Bosnian Special Delivery Stamps Overprinted in Black

1918		Unwmk.		Perf. 12½, 13	
1LE1	SD1	2h vermilion	6.00	6.00
a.		Inverted overprint	35.00	
b.		Overprinted as No. 1LE2	47.50	47.50
1LE2	SD2	5h deep green	3.25	3.25
a.		Inverted overprint	18.00	
b.		Overprinted as No. 1LE1	47.50	47.50

POSTAGE DUE STAMPS ISSUES FOR BOSNIA AND HERZEGOVINA

Postage Due Stamps of Bosnia and Herzegovina, 1916, Overprinted in Black or Red

a

b

1918		Unwmk.		Perf. 12½, 13	
1LJ1	D2 (a)	2h red	.25	.25
1LJ2	D2 (b)	4h red	.55	.55
1LJ3	D2 (b)	5h red	.25	.25
1LJ4	D2 (b)	6h red	.90	.90
1LJ5	D2 (a)	10h red	.25	.25
1LJ6	D2 (b)	15h red	6.75	6.75
1LJ7	D2 (a)	20h red	.25	.25
1LJ8	D2 (b)	25h red	.55	.55
1LJ9	D2 (a)	30h red	.55	.55
1LJ10	D2 (a)	40h red	.25	.25
1LJ11	D2 (a)	50h red	1.20	1.20

c

d

1LJ12	D2 (c)	1k dark blue (R)	.55	.55
1LJ13	D2 (d)	3k dark blue (R)	.40	.40
		Nos. 1LJ1-1LJ13 (13)	12.70	12.70

Nos. 1LJ1-1LJ13 exist with overprint double or inverted. Value $3 to $7.
Nos. 1LJ1-1LJ11 exist with type "b" overprint instead of type "a," and vice versa. Value, each $10.

Stamps of Bosnia and Herzegovina, 1900-04, Surcharged

e

f

1919				
1LJ14	A2 (e)	2h on 35h blue	.55	.80
1LJ15	A2 (e)	5h on 45h grnsh bl	.95	1.20
1LJ16	A2 (f)	10h on 10 red	.40	.50
1LJ17	A2 (f)	15h on 40h org	.40	.50
1LJ18	A2 (f)	20h on 5h green	.25	.25
1LJ19	A2 (f)	25h on 20h pink	.40	.55
1LJ20	A2 (f)	30h on 30h bis brn	.40	.55
1LJ21	A2 (e)	1k on 50h red lil	.25	.55
1LJ22	A2 (e)	3k on 25h blue	.50	.55

Postage Due Stamps of Bosnia and Herzegovina, 1904 Surcharged

g   h

1LJ23	D1 (g)	40h on 6h blk, red & yel	.25	.25
1LJ24	D1 (h)	50h on 6h blk, red & yel	.25	.25
1LJ25	D1 (h)	200h blk, red & grn	8.00	6.75
1LJ26	D1 (h)	4k on 7h blk, red & yel	.40	.55
		Nos. 1LJ14-1LJ26 (13)	12.85	13.00

Nos. 1LJ14-1LJ26 exist with overprint double or inverted. Value, $3 to $6.

CROATIA-SLAVONIA

Stamps of Hungary Overprinted in Blue

A1

1918		Wmk. 137	Perf. 15

On Stamps of 1913
2L1	A1	6f olive green	1.10	2.00
2L2	A1	50f lake, *blue*	1.20	2.00

A2   A3

On Stamps of 1916
2L3	A2	10f violet	100.00	140.00
2L4	A3	15f red	100.00	140.00

A4

On Hungary Nos. 106-107 White Numerals
2L4A	A4	10f rose	1,600.	1,600.
2L5	A4	15f violet	150.00	150.00
	a.	Inverted overprint	—	

On Stamps of 1916-18 Colored Numerals
2L6	A4	2f brown orange	.40	.40
2L7	A4	3f red lilac	.40	.40
2L8	A4	5f green	.40	.40
2L9	A4	6f greenish blue	.40	.40
2L10	A4	10f rose red	16.00	12.00
2L11	A4	15f violet	.40	.40
2L12	A4	20f gray brown	.40	.40
2L13	A4	25f dull blue	.40	.40
2L14	A4	35f brown	.40	.40
2L15	A4	40f olive green	.40	.80

The overprints and surcharges for Croatia-Slavonia exist inverted, double, double inverted, in wrong colors, on wrong stamps, on back, in pairs with one lacking overprint, etc.

A5

A6

2L16	A5	50f red vio & lilac	.40	.40
2L17	A5	75f brt bl & pale bl	.40	.40
2L18	A5	80f grn & pale grn	.40	.40
2L19	A6	1k red brown & cl	.40	.40
2L20	A6	2k olive brn & bis	.40	.40
2L21	A6	3k dark vio & ind	.40	.40
2L22	A6	5k dk brn & lt brn	2.50	3.00
2L23	A6	10k vio brn & vio	16.00	16.00

Stamps of Hungary Overprinted in Blue, Black or Red

A7   A8

2L24	A7	10f scarlet (Bl)	.40	.40
2L25	A7	20f dark brown (Bk)	.40	.40
2L26	A7	25f deep blue (R)	.40	.80
2L27	A8	40f olive green (Bl)	.40	.40
		Nos. 2L6-2L27 (22)	42.10	39.40

Many other stamps of the 1913-18 issues of Hungary, the Semi-Postal Stamps of 1915-16 and Postage Due Stamps were surreptitiously overprinted but were never sold through the post office.

Freedom of Croatia-Slavonia
A9

1918		Unwmk.	Litho.	Perf. 11½
2L28	A9	10f rose	6.50	4.00
2L29	A9	20f rose	6.50	4.00
2L30	A9	25f blue	12.00	8.00
2L31	A9	45f greenish blk	95.00	55.00
		Nos. 2L28-2L31 (4)	120.00	71.00

Independence of Croatia, Slavonia and Dalmatia.
#2L28-2L31 exist imperforate, but were not officially issued in this condition.
Excellent counterfeits of #2L28-2L31 exist.

Allegory of Freedom
A10

Youth with Standard
A11

Falcon, Symbol of Liberty — A12

1919			Perf. 11½
2L32	A10	2f brn orange	.25	.40
2L33	A10	3f violet	.25	.50
2L34	A10	5f green	.25	.25
2L35	A11	10f red	.25	.25
2L36	A11	20f black brown	.25	.25
2L37	A11	25f deep blue	.25	.25
2L38	A11	45f dark ol grn	.25	.25
2L39	A12	1k carmine rose	.25	.25
2L40	A12	3k dark violet	.80	.95
2L41	A12	5k deep brown	1.20	.80
		Nos. 2L32-2L41 (10)	4.00	4.15

			Perf. 12½
2L32a	A10	2f	2.90	2.90
2L33a	A10	3f	2.90	2.90
2L34a	A10	5f	15.00	15.00
2L35a	A11	10f	2.90	2.90
2L36a	A11	20f	2.90	2.90
		Nos. 2L32a-2L36a (5)	26.60	26.60

#2L32-2L41 exist imperf. Value, set $25.

SEMI-POSTAL STAMPS ISSUES FOR CROATIA-SLAVONIA

SP1   SP2

SP3

1918		Wmk. 137	Perf. 15
2LB1	SP1	10f + 2f rose red	.40	2.75
2LB2	SP2	15f + 2f dull violet	.40	.40
2LB3	SP3	40f + 2f brn carmine	.40	.85
		Nos. 2LB1-2LB3 (3)	1.20	4.00

SPECIAL DELIVERY STAMP ISSUE FOR CROATIA-SLAVONIA

SD1

Hungary No. E1 Overprinted in Black
1918		Wmk. 137	Perf. 15
2LE1	SD1	2f gray green & red	.25	.25

POSTAGE DUE STAMPS ISSUES FOR CROATIA-SLAVONIA

D1

Postage Due Stamps of Hungary Overprinted in Blue
1918		Wmk. Crown (136)	Perf. 15
2LJ1	D1	50f green & blk	650.00	650.00

		Wmk. Double Cross (137)	
2LJ2	D1	1f green & red	40.00	40.00
	a.	Inverted overprint		
2LJ3	D1	2f green & red	1.20	1.20
2LJ4	D1	10f green & red	1.20	1.20
2LJ5	D1	12f green & red	180.00	180.00
2LJ6	D1	15f green & red	.80	.80
2LJ7	D1	20f green & red	.80	.80
2LJ8	D1	30f green & red	2.00	2.00
2LJ9	D1	50f green & red	65.00	65.00
		Nos. 2LJ2-2LJ9 (8)	271.00	271.00

NEWSPAPER STAMPS ISSUES FOR CROATIA-SLAVONIA

N1   N2

Hungary No. P8 Overprinted in Black
1918		Wmk. 137	Imperf.
2LP1	N1	(2f) orange	.40	.40

1919		Litho.	Unwmk.
2LP2	N2	2f yellow orange	.25	1.20

SLOVENIA

Chain Breaker
A1   A2

3, 5, 10, 15f: Chain on right wrist is short, extending only about half way to the frame.
10f: Numerals are 8½mm high.
20, 25, 30, 40f: Distant mountains show faintly between legs of male figure.
40f: Numerals 7mm high. The upright strokes of the "4" extend to the same height; the "0" is 3mm wide.

1919		Unwmk.	Perf. 11½

Lithographed at Ljubljana Fine Impression
3L1	A1	3f violet	.25	.25
3L2	A1	5f green	.25	.25
3L3	A1	10f carmine rose	.40	.25
3L4	A1	15f blue	.25	.25
3L5	A2	20f brown	.65	.25
3L6	A2	25f blue	.30	.25
3L7	A2	30f lilac rose	.30	.25
3L8	A2	40f bister	.30	.25
		Nos. 3L1-3L8 (8)	2.70	2.00

Various stamps of this series exist imperforate and part perforate. Many shades exist.
See Nos. 3L9-3L17, 3L24-3L28. For surcharges see Nos. 3LJ15-3LJ32.

Allegories of Freedom
A3   A4

King Peter I — A5

3, 5, 15f: The chain on the right wrist touches the bottom tablet.
10f: Numerals are 7½mm high.
15f: Curled end of loin cloth appears above letter "H" in the bottom tablet.
20, 25, 30, 40f: The outlines of the mountains have been redrawn and they are more distinct than on the lithographed stamps.
40f: Numerals 8mm high. The left slanting stroke of the "4" extends much higher than the main vertical stroke. The "0" is 2½mm wide and encloses a much narrower space than on the lithographed stamp.

1919-20			Perf. 11½

Typographed at Ljubljana and Vienna Coarse Impression
3L9	A1	3f violet	.25	.25
3L10	A1	5f green	.30	.25
3L11	A1	10f red	.25	.25
3L12	A1	15f blue	1.60	.25
3L13	A2	20f brown	.55	.25
3L14	A2	25f blue	.50	.25
3L15	A2	30f carmine rose	.55	.25
3L16	A2	30f dp red	2.75	.90
3L17	A2	40f orange	.55	.25
3L18	A3	50f green	.55	.25
	a.	50f dark green	.55	.25
	b.	50f olive green	3.50	1.10
3L19	A3	60f dark blue	.85	.25
	a.	60f violet blue	.85	.25
3L20	A4	1k vermilion	.55	.25
	a.	1k red orange	.55	.25
3L21	A4	2k blue	.55	.25
	a.	2k dull ultramarine	.90	.25

3L22 A5 5k brown lake   .80   .25
  a. 5k lake   12.00 1.60
  b. 5k dull red   .60   .25
3L23 A5 10k deep ultra   3.25   .90
    Nos. 3L9-3L23 (15)   13.85 5.05

Nos. 3L9-3L23 exist imperf. Value, set $90.
Many of the series exist part perforate.
Many shades exist of lower values.
See Nos. 3L29-3L32, 3L40-3L41.

Serrate Roulette 13½

3L24 A1 5f light grn   .25   .25
3L25 A1 10f carmine   .25   .25
3L26 A1 15f slate blue   .30   .25
3L27 A2 20f dark brown   .65   .25
  a. Serrate x straight roul.   .65   .25
3L28 A2 30f car rose   .30   .25
  a. Serrate x straight roul.   .70   .25
3L29 A3 50f green   .30   .25
3L30 A3 60f dark blue   .95   .40
  a. 60f violet blue   2.25 1.10
3L31 A4 1k vermilion   1.40   .40
  a. 1k rose red   1.40   .40
3L32 A4 2k blue   9.00 2.75
    Nos. 3L24-3L32 (9)   13.40 5.05

Roulette x Perf. 11½

3L24a A1 5f   150.00 150.00
3L25a A1 10f   55.00   55.00
3L26a A1 15f   175.00 175.00
3L28b A2 30f   55.00   55.00
3L29a A3 50f   5.25   4.00
3L30b A3 60f   55.00   55.00
3L31b A4 1k   55.00   55.00

Thick Wove Paper

1920   **Litho.**   **Perf. 11½**
3L40 A5 15k gray green   7.25 14.50
3L41 A5 20k dull violet   1.40   2.40

On Nos. 3L40-3L41 the horizontal lines
have been removed from the value tablets.
They are printed over a background of pale
brown wavy lines.

Chain
Breaker
A7

Freedom
A8

King Peter
I — A9

Pale red wavy
lines

Dinar Values:
Type I — Size: 21x30½mm.
Type II — Size: 22x32½mm.

Thin to Thick Wove Paper

1920   *Serrate Roulette 13½*
3L42 A7 5p olive green   .25   .25
3L43 A7 10p green   .25   .25
3L44 A7 15p brown   .25   .25
3L45 A7 20p carmine   .40   .40
3L46 A7 25p chocolate   .40   .25
3L47 A8 40p dark violet   .25   .25
3L48 A8 45p yellow   .25   .25
3L49 A8 50p dark blue   .25   .25
3L50 A8 60p red brown   .25   .25
3L51 A9 1d dark brown (I)   .25   .25

    Perf. 11½
3L52 A9 2d gray vio (II)   .25   .25
3L53 A9 4d grnsh black (I)   .30   .30
3L54 A9 6d olive brn (II)   .25   .25
3L55 A9 10d brown red (II)   .30   .80
    Nos. 3L42-3L55 (14)   3.90 4.25

The 2d and 6d have a background of pale
red wavy lines, the 10d of gray lines.
Counterfeits exist of No. 3L45.

POSTAGE DUE STAMPS ISSUES
FOR SLOVENIA

D1

1919   Litho.   Unwmk.   Perf. 11½
Ljubljana Print
Numerals 9½mm high

3LJ1 D1 5f carmine   .25   .25
3LJ2 D1 10f carmine   .25   .25
3LJ3 D1 20f carmine   .25   .25
3LJ4 D1 50f carmine   .25   .25

Nos. 3LJ1-3LJ4 were also printed in scarlet
and dark red.

Numerals 8mm high

3LJ5 D1 1k dark blue   .45   .30
3LJ6 D1 5k dark blue   .65   .50
3LJ7 D1 10k dark blue   .90   .75
    Nos. 3LJ1-3LJ7 (7)   3.00 2.55

1920

Vienna Print
Numerals 11 to 12 mm high

3LJ8 D1 5f red   .25   .25
3LJ9 D1 10f red   .25   .25
3LJ10 D1 20f red   .25   .25
3LJ11 D1 50f red   1.25   .85

Numerals 7mm high

3LJ12 D1 1k Prussian blue   1.10   .70
  a. 1k dark blue   5.00   4.50
3LJ13 D1 5k Prussian blue   1.60 1.25
  a. 5k dark blue   8.00   6.75
3LJ14 D1 10k Prussian blue   3.75 3.25
  a. 10k dark blue   14.00 15.00
    Nos. 3LJ8-3LJ14 (7)   8.45 6.80

Nos. 3LJ8-3LJ14 exist imperf. Value, set
$40.

No. 3L4 Surcharged
in Red

1920   **Perf. 11½**
On Litho. Stamps

3LJ15 A1 5p on 15f blue   .25   .25
3LJ16 A1 10p on 15f blue   .60   .80
3LJ17 A1 20p on 15f blue   .25   .25
3LJ18 A1 50p on 15f blue   .25   .25
    Nos. 3LJ15-3LJ18 (4)   1.35 1.55

Nos. 3L7, 3L12,
3L26, 3L28, 3L28a
Surcharged in Dark
Blue

3LJ19 A2 1d on 30f lil rose   .25   .25
3LJ20 A2 3d on 30f lil rose   .25   .25
3LJ21 A2 8d on 30f lil rose   1.60   .80
    Nos. 3LJ19-3LJ21 (3)   2.10 1.30

On Typographed Stamps

3LJ22 A1 5p on 15f pale bl   12.00   2.50
3LJ23 A1 10p on 15f pale bl 35.00 25.00
3LJ24 A1 20p on 15f pale bl 11.00   4.00
3LJ25 A1 50p on 15f pale bl   6.00   7.00
    Nos. 3LJ22-3LJ25 (4)   64.00 38.50

3LJ26 A1 5p on 15f slate bl   2.75   .50
3LJ27 A1 10p on 15f slate bl 8.50 3.25
3LJ28 A1 20p on 15f slate bl 2.75   .50
3LJ29 A1 30p on 15f slate bl 2.75   .50
3LJ30 A2 1d on 30f dp
     rose   2.75   .65
  a. Serrate x straight roulette 7.00 4.50
3LJ31 A2 3d on 30f dp
     rose   5.75 1.75
  a. Serrate x straight roulette 8.00 5.50
3LJ32 A2 8d on 30f dp
     rose   125.00 6.50
  a. Serrate x straight roulette 75.00 7.50
    Nos. 3LJ26-3LJ32 (7) 150.25 13.65

The para surcharges were printed in sheets
of 100, ten horizontal rows of ten. There were:

5p three rows, 10p one row, 20p three rows,
50p three rows. The dinar surcharges were in
a setting of 50, arranged in vertical rows of
five. There were: 1d five rows, 3d three rows,
8d two rows.

NEWSPAPER STAMPS ISSUES FOR
SLOVENIA

Eros — N1

1919   Unwmk.   Litho.   Imperf.
Ljubljana Print

3LP1 N1 2f gray   .25   .25
3LP2 N1 4f gray   .25   .40
3LP3 N1 6f gray   3.50 4.00
3LP4 N1 10f gray   .25   .25
3LP5 N1 30f gray   .25   .40
    Nos. 3LP1-3LP5 (5)   4.50 5.30

See Nos. 3LP6-3LP13. For surcharges see
Nos. 3LP14-3LP23, 4LB1-4LB5.

N2

1920

Vienna Print

3LP6 N2 2f gray   .25   .25
3LP7 N2 4f gray   6.50 10.00
3LP8 N2 6f gray   1.75   2.75
3LP9 N2 10f gray   14.00 21.00
3LP10 N2 2f blue   .25   .30
3LP11 N2 4f blue   .25   .25
3LP12 N2 6f blue   125.00 125.00
3LP13 N2 10f blue   .25   .25
    Nos. 3LP6-3LP13 (8) 148.25 159.80

Nos. 3LP1, 3LP10 Surcharged

a   b

On Ljubljana Print

3LP14 N1 (a) 2p on 2f gray   .25   .40
3LP15 N1 (a) 4p on 2f gray   .25   .40
3LP16 N1 (a) 6p on 2f gray   .40   .65
3LP17 N1 (b) 10p on 2f gray   .65   .65
3LP18 N1 (b) 30p on 2f gray   .65   .85

On Vienna Print

3LP19 N1 (a) 2p on 2f blue   .25   .25
3LP20 N1 (a) 4p on 2f blue   .25   .25
3LP21 N1 (a) 6p on 2f blue   .25   .25
3LP22 N1 (b) 10p on 2f blue   .25   .25
3LP23 N1 (b) 30p on 2f blue   .25   .25
    Nos. 3LP14-3LP23 (10)   3.45 4.35

The five surcharges were arranged in a setting of 100, in horizontal rows of ten. There
were: 2p three rows, 4p three rows, 6p two
rows, 10p one row and 30p one row. The
sheets were perforated 11½ horizontally
between the groups of the different values.

SEMI-POSTAL STAMPS ISSUE FOR
CARINTHIA PLEBISCITE

SP1

Nos. 3LP2, 3LP1 Surcharged With
Various Designs in Dark Red

1920
4LB1 SP1 5p on 4f gray   .25   .25
4LB2 SP1 15p on 4f gray   .25   .25
4LB3 SP1 25p on 4f gray   .25   .55
4LB4 SP1 45p on 2f gray   .25 1.20
4LB5 SP1 50p on 2f gray   .25 1.40
4LB6 SP1 2d on 2f gray   2.00 6.00
    Nos. 4LB1-4LB6 (6)   3.25 9.65

Nos. 4LB1 to 4LB6 have a different
surcharge on each stamp but each includes
the letters "K.G.C.A." which signify Carinthian
Governmental Commission, Zone A.
Sold at three times face value for the benefit
of the Plebiscite Propaganda Fund.

GENERAL ISSUES

For Use throughout the Kingdom

King
Alexander — A1

King Peter
I — A2

Unwmk.
1921, Jan. 16   Engr.   Perf. 12
1 A1 2p olive brown   .25   .25
2 A1 5p deep green   .25   .25
3 A1 10p carmine   .25   .25
4 A1 15p violet   .25   .25
5 A1 20p black   .25   .25
6 A1 25p dark blue   .25   .25
7 A1 50p olive green   .25   .25
8 A1 60p vermilion   .25   .25
9 A1 75p purple   .25   .25
10 A2 1d orange   .25   .25
11 A2 2d olive bister   .30   .25
12 A2 4d dark green   .60   .25
13 A2 5d carmine rose   2.50   .25
14 A2 10d red brown   12.00   .55
    Nos. 1-14 (14)   17.90 3.80
  Set, never hinged   32.50

  Exist imperf. Value, set $125.
For surcharge see No. 27.

Nos. B1-B3 Surcharged in Black,
Brown, Green or Blue

a

b

1922-24
15 SP1(a) 1d on 10p   .25   .25
16 SP2(b) 1d on 15p ('24)   .25   .25
17 SP3(a) 1d on 25p (Br)   .25   .25
18 SP2(b) 3d on 15p (G)   .80   .25
  a. Blue surcharge   1.20   1.20
19 SP2(b) 8d on 15p (G)   1.60   .25
  a. Double surcharge   35.00 30.00
  b. 9d on 15p (error)   130.00
20 SP2(b) 20d on 15p   10.00 1.00
21 SP2(b) 30d on 15p (Bl)   27.50 2.50
    Nos. 15-21 (7)   40.65 4.75
  Set, never hinged   60.00

A3

1923, Jan. 23   **Engr.**

22	A3	1d red brown	1.75	.25
23	A3	5d carmine	3.50	.25
24	A3	8d violet	7.00	.25
25	A3	20d green	24.00	.75
26	A3	30d red orange	70.00	2.75
		Nos. 22-26 (5)	106.25	4.25
		Set, never hinged	240.00	

For surcharge see No. 28.

Nos. 8 and 24
Surcharged in Black
or Blue

1924, Feb. 18

27	A1	20p on 60p ver	.25	.25
28	A3	5d on 8d violet (Bl)	8.00	.60
		Set, never hinged	17.50	

The color of the surcharge on No. 28 varies, including blue, blue black, greenish black and black.

A4   A5

1924, July 1   **Perf. 14**

29	A4	20p black	.25	.25
30	A4	50p dark brown	.25	.25
31	A4	1d carmine	.25	.25
32	A4	2d myrtle green	.25	.25
33	A4	3d ultramarine	.25	.25
34	A4	5d orange brown	1.40	.25
35	A5	10d dark violet	12.50	.25
36	A5	15d olive green	7.50	.25
37	A5	20d vermilion	7.50	.25
38	A5	30d dark green	7.50	1.25
		Nos. 29-38 (10)	37.65	3.50
		Set, never hinged	80.00	

No. 33 Surcharged

п 50 Р

1925, June 5

39	A4	25p on 3d ultramarine	.35	.25
40	A4	50p on 3d ultramarine	.35	.25
		Set, never hinged	1.60	

King Alexander
A6   A7

1926-27   **Typo.**   **Perf. 13**

41	A6	25p deep green	.25	.25
42	A6	50p olive brown	.25	.25
43	A6	1d scarlet	.25	.25
44	A6	2d slate black	.25	.25
45	A6	3d slate blue	.30	.25
46	A6	4d red orange	.50	.25
47	A6	5d violet	.80	.25
48	A6	8d black brown	5.25	.25
49	A6	10d olive brown	4.00	.25
50	A6	15d brown ('27)	15.00	.25

51	A6	20d dark vio ('27)	17.50	.25
52	A6	30d orange ('27)	65.00	.45
		Nos. 41-52 (12)	109.35	3.20
		Set, never hinged	240.00	

For overprints and surcharges see Nos. 53-62, 87-101, B5-B16.

Nos. B7-B16
Overprinted over the
Red Surcharge

1928, July

53	A6	1d scarlet	.25	.25
a.		Surcharge "0.50" inverted		
54	A6	2d black	.50	.25
55	A6	3d deep blue	.80	.50
56	A6	4d red orange	2.00	.60
57	A6	5d bright vio	1.60	.25
58	A6	8d black brown	6.50	.95
59	A6	10d olive brown	12.50	.25
60	A6	15d brown	95.00	3.00
61	A6	20d violet	47.50	3.00
62	A6	30d orange	125.00	9.50
		Nos. 53-62 (10)	291.65	18.55
		Set, never hinged	725.00	

With Imprint at Foot

1931-34   **Perf. 12½**

63	A7	25p black	.25	.25
64	A7	50p green	.25	.25
65	A7	75p slate green	.40	.25
66	A7	1d red	.25	.25
67	A7	1.50d pink	.80	.25
68	A7	1.75d dp rose ('34)	1.60	.35
69	A7	3d slate blue	6.00	.35
70	A7	3.50d ultra ('34)	2.40	.35
71	A7	4d deep orange	3.00	.25
72	A7	5d purple	4.50	.25
73	A7	10d dark olive	12.00	.25
74	A7	15d deep brown	12.00	.25
75	A7	20d dark violet	24.00	.25
76	A7	30d rose	12.00	.25
		Nos. 63-76 (14)	77.95	3.90
		Set, never hinged	175.00	

**Type of 1931 Issue
Without Imprint at Foot**

1932-33

77	A7	25p black	.25	.25
78	A7	50p green	.25	.25
79	A7	1d red	.25	.25
80	A7	3d slate bl ('33)	1.00	.25
81	A7	4d deep org ('33)	3.50	.25
82	A7	5d purple ('33)	5.25	.25
83	A7	10d dk olive ('33)	17.00	.25
84	A7	15d deep brn ('33)	27.50	.25
85	A7	20d dark vio ('33)	35.00	.25
86	A7	30d rose ('33)	45.00	.35
		Nos. 77-86 (10)	135.00	2.60
		Set, never hinged	225.00	

See Nos. 102-115.

Nos. 41 to 52
Overprinted

1933, Sept. 5   **Perf. 13**

87	A6	25p deep green	.25	.25
88	A6	50p olive brown	.25	.25
89	A6	1d scarlet	.75	.25
90	A6	2d slate black	3.25	.70
91	A6	3d slate blue	3.00	.25
92	A6	4d red orange	2.00	.25
93	A6	5d violet	4.00	.25
94	A6	8d black brown	9.25	1.40
95	A6	10d olive brown	16.00	.25
96	A6	15d brown	24.00	1.75
97	A6	20d dark violet	32.50	.80
98	A6	30d orange	32.50	.80
		Nos. 87-98 (12)	127.75	7.20
		Set, never hinged	240.00	

**Semi-Postal Stamps of 1926
Overprinted like Nos. 87 to 98 and
Four Bars over the Red Surcharge of
1926**

1933, Sept. 5

99	A6	25p green	.80	.25
100	A6	50p olive brown	.80	.25
101	A6	1d scarlet	2.40	.50
		Nos. 99-101 (3)	4.00	1.00
		Set, never hinged	8.00	

Nos. 99-101 exist with double impression of bars. Value, each $5.50 unused, $4.50 used.

King Alexander Memorial Issue
Type of 1931-34 Issues
Borders in Black

1934, Oct. 17

102	A7	25p black	.25	.25
103	A7	50p green	.25	.25
104	A7	75p slate green	.25	.25
105	A7	1d red	.25	.25
106	A7	1.50d pink	.25	.25
107	A7	1.75d deep rose	.25	.25
108	A7	3d slate blue	.25	.25
109	A7	3.50d ultramarine	.25	.25
110	A7	4d deep orange	.40	.25
111	A7	5d purple	.60	.25
112	A7	10d dark olive	2.00	.25
113	A7	15d deep brown	4.00	.25
114	A7	20d dark violet	12.00	.25
115	A7	30d rose	10.00	.40
		Nos. 102-115 (14)	31.00	3.65
		Set, never hinged	50.00	

Cyrillic Characters
Latin and Cyrillic inscriptions are transposed within some sets. In some sets some stamps are inscribed in Latin, others in Cyrillic. This will be mentioned only if it is necessary to identify otherwise identical stamps.

King Peter II — A10

1935-36   **Perf. 13x12½**

116	A10	25p brown black	.25	.25
117	A10	50p yel orange	.25	.25
118	A10	75p turq green	.25	.25
119	A10	1d brown red	.25	.25
120	A10	1.50d scarlet	.25	.25
121	A10	1.75d cerise	.25	.25
122	A10	2d magenta ('36)	.25	.25
123	A10	3d brn orange	.25	.25
124	A10	3.50d ultramarine	.40	.25
125	A10	4d yellow grn	1.20	.25
126	A10	4d slate blue ('36)	1.20	.25
127	A10	10d bright vio	1.20	.25
128	A10	15d brown	1.20	.25
129	A10	20d bright blue	4.75	.25
130	A10	30d rose pink	2.40	.25
		Nos. 116-130 (15)	13.40	3.75
		Set, never hinged	25.00	

For overprints see Nos. N12, N14, N29.

King   Nikola
Alexander — A11   Tesla — A12

1935, Oct. 9   **Perf. 12½x11½, 11½**

131	A11	75p turq green	.25	.40
132	A11	1.50d scarlet	.25	.40
133	A11	1.75d dark brown	.30	.80
134	A11	3.50d ultramarine	1.60	2.40
135	A11	7.50d rose carmine	1.00	2.00
		Nos. 131-135 (5)	3.40	6.00

Death of King Alexander, 1st anniv.

1936, May 28 Litho. Perf. 12½x11½

136	A12	75p yel grn & dk brn	.40	.25
137	A12	1.75d dull blue & indigo	.40	.25
		Set, never hinged	5.00	

80th birthday of Nikola Tesla (1856-1943), electrical inventor.

Memorial   Coats of Arms of
Church,   Yugoslavia, Greece,
Oplenac — A13   Romania and
                   Turkey — A14

1937, July 1

138	A13	3d Prussian grn	1.00	.50
a.		Perf. 12½	15.00	24.00
		Never hinged	30.00	
139	A13	4d dark blue	1.00	1.20
		Set, never hinged	4.00	

"Little Entente," 16th anniversary.

Perf. 11, 11½, 12½

1937, Oct. 29   **Photo.**

140	A14	3d peacock grn	1.00	.35
141	A14	4d ultramarine	1.00	.85
		Set, never hinged	5.50	

Balkan Entente.

King Peter II — A16

1939-40   **Typo.**   **Perf. 12½**

142	A16	25p black ('40)	.25	.25
143	A16	50p orange ('40)	.25	.25
144	A16	1d yellow grn	.25	.25
145	A16	1.50d red	.25	.25
146	A16	2d dp mag ('40)	.25	.25
147	A16	3d dull red brn	.25	.25
148	A16	4d ultra	.25	.25
148A	A16	5d dk blue ('40)	.25	.25
148B	A16	5.50d dk vio brn ('40)	.50	.25
149	A16	6d slate blue	1.00	.25
150	A16	8d sepia	1.20	.25
151	A16	12d bright vio	1.75	.25
152	A16	16d dull violet	2.40	.25
153	A16	20d blue ('40)	2.40	.25
154	A16	30d brt pink ('40)	5.50	.55
		Nos. 142-154 (15)	16.75	4.05
		Set, never hinged	35.00	

For overprints and surcharges see Nos. N1-N11, N13, N15-N28, N30-N35, Croatia 1-25.

Arms of Yugoslavia, Greece, Romania
and Turkey
A17   A18

1940, June 1

155	A17	3d ultramarine	.80	.50
156	A18	3d ultramarine	.80	.50
a.		Pair, #155-156	6.00	12.00
157	A17	4d dark blue	.80	.50
158	A18	4d dark blue	.80	.50
a.		Pair, #157-158	6.00	12.00
		Nos. 155-158 (4)	3.20	2.00
		Set, never hinged	7.50	
		Pairs, never hinged	30.00	

Balkan Entente.

Bridge at
Obod
A19

1940, Sept. 29   **Litho.**

159	A19	5.50d slate grn & dull grn	2.00	3.25
		Never hinged	3.75	

Zagreb Phil. Exhib.; 500th anniv. of Johann Gutenberg's invention of printing. The first press in the Yugoslav area was located at Obod in 1493.

Issues for Federal Republic
Serbia Nos. 2N37, 2N39 Surcharged
in Green or Vermilion

**1944, Dec.   Unwmk.   Perf. 11½
Overprinted with Pale Green
Network**

159A	OS4	5d (3d + 2d) rose pink	.25	.25
159B	OS4	10d (7d + 3d) dk sl grn (V)	.25	.25

Similar Srch. on Serbia Nos. 2N37-2N39

1945, Jan. 24   **Without Network**
159C OS4 5d (3d + 2d) rose pink   .25 .25
159D OS4 10d (7d + 3d) dk sl grn (V)   .25 .25
159E OS4 25d (4d + 21d) ultra (Bk)   .25 .25
    Nos. 159C-159E (3)   .75 .75

Marshal Tito (Josip Broz) — A20

1945	**Photo.**	**Perf. 12½**	
160 A20	25p bright bl grn	.25	.25
161 A20	50p deep green	.25	.25
162 A20	1d crimson rose	1.20	.25
163 A20	2d dark car rose	.25	.25
164 A20	4d deep blue	.25	.25
165 A20	5d deep green	.25	.40
166 A20	6d dark purple	.25	.25
167 A20	9d orange brown	.35	.25
168 A20	10d deep rose	.25	.40
169 A20	20d orange	1.75	1.60
170 A20	25d dark purple	.25	.25
171 A20	30d deep blue	.25	.25
	Nos. 160-171 (12)	5.55	4.65
	Set, never hinged	9.00	

Prohor Pcinski Monastery — A21

1945, Aug. 2   **Typo.**   **Perf. 11½**
172 A21 2d red   2.00 2.00
    Never hinged   4.00

Formation of the Popular Antifascist Chamber of Deputies of Macedonia, Aug. 2, 1944.

Partisans
A22   A23

Marshal Tito — A24   City of Jajce — A25

Partisan Girl and Flag — A26

1945, Oct. 10	**Litho.**	**Perf. 12½**	
173 A22	50p olive gray	.25	.25
174 A22	1d blue green	.25	.25
175 A23	1.50d orange brown	.25	.25
176 A24	2d scarlet	.25	.25
177 A25	3d red brown	1.75	.25
178 A24	4d dark blue	.30	.25
179 A25	5d dark yel grn	1.00	.25
180 A26	6d black	.25	.25
181 A26	9d deep plum	.40	.25
182 A23	12d ultramarine	.90	.25
183 A22	16d blue	.70	.25
184 A23	20d orange ver	1.60	.25
	Nos. 173-184 (12)	8.10	3.00
	Set, never hinged	17.50	

See Nos. 211-214. For surcharges and overprints see Nos. 202-203, 273-292, 286-289, Istria 42, 44, 46, 48, 50, Trieste 5-14.

"Labor" and "Agriculture"
A27   A28

1945, Nov. 29	**Photo.**	**Perf. 12**	
185 A27	2d brn carmine	1.60	3.25
186 A27	2d brn carmine	1.60	3.25
187 A27	4d deep blue	1.60	3.25
188 A28	4d deep blue	1.60	3.25
189 A27	6d dk slate grn	1.60	3.25
190 A28	6d dk slate grn	1.60	3.25
191 A27	9d red orange	1.60	3.25
192 A28	9d red orange	1.60	3.25
193 A27	16d bright ultra	1.60	3.25
194 A28	16d bright ultra	1.60	3.25
195 A27	20d dark brown	1.60	3.25
a.	Souv. sheet of 2, #191, 195, perf. 11½	12.00	24.00
196 A28	20d dark brown	1.60	3.25
a.	Souv. sheet of 2, #192, 196, perf. 11½	12.00	24.00
	Nos. 185-196 (12)	19.20	39.00
	Set, never hinged	40.00	
	Se-tenant pairs, #185-196 (6)	22.50	22.50
	Se-tenant pairs, never hinged	45.00	

Constitution for the Democratic Federation of Yugoslavia, Nov. 29, 1945.

Parade of Armed Forces — A31

1946, May 9	**Unwmk.**	**Perf. 12½**	
199 A31	1.50d org yel & red	.40	.55
200 A31	2.50d cerise & red	.80	.25
201 A31	5d blue & red	2.75	1.60
	Nos. 199-201 (3)	3.95	2.95

Victory over fascism, 1st anniv.

Type of 1945 Surcharged with New Values in Black

1946, Apr. 1
202 A26 2.50d on 6d bright red   .40 .25
203 A26 8d on 9d orange   .50 .25
    Set, never hinged   1.75

Svetozar Markovic — A32

1946, Sept. 22
204 A32 1.50d blue green   .75 .35
205 A32 2.50d dp red lilac   .85 .50
    Set, never hinged   2.50

Markovic, Serbian socialist, birth cent.

People's Theater, Sofia A33

Sigismund Monument, Warsaw — A35

Designs: 1d, Prague. 2½d, Victory Monument, Belgrade. 5d, Spassky Tower, Kremlin.

1946, Dec. 8	**Litho.**	**Perf. 11½**	
206 A33	½d dk brn & yel brn	2.00	4.00
207 A33	1d grnsh blk & emer	2.00	4.00
208 A35	1½d dk car rose & rose	2.00	4.00
209 A35	2½d hn brn & brn org	2.00	4.00
210 A35	5d dark bl & blue	2.00	4.00
	Nos. 206-210 (5)	10.00	20.00
	Set, never hinged	20.00	

Pan-Slavic Congress, Belgrade, Dec. 1946.

Types of 1945

1947, Jan. 15	**Litho.**	**Perf. 12½**	
211 A26	2.50d red orange	.35	.25
212 A25	3d dull red	.50	.25
213 A25	5d dark blue	1.40	.25
214 A26	8d orange	.90	.25
	Nos. 211-214 (4)	3.15	1.00
	Set, never hinged	6.00	

Gorski Vijenac — A38   Peter P. Nyegosh — A39

1947, June 8		**Typo.**	
215 A38	1.50d Prus grn & blk	.40	.80
216 A39	2.50d ol bis & dk car	.40	.80
217 A38	5d blue & black	.40	.80
	Nos. 215-217 (3)	1.20	2.40
	Set, never hinged	2.40	

Centenary of the Montenegrin national epic "Gorski Vijenac" (Wreath of Mountains) by Nyegosh.

Girls' Physical Training Classes — A40

Girl Runner — A41

Physical Culture Parade A42

1947, June 15	**Litho.**	**Perf. 11**	
218 A40	1.50d brown	1.00	1.00
219 A41	2.50d red	1.00	1.00
220 A42	4d violet blue	1.00	1.00
	Nos. 218-220 (3)	3.00	3.00
	Set, never hinged	6.00	

Natl. sports meet, Belgrade, 6/15-22/47.

Map and Star — A43

1947, Sept. 16   **Typo.**
231 A43 2.50d dp car & dark bl   .40 .80
232 A43 5d org brn & dk grn   .40 .80
    Set, never hinged   1.60

Annexation of Julian Province.

Music and One-string Gusle A44

Vuk Karadzic — A45

1947, Sept. 27   **Perf. 11½x12, 12½**
233 A44 1.50d green   .40 .80
234 A45 2.50d orange red   .40 .80
235 A44 5d violet blue   .40 .80
    Nos. 233-235 (3)   1.20 2.40
    Set, never hinged   2.40

Centenary of Serbian literature.

Symbols of Industry and Agriculture, Map and Flag — A46

1948, Apr. 8	**Litho.**	**Perf. 12½**	
236 A46	1.50d grn, bl & salmon	1.40	2.00
237 A46	2.50d red brn, bl & salmon	1.40	2.00
238 A46	5d dk bl, bl & salmon	1.40	2.00
	Nos. 236-238 (3)	4.20	6.00
	Set, never hinged	8.00	

International Fair, Zagreb, May 8-17.

Danube River Scene — A47

1948, July 30		**Unwmk.**	
239 A47	2d green	2.25	4.00
240 A47	3d carmine	2.25	4.00
241 A47	5d blue	2.25	4.00
242 A47	10d brown orange	2.25	4.00
	Nos. 239-242 (4)	9.00	16.00
	Set, never hinged	16.00	

Danube Conference, Belgrade.

Marchers with
Party
Flag — A48

Laurent
Kosir — A49

1948, July 21   *Perf. 11½, 12½*
243 A48 2d dark green .40 .40
244 A48 3d dark red .60 1.20
245 A48 10d dark blue vio .60 .80
   Nos. 243-245 (3) 1.60 2.40
Set, never hinged 3.25

5th Congress of the Communist Party in Yugoslavia, July 21, 1948.

1948, Aug. 21   *Perf. 12½*
246 A49 3d claret .40 .40
247 A49 5d blue .40 .40
248 A49 10d red orange .40 .40
249 A49 12d dull green .40 .40
   Nos. 246-249 (4) 1.60 1.60
Set, never hinged 3.25

80th death anniv. of Laurent Kosir, recognized by Yugoslavia as inventor of the postage stamp.

Arms of Bosnia
and
Herzegovina
A50

Arms of
Yugoslavia
A51

1948, Nov. 29   *Perf. 12½, 12x11½*
Arms of Yugoslav Peoples Republics
250 A50 3d green .40 .80
251 A50 3d rose lil (Macedonia) .40 .80
252 A50 3d gray bl (Serbia) .40 .80
253 A50 3d gray (Montenegro) .40 .80
254 A50 3d rose (Croatia) .40 .80
255 A50 3d orange (Slovenia) .40 .80
256 A51 10d deep carmine .60 1.40
   Nos. 250-256 (7) 3.00 6.20
Set, never hinged 6.00

The Cyrillic and Latin inscriptions are transposed on Nos. 252, 253 and 255.

Franc
Presern — A52

1949, Feb. 8   **Photo.**   *Perf. 11½*
257 A52 3d dark blue .30 .25
258 A52 5d brown orange .30 .25
259 A52 10d olive black 1.00 .80
   Nos. 257-259 (3) 1.60 1.30
Set, never hinged 2.75

Death cent. of Franc Presern, poet.

Ski Jump,
Planica — A53

Ski
Jumper — A54

     Perf. 12½x11½
1949, Mar. 20   **Litho.**
260 A53 10d magenta .40 1.00
261 A54 12d slate gray .80 1.10
   Set, never hinged 2.40

Intl. Ski Championships, Planica, Mar. 13-20.

Soldiers — A55

Farmers — A56

Arms and Flags
of Macedonia
and
Yugoslavia — A57

1949, Aug. 2   *Perf. 12½*
262 A55 3d carmine rose .30 .65
263 A56 5d dull blue .40 .80
264 A57 12d red brown 2.00 2.75
   Nos. 262-264 (3) 2.70 4.20
Set, never hinged 4.00

Liberation of Macedonia, 5th anniv.
It is reported that No. 264 was not sold to the public at post offices.
For overprints see Nos. C30-C32.

Postal
Communications
A58

UPU, 75th anniversary: 5d, Plane, locomotive and stagecoach, horiz.

1949, Sept. 8   **Unwmk.**
265 A58 3d red 1.60 3.25
266 A58 5d blue .40 .80
267 A58 12d brown .40 .80
   Nos. 265-267 (3) 2.40 4.85
Set, never hinged 4.75

For overprints see Trieste Nos. 15-16.

Locomotives
A60

1949, Dec. 15   **Photo.**
269 A60 2d Early steam 1.00 2.00
270 A60 3d Modern steam 1.00 2.00
271 A60 5d Diesel 1.00 2.00
272 A60 10d Electric 22.50 24.00
   Nos. 269-272 (4) 25.50 30.00
Set, never hinged 50.00

Centenary of Yugoslav railroads.
For overprints see Trieste Nos. 17-20.

Official Stamps
Nos. O7 and O8
Surcharged:

1949   **Typo.**
272A O1 3d on 8d chocolate .50 .40
272B O1 3d on 12d violet .50 .40
   Set, never hinged 2.00

Stamps of 1945 and 1947 Overprinted
or Surcharged in Black

a   b

c   d

1949   **Litho.**
273 A22 (a) 50p olive gray .25 .25
274 A22 (a) 1d blue green .25 .25
275 A24 (b) 2d scarlet .25 .25
276 A26 (c) 3d on 8d orange .25 .25
277 A25 (d) 3d dull red .25 .25
278 A25 (d) 5d dark blue .25 .25
279 A23 (a) 10d on 20d org ver .45 .25
280 A23 (a) 12d ultramarine .40 .25
281 A22 (a) 16d blue .60 .25
282 A23 (a) 20d orange ver .60 .25
   Nos. 273-282 (10) 3.55 2.50
Set, never hinged 6.00

On No. 279 the surcharge includes a rule below "JUGOSLAVIJA" and "D 10" with two bars over "20D."
See Nos. 286-289.

Surveying for
Highway
A61

Bridge, Map
and
Automobile
A62

Highway
Completion
Symbolized
A63

1950, Jan. 16   **Photo.**   *Perf. 12½*
283 A61 2d blue green .55 .80
284 A62 3d rose brown .55 .80
285 A63 5d violet blue .80 1.20
   Nos. 283-285 (3) 1.90 2.80
Set, never hinged 3.75

Completion of Belgrade-Zagreb highway, Dec. 1949.

Types of 1945 Overprinted in Black
1950   **Unwmk.**   *Perf. 12½*
286 A22 (a) 1d brownish org .40 .25
287 A24 (b) 2d blue green .40 .25
288 A25 (d) 3d rose pink .60 .25
289 A25 (d) 5d blue .60 .25
   Nos. 286-289 (4) 2.00 1.00
Set, never hinged 4.00

Marshal
Tito — A64

Child
Eating — A65

1950, Apr. 30   **Engr.**
290 A64 3d red 1.00 .80
291 A64 5d dull blue 1.00 .80
292 A64 10d brown 10.00 20.00
293 A64 12d olive black 1.25 2.40
   Nos. 290-293 (4) 13.25 24.00
Set, never hinged 24.00

Labor Day, May 1.

1950, June 1   **Photo.**
294 A65 3d brown red .80 .45
   Never hinged 1.60

Issued to publicize Children's Day, June 1.

Boy and Model
Plane — A66

Map and Chess
Symbols — A67

Designs: 3d, Glider aloft. 5d, Parachutists. 10d, Aviatrix. 20d, Glider on field.

1950, July 2   **Engr.**
295 A66 2d dark green 1.60 3.25
296 A66 3d brown red 1.60 3.25
297 A66 5d violet 1.60 3.25
298 A66 10d chocolate 1.60 3.25
299 A66 20d ultramarine 12.00 24.00
   Nos. 295-299 (5) 18.40 37.00
Set, never hinged 37.50

Third Aviation Meet, July 2-11.

1950, Aug. 20   **Photo.**   *Perf. 11½*
3d, Rook and ribbon. 5d, Globe and chess board. 10d, Allegory of international chess. 20d, View of Dubrovnik, knight and ribbon.
300 A67 2d red brn & rose
     brown .45 .80
301 A67 3d blk brn, gray brn
     & dl yellow .45 .80
302 A67 5d dk grn, bl & buff 1.10 .80
303 A67 10d cl, bl & org yel 1.10 2.00
304 A67 20d dk bl, bl & org
     yellow 22.00 22.50
   Nos. 300-304 (5) 25.10 26.90
Set, never hinged 50.00

Intl. Chess Matches, Dubrovnik, Aug. 1950.

Electrification
A68

Coal and Logs for
Export
A69

Designs: 50p, Metallurgy. 2d, Agriculture. 3d, Construction. 5d, Fishing. 7d, Mining. 10d, Fruitgrowing. 12d, Lumbering. 16d, Gathering sunflowers. 20d, Livestock raising. 30d, Book manufacture. 50d, Loading ship.

1950-51   **Unwmk.**   **Engr.**   *Perf. 12½*
305 A68 50p dk brn ('51) .25 .25
306 A68 1d blue green .25 .25
307 A68 2d orange .25 .25
308 A68 3d rose red .25 .25
309 A68 5d ultramarine .60 .25
310 A68 7d gray .60 .25
311 A68 10d chocolate .60 .25
312 A68 12d vio brn ('51) 2.00 .25
313 A68 16d vio bl ('51) 1.75 .30
314 A68 20d ol grn ('51) 1.75 .25

314A A68 30d red brn ('51)   4.00   .55
315   A68 50d violet ('51)   21.00 24.00
      Nos. 305-315 (12)   33.30 27.10
      Set, never hinged   55.00

See Nos. 343-354, 378-384A. For overprints see Trieste Nos. 68-75, 90-92.

1950, Sept. 23   **Photo.**
316 A69 3d red brown   .80   .25
    Never hinged   1.60

Zagreb International Fair, 1950.

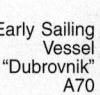

Early Sailing Vessel "Dubrovnik" A70

Designs: 3d, Partisans in boat. 5d, Loading freighter. 10d, Transatlantic ship "Zagreb." 12d, Sailboats. 20d, Naval gun and ship.

1950, Nov. 29
317 A70 2d brown violet   .25   .25
318 A70 3d orange brown   .25   .25
319 A70 5d dull green   .25   .25
320 A70 10d chalky blue   .30   .25
321 A70 12d dark blue   .80   .30
322 A70 20d red brown   10.00   2.90
    Nos. 317-322 (6)   11.85   4.20
    Set, never hinged   20.00

Yugoslav navy.

Partisans with Flag — A71

1951, Mar. 27   **Engr.**
323 A71 3d red & red brn   3.50 3.50
    Never hinged   7.50

Yugoslavia's resistance to Nazi Germany, 10th anniv.

Stane Rozman A72

5d, Post-boy during Slovene insurrection.

1951, Apr. 27   **Photo.**
324 A72 3d brown red   .25   .25
325 A72 5d dark blue   .60   .40
    Set, never hinged   1.60

Slovene insurrection, 10th anniv.

Children Painting A73

1951, June 3
326 A73 3d red   .80   .25
    Never hinged   1.60

Issued to publicize Children's Day, June 3.

Zika Jovanovich — A74

Serbian Revolutionists A75

1951, July 7
327 A74 3d brown red   .30   .45
328 A75 5d deep blue   .55   .90
    Set, never hinged   1.60

Serbian insurrection, 10th anniv.

Sava Kovacevich A76

Kovacevich Leading Revolutionists A77

1951, July 13
329 A76 3d rose pink   .40   .50
330 A77 5d light blue   1.00 1.10
    Set, never hinged   2.60

Montenegrin insurrection, 10th anniv.

Monument to Marko Oreskovich A78

1951, July 27
331 A78 3d shown   .45   .50
332 A78 5d Monument to wounded   .70   .90
    Set, never hinged   2.00

Croatian insurrection, 10th anniv.

Sium Bolaj — A79

Revolutionists A80

1951, July 27
333 A79 3d rose brown   .40   .50
334 A80 5d blue   .75   .90
    Set, never hinged   2.00

Revolution in Bosnia and Herzegovina, 10th anniv.

Primoz Trubar — A81

12d, Marko Marulic. 20d, Tsar Stefan Duschan.

1951, Sept. 9   **Engr.**
335 A81 10d slate gray   3.25   6.50
336 A81 12d brown orange   3.25   6.50
337 A81 20d violet   10.00 20.00
    Nos. 335-337 (3)   16.50 33.00
    Set, never hinged   32.50

Yugoslav cultural anniversaries.
For overprints see Trieste Nos. 40-41.

National Handicrafts — A82

1951, Sept. 15 **Litho.** **Perf. 11½**
338 A82 3d multicolored   1.75 1.20
    Set, never hinged   2.50

Zagreb International Fair, 1951.

Mirce Acev — A83

Monument at Skopje A84

1951, Oct. 11
339 A83 3d deep plum   .40   .40
340 A84 5d indigo   .80 1.20
    Set, never hinged   2.50

Macedonian insurrection, 10th anniv.

Soldier and Emblem — A85

1951, Dec. 22 **Photo.** **Perf. 12½**
341 A85 15d deep carmine   .25   .25
    Never hinged   .50

Army Day. See No. C54.

Peter P. Nyegosh — A86

1951, Nov. 29   **Engr.**
342 A86 15d deep claret   2.00   .80
    Never hinged   3.25

Death centenary of Nyegosh. See note after No. 217.

Types of 1950-51

Designs: 15d, Gathering sunflowers. 25d, Agriculture. 35d, Construction. 75d, Lumbering. 100d, Metallurgy.

1951-52   **Engr.**
343 A68 1d gray ('52)   .25   .25
344 A68 2d rose car ('52)   .25   .25
345 A68 5d orange ('52)   .80   .25
346 A68 10d emerald ('52)   4.00   .25
347 A68 15d rose car ('52)   20.00   .25
348 A68 20d purple   2.00   .25
349 A68 25d yel brn ('52)   8.75   .25
350 A68 30d blue   1.00   .25
351 A68 35d red brn ('52)   1.50   .25
352 A68 50d greenish bl   .80   .25
353 A68 75d purple ('52)   2.00   .25
354 A68 100d sepia ('52)   4.00   .25
     Nos. 343-354 (12)   45.35 3.00
     Set, never hinged   90.00

No. 349 exists with and without printer's inscriptions at bottom, with stamps differing slightly.

Marshal Tito
A87   A88

1952, May 25 **Photo.** **Perf. 11½**
355 A87 15d shown   .40   .80
356 A88 28d shown   .40   .80
357 A87 50d Tito facing left   19.00 30.00
    Nos. 355-357 (3)   19.80 31.60
    Set, never hinged   40.00

60th birthday of Marshal Tito.

Child with Ball — A89

1952, June 1 **Litho.** **Perf. 12½**
358 A89 15d bright rose   3.00 3.00
    Never hinged   6.00

Issued to publicize Children's Day, June 1.
For overprint see Trieste No. 60.

Girl Gymnast — A90

1952, July 10   **Perf. 12½**
359 A90 5d shown   .40   .25
360 A90 10d Runner   .60   .25
361 A90 15d Swimmer   .60   .25
362 A90 28d Boxer   1.40   .80
363 A90 50d Basketball   2.00   4.50
364 A90 100d Soccer   24.00 27.50
     Nos. 359-364 (6)   29.00 33.55
     Set, never hinged   55.00

15th Olympic Games, Helsinki, 1952.
Nos. 359-364 exist imperf. Value $800.
For overprints see Trieste Nos. 51-56.

Split,
Dalmatia — A91

1952, Sept. 10 **Litho.**
365 A91 15d shown .40 .80
366 A91 28d Naval scene .80 1.75
367 A91 50d St. Stefan 9.00 14.00
Nos. 365-367 (3) 10.20 16.55
Set, never hinged 20.00

Yugoslav navy, 10th anniv.
For overprints see Trieste Nos. 57-59.

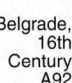

Belgrade,
16th
Century
A92

1952, Sept. 14 **Engr.** **Perf. 11½**
368 A92 15d violet brn 6.00 10.00
Never hinged 10.00

1st Yugoslav Phil. Exhib., Sept. 14-20. Sold
only at the exhibition.

Marching
Workers and
Congress
Flag — A93

1952, Nov. 2 **Perf. 11½**
369 A93 15d red brown .60 1.20
370 A93 15d dark vio blue .60 1.20
371 A93 15d dark brown .60 1.20
372 A93 15d blue green .60 1.20
Nos. 369-372 (4) 2.40 4.80
Set, never hinged 5.00

6th Yugoslav Communist Party Congress,
Zagreb.
For overprints see Trieste Nos. 61-64.

Nikola
Tesla — A94

Woman Pouring
Water — A95

1953, Jan. 7 **Unwmk.**
373 A94 15d brown carmine .40 .25
374 A94 30d chalky blue 2.00 .65
Set, never hinged 4.00

Death of Nikola Tesla, 10th anniv.
For overprints see Trieste Nos. 66-67.

1953, Mar. 24 **Litho.** **Perf. 11½**
Designs: 30d, Hands holding two birds.
50d, Woman holding Urn.
375 A95 15d dk olive green .40 .65
376 A95 30d chalky blue .90 .65
377 A95 50d henna brown 8.75 4.50
Nos. 375-377 (3) 10.05 5.80
Set, never hinged 20.00

Issued to honor the United Nations.
See Nos. RA19 and RAJ16. For overprints
see Trieste Nos. 76-78.

Types of 1950-52
1953-55 **Litho.** **Perf. 12½**

8d, Mining. 17d, Livestock raising.

378 A68 1d dull gray .40 .25
379 A68 2d carmine 1.00 .25
380 A68 5d orange 3.50 .25

381 A68 8d blue 2.50 .25
382 A68 10d yellow green 4.00 .25
383 A68 12d lt vio brown 20.00 .25
384 A68 15d rose red 8.00 .25
384A A68 17d vio brn ('55) 1.50 .25
Nos. 378-384A (8) 40.90 2.00
Set, never hinged 75.00

For overprints see Trieste Nos. 68-75, 90-92.

Automobile
Climbing Mt.
Lovcen — A96

30d, Motorcycle & auto at Opatija. 50d, Racers leaving Belgrade. 70d, Auto near Mt.
Triglav.

1953, May 10 **Photo.** **Perf. 12½**
385 A96 15d sal & dp plum .25 .25
386 A96 30d bl & dark blue .25 .25
387 A96 50d ocher & choc .60 .40
388 A96 70d lt bl grn & ol grn 15.00 4.75
Nos. 385-388 (4) 16.10 5.65
Set, never hinged 35.00

Intl. Automobile & Motorcycle Races, 1953.

President
Tito — A97

Star and Flag-
encircled
Globe — A98

1953, June 28 **Engr.** **Unwmk.**
389 A97 50d deep purple 6.00 8.00
Never hinged 12.00

Marshal Tito's election to the presidency,
Jan. 14, 1953.
For overprint see Trieste No. 83.

1953, July 25 **Engr.; Star Typo.**
390 A98 15d gray & green 1.50 2.40
Never hinged 3.00

38th Esperanto Cong., Zagreb, 7/25-8/1.
For overprint see Trieste No. 84.

Macedonian
Revolutionary
A99

Nicolas Karev
A100

1953, Aug. 2 **Litho.**
391 A99 15d dark red brown .30 .65
392 A100 30d dull green 1.75 3.50
Set, never hinged 4.00

Macedonian Insurection of 1903, 50th anniv.

Family — A101

1953, Sept. 6 **Photo.**
393 A101 15d deep green 40.00 40.00
Never hinged 100.00

Liberation of Istria and the Slovene coast,
10th anniv.
For overprint see Trieste No. 85.

Branko
Radicevic — A102

1953, Oct. 1 **Engr.**
394 A102 15d lilac 2.50 2.00
Never hinged 5.00

10th death anniv. of Branko Radicevic, poet.
For overprint see Trieste No. 86.

View of
Jajce — A103

Designs: 30d, First meeting place. 50d,
Marshal Tito addressing Assembly.

1953, Nov. 29 **Perf. 12½x12**
395 A103 15d dark green .40 .80
396 A103 30d rose car .60 1.20
397 A103 50d dark brown 4.00 8.00
Nos. 395-397 (3) 5.00 10.00
Set, never hinged 10.00

2nd Assembly of the Natl. Republic of Yugoslavia, 10th anniv.
For overprints see Trieste Nos. 87-89.

Wildlife
A104

Lammergeier
A105

1954, June 30 **Photo.** **Perf. 11½**
398 A104 2d Ground squir-
rel .25 .25
399 A104 5d Lynx .25 .25
400 A104 10d Red deer .40 .25
401 A104 15d Brown bear .50 .25
402 A104 17d Chamois .80 .25
403 A104 25d White pelican 1.20 .40
404 A105 30d shown 1.20 .40
405 A105 35d Black beetle 1.60 .55
406 A105 50d Bush cricket 6.00 2.00
407 A105 65d Adriatic lizard 10.00 10.00
408 A105 70d Salamander 8.00 10.00
409 A105 100d Trout 24.00 32.50
Nos. 398-409 (12) 54.20 57.10
Set, never hinged 125.00

See Nos. 497-505. For overprints see Trieste Nos. 93-104.

**Catalogue values for unused
stamps in this section, from this
point to the end of the section, are
for Never Hinged items.**

Ljubljana,
17th
Century
A106

1954, July 29 **Engr.**
410 A106 15d multicolored 13.00 13.00

2nd Yugoslav Phil. Exhib., July 29-Aug. 8.
Sold for 50d, which included admission to the
exhibition.

Revolutionary
Flag — A107

Engr. & Typo.
1954, Oct. 3 **Perf. 12½**
411 A107 15d shown 1.60 .45
412 A107 30d Cannon 2.25 .80
413 A107 50d Revolutionary
seal 5.00 1.10
414 A107 70d Karageorge 32.50 15.00
Nos. 411-414 (4) 41.35 17.35

1st Serbian insurrection, 150th anniv.
For overprints see Trieste Nos. 105-108.

Vatroslav
Lisinski — A108

30d, Andrea Kacic-Miosic. 50d, Jure Vega.
70d, Jovan Jovanovic-Zmaj. 100d, Philip
Visnic.

1954, Dec. 25 **Engr.**
415 A108 15d dark green 2.75 1.00
416 A108 30d chocolate 2.75 1.60
417 A108 50d dp claret 3.75 3.00
418 A108 70d indigo 7.50 7.00
419 A108 100d purple 19.00 19.00
Nos. 415-419 (5) 35.75 31.60

Scene from
"Robinja" — A109

"A
Midsummer
Night's
Dream"
A110

1955 **Photo.** **Perf. 12x11½, 12½**
Glazed Paper

420 A109 15d brown lake 1.00 .55
421 A110 30d dark blue 3.50 2.00

Festival at Dubrovnik.

Dragon Emblem of Ljubljana — A111

1955   Engr.   Perf. 12½
422 A111 15d dk grn & brn   6.00 4.00
1st Intl. Exhib. of Graphic Arts, Ljubljana, July 3-Sept. 3.

Symbol of Sign Language — A112

Hops — A113

1955, Aug. 23
423 A112 15d rose lake   2.00 .45
2nd World Congress of Deaf Mutes, Zagreb, Aug. 23-27.

1955, Sept. 24   Photo.   Perf. 11½
Medicinal Plants.
424 A113 5d shown   .25 .25
425 A113 10d Tobacco   .25 .25
426 A113 15d Poppy   .25 .25
427 A113 17d Linden   .25 .25
428 A113 25d Chamomile   .25 .25
429 A113 30d Salvia   .40 .25
430 A113 50d Dog rose   2.50 1.75
431 A113 70d Gentian   5.00 2.75
432 A113 100d Adonis   21.00 15.00
   Nos. 424-432 (9)   30.15 21.00

"Peace" Statue, New York — A114

1955, Oct. 24   Litho.   Perf. 12½
433 A114 30d lt bl & blk   1.50 1.10
United Nations, 10th anniversary.

Woman and Dove — A115

1955, Nov. 29   Engr.
434 A115 15d dull violet   .80 .55
10th anniv. of the "New Yugoslavia."

St. Donat, Zadar — A116

Cornice, Cathedral at Sibenik A117

Yugoslav Art: 10d, Relief of a King, Split. 15d, Griffin, Studenica Monastery. 20d, Figures, Trogir Cathedral. 25d, Fresco, Sopocani Monastery. 30d, Tombstone, Radimlje. 40d, Ciborium, Kotor Cathedral. 50d, St. Martin from Tryptich, Dubrovnik. 70d, Figure, Belec Church. 100d, Rihard Jakopic, self-portrait. 200d, "Peace" Statue, New York.

1956, Mar. 24   Photo.   Perf. 11½
435 A116 5d blue vio   .45 .25
436 A116 10d slate grn   .45 .25
437 A116 15d olive brn   .45 .25
438 A116 20d brown car   .45 .25
439 A116 25d black brn   .45 .25
440 A116 30d dp claret   .45 .25
441 A117 35d olive grn   1.00 .25
442 A117 40d red brown   1.75 .50
443 A116 50d olive brn   2.50 .70
444 A116 70d dk green   9.25 6.75
445 A116 100d dark pur   32.50 20.00
446 A116 200d deep blue   77.50 32.50
   Nos. 435-446 (12)   127.20 62.20

13th Century Tower, Zagreb A118

1956, Apr. 20   Engr.   Perf. 11½
Chalky Paper
447 A118 15d vio brn, bis brn & gray   1.00 .25
a.   Miniature sheet of 4   9.00 —
3rd Yugoslavia Phil. Exhib. (JUFIZ III), Zagreb, May 20-27. No. 447a was sold at the exhibition, tipped into a folder, for 75 dinars. See No. C56.

Induction Motor — A119

Perf. 11½x12½
1956, July 10   Photo.
448 A119 10d shown   .50 .25
449 A119 15d Transformer   .60 .25
450 A119 30d Electronic controls   1.10 .50
451 A119 50d Nikola Tesla   4.00 2.00
   Nos. 448-451 (4)   6.20 3.00
Birth cent. of Nikola Tesla, inventor.

Sea Horse — A120

Paper Nautilus A121

Designs: 20d, European rock lobster. 25d, "Sea Prince." 30d, Sea perch. 35d, Red mullet. 50d, Scorpion fish. 70d, Wrasse. 100d, Dory.

1956, Sept. 10   Perf. 11½
Granite Paper
Animals in Natural Colors
452 A120 10d bright grn   .50 .30
453 A121 15d ultra & blk   .50 .30
454 A121 20d deep blue   .50 .30
455 A121 25d violet blue   .80 .30
456 A121 30d brt grnsh bl   .85 .30
457 A121 35d dk bl green   1.75 .30
458 A121 50d indigo   6.50 1.90
459 A121 70d slate grn   8.00 4.00
460 A121 100d dark blue   32.50 20.00
   Nos. 452-460 (9)   51.90 27.70

Runner A122

Designs: 15d, Paddling kayak. 20d, Skiing. 30d, Swimming. 35d, Soccer. 50d, Water polo. 70d, Table tennis. 100d, Sharpshooting.

1956, Oct. 24   Litho.   Perf. 12½
Design and Inscription in Bister
461 A122 10d dk carmine   .80 .35
462 A122 15d dark blue   .80 .35
463 A122 20d ultramarine   1.50 .70
464 A122 30d olive grn   1.50 .70
465 A122 35d dark brown   1.50 .70
466 A122 50d green   1.50 .70
467 A122 70d brn violet   50.00 22.50
468 A122 100d dark red   50.00 22.50
   Nos. 461-468 (8)   107.60 48.50
16th Olympic Games, Melbourne, 11/22-12/8.

Centaury — A123

Medicinal Plants: 15d, Belladonna. 20d, Autumn crocus. 25d, Marsh mallow. 30d, Valerian. 35d, Woolly Foxglove. 50d, Aspidium. 70d, Green Winged Orchid. 100d, Pyrethrum.

Granite Paper
Flowers in Natural Colors
1957, May 25   Photo.   Perf. 11½
469 A123 10d dk bl & grn   .25 .25
470 A123 15d violet   .25 .25
471 A123 20d lt ol grn & brn   .25 .25
472 A123 25d dp cl & dk bl   .50 .25
473 A123 30d lil rose & claret   .90 .25
474 A123 35d dk gray & dl pur   1.50 .25
475 A123 50d dp grn & choc   2.50 .75
476 A123 70d pale brn & grn   4.50 1.60
477 A123 100d gray & brown   14.00 6.00
   Nos. 469-477 (9)   24.65 9.85
See #538-546, 597-605, 689-694, 772-777.

Hand Holding Factory A124

1957, June 25   Engr.   Perf. 12½
478 A124 15d dark car rose   .40 .25
479 A124 30d violet blue   1.40 .80
Congress of Workers' Councils, Belgrade, June 25. Exist imperf.

2nd Gymnastic Meet, Zagreb, July 10-14 — A125

Various gymnastic positions.

1957, July 1   Photo.
480 A125 10d ol grn & blk   .25 .25
481 A125 15d brn red & blk   .25 .25
482 A125 30d Prus bl & blk   .80 .25
483 A125 50d brn & black   3.75 1.25
   Nos. 480-483 (4)   5.05 2.00

Montenegro A126

Natl. Costumes: 15d, Macedonia. 30d, Croatia. 50d, Serbia. 70d, Bosnia and Herzegovina. 100d, Slovenia. 50d, 70d, 100d vert.

1957, Sept. 24   Typo.   Perf. 12½
Background in Bister Brown
484 A126 10d dk brn, ultra & red   .40 .25
485 A126 15d dk brn, blk & red   .40 .25
486 A126 30d dk brn, grn & red   .40 .25
487 A126 50d dk brn & green   1.00 .25
488 A126 70d dk brn & black   1.40 .50
489 A126 100d dk brn, grn & red   6.50 3.25
   Nos. 484-489 (6)   10.10 4.75

Revolutionists A127

Lithographed and Engraved
1957, Nov. 7   Perf. 11½x12½
490 A127 15d ocher & red   .65 .45
Russian Revolution, 40th anniv.

Simon Gregorcic — A128

Famous Yugoslavs: 30d, Anton Linhart, dramatist and historian. 50d, Oton Kucera, physicist. 70d, Stevan Mokranjac, composer. 100d, Jovan Sterija Popovic, writer

1957, Dec. 3   Engr.   Perf. 12½
491 A128 15d sepia   .45 .40
492 A128 30d indigo   .60 .40
493 A128 50d reddish brn   1.25 .40
494 A128 70d dl violet   9.00 4.75
495 A128 100d olive grn   15.00 8.00
   Nos. 491-495 (5)   26.30 13.95

"Young Man on Fire" — A129

1958, Apr. 22   Photo.
496 A129 15d deep plum   .80 .25
Union of Yugoslav Communists, 7th congress, Ljubljana, Apr. 22.

Types of 1954
Game birds.

1958, May 25   Perf. 11½
Granite Paper
Birds in Natural Colors

497	A104	10d Mallard	.30	.25
498	A104	15d Capercaillie	.30	.25
499	A104	20d Ring-necked pheasant	.30	.25
500	A104	25d Coot	.30	.25
501	A104	30d Water rail	.70	.25
502	A105	35d Great bustard	1.25	.25
503	A105	50d Rock partridge	4.50	1.25
504	A104	70d Woodcock	8.25	3.25
505	A105	100d Eurasian crane	17.50	7.50
		Nos. 497-505 (9)	33.40	13.50

Stylized Bird — A130

1958, June 14   Engr.   Perf. 12½
506   A130   15d bluish black   .80   .25

Opening of Postal Museum, Belgrade. Exists imperf.

Flag and Laurel A131

1958, July 1   Unwmk.
507   A131   15d brn carmine   .50   .30

15th anniv. of victory over Germans at Sutjeska, Bosnia.

Onufrio Well, Dubrovnik A132

1958, Aug. 10   Litho.   Perf. 12½
508   A132   15d black & brn   1.50   .30

Marin Drzic, dramatist, 450th birth anniv.

Sisak Steel Works — A133   Titograd Hotel and Open-Air Theater — A134

Industrial Progress Designs: 2d, Crude oil production. 5d, Shipbuilding. 10d, Sisak steel works. 15d, Jablanica hydroelectric works. 17d, Lumber industry. 25d, Overpass, Zagreb-Ljubljana highway. 30d, Litostroy turbine factory. 35d, Lukavac coke plant. 50d, Bridge at Skopje. 70d, Railroad station, Sarajevo. 100d, Triple bridge, Ljubljana. 200d, Mestrovic station, Zagreb. 500d, Parliament, Belgrade.

1958   Typo.   Perf. 12½ Horiz.
509	A133	10d green	14.00	6.00
510	A133	15d orange ver	14.00	6.00

		Engr.	Perf. 12½	
511	A133	2d olive	.25	.25
512	A133	5d brown red	.25	.25
513	A133	10d green	.40	.25
514	A133	15d orange ver	.40	.25
515	A133	17d deep claret	.40	.25
516	A133	25d slate	.40	.25
517	A133	30d blue black	.40	.25
518	A133	35d rose red	.40	.25
519	A133	40d car rose	.45	.25
520	A134	50d bright bl	.50	.25

521	A134	70d orange ver	1.25	.25
522	A134	100d green	4.75	.25
523	A134	200d red brown	4.50	.25
524	A134	500d intense bl	8.50	.30
		Nos. 511-524 (14)	22.85	3.55

Nos. 509-510 are coil stamps.
See #555-562, 627-645, 786-789, 830-840.

Ocean Exploration A135

1958, Oct. 24   Unwmk.
525   A135   15d brown violet   .50   .25

Intl. Geophysical Year, 1957-58. Exists imperf. See #C58.

White and Black Hands Holding Scales A136

1958, Dec. 10   Perf. 12½
526   A136   30d steel blue   1.10   .80

Universal Declaration of Human Rights, 10th anniv.

Dubrovnik A137

Tourist attractions: #528, Bled. #529, Postojna grotto. #530, Ohrid. #531, Opatija. #532, Plitvice National Park. #533, Split. #534, Sveti Stefan. #535, Exhibition Hall, Belgrade.

1959, Feb. 16   Litho.   Perf. 12½
527	A137	10d crim rose & cit	.25	.25
528	A137	10d lt grn & lt vio bl	.25	.25
529	A137	15d grnsh bl & pur	.25	.25
530	A137	15d grn & bright bl	.25	.25
531	A137	20d lt grn & grnsh bl	.25	.25
532	A137	20d ol bis & brt grn	.25	.25
533	A137	30d yel org & purple	1.40	.25
534	A137	30d lt vio bl & gray ol	1.40	.25
535	A137	70d gray & grnsh bl	4.50	2.25
		Nos. 527-535 (9)	8.80	4.25

Nos. 527, 530, 532 and 534 are inscribed in Cyrillic characters. See #650-658, 695-700.

Red Flags — A138

1959, Apr. 20   Unwmk.   Perf. 12½
536   A138   20d multicolored   .50   .25

Yugoslav Communist Party, 40th anniv.

Dubrovnik, 15th Century A139

1959, May 24   Engr.   Perf. 11½
537   A139   20d yel grn, dk grn & bl   10.00   3.50

4th Yugoslavia Phil. Exhib. (JUFIZ IV), Dubrovnik.

Flower Type of 1957

Medicinal Plants: 10d, Lavender. 15d, Black Alder. 20d, Scopolia. 25d, Monkshood. 30d, Bilberry. 35d, Juniper. 50d, Primrose. 70d, Pomegranate. 100d, Jimson weed.

1959, May 25   Photo.
Granite Paper
Flowers in Natural Colors

538	A123	10d lt bl & dk blue	.25	.25
539	A123	15d brt yel & car	.25	.25
540	A123	20d dk ol bis & mar	.25	.25
541	A123	25d ap grn & dk pur	.25	.25
542	A123	30d pink & dk bl	.25	.25
543	A123	35d bis brn & vio bl	1.25	.25
544	A123	50d brn & green	3.00	.40
545	A123	70d yel & ocher	4.00	.65
546	A123	100d lt brn & brn	8.50	4.00
		Nos. 538-546 (9)	18.00	6.55

Tug of War — A140

Sports: 15d, High jump and runners. 20d, Ring and parallel bar exercises. 35d, Women gymnasts. 40d, Sailors doing gymnastics. 55d, Field ball and basketball. 80d, Swimming. 100d, Festival emblem, vert.

1959, June 26   Litho.   Perf. 12½
547	A140	10d dk sl grn & ocher	.25	.25
548	A140	15d vio bl & sepia	.25	.25
549	A140	20d ol bis & dl lil	.25	.25
550	A140	35d deep cl & gray	.25	.25
551	A140	40d violet & gray	.25	.25
552	A140	55d sl grn & ol bis	.50	.25
553	A140	80d indigo & olive	3.25	.50
554	A140	100d pur & bister	7.00	3.50
		Nos. 547-554 (8)	12.00	5.50

Physical Culture Festival. Exist imperf.

Types of 1958; Designs as before

Designs: 8d, Lumber industry. 15d, Overpass, Zagreb-Ljubljana highway. 20d, Jablanica hydroelectric works. 40d, Titograd Hotel. 55d, Bridge at Skopje. 80d, Railroad Station, Sarajevo.

1959   Typo.   Perf. 12½ Horizontally
555	A133	15d green	2.50	1.10
556	A133	20d orange ver	3.00	1.10

		Engr.	Perf. 12½	
557	A133	8d deep claret	.40	.25
558	A133	15d green	.55	.25
559	A133	20d orange ver	.95	.25
560	A134	40d bright blue	2.25	.25
561	A134	55d carmine rose	3.50	.25
562	A134	80d orange ver	6.00	.25
		Nos. 557-562 (6)	13.65	1.50

Nos. 555-556 are coil stamps.

Fair Emblem — A141

1959, Sept. 5   Litho.   Unwmk.
563   A141   20d lt vio bl & blk   2.00   1.00

50th International Fair at Zagreb.

Athletics — A142

1960, Apr. 25   Perf. 12½
564	A142	15d shown	.40	.40
565	A142	20d Swimming	.40	.40
566	A142	30d Skiing	.40	.40
567	A142	35d Wrestling	.40	.40
568	A142	40d Bicycling	.40	.40
569	A142	55d Yachting	.40	.40
570	A142	80d Horseback riding	5.00	3.50
571	A142	100d Fencing	5.00	3.50
		Nos. 564-571 (8)	12.40	9.40

17th Olympic Games.

Hedgehog A143

1960, May 25   Photo.   Perf. 12x11½
Animals in Natural Colors

572	A143	15d shown	.30	.30
573	A143	20d Red squirrel	.30	.30
574	A143	25d Pine marten	.30	.30
575	A143	30d Hare	.70	.70
576	A143	35d Red fox	.70	.70
577	A143	40d Badger	.70	.70
578	A143	55d Wolf	1.50	1.50
579	A143	80d Roe deer	1.50	1.50
580	A143	100d Wild boar	4.00	4.00
		Nos. 572-580 (9)	10.00	10.00

See Nos. 663-671.

Lenin, 90th Birth Anniv. — A144

1960, June 22   Engr.   Perf. 12½
581   A144   20d dk grn & slate grn   .25   .25

Atomic Accelerator A145

1960, Aug. 23   Unwmk.
582	A145	15d shown	8.00	8.00
583	A145	20d Generator	8.00	8.00
584	A145	40d Nuclear reactor	8.00	8.00
		Nos. 582-584 (3)	24.00	24.00

Nuclear energy exposition, Belgrade. Exist imperf.

Serbian National Theater, Novi Sad — A146

Designs: 20d, Woman from Croatian play. 40d, Edward Rusijan and early plane. 55d, Symbolic hand holding fruit. 80d, Atom and UN emblem.

1960, Oct. 24   Perf. 12½
585	A146	15d gray black	.75	.75
586	A146	20d brown	.75	.75
587	A146	40d dark gray blue	.75	.75
588	A146	55d dull claret	1.00	1.00
589	A146	80d dark green	1.00	1.00
		Nos. 585-589 (5)	4.25	4.25

Serbian Natl. Theater, Novi Sad, cent. (#585); Croatian Natl. Theater, Zagreb, cent. (#586); 1st flight in Yugoslavia, 50th anniv. (#587); 15th anniv. of the Yugoslav Republic (#588); UN, 15th anniv. (#589). Exist imperf.

Ivan Cankar, Writer — A147

Famous Yugoslavs: 20d, Silvije Strahimir Kranjcevic, poet. 40d, Paja Jovanovic, painter. 55d, Dura Jaksic, writer and painter. 80d, Mihajlo Pupin, electro-technician. 100d, Rudjer Boscovich, mathematician.

1960, Dec. 24   Engr.   Perf. 12½

590	A147	15d dark green	.35	.30
591	A147	20d henna brown	.35	.30
592	A147	40d olive bister	.35	.30
593	A147	55d magenta	.35	.30
594	A147	80d dark blue	.35	.30
595	A147	100d Prussian bl	.35	.30
		Nos. 590-595 (6)	2.10	1.80

Exist imperf.

International Atomic Energy Commission Emblem A148

Victims' Monument, Kragujevac A149

Engr. & Litho.

1961, May 15   Perf. 12½

596	A148	25d multicolored	.50	.25

Intl. Nuclear Electronic Conf., Belgrade.

Flower Type of 1957

Medicinal plants: 10d, Yellow foxglove. 15d, Marjoram. 20d, Hyssop. 25d, Scarlet haw. 40d, Rose mallow. 50d, Soapwort. 60d, Clary. 80d, Blackthorn. 100d, Marigold.

1961, May 25   Photo.   Perf. 11½
Granite Paper
Flowers in Natural Colors

597	A123	10d lt bl & grnsh bl	.30	.30
598	A123	15d gray & chnt	.30	.30
599	A123	20d buff & green	.30	.30
600	A123	25d lt vio & vio	.30	.30
601	A123	40d lt ultra & ultra	.30	.30
602	A123	50d lt bl & blue	.30	.30
603	A123	60d beige & dk car rose	.30	.30
604	A123	80d lt grn & green	.30	.30
605	A123	100d redsh brn & choc	12.00	9.00
		Nos. 597-605 (9)	14.40	11.40

1961, July 3   Perf. 12x12½

Monuments: 15d, Stevan Filipovic, Valjevo. 20d, Relief from Insurrection, Bozansko Grahovo. 60d, Victory, Nova Gradiska. 100d, Marshal Tito, Titovo Uzice.

Granite Paper
Gold Frames and Inscriptions

606	A149	15d crimson & brn	.25	.25
607	A149	20d brn & ol bis	.25	.25
608	A149	25d bl grn & gray olive	.25	.25
609	A149	60d violet	.25	.25
610	A149	100d indigo & black	.25	.25
		Nos. 606-610 (5)	1.25	1.25

Souvenir Sheet
Imperf

611	A149	500d indigo & black	125.00 125.00

Natl. Insurrection, 20th anniv.

Men of Five Races A150

National Assembly Building, Belgrade — A151

1961, Sept. 1   Litho.   Perf. 11½

613	A150	25d brown	.25	.25

Engr.

614	A151	50d blue green	.25	.25
		Nos. 613-614,C59-C60 (4)	3.40	2.35

Miniature Sheet
Imperf

615	A150	1000d claret	20.00 17.50

Conference of Non-aligned Nations, Belgrade, Sept. 1961.

St. Clement, 14th Century Wood Sculpture — A152

1961, Sept. 10   Engr.   Perf. 12½

616	A152	25d sepia & olive	2.00	.65

12th Intl. Congress for Byzantine Studies.

Serbian Women A153

Regional Costumes: 25d, Montenegro. 30d, Bosnia and Herzegovina. 50d, Macedonia. 65d, Croatia. 100d, Slovenia.

1961, Nov. 28   Litho.

617	A153	15d beige, brn & red	.25	.25
618	A153	25d beige, red brn & black	.25	.25
619	A153	30d beige, brn & dk red	.25	.25
620	A153	50d multicolored	.25	.25
621	A153	65d brn, red & yel	.60	.25
622	A153	100d multicolored	1.60	.75
		Nos. 617-622 (6)	3.20	2.00

Luka Vukalovic — A154

1961, Dec. 15   Engr.

623	A154	25d slate blue	.25	.25

Centenary of Herzegovina insurrection.

Hands with Flower and Rifle — A155

1961, Dec. 22

624	A155	25d red & vio blue	.25	.25

20th anniversary of Yugoslav army.

Miladinov Brothers A156

1961, Dec. 25   Litho.

625	A156	25d buff & claret	.25	.25

Centenary of Macedonian folksong "Koder"; Dimitri and Konstantin Miladinov, brothers who collected and published folksongs. Monument is at Struga.

Types of 1958; Designs as before

Designs: 5d, Shipbuilding. 8d, Lumber industry. 10d, Sisak steel works. 15d, Overpass. 20d, Jablanica hydroelectric works. 25d, Cable factory, Svetozarevo. 30d, Litostroy turbine factory. 40d, Lukavac coke plant. 50d, Zenica steel works. 65d, Sevojno copper works. 100d, Crude oil production. 150d, Titograd hotel. 200d, Bridge, Skopje. 300d, Railroad station, Sarajevo. 500d, Triple bridge, Ljubljana. 1000d, Mestrovic station, Zagreb. 2000d, Parliament, Belgrade.

1961-62   Typo.   Perf. 12½ Horiz.

627	A133	10d dark red brn	7.50	.55
628	A133	15d emerald	12.00	.30

Engr.   Perf. 12½

629	A133	5d dull orange	.25	.25
630	A133	8d gray	.25	.25
631	A133	10d dk red brn	.25	.25
632	A133	15d emerald	.25	.25
633	A133	20d violet blue	.50	.25
634	A133	25d vermilion	.25	.25
635	A133	30d red brown	6.50	.25
636	A133	40d dp cl ('62)	.25	.25
637	A133	50d gray blue	1.60	.25
638	A133	65d green	.25	.25
639	A133	100d yel olive	3.25	.25
640	A134	150d carmine ('62)	.75	.25
641	A134	200d slate grn ('62)	.75	.25
642	A134	300d olive ('62)	1.50	.25
643	A134	500d dull violet	1.25	.25
644	A134	1000d bister brn	4.50	.25
645	A134	2000d claret	10.00	.40
		Nos. 629-645 (17)	32.35	4.40

Nos. 627-628 are coil stamps. For surcharges see Nos. 786, 789.

Isis of Kalabsha — A157

Design: 50d, Ramses II, Abu Simbel.

1962, Apr. 7   Engr.   Perf. 12½

646	A157	25d grnsh blk, cream	.25	.25
647	A157	50d brown, buff	.25	.25

15th anniv. (in 1961) of UNESCO.

Joy of Motherhood by Frano Krsinic — A158

1962, Apr. 7

648	A158	50d black, cream	.30	.25

15th anniv. (in 1961) of UNICEF.

Anopheles Mosquito — A159

1962, Apr. 7   Unwmk.

649	A159	50d black, gray	.40	.25

WHO drive to eradicate malaria.

Scenic Type of 1959

Tourist attractions: #650, Portoroz. #651, Jajce. #652, Zadar. #653, Popova Sapka. #654, Hvar. #655, Bay of Kotor. #656, Danube, Iron Gate. #657, Rab. #658, Zagreb.

1962, Apr. 24   Litho.

650	A137	15d ol & chlky bl	.25	.25
651	A137	15d blue grn & bis	.25	.25
652	A137	25d blue & red brn	.25	.25
653	A137	25d dk bl & pale bl	.25	.25
654	A137	30d blue & brn org	.25	.25
655	A137	30d gray & chlky bl	.25	.25
656	A137	50d ol & grnsh bl	.90	.25
657	A137	50d blue & olive	.90	.25
658	A137	100d dk grn & gray bl	7.50	3.00
		Nos. 650-658 (9)	10.80	5.00

#651, 653, 655-656 are inscribed in Cyrillic. Exist imperf.

Marshal Tito, by Augustincic A160

Design: 50d, 200d, Sideview of bust by Antun Augustincic.

1962, May 25   Engr.   Perf. 12½

659	A160	25d dark green	1.00	.80
660	A160	50d dark brown	1.00	.80
661	A160	100d dark blue	1.00	.80
662	A160	200d greenish blk	1.00	.80
a.		Souv. sheet of 4, #659-662, imperf.	35.00	35.00
		Nos. 659-662 (4)	4.00	3.20

70th birthday of Pres. Tito (Josip Broz).

Animal Type of 1960

Designs: 15d, Crested newt. 20d, Fire salamander. 25d, Yellow-bellied toad. 30d, Pond frog. 50d, Pond turtle. 65d, Lizard. 100d, Emerald lizard. 150d, Leopard snake. 200d, European viper (adder).

1962, June 8   Photo.   Perf. 12x11½
Animals in Natural Colors

663	A143	15d green	.50	.50
664	A143	20d purple	.50	.50
665	A143	25d chocolate	.50	.50
666	A143	30d violet blue	.50	.50
667	A143	50d dark red	.50	.50
668	A143	65d bright grn	.50	.50
669	A143	100d black	1.25	1.25
670	A143	150d brown	1.25	1.25
671	A143	200d car rose	12.50	7.00
		Nos. 663-671 (9)	18.00	12.50

Pole
Vault — A161

Sports: 25d, Woman discus thrower, horiz. 30d, Long distance runners. 50d, Javelin thrower, horiz. 65d, Shot put. 100d, Women runners, horiz. 150d, Hop, step and jump. 200d, High jump, horiz.

Athletes in Black

1962, July 10　　Litho.　　Perf. 12½

672	A161	15d blue	.35	.25
673	A161	25d magenta	.35	.25
674	A161	30d emerald	.35	.25
675	A161	50d red	.35	.25
676	A161	65d vio blue	.35	.25
677	A161	100d green	.70	.25
678	A161	150d orange	3.50	.40
679	A161	200d orange brn	9.50	.80
		Nos. 672-679 (8)	15.45	2.70

7th European Athletic Championships, Belgrade, Sept. 12-16. See No. C61.

Child at
Play — A162

Litho. & Engr.
1962, Oct. 1　　　　　　　Perf. 12½

680	A162	25d red & black	.30	.25

Issued for Children's Week.

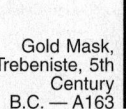

Gold Mask,
Trebeniste, 5th
Century
B.C. — A163

Bathing the Infant
Christ, Fresco,
Decani
Monastery — A164

Yugoslav Art Treasures: 25d, Horseman and bird, bronze vase (5th cent. B.C.). 50d, God Kairos, marble relief. 65d, "The Pigeons of Nerezi," fresco (12th cent.). 150d, Archangel Gabriel, icon (14th cent.).

1962, Nov. 28　　　　　　　Photo.

681	A163	25d Prus bl, blk & gold	.25	.25
682	A163	30d gold, saph & blk	.25	.25
683	A164	50d dk grn, brn & gold	.25	.25
684	A164	65d multicolored	.25	.25
685	A164	100d multicolored	.50	.50
686	A163	150d multicolored	1.00	1.00
		Nos. 681-686 (6)	2.50	2.50

Parched Earth
and
Wheat — A165

1963, Mar. 21　　Engr.　　Perf. 12½

687	A165	50d dark brn, tan	.40	.40

FAO "Freedom from Hunger" campaign.

Dr. Andrija
Mohorovicic and
UN
Emblem — A166

1963, Mar. 23　　　　　　　Unwmk.

688	A166	50d dk blue, gray	.40	.40

UN 3rd World Meteorological Day, Mar. 23. Dr. Mohorovicic (1857-1936) was director of the Zagreb meteorological observatory.

Flower Type of 1957

Medicinal Plants: 15d, Lily of the valley. 25d, Iris. 30d, Bistort. 50d, Henbane. 65d, St. John's wort. 100d, Caraway.

1963, May 25　　Photo.　　Perf. 11½
Granite Paper
Flowers in Natural Colors

689	A123	15d gray grn & grn	.25	.25
690	A123	25d lt bl, ultra & pur	.25	.25
691	A123	30d gray & black	.25	.25
692	A123	50d redsh brn & red brn	.25	.25
693	A123	65d pale brn & brn	.65	.65
694	A123	100d slate & blk	3.50	2.75
		Nos. 689-694 (6)	5.15	4.40

Scenic Type of 1959

Tourist attractions: 15d, Pula. 25d, Vrnjacka Banja. 30d, Crikvenica. 50d, Korcula. 65d, Durmitor mountain. 100d, Ljubljana.

1963, June 6　　Litho.　　Perf. 12½

695	A137	15d multicolored	.25	.25
696	A137	25d multicolored	.25	.25
697	A137	30d multicolored	.25	.25
698	A137	50d multicolored	.25	.25
699	A137	65d multicolored	.25	.25
700	A137	100d multicolored	1.50	.40
		Nos. 695-700 (6)	2.75	1.65

Partisans on the March, by Djordje
Andrejevic-Kun — A167

Sutjeska
(Gorge) — A168

Design: No. 702A, As 15d, but inscribed "Vis 1944-1964." 50d, Partisans in battle.

Engr. & Litho.; Litho. (No. 702)
1963-64　　　　　Perf. 12½, 11½

701	A167	15d gray & dk sl grn	.25	.25
702	A168	25d dark slate grn	.25	.25
702A	A167	25d gray & dark car rose	.45	.45
703	A167	50d tan & purple	.25	.25
		Nos. 701-703 (4)	1.20	1.20

20th anniv. of the Partisan Battle of Sutjeska (Nos. 701, 702-703); 20th anniv. of the arrival of the Yugoslav General Staff on the island of Vis (No. 702A).
Issued: #702A, 7/27/64; others, 7/3/63.

Gymnast on
Vaulting
Horse — A169

1963, July 6　　Litho.　　Perf. 12½

704	A169	25d shown	.40	.40
705	A169	50d Parallel bars	.80	.40
706	A169	100d Rings	1.20	.40
		Nos. 704-706 (3)	2.40	1.20

5th Gymnastics Europa Prize.

Mother, by Ivan
Mestrovic
A170

Sculptures by Mestrovic (1883-1962): 50d, "Reminiscences" (woman). 65d, Head of Kraljevic Marko. 100d, Indian on Horseback.

1963, Sept. 28　　　　　　Engr.

707	A170	25d brown, buff	.25	.25
708	A170	50d sl green, grnsh	.25	.25
709	A170	65d grnsh blk, grysh	.25	.25
710	A170	100d black, grayish	1.00	.75
		Nos. 707-710 (4)	1.75	1.50

Children with
Toys — A171

1963, Oct. 5　　　　　　　Litho.

711	A171	25d multicolored	.40	.25

Issued for Children's Week.

Soldier with
Gun and
Flag — A172

Litho. & Engr.
1963, Oct. 20　　　　　　Perf. 12½

712	A172	25d ver, tan & gold	.25	.25

Yugoslavian Democratic Federation, 20th anniv.

Relief from
Tombstone,
Herzegovina
A173

Dositej Obradovic
A174

Art through the centuries: 30d, Horseback trio, Split Cathedral. 50d, King & queen on horseback, Beram Church, Istria. 65d, Archangel Michael, Dominican monastery, Dubrovnik. 100d, Man pouring water, fountain, Ljubljana. 150d, Archbishop Eufrasie, mosaic, Porec Basilica, Istria.

1963, Nov. 29　　　　　　Photo.

713	A173	25d multi	.25	.25
714	A173	30d multi, horiz.	.25	.25
715	A173	50d multi, horiz.	.25	.25
716	A173	65d multi	.25	.25
717	A173	100d multi	.25	.25
718	A173	150d multi	.95	.75
		Nos. 713-718 (6)	2.20	2.00

Issued for the Day of the Republic.

1963, Dec. 10　　　　　　Engr.

Famous Yugoslavians: 30d, Vuk Stefanovic Karadzic, reformer of Serbian language. 50d, Franc Miklosic, Slovenian philologist. 65d,

Ljudevit Gaj, reformer of Croatian language. 100d, Peter Petrovich Nyegosh, Montenegrin prince, bishop and poet.

Variously Toned Paper

719	A174	25d black	.25	.25
720	A174	30d black	.25	.25
721	A174	50d black	.25	.25
722	A174	65d black	1.00	.25
723	A174	100d black	1.00	.50
		Nos. 719-723 (5)	2.75	1.50

Vanessa
Io — A175

Fireman Rescuing
Child — A176

Butterflies & Moths: 30d, Vanessa antiopa. 40d, Daphnis nerii. 50d, Parnassius apollo. 150d, Saturnia pyri. 200d, Papilio machaon.

1964, May 25　　Photo.　　Perf. 12½

724	A175	25d multicolored	.40	.40
725	A175	30d multicolored	.40	.40
726	A175	40d multicolored	.40	.40
727	A175	50d multicolored	.40	.40
728	A175	100d multicolored	4.00	4.00
729	A175	200d multicolored	4.00	4.00
		Nos. 724-729 (6)	9.60	9.60

1964, June 14　　　　　　Litho.

730	A176	25d red & black	.25	.25

Centenary of voluntary firemen. Exists imperf.

Runner
A177

1964, July 1　　Unwmk.　　Perf. 12½

731	A177	25d shown	.25	.25
732	A177	30d Boxing	.25	.25
733	A177	40d Rowing	.25	.25
734	A177	50d Basketball	.25	.25
735	A177	150d Soccer	5.00	1.00
736	A177	200d Water polo	5.00	1.00
		Nos. 731-736 (6)	11.00	3.00

18th Olympic Games, Tokyo, Oct. 10-25.

UN Flag over
Scaffolding
A178

25d, Upheaval of the earth & scaffolding.

1964, July 26　　　　　　Engr.

737	A178	25d red brown	.25	.25
738	A178	50d blue	.25	.25

Earthquake at Skopje; 1st anniv.

Serbian
Women — A179

Regional Costumes: 30d, Slovenia. 40d, Bosnia and Herzegovina. 50d, Croatia. 150d, Macedonia. 200d, Montenegro.

Costumes Multicolored

1964, Aug. 5		Litho.	
740	A179 25d violet & brn	.65	.65
741	A179 30d slate & green	.65	.65
742	A179 40d redsh brn & blk	.65	.65
743	A179 50d blue & black	.65	.65
744	A179 150d dl grn & sepia	2.75	2.75
745	A179 200d tan, red & brn	2.75	2.75
	Nos. 740-745 (6)	8.10	8.10

Exist imperf.

Friedrich Engels — A180

Litho. & Engr.

1964, Sept. 27		Perf. 11½	
746	A180 25d shown	.25	.25
747	A180 50d Karl Marx	.25	.25

1st Socialist Intl., London, Sept. 28, 1864. Exist imperf.

Children at Play — A181

1964, Oct. 4		Litho.	Perf. 12½
748	A181 25d ver, pink & gray grn	.40	.40

Issued for Children's Week. Exists imperf.

The Victor by Ivan Mestrovic — A182

1964, Oct. 20		Engr.	Perf. 11½
749	A182 25d gold & blk, pnksh	.25	.25

Liberation of Belgrade, 20th anniv.

Initial from Evangel of Hilandar — A183   Hand, "Liberty and Equality" — A184

Art through the centuries: 30d, Initial from Evangel of Miroslav (musician). 40d, Detail from Cetigne octavo, 1494 (saint with scroll). 50d, Miniature from Evangel of Trogir, 13th cent. (female saint). 150d, Miniature from Hrovoe Missal, 15th cent. (knight on horseback). 200d, Miniature from 14th cent. manuscript (symbolic fight), horiz.

Perf. 11½x12, 12x11½

1964, Nov. 29		Photo.	Unwmk.
750	A183 25d multicolored	.25	.25
751	A183 30d multicolored	.25	.25
752	A183 40d multicolored	.25	.25
753	A183 50d multicolored	.25	.25
754	A183 150d multicolored	.25	.25
755	A183 200d multicolored	.25	.25
	Nos. 750-755 (6)	1.50	1.50

Issued for Day of the Republic.

1964, Dec. 7			Perf. 12
50d, Dove over factory, "Peace and Socialism." 100d, Smokestacks, "Building Socialism."

756	A184 25d multicolored	.25	.25
757	A184 50d multicolored	.25	.25
758	A184 100d multicolored	.40	.25
	Nos. 756-758 (3)	.90	.75

Yugoslav Communist League, 8th congress.

Table Tennis Player — A185

1965, Apr. 15		Litho.	Perf. 12½
759	A185 50d shown	4.00	4.00
760	A185 150d Player at left	4.00	4.00

28th Table Tennis Championships, Ljubljana, Apr. 15-25. Exist imperf.

Titograd — A186

1965, May 8			Engr.
761	A186 25d shown	.25	.25
762	A186 30d Skopje	.25	.25
763	A186 40d Sarajevo	.25	.25
764	A186 50d Ljubljana	.50	.50
765	A186 150d Zagreb	.50	.50
766	A186 200d Belgrade	.65	.65
	Nos. 761-766 (6)	2.40	2.40

Liberation of Yugoslavia from the Nazis, 20th anniv. Exist imperf.

Young Pioneer — A187

1965, May 10		Litho. & Engr.	
767	A187 25d blk & tan, buff	.25	.25

Young Pioneer Games "20 Years of Freedom." Exists imperf.

ITU Emblem and Television Tower — A188

1965, May 17			Engr.
768	A188 50d dark blue	.25	.25

ITU, centenary.

Iron Gate, Danube — A189

Arms of Yugoslavia and Romania and Djerdap Dam — A190

50d, Iron Gate hydroelectric plant and dam.

1965, May 20		Litho.	Perf. 12½x12
769	A189 25d (30b) lt bl & grn	.25	.25
770	A189 50d (55b) lt bl & dk red	.40	.25

Miniature Sheet
Perf. 13½x13

771	A190	Sheet of 4	4.25	4.25
a.		100d multicolored	.35	.35
b.		150d multicolored	.70	.70

Nos. 769-771 were issued simultaneously by Yugoslavia and Romania to commemorate the start of the construction of the Iron Gate hydroelectric plant. Nos. 769-770 were valid for postage in both countries.

No. 771 contains one each of Nos. 771a, 771b and Romania Nos. 1747a and 1747b. Only Nos. 771a and 771b were valid in Yugoslavia. Sold for 500d.

See Romania Nos. 1745-1747.

Flower Type of 1957

Medicinal Plants: 25d, Milfoil. 30d, Rosemary. 40d, Inula. 50d, Belladonna. 150d, Mint. 200d, Foxglove.

1965, May 25		Photo.	Perf. 11½

Granite Paper
Flowers in Natural Colors

772	A123 25d deep carmine	.30	.30
773	A123 30d olive bister	.30	.30
774	A123 40d red brown	.30	.30
775	A123 50d dark blue	.30	.30
776	A123 150d violet blue	.35	.35
777	A123 200d purple	2.00	2.00
	Nos. 772-777 (6)	3.55	3.55

Intl. Cooperation Year Emblem — A191

1965, June 26		Litho.	Perf. 12½
778	A191 50d dk bl & dull bl	.25	.25

Sibenik — A192

1965, July 6		Unwmk.	Perf. 12½
779	A192 25d Rogaska Slatina	.40	.40
780	A192 30d shown	.40	.40
781	A192 40d Prespa Lake	.40	.40
782	A192 50d Prizren	.40	.40
783	A192 150d Scutari	1.20	1.20
784	A192 200d Sarajevo	2.00	2.00
	Nos. 779-784 (6)	4.80	4.80

Cat — A193

1965, Oct. 3		Litho.	Perf. 12½
785	A193 30d maroon & brt yel	.45	.25

Issued for Children's Week. Exists imperf.

Nos. 630 and 634 Surcharged in Maroon and Type of 1958

Designs: 20d, Jablanica hydroelectric works. 30d, Litostroy turbine factory.

1965		Engr.	Perf. 12½
786	A133 5d on 8d gray	.60	.25
787	A133 20d emerald	.50	.25
788	A133 30d red orange	.80	.25
789	A133 50d on 25d vermilion	.60	.25
	Nos. 786-789 (4)	2.50	1.00

Branislav Nusic — A194   Marshal Tito — A195

Famous Yugoslavs: 50d, Antun Gustav Matos, poet. 60d, Ivan Mazuranic, writer. 85d, Fran Levstik, writer. 200d, Josif Pancic, physician and botanist. 500d, Dimitrije Tucovic, political writer.

1965, Nov. 28			Engr.

Variously Toned Paper

790	A194 30d dull red	.25	.25
791	A194 50d indigo	.25	.25
792	A194 60d brown	.25	.25
793	A194 85d dark blue	.25	.25
794	A194 200d dk olive grn	.25	.25
795	A194 500d deep claret	.60	.45
	Nos. 790-795 (6)	1.85	1.70

1966, Feb. 4		Litho.	Perf. 12½
796	A195 20p bluish grn	.40	.25
797	A195 30p rose pink	.55	.25

Exists imperf.

Rowing A196

30p, Long jump. 50p, Ice hockey. 3d, Hockey sticks, puck. 5d, Oars, scull.

1966, Mar. 1			Engr.
798	A196 30p dk car rose	.25	.25
799	A196 50p dk purple	.25	.25
800	A196 1d gray green	.25	.25
801	A196 3d dk red brn	1.75	1.75
802	A196 5d dark blue	1.75	1.75
	Nos. 798-802 (5)	4.25	4.25

25th Balkan Games; World ice hockey championship; 2nd rowing championships.

"T" from 15th Century Psalter — A197   Radio Amateurs' Emblem — A198

Art through the Centuries (Initials from Medieval Manuscripts): 50p, Cyrillic "V," Divosh Evangel, 14th cent. 60p, "R," Gregorius I, Libri moralium, 12th cent. 85p, Cyrillic "P," Miroslav Evangel, 12th cent. 2d, Cyrillic "B," Radomir Evangel, 13th cent. 5d, "F," Passional, 11th cent.

1966, Apr. 25		Photo.	Perf. 12
803	A197 30p multicolored	.25	.25
804	A197 50p multicolored	.25	.25
805	A197 60p multicolored	.25	.25
806	A197 85p multicolored	.25	.25

807 A197 2d multicolored   .25   .25
808 A197 5d multicolored   .80   .40
    Nos. 803-808 (6)   2.05 1.65

1966, May 23   Engr.   Perf. 12½x12
809 A198 85p dark blue   2.50 1.20
Union of Yugoslav Radio Amateurs, 20th
anniv.; Intl. Congress of Radio Amateurs,
Opatija, 5/23-28.

Stag
Beetle — A199

Serbia No. 2,
1866 — A200

Beetles: 50p, Floral beetle. 60p, Oil beetle.
85p, Ladybird. 2d, Rosalia alpina. 5d, Aquatic
beetle.

1966, May 25   Photo.   Perf. 12x12½
810 A199 30p gray, blk & bis   .30   .25
811 A199 50p gray, emer & blk   .30   .25
812 A199 60p bluish blk, sl grn &
                gray   .30   .25
813 A199 85p dl org, dp org &
                black   .30   .25
814 A199 2d gray, ultra & blk   .30   .25
815 A199 5d tan, brn & blk   .55   .25
    Nos. 810-815 (6)   2.05 1.50

Litho. & Engr.

1966, June 25   Perf. 12½
816 A200 30p shown   .25   .25
817 A200 50p No. 3   .25   .25
818 A200 60p No. 4   .25   .25
819 A200 85p No. 5   .25   .25
820 A200 2d No. 6   .45   .35
    Nos. 816-820 (5)   1.45 1.35

Souvenir Sheet

Imperf
821 A200 10d No. 1   2.00 2.00
Serbia's first postage stamps, cent.

Leather Shield
with Farmer,
Soldier and
Woman — A201

1966, July 2   Perf. 12½
822 A201 20p pale grn, gold &
                red brown   .25   .25
823 A201 30p buff, gold & dp
                mag   .25   .25
824 A201 85p lt gray, gold &
                Prus bl   .25   .25
825 A201 2d lt bl, gold & vio   .25   .25
    Nos. 822-825 (4)   1.00 1.00
25th anniversary of National Revolution.

Bishop
Strossmayer and
Franjo
Racki — A202

1966, July 15
826 A202 30p dl ol, blk & buff   .25   .25
Centenary of Academy of Arts and Sciences, founded by Bishop Josip Juraj Strossmayer with Racki as first president.

Mostar Bridge,
Neretva
River — A203

1966, Sept. 24   Engr.   Perf. 12½
827 A203 30p rose claret   4.00 1.60
400th anniversary of Mostar Bridge.

Medieval
View of
Sibenik
A204

1966, Sept. 24
828 A204 30p deep plum   .25   .25
900th anniversary of Sibenik.

Girl
A205

Shipbuilding
A206

1966, Oct. 2   Litho.
829 A205 30p ultra, org, red &
                blk   1.50 1.50
Issued for Children's Week.

1966   Engr.   Perf. 12½
Designs: 10p, Sisak steel works. 15p, Overpass. 20p, Jablonica hydroelectric works. 30p,
Litostroy turbine factory. 40p, Lukavac coke
factory. 50p, Zenica steel works. 60p, Cable
factory, Svetozarevo. 65p, Sevojno copper
works. 85p, Lumber industry. 1d, Crude oil
production.

830 A206 5p dull orange   1.00 1.00
831 A206 10p brown   1.00 1.00
832 A206 15p vio blue   1.00 1.00
833 A206 20p emerald   .25   .25
834 A206 30p vermilion   .75   .25
835 A206 40p dp claret   1.00 1.00
836 A206 50p gray blue   1.00 1.00
837 A206 60p red brown   1.00 1.00
838 A206 65p green   1.00 1.00
839 A206 85p dl purple   1.00 1.00
840 A206 1d yel olive   2.00 2.00
    Nos. 830-840 (11)   11.00 10.50

Iooud: 5, 15p, 6/10; 10, 40, 50p, 6/8; 20,
30p, 4/28; 60, 65, 85p, 5/12; 1d, 6/18.
Nos. 830, 832 and 840 exist imperf.
For surcharge see No. 1322.

UNESCO
Emblem — A207

Santa
Claus — A208

1966, Nov. 4   Litho.
841 A207 85p violet blue   .25   .25
20th anniversary of UNESCO.

1966, Nov. 25   Litho.   Perf. 12½
Designs: 15p, Stylized winter landscape.
30p, Stylized Christmas tree.

842 A208 15p org & dk bl   .25   .25
843 A208 20p org & purple   .25   .25
844 A208 30p org & sl grn   .25   .25

1966, Dec. 23   Photo.   Perf. 12½
845 A208 15p gold & dk bl   .30   .25
846 A208 20p gold & red   .30   .25
847 A208 30p gold & green   .30   .25
    Nos. 842-847 (6)   1.65 1.50
Nos. 842-847 issued for New Year, 1967.

Wolf's Head
Coin of Durad
I, 1373 — A209

Medieval Coins: 50p, ½d of King Stefan, c.
1461 (arms of Bosnia). 60d, Dinar of Serbia
(portrait of Durad Brankovic). 85p, Dinar of
Ljubljana, c. 1250 (heraldic eagle). 2d, Dinar
of Split, c. 1403-1413 (shield with arms of
Duke Hrvoje Vukcic). 5d, Dinar of Emperor
Stefan Dusan, c. 1346-1355 (Emperor on
horseback).

1966, Nov. 28   Photo.
Coins in Silver, Gray and Black
848 A209 30p ver & blk   .25   .25
849 A209 50p ultra & blk   .25   .25
850 A209 60p magenta & blk   .25   .25
851 A209 85p violet & blk   .25   .25
852 A209 2d dk ol bis & blk   .25   .25
853 A209 5d brt grn & blk   .55   .35
    Nos. 848-853 (6)   1.80 1.60

Medicinal
Plants — A210

Marshal
Tito — A211

1967, May 25   Photo.   Perf. 11½
Granite Paper
854 A210 30p Arnica   .25   .25
855 A210 50p Flax   .25   .25
856 A210 85p Oleander   .25   .25
857 A210 1.20d Gentian   .25   .25
858 A210 3d Laurel   .25   .25
859 A210 5d African rue   .80   .80
    Nos. 854-859 (6)   2.05 2.05
Youth Day, May 25.

1967, May 25   Engr.   Perf. 12½
Size: 20x27½mm
860 A211 5p orange   .25   .25
861 A211 10p dk red brown   .25   .25
862 A211 15p dk vio blue   .25   .25
863 A211 20p green   .25   .25
864 A211 30p vermilion   .25   .25
865 A211 40p black   .25   .25
866 A211 50p Prussian grn   .25   .25
867 A211 60p lilac   .25   .25
868 A211 85p deep blue   .25   .25
869 A211 1d plum   .25   .25
    Nos. 860-869 (10)   2.50 2.50
75th birthday of Pres. Tito. Sheets of 15.
Nos. 860-869 were reissued in 1967 with
slight differences including thinner paper and
slightly darker shades.
See #924-939. For surcharge see #1414.

Coil Stamps
1968-69   Photo.   Perf. 12½ Horiz.
869A A211 20p green   .30   .25
869B A211 30p vermilion   .40   .25
869C A211 50p vermilion ('69)   .30   .25
    Nos. 869A-869C (3)   1.00   .75

EXPO Emblem,
Sputnik 1 and
Explorer 1 — A212

ITY Emblem, St.
Tripun's Church,
Kotor — A213

Spacecraft: 50p, Tiros, Telstar and Molniya.
85p, Luna 9 and lunar satellite. 1.20d, Mariner
4, and Venus 3. 3d, Vostok, Gemini and
Agena Rocket. 5d, Astronaut walking in
space.

1967, June 26   Photo.   Perf. 11½
870 A212 30p ultra & multi   .25   .25
871 A212 50p yel & multi   .25   .25
872 A212 85p slate & multi   .25   .25
873 A212 1.20d multicolored   .25   .25
874 A212 3d vio & multi   .25   .25
875 A212 5d blue & multi   2.75 2.75
    Nos. 870-875 (6)   4.00 4.00
EXPO '67, Montreal, Apr. 28-Oct. 27; 18th
Congress of the Intl. Astronautical Federation,
Belgrade. Exist imperf.

1967, July 17   Engr.
Designs (ITY Emblem and): 50p, Municipal
Building, Maribor. 85p, Cathedral, Trogir.
1.20d, Fortress gate, Nis. 3d, Drina Bridge,
Visegrad. 5d, Daut-pasha's Bath, Skopje.

876 A213 30p slate bl & lt ol   .25   .25
877 A213 50p brn & dl vio   .25   .25
878 A213 85p dk bl & dp claret   .25   .25
879 A213 1.20d dp claret & brn   .25   .25
880 A213 3d brn & slate grn   .35   .25
881 A213 5d slate grn & brn   3.00   .45
    Nos. 876-881 (6)   4.35 1.70
Issued for International Tourist Year, 1967.

Partridge — A214

1967, Sept. 22   Photo.   Perf. 14
882 A214 30p shown   .30   .30
883 A214 50p Pike   .30   .30
884 A214 1.20d Red deer   .50   .50
885 A214 5d Peregrine falcon   1.25 1.25
    Nos. 882-885 (4)   2.35 2.35
Intl. Fishing and Hunting Exposition and
Fair, Novi Sad.

Congress
Emblem with
Sputnik 1
A215

Litho. & Engr.
1967, Sept. 25   Perf. 12½
886 A215 85p dk bl, lt bl & gold .25   .25
18th Congress of the Intl. Astronautical Federation, Belgrade, Sept. 25-30.

Old Theater and
Castle,
Ljubljana — A216

1967, Sept. 29   Engr.   Perf. 12½
887 A216 30p sepia & dk grn   .25   .25
Centenary of Slovene National Theater.

Child's Drawing:
Winter
Scene — A217

1967, Oct. 2   Litho.
888 A217 30p multicolored   .50   .25
International Children's Week, Oct. 2-8.

Lenin by Mestrovic
A218

4-Leaf Clover
A219

1967, Nov. 7   Engr.   Perf. 12½
889 A218 30p dark purple .25 .25
890 A218 85p olive gray .25 .25

Souvenir Sheet
Imperf
891 A218 10d magenta 8.00 8.00

Russian October Revolution, 50th anniv.
Nos. 889-890 exist imperf.

1967, Nov. 15   Photo.   Perf. 14
30p, Chimney sweep. 50p, Horseshoe & flower.

Dated "1968"
892 A219 20p shown .25 .25
893 A219 30p Chimney sweep .25 .25
894 A219 50p Horseshoe, flower .25 .25
        Nos. 892-894 (3) .75 .75

New Year 1968. See Nos. 957-959.

The Young Sultana, by Vlaho
Bucovac — A220

Paintings: 85p, The Watchtower, by Dura Jaksic. 2d, Visit to the Family, by Josip Petkovsek. 3d, The Cock Fight, by Paja Jovanovic. 5d, "Spring" (woman and children), by Ivana Kobilca.

Perf. 11½x12, 12x11½
1967, Nov. 28   Engr. & Litho.
895 A220 85p multi, vert. 1.50 .35
896 A220 1d multi 1.50 .35
897 A220 2d multi 1.50 .35
898 A220 3d multi 1.50 .35
899 A220 5d multi, vert. 6.00 3.00
        Nos. 895-899 (5) 12.00 4.40

Issued for the Day of the Republic, Nov. 29.
See Nos. 942-946, 995-1000.

Ski Jump — A221

Sport: 1d, Figure skating pair. 2d, Downhill skiing. 5d, Ice hockey.

1968, Feb. 5   Engr.   Perf. 12½
900 A221 50p dk bl & dk pur .40 .25
901 A221 1d brn & sl green .40 .25
902 A221 2d sl grn & lake .70 .40
903 A221 5d sl grn & dk bl 5.50 3.00
        Nos. 900-903 (4) 7.00 3.90

10th Winter Olympic Games, Grenoble, France, Feb. 6-18.

Annunciation
A222

Medieval Icons: 50p, Madonna, St. George's Church, Prizren. 1.50d, St. Sava and St. Simeon. 2d, Christ's descent into hell, Ohrid. 3d, Crucifixion, St. Clement's Church, Ohrid. 5d, Madonna, Church of Our Lady of the Bell Tower, Split.

1968, Apr. 20   Photo.   Perf. 13½
906 A222 50p gold & multi .25 .25
907 A222 1d gold & multi .25 .25
908 A222 1.50d gold & multi .25 .25
909 A222 2d gold & multi .35 .25
910 A222 3d gold & multi .50 .40
911 A222 5d gold & multi 1.10 1.00
        Nos. 906-911 (6) 2.70 2.40

European
Bullfinch — A223

800-meter Race for
Women — A224

Finches: 1d, Goldfinch. 1.50d, Chaffinch. 2d, European greenfinch. 3d, Red crossbill. 5d, Hawfinch.

1968, May 25   Photo.   Perf. 11½
Birds in Natural Colors
912 A223 50p bister .40 .40
913 A223 1d rose lake .40 .40
914 A223 1.50d gray blue .40 .40
915 A223 2d deep orange .40 .40
916 A223 3d olive green .45 .45
917 A223 5d pale violet 6.50 3.25
        Nos. 912-917 (6) 8.55 5.30

Issued for Youth Day. Exist imperf.

Litho. & Engr.
1968, June 28   Perf. 12½

1d, Basketball. 1.50d, Gymnast on vaulting horse. 2d, Rowing. 3d, Water polo. 5d, Wrestling.

918 A224 50p dk brn & dk red
                brown .40 .40
919 A224 1d Prus bl & blk .40 .40
920 A224 1.50d slate & dk brn .40 .40
921 A224 2d bis & sl grn 1.50 .40
922 A224 3d blk brn & ind 1.50 .40
923 A224 5d dk grn & vio blk 16.00 5.00
        Nos. 918-923 (6) 20.20 7.00

19th Olympic Games, Mexico City, 10/12-27.

Tito Type of 1967
1968-72   Engr.   Perf. 12½
Size: 20x27½mm
924 A211 20p dark blue 1.25 .25
925 A211 25p lake .25 .25
926 A211 30p green .25 .25
927 A211 50p vermilion .75 .25
928 A211 70p black .30 .25
929 A211 75p slate grn .40 .25
930 A211 80p olive 2.00 .25
930A A211 80p red org ('72) .40 .25
931 A211 90p olive .30 .25
932 A211 1.20d dark blue .50 .25
932A A211 1.20d sl grn ('72) .40 .25
933 A211 1.25d deep blue .40 .25
934 A211 1.50d slate grn .40 .25

Size: 20x30½mm
935 A211 2d sepia 2.50 .25
936 A211 2.50d Prussian grn 1.60 .25
937 A211 5d deep plum 1.40 .25
938 A211 10d violet blk 3.00 .35
939 A211 20d bluish black 4.25 .45
        Nos. 924-939 (18) 20.20 4.80

The shading of the background of Nos. 924-939 has been changed from the 1967 issue to intensify the contrast around the portrait.

Cannon and
Laurel
Wreath — A225

1968, Aug. 2   Photo.   Perf. 12½
940 A225 50p org brn & gold .25 .25

65th anniversary of the Ilinden uprising.

Mother Nursing
Twins, Fresco by
Jan of
Kastav — A226

1968, Sept. 9   Litho.
941 A226 50p black & multi .25 .25

Annexation of Istria and the Slovene Coast to Yugoslavia, 25th anniv. Exists imperf.

Painting Type of 1967

Paintings: 1d, Lake Klansko, by Marko Pernhart. 1.50d, Bavarian Landscape, by Milan Popovic. 2d, Porta Terraferma, Zadar, by Ferdo Quiquerez. 3d, Mt. Triglav seen from Bohinj, by Anton Karinger. 5d, Studenica Monastery, by Djordje Krstic.

Engr. & Litho.
1968, Oct. 3   Perf. 14x13½
942 A220 1d gold & multi .25 .25
943 A220 1.50d gold & multi .25 .25
944 A220 2d gold & multi .25 .25
945 A220 3d gold & multi .30 .25
946 A220 5d gold & multi 2.40 .70
        Nos. 942-946 (5) 3.45 1.70

Exist imperf.

Aleksa Santic
(1868-1924),
Poet — A227

1968, Oct. 5   Engr.   Perf. 12½
947 A227 50p dark blue .25 .25

"Going for a
Walk" — A228

1968, Oct. 6   Litho.
948 A228 50p multicolored .25 .25

Issued for Children's Week.

Karl Marx (1818-
1883), by N.
Mitric — A229

1968, Oct. 11   Engr.
949 A229 50d dk car rose .25 .25

Old Theater and
Belgrade
Castle — A230

1968, Nov. 22   Engr.   Perf. 12½
950 A230 50p ol brn & sl grn .25 .25

Serbian National Theater, Belgrade, cent.

Hasan
Brkic — A231

Portraits: 75p, Ivan Milutinovic. 1.25d, Rade Koncar. 2d, Kuzman Josifovski. 2.50d, Tone Tomsic. 5d, Mosa Pijade.

1968, Nov. 28   Engr.   Perf. 12½
951 A231 50p violet black .25 .25
952 A231 75p black .25 .25
953 A231 1.25d red brown .25 .25
    a. Souv. sheet, 2 ea #951-953 15.00 15.00
954 A231 2d bluish black .25 .25
955 A231 2.50d slate green .25 .25
956 A231 5d claret 1.25 .50
    a. Souv. sheet, 2 ea #954-956 15.00 15.00
        Nos. 951-956 (6) 2.50 1.75

2nd Assembly of the National Republic of Yugoslavia, 25th anniv.
No. 954 exists imperf. Value $100.
Nos. 953a and 956a exist imperf.

New Year's Type of 1967
1968, Nov. 25   Photo.   Perf. 14
Dated "1969"
957 A219 20p Four-leaf clover .25 .25
958 A219 30p Chimney sweep .25 .25
959 A219 50p Horseshoe, flower .25 .25
        Nos. 957-959 (3) .75 .75

Issued for New Year 1969.

The Family, by J.
Soldatovic
A232

1968, Dec. 10   Engr.   Perf. 12½
960 A232 1.25d dark blue .25 .25

International Human Rights Year.

ILO
Emblem — A233

Litho. & Engr.
1969, Jan. 27   Perf. 12½
961 A233 1.25d red & black .25 .25

ILO, 50th anniv.

Dove, Hammer and Sickle Emblem — A234

75p, Graffiti "TITO" & 5-pointed star. 1.25d, 5-pointed crystal. 10d, Marshal Tito in 1943.

Engr. & Photo.

1969, Mar. 11			**Perf. 12½**	
962	A234	50p black & red	.25	.25
963	A234	75p ol bis & blk	.25	.25
964	A234	1.25d red & black	.25	.25
		Nos. 962-964 (3)	.75	.75

Souvenir Sheet

964A		Sheet of 9	9.00 9.00
b.	A234 10d brown, engr.		5.00 5.00

Communist Federation of Yugoslavia, 50th anniv.; 9th party congress.
#964A contains 4 #962, 2 each #963-964, 964b.
Nos. 962-964A exist imperf.

St. Nikita, from Manasija Monastery A235

Frescoes from Monasteries: 75p, Apostles, Zakopani. 1.25d, Crucifixion, Studenica. 2d, Wedding at Cana, Kalenic. 3d, Angel at the Grave, Milseva. 5d, Pieta, Nerezi.

1969, Apr. 7		**Photo.**	**Perf. 13½**	
965	A235	50p gold & multi	.25	.25
966	A235	75p gold & multi	.25	.25
967	A235	1.25d gold & multi	.25	.25
968	A235	2d gold & multi	.25	.25
969	A235	3d gold & multi	.45	.45
970	A235	5d gold & multi	2.00	.90
		Nos. 965-970 (6)	3.45	2.35

Roman Memorial and View of Ptuj A236

1969, Apr. 23		**Engr.**	**Perf. 11½**	
971	A236	50p violet brown	.25	.25

1900th anniv. of Ptuj, the Roman Petovio. Issued in sheets of 9 (3x3).

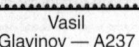

Vasil Glavinov — A237   Thin-leafed Peony — A238

1969, May 8			**Perf. 12x12½**	
972	A237	50p ocher & rose lilac	.25	.25

Vasil Glavinov, Macedonian socialist, birth cent. Issued in sheets of 9 (3x3).

1969, May 25   Photo.   Perf. 11½

Medicinal Plants: 75p, Coltsfoot. 1.25d, Primrose. 2d, Hellebore. 2.50d, Violets. 5d, Anemones.

Flowers in Natural Colors

973	A238	50p yellow brn	.25	.25
974	A238	75p dull purple	.25	.25
975	A238	1.25d blue	.25	.25
976	A238	2d brown	.25	.25

977	A238	2.50d plum	.25	.25
978	A238	5d green	2.75	2.75
		Nos. 973-978 (6)	4.00	4.00

Exist imperf.
See Nos. 1056-1061, 1140-1145.

Eber, by Vasa Ivankovic — A239

Paintings of Sailing Ships: 1.25d, Tare, by Franasovic. 1.50d, Brig Sela, by Vasa Ivankovic. 2.50d, Dubrovnik galleon, 16th century. 3.25d, Madre Mimbelli, by Antoine Roux. 5d, The Virgin Saving Seamen from Disaster, 16th century ikon.

1969, July 10		**Photo.**	**Perf. 11½**	
979	A239	50p gold & multi	.25	.25
980	A239	1.25d gold & multi	.25	.25
981	A239	1.50d gold & multi	.25	.25
982	A239	2.50d gold & multi	.25	.25
983	A239	3.25d gold & multi	.25	.25
984	A239	5d gold & multi	2.00	2.00
		Nos. 979-984 (6)	3.25	3.25

Dubrovnik Summer Festival, 20th anniv. Exist imperf.

11th World Games for the Deaf, Belgrade, Aug. 9-16 — A240

1969, Aug. 9		**Engr.**	**Perf. 12½**	
985	A240	1.25d dp claret & dl vio	.40	.25

Lipice Horse A241

Horses: 75p, Bosnian mountain horse. 3.25d, Ljutomer trotter. 5d, Half-breed.

1969, Sept. 26		**Photo.**	**Perf. 11½**	
986	A241	75p multicolored	.25	.25
987	A241	1.25d olive & multi	.25	.25
988	A241	3.25d brn & multi	.30	.25
989	A241	5d multicolored	3.00	1.50
		Nos. 986-989 (4)	3.80	2.25

Zagreb Veterinary College, 50th anniv. Exist imperf.

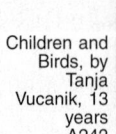

Children and Birds, by Tanja Vucanik, 13 years A242

1969, Oct. 5		**Litho.**	**Perf. 12½**	
990	A242	50p org, blk & gray	.25	.25

Issued for Children's Week.

Arms of Belgrade — A243

Arms: #992, Skopje (bridge & mountain). #993, Titograd (bridge & fortifications).

1969		**Litho.**	**Perf. 12½**	
991	A243	50p gold & multi	.25	.25
992	A243	50p gold & multi	.25	.25
993	A243	50p gold & multi	.25	.25
		Nos. 991-993 (3)	.75	.75

Liberation of capitals of the Federated Republics, 25th anniv. See Nos. 1017-1020.

Josip Smodlaka A244

1969, Nov. 9			**Engr.**	
994	A244	50p dark blue	.25	.25

Smodlaka (1869-1956), leader in Yugoslavia's fight for independence.

Painting Type of 1967

Paintings of Nudes: 50p, The Little Gypsy with the Rose, by Nikola Martinoski. 1.25d, Girl on a Red Chair, by Sava Sumanovic. 1.50d, Woman Combing her Hair, by Marin Tartaglia. 2.50d, Olympia, by Miroslav Kraljevic. 3.25d, The Bather, by Jovan Bijelic. 5d, Woman on a Couch, by Matej Sternen.

Photo. & Engr.

1969, Nov. 29			**Perf. 13½**	
995	A220	50p multi, vert.	.25	.25
996	A220	1.25d multi, vert.	.25	.25
997	A220	1.50d multi, vert.	.25	.25
998	A220	2.50d multi	.30	.30
999	A220	3.25d multi, vert.	.40	.40
1000	A220	5d multi	2.50	2.50
		Nos. 995-1000 (6)	3.95	3.95

Exist imperf.

University of Ljubljana, 50th Anniv. A245

1969, Dec. 9		**Engr.**	**Perf. 11½**	
1001	A245	50p slate grn	.25	.25

Seal of Zagreb University A246

Photo. & Engr.

1969, Dec. 17			**Perf. 12½**	
1002	A246	50p gold, bl & brn	.25	.25

University of Zagreb, 300th anniv.

Common Design Types pictured following the introduction.

Europa Issue, 1969
Common Design Type

1969, Dec. 20		**Photo.**	**Perf. 11½**	
1003	CD12	1.25d grnsh gray, buff & brn	1.25	1.25
1004	CD12	3.25d rose lil, gray & dk bl	2.75	2.75

Yugoslavia's admission to CEPT. Exist imperf.

Jovan Cvijic, Geographer A247

Famous Yugoslavs: 1.25d, Dr. Andrija Stampar, hygienist. 1.50d, Joakim Krcovski, author. 2.50d, Marko Miljanov, Montenegrin patriot-hero. 3.25d, Vaca Pelagic, socialist. 5d, Oton Zupancic, Slovenian poet.

1970, Feb. 16		**Engr.**	**Perf. 12½**	
1005	A247	50p reddish brn	.25	.25
1006	A247	1.25d brnsh black	.25	.25
1007	A247	1.50d lilac	.25	.25
1008	A247	2.50d slate grn	.25	.25
1009	A247	3.25d reddish brn	.25	.25
1010	A247	5d blue vio	.25	.25
		Nos. 1005-1010 (6)	1.50	1.50

Punishment of Dirce, Pulj — A248

Mosaics from the 1st-4th Centuries: 1.25d, Cerberus, Bitola, horiz. 1.50d, Angel of the Annunciation, Porec. 2.50d, Hunters, Gamzigard. 3.25d, Bull and cherry tree, horiz. 5d, Virgin and Child enthroned, Porec.

1970, Mar. 16		**Photo.**	**Perf. 13½**	
1011	A248	50p gold & multi	.25	.25
1012	A248	1.25d gold & multi	.25	.25
1013	A248	1.50d gold & multi	.25	.25
1014	A248	2.50d gold & multi	.30	.25
1015	A248	3.25d gold & multi	.55	.35
1016	A248	5d gold & multi	1.50	1.50
		Nos. 1011-1016 (6)	3.10	2.85

Exist imperf.

Arms Type of 1969

#1017, Sarajevo (arcade). #1018, Zagreb (castle). #1019, Ljubljana (dragon and tower). #1020a, Yugoslavia (embossed coat of arms.)

1970		**Litho.**	**Perf. 12½**	
1017	A243	50p gold & multi	.25	.25
1018	A243	50p gold & multi	.25	.25
1019	A243	50p gold & multi	.25	.25
		Nos. 1017-1019 (3)	.75	.75

Souvenir Sheet

1020		Sheet of 7	15.00 15.00
a.	A243 12d gold & black		12.50 12.50

Liberation of Yugoslavia, 25th anniv. No. 1020 contains Nos. 991-993, 1017-1019, 1020a + 2 labels.
Issued: #1017, Apr. 6; #1018, May 8; #1019, May 9; #1020, May 15.

Lenin (1870-1924), by S. Stojanovic A249

Design: 1.25d, Lenin sculpture facing left.

1970, Apr. 22			**Engr.**	
1021	A249	50p rose lilac	.25	.25
1022	A249	1.25d blue gray	.25	.25

Basketball
A250

1970, Apr. 25
1023 A250 1.25d plum   .25 .25
6th World Basketball Championships, Ljubljana, May 10-23.
Exists imperf.

Europa Issue, 1970
Common Design Type
1970, May 4   **Photo.**   *Perf. 11½*
Size: 32½x23mm
1024 CD13 1.25d lt bl, dk bl & lt grnsh bl   .40 .40
1025 CD13 3.25d rose lil, plum & gray   .40 .40
Exist imperf.

Istrian Shorthaired Hound
A251

Yugoslav Breeds of Dogs: 1.25d, Yugoslav tricolor hound. 1.50d, Istrian hard-haired hound. 2.50d, Balkan hound. 3.25d, Dalmatian. 5d, Shara mountain dog.

1970, May 25   **Photo.**   *Perf. 11½*
Granite Paper
1026 A251 50p tan & multi   .25 .25
1027 A251 1.25d olive & multi   .25 .25
1028 A251 1.50d violet & multi   .25 .25
1029 A251 2.50d slate & multi   .25 .25
1030 A251 3.25d multi   .45 .25
1031 A251 5d multi   2.00 2.00
Nos. 1026-1031 (6)   3.45 3.25
Exist imperf.

Telegraph Circuit — A252

1970, June 20   **Litho.**   *Perf. 12½*
1032 A252 50p henna brn, gold & blk   .25 .25
Telegraph service in Montenegro, cent.

Bird — A253

1970, Oct. 5
1033 A253 50p multicolored   .25 .25
Issued for Children's Week, Oct. 5-11.

Stylized Gymnast — A254

1970, Oct. 22   **Engr.**
1034 A254 1.25d car & slate   .25 .25
17th World Gymnastics Championships, Ljubljana, Oct. 22-27.

UN Emblem and Hand Holding Dove, by Makoto A255

Litho. & Engr.
1970, Oct. 24   *Perf. 11½*
1035 A255 1.25d dk brn, blk & gold .25 .25
25th anniversary of the United Nations.

Ascension, by Teodor D. Kracum A256

Baroque Paintings: 75p, Abraham's Sacrifice, by Federiko Benkovic. 1.25d, Holy Family, by Francisek Jelovsek. 2.50d, Jacob's Ladder, by Hristofor Zefarovic. 3.25d, Baptism of Christ, by unknown Serbian painter. 5.75d, The Coronation of Mary, by Tripo Kokolja.

Engr. & Photo.
1970, Nov. 28   *Perf. 13½x14*
1036 A256 50p gold & multi   .25 .25
1037 A256 75p gold & multi   .25 .25
1038 A256 1.25d gold & multi   .25 .25
1039 A256 2.50d gold & multi   .25 .25
1040 A256 3.25d gold & multi   .45 .25
1041 A256 5.75d gold & multi   .75 .70
Nos. 1036-1041 (6)   2.20 1.95
Exist imperf.

Alpine Rhododendron — A257

European Nature Protection Year emblem and: 3.25d, Bearded vulture.

1970, Dec. 14   **Photo.**   *Perf. 11½*
1042 A257 1.25d multi   3.00 3.00
1043 A257 3.25d multi   10.00 10.00
Sheets of 9.

Frano Supilo — A258

Litho. & Engr.
1971, Jan. 25   *Perf. 12½*
1044 A258 50p black & buff   .25 .25
Supilo (1870-1917), Croat leader for independence from Austria-Hungary. Sheets of 9.

British, French, Canadian, Italian Satellites A259

75p, Satellite. 1.25d, Automated moon exploration. 2.50d, Various spacecraft. 3.25d, 1st experimental space station. 5.75d, Astronauts on moon.

1971, Feb. 8   **Photo.**   *Perf. 13½*
1045 A259 50p multi   .25 .25
1046 A259 75p multi   .25 .25
1047 A259 1.25d multi   .25 .25
1048 A259 2.50d multi, horiz.   .25 .25
1049 A259 3.25d multi, horiz.   .25 .25
1050 A259 5.75d multi, horiz.   1.10 1.10
Nos. 1045-1050 (6)   2.35 2.35
"Space in the service of science." Sheets of 9.

Proclamation of the Commune, Town Hall, Paris — A260

Litho. & Engr.
1971, Mar. 18   *Perf. 11½*
1051 A260 1.25d bis brn & gray brn .25 .25
Centenary of the Paris Commune. Exist imperf.

Europa Issue, 1971
Common Design Type
1971, May 4   **Photo.**   *Perf. 11½*
Size: 33x23mm
1052 CD14 1.50d Prus bl, pale grn & dk bl   .25 .25
1053 CD14 4d mag, pink & dk mag   .25 .25
Exist imperf.

Circles — A261

1971, May 5   *Perf. 13½*
1054 A261 50p shown   .50 .25
1055 A261 1.25d 20 circles   1.40 .70
2nd Congress of Managers of Autonomous States.

Flower Type of 1969
Medicinal Plants: 50p, Common mallow. 1.50d, Common buckthorn. 2d, Water lily. 2.50d, Poppy. 4d, Wild chicory. 6d, Physalis.

1971, May 25   **Photo.**   *Perf. 11½*
Flowers in Natural Colors
1056 A238 50p lt ultra   .25 .25
1057 A238 1.50d olive bis   .25 .25
1058 A238 2d dull blue   .25 .25
1059 A238 2.50d dark car   .30 .25
1060 A238 4d dp bister   .65 .65
1061 A238 6d org brown   4.00 4.00
Nos. 1056-1061 (6)   5.70 5.65
Exist imperf.

Prince Lazar, Fresco, Lazarica Church — A262

1971, June 28   **Photo.**   *Perf. 13½*
1062 A262 50p gray & multi   .25 .25
600th anniversary of founding of Krusevac by Prince Lazar Hrebeljanovic (1329-1389).

View of Krk — A263

Views: 5p, Krusevo. 10p, Castle & mosque, Gradacac. 20p, Church & bridge, Bohinj. 35p, Shore & mountains, Omis. 40p, Peje. 50p, Memorial column, Krusevac. 60p, Logar Valley. 75p, Bridge & church, Bohinj. 80p, Church, Piran. 1d, Street, Bitolj. 1.20d, Minaret, Pocitelj. 1.25d, 1.50d, Gate tower, Hercegnovi. 2d, Cathedral & City Hall Square, Novi Sad. 2.50d, Crna River.

1971-73   **Engr.**   *Perf. 13*
1063 A263 5p orange ('73)   .25 .25
1064 A263 10p brown ('72)   .25 .25
1065 A263 20p vio blk ('73)   .25 .25
1066 A263 30p ol gray ('72)   .25 .25
    a.   30p green   1.00 .25
1067 A263 35p brn car ('73)   .25 .25
1068 A263 40p black ('72)   .25 .25
1069 A263 50p vermilion   1.50 .25
1070 A263 50p green ('72)   .25 .25
1071 A263 60p purple ('72)   .25 .25
1072 A263 75p slate green   .25 .25
1073 A263 80p rose red ('72)   1.50 .25
1073A A263 1d violet brn   1.50 .45
1073B A263 1.20d sl grn ('72)   2.00 .25
1073C A263 1.25d deep blue   1.10 .25
1073D A263 1.50d bluish blk ('73)   .25 .25
1073E A263 2d blue ('72)   1.00 .25
1073F A263 2.50d dl pur ('73)   1.00 .25
Nos. 1063-1073F (17)   12.10 4.45

Issued with and without fluorescent bars. See type A323. See Nos. 1482-1486, 1599-1600, 1602-1603, 1717. For surcharges see Nos. 1413, 1711-1712, 1765-1766, 1769.

Tourist Issue

Emperor Constantine, 4th Century — A264

Antique Bronzes excavated in Yugoslavia: 1.50d, Boy with fish. 2d, Hercules, replica after Lysippus. 2.50d, Satyr. 4d, Head of Aphrodite. 6d, Citizen of Emona, 1st century tomb.

1971, Sept. 20   **Photo.**   *Perf. 13½*
1074 A264 50p rose & multi   .25 .25
1075 A264 1.50d multicolored   .25 .25
1076 A264 2d multicolored   .25 .25
1077 A264 2.50d lem & multi   .25 .25

1078	A264	4d ocher & multi	.25	.25
1079	A264	6d multicolored	.25	.25
		Nos. 1074-1079 (6)	1.50	1.50

Sheets of 9.

UNICEF Emblem, Children in Balloon — A265

1971, Oct. 4 Litho. Perf. 13x13½

1080	A265	50p multicolored	.25	.25

Children's Week, Oct. 3-10.

Woman in Serbian Costume, by Katarina Ivanovic A266

Portraits, 19th Century: 1.50d, The Merchant Ivanisevic, by Anastasije Bocaric. 2d, Ana Kresic, by Vjekoslav Karas. 2.50d, Pavle Jagodic, by Konstantin Danil. 4r, Luiza Pesjakova, by Mihael Stroj. 6d, Old Man and view of Ljubljana, by Matevz Langus.

Engraved and Photogravure

1971, Nov. 29 Perf. 13½x14

1081	A266	50p gold & multi	.25	.25
1082	A266	1.50d gold & multi	.25	.25
1083	A266	2d gold & multi	.25	.25
1084	A266	2.50d gold & multi	.25	.25
1085	A266	4d gold & multi	.25	.25
1086	A266	6d gold & multi	.80	.80
		Nos. 1081-1086 (6)	2.05	2.05

See Nos. 1120-1125.

Letter with Postal Code, Map of Yugoslavia — A267

1971, Dec. 15 Photo. Perf. 13½x14

1087	A267	50p ultra & multi	.25	.25

Introduction of postal code system.

Damjan Gruev (1871-1906), Macedonian Revolutionist A268

1971, Dec. 22 Engr. Perf. 12½

1088	A268	50p dark blue	.25	.25

11th Winter Olympic Games, Sapporo, Japan, Feb. 3-13 A269

1972, Feb. 3 Perf. 11½

1089	A269	1.25d Speed skating	.25	.25
1090	A269	6d Slalom	2.50	1.25

Sheets of 9.

First Page of Statute of Dubrovnik A270

Lithographed and Engraved

1972, Mar. 15 Perf. 13½

1091	A270	1.25d gold & multi	.25	.25

700th anniversary of the Statute of Dubrovnik, a legal code given by Prince Marko Justiniani.

Ski Jump Track, Planica — A271

1972, Mar. 21 Perf. 11½

1092	A271	1.25d blk, lt bl & grn	.25	.25

World Ski Jump Championships, Planica, Mar. 22-26.

Water Polo and Olympic Rings — A272

1972, Apr. 17 Litho. Perf. 12½x12

1093	A272	50p shown	.25	.25
1094	A272	1.25d Basketball	.25	.25
1095	A272	2.50d Butterfly stroke	.25	.25
1096	A272	3.25d Boxing	.25	.25
1097	A272	5d Running	.25	.25
1098	A272	6.50d Yachting	.40	.40
		Nos. 1093-1098 (6)	1.65	1.65

20th Olympic Games, Munich, Aug. 26-Sept. 10. Sheets of 9.

Europa Issue 1972

Common Design Type

1972, May 4 Photo. Perf. 11½

1100	CD15	1.50d bl, grn & yel	.60	.60
1101	CD15	5d brt rose, mag & org	.60	.60

Wall Creeper — A275

Marshal Tito, by Bozidar Jakac — A276

Birds: 1.25d, Little bustard. 2.50d, Red-billed chough. 3.25d, Spoonbill. 5d, Eagle owl. 6.50d, Rock ptarmigan.

1972, May 8

Birds in Natural Colors

1102	A275	50p gray violet	.25	.25
1103	A275	1.25d ocher	.25	.25
1104	A275	2.50d gray olive	.25	.25
1105	A275	3.25d light plum	.35	.35
1106	A275	5d red brown	.65	.65
1107	A275	6.50d violet	2.50	2.50
		Nos. 1102-1107 (6)	4.25	4.25

Nature protection.

1972, May 25 Litho. Perf. 12½

1108	A276	50p cream & dk brn	.25	.25
1109	A276	1.25d gray & indigo	.50	.50

Souvenir Sheet

Imperf

1110	A276	10d gray & blk brn	2.75	2.75

80th birthday of Pres. Tito. Sheets of 9. No. 1110 printed in blocks of 4.

First Locomotive Built in Serbia, 1882 — A277

5d, Modern Yugoslavian electric locomotive.

1972, June 12 Photo. Perf. 11½

1111	A277	1.50d multicolored	.25	.25
1112	A277	5d multicolored	.80	.30

Intl. Railroad Union, 50th anniv. Exist imperf.

Glider A278

1972, July 8 Photo. Perf. 12½

1113	A278	2d bl gray, gold & blk	.25	.25

13th World Gliding Championships, Vrsac Airport, July 9-23. Sheets of 9. Exists imperf.

Pawn on Chessboard — A279

6d, Chessboard, emblems of King and Queen.

1972, Sept. 18 Perf. 11½

1114	A279	1.50d multi	.25	.25
1115	A279	6d multi	1.25	.70

20th Men's and 5th Women's Chess Olympiad, Skopje, Sept.-Oct. Sheets of 9.

Boy on Rocking Horse — A280

1972, Oct. 2 Litho. Perf. 12½

1116	A280	80p org & multi	.25	.25

Children's Week, Oct. 2-8.

Goce Delchev — A281

1972, Oct. 16 Perf. 13

1117	A281	80p yel grn & blk	.25	.25

Delchev (1872-1903), Macedonian freedom fighter.

Grga Martic, by Ivan Mestrovic A282

1972, Nov. 3 Perf. 12½

1118	A282	80p red, yel grn & blk	.25	.25

Brother Grga Martic (1822-1905), Franciscan administrator, educator and poet.

Serbian National Library, Belgrade A283

1972, Nov. 25 Engr. Perf. 11½x12

1119	A283	50p chocolate	.25	.25

140th anniversary of the Serbian National Library and opening of new building.

Painting Type of 1971

Still-Life Paintings: 50p, by Milos Tenkovic. 1.25d, by Jozef Pekovsek. 2.50d, by Katarina Jovanovic, horiz. 3.25d, by Konstantin Danil, horiz. 5d, by Nikola Masic. 6.50d, by Celestin Medovic, horiz.

Perf. 14x13½, 13½x14

1972, Nov. 28 Engr. & Photo.

1120	A266	50p gold & multi	.25	.25
1121	A266	1.25d gold & multi	.25	.25
1122	A266	2.50d gold & multi	.25	.25
1123	A266	3.25d gold & multi	.25	.25
1124	A266	5d gold & multi	.25	.25
1125	A266	6.50d gold & multi	.70	.50
		Nos. 1120-1125 (6)	1.95	1.75

Exist imperf.

Battle of Stubica, by Krsto Hegedusic — A284

6d, Battle of Krsko, by Gojmir Anton Kos.

1973, Jan. 29 Photo. Perf. 11½

1126	A284	2d gold & multi	.30	.25
1127	A284	6d gold & multi	1.25	.70

Croatian-Slovenian Rebellion, 400th anniv. (2d); Beginning of the peasant rebellions in Slovenia, 500th anniv. (6d). Sheets of 9.

Radoje
Domanovic
(1873-1908),
Serbian
Writer — A285

1973, Feb. 3   Litho.   Perf. 12½
1128 A285 80p tan & brn   .40 .25
Sheets of 9.

Skofja Loka
A286

1973, Feb. 15   Perf. 11½
1129 A286 80p brown & buff   .30 .25
Millennium of the founding of Skofja Loka.
Sheets of 9.

Novi Sad, by Peter
Demetrovic — A287

Old Engravings: 1.25d, Zagreb, by Josef
Szeman. 2.50d, Kotor, by Pierre Mortier.
3.25d, Belgrade, by Mancini. 5d, Split, by
Louis-Francois Cassas. 6.50d, Kranj, by Matthaus Merian.

Engraved and Photogravure
1973, Mar. 15   Perf. 13½
1130 A287 50p gold, buff & blk   .25 .25
1131 A287 1.25d gold, gray &
             black   .25 .25
1132 A287 2.50d gold & blk   .25 .25
1133 A287 3.25d gold & blk   .25 .25
1134 A287 5d gold, buff & blk   .25 .25
1135 A287 6.50d gold & blk   .25 .25
       Nos. 1130-1135 (6)   1.50 1.50

Nos. 1130-1131, 1133-1135 exist imperf.

Championship
Poster
A288

1973, Apr. 5   Litho.   Perf. 13½x13
1136 A288 2d multicolored   .40 .40
32nd Intl. Table Tennis Championships,
Sarajevo, Apr. 5-15. Sheets of 9.

Europa Issue, 1973
Common Design Type
1973, Apr. 30   Photo.   Perf. 11½
Size: 32½x23mm
1138 CD16 2d dk bl, lil & lt
             grn   .35 .30
1139 CD16 5.50d pur, cit & sal
             pink   .80 .80
       Sheets of 9.

Flower Type of 1969
Medicinal Plants: 80p, Birthwort. 2d, Globe
thistles. 3d, Olive branch. 4d, Corydalis. 5d,
Mistletoe. 6d, Comfrey.

1973, May 25   Photo.   Perf. 11½
Flowers in Natural Colors
1140 A238 80p orange & grn   .25 .25
1141 A238 2d dl bl & blue   .25 .25
1142 A238 3d olive & blk   .25 .25
1143 A238 4d yel grn & grn   .25 .25

1144 A238 5d org & sepia   .40 .40
1145 A238 6d lilac & grn   1.75 1.75
       Nos. 1140-1145 (6)   3.15 3.15

Anton Jansa
(1734-1773),
Teacher,
Apiculturist and
Bee — A291

1973, Aug. 25   Engr.   Perf. 12½
1147 A291 80p black   .40 .25
Sheets of 9.

Championship
Badge
A292

1973, Sept. 1   Litho.   Perf. 13½x13
1148 A292 2d multicolored   .30 .25
World water sport championships (swimming, water polo, water jumps, figure swimming), Belgrade, Sept. 1-9. Sheets of 9.

"Greeting the
Sun," by Ivan
Vucovic
A293

1973, Oct. 1   Perf. 12½
1149 A293 80p multicolored   1.20 .80
Children's Week, Oct. 1-7. Sheets of 9.

Post Horn — A294

Coil Stamps
1973-77   Photo.   Perf. 14½x14
1150 A294 30p brown   .25 .25
1151 A294 50p gray blue   .25 .25
1152 A294 80p rose red ('74)   .40 .25
1153 A294 1d yel grn ('77)   .40 .25
1154 A294 1.20d pink ('74)   .30 .25
1155 A294 1.50d rose ('77)   .40 .25
       Nos. 1150-1155 (6)   2.00 1.50

Juraj Dalmatinac,
Sculptor,
Architect, 500th
Anniv. of
Death — A295

1973, Oct. 8   Litho.   Perf. 12½
1158 A295 80p grnsh gray & ol
             blk   .25 .25
Sheets of 9.

Nadezda Petrovic (1873-1915), Self-
Portrait — A296

Lithographed and Engraved
1973, Oct. 12   Perf. 11½
1159 A296 2d gold & multi   .30 .25
Sheets of 9.

Interior, by Marko
Celebonovic — A297

Paintings of Interiors by Yugoslav artists:
2d, St. Duja, by Emanuel Vidovic. 3d, Room
with Slovak Woman, by Marino Tartaglia. 4d,
Painter with Easel, by Miljenko Stancic. 5d,
Studio, by Milan Konjovic. 6d, Tavern in Stara
Loka, by France Slana.

1973, Oct. 20   Photo.   Perf. 13½
1160 A297 80p gold & multi   .25 .25
1161 A297 2d gold & multi   .25 .25
1162 A297 3d gold & multi   .25 .25
1163 A297 4d gold & multi   .25 .25
1164 A297 5d gold & multi   .25 .25
1165 A297 6d gold & multi   .45 .40
       Nos. 1160-1165 (6)   1.70 1.65
       Sheets of 9.

Dragojlo Dudic — A298

Lithographed and Engraved
1973, Nov. 29   Perf. 12½
Gray and Indigo
1166 A298 80p shown   .25 .25
1167 A298 80p Strahil Pindzur   .25 .25
1168 A298 80p Boris Kidric   .25 .25
1169 A298 80p Radoje Dakic   .25 .25
Gray and Plum
1170 A298 2d Josip Mazar-
             Sosa   .25 .25
1171 A298 2d Zarko Zrenjanin   .25 .25
1172 A298 2d Emin Duraku   .25 .25
1173 A298 2d Ivan-Lola Ribar   .25 .25
   a. Sheet of 8, #1166-1173   2.00 2.00
Republic Day, Nov. 29, honoring national
heroes who perished during WWII.

Memorial, by   Winged Globe, by D.
O. Boljka,   Dzamonja, at
Ljubljana   Podgaric
A299   A300

Sculptures: 4.50d, Tower by D. Dzamonja,
at Kozara. 5d, Memorial, by B. Grabulovski, at
Belcista. 10d, Abstract, by M. Zivkovic, at
Sutjeska. 50d, Stone "V," by Zivkovic, at
Kragujevac.

1974   Engr.   Perf. 12½
1174 A299 3d slate grn   .65 .25
1175 A299 4.50d brn lake   1.00 .25
1176 A299 5d dark vio   .90 .25
   b. Perf. 13½   6.00 .40
1177 A300 10d slate grn   1.60 .40
1178 A300 20d dull pur   3.25 .25
1179 A300 50d indigo   4.00 1.00
       Nos. 1174-1179 (6)   11.40 2.40
       Exist imperf.

1978-82   Litho.
1176a A299 5d   2.25 .25
1177a A300 10d ('81)   2.25 .50
1178a A300 20d ('81)   3.25 .50
1179a A300 50d ('82)   4.00 1.00
       Nos. 1176a-1179a (4)   11.75 2.25

Metric
Measure
A301

1974, Jan. 10   Litho.   Perf. 13
1180 A301 80p plum & multi   .25 .25
Centenary of introduction of metric system.

European Ice
Skating
Championships,
Jan. 29-Feb. 2,
Zagreb — A302

1974, Jan. 29
1181 A302 2d multicolored   .65 .25
       Exists imperf.

Diligence,
1874
A303

1974, Feb. 25   Litho. & Engr.
**   Perf. 11½**
1182 A303 80p shown   .25 .25
1183 A303 2d New UPU head-
             quarters   .25 .25
1184 A303 8d Jet plane   .25 .25
       Nos. 1182-1184 (3)   .75 .75
Centenary of the Universal Postal Union.

Montenegro
No.
1 — A304

Litho. & Engr.
1974, Mar. 11   **Perf. 13**
1185 A304 80p shown   .25 .25
1186 A304 6d Montenegro No. 7   .30 .25
Centenary of first Montenegrin postage stamps.

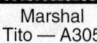

Marshal Tito — A305   Lenin, by Nandor Glid — A306

1974   **Litho.**   **Perf. 13**
1193 A305 50p green   .25 .25
  a.   Perf. 13x12½   .40 .25
1196 A305 80p vermilion   .25 .25
1198 A305 1.20d slate green   .25 .25
1201 A305 2d gray blue   .25 .25
  a.   Perf. 13x12½   .40 .25
    Nos. 1193-1201 (4)   1.00 1.00

Issued with and without fluorescence.
For surcharge see No. 1415.

1974, Apr. 20   **Litho.**   **Perf. 13**
1204 A306 2d blk & silver   .25 .25
50th death anniv. of Lenin.

Lepenski Vir Statue, c. 4950 B.C. — A307

Europa: 6d, Widow & Child, by Ivan Mestrovic.

1974, Apr. 29   **Photo.**   **Perf. 11½**
1205 A307 2d multicolored   .40 .40
1206 A307 6d multicolored   1.20 1.20
Exist imperf.

Great Tit — A308   Congress Poster — A309

1974, May 25   **Photo.**   **Perf. 11½**
1207 A308 80p shown   .25 .25
1208 A308 2d Rose   .25 .25
1209 A308 6d Cabbage butterfly   1.40 1.10
    Nos. 1207-1209 (3)   1.90 1.60
Youth Day. Issued in sheets of 9.

1974, May 27   **Litho.**   **Perf. 11½**
1210 A309 80p gold & multi   .25 .25
1211 A309 2d silver & multi   .25 .25
1212 A309 6d ocher & multi   .40 .40
    Nos. 1210-1212 (3)   .90 .90
10th Congress of Yugoslav League of Communists, Belgrade, May 27-30.

Radar Ground Station, Ivanjica — A311

1974, June 7   **Engr.**   **Perf. 13**
1214 A311 80p shown   .25 .25
1215 A311 6d Intelsat IV   .50 .25
Opening of first satellite ground station in Yugoslavia at Ivanjica. Sheets of 9.

Games Emblem and Soccer Cup — A312

1974, June 13   **Litho.**   **Perf. 13**
1216 A312 4.50d vio bl & multi   1.25 .90
World Cup Soccer Championship, Munich, June 13-July 7. Sheets of 9.

Klek Mountain, Edelweiss, Mountaineers' Emblem — A313

1974, June 15
1217 A313 2d grn & multi   .25 .25
Mountaineering in Yugoslavia, cent. Sheets of 9. Exists imperf. Value $40.

Children's Dance, by Jano Knjazovic — A314

Paintings: 2d, "Crucified Rooster," by Ivan Generalic, vert. 5d, Laundresses, by Ivan Lackovic, vert. 8d, Dance, by Janko Brasic.

1974, Sept. 9   **Photo.**   **Perf. 11½**
1218 A314 80p multi   .30 .30
1219 A314 2d multi   .30 .30
1220 A314 4d multi   .30 .30
1221 A314 8d multi   .75 .75
    Nos. 1218-1221 (4)   1.65 1.65
Yugoslav primitive art.

Cock and Flower, by Kaca Milinojsin A315

Designs (Children's Paintings): 3.20d, Girl and Boy, by Ewa Medrzecka, vert. 5d, Cat and Kitten, by Jelena Anastasijevic.

1974, Oct. 7   **Litho.**   **Perf. 13**
1222 A315 1.20d multi   .25 .25
1223 A315 3.20d multi   .25 .25
1224 A315 5d multi   .25 .25
    Nos. 1222-1224 (3)   .75 .75
Children's Week, Oct. 1-7, and Joy of Europe meeting in Belgrade. Sheets of 9.

Library and Primoz Trubar Statue A316

1974, Oct. 21   **Engr.**   **Perf. 13**
1225 A316 1.20d black   .25 .25
Natl. University Library, Ljubljana, 200th anniv. Exists imperf.

White Peonies, by Petar Dobrovic A317

Paintings of Flowers by Yugoslav artists: 2d, Carnations, by Vilko Gecan. 3d, Flowers, still-life, by Milan Konjovic. 4d, White Vase, by Sava Sumanovic. 5d, Larkspur, by Stane Kregar. 8d, Roses, by Petar Lubarda.

1974, Nov. 28   **Photo.**   **Perf. 11½**
1226 A317 80p gold & multi   .25 .25
1227 A317 2d gold & multi   .25 .25
1228 A317 3d gold & multi   .25 .25
1229 A317 4d gold & multi   .25 .25
1230 A317 5d gold & multi   .25 .25
1231 A317 8d gold & multi   .80 .80
    Nos. 1226-1231 (6)   2.05 2.05
Sheets of 9.

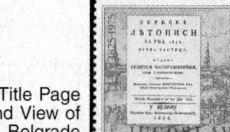

Title Page and View of Belgrade A318

1975, Jan. 8   **Litho.**   **Perf. 13**
1232 A318 1.20d citron   .25 .25
  a.   Perf. 12½   30.00 30.00
Sesquicentennial of the first publication of Matica Srpska, literary journal.

Map of Europe and Dove — A319

1975, Jan. 30   **Perf. 12x11½**
1233 A319 3.20d bl & multi   .25 .25
1234 A319 8d multi   .50 .25
Interparliamentary Union for European Cooperation and Security, 2nd Conference, Belgrade, Jan. 31-Feb. 6. Exist imperf.

Gold-plated Bronze Earring A320

Antique jewelry in Yugoslav museums: 2.10d, Silver bracelet, 18th cent. 3.20d, Silver gilt belt buckle, 18th cent. 5d, Silver ring with Nike cameo, 14th cent. 6d, Silver necklace, 17th cent. 8d, Bronze gilt bracelet, 14th cent.

1975, Feb. 25   **Photo.**   **Perf. 14x13**
1235 A320 1.20d multi   .25 .25
1236 A320 2.10d multi   .25 .25
1237 A320 3.20d multi   .25 .25
1238 A320 5d multi   .25 .25
1239 A320 6d multi   .25 .25
1240 A320 8d multi   .40 .40
    Nos. 1235-1240 (6)   1.65 1.65

Svetozar Markovic, by Stevan Bodnarov A321

1975, Feb. 26   **Engr.**   **Perf. 13**
1241 A321 1.20d blue blk   .50 .25
Markovic (1846-1875), writer and poet.

Fettered Woman, by Frano Krsinic A322

1975, Mar. 8   **Photo.**   **Perf. 14½x14**
1242 A322 3.20d gold & sepia   .25 .25
International Women's Year.

Street, Ohrid — A323

Views: 25p, Budva. 75p, City Hall, Rijeka (Fiume). Nos. 1245, 1246, Street, Ohrid. 1.50d, Church, Bihac. 2.10d, Street and fountain, Hvar. 3.20d, Skofja Loka. 3.40d, Main Square, Vranje. 4.90d, Mosque, Perast.

No Inscription at Bottom
1975-77   **Litho.**   **Perf. 13**
1243 A323 25p carmine ('76)   1.20 .25
1244 A323 75p purple ('76)   .80 .25
1245 A323 1d dull purple   .25 .25
1246 A323 1d dl grn ('76)   .40 .25
  a.   Perf. 13x12½   .40 .25
1247 A323 1.50d rose red ('76)   1.20 .25
  a.   Perf. 13x12½   24.00 24.00
1248 A323 2.10d gray green   .25 .25
1249 A323 3.20d dull blue   .25 .25
1250 A323 3.40d gray grn ('77)   .80 .25
  a.   Perf. 13x12½   1.60 .25
1251 A323 4.90d dl bl ('76)   2.75 .25
    Nos. 1243-1251 (9)   7.90 2.25

See Nos. 1487-1491, 1598, 1601, 1603A, 1713, 1718-1719. For surcharges see Nos. 1382-1383, 1481, 1502, 1545, 1550, 1594-1597A, 1764, 1767-1768, 1770-1771, 1864, 1973.
Nos. 1243, 1246, 1247 exist imperf. Value each, $20.

Europa Issue 1975

Still Life with Eggs, by Mosa Pijade A325

Painting: 8d, Three Graces, by Ivan Radovic.

1975, Apr. 28
1252 A325 3.20d gold & multi   .40 .40
1253 A325 8d gold & multi   .40 .40
Exist imperf.

Srem Front
Fighters'
Monument,
by Dusan
Dzamonja
A326

1975, May 9　　Litho.　　Perf. 13½
1254 A326 3.20d red & multi　　　　.30 .25
　Victory over Fascism in WWII; liberation of
Yugoslavia, 30th anniv.

Garland
Flower — A327

Kayak — A328

1975, May 24　Photo.　Perf. 14x14½
1255 A327 1.20d shown　　　　　.25 .25
1256 A327 2.10d Garden balsam　.25 .25
1257 A327 3.20d Rose mallow　　.25 .25
1258 A327　5d Geranium　　　　.25 .25
1259 A327　6d Crocus　　　　　.25 .25
1260 A327　8d Oleander　　　　1.00 1.00
　　Nos. 1255-1260 (6)　　　　2.25 2.25
　　　　　　Youth Day.

1975, June 20　Litho.　Perf. 13½
1261 A328 3.20d grnsh bl & multi　.25 .25
　9th World Championship of Wild Water Racing, Radika River, June 24-25, and 14th World
Championship of Canoe-Slalom, Treska River,
June 28-29.

Ambush, Herzegovinian Insurgents, by
Ferdo Quiquerez — A329

1975, July 9　Photo.　Perf. 13½x14½
1262 A329 1.20d gold & multi　　.25 .25
　Bosnian & Herzegovinian Uprising, cent.

Stjepan Mitrov
Ljubisa (1824-
1878)
A330

　Yugoslav writers:　2.10d, Ivan Prijatelj
(1875-1937). 3.20d, Jakov Ignjatovic (1824-
1889). 5d, Dragojla Jarnevic (1824-1889). 6d,
Svetozar Corovic (1875-1919). 8d, Ivana Brlic-
Mazuranic (1874-1938).

1975, Sept. 16　Litho.　Perf. 13
1263 A330 1.20d brick red & blk　.25 .25
1264 A330 2.10d dl grn & blk　　.25 .25
1265 A330 3.20d ol bis & blk　　.25 .25
1266 A330　5d brn org & blk　　.25 .25
1267 A330　6d yel grn & blk　　.25 .25
1268 A330　8d Prus bl & blk　　.30 .30
　　Nos. 1263-1268 (6)　　　　1.55 1.55

"Joy of
Europe"
Children's
Meeting, Oct.
2-7, Belgrade
A331

Children's drawings.

1975, Oct. 1　　Litho.　　Perf. 13½
1269 A331 3.20d Young Lion　　.25 .25
1270 A331　6d Baby Carriage　.70 .65

Peace Dove
A332

1975, Oct. 10
1271 A332 3.20d multi　　　　.25 .25
1272 A332　8d multi　　　　.45 .45
　European Security and Cooperation Conference, Helsinki, July 30-Aug. 1. Exist imperf.

Red Cross,
"100", Map of
Yugoslavia
A333

　8d, Red Cross, people seeking help.

1975, Nov. 1　Litho.　Perf. 13½x13
1273 A333 1.20d red & multi　.25 .25
1274 A333　8d red & multi　.25 .25
　Centenary of Red Cross in Yugoslavia.

Soup Kitchen,
by Dorde
Andrejevic-Kun
A334

　Social paintings by 20th century Yugoslav
artists:　2.10d, People at the Door, by Vinko
Grdan. 3.20d, Drunks in Coach, by Marijan
Detoni, horiz. 5d, Workers' Lunch, by Tone
Kralj, horiz. 6d, Water Wheel, by Lazar Lice-
noski. 8d, The Hanging, by Krsto Hegedusic.

Perf. 14½x13½, 13½x14½
1975, Nov. 28　　　　　　Photo.
1275 A334 1.20d gold & multi　.25 .25
1276 A334 2.10d gold & multi　.25 .25
1277 A334 3.20d gold & multi　.25 .25
1278 A334　5d gold & multi　.25 .25
1279 A334　6d gold & multi　.25 .25
1280 A334　8d gold & multi　.30 .30
　　Nos. 1275-1280 (6)　　1.55 1.55
　Sheets of 9. No. 1277 exists imperf.

Diocletian's
Palace, 304
A.D. — A335

　3.20d, House of Ohrid, 19th cent., vert. 8d,
Gracanica Monastery, Kosovo, 1321.

1975, Dec. 10　Engr.　Perf. 13½
1281 A335 1.20d dark brown　　.25 .25
1282 A335 3.20d bluish black　　.25 .25
1283 A335　8d dk vio brown　.25 .25
　　Nos. 1281-1283 (3)　　　.75 .75
　European Architectural Heritage Year 1975.
Sheets of 9. Exist imperf.

12th Winter
Olympic
Games, Feb.
4-15,
Innsbruck,
Austria
A336

1976, Feb. 4　　Engr.　　Perf. 13½
1284 A336 3.20d Ski jump　　.25 .25
1285 A336　8d Pair figure skat-
　　　　　　ing　　　　.70 .40
　　　　Exist imperf.

Red
Flag — A337

1976, Feb. 14　　　　　　　Litho.
1286 A337 1.20d red & multi　.25 .25
　"Red Flag" workers demonstration,
Kragujevac, Feb. 15, 1876.
　Exists imperf. Value $32.50.

Svetozar
Miletic (1826-
1901),
Lawyer,
Founder of
United
Serbian
Youth — A338

1976, Feb. 23　　　　Perf. 13½x13
1287 A338 1.20d grnsh gray & dl
　　　　　　grn　　　　.25 .25

Borislav
"Bora"
Stankovic,
(1876-1927),
Writer
A339

1976, Mar. 31　Litho.　Perf. 13½x13
1288 A339 1.20d lem, ol & mar　.25 .25
　　　　　Sheets of 9.

Europa Issue 1976

King
Matthias, by
Jakob
Pogorelec,
1931 — A340

1976, Apr. 26　Photo.　Perf. 11½
1289 A340 3.20d shown　　　.25 .25
1290 A340　8d Bowl, 14th cent　.25 .25

Ivan Cankar
(1876-1918),
Slovenian
Writer
A341

1976, May 8　Litho.　Perf. 13½x13
1291 A341 1.20d orange & plum　.25 .25

Train on
Viaduct in
Bosnia
A342

　Design: 8d, Train on viaduct in Montenegro.

1976, May 15　　Engr.　　Perf. 13½
1292 A342 3.20d deep magenta　.25 .25
1293 A342　8d deep blue　　.40 .40
　Inauguration of the Belgrade-Bar railroad.

Hawker
Dragonfly
A343

　Fresh-water Fauna:　2.10d, Winkle. 3.20d,
Rudd. 5d, Green frog. 6d, Ferruginous duck.
8d, Muskrat.

1976, May 25　　　　　　Litho.
1294 A343 1.20d yel & multi　.40 .40
1295 A343 2.10d bl & multi　.40 .40
1296 A343 3.20d vio & multi　.40 .40
1297 A343　5d multicolored　.80 .80
1298 A343　6d multicolored　.80 .80
1299 A343　8d multicolored　2.75 2.75
　　Nos. 1294-1299 (6)　5.55 5.55
　　Youth Day. Exist imperf.

Vladimir Nazor,
Croatian Writer,
Birth
Cent. — A344

1976, May 29　　　　　Perf. 13
1300 A344 1.20d pale lil & dl bl　.25 .25

Battle
of
Vucji
Dol,
1876
A345

1976, June 16　　Litho.　　Perf. 13
1301 A345 1.20d gold, brn & buff　.25 .25
　Liberation of Montenegro from Turkey, cent.
Exists imperf.

Serbian
Pitcher
A346

　Water Pitchers:　2.10d, Slovenia. 3.20d,
Bosnia-Herzegovina. 5d, Vojvodina 6d, Macedonia. 8d, Kosovo.

1976, June 22　Photo.　Perf. 14x13
1302 A346 1.20d dk car & multi　.25 .25
1303 A346 2.10d olive & multi　.25 .25
1304 A346 3.20d red & multi　.25 .25
1305 A346　5d brown & multi　.25 .25
1306 A346　6d dk grn & multi　.25 .25
1307 A346　8d dk bl & multi　.35 .35
　　Nos. 1302-1307 (6)　1.60 1.60
　　　　Exist imperf.

Tesla
Monument,
Belgrade,
and Niagara
Falls — A347

1976, July 10　　Engr.　　Perf. 13
1308 A347 5d slate grn & indigo　.50 .25
　Nikola Tesla (1856-1943), electrical engineer and inventor. Sheets of 9. Exists imperf.

21st Olympic Games, July 17-Aug. 1, Montreal, Canada, A348

1976, July 17
1309	A348	1.20d	Long jump	.25 .25
1310	A348	3.20d	Team handball	.25 .25
1311	A348	5d	Target shooting	.25 .25
1312	A348	8d	Single scull rowing	2.00 1.50
		Nos. 1309-1312 (4)		2.75 2.25

Sheets of 9.

World Map and Peace Dove A349

1976, Aug. 16   Litho.   Perf. 13
1313 A349 4.90d multi .30 .25

5th Summit Conference of Non-Aligned Countries, Colombo, Sri Lanka, Aug. 9-19. Sheets of 9.
Exists imperf. Value $25.

Children's Train — A350

Children's drawings: 4.90d, Navy Day (submarine).

1976, Oct. 2   Litho.   Perf. 13
1314 A350 4.90d multi .25 .25
1315 A350 8d multi .30 .30

"Joy of Europe" Children's Meeting, Belgrade, Oct. 2-7.
No. 1315 exists imperf.

Herzegovinian Fugitives, by Uros Predic — A351

Historical paintings by 19th-20th century Yugoslav painters: 1.20d, Battle of the Montenegrins, by Djura Jaksic, vert. 2.10d, Nikola S. Zrinjski at Siget, by Oton Ivekovic, vert. 5d, Uprising at Razlovci, by Borko Lazeski. 6d, Enthroning of Slovenian Duke at Gospovetsko Field, by Anton Gojmir Kos. 8d, Break-through at Solun Front, by Veljko Stanojevic.

Perf. 13½x12½, 12½x13½
1976, Nov. 29   Photo.
1316	A351	1.20d	gold & multi	.25 .25
1317	A351	2.10d	gold & multi	.25 .25
1318	A351	3.20d	gold & multi	.25 .25
1319	A351	5d	gold & multi	.25 .25
1320	A351	6d	gold & multi	.25 .25
1321	A351	8d	gold & multi	.80 .80
		Nos. 1316-1321 (6)		2.05 2.05

Sheets of 9.

No. 839 Surcharged with New Value and 3 Bars in Rose

1976, Dec. 8   Engr.   Perf. 12½
1322 A206 1d on 85p dl pur .40 .25

Mateja Nenadovic A352

1977, Feb. 4   Photo.   Perf. 13½x14
1323 A352 4.90d multicolored .30 .25

Prota Mateja Nenadovic (1777-1854), Serbian Duke, archbishop and writer.

Rajko Zinzifov — A353

1977, Feb. 10   Litho.   Perf. 13x13½
1324 A353 1.50d brn & sepia .25 .25

Rajko Zinzifov (1839-1877), writer.

Phlox — A354

Flowers: 3.40d, Lily. 4.90d, Bleeding heart. 6d, Zinnia. 8d, Spreading marigold. 10d, Horseshoe geranium.

1977, Mar. 8   Perf. 13½x13
1325	A354	1.50d	multi	.25 .25
1326	A354	3.40d	multi	.25 .25
1327	A354	4.90d	multi	.25 .25
1328	A354	6d	multi	.30 .25
1329	A354	8d	multi	.30 .25
1330	A354	10d	multi	1.00 .80
		Nos. 1325-1330 (6)		2.35 2.05

Exists imperf.

Croatian Music Institute, Zagreb, 150th Anniv. A355

1977, Apr. 4   Engr.   Perf. 13
1331 A355 4.90d bl & sepia .40 .40

Alojz Kraigher — A356

1977, Apr. 11   Litho.   Perf. 13½
1332 A356 1.50d lemon & brn .30 .25

Kraigher (1877-1959), Slovenian writer.

Boka Kotorska, by Milo Milunovic A357

10d, Zagorje in November, by Ljubo Babic.

1977, May 4   Photo.   Perf. 11½
1333 A357 4.90d gold & multi .40 .40
1334 A357 10d gold & multi .40 .40

Europa. Issued in sheets of 9.

Marshal Tito, by Omer Mujadzic A358

1977, May 25   Perf. 11½x12
1335 A358 1.50d gold & multi .25 .25
1336 A358 4.90d gold & multi .25 .25
1337 A358 8d gold & multi .30 .30
     Nos. 1335-1337 (3) .80 .80

85th birthday of Pres. Tito. Sheets of 9. Exists imperf.

Mountain Range and Gentian — A359

Design: 10d, Plitvice Lakes Falls, trees, robin and environmental protection emblem.

1977, June 6   Litho.   Perf. 13x13½
1338 A359 4.90d multicolored .25 .25
1339 A359 10d multicolored .70 .50

World Environment Day.

Petar Kocic (1877-1916), Writer A360

1977, June 15   Perf. 13½
1340 A360 1.50d pale grn & brn .30 .25

Map of Europe and Peace Dove A361

1977, June 15   Litho.   Perf. 13½
1341 A361 4.90d multi .25 .25
1342 A361 10d multi 1.00 1.00

Security and Cooperation Conference, Belgrade, June 15.

Child on Float — A362

Children's drawings: 10d, Fruit picking.

1977, Oct. 3   Litho.   Perf. 13½
1343 A362 4.90d multi .25 .25
1344 A362 10d multi .50 .40

"Joy of Europe" Children's Meeting.

Sava Congress Center, Belgrade A363

1977, Oct. 4   Litho.   Perf. 13½
1345 A363 4.90d bl & multi .25 .25
1346 A363 10d car & multi 1.00 1.00

European Security and Cooperation Conference, Belgrade.
Exist imperf. Value, each $125.

Exhibition Emblem — A364

1977, Oct. 20   Litho.   Perf. 13½
1347 A364 4.90d gold & multi .30 .25

Balkanfila 1977, 6th Intl. Phil. Exhib. of Balkan Countries, Belgrade, Oct. 24-30.

Double Flute and Shepherd A365

Landscape and Musician: 3.40d, 4.90d, 6d, Various string instruments. 8d, Bagpipes. 10d, Panpipes.

1977, Oct. 25   Engr.   Perf. 13½
1348	A365	1.50d	och & red brn	.25 .25
1349	A365	3.40d	green & brn	.25 .25
1350	A365	4.90d	dk brn & yel	.25 .25
1351	A365	6d	bl & red brn	.25 .25
1352	A365	8d	brick red & sep	.25 .25
1353	A365	10d	sl grn & bis	.50 .50
		Nos. 1348-1353 (6)		1.75 1.75

Musical instruments from Belgrade Ethnographical Museum.

Ivan Vavpotic, Self-portrait A366

Self-portraits of Yugoslav artists: 3.40d, Mihailo Vukotic. 4.90d, Kosta Hakman. 6d, Miroslav Kraljevic. 8d, Nikola Martinovski. 10d, Milena Pavlovic-Barili.

Perf. 13½x12½
1977, Nov. 26   Photo.
1354	A366	1.50d	gold & multi	.25 .25
1355	A366	3.40d	gold & multi	.25 .25
1356	A366	4.90d	gold & multi	.25 .25
1357	A366	6d	gold & multi	.25 .25
1358	A366	8d	gold & multi	.25 .25
1359	A366	10d	gold & multi	.65 .65
		Nos. 1354-1359 (6)		1.90 1.90

Festival of Testaccio, by Klovic — A367

Julija Klovic, by El Greco — A368

1978, Jan. 14 Photo. Perf. 13½
1360 A367 4.90d multicolored .25 .25
1361 A368 10d multicolored .25 .25

Julija Klovic (1498-1578), Croat miniaturist.

Stampless Cover, Banaviste to Kubin, 1869 — A369

Designs: 3.40d, Mailbox. 4.90d, Ericsson telephone, 1900. 10d, Morse telegraph, 1844.

1978, Jan. 28 Perf. 13x14
1362 A369 1.50d multicolored .25 .25
1363 A369 3.40d multicolored .25 .25
1364 A369 4.90d multicolored .25 .25
1365 A369 10d multicolored .25 .25
  Nos. 1362-1365 (4) 1.00 1.00

Post Office Museum, Belgrade.

Battle of Pirot A370

1978, Feb. 20 Litho. Perf. 13½
1366 A370 1.50d gold, blk & sl grn 1.75 1.75

Centenary of Serbo-Turkish War.
Exists imperf. Value $40.

Airplanes A371

1978, Apr. 24 Litho. Perf. 13½
1367 A371 1.50d S-49A, 1949 .25 .25
1368 A371 3.40d Galeb, 1961 .25 .25
1369 A371 4.90d Utva-75, 1976 .25 .25
1370 A371 10d Orao, 1974 .80 .80
  Nos. 1367-1370 (4) 1.55 1.55

Aeronautical Day.
Exist imperf. Value, each $35.

Europa Issue

View of Golubac A372

1978, May 3 Photo. Perf. 11½
1371 A372 4.90d shown .25 .25
1372 A372 10d St. Naum Monastery, Ohrid .40 .40

Exist imperf.

Boxing Glove A373   Honeybee A374

1978, May 5 Litho. Perf. 13½
1373 A373 4.90d multicolored .35 .25

Amateur Boxing Championships.
Exists imperf. Value $35.

1978, May 25 Photo. Perf. 11½
Bees of Yugoslavia: 3.40d, Halictus scabiosae. 4.90d, Blue carpenter bee. 10d, Large earth bumblebee.

1374 A374 1.50d multi .25 .25
1375 A374 3.40d multi .25 .25
1376 A374 4.90d multi .25 .25
1377 A374 10d multi .95 .95
  Nos. 1374-1377 (4) 1.70 1.70

Exist imperf.

Filip Filipovic (1878-1938), Radovan Radovic (1878-1906), Revolutionaries — A375

1978, June 19 Litho. Perf. 13½
1378 A375 1.50d dk pur & dl ol .25 .25

Marshal Tito — A376

Congress Emblem — A377

1978, June 20
1379 A376 2d red & multi .25 .25
1380 A377 4.90d red & multi .30 .25

Souvenir Sheet
Imperf
1381 A376 15d red & multi 3.00 3.00

11th Congress of Yugoslav League of Communists, Belgrade, June 20-23.
Nos. 1379-1380 exist imperf. Value, each $35.

Nos. 1246, 1248 Surcharged with New Value and Two Bars in Brown
1978 Litho. Perf. 13
1382 A323 2d on 1d 10.00 .25
1383 A323 3.40d on 2.10d .40 .25

Issue dates: #1382, July 17; #1383, Aug. 1.

Conference Emblem over Belgrade — A378

1978, July 25 Photo. Perf. 13½
1384 A378 4.90d bl & lt blue .30 .25

Conference of Foreign Ministers of Nonaligned Countries, Belgrade, July 25-29.
Exists imperf. Value $35.

Championship Emblem — A379

1978, Aug. 10 Litho. Perf. 13½x13
1385 A379 4.90d multicolored .30 .25

14th Kayak and Canoe Still Water Championships, Lake Sava, Aug. 10-14.

Mt. Triglav, North Rock — A380

1978, Aug. 26 Photo. Perf. 14
1386 A380 2d multicolored .25 .25

Bicentenary of first ascent of Mt. Triglav by Slovenian climbers.

Black Lake, Mt. Durmitor A381

1978, Sept. 20
1387 A381 4.90d shown .25 .25
1388 A381 10d Tara River .55 .30

Protection of the environment.

Night Sky A382

1978, Sept. 30 Litho. Perf. 13x12½
1389 A382 4.90d bl blk, blk & gold .30 .25

29th Congress of International Astronautical Federation, Dubrovnik, Oct. 1-8.

People in Forest A383

Children's drawings: 10d, Family around pond.

1978, Oct. 2 Perf. 13½x13
1390 A383 4.90d multi .35 .25
1391 A383 10d multi .65 .45

"Joy of Europe" Children's Meeting.

Seal on Insurrection Declaration A384

1978, Oct. 5 Perf. 13½
1392 A384 2d gold, brn & blk .25 .25

Centenary of Kresna uprising.
Exists imperf. Value $40.

Teachers' Training Institute, Sombor, Bicent. A385

1978, Oct. 16
1393 A385 2d multicolored .25 .25

Exists imperf.

Croatian Red Cross, Cent. A386

1978, Oct. 21
1394 A386 2d lt bl, blk & red .25 .25

Metallic Sculpture XXII, by Dusan Dzamonja A387

Modern Sculptures: 3.40d, Circulation in Space I, by Vojin Bakic, vert. 4.90d, Tectonic Octopode, by Olga Jevric, vert. 10d, Tree of Life, by Drago Trsar.

Perf. 13½x13, 13x13½
1978, Nov. 4 Litho.
1395 A387 2d multicolored .25 .25
1396 A387 3.40d multicolored .25 .25
1397 A387 4.90d multicolored .25 .25
1398 A387 10d multicolored .35 .35
  Nos. 1395-1398 (4) 1.10 1.10

Crossing of Neretva Pass, by Ismet Mujezinovic A388

1978, Nov. 10 Litho. Perf. 13
1399 A388 2d multicolored .25 .25

35th anniversary of Battle of Neretva. Exists imperf.

Workers Leaving
Factory, by Marijan
Detoni — A389

Larch
Cone — A390

Engravings: 3.40d, Workers, by Maksim
Sedej. 4.90d, Lumberjacks, by Daniel Ozmo.
6d, Meal Break, by Pivo Karamatijevic. 10d,
Hanged Man and Raped Woman, by Djordje
Andrejevic Kun.

1978, Nov. 28 Photo. Perf. 14x13½

1400	A389	2d gold, blk & buff	.25	.25
1401	A389	3.40d gold & black	.25	.25
1402	A389	4.90d gold, yel & blk	.25	.25
1403	A389	6d gold, buff & blk	.25	.25
1404	A389	10d gold, cr & blk	.70	.50
	Nos. 1400-1404 (5)		1.70	1.50

Republic day.

1978, Dec. 11 Photo. Perf. 13x12½

1405	A390	1.50d shown	.25	.25
1406	A390	1.50d Red squirrel	.25	.25
1407	A390	2d Sycamore leaves	.25	.25
1408	A390	2d Red deer	.25	.25
a.		Bklt. pane of 8	1.25	
1409	A390	3.40d Alder leaves	.25	.25
1410	A390	3.40d Partridge	.25	.25
1411	A390	4.90d Oak leaves	.25	.25
1412	A390	4.90d Grouse	.25	.25
a.		Bklt. pane of 8	3.25	
	Nos. 1405-1412 (8)		2.00	2.00

New Year 1979. Nos. 1405-1412 printed
se-tenant in sheets of 25.
No. 1408a contains 4 each of Nos. 1407-
1408; No. 1412a 2 each of Nos. 1409-1412,
with background colors changed. Exist imperf.

**Nos. 1064, 868, 1198 Surcharged with
New Value and Bars**

1978 Engr.; Litho. Perf. 12½, 13½

1413	A263	35p on 10p brown	1.60	.30
1414	A211	60p on 85p dp bl	1.60	.30
1415	A305	80p on 1.20d sl grn	1.60	.30
	Nos. 1413-1415 (3)		4.80	.90

First
Masthead of
Politika
A391

1979, Jan. 25 Litho. Perf. 13½

1416	A391	2d gold & black	.25	.25

Politika daily newspaper, 75th anniv.
Exists imperf. Value $35.

Red Flags and
Emblem
A392

Child and IYC
Emblem
A393

1979, Feb. 15

1417	A392	2d red & gold	.25	.25

11th Meeting of Self-managers, Kragujevac,
Feb. 15-16.
Exists imperf. Value $40.

1979, Mar. 1 Photo. Perf. 11½x12

1418	A393	4.90d gold vio & bl	.45	.30

International Year of the Child. Exists imperf.

Sabre,
Mace,
Koran
Pouch
A394

Old Weapons: 3.40d, Pistol and ramrod,
Montenegro. 4.90d, Short carbine and powder horn, Slovenia and Croatia. 10d, Oriental
rifle and cartridge pouch.

1979, Mar. 26 Photo. Perf. 14

1419	A394	2d multicolored	.25	.25
1420	A394	3.40d multicolored	.25	.25
1421	A394	4.90d multicolored	.25	.25
1422	A394	10d multicolored	.50	.50
	Nos. 1419-1422 (4)		1.25	1.25

5-Pointed Star,
Hammer and
Sickle — A395

1979, Apr. 20 Photo. Perf. 13½

1423	A395	2d multicolored	.25	.25
1424	A395	4.90d multicolored	.25	.25

Communist and Communist Youth Leagues,
60th anniversary.
Exist imperf. Value, each used, $25.

Cyril and
Methodius
University
and Emblem
A396

1979, Apr. 24 Litho.

1425	A396	2d multicolored	.25	.25

Sts. Cyril and Methodius University, Skopje,
30th anniv.

19th Century
Belgrade, by
C. Goebel
A397

Europa: 10d, Postilion and Ljubljana, 17th
century, by Jan van der Heyden.

1979, Apr. 30 Photo. Perf. 11½

1426	A397	4.90d multicolored	.40	.40
1427	A397	10d multicolored	.40	.40

Blue Sow Thistles
A398

Milutin
Milankovic, by
Paja Jovanovic
A399

Flowers: 3.40d, Anemones. 4.90d, Astragalus. 10d, Alpine trifolium.

1979, May 25 Photo. Perf. 13½

1428	A398	2d multicolored	.25	.25
1429	A398	3.40d multicolored	.25	.25
1430	A398	4.90d multicolored	.25	.25
1431	A398	10d multicolored	.75	.75
	Nos. 1428-1431 (4)		1.50	1.50

1979, May 28

1432	A399	4.90d multi	.35	.25

Milutin Milankovic (1879-1958), scientist.

Kosta Abrasevic
(1879-1898),
Poet — A400

1979, May 29 Litho. Perf. 13½x13

1433	A400	2d org, blk & gray	.25	.25

Exists imperf. Value, used $40.

Eight-Oared
Shell
A401

1979, Aug. 28 Litho. Perf. 13

1434	A401	4.90d multicolored	.40	.25

9th World Rowing Championship, Lake Bled.
Exist imperf. Value $40.

8th Mediterranean Games, Sept. 15-
29, Split — A402

1979, Sept. 10

1435	A402	2d Games Emblem	.25	.25
1436	A402	4.90d Mascot	.25	.25
1437	A402	10d Map, Flags	.30	.30
	Nos. 1435-1437 (3)		.80	.80

Exist imperf. Value, each $30.

Seal, 15th
Century
A403

1979, Sept. 14 Perf. 12½

1438	A403	2d multicolored	.25	.25

Zagreb Postal Service, 450th anniversary.
Exists imperf. Value $35.

Lake
Palic — A404

Environment Protection: 10d, Lakefront,
Prokletije Mountains.

1979, Sept. 20 Photo. Perf. 14x13½

1439	A404	4.90d multicolored	.25	.25
1440	A404	10d multicolored	.65	.40

Bank and
Fund
Emblems
A405

Engr. & Photo.

1979, Oct. 1 Perf. 13½

1441	A405	4.90d multicolored	.25	.25
1442	A405	10d multicolored	.40	.40

Meeting of the World Bank and International
Monetary Fund, Belgrade, Oct. 2-5.
Exist imperf. Value, each $25.

"Joy of
Europe"
A406

Children's drawings.

1979, Oct. 2 Litho.

1443	A406	4.90d shown	.25	.25
1444	A406	10d Child in yard	.45	.45

Exist imperf. Value, each $40.

Mihailo Pupin
(1854-1935),
Physicist,
Inventor — A407

1979, Oct. 9 Perf. 13x13½

1445	A407	4.90d multicolored	.40	.25

Marko Cepenkov
A408

1979, Nov. 15 Litho. Perf. 13½

1446	A408	2d multicolored	.25	.25

Cepenkov (1829-1920), Macedonian folklor-
ist. Exists imperf.

Pristina
University,
10th
Anniversary
A409

1979, Nov. 17

1447	A409	2d multicolored	.25	.25

Exists imperf. Value, used $40.

Radovan Portal,
Trogir Cathedral
A410

Romanesque Sculptures: 3.40d, Choir stall,
Cathedral of Split. 4.90d, Triforium, Church of
the Resurrection, Decani. 6d, Buvina Portal,
Cathedral of Split. 10d, Western portal,
Church of Our Lady, Studenica.

1979, Nov. 28 Photo.

1448	A410	2d multi	.25	.25
1449	A410	3.40d multi	.25	.25
1450	A410	4.90d multi	.25	.25
1451	A410	6d multi	.25	.25
1452	A410	10d multi	.35	.35
	Nos. 1448-1452 (5)		1.35	1.35

Exist imperf.

Sarajevo University, 30th Anniversary A411

1979, Dec. 1 **Litho.**
1453 A411 2d multicolored .25 .25

Exists imperf. Value, used $40.

Duro Dakovic and Nikola Hecimovic, Communist Revolutionaries, 50th Death Annivs. — A412

1979, Dec. 10
1454 A412 2d multicolored .25 .25

Exists imperf. Value, used $40.

Sidewheeler Deligrad, 1862-1914 — A413

1979, Dec. 14
1455 A413 4.90d shown .50 .60
1456 A413 10d Sidewheeler Serbia, 1917-72 1.00 1.00

Danube Conference.
Exist imperf. Value, each $60.

Milton Manaki and Camera A414

1980, Jan. 21 **Litho.** **Perf. 13½**
1457 A414 2d deep bister & plum .25 .25

Manaki (1880-1964), photographer and documentary film maker.

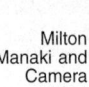

Edward Kardelj, by Zdenko Kalin — A415

1980, Jan. 26
1458 A415 2d multicolored .25 .25

Kardelj (1910-1979), labor movement leader.
Exists imperf. Value, used $40.

No. 1458 Overprinted in Red

1980, Jan. 26
1459 A415 2d multicolored .25 .25

Ploce renamed Kardeljevo.
Exists imperf. Value, used $40.

13th Winter Olympic Games, Feb. 12-24, Lake Placid, NY — A416

1980, Feb. 13
1460 A416 4.90d Speed skating .25 .25
1461 A416 10d Cross-country skiing 1.40 1.40

Exist imperf.

University of Belgrade, 75th Anniversary A417

1980, Feb. 27
1462 A417 2d multicolored .25 .25

22nd Summer Olympic Games, July 19-Aug. 3, Moscow A418

1980, Apr. 21
1463 A418 2d Fencing .25 .25
1464 A418 3.40d Bicycling .25 .25
1465 A418 4.90d Field hockey .25 .35
1466 A418 10d Archery .50 .50
Nos. 1463-1466 (4) 1.25 1.35

Marshal Tito, by Antun Augustincic A419

Europa: 13d, Tito, by Djordje Prudnikov.

1980, Apr. 28 **Photo.** **Perf. 11½**
Granite Paper
1467 A419 4.90d multi .25 .25
1468 A419 13d multi 1.00 1.00

Exist imperf. Value, each $15.

Marshal Tito, by Bozidar Jakac — A420

1980, May 4 **Litho.** **Perf. 13½**
1469 A420 2.50d purplish blk .25 .25
a. Perf. 10½ .30 .25
1470 A420 4.90d gray black .60 .60

Marshal Tito (1892-1980) memorial. Issued in sheets of 8 plus label.

Exist imperf. Value, each $25.

Sava Kovacevic (1905-1943), Revolutionary — A421

1980, May 11 **Litho.** **Perf. 13½**
1471 A421 2.50d multicolored .25 .25

Wood Baton and Letter A422

1980, May 14
1472 A422 2d multicolored .25 .25

1st Tito Youth Relay Race, 35th anniv.
Exists imperf. Value $35.

Flying Gunard — A423

Emperor Trajan Decius Coin, 3rd Cent. — A424

1980, May 24 **Photo.** **Perf. 12**
1473 A423 2d shown .25 .25
1474 A423 3.40d Loggerhead turtle .25 .25
1475 A423 4.90d Sea swallow .30 .30
1476 A423 10d Dolphin 2.25 2.25
Nos. 1473-1476 (4) 3.05 3.05

1980, June 10

3rd Century Roman Coins (Illyrian Emperors): 3.40d, Aurelianus. 4.90d, Probus. 10d, Diocletianus.

1477 A424 2d multicolored .25 .25
1478 A424 3.40d multicolored .25 .25
1479 A424 4.90d multicolored .30 .25
1480 A424 10d multicolored .50 .30
Nos. 1477-1480 (4) 1.30 1.05

No. 1247 Surcharged with New Value and Bars

1980, June 17 **Litho.** **Perf. 13½**
1481 A323 2.50d on 1.50d .40 .25

Types of 1971-77

Views: 5p, Krusevac. 10p, Gradacac. 20p, Church and bridge, Bohinj. 30p, Krk. 35p, Omis. 40p, Pec. 60p, Logar Valley. 2.50d, Kragujevac. 3.50d, Vrsac. 5.60d, Travnik. 8d, Dubrovnik.

Perf. 13½, 13¼x12½ (#1487), 13¼ (#1486A)

1978-81
1482 A263 5p deep orange .40 .25
1483 A263 10p brown .40 .40
1483A A263 20p purple ('78) .80 .55
1484 A263 30p olive gray .40 .25
1485 A263 35p brown red .80 .55
1486 A263 40p gray .40 .25
1486A A263 60p purple .40 .25
1487 A323 2.50d rose red .80 .25
1488 A323 2.50d bl gray ('81) .35 .25
1489 A323 3.50d red org ('81) .25 .25
1490 A323 5.60d gray grn ('81) .25 .25
1491 A323 8d gray ('81) .25 .25
Nos. 1482-1491 (12) 5.50 3.75

No. 1483A has all three numerals in denomination the same size. On No. 1065 "20" is taller than first "0."

Perf. 13¼x12½
1482a A263 5p 1.25 .25
1483b A263 10p .60 .60
1483Ac A263 20p .80 .55
1484a A263 30p .80 .40
1485a A263 35p 1.25 .80
1486b A263 40p .55 .25

1486Ac A263 60p .55 .40
1487a A323 2.50d .50 .25
1488a A323 2.50d .25 .25
1489a A323 3.50d .25 .25
1490a A323 5.60d .25 .25
1491a A323 8d .60 .25
Nos. 1482a-14891a (12) 7.65 4.50

400th Anniversary of Lipica Stud Farm — A425

1980, June 25
1493 A425 2.50d black .25 .25

A426

1980, June 27 **Perf. 13½**
1494 A426 2.50d magenta & red .25 .25

Tito, Basic Law of Self-management, 30th anniv.

A427

1980, June 28 **Perf. 13**
1495 A427 2.50d light green .25 .25

University of Novi Sad, 20th anniv.

Mljet National Park — A428

1980, Sept. 5 **Photo.** **Perf. 14**
1496 A428 4.90d shown .25 .25
1497 A428 13d Galicica Natl. Park .25 .25

European Nature Protection Year.

Minerals — A429

1980, Sept. 10 **Litho.** **Perf. 13½**
1498 A429 2.50d Pyrrhotine .35 .35
1499 A429 3.40d Dolomite .35 .35
1500 A429 4.90d Sphalerite .35 .35
1501 A429 13d Wulfenite .80 .80
Nos. 1498-1501 (4) 1.85 1.85

No. 1244 Surcharged with New Value and Bars

1980, Oct. 15 **Litho.** **Perf. 13**
1502 A323 5d on 75p purple 2.00 .25

View of Kotor, UNESCO Emblem A430

1980, Sept. 23　　　　**Perf. 13½**
1503 A430 4.90d multicolored　　.25 .25
21st UNESCO General Conf., Belgrade,

Children in Garden A431

Joy of Europe Children's Festival: 13d, 3 faces.

1980, Oct. 2　　　　**Perf. 13½x13**
1504 A431 4.90d multi　　　　.25 .25
1505 A431 13d multi　　　　.35 .35

Dove over Madrid Meeting Hall — A432

Lithographed and Engraved
1980, Nov. 11　　　　**Perf. 13½**
1506 A432 4.90d dk grn & bl grn .25 .25
1507 A432 13d dk brn & yel brown　　.40 .40
European Security Conference, Madrid.

Federal Flag of Yugoslavia A433

Republic Day: Socialist Republic flags. Nos. 1508-1515 se-tenant. No. 1511 has Latin letters.

1980, Nov. 28　　**Litho.**　　**Perf. 12½**
1508 A433 2.50d Bosnia & Her-
　　　　zegovina　　　　.25 .25
1509 A433 2.50d Croatia　　.25 .25
1510 A433 2.50d shown　　.25 .25
1511 A433 2.50d Yugoslavia　.25 .25
1512 A433 2.50d Macedonia　.25 .25
1513 A433 2.50d Montenegro　.25 .25
1514 A433 2.50d Serbia　　.25 .25
1515 A433 2.50d Slovenia　.25 .25
　　Nos. 1508-1515 (8)　2.00 2.00

Woman with Straw Hat — A434

Paintings: 3.40d, Atelier No. 1, by Gabriel Stupica. 4.90d, To the Glory of the Sutjeska Fighters, by Ismet Mujezinovic. 8d, Serenity, by Marino Tartaglia. 13d, Complaint, by Milos Vuskovic.

1980, Dec. 16　　　　**Perf. 13½**
1516 A434 2.50d multi　　　.25 .25
1517 A434 3.40d multi　　　.25 .25
1518 A434 4.90d multi　　　.25 .25
1519 A434 8d multi, vert.　.25 .25
1520 A434 13d multi, vert.　.80 .80
　　Nos. 1516-1520 (5)　1.80 1.80

Ivan Ribar (1881-1968), Politician — A435

1981, Jan. 21　　**Litho.**　　**Perf. 13½**
1521 A435 2.50d rose red & blk　.25 .25

Cementusa Hand Bomb A436

Partisan Weapons: 5.60d, Rifle. 8d, 52-mm Cannon. 13d, Man-powered tank.

1981, Feb. 16
1522 A436 3.50d brick red & blk　.25 .25
1523 A436 5.60d grn & blk　.25 .25
1524 A436 8d bis brn & blk　.25 .25
1525 A436 13d rose vio & blk　.50 .50
　　Nos. 1522-1525 (4)　1.25 1.25

Monastery of the Virgin, Eleousa, 900th Anniversary A437

1981, Mar. 3
1526 A437 3.50d multicolored　1.10 1.10
Exists imperf. Value $35.

36th World Table Tennis Championship, Novi Sad, Apr. 14-26 — A438

1981, Apr. 14　　**Litho.**　　**Perf. 13½**
1527 A438 8d multicolored　.25 .25
Exists imperf.

Europa Issue

Wedding in Herzegovina, by Nikola Arsenovic A439

Paintings by Nikola Arsenovic (1823-85): 13d, Witnesses at a Wedding.

1981, May 5　　**Photo.**　　**Perf. 12**
Granite Paper
1528 A439 8d multicolored　.30 .25
1529 A439 13d multicolored　.30 .25

Dimitrije Tucovic and Slavija Square, Belgrade A440

1981, May 13　　**Litho.**　　**Perf. 13½**
1530 A440 3.50d bl vio & red　.25 .25
Tucovic (1881-1914), Socialist leader. Exists imperf.

Marshal Tito, by Milivoje Unkovic — A441

1981, May 25　**Photo.**　**Perf. 11½x12**
Granite Paper
1531 A441 3.50d gold & dk brn　.40 .40
Marshal Tito's 89th birth anniversary. Exists imperf.

Sunflower A442

3rd Autonomous Enterprises Cong. A443

1981, May 28　　**Photo.**　　**Perf. 11½**
Granite Paper
1532 A442 3.50d shown　　.25 .25
1533 A442 5.60d Hops　　.25 .25
1534 A442 8d Corn　　.30 .25
1535 A442 13d Wheat　　.55 .35
　　Nos. 1532-1535 (4)　1.35 1.10
Exist imperf.

1981, June 16　　**Litho.**　　**Perf. 13½**
1536 A443 3.50d multicolored　.25 .25

Djordje Petrov (1864-1921), Macedonian Revolutionary A444

1981, June 22
1537 A444 3.50d bister & black　.25 .25

National Insurrection, 40th Anniv. A445

1981, July 4　　　　**Perf. 12½**
1538 A445 3.50d red org & tan　.25 .25
1539 A445 8d red org & tan　.25 .25
Souvenir Sheet
Imperf
1540 A445 30d Tito monument　1.25 1.25

800th Anniv. of Varazdin A446

1981, Aug. 20　　**Litho.**　　**Perf. 13½**
1541 A446 3.50d multicolored　.25 .25

Parliament Building, Belgrade — A447

1981, Sept. 1
1542 A447 8d red & blue　　.25 .25
Belgrade Conference of Non-Aligned Countries, 20th anniv.

Serbian Printing Office, 150th Anniv. A448

1981, Sept. 15
1543 A448 3.50d pale rose & dk bl .25 .25

Fran Levstik (1831-1887), Writer A449

1981, Sept. 28　　　　**Perf. 12x11½**
1544 A449 3.50d dl red & gray　.25 .25

No. 1251 Surcharged with New Value and Bars

1981, Oct.　　　　**Perf. 13**
1545 A323 5d on 4.90d dl bl　.80 .25
　a.　Perf. 13x12½　　1.60 .40

Joy of Europe Children's Festival A450

1981, Oct. 2
1546 A450 8d Barnyard　.25 .25
1547 A450 13d Skiers　　.25 .25

125th Anniv. of European Danube Commission — A451

1981, Oct. 28　　**Litho.**　　**Perf. 13½**
1548 A451 8d Tugboat Karlovac .25 .25
1549 A451 13d Train hauling boat, Sip Canal　.70 .70
Nos. 1548-1549 exist imperf. Value, set $75.

No. 1250a Surcharged with New Value and Bars
1981, Oct. 9　　**Litho.**　　**Perf. 13x12½**
1550 A323 3.50d on 3.40d gray grn　　1.75 .30
　a.　on #1250　　　.40 .25

Savings Bank of Yugoslavia, 60th Anniv. — A452

Intl. Inventions Conference — A453

1981, Oct. 31   *Perf. 11½x12*
1551 A452 3.50d multicolored   .25 .25

1981, Nov. 4   *Perf. 13½*
1552 A453 8d red & gold   .25 .25

Nature Protection — A454

1981, Nov. 14
1553 A454 8d Plant, Ruguvo Gorge   .25 .25
1554 A454 13d Lynx, Prokletjie Mountains   .75 .75

August Senoa (1838-1881), Writer — A455

1981, Dec. 12   *Perf. 11½x12*
1555 A455 3.50d dl gray vio & gldn brn   .25 .25

Still Life with a Fish, by Jovan Bijelic (1886-1964) — A456

Paintings of Animals: 5.60d, Raven, by Milo Milunovic (1897-1967). 8d, Bird on Blue Background, by Marko Celebonovic (b. 1902). 10d, Horses, by Peter Lubarda (1907-1974). 13d, Sheep, by Nikola Masic (1852-1902).

1981, Dec. 29   Photo.   *Perf. 13½*
1556 A456 3.50d multi   .25 .25
1557 A456 5.60d multi   .25 .25
1558 A456 8d multi   .25 .25
1559 A456 10d multi   .25 .25
1560 A456 13d multi   .55 .55
Nos. 1556-1560 (5)   1.55 1.55

40th Anniv. of Foca Regulations A457

1982, Jan 14   Litho.   *Perf. 13½*
1561 A457 3.50d Mosa Pijade   .25 .25

60th Anniv. of Communist Newspaper Borba A458

1982, Feb. 19   Litho.
1562 A458 3.50d red & blk   .25 .25

500th Anniv. of City of Cetinje — A459

1982, Mar. 10
1563 A459 3.50d dull red brn   .25 .25

Capt. Ivo Visin (1806-1868), Boka Kotorska's Map — A460

1982, May 5   Photo.   *Perf. 11½*
1564 A460 8d shown   .40 .40
1565 A460 15d Ship Splendido   .40 .40
Europa, 1st Yugoslavian circumnavigation, 1852-1859.

Male House Sparrow A461

1982, May 24   Litho.   *Perf. 13½*
1566 A461 3.50d shown   .25 .25
1567 A461 5.60d Female house sparrow   .25 .25
1568 A461 8d Male field sparrow   .25 .25
1569 A461 15d Female field sparrow   2.40 2.40
Nos. 1566-1569 (4)   3.15 3.15
See Nos. 1687-1690.

90th Birth Anniv. of Marshal Tito — A462

1982, May 25   Photo.   *Perf. 11½x12*
Granite Paper
1570 A462 3.50d multicolored   .25 .25

1982 World Cup — A463

Designs: Soccer ball in various positions.

1982, June 12   *Perf. 11½*
Granite Paper
1571 Sheet of 4   1.60 1.60
a. A463 3.50d multicolored   .25 .25
b. A463 5.60d multicolored   .25 .25
c. A463 8d multicolored   .25 .25
d. A463 15d multicolored   .25 .25

12th Congress of Yugoslavian Communists' League, Belgrade, June 26-29 A464

1982 June 26   Litho.   *Perf. 13½*
1572 A464 3.50d orange & red   .25 .25
1573 A464 8d gray & red   .25 .25
Souvenir Sheet
Perf. 12½
1574 Sheet of 2   .80 .80
a. A464 10d like 3.50d   .25 .25
b. A464 20d like 8d   .55 .55
Exists imperf. Value $250.

Dura Jaksic (1832-1878), Writer, Painter A465

1982, July 27   Litho.   *Perf. 14*
1575 A465 3.50d Self-portrait   .25 .25

1982 World Championships Held in Yugoslavia — A466

1982, July 30   *Perf. 13½*
1576 A466 8d Gymnastics   .80 .25
1577 A466 8d Kayak   .80 .25
1578 A466 8d Weightlifting   .80 .25
Nos. 1576-1578 (3)   2.40 .75

Ivan Zajc (1832-1914), Composer and Conductor A467

1982, Aug. 3
1579 A467 4d brown   .25 .25

Breguet XIX and Potez XXV A468

1982, Sept. 1   Litho.   *Perf. 13½*
1580 A468 4d shown   .25 .25
1581 A468 6.10d Super Galeb G-4   .25 .25
1582 A468 8.80d Armed boat   .25 .25
1583 A468 15d Rocket gun boat   .50 .50
Nos. 1580-1583 (4)   1.25 1.25
40th anniv. of Air Force/Anti-aircraft Defense and Navy.

Spruce Branch, Tara Natl. Park A469

1982, Sept. 3
1584 A469 8.80d shown   .25 .25
1585 A469 15d Mediterranean monk seal, Kornati   .60 .60

14th Joy of Europe Children's Festival — A470

1982, Oct. 2
1586 A470 8.80d Traffic   .25 .25
1587 A470 15d In the Bath   .55 .55

Small Onofrio's Fountain, 15th Cent. A471

1982, Oct. 23
1588 A471 8.80d multi   .25 .25
16th Universal Federation of Travel Agents' Assoc. Cong., Dubrovnik, Oct. 24-30.

600th Anniv. of Hercegnovi A472

1982, Oct. 28
1589 A472 4d multicolored   .50 .50

14th Winter Olympic Games, Sarajevo, Feb. 8-19, 1984 — A473

1982, Nov. 20   *Perf. 12½*
1590 A473 4d Bridge, Miljacka River   .25 .25
1591 A473 6.10d Minaret, Mosque   .25 .25
1592 A473 8.80d Evangelical Church   .50 .50
1593 A473 15d Street   1.10 1.10
Nos. 1590-1593 (4)   2.10 2.10

Nos. 1488a and 1489a Surcharged In Red, Blue, Black or Red Violet with Two Bars or Shield

1982-83   Litho.   *Perf. 13x12½*
1594 A323 30p on 2.50d (R)   .50 .25
1595 A323 50p on 2.50d (Bl)   1.20 .25
1596 A323 60p on 2.50d ('83)   .50 .25
1597 A323 1d on 3.50d   .25 .25
1597A A323 2d on 2.50d (RV)   1.60 .25
Nos. 1594-1597A (5)   4.05 1.25

Perf. 13
1594a A323 30p on #1488   .40 .25
1595a A323 50p on #1488   .25 .25
1596a A323 60p on #1488   1.00 .25
1597b A323 1d on #1489   .65 .25
Nos. 1594a-1597b (4)   2.30 1.00

Types of 1971-77

Designs: 3d, Skofja Loka. 4d, Pocitelj. 5d, Osijek. 6.10d, like 2.10d. 8.80d, Hercegnovi. 10d, Sarajevo. 16.50d, Ohrid.

1982-83 Litho. Perf. 13x12½
1598	A323	3d gray bl	.25	.25
1599	A263	4d red org	.25	.25
1600	A263	5d grnsh bl ('83)	.40	.25
1601	A323	6.10d olive grn	.60	.25
1602	A263	8.80d gray	.40	.25

Perf. 13½
1603	A263	10d red lil ('83)	.25	.25
1603A	A323	16.50d dl bl ('83)	.25	.25
		Nos. 1598-1603A (7)	2.40	1.75

Type styles of Nos. 1600, 1603-1603A differ
somewhat from illustrations.
No. 1600 exists imperf. Value $35.

Perf. 13
1598a	A323	3d	.50	.25
1599a	A323	4d	.50	.25
1600a	A323	5d	.40	.25
1601a	A323	6.10d	.80	.25
1602a	A323	8.80d	1.20	.25
1603b	A323	10d	1.10	.25
1603c	A323	16.50d	1.25	.30
		Nos. 1598a-1603c (7)	5.75	1.80

40th Anniv.
of Anti-
Fascist
Council
A474

1982, Nov. 26 Perf. 13½
1604	A474	4d Bihac, 1942	.25	.25

The Manuscript, by Janez Bernik (b.
1933) — A475

4d, Prophet on Golden Background, by Joze
Ciuha (b. 1924). 6.10d, Journey to the West,
by Andrej Jemec (b. 1934). 8.80d, Black Comb
with Red Band, by Riko Debenjak (b. 1908).
15d, The Vitrine, by Adriana Maraz (b. 1931).

1982, Nov. 27
1605	A475	4d multi, vert.	.25	.25
1606	A475	6.10d multi, vert.	.25	.25
1607	A475	8.80d multi, vert.	.25	.25
1608	A475	10d multi	.25	.25
1609	A475	15d multi	.55	.55
		Nos. 1605-1609 (5)	1.55	1.55

Uros Predic (1857-
1953),
Painter — A476

Union of
Pioneers, 40th
Anniv. — A477

1982, Dec. 7
1610	A476	4d multicolored	.25	.25

1982, Dec. 27 Perf. 12
1611	A477	4d multicolored	.25	.25

Articles from
Museum of
Applied Art,
Belgrade
A478

Designs: 4d, Lead pitcher, Gnjilane, 16th
cent. 6.10d, Silver-plated jug, Macedonia, 18th
cent. 8.80d, Goblet, 16th cent., Dalmatia. 15d,
Mortar, 15th cent., Kotor.

1983, Feb. 19
1612	A478	4d multicolored	.25	.25
1613	A478	6.10d multicolored	.25	.25
1614	A478	8.80d multicolored	.25	.25
1615	A478	15d multicolored	.40	.30
		Nos. 1612-1615 (4)	1.15	1.05

Mount
Jalovec — A479

Serbian Telephone
Service
Centenary — A480

1983, Feb. 26
1616	A479	4d blue & lt bl	.25	.25

Slovenian Mountaineering Soc., 90th anniv.

1983, Mar. 15
1617	A480	3d Ericsson phone	.25	.25

25th Anniv. of
Intl. Org. for
Maritime
Navigation
(OMI) — A481

1983, Mar. 17 Perf. 13½x14
1618	A481	8.80d multi	.25	.25

Edible
Mushrooms
A482

1983, Mar. 21 Perf. 14
1619	A482	4d Agaricus campestris	.30	.30
1620	A482	6.10d Morchella vulgaris	.30	.30
1621	A482	8.80d Boletus edulis	.30	.30
1622	A482	15d Cantharellus cibarius	1.20	1.20
		Nos. 1619-1622 (4)	2.10	2.10

Rijeka Railway,
110th
Anniv. — A483

1983, Apr. 5
1623	A483	4d Steam engine series 401	.25	.25
1624	A483	23.70d on 8.80d Thyristor locomotive 442	.50	.50

No. 1624 not issued without surcharge.

Boro and Ramiz
Monument,
Landovica
A484

1983, Apr. 10
1625	A484	4d multi	.25	.25

Boro Vukmirovic and Ramiz Sadiku, revolutionary martyrs, 40th death anniv.

Ivo Andric
(1892-1975),
Poet, 1961
Nobel Prize
Winner
A485

1983, May 5 Photo. Perf. 11½
Granite Paper
1626	A485	8.80d Medal, Travnik Chronicle text	.40	.40
1627	A485	20d Portrait, Bridge, Drina River	.40	.40

Europa.

50th Intl.
Agricultural
Fair, Novi
Sad — A486

1983, May 13 Litho. Perf. 14
1628	A486	4d Combine harvester	.25	.25

40th Anniv. of
Battle of
Sutjeska
A487

1983, May 14 Perf. 12½
1629	A487	3d Assault, by Pivo Karamatijevic	.25	.25

A488

1983, May 25 Perf. 13½
1630	A488	4d Tito, Parliament	.25	.25
a.		Perf. 12½	1.00	1.00

30th anniv. of election of Pres. Tito.

A489

1983, May 27
1631	A489	4d First mail and passenger car	.25	.25
1632	A489	16.50d Mountain road, Kotor	.25	.25

80th anniv. of automobile service in
Montenegro.

A490

1983, June 5 Perf. 14
1633	A490	23.70d multi	.25	.25

UN Conference on Trade and Development,
6th session, Belgrade, June 6-30.

A491

1983, June 7 Perf. 12½
1634	A491	4d Engraving by Valvasor	.25	.25

Town of Pazin millennium.

Triumphal
Arch,
Titograd
A492

1983, June 9 Perf. 12½
1635	A492	100d Memorial to S. Filipovic, Valjevo, vert.	2.50	.25
a.		Perf. 13x13½	1.40	.25
1636	A492	200d shown	2.00	.95
a.		Perf. 13½x13	3.75	.95

Skopje
Earthquake,
20th
Anniv. — A493

1983, July 26 Litho. Perf. 12½
1637	A493	23.70d deep magenta	.25	.25
a.		Perf. 13½	.80	.45

For surcharge, see No. 1715.

Sculpture by Ivan
Mestrovic — A494

1983, Aug. 15
1638	A494	6d multicolored	.25	.25

European Nature Protection — A495

16.50d, Gentian, Kopaonik National Park.
23.70d, Chamois, Perucica Gorge.

1983, Sept. 10 Litho. Perf. 13
1639	A495	16.50d multi	.35	.35
1640	A495	23.70d multi	.65	.65

See Nos. 1685-1686.

Joy of
Europe — A496

Children's Paintings: 16.50d, Bride and
Bridegroom by Verna Paunkonik. 23.70d,
Andres and his Mother by Marta Lopez-Ibor.

1983, Oct. 3 Litho. Perf. 13½
1641	A496	16.50d multi	.25	.25
1642	A496	23.70d multi	.65	.65

A497

A498

1983, Oct. 17 Litho. Perf. 12½
1643 A497 5d multicolored .25 .25
Kragujevac High School sesquicentenary.

1983, Oct. 17 Litho. Perf. 13½
1644 A498 5d multicolored .25 .25
Timok Uprising centenary.

14th Winter Olympic Games, Sarajevo, Feb. 8-19, 1984
A499

1983, Nov. 25 Engr. Perf. 13½
1645 A499 4d Ski jump .25 .25
1646 A499 4d Slalom .25 .25
1647 A499 16.50d Bobsledding .25 .25
1648 A499 16.50d Downhill skiing .25 .25
1649 A499 23.70d Speed skating .50 .50
1650 A499 23.70d Hockey .50 .50
Nos. 1645-1650 (6) 2.00 2.00

Souvenir Sheet
Imperf
1651 A499 50d Emblem 1.75 1.75
Nos. 1645-1651 exist imperf.

Jovan Jovanovic Zmaj (1833-1904), Poet, Neven Masthead
A500

1983, Nov. 24 Litho. Perf. 12½
1652 A500 5d multicolored .25 .25

Peasant Wedding, by Pieter Brueghel
A501

Paintings: No. 1654, Susanna with the Old Men, by the "Master of the Prodigal Son." No. 1655, Allegory of Wisdom and Strength, by Paolo Veronese (1528-1588). No. 1656, Virgin Mary from Salamanca, by Robert Campin (1375-1444). No. 1657, St. Ann with Madonna and Jesus, by Albrecht Dürer (1471-1528).

1983, Nov. 26 Perf. 14
1653 A501 4d multi .25 .25
1654 A501 16.50d multi .25 .25
1655 A501 16.50d multi .25 .25
1656 A501 23.70d multi .55 .55
1657 A501 23.70d multi .80 .80
Nos. 1653-1657 (5) 2.10 2.10

View of Jajce — A502

1983, Nov. 28 Perf. 13x12½
1658 A502 5d multicolored .25 .25
Souvenir Sheet
Imperf
1659 A502 30d Tito .80 .80
40th anniv. of Second Session of the Antifascist Council of the Natl. Liberation of Yugoslavia, Jajce, Nov. 29-30.

World Communications Year — A503

1983, Dec. 10 Perf. 13½
1660 A503 23.70d multi .25 .25

Koco Racin (1908-1943), Writer — A504

1983, Dec. 22
1661 A504 5d multicolored .25 .25

Politika Front Page, Oct. 28, 1944 — A505

1984, Jan. 25 Litho. Perf. 12½
1662 A505 5d red & black .25 .25
80th anniv. of Politika newspaper and 40th anniv. in Yugoslavia.

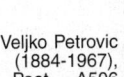
Veljko Petrovic (1884-1967), Poet — A506

1984, Feb. 4 Litho. Perf. 13½
1663 A506 5d multicolored .25 .25

1984 Winter Olympics
A507

1984, Feb. 8
1664 A507 4d Biathlon .25 .25
1665 A507 4d Giant slalom .25 .25
1666 A507 5d Bobsledding .25 .25
1667 A507 5d Slalom .25 .25
1668 A507 16.50d Speed skating .25 .25
1669 A507 16.50d Hockey .25 .25
1670 A507 23.70d Ski jumping .25 .25
1671 A507 23.70d Downhill skiing .25 .25
Nos. 1664-1671 (8) 2.00 2.00

Souvenir Sheets
Imperf
1672 A507 50d Flame, rings 1.40 1.40
1673 A507 100d Flame, map 2.75 2.75
No. 1664-1671 exist imperf.

Natl. Heroines
A508

Designs: a, Marija Bursac (1902-43). b, Jelena Cetkovic (1916-43). c, Nada Dimic (1923-42). d, Elpida Karamandi (1920-42). e, Toncka Cec Olga (1896-1943). f, Spasenija Babovic Cana (1907-77). g, Jovanka Radivojevic Kica (1922-43). h, Sonja Marinkovic (1916-41).

1984, Mar. 8 Litho. Perf. 14
1674 Sheet of 8 + label 3.50 3.50
a.-h. A508 5d any single .25 .25

Slovenia Monetary Institute, 40th Anniv.
A509

1984, Mar. 12 Perf. 12½
1675 A509 5d Bond, note .25 .25

Railroad Service in Serbia (Belgrade-Nis) Centenary — A510

1984, Apr. 9 Perf. 13
1676 A510 5d Train, Central Belgrade Station .25 .25

Jure Franko, Giant Slalom Silver Medalist, 1984 — A511

1984, Apr. 28
1677 A511 23.70d multi .80 .80
Yugoslavia's first Winter Olympic medalist.

Europa (1959-84)
A512

1984, Apr. 30 Perf. 13½
1678 A512 23.70d multi .40 .40
1679 A512 50d multi .80 .80

1984 Summer Olympics, Los Angeles
A513

1984, May 14
1680 A513 5d Basketball .55 .55
1681 A513 16.50d Diving .55 .55
1682 A513 23.70d Equestrian .55 .55
1683 A513 50d Running 2.00 2.00
Nos. 1680-1683 (4) 3.65 3.65

Marshal Tito — A514

1984, May 25 Perf. 13
1684 A514 5d brown red .25 .25

Nature Type of 1983
Designs: 26d, Centaurea gloriosa (flower), Biokovo Mountain Park. 40d, Anophthalmus (insect), Pekel Cave, Savinja Valley.

1984, June 11 Litho. Perf. 13½
1685 A495 26d multicolored .50 .25
1686 A495 40d multicolored .80 .40

Bird Type of 1982
1984, June 28
1687 A461 4d Great black-backed gull .40 .40
1688 A461 5d Black-headed gull .40 .40
1689 A461 16.50d Herring gull .40 .40
1690 A461 40d Common tern 3.50 1.50
Nos. 1687-1690 (4) 4.70 2.70

19th Cent. Cradles
A515

1984, Sept. 1 Litho. Perf. 12½
1691 A515 4d Bosnia & Herzegovina .25 .25
1692 A515 5d Montenegro .25 .25
1693 A515 26d Macedonia .40 .40
1694 A515 40d Serbia .65 .65
Nos. 1691-1694 (4) 1.55 1.55

Olive Tree, Mirovica
A516

1984, Sept. 1
1695 A516 5d multi .25 .25

Joy of Europe — A517

Children's Drawings.

1984, Oct. 2 Litho. Perf. 14
1696 A517 26d Traditional costumes .35 .35
1697 A517 40d Girl with doll carriage .90 .90

City of Virovitica, 750th Anniv.
A518

1984, Oct. 4 Perf. 13½
1698 A518 5d Engraving, 17th cent. .25 .25

Map, Concentric Waves — A519

1984, Oct. 10
1699 A519 6d Prus bl & brt grn .25 .25
Radio and telegraph service in Montenegro, 80th anniv.

Veterans Conference A520

1984, Oct. 18
1700 A520 26d multicolored .90 .90
1701 A520 40d multicolored 1.20 1.20

Conf. of Veterans on Security, Disarmament & Cooperation in Europe, Belgrade, 10/18-20.

Liberation of Belgrade, 40th Anniv. — A521

1984, Oct. 20
1702 A521 6d "40," arms .25 .25

Miloje Milojevic (1884-1946), Composer A522

1984, Oct. 27
1703 A522 6d Portrait, score .25 .25

Medals Events, 1984 Summer Olympics A522a

Designs: a, Wrestling. b, Running. c, Field hockey. d, Shot put. e, Soccer. f, Basketball. g, Netball. h, Rowing.

1984, Nov. 14   Litho.   Perf. 13½
1704   Sheet of 8   4.00 4.00
a.-h. A522a 26d any single .25 .25

The Tahitians, by Gauguin — A523

Paintings by Foreign Artists in Yugoslav Museums: 6d, Portrait of Madame Tatichek, by Ferdinand Waldmuller (1793-1865). No. 1706, The Bathers, by Renoir (1841-1919). No. 1707, At the Window, by Henri Matisse (1869-1954). 40d, Ballerinas, by Edgar Degas (1834-1917).

Perf. 13½x14, 14x13½
1984, Nov. 15
1705 A523 6d multi, vert. .25 .25
1706 A523 26d multi, vert. .25 .25
1707 A523 26d multi, vert. .25 .25
1708 A523 38d multi .50 .50
1709 A523 40d multi .80 .80
   Nos. 1705-1709 (5) 2.05 2.05

Nova Macedonia Newspaper, 40th Anniv. A523a

1984, Nov. 29   Perf. 13½
1710 A523a 6d 1st & recent editions .25 .25

Nos. 1602, 1599 and 1637 Surcharged with Three Bars in Red Brown or Black, Types of 1975 and

Exhibition Center, Zagreb A524

Bird, Jet, Landscape A525

Designs: 6d, Kikinda. 26d, Korcula. 38d, Maribor. 70d, Trumpeter monument, riverside buildings in Zagreb. 1000d, bird, tail of jet on airfield.

Perf. 13½x12½, 13 (#1713, 1717), 12½ (#1715)
1984-86   Litho.
1711 A263 2d on 8.80d 1.75 1.75
  a.   on #1602a .40 .25
1712 A263 6d on 4d (RBr) .40 .25
  a.   on #1599a .55 .40
1713 A323 6d lt red brn .40 .25
  a.   Perf. 13x12½ .80 .25
1715 A493 20d on 23.70d .40 .25
1717 A263 26d dp ultra .40 .25
  a.   Perf. 13x12½ .50 .25
1718 A323 38d dp lil rose 1.60 .25
  a.   Perf. 13 .40 .25
1719 A323 70d brt ultra ('85) 1.25 .55
  b.   Perf. 13 .55 .45
      Perf. 14
1719A A524 100d brt org yel & vio .65 .35
      Perf. 12½
1720 A525 500d redsh brn & multi ('85) 3.75 1.40
  a.   Perf. 13¼ 1.75 .65
1721 A525 1000d org brn & multi ('85) 5.50 2.90
  a.   Perf. 13½ 2.10 1.25
   Nos. 1711-1721 (10) 16.10 8.20

Type styles for Nos. 1717-1718 differ somewhat from illustration.
For surcharge, see No. 1973.

Museum Exhibits - Fossils A526

1985, Feb. 4   Litho.   Perf. 12½
1722 A526 5d Aturia aturi .25 .25
1723 A526 6d Pachyophis woodwardi .25 .25
1724 A526 33d Chactodon hoeferi .40 .40
1725 A526 60d Homo sapiens neanderthalensis .90 .90
   Nos. 1722-1725 (4) 1.80 1.80

40th Anniv., Monument Protection A527

1985, Feb. 20   Litho.   Perf. 12½
1726 A527 6d Hopovo church .25 .25

Ski Jumping at Planica, 50th Anniv. A528

European Nature Conservation A529

1985, Mar. 15   Litho.   Perf. 13½
1727 A528 6d Three herons in flight 4.75 2.40

1985, Mar. 30   Perf. 14
1728 A529 42d Pandion haliaetus 1.25 .80
1729 A529 60d Upupa epops 2.40 1.25

Audubon birth bicentenary, European Information Center for Nature Protection.

A530

Fresco of St. Methodius, St. Naum Monastery, Ohrid.

1985, Apr. 6   Litho.   Perf. 11½x12
1730 A530 10d multicolored 1.75 .80

St. Methodius (d. 885), archbishop of Pannonia and Moravia.

A531

1985, Apr. 16   Litho.   Perf. 12½
1731 A531 6d Clasped hands .25 .25

Osimo Agreements, 10th anniv. Yugoslavia-Italy political and economic cooperation.

Josip Slavenski (1896-1955), Composer A532

Europa. 60d, Portrait, block flute, darabukka, 80d, Balkanophonia coord, signature.

1985, Apr. 29   Perf. 14
1732 A532 60d multi .40 .40
1733 A532 80d multi .80 .80

Joachim Vujic, by Dimitrije Avramovic (1815-1855) A533

1985, May 8   Perf. 12x11½
1734 A533 10d multi .25 .25

Joachim Vujic Theater, Kragujevac, 150th anniv.

Liberation from German Occupation Forces, 40th Anniv. — A534

1985, May 9   Perf. 13½
1735 A534 10d shown .25 .25
1736 A534 10d Order of Natl. Liberation .25 .25

Franjo Kluz (1912-1944), Rudi Cajavec (1911-1942), Breguet-19 Fighter — A535

1985, May 21   Perf. 13x12½
1737 A535 10d multi .25 .25

Air Force Day.

Pres. Tito (1892-1980) A536

1985, May 25   Perf. 13½
1738 A536 10d Portrait .50 .25

Cres-Losinj Municipal Tourism Bureau, Cent. — A537

1985, June 12
1739 A537 10d Map, town arms, villa .65 .65

UN 40th Anniv. — A538

Rowing — A539

1985, June 26   Litho.   Perf. 12½
1740 A538 70d Emblem, rainbow .25 .25

1985, June 29   Litho.   Perf. 13½
1741 A539 70d multicolored .40 .40
        Souvenir Sheet
1742 A539 100d Course map, arms 1.40 1.40

Intl. European-Danube Rowing Regatta, 30th anniv.

Nautical Tourism — A540

1985, July 1 **Litho.**
1743 A540 8d Sailboat .80 .80
1744 A540 10d Windsurfing .80 .80
1745 A540 50d Sailboat, diff. .80 .80
1746 A540 70d Sailboat, diff. 2.50 2.50
Nos. 1743-1746 (4) 4.90 4.90

F1B Class Motorized Model Plane A541

1985, Aug. 10 Litho. Perf. 12½x13
1747 A541 70d multicolored .50 .40
Free Flight World Championships, Livno, Aug. 12-18.

Algae — A542

1985, Sept. 20 **Perf. 14**
1748 A542 8d Corallina officinalis .25 .25
1749 A542 10d Desmarestia viridis .25 .25
1750 A542 50d Fucus vesiculosus .30 .30
1751 A542 70d Padina pavonia 1.50 1.50
Nos. 1748-1751 (4) 2.30 2.30

Intl. Federation of Stomatologists, 73rd Congress, Belgrade, Sept. 21-28 — A543

1985, Sept. 21 **Perf. 12x11½**
1752 A543 70d multicolored .40 .40

Children's Drawings A544

Designs: 50d, Children in a Horse-drawn Cart, by Branka Lukic, age 14, Yugoslavia. 70d, Children in Field, by Suzanne Straathof, age 9, Netherlands.

1985, Oct. 2 **Perf. 14**
1753 A544 50d multicolored .40 .40
1754 A544 70d multicolored 1.25 1.25

Croatian Natl. Theater, Zagreb, 125th Anniv. A545

1985, Nov. 23 **Perf. 12½**
1755 A545 10d Facade detail .25 .25

Miladin Popovic A546 — Natl. Coat of Arms A547

1985, Nov. 26 **Perf. 11½x12**
1756 A546 10d Portrait .25 .25
Popovic (1910-1945), revolutionary.

1985, Nov. 28 **Perf. 13½**
1757 A547 10d multicolored .25 .25
Souvenir Sheet
Imperf
1758 A547 100d multicolored 1.00 1.00
Socialist Federal Republic of Yugoslavia, 40th anniv. No. 1758 contains one stamp 18x27mm.

Royal Procession, by Iromie Wijewardena, Sri Lanka — A548

Paintings from the Art Gallery of Non-aligned Countries, Titograd: 10d, Return from Hunting, by Mama Cangare, Mali. No. 1761, Drum of Coca, by Agnes Ovando Sanz De Franck, Bolivia. No. 1762, The Cock, by Mariano Rodriguez, Cuba. 70d, Three Women, by Quamrul Hassan, Bangladesh.

1985, Dec. 2 **Perf. 14**
1759 A548 8d multicolored .25 .25
1760 A548 10d multicolored .25 .25
1761 A548 50d multicolored .25 .25
1762 A548 50d multicolored .25 .25
1763 A548 70d multicolored 1.40 1.40
Nos. 1759-1763 (5) 2.40 2.40

Nos. 1243, 1482, 1485a, 1490, 1491, 1713a, 1717a, 1603A and 1718 Surcharged in Light Red Brown, Brown or Dark Brown
1985-86 Litho. Perf. 13½, 13½x12½
1764 A323 1d on 25p (B) .80 .25
1765 A263 2d on 5p (DB) .40 .25
a. on #1482a .40
1766 A263 3d on 35p (DB) .25 .25
a. on #1485a .25 .25
1767 A323 4d on 5.60d (B) .25 .25
b. on #1490 .80 .50
1767A A323 5d on 8d (B) .40 .25
c. on #1491a .80 .80
1768 A323 8d on 6d .25 .25
a. on #1713 .25 .25
1769 A263 20d on 26d .25 .25
a. on #1717 7.00 4.00
1770 A323 50d on 16.50d (B) .80 .40
a. on #1603c .80 .80
1771 A323 70d on 38d .80 .50
Nos. 1764-1771 (9) 4.20 2.65
Issued: #1767A, 3/17/86; others, 12/85.

Natl. Automobile Assoc., 40th Anniv. A549

1986, Feb. 25 **Perf. 12½**
1772 A549 10d Car .25 .25
1773 A549 70d Helicopter .80 .80

Tara River, Montenegro A550

1986, Mar. 3 **Perf. 14**
1774 A550 100d Canyon .40 .40
1775 A550 150d Bridge .80 .80
European nature protection. Sheets of 9.

Studenica Monastery, 800th Anniv. — A551

1986, Mar. 15 **Perf. 13½**
1776 A551 10d Chapel of Our Lady .55 .40

A552

Various soccer plays.

1986, Apr. 5 Litho. Perf. 14
1777 A552 70d multi .65 .65
1778 A552 150d multi .80 .80
1986 World Cup Soccer Championships, Mexico.

Arrival of St. Clement in Ohrid, 1100th Anniv. A553

1986, Apr. 12 **Perf. 12½**
1779 A553 10d Township model 5.00 5.00

Europa Issue

Brain, Mushroom Cloud — A554

1986, Apr. 28 **Perf. 14**
1780 A554 100d shown .40 .40
1781 A554 200d Injured deer 1.20 .80

European Men's Senior Judo Championships, Belgrade, May 8-11 — A555

1986, May 7 **Perf. 12½**
1782 A555 70d multi .50 .40

Natl. Costumes A556 — Yachts, Moscenika Draga Bay A557

a, Slovenia. b, Vojvodina. c, Croatia. d, Macedonia. e, Serbia. f, Montenegro. g, Kosovo. h, Bosnia & Herzegovina.

1986, May 22 Litho. Perf. 12x13
Booklet Stamps
1783 Bklt. pane of 8 4.50
a.-h. A556 50d any single .55 .55

1986, May 23 **Perf. 14**
1784 A557 50d multi .25 .25
1785 A557 80d multi, diff. .40 .40
Souvenir Sheet
Imperf
1786 A557 100d multi 3.25 3.25
European Sailing Championships, Croatia, May 29-June 7, Flying Dutchman Class. No. 1786 contains one stamp 22x28mm.

Marshal Tito — A557a

1986, May 24 **Perf. 13x12½**
1787 A557a 10d multicolored .25 .25

Moths and Butterflies A558

1986, May 26 **Perf. 14**
1788 A558 10d Eudia pavonia .80 .80
1789 A558 20d Inachis io .80 .80
1790 A558 50d Parnassius apollo .80 .80
1791 A558 100d Apatura iris 1.60 1.60
Nos. 1788-1791 (4) 4.00 4.00

Ancient Manuscripts A558a

Designs: 10d, Evangelical, 18th cent. 20d, Leontijevo Evangelical, 16th cent. 50d, Astrological, Mesopotamia, 15th cent. 100d, Hebrew Haggadah, Spain, 14th cent.

1986, June 12 Litho. Perf. 14
1792 A558a 10d multicolored .25 .25
1793 A558a 20d multicolored .25 .25
1794 A558a 50d multicolored .40 .40
1795 A558a 100d multicolored .80 .65
Nos. 1792-1795 (4) 1.70 1.55

A559

A560

Designs: 20d, Postman on motorcycle. 30d, Postman, resident. 40d, Forklift, mail pallets. 50d, Mail train. 60d, Man posting letters in mailbox. 93d, Open envelope and greetings telegram form. 100d, Postman, mail van. No. 1803, Computer operator facing right. No. 1804, 140d, Computer operator facing left. 120d, Woman sending love letter. 200d, Freighter in high seas. 500d, Postal employee sorting mail. 1000d, Woman at telephone station. 2000d, Aircraft, hemispheres on world map. 30d, 60d, 93d, 106d, 120d, 140d, 500d, 1000d vert.

Perf. 13½, 12½x13½ (20d, 40d, 50d), 14 (100d)

1986-88			Litho.	
1796	A559	20d brt pink	.40	.25
a.		Perf. 13	.40	.25
1797	A559	30d lt brn vio	.40	.25
a.		Perf. 13x12½	.80	.25
1798	A559	40d brt red	.40	.25
a.		Perf. 13	.40	.25
1799	A559	50d violet	.40	.25
a.		Perf. 13	.25	.25
1800	A559	60d lt sage grn	.40	.25
1801	A559	93d ultra	.40	.25
1802	A559	100d dl magenta	.80	.30
1803	A559	106d rose red	.40	.25
1804	A559	106d brn org	.40	.25
1805	A559	120d dull blue grn	.25	.25
1806	A559	140d dull rose	.25	.25
1807	A559	200d greenish bl	1.00	.40
a.		Perf. 12½	2.00	1.60
b.		Perf. 12½x13½	6.00	2.00
1808	A559	500d deep blue & beige	.40	.40
1809	A559	500d chalky blue & yel	.25	.25
1810	A559	1000d vio & blue grn	.25	.25
b.		Perf. 12½	.55	.50
1810A	A560	2000d brt blue, red & brt vio	1.00	.50
Nos. 1796-1810A (16)			7.40	4.60

Size of No. 1802: 19½x18mm.
Issued: 20d, 3/17; 50d, 200d, 6/4; 40d, 7/17; 100d, 6/12; 30d, 7/26; 60d, 6/5/87; #1803, 12/10/87; 93d, 12/16/87; #1804, 1/22/88; #1808, 4/29/88; 1000d, 7/21/88; 20d, 140d, 2000d, #1809, 9/5/88.
See Nos. 1935-1945, 2004-2007, 2013-2015, 2021. For surcharges see Nos. 1877, 1912-1913, 1947-1948, 1972, 1974-1975, 2017, 2019, 2048-2051, 2053.

13th Communist Federations Congress (SKJ) A561

1986, June 25			**Perf. 12½**	
1811	A561	10d shown	.25	.25
1812	A561	20d Star	.25	.25

Souvenir Sheet
Imperf

1813	A561	100d Tito	.80	.80

Trubar, Abecedarian Manuscript Title Page A562

1986, June 28	Litho.	**Perf. 12½x13**		
1814	A562	20d multi	.55	.40

Primoz Trubar (1508-1568), Slovenian philologist and religious reformer.

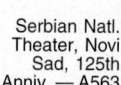

Serbian Natl. Theater, Novi Sad, 125th Anniv. — A563

1986, July 28			**Perf. 14**	
1815	A563	40d Thalia	.25	.25

Rugovo Dance, Kosovo Province — A564

1986, Sept. 10				
1816	A564	40d multi	.25	.25

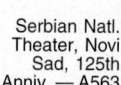

1987 Universiade Games, Zagreb, July 8-19 — A565

1986, Sept. 22			**Perf. 13½**	
1817	A565	30d Volleyball	.35	.35
1818	A565	40d Canoeing	.35	.35
1819	A565	100d Gymnastics	.55	.55
1820	A565	150d Fencing	.80	.80
Nos. 1817-1820 (4)			2.05	2.05

18th Joy of Europe Youth Conference A566

Children's drawings: 100d, Dove, by Tanja Faletic, 14. 150d, Buildings, by Johanna Kraus, 12, DDR.

1986, Oct. 2			**Perf. 14**	
1821	A566	100d multicolored	.55	.55
1822	A566	150d multicolored	.80	.80

Rotary Switching Apparatus, Village of Bled — A567

1986, Oct. 4			**Perf. 13½**	
1823	A567	40d multicolored	.25	.25

Telephone exchanges connected with automatic switching equipment, 50th anniv.

INTERPOL 55th General Assembly, Belgrade, Oct. 6-13 — A568

1986, Oct. 6			**Perf. 14**	
1824	A568	150d multicolored	.40	.40

Intl. Brigades, 50th Anniv. — A569

1986, Oct. 21			**Perf. 13½**	
1825	A569	40d multicolored	.25	.25

Intl. Peace Year — A570

1986, Nov. 20				
1826	A570	150d multicolored	.50	.50

Serbian Academy of the Arts and Sciences, Cent. A571

1986, Nov. 1		Photo.	**Perf. 13½**	
1827	A571	40d multicolored	.25	.25

Paintings by Foreign Artists in the Museum of Contemporary Art, Skopje — A572

No. 1828, Still Life, by Frantisek Muzika, Czechoslovakia. #1829, Disturbance, by Rafael Canogar, England. #1830, Iol, by Victor Vasarely, France. #1831, Portrait, by Bernard Buffet, France. #1832, Woman's Head, by Pablo Picasso, Spain.

1986, Dec. 10		Litho.	**Perf. 14**	
1828	A572	30d multi	.25	.25
1829	A572	40d multi	.25	.25
1830	A572	100d multi, vert.	.40	.40
1831	A572	100d multi, vert.	.40	.40
1832	A572	150d multi, vert.	.65	.65
Nos. 1828-1832 (5)			1.95	1.95

Wildlife Conservation A573

30d, Lutra lutra. 40d, Ovis musimon. 100d, Cervus elaphus. 150d, Ursus arctos.

1987, Jan. 22	Litho.	**Perf. 13½x14**		
1833		Strip of 4 + label	8.00	8.00
a.	A573	30d multi	.65	.65
b.	A573	40d multi	.65	.65
c.	A573	100d multi	.65	.65
d.	A573	150d multi	.65	.65

Label pictures nature reserve.

Rudjer Boscovich (1711-1787), Scientist, and Solar Eclipse over Brera Observatory, Italy — A574

1987, Feb. 13			**Perf. 14**	
1834	A574	150d multicolored	.50	.40

European Nature Protection — A575

1987, Mar. 9				
1835	A575	150d shown	1.00	1.00
1836	A575	400d Triglav glacial lake	1.50	1.50

1987 World Alpine Skiing Championships, Crans Montana — A576

1987, Mar. 20		Litho.	**Perf. 14**	
1837	A576	200d multicolored	2.40	2.40

No. 1837 printed in sheets of 8 plus center label.

Natl. Civil Aviation, 60th Anniv. A577

1987, Mar. 20			**Perf. 14**	
1838	A577	150d POTEZ-29	.55	.55
1839	A577	400d DC-10	1.20	1.20

Each printed in sheets of 8 plus center label.

Kole Nedelkovski (1912-1941), Poet, Revolutionary A578

1987, Apr. 2			**Perf. 13½**	
1840	A578	40d multicolored	.25	.25

Liberation of Montenegro from Turkey, 125th Anniv. A579

1987, Apr. 16			**Perf. 13½**	
1841	A579	40d Battle flags, folk guitar	.25	.25

Slovenian Communist Party, Cebine, 50th Anniv. — A580

1987, Apr. 18   **Perf. 14**
1842 A580 40d multicolored   .25 .25

Europa Issue

Tito Bridge, Krk — A581

1987, Apr. 30   **Litho.**   **Perf. 14**
1843 A581 200d shown   .40 .40
1844 A581 400d Bridges over canal   .80 .80

Fruit Trees — A582

1987, May 15   **Litho.**   **Perf. 14**
1845 A582 60d Almond   .25 .25
1846 A582 150d Pear   .65 .65
1847 A582 200d Apple   .80 .80
1848 A582 400d Plum   1.60 1.60
   Nos. 1845-1848 (4)   3.30 3.30

Tito, 1930, by Mosa Pijade — A583

1987, May 25
1849 A583 60d multi   .30 .25
   50th anniv. of Tito's assumption of Yugoslavian communist party leadership.

Vuk Stefanovik Karadzic (1787-1864), Linguist and Historian — A584

   60d, Bust by Petar Ubavkic, his Trsic residence & Vienna. 200d, Portrait by Uros Knezevic, & alphabet from Karadzic's Serbian Dictionary, 1818.

1987, June 10
1850 A584 60d multi   .25 .25
1851 A584 200d multi   .40 .40

Zrenjanin Postal Service, 250th Anniv. A585

1987, June 22   **Perf. 13½**
1852 A585 60d multi   .25 .25

UNIVERSIADE '87, Zagreb, July 8-19 — A586

1987, July 8   **Litho.**   **Perf. 13½**
1853 A586 60d Hurdling   .25 .25
1854 A586 150d Basketball   .40 .40
1855 A586 200d Balance beam   .55 .55
1856 A586 400d Swimming   1.25 1.25
   Nos. 1853-1856 (4)   2.45 2.45
   Each printed in sheets of eight plus label.

Fire Fighting A587

1987, July 20   **Perf. 14**
1857 A587 60d Canadair CL-215 spraying forest   .25 .25
1858 A587 200d Fire boat   .25 .25
   Each printed in sheets of eight plus label.

Monument, Anindol Park, Samobor — A588

1987, Aug. 1   **Perf. 13½**
1859 A588 60d multi   .25 .25
   Communist Party of Croatia, 50th anniv.

Sabac High School, 150th Anniv. A589

1987, Sept. 10   **Litho.**   **Perf. 13½**
1860 A589 80d multi   .25 .25

Exhibition Emblem, Balkan Peninsula, Flowers A590

XI FILATELISTIČKA IZLOŽBA
BALKANSKIH ZEMALJA
NOVI SAD · JUGOSLAVIJA

Clock Tower, Petrovaradin Fortress and Novi Sad — A591

1987, Sept. 19   **Perf. 14**
1861 A590 250d multi   .40 .40

Souvenir Sheet
Imperf
1862 A591 400d multi   1.00 1.00
   BALKANFILA XI, Novi Sad, Sept. 19-26.

19th Joy of Europe Conference A592

   Children's drawings: 250d, Girls in forest, by Bedic Aranka, Juguoslavia. 400d, Scarecrow, by Schaffer Ingeborg, Austria.

1987, Oct. 2   **Litho.**   **Perf. 14**
1863 A592 250d multi   .75 .75
1864 A592 400d multi   .80 .80
   Printed in sheets of nine.

Bridges A593

1987, Oct. 15
1865 A593 80d Arslanagica, Trebinje, 16th cent.   .40 .40
1866 A593 250d Terzija, Djakovica, 15th cent.   .40 .40

Ship, Dunav-Tisa Channel A594

1987, Oct. 20   **Perf. 13½**
1867 A594 80d multi   .25 .25
   City of Titov Vrbas, 600th anniv.

Astronomical and Meteorological Observatory, Belgrade, Cent. — A595

1987, Nov. 21   **Perf. 14**
1868 A595 80d multi   .25 .25

St. Luke the Evangelist, by Raphael A596

   Paintings by foreign artists in national museums: 200d, Infanta Maria Theresa, by Velazquez. 250d, Nicholas Rubens, Painter's Son, by Rubens. 400d, Louis Laure Sennegon, Painter's Niece, by Jean-Baptiste-Camille Corot (1796-1875).

1987, Nov. 28
1869 A596 80d shown   .25 .25
1870 A596 200d multi   .40 .40
1871 A596 250d multi   .40 .40
1872 A596 400d multi   1.10 1.10
   Nos. 1869-1872 (4)   2.15 2.15

Traditional Competitions A597

   80d, Bull fighting. 200d, Ljubicevo Horse Games. 250d, Moresca game. 400d, Sinj iron ring.

1987, Dec. 10
1873 A597 80d multi   .25 .25
1874 A597 200d multi   .40 .40
1875 A597 250d multi   .40 .40
1876 A597 400d multi   1.50 1.50
   Nos. 1873-1876 (4)   2.55 2.55

No. 1800 Surcharged

1987, Sept. 22   **Perf. 13½**
1877 A559 80d on 60d sg grn   .40 .25

Vinodol Codex, City of Vinodolski, Coat of Arms — A598

1988, Jan. 6   **Litho.**   **Perf. 14**
1878 A598 100d multi   .25 .25
   Vinodol Codex, 700th anniv.

Intl. Women's Golden Fox Skiing Championships, 25th Anniv. — A599

1988, Jan. 30
1879 A599 350d Slalom, emblem, Mirobor City   .25 .25
   Printed in sheets of eight plus center label.

World Wildlife Fund — A600

Brown bears (Ursus arctos).

1988, Feb. 1
1880	A600	70d Cub	2.40	1.60
1881	A600	80d Cubs	2.40	1.60
1882	A600	200d Adult, head	2.40	1.60
1883	A600	350d Adult	9.00	4.75
		Nos. 1880-1883 (4)	16.20	9.55

1988 Winter Olympics, Calgary — A601

1988, Feb. 13   **Perf. 14x13½**
1884	A601	350d Slalom	.85	.85
1885	A601	1200d Ice hockey	1.25	1.25

Each printed in sheets of 8 plus center label.

Souvenir Sheet

Map of Europe Highlighting Balkan Nations — A602

1988, Feb. 24   **Litho.**   **Imperf.**
1886	A602	1500d multi	1.75	1.75

Congress of Foreign Affairs Ministers from the Balkan Countries, Belgrade, Feb. 24-26.

1988 Summer Olympics, Seoul — A603

South Korean Landscape — A604

1988, Mar. 21   **Perf. 14x13½**
1887	A603	106d Basketball	.55	.55
1888	A603	450d High jump	.55	.55
1889	A603	500d Pommel horse	.55	.55
1890	A603	1200d Boxing	.55	.55
		Nos. 1887-1890 (4)	2.20	2.20

Souvenir Sheet
Imperf
1891	A604	1500d multi	2.00	2.00

Nos. 1887-1890 printed in sheets of 8 plus center label.

Europa Issue

Telecommunications — A605

1988, Apr. 30   **Litho.**   **Perf. 13½x14**
1892	A605	450d shown	.45	.45
1893	A605	1200d Transportation	.80	.80

Sea Shells — A606

1988, May 14
1894	A606	106d Gibbula magus	.65	.50
1895	A606	550d Pecten jacobaeus	.65	.50
1896	A606	600d Tonna galea	1.00	.80
1897	A606	1000d Argonauta argo	1.50	.80
		Nos. 1894-1897 (4)	3.80	2.60

Trial of Tito and Five Comrades, 60th Anniv. — A607

1988, May 25
1898	A607	106d black & brn	.25	.25

Palace of Princess Ljubica of Serbia, 1st University Building A608

1988, June 14   **Litho.**   **Perf. 13½**
1899	A608	106d multi	.25	.25

Belgrade University, 150th anniv.

Flowers — A609

1988, July 2   **Perf. 14**
1900	A609	600d Phelypaea boissieri	.80	.80
1901	A609	1000d Campanula formanekiana	1.25	1.25

European Nature Protection.

Esperanto, Cent. — A610

1988, July 14   **Perf. 13½**
1902	A610	600d dull vio & ol grn	.80	.55

Printed in sheets of 8 plus center label.

Cargo Ships — A611

Map of the Danube Basin — A612

1988, Aug. 18   **Litho.**   **Perf. 14**
1903	A611	1000d multi	.50	.50

Souvenir Sheet
Imperf
1904	A612	2000d multi	3.25	3.25

Danube Conference, 40th anniv.

13th European Junior Basketball Championships, Aug. 21-28 — A613

1988, Aug. 20   **Perf. 14**
1905	A613	600d multi	.40	.40

1st Horse Race in Belgrade, 125th Anniv. — A614

1988, Aug. 27
1906	A614	140d Thoroughbred racing	.40	.40
1907	A614	600d Steeplechase	.80	.80
1908	A614	1000d Harness racing	1.20	1.20
		Nos. 1906-1908 (3)	2.40	2.40

Museum of Bosnia and Herzegovina, Sarajevo, Cent. — A615

1988, Sept. 10   **Perf. 13½**
1909	A615	140d Museum, Bosnian bellflower	.25	.25

Anti-Cancer and AIDS Campaigns A616

1988, Sept. 24   **Perf. 14**
1910	A616	140d Arm, lobster claw	.25	.25
1911	A616	1000d Blood, scream	.65	.65

Nos. 1801 and 1804 Surcharged
1988, July   **Litho.**   **Perf. 13½**
1912	A559	120d on 93d ultra	.25	.25
1913	A559	140d on 106d brn org	.25	.25

Joy of Europe Youth Conference A617

Portraits of girls by: 1000d, P. Ranosovic. 1100d, Renoir.

1988, Oct. 1   **Litho.**   **Perf. 14**
1914	A617	1000d multi	.65	.65
1915	A617	1100d multi	.80	.80

See Nos. 1987-1988.

Slovenski Academy, 50th Anniv. — A618

1988, Oct. 13   **Litho.**   **Perf. 14**
1916	A618	200d multi	.25	.25

Museum Exhibits and Places of Origin A618a

200d, Wood bassinet, traditional wedding (Galicka). #1918, Embroidery, man and woman wearing folk costumes of Vojvodina. #1919, Scimitar, flintlock, man & woman wearing folk costumes of Kotor (Bokelji). 1100d, Masks (Kurenti).

1988, Oct. 18
1917	A618a	200d multi, vert.	.65	.65
1918	A618a	1000d shown	.65	.65
1919	A618a	1000d multi, vert.	.65	.65
1920	A618a	1100d multi	.65	.65
		Nos. 1917-1920 (4)	2.60	2.60

Woman with Lyre, 4th Cent. B.C. — A618b

Grecian terra cotta figurines: #1922, Eros & Psyche, 2nd cent. BC. #1923, Seated woman, 3rd cent. BC. 1100d, Woman by Stele, 3rd cent. BC.

1988, Oct. 28

1921	A618b	200d multi	.50	.50
1922	A618b	1000d multi	.50	.50
1923	A618b	1000d multi	.50	.50
1924	A618b	1100d multi	.50	.50
		Nos. 1921-1924 (4)	2.00	2.00

Peter II (1813-1851), Prince Bishop and Poet — A618c

Portraits and: 200d, Cetinje Monastery and frontispiece of his principal work. 1000d, Njegos Mausoleum.

1988, Nov. 1

1925	A618c	200d multi	.25	.25
1926	A618c	1000d multi	.55	.55

Postal Service Types of 1986 and:

Telephone Receiver and Telephone Card — A619

Bird, Posthorn, Simulated Stamp — A620

Propeller Plane, Two Arrows and Map — A621

Designs: 170d, 300d, Flower, envelope, mailbox and simulated stamp. 220d, PTT emblem on simulated stamp, mail coach. 800d, Postman on motorcycle. No. 1941, Postman, resident. No. 1942, Mail train. No. 1943, Envelopes, satellite dish. No. 1944, Earth, telecommunications satellite. 100,000d, Bird, open envelope, flower. 170d, 220d, 300d, 2000d, 5000d, No. 1941 vert.

1988-89 **Litho.** **Perf. 13¼**

1935	A559	170d dl grn	.40	.25
1936	A559	220d brn org	.40	.25
1937	A559	300d ver	.40	.25
1938	A559	800d brt ultra	.25	.25
1939	A619	2000d multi	.25	.25
1940	A620	5000d dk red & ultra	.80	.40
1941	A559	10,000d org & brt lil	.55	.55
1942	A559	20,000d lt ol grn & lt red brn	.55	.55

Perf. 13½

1943	A560	10,000d multi	1.25	.55
1944	A560	20,000d multi	.80	.55
1944A	A621	50,000d org & dl bl	1.00	.40
1945	A560	100,000d org & dl grn	.25	.25
		Nos. 1935-1945 (12)	6.90	4.50

Perf. 12½

1937a	A559	300d	.40	.25
1938a	A559	800d	.25	.25
1939a	A619	2000d	.25	.25
1940a	A620	5000d	.80	.40
1941a	A559	10,000d	.25	.25
1942a	A559	20,000d	.25	.25
		Nos. 1937a-1941a (5)	1.95	1.40

Issued: 1988 — 170d, 11/17; 220d, 12/6; 1989 — 300d, 5/11; 800d, 2000d, 7/20; 5000d, 1/20; #1941, 11/28; #1942, 12/8; #1943, 3/20; #1944, 7/19; 50,000d, 11/8; 100,000d, 12/4.
See Nos. 2008-2009, 2017, 2052. For surcharges see Nos. 1972, 1974, 2048.

Yugoslavia, 70th Anniv. — A622

1988, Dec. 1 **Litho.** **Perf. 14**
1946 A622 200d Krsmanovic Hall, Belgrade   .25 .25

Nos. 1805-1806 Surcharged

1988 **Litho.** **Perf. 13½**
1947	A559	170d on 120d	.80	.25
1948	A559	220d on 140d	.80	.25

Issued: #1947, Dec. 21; #1948, Dec. 15.

Miniature Sheet

Victory of Yugoslavian Athletes at the 1988 Summer Olympics, Seoul — A623

Medals and events: a, Women's air pistol. b, Team handball. c, Table tennis. d, Wrestling. e, Double sculls. f, Basketball. g, Water polo. h, Boxing.

1988, Dec. 31 **Litho.** **Perf. 14**
1949   Sheet of 8 + label   3.00 3.00
a.-h.   A623 500d any single   .30 .25

Ivan Gundulic (1589-1638), Poet — A624

1989, Jan. 7 **Perf. 13½**
1950 A624 220d multi   .40 .25

World Wildlife Fund — A625

Ducks.

1989, Feb. 23 **Litho.** **Perf. 14**
1951		Strip of 4 + label	14.00	8.00
a.	A625	300d Anas platyrhynchos	1.25	.50
b.	A625	2100d Anas crecca	3.50	1.75
c.	A625	2200d Anas acuta	3.50	1.75
d.	A625	2200d Anas clypeata	3.50	1.75

Printed in sheets of 20+5 labels. Label pictures WWF emblem.

Publication of The Glory of the Duchy of Kranjska, by Johann Valvasor (1641-1693), 300th Anniv. A626

1989, Mar. 10 **Perf. 13½**
1952 A626 300d Portrait   .25 .25

Flowering Plants — A627

1989, Mar. 20 **Perf. 14**
1953	A627	300d Bulbocodium vernum	1.00	1.00
1954	A627	2100d Nymphaea al-ba	1.00	1.00
1955	A627	2200d Fritillaria degeniana, vert.	1.00	1.00
1956	A627	3000d Orchis simia, vert.	1.00	1.00
		Nos. 1953-1956 (4)	4.00	4.00

6th World Air-Gun Championships, Sarajevo, Apr. 27-30 — A628

1989, Apr. 26
1957 A628 3000d multi   .50 .50

Europa 1989 — A629

1989, Apr. 29
1958	A629	3000d shown	.80	.80
1959	A629	6000d Marbles	.80	.80

15th European Trophy for Natl. Athletic Club Champions, Belgrade, June 3-4 — A630

1989, June 1 **Litho.** **Perf. 13½**
1960 A630 4000d Pole vault   .80 .80

Printed in sheets of 8+label picturing flags of participating nations.

Yugoslavia Motorcycle Grand Prix, Rijeka, June 9-11 — A631

Various race scenes.

1989, June 9 **Perf. 14**
1961	A631	500d multi	.25	.25
1962	A631	4000d multi	.40	.40

Souvenir Sheet
Perf. 14x13½
1963 A631 6000d multi   1.50 1.50
No. 1963 contains one 54x35 stamp.

No. 1246 Surcharged

1989, Apr. 6 **Litho.** **Perf. 13**
1964 A323 100d on 1d dull grn   .40 .25
a.   Perf. 13x12½   .40 .40

Tito — A632

1989, May 25 **Perf. 13½x14**
1965 A632 300d multi   .25 .25

Early Adriatic Ships A633

a, Ancient Greek galley. b, Roman galley. c, Crusade galleon, 13th cent. d, Nava of Dubrovnik, 16th cent. e, French ship, 17th cent. f, Vessels, 18th cent. 3000d, View of Dubrovnik seaport, called Ragusa in Italian, from a 17th cent. engraving.

1989, June 10 **Perf. 13½**
1966   Block of 6   2.00 1.50
a.-f.   A633 1000d any single   .30 .25

Souvenir Sheet
1967 A633 3000d multi   .75 .35
No. 1967 contains one 75x32mm stamp. Nos. 1966-1967 printed se-tenant and sold folded in booklet cover.

26th European Basketball Championships — A634

Map of Europe, basketball and flags of: No. 1968, France, Yugoslavia, Greece, Bulgaria. No. 1969, Netherlands, Italy, Russia, Spain.

1989, June 20 **Litho.** **Perf. 13½x14**
1968	A634	2000d multi	.25	.25
1969	A634	2000d multi	.25	.25

Nos. 1968-1969 exist with setenant label.

Defeat of the Serbians at the Battle of Kosovo, 1389 — A635

1989, June 28
1970 A635 500d multi   .25 .25

Danilovgrad Library, Cent. A636

1989, July 15 **Litho.** **Perf. 13½**
1971 A636 500d multi   .25 .25

Nos. 1797, 1719, 1935, 1936
Surcharged

1989
1972	A559	400d on 30d lt brn vio	.80	.25
1973	A323	700d on 70d brt ultra	.80	.25
1974	A559	700d on 170d dull green	.80	.25
1975	A559	700d on 220d brn org	.80	.25
		Nos. 1972-1975 (4)	3.20	1.00

Issued: #1975, 7/19; #1974, 8/10; #1972, 8/23; #1973, 12/13.

Kulin Ban Charter, 800th Anniv. — A638

1989, Aug. 29   Litho.   Perf. 14
1976	A638	500d multi	.25	.25

World Rowing Championships — A639

1989, Sept. 2   Perf. 13½
1977	A639	10,000d multi	.50	.50

Interparliamentary Union, Cent. — A640

Architecture: No. 1978, Parliament, London (emblem at R). No. 1979, Notre Dame Cathedral (emblem at L).

1989, Sept. 4   Perf. 13½x14
1978	A640	10,000d multi	.40	.40
1979	A640	10,000d multi	.40	.40

A641

View of Belgrade and Maps
BEOGRAD '89 — A642

Architecture & antiquities of non-aligned summit host cities: #1980, Belgrade '61, Cairo

---

'64. #1981, Lusaka '70, Algiers '73. #1982, Colombo '76, Havana '79. #1983, New Delhi '83, Harare '76.

1989, Sept. 4
1980	A641	10,000d multi	.25	.25
1981	A641	10,000d multi	.25	.25
1982	A641	10,000d multi	.25	.25
1983	A641	10,000d multi	.25	.25
		Nos. 1980-1983 (4)	1.00	1.00

Souvenir Sheet
Perf. 14
1984	A642	20,000d multi	1.25	1.25

European Nature Protection — A643

8000d, Paeonia officinalis, Brezovica-Jazinac Lake. 10,000d, Paeonia corallina, Mirusa Canyon.

1989, Sept. 11   Perf. 14
1985	A643	8000d multi	.40	.40
1986	A643	10,000d multi	.40	.40

Joy of Europe Type of 1988
Portraits of children: No. 1987, Child with Lamb, by Jovan Popovic. No. 1988, Girl Feeding Dog, by Albert Cuyp (1620-1691).

1989, Oct. 2   Litho.   Perf. 14
1987	A617	10,000d multi	.50	.50
1988	A617	10,000d multi	.50	.50

Karpos Uprising, 300th Anniv. — A644

1989, Oct. 20   Litho.   Perf. 13½
1989	A644	1200d ver & dark brn	.25	.25

No. 1833c, Cancellation, Quill Pen, Wax Seals and Seal Device on Parchment A645

1989, Oct. 31   Perf. 14
1990	A645	1200d multicolored	.25	.25

Stamp Day.

Museum Exhibits A646

1989, Nov. 2
1991	A646	1200d Pack-saddle maker	.25	.25
1992	A646	14,000d Cooper	.55	.55
1993	A646	15,000d Winegrower	.80	.80
1994	A646	30,000d Weaver	1.40	1.40
		Nos. 1991-1994 (4)	3.00	3.00

Religious Paintings — A647

2100d, Apostle Matthew, vert. 21,000d, St. Barbara, vert. 30,000d, The Fourth Day of Creation. 50,000d, The Fifth Day of Creation.

1989, Nov. 28   Litho.   Perf. 14
1997	A647	2100d multicolored	.25	.25
1998	A647	21,000d multicolored	.40	.40
1999	A647	30,000d multicolored	.80	.80
2000	A647	50,000d multicolored	1.25	1.25
		Nos. 1997-2000 (4)	2.70	2.70

A648

League of Communists 14th Congress — A649

1990, Jan. 20   Litho.   Perf. 13½x14
2001	A648	10,000d Star	.30	.25
2002	A648	50,000d Computer	.55	.55

Souvenir Sheet
Imperf
2003	A649	100,000d Star, diff.	1.25	1.25

Postal Service Types of 1986-88
10p, Man posting letters in mailbox. 20p, Postal employee sorting mail. 30p, Postman, resident. 40p, Woman at telephone station. 1d, Mail train. 2d, Ship & envelope. 3d, Flower, mailbox, envelope & simulated stamp. 5d, Airplane, letters, map of Europe. 10d, Bird, open envelope, flower. 20d, Woman at telephone station.

Designs for other values as before.
10p, 20p, 30p, 40p, 3d, 5d vert.

1990   Perf. 12½
2004	A559	10p br yel grn & vio	.50	.25
2005	A559	20p red vio & org	.50	.25
2006	A559	30p org & yel grn	.25	.25
2007	A559	40p blue grn & red vio	.25	.25
2008	A620	50p pur & blue grn	.30	.25
2009	A619	60p red org & brt vio	.30	.25
2013	A559	1d rose lil & green-ish bl	.50	.25
2014	A559	2d red lil & blue	.90	.25
2015	A559	3d org & dl blue	.90	.30
2017	A619	5d ultra & grnsh blue	.90	.45
2019	A559	10d red org & vio bl	1.75	1.40
		Nos. 2004-2019 (11)	7.05	4.15

Issued: 10p, 20p, 2/9; 30p, 40p, 1/24; 50p, 1/29; 60p, 2/6; 2d, 2/14; 3d, 2/22; 5d, 1/31; 1d, 5/24; 10d, 6/12.
For surcharges see Nos. 2049-2053, 2168//2176.

1990-92   Perf. 13¼
2004a	A559	10p br yel grn & vio	.50	.25
2005a	A559	20p red vio & org	1.40	.70
2006a	A559	30p org & yel grn	.25	.25
2007a	A559	40p blue grn & red vio	.25	.25

2008a	A620	50p pur & blue grn	.30	.25
2009a	A619	60p red org & brt vio	.30	.30
2013a	A559	1d rose lil & green-ish bl	1.75	1.25
2014a	A559	2d red lil & blue	.65	.45
2015a	A559	3d org & dl blue>	2.50	2.25
2017a	A619	5d ultra & grnsh blue	1.25	1.00
2019a	A559	10d red org & vio bl	7.50	5.50
2021	A559	20d car rose & org	.45	.25
		Nos. 2004a-2021 (12)	17.10	12.70

Issued: 30p, 40p, 1/24; 50p, 1/29; 5d, 1/31; 60p, 2/6; 10p, 20p, 2/9; 2d, 2/14; 3d, 2/22; 10d, 6/12; 1d, 7/2; 20d, 1/27/92.
For surcharges see Nos. 2049a-2053a, 2168//2176.

Anti-smoking Campaign A650

1990, Jan. 31   Litho.   Perf. 13½x13
2034	A650	10d gry & yel brn	.90	.90

Protected Fish — A651

1990, Feb. 15   Perf. 13½
2035		Strip of 4 + label	8.00	8.00
a.	A651	1d *Esox lucius*	1.25	1.25
b.	A651	5d *Silurus glanis*	1.25	1.25
c.	A651	10d *Lota lota*	1.25	1.25
d.	A651	15d *Perca fluviatilis*	1.25	1.25

Zabljak Fortress, Illuminated Manuscript, Coat of Arms — A652

1990, Mar. 9   Perf. 14x13½
2036	A652	50p multicolored	1.20	1.20

Enthronement of Djuradj Crnojevic, 500th anniv.

ITU, 125th Anniv A653

1990, Mar. 23
2037	A653	6.50d Telegrapher, computer	.90	.90

1990 World Cup Soccer Championships, Italy — A654

1990, Apr. 16
2038	A654	6.50d shown	1.40	1.40
2039	A654	10d multi, diff.	1.40	1.40

Europa
1990 — A655

Post offices: 6.50d, PTT Central, Skopje. 10d, Telecommunications Central, Belgrade.

1990, Apr. 23   **Perf. 13½x14**
2040 A655 6.50d multicolored   1.60 1.60
2041 A655 10d multicolored   1.60 1.60

A656

1990, Apr. 30   **Litho.**   **Perf. 13½**
2042 A656 6.50d multicolored   1.00 1.00

Labor Day, cent.

A657

Eurovision Song Contest: 10d, Conductor, musical score.

1990, May 5   **Perf. 14x13½**
2043 A657 6.50d multicolored   1.10 1.10
2044 A657 10d multicolored   1.20 1.20

No. 2043 exists with setenant label.

Tennis — A658

1990, May 15   **Litho.**   **Perf. 14**
2045 A658 6.50d multicolored   1.40 1.40
2046 A658 10d multicolored   1.40 1.40

Tito — A659

1990, May 25   **Perf. 13½x14**
2047 A659 50p multicolored   .30 .30

Nos. 1938, 2004-2009a Surcharged

No. 2048   No. 2049

1990-91   **Litho.**   **Perf. 12½**
2048 A559 50p on 800d (#1938a)   .45 .25
    a.   Perf 13¼ (#1938)   .45 .25
2049 A559 50p on 20p (#2005)   .45 .25
    a.   Perf 13¼ (#2005a) ('91)   3.50 2.75

2050 A559 1d on 30p (#2006)   .45 .25
    a.   Perf 13¼ (#2006a)   3.50 3.25
2051 A559 2d on 40p (#2007), I   .90 .45
    a.   Type II, perf. 13¼ (#2007a)   1.40 .90
    b.   Type I, perf. 13¼ (#2007a)   2.25 2.25
2052 A619 5d on 60p (#2009)   .45 .25
    a.   Perf 13¼ (#2009a)   4.50 1.75
2053 A559 10d on 10p (#2004)   .45 .25
    a.   Perf 13¼ (#2004a)   1.00 .55
    Nos. 2048-2053 (6)   3.15 1.70

Type II surcharge has 3 instead of 2 bars obliterating old value, new denomination is at bottom of stamp.
Issued: #2048, 2048a, 5/24; #2050, 8/7; #2049, 2049a, 9/18; #2051-2051b, 10/2; #2050a, 1/4/91; #2053, 2053a, 12/12/91; #2052, 2052a, 12/17/91.

Public Postal Service in Serbia, 150th Anniv. A660

1990, May 25
2056 A660 50p multicolored   2.25 1.50

Pigeons A661

1990, June 8   **Perf. 13½**
2057 A661 50p multicolored   .55 .55
2058 A661 5d multicolored   1.10 1.10
2059 A661 6.50d multi, vert.   1.10 1.10
2060 A661 10d multi, vert.   2.75 2.75
    Nos. 2057-2060 (4)   5.50 5.50

Mercury Mine at Idrija, 500th Anniv. — A662

Designs: 6.50d, Miners at work, ca. 1490.

1990, June 22   **Perf. 13½x14**
2061 A662 50p multicolored   .25 .25
2062 A662 6.50d multicolored   1.00 1.00

Newspaper "Vjesnik," 50th Anniv. — A663

1990, June 23   **Perf. 13½**
2063 A663 60p multicolored   .70 .70

Serbian Migration, 300th Anniv. — A664

1990, Sept. 20   **Perf. 14**
2064 A664 1d shown   .25 .25
2065 A664 6.50d Caravan   .90 .90

European Track & Field Championships, Split — A665

1990, Aug. 27   **Perf. 13½**
2067 A665 1d Start of race   .60 .60
2068 A665 6.50d Runners' feet   .90 .90

Souvenir Sheet

2069 A665 10d Runners   2.25 2.25

No. 2069 contains one 54x35mm stamp. A 50p exists but no information on its postal category is available.

Joy of Europe A666

Paintings: 6.50d, Children by I. Kobilca. 10d, William III of Orange as a Child by A. Hanneman, vert.

1990, Oct. 2   **Litho.**   **Perf. 14**
2070 A666 6.50d multicolored   1.10 1.10
2071 A666 10d multicolored   1.50 1.50

Souvenir Sheets

29th Chess Olympics, Novi Sad — A667

1990, Oct. 2   **Perf. 11½**

Granite Paper

2072 Sheet of 4   8.00 8.00
    a.   A667 1d shown   1.10 1.10
    b.   A667 5d Rook, bishop, knight   1.10 1.10
    c.   A667 6.50d King, bishop, knght, pawn   1.10 1.10
    d.   A667 10d Chess pieces   1.10 1.10

Imperf

2073 Sheet of 4   8.00 8.00
    a.   A667 1d like No. 2072a   1.10 1.10
    b.   A667 5d like No. 2072b   1.10 1.10
    c.   A667 6.50d like No. 2072c   1.10 1.10
    d.   A667 10d like No. 2072d   1.10 1.10

No. 2073 has blue margin inscriptions. Emblems on Nos. 2072a-2072d are in silver, those on Nos. 2073a-2073d are in gold.

Stamp Day A668

1990, Oct. 2   **Perf. 14**
2074 A668 2d multicolored   .60 .55

150th anniv. of the Penny Black.

European Nature Protection A669

1990, Nov. 16   **Litho.**   **Perf. 14**
2075 A669 6.50d Vransko Lake   1.10 1.10
2076 A669 10d Gyps fulvus   1.50 1.50

Frescoes — A670

Designs: 2d, King Milutin, Monastery of Our Lady, Ljeviska. 5d, Saint Sava, Mileseva Monastery. 6.50d, Saint Elias, Moraca Monastery. 10d, Jesus Christ, Sopocani Monastery.

1990, Nov. 28
2077 A670 2d multicolored   .45 .45
2078 A670 5d multicolored   .95 .95
2079 A670 6.50d multicolored   .95 .95
2080 A670 10d multicolored   1.40 1.40
    Nos. 2077-2080 (4)   3.75 3.75

Dr. Bozo Milanovic (1890-1980), Religious and Political Leader A671

1990, Dec. 20   **Litho.**   **Perf. 13½**
2081 A671 2d multicolored   .30 .30

Religious Carvings A672

Designs: 2d, Christ in the temple. 5d, Nativity scene. 6.50d, Flight from Egypt, horiz. 10d, Entry into Jerusalem, horiz.

1990, Dec. 24   **Perf. 13½x14, 14x13½**
2082 A672 2d gld, brn, & blk   .45 .45
2083 A672 5d gld, brn, & blk   .70 .70
2084 A672 6.50d gld, brn, & blk   .90 .90
2085 A672 10d gld, brn, & blk   1.10 1.10
    Nos. 2082-2085 (4)   3.15 3.15

Protected Birds — A673

1991, Jan. 31   **Litho.**   **Perf. 14x13½**
2086 Strip of 4 + label   9.00 9.00
    a.   A673 2d Vanellus vanellus   1.10 1.10
    b.   A673 5d Lanius senator   1.10 1.10
    c.   A673 6.50d Grus grus   1.10 1.10
    d.   A673 10d Mergus merganser   1.10 1.10

Flora — A674

1991, Feb. 20
2087 A674 2d Crocus kosaninii   .45 .45
2088 A674 6d Crocus scardicus   .55 .55
2089 A674 7.50d Crocus rujanesis   .60 .60
2090 A674 15d Crocus adamii   2.00 2.00
    Nos. 2087-2090 (4)   3.60 3.60

Bishop Josip J. Strossmayer (1815-1905), Founder of Academy of Arts and Sciences A675

1991, Mar. 4   Litho.   Perf. 13½x14
2091 A675 2d multicolored   1.10   .60
Academy of Arts and Sciences, 125th Anniv.

Wolfgang Amadeus Mozart, Composer A676

1991, Mar. 20   Perf. 14
2092 A676 7.50d multicolored   .90   .60

Otto Lilienthal's First Glider Flight, Cent. — A677

Designs: 7.50d, Edvard Rusjan (1886-1911), pilot, aircraft designer. 15d, Otto Lilienthal (1848-1896), aviation pioneer.

1991, Apr. 1
2093 A677 7.50d multicolored   1.10 1.10
2094 A677 15d multicolored   1.40 1.40
Printed in sheets of 8 plus label.

Lhotse I, Himalayas, South Face First Climbed by Tomo Cesen, 1990 — A678

1991, Apr. 24   Perf. 14x13½
2095 A678 7.50d multicolored   .90   .55

Europa A679

Designs: 7.50d, Telecommunications satellite. 15d, Satellite, antenna, telephone.

1991, May 6   Perf. 14
2096 A679 7.50d multicolored   .90   .90
2097 A679 15d multicolored   1.75 1.75

Franciscan Monastery, Trsat, 700th Anniv. — A680

1991, May 10   Litho.   Perf. 13½x14
2098 A680 3.50d multicolored   .80   .25

Governments of Danube River Region Conf., Belgrade — A681

15d, Danube River shipping. 20d, Course of Danube, landmarks, regional animals.

1991, May 15   Perf. 13½
2099 A681 7.50d multicolored   1.00 1.00
2100 A681 15d multicolored   1.50 1.50
Souvenir Sheet
2101 A681 20d multicolored   9.00 9.00
No. 2101 contains one 55x35mm stamp.

Opening of Karavanke Tunnel — A682

Designs: 4.50d, Passage Over Karavanke by J. Valvasor, 17th century. 11d, Entrance to new Karavanke Tunnel.

1991, June 1   Perf. 14x13½
2102 A682 4.50d multicolored   .60   .60
2103 A682 11d multicolored   .90   .90

Basketball, Cent. — A683

1991, June 15   Perf. 13½x14
2104 A683 11d shown   1.10 1.10
2105 A683 15d Nets, "100"   1.10 1.10

Yugoslavian Insurrection, 50th Anniv. — A684

Tin Ujevic (1891-1955), Writer — A685

Designs: 4.50d, Partisan Memorial Medal, 1941. 11d, Medal for Courage.

1991, July 4   Litho.   Perf. 14
2106 A684 4.50d multicolored   .35   .35
2107 A684 11d multicolored   .70   .70
Yugoslav Natl. Army, 50th Anniv.

1991, July 5   Perf. 13½
2108 A685 4.50d multicolored   .60   .45

Jacobus Gallus (1550-1591), Composer A686

1991, July 18
2109 A686 11d multicolored   .60   .60

Lighthouses of Adriatic and Danube — A687

Designs: a, Savudrija, 1818. b, Sveti Ivan na pucini, 1853. c, Porer, 1833. d, Stoncica, 1865. e, Olipa, c. 1842. f, Glavat, 1884. g, Veli rat, 1849. h, Vir, 1881. i, Tajerske sestrice, 1876. j, Razanj, 1875. k, Derdap-Danube. l, Tamis-Danube.

1991, July 25   Litho.   Perf. 13½
2110 A687 10d Bklt. pane of 12, #a.-l.   12.00 12.00

Sremski Karlovci High School, Bicent. — A688

1991, Sept. 12   Litho.   Perf. 14
2111 A688 4.50d multicolored   .45   .30

European Nature Protection A689

1991, Sept. 24   Perf. 13½x14
2112 A689 11d Palingenia longicauda   .90   .90
2113 A689 15d Phalacrocorax pygmaeus   .90   .90

A690

1991, Sept. 28   Perf. 14
2114 A690 4.50d multicolored   .45   .30
Town of Subotica, 600th anniv.

A691

Paintings: 15d, Little Dubravka, by Jovan Bijelic (1886-1964). 30d, Little Girl with a Cat by Mary Cassatt (1845-1926).

1991, Oct. 2
2115 A691 15d multicolored   .70   .70
2116 A691 30d multicolored   1.10 1.10
Joy of Europe.

33rd Intl. Apicultural Congress, APIMONDIA '91 — A692

1991, Sept. 28   Litho.   Perf. 13½x14
2117 A692 11d multicolored   1.10   .90

Stamp Day, Monument to Prince Michael Obrenovich, Serbia #1 — A693

1991, Oct. 31   Perf. 14
2118 A693 4.50d multicolored   .60   .25
First Serbia Postage Stamps, 125th Anniv.

Museum Exhibits A694

Flags and medals: 20d, Vucjido battle flag, medal for courage. 30d, Grahovac battle flag and medal. 40d, Montenegrin state flag, medal for bravery. 50d, Montenegrin court flag, medal of Petrovich Nyegosh Dynasty.

1991, Nov. 28   Perf. 13½x14
2119 A694 20d multicolored   .25   .25
2120 A694 30d multicolored   .45   .45
2121 A694 40d multicolored   .60   .60
2122 A694 50d multicolored   .90   .90
   Nos. 2119-2122 (4)   2.20 2.20

Illustrations from Ancient Manuscripts A695

Designs: 20d, Angel carrying Sun around Earth, 17th cent. 30d, Celnica Gospel, menology for April, 14th cent. 40d, Angel from the Annunciation, 13th cent. 50d, Mary Magdalene, 12th cent.

1991, Dec. 12
2123 A695 20d multicolored   .25   .25
2124 A695 30d multicolored   .45   .45
2125 A695 40d multicolored   .60   .60
2126 A695 50d multicolored   .90   .90
   Nos. 2123-2126 (4)   2.20 2.20

Gotse Deltchev
(1872-1903),
Macedonian
Revolutionary
A696

1992, Jan. 29   Litho.   Perf. 13½
2127 A696 5d multicolored   2.25 2.25

Red Star,
European and
World Soccer
Champions
A697

1992, Jan. 29   Litho.   Perf. 14x13½
2128 A697 17d multicolored   2.00 2.00

A698   A699

1992, Feb. 8   Perf. 14x13½
2129 A698 80d Ski jumping   1.75 1.75
2130 A698 100d Freestyle skiing 1.75 1.75
1992 Winter Olympics, Albertville.

1992, Mar. 10   Litho.   Perf. 14
Protected Animals: a, 50d, Lepus
europaeus. b, 60d, Pteromys volans. c, 80d,
Dryomys nitedula. d, 100d, Cricetus cricetus.
2131 A699 Strip of 4, #a.-d. +
            label   8.00 8.00

Madonna and
Child, 14th
century,
Pec — A700

1992, Mar. 14   Perf. 13½x14
2132 A700 80d multicolored   1.00 1.00
Promotion of Breastfeeding.

Ski Association of Montenegro — A701

1992, Mar. 25   Perf. 14x13½
2133 A701 8d multicolored   5.00 5.00
Skiing in Montenegro, cent.

1860 Fountain,
Belgrade —
A702

 A702a

A702b   A702c

A702d   A702e

A702f   A702g

A702h   A702i

A702j

5d, Griffins, 14th cent. #2136, #2139, Fisherman Fountain, Belgrade. #2138, like #2137.
300d, Kalemgdan Fountain, Belgrade. 500d,
Fountain, Sremski Karlovci. #2142, Symbols
of Miroslav-Evangelium, 12th cent. 3000d,
Fountain, Studenica. 5000d, Fountain,
Oplenzu. 10,000d, 500,000d, Health spa,
Vrnjacka Banja. 50,000d, Envelopes over map
of Europe. #2147, Airplane. #2148, Health
spa, Bukovacka Banja.

Inscribed "1992" or "1993"
1992-93   Litho.   Perf. 13¼
2135 A702a 5d brn & olive   1.00   .25
2136 A702   50d dk bl & lt bl .45   .25
2137 A702   50d violet   .45   .35
2138 A702   100d lil rose &
             pink   .45   .25
2139 A702   100d dk grn & lt
             grn   .25   .25
2140 A702b 300d brn & red
             brn   .45   .25
2141 A702c 500d dk ol & pale
             org   .90   .25
   a. Perf. 12½   1.75 1.75
2142 A702d (A) red,
             18x22mm   1.75   .45
   a. Perf. 12½   4.00   .45
   b. Inscribed "1996," Perf. 13¼ 2.25 2.25
   c. Inscribed "1996," perf. 12½ .90   .25
   d. Inscribed "1997," perf. 12½ 1.50 .25
   e. Inscribed "2002," perf. 12½ 5.00 1.50
2143 A702e 3000d red brn   .45   .25
   a. Perf. 12½   2.75 2.25
2144 A702f 5000d vio &
             yel brn   .45   .25
   a. Perf 12½   3.50 2.75
2145 A702g 10,000d vio bl &
             grn bl   1.00   .25
2146 A702h 50,000d gray &
             gray bl   .45   .25
   a.   1.10   .90
2147 A702i 100,000d red & bl .90   .45
   a.   1.10   .90
2148 A702j 100,000d brn red
             & brn   .90   .25
2149 A702g 500,000d bl & vio .45   .25
   Nos. 2135-2149 (15)   10.30 4.25

Issued: #2137, 4/1/92; #2139, 5/6/92; 5d,
11/24/92; #2136, 12/15/92; #2138, 12/22/92;
300d, 12/3/92; 500d, 1/14/93; #2142, 4/5/93;

#2142a, 1993; #2143, 4/23/93; 5000d,
3/18/93; 10,000d, 11/9/93; 50,000d, 6/10/93;
100,000d, 6/28/93; 100,000d, 12/6/93;
500,000d, 8/10/93.
   No. 2142 was valued at 3000d on day of
issue.
   See No. 2386. For surcharges see Nos.
2220a-2220l, 2253-2254.

Sinking of the
Titanic, 80th
Anniv. — A703

1992, Apr. 14   Perf. 14
2152 A703 150d multicolored   .90 .90

Expo
'92,
Seville
A704

1992, Apr. 20
2153 A704 150d multicolored   .90 .90

Discovery of
America,
500th
Anniv. — A705

1992, May 5   Litho.   Perf. 13½x14
2154 A705 300d Columbus,
            ship   4.50 4.50
2155 A705 500d Columbus'
            fleet   4.50 4.50
Souvenir Sheet
Perf. 14x13½
2156 A705 1200d Ships in port 13.50 13.50
   Europa. No. 2156 contains one 54x34mm
stamp.

1992 Summer
Olympics,
Barcelona — A706

1992, May 20   Perf. 14x13½
2157 A706 500d Pistol shoot-
            ing   .90 .90
2158 A706 500d Water polo   .90 .90
2159 A706 500d Tennis   .90 .90
2160 A706 500d Handball   .90 .90
   Nos. 2157-2160 (4)   3.60 3.60

European Soccer
Championships — A707

Various soccer plays.

1992, June 1   Perf. 13½
2161 A707 1000d shown   1.60 1.60
2162 A707 1000d multicolored 1.60 1.60

Domestic
Cats — A708

Designs: No. 2163, Red Persian. No. 2164,
White Persian. No. 2165, Yellow tabby. No.
2166, British blue short-hair.

1992, June 25   Litho.   Perf. 13½x14
Background Color
Cyrillic Letters
2163 A708 1000d blue   1.60 1.60
2164 A708 1000d purple   1.60 1.60
Latin Letters
2165 A708 1000d dark purple 1.60 1.60
2166 A708 1000d brown   1.60 1.60
   Nos. 2163-2166 (4)   6.40 6.40

Steam
Locomotives
A709

Designs: a, JDZ 162. b, JDZ 151. c, JDZ 73.
d, JDZ 83. e, JDZ 16. f, Prince Nicholas'
coach.

1992, July 3   Litho.   Perf. 14
2167 A709 1000d Booklet
            pane of 6,
            #a.-f.   15.00 15.00

Nos. 2005//2017a
Surcharged

1992   Perfs., Etc. as Before
2168 A559 2d on 30p #2006   .90 .50
   a. Perf 13¼ (#2006a)   1.75 1.00
2169 A559 5d on 20p #2005 1.75 .25
   a. Perf 13¼ (#2007a)   1.75 1.00
2170 A559 5d on 40p #2007   .90 .50
2171 A620 10d on 50p #2008 1.75 .25
2172 A621 10d on 5d #2017a .90 .25
2173 A559 20d on 1d #2013 3.00 .90
   a. Perf 13¼ (#2013a)   1.75 .90
2174 A621 20d on 5d type of
            #2017, yel,
            bl & grn bl   1.00 .50
2175 A559 50d on 2d #2014 10.00 5.00
   a. Perf 13¼ (#2014a)   1.75 .25
2176 A559 100d on 3d #2015 6.00 2.00
   a. Perf 13¼ (#2015a)   3.50 .25
   Nos. 2168-2176 (9)   26.20 10.15

Issued: #2168, 2170, 10/26; #2169, 9/12;
#2171, 9/17; #2172, 10/29; #2173, 2175-2176,
8/6; #2174, 11/9.

World Chess
Champions
A710

1992, Sept. 14   Litho.   Perf. 14
2177 A710 500d Bobby Fischer 1.75 1.75
2178 A710 500d Boris Spassky 1.75 1.75

Telephone
Service in
Vojvodina,
Cent.
A711

1892 Telephone, buildings of Novi Sad, Subotica and Zrenjanin.

1992, Oct. 1
2179 A711 10d multicolored   1.40 1.40

Stamp Day A712

Design: Montenegro #7, musician.

1992, Oct. 2
2180 A712 50d multicolored   1.00 .90

European Art — A713

Europa: No. 2181, Ballet Dancer, by Edgar Degas (1834-1917). No. 2182, Painting of young man, by U. Knezevic.

1992, Oct. 2
2181 A713 500d multicolored   1.40 1.40
2182 A713 500d multicolored   1.40 1.40

European Nature Protection A714

1992, Nov. 14   **Perf. 13½**
2183 A714 500d Tetrao urogallus   4.00 4.00
2184 A714 500d Pelecanus onocrotalus   4.00 4.00

Publisher Srpska Knjizevna Zadruga, Cont. — A715

1992, Nov. 20   **Perf. 14**
2185 A715 100d multicolored   1.00 1.00

Traditional Architecture — A716

Designs: No. 2186, Ancient hut, Zlatibor region. No. 2187, Round house, Morava region. No. 2188, House, on stone cliff, Metohija region. No. 2189, Large estate house, Vojvodina region.

1992, Dec. 12
2186 A716 500d multicolored   .80 .80
2187 A716 500d multicolored   .80 .80
2188 A716 500d multicolored   .80 .80
2189 A716 500d multicolored   .80 .80
    Nos. 2186-2189 (4)   3.20 3.20

Icons, Mosaics — A717

#2190, St. Petka, St. Petka Church, Belgrade. #2191, St. Vasilije-Ostronoski, St. Vasilije-Ostronoski Church, Montenegro. #2192, Mosaic of Simeon Nemanja with model of Blessed Virgin Church, Studenica. #2193, Mosaic of St. Lazar with model of Ravanica Monastery.

1992, Dec. 15
2190 A717 500d multi   1.00 1.00
2191 A717 500d multi   1.00 1.00
2192 A717 500d multi, vert.   1.00 1.00
2193 A717 500d multi, vert.   1.00 1.00
    Nos. 2190-2193 (4)   4.00 4.00

Aviation in Yugoslavia, 80th Anniv. — A718

1992, Dec. 24
2194 A718 500d Bleriot XI   1.10 1.10

Diocletian's Reformation of the Roman Empire, 1700th Anniv. — A719

Design: Detail of Roman fresco.

1993, Jan. 28   Litho.   Perf. 13½
2195 A719 1500d multicolored   1.10 1.10

State Museum, Cetinje, Cent. — A720

1993, Feb. 12   **Perf. 14**
2196 A720 2500d multicolored   1.10 1.10

Marine Life — A721

Designs: a, Acipenser sturio. b, Scorpaena scrofa. c, Xiphias gladius. d, Tursiops truncatus.

1993, Mar. 20   **Perf. 13½**
2197 A721 10,000d Strip of 4, #a.-d. + label   8.00 8.00

Serbian Money — A722

#2198, Ancient document, 10 para coins. #2199, 5 dinar banknotes, 5 dinar coins.

1993, Mar. 30
2198 A722 10,000d multicolored   1.40 1.40
2199 A722 10,000d multicolored   1.40 1.40
    Restablishment of Serbian monetary system, 125th anniv. (No. 2198). Restoring dinars as Serbian currency, 120th anniv. (No. 2199).

Famous People A723

Designs: No. 2200, Milos Crnjanski (1893-1977), writer, journalist. No. 2201, Nicola Tesla (1856-1943), physicist. No. 2202, Mihailo Petrovic (1868-1943), mathematician. No. 2203, Aleksa Santic (1868-1924), poet.

1993, Apr. 1
2200 A723 40,000d multicolored   1.40 1.40
2201 A723 40,000d multicolored   1.40 1.40
2202 A723 40,000d multicolored   1.40 1.40
2203 A723 40,000d multicolored   1.40 1.40
    Nos. 2200-2203 (4)   5.60 5.60

Joy of Europe — A724

Children's paintings: No. 2204, Girl holding flowers, children, dove, by M. Markovski. No. 2205, Angels, birds, by J. Rugovac.

1993, Apr. 5
2204 A724 50,000d multicolored   1.40 1.40
2205 A724 50,000d multicolored   1.75 1.75

Contemporary Art — A725

Europa: No. 2206, Nude with a Mirror, by M. Milunovic. No. 2207, Composition, by M.P. Barili.

1993, May 5
2206 A725 95,000d multicolored   2.75 2.75
2207 A725 95,000d multicolored   2.75 2.75

A726

A727

A728

A729

A730

Ancient Fortresses: No. 2208, Sutorina, Montenegro. No. 2209, Kalemegdan, Belgrade. No. 2210, Medun, Montenegro. No. 2211, Petrovaradin, near Novi Sad. No. 2212, Bar, Montenegro. No. 2213, Golubac.

1993, July 9
Booklet Stamps
2208 A726 900,000d multi   1.00 1.00
2209 A727 900,000d multi   1.00 1.00
2210 A728 900,000d multi   1.00 1.00
2211 A729 900,000d multi   1.00 1.00
2212 A730 900,000d multi   1.00 1.00
2213 A730 900,000d multi   1.00 1.00
    a.   Booklet pane, #2208-2213   6.00
        Complete booklet, #2213a   6.00

Flowers A731

Colors of various flowers in vases: No. 2214, Yellow, white. No. 2215, Orange, red. No. 2216, Purple, pink, white. No. 2217, Mixed.

1993, July 10   **Perf. 14**
2214 A731 1,000,000d multi   1.40 1.40
2215 A731 1,000,000d multi   1.40 1.40
2216 A731 1,000,000d multi   1.40 1.40
2217 A731 1,000,000d multi   1.40 1.40
    Nos. 2214-2217 (4)   5.60 5.60

Electrification of Serbia, Cent. A732

1993, July 28   **Perf. 13½**
2218 A732 2,500,000d multi   .70 .65

European Nature Protection A733

Designs: No. 2219, Garrulus glandarius. No. 2220, Oriolus oriolus.

1993, Sept. 30
2219 A733 300,000,000d multi   6.25 6.25
2220 A733 300,000,000d multi   6.25 6.25

Nos. 2147a, 2135, 2144, 2136 and 2140 Srchd.

No. 2143 Surcharged

1993 **Perf 13¼**
2220A A702i 10d on
       100,000d   .90   .90
  b.   Perf 12½   1.75   .25
2220B A702a 50d on 5d   1.00   .25
2220C A702f 100d on 5000d   1.00   .25
2220D A702 500d on 50d   1.00   .25
2220E A702e 1000d on 3000d 1.00   .60
  b.   Perf 12½   1.00   .25
2220F A702b 10,000d on 300d 1.00   .25
2220G A702a 50,000d on 50d
       on 5d   2.75   .75
   Nos. 2220A-2220G (7)   8.65 3.25

Issued: 50,000d, 11/9/93; others, 10/18/93.
Size and location of surcharge varies.
No 2220G was created by applying three additional "0"s to the "50" surcharge on No. 2220B.

A734

Cooperation on the Danube River — A735

Designs: No. 2221, Ships on river. No. 2222, Ship going down river. 20,000d, Map showing location of Danube River.

1993, Oct. 20   **Perf. 14**
2221 A734 15,000d multicolored 1.40 1.40
2222 A734 15,000d multicolored 1.40 1.40

Souvenir Sheet
2223 A735 20,000d multicolored 2.75 2.75

Post Office in Jagodina, 150th Anniv. A736

1993, Oct. 30   **Perf. 13½**
2224 A736 12,000d multicolored 1.50 1.00

Stamp Day.

Joy of Europe — A737

Paintings: No. 2225, Boy with Cat, by Sava Sumanovic (1896-1942). No. 2226, Circus Rider, by Georges Rouault (1871-1958).

1993, Nov. 26
2225 A737 2,000,000d multi 1.40 1.40
2226 A737 2,000,000d multi 1.40 1.40

Icons in Monasteries A738

Designs: No. 2227, The Annunciation, Mileseva. No. 2228, Nativity, Studenica. No. 2229, Madonna and Child, Bogorodica Ljeviska. No. 2230, Flight into Egypt, Oplenac.

1993, Dec. 15
2227 A738 400,000,000d multi 1.00 1.00
2228 A738 400,000,000d multi 1.00 1.00
2229 A738 400,000,000d multi 1.00 1.00
2230 A738 400,000,000d multi 1.00 1.00
   Nos. 2227-2230 (4)   4.00 4.00

Traditional Houses — A739

#2231, A-frame huts, Savardak, horiz. #2232, Watchtower. #2233, Stone house on edge of river. #2234, Crmnicka house, Bar, horiz.

1993, Dec. 31
2231 A739 50d multicolored 1.00 1.00
2232 A739 50d multicolored 1.00 1.00
2233 A739 50d multicolored 1.00 1.00
2234 A739 50d multicolored 1.00 1.00
   Nos. 2231-2234 (4)   4.00 4.00

Publication of Oktoechos, 500th Anniv. — A740

1994, Jan. 17 **Litho.** **Perf. 13½**
2235 A740 1000d Text   .80 .80
2236 A740 1000d Liturgists .80 .80

Raptors A741

Designs: a, Neophron percnopterus. b, Falco cherrug. c, Buteo rufinus. d, Falco naumanni.

1994, Feb. 7
2237 A741 80p Strip of 4, #a.-
          d. + label   22.50 22.50

Intl. Mimosa Festival, Herceg-Novi A742

1994, Feb. 28
2238 A742 80p multicolored 1.40 1.40

Natl. Museum, Belgrade, 150th Anniv. A743

Design: No. 2240, National Theater, Belgrade, 125th anniv., portrait of Prince Milos Obrenovic.

1994, Mar. 19
2239 A743 80p multicolored 1.40 1.40
2240 A743 80p multicolored 1.40 1.40

1994 Winter Olympics, Lillehammer — A744

a, Speed skater. b. Olympic rings, flame. c, Skier.

1994, Apr. 11
2241 A744 60p Strip of 3, #a.-c. 3.25 3.25

Europa A745

Map of flight route and: 60p, Kodron C61, automobile. 1.80d, Kodron C61 in air over Belgrade.

1994, May 5
2242 A745 60p multicolored   1.75 1.75
2243 A745 1.80d multicolored 2.25 2.25

First night flight Paris-Belgrade-Bucharest-Istanbul, piloted by Louis Guidon, 1923.

Burning of Relics of Holy Sava, 400th Anniv. A746

1994, May 10   **Perf. 14**
2244 A746 60p multicolored 1.75 1.75

1994 World Cup Soccer Championships, U.S. — A747

60p, Three players with arms raised in victory. 1d, Three players down on ground.

1994, June 10   **Perf. 13½**
2245 A747 60p multicolored 1.40 1.40
2246 A747 1d multicolored   1.40 1.40

A748

1994, July 8
2247 A748 60p Basset hound 1.40 1.40
2248 A748 60p Maltese   1.40 1.40
2249 A748 60p Welsh terrier 1.40 1.40
2250 A748 1d Husky   1.40 1.40
   Nos. 2247-2250 (4)   5.60 5.60

A749

1994, July 20
2251 A749 60p multicolored 1.40 1.40

Assembly of Eastern Orthodox Christian nations.

Protecting the Ecology of Montenegro A750

1994, July 28
2252 A750 50p Tcherna Gora
          Park   1.40 1.40

Nos. 2148, 2145 Surcharged

1994, July 15   **Perf. 13½**
2253 A702j 10p on 100,000d .50 .50
2254 A702g 50p on 10,000d   .90 .65

A751

Monasteries: 1p, Moraca, 13th cent. 5p, Gracanica, 14th cent. 10p, Ostrog. No. 2258-2259, Lazarica, 14th cent. 50p, Studenica, 12th cent. 1d, Sopocani, 13th cent.

Inscribed "1994"

1994 **Litho.** **Perf. 13¼**
2255 A751 1p bister & purple   1.40 .25
  a.   Perf 12½, Inscr. "1997" 1.40 .25
2256 A751 5p yel brn & blue   1.40 .25
  a.   Perf 12½, Inscr. "1998" 1.40 .25
2257 A751 10p magenta & slate   .55 .25
  a.   Perf 12½, Inscr. "1998"   .55 .25
2258 A751 20p lil rose & pale
          vio   .90 .25
2259 A751 20p pale car & gray 35.00 .25
  a.   Perf 12½, Inscr. "1998" 1.75 .25
2260 A751 50p deep pur & mag   .55 .25
  a.   Inscribed "1997"   .55 .25
  b.   As "a," perf 12½   .55 .25
2261 A751 1d blue & org
          brown   1.40 .50
  a.   Perf 12½, Inscr. "1997" 1.40 .50
   Nos. 2255-2261 (7)   41.20 2.00

UNESCO (#2260-2261).
Issued: 1p, 5p, #2258, 1d, 8/15; #2259, 9/10; 10p, 50p, 11/10.
Nos. 2262-2271 are unassigned.
For surcharges, see Serbia Nos. 195, 260-261.

A752

1994, Sept. 10
2272 A752 50p multicolored   .90 .90
St. Arsenius Seminary, Sremski Karlovci,
bicent.

European
Nature
Protection
A753

Designs: 1d, Fishing pier, Reka Bojana.
1.50d, Lake, Belgrade.

1994, Sept. 20
2273 A753   1d multicolored   2.75 2.75
2274 A753   1.50d multicolored   2.75 2.75

Painting by U.
Knezevic — A754

1994, Oct. 5   **Perf. 14**
2275 A754 1d multicolored   1.75 1.75
Joy of Europe.

Sailing Ships in Bottles — A755

a, Revenge, 1585. b, Grand yacht, 1678. c,
Santa Maria, 15th cent. d, Nava, 15th cent. e,
Mayflower, 1615. f, Carrack, 14th cent.

1994, Oct. 27   **Perf. 13½**
2276 A755 50p Bklt. pane of 6,
       #a.-f.   6.00 6.00
    Complete booklet, #2276   6.00

Stamp
Day — A756

1994, Oct. 31
2277 A756 50p multicolored   4.00 4.00

Drawings on
Gravestones
A757

#2278, Man holding umbrella, purse. #2279,
2 men. #2280, Cemetery, stone with man on
horse, inscriptions. #2281, Fence, 2 gravestones, cross, man.

1994, Nov. 25
2278 A757 50p multicolored   .80   .80
2279 A757 50p multicolored   .80   .80
2280 A757 50p multicolored   .80   .80
2281 A757 50p multicolored   .80   .80
       Nos. 2278-2281 (4)   3.20 3.20

Religious
Art — A758

#2282, The Annunciation, by D. Bacevic.
#2283, Adoration of the Magi, by N. Neskovic.
#2284, Madonna and Child, by T.N. Cesljar.
#2285, St. John Baptizing Christ, by T.
Kracun.

1994, Dec. 15
2282 A758 60p multicolored   .80   .80
2283 A758 60p multicolored   .80   .80
2284 A758 60p multicolored   .80   .80
2285 A758 60p multicolored   .80   .80
       Nos. 2282-2285 (4)   3.20 3.20

Natl.
Symbols
A759

1995, Jan. 26   Litho.   Perf. 13½
2286 A759 1d Flag   1.50 1.50
2287 A759 1d Arms   1.50 1.50

Sheets of 8

World Chess
Champions
A760

#2288: a, Wilhelm Steinitz (1836-1900),
Austria. b, Silhouettes of chessman. c,
Emmanuel Lasker (1868-1941), Germany. d,
Knight. e, Chessman, row of pawns at top. f,
José Raúl Capablanca (1888-1942), Cuba. g,
Chessman, rook at left. h, Alexander Alekhine
(1892-1946), Russia.
#2289: a, Max Euwe, Netherlands. b,
Board, pawn in center. c, Mikhail M. Botvinik,
Soviet Union. d, Board, queen in middle. e,
Board, bishop, knight. f, Vassili Smyslov,
Soviet Union. g, Silhouette of knight, rook
queen, chessboard. h, Mikhail N. Tal, Soviet
Union.

1995
2288 A760 60p #a.-h. + label 10.00 10.00
2289 A760 60p #a.-h. + label 10.00 10.00
    Issued: No. 2288, 2/28; No. 2289, 9/1.

Red Star
Army Sport
Club, 50th
Anniv.
A761

1995, Mar. 4
2290 A761 60p bl, red & bister 1.75 1.75

Protection of
Nature
A762

a, Salamandra salamandra. b, Triturus
alpestris. c, Rana graeca. d, Pelobates
syriacus balcanicus.

1995, Mar. 23
2291 A762 60p Strip of 4, #a.-
       d. + label   10.00 10.00

A763

1995, Apr. 20
2292 A763 60p multicolored   1.50 1.50
Radnicki Soccer Club, Belgrade, 75th anniv.

A764

Europa: 60p, Eagle, mountains. 1.90d, Girl
on tricycle, elderly man, woman on park
bench, horiz.

1995, May 6
2293 A764 60p multicolored   3.00 2.50
2294 A764 1.90d multicolored 3.00 2.50

A765

1995, May 9
2295 A765 60p multicolored   1.50 1.50
End of World War II, 50th anniv.

A766

1995, May 28
2296 A766 60p multicolored   2.00 2.00
Opening of Vukov-Denkmal Subway Station,
Belgrade.

Draba
Bertiscea
A767

a, shown. b, Plants, diff. c, Flowers, mountain. d, Plants on rock, stems at right.

1995, June 12
2297 A767 60p Strip of 4, #a.-
       d. + label   10.00 10.00

European
Nature
Protection
A768

Designs: 60p, Eremophila alpestris balcan-
ica. 1.90d, Rhinolophus blasii.

1995, July 10
2298 A768 60p multicolored   2.00 2.00
2299 A768 1.90d multicolored 2.50 2.50

Slovakian Folk Festival, by Zuzka
Medvedova (1897-1985),
Painter — A769

1995, Aug. 3
2300 A769 60p multicolored   1.25 1.25

Volleyball,
Cent. — A770

1995, Sept. 10
2301 A770 90p multicolored   1.25 1.25

Church of St.
Luke, Kotor,
800th
Anniv. — A771

1995, Sept. 20
2302 A771 80p multicolored   1.25 1.25

Motion
Pictures,
Cent.
A772

Designs: 1.10d, Newsreel showing coronation of King Peter II. 2.20d, Auguste and Louis
Jean Lumière, film projector.

1995, Oct. 3
2303 A772 1.10d dk brn, lt red
              brn   1.50 1.50
2304 A772 2.20d dk brn, lt red
              brn   1.50 1.50

Army Sports Club "Partisan," 50th
Anniv. — A773

1995, Oct. 4
2305 A773 80p multi + label   1.25 1.25

UN, 50th Anniv. — A774

1995, Oct. 24
2306 A774 1.10d multicolored   1.25 1.25

Stamp Day — A775

1995, Oct. 31
2307 A775 1.10d multicolored   1.00 1.00

Joy of Europe — A776

Paintings: 1.10d, Young boy by Milos Tenkovic. 2.20d, Young girl by Pierre Bonnard.

1995, Nov. 26
2308 A776 1.10d multicolored   1.50 1.50
2309 A776 2.20d multicolored   1.50 1.50
Children's Day.

Souvenir Sheet

JUFIZ VIII, Natl. Philatelic Exhibition, Budva — A777

Design: Montenegro #37, Serbia #6.

1995, Dec. 13   **Perf. 14**
2310 A777 2.50d Sheet of 1 + label   2.00 2.00

Christmas A778

Contemporary religious paintings: No. 2311, Flight into Egypt, by Z. Halupova. No. 2312, Nativity, by D. Milojevic, vert. No. 2313, Outdoor Christmas scene, by M. Rasic, vert. No. 2314, Indoor traditional Christmas scene, by J. Brasic.

1995, Dec. 26   **Perf. 13½**
2311 A778 1.10d multicolored   .50 .50
2312 A778 1.10d multicolored   .50 .50
2313 A778 2.20d multicolored   1.00 1.00
2314 A778 2.20d multicolored   1.00 1.00
Nos. 2311-2314 (4)   3.00 3.00

Airplanes A779

1995, Dec. 26
2315 A779 1.10d Saric No. 1   .50 .50
2316 A779 1.10d Douglas DC-3   .50 .50
2317 A779 2.20d Fizir FN   1.00 1.00
2318 A779 2.20d Caravelle   1.00 1.00
Nos. 2315-2318 (4)   3.00 3.00

Battle of Mojkovac, 80th Anniv. — A780

Design: Montenegrins on mountain.

1996, Jan. 6
2319 A780 1.10d multicolored   .50 .50

Birth of Sava Sumanovic, Cent. A781

Design: 1927 Painting, "Drink Boat."

1996, Jan. 22
2320 A781 1.10d multicolored   .50 .50

A782   A783

Insects: a, Pyrgomorphela serbica. b, Calosoma sycopanta. c, Formica rufa. d, Ascalaphus macaronius.

1996, Feb. 15
2321 A782 2.20d Strip of 4, #a.-d. + label   7.00 7.00
Protection of nature.

1996, Feb. 29   **Litho.**   **Perf. 12½**
Churches.
2322 A783   5d Ljeviska   2.00 1.50
2323 A783 10d Zica   4.00 3.00
2324 A783 20d Decani   8.00 6.00
Nos. 2322-2324 (3)   14.00 10.50

Chess Champions — A784

Designs: a, Tigran Petrosian, Soviet Union. b, Chess pieces, sundial, chess board. c, Boris Spassky, Soviet Union. d, Chess pieces, board, clock showing two time zones. e, Garry Kasparov, Soviet Union. f, Chess pieces, hand holding hour glass. g, Bobby Fischer, US. h, Chess pieces, six clocks. i, Anatoly Karpov, Soviet Union.

1996, Mar. 15   **Litho.**   **Perf. 13½**
2325 A784 1.50d Sheet of 9, #a.-i.   6.00 6.00

Olympic Games, Cent. A786

1.50d, Discus throwers. 2.50d, Runners.

Perf. 13½x13¼
1996, Mar. 30   **Litho.**
2326 A786 1.50d multi   .75 .75
2327 A786 2.50d multi   1.25 1.25

1996 Summer Olympics, Atlanta — A787

1996, Apr. 12
2328 A787 1.50d shown   1.50 1.50
2329 A787 1.50d Basketball   1.50 1.50
2330 A787 1.50d Handball   1.50 1.50
2331 A787 1.50d Volleyball   1.50 1.50
2332 A787 1.50d Shooting   1.50 1.50
2333 A787 1.50d Water polo   1.50 1.50
Nos. 2328-2333 (6)   9.00 9.00

1996 Summer Olympic Games, Atlanta — A787a

1996, Apr. 12   **Litho.**   **Perf. 13**
2334 A787 5d Sheet of 1 + label   2.00 2.00

Stamp Day — A788

1996, Apr. 30   **Litho.**   **Perf. 13½**
2335 A788 1.50d Railway mail car   .60 .60

Famous Women Writers — A789

Europa: 2.50d, Isidora Sekulic (1877-1958). 5d, Desanka Maksimovic (1898-1993).

1996, May 7   **Litho.**   **Perf. 13½**
2336 A789 2.50d multicolored   2.00 2.00
2337 A789   5d multicolored   2.00 2.00

Serbian Red Cross, 120th Anniv. A790

1996, May 8
2338 A790 1.50d Dr. Vladan Djordjevic   .60 .60

Architectural Education in Yugoslavia, 150th Anniv. — A791

1996, June 1   **Litho.**   **Perf. 13½**
2339 A791 1.50d multicolored   .60 .60

European Nature Protection A792

1996, June 28
2340 A792 2.50d Platalea leucorodia   1.00 1.00
2341 A792   5d Plegadis falcinellus   2.00 2.00

Prince Peter I Petrovic at Battle of Martinici, 1796 — A793

Design: 2.50d, Prince's Guard at Battle of Kruse (1796), by Valerio, vert.

1996, July 22
2342 A793 1.50d multicolored   .50 .50
2343 A793 2.50d multicolored   1.00 1.00

Horse Racing, Ljubicevo A794

1996, Sept. 2   **Litho.**   **Perf. 13½**
2344 A794 1.50d shown   .50 .50
2345 A794 2.50d 3 horses racing   1.00 1.00

Fauna A795

Designs: a, 1.50d, Probosciger aterrimus. b, 2.50d, Goura scheepmakeri. c, 1.50d, Equus burchelli. d, 2.50d, Panthera tigris.

1996, Sept. 25
2346 A795 Strip of 4, #a.-d. + label   8.00 8.00
Belgrade Zoo, 60th anniv.

Children's Day — A796

1996, Oct. 2
2347 A796 1.50d multicolored .70 .70
2348 A796 2.50d Bird 1.25 1.25

Medalists, 1996 Summer Olympic Games A797

Designs: No. 2349, Shooting, bronze. No. 2350, Shooting, gold. No. 2351, Volleyball, bronze. No. 2352, Basketball, silver.

1996, Oct. 31   Litho.   Perf. 13½
2349 A797 2.50d multicolored 1.40 1.40
2350 A797 2.50d multicolored 1.40 1.40
2351 A797 2.50d multicolored 1.40 1.40
2352 A797 2.50d multicolored 1.40 1.40
    Nos. 2349-2352 (4) 5.60 5.60

Savings Accounts, 75th Anniv. — A798

1996, Oct. 31   Litho.   Perf. 13½
2353 A798 1.50d multicolored .70 .70

Soccer in Yugoslavia, Cent. — A799

1996, Nov. 8   Litho.   Perf. 13½
2354 A799 1.50d multicolored .70 .70

Archaeological Finds — A800

Sculptures: No. 2355, God of Autumn. No. 2356, Mother with child. No. 2357, Head of woman. No. 2358, Redheaded goddess.

1996, Nov. 25
2355 A800 1.50d multicolored .60 .50
2356 A800 1.50d multicolored .60 .50
2357 A800 2.50d multicolored 1.00 .75
2358 A800 2.50d multicolored 1.00 .75
    Nos. 2355-2358 (4) 3.20 2.50

A801

Christmas (Paintings): No. 2359, Annunciation. No. 2360, Mother of God with Christ. No. 2361, Birth of Christ. No. 2362, Palm Sunday.

1996, Dec. 10
2359 A801 1.50d multicolored .60 .50
2360 A801 1.50d multicolored .60 .50
2361 A801 2.50d multicolored 1.00 .75
2362 A801 2.50d multicolored 1.00 .75
    Nos. 2359-2362 (4) 3.20 2.50

A802

1997, Jan. 24   Litho.   Perf. 13½
2363 A802 1.50d multicolored .60 .60
Radomir Putnik Voivode, 150th birth anniv.

25th Intl. Film Festival, Belgrade A803

1997, Jan. 31
2364 A803 1.50d multicolored .70 .70

Protected Birds — A804

Designs: No. 2365, Dendrocopos major. No. 2366, Nucifraga caryocatactes. No. 2367, Parus cristatus. No. 2368, Erithacus rubecula.

1997, Feb. 21
2365 A804 1.50d multicolored .60 .60
2366 A804 2.50d multicolored .60 .60
2367 A804 1.50d multicolored .90 .90
2368 A804 2.50d multicolored .90 .90
a.   Strip of 4, #2365-2368 + label 7.00 7.00

A805

1997, Mar. 17   Litho.   Perf. 13
2369 A805 1.50d multicolored 1.00 1.00
St. Achilleus Church, 700th Anniv.

A806

Design: Prince Peter I Petrovic (1747-1830), Bishop of Montenegro.

1997, Apr. 3   Perf. 13½
2370 A806 1.50d multicolored 1.00 1.00

A807

1997, Apr. 19
2371 A807 2.50d multicolored 1.25 1.25
10th Belgrade Marathon.

A808

1997, Apr. 22   Litho.   Perf. 13½
2372 A808 2.50d multicolored 1.25 1.25
Serbian Medical Assoc., 125th anniv.

Air Mail Being Loaded at Night A809

1997, May 3
2373 A809 2.50d multicolored 1.25 1.25
Stamp Day.

Tennis Tournaments in Yugoslavia — A810

Stylized designs: No. 2374, Player, large racket overhead, Budva. No. 2375, Player with ball flying from racket, Belgrade. No. 2376, Player with racket out in front, Novi Sad.

1997, May 8
2374 A810 2.50d multi + label 1.25 1.25
2375 A810 2.50d multi + label 1.25 1.25
2376 A810 2.50d multi + label 1.25 1.25
    Nos. 2374-2376 (3) 3.75 3.75

Stories and Legends A811

Europa: 2.50d, Shackled Bach Chelik surrounded by creatures. 6d, Bach Chelik in chains, prince fighting with him, princess, castle.

1997, May 30   Perf. 11½
2377 A811 2.50d multicolored 2.00 2.00
2378 A811 6d multicolored 2.00 2.00
Each issued in sheets of 8 + label.

European Nature Protection A812

1997, June 5
2379 A812 2.50d Cerambyx cerdo 1.00 1.00
2380 A812 6d Quercus robur 2.00 2.00

Stanislav Binicki (1872-1947) A813

1997, June 7   Perf. 13½
2381 A813 2.50d multicolored 1.00 1.00

Printing of Gorski Vijenac, 150th Anniv. — A814

1997, June 7
2382 A814 2.50d multicolored 1.00 1.00

Flowers — A815

Designs: a, 1.50d, Pelargonium grandiflorum. b, 2.50d, Saintpaulia ionantha. c, 1.50d, Hydrangea macrophylla. d, 2.50d, Oncidium varicosum.

1997, Sept. 10   Litho.   Perf. 13
2383 A815 Strip of 4, #a.-d. + label 7.00 7.00

Souvenir Sheet

JUFIZ IX, 9th Natl. Philatelic Exhibition — A816

Design: Sculpture, by Dragomir Arambasic, in front of art gallery.

1997, Sept. 10   Perf. 14
2384 A816 5d multicolored 2.50 2.50

A817

1997, Sept. 24   Perf. 13½x14
2385 A817 2.50d multicolored 1.00 1.00
Serbian Chemical Society, cent.

**Type of 1993
Size: 18x18mm**

1997, Oct. 2   Perf. 14
2386 A702d (A) like #2142 1.00 .25
a.   Dated "1999" 1.00 .25

A818

Joy of Europe children's art works: 2.50d, 5d, Busts of people formed from collage of various food products.

1997, Oct. 2
2387 A818 2.50d multicolored 1.00 1.00
2388 A818 5d multicolored 2.00 2.00

"May Assembly in Sremski Karlivoci," by Pavle Simic — A819

1997, Oct. 10   Litho.   Perf. 14
2389 A819 2.50d multicolored 1.00 1.00

Matica Srpska Gallery, 150th anniv.

A820

Museum exhibits: No. 2390, Two-headed statuette. No. 2391, Parade helmet. No. 2392, Terra cotta statuette. No. 2393, Virgin icon.

1997, Nov. 12
2390 A820 1.50d multicolored .50 .50
2391 A820 1.50d multicolored .50 .50
2392 A820 2.50d multicolored 1.00 1.00
2393 A820 2.50d multicolored 1.00 1.00
Nos. 2390-2393 (4) 3.00 3.00

A821

Icons (Chelandari Serbian Monastery, Mount Athos): No. 2394, Christ. No. 2395, Madonna and Child, 12th cent. No. 2396, Madonna and Child, 13th cent. No. 2397, 3-handed Madonna.

Granite Paper
1997, Dec. 2   Perf. 11½
2394 A821 1.50d multicolored .50 .50
2395 A821 1.50d multicolored .50 .50
2396 A821 2.50d multicolored 1.00 1.00
2397 A821 2.50d multicolored 1.00 1.00
Nos. 2394-2397 (4) 3.00 3.00

A822

1998, Jan. 20   Litho.   Perf. 13½
2398 A822 1.50d Savina 1.00 1.00
2399 A822 2.50d Donji Brceli 1.00 1.00

Monasteries of Montenegro.

A823

1998, Feb. 6   Perf. 14
2400 A823 2.50d Figure skater 2.00 2.00
2401 A823 6d Skier 2.00 2.00

1998 Winter Olympic Games, Nagano.

Horses A824

Designs: a, 1.50d, Two running. b, 2.50d, Arabian up close. c, 1.50d, Thoroughbred. d, 2.50d, Thoroughbred running on race track.

1998, Feb. 26   Litho.   Perf. 12x11½
2402 A824 Strip of 4, #a.-d. + label 10.00 10.00

Intl. Women's Day A825

1998, Mar. 7   Perf. 13½
2403 A825 2.50d multicolored 1.00 1.00

Yugoslav Airlines Assoc., 50th Anniv. A826

1998, Apr. 24
2404 A826 2.50d multicolored 1.00 1.00

Europa — A827

Paintings: 6d, "Dressing the Bride," by Paja Jovanovic (1859-1957). 9d, "Bishop's Congratulations," by Pero Pocek (1878-1963).

1998, May 4   Litho.   Perf. 12
Granite Paper
2405 A827 6d multicolored 3.00 3.00
2406 A827 9d on 2.50d, multi 3.00 3.00

No. 2406 was not issued without the silver surcharge.

1998 World Cup Soccer Championships, France — A828

1998, May 15   Litho.   Perf. 13½
2407 A828 6d shown 1.75 1.75
2408 A828 9d Soccer players, diff. 2.75 2.75

Souvenir Sheet

Danube Commission, 50th Anniv. — A829

1998, May 19   Perf. 14
2409 A829 9d multicolored 4.00 4.00

European Nature Protection A830

Designs: 6d, Heracium blecicii. 9d, Mola mola, vert.

1998, June 17   Litho.   Perf. 13¾
2410 A830 6d multi 1.25 1.25
2411 A830 9d multi 1.75 1.75

Each stamp was printed in sheets of 8 + label.

Famous People of Serbia — A831

a, Djura Jaksic (1832-78), poet, painter. b, Nadezda Petrovic (1873-1915), painter. c, Radoje Domanovic (1873-1908), writer. d, Vasilije Mokranjac (1923-1984), composer. e, Streten Stojanovic (1898-1960), sculptor. f, Milan Konjovic (1898-1993), painter. g, Desanka Maksimovic (1898-1993), poet. h, Ivan Tabakovic (1898-1977), painter.

1998, June 30   Litho.   Perf. 12
Granite Paper
Sheet of 8
2412 A831 1.50d #a.-h. + label 3.25 3.25

Souvenir Sheet

Yugoslavia, Winner of World Basketball Championships — A832

1998, Aug. 21   Perf. 13½
2413 A832 10d multicolored 8.00 8.00

Protected Animals — A833

a, 2d, Martes martes. b, 2d, Anthropoides virgo. c, 5d, Lynx lynx. d, 5d, Loxia curvirostra.

1998, Sept. 2
2414 A833 Strip of 4, #a.-d. + label 9.00 9.00

Breaking of the Thessaloniki Front, 80th Anniv. A834

Designs: No. 2415, 5d, Soldiers and cannons. No. 2416, 5d, Soldiers with machine guns, binoculars.

1998, Sept. 15   Engr.   Perf. 13½
2415-2416 A834 Set of 2 3.50 3.50

Stamp Day — A835

1998, Sept. 28
2417 A835 6d Prussian blue 1.40 1.40

Serbian Philatelic Society, 50th anniv.

Joy of Europe Children's Drawings A836

Designs: 6d, Fish. 9d, Fish, diff.

1998, Oct. 2   Litho.   Perf. 13¾
2418-2419 A836 Set of 2 3.50 3.50

Development of the Railway — A837

Trains: a, 1847. b, 1900. c, 1920. d, 1930. e, Diesel locomotive. f, 1990.

1998, Nov. 3   Litho.   Perf. 13½
2420 A837 2.50d Booklet pane of
6, #a.-f.   9.00 9.00
Complete booklet, #2420   9.50

Paintings of Sailing Ships, Maritime Museum, Kotor A838

#2421, Veracruz, 1873. #2422, Pierino, 1883. #2423, Draghetto, 1865. #2424, Group of ships.

1998, Nov. 11   Perf. 12
Granite Paper
2421 A838 2d multicolored   .50   .50
2422 A838 2d multicolored   .50   .50
2423 A838 5d multicolored   1.50 1.50
2424 A838 5d multicolored   1.50 1.50
   Nos. 2421-2424 (4)   4.00 4.00

Chelandari Monastery, 800th Anniv. — A839

Views of monastery: No. 2425, Looking from center of complex, two trees. No. 2426, Group of taller buildings. No. 2427, Aerial view. No. 2428, Looking across group of buildings, crosses on turrets.

1998, Dec. 9   Perf. 14
2425 A839 2d multicolored   .50   .50
2426 A839 2d multicolored   .50   .50
2427 A839 5d multicolored   1.25 1.25
2428 A839 5d multicolored   1.25 1.25
   Nos. 2425-2428 (4)   3.50 3.50

Third Meeting of Southeast European Postal Ministers A840

1998, Dec. 17   Litho.   Perf. 14
2429 A840 5d multicolored   3.00 3.00

Souvenir Sheet

Yugoslavia, Silver Medalists at 1998 World Volleyball Championships — A841

1998, Dec. 19   Perf. 13½
2430 A841 10d multicolored   50.00 50.00

Post and Telecommunications Museum, Belgrade, 75th Anniv. — A842

#2431, Postrider. #No. 2432, Antique telegraph equipment, museum building.

1998, Dec. 21   Engr.
2431 A842 5d olive brown & slate 1.00 1.00
2432 A842 5d red & brown   1.00 1.00

Serbian Monasteries A843

1999, Jan. 14   Litho.   Perf. 13¾
2433 A843 2d Visoki Decani   .60   .60
2434 A843 5d Grachanica   1.60 1.60

Farm Animals A844

Designs: a, 2d, Pigs. b, 6d, Goat. c, 2d, Oxen. d, 6d, Long-horn sheep.

1999, Feb. 5   Litho.   Perf. 13½
2435 A844 Strip of 4, #a.-d. +
label   7.00 7.00

A845

1999, Feb. 24   Litho.   Perf. 13¼
2436 A845 6d Scouting   2.00 2.00

A846

1999, Mar. 27
2437 A846 6d brown & buff   1.40 1.40
Yugoslav Bar Association, 70th anniv.

Target
A847   A848

1999   Perf. 12¼x12½
2438 A847 (A) black   5.00 3.00
2439 A848 (A) black & red   20.00 12.00
   Issued: No. 2438, 3/27; No. 2439, 4/7. Nos. 2438-2439 sold for 2.04d when issued.

World Table Tennis Championships, Belgrade — A849

1999, Apr. 9   Perf. 13¼
Player colors
2440 A849 6d blue & red   2.00 2.00
2441 A849 6d green & red   2.00 2.00

A850

Europa, National Parks and Reserves: 6d, Falcon, trees, mountains, Kopaonik Natl. Park. 15d, Flowers, mountains, Lovcen Natl. Park.

1999, May 5   Photo.   Perf. 11¾
Granite Paper
2442 A850 6d multicolored   6.00 6.00
2443 A850 15d multicolored   6.00 6.00
Each printed in sheets of 8 + 1 central label

A851

European Nature Protection.

1999, May 13   Perf. 11¾x12
2444 A851 6d Shovel, spider
web   2.50 2.50
2445 A851 15d Thumb squeezing
earth   2.50 2.50

Mushrooms A852

Designs: a, Amanita virosa. b, Amanita pantherina. c, Hypholoma fasciculare. d, Ramaria pallida.

1999, June 18   Litho.   Perf. 11¾x12
Granite Paper
2446 A852 6d Strip of 4, #a.-
d., + central la-
bel   10.00 10.00
   Central labels differ on sheet.

Famous Montenegrins — A853

Designs: a, Stjepan Mitrov Ljubisa (1824-78). b, Marko Milanov (1833-1901). c, Pero Pocek (1878-1963). d, Risto Stijovic (1894-1974). e, Milo Milunovic (1897-1967). f, Petar Lubarda (1907-74). g, Vuko Radovic (1911-96). h, Mihailo Lalic (1914-92).

1999, June 30   Perf. 13¼
2447 A853 2d Sheet of 8, #a.-h.,
+ central label   3.25 3.25

UPU, 125th Anniv. A854

1999, Sept. 15   Perf. 13¼
2448 A854 6d shown   1.00 1.00
2449 A854 12d Envelopes cir-
cling globe   2.00 2.00

Joy of Europe Children's Drawings A855

1999, Oct. 1   Perf. 13¾
2450 A855 6d Lion   1.00 1.00
2451 A855 15d Family, vert.   2.50 2.50

Frédéric Chopin (1810-49), Composer A856

1999, Oct. 15   Perf. 13¼
2452 A856 10d multi   2.25 2.25

No. 2438,
Mastheads of
"Filatelista"
A857

1999, Oct. 18
2453　A857　10d multi　　　1.50　1.50
Stamp Day.

A858

Bridges
Destroyed by
NATO Air
Strikes
A859

Bridges: #2454, Varadinski. #2455,
Ostruznica. #2456, Murino. #2457, Grdelica.
#2458, Bistrica. #2459, Zezeljev.

1999, Oct. 29　　　**Perf. 13¾**
2454　A858　2d shown　　　　.90　.90
2455　A859　2d shown　　　　.90　.90
2456　A859　2d multi　　　　.90　.90
2457　A859　6d multi　　　　.90　.90
2458　A859　6d multi　　　　.90　.90
2459　A859　6d multi　　　　.90　.90
　　　Nos. 2454-2459 (6)　　5.40　5.40

Millennium
A860

a, 6d, Roman altars, statue of Jupiter. b, 6d,
Sculpture of Emperor Trajan and army leaders, mosaic, lamp, lead mirror. c, 6d, Mosaic
of Dionysius, arch. d, 6d, Hagia Sophia,
mosaic of Madonna and Child, Emperor Constantine. e, 6d, Large cross, candle, fibula,
pot. f, 6d, Church, boats, manuscript. g, 15d,
Nativity and crucifixion of Christ, boats,
farmers.

1999, Nov. 19
2460　A860　Booklet pane of 7,
　　　#a.-g., + 2 labels　　　9.00　9.00
　　　Complete booklet, #2460　　9.00
　　　Size of #2460g: 105x55mm.

A861

Bomb Damage
A862

#2461, Bolnice. #2462, Telecommunications
complex. #2463, Refinery. #2464, Bolnice.
#2465, Telecommunications complex, diff.
#2466, Television complex.

1999, Nov. 27　Litho.　Perf. 13¾
2461　A861　2d shown　　　　.50　.50
2462　A862　2d shown　　　　.50　.50
2463　A862　2d multi　　　　.50　.50
2464　A862　6d multi　　　1.00　1.00
2465　A862　6d multi　　　1.00　1.00
2466　A862　6d multi　　　1.00　1.00
　　　Nos. 2461-2466 (6)　　4.50　4.50

A863

Frescoes of Poganovo Monastery,
500th Anniv. — A864

Design A863 has Latin letters, A864 has
Cyrillic letters.

1999, Dec. 23
2467　A863　6d shown　　　　.80　.80
2468　A864　6d shown　　　　.80　.80
2469　A863　6d Fresco, diff.　.80　.80
2470　A864　6d Fresco, diff.　.80　.80
　　　Nos. 2467-2470 (4)　　3.20　3.20

A865

Gold
Prospectors in
Pec
River — A866

Design A865 has Latin letters, A866 has
Cyrillic letters.

1999, Dec. 30
2471　A865　6d shown　　　　.80　.80
2472　A866　6d shown　　　　.80　.80
2473　A865　6d Prospectors, diff.　.80　.80
2474　A866　6d Prospectors, diff.　.80　.80
　　　Nos. 2471-2474 (4)　　3.20　3.20

Krusedol
Monastery
A867

2000, Jan. 13　　　Perf. 13¼
2475　A867　10d shown　　　1.50　1.50
2476　A867　10d Rakovac Monas-
　　　tery　　　　　　　1.50　1.50

Yugoslavian
Archives,
50th Anniv.
A868

2000, Jan. 21
2477　A868　10d multi　　　25.00　25.00

Butterflies — A869

No. 2478: a, Nymphalis antiopa. b,
Parnalius polyxena. c, Limenitis populi. d,
Melanargia galathea.

2000, Feb. 25　Litho.　Perf. 13¾
2478　Horiz. strip of 4 + cen-
　　　tral label　　　　18.00　18.00
　a.-d.　A869　10d Any single　2.50　2.50

Worldwide
Fund for
Nature
A870

Perdix perdix: a, Pair in snow. b, Pair facing
right. c, Bird on nest. d, Pair, one facing left.

2000, Mar. 14　Litho.　Perf. 12x11¾
2479　A870　10d Strip of 4, #a.-
　　　d., + central
　　　label　　　　　　12.00　12.00

Damage
from NATO
Airstrikes
A871

Various destroyed buildings. Colors: 10d,
Blue. 20d, Brown.

2000, Mar. 24　Engr.　Perf. 13¼
2480-2481　A871　Set of 2　5.00　5.00

Souvenir Sheet

JUFIZ X Philatelic Exhibition,
Belgrade — A872

2000, May 2　　　　Litho.
2482　A872　15d multi　　　50.00　50.00

Nature
Protection
A873

Designs: No. 2483, 30d, Feeding chicks by
hand. No. 2484, 30d, Map of Europe in tree's
leaves, vert.

Perf. 12x11¾, 11¾x12

2000, May 4　　　　　　Litho.
2483-2484　A873　Set of 2　4.00　4.00

Europa — A874

"2000" and: No. 2485, 30d, Astronaut on
moon. No. 2486, 30d, Star and mountains.

2000, May 9　　　Perf. 11¾x12
2485-2486　A874　Set of 2　8.00　8.00

European Soccer
Championships
A875

Inscriptions in: No. 2487, 30d, Cyrillic letters. No. 2488, 30d, Latin letters.

2000, May 20　Litho.　Perf. 13¾
2487-2488　A875　Set of 2　6.00　6.00

Postal
Services in
Serbia, 160th
Anniv. — A876

2000, June 7　Litho.　Perf. 13¾
2489　A876　10d multi　　　2.00　2.00

2000 Summer
Olympics,
Sydney — A877

Map of Australia and: 6d, Kangaroo. 12d,
Emu. 24d, Koala and soccer ball. 30d, Parrot.

2000, June 28
2490-2493　A877　Set of 4　7.00　7.00

Stamp
Day — A878

2000, Sept. 26　　　Perf. 13¼
2494　A878　10d multi　　　4.50　4.50

"Joy of
Europe"
A879

Children's art: 30d, Cows. 40d, Cranes,
vert.

2000, Oct. 2
2495-2496　A879　Set of 2　3.50　3.50

World Teachers' Day — A880

2000, Oct. 5
2497 A880 10d multi   20.00 20.00

13th Apiarists Congress A881

2000, Oct. 6
2498 A881 10d multi   5.00 5.00

Medals Won at 2000 Summer Olympics A882

Designs: No. 2499, 20d, Water polo (bronze). No. 2500, 20d, Shooting (silver). 30d, Volleyball, vert.

2000, Oct. 23   **Perf. 13¾**
2499-2500 A882   Set of 2   3.00 3.00
        Souvenir Sheet
2501 A882 30d multi   20.00 20.00
No. 2501 contains one 35x46mm stamp.

Millennium A883

No. 2502: a, Ships. b, Papermaking. c, Galileo and telescopes. d, Steam locomotive and steamship. e, Nikola Tesla, invention of the telephone. f, Astronaut, outer space settlement. g, Ships, airplanes, balloons, horses.

2000, Nov. 2   **Litho.**   **Perf. 13¾**
2502   Booklet pane of 7 + 2
        labels   6.00 —
  a.-f. A883 12d any single   .60 .60
  g. A883 40d multi   2.00 2.00
    Booklet, #2502   6.00
    Size of No. 2502g: 105x55mm.

Nativity Fresco, Pec — A884

2000, Nov. 7   **Litho.**   **Perf. 13¾**
2503 A884 A multi   3.50 .50
No. 2503 sold for 3.56d on day of issue.

Serb Clothing From the 1900s — A885

Designs: 6d, Vest, Jagodina. 12d, Dresses, Metochija. 24d, Blouse, Pec. 30d, Vest, Kupres.

2000, Dec. 7
2504-2507 A885   Set of 4   3.00 3.00

Montenegrin Religious Art — A886

Designs: 6d, Madonna and Child, 1573-74. 12d, Nativity, 1666-67. 24d, St. Luke, 1672-73. 30d, Madonna and Child, 1642.

2000, Dec. 19
2508-2511 A886   Set of 4   3.00 3.00

A887

A887a

2000, Dec. 29   **Litho.**   **Perf. 13¾**
2512 A887   6d multi   .50 .50
2513 A887a 12d multi   .50 .50
Resumption of Yugoslavia's membership in Organization for Security and Cooperation in Europe (#2512), and United Nations (#2513).

Vatoped Monastery, Mount Athos, Greece A888

Esfigmen Monastery, Mount Athos, Greece A889

2001, Jan. 26   **Litho.**   **Perf. 13¼**
2514 A888 10d multi   .55 .55
2515 A889 27d multi   1.60 1.60

Matica Srpska, 175th Anniv. — A890

2001, Feb. 16   **Perf. 13¾**
2516 A890 15d multi   1.10 1.10

Animals — A891

No. 2517: a, Felis leo. b, Ursus maritimus. c, Macaca fuscata. d, Spheniscus humboldti.

2001, Feb. 23
2517   Horiz. strip of 4 + cen-
      tral label   7.25 7.25
  a. A891 6d multi   .45 .45
  b. A891 12d multi   .90 .90
  c. A891 24d multi   1.10 1.10
  d. A891 30d multi   1.40 1.40

Women's World Chess Champions — A892

No. 2518: a, Vera Menchik (1927-44). b, Lyudmila Rudenko (1950-53). c, Yelisavyeta Bykova (1953-56, 1958-62). d, Olga Rubtsova (1956-58). e, Nona Gaprindashvili (1962-78). f, Maia Chiburdanidze (1978-91). g, Zsuzsa Polgar (1996-99). h, Xie Jun (1991-96, 1999-2000).

2001, Mar. 8   **Perf. 13¼**
2518 A892 10d Sheet of 8, #a-h,
    + label   4.50 4.50

Famous Men — A893

Designs: 50d, Stevan Mokranjac (1856-1914), composer. 100d, Nikola Tesla (1856-1943), inventor.

2001, Mar. 19   **Perf. 13¾**
2519-2520 A893   Set of 2   7.25 7.25

Flowers A894

No. 2521: a, Hibiscus syriacus. b, Nerium oleander. c, Lapageria rosea. d, Sorbus aucuparia.

2001, Apr. 13   **Perf. 12x11¾**
2521   Horiz. strip of 4 + cen-
      tral label   6.50 6.50
  a. A894 6d multi   .35 .35
  b. A894 12d multi   .55 .55
  c. A894 24d multi   1.00 1.00
  d. A894 30d multi   1.40 1.40

Europa — A895

Designs: 30d, Vratna River. 45d, Jerme Canyon.

2001, May 4   **Perf. 11¾x12**
2522-2523 A895   Set of 2   5.50 5.50

Serbian Mountaineering Association, Cent. — A896

2001, June 8   **Perf. 13¼**
2524 A896 15d multi   1.25 1.25

European Nature Protection A897

Designs: 30d, Bird on branch, Lake Ludasko. 45d, Stork flying above Begej River.

2001, June 22   **Perf. 12x11¾**
2525-2526 A897   Set of 2   3.75 3.75

14th Cent. Book Illumination A898

2001, July 2   **Perf. 13¼**
2527 A898 E multi   1.60 1.60
Sold for 28.70d on day of issue.

Souvenir Sheet

Yugoslavian Victory in European Water Polo Championships — A899

2001, July 5   **Perf. 13¾**
2528 A899 30d multi   6.50 6.50

Souvenir Sheet

Serbiafila XII Stamp Exhibition — A900

2001, Sept. 8
2529 A900 30d multi   2.50 2.50

Solar Energy — A901

2001, Sept. 19 **Perf. 13¼**
2530 A901 15d multi 1.60 1.60

Danube Commission A902

Designs: 30d, Ships, hands raising bridge. 45d, Ship, hand, clock.

2001, Sept. 20 **Perf. 13¾**
2531-2532 A902 Set of 2 5.50 5.50

Joy of Europe — A903

Paintings: 30d, Child, by Marko Chelebonovic. 45d, Girl Under a Fruit Tree, by Beta Vukanovic.

2001, Oct. 2 **Perf. 13¼**
2533-2534 A903 Set of 2 5.50 5.50

Yugoslavian Victories in European Sports Championships A904

Designs: No. 2535, 30d, Men's basketball. No. 2536, 30d, Men's volleyball.

2001, Oct. 11
2535-2536 A904 Set of 2 45.00 45.00

Intl. Federation of Philately (FIP), 75th Anniv. A905

2001, Oct. 24
2537 A905 15d multi 1.60 1.60

Stamp Day.

Minerals A906

2001, Nov. 2 **Perf. 13¾**
2538 Horiz. strip of 4 + central label 5.00 5.00
a. A906 7d Antimonite 1.10 1.10
b. A906 14d Calcite 1.10 1.10
c. A906 26.20d Quartz 1.10 1.10
d. A906 28.70d Calcite and galenite 1.10 1.10

Pljevlja Gymnasium, Cent. — A907

2001, Nov. 18 **Perf. 13¼**
2539 A907 15d multi 2.25 2.25

Public Telephone Booths in Serbia, Cent. — A908

2001, Nov. 20
2540 A908 15d multi 1.40 1.40

Christmas A910

Paintings of the Birth of Jesus Christ: 7d, 14d, 26.20d, 28.70d.

2001, Dec. 1 **Perf. 13¾**
2541-2544 A910 Set of 4 4.50 4.50

Junior World Ice Hockey Championships, Belgrade — A911

2002, Jan. 5 **Perf. 13¼**
2545 A911 14d multi 10.00 10.00

2002 Winter Olympics, Salt Lake City — A912

Designs: 28.70d, Skier. 50d, Four-man bobsled, vert.

2002, Jan. 25 **Perf. 13¼**
2546-2547 A912 Set of 2 25.00 25.00

Jovan Karamata (1902-67), Mathematician A913

2002, Feb. 1
2548 A913 14d multi 10.00 10.00

Birds — A914

No. 2549: a, Saxicola torquata. b, Saxicola rubetra. c, Parus caeruleus. d, Turdus philomelos.

2002, Feb. 22
2549 Horiz. strip of 4 + central label 10.00 10.00
a. A914 7d multi .65 .65
b. A914 14d multi 1.50 1.50
c. A914 26.20d multi 3.00 3.00
d. A914 28.70d multi 3.50 3.50

Easter — A915

Designs: 7d, Crucifixion, fresco from Studenica Monastery, 1208. 14d, King Milutin's Veil, 1300. 26.20d, Christ's Descent to Hell, silverwork, 1540. 28.70d, Easter egg, Pec Patriarchy, 1980.

2002, Mar. 7 **Perf. 13¾**
2550-2553 A915 Set of 4 9.00 9.00

Bunjevac Women's Clothing — A916

Woman with: 7d, White blouse. 28.70d, Kerchief.

2002, Mar. 29 **Perf. 13¼**
2554-2555 A916 Set of 2 4.50 4.50

Zarko Tomic-Sremac (b. 1900), World War II Hero — A917

2002, Apr. 15
2556 A917 14d multi 12.50 12.50

Danube Fish — A918

No. 2557: a, Rutilus rutilus. b, Acipenser ruthenus. c, Huso huso. d, Stizostedion lucioperca.

2002, Apr. 25 **Litho.** **Perf. 13¼**
2557 Horiz. strip of 4 + central label 18.00 18.00
a. A918 7d multi 1.50 1.50
b. A918 14d multi 2.50 2.50
c. A918 26.20d multi 5.00 5.00
d. A918 28.70d multi 5.00 5.00

Europa A919

Designs: 28.70d, Trapeze artists. 50d, Tiger trainer.

2002, May 3 **Perf. 13¾**
2558-2559 A919 Set of 2 11.00 11.00

Europa Type of 2002
Souvenir Sheet

Design: 45d, Trained horse act.

2002, May 3 **Litho.** **Perf. 13¾**
2560 A919 45d multi 60.00 60.00

No. 2560 contains one 46x35mm stamp.

Civil Aviation in Yugoslavia, 75th Anniv. A920

Designs: 7d, Potez-29. 28.70d, Boeing 737-300.

Perf. 13¼ Syncopated
2002, June 17 **Litho.**
2561-2562 A920 Set of 2 30.00 30.00

Types of 1993 and 2001
Size: 19x21mm (#2563)

2002, July 25 **Litho.** **Perf. 12½**
2563 A702d A blue 3.00 1.50

Perf. 13¼
"E" in Green
2564 A898 E multi 7.50 4.50

Nos. 2563-2564 were intended for use in Montenegro and were sold there for 13c and 52c in euro currency respectively. The stamps were valid for use in the Serbian section of Yugoslavia.

European Nature Protection A921

Designs: 28.70d, Tara National Park. 50d, Golija Nature Park.

Perf. 13¼ Syncopated
2002, June 28 **Litho.**
2565-2566 A921 Set of 2 9.00 9.00

Mills — A922

Designs: 7d, Windmill, Melenci. 28.70d, Water mill, Lyuberada.

2002, Sept. 14
2567-2568 A922 Set of 2 9.00 9.00

Liberation of Niskic, 125th Anniv. — A923

2002, Sept. 18 **Perf. 13¾**
2569 A923 14d multi 10.00 9.00

Souvenir Sheet

Victory in 2002 World Basketball
Championships — A924

2002, Sept. 20
2570 A924 30d multi   10.00 10.00

Souvenir Sheet

JUFIZ XI Philatelic Exhibition — A925

2002, Sept. 23
2571 A925 30d multi   8.00 8.00

Joy of
Europe — A926

Children's art: 28.70d, Boat. 50d, Bird.

2002, Oct. 2
2572-2573 A926   Set of 2   8.50 8.50

Moraca
Monastery,
750th
Anniv. — A927

2002, Oct. 10
2574 A927 16d multi   20.00 12.00

Nos. 2255-2256 Srchd.
in Black or Violet

2002   *Perfs, etc., as Before*
2575 A751 50p on 5p #2256
              multi   2.50 1.25
2576 A702g 10d on 10,000d
              #2145   7.50 6.00
2577 A751 12d on 1p #2255
              multi (V)   6.00 4.00
      Nos. 2575-2577 (3)   16.00 11.25
    Issued: No. 2575, 10/17; No. 2576, 11/28;
No. 2577, 12/19.
    For stamp like No. 2577, but with black
surcharge, see Serbia and Montenegro No.
260.

Intl. Federation
of Stamp
Dealers
Associations,
50th
Anniv. — A928

2002, Oct. 24 Litho.   *Perf. 13¾*
2578 A928 16d multi   7.50 7.50

Serbian Folk
Costumes — A929

Paintings of costumes by Olga Benson in
Ethnographic Institute of Serbian Academy of
Sciences and Arts: a, Man, Kusadak. b,
Woman with red headdress, Belgrade. c, Man,
Novo Selo. d, Woman in profile, Belgrade.

2002, Nov. 8   *Perf. 13¾*
2579   Horiz. strip of 4, + cen-
            tral label   8.00 8.00
  a. A929 16d multi   1.00 1.00
  b. A929 24d multi   2.00 2.00
  c. A929 26.20d multi   2.00 2.00
  d. A929 28.70d multi   2.00 2.00

Christmas
A930

Religious art: 12d, Nativity, Stavronikita
Monastery, Mount Athos, Greece, 1546. 16d,
Nativity, Chilandari Monastery, Mount Athos,
Greece, c. 1618. 26.20d, Nativity, Tretyakov
Gallery, Moscow, 15th cent. 28.70d, Adoration
of the Magi, by Sandro Botticelli.

2002, Dec. 2   Set of 4   7.00 7.00

Abandoned
Dogs — A931

Various dogs.

2003, Jan. 31   *Perf. 13¾*
2584   Horiz. strip of 4, + cen-
            tral label   5.00 5.00
  a. A931 16d multi   .50 .50
  b. A931 24d multi   1.25 1.25
  c. A931 26.20d multi   1.25 1.25
  d. A931 28.70d multi   1.25 1.25

Yugoslavia became Serbia & Montenegro on Feb. 4, 2003. See Serbia
& Montenegro for subsequent issues.

SEMI-POSTAL STAMPS

Giving Succor
to Wounded
SP1

Wounded
Soldier
SP2

Symbolical of
National
Unity — SP3

Unwmk.
1921, Jan. 30 Engr.   *Perf. 12*
B1 SP1 10p carmine   .25 .25
B2 SP2 15p violet brown   .25 .25
B3 SP3 25p light blue   .25 .25
    Nos. B1-B3 (3)   .75 .75
    Nos. B1-B3 were sold at double face value,
the excess being for the benefit of invalid
soldiers.
    Exist imperf. Value $35.
    For surcharges see Nos. 15-21.

    This overprint was applied to 500,000
examples of No. B1 in 1923 and they
were given to the Society for Wounded
Invalids (Uprava Ratnih Invalida) which
sold them for 2d a piece. These overprinted stamps had no franking power,
but some were used through ignorance.

Regular Issue of
1926-27 Surcharged
in Dark Red

1926, Nov. 1   *Perf. 13*
B5 A6 25p + 25p green   .25   .25
B6 A6 50p + 50p olive brn   .25   .25
B7 A6 1d + 50p scarlet   .25   .25
B8 A6 2d + 50p black   .25   .25
B9 A6 3d + 50p slate blue   .25   .25
B10 A6 4d + 50p red org   .30   .25
B11 A6 5d + 50p brt vio   .50   .25
B12 A6 8d + 50p black brn   1.00   .25
B13 A6 10d + 1d olive brn   2.00   .25
B14 A6 15d + 1d brown   8.00 1.00
B15 A6 20d + 1d dark vio   12.00   .55
B16 A6 30d + 1d orange   27.50 3.25
  a. Double surcharge
      Nos. B5-B16 (12)   52.55 7.05
    Set, never hinged   105.00

    The surtax on these stamps was intended
for a fund for relief of sufferers from floods.
    For overprints see Nos. 99-101.

Cathedral at
Duvno
SP4

King Tomislav
SP6

Kings
Tomislav
and
Alexander
SP5

Perf. 12½, 11½x12
1929, Nov. 1   Typo.
B17 SP4 50p (+ 50p) olive green   .25   .25
B18 SP5 1d (+ 50p) red   .60   .40
B19 SP6 3d (+ 1d) blue   1.60 1.10
    Nos. B17-B19 (3)   2.45 1.75
    Set, never hinged   4.75

    Millenary of the Croatian kingdom. The sur-
tax was used to create a War Memorial Cemetery in France and to erect a monument to
Serbian soldiers who died there.
    No. B18 exists imperf. Value $400.

View of
Dobropolje
SP7

War
Memorial — SP8

View of
Kajmaktchalan
SP9

1931, Apr. 1   *Perf. 12½, 11½*
B20 SP7 50p + 50p blue grn   .25   .25
B21 SP8 1d + 1d scarlet   .25   .25
B22 SP9 3d + 3d deep blue   .25   .25
    Nos. B20-B22 (3)   .75   .75

    The surtax was added to a fund for a War
Memorial to Serbian soldiers who died in
France during World War I.

SP10

SP12

SP11

Black Overprint
1931, Nov. 1   *Perf. 12½, 11½x12*
B23 SP10 50p (+ 50p) olive grn   .25   .25
B24 SP11 1d (+ 50p) red   .25   .25
B25 SP12 3d (+ 1d) blue   .30   .30
    Nos. B23-B25 (3)   .80   .80

    Surtax for War Memorial fund.

Rower on
Danube at
Smederevo
SP13

Bled Lake
SP14

Danube near Belgrade SP15

View of Split Harbor SP16

Zagreb Cathedral — SP17

Prince Peter — SP18

1932, Sept. 2   Litho.   Perf. 11½

B26	SP13	75p + 50p dl grn & lt blue	.60	1.20
B27	SP14	1d + ½d scar & lt blue	.60	1.20
B28	SP15	1½d + ½d rose & green	.80	1.60
B29	SP16	3d + 1d bl & lt bl	1.60	2.40
B30	SP17	4d + 1d red org & lt blue	7.25	16.00
B31	SP18	5d + 1d dl vio & li-lac	7.25	13.50
		Nos. B26-B31 (6)	18.10	35.90
		Set, never hinged	35.00	

European Rowing Championship Races, Belgrade.

King Alexander SP19

Prince Peter SP20

1933, May 25   Typo.   Perf. 12½

B32	SP19	50p + 25p black	6.00	12.00
B33	SP19	75p + 25p yel grn	6.00	12.00
B34	SP19	1.50d + 50p rose	6.00	12.00
B35	SP19	3d + 1d bl vio	6.00	12.00
B36	SP19	4p + 1d dk grn	6.00	12.00
B37	SP19	5d + 1d orange	6.00	12.00
		Nos. B32-B37 (6)	36.00	72.00
		Set, never hinged	72.50	

11th Intl. Congress of P.E.N. (Poets, Editors and Novelists) Clubs, Dubrovnik, May 25-27.

The labels at the foot of the stamps are printed in either Cyrillic or Latin letters and each bears the amount of a premium for the benefit of the local P.E.N. Club at Dubrovnik.

1933, June 28

B38	SP20	75p + 25p slate grn	.25	.25
B39	SP20	1½d + ½d deep red	.25	.25

60th anniv. meeting of the National Sokols (Sports Associations) at Ljubljana, July 1.

Eagle Soaring over City — SP22

Athlete and Eagle — SP23

1934, June 1   Perf. 12½

B40	SP22	75p + 25p green	4.00	9.00
B41	SP22	1.50d + 50p car	6.00	9.50
B42	SP22	1.75d + 25p brown	10.00	9.50
		Nos. B40-B42 (3)	20.00	28.00
		Set, never hinged	40.00	

20th anniversary of Sokols of Sarajevo.

1934, June 1

B43	SP23	75p + 25p Prus grn	2.40	4.75
B44	SP23	1.50d + 50p car	2.40	4.75
B45	SP23	1.75d + 25p choc	10.00	14.50
		Nos. B43-B45 (3)	14.80	24.00
		Set, never hinged	27.50	

60th anniversary of Sokols of Zagreb.

Mother and Children
SP24   SP25

Perf. 12½x11½

1935, Dec. 25   Photo.

B46	SP24	1.50d + 1d dk brn & brown	1.25	1.20
a.		Perf. 11½	12.00	14.50
B47	SP25	3.50d + 1.50d bright ultra & bl	2.00	2.90
		Set, never hinged	6.50	

The surtax was for "Winter Help."

Queen Mother Marie SP26

Prince Regent Paul SP27

1936, May 3   Litho.

B48	SP26	75p + 25p grnsh bl	.25	.40
B49	SP26	1.50d + 50p rose pink	.25	.45
B50	SP26	1.75d + 75p brown	1.25	1.25
B51	SP26	3.50d + 1d brt bl	1.60	2.75
		Nos. B48-B51 (4)	3.35	4.85
		Set, never hinged	6.50	

1936, Sept. 20   Typo.

B52	SP27	75p + 50p turq grn & red	.40	*.35*
B53	SP27	1.50d + 50p cer & red	.40	*.35*
		Set, never hinged	1.60	

Surtax for the Red Cross.

Princes Tomislav and Andrej
SP28   SP29

Perf. 11½x12½, 12½x11½

1937, May 1

B54	SP28	25p + 25p red brn	.25	.25
B55	SP28	75p + 75p emerald	.25	.40
B56	SP29	1.50d + 1d org red	.30	.65
B57	SP29	2d + 1d magenta	.60	1.20
		Nos. B54-B57 (4)	1.40	2.50
		Set, never hinged	2.40	

Souvenir Sheet

National Costumes — SP30

1937, Sept. 12   Perf. 14

B57A	SP30	Sheet of 4	4.75	10.00
		Never hinged	9.50	
b.		1d blue green	1.00	1.75
c.		1.50d bright violet	1.00	1.75
d.		2d rose red	1.00	1.75
e.		4d dark blue	1.00	1.75

1st Yugoslavian Phil. Exhib., Belgrade. Sold only at the exhibition post office at 15d each.

SP31   SP32

Perf. 11½x12½, 12½x11½

1938, May 1   Photo.

B58	SP31	50p + 50p dark brn	.25	.30
B59	SP32	1d + 1d dk green	.25	.35
B60	SP31	1.50d + 1.50d scar	.50	.40
B61	SP32	2d + 2d magenta	1.25	.80
		Nos. B58-B61 (4)	2.25	1.85
		Set, never hinged	4.00	

Surtax for the benefit of Child Welfare.
For overprints see Nos. B75-B78.

Bridge and Anti-aircraft Lights — SP33

1938, May 28   Perf. 11½x12½

B62	SP33	1d + 50p dk grn	.40	.80
B63	SP33	1.50d + 1d scarlet	.60	1.20
a.		Perf. 11½	17.50	27.50
B64	SP33	2d + 1d rose vio	1.25	2.40
a.		Perf. 11½	18.00	35.00
B65	SP33	3d + 1.50d dp bl	2.00	4.00
		Nos. B62-B65 (4)	4.25	8.40
		Set, never hinged	8.00	

Intl. Aeronautical Exhib., Belgrade.

Cliff at Demir-Kapija — SP34

Modern Hospital SP35

Runner Carrying Torch — SP36

Alexander I — SP37

Perf. 11½x12½, 12½x11½

1938, Aug. 1

B66	SP34	1d + 1d slate grn & dp grn	.45	.40
B67	SP35	1.50d + 1.50d scar	.70	.55
B68	SP36	2d + 2d claret & dp rose	1.60	3.25
B69	SP37	3d + 3d dp bl	1.60	3.25
		Nos. B66-B69 (4)	4.35	7.45
		Set, never hinged	9.00	

The surtax was to raise funds to build a hospital for railway employees.

Runner SP38

Shot-Putter SP41

Hurdlers SP39

Pole Vaulter SP40

1938, Sept. 11

B70	SP38	50p + 50p org brn	1.25	2.40
B71	SP39	1d + 1d sl grn & dp grn	1.25	2.40
B72	SP40	1.50d + 1.50d rose & dk mag	1.25	2.40
B73	SP41	2d + 2d dk blue	2.50	4.75
		Nos. B70-B73 (4)	6.25	11.95
		Set, never hinged	12.00	

Ninth Balkan Games.

Stamps of 1938 Overprinted in Black

a   b

1938, Oct. 1

B75	SP31(a)	50p + 50p dk brn	.40	.55
B76	SP32(b)	1d + 1d dk grn	.40	.80
B77	SP31(a)	1.50d + 1.50d scar	.60	1.20
B78	SP32(b)	2d + 2d mag	1.25	2.40
		Nos. B75-B78 (4)	2.65	4.95
		Set, never hinged	5.25	

Surtax for the benefit of Child Welfare.

Postriders
SP43

1d+1d, Rural mail delivery. 1.50d+1.50d,
Mail train. 2d+2d, Mail bus. 4d+4d, Mail plane.

1939, Mar. 15   Photo.   Perf. 11½
B79	SP43	50p + 50p buff, bis & brown	.30	.55
B80	SP43	1d + 1d sl grn & dp green	.30	.55
B81	SP43	1.50d + 1.50d red, cop red & brn car	2.00	2.00
B82	SP43	2d + 2d dp plum & rose lilac	2.00	2.75
B83	SP43	4d + 4d ind & sl bl	2.40	4.00
		Nos. B79-B83 (5)	7.00	9.85
		Set, never hinged	14.00	

Centenary of the present postal system in
Yugoslavia. The surtax was used for the Railway Benevolent Association.
The Cyrillic and Latin inscriptions are transposed on Nos. B82 and B83.

Child Eating
SP48

Children at
Seashore — SP49

Boy
Planing
Board
SP50

Children in
Crib — SP51

1939, May 1   Perf. 12½
B84	SP48	1d + 1d blk & dp bl green	.50	1.00
B85	SP49	1.50d + 1.50d org brn & sal	2.00	3.25
a.	Perf. 11½		80.00	160.00
B86	SP50	2d + 2d mar & vio rose	1.40	2.90
B87	SP51	4d + 4d ind & royal blue	1.40	2.90
		Nos. B84-B87 (4)	5.30	10.05
		Set, never hinged	10.50	

The surtax was for the benefit of Child
Welfare.

Czar Lazar of
Serbia — SP52

Milosh
Obilich — SP53

1939, June 28   Perf. 11½
B88	SP52	1d + 1d sl grn & bl grn	1.60	1.60
B89	SP53	1.50d + 1.50d mar & brt car	1.60	1.60
		Set, never hinged	6.50	

Battle of Kosovo, 550th anniversary.

Training
Ship
"Jadran"
SP54

Designs: 1d+50p, Steamship "King Alexander." 1.50d+1d, Freighter "Triglan." 2d+1.50d,
Cruiser "Dubrovnik."

1939, Sept. 6   Engr.
B90	SP54	50p + 50p brn org	.40	.80
B91	SP54	1d + 50p dull grn	.80	1.60
B92	SP54	1.50d + 1d dp rose	1.25	2.40
B93	SP54	2d + 1.50d dark bl	2.00	4.00
		Nos. B90-B93 (4)	4.45	8.80
		Set, never hinged	9.00	

Yugoslav Navy and Merchant Marine. The
surtax aided a Marine Museum.

Motorcycle and
Sidecar — SP58

Racing Car
SP59

Motorcycle
SP60

Racing Car
SP61

1939, Sept. 3   Photo.
B94	SP58	50p + 50p multi	.50	.80
B95	SP59	1d + 1d multi	1.00	1.60
B96	SP60	1.50d + 1.50d multi	1.40	2.40
B97	SP61	2d + 2d multi	2.50	4.00
		Nos. B94-B97 (4)	5.40	8.80
		Set, never hinged	10.50	

Automobile and Motorcycle Races, Belgrade. The surtax was for the Race Organization and the State Treasury.

Unknown
Soldier
Memorial
SP62

1939, Oct. 9   Perf. 12½
B98	SP62	1d + 50p sl grn & green	1.00	1.60
B99	SP62	1.50d + 1d red & rose red	1.00	1.60
B100	SP62	2d + 1.50d dp cl & vio rose	1.25	2.40
B101	SP62	3d + 2d dp bl & bl	2.50	4.00
		Nos. B98-B101 (4)	5.75	9.60
		Set, never hinged	11.00	

Assassination of King Alexander, 5th anniv.
The surtax was used to aid World War I
invalids.

Postman
Delivering
Mail — SP64

Postman Emptying
Mail Box — SP65

Parcel Post
Delivery
Wagon
SP66

Parcel Post
SP67

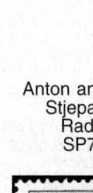

Repairing
Telephone
Wires — SP68

1940, Jan. 1
B102	SP64	50p + 50p brn & deep org	.60	1.00
B103	SP65	1d + 1d sl grn & blue grn	.60	1.00
B104	SP66	1.50d + 1.50d red brn & scar	1.00	2.40
B105	SP67	2d + 2d dl vio & red lilac	1.25	2.40
B106	SP68	4d + 4d sl bl & bl	4.00	6.50
		Nos. B102-B106 (5)	7.45	13.30
		Set, never hinged	14.50	

The surtax was used for the employees of
the Postal System in Belgrade.

Croats'
Arrival at
Adriatic in
640
SP69

King
Tomislav — SP70

Death of Matija
Gubec — SP71

Anton and
Stjepan
Radic
SP72

Map of
Yugoslavia
SP73

1940, Mar. 1   Typo.   Perf. 11½
B107	SP69	50p + 50p brn org	.40	.55
B108	SP70	1d + 1d green	.40	.55
B109	SP71	1.50d + 1.50d brt red	1.25	.55
B110	SP72	2d + 2d dk cerise	2.00	2.40
B111	SP73	4d + 2d dark blue	2.00	2.75
		Nos. B107-B111 (5)	6.05	6.80
		Set, never hinged	12.00	

The surtax was used for the benefit of postal
employees in Zagreb.

Children
Playing in
Snow
SP74

Children at
Seashore — SP75

1940, May 1 Photo. Perf. 11½, 12½
B112	SP74	50p + 50p brn org & org yellow	.25	.40
B113	SP75	1d + 1d sl grn & dk green	.25	.40
B114	SP74	1.50d + 1.50d brn red & scarlet	.60	.80
B115	SP75	2d + 2d mar & vio rose	1.00	1.60
		Nos. B112-B115 (4)	2.10	3.20
		Set, never hinged	4.00	

The surtax was for Child Welfare.

Nos. C11-C14
Surcharged in
Carmine

Perf. 11½x12½, 12½x11½
1940, Dec. 23
B116	AP6	50p + 50p on 5d	.25 .25
B117	AP7	1d + 1d on 10d	.25 .40
a.		Perf. 12½	40.00 40.00
B118	AP8	1.50d + 1.50d on 20d	.80 1.40
B119	AP9	2d + 2d on 30d	.90 1.75
		Nos. B116-B119 (4)	2.20 3.80
		Set, never hinged	4.00

The surtax was used to fight tuberculosis.
For surcharges see Nos. NB1-NB4.

Croatian, Serbian
and Slovenian
SP77

Chapel at
Kajmaktchalan
SP78

St. Peter's Cemetery,
Ljubljana — SP76

St. Peter's Cemetery,
Ljubljana — SP76

Memorial
at Brezje
SP79

1941, Jan. 1   **Perf. 12½**
B120	SP76	50p + 50p gray grn & yel green	.25 .40
B121	SP77	1d + 1d brn car & dl rose	.25 .40
B122	SP78	1.50d + 1.50d myr grn & bl green	.60 1.25
B123	SP79	2d + 2d gray bl & pale lilac	1.00 2.00
		Nos. B120-B123 (4)	2.10 4.05
		Set, never hinged	4.00

Surtax for the Ljubljana War Veterans Assoc.

Kamenita Gate,
Zagreb — SP80

13th Century
Cathedral,
Zagreb — SP81

1941, Mar. 16   Engr.   Perf. 11½
B124	SP80	1.50d + 1.50d choc	.60 1.25
B125	SP81	4d + 3d blue blk	.60 1.25
		Set, never hinged	2.75

2nd Philatelic Exhibition of Croatia, at
Zagreb, Mar. 16-27.

Nos. B124-B125 exist perf. 9½ on right side.
Value, each $32.50.

1941, Apr.
B126	SP80	1.50d + 1.50d bl black	12.00 24.00
B127	SP81	4d + 3d choc	12.00 24.00
		Set, never hinged	55.00

Regional philatelic exhibition at Slavonski
Brod. Nos. B126-B127 with gold overprint,
"Nezavisna Drzava Hrvatska," are Croatia
Nos. B1-B2.

Nos. B126-B127 exist perf. 9½ on right side.
Value, each $40 unused, $80 never hinged,
$80 used.

Issues for Federal Republic

Carrying
Wounded
Soldier — SP82

Child — SP83

1945, Sept. 15   Typo.   Perf. 11½
B131	SP82	1d + 4d deep ultra	.50 .80
B132	SP83	2d + 6d scarlet	.50 .80
		Set, never hinged	1.90

The surtax was for the Red Cross.

Russia,
Yugoslavia
Flags
SP84

1945, Oct. 20   Photo.   Unwmk.
B133	SP84	2d + 5d multi	.80 1.60
		Never hinged	1.60

Liberation of Belgrade, 1st anniv.
Exist imperf. Value $50 unused, $100 never hinged.

Communications
Symbols — SP85

1946, May 10   Perf. 12½
B134	SP85	1.50d + 1d emer	1.60 3.25
B135	SP85	2.50d + 1.50d car rose	1.60 3.25
B136	SP85	5d + 2d gray bl	1.60 3.25
B137	SP85	8d + 3.50d dl brn	1.60 3.25
		Nos. B134-B137 (4)	6.40 13.00
		Set, never hinged	12.00

1st PTT Congress since liberation, May 10.

Flag and Young
Laborers
SP86

Handstand on
Horizontal Bar
SP87

1946, Aug. 1   Litho.
Flag in Red or Carmine and Deep or
Dark Blue
B138	SP86	50p + 50p brn & buff	1.00 1.60
B139	SP86	1.50d + 1d dk grn & lt green	1.00 1.60
B140	SP86	2.50d + 2d rose vio & rose lilac	1.00 1.60
B141	SP86	5d + 3d gray bl & blue	1.00 1.60
		Nos. B138-B141 (4)	4.00 6.40
		Set, never hinged	8.00

The surtax aided railroad reconstruction
carried out by Yugoslav youths.

1947, Sept. 5   Perf. 11½
B142	SP87	1.50d + 50p dark grn	2.00 4.00
B143	SP87	2.50d + 50p carmine	2.00 4.00
B144	SP87	4d + 50p brt blue	2.00 4.00
		Nos. B142-B144 (3)	6.00 12.00
		Set, never hinged	12.00

1947 Balkan Games, Sept. 5-7, Ljubljana.

Young
Railway
Laborers
SP88

1947, Sept. 25   Typo.   Perf. 11½x12
B145	SP88	1d + 50p orange	.50 1.00
B146	SP88	1.50d + 1d yel green	.50 1.00
B147	SP88	2.50d + 1.50d car lake	.50 1.00
B148	SP88	5d + 2d deep blue	.50 1.00
		Nos. B145-B148 (4)	2.00 4.00
		Set, never hinged	4.00

The surtax was for youth brigades employed
in the construction of the Samac-Sarajevo
railway.

Symbolizing
Protection of
"B.C.G."
Vaccine
SP89

Dying Serpent
SP91

"Illness" and
"Recovery"
SP90

1948, Apr. 1   Litho.   Perf. 12½
B149	SP89	1.50d + 1d sl blk & red	.40 .80
B150	SP90	2.50d + 2d grnsh gray, ol blk & red	.40 .80
B151	SP91	5d + 3d dk bl & car	.40 .80
		Nos. B149-B151 (3)	1.20 2.40
		Set, never hinged	2.40

Fight against tuberculosis. The surtax was
for the Yugoslav Red Cross.

Juro
Danicic
SP92

Portraits: 2.50d+1d, Franjo Racki. 4d+2d,
Josip J. Strossmayer.

1948, July 28   Perf. 11
B152	SP92	1.50d + 50p blk green	.40 .80
B153	SP92	2.50d + 1d dark red	.40 .80
B154	SP92	4d + 2d dark blue	.40 .80
		Nos. B152-B154 (3)	1.20 2.40
		Set, never hinged	2.40

Yugoslav Academy of Arts and Sciences,
Zagreb, 80th anniv. The surtax was for the
Academy.

Shot Put — SP93

1948, Sept. 10   Perf. 12½
B155	SP93	2d + 1d shown	.40 .80
B156	SP93	3d + 1d Hurdles	.40 .80
B157	SP93	5d + 2d Pole vault	1.00 1.50
		Nos. B155-B157 (3)	1.80 2.85
		Set, never hinged	3.50

Balkan and Central Europe Games, 1948.
On sale 4 days.

AIR POST STAMPS

Dubrovnik
AP1

Lake Bled
AP2

Falls of
Jaice — AP3

Church at
Oplenac — AP4

Bridge at
Mostar — AP5

Perf. 12½
1934, June 15   Typo.   Unwmk.
C1	AP1	50p violet brown	.25 .25
C2	AP2	1d green	.25 .25
C3	AP3	2d rose red	.45 .30
C4	AP4	3d ultramarine	1.00 1.00
C5	AP5	10d vermilion	2.40 3.75
		Nos. C1-C5 (5)	4.35 4.95
		Set, never hinged	8.00

King Alexander Memorial Issue
1935, Jan. 1
Border in Black
C6	AP4	3d ultramarine	3.25 4.75
		Never hinged	6.50

St. Naum
Convent — AP6

Port of
Rab — AP7

Sarajevo
AP8

Ljubljana
AP9

Perf. 11½x12½, 12½x11½

1937, Sept. 12			Photo.	
C7	AP6	50p brown	.25	.25
a.	Perf. 12½		.25	.25
C8	AP7	1d yellow grn	.25	.25
a.	Perf. 12½		.25	.25
C9	AP8	2d blue gray	.25	.25
a.	Perf. 12½		.25	.25
C10	AP9	2.50d rose red	.25	.25
a.	Perf. 12½		.25	.25
C11	AP6	5d brn violet	.25	.25
a.	Perf. 12½		.25	.25
C12	AP7	10d brown lake	.50	.25
a.	Perf. 12½		.70	.25
C13	AP8	20d dark green	5.25	8.00
a.	Perf. 12½		.70	1.00
C14	AP9	30d ultramarine	18.00	27.50
a.	Perf. 12½		1.00	1.75
	Nos. C7-C14 (8)		25.00	37.00
	Nos. C7-C14, never hinged		47.50	
	Nos. C7a-C14a, never hinged		5.50	

For surcharges see Nos. B116-B119, NB1-NB4, NC1-NC8.

Cathedral
of Zagreb
AP10

Bridge at
Belgrade
AP11

1940, Aug. 15		Litho.	Perf. 12½	
C15	AP10	40d Prus grn & pale green	4.00	3.25
C16	AP11	50d slate bl & gray bl	4.00	4.75
	Set, never hinged		16.00	

For overprints see Nos. NC9-NC10.

Issues for Federal Republic

Plane over
Terrace of
Kalimegdan,
Belgrade
AP12

Plane over
Dubrovnik
AP13

1947, Apr. 21		Typo.	Perf. 11½	
Cyrillic Inscription at Top				
C17	AP12	50p ol gray & brn vio	.25	.25
C18	AP13	1d mag & ol gray	.25	.25
C19	AP12	2d blue & black	.25	.25
C20	AP13	5d green & gray	.25	.25
C21	AP12	10d olive bis & choc	.25	.25
C22	AP13	20d ultra & olive	.60	1.25
Roman Inscription at Top				
C23	AP12	50p ol gray & brn vio	.25	.25
C24	AP13	1d mag & ol gray	.25	.25
C25	AP12	2d blue & black	.25	.25
C26	AP13	5d green & gray	.25	.25

C27	AP12	10d olive bis & choc	.25	.25
C28	AP13	20d ultra & olive	.60	1.25
	Nos. C17-C28 (12)		3.70	5.00
	Set, never hinged		4.75	

Sheets of each denomination contain alternately stamps with Cyrillic or Roman inscription at top. Value, 6 se-tenant pairs: unused $24; never hinged $47.50.

Laurent
Kosir and
Birthplace
AP14

1948, Aug. 27			Engr.	
C29	AP14	15d red violet	.60	1.25
	Never hinged		1.25	

Kosir, recognized by Yugoslavia as inventor of the postage stamp, 80th death anniv. Issued in sheets of 25 stamps and 25 labels.

Nos. 262 to 264
Overprinted in
Blue or Carmine

1949, Aug. 25		Unwmk.	Perf. 12½	
C30	A55	3d carmine rose	5.50	8.00
C31	A56	5d dull blue (C)	5.50	8.00
C32	A57	12d red brown	5.50	8.00
	Nos. C30-C32 (3)		16.50	24.00
	Never hinged		32.50	

Liberation of Macedonia, 5th anniv. It is reported that No. C32 was not sold to the public at the post office.

Souvenir Sheet

Electric
Train
AP15

Perf. 11½x12½

1949, Dec. 15			Photo.	
C33	AP15	10d lilac rose	90.00	105.00
	Never hinged		175.00	
a.	Imperf.		90.00	105.00
	Never hinged		175.00	

Centenary of Yugoslav railroads. For overprint see Trieste No. C17.

Iron Gate,
Derdap
AP16

Belgrade
AP17

Designs: 2d, Cascades, Plitvice. 3d, Carniola. 6d, Roman bridge, Mostar. 10d, Ohrid. 20d, Gulf of Kotor. 30d, Dubrovnik. 50d, Bled.

Perf. 12½

1951, June 16		Unwmk.	Engr.	
C34	AP16	1d deep org	.25	.25
C35	AP16	2d dk green	.25	.25
C36	AP16	3d dark red	.25	.25
C37	AP16	6d ultra	2.00	4.00
C38	AP16	10d dark brn	.25	.25
C39	AP16	20d grnsh blk	.40	.25
C40	AP16	30d dp claret	1.00	.25
C41	AP16	50d dk purple	1.40	.25
C42	AP17	100d dk gray bl	27.50	9.00
	Nos. C34-C42 (9)		33.30	14.75
	Set, never hinged		65.00	

Souvenir Sheet

Imperf

C43	AP17	100d red brn	90.00	175.00
	Never hinged		175.00	

See Nos. C50-C53. For overprints see Nos. C44, C49, Trieste C22-C32.

Roman Bridge Type of 1951 Overprinted "ZEFIZ 1951" in Carmine

1951, June 16			Perf. 12½	
C44	AP16	6d dark green	4.00	3.75
	Never hinged		8.00	

Nos. C43-C44 were issued for Zagreb Philatelic Exhibition, June 16-26.

View on Mt.
Kopaonik
AP18

Plane and
Parachutists
AP19

Perf. 12½

1951, July		Unwmk.	Photo.	
C45	AP18	3d shown	1.00	2.00
C46	AP18	5d Mt. Triglav	1.00	2.00
C47	AP18	20d Mt. Kalnik	32.50	47.50
	Nos. C45-C47 (3)		34.50	51.50
	Set, never hinged		65.00	

Intl. Union of Mountaineers, 12th Assembly, Bled, July 13-18.

1951, Aug. 16			Engr.	
C48	AP19	6d carmine	2.00	2.00

Type of
1951
Overprinted
in Carmine

C49	AP16	50d blue	32.50	40.00

First World Parachute Championship, Bled, Aug. 16-20. Nos. C48-C49, never hinged $65.

> **Catalogue values for unused stamps in this section, from this point to the end of the section, are for Never Hinged items.**

Types of 1951

Designs: 5d, Cascades, Plitvice. 100d, Carniola. 200d, Roman bridge, Mostar.

1951-52				
C50	AP16	5d yel brn ('52)	.40	.25
C51	AP16	100d green	1.75	.25
C52	AP16	200d deep car ('52)	2.50	.30
C53	AP17	500d blue vio ('52)	8.00	.40
	Nos. C50-C53 (4)		12.65	1.20

Marshal Tito,
Tank, Factory
and Planes
AP20

1951, Dec. 22			Unwmk.	
C54	AP20	150d deep blue	10.00	10.00

Army Day, Dec. 22; 10th anniv. of the formation of the 1st military unit of "New" Yugoslavia.

Star and Flag-encircled
Globe — AP21

1953, July 30			Engr.	
C55	AP21	300d bl & grn	160.00	160.00

38th Esperanto Congress, Zagreb, 7/25-8/1. For overprint see Trieste No. C21.

13th
Century
Tower,
Zagreb
AP22

1956, May 20			Perf. 11½	
Chalky Paper				
C56	AP22	30d gray, vio bl & org red		3.25	1.40

Yugoslav Intl. Phil. Exhib., JUFIZ III, Zagreb, May 20-27.

Workers and
Cogwheel — AP23

1956, June 15			Photo.	
Glossy Paper				
C57	AP23	30d car rose & blk	1.60	1.60

10th anniversary of technical education.

Moon and Earth
with
Satellites — AP24

1958, Oct. 24		Engr.	Perf. 12½	
C58	AP24	300d dark blue	7.50	3.50

Intl. Geophysical Year, 1957-58.

Types of Regular Issue, 1961

1961, Sept. 1			Perf. 11½	
C59	A150	250d dark purple	.90	.60
C60	A151	500d violet blue	2.00	1.25

Type of Athletic Regular Issue, 1962
Souvenir Sheet
Design: Army Stadium, Belgrade.

1962, Sept. 12   Litho.   Imperf.
C61 A161 600d vio & blk   16.00 16.00

7th European Athletic Championships, Belgrade, Sept. 12-16.

REGISTERED LETTER STAMPS

> Catalogue values for unused stamps in this section are for Never Hinged items.

RL1

1993, June 28   Litho.   Perf. 13¼
F1 RL1 (R) ultra   1.60 .40
  a. Perf. 12½   6.50 .55
  b. Dated "1997"   6.50 .40

No. F1 was valued at 11,000d on day of issue. No. F1b issued 2/97.
For surcharge, see Serbia No. 194.

Type of 1993
2002, July 25   Litho.   Perf. 12½
F2 RL1 R red   2.00 1.50

No. F2 was intended for use in Montenegro and was sold there for 39c in euro currency. The stamp was valid for use in the Serbian section of Yugoslavia.

POSTAGE DUE STAMPS

King Alexander — D1

1921   Typo.   Unwmk.   Perf. 11½
Red or Black Surcharge
J1 D1 10p on 5p green (R)   .25 .25
J2 D1 30p on 5p green (Bk)   .25 .25
  Set, never hinged   .65

D2   D3

1921-22   Typo.   Perf. 11½, Rough
J3 D2 10p rose   .25 .25
J4 D2 30p yellow green   .25 .25
J5 D2 50p violet   .25 .25
J6 D2 1d brown   .30 .25
J7 D2 2d blue   .40 .25
J8 D3 5d orange   2.00 .25
J9 D3 10d violet brown   6.00 .45
  a. Cliche of 10p in sheet of
    10d   190.00 —
J10 D3 25d pink   35.00 1.60
J11 D3 50d green   30.00 1.60
  Nos. J3-J11 (9)   74.45 5.15
  Set, never hinged   140.00

1924   Perf. 9, 10½, 11½, Clean-cut
J12 D3 10p rose red   .25 .25
J13 D3 30p yellow green   .35 .40
J14 D3 50p violet   .25 .25
J15 D3 1d brown   .25 .25
J16 D3 2d deep blue   .50 .25
J17 D3 5d orange   1.60 .25
J18 D3 10d violet brown   10.00 .25
J19 D3 25d pink   65.00 1.25
J20 D3 50d green   47.50 1.25
  Nos. J12-J20 (9)   125.70 4.40
  Set, never hinged   240.00

Nos. J19-J20 do not exist perf 9. Nos. J18-J20 do not exist perf 11½.

Nos. J19-J20 Surcharged

1928
J21 D3 10d on 25d pink   3.25 .40
J22 D3 10d on 50d green   3.25 .40
  a. Inverted surcharge   30.00 18.00
  Set, never hinged   13.00

A second type of "1" in surcharge has flag projecting horizontally. Value, each: $24 never hinged; $12 unused; $3.25 used.

Coat of   Numeral of
Arms — D4   Value — D5

1931   Typo.   Perf. 12½
With Imprint at Foot
J23 D4 50p violet   1.40 .25
J24 D4 1d deep magenta   3.00 .25
J25 D4 2d deep blue   9.50 .25
J26 D4 5d orange   2.00 .25
J27 D4 10d chocolate   10.00 1.25
  Nos. J23-J27 (5)   25.90 2.25
  Set, never hinged   47.50

For overprints see Nos. NJ1-NJ13, Croatia 26-29, J1-J5.

1932   Without Imprint at Foot
J28 D4 50p violet   .25 .25
J29 D4 1d deep magenta   .25 .25
J30 D4 2d deep blue   .25 .25
J31 D4 5d orange   .25 .25
J32 D4 10d chocolate   .25 .25
  Nos. J28-J32 (5)   1.25 1.25

Overprint in Green, Blue or Maroon
1933   Perf. 9, 10½, 11½
J33 D5 50p vio (G)   .25 .25
  a. Perf. 10½   .30
J34 D5 1d brown (Bl)   .25 .25
  a. Perf. 10½   2.00 1.40
J35 D5 2d blue (M)   .25 .25
  a. Perf. 10½   1.00 1.25
J36 D5 5d orange (Bl)   .80 .25
J37 D5 10d violet brn (Bl)   4.00 .25
  Nos. J33-J37 (5)   5.55 1.25
  Set, never hinged   10.50

Issues for Federal Republic

Redrawn Type OD5, German Occupation of Serbia, Overprinted in Black

1945   Unwmk.   Perf. 12½
J37A OD5 10d red   .60 .55
J37B OD5 20d ultramarine   .60 .55
  Set, never hinged   2.40

In the redrawn design the eagle is replaced by a colorless tablet.

Coat of   Torches and
Arms — D6   Star — D7

1945   Litho.   Perf. 12½
Numerals in Black
J38 D6 2d brown violet   .25 .25
J39 D6 3d violet   .25 .25
J40 D6 5d green   .25 .25
J41 D6 7d orange brown   .25 .25
J42 D6 10d rose lilac   .25 .25
J43 D6 20d blue   .25 .25

J44 D6 30d light bl grn   .40 .35
J45 D6 40d rose red   .40 .40
Numerals in Color of Stamp
J46 D6 1d blue green   .25 .25
J47 D6 1.50d blue   .25 .25
J48 D6 2d vermilion   .40 .25
J49 D6 3d violet brown   .40 .25
J50 D6 4d rose violet   .60 .25
  Nos. J38-J50 (13)   4.20 3.50
  Set, never hinged   6.50

For overprints see Nos. J64-J66.

1946-47   Typo.   Unwmk.
J51 D7 50p dp orange ('47)   .25 .25
J52 D7 1d orange   .25 .25
J53 D7 2d dark blue   .25 .25
J54 D7 3d yellow green   .25 .25
J55 D7 5d bright purple   .25 .25
J56 D7 7d crimson   .80 .25
J57 D7 10d brt pink ('47)   .80 .25
J58 D7 20d rose lake ('47)   2.00 .55
  Nos. J51-J58 (8)   4.85 2.30
  Set, never hinged   8.00

See Nos. J67-J79. For overprints see Trieste Nos. J1-J5, J11-J18.

Nos. J47, J49 and J50 Overprinted in Black

1950   Litho.
J64 D6 1.50d blue   .25 .25
J65 D6 3d violet brown   .25 .25
J66 D6 4d rose violet   .25 .30
  Nos. J64-J66 (3)   .75 .80
  Set, never hinged   1.25

> Catalogue values for unused stamps in this section, from this point to the end of the section, are for Never Hinged items.

Type of 1946-47
1951-52   Typo.   Perf. 12½
J67 D7 1d brown ('52)   .40 .25
J68 D7 2d emerald   .40 .25
J69 D7 5d blue   .55 .25
J70 D7 10d scarlet   1.25 .25
J71 D7 20d purple   2.00 .25
J72 D7 30d org yel ('52)   4.00 .25
J73 D7 50d ultramarine   16.00 .40
J74 D7 100d dp plum ('52)   55.00 2.00
  Nos. J67-J74 (8)   79.60 3.90

For overprints see Istria Nos. J20-J24, Trieste J11-J18.

1962   Litho.   Perf. 12½
J75 D7 10d red orange   3.25 .25
J76 D7 20d purple   3.25 .25
J77 D7 30d orange   6.75 .25
J78 D7 50d ultramarine   32.50 .80
J79 D7 100d rose lake   20.00 1.25
  Nos. J75-J79 (5)   65.75 2.80

OFFICIAL STAMPS

Issues for Federal Republic

Arms of the Federated People's Republic — O1

Perf. 12½
1946, Nov. 1   Unwmk.   Typo.
O1 O1 50p orange   .25 .25
O2 O1 1d blue green   .25 .25
O3 O1 1.50d olive green   .25 .25
O4 O1 2.50d red   .25 .25
O5 O1 4d yellow brown   .40 .25
O6 O1 5d deep blue   .60 .25
O7 O1 8d chocolate   1.25 .25
O8 O1 12d violet   1.40 .25
  Nos. O1-O8 (8)   4.65 2.00
  Set, never hinged   8.00

For surcharges see Nos. 272A-272B, Istria 43, 45, 47, 49, 51.

POSTAL TAX STAMPS

> Catalogue values for unused stamps in this section are for Never Hinged items.

The tax was for the Red Cross or The Olympic Fund unless otherwise noted.

Red Cross   Dr. Vladen
Emblem   Djordjevic
PT1   PT2

Unwmk.
1933, Sept. 17   Litho.   Perf. 13
RA1 PT1 50p dark blue & red   .65 .25

Obligatory on inland letters during Red Cross Week, Sept. 17-23.
See No. RAJ1.

1936, Sept. 20   Typo.   Perf. 12
RA2 PT2 50p brn blk & red   .40 .25

Obligatory on inland letters during Red Cross Week, Sept. 20-26.

Aiding the Wounded PT3

1938, Sept. 18   Litho.   Perf. 12½
RA3 PT3 50p dk bl, red, yel &
    grn   .40 .25

1940, Sept. 15   Redrawn
RA4 PT3 50p slate blue & red   .55 .25

The inscription at the upper right of this stamp and the numerals of value are in smaller characters.
Obligatory on all letters during the second week of September.

Issues for Federal Republic

Ruined   Red Cross
Dwellings — PT4 Nurse — PT5

1947, Jan. 1   Litho.   Perf. 12½
RA5 PT4 50p brn & scarlet   .25 .25

See No. RAJ2. For overprints see Trieste Nos. RA1, RAJ1.

1948, Oct. 1
RA6 PT5 50p dk vio bl & red   .25 .25

See No. RAJ3.

Nurse and Child — PT6

Nurse Holding Book — PT7

Girl PT12

Nurse Opening Window PT13

1949, Nov. 5
RA7 PT6 50p red & brown .25 .25
See No. RAJ4. For overprints see Trieste Nos. RA2, RAJ2.

1950, Oct. 1
RA8 PT7 50p dark green & red .25 .25
Obligatory Oct. 1-8, 1950.
See No. RAJ6.

Hands Raising Red Cross Flag — PT8

Nurse — PT9

1951, Oct. 7
RA9 PT8 50p vio bl & red .25 .25
Obligatory Oct. 7-14.
For overprints see Trieste Nos. RA3, RAJ3.

1952, Oct. 5 Photo. Perf. 12½
RA10 PT9 50p gray & carmine .25 .25
For overprint see Trieste No. RA4.

Child Receiving Blood Transfusion PT10

Youths Carrying Flags PT11

1953, Oct. 25 Litho.
RA11 PT10 2d red vio & red .40 .25
See No. RAJ8. For overprints see Trieste Nos. RA5, RAJ5.

1954, Nov. 1
RA12 PT11 2d gray grn & red .40 .25
See Nos. RAJ9.

Infant — PT11a

1954, Oct. 4
RA12A PT11a 2d brn & salmon 1.25 .65
The tax was for Children's Week.

1955, Oct. 2 Unwmk. Perf. 12½
RA13 PT12 2d dull red .40 .25
The tax was for child welfare.
See No. RAJ10.

1955, Oct. 31
RA14 PT13 2d vio blk & red .25 .25
See No. RAJ11.

Ruins in the Snow — PT14

Children and Goose — PT15

1956, May 6 Perf. 12½
RA15 PT14 2d sepia & red .30 .25
See No. RAJ12.

1956, Sept. 30
RA16 PT15 2d gray green .40 .25
The tax was for child welfare.
See No. RAJ13.

Plane over Temporary Shelter — PT16

1957, May 5 Litho.
RA17 PT16 2d lt bl, blk & car .30 .25
See No. RAJ14.

Girl and Boy Pioneers PT17

1957, Sept. 30 Unwmk. Perf. 12½
RA18 PT17 2d rose & gray .30 .25
Children's Week. Obligatory Oct. 2-6.
See No. RAJ15.

Redrawn Type of Regular Issue, 1953

1958, May 4 Perf. 12½x12
RA19 A95 2d multicolored .40 .25
On No. RA19 the UN emblem has been left out, Cyrillic inscriptions at left added, country name in Latin letters.

Playing Children — PT18

1958, Oct. 5 Litho. Perf. 12½
RA20 PT18 2d brt yel & black .25 .25
Children's Week, Oct. 5-11.

Helping Hand and Family — PT19

1959, May 3
RA21 PT19 2d blue vio & red .30 .25
Red Cross centenary. Obligatory May 3-9.
See No. RAJ18.

Blackboard, Flower and Fish — PT20

1959, Oct. 5 Unwmk.
RA22 PT20 2d ocher & Prus grn .30 .25
Children's Week. Obligatory on domestic mail, Oct. 5-11.
See No. RAJ19.

"Reconstruction" PT21

1960, May 8 Perf. 12½
RA23 PT21 2d slate & red .30 .25
Obligatory May 8-14. See No. RAJ20.

Girl and Toys — PT22

1960, Oct. 2 Litho. Perf. 12½
RA24 PT22 2d red .25 .25
Issued for Children's Week. Obligatory on domestic mail Oct. 2-8.
See No. RAJ21.

Blood Donor Symbolism PT23

1961, May 7
RA25 PT23 2d multicolored .30 .25
Obligatory May 7-13. Exists imperf. Value $14.
See No. RAJ22.

Bird Holding Flower PT24

1961, Oct. 1
RA26 PT24 2d orange & violet .25 .25
Children's Week. Exists imperf. Obligatory on domestic mail, Oct. 1-7.
See No. RAJ23.

Bandages and Symbols of Home, Industry, Weather, Transportation, Fire and Flood — PT25

1962, Apr. 30 Perf. 12½
RA27 PT25 5d red brn, gray & red .25 .25
Obligatory on domestic mail May 6-12.
See No. RAJ24.

Centenary Emblem — PT26

1963, May 5 Unwmk. Perf. 12½
RA28 PT26 5d dl yel, red & gray .30 .25
Intl. Red Cross, centenary. Exists imperf. Obligatory on all domestic mail during Red Cross Week, May 5-11.
See No. RAJ25.

Parachute Drop of Supplies, Yugoslav Flag — PT27

1964, Apr. 27 Litho.
RA29 PT27 5d blue, rose & dk bl .25 .25
Obligatory on domestic mail, May 3-9.

Children in Circle — PT28

1965, May 2   Litho.   Perf. 12½
RA30 PT28 5d tan & red   .25   .25
Obligatory on domestic mail, May 2-8.

Arrows
PT29

1966, Apr. 28   Litho.   Perf. 12½
RA31 PT29 5p gray & multi   .25   .25
Obligatory on domestic mail, May 1-7.

Crosses and Flower
PT30

1967, Apr. 28   Litho.   Perf. 12½
RA32 PT30 5p vio, red & yel grn   .25   .25
Exists imperf.

Honeycomb and Red Cross — PT31

1968, Apr. 30   Litho.   Perf. 12
RA33 PT31 5p multicolored   .25   .25
Obligatory on all domestic mail May 5-11.

Aztec Calendar Stone and Olympic Rings — PT32

1968, Oct. 12   Perf. 12½
RA34 PT32 10p black & multi   .25   .25

Red Cross, Hands and Globe — PT33

1969, May 18   Litho.   Perf. 12
RA35 PT33 20p red org, dl red & blk   .25   .25

Globe, Olympic Torch and Rings — PT34

1969, Nov. 24   Litho.   Perf. 11¼
RA36 PT34 10p gold & multi   4.50   .25
a.   Perf. 9   12.00   1.90
Yugoslav Olympic Committee, 50th anniv. Exists imperf. Value $125.

Symbolic Flower and People
PT35

1970, Apr. 27   Litho.   Perf. 13
RA37 PT35 20p vio bl, org & red   .25   .25

Olympic Flag — PT36

1970, June 10   Litho.   Perf. 13x13½
RA38 PT36 10p multicolored   .25   .25

Red Cross Encircling Globe
PT37

1971, Apr. 26   Litho.   Perf. 12½
RA39 PT37 20p blue, yel & red   .25   .25

Olympic Rings and Disk — PT38

1971, June 15   Litho.   Perf. 12½
RA40 PT38 10p blue & black   .25   .25

Red Cross and Hemispheres
PT39

1972, Apr. 27   Perf. 13½x13
RA41 PT39 20p red & multi   .25   .25

Olympic Rings, TV Tower, Munich and Sapporo Emblems — PT40

1972, May   Perf. 13x13½
RA42 PT40 10p ultra & multi   .25   .25

Red Cross, Crescent and Lion Emblems — PT41

1973, Apr. 24   Litho.   Perf. 13x13½
RA43 PT41 20p blue & multi   .25   .25

Globe and Olympic Rings — PT42

1973, June 1   Litho.   Perf. 13x13½
RA44 PT42 10p multicolored   .25   .25

Drop of Blood, Red Cross Emblems
PT43

1974, Apr. 25   Litho.   Perf. 13
RA45 PT43 20p red & multi   .25   .25

Olympic Rings
PT44

1974, June 1   Litho.   Perf. 13
RA46 PT44 10p blue & multi   .25   .25

Red Cross, Hands
PT45

1975, Apr. 23   Photo.   Perf. 11½
RA47 PT45 20p blue, car & blk   .25   .25

Olympic Rings — PT46

1975, June 2   Litho.   Perf. 13½
RA48 PT46 10p multicolored   .25   .25

Ruin and Clock — PT47

1975, July 26   Litho.   Perf. 13x13½
RA49 PT47 30p blk & dk bl   .25   .25
Solidarity Week, July 26-Aug. 1. See Nos. RA61-RA62.

Red Crescent, Red Cross, Red Lion — PT48

1976, May 8   Photo.   Perf. 12½x13
RA50 PT48 20p multicolored   .80   .55

1984 Olympics
PT49

1976, July 26   Litho.   Perf. 13½
RA51 PT49 10p intense blue   .25   .25

Fight Tuberculosis, Red Cross — PT50

1977, Sept. 14   Photo.
RA52 PT50 50p multicolored   2.00   .80
RA53 PT50 1d multicolored   2.00   .80
Exist imperf.

1984 Olympics
PT51

1977, Dec. 17   Perf. 13½x13
RA54 PT51 10p multicolored   .25   .25

Postal Tax Stamps for use in a particular republic or republics fall beyond the scope of this catalogue and are not listed. These stamps, issued since 1977, were not intended for nationwide use. Some of these issues have designs which are similar to stamps used nationwide, most notably those using variations of the Ruin and Clock (PT47) design. Most others show the Red Cross or the Tuberculosis Cross.

Red Crescent, Red Cross, Red Lion — PT52

1978, May 7   Litho.   Perf. 13½
RA55 PT52 20p on 1d bl & red   .50   .25
RA56 PT52 1d blue & red   .30   .25

1984
Olympics
PT53

1978, Sept.
RA57 PT53 30p multicolored   .35   .25

8th Mediterranean Games, Split, Sept.
15-29 — PT54

1979, Mar. 1   Photo.   Perf. 13½x13
RA58 PT54 1d violet   .25   .25
RA59 PT54 1d greenish blue   .25   .25

Red Cross
Week
PT55

1979, May 6   Perf. 13½
RA60 PT55 1d multicolored   .25   .25

**Ruin and Clock Type of 1975
Inscribed "1.-7.VI"**

1979, June 1
RA61 PT47 30p blk & intense bl   .25   .25
Solidarity Week.

**Ruin and Clock Type of 1975
Inscribed "1.-7.VI"**

1980, June 1   Litho.   Perf. 13x13½
RA62 PT47 1d black & blue   .25   .25
Solidarity Week, June 1-7.

Olympic
Week — PT57

1979, Oct. 15   Photo.   Perf. 14
RA63 PT57 30p blue & red   .25   .25

Sculpture, Red
Cross — PT58

1980, May 4   Litho.   Perf. 13½
RA64 PT58 1d multicolored   .35   .30

Olympic
Week — PT59

1980, Oct. 20   Perf. 14
RA65 PT59 50p multicolored   .40   .25

SPENS '81,
Novi
Sad — PT60

1980, Dec. 20   Perf. 13½
RA66 PT60 1d multicolored   .25   .25

Red
Cross — PT61

1981, May 4   Photo.
RA67 PT61 1d multicolored   .25   .25

Fight
Tuberculosis, Red
Cross — PT62

1981, Sept. 14
RA68 PT62 1d multicolored   .25   .25

Handshake
PT63

1982, May   Litho.   Perf. 13
RA69 PT63 1d black & red   .25   .25

Robert Koch
PT64

1983, Sept. 18   Litho.   Perf. 13
RA70 PT64 1d multicolored   .25   .25
For surcharge see No. RA76.

Fight
Tuberculosis, Red
Cross — PT65

1983, Sept. 14   Litho.   Perf. 13½
RA71 PT65 1d bluish grn, blk &
            red   .25   .25
RA72 PT65 2d bluish grn, blk &
            red   .25   .25

1984 Winter
Olympics,
Sarajevo
PT66

1983, Oct. 20   Litho.   Perf. 12½
RA73 PT66 2d greenish blue   .25   .25

PLANICA
50 — PT67

1985, Apr. 1   Photo.   Perf. 14
RA74 PT67 2d brt ultra & blue   .25   .25

Ruin, Clock and
Red Cross — PT68

1987, June 1   Litho.   Perf. 10
RA75 PT68 30p multicolored   .25   .25
Solidarity Week, June 1-7.

No. RA70
Surcharged
in Silver

1988, Sept. 14   Litho.   Perf. 13
RA76 PT64 12d on 1d multi   8.00 8.00

Intl. Red Cross, 125th
Anniv. — PT69

**1989, May 8   Litho.   Perf. 12x11
Without Gum**
RA77 PT69 20d bl, sil & red   .40   .40
RA78 PT69 80d bl, sil & red   .40   .40
RA79 PT69 150d bl, sil & red   .40   .40
RA80 PT69 160d bl, sil & red   .40   .40
Nos. RA77-RA80 (4)   1.60 1.60

Souvenir folders with perf. or imperf. miniature sheets of 4 sold for 3200d.

Ruin, Clock
and Red
Cross — PT70

Building, Clock
and Red
Cross — PT71

**1989, June 1   Perf. 10
Without Gum**
RA81 PT70 250d red & silver   .55   .40

Roulette 10
RA82 PT71 400d brt bl gray &
            red   1.00 .50

Souvenir folders with perf. or imperf. miniature sheets containing one 45x65mm stamp
like RA81 sold for 3200d.

Fight TB, Red   Red
Cross — PT72   Cross — PT73

**1989, Sept. 14   Rough Perf. 10½
Without Gum**
RA83 PT72 20d black & red   .30   .30
RA84 PT72 200d black & red   .30   .30
RA85 PT72 250d black & red   .30   .30
RA86 PT72 400d black & red   .30   .30
RA87 PT72 650d black & red   .30   .30
Nos. RA83-RA87 (5)   1.50 1.50

**1990, May 8   Perf. 13½
Without Gum**
RA88 PT73 10p green & red   .80   .25

Perf. 12½
RA89 PT73 20p green & red   .80   .25
  a.   Perf. 13½   .80   .25
RA90 PT73 30p green & red   .80   .25
Nos. RA88-RA90 (3)   2.40 .75

Flowers — PT74

Macedonian Red
Cross, 45th
Anniv. — PT75

**1990, May 8   Perf. 10
Without Gum**
RA91 PT74 20p shown   .25   .25
RA92 PT74 20p multi, diff.   .25   .25
RA93 PT75 20p multicolored   .25   .25
  a.   Block of 3 + label, #RA91-
        RA93   .80   .80

Souvenir folders with perf. or imperf. miniature sheets of 3 + label sold for 4d.

PT76   PT77

**1990, Sept. 14   Litho.   Perf. 10
Without Gum**
RA94 PT76 20p blue, org & red   .40   .40
RA95 PT76 25p blue, yel & red   .40   .40
RA96 PT76 50p blue, yel & red   .40   .40
Nos. RA94-RA96 (3)   1.20 1.20

Fight tuberculosis, Red Cross.

**1991, Sept. 14   Litho.   Perf. 12½
Without Gum**
RA97 PT77 1.20d dk bl, yel & red   .30   .30
RA98 PT77 2.50d multicolored   .30   .30
Required on mail 9/14-21/91.

PT78

PT79

1994, May 8 Litho. Perf. 13½
RA99 PT78 10p multicolored 1.00 .50
No. RA99 was required on mail 5/8-15/94.

1994, Sept. 14 Litho. Perf. 13x13½
RA100 PT79 10p multicolored 1.00 .50
No. RA100 was required on mail 9/14-21/94.

PT80

PT81

1995, May 8 Litho. Perf. 13½x13
RA101 PT80 10p multicolored 1.00 .50
No. RA101 was required on mail 5/8-15/95.

1995, Sept. 9 Litho. Perf. 13½x13
RA102 PT81 10p Wilhelm Röntgen 1.00 .50
Fight Tuberculosis. No. RA102 was required on mail 9/9-14/95.

PT82 PT83

1996, May 8 Litho. Perf. 12x12½
RA103 PT82 15p multicolored .40 .30
No. RA103 was required on mail 5/8-15/96.

1996, Sept. Litho. Perf. 12x12½
RA104 PT83 20p multicolored 2.00 .40

PT84

1997, May 8 Litho. Perf. 13
RA105 PT84 20p multicolored 5.00 1.00
No. RA105 was required on mail 5/8-15/97.

Milutin Rankovic (1880-1967), Artist — PT85

1997, Sept. 14 Litho. Perf. 14
RA106 PT85 20p multicolored .40 .40
Fight Tuberculosis. No. RA106 was required on mail 9/14-21/97.

PT86

1998, May 8 Litho. Perf. 13¾
RA107 PT86 20p multicolored .40 .40
No. RA107 was required on mail 5/8-15/98.

Red Cross — PT87

1999, May 8 Litho. Perf. 13¾
RA108 PT87 1d multi 2.00 .50
No. RA108 was required on mail 5/8-5/15/99.

Red Cross — PT88

1999, Sept. 14
RA109 PT88 1d multi 7.00 .70
No. RA109 was required on mail 9/14-9/21/99.

POSTAL TAX DUE STAMPS

Catalogue values for unused stamps in this section are for Never Hinged items.

The tax of Nos. RAJ1-RAJ9, RAJ11-RAJ12, RAJ14 and RAJ18 was for the Red Cross.

Inscribed "PORTO."

Type of Postal Tax Stamp, 1933
1933 Unwmk. Litho. Perf. 12½
RAJ1 PT1 50p dull grn & red 1.00 .25
a. Perf. 11½ 20.00 8.00

Type of Postal Tax Stamp, 1947
1947
RAJ2 PT4 50p blue grn & scar .50 .25
For surcharge see Trieste No. RAJ1.

Type of Postal Tax Stamp, 1948
1948
RAJ3 PT5 50p dark grn & red .40 .25

Type of Postal Tax Stamp, 1949
1949
RAJ4 PT6 50p red & violet .55 .25
For overprint see Trieste No. RAJ2.

Cross and Map of Yugoslavia — PTD2

1950 Unwmk. Perf. 12½
RAJ5 PTD2 50p red brown & red .40 .25
Exists imperf.

Type of Postal Tax Stamp, 1951
1951
RAJ6 PT8 50p emerald & red .40 .25
For overprint see Trieste No. RAJ3.

Red Cross — PTD3

1952 Unwmk. Photo. Perf. 12½
RAJ7 PTD3 50p gray & car .65 .25
For overprint see Trieste No. RAJ4.

Types of Postal Tax Stamps, 1953-57
1953-57 Litho.
RAJ8 PT10 2d yel brown & red .80 .40
RAJ9 PT11 2d lilac & red ('54) .75 .30
RAJ10 PT12 2d yel grn ('55) .55 .25
RAJ11 PT13 2d dk vio brn & red ('55) .80 .25
RAJ12 PT14 2d blue grn & red ('56) .55 .25
RAJ13 PT15 2d violet brn ('56) .55 .25
RAJ14 PT16 2d gray, blk & car ('57) .55 .25
RAJ15 PT17 2d lt bl, bis & grn ('57) .55 .25
Nos. RAJ8-RAJ15 (8) 5.10 2.20
For overprints see Trieste Nos. RAJ5-RAJ5.

Redrawn Type of Regular Issue, 1953
1958 Perf. 12½x12
RAJ16 A95 2d multicolored .80 .40

Child With Toy — PTD4

1958 Litho. Perf. 12½
RAJ17 PTD4 2d lt ultra & blk .55 .25
Issued for Children's Week, Oct. 5-11.

Type of Postal Tax Stamp, 1959
1959
RAJ18 PT19 2d yel org & red .55 .25

Type of Postal Tax Stamp, 1959
Design: Tree, cock and wheat.
1959
RAJ19 PT20 2d ocher & mar .40 .25

Type of Postal Tax Stamp, 1960
1960
RAJ20 PT21 2d vio brn & red .50 .25

Type of Postal Tax Stamp, 1960
Design: Boy, tools and ball.
1960
RAJ21 PT22 2d Prussian blue .30 .25

Type of Postal Tax Stamp, 1961
1961, May 7
RAJ22 PT23 2d multicolored .30 .25

Type of Postal Tax Stamp, 1961
1961, Oct. 1
RAJ23 PT24 2d apple grn & brn .30 .25

Type of Postal Tax Stamp, 1962
1962, Apr. 30
RAJ24 PT25 5d brn red, bl & red .30 .25

Type of Postal Tax Stamp, 1963
1963, May 5
RAJ25 PT26 5d red org, red & gray .50 .25

OFFICES ABROAD

Catalogue values for unused stamps in this section are for Never Hinged items.

King Peter II — A1

1943 Unwmk. Typo. Perf. 12½
1K1 A1 2d dark blue .40 4.00
1K2 A1 3d slate .40 4.00
1K3 A1 5d carmine .40 4.00
1K4 A1 10d black .40 4.00
Nos. 1K1-1K4 (4) 1.60 16.00
For surcharges see Nos. 1KB1-1KB4.

V. Vodnik — A2
Peter Nyegosh — A3

3d, Ljudovit Gaj. 4d, Vuk Stefanovic Karadzic. 5d, Bishop Joseph Strossmayer. 10d, Karageorge.

1943, Dec. 1 Engr. Perf. 12½x13
1K5 A2 1d red org & black .40 8.25
1K6 A3 2d yel green & blk .80 8.50
1K7 A2 3d dp ultra & blk .80 8.75
1K8 A3 4d dk pur & brn blk 1.60 9.25
1K9 A2 5d brn vio & brn blk 1.60 9.75
1K10 A3 10d brn & brown blk 5.50 10.00
Nos. 1K5-1K10 (6) 10.70 54.50

Souvenir Sheet Center in Black
1K11 Sheet of 6, #1K5-1K10 65.00

25th anniv. of the Union of Liberated Yugoslavia. Valid on ships of the Yugoslav Navy and Mercantile Marine.
Nos. 1K5-1K10 overprinted diagonally "1945" in London were not issued. In 1950, they were sold by the Yugoslav Government without postal validity. Later they appeared with the additional overprint of the outline of a plane at upper left in carmine or black.

OFFICES ABROAD SEMI-POSTAL STAMPS

Nos. 1K1-1K4 Surcharged in Orange or Black

1943 Unwmk. Perf. 12½
1KB1 A1 2d + 12.50d dk bl 2.40 8.25
1KB2 A1 3d + 12.50d slate 2.40 8.25
1KB3 A1 5d + 12.50d car (Bk) 2.40 8.25
1KB4 A1 10d + 12.50d black 2.40 8.25
Nos. 1KB1-1KB4 (4) 9.60 33.00
The surtax was for the Red Cross.

LJUBLJANA
(Lubiana, Laibach)
Italian Occupation

Under Italian occupation in 1941, the western half of Slovenia was known as the Province of Ljubljana (Lubiana to the Italians, Laibach to the Germans) and a quisling administration was set up under the profascist General Rupnik.

100 Centesimi = 1 Lira

Yugoslavia Nos. 127, 128, 142-154 Overprinted in Black

1941		**Unwmk.**	**Perf. 12½, 13x12½**	
N1	A16	25p black	3.25	4.00
N2	A16	50p orange	3.25	4.00
N3	A16	1d yellow grn	3.25	4.00
N4	A16	1.50d red	3.25	4.00
N5	A16	2d dp magenta	3.25	4.00
N6	A16	3d dl red brn	3.25	4.00
N7	A16	4d ultra	3.25	4.00
N8	A16	5d dark blue	3.25	4.00
N9	A16	5.50d dk vio brn	3.25	4.00
N10	A16	6d slate blue	4.75	9.50
N11	A16	8d sepia	4.75	9.50
N12	A10	10d bright vio	4.75	9.50
N13	A16	12d brt violet	12.00	14.50
N14	A10	15d brown	325.00	525.00
N15	A16	16d dl violet	12.00	14.50
N16	A16	20d blue	24.00	32.50
N17	A16	30d brt pink	52.50	95.00
		Nos. N1-N17 (17)	469.00	746.00
		Set, never hinged	1,100.	

Yugoslavia Nos. 127, 142-154 Overprinted in Black

N18	A16	25p black	3.25	3.25
N19	A16	50p orange	3.25	3.25
N20	A16	1d yellow grn	3.25	3.25
N21	A16	1.50d red	3.25	3.25
N22	A16	2d dp magenta	3.25	3.25
N23	A16	3d dl red brn	3.25	3.25
N24	A16	4d ultra	3.25	3.25
N25	A16	5d dark blue	3.25	3.25
N26	A16	5.50d dk vio brn	3.25	3.25
N27	A16	6d slate blue	3.25	3.25
N28	A16	8d sepia	3.25	3.25
N29	A10	10d brt violet	6.50	4.00
N30	A16	12d bright vio	3.25	3.25
N31	A16	16d dl violet	6.50	4.00
N32	A16	20d blue	20.00	27.50
N33	A16	30d brt pink	110.00	140.00

Yugoslavia Nos. 145, 148 Surcharged in Black

N34	A16	50p on 1.50d red	1.60	2.00
N35	A16	1d on 4d ultra	1.60	2.00
		Nos. N18-N35 (18)	185.20	218.50
		Set, never hinged	400.00	

German Occupation
Stamps of Italy, 1929-42, Overprinted or Surcharged in Blue, Carmine, Black or Green

a   b

---

c

1944		**Wmk. 140**	**Perf. 14**	
N36	A90(a)	5c ol brown	.25	5.50
N37	A92(b)	10c dark brn	.25	5.50
N38	A93(a)	15c sl grn (C)	.25	5.50
N39	A91(b)	20c rose red	.25	5.50
N40	A94(a)	25c dp grn (C)	.25	5.50
N41	A95(b)	30c ol brown	.25	5.50
N42	A93(a)	35c dp bl (C)	.40	5.50
N43	A95(b)	50c purple (C)	.25	7.00
N44	A94(a)	75c rose red	.25	10.50
N45	A91(b)	1 l deep vio	.25	10.50
N46	A94(a)	1.25 l dp bl (C)	.25	4.00
N47	A92(b)	1.75 l red org	6.00	24.00
N48	A93(a)	2 l car lake	.25	7.00
N49	A90(c)	2.55 l on 5c ol brn (Bk)	2.40	12.00
N50	A94(a)	5 l on 25c dp grn	2.40	20.00
N51	A93(b)	10 l purple	10.00	55.00
N52	A91(a)	20 l on 20c rose red (G)	12.00	65.00
N53	A93(b)	25 l on 2 l car lake (G)	10.00	125.00
N54	A92(a)	50 l on 1.75 l red org (C)	40.00	400.00
		Nos. N36-N54 (19)	85.95	778.50
		Set, never hinged	175.00	

Krizna Jama — A1

Cerknica Lake — A2

Designs: 20c, Railroad Bridge, Borovnica. 25c, Landscape near Ljubljana. 50c, Church, Ribnica. 75c, View, Ljubljana. 1 l, Old Castle, Ljubljana. 1.25 l, Kocevje (Gottschee). 1.50 l, Borovnica Falls. 2 l, Castle, Konstanjevnica. 2.50 l, Castle, Turjak. 3 l, Castle, Zuzemperk. 5 l, View of Krk. 10 l, View of Otolac. 20 l, Farm, Carniola. 30 l, Castle and church, Tabor.

Perf. 10½x11½, 11½x10½				
1945		**Photo.**	**Unwmk.**	
N55	A1	5c black	.40	4.00
N56	A2	10c red orange	.40	4.00
N57	A2	20c brn carmine	.40	4.00
N58	A2	25c dk sl green	.40	4.00
N59	A1	50c deep violet	.40	4.00
N60	A2	75c vermilion	.40	4.00
N61	A2	1 l dark ol grn	.40	4.00
N62	A1	1.25 l dark bluc	.40	8.00
N63	A1	1.50 l olive black	.40	8.00
N64	A2	2 l ultramarine	.60	9.50
N65	A2	2.50 l brown	.60	9.50
N66	A1	3 l brt red vio	1.50	16.00
N67	A2	5 l dk red brn	1.60	16.00
N68	A2	10 l slate green	3.25	72.50
N69	A2	20 l sapphire	20.00	250.00
N70	A1	30 l rose pink	95.00	950.00
		Nos. N55-N70 (16)	126.15	1,367.
		Set, never hinged	240.00	

SEMI-POSTAL STAMPS

Italian Occupation

Yugoslavia Nos. B116-B119 with Additional Ovpt. in Black

Perf. 11½x12½, 12½x11½				
1941			**Unwmk.**	
NB1	AP6	50p + 50p on 5d	9.50	14.50
NB2	AP7	1d + 1d on 10d	9.50	14.50
NB3	AP8	1.50d + 1.50d on 20d	9.50	14.50
NB4	AP9	2d + 2d on 30d	9.50	14.50
		Nos. NB1-NB4 (4)	38.00	58.00
		Set, never hinged	90.00	

German Occupation

Italy Nos. E14 & E15 Srchd. in Red

1944			**Wmk. 140**	
NB5	SD4	1.25 l + 50 l green	35.00	600.00
NB6	SD4	2.50 l + 50 l dp org	35.00	600.00

The surtax aided the Red Cross.

Italy Nos. E4 & E15 Srchd. in Blue or Green

NB7	SD4	1.25 l + 50 l grn (B)	35.00	600.00
NB8	SD4	2.50 l + 50 l dp org	35.00	600.00
		Nos. NB5-NB8 (4)	140.00	2,400.
		Set, never hinged	275.00	

The surtax aided the Homeless Relief Fund. The German and Slovenian inscriptions in the surcharges are transposed on Nos. NB6 and NB8.

Italy Nos. C12-C14, C16-C18 Surcharged "DEN WAISEN," "SIROTAM," Heraldic Eagle and Surtax in Blue or Red

1944			**Wmk. 140**	
NB9	AP4	25c + 10 l dk grn	14.00	400.00
NB10	AP3	50c + 10 l ol brn	14.00	400.00
NB11	AP5	75c + 20 l org brn	14.00	400.00
NB12	AP5	1 l + 20 l purple	14.00	400.00
NB13	AP6	2 l + 20 l dp bl (R)	14.00	400.00
NB14	AP3	5 l + 20 l dk grn	14.00	400.00
		Nos. NB9-NB14 (6)	84.00	2,400.
		Set, never hinged	175.00	

The surcharge aided orphans.

Same, Surcharged "WINTERHILFE," "ZIMSKA POMOC," Heraldic Eagle and Surtax in Blue or Red

NB15	AP4	25c + 10 l dk grn	14.00	400.00
NB16	AP3	50c + 10 l ol brn	14.00	400.00
NB17	AP5	75c + 20 l org brn	14.00	400.00
NB18	AP5	1 l + 20 l purple	14.00	400.00
NB19	AP6	2 l + 20 l dp bl (R)	14.00	400.00
NB20	AP3	5 l + 20 l dk grn	14.00	400.00
		Nos. NB15-NB20 (6)	84.00	2,400.
		Set, never hinged	175.00	

The surcharge was for winter relief.

AIR POST STAMPS

Italian Occupation
Yugoslavia Nos. C7-C16 Ovptd. like Nos. NB1-NB4

Perf. 12½, 12½x11½, 11½x12½				
1941			**Unwmk.**	
NC1	AP6	50p brown	11.00	11.00
NC2	AP7	1d yel grn	11.00	11.00
NC3	AP8	2d bl gray	12.50	12.50
NC4	AP9	2.50d rose red	12.50	12.50
NC5	AP6	5d brn vio	20.00	20.00
NC6	AP7	10d brn lake	20.00	20.00
NC7	AP8	20d dark grn	55.00	55.00
NC8	AP9	30d ultra	87.50	95.00

NC9	AP10	40d Prus grn & pale grn	300.00	360.00
NC10	AP11	50d sl bl & gray bl	240.00	240.00
a.		Inverted overprint	950.00	
		Nos. NC1-NC10 (10)	769.50	837.00
		Set, never hinged	1,800.	

German Occupation
Italy Nos. C12-C14, C16-C19 Overprinted Types "a" and "b" in Carmine, Green or Blue

1944		**Wmk. 140**	**Perf. 14**	
NC11	AP4(a)	25c dk grn (C)	10.00	40.00
NC12	AP3(b)	50c ol brn (C)	10.00	125.00
NC13	AP5(a)	75c org brn (G)	10.00	40.00
NC14	AP5(b)	1 l pur (C)	10.00	125.00
NC15	AP6(a)	2 l dp bl (Bl)	10.00	87.50
NC16	AP3(b)	5 l dk grn (C)	10.00	125.00
NC17	AP3(a)	10 l dp car (G)	10.00	87.50
		Nos. NC11-NC17 (7)	70.00	630.00

AIR POST SPECIAL DELIVERY STAMP

German Occupation
Italy #CE3 Ovptd. Type "b" in Blue

1944		**Wmk. 140**	**Perf. 14**	
NCE1	APSD2	2 l gray blk	10.00	87.50

SPECIAL DELIVERY STAMP

German Occupation
Italy #E14 Ovptd. Type "b" in Green

1944		**Wmk. 140**	**Perf. 14**	
NE1	SD4	1.25 l green	10.00	24.00

POSTAGE DUE STAMPS

Italian Occupation
Yugoslavia Nos. J28-J32 Overprinted in Black Like Nos. N1-N17

1941		**Unwmk.**	**Perf. 12½**	
NJ1	D4	50p violet	4.00	4.00
NJ2	D4	1d rose	4.00	4.00
NJ3	D4	2d deep blue	4.00	4.00
NJ4	D4	5d orange	12.00	22.50
NJ5	D4	10d chocolate	12.00	22.50
		Nos. NJ1-NJ5 (5)	36.00	57.00
		Set, never hinged	80.00	

Same Overprinted in Black

NJ6	D4	50p violet	4.00	8.00
NJ7	D4	1d deep magenta	4.00	8.00
NJ8	D4	2d deep blue	8.00	9.50
NJ9	D4	5d orange	55.00	110.00
NJ10	D4	10d chocolate	21.00	40.00
		Nos. NJ6-NJ10 (5)	92.00	175.50

Same Overprinted in Black

NJ11	D4	50p violet	4.00	4.00
NJ12	D4	1d deep magenta	6.50	6.50
NJ13	D4	2d deep blue	55.00	110.00
		Nos. NJ11-NJ13 (3)	65.50	120.50

German Occupation
Postage Due Stamps of Italy, 1934, Overprinted or Surcharged in Various Colors

d   e

f   g

1944		**Wmk. 140**	**Perf. 14**		
NJ14	D6(d)	5c brown (Br)		2.40	80.00
NJ15	D6(e)	10c blue (Bl)		2.40	80.00
NJ16	D6(d)	20c rose red (R)		1.25	8.00
NJ17	D6(e)	25c green (G)		1.25	8.00
NJ18	D6(f)	30c on 50c vio (Bk)		1.25	8.00
NJ19	D6(g)	40c on 5c brn (Bl)		1.25	8.00
NJ20	D6(d)	50c violet (V)		1.25	8.00
NJ21	D7(e)	1 l red orange (R)		2.40	80.00
NJ22	D7(d)	2 l green (Bl)		2.40	80.00
		Nos. NJ14-NJ22 (9)		15.85	360.00

Fiume-Kupa Zone
Italian Occupation

Four issues of 1941-42 consist of overprints on Yugoslav stamps of 1939-41: (a.) 14 stamps overprinted "ZONA OCCUPATO FIUMANO KUPA" and "ZOFK ZOFK ZOFK." (b.) 3 stamps overprinted as illustrated. (c.) 1 stamp surcharged "MEMENTO AVDERE SEMPER." "L1," etc. (d.) 3 stamps overprinted in arch: "Pro Maternite e Infanzia."

ISSUES FOR ISTRIA AND THE SLOVENE COAST (ZONE B)

Grapes — A1

Olive Branch — A2

Sailboat, Pola — A3

Designs: 50c, Donkey. Nos. 25-26, Ruined home. 2 l, Duino Castle. 5 l, Birthplace of Vladimir Gortan. 10 l, Plowing. Nos. 33-34, Tuna. 30 l, Viaduct at Solkan, Soca River.

		Perf. 11½, 12, 10½x11½		
1945-46				**Photo.**
23	A1	25c dark green	.40	1.00
24	A1	50c red brown	.25	.25
25	A1	1 l green	.25	.25
26	A1	1 l red	.25	.25
27	A2	1.50 l olive brown	.25	.25
28	A2	2 l dk Prus grn	.25	.25
29	A3	4 l red	.25	.25
30	A3	4 l bright blue	.25	.40
31	A3	5 l gray black	.25	.25
32	A3	10 l brown	.25	.40
33	A3	20 l blue	1.60	.85
34	A3	20 l dark violet	3.50	5.25
35	A3	30 l magenta	1.40	.80
		Nos. 23-35 (13)	9.15	10.30
		Set, never hinged	16.00	

The first (Ljubljana) printing is perf. 10½x11½ and consists of Nos. 23-24, 26-28, 30-32, 34-35. The second (Zagreb) printing is perf. 12 and consists of Nos. 23-25, 27-29, 31-33, 35. The third (Belgrade) printing is perf. 11½ and consists of Nos. 25, 28, 40-41.

See Nos. 40-41. For surcharges see Nos. 36-37, J1-J19.

Nos. 33 and 35 Surcharged with New Values and Bars in Black

1946		**Unwmk.**	**Perf. 11½**		
36	A3	1 l on 20 l blue		.60	1.25
37	A3	2 l on 30 l magenta		.60	1.25
		Set, never hinged		2.40	

Types of 1945

Design: 3 l, Duino Castle

1946, Nov. 30				
40	A2	3 l crimson	1.50	1.75
41	A3	6 l ultra	3.25	4.00
		Set, never hinged	9.25	

Types of Yugoslavia and of Official Stamps of 1946 Surcharged in Black

On A26

On O1

1947		**Unwmk.**	**Perf. 12½**		
42	A26	1 l on 9d lilac rose		.25	.40
43	O1	1.50 l on 50p blue		.25	.40
44	A26	2 l on 9d lilac rose		.25	.40
45	O1	3 l on 50p blue		.25	.40
46	A26	5 l on 9d lilac rose		.25	.40
47	O1	6 l on 50p blue		.25	.40
48	A26	10 l on 9d lilac rose		.25	.40
49	O1	15 l on 50p blue		.25	.55
50	A26	35 l on 9d lilac rose		.25	.90
51	O1	50 l on 50p blue		.25	.90
		Nos. 42-51 (10)			5.15
		Set, never hinged			2.00

POSTAGE DUE STAMPS

Nos. 23, 24, 34 and 35 Surcharged in Black

1945		**Unwmk.**	**Perf. 10½x11½**		
J1	A3	50c on 20 l dk vio		.30	1.00
J2	A1	1 l on 25c dk grn		6.00	2.00
J3	A3	2 l on 30 l magenta		.90	2.40
J4	A1	4 l on 50c red brn		.70	.65
J5	A1	8 l on 50c red brn		.70	.65
J6	A1	10 l on 50c red brn		4.00	1.90
J7	A1	20 l on 50c red brn		4.50	3.25
		Nos. J1-J7 (7)		17.10	11.85
		Set, never hinged		32.50	

Nos. 25 and 35 Surcharged in Black

1945			**Perf. 12**		
J8	A1	1 l on 1 l green		.25	.40
J9	A1	2 l on 1 l green		.25	.40
J10	A1	4 l on 1 l green		.30	.40
J11	A3	10 l on 30 l magenta		2.50	2.00
J12	A3	20 l on 30 l magenta		4.00	4.50
J13	A3	30 l on 30 l magenta		4.00	4.50
		Nos. J8-J13 (6)		11.30	12.20

The surcharges are arranged to fit the designs of the stamps.

No. 23 Surcharged in Black

1946					
J14	A1	1 l on 25c dark green		.40	.55
J15	A1	2 l on 25c dark green		.70	.80
J16	A1	4 l on 25c dark green		.40	.55

No. 33 Surcharged in Black

J17	A3	10 l on 20 l blue		2.25	1.75
J18	A3	20 l on 20 l blue		5.50	4.50
J19	A3	30 l on 20 l blue		5.25	5.25
		Nos. J14-J19 (6)		14.50	13.40
		Set, never hinged		25.00	

Type of Yugoslavia Postage Due Stamps, 1946, Surcharged in Black

1947					
J20	D7	1 l on 1d brt blue grn		.25	.50
J21	D7	2 l on 1d brt blue grn		.25	.50
J22	D7	6 l on 1d brt blue grn		.25	.50
J23	D7	10 l on 1d brt blue grn		.25	.50
J24	D7	30 l on 1d brt blue grn		.25	.65
		Nos. J20-J24 (5)		1.25	2.65
		Set, never hinged		1.75	

TRIESTE, ZONE A
See listing under Italy, Vol. 3.

TRIESTE

A free territory (1947-1954) on the Adriatic Sea between Italy and Yugoslavia. In 1954 the territory was divided, Italy acquiring the northern section and seaport, Yugoslavia the southern section (Zone B).

> Catalogue values for all unused stamps in this country are for Never Hinged items.

ZONE B

Issued by the Yugoslav Military Government

100 Centesimi = 1 Lira
100 Paras = 1 Dinar (1949)

See Istria and the Slovene Coast (Zone B) for preceding issues of 1945-47.

Stylized Gymnast and Arms of Trieste — A1

1948	**Unwmk. Litho.**	**Perf. 10½x11**		
Inscriptions in:				
1	A1	100 l Italian	8.00	4.00
2	A1	100 l Croatian	8.00	4.00
3	A1	100 l Slovene	8.00	4.00
a.		Strip of 3, #1-3	95.00	65.00
		Nos. 1-3 (3)	24.00	12.00

May Day.

Clasped Hands, Hammer and Sickle — A2

1949	**Photo.**	**Perf. 11½x12½**		
4	A2	10 l grnsh blk & ol grn	.80	.80

Labor Day, May 1, 1949.
"V.U.J.A. S.T.T." are the initials of "Vojna Uprava Jugoslovenske Armije, Slobodna Teritorija Trsta" (Military Administration Yugoslav Army, Free Territory of Trieste).

Stamps of Yugoslavia, 1945-47 Overprinted in Carmine or Ultramarine

1949, Aug. 15		**Perf. 12½**		
5	A22	50p ol gray	.40	.30
6	A22	1 d bl grn	.40	.30
7	A24	2 d scar (U)	.40	.30
8	A25	3 d dl red (U)	.40	.30
9	A24	4 d dk bl	.80	.30
10	A25	5 d dk bl	.80	.30
11	A26	9 d rose vio (U)	5.50	.30
12	A23	12 d ultra	5.50	4.00
13	A22	16 d blue	8.00	4.75
14	A23	20 d org ver (U)	16.00	6.50
		Nos. 5-14 (10)	38.20	17.85

The letters of the overprint are set closer and in one line on Nos. 7 and 9.

Yugoslavia Nos. 266 and 267 Overprinted in Carmine

Burelage in Color of Stamp

1949				
15	A58	5 d blue	10.50	8.00
16	A58	12 d brown	10.50	8.00

75th anniv. of the UPU.

Yugoslavia, Nos. 269 to 272, Overprinted in Carmine

1950				
17	A60	2 d bl grn	4.00	.80
18	A60	3 d car rose	4.00	.80
19	A60	8 d blue	4.00	2.40
20	A60	10 d dp org	16.00	8.00
		Nos. 17-20 (4)	28.00	12.00

Workers Carrying Tools and Flag — A3

1950, May 1 **Photo.**
21	A3	3d violet	.55	.55
22	A3	10d carmine	1.00	1.00

Labor Day, May 1, 1950.

Peasant on Ass — A4

Designs: 1d, Cockerel. 2d, Goose. 3d, Bees and honeycomb. 5d, Oxen. 10d, Turkey. 15d, Goats. 20d, Silkworms.

1950 **Unwmk.** **Perf. 12½**
23	A4	50p dk gray	.40	.40
24	A4	1d brn car	.40	.40
25	A4	2d dp bl	.40	.40
26	A4	3d org brn	.40	.40
27	A4	5d aqua	3.25	.40
28	A4	10d brown	3.25	.40
29	A4	15d violet	20.00	8.00
30	A4	20d dk grn	8.00	4.00
		Nos. 23-30 (8)	36.10	14.40

1951
31	A4	1d orange brown	1.25	.40
32	A4	3d rose brown	1.60	.40

Worker A5

1951, May 1
33	A5	3d dark red	.80	.40
34	A5	10d brown olive	1.25	.80

Labor Day.

Pietro Paolo Vergerio — A7

1951, Oct. 21 **Litho.**
37	A7	5d blue	1.00	1.00
38	A7	10d claret	1.00	1.00
39	A7	20d sepia	1.00	1.00
		Nos. 37-39 (3)	3.00	3.00

Types of Yugoslavia, 1951, Overprinted "STT VUJA"

1951, Nov.
40	A81	10d brn org (V)	1.00	.70
41	A81	12d grnsh blk (C)	1.00	.70

Bicycle Race — A8

1952 **Photo.**
42	A8	5d shown	.40	.40
43	A8	10d Soccer	.40	.40
44	A8	15d Rowing	.40	.40
45	A8	28d Sailing	1.60	1.25
46	A8	50d Volleyball	3.25	2.40
47	A8	100d Diving	10.00	4.00
		Nos. 42-47 (6)	16.05	8.85

Marshal Tito
A9   A10

1952, May 25 **Perf. 11½**
48	A9	15d dk brn	2.50	1.25
49	A10	28d red brn	2.50	2.00
50	A9	50d dk gray grn	4.75	2.75
		Nos. 48-50 (3)	9.75	6.00

60th birthday of Marshal Tito.

Types of Yugoslavia 1952 Overprinted in Carmine "STT VUJNA"

1952, July 26 **Perf. 12½**
51	A90	5d dk brn & sal, *cr*	1.60	.40
52	A90	10d dk grn & grn	1.60	.40
53	A90	15d dk brn & bl, *lil*	1.60	.40
54	A90	28d dk brn & buff, *cr*	1.60	1.60
55	A90	50d dk brn & buff, *yel*	14.00	9.50
56	A90	100d ind & lil, *pink*	32.50	27.50
		Nos. 51-56 (6)	52.90	39.80

15th Olympic Games, Helsinki, 1952. Nos. 52, 54, 56 inscribed in Cyrillic characters. The added "N" in "VUJNA" stands for "Narodna" (Peoples'). See note after No. 4. Nos. 51-56 exist imperf. Value of set, $950, unused or used.

Yugoslavia Nos. 365 to 367 Overprinted in Carmine "STT VUJNA"

1952, Sept. 13
57	A91	15d deep claret	3.25	2.75
58	A91	28d dark brown	4.00	2.75
59	A91	50d gray	4.75	2.75
		Nos. 57-59 (3)	12.00	8.25

Formation of the Yugoslav navy, 10th anniv.

Yugoslavia No. 358 Overprinted "STT VUJA" in Blue

1952, June 22
60	A89	15d bright rose	1.60	.80

Children's Week.

Yugoslavia Nos. 369-372 Overprinted "VUJNA STT" in Blue or Carmine

1952, Nov. 4
61	A93	15d red brn (Bl)	1.00	.65
62	A93	15d dk vio bl	1.00	.65
63	A93	15d dk brn	1.00	.65
64	A93	15d bl grn	1.00	.65
		Nos. 61-64 (4)	4.00	2.60

Issued to publicize the 6th Yugoslavia Communist Party Congress, Zagreb, 1952.

Anchovies and Starfish — A11

1952 Unwmk. Photo. Perf. 11x11½
65	A11	15d red brown	4.00	4.00
a.		Souvenir sheet, imperf.	55.00	55.00

Capodistria Phil. Exhib., Nov. 29-Dec. 7. No. 65a contains a 50d dark blue green stamp. Sold for 85d.

Stamps or Types of Yugoslavia Overprinted "STT VUJNA" in Various Colors

1953, Feb. 3 **Perf. 12½**
66	A94	15d brn carmine (Bl)	.40	.40
67	A94	30d chalky blue (R)	1.60	1.60

10th anniv. of the death of Nikola Tesla.

1953
68	A68	1d gray	9.50	7.25
69	A68	2d car (V)	.80	.40
70	A68	3d rose red (R)	.80	.40
71	A68	5d orange	.40	.40
72	A68	10d emerald (G)	.80	.40
73	A68	15d rose red (V)	1.60	.80
74	A68	30d blue (Bl)	4.00	2.40
75	A68	50d grnsh bl (Bl)	8.00	4.00
		Nos. 68-75 (8)	25.90	16.05

Nos. 69, 71 and 73 are lithographed. See Nos. 90-92.

1953, Apr. 21 **Perf. 11½**
76	A95	15d dk ol grn (O)	.25	.25
77	A95	30d chalky blue (O)	.40	.40
78	A95	50d henna brown	1.10	1.10
		Nos. 76-78 (3)	1.75	1.75

Issued in honor of the United Nations.

Automobile Climbing Mt. Lovcen — A12

Various automobiles and motorcycles.

1953, June 2 **Perf. 12½**
79	A12	15d ocher & choc	.40	.40
80	A12	30d lt bl grn & ol grn	.40	.40
81	A12	50d salmon & dp plum	.40	.40
82	A12	70d bl & dk bl	2.75	2.00
		Nos. 79-82 (4)	3.95	3.20

Intl. Automobile and Motorcycle Races, 1953.

Stamps or Types of Yugoslavia Overprinted "STT VUJNA" in Various Colors

1953, July 8 **Engr.**
83	A97	50d grnsh gray (C)	4.00	4.00

Tito's election to the presidency, 1/14/53.

1953, July 31
84	A98	15d gray & grn (C)	2.00	2.00

38th Esperanto Cong., Zagreb, July 25-Aug. 1, 1953. See No. C21.

1953, Sept. 5
85	A101	15d blue (C)	4.00	4.00

Liberation of Istria & the Slovene coast, 10th anniv.

1953, Oct. 3
86	A102	15d gray	1.60	1.25

Cent. of the death of Branko Radicevic, poet.

1953, Nov. 29 **Perf. 12½x12**
87	A103	15d gray vio (V)	1.10	.80
88	A103	30d claret (Br)	1.10	.80
89	A103	50d dl bl grn (Dk Bl)	1.10	.80
		Nos. 87-89 (3)	3.30	2.40

10th anniv. of the 1st republican legislative assembly of Yugoslavia.

1954, Mar. 5 **Perf. 12½**
90	A68	5d org (V)	1.00	.40
91	A68	10d yel grn (C)	.80	.40
92	A68	15d rose red (G)	1.00	.40
		Nos. 90-92 (3)	2.80	1.20

Overprinted in Carmine

1954 **Photo.** **Perf. 11½**
93	A104	2d red brn, sl & cr	.80	.40
94	A104	5d gray & dk yel brn	.80	.40
95	A104	10d ol grn & dk org brn	.80	.40
96	A104	15d dp bl grn & dk org brn	.80	.40
97	A104	17d gray brn, dk brn & cr	.80	.40
98	A104	25d bis, gray bl & org yel	.80	.40
99	A105	30d lil & dk brn	.80	.40
100	A105	35d rose vio & bl blk	.80	.80
101	A105	50d yel grn & vio brn	1.60	1.25
102	A105	65d org brn & gray blk	4.75	3.25
103	A105	70d bl & org brn	12.00	6.50
104	A105	100d brt bl & blk brn	32.50	25.00
		Nos. 93-104 (12)	57.25	39.60

Overprinted in Various Colors

1954, Oct. 8 **Perf. 12½**
105	A107	15d mar, red, ocher & dk bl (Bk)	.80	.55
106	A107	30d dk bl, grn, sal buff & choc (G)	.80	.55
107	A107	50d brn, bis & red (G)	.80	.55
108	A107	70d dk grn, gray grn & choc (R)	1.60	1.25
		Nos. 105-108 (4)	4.00	2.90

150th anniv. of the 1st Serbian insurrection.

AIR POST STAMPS

AP1

1948, Oct. 17 **Photo.** **Unwmk.**
C1	AP1	25 l gray	1.10	.80
C2	AP1	50 l orange	1.10	.80

Economic Exhib. at Capodistria, Oct. 17-24.

Fishermen — AP2   Farmer and Pack Mule — AP3

Mew over Chimneys AP4

1949, June 1 **Perf. 11½**
C3	AP2	1 l grnsh bl	.40	.40
C4	AP3	2 l red brn	.80	.40
C5	AP2	5 l blue	.80	.40
C6	AP3	10 l purple	2.40	2.00
C7	AP2	25 l brown	6.50	4.00
C8	AP3	50 l ol grn	8.00	4.00
C9	AP4	100 l dk vio brn	14.50	6.50
		Nos. C3-C9 (7)	33.40	17.70

Italian inscriptions on Nos. C5 and C6, Croatian on No. C7, Slavonic on No. C8. Nos. C3-C4 exist imperf. Value, each $150.

Nos. C3-C9 Surcharged "DIN," or New Value and "DIN" in Various Colors

1949, Nov. 5
C10	AP2	1d on 1 l (Bk)	.40	.40
C11	AP3	2d on 2 l (Br)	.80	.40
C12	AP2	5d on 5 l (Bl)	.80	.40
C13	AP3	10d on 10 l (V)	.80	.40
C14	AP2	15d on 25 l (Br)	16.00	9.50
C15	AP3	20d on 50 l (Gr)	8.00	3.25
C16	AP4	30d on 100 l (Bk)	9.50	4.00
		Nos. C10-C16 (7)	36.30	18.35

On Nos. C14 and C15 the original value is obliterated by a framed block, on No. C16 by four parallel lines.

Yugoslavia No. C33 Overprinted in Carmine and Lilac Rose Network

Souvenir Sheet

1950		Perf. 11½x12½
C17	AP15 10d lilac rose	200.00 160.00
a.	Imperf.	200.00 160.00

Main Square, Capodistria AP5

Lighthouse, Pirano — AP6

Design: 25d, Hotel, Portorose.

1952	Unwmk.	Photo.	Perf. 12½
C18	AP5	5d brown	12.00 12.00
C19	AP6	15d brt bl	8.00 8.00
C20	AP5	25d green	8.00 8.00
	Nos. C18-C20 (3)		28.00 28.00

75th anniv. (in 1949) of the UPU.

Type of Yugoslavia, 1953 Overprinted "STT VUJNA" in Carmine

1953, July 31

C21	AP21 300d vio & grn	250.00 250.00

38th Esperanto Cong., Zagreb, 7/25-8/1. Sheets of 12 (12,000 stamps) and sheets of 8 (3,000 stamps in light violet and green). A private red overprint was applied marginally to 250 sheets of 8: "Esperantski Kongres — 38 — a Universala Kongreso de Esperanto — Congresso del Esperanto."

Air Post Stamps of Yugoslavia in New Colors Overprinted "STT VUJNA" in Various Colors

1954			Engr.
C22	AP16	1d dp pur gray	.80 .40
C23	AP16	2d brt grn (G)	.80 .40
C24	AP16	3d red brn (Br)	.80 .40
C25	AP16	5d chocolate	.80 .40
C26	AP16	10d bl grn	.80 .40
C27	AP16	20d brn (Br)	.80 .40
C28	AP16	30d blue	.80 .40
C29	AP16	50d olive blk	.80 .60
C30	AP16	100d scar (R)	2.50 2.50
C31	AP16	200d dk bl vio (Bl)	4.75 4.00
		Perf. 11x11½	
C32	AP17	500d orange (Br)	27.50 20.00
	Nos. C22-C32 (11)		41.15 29.90

POSTAGE DUE STAMPS

Yugoslavia Nos. J51 to J55 Overprinted "S T T VUJA" in Two Lines in Ultramarine or Carmine

1949		Unwmk.	Perf. 12½
J1	D7	50p dp org	.80 .40
J2	D7	1d orange	.80 .40
J3	D7	2d dk bl (C)	.80 .40
J4	D7	3d yel grn (C)	1.60 .40
J5	D7	5d brt pur (C)	4.00 1.60
	Nos. J1-J5 (5)		8.00 3.20

Croakers
D1

Anchovies
D2

1950			Photo.
J6	D1	50p brn org	4.00 .80
J7	D1	1d dp ol grn	4.00 1.60
J8	D2	2d dk grnsh bl	4.00 1.60
J9	D2	3d dk vio bl	4.00 1.60
J10	D2	5d plum	20.00 6.50
	Nos. J6-J10 (5)		36.00 12.10

Yugoslavia Nos. J67-J74 Overprinted "STT VUJNA" in Blue or Carmine

1952			
J11	D7	1d brown (Bl)	.40 .40
J12	D7	2d emerald	.40 .40
J13	D7	5d blue	.40 .40
J14	D7	10d scar (Bl)	.40 .40
J15	D7	20d purple	.40 .40
J16	D7	30d org yel (Bl)	.40 .40
J17	D7	50d ultra	.40 .40
J18	D7	100d dp plum (Bl)	13.50 8.00
	Nos. J11-J18 (8)		16.30 10.80

POSTAL TAX STAMPS

Yugoslavia No. RA5 Surcharged in Blue

1948	Unwmk.	Perf. 12½
RA1	PT4 2 l on 50p brn & scar	32.50 32.50

Obligatory on all mail from May 22-30.

Yugoslavia No. RA7 Overprinted "VUJA STT" in Black

1950, July 3

RA2	PT6 50p red & brn	2.40 1.25

Yugoslavia No. RA9 Overprinted "STT VUJA" in Black

1951

RA3	PT8 50p vio bl & red	24.00 16.00

Yugoslavia No. RA10 Overprinted "STT VUJNA" in Carmine

1952

RA4	PT9 50p gray & carmine	1.60 .80

Type of Yugoslavia, 1953, Overprinted "STT VUJNA" in Blue

1953

RA5	PT10 2d org brn & red	1.60 .80

The tax of Nos. RA1-RA5 was for the Red Cross.

POSTAL TAX DUE STAMPS

Yugoslavia No. RAJ2 Surcharged Like No. RA1 in Scarlet

1948	Unwmk.	Perf. 12½
RAJ1	PT4 2 l on 50p bl grn & scar	260.00 240.00

Yugoslavia No. RAJ4 Overprinted "VUJA STT" in Black

1950, July 3

RAJ2	PT6 50p red & vio	2.40 1.25

Yugoslavia No. RAJ6 Overprinted "STT VUJA" in Black

1951

RAJ3	PT8 50p emer & red	240.00 225.00

Yugoslavia No. RAJ7 Overprinted "STT VUJNA" in Carmine

1952

RAJ4	PTD3 50p gray & car	1.60 1.00

Type of Yugoslavia, 1953, Overprinted "STT VUJNA" in Blue

1953

RAJ5	PT10 2d lilac rose & red	1.60 1.00

ZAIRE

zä-'ir

(Congo Democratic Republic)

LOCATION — Central Africa
GOVT. — Republic
AREA — 905,365 sq. mi.
POP. — 50,481,305 (1999 est.)
CAPITAL — Kinshasa

Congo Democratic Republic changed its name to Republic of the Zaire in November 1971. Issues before that date are listed in Vol. 2 under Congo Democratic Republic.

100 Sengi = 1 Li-Kuta
100 Ma-Kuta = 1 Zaire
100 Centimes = 1 Franc (July 1998)

> Catalogue values for all unused stamps in this country are for Never Hinged items.

> From 1971 through 1997, imperforates exist of almost all issues. Exceptions are Nos. 756-772, 850-860, 991-999 and 1259-1442.

UNICEF Emblem, Child Care — A143

UNICEF Emblem and: 14k, Map of Africa showing Zaire. 17k, Boy in African village.

		Perf. 14x13½	
1971, Dec. 18			**Unwmk.**
750	A143	4k gold & multi	.50 .25
751	A143	14k lt bl, gold, red & grn	1.25 .65
752	A143	17k gold & multi	2.00 .60
	Nos. 750-752 (3)		3.75 1.50

25th anniv. of UNICEF. For surcharge see No. 1327.

Pres. Mobutu, MPR Emblem A144

1972		Photo.	Perf. 11½
753	A144	4k multi	4.00 3.00
754	A144	14k multi	4.00 3.00
755	A144	22k multi	4.00 3.00
	Nos. 753-755 (3)		12.00 9.00

5th anniv. of the People's Revolutionary Movement (MPR). For surcharge see #1308.

Zaire Arms — A145

Pres. Joseph D. Mobutu — A146

1972		Litho.	Perf. 14
756	A145	10s red org & blk	.25 .25
757	A145	40s brt bl & multi	.25 .25
758	A145	50s citron & multi	.25 .25
			Perf. 13
759	A146	1k sky bl & multi	.25 .25
760	A146	2k org & multi	.25 .25
761	A146	4k multi	.25 .25
762	A146	4k emer & multi	.25 .25
763	A146	5k multi	.25 .25
764	A146	6k multi	.25 .25
765	A146	8k cit & multi	.60 .25
766	A146	9k multi	.70 .25
767	A146	10k lt lil & multi	.70 .25
768	A146	14k multi	.90 .45
769	A146	17k multi	1.00 .60
770	A146	20k yel & multi	1.40 .65
771	A146	50k multi	3.25 1.40
772	A146	100k fawn & multi	5.25 3.00
	Nos. 756-772 (17)		16.05 9.10

For surcharges and overprints see Nos. 860, 1328, O1-O11.

Same, Denominations in Zaires

1973, Feb. 21			
773	A146	0.01z sky bl & multi	.25 .25
774	A146	0.02z org & multi	.25 .25
775	A146	0.03z multi	.25 .25
776	A146	0.04z multi	.25 .25
777	A146	0.10z multi	.40 .25
778	A146	0.14z multi	.60 .55
	Nos. 773-778 (6)		2.00 1.80

Inga Dam A147

1973, Jan. 25		Litho.	Perf. 13½
790	A147	0.04z multi	.35 .35
791	A147	0.14z pink & multi	.45 .40
792	A147	0.18z yel & multi	.80 .65
	Nos. 790-792 (3)		1.60 1.40

Completion of first section of Inga Dam Nov. 24, 1972.

World Map A148

1973, June 23	Photo.	Perf. 12½x12	
793	A148	0.04z lil & multi	.25 .25
794	A148	0.07z multi	.35 .25
795	A148	0.18z multi	.85 .40
	Nos. 793-795 (3)		1.45 .90

3rd Intl. Fair at Kinshasa, June 23-July 8. The dark brown ink of the inscription was applied by a thermographic process and varnished, producing a shiny, raised effect.

Hand and INTERPOL Emblem — A149

1973, Sept. 28   Litho.   Perf. 12½
796 A149 0.06z multi   .45 .25
797 A149 0.14z multi   .95 .45

50th anniversary of International Criminal Police Organization.

Leopard with Soccer Ball on Globe A150

1974, July 17   Photo.   Perf. 11½x12
798 A150 1k multi   .25 .25
799 A150 2k multi   .25 .25
800 A150 3k multi   .90 .50
801 A150 4k multi   1.25 .65
802 A150 5k multi   1.40 .75
803 A150 14k multi   4.00 1.50
 a.   Souvenir sheet, 1 #803   36.00
      Nos. 798-803 (6)   8.05 3.90

World Cup Soccer Championship, Munich, June 13-July 7.

Foreman-Ali Fight — A151

1974, Nov. 9   Litho.   Perf. 12x12½
804 A151 1k multi   .25 .25
805 A151 2k multi   .25 .25
806 A151 4k multi   .35 .30
807 A151 14k multi   .75 .55
808 A151 20k multi   1.10 1.00
      Nos. 804-808 (5)   2.70 2.35

World Heavyweight Boxing Championship match between George Foreman and Muhammad Ali, Kinshasa, Oct. 30 (postponed from Sept. 25).

Same, Type of 1974, Denominations in Zaires and Inscribed in Various Colors

1975, Aug.   Litho.   Perf. 12x12½
809 A151 0.01z multi (R)   .25 .25
810 A151 0.04z multi (Br)   .25 .25
811 A151 0.06z multi (Bk)   .30 .30
812 A151 0.14z multi (G)   .65 .55
813 A151 0.20z multi (Bk) 1.25 1.10
      Nos. 809-813 (5)   2.70 2.45

Judge, Lawyers, IWY Emblem A152

1975, Dec.   Photo.   Perf. 11½
814 A152 1k dull blk & multi   .25 .25
815 A152 2k dp rose & multi   .25 .25
816 A152 4k dull grn & multi   1.00 .45
817 A152 14k violet & multi   2.00 .80
      Nos. 814-817 (4)   3.50 1.75

International Women's Year 1975.

Waterfall — A153

1975   Photo.   Perf. 11½
818 A153 1k multicolored   .25 .25
819 A153 2k lt blue & multi .30 .25
820 A153 3k multicolored   .50 .30
821 A153 4k salmon & multi 1.25 .65
822 A153 5k green & multi 1.25 .65
      Nos. 818-822 (5)   3.55 2.10

12th General Assembly of the Intl. Union for Nature Preservation (U.I.C.N.), Kinshasa, Sept. 1975.

Okapis A154

1975
823 A154 1k blue & multi   .60 .25
824 A154 2k yellow grn & multi .90 .25
825 A154 3k brown red & multi 1.50 .30
826 A154 4k green & multi   2.40 .50
827 A154 5k yellow & multi   3.25 .60
      Nos. 823-827 (5)   8.65 1.90

Virunga National Park, 50th anniversary.

Siderma Maluku Industry A155

Designs: 1k, Sozacom apartment building, vert. 3k, Matadi flour mill, vert. 4k, Women parachutists. 8k, Pres. Mobutu visiting Chairman Mao, vert. 10k, Soldiers working along the Salongo. 14k, Pres. Mobutu addressing UN Gen. Assembly, Oct. 1974. 15k, Celebrating crowd.

1975
828 A155 1k ocher & multi   .40 .25
829 A155 2k yel grn & multi .40 .25
830 A155 3k multi   .75 .25
831 A155 4k multi   1.00 .25
832 A155 8k dk brn & multi 1.50 .35
833 A155 10k sep & multi   2.25 .50
834 A155 14k bl & multi   4.50 .75
835 A155 15k org & multi   6.50 1.00
      Nos. 828-835 (8)   17.30 3.60

10th anniversary of new government.

Tshokwe Mask — A156   Map of Zaire, UPU Emblem — A157

Designs: 2k, 4k, Seated woman, Pende. 7k, like 5k. 10k, 14k, Antelope mask, Suku. 15k, 18k, Kneeling woman, Kongo. 20k, 25k, Kuba mask.

1977, Jan. 8   Photo.   Perf. 11½
836 A156 2k multi   .25 .25
837 A156 4k multi   .25 .25
838 A156 5k gray & multi   .25 .25

839 A156 7k multi   .25 .25
840 A156 10k multi   .30 .25
841 A156 14k multi   .40 .25
842 A156 15k multi   .50 .25
843 A156 18k multi   .60 .30
844 A156 20k multi   1.25 .40
845 A156 25k vio & multi   1.40 .55
      Nos. 836-845 (10)   5.45 3.00

Wood carving and masks of Zaire.

1977, Apr.   Litho.   Perf. 13½
846 A157 1k org & multi   .30 .25
847 A157 4k dk bl & multi   .90 .25
848 A157 7k ol grn & multi 1.40 .30
849 A157 50k brn & multi   6.25 4.00
      Nos. 846-849 (4)   8.85 4.80

Cent. of UPU (in 1974).

Congo Stamps of 1968-1971
Surcharged with New Value, Bars and
"RÉPUBLIQUE DU ZAIRE"

1977
850 A126 1k on 10s (#642)   .70 .70
851 A122 2k on 9.6k (#618)   .70 .70
852 A140 10k on 10s (#735)   .85 .70
853 A134 25k on 10s (#703) 2.25 1.60
854 A127 40k on 9.6k (#652) 3.75 2.40
855 A135 48k on 10s (#713) 5.00 3.00
      Nos. 850-855 (6)   13.25 9.10

Congo Nos. 644, 643, 635, 746
Surcharged with New Value, Bars and
"RÉPUBLIQUE DU ZAIRE" in Black or
Carmine, Zaire No. 757 Surcharged

1977
856 A126 5k on 30s   .70 .70
857 A126 10k on 15s (C)   .70 .70
858 A124 20k on 9.60k   1.75 .70
859 A141 30k on 12k   3.25 1.25
860 A145 100k on 40s (C)   9.50 5.25
      Nos. 856-860 (5)   15.90 8.60
      Nos. 850-860 (11)   29.15 17.70

Souvenir Sheet

Adoration of the Kings, by Rubens — A158

1977, Dec. 19   Photo.   Perf. 13½
861 A158 5z multi   150.00 110.00

Christmas 1977.

Pantodon Buchholzi A159

Fish: 70s, Aphyosemion striatum. 55, Ctenopoma fasciolatum. 8k, Malapterurus electricus. 10k, Hemichromis bimaculatus. 30k, Marcusenius isidori. 40k, Synodontis nigriventris. 48k, Julidochromis ornatus. 100k, Nothobranchius brieni. 250k, Micralestes interruptus.

1978, Jan. 23   Litho.   Perf. 14
862 A159 30s multi   .25 .25
863 A159 70s multi   .25 .25
864 A159 5k multi   .25 .25
865 A159 8k multi   .40 .30
866 A159 10k multi   .70 .70
867 A159 30k multi   1.25 .90
868 A159 40k multi   1.75 1.00
869 A159 48k multi   2.25 1.25
870 A159 100k multi   7.00 2.75
      Nos. 862-870 (9)   14.10 7.65

Souvenir Sheet
Perf. 13½
871 A159 250k multi   10.00 10.00

No. 871 contains one 46x35mm stamp. For surcharges see Nos. 1294, 1311.

Soccer Game, Argentina-France A160

Various Soccer Games and Jules Rimet Cup: 3k, Austria-Brazil. 7k, Scotland-Iran. 9k, Netherlands-Peru. 10k, Hungary-Italy. 20k, Fed. Rep. of Germany-Mexico. 50k, Tunisia-Poland. 100k, Spain-Sweden. 500k, Rimet Cup, Games' emblem and cartoon of soccer player, horiz.

1978, Aug. 7   Litho.   Perf. 12½
872 A160 1k multi   .25 .25
873 A160 3k multi   .25 .25
874 A160 7k multi   .25 .25
875 A160 9k multi   .25 .25
876 A160 10k multi   .25 .25
877 A160 20k multi   .40 .25
878 A160 50k multi   1.10 .60
879 A160 100k multi   2.25 1.25
      Nos. 872-879 (8)   5.00 3.35

Souvenir Sheets
880 A160 500k blue & multi 25.00 25.00
881 A160 500k red & multi 25.00 25.00

11th World Cup Soccer Championship, Argentina, June 1-25. Nos. 880-881 contain one stamp each (47x36mm). Stamp of No. 880 has blue frameline. Stamp of No. 881 has red frame line.

For surcharge see No. 1259.

Mama Mobutu — A161

1978, Oct. 23   Photo.   Perf. 12
882 A161 8k multi   .30 .30

Mama Mobutu (1941-77), wife of Pres. Mobutu.

Pres. Joseph D. Mobutu — A162

Frame Color
Granite Paper

1978   Photo.   Perf. 12
883 A162 2k blue   .25 .25
884 A162 5k bister   .25 .25
885 A162 6k Prussian blue   .25 .25
886 A162 8k red brown   .25 .25
887 A162 10k emerald   .25 .25
888 A162 25k red   .25 .25
889 A162 48k purple   .50 .30
890 A162 1z green   .95 .70
      Nos. 883-890 (8)   2.95 2.50

See Nos. 1053, 1055-1056. For surcharges see Nos. 1313, 1333-1336.

Souvenir Sheet

Elizabeth II in Westminster Abbey — A163

1978, Dec. 11 Photo. Perf. 13½
891 A163 5z multi 12.00 12.00
Coronation of Queen Elizabeth II, 25th anniv.

Souvenir Sheet

Albrecht Dürer, Self-portrait — A164

1978, Dec. 18 Perf. 13
892 A164 5z multi 12.00 12.00
Albrecht Dürer (1471-1528), German painter and engraver.

Leonardo da Vinci and his Drawings — A165

History of Aviation: 70s, Planes of Wright Brothers, 1905, and Santos Dumont, 1906. 1k, Bleriot XI, 1909, and Farman F-60, 1909. 5k, Junkers G-38, 1929, and Spirit of St. Louis, 1927. 8k, Sikorsky S-42B, 1934 and Macchi-Castoldi MC-72, 1934. 10k, Boeing 707, 1960, and Fokker F-VII, 1935. 50k, Apollo XI, 1969, and Concorde, 1976. 75k, Helicopter and Douglas DC-10, 1971. 5z, Giffard's balloon, 1852, and Hindenburg LZ 129, 1936.

1978, Dec. 28 Litho. Perf. 13
893 A165 30s multi .25 .25
894 A165 70s multi .25 .25
895 A165 1k multi .25 .25
896 A165 5k multi .35 .25
897 A165 8k multi .35 .25
898 A165 10k multi .70 .25
899 A165 50k multi 3.00 1.25
900 A165 75k multi 4.00 1.50
  Nos. 893-900 (8) 9.15 4.25

Souvenir Sheet
Perf. 11½
901 A165 5z multi 12.00 12.00
For overprint and surcharges see Nos. 993, 1173-1181, 1291, 1295.

Pres. Mobutu, Map of Zaire, N'tombe Dancer — A166

Pres. Mobutu & Map: 3k, Bird. 4k, Elephant. 10k, Diamond and cotton boll. 14k, Hand holding torch. 17k, Leopard's head and Victoria Regia lily. 25k, Finzia waterfall. 50k, Wagenia fishermen.

1979, Feb. Litho. Perf. 14x13½
902 A166 1k multicolored .25 .25
903 A166 3k multicolored .25 .25
904 A166 4k multicolored .25 .25
905 A166 10k multicolored .25 .25
  a. Souvenir sheet of 4, #902-905 13.00 —
906 A166 14k multicolored .25 .25
907 A166 17k multicolored .40 .25
908 A166 25k multicolored .60 .40
909 A166 50k multicolored 1.25 .85
  a. Souvenir sheet of 4, #906-909 13.00 —
  Nos. 902-909 (8) 3.50 2.75
Zaire (Congo) River expedition.

Phylloporus Ampliporus A167

Mushrooms: 5k, Engleromyces goetzei. 8k, Scutellinia virungae. 10k, Pycnoporus sanguineus. 30k, Cantharellus miniatescens. 40k, Lactarius phlebonemus. 48k, Phallus indusiatus. 100k, Ramaria moelleriana.

1979, Mar. Photo. Perf. 13½x13
910 A167 30s multicolored .25 .25
911 A167 5k multicolored .30 .25
912 A167 8k multicolored .55 .35
913 A167 10k multicolored .80 .45
914 A167 30k multicolored 1.75 1.25
915 A167 40k multicolored 2.10 1.40
916 A167 48k multicolored 4.25 2.00
917 A167 100k multicolored 6.00 3.50
  Nos. 910-917 (8) 16.00 9.45

For surcharges see Nos. 1296, 1298, 1312, 1361-1362, 1365-1366, 1368-1369, 1372, 1375.

Souvenir Sheets

Pope John XXIII (1881-1963) A168

Popes: No. 919, Paul VI (1897-1978). No. 920, John Paul I (1912-78).

1979, June 25 Litho. Perf. 11½
918 A168 250k multi 5.00 5.00
919 A168 250k multi 5.00 5.00
920 A168 250k multi 5.00 5.00
  Nos. 918-920 (3) 15.00 15.00

Boy Beating Drum — A169

IYC Emblem on Map of Zaire and: 10k, 20k, Girl, diff. 50k, Boy. 100k, Boys. 300k, Mother and child. 10z, Mother and children, horiz.

1979, July 23 Litho. Perf. 12½
921 A169 5k multi .25 .25
922 A169 10k multi .25 .25
923 A169 20k multi .40 .25
924 A169 50k multi .90 .50
925 A169 100k multi 1.90 1.00
926 A169 300k multi 5.25 2.50
  Nos. 921-926 (6) 8.95 4.75

Souvenir Sheet
927 A169 10z multi 14.00 10.50
International Year of the Child.
For surcharges see Nos. 997, 999, 1299, 1306.

Globe and Drummer A170

1979, July 23
928 A170 1k multi .25 .25
929 A170 9k multi .25 .25
930 A170 90k multi .70 .50
931 A170 100k multi .80 .55
  Nos. 928-931 (4) 2.00 1.55

Souvenir Sheet
932 A170 500k multi 4.75 2.75
6th International Fair, Kinshasa. No. 932 contains one 52x31mm stamp.
For overprint & surcharge see #996, 1320.

Globe and School Desk — A171

1979, Dec. 24 Litho. Perf. 13
933 A171 10k multi .25 .25
Intl. Bureau of Education, Geneva, 50th anniv.

Adoration of the Kings, by Memling — A172

1979, Dec. 24 Imperf.
934 A172 5z multi 6.00 3.00
Christmas 1979.

"Puffing Billy," 1814, Gt. Britain A173

1980, Jan. 14 Litho. Perf. 13½x13
935 A173 50s shown .25 .25
936 A173 1.50k Buddicom No. 33, 1843, France .25 .25
937 A173 5k "Elephant," 1835, Belgium .25 .25
938 A173 8k No. 601, 1906, Zaire .25 .25
939 A173 50k "Slieve Gullion 440," Ireland .75 .25
940 A173 75k "Black Elephant," Germany 1.10 .75
941 A173 2z Type 1-15, Zaire 2.25 1.90
942 A173 5z "Golden State," US 6.00 6.00
  Nos. 935-942 (8) 11.10 9.90

Souvenir Sheet
943 A173 10z Type E.D.75, Zaire 15.00 15.00
For overprints and surcharges see Nos. 991-992, 994, 1325.

Hill, Belgian Congo No. 257 A174

1980, Jan. 28 Perf. 13½x14
944 A174 2k No. 5 .25 .25
945 A174 4k No. 13 .25 .25
946 A174 10k No. 24 .25 .25
947 A174 20k No. 38 .25 .25
948 A174 40k No. 111 .40 .25
949 A174 150k No. B29 1.25 .85
950 A174 200k No. 198 1.50 1.00
951 A174 250k shown 1.90 1.25
  Nos. 944-951 (8) 6.05 4.35

Souvenir Sheet
952 A174 10z No. 198 11.00 11.00
Sir Rowland Hill (1795-1879), originator of penny postage.
For overprint and surcharge see Nos. 998, 1329.

Albert Einstein (1879-1955), Theoretical Physicist A175

1980, Feb. 18 Perf. 13
953 A175 40s multi .25 .25
954 A175 2k multi .25 .25
955 A175 4k multi .25 .25
956 A175 15k multi .25 .25
957 A175 50k multi .40 .25
958 A175 300k multi 1.50 .75
  Nos. 953-958 (6) 2.90 2.00

Souvenir Sheet
959 A175 5z multi, diff. 4.50 2.50
For surcharges see Nos. 1285, 1290, 1304.

Salvation Army Brass Players — A176

50s, Booth Memorial Hospital, NYC. 4.50k, Commissioner George Railton sailing for US mission. 10k, Mobile dispensary, Masina. 20k, Gen. Evangeline Booth, officer holding infant, vert. 75k, Outdoor well-baby clinic. 1.50z, Disaster relief. 2z, Parade, vert. 10z, Gen. & Mrs. Arnold Brown.

1980, Mar. 3 Perf. 11
960 A176 50s multi .25 .25
961 A176 4.50k multi .25 .25
962 A176 10k multi .25 .25
963 A176 20k multi .25 .25
964 A176 40k multi .35 .25
965 A176 75k multi .55 .25
966 A176 1.50z multi 1.10 .55
967 A176 2z multi 1.60 .80
  Nos. 960-967 (8) 4.60 2.85

Souvenir Sheet
968 A176 10z multi 7.50 5.00
Salvation Army cent. in US. No. 968 contains one 53x38mm stamp and 2 labels.

Souvenir Sheets

Visite de Sa Sainteté le Pape Jean Paul II
au Zaïre — Mai 1980

Pope John Paul II — A177

1980, May 2   Litho.   Perf. 11½
969 A177 10z multi   17.50 17.50
Visit of Pope John Paul II to Zaire, May.

Baia Castle, by Antonio Pitloo — A178

1980, May 5
970 A178 10z multi   5.50 5.50
20th International Philatelic Exhibition,
Europa '80, Naples, Apr. 26-May 4.

A179

Perf. 12½x13, 13x12½
1980, May 24   Litho.
971 A179 50k Woman, line-
            drawing   .25 .25
972 A179 100k Plutiarch   .50 .40
973 A179 500k Kneeling man,
            sculpture, vert.   2.50 1.75
  a.   Souvenir sheet of 3   6.00 4.25
      Nos. 971-973 (3)   3.25 2.40
Rotary Intl., 75th anniv. No. 973a contains 3
stamps similar to Nos. 971-973, size: 55x35,
35x55mm. Exists imperf.
For surcharge see No. 1313.

Tropical Fish — A180

1980, Oct. 20   Litho.   Perf. 14x13½
974 A180 1k Chaetodon col-
            laris   .25 .25
975 A180 5k Zebrasoma ve-
            liferum   .25 .25
976 A180 10k Euxiphipops
            xanthometapon   .25 .25
977 A180 20k Pomacanthus
            annularis   .25 .25
978 A180 50k Centropyge
            oriculus   .60 .50

---

979 A180 150k Oxymona-
            canthus
            longirostris   1.40 .65
980 A180 200k Balistoides niger 1.90 .80
981 A180 250k Rhinecanthus
            aculeatus   2.25 1.10
      Nos. 974-981 (8)   7.15 4.05
      Souvenir Sheet
981A A180 5z Baliste ondule   4.50 4.50
For surcharge see No. 1307.

Exhibition Emblem, Congo
#365 — A181

1980, Dec. 6   Litho.   Perf. 13
982   Block of 4   2.00 1.60
  a. A181 1z, UR shown   .45 .35
  b. A181 1z, UL Belgium #511   .45 .35
  c. A181 1z, UR like #982b   .45 .35
  d. A181 1z, UL like #982a   .45 .35
983   Block of 4   4.00 2.50
  a. A181 2z, UR Congo #432   .95 .60
  b. A181 2z, UL Belgium # B835   .95 .60
  c. A181 2z, UR like #983b   .95 .60
  d. A181 2z, UL like #983a   .95 .60
984   Block of 4   5.75 4.00
  a. A181 3z, UR Zaire #755   1.40 .90
  b. A181 3z, UL Belgium # B878   1.40 .90
  c. A181 3z, UR like #984b   1.40 .90
  d. A181 3z, UL like #984a   1.40 .90
985   Block of 4   8.00 5.00
  a. A181 4z, UR Congo #572   1.75 1.10
  b. A181 4z, UL Belgium # B996   1.75 1.10
  c. A181 4z, UR like #985b   1.75 1.10
  d. A181 4z, UL like #985a   1.75 1.10
      Nos. 982-985 (4)   19.75 13.10
PHIBELZA, Belgium-Zaire Phil. Exhib.
#982-985 can be collected as strips of 4.
For surcharge see No. 1342.

Map of
Africa,
King
Leopold I
A182

Belgian independence sesquicentennial:
75k, Stanley expedition, Leopold II. 100k,
Colonial troops, Albert I. 270k, 145k, protected animals, Leopold III. Visit of King
Baudouin and Queen Fabiola.

1980, Dec. 13   Photo.   Perf. 14
986 A182 10k multi   .30 .25
987 A182 75k multi   1.10 .50
988 A182 100k multi   1.75 .65
989 A182 145k multi   2.40 .85
990 A182 270k multi   4.25 1.50
      Nos. 986-990 (5)   9.80 3.75
For surcharges see Nos. 1326, 1331, 1345,
1357, 1408-1412, 1426.

Nos. 935, 936, 898, 939, 900, 931,
925, 951, Overprinted in Red, Silver or
Black: 20e Anniversaire-Independence
/ 1960-1980

1980, Dec. 13   Litho.
991 A173 50s multi   .25 .25
992 A173 1.50k multi   .25 .25
993 A165 10k multi   .25 .25
994 A173 50k multi   .55 .25
995 A165 75k multi   .70 .25
996 A170 100k multi (S)   1.00 .65
997 A169   1z on 5z on 100k
               multi (B)   1.25 .65
998 A174 250k multi   2.50 1.40
999 A169   5z on 100k multi
               (B)   5.00 2.75
      Nos. 991-999 (9)   11.75 6.70
20th anniversary of independence. For
surcharges see Nos. 1300, 1316.

Nativity
A183

1980, Dec. 24   Perf. 13
1000 A183 10k Shepherds and
            angels   .25 .25
1001 A183 75k Flight into Egypt   1.00 .50
1002 A183 80k Three kings   1.00 .50
1003 A183 145k shown   1.75 .95
      Nos. 1000-1003 (4)   4.00 2.00
      Souvenir Sheet
1004 A183 10z Church, nativity   5.50 5.50
Christmas 1980. No. 1004 contains one
49x33mm stamp. Exists imperf. For
surcharges see Nos. 1301, 1317-1318.

Postal Clerk
Sorting Mail,
by Norman
Rockwell
A184

Designs: Saturday Evening Post covers by
Norman Rockwell.

1981, Apr. 27   Litho.   Perf. 14
1005 A184 10k multi   .25 .25
1006 A184 20k multi   .25 .25
1007 A184 50k multi   .40 .25
1008 A184 80k multi   .65 .40
1009 A184 100k multi   .70 .45
1010 A184 125k multi   1.10 .50
1011 A184 175k multi   1.25 .70
1012 A184 200k multi   1.40 .80
      Nos. 1005-1012 (8)   6.00 3.60
For surcharges see Nos. 1262, 1265, 1269,
1275, 1281, 1354.

First
Anniv.
of Visit
of Pope
John
Paul II
A185

Scenes of Pope's visit. 50k, 500k, vert.

1981, May 2   Perf. 13
1013 A185 5k multi   .25 .25
1014 A185 10k multi   .25 .25
1015 A185 50k multi   .35 .35
1016 A185 100k multi   1.00 .60
1017 A185 500k multi   5.50 2.75
1018 A185 800k multi   7.75 4.75
      Nos. 1013-1018 (6)   15.10 8.95
For surcharges see #1190-1194, 1292,
1302, 1343.

Soccer
Players — A186

Designs: Soccer scenes.

1981, July 6   Litho.   Perf. 12½
1019 A186 2k multi   .25 .25
1020 A186 10k multi   .25 .25
1021 A186 25k multi   .25 .25
1022 A186 90k multi   .50 .25
1023 A186 2z multi   1.00 .65
1024 A186 3z multi   1.60 1.00
1025 A186 6z multi   2.75 1.75
1026 A186 8z multi   4.50 3.25
      Nos. 1019-1026 (8)   11.10 7.65
      Souvenir Sheet
1027   Sheet of 2   6.00 6.00
  a. A186 5z like #1019   2.75 2.75
  b. A186 5z like #1025   2.75 2.75
ESPANA '82 World Cup Soccer Championship. For surcharges see Nos. 1287, 1303,
1309, 1321.

Intl. Year of the Disabled — A187

1981, Nov. 2   Litho.   Perf. 14x14½
1028 A187 2k Archer   .25 .25
1029 A187 5k Ear, sound
            waves   .25 .25
1030 A187 10k Amputee   .25 .25
1031 A187 18k Cane braille,
            sunglasses   .25 .25
1032 A187 50k Boy with leg
            braces   .25 .25
1033 A187 150k Sign language   .55 .30
1034 A187 500k Hands   1.40 1.25
1035 A187 800k Dove   2.25 2.25
      Nos. 1028-1035 (8)   5.45 5.05
For surcharges see Nos. 1288, 1293, 1305,
1314.

Souvenir Sheet

Birth Sesqui. of Heinrich von
Stephan, UPU Founder — A188

Photogravure and Engraved
1981, Dec. 21   Perf. 11½x12
1036 A188 15z purple   8.00 8.00

Christmas
1981 — A189

Designs: 25k, 1z, 1.50z, 3z, 5z, Various
children. 10z, Holy Family, horiz.

1981, Dec. 21   Litho.   Perf. 14
1037 A189 25k multi   .25 .25
1038 A189 1z multi   .65 .25
1039 A189 1.50z multi   .75 .35
1040 A189 3z multi   1.50 .75
1041 A189 5z multi   2.75 1.40
      Nos. 1037-1041 (5)   5.90 3.00
      Souvenir Sheet
1042 A189 10z multi   5.50 5.50

13th World Telecommunications Day
(1981) — A190

Designs: Symbols of communications and health care delivery.

1982, Feb. 8   **Litho.**   *Perf. 13*

1043	A190	1k multi	.25	.25
1044	A190	25k multi	.25	.25
1045	A190	90k multi	.30	.25
1046	A190	1z multi	.30	.25
1047	A190	1.70z multi	.55	.45
1048	A190	3z multi	1.10	.75
1049	A190	4.50z multi	1.60	1.10
1050	A190	5z multi	1.75	1.25
		Nos. 1043-1050 (8)	6.10	4.55

For surcharges see Nos. 1270, 1282.

Pres. Mobutu Type of 1978
Frame Color
Granite Paper

1982   **Photo.**   *Perf. 12*

1053	A162	50k purple	.25	.25
1055	A162	2z bister	.40	.25
1056	A162	5z Prussian blue	2.25	1.40
		Nos. 1053-1056 (3)	2.90	1.90

20th Anniv. of African Postal Union
(1981) — A191

1982, Mar. 8   **Litho.**   *Perf. 13*

1057	A191	1z yel grn & gold	.50	.25

For surcharges see Nos. 1348, 1352.

1982 World Cup A192

Designs: Flags and players of finalists.

1982

1058	A192	2k multi	.25	.25
1059	A192	8k multi	.25	.25
1060	A192	25k multi	.25	.25
1061	A192	50k multi	.25	.25
1062	A192	90k multi	.30	.25
1063	A192	1z multi	.45	.30
1064	A192	1.45z multi	.55	.45
1065	A192	1.70z multi	.85	.70
1066	A192	3z multi	1.40	1.10
1067	A192	3.50z multi	1.90	1.40
1068	A192	5z multi	3.00	2.10
1069	A192	6z multi	3.25	2.50
		Nos. 1058-1069 (12)	12.70	9.80

Souvenir Sheet

1070	A192	10z multi	7.50	7.50

Issued: #1058-1069, July 6; #1070, Sept. 21.
For surcharges see #1289, 1315, 1322, 1344, 1435 and footnote after #1336.

9th Conference of Heads of State of Africa and France, Kinshasa, Oct. — A193

1982, Oct. 8   **Litho.**   *Perf. 13*

1071	A193	75k multi	.25	.25
1072	A193	90k multi	.25	.25
1073	A193	1z multi	.25	.25
1074	A193	1.50z multi	.25	.25
1075	A193	3z multi	.75	.60
1076	A193	5z multi	1.10	.90
1077	A193	8z multi	1.90	1.50
		Nos. 1071-1077 (7)	4.75	4.00

For surcharges see Nos. 1268, 1271, 1280, 1283, 1347, 1351.

Animals from Virunga Natl. Park — A194

1982, Nov. 5

1078	A194	1z Lions	.25	.25
1079	A194	1.70z Buffalo	.90	.60
1080	A194	3.50z Elephants	2.10	1.40
1081	A194	6.50z Antelope	3.50	2.25
1082	A194	8z Hippopotamus	5.00	3.25
1083	A194	10z Monkeys	5.75	3.75
1084	A194	10z Leopard	5.75	3.75
a.		Pair, #1083-1084 + label	12.00	12.00
		Nos. 1078-1084 (7)	23.25	15.25

#1084a has continuous design.
For surcharge see No. 1430.

Scouting Year — A195

1982, Nov. 29   **Photo.**   *Perf. 11½*
Granite Paper

1085	A195	90k Camp	.35	.30
1086	A195	1.70z Campfire	.90	.65
1087	A195	3z Scout	1.50	1.10
1088	A195	5z First aid	3.25	1.90
1089	A195	8z Flag signals	6.00	3.50
		Nos. 1085-1089 (5)	12.00	7.45

Souvenir Sheet

1090	A195	10z Baden-Powell	11.00	11.00

For surcharges see Nos. 1207-1214.

Local Birds — A196

1982, Dec. 6   **Litho.**   *Perf. 13*

1091	A196	25k Quelea quelea	.25	.25
1092	A196	50k Ceyx picta	.25	.25
1093	A196	90k Tauraco persa	.60	.25
1094	A196	1.50z Charadrius tricollaris	.65	.40
1095	A196	1.70k Cursorius temminckii	.70	.40
1096	A196	2z Campethera bennettii	.95	.60
1097	A196	3z Podiceps ruficollis	1.40	.80
1098	A196	3.50z Kaupifalco monogrammicus	1.50	.85
1099	A196	5z Limnocorax flavirostris	2.25	1.25
1100	A196	8z White-headed vulture	3.50	2.10
		Nos. 1091-1100 (10)	12.05	7.15

All except 3.50z, 8z horiz.
For surcharges see Nos. 1263, 1266, 1272, 1276, 1278, 1284, 1425, 1432, 1438, 1440.

Souvenir Sheet

Christmas — A197

1982, Dec. 20   **Photo.**   *Perf. 13½*

1101	A197	15z Adoration of the Magi, by van der Goes	8.00	8.00

Quartz A198

1983, Feb. 13   **Photo.**   *Perf. 11½*
Granite Paper

1102	A198	2k Malachite, vert.	.25	.25
1103	A198	45k shown	.25	.25
1104	A198	75k Gold	.55	.25
1105	A198	1z Uraninite	1.00	.25
1106	A198	1.50z Bournonite, vert.	1.50	.80
1107	A198	3z Cassiterite	3.00	1.50
1108	A198	6z Dioptase, vert.	6.00	3.00
1109	A198	8z Cuprite, vert.	7.50	4.00
		Nos. 1102-1109 (8)	20.05	10.30

Souvenir Sheet

1110	A198	10z Diamonds	10.00	10.00

For surcharges see Nos. 1324, 1330, 1332, 1346.

TB Bacillus Centenary — A199

1983, Feb. 21   **Litho.**   *Perf. 13*

1111	A199	80k multi	.25	.25
1112	A199	1.20z multi	.40	.25
1113	A199	3.60z multi	1.40	.65
1114	A199	9.60z multi	4.00	1.90
		Nos. 1111-1114 (4)	6.05	3.05

For surcharges see Nos. 1319, 1356, 1358, 1360, 1433, 1436, 1441.

Kinshasa Monuments — A200

1983, Apr. 25

1115	A200	50k Zaire Diplomat, vert.	.25	.25
1116	A200	1z Echo of Zaire	.25	.25
1117	A200	1.50z Messengers, vert.	.35	.25
1118	A200	3z Shield of Revolution, vert.	.65	.35
1119	A200	5z Weeping Woman	1.10	.55
1120	A200	10z Militant, vert.	2.40	1.10
		Nos. 1115-1120 (6)	5.00	2.75

For surcharges see Nos. 1267, 1279, 1349-1350.

ITU Plenipotentiaries Conference, Nairobi, Sept. 1982 — A201

Various satellites, dish antennae and maps.

1983, June 13   **Litho.**   *Perf. 13*

1121	A201	2k multi	.25	.25
1122	A201	4k multi	.25	.25
1123	A201	25k multi	.25	.25
1124	A201	1.20z multi	.40	.25
1125	A201	2.05z multi	.65	.35
1126	A201	3.60z multi	1.25	.60
1127	A201	6z multi	2.00	1.00
1128	A201	8z multi	2.50	1.40
		Nos. 1121-1128 (8)	7.55	4.35

For surcharges see Nos. 1260-1261, 1264, 1273-1274, 1277, 1355, 1359, 1429, 1434, 1437, 1439, 1442.

Christmas 1983 — A202

Raphael Paintings; No. 1129: a, Virgin and Child. b, Holy Family. c, Esterhazy Madonna. d, Sistine Madonna. No. 1130: a, La Belle Jardiniere. b, Virgin of Alba. c, Holy Family, diff. d, Virgin and Child, diff.

1983, Dec. 26   **Photo.**   *Perf. 13½x13*

1129		Sheet of 4	3.50	3.50
a.-d.		A202 10z, any single	.85	.85
1130		Sheet of 4	5.25	5.25
a.-d.		A202 15z, any single	1.25	1.25

Garamba Park — A203

1984, Apr. 2   **Litho.**   *Perf. 13*

1131	A203	10k Darby's Eland	.25	.25
1132	A203	15k Eagles	.25	.25
1133	A203	3z Servals	.25	.25
1134	A203	10z White rhinoceros	1.75	1.75
1135	A203	15z Lions	2.50	2.50
1136	A203	37.50z Warthogs	6.00	6.00
1137	A203	40z Koris bustards	6.75	6.75
1138	A203	40z Crowned cranes	6.75	6.75
a.		Pair, #1137-1138 + label	13.50	13.50
		Nos. 1131-1138 (8)	24.50	24.50

Nos. 1137-1138 are narrower, 49x34mm, with continuous design.
For surcharge see No. 1428.

World Communications Year — A204

Designs: 10k, Computer operator, Congo River ferry. 15k, Communications satellite. 8.50z, Engineer, Congo River Bridge. 10z, Satellite, ground receiving station. 15z, TV camerawoman filming crowed crane. 37.50z, Satellite, dish antennas. 80z, Switchboard operator, bus.

1984, May 14   **Litho.**   *Perf. 13x12½*

1139	A204	10k multi	.25	.25
1140	A204	15k multi	.25	.25
1141	A204	8.50z multi	.65	.65
1142	A204	10z multi	.70	.70
1143	A204	15z multi	1.10	1.10
1144	A204	37.50z multi	2.75	2.75
1145	A204	80z multi	5.75	5.75
		Nos. 1139-1145 (7)	11.45	11.45

Hypericum
Revolutum
A205

Local flowers: 15k, Borreria dibrachiata. 3z,
Disa erubescens. 8.50z, Scaevola plumieri.
10z, Clerodendron thompsonii. 15z,
Thumbergia erecta. 37.50z, Impatiens
niamniamensis. 100z, Canarina eminii.

1984, May 28   Photo.   Perf. 14x13½
1146	A205	10k multi	.25	.25
1147	A205	15k multi	.25	.25
1148	A205	3z multi	.25	.25
1149	A205	8.50z multi	.80	.80
1150	A205	10z multi	.90	.90
1151	A205	15z multi	1.25	1.25
1152	A205	37.50z multi	3.25	3.25
1153	A205	100z multi	9.00	9.00
		Nos. 1146-1153 (8)	15.95	15.95

1984 Summer
Olympics
A206

1984, June 5   Litho.   Perf. 13
1154	A206	2z Basketball	.25	.25
1155	A206	3z Equestrian	.35	.35
1156	A206	10z Running	1.10	1.10
1157	A206	15z Long jump	1.60	1.60
1158	A206	20z Soccer	2.75	2.75
		Nos. 1154-1158 (5)	6.05	6.05

Souvenir Sheet
Perf. 11½
1159	A206	50z Kayak	5.50	5.50

No. 1159 contains one 31x49mm stamp.
For surcharge see No. 1427.

Manned Flight
Bicent. — A207

10k, Montgolfiere, 1783. 15k, Charles &
Robert, 1783. 3z, Gustave, 1783. 5z, Santos-
Dumont III, 1899. 10z, Stratospheric balloon,
1934. 15z, Zeppelin LZ-129, 1936. 37.50z,
Double Eagle II, 1978. 80z, Hot air balloons.

1984, June 28   Litho.   Perf. 14
1160	A207	10k multi	.25	.25
1161	A207	15k multi	.25	.25
1162	A207	3z multi	.25	.25
1163	A207	5z multi	.50	.50
1164	A207	10z multi	.90	.90
1165	A207	15z multi	1.40	1.40
1166	A207	37.50z multi	3.25	3.25
1167	A207	80z multi	7.25	7.25
		Nos. 1160-1167 (8)	14.05	14.05

For surcharges see Nos. 1413-1420.

Okapi — A208

1984, Oct. 15   Litho.   Perf. 13
1168	A208	2z Grazing	1.25	.60
1169	A208	3z Resting	2.00	.70
1170	A208	8z Mother and young	3.25	2.25
1171	A208	10z In water	5.50	4.25
		Nos. 1168-1171 (4)	12.00	7.80

Souvenir Sheet
Perf. 11½
1172	A208	50z like 10z	5.25	5.25

World Wildlife Fund. No. 1172 contains one
36x51mm stamp, margin continues the design
of the 10z without emblem.

**Nos. 893-900 Surcharged in Silver
Over Black Bar and With One of
Three Different Sabena Airlines
Emblems and "1925 1985" in Silver**

1985, Feb. 19   Perf. 13
1173	A165	2.50z on 30s #893	.25	.25
1174	A165	5z on 5k #896	.40	.40
1175	A165	6z on 70s #894	.40	.40
1176	A165	7.50z on 1k #895	.60	.60
1177	A165	8.50z on 10k #898	.60	.60
1178	A165	10z on 8k #897	.75	.75
1179	A165	12.50z on 75k #900	.95	.95
1180	A165	30z on 50k #899	2.25	2.25
		Nos. 1173-1180 (8)	6.20	6.20

**No. 901 Surcharged in Silver Over
Black Bar and With Silver Text "60e
ANNIVERSAIRE/1re LIASON
AERIENNE/BRUXELLES-
KINSHASAL/PAR EDMOND
THIEFFRY"**
Souvenir Sheet
1985, Feb. 19   Perf. 11½
1181	A165	50z on 5z #901	60.00	60.00

OLYMPHILEX '85, Lausanne — A209

1985, Apr. 19   Perf. 13
1182	A209	1z Swimming	.25	.25
1183	A209	2z Soccer, vert.	.25	.25
1184	A209	3z Boxing	.25	.25
1185	A209	4z Basketball, vert.	.25	.25
1186	A209	6z Equestrian	.40	.40
1187	A209	10z Volleyball, vert.	.75	.75
1188	A209	15z Running	1.25	1.25
1189	A209	30z Cycling, vert.	2.50	2.50
		Nos. 1182-1189 (8)	5.90	5.90

**Nos. 1013-1018, 969 Ovptd. and
Surcharged with 1 or 2 Gold Bars and
"AOUT 1985" in Gold or Black**
1985, Aug. 15   Perf. 13, 11½
1190	A185	2z on 5k	.25	.25
1191	A185	3z on 10k	.35	.35
1192	A185	5z on 50k	.60	.60
1192A	A185	10z on 100k	1.40	1.40
1192B	A185	15z on 500k	1.90	1.90
1193	A185	40z on 800k	5.50	5.50
		Nos. 1190-1193 (6)	10.00	10.00

Souvenir Sheet
1194	A177	50z on 10z (B)	12.00	12.00

Second visit of Pope John Paul II.

Audubon Birth Bicent. — A210

Illustrations of North American bird species
by John Audubon.

1985, Oct. 1   Perf. 13
1195	A210	5z Great egret	.85	.60
1196	A210	10z Yellow-beaked duck	1.90	1.10
1197	A210	15z Small heron	3.00	1.90
1198	A210	25z White-fronted duck	5.25	3.25
		Nos. 1195-1198 (4)	11.00	6.85

For surcharges see Nos. 1421-1424.

Natl.
Independence,
25th
Anniv. — A211

1985, Oct. 23   Photo.   Perf. 12
Granite Paper
1200	A211	5z multi	.25	.25
1201	A211	10z multi	.45	.45
1202	A211	15z multi	.70	.70
1203	A211	20z multi	1.10	1.10
		Nos. 1200-1203 (4)	2.50	2.50

Souvenir Sheet
Perf. 11½
1204	A211	50z multi	2.25	2.25

UN,
40th
Anniv.
A212

1985, Nov. 26
1205	A212	10z Flags, vert.	.50	.50
1206	A212	50z Emblem, UN building	2.50	2.50

Nos. 1087-1088,
1085-1086, 1089-
1090 Surcharged

1985, Dec. 2   Perf. 11½
Granite Paper
1207	A195	3z on 3z multi	.55	.55
1208	A195	5z on 5z multi	.75	.75
1209	A195	7z on 90k multi	1.00	1.00
1210	A195	10z on 90k multi	1.40	1.40
1211	A195	15z on 1.70z multi	2.25	2.25
1212	A195	20z on 8z multi	3.00	3.00
1213	A195	50z on 90k multi	8.00	8.00
		Nos. 1207-1213 (7)	16.95	16.95

Souvenir Sheet
1214	A195	50z on 10z multi	12.00	12.00

Intl. Youth Year.

Souvenir Sheet

Virgin and Child, by Titian — A213

Photogravure and Engraved
1985, Dec. 23   Perf. 13½
1215	A213	100z brown	7.00	7.00

Christmas 1985.

Natl. Transit Authority, 50th
Anniv. — A214

1985, Dec. 31   Perf. 13
1216	A214	7z Kokolo mail ship	.25	.25
1217	A214	10z Steam locomotive	.40	.40
1218	A214	15z Luebo ferry	.60	.60
1219	A214	50z Stanley locomotive	2.00	2.00
		Nos. 1216-1219 (4)	3.25	3.25

Postage
Stamp,
Cent.
A215

Stamps on stamps: 7z, Belgian Congo No.
30. 15z, Belgian Congo No. B28. 20z, Belgian
Congo No. 226. 25z, Zaire No. 1059. 40z,
Zaire No. 1152. 50z, Zaire No. 883 and
Belgium No. 1094.

1986, Feb. 23   Perf. 13
1220	A215	7z multi	.50	.50
1221	A215	15z multi	1.00	1.00
1222	A215	20z multi	1.40	1.40
1223	A215	25z multi	1.60	1.60
1224	A215	40z multi	2.75	2.75
		Nos. 1220-1224 (5)	7.25	7.25

Souvenir Sheet
Perf. 11½
1225	A215	50z multi	2.50	2.50

No. 1225 contains one 50x35mm stamp.

Beatification of Sister Anuarite
Nengapeta, Aug. 15, 1985 — A216

1986, Feb. 21   Litho.   Perf. 13
1226	A216	10z Pope John Paul II	.80	.60
1227	A216	15z Sr. Anuarite	1.10	.80
1228	A216	25z Both portraits	1.60	1.25
		Nos. 1226-1228 (3)	3.50	2.65

Souvenir Sheet
Imperf

1229 A216 100z Both portraits,
triangular   5.00 5.00

Nos. 1226-1227 vert. No. 1229 contains
one quadrilateral stamp, size: 30x36x60mm.
For surcharges see Nos. 1370-1371, 1373,
1376-1377.

Congo Stamp
Cent. — A217

1986, Feb. 22   **Litho.**   **Perf. 13**
1230 A217 25z Belgian Congo
No. 3   1.25 1.25

Imperfs exist. Value $5.
See Belgium No. 1236.

Indigenous
Reptiles
A218

1987, Feb. 11   **Litho.**   **Perf. 13**
1231 A218 2z Dasypeltis scaber .25 .25
1232 A218 5z Agama agama .25 .25
1233 A218 10z Python regius .50 .50
1234 A218 15z Chamaeleo
dilepis   1.00 1.00
1235 A218 25z Dendroaspis
jamesoni   1.40 1.40
1236 A218 50z Naja nigricolis   2.50 2.50
   Nos. 1231-1236 (6)   5.90 5.90

Christmas
1987 — A219

Paintings (details) by Fra Angelico: 50z, Virgin and Child, center panel of the Triptych of Cortona, 1435. 100z, The Nativity. 120z, Virgin and Child with Angels and Four Saints, Fiesole Retable. 180z, Virgin and Child with Six Saints, Annalena Retable.

1987, Dec. 24   **Litho.**   **Perf. 13**
1237 A219 50z multi   .75 .75
1238 A219 100z multi   1.75 1.75
1239 A219 120z multi   2.25 2.25
1240 A219 180z multi   3.25 3.25
   Nos. 1237-1240 (4)   8.00 8.00

French Revolution, Bicent. — A220

Designs: 50z, Declaration of the Rights of Man and Citizen. 100z, Abstract art. 120z, Globe showing Africa, South America.

1989   **Litho.**   **Perf. 13½x14½**
1241 A220 40z multicolored   .50 .50
1242 A220 50z multicolored   .60 .60
1243 A220 100z multicolored   1.25 1.25
1244 A220 120z multicolored   1.60 1.60
   Nos. 1241-1244 (4)   3.95 3.95

REGIDESCO, 50th Anniv. — A221

1989
1245 A221 40z Administration
bldg.   .40 .40
1246 A221 50z Modern factory   .50 .50
1247 A221 75z Water works   .75 .75
1248 A221 120z Woman drawing
water   1.25 1.25
   Nos. 1245-1248 (4)   2.90 2.90

Fight Against AIDS — A222

Designs: 40z, Bowman firing arrow through SIDA. 80z, "SIDA" on Leopard. 150z, World map with AIDS symbols.

1989
1249 A222 30z multicolored   .90 .90
1250 A222 40z multcolored   1.25 1.25
1251 A222 80z multicolored   2.50 2.50
   Nos. 1249-1251 (3)   4.65 4.65

Souvenir Sheet
Perf. 14

1252 A222 150z multicolored   4.50 4.50

Tourist Attractions — A223

1990   **Litho.**   **Perf. 13½x14½**
1253 A223 40z Waterfalls of Venus   .55 .55
1254 A223 60z Rural village   .85 .85
1255 A223 100z Kivu Lake   1.40 1.40
1256 A223 120z Niyara Gongo
Volcano   1.75 1.75
   Nos. 1253-1256 (4)   4.55 4.55

Souvenir Sheet
Perf. 14½

1257 A223 300z Kisantu Botanical Gardens,
vert.   4.25 4.25

Souvenir Sheet

Christmas — A224

1990   **Litho.**   **Perf. 14**
1258 A224 500z multicolored   5.00 5.00

Various 1971-1983
Stamps Surcharged
in Gold

1990		**Perfs., Etc. as Before**		
1259	A160	20z on 20k		
		#877	.60	.60
1260	A201	40z on 2k		
		#1121	.60	.60
1261	A201	40z on 4k		
		#1122	.60	.60
1262	A184	40z on 10k		
		#1005	.60	.60
1263	A196	40z on 25k		
		#1091	.60	.60
1264	A201	40z on 25k		
		#1123	.60	.60
1265	A184	40z on 50k		
		#1007	.60	.60
1266	A196	40z on 50k		
		#1092	.60	.60
1267	A200	40z on 50k		
		#1115	.60	.60
1268	A193	40z on 75k		
		#1071	.60	.60
1269	A184	40z on 80k		
		#1008	.60	.60
1270	A190	40z on 90k		
		#1045	.60	.60
1271	A193	40z on 90k		
		#1072	.60	.60
1272	A196	40z on 90k		
		#1093	.60	.60
1273	A201	80z on 2k		
		#1121	1.50	1.50
1274	A201	80z on 4k		
		#1122	1.50	1.50
1275	A184	80z on 10k		
		#1005	1.50	1.50
1276	A196	80z on 25k		
		#1091	1.50	1.50
1277	A201	80z on 25k		
		#1123	1.50	1.50
1278	A196	80z on 50k		
		#1092	1.50	1.50
1279	A200	80z on 50k		
		#1115	1.50	1.50
1280	A193	80z on 75k		
		#1071	1.50	1.50
1281	A184	80z on 80k		
		#1008	1.50	1.50
1282	A190	80z on 90k		
		#1045	1.50	1.50
1283	A193	80z on 90k		
		#1072	1.50	1.50
1284	A196	80z on 90k		
		#1093	1.50	1.50
1285	A175	100z on 40s		
		#953	2.10	2.10
1287	A186	100z on 2k		
		#1019	2.10	2.10
1288	A187	100z on 2k		
		#1028	2.10	2.10
1289	A192	100z on 2k		
		#1058	2.10	2.10
1290	A175	100z on 4k #955	2.10	2.10
1291	A165	100z on 5k #896	2.10	2.10
1292	A185	100z on 5k		
		#1013	2.10	2.10
1293	A187	100z on 5k		
		#1029	2.10	2.10
1294	A159	100z on 8k #865	2.10	2.10
1295	A165	100z on 8k #897	2.10	2.10
1296	A167	100z on 8k #912	2.10	2.10
1298	A167	100z on 10k		
		#913	2.10	2.10
1299	A169	100z on 10k		
		#922	2.10	2.10
1300	A165	100z on 10k		
		#993	2.10	2.10
1301	A183	100z on 10k		
		#1000	2.10	2.10
1302	A185	100z on 10k		
		#1014	2.10	2.10
1303	A186	100z on 10k		
		#1020	2.10	2.10
1304	A175	100z on 15k		
		#956	2.10	2.10
1305	A187	100z on 18k		
		#1031	2.10	2.10
1306	A169	100z on 20k		
		#923	2.10	2.10
1307	A180	100z on 20k		
		#977	2.10	2.10
1308	A144	100z on 22k		
		#755	2.10	2.10
1309	A186	100z on 25k		
		#1021	2.10	2.10
1311	A159	100z on 48k		
		#869	2.10	2.10
1312	A167	100z on 48k		
		#916	2.10	2.10
1313	A179	100z on 50k		
		#971	2.10	2.10
1314	A187	100z on 50k		
		#1032	2.10	2.10
1315	A192	100z on 50k		
		#1061	2.10	2.10
1316	A165	100z on 75k		
		#995	2.10	2.10
1317	A183	100z on 75k		
		#1001	2.10	2.10
1318	A183	100z on 80k		
		#1002	2.10	2.10
1319	A199	100z on 80k		
		#1111	2.10	2.10
1320	A170	100z on 90k		
		#930	2.10	2.10
1321	A186	100z on 90k		
		#1022	2.10	2.10
1322	A192	100z on 90k		
		#1062	2.10	2.10
1324	A198	300z on 2k		
		#1102	6.50	6.50
1325	A173	300z on 8k #938	6.50	6.50
1326	A182	300z on 10k		
		#986	6.50	6.50
1327	A143	300z on 14k		
		#751	6.50	6.50
1328	A146	300z on 17k		
		#769	6.50	6.50
1329	A174	300z on 20k		
		#947	6.50	6.50
1330	A198	300z on 45k		
		#1103	6.50	6.50
1331	A182	300z on 75k		
		#987	6.50	6.50
1332	A198	300z on 75k		
		#1104	6.50	6.50
1333	A162	500z on 8k #886	11.50	11.50
1334	A162	500z on 10k		
		#887	11.50	11.50
1335	A162	500z on 25k		
		#888	11.50	11.50
1336	A162	500z on 48k		
		#889	11.50	11.50
		Nos. 1259-1336 (74)	204.40	204.40

Size and location of surcharge varies. Some surcharges show "z" before numeral.
100z on #1060 was surcharged in error.
Numbers have been reserved for additional values in this set.

Various 1980-1983 Stamps
Surcharged

1991		**Perfs., Etc., as Before**		
1342	A181	1000z on 1z		
		#982a-982d	2.00	2.00
1343	A185	1000z on 100k		
		#1016	.35	.35
1344	A192	1000z on 1z		
		#1063	.35	.35
1345	A182	2000z on 100k		
		#988	.70	.70
1346	A198	2000z on 1z		
		#1105	.70	.70
1347	A193	2500z on 1z		
		#1073	1.40	1.40
1348	A191	3000z on 1z		
		#1057	2.00	2.00
1349	A200	4000z on 1z		
		#1116	2.75	2.75
1350	A200	5000z on 1z		
		#1116	4.00	4.00
1351	A193	10,000z on 1z		
		#1073	5.25	5.25
1352	A191	15,000z on 1z		
		#1057	8.00	8.00
		Nos. 1342-1352 (11)	27.50	27.50

Size and location of surcharge varies.

The editors have received from a collector mint stamps bearing the surcharges shown below. There is conflicting data as to the validity of these surcharges, and anyone with information on them is asked to contact the new issues editor.

12 - 6 - 92
6° ANNIVERSAIRE DE
OFFICE NATIONAL
DU TOUR.SME

1.000 000 Z

12 - 3 - 92
INAUGURATION
STATION POMPAGE

600.000 Z.

Du 8 au 15 - 6 - 92
2° Conférence Addis - Abeba
Virus VIH 1 - et VIH 2
EN AFRIQUE

10.000.000 Z

5.000.000 Z

Conférence
Nationale
Souveraine
3 mars - 4 decembre
1991 - 1992

15.000.000 Z.

Conférence
Nationale
Souveraine
3 mars - 4
décembre
1991 - 1992

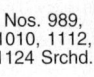

Nos. 989,
1010, 1112,
1124 Srchd.

1992, Aug. 18   Perfs., Etc. as Before
1354 A184 50th z on 125k
              #1010   .30   .30
1355 A201 100th z on 1.20z
              #1124   .70   .70
1356 A199 150th z on 1.20z
              #1112   1.25   1.25
1357 A182 200th z on 145k
              #989   1.75   1.75
1358 A199 250th z on 1.20z
              #1112   2.25   2.25
1359 A201 300th z on 1.20z
              #1124   2.75   2.75
1360 A199 500th z on 1.20z
              #1112   4.50   4.50
    Nos. 1354-1360 (7)   13.50 13.50

Size and location of surcharge varies. Numbers have been reserved for additional values
in this set.

#1361-1366

#1368-1374

1993, Oct. 29   Photo.   Perf. 13½x13
1361 A167 500th z on 30s
              #910   .70   .70
1362 A167 500th z on 5k
              #911   .70   .70
1365 A167 750th z on 8k
              #912   1.00   1.00
1366 A167 750th z on 10k
              #913   1.00   1.00
1368 A167 1 mil z on 30k
              #914   1.40   1.40
1369 A167 1 mil z on 40k
              #915   1.40   1.40

1370 A167 5 mil z on 48k
              #916   7.00   7.00
1371 A167 10 mil z on 100k
              #917   14.00 14.00
    Nos. 1361-1371 (8)   27.20 27.20

Nos. 1226-
1229 Srchd. in
Black or Red

1993, Oct. 29   Litho.   Perf. 13
1373 A216 3 mil z on 10z
              #1226   2.75   2.75
1374 A216 3 mil z on 10z
              #1226 (R)
1375 A216 5 mil z on 15z
              #1227   4.50   4.50
1376 A216 10 mil z on 25z
              #1228   8.75   8.75

Souvenir Sheet
1377 A216 10 mil z on 100z
              #1229   12.00 12.00
Size and location of surcharge varies.

Natl.
Game
Parks,
50th
Anniv.
A225

1993   Litho.   Perf. 13
1403 A225 30k Cape eland   .25   .25
1404 A225 50k Elephants   .25   .25
1405 A225 1.50z Giant eland 1.00   1.00
1406 A225 3.50z White rhinoc-
              eros   2.50   2.50
1407 A225 5z Bongo   3.50   3.50
    Nos. 1403-1407 (5)   7.50   7.50

For surcharge see No. 1431.

Nos. 986-900 Surcharged

1994, Apr. 23   Photo.   Perf. 14
1408 A182 30k on 10k   .45   .45
1409 A182 50k on 75k   1.10   1.10
1410 A182 1.50z on 100k   3.00   3.00
1411 A182 3.50z on 145k   6.00   6.00
1412 A182 5z on 270k   9.50   9.50
    Nos. 1408-1412 (5)   20.05 20.05

Nos. 1160-1167 Surcharged

1994, Apr. 23   Litho.   Perf. 14
1413 A207 30k on 10k   .40   .40
1414 A207 50k on 15k   .55   .55
1415 A207 1.50z on 3z   1.60   1.60
1416 A207 2.50z on 5z   2.50   2.50
1417 A207 3.50z on 10z   3.75   3.75
1418 A207 5z on 15z   5.25   5.25
1419 A207 7.50z on 37.50z   8.50   8.50
1420 A207 10z on 80z   10.50 10.50
    Nos. 1413-1420 (8)   33.05 33.05

Nos. 1195-1198 Surcharged

1994, Apr. 23   Litho.   Perf. 13
1421 A210 50k on 5z   1.50   1.50
1422 A210 1.50z on 10z   4.25   4.25
1423 A210 3.50z on 15z   8.00   8.00
1424 A210 5z on 25z   16.00 16.00
    Nos. 1421-1424 (4)   29.75 29.75

Nos. 990, 1079, 1094, 1097, 1113,
1125-1126, 1133, 1155, & 1404
Surcharged in Gold

1994, Aug. 31   Perfs., Etc. as Before
1425 A196 20z on 3z #1097   .25   .25
1426 A182 40z on 270k #990   .25   .25
1427 A203 50z on 3z #1133   .40   .40
1428 A206 75z on 3z #1155   .40   .40
1429 A201 100z on 2.05z
              #1125   .55   .55
1430 A194 150z on 1.70z
              #1079   .95   .95
1431 A225 200z on 50k #1404 1.25   1.25
1432 A196 250z on 1.50z
              #1094   1.50   1.50
1433 A199 300z on 3.60z
              #1113   1.75   1.75
1434 A201 500z on 3.60z
              #1126   2.75   2.75
    Nos. 1425-1434 (10)   10.05 10.05

Size and location of surcharge varies.

Nos. 1067, 1094, 1113, 1125-1126
Surcharged in Gold

No.
1435

No. 1437

1996   Perfs., Etc. as Before
1435 A192 100z on 3.50z
              #1067   .25   .25
1436 A199 500z on 3.60z
              #1113   .25   .25
1437 A201 1000z on 2.05z
              #1125   .25   .25
1438 A196 2500z on 1.50z
              #1094   1.10   1.10
1439 A201 5000z on 3.60z
              #1126   2.40   2.40
1440 A196 6000z on 1.50z
              #1094   3.25   3.25
1441 A199 15,000z on 3.60z
              #1113   7.50   7.50
1442 A201 25,000z on 3.60z
              #1126   13.00 13.00
    Nos. 1435-1442 (8)   28.00 28.00

1996
Summer
Olympic
Games,
Atlanta
A226

1996, July 29   Litho.   Perf. 11½
1444 A226 1000z Equestrian   .25   .25
1445 A226 12,500z Boxing   1.00   1.00
1446 A226 25,000z Table ten-
              nis   3.00   3.00
1447 A226 35,000z Basketball,
              vert.   4.00   4.00
1448 A226 50,000z Tennis   4.75   4.75
    Nos. 1444-1448 (5)   13.00 13.00

Insects &
Spiders
A227

No. 1449: a, Lasius niger. b, Caloptery-
gides. c, Peucetia. d, Sphecides.

1996   Litho.   Perf. 13½
1449 A227 15,000z Sheet of 4,
              #a.-d.   12.00 12.00

Minerals
A228

No. 1450: a, Uraninite. b, Malachite. c,
Ruby. d, Diamond.
No. 1452, Uranotile, cuprosklodowskite,
horiz.

1996
1450 A228 40,000z Sheet of
              4, #a.-d.   25.00 25.00

Souvenir Sheet
1452 A228 105,000z multi   11.00 11.00
A number has been reserved for an additional sheet with this set.

Raptors
A229

No. 1453: a, Congo eagle. b, Crowned
eagle. c, Melierax metabates. d, Urotriorchis
macrourus.

1996
1453 A229 50,000z Sheet of 4,
              #a.-d.   20.00 20.00

Butterflies
A230

No. 1454: a, Cymothoe sangaris. b, Colotis
zoe. c, Physcaeneura leda. d, Charaxes
candiope.

1996

Sheet of 4
1454 A230 70,000z #a.-d.   27.50 27.50

The validity of Nos. 1455-1481 and other stamps from the same time period has been questioned. The editors are attempting to find out more about these stamps.

1998 World Cup Soccer Championships, France — A231

Numbers on players: No. 1455, #12. No. 1456, none. No. 1457, #7. No. 1458, #3. No. 1459: a, British player. b, Brazilian player.
No. 1460: a-d, Like #1455-1458, but with part of World Cup Trophy behind each player.

1996
1455-1458 A231 35,000z Set
of 4 14.00 14.00
Souvenir Sheets
1459 A231 10,500z Sheet of 2,
#a.-b. 1.25 1.25
1460 A231 35,000z Sheet of 4,
#a.-d. 14.00 14.00

No. 1459 contains 2 42x39mm stamps.
See Nos. 1467-1476.

World Wildlife Fund — A231a

No. 1466 — Pan paniscus: a, With young. b, Two in trees. c, Holding vines. d, Head.

1997
1466 A231a 20,000z Block of
4, #a.-d. 18.00 18.00

1998 World Cup Soccer Championships Type of 1996

African soccer players: No. 1467, 20,000z, Soccer ball at his right. No. 1468, 20,000z, Ball at head. No. 1469, 20,000z, Yellow uniform. No. 1470, 20,000z, Ball on knee.
German soccer players, soccer ball on stamp at: No. 1471, 50,000z, UR. No. 1472, 50,000z, LL. No. 1473, 50,000z, LR. No. 1474, 50,000z, UL.
Nos. 1475a-1475d, 1476a-1476d are like Nos. 1467-1474 but with part of World Cup Trophy behind each player.

1996 **Litho.** **Perf. 13½**
1467-1470 A231 Set of 4 9.00 9.00
1471-1474 A231 Set of 4 20.00 20.00
Souvenir Sheets
1475 A231 20,000z Sheet of 4,
#a.-d. 9.00 9.00
1476 A231 50,000z Sheet of 4,
#a.-d. 20.00 20.00

Boy Scouts and Lions Intl. Clubs A232

No. 1477 — Diceros bicornis: a, Walking forward. b, Walking left, left leg up. c, Facing left. d, Holding head up.
No. 1478 — Panthera leo: a, Cubs. b, Adult male. c, Adult male facing forward, mouth open. d, Adult female on fallen tree.
No. 1479 — Loxodonta africana: a, Walking right, trunk in air. b, Reaching up to tree limb with trunk. c, Walking right, trunk down. d, Mother with calf.
105,000z, Hippopotamus amphibus.

1997 **Litho.** **Perf. 13x13½**
1477 A232 40,000z Sheet of
4, #a.-d. 9.50 9.50
1478 A232 50,000z Sheet of
4, #a.-d. 11.75 11.75
1479 A232 70,000z Sheet of
4, #a.-d. 19.00 19.00
Souvenir Sheet
1480 A232 105,000z multi 6.25 6.25
Boy Scouts (#1477, 1479-1480). Lions Intl. Clubs (#1478).

Jacqueline Kennedy Onassis (1929-94) A233

Various portraits.

1997 **Litho.** **Perf. 13½**
1481 A233 15,000z Sheet of 9,
#a.-i. 17.50 17.50
No. 1481 also exists imperf.

Stamps from this country are now being released under the previous name, "Republique Democratique du Congo," or Congo Democratic Republic, despite the resumption of civil war. We will continue to list these stamps under the country's name of Zaire until the situation is resolved.

Diana, Princess of Wales (1961-97) — A234

Mother Teresa (1910-97) — A235

No. 1482: a, Wearing tiara. b, In white jacket. c, In white hat. d, In polka dotted dress. e, Scarf around neck. f, Low cut evening dress.
No. 1483: a, Wearing tiara. b, Hand under chin. c, Leaning chin on both hands. d, One-shoulder-covered outfit.
No. 1484: a, Red & black dress. b, White jacket, pearls. c, Profile view. d, Wearing tiara.
No. 1485, 400,000z, In black evening dress.
No. 1486, 400,000z, Holding flowers.

1998, Aug. 6 **Litho.** **Perf. 14**
1482 A234 50,000z Sheet of
6, #a.-f. 13.50 7.75
1483 A234 100,000z Sheet of
4, #a.-d. 17.50 10.50
1484 A234 125,000z Sheet of
4, #a.-d. 24.00 14.50
Souvenir Sheets
1485-1486 A234 Set of 2 50.00 25.00

1998, Aug. 6
1487 A235 50,000z shown 2.25 1.50
Souvenir Sheet
1488 A235 325,000z Portrait,
diff. 11.50 7.50
No. 1487 was issued in sheets of 6.

---

100 Centimes = 1 Franc (1998)

Native Dwelling — A236

Arms — A237

Inauguration of Pres. Laurent Kabila — A238

Designs: 1.25fr, Troops and civilians in Kinshasa. 3fr, Flag, crowd, Pres. Kabila breaking chain with sword, horiz.
2.50fr, Gun, arrow, handshake, tractor. 3.50fr, Pres. Kabila.

1999, May 12 **Litho.** **Perf. 14**
1489 A236 25c multi .25 .25
1490 A237 50c multi .55 .55
1491 A238 75c multi .80 .80
1492 A238 1.25fr multi 1.40 1.40
1493 A238 3fr multi 3.25 3.25
Nos. 1489-1493 (5) 6.25 6.25
Souvenir Sheets
1494 A238 2.50fr multi 2.60 2.60
1495 A238 3.50fr multi 3.75 3.75
Conquest of Kinshasa by troops of Laurent Kabila, 2nd anniv.

Chinese Zodiac Animals — A239

No. 1496: a, Rat. b, Ox. c, Tiger. d, Rabbit. e, Dragon. f, Snake. g, Horse. h, Ram. i, Monkey. j, Cock. k, Dog. l, Boar.

1999, Aug. 20 **Perf. 13¼x13½**
1496 A239 78c Sheet of 12,
#a-l 27.50 27.50

A240

A241

A242

A243

Outlaws of the Marsh — A244

No. 1497 — Sheet with text starting with "The historical novel. . .": a, 1.45fr, Men fighting. b, 1.50fr, Man uprooting tree. c, 1.60fr, Man with sword in snowstorm. d, 1.70fr, Man with sword, other men at bridge. e, 1.80fr, Three men at table.
No. 1498 — Sheet with text starting with "The main theme. . .": a, 1.45fr, Men and baskets. b, 1.50fr, Man threatening another man with sword. c, 1.60fr, Man attacking tiger. d, 1.70fr, People watching men in martial arts battle. e, 1.80fr, Battling horsemen.
No. 1499 — Sheet with text starting with "The common people. . .": a, 1.45fr, Men fighting in boat. b, 1.50fr, Man with sword fighting man with hatchets. c, 1.60fr, Men near fortified wall. d, 1.70fr, Men fighting on cobblestone street. e, 1.80fr, Archer on horseback at doorway.
No. 1500 — Sheet with text starting with "Today, it is thought. . .": a, 1.45fr, Man seated and other man standing near table. b, 1.50fr, Man setting fire to building. c, 1.60fr, Man in room. d, 1.70fr, Man lifting another man in a battle. e, 1.80fr, Man holding torn scroll.

1999, Aug. 20 **Perf. 13¼**
Sheets of 5, #a-e
1497-1500 A240 Set of 4 55.00 55.00
Souvenir Sheets
Perf. 13¼x13½
1501 A241 10fr multi 17.50 17.50
1502 A242 10fr multi 17.50 17.50
1503 A243 10fr multi 17.50 17.50
1504 A244 10fr multi 17.50 17.50

A245

A246

African Flora and Fauna — A247

Designs: 1fr, Telophorus quadricolor. 1.50fr, Panthera pardus. No. 1507, 2fr, Colotis protomedia. No. 1508, 2fr, Kobus vardoni. No. 1509, 3fr, Canarina abyssinica. No. 1510, 3fr, Smutsia temminckii.

7.80fr, Lion.

No. 1512: a, Okapi. b, Bird, rainbow, waterfalls. c, Giraffe, rainbow, waterfalls. d, Giraffe, waterfall mist. e, Mandrill. f, Chimpanzee. g, Leopard. h, Butterflies. i, Hippopotamus. j, Bird in water. k, Flowers. l, Antelope.

No. 1513: a, Sun. b, Pieris citrina. c, Merops apiaster. d, Lanius collurio. e, Ploceus cucullatus. f, Charaxes pelias. g, Charaxes eupale. h, Giraffa camelopardalis. i, Galago moholi. j, Strelitzia reginae. k, Gazella thomsoni. l, Upupa epops.

No. 1514, 10fr, Taurotragus oryx. No. 1515, 10fr, Hippopotamus amphibius.

No. 1516, 10fr, Warthog.

Perf. 14, 14¼x14¾ (#1511), 14¼x14 (#1516)

2000, Feb. 28
1505-1510	A245	Set of 6	13.50	13.50
1511	A246	7.80fr multi	7.00	7.00
1512	A247	1fr Sheet of 12, #a-l	12.50	12.50
1513	A245	1.50fr Sheet of 12, #a-l	20.00	20.00

Souvenir Sheets
1514-1515	A245	Set of 2	20.00	20.00
1516	A247	10fr multi	10.00	10.00

No. 1516 contains one 42x57mm.

Wild Felines and Canines — A248

No. 1517, 1.50fr: a, Felis bengalensis. b, Felis aurata. c, Felis caracal. d, Felis conocolor. e, Felis nigripes. f, Panthera leo. g, Neofelis nebulosa. h, Felis wiedii. i, Acinonyx jubatus. j, Felis pardina. k, Felis yagouaroundi. l, Felis serval.

No. 1518, 2fr: a, Canis mesomelas. b, Otocyon megalotis. c, Speothos venaticus. d, Canis latrans. e, Cuon alpinus. f, Fennecus zerda. g, Urocyon cinereoargenteus. h, Canis lupus. i, Vulpes macrotis. j, Chrysocyon brachyurus. k, Nyctereutes procyonoides. l, Vulpes vulpes.

No. 1519, 10fr, Panthera pardus. No. 1520, 10fr, Alopex lagopus.

2000, Feb. 28 **Perf. 14**
Sheets of 12, #a-l
1517-1518	A248	Set of 2	40.00	40.00

Souvenir Sheets
1519-1520	A248	Set of 2	17.00	17.00

Millennium
A249

2000, June 10
1521		Horiz. strip of 3	16.00	16.00
a.		A249 4.50fr multi	2.25	2.25
b.		A249 9fr multi	4.50	4.50
c.		A249 15fr multi	8.00	8.00

Printed in sheets containing two strips.

A250　　　A251

Birds
A252

Designs: No. 1522, 3fr, Alopochen aegyptiacus. No. 1523, 3fr, Ardeola ibis. No. 1524, 4.50fr, Oena capensis. No. 1525, 4.50fr, Lybius torquatus. No. 1526, 9fr, Falco tinnunculus. No. 1527, 9fr, Corythaelo cristata.

No. 1528, 4.50fr, Psephotus chrysopterygius chrysopterygius. 8fr, Amazona aestiva. No. 1530, 8.50fr, Are nobilis cumanensis. No. 1531, 9fr, Agapornis roseicollis.

No. 1532, 8.50fr, Lophornis ornata. No. 1533, 9fr, Polytrus guauvunibi.

No. 1534, 9fr: a, Euplectes orix. b, Euplectes ardens. c, Oriolus auratus. d, Plocens cucullatus. e, Amandava subflava. f, Nectarina senegalensis.

No. 1535, 9fr: a, Halcyon malimbicus. b, Tachymarptis melba. c, Haliaeetus vocifer. d, Ardea purpurea. e, Balaeniceps rex. f, Balearica regulorum.

No. 1536: a, Ertoxeres aquila. b, Aglaiolepus kinde. c, Archilochus calobris. d, Trochlus polytaus. e, Chaliostigna herrani. f, Ensifera. g, Chrysolampus mosquitus. h, Phorethornus syrmatophorus. i, Calypre hetervare.

No. 1537, 5fr: a, Eos squamata squamata. b, Aratinga guarouba. c, Aratinga aurea. d, Psuedeos fuscata. e, Agapornis fischeri. f, Aratinga nana nana. g, Aratinga mitrata. h, Trichoglossus haematodus rubitorquis. i, Cacatua galerita galerita.

No. 1538, 5fr: a, Ara macao. b, Neophema elegans. c, Loriculus vernalis. d, Aratinga solstitialis. e, Pionites melancephala. f, Bolborhynchus lineola. g, Ara severa. h, Psephotus chrysopterygius dissimilis. i, Ara militaris.

No. 1539, 15fr, Actophilornis africanus, horiz. No. 1540, 20fr, Ceryle rudis, horiz.

No. 1541, 15fr, Opopsitta diophthalma. No. 1542, 15fr, Ara ararrauna, horiz.

No. 1543, 15fr, Coeligena torgoata. No. 1544, 20fr, Campylopterus hemileicurus.

2000, Aug. 16 **Perf. 14**
1522-1527	A250	Set of 6	15.00	15.00
1528-1531	A251	Set of 4	13.50	13.50
1532-1533	A252	Set of 2	7.75	7.75

Sheets of 6, #a-f
1534-1535	A250	Set of 2	47.50	47.50
1536	A252	4.50fr Sheet of 9, #a-i	18.00	18.00

Sheets of 9, #a-l
1537-1538	A251	Set of 2	40.00	40.00

Souvenir Sheets
1539-1540	A250	Set of 2	16.00	16.00
1541-1542	A251	Set of 2	13.50	13.50
1543-1544	A252	Set of 2	16.00	16.00

Surcharges on
Unissued
Stamps
A253

Designs: 10fr on 70,000z, Colotis zoe. 15fr on 25,000z, Bulbophyllum falcatum. 25fr on 20,000z, Scutellosaurus. 35fr on 15,000z, Sphecides. 45fr on 100,000z, Diamond. 50fr on 35,000z, Termitomyces aurantiacus. 70fr on 50,000z, Melierax metabates. 100fr on 40,000z, Malachite. 150fr on 25,000z, Panda.

2000 **Litho.** **Perf. 13¼**
1545	A253	10fr on 70,000z multi	7.25	7.25
1546	A253	15fr on 25,000z multi	7.25	7.25
1547	A253	25fr on 20,000z multi	7.25	7.25
1548	A253	35fr on 15,000z multi	7.25	7.25
1549	A253	45fr on 100,000z multi	7.25	7.25
1550	A253	50fr on 35,000z multi	7.25	7.25
1551	A253	70fr on 50,000z multi	7.25	7.25
1552	A253	100fr on 40,000z multi	7.25	7.25
1553	A253	150fr on 25,000z multi	7.25	7.25

Location of surcharges varies. All surcharged stamps have white margins.

A254

Trains — A255

Designs: 1fr, Missouri-Kansas-Texas Line locomotive. 2fr, Spremberg steam locomotive. No. 1556, 3fr, King Class, Great Western Railway. No. 1557, 3fr, Crocodile locomotive. 5fr, Inner-city trains, Great Britain. 6fr, Big Boy, Union Pacific.

No. 1560, 4.50fr: a, Class SU, 2-6-2, Russia. b, Prussian locomotive. c, Zimbabwe locomotive. d, Hunslet 2-8-2, Peru. e, London, Midland & Scottish Railway locomotive. f, London Northeastern Railway locomotive.

No. 1561, 8fr: a, Denver & Rio Grande Western Railroad locomotive. b, Mikado 2-8-2, Louisville & Nashville. c, Mogul, Rio Grande. d, New York Central Railway locomotive. e, Sumpter Valley Railway steam locomotive. f, Three-truck Shay No. 7.

No. 1562, 9.50fr: a, Compagnie du Nord locomotive, France. b, Union Pacific locomotive. c, Great Northern Railway locomotive. d, Liverpool & Manchester Railway locomotive. e, Patentee 2-2-2, London & Birmingham. f, Puffing Billy.

No. 1563, 10fr: a, Chicago, Rock Island & Pacific Railway locomotive. b, Powhattan Arrow, Norfolk & Western. c, Class S-1, New York Central Hudson River Railway. d, Reading Railroad locomotive. e, Great Bear, Great Western Railway. f, Bi-polar, Chicago, Milwaukee, St. Paul & Pacific Railway.

No. 1564, 5fr: a, Beyer-Garratt 50 4-8-2+2-8-4 locomotive. b, Locomotive Express 4-0-2. c, 780CV electric locomotive. d, Electric locomotive on curve. e, Class 2-10-0 Locomotive 56001. f, Electric locomotive on straight track. g, Class 2-8-4 Locomotive 284. h, Class G 6/6 electric locomotive.

No. 1565, 8.50fr: a, Class B-B electric locomotive AE4/4. b, Class EX, Paris-Lyon-Mediterranean. c, Big Boy. d, Tourist car. e, Class 4-8-4 GS-4. f, Class 46 electric locomotive. g, Class-4-6-0 County. h, Class DA Diesel-electric locomotive.

No. 1566, 15fr, New York Central & Hudson River Railway locomotive. No. 1567, 20fr, Mohawk & Hudson Railroad locomotive. No. 1568, 20fr, Broadway Limited, Pennsylvania Railroad. No. 1569, 20fr, Trans-Europe Express.

No. 1570, 20fr, Deltic electric locomotive, Great Britain. No. 1571, 20fr, Diesel-electric locomotive, Canada Pacific.

2001, Jan. 15 **Litho.** **Perf. 14**
1554-1559	A254	Set of 6	11.50	11.50

Sheets of 6, #a-f
1560-1563	A254	Set of 4	65.00	65.00

Sheets of 8, #a-h
1564-1565	A255	Set of 2	45.00	45.00

Souvenir Sheets
1566-1569	A254	Set of 4	32.50	32.50
1570-1571	A255	Set of 2	14.00	14.00

Ships
A256

Designs: 2.50fr, Clipper. 5fr, Arab bum. 20fr, Flemish galley. 21.70fr, Trabaccolo, vert. 30fr, Dutch galliot. 45.80fr, Japanese coaster.

No. 1578, 10fr: a, Trireme. b, Roman caudicaria. c, 13th cent. warship. d, Byzantine galley. e, Lateneer. f, 14th century cog. g, Arab dhow. h, Hanseatic cog. i, Portuguese galley.

No. 1579, 10fr: a, Egyptian sailing ship. b, Egyptian rowing craft. c, Egyptian seagoing ship. d, Greek galley. e, Etruscan merchantman f, Etruscan fishing skiff. g, Greek merchantman. h, Minoan passenger ship. i, Roman harbor boat.

No. 1580, 10fr: a, Flemish galleon. b, English galleon. c, Carrack. d, Chinese war galley. e, Venetian galley. f, Polacre. g, Hemmena. h, Venetian bragozzo. i, Schooner.

No. 1581, 25fr, Viking drakkar. No. 1582, 25fr, Portuguese caravel. vert. No. 1583, 25fr, HMS Endeavour, vert.

2001, June 22 **Perf. 14**
1572-1577	A256	Set of 6	14.00	14.00

Sheets of 9, #a-i
1578-1580	A256	Set of 3	30.00	30.00

Souvenir Sheets
Perf. 13¾
1581-1583	A256	Set of 3	16.00	16.00

No. 1581 contains one 50x38mm stamp; Nos. 1582-1583 each contain one 38x50mm stamp.

History of Aviation — A257

No. 1584: a, Montgolfier balloon (36x61mm). b, Boxkite and Tiger Moth airplanes (36x61mm). c, Gladiator. d, Eurofighter. e, Mosquito. f, Chipmunk.

No. 1585: a, Blackburn and Spartan Arrow airplanes (36x61mm). b, Tiger Moth. c, Lightning. d, Vulcan B2. e, Tornado.

No. 1586, 25fr, Fox Moth and Avro 540K airplanes. No. 1587, 25fr, Avro 504K and Fox Moth airplanes.

2001, June 22 **Perf. 14¼**
1584	A257	10fr Sheet of 6, #a-f	10.00	10.00
1585	A257	10fr Sheet of 6, #1584a, 1585a-1585e	10.00	10.00

Souvenir Sheets
Perf. 14¼x14½
1586-1587	A257	Set of 2	12.00	12.00

First Zeppelin Flight, Cent. — A258

No. 1588: a, LZ-6. b, LZ-7. c, US Navy airship Akron. c, Lindstrand HS-110 Pittsburgh Tribune-Review airship.
No. 1589, 100fr, LZ-130 Graf Zeppelin II. No. 1590, 100fr, LZ-1.

2001, June 22   **Perf. 14**
1588 A258 60fr Sheet of 4, #a-d   27.50 27.50
Souvenir Sheets
1589-1590 A258 Set of 2   22.50 22.50

Butterflies — A259

Designs: 5fr, Striped policeman. 21.70fr, Brown-veined white. 45fr, Common dotted border. 45.80fr, Cabbage. 50fr, African migrant. 51.80fr, Mocker swallowtail.
No. 1597, 6fr, horiz.: a, Common grass blue. b, Golden tiger. c, Palla. d, Blue diadem. e, African giant swallowtail. f, African leaf. g, Gold-banded forester. h, Small harvester.
No. 1598, 6fr, horiz.: a, Guinea fowl. b, Forest queen. c, Sweet potato acraea. d, Wanderer. e, Evening brown. f, African ringlet. g, Plain tiger. h, Monarch.
No. 1599, 8fr, horiz.: a, Broad-bordered grass yellow. b, Crimson tip. c, Orange-banded protea. d, Azure hairstreak. e, Marshall's false monarch. f, Blue swallowtail. g, Figtree blue. h, Grass jewel.
No. 1600, 25fr, Long-tailed blue, horiz. No. 1601, 25fr, Chief, horiz. No. 1602, 25fr, Large spotted acraea, horiz.

2001, June 22
1591-1596 A259 Set of 6   25.00 25.00
Sheets of 8, #a-h
1597-1599 A259 Set of 3   37.50 37.50
Souvenir Sheets
1600-1602 A259 Set of 3   16.00 16.00

Flowers and Insects — A260

Designs; 20fr, Aconite, Brazilian frog-hopper. 21.70fr, Larkspur, Mexican cicada. 25fr, Blue orchid, dragonfly. 45.80fr, Spotted blossom orchid, buck moth.
No. 1607, 10fr, horiz.: a, Rein orchids, tiger moth. b, Ivy, Siamese wasp. c, Pink lady's slipper, goat weed emperor. d, Gletscherpetersbart, velvet ant. e, Licorice, viceroy butterfly. f, Grass pink, aphid. g, Ranunculus, spider wasp. h, Clamshell orchid, tropical bee. i, Bog orchids, mayfly.
No. 1608, 10fr, horiz.: a, Common lantana, red-spotted purple butterfly. b, Deep purple lilac, zebra swallowtail. c, Mt. Fujiyama, ruddy copper butterfly. d, Pinafore pink, red admiral butterfly. e, Argemone mexicana, purple hairstreak butterfly. f, Soapwort, sulphur butterfly. g, Lungwort, Buckeye butterfly. h, Wild thyme, pipevine swallowtail. i, Loeselia mexicana, banded purple butterfly.
No. 1609, 10fr, horiz.: a, Cymbidium Stanley Fouraker Highlander, scarlet tiger moth. b, Cymbidium Sparkle "Ruby Lips," Sumatran carpenter bee. c, Dendrobium Sussex, ant lion. d, Cymbidium Vieux Rose Loch Lomond, nachahmend butterfly. e, Cymbidium, cicada-killer wasp. f, Dendrobium Mousmee, spechosoma wasp. g, Arachnis flos-aeris, green lacewing. h, Paphiopedilum, seven-spot ladybug. i, Eulophia quartiniana, damselfly.
No. 1610, 25fr, Jolly Jocker pansy, monarch butterfly, horiz. No. 1611, 25fr, Pink peony, wasp (inscribed erroneously like No. 1610), horiz. No. 1612, 25fr, Plumbago capensis, honey bee, horiz.

2001, June 22   **Perf. 14**
1603-1606 A260 Set of 4   13.00 13.00

Sheets of 9, #a-i
Perf. 14¼x14½
1607-1609 A260 Set of 3   30.00 30.00
Souvenir Sheets
1610-1612 A260 Set of 3   16.00 16.00
Nos. 1607-1609 each contain nine 37x30mm stamps; Nos. 1610-1612 each contain one 50x37mm stamp.

Tintin in Africa — A261

Designs: 190fr, Tintin with hand above eyes. 461fr, Tintin in car with dog and native.

2001, Dec. 31   **Photo.**   **Perf. 11½**
1613 A261 190fr multi   2.50 2.50
Souvenir Sheet
1614 A261 461fr multi   7.00 7.00
No. 1614 contains one 48x38mm stamp. Imperfs exist. Value: 1613, $15; 1614, $30. See Belgium Nos. 1875-1876.

Native Handicrafts A262

Designs: 10fr, Tabwa buffalo mask. 50fr, Kongo bedpost. 60fr, Loi drum. 150fr, Kuba royal statue, vert. 200fr, Tshokwe mask, vert. 300fr, Luba mask, vert.

2002, Mar. 7   **Litho.**   **Perf. 11½**
1615-1620 A262 Set of 6   13.00 13.00

Lions A263

Designs: 50fr, Lioness and cub. 75fr, Lion and dead animal. 150fr, Lioness and cubs at water's edge. 250fr, Lion and lioness. 300fr, Lion leaping in water.

2002, Mar. 7   **Litho.**   **Perf. 11½**
1621-1625 A263 Set of 5   13.50 13.50

Flowers — A264

Designs: 25fr, Gloriosa rothschildiana. 50fr, Aworthia cooperi. 125fr, Lithops aucampiae. 250fr, Angraecum sesquipedale. 500fr, Lampranthus coccineus.

2002   **Litho.**   **Perf. 11½**
1626-1629 A264 Set of 4   4.75 4.75
Souvenir Sheet
1630 A264 500fr multi   5.75 5.75

Minerals A265

Designs: 190fr, Beryl, vert. 340fr, Willemite mimetite. 410fr, Quartz chlorite. 445fr, Allophane copper. 455fr, Rhodochrosite, vert. 480fr, Zircon.

Perf. 11½x11¼
2002, Aug. 30   **Litho.**
1631 A265 190fr multi   2.25 2.25
1632 A265 340fr multi   4.00 4.00
1633 A265 410fr multi   5.00 5.00
1634 A265 445fr multi   5.25 5.25
1635 A265 455fr multi   5.25 5.25
1636 A265 480fr multi   5.75 5.75
An additional stamp was issued in the set. The editors would like to examine it.

Worldwide Fund for Nature (WWF) — A266

Designs: 20fr, Head of gorilla. 190fr, Adult and juvenile gorillas. 390fr, Gorilla in grass, vert. 455fr, Gorilla eating grass, vert.

2002, Aug. 30   **Litho.**   **Perf. 11¾**
1638-1641 A266 Set of 4   — —
An additional stamp was issued in this set. The editors would like to examine any example of it.

Pres. Joseph Kabila A267

Background color: 195fr, Blue green. 350fr, 800fr, Light blue. 1500fr, Gold.

2002, Dec. 10   **Litho.**   **Perf. 13¼**
1643-1644 A267 Set of 2   — —
Souvenir Sheets
1645 A267 800fr multi   — —
Litho. & Embossed With Foil Application
1646 A267 1500fr gold & multi   — —
Nos. 1645-1646 each contain one 42x50mm stamp.

OFFICIAL STAMPS

Nos. 756-772 Overprinted

1975   **Litho.**   **Perf. 14**
O1 A145 10s red org & blk   .25 .25
O2 A145 40s multi   .25 .25
O3 A145 50s multi   .25 .25
     Perf. 13
O4 A146 1k multi   .25 .25
O5 A146 2k multi   .25 .25
O6 A146 3k multi   .25 .25
O7 A146 4k multi   .30 .25
O8 A146 5k multi   .30 .25
O9 A146 6k multi   .45 .25
O10 A146 8k multi   .60 .25
O11 A146 9k multi   .60 .25
O12 A146 10k multi   .70 .25
O13 A146 14k multi   1.00 .40
O14 A146 17k multi   1.10 .45
O15 A146 20k multi   1.10 .45
O16 A146 50k multi   3.00 1.40
O17 A146 100k multi   10.00 3.50
   Nos. O1-O17 (17)   20.65 9.20
"SP" are the initials of "Service Public."

ZAMBEZIA

zam-'bē-zē-ə

LOCATION — A former district of the Mozambique Province in Portuguese East Africa
GOVT. — Part of the Portuguese East Africa Colony

The districts of Quelimane and Tete were created from Zambezia. Eventually stamps of Mozambique came into use. See Quelimane and Tete.

1000 Reis = 1 Milreis

King Carlos
A1   A2

Perf. 11½, 12½, 13½
1894   **Typo.**   **Unwmk.**
1 A1 5r yellow   .25 .25
2 A1 10r red violet   .75 .45
3 A1 15r chocolate   1.00 .65
a.   Perf. 12½   27.50 19.00
4 A1 20r lavender   1.00 .65
5 A1 25r blue green   2.00 1.25
a.   Perf. 11½
6 A1 50r lt blue   2.00 1.25
7 A1 75r carmine   4.50 3.25
a.   Perf. 11½   50.00 35.00
8 A1 80r yellow grn   5.00 2.50
9 A1 100r brown, buff   4.00 1.75
10 A1 150r car, rose   7.00 3.00
11 A1 200r dk blue, bl   8.00 3.00
a.   Perf. 11½   200.00 150.00
b.   Perf. 13½   32.50 24.00
12 A1 300r dk bl, salmon   10.00 4.50
a.   Perf. 11½   25.00 20.00
   Nos. 1-12 (12)   45.50 22.50
For surcharges and overprints see Nos. 36-47, 73-74, 77-81, 84-88.

1898-1903   **Perf. 11½**
Name and Value in Black or Red (500r)
13 A2 2½r gray   .45 .45
14 A2 5r orange   .45 .45
15 A2 10r lt green   .75 .50
16 A2 15r brown   1.25 1.00
17 A2 15r gray grn ('03)   1.60 1.40
18 A2 20r gray violet   1.25 1.00
19 A2 25r sea green   1.25 1.00
20 A2 25r carmine ('03)   1.00 .85
21 A2 50r blue   1.25 1.10
22 A2 50r brown ('03)   2.75 2.25
23 A2 65r dull bl ('03)   8.00 5.50
24 A2 75r rose   10.00 5.25
25 A2 75r lilac ('03)   3.25 2.75
26 A2 80r violet   5.00 3.00
27 A2 100r dk bl, bl   2.00 2.00
28 A2 115r org brn, pink ('03)   10.00 7.25
29 A2 130r brn, straw ('03)   10.00 7.25
30 A2 150r brn, buff   6.00 3.50
31 A2 200r red vio, pnksh   6.00 3.50
32 A2 300r dk bl, rose   8.00 3.50
33 A2 400r dull bl, straw ('03)   10.00 8.50
34 A2 500r blk, bl ('01)   12.00 6.75
35 A2 700r vio, yelsh ('01)   15.00 8.75
   Nos. 13-35 (23)   117.25 77.50
For surcharges and overprints see Nos. 49-68, 72, 82-83, 93-107.

Stamps of 1894 Surcharged

1902   **Perf. 11½, 12½**
36 A1 65r on 10r red vio   9.00 7.00
37 A1 65r on 15r choc   9.00 7.00
38 A1 65r on 20r lav   9.00 7.00
39 A1 65r on 300r bl, sal   9.00 7.00
40 A1 115r on 5r yel   9.00 7.00
41 A1 115r on 25r bl grn   9.00 7.00
42 A1 115r on 80r yel grn   9.00 7.00
43 A1 130r on 75r car   7.00 7.00
44 A1 130r on 150r car, rose   5.25 5.25
45 A1 400r on 50r lt bl   2.00 3.25
46 A1 400r on 100r brn, buff   2.00 3.50

47 A1 400r on 200r bl, *bl*   2.00   3.50

Same Surcharge on No. P1

48 N1 130r on 2½r brn   9.00   7.00
Nos. 36-48 (13)   90.25   78.50

Stamps of 1898
Overprinted

1902   Perf. 11½
49 A2 15r brown   2.00   1.40
50 A2 25r sea green   2.00   1.40
51 A2 50r blue   2.00   1.40
52 A2 75r rose   6.00   3.75
Nos. 49-52 (4)   12.00   7.95

No. 23 Surcharged in
Black

1905
53 A2 50r on 65r dull blue   5.75   4.00

Stamps of 1898-1903
Overprinted in
Carmine or Green

1911
54 A2 2½r gray   .35   .25
55 A2 5r orange   .35   .25
56 A2 10r light green   .40   .25
a. Inverted overprint   15.00   12.50
57 A2 15r gray green   .40   .25
58 A2 20r gray violet   .50   .30
59 A2 25r carmine (G)   1.50   .50
60 A2 50r brown   .40   .35
61 A2 75r lilac   1.25   .90
62 A2 100r dk bl, *bl*   1.25   .90
63 A2 115r org brn, *pink*   1.25   .90
64 A2 130r brown, *straw*   1.25   .90
65 A2 200r red vio, *pnksh*   1.25   .90
66 A2 400r dull bl, *straw*   2.10   1.10
67 A2 500r blk & red, *bl*   2.10   1.10
68 A2 700r violet, *yelsh*   2.25   1.50
Nos. 54-68 (15)   16.60   10.35

Stamps of 1902-05
Overprinted in
Carmine or Green

1914
Without Gum
72 A2 50r on 65r dl bl   4,000.   1,200.
73 A1 115r on 5r yellow   1.25   1.50
74 A1 115r on 25r bl grn   1.25   1.50
75 A1 115r on 80r yel grn   1.25   1.50
76 N1 130r on 2½r brn (G)   1.25   1.50
a. Carmine overprint   22.50   22.50
77 A1 130r on 75r car   1.75   1.50
a. Perf. 12½   5.50   7.00
78 A1 130r on 150r car,
rose   1.75   1.50
79 A1 400r on 50r lt bl   2.50   3.00
a. Perf. 12½   11.00   11.00
80 A1 400r on 100r brn, *buff*   2.50   2.50
81 A1 400r on 200r bl, *bl*   2.50   2.50

On Nos. 51-52
82 A2 50r blue   1.50   1.50
83 A2 75r rose   1.50   1.50
Nos. 73-83 (11)   19.00   20.00

Preceding Issues
Overprinted in
Carmine

1915
On Surcharged Issue of 1902
84 A1 115r on 5r yellow   .85   .45
85 A1 115r on 25r bl grn   .85   .45
86 A1 115r on 80r lt grn   .85   .45
87 A1 130r on 75r carmine   .85   .45
a. Perf. 12½   4.50   2.25
88 A1 130r on 150r car,
rose   .85   .45
92 N1 130r on 2½r (down)   .85   .45

On Nos. 51, 53
93 A2 50r blue   .85   .50
a. "Republica" inverted   15.00   15.00
94 A2 50r on 65r dull bl   3.50   4.50
Nos. 84-94 (8)   9.45   7.70

Stamps of 1898-1903
Overprinted Locally
in Carmine

1917
Without Gum
95 A2 2½r gray   1.50   3.00
96 A2 5r orange   7.00   6.50
97 A2 10r light green   7.00   6.00
98 A2 15r gray green   6.50   6.50
99 A2 20r gray violet   7.25   6.50
100 A2 25r sea green   13.50   15.00
101 A2 100r blue, *blue*   4.00   2.75
102 A2 115r org brn, *pink*   4.00   2.75
103 A2 130r brown, *straw*   4.00   2.75
104 A2 200r red vio, *pnksh*   4.00   2.75
105 A2 400r dull bl, *straw*   4.50   3.50
106 A2 500r blk & red, *bl*   5.50   3.75
107 A2 700r vio, *yelsh*   9.00   5.25
Nos. 95-107 (13)   77.75   67.00

NEWSPAPER STAMP

 N1

1894   Unwmk.   Typo.   Perf. 12½
P1 N1 2½r brown   .60   .35
For overprints and surcharges see Nos. 76, 92.

ZAMBIA

ˈzam-bē-ə

LOCATION — Southern Africa
GOVT. — Republic
AREA — 290,586 sq. mi.
POP. — 9,663,535 (1999 est.)
CAPITAL — Lusaka

The former British protectorate of Northern Rhodesia became an independent republic Oct. 24, 1964, taking the name Zambia. See Northern Rhodesia; see Rhodesia and Nyasaland.

12 Pence = 1 Shilling
20 Shillings = 1 Pound
100 Ngwee = 1 Kwacha (1968)

**Catalogue values for all unused
stamps in this country are for
Never Hinged items.**

Pres. Kenneth D.
Kaunda, Victoria
Falls — A1

College of
Further
Education,
Lusaka — A2

Perf. 14½x14, 14x14½
1964, Oct. 24   Photo.   Unwmk.
1 A1 3p shown   .25   .25
2 A1 6p shown   .30   .25
3 A1 1sh3p Barotse dancer   .50   .30
Nos. 1-3 (3)   1.05   .80
Zambia's independence, Oct. 24, 1964.

Farmer and Silo
A3

X-Ray
Technician
A4

Designs: 2p, Chinyau dancer. 3p, Woman picking cotton. 4p, Angoni bull. 6p, Communications by drum and teletype. 9p, Redwood blossoms and factory. 1sh, Night fishing on Lake Tanganyika. 1sh3p, Woman tobacco worker. 2sh, Tonga basket maker and child. 2sh6p, Elephants in Luangwa Valley Game Reserve. 5sh, Child and school. 10sh, Copper mining. £1, Makishi dancer.

1964, Oct. 24   Photo.   Perf. 14½
Size: 23x19mm, 19x23mm
4 A3 ½p emerald, blk &
red   .25   .25
5 A4 1p ultra, blk & brn   .25   .25
6 A4 2p orange, brn & red   .25   .25
7 A4 3p red & black   .25   .25
8 A3 4p orange & black   .25   .25

Perf. 13½x14½, 14½x13½
Size: 32x23mm, 23x32mm
9 A3 6p Prus grn, brn &
org   .25   .25
10 A3 9p ultra, brn & dk
car rose   .25   .25
11 A3 1sh blue, bis & blk   .25   .25
12 A4 1sh3p dk bl, ver, blk &
yel   .30   .25
13 A4 2sh org, blk, brn & ultra   .35   .25
14 A3 2sh6p org yel & blk   .85   .45
15 A3 5sh emerald, blk & yel   1.40   .65
16 A3 10sh orange & blk   4.00   4.00
17 A4 £1 red, blk, brn & yel   3.00   4.00
Nos. 4-17 (14)   11.90   11.60

ITU Emblem, Old
and New
Communication
Equipment — A5

1965, July 20   Photo.   Perf. 14
18 A5 6p brt lilac & gold   .25   .25
19 A5 2sh6p gray & gold   1.25   1.50
Cent. of the ITU.

ICY
Emblem
A6

1965, July 26   Perf. 14
20 A6 3p grnsh blue & gold   .25   .25
21 A6 1sh3p ultra & gold   .70   .65
International Cooperation Year, 1965.

Pres. Kaunda
and State
House,
Lusaka — A7

Clematopsis — A8

Designs: 6p, Fireworks over Independence Stadium. 2sh6p, Tithonia diversifolia.

Perf. 13½x14½
1965, Oct. 18   Unwmk.
22 A7 3p multicolored   .25   .25
23 A7 6p ind, yel & brt pink   .25   .25
Perf. 14
24 A8 1sh3p pink, yel & brn   .25   .25
25 A8 2sh6p brt grn, dp org &
brn   .25   .25
Nos. 22-25 (4)   1.00   1.00
1st anniv. of independence, Oct. 24.

Inauguration of WHO Headquarters,
Geneva — A9

1966, May 18   Perf. 14
26 A9 3p rose brn, brt bl &
gold   .25   .25
27 A9 1sh3p vio bl, brt bl & gold   1.25   1.00

University of
Zambia — A10

1966, July 12   Photo.   Perf. 14
28 A10 3p brt green & gold   .25   .25
29 A10 1sh3p brt purple & gold   .35   .25
University of Zambia opening, Mar. 17.

National Assembly Building — A11

1967, May 2   Unwmk.   Perf. 14
30 A11 3p slate & bronze   .25   .25
31 A11 6p yellow grn & bronze   .35   .25
Completion of National Assembly Building.

Lusaka
Airport — A12

1967, Oct. 2   Photo.   Perf. 13½x14½
32 A12 6p vio blue & bronze   .25   .25
33 A12 2sh6p brown & bronze   .85   .85
Opening of Lusaka International Airport.

Symbols of
Agriculture
A13

Radio, Telephone
and
Television — A14

Designs: 4p, Emblem of Zambia Youth Service. 1sh, Map showing locations of Zambia coalfields. 1sh6p, Map showing Zambia-Tanzania Road.

Perf. 14½x13½, 13½x14½
1967, Oct. 23

34	A14	4p gray, red & gold	.25	.25
35	A13	6p lt vio bl, gold & blk	.25	.25
36	A14	9p dull blue, sil & blk	.35	.35
37	A14	1sh gold, red, blk & vio bl	.60	.25
38	A13	1sh6p bl grn, ultra, gold & blk	.90	1.25
		Nos. 34-38 (5)	2.35	2.35

Issued to publicize National Development.

Lusaka
Cathedral — A15

Baobab
Tree — A16

Designs: 3n, Zambia Airways plane. 5n, National Museum, Livingstone. 8n, Vimbuza dancer. 10n, Woman tobacco picker. 15n, Nudaurelia zambesina butterfly. 20n, Crowned cranes. 25n, Angoni warrior. 50n, Chokwe dancer. 1k, Railroad bridge, Kafue River. 2k, Eland.

Perf. 13½x14½, 14½x13½
1968, Jan. 16   **Photo.**
Size: 26x22mm, 22x26mm

39	A15	1n bronze & multi	.25	.25
a.		Booklet pane of 6	1.40	
b.		Booklet pane of 4	1.40	
40	A16	2n bronze & multi	.25	.25
41	A16	3n bronze & multi	.25	.25
a.		Booklet pane of 6	1.40	
b.		Booklet pane of 4	1.40	
42	A16	5n sepia & bronze	.25	.25
43	A16	8n bronze & multi	.25	.25
44	A16	10n bronze & multi	.25	.25

Size: 32x26mm, 26x32mm

45	A15	15n bronze & multi	3.00	.25
46	A16	20n bronze & multi	5.00	.25
47	A16	25n bronze & multi	.55	.25
48	A16	50n bronze, org & blk	.50	.25
49	A15	1k dk blue & brnz	.50	.30
50	A15	2k copper & blk	3.50	1.25
		Nos. 39-50 (12)	19.05	4.05

Used values of Nos. 48-50 are for canceled-to-order stamps. Postally used examples sell for more.

Map of
Zambia, Arrow
Pointing to
Ndola — A17

Perf. 14½x14
1968, June 29   **Photo.**   **Unwmk.**

51	A17	15n brt green & gold	.40	.40

Zambia Trade Fair at Ndola.

Children and
Human Rights
Flame — A18

WHO Emblem
A19

Children
A20

Photogravure; Gold Impressed
1968, Oct. 23   **Perf. 14½x14**

52	A18	3n ultra, dk bl & gold	.40	.40
53	A19	10n brt violet & gold	.40	.40
54	A20	25n brt blue, blk & gold	.50	.70
		Nos. 52-54 (3)	1.30	1.50

Intl. Human Rights Year; 20th anniv. of WHO; 21st anniv. of UNICEF (25n).

Copper
Miner — A21

Design: 25n, Worker poling furnace, horiz.

Perf. 14½x13½
1969, June 18   **Photo.**

55	A21	3n dp violet & copper	.30	.25
56	A21	25n yellow, blk & copper	1.50	1.10

50th anniv. of the ILO.

Map of Africa with
Zambia — A22

10n, Waterbucks, Kafue National Park, horiz. 15n, Golden perch, Kasaba Bay, horiz. 25n, Carmine bee-eater, Luangwa Valley.

Perf. 13½x14, 14x13½
1969, Oct. 23   **Photo.**

57	A22	5n ultra, yel & copper	.25	.25
58	A22	10n copper & multi	.35	.25
59	A22	15n copper & multi	.70	.40
60	A22	25n copper & multi	1.75	1.75
		Nos. 57-60 (4)	3.05	2.65

International Year of African Tourism.

Nimbus III
Weather
Satellite — A23

1970, Mar. 23   **Litho.**   **Perf. 13x11**

61	A23	15n multicolored	.65	.65

Issued for World Meteorological Day.

"Clean
Water" — A24

Designs: 15n, "Nutrition" (infant on scale). 25n, Children's immunization and Edward Jenner, M.D.

1970, July 4   **Litho.**   **Perf. 13x12½**

62	A24	3n multicolored	.25	.25
63	A24	15n multicolored	.70	.70
64	A24	25n multicolored	1.25	1.25
		Nos. 62-64 (3)	2.20	2.20

Issued to publicize preventive medicine and the "Under Five" children's clinics.

Mural by
Gabriel
Ellison
A25

1970, Sept. 8   **Litho.**   **Perf. 14x14½**

65	A25	15n multicolored	.70	.70

Opening of the Conf. of Non-Aligned Nations in Mulungushi Hall (decorated with murals by Mrs. Ellison) in Zambia.

Ceremonial
Axe — A26

Traditional Crafts: 5n, Clay pipe bowl with antelope head. 15n, Makishi mask, vert. 25n, The Kuomboka Ceremony (dancers and ceremonial boat).

1970, Nov. 30   **Litho.**   **Perf. 14x14½**
Size: 34x25mm

66	A26	3n dp lil rose & multi	.30	.30
67	A26	5n dp org, blk & sepia	.30	.30

Perf. 13x13½
Size: 30x45½mm

68	A26	15n dp lil rose & multi	.80	.80

Perf. 12½
Size: 71½x23½mm

69	A26	25n violet, blue & multi	1.25	1.25
a.		Souvenir sheet of 4, #66-69	12.00	12.00
		Nos. 66-69 (4)	2.65	2.65

Dag Hammarskjold and UN General
Assembly — A27

Hammarskjold and: 10n, Downed plane. 15n, Dove with olive branch. 25n, Plaque and flowers.

1971, Sept. 18   **Perf. 13½**

70	A27	4n brown & multi	.25	.25
71	A27	10n yellow grn & multi	.25	.25
72	A27	15n blue & multi	.50	.50
73	A27	25n plum & multi	.75	.75
		Nos. 70-73 (4)	1.75	1.75

10th anniv. of the death of Dag Hammarskjold, (1905-61) Secretary-General of the UN, near Ndola, Zambia.

Red-Breasted Bream — A28

1971, Dec. 10

74	A28	4n shown	.30	.30
75	A28	10n Green-headed bream	1.00	.80
76	A28	15n Tiger fish	2.40	1.10
		Nos. 74-76 (3)	3.70	2.20

Christmas.

Cheetah — A29

Soil
Conservation
A30

1972, Mar. 15   **Perf. 13½x14**

77	A29	4n shown	.25	.25
78	A29	10n Lechue	.65	.55

Perf. 14x13½

79	A30	15n Cape porcupine	1.00	.85
80	A30	25n Elephant	2.50	1.40
		Nos. 77-80 (4)	4.40	3.05

Conservation Year.

1972, June 30   **Litho.**   **Perf. 14x13½**
Size: 18½x45mm

81	A30	4n shown	.25	.25
82	A30	10n Forest conservation	.30	.30

Perf. 13½x14

83	A29	15n Water conservation (river view)	.50	.50
84	A29	25n Woman in corn field	.95	.95
		Nos. 81-84 (4)	2.00	2.00

Souvenir Sheet

85		Sheet of 4	11.00	13.50
a.		A30 10n Giraffe and zebra	1.50	1.90
b.		A30 10n Rhinoceros	1.50	1.90
c.		A30 10n Hippopotamus and deer	1.50	1.90
d.		A30 10n Lion	1.50	1.90

Conservation Year. Stamp size: 27x50mm.

1972, Sept. 22   **Perf. 13½x14**

Designs: All horizontal.

Size: 48x35mm

86	A30	4n Zambian flowers	1.40	.75
87	A30	10n Citrus swallowtails and roses	2.40	2.10
88	A30	15n Bee	4.50	3.00
89	A30	25n Locusts in corn field	6.75	4.50
		Nos. 86-89 (4)	15.05	10.35

Conservation Year.

Mary and Joseph Going to
Bethlehem — A31

1972, Dec. 1   Litho.   *Perf. 14*

90	A31	4n shown	.25	.25
91	A31	9n Holy Family	.25	.25
92	A31	15n Adoration of the shepherds	.35	.35
93	A31	25n Kings following the star	.65	.65
		Nos. 90-93 (4)	1.50	1.50

Christmas.

Broken Hill Man A32

Designs: 4n, Oudenodon and rubidgea (artist's conception; vert.). 10n, Zambiasaurus. 15n, Skull of Luangwa Drysdalli. 25n, Glossopteris (seed).

Perf. 14x13½, 14

1973, Feb. 1   Litho.

Size: 29x45mm

94	A32	4n org ver & multi	.75	.35

Size: 37½x21mm

95	A32	9n org ver & multi	1.10	.75
96	A32	10n apple grn & multi	1.25	.95
97	A32	15n lilac & multi	1.75	1.25
98	A32	25n orange brn & multi	2.75	2.75
		Nos. 94-98 (5)	7.60	6.05

Fossils from Luangwa area (except 9n), over 200 million years old.

Meeting of Stanley and Livingstone at Ujiji — A33

4n, Livingstone, the missionary. 9n, Livingstone at Victoria Falls. 10n, Livingstone stopping slave traders. 15n, Livingstone, the physician. 25n, Portrait & tree in Chitumbu, marking burial place of heart.

1973, May 1   *Perf. 13x13½*

99	A33	3n multicolored	.25	.25
100	A33	4n multicolored	.25	.25
101	A33	9n multicolored	.50	.50
102	A33	10n multicolored	.60	.60
103	A33	15n multicolored	.90	.90
104	A33	25n multicolored	1.50	1.50
		Nos. 99-104 (6)	4.00	4.00

Dr. David Livingstone (1813-73), medical missionary and explorer.

Parliamentary Mace — A34

1973, Sept. 24   Litho.   *Perf. 13½x14*

105	A34	9n tan & multi	.35	.35
106	A34	15n gray & multi	.70	.70
107	A34	25n brt green & multi	.95	.95
		Nos. 105-107 (3)	2.00	2.00

Third Commonwealth Conference of Speakers and Presiding Officers, Lusaka.

Vaccination — A35

WHO Emblem and: 4n, Mother washing infant, vert. 9n, Nurse weighing infant, vert. 15n, Child eating cereal and fruit.

1973, Oct. 16   Litho.   *Perf. 14*

108	A35	4n blue & multi	65.00	40.00
109	A35	9n orange & multi	.30	.30
110	A35	10n brt grn & multi	.40	.40
111	A35	15n violet & multi	.50	.50
		Nos. 108-111 (4)	66.20	41.20

WHO, 25th anniv.

A36

A37

Birth of the Second Republic: 4n, UNIP flag. 9n, United National Independence Party Headquarters, Lusaka. 10n, Army band. 15n, Women dancing and singing. 25n, President's parliamentary chair.

1973, Dec. 13   Litho.   *Perf. 14x13½*

112	A36	4n multicolored	12.00	7.50
113	A36	9n multicolored	.25	.25
114	A36	10n multicolored	.30	.30
115	A36	15n multicolored	.45	.45
116	A37	25n multicolored	.75	.75
		Nos. 112-116 (5)	13.75	9.25

Pres. Kaunda and his Home During Struggle for Independence — A38

4n, Pres. Kaunda at Mulungushi. 15n, Pres. Kaunda holding torch of freedom.

1974, Apr. 28   Litho.   *Perf. 14½x14*

117	A38	4n multi, vert.	.50	.50
118	A38	9n multi	.60	.60
119	A38	15n multi	.90	.90
		Nos. 117-119 (3)	2.00	2.00

50th birthday of Pres. Kenneth Kaunda.

Nakambla Sugar Estate — A39

Designs: 4n, Local market. 9n, Kapiri glass factory. 10n, Kafue hydroelectric plant. 15n, Kafue Bridge. 25n, Conference of Non-aligned Nations, Lusaka, 1970.

1974, Oct. 24   Litho.   *Perf. 13½x14*

120	A39	3n multicolored	.25	.25
121	A39	4n multicolored	.25	.25
122	A39	9n multicolored	.35	.35
123	A39	10n multicolored	.40	.40
124	A39	15n multicolored	.60	.60
125	A39	25n multicolored	.90	.90
		Nos. 120-125 (6)	2.75	2.75

Souvenir Sheet

126		Sheet of 4	7.00	10.00
a.	A39	15n Academic education	1.40	1.90
b.	A39	15n Teacher Training College	1.40	1.90
c.	A39	15n Technical education	1.40	1.90
d.	A39	15n University of Zambia	1.40	1.90

10th anniversary of independence.

Mobile Post Office — A40

UPU Emblem and: 9n, Rural mail service by Zambia Airways. 10n, Modern Post Office, Chipata. 15n, Ndola Postal Training Center.

1974, Nov. 15

127	A40	4n multicolored	.25	.25
128	A40	9n multicolored	.25	.25
129	A40	10n multicolored	.30	.25
130	A40	15n multicolored	.45	.30
		Nos. 127-130 (4)	1.25	1.05

Centenary of Universal Postal Union.

Radar by Day A41

1974, Dec. 16

131	A41	4n shown	.25	.25
132	A41	9n Radar by night	.50	.40
133	A41	15n Radar at dawn	.80	.70
134	A41	25n Radar station	1.40	1.40
		Nos. 131-134 (4)	2.95	2.75

Inauguration of Mwembeshi Earth Station, Oct. 21, 1974.

Rhinoceros and Calf — A42

Peanut Harvest — A43

1975, Jan. 3   Litho.   *Perf. 13½x14*

135	A42	1n shown	.55	.55
136	A42	2n Guinea fowl	.55	.55
137	A42	3n Zambian dancers	.25	.40
138	A42	4n Fish eagle	1.00	.25
139	A42	5n Bridge, Victoria Falls	1.00	1.00
140	A42	8n Sitatunga	1.00	.90
141	A42	9n Elephant, Kasaba Bay Resort	1.25	.85
142	A42	10n Giant pangolin	.25	.25

Perf. 13

143	A43	15n Zambezi River source, Monument	.35	.25
144	A43	20n shown	1.00	1.40
145	A43	25n Tobacco field	1.60	.65
146	A43	50n Flying doctor service	4.00	3.00
147	A43	1k Lady Ross's touraco	5.75	2.50
148	A43	2k Village scene	4.00	6.00
		Nos. 135-148 (14)	22.55	18.55

For surcharges see #188-191, 319.

Map of Namibia (South-West Africa) — A44

1975, Aug. 26   Litho.   *Perf. 14x13½*

149	A44	4n green & dk green	.25	.25
150	A44	9n dk blue & gray bl	.30	.25
151	A44	15n yellow & orange	.40	.55
152	A44	25n orange & dp orange	.50	1.10
		Nos. 149-152 (4)	1.45	2.15

Namibia Day.

Sprinkler Irrigation — A45

Designs: 9n, Sprinkler irrigation over rows of vegetables. 15n, Furrow irrigation.

1975, Dec. 16   Litho.   *Perf. 13*

153	A45	4n multicolored	.25	.25
154	A45	9p multicolored	.45	.50
155	A45	15n multicolored	.75	1.10
		Nos. 153-155 (3)	1.45	1.85

Intl. Commission on Irrigation and Drainage, 25th anniv.

Julbernardia Paniculata — A46

Trees of Zambia: 4n, Sycamore fig. 9n, Baikiaea plurijuga. 10n, Colophospermum. 15n, Uapaca kirkiana. 25n, Pterocarpus angolensis.

1976, Mar. 22   Litho.   *Perf. 13*

156	A46	3n multicolored	.35	.35
157	A46	4n multicolored	.35	.35
158	A46	9n multicolored	.50	.50
159	A46	10n multicolored	.50	.50
160	A46	15n multicolored	.80	.80
161	A46	25n multicolored	1.00	1.00
		Nos. 156-161 (6)	3.50	3.50

World Forestry Day, Mar. 21.

TAZARA Passenger Train — A47

9n, Train carrying copper. 10n, Clearing the bush. #164, Train carrying heavy machinery. #166b, Track laying. 20n, Reinforcing railroad track. #165, Train carrying various goods. #166d, Completed tracks.

1976, Dec. 10   Litho.   *Perf. 13*

162	A47	4n multicolored	.25	.25
163	A47	9n multicolored	.65	.65
164	A47	15n multicolored	1.10	1.10
165	A47	25n multicolored	1.75	1.75
		Nos. 162-165 (4)	3.75	3.75

Souvenir Sheet
Perf. 13½x14

166	Sheet of 4		4.50	4.50
a.	A47 10n multicolored		.45	.35
b.	A47 15n multicolored		.65	.50
c.	A47 20n multicolored		.75	.55
d.	A47 25n multicolored		1.10	.70

Completion of Tanzania-Zambia Railroad.

Kayowe Dance — A48

1977, Jan. 18   Litho.   Perf. 13½x14

167	A48	4n shown	.25	.25
168	A48	9n Lilombola dance	.25	.25
169	A48	15n Initiation ceremony	.45	.40
170	A48	25n Munkhwele dance	.75	.50
		Nos. 167-170 (4)	1.70	1.40

2nd World Black and African Festival, Lagos, Nigeria, Jan. 15-Feb. 12.

Grimwood's Longclaw — A49

Birds of Zambia: 9n, Shelley's sunbird. 10n, Black-cheeked lovebird. 15n, Locust finch. 20n, White-chested tinkerbird. 25n, Chaplin's barbet.

1977, July 1   Litho.   Perf. 14½

171	A49	4n multicolored	.45	.25
172	A49	9n multicolored	.80	.60
173	A49	10n multicolored	.95	.60
174	A49	15n multicolored	1.90	1.90
175	A49	20n multicolored	2.00	2.25
176	A49	25n multicolored	2.50	2.75
		Nos. 171-176 (6)	8.60	8.35

Children Playing with Blocks A50

Designs: 9n, Women of various races dancing in circle. 15n, Black and white girls with young bird.

1977, Oct. 20   Litho.   Perf. 14x14½

177	A50	4n multicolored	.25	.25
178	A50	9n multicolored	.25	.25
179	A50	15n multicolored	.45	.45
		Nos. 177-179 (3)	.95	.95

Combat racism and racial discrimination.

"Glory to God in the Highest" A51

Christmas: 9n, Nativity. 10n, Three Kings and camel. 15n, Presentation at the Temple.

1977, Dec. 20   Litho.   Perf. 14

180	A51	4n multicolored	.25	.25
181	A51	9n multicolored	.25	.25
182	A51	10n multicolored	.25	.25
183	A51	15n multicolored	.25	.25
		Nos. 180-183 (4)	1.00	1.00

Elephant and Road Check A52

Designs: 18n, Waterbuck and Kafue River boat patrol. 28n, Warthog and helicopter surveillance of National Parks. 32n, Cheetah and armed wildlife guards in Parks and Game Management Areas.

1978, Aug. 1   Litho.   Perf. 14x14½

184	A52	8n multicolored	.35	.35
185	A52	18n multicolored	.65	.65
186	A52	28n multicolored	1.10	1.10
187	A52	32n multicolored	1.40	1.40
		Nos. 184-187 (4)	3.50	3.50

Anti-poaching Campaign of Zambia Wildlife Conservation Society, Aug. 1978.

Nos. 141, 137, 145 and 143 Surcharged with New Value and 2 Bars

1979, Mar. 15   Perf. 13½x14, 13

188	A42	8n on 9n multi	.60	.25
189	A42	10n on 3n multi	.25	.25
190	A43	18n on 25n multi	.25	.25
191	A43	28n on 15n multi	.25	.25
		Nos. 188-191 (4)	1.35	1.00

Kayowe Dance A53

Designs: 32n, Kutambala dance. 42n, Chitwansombo drummers. 58n, Lilombola dance.

1979, Aug. 1

192	A53	18n multicolored	.30	.30
193	A53	32n multicolored	.35	.35
194	A53	42n multicolored	.35	.35
195	A53	58n multicolored	.50	.50
		Nos. 192-195 (4)	1.50	1.50

Commonwealth Summit Conf., Lusaka, Aug. 1-9.

"Why the Zebra is Hornless" — A54

Children's Stories: 18n, Kalulu and the Tug of War. 42n, How the Tortoise got his Shell. 58n, Kalulu and the Lion.

1979, Sept. 21   Litho.   Perf. 14

196	A54	18n multicolored	.30	.25
197	A54	32n multicolored	.45	.55
198	A54	42n multicolored	.55	.75
199	A54	58n multicolored	.70	1.00
a.	Souvenir sheet of 4, #196-199		3.00	3.00
		Nos. 196-199 (4)	2.00	2.55

International Year of the Child.

Girls of Different Races Holding Emblem A55

Anti-Apartheid Year (1978): 32n, Boys and toy car. 42n, Infants and butterfly. 58n, Children and microscope.

1979, Nov. 16   Litho.   Perf. 14½x15

200	A55	18n multicolored	.25	.25
201	A55	32n multicolored	.45	.45
202	A55	42n multicolored	.65	.65
203	A55	58n multicolored	.90	.90
		Nos. 200-203 (4)	2.25	2.25

Hill, Zambia No. 13 A56

Hill and: 32n, Mailman & bicycle. 42n, No. Rhodesia #75. 58n, Mailman & oxcart.

1979, Dec. 20   Litho.   Perf. 14½

204	A56	4n multicolored	.40	.25
205	A56	32n multicolored	.50	.50
206	A56	42n multicolored	.50	.65
207	A56	58n multicolored	.60	1.10
a.	Souvenir sheet of 4, #204-207		2.75	3.25
		Nos. 204-207 (4)	2.00	2.50

Sir Rowland Hill (1795-1879), originator of penny postage.

Nos. 204-207a Overprinted "LONDON 1980"

1980, Mar 6   Litho.   Perf. 15

208	A56	18n multicolored	.25	.40
209	A56	32n multicolored	.35	.55
210	A56	42n multicolored	.45	.70
211	A56	58n multicolored	.70	.85
a.	Souvenir sheet of 4		3.50	4.00
		Nos. 208-211 (4)	1.75	2.50

London 80 Intl. Stamp Exhib., May 6-14.

Anniverary Emblem on Map of Zambia — A57

1980, June 18   Litho.   Perf. 14

212	A57	8n multicolored	.25	.25
213	A57	32n multicolored	.55	.55
214	A57	42n multicolored	.70	.70
215	A57	58n multicolored	.85	.85
a.	Souvenir sheet of 4, #212-215		2.75	2.75
		Nos. 212-215 (4)	2.35	2.35

Rotary International, 75th anniversary.

Running A58

1980, July 19   Litho.   Perf. 13

216	A58	18n shown	.30	.30
217	A58	32n Boxing	.55	.55
218	A58	42n Soccer	.65	.65
219	A58	58n Swimming	1.00	1.00
a.	Souvenir sheet of 4, #216-219		3.25	3.25
		Nos. 216-219 (4)	2.50	2.50

22nd Summer Olympic Games, Moscow, July 19-Aug. 3.

Zaddach's Forester — A59

1980, Sept. 22

220	A59	18n shown	.50	.25
221	A59	32n Northern highflier	.85	.60
222	A59	42n Zambezi skipper	1.25	1.25
223	A59	58n Modest blue	1.75	2.50
a.	Souvenir sheet of 4, #220-223		10.00	10.00
		Nos. 220-223 (4)	4.35	4.60

Coat of Arms — A60

1980, Sept. 27   Litho.   Perf. 14½

224	A60	18n multicolored	.30	.25
225	A60	32n multicolored	.50	.55
226	A60	42n multicolored	.60	.75
227	A60	58n multicolored	.85	1.50
		Nos. 224-227 (4)	2.25	3.05

26th Commonwealth Parliamentary Association Conference, Lusaka.

A61

Nativity and St. Francis of Assisi (stained glass window), Ndola Church.

1980, Oct.   Litho.   Perf. 14

228	A61	8n multicolored	.25	.25
229	A61	18n multicolored	.70	1.00
230	A61	32n multicolored	.70	1.00
231	A61	42n multicolored	1.10	1.50
		Nos. 228-231 (4)	2.75	3.75

Christmas and 50th anniv. of Catholic Church in Copperbelt (central Zambia).

Trichilia Emetica Seed Pods, Musikili A62

Designs: Seed Pods.

1981, Mar. 21   Litho.   Perf. 14

232	A62	8n shown	.25	.25
233	A62	18n Afzelia quanzensis, Mupapa	.40	.45
234	A62	28n Erythrina abyssinica, Mulunguti	.45	.80
235	A62	32n Combretum collinum, Mulama	.45	1.25
		Nos. 232-235 (4)	1.55	2.75

World Forestry Day.

ITU Emblem — A63   Mask Maker — A64

Designs: 18n, 32n, WHO emblem.

1981, May 15   Litho.   Perf. 14½

236	A63	8n multicolored	.50	.50
237	A63	18n multicolored	.65	.65
238	A63	28n multicolored	.75	.75
239	A63	32n multicolored	.85	.85
		Nos. 236-239 (4)	2.75	2.75

13th World Telecommunications Day (8n, 28n).

1981-83

240	A64	1n shown	.25	.25
241	A64	2n Blacksmiths	.25	.25
242	A64	5n Potter	.25	.25

243	A64	8n	Straw basket fishing	.25 .25
244	A64	10n	Roof thatching	.25 .25
244A	A64	12n	Picking mushrooms ('83)	3.50 2.75
245	A64	18n	Millet grinding	.50 .25
246	A64	28n	Royal Barge paddler	.70 .25
247	A64	30n	Makishi tightrope dancer	.70 .25
248	A64	35n	Tonga-ila granary, house	.75 .25
249	A64	42n	Cattle herding	.75 1.50

Perf. 14
Size: 37x25mm

250	A64	50n	Traditional healer	.75 .25
251	A64	75n	Carrying water jugs ('83)	.75 .90
252	A64	1k	Grinding corn ('83)	.75 .90
253	A64	2k	Woman smoking pipe	.75 .90
			Nos. 240-253 (15)	11.15 9.45

For surcharges see Nos. 358, 372, 499-506, 596.

Kankobele — A65   Bornite — A66

Designs: Traditional musical instruments.

1981, Sept. 30   Litho.   Perf. 14½

254	A65	8n	shown	.55 .25
255	A65	18n	Inshingili	.65 .55
256	A65	28n	Ilimba	.90 1.50
257	A65	32n	Bango	.90 1.75
			Nos. 254-257 (4)	3.00 4.05

Designs: Rocks and minerals.

1982, Jan. 5   Litho.   Perf. 14

258	A66	8n	Banded Ironstone	1.50 .30
259	A66	18n	Cobaltocalcite	3.00 1.10
260	A66	28n	Amazonite	4.00 3.00
261	A66	32n	Tourmaline	4.25 4.00
262	A66	42n	Uranium ore	4.75 5.25
			Nos. 258-262 (5)	17.50 13.65

1982, July 1   Litho.   Perf. 14

263	A66	8n	shown	1.20 .35
264	A66	18n	Chalcopyrite	2.75 1.40
265	A66	28n	Malachite	3.50 3.75
266	A66	32n	Azurite	3.50 3.75
267	A66	42n	Vanadinite	4.25 4.50
			Nos. 263-267 (5)	15.20 13.75

Scouting Year A67

1982, Mar. 30   Litho.   Perf. 14

268	A67	8n	Scouts, flag	.40 .40
269	A67	18n	Baden-Powell	.80 .80
270	A67	28n	Horned buffalo, patrol pennant	.80 .80
271	A67	1k	Eagle, conservation badge	2.50 3.00
a.			Souvenir sheet of 4, #268-271	5.50 6.25
			Nos. 268-271 (4)	4.50 5.00

Drilling Rig, 1926 A68

Steam locomotives.

1983, Jan. 26   Perf. 14x14½

272	A68	8n	shown	.65 .30
273	A68	18n	Class B6, 1910	1.00 1.00
274	A68	28n	Borsig engine, 1925	1.60 2.50
275	A68	32n	7th class, 1900	2.00 2.75
			Nos. 272-275 (4)	5.25 6.55

Commonwealth Day — A68a

1983, Mar. 10   Litho.   Perf. 14

276	A68a	12n	Cotton picking	.25 .25
277	A68a	18n	Miners	.30 .25
278	A68a	28n	Ritual pot, dancers	.25 .35
279	A68a	1k	Victoria Falls, purple-crested lorie	3.25 4.25
			Nos. 276-279 (4)	4.05 5.10

Local Flowers — A69

1983, May 26   Litho.   Perf. 14

280	A69	12n	Eulophia cucullata	.25 .25
281	A69	28n	Kigelia africana	.50 .60
282	A69	35n	Protea gaguedi	.60 .75
283	A69	50n	Leonotis nepotifolia	1.20 2.25
a.			Souvenir sheet of 4, #280-283, perf. 12x12½	3.25 4.50
			Nos. 280-283 (4)	2.55 3.85

Thornicroft's Giraffes — A70

1983, July 21   Litho.   Perf. 14

284	A70	12n	shown	.80 .80
285	A70	28n	Cookson's wildebeest	1.10 1.10
286	A70	35n	Black lechwe	1.50 1.50
287	A70	1k	Yellow-backed duiker	3.00 3.75
			Nos. 284-287 (4)	6.40 7.15

Tiger Fish A71

1983, Sept. 29   Litho.   Perf. 14

288	A71	12n	shown	.60 .25
289	A71	28n	Silver Barbel	1.00 .70
290	A71	35n	Spotted Squeaker	1.10 2.00
291	A71	38n	Red Breasted Bream	1.25 2.00
			Nos. 288-291 (4)	3.95 4.95

For surcharge see No. 597.

Christmas — A72

1983, Dec. 12   Litho.   Perf. 14x14½

292	A72	12n	Annunciation	.25 .25
293	A72	28n	Shepherds	.35 .30
294	A72	35n	Three Kings	.45 .75
295	A72	38n	Flight into Egypt	.50 1.00
			Nos. 292-295 (4)	1.55 2.30

40th Anniv. of Intl. Civil Aviation Org. — A73

1984, Jan. 26   Litho.   Perf. 14

296	A73	12n	Boeing 737, 1983	.25 .25
297	A73	28n	Beaver, 1954	.55 .55
298	A73	35n	Short Solent Flying Boat, 1948	.70 .70
299	A73	1k	DH-66, 1931	2.00 2.75
			Nos. 296-299 (4)	3.50 4.25

60th Birthday of Pres. Kaunda A74

Perf. 14½x14, 14x14½

1984, Apr. 28   Litho.

300	A74	12n	Receiving greetings	.30 .30
301	A74	28n	Swearing in, 1983, vert.	.45 .45
302	A74	60n	Planting cherry tree	.90 2.00
303	A74	1k	Opening Natl. Assembly, vert.	1.10 2.50
			Nos. 300-303 (4)	2.75 5.25

1984 Summer Olympics — A75

1984, July 18   Litho.   Perf. 14

304	A75	12n	Soccer	.25 .25
305	A75	28n	Running	.60 .60
306	A75	35n	Hurdles	.70 .80
307	A75	50n	Boxing	1.00 1.50
			Nos. 304-307 (4)	2.55 3.15

Reptiles A76

1984, Sept. 5   Litho.   Perf. 14

308	A76	12n	Gabon viper	.40 .20
309	A76	28n	Chameleon	.75 .65
310	A76	35n	Nile crocodile	.90 .80
311	A70	1k	Blue headed agama	2.00 2.50
a.			Souvenir sheet of 4, #308-311	5.25 5.25
			Nos. 308-311 (4)	4.05 4.25

20th Anniv. of Independence — A77

1984, Oct. 22   Litho.   Perf. 14

312	A77	12n	Pres. Kaunda, Mulungushi Rock	.35 .35
313	A77	28n	Freedom Statue	.50 .60
314	A77	1k	Produce	1.60 2.25
			Nos. 312-314 (3)	2.45 3.20

Local Mushrooms A78

1984, Dec. 12   Litho.   Perf. 14x14½

315	A78	12n	Amanita flammeola	1.45 1.45
316	A78	28n	Amanita zambiana	1.60 1.60
317	A78	32n	Termitomyces letestui	2.50 2.50
318	A78	75n	Cantharellus miniatescens	4.50 4.50
			Nos. 315-318 (4)	10.05 10.05

For surcharge see No. 600.

No. 146 Surcharged with New Value and Two Bars

1985, Mar. 5   Litho.   Perf. 13½

319	A43	5k on 50n multi		2.50 3.00

Primates A79

1985, Apr. 25   Litho.   Perf. 14

320	A79	12n	Chacma baboon	.75 .75
321	A79	20n	Moloney's monkey	1.00 1.00
322	A79	45n	Blue monkey	2.10 2.10
323	A79	1k	Vervet monkey	3.25 4.00
			Nos. 320-323 (4)	7.10 7.85

For surcharge see No. 604.

SADCC, 5th Anniv. A80

1985, July 9   Litho.   Perf. 14

324	A80	20n	Map	.95 .95
325	A80	45n	Mining	2.40 2.40
326	A80	1k	Mulungushi Hall	2.50 3.00
			Nos. 324-326 (3)	5.85 6.35

Southern African Development Coordination Conference.
For surcharge see No. 605.

Queen Mother, 85th Birthday — A81

25n, Portrait in blue, age 80. 45n, Queen Consort at Clarence House, 1963. 55n, With Elizabeth II and Princess Margaret. 5k, With royal family, christening of Prince Henry, 1984.

1985, Aug. 2

327	A81	25n	multi, vert.	.25 .25
328	A81	45n	multi, vert.	.25 .25
329	A81	55n	multi	.25 .25
330	A81	5k	multi	1.40 2.00
			Nos. 327-330 (4)	2.15 2.75

For surcharges see Nos. 401, 406, 410, 414, 595, 606, 611.

National Anniversaries — A81a

#330A, Pres. Kenneth Kaunda, Mulungushi Rock. #330B, Kaunda, agricultural products. #330C, Freedom statue, flags.

Die Cut Perf. 10
1985, Oct. 23   **Embossed**
330A-330C   A81a 5k gold   25.00 25.00

United National Independence Party, 26th anniv. (No. 330A); Independence, 20th anniv. (Nos. 330B-330C).

Postal and Telecommunications Corp., 10th Anniv. — A82

1985, Dec. 12   **Perf. 13½x13**
331 A82 20n Lusaka P.O., 1958   .65 .65
332 A82 45n Livingstone P.O., 1950   .95 .95
333 A82 55n Kalomo P.O., 1902   1.10 1.10
334 A82 5k Transcontinental Telegraph, 1900   3.50 4.50
   Nos. 331-334 (4)   6.20 7.20

For surcharges see Nos. 590-593.

UN, 40th Anniv. — A83

1985, Dec. 19   **Perf. 14**
335 A83 20n Boy in cornfield   .40 .40
336 A83 45n Emblem   .70 .70
337 A83 1k Pres. Kaunda, 1970   1.40 1.75
338 A83 2k Charter signing, 1945   2.00 2.50
   Nos. 335-338 (4)   4.50 5.35

For surcharges see #594, 607.

Beetles A84

1986, Mar. 20
339 A84 35n Mylabris tricolor   .25 .25
340 A84 1k Phasgonocnema melananthe   .50 .55
341 A84 1.70k Amarodes passerinii   .85 .95
342 A84 5k Ranzania petersiana   2.75 3.00
   Nos. 339-342 (4)   4.35 4.75

For surcharges see #609, 612.

> Common Design Types pictured following the introduction.

Queen Elizabeth II 60th Birthday
Common Design Type

Designs: 35n, At the Flower Ball, Savoy Hotel, London, 1951. 1.25k, With Prince Andrew at Lusaka Airport, Commonwealth Conf., 1979. 1.70k, With Dr. Kaunda observing natl. anthem. 1.95k, Wearing Queen Mary tiara, state visit to Luxembourg, 1976. 5k, Visiting Crown Agents' offices, 1983.

1986, Apr. 21   **Wmk. 384**   **Perf. 14**
343 CD337 35n scar, blk & sil   .30 .30
344 CD337 1.25k ultra & multi   .40 .40
345 CD337 1.70k grn, blk & sil   .45 .45
346 CD337 1.95k vio & multi   .45 .45
347 CD337 5k rose vio & multi   .65 .65
   Nos. 343-347 (5)   2.25 2.25

For surcharges see Nos. 402, 405, 407, 411, 415.

Royal Wedding Issue, 1986
Common Design Type
Designs: 1.70k, Sarah Ferguson kissing Prince Andrew. 5k, Andrew in informal dress.

1986, July 23   **Litho.**   **Perf. 14**
348 CD338 1.70k multicolored   .35 .35
349 CD338 5k multicolored   .95 1.10

1986 World Cup Soccer Championships, Mexico — A85

Various soccer plays.

1986, June 27   **Litho.**   **Perf. 14½**
350 A85 35n multicolored   1.00 1.00
351 A85 1.25k multicolored   2.25 2.25
352 A85 1.70k multicolored   2.60 2.60
353 A85 5k multicolored   3.75 3.75
   Nos. 350-353 (4)   9.60 9.60

For surcharges see Nos. 403, 408, 412, 416.

Halley's Comet A86

Designs: 1.25k, Edmond Halley (1656-1742), by Henry Pegram. 1.70k, Giotto space probe approaching comet. 2k, Youth, astronomer. 5k, Halley's map of the southern constellations.

1986, July 4
354 A86 1.25k multicolored   1.00 1.00
355 A86 1.70k multicolored   1.20 1.20
356 A86 2k multicolored   1.75 1.75
357 A86 5k multicolored   3.50 3.50
   Nos. 354-357 (4)   7.45 7.45

For surcharges see Nos. 404, 409, 413, 417.

#244A Surcharged in Light Red Brown
1986, July   **Litho.**   **Perf. 14½**
358 A64 20n on 12n multi   15.00 .50

Christmas A87

Children's drawings.

1986, Dec. 15   **Litho.**   **Perf. 14**
359 A87 35n Nativity   .45 .45
360 A87 1.25k Magi   1.60 1.60
361 A87 1.60k Nativity   2.00 2.00
362 A87 5k Angel, house, tree   4.00 4.00
   Nos. 359-362 (4)   8.05 8.05

For surcharges see #602, 608.

Tazara Railroad, 10th Anniv. A88

Locomotive traveling various railway lines.

1986, Dec. 22
363 A88 35n Overpass, Kasama   .30 .30
364 A88 1.25k Tunnel 21 vicinity   .50 .50
365 A88 1.70k Tunnels 6-7   .65 .65
366 A88 5k Mpika Station grade separation   1.30 1.30
   Nos. 363-366 (4)   2.75 2.75

University of Zambia A89

Designs: 35n, Pres. Kaunda shaking council member's hand. 1.25k, University crest, vert. 1.60k, University statue. 5k, Kaunda laying university building cornerstone, vert.

1987, Jan. 27   **Litho.**   **Perf. 14**
367 A89 35n multicolored   .40 .40
368 A89 1.25k multicolored   .85 .85
369 A89 1.60k multicolored   .95 .95
370 A89 5k multicolored   3.25 4.50
   Nos. 367-370 (4)   5.45 6.70

No. 137 Surcharged in Blue
1987   **Perf. 14½**
372 A64 25n on 8n multi   .65 .45

Municipal Arms — A90

Birds — A91

1987, Mar. 26   **Perf. 14**
373 A90 35n Kitwe   .25 .25
374 A90 1.25k Ndola   .35 .35
375 A90 1.70k Lusaka   .45 .45
376 A90 20k Livingstone   3.25 3.25
   Nos. 373-376 (4)   4.30 4.30

For surcharge see No. 603.

1987-88   **Perf. 11x13**
Size: 20x25½mm
377 A91 25n Long-toed fluff tail   3.00 3.00
378 A91 30n Miombo pied barbet   .25 .25
379 A91 35n Black-and-rufous swallow   3.00 3.00
Size: 25x38½mm
Perf. 14
380 A91 50n Slaty egret   .25 .25
381 A91 1k Bradfield's hornbill   3.00 3.00
382 A91 1.25k Margaret's batis   3.00 3.00
383 A91 1.60k Red-and-blue sunbird   3.00 3.00
384 A91 1.70k Boehm's bee-eater   3.25 3.25
385 A91 1.95k Gorgeous bush shrike   3.25 3.25
386 A91 2k Shoebill   .40 .40
387 A91 5k Taita falcon   3.75 3.75

Surcharged

Size: 20x25½mm
Perf. 11x13
388 A91 20n on 1n Yellow swamp warbler   .30 .30
389 A91 75n on 2n Olive-flanked robin   .30 .30
390 A91 1.65k on 30n #378   .30 .30
Size: 25x38½mm
Perf. 14
391 A91 10k on 50n #380   1.90 1.90
392 A91 20k on 2k #386   2.40 2.40
   Nos. 377-392 (16)   31.35 31.35

Issued: #377, 379, 381-385, 387, 9/14/87; #391-392, 3/10/88; others 10/8/87.
Nos. 388-389 not issued without overprint.
See Nos. 433-435, 527-547. For surcharges see Nos. 490, 492-498.

Look-out Tree, Livingstone — A92

1987, June 30   **Perf. 14**
393 A92 35n shown   .35 .35
394 A92 1.25k Rafting, Zambezi River   .40 .40
395 A92 1.70k Walking safari, Luangwa Valley   1.75 1.75
396 A92 10k White pelicans   6.75 6.75
   Nos. 393-396 (4)   9.25 9.25

Zambia Airways, 20th Anniv. A93

1987, Sept. 21
397 A93 35n De Havilland Beaver   .85 .85
398 A93 1.70k DC-10   2.00 2.00
399 A93 5k DC-3   4.50 4.50
400 A93 10k Boeing 707   6.75 6.75
   Nos. 397-400 (4)   14.10 14.10

Issues of 1985-86 Surcharged in Gold or Black
1987, Sept. 14   **Perfs. as Before**
401 A81 3k on 25n #327   1.20 1.20
402 CD337 (G) 3k on 35n #343   .95 .95
403 A85 3k on 35n #350   1.20 1.20
404 A86 3k on 1.25k #354   2.10 2.10
405 CD337 (G) 4k on 1.25k #344   1.15 1.15
406 A81 6k on 45n #328   2.10 2.10
407 CD337 6k on 1.70k #345   1.60 1.60
408 A85 6k on 1.25k #351   2.10 2.10
409 A86 6k on 1.70k #355   3.25 3.25
410 A81 (G) 10k on 55n #329   3.00 3.00
411 CD337 10k on 1.95k #346   3.00 3.00
412 A85 10k on 1.70k #352   3.00 3.00
413 A86 10k on 2k #356   5.75 5.75
414 A81 (G) 20k on 5k #330   6.00 6.00
415 CD337 20k on 5k #347   6.00 6.00
416 A85 20k on 5k #353   6.00 6.00
417 A86 20k on 5k #357   10.50 10.50
   Nos. 401-417 (17)   58.90 58.90

World Food Day — A94

Cattle.

1987, Oct. 1   **Perf. 14½x15**
418 A94 35n Friesian-Holstein   .25 .25
419 A94 1.25k Simmental   .50 .50
420 A94 1.70k Sussex   .50 .50
421 A94 20k Brahma   2.50 2.50
   Nos. 418-421 (4)   3.75 3.75

Traditional Heritage — A95

Zambian people.

1987, Oct. 20   **Perf. 13x12½**
422 A95 35n Mpoloto Ne Mikobango   .25 .25
423 A95 1.25k Zintaka   .40 .40
424 A95 1.70k Mufuluhi   .60 .60
425 A95 10k Ntebwe   1.50 1.50

426 A95 20k Kubangwa Aa
Mbulunga 2.75 2.75
Nos. 422-426 (5) 5.50 5.50

World Wildlife
Fund — A96

Wild Cats — A97

1987, Dec. 21 Litho. Perf. 14
427 A96 50n Black lechwe
drinking water 1.50 1.50
428 A96 2k Adults and
young, horiz. 2.75 2.75
429 A96 2.50k Running, horiz. 2.75 2.75
430 A96 10k Male, diff. 6.00 6.00
Nos. 427-430 (4) 13.00 13.00

Souvenir Sheets

431 A97 20k Cheetah 8.00 8.00
432 A97 20k Caracal 8.00 8.00

Bird Type of 1987

1987 Litho. Perf. 11x13
433 A91 5n Black-tailed cisticola .25 .25
434 A91 10n White-winged starling .25 .25
435 A91 40n Wattled crane .25 .25
Nos. 433-435 (3) .75 .75

For surcharge see No. 491.

Intl. Fund for Agricultural Development
(IFAD), 10th Anniv. — A98

1988, Apr. 2 Perf. 14
436 A98 50n Cassava crop .25 .25
437 A98 2.50k Net fishing .65 .65
438 A98 2.85k Cattle breeding .75 .75
439 A98 10k Coffee picking 2.50 2.50
Nos. 136 130 (1) 4.15 4.15

A99

1988, Sept. 12 Litho. Perf. 12½
440 A99 50n Breast-feeding .25 .25
441 A99 2k Growth monitoring .55 .55
442 A99 2.85k Immunization .75 .75
443 A99 10k Oral rehydration 2.50 2.50
Nos. 440-443 (4) 4.05 4.05

UN child survival campaign.

A100

1988, Oct. 10 Litho. Perf. 12½x13
444 A100 50n Asbestos cement .25 .25
445 A100 2.35k Textiles .60 .60
446 A100 2.50k Tea .70 .70
447 A100 10k Poultry 2.50 2.50
Nos. 444-447 (4) 4.05 4.05

Preferential Trade Area Fair.

Intl. Red Cross and Red Crescent
Organizations, 125th Annivs. — A101

1988, Oct. 20 Perf. 14
448 A101 50n Famine relief .25 .25
449 A101 2.50k Giving first aid .70 .70
450 A101 2.85k Teaching first aid .85 .85
451 A101 10k Jean-Henri Du-
nant 3.25 3.25
Nos. 448-451 (4) 5.05 5.05

Endangered Species — A102

1988, Dec. 5 Litho. Perf. 14
452 A102 50n Aardvark .35 .30
453 A102 2k Pangolin .75 .75
454 A102 2.85k Wild dog 1.00 1.00
455 A102 20k Black rhinoceros 8.25 8.25
Nos. 452-455 (4) 10.35 10.30

1988
Summer
Olympics,
Seoul
A103

1988, Dec. 30 Litho. Perf. 14
456 A103 50n Boxing .25 .25
457 A103 2k Running .50 .50
458 A103 2.50k Hurdling .65 .65
459 A103 20k Soccer 4.75 4.75
Nos. 456-459 (4) 6.15 6.15

Souvenir Sheets

460 A103 30k Tennis 6.00 6.00
461 A103 30k Martial arts 6.00 6.00

Frogs and
Toads
A104

1989, Jan. 25 Litho. Perf. 12½
462 A104 50n Red toad .25 .25
463 A104 2.50k Puddle frog .90 .90
464 A104 2.85k Marbled reed
frog 1.10 1.10
465 A104 10k Young reed frogs 3.50 3.50
Nos. 462-465 (4) 5.75 5.75

Bats
A105

1989, Mar. 22 Litho. Perf. 12½x13
466 A105 50n Common slit-
faced .25 .25
467 A105 2.50k Little free-tailed .90 .90
468 A105 2.85k Hildebrandt's
horseshoe 1.10 1.10
469 A105 10k Peters' epauletted fruit 3.50 3.50
Nos. 466-469 (4) 5.75 5.75

A106 A107

1989, May 2 Litho. Perf. 12½
470 A106 50n Map of
Zambia 1.00 .25
471 A106 6.85k Peace dove 4.00 4.00
472 A106 7.85k Papal arms 4.50 4.50
473 A106 10k Victoria Falls 6.50 6.50
Nos. 470-473 (4) 16.00 15.25

State visit of Pope John Paul II, May 2-4.
For surcharges see #614, 616.

1989, July 26 Litho. Perf. 14½x15

Edible wild fruits.

474 A107 50n Parinari curatel-
lifolia .25 .25
475 A107 6.50k Uapaca kirkiana 1.75 2.25
476 A107 6.85k Ficus capensis 1.75 2.25
477 A107 10k Borassus aethi-
opum 3.25 3.75
Nos. 474-477 (4) 7.00 8.50

For surcharges see #613, 615.

Grasshoppers — A108

1989, Nov. 8 Litho. Perf. 14x13½
478 A108 70n Phamphagid .25 .25
479 A108 10.40k Pyrgomorphid 2.25 2.40
480 A108 12.50k Brown katydid 2.75 3.00
481 A108 15k Bush locust 3.50 4.25
Nos. 478-481 (4) 8.75 9.90

No. 480 misspelled "Catydid."

Christmas — A109

Flowers.

1989, Dec. 6 Litho. Perf. 14½
482 A109 70n Fireball .30 .25
483 A109 10.40k Flame lily 1.50 1.60
484 A109 12.50k Foxglove lily 2.10 2.25
485 A109 20k Vlei lily 3.50 4.00
Nos. 482-485 (4) 7.40 8.10

Stamp
World
London
'90
A110

Designs: 1.20k, Lusaka Main P.O., van,
mailman, bicycle. 19.50k, Zambia #220.
20.50k, Rhodesia and Nyasaland #164A,
Northern Rhodesia #1. 50k, Great Britain #1,
Maltese Cross cancel in red.

Unwmk.

1990, May 2 Litho. Perf. 14
486 A110 1.20k multicolored .30 .30
487 A110 19.50k multicolored 3.25 3.25
488 A110 20.50k multicolored 3.25 3.25
489 A110 50k multicolored 6.50 6.50
Nos. 486-489 (4) 13.30 13.30

Nos. 379, 381-
387, 433
Surcharged

1989, July 1 Perf. 11x13
490 A91 70n on 35n #379 1.00 .25
491 A91 3k on 5n #433 1.25 .40

Size: 25x38½mm
Perf. 14
492 A91 8k on 1.25k #382 1.50 1.00
493 A91 9.90k on 1.70k #384 1.75 1.75
494 A91 10.40k on 1.60k #383 1.75 1.75
495 A91 12.50k on 1k #381 2.00 2.00
496 A91 15k on 1.95k #385 2.00 2.00
497 A91 20k on 3k #386 3.00 3.00
498 A91 20.35k on 5k #387 3.00 3.00
Nos. 490-498 (9) 17.25 15.15

Nos. 242, 244-245, 247-248 251, 253
Surcharged in Black, Orange Brown,
Red Brown, or Violet

a b

c

1989 Perf. 14½
Size: 22x26mm
499 A64(a) 1.20k on 35n
#248 (OB) .25 .25
500 A64(b) 3.75k on 5n #242 .40 .40
501 A64(b) 8.11k on 10n
#244 1.00 1.00
502 A64(b) 9k on 30n
#247 1.00 1.00
Size: 37x25mm
Perf. 14
503 A64(b) 10k on 75n
#251 1.00 1.00
504 A64(c) 18.50k on 2k #253 2.00 2.00
Size: 22x26mm
Perf. 14½
505 A64(a) 19.50k on 12n
#244A
(RB) 4.00 4.00
506 A64(a) 20.50k on 18n
#245 (V) 2.00 1.75
Nos. 499-506 (8) 11.65 11.40

Issued: #500-504, 7/1; others, 11/1.

ZAMBIA
K1.20

World Cup Soccer
Championships,
Italy — A111

Soccer players in various positions.

1990, July 7   Litho.   Perf. 14
507 A111 1.20k multicolored   .25   .25
508 A111 18.50k multicolored   2.50   2.50
509 A111 19.50k multicolored   2.50   2.50
510 A111 20.50k multicolored   2.50   2.50
    Nos. 507-510 (4)   7.75   7.75

Souvenir Sheet
510A A111 50k multicolored   11.00 12.00

K1.20

ZAMBIA

Southern African Development Coordination Conf. (SADCC), 10th
Anniv. — A112

Map of SADCC members and: 1.20k, Truck.
19.50k, Telecommunications. 20.50k,
Regional cooperation. 50k, Coal transport by
cable car.

1990, July 23   Perf. 12½
511 A112 1.20k multicolored   .30   .25
512 A112 19.50k multicolored   2.25   2.25
513 A112 20.50k multicolored   2.25   2.25
514 A112 50k multicolored   7.50   7.50
    Nos. 511-514 (4)   12.30 12.25

ZAMBIA K1.20

Independence, 26th Anniv. — A113

1990, Oct. 23   Litho.   Perf. 14
515 A113 1.20k Agriculture   .25   .25
516 A113 19.50k Shoe factory   1.25   1.25
517 A113 20.50k Satellite com-
        munications   1.40   1.40
518 A113 50k Mother and
        child statue   3.00   3.00
    Nos. 515-518 (4)   5.90   5.90

ZAMBIA K1.20

Small Carnivores — A114

1990, Nov. 12
519 A114 1.20k Genet   .30   .30
520 A114 18.50k Civet   3.00   3.00
521 A114 19.50k Serval   3.25   3.25
522 A114 20.50k African wild
        cat   3.50   3.50
    Nos. 519-522 (4)   10.05 10.05

ZAMBIA K1.20

Intl. Literacy
Year — A115

COOK
SOYA BEANS

ZAMBIA K1.00

Soy
Beans — A116

Children's stories.

1991, Jan. 11   Litho.   Perf. 14
523 A115 1.20k Bird and the
        Snake   .30   .30
524 A115 18.50k Hare and the
        Leopard   2.10   2.10
525 A115 19.50k Mouse and Lion 3.00   3.00
526 A115 20.50k Hare and the
        Hippo   3.25   3.25
    Nos. 523-526 (4)   8.65   8.65

Bird Type of 1987

1990-91   Litho.   Perf. 11x13
527 A91 10n Livingstone's fly-
        catcher   .85   .45
528 A91 15n Bar-winged weav-
        er   .85   .45
529 A91 30n Purple-throated
        cuckoo shrike   1.40   .45
530 A91 50n Red-billed helmet
        shrike   1.40   .50
531 A91 50n like #527   1.40   .60
532 A91 1k like #528   1.60   .25
533 A91 1.20k Western
        bronze-naped
        pigeon   1.60   .25
534 A91 2k like #529   1.60   .65
535 A91 3k like #530   1.60   .65
536 A91 5k like #533   1.90   .65

Size: 25x38½mm
Perf. 14
537 A91 15k Corn crake   1.40   .60
538 A91 20k Dickinson's grey
        kestrel   2.75   1.75
539 A91 20.50k like #538   1.40   .85
540 A91 50k Denham's bus-
        tard   2.25   2.00
    Nos. 527-540 (14)   22.00 10.10

   Issued: #533, 1k, 2k, 3k, 5k, 20k, 5/7/91;
others, 10/30.

1991, June 28   Litho.   Perf. 13½
548 A116 1k Woman cooking   .25   .25
549 A116 2k Soy bean seed   .25   .25
550 A116 5k Woman feeding
        child   .35   .25
551 A116 20k Malnourished,
        healthy children   2.00   2.00
552 A116 50k Pres. Kaunda,
        child   3.75   3.75
    Nos. 548-552 (5)   6.60   6.50

United Church of Zambia / Rotary Foundation Project.

ZAMBIA K1.00

St. Ignatius of
Loyola (1491-
1556), Founder of
Jesuit
Order — A117

1k, Chilubula Church near Kasama. 2k,
Chikuni Church near Monze. 20k, Bishop
Joseph Du Pont.

1991, July 18   Litho.   Perf. 13½
553 A117 1k multicolored   .30   .30
554 A117 2k multicolored   .30   .30
555 A117 20k multicolored   3.00   3.00
556 A117 50k shown   5.50   5.50
    Nos. 553-556 (4)   9.10   9.10

BAOBAB Adansonia Digitata

ZAMBIA K1.00

Flowering
Trees
A118

1991, Nov. 29   Litho.   Perf. 13½
557 A118 1k Baobab   .25   .25
558 A118 2k Dichrostachys
        cinerea   .35   .25
559 A118 10k Sterospermum
        kunthianum   2.00   1.50
560 A118 30k Azanza garckeana 3.75   3.75
    Nos. 557-560 (4)   6.35   5.75

**Queen Elizabeth II's Accession to
the Throne, 40th Anniv.**
Common Design Type
Perf. 14x13½
1992, Feb. 2   Litho.   Wmk. 373
561 CD349 4k multicolored   .25   .25
562 CD349 32k multicolored   1.25   1.25
563 CD349 35k multicolored   1.40   1.40

---

564 CD349 38k multicolored   1.50   1.50
565 CD349 50k multicolored   2.00   2.00
    Nos. 561-565 (5)   6.40   6.40

  For surcharges see Nos. 690-692.

DISA HAMATOPETALA

ZAMBIA K1.00

Orchids — A119

Perf. 13x13½
1992, Feb. 28   Unwmk.
566 A119 1k Disa hamatopetala .70   .25
567 A119 2k Eulophia paivae-
        ana   .70   .25
568 A119 5k Eulophia quartini-
        ana   1.25   .60
569 A119 20k Aerangis verdickii 5.25 5.25
    Nos. 566-569 (4)   7.90   6.35

ZAMBIA K1.00

Masks — A120

1992, Mar. 10
570 A120 1k Kasinja   .30   .30
571 A120 2k Chizaluke   .30   .30
572 A120 10k Mwanapweu   1.25   1.00
573 A120 30k Maliya   3.25   3.75
    Nos. 570-573 (4)   5.10   5.35

BUSHBUCK ZAMBIA
K4 Tragelaphus scriptus

Antelopes
A121

1992, Sept. 14   Litho.   Perf. 14
574 A121 4k Bushbuck   .25   .25
575 A121 40k Eland   1.50   .95
576 A121 45k Roan antelope   1.50   .95
577 A121 100k Sable antelope 3.00   4.00
    Nos. 574-577 (4)   6.25   6.15

DH66 HERCULES

Zambia K4

Airmail
Services,
75th
Anniv.
A122

1992, Nov. 24   Litho.   Perf. 14
578 A122 4k DH66 Hercules   .40   .30
579 A122 40k VC10   2.40   .95
580 A122 45k C Class flying
        boat   2.40   .95
581 A122 100k DC10   4.25   5.50
    Nos. 578-581 (4)   9.45   7.70

OLYMPIC GAMES
BARCELONA 1992

ATHLETICS - 400 metres hurdles
ZAMBIA K10

1992 Summer
Olympics,
Barcelona — A123

1992, Dec. 28
582 A123 10k 400-meter hur-
        dles   .25   .25
583 A123 40k Boxing   .85   .55
584 A123 80k Judo   1.75   1.75
585 A123 100k Cycling   4.25   4.25
    Nos. 582-585 (4)   7.10   6.80

ZAMBIA

Christmas — A124

1992, Dec. 23   Litho.   Perf. 14
586 A124 10k Wise men   .25   .25
587 A124 80k Nativity scene 2.00   2.00
588 A124 90k Angels singing 2.25   2.25
589 A124 100k Angel, shep-
        herds   2.25   2.25
  a. Souvenir sheet of 4, #586-
        589   12.00 12.00
    Nos. 586-589 (4)   6.75   6.75

  For surcharges see Nos. 658-659.

Nos. 331-334 Surcharged

PTC 10th Anniversary

K2

ZAMBIA

1991, Mar. 4   Litho.   Perf. 13½x13
590 A82 2k on 20n #331   35.00   5.75
591 A82 2k on 45n #332   .75   5.75
592 A82 2k on 55n #333   —   5.75
593 A82 2k on 5k #334   17.50   5.75

40th Anniversary of
United Nations

K2

ZAMBIA

Stamps of 1981-89
Surcharged in
Black or Gold

Perfs. as Before
1991, July 5   Litho.
594 A83 2k on 20n #335   10.00   6.00
595 A81 2k on 25n #327
        (G)   10.00   6.00
596 A64 2k on 28n #246   —
597 A71 2k on 28n #289   —
598 A73 2k on 28n #297   —
600 A78 2k on 32n #317   30.00   8.00
601 CD337 2k on 35n #343   20.00
602 A87 2k on 35n #359   75.00   6.00
603 A90 2k on 35n #373   45.00   6.00
604 A79 2k on 45n #325   45.00   6.00
605 A80 2k on 45n #328   60.00   6.00
606 A81 2k on 45n #336   47.50   6.00
607 A83 2k on 45n #336   47.50   6.00
608 A87 2k on 1.60k #361   80.00   6.00
609 A84 2k on 1.70k #341   47.50   6.00
611 A81 2k on 5k #330   17.50   6.00
612 A84 2k on 5k #342   17.50   6.00
613 A107 2k on 6.50k #475   47.50   6.00
614 A106 2k on 6.85k #471   62.50   6.00
615 A107 2k on 6.85k #476   17.50   6.00
616 A106 2k on 7.85k #472   90.00   6.00

  Numbers have been reserved for additional
surcharges in this set.

ZAMBIA K50.00

Waterfalls
A125

1993, Sept. 30   Litho.   Perf. 13½
617 A125 50k Nkundalila   .35   .35
618 A125 200k Chishimba   1.40   1.40
619 A125 250k Chipoma   1.75   1.75
620 A125 300k Lumangwe   2.50   2.50
    Nos. 617-620 (4)   6.00   6.00

  For surcharges, see Nos. 1011-1014.

Healthy
Hearts — A126

1993, Oct. 20　　Litho.　　Perf. 14½
621	A126	O Runner	1.25	1.25
622	A126	P Heart	1.25	1.25

No. 621 sold for 50k and No. 622 sold for 80k on date of issue.

Sunbirds
A127

Designs: 20k, Bronze. 50k, Violet-backed. No. 625, Marico. No. 626, Eastern double-collared. 100k, Scarlet-chested. 150k, Bannerman's blue-headed. 200k, Oustalet's. 250k, Red and blue. 300k, Olive. 350k, Greenheaded. 400k, Scarlet tufted malachite. 500k, Yellow-bellied. 800k, Copper. 1000k, Orangetufted. 1500k, Black. 2000k, Green-throated.

1993, May 30　　Litho.　　Perf. 13
623	A127	20k multicolored	.25	.25
624	A127	50k multicolored	.25	.25
625	A127	O multicolored	.25	.25
626	A127	P multicolored	.30	.30
627	A127	100k multicolored	.35	.35
628	A127	150k multicolored	.55	.55
629	A127	200k multicolored	.65	.65
630	A127	250k multicolored	.80	.80
631	A127	300k multicolored	.90	.90
632	A127	350k multicolored	1.10	1.10
633	A127	400k multicolored	1.25	1.25
634	A127	500k multicolored	1.50	1.50
635	A127	800k multicolored	2.50	2.50
636	A127	1000k multicolored	3.25	3.25
637	A127	1500k multicolored	5.00	5.00
638	A127	2000k multicolored	6.75	6.75
		Nos. 623-638 (16)	25.65	25.65

Nos. 625 sold for 50k and 626 sold for 80k on date of issue.
For surcharge, see Nos. 997, 1090.

Snakes — A128

1994, Sept. 28　　Litho.　　Perf. 14
639	A128	50k Tiger snake	.25	.25
640	A128	200k Egyptian cobra	1.75	1.75
641	A128	300k African python	2.75	2.75
642	A128	500k Green mamba	4.50	4.50
		Nos. 639-642 (4)	9.25	9.25

For surcharges, see Nos. 996, 1007-1010.

ILO, 75th
Anniv.
A129

1995, Apr. 3　　Litho.　　Perf. 14
643	A129	100k Road rehabilitation	.50	.50
644	A129	450k Block making	2.50	2.50

For surcharge see No. 781A.

Christmas Angels — A130

1995, Aug. 29　　　　Perf. 14½x14
645	A130	100k shown	.45	.45
646	A130	300k With animals	1.25	1.25
647	A130	450k Blowing horn, birds	1.90	1.90
648	A130	500k Playing drum	2.10	2.10
		Nos. 645-648 (4)	5.70	5.70

For surcharge, see No. 998.

UN, 50th
Anniv.
A131

1995, Dec. 30　　Litho.　　Perf. 11½
Granite Paper
649	A131	700k multicolored	2.25	2.25

For surcharges, see Nos. 1038, 1121.

Natl. Monuments
A132

Designs: 100k, David Livingstone. 300k, Mbereshi Mission. 450k, Von Lettow-Vorbeck. 500k, Niamkolo Church.

1996, Feb. 21　　Litho.　　Perf. 14
650	A132	100k multicolored	.40	.25
651	A132	300k multicolored	1.25	1.25
652	A132	450k multicolored	1.60	1.60
653	A132	500k multicolored	1.90	1.90
		Nos. 650-653 (4)	5.15	5.00

For surcharges, see Nos. 870A, 1015-1018.

World
Wildlife
Fund
A133

Designs: 200k, Saddle-billed stork. 300k, Black-cheeked lovebird. 500k, Two black-cheeked lovebirds. 900k, Saddle-billed stork with young.

1996, Nov. 27　　Litho.　　Perf. 14x14½
654	A133	200k multicolored	.70	.70
655	A133	300k multicolored	1.00	1.00
656	A133	500k multicolored	1.30	1.30
657	A133	900k multicolored	2.00	2.00
		Nos. 654-657 (4)	5.00	5.00

For surcharges, see Nos. 1003-1006.

Nos. 587-588 Surcharged

1996　　　　　Litho.　　　Perf. 14
658	A124	(0) on 90k #588	1.75	1.75
659	A124	900k on 80k #587	3.00	3.00

No. 658 was valued at 500k on day of issue.
Size and location of surcharge varies.

New Year 1997 (Year of the
Ox) — A134

Disney characters posing for portrait in Chinese scene, vert.: #660: a, Clarabelle seated. b, Holding scroll. c, Playing musical instrument. d, On bicycle. e, Minnie, Mickey, Clarabelle. f, Holding mirror.
No. 661: a, 250k, Faces of Minnie, Mickey, Clarabelle Cow. b, 400k, Clarabelle seated. c, 500k, Clarabelle standing. d, 600k, Mickey, Clarabelle, Minnie dressed in Chinese outfits. e, 750k, Minnie, Clarabelle, Mickey dancing. f, 1000k, Clarabelle with parasol.

1997, Jan. 28　　Litho.　　Perf. 14x13½
660	A134	500k Sheet of 6, #a.-f.	8.00	8.00
661	A134	Sheet of 6, #a.-f.	8.00	8.00

No. 660 contains six 35x61mm stamps.

Endangered Species — A135

Species of the world, each 500k: No. 662: a, Spider monkey. b, Manatee. c, Jaguar. d, Puerto Rican parrot. d, Green sea turtle. e, Harpy eagle.
Species of Africa, each 1000k: No. 663a, Black rhinoceros. b, Leopard. c, Chimpanzee. d, Zebra (Grants). e, Mountain gorilla. f, African elephant.
Each, 3000k: No. 664, Lion (African). No. 665, Margay cat.

1997, Feb. 12　　　　　Perf. 14
662	A135	Sheet of 6, #a.-f.	8.00	8.00
663	A135	Sheet of 6, #a.-f.	16.00	16.00

Souvenir Sheets
664-665	A135	Set of 2	11.50	11.50

Deng Xiaoping (1904-97) — A136

Various portraits of Deng Xiaoping and: 800k, Flags, map of Hong Kong. 1000k, Flag, Hong Kong harbor. 2000k, Hong Kong at night, countdown clock. 2500k, World map with China highlighted.

1997, May 26　　Litho.　　Perf. 14
666	A136	800k multicolored	2.50	2.50
667	A136	1000k multicolored	3.50	3.50

Souvenir Sheets
668	A136	2000k multicolored	4.75	4.75
669	A136	2500k multicolored	5.75	5.75

Nos. 666-667 were issued in sheets of 3 each. No. 669 contains one 72x47mm stamp.

Trains — A137　　　　　A138

Locomotives: 200k, Suburban tank, Eastern Railway, France. 300k, Streamlined express, Belgian Natl. Railways. 500k, "Mountain" type express, Union Pacific Railraod. 900k, 2-8-2 "Mikado," Kenya & Uganda Railway. 1000k, 4-6-0 "Royal Scot," LM & S Railway. 1500k, 4-6-0 "Lord Nelson" type, Southern Railway.
No. 676, each 500k: a, Express, German State Railways. b, Express, "Duke of Abercorn," NCC (LMSR), Ireland. c, Heavy freight tank, Netherlands Railways. d, Express, Austrian Federal Railways. e, "Governor" class, Gold Coast Railways. f, 4-8-4 Express, Canadian Natl. Railways.
Each 3000k: No. 677, Diesel-electric passenger, Royal Siamese State Railways. No. 678, "Pacific" type, South African Railways.

1997, June 2
670-675	A137	Set of 6	7.25	7.25
676	A137	Sheet of 6, #a.-f.	6.50	6.50

Souvenir Sheets
677-678	A137	Set of 2	11.00	11.00

1997, Aug. 8　　Litho.　　Perf. 14
Butterflies and Moths: 300k, No. 683a, Gaudy commodore. 500k, No. 683b, African moon moth. 700k, No. 683c, Emperor moth. No. 682, 900k, Emperor swallowtail.
679-682	A138	Set of 4	9.75	9.75
683	A138	900k Sheet of 4, #a.-c., #682	15.00	15.00

Queen Elizabeth II and Prince Philip,
50th Wedding Anniv.
A139

No. 684, each 500k: a, Queen Elizabeth II. b, Royal arms. c, Queen wearing crown, Prince in uniform. d, Queen, Prince riding in open carriage. e, Buckingham Palace. f, Prince waving.
3200k, Queen, Prince waving from balcony.

1997, Aug. 26　　Litho.　　Perf. 14
684	A139	Sheet of 6, #a.-f.	8.00	8.00

Souvenir Sheet
685	A139	3200k multicolored	8.00	8.00

Paul P. Harris (1868-1947), Founder
of Rotary, Intl. — A140

1000k, First Rotarians, Silvester Schiele, Harris, Hiram Shorey, Gus Loehr, portrait of Harris.
3200k, Zambian interactors with retirees.

1997, Aug. 27
686	A140	1000k multicolored	4.75	4.75

Souvenir Sheet
687	A140	3200k multicolored	6.25	6.25

Heinrich
von
Stephan
(1831-97),
Founder
of UPU
A141

Each 1000k, Portrait of Von Stephan and: #688a, World Postal Congress, Berne, 1874. #688b, UPU emblem. #688c, Savannah, paddle steamer, 1819.

3200k, Von Stephan, Prussian postilion, 1715.

1997, Aug. 28
688 A141 Sheet of 3, #a.-c. 7.25 7.25
Souvenir Sheet
689 A141 3200k multicolored 6.25 6.25

Nos. 562-564 Surcharged

1997, Sept. 19 Litho. Perf. 14x13½
690 CD349 500k on 35k 2.00 .75
691 CD349 (0) on 32k 2.00 .90
692 CD349 900k on 38k 4.00 4.00
Nos. 690-692 (3) 8.00 5.65
No. 691 was valued at 600k on day of issue.

Owls — A142

300k, #697b, Verreaux's eagle owl. 500k, #697c, Pel's fishing owl. 700k, #697a, Barn owl. #696, Spotted eagle owl.

1997, Dec. 18 Litho. Perf. 14
693 A142 300k multicolored .80 .80
694 A142 500k multicolored 1.40 1.40
695 A142 700k multicolored 2.00 2.00
696 A142 900k multicolored 2.40 2.40
Nos. 693-696 (4) 6.60 6.60
Sheet of 4
697 A142 900k #a.-c., #696 10.00 10.00

Christmas A143

Entire paintings or details, sculpture: No. 698, 50k, Winged Victory of Samothrace. No. 699, 50k, Ognissanti Madonna, by Giotto. No. 700, 100k, Angel, by Antonio Pollaiuolo. No. 701, 100k, Angel of the Annunciation, by Jacopo da Pontormo. No. 702, 500k, No. 703, 1000k, The Virgin and Child Enthroned Among Angels and Saints, by Benozzo Gozzoli.

Each 3200k: No. 704, All of the Rebel Angels, detail, by Rubens. No. 705, The Resurrection of the Dead, by Joseph Christian.

1997, Dec. 18 Litho. Perf. 14
698-703 A143 Set of 6 5.75 5.75
Souvenir Sheets
704-705 A143 Set of 2 11.50 11.50
No. 704 incorrectly inscribed "The Virgin and Child Enthroned Among Angels and Saints, by Bonozzo Gozzoli."

Diana, Princess of Wales (1961-97) — A144

Various portraits with color of sheet margin: No. 706, Pale green. No. 707, Pale yellow.

Each 2500k: No. 708, Touching hand of blind man (in sheet margin). No. 709, With Barbara Bush (in sheet margin).

1997
706 A144 500k Sheet of 6, #a.-f. 9.00 9.00
707 A144 700k Sheet of 6, #a.-f. 11.00 11.00
Souvenir Sheets
708-709 A144 Set of 2 10.50 10.50

PAPU (Pan African Postal Union), 18th Anniv. A145

Designs: 500k, Kobus leche kafuensis. (O), Dove carrying letter over map. 900k, Emblem of dove carrying letter.

1998 Perf. 14½
710 A145 500k multicolored 1.40 1.40
711 A145 (O) multicolored 1.75 1.75
712 A145 900k multicolored 2.25 2.25
Nos. 710-712 (3) 5.40 5.40
No. 711 was valued at 600k on day of issue. For surcharges, see Nos. 1019-1021.

Mahatma Gandhi (1869-1948) — A146

Portraits of Gandhi: 250k, As law student in London, 1888. 500k, With Nehru, 1946. No. 715, (O), In front of Red Fort, New Delhi. 900k, At prayer.

2000k, Gandhi at 2nd Round Table Conference, London, 1931.

1998, Jan. 30 Litho. Perf. 13½
713-716 A146 Set of 4 7.50 7.50
Souvenir Sheet
717 A146 2000k multicolored 6.50 6.50
No. 715 was valued at 600k on day of issue. Nos. 713, 715-717 are vert. For surcharges, see Nos. 911-912.

Flowers — A147

Designs: No. 718, Lantana camara. No. 719, Clusia rosea. No. 720, Nymphaea hybrids. No. 721, Portulaca grandiflora.

No. 722: a, Hibiscus rosa-sinensis. b, Plumeria. c, Erythrina variegata. d, Bauhinia blakeana. e, Carissa grandiflora. f, Cordia sebestena. g, Couroupita guianensis. h, Eustoma grandiflorum. i, Passiflora.

3200k, Strelitzia reginae, horiz.

1998, Feb. 27 Litho. Perf. 14
718-721 A147 500k Set of 4 3.25 3.25

722 A147 500k Sheet of 9, #a.-i. 7.50 7.50
Souvenir Sheet
723 A147 3200k multicolored 5.25 5.25

New Year 1998 (Year of the Tiger) A148

Chinese symbols and stylized tigers, each 700k: No. 724: a, Looking right. b, Looking left. c, Facing forward, denomination UL. d, Facing forward, denomination UR.

1500k, Tiger, symbols on both sides.

1998 Litho. Perf. 14
724 A148 Sheet of 4, #a.-d. 6.25 6.25
Souenir Sheet
725 A148 1500k multicolored 4.00 4.00

Sites of India A149

Designs: a, Taj Mahal, Agra. b, Gateway to India, Calcutta. c, Great Imambara Mosque, Lucknow.

1998
726 A149 900k Sheet of 3, #a.-c. 7.25 7.25

Art of India A150

No. 727, each 700k: a, Ragmala, School of Mewar, 17th cent. b, Babur Nama, Mogul School, 16th cent. c, Hamza Nama, Mogul School, 16th cent. d, Meghamallar, School of Mewar, 16th cent.

2500k, Hindola Raga, School of Deccan, 17th-18th cent.

1998
727 A150 Sheet of 4, #a.-d. 8.25 8.25
Souvenir Sheet
728 A150 2500k multicolored 8.00 8.00

1998 World Cup Soccer Championships, France — A151

No. 729, each 450k: a, Albert, Belgium. b, Bebeto, Brazil. c, Beckenbauer, W. Germany. d, Littbarski, W. Germany. e, Juninho, Brazil. f, Lineker, England. g, Lato, Poland. h, McCoist, Scotland.

No. 730, each 500k: a, Maier, W. Germany, 1974. b, Bellini, Brazil, 1958. c, Kempes, Argentina, 1978. d, Nazassi, Uruguay, 1930. e, Pele, Brazil, 1970. f, Beckenbauer, W. Germany, 1974. g, Combi, Italy, 1934. h, Zoff, Italy, 1982.

No. 731, each 500k: a, Keane, Rep. of Ireland. b, Seaman, England. c, Like #729b. d, Futre, Portugal. e, Ravanelli, Italy. f, Weah, Liberia. g, Bergkamp, Holland. h, Raducioiu, Romania.

Each 3200k: No. 732, Juninho, Brazil. No. 733, Romario, Brazil, horiz. No. 734, McCoist, Scotland, horiz.

1998, Apr. 17 Perf. 13½x14, 14x13½ Sheets of 8, #a-h, + Label
729 A151 multi 5.25 5.25
730-731 A151 Set of 2 13.00 13.00
Souvenir Sheets
732-734 A151 Set of 3 13.50 13.50

Parrots — A152

No. 735, each 500k: a, Rainbow lorikeet. b, Budgerigar, blossom-headed parakeet. c, Blue-yellow macaw. d, Blue-crowned parrot. e, Golden conure. f, Sulphur-crested cockatoo.

No. 736, each 1000k: a, Ara ararauna. b, Ara chloropterd. c, Pale-headed rosellas. d, Northern rosella. e, Gang-gang cockatoo. f, Palm cockatoo.

Each 3200k: No. 737, Mulga parakeet. No. 738, Major Mitchell cockatoo, horiz.

1998, June 1 Litho. Perf. 14
735 A152 Sheet of 6, #a.-f. 4.25 4.25
736 A152 Sheet of 6, #a.-f. 8.50 8.50
Souvenir Sheets
737-738 A152 Set of 2 9.50 9.50

Mushrooms — A153

No. 739, 250k, Red-tufted wood tricholoma. No. 740, 250k, Chlorophyllum molybdites. No. 741, 450k, Stuntz's psilocybe. No. 742, 450k, Lepista sordida. No. 743, 500k, Lepiota. No. 744, 500k, Rosy gomphidius. No. 745, 900k, Cantharellus cybrina. No. 746, 900k, Olive-capped boletus. No. 747, 1000k, Showy volvaria. No. 748, 1000k, Sooty brown waxy cap.

No. 749, each 900k: a, Leller's boletus. b, Short-stemmed russula. c, Anise-scented clitocybe. d, Dung roundhead. e, Oak-loving collybia. f, Wine-red stropharia.

No. 750, each 900k: a, Flat-topped mushroom. b, Alice Eastwood's boletus. c, Pitted milky cap. d, Short-stemmed slippery jask. e, Rose-red russula. f, Zeller's tricholoma.

Each 3200k: No. 751, Honey mushroom. No. 752, Velvet-stemmed flammulina.

1998, July 1
739-748 A153 Set of 10 8.00 8.00
Sheets of 6
749-750 A153 Set of 2 15.50 15.50
Souvenir Sheets
751-752 A153 Set of 2 9.00 9.00
Nos. 749-752 are continuous designs.

Traditional Stories — A154

No. 755, each 2000k: a, like #753. b, like #754.

1998, Dec. 2 Litho. Perf. 14
753 A154 300k Luchela nganga .90 .90
754 A154 500k Kasuli 1.40 1.40
Souvenir Sheet
755 A154 Sheet of 2, #a.-b. 6.00 6.00
Christmas.

Orchids
A155

Designs, vert: No. 756, 100k, Paphiopedilum callosum. No. 757, 100k, Phaius tankervilleae. No. 758, 500k, Paphiopedilum fairrieanum. No. 759, 500k, Barkeria lindleyana. No. 760, 1000k, Laelia flava. No. 761, 1000k, Masdervallia unifloria, masdervallia angulifera.

No. 762, each 900k: a, Acacallis cyanea. b, Miltoniopsis phalaenopsis. c, Dendrobium bellatulum. d, Polystachya campyloglossa. e, Pleione bulbocodioides. f, Rhynchostylis gigantea. g, Cattleya lawrenceana. h, Sopbrolaelia. i, Laelia tenebrosa.

No. 763, each 900k: a, Acacallis cyanea, diff. b, Epidendrum gastropodium. c, Laelia rubescens. d, Paphiopedilum dayanum. e, Laelia lobata. f, Dendrobium crepidatum. g, Cattleya nobilior. h, Dendrobium johnsoniae. i, Trichopilia fragrans.

Each 4000k: No. 764, Cattleya maxima, vert. No. 765, Cattleya violacea.

1998, Dec. 23
756-761 A155 Set of 6   5.50 5.50
Sheets of 9
762-763 A155 Set of 2   17.50 17.50
Souvenir Sheets
764-765 A155 Set of 2   13.00 13.00

Classic
Cars
A156

Designs: 300k, Ferrari Daytona 365 GTB/4. 500k, Austin Healey Sprite. 900k, Gordon Keeble. 1000k, Alvis TD.

No. 770: a, Mercedes-Benz 300Sl. b, Chevrolet Corvair. c, AC Cobra 427. d, Aston Martin DB5. e, BMW 2002 Turbo. f, Cadillac Eldorado Brougham.

No. 771: a, Mercedes-Benz 280SE 3.5. b, Aston Martin DB2. c, Volkswagen Beetle. d, Lancia Aurelia B20 GT. e, Lamborghini 350 GT. f, Cisitalia 202 Coupe.

No. 771G: h, 1995 Ferrari 750 Pinnafarina. i, 1997 Federrari 312T2/77. j, 1983 Ferrari 208 Turbo. k, 1962 Ferrari Dino 268 SP. l, 1994 Ferrari F355 Berlinetta. m, Ferrari 250 GTE Coupe 2+2 California.

Each 4000k: No. 772, Citroen Light 15. No. 773, Austin Healey MKII 3000.

1998, Dec. 23
766-769 A156 Set of 4   4.75 4.75
Sheets of 6, #a-f
770-771G A156 900k Set of 3 17.50 17.50
Souvenir Sheets
772-773 A156 Set of 2   13.50 13.50

New Year
1999
(Year of
the
Rabbit)
A157

Various rabbits, denomination at — #774 (each 700k): a, LL. b, LR. c, LL (scratching). d, LR (nose near ground).
2000k, Rabbit, vert.

1999, Jan. 4
774 A157 Sheet of 4, #a.-d.   4.75 4.75
Souvenir Sheet
775 A157 2000k multicolored   4.50 4.50

Trains
A158

Locomotives: No. 776, (0), U20C Diesel electric, 1967. No. 777, 800k, 7th Class No. 70, 1900. No. 778, 800k, 15A Class Beyer-

Garrat No. 401, 1950. No. 779, 900k, HP diesel electric, 1966. No. 780, 900k, 20th Class No. 708, 1954.
4000k, 7th Class No. 955, 1892.

1999, Feb. 1   Litho.   Perf. 14½
776-780 A158 Set of 5   6.00 6.00
Souvenir Sheet
781 A158 4000k multicolored   4.50 4.50
No. 776 was valued at 600k on day of issue.

No. 643 Surcharged

Methods and Perfs as Before
1999, June 1
781A A129 500k on 100k multi

Queen Mother (b.
1900) — A159

No. 782: a, With Princess Elizabeth, 1936. b, Lady of the Garter. c, With Prince Andrew, 1960. d, At Ascot.
5000k, Wedding photograph, 1923.

1999, Sept. 1   Perf. 14
782 A159 2000k Sheet of 4, #a.-d., + label   9.00 9.00
Souvenir Sheet
Perf. 13¾
783 A159 5000k multicolored   6.00 6.00
No. 783 contains one 38x51mm stamp.

Dinosaurs
A160

Designs: 50k, Dimetrodon. 100k, Deinonychus. 500k, Protoceratops. 900k, Heterodontosaurus. 1000k, Oviraptor. 1800k, Psittacosaurus.

No. 700, each 900k: a, Stegosaurus. b, Triceratops. c, Brontosaurus. d, Gallimimus. e, Saurolophus. f, Lambeosaurus. g, Centrosaurus. h, Edmontonia. i, Parasaurolophus.

No. 791, each 900k: a, Ceratosaurus. b, Daspletosaurus. c, Baryonyx. d, Ornitholestes. e, Troodon. f, Coelophysis. g, Tyrannosaurus. h, Allosaurus. i, Compsognathus.

Each 4000k: No. 792, Saltasaurus, vert. No. 793, Stygimoloch, vert.

1999, Sept. 27   Litho.   Perf. 14
784-789 A160 Set of 6   3.75 3.75
Sheets of 9
790-791 A160 Set of 2   13.50 13.50
Souvenir Sheets
792-793 A160 Set of 2   7.00 7.00

Johann Wolfgang von Goethe (1749-1832), German Poet — A161

No. 794, each 2000k: a, A drinking party in Amerbach's cellar. b, Goethe and Friedrich von Schiller. c, Faust falls in love with Margaret.

5000k, Angel.

1999, Oct. 4   Litho.   Perf. 14
794 A161 Sheet of 3, #a.-c.   4.25 4.25
Souvenir Sheet
795 A161 5000k org brn & brn 3.75 3.75

A162

Cats: 50k, White Devon Rex. 100k, Red Persian. 500k, Chartreux. 900k, Brown tabby Maine Coon.

No. 800, each 1000k, horiz.: a, Tortie point Himalayan. b, Blue mackerel tabby Scottish Fold. c, Chocolate lynx point Balinese. d, Havana Brown. e, Seal point Ragdoll. f, Silver shaded Persian.

No. 801, each 1000k, horiz.: a, Red spotted tabby Exotic Shorthair. b, Blue tortie smoke Persian. c, Brown classic tabby longhaired Scottish Fold. d, Spotted tabby American Bobtail. e, Silver spotted tabby Ocicat. f, Blue British Shorthair.

Each 4000k: No. 802, Silver tabby longhair Persian, horiz. No. 803, Tabby point Siamese.

1999, Oct. 18
796-799 A162 Set of 4   1.10 1.10
Sheets of 6, #a.-f.
800-801 A162 Set of 2   8.50 8.50
Souvenir Sheets
802-803 A162 Set of 2   6.00 6.00

A163

Dogs: 100k, Welsh corgi. 500k, Shetland sheepdog. 900k, Italian greyhound. 1000k, Tibetan spaniel.

No. 808, each 1000k, horiz.: a, Dalmatian. b, Shetland sheepdogs. c, Bearded collie. d, Eskimo. e, Basenji. f, Saluki.

No. 809, each 1000k, horiz.: a, Norwegian elkhound. b, Flat-coated retriever. c, St. Bernard. d, Basset hound, Pembroke Welsh corgi. e, Pembroke Welsh corgi, Pointer. f, Petit Basset Griffon Vendeen.

Each 4000k: No. 810, Whippet. No. 811, Rottweiler.

1999, Oct. 18
804-807 A163 Set of 4   1.75 1.75
Sheets of 6, #a.-f.
808-809 A163 Set of 2   8.50 8.50
Souvenir Sheets
810-811 A163 Set of 2   6.00 6.00

11th Intl. Conference on AIDS in
Africa, Lusaka — A164

Designs: 500k, Emblem, waterfalls. 900k, Emblem, close-up view of waterfalls.

1999, Oct. 20
812-813 A164 Set of 2   2.00 2.00

Paintings by
Zhang Daqian
(1899-1983)
A165

No. 814, each 500k: a, Water Lily in the Rain. b, Chinghai Tribal Girl and a Black Hound. c, Taking a Nap. d, Monkey and Old Tree. e, Bird and Tree of Chin-Chang Mountain. f, Watching Waterfalls. g, On the Way to Switzerland and Austria. h, A Boat Brings the Wine. i, Brown Landscape. j, Nice Autumn.

No. 815: a, 1000k, White Water Lily, horiz. b, 2000k, Cloudy Waterfalls and Summer Mountain, horiz.

1999, Oct. 21   Perf. 13
814 A165 Sheet of 10, #a.-j. 3.75 3.75
815 A165 Sheet of 2, #a.-b.   2.10 2.10
China 1999 World Philatelic Exhibition, 22nd UPU Congress, Beijing. #815 contains two 52x39mm stamps.

A166

Flora &
Fauna
A167

Designs: 50k, Leatherback turtle. 100k, American kestrel. No. 818, 500k, Great blue heron. 900k, Mesene phareus. 1000k, Laeliocattleya. 1800k, Papilio cresphontes.

Each 500k: No. 822, Cairn's birdwing. No. 823, Pintail. No. 824, Rose. No. 825, Gray tree frog.

No. 826, each 700k: a, White-tailed tropicbird. b, Sooty tern. c, Laughing gull. d, Black skimmer. e, Brown pelican. f, Bottle nosed dolphin. g, Common dolphin. h, Man in sailboat. i, Blue tang. j, Southern stingray. k, Hammerhead shark. l, Mako shark.

No. 827, each 700k: a, Heliconia. b, Purple-throated Carib. c, St. Vincent parrot. d, Bananaquit. e, prepona meander. f, Unidentified butterfly. g, Hawksbill turtle. h, Black-necked stilt. i, Banded butterflyfish. j, Porkfish. k, Seahorse. l, Chain moray eel.

No. 828: a, Baltimore oriole. b, Chipmunk. c, Blue jay. d, Monarch butterfly. e, Gray heron. f, Mallard. g, Canadian otter. h, American lotus. i, Fowler's toad. j, Bluegill sunfish. k, Rainbow trout. l, Terrapin.

Each 4000k: No. 829, Amazona guildingii. No. 830, Bottle-nosed dolphin, diff. No. 831, Fuchsia. No. 832, Red-banded pereute.

1999, Oct. 27
816-821 A166 Set of 6   3.25 3.25
822-825 A167 Set of 4   1.40 1.40
Sheets of 12, #a.-l.
826-827 A166 Set of 2   12.00 12.00
828 A167 700k multi   6.00 6.00
Souvenir Sheets
829-830 A166 Set of 2   6.00 6.00
831-832 A167 Set of 2   6.00 6.00

IBRA '99 — A168

Trains: 1000k, Crampton. 3200k, Post standard 2-8-4 tank locomotive.

1999   **Perf. 14x14¾**
833-834 A168 Set of 2   3.00 3.00

Souvenir Sheets

PhilexFrance '99 — A169

Each 5000k: #835, Paris-Orleans Railway 4-4-0. #836, paris, Lyon & Mediterranean Railway 2-4-2.

1999   **Perf. 14¼**
835-836 A169 Set of 2   7.50 7.50

Wedding of Prince Edward and Sophie Rhys-Jones A170

No. 837: a, 500k, Sophie. b, 900k, Couple. c, 100k, Edward. 3000k, Couple kissing.

1999   **Perf. 14**
837 A170 Sheet of 3, #a.-c.   1.75 1.75
Souvenir Sheet
838 A170 3000k multi   2.10 2.10

Birds — A171

Designs: 50k, Blacksmith plover. 100k, Sacred ibis. 200k, Purple gallinule. 250k, Purple heron. 300k, Glossy ibis. 400k, Marabou stork. 450k, African spoonbill. 500k, African finfoot. O, No. 847, Knot-billed duck. 600k, Darter. 700k, African skimmer. 800k, Spurwinged goose. 900k, Hammerkop. 1000k, White pelican. 1500k, Black-winged stilt. 2000k, Black-crowned night heron.

1999, Dec. 20 Litho. Perf. 14½x15
839-854 A171 Set of 16   12.00 12.00

No. 847 sold for 500k on day of issue. Design size of No. 847 is 30½mm wide. See Nos. 927-930.

Flowers A172

Various flowers making up a photomosaic of Princess Diana, each 1000k.

1999, Dec. 31   **Perf. 13¾**
855 A172 Sheet of 8, #a.-h.   6.25 6.25

Millennium A173

Highlights of 1950-2000: a, Venice Biennale shows Jackson Pollock and Abstract Expressionism. b, James Watson and Francis Crick piece together the structure of DNA. c, Edmund Hillary reaches the summit of Mount Everest. d, Jonas Salk's polio vaccine. e, Ghana achieves independence. f, Yuri Gagarin becomes 1st man in space. g, Rachel Carson and the beginning of the environmental movement. h, Indira Gandhi becomes Prime Minister of India. i, 1st successful heart transplant. j, Apollo 11 lands on moon. k, Microprocessor developed. l, Richard Nixon visits People's Republic of China. m, Qin Shi Huang Mausoleum discovered. n, Stephen Hawking proposes new ideas about the universe and black holes. o, Margaret Thatcher elected 1st female Prime Minister of Great Britain. p, Mikhail Gorbachev becomes leader of Soviet Union. q, Fall of the Berlin Wall. r, Nelson Mandela elected Pres. of South Africa.

2000, Feb. 7   **Perf. 12¾x12½**
856 A173 500k Sheet of 18, #a.-r., + label   6.25 6.25

Butterflies A174

400k, Papilio antimachus. 450k, Amauris niavius. 500k, Charaxes smaragdalis. 800k, Charaxes zelica. 900k, Cymothoe confusa. 1000k, #862, Labobunea ansorgei.
No. 863, each 1000k: a, Palla ussheri. b, Euphaedra aureola. c, Graphium cyrnus nuscyrus. d, Salamis cacta. e, Salamis parhassus. f, Charaxes pelias.
No. 864, each 1000k: a, Large Spotted Acraea. b, Palla (orange wings). c, Palla (blue wings). d, Gold-banded Forester (white wings). e, Figtree blue. f, Gold-banded Forester (pink wings).
No. 865, each 1500k: a, Colotis ione. b, Charaxes acraeoides. c, Euphaedra edwardsi. d, Colotis phisadia. e, Charaxes lydiae. f, Euphaedra eupaulus.
No. 866, each 1500k: a, Papilio zalmoxis. b, Amauris niavius. c, Salamis cytora. d, Salamis temora. e, Charaxes eupale. f, Cymothoe hypatha.
Each 5000k: No. 867, Euphaedra ceres. No. 868, Cymothoe fumana. No. 869, Euphaedra spatiosa. No. 870, Euryphene gambiae.

2000, Feb. 8   **Perf. 14**
857-862 A174 Set of 6   2.75 2.75
Sheets of 6, #a.-f.
863-864 A174 Set of 2   8.50 8.50
865-866 A174 Set of 2   12.50 12.50
Souvenir Sheets
867-870 A174 Set of 4   14.00 14.00

No. 650 Surcharged

Method and Perf. as Before
2000, Apr. 11
870A A132 700k on 100k multi

Orchids — A175

No. 871, each 1500k: a, Paphiopedilum sioux. b, Phalaenopsis amabilis hybrid. c, Thelymitza ixioides. d, Phalaenopsis schilleriana.
No. 872, each 1500k: a, Miltoniopsis pansy orchid. b, Paphiopedilum venustum. c, Odontoglossum grande. d, Vanda sanderiana alba. e, Phalaenopsis violacea. f, Pleione alishan.
No. 873, each 1500k: a, Cyrtorchis arcuata. b, Cymbioiella rhodochila. c, Unidentified orchid. d, Eulophia quartiana. e, Augraecum montanum. f, Polystacha vulcanica.
No. 874, each 1500k, vert.: a, Catasetum splendens. b, Miltonia spectabilis. c, Stenia pallida. d, Cozacias spatulata. e, Eriopsis sceptzum. f, Paphinia cristata.
Each 6000k: No. 875, Cattleya hybrid. No. 876, Brachycorythis kalbreyeri.

2000, May 16 Litho. Perf. 14
871 A175 Sheet of 4, #a.-d.   4.00 4.00
Sheets of 6, #a.-f.
872-874 A175 Set of 3   18.00 18.00
Souvenir Sheets
875-876 A175 Set of 2   8.00 8.00
The Stamp Show 2000, London.

Popes — A176

No. 877: a, Liberius, 352-66. b, Linus, 67-76. c, Lucius I, 253-54. d, Marcellinus, 296-304. e, Mark, 336. f, Pius I, 140-155.
No. 878: a, Simplicius, 468-83. b, Siricius, 384-99. c, Stephen I, 254-57. d, Urban I, 222-30. e, Zephyrinus, 199-217. f, Zosimus, 417-18.
No. 879, Silverius, 536-37. No. 880, Vigilius, 537-55.

2000, July 7 Litho. Perf. 13¾
Sheets of 6, #a-f
877-878 A176 1500k Set of 2   11.00 11.00
Souvenir Sheets
879-880 A176 5000k Set of 2   8.00 8.00

Birds — A177

400k, Great Indian hornbill. 500k, Cockatiel. 600k, Amazonian umbrellabird. 1000k, Unidentified bird. 2000k, Rainbow lorikeet.
No. 886: a, Green aracari. b, Eclectus parrot. c, Crimson topaz. d, King bird of paradise. e, keel-billed toucan. f, Australian king parrot. g, Sailboat. h, Hyacinth macaw.
No. 887: a, Resplendent quetzal. b, Carmine bee-eater. c, Wattled false sunbird. d, Palm trees. e, Sulphur-crested cockatoo. f, Great blue turaco. g, Crimson rosella. h, Malabar pied hornbill.
No. 888: a, Yellow-crowned amazon. b, Green turaco. c, Butterfly and palm trees. d, Plate-billed mountain toucan. e, Scarlet macaw. f, Blue and yellow macaw. g, Guianan cock of the rock. h, Palm cockatoo.
No. 889, Red-crested pochard. No. 890, Toco toucan, horiz. No. 891, Blue and yellow macaw, horiz.

2000, Sept. 8   **Perf. 14**
881-885 A177 Set of 5   2.75 2.75
Sheets of 8, #a-h
886-888 A177 1500k Set of 3   21.00 21.00
Souvenir Sheets
889-891 A177 5000k Set of 3   9.00 9.00

Birds — A178

Designs: 700k, Red-backed shrike. 800k, Golden pipet. No. 894, 1200k, Orange-breasted sunbird. No. 895, 1400k, Eurasian goldfinch. 1500k, Red-crested turaco. 3000k, Carmine bee-eater.
No. 898, 1000k: a, Gouldian finch. b, Parrot finch. c, Purple grenadier. d, Red bishop. e, Red-crested cardinal. f, Spectacled monarch. g, Crimson chat. h, Necklaced laughing thrush. i, Chestnut-backed jewel babbler.
No. 899, 1200k: a, Lovely cotinga. b, Andean cock-of-the-rock. c, Orange-bellied leafbird. d, Pin-tailed manakin. e, Pin-tailed broadbill. f, Rufous motmot. g, American goldfinch. h, Double-barred finch. i, Golden-breasted starling.
No. 900, 1400k: a, Campo oriole. b, Hooded warbler. c, Purple honeycreeper. d, Blue-faced honeyeater. e, Scarlet tanager. f, Green-headed tanager. g, Blue-breasted fairy wren. h, Banded pitta. i, Wire-tailed manakin.
No. 901, 5000k, Pin-tailed sandgrouse. No. 902, 5000k, Black bustard.

2000, Sept. 8 Litho. Perf. 14
892-897 A178 Set of 6   4.75 4.75
Sheets of 9, #a-i
898-900 A178 Set of 3   18.00 18.00
Souvenir Sheets
901-902 A178 Set of 2   5.75 5.75

African Creation Legends A179

Designs: Nos, 903, 906a, 600k, Creation in Clay. Nos. 904, 906b, 1000k, The Chameleon and the Lizard. Nos. 905, 906c, 1400k, Why the Stones Do Not Die.

Perf. 14¼x14½

2000, Nov. 10   Litho.
903-905 A179 Set of 3   1.40 1.40

With Brown Frame

906 A179 Horiz. strip of 3, #a-c 1.40 1.40

Souvenir Sheet

No Frame Around Stamp

907 A179 3500k The Rooster in
         the Sky   1.60 1.60

No. 906 issued in sheets of 9 stamps.
For surcharge, see No. 1106.

Common Market for Eastern and Southern Africa A180

Designs: 600k, Map of member nations. 700k, Truck crossing border. 1000k, Exchange of money and sale of goods at border.

2000
908-910 A180 Set of 3   1.10 1.10

Nos. 713-714 Surcharged

2000   Method and Perf. as Before
911 A146 1200k on 250k multi
912 A146 1500k on 500k multi

UN High Commissioner for Refugees, 50th Anniv. — A181

Designs: 700k, Children receiving food. 1500k, Woman carrying child.

Perf. 13¾x14¼

2001, Mar. 13   Litho.
915-916 A181 Set of 2   1.40 1.40

A182

Animals — A183

Designs: 500k, African buffalo. 1000k, Cheetah, vert. No. 919, 2000k, Female elephant. 3200k, Ruffed lemur, vert.

No. 921, 2000k: a, Crimson-breasted shrike. b, Common bee-eater. c, Blue monkey. d, Chimpanzee. e, Bush baby. f, Genet.

No. 922, 2000k, horiz.: a, Defassa waterbuck. b, Crowned crane. c, Red hartebeest. d, Pygmy hippopotamus. e, White rhinoceros. f, Giant forest hog.

No. 923, 2000k, horiz.: a, Cheetah. b, Three adult, one young impala. c, Four adult impalas. d, Warthog. e, Two lions. f, Four lions.

No. 924, 6000k, Bull elephant. No. 925, 6000k, Black rhinoceros. No. 926, 6000k, Zebras, vert.

Perf. 13¼x13½, 13½x13¼

2001, Mar. 30
917-920 A182 Set of 4   4.00 4.00

Sheets of 6, #a-f

921-923 A183 Set of 3   22.50 22.50

Souvenir Sheets

924-926 A182 Set of 3   11.00 11.00

Bird Type of 1999

Designs: No. 927, O, Knob-billed duck. No. 928, A, Blacksmith plover. No. 929, B, Sacred ibis. No. 930, C, Purple gallinule.

Perf. 14½x14¾

2001, Mar. 19   Litho.
927-930 A171 Set of 4   3.00 3.00

Nos. 927-930 each sold for 700k, 1200k, 1400k, and 1500k respectively on day of issue. No. 927 is dated "2000" and has a design width of 31½mm. No. 847 has no date and has a design width of 30½mm.
For surcharge, see No. 1119.

Total Solar Eclipse, June 21 — A184

Eclipse and: 1000k, Woman. 1500k, Bird. 1700k, Lizard. 1800k, Elephant and man. 2200k, Man.

2001, June 1   Litho.   **Perf. 13¾**
931-935 A184 Set of 5   4.50 4.50

Phila Nippon '01, Japan — A185

Designs: No. 936, 500k, Senya Nakamura as Toknatsu, by Kiyomasu Torii I. No. 937, 500k, Kantaro Sanjo II and Monosuke Ichikawa I, by Okumura Masanobu, 1720. No. 938, 1000k, Kantaro Sanjo and Monosuke Ichikawa, by Masanobu, c. 1730. No. 939, 1000k, Standing Figure of a Woman, by Kiyomasu Torii I. 1500k, Ono no Komachi, by Masanobu. 1800k, Dog Bringing a Love Letter, by Shigenaga.

No. 942, 3200k: a, Matsue Nakamura as a Cat Woman, by Shunsho. b, Kantaro Sanjo With Branch of Bamboo, by Kiyomasu Torii I. c, Kinsaku Yamashika I as Peddler, by Kiyomasu Torii I. d, Portrait of an Actor, by Shunsho.

No. 943, 3200k: a, Kumetaro Nakamura I, by Shunsho. b, Actor in Female Role, by Kiyomasu Torii I. c, Kikunojo Segawa Leaning on Sugoroku Board, by Kiyomasu Torii I. d, Gennosuke Ichikawa as a Wakashu, by Kiyomasu Torii I.

No. 944, 6000k, Akashi of the Tamaya, by Ryukoku Hishikawa. No. 945, 6000k, Events of Year in the Floating World, by Moroshige, horiz.

2001, July 4   Perf. 14
936-941 A185 Set of 6   3.50 3.50

Sheets of 4, #a-d

942-943 A185 Set of 2   14.00 14.00

Souvenir Sheets

944-945 A185 Set of 2   6.50 6.50

SOS Children's Village A186

2001, July 30
946 A186 2500k multi   1.40 1.40

Royal Navy Submarines, Cent. — A187

No. 947, horiz.: a, HMS Tabard. b, HMS Opossum. c, HMS Unicorn. d, HMS Churchill. e, HMS Victorious. f, HMS Triumph.
6000k, Lieutenant Commander Malcolm David Wanklyn.

2001, July 30
947 A187 2000k Sheet of 6, #a-f 6.75 6.75

Souvenir Sheet

948 A187 6000k multi   3.50 3.50

Giuseppe Verdi (1813-1901), Opera Composer — A188

No. 949 — Actors in Falstaff: a, Benjamin Luxon (without hat). b, Luxon (with hat). c, Paul Plishka. d, Anne Collin.
8000k, Falstaff.

2001, July 30
949 A188 4000k Sheet of 4, #a-d 9.00 9.00

Souvenir Sheet

950 A188 8000k multi   4.50 4.50

Monet Paintings — A189

No. 951, horiz.: a, The Promenade at Argenteuil. b, View of the Argenteuil Plain from the Sannois Hills. c, The Seine at Argenteuil. d, The Basin at Argenteuil.
6000k, Rouen Cathedral Portal, Overcast Weather.

2001, July 30   Perf. 13¾
951 A189 1500k Sheet of 4, #a-d 6.00 6.00

Souvenir Sheet

952 A189 6000k multi   6.00 6.00

Mao Zedong (1893-1976) — A190

No. 953 — Mao in: a, 1918. b, 1945. c, 1937.
4000k, Portrait.

2001, July 30
953 A190 3200k Sheet of 3, #a-c 7.00 7.00

Souvenir Sheet

954 A190 4000k multi   3.25 3.25

Queen Victoria (1819-1901) — A191

No. 955: a, As child. b, Wearing black dress. c, With child. d, With Prince Albert. e, Wearing crown and red sash. f, Wearing red dress. 7000k, Portrait.

2001, July 30   *Perf. 14*
955 A191 2000k Sheet of 6, #a-f   7.25 7.25
Souvenir Sheet
956 A191 7000k multi   5.25 5.25

Queen Elizabeth II, 75th Birthday — A192

No. 957: a, As infant. b, As child. c, As child, in garden. d, Wearing hat.
8000k, Wearing green and black hat.

2001, July 30
957 A192 4000k Sheet of 4, #a-d   9.00 9.00
Souvenir Sheet
958 A192 8000k multi   6.00 6.00
No. 957 contains four 28x42mm stamps.

First Zeppelin Flight, Cent. — A193

No. 959: a, LZ-1. b, Parseval PL25. c, LZ-3. d, Baldwin. e, LZ-129. f, Norge Nobile N1.
No. 960, 700k, Graf Zeppelin, vert.

2001, July 30
959 A193 2000k Sheet of 6, #a-f   6.75 6.75
Souvenir Sheet
960 A173 700k multi   .40 .40
No. 960 contains one 38x51mm stamp.

Pres. F. J. T. Chiluba — A194

Chiluba: 1000k, Recieving Master's degree. 1500k, Signing forms. 1700k, With arm raised, horiz.
6000k, Receiving Master's degree, diff.

2001   Litho.   *Perf. 14*
961-963 A194   Set of 3   3.50 3.50
Souvenir Sheet
964 A194 6000k multi   4.75 4.75

Nobel Prizes, Cent. (in 2001) — A195

No. 965, 2000k — Peace laureates: a, Norman E. Borlaug, 1970. b, Lester B. Pearson, 1957. c, Intl. Red Cross, 1944. d, Anwar Sadat, 1978. e, Georges Pire, 1958. f, Linus Pauling, 1962.
No. 966, 2000k — Literature laureates: a, Isaac Bashevis Singer, 1978. b, Gao Xingjian, 2000. c, Claude Simon, 1985. d, Naguib Mahfouz, 1988. e, Camilo Jose Cela, 1989. f, Czeslaw Milosz, 1980.
No. 967, 2000k — Literature laureates: a, Seamus Heaney, 1995. b, Toni Morrison, 1993. c, Günter Grass, 1999. d, Wislawa Szymborska, 1996. e, Dario Fo, 1997. f, José Saramago, 1998.
No. 968, 6000k, George C. Marshall, Peace, 1953. No. 969, 6000k, Gerard Debreu, Economics, 1983. No. 970, 6000k, Robert W. Fogel, Economics, 1993.

2002, Feb. 11   Litho.   *Perf. 14*
Sheets of 6, #a-f
965-967 A195   Set of 3   16.00 16.00
Souvenir Sheets
968-970 A195   Set of 3   8.25 8.25

Souvenir Sheet

New Year 2002 (Year of the Horse) — A196

2002, Feb. 18   *Perf. 13¼*
971 A196 5000k multi   2.40 2.40

2002 World Cup Soccer Championships, Japan and Korea — A197

No. 972, 2000k: a, Poster from 1954 World Cup, Switzerland. b, Stanly Matthews and English flag. c, Scottish player and flag. d, Belgian player and flag. e, Player and Daejon World Cup Stadium, Korea, horiz.
No. 973, 2000k: a, Ferenc Puskas and Hungarian flag. b, Poster from 1962 World Cup, Chile. c, Spanish player and flag. d, English player and flag. e, Player and Jeonju World Cup Stadium, Korea, horiz.
No. 974, 8000k, Bryan Robson's goal against France, 1982. No. 975, 8000k, Salenko's fifth goal against Cameroon, 1994, horiz.

2002, Feb. 26   *Perf. 14*
Sheets of 5, #a-e
972-973 A197   Set of 2   8.75 8.75
Souvenir Sheets
974-975 A197   Set of 2   7.00 7.00
Size of Nos. 972a-972d, 973a-973d: 28x42mm.

United We Stand — A198

2002, Feb.   *Perf. 13½x13¼*
976 A198 3200k multi   1.40 1.40
Issued in sheets of 4.

Reign of Queen Elizabeth, 50th Anniv. — A199

No. 977: a, Wearing blue and white hat. b, Without hat. c, Wearing scarf. d, Wearing tiara.
7500k, With Prince Philip.

2002, July 15   Litho.   *Perf. 14¼*
977 A199 3200k Sheet of 4, #a-d   5.75 5.75
Souvenir Sheet
978 A199 7500k multi   3.50 3.50

2002 Winter Olympics, Salt Lake City A200

Designs: 1000k, Ice hockey. 3200k, Cross-country skiing.

2002, July 30   *Perf. 13¼x13¾*
979-980 A200   Set of 2   1.90 1.90

20th World Scout Jamboree, Thailand — A201

No. 981, horiz.: a, Troop hiking. b, Knot tying. c, Archery. d, Fire making.
8000k, Camping.

2002, July 30   *Perf. 14*
981 A201 3200k Sheet of 4, #a-d   5.75 5.75
Souvenir Sheet
982 A201 8000k multi   3.50 3.50

Intl. Year of Mountains — A202

No. 983: a, Mt. Whitney, US. b, Mt. Aconcagua, Argentina and Chile. c, Mt. Mönch, Switzerland. d, Mt. Ararat, Turkey.
9000k, Mt. Everest, Nepal and China.

2002, July 30
983 A202 1500k Sheet of 4, #a-d   2.75 2.75
Souvenir Sheet
984 A202 9000k multi   4.00 4.00

Birds — A203

Designs: 700k, Bee-eater. 1200k, Blue-cheeked bee-eater. 1400k, Boehm's bee-eater. 1500k, Little bee-eater.

2002, Aug. 12
985-988 A203   Set of 4   2.10 2.10
See Nos. 1027-1030. For surcharge, see No. 1091.

Flowers, Butterflies and
Mushrooms — A204

No. 989, 2500k — Flowers: a, Camel's foot.
b, Christmas bells. c, Impala lily. d, Everlasting. e, Anomatheca grandiflora. f, Soldier lily.
No. 990, 2500k — Butterflies: a, False monarch. b, Golden piper. c, Blue pansy. d, Christmas tree acraea. e, Grass yellow. f, Gold-spot-
ted sylph.
No. 991, 2500k — Mushrooms: a, Copper
trumpet. b, King bolete. c, Death cap. d, Fly
agaric. e, Chanterelle. f, Deadly fiber cap.
No. 992, 8000k, Arum lily. No. 993, 8000k,
African monarch butterfly. No. 994, 8000k,
Stump brittle-head mushrooms.

2002, Sept. 9   Litho.
Sheets of 6, #a-f
989-991 A204   Set of 3   20.00 20.00
Souvenir Sheets
992-994 A204   Set of 3   11.00 11.00

Nos. 624, 629, 645 Surcharged

Methods & Perfs as Before
2002, July 1
996 A128 250k on 50k #639   —   —
997 A127 300k on 50k #624   —   —
998 A130 1000k on 100k #645   —   —

Coronation of Queen Elizabeth II, 50th
Anniv. — A205

No. 999: a, Wearing crown and pearl necklace. b, Wearing tiara and jeweled necklace. c,
Wearing pink and black hat.
10,000k, Wearing flowered dress and hat.

2003, May 19   Litho.   **Perf. 14**
999 A205 5000k Sheet of 3,
#a-c   6.25 6.25
Souvenir Sheet
1000 A205 10,000k multi   4.25 4.25

Prince William, 21st Birthday — A206

No. 1001: a, Wearing bow tie. b, Wearing
blue shirt and tie. c, Wearing yellow and black
sports shirt.
10,000k, Wearing sweater.

2003, May 19
1001 A206 5000k Sheet of 3,
#a-c   6.25 6.25
Souvenir Sheet
1002 A206 10,000k multi   4.25 4.25

Nos. 654-657 Surcharged

Nos. 639-642
Surcharged

Nos. 617-
620
Surcharged

Nos. 650-653
Surcharged

Nos. 710-
712
Surcharged

Methods & Perfs. as Before
2003, June 26
1003 A133 1000k on 200k
#654   25.00 25.00
1004 A133 1000k on 300k
#655   25.00 25.00
1005 A133 1000k on 900k
#656   25.00 25.00
1006 A133 1000k on 900k
#657   25.00 25.00
1007 A128 1700k on 50k
#639   1.00   1.00
1008 A128 1700k on 200k
#640   1.00   1.00
1009 A128 1700k on 300k
#641   1.00   1.00
1010 A128 1700k on 500k
#642   1.00   1.00
1011 A125 1800k on 50k
#617   1.10   1.10
1012 A125 1800k on 200k
#618   1.10   1.10
1013 A125 1800k on 250k
#619   1.10   1.10
1014 A125 1800k on 300k
#620   1.10   1.10
1015 A132 2200k on 100k
#650   1.25   1.25
1016 A132 2200k on 300k
#651   1.25   1.25
1017 A132 2200k on 450k
#652   1.25   1.25
1018 A132 2200k on 500k
#653   1.25   1.25
1019 A145 2500k on 500k
#710   1.50   1.50
1020 A145 2500k on (O)
#711   1.50   1.50
1021 A145 2500k on 900k
#712   1.50   1.50
Nos. 1003-1021 (19)   117.90 117.90
Location of surcharges vary on Nos. 1019-
1021.

Miniature Sheet

New Year 2003 (Year of the
Ram) — A207

No. 1022 — Background colors: a, Green.
b, Blue violet. c, Maroon. d, Purple.

2003, July 30   Litho.   **Perf. 13¼**
1022 A207 3200k Sheet of 4,
#a-d   5.50 5.50

Intl. Year of Fresh Water — A208

No. 1023: a, Cabora Bassa Dam. b, Lake
Kariba. c, Mana Pools National Park.
10,000k, Victoria Falls.

2003, July 30   **Perf. 13½x13¼**
1023 A208 5000k Sheet of 3,
#a-c   6.50 6.50
Souvenir Sheet
1024 A208 10,000k multi   4.25 4.25

Powered Flight, Cent. — A209

No. 1025: a, Avro 547A. b, Avro 504O with
floats. c, Avro 584 Avrocet. d, Avro 504M.
10,000k, Avro 621 Tutor Replica.

2003, July 30   **Perf. 14**
1025 A209 4000k Sheet of 4, #a-
d   6.75 6.75
Souvenir Sheet
1026 A209 9000k multi   4.00 4.00

Bird Type of 2002

Designs: 1000k, White-fronted bee-eaters.
1200k, Little bee-eaters. 1500k, Blue-cheeked
bee-eater. 1800k, Boehn's bee-eater.

2003, Dec. 26   **Perf. 13¼**
Size: 25x20mm
1027-1030 A203 Set of 4   2.50 2.50
For surcharges, see Nos. 1089, 1109.

Rotary
International in
Zambia, 50th
Anniv. — A210

Design: 1000k, Rotary emblem and hands.
1200k, Rotary emblem.

2003, Nov. 21   Litho.   **Perf. 13**
1031 A210 1000k multi   —   —
1032 A210 1200k multi   —   —

For surcharge, see No. 1107.

Miniature Sheet

Birds — A211

No. 1033: a, 500k, African fish eagles,
national bird of Zimbabwe. b, 750k, Cattle
egrets, national bird of Botswana. c, 1000k,
African fish eagles, national bird of Zambia. d,
1100k, Peregrine falcons, national bird of
Angola. e, 1500k, Bar-tailed trogons. f, 1700k,
African fish eagles, national bird of Namibia. g,
1800k, Purple-crested louries, national bird of
Swaziland. h, 2200k, Blue cranes, national
bird of South Africa.

2004, Oct. 11   Litho.   **Perf. 14**
1033 A211 Sheet of 8, #a-h   4.50 4.50

See Botswana Nos. 792-793, Malawi No. ,
Namibia No. 1052, South Africa No. 1342,
Swaziland Nos. 727-735, and Zimbabwe No.
975.

Independence,
40th
Anniv. — A212

Design: 1500k, Vimbuza dancer. 1800k,
Kayowe dancer. 2700k, Ngoma dancer.
3300k, Ukishi dancer.

2004, Oct. 23   Litho.   Perf. 13x13¼
1034	A212	1500k multi	—	—
1035	A212	1800k multi	—	—
1036	A212	2700k multi	—	—
1037	A212	3300k multi	—	—

No. 649
Surcharged

Methods and Perfs As Before
2004, Dec. 28
Granite Paper
1038	A131	1000k on 700k #649	1.50	1.50

Mammals
A213

Designs: No. 1039, 2250k, Acionyx jubatus. No. 1040, 2250k, Phacochoerus aethiopicus. No. 1041, 2250k, Giraffa camelopardalis. 2700k, Syncerus caffer.
No. 1043, vert.: a, Panthera pardus. b, Pan troglodytes. c, Lycaon pictus. d, Equus burchelli.
10,000k, Diceros bicornis, vert.

2005, June 27   Litho.   Perf. 14
1039-1042	A213	Set of 4	4.25	4.25
1043	A213	3300k Sheet of 4, #a-d	5.75	5.75

Souvenir Sheet
1044	A213	10,000k multi	4.50	4.50

Insects — A214

Designs: 1500k, Fornasinius russus. No. 1046, 2250k, Goliathus giganteus. No. 1047, 2250k, Macrorhina. 2700k, Chelorrhina polyphemus.
No. 1048: a, Sternotomis virescens. b, Cicindela regalis. c, Goliathus meleagris. d, Mecosasms explanta.
10,000k, Meloid.

2005, June 27
1045-1048	A214	Set of 4	3.75	3.75
1049	A214	3300k Sheet of 4, #a-d	5.75	5.75

Souvenir Sheet
1050	A214	10,000k multi	4.50	4.50

Butterflies — A215

Designs: No. 1051, 2250k, Ropalo ceres. No. 1052, 2250k, Morpho portis nymphalidae. No. 1053, 2250k, Phyllocnistis citrella. 2700k, H. misippus.
No. 1055: a, Colotis evippe. b, Papilio lormieri. c, Papilio dardanus. d, Papilio zalmoxis.
10,000k, Epiphora albida druce.

2005, June 27
1051-1054	A215	Set of 4	4.25	4.25

1055	A215	3300k Sheet of 4, #a-d	5.75	5.75

Souvenir Sheet
1056	A215	10,000k multi	4.50	4.50

Orchids — A216

Designs: No. 1057, 1500k, Disa draconis. No. 1058, 1500k, Disa uniflora. No. 1059, 1500k, Disa uniflora orange. 2700k, Phalaenopsis penetrate.
No. 1061: a, Ansellia africana (yellow flower). b, Ansellia africana (spotted flower). c, Cattleya lueddemanniana. d, Laelia tenebrosa.
10,000k, Cymbidium.

2005, June 27
1057-1060	A216	Set of 4	3.25	3.25
1061	A216	3300k Sheet of 4, #a-d	5.75	5.75

Souvenir Sheet
1062	A216	10,000k multi	4.50	4.50

Jesuits in Zambia, Cent. A217

Designs: 1500k, Bishop Paul Lungu, Map of Zambia. 2550k, Father Torrend, Kasisi Church. 2700k, Father Moreau, Chikuni Church. 3300k, St. Ignatius of Loyola.

2005, June 25   Litho.   Perf. 13¼x13
1063-1066	A217	Set of 4	4.50	4.50
1066a		Souvenir sheet, #1063-1066	4.50	4.50

Dag Hammarskjöld (1905-61), UN Secretary General A218

Background color: 1500k, Dark blue. 2700k, Blue green.

2005, July 29   Litho.   Perf. 13½
1067-1068	A218	Set of 2	6.50	6.50
1068a		Souvenir sheet of 2, #1067-1068	6.50	6.50

Pope John Paul II (1920-2005) and Pres. Jimmy Carter — A219

Pope John Paul II — A220

No. 1070: a, With Sri Chinmoy. b, With boy and dove. c, With Schneider brothers. d, Visiting Ukraine.

2005, Aug. 22   Litho.   Perf. 12¾
1069	A219	7000k multi	3.00	3.00
1070	A220	3300k Sheet of 4, #a-d	5.75	5.75

No. 1069 was printed in sheets of 4.

A221

Railroads, 200th Anniv. — A222

No. 1071: a, Chinese Class KF 4-8-4. b, Indian Class WP 4-6-2. c, Irish 800 Class 4-6-0. d, French 241A Class 4-8-2.
No. 1072, 1700k: a, British Rail Class 4MT 2-6-4T. b, South African Railways Class 12A. c, Cuban sugar plantation locomotive. d, LNER A4 Pacific facing right. e, LNER A4 Pacific facing left. f, GWR City of Truro 4-4-0. g, British Rail HST Intercity 125. h, Eurostar. i, LNER A3 Flying Scotsman.
No. 1073, 1700k: a, Southern Railway King Arthur Class 4-6-0. b, Berkshire at Kaiiman's Bridge. c, Indian Railways WT Class 2-84 Suburban Tank steam locomotive. d, Ladders on shell of railway car being built. e, Worker on knees inside railway car. f, Yellow staircase next to railway car. g, Workers looking at undercarriage of raised railway car. h, Railway car between blue machinery. i, Model of steam locomotive.
No. 1074, 1700k: a, Great Western Hall Class 4-6-0. b, Argentinian 15B Class 4-8-0. c, Mallet Meter Gauge steam locomotive. d, Worker cutting track. e, Worker and pulley. f, Workers in cherrypicker. g, Workers on tracks and in cherrypickers. h, Workers pouring cement. i, Track workers.
No. 1075, Finnish Class HV2 4-6-0.
No. 1076, 8000k, Orient Express. No. 1077, 8000k, Edinburgh to London train. No. 1078, 800k, Bernina Express.

2005, Aug. 22
1071	A221	4200k Sheet of 4, #a-d	7.50	7.50

Sheets of 9, #a-i
1072-1074	A222	Set of 3	20.00	20.00

Souvenir Sheets
1075	A221	8000k multi	3.50	3.50
1076-1078	A222	Set of 3	10.50	10.50

David Livingstone at Victoria Falls, 150th Anniv. A223

Designs: 1500k, Livingstone, Victoria Falls. 2700k, Statue of Livingstone, railroad bridge.

2006, Jan. 20   Litho.   Perf. 13x13¼
1079-1080	A223	Set of 2	2.60	2.60

Franciscan Conventuals in Zambia, 75th Anniv. A224

Design: 3300k, Sister Water.

2006, July 8   Litho.   Perf. 13¼x13
1084	A224	3300k multi		

Three additional stamps were issued in this set. The editors would like to examine any examples.

Queen Elizabeth II, 80th Birthday — A225

No. 1085 — Queen: a, Wearing crown. b, Wearing necklace. c, Wearing necklace and jacket. d, With Princess Anne.
6500k, Wearing green hat.

2006, Aug. 8   Litho.   Perf. 13¼
1085	A225	3200k Sheet of 4, #a-d	6.50	6.50

Souvenir Sheet
1086	A225	6500k multi	3.25	3.25

Scouting, Cent. (in 2007) — A226

No. 1087, vert. — Scouting emblem, doves, Lord Robert Baden-Powell and background colors of: a, Pink and lilac. b, Yellow and orange. c, Blue and light blue. d, Light green and green.
6500k, Purple and red.

2006, Aug. 8
1087	A226	3200k Sheet of 4, #a-d	6.50	6.50

Souvenir Sheet
1088	A226	6500k multi	3.25	3.25

Nos. 623, 987 and 1028 Surcharged

Methods and Perfs As Before
2007
1089	A203	1500k on 1200k #1028	.70	.70
1090	A127	1850k on 20k #623	.95	.95
1091	A203	3300k on 1400k #987	1.60	1.60
		Nos. 1089-1091 (3)	3.25	3.25

Issued: Nos. 1089, 1091, 3/19; No. 1090, 5/30.

Miniature Sheet

Tazara Railway, 30th Anniv. (in 2006) — A227

No. 1092: a, Map of Tanzania and Zambia, waterfall, mountain, people waving, and men signing agreement. b, Men and train, elephant and antelope. c, Dar es Salaam Station, sign and wreaths with Chinese inscriptions. d, New Kapiri Mposhi Station, people near train. e, Train, bridge and tunnel, zebra and giraffe. f, Train on bridge, lion and lioness.

2007, May 28   Litho.   Perf. 12
1092 A227 1500k Sheet of 6, #a-
f   4.75 4.75

Mammals
A228

Designs: 1500k, Bat-eared fox. 2250k, Spotted hyena. 2700k, Aardwolf. 3300k, Side-striped jackal.

2007, June 29   Perf. 13¼x13
1093-1096 A228 Set of 4   5.25 5.25
1096a   Souvenir sheet, #1093-1096   5.25 5.25

For surcharges, see Nos. 1110, 1114, 1122.

National Animals
A229

Designs: 1500k, Buffalo (Zambia). 1800k, Nyala (Malawi). 2250k, Nyala (Zimbabwe). 2700k, Burchell's zebra (Botswana). 3300k, Oryx (Namibia).

Litho. With Foil Application
2007, Oct. 9   Perf. 13¾
1097-1101 A229 Set of 5   6.25 6.25

See Botswana No. 838, Malawi No. , Namibia Nos. 1141-1142, Zimbabwe Nos. 1064-1068.

Miniature Sheet

2008 Summer Olympics, Beijing — A230

No. 1102: a, Soccer. b, Hurdles. c, Boxing. d, Swimming.

2008, June 8   Litho.   Perf. 12
1102 A230 2000k Sheet of 4, #a-
d   5.00 5.00

Worldwide Fund for Nature (WWF) — A231

No. 1103 — Greater kudu: a, Two males battling. b, Female and calf. c, Male drinking. d, Female and tree branches.

2008, June 30   Perf. 13¼
1103   Horiz. strip or block
        of 4   7.25 7.25
a.-d. A231 3000k Any single   1.75 1.75
e.   Miniature sheet of 8, 2 each
      #1103a-1103d   14.50 14.50

Muhammad Ali, Boxer — A232

No. 1104 — Ali: a, In fighting stance without boxing gloves. b, Looking right. c, With gloved fist at chest level. d, With gloved fist near head. e, Pointing. f, Holding Olympic torch.
3200k, Ali wearing crown, with arms raised, and boxing.

2008   Perf. 14
1104 A232 500k Sheet of 6, #a-
f   1.90 1.90

Souvenir Sheet
Perf. 13½x13¾
1105 A232 3200k multi   1.90 1.90

No. 1105 contains one 38x50mm stamp. Nos. 1104-1105 were said to have been released in 1998, but did not appear in the marketplace until 2008.

No. 905 Surcharged

Method and Perf. As Before
2008, July 22
1106 A179 1500k on 1400k #905 .90 .90

No. 1032 Surcharged

Method and Perf. As Before
2009, Feb. 17
1107 A210 1500k on 1200k
            #1032   1.50 1.50

Peonies
A233

2009, Apr. 10   Litho.   Perf. 13¼
1108 A233 2000k multi   .75 .75
Printed in sheets of 8.

No. 1030 Surcharged

Method and Perf. As Before
2009, May 29
1109 A203 1500k on 1800k
            #1030   1.50 1.50

No. 1094 Surcharged

No. 1068 Surcharged

No. 1080 Surcharged

No. 1095 Surcharged

2009   Method and Perf. As Before
1110 A228 3300k on 2250k
            #1094   7.75 7.75
1111 A218 3500k on 2700k
            #1068   —
1113 A223 4050k on 2700k
            #1080   —
1114 A228 4950k on 2700k
            #1095   —
Issued: Nos. 1110-1111, 1113, 5/29, No. 1114, 12/1.
One additional surcharge was issued in this set. The editors would like to examine an example.

2010 World Cup Soccer Championships, South Africa — A234

Soccer players, ball, 2010 World Cup mascot and flag of: Nos. 1115, 1118e, 2500k, Zambia. Nos. 1116, 1118h, 4050k, Namibia. Nos. 1117, 1118i, 4950k, South Africa.
No. 1118: a, 900k, Lesotho. b, 1000k, Mauritius. c, 2050k, Botswana. d, 2250k, Zimbabwe. f, 3500k, Malawi. g, 3800k, Swaziland.

2010, Apr. 9   Litho.   Perf. 13½
On Plain Paper With Olive Brown Background
1115-1117 A234 Set of 3   5.00 5.00
On Gold-faced Paper
1118 A234 Sheet of 9, #a-i 11.00 11.00

See Botswana Nos. 896-905, Lesotho No. , Malawi No. , Mauritius No. , Namibia No. 1188, South Africa No. 1403, Swaziland Nos. 794-803, and Zimbabwe Nos.1112-1121.

Nos. 649, 928 and 1094 Surcharged

Methods and Perfs As Before
2010 ?
1119 A171 2500k on A #928   — —
1121 A131 5000k on 700k
            #649   — —
1122 A228 10,000k on 2250k
            #1094   — —

An additional surcharge was issued in this set. The editors would like to examine any example of it.

POSTAGE DUE STAMPS

Type of Northern Rhodesia
Perf. 12½

				Unwmk.
1964, Oct. 24		**Litho.**		
J1	D2	1p orange	.25	1.00
J2	D2	2p dark blue	.25	1.00
J3	D2	3p rose claret	.25	1.25
J4	D2	4p violet blue	.35	1.60
J5	D2	6p purple	.50	2.50
J6	D2	1sh emerald	1.50	7.50
		Nos. J1-J6 (6)	3.10	14.85

ZANZIBAR

ˈzan-zə-ˌbär

LOCATION — Group of islands about twenty miles off the coast of Tanganyika in East Africa
GOVT. — Republic
AREA — 1,044 sq. mi. (approx.)
POP. — 354,360 (est. 1967)
CAPITAL — Zanzibar

Before 1895, unoverprinted stamps of India were used in Zanzibar.
Zanzibar was a British protectorate until Dec. 10, 1963, when it became independent. After a revolt in January, 1964, a republic was established. Zanzibar joined Tanganyika Apr. 26, 1964, to form the United Republic of Tanganyika and Zanzibar (later renamed Tanzania). See Tanzania.

12 Pies = 1 Anna
16 Annas = 1 Rupee
100 Cents = 1 Rupee (1908)
100 Cents = 1 Shilling (1935)

Catalogue values for unused stamps in this country are for Never Hinged items, beginning with Scott 201 in the regular postage section and Scott J18 in the postage due section.

Watermarks

Wmk. 47 — Multiple Rosette | Wmk. 71 — Rosette

Stamps of British India Overprinted

On Stamps of 1882-95

1895 Wmk. Star (39) Perf. 14
Blue Overprint

1	A17	½a green	22,500.	5,500.
2	A19	1a violet brn	2,750.	600.
a.	"Zanzibar"		25,000.	

1895-96
Black Overprint

3	A17	½a green	4.75	4.00
a.	"Zanzibar"		1,350.	725.00
b.	"Zanibar"		1,350.	1,800.
c.	"Zapzibar"			
4	A19	1a violet brn	4.75	4.00
a.	"Zanzibar"			3,500.
b.	"Zanibar"		1,750.	2,000.
5	A20	1a6p bister brn	5.25	4.50
a.	"Zanzibar"		4,000.	1,200.
b.	"Zanibar"		1,750.	
c.	"Zanibar"		1,600.	1,750.
d.	"Zapzibar"			
6	A21	2a ultra	7.00	6.50
a.	"Zanzibar"		7,000.	3,000.
b.	"Zanibar"		6,000.	2,750.
c.	"Zapzibar"			
d.	Double overprint		280.00	
7	A28	2a6p green	9.00	5.50
a.	"Zanzibar"		7,500.	1,800.
b.	"Zanibar"		700.00	1,400.
c.	"Zapzibar"			
d.	"Zanzipar"		1,250.	
8	A22	3a orange	12.50	12.00
a.	"Zanzibar"		1,000.	1,900.
b.	"Zanibar"		6,000.	6,500.
9	A23	4a olive grn	19.50	17.50
a.	"Zanzibar"		10,000.	4,250.
10	A25	8a red vio	32.50	24.00
a.	"Zanzibar"		9,500.	8,000.
11	A26	12a vio, red	18.00	11.50
a.	"Zanzibar"		9,500.	4,250.
12	A27	1r gray	100.00	85.00
a.	"Zanzibar"		9,000.	5,500.
13	A29	1r car rose & grn	22.50	30.00
a.	Vertical overprint		475.00	

14	A30	2r brn & rose	100.00	110.00
a.	"Zanziba"		27,000.	5,000.
b.	Inverted "r"		4,000.	5,000.
c.	Pair, one without overprint			
15	A30	3r grn & brn	75.00	90.00
a.	"Zanziba"		27,000.	
b.	Inverted "r"		5,500.	5,500.
16	A30	5r vio & blue	85.00	120.00
a.	"Zanziba"		27,000.	
b.	Inverted "r"		4,500.	7,000.
c.	Dbl. ovpt., one invtd.		950.00	

On Stamp of 1873-76
Wmk. Elephant's Head (38)

17	A14	6a bister	21.00	12.50
a.	"Zanzidar"		10,000.	4,250.
b.	"Zanzibarr"		6,000.	4,750.
c.	"Zanzbar"		800.00	1,400.
d.	"Zapzibar"			
e.	Double overprint		175.00	
	Nos. 3-17 (15)		516.75	537.00

Nos. 4-6 Surcharged

a | b

c | d

e | f

1896 Wmk. Star (39)
Black Surcharge

18	(a)	2½a on 1a	175.00	110.00
19	(b)	2½a on 1a	450.00	350.00
20	(c)	2½a on 1a	180.00	125.00

Red Surcharge

21	(a)	2½a on 1a	275.00	675.00
22	(b)	2½a on 1a	500.00	1,000.
23	(c)	2½a on 1a	275.00	675.00
24	(a)	2½a on 1a6p	65.00	50.00
a.	"Zanziba"		1,600.	1,400.
b.	"Zanziba"		4,500.	2,250.
24C	(b)	2½a on 1a6p	250.00	650.00
25	(c)	2½a on 1a6p	130.00	300.00
26	(d)	2½a on 1a6p	170.00	150.00
27	(e)	2½a on 1a6p	450.00	550.00
27A	(f)	2½a on 1a6p	21,000.	14,000.
28	(a)	2½a on 2a	125.00	325.00
28A	(b)	2½a on 2a	250.00	550.00
29	(c)	2½a on 2a	140.00	375.00
30	(d)	2½a on 2a	65.00	40.00
31	(e)	2½a on 2a	200.00	125.00
31A	(f)	2½a on 2a	5,000.	2,500.

Certain type varieties are found in the word "Zanzibar" on Nos. 1 to 31A viz: Inverted "q" for "b," broken "p" for "n," "i" without dot, small second "z" and tall second "z." These varieties are found on all values from ½a to 1r inclusive and the tall "z" is also found on the 2r, 3r and 5r.

Stamps of British East Africa, 1896, Overprinted in Black or Red

1896 Wmk. Crown and C A (2)

32	A8	½a yellow grn	37.50	22.50
33	A8	1a carmine	37.50	18.00
34	A8	2½a dk blue (R)	85.00	50.00
35	A8	4½a orange	50.00	60.00
36	A8	5a dark ocher	60.00	37.50
37	A8	7½a lilac	50.00	60.00
	Nos. 32-37 (6)		320.00	248.00

Sultan Seyyid Hamed-bin-Thwain
A2 | A3

1896, Sept. 20 Engr. Wmk. 71

38	A2	½a yel grn & red	4.50	2.00
39	A2	1a indigo & red	3.75	1.75
40	A2	2a red brn & red	3.50	.85
41	A2	2½a ultra & red	16.00	1.60
42	A3	3a slate & red	15.00	9.50
43	A2	4a dk green & red	9.50	4.75
44	A2	4½a orange & red	8.00	6.75
45	A2	5a bister & red	7.50	3.00
a.	Half used as 2½a on cover			4,750.
46	A2	7½a lilac & red	4.75	4.75
47	A2	8a ol gray & red	13.50	9.00
48	A3	1r ultra & red	22.50	12.00
49	A3	2r green & red	30.00	13.00
50	A3	3r violet & red	36.00	13.00
51	A3	4r lake & red	27.50	20.00
52	A3	5r blk brn & red	38.00	20.00
	Nos. 38-52 (15)		240.00	121.95

No. 43 Surcharged in Red
1897

53	A2	(a) 2½a on 4a	85.00	47.50
54	A2	(b) 2½a on 4a	275.00	250.00
55	A2	(c) 2½a on 4a	100.00	70.00
	Nos. 53-55 (3)		460.00	367.50

1898 Engr. Wmk. 47

56	A2	½a yel grn & red	1.75	.45
57	A2	1a indigo & red	5.00	.75
58	A2	2a red brn & red	7.00	2.25
58A	A2	2½a ultra & red	5.00	.45
59	A2	3a slate & red	7.00	.75
60	A2	4a dk grn & red	4.25	1.25
60A	A2	4½a orange & red	12.00	1.25
61	A2	5a bister & red	20.00	2.25
61A	A2	7½a lilac & red	14.50	3.50
61B	A2	8a ol gray & red	18.00	3.25
	Nos. 56-61B (10)		94.50	16.15

Sultan Seyyid Hamoud-bin-Mahommed-bin-Said
A4 | A5

1899-1901

62	A4	½a yel grn & red	2.75	.65
63	A4	1a indigo & red	5.00	.25
64	A4	1a car & red ('01)	3.00	.25
65	A4	2a red brn & red	3.75	.75
66	A4	2½a ultra & red	3.75	.75
67	A4	3a slate & red	4.75	2.50
68	A4	4a dk green & red	4.50	2.50
69	A4	4½a orange & red	17.50	7.00
70	A4	4½a ind & red ('01)	19.00	13.50
71	A4	5a bister & red	4.75	1.75
72	A4	7½a lilac & red	4.75	5.50
73	A4	8a ol gray & red	4.75	5.00

Wmk. 71

74	A5	1r ultra & red	21.00	17.50
75	A5	2r green & red	22.50	21.00
76	A5	3r violet & red	45.00	52.50
77	A5	4r lilac rose & red	75.00	77.50
78	A5	5r gray brown & red	85.00	87.50
	Nos. 62-78 (17)		326.75	296.40

For surcharges see Nos. 94-98.

A6 | Monogram of Sultan Ali bin Hamoud — A7

1904, June 8 Typo. Wmk. 47

79	A6	½a emerald	2.25	1.00
80	A6	1a rose red	2.25	.25

81	A6	2a bister brown	4.25	.50
82	A6	2½a ultra	4.25	.40
83	A6	3a gray	4.50	2.50
84	A6	4a blue green	3.50	1.75
85	A6	4½a black	4.25	2.75
86	A6	5a ocher	6.00	1.00
87	A6	7½a violet	7.50	8.00
88	A6	8a olive green	5.00	4.25
89	A7	1r ultra & red	32.50	22.50
90	A7	2r green & red	37.50	47.50
91	A7	3r violet & red	55.00	85.00
92	A7	4r magenta & red	75.00	120.00
93	A7	5r olive & red	75.00	132.50
	Nos. 79-93 (15)		318.75	430.30

Nos. 69-70, 72-73 Surcharged in Black or Lake

g | h

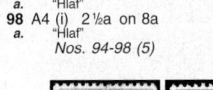
i

1904

94	A4	(g) 1a on 4½a	5.00	6.00
95	A4	(g) 1a on 4½a (L)	5.75	24.00
96	A4	(h) 2a on 4a (L)	19.00	24.00
97	A4	(i) 2½a on 7½a	17.50	25.00
a.	"Hlaf"		16,000.	
98	A4	(i) 2½a on 8a	27.50	37.50
a.	"Hlaf"		15,000.	10,000.
	Nos. 94-98 (5)		74.75	116.50

Sultan Ali bin Hamoud
A8 | A9

A10

Palace of the Sultan — A11

1908-09 Engr. Wmk. 47

99	A8	1c gray ('09)	2.75	.35
100	A8	3c yellow grn	8.50	.25
101	A8	6c carmine	11.00	.25
102	A8	10c org brn ('09)	6.50	2.25
103	A8	12c violet	17.50	2.00
104	A9	15c ultra	16.00	.45
105	A9	25c brown	8.00	1.10
106	A9	50c dp green	10.00	6.00
107	A9	75c slate ('09)	16.00	17.50
108	A10	1r yellow green	37.50	14.00
109	A10	2r violet	21.00	18.00
110	A10	3r yellow brown	30.00	57.50
111	A10	4r red	75.00	100.00
112	A10	5r blue	65.00	90.00
113	A11	10r brn & dk grn	190.00	350.00
114	A11	20r yel grn & blk	475.00	750.00
115	A11	30r dk brn & blk	550.00	900.00
116	A11	40r org brn & blk	750.00	
117	A11	50r lilac & blk	650.00	
118	A11	100r blue & blk	900.00	
119	A11	200r black & brn	1,300.	
	Nos. 99-112 (14)		324.75	309.65

It is probable that Nos. 118 and 119 were used only for fiscal purposes.

Sultan
Khalifa bin
Harub — A12

Dhow — A13

Dhow — A14

1913			**Perf. 14**
120	A12	1c gray	.50	.50
121	A12	3c yellow grn	1.50	.60
122	A12	6c carmine	1.75	.25
123	A12	10c brown	1.25	3.25
124	A12	12c violet	1.40	.40
125	A12	15c ultra	2.25	.40
126	A12	25c black brn	1.40	2.50
127	A12	50c dk green	3.25	6.50
128	A12	75c dk gray	2.75	5.00
129	A13	1r yellow grn	16.00	16.00
130	A13	2r dk violet	14.00	30.00
131	A13	3r orange	20.00	47.50
132	A13	4r red	32.50	80.00
133	A13	5r blue	47.50	50.00
134	A14	10r brown & grn	170.00	350.00
135	A14	20r yel grn & blk	300.00	550.00
136	A14	30r dk brn & blk	300.00	700.00
137	A14	40r orange & blk	500.00	900.00
138	A14	50r dull vio & blk	475.00	950.00
139	A14	100r blue & blk	650.00
140	A14	200r black & brn	1,000.
	Nos. 120-134 (15)	316.05	592.90

1914-22			**Wmk. 3**
141	A12	1c gray	.90	.30
142	A12	3c yellow grn	1.40	.25
143	A12	6c carmine	1.00	.25
144	A12	8c vio, *yel* ('22)	1.00	5.50
145	A12	10c dk grn, *yel* ('22)	.85	.40
146	A12	15c ultra	1.50	6.50
148	A12	50c dark green	5.00	5.00
149	A12	75c deep gray	3.50	27.50
150	A13	1r yellow grn	5.00	4.00
151	A13	2r dark violet	9.50	11.50
152	A13	3r brown org	22.50	45.00
153	A13	4r red	20.00	95.00
154	A13	5r blue	19.00	72.50
155	A14	10r brown & grn	180.00	650.00
	Nos. 141-155 (14)	271.15	923.70

1921-29			**Wmk. 4**
156	A12	1c gray	.30	9.00
157	A12	3c yellow grn	2.50	4.75
158	A12	3c orange ('22)	.40	.25
159	A12	4c green ('22)	.60	2.00
160	A12	6c carmine	.40	.55
161	A12	6c vio, *bl* ('22)	.45	.25
162	A12	10c lt brown	.80	13.00
163	A12	12c violet	.50	.35
164	A12	12c carmine ('22)	.50	.50
165	A12	15c ultra	.80	12.00
166	A12	20c dk blue ('22)	1.25	.40
167	A12	25c black brn	.90	20.00
168	A12	50c blue green	2.00	5.50
169	A12	75c dark gray	3.25	65.00
170	A13	1r yellow grn	7.00	4.00
171	A13	2r dk violet	4.50	13.50
172	A13	3r ocher	5.50	8.50
173	A13	4r red	17.50	40.00
174	A13	5r blue	24.00	72.50
175	A14	10r brown & grn	170.00	400.00
176	A14	20r green & blk	350.00	700.00
177	A14	30r dk brn & blk ('29)	300.00	750.00
	Nos. 156-175 (20)	243.15	672.05

Sultan Khalifa bin
Harub ("CENTS" with
Serifs) — A15

1926-27
--- | --- | --- | ---
184 | A15 | 1c brown | 1.00 | .25
185 | A15 | 3c yellow org | .30 | .25
186 | A15 | 4c deep green | .30 | .35
187 | A15 | 6c dark violet | .35 | .25
188 | A15 | 8c slate | 1.10 | 5.50
189 | A15 | 10c olive green | 1.10 | .45
190 | A15 | 12c deep red | 2.75 | .25
191 | A15 | 20c ultra | .65 | .40
192 | A15 | 25c violet, *yel* | 9.00 | 3.00

---

193 | A15 | 50c claret | 3.75 | .50
--- | --- | --- | ---
194 | A15 | 75c olive brown | 29.00 | 35.00
| | *Nos. 184-194 (11)* | 49.30 | 46.20

> **Catalogue values for unused stamps in this section, from this point to the end of the section, are for Never Hinged items.**

"CENTS"
without
Serifs — A16

Dhow — A17

Dhow — A18

1936			**Perf. 14**
201	A16	5c deep green	.25	.25
202	A16	10c black	.25	.25
203	A16	15c carmine	.30	1.25
204	A16	20c brown org	.25	.25
205	A16	25c violet, *yel*	.25	.25
206	A16	30c ultra	.25	.25
207	A16	40c black brown	.25	.25
208	A16	50c claret	.50	.25
209	A17	1sh yellow grn	.75	.25
210	A17	2sh dark violet	1.50	2.50
211	A17	5sh red	22.50	8.00
212	A17	7.50sh blue	35.00	32.50
213	A18	10sh brn & grn	37.50	27.50
	Nos. 201-213 (13)	99.55	73.75

For overprints see Nos. 222-223.

A19

1936, Dec. 9
--- | --- | --- | ---
214 | A19 | 10c olive grn & blk | 4.25 | .35
215 | A19 | 20c red violet & blk | 6.50 | 2.75
216 | A19 | 30c deep ultra & blk | 19.00 | .65
217 | A19 | 50c red orange & blk | 20.00 | 5.50
| | *Nos. 214-217 (4)* | 49.75 | 9.25

Reign of Sultan Khalifa bin Harub, 25th
anniv.

A20

Dhow & Map Showing Zanzibar & Muscat.

Perf. 14

1944, Nov. 20		**Engr.**		**Wmk. 4**
218	A20	10c violet blue	1.00	3.75
219	A20	20c brown orange	1.25	3.50
220	A20	50c Prus green	1.25	.40
221	A20	1sh dull purple	1.25	.80
	Nos. 218-221 (4)	4.75	8.45

200th anniv. of the Al Busaid Dynasty.

Nos. 202 and 206
Overprinted in Red

1946, Nov. 11
--- | --- | --- | ---
222 | A16 | 10c black | .25 | .50
223 | A16 | 30c ultra | .40 | .50

Victory of the Allied Nations in WW II.

Common Design Types
pictured following the introduction.

Silver Wedding Issue
Common Design Types
1949, Jan. 10　Photo.　Perf. 14x14½
224	CD304	20c orange	.60	1.50

Engraved; Name Typographed
Perf. 11½x11
225	CD305	10sh light brown	29.00	36.50

UPU Issue
Common Design Types
Engr.; Name Typo. on 30c, 50c
Perf. 13½, 11x11½
1949, Oct. 10 | | | **Wmk. 4**
--- | --- | --- | --- | ---
226 | CD306 | 20c red orange | .45 | 3.75
227 | CD307 | 30c indigo | 3.00 | 2.00
228 | CD308 | 50c red lilac | 1.40 | 3.25
229 | CD309 | 1sh blue green | 1.40 | 4.50
| | *Nos. 226-229 (4)* | 6.25 | 13.50

Sultan Khalifa bin
Harub — A21

Seyyid
Khalifa
Schools
A22

Perf. 12x12½, 13x12½
1952, Aug. 26 | | | **Engr.**
--- | --- | --- | --- | ---
230 | A21 | 5c black | .25 | .25
231 | A21 | 10c red orange | .25 | .25
232 | A21 | 15c green | 1.50 | 2.50
233 | A21 | 20c carmine | .75 | .75
234 | A21 | 25c plum | 1.10 | .25
235 | A21 | 30c blue green | 1.10 | .25
236 | A21 | 35c ultra | .75 | 5.00
237 | A21 | 40c chocolate | .75 | 2.00
238 | A21 | 50c purple | 3.25 | .25
239 | A22 | 1sh choc & bl grn | .75 | .25
240 | A22 | 2sh claret & ultra | 3.00 | 2.75
241 | A22 | 5sh carmine & blk | 3.00 | 5.00
242 | A22 | 7.50sh emer & gray | 25.00 | 27.50
243 | A22 | 10sh gray blk & rose red | 12.00 | 15.00
| | *Nos. 230-243 (14)* | 53.45 | 62.00

Sultan Khalifa bin
Harub — A23

1954, Aug. 26 | | **Perf. 12½x12**
--- | --- | --- | --- | ---
244 | A23 | 15c green | .25 | .25
245 | A23 | 20c scarlet | .25 | .25
246 | A23 | 30c ultra | .25 | .25
247 | A23 | 50c purple | .30 | .30
248 | A23 | 1.25sh brown orange | .75 | .75
| | *Nos. 244-248 (5)* | 1.80 | 1.80

The frames differ on Nos. 245 and 247. Sultan Khalifa bin Harub, 75th birth anniv.

Cloves — A24

Dhows
A25

Sultan's
Barge — A26

Malindi Minaret
Mosque — A27

Kibweni
Palace — A28

Sultan Khalifa bin Harub and: 25c, 35c, and
50c Map showing location of Zanzibar. 1sh,
2sh, Dimbani Mosque.

Perf. 11½ (A24), 11x11½ (A25),
14x13½ (A26), 13½x14 (A27),
13x13½ (A28)
1957, Aug. 26 | | **Engr.** | **Wmk. 314**
--- | --- | --- | --- | ---
249 | A24 | 5c dull grn & org | .25 | .25
250 | A24 | 10c rose car & brt grn | .25 | .25
251 | A25 | 15c dk brn & grn | .25 | 3.25
252 | A26 | 20c ultra | .25 | .25
253 | A26 | 25c blk & brn org | .25 | 1.50
254 | A25 | 30c int blk & rose car | .25 | 1.50
255 | A26 | 35c brt grn & ind | .30 | .25
256 | A27 | 40c int blk & redsh brn | .25 | .25
257 | A26 | 50c dull grn & bl | .35 | .30
258 | A27 | 1sh int blk & brt car | .30 | .30
259 | A25 | 1.25sh rose car & dk grn | 4.00 | .45
260 | A27 | 2sh dull grn & org | 4.00 | 2.50
261 | A28 | 5sh vio | 6.00 | 2.50
262 | A28 | 7.50sh green | 13.00 | 4.50
263 | A28 | 10sh rose carmine | 14.00 | 6.50
| | *Nos. 249-263 (15)* | 43.70 | 24.55

Sultan Seyyid
Abdulla bin
Khalifa — A29

Designs as before with portrait of Sultan
Seyyid Abdulla bin Khalifa.

Perf. 11½ (A29), 11x11½ (A25),
14x13½ (A26), 13½x14 (A27)
1961, Oct. 17 | | **Engr.** | **Wmk. 314**
--- | --- | --- | --- | ---
264 | A29 | 5c dull grn & org | .40 | 1.10
265 | A29 | 10c rose car & brt grn | .40 | .25
266 | A25 | 15c dk brn & grn | .90 | 3.75
267 | A26 | 20c ultra | .40 | .45
268 | A26 | 25c blk & brn org | 1.00 | 1.75
269 | A25 | 30c int blk & rose car | 3.25 | 2.75
270 | A26 | 35c brt grn & indigo | 3.00 | 5.00
271 | A27 | 40c int blk & redsh brn | .40 | .25
272 | A26 | 50c dull grn & bl | 2.75 | .25
273 | A27 | 1sh int blk & brt car | .50 | 1.25
274 | A25 | 1.25sh rose car & dk grn | 3.00 | 5.00
275 | A27 | 2sh dull grn & org | 1.00 | 3.75

Perf. 13x13½
276	A28	5sh ultra	4.00	9.00
277	A28	7.50sh green	3.75	18.00
278	A28	10sh rose carmine	3.75	10.00
279	A28	20sh dk brown	19.00	30.00
	Nos. 264-279 (16)	47.50	92.55

For overprints see Nos. 285-300.

Freedom from Hunger Issue
Common Design Type with Portrait of Sultan Seyyid Abdulla bin Khalifa

1963, June 4   Photo.   Perf. 14x14½
280 CD314 1.30sh sepia   1.50   .80

Independent State

Sultan Seyyid Jamshid bin Abdulla and Zanzibar Clove — A30

Designs: 50c, "To Prosperity," arch and sun. 1.30sh, "Religious Tolerance," composite view of churches and mosques, horiz. 2.50sh, "Towards the Light," Mangapwani Cave.

Perf. 12½

1963, Dec. 10   Photo.   Unwmk.
281 A30 30c multicolored   .25   .25
282 A30 50c multicolored   .30   .30
283 A30 1.30sh multicolored   .40   2.00
284 A30 2.50sh multicolored   .50   2.00
  Nos. 281-284 (4)   1.45   4.55

Zanzibar's independence, Dec. 10, 1963. For overprints see Nos. 301-304.

Republic

Nos. 264-279 Overprinted

1964, Feb. 28   As Before
285 A29 5c dull grn & org   .25   .25
286 A29 10c rose car & brt grn   .25   .25
287 A29 15c dk brn & grn   .25   .25
288 A26 20c ultra   .25   .25
289 A25 25c blk & brn org   .35   .25
290 A25 30c int blk & rose car   .25   .25
291 A26 35c brt grn & ind   .35   .25
292 A27 40c int blk & redsh brn   .25   .25
293 A26 50c dull grn & blue   .35   .25
294 A27 1sh int blk & brt car   .30   .25
295 A25 1.25sh rose car & dk grn   2.25   .90
296 A27 2sh dull grn & org   .85   .45
297 A28 5sh ultra   .85   .50
298 A28 7.50sh green   1.25   7.00
299 A28 10sh rose carmine   2.00   7.00
300 A28 20sh dark brown   3.00   8.50
  Nos. 285-300 (16)   13.05   26.85

The overprint was applied in England. It is in 2 lines on 40c and 1sh to 20sh. "Jamhuri" means "republic."

Overprint Handstamped

285a A29 5c   1.00   .60
286a A29 10c   1.00   .25
287a A25 15c   1.50   2.00
288a A26 20c   1.00   .50
289a A26 25c   1.75   .25
290a A25 30c   1.00   .50
291a A26 35c   1.75   1.00
292a A27 40c   1.00   1.00
293a A26 50c   1.75   .25
294a A27 1sh   1.00   1.25
295a A25 1.25sh   1.00   1.50
296a A27 2sh   2.50   1.50
297a A28 5sh   2.00   1.75
298a A28 7.50sh   2.50   1.75
299a A28 10sh   2.50   2.50
300a A28 20sh   3.00   8.00
  Nos. 285a-300a (16)   26.25   24.60

This overprint was applied locally. It has one line of serifed letters. These are found diagonal, vertical, horizontal, double and inverted. See Nos. 301a-304b. Other stamps with this overprint, including postage dues, were unofficial.

Nos. 281-284 Overprinted

1964, Feb. 28   As Before
301 A30 30c multi   .25   .25
302 A30 50c multi   .30   .30
303 A30 1.30sh multi   .40   .40
304 A30 2.50sh multi   .60   .60
  a. Green omitted   140.00
  Nos. 301-304 (4)   1.55   1.55

One-line overprint on 1.30sh.

Overprint Handstamped

301a A30 30c   .60   .30
302a A30 50c   .40   .35
303a A30 1.30sh   1.00   .80
304b A30 2.50sh   1.50   1.50
  c. Green omitted   350.00
  Nos. 301a-304b (4)   3.50   2.95

See note after No. 300a.

Moorish Arch, Ax, Sword and Spear — A31

Designs: 10c, 20c, Arch and arrow piercing chain. 25c, 40c, Man with rifle. 30c, 50c, Man breaking chain. 1sh, Man, flag and sun. 1.30sh, Hands breaking chain and cloves, horiz. 2sh, Hands waving flag, horiz. 5sh, Map of Zanzibar and Pemba and flag, horiz. 10sh, Flag and map of Zanzibar and Pemba, horiz. 20sh, Flag of Zanzibar, horiz

Perf. 13x13½, 13½x13

1964, June 21   Litho.   Unwmk.
305 A31 5c multicolored   .40   .25
306 A31 10c multicolored   .40   .25
307 A31 15c multicolored   .40   .25
308 A31 20c multicolored   .50   .25
309 A31 25c multicolored   .50   .25
310 A31 30c multicolored   .40   .25
311 A31 40c multicolored   .60   .25
312 A31 50c multicolored   .40   .25
313 A31 1sh multicolored   .50   .25
314 A31 1.30sh multicolored   .30   1.25
315 A31 2sh multicolored   .50   .50
316 A31 5sh multicolored   1.25   3.00
317 A31 10sh multicolored   5.25   4.00
318 A31 20sh multicolored   5.00   20.00
  Nos. 305-318 (14)   16.40   31.00

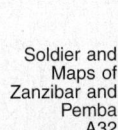

Soldier and Maps of Zanzibar and Pemba A32

Reconstruction A33

Perf. 13½x13, 13x13½

1965, Jan. 12   Unwmk.
319 A32 20c green & yel grn   .25   .25
320 A33 30c dk brn & ocher   .25   .25
321 A32 1.30sh vio blue & blue   .25   .25
322 A33 2.50sh purple & rose   .75   .50
  Nos. 319-322 (4)   1.50   1.25

First anniversary of the revolution.

Zanzibar and Tanzania

Rice Planting A34

Design: 30c, 1.30sh, Hands holding rice.

Perf. 13x12½

1965, Oct. 17   Litho.   Unwmk.
323 A34 20c blue & blk brn   .25   1.00
324 A34 30c brt pink & blk brn   .25   1.00
325 A34 1.30sh org & blk brn   .35   2.25
326 A34 2.50sh emer & blk brn   .55   4.00
  Nos. 323-326 (4)   1.40   8.25

Issued to publicize agricultural development.

Symbols of Trade, Agriculture, Industry and Education A35

Pres. Abeid Amani Karume and Vice-Pres. Abdulla Kassim Hanga A36

Designs: 50c, 2.50sh, Soldier and sunburst.

1966, Jan. 12   Litho.   Perf. 12½x13
327 A35 20c ultra, red & gray   .25   .25
328 A35 50c black & yel   .25   .25
329 A35 1.30sh multicolored   .30   .35
330 A35 2.50sh black & org   .60   1.00
  Nos. 327-330 (4)   1.40   1.85

2nd anniv. of the revolution of Jan. 12, 1964.

1966, Apr. 26   Photo.   Perf. 13½x13
Design: 50c, 1.30sh, Flag, laurel and hands holding Flame of the Union (inscribed: Jamhuri Tanzania Zanzibar).
331 A36 30c multicolored   .25   .25
332 A36 50c multicolored   .25   .25
333 A36 1.30sh multicolored   .35   .30
334 A36 2.50sh multicolored   .60   1.25
  Nos. 331-334 (4)   1.45   2.05

Union of Tanganyika and Zanzibar, 2nd anniv.

Logging A37

10c, 1sh, Clove trees & man. 15c, 40c, Cabinetmaker. 20c, 5sh, Lumumba College & book. 25c, 1.30sh, Farmer & tractor. 30c, 2sh, Volunteer farm workers. 50c, 10sh, Street scene, vert.

Perf. 13x12½, 12½x13

1966, June 5   Litho.
335 A37 5c lemon & vio brn   .70   .80
336 A37 10c brt grn & vio brn   .70   .80
337 A37 15c vio brn & bl   .70   .80
338 A37 20c vio bl & org   .70   .25
339 A37 25c vio brn & yel   .70   .25
340 A37 30c vio brn & dl yel   .80   .25
341 A37 40c vio brn & rose   .90   .25
342 A37 50c green & yel   .90   .25
343 A37 1sh ultra & vio brn   .90   .25
344 A37 1.30sh lt bl grn & vio brn   1.00   3.25
345 A37 2sh brt grn & vio brn   1.00   .60
346 A37 5sh ver & gray   1.50   6.00
347 A37 10sh red brn & yel   2.50   20.00
348 A37 20sh brt pink & vio brn   5.00   35.00
  Nos. 335-348 (14)   18.00   68.80

Symbols of Education — A38

1966, Sept. 25   Perf. 13½x13
349 A38 50c blue, blk & org   .25   1.00
350 A38 1.30sh blue, blk & yel grn   .30   1.75
351 A38 2.50sh blue, blk & pink   .80   4.00
  Nos. 349-351 (3)   1.35   6.75

Introduction of free education.

People and Flag A39

Design: 50c, 1.30sh, Vice-President Abdulla Kassim Hanga, flag and crowd, vert.

Perf. 14x14½, 14½x14

1967, Feb. 5   Litho.   Unwmk.
352 A39 30c multicolored   .25   1.00
353 A39 50c multicolored   .25   1.00
354 A39 1.30sh multicolored   .25   1.25
355 A39 2.50sh multicolored   .40   3.00
  Nos. 352-355 (4)   1.15   6.25

10th anniversary of Afro-Shirazi Party.

Volunteer Workers A40

Perf. 12½x12

1967, Aug. 20   Photo.   Unwmk.
356 A40 1.30sh multicolored   .30   2.50
357 A40 2.50sh multicolored   .55   6.50

Volunteer (Young) Workers Brigade.
All Zanzibar stamps were withdrawn July 1, 1968, and replaced with current Kenya, Uganda and Tanzania stamps.

POSTAGE DUE STAMPS

D1

Rouletted 10

1931   Typeset   Unwmk.
Thin Paper
Without Gum

J1 D1 1c blk, orange   12.50   150.00
J2 D1 2c blk, orange   5.50   80.00
J3 D1 3c blk, orange   5.75   65.00
J3A D1 6c blk, orange   8,000.
J4 D1 9c blk, orange   3.25   35.00
J4A D1 12c blk, orange   13,000.   11,000.
J4B D1 12c blk, green   1,600.   675.00
J5 D1 15c blk, orange   3.25   37.50
J6 D1 18c blk, orange   27.50   85.00
  a. 18c black, salmon   5.00   55.00
J7 D1 20c blk, orange   4.50   80.00
J8 D1 21c blk, orange   4.00   50.00
J8A D1 24c blk, orange   17,000.   16,000.
J8B D1 25c blk, magenta   3,250.   1,500.

J9	D1 31c blk, *orange*	11.00	100.00
J10	D1 50c blk, *orange*	24.00	250.00
J11	D1 75c blk, *orange*	75.00	600.00

The variety "cent.s" occurs once on each sheet of Nos. J3 to J11 inclusive.

Insufficiently prepaid
Postage due.
25 cents.
D2

1931-33   Rouletted 5
Thick Paper

J12	D2 2c blk, *salmon*	23.00	37.50
J13	D2 3c blk, *rose*	4.00	60.00
J14	D2 6c blk, *yellow*	4.00	40.00
J15	D2 12c blk, *blue*	5.00	32.50
J16	D2 25c blk, *pink*	11.00	110.00
J17	D2 25c blk, *dull violet*	22.50	75.00
	Nos. J12-J17 (6)	69.50	355.00

Catalogue values for unused stamps in this section, from this point to the end of the section, are for Never Hinged items.

D3

1936   Typo.   Wmk. 4   Perf. 14

J18	D3 5c violet	8.00	13.00
J19	D3 10c carmine	6.00	3.25
J20	D3 20c green	2.50	6.50
J21	D3 30c brown	15.00	22.50
J22	D3 40c ultra	10.00	30.00
J23	D3 1sh gray	14.00	37.50
	Nos. J18-J23 (6)	55.50	112.75

Chalky paper was introduced in 1956 for the 5c, 30c, 40c, 1sh, and in 1962 for the 10c, 20c. Value for set of 6, unused $3.25, used $110. See note after No. 300a.

ZIMBABWE

zim-'bä-bwē

LOCATION — Southeastern Africa, bordered by Zambia, Mozambique, South Africa, and Botswana
GOVT. — Republic
AREA — 150,872 sq. mi.
POP. — 11,163,160 (1999 est.)
CAPITAL — Harare

Formerly Rhodesia, the Republic of Zimbabwe was established April 18, 1980.

100 Cents = 1 Dollar

Catalogue values for all unused stamps in this country are for Never Hinged items.

Morganite
A69

Black Rhinoceros
A70

Odzani
Falls — A71

Perf. 14½, 14½x14 (A70)
1980   Litho.

414	A69 1c shown	.25	.35
415	A69 3c Amethyst	.40	.35
416	A69 4c Garnet	.40	.25
417	A69 5c Citrine	.40	.25
418	A69 7c Blue topaz	.40	.25
419	A70 9c shown	.25	.25
420	A70 11c Lion	.25	.25
421	A70 13c Warthog	.25	.25
422	A70 15c Giraffe	.25	.25
423	A70 17c Zebra	.25	.25
424	A71 21c shown	.25	.25
425	A71 25c Goba Falls	.35	.35
426	A71 30c Inyangombe Falls	.40	.55
426A	A71 40c Bundi Falls	7.75	5.25
427	A71 $1 Bridal Veil Falls	.55	2.25
428	A71 $2 Victoria Falls	.95	4.00
	Nos. 414-428 (16)	13.35	15.35

Rotary
International, 75th
Anniversary — A72

1980, June 18   Perf. 14½

429	A72 4c multicolored	.25	.25
430	A72 13c multicolored	.25	.30
431	A72 21c multicolored	.25	.50
432	A72 25c multicolored	.35	.75
a.	Souvenir sheet of 4, #429-432	1.40	1.40
	Nos. 429-432 (4)	1.10	1.80

Olympic
Rings
A73

1980, July 19

433	A73 17c multicolored	.35	.35

22nd Summer Olympic Games, Moscow, July 19-Aug. 3.

Gatooma
Post
Office,
1912
A74

Post Offices: 7c, Salisbury, 1912. 9c, Umtali, 1901. 17c, Bulawayo, 1895.

1980   Litho.   Perf. 14½

434	A74 5c multicolored	.25	.25
435	A74 7c multicolored	.25	.25
436	A74 9c multicolored	.25	.25
437	A74 17c multicolored	.25	.25
a.	Souvenir sheet of 4, #434-437	1.00	1.00
	Nos. 434-437 (4)	1.00	1.00

Post Office Savings Bank, 75th anniv.

Intl. Year of the
Disabled — A75

Natl. Tree
Day — A76

Designs: Various disabilities. Nos. 438-441 form a continuous design.

1981, Sept. 23   Litho.   Perf. 14½

438	A75 5c multicolored	.25	.25
439	A75 7c multicolored	.25	.25
440	A75 13c multicolored	.25	.25
441	A75 17c multicolored	.50	.50
	Nos. 438-441 (4)	1.25	1.25

1981, Dec. 4

442	A76 5c Msasa	.25	.25
443	A76 7c Mopane	.25	.25
444	A76 21c Flat-crowned acacia	.70	.70
445	A76 30c Pod mahogany	.90	.90
	Nos. 442-445 (4)	2.10	2.10

Rock
Paintings
A77

Designs: 9c, Khoisan figures, Gwamgwadza Cave. 11c, Kudus, human figures, Epworth Mission. 17c, Diana's Vow, Rusape. 21c, Giraffes, Gwamgwadza Cave. 25c, Warthog, Mucheka Cave. 30c, Hunters, Shinzwini Shelter.

1982, Mar. 17   Litho.   Perf. 14½

446	A77 9c multicolored	.75	.75
447	A77 11c multicolored	.90	.90
448	A77 17c multicolored	1.25	1.25
449	A77 21c multicolored	1.75	1.75
450	A77 25c multicolored	1.75	1.75
451	A77 30c multicolored	2.75	2.75
	Nos. 446-451 (6)	9.15	9.15

Scouting
Year — A78

1982, July 21

452	A78 9c Emblem	.35	.35
453	A78 11c Campfire	.40	.40
454	A78 21c Map reading	.75	.75
455	A78 30c Baden Powell	1.00	1.00
	Nos. 452-455 (4)	2.50	2.50

TB
Bacillus
Centenary
A79

1982, Nov. 17   Perf. 14½

456	A79 11c Koch	1.00	1.25
457	A79 30c Scientist examining slide	2.00	2.25

Commonwealth Day — A80

Sculptures: 9c, Wing Woman, by Henry Mudzengerere, vert. 11c, Telling Secrets, by Joseph Ndandarika. 30c, Hornbill Man, by John Takawira. $1, The Chief, by Nicholas Mukomberanwa, vert.

1983, Mar. 14   Perf. 14½

458	A80 9c multicolored	.25	.25
459	A80 11c multicolored	.25	.25
460	A80 30c multicolored	.30	.35
461	A80 $1 multicolored	.80	1.50
	Nos. 458-461 (4)	1.60	2.35

World Plowing Contest, May — A81

No. 463, mechanized plowing.

1983, May 13   Litho.   Perf. 14½

462	A81 Pair	.70	.70
a.-b.	21c, any single	.35	.35
463	A81 Pair	.90	.90
a.-b.	30c, any single	.45	.45

World Communications Year — A82

Means of communication and transportation. Nos. 464-467 vert.

1983, Oct. 12   Litho.   Perf. 14½

464	A82 9c Mailman	.25	.25
465	A82 11c Signaling airplane	.30	.30
466	A82 15c Telephone operators	.45	.45
467	A82 17c Reading newspapers	.60	.60
468	A82 21c Truck on highway	.70	.70
469	A82 30c Train	1.00	1.00
	Nos. 464-469 (6)	3.30	3.30

Zimbabwe Intl.
Trade Fair,
Bulawayo, May 5-
13 — A83

1984, Apr. 11   Litho.   Perf. 14½

470	A83 9c shown	.25	.25
471	A83 11c Globe	.25	.25
472	A83 30c Emblem	.70	.70
	Nos. 470-472 (3)	1.20	1.20

1984
Summer
Olympics
A84

Children's Drawings.

1984, July 18   Litho.   Perf. 14½

473	A84 9c Bicycling	.30	.25
474	A84 21c Swimming	.65	.65
475	A84 30c Running	1.00	1.00
476	A84 40c Hurdles	1.40	2.25
	Nos. 473-476 (4)	3.35	4.15

Heroes'
Day
A85

1984, Aug. 8   Litho.   Perf. 14½

477	A85 9c Heroes	.25	.25
478	A85 11c Monument, vert.	.25	.25
479	A85 17c Statue, vert.	.45	.45
480	A85 30c Bas-relief	.75	.75
	Nos. 477-480 (4)	1.70	1.70

Fish Eagle — A86

1984, Oct. 10   Litho.   Perf. 14½

481	A86 9c shown	.75	.75
482	A86 11c Long crested eagle	.80	.80
483	A86 13c Bateleur	.90	.90
484	A86 17c Black eagle	1.25	1.25

485	A86	21c Martial eagle	1.50 1.50
486	A86	30c African hawk eagle	2.10 2.10
		Nos. 481-486 (6)	7.30 7.30

Superheat Engine No. 86,
Mashonaland Railways, 1918 — A87

Steam locomotives: 11c, Engine No. 190, North British Locomotive Co., 1926. 17c, Engine No. 424, Beyer Peacock & Co., 1950. Engine No. 726, Beyer Peacock & Co., 1957.

1985, May 15 **Litho.**

487	A87	9c multicolored	1.00 1.00
488	A87	11c multicolored	1.40 1.40
489	A87	17c multicolored	2.10 2.10
490	A87	30c multicolored	3.75 3.75
		Nos. 487-490 (4)	8.25 8.25

INTELSAT V
A88

57c, Mazowe Earth Satellite Station.

Perf. 14½x14, 14½

1985, July 8 **Litho.**

491	A88	26c multicolored	2.10 2.40

Size: 62x23mm

492	A88	57c multicolored	4.25 4.75

Zimbabwe Bird
and
Tobacco — A89

Agriculture and industry.

Perf. 14¾x14½

1985, Aug. 21 **Litho.**

493	A89	1c shown	.25 .25
a.		Perf 14¼x13¾ ('88)	— 2.00
494	A89	3c Corn	.25 .25
a.		Perf 14¼x13¾ ('88)	— 2.00
495	A89	4c Cotton	.25 .25
a.		Perf 14¼x13¾ ('88)	— 2.00
496	A89	5c Tea	.45 .45
a.		Perf 14¼x13¾ ('88)	— 2.00
497	A89	10c Cattle	.45 .25
a.		Perf 14¼x13¾ ('88)	— 2.00
498	A89	11c Birchenough Bridge	1.10 .25
499	A89	12c Stamp mill	1.75 .25
500	A89	13c Gold production	3.25 .25
a.		Perf 14¼x13¾ ('88)	— 4.00
501	A89	15c Coal mining	2.50 .25
a.		Perf 14¼x13¾ ('88)	— 4.00
502	A89	17c Amethyst mining	3.25 .45
503	A89	18c Electric train	3.25 .45
504	A89	20c Kariba Dam	2.25 .45
a.		Perf 14¼x13¾ ('88)	— 4.00
505	A89	23c Elephants	3.50 .45
506	A89	25c Zambezi River sunset	.90 .45
a.		Perf 14¼x13¾ ('88)	— 5.00
507	A89	26c Baobab tree	.90 .30
508	A89	30c Great Zimbabwe ruins	1.10 .45
509	A89	35c Folk dancing	.90 .45
510	A89	45c Crushing corn	1.10 .60
511	A89	57c Wood carving	1.10 1.00
512	A89	$1 Mbira drum	1.75 1.25
a.		Perf 14¼x13¾ ('88)	— 25.00
513	A89	$2 Mule-drawn scotch cart	3.00 4.00
514	A89	$5 Natl. coat of arms	5.50 7.00
		Nos. 493-514 (22)	38.75 19.35

Natl.
Archives,
50th
Anniv.
A90

Designs: 12c, Gatsi Rusere (c. 1589-1623), ruler of Mashonaland and Zambezi area;

mutapa, 17th cent. 18c, Lobengula, ruler of Ndebele State (1870-94), sketch by E. A. Maund, 1889; 1888 Moffat Treaty and elephant seal. 26c, Archives exhibition hall. 35c, Archives building.

1985, Sept. 18 **Perf. 14½**

515	A90	12c multicolored	.25 .25
516	A90	18c multicolored	.30 .30
517	A90	26c multicolored	.45 .45
518	A90	35c multicolored	.65 .65
		Nos. 515-518 (4)	1.65 1.65

UN
Decade
for
Women
A91

1985, Nov. 13

519	A91	10c Computer operator	.70 .70
520	A91	17c Nurse, child	1.00 1.00
521	A91	26c Engineer	1.75 1.75
		Nos. 519-521 (3)	3.45 3.45

Harare Conference Center — A92

1986, Jan. 29 **Litho.** **Perf. 14½**

523	A92	26c Facade	.90 .90
524	A92	35c Interior	1.60 1.60

Southern African Development
Coordination Conference — A93

1986, Apr. 1 **Perf. 14½**

525	A93	12c Grain elevators	.50 .50
526	A93	18c Rhinoceros	2.60 2.60
527	A93	26c Map, jet	2.60 2.60
528	A93	35c Map, flags	2.75 2.75
		Nos. 525-528 (4)	8.45 8.45

Moths — A94

1986, June 18 **Litho.** **Perf. 14½x14**

529	A94	12c Jackson's emperor	1.60 1.60
530	A94	18c Oleander hawk	2.10 2.10
531	A94	26c Zaddach's emperor	2.75 2.75
532	A94	35c Southern marbled emperor	3.25 3.25
		Nos. 529-532 (4)	9.70 9.70

8th Non-
aligned
Summit
Conference
A95

1986, Aug. 28 **Litho.** **Perf. 14½x14**

533	A95	26c Victoria Falls	2.75 2.75

Size: 66x26mm

Perf. 14½

534	A95	$1 Great Zimbabwe Enclosure	6.50 6.50

Motoring
Cent.
A96

1986, Oct. 8 **Perf. 14½**

535	A96	10c Sopwith, 1921	.75 .75
536	A96	12c Gladiator, 1902	.75 .75
537	A96	17c Douglas, 1920	1.10 1.10
538	A96	26c Ford Model-A, 1930	1.75 1.75
539	A96	35c Schacht, 1909	2.25 2.25
540	A96	40c Benz Velocipede, 1886	2.25 2.25
		Nos. 535-540 (6)	8.85 8.85

A97

UN Child Survival Campaign: a, Growth monitoring. b, Breast-feeding. c, Oral rehydration. d, Immunization.

1987, Feb. 11 **Litho.** **Perf. 14x14½**

541		Block of 4	8.50 8.50
a.-d.		A97 12c any single	1.90 1.90

A98

Indigenous owls.

1987, Apr. 15 **Perf. 14½**

542	A98	12c Barred	2.75 2.75
543	A98	18c Pearl-spotted	3.50 3.50
544	A98	26c White-faced	4.00 4.00
545	A98	35c Scops	6.25 6.25
		Nos. 542-545 (4)	16.50 16.50

Natl. Girl Guides Movement, 75th
Anniv. — A99

1987, June 24

546	A99	15c Commitment	.75 .75
547	A99	23c Adventure	.90 .90
548	A99	35c Service	1.10 1.10
549	A99	$1 Intl. friendship	2.60 2.60
		Nos. 546-549 (4)	5.35 5.35

Duikers and
Population
Maps — A100

1987, Oct. 7 **Perf. 14½x14**

550	A100	15c Common gray	1.00 1.00
551	A100	23c Zebra	1.10 1.10
552	A100	25c Yellow-backed	1.10 1.10
553	A100	30c Blue	1.40 1.40
554	A100	35c Jentink's	1.40 1.40
555	A100	38c Red	1.40 1.40
		Nos. 550-555 (6)	7.40 7.40

Insects
A101

1988, Jan. 12 **Litho.** **Perf. 14½**

556	A101	15c Praying mantis	.90 .25
557	A101	23c Scarab beetle	1.25 .50
558	A101	35c Short-horned grasshopper	1.75 1.50
559	A101	45c Giant shield bug	2.00 3.75
		Nos. 556-559 (4)	5.90 6.00

Natl. Gallery of
Art, 30th
Anniv. — A102

Sculpture and paintings: 15c, Cockerel, by Arthur Azevedo. 23c, Changeling, by Bernard Matemera. 30c, Spirit Python, by Henry Munyaradzi. 35c, Spirit Bird Carrying People, by Thomas Mukarobgwa, horiz. 38c, The Song of the Shepherd Boy, by George Nene, horiz. 45c, War Victim, by Joseph Muzondo, horiz.

Perf. 14x14½, 14½x14

1988, Apr. 14 **Litho.**

560	A102	15c multicolored	.25 .25
561	A102	23c multicolored	.40 .40
562	A102	30c multicolored	.50 .50
563	A102	35c multicolored	.70 .70
564	A102	38c multicolored	.70 .70
565	A102	45c multicolored	.85 .85
		Nos. 560-565 (6)	3.40 3.40

Aloes and
Succulents
A103

1988, July 14 **Perf. 14½**

566	A103	15c Aloe cameronii bondana	.40 .40
567	A103	23c Orbeopsis caudata	.75 .75
568	A103	25c Euphorbia wildii	.75 .75
569	A103	30c Euphorbia fortissima	.85 .85
570	A103	35c Aloe aculeata	.85 .85
571	A103	38c Huernia zebrina	1.10 1.10
		Nos. 566-571 (6)	4.70 4.70

A104

1988, Oct. 6 **Litho.** **Perf. 14½x14**

572	A104	15c White-faced duck	1.00 .25
573	A104	23c Pygmy goose	1.10 .45
574	A104	30c Hottentot teal	1.25 1.25
575	A104	35c Knob-billed duck	1.40 1.40
576	A104	38c White-backed duck	1.50 1.50
577	A104	45c Maccoa	2.10 3.00
		Nos. 572-577 (6)	8.35 7.85

Geckos
A105

1989, Jan. 10 **Litho.** **Perf. 14½**

578	A105	15c O'Shaughnessy's banded	1.10 1.10
579	A105	23c Tiger rock	1.25 1.25

580 A105 35c Tasman's 2.00 2.00
581 A105 45c Bibron's 2.25 2.25
Nos. 578-581 (4) 6.60 6.60

Wildflowers
A106

1989, Apr. 12 Litho. Perf. 14½
582 A106 15c Spotted-leaved
arum-lily .60 .60
583 A106 23c Grassland vlei-lily .75 .75
584 A106 30c Manica protea .75 .75
585 A106 35c Flame lily .90 .90
586 A106 38c Poppy hibiscus 1.00 1.00
587 A106 45c Blue sesbania 1.10 1.10
Nos. 582-587 (6) 5.10 5.10

Fish
A107

1989, July 12 Litho. Perf. 14½
588 A107 15c Red-breasted
bream .90 .25
589 A107 23c Chessa 1.10 .25
590 A107 30c Eastern bottlenose 1.25 1.00
591 A107 35c Vundu 1.25 1.00
592 A107 38c Largemouth black
bass 1.50 1.50
593 A107 45c Tiger fish 2.00 2.40
Nos. 588-593 (6) 8.00 6.40
See Nos. 696-701.

Endangered
Species
A108

1989 Litho. Perf. 14½x14
594 A108 15c Black rhinoceros 1.75 1.75
595 A108 23c Cheetah 2.10 2.10
596 A108 30c Wild dog 2.25 2.25
597 A108 35c Pangolin 2.25 2.25
598 A108 38c Brown hyena 2.25 2.25
599 A108 45c Roan antelope 2.50 2.50
Nos. 594-599 (6) 13.10 13.10

Achievements,
1980-1990
A109

1990, Apr. 17 Litho. Perf. 14½x14
600 A109 15c Unity accord .60 .25
601 A109 23c Conference center .70 .25
602 A109 30c Education .80 .80
603 A109 35c Satellite dish .90 .90
604 A109 38c Sports stadium .90 .90
605 A109 45c Agriculture 1.40 2.50
Nos. 600-605 (6) 5.30 5.60

City of
Harare,
Cent.
A110

1990, July 11 Litho. Perf. 14½
606 A110 15c Runhare house,
1986 .55 .55
607 A110 23c Market hall, 1894 .80 .80
608 A110 30c Charter house,
1959 .85 .85

---

609 A110 35c Supreme Court,
1927 .90 .90
610 A110 38c Standard
Chartered Bank,
1911 .90 .90
611 A110 45c Town house, 1933 1.30 1.30
Nos. 606-611 (6) 5.30 5.30

36th
Commonwealth
Parliamentary
Conf. — A111

1990, Sept. 17
612 A111 35c Speaker's mace .75 .75
613 A111 $1 Speaker's chair 2.25 2.25

Animals — A112

Hand
Crafts — A113

Transportation — A114

**Perf. 14, 14½x14 (#620-625), 14¼
(#626-631)**

1990, Jan. 2 Litho.
614 A112 1c Tiger fish .25 .25
a. Perf 14¾x14½ 1.25 .25
615 A112 2c Helmeted
guineafowl 1.25 .25
a. Perf 14¾x14½ 1.75 .25
616 A112 3c Scrub hare .25 .25
a. Perf 14¾x14½ 1.25 .25
617 A112 4c Pangolin .45 .25
a. Perf 14x13½ .90 .25
618 A112 5c Greater kudu .75 .75
a. Perf 14¾x14½ 1.25 .25
619 A112 9c Black rhinoceros 2.00 .40
a. Perf 14¾x14½ 2.00 .40
620 A113 15c Head rest .25 .25
621 A113 20c Hand axe .25 .25
622 A113 23c Gourd, water
pot .25 .25
623 A113 25c Snuff box .25 .25
624 A113 26c Winnowing basket .60 .60
625 A113 30c Grinding stone .60 .60
626 A114 33c Riding bicycles 1.30 1.30
627 A114 35c Buses 2.00 2.00
628 A114 38c Train 2.00 2.00
629 A114 45c Motorcycle, trailer 2.00 2.00
630 A114 $1 Jet 3.00 3.00
631 A114 $2 Tractor-trailer
truck 3.00 3.00
Nos. 614-631 (18) 20.45 17.65

Animals
A115

1991, Jan. 15 Litho. Perf. 14½x14
632 A115 15c Small-spotted genet 1.40 1.40
633 A115 23c Red squirrel 1.50 1.50
634 A115 35c Night ape 2.10 2.10
635 A115 45c Bat-eared fox 3.00 3.00
Nos. 632-635 (4) 8.00 8.00

A116

Traditional musical instruments.

1991, Apr. 16 Litho. Perf. 14½
636 A116 15c Hosho .80 .25
637 A116 23c Mbira .85 .25
638 A116 30c Ngororombe .95 .95
639 A116 35c Chipendani 1.25 1.25
640 A116 38c Marimba 1.25 1.25
641 A116 45c Ngoma 1.40 1.90
Nos. 636-641 (6) 6.50 5.85

Wild
Fruits — A117

1991, July 17 Litho. Perf. 14x14½
642 A117 20c Snot-apple .75 .75
643 A117 39c Marula .90 .90
644 A117 51c Mobola plum 1.00 1.00
645 A117 60c Water berry 1.10 1.10
646 A117 65c Northern dwaba
berry 1.25 1.25
647 A117 77c Mahobohobo 1.50 1.50
Nos. 642-647 (6) 6.50 6.50
See Nos. 870-875.

A118

1991, Oct. 16 Litho. Perf. 14½
648 A118 20c Bridal Veil Falls 1.15 1.15
649 A118 39c Conference Em-
blem 1.15 1.15
650 A118 51c Chinhoyi Caves 1.50 1.50
651 A118 60c Kariba Dam
Wall 1.75 1.75
652 A118 65c Victoria Falls 1.90 1.90
653 A118 77c Balancing
Rocks 1.90 1.90
Nos. 648-653 (6) 9.35 9.35
Commonwealth Heads of Government
meeting, Harare.

Wild Cats
A119

1992, Jan. 8 Litho. Perf. 14½
654 A119 20c Lion 1.25 .25
655 A119 39c Leopard 2.00 .90
656 A119 60c Cheetah 3.00 3.00
657 A119 77c Serval 4.00 3.75
Nos. 654-657 (4) 10.25 7.90

Mushrooms
A120

Designs: 20c, Amanita zambiana. 39c,
Boletus edulis. 51c, Termitomyces. 60c,
Cantharellus densifolius. 65c, Cantharellus
longisporus. 77c, Cantharellus cibarius.

1992, Apr. 8 Litho. Perf. 14x14½
658 A120 20c multicolored 1.10 1.10
659 A120 39c multicolored 1.40 1.40
660 A120 51c multicolored 1.50 1.50
661 A120 60c multicolored 1.60 1.60
662 A120 65c multicolored 2.00 2.00
663 A120 77c multicolored 2.50 2.50
Nos. 658-663 (6) 10.10 10.10

Birds — A121

1992, July 17 Litho. Perf. 14½
664 A121 25c Blackeyed bulbul 1.10 1.10
665 A121 59c Fiscal shrike 1.50 1.50
666 A121 77c Forktailed
drongo 1.60 1.60
667 A121 90c Cardinal
woodpecker 1.90 1.90
668 A121 98c Yellowbilled
hornbill 1.90 1.90
669 A121 $1.16 Crested fran-
colin 2.00 2.00
Nos. 664-669 (6) 10.00 10.00

Butterflies
A122

1992, Oct. 15 Litho. Perf. 14½x14
670 A122 25c Foxy charaxes 1.30 1.30
671 A122 59c Orange & lem-
on 2.25 2.25
672 A122 77c Emperor swallowtail 2.75 2.75
673 A122 90c Blue pansy 3.25 3.25
674 A122 98c African mon-
arch 3.50 3.50
675 A122 $1.16 Gaudy com-
modore 4.00 4.00
Nos. 670-675 (6) 17.05 17.05

Minerals
A123

1993, Jan. 12 Litho. Perf. 14½x14
676 A123 25c Autunite 2.00 2.00
677 A123 59c Chromite 2.75 2.75
678 A123 77c Azurite 2.50 2.50
679 A123 90c Coal 4.00 4.00
680 A123 98c Gold 4.25 4.25
681 A123 $1.16 Emerald 5.50 5.50
Nos. 676-681 (6) 21.00 21.00

Owls — A124

1993, Apr. 6 Litho. Perf. 14½
682 A124 25c Wood owl 2.40 2.40
683 A124 59c Pels fishing
owl 3.00 3.00
684 A124 90c Spotted eagle
owl 4.50 4.50
685 A124 $1.16 Giant eagle
owl 5.50 5.50
Nos. 682-685 (4) 15.40 15.40

Household
Pottery
A125

1993, July 13 Litho. Perf. 14½x14
686 A125 25c Hadyana .80 .80
687 A125 59c Chirongo 1.00 1.00
688 A125 77c Mbiya 1.20 1.20
689 A125 90c Pfuko 1.40 1.40
690 A125 98c Tsaya 1.60 1.60
691 A125 $1.16 Gate 1.90 1.90
Nos. 686-691 (6) 7.90 7.90

Orchids — A126

1993, Oct. 12 Litho. Perf. 14½
692 A126 35c Polystachya
dendrobiflora 1.00 1.00
693 A126 $1 Diaphananthe
subsimplex 2.10 2.10
694 A126 $1.50 Ansellia gi-
gantea 3.25 3.25
695 A126 $1.95 Vanilla poly-
epis 4.25 4.25
Nos. 692-695 (4) 10.60 10.60

Fish Type of 1989
1994, Jan. 20 Litho. Perf. 14½
696 A107 35c Hunyani salmon .45 .45
697 A107 $1 Barbel .85 .85
698 A107 $1.30 Rainbow trout 1.10 1.10
699 A107 $1.50 Mottled eel 1.30 1.30
700 A107 $1.65 Mirror carp 1.50 1.50
701 A107 $1.95 Robustus bream 1.75 1.75
Nos. 696-701 (6) 6.95 6.95

City of
Bulawayo,
Cent.
A127

1994, Apr. 5 Litho. Perf. 14½
702 A127 35c City Hall .50 .50
703 A127 80c Cresta Churchill
Hotel .50 .50
704 A127 $1.15 High Court .80 .80
705 A127 $1.75 Douslin House 1.00 1.00
706 A127 $1.95 Goldfields Build-
ing 1.25 1.25
707 A127 $2.30 Parkade Centre 1.40 1.40
Nos. 702-707 (6) 5.45 5.45

Export
Flowers — A128
Christmas — A129

1994, July 12 Litho. Perf. 14½
708 A128 35c Strelitzia .65 .65
709 A128 80c Protea .65 .65
710 A128 $1.15 Phlox 1.10 1.10
711 A128 $1.75 Chrysanthemum 1.60 1.60
712 A128 $1.95 Lillum 1.75 1.75
713 A128 $2.30 Rose 2.00 2.00
Nos. 708-713 (6) 7.75 7.75

1994, Oct. 11 Litho. Perf. 14½
Designs: 35c, Archangel Gabriel, Virgin Mary. 80c, Mary, Joseph on way to Bethlehem. $1.15, Nativity scene. $1.75, Angel

pointing way to shepherds. $1.95, Magi following star. $2.30, Madonna and child.
714 A129 35c multicolored .70 .70
715 A129 80c multicolored .70 .70
716 A129 $1.15 multicolored 1.05 1.05
717 A129 $1.75 multicolored 1.30 1.30
718 A129 $1.95 multicolored 1.75 1.75
719 A129 $2.30 multicolored 1.90 1.90
Nos. 714-719 (6) 7.40 7.40

A130

1995-96 Litho. Perf. 14
720 A130 1c Corn .40 .40
721 A130 2c Sugar cane .40 .40
722 A130 3c Sunflowers .40 .40
723 A130 4c Sorghum .40 .40
724 A130 5c Mine workers .40 .40
725 A130 10c Underground
mining .40 .40
726 A130 20c Coal mining .40 .40
727 A130 30c Chrome
smelting .40 .40
728 A130 40c Opencast
mining .40 .40
728A A130 45c Underground
drilling .40 .40
729 A130 50c Gold smelting .40 .40
730 A130 70c Boggie Clock
Tower .40 .40
731 A130 80c Masvingo
Watchtower .40 .40
732 A130 $1 Hanging tree .50 .50
733 A130 $2 Cecil House .95 .95
734 A130 $5 The To-
poscope 2.40 2.40
735 A130 $10 Paper House 4.75 4.75
Nos. 720-735 (17) 13.80 13.80
Issued: 45c, 6/3/96; others, 1/17/95.

Insects
A131

1995, Apr. 4 Litho. Perf. 14½
736 A131 35c Spider-hunting
wasp 1.00 1.00
737 A131 $1.15 Emperor drag-
onfly 1.50 1.50
738 A131 $1.75 Foxy charaxes 2.00 2.00
739 A131 $2.30 Antlion 2.75 2.75
Nos. 736-739 (4) 7.25 7.25

6th All Africa
Games,
Harare — A132

1995, July 11 Litho. Perf. 14x14½
740 A132 35c Soccer .70 .70
741 A132 80c Track .70 .70
742 A132 $1.15 Boxing 1.05 1.05
743 A132 $1.75 Swimming 1.40 1.40
744 A132 $1.95 Field hockey 1.60 1.60
745 A132 $2.30 Volleyball 2.00 2.00
Nos. 740-745 (6) 7.45 7.45

UN, 50th
Anniv. — A133

1995, Oct. 17 Litho. Perf. 14½
746 A133 35c Health .35 .35
747 A133 $1.15 Environment .60 .60
748 A133 $1.75 Food distribution .70 .70
749 A133 $2.30 Education .95 .95
Nos. 746-749 (4) 2.60 2.60

Flowering
Trees — A134

1996, Jan. 24 Litho. Perf. 14½
750 A134 45c Fernandoa .40 .40
751 A134 $1 Round leaf
mukwa .40 .40
752 A134 $1.50 Luckybean tree .80 .80
753 A134 $2.20 Winter cassia 1.25 1.25
754 A134 $2.50 Sausage tree 1.40 1.40
755 A134 $3 Sweet thorn 1.75 1.75
Nos. 750-755 (6) 6.00 6.00

Dams of
Zimbabwe
A135

1996, Apr. 9 Litho. Perf. 14½
756 A135 45c Mazvikadei .45 .45
757 A135 $1.50 Mutirikwi .80 .80
758 A135 $2.20 Ncema 1.25 1.25
759 A135 $3 Odzani 1.50 1.50
Nos. 756-759 (4) 4.00 4.00

Scenic
Views
A136

Designs: 45c, Matusadonha Natl. Park. $1.50, Juliasdale Rocky Outcrops. $2.20, Honde Valley. $3, Finger Rocks, Morgenster Mission.

1996, July 18 Litho. Perf. 14½
760 A136 45c multicolored .45 .45
761 A136 $1.50 multicolored .65 .65
762 A136 $2.20 multicolored 1.00 1.00
763 A136 $3 multicolored 1.40 1.40
Nos. 760-763 (4) 3.50 3.50

Wood
Carvings
A137

1996, Oct. 15 Litho. Perf. 14½
764 A137 45c Frog .35 .35
765 A137 $1.50 Tortoise .50 .50
766 A137 $1.70 Kudu .60 .60
767 A137 $2.20 Chimpanzee .75 .75
768 A137 $2.50 Porcupine .90 .90
769 A137 $3 Rhinoceros 1.00 1.00
Nos. 764-769 (6) 4.10 4.10

Cattle
A138

1997, Jan. 7 Litho. Perf. 14½
770 A138 45c Mashona cow .50 .50
771 A138 $1.50 Tuli cow .75 .75
772 A138 $2.20 Nkoni bull .95 .95
773 A138 $3 Brahman bull 1.35 1.35
Nos. 770-773 (4) 3.55 3.55

Convention on Intl. Trade in
Endangered Species of Flora and
Fauna (CITES) — A139

1997, Apr. 15 Litho. Perf. 14½
774 A139 45c Cycad .55 .55
775 A139 $1.50 Peregrine falcon .70 .70
776 A139 $1.70 Pangolin .80 .80
777 A139 $2.20 Black rhinoceros 1.10 1.10
778 A139 $2.50 Elephant 1.25 1.25
779 A139 $3 Python 1.50 1.50
Nos. 774-779 (6) 5.90 5.90

Aspects of
Rural Life
A140

1997, July 22 Litho. Perf. 14½
780 A140 65c Carving .25 .25
781 A140 $1 Winnowing .25 .25
782 A140 $1.50 Dancing .60 .60
783 A140 $2.50 Plowing .70 .70
784 A140 $3.10 Stamping .90 .90
785 A140 $4.20 Fetching water 1.30 1.30
Nos. 780-785 (6) 4.00 4.00

Zimbabwe
Railway,
Cent.
A141

1997, Oct. 28 Litho. Perf. 14½
786 A141 65c Passenger coach .35 .35
787 A141 $1 12th Class, No.
257 .35 .35
788 A141 $2.40 16A Class, No.
605 .80 .80
789 A141 $2.50 El 1, No. 4107 .80 .80
790 A141 $3.10 Jack Tar 1.00 1.00
791 A141 $4.20 DE 2, No. 1211 1.25 1.25
Nos. 786-791 (6) 4.55 4.55

Wildlife
A142

1998, Jan. 20 Litho. Perf. 14½
792 A142 65c Aardwolf .55 .55
793 A142 $2.40 Large gray mon-
goose .70 .70
794 A142 $3.10 Clawless otter 1.00 1.00
795 A142 $4.20 Antbear (Aard-
vark) 1.25 1.25
Nos. 792-795 (4) 3.50 3.50

Apiculture
A143

Designs: $1.20, Honeybee on flower. $4.10, Queen, worker, drone. $4.70, Queen, retinue. $5.60, Rural beekeeper. $7.40, Commercial beekeepers. $9.90, Products of the hive.

1998, Apr. 14 Litho. Perf. 14
796 A143 $1.20 multicolored .35 .35
797 A143 $4.10 multicolored .90 .90
798 A143 $4.70 multicolored 1.00 1.00
799 A143 $5.60 multicolored 1.25 1.25
800 A143 $7.40 multicolored 1.50 1.50
801 A143 $9.90 multicolored 2.00 2.00
Nos. 796-801 (6) 7.00 7.00

Fossils
A144

1998, July 21   Litho.   Perf. 14½
802	A144	$1.20	Fossil fish	1.10	.45
803	A144	$5.60	Allosaurus foot-prints	1.60	.95
804	A144	$7.40	Massospondylus	1.90	1.60
805	A144	$9.90	Fossil wood	2.40	2.40
		Nos. 802-805 (4)		7.00	5.40

Birds — A145

Designs: $1.20, Yellow-bellied sunbird. $4.10, Lesser blue-eared starling. $4.70, Greyhooded kingfisher. $5.60, Mombo gray tit. $7.40, Chirinda apalis. $9.90, Swynnerton's robin.

1998, Oct. 20   Litho.   Perf. 14
806	A145	$1.20	multicolored	.85	.85
807	A145	$4.10	multicolored	1.00	1.00
808	A145	$4.70	multicolored	1.25	1.25
809	A145	$5.60	multicolored	1.60	1.60
810	A145	$7.40	multicolored	1.90	1.90
811	A145	$9.90	multicolored	2.40	2.40
		Nos. 806-811 (6)		9.00	9.00

UPU, 125th
Anniv. — A146

$1.20, Counter services at Post Office and Philatelic Bureau. $5.60, Postman delivering mail on bicycle. $7.40, 19th cent. runner, EMS, PTC delivery today. $9.90, Harare Central Sorting Office.

1999, Jan. 19   Litho.   Perf. 14
812	A146	$1.20	multicolored	.45	.45
813	A146	$5.60	multicolored	.65	.65
814	A146	$7.40	multicolored	.85	.85
815	A146	$9.90	multicolored	1.05	1.05
		Nos. 812-815 (4)		3.00	3.00

A147

Wild cats of Zimbabwe.

1999, Mar. 16   Litho.   Perf. 14
816	A147	$1.20	Serval	.50	.50
817	A147	$5.60	Cheetah	.75	.75
818	A147	$7.40	Caracal	1.05	1.05
819	A147	$9.90	Leopard	1.40	1.40
		Nos. 816-819 (4)		3.70	3.70

A148

Owls.

1999, June 8   Litho.   Perf. 14¼
820	A148	$1.20	Cape eagle owl	.85	.85
821	A148	$5.60	Grass owl	1.35	1.35
822	A148	$7.40	Barn owl	1.75	1.75
823	A148	$9.90	Marsh owl	2.10	2.10
		Nos. 820-823 (4)		6.05	6.05

Tourist
Activities
A149

1999, Aug. 10   Litho.   Perf. 14¼x14
824	A149	$2	Canoeing	.40	.40
825	A149	$6.70	Rock climbing	.65	.65
826	A149	$7.70	Microlighting	.75	.75
827	A149	$9.10	White water rafting	.90	.90
828	A149	$12	Scenic view	1.25	1.25
829	A149	$16	Viewing game	1.75	1.75
		Nos. 824-829 (6)		5.70	5.70

A150

Christmas: $2, Christmas time — Family time. $6.70, Christmas tree in Africa. $7.70, Joy to you this Christmas. $9.10, Christmas time — Flame lily time. $12, Glory to God & Peace on Earth. $16, The House of Christmas.

1999, Oct. 12   Litho.   Perf. 14x14¼
830	A150	$2	multi	.35	.35
831	A150	$6.70	multi	.65	.65
832	A150	$7.70	multi	.70	.45
833	A150	$9.10	multi	.95	.95
834	A150	$12	multi	1.25	1.25
835	A150	$16	multi	1.60	1.60
		Nos. 830-835 (6)		5.50	5.25

A151

Designs: 1c, Nyala. 10c, Construction. 30c, Timber. 50c, Tobacco auction floors. 70c, Harare Central Sorting Office. 80c, New international airport, Harare. $1, Westgate Shopping Complex. $2, Nile crocodile. $3, Pungwe water project. $4, Zebra. $5, Mining. $7, National University of Science and Technology. $10, Ostrich. $15, Cape parrot. $20, Leather products. $30, Lilac-breasted roller. $50, Victoria Falls. $100, Tokwe Mukorsi Dam.

2000, Jan. 25   Litho.   Perf. 14¾
836	A151	1c	multi	.25	.25
837	A151	10c	multi	.25	.25
838	A151	30c	multi	.25	.25
839	A151	50c	multi	.25	.25
840	A151	70c	multi	.25	.25
841	A151	80c	multi	.25	.25
842	A151	$1	multi	.25	.25
843	A151	$3	multi	.25	.25
844	A151	$4	multi	.25	.25
845	A151	$5	multi	.30	.30
846	A151	$7	multi	.40	.40
847	A151	$10	multi	.65	.65
848	A151	$15	multi	1.10	1.10
849	A151	$20	multi	1.25	1.25
850	A151	$30	multi	1.90	1.90
851	A151	$50	multi	3.00	3.00
852	A151	$100	multi	6.25	6.25
853	A151				
		Nos. 836-853 (18)		17.35	17.35

Sports — A152

2000, Apr. 25   Litho.   Perf. 14
854	A152	$2	Basketball	.40	.40
855	A152	$6.70	Lawn tennis	.65	.65
856	A152	$7.70	Netball	.85	.85
857	A152	$9.10	Weight lifting	.95	.95
858	A152	$12	Taekwondo	1.25	1.25
859	A152	$16	Diving	1.75	1.75
		Nos. 854-859 (6)		5.85	5.85

Dr. Joshua
Nkomo (1917-
99), Vice-
President
A153

Designs: $2, $12, Wearing suit. $9.10, $16, Wearing headdress.

2000, June 27   Litho.   Perf. 14x14¼
Background Color
860	A153	$2	blue	.55	.55
861	A153	$9.10	green	1.40	1.40
862	A153	$12	red	1.75	1.75
863	A153	$16	orange	2.25	2.25
		Nos. 860-863 (4)		5.95	5.95

Organizations
Combatting
Disease
A154

Designs: $2, Ministry of Health. $6.70, Rehabilitation and Prevention of Tuberculosis (RAPT). $7.70, New Start centers. $9.10, Riders for Health. $12, Natl. Aids Coordination Program (NACP). $16, Rotary Intl.

2000, July 18   Litho.   Perf. 14¼x14
864	A154	$2	multi	.30	.30
865	A154	$6.70	multi	.55	.55
866	A154	$7.70	multi	.65	.65
867	A154	$9.10	multi	.90	.90
868	A154	$12	multi	1.05	1.05
869	A154	$16	multi	1.50	1.50
		Nos. 864-869 (6)		4.95	4.95

Wild Fruits Type of 1991

$2, Masawu. $6.70, Spiny monkey orange. $7.70, Bird plum. $9.10, Shakama plum. $12, Wild medlar. $16, Wild custard apple.

2000, Oct. 24   Litho.   Perf. 14x14½
870-875	A117	Set of 6		4.50	4.50

Aviation
A155

Designs: $8, Boeing 737-200. $12, BAe Hawk MK 60. $14, Hawker Hunter FGA-9. $16, Cessna/Reims F-337. $21, Aerospatiale Alouette III helicopter. $28, Boeing 767-200ER.

2001, Jan. 31   Litho.   Perf. 14¼
876-881	A155	Set of 6		6.50	6.50

Total Solar
Eclipse, June
21,
2001 — A156

Designs: $8, Solar prominences. $21, Eclipse path over Africa. $28, Eclipse phases (62x24mm).

Perf. 14¼x14, 14½ ($28)
2001, Apr. 24   Litho.
882-884	A156	Set of 3		4.50	4.50

Folklore — A157

Designs: $8, The Hare Who Rode Horseback. $12, The Hippo Who Lost His Hair. $13, The Lion Who Was Saved by a Mouse. $16, The Bush Fowl Who Wakes the Sun. $21, The Chameleon Who Came Too Late. $28, The Tortoise Who Collected Wisdom.

2001, July 24   Litho.   Perf. 14x14¼
885-890	A157	Set of 6		6.00	6.00
a.	Souvenir sheet, #885-890			8.00	8.00

Heroes'
Acre — A158

Designs: $8, Main entrance gate. $16, Statue of the Unknown Soldier. $21, General view. $28, Aerial view.

2001, Aug. 7   Litho.   Perf. 14¼x14
891-894	A158	Set of 4		5.00	5.00

Year of Dialogue
Among Civilizations
A159

Winning stamp design entry in: $8, National competition (Three Faces, by Nation Mandla Mguni). $21, International competition.

2001, Oct. 16   Litho.   Perf. 14¼
895-896	A159	Set of 2		4.00	4.00

Butterflies
A160

Designs: $12, Large blue charaxes. $20, Painted lady. $25, Yellow pansy. $30, Gold-banded forester. $35, Sapphire. $45, Clear-spotted acrea.

2001, Dec. 6   Litho.   Perf. 14¼x14
897-902	A160	Set of 6		12.00	12.00
902a	Souvenir sheet, #897-902			12.00	12.00

Craftsmanship
A161

Designs: $12, Knitting and crocheting. $20, Art and design. $25, Basket making. $30, Pottery. $35, Wood carving. $45, Sculpture.

2002, Jan. 22
903-908	A161	Set of 6		10.00	10.00

Gemstones
A162

Designs: $12, Agate. $25, Aquamarine. $35, Diamond. $45, Emerald.

2002, Apr. 23　Litho.　Perf. 14¼x14
909-912　A162　Set of 4　　12.00 12.00

Childline
A163

Children's art: $12, Children embracing. $25, Girl on phone. $35, Teddy bear. $45, Arm with phone receiver.

2002, June 4　Litho.　Perf. 14¼x14
913-916　A163　Set of 4　　7.75 7.75

First Lady Sally
Mugabe (1931-92) — A164

Various portraits: $20, $50, $70, $90.

2002, Aug. 6　　　Perf. 14x14¼
917-920　A164　Set of 4　　12.00 12.00

Children's Stamp Design Contest Winners A165

Designs: $20, Mail runner and bicycle at post office, by Agreement Ngwenya. $70, Mail runner and airplane, by Kudzai Chikomo.

2002, Oct. 8　Litho.　Perf. 14¼
921-922　A165　Set of 2　　6.00 6.00

Wild Flowers
A166

Designs: $20, Dissotis princeps. $35, Leonotis nepetifolia. $40, Hibiscus vitifolius. $50, Boophane disticha. $70, Pycnostachys urticifolia. $90, Gloriosa superba.

2002, Oct. 22　　　Perf. 14¼x14
923-928　A166　Set of 6　　16.50 16.50
928a　　　Souvenir sheet, #923-928　18.00 18.00

History Society of Zimbabwe, 50th Anniv. — A167

Map of Zimbabwe and: $30, Society emblem. $80, Hourglass, books, diploma. $110, People listening to speaker. $140, Old building.

2003, Jan. 28　Litho.　Perf. 14x14¼
929-932　A167　Set of 4　　8.50 8.50

Harare Intl. Festival of the Arts — A168

Designs: $30, Festival emblem. $80, Emblem and flower. $110, Eye and flowers. $140, Emblem and flowers.

2003, Apr. 22　Litho.　Perf. 14x14¼
933-936　A168　Set of 4　　4.25 4.25

Type of 2000

Designs: ($100), Bateleur eagle. $500, Goliath heron. $1000, White rhinoceros. $5000, Cheetah.

2003, June 24　Litho.　Perf. 14¾
937　A151　($100) multi　　.25 　.25
938　A151　$500 multi　　1.00 1.00
939　A151　$1000 multi　　2.00 2.00
940　A151　$5000 multi　　10.00 10.00
　　　Nos. 937-940 (4)　　13.25 13.25

Spiders
A169

Designs: $150, Baboon spider. $200, Rain spider. $600, Black widow spider. $900, Wolf spider. $1250, Violin spider. $1600, Wall spider.

2003, July 30　　　Perf. 14¼
941-946　A169　Set of 6　　8.50 8.50
946a　　　Souvenir sheet, #941-946　8.50 8.50

Women Empowerment A170

Woman in cap and gown with: $300, Globe, hoe and briefcase. $2100, Traditional woman.

2003, Oct. 14　Litho.　Perf. 14¼
947-948　A170　Set of 2　　4.75 4.75

Endangered Medicinal Herbs — A171

Designs: $200, Wild verbena. $500, Pimpernel. $1000, African arrowroot. $3000, Bird pepper. $4200, Wild garlic. $5400, Cleome.

2003, Oct. 28　　　Perf. 14¼x14¼
949-954　A171　Set of 6　　24.50 24.50
　a.　Miniature sheet, #949-954　24.50 24.50

Environmental Awareness A172

Designs: $500, Environment Africa. $3000, Sondela. $4200, Water Africa. $5400, Tree Africa.

2004, Feb. 17　Litho.　Perf. 14x14¼
955-958　A172　Set of 4　　22.50 22.50

Medals — A173

Designs: $1500, Zimbabwe Independence Medal. $9000, Bronze Cross of Zimbabwe. $13,000, Silver Cross of Zimbabwe. $16,500, Gold Cross of Zimbabwe.

2004, Apr. 6　Litho.　Perf. 14¼
959-962　A173　Set of 4　　65.00 65.00

Aloes — A174

Designs: $1500, Aloe ballii. $3,000, Aloe rhodesiana. $9000, Aloe greatheadii. $10,000, Aloe ortholopha. $13,000, Aloe inyangensis. $16,500, Aloe arborescens.

2004, July 20　Litho.　Perf. 14x14¼
963-968　A174　Set of 6　　30.00 30.00
968a　　　Miniature sheet, #963-968　30.00 30.00

Co-Vice President Simon Vengai Muzenda (1922-2003) A175

Background colors: $2300, Red. $12,000, Yellow. $17,000, Green. $22,000, Gray.

2004, Sept. 20　Litho.　Perf. 14x14¼
969-972　A175　Set of 4　　40.00 40.00

Conservation A176

Winning art in conservation stamp design contest: $4600, Butterfly, by Kingston Chigidhani. $33,500, Hands and wildlife, by Kudzai Chikomo.

2004, Oct. 26　Litho.　Perf. 14¼x14¼
973-974　A176　Set of 2　　14.00 14.00

Miniature Sheet

FIRST SAPOA JOINT STAMP ISSUE

Birds — A177

No. 975: a, $500, African fish eagles, national bird of Zambia. b, $1000, Purple-crested louries, national bird of Swaziland. c, $2300, African fish eagles, national bird of Zimbabwe. d, $3000, Blue cranes, national bird of South Africa. e, $5000, Cattle egrets, national bird of Botswana. f, $9000, Peregrine falcons, national bird of Angola. g, $12,000,

Bar-tailed trogons. h, $17,000, African fish eagles, national bird of Namibia.

2004, Oct. 11　Litho.　Perf. 14
975　A177　Sheet of 8, #a-h　70.00 70.00

See Botswana Nos. 792-793, Malawi No. Namibia No. 1052, South Africa No. 1342, Swaziland Nos. 727-735, and Zambia No. 1033.

Birds — A178

Designs: $500, Black-collared barbet. $5000, Gray-headed bush shrike. Z, Red-headed weaver. $10,000, Golden-breasted bunting. $20,000, Cut-throat finch. A, Cabanis's bunting. E, Miombo double-collared sunbird. R, Crested barbet. $50,000, Heuglin's robin. $100,000, Giant kingfisher.

2005, Feb. 8　Litho.　Perf. 14¾x14½
976　A178　$500 multi　　.25 　.25
977　A178　$5000 multi　　1.40 1.40
978　A178　Z multi　　1.75 1.75
979　A178　$10,000 multi　　2.75 2.75
980　A178　$20,000 multi　　5.50 5.50
981　A178　A multi　　8.00 8.00
982　A178　E multi　　10.50 10.50
983　A178　R multi　　13.00 13.00
984　A178　$50,000 multi　　13.00 13.00
985　A178　$100,000 (10)　　26.00 26.00
　　　Nos. 976-985 (10)　　82.15 82.15

On day of issue No. 978 sold for $6900, No. 981 sold for $30,000, No. 982 sold for $40,000, and No. 983 sold for $50,000.

Clouds A179

Designs: $6900, Cirrus. $13,800, Nimbostratus. $30,000, Altocumulus. $40,000, Cumulonimbus.

2005, Apr. 26　　　Perf. 14¼
986-989　A179　Set of 4　　17.50 17.50

Snakes A180

Designs: $6900, Banded Egyptian cobra. $13,800, Puff adder. $20,000, Boomslang. $25,000, Mozambique spitting cobra. $30,000, Gaboon viper. $40,000, Black mamba.

2005, July 12　Litho.　Perf. 14¼x14
990-995　A180　Set of 6　　16.00 16.00
995a　　　Miniature sheet, #990-995　16.00 16.00

Governmental Officials — A181

Designs: $6900, Josiah Tongogara (1940-79), Chief of Defense. $13,800, Herbert Chitepo (1923-75), Director of Public Prosecutions. $30,000, Bernard Chidzero (1927-2002), Minister of Economic Planning. $50,000, Moven Mahachi (1948-2001), Minister of various departments.

2005, Aug. 4　Litho.　Perf. 14x14¼
996-999　A181　Set of 4　　16.00 16.00

UNESCO World Heritage Sites A182

Designs: Z, Soapstone Zimbabwe bird, Great Zimbabwe National Park. $15,500, Wall, Khami Ruins. $52,000, Elephant, Mana Pools National Park. $62,000, Victoria Falls.

2005, Oct. 6   **Litho.**   **Perf. 14¼**
1000-1003 A182   Set of 4   30.00 30.00
1003a   Souvenir sheet, #1000-1003   11.00 11.00

No. 1000 sold for $10,250 on day of issue.

World AIDS Day — A183

Designs: $18,000, Cooking pot, field tender, care for the ill. $80,000, Children teaching AIDS prevention.

2005, Dec. 1   **Litho.**   **Perf. 14¼x14**
1004-1005 A183   Set of 2   15.00 15.00

Food — A184

Designs: $25,000, Mushrooms. $35,000, Rapoko, corn and sorghum. $50,000, Pumpkin, watermelon, spiny cucumber. $150,000, Wild fruits. $250,000, Herbs. $300,000, Sweet potato, cassava, peanuts.

2006, Jan. 17   **Litho.**   **Perf. 14x14¼**
1006-1011 A184   Set of 6   16.50 16.50
1011a   Miniature sheet, #1006-1011   16.50 16.50

Pope John Paul II (1920-2005) A185

Pope: $25,000, Wearing crucifix. $250,000, Holding crucifix.

2006, Feb. 9
1012-1013 A185   Set of 2   15.00 15.00
1013a   Souvenir sheet, #1012-1013   15.00 15.00

Water Conservation A186

Designs: $30,000, Faucet and pail. $225,000, Flood irrigation system. $375,000, Lions at waterhole. $450,000, Kariba Dam.

2006, Apr. 25   **Litho.**   **Perf. 14x14¼**
1014-1017 A186   Set of 4   21.00 21.00

National Heroes — A187

Flag and: $60,000, Leopold T. Takawira (1916-70), first vice-president of Zimbabwe African National Union. $350,000, Simon C. Mazorodze (1933-81), health minister. $500,000, Herbert M. Ushewokunze (1933-95), government minister. $650,000, Tichafa S. Parirenyatwa (1927-62), deputy president of Zimbabwe African People's Union.

2006, July 25   **Litho.**   **Perf. 14x14¼**
1018-1021 A187   Set of 4   30.00 30.00

Huts — A188

Designs: $100, One hut. $800, Three huts.

2006, Oct. 24   **Litho.**   **Perf. 14¼x14**
1022-1023 A188   Set of 2   12.00 12.00
1023a   Souvenir sheet, #1022-1023   7.25 7.25

Bridges A189

Designs: Z, Mpudzi River Bridge. $450, Victoria Falls Bridge. $600, Limpopo River Bridge. $750, Otto Beit Bridge. $800, Kariba Barrage Bridge. $1000, Birchenough Bridge.

2006, Oct. 24
1024-1029 A189   Set of 6   22.50 22.50
1029a   Souvenir sheet, #1024-1029   30.00 30.00

No. 1024 sold for $100 on day of issue.

Trees — A190

Designs: $150, Ziziphuus mauritania. $600, Schlerochra birrea. $750, Jatropha carcus. $1000, Uaparca kirkiana.

2006, Dec. 1   **Litho.**   **Perf. 14x14¼**
1030-1033 A190   Set of 4   21.00 21.00
1033a   Souvenir sheet, #1030-1033   20.00 20.00

Birds — A191

Designs: $50, Hoopoe. $100, Cattle egret. $500, Malachite kingfisher. $1000, Little bee-eater. $2000, Purple-crested lorie. $5000, Purple gallinule. $10,000, African jacana. $20,000, Ground hornbill. $50,000, Gorgeous bush shrike. $100,000, Secretary bird.

Perf. 14¾x14½

2007, Feb. 20   **Litho.**
1034 A191 $50 multi   .25 .25
1035 A191 $100 multi   .25 .25
1036 A191 $500 multi   .25 .25
1037 A191 $1000 multi   .35 .35
1038 A191 $2000 multi   .65 .65

1039 A191 $5000 multi   1.75 1.75
1040 A191 $10,000 multi   3.25 3.25
1041 A191 $20,000 multi   6.75 6.75
1042 A191 $50,000 multi   17.00 17.00
1043 A191 $100,000 multi   35.00 35.00
a.   Souvenir sheet, #1034-1043   67.50 67.50
   Nos. 1034-1043 (10)   65.50 65.50

Scouting, Cent. — A192

Scouting emblem and: $400, Great Zimbabwe Ruins. $1500, Map of Zimbabwe. $2000, Centenary emblem. $2500, Map of Africa.

2007, Feb. 20   **Perf. 14x14¼**
1044-1047 A192   Set of 4   15.00 15.00

Women A193

Designs: $7500, Mbuya Nehanda (?-1898), colonial resistance organizer. $29,000, Queen Lozikeyi (c. 1855-1919). $35,000, Mother Patrick (1863-1900), educator. $45,000, Amai Sally Mugabe (1932-92), First Lady.

2007, July 10   **Perf. 14¼**
1048-1051 A193   Set of 4   7.75 7.75

Beginning in 2007, Zimbabwean currency began to experience extreme hyperinflation. Starting with Nos. 1052-1055, most stamps are non-denominated, inscribed "Z" for surface-rate letters sent within Zimbabwe, "A" for letters sent to the rest of Africa by air, "E" for letters sent to Europe by air, and "R" for letters sent to the rest of the world by air, with letters being up to 20 grams in weight. Press release information about these stamps probably was printed in advance of their issuance, so it is unknown if the stamps were actually sold to local customers at the rates implied by the release on the stated day of issue at post offices in Zimbabwe. As the Zimbabwean dollar and denominated stamps daily became more and more worthless (with a reissuance of new Zimbabwe dollars eliminating 10 zeroes on Aug. 1, 2008, and yet again eliminating 12 zeroes on Feb. 2, 2009), the editors cannot easily determine selling prices for these stamps.

National Heroes — A194

Designs: Z, Jason Ziyaphapha Moyo (1927-77), second vice-president of Zimbabwe African People's Union. A, Maurice T. Nyagumbo (1924-89), Zimbabwe African National Union senior minister of political affairs. E, Guy Clutton-Brock (1906-95), founder of Cold Comfort Farm Society. R, Chief Rekayi Tangwena (c. 1910-84), senator.

2007, Aug. 9   **Litho.**   **Perf. 14x14¼**
1052-1055 A194   Set of 4   — —
On day of issue, Nos. 1052-1055 reportedly sold for $3,000, $12,000, $17,000, and $20,000, respectively.

Butterflies A195

Designs: Z, Mother-of-pearl. A, Citrus swallowtail. E, Orange tip. R, Blue charaxes. $50,000, Crimson tip. $100,000, Painted lady.

2007, Sept. 18
1056-1061 A195   Set of 6   — —
On day of issue, Nos. 1056-1059 reportedly sold for $7,500, $29,000, $35,000, and $45,000, respectively.

Life of Children — A196

Winning art in stamp design contest: Z, Boy studying, by John Ndhlovu. $100,000, Mother feeding baby, by Fungai Madzima.

2007, Oct. 9
1062-1063 A196   Set of 2   — —
On day of issue, Nos. 1062 reportedly sold for $7,500.

National Animals A197

Designs: Z, Buffalo (Zambia). A, Nyala (Malawi). E, Burchell's zebra (Botswana). R, Oryx (Namibia). $100,000, Nyala (Zimbabwe).

Litho. With Foil Application
2007, Oct. 9   **Perf. 13¾**
1064-1068 A197   Set of 5   — —
On day of issue, Nos. 1064-1067 reportedly sold for $7,500, $29,000, $35,000, and $45,000, respectively. See Botswana No. 838, Malawi No. , Namibia Nos. 1141-1142, Zambia Nos. 1097-1101.

St. Valentine's Day — A198

Designs: Z, Heart. A, Cupid. E, Card (5 hearts). R, Rose.

2008, Jan. 24   **Litho.**   **Perf. 14x14¼**
1069-1072 A198   Set of 4   — —
1072a   Souvenir sheet, #1069-1072   — —
On day of issue, Nos. 1069-1072 reportedly sold for $25,000, $100,000, $170,000, and $240,000, respectively.

Rodents A199

Designs: Z, Striped mouse. A, Water rat. E, Angoni vlei rat. R, Woodland dormouse.

$5,000,000, Bushveld gerbil. $10,000,000, Namaqua rock mouse.

2008, Apr. 24   *Perf. 14¼*
1073-1078 A199   Set of 6

On day of issue, Nos. 1073-1076 reportedly sold for $550,000, $1,900,000, $3,150,000, and $4,600,000, respectively.

National Heroes — A200

Designs: Z, Johanna Nkomo (1927-2003), wife of Joshua Nkomo. A, Ruth Lottie Nomonde Chinamano (1925-2005), political activist. E, Dr. Swithun Tachiona Mombeshora (1945-2003), National president of Red Cross. R, Willie Dzawanda Musarurwa (1927-90), journalist.

2008, Aug. 5   *Perf. 14x14¼*
1079-1082 A200   Set of 4

On day of issue, release information states that Nos. 1079-1082 were to be sold for $250,000,000, $50,000,000, $90,000,000,000,   and $110,000,000,000, respectively, but the stamps were issued after the Aug. 1 revaluation of the currency eliminating 10 zeroes from the denominations.

In December 2008, Zimbabwe's hyperinflation was calculated by *Forbes Asia* at 6.5 times 10 to the 108th power. By the middle of January 2009, virtually all transactions in Zimbabwe were being conducted in foreign currencies, despite law that mandated that the Zimbabwe dollar be used in transactions between parties not having a government license allowing them to conduct transactions in foreign currencies. On January 29, Zimbabwe's finance minister finally made the use of foreign currencies legal for any transactions in Zimbabwe. On February 2, the government revalued the Zimbabwe dollar for the final time, and finally suspended its use on April 12. Selling prices for stamps listed below are stated in US currency, the primary foreign currency used in the country, as well as the currency used in philatelic press releases.

2008 Summer Olympics, Beijing A201

Emblem of the Zimbabwe Olympic Committee and: Z, Water Cube. A, National Stadium (Bird's Nest). E, Olympic pool. R, Flag of Zimbabwe, medals won by Zimbabwe Olympic athletes.

2009, Jan. 20   **Litho.**   *Perf. 14¼*
1083-1086 A201   Set of 4   10.00 10.00

On day of issue, Nos. 1083-1086 reportedly sold in US currency for 50c, $1, $1.50, and $2. respectively.

Paintings A202

Designs: Zb, Cardoor Scape, bu Cosmos Shiridzinomwa. Zs, Countryside, by James Jali. No. 1089, A, Mountains, by George Churu. No. 1090, A, Barn, by Hilary Kashiri. E, Backyard 1, by Freddy Tauro. R, X in the Land, by Admire Kamudzengere.

2009, Apr. 21
1087-1092 A202   Set of 6   6.50 6.50
1092a   Souvenir sheet of 6,
    #1087-1092   6.50 6.50

On day of issue, Nos. 1087-1092 sold in US currency for 20c, 25c, 50c, 50c, 75c and $1, respectively.

Wildlife A203

Designs: Zb, Leopard. Zs, Black rhinonceros. No. 1095, A, African buffalo. No. 1096, A, Lion. E, African elephant. R, All five animals.

2009, June 23
1093-1098 A203   Set of 6   6.50 6.50
1098a   Souvenir sheet of 6,
    #1093-1098   6.50 6.50

On day of issue, Nos. 1093-1098 sold in US currency for 20c, 25c, 50c, 50c, 75c and $1, respectively.

National Heroes — A204

Flag of Zimbabwe and: Zb, Vitalis Musungwa Gava Zvinavashe (1943-2009), commander of Zimbabwe Defense Forces. Zs, Garikayi Hlomayi Settled Magadzire (1937-96), leader of Zimbabwe National Farmers' Union. A, George Bodzo Nyandoro (1926-94), Minister of Lands, Natural Resources and Rural Development. E, Border "Madzibaba" Gezi (1964-2001), Minister of Youth, Gender and Employment Creation. R, Seugeant Masotsha Ndlovu (1890-1982), union leader.

2009, Aug. 4   *Perf. 14x14¼*
1099-1103 A204   Set of 5   5.50 5.50

On day of issue, Nos. 1099-1103 sold in US currency for 20c, 25c, 50c, 75c and $1, respectively.

Christmas A205

Rural churches: Z, St. Barbara's Catholic Church, Kariba. A, Regina Coeli Catholic Church. E, Elim Evangelical Church, Katerere. R, Free Presbyterian Church, Mbuma.

2009, Dec. 15   *Perf. 14¼*
1104-1107 A205   Set of 4   5.00 5.00

On day of issue, Nos. 1104-1107 sold in US currency for 25c, 50c, 75c and $1, respectively.

Zimbabwe, Africa's Paradise — A206

Winning art in stamp design contest by: Z, Fredy Tembo. A, Munashe M. Patsanza. E, Methembe Dhlamini. R, Kudzai Chikomo.

2010, Jan. 19
1108-1111 A206   Set of 4   5.00 5.00
1111a   Souvenir sheet of 4,
    #1108-1111   5.00 5.00

On day of issue, Nos. 1108-1111 sold in US currency for 25c, 50c, 75c and $1 respectively.

2010 World Cup Soccer Championships, South Africa — A207

Soccer players, ball, 2010 World Cup mascot and flag of: Nos. 1112, 1121a, 10c, Namibia. Nos. 1113, 1121b, 15c, South Africa. Nos. 1114, 1121c, 25c, Zimbabwe. Nos. 1115, 1121d, Z, Botswana. Nos. 1116, 1121e, 50c, Malawi. Nos. 1117, 1121f, A, Mauritius. Nos. 1118, 1121g, 75c, Swaziland. Nos. 1119, 1121h, E, Lesotho. Nos. 1120, 1120i, R, Zambia.

2010, Apr. 9   **Litho.**   *Perf. 13½*
On Plain Paper With Olive Brown Background
1112-1120 A207   Set of 9   8.50 8.50
On Gold-faced Paper
1121 A207   Sheet of 9, #a-i   8.50 8.50

On day of issue, Nos. 1115 and 1121d sold for 25c, Nos. 1117 and 1121f sold for 50c, Nos. 1119 and 1121h sold for 75c, and Nos. 1120 and 1121i sold for $1.
See Botswana Nos. 896-905, Lesotho No. , Malawi No. , Mauritius No. , Namibia No. 1188, South Africa No. 1403, Swaziland Nos. 794-803, and Zambia Nos. 1115-1118.

Vice-President Joseph Wilfred Msika (1923-2009) A208

Zimbabwe flag and various photographs of Msika with panel color of: Z, Yellow. A, Black. E, Dark red. R, Green.

2010, July 27   **Litho.**   *Perf. 14x14¼*
1122-1125 A208   Set of 4   5.00 5.00

On day of issue, Nos. 1122-1125 sold for 25c, 50c, 75c and $1, respectively.

Pan-African Postal Union, 30th Anniv. — A209

2010, Dec. 28   *Perf. 14¼*
1126 A209   Z multi   .50   .50

No. 1126 sold for 50c on day of issue.

Railroad Stations A210

Station in: 25c, Harare. 30c, Kadoma. 85c, Bulawayo. $1, Mutare.

2011, May 26   *Perf. 14¼x14*
1127-1130 A210   Set of 4   5.00 5.00

National Heroes — A211

Designs: 25c, Tarcissius Malan George Silundika (1929-81), governmental minister. 30c, Julia Zvobgo (1937-2004), politician. 85c, Ariston Maguranyanga Chambati (1934-95), politician. $1, Joseph Luke Culverwell (1918-93), governmental minister.

2011, July 27   *Perf. 14x14¼*
1131-1134 A211   Set of 4   5.00 5.00

Huts — A212

Designs: 25c, Shona hut. 30c, Ndebele hut. 85c, Manyika hut. $1, Tonga hut.

2011, Nov. 29   *Perf. 14½x14*
1135-1138 A212   Set of 4   5.00 5.00
1138a   Sheet of 4, #1135-1138   5.00 5.00

POSTAGE DUE STAMPS

D1

1981   **Litho.**   *Perf. 14½*

J20	D1	1c emerald	.40	1.10
J21	D1	2c ultramarine	.40	1.10
J22	D1	5c lilac	.50	1.40
J23	D1	6c yellow	.65	2.00
J24	D1	10c red	1.40	4.25
		Nos. J20-J24 (5)	3.35	9.85

For surcharge see No. J30.

D2

1985, Aug. 21   **Litho.**   *Perf. 14½*

J25	D2	1c pale orange	.40	.75
J26	D2	2c lilac rose	.40	.75
J27	D2	6c light green	.40	.75
J28	D2	10c tan	.40	.75
J29	D2	13c bright blue	.40	.75
		Nos. J25-J29 (5)	2.00	3.75

No. J24 Surcharged

1990, Jan. 2   **Litho.**   *Perf. 14½*
J30 D1 25c on 10c #J24   11.00 11.00

D3

1995, Jan. 17   **Litho.**   *Perf. 14½*

J31	D3	1c yellow	.35	.35
J32	D3	2c yellow orange	.35	.35
J33	D3	5c rose lilac	.35	.35
J34	D3	10c pale blue	.35	.35

J35	D3	25c violet	.35	.35
J36	D3	40c green	.35	.35
J37	D3	60c orange	.35	.35
J38	D3	$1 brown	.55	.55
		Nos. J31-J38 (8)	3.00	3.00

D4

Bird sculpture.

2000, Jan. 25		**Litho.**	**Perf. 14½**	
J39	D4	1c blk, lt grn & grn	.25	.25
J40	D4	10c blk, lt blue & blue	.25	.25
J41	D4	50c blk, lt brn & brn	.25	.25
J42	D4	$1 blk, pink & red	.25	.25
J43	D4	$2 blk, lt yel & yel	.25	.25
J44	D4	$5 blk, lil & red vio	.25	.25
J45	D4	$10 blk, lt ver & ver	.55	.55
		Nos. J39-J45 (7)	2.05	2.05

ZULULAND

'zü-ₒlü-ₗland

LOCATION — Northeastern part of Natal, South Africa
GOVT. — British Colony, 1887-1897
AREA — 10,427 sq. mi.
POP. — 230,000 (estimated 1900)
CAPITAL — Eshowe

12 Pence = 1 Shilling
20 Shillings = 1 Pound

Stamps of Great Britain
Overprinted

1888-93		**Wmk. 30**	**Perf. 14**	
1	A54	½p vermilion	6.00	3.00
2	A40	1p violet	31.00	5.00
3	A56	2p green & red	24.00	45.00
4	A57	2½p vio, bl ('91)	27.50	22.50
5	A58	3p violet, yel	29.00	25.00
6	A59	4p green & brn	55.00	75.00
7	A61	5p lil & bl ('93)	100.00	150.00
8	A62	6p vio, rose	19.00	20.00
9	A63	9p blue & lil ('92)	110.00	115.00
10	A65	1sh green ('92)	130.00	150.00
		Wmk. 31		
11	A51	5sh rose ('92)	700.00	750.00
		Nos. 1-10 (10)	531.50	610.50

Natal No. 66
Overprinted

1888-94			**Wmk. 2**	
12	A14	½p green, no period	28.50	47.50
a.		Period after "Zululand"	62.50	95.00
b.		As "a," double overprint	1,500.	1,750.
c.		As "a," invtd. overprint	1,400.	
d.		As "a," pair, one without ovpt.	7,500.	
e.		As No. 12, double over-print	1,600.	1,750.

Natal No. 71 Ovptd. Like Nos. 1-11

13	A11	6p violet ('94)	70.00	62.50

A1

A2

1891

14	A1	1p lilac	3.75	3.50

By proclamation of the Governor of Zululand, dated June 27th, 1891, No. 14 was declared to be a postage stamp.

1894-96				**Typo.**
15	A2	½p lilac & grn	5.00	5.50
16	A2	1p lilac & rose	6.00	3.00
17	A2	2½p lilac & blue	16.00	9.75
18	A2	3p lilac & brn	10.00	4.00
19	A2	6p lilac & blk	22.50	25.00
20	A2	1sh green	45.00	45.00
21	A2	2sh6p grn & blk ('96)	85.00	100.00
22	A2	4sh grn & car rose	140.00	190.00
23	A2	£1 violet, red	600.00	625.00
24	A2	£5 vio & blk, red	5,750.	1,900.
		Nos. 15-23 (9)	929.50	1,007.

Numerals of Nos. 19-24 are in color on plain tablet. Dangerous forgeries of No. 24 exist.
Purple or violet cancellations are not necessarily revenue cancels. 14 of the 17 post offices and agencies used violet as well as black postal cancellations.
Zululand was annexed to Natal in Dec. 1897 and separate stamps were discontinued June 30, 1898.

Vol. 6 Number Additions, Deletions & Changes

Number in 2012 Catalogue	Number in 2013 Catalogue	Number in 2012 Catalogue	Number in 2013 Catalogue	Number in 2012 Catalogue	Number in 2013 Catalogue	Number in 2012 Catalogue	Number in 2013 Catalogue
Saudi Arabia		**Yemen**		**Yemen**		**Yemen**	
504a (wmk. 361)	504c	new	220	new	257	new	296A-296E
889a	1300A	new	220A-220F	new	257A-257F	new	296f
		new	221	new	258	new	297
Serbia		new	221A-221B	new	258A-258F	new	297A
new	260a	221	222	new	259	new	298
new	261a	222	222A	new	259A-259F	new	298A
		new	223	new	260	new	299
Singapore		new	223A-223H	new	260A-260G	new	299A-299E
821A	deleted	new	224	new	261	new	299f
		new	224A-224F	new	261A-261G	new	300
South Russia		new	225	new	262	new	300A
new	8a	new	225A-225H	new	262A-262F	new	301
new	45a	new	226	new	263	new	301A-301E
		new	226A-226G	new	263A-263G	new	304
South West Africa		223	227	new	264	new	304A-304D
new	7b	224	228	new	264A-264G	new	305
new	13d	new	229	new	265	new	305A-305F
new	14d	new	229A-229D	new	265A-265G	301	306
new	15d	new	230	new	266	302	307
		new	230A-230B	new	266A-266F	303	308
Sudan		new	231	new	267	304	308A
new	590a	new	231A-231E	new	267A-267F	305	308B
		new	232	new	268	306	309
Togo		new	232A-232G	new	268A-268G	307	309A
1990G	1990H	new	233	new	269	308	310
1990H	1990I	new	233A-233G	new	269A-269E	309	310A
1990I	1990J	new	234	new	270	310	311
new	1990G	new	234A-234I	new	270A-270E	311	311A
		new	235	new	271	312	311B
Uruguay		new	235A-235D	new	271A-271E	new	623A
1413a	1413c	new	236		271f	new	C29E-C29I
1413b	1413d	new	236A-236C	new	272	new	C29J-C29N
1414a	1413a	new	237	new	272A-272E	new	C33A-C33D
1414b	1413b	new	237A-237I	new	273	new	C33E-C33G
1414	deleted	new	239	new	273A-273B	new	C33H-C33J
		new	239A-239D	new	274	new	C33K-C33M
Yemen		new	240	new	274A	new	C33N-C33P
new	188A-188F	new	240A-240D	new	275	new	C33T-C33V
new	192A-192H	new	241	new	275A	new	C33W-C33Y
new	192i	new	241A-241D	new	276	new	J9-J11
194	193A	new	242	new	276A-276B	new	J12-J14
195	193B	new	242A-242D	new	278	new	J15-J19
196	193C	new	243	new	278A	new	J23-J25
197	194	new	243A-243D	new	279		
198	194A	new	244	new	279A	**Yugoslavia**	
199	194B	new	244A-244D	new	280	new	1720a
new	195	new	245	new	280A	new	2386a
new	195A-195F	new	245A-245D	new	281	new	B117a
new	196	new	246	new	281A	new	C7a
new	196A-196H	new	246A-246P	276	282	new	C8a
new	196i	new	247	277	282A	new	C9a
new	197	new	247A-247D	278	282B	new	C10a
new	197A-197H	new	248	new	283, 283A	new	C11a
new	197i	new	248A-248D	new	284, 284A	new	C12a
new	198	new	248e	new	285, 285A-285E	new	C13a
new	198A-198G	new	249	new	286, 286A-286L	new	C14a
new	199	new	249A-249D	new	287, 287A-287F	F1	F1a
new	199A-199G	new	249e	new	288, 288A	new	F1
new	209A-209L	new	250	new	289, 289A	new	F1b
214	213	new	250A-250B	new	290, 290A-E	new	J33a
215	214	new	251	282	291	new	RA36a
216	214A	new	251A-251E	283	291A	new	RAJ1a
217	215	new	252	284	291B		
218	215A	new	252A-252F	new	292		
new	216	new	253	new	292A		
new	216A-216G	new	253A-253E	new	293		
new	217	new	254	new	293A		
new	217A-217H	new	254A-254E	new	294		
219	218	new	255	new	294A		
220	218A	new	255A-255E	new	295		
new	219	new	256	new	295A-295G		
new	219A-219G	new	256A-256K	new	296		

scott**mounts**

For stamp presentation unequaled in beauty and clarity, insist on ScottMounts. Made of 100% inert polystyrol foil, ScottMounts protect your stamps from the harmful effects of dust and moisture. Available in your choice of clcar or black backs, ScottMounts are center-split across the back for easy insertion of stamps and feature crystal clear mount faces. Double layers of gum assure stay-put bonding on the album page. Discover the quality and value ScottMounts have to offer. ScottMounts are available from your favorite stamp dealer or direct from:

SCOTT®

Scott Publishing Co.
1-800-572-6885
P.O. Box 828 Sidney OH 45365-0828
www.amosadvantage.com

Discover the quality and value ScottMounts have to offer. For a complete list of ScottMount sizes visit www.amosadvantage.com

AMOS PUBLISHING

Publishers of:
Coin World, Linn's Stamp News and Scott Publishing Co.

Illustrated Identifier

This section pictures stamps or parts of stamp designs that will help identify postage stamps that do not have English words on them.

Many of the symbols that identify stamps of countries are shown here as well as typical examples of their stamps.

See the Index and Identifier on the previous pages for stamps with inscriptions such as "sen," "posta," "Baja Porto," "Helvetia," "K.S.A.", etc.

Linn's Stamp Identifier is now available. The 144 pages include more than 2,000 inscriptions and more than 500 large stamp illustrations. Available from Linn's Stamp News, P.O. Box 29, Sidney, OH 45365-0029.

1. HEADS, PICTURES AND NUMERALS

GREAT BRITAIN

Great Britain stamps never show the country name, but, except for postage dues, show a picture of the reigning monarch.

Victoria

Edward VII   George V   Edward VIII

George VI

Elizabeth II

Some George VI and Elizabeth II stamps are surcharged in annas, new paisa or rupees. These are listed under Oman.

Silhouette (sometimes facing right, generally at the top of stamp)

The silhouette indicates this is a British stamp. It is not a U.S. stamp.

VICTORIA

Queen Victoria

INDIA

Other stamps of India show this portrait of Queen Victoria and the words "Service" (or "Postage") and "Annas."

AUSTRIA

YUGOSLAVIA

(Also BOSNIA & HERZEGOVINA if imperf.)

BOSNIA & HERZEGOVINA

Denominations also appear in top corners instead of bottom corners.

HUNGARY

Another stamp has posthorn facing left

BRAZIL

AUSTRALIA

Kangaroo and Emu

GERMANY

Mecklenburg-Vorpommern

SWITZERLAND

PALAU

---

2. ORIENTAL INSCRIPTIONS

CHINA

Any stamp with this one character is from China (Imperial, Republic or People's Republic). This character appears in a four-character overprint on stamps of Manchukuo. These stamps are local provisionals, which are unlisted. Other overprinted Manchukuo stamps show this character, but have more than four characters in the overprints. These are listed in People's Republic of China.

Some Chinese stamps show the Sun.

Most stamps of Republic of China show this series of characters.

Stamps with the China character and this character are from People's Republic of China.

Calligraphic form of People's Republic of China

(一)	(二)	(三)	(四)	(五)	(六)
1	2	3	4	5	6
(七)	(八)	(九)	(十)	(一十)	(二十)
7	8	9	10	11	12

Chinese stamps without China character

REPUBLIC OF CHINA

PEOPLE'S REPUBLIC OF CHINA

Mao Tse-tung

MANCHUKUO

Temple   Emperor Pu-Yi

The first 3 characters are common to many Manchukuo stamps.

The last 3 characters are common to other Manchukuo stamps.

Orchid Crest

Manchukuo stamp without these elements

JAPAN

Chrysanthemum Crest   Country Name

Japanese stamps without these elements

The number of characters in the center and the design of dragons on the sides will vary.

RYUKYU ISLANDS

Country Name

PHILIPPINES
(Japanese Occupation)

Country Name

NETHERLANDS INDIES
(Japanese Occupation)

JAVA   SUMATRA

Java   Sumatra

MOLUCCAS, CELEBES AND SOUTH BORNEO

NORTH BORNEO
(Japanese Occupation)

Indicates Japanese Occupation   Country Name

MALAYA
(Japanese Occupation)

Indicates Japanese Occupation   Country Name

BURMA
Union of Myanmar

ပြည်ထောင်စုမြန်မာနိုင်ငံတော်

Union of Myanmar
(Japanese Occupation)

Indicates Japanese   Country
Occupation   Name

Other Burma Japanese Occupation stamps
without these elements

Burmese Script

KOREA

These two characters, in any order,
are common to stamps from the
Republic of Korea (South Korea) or of
the People's Democratic Republic of
Korea (North Korea).

This series of four characters can be found
on the stamps of both Koreas.
Most stamps of the Democratic People's
Republic of Korea (North Korea)
have just this inscription.

Indicates Republic of Korea (South Korea)

South Korean postage stamps issed after
1952 do not show currency expressed
in Latin letters. Stamps wiith "
HW," "HWAN," "WON,"
"WN," "W" or "W" with two lines through it,
if not illustrated in listings of stamps
before this date, are revenues.
North Korean postage stamps do not have
currency expressed in Latin letters.

Yin Yang appears on some stamps.

South Korean stamps show Yin Yang and
starting in 1966, 'KOREA' in Latin letters

Example of South Korean stamps lacking
Latin text, Yin Yang and standard Korean
text of country name. North Korean stamps
never show Yin Yang and starting in 1976
are inscribed "DPRK" or "DPR KOREA" in
Latin letters.

THAILAND

Country Name

King Chulalongkorn

King Prajadhipok and
Chao P'ya Chakri

---

3. CENTRAL AND EASTERN ASIAN INSCRIPTIONS

INDIA - FEUDATORY STATES

Alwar

Bhor

Bundi

Similar stamps come with
different designs in corners
and differently drawn daggers
(at center of circle).

Dhar   Duttia

Faridkot

Hyderabad

Similar stamps exist with
different central design which is
inscribed "Postage"
or "Post & Receipt."

Indore

Jammu & Kashmir

Text varies.

Jasdan

Jhalawar

Kotah

Size and text varies

Nandgaon

Nowanuggur

Poonch

Similar stamps exist
in various sizes with different text

Rajasthan

Rajpeepla

Soruth

Tonk

BANGLADESH

Country Name

NEPAL

Similar stamps are smaller, have squares in
upper corners and have five or nine
characters in central bottom panel.

TANNU TUVA   ISRAEL

GEORGIA

This inscription
is found on other
pictorial stamps.

Country Name

ARMENIA

The four characters are found somewhere
on pictorial stamps. On some stamps only
the middle two are found.

4. AFRICAN INSCRIPTIONS

ETHIOPIA

5. ARABIC INSCRIPTIONS

١ ٢ ٣ ٤ ٥
1 2 3 4 5

٧ ٨ ٩ ٠
6 7 8 9 0

AFGHANISTAN

Many early Afghanistan stamps show Tiger's head, many of these have ornaments protruding from outer ring, others show inscriptions in black.

Arabic Script

Crest of King Amanullah

Mosque Gate & Crossed Cannons

The four characters are found somewhere on pictorial stamps. On some stamps only the middle two are found.

BAHRAIN

EGYPT

Postage

IRAN

Country Name

Royal Crown

Lion with Sword

Symbol

Emblem

IRAQ

JORDAN

LEBANON

Similar types have denominations at top and slightly different design.

LIBYA

Country Name in various styles

Other Libya stamps show Eagle and Shield (head facing either direction) or Red, White and Black Shield (with or without eagle in center).

Without Country Name

SAUDI ARABIA

Tughra (Central design)

← Palm Tree and Swords

20H ٥٢٠

SYRIA

Arab Government Issues

THRACE   **YEMEN**

PAKISTAN

PAKISTAN - BAHAWALPUR

Country Name in top panel, star and crescent

TURKEY

Star & Crescent is a device found on many Turkish stamps, but is also found on stamps from other Arabic areas (see Pakistan-Bahawalpur)

Tughra (similar tughras can be found on stamps of Turkey in Asia, Afghanistan and Saudi Arabia)

Mohammed V

Mustafa Kemal

Plane, Star and Crescent

TURKEY IN ASIA

Other Turkey in Asia pictorials show star & crescent. Other stamps show tughra shown under Turkey.

6. GREEK INSCRIPTIONS

GREECE

Country Name in various styles (Some Crete stamps overprinted with the Greece country name are listed in Crete.)

Lepta

Drachma   Drachmas   Lepton

Abbreviated Country Name

Other forms of Country Name

No country name

CRETE

Country Name

Crete stamps with a surcharge that have the year "1922" are listed under Greece.

EPIRUS

Similar stamps have text above the eagle.

IONIAN IS.

---

7. CYRILLIC INSCRIPTIONS

RUSSIA

Postage Stamp   Imperial Eagle

Postage in various styles

Abbreviation   Abbreviation   Russia
for Kopeck   for Ruble

Abbreviation for Russian Soviet
Federated Socialist Republic
RSFSR stamps were overprinted
(see below)

Abbreviation for Union of Soviet
Socialist Republics

This item is footnoted in Latvia

RUSSIA - Army of the North

"OKCA"

RUSSIA - Wenden

RUSSIAN OFFICES IN THE TURKISH EMPIRE

These letters appear
on other stamps of the
Russian offices.

The unoverprinted ver-
sion of this stamp and a
similar stamp were over-
printed by various coun-
tries (see below).

ARMENIA

BELARUS

FAR EASTERN REPUBLIC

Country Name

SOUTH RUSSIA

Country Name

FINLAND

Circles and Dots
on stamps similar
to Imperial
Russia issues

BATUM

Forms of Country Name

TRANSCAUCASIAN FEDERATED REPUBLICS

  Abbreviation for
Country Name

KAZAKHSTAN

Country Name

KYRGYZSTAN

КЫРГЫЗСТАН

КЫРГЫЗСТАН   Country Name

ROMANIA

TAJIKISTAN

Country Name & Abbreviation

UKRAINE

Country Name in various forms

The trident appears   Abbreviation for
on many stamps,   Ukrainian
usually as   Soviet
an overprint.   Socialist
                      Republic

WESTERN UKRAINE

Abbreviation for
Country Name

AZERBAIJAN

AZƏRBAYCAN

Country Name

A.C.C.P.

Abbreviation for Azerbaijan
Soviet Socialist Republic

MONTENEGRO

ЦРНА ГОРА

Country Name in various forms

Abbreviation
for country
name

No country name
(A similar Montenegro
stamp without coun-
try name has same
vignette.)

SERBIA

СРБИЈА

Country Name in various forms

Abbreviation for country name

No country name

SERBIA & MONTENEGRO

YUGOSLAVIA

ЈУГОСЛАВИЈА

Showing country name

No Country Name

MACEDONIA

МАКЕДОНИЈА

Country Name

МАКЕДОНСКИ ПОШТИ

МАКЕДОНСКИ

Different form of Country Name

BOSNIA & HERZEGOVINA
(Serb Administration)

РЕПУБЛИКА СРПСКА

Country Name

РЕПУБЛИКЕ СРПСКЕ

Different form of Country Name

No Country Name

BULGARIA

Country Name Postage

Stotinka

Stotinki (plural) Abbreviation for Stotinki

Country Name in various forms and styles

No country name

 Abbreviation for Lev, leva

MONGOLIA

ШУУДАН твгрвг

Country name in Tugrik in Cyrillic
one word

МОНГОЛ ШУУДАН мөнгө

Country name in Mung in Cyrillic
two words

Mung
in Mongolian

Tugrik
in Mongolian

Arms

No Country Name

INDEX AND IDENTIFIER

All page numbers shown are those in this Volume 6.

Postage stamps that do not have English words on them are shown in the Illustrated Identifier.

Pronunciation Symbols

ə	....	banana, collide, abut
'ə, ˌə	....	humdrum, abut
ə	....	immediately preceding \l\, \n\, \m\, \ŋ\, as in battle, mitten, eaten, and sometimes open \'ō-pᵊm\, lock and key \-ᵊŋ-\; immediately following \l\, \m\, \r\, as often in French table, prisme, titre
ər	....	further, merger, bird
'ər- 'ə-r	....	as in two different pronunciations of hurry \'hər-ē, 'hə-rē\
a	....	mat, map, mad, gag, snap, patch
ā	....	day, fade, date, aorta, drape, cape
ä	....	bother, cot, and, with most American speakers, father, cart
à	....	father as pronounced by speakers who do not rhyme it with bother; French patte
aů	....	now, loud, out
b	....	baby, rib
ch	....	chin, nature \'nā-chər\
d	....	did, adder
e	....	bet, bed, peck
'ē, ˌē	....	beat, nosebleed, evenly, easy
ē	....	easy, mealy
f	....	fifty, cuff
g	....	go, big, gift
h	....	hat, ahead
hw	....	whale as pronounced by those who do not have the same pronunciation for both whale and wail
i	....	tip, banish, active
ī	....	site, side, buy, tripe
j	....	job, gem, edge, join, judge
k	....	kin, cook, ache
k̲	....	German ich, Buch; one pronunciation of loch
l	....	lily, pool
m	....	murmur, dim, nymph
n	....	no, own
ⁿ	....	indicates that a preceding vowel or diphthong is pronounced with the nasal passages open, as in French un bon vin blanc \œⁿ -bōⁿ -vaⁿ -bläⁿ\
ŋ	....	sing \'siŋ\, singer \'siŋ-ər\, finger \'fiŋ-gər\, ink \'iŋk \
ō	....	bone, know, beau
ȯ	....	saw, all, gnaw, caught
œ	....	French boeuf, German Hölle
ōœ	....	French feu, German Höhle
ȯi	....	coin, destroy
p	....	pepper, lip
r	....	red, car, rarity
s	....	source, less
sh	....	as in shy, mission, machine, special (actually, this is a single sound, not two); with a hyphen between, two sounds as in grasshopper \'gras-ˌhä-pər\
t	....	tie, attack, late, later, latter
th	....	as in thin, ether (actually, this is a single sound, not two); with a hyphen between, two sounds as in knighthood \'nīt-ˌhůd\
t̲h̲	....	then, either, this (actually, this is a single sound, not two)
ü	....	rule, youth, union \'yün-yən\, few \'fyü\
ů	....	pull, wood, book, curable \'kyůr-ə-bəl\, fury \'fyůr-ē\
ue	....	German füllen, hübsch
ūe	....	French rue, German fühlen
v	....	vivid, give
w	....	we, away
y	....	yard, young, cue \'kyü\, mute \'myüt\, union \'yün-yən\
ʸ	....	indicates that during the articulation of the sound represented by the preceding character the front of the tongue has substantially the position it has for the articulation of the first sound of yard, as in French digne \dēnʸ\
z	....	zone, raise
zh	....	as in vision, azure \'a-zhər\ (actually, this is a single sound, not two); with a hyphen between, two sounds as in hogshead \'hȯgz-ˌhed, 'hägz-\
\	....	slant line used in pairs to mark the beginning and end of a transcription: \'pen\
'	....	mark preceding a syllable with primary (strongest) stress: \'pen-mən-ˌship\
ˌ	....	mark preceding a syllable with secondary (medium) stress: \'pen-mən-ˌship\
-	....	mark of syllable division
( )	....	indicate that what is symbolized between is present in some utterances but not in others: factory \'fak-t(ə-)rē\
÷	....	indicates that many regard as unacceptable the pronunciation variant immediately following: cupola \'kyü-pə-lə, ÷-ˌlō\

The system of pronunciation is used by permission from Merriam-Webster's Collegiate® Dictionary, Tenth Edition ©1993 by Merriam-Webster Inc., publisher of the Merriam-Webster® dictionaries.

STOCKBOOKS

Stockbooks are a classic and convenient storage alternative for many collectors. These 9" x 12" Lighthouse stockbooks feature heavyweight archival quality paper with 9 pockets on each page and include double glassine interleaving between the pages for added protection.

Item	Color	Pg Count	Retail	AA*
LS4/8BK	Black	16 pgs	$17.95	**$15.95**
LS4/8BL	Blue	16 pgs	$17.95	**$15.95**
LS4/8GR	Green	16 pgs	$17.95	**$15.95**
LS4/8RD	Red	16 pgs	$17.95	**$15.95**
LS4/16BK	Black	32 pgs	$27.95	**$23.95**
LS4/16BL	Blue	32 pgs	$27.95	**$23.95**
LS4/16GR	Green	32 pgs	$27.95	**$23.95**
LS4/16RD	Red	32 pgs	$27.95	**$23.95**

Item	Color	Pg Count	Retail	AA*
LS4/24GR	Green	48 pgs	$38.95	**$33.99**
LS4/24RD	Red	48 pgs	$38.95	**$33.99**
LS4/32BK	Black	64 pgs	$53.95	**$46.95**
LS4/32BL	Blue	64 pgs	$53.95	**$46.95**
LS4/32GR	Green	64 pgs	$53.95	**$46.95**
LS4/32RD	Red	64 pgs	$53.95	**$46.95**

AMOS HOBBY PUBLISHING

1. *AA prices apply to paid subscribers of Amos Hobby publications, or orders placed online.
2. Prices, terms and product availability subject to change.
3. **Shipping & Handling:**
   United States: 10% of order total.
   Minimum charge $6.99 Maximum charge $45.00.
   Canada: 15% of order total.
   Minimum charge $19.99 Maximum charge $50.00.

   Foreign orders are shipped via FedEx Intl. and billed actual freight. Credit cards only.

To Order Call:
1-800-572-6885

www.amosadvantage.com

INDEX TO ADVERTISERS
2013 VOLUME 6

2013
VOLUME 6
DEALER DIRECTORY
YELLOW PAGE LISTINGS

This section of your Scott Catalogue contains
advertisements to help you conveniently find
what you need, when you need it...!

Accessories

BROOKLYN GALLERY COIN & STAMP, INC.
8725 4th Ave.
Brooklyn, NY 11209
PH: 718-745-5701
FAX: 718-745-2775
info@brooklyngallery.com
www.brooklyngallery.com

Appraisals

COLONIAL STAMP COMPANY
5757 Wilshire Blvd. PH #8
Los Angeles, CA 90036
PH: 323-933-9435
FAX: 323-939-9930
Toll Free in North America
PH: 877-272-6693
FAX: 877-272-6694
info@colonialstampcompany.com
www.colonialstampcompany.com

NATICK STAMPS & HOBBIES
PO Box 80613
San Marino, CA 91118
PH: 626-285-1384
natickco@hotmail.com
Ebay ID: attickmwj

PHILIP WEISS AUCTIONS
1 Neil Ct.
Oceanside, NY 11572
PH: 516-594-0731
FAX: 516-594-9414
phil@prwauctions.com
www.prwauctions.com

Asia

MICHAEL ROGERS, INC.
Suite 4-1
415 S. Orlando Ave.
Winter Park, FL 32789-3683
PH: 407-644-2290
PH: 800-843-3751
FAX: 407-645-4434
Stamps@michaelrogersinc.com
www.michaelrogersinc.com

THE STAMP ACT
PO Box 1136
Belmont, CA 94002
PH: 650-703-2342
PH: 650-592-3315
FAX: 650-508-8104
thestampact@sbcglobal.net
www.thestampact.com

Auctions

COLONIAL STAMP COMPANY
5757 Wilshire Blvd. PH #8
Los Angeles, CA 90036
PH: 323-933-9435
FAX: 323-939-9930
Toll Free in North America
PH: 877-272-6693
FAX: 877-272-6694
info@colonialstampcompany.com
www.colonialstampcompany.com

DANIEL F. KELLEHER AUCTIONS LLC
PMB 44
60 Newtown Rd
Danbury, CT 06810
PH: 203-297-6056
FAX: 203-297-6059
info@kelleherauctions.com
www.kelleherauctions.com

Auctions

DUTCH COUNTRY AUCTIONS
4115 Concord Pike
Wilmington, DE 19803
PH: 302-478-8740
FAX: 302-478-8779
auctions@thestampcenter.com
www.thestampcenter.com

JACQUES C. SCHIFF, JR., INC.
195 Main St.
Ridgefield Park, NJ 07660
PH: 201-641-5566
FAX: 201-641-5705

MICHAEL ROGERS, INC.
Suite 4-1
415 S. Orlando Ave.
Winter Park, FL 32789-3683
PH: 407-644-2290
PH: 800-843-3751
FAX: 407-645-4434
Stamps@michaelrogersinc.com
www.michaelrogersinc.com

PHILIP WEISS AUCTIONS
1 Neil Ct.
Oceanside, NY 11572
PH: 516-594-0731
FAX: 516-594-9414
phil@prwauctions.com
www.prwauctions.com

R. MARESCH & SON LTD.
5th Floor - 6075 Yonge St.
Toronto, ON M2M 3W2
CANADA
PH: 416-363-7777
FAX: 416-363-6511
www.maresch.com

Auctions - Public

ALAN BLAIR AUCTIONS, L.L.C.
Suite 1
5405 Lakeside Ave.
Richmond, VA 23228-6060
PH: 800-689-5602
FAX: 804-262-9307
alanblair@verizon.net
www.alanblairstamps.com

British Commonwealth

ARON R. HALBERSTAM PHILATELISTS, LTD.
PO Box 150168
Van Brunt Station
Brooklyn, NY 11215-0168
PH: 718-788-3978
FAX: 718-965-3099
arh@arhstamps.com
www.arhstamps.com

Central America

GUY SHAW
PO Box 27138
San Diego, CA 92198
PH/FAX: 858-485-8269
guyshaw@guyshaw.com
www.guyshaw.com

Auctions

British Commonwealth

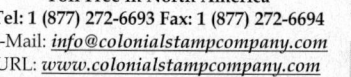

China

MICHAEL ROGERS, INC.
Suite 4-1
415 S. Orlando Ave.
Winter Park, FL 32789-3683
PH: 407-644-2290
PH: 800-843-3751
FAX: 407-645-4434
Stamps@michaelrogersinc.com
www.michaelrogersinc.com

Ducks

MICHAEL JAFFE
PO Box 61484
Vancouver, WA 98666
PH: 360-695-6161
PH: 800-782-6770
FAX: 360-695-1616
mjaffe@brookmanstamps.com
www.brookmanstamps.com

German Colonies

COLONIAL STAMP COMPANY
5757 Wilshire Blvd. PH #8
Los Angeles, CA 90036
PH: 323-933-9435
FAX: 323-939-9930
Toll Free in North America
PH: 877-272-6693
FAX: 877-272-6694
info@colonialstampcompany.com
www.colonialstampcompany.com

Germany

HENRY GITNER PHILATELISTS, INC.
PO Box 3077-S
Middletown, NY 10940
PH: 845-343-5151
PH: 800-947-8267
FAX: 845-343-0068
hgitner@hgitner.com
www.hgitner.com

Japan

MICHAEL ROGERS, INC.
Suite 4-1
415 S. Orlando Ave.
Winter Park, FL 32789-3683
PH: 407-644-2290
PH: 800-843-3751
FAX: 407-645-4434
Stamps@michaelrogersinc.com
www.michaelrogersinc.com

Korea

MICHAEL ROGERS, INC.
Suite 4-1
415 S. Orlando Ave.
Winter Park, FL 32789-3683
PH: 407-644-2290
PH: 800-843-3751
FAX: 407-645-4434
Stamps@michaelrogersinc.com
www.michaelrogersinc.com

Latin America

GUY SHAW
PO Box 27138
San Diego, CA 92198
PH/FAX: 858-485-8269
guyshaw@guyshaw.com
www.guyshaw.com

Manchukuo

MICHAEL ROGERS, INC.
Suite 4-1
415 S. Orlando Ave.
Winter Park, FL 32789-3683
PH: 407-644-2290
PH: 800-843-3751
FAX: 407-645-4434
Stamps@michaelrogersinc.com
www.michaelrogersinc.com

Middle East-Arab

MICHAEL ROGERS, INC.
Suite 4-1
415 S. Orlando Ave.
Winter Park, FL 32789-3683
PH: 407-644-2290
PH: 800-843-3751
FAX: 407-645-4434
Stamps@michaelrogersinc.com
www.michaelrogersinc.com

New Issues

DAVIDSON'S STAMP SERVICE
PO Box 36355
Indianapolis, IN 46236-0355
PH: 317-826-2620
ed-davidson@earthlink.net
www.newstampissues.com

South Africa

ARON R. HALBERSTAM PHILATELISTS, LTD.
PO Box 150168
Van Brunt Station
Brooklyn, NY 11215-0168
PH: 718-788-3978
FAX: 718-965-3099
arh@arhstamps.com
www.arhstamps.com

South America

GUY SHAW
PO Box 27138
San Diego, CA 92198
PH/FAX: 858-485-8269
guyshaw@guyshaw.com
www.guyshaw.com

Sri Lanka

COLONIAL STAMP COMPANY
5757 Wilshire Blvd. PH #8
Los Angeles, CA 90036
PH: 323-933-9435
FAX: 323-939-9930
Toll Free in North America
PH: 877-272-6693
FAX: 877-272-6694
info@colonialstampcompany.com
www.colonialstampcompany.com

STAMP STORES

Arizona

A TO Z STAMPS & COINS
4950 E. Thomas Rd.
Phoenix, AZ 85018
OFFICE: 480-844-9878
CELL: 248-709-8939
michael@azstampcoin.com
www.WorldwideStamps.com

California

BROSIUS STAMP, COIN & SUPPLIES
2105 Main St.
Santa Monica, CA 90405
PH: 310-396-7480
FAX: 310-396-7455
brosius.stamp.coin@hotmail.com

COAST PHILATELICS
Suite D
1113 Baker St.
Costa Mesa, CA 92626
PH: 714-545-1791
chizz5@aol.com

COLONIAL STAMP COMPANY
5757 Wilshire Blvd. PH #8
Los Angeles, CA 90036
PH: 323-933-9435
FAX: 323-939-9930
Toll Free in North America
PH: 877-272-6693
FAX: 877-272-6694
info@colonialstampcompany.com
www.colonialstampcompany.com

STAMP STORES

California

FISCHER-WOLK PHILATELICS
Suite 211
22762 Aspan St.
Lake Forest, CA 92630
PH: 949-837-2932
fischerwolk@fw.occoxmail.com

NATICK STAMPS & HOBBIES
PO Box 80613
San Marino, CA 91118
PH: 626-285-1384
natickco@hotmail.com
Ebay ID: attiekmwj

Connecticut

SILVER CITY COIN & STAMP
41 Colony St.
Meriden, CT 06451
PH: 203-235-7634
FAX: 203-237-4915

Georgia

STAMPS UNLIMITED OF GEORGIA, INC.
Suite 1460
100 Peachtree St. NW
Atlanta, GA 30303
PH: 404-688-9161
tonyroozen@yahoo.com
www.stampsunlimitedofga.com

Illinois

DR. ROBERT FRIEDMAN & SONS
2029 W. 75th St.
Woodridge, IL 60517
PH: 800-588-8100
FAX: 630-985-1588
drbobstamps@yahoo.com
www.drbobfriedmanstamps.com

Indiana

KNIGHT STAMP & COIN CO.
237 Main St.
Hobart, IN 46342
PH: 219-942-4341
PH: 800-634-2646
knight@knightcoin.com
www.knightcoin.com

British Commonwealth

Stamp Shows

STAMP STORES

Missouri

DAVID SEMSROTT STAMPS
Greater St. Louis Area
CELL: 314-813-4224
PH: 314-984-8361
fixodine@sbcglobal.net
www.DavidSemsrott.com

New Jersey

BERGEN STAMPS & COLLECTIBLES
306 Queen Anne Rd.
Teaneck, NJ 07666
PH: 201-836-8987

TRENTON STAMP & COIN CO
Thomas DeLuca
Store: Forest Glen Plaza
1804 Route 33
Hamilton Square, NJ 08690
Mail: PO Box 8574
Trenton, NJ 08650
PH: 800-446-8664
PH: 609-584-8100
FAX: 609-587-8664
TOMD4TSC@aol.com

New York

CHAMPION STAMP CO., INC.
432 W. 54th St.
New York, NY 10019
PH: 212-489-8130
FAX: 212-581-8130
championstamp@aol.com
www.championstamp.com

Ohio

HILLTOP STAMP SERVICE
Richard A. Peterson
PO Box 626
Wooster, OH 44691
PH: 330-262-8907 (0)
PH: 330-262-5378
hilltop@bright.net

THE LINK STAMP CO.
3461 E. Livingston Ave.
Columbus, OH 43227
PH/FAX: 614-237-4125
PH/FAX: 800-546-5726

Virginia

LATHEROW & CO., INC.
5054 Lee Hwy.
Arlington, VA 22207
PH: 703-538-2727
PH: 800-647-4624
FAX: 703-538-5210
latherows@gmail.com

Straits Settlements

COLONIAL STAMP COMPANY
5757 Wilshire Blvd. PH #8
Los Angeles, CA 90036
PH: 323-933-9435
FAX: 323-939-9930
Toll Free in North America
PH: 877-272-6693
FAX: 877-272-6694
info@colonialstampcompany.com
www.colonialstampcompany.com

Thailand

THE STAMP ACT
PO Box 1136
Belmont, CA 94002
PH: 650-703-2342
PH: 650-592-3315
FAX: 650-508-8104
thestampact@sbcglobal.net
www.thestampact.com

Togo

COLONIAL STAMP COMPANY
5757 Wilshire Blvd. PH #8
Los Angeles, CA 90036
PH: 323-933-9435
FAX: 323-939-9930
Toll Free in North America
PH: 877-272-6693
FAX: 877-272-6694
info@colonialstampcompany.com
www.colonialstampcompany.com

Tonga

COLONIAL STAMP COMPANY
5757 Wilshire Blvd. PH #8
Los Angeles, CA 90036
PH: 323-933-9435
FAX: 323-939-9930
Toll Free in North America
PH: 877-272-6693
FAX: 877-272-6694
info@colonialstampcompany.com
www.colonialstampcompany.com

Worldwide

Topicals

E. JOSEPH McCONNELL, INC.
PO Box 683
Monroe, NY 10949
PH: 845-783-9791
FAX: 845-782-0347
ejstamps@gmail.com
www.EJMcConnell.com

HENRY GITNER PHILATELISTS, INC.
PO Box 3077-S
Middletown, NY 10940
PH: 845-343-5151
PH: 800-947-8267
FAX: 845-343-0068
hgitner@hgitner.com
www.hgitner.com

Topicals-Columbus

MR. COLUMBUS
PO Box 1492
Fennville, MI 49408
PH: 269-543-4755
David@MrColumbus1492.com
MrColumbus1492.com

Transvaal

COLONIAL STAMP COMPANY
5757 Wilshire Blvd. PH #8
Los Angeles, CA 90036
PH: 323-933-9435
FAX: 323-939-9930
Toll Free in North America
PH: 877-272-6693
FAX: 877-272-6694
info@colonialstampcompany.com
www.colonialstampcompany.com

Uganda

COLONIAL STAMP COMPANY
5757 Wilshire Blvd. PH #8
Los Angeles, CA 90036
PH: 323-933-9435
FAX: 323-939-9930
Toll Free in North America
PH: 877-272-6693
FAX: 877-272-6694
info@colonialstampcompany.com
www.colonialstampcompany.com

United Nations

BRUCE M. MOYER
Box 99
East Texas, PA 18046
PH: 610-395-8410
FAX: 610-395-8537
moyer@unstamps.com
www.unstamps.com

United States

ACS STAMP COMPANY
10831 Chambers Way
Commerce City, CO 80022
PH: 303-841-8666
ACS@ACSStamp.com
www.acsstamp.com

BROOKMAN STAMP CO.
PO Box 90
Vancouver, WA 98666
PH: 360-695-1391
PH: 800-545-4871
FAX: 360-695-1616
larry@brookmanstamps.com
www.brookmanstamps.com

U.S.-Classics/Moderns

A TO Z STAMPS & COINS
4950 E. Thomas Rd.
Phoenix, AZ 85018
OFFICE: 480-844-9878
CELL: 248-709-8939
michael@azstampcoin.com
www.WorldwideStamps.com

U.S.-Collections Wanted

DR. ROBERT FRIEDMAN & SONS
2029 W. 75th St.
Woodridge, IL 60517
PH: 800-588-8100
FAX: 630-985-1588
drbobstamps@yahoo.com
www.drbobfriedmanstamps.com

Want Lists-British Empire 1840-1935 German Cols./Offices

COLONIAL STAMP COMPANY
5757 Wilshire Blvd. PH #8
Los Angeles, CA 90036
PH: 323-933-9435
FAX: 323-939-9930
Toll Free in North America
PH: 877-272-6693
FAX: 877-272-6694
info@colonialstampcompany.com
www.colonialstampcompany.com

Wanted-Estates

A TO Z STAMPS & COINS
4950 E. Thomas Rd.
Phoenix, AZ 85018
OFFICE: 480-844-9878
CELL: 248-709-8939
michael@azstampcoin.com
www.WorldwideStamps.com

Wanted-Worldwide Collections

DANIEL F. KELLEHER AUCTIONS LLC
PMB 44
60 Newtown Rd
Danbury, CT 06810
PH: 203-297-6056
FAX: 203-297-6059
info@kelleherauctions.com
www.kelleherauctions.com

DR. ROBERT FRIEDMAN & SONS
2029 W. 75th St.
Woodridge, IL 60517
PH: 800-588-8100
FAX: 630-985-1588
drbobstamps@yahoo.com
www.drbobfriedmanstamps.com

DUTCH COUNTRY AUCTIONS
4115 Concord Pike
Wilmington, DE 19803
PH: 302 478 8710
FAX: 302-478-8779
auctions@thestampcenter.com
www.thestampcenter.com

Websites

ACS STAMP COMPANY
10831 Chambers Way
Commerce City, CO 80022
PH: 303-841-8666
ACS@ACSStamp.com
www.acsstamp.com

Worldwide Stamps

A TO Z STAMPS & COINS
4950 E. Thomas Rd.
Phoenix, AZ 85018
OFFICE: 480-844-9878
CELL: 248-709-8939
michael@azstampcoin.com
www.WorldwideStamps.com